W9-CQU-582

THE BETHANY PARALLEL COMMENTARY ON THE NEW TESTAMENT

THE BETHANY PARALLEL COMMENTARY ON THE NEW TESTAMENT

FROM THE CONDENSED EDITIONS OF
MATTHEW HENRY • JAMIESON/FAUSSET/BROWN • ADAM CLARKE

THREE CLASSIC COMMENTARIES IN ONE VOLUME

Also includes supplementary commentary from A.T. Robertson ■ Alexander Maclaren ■ W.E. Vine ■ Charles H. Spurgeon ■ A.B. Simpson ■ Albert Barnes ■ G. Campbell Morgan ■ F.B. Meyer ■ Martin Luther ■ John Wesley ■ and J.A. Seiss.

BETHANY HOUSE PUBLISHERS
MINNEAPOLIS, MINNESOTA 55438

THE BETHANY PARALLEL COMMENTARY
ON THE NEW TESTAMENT

ISBN 0-87123-474-2

Published by Bethany House Publishers
A Division of Bethany Fellowship, Inc.
6820 Auto Club Road, Minneapolis, MN 55438

Printed in the United States of America

PUBLISHER'S PREFACE

The idea for *The Bethany Parallel Commentary on the New Testament* was generated and developed to provide a convenient method for comparing the comments and opinions of several Bible scholars without having to resort to many different volumes. Meeting the needs of pastors, Bible teachers and students for a manageable, convenient, practical and inspiring reference tool, here are three classic commentaries in one volume for easy comparison and helpful insight on specific texts.

The Bethany Parallel Commentary on the New Testament gives background information, original word definitions, inspirational insights and interesting notations on every passage of the New Testament from a wide spectrum of evangelical Christian thought.

When Matthew Henry's pastoral view, including practical application of the text to personal experience, is compared with Adam Clarke's and the Jamieson/Fausset/Brown more technical and linguistic approach, the researcher will find this book to be an invaluable aid in discovering background information and interpreting particular scriptures. The three commentaries complement each other, giving the reader a more complete understanding and new insights on a certain passage or verse.

Though working from the condensed editions of these three commentaries, further condensation was necessary to shorten some of the material on the Jamieson/Fausset/Brown commentary. Deletions were made from 1 Corinthians to Revelation in places where their material was far more extensive than the other commentaries. Some minor points, especially when this material included various opinions from outside sources, were cut from the condensed commentary, but only after their main concepts on that passage of scripture had been clearly defined. Thus, material nonessential to the central arguments was eliminated in the interest of length in some places without disturbing the primary statement of the commentators. These modifications involved only a few sentences or a short paragraph.

Nearly five hundred additional notes are included in appropriate sections throughout the book. Outstanding Bible scholars such as Charles Spurgeon, Alexander Maclaren, G. Campbell Morgan, W. E. Vine, F. B. Meyer, A. B. Simpson, A. T. Robertson, Albert Barnes, John Wesley, Martin Luther and J. A. Seiss give additional amplification to the scripture texts. These further notes are a very effective introduction to some of the great Bible scholars, and many of these also would make excellent quotations in sermons or Bible studies.

It is the publisher's hope that *The Bethany Parallel Commentary* will help pastors, Bible teachers, and laymen better to understand and apply the eternal truths of God's Word.

PUBLISHER'S NOTE

Throughout the gospels, both the JAMIESON, FAUSSET AND BROWN COMMENTARY and ADAM CLARKE'S COMMENTARY incorporated a cross-reference system when the same material was covered by more than one of the Gospel writers. An example from page 169 of this volume appears below. Note the underlined sentence in the middle column. In the original commentary, the following section was blank and the reader turned to the indicated passage. As a further convenience, we have inserted that material from the other Gospel portion instead of referring you to another page. In some cases, though, the amount of commentary in those cross-referenced sections was much more than the space available for the Gospel being studied. When that occurred, we inserted the major points of the material, but you still may wish to turn to those sections for complete commentary on the passage. The reader should also be aware of the fact that the cross-referenced material which is now included below that reference indication will at times be slightly different from the material in the actual Gospel being studied, since details vary slightly with each Gospel writer.

169 — MATTHEW 20:17-21

MATTHEW HENRY	JAMIESON, FAUSSET, BROWN	ADAM CLARKE
are called but few chosen. As to the outward call; *many are called,* and yet refuse (Prov. i. 24). There are but few *chosen* Christians, in comparison with the many that are only *called* Christians. **Verses 17–19** This is the third time that Christ gave his disciples notice of his approaching sufferings. I. The privacy of this prediction; *He took the twelve disciples apart in the way.* His secret was with them, as his friends. It was a hard saying, and if any could bear it, they could. It was requisite that they should know of it, that, being fore-warned, they might be fore-armed. It was not fit to be spoken publicly as yet, because many that were cool toward him, would hereby have been driven to turn their	service all their days may, by the spirit which they manifest at the last, make it too evident that, as between God and their own souls, they never were chosen workmen at all. 17-28. THIRD EXPLICIT ANNOUNCEMENT OF HIS APPROACHING SUFFERINGS, DEATH, AND RESURRECTION—THE AMBITIOUS REQUEST OF JAMES AND JOHN, AND THE REPLY. (=Mark 10:32-45; Luke 18:31-34.) For the exposition, see on Mark 10:32-45. **And they were in the way**—on the road. **going up to Jerusalem**—in Perea, and probably somewhere between Ephraim and Jericho, on the farther side of the Jordan, and to the northeast of Jerusalem.	17. *And Jesus going up.* From Jericho to Jerusalem, chap. xix. 15.

THE COMMENTATORS

MATTHEW HENRY (1662-1714)

Born in a Welsh farmhouse at Iscoid, Flintshire, Matthew Henry was the son of an evangelical Church of England minister who had recently been ejected from the Anglican Church along with two thousand Presbyterian, Independent, and Baptist ministers. They had resisted universal adoption of the Elizabethan Prayer Book. A studious boy, Matthew Henry dated his conversion from 1672. In 1680 he was sent to the Academy (a Nonconformist school) at Islington, London, and went on to study law at Gray's Inn. His remarkable memory and eloquence showed the promise of a great future. In 1687 he received a private ordination, but in 1702 he obtained a document certifying the regularity of his Presbyterian ordination fifteen years earlier. His first pastorate was in Chester (1687-1712), followed by Hackney (1712-1714).

Greatly influenced by the Puritans, he made exposition of Scripture and its practical application to life the central concern of his ministry. In November of 1704 he began his commentary of the Bible and finished to the end of Acts before his death in 1714. The Epistles and Revelation were prepared by thirteen Nonconformist ministerial friends. His commentary set a style in detailed, often highly spiritualized exposition of Scripture which has shaped evangelical ministry ever since.

For two hundred and fifty years, this commentary has been the most widely used of all Bible commentaries. Charles Spurgeon is reported to have said that "every minister ought to read Matthew Henry entirely and carefully through once at least."

ADAM CLARKE (1762?-1832)

Born at Moybeg in County Londonderry, Ireland, no conclusive record of his birth is now available. His father was a man of English extraction who studied at the universities of Edinburgh and Glasgow (M.A.), and his mother was a devout Scottish Presbyterian. He received a local education through the influence of John Wesley at Kingswood School, Bristol. Becoming a Methodist in 1778, he was appointed a Methodist circuit rider by Wesley in 1782. Thirty-one towns and villages were covered regularly by horseback, and he often preached in the open air. From 1805 he lived chiefly in London and was three times president of the Methodist conference. Awarded an Aberdeen LL.D., his scholarship encompassed classics, patristics, oriental languages and literature, history, geology and natural science.

Actual work on his commentary began in May of 1798. The project was completed in March 1825. Clarke worked long hours before daybreak and after sunset during those years before the whole set, in eight large volumes, was published in 1826. For over one hundred and fifty years, its authoritative scholarship has been recognized by scholars from all evangelical backgrounds.

ROBERT JAMIESON (1802-1880)

He was born in Edinburgh, Scotland, and his father was a baker. Graduating from Edinburgh University, Jamieson was licensed as a Presbyterian preacher in 1827. He served a parish in Weststruther (1830-1837), in the presbytery of Laudes, and, for seven more years, the parish of Currie in the presbytery of Edinburgh. From 1844-1880 he served as minister of St. Paul's, Glasgow. In 1848 the University of Glasgow conferred on him the degree of Doctor of Divinity, and his church made him moderator of the General Assembly in 1872. Since his material for the JFB Commentary includes only Old Testament writings, his actual notes do not appear in this volume.

ANDREW FAUSSET (1821-1910)

Born in County Fermanagh, Ireland, he was a brilliant Anglican scholar. Graduating from Trinity College, Dublin, in 1843, he went on to excel in Latin and Greek. He was ordained a priest in 1848 and from then to 1859 was the curate in Bishop Middleham, County Durham. From 1859-1910 he was of St. Cuthbert's, York.

He was a prolific writer, especially interested in prophecy. His works include *Scripture and the Prayer Book in Harmony* (1854); the editorship of the first ET of Bengel's *Gnomon of the New Testament* (1886); *The Englishman's Critical and Expository Bible Cyclopedia* (1878); and the JFB commentary. He wrote the sections from Job to Malachi and 1 Corinthians to Revelation, approximately half of the entire work.

DAVID BROWN (1803-1897)

He was born in Aberdeen, Scotland. Graduating from Aberdeen University, M.A., in 1821, he served as an assistant to Edward Irving from 1830-1832 and was influenced by Irving's prophetic teaching. In 1857 he was appointed professor of apologetics and the exegesis of the Gospels in the Free Church College of Aberdeen, a professorship which he held for thirty years. In 1876 he was made principal of the college and remained in this office until his death. In 1885 he was appointed moderator of the General Assembly of the Free Church.

He was an industrious writer. His works include *Christ's Second Coming: Will it be Premillennial?* (from a postmillennial standpoint); *The Handbook for Bible Classes* (a volume on Romans); *The Apocalypse: It's Structure and Preliminary Predictions*. In the JFB commentary, he wrote the Gospels, Acts, and Romans—which many have felt are the most important section of the work.

Combined as one effort, the JFB commentary came from differing positions and attitudes. Jamieson and Brown were Presbyterians, while Fausset was a clergyman in the Church of England. All three served as ministers of congregations in England and knew the needs of a minister's life. All were conservative in their theology.

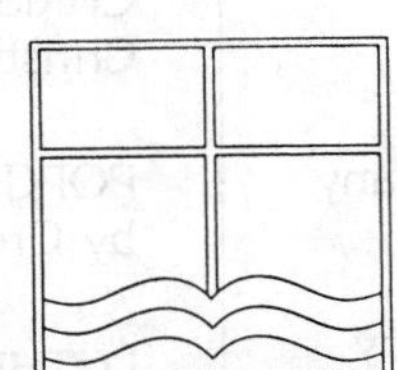

TABLE OF CONTENTS

ACKNOWLEDGMENTS

WORD PICTURES IN THE NEW TESTAMENT, VOL. 1-6, by A. T. Robertson. Copyright © 1933, Broadman Press, Renewal 1960. All rights reserved. Used by permission.

GREAT VERSES THROUGH THE BIBLE by F. B. Meyer. Copyright © 1966, Marshall, Morgan and Scott, Ltd. Published by the Zondervan Corporation. Used by permission.

THE GOSPEL ACCORDING TO MATTHEW/MARK/LUKE/JOHN. Four volumes by G. Campbell Morgan. Copyright © 1929, 1929, 1931, Fleming H. Revell Company. Used by permission.

THE ACTS OF THE APOSTLES by G. Campbell Morgan. Copyright © 1924, Fleming H. Revell Company. Used by permission.

BIBLE COMMENTARY by F. B. Meyer. Published by Tyndale House.

TODAY'S DICTIONARY OF THE BIBLE compiled by T. A. Bryant. Copyright © 1982, Bethany House Publishers. All rights reserved.

AN EXPOSITORY DICTIONARY OF NEW TESTAMENT WORDS by W. E. Vine. Published by Marshall, Morgan & Scott, Ltd. Used by permission.

MACLAREN'S EXPOSITIONS OF HOLY SCRIPTURE by Alexander Maclaren. Copyright © 1905, Hodder & Stoughton. Published by Wm. B. Eerdmans Publishing Company.

THE TREASURY OF THE NEW TESTAMENT by Charles H. Spurgeon. Published by Zondervan Corporation.

SPURGEON'S DEVOTIONAL BIBLE by Charles H. Spurgeon. Published by Baker Book House.

CHRIST IN THE BIBLE by A. B. Simpson. Published by Christian Publications, Inc.

POPULAR COMMENTARY by Albert Barnes. Published by Gresham Publishing Company.

LUTHER'S WORKS by Martin Luther. Copyright © 1964, Concordia Publishing House.

THE NEW TESTAMENT WITH EXPLANATORY NOTES by John Wesley. Published by W. Nicholson and Sons.

THE APOCALYPSE by J. A. Seiss. Published by Zondervan Corporation.

THE GOSPEL ACCORDING TO MATTHEW

I. His person (1:1-4:16)
- *A. His relation to earth (1:1-3:12)*
  - 1. Genealogy (1:1-7)
  - 2. Birth (1:18-2:23)
  - 3. Herald (3:1-12)
- *B. His relation to heaven (3:13-17)*
  - 1. Attestation (3:13-16)
  - 2. Anointing (3:17)
- *C. His relation to hell (4:1-11)*
  - 1. Testing (4:1-10)
  - 2. Triumph (4:11)
- *D. Bridge between 3:17 and 11:2 (4:12-16)*

II. His propaganda (4:17-16:20)
- *A. His enunciation of laws (4:17-7:29)*
  - 1. A nucleus gathered (4:17-25)
  - 2. The manifesto (5:1-7:29)
    - a. The nature—character (5:1-12)
    - b. The purpose—influence (5:13-16)
    - c. The laws (5:17-6:34)
    - d. The dynamic (7:1-12)
    - e. The final words (7:13-29)
- *B. His exhibition of benefits (8:1-9:34)*
  - 1. First manifestation and result (8:1-22)
  - 2. Second manifestation and result (8:23-9:17)
  - 3. Third manifestation and result (9:18-34)
- *C. His enforcement of claims (9:35-16:20)*
  - 1. The twelve (9:35-11:30)
  - 2. Conflict with rulers (12:1-50)
  - 3. Parables of the Kingdom (13:1-52)
  - 4. Increasing opposition (13:53-16:12)
  - 5. The confession of Peter (16:13-20)

III. His passion (16:21-28:20)
- *A. His cross and His subjects (16:21-20:28)*
  - 1. The cross and the glory (16:21-28)
  - 2. The glory and the cross (17:1-21)
  - 3. The cross and the Resurrection (17:22, 23)
  - 4. Instructions to His disciples (17:24-18:35)
  - 5. The multitudes (19:1-22)
  - 6. Instructions to His disciples (19:23-20:28)
- *B. His rejection of the Hebrew nation (21:1-24:2)*
  - 1. The entry (21:1-17)
  - 2. Opposition and parabolic denunciation (21:18-22:46)
  - 3. The final woes (23:1-36)
  - 4. Withdrawal (23:37-24:2)
- *C. His predictions to His subjects (24:3-25:46)*
  - 1. The disciples' questions (24:3)
  - 2. The detailed answers (24:4-25:46)
- *D. His passion (26:1-28:20)*
  - 1. Preliminary (26:1-30)
  - 2. The suffering (26:31-27:66)
  - 3. The Triumph (28:1-20)

The New Testament of our Lord and Savior Jesus Christ; so this second part of the Holy Bible is entitled: The *new covenant.* But, when it is (as here) spoken of as Christ's act and deed, it is most properly rendered a *testament,* for he is the testator, and it becomes of force by his death (Heb. 9:16, 17). All the grace contained in this book is owing to Jesus Christ as our Lord and Savior; and, unless we consent to him as our Lord, we cannot expect any benefit by him as our Savior. This is called a *new* testament, to distinguish it from that which was given by Moses. How carefully do we preserve, and with what attention and pleasure do we read, the last will and testament of a friend, who has therein left us a fair estate, and, with it, high expressions of his love to us! How precious then should this testament of our blessed Savior be to us, which secures to us all his unsearchable riches! It is *his* testament; for though, as is usual, it was written by others, yet he dictated it; and the night before he died, in the institution of his supper, he signed, sealed, and published it in the presence of twelve witnesses. In it is declared the whole counsel of God concerning our salvation (Acts 20:27).

The Four Gospels. Gospel signifies *good news,* or *glad tidings;* and this history of Christ's coming into the world to save sinners is, without doubt, the best news that ever came from heaven to earth; the angel gave it this title (Luke 2:10), "I bring you good tidings; I bring the gospel to you." And the prophet Isaiah foretold it (Isa. 52:7; 61:1). *Gospel* is an old Saxon word; it is *God's spell* or *word.* The four books which contain the history of the Redeemer we commonly call *the four gospels,* and the inspired penmen of them *evangelists,* or *gospel writers.* These four gospels were early and constantly received by the primitive church, and read in Christian assemblies, as appears by the writings of Justin Martyr and Irenaeus, who lived little more than a hundred years after the ascension of Christ. A Harmony of these four evangelists was compiled by Tatian about that time, which he called, *The Gospel out of the four.* In the third and fourth centuries there were gospels forged by various sects, and published, one under the name of St. Peter, another of St. Thomas, another of St. Philip, etc. But they were never owned by the church.

The Gospel according to St. Matthew. The penman was by birth a Jew, by calling a publican, till Christ commanded his attendance, and then he left *the receipt of custom,* to follow him, and was one of those that accompanied him all the time that the Lord Jesus went in and out, beginning from the baptism of John unto the day that he was taken up (Acts 1:21, 22). He was therefore a competent witness of what he has here recorded. Doubtless, it was written in Greek, as the other parts of the New Testament were; not in that language which was peculiar to the Jews, whose church and state were near a period, but in that which was common to the world, and in which the knowledge of Christ would be most effectually transmitted to the nations of the earth.

MATTHEW HENRY

CHAPTER 1

Verses 1–17

Concerning this genealogy of our Saviour,

I. The title of it. It is *the book of the generation of Jesus Christ,* of his ancestors according to the flesh; or, It is the narrative of his birth. It is *Βίβλος Γενέσεως—a book of Genesis.* The Old Testament begins with the book of the generation of the world, but the glory of the New Testament *herein* excelleth, that it begins with *the book of the generation of* him that made the world.

II. The principal intention of it. It is not an endless or needless genealogy. It is like a pedigree given in evidence, to prove a title, and make out a claim; the design is to prove that our Lord Jesus is *the son of David,* and *the son of Abraham,* of that nation and family out of which the Messiah was to arise. Abraham and David were, in their day, the great trustees of the promise relating to the Messiah. It was promised to Abraham that Christ should descend from him (Gen. xii. 3; xxii. 18), and to David that he should

JAMIESON, FAUSSET, BROWN

CHAPTER 1

Vss. 1-17. GENEALOGY OF CHRIST. (—Luke 3:23-38). **1. The book of the generation**—an expression purely Jewish; meaning, "table of the genealogy." In Genesis 5:1 the same expression occurs in this sense. We have here, then, the title, not of this whole Gospel of Matthew, but only of the first seventeen verses. **of Jesus Christ**—For the meaning of these glorious words, see on vss. 16, 21. "Jesus," the name given to our Lord at His circumcision (Luke 2:21), was that by which He was familiarly known while on earth. The word "Christ"—though applied to Him as a proper name by the angel who announced His birth to the shepherds (Luke 2:11), and once or twice used in this sense by our Lord Himself (ch. 23:8, 10; Mark 9:41)—only began to be so used by others about the very close of His earthly career (ch. 26:68; 27:17). The full form, "Jesus Christ," though once used by Himself in His Intercessory Prayer (John 17:3), was

ADAM CLARKE

CHAPTER 1

1. ***The book of the generation of Jesus Christ.*** I suppose these words to have been the original title to this Gospel; and that they signify, according to the Hebrew phraseology, not only the account of the genealogy of Christ, but the history of His birth, acts, sufferings, death, resurrection, and ascension.

The phrase, "book of the generation," *sepher toledoth,* is frequent in the Jewish writings, and is translated by the Septuagint, *biblos geneseos,* as here, by the Evangelist; and regularly conveys the meaning given to it above. E.g., "This is the book of the generations of Adam," Gen. v. 1; that is, the account of the life of Adam and certain of his immediate descendants. Again, "These are the generations of Jacob," Gen. xxxvii. 2; that is, the account or history of Jacob, his son Joseph, and the other remarkable branches of the family. And again, "These

MATTHEW HENRY

descend from him (2 Sam. vii. 12; Ps. lxxxix. 3, &c.; cxxxii. 11). Christ is here first called *the son of David*, because under that title he was commonly spoken of, and expected, among the Jews. They who owned him to be *the Christ*, called him *the son of David, ch.* xv. 22; xx. 31; xxi. 15. This, therefore, the evangelist undertakes to make out, that he is not only a *son of David*, but that *son of David* on whose *shoulders the government was to be*; not only *a son of Abraham*, but that *son of Abraham* who was to be *the father of many nations*.

In calling Christ *the son of David*, and *the son of Abraham*, he shows that God is faithful to his promise, and will make good every word that he has spoken; and this, 1. Though the performance be long deferred. Delays of promised mercies, though they exercise our patience, do not weaken God's promise. 2. Though it begin to be despaired of. This *son of David*, and *son of Abraham*, who was to be the glory of his Father's house, was born when the seed of Abraham was a despised people, recently become tributary to the Roman yoke, and when the house of David was buried in obscurity; for Christ was to be *a root out of a dry ground*.

III. The particular series of it, drawn in the direct line from Abraham downward, according to the genealogies recorded in the beginning of the books of Chronicles.

Some particulars in this genealogy.

1. Among the ancestors of Christ who had brethren, generally he descended from a younger brother; such Abraham himself was, and Jacob, and Judah, and David, and Nathan, and Rhesa; to show that the pre-eminence of Christ came not from the primogeniture of his ancestors, but from the will of God, who *exalteth them of low degree*, and puts *more abundant honour upon that part which lacked*.

2. Among the sons of Jacob, besides Judah from whom Shiloh came, notice is here taken of *his brethren: Judas and his brethren*. No mention is made of Ishmael the son of Abraham, or of Esau the son of Isaac; because they were shut out of the church; whereas all the children of Jacob were taken in and therefore are mentioned in this genealogy.

3. Phares and Zara, the twin-sons of Judah, are likewise both named, though Phares only was Christ's ancestor, for the same reason that the brethren of Judah are taken notice of.

4. There are four women, and but four, named in this genealogy; two of them were originally *strangers to the commonwealth of Israel*, Rachab a Canaanitess, and a harlot besides, and Ruth the Moabitess; for *in Jesus Christ there is neither Greek nor Jew*; those that are *strangers and foreigners* are welcome, in Christ, to *the citizenship of the saints*. The other two were adulteresses, Thamar and Bathsheba; which was a further mark of humiliation put upon our Lord Jesus. He took upon him *the likeness of sinful flesh* (Rom. viii. 3), and takes even great sinners, upon their repentance, into the nearest relation to himself.

5. Though divers kings are here named, yet none is expressly called a king but David (*v.* 6), because with him the covenant of royalty was made. The Messiah is therefore said to inherit *the throne of his father David*, Luke i. 32.

6. In the pedigree of the kings of Judah, between Joram and Ozias (*v.* 8), there are three left out, namely, Ahaziah, Joash, and Amaziah; and therefore when it is said, *Joram begat Ozias*, it is meant, according to the usage of the Hebrew tongue, that Ozias was lineally descended from him.

7. Some observe what a mixture there was of good and bad in the succession of these kings; as for instance (*v.* 7, 8), wicked *Roboam begat* wicked *Abia*; wicked *Abia begat* good *Asa*; good *Asa begat* good *Josaphat*; good *Josaphat begat* wicked *Joram*. Grace does not run in the blood, neither does reigning sin. God's grace is his own, and he gives or withholds it as he pleases.

8. The captivity in Babylon is mentioned as a remarkable period in this line, *v.* 11, 12. All things considered, it was a wonder that the Jews were not lost in that captivity, as other nations have been; but this intimates the reason why the streams of that people were kept to run pure through that dead sea, because from them, as *concerning the flesh*, *Christ* was to *come*.

9. *Josias* is said to *beget Jechonias and his brethren* (*v.* 11); by Jechonias here is meant Jehoiakim, who was the first-born of Josias. When Jechonias is said to have been written *childless* (Jer. xxii. 30), it is explained thus: *No man of his seed shall prosper. Salathiel* is here said to *beget Zerubbabel*, whereas Salathiel begat Pedaiah, and he begat Zerubbabel (1 Chron. iii. 19): but, as before, the grandson is often called the son.

JAMIESON, FAUSSET, BROWN

never used by others till after His ascension and the formation of churches in His name. Its use, then, in the opening words of this Gospel (and in vss. 17, 18) is in the style of the late period when our Evangelist wrote, rather than of the events he was going to record. **the son of David, the son of Abraham**—As Abraham was the *first* from whose family it was predicted that Messiah should spring (Gen. 22:18), so David was the *last*. To a Jewish reader, accordingly, these behooved to be the two great starting-points of any true genealogy of the promised Messiah; and thus this opening verse, as it stamps the first Gospel as one peculiarly Jewish, would at once tend to conciliate the writer's people. From the nearest of those two fathers came that familiar name of the promised Messiah, "the son of David" (Luke 20:41), which was applied to Jesus, either in devout acknowledgment of His rightful claim to it (ch. 9:27; 20:31), or in the way of insinuating inquiry whether such were the case (see on John 4:29; ch. 12:23). **2. Abraham begat Isaac; and Isaac begat Jacob; and Jacob begat Judas and his brethren**—Only the fourth son of Jacob is here named, as it was from his loins that Messiah was to spring (Gen. 49:10). **3. And Judas begat Phares and Zara of Thamar; and Phares begat Esrom; and Esrom begat Aram; 4. And Aram begat Aminadab; and Aminadab begat Naasson; and Naasson begat Salmon; 5. And Salmon begat Booz of Rachab; and Booz begat Obed of Ruth; and Obed begat Jesse; 6. And Jesse begat David the king; and David the king begat Solomon of her of Urias**—Four women are here introduced; two of them Gentiles by birth—*Rachab* and *Ruth;* and three of them with a blot at their names in the Old Testament—*Thamar, Rachab*, and *Bath-sheba*. This feature in the present genealogy—herein differing from that given by Luke—comes well from him who styles himself in his list of the Twelve, what none of the other lists do, "Matthew *the publican*"; as if thereby to hold forth, at the very outset, the unsearchable riches of that grace which could not only fetch in "them that are afar off," but reach down even to "publicans and harlots," and raise them to "sit with the princes of his people." David is here twice emphatically styled "David the king," as not only the first of that royal line from which Messiah was to descend, but the one king of all that line from which the throne that Messiah was to occupy took its name—"the throne of David." The angel Gabriel, in announcing Him to His virgin-mother, calls it "the throne of David His father," sinking all the intermediate kings of that line, as having no importance save as links to connect the first and the last king of Israel as father and son. It will be observed that Rachab is here represented as the great-grandmother of David (see Ruth 4:20-22; and I Chron. 2:11-15)—a thing not beyond possibility indeed, but extremely improbable, there being about four centuries between them. There can hardly be a doubt that one or two intermediate links are omitted. **7. And Solomon begat Roboam; and Roboam begat Abia; and Abia begat Asa; 8. And Asa begat Josaphat; and Josaphat begat Joram; and Joram begat Ozias** [or Uzziah]—Three kings are here omitted—*Ahaziah, Joash*, and *Amaziah* (I Chron. 3:11, 12). Some omissions behooved to be made, to compress the whole into three fourteens (vs. 17). The reason why these, rather than other names, are omitted, must be sought in *religious* considerations—either in the connection of those kings with the house of Ahab (as LIGHTFOOT, EBRARD, and ALFORD view it); in their slender right to be regarded as true links in the theocratic chain (as LANGE takes it); or in some similar disqualification. **11. And Josias begat Jechonias and his brethren**—Jeconiah was Josiah's grandson, being the son of Jehoiakim, Josiah's second son (I Chron. 3:15); but Jehoiakim might well be sunk in such a catalogue, being a mere puppet in the hands of the king of Egypt (II Chron. 36:4). The "brethren" of Jechonias here evidently mean his uncles—the chief of whom, Mattaniah or Zedekiah, who came to the throne (II Kings 24:17), is, in II Chronicles 36:10, as well as here, called "his brother." **about the time they were carried away to Babylon**—lit., "of their migration," for the Jews avoided the word "captivity" as too bitter a recollection, and our Evangelist studiously respects the national feeling. **12. And after they were brought to** [after the migration of] **Babylon, Jechonias begat Salathiel**—So I Chron. 3:17. Nor does this contradict Jeremiah 22:30, Thus saith the Lord, Write ye this man [Coniah, or Jeconiah] childless"; for what follows explains in what sense this was meant—"for no man of his seed shall prosper, sitting upon the throne of David." He *was* to have seed, but no *reigning* child. **and Salathiel** [or Shealtiel] **begat Zorobabel**

ADAM CLARKE

are the generations of Aaron and Moses," Num. 3:1; that is, the history of the life and acts of these persons and some of their immediate descendants. The same form of expression is also used in Gen. ii. 4, when giving the history of the creation of heaven and earth. *The son of David, the son of Abraham.* No person ever born could boast, in a direct line, a more illustrious ancestry than Jesus Christ. David, the most renowned of sovereigns, was king and prophet; Abraham, the most perfect character in all antiquity, was priest and prophet. But the three offices were never united except in the person of Christ; He alone was Prophet, Priest, and King. This threefold office Christ executes not only in a general sense, in the world at large, but in a particular sense, in every Christian soul. He is first a Prophet, to teach the heart of man the will of God. He is next a Priest, to apply that atonement to the guilty conscience, the necessity of which, as a Prophet, He had previously made known. And lastly, as a King, He leads captivity captive, subdues and destroys sin, and reigns Lord over all the powers and faculties of the human soul. It is remarkable that the Evangelist names David before Abraham, though the latter was many generations older. The reason seems to be this, not only that David was not only the most illustrious of our Lord's predecessors, as being both king and prophet, but that promise which at first was given to Abraham was at last determined and restricted to the family of David. Son of David was an epithet by which the Messiah was afterwards known among the Jews.

8. *Joram begat Ozias.* Ozias was not the immediate son of Joram; there were three kings between them, Ahaziah, Joash, and Amaziah, which swell the fourteen generations to seventeen. But it is observed that omissions of this kind are not uncommon in the Jewish genealogies. Matthew took up the genealogies just as he found them in the public Jewish records, which, though they were in the main correct, yet were deficient in many particulars.

11. *Josias begat Jechonias.* There are three considerable difficulties in this verse: (1) Josias was not the father of Jechonias; he was only the grandfather of that prince, I Chron. iii. 14-16. (2) Jechonias had no brethren; at least, none are on record. (3) Josias died twenty years before the Babylonish captivity took place, and therefore Jechonias and his brethren could not have been begotten about the time they were carried away to Babylon. To this may be added a fourth difficulty, viz., there are only thirteen in this second class of generations; or forty-one, instead of forty-two, in the whole. But all these difficulties disappear by adopting a reading found in many manuscripts: And Josias begat Jehoiakim (or Joakim), and Joakim begat Jechonias.

12. *Jechonias begat Salathiel.* After Jechonias was brought to Babylon, he was put in prison by Nebuchadnezzar, where he continued till the death of this prince and the accession of Evil-merodach, who brought him out of prison, in which he had been detained thirty-seven years, and restored him to such favor that his throne (seat) was exalted above all the kings which were with him in Babylon, Jer. 3:31-32. But though he thus became a royal favorite, he was never restored in his kingdom. The term "carrying away to Babylon" would be more properly translated by the word transportation, which is here peculiarly appropriate. The change was not voluntary; they were forced away.

MATTHEW HENRY

10. The line is brought down, not to Mary the mother of our Lord, but to *Joseph the husband of Mary* (*v.* 16); for the Jews always reckoned their genealogies by the males; yet Mary was of the same tribe and family with Joseph, so that, both by his mother and by his supposed father, he was of the house of David.

11. The centre in whom all these lines meet is *Jesus, who is called Christ*, *v.* 16. This is he that was so importunately desired, so impatiently expected. They who do the will of God are in a more honourable relation to Christ than those who were akin to him according to the flesh, *ch.* xii. 50. *Jesus* is called *Christ*, that is, the *Anointed*, the same with the *Hebrew* name *Messiah*.

Lastly, The general summary of all this genealogy we have, *v.* 17, where it is summed up in three fourteens, signalised by remarkable periods. In the first fourteen, we have the family of David rising, and looking forth as the morning; in the second, we have it flourishing in its meridian lustre; in the third, we have it declining and growing less and less, dwindling into the family of a poor carpenter, and then Christ *shines forth* out of it, the *glory of his people Israel*.

Verses 18–25

The mystery of Christ's incarnation is to be adored, not pried into. If we *know not the way of the Spirit* in the formation of common persons, nor *how the bones are formed in the womb of* anyone *that is with child* (Eccles. xi. 5), much less do we know how the blessed Jesus was formed in the womb of the blessed virgin. Some circumstances attending the birth of Christ are not in Luke, though it is more largely recorded there. Here we have,

I. Mary's espousals to Joseph. Mary, the mother of our Lord, *was espoused to Joseph*, not completely married, but contracted. We read of a man who *has betrothed a wife and has not taken her*, Deut. xx. 7. Christ was born of a virgin, but a betrothed virgin, 1. To put respect upon the marriage state, and to recommend it as *honourable among all*. Who more highly favoured than Mary was in her espousals? 2. To save the credit of the blessed virgin, which otherwise would have been exposed. It was fit that her conception should be protected by a marriage, and so justified in the eye of the world. 3. That the blessed virgin might have one to be a help-meet for her. Some think that Joseph was now a widower, and that those who are called the *brethren of Christ* (*ch.* xiii. 55), were Joseph's children by a former wife. Joseph was a *just man*, she a *virtuous woman*. We may also learn, from this example, that it is good to enter into the married state with deliberation, and not hastily —to preface the nuptials with a contract. It is better to *take* time to consider before than to *find* time to repent after.

II. Her pregnancy of the promised seed; *before they came together*, she was *found with child*, which really was *of the Holy Ghost*. Now we may well imagine, what a perplexity this might justly occasion to the blessed virgin. She herself knew the divine original

JAMIESON, FAUSSET, BROWN

—So Ezra 3:2; Nehemiah 12:1; Haggai 1:1. But it would appear from I Chronicles 3:19 that Zerubbabel was Salathiel's grandson, being the son of Pedaiah, whose name, for some reason unknown, is omitted. **13-15. And Zorobabel begat Abiud . . .** —None of these names are found in the Old Testament; but they were doubtless taken from the public or family registers, which the Jews carefully kept, and their accuracy was never challenged. **16. And Jacob begat Joseph, the husband of Mary, of whom was born Jesus**—From this it is clear that the genealogy here given is not that of Mary, but of Joseph; nor has this ever been questioned. And yet it is here studiously proclaimed that Joseph was not the natural, but only the legal father of our Lord. His birth of a virgin was known only to a few; but the acknowledged descent of his legal father from David secured that the descent of Jesus Himself from David should never be questioned. See on vs. 20. **who is called Christ**—signifying "anointed." It is applied in the Old Testament to the *kings* (I Sam. 24:6, 10); to the *priests* (Lev. 4:5, 16, etc.); and to the *prophets* (I Kings 19:16)—these all being anointed will oil, the symbol of the needful spiritual gifts to consecrate them to their respective offices; and it was applied, in its most sublime and comprehensive sense, to the promised Deliverer, inasmuch as He was to be consecrated to an office embracing all three by the immeasurable anointing of the Holy Ghost (Isa. 61:1; cf. John 3:34). **17. So all the generations from Abraham to David are fourteen generations; and from David until the carrying away** [or migration] **into Babylon are fourteen generations; and from the carrying away into** [the migration of] **Babylon unto Christ are fourteen generations**—that is, the whole may be conveniently divided into three fourteens, each embracing one marked era, and each ending with a notable event, in the Israelitish annals. Such artificial aids to memory were familiar to the Jews, and much larger gaps than those here are found in some of the Old Testament genealogies. In Ezra 7:1-5 no fewer than six generations of the priesthood are omitted, as will appear by comparing it with I Chronicles 6:3-15. It will be observed that the last of the three divisions of fourteen appears to contain only thirteen distinct names, including Jesus as the last. LANGE thinks that this was meant as a tacit hint that *Mary* was to be supplied, as the thirteenth link of the last chain, as it is impossible to conceive that the Evangelist could have made any mistake in the matter. But there is a simpler way of accounting for it. As the Evangelist himself (vs. 17 reckons David twice—as the last of the first fourteen and the first of the second—so, if we reckon the second fourteen to end with Josiah, who was coeval with the "carrying away into captivity" (vs. 11), and the third to begin with Jeconiah, it will be found that the last division, as well as the other two, embraces fourteen names, including that of our Lord.

13-25. BIRTH OF CHRIST. **18. Now the birth of Jesus Christ was on this wise** [or, thus]:

When as his mother Mary was espoused [rather, betrothed] **to Joseph, before they came together,**

she was found [discovered to be] **with child of the Holy Ghost**—It was, of course, the fact only that was discovered; the explanation of the fact here given is the Evan-

ADAM CLARKE

16. *Jesus, who is called Christ*. As the word *Christos*, Christ, signifies "the anointed or anointer," from *chrio*, "to anoint," it answers exactly to the Hebrew *mashiach*, which we pronounce Messiah or Messias. As the same Person is intended by both the Hebrew and Greek appellation, it should be regularly translated the Messiah, or the Christ.

17. *Fourteen generations*. The Jews had a sort of technical method of summing up generations in this way. In Synopsis, *Sohar*, p. 132, n. 18, we have the following words, "From Abraham to Solomon were fifteen generations and then the moon was at the full. From Solomon to Zedekiah were other fifteen generations; the moon was then in the wane, and Zedekiah's eyes were put out." That is, the regal state came to its zenith of light and glory in the time of Solomon, but decreased gradually, till it became nearly extinct in the days of Zedekiah.

18. *Espoused to Joseph*. The word refers to the previous marriage agreement, in which the parties mutually bound themselves to each other, without which no woman was ever married among the Jews. *Before they came together*. The woman was espoused at her own or her father's house, and generally some time elapsed before she was taken home to the house of her husband, Deut. xxii. 7; Judg. xiv. 7-8. Among the Jews the espousal, though the marriage had not been consummated, was considered as perfectly legal and binding on both sides; and hence a breach of this contract was considered as a case of adultery, and punished exactly in the same way. See Deut. xxii. 25-28.

She was found with child. Her situation was the most distressing and humiliating that can be conceived. Nothing but the fullest consciousness of her own integrity and the strongest confi-

MATTHEW HENRY

of this conception; but how could she prove it? She would be *dealt with as a harlot*. Never was any daughter of Eve so dignified as the Virgin Mary was, and yet in danger of falling under the imputation of one of the worst of crimes; yet we do not find that she tormented herself about it; but, being conscious of her own innocence, she kept her mind calm and easy, and committed her cause to *him that judgeth righteously*.

III. Joseph's perplexity, and his care what to do in this case. He is loth to believe so ill a thing of one whom he believed to be so good a woman; and yet the matter, as it is too bad to be excused, is also too plain to be denied.

1. The extremity which he studied to avoid. He was *not willing to make her a public example*. He might have done so, Deut. xxii. 23, 24. How different was the spirit which Joseph displayed from that of Judah, who in a similar case hastily passed that severe sentence, *Bring her forth and let her be burnt!* Gen. xxxviii. 24. How good is it to *think on things*, as Joseph did here! Were there more of deliberation in our censures and judgments, there would be more of mercy and moderation in them.

Some persons of a rigorous temper would blame Joseph for his clemency: but it is here spoken of to his praise; because *he was a just man*, therefore he was not willing to expose her. He was a *religious, good man*; and therefore inclined to be merciful as God is, and to *forgive* as one that was *forgiven*. It becomes us, in many cases, to be gentle towards those that come under suspicion of having offended. That court of conscience which moderates the rigour of the law we call a *court of equity*. Those who are found faulty were perhaps *overtaken in the fault*, and are therefore to be *restored with the spirit of meekness*.

2. The expedient he found out for avoiding this extremity. He was *minded to put her away privily*, that is, to give a bill of divorce into her hand before two witnesses, and so to hush up the matter among themselves. The necessary censures of those who have offended ought to be managed without noise. Christian love and Christian prudence will *hide a multitude of sins*, and great ones, as far as may be done without having fellowship with them.

IV. Joseph's discharge from this perplexity by an express sent from heaven, *v.* 20, 21. *While he thought on these things* and knew not what to determine, God graciously directed him what to do, and made him easy. Those who would have direction from God must *think on things* themselves, and consult with themselves. It is the *thoughtful*, not the *unthinking*, whom God will guide. When he was at a loss, and had carried the matter as far as he could in his own thoughts, then God came in with advice. God's time to come in with instruction to his people is when they are *nonplussed* and at a stand. The message was sent to Joseph by an *angel of the Lord*. How far God may now, in an invisible way, make use of the ministration of angels, for extricating his people out of their straits, we cannot say; but this we are sure of, they are all *ministering spirits* for their good. This angel appeared to Joseph *in a dream* when he was asleep. When we are most quiet and composed we are in the best frame to receive the notices of the divine will.

1. Joseph is here *directed* to proceed in his intended marriage. It was requisite to put this poor carpenter in mind of his high birth: "Value thyself. Joseph, thou art that *son of David* through whom the line of the Messiah is to be drawn." We may thus say to every true believer, "Fear not, thou son of Abraham, thou child of God; forget not the dignity of thy birth, thy new birth." *Fear not to take Mary for thy wife;* so it may be read.

2. He is here *informed* concerning that *holy thing* with which his espoused wife was now pregnant. That which is conceived in her is of a divine original. Two things he is told,

(1) That she had conceived *by the power of the Holy Ghost*; not by the power of nature. The Holy Spirit, who produced the world, now produced the Saviour of the world, and *prepared him a body*, as was promised him, when he said, *Lo, I come*, Heb. x. 5. He is the *Son of God*, and yet so far partakes of the substance of his mother as to be called *the fruit of her womb*, Luke i. 42. Histories tell us of some who vainly pretended to have conceived by a divine power, as the mother of Alexander; but none ever really did so, except the mother of our Lord. We do not read that the virgin Mary did herself proclaim the honour done to her; but she hid it in her heart, and therefore God sent an angel to attest it.

(2) That she should bring forth *the Saviour of the world* (*v.* 21).

[1] In the name that should be given to her Son: *Thou shalt call his name Jesus, a Saviour*. Jesus is

JAMIESON, FAUSSET, BROWN

gelist's own. That the Holy Ghost is a living conscious Person is plainly implied here, and is elsewhere clearly taught (Acts 5:3, 4, etc.): and that, in the unity of the Godhead, He is distinct both from the Father and the Son, is taught with equal distinctness (Matt. 28:19; II Cor. 13:14). On the miraculous conception of our Lord, see on Luke 1:35.

19. Then Joseph her husband—Cf. vs. 20, "Mary, thy wife." Betrothal was, in Jewish law, valid marriage. In giving Mary up, therefore, Joseph had to take legal steps to effect the separation. **being a just man, and not willing to make her a public example** to expose her (see Deut. 22: 23, 24)

was minded to put her away privily—i.e., privately by giving her the required writing of divorcement (Deut. 24:1), in presence of only two or three witnesses, and without cause assigned, instead of having her before a magistrate. That some communication had passed between him and his betrothed, directly or indirectly, on the subject, after she returned from her three months' visit to Elizabeth, can hardly be doubted. Nor does the purpose to divorce her necessarily imply disbelief, on Joseph's part, of the explanation given him. Even supposing him to have yielded to it some reverential assent—and the Evangelist seems to convey as much, by ascribing the proposal to screen her to the *justice* of his character—he might think it altogether unsuitable and incongruous in such circumstances to follow out the marriage. **20. But while he thought on these things**—Who would not feel for him after receiving such intelligence, and before receiving any light from above? As he brooded over the matter alone, in the stillness of the night, his domestic prospects darkened and his happiness blasted for life, his mind slowly making itself up to the painful step, yet planning how to do it in the way least offensive—at the last extremity the Lord Himself interposes.

behold, the angel of the Lord appeared to him in a dream, saying, Joseph thou son of David—This style of address was doubtless advisedly chosen to remind him of what all the families of David's line so early coveted, and thus it would prepare him for the marvellous announcement which was to follow. **fear not to take unto thee Mary thy wife**—Though a dark cloud now overhangs this relationship, it is unsullied still. **for that which is conceived in her is of the Holy Ghost.**

ADAM CLARKE

dence in God could have supported her in such trying circumstances, where her reputation, her honor, and her life were at stake. What conversation passed between her and Joseph on this discovery we are not informed; but the issue proves that it was not satisfactory to him, nor could he resolve to consider her as his wife till God had sent His angel to bear the most unequivocal testimony to the Virgin's innocence. His whole conduct, on this occasion, was exceedingly benevolent and humane. He might at once have taken the advantage of the law, Deut. xxii. 23-24, and had her stoned to death.

19. *To make her a publick example*. Though Joseph was a righteous man, and knew that the law required that such persons as he supposed his wife to be should be put to death, yet, as righteousness is ever directed by mercy, he determined to put her away or divorce her privately, i.e., without assigning any cause, that her life might be saved. And as the offense was against himself, he had a right to pass it by if he chose.

A. T. ROBERTSON:

20. "An angel of the Lord appeared unto him in a dream" (*aggelos kuriou kat onar ephane autoi*). This expression (*aggelos kuriou*) is without the article in the New Testament except when, as in 1:24, there is reference to the angel previously mentioned. Sometimes in the Old Testament Jehovah himself is represented by this phrase. Surely Joseph needed God's help if ever man did. If Jesus was really God's Son, Joseph was entitled to know this supreme fact that he might be just to both Mary and her child. It was in a dream, but the message was distinct and decisive for Joseph. He is called "Son of David" as had been shown by Matthew in 1:16. Mary is called his "wife" (*ten gunaika sou*). He is told "not to become afraid" (ingressive first aorist passive subjunctive in prohibition, *me phobetheis*) "to take to his side" (*paralabein,* ingressive aorist active infinitive) her whom he had planned (*enthumethentos,* genitive absolute again, from *en* and *thumos*) to send away with a writ of divorce. He had pondered and had planned as best he knew, but now God had called a halt, and he had to decide whether he was willing to shelter Mary by marrying her and, if necessary, take upon himself whatever stigma might attach to her. Joseph was told that the child was begotten of the Holy Spirit and thus that Mary was innocent of any sin. But who would believe it now if he told it of her? Mary knew the truth and had not told him because she could not expect him to believe it.—*Word Pictures in the New Testament*

20. *That which is conceived* (or formed) *in her*. It appears that the human nature of Jesus Christ was a real creation in the womb of the Virgin by the power of the Holy Spirit. *The angel of the Lord* mentioned here was probably the angel Gabriel, who six months before had been sent to Zacharias and Elisabeth to announce the birth of Christ's forerunner, John the Baptist. See Luke i. 36.

MATTHEW HENRY

the same name with Joshua, the termination only being changed, for the sake of conforming it to the Greek. Joshua is called *Jesus* (Acts vii. 45; Heb. iv. 8), from the Seventy. Christ is our Joshua; both the *Captain of our salvation*, and the *High Priest of our profession*, and, in both, our Saviour—a Joshua who comes in the stead of Moses, and does that for us which *the law could not do, in that it was weak.* Joshua had been called *Hosea*, but Moses prefixed the first syllable of the name *Jehovah*, and so made it *Jehoshua* (Num. xiii. 16), to intimate that the Messiah, who was to bear that name, should be *Jehovah*; he is therefore *able to save to the uttermost*, neither is there *salvation in any other*.

[2] In the reason of that name: *For he shall save his people from their sins.* Those whom Christ saves he saves *from their sins*; from the guilt of sin by the *merit of his death*, from the dominion of sin by the *Spirit of his grace*. In saving them from sin, he saves them from wrath and the curse, and all misery here and hereafter. Those who leave their sins, and give up themselves to Christ as *his people*, are interested in the Saviour, and the great salvation which he has *wrought out*, Rom. xi. 26.

V. The fulfilling of the scripture in all this. This evangelist, writing among the Jews, more frequently observes this than any other of the evangelists. Here the Old Testament prophecies had their accomplishment in our Lord Jesus. Now the scripture that was fulfilled in the birth of Christ was that promise of a sign which God gave to king Ahaz (Isa. vii. 14), *Behold a virgin shall conceive;* where the prophet, encouraging the people of God to hope for the promised deliverance from Sennacherib's invasion, directs them to look forward to the Messiah, who was to come of the people of the Jews, and the house of David.

1. The sign given is that the Messiah shall be *born of a virgin. A virgin shall conceive*, and, by her, he shall be manifested *in the flesh*. The word *Almah* signifies a *virgin* in the strictest sense, such as Mary professes herself to be (Luke i. 34), *I know not a man.* Christ would be born, not of an *empress* or *queen*, for he appeared not in outward pomp or splendour, but of a virgin, to teach us spiritual purity.

2. The truth proved by this sign is, that he is the Son of God, and the Mediator between God and man; for *they shall call his name Immanuel. Immanuel* signifies *God with us;* a mysterious name, but very precious; God *incarnate* among us, and so God *reconcilable* to us, at peace with us, and taking us into covenant and communion with himself. The people of the Jews had *God with them*, in types and shadows, dwelling between the cherubim; but never so as when the *Word was made flesh*—that was the blessed *Shechinah*. By the light of *nature*, we see God as a God *above us*; by the light of the *law*, we see him as a God *against us*; but by the light of the gospel, we see him as *Immanuel*, God *with us*, in our own nature, and in our interest. Herein consists the salvation he wrought out, in the *bringing of God and man together*; this was what he designed, to bring *God* to be *with us*, which is our great happiness, and to bring *us* to *be with God*, which is our great duty.

VI. Joseph's obedience to the divine precept (*v.* 24). *Being raised from sleep* by the impression which the dream made upon him, *he did as the angel of the Lord had bidden him. He took unto him his wife.* God has still ways of making known his mind in doubtful cases, by hints of providence, debates of conscience, and advice of faithful friends; by each of these, applying the general rules of the written word, we should take direction from God.

VII. The accomplishment of the divine promise (*v.* 25). *She brought forth her first-born* son. The circumstances of it are more largely related, Luke ii. 1, &c. If Christ be *formed* in the soul, God himself has begun the good work which he will perform; what is *conceived* in grace will no doubt be *brought forth* in glory.

Joseph, though he solemnized the marriage with Mary, his espoused wife, *knew her not till she had brought him forth.* Much has been said concerning the perpetual virginity of the mother of our Lord: Jerome was very angry with Helvidius for denying it. It is certain that it cannot be proved from scripture. Dr. *Whitby* inclines to think that when it is said, *Joseph knew her not till she had brought forth her first-born*, it is intimated that, afterward he lived with her, according to the law, Exod. xxi. 10. *Joseph called his name Jesus*, according to the direction given him.

JAMIESON, FAUSSET, BROWN

21. And she shall bring forth a son—Observe, it is not said, "she shall bear *thee* a son," as was said to Zacharias of his wife Elizabeth (Luke 1:13). **and thou** [as his legal father] **shalt call his name JESUS** from the *Hebrew* meaning "Jehovah the Saviour"; in *Greek* JESUS—to the awakened and anxious sinner sweetest and most fragrant of all names, expressing so melodiously and briefly His whole saving office and work!

for he shall save—The "He" is here emphatic—He it is that shall save; He personally, and by personal acts (as WEBSTER and WILKINSON express it). **his people**—the lost sheep of the house of Israel, in the first instance; for they were the only people He then had. But, on the breaking down of the middle wall of partition, the saved people embraced the "redeemed unto God by His blood out of every kindred and people and tongue and nation." **from their sins**—in the most comprehensive sense of salvation from sin (Rev. 1:5; Eph. 5:25-27). **22. Now all this was done, that it might be fulfilled which was spoken of the Lord by the prophet** [Isa. 7:14], **saying,**

23. Behold, a virgin—It should be "*the* virgin" meaning that particular virgin destined to this unparalleled distinction. **shall be with child, and shall bring forth a son, and they shall call his name Emmanuel, which, being interpreted, is, God with us**—Not that He was to have this for a proper name (like "Jesus"), but that He should come to be known *in this character*, as God manifested in the flesh, and the living bond of holy and most intimate fellowship between God and men from henceforth and for ever.

24. Then Joseph, being raised from sleep [and all his difficulties now removed], **did as the angel of the Lord had bidden him, and took unto him his wife**—With what deep and reverential joy would this now be done on his part; and what balm would this minister to his betrothed one, who had till now lain under suspicions of all others the most trying to a chaste and holy woman—suspicions, too, arising from what, though to her an honor unparalleled, was to all around her wholly unknown!

25. And knew her not till she had brought forth her first-born son: and he called his name JESUS—The word "till" does not necessarily imply that they lived on a different footing afterwards (as will be evident from the use of the same word in I Sam. 15:35; II Sam. 6:23; Matt. 12:20); nor does the word "first-born" decide the much-disputed question, whether Mary had any children to Joseph after the birth of Christ; for, as LIGHTFOOT says, "The law, in speaking of the first-born, regarded not whether any were born *after* or no, but only that none were born before." (See on ch. 13:55, 56).

ADAM CLARKE

21. *Jesus.* The same as Joshua, *Yehoshua*, from *yasha*, "he saved, delivered, put to a state of safety." *He shall save his people from their sins.* This shall be His great business in the world, the great errand on which He is come, viz., to make an atonement for, and to destroy, sin. Deliverance from all the power, guilt, and pollution of sin is the privilege of every believer in Christ Jesus. The perfection of the gospel system is not that it makes allowances for sin, but that it makes an atonement for it; not that it tolerates sin, but that it destroys it.

23. *Behold, a virgin shall be with child.* Both the divine and human nature of our Lord, as well as the miraculous conception, appear to be pointed out in the prophecy quoted here by the Evangelist: He shall be called *Im-Menu-El;* literally, "The strong God with us." "The Word" which "was God . . . was made flesh, and dwelt among us . . . full of grace and truth," John i. 1-14. So that we are to understand "God with us" to imply God incarnated—God in human nature. This seems further evident from the words of the prophet, Isa. 7:15, "Butter and honey shall he eat"—He shall be truly man, grow up and be nourished in a human, natural way; which refers to His being "with us," i.e., incarnated. To which the prophet adds, "That he may know to refuse the evil, and choose the good"—or rather, "According to His knowledge, reprobating the evil, and choosing the good." This refers to Him as God. Now this union of the divine and human nature is termed a sign or miracle, i.e., something which exceeds the power of nature to produce. And this miraculous union was to be brought about in a miraculous way: "Behold, a virgin shall conceive"—the only one that ever was, or ever shall be, a mother in this way. In what sense, then, is Christ "God with us"? Jesus is called Immanuel, or God with us, in His incarnation—God united to our nature, God with man, God in man; God with us by His continual protection; God with us by the influences of His Holy Spirit—in the Holy Sacrament—in the preaching of His Word—in private prayer; and God with us through every action of our lives that we begin, continue, and end in His name. He is God with us to comfort, enlighten, protect, and defend us in every time of temptation and trial, in the hour of death, in the day of judgment; and God with us and in us, and we with and in Him, to all eternity.

25. *Her firstborn son.* Literally, "That Son of hers, the firstborn One." That Mary might have had other children, any person may reasonably and piously believe; that she had others, many think exceedingly probable, and that this text is at least an indirect proof of it. *He knew her not.* Had no matrimonial intercourse with her—till she had brought forth that Son of hers of whom the Evangelist had been just speaking, the firstborn, the eldest of the family, to whom the birthright belonged, and who was miraculously born before she knew any man, being yet in a state of virginity. *He called his name Jesus.* This name was given by the command of God, see v. 16, and was imposed on Christ when eight days old; for then, according to the Jewish law, He was circumcised. The goodness of God is manifested, not only in His giving His Son to save a lost world, but also in the choice of the persons who were His progenitors; among whom we find, first, saints, to excite our courage: Abraham, remarkable for his faith; Isaac, for his obedience; and Jacob, for his fervor and constancy. Secondly, penitent sinners, to excite our confidence, such as David, Manasses, etc. Thirdly, sinners, of whose repentance and salvation we hear nothing, to put us on our guard. Four women are mentioned in this genealogy; two of these were adulteresses, Tamar and Bathsheba; and two were Gentiles, Rahab and Ruth, and strangers to the covenant of promise; to teach us that Jesus Christ came to save sinners, and that, though strangers to His people, we are not on that account excluded from a salvation which God has designed for all men. He is not the God of the Jews only; He is also the God of the Gentiles.

MATTHEW HENRY

CHAPTER 2

It was a *mark of humiliation* put upon the Lord Jesus that, though he was the *Desire of all nations*, yet his coming into the world was little observed and taken notice of, his birth was obscure and unregarded. He *came into the world*, and the *world knew him not*; nay, he *came to his own*, and *his own received him not*. Yet, as afterward, so in his birth, some rays of glory darted forth in the midst of the greatest instances of his abasement.

The first who took notice of Christ after his birth were the shepherds (Luke ii. 15, &c.), who saw and heard glorious things concerning him, and *made them known abroad*, to the amazement of all that heard them, *v.* 17, 18. After that, Simeon and Anna spoke of him, by the Spirit, to all that were disposed to heed what they said, Luke ii. 38. Now, one would think, these hints should have been taken by the men of Judah and the *inhabitants of Jerusalem*, and they should with both arms have embraced the long-looked-for Messiah; but, for aught that appears, he continued nearly two years after at Bethlehem, and no further notice was taken of him till these wise men came. Nothing will awaken those that are resolved to be regardless. Observe,

I. When this enquiry was made concerning Christ. It was *in the days of Herod the king*. This Herod was an Edomite, made king of Judæa by Augustus and Antonius, the then chief rulers of the Roman state, a man made up of falsehood and cruelty; yet he was complimented with the title of *Herod the Great*.

II. Who and what these *wise men* were; they are here called *Magicians*. Some take it in a good sense; the *Magi* among the *Persians* were their philosophers and their priests; others think they dealt in unlawful arts; the word is used of Simon, the sorcerer (Acts viii. 9, 11), and of Elymas, the sorcerer (Acts xiii. 6), nor does the scripture use it in any other sense. Well, whatever sort of wise men they were before, now they began to be *wise men* indeed when they set themselves to enquire after Christ.

This we are sure of, 1. That they were Gentiles, and not belonging to the commonwealth of Israel. The Jews regarded not Christ, but these Gentiles enquired him out. Note, Many times those who are nearest to the means, are furthest from the end. See *ch.* viii. 11, 12. 2. That they were *scholars*. They dealt in arts, curious arts; good scholars should be good Christians, and *then* they complete their *learning* when they *learn Christ*. 3. That they were *men of the east*, who were noted for their *soothsayings*, Isa. ii. 6. Arabia is called the land of *the east* (Gen. xxv. 6), and the *Arabians* are called *men of the east*, Judges vi. 3. The presents they brought were the products of that country.

III. What induced them to make this enquiry. They, in their country, which was in the *east*, had seen an *extraordinary star*, such as they had not seen before; which they took to be an indication of an extraordinary person born in the land of *Judæa*, over which land this star was seen to hover. This differed so much from anything that was common that they concluded it to signify something uncommon. The birth of Christ was notified to the Jewish shepherds by *an angel*, to the Gentile philosophers by a *star*: to both God spoke in their own language, and in the way they were best acquainted with. The same star which they had seen in the *east* they saw a great while after, leading them to the house where Christ lay, was a candle set up on purpose to guide them to Christ. The idolaters worshipped the stars as the *host of heaven*, especially the *eastern* nations. Thus the stars that had been misused came to be put to the right use, to lead men to Christ; the gods of the heathen became his servants. Others impute their enquiry to the general expectation entertained at that time, in those *eastern* parts, of some great prince to appear. We may suppose a divine impression made upon their minds, enabling them to interpret this star as a signal given by Heaven of the birth of Christ.

IV. How they prosecuted this enquiry. *They came from the* east to Jerusalem, in further quest of this prince. They might have said, "If such a prince be born, we shall hear of him shortly in our own country, and it will be time enough then to pay our homage to him." But so impatient were they to be better acquainted with him, that they took a long journey on purpose to enquire after him. Those who truly desire to know Christ, and find him, will not regard pains or perils in seeking after him.

Their question is, *Where is he that is born king of the* Jews? They do not ask, *whether there were such a one born?* but, *Where is he born?* Those who know *something* of Christ cannot but covet to *know more* of him.

To this question they doubted not but to have a ready answer, and to find all Jerusalem worshipping

JAMIESON, FAUSSET, BROWN

CHAPTER 2

Vss. 1-12. VISIT OF THE MAGI TO JERUSALEM AND BETHLEHEM. *The Wise Men Reach Jerusalem—The Sanhedrim, on Herod's Demand, Pronounce Bethlehem to Be Messiah's Predicted Birthplace* (vss. 1-6). **1. Now when Jesus was born in Bethlehem of Judea**—so called to distinguish it from another Bethlehem in the tribe of Zebulun, near the Sea of Galilee (Josh. 19:15); called also *Beth-le-hem-judah*, as being in that tribe (Judg. 17:7); and *Ephrath* (Gen. 35:16); and combining both, *Beth-lehem Ephratah* (Mic. 5:2). It lay about six miles southwest of Jerusalem. But how came Joseph and Mary to remove thither from Nazareth, the place of their residence? Not of their own accord, and certainly not with the view of fulfilling the prophecy regarding Messiah's birthplace; nay, they stayed at Nazareth till it was almost too late for Mary to travel with safety; nor would they have stirred from it at all, had not an order which left them no choice forced them to the appointed place. A high hand was in all these movements. (See on Luke 2:1-6.) **in the days of Herod the king**—styled the Great; son of Antipater, an *Edomite*, made king by the Romans. Thus was "the sceptre departing from Judah" (Gen. 49:10), a sign that Messiah was now at hand. As Herod is known to have died in the year of Rome 750, in the fourth year before the commencement of our Christian era, the birth of Christ must be dated four years before the date usually assigned to it, even if He was born within the year of Herod's death, as it is next to certain that He was. **there came wise men**—lit., "Magi" or "Magians," probably of the learned class who cultivated astrology and kindred sciences. Balaam's prophecy (Num. 24:17), and perhaps Daniel's (ch. 9:24, etc.), might have come down to them by tradition; but nothing definite is known of them. **from the east**—but whether from Arabia, Persia, or Mesopotamia is uncertain. **to Jerusalem**—as the Jewish metropolis.

F. B. MEYER:

The wise men follow the star. The expectation of the advent of a great king was far-spread at the time of the Nativity. It was probably founded, so far as the East was concerned, on the prophecies of Balaam and Daniel (see Num. 24:17; Dan. 7:13, 14). There are evidences of the same expectation in the classic literature of the West. Our Lord was the desire of all nations, and the corruption and anarchy of the Roman Empire made the longing still more intense.

God comes to men in the spheres with which they are most familiar: to Zacharias in the temple, to the shepherds in the fields, to the wise men by a portent in the heavens. He knows just where to find us. Be sure to follow your star, whatever it be; only remember that it must ultimately receive the corroboration of Scripture, as in the present case (v. 5). A miracle may be wrought to awaken and start us on our great quest, but the miraculous is withdrawn where the ordinary methods of inquiry will serve. The news of Jesus always disquiets the children of the world; they know that it means division.—*Bible Commentary*

ADAM CLARKE

CHAPTER 2

1. *Bethlehem of Judaea.* This city is mentioned in Judg. xvii. 7. It is situated on the declivity of a hill about six miles from Jerusalem. *Beth-lechem* in Hebrew signifies "the house of bread." The name may be considered as very properly applied to that place where Jesus, the Messiah, the True Bread that came down from heaven, was manifested to give life to the world. *In the days of Herod the king.* This is Herod, improperly denominated "the Great," the son of Antipater, an Idumean. He reigned thirty-seven years in Judea, reckoning from the time he was created king of that country by the Romans. Our blessed Lord was born in the last year of his reign; and at this time the sceptre had literally departed from Judah, a foreigner being now upon the throne.

There came wise men from the east. Or Magi "came from the Eastern countries." That many Jews were mixed with this people there is little doubt; and that these Eastern Magi, or philosophers, astrologers, or whatever else they were, might have been originally of that class there is room to believe. These, knowing the promise of the Messiah, were now probably, like other believing Jews, waiting for "the consolation of Israel." It is very probable that the persons mentioned by the Evangelist were a sort of astrologers, probably of Jewish extraction, that they lived in Arabia Felix, and came to worship their newborn Sovereign.

2. *We have seen his star.* Having discovered an unusual luminous appearance or meteor in the heavens, supposing these persons to have been Jews, and knowing the prophecies relative to the redemption of Israel, they probably considered this to be the star mentioned by Balaam, Num. xiv. 17. *In the east.* "At its rise."

MATTHEW HENRY

at the feet of this new king; but no man can give them any information. There is more gross ignorance in the world, and in the church too, than we are aware of. Many that we think should direct us to Christ are themselves strangers to him. They pursue the enquiry, *Where is he that is born king of the Jews?* Are they asked, "Why do ye make this enquiry?" It is because they have *seen his star in the east*. Are they asked, "What business have ye with him? What have the men of the *east* to do with the *King of the Jews?*" They have their answer ready, *We are come to worship him*. Those in whose hearts the day-star is risen, to give them anything of the knowledge of Christ, must make it their business to worship him.

V. How this enquiry was treated at Jerusalem. News of it at last came to court; and *when Herod heard it he was troubled*, *v.* 3. He could not be a stranger to the prophecies of the *Old Testament*, concerning the Messiah and his kingdom, and the times fixed for his appearing by Daniel's weeks; but, having himself reigned so long and so successfully, he began to hope that those promises would for ever fail, and that his kingdom would be established and perpetuated in spite of them. What a damp therefore must it needs be upon him, to hear talk of this king being born.

But though Herod, an Edomite, was troubled, one would have thought Jerusalem should rejoice greatly to hear that her King comes; yet, it seems, *all Jerusalem were troubled with* Herod, and were apprehensive of I know not what ill consequences of the birth of this new king. The slavery of sin is foolishly preferred by many to the glorious liberty of the children of God, only because they apprehend some present difficulties attending that necessary revolution of the government in the soul. Herod and Jerusalem were thus troubled, from a mistaken notion that the kingdom of the Messiah would clash and interfere with the secular powers; whereas the star that proclaimed him king plainly intimated that his kingdom was heavenly, and not of this lower world.

VI. What assistance they met with in this enquiry from the scribes and the priests, *v.* 4-6. Nobody can pretend to tell where the King of the Jews is, but Herod enquires where it was expected *he should be born*. It was generally known that Christ should be *born at Bethlehem* (John vii. 42); but Herod would have counsel's opinion upon it, and therefore applies himself to the proper persons; *all the chief priests, and all the scribes*; and *demands of them* what was the place, *where Christ should be born?* Many a good question is put with an ill design.

The priests and scribes need not take any long time to give an answer to this query; nor do they differ in their opinion, but all agree that the Messiah must be *born in Bethlehem, the city of David*, here called *Bethlehem of Judæa*. *Bethlehem* signifies *the house of bread;* the fittest place for him to be born in who is the true manna, *the bread which came down from heaven*, which was *given for the life of the world*. Bethlehem's honour lay not, as that of other cities, in the multitude of the people, but in the magnificence of the princes it produced. Herein it had the pre-eminence above all the cities of Israel, that *the Lord shall count, when he writes up the people, that this man*, even *the man Christ Jesus, was born there*, Ps. lxxxvii. 6. *Out of thee shall come a Governor*, the *King of the Jews*. Bethlehem was the *city of David*, and David the glory of Bethlehem; there, therefore, must David's son and successor be born. There was a famous well at *Bethlehem*, by the gate, which David longed to drink of (2 Sam. xxiii. 15); in Christ we have not only bread enough and to spare, but may come and take also *of the water of life freely*.

JAMIESON, FAUSSET, BROWN

2. Saying, Where is he that is born King of the Jews?—From this it would seem they were not themselves Jews. (Cf. the language of the Roman governor, John 18:33, and of the Roman soldiers, ch. 27:29, with the very different language of the Jews themselves, ch. 27:42, etc.). The Roman historians, SUETONIUS and TACITUS, bear witness to an expectation, prevalent in the East, that out of Judea should arise a sovereign of the world. **for we have seen his star in the east**—Much has been written on the subject of this star; but from all that is here said it is perhaps safest to regard it as simply a luminous meteor, which appeared under special laws and for a special purpose. **and are come to worship him**—to do Him homage, as the word signifies; the nature of that homage depending on the circumstances of the case. That not civil but religious homage is meant here is plain from the whole strain of the narrative, and particularly vs. 11. Doubtless these simple strangers expected all Jerusalem to be full of its new-born King, and the time, place, and circumstances of His birth to be familiar to every one. Little would they think that the first announcement of His birth would come from themselves, and still less could they anticipate the startling, instead of transporting, effect which it would produce—else they would probably have sought their information regarding His birthplace in some other quarter. But God overruled it to draw forth a noble testimony to the predicted birthplace of Messiah from the highest ecclesiastical authority in the nation. **3. When Herod the king had heard these things, he was troubled**—viewing this as a danger to his own throne: perhaps his guilty conscience also suggested other grounds of fear. **and all Jerusalem with him**—from a dread of revolutionary commotions, and perhaps also of Herod's rage. **4. And when he had gathered all the chief priests and scribes of the people together**—The class of the "chief priests" included the high priest for the time being, together with all who had previously filled this office; for though the then head of the Aaronic family was the only rightful high priest, the Romans removed them at pleasure, to make way for creatures of their own. In this class probably were included also the heads of the four-and-twenty courses of the priests. The "scribes" were at first merely transcribers of the law and synagogue-readers; afterwards interpreters of the law, both civil and religious, and so both lawyers and divines. The first of these classes, a proportion of the second, and "the elders"—that is, as LIGHTFOOT thinks, "those elders of the laity that were not of the Levitical tribe"—constituted the supreme council of the nation, called the *Sanhedrim*, the members of which, at their full complement, numbered seventy-two. That this was the council which Herod now convened is most probable, from the solemnity of the occasion; for though the elders are not mentioned, we find a similar omission where all three were certainly meant (cf. ch. 26:59; 27:1). As MEYER says, it was all the theologians of the nation whom Herod convened, because it was a theological response that he wanted. **he demanded of them**—as the authorized interpreters of Scripture. **where Christ**—the Messiah. **should be born**—according to prophecy. **5. And they said unto him, In Bethlehem of Judea**—a prompt and involuntary testimony from the highest tribunal; which yet at length condemned Him to die. **for thus it is written by the prophet**—(Mic. 5:2). **6. And thou, Bethlehem,** [in] **the land of Juda**—the "in" being familiarly left out, as we say, "London, Middlesex." **art not the least among the princes of Juda: for out of thee shall come a Governor . . .**—This quotation, though differing verbally, agrees substantially with the *Hebrew* and LXX. For says the prophet, "Though thou be little, yet out of thee shall come the Ruler"—this honor more than compensating for its natural insignificance; while our Evangelist, by a lively turn, makes him say, "Thou art *not the least:* for out of thee shall come a Governor"—this distinction lifting it from the lowest to the highest rank. The "thousands of Juda," in the prophet, mean the subordinate divisions of the tribe: our Evangelist, instead of these, merely names the "princes" or heads of these families, including the districts which they occupied **that shall rule**—or "feed," as in the margin. **my people Israel**—In the Old Testament, kings are, by a beautiful figure, styled "shepherds" (Ezek. 31, etc.). The classical writers use the same figure. The pastoral rule of Jehovah and Messiah over His people is a representation pervading all Scripture, and rich in import. (See Ps. 23; Isa 40:11; Ezek. 37:24; John 10:11; Rev. 7:17). That this prophecy of Micah referred to the Messiah, was admitted by the ancient Rabbins.

ADAM CLARKE

To worship him. Or "to do Him homage." The word signifies to crouch and fawn like a dog at his master's feet. It means to prostrate oneself to another, according to the Eastern custom which is still in use. As to what is here called a *star*, some make it a meteor, others a luminous appearance like an aurora borealis, others a comet. There is no doubt the appearance was very striking, but it seems to have been a simple meteor provided for the occasion.

3. *When Herod . . . heard these things, he was troubled*. Herod's consternation was probably occasioned by the agreement of the account of the Magi with an opinion predominant throughout the East, and particularly in Judea, that some great personage would soon make his appearance for the deliverance of Israel from their enemies, and would take upon himself universal empire.

4. *The chief priests*. Not only the high priest for the time being, and his deputy, with those who had formerly borne the high priest's office —but also the chiefs or heads of the twenty-four sacerdotal families, which David distributed into so many courses, 1 Chronicles xxiv. *Scribes*. The word in the Septuagint is used for a political officer, whose business it was to assist kings and civil magistrates, and to keep an account in writing of public acts and occurrences. Such an officer is called in Hebrew the king's scribe or secretary. See the Septuagint, II Kings 7:10. The word is often used by the Septuagint for a man of learning, especially for one skilled in the Mosaic law; and in the same sense it is used by the New Testament writers. It is therefore to be understood as always implying a man of letters, or learning, capable of instructing the people. The word is used in Acts xix. 35 for a civil magistrate at Ephesus, probably such a one as we would term recorder. It appears that Herod at this time gathered the whole Sanhedrin, in order to get the fullest information on a subject by which all his jealous fears had been alarmed.

6. *And thou Bethlehem, in the land of Juda*. To distinguish it from Bethlehem in the tribe of Zebulon, Josh. xix. 15. *Among the princes of Juda*. In Mic. v. 2 it is "the thousands of Judah." There is reason to believe that each tribe was divided into small portions called thousands. These thousands being petty governments, Matthew renders them by the word *hegemosin*, because the word princes or governors was more intelligible in the Greek tongue than thousands, though in this case they both signify the same.

That shall rule my people Israel. Who shall feed My people—that is, as a shepherd feeds his flock. Among the Greeks, kings are called, by Homer, shepherds of the people.

MATTHEW HENRY

VII. The bloody project and design of Herod, occasioned by this enquiry, *v.* 7, 8. Herod was now an old man, and had reigned thirty-five years; this king was but newly born, and not likely to enterprise anything considerable for many years; yet Herod is jealous of him. Crowned heads cannot endure to think of successors, much less of rivals; and therefore nothing less than the blood of this infant king will satisfy him. Passion has got the mastery of reason and conscience.

1. See how cunningly he laid the project (*v.* 7, 8). *He privily called the wise men,* to talk with them about this matter. He would not openly own his fears and jealousies. Sinners are often tormented with secret fears, which they keep to themselves. Herod learns of the wise men the *time when the star appeared,* and then employs them to enquire further, and bids them bring him an account. All this might look suspicious, if he had not covered it with a show of religion: *that I may come and worship him also.* The greatest wickedness often conceals itself under a mask of piety.

2. See how strangely he was befooled and infatuated in this, that he trusted it with the wise men. It was but seven miles from Jerusalem; how easily might he have sent spies to watch the wise men, who might have been as soon there to destroy the child as they to worship him!

Verses 9–12

We have here the wise men's humble attendance upon this new-born *King of the Jews,* and the honours they paid him. From Jerusalem they went to Bethlehem, resolving to *seek till they should find;* but it is very strange that they went alone. They *came from a far country,* to worship Christ while the Jews, his kinsmen, would not stir a step, would not go to the next town to bid him welcome. We must continue our attendance upon Christ, though we be alone in it; whatever others do, we must *serve the Lord.*

I. See how they found out Christ by the same star that they had seen in their own country, *v.* 9, 10. Observe, 1. How graciously God directed them. By the first appearance of the star they were given to understand where they might enquire for this King, and then it disappeared, and they were left to take the usual methods for such an enquiry. Extraordinary helps are not to be expected where ordinary means are to be had. Well, they had traced the matter as far as they could; they were upon their journey to Bethlehem, but that is a populous town. Where shall they find him when they come thither? Here they were at a loss, at their wit's end, but not at their faith's end; they believed that God would not leave them there; nor did he; for, behold, *the star which they saw in the east went before them.* If we go on as far as we can in the way of our duty, God will direct and enable us to do that which of ourselves we cannot do. The star had left them a great while, yet now returns. They who follow God in the dark shall find that light is sown, is reserved, for them. This star was the token of God's presence with them; for he is light, and goes before his people as their Guide. There is a day-star that arises in the hearts of those that enquire after Christ, 2 Peter i. 19. 2. Observe how joyfully they followed God's direction (*v.* 10). *When they saw the star, they rejoiced with exceeding great joy.* Now they saw they were not deceived, and had not taken this long journey in vain. Now they were sure that God was with them, and the tokens of his presence and favour cannot but fill with joy unspeakable the souls of those that know how to value them. We cannot expect too little from man, nor too much from God. What a transport of joy these wise men were in upon this sight of the star. Now they had reason to hope for a sight of *the Lord's Christ* speedily, of *the Sun of righteousness,* for they see *the Morning Star.* We should be glad of everything that will show us the way to Christ. This star was sent to meet the wise men, and to conduct them into the presence chamber of the King. Now God fulfills his promise of meeting those that are disposed to *rejoice and work righteousness* (Isa. lxiv. 5). God is pleased sometimes to favour young converts with such tokens of his love as are very encouraging to them, in reference to the difficulties they meet with at their setting out in the ways of God.

II. See how they made their address to him when they had found him, *v.* 11. We may well imagine what a disappointment it was to them when they found a cottage was his palace, and his own poor mother all the retinue he had! However, these wise men were so wise as to see through this veil. They did not think themselves baulked or baffled in their enquiry; but, as having found the King they sought, they presented themselves first, and then their gifts, to him.

1. They presented themselves to him: *they fell*

JAMIESON, FAUSSET, BROWN

The Wise Men, Despatched to Bethlehem by Herod to See the Babe, and Bring Him Word, Make a Religious Offering to the Infant King, but Divinely Warned, Return Home by Another Way (vss. 7-12). **7. Then Herod, when he had privily called the wise men**—Herod has so far succeeded in his murderous design: he has tracked the spot where lies his victim, an unconscious babe. But he has another point to fix—the date of His birth—without which he might still miss his mark. The one he had got from the Sanhedrim; the other he will have from the sages; but secretly, lest his object should be suspected and defeated. So he **inquired of them diligently**—rather, "precisely." **what time the star appeared**—presuming that this would be the best clue to the age of the child. The unsuspecting strangers tell him all. And now he thinks he is succeeding to a wish, and shall speedily clutch his victim; for at so early an age as they indicate, He would not likely have been removed from the place of His birth. Yet he is wary. He sends them as messengers from himself, and bids them come to *him,* that he may follow their pious example. **8. And he sent them to Bethlehem, and said, Go and search diligently**—"Search out carefully." **for the young child; and when ye have found him, bring me word again, that I may come and worship him also**—The cunning and bloody hypocrite! Yet this royal mandate would meantime serve as a safe-conduct to the strangers.

9. When they had heard the king, they departed—But where were ye, O Jewish ecclesiastics, ye chief priests and scribes of the people? Ye could tell Herod where Christ should be born, and could hear of these strangers from the far East that the Desire of all nations had actually come; but I do not see you trooping to Bethlehem—I find these devout strangers journeying thither all alone. Yet God ordered this too, lest the news should be blabbed, and reach the tyrant's ears, before the Babe could be placed beyond his reach. Thus are the very errors and crimes and cold indifferences of men all overruled.

and, lo, the star, which they saw in the east—implying apparently that it had disappeared in the interval. **went before them, and stood over where the young child was**—Surely this could hardly be but by a luminous meteor, and not very high.

10. When they saw the star, they rejoiced with exceeding great joy—The language is very strong, expressing exuberant transport.

11. And when they were come into the house—not the stable; for as soon as Bethlehem was emptied of its strangers, they would have no difficulty in finding a dwelling-house. **they saw**—The received text has "found"; but here our translators rightly depart from it, for it has no authority. **the young child with Mary his mother**—The blessed Babe is naturally mentioned first, then the mother; but Joseph, though doubtless present, is not noticed, as being but the head of the house. **and fell down**

ADAM CLARKE

8. *That I may come and worship him also.* See v. 2, and on Gen. xvii. 3 and Exod. iv. 31. What exquisite hypocrisy was here! He only wished to find out the Child that he might murder Him; but see how that God who searches the heart prevents the designs of wicked men from being accomplished!

9. *In the east.* Or "at its rise."

MATTHEW HENRY

down, and worshipped him. We do not read that they gave such honour to Herod, though he was in the height of his royal grandeur; but to this babe they gave this honour, not only as to a king, but as to a God. All that have found Christ fall down before him; they adore him, and submit themselves to him. *He is thy Lord, and worship thou him.*

2. *They presented their gifts to him.* In the eastern nations, when they did homage to their kings, they made them presents. With ourselves, we must give up all that we have to Jesus Christ. Nor are our gifts accepted, unless we first present ourselves to him living sacrifices. The gifts they presented were, *gold, frankincense, and myrrh,* money, and money's-worth. Providence sent this for a seasonable relief to Joseph and Mary in their present poor condition. These were the products of their own country; what God favours us with, we must honour him with. They offered him *gold,* as a king, paying him tribute; *frankincense,* as God, for they honoured God with the smoke of incense; and *myrrh,* as a Man that should die, for *myrrh* was used in embalming dead bodies.

III. See how they left him when they had made their address to him, *v.* 12. Herod appointed them to *bring him word.* They would have done so, if they had not been countermanded, not suspecting their being thus made his tools in a wicked design. Those that mean honestly and well themselves are easily made to believe that others do so too, and cannot think the world is so bad as really it is. God prevented the mischief Herod designed to the Child Jesus. They were *warned not to return to Herod,* nor to Jerusalem; those were unworthy to have reports brought them concerning Christ, that might have seen with their own eyes, and would not. *They departed into their own country another way,* to bring the tidings to their countrymen; but it is strange that we never hear any more of them.

Verses 13–15

We have here Christ's flight into Egypt to avoid the cruelty of Herod. It was but little respect (compared with what should have been) that was paid to Christ in his infancy: yet even that, instead of honouring him among his people, did but expose him.

I. The command given to Joseph concerning it, *v.* 13. Joseph knew neither the danger the child was in, nor how to escape it; but God, by *an angel,* tells him both *in a dream,* as before he directed him in like manner what to do, *ch.* i. 20. Joseph is here told what their danger was: *Herod will seek the young child to destroy him.* God is acquainted with all the cruel projects and purposes of the enemies of his church. How early was the blessed Jesus involved in trouble! Usually, even those whose riper years are attended with toils and perils have a peaceable and quiet infancy; but it was not so with the blessed Jesus: his life and sufferings began together. He is directed what to do, to escape the danger; *Take the young child, and flee into Egypt.* Thus early must Christ give an example to his own rule (*ch.* x. 23): *When they persecute you in one city, flee to another.* Self-preservation, being a branch of the law of nature, is eminently a part of the law of God. *Flee;* but why *into Egypt*? Egypt was infamous for idolatry, tyranny, and enmity to the people of God. Yet that is appointed to be a place of refuge to the holy child Jesus. God, when he pleases, can make the worst of places serve the best of purposes. This may be considered,

1. As a trial of the faith of Joseph and Mary. They might be tempted to think, "If this child be the Son of God, as we are told he is, has he no other way to secure himself from a man that is a worm, than by such a mean and inglorious retreat as this? They had been lately told that he should be *the glory of his people Israel*; and is the land of Israel so soon become too hot for him? Now it appeared how well God had provided for *the young child and his mother,* in appointing Joseph to stand in so near a relation to them; now the gold which the wise men brought would stand them in stead to bear their charges. God foresees his people's distresses, and provides against them beforehand. God intimates the continuance of his care and guidance, when he saith, *Be thou there until I bring thee word,* so that he must expect to hear from God again, and not stir without fresh orders.

2. As an instance of the humiliation of our Lord Jesus. As there was no room for him in the inn at Bethlehem, so there was no quiet room for him in the land of Judæa. If we and our infants be at any time in straits, let us remember the straits Christ in his infancy was brought into.

3. As a token of God's displeasure against the Jews, who took so little notice of him; justly does he leave those who had slighted him.

II. Joseph's obedience to this command, *v.* 14.

JAMIESON, FAUSSET, BROWN

and worshipped him—Clearly this was no civil homage to a petty Jewish king, whom these starguided strangers came so far, and inquired so eagerly, and rejoiced with such exceeding joy, to pay, but a lofty spiritual homage. The next clause confirms this. **and when they had opened their treasures they presented**—rather, "offered." **unto him gifts**—This expression, used frequently in the Old Testament of the oblations presented to God, is in the New Testament employed seven times, and always in *a religious* sense of *offerings to God.* Beyond doubt, therefore, we are to understand the presentation of these gifts by the Magi as *a religious offering.* **gold, frankincense, and myrrh**—Visits were seldom paid to sovereigns without a present (I Kings 10:2, etc.); cf. Ps. 72:10, 11, 15; Isa. 60:3, 6). "Frankincense" was an aromatic used in sacrificial offerings: "myrrh" was used in perfuming ointments. These, with the "gold" which they presented, seem to show that the offerers were persons in affluent circumstances. That the gold was presented to the infant King in token of His royalty; the frankincense in token of His divinity, and the myrrh, of His sufferings; or that they were designed to express His divine and human natures; or that the prophetical, priestly, and kingly offices of Christ are to be seen in these gifts; or that they were the offerings of three individuals respectively, each of them kings, the very names of whom tradition has handed down—all these are, at the best, precarious suppositions. But that the feelings of these devout givers are to be seen in the richness of their gifts, and that the gold, at least, would be highly serviceable to the parents of the blessed Babe in their unexpected journey to Egypt and stay there—that much at least admits of no dispute. **12. And being warned of God in a dream that they should not return to Herod, they departed** [or, withdrew] **to their own country another way**—What a surprise would this vision be to the sages, just as they were preparing to carry the glad news of what they had seen to the *pious* king! But the Lord knew the bloody old tyrant better than to let him see their face again.

13-25. The Flight into Egypt—The Massacre at Bethlehem—The Return of Joseph and Mary with the Babe, after Herod's Death, and Their Settlement at Nazareth. (= Luke 2:39). *The Flight into Egypt* (vss. 13-15). **13. And when they were departed, behold, the angel of the Lord appeareth to Joseph in a dream, saying, Arise, and take the young child and his mother**—Observe this form of expression, repeated in the next verse—another indirect hint that Joseph was no more than the Child's *guardian.* Indeed, personally considered, Joseph has no spiritual significance, and very little place at all, in the Gospel history. **and flee into Egypt**—which, being near, as Alford says, and a Roman province independent of Herod, and much inhabited by Jews, was an easy and convenient refuge. Ah! blessed Saviour, on what a checkered career hast Thou entered here below! At Thy birth there was no room for Thee in the inn; and now all Judea is too hot for Thee. How soon has the sword begun to pierce through the Virgin's soul (Luke 2:35)! How early does she taste the reception which this mysterious Child of hers is to meet with in the world! And whither is He sent? To "the house of bondage?" Well, it once was that. But Egypt was a house of refuge before it was a house of bondage, and now it has but returned to its first use.

and be thou there until I bring thee word; for Herod will seek the young child to destroy him—Herod's murderous purpose was formed before the Magi had reached Bethlehem.

ADAM CLARKE

11. *They presented unto him gifts.* The people of the East never approach the presence of kings and great personages without a present in their hands. *Gold, and frankincense, and myrrh.* Some will have these gifts to be emblematic of the divinity, regal office, and manhood of Christ. "They offered Him incense as their God; gold as their King; and myrrh as united to a human body, subject to suffering and death." Rather, they offered Him the things which were in most esteem among themselves and which were productions of their own country. The gold was probably a very providential supply, as on it, it is likely, they subsisted while in Egypt.

13. *Flee into Egypt.* Many Jews had settled in Egypt; not only those who had fled thither in the time of Jeremiah, see chap. 48, but many others who had settled there also on account of the temple which Onias IV had built at Heliopolis.

MATTHEW HENRY

The journey would be inconvenient and perilous both to the young child and to his mother; yet Joseph *was not disobedient to the heavenly vision*, made no objection, nor was dilatory in his obedience. As soon as he had received his orders, he immediately *arose*, and went away *by night*. Those that would make *sure* work of their obedience, must make *quick* work of it. Now Joseph went out, as his father Abraham did, with an implicit dependence upon God, *not knowing whither he went*, Heb. xi. 8.

Joseph took the young child and his mother. Some observe, that *the young child* is put first, as the principal person, and Mary is called, not *the wife of Joseph*, but, which was her greater dignity, *the mother of the young child*. They continued in Egypt till the death of Herod. There they were at a distance from the temple and the service of it, and in the midst of idolaters. Though they were far from the temple of the Lord, they had with them the Lord of the temple. A forced absence from God's ordinances, and a forced presence with wicked people, may be the lot, are not the sin, yet cannot but be the grief, of good people.

III. The fulfilling of the scripture in all this—that scripture (Hos. xi. 1), *Out of Egypt have I called my son*. Of all the evangelists, Matthew takes most notice of the fulfilling of the scripture in what concerned Christ. Now this word of the prophet undoubtedly referred to the deliverance of Israel out of Egypt, in which God owned them for his son, his first-born (Exod. iv. 22); but it is here applied, by way of analogy, to Christ, the Head of the church. The scripture has many accomplishments. God is every day fulfilling the scripture. It is no new thing for God's sons to be in Egypt, in a strange land, in a house of bondage; but they shall be fetched out. They may be hid in Egypt, but they shall not be left there.

Verses 16–18

I. Herod's resentment of the departure of the wise men. He waited long for their return; but he hears, upon enquiry, that they are gone off another way, which made him *exceeding wroth*; and he is the more desperate and outrageous for his being disappointed.

II. His politic contrivance, notwithstanding this, to take off him that is *born King of the Jews*. If he could not reach him by a particular execution, he doubted not but to involve him in a general stroke. It was strange that Herod could find any so inhuman as to be employed in such a bloody and barbarous piece of work; but wicked hands never want wicked tools to work with. Herod was now about seventy years old, so that an infant, at this time *under two years old*, was not likely ever to give him any disturbance. It was purely to gratify his own brutish lusts of pride and cruelty that he did this.

Observe, What large measures he took, 1. As to time; He *slew all from two years old and under*. It is probable that the blessed Jesus was at this time not a year old; yet Herod took in all the infants *under two years old*, that he might be sure not to miss his prey. 2. As to place; he kills all the male children, not only *in Bethlehem*, but *in all the coasts thereof*, in all the villages of that city. This was being *overmuch wicked*, Eccles. vii. 17. An unbridled wrath, armed with an unlawful power, often transports men to the most absurd and unreasonable instances of cruelty. We are not to suppose that these children *were sinners above all that were in Israel*, because they suffered such things. But we must look upon this murder of the infants under another character: it was their martyrdom. They shed their blood for him, who afterwards shed his for them. These were the infantry of *the noble army of martyrs*.

JAMIESON, FAUSSET, BROWN

14. When he arose, he took the young child and his mother by night—doubtless the same night. **and departed into Egypt; 15. And was there until the death of Herod**—which took place not very long after this of a horrible disease; the details of which will be found in JOSEPHUS (*Antiquities*, 17. 6. 1, 5, 7, 8). **that it might be fulfilled which was spoken of the Lord by the prophet, saying** [Hos. 11:1], **Out of Egypt have I called my son**—Our Evangelist here quotes directly from the *Hebrew*, warily departing from the LXX, which renders the words, "From Egypt have I recalled his children," meaning Israel's children. The prophet is reminding his people how dear Israel was to God in the days of his youth; how Moses was bidden to say to Pharaoh, "Thus saith the Lord, Israel is My *son*, My first-born; and I say unto thee, Let *My* son go, that he may serve Me; and if thou refuse to let him go, behold, I will slay *thy* son, even thy first-born" (Exod. 4:22, 23); how, when Pharaoh refused, God having slain all *his* first-born, "called His own son out of Egypt," by a stroke of high-handed power and love. Viewing the words in this light, even if our Evangelist had not applied them to the recall from Egypt of God's own beloved, Only-begotten Son, the application would have been irresistibly made by all who have learnt to pierce beneath the surface to the deeper relations which Christ bears to His people, and both to God; and who are accustomed to trace the analogy of God's treatment of each respectively. **16. Then Herod . . .**—As Deborah sang of the mother of Sisera: "She looked out at a window, and cried through the lattice, Why is his chariot so long in coming? why tarry the wheels of his chariots? Have they not sped?" so Herod wonders that his messengers, with pious zeal, are not hastening with the news that all is ready to receive him as a worshipper. What can be keeping them? Have they missed their way? Has any disaster befallen them? At length his patience is exhausted. He makes his inquiries and finds they are already far beyond his reach on their way home. **when he saw that he was mocked** [was trifled with] **of the wise men**—No, Herod, thou art not mocked of the wise men, but of a Higher than they. He that sitteth in the heavens doth laugh at thee; the Lord hath thee in derision. He disappointeth the devices of the crafty, so that their hands cannot perform their enterprise. He taketh the wise in their own craftiness, and the counsel of the froward is carried headlong (Ps. 2:4; Job 5:12, 13). That blessed Babe shall die indeed, but not by thy hand. As He afterwards told that son of thine—as cunning and as unscrupulous as thyself—when the Pharisees warned Him to depart, for *Herod would seek to kill Him*—"Go ye, and tell that *fox*, Behold, I cast out devils, and I do cures to-day and to-morrow, and the third day I shall be perfected. Nevertheless I must walk to-day, and to-morrow, and the day following: for it cannot be that a prophet perish out of Jerusalem" (Luke 13:32, 33). Bitter satire! **was exceeding wroth**—To be made a fool of is what none like, and proud kings cannot stand. Herod burns with rage and is like a wild bull in a net. So he **sent forth** [a band of hired murderers], **and slew all the** [male] **children that were in Bethlehem, and in all the coasts** [environs] **thereof, from two years old and under, according to the time which he had diligently** [carefully] **inquired of the wise men**—In this ferocious step Herod was like himself—as crafty as cruel. He takes a large sweep, not to miss his mark. He thinks this will surely embrace his victim. And so it had, if He had been there. But He is gone. Heaven and earth shall sooner pass away than thou shalt have that Babe into thy hands. Therefore, Herod, thou must be content to want Him: to fill up the cup of thy bitter mortifications, already full enough—until thou die not less of a broken heart than of a loathsome and excruciating disease. Why, ask skeptics and skeptical critics, is not this massacre, if it really occurred, recorded by JOSEPHUS, who is minute enough in detailing the cruelties of Herod? To this the answer is not difficult. If we consider how small a town Bethlehem was, it is not likely there would be many male children in it from two years old and under; and when

ADAM CLARKE

15. *Out of Egypt have I called my son*. This is quoted from Hos. 11:1, where the deliverance of Israel, and that only, is referred to. But as that deliverance was extraordinary, it is very likely that it had passed into a proverb, so that "Out of Egypt have I called my son" might have been used to express any signal deliverance.

CHARLES H. SPURGEON

Thus did our Lord narrowly escape a cruel death. He had poor welcome among men, whom he came to redeem. Angels celebrated his birth with songs, but among men the malice of the wicked greeted him with the blood of infants and the wailings of bereaved mothers. O dear Redeemer, how sorrowfully did thy life for us begin! Alas! how sorrowfully did it end!

As with gladness men of old
Did the guiding star behold,
As with joy they hailed its light,
Leading onward, beaming bright,
So, most gracious God, may we
Evermore be led by thee!

As with joyful steps they sped
To that lowly manger-bed
There to bend the knee before
Him whom heaven and earth adore,
So may we, with willing feet,
Ever seek thy mercy-seat.

—*Spurgeon's Devotional Bible*

16. *Slew all the children*. This cruelty of Herod seems alluded to in very decisive terms by Macrobius, who flourished toward the conclusion of the fourth century: "When he heard that among those male infants about two years old, which Herod, the king of the Jews, ordered to be slain in Syria, one of his sons was also murdered, he said: 'It is better to be Herod's hog than his son.' "

MATTHEW HENRY

III. The fulfilling of the scripture in this (*v.* 17, 18); *Then was fulfilled* that prophecy (Jer. xxxi. 15), *A voice was heard in Ramah.* That prediction was accomplished in Jeremiah's time. But now the prophecy is again fulfilled in the great sorrow that was for the death of these infants. The scripture was fulfilled.

1. In the place of this mourning. The noise of it was heard from Bethlehem to Ramah; for Herod's cruelty extended itself to *all the coasts of Bethlehem*, even into the lot of Benjamin, among the children of Rachel. Rachel's sepulchre was hard by Bethlehem, Gen. xxxv. 16, 19. Compare 1 Sam. x. 2. These mothers were like Rachel, lived near Rachel's grave, and many of them descended from Rachel; and therefore their lamentations are elegantly represented by *Rachel's weeping*.

2. In the degree of this mourning. It was *lamentation and weeping, and great mourning*; all little enough to express the sense they had of this aggravated calamity. There was a great cry in Egypt when the first-born were slain, and so there was here when the youngest was slain; for whom we naturally have a particular tenderness. This sorrow was so great, that they *would not be comforted*. Blessed be God, there is no occasion of grief in this world, no, not that which is supplied by sin itself, that will justify us in refusing to *be comforted*! They *would not be comforted, because they are not*, that is, *they are not* in the land of the living, *are not* as they were, in their mothers' embraces. If, indeed, *they were not*, there might be some excuse for sorrowing as though we had no hope; but we know they are not lost, but gone before; if we forget that *they are*, we lose the best ground of our comfort, 1 Thess. iv. 13. If we look further into this prophecy, we shall find that *the bitter weeping* in Ramah was but a prologue to the greatest joy, for it follows, *Thy work shall be rewarded, and there is hope in thy end.* The worst things are, the sooner they will mend.

Verses 19–23

We have here Christ's return out of Egypt into the *land of Israel* again. Egypt may serve to sojourn in, or take shelter in, for a while, but not to abide in. Christ was *sent to the lost sheep of the house of Israel*, and therefore to them he must return.

I. What it was that made way for his return—the death of Herod, which happened not long after the murder of the infants. Such quick work did divine vengeance make! Of all sins, the guilt of innocent blood fills the measure soonest. So passionate and impatient was he, that he was a torment to himself, and a terror to all that attended him. See what kind of men have been the enemies and persecutors of Christ and his followers! Few have opposed Christianity but such as have first divested themselves of humanity.

II. The orders given from heaven concerning their return, and Joseph's obedience to those orders, *v.* 19–21. God had sent Joseph into Egypt, and there he stayed till the same that brought him thither ordered him thence. In all our removes, it is good to see our way plain, and God going before us; we should not move either one way or the other without order. No place can exclude God's gracious visits. **Angels come to Joseph in Egypt, to Ezekiel in Babylon, and to John in Patmos. 1. The angel informs him of the death of Herod and his accomplices:** *They are dead, which sought the young Child's life.* They are dead, but the young Child lives. Persecuted saints sometimes live to tread upon the graves of their persecutors. Thus did the church's King weather the storm, and many a one has the church in like manner weathered. 2. He directs him what to do. He must *go* and return *to the land of Israel*; and he did so without delay. God's people follow his direction whithersoever he leads them, wherever he lodges them.

III. The further direction he had from God, which way to steer, and where to fix in the land of Israel, *v.* 22, 23. God could have given him these instructions with the former, but God reveals his mind to his people by degrees, to keep them still waiting on him, and expecting to hear further from him. These orders Joseph received *in a dream*, probably, as those before, by the ministration of an angel.

Now the direction given this holy, royal family, is,

1. That it might not settle in Judæa, *v.* 22. Joseph might think that Jesus, being *born in Bethlehem*, must be brought up there; yet he is prudently *afraid* for *the young Child*, because *he hears that Archelaus reigns in* Herod's stead, but only over Judæa. See what a succession of enemies there is to fight against Christ and his church! If one drop off, another presently appears, to keep up the old enmity. But for this reason Joseph must not take the young Child into Judæa. God will not thrust his children into the mouth of danger, but when it is for his own glory and their trial.

JAMIESON, FAUSSET, BROWN

we think of the number of fouler atrocities which JOSEPHUS has recorded of him, it is unreasonable to make anything of his silence on this. **17. Then was fulfilled that which was spoken by Jeremy the prophet, saying**—(Jer. 31:15, from which the quotation differs but verbally). **18. In Rama was there a voice heard, lamentation, and weeping, and great mourning, Rachel weeping for her children, and would not be comforted, because they are not**—These words, as they stand in Jeremiah, undoubtedly relate to the Babylonish captivity. Rachel, the mother of Joseph and Benjamin, was buried in the neighborhood of Bethlehem (Gen. 35:19), where her sepulchre is still shown. She is figuratively represented as rising from the tomb and uttering a double lament for the loss of her children—first, by a bitter captivity, and now by a bloody death. And a foul deed it was. O ye mothers of Bethlehem! methinks I hear you asking why your innocent babes should be the ram caught in the thicket, while Isaac escapes. I cannot tell you, but one thing I know, that ye shall, some of you, live to see a day when that Babe of Bethlehem shall be Himself the Ram, caught in another sort of thicket, in order that your babes may escape a worse doom than they now endure. And if these babes of yours be now in glory, through the dear might of that blessed Babe, will they not deem it their honor that the tyrant's rage was exhausted upon themselves instead of their infant Lord?

19. But when Herod was dead—Miserable Herod! Thou thoughtest thyself safe from a dreaded Rival; but it was He only that was safe from thee; and thou hast not long enjoyed even this fancied security. See on vs. 15. **behold, an angel of the Lord**—Our translators, somewhat capriciously, render the same expression "*the* angel of the Lord," ch. 1:20; 2:13; and "*an* angel of the Lord," as here. As the same angel appears to have been employed on all these high occasions—and most likely he to whom in Luke is given the name of "Gabriel," ch. 1:19, 26—perhaps it should in every instance except the first, be rendered "*the* angel." **appeareth in a dream to Joseph in Egypt, 20. Saying, Arise, and take the young child and his mother, and go into the land of Israel**—not to the land of Judea, for he was afterward expressly warned not to settle there, nor to Galilee, for he only went thither when he found it unsafe to settle in Judea but to "the land of Israel," in its most general sense; meaning the Holy Land at large—the particular province being not as yet indicated. So Joseph and the Virgin had, like Abraham, to "go out, not knowing whither they went," till they should receive further direction. **for they are dead which sought the young child's life**—a common expression in most languages where only one is meant, who here is Herod. But the words are taken from the strikingly analogous case in Exodus 4:19, which probably suggested the plural here; and where the command is given to Moses to return *to* Egypt for the same reason that the greater than Moses was now ordered to be brought back *from* it—the death of him who sought his life. Herod died in the seventieth year of his age, and thirty-seventh of his reign. **21. And he arose, and took the young child and his mother, and came into the land of Israel**—intending, as is plain from what follows, to return to Bethlehem of Judea, there, no doubt, to rear the Infant King, as at His own royal city, until the time should come when they would expect Him to occupy Jerusalem, "the city of the Great King." **22. But when he heard that Archelaus did reign in Judea in the room of his father Herod**—Archelaus succeeded to Judea, Samaria, and Idumea; but Augustus refused him the title of *king* till it should be seen how he conducted himself; giving him only the title of *ethnarch* [JOSEPHUS, *Antiquities*, 17., 11, 4]. Above this, however, he never rose. The people, indeed, recognized him as his father's successor; and so it is here said that he "*reigned* in the room of his father Herod." But, after ten years' defiance of the Jewish law and cruel tyranny, the people lodged heavy complaints against him, and the emperor banished him to Vienne in Gaul, reducing

ADAM CLARKE

18. *In Rama was there a voice heard.* These words, quoted from Jer. xxxi. 15, were originally spoken concerning the captivity of the ten tribes, but are here elegantly applied to the murder of the innocents at Bethlehem. As Rachel might be said to weep over her children which were slaughtered or gone into captivity, so in Bethlehem the mothers bitterly lamented their children because they were slain.

20. *They are dead.* Both Herod and Antipater, his son; though some think the plural is here used for the singular, and that the death of Herod alone is here intended. But as Herod's son Antipater was at this time heir apparent to the throne, and he had cleared his way to it by procuring the death of both his elder brothers, he is probably alluded to here, as doubtless he entered into his father's designs. *They are dead* —Antipater was put to death by his father's command, five days before this execrable tyrant went to his own place.

22. *When he heard that Archelaus did reign.* This son partook of the cruel and bloodthirsty disposition of his father. At one of the Passovers he caused 3,000 of the people to be put to death in the Temple and city. For his tyranny and cruelty Augustus deprived him of the government and banished him. His character considered, Joseph, with great propriety, forbore to settle under his jurisdiction. He turned aside into the parts of Galilee. Here Antipas governed, who is allowed to have been of comparatively mild disposition. He was besides in a state of enmity with his brother Archelaus.

TODAY'S DICTIONARY OF THE BIBLE:

Herod the Great (Matt. 2:1-22; Luke 1:5; Acts 23:35), the son of Antipater, an Idumaean, and Cypros, an Arabian of noble descent. In the year 47 B.C. Julius Caesar made Antipater, a "wily Idumaean," procurator of Judea, who divided his territories between his four sons, Galilee falling to the lot of Herod, who was afterward appointed tetrarch of Judea by Mark Antony (40 B.C.), and also king of Judea by the Roman senate.

Of a stern and cruel disposition, "he was brutish and a stranger to all humanity." Alarmed by the tidings of one "born King of the Jews," he sent out soldiers who "slew all the children that were in Bethlehem, and in all the coasts thereof, from two years old and under" (Matt. 2:16). Herod was fond of splendor and lavished great sums in rebuilding and adorning the cities of his empire. He rebuilt the city of Caesarea on the coast, and also the city of Samaria which he called Sebaste, in honor of Augustus. The king also restored the ruined temple of Jerusalem, a work which was begun 20 B.C., but was not finished till after Herod's death, probably not till about A.D. 50 (John 2:20). After a troubled reign of thirty-seven years, he died at Jericho amid great agonies both of body and mind, 4 B.C., the latest possible date for the birth of Christ.

After his death his kingdom was divided among three of his sons. Of these, Philip had the land east of Jordan, between Caesarea Philippi and Bethadara, Antipas had Galilee and Peraea, while Archelaus had Judea and Samaria.

MATTHEW HENRY

2. That it must settle in Galilee, *v.* 22. There Philip now ruled, who was a mild, quiet man. Note, The providence of God commonly so orders it, that his people shall not want a quiet retreat from the storm and from the tempest. Thither they were sent, to Nazareth, a city upon a hill, in the centre of the lot of Zebulun; there the mother of our Lord lived, when she conceived that *holy thing*; and, probably, Joseph lived there too, Luke i. 26, 27. Thither they were sent, and there they were well known, and were among their relations; the most proper place for them to be in. There they continued, and from thence our Saviour was called *Jesus of Nazareth*, which was to *the Jews a stumbling-block*, for, *Can any good thing come* out of *Nazareth?*

In this is said to be fulfilled what was *spoken by the prophets, He shall be called a Nazarene*, which may be looked upon, (1) As a name of honour and dignity, though primarily it signifies no more than a *man of Nazareth*; there is an allusion or mystery in it, speaking Christ to be, [1] The *Man, the Branch*, spoken of, Isa. xi. 1. [2] It speaks him to be the *great Nazarite*. Not that Christ was, *strictly, a Nazarite*, for he drank wine, and touched dead bodies; but he was *eminently* so, both as he was singularly holy, and as he was by a solemn designation and dedication set apart to the honour of God in the work of our redemption, as Samson was to save Israel. Or, (2) As a name of reproach and contempt. To be called a *Nazarene*, was to be called a *despicable man*, a man from whom no good was to be expected, and to whom no respect was to be paid. It stuck as a nickname to him and his followers. Let no name of reproach for religion's sake seem hard to us, when our Master was himself called a *Nazarene*.

JAMIESON, FAUSSET, BROWN

Judea again to a Roman province. Then the "scepter" clean "departed from Judah." **he was afraid to go thither**—and no wonder, for the reason just mentioned. **notwithstanding** [or more simply, "but"] **being warned of God in a dream, he turned aside** [withdrew] **into the parts of Galilee,** or the Galilean parts. The whole country west of the Jordan was at this time, as is well known, divided into three provinces—GALILEE being the northern, JUDEA the southern, and SAMARIA the central province. The province of Galilee was under the jurisdiction of Herod Antipas, the brother of Archelaus, his father having left him that and Perea, on the east side of the Jordan, as his share of the kingdom, with the title of *tetrarch,* which Augustus confirmed. Though crafty and licentious, according to JOSEPHUS —precisely what the Gospel history shows him to be (see on Mark 6:14-30, and on Luke 13:31-35)—he was of a less cruel disposition than Archelaus; and Nazareth being a good way off from the seat of government, and considerably secluded, it was safer to settle there. **23. And he came and dwelt in a city called Nazareth**—a small town in Lower Galilee, lying in the territory of the tribe of Zebulun, and about equally distant from the Mediterranean Sea on the west and the Sea of Galilee on the east. N.B. —If, from Luke 2:39, one would conclude that the parents of Jesus brought Him straight back to Nazareth after His presentation in the temple—as if there had been no visit of the Magi, no flight to Egypt, no stay there, and no purpose on returning to settle again at Bethlehem—one might, from our Evangelist's way of speaking here, equally conclude that the parents of our Lord had never been at Nazareth until now. Did we know exactly the sources from which the matter of each of the Gospels was drawn up, or the mode in which these were used, this apparent discrepancy would probably disappear at once. In neither case is there any inaccuracy. At the same time it is difficult, with these facts before us, to conceive that either of these two Evangelists wrote his Gospel with that of the other before him—though many think this a precarious inference. **that it might be fulfilled which was spoken by the prophets, He shall be called a Nazarene**—better, perhaps, "Nazarene." The best explanation of the origin of this name appears to be that which traces it to the word *netzer* in Isaiah 11: 1—the small *twig, sprout,* or sucker, which the prophet there says, "shall come forth from the stem (or rather, 'stump') of Jesse, the branch which should fructify from his roots." The little town of Nazareth, mentioned neither in the Old Testament nor in JOSEPHUS, was probably so called from its insignificance: a weak twig in contrast to a stately tree; and a special contempt seemed to rest upon it —"Can any good thing come out of Nazareth?" (John 1:46)—over and above the general contempt in which all Galilee was held, from the number of Gentiles that settled in the upper territories of it, and, in the estimation of the Jews, debased it. Thus, in the providential arrangement by which our Lord was brought up at the insignificant and opprobrious town called *Nazareth,* there was involved, first, a local humiliation; next, an allusion to Isaiah's prediction of His lowly, twig-like upspringing from the branchless, dried-up stump of Jesse; and yet further, a standing memorial of that humiliation which the prophets," in a number of the most striking predictions, had attached to the Messiah.

ADAM CLARKE

23. *That it might be fulfilled which was spoken by the prophets.* It is difficult to ascertain by what prophets this was spoken. The margin usually refers to Judg. 13:5, where the angel, foretelling the birth of Samson, says, "No razor shall come on his head: for the child shall be a Nazarite [*nezir*] unto God from the womb." The second passage usually referred to is Isa. 11:1: "There shall come forth a rod out of the stem of Jesse, and a Branch [*netser*] shall grow out of his roots." That this refers to Christ, there is no doubt. Jer. xxiii. 5 is supposed to speak in the same language, "I will raise unto David a righteous Branch." But here the word is *tsemach,* not *netser;* and it is the same in the parallel place, Zech. iii. 8; vi. 12. Therefore these two prophets cannot be referred to. But the passages in Judges and Isaiah may have been in the eye of the Evangelist, as well as the whole institution relative to the Nazarite. Gusset, Wolf, Rosenmuller, and others give four rules according to which the phrase *that it might be fulfilled* may be applied in the New Testament: (1) When the thing predicted is literally accomplished; (2) When that is done, of which the Scripture has spoken, not in a literal sense, but in a spiritual sense; (3) When a thing is done neither in a literal nor spiritual sense, according to the fact referred to in the Scripture, but is similar to that fact; (4) When that which has been mentioned in the Old Testament as formerly done is accomplished in a larger and more extensive sense in the New Testament. Matthew seems to quote according to all these rules, and it will be useful to the reader to keep them constantly in view.

MATTHEW HENRY

CHAPTER 3

We have here an account of the preaching and baptism of John.

I. The time when he appeared. *In those days* (*v.* 1), or, *after those days*, long after what was recorded in the foregoing chapter, which left the child Jesus in his infancy; *in those days*, in the time appointed of the Father for the beginning of the gospel, when the *fulness of time* was come. Glorious things were spoken both of John and Jesus, at and before their births, which would have given occasion to expect some extraordinary appearances of a divine presence and power with them when they were very young; but it is quite otherwise. Except Christ's disputing with the doctors at twelve years old, nothing appears remarkable concerning either of them, till they were about thirty years old. And this was to show, 1. That even when God is acting as the God of Israel, the *Saviour*, yet *verily he is a God that hideth himself* (Isa. xlv. 15). 2. That our faith must principally have an eye to Christ in his office and undertaking, for there is the *display* of his power; but in his person is the *hiding* of his power.

Matthew says nothing of the conception and birth of John the Baptist, which is largely related by St. Luke, but finds him at full age, as if dropt from the clouds to preach in the wilderness. After Malachi there was no prophet, nor any pretender to prophecy, till John the Baptist.

II. The place where he appeared first. *In the wilderness of Judæa.* It was not an uninhabited desert, but a part of the country not so thickly peopled as other parts were; it was such a wilderness as had six cities and their villages in it. In these cities and villages John preached, for thereabouts he had hitherto lived. The *word of the Lord* found John here in a *wilderness.* No place is so remote as to shut us out from the visits of divine grace. It was in this *wilderness* of Judah that David penned the 63rd Psalm, which speaks so much of the sweet communion he then had with God, Hos. ii. 14. John Baptist was a priest of the order of Aaron, yet we find him preaching in a *wilderness*, and never officiating in the *temple*; but Christ, who was not a son of Aaron, is yet often found in the temple, and sitting there as one having authority. *The Lord whom ye seek shall suddenly come to his temple;* not the *messenger* that was to prepare his way.

The beginning of the gospel in a wilderness, speaks comfort to the deserts of the Gentile world. *The desert shall rejoice*, Isa. xxxv. 1, 2.

III. His preaching. This he made his business. By the foolishness of preaching, Christ's kingdom must be set up.

1. The doctrine he preached was that of repentance (*v.* 2); *Repent ye.* He preached it, not in Jerusalem, but in the wilderness of Judæa, among the plain country people; for even those who think themselves most out of the way of temptation, and furthest from the vanities and vices of the town, cannot wash their hands in innocency, but must do it in repentance. John Baptist's business was to call men to *repent* of their sins. "*Change your minds;* you have thought amiss; *think again*, and *think aright*." The change of the *mind* produces a change of the *way.* Those who are truly sorry for what they have done amiss, will be careful to do so no more. This repentance is a necessary duty, in obedience to the command of God (Acts xvii. 30); and a necessary preparative and qualification for the comforts of the gospel of Christ. The sore must be searched, or it cannot be cured. *I wound* and *I heal.*

2. The argument he used to enforce this call was, *For the kingdom of heaven is at hand.* It is a *kingdom* of which Christ is the Sovereign. It is a kingdom of *heaven*, not of this world. John preached this as *at hand*; then it was at the door; to us it is come. (1) This is a great *inducement* to us *to repent.* There is nothing like the consideration of divine grace to break the heart, both *for sin* and *from sin.* Kindness is conquering; abused kindness, humbling and melting. What a wretch was I to sin against such grace, against the law and love of such a kingdom! (2) It is a *great encouragement* to us *to repent.* The proclamation of pardon discovers, and fetches in, the malefactor who before fled and absconded. Thus are we drawn to it with the cords of a man, and the bands of love.

IV. The *prophecy* that was fulfilled in him, *v.* 3. This is he that was spoken of in the beginning of that part of the prophecy of Esaias, which is mostly evangelical, and which points at gospel-times and gospel-grace; see Isa. xl. 3, 4. John is here spoken of,

1. As the *voice of one crying in the wilderness.* John owned it himself (John i. 23); *I am the voice*, and that

JAMIESON, FAUSSET, BROWN

CHAPTER 3

Vss. 1-12. PREACHING AND MINISTRY OF JOHN. (= Mark 1:1-8; Luke 3:1-18.) For the proper introduction to this section, we must go to Luke 3:1, 2. Here, as BENGEL well observes, the curtain of the New Testament is, as it were, drawn up, and the greatest of all epochs of the Church commences. Even our Lord's own age is determined by it (vs. 23). No such elaborate chronological precision is to be found elsewhere in the New Testament, and it comes fitly from him who claims it as the peculiar recommendation of his Gospel, that "he had traced down all things with precision from the very first" (ch. 1: 3). Here evidently commences his proper narrative. Vs. 1: "Now in the fifteenth year of the reign of Tiberius Cæsar"—not the fifteenth from his full accession on the death of Augustus, but from the period when he was associated with him in the government of the empire, three years earlier, about the end of the year of Rome 779, or about four years before the usual reckoning. "Pontius Pilate being governor of Judea." His proper title was *procurator*, but with more than the usual powers of that office. After holding it for about ten years, he was summoned to Rome to answer to charges brought against him; but ere he arrived, Tiberius died (A.D. 35), and soon after miserable Pilate committed suicide. "And Herod being tetrarch of Galilee [see on Mark 6:14], and his brother Philip"—a very different and very superior Philip to the one whose name was *Herod Philip*, and whose wife, Herodias, went to live with Herod Antipas (see on Mark 6:17)—"tetrarch of Iturea"—lying to the northeast of Palestine, and so called from *Itur* or *Jetur*, Ishmael's son (I Chron. 1:31), and anciently belonging to the half-tribe of Manasseh. "and of the region of Trachonitis"—lying farther to the northeast, between Iturea and Damascus; a rocky district infested by robbers, and committed by Augustus to Herod the Great to keep in order. "and Lysanias the tetrarch of Abilene"—still more to the northwest; so called, says ROBINSON, from *Abila*, eighteen miles from Damascus. Vs. 2: "Annas and Caiaphas being the high priests." The former, though deposed, retained much of his influence, and, probably, as *sagan* or deputy, exercised much of the power of the high priesthood along with Caiaphas, his son-in-law (John 18:13; Acts 4:6). In David's time both Zadok and Abiathar acted as high priests (II Sam. 15:35), and it seems to have been the fixed practice to have two (II Kings 25:18). "the word of God came unto John the son of Zacharias in the wilderness." Such a way of speaking is never once used when speaking of Jesus, because He was Himself *The Living Word;* whereas to all merely creature-messengers of God, the word they spoke was a foreign element. See on John 3:31. We are now prepared for the opening words of Matthew. **1. In those days**—of Christ's secluded life at Nazareth, where the last chapter left Him. **came John the Baptist, preaching**—about six months before his Master. **in the wilderness of Judea**—the desert valley of the Jordan, thinly peopled and bare in pasture, a little north of Jerusalem.

2. And saying, Repent ye—Though the word strictly denotes a *change of mind*, it has respect here (and wherever it is used in connection with salvation) primarily to that *sense of sin* which leads the sinner to flee from the wrath to come, to look for relief only from above, and eagerly to fall in with the provided remedy. **for the kingdom of heaven is at hand**—This sublime phrase, used in none of the other Gospels, occurs in this peculiarly Jewish Gospel nearly thirty times; and being suggested by Daniel's grand vision of the Son of man coming in the clouds of heaven to the Ancient of days, to receive His investiture in a world-wide kingdom (Dan. 7:13, 14), it was fitted at once both to meet the national expectations and to turn them into the right channel. A kingdom for which *repentance* was the proper preparation behooved to be essentially spiritual. Deliverance from sin, the great blessing of Christ's kingdom (ch. 1:21), can be valued by those only to whom sin is a burden (ch. 9:12). John's great work, accordingly, was to awaken this feeling and hold out the hope of a speedy and precious remedy. **3. For this is he that was spoken of by the prophet Esaias** [ch. 11:3], **saying. The voice of one crying in the wilderness**—(see on Luke 3:2); the scene of his ministry corresponding to its rough nature. **Prepare ye the way of the Lord, make his paths straight**—This prediction is quoted in all the four Gospels, showing that it was regarded as a great outstanding

ADAM CLARKE

CHAPTER 3

1. *John the Baptist.* John, surnamed the Baptist because he required those to be baptized who professed to be contrite because of their sins, was the son of a priest named Zacharias, and his wife, Elisabeth, and was born about six months before our blessed Lord. *Came . . . preaching. Kerysson*, "proclaiming," as a herald, a matter of great and solemn importance to men; the subject not his own, nor of himself, but from that God from whom alone he had received his commission. *The wilderness of Judaea.* That is, the country parts, as distinguished from the city.

2. *Repent.* This was the matter of the preaching. The sinner is led to understand that the way he has walked in is the way of misery, death, and hell. *The kingdom of heaven is at hand.* Referring to the prophecy of Daniel (vii. 13-14) where the reign of Christ among men is expressly foretold. This phrase and "the kingdom of God" mean the same thing—the dispensation of infinite mercy and manifestation of eternal truth by Christ Jesus, producing the true knowledge of God, accompanied with that worship which is pure and holy, worthy of that God who is its Institutor and its Object. But why is this called a Kingdom? Because it has its laws, all the moral precepts of the gospel; its subjects, all who believe in Christ Jesus; and its King, the Sovereign of heaven and earth. Jesus Christ never saved a soul which He did not govern, nor is this Christ precious or estimable to any man who does not feel a spirit of subjection to the divine will. But why is it called the kingdom of Heaven? Because God designed that His kingdom of grace here should resemble the Kingdom of glory above. It is further added, This Kingdom *is at hand.* The dispensation of the glorious gospel was now about to be fully opened, and the Jews were to have the first offers of salvation. This Kingdom is also at hand to us; and wherever Christ crucified is preached, there is salvation to be found.

3. *The voice of one crying in the wilderness.* Or a voice of a crier in the wilderness. This

MATTHEW HENRY

is all, God is the Speaker, who makes known his mind by John, as a man does by his voice. John is called the *voice of one crying* aloud, which is startling and awakening. Christ is called *the Word*, which, being distinct and articulate, is more instructive. John as the *voice*, roused men, and then Christ, as the *Word*, taught them.

2. As one whose business it was to *prepare the way of the Lord, and to make his paths straight*. So John prepares the way of the Lord. (1) He himself did so among the men of that generation. In the Jewish church and nation, at that time, all was out of course. The people were, generally, extremely proud of their privileges, insensible of sin; and, though now under the most *humbling* providences, being lately made a province of the Roman Empire, yet they were *unhumbled*. Now John was sent to level these mountains, to take down their high opinion of themselves. (2) His doctrine of repentance and humiliation is still as necessary as it was then. There is a great deal to be done, to make way for Christ into a soul, and nothing is more needful, in order to this, than the discovery of sin, and a conviction of the insufficiency of our own righteousness. That which lets will let, until it be taken out of the way. The way of sin and Satan is a *crooked way*; to prepare a way for Christ, the paths must be *made straight*.

V. The garb in which he appeared, the figure he made, and the manner of his life, *v.* 4. He shall be *great in the sight of the Lord*, but mean in the eye of the world; and, as Christ himself, having *no form or comeliness*.

1. His *dress* was *plain*. This same John had *his raiment of camel's hair, and a leathern girdle about his loins*; for he lived in a country place, and suited his *habit* to his *habitation*. It is good for us to accommodate ourselves to the place and condition which God, in his providence, has put us in. John appeared in this dress, (1) To show that, like Jacob, he was a *plain man*, and mortified to this world, and the delights and gaieties of it. (2) To show that he was a *prophet*, for prophets wore *rough garments*, as mortified men (Zech. xiii. 4). (3) To show that he was a man of resolution; his girdle was not *fine*, such as were then commonly worn, but it was *strong*.

2. His *diet* was *plain*; his *meat* was locusts and *wild honey*. *Locusts* were a sort of flying insect, very good for food, and allowed as clean (Lev. xi. 22). *Wild honey* was that which *Canaan* flowed with, 1 Sam. xiv. 26. This intimates that he ate *sparingly*, a little served his turn; a man would be long ere he filled his belly with locusts and wild honey. He was so entirely taken up with spiritual things, that he could seldom find time for a set meal. Those whose business it is to call others to mourn for sin, and to mortify it, ought themselves to live a serious life, a life of self-denial. Every day was a *fast-day* with him. A conviction of the vanity of the world, and everything in it, is the best preparative for the entertainment of the kingdom of heaven in the heart. *Blessed are the poor in spirit*.

VI. The people who attended upon him, and flocked after him (*v.* 5); *Then went out to him Jerusalem, and all Judæa*. Great multitudes came to him from the city, and from all parts of the country. This was a great *honour* put upon John. Frequently those have most real honour done them, who least court the shadow of it. Men have a secret value and reverence for them, more than one would imagine. This gave John a great opportunity of doing good, and was an evidence that God was with him. It was generally thought that the *kingdom of God* would presently *appear*. They were ready to say of him, that he was *the Christ* (Luke iii. 15). Those who would have the benefit of John's ministry must *go out* to him in the wilderness, sharing in his reproach. They who would learn the doctrine of repentance must *go out* from the hurry of this world, and be still. It appears by the issue, that of the many who came to John's Baptism, there were but few that adhered to it. There may be a multitude of forward hearers, where there are but a few true believers.

VII. The rite, or ceremony, by which he admitted disciples, *v.* 6. Those who received his doctrine, and submitted to his discipline, were *baptized of him in Jordan*. They testified their repentance by *confessing their sins*. The Jews had been taught to *justify* themselves; but John teaches them to *accuse* themselves. A penitent confession of sin is required in order to peace and pardon; and those only are ready to receive Jesus Christ as their Righteousness, who are brought with sorrow and shame to own their guilt, 1 John i. 9. The benefits of the *kingdom of heaven*, now *at hand*, were thereupon sealed to them by baptism. He washed them with water, in token of this—that from all their iniquities God would *cleanse them*. It was *the baptism of repentance*, Acts xix. 4. All Israel

JAMIESON, FAUSSET, BROWN

one, and the predicted forerunner as the connecting link between the old and the new economies. Like the great ones of the earth, the Prince of peace was to have His immediate approach proclaimed and His way prepared; and the call here—taking it generally—is a call to put out of the way whatever would obstruct His progress and hinder His complete triumph, whether those hindrances were public or personal, outward or inward. In Luke (3:5, 6) the quotation is thus continued: "Every valley shall be filled, and every mountain and hill shall be brought low; and the crooked shall be made straight, and the rough ways shall be made smooth; and all flesh shall see the salvation of God." Levelling and smoothing are here the obvious figures whose sense is conveyed in the first words of the proclamation—"*Prepare ye the way of the Lord.*" The idea is that every obstruction shall be so removed as to reveal to the whole world the salvation of God in Him whose name is the "Saviour." (Cf. Ps. 98:3; Isa. 11:10; 49:6; 52:10; Luke 2:31, 32; Acts 13:47.)

4. And the same John had his raiment of camel's hair [woven of it] **and a leathern girdle about his loins**—the prophetic dress of Elijah (II Kings 1:8; and see Zech. 13:4). **and his meat was locusts**—the great, well-known Eastern locust, a food of the poor (Lev. 11:22). **and wild honey**—made by wild bees (I Sam. 14:25, 26). This dress and diet, with the shrill cry in the wilderness, would recall the stern days of Elijah.

5. Then went out to him Jerusalem, and all Judea, and all the region round about Jordan—From the metropolitan center to the extremities of the Judean province the cry of this great preacher of repentance and herald of the approaching Messiah brought trooping penitents and eager expectants.

6. And were baptized of him in Jordan, confessing [probably confessing aloud] **their sins**—This baptism was at once a public seal of their felt need of deliverance from sin, of their expectation of the coming Deliverer, and of their readiness to welcome Him when He appeared. The baptism itself startled, and was intended to startle, them. They were familiar enough with the *baptism of proselytes* from heathenism; but this *baptism of Jews* themselves was quite new and strange to them.

ADAM CLARKE

is quoted from Isa. xi. 3, which clearly proves that John the Baptist was the person of whom the prophet spoke. The idea is taken from the practice of Eastern monarchs, who, whenever they entered upon an expedition or took a journey through a desert country, sent harbingers before them to prepare all things for their passage; and pioneers to open the passes, to level the ways, and to remove all impediments. The Jewish church was that desert country to which John was sent to announce the coming of the Messiah. It was destitute at that time of all religious cultivation, and of the spirit and practice of piety; and John was sent to prepare the way of the Lord, by preaching the doctrine of repentance.

4. *His raiment of camel's hair.* A sort of coarse or rough covering, which it appears was common to the prophets, Zech. xiii. 4. In such a garment we find Elijah clothed, 2 Kings 1:8. And as John had been designed under the name of this prophet, Mal. iv. 5, whose spirit and qualifications he was to possess, Luke i. 17, he took the same habit and lived in the same state of self-denial. *His meat was locusts.* May either signify the insect called the locust, which still makes a part of the food in the land of Judea, or the top of a plant. Many eminent commentators are of the latter opinion, but the first is the most likely. *Wild honey.* Such as he got in the rocks and hollows of trees, and which abounded in Judea; see 1 Sam. xiv. 26. It is most likely that the dried locusts, which are an article of food in Asiatic countries to the present day, were fried in the honey, or compounded in some manner with it.

6. *Were baptized.* Were the people dipped or sprinkled? Those who are dipped or immersed in water, in the name of the Holy Trinity, I believe to be evangelically baptized; those who are washed or sprinkled with water in the name of the Father, and of the Son, and of the Holy Ghost, I believe to be equally so. *Confessing their sins.* Earnestly acknowledging that their sins were their own, thus taking the whole blame upon themselves, and laying nothing to the charge of God or man. This is essential to true repentance; and till a man take the whole blame on himself, he cannot feel the absolute need he has of casting his soul on the mercy of God, that he may be saved.

MATTHEW HENRY

were baptized unto Moses, 1 Cor. x. 2. The *ceremonial law* consisted in *divers washings or baptisms* (Heb. ix. 10); but John's baptism refers to the remedial law, the law of repentance and faith. By baptism he obliged them to live a holy life, according to the profession they took upon themselves. Confession of sin must always be accompanied with holy resolutions.

Verses 7-12

The doctrine John preached was that of repentance. Here we have the use of that doctrine. Application is the life of preaching, so it was of John's preaching. To whom he applied it; to the Pharisees and Sadducees that came to his baptism, *v.* 7. The Pharisees were zealots for the ceremonies, and the traditions of the elders; the Sadducees ran into the other extreme, and were little better than deists, denying the existence of spirits and a future state. Many come to ordinances, who come not under the power of them. Note the application was plain and home, and directed to their consciences; he speaks as one that came not to preach *before* them, but to preach *to* them. He was not bashful when he appeared in public, nor did he fear the face of man.

I. Here is a word of conviction and awakening. He begins harshly, calls them not Rabbi, gives them not the titles, much less the applauses, they had been used to. 1. The *title* he gives them is, *O generation of vipers.* Christ gave them the same title; *ch.* xii. 34; xxiii. 33. They were a *viperous brood,* the seed and offspring of such as had been of the same spirit; it was bred in the bone with them. They were a *viperous gang,* they were all alike; though enemies to one another, yet confederate in mischief. It becomes the ministers of Christ to be bold in showing sinners their true character. 2. The *alarm* he gives them is, *Who has warned you to flee from the wrath to come?* This intimates that they were in danger of the wrath to come; that it was next to a miracle to effect anything hopeful among them. "What brings you hither? Who thought of seeing you here? What fright have you been put into, that you enquire after the kingdom of heaven?" (1) There is a *wrath to come.* (2) It is the great concern of everyone of us to flee from this wrath. (3) It is wonderful mercy that we are fairly warned to flee from this wrath; think—*Who has warned us?* God has warned us, who delights not in our ruin. (4) These warnings sometimes startle those who seemed to have been very much hardened in their security and good opinion of themselves.

II. Here is a word of *exhortation* and *direction* (*v.* 8); "*Bring forth therefore fruits meet for repentance. Therefore,* because you profess repentance, and attend upon the doctrine and baptism of repentance, evidence that you are true penitents." Repentance is seated in the heart. There it is as a root; but in vain do we pretend to have it there, if we do not *bring forth the fruits.* Those are not worthy the name of penitents, or their privileges, who say they are sorry for their sins, and yet persist in them. They that profess repentance, as all that are baptized do, must be and act as becomes penitents.

III. Here is a word of caution, not to trust to their external privileges (*v.* 9); *Think not to say within yourselves, We have Abraham to our father.* There is a great deal which carnal hearts are apt to say within themselves, to put by the convincing, commanding power of the word of God. *Please not yourselves* with saying this (so some read it); "rock not yourselves asleep with this, nor flatter yourselves into a fool's paradise." God takes notice of what we say *within* ourselves. Many hide the lie that ruins them, in *their right hand,* and roll it *under their tongue,* because they are ashamed to own it. Now John shows them,

1. What their pretence was; "*We have Abraham to our father;* we are not sinners of the Gentiles; what is this to us?" The word does us no good, when we will not take it as spoken to us, and belonging to us. "Think not that because you are the seed of Abraham, therefore," (1) "You *need not repent,* that there is no occasion for you to change your mind or way." (2) "That therefore you shall *fare well enough,* though you do not *repent.*" It is vain presumption to think that our having good relations will save us, though we be not good ourselves. What will all this avail us, if we do not repent, and live a life of repentance? Multitudes, by resting in the honours and advantages of their visible church-membership, take up short of heaven.

2. How foolish and groundless this pretence was; they thought that being the seed of Abraham, they were the only people God had in the world. John shows them the folly of this conceit; *I say unto you* (whatever you say within yourselves), that *God is able of these stones to raise up children unto Abraham.* He was now baptizing in Jordan at Bethabara (John i. 28), *the house of passage,* where the children of

JAMIESON, FAUSSET, BROWN

7. But when he saw many of the Pharisees and Sadducees come to his baptism, he said unto them [astonished at such a spectacle]; **O generation of vipers**—"Viper-brood," expressing the deadly influence of both sects alike upon the community. Mutually and entirely antagonistic as were their religious principles and spirit, the stern prophet charges both alike with being the poisoners of the nation's religious principles. In ch. 12:34, and 23:33, this strong language of the Baptist is anew applied by the faithful and true Witness to the Pharisees specifically—the only party that had zeal enough actively to diffuse this poison. **who hath warned you** [given you the hint, as the idea is] **to flee from the wrath to come?**—"What can have brought *you* hither?" John more than suspected it was not so much their own spiritual anxieties as the popularity of his movement that had drawn them thither. What an expression is this, "The wrath to come!" God's "wrath," in Scripture, is His righteous displeasure against sin, and consequently against all in whose skirts sin is found, arising out of the essential and eternal opposition of His nature to all moral evil. This is called "the *coming* wrath," not as being wholly future—for as a merited sentence it lies on the sinner already, and its effects, both inward and outward, are to some extent experienced even now—but because the impenitent sinner will not, until "the judgment of the great day," be concluded under it, will not have sentence publicly and irrevocably passed upon him, will not have it discharged upon him and experience its effects without mixture and without hope. In this view of it, it is a wrath *wholly* to come, as is implied in the noticeably different form of the expression employed by the apostle in I Thessalonians 1:10. Not that even true penitents came to John's baptism with all these views of "the wrath to come." But what he says is that this was the *real import of the step itself.* In this view of it, how striking is the word he employs to express that step—*fleeing* from it—as of one who, beholding a tide of fiery wrath rolling rapidly towards him, sees in instant flight his only escape! **8. Bring forth therefore fruits** [the true reading clearly is "fruit" **meet for repentance**—that is, such fruit as *befits* a true penitent. John now being gifted with a knowledge of the human heart, like a true minister of righteousness and lover of souls here directs them how to evidence and carry out their repentance, supposing it genuine; and in the following verses warns them of their danger in case it were not.

9. And think not to say within yourselves, We have Abraham to our father—that pillow on which the nation so fatally reposed, that rock on which at length it split.

for I say unto you, that God is able of these stones to raise up children unto Abraham—i.e., "Flatter not yourselves with the fond delusion that God stands in need of you, to make good His promise of a seed to Abraham; for I tell you that, though you were all to perish, God is as able to raise up a seed to Abraham out of those stones as He was to take Abraham himself out of the rock whence he was hewn, out of the hole of the pit whence he was digged" (Isa. 51:1). Though the stern speaker may have pointed as he spoke to the pebbles of the bare clay hills that lay around (so STANLEY's *Sinai and Palestine*), it was clearly the calling of the *Gentiles* at that time stone-dead in their sins, and quite as unconscious of it—into the room of unbelieving and disinherited Israel that he meant thus to indicate (see ch. 21:43; Rom. 11:20, 30).

ADAM CLARKE

7. *Pharisees.* A very numerous sect among the Jews, who, in their origin, were very probably a pure and holy people. It is likely that they got the name of Pharisees, i.e., Separatists (from *pharash,* "to separate"), from their separating themselves from the pollution of the Jewish national worship. But in process of time, like all religious sects and parties, they degenerated; they lost the spirit of their institution. They ceased to recur to first principles, and had only the form of godliness, when Jesus Christ preached in Judea; for He bore witness that they did make the outside of the cup and platter clean—they observed the rules of their institution but the spirit was gone. *Sadducees.* A sect who denied the existence of angels and spirits, consequently all divine influence and inspiration, and also the resurrection of the dead. The Sadducees of that time were the materialists and deists of the Jewish nation. When the sect of the Pharisees arose cannot be distinctly ascertained, but it is supposed to have been some time after the Babylonish captivity. The sect of the Sadducees were the followers of one Sadok, a disciple of Antigonus Sochaeus, who flourished about three centuries before Christ. *O generation of vipers.* A terribly expressive speech. A serpentine brood, from a serpentine stock. As their fathers were, so were they, children of the wicked one. This is God's estimate of a sinner, whether he wade in wealth or soar in fame. *The wrath to come.* The desolation which was about to fall on the Jewish nation for their wickedness, and threatened in the last words of their own Scriptures. See Mal. iv. 6. "Lest I come and smite the earth with a curse." This wrath or curse was coming; they did not prevent it by turning to God, and receiving the Messiah, and therefore the wrath of God came upon them to the uttermost.

JOHN WESLEY:

8. *Repentance* is of two sorts: that which is termed legal, and that which is styled evangelical repentance. The former (which is the same that is spoken of here) is a thorough conviction of sin. The latter is a change of heart (and consequently of life) from all sin to all holiness.

9. "And say not confidently"—The word in the original, vulgarly rendered, "Think not," seems here, and in many places, not to diminish, but rather add to the force of the word to which it is joined. "We have Abraham to our father"—It is almost incredible how great the presumption of the Jews was, on this their relation to Abraham. One of their famous sayings was, "Abraham sits near the gates of hell, and suffers no Israelite to go down into it." "I say unto you"—This preface always denotes the importance of what follows. "Of these stones"—Probably pointing to those which lay before them.

—*Wesley's Notes on the New Testament*

MATTHEW HENRY

Israel passed over; and there were the twelve stones, one for each tribe, which Joshua set up for a memorial, Joshua iv. 20. It is not unlikely that he pointed to those stones, which God could raise to be, more than in representation, the *twelve tribes of Israel.* Whatever comes of the present generation, God will never want a church in the world.

IV. Here is a word of terror to the careless and secure Pharisees and Sadducees, and other Jews, that knew not the signs of the times, nor the day of their visitation, *v.* 10. "Now look about you, now that *the kingdom of God is at hand*, and be made sensible."

1. "How strict and short your trial is; *Now the axe* is *laid to the root of the tree*; now you are marked for ruin, and cannot avoid it but by a speedy and sincere repentance. *Behold, I come quickly.*" Now they were put upon their last trial; now or never.

2. "How sore and severe your doom will be, if you do not improve this." It is now declared with the axe at the root, that *every tree*, however *high* in gifts and honours, however *green* in external professions and performances, if it *bring not forth good fruit*, the fruits meet for repentance, is *hewn down*, disowned as a tree in God's vineyard, unworthy to have room there, and is *cast into the fire* of God's wrath—the fittest place for barren trees: what else are they good for? If not fit for fruit, they are fit for fuel.

V. A word of instruction concerning Jesus Christ. Christ's ministers preach, not themselves, but him.

1. The dignity and pre-eminence of Christ above John. See how meanly he speaks of himself, that he might magnify Christ (*v.* 11); "*I indeed baptize you with water*, that is the utmost I can do. But *he that comes after me is mightier than I.*" John was truly great, great in the sight of the Lord (not a greater was born of woman), yet he thinks himself unworthy to be in the meanest place of attendance upon Christ, *whose shoes I am not worthy to bear.* He sees, (1) How mighty Christ is, in comparison with him. It is a great comfort to faithful ministers, to think that Jesus Christ is mightier than they, his strength is perfected in their weakness. (2) How mean he is in comparison with Christ, not worthy to carry his shoes after him! Those whom God puts honour upon, are thereby made very humble and low in their own eyes, so that Christ may be all.

2. The design and intention of Christ's appearing, which they were now speedily to expect. Christ will come to make a distinction.

(1) By the powerful working of his grace; *He shall baptize you*, that is, some of you, *with the Holy Ghost and with fire.* Note, [1] It is Christ's prerogative to baptize *with the Holy Ghost.* This he did in the extraordinary gifts of the Spirit conferred upon the apostles. This he does in the graces and comforts of the Spirit given to them that ask him. [2] They who are baptized with the Holy Ghost are baptized as *with fire.* Is fire enlightening? So the Spirit is a Spirit of illumination. Is it warming? And do not their hearts burn within them? Is it consuming? And does not the Spirit of judgment, as a *Spirit of burning*, consume the dross of their corruptions? Does fire make all it seizes like itself? And does it move upwards? So does the Spirit make the soul holy like itself, and its tendency is heaven-ward.

JAMIESON, FAUSSET, BROWN

10. And now also [And even already] **the axe is laid unto** [lieth at] **the root of the trees**—as it were ready to strike: an expressive figure of impending judgment, only to be averted in the way next described. **therefore every tree which bringeth not forth good fruit is hewn down, and cast into the fire**—Language so personal and individual as this can scarcely be understood of any national judgment like the approaching destruction of Jerusalem, with the breaking up of the Jewish polity and the extrusion of the chosen people from their peculiar privileges which followed it; though this would serve as the dark shadow, cast before, of a more terrible retribution to come. The "fire," which in another verse is called "unquenchable," can be no other than that future "torment" of the impenitent whose "smoke ascendeth up for ever and ever," and which by the Judge Himself is styled "everlasting punishment" (Matt. 25:48). What a strength, too, of just indignation is in that word "cast" or "flung into the fire!" The third Gospel here adds the following important particulars in Luke 3:10 16. Vs. 10: "And the people [the multitudes] asked him, saying, What shall we do then?"—that is, to show the sincerity of our repentance. Vs. 11: "He answereth and saith unto them, He that hath two coats, let him impart to him that hath none; and he that hath meat [provisions, victuals] let him do likewise." This is directed against the reigning avarice and selfishness. (Cf. the corresponding precepts of the Sermon on the Mount, ch. 5:40-42.) Vs. 12: "Then came also the publicans to be baptized, and said unto him, Master [Teacher] what shall we do?"—In what special way is the genuineness of our repentance to be manifested? Vs. 13: "And he said unto them, Exact no more than that which is appointed you." This is directed against that extortion which made the publicans a byword. (See on ch. 5:46; and on Luke 15:1.) Vs. 14: "And the soldiers [rather, 'And soldiers'—the word means 'soldiers on active duty'] likewise demanded [asked] of him, saying, And what shall we do? And he said unto them, Do violence to [Intimidate] no man." The word signifies to "shake thoroughly," and refers probably to the extorting of money or other property. "neither accuse any falsely"—by acting as informers vexatiously on frivolous or false pretexts—"and be content with your wages," or "rations." We may take this, say Webster and Wilkinson, as a warning against mutiny, which the officers attempted to suppress by largesses and donations. And thus the "fruits" which would evidence their repentance were just resistance to the reigning sins—particularly of the *class* to which the penitent belonged—and the manifestation of an opposite spirit. Vs. 15: "And as the people were in expectation"—in a state of excitement, looking for something new—"and all men mused in their hearts of John, whether he were the Christ, or not"—rather, "whether he himself might be the Christ." The structure of this clause implies that they could hardly think it, but yet could not help asking themselves whether it might not be; showing both how successful he had been in awakening the expectation of Messiah's immediate appearing, and the high estimation and even reverence, which his own character commanded. Vs. 16: "John answered,"—either to that deputation from Jerusalem, of which we read in John 1:19, etc., or on some other occasion, to remove impressions derogatory to his blessed Master, which he knew to be taking hold of the popular mind—"saying unto them all"—in solemn protestation: (We now return to the first Gospel). **11. I indeed baptize you with water unto repentance** [see on vs. 6]: **but he that cometh after me is mightier than I**—In Mark and Luke this is more emphatic—"But there cometh the Mightier than I," **whose shoes** [sandals] **I am not worthy to bear**—The sandals were tied and untied, and borne about by the meanest servants. **he shall baptize you**—the emphatic "He": "He it is," to the exclusion of all others, "that shall baptize you." **with the Holy Ghost**—"So far from entertaining such a thought as laying claim to the honors of Messiahship, the meanest services I can render to that "Mightier than I that is coming after me" are too high an honor for me; I am but the servant, but the Master is coming; I administer but the outward symbol of purification; His it is, as His sole prerogative, to dispense the inward reality. Beautiful spirit, distinguishing this servant of Christ throughout! **and with fire**—To take this as a distinct baptism from that of the Spirit—a baptism of the impenitent with hell-fire—is exceedingly unnatural. Yet this was the view of Origen among the Fathers; and among moderns, of Neander, Meyer, De Wette, and Lange. Nor is it much better to refer

ADAM CLARKE

10. *And now also the ax is laid.* Or, Even now the ax lieth. As if he had said, There is not a moment to spare—God is about to cut off every impenitent soul—you must therefore either turn to God immediately or be utterly and finally ruined. It was customary with the prophets to represent the kingdoms, nations, and individuals, whose ruin they predicted, under the notion of forests and trees doomed to be cut down. See Jer. xlvi. 22-23; Ezek. xxxi. 3, 11-12. The Baptist follows the metaphor; the Jewish nation is the tree, and the Romans the ax which, by the just judgment of God, was speedily to cut it down.

G. CAMPBELL MORGAN:

Listen to what John says about Jesus' methods. This is to be a strange and wonderful King who is coming. He is to be destructive and constructive in His method; and His victories are to be destructive and constructive.

His methods of destruction are: "the axe," "the fan," and "the fire." "The axe lieth at the root of the trees," said John. It is ready. He is coming, and His "fan is in his hand," the fan that winnows. And the fire will burn.

But His methods are constructive. He shall baptize you with fire; He shall cleanse the threshing floor, not destroy it, and "He will gather his wheat into the garner." Mark the contrast. The axe at the root of the trees for destruction—for the cutting off of the fruitless; the fan for scattering the chaff; the fire for immediately devouring the chaff. But mark the constructive work. The fire is for cleansing and energy; the cleansing of the threshing floor, that perfect work may go forward, and the garnering and the gathering in of the wheat. It is the same thing, and the same instrument that does two opposite things. The fan drives away the chaff, leaving the wheat. The fire burns up the thing that cannot stand its fierce flame, and perfects that which can bear the flame. And so the King who comes is to be destructive and constructive—destructive, for the fruitless tree is to be hewn down, the chaff is to be driven away and burnt; constructive, for the threshing floor is to be cleansed, the wheat is to be gathered and garnered, and men are to be fire-baptized.

—*The Gospel According to Matthew*

11. *But he that cometh after me*, or, is coming after me, who is now on His way, and will shortly make His appearance. Jesus Christ began His ministry when He was thirty years of age, Luke 3:23, which was the age appointed by the law, Num. iv. 3. John the Baptist was born about six months before Christ; and as he began his public ministry when thirty years of age, then this coming after refers to six months after the commencement of John's public preaching, at which time Christ entered upon His. *Whose shoes I am not worthy to bear.* This saying is expressive of the most profound humility and reverence. To put on, take off, and carry the shoes of their masters was not only among the Jews but also among the Greeks and Romans the work of the vilest slaves. *With the Holy Ghost, and with fire.* That the influences of the Spirit of God are here designed needs but little proof. Christ's religion was to be a spiritual religion, and was to have its seat in the heart. Outward precepts, however well they might describe, could not produce inward spirituality. This was the province of the Spirit

MATTHEW HENRY

(2) By the final determinations of his judgment (*v.* 12); *Whose fan is in his hand.* Now he sits as a Refiner. Observe here, [1] The visible Church is Christ's floor. The temple, a type of the church, was built, upon a threshing-floor. [2] In this floor there is a mixture of wheat and chaff. True believers are as wheat, hypocrites are as chaff; these are now mixed, good and bad, under the same external profession. [3] There is a day coming when the floor shall be purged, and the wheat and chaff shall be separated. But it is the day of the last judgment that will be the great winnowing, distinguishing day, when saints and sinners shall be parted for ever. [4] Heaven is the garner into which Jesus Christ will shortly gather all his wheat, and not a grain of it shall be lost: and there is no chaff among them. They are not only gathered into *the barn* (*ch.* xiii. 30), but into *the garner*, where they are thoroughly purified. [5] Hell is the *unquenchable fire*, which will burn up the chaff. As we now are in the *field*, we shall be then in the *floor*.

Verses 13–17

Behold, *the Sun of righteousness* rises in glory. *The fulness of time was come* that Christ should enter upon his prophetical office; and he chooses to do it, not at Jerusalem, but there *where John was baptizing*; for to him resorted those who *waited for the consolation of Israel*, to whom alone he would be welcome. Christ's coming from Galilee *to Jordan, to be baptized*, teaches us not to shrink from pain and toil, that we may have an opportunity of drawing nigh to God in an ordinance. We should be willing to go far, rather than come short of communion with God. They who will find must seek.

Now in this story of Christ's baptism we may observe,

I. How hardly John was persuaded to admit of it, *v.* 14, 15. It was an instance of Christ's great humility, that he would offer himself *to be baptized of John*. As soon as ever Christ began to preach, he preached humility. Christ was designed for the highest honours, yet in his first step he thus abases himself. Those who would rise high must begin low. *Before honour is humility*. Those that honour God he will honour. Now here we have,

1. The objection that John made against baptizing Jesus, *v.* 14. *John forbade him*, as Peter did, when Christ went about to wash his feet, John xiii. 6, 8. Christ's gracious condescensions are so surprising, so deep and mysterious, that even they who know his mind well cannot soon find out the meaning of them. John's modesty thinks this an honour too great for him to receive. John had now obtained a great name, and was universally respected: yet see how humble he is still! God has further honours in reserve for those whose spirits continue low when their reputation rises.

(1) John thinks it necessary that he should be baptized of Christ; *I have need to be baptized of thee* with the baptism of the Holy Ghost, as of fire. [1] Though *John was filled with the Holy Ghost from*

JAMIESON, FAUSSET, BROWN

it to the fire of the great day, by which the earth and the works that are therein shall be burned up. Clearly, as we think, it is but the *fiery* character of the Spirit's operations upon the soul—searching, consuming, refining, sublimating—as nearly all good interpreters understand the words. And thus, in two successive clauses, the two most familiar emblems—*water* and *fire*—are employed to set forth the same purifying operations of the Holy Ghost upon the soul. **12. Whose** [winnowing] **fan is in his hand** —ready for use. This is no other than the preaching of the Gospel, even now beginning, the effect of which would be to separate the solid from the spiritually worthless, as wheat, by the winnowing fan, from the chaff. (Cf. the similar representation in Mal. 3:1-3.) **and he will throughly purge his** [threshing] **floor**—that is, the visible Church. **and gather his wheat**—His true-hearted saints; so called for their solid worth (cf. Amos 9:9; Luke 22:31). **into the garner**—"the kingdom of their Father," as this "garner" or "barn" is beautifully explained by our Lord in the parable of the wheat and the tares (ch. 13:30, 43). **but he will burn up the chaff**—empty, worthless professors of religion, void of all solid religious principle and character (see Ps. 1:4). **with unquenchable fire**—Singular is the strength of this apparent contradiction of figures:—to be burnt up, but with a fire that is unquenchable; the one expressing the *utter destruction* of all that constitutes one's true life, the other the *continued consciousness of existence* in that awful condition. Luke adds the following important particulars (3: 18-20): Vs. 18: "And many other things in his exhortation preached he unto the people," showing that we have here but an abstract of his teaching. Besides what we read in John 1: 29, 33, 34; 3:27-36, the incidental allusion to his having taught his disciples to pray (Luke 11:1)—of which not a word is said elsewhere—shows how varied his teaching was. Vs. 19: "But Herod the tetrarch, being reproved by him for Herodias his brother Philip's wife, and for all the evils which Herod had done." In this last clause we have an important fact, here only mentioned, showing how *thoroughgoing* was the fidelity of the Baptist to his royal hearer, and how strong must have been the workings of conscience in that slave of passion when, notwithstanding such plainness, he "did many things, and heard John gladly" (Mark 6:20). Vs. 20: "Added yet this above all, that he shut up John in prison." This imprisonment of John, however, did not take place for some time after this; and it is here recorded merely because the Evangelist did not intend to recur to his history till he had occasion to relate the message which he sent to Christ from his prison at Machærus (Luke 7:18, etc.).

13-17. Baptism of Christ, and Descent of the Spirit upon Him Immediately Thereafter. (= Mark 1:9-11; Luke 3:21, 22; John 1:31-34.) *Baptism of Christ* (vss. 13-15). **13. Then cometh Jesus from Galilee to Jordan unto John, to be baptized of him**—Moses rashly anticipated the divine call to deliver his people, and for this was fain to flee the house of bondage, and wait in obscurity for forty years more (Exod. 2:11, etc.). Not so this greater than Moses. All but thirty years had He now spent in privacy at Nazareth, gradually ripening for His public work, and calmly awaiting the time appointed of the Father. Now it had arrived; and this movement from Galilee to Jordan is the step, doubtless, of deepest interest to all heaven since that first one which brought Him into the world. Luke (3:21) has this important addition—"Now *when all the people were baptized,* it came to pass, that Jesus being baptized, . . ."—implying that Jesus waited till all other applicants for baptism that day had been disposed of, ere He stepped forward, that He might not seem to be merely one of the crowd. Thus, as He rode into Jerusalem upon an ass "whereon yet never man sat" (Luke 19:30), and lay in a sepulchre "wherein was never man yet laid" (John 19:41), so in His baptism, too. He would be "separate from sinners." **14. But John forbade him**—rather, "was [in the act of] hindering him," or "attempting to hinder him." **saying, I have need to be baptized of thee, and comest thou to me?**—(How John came to recognize Him, when he says he knew Him not, see on John 1:31-34). The emphasis of this most remarkable speech lies all in the pronouns: "What! Shall the Master come for baptism to the servant—the sinless Saviour to a sinner?" That thus much is in the Baptist's words will be clearly seen if it be observed that he evidently regarded Jesus as *Himself needing no purification* but rather *qualified to impart it to those who did*. And do not all his other testimonies to Christ fully bear out this sense of the words? But it were a pity if, in the glory of

ADAM CLARKE

of God, and of Him alone; therefore He is represented here under the similitude of fire, because He was to illuminate and invigorate the soul, penetrate every part, and assimilate the whole to the image of the God of glory.

12. *Whose fan is in his hand.* The Romans are here termed God's fan, as in v. 10 they were called His ax, and as in 12:7, they are termed His troops or armies. *His floor.* Does not this mean the land of Judea, which had been long, as it were, the threshing floor of the Lord? God says He will now, by the winnowing fan (viz., the Romans), throughly cleanse this floor. The *wheat*, those who believe in the Lord Jesus, He *will gather* into His *garner*, either take to heaven from the evil to come, or put in a place of safety, as He did the Christians by sending them to Pella previously to the destruction of Jerusalem. *But he will burn up the chaff*—the disobedient and rebellious Jews, who would not come unto Christ, that they might have life. *Unquenchable fire.* That cannot be extinguished by man.

F. B. MEYER:

John the Baptist is sadly needed today. Much of what we call Christianity is but christianized heathenism. It glosses over covetousness, luxurious self-indulgence, compliance with fashion and worldliness; it admits into its high places men who thrive on the oppression of the poor; it condones the oppression of the native races, the sale of opium and spirits, and shameless traffic in impurity; it rears the ideals of the world in the place of the changeless cross of the slain Christ with its divine sorrow and blood. Ah, we need that John the Baptist should come with his stern words about the axe, the winnowing-fan, and the fire. Nothing less will avail to prepare the way for a new coming of Christ.

Each age has had its John the Baptist. Now St. Bernard; now Savonarola; now John Knox. With sonorous, ringing voice the herald has prepared the way of the King: "He cometh to judge the world!"

—*Great Verses Through the Bible*

14. *John forbad him.* Earnestly and pressingly opposed Him; this is the proper import of the words.

MATTHEW HENRY

the womb (Luke i. 15), yet he acknowledges he had need to be baptized with that baptism. They who have much of the Spirit of God, see that they have need of more. [2] *John has need to be baptized,* though he was the *greatest that ever was born of woman.* The purest souls are most sensible of their own remaining impurity, and seek most earnestly for spiritual washing. [3] He has *need to be baptized of* Christ. The best and holiest of men *have need of* Christ, and the better they are, the more they see of that need. [4] This was said before the multitude, who had a great veneration for John, and were ready to embrace him for the Messiah. It is no disparagement to the greatest of men, to confess that they are undone without Christ and his grace. [5] John was Christ's forerunner, and yet owns that he had *need to be baptized of* him. Even they who were before Christ in time depended on him. [6] While John was dealing with others about their souls, observe how feelingly he speaks of the case of his own soul, *I have need to be baptized of thee.* Take heed to thyself first; *save thyself,* 1 Tim. iv. 16.

(2) He therefore thinks it very preposterous and absurd, that Christ should be baptized by him; *Comest thou to me?* Christ's coming to us may well be wondered at.

2. The overruling of this objection (*v.* 15); *Jesus said, Suffer it to be so now.* Christ accepted his humility, but not his refusal. See,

(1) How Christ insists upon it; It must *be so now.* Everything is beautiful in its season. But why *now*? Why yet? [1] Christ is *now* in a state of humiliation. He is not only *found in fashion as a man,* but is *made in the likeness of sinful flesh,* and thus he *was made sin for us,* though he *knew no sin.* [2] John's baptism is now in reputation, it is that by which God is now doing his work. What we see God owns, and while we see he does so, we must own. [3] It must *be so now,* because now is the time for Christ's appearing in public, and this will be a fair opportunity for it.

(2) The reason he gives for it; *Thus it becomes us to fulfil all righteousness.* [1] There was a propriety in everything that Christ did for us: it was all graceful, *lovely, and of good report.* [2] Our Lord Jesus looked upon it as a thing well becoming him, *to fulfil all righteousness. Thus it becomes* him to justify God, and approve his wisdom. *Thus it becomes us* to countenance and encourage everything that is good, by pattern as well as precept. Thus Jesus began *first to do, and then to teach;* and his ministers must take the same method. It became Christ to submit to John's washing with water, because it was a divine appointment.

With the will of Christ, and this reason for it, John was entirely satisfied, and *then he suffered him.* The same modesty which made him at first decline the honour Christ offered him, now made him do the service Christ enjoined him. No pretence of humility must make us decline our duty.

II. How solemnly Heaven was pleased to grace the baptism of Christ with a special display of glory (*v.* 16, 17); *Jesus when he was baptized, went up straightway out of the water.* Others that were baptized stayed to *confess their sins* (*v.* 6); but Christ, having no sins to confess, *went up* immediately. *He went up straightway,* as one that entered upon his work with the utmost cheerfulness and resolution; he would lose no time. *How was he straightened till it was accomplished!*

1. *Lo! the heavens were opened unto him,* so as to discover something above and beyond the starry firmament, at least, to him. This was, (1) To encourage him to go on in his undertaking, with the prospect of the glory and *joy that were set before him.* (2) To encourage us to receive him, and submit to him. Sin shut up heaven, put a stop to all friendly intercourse between God and man; but now Christ *has opened the kingdom of heaven to all believers.* Divine light and love are darted down upon the children of men, and all by Jesus Christ, who is the ladder that has its foot on earth and its top in heaven.

2. *He saw the Spirit of God descending like a dove,* or *as a dove, and* coming or *lighting upon him.* Christ saw it (Mark i. 10), and John saw it (John i. 33, 34), and it is probable that all the standers-by saw it; for this was intended to be his public inauguration.

(1) *The Spirit of God descended, and lighted on him.* In the beginning of the old world, *the Spirit of God moved upon the face of the waters* (Gen. i. 2), *hovered* as a bird upon the nest. So here, in the beginning of this new world *the Spirit of the Lord should rest upon him* (Isa. xi. 2; lxi. 1), and here he did so. [1] He was to be a Prophet; and prophets always spoke by the Spirit of God, who came upon them. [2] He was to be the Head of the church. Christ *received gifts for men,* that he might give *gifts to men.*

JAMIESON, FAUSSET, BROWN

this testimony to Christ, we should miss the beautiful spirit in which it was borne—"Lord, must *I* baptize *Thee?* Can I bring myself to do such a thing?"—reminding us of Peter's exclamation at the supper table, "Lord, dost Thou wash my feet?" while it has nothing of the false humility and presumption which dictated Peter's next speech. "Thou shalt never wash my feet" (John 13:6, 8).

15. And Jesus answering said unto him, Suffer it to be so now—"Let it pass for the present"; i.e., "Thou recoilest, and no wonder, for the seeming incongruity is startling; but in the present case do as thou art bidden." **for thus it becometh us**—"us," not in the sense of me and thee," or "men in general," but as in John 3:11. **to fulfil all righteousness**—If this be rendered, with SCRIVENER, "every ordinance," or, with CAMPBELL, "every institution," the meaning is obvious enough; and the same sense is brought out by "all righteousness," or compliance with everything enjoined, baptism included. Indeed, if this be the meaning, our version perhaps best brings out the force of the opening word "Thus." But we incline to think that our Lord meant more than this. The import of circumcision and of baptism seems to be radically the same. And if our remarks on the circumcision of our Lord (on Luke 2:21-24) are well founded, He would seem to have said, "Thus do I impledge Myself to the whole righteousness of the Law—thus symbolically do enter on and engage to fulfil it all." Let the thoughtful reader weigh this. **Then he suffered him**—with true humility, yielding to higher authority than his own impressions of propriety.

Descent of the Spirit upon the Baptized Redeemer (vss. 16, 17). **16. And Jesus when he was baptized, went up straightway out of** [rather, "from"] **the water.** Mark has "out of the water." "and"—adds Luke (3:21), "while He was praying"; a grand piece of information. Can there be a doubt about the burden of that prayer; a prayer sent up, probably, while yet in the water—His blessed head suffused with the baptismal element; a prayer continued likely as He stepped out of the stream, and again stood upon the dry ground; the work before Him, the needed and expected Spirit to rest upon Him for it, and the glory He would then put upon the Father that sent Him—would not these fill His breast, and find silent vent in such form as this?—"Lo, I come; I delight to do Thy will, O God. Father, glorify Thy name. Show Me a token for good. Let the Spirit of the Lord God come upon Me, and I will preach the Gospel to the poor, and heal the broken-hearted, and send forth judgment unto victory." While He was yet speaking—**lo, the heavens were opened**—Mark says, sublimely, "He saw the heavens cleaving." **and he saw the Spirit of God descending**—that is, He only, with the exception of His honored servant, as he tells us himself (John 1:32-34); the bystanders apparently seeing nothing. **like a dove, and lighting upon him**—Luke says, "in a bodily shape" (3:22); that is, the blessed Spirit, assuming the corporeal form of a dove, descended thus upon His sacred head. But why in this form? The Scripture use of this emblem will be our best guide here. "My dove, *my undefiled* is one," says the Song of Solomon (6:9). This is chaste purity. Again, "Be ye *harmless* as doves," says Christ Himself (Matt. 10:16). This is the same thing, in the form of inoffensiveness towards men. "A conscience void of offense toward God and toward men" (Acts 24:16) expresses both.

ADAM CLARKE

15. *To fulfil all righteousness.* That is, "every righteous ordinance"; so I think the words should be translated. But was this an ordinance? Undoubtedly; it was the initiatory ordinance of the Baptist's dispensation. Now as Christ had submitted to circumcision, which was the initiatory ordinance of the Mosaic dispensation, it was necessary that He should submit to this, which was instituted by no less an authority, and was the introduction to His own dispensation of eternal mercy and truth. But it was necessary on another account. Our Lord represented the high priest, and was to be the High Priest over the house of God. As the high priest was initiated into his office by washing and anointing, so must Christ; and hence He was baptized, washed, and anointed by the Holy Ghost. Thus He fulfilled the righteous ordinance of His initiation into the office of High Priest, and thus was prepared to make an atonement for the sins of mankind.

16. *The heavens were opened unto him.* That is, to John the Baptist—*and he,* John, *saw the Spirit of God . . . lighting upon him,* i.e., Jesus. This passage affords no mean proof of the doctrine of the Trinity. That three distinct Persons are here represented there can be no dispute: (1) The person of Jesus Christ, baptized by John in Jordan; (2) The person of the Holy Ghost in a bodily shape (Luke iii. 22) like a dove; (3) The person of the Father—a voice came out of heaven, saying, "This is my beloved Son." The voice is here represented as proceeding from a different place to that in which the persons of the Son and Holy Spirit were manifested; and merely, I think, more forcibly to mark this divine Personality.

MATTHEW HENRY

(2) He *descended on him like a dove*. If there must be a bodily shape (Luke iii. 22), it must not be that of a man. None therefore was more fit than the shape of one of the fowls of heaven (heaven being now opened), and of all fowl none was so significant as the dove. [1] The Spirit of Christ is a dove-like spirit. *The Spirit descended*, not in the shape of an eagle, which is, though a royal bird, yet a bird of prey, but *in the shape of a dove*, than which no creature is more harmless and inoffensive. Such must Christians be, *harmless as doves*. The dove mourns much (Isa. xxxviii. 14). Christ wept oft; and penitent souls are compared to *doves of the valleys*. [2] The dove was the only fowl that was offered in sacrifice (Lev. i. 14), and Christ *offered himself without spot to God*. [3] The tidings of the decrease of Noah's flood were brought by a dove, with an olive-leaf in her mouth; fitly therefore are the glad tidings of peace with God brought by the Spirit as *a dove*. That God is in Christ reconciling the world unto himself, is a joyful message, which comes to us upon the wing, *the wings of a dove*.

3. To explain and complete this solemnity, *there came a voice from heaven*. The Holy Spirit manifested himself in the likeness of a *dove*, but God the Father by *a voice*.

(1) See here how God owns our Lord Jesus; *This is my beloved Son*. Observe, [1] The relation he stood in to him; He *is my Son*. He is the Son of God by special designation to the work and office of the world's Redeemer. He was sanctified and sealed, and went upon that errand, *brought up with* the Father for it. [2] The affection the Father had for him; He *is my beloved Son*. Particularly as Mediator, and in undertaking the work of man's salvation, he was his *beloved Son*. Because he consented to the covenant of redemption, and delighted to do that *will of God*, *therefore the Father loved him*. Now know we that he loved us, *seeing he has not withheld his Son, his only Son, his Isaac whom he loved*, but *gave him to be a sacrifice for our sin*.

(2) See here how ready he is to own us in him: He *is my beloved Son*, not only *with* whom, but *in* whom, I am well pleased. He is pleased with all that are in him, and are united to him by faith. Hitherto God had been displeased with the children of men, but now his anger is turned away, and he has made us *accepted in the Beloved*, Eph. i. 6. Out of Christ, God *is a consuming Fire*, but, in Christ, a reconciled Father. This is the sum of the whole gospel. We must by faith cheerfully concur, and say, that he *is our beloved* Saviour, *in whom we are well pleased*.

JAMIESON, FAUSSET, BROWN

Further, when we read in the Song (2:14), "O my dove, that art in the *clefts* of the rocks, in the *secret places* of the stairs (see Isaiah 60:8), let me see thy countenance, let me hear thy voice; for sweet is thy voice, and thy countenance is comely"—it is shrinking modesty, meekness, gentleness, that is thus charmingly depicted. In a word—not to allude to the historical emblem of the dove that flew back to the ark, bearing in its mouth the olive leaf of *peace* (Gen. 8:11)—when we read (Ps. 68:13), "Ye shall be as the wings of a dove covered with silver, and her feathers with yellow gold," it is *beauteousness* that is thus held forth. And was not such that "holy, harmless, undefiled One," the "separate from sinners"? "Thou art fairer than the children of men; grace is poured into Thy lips; therefore God hath blessed Thee for ever!" But the fourth Gospel gives us one more piece of information here, on the authority of one who saw and testified of it: "John bare record, saying, I saw the Spirit descending from heaven like a dove, and IT ABODE UPON HIM." And lest we should think that this was an accidental thing, he adds that this last particular was expressly given him as part of the sign by which he was to recognize and identify Him as the Son of God: "And I knew Him not: but He that sent me to baptize with water, the same said unto me, Upon whom thou shalt see the Spirit descending AND REMAINING ON HIM, the same is He which baptizeth with the Holy Ghost. And I saw and bare record that this is the Son of God" (John 1:32-34). And when with this we compare the predicted descent of the Spirit upon Messiah (Isa. 11:2), "And *the Spirit of the Lord shall rest upon Him*," we cannot doubt that it was this permanent and perfect resting of the Holy Ghost upon the Son of God—now and henceforward in His *official* capacity—that was here visibly manifested. **17. And lo a voice from heaven, saying, This is**—Mark and Luke give it in the direct form, "Thou art." **my beloved Son, in whom I am well pleased**—The verb is put in the aorist to express absolute complacency, once and for ever felt towards Him. The English here, at least to modern ears, is scarcely strong enough. "I delight" comes the nearest, perhaps, to that ineffable *complacency* which is manifestly intended; and this is the rather to be preferred, as it would immediately carry the thoughts back to that august Messianic prophecy to which the voice from heaven plainly alluded (Isa. 42:1), "Behold My Servant, whom I uphold; Mine Elect, IN WHOM MY SOUL DELIGHTETH." Nor are the words which follow to be overlooked, "I have put My Spirit upon Him; He shall bring forth judgment to the Gentiles." (The LXX perverts this, as it does most of the Messianic predictions, interpolating the word "Jacob," and applying it to the Jews.) Was this voice heard by the bystanders? From Matthew's form of it, one might suppose it so designed; but it would appear that it was not, and probably John only heard and saw anything peculiar about that great baptism. Accordingly, the words, "Hear ye Him," are not added, as at the Transfiguration.

ADAM CLARKE

F. B. MEYER:

Baptized with the Spirit. While John was denouncing the sins of others, he was very conscious of his own. He melted in holy humility before the one nature in which his keen eye detected no trace of impurity, and he strenuously strove to forbid the incongruity of his polluted hands baptizing so pure a being as he felt Christ to be.

Our Lord accepted the disclaimer, but overruled it. He alone of all holy men had no consciousness of sin. He "did no sin, neither was guile found in his mouth" (1 Pet. 2:22). As God's designated Lamb, he was carefully scrutinized, but those who knew the most about him were compelled to attest his innocence and purity. Yet he was baptized that he might assume the sinner's guilt, standing with him and for him and identifying himself with his lot. Then he was anointed by the Spirit and attested by the Father's voice. Probably only John and he were aware of these celestial tokens (see John 1:32). But let us stand beneath the same chrism as did Christ (see 1 John 2:20, 27).
—*Bible Commentary*

17. *In whom I am well pleased.* "In whom I have delighted"—though it is supposed that the past tense is here used for the present. By this voice, and overshadowing of the Spirit, the mission of the Lord Jesus was publicly and solemnly accredited, God intimating that He had before delighted in Him; the law, in all its ordinances, having pointed Him out, for they could not be pleasing to God but as they were fulfilled in, and showed forth, the Son of Man, till He came.

MATTHEW HENRY — CHAPTER 4

Verses 1–11

We have here the story of a famous duel, fought hand to hand, between Michael and the dragon, the Seed of the woman and the seed of the serpent, nay, the serpent himself in which the seed of the woman suffers, being *tempted*, and so has his heel bruised but the serpent is quite baffled in his temptations, and so has his head broken.

I. The time when it happened. Immediately after *the heavens were opened* to him, and *the Spirit descended on him*. The next news we hear of him is, he is *tempted*; for *then* he is best able to grapple with the temptation. 1. Great privileges, and special tokens of divine favour, will not secure us from being *tempted*. Nay, 2. After great honours put upon us, we must expect something that is humbling. 3. God usually prepares his people for temptation before he calls them to it. 4. The assurance of our sonship is the best preparative for temptation.

Then, when he was baptized, *then* he was *tempted*. After we have been admitted into communion with God, we must expect to be set upon by Satan. The enriched soul must double its guard. The Devil has a particular spite at useful persons, who are not only good, but given to do good, especially at their first setting out. Let young ministers know what to expect, and arm accordingly.

II. The place where it was; *in the wilderness*. After communion with God, it is good to be private awhile,

JAMIESON, FAUSSET, BROWN — CHAPTER 4

Vss. 1-11. TEMPTATION OF CHRIST. (= Mark 1:12, 13; Luke 4:1-13.) **1. Then**—an indefinite note of sequence. But Mark's word (1:12) fixes what we should have presumed was meant, that it was "immediately" after His baptism; and with this agrees the statement of Luke (4:1). **was Jesus led up**—i.e., from the low Jordan valley to some more elevated spot. **of the Spirit**—that blessed Spirit immediately before spoken of as descending upon Him at His baptism, and abiding upon Him. Luke, connecting these two scenes, as if the one were but the sequel of the other, says, "Jesus, being full of the Holy Ghost, returned from Jordan, and was led . . . ." Mark's expression has a startling sharpness about it—"Immediately the Spirit driveth Him," "putteth," or "hurrieth Him forth," or "impelleth Him." (See the same word in Mark 1:43; 5:40; Matt. 9:25; 13:52; John 10:4.) The thought thus strongly expressed is the mighty constraining impulse of the Spirit under which He went; while Matthew's more gentle expression, "was led up," intimates how purely voluntary on His own part this action was. **into the wilderness**—probably the wild Judean desert. The particular spot which tradition has fixed upon has hence got the name of *Quarantana* or *Quarantaria,* from the forty days, —"an almost perpendicular wall of rock twelve or fifteen hundred feet above the plain" [ROBINSON'S *Palestine*]. The supposition of those who incline

ADAM CLARKE — CHAPTER 4

1. *Then was Jesus led up of the spirit.* This transaction appears to have taken place immediately after Christ's baptism; and this bringing up of Christ was through the influence of the Spirit of God, that Spirit which had rested upon Him in His baptism. *To be tempted.* The first act of the ministry of Jesus Christ was a combat with Satan. Does not this receive light from Gen. iii. 15: "I will put enmity between" the woman's Seed and thy seed; "it shall bruise thy head, and thou shalt bruise his heel."

MATTHEW HENRY

lest we lose what we have received, in the crowd, and hurry of worldly business. Christ withdrew into the wilderness, 1. To gain advantage to himself. Retirement gives an opportunity for meditation and communion with God; even they who are called to the most active life must yet have their contemplative hours, and must find time to be alone with God. Those are not fit to speak of the things of God in public to others, who have not first conversed with those things in secret by themselves. 2. To give advantage to the tempter. Though solitude is a friend to a good heart, yet Satan knows how to improve it against us. Those who, under pretence of sanctity and devotion, retire into dens and deserts, find that they are not out of the reach of their spiritual enemies, and that there they want the benefit of the communion of saints. Christ retired, (1) That Satan might have leave to do his worst. To make his victory the more illustrious, he gave the enemy sun and wind on his side, and yet baffled him. (2) That he might have an opportunity to do his best himself, that he might be exalted in his own strength. Christ entered the lists without a second.

III. The preparatives for it, which were two.

1. He was directed to the combat; he *was led up of the Spirit to be tempted of the Devil.* The Spirit that *descended upon him like a dove* made him meek, and yet made him bold. If God, by his providence, order us into circumstances of temptation, for our trial, we must not think it strange, but double our guard. *Be strong in the Lord, resist steadfast in the faith*, and all shall be well. Whithersoever God leads us, we may hope he will go along with us, and bring us off *more than conquerors.*

Christ *was led to be tempted of the Devil*, and of him only. Others are tempted, *when they are drawn aside of their own lust and enticed* (James i. 14); but our Lord Jesus had no corrupt nature, and therefore he was led, as a champion into the field, *to be tempted* purely by *the Devil.*

Now Christ's temptation is, (1) An instance of his own condescension and humiliation. Christ submitted because he would humble himself, *in all things to be made like unto his brethren.* (2) An occasion of Satan's confusion. There is no conquest without a combat. Christ was tempted, that he might overcome the tempter. (3) Matter of comfort to all the saints. In the temptation of Christ it appears, that our enemy is not invincible. Though he is *a strong man armed*, yet the Captain of our salvation is *stronger than he.* It is some comfort to us to think that Christ suffered, being *tempted*; for thus it appears that temptations, if not yielded to, are not sins, they are afflictions only. And we have a High Priest who knows, by experience, what it is to be *tempted*, and who therefore is the more tenderly touched with *the feeling of our infirmities* in an hour of temptation.

2. He was dieted for the combat, as wrestlers, who are *temperate in all things* (1 Cor. ix. 25); but Christ beyond any other, for he *fasted forty days and forty nights.* Christ needed not to fast for mortification (he had no corrupt desires to be subdued); yet he *fasted.* If good people are brought low, if they want friends and succours, this may comfort them, that their Master himself was in like manner exercised. A man may want bread, and yet be a favourite of heaven, and under the conduct of the spirit. *When he fasted forty days he was* never hungry; converse with heaven was instead of meat and drink to him, but *he was afterwards an hungred*, to show that he was really and truly man. Man fell by eating, and that way we often sin, and therefore Christ *was an hungred.*

IV. The temptations themselves. That which Satan aimed at, in all his temptations, was, to bring him to *sin against God*, and so to render him for ever incapable of being a Sacrifice for the sin of others. That which he aimed at was, to bring him, 1. To despair of his Father's goodness. 2. To presume upon his Father's power. 3. To alienate his Father's honour, by giving it to Satan. The two former are artful temptations, which there was need of great wisdom to discern; the last was a strong temptation, which there was need of great resolution to resist.

1. He tempted him to despair of his Father's goodness, and to distrust his Father's care concerning him.

(1) See how the temptation was managed (*v.* 3); *The tempter came to him. The tempter came to* Christ in a visible appearance. If ever the Devil *transformed himself into an angel of light*, he did so now, and pretended to be a good genius, a guardian angel.

Observe the subtlety of *the tempter*, in joining this first temptation with what went before, to make it the stronger. [1] Christ began to be hungry, and therefore the motion seemed very proper, to turn *stones* into *bread* for his necessary support. Want

JAMIESON, FAUSSET, BROWN

to place the temptation amongst the mountains of Moab is, we think, very improbable. **to be tempted**—The *Greek* word (*peirazein*) means simply to *try* or make proof of; and when ascribed to God in His dealings with men, it means, and can mean no more than this. Thus, Genesis 22:1, "It came to pass that God did tempt Abraham," or put his faith to a severe proof. (See Deut. 8:2.) But for the most part in Scripture the word is used in a bad sense, and means to entice, solicit, or provoke to sin. Hence the name here given to the wicked one—"the tempter" (vs. 3). Accordingly "to be tempted" here is to be understood both ways. The Spirit conducted Him into the wilderness simply to have His faith *tried;* but as the agent in this trial was to be the wicked one, whose whole object would be to seduce Him from His allegiance to God, it was a *temptation* in the bad sense of the term. The unworthy inference which some would draw from this is energetically repelled by an apostle (Jas. 1:13-17). **of the devil.** The word signifies a slanderer—one who casts imputations upon another. Hence that other name given him (Rev. 12:10), "The accuser of the brethren, who accuseth them before our God day and night." Mark (1:13) says, "He was forty days tempted of *Satan*," a word signifying an *adversary*, one who lies in wait for, or sets himself in opposition to another. These and other names of the same fallen spirit point to different features in his character or operations. What was the high design of this? First, as we judge, to give our Lord a taste of what lay before Him in the work He had undertaken; next, to make trial of the glorious equipment for it which He had just received; further, to give Him encouragement, by the victory now to be won, to go forward spoiling principalities and powers, until at length He should make a show of them openly, triumphing over them in His cross; that the tempter, too, might get a taste, at the very outset, of the new kind of material in *man* which he would find he had here to deal with; finally, that He might acquire experimental ability "to succor them that are tempted" (Heb. 2:18). The temptation evidently embraced two stages: the one continuing throughout the forty days' fast; the other, at the conclusion of that period. FIRST STAGE: **2. And when he had fasted forty days and forty nights**—Luke says, "When they were quite ended." **he was afterward an hungered**—evidently implying that the sensation of hunger was unfelt during all the forty days; coming on only at their close. So it was apparently with Moses (Exod. 34:28) and Elijah (I Kings 19:8) for the same period. A supernatural power of endurance was of course imparted to the body, but this probably operated through a natural law—the absorption of the Redeemer's Spirit in the dread conflict with the tempter. (See on Acts 9:9.) Had we only this Gospel, we should suppose the temptation did not begin till after this. But it is clear, from Mark's statement, that "He was in the wilderness forty days tempted of Satan," and Luke's, "being forty days tempted of the devil," that there was a forty days' temptation *before* the three specific temptations afterwards recorded. And this is what we have called the First Stage. What the precise nature and object of the forty days' temptation were is not recorded. But two things seem plain enough. First, the tempter had utterly failed of his object, else it had not been renewed; and the terms in which he opens his second attack imply as much. But further, the tempter's whole object during the forty days evidently was to get Him to distrust the heavenly testimony borne to Him at His baptism as THE SON OF GOD—to persuade Him to regard it as but a splendid illusion—and, generally, to dislodge from His breast the consciousness of His Sonship. With what plausibility the events of His previous history from the beginning would be urged upon Him in support of this temptation it is easy to imagine. And it makes much in support of this view of the forty days' temptation that the particulars of it are not recorded; for how the details of such a purely internal struggle could be recorded it is hard to see. If this be correct, how naturally does the SECOND STAGE of the temptation open! In Mark's brief notice of the temptation there is one expressive particular not given either by Matthew or by Luke—that "He was with the wild beasts," no doubt to add terror to solitude, and aggravate the horrors of the whole scene. **3. And when the tempter came to him**—Evidently we have here a new scene. **he said, if thou be the Son of God, command that these stones be made bread**—rather, "loaves," answering to "stones" in the plural; whereas Luke, having said, "Command this stone," in the singular, adds, "that it be made bread," in

ADAM CLARKE

W. E. VINE:

PEIRAZO signifies (1) to try, attempt, assay; (2) to test, try, prove, in a good sense, said of Christ and of believers, Heb. 2:18, where the context shows that the temptation was the cause of suffering to Him, and only suffering, not a drawing away to sin, so that believers have the sympathy of Christ as their High Priest in the suffering which sin occasions to those who are in the enjoyment of communion with God; so in the similar passage in 4:15; in all the temptations which Christ endured, there was nothing within Him that answered to sin. There was no sinful infirmity in Him. While He was truly man, and His divine nature was not in any way inconsistent with His manhood, there was nothing in Him such as is produced in us by the sinful nature which belongs to us; in Heb. 11:37, of the testing of O.T. saints; in 1 Cor. 10:13, where the meaning has a wide scope, the verb is used of testing as permitted by God, and of the believer as one who should be in the realization of his own helplessness and his dependence upon God; in a bad sense, to tempt (a) of attempts to ensnare Christ in His speech (Matt. 16:1; 19:3; 22:18, 35, and parallel passages; John 8:6); (b) of temptations to sin, e.g., Gal. 6:1, where one who would restore an erring brother is not to act as his judge, but as being one with him in liability to sin, with the possibility of finding himself in similar circumstances, James 1:13, 14; of temptations mentioned as coming from the devil (Matt. 4:1, and parallel passages; 1 Cor. 7:5; 1 Thess. 3:5); (c) of trying or challenging God (Acts 15:10; 1 Cor. 10:9; Heb. 3:9); the Holy Spirit (Acts 5:9).
—*Vine's Expository Dictionary*

2. *And when he had fasted forty days.* **It is remarkable that Moses, the great lawgiver of the Jews, previous to his receiving the law from God, fasted forty days in the mount; that Elijah, the chief of the prophets, fasted also forty days; and that Christ, the Giver of the new covenant, should act in the same way. Was not all this intended to show that God's kingdom on earth was to be spiritual and living? That it should not consist "in meat and drink; but righteousness, and peace, and joy in the Holy Ghost," Rom. xiv. 17?**

3. *And when the tempter.* **This onset of Satan was made (speaking after the manner of men) judiciously; he came when Jesus, after having fasted forty days and forty nights, was hungry. Now as hunger naturally diminishes the strength of the body, the mind gets enfeebled, and be-**

MATTHEW HENRY

and poverty are a great temptation to discontent and unbelief, and the use of unlawful means for our relief, under pretence that necessity has no law. Those therefore who are reduced to straits, have need to double their guard; it is better to starve to death, than live and thrive by sin. [2] Christ was lately declared to be *the Son of God*, and here the Devil tempts him to doubt of that; *If thou be the Son of God.*

First, "Thou hast now an occasion to question whether *thou be the Son of God* or no; for can it be, that *the Son of God*, who is *Heir of all things*, should be reduced to such straits? Either God is not thy Father, or he is a very unkind one." *a.* The great thing Satan aims at, in tempting good people, is to overthrow their relation to God as a Father. *b.* Outward afflictions, wants and burdens, are the great arguments Satan uses to make the people of God question their sonship. They know how to answer this temptation, who can say with holy Job, *Though he slay me, though he* starve me, *yet I will trust in him*, and love him as a Friend. *c.* The Devil aims to shake our faith in the word of God. *Has God said* that thou art his *beloved Son?* Surely he did not say so; or if he did it is not true. *d.* The Devil carries on his designs very much by possessing people with hard thoughts of God, as if he were unkind, or unfaithful.

Secondly, "Thou hast now an opportunity to show that thou art *the Son of God. If thou* art *the Son of God*, prove it by this, *command that these stones*" (a heap of which, probably, lay now before him) "*be made bread*," *v.* 3. He does not say, *Pray to thy Father* that he would turn them into *bread*; but *command* it to be done; thy Father hath forsaken thee, set up for thyself, and be not beholden to him. The Devil is for nothing that is humbling, but everything that is assuming.

(2) See how this temptation was resisted and overcome.

[1] Christ refused to comply with it. He would not *command these stones to be made bread*; not because he could not; but he would not. And why would he not? At first view, the thing appears justifiable enough, and the truth is, the more plausible a temptation is, and the greater appearance there is of good in it, the more dangerous it is. This matter would bear a dispute, but Christ was soon aware of the snake in the grass, and would not do anything, *First*, That looked like questioning the truth of the voice he heard from heaven. *Secondly*, That looked like distrusting his Father's care of him. *Thirdly*, That looked like setting up for himself, and being his own carver; or, *Fourthly*, That looked like gratifying Satan, by doing a thing at his motion.

[2] He was ready to reply to it (*v.* 4); *He answered and said, It is written.* This is observable, that Christ answered and baffled all the temptations of Satan with, *It is written.* He put honour upon the scripture, and, to set us an example, he appealed to what was written in the law. The word of God is *the sword of the Spirit*, the only offensive weapon in all the Christian armoury (Eph. vi. 17).

This answer, as all the rest, is taken out of the book of *Deuteronomy*, which signifies *the second law*, and in which there is very little ceremonial; the Levitical sacrifices and purifications, though of divine institution, could not drive away Satan, but moral precepts and evangelical promises, mixed with faith, these are *mighty, through God*, for the vanquishing of Satan. The reason given why God fed the Israelites with manna is, because he would teach them that *man shall not live by bread alone*. This Christ applies to his own case. The Devil would have him question his sonship, because he was in straits; no, says he, Israel was God's son, and it follows there (Deut. viii. 5), *As a man chasteneth his son, so the Lord thy God chasteneth thee.* Christ, *being a Son*, thus *learns obedience*. The Devil would have him distrust his Father's love and care. The Devil would have him, as soon as he began to be hungry, immediately look out for supply. God will have his children, when they want, not only to wait on him, but to wait for him. The Devil would have him to supply himself with bread. "No," says Christ, "what need is there of that? Man may live without bread, as Israel in the wilderness lived forty years upon manna." *Any word proceeding out of the mouth of God*, anything that God shall order and appoint for that end, will be as good a livelihood for man as bread, and will maintain him as well. As we may *have bread*, and yet not be nourished, if God deny his blessing (for though bread is *the staff of life*, it is God's blessing that is *the staff of bread*), so we may *want bread*, and yet be nourished some other way. As in our greatest abundance we must not think to live *without* God, so in our greatest straits we must learn to live *upon* God. Let us learn of Christ here to be at God's finding, rather than at our own. *Jehovah-jireh;* some

JAMIESON, FAUSSET, BROWN

the singular. The sensation of hunger, unfelt during all the forty days, seems now to have come on in all its keenness—no doubt to open a door to the tempter, of which he is not slow to avail himself; "Thou still clingest to that vainglorious confidence that Thou art the Son of God, carried away by those illusory scenes at the Jordan. Thou wast born in a stable; but Thou art the Son of God! hurried off to Egypt for fear of Herod's wrath; but Thou art the Son of God! a carpenter's roof supplied Thee with a home, and in the obscurity of a despicable town of Galilee Thou hast spent thirty years, yet still Thou art the Son of God! and a voice from heaven, it seems, proclaimed it in Thine ears at the Jordan! Be it so; but after *that*, surely Thy days of obscurity and trial should have an end. Why linger for weeks in this desert, wandering among the wild beasts and craggy rocks, unhonored, unattended, unpitied, ready to starve for want of the necessaries of life? Is this befitting "the Son of God"? At the bidding of "the Son of God" surely those stones shall all be turned into loaves, and in a moment present an abundant repast."

4. But he answered and said, It is written—(Deut. 8:3). **Man shall not live by bread alone**—more emphatically, as in the *Greek*, "Not by bread alone shall man live." **but by every word that proceedeth out of the mouth of God**—Of all passages in Old Testament Scripture, none could have been pitched upon more apposite, perhaps not one so apposite, to our Lord's purpose. "The Lord . . . led thee [said Moses to Israel, at the close of their journeyings] these forty years in the wilderness, to humble thee, and to prove thee, to know what was in thine heart, whether thou wouldest keep His commandments, or no. And He humbled thee, and suffered thee to hunger, and fed thee with manna, which thou knewest not, neither did thy fathers know; that He might make thee know that man doth not live by bread only . . .", "Now, if Israel spent, not forty days, but forty years in a waste, howling wilderness, where there were no means of human subsistence, not starving, but divinely provided for, on purpose to prove to every age that human support depends not upon bread, but upon God's unfailing word of promise and pledge of all needful providential care, am I, distrusting this word of God, and despairing of relief, to take the law into My own hand? True, the Son of God is able enough to turn stones into bread: but what the Son of God is able to do is not the present question, but what is *man's duty* under want of the necessaries of life. And as Israel's condition in the wilderness did not justify their unbelieving murmurings and frequent desperation, so neither would Mine warrant the exercise of the power of the Son of God in snatching despairingly at unwarranted relief. As man, therefore, I will await divine supply, nothing doubting that at the fitting time it will arrive." The *second* temptation in this Gospel is in Luke's the *third*. That Matthew's order is the right one will appear, we think, quite clearly in the sequel.

ADAM CLARKE

comes easily irritated; and if much watching and prayer be not employed, the uneasiness which is occasioned by a lack of food may soon produce impatience, and in this state of mind the tempter has great advantages. *Command that these stones.* The meaning of this temptation is: "Distrust the divine providence and support, and make use of illicit means to supply Thy necessities."

4. *But by* (or upon,) *every word. Rhema* in Greek answers to *dabar* in Hebrew, which means not only "a word spoken" but also "thing, purpose, appointment." Our Lord's meaning seems to be this: God purposes the welfare of His creatures—all His appointments are calculated to promote this end. Some of them may appear to man to have a contrary tendency; but even *fasting* itself, when used in consequence of a divine injunction, becomes a means of supporting that life which it seems naturally calculated to impair or destroy.

W. E. VINE:

RHEMA denotes that which is spoken, what is uttered in speech or writing; in the singular, a word (Matt. 12:36; 27:14; 2 Cor. 12:4; 13:1; Heb. 12:19); in the plural, speech, discourse (John 3:34; 8:20; Acts 2:14; 6:11, 13; 11:14; 13:42; 26:25; Rom. 10:18; 2 Pet. 3:2; Jude 17); it is used of the gospel in Rom. 10:8 (twice), 17, R.V., "the word of Christ" (i.e., the word which preaches Christ); 10:18; 1 Pet. 1:25 (twice); of a statement, command, instruction (Matt. 26:75; Luke 1:37, R.V., "[no] word [from God shall be void of power];" v. 38; Acts 11:16; Heb. 11:3).

The significance of *rhema* (as distinct from *logos*) is exemplified in the injunction to take "the sword of the Spirit, which is the word of God" (Eph. 6:17); here the reference is not to the whole Bible as such, but to the individual scripture which the Spirit brings to our remembrance for use in time of need, a prerequisite being the regular storing of the mind with Scripture.
—Vine's Expository Dictionary

MATTHEW HENRY

way or other *the Lord will provide*. It is better to live poorly upon the fruits of God's goodness, than live plentifully upon the products of our own sin.

2. He tempted him to presume upon his Father's power and protection. See what a restless unwearied adversary the Devil is!

Now in this second attempt we may observe,

(1) What the temptation was, and how it was managed. In general, finding Christ so confident of his Father's care of him, in point of nourishment, he endeavours to draw him to presume upon that care in point of safety. Nor are any extremes more dangerous than those of despair and presumption, especially in the affairs of our souls. Some who have obtained a persuasion that Christ is able and willing to save them *from* their sins, are then tempted to presume that he will save them *in* their sins.

Now in this temptation we may observe,

[1] How he made way for it. He took Christ, not by force and against his will, but moved him to go, and went along with him, to Jerusalem. He was *set upon a pinnacle of the temple*. Now observe, *First*, How submissive Christ was, in suffering himself to be hurried thus, that he might let Satan do his worst and yet conquer him. How comfortable is it, that Christ, who let loose this power of Satan against himself, does not in like manner let it loose against us, but restrains it, for he *knows our frame*! *Secondly*, How subtle the Devil was, in the choice of the place for his temptations. He fixes him on a public place in Jerusalem, a populous city, and *the joy of the whole earth*; and in the temple, one of the wonders of the world, continually gazed upon with admiration by some one or other. There he might make himself remarkable, and prove himself the Son of God; not, in the obscurities of a wilderness, but before multitudes.

Observe, *a*. That Jerusalem is here called the *holy city*; for so it was in name and profession. There is no city on earth so holy as to exempt and secure us from the Devil and his temptations. The *holy city* is the place where he does, with the greatest advantage and success, tempt men to pride and presumption; but, blessed be God, into the Jerusalem above, that holy city, no unclean thing shall enter; there we shall be for ever out of temptation. *b*. That he *set him upon a pinnacle of the temple*. Pinnacles of the temple are places of temptation. (*a*) High places are so; they are slippery places. God casts down, that he may raise up; the Devil raises up, that he may cast down. (*b*) High places *in the church* are, in a special manner, dangerous. They who excel in gifts, who are in eminent stations, and have gained great reputation, have need to keep humble. Those that *stand high* are concerned to *stand fast*.

[2] How he moved it; "*If thou be the Son of God*, now show thyself to the world, and prove thyself to be so; *cast thyself down*, and then," *First*, "Thou wilt be admired, as *under the special protection of heaven*." *Secondly*, "Thou wilt be received, as coming *with a special commission from heaven*. All Jerusalem will see and acknowledge, not only that thou art more than a man, but that thou art that *Messenger*, that *Angel of the covenant*, that should *suddenly come to the temple* (Mal. iii. 1)."

Observe, The Devil said, *Cast thyself down*. The Devil could not cast him down. The power of Satan is a limited power; *hitherto he shall come, and no further*. The Devil can but persuade, he cannot compel; he can but say, *Cast thyself down*; he cannot cast us down. Therefore let us not *hurt ourselves*, and then, blessed be God, no one else can hurt us, Prov. ix. 12.

[3] How he backed this motion with a scripture; *For it is written, He shall give his angels charge concerning thee*. But *is Saul also among the prophets*? Is Satan so well versed in scripture, as to be able to quote it so readily? It seems, he is. Note, It is possible for a man to have his head full of scripture-notions, and his mouth full of scripture-expressions, while his heart is full of reigning enmity to God and all goodness.

First, There was *something right*. It is true, there is such a promise of the ministration of the angels, for the protection of the saints. The devil knows it by experience. The angels guard the saints for Christ's sake, Rev. vii. 5, 11.

Secondly, There was a great deal *wrong in it*; and perhaps the devil had a particular spite against this promise, and perverted it, because it often stood in his way, and baffled his mischievous designs against the saints. See here, 1. How he *misquoted* it; and that was *bad*. The promise is, They shall *keep thee*; but how? *In all thy ways;* not otherwise; if we go *out of our way*, out of the way of our duty, we forfeit the promise, and put ourselves out of God's protection. It is good for us upon all occasions to consult the scriptures themselves, and not to take things upon trust. 2. How he *misapplied* it; and that was *worse*.

JAMIESON, FAUSSET, BROWN

5. Then the devil taketh him up—rather, "conducteth Him." **into the holy city**—so called (as in Isa. 48:2; Neh. 11:1) from its being "the city of the Great King," the seat of the temple, the metropolis of all Jewish worship. **and setteth him on a pinnacle** [rather, the pinnacle] **of the temple**—a certain well-known projection. Whether this refers to the highest summit of the temple, which bristled with golden spikes (JOSEPHUS, *Antiquities*, 5. 5, 6); or whether it refers to another peak, on Herod's royal portico, overhanging the ravine of Kedron, at the valley of Hinnom—an immense tower built on the very edge of this precipice, from the top of which dizzy height JOSEPHUS says one could not look to the bottom (*Antiquities*, 15. 11, 5)—is not certain; but the latter is probably meant.

6. And saith unto him, If thou be the Son of God—As this temptation starts with the same point as the first—our Lord's determination not to be disputed out of His Sonship—it seems to us clear that the one came directly after the other; and as the remaining temptation shows that the hope of carrying that point was abandoned, and all was staked upon a desperate venture, we think that remaining temptation is thus shown to be the last; as will appear still more when we come to it. **cast thyself down**—"from hence" (Luke 4:9). **for it is written**—(Ps. 91:11, 12). "But what is this I see?" exclaims stately BISHOP HALL—"Satan himself with a Bible under his arm and a text in his mouth!" Doubtless the tempter, having felt the power of God's Word in the former temptation, was eager to try the effect of it from his own mouth (II Cor. 11: 14). **He shall give his angels charge concerning thee: and in** [rather, on] **their hands they shall bear thee up, lest at any time thou dash thy foot against a stone**—The quotation is precisely as it stands in the *Hebrew* and LXX, save that after the first clause the words, "to keep thee in all thy ways," are here omitted. Not a few good expositors have thought that this omission was intentional, to conceal the fact that this would *not* have been one of "His ways," i.e., of duty. But as our Lord's reply makes no allusion to this, but seizes on the great principle involved in the promise quoted, so when we look at the promise itself, it is plain that the sense of it is precisely the same whether the clause in question be inserted or not. **7. Jesus said unto him, It is written again**—(Deut. 6:16), q.d., "True, it is so written, and on that promise I implicitly rely; but in using it there is another Scripture which must not be forgotten. **Thou shalt not tempt the Lord thy God**—Preservation in danger is divinely pledged: shall I then *create* danger, either to put the promised security skeptically to the proof, or wantonly to demand a display of it? That were "to tempt the Lord my God," which, being expressly forbidden, would forfeit the right to expect preservation."

ADAM CLARKE

5. *Pinnacle of the temple*. It is very likely that this was what was called the king's gallery; which, as Josephus says, "deserves to be mentioned among the most magnificent things under the sun: for upon a stupendous depth of a valley, scarcely to be fathomed by the eye of him that stands above, Herod erected a gallery of a vast height, from the top of which if any looked down, he would grow dizzy, his eyes not being able to reach so vast a depth."

6. *Cast thyself down*. Our Lord had repelled the first temptation by an act of confidence in the power and goodness of God, and now Satan solicits Him to make trial of it. Through the unparalleled subtlety of Satan, the very means we made use of to repel one temptation may be used by him as the groundwork of another.

He shall give his angels charge. This is a mutilated quotation of Ps. xci. 11. The clause "to keep thee in all thy ways," Satan chose to leave out, as quite unsuitable to his design. That God has promised to protect and support His servants admits of no dispute; but as the path of duty is the way of safety, they are entitled to no good when they walk out of it. *In their hands they shall bear thee up*. This quotation from Ps. xci. 11 is a metaphor taken from a nurse's management of her child. In teaching it to walk, she guides it along plain ground; but when stones or other obstacles occur, she lifts up the child and carries it over them, and then sets it down to walk again.

7. *Thou shalt not tempt*. To expose myself to any danger naturally destructive, with the vain presumption that God will protect and defend me from the ruinous consequences of my imprudent conduct, is to tempt God.

MATTHEW HENRY

This promise is firm, and stands good; but the devil made an ill use of it, when he used it as an encouragement to presume upon the divine care. But *shall we continue in sin, that grace may abound*? throw ourselves down, that the angels may bear us up? God forbid.

(2) How Christ overcame this temptation; he resisted and overcame it, as he did the former, with, *It is written.* The Devil's *abusing* of scripture did not prevent Christ from using it, but he presently urges, Deut. vi. 16, *Thou shalt not tempt the Lord thy God.* In the place whence it is quoted, it is in the plural number, *You shall not tempt*; here it is singular, *Thou shalt not.* We are *then* likely to get good by the word of God, when we hear and receive general promises as speaking to us in particular.

If Christ should *cast himself down*, it would be the tempting of God, [1] As it would be *requiring a further confirmation* of that which was so well confirmed. Christ was abundantly satisfied that God was already his Father, and took care of him. [2] As it would be *requiring a special preservation* of him, in doing that which he had no call to. If we expect that because God has promised not to forsake us, therefore he should follow us out of the way of our duty; that because he has promised to supply our wants, therefore he should humour us, and please our fancies; this is presumption, this is tempting God. This is to affront him whom we ought to honour. We must never promise ourselves any more than God has promised us.

3. He tempted him to the most *black and horrid idolatry*, with the proffer of the *kingdoms of the world, and the glory of them.* (1) The worst temptation was reserved for the last. Whatever temptation we have been assaulted by, still we must prepare for worse.

In this temptation, we may observe,

[1] What he *showed him—all the kingdoms of the world.* In order to this, he took him to an *exceeding high mountain.* The pinnacle of the temple is not high enough; the prince of the power of the air must have him further up into his territories. Hither the blessed Jesus was carried for the advantage of a prospect; as if the devil could show him more of the world than he knew already, who made and governed it. His taking him up into a high mountain, was but to *humour the thing*, and to colour the delusion; in which yet the blessed Jesus did not suffer himself to be imposed upon, but saw through the cheat. Hence, observe, concerning *Satan's temptations*, that, *First*, They often *come in at the eye.* The first sin began in the eye, Gen. iii. 6. We have therefore need to make a covenant with our eyes, and to pray that God would *turn them away from beholding vanity. Secondly*, That temptations commonly take rise from the world, and the things of it. *Thirdly*, That it is a *great cheat* which the devil puts upon poor souls, in his temptations. He deceives, and so destroys; he imposes upon men with shadows and false colours; shows the world and the glory of it, and hides from men's eyes the sin and sorrow and death which stain the pride of all this glory. *Fourthly*, That the *glory of the world* is the most *charming* temptation to the *unthinking* and *unwary*, and that by which men are most imposed upon. The *pride of life* is the most dangerous snare.

[2] What he *said to him* (*v.* 9); *All these things will I give thee, if thou wilt fall down and worship me.* See,

First, How *vain the promise* was. *All these things will I give thee.* He seems to take it for granted, that in the former temptations he had in part gained his point. "Come," says he, "it seems that the God whose Son thou thinkest thyself to be deserts thee, and starves thee—a sign that he is not thy Father; but if thou wilt be ruled by me, I will provide better for thee than so: own me for thy father, and ask my blessing, and *all this will I give thee.*" Satan makes an easy prey of men, when he can persuade them to think themselves abandoned of God. The fallacy of this promise lies in that, *All this will I give thee.* The devil's baits are all a sham; they are shows and shadows with which he deceives. The *nations of the earth* had been, long before, promised to the Messiah; if he be *the Son of God*, they belong to him. We must take heed of receiving even that which God hath promised, out of the devil's hand.

Secondly, How *vile* the *condition* was; *If thou wilt fall down*, and *worship me.* The devil is fond of being worshipped. What temptation could be more hideous, more black? The best of saints may be tempted to the worst of sins. This is their affliction, but while there is no consent to it, nor approbation of it, it is not their sin; Christ was tempted to worship Satan.

(2) See how Christ warded off the thrust. He rejected the proposal,

G. CAMPBELL MORGAN:

Then once again, in the third temptation, Jesus is seen as existing for a purpose. He was born to serve. He was equipped in His being for service. He knew that service could only be rendered as He worshiped God. "Thou shalt worship the Lord thy God, and him only shalt thou serve."

Here, then, is revealed the Man whom God ordained to be King—God's archetypal Man, the perfect Man—and as we look at Him, we see that the supreme end of life is vocation; that the essence of life is spiritual; that the present expression of the spiritual fact and vocation is physical. Temptation commences in the external, which is physical; passes to the internal, which is spiritual; attacks finally the vocational, which is the supreme thing in the life of every man. This is the picture of human life according to the purpose of God.

The government of such beings is placed by God in the authority of One of them; but the King must be unimpaired in realization of the Divine Ideal. A man who has failed at any point cannot govern men. He cannot govern those who have not failed, and he certainly cannot redeem those who have failed. A man who has prostituted his physical nature to base uses; a man who has silenced and stifled and dwarfed his spiritual nature; a man who has failed to realize his vocation cannot be king. An imperfect being cannot demand our loyalty; we cannot be loyal to inferiority; we cannot bow the knee and worship in the presence of anything other than perfection.

—The Gospel According to Matthew

JAMIESON, FAUSSET, BROWN

8. Again, the devil taketh him up ["conducteth him," as before] **into** [or unto] **an exceeding high mountain, and showeth him all the kingdoms of the world, and the glory of them**—Luke (4:5) adds the important clause, "in a moment of time"; a clause which seems to furnish a key to the true meaning. That a scene was presented to our Lord's natural eye seems plainly expressed. But to limit this to the most extensive scene which the natural eye could take in, is to give a sense to the expression, "all the kingdoms of the world," quite violent. It remains, then, to gather from the expression, "in a moment of time"— which manifestly is intended to intimate some supernatural operation—that it was permitted to the tempter to extend preternaturally for a moment our Lord's range of vision, and throw a "glory" or glitter over the scene of vision: a thing not inconsistent with the analogy of other scriptural statements regarding the permitted operations of the wicked one. In this case, the "exceeding height" of the "mountain" from which this sight was beheld would favor the effect to be produced.

9. And saith unto him, All these things will I give thee—"and the glory of them," adds Luke. But Matthew having already said that this was "showed Him," did not need to repeat it here. Luke (4:6) adds these other very important clauses, here omitted—"for that is," or "has been," "delivered unto me, and to whomsoever I will I give it." Was this wholly false? That were not like Satan's unusual policy, which is to insinuate his lies under cover of some truth. What truth, then, is there here? We answer, Is not Satan thrice called by our Lord Himself, "the prince of this world" (John 12:31; 14:30; 16:11)? Does not the apostle call him "the god of this world" (II Corinthians 4:4)? And still further, is it not said that Christ came to destroy by His death "him that *hath the power of death,* that is, the devil" (Heb. 2:14)? No doubt these passages only express men's voluntary subjection to the rule of the wicked one while they live, and his power to surround death to them, when it comes, with all the terrors of the wages of sin. But as this is a real and terrible sway, so all Scripture represents men as righteously sold under it. In this sense he speaks what is not devoid of truth, when he says, "All this is delivered unto me." But how does he deliver this "to whomsoever he will?" As employing whomsoever he pleases of his willing subjects in keeping men under his power. In this case his offer to our Lord was that of a *deputed* supremacy commensurate with his own, though as *his gift* and for *his ends.* **if thou wilt fall down and worship me**—This was the sole but monstrous condition. No Scripture, it will be observed, is quoted now, because none could be found to support so blasphemous a claim. In fact, he has ceased now to present his temptations under

ADAM CLARKE

8. *An exceeding high mountain, and sheweth him.* If the words *all the kingdoms of the world* be taken in a literal sense, then this must have been a visionary representation, as the highest mountain on the face of the globe could not suffice to make evident even one hemisphere of the earth, and the other must of necessity be in darkness. But if we take *the world* to mean only the land of Judea and some of the surrounding nations, as it appears sometimes to signify, then the mountain described by the Abbe Mariti (*Travels Through Cyprus*, etc.) could have afforded the prospect in question. Speaking of it, he says, "Here we enjoyed the most beautiful prospect imaginable. This part of the mountain overlooks the mountains of Arabia, the country of Gilead, the country of the Amorites, the plains of Moab, the plains of Jericho, the river Jordan, and the whole extent of the Dead Sea. It was here that the devil said to the Son of God, 'All these kingdoms will I give thee, if thou wilt fall down and worship me.'"

9. *If thou wilt fall down and worship me.* As if he had said, "The whole of this land is now under my government; do me homage for it, and I will deliver it into Thy hand."

MATTHEW HENRY

[1] With *abhorrence* and *detestation*; Get thee hence, *Satan*. It appears abominable at the first sight, and therefore is immediately rejected. While Satan tempted Christ to do himself a mischief, by casting himself down, though he yielded not, yet he heard it; but now that the temptation flies in the face of God, he cannot bear it; *Get thee hence, Satan*. It is good to be *peremptory* in resisting temptation, and to *stop our ears* to Satan's charms.

[2] With an argument fetched from scripture. The argument is very suitable, and exactly to the purpose, taken from Deut. vi. 13, and x. 20. *Thou shalt worship the Lord thy God, and him only shalt thou serve*. Our Saviour has recourse to the fundamental law in this case, which is indispensable, and universally obligatory. Religious worship is due to God only. Christ quotes this law concerning religious worship, and quotes it with application to himself; *First*, To show that in his estate of humiliation as man, he did worship God, both publicly and privately. Thus it became him to fulfil all righteousness. *Secondly*, To show that the law of religious worship is of eternal obligation.

V. We have here the end and issue of this combat, *v*. 11.

1. The devil was baffled, and quitted the field; *Then the devil leaveth him*, forced to do so by the power that went along with that word of command, *Get thee hence, Satan*. He made a shameful and inglorious retreat, and came off with disgrace. He despairs of moving him, and begins to conclude that he is the *Son of God*, and that it is in vain to tempt him any further. If we resist the devil, he will flee from us; he will yield, if we keep our ground. When the devil left our Saviour, he owned himself fairly beaten. The devil, though he is an enemy to all the saints, is a conquered enemy. The Captain of our salvation has defeated and disarmed him; we have nothing to do but to *pursue the victory*.

2. The holy angels came and attended upon our victorious Redeemer; *Behold, angels came and ministered unto him*. One angel might have served to bring him food, but here are many attending him, to testify their respect to him, and their readiness to receive his commands. Behold this! It is worth taking notice of; (1) That as there is a world of wicked, malicious spirits that fight against Christ and his church, and all particular believers, so there is a world of holy, blessed spirits engaged and employed for them. (2) That Christ's victories are the angels' triumphs. (3) That the angels ministered to the Lord Jesus, not only food, but whatever else he wanted after this great fatigue. Though God may suffer his people to be brought into wants and straits, yet he will take effectual care for their supply, and will rather send angels to feed them, than see them perish.

Christ was thus succoured after the temptation, [1] For his encouragement to go on in his undertaking. [2] For our encouragement to trust in him. We may expect, not only that he will sympathize with his tempted people, but that he will come in with seasonable relief to them.

Verses 12–17

We have here an account of Christ's preaching in the synagogues of Galilee.

Several passages in the other gospels, especially in that of St. John, are supposed, in the order of the story of Christ's life, to intervene between his temptation and his preaching in Galilee. But Matthew, having had his residence in Galilee, begins his story of Christ's public ministry with his preaching there.

JAMIESON, FAUSSET, BROWN

the mask of piety, and he stands out unblushingly as the rival of God Himself in his claims on the homage of men. Despairing of success as an angel of light, he throws off all disguise, and with a splended bribe solicits divine honor. This again shows that we are now at the last of the temptations, and that Matthew's order is the true one. **10. Then saith Jesus unto him, Get thee hence, Satan**—Since the tempter has now thrown off the mask, and stands forth in his true character, our Lord no longer deals with him as a pretended friend and pious counsellor, but calls him by his right name—His knowledge of which from the outset He had carefully concealed till now—and orders him off. This is the final and conclusive evidence, as we think, that Matthew's must be the right order of the temptations. For who can well conceive of the tempter's returning to the assault after this, in the pious character again, and hoping still to dislodge the consciousness of His Sonship, while our Lord must in that case be supposed to quote Scripture to one He had called the devil to his face—thus throwing His pearls before worse than swine? **for it is written**—(Deut. 6:13). Thus does our Lord part with Satan on the rock of Scripture. **Thou shalt worship**—In the *Hebrew* and LXX it is, "Thou shalt *fear*"; but as the sense is the same, so "worship" is here used to show emphatically that what the tempter claimed was precisely what God had forbidden. **the Lord thy God, and him only shalt thou serve**—The word "serve" in the second clause, is one never used by the LXX of any but *religious* service; and in this sense exclusively is it used in the New Testament, as we find it here. Once more the word "only," in the second clause—not expressed in the *Hebrew* and LXX—is here added to bring out emphatically the *negative* and *prohibitory* feature of the command. (See Gal. 3:10 for a similar supplement of the word "all" in a quotation from Deut. 27:26). **11. Then the devil leaveth him**—Luke says, "And when the devil had exhausted"—or "quite ended," as in Luke 4:2—"every [mode of] temptation, he departed from him till a season." The definite "season" here indicated is expressly referred to by our Lord in John 14:36 and Luke 22:52, 53. **and, behold, angels came and ministered unto him**—or supplied Him with food, as the same expression means in Mark 1:31 and Luke 8:3. Thus did angels to Elijah (I Kings 19:5-8). Excellent critics think that they ministered, not food only, but supernatural support and cheer also. But this would be the natural *effect* rather than the direct *object* of the visit, which was plainly what we have expressed. And after having refused to claim the *illegitimate* ministration of angels in His behalf, oh, with what deep joy would He accept their services when sent, unasked, at the close of all this temptation, direct from Him whom He had so gloriously honored! What "angels' food" would this repast be to Him! and as He partook of it, might not a Voice from heaven be heard again, by any who could read the Father's mind, "Said I not well, This is my beloved Son, in whom I am well pleased?"

12-25. Christ Begins His Galilean Ministry—Calling of Peter and Andrew, James and John—His First Galilean Circuit. (= Mark, 1:14-20, 35-39; Luke 4:14, 15). *There is here a notable gap in the history*, which but for the fourth Gospel we should never have discovered. From the former Gospels we should have been apt to draw three inferences, which from the fourth one we know to be erroneous: First, that our Lord awaited the close of John's ministry, by his arrest and imprisonment, before beginning His own; next, that there was but a brief interval between the baptism of our Lord and the imprisonment of John; and further, that our Lord not only opened His work in Galilee, but never ministered out of it, and never visited Jerusalem at all nor kept a passover till He went thither to become "our Passover, sacrificed for us." The fourth Gospel alone gives the true succession of events; not only recording those important openings of our Lord's public work which preceded the Baptist's imprisonment—extending to the end of the third chapter—but so specifying the passover which occurred during our Lord's ministry as to enable us to line off, with a large measure of certainty, the events of the first three Gospels according to the successive passover which they embraced. Eusebius, the ecclesiastical historian, who, early in the fourth century, gave much attention to this subject, in noticing these features of the Evangelical Records, says (3:24) that John wrote his Gospel at the entreaty of those who knew the important materials he possessed, and filled up what is wanting in the first three Gospels. Why it was reserved for the fourth Gospel, published at so late a period, to

ADAM CLARKE

10. *Get thee hence*. This temptation savoring of nothing but diabolical impudence, Jesus did not treat it as the others, but with divine authority commanded the tempter to return to his own place. In the course of this trial it appears that our blessed Lord was tempted: (1) to distrust—"command that these stones be made bread"; (2) to presumption, "Cast thyself down"; (3) to worldly ambition, "All these things will I give thee"; and (4) to idolatry, "Fall down and worship me," or do me homage. There is probably not a temptation of Satan but is reducible to one or other of these four articles. From the whole we may learn that: (1) No man, howsoever holy, is exempted from temptation; for God manifested in the flesh was tempted by the devil. (2) The best way to foil the adversary is by "the sword of the Spirit, which is the word of God," Eph. vi. 17. (3) To be tempted even to the greatest abominations (while a person resists) is not sin, for Christ was tempted to worship the devil. (4) There is no temptation which is from its own nature, or favoring circumstances, irresistible. God has promised to bruise even Satan under our feet. As I wish to speak what I think most necessary on every subject when I first meet it, and once for all, I would observe: (1) That the fear of being tempted may become a most dangerous snare; (2) That when God permits a temptation or trial to come, He will give grace to bear or overcome it; (3) That our spiritual interests shall be always advanced in proportion to our trials and faithful resistance; (4) That a more than ordinary measure of divine consolation shall be the consequence of every victory.

11. *Behold, angels came and ministered unto him*. That is, brought that food which was necessary to support nature.

CHARLES H. SPURGEON:

11. "Then the devil leaveth him, and, behold, angels came and ministered unto him."

After the devil the angels. Only let us be steadfast, and, like our Lord, we shall receive celestial consolations. O thou who wast tempted for us, help us in temptation. Amen.

Jesus, more than conqueror
O'er the thrice-embattled foe,
Fill'd with thine own Spirit's power,
Thou wilt power on us bestow.

By thy conquering Spirit led,
We shall put the fiend to flight;
Bruise again the serpent's head,
Triumph in Messiah's might.

—*Spurgeon's Devotional Bible*

MATTHEW HENRY

I. The time; *When Jesus had heard that John was cast into prison,* then he *went into Galilee, v.* 12. The cry of the saints' sufferings comes up into the ears of the Lord Jesus. If John be cast into prison, Jesus hears it, takes cognizance of it, and steers his course accordingly. 1. Christ did *not* go into the country, *till he heard of* John's imprisonment; for he must have time given him to *prepare the way of the Lord,* before the Lord himself appear. John must be Christ's harbinger, but not his rival. The moon and stars are lost when the sun rises. 2. He *did* go into the country as soon as he heard of John's imprisonment; not only to provide for his own safety, but to supply the want of John Baptist, and to build upon the good foundation he had laid. God will not leave himself without witness, nor his church without guides.

II. The place where he preached; in Galilee, a remote part of the country, that lay furthest from Jerusalem, and was there looked upon with contempt, as rude and boorish. The inhabitants of that country were reckoned stout men, fit for soldiers, but not polite men, or fit for scholars. Observe,

1. The particular city he chose for his residence; not Nazareth, where he had been bred up; no, he left Nazareth; particular notice is taken of that, *v.* 13. And with good reason did he leave Nazareth; for the men of that city *thrust him out* from among them, Luke iv. 29. Christ will not stay long where he is not welcome. Unhappy Nazareth!

But he *came and dwelt in Capernaum,* which was a city of Galilee, but many miles distant from Nazareth, a great city and of much resort. It is said here to be *on the sea coast,* not the *great sea,* but the sea of Tiberias. Hither Christ came, and here he dwelt. However, here he fixed not constantly, for he went about doing good; but this was for some time his headquarters: what little rest he had, was here. And at Capernaum, it should seem, he was welcome. If some reject Christ, yet others will receive him, and bid him welcome. Capernaum is glad of Nazareth's leavings.

2. The prophecy that was fulfilled in this, *v.* 14–16. It is quoted from Isa. ix. 1, 2, but with some variation. The evangelist here takes only the latter clause, which speaks of the return of the light of liberty and prosperity to those countries that had been in the darkness of captivity, and applies it to the appearing of the gospel among them.

The places are spoken of, *v.* 15. Christ came to Capernaum, the gospel came to all those places round about; such diffusive influences did the Sun of righteousness cast.

JAMIESON, FAUSSET, BROWN

supply such important particulars in the life of Christ, it is not easy to conjecture with any probability. It may be, that though not unacquainted with the general facts, they were not furnished with reliable details. But one thing may be affirmed with tolerable certainty, that as our Lord's teaching at Jerusalem was of a depth and grandeur scarcely so well adapted to the prevailing character of the first three Gospels, but altogether congenial to the fourth; and as the bare mention of the successive passovers, without any account of the transactions and discourses they gave rise to, would have served little purpose in the first three Gospels, there may have been no way of preserving the unity and consistency of each Gospel, so as to furnish by means of them all the precious information we get from them, save by the plan on which they are actually constructed.

Entry into Galilee (vss. 12-17). **12. Now when Jesus had heard that John was cast into prison**—more simply, "was delivered up", as recorded in ch. 14:3-5; Mark 6:17-20; Luke 3:19, 20. **he departed**—rather, "withdrew." **into Galilee**—as recorded, in its proper place, in John 4:1-3. **13. And leaving Narazeth**—The prevalent opinion is that this refers to a *first* visit to Nazareth after His baptism, whose details are given by Luke (4:16, etc.); a *second* visit being that detailed by our Evangelist (ch. 13:54-58), and by Mark (ch. 6:1-6). But to us there seem all but insuperable difficulties in the supposition of two visits to Nazareth after His baptism; and on the grounds stated in Luke 4:16, etc., we think that the *one only visit* to Nazareth is that recorded by Matthew (13), Mark (6), and Luke (4). But how, in that case, are we to take the word "*leaving* Nazareth" here? We answer, just as the same word is used in Acts 21:3, "Now when we had sighted Cyprus, and *left* it on the left, we sailed into Syria,"—i.e., without entering Cyprus at all, but merely "sighting" it, as the nautical phrase is, they steered southeast of it, leaving it on the northwest. So here, what we understand the Evangelist to say is, that Jesus, on His return to Galilee, did not, as might have been expected, make Nazareth the place of His stated residence, but, "leaving [or passing by] Nazareth," **he came and dwelt in Capernaum, which is upon the seacoast**—maritime Capernaum, on the northwest shore of the Sea of Galilee; but the precise spot is unknown. (See on ch. 11:23). Our Lord seems to have chosen it for several reasons. Four or five of the Twelve lived there; it had a considerable and mixed population, securing some freedom from that intense bigotry which even to this day characterizes all places where Jews in large numbers dwell nearly alone; it was centrical, so that not only on the approach of the annual festivals did large numbers pass through it or near it, but on any occasion multitudes could easily be collected about it; and for crossing and recrossing the lake, which our Lord had so often occasion to do, no place could be more convenient. But one other high reason for the choice of Capernaum remains to be mentioned, the only one specified by our Evangelist. **in the borders of Zabulon and Nephthalim**—the one lying to the west of the Sea of Galilee, the other to the north of it; but the precise boundaries cannot now be traced out. **14. That it might be fulfilled which was spoken by Esaias the prophet**—(ch. 9:1, 2 or, as in *Hebrew,* ch. 8:23, and 9:1). **saying, 15. The land of Zabulon, and the land of Nephthalim,** [by] **the way of the sea**—the coast skirting the Sea of Galilee westward—beyond Jordan—a phrase commonly meaning eastward of Jordan; but here and in several places it means westward of the Jordan. The word seems to have got the general meaning of "the other side"; the nature of the case determining which side that was. **Galilee of the Gentiles**—so called from its position, which made it the frontier between the Holy Land and the external world. While Ephraim and Judah, as STANLEY says, were separated from the world by the Jordan valley on one side and the hostile Philistines on another, the northern tribes were in the direct highway of all the invaders from the north, in unbroken communication with the promiscuous races who have always occupied the heights of Lebanon, and in close and peaceful alliance with the most commercial nation of the ancient world, the Phœnicians. Twenty of the cities of Galilee were actually annexed by Solomon to the adjacent kingdom of Tyre, and formed, with their territory, the "boundary" or "offscouring" (*Gebul* or *Cabul*) of the two dominions—at a later time still known by the general name of "the boundaries (coasts or borders) of Tyre and Sidon." In the first great transportation of the Jewish population, Naphtali and Galilee suffered the same fate as the transjor-

ADAM CLARKE

13. *And leaving Nazareth.* Or entirely leaving Nazareth. It seems that, from this time, our blessed Lord made Capernaum His ordinary place of residence and utterly forsook Nazareth, because they had wholly rejected His word, and even attempted to take away His life (see Luke iv. 29). Galilee was bounded by Mount Lebanon on the north, by the river Jordan and the Sea of Galilee on the east, by Chison on the south, and by the Mediterranean on the west. *Nazareth,* a little city in the tribe of Zebulun, in lower Galilee, with Tabor on the east and Ptolemais on the west. It is supposed that this city was the usual residence of our Lord for the first thirty years of His life.

Capernaum, a city famous in the New Testament but never mentioned in the Old. Probably it was one of those cities which the Jews built after their return from Babylon. Capernaum is well known to have been the principal scene of our Lord's miracles during the three years of His public ministry.

Zabulon, the country of this tribe, in which Nazareth and Capernaum were situated, bordered on the Lake of Gennesaret, stretching to the frontiers of Sidon, Gen. xlix. 13. *Nepthalim* was contiguous to it, and both were on the east side of Jordan, Josh. 19:34.

15. *Galilee of the Gentiles.* Or of the nations. So called because it was inhabited by Egyptians, Arabians, and Phoenicians, according to the testimony of Strabo and others. The Hebrew *goyim* and the Greek *ethnon* signify "nations," and in the Old and New Testaments mean those people who were not descendants of any of the twelve tribes. The word *Gentiles,* from *gens,* "a nation," signifies the same. It was a regular tradition among the ancient Jews that the Messiah should begin His ministry in Galilee.

MATTHEW HENRY

(1) They were *in darkness.* Those that are without Christ, are in the dark, nay, they are darkness itself. They were *sitting* in this condition. Sitting is a continuing posture; where we sit, we mean to stay. And it is a contented posture; they were in the dark, and they loved darkness. He that is in the dark because it is night, may be sure that the sun will shortly arise; but he that is in the dark because he is blind, will not so soon have his eyes opened. We have the light, but what will that avail us, if we be not light in the Lord? (2) When the gospel comes, light comes; when it comes to any place, when it comes to any soul, it makes day there. Light is discovering, it is directing; so is the gospel.

It is a *great* light. *Great* in comparison with the light of the law, the shadows of which were now done away. It is a *great light*, for it discovers great things and of vast consequence; it will last long, and spread far. And it is a *growing light*, intimated in that word, It is *sprung up.* It was but *spring of day* with them; now the day dawned, which afterward *shone more and more.* The gospel-kingdom, like a grain of mustard-seed or the morning light, was small in its beginnings, gradual in its growth, but great in its perfection.

Observe, The light *sprang up to them*; they did not go to seek it. It came upon them ere they were aware.

III. The text he preached upon (*v.* 17): *From that time* he began to preach.

The subject which Christ dwelt upon now in his preaching (and it was indeed the sum and substance of all his preaching), was the very same that John had preached upon (*ch.* iii. 2); *Repent, for the kingdom of heaven is at hand;* for the gospel is the same for substance under various dispensations; for it is the *everlasting gospel. Fear God, and,* by repentance, *give honour to him,* Rev. xiv. 6, 7. Christ put a great respect upon John's ministry, when he preached to the same purport that John had preached before him. Thus did God confirm the word of his messenger, Isa. xliv. 26. He pitches upon this old, plain text, *Repent, for the kingdom of heaven is at hand.* 1. This he preached *first* upon; he began with this. We need not go up to heaven, nor down to the deep, for matter or language in our preaching. As John prepared Christ's way, so Christ prepared his own, and made way for the further discoveries he designed, with the doctrine of repentance. 2. This he preached *often* upon; wherever he went, this was his subject, and neither he nor his followers ever reckoned it worn threadbare. That which has been preached and heard before, may yet very profitably be preached and heard again; but then it should be preached and heard better. 3. This he preached as gospel. Not only the austere Baptist, who was looked upon as a melancholy, morose man, but the sweet and gracious Jesus, whose lips dropped as a honey-comb, preached repentance. 4. The reason is still the same; The *kingdom of heaven is at hand.* Now that it was so much nearer, the argument was so much the stronger; now is the *salvation nearer,* Rom. xiii. 11.

Verses 18–22

When Christ began to preach, he began to *gather disciples,* who should now be the *hearers,* and hereafter the *preachers.* Now, in these verses, we have an account of the first disciples that he called into fellowship with himself.

And this was an instance, 1. Of *effectual calling* to Christ. In all his preaching he gave a common call to all the country, but in this he gave a special and particular call to those that were given him by the Father. All the country was *called,* but these were *called out.* 2. It was an instance of *ordination,* and appointment to the work of the ministry. When Christ, as a Teacher, set up his great school, one of his first works was to appoint ushers, or under masters, to be employed in the work of instruction.

Now we may observe here,

I. *Where* they were called—by the *sea of Galilee,* where Jesus was walking. Hither he went to call disciples; not to Herod's court (for few mighty or noble are called), not to Jerusalem, among the chief priests and the elders, but to the sea of Galilee; surely Christ sees not as man sees. Galilee was a remote part of the nation, the inhabitants were less cultivated and refined, their very language was broad and uncouth to the curious, their *speech betrayed them.* Yet thither Christ went, to call his apostles that were to be the prime ministers of state in his kingdom, for he *chooses the foolish things of the world, to confound the wise.*

II. *Who* they were. We have an account of the call of two pairs of brothers in these verses—Peter and Andrew, James and John. They had been

JAMIESON, FAUSSET, BROWN

danic tribes before Ephraim or Judah had been molested (II Kings 15:29). In the time of the Christian era this original disadvantage of their position was still felt; the speech of the Galileans "bewrayed them" by its uncouth pronunciation (Matt. 26:73); and their distance from the seats of government and civilization at Jerusalem and Cæsarea gave them their character for turbulence or independence, according as it was viewed by their friends or their enemies. **16. The people which sat in darkness saw great light; and to them which sat in the region and shadow of death light is sprung up.** The prophetic strain to which these words belong commences with Isaiah 7, to which ch. 6 is introductory, and goes down to the end of ch. 12, which hymns the spirit of that whole strain of prophecy. It belongs to the reign of Ahaz and turns upon the combined efforts of the two neighboring kingdoms of Syria and Israel to crush Judah. In these critical circumstances Judah and her king were, by their ungodliness, provoking the Lord to sell them into the hands of their enemies. What, then, is the burden of this prophetic strain, on to the passage here quoted? First, Judah shall not, cannot perish, because IMMANUEL, the Virgin's Son, is to come forth from his loins. Next, one of the invaders shall soon perish, and the kingdoms of neither be enlarged. Further, while the Lord will be the Sanctuary of such as confide in these promises and await their fulfilment, He will drive to confusion, darkness, and despair the vast multitude of the nation who despised His oracles, and, in their anxiety and distress, betook themselves to the lying oracles of the heathen. This carries us down to the end of the eighth chapter. At the opening of the ninth chapter a sudden light is seen breaking in upon one particular part of the country, the part which was to suffer most in these wars and devastations—"the land of Zebulun, and the land of Naphtali, the way of the sea, beyond Jordan, Galilee and the Gentiles." The rest of the prophecy stretches over both the Assyrian and the Chaldean captivities and terminates in the glorious Messianic prophecy of ch. 11 and the choral hymn of ch. 12. Well, this is the point seized on by our Evangelist. By Messiah's taking up His abode in those very regions of Galilee, and shedding His glorious light upon them, this prediction, He says, of the Evangelical prophet was now fulfilled; and if it was not thus fulfilled, we may confidently affirm it was not fulfilled in any age of the Jewish ceremony, and has received no fulfilment at all. Even the most rationalistic critics have difficulty in explaining it in any other way. **17. From that time Jesus began to preach, and to say, Repent; for the kingdom of heaven is at hand**—Thus did our Lord not only take up the strain, but give forth the identical summons of His honored forerunner. Our Lord sometimes speaks of the new kingdom as already come—in His own Person and ministry; but the *economy* of it was only "at hand" until the blood of the cross was shed, and the Spirit on the day of Pentecost opened the fountain for sin and for uncleanness to the world at large.

Calling of Peter and Andrew, James and John (vss. 18-22). **18. And Jesus, walking**—The word "Jesus" here appears not to belong to the text, but to have been introduced from those portions of it which were transcribed to be used as church lessons; where it was naturally introduced as a connecting word at the commencement of a lesson. **by the Sea of Galilee, saw two brethren, Simon called Peter**—for the reason mentioned in ch. 16:18. **and Andrew his brother, casting a net into the sea; for they were fishers.**

ADAM CLARKE

16. *The people which sat in darkness.* This is quoted from Isa. ix. 2, where, instead of sitting, the prophet used the word "walked." The Evangelist might change the term on purpose, to point out the increased misery of the state of these persons. Sitting in darkness expresses a greater degree of intellectual blindness than walking in darkness does. In the time of Christ's appearing the people were in a much worse state than in the time of the prophet, nearly seven hundred years before. *The region and shadow of death.* These words are amazingly descriptive. A region of death—death's country, where, in a peculiar manner, Death lived, reigned, and triumphed, subjecting all the people to his sway. *Shadow of death.* Used only here and in Luke 1:79, but often in the old covenant. As in the former clause death is personified, so here. Death is here represented as standing between the land above mentioned and the light of light, or Sun of righteousness; in consequence of which all the inhabitants were involved in a continual cloud of intellectual darkness, misery, and sin. The heavenly Sun was continually eclipsed to them till this glorious time when Jesus Christ, the true Light, shone forth in the beauty of holiness and truth. Christ began His ministry in Galilee, and frequented this uncultivated place more than He did Jerusalem and other parts of Judea; here His preaching was peculiarly needful, and by this was the prophecy fulfilled.

17. *Jesus began to preach, and to say, Repent.* Every preacher commissioned by God to proclaim salvation to a lost world begins his work with preaching the doctrine of repentance. This was the case with all the prophets, John the Baptist, Jesus Christ, all the apostles, and all their genuine successors in the Christian ministry.

18. *Simon called Peter, and Andrew his brother.* Why did not Jesus Christ call some of the eminent scribes or Pharisees to publish His gospel, and not poor, unlearned fishermen, without credit or authority? Because it was the kingdom of Heaven they were to preach, and their teaching must come from above. Besides, the conversion of sinners, though it be effected instrumentally by the preaching of the gospel, yet the Grand Agent in it is the Spirit of God.

MATTHEW HENRY

disciples of John, and so were the better disposed to follow Christ. Those who have submitted to the discipline of repentance, shall be welcome to the joys of faith. We may observe concerning them,

1. That they were *brothers*. It is the honour and comfort of a house, when those that are of the *same* family, are of *God's* family.

2. That they were *fishers*. Being fishers, (1) They were *poor men*: if they had had estates, or any considerable stock in trade, they would not have made fishing their trade, however they might have made it their recreation. Christ does not despise the poor, and therefore we must not. (2) They were *unlearned men*. Yet this will not justify the bold intrusion of ignorant and unqualified men into the work of the ministry. (3) They were *men of business*, who had been bred up to labour. Diligence in an honest calling is pleasing to Christ, and no hindrance to a holy life. Idle people lie more open to the temptations of Satan than to the calls of God. (4) They were men that were accustomed to *hardships* and hazards; the fisher's trade, more than any other, is laborious and perilous; fishermen must be often wet and cold; they must watch, and wait, and toil, and be often in *peril by waters*. Those who have learned to bear hardships, and to run hazards, are best prepared for the fellowship and discipleship of Jesus Christ. Good soldiers of Christ must endure hardness.

III. *What they were doing*. Peter and Andrew were then using their nets, they were fishing; and James and John were *mending their nets*, which was an instance of their industry and good husbandry. They did not go to their father for money to buy new nets, but took pains to mend their old ones. It is commendable to make what we have go as far, and last as long, as may be. James and John were *with their father Zebedee*, ready to assist him. It is a happy and hopeful presage, to see children careful of their parents, and dutiful to them. Observe, 1. They were *all* employed, all very busy, and none idle. When Christ comes, it is good to be found doing. 2. They were *differently* employed; two of them were fishing, and two of them *mending their nets*. Ministers should be always employed, either in teaching or studying; and *mending their nets*, is in its season, as necessary work as fishing.

IV. *What the call was* (*v.* 19); *Follow me, and I will make you fishers of men*. Even they who have been called to follow Christ, have need to be called to follow on, and to follow nearer. Observe,

1. What Christ intended them for; *I will make you fishers of men*. Let them not be proud of the new honour designed them, they are still but fishers; let them not be afraid of the new work cut out for them, for they have been used to fishing, and fishers they are still. (1) Ministers are *fishers of men*, not to destroy them, but to save them, by bringing them into another element. (2) It is Jesus Christ that makes them so; *I will make you fishers of men*. It is he that qualifies men for this work, calls them to it, authorizes them in it, and gives them success in it.

2. What they must do in order to this; *Follow me*. They must separate themselves to a diligent attendance on him. (1) Those whom Christ employs in any service for him, must first be fitted and qualified for it. (2) Those who would *preach Christ*, must first *learn* Christ, and learn of him. (3) Those who would get an acquaintance with Christ, must be diligent and constant in their attendance on him. There is no learning comparable to that which is got by following Christ. (4) Those who are to fish for men, must therein follow Christ, and do it as he did, with diligence, faithfulness, and tenderness.

V. What was the *success* of this call. Peter and Andrew *straightway left their nets* (*v.* 20); and James and John *immediately left the ship and their father* (*v.* 22); *and they* all *followed him*. Those who would follow Christ aright, must *leave all* to follow him.

1. This instance of the power of the Lord Jesus gives us good encouragement to depend upon the sufficiency of his grace. How strong and effectual is his word! *He speaks, and it is done.*

2. This instance of the pliableness of the disciples, gives us a good example of obedience to the command of Christ. It is the good property of all Christ's faithful servants to come when they are called, and to follow their Master wherever he leads them. Being called, they obeyed, and, like Abraham, *went out not knowing whither they went*, but knowing very well whom they followed.

Verses 23–25

I. What an industrious preacher Christ was; He *went about all Galilee, teaching in their synagogues, and preaching the gospel of the kingdom*. Observe,

JAMIESON, FAUSSET, BROWN

ADAM CLARKE

G. CAMPBELL MORGAN:

When our Lord calls men away from their daily vocation into a new vocation, He calls them with infinite simplicity, and great sublimity, by suggesting to them that all they have been using for themselves they can now use for Him. "I will make you fishers of men."

The principle here is not that Jesus is going to make us all fishers of men. He is going to make us all workers, and turn any capacity we have into account. Jesus found me at my desk with boys about me, teaching them, and He passed me one day and said, "Come with Me, and I will make you a teacher of men." He took hold of that which I could do, and said, "Do it for Me." If He had said "fishers," He never would have won me. He took fishermen, and He said, "Fish." He will take soldiers if they will hear, and He will say to them, "Fight for Me." He will take the teacher and say to him, "Teach for Me." What He wants is men who will give Him the capacity they have, and let Him lift it into a higher realm, and He will use it, never mind what it is. He said to these men, "Come with Me and I will make you fishers of men; I will take the training you have, and use it on higher levels."

And how beautiful is the answer! It is the same in each case. "Straightway" for Andrew and Simon; and "straightway" for James and John. Straightway they dropped their nets and went out after Him. They left their nets and their father, and went out after Him to follow Him. At His command for service, they abandoned their daily calling. They did not do this until He ordered them to. The vast multitude of Christian people are not called to leave their fishing nets. They are called to abide in their calling with God; which is quite as honorable as leaving it. The honorable thing is to obey Christ, and the despicable thing is to disobey. What He wants is men who can keep hold of the things of the daily calling until He calls. Has He called you? If He has called you to the ministry, drop the things in your hands straightway; the Kingdom waits for violent hands. If He has not called you, keep hold of the fishing nets and you will find when the glory breaks upon your vision by and by that the fishing nets, and the fishing, were parts of God's work for winning the world. He called them and they went straightway.—*The Gospel According to Matthew*

19. And he saith unto them, Follow me—rather, as the same expression is rendered in Mark, "Come ye after Me." **and I will make you fishers of men**—raising them from a lower to a higher *fishing*, as David was from a lower to a higher *feeding* (Ps. 78:70-72). **20. And they straightway left their nets, and followed him. 21. And going on from thence, he saw other two brethren, James the son of Zebedee, and John his brother, in a ship**—rather, "in the ship," their fishing boat. **with Zebedee their father, mending their nets: and he called them. 22. And they immediately left the ship and their father**—Mark adds an important clause: "They left their father Zebedee in the ship with the *hired servants*"; showing that the family were in easy circumstances. **and followed him**—Two harmonistic questions here arise: *First*, Was this the same calling as that recorded in John 1:35-42? Clearly not. For, (1) That call was given while Jesus was yet in Judea: this, after His return to Galilee. (2) Here, Christ calls Andrew: there, Andrew solicits an interview with Christ. (3) Here, Andrew and Peter are called together: there, Andrew having been called, with an unnamed disciple, who was clearly the beloved disciple (see on John 1:40), goes and fetches Peter his brother to Christ, who then calls him. (4) Here, John is called along with James his brother: there, John is called along with Andrew, after having at their own request had an interview with Jesus; no mention being made of James, whose call, if it then took place, would not likely have been passed over by his own brother. Thus far nearly all are agreed. But on the *next* question opinion is divided: Was this the same calling as that recorded in Luke 5:1-11? Many able critics think so. But the following considerations are to us decisive against it. First here, the four are called separately, in pairs: in Luke, all together. Next, in Luke, after a glorious miracle: here, the one pair are casting their net, the other are mending theirs. Further, here, our Lord had made no public appearance in Galilee, and so had gathered none around Him; He is walking solitary by the shores of the lake when He accosts the two pairs of fishermen: in Luke, the multitude are pressing upon Him, and hearing the word of God, as He stands by the Lake of Gennesaret—a state of things implying a somewhat advanced stage of His early ministry, and some popular enthusiasm. Regarding these successive callings, see on Luke 5:1.

First Galilean Circuit (vss. 23-35). **23. And Jesus went about all Galilee, teaching in their synagogues**—These were houses of local worship. It cannot be proved that they existed before the Babylonish

19. *Follow me*. Come after Me. Receive My doctrines, imitate Me in My conduct—in every respect be My disciples. Following a person, in the Jewish phrase, signifies being his disciple or scholar.

20. *They straightway left their nets*. A change, as far as it respected secular things, every way to their disadvantage.

22. *Left the ship and their father*. By *the ship* we are to understand the fishing boat used for extending their nets in the water and bringing the hawser or rope of the farther end to shore, by which the net was pulled to land.

23. *Teaching in their synagogues*. Synagogue, from *syn*, "together," and *ago*, "I bring," a public assembly of persons, or the place where such persons publicly assembled. Synagogues, among

MATTHEW HENRY

1. *What* Christ preached—*the gospel of the kingdom. The kingdom of heaven*, that is, of grace and glory, is emphatically *the kingdom. The gospel* is the charter of that kingdom, containing the King's coronation oath, by which he has graciously obliged himself to pardon, protect, and save the subjects of that kingdom. 2. *Where* he preached—*in the synagogues*; not there only, but there chiefly, because those were *the places of concourse*, where *wisdom* was to *lift up her voice* (Prov. i. 21). 3. *What pains he took* in preaching; He *went about all Galilee, teaching*. He *waits to be gracious*, and comes *to seek and save*. He *went about doing good*. Never was there such an itinerant preacher, such an indefatigable one, as Christ was.

II. What a powerful physician Christ was; he *went about* not only *teaching*, but *healing*,

1. What diseases he cured—all without exception. He *healed all manner of sickness, and all manner of disease*. There are diseases which are called *the reproach of physicians. He healed them*, all, however inveterate.

Three general words are here used to intimate this; he healed every sickness, every *disease*, or languishing, and all *torments*. None was too bad, none too hard, for Christ to heal with a word's speaking.

Three particular diseases are specified; *the palsy*, which is the greatest weakness of the body; *lunacy*, which is the greatest malady of the mind, and *possession of the Devil*, which is the greatest misery and calamity of both, yet Christ healed all.

2. What patients he had. See here, what flocking there was to him from all parts; great multitudes of people came, not only *from Galilee* and the country about, but even *from Jerusalem* and *from Judæa*, which lay a great way off; for *his fame went throughout all Syria. This* is given as the reason why such multitudes came to him, because his fame had spread so widely. What we hear of Christ from others, should invite us to him. The voice of fame is "Come and see." Christ both *taught and healed*. It is well if anything will bring people to Christ; and they who come to him will find more in him than they expected.

Now concerning the cures which Christ wrought, let us, once for all, observe the *miracle*, the *mercy*, and the *mystery*, of them.

(1) The *miracle* of them. They were wrought in such a manner, as plainly spake them to be the immediate products of a divine and supernatural power, and they were God's seal to his commission. Nature could not do these things. All which proves him *a Teacher come from God*, for, otherwise, none could have done the works that he did, John iii. 2. His healing and his preaching generally went together, for the former confirmed the latter; thus here he *began to* do *and to* teach, Acts i. 1.

(2) The *mercy* of them. The miracles that Christ wrought, were most of them cures, and all of them (except the cursing of the barren fig-tree) blessings and favours; for the gospel dispensation is founded, and built up in love, and grace, and sweetness. Christ designed by his cures to win people, and so to draw them with the bands of love, Hos. xi. 4. The miracle of them proved his doctrine *a faithful saying*, and convinced men's judgments; the mercy of them proved it *worthy of all acceptation*, and wrought upon their affections. They were not only *great works*, but *good works*, that he *showed them from* his *Father* (John x. 32).

(3) The *mystery* of them. Christ, by curing *bodily diseases*, intended to show, that his great errand into the world was to cure *spiritual maladies*. Sin is the *sickness, disease*, and *torment* of the soul; Christ *came to take away sin*, and so to heal these. And the particular stories of the cures Christ wrought are therefore so to be explained and improved, to the honour and praise of that glorious Redeemer, *who forgiveth all our iniquities, and so healeth all our diseases*.

JAMIESON, FAUSSET, BROWN

captivity; but as they began to be erected soon after it, probably the idea was suggested by the religious inconveniences to which the captives had been subjected. In our Lord's time, the rule was to have one wherever ten learned men or professed students of the law resided; and they extended to Syria, Asia Minor, Greece, and most places of the dispersion. The larger towns had several, and in Jerusalem the number approached 500. In point of officers and mode of worship, the Christian congregations are modelled after the synagogue.

and preaching the gospel [proclaiming the glad tidings] **of the kingdom, and healing all manner of sickness** [every disease] **and all manner of disease** [every complaint]—The word means any incipient malady causing "softness"—**among the people.**

24. And his fame went throughout all Syria—reaching first to the part of it adjacent to Galilee, called Syro-phœnicia (Mark 7:26), and thence extending far and wide. **and they brought unto him all sick people**—all that were ailing or unwell [those] **that were taken**—for this is a distinct class, not an explanation of the "unwell" class, as our translators understood it. **with divers diseases and torments**—i.e., acute disorders. **and those which were possessed with devils**—that were demonized or possessed with demons. **and those which were lunatic**—moon-struck. **and those that had the palsy**—paralytics, a word not naturalized when our version was made. **and he healed them**—These healings were at once His credentials and illustrations of "the glad tidings" which He proclaimed. After reading this account of our Lord's first preaching tour, can we wonder at what follows?

25. And there followed him great multitudes of people from Galilee, and from Decapolis—a region lying to the east of the Jordan, so called as containing ten cities, founded and chiefly inhabited by Greek settlers. **and from Jerusalem, and from beyond Jordan**—meaning from Perea. Thus not only was all Palestine upheaved, but all the adjacent regions. But the more immediate object for which this is here mentioned is, to give the reader some idea both of the vast concourse and of the varied complexion of eager attendants upon the great Preacher, to whom the astonishing discourse of the next three chapters was addressed. On the importance which our Lord Himself attached to this first preaching circuit, and the preparation which He made for it, see on Mark 1:35-39.

ADAM CLARKE

the Jews, were probably not older than the return from the Babylonish captivity. They were erected not only in cities and towns, but in the country, and especially by rivers, that they might have water for the convenience of their frequent washings. Not less than ten persons of respectability composed a synagogue, as the rabbins supposed that this number of persons, of independent property and well-skilled in the law, were necessary to conduct the affairs of the place and keep up the divine worship. The chief things belonging to a synagogue were: (1) the ark or chest, made after the mode of the ark of the covenant, containing the Pentateuch; (2) the pulpit and desk, in the middle of the synagogue, on which he stood who read or expounded the law; (3) the seats or pews for the men below, and the galleries for the women above; (4) the lamps to give light in the evening service, and at the Feast of the Dedication; (5) apartments for the utensils and alms-chests. The synagogue was governed by a council or assembly, over whom was a president, called in the Gospels the ruler of the synagogue. These are sometimes called chiefs of the Jews, the rulers, the priests or elders, the governors, the overseers, the fathers of the synagogue. Service was performed in them three times a day—morning, afternoon, and night. *Preaching the gospel of the kingdom*. Or proclaiming the glad tidings of the Kingdom. Behold here the perfect pattern of an evangelical preacher: (1) He goes about seeking sinners on every side, that he may show them the way to heaven. (2) He proclaims the glad tidings of the Kingdom, with a freedom worthy of the King whom he serves. (3) He makes his reputation and the confidence of the people subservient not to his own interest, but to the salvation of souls. (4) To his preaching he joins, as far as he has ability, all works of mercy and temporal assistance to the bodies of men. (5) He takes care to inform men that diseases and all kinds of temporal evils are the effects of sin, and their hatred to iniquity should increase in proportion to the evils they endure through it. (6) And that nothing but the power of God can save them from sin and its consequences.

24. *Possessed with devils* (demoniacs). Persons possessed by evil spirits. This is certainly the plain, obvious meaning of *demoniac* in the Gospels. Our common version, which renders the word "those . . . possessed with devils," is not strictly correct, as the word devil is not found in the plural in any part of the Sacred Writings when speaking of evil spirits; for though there are multitudes of demons (Mark v. 9), yet it appears there is but one devil, who seems to be supreme, or head, over all the rest. *Diabolos* signifies an accuser or slanderer (1 Tim. iii. 11; 2 Tim. iii. 3; Titus ii. 3). Perhaps Satan was called so (1) because he accused or slandered God in paradise (Gen. iii. 5), and (2) because he is the accuser of men (Rev. vii. 9-10). See also Job i. 2. *He healed them*. Either with a word or a touch; and thus proved that all nature was under His control.

25. This verse is immediately connected with the fifth chapter, and should not be separated from it. *Great multitudes*. This, even according to the Jews, was one proof of the days of the Messiah. *Decapolis*. A small country situated between Syria and Galilee of the nations. It was called *Decapolis* (from *deka*, "ten," and *polis*, a "city") because it contained only ten cities, the metropolis and most ancient of which was Damascus. *From beyond Jordan*. Or from the side of Jordan. Probably this was the country which was occupied anciently by the two tribes of Reuben and Gad, and the half-tribe of Manasseh.

MATTHEW HENRY — CHAPTER 5

Verses 1–2

We have here a general account of this sermon.

I. *The Preacher* was our Lord Jesus, the Prince of preachers. The prophets and John had *done virtuously* in preaching, *but Christ excelled them all*. He is the eternal Word, by whom God *has in these last days spoken to us*. The many miraculous cures wrought by Christ in Galilee were intended to dispose people to receive instructions from one in whom there

JAMIESON, FAUSSET, BROWN — CHAPTER 5

Vss. 1-16. THE BEATITUDES, AND THEIR BEARING UPON THE WORLD. **1. And seeing the multitudes**—those mentioned in ch. 4:25—**he went up into a mountain**—one of the dozen mountains which ROBINSON says there are in the vicinity of the Sea of Galilee, any one of them answering about equally well to the occasion. So charming is the whole landscape that the descriptions of it, from JOSEPHUS downwards (*J. W.*, 4. 10, 8), are apt to be thought

ADAM CLARKE — CHAPTER 5

1. *And seeing the multitudes*. These *multitudes*, viz., those mentioned in the preceding verse, which should make the first verse of this chapter. *He went up into a mountain*. That He might have the greater advantage of speaking, so as to be heard by that great concourse of people which followed Him. Probably nothing more is meant here than a small hill or eminence. *And when he was set*. The usual posture

MATTHEW HENRY

appeared so much of a divine power and goodness; and, probably, this sermon was the summary, of what he had preached in the synagogues. His text was, *Repent, for the kingdom of heaven is at hand.*

II. *The place* was a mountain in Galilee. Our Lord Jesus was but ill accommodated; he had no convenient place to preach in, any more than *to lay his head* on. Our Lord Jesus, the great Teacher of truth, is driven out to the desert, and finds no better a pulpit than *a mountain* can afford; and not one of the *holy mountains of Zion*, but a common *mountain*; by which Christ would intimate that it is *the will of God that men should pray* and preach *everywhere*, anywhere, provided it be decent and convenient. Christ preached this sermon, which was an exposition of the law, upon a mountain, because upon *a mountain* the law was given. But observe the difference: when *the law was given*, the Lord *came down* upon the *mountain*; now the Lord *went up*; then, he spoke *in thunder and lightning*; now, *in a still small voice*: then the people were ordered to keep their distance; now they are invited to draw near: a blessed change!

III. *The auditors* were *his disciples*. They followed him for love and learning, while others attended him only for cures. *He taught them*, because they were willing to be *taught*; because they would *understand* what he taught, and because they were to teach others. Though this discourse was directed to the disciples, it was in the hearing of *the multitude*. No bounds were set about *this mountain*, to keep the people off, for, through Christ, we have access to God. Nay, he had an eye to *the multitude*, in preaching this sermon. It is an encouragement to a faithful minister to cast the net of the gospel where there are a great many fishes, in hope that some will be caught. The sight of a *multitude* puts life into a preacher, which yet must arise from a desire of their profit, not his own praise.

IV. *The solemnity* of his sermon is intimated in that word, *when he was set*. This was a set sermon, when he had placed himself so as to be best heard. That phrase, *He opened his mouth*, is only a Hebrew periphrasis of speaking. Yet some think it intimates the solemnity of this discourse; the congregation being large, he raised his voice, and spoke louder than usual. One of the ancients has this remark upon it; Christ *taught* much without *opening his mouth*, that is, by his holy and exemplary life; nay, he *taught*, when, being *led as a lamb to the slaughter, he opened not his mouth*, but now *he opened his mouth, and taught*. *He taught them*, what was the evil they should abhor, and what the good they should abide and abound in; for Christianity is designed to regulate the temper of our minds and the tenor of our conversations; gospel-time is a time of reformation (Heb. ix. 10); and by the gospel we must be reformed, must be made good, must be made better.

Verses 3–12

Christ begins his sermon with blessings, for *he came into the world to bless us* (Acts iii. 26). He does it *as one having authority*, as one that can *command the blessing, even life for evermore*. The Old Testament ended with a curse (Mal. iv. 6), the gospel begins with a blessing. Each of the blessings Christ here pronounces has a double intention: 1. To show who they are that are to be accounted. 2. What this is wherein true happiness consists.

1. This is designed to rectify the ruinous mistakes of a blind and carnal world. Blessedness is the thing which men pretend to pursue; *Who will make to see good?* Ps. iv. 6. But most mistake the end, and form a wrong notion of happiness; and then no wonder that they miss the way. The general opinion is, *Blessed are they* that are rich, and great, and honourable in the world; that spend their days in mirth, and their years in pleasure; that eat the fat, and drink the sweet, and carry all before them with a high hand. Now our Lord Jesus comes to give us quite another notion of blessedness and blessed people. The beginning of a Christian's practice must be to take his measures of happiness from those maxims, and to direct his pursuits accordingly.

2. It is designed to remove the discouragements of the weak and poor who receive the gospel. Even *the least in the kingdom of heaven*, whose heart was upright with God, was happy in the honours and privileges of that kingdom.

3. It is designed to invite souls to Christ. And those who had seen the gracious cures wrought by his hand (*ch.* iv. 23, 24), and now heard *the gracious words proceeding out of his mouth*, would say that he was all of a piece, made up of love and sweetness.

4. It is designed to settle and sum up the articles of agreement between God and man. The scope of the divine revelation is to let us know what God

JAMIESON, FAUSSET, BROWN

a little colored. **and when he was set** [had sat or seated Himself] **his disciples came unto him**—already a large circle, more or less attracted and subdued by His preaching and miracles, in addition to the smaller band of devoted adherents. Though the latter only answered to the subjects of His kingdom, described in this discourse, there were drawn from time to time into this inner circle souls from the outer one, who, by the power of His matchless word, were constrained to forsake their all for the Lord Jesus.

2. And he opened his mouth—a solemn way of arousing the reader's attention, and preparing him for something weighty (Job 9:1; Acts 8: 35; 10:34). **and taught them, saying, 3. Blessed . . .** —Of the two words which our translators render "blessed," the one here used points more to what is *inward*, and so might be rendered "happy," in a lofty sense; while the other denotes rather what comes to us *from without* (as Matt. 25:34). But the distinction is not always clearly carried out. One Hebrew word expresses both. On these precious Beatitudes, observe that though eight in number, there are here but *seven* distinct features of character. The eighth one—the "persecuted for righteousness' sake"—denotes merely the possessors of the seven preceding features, on account of which it is that they are persecuted (II Tim. 3:12). Accordingly, instead of any distinct promise to this class, we have merely a repetition of the first promise. This has been noticed by several critics, who by the *sevenfold* character thus set forth have rightly observed that a *complete* character is meant to be depicted, and by the *sevenfold* blessedness attached to it, a *perfect* blessedness is intended. Observe, again, that the language in which these Beatitudes are couched is purposely fetched from the Old Testament, to show that the new kingdom is but the old in a new form; while the characters described are but the varied forms of that *spirituality* which was the essence of real religion all along, but had well-nigh disappeared under corrupt teaching. Further, the things here promised, far from being mere arbitrary rewards, will be found in each case to grow out of the characters to which they are attached, and in their completed form are but the appropriate coronation of them. Once more, as "the kingdom of heaven," which is the first and the last thing here promised, has two stages—a present and a future, an initial and a consummate stage—so the fulfilment of each of these promises has two stages —a present and a future, a partial and a perfect stage.

ADAM CLARKE

of public teachers among the Jews, and among many other people. *His disciples.* Literally, a scholar. Those who originally followed Christ, considered Him in the light of a divine Teacher.

CHARLES H. SPURGEON:

1. "And seeing the multitudes, he went up into a mountain": where he could find a suitable position for an audience. How different was this hill of the gospel from the Sinai of the law! Israel trembled before a mountain of curses; we rejoice in the mount of Beatitudes. "And when he was set, his disciples came unto him." Sitting was the usual posture of an oriental teacher; he spake as from the chair of authority, and his learners gathered at his feet.

2. "And he opened his mouth, and taught them." Now was opened the richest fountain of instruction which had ever flowed for the good of mankind. He who had aforetime opened the mouths of prophets now opened his own mouth. Speaking distinctly and earnestly, as all should do who have an important message to deliver, he went on to pronounce seven benedictions upon seven sorts of persons. These seven descriptions make up a perfect character, and the seven blessings appended thereto when combined constitute perfect bliss. The whole seven rise one above another like the steps of a ladder of light, and the blessings appropriate to each grow out of the virtues described. At the close of the seven beatitudes of character comes an eighth and double benediction bestowed upon that persecuted condition which is the present result of holiness. The whole make up a celestial octave of benediction.—*Spurgeon's Devotional Bible*

MATTHEW HENRY

expects from us, and what we may then expect from him; and nowhere is this more fully set forth in a few words than here. The way to happiness is here opened, and made a *highway* (Isa. xxxv. 8). Some of the wiser heathen had notions of blessedness different from the rest of mankind, and looking toward this of our Saviour. Seneca, undertaking to describe a blessed man, makes it out, that it is only an honest, good man that is to be so called: *In whose estimations nothing is good or evil, but a good or evil heart.*

Our Saviour here gives us eight characters of blessed people; which represent to us the principal graces of a Christian. On each of them a present blessing is pronounced; *Blessed are* they; and to each a future blessedness is promised.

I. *The poor in Spirit* are happy, *v.* 3. There is a poor-spiritedness that is so far from making men blessed that it is a sin and a snare—cowardice and base fear. To be *poor in spirit* is, 1. To be contentedly poor, willing to be empty of worldly wealth, if God orders that to be our lot. Many are poor in the world, but high in spirit, poor and proud, but we must accommodate ourselves to our poverty, must *know how to be abased*, Phil. iv. 12. It is to sit loose to all worldly wealth, and not set our hearts upon it. It is not, in pride or pretence, to make ourselves poor, by throwing away what God has given us. If we be rich in the world we must be *poor in spirit*, that is, we must condescend to the poor and sympathize with them, as being touched with the feeling of their infirmities; we must expect and prepare for poverty; must not inordinately fear or shun it, but must bid it welcome, especially when it comes upon us for keeping a good conscience, Heb. x. 34. Job was *poor in spirit*, when he blessed God in *taking away*, as well as giving. 2. To be humble and lowly in our own eyes. To be *poor in spirit*, is to think meanly of ourselves, of what we are, and have, and do; it is to be as little children in our opinion of ourselves. Paul was rich in *spirituals*, excelling most in gifts and graces, and yet *poor in spirit*, *the least of the apostles*, less than the least of all saints, and *nothing* in his own account. It is to be willing to make ourselves cheap, and mean, and little, to do good; to *become all things to all men.* It is to acknowledge that God is great, and we are mean; that he is holy and we are sinful; that he is all and we are nothing. 3. To come off from all confidence in our own righteousness and strength, that we may depend only upon the merit of Christ and the spirit and grace of Christ. That *broken and contrite spirit* with which the publican cried for mercy to a poor sinner, is this poverty of spirit. We must call ourselves poor, because always in want of God's grace, always begging at God's door, always hanging on in his house.

(1) This poverty in spirit is put first among the Christian graces. The philosophers did not reckon humility among their moral virtues, but Christ puts it first. The foundation of all other graces is laid in humility. Those who would build high must begin low. Those *who are weary and heavy laden*, are *the poor in spirit*, and they shall find rest with Christ.

(2) They are *blessed.* Now they are so, in this world. God looks graciously upon them. Nothing comes amiss to them; while high spirits are always uneasy.

(3) *Theirs is the kingdom of heaven.* The kingdom of *grace* is composed of such; the kingdom of *glory* is prepared for them. The great, high spirits go away with the glory of *the kingdoms of the earth*; but the humble, mild, and yielding souls obtain the glory of *the kingdom of heaven.* The same happiness is promised to those who are contentedly poor, as to those who are usefully rich. If I am not able to *spend* cheerfully for his sake, if I can but *want* cheerfully for his sake, even that shall be recompensed.

II. *They that mourn* are happy (*v.* 4); *Blessed are they that mourn.* This is another strange blessing. We are apt to think, Blessed are the *merry*; but Christ, who was himself a great mourner, says, Blessed are the *mourners.* There is a sinful mourning, which is an enemy to blessedness—*the sorrow of the world.* There is a natural mourning, which may prove a friend to blessedness, by the grace of God working with it. But there is a gracious mourning, which qualifies for blessedness. 1. A penitential mourning for our own sins; this is *godly sorrow*, a sorrow according to God; sorrow for sin, with an eye to Christ. Those are God's mourners, who live a life of repentance, who, out of regard to God's honour, mourn also for the sins of others. 2. A sympathising mourning for the afflictions of others; the mourning of those who *weep with them that weep*, who look with compassion on perishing souls, and *weep over* them, as Christ *over Jerusalem.*

Now these gracious mourners, (1) *Are blessed.* As in vain and sinful *laughter the heart is sorrowful*, so

JAMIESON, FAUSSET, BROWN

3. Blessed are the poor in spirit—All familiar with Old Testament phraseology know how frequently God's true people are styled "the poor" (the "oppressed," "afflicted," "miserable") or "the needy"—or both together (as in Ps. 40:17; Isa. 41:17). The explanation of this lies in the fact that it is generally "the poor of this world" who are "rich in faith" (Jas. 2:5; cf. II Cor. 6:10, and Rev. 2:9); while it is often "the ungodly" who "prosper in the world" (Ps. 73:12). Accordingly, in Luke (6:20, 21). it seems to be this class—the literally "poor" and "hungry"—that are specially addressed. But since God's people are in so many places styled "the poor" and "the needy," with no evident reference to their temporal circumstances (as in Ps. 68: 10; 69:29-33; 132:15; Isa. 61:1; 66:2), it is plainly a *frame of mind* which those terms are meant to express. Accordingly, our translators sometimes render such words "the humble" (Ps. 10:12, 17), "the meek" (Ps. 22:26), "the lowly" (Prov. 3:34), as having no reference to outward circumstances. But here the explanatory words, "in spirit," fix the sense to "those who in their deepest consciousness realize their entire need" (cf. the *Greek* of Luke 10: 21; John 11:33; 13:21; Acts 20:22; Rom. 12:11; I Cor. 5:3; Phil. 3). This self-emptying conviction, that "before God we are void of everything," lies at the foundation of all spiritual excellence, according to the teaching of Scripture. Without it we are inaccessible to the riches of Christ; with it we are in the fitting state for receiving all spiritual supplies (Rev. 3:17, 18; Matt. 9:12, 13). **for theirs is the kingdom of heaven.** (See on ch. 3:2). The poor in spirit not only shall have—they already have—the kingdom. The very sense of their poverty is begun riches. While others "walk in a vain show"—"in a shadow," "an image"—in an unreal world, taking a false view of themselves and all around them—the poor in spirit are rich in the knowledge of their real case. Having courage to look this in the face, and own it guilelessly, they feel strong in the assurance that "unto the upright there ariseth light in the darkness" (Ps. 112:4); and soon it breaks forth as the morning. God wants nothing from us as the price of His saving gifts; we have but to feel our universal destitution, and cast ourselves upon His compassion (Job 33:27, 28; I John 1:9). So the poor in spirit are enriched with the fulness of Christ, which is the kingdom in substance; and when He shall say to them from His great white throne, "Come, ye blessed of My Father, inherit the kingdom *prepared for you,*" He will invite them merely to the full enjoyment of an already possessed inheritance.

4. Blessed are they that mourn: for they shall be comforted—This "mourning" must not be taken loosely for that feeling which is wrung from men under pressure of the ills of life, nor yet strictly for sorrow on account of committed sins. Evidently it is that entire feeling which the sense of our spiritual poverty begets; and so the second beatitude is but the complement of the first. The one is the intellectual, the other the emotional aspect of the same thing. It is poverty of spirit that says, "I am undone"; and it is the mourning which this causes that makes it break forth in the form of a lamentation—"Woe is me! for I am undone." Hence this class are termed "mourners *in Zion,*" or, as we might express it, religious mourners, in sharp contrast with all other sorts (Isa. 61:1-3; 66:2). Religion, according to the Bible, is neither a set of intellectual convictions nor a bundle of emotional feelings, but a compound of both, the former giving birth to the latter. Thus closely do the first two beatitudes cohere. The mourners shall be "com-

ADAM CLARKE

3. *Blessed.* Or, happy. Homer, *Iliad* i. 339, calls the supreme gods *theon makaron,* "the ever happy and immortal gods," and opposes them to mortal men. *Poor in spirit.* One who is deeply sensible of his spiritual poverty and wretchedness. In the original this means someone who trembles or shrinks with fear. Being destitute of the true riches, he is tremblingly alive to the necessities of his soul, shrinking with fear lest he should perish without the salvation of God. Such Christ pronounces happy, because there is but a step between them and that Kingdom which is here promised.

Kingdom of heaven. Or, "of the heavens." A participation of all the blessings of the new covenant here, and the blessings of glory above. See this phrase explained, chap. iii. 2.

4. *Blessed are they that mourn.* That is, those who, feeling their spiritual poverty, mourn after God, lamenting the iniquity that separates them from the Fountain of blessedness.

MATTHEW HENRY

in gracious mourning *the heart* has a serious joy, a secret satisfaction, which *a stranger does not intermeddle with.* (2) *They shall be comforted.* Light is sown for them; and in heaven, it is certain, *they shall be comforted*, as Lazarus, Luke xvi. 25. The happiness of heaven consists in being perfectly and eternally comforted, and in the *wiping away of all tears from their eyes.* Heaven will be heaven indeed to those who go mourning thither; it will be a harvest of joy, the return of a seed-time of tears (Ps. cxxvi. 5, 6).

III. *The meek* are happy (*v.* 5); *Blessed are the meek.* The meek are those who quietly submit themselves to God, and are *gentle towards all men* (Titus iii. 2); who can bear provocation without being inflamed by it; are either silent, or return a soft answer; who can be cool when others are hot; and in their patience keep possession of their own souls, when they can scarcely keep possession of anything else. *They* are the meek, who would rather forgive twenty injuries than revenge one.

These meek ones are here represented as happy, even in this world. 1. They are *blessed*, for they are like the blessed Jesus. They are *blessed*, for they have the most comfortable, undisturbed enjoyment of themselves, their friends, their God; they are fit to live, and fit to die.

2. *They shall inherit the earth.* Not that they shall always have much of *the earth*, much less that they shall be put off with that only; but this branch of godliness has, in a special manner, *the promise of that life that now is.* Meekness, however ridiculed and run down, has a real tendency to promote our health, wealth, comfort, and safety, even in this world. Or, *They shall inherit the land* (so it may be read), *the land of Canaan*, a type of heaven. So that all the blessedness of heaven above, and all the blessings of earth beneath, are the portion of the meek.

IV. *They that hunger and thirst after righteousness* are happy, *v.* 6. Some understand this as a further instance of outward poverty, and a low condition in this world. Yet, *blessed are they*, if they suffer these hardships for and with a good conscience; let them hope in God. Those who contentedly bear oppression, and quietly refer themselves to God to plead their cause, shall in due time be satisfied, abundantly satisfied, in the wisdom and kindness, which shall be manifested in his appearances for them. 1. *Righteousness* is here put for all spiritual blessings. They are purchased for us by *the righteousness of Christ.* To become *a new man*, and to bear the image of God; to have an interest in Christ and the promises —this is *righteousness.* 2. These we must *hunger and thirst after.* We must truly and really desire them. Our desires of spiritual blessings must be earnest and importunate; "*Give me these, or else I die*; give me these, and I have enough, though I had nothing else." *Hunger and thirst* are appetites that return frequently, and call for fresh satisfactions. The quickened soul calls for constant meals of righteousness, grace to do the work of every day in its day. Those who *hunger and thirst* will labour for supplies;

JAMIESON, FAUSSET, BROWN

forted." Even now they get beauty for ashes, the oil of joy for mourning, the garment of praise for the spirit of heaviness. Sowing in tears, they reap even here in joy. Still, all present comfort, even the best, is partial, interrupted, short-lived. But the days of our mourning shall soon be ended, and then God shall wipe away all tears from our eyes. Then, in the fullest sense, shall the mourners be "comforted." **5. Blessed are the meek: for they shall inherit the earth**—This promise to the meek is but a repetition of Psalm 37:11; only the word which our Evangelist renders "the meek," after the LXX, is the same which we have found so often translated "the poor," showing how closely allied these two features of character are. It is impossible, indeed, that "the poor in spirit" and "the mourners" in Zion should not at the same time be "meek"; that is to say, persons of a lowly and gentle carriage. How fitting, at least, it is that they should be so, may be seen by the following touching appeal: "Put them in mind to be subject to principalities and powers, to obey magistrates, to be ready to every good work, to speak evil of no man, to be no brawlers, *but gentle, showing all meekness unto all men:* FOR WE OURSELVES WERE ONCE FOOLISH, disobedient, deceived, serving divers lusts and pleasures . . . But after that the kindness and love of God our Saviour toward man appeared: . . . according to His mercy He saved us . . ." (Titus 3:1-7). But He who had no such affecting reasons for manifesting this beautiful carriage, said, nevertheless, of Himself, "Take My yoke upon you, and learn of Me; for I am meek and lowly in heart: and ye shall find rest unto your souls" (Matt. 11:29); and the apostle besought one of the churches by "the meekness and gentleness of Christ" (II Cor. 10:1). In what esteem this is held by Him who seeth not as man seeth, we may learn from I Peter 3:4, where the true adorning is said to be that of "a meek and quiet spirit, which in the sight of God is of great price." Towards men this disposition is the opposite of high-mindedness, and a quarrelsome and revengeful spirit; it "rather takes wrong, and suffers itself to be defrauded" (I Cor. 6:7); it "avenges not itself, but rather gives place unto wrath" (Rom. 12: 19); like the meek One, "when reviled, it reviles not again; when it suffers, it threatens not: but commits itself to Him that judgeth righteously" (I Pet. 2:19-22). "The earth" which the meek are to inherit might be rendered "the land"—bringing out the more immediate reference to Canaan as the promised land, the secure possession of which was to the Old Testament saints the evidence and manifestation of God's favor resting on them, and the ideal of all true and abiding blessedness. Even in the Psalm from which these words are taken the promise to the meek is not held forth as an arbitrary reward, but as having a kind of natural fulfilment. When they delight themselves in the Lord, He gives them the desires of their heart: when they commit their way to Him, He brings it to pass; bringing forth their righteousness as the light, and their judgment as the noonday: the little that they have, even when despoiled of their rights, is better than the riches of many wicked (Ps. 37). All things, in short, are theirs—in the possession of that favor which is life, and of those rights which belong to them as the children of God—whether the world, or life, or death, or things present, or things to come; all are theirs (I Cor. 3:21, 22); and at length, overcoming, they "inherit all things" (Rev. 21:7). Thus are the meek the only rightful occupants of a foot of ground or a crust of bread here, and heirs of all coming things. **6. Blessed are they which do hunger and thirst after righteousness: for they shall be filled**—"shall be saturated." "From this verse," says THOLUCK, "the reference to the Old Testament background ceases." Surprising! On the contrary, none of these beatitudes is more manifestly dug out of the rich mine of the Old Testament. Indeed, how could any one who found in the Old Testament "the poor in spirit," and "the mourners in Zion," doubt that he would also find those same characters also *craving* that righteousness which they feel and mourn their want of? But what is the precise meaning of "righteousness" here? Lutheran expositors, and some of our own, seem to have a hankering after that more restricted sense of the term in which it is used with reference to the sinner's justification before God. (See Jer. 23:6; Isa. 45:24; Rom. 4:6; II Cor. 5:21). But, in so comprehensive a saying as this, it is clearly to be taken —as in vs. 10 also—in a much wider sense, as denoting that spiritual and entire conformity to the law of God, under the want of which the saints groan, and the possession of which constitutes the only true saintship. The Old Testament dwells

ADAM CLARKE

5. *Blessed are the meek.* Happy are those who are of a quiet, gentle spirit, in opposition to the proud and supercilious scribes and Pharisees, and their disciples. *For they shall inherit the earth.* Or "the land." Under this expression, which was commonly used by the prophets to signify the land of Canaan, in which all temporal good abounded, Judg. xviii. 9-10, Jesus Christ points out that abundance of spiritual good which was provided for men in the gospel. Besides, Canaan was a type of the kingdom of God; and who is so likely to inherit glory as the man in whom the meekness and gentleness of Jesus dwell?

W. E. VINE:

PRAUTES, or *PRAOTES*, an earlier form, denotes meekness. In its use in Scripture, in which it has a fuller, deeper significance than in nonscriptural Greek writings, it consists not in a person's "outward behavior only; nor yet in his relations to his fellowmen; as little in his more natural disposition. Rather, it is an inwrought grace of the soul; and the exercises of it are first and chiefly toward God. It is that temper of spirit in which we accept His dealings with us as good, and therefore without disputing or resisting; it is closely linked with the word *tapeinophrosune* (humility), and follows directly upon it (Eph. 4:1; Col. 3:12; cf. the adjectives in the LXX of Zeph. 3:12, 'meek and lowly') . . . it is only the humble heart which is also the meek, and which, as such, does not fight against God and more or less struggle and contend with Him. This meekness, however, being first of all a meekness before God, is also such in the face of men, even of evil men, out of a sense that these, with the insults and injuries which they may inflict, are permitted and employed by Him for the chastening and purifying of His elect." In Gal. 5:23 it is associated with self-control.

— Vine's Expository Dictionary

6. *They which do hunger and thirst.* As the body has its natural appetites of hunger and thirst for the food and drink suited to its nourishment, so has the soul. When the soul is awakened to a sense of its wants, and begins to hunger and thirst after righteousness or holiness, which is its proper food, we know that it must be purified by the Holy Spirit, and be made a partaker of that living bread, John viii. 48, or perish everlastingly. Now, as God never inspires a prayer but with a design to answer it, he who hungers and thirsts after the full salvation of God may depend on being speedily and effectually blessed or satisfied, well-fed.

MATTHEW HENRY	JAMIESON, FAUSSET, BROWN	ADAM CLARKE

MATTHEW HENRY

so we must not only desire spiritual blessings, but take pains for them in the use of the appointed means.

Those who thus *hunger and thirst shall be filled* with those blessings. (1) They are *blessed* in those desires. Though all desires of grace are not grace (feigned, faint desires are not), yet such a desire as this is; it is an *evidence* of something *good*, and an *earnest* of something *better*. It is a desire of God's own raising. (2) They *shall be filled* with those blessings. God will give them what they desire to their complete satisfaction. It is God only who can *fill a soul*, whose grace and favour are adequate to its just desires. He *fills the hungry* (Luke i. 53), *satiates* them, Jer. xxxi. 25.

V. The *merciful* are happy, *v.* 7. This, like the rest, is a paradox; for the merciful are not taken to be the wisest, nor are likely to be the richest; yet Christ pronounces them *blessed.* A man may be truly *merciful*, who has not wherewithal to be bountiful or liberal; and then God accepts the willing mind. We must not only bear our own afflictions patiently, but we must, by Christian sympathy, partake of the afflictions of our brethren; pity must be shown (Job vi. 14), and *bowels of mercy put on* (Col. iii. 12). We must have compassion on the souls of others, and help them; pity the ignorant, and instruct them; the careless, and warn them; those who are in a state of sin, and snatch them as *brands out of the burning*. Nay, a *good man is merciful to his beast*.

1. They are *blessed*; so it was said in the Old Testament; *Blessed is he that considers the poor*, Ps. xli. 1. Herein they resemble God, whose goodness is his glory. One of the purest and most refined delights in this world, is that of *doing good*. In this word, *Blessed are the merciful*, is included that saying of Christ, which otherwise we find not in the gospels, *It is more blessed to give than to receive*, Acts xx. 35. 2. *They shall obtain mercy*; mercy *with men*, when they need it (we know not how soon we may stand in need of kindness, and therefore should be kind); but especially mercy *with God*, for *with the merciful he will show himself merciful*, Ps. xviii. 25. The most *merciful* and charitable cannot pretend to *merit*, but must fly to mercy. Whereas *they* shall have *judgment without mercy* who have *shown no mercy*.

VI. The *pure in heart* are happy (*v.* 8); *Blessed are the pure in heart, for they shall see God*. This is the most comprehensive of all the beatitudes.

1. Here is the most *comprehensive character* of the blessed; they are the *pure in heart*. True Christianity lies in the heart, in the *purity of the heart*; the *washing* of that *from wickedness*, Jer. iv. 14. We must lift up to God, not only clean hands, but a pure heart, Ps. xxiv. 4, 5; 1 Tim. i. 5. The heart must be *pure*, in opposition to *mixture*—an honest heart that aims well; and pure, in opposition to *pollution* and *defilement*; as wine *unmixed*, as water *unmuddied*. The heart must be kept *pure* from all filthiness of flesh

JAMIESON, FAUSSET, BROWN

much on this righteousness, as that which alone God regards with approbation (Ps. 11:7; 23:3; 106: 3; Prov. 12:28; 16:31; Isa. 64:5, etc.). As hunger and thirst are the keenest of our appetites, our Lord, by employing this figure here, plainly means "those whose deepest cravings are after spiritual blessings." And in the Old Testament we find this craving variously expressed: "Hearken unto Me, ye that follow after righteousness, ye that seek the Lord" (Isa. 51: 1); "I have waited for Thy salvation, O Lord," exclaimed dying Jacob (Gen. 49:18); "My soul," says the sweet Psalmist, "breaketh for the longing that it hath unto Thy judgments at all times" (Ps. 119: 20): and in similar breathings does he give vent to his deepest longings in that and other Psalms. Well, our Lord just takes up here this blessed frame of mind, representing it as the surest pledge of the coveted supplies, as it is the best preparative, and indeed itself the beginning of them. "They shall be saturated," He says; they shall not only have what they so highly value and long to possess, but they shall have their fill of it. Not here, however. Even in the Old Testament this was well understood. "Deliver me," says the Psalmist, in language which, beyond all doubt, stretches beyond the present scene, "from men of the world, which have their portion in this life: as for me, I shall behold Thy face in righteousness: I shall be satisfied, when I awake, with Thy likeness" (Ps. 17:13-15). The foregoing beatitudes—the first four—represent the saints rather as *conscious of their need of salvation*, and acting suitably to that character, than as possessed of it. The next three are of a different kind —representing the saints as *having now found salvation*, and conducting themselves accordingly. **7. Blessed are the merciful: for they shall obtain mercy.** Beautiful is the connection between this and the preceding beatitude. The one has a natural tendency to beget the other. As for the words, they seem directly fetched from Psalm 18:25, "With the merciful Thou wilt show Thyself merciful." Not that our mercifulness comes absolutely first. On the contrary, our Lord Himself expressly teaches us that God's method is to awaken in us compassion towards our fellow men by His own exercise of it, in so stupendous a way and measure, towards ourselves. In the parable of the unmerciful debtor, the servant to whom his lord forgave ten thousand talents was naturally expected to exercise the small measure of the same compassion required for forgiving his fellow servant's debt of a hundred pence; and it is only when, instead of this, he relentlessly imprisoned him till he should pay it up, that his lord's indignation was roused, and he who was designed for a vessel of mercy is treated as a vessel of wrath (ch. 18:23-35; and see ch. 5:23, 24; 6:15; Jas. 2:13). "According to the view given in Scripture," says TRENCH most justly, "the Christian stands in a middle point, between a mercy received and a mercy yet needed." Sometimes the first is urged upon him as an argument for showing mercy—"forgiving one another, as Christ forgave you" (Col. 3:13; Eph. 4:32): sometimes the last—"Blessed are the merciful: for they shall obtain mercy"; "Forgive, and ye shall be forgiven" (Luke 6:37; Jas. 5: 9). And thus, while he is ever to look back on the mercy received as the source and motive of the mercy which he shows, he also looks forward to the mercy which he yet needs, and which he is assured that the merciful—according to what BENGEL beautifully calls the *benigna talio* (the gracious requital) of the kingdom of God—shall receive, as a new provocation to its abundant exercise. The foretastes and beginnings of this judicial recompense are richly experienced here below: its perfection is reserved for that day when, from His great white throne, the King shall say, "Come, ye blessed of My Father, inherit the kingdom prepared for you from the foundation of the world; for I was an hungered, and thirsty, and a stranger, and naked, and sick, and in prison, and ye ministered unto Me." Yes, thus He acted towards us while on earth, even laying down His life for us; and He will not, He cannot disown, in the merciful, the image of Himself. **8. Blessed are the pure in heart: for they shall see God.** Here, too, we are on Old Testament ground. There the difference between outward and inward purity, and the acceptableness of the latter only in the sight of God, are everywhere taught. Nor is the "vision of God" strange to the Old Testament; and though it was an understood thing that this was not possible in the present life (Exod. 33:20; and cf. Job 19:26, 27; Isa. 6:5) yet spiritually it was known and felt to be the privilege of the saints even here (Gen. 5: 24; 6:9; 17:1; 48:15; Ps. 27:4; 36:9; 63:2; Isa. 38:3, 11, etc.). But oh, with what grand simplicity, brevity, and power is this great fundamental

ADAM CLARKE

Righteousness here is taken for all the blessings of the new covenant—all the graces of the Messiah's kingdom—a full restoration to the image of God!

7. *The merciful.* The word *mercy*, among the Jews, signified two things: the pardon of injuries, and almsgiving. Our Lord undoubtedly takes it in its fullest latitude here.

They shall obtain mercy. Mercy is not purchased but at the price of mercy itself, and even this price is a gift of the mercy of God.

8. *Pure in heart.* In opposition to the Pharisees, who affected outward purity, while their hearts were full of corruption and defilement. A principal part of the Jewish religion consisted in outward washings and cleansings; on this ground they expected to *see* God, to enjoy eternal glory. But Christ here shows that a purification of the *heart* from all vile affections and desires is essentially requisite in order to enter into the kingdom of God. He whose soul is not delivered from all sin, through the Blood of the covenant, can have no scriptural hope of ever being with God. *Shall see God.* This is a Hebraism which

MATTHEW HENRY

and spirit, all that which comes *out of the heart*, and *defiles the man*. The heart must be *purified by faith*, and entire for God. *Create in me such a clean heart, O God!*

2. Here is the most *comprehensive comfort* of the blessed; They shall see God. (1) It is the perfection of the soul's happiness to *see God*; *seeing him*, as we may by faith in our present state, is a *heaven upon earth*; and seeing him as we shall in the future state, is the *heaven of heaven*. (2) The happiness of seeing God is promised to those, and those only who are *pure in heart*. None but the *pure* are capable of *seeing* God. What pleasure could an unsanctified soul take in the vision of a holy God? But all that are *pure in heart*, all that are truly sanctified, have desires wrought in them, which nothing but the sight of God will satisfy.

VII. The *peace-makers* are happy, *v.* 9. The wisdom that is from above is first *pure*, and then *peaceable*; the blessed ones are *pure* toward God, and *peaceable* toward men. The *peace-makers* are those who have, 1. *A peaceable disposition*. It is to love, and desire, and delight in peace; to be in it as in our element. 2. A *peaceable conversation*; industriously, as far as we can, to preserve the peace that it be not broken, and to recover it when it is broken. The *making of peace* is sometimes a *thankless office*, and it is the lot of him who parts a fray, to have *blows on both sides*; yet it is a good office, and we must be forward to it. (1) Such persons are *blessed*. They are working together with Christ, who came into the world to *slay all enmities*, and to proclaim *peace on earth*. (2) *They shall be called the children of God*. God will own them as such. If the peacemakers are blessed, woe to the peace-breakers!

VIII. Those who are *persecuted for righteousness' sake*, are happy. This is the greatest paradox of all, and peculiar to Christianity. This beatitude, like Pharaoh's dream, is doubled, because hardly credited, and yet *the thing is certain*.

1. The case of suffering saints described.

(1) They are persecuted, hunted, pursued, run down, as noxious beasts are, that are sought for to be destroyed; they are abandoned as the *offscouring of all things*.

(2) They are *reviled, and have all manner of evil said against them falsely*. Nicknames, and names of reproach, are fastened upon them, sometimes to make them formidable, that they may be powerfully assailed. Those who have had no power in their

JAMIESON, FAUSSET, BROWN

truth here expressed! And in what striking contrast would such teaching appear to that which was then current, in which exclusive attention was paid to ceremonial purification and external morality! This heart-purity begins in a "heart sprinkled from an evil conscience," or a "conscience purged from dead works" (Heb. 10:22; 9:14; and see Acts 15:9); and this also is taught in the Old Testament (Ps. 32:1, 2; cf. Rom. 4:5-8; and Isa. 6:5-8). The conscience thus purged—the heart thus sprinkled—there is light within wherewith to see God. "If we say that we have fellowship with Him, and walk in darkness, we lie, and do not the truth: but if we walk in the light, as He is in the light, we have fellowship one with the other"—He with us and we with Him—"and the blood of Jesus Christ His Son cleanseth us"—us who have this fellowship, and who, without such continual cleansing, would soon lose it again—"from all sin" (I John 1:6, 7). "Whosoever sinneth hath not seen Him, neither known Him" (I John 3:6); "He that doeth evil hath not seen God" (III John 11). The inward vision thus clarified, and the whole inner man in sympathy with God, each looks upon the other with complacency and joy, and we are "changed into the same image from glory to glory." But the full and beatific vision of God is reserved for that time to which the Psalmist stretches his views—"As for me, I shall behold Thy face in righteousness: I shall be satisfied, when I awake, with Thy likeness" (Ps. 17:15). Then shall His servants serve Him: and they shall see His face; and His name shall be in their foreheads (Rev. 22:3, 4). They shall see Him as He is (I John 3:2). But, says the apostle, expressing the converse of this beatitude—"Follow holiness, without which no man shall see the Lord" (Heb. 12:14). **9. Blessed are the peacemakers**—who not only study peace, but diffuse it—**for they shall be called the children** [shall be called sons] **of God**—Of all these beatitudes this is the only one which could hardly be expected to find its definite ground in the Old Testament; for that most glorious character of God, the likeness of which appears in the peacemakers, had yet to be revealed. His glorious name, indeed—as "The Lord, the Lord God, merciful and gracious, long-suffering, and abundant in goodness and truth, forgiving iniquity and transgression and sin"—had been proclaimed in a very imposing manner (Exod. 34: 6), and manifested in action with affecting frequency and variety in the long course of the ancient economy. And we have undeniable evidence that the saints of that economy felt its transforming and ennobling influence on their own character. But it was not till Christ "made peace by the blood of the cross" that God could manifest Himself as "the God of peace, that brought again from the dead our Lord Jesus, that great Shepherd of the sheep, through the blood of the everlasting covenant" (Heb. 13:20)—could reveal Himself as "in Christ reconciling the world unto Himself, not imputing their trespasses unto them," and hold Himself forth in the astonishing attitude of beseeching men to be "reconciled to Himself" (II Cor. 5:19, 20). When this reconciliation actually takes place, and one has "peace with God through our Lord Jesus Christ"—even "the peace of God which passeth all understanding"—the peace-receivers become transformed into peace-diffusers. God is thus seen reflected in them; and by the family likeness these peacemakers are recognized as the children of God. In now coming to the eighth, or supplementary beatitude, it will be seen that all that the saints are *in themselves* has been already described, in seven features of character; that number indicating *completeness* of delineation. The last feature, accordingly, is a passive one, representing the treatment that the characters already described may expect from the world. He who shall one day fix the destiny of all men here pronounces certain characters "blessed"; but He ends by forewarning them that the world's estimation and treatment of them will be the reserve of His. **10. Blessed are they which are persecuted for righteousness' sake . . .**—How entirely this final beatitude has its ground in the Old Testament, is evident from the concluding words, where the encouragement held out to endure such persecutions consists in its being but a continuation of what was experienced by the Old Testament servants of God. But how, it may be asked, could such beautiful features of character provoke persecution? To this the following answers should suffice: "Every one that doeth evil hateth the light, neither cometh to the light, lest his deeds should be reproved." "The world cannot hate you; but Me it hateth, because I testify of it, that the works thereof are evil." "If

ADAM CLARKE

signifies "possess God, enjoy His felicity," as seeing a thing was used among the Hebrews for possessing it.

9. *The peacemakers*. A peacemaker is a man who, being endowed with a generous public spirit, labors for the public good, and feels his own interest promoted in promoting that of others. Therefore, instead of fanning the fire of strife, he uses his influence and wisdom to reconcile the contending parties, adjust their differences, and restore them to a state of unity.

10. *They which are persecuted*. They who are hard pressed upon, and pursued with repeated acts of enmity. They are happy who suffer seems a strange saying; and that the righteous should suffer merely because they are such seems as strange. But such is the enmity of the human heart to everything of God and goodness that all those who live godly in Christ Jesus shall suffer persecution in one form or other.

MATTHEW HENRY

hands to do them any other mischief, could yet do this; and those who have had power to *persecute*, have found it necessary to *do this too*, to justify themselves in their barbarous usage of them. *Reviling* the saints is *persecuting* them, and will be found so shortly when *hard speeches* must be accounted for (Jude 15), and *cruel mockings*, Heb. xi. 36. They will say all *manner of evil of you falsely*. There is no evil so black and horrid, which, at one time or other, has not been said falsely, of Christ's disciples and followers.

(3) All this is *for righteousness' sake* (*v.* 10); *for my sake*, *v.* 11. This precludes those from this blessedness who suffer *justly*, and are evil spoken of *truly* for their real crimes; it is not the suffering, but the cause, that makes the martyr. Those suffer *for righteousness' sake*, who suffer for doing that which is good.

2. The comforts of suffering saints laid down.

(1) They *are blessed*; for they now, in their lifetime, receive *their evil things* (Luke xvi. 25), and receive them upon a good account. They are *blessed*, for it is an honour to them; it is an opportunity of glorifying Christ, and of experiencing special comforts and tokens of his presence.

(2) They shall be *recompensed*; Theirs is *the kingdom of heaven*. They have at present a sure title to it, and sweet foretastes of it; and shall ere long be in possession of it. *Great is your reward in heaven:* so great, as far to transcend the service. God will provide that those who lose *for* him, though it be life itself, shall not lose *by* him in the end. This is that which has borne up the suffering saints in all ages—this *joy is set before them*.

(3) "*So persecuted they the prophets that were before you*, *v.* 12. They were *before you* in excellency, above what you are yet arrived at; they were *before you* in time, that they might be examples to you of *suffering affliction* and *of patience*, James v. 10. Can you expect to go to heaven in a way by yourselves? It is a comfort to see the way of suffering a beaten road, and an honour to follow such leaders. That grace which was *sufficient for them*, to carry them through their sufferings, shall not be *deficient to you*."

(4) Therefore *rejoice and be exceeding glad*, *v.* **12.** It is not enough to be patient and content under these sufferings, but we must rejoice. Not that we must take a *pride* in our sufferings, (that spoils all), but we must take *a pleasure* in them, as knowing that Christ is herein *beforehand* with us, and that he will not be *behindhand* with us.

Verses 13–16

Christ had lately called his disciples, and told them that they should be *fishers of men*; here he tells them further what he designed them to be—*the salt of the earth*, and *lights of the world*.

I. *Ye are the salt of the earth*. The prophets, who went before them, were the salt of the land of Canaan; but the apostles were the salt of *the whole earth*, for they must *go into all the world to preach the gospel*. What could they do in so large a province as *the whole earth?* But, being to work silently as salt, one handful of that salt would diffuse its savour far and wide; would go a great way, and work insensibly and irresistibly as leaven, *ch.* xiii. 33. The doctrine of the gospel is as *salt*; it is penetrating, it reaches *the heart*, Acts ii. 37. It is cleansing, it is relishing, and preserves from putrefaction. An everlasting covenant is called a *covenant of salt* (Num. xviii. 19); and the gospel is an everlasting gospel. Salt was required in all the sacrifices. Christians, and especially ministers, are the salt of the earth.

1. If they be such as they should be they are *as good salt*, white, and small, and broken into many grains, but very useful and necessary. See in this, (1) What they are to be in themselves—seasoned with the gospel, with the salt of grace. *Have salt in yourselves*, else you cannot diffuse it among others, Mark

JAMIESON, FAUSSET, BROWN

ye were of the world, the world would love his own: but because ye are not of the world, but I have chosen you out of the world, therefore the world hateth you." "There is yet one man (said wicked Ahab to good Jehoshaphat) by whom we may inquire of the Lord: but I hate him; for he never prophesied good unto me, but always evil" (John 3: 20; 7:7; 15:19; II Chron. 18:7). But more particularly, the seven characters here described are all in the teeth of the spirit of the world, insomuch that such hearers of this discourse as breathed that spirit must have been startled, and had their whole system of thought and action rudely dashed. Poverty of spirit runs counter to the pride of men's heart; a pensive disposition, in the view of one's universal deficiencies before God, is ill relished by the callous, indifferent, laughing, self-satisfied world; a meek and quiet spirit, taking wrong, is regarded as pusillanimous, and rasps against the proud, resentful spirit of the world; that craving after spiritual blessings rebukes but too unpleasantly the lust of the flesh, the lust of the eye, and the pride of life; so does a merciful spirit the hardheartedness of the world; purity of heart contrasts painfully with painted hypocrisy; and the peacemaker cannot easily be endured by the contentious, quarrelsome world. Thus does "righteousness" come to be "persecuted." But blessed are they who, in spite of this, dare to be righteous. **for theirs is the kingdom of heaven**—As this was the reward promised to the poor in spirit—the leading one of these seven beatitudes—of course it is the proper portion of such as are persecuted for exemplifying them. **11. Blessed are ye when men shall revile you**—or abuse you to your face, in opposition to backbiting. (See Mark 15: 32). **and persecute you, and shall say all manner of evil against you, falsely, for my sake.** Observe this. He had before said, "for righteousness' sake." Here He identifies Himself and His cause with that of righteousness, binding up the cause of righteousness in the world with the reception of Himself. Would Moses, or David, or Isaiah, or Paul have so expressed themselves? Never. Doubtless they suffered for righteousness' sake. But to have called this "their sake," would, as every one feels, have been very unbecoming. Whereas He that speaks, being Righteousness incarnate (see Mark 1: 24; Acts 3:14; Rev. 3:7), when He so speaks, speaks only like Himself. **12. Rejoice, and be exceeding glad**—"exult." In the corresponding passage of Luke (6:22, 23), where every indignity trying to flesh and blood is held forth as the probable lot of such as were faithful to Him, the word is even stronger than here: "leap," as if He would have their inward transport to overpower and absorb the sense of all these affronts and sufferings; nor will anything else do it. **for great is your reward in heaven: for so persecuted they the prophets which were before you:**—i.e., "You do but serve yourselves heirs to their character and sufferings, and the reward will be common." **13-16.** We have here the practical application of the foregoing principles to those disciples who sat listening to them, and to their successors in all time. Our Lord, though He began by pronouncing certain *characters* to be blessed—without express reference to any of His hearers—does not close the beatitudes without intimating that such characters were in existence, and that already they were before Him. Accordingly, from characters He comes to *persons* possessing them, saying, "Blessed are ye when men shall revile you . . ." And now, continuing this mode of direct personal address, He startles those humble, unknown men by pronouncing them the exalted benefactors of their whole species. **13. Ye are the salt of the earth**—to preserve it from corruption, to season its insipidity, to freshen and sweeten it. The value of salt for these purposes is abundantly referred to by classical writers as well as in Scripture; and hence its symbolical significance in the religious offerings as well of those without as of those within the pale of revealed religion. In Scripture, mankind, under the unrestrained workings of their own evil nature, are represented as entirely corrupt. Thus, before the flood (Gen. 6:11, 12); after the flood (Gen. 8:21); in the days of David (Ps. 14:2, 3); in the days of Isaiah (Isa. 1:5, 6); and in the days of Paul (Eph. 2:1-3; see also Job 14:4; 15:15, 16; John 3:6; compared with Rom. 8:8; Titus 3:2, 3). The remedy for this, says our Lord here, is the active presence of His disciples among their fellows. The character and principles of Christians, brought into close contact with it, are designed to arrest the festering corruption of humanity and season its insipidity. But how, it may be asked, are Christians to do this office for their fellow men, if their righteousness only exasperate them, and recoil, in every

ADAM CLARKE

For theirs is the kingdom of heaven. That spiritual Kingdom, explained in chap. iii. 2, and that Kingdom of glory which is its counterpart and consequence.

11. *When men shall revile you, and persecute.* The persecution mentioned in the preceding verse comprehends all outward acts of violence—all that the hand can do. This comprehends also all calumny, slander, etc.—all that the tongue can effect.

12. *Rejoice.* In the testimony of a good conscience; for, without this, suffering has nothing but misery in it. *Be exceeding glad.* "Leap for joy." There are several cases on record where this was literally done by martyrs.

13. *Ye are the salt of the earth.* Our Lord shows here what the preachers of the gospel, and what all who profess to follow Him, should be: the *salt*, to preserve the world from putrefaction and destruction. *But if the salt have lost his savour.* A preacher, or private Christian, who has lost the life of Christ, and the witness of His Spirit, out of his soul may be likened to such salt. He may have the sparks and glittering particles of true wisdom, but without its unction or comfort. Only that which is connected with the Rock, the soul that is in union with Christ Jesus by the Holy Spirit, can preserve its *savor*, and be instrumental of good to others.

MATTHEW HENRY

ix. 50. (2) What they are to be to others; they must not only *be* good but *do* good. (3) What great blessings they are to the world. Mankind, lying in ignorance and wickedness, were a vast heap of unsavoury stuff, ready to putrefy; but Christ sent forth his disciples, by their lives and doctrines, to season it with knowledge and grace, and so to render it acceptable to God. (4) How they must expect to be disposed of. They must be scattered as salt upon the meat, here a grain and there a grain. Some have observed, that whereas it is foolishly called an ill omen to have the salt fall towards us, it is really an ill omen to have this salt fall from us.

2. If they be not, they are as *salt* that has *lost its savour*. If a Christian be so, especially if a minister be so, his condition is very sad; for, (1) He is *irrecoverable*: *Wherewith shall it be salted?* There is no remedy for *unsavoury salt*.

(2) He is *unprofitable*: *It is thenceforth good for nothing*. As a man without reason, so is a Christian without grace. (3) He is doomed to ruin and rejection; He shall be *cast out*. He shall be *trodden under foot of men*.

II. *Ye are the light of the world*, *v.* 14. This also bespeaks them useful, as the former. (*Nothing more useful than the sun and salt*), but more glorious. Truly *the light is sweet*, it is welcome; the light of the first day of the world was so, so is the morning light of every day; so is the gospel, and those that spread it.

1. As *the lights of the world*, they are illustrious and conspicuous, and have many eyes upon them. A city that is *set on a hill cannot be hid*. They are for *signs* (Isa. viii. 18), *men wondered at* (Zech. iii. 8); all their neighbours have an eye upon them. Some admire them, commend them, rejoice in them, and study to imitate them; others envy them, hate them, censure them, and study to blast them. They are concerned therefore to *walk circumspectly*, because of *their observers*.

2. As the *lights of the world*, they are intended to illuminate and give light to others (*v.* 15), and therefore, (1) They shall be *set up* as lights. Christ having lighted these candles, they shall not be put under a bushel. The gospel is so strong a light, and carries with it so much of its own evidence, that, *like a city on a hill, it cannot be hid*, it cannot but appear to be from God. It will *give light to all that are in the house*, to all that will draw near to it, and come where it is. Those to whom it does not give light, must thank themselves; they will not be in the house with it. (2) They must *shine* as lights, [1] By their *good preaching*. The knowledge they have, they must communicate for the good of others; not put it *under a bushel*, but spread it. The disciples of Christ must not muffle themselves up in privacy and obscurity, under pretence of contemplation, modesty, or self-preservation. [2] By their *good living*. They must be *burning and shining lights*.

First, How our light must shine—by doing such *good works* as men *may see*. We must do good works *that may be seen* to the edification of others, but not *that they may be seen* to our own ostentation. Those about us must not only *hear* our good words, but *see* our good works.

Secondly, For what *end* our light must shine—"That those who see your good works may be brought, not to glorify *you*, but to *glorify your Father which is in heaven*." The glory of God is the great thing we must aim at in everything we do in religion. We must do all we can to bring others to glorify him. The sight of our *good works* will do this, by furnishing them, 1. With *matter for praise*. 2. With *motives to piety*. The holy, regular, and exemplary conversation of the saints, may do much towards the conversion of sinners. Examples teach. There is a winning virtue in a godly conversation.

JAMIESON, FAUSSET, BROWN

form of persecution, upon themselves? The answer is: That is but the first and partial effect of their Christianity upon the world: though the great proportion would dislike and reject the truth, a small but noble band would receive and hold it fast; and in the struggle that would ensue, one and another even of the opposing party would come over to His ranks, and at length the Gospel would carry all before it. **but if the salt have lost his savour**—"become unsavory" or "insipid"; losing its saline or salting property. The meaning is: If that Christianity on which the health of the world depends, does in any age, region, or individual, exist only in *name*, or if it contain not those *saving elements* for want of which the world languishes, **wherewith shall it be salted?**—How shall the salting qualities be restored it? (Cf. Mark 9:50.) Whether salt ever does lose its saline property—about which there is a difference of opinion—is a question of no moment here. The point of the case lies in the supposition—that *if it should lose it*, the consequence would be as here described. So with Christians. The question is not: Can, or do, the saints ever totally lose that grace which makes them a blessing to their fellow men? But, What is to be the issue of that Christianity which is found wanting in those elements which can alone stay the corruption and season the tastelessness of an all-pervading carnality? The restoration or non-restoration of *grace*, or true living Christianity, to those who have lost it, has, in our judgment, nothing at all to do here. The question is not, If a man lose his grace, how shall *that* grace be restored to him? but, Since living Christianity is the only "salt of the earth," if men lose that, *what else* can supply its place? What follows is the appalling answer to this question. **it is thenceforth good for nothing, but to be cast out**—a figurative expression of indignant exclusion from the kingdom of God (cf. ch. 8:12; 22:13; John 6:37; 9:34). **and to be trodden under foot of men**—expressive of contempt and scorn. It is not the mere want of a certain character, but the want of it in those whose *profession* and *appearance* were fitted to beget expectation of finding it. **14. Ye are the light of the world**—This being the distinctive title which our Lord appropriates to Himself (John 8:12; 9:5; and see John 1:4, 9; 3:19; 12:35, 36)—a title expressly said to be unsuitable even to the highest of all the prophets (John 1:8)—it must be applied here by our Lord to His disciples only as they shine with His light upon the world, in virtue of His Spirit dwelling in them, and the same mind being in them which was also in Christ Jesus. Nor are Christians anywhere else so called. Nay, as if to avoid the august title which the Master has appropriated to Himself, Christians are said to "shine"—not as "lights," as our translators render it, but—"as *luminaries* in the world" (Phil. 2:15); and the Baptist is said to have been "the burning and shining"—not "light," as in our translation, but "*lamp*" of his day (John 5:35). Let it be observed, too, that while the two figures of salt and sunlight both express the same function of Christians—their blessed influence on their fellow men—they each set this forth under a different aspect. Salt operates *internally*, in the mass with which it comes in contact; the sunlight operates *externally*, irradiating all that it reaches. Hence Christians are warily styled "the salt of the *earth*"—with reference to the masses of mankind with whom they are expected to mix; but "the light of the *world*"—with reference to the vast and variegated surface which feels its fructifying and gladdening radiance. The same distinction is observable in the second pair of those seven parables which our Lord spoke from the Galilean Lake—that of the "mustard seed," which grew to be a great overshadowing tree, answering to the sunlight which invests the world, and that of the "leaven," which a woman took and, like the salt, *hid* in three measures of meal, till the whole was leavened (ch. 13:31-33). **A city that is set on an hill cannot be hid**—nor can it be supposed to have been so built except to be seen by many eyes. **15. Neither do men light a candle** [or, lamp] **and put it under a bushel** [a dry measure] **but on a candlestick**—rather, under the bushel, but on the lampstand." The article is inserted in both cases to express the familiarity of everyone with those household utensils. **and it giveth light** [shineth] **unto all that are in the house. 16. Let your light so shine before men, that they may see your good works, and glorify your Father which is in heaven**—As nobody lights a lamp only to cover it up, but places it so conspicuously as to give light to all who need light, so Christians, being the light of the world, instead of hiding their light, are so to hold it forth before men that they may see what a life the dis-

ADAM CLARKE

TODAY'S DICTIONARY OF THE BIBLE:

In Matt. 5:13 Jesus refers to salt, with the symbolic meaning of zest or flavor. But how, we ask, is it possible for salt to lose its flavor? The answer relates to the method whereby Jews in Jesus' day secured salt. During the late summer, when the Dead Sea was at its lowest, the salt-charged adobe shards on the perimeter of the Sea were carried to Jerusalem and submerged in water, thus dissolving the salt from them. The shards, as Jesus points out, would thereafter be useless.

14. *Ye are the light of the world.* That is, the instruments which God chooses to make use of to illuminate the minds of men, as He uses the sun to enlighten the world.

15. *Neither do men light a candle, and put it under a bushel.* A measure among both Greeks and Romans, containing a little more than a peck. From some ancient writers we learn that only those who had bad designs hid a candle under a bushel; that, in the dead of the night, when all were asleep, they might rise up, and have light at hand to help them to effect their horrid purposes of murder, etc.

16. *Let your light so shine.* Or more literally, "Thus let your light shine." As the sun is lighted up in the firmament of heaven to diffuse its light and heat freely to every inhabitant of the earth; and as the lamp is not set under the bushel, but placed upon the lamp-

MATTHEW HENRY

Verses 17–20

Those to whom Christ preached had an eye, 1. To the *scriptures* of the *Old Testament* as their *rule*, and therein Christ here shows them they were in the right: 2. To the scribes and Pharisees as their *example*, and therein Christ here shows them they were in the wrong; for,

I. The rule which Christ came to establish exactly agreed with the scriptures of the *Old Testament*, here called *the law* and *the prophets*.

1. He protests against the thought of cancelling and weakening the *Old Testament*; *Think not that I am come to destroy the law and the prophets.* (1) "Let not the pious Jews, who have an affection for the *law and the prophets, fear* that I come to *destroy* them." (2) "Let not the profane Jews, who have a disaffection to the law and the prophets, and are weary of that yoke, hope that I am come to destroy them." The Saviour of souls is the *destroyer* of nothing that comes from God, much less of those excellent dictates which we have from Moses and the prophets. No, he came to *fulfil* them. That is, [1] To obey the commands of the law. He in all respects yielded obedience to the law, and never broke the law in anything. [2] To make good the promises of the law, and the predictions of the prophets. [3] To answer the types of the law. [4] To fill up the defects of it, and so to complete and perfect it. As a picture that is first rough-drawn, displays some outlines only of the piece intended, which are afterwards filled up; so Christ made an improvement of the law and the prophets by his additions and explications. [5] To carry on the same design. The gospel is the *time of reformation* (Heb. ix. 10), not the repeal of the law, but the amendment of it, and, consequently, its establishment.

2. He asserts the perpetuity of it. "*Verily I say unto you, I*, the *Amen*, the faithful Witness, solemnly declare it, that *till heaven and earth pass, one jot, or one tittle, shall in no wise pass from the law till all be fulfilled*." *The word of the Lord endures for ever*, both that of the law, and that of the gospel. The care of God concerning his law extends itself even to those things that seem to be of least account on it, for whatever belongs to God, and bears his stamp, be it ever so little, shall be preserved.

3. He gives it in charge to his disciples, carefully to preserve the law, and shows them the danger of the neglect and contempt of it (*v.* 19); *Whosoever therefore shall break one of the least commandments of the law of Moses he shall be called the least in the kingdom of heaven. Whosoever shall do and teach them* shall be *called great in the kingdom of heaven.* (1) Among the commands of God there are some less than others; none absolutely little, but comparatively so. (2) It is a dangerous thing, in doctrine or practice, to disannul the least of God's commands. It is something more than transgressing the law, it is making void the law, Ps. cxix. 126. (3) That the further such corruptions as these spread, the worse they are. It is impudence enough to break the command, but it is a greater degree of it to teach men so. He that does so, shall be called *least in the kingdom of heaven*, in the kingdom of glory. Those are truly honourable, and of great account in the church of Christ, who both do and teach that which is good; for those who do not as they teach, pull down with one hand what they build up with the other. Those who speak from experience, who live up to what they preach, are truly great; hereafter they shall shine as the *stars in the kingdom of our Father*.

JAMIESON, FAUSSET, BROWN

ciples of Christ lead, and seeing this, may glorify their Father for so redeeming, transforming, and ennobling earth's sinful children, and opening to themselves the way to like redemption and transformation.

17-48. Identity of These Principles with Those of the Ancient Economy, in Contrast with the Reigning Traditional Teaching. *Exposition of Principles* (vss. 17-20). **17. Think not that I am come** [that I came] **to destroy the law, or the prophets**–i.e., "the authority and principles of the Old Testament." (On the phrase, see ch. 7:12; 22:40; Luke 16:16; Acts 13:15). This general way of taking the phrase is much better than understanding "the law" and "the prophets" separately, and inquiring, as many good critics do, in what sense our Lord could be supposed to meditate the subversion of each. To the various classes of His hearers, who might view such supposed abrogation of the law and the prophets with very different feelings, our Lord's announcement would, in effect, be such as this–"Ye who tremble at the word of the Lord, *fear* not that I am going to sweep the foundation from under your feet: Ye restless and revolutionary spirits, *hope* not that I am going to head any revolutionary movement: And ye who hypocritically affect great reverence for the law and the prophets, *pretend* not to find anything in My teaching derogatory to God's living oracles." **I am not come to destroy, but to fulfil**–Not to subvert, abrogate, or annul, but to establish the law and the prophets –to unfold them, to embody them in living form, and to enshrine them in the reverence, affection, and character of men, am I come. **18. For verily I say unto you**–Here, for the first time, does that august expression occur in our Lord's recorded teaching, with which we have grown so familiar as hardly to reflect on its full import. It is the expression manifestly, of *supreme legislative authority;* and as the subject in connection with which it is uttered is the Moral Law, no higher claim to an authority *strictly divine* could be advanced. For when we observe how jealously Jehovah asserts it as His exclusive prerogative to give law to men (Lev. 18:1-5; 19:37; 26:1-4; 13-16, etc.), such language as this of our Lord will appear totally unsuitable, and indeed abhorrent, from any creature-lips. When the Baptist's words–"I say unto you" (ch. 3:9)–are compared with those of his Master here, the difference of the two cases will be at once apparent. **Till heaven and earth pass**–Though even the Old Testament announces the ultimate "perdition of the heavens and the earth," in contrast with the immutability of Jehovah (Ps. 102:24-27), the prevalent representation of the heavens and the earth in Scripture, when employed as a popular figure, is that of their *stability* (Ps. 119:89-91; Eccles. 1:4; Jer. 33:25, 26). It is the enduring stability, then, of the great truths and principles, moral and spiritual, of the Old Testament revelation which our Lord thus expresses. **one jot**–the smallest of the Hebrew letters. **one tittle**–one of those little strokes by which alone some of the Hebrew letters are distinguished from others like them. **shall in no wise pass from the law, till all be fulfilled**–The meaning is that "not so much as the smallest loss of authority or vitality shall ever come over the law." The expression, "till all be fulfilled," is much the same in meaning as "it *shall* be had in undiminished and enduring honor, from its greatest to its least requirements." Again, this general way of viewing our Lord's words here seems far preferable to that *doctrinal* understanding of them which would require us to determine the different kinds of "fulfilment" which the *moral* and the *ceremonial* parts of it were to have. **19. Whosoever therefore shall break**–rather, dissolve, annul, or make invalid. **one of these least commandments**–an expression equivalent to "one of the least of these commandments." **and shall teach men so**–referring to the Pharisees and their teaching, as is plain from the next verse, but of course embracing all similar schools and teaching in the Christian Church. **he shall be called the least in the kingdom of heaven**–As the thing spoken of is not the practical breaking, or disobeying, of the law, but annulling or enervating its obligation by a vicious system of interpretation, and teaching others to do the same; so the thing threatened is not exclusion from heaven, and still less the lowest place in it, but a degraded and contemptuous position in the present stage of the kingdom of God. In other words, they shall be reduced by the retributive providence that overtakes them, to the same condition of dishonor to which, by their system and their teaching, they have brought down those eternal principles of God's law. **but whosoever shall do and teach them**–whose

ADAM CLARKE

stand, that it may give light to all in the house, thus let every follower of Christ, and especially every preacher of the gospel, diffuse the light of heavenly knowledge and the warmth of divine love through the whole circle of their acquaintance.

17. *Think not that I am come to destroy the law.* "Do not imagine that I am come to violate the law." I am not come to make the law of none effect—to dissolve the connection which subsists between its several parts, or the obligation men are under to have their lives regulated by its moral precepts; nor am I come to dissolve the connecting reference it has to the promised. But I am come to complete—to perfect its connection and reference, to accomplish everything shadowed forth in the Mosaic ritual, to fill up its great design; and to give grace to all My followers, "to fill up, or complete" every moral duty. Christ completed the law: (1) *In itself,* it was only the shadow, the typical representation, of good things to come; and He added to it that which was necessary to make it perfect, His own sacrifice, without which it could neither satisfy God nor sanctify men. (2) He completed it *in himself,* by submitting to its types with an exact obedience, and verifying them by His death upon the Cross. (3) He completes this law, and the sayings of His prophets, *in his members,* by giving them grace to love the Lord with all their heart, soul, mind, and strength, and their neighbor as themselves; for this is all the *law* and the *prophets.*

18. *Till heaven and earth pass away.* From the very beginning of His ministry, Jesus Christ teaches the instability of all visible things. *One jot or one tittle.* One *yod,* the smallest letter in the Hebrew alphabet. One *tittle* or "point," meaning either those points which serve for vowels in this language, if they then existed, or the points of certain letters. *Till all be fulfilled.* Or "accomplished." Though all earth and hell should join together to hinder the accomplishment of the great designs of the Most High, yet it shall all be in vain—even the sense of a single letter shall not be lost. The words of God, which point out His designs, are as unchangeable as His nature itself.

19. *Whosoever therefore shall break one of these least commandments.* The Pharisees were remarkable for making a distinction between weightier and lighter matters in the law, and between what has been called, in a corrupt part of the Christian Church, *mortal* and *venial sins.*

MATTHEW HENRY

II. The righteousness which Christ came to establish by this rule, must exceed that of the scribes and Pharisees, *v.* 20. This was strange doctrine to those who looked upon the scribes and Pharisees as having arrived at the highest pitch of religion. It was therefore a great surprise to them, to hear that they must be better than they. The scribes and Pharisees were enemies to Christ and his doctrine, and were great oppressors; and yet it must be owned, that there was something commendable in them. Yet our Lord Jesus here tells his disciples, that the religion he came to establish, did not only exclude the badness, but excel the goodness, of the scribes and Pharisees. We must do more than they, and better than they. They minded only the *outside*, but we must make conscience of *inside* godliness. They aimed at the *praise* and *applause of men*, but we must aim at *acceptance with God*: but we, when we have done all, must *deny ourselves*, and say, We are *unprofitable servants*, and trust only to the *righteousness of Christ*.

Verses 21–26

Christ proceeds to expound the law in some particular instances. He adds not anything new, only limits and restrains some permissions which had been abused: and as to the precepts, shows the breadth, strictness, and spiritual nature of them. In these verses, he explains the law of the sixth commandment, according to the true intent and full extent of it.

I. Here is the *command itself* laid down (*v.* 12). The laws of God are not novel, upstart laws, but were delivered to them of old time; they are ancient laws, but of that nature as never to be *antiquated* nor grow *obsolete*. *Killing* is here forbidden, killing ourselves, killing any other, directly or indirectly, or being any way accessory to it. The law of God, the God of life, is a hedge of protection about our lives.

II. The exposition of this command which the Jewish teachers contented themselves with; their comment upon it was, *Whosoever shall kill, shall be in danger of the judgment*. Now this gloss of theirs upon this commandment was faulty, for it intimated, That the law of the sixth commandment was only external, and forbade no more than the act of murder, and laid no restraint upon the inward lusts, from which *wars and fightings come*. This was indeed the *fundamental error* of the Jewish teachers, that the divine law prohibited only the sinful act, not the sinful thought.

III. The exposition which Christ gave of this commandment.

1. Christ tells them that *rash anger is heart-murder* (*v.* 22); *Whosoever is angry with his brother without a cause*, breaks the sixth commandment. Anger is a natural passion; there are cases in which it is lawful and laudable; but it is then *sinful*, when we are angry without cause. When it is without any just provocation given; either for no cause, or no good cause, or no great and proportionable cause; when we are angry upon groundless surmises, or for trivial affronts not worth speaking of. When it is without any good end aimed at, then it is in vain, it is to do hurt; whereas if we are at any time angry, it should be to

JAMIESON, FAUSSET, BROWN

principles and teaching go to exalt the authority and honor of God's law, in its lowest as well as highest requirements. **the same shall be called great in the kingdom of heaven**—shall, by that providence which watches over the honor of God's moral administration, be raised to the same position of authority and honor to which they exalt the law. **20. For I say unto you, That except your righteousness shall exceed the righteousness of the scribes and Pharisees**—The superiority to the Pharisaic righteousness here required is plainly in *kind*, not *degree;* for all Scripture teaches that entrance into God's kingdom, whether in its present or future stage, depends, not on the degree of our excellence in anything, but solely on our having the character itself which God demands. Our righteousness, then—if it is to contrast with the *outward* and *formal* righteousness of the scribes and Pharisees—must be *inward, vital, spiritual*. Some, indeed, of the scribes and Pharisees themselves might have the very righteousness here demanded; but our Lord is speaking, not of persons, but of the *system* they represented and taught. **ye shall in no case enter into the kingdom of heaven**—If this refer, as in the preceding verse, rather to the earthly stage of this kingdom, the meaning is that without a righteousness exceeding that of the Pharisees, we cannot be members of it at all, save in name. This was no new doctrine (Rom. 2:28, 29; 9:6; Phil. 3:3). But our Lord's teaching here stretches beyond the present scene, to that everlasting stage of the kingdom, where without "purity of heart" none "shall see God."

The Spirituality of the True Righteousness, in Contrast with That of the Scribes and Pharisees, Illustrated from the Sixth Commandment (vss. 21-26). **21. Ye have heard that it was said by them of old time**—or, as in the margin, "to them of old time." Which of these translations is the right one has been much controverted. Either of them is grammatically defensible, though the latter—"*to* the ancients"—is more consistent with New Testament usage (see the *Greek* of Rom. 9:12, 26; Rev. 6:11; 9:4); and most critics decide in favor of it. But it is not a question of Greek only. Nearly all who would translate "to the ancients" take the speaker of the words quoted to be *Moses in the law*; "the ancients" to be *the people* to whom Moses gave the law; and the intention of our Lord here to be to contrast His own teaching, more or less, with that of Moses; either as opposed to it—as some go the length of affirming—or at least as modifying, enlarging, elevating it. But who can reasonably imagine such a thing, just after the most solemn and emphatic proclamation of the perpetuity of the law, and the honor and glory in which it was to be held under the new economy? To us it seems as plain as possible that our Lord's one object is to contrast the traditional perversions of the law with the true sense of it as expounded by Himself. A few of those who assent to this still think that "to the ancients" is the only legitimate translation of the words; understanding that our Lord is reporting what had been said to the ancients, not by Moses, but by the perverters of his law. We do not object to this; but we incline to think (with BEZA, and after him with FRITZSCHE, OLSHAUSEN, STIER, and BLOOMFIELD) that "by the ancients" must have been what our Lord meant here, referring to the corrupt teachers rather than the perverted people. **Thou shalt not kill:**—i.e., This being all that the law requires, whosoever has imbrued his hands in his brother's blood, but he only, is guilty of a breach of this commandment. **and whosoever shall kill shall be in danger of** [liable to] **the judgment**—i.e., of the sentence of those inferior courts of judicature which were established in all the principal towns, in compliance with Deuteronomy 16:16. Thus was this commandment reduced, from a holy law of the heart-searching God, to a mere criminal statute, taking cognizance only of outward actions, such as that which we read in Exodus 21:12; Leviticus 24:17. **22. But I say unto you**—Mark the authoritative tone in which—as Himself the Lawgiver and Judge—Christ now gives the true sense, and explains the deep reach, of the commandment. **That whosoever is angry with his brother without a cause shall be in danger of the judgment; and whosoever shall say to his brother, Raca! shall be in danger of the council; but whosoever shall say, Thou fool! shall be in danger of hell fire**—It is unreasonable to deny, as ALEXANDER does, that three degrees of punishment are here meant to be expressed, and to say that it is but a threefold expression of one and the same thing. But Romish expositors greatly err in taking the first two—"the judgment" and "the council"—to refer to degrees of *temporal* punishment with which

ADAM CLARKE

20. *Except your righteousness shall exceed.* "Unless your righteousness abound more"—unless it take in not only the letter but the spirit and design of the moral and ritual precept (the one directing you how to walk so as to please God; the other pointing out Christ, the great Atonement, through and by which a sinner is enabled to do so)—more than that *of the scribes and Pharisees*, who only attend to the letter of the law, and had indeed made even that of no effect by their traditions—*ye shall not enter into the kingdom of heaven.*

21. *Ye have heard that it was said by them of old time.* "To or by the ancients." By the "ancients" we may understand those who lived before the law, and those who lived under it.

Thou shalt not kill. Murder was, in the most solemn manner, forbidden before, as well as under, the law, Gen. xi. 5-6.

22. *Whosoever is angry with his brother without a cause.* What our Lord seems here to prohibit is not merely that miserable facility which some have of being angry at every trifle, continually taking offense against their best friends, but that anger which leads a man to commit outrages against another. *Shall be in danger of the judgment.* "Shall be liable to the judgment."

MATTHEW HENRY

awaken the offender to repentance, and prevent his doing so again. When it exceeds due bounds; when we are outrageous and mischievous, and when we seek the hurt of those we are displeased at. This is a breach of the sixth commandment, for he that is thus angry, would kill if he could and durst; he has taken the first step towards it.

2. He tells them, that giving opprobrious language to our brother is tongue-murder, calling him, *Raca*, and *Thou fool*. When this is done with mildness and for a good end, to convince others of their vanity and folly, it is not sinful. But when it proceeds from anger and malice within, it is the smoke of that fire which is kindled from hell. (1) *Raca* is a scornful word, and comes from pride, "Thou empty fellow." *This people who knoweth not the law, is cursed*, is such language, John vii. 49. (2) *Thou fool*, is a spiteful word, and comes from hatred; looking upon him, not only as mean and not to be honoured, but as vile and not to be loved. The former speaks a man without sense, this (in scripture language) speaks a man without grace; the more the reproach touches his spiritual condition, the worse it is. Malicious slanders and censures are *poison under the tongue*, that kills secretly and slowly. It is an evidence of such an ill-will to our neighbour as would strike at his life, if it were in our power.

3. He tells them, that how light soever they made of these sins, they would certainly be reckoned for; he *that is angry with his brother shall be in danger of the judgment* and anger of God; he that calls him *Raca, shall be in danger of the council*, of being punished by the Sanhedrim for reviling an Israelite; *but whosoever saith, Thou fool*, thou profane person, thou child of hell, *shall be in danger of hell-fire*, to which he condemns his brother. Christ would thus show which sin was most sinful, by showing which it was the punishment whereof was most dreadful.

IV. From all this it is here inferred, that we ought carefully to preserve Christian love and peace with all our brethren, and that if at any time a breach happens, we should labour for a reconciliation.

1. Because, till this be done, we are utterly unfit for communion with God in holy ordinances, *v.* 23, 24. If thou *have aught against thy brother*, make short work of it; no more is to be done but to forgive him (Mark xi. 25), and forgive the injury; but if the quarrel began on thy side, and the fault was either at first or afterwards thine, so *that thy brother* has a controversy with *thee, go* and *be reconciled to* him before thou *offer thy gift at the altar*, before thou approach solemnly to God. When we are addressing ourselves to any religious exercises, it is good for us to take that occasion of serious reflection and self-examination. Religious exercises are not acceptable to God, if they are performed when we are in wrath. Prayers made in wrath are written in gall, Isa. i. 15; lviii. 4. Love or charity is so much *better than all burnt-offerings and sacrifice*, that God is content to stay for the gift, rather than have it offered while we are under guilt and engaged in a quarrel. Though we are unfitted for communion with God, by a continual quarrel with a brother, yet that can be no excuse for the omission or neglect of our duty. Many give this as a reason why they do not come to church or to the communion, because they are at variance with some neighbour; and whose fault is that? One sin will never excuse another, but will rather double the guilt. Want of charity cannot justify the want of piety. *Therefore* we must *not let the sun go down upon our wrath* any day, because we must go to prayer before

JAMIESON, FAUSSET, BROWN

lesser sins were to be visited under the Gospel, and only the last—"hell fire"—to refer to the future life. All three clearly refer to *divine retribution*, and that alone, for breaches of this commandment; though this is expressed by an *allusion* to Jewish tribunals. The "judgment," as already explained, was the lowest of these; the "council," or "Sanhedrim,"—which sat at Jerusalem—was the highest; while the word used for "hell fire" contains an allusion to the "valley of the son of Hinnom" (Josh. 18:16). In this valley the Jews, when steeped in idolatry, went the length of burning their children to Molech "on the high places of Tophet"—in consequence of which good Josiah defiled it, to prevent the repetition of such abominations (II Kings 23:10); and from that time forward, if we may believe the Jewish writers, a fire was kept burning in it to consume the carrion and all kinds of impurities that collected about the capital. Certain it is, that while the final punishment of the wicked is described in the Old Testament by allusions to this valley of Tophet or Hinnom (Isa. 30:33; 66:24), our Lord Himself describes the same by merely quoting these terrific descriptions of the evangelical prophet (Mark 9:43-48). What precise degrees of unholy feeling towards our brothers are indicated by the words "Raca" and "fool" it would be as useless as it is vain to inquire. Every age and every country has its modes of expressing such things; and no doubt our Lord seized on the then current phraseology of unholy disrespect and contempt, merely to express and condemn the different degrees of such feeling when brought out in words, as He had immediately before condemned the feeling itself. In fact, so little are we to make of mere *words*, apart from the feeling which they express, that as *anger* is expressly said to have been borne by our Lord towards His enemies though mixed with "grief for the hardness of their hearts" (Mark 3:5), and as the apostle teaches us that there is an anger which is not sinful (Eph. 4:26); so in the Epistle of James (2:20) we find the words, "O vain [or, empty] man"; and our Lord Himself applies the very word "fools" twice in one breath to the blind guides of the people (ch. 23:17, 19)—although, in both cases, it is to *false reasoners* rather than persons that such words are applied. The spirit, then, of the whole statement may be thus given: "For ages ye have been taught that the sixth commandment, for example, is broken only by the murderer, to pass sentence upon whom is the proper business of the recognized tribunals. But I say unto you that it is broken even by causeless anger, which is but hatred in the bud, as hatred is incipient murder (I John 3:15); and if by the feelings, much more by those *words* in which all ill feeling, from the slightest to the most envenomed, are wont to be cast upon a brother: and just as there are gradations in human courts of judicature, and in the sentences which they pronounce according to the degrees of criminality, so will the judicial treatment of all the breakers of this commandment at the divine tribunal be according to their real criminality before the heart-searching Judge." Oh, what holy teaching is this! **23. Therefore**—to apply the foregoing, and show its paramount importance. **if thou bring thy gift to the altar, and there rememberest that thy brother hath aught** [of just complaint] **against thee; 24. Leave there thy gift before the altar, and go thy way; first be reconciled to thy brother**—The meaning evidently is—not, "dismiss from thine own breast all ill feeling, "but" get thy brother to dismiss from his mind all grudge against thee." **and then come and offer thy gift**—"The picture," says THOLUCK," is drawn from life. It transports us to the moment when the Israelite, having brought his sacrifice to the court of the Israelites, awaited the instant when the priest would approach to receive it at his hands. He waits with his gift at the rails which separate the place where he stands from the court of the priests, into which his offering will presently be taken, there to be slain by the priest, and by him presented upon the altar of sacrifice." It is at this solemn moment, when about to cast himself upon divine mercy, and seek in his offering a seal of divine forgiveness, that the offerer is supposed, all at once, to remember that some brother has a just cause of complaint against him through breach of this commandment in one or other of the ways just indicated. What then? Is he to say, As soon as I have offered this gift I will go straight to my brother, and make it up with him? Nay; but before another step is taken—even before the offering is presented—this reconciliation is to be sought, though the gift have to be left unoffered before the altar. The converse of the truth here taught is very strikingly expressed in Mark 11:25, 26: "And *when*

ADAM CLARKE

Raca. From the Hebrew *rak*, "to be empty." It signifies a "vain, empty, worthless fellow, shallow brains." a term of great contempt. *The council*. The famous council, known among the Jews by the name of Sanhedrin. It was composed of seventy-two elders. This grand Sanhedrin not only received appeals from the inferior Sanhedrins, or court of twenty-three, but could alone take cognizance, in the first instance, of the highest crimes, and alone inflict the punishment of stoning. *Thou fool. Moreh*, probably from *marah*, "to rebel," a "rebel against God," apostate from all good. This term implied, among the Jews, the highest enormity and most aggravated guilt. *Shall be in danger of hell fire*. Our Lord here alludes to the valley of the son of Hinnom. This place was near Jerusalem, and had been formerly used for those abominable sacrifices, in which the idolatrous Jews had caused their children to pass through the fire to Molech. See 2 Kings xxiii. 10; 2 Chron. xxviii. 3; Jer. vii. 31-32. From the circumstance of this valley having been the scene of those infernal sacrifices, the Jews, in our Saviour's time, used the word for "hell," the place of the damned. There are *three* kinds of offences here, which exceed each other in their degrees of guilt: (1) *Anger* against a man, accompanied with some injurious act. (2) *Contempt,* expressed by the opprobrious epithet *raka, or shallow brains*. (3) *Hatred and mortal enmity*, expressed by the term *moreh*, or *apostate*, where such apostasy could not be proved. Now, proportioned to these *three* offenses were *three* different degrees of punishment, each exceeding the other in its severity, as the offenses exceeded each other in their different degrees of guilt: (1) The *judgment*, the council of *twenty-three*, which could inflict the punishment of *strangling*. (2) The *Sanhedrin*, or great council, which could inflict the punishment of *stoning*. (3) The being *burnt alive* in the valley of the son of Hinnom. This appears to be the meaning of our Lord.

23. *Therefore if thou bring thy gift*. Evil must be nipped in the bud. An unkind thought of another may be the foundation of that which leads to actual murder.

24. *Leave there thy gift before the altar*. This is as much as to say, "Do not attempt to bring any offering to God while you are in a spirit of enmity against any person; or have any difference with your neighbor, which you have not used your diligence to get adjusted." It is our duty and interest, both to bring our gift and offer it too; but God will not accept any act of religious worship from us while any enmity subsists in our hearts towards any soul of man, or while any subsists in our neighbor's heart towards us which we have not used the proper means to remove.

MATTHEW HENRY

we go to sleep; much less let the sun rise *upon our wrath* on a sabbath-day, because it is a day of prayer.

2. Because, till this be done, we lie exposed to much danger, *v.* 25, 26.

(1) Upon a temporal account. If the offence we have done to our brother, in his body, goods, or reputation, be such as will bear an action, in which he may recover considerable damages, it is our wisdom, and it is our duty to our family, to prevent that by a humble submission and a just and peaceable satisfaction; lest otherwise he recover it by law, and put us to the extremity of a prison. It is in vain to contend with the law, and there is danger of our being crushed by it. It is good to agree, for the law is costly. Though we must be merciful to those we have advantage against, yet we must be just to those that have advantage against us. A prison is an uncomfortable place to those who are brought to it by their own pride, and prodigality, their own wilfulness and folly.

(2) Upon a spiritual account. "*Go,* and be *reconciled to thy brother,* be just to him, be friendly with him, because while the quarrel continues, as thou art unfit to *bring thy gift to the altar,* unfit to come to *the table of the Lord,* so thou art unfit to die."

This is very applicable to the great business of our reconciliation to God through Christ; *Agree with him quickly, whilst thou art in the way.* Note, [1] The great God is an Adversary to all sinners. [2] It is our concern to *agree with him.* [3] It is our wisdom to do this *quickly, while we are in the way.* While we are alive, *we are in the way*; after death, it will be too late to do it. [4] They who continue in a state of enmity to God, are continually exposed to the arrests of his justice. Hell is the prison, into which those will be cast that continue in a state of enmity to God. Sinners must remain in it to eternity; they shall not *depart till they have paid the uttermost farthing.*

Verses 27–32

We have here an exposition of the seventh commandment. It is the law against uncleanness, which fitly follows upon the former; *that* laid a restraint upon sinful passions, *this* upon sinful appetites.

I. The command is here laid down (*v.* 17), *Thou shalt not commit adultery*; which includes a prohibition of all other acts of uncleanness, and the desire of them.

II. It is here explained in the strictness of it, in three things.

1. We are here taught, that there is such a thing as *heart-adultery,* adulterous thoughts and dispositions which never proceed to the act of adultery or fornication. *Whosoever looketh on a woman* (not only another man's wife, as some would have it, but any woman), *to lust after her, has committed adultery with her in his heart, v.* 28. This command forbids not only the acts of fornication and adultery, but, (1) All appetites to them. Lust is conscience baffled or biassed: biassed, if it say nothing against the sin; baffled, if it prevail not in what it says. (2) All approaches towards them; feeding the eye with the sight of the forbidden fruit. The eye is both the inlet

JAMIESON, FAUSSET, BROWN

ye stand praying [in the very act], forgive, if ye have aught [of just complaint] against any; that your Father also which is in heaven may forgive you your trespasses. But if ye do not forgive, neither will your Father which is in heaven forgive you . . ." Hence the beautiful practice of the early Church, to see that all differences amongst brethren and sisters in Christ were made up, in the spirit of love, before going to the Holy Communion; and the Church of England has a rubrical direction to this effect in her Communion service. Certainly, if this be the highest act of worship on earth, such reconciliation—though obligatory on all other occasions of worship—must be peculiarly so then. **25. Agree with thine adversary**—thine opponent in a matter cognizable by law. **quickly, whiles thou art in the way with him**—"to the magistrate," as in Luke 12:58. **lest at any time**—here, rather, "lest at all," or simply "lest." **the adversary deliver thee to the judge, and the judge** [having pronounced thee in the wrong] **deliver thee to the officer**—the official whose business it is to see the sentence carried into effect. **26. Verily I say unto thee, Thou shalt by no means come out thence, till thou hast paid the uttermost farthing**—a fractional Roman coin, worth about half a cent. That our Lord meant here merely to give a piece of prudential advice to his hearers, to keep out of the hands of the law and its officials by settling all disputes with one another privately, is not for a moment to be supposed, though there are critics of a school low enough to suggest this. The concluding words—"Verily I say unto thee, Thou shalt by no means come out . . ."—manifestly show that though the *language* is drawn from human disputes and legal procedure, He is dealing with a higher than any human quarrel, a higher than any human tribunal, a higher than any human and temporal sentence. In this view of the words—in which nearly all critics worthy of the name agree—the spirit of them may be thus expressed: "In expounding the sixth commandment, I have spoken of offenses between man and man; reminding you that the offender has another party to deal with besides him whom he has wronged on earth, and assuring you that all worship offered to the Searcher of hearts by one who knows that a brother has just cause of complaint against him, and yet takes no steps to remove it, is vain: But I cannot pass from this subject without reminding you of One whose cause of complaint against you is far more deadly than any that man can have against man: and since with that Adversary you are already on the way to judgment, it will be your wisdom to make up the quarrel without delay, lest sentence of condemnation be pronounced upon you, and then will execution straightway follow, from the effects of which you shall never escape as long as any remnant of the offense remains unexpiated." It will be observed that as the *principle* on which we are to "agree" with this "Adversary" is not here specified, and the precise *nature* of the retribution that is to light upon the despisers of this warning is not to be gathered from the mere use of the word "prison"; so, the *remedilessness* of the punishment is not in so many words expressed, and still less is its actual *cessation* taught. The language on all these points is designedly general; but it may safely be said that the *unending duration* of future punishment—elsewhere so clearly and awfully expressed by our Lord Himself, as in vss. 29 and 30, and Mark 9:43, 48—is the only doctrine with which His language here quite naturally and fully accords. (Cf. ch. 18:30, 34).

The Same Subject Illustrated from the Seventh Commandment (vss. 27-32). **27. Ye have heard that it was said**—The words by," or "to them of old time," in this verse are insufficiently supported, and probably were not in the original text. **Thou shalt not commit adultery**—Interpreting this seventh, as they did the sixth commandment, the traditional perverters of the law restricted the breach of it to *acts* of criminal intercourse between, or with, married persons exclusively. Our Lord now dissipates such delusions. **28. But I say unto you, That whosoever looketh on a woman to lust after her**—with the intent to do so, as the same expression is used in ch. 6:1; or, with the full consent of his will, to feed thereby his unholy desires. **hath committed adultery with her already in his heart**—We are not to suppose, from the word here used—"adultery"—that our Lord means to restrict the breach of this commandment to married persons, or to criminal intercourse with such. The expressions, "*whosoever* looketh," and "looketh upon a *woman,*" seem clearly to extend the range of this commandment to all forms of impurity, and the counsels which follow—as they most certainly were intended

ADAM CLARKE

25. *Agree with thine adversary quickly. Adversary,* properly a plaintiff in law—a perfect law term. Our Lord enforces the exhortation given in the preceding verses, from the consideration of what was deemed prudent in ordinary lawsuits. A good use of this very prudential advice of our Lord is this: You are a sinner; God has a controversy with you. There is but a step between you and death. Now is the accepted time. You are invited to return to God by Christ Jesus. Come immediately at His call, and He will save your soul.

26. *The uttermost farthing.* This was the smallest coin among the Romans.

G. CAMPBELL MORGAN:

It would seem that Jesus is here passing behind the feeling that may be in a man's heart against his brother, and is dragging the archenemy into the light. Probably this term adversary refers here, as everywhere, to Satan. This is a figure of law. The adversary is the antagonist. It is strictly a legal word, and yet it is a curious fact that it occurs only four times in the New Testament, and every time it is used of an antagonist in law in a bad sense, and never in a good. It is the one word Peter uses concerning the great enemy, "Your adversary the devil." And the Greek word very bluntly translated means "against right." It is the adversary in law, who is not on the side of righteousness.

But you say, "Surely Jesus was not advising us to agree with the devil?" Yes, exactly that. Let us follow it carefully. Here again in a flash He reveals the relation Satan bears to all such as are in His Kingdom. Satan is not powerful over such as put their trust in God. Jesus said on another occasion, "Satan asked to have you, that he might sift you as wheat." Now He says: "If there is evil in your heart toward your brother, if you have wronged your brother, and he has that against you, then the adversary himself has a claim upon you; he can claim you to deliver you to punishment. His claim is established because of your wrong-doing. Haste from the altar, be reconciled to your brother; have the evil put away; agree with your brother; and so have done with the adversary that he may have no complaint." Remember, Satan is the accuser of the brethren, the one who charges us with sin. So long as we are living in sin, he has right over us, even though we be in God's Kingdom; we give him the right to lead us into the place of ultimate penalty. Thus the King safeguards human life.

—*The Gospel According to Matthew*

28. *Whosoever looketh on a woman to lust after her.* "Earnestly to covet her." The verb is undoubtedly used here by our Lord in the sense of coveting through the influence of impure desire. *Hath committed adultery with her already in his heart.* It is the earnest wish or desire of the soul which, in a variety of cases, constitutes the good or evil of an act. If a man earnestly wish to commit an evil, but cannot because God puts time, place, and opportunity out of his power, he is fully chargeable with the iniquity of the act by that God who searches and judges the heart. If voluntary and delib-

MATTHEW HENRY

and outlet of a great deal of wickedness of this kind. What have we the covering of the eyes for, but to restrain corrupt glances, and to keep out their defiling impressions? This forbids also the using of any other of our senses to stir up lust. If ensnaring looks are forbidden fruit, much more unclean discourses, and wanton dalliances, the fuel and bellows of this hellish fire. These precepts are hedges about the law of heart-purity, *v.* 8. And if looking be lust, they who dress and deck, and expose themselves, with design to be looked at and lusted after are no less guilty. Men sin, but devils tempt to sin.

2. That such looks and such dalliances are so very dangerous and destructive to the soul, that it is better to lose the eye and the hand that thus offend than to give way to the sin. "*It is a hard saying, who can bear it?* Flesh and blood cannot but look with pleasure upon a beautiful woman; and it is impossible to forbear lusting after and dallying with such an object." Such pretences as these will scarcely be overcome by reason, and therefore must be argued against with *the terrors of the Lord.*

(1) It is a severe operation that is here prescribed for the preventing of these fleshly lusts. *If thy right eye offend thee,* or *cause thee to offend,* by wanton glances, or wanton gazings, upon forbidden objects; *if thy right hand offend thee,* or *cause thee to offend,* by wanton dalliances; if there were no other way to restrain them (which, blessed be God, through his grace, there is), it were better for us to *pluck out the eye,* and *cut off the hand* than to indulge them in sin to the ruin of the soul. And if this must be submitted to, at the thought of which nature startles, much more must we resolve to keep a constant watch over our own hearts, and to suppress the first rising of lust and corruption there; to avoid the occasions of sin, to resist the beginnings of it, and to decline the company of those who will be a snare to us, though ever so pleasing; to keep out of harm's way, and abridge ourselves in the use of lawful things, when we find them temptations to us; and to seek unto God for his grace, and depend upon that grace daily, and so to *walk in the Spirit,* as that we may not *fulfil the lusts of the flesh;* and this will be as effectual as *cutting off a right hand or pulling out a right eye;* and perhaps as much against the grain to flesh and blood; it is the destruction of the old man.

(2) It is a startling argument that is made use of to enforce this prescription (*v.* 29). *It is profitable for thee that one of thy members should perish, and not that thy whole body should be cast into hell.* It is not unbecoming a minister of the gospel to preach of hell and damnation; nay, he *must* do it, for Christ himself did it; and we are unfaithful to our trust, if we give not warning of *the wrath to come.* [1] There are some sins from which we need to be *saved with fear,* particularly *fleshly lusts,* which are such *natural brute beasts* as cannot be checked, but by being frightened. [2] Those do not know or do not believe what hell is, that will rather venture their eternal ruin than deny themselves the gratification of a base and brutish lust. [3] Even those duties that are most unpleasant to flesh and blood, are *profitable for us;* and our Master requires nothing from us but what he knows to be for our advantage.

3. That men's divorcing their wives upon dislike, or for any other cause except adultery, was a violation of the seventh commandment, as it opened a door to adultery, *v.* 31, 32. Here observe,

(1) How the matter now stood with reference to divorce. "*Whosoever shall put away his wife, let him give her a bill of divorce;* let him not think to do it by word of mouth, when he is in a passion; let him do it solemnly." Thus the law had prevented rash and hasty divorces.

(2) How this matter was rectified and amended by our Saviour. He reduced the ordinance of marriage to its primitive institution: *They two shall be one flesh,* not to be easily separated, and therefore divorce is not to be allowed, except in case of adultery, which breaks the marriage covenant; but he that puts away his wife upon any other pretence, *causeth her to commit adultery,* and him also that shall marry her when she is thus divorced.

Verses 33–37

We have here an exposition of the third commandment. *God will not hold him guiltless,* however he may hold himself, who breaks this commandment, by *taking the name of the Lord God in vain.*

I. It is agreed on all hands that it forbids perjury, forswearing, and the violation of oaths and vows, *v.* 33. Perjury is a sin condemned by the light of nature, as a complication of impiety toward God and injustice toward man, and as rendering a man highly obnoxious to the divine wrath. *So help me God;* wishing I may never have any help from God,

JAMIESON, FAUSSET, BROWN

for all, whether married or unmarried—seem to confirm this. As in dealing with the sixth commandment our Lord first expounds it, and then in the four following verses applies His exposition, so here He first expounds the seventh commandment, and then in the four following verses applies His exposition. **29. And if thy right eye**—the readier and the dearer of the two. **offend thee**—be a "trap-spring," or as in the New Testament, be "an occasion of stumbling" to thee. **pluck it out and cast it from thee**—implying a certain indignant promptitude, heedless of whatever cost to feeling the act may involve. Of course, it is not *the eye simply* of which our Lord speaks—as if execution were to be done upon the bodily organ—though there have been fanatical ascetics who have both advocated and practiced this, showing a very low apprehension of spiritual things—but *the offending eye,* or the eye considered as the occasion of sin; and consequently, only the *sinful exercise* of the organ which is meant. For as one might put out his eyes without in the least quenching the lust to which they ministered, so, "if thine eye be single, thy whole body shall be full of light," and, when directed by a holy mind, becomes an "instrument of righteousness unto God." At the same time, just as by cutting off a hand, or plucking out an eye, the *power* of acting and of seeing would be destroyed, our Lord certainly means that we are to *strike at the root* of such unholy dispositions, as well as cut off the occasions which tend to stimulate them. **for it is profitable for thee that one of thy members should perish, and not that thy whole body should be cast into hell**—He who despises the warning to cast from him, with indignant promptitude, an offending member, will find his whole body "cast," with a retributive promptitude of indignation, "into hell." Sharp language, this, from the lips of Love incarnate! **30. And if thy right hand** [the organ of *action,* to which the eye excites] **offend thee. cut it off, and cast it from thee; for it is profitable . . .**—See on vs. 29. The repetition, in identical terms, of such stern truths and awful lessons seems characteristic of our Lord's manner of teaching. Cf. Mark 9:43-48. **31. It hath been said**—This shortened form was perhaps intentional, to mark a transition from the commandments of the Decalogue to a civil enactment on the subject of divorce, quoted from Deuteronomy 24:1. The law of divorce—according to its strictness or laxity—has so intimate a bearing upon purity in the married life, that nothing could be more natural than to pass from the seventh commandment to the loose views on that subject then current. **Whosoever shall put away his wife, let him give her a writing of divorcement**—a legal check upon reckless and tyrannical separation. The one legitimate ground of divorce allowed by the enactment just quoted was "some uncleanness"—in other words, conjugal infidelity. But while one school of interpreters (that of Shammai) explained this quite correctly, as prohibiting divorce in every case save that of adultery, another school (that of Hillel) stretched the expression so far as to include everything in the wife offensive or disagreeable to the husband—a view of the law too well fitted to minister to caprice and depraved inclination not to find extensive favor. And, indeed, to this day the Jews allow divorces on the most frivolous pretexts. It was to meet this that our Lord uttered what follows: **32. But I say unto you, That whosoever shall put away his wife, saving for the cause of fornication, causeth her to commit adultery**—i.e., drives her into it in case she marries again. **and whosoever shall marry her that is divorced** [for anything short of conjugal infidelity] **committeth adultery**—for if the commandment is broken by the one party, it must be by the other also. But see on ch. 19:4-9. Whether the innocent party, after a just divorce, may lawfully marry again, is not treated of here. The Church of Rome says, No; but the Greek and Protestant Churches allow it.

Same Subject Illustrated from the Third Commandment (vss. 33-37). **33. Again, ye have heard that it hath been said by them of old time, Thou shalt not forswear thyself**—These are not the precise words of Exodus 20:7; but they express all that it was currently understood to condemn, viz., false swearing (Lev. 19:12, etc.). This is plain from what follows.

ADAM CLARKE

erate looks and desires make adulterers and adulteresses, how many persons are there whose whole life is one continued crime!

29. *And if thy right eye offend thee.* The *right eye* and the *right hand* are used here to point out those sins which appear most pleasing and profitable to us; from which we must be separated, if we desire ever to see the kingdom of God.

29-30. *Pluck it out . . . cut it off.* We must shut our senses against dangerous objects to avoid the occasions of sin, and deprive ourselves of all that is most dear and profitable to us in order to save our souls, when we find that these dear and profitable things, however innocent in themselves, cause us to sin against God.

It is profitable for thee that one of thy members. Men often part with some members of the body, at the discretion of a surgeon, that they may preserve the trunk, and die a little later; and yet they will not deprive themselves of a look, a touch, a small pleasure, which endanger the eternal death of the soul.

31. *Whosoever shall put away his wife.* The Jewish doctors gave great license in the matter of divorce. Among them a man might divorce his wife if she displeased him even in the dressing of his victuals!

32. *Saving for the cause of fornication.* As fornication signifies no more than the unlawful connection of unmarried persons, it cannot properly be used when speaking of those who are married. I have therefore translated "on account of whoredom." It does not appear that there is any other case in which Jesus Christ admits of divorce. A real Christian ought rather to beg of God the grace to bear patiently and quietly the imperfections of his wife than to think of the means of being parted from her.

33. *Thou shalt not forswear thyself.* They dishonor the great God and break this commandment who use frequent oaths and imprecations, even in reference to things that are true; and those who make vows and promises which they either cannot perform or do not design to fulfill are not less criminal. *Perform unto the Lord thine oaths.* The morality of the Jews on this point was truly detestable; they maintained that a man might swear with his

MATTHEW HENRY

if I swear falsely. Thus, by the consent of nations, have men cursed themselves, not doubting but that God would curse them, if they lied against the truth then when they solemnly called God to witness to it.

II. It is here added, that the commandment does not only forbid false swearing, but all rash, unnecessary swearing: *Swear not at all, v.* 34. Not that all swearing is sinful; so far from that, if rightly done, it is a part of religious worship, and we in it *give unto God the glory due to his name.* In swearing, we pawn the truth of something known, to confirm the truth of something doubtful or unknown; we appeal to a greater knowledge, to a higher court.

Now the mind of Christ in this matter is,

1. That we must *not swear at all,* but when we are duly called to it, and justice or charity to our brother, or respect to the commonwealth, make it necessary for *the end of strife* (Heb. vi. 16). We may be sworn, but we must not swear.

2. That we must not swear lightly and irreverently, in common discourse: it is a very great sin to make a ludicrous appeal to the glorious Majesty of heaven. It is a sin that has no cloak, no excuse for it, and therefore a sign of a graceless heart.

3. That we must in a special manner avoid promissory oaths, of which Christ more particularly speaks here, for they are oaths that are to be performed. The frequent requiring and using of oaths, is a reflection upon Christians, who should be of such acknowledged fidelity, as that their sober words should be as sacred as their solemn oaths.

4. That we must not swear by any creature. It should seem there were some, who, in civility (as they thought) to the name of God, would not make use of that in swearing, but would swear *by heaven* or *earth,* &c. There is nothing we can swear by, but it is some way or other related to God, who is the Fountain of all beings, and therefore it is as dangerous to swear by them, as it is to swear by God himself: it is the verity of the creature that is laid at stake; now that cannot be an instrument of testimony, but as it has regard to God.

(1) *Swear not by the heaven;* "As sure as there is a heaven, this is true;" *for it is God's throne,* where he resides. You cannot *swear by heaven,* but you swear by God himself.

(2) *Nor by the earth, for it is his footstool. The earth is the Lord's;* so that in swearing by it, you swear by its Owner.

(3) *Neither by Jerusalem,* a place for which the Jews had such a veneration, that they could not speak of anything more sacred to *swear by. It is the city of the great King* (Ps. xlviii. 2), *the city of God* (Ps. xlvi. 4), he is therefore interested in it, and in every oath taken by it.

(4) "*Neither shalt thou swear by thy head.* It is more God's than thine; for he made it, and formed all the springs and powers of it; whereas thou thyself canst not, from any natural intrinsic influence, change the colour of *one hair,* so as to make *it white or black;* so that thou canst not *swear by thy head,* but thou swearest by him who is *the Life of thy head,* and *the Lifter up of it.*" Ps. iii. 3.

5. That therefore in all our communications we must content ourselves with, *Yea, yea,* and *Nay, nay, v.* 37. *Verily, verily,* was our Saviour's *yea, yea.* So if we deny a thing, let it suffice to say, No. If our fidelity be known, that will suffice to gain us credit; and if it be questioned, to back what we say with swearing and cursing, is but to render it more suspicious. They who can *swallow* a profane oath, will not *strain at a lie.*

The reason is observable; *For whatsoever is more than these cometh of evil,* though it do not amount to the iniquity of an oath. It comes from that deceitfulness which is in men, *All men are liars;* therefore men use these protestations, because they are distrustful one of another, and think they cannot be believed without them. An oath is physic, which supposes a disease.

Verses 38–42

In these verses the law of retaliation is expounded. Observe,

I. What the *Old Testament permission* was, in case of injury. It was not a command, that everyone should of necessity require such satisfaction; but they might lawfully insist upon it, if they pleased;

JAMIESON, FAUSSET, BROWN

But I say unto you, Swear not at all—That this was meant to condemn swearing of every kind and on every occasion—as the Society of Friends and some other ultra-moralists allege—is not for a moment to be thought. For even Jehovah is said once and again to have sworn by Himself; and our Lord certainly answered upon oath to a question put to Him by the high priest; and the apostle several times, and in the most solemn language, takes God to witness that he spoke and wrote the truth; and it is inconceivable that our Lord should here have quoted the precept about not forswearing ourselves, but performing to the Lord our oaths, only to give a precept of His own directly in the teeth of it. Evidently, it is swearing in common intercourse and on frivolous occasions that is here meant. Frivolous oaths were indeed severely condemned in the teaching of the times. But so narrow was the circle of them that a man might swear, says LIGHTFOOT, a hundred thousand times and yet not be guilty of vain swearing. Hardly anything was regarded as an oath if only the name of God were not in it; just as among ourselves, as TRENCH well remarks, a certain lingering reverence for the name of God leads to cutting off portions of His name, or uttering sounds nearly resembling it, or substituting the name of some heathen deity, in profane exclamations or asseverations. Against all this our Lord now speaks decisively; teaching His audience that every oath carries an appeal to God, whether named or not. **neither by heaven; for it is God's throne: 35. Nor by the earth; for it is his footstool** [quoting Isa. 66: 1]; **neither by Jerusalem for it is the city of the great King** [quoting Ps. 48:2]. **36. Neither shalt thou swear by thy head, because thou canst not make one hair white or black**—In the other oaths specified, God's name was profaned quite as really as if His name had been uttered, because it was instantly *suggested* by the mention of His "throne," His "footstool," His "city." But in swearing by our own *head* and the like, the objection lies in their being "beyond our control," and therefore profanely assumed to have a stability which they have not. **37. But let your communication**—"your word," in ordinary intercourse, be, **Yea, yea; Nay, nay**—Let a simple *Yes* and *No* suffice in affirming the truth or the untruth of anything. (See Jas 5:12, and II Cor. 1:17, 18). **for whatsoever is more than these cometh of evil**—not "of the evil one"; though an equally correct rendering of the words, and one which some expositors prefer. It is true that all evil in our world is originally of the devil, that it forms a kingdom at the head of which he sits, and that, in every manifestation of it he has an active part. But any reference to this here seems unnatural, and the allusion to this passage in the Epistle of James (5:12) seems to show that this is not the sense of it: "Let your yea be yea; and your nay, nay; *lest ye fall into condemnation.*" The untruthfulness of our corrupt nature shows itself not only in the tendency to deviate from the strict truth, but in the disposition to suspect others of doing the same; and as this is not diminished, but rather aggravated, by the habit of confirming what we say by an oath, we thus run the risk of having all reverence for God's holy name, and even for strict truth, destroyed in our hearts, and so "fall into condemnation." The practice of going beyond Yes and No in affirmations and denials —as if our word for it were not enough, and we expected others to question it—springs from that vicious root of untruthfulness which is only aggravated by the very effort to clear ourselves of the suspicion of it. And just as swearing to the truth of what we say begets the disposition it is designed to remove, so the love and reign of truth in the breasts of Christ's disciples reveals itself so plainly even to those who themselves cannot be trusted, that their simple Yes and No come soon to be more relied on than the most solemn asseverations of others. Thus does the grace of our Lord Jesus Christ, like a tree cast into the bitter waters of human corruption, heal and sweeten them.

Same Subject—Retaliation (vss. 38-42). We have here the converse of the preceding lessons. They were *negative:* these are *positive.* **38. Ye have heard that it hath been said** [Exod. 21:23-25; Lev. 24:19, 20; Deut. 19:21], **An eye for an eye, and a tooth for a tooth**—i.e., whatever penalty was regarded as a proper equivalent for these. This law of retribution—designed to take vengeance out of the hands of private persons, and commit it to the

ADAM CLARKE

lips and annul it in the same moment in his heart.

34. *Swear not at all.* Much has been said in vindication of the propriety of swearing in civil cases before a magistrate, and much has been said against it. The best way is to have as little as possible to do with oaths. An oath will not bind a dishonest person nor a liar; and an honest man needs none, for his character and conduct swear for him.

34-35. *Neither by heaven . . . nor by the earth.* It was a custom among the ancient Scythians, when they wished to bind themselves in the most solemn manner, to swear by the king's throne; and if the king was at any time sick, they believed it was occasioned by someone's having taken the oath falsely.

36. *Neither shalt thou swear by thy head.* For these plain reasons: (1) God commands you not to do it. (2) You have nothing which is your own, and you should not pledge another's property. (3) It never did, and never can, answer any good purpose. (4) Being a breach of the law of God, it is the way to everlasting misery.

37. *Let your communication be, Yea, yea; Nay, nay.* That is, a positive and forthright affirmation or negation, according to your knowledge of the matter concerning which you are called to testify. Do not equivocate; mean what you assert, and adhere to your assertion. *Whatsoever is more than these.* That is, more than a bare affirmation or negation, according to the requirements of Eternal Truth, cometh of evil; or "is of the wicked one", i.e., the devil, the father of superfluities and lies.

38. *An eye for an eye.* Our Lord refers here to the law of retaliation mentioned in Exod. xxi. 24, which obliged the offender to suffer the same injury he had committed. The Greeks and Romans had the same law.

MATTHEW HENRY

an eye for an eye, and a tooth for a tooth. It was a direction, and a restraint to such as have mischief done to them that they may not insist on a greater punishment than is proper: it is not *a life for an eye,* nor *a limb for a tooth,* but observes a proportion.

Now, so far this is in force with us, as a direction to magistrates, to use the sword of justice according to the good and wholesome laws of the land, for the terror of evil-doers, and the vindication of the oppressed. And it is in force as a rule to lawgivers, to provide accordingly, and wisely to apportion punishments to crimes.

II. What the *New Testament precept* is, as to the complainant himself, his duty, is to *forgive the injury* as done to himself, and no further to insist upon the punishment of it than is necessary to the public good.

Two things Christ teaches us here:

1. We must not be revengeful (*v.* 39); *I say unto you, that ye resist not evil;*—the evil person that is injurious to you. We may *avoid evil,* and may *resist* it, so far as is necessary to our own security; but we must not *render evil for evil,* must not bear a grudge, nor avenge ourselves, nor study to be even with those that have treated us unkindly, but we must go beyond them by forgiving them. The law of retaliation must be made consistent with the law of love. It will not justify us in hurting our brother to say that he began, for it is the second blow that makes the quarrel.

Three things our Saviour specifies, to show that Christians must patiently yield to those who bear hard upon them.

(1) A blow on the cheek, which is an injury to me in my body; "*Whosoever shall smite thee on thy right cheek,* which is not only a hurt, but an affront and indignity, *turn to him the other cheek.*" Bear it patiently: give not the rude man as good as he brings. Pass it by, and take no further notice of it: there are no bones broken, no great harm done, forgive it and forget it; and if proud fools think the worse of thee, and laugh at thee for it, all wise men will value and honour thee for it, as a follower of the blessed Jesus. Though this may perhaps, with some base spirits, expose us to the like affront another time, and so it is, in effect, to *turn the other cheek,* yet let not that disturb us. Perhaps, the forgiving of one injury may prevent another, when the avenging of it would but draw on another; some will be overcome by submission, who by resistance would but be the more exasperated.

(2) The loss of a coat, which is a wrong to me in my estate (*v.* 40); *If any man will sue thee at the law, and take away thy coat.* Though judges be just and circumspect, yet it is possible for bad men who make no conscience of oaths and forgeries, by course of law to force off the coat from a man's back. *Marvel not at the matter* (Eccles. v. 8), but *let him* even *take thy cloak also.* If the matter be small it is good to submit to it for peace' sake. "It will not cost thee so much to buy another cloak, as it will cost thee by course of law to recover that."

(3) The going a mile by constraint, which is a wrong to me in my liberty (*v.* 41); "*Whosoever shall compel thee to go a mile, go with him two miles.*" Say, "Therefore I will do it, for otherwise there will be a quarrel;" and it is better to serve him, than to serve thy own lusts of pride and revenge. The sum of all is, that Christians must not be litigious; small injuries must be submitted to, and no notice taken of them; and if the injury be such as requires us to seek reparation, it must be for a good end, and without thought of revenge.

2. We must be charitable and beneficent (*v.* 42); must not only do no hurt to our neighbours, but labour to do them all the good we can. (1) We must be ready to give; "*Give to him that asketh thee.* If thou hast an ability, look upon the request of the poor as giving thee an opportunity for the duty of almsgiving." Yet the affairs of our charity must be *guided with discretion,* lest we give that to the idle and unworthy, which should be given to those that are necessitous, and deserve well. What God says to us, we should be ready to say to our poor brethren, *Ask, and it shall be given you.* (2) We must be ready to lend. This is sometimes as great a piece of charity as giving; as it not only relieves the present exigence, but obliges the borrower to providence, industry, and honesty. Be easy of access to him *that would borrow*: though he be bashful, and have not confidence to make known his case and beg the favour, yet thou knowest both his need and his desire, and therefore offer him the kindness. It becomes us to be thus forward in acts of kindness, for before we call, God hears us, and *prevents us with the blessings of his goodness.*

JAMIESON, FAUSSET, BROWN

magistrate—was abused in the opposite way to the commandments of the Decalogue. While they were reduced to the level of civil enactments, this judicial regulation was held to be a warrant for taking redress into their own hands, contrary to the injunctions of the Old Testament itself (Prov. 20:22; 24:29).

39. But I say unto you, That ye resist not evil; but whosoever shall smite thee on thy right cheek, turn to him the other also—Our Lord's own meek, yet dignified bearing, when smitten rudely on the cheek (John 18:22, 23), and *not* literally presenting the other, is the best comment on these words. It is the preparedness, after one indignity, not to invite but to submit meekly to another, without retaliation, which this strong language is meant to convey.

40. And if any man will sue thee at the law, and take way thy coat—the inner garment; in pledge for a debt (Exod. 22:26, 27). **let him have thy cloak also**—the outer and more costly garment. This overcoat was not allowed to be retained over night as a pledge from the poor because they used it for a bed-covering. **41. And whosoever shall compel thee to go a mile, go with him twain**—an allusion, probably, to the practice of the Romans and some Eastern nations, who, when government despatches had to be forwarded, obliged the people not only to furnish horses and carriages, but to give personal attendance, often at great inconvenience, when required. But the thing here demanded is a readliness to submit to unreasonable demands of whatever kind, rather than raise quarrels, with all the evils resulting from them. What follows is a beautiful extension of this precept. **42. Give to him that asketh thee**—The sense of *unreasonable* asking is here implied (cf. Luke 6:30). **and from him that would borrow of thee turn not thou away**—Though the word signifies classically "to have money lent to one on security," or "with interest," yet as this was not the original sense of the word, and as usury was forbidden among the Jews (Exod. 22:25, etc.), it is doubtless simple borrowing which our Lord here means, as indeed the whole strain of the exhortation implies. This shows that such counsels as "Owe no man anything" (Rom. 13:8), are not to be taken absolutely; else the Scripture commendations of the righteous for "lending" to his necessitous brother (Ps. 37:36; 112:5; Luke 6: 37) would have no application. **turn not thou away**—a graphic expression of unfeeling refusal to relieve a brother in extremity.

ADAM CLARKE

39. *Resist not evil.* Or "the evil person." Our Lord's meaning is, "Do not repel one outrage by another." *Turn to him the other also.* That is, rather than avenge yourself, be ready to suffer patiently a repetition of the same injury. But these exhortations belong principally to those who are persecuted for righteousness' sake.

40. *And if any man will sue thee at the law.* Everywhere our blessed Lord shows the utmost disapprobation of such litigations as tended to destroy brotherly kindness and charity. It is evident He would have His followers to suffer rather the loss of all their property than to have recourse to such modes of redress at so great a risk. *Coat.* See on Luke vi. 29.

41. *Shall compel thee to go a mile, go with him twain.* This derives its meaning from reference to the Persians. The Persian messengers had the royal authority for pressing horses, ships, and even men to assist them in the business on which they were employed. We are here exhorted to patience and forgiveness: (1) when we receive in our persons all sorts of insults and affronts, v. 39; (2) when we are despoiled of our goods, v. 40; (3) when our bodies are forced to undergo all kinds of toils, vexations, and torments, v. 41. The proper way to face the injustice of man is to exercise under it meekness, gentleness, and long-suffering, without which disposition of mind no man can be happy either here or hereafter; for he that avenges himself must lose the mind of Christ, and thus suffer an injury ten thousand times greater than he can ever receive from man. Revenge at such an expense is dear indeed.

42. *Give to him that asketh thee, and from him that would borrow.* To give and lend freely to all who are in need is a general precept from which we are excused only by our inability to perform it.

A. T. ROBERTSON:

39. "Resist not him that is evil" (*me antistenai toi poneroi*). Here again it is the infinitive (second aorist active) in indirect command. But is it "the evil man" or the "evil deed"? The dative case is the same form for masculine and neuter. Weymouth puts it "not to resist a [the] wicked man"; Moffat, "not to resist an injury"; Goodspeed, "not to resist injury." The examples will go with either view. Jesus protested when smitten on the cheek (John 18:22). And Jesus denounced the Pharisees (Matt. 23) and fought the devil always. The language of Jesus is bold and picturesque and is not to be pressed too literally. Paradoxes startle and make us think. We are expected to fill in the other side of the picture. One thing certainly is meant by Jesus and that is that personal revenge is taken out of our hands, and that applies to "lynch-law." Aggressive or offensive war by nations is also condemned, but not necessarily defensive war or defense against robbery and murder. Professional pacifism may be mere cowardice.—*Word Pictures in the New Testament*

MATTHEW HENRY

Verses 43–48

We have here, lastly, an exposition of that great fundamental law of the second table, *Thou shalt love thy neighbour.*

I. See here how this law was corrupted by the comments of the Jewish teachers, *v.* 43. God said, *Thou shalt love thy neighbour;* and by *neighbour* they understood those only that they were pleased to look upon as their friends. They were willing to infer what God never designed; *Thou shalt hate thine enemy;* and they looked upon whom they pleased as their enemies. See how willing corrupt passions are to fetch countenance from the word of God, and to *take occasion by the commandment* to justify themselves.

II. See how it is cleared by the command of the Lord Jesus, who teaches us another lesson: "*But I say unto you, Love your enemies*," *v.* 44. Though men are ever so bad themselves, and carry it ever so basely towards us, yet that does not discharge us from the great debt we owe them, of love to our kind, love to our kin. It is the great duty of Christians to *love their enemies;* whilst we cannot have complacency in one that is openly wicked and profane, yet we must take notice, with pleasure, of that even in our enemies which is amiable and commendable; and love that, though they are our enemies. We must have a compassion for them, and a goodwill toward them. We are here told,

1. That we must *speak* well of them: *Bless them that curse you.* When we speak to them, we must answer their revilings with courteous and friendly words, and *not render railing for railing.* They, in whose tongues is *the law of kindness,* can give good words to those who give bad words to them.

2. That we must *do* well to them: *Do good to them that hate you,* and that will be a better proof of love than good words. Be ready to do them all the real kindness that you can, and glad of an opportunity to do it.

3. We must *pray for them*: *Pray for them that despitefully use you, and persecute you.* Christ himself was so treated. When at any time we meet with such usage, we have an opportunity of showing our conformity both to the precept and to the example of Christ, by praying for them who thus abuse us. We must pray that God will forgive them, that they may never fare the worse for anything they have done against us, and that he would make them to be at peace with us. This is *heaping coals of fire on their heads.*

We must do it,

[1] That we may be *like God our Father;* "that ye may be, may approve yourselves to be, *the children of your Father which is in heaven.*" Can we write after a better copy? God *maketh his sun to rise,* and *sendeth rain,* on *the just and unjust, v.* 45. *Sunshine* and *rain* are great blessings to the world, and they come from God. Common mercies must be valued as instances and proofs of the goodness of God, who in them shows himself a bountiful Benefactor. These gifts of common providence are dispensed indifferently to *good* and *evil, just* and *unjust.* The worst of men partake of the comforts of this life in common with others. which is an amazing instance of God's patience and bounty. The gifts of God's bounty to wicked men that are in rebellion against him, teach us to *do good to those that hate us.* Those only will be accepted as the children of God, who study to resemble him, particularly in his goodness.

[2] That we may herein *do more than others, v.* 46, 47. *First, Publicans love their friends.* Nature inclines them to it; interest directs them to it. To do good to them who do good to us, is a common piece of humanity. *Secondly,* We must therefore love our enemies, that we may exceed them. Christianity is something more than humanity. It is a serious question, and which we should frequently put to ourselves, "*What do we more than others? What excelling thing do we do?* God has done more for us, and therefore justly expects more from us than from others; but *what do we more than others?* Wherein do we live above the rate of the children of this world? We cannot expect the reward of Christians, if we rise no higher than the virtue of publicans." Those who promise themselves a reward above others must study to *do more than others.*

Our Saviour concludes this subject with this exhortation (*v.* 48), *Be ye therefore perfect, as your Father which is in heaven is perfect.* Which may be understood, 1. In general, including all those things wherein we must be *followers of God as dear children.* It is the duty of Christians to desire, and aim at, and press towards a perfection in grace and holiness. Or, 2. In this particular before mentioned, of *doing good to our enemies;* see Luke vi. 36. It is God's perfection to *forgive injuries* and to *entertain strangers,*

JAMIESON, FAUSSET, BROWN

Same Subject—Love to Enemies (vss. 43-48). **43. Ye have heard that it hath been said**—(Lev. 19:18). **Thou shalt love thy neighbour**—To this the corrupt teachers added, **and hate thine enemy**—as if the one were a legitimate inference from the other, instead of being a detestable gloss, as BENGEL indignantly calls it. LIGHTFOOT quotes some of the cursed maxims inculcated by those traditionists regarding the proper treatment of all Gentiles. No wonder that the Romans charged the Jews with hatred of the human race.

44. But I say unto you, Love your enemies—The word here used denotes *moral* love, as distinguished from the other word, which expresses *personal* affection. Usually, the former denotes "complacency in the character" of the person loved; but here it denotes the benignant, compassionate outgoings of desire for anothers' good. **bless them that curse you, do good to them that hate you, and pray for them which despitefully use you, and persecute you**—The best commentary on these matchless counsels is the bright example of Him who gave them. (See I Pet. 2:21-24; and cf. Rom. 12:20, 21; I Cor. 4:12; I Pet. 3:9). But though such precepts were never before expressed—perhaps not even conceived—with such breadth, precision, and sharpness as here, our Lord is here only the incomparable Interpreter of the law in force from the beginning; and this is the only satisfactory view of the entire strain of this discourse.

45. That ye may be the children [sons] **of your Father which is in heaven**—The meaning is, "that ye may show yourselves to be such by *resembling* Him" (cf. vs. 9 and Eph. 5:1). **for he maketh his sun**—"your Father's sun." Well might BENGEL exclaim, "Magnificent appellation!"—**to rise on the evil and on the good, and sendeth rain on the just and on the unjust**—rather (without the article) "on evil and good, and on just and unjust." When we find God's own procedure held up for imitation in the law, and much more in the prophets (Lev. 19:2; 20:26; and cf. I Pet. 1:15, 16), we may see that the principle of this surprising verse was nothing new: but the form of it certainly is that of One who spake as never man spake. **46. For if ye love them which love you, what reward have ye? do not even the publicans the same?**—The publicans, as collectors of taxes due to the Roman government, were ever on this account obnoxious to the Jews, who sat uneasy under a foreign yoke, and disliked whatever brought this unpleasantly before them. But the extortion practiced by this class made them hateful to the community, who in their current speech ranked them with "harlots." Nor does our Lord scruple to speak of them as others did, which we may be sure He never would have done if it had been calumnious. The meaning, then, is, "In loving those who love you, there is no evidence of superior principle; the worst of men will do this: even a publican will go that length." **47. And if ye salute your brethren only**—of the same nation and religion with yourselves. **what do ye more [than others]?**—what do ye uncommon or extraordinary? i.e, wherein do ye *excel*? **do not even the publicans so?**—The true reading here appears to be, "Do not even the heathens the same?" Cf. ch. 18:17, where the excommunicated person is said to be "as an heathen man and a publican." **48. Be ye therefore**—rather, "Ye shall therefore be," or "Ye are therefore to be," as My disciples and in My kingdom—**perfect,** or complete. Manifestly, our Lord here speaks, not of *degrees* of excellence, but of the *kind* of excellence which was to distinguish His disciples and characterize His kingdom. When therefore He adds,

ADAM CLARKE

43. *Thou shalt love thy neighbour, and hate thine enemy.* You shall love your friend and hate your enemy. This was certainly the meaning which the Jews put on it; for neighbor, with them, implied those of the Jewish race, and all others were considered by them as natural enemies.

44. *Love your enemies.* This is the most sublime piece of morality ever given to man. But who can obey it? None but he who has the mind of Christ. *Bless them that curse you.* "Give them good words" for their bad words. *Do good to them that hate you.* Give your enemy every proof that you love him. We must not love in tongue, but in deed and in truth. *Pray for them which despitefully use you.* Those who constantly harass and slander you. *Pray for them.* I cannot change that wicked man's heart, and while it is unchanged he will continue to harass me, God alone can change it. Then I must implore Him to do that which will at once secure the man's salvation and contribute so much to my own peace. *And persecute you.* Those who "press hard on" and "pursue" you with hatred and malice accompanied with repeated acts of enmity. In this verse our Lord shows us that a man may be our enemy in *three* different ways: (1) in his heart, by hatred; (2) in his words, by cursing or using direful imprecations against us; (3) in his actions, by continually harassing and abusing us. He shows us also how we are to behave to those. The hatred of the first we are to meet with love. The cursings or evil words of the second we are to meet with good words and blessings. And the repeated injurious acts of the third we are to meet with continual prayer to God for the man's salvation.

45. *That ye may be the children of your Father.* As a man's child is called his, because a partaker of his own nature, so a holy person is said to be a child of God, because he is a partaker of the divine nature. If God had not loved us while we were His enemies, we could never have become His children, and we shall cease to be such as soon as we cease to imitate Him.

46. *For if ye love them which love you.* He who loves only his friends does nothing for God's sake. He who loves for the sake of pleasure or interest pays himself. God has no enemy which He hates but sin; we should have no other. *The publicans.* That is, "taxgatherers." A farmer or collector of the taxes or public revenues. This class of men were detestable among the Romans, the Greeks, and the Jews for their intolerable rapacity and avarice. They were abhorred in an especial manner by the Jews, to whom the Roman government was odious. These, assisting in collecting the Roman tribute, were considered as betrayers of the liberties of their country, and abettors of those who enslaved it.

47. *And if ye salute your brethren only.* Instead of *brethren,* upwards of one hundred MSS., and several of them of great authority and antiquity, have "friends." As *brother* is more conformable to the Jewish mode of address, it should be retained in the text.

48. *Be ye therefore perfect, even as your Father.* God himself is the only Pattern of the perfection which He recommends to His children. The words are very emphatic: "Ye shall be therefore *perfect*"—you shall be filled with the spirit of that God whose name is Mercy, and whose nature is love. These words of our Lord

MATTHEW HENRY

and to do good to the evil and unthankful, and it will be ours to be like him. We that owe *so much*, that owe *our all*, to the divine bounty, ought to copy it out as well as we can.

JAMIESON, FAUSSET, BROWN

even as your Father which is in heaven is perfect, He refers to that fullorbed glorious completeness which is in the great Divine Model, "their Father which is in heaven."

ADAM CLARKE

include both a *command* and a *promise*. Can we be fully saved from sin in this world? This is an important question, to which this text gives a satisfactory answer: "Ye shall be perfect, as your Father, who is in heaven, is perfect." As in His infinite nature there is no sin, nothing but goodness and love, so in your finite nature there shall dwell no sin, for the law of the spirit of life in Christ Jesus shall make you free from the law of sin and death, Rom. viii. 2. God shall live in, fill, and rule your hearts; and, in what He fills and influences, neither Satan nor sin can have any part. But where is the person thus saved? Wherever he is found who loves God with all his heart, soul, mind, and strength, and his neighbor as himself.

MATTHEW HENRY

CHAPTER 6

Verses 1–4

We must watch against hypocrisy, which was the leaven of the Pharisees, as well as against their doctrine, Luke xii. 1. *Almsgiving, prayer*, and *fasting*, are three great Christian duties. Thus we must not only *depart from evil*, but *do good*, and do it well, and so *dwell for evermore*.

We are cautioned against hypocrisy in giving alms. *Take heed* of it. It is a subtle sin; vain-glory insinuates itself into what we do ere we are aware. It is a sin we are in *great danger by*. Take heed of hypocrisy, for if it reign in you, it will ruin you. It is the dead fly that spoils the whole box of precious ointment.

Two things are here supposed,

I. The *giving of alms* is a great duty, and a duty which all the disciples of Christ, according to their ability, must abound in. The Jews called the *poor's box* the *box of righteousness*. It is true, our alms-deeds do not deserve heaven; but it is as true that we cannot go to heaven without them. Christ here takes it for granted that his disciples *give alms*, nor will he own those that do not.

II. That it is such a duty as has a great reward attending it, which is lost if it be done in hypocrisy. It shall be recompensed in the resurrection of the just (Luke xiv. 14), in *eternal riches*.

The riches you impart form the only wealth you will always retain.

1. What was the *practice of the hypocrites* about this duty. They did it indeed, but not from any principle of obedience to God, or love to man, but in pride and vain-glory; not in compassion to the poor, but purely for ostentation. Pursuant to this intention, they chose to give their alms *in the synagogues, and in the streets*, where there was the greatest concourse of people to observe them. Not that it is unlawful to give alms *when men see us*; we may do it, we must do it, but not *that men may see us*. The hypocrites, if they gave alms at their own houses, *sounded a trumpet*, to proclaim their charity, and to have that taken notice of and made the subject of discourse.

Now the doom that Christ passes upon this is very observable: *Verily I say unto you, they have their reward*. Two words in it make it a threatening.

(1) It is a reward, but it is *their* reward; not the reward which God promises to them that do good, but the reward which they promise themselves, and a poor reward it is; they did it to be *seen of men*, and they *are* seen of men.

(2) It is a reward, that it is a *present reward*, they *have* it; and there is none reserved for them in the future state. They now have all that they are likely to have from God. It signifies a *receipt in full*. The world is but for *provision* to the saints, it is their spending-money; but it is *pay* to hypocrites, it is their portion.

2. What is the *precept of our Lord Jesus* about it, *v.* 3, 4. "*Let not thy left hand know what thy right hand doeth* when thou givest alms." The giving of alms with the *right hand*, intimates readiness to it and resolution in it; do it dexterously. But, "whatever kindness thy right hand doeth to the poor, *let not thy left hand know it*; conceal it as much as possible; industriously keep it private. Do it because it is a good work, not because it will give thee a good name." It is intimated, (1) That we must not let *others* know what we do. (2) That we must not observe it too much *ourselves*. Self-conceit and self-complacency, and an adoring of our own shadow, are branches of pride. We find those had their good works remembered to their honour, who had themselves forgotten them: *When saw we thee an hungered, or athirst?*

3. What is the *promise to those who are thus sincere*

JAMIESON, FAUSSET, BROWN

CHAPTER 6

SERMON ON THE MOUNT—*continued*. Vss. 1-18. FURTHER ILLUSTRATION OF THE RIGHTEOUSNESS OF THE KINGDOM—ITS UNOSTENTATIOUSNESS. *General Caution against Ostentation in Religious Duties* (vs. 1). **1. Take heed that ye do not your alms**—But the true reading seems clearly to be "your righteousness." The external authority for both readings is pretty nearly equal; but internal evidence is decidedly in favor of "righteousness." The subject of the second verse being "almsgiving" that word—so like the other in Greek—might easily be substituted for it by the copyist: whereas the opposite would not be so likely. But it is still more in favor of "righteousness," that if we so read the first verse, it then becomes a general heading for this whole section of the discourse, inculcating unostentatiousness in *all* deeds of righteousness—Almsgiving, Prayer, and Fasting being, in that case, but selected examples of this righteousness; whereas, if we read, "Do not your *alms* . . . ", this first verse will have no reference but to that one point. By "righteousness," in this case, we are to understand that same righteousness of the kingdom of heaven, whose leading features—in opposition to traditional perversions of it—it is the great object of this discourse to open up: that righteousness of which the Lord says, "Except your righteousness shall exceed the righteousness of the scribes and Pharisees, ye shall in no case enter into the kingdom of heaven" (ch. 5:20). To "*do*" this righteousness, was an old and well-understood expression. Thus, "Blessed is he that doeth righteousness at all times" (Ps. 106:3). It refers to the *actings* of righteousness in the life—the outgoings of the gracious nature—of which our Lord afterwards said to His disciples, "Herein is My Father glorified, that ye bear much fruit; so shall ye be My disciples" (John 15:8). **before men, to be seen of them**—with the view or intention of being beheld of them. See the same expression in ch. 5:28. True, He had required them to let their light so shine before men that they might see their good works, and glorify their Father which is in heaven (ch. 5:16). But this is quite consistent with not making a display of our righteousness for self-glorification. In fact, the doing of the former necessarily implies our *not* doing the latter. **otherwise ye have no reward of your Father which is in heaven**—When all duty is done to God—as primarily enjoining and finally judging of it—He will take care that it be duly recognized; but when done purely for ostentation, God cannot own it, nor is His judgment of it even thought of—God accepts only what is done to Himself. So much for the general principle. Now follow three illustrations of it.

Almsgiving (vss. 2-4). **2. Therefore, when thou doest thine alms, do not sound a trumpet before thee**—The expression is to be taken figuratively for *blazoning* it. Hence our expression to "trumpet." **as the hypocrites do**—This word—of such frequent occurrence in Scripture, signifying primarily "one who acts a part"—denotes one who either *pretends* to be what he is not (as here), or *dissembles* what he really is (as in Luke 12:1, 2). **in the synagogues and in the streets**—the places of religious and secular resort. **that they may have glory of men. Verily I say unto you**—In such august expressions, it is the Lawgiver and Judge Himself that we hear speaking to us. **They have their reward**—All they wanted was human applause, and they have it—and with it, all they will ever get. **3. But when thou doest alms, let not thy left hand know what thy right hand doeth**—So far from making a display of it, dwell not on it even in thine own thoughts, lest it minister to spiritual pride.

ADAM CLARKE

CHAPTER 6

1. *That ye do not your alms.* "Perform not your acts of righteousness"—such as almsgiving, fasting, and prayer, mentioned immediately after. "Righteousness" was a common word for *alms* among the Jews. Dr. Lightfoot shows that it was thus commonly used among the Jewish writers: "It is questioned," says he, "whether *Matthew* writ *alms* or *righteousness*. I answer: That our Saviour certainly said *righteousness*, I make no doubt at all; but that that word could not be otherwise understood by the common people than of *alms*, there is as little doubt to be made."

Before men. Our Lord does not forbid public almsgiving, fasting, and prayer, but simply censures those vain and hypocritical persons who do these things publicly in order that they may be seen of men, and receive from them the reputation of saints.

2. *Therefore when thou doest thine alms.* In the first verse the exhortation is general: "Take heed." In this verse the address is pointed—*thou. Do not sound a trumpet.* It may be that this was literally practiced among the Pharisees, who seemed to live on the public esteem, and were excessively self-righteous and vain. Having something to distribute by way of alms, it is very probable they caused this to be published by blowing a trumpet or horn, under pretense of collecting the poor, though with no other design than to gratify their own ambition. It must be granted that in the Jewish writings there is no such practice referred to. *They have their reward.* That is, the honor and esteem of men, which they sought. God is under no obligation to them—they did nothing with an eye to His glory, and from Him they can expect no recompense. They had their recompense in this life, and could expect none in the world to come.

3. *Let not thy left hand know.* In many cases, works of charity must be hidden from even our nearest relatives, who, if they knew, would hinder us from doing what God has given us power and inclination to perform. We must go even further and conceal them as far as is possible from ourselves, by not thinking of them, or eyeing them with complacency.

MATTHEW HENRY

and humble in their alms-giving. Let *thine alms be in secret*, and then *thy Father who seeth in secret* will observe them. When we take least notice of our good deeds ourselves, God takes most notice of them. It is a comfort to sincere Christians, that God *sees in secret*. Observe how emphatically it is expressed; *himself shall reward*, he will himself be the Rewarder. Nay, he will *himself be the Reward* (Gen. xv. 1), thine *exceeding great reward*. He will reward thee as thy Father, not as a master who gives his servant just what he earns and no more, but as a father who gives abundantly more, and without stint, to his son that serves him. If the work be not open, the reward shall, and that is better.

Verses 5-8

When thou prayest (*v.* 5). It is taken for granted that all the disciples of Christ *pray*. You may as soon find a living man that does not breathe, as a living Christian that does not pray. If prayerless, then graceless.

Now there were two great faults they were guilty of in prayer—vain-glory (*v.* 5, 6); and vain repetitions, *v.* 7, 8.

I. We must not be *proud* and *vain-glorious* in prayer, nor aim at the praise of men. And here observe,

1. What was the *way and practice of the hypocrites*. In all their exercises of devotion, it was plain, the chief thing they aimed at was to be commended by their neighbours. When they seemed to *soar upwards* in prayer then their eye was *downwards* upon this as their *prey*. Observe,

(1) What the *places* were which they chose for their devotion; they prayed in the *synagogues*, which were indeed proper places for public prayer, but not for personal. They prayed in *the corners of the streets*, the broad streets (so the word signifies), which were most frequented. It was to cause themselves to be taken notice of.

(2) The *posture* they used in prayer; they prayed standing; this is a lawful and proper posture for prayer, but kneeling being the more humble and reverent gesture, their standing seemed to savour of pride and confidence in themselves (Luke xviii. 11).

(3) Their *pride* in choosing those public places, which is expressed in two things: [1] They *love* to pray there. They did not love prayer for its own sake, but they loved it when it gave them an opportunity of making themselves noticed. [2] It is that they may be *seen of men*; not that God might accept them, but that men might admire and applaud them.

(4) The *product* of all this, *they have their reward*; they have all the recompence they must ever expect from God for their service, and a poor recompence it is. What will it avail us to have the good word of our fellow-servants, if our Master do not say, *Well done?* They did it to be *seen of men*, and they are so; and much good may it do them. What passes between God and our own souls must be out of sight. Public places are not proper for private solemn prayer.

2. What is the *will of Jesus Christ* in opposition to this. *Thou, when thou prayest*, do so and so (*v.* 6). Personal prayer is here supposed to be the duty and practice of all Christ's disciples.

Observe, (1) The directions here given about it.

[1] Instead of praying in *the synagogues* and in the *corners of the streets*, *enter into thy closet*, into some place of privacy and retirement. Isaac went into the field (Gen. xxiv. 63), Christ to a mountain, Peter to the house-top. No place amiss in point of ceremony, if it do but answer the end. Yet if the circumstances be such that we cannot possibly avoid being taken notice of, we must not therefore neglect the duty, lest the omission be a greater scandal than the observation of it.

[2] Instead of doing it to be *seen of men*, *pray to thy Father who is in secret*. The Pharisees prayed rather to men than to God. Do you pray to God, and let that be enough for thee. Pray to him as a Father, as thy Father, ready to hear and answer, graciously inclined to pity, help, and succour thee. Pray to thy Father *who is in secret*. He is there in thy closet when no one else is there; there especially nigh to thee in what thou *callest upon him for*.

(2) The encouragements here given us to it.

[1] Thy Father *seeth in secret*. There is not a secret sudden breathing after God, but he observes it.

[2] He *will reward thee openly*; they have their reward that do it openly, and thou shalt not lose thine for thy doing it in secret. It is called a *reward*, but it is *of grace*, not *of debt*. Sometimes secret prayers are rewarded openly in this world by signal answers to them, which manifests God's praying people in the consciences of their adversaries.

II. We must not *use vain repetitions* in prayer, *v.* 7, 8. Though the life of prayer lies in *lifting up the*

JAMIESON, FAUSSET, BROWN

4. That thine alms may be in secret, and thy Father which seeth in secret [himself] shall reward thee openly—The word "Himself" appears to be an unauthorized addition to the text, which the sense no doubt suggested. (See I Tim. 5:25; Rom. 2:16; I Cor. 4:5).

Prayer (vss. 5, 6). **5. And when thou prayest, thou shalt** [or, preferably, when ye pray ye shall] **not be as the hypocrites are: for they love to pray standing in the synagogues and in the corners of the streets** [see on vs. 2], **that they may be seen of men.**

Verily I say unto you, They have . . . The *standing* posture in prayer was the ancient practice, alike in the Jewish and in the early Christian Church. But of course this conspicuous posture opened the way for the ostentatious.

6. But thou, when thou prayest, enter into thy closet [a place of retirement] **and when thou hast shut thy door, pray to thy Father which is in secret; and thy Father which seeth in secret shall reward thee openly**—Of course, it is not the simple publicity of prayer which is here condemned. It may be offered in any circumstances, however open, if not prompted by the spirit of ostentation, but dictated by the great ends of prayer itself. It is the *retiring* character of true prayer which is here taught.

ADAM CLARKE

4. *Which seeth in secret.* We should ever remember that the eye of the Lord is upon us, and that He sees not only the act, but also every motive that led to it.

5. *And when thou prayest.* Signifies "to pour out prayers or vows," probably alluding to the offerings or libations which were poured out before, or on, the altar. A proper idea of prayer is a pouring out of the soul unto God, as a freewill offering (solemnly and eternally dedicated to Him), accompanied with the most earnest desire that it may know, love, and serve Him alone. He that comes thus to God will ever be heard and blessed. Prayer is the language of dependence; he who prays not is endeavoring to live independently of God. This was the first curse, and continues to be the great curse of mankind. *Thou shalt not be as the hypocrites.* Properly a stage-player who acts under a mask, personating a character different from his own; a counterfeit, a dissembler; one who would be thought to be different from what he really is. A person who wishes to be taken for a follower of God but who has nothing of religion except the outside.

Love to pray standing in the synagogues and in the corners of the streets. The Jewish phylacterical prayers were long, and the canonical hours obliged them to repeat these prayers wherever they happened to be; and the Pharisees, who were full of vainglory, contrived to be overtaken in the streets at the canonical hour, that they might be seen by the people and be applauded for their great and conscientious piety.

6. *But thou, when thou prayest.* Prayer is the most secret intercourse of the soul with God, and as it were the conversation of one heart with another. The world is too profane and treacherous to be of the secret. We must *shut the door* against it; endeavor to forget it, with all the affairs which busy and amuse it. Prayer requires retirement, at least of the heart; for this may be fitly termed the *closet* in the house of God, which house the body of every real Christian is, I Cor. iii. 16.

MATTHEW HENRY

soul and pouring out the heart, yet there is some interest which words have in prayer, especially in joint prayer; for in that, words are necessary. *Use not vain repetitions*, either alone or with others. Now observe,

1. What the *fault* is that is here reproved and condemned; it is making a mere lip-labour of the duty of prayer. (1) *Vain repetitions*—tautology. It is not all repetition in prayer that is here condemned, but vain repetitions. Christ himself prayed, saying the same words (*ch.* xxvi. 44), out of a more than ordinary fervour and zeal, Luke xxii. 44. When we would fain say much, but cannot say much to the purpose; this is displeasing to God and all wise men. (2) *Much speaking*, an affectation of prolixity in prayer, because men love to *hear themselves talk*. Not that all long prayers are forbidden; Christ prayed all night, Luke vi. 12. It is not much *praying* that is condemned; no, we are bid to *pray always*, but much *speaking*; the danger of this error is when we only *say* our prayers, not when we *pray* them.

2. What reasons are given against this.

(1) This is the way of the heathen, *as the heathen do*; and it ill becomes Christians to worship their God as the Gentiles worship theirs. Thinking God altogether such a one as themselves, they thought he needed many words to make him understand what was said to him, or to bring him to comply with their requests. *Lip-labour* in prayer, though ever so well *laboured*, if that be all, is but *lost labour*.

(2) "It need not be your way, *for your Father* in heaven *knoweth what things ye have need of before ye ask him*, and therefore there is no occasion for such abundance of words. It does not follow that therefore ye need not pray; for God requires you by prayer to own your need of him. Open your case, and pour out your hearts before him, and then leave it with him." [1] The God we pray to is our Father. Children do not make long speeches to their parents when they want anything. They need not say many words, that are taught by the Spirit of adoption to say that one aright, *Abba Father*. [2] He is a Father that knows our case and knows our wants better than we do ourselves. *He knows what things we have need of.* He often gives *before we call* (Isa. lxv. 24), and *more than we ask for* (Eph. iii. 20). We need not be long, nor use many words in representing our case; God knows it better than we can tell him, only he will know it *from us* (*what will ye that I should do unto you?*). The most powerful intercessions are those which are made with *groanings that cannot be uttered*, Rom. viii. 26.

Verses 9–15

Because we know not what to pray for as we ought, he here helps our infirmities, by putting words into our mouths; *after this manner therefore pray ye, v.* 9. Not that we are tied up to the use of this form only, or of this always, as if this were necessary to the consecrating of our other prayers; we are here bid to pray after this manner, with these words, or to this effect. Yet, without doubt, it is very good to use it as a form, and it is a pledge of the communion of saints, it having been used by the church in all ages. It is used acceptably no further than it is used with understanding and without vain repetition.

The Lord's prayer (as indeed every prayer) is a letter sent from earth to heaven. Here is the inscription of the letter, the person to whom it is directed, *our Father*; the place where, *in heaven*; the contents of it in several errands of request; the close, *for thine is the kingdom*; the seal, *Amen*; and if you will, the date, too, *this day*.

JAMIESON, FAUSSET, BROWN

Supplementary Directions, and Model Prayer (vss. 7-15). **7. But when ye pray, use not vain repetitions**—"Babble not" would be a better rendering, both for the form of the word—which in both languages is intended to imitate the sound—and for the sense, which expresses not so much the repetition of the same words as a senseless multiplication of them; as appears from what follows. **as the heathen do: for they think that they shall be heard for their much speaking**—This method of heathen devotion is still observed by Hindoo and Mohammedan devotees. With the Jews, says LIGHTFOOT, it was a maxim, that "Every one who multiplies prayer is heard." In the Church of Rome, not only is it carried to a shameless extent, but, as THOLUCK justly observes, the very prayer which our Lord gave as an antidote to vain repetitions is the most abused to this superstitious end; the number of times it is repeated counting for so much more merit. Is not this just that characteristic feature of heathen devotion which our Lord here condemns? But praying much, and using at times the same words, is *not* here condemned, and has the example of our Lord Himself in its favor. **8. Be not ye therefore like unto them: for your Father knoweth what things ye have need of before ye ask him**—and so needs not to be *informed* of our wants, any more than to be *roused* to attend to them by our incessant speaking. What a view of God is here given, in sharp contrast with the gods of the heathen! But let it be carefully noted that it is not as *the general Father of mankind* that our Lord says, "Your Father" knoweth what ye need before ye ask it; for it is not men, as such, that He is addressing in this discourse, but His own disciples—the poor in spirit, the mourners, the meek, hungry and thirsty souls, the merciful, the pure in heart, the peacemakers, who allow themselves to have all manner of evil said against them for the Son of man's sake—in short, the newborn children of God, who, making their Father's interests their own, are here assured that their Father, in return, makes their interests His, and needs neither to be told nor to be reminded of their wants. Yet He will have His children pray to Him, and links all His promised supplies to their petitions for them; thus encouraging us to draw near and keep near to Him, to talk and walk with Him, to open our every case to Him, and assure ourselves that thus asking we shall receive—thus seeking we shall find—thus knocking it shall be opened to us.

9. After this manner [more simply "Thus"] **therefore pray ye**—The "ye" is emphatic here, in contrast with the heathen prayers. That this matchless prayer was given not only as a *model*, but as a *form*, might be concluded from its very nature. Did it consist only of hints or directions for prayer, it could only be used as a directory; but seeing it is an actual prayer—designed, indeed, to show how much real prayer could be compressed into the fewest words, but still, as a prayer, only the more incomparable for that—it is strange that there should be a doubt whether we ought to pray that very prayer. Surely the words with which it is introduced, in the second utterance and varied form of it which we have in Luke 11:2, ought to set this at rest: "When ye pray, *say*, Our Father." Nevertheless, since the second form of it varies considerably from the first, and since no example of its actual use, or express quotation of its phraseology, occurs in the sequel of the New Testament, we are to guard against a superstitious use of it. How early this began to appear in the church services, and to what extent it was afterwards carried, is known to every one versed in Church History. Nor has the spirit which bred this abuse quite departed from some branches of the Protestant Church, though the opposite and equally condemnable extreme is to be found in other branches of it.

Model Prayer (vss. 9-13). According to the Latin fathers and the Lutheran Church, the petitions of the Lord's Prayer are *seven* in number; according to the Greek fathers, the Reformed Church and the Westminster divines, they are only *six;* the two last being regarded—we think, less correctly—as one. The first three petitions have to do exclusively with God: "*Thy* name be hallowed"—"*Thy* kingdom come"—"*Thy* will be done." And they occur in a *descending* scale—from Himself down to the manifestation of Himself in His kingdom; and from His kingdom to the entire subjection of its subjects, or the complete doing of His will. The remaining four petitions have to do with OURSELVES: "Give *us*

ADAM CLARKE

7. *Use not vain repetitions.* Prayer requires more of the heart than of the tongue. The eloquence of prayer consists in the fervency of desire and the simplicity of faith. Our trust and confidence ought to proceed from that which God is able to do in us, and not from that which we can say to Him.

8. *Your Father knoweth what things ye have need of.* Prayer is not designed to inform God, but to give man a sight of his misery; to humble his heart, to excite his desire, to inflame his faith, to animate his hope, to raise his soul from earth to heaven, and to put him in mind that there is his Father, his country, and inheritance. In the preceding verses we may see three faults which our Lord commands us to avoid in prayer: (1) Hypocrisy. *Be not as the hypocrites,* v. 5. (2) Dissipation. *Enter into thy closet,* v. 6. (3) Much speaking, or unmeaning repetition. *Be not like the heathen,* v. 7.

9. *After this manner therefore pray ye.* **Forms** of prayer were frequent among the Jews, and every public teacher gave one to his disciples. Some forms were drawn out to a considerable length, and from these abridgments were made. To the latter sort the following prayer properly belongs, and consequently, besides its own very important use, it is a plan for a more extended devotion.

MATTHEW HENRY

I. *The preface, Our Father who art in heaven. Our Father.* Intimating, that we must pray, not only alone and for ourselves, but with and for others. We are here taught *to whom to pray*, to God only, and not to saints and angels. We are taught how to address ourselves to God, and what title to give him, that which speaks him rather beneficent than magnificent, for we are to come boldly to the throne of grace.

1. We must address ourselves to him as *our Father*, and must call him so. Nothing more pleasing to God, nor pleasant, to ourselves, than to call God *Father*. Christ in prayer mostly called God *Father*. If he be our Father, he will pity us under our weaknesses and infirmities (Ps. ciii. 13), will spare us (Mal. iii. 17), will make the best of our performances, though very defective, will deny us nothing that is good for us, Luke xi. 11-13. When we come repenting of our sins, we must eye God as a Father, as the prodigal did (Luke xv. 18), as a loving, gracious, reconciled Father in Christ.

2. As our Father *in heaven*: so in heaven as to be everywhere else, for the heaven cannot contain him; yet so in heaven as there to manifest his glory, for it is his throne (Ps. ciii. 19), and it is to believers a throne of grace: thitherward we must direct our prayers. Thence he has a full and clear view of all our wants and burdens and desires, and all our infirmities. He is not only, as a Father, willing to help us, but as a heavenly Father, able to help us, able to do great things for us, more than we can ask or think; he has wherewith to supply our needs, for every good gift is from above. He is a Father, and therefore we may come to him with boldness, but a Father in heaven, and therefore we must come with reverence. By prayer, we send before us thither, where we profess to be going.

II. *The petitions*, and those are six; the three first relating more immediately to God and his honour, the three last to our own concerns. The method of this prayer teaches us to seek first the *kingdom of God and his righteousness*, and then to hope that *other things shall be added*.

1. *Hallowed be thy name.* (1) We give glory to God. We should give glory to God, before we expect to receive mercy and grace from him. Let him have the praise of his perfections, and then let us have the benefit of them. (2) We fix our end, that God may be glorified; all our other requests must be in subordination to this, and in pursuance of it. "*Father, glorify thyself* in giving me my daily bread and pardoning my sins," &c. Since all is of him and through him, all must be to him and for him. In prayer our thoughts and affections should be carried out most to the glory of God. "Do so and so for me, *for the glory of thy name*, and as far as is for the glory of it." (3) We desire and pray that the name of God, that is, God himself, in all that whereby he has made himself known, may be sanctified and glorified both by us and others, and especially by himself. "Father, let thy name be glorified as a Father, and a Father in heaven; glorify thy goodness and thy highness, thy majesty and mercy.

2. *Thy kingdom come.* This petition has plainly a reference to the doctrine which Christ preached at this time, *the kingdom of heaven is at hand.* The kingdom of your Father, who is in heaven, this is at hand, pray that it may come. We should turn the word we hear into prayer, our hearts should echo to it; does Christ promise, *surely I come quickly?* our hearts should answer, *Even so, come.* What God has promised we must pray for; for promises are given, not to supersede, but to quicken and encourage prayer.

JAMIESON, FAUSSET, BROWN

our daily bread"—"Forgive *us* our debts"—"Lead *us* not into temptation"—"Deliver *us* from evil." But these latter petitions occur in an *ascending* scale—from the bodily wants of every day up to our final deliverance from all evil.

Invocation: **Our Father which art in heaven.** In the former clause we express His nearness to us; in the latter, His distance from us. (See Eccles. 5:2; Isa. 66:1). Holy, loving familiarity suggests the one; awful reverence the other. In calling Him "Father" we express a relationship we have all known and felt surrounding us even from our infancy; but in calling Him our Father "who art in heaven," we contrast Him with the fathers we all have here below, and so raise our souls to that "heaven" where He dwells, and that Majesty and Glory which are there as in their proper home. These first words of the Lord's Prayer—this invocation with which it opens—what a brightness and warmth does it throw over the whole prayer, and into what a serene region does it introduce the praying believer, the child of God, as he thus approaches Him! It is true that the paternal relationship of God to His people is by no means strange to the Old Testament. (See Deut. 32:6; Ps. 103: 13; Isa. 63:16; Jer. 3:4, 19; Mal. 1:6; 2:10.) But these are only glimpses—the "back parts" (Exod. 33:23), if we may so say, in comparison with the "open face" of our Father revealed in Jesus. (See on II Cor. 3:18). Nor is it too much to say, that the view which our Lord gives, throughout this His very first lengthened discourse, of "our Father in heaven," beggars all that was ever taught, even in God's own Word, or conceived before by His saints, on this subject.

First Petition: **Hallowed be**—i.e., "Be held in reverence"; *regarded* and *treated* as holy. **thy name**—God's name means "Himself as revealed and manifested." Everywhere in Scripture God defines and marks off the faith and love and reverence and obedience He will have from men by the disclosures which He makes to them of what He is; both to shut out false conceptions of Him, and to make all their devotion take the shape and hue of His own teaching. Too much attention cannot be paid to this.

Second Petition: **10. Thy kingdom come**—The kingdom of God is that moral and spiritual kingdom which the God of grace is setting up in this fallen world, whose subjects consist of as many as have been brought into hearty subjection to His gracious scepter, and of which His Son Jesus is the glorious Head. In the inward reality of it, this kingdom existed ever since there were men who "walked with God" (Gen. 5:24), and "waited for His salvation" (Gen. 49:18); who were "continually with Him, holden by His right hand" (Ps. 73:23), and who, even in the valley of the shadow of death, feared no evil when He was with them (Ps. 23:4). When Messiah Himself appeared, it was, as a visible kingdom, "at hand." His death laid the deep foundations of it. His ascension on high, "leading captivity captive and receiving gifts for men, yea, for the rebellious, that the Lord God might dwell among them," and the Pentecostal effusion of the Spirit, by which those gifts for men descended upon the rebellious, and the Lord God was beheld, in the persons of thousands upon thousands, "dwelling" among men—was a glorious "coming" of this kingdom. But it is still to come, and this petition, "Thy kingdom come," must not cease to ascend so long as one subject of it remains to be brought in. But does not this prayer stretch further forward—to

ADAM CLARKE

Our Father. It was a maxim of the Jews that a man should not pray alone, but join with the church; by which they particularly meant that he should, whether alone or with the synagogue, use the plural number as comprehending all the followers of God. The word *Father*, placed here at the beginning of this prayer, includes two grand ideas which should serve as a foundation to all our petitions: (1) That tender and respectful love which we should feel for God, such as that which children feel for their fathers; (2) That strong confidence in God's love to us, such as fathers have for their children. Thus all the petitions in this prayer stand in strictest reference to the word *Father*, the first three referring to the love we have for God, and the last three to that confidence which we have in the love He bears to us.

Which art in heaven. The phrase, *Our Father which art in heaven* was very common among the ancient Jews, and was used by them precisely in the same sense as it is used here by our Lord. This phrase in the Scriptures seems used to express: (1) His omnipresence. "The . . . heaven of heavens cannot contain thee," 1 Kings viii. 27. (2) His majesty and dominion over His creatures. "Art not thou God in heaven? and rulest not thou over all the kingdoms of the heathen?" 2 Chron. xx. 6 (3) His power and might. "Art not thou God in heaven? . . . and in thine hand is there not power and might, so that none is able to withstand thee?" 2 Chron. xx. 6 (4) His omniscience. "The Lord's throne is in heaven: his eyes behold, his eyelids try, the children of men," Ps. xi. 4. (5) His infinite purity and holiness. Thou art "the high and lofty One that inhabiteth eternity, whose name is Holy," Isa. lvii. 15.

Hallowed. Hagiazo from a negative, and *ge, the earth*, a thing *separated from the earth*, or from earthly purposes and employments. As the word *sanctified* or *hallowed*, in Scripture, is frequently used for the consecration of a thing or person to a holy use or office, as the Levites, firstborn, Tabernacle, Temple, and their utensils, which were all set apart from every earthly, common, or profane use, and employed wholly in the service of God, so the Divine Majesty may be said to be sanctified by us, in analogy to those things, viz., when we separate Him from, and in our conceptions and desires exalt Him above, earth and all things. *Thy name.* That is, God himself, with all the attributes of His divine nature—His power, wisdom, justice, mercy. We hallow God's name: (1) with our *lips*, when all our conversation is holy, and we speak of those things which are meet to minister grace to the hearers; (2) in our *thoughts*, when we suppress every rising evil, and have our tempers regulated by His grace and Spirit; (3) in our *lives*, when we begin, continue, and end our works to His glory; (4) in our *families*, when we endeavor to bring up our *children* in the discipline and admonition of the Lord; (5) in a particular *calling* or *business*, when we separate the falsity, deception, and lying, commonly practiced, from it, buying and selling as in the sight of the holy and just God.

10. *Thy kingdom come.* The ancient Jews scrupled not to say: "He prays not at all, in whose prayers there is no mention of the kingdom of God."

MATTHEW HENRY

3. *Thy will be done in earth as it is in heaven.* We pray that God's kingdom being come, we and others may be brought into obedience to all the laws and ordinances of it. We make Christ but a titular Prince, if we call him King, and do not do his will: having prayed that he may rule us, we pray that we may in everything be ruled by him. (1) The thing prayed for, *thy will be done.* In this sense Christ prayed, *not my will, but thine be done.* "Enable me to do what is pleasing to thee; give me that grace that is necessary to the right knowledge of thy will, and an acceptable obedience to it, that we may neither displease God in anything we do nor be displeased at anything God does." (2) The pattern of it, that it may *be done on earth* (where our work must be done, or it never will be done), *as it is done in heaven.* We pray that earth may be made more like heaven by the observance of God's will.

4. *Give us this day our daily bread.* Because our natural being is necessary to our spiritual well-being in this world, therefore, after the things of God's glory, kingdom, and will, we pray for the necessary supports and comforts of this present life.

Every word here has a lesson in it: (1) We ask for *bread*; not dainties, not superfluities; that which is wholesome. (2) We ask for *our* bread; that teaches us honesty and industry. (3) We ask for our *daily* bread; which teaches us not to *take thought for the morrow* (*v.* 34), but constantly to depend upon divine Providence. (4) We beg of God to *give* it us. The greatest of men must be beholden to the mercy of God for their *daily bread,* (5) We pray, "Give it to us; not to me only, but to others in common with me." This teaches us charity, and a compassionate concern for the poor and needy. (6) We pray that God would give it us *this day*; which teaches us to renew the desire of our souls toward God, as the wants of our bodies are renewed. We could as well go a day without meat, as without prayer.

5. *And forgive us our debts, as we forgive our debtors.* This is connected with the former. *Our daily bread* does but feed us *as lambs for the slaughter*, if our sins be not pardoned. It intimates, likewise, that we must pray for daily *pardon*, as duly as we pray for daily *bread.*

(1) A petition; *Father in heaven forgive us our debts,* our debts to thee. Our sins are our debts; there is a debt of duty, which, as creatures, we owe to our Creator; we do not pray to be discharged from that, but upon the non-payment of that there arises a debt of punishment. Our hearts' desire and prayer to our heavenly Father every day should be, that he would *forgive us our debts*; that we may be discharged and have the comfort of it.

JAMIESON, FAUSSET, BROWN

"the glory to be revealed," or that stage of the kingdom called "the everlasting kingdom of our Lord and Saviour Jesus Christ" (II Peter 1:11)? Not directly, perhaps, since the petition that follows this—"Thy will be done in earth, as it is in heaven"—would then bring us back to this present state of imperfection. Still, the mind refuses to be so bounded by stages and degrees, and in the act of praying, "Thy kingdom come," it irresistibly stretches the wings of its faith, and longing, and joyous expectation out to the final and glorious consummation of the kingdom of God.

Third Petition: **Thy will be done in earth, as it is in heaven**—or, as the same words are rendered in Luke, "as in heaven, so upon earth"—as *cheerfully*, as *constantly*, as *perfectly*. But some will ask, Will this ever be? We answer, If the "new heavens and new earth" are to be just our present material system purified by fire and transfigured, of course it will. But we incline to think that the aspiration which we are taught in this beautiful petition to breathe forth has no direct reference to any such *organic* fulfilment, and is only the spontaneous and resistless longing of the renewed soul—put into words—to see the whole inhabited earth in entire conformity to the will of God. It asks not if ever it shall be—or if ever it can be—in order to pray this prayer. It *must* have its holy yearnings breathed forth, and this is just the bold yet simple expression of them. Nor is the Old Testament without prayers which come very near to this (Ps. 7:9; 67; 72:19, etc.).

Fourth Petition: **11. Give us this day our daily bread**—The compound word here rendered "daily" occurs nowhere else, either in classical or sacred Greek, and so must be interpreted by the analogy of its component parts. But on this critics are divided. To those who would understand it to mean, "Give us this day the bread of to-morrow"—as if the sense thus slid into that of Luke "Give us *day by day*" (as BENGEL, MEYER, etc.)—it may be answered that the sense thus brought out is scarcely intelligible, if not something less; that the expression "bread of to-morrow" is not at all the same as bread "from day to day," and that, so understood, it would seem to contradict vs. 34. The great majority of the best critics (taking the word to be compounded of *ousia, "substance,"* or "being") understand by it the "staff of *life,*" the bread of *subsistence,* and so the sense will be, "Give us this day the bread which this day's necessities require." In this case, the rendering of our authorized version (after the *Vulgate*, LUTHER and some of the best modern critics)—"our daily bread"—is, in sense, accurate enough. (See Prov. 30:8.) Among commentators, there was early shown an inclination to understand this as a prayer for the heavenly bread, or spiritual nourishment; and in this they have been followed by many superior expositors, even down to our own times. But as this is quite unnatural, so it deprives the Christian of one of the sweetest of his privileges—to cast his bodily wants in this short prayer, by one simple petition, upon his heavenly Father. No doubt the spiritual mind will, from "the meat that perisheth," naturally rise in thought to "that meat which endureth to everlasting life." But let it be enough that the petition about bodily wants irresistibly *suggests* a higher petition; and let us not rob ourselves—out of a morbid spirituality—of our one petition in this prayer for that bodily provision which the immediate sequel of this discourse shows that our heavenly Father has so much at heart. In limiting our petitions, however, to provision *for the day*, what a spirit of childlike dependence does the Lord both demand and beget!

Fifth Petition: **12. And forgive us our debts**—A vitally important view of sin, this—as an offense against God demanding reparation to His dishonored claims upon our absolute subjection. As the debtor in the creditor's hand, so is the sinner in the hands of God. This idea of sin had indeed come up before in this discourse—in the warning to agree with our adversary quickly, in case of sentence being passed upon us, adjudging us to payment of the last farthing, and to imprisonment till then (ch. 5:25, 26). And it comes up once and again in our Lord's subsequent teaching—as in the parable of the creditor and his two debtors (Luke 7: 41, etc.), and in the parable of the unmerciful debtor (ch. 18:23, etc.). But by embodying it in this brief model of acceptable prayer, and as the first of three petitions more or less bearing upon sin, our Lord teaches us, in the most emphatic manner conceivable, to regard this view of sin as the primary and fundamental one. Answering to this is the "forgiveness" which it directs us to seek—not the removal

ADAM CLARKE

Thy will be done. This petition is properly added to the preceding; for when the Kingdom of righteousness, peace, and joy, in the Holy Spirit, is established in the heart, there is then an ample provision made for the fulfillment of the divine will. *As it is in heaven.* The Jews maintained that they were the angels of God upon earth, as those pure spirits were angels of God in heaven; hence they said, "As the angels sanctify the divine name in heaven, so the Israelites sanctify the divine name upon earth." Observe: (1) The salvation of the soul is the result of two wills conjoined: the will of God and the will of man. If God will not the salvation of man, he cannot be saved. If man will not the salvation God has prepared for him, he cannot be delivered from his sins. (2) This petition certainly points out a deliverance from all sin. For nothing that is unholy can consist with the divine will; and if this be fulfilled in man, surely sin shall be banished from his soul. (3) This is further evident from these words, *as it is in heaven;* i.e., as the angels do it, that is, with all zeal, diligence, love, delight, and perseverance. (4) Does not the petition plainly imply we may live without sinning against God?

11. *Give us this day our daily bread.* The word *epiousion* has greatly perplexed critics and commentators. I find upwards of thirty different explanations of it. It is found in no Greek writer before the Evangelists. The interpretation of Theophylact, one of the best of the Greek fathers, has ever appeared to me to be the most correct, "Bread, sufficient for our substance and support," i.e., that quantity of food which is necessary to support our health and strength, by being changed into the substance of our bodies.

12. *And forgive us our debts.* Sin is represented here under the notion of a debt, and as our sins are many, they are here called *debts.* God made man that he might live to His glory, and gave him a law to walk by; and if, when he does anything that tends not to glorify God, he contracts a debt with divine justice, how much more is he debtor when he breaks the law by actual transgression! *Forgive us.* Man has nothing to pay; if his debts are not forgiven, they must stand charged against him forever, as he is absolutely insolvent. Forgiveness, therefore, must come from the free mercy of God in Christ.

MATTHEW HENRY

(2) An argument to enforce this petition; *as we forgive our debtors.* This is not a plea of merit, but a plea of grace. Our duty is to *forgive our debtors.* We must forbear, and forgive, and forget the affronts put upon us, and the wrongs done us; and this is a moral qualification for pardon and peace; it encourages to hope, that God will *forgive us*; it will be an evidence to us that he has forgiven us, having wrought in us the condition of forgiveness.

6. *And lead us not into temptation, but deliver us from evil. Lead us not into temptation.* Having prayed that the guilt of sin may be removed, we pray, as is fit, that we may never return again to folly, that we may not be tempted to it.

But deliver us from evil; ἀπὸ τοῦ πονηροῦ—*from the evil one,* the devil, the tempter; keep us, that we may not be assaulted: Or *from the evil thing,* sin, the worst of evils; an evil, an only evil; that evil thing which God hates, and which Satan tempts men to and destroys them by.

III. The conclusion: *For thine is the kingdom, and the power and the glory, for ever. Amen.*

1. It is our duty to plead with God in prayer, to fill our mouth with arguments not to move God, but to affect ourselves; to encourage our faith, to excite our fervency, and to evidence both. Now the best pleas in prayer are those that are taken from God himself, and from that which he has made known of himself. We must wrestle with God in his own strength. "*Thine is the kingdom*"; God gives and saves like a king. "*Thine is the power,* to maintain and support that kingdom, and to make good all thine

JAMIESON, FAUSSET, BROWN

from our own hearts of the stain of sin, nor yet the removal of our just dread of God's anger, or of unworthy suspicions of His love, which is all that some tell us we have to care about—but the removal from God's own mind of His displeasure against us on account of sin, or, to retain the figure, the wiping or crossing out from His "book of remembrance" of all entries against us on this account. **as we forgive our debtors**—the same view of sin as before; only now transferred to the region of offenses given and received between man and man. After what has been said on ch. 5:7, it will not be thought that our Lord here teaches that our exercise of forgiveness towards our offending fellow men absolutely precedes and is the proper ground of God's forgiveness of us. His whole teaching, indeed—as of all Scripture—is the reverse of this. But as no one can reasonably imagine himself to be the object of divine forgiveness who is deliberately and habitually unforgiving towards his fellow men, so it is a beautiful provision to make our right to ask and expect daily forgiveness of our daily shortcomings and our final absolution and acquittal at the great day of admission into the kingdom, dependent upon our consciousness of a forgiving disposition towards our fellows, and our preparedness to protest before the Searcher of hearts that we do actually forgive them. (See Mark 11:25, 26). God sees His own image reflected in His forgiving children; but to ask God for what we ourselves refuse to men, is to insult Him. So much stress does our Lord put upon this, that immediately after the close of this prayer, it is the one point in it which He comes back upon (vss. 14, 15), for the purpose of solemnly assuring us that the divine procedure in this matter of forgiveness will be exactly what our own is.

Sixth Petition: **13. And lead us not into temptation**—He who honestly seeks, and has the assurance of, forgiveness for past sin, will strive to avoid committing it for the future. But conscious that "when we would do good evil is present with us," we are taught to offer this sixth petition, which comes naturally close upon the preceding, and flows, indeed, instinctively from it in the hearts of all earnest Christians. There is some difficulty in the form of the petition, as it is certain that God does bring His people—as He did Abraham, and Christ Himself—into circumstances both fitted and designed to try them, or test the strength of their faith. Some meet this by regarding the petition as simply an humble expression of self-distrust and instinctive shrinking from danger; but this seems too weak. Others take it as a prayer against yielding to temptation, and so equivalent to a prayer for support and deliverance when we are tempted; but this seems to go beyond the precise thing intended. We incline to take it as a prayer against being *drawn* or sucked, *of our own will,* into temptation, to which the word here used seems to lend some countenance—"Introduce us not." This view, while it does not put into our mouths a prayer against being tempted—which is more than the divine procedure would seem to warrant—does not, on the other hand, change the sense of the petition into one for support *under* temptation, which the words will hardly bear; but it gives us a subject for prayer, in regard to temptation, most *definite,* and of all others most *needful.* It was precisely this which Peter needed to ask, but did not ask, when—of his own accord, and in spite of difficulties—he pressed for entrance into the palace-hall of the high priest, and where, once sucked into the scene and atmosphere of temptation, he fell so foully. And if so, does it not seem pretty clear that this was exactly what our Lord meant His disciples to pray against when He said in the garden—"Watch and pray, that ye *enter not into* temptation?" (ch. 26:41).

Seventh Petition: **But deliver us from evil**—We can see no good reason for regarding this as but the second half of the sixth petition. With far better ground might the second and third petitions be regarded as one. The "but" connecting the two petitions is an insufficient reason for regarding them as one, though enough to show that the one thought naturally follows close upon the other. As the expression "from evil" may be equally well rendered "from the evil one," a number or superior critics think the devil is intended, especially from its following close upon the subject of "temptation." But the comprehensive character of these brief petitions, and the place which this one occupies, as that on which all our desires die away, seems to us against so contracted a view of it. Nor can there be a reasonable doubt that the apostle, in some of the last sentences which he penned before he was

ADAM CLARKE

As we forgive our debtors. It was a maxim among the ancient Jews that no man should lie down in his bed without forgiving those who had offended him. That man condemns himself to suffer eternal punishment who makes use of this prayer with revenge and hatred in his heart.

13. *And lead us not into temptation.* That is, "Bring us not into sore trial." *Peirasmon,* which may be here rendered "sore trial," comes from *peiro,* "to pierce through," as with a spear, or spit, used so by some of the best Greek writers. The word not only implies violent assaults from Satan, but also sorely afflictive circumstances, none of which we have as yet grace or fortitude sufficient to bear. "Bring us not in," or *lead us not into.* This is a mere Hebraism. God is said to do a thing which He only permits or suffers to be done. The process of *temptation* is often as follows: (1) a simple evil thought; (2) a strong imagination, or impression made on the imagination, by the thing to which we are tempted; (3) delight in viewing it; (4) consent of the will to perform it. A man may be tempted without entering *into* the temptation: *entering into it* implies giving way, closing in with, and embracing it.

But deliver us from evil. "From the wicked one." Satan is expressly called "the wicked one." *Deliver us.* A very expressive word—"Break our chains, and loose our bands"—snatch, pluck us from the evil, and its calamitous issue. *For thine is the kingdom . . . forever. Amen.* The whole of this doxology is rejected by Wetstein, Griesbach, and the most eminent critics. It is variously written in several MSS., and omitted by most of the fathers, both Greek and Latin. *For ever.* "To the for evers." Well-expressed by our common translation "for ever and ever"—the first *ever* in our ancient use of the word taking in the whole duration of time, and the second *ever* the whole of eternity. *Amen.* This word is Hebrew and signifies "faithful" or "true." The word itself implies a confident resting of the

MATTHEW HENRY

engagements to thy people." *Thine is the glory*, as the end of all that which is given to, and done for, the saints, in answer to their prayers.

2. It is a form of praise and thanksgiving. The best pleading with God is praising of him; it is the way to obtain further mercy, as it qualifies us to receive it. We praise God, and give him glory, not because he needs it—he is praised by a world of angels, but because he deserves it. Praise is the work and happiness of heaven; and all that would go to heaven hereafter, must begin their heaven now. It becomes us to be copious in praising God. A true saint never thinks he can speak honourably enough of God. Ascribing glory to God *for ever*, intimates an acknowledgment, that it is eternally due, and an earnest desire to be eternally doing it, with angels and saints above, Ps. lxxi. 14.

Lastly, To all this we are taught to affix our *Amen*, so be it. God's *Amen* is a grant; it shall be so: our *Amen* is only a summary desire; let it be so: it is in token of our desire and assurance to be heard, that we say *Amen*. It is good to conclude religious duties with some warmth and vigour, that we may go from them with a sweet savour upon our spirits.

Most of the petitions in the Lord's prayer had been commonly used by the Jews in their devotions, or words to the same effect: but that clause in the fifth petition, *As we forgive our debtors*, was perfectly new, and therefore our Saviour here shows for what reason he added it, from the necessity and importance of the thing itself. God, in forgiving us, has a peculiar respect to our forgiving those that have injured us; and therefore, when we pray for pardon, we must mention our making conscience of that duty, not only to remind ourselves of it, but to bind ourselves to it. Selfish nature is loth to comply with this, and therefore it is here inculcated, *v.* 14, 15.

1. In a promise. *If ye forgive, your heavenly Father will also forgive*. Not as if this were the only condition required; there must be repentance and faith, and new obedience. He that relents toward his brother thereby shows that he repents toward his God. It is a good evidence, and a good help of our forgiving others, to call the injuries done us by a mollifying, excusing name. Call them not wilful injuries, but casual inadvertencies; *peradventure it was an oversight*, therefore make the best of it. We must forgive, as we hope to be forgiven; must not upbraid our brother with the injuries he has done us, nor rejoice in any hurt that befalls him, but must be ready to help him and do him good, and if he repent and desire to be friends again, we must be free and familiar with him, as before.

2. In a threatening. *"But if you forgive not"* those that have injured you, that is a bad sign you have not the other requisite conditions, but are altogether unqualified for pardon; and therefore *your Father* will *not forgive you*. And if other graces be sincere, and yet you be defective greatly in forgiving, you cannot expect the comfort of your pardon Those that would find mercy with God must show mercy to their brethren. If we pray in anger, we have reason to fear God will answer in anger. It has been said, Prayers made in wrath are written in gall. What reason is it that God should forgive us the talents we are indebted to him, if we forgive not our brethren the pence they are indebted to us? Christ *came into the world* as the great *Peace-Maker*, not only *to reconcile us to God*, but one to another. It is great presumption and of dangerous consequence, for any to make a light matter of that which Christ here lays such a stress upon. Men's passions shall not frustrate God's word.

Verses 16–18

We are here cautioned against hypocrisy in fasting.

I. It is here supposed that religious fasting is a duty required of the disciples of Christ, when God, in his providence, calls to it, and when the case of their own souls upon any account requires it. Fasting is here put last, because it is not so much a duty for its own sake, as a means to dispose us for other duties. Prayer comes in between almsgiving and fasting, as being the life and soul of both. It was not the Pharisee's fasting *twice in the week*, but his boasting of it, that Christ condemned. It is a laudable practice, and we have reason to lament it, that it is so generally neglected among Christians. It is an act of self-denial and humiliation under the hand of God. The most grown Christians must hereby own, they are so far from having anything to be proud of, that they are unworthy of their daily bread.

II. We are cautioned not to do this *as the hypocrites* did it, lest we lose the reward of it.

Now, 1. The *hypocrites* pretended fasting, when there was nothing of that contrition or humiliation of soul in them, which is the life and soul of the duty. Theirs were mock-fasts, the show and shadow without

JAMIESON, FAUSSET, BROWN

brought forth to suffer for his Lord, alludes to this very petition in the language of calm assurance—"And the Lord shall deliver me from every evil work [cf. the *Greek* of the two passages], and will preserve me unto his heavenly kingdom" (II Tim. 4:18). The final petition, then, is only rightly grasped when regarded as a prayer for deliverance from all evil of whatever kind—not only from sin, but from all its consequences—fully and finally. Fitly, then, are our prayers ended with this. For what can we desire which this does not carry with it? **For thine is the kingdom, and the power, and the glory, for ever. Amen**—If any reliance is to be placed on external evidence, this doxology, we think, can hardly be considered part of the original text. It is wanting in all the most ancient MSS.; it is wanting in the *Old Latin* version and in the *Vulgate:* the former mounting up to about the middle of the second century, and the latter being a revision of it in the fourth century by JEROME, a most reverential and conservative as well as able and impartial critic. As might be expected from this, it is passed by in silence by the earliest Latin fathers; but even the Greek commentators, when expounding this prayer, pass by the doxology. On the other hand, it is found in a majority of MSS., though not the oldest; it is found in all the Syriac versions, even the *Peshito*—dating probably as early as the second century—although this version lacks the "Amen," which the doxology, if genuine, could hardly have wanted; it is found in the *Sahidic* or *Thebaic* version made for the Christians of Upper Egypt, possibly as early as the Old Latin; and it is found in perhaps most of the later versions. On a review of the evidence, the strong probability, we think, is that it was no part of the original text. **14. For if ye forgive men . . . 15. But if ye forgive not . . .**—See on vs. 12.

ADAM CLARKE

soul in God, with the fullest assurance that all these petitions shall be fulfilled to everyone who prays according to the directions given before by our blessed Lord.

14. *If ye forgive men.* He who shows mercy to men receives mercy from God.

15. *But if ye forgive not.* A vindictive man excludes himself from all hope of eternal life, and himself seals his own damnation. *Trespasses. Paraptomata*, from *para* and *pipto*, "to fall off." What a remarkable difference there is between this word and "debts" in v. 12! Men's sins against us are only their stumblings, or fallings off from the duties they owe us, but ours are debts to God's justice, which we can never discharge.

G. CAMPBELL MORGAN:

We are perpetually insisting upon the necessity for self-denial, and we do well to insist upon it. It is at the very heart and center of Christian life. That is the process by which the life is made strenuous. The athlete denies himself a great many things, in themselves harmless and proper, in order to win. There must be self-denial, there must be restraint, there must be fasting. But the mistake is that we fast in order that men may think how good we are. We get our reward, and there is nothing beyond. But if fasting is for the purpose of finding the stronger, the truer, the nobler; in order to create larger room for the coming and going and sweep of the Spirit—then it is true. But what are to be the outward signs of fasting? The sad countenance and the disfigured face? Rather, the washed face and the anointed head. Is it not time that we in the Christian Church talked a little less about self-denial, and lived it more? Have we not by overemphasizing in our conventions on the one hand, and on the other, in the new ascetic ideal manifesting itself in scourging, been false to this word of Jesus, "Anoint thy head and wash thy face"? Oh, my life, thou shouldest keep perpetual Lent within the secret chamber of thy being, and everlasting Easter on thy face! The inner life must always be a denial of self, but we must come to the world with a smile and a song, and the anointed head, and the washed face. This is religion, this is life.—*The Gospel According to Matthew*

Fasting (**vss. 16-18**). **Having concluded His supplementary directions on the subject of prayer with this Divine Pattern, our Lord now returns to the subject of** *Unostentatiousness* **in our deeds of righteousness, in order to give one more illustration of it, in the matter of fasting. 16. Moreover, when ye fast**—referring, probably, to private and voluntary fasting, which was to be regulated by each individual for himself; though in spirit it would apply to any fast—**be not, as the hypocrites, of a sad countenance: for they disfigure their faces**—lit., "make unseen"; very well rendered "disfigure." They went about with a slovenly appearance, and ashes sprinkled on their head. **that they may appear unto men to fast**—It was not the *deed*, but *reputation* for the deed which they sought; and with this view those hypocrites multiplied their fasts. And are the exhausting fasts of the Church of Rome, and of Romanizing Protestants, free from this taint?

16. *When ye fast.* A total abstinence from food for a certain time. Abstaining from flesh, and living on fish, vegetables, etc., is no fast, but may be rather considered a burlesque on fasting. *As the hypocrites, of a sad countenance.* A hypocrite has always a difficult part to act. When he wishes to appear as a penitent, not having any godly sorrow at heart, he is obliged to counterfeit it the best way he can, by a gloomy and austere look.

MATTHEW HENRY

the substance.

2. They proclaimed their fasting, and managed it so that all who saw them might take notice that it was a fasting-day with them. Even on these days they appeared in the streets, that men might see how often they fasted, and might extol them as devout, mortified men. It is sad that men, who have, in some measure, mastered their pleasure, which is sensual wickedness, should be ruined by their pride, which is spiritual wickedness, and no less dangerous. Here also *they have their reward*, and it is their all.

III. We are directed how to manage a private fast. He does not tell us how often we must fast; the Spirit in the word has left that to the Spirit in the heart; but take this for a rule, whenever you undertake this duty, study therein to approve yourselves to God, and not to recommend yourselves to the good opinions of men. Christ does not direct to abate anything of the reality of the fast; he does not say, "take a little meat, or a little drink, or a little cordial;" no, "let the body suffer, but lay aside the show and appearance of it. Look pleasant, *anoint thine head and wash thy face*, as thou dost on ordinary days, on purpose to conceal thy devotion; and thou shalt be no loser in the praise of it at last; for though it be not of men, it shall be of God." Fasting is the humbling of the soul; let that therefore be thy principal care. If we be sincere in our solemn fasts, and humble, and trust God's omniscience for our witness, and his goodness for our reward, we shall find, both that he did *see in secret*, and will *reward openly*. Religious fasts, if rightly kept, will shortly be recompensed with an everlasting feast.

Verses 19–24

Christ, having warned us against coveting *the praise of men*, proceeds next to warn us against coveting the wealth of the world; in this also we must take heed, lest we be as the hypocrites are, and do as they do: the fundamental error that they are guilty of is, that they choose the world for *their reward*.

I. In choosing the *treasure* we *lay up*. Something or other every man has which he makes his *treasure*, his portion, which his heart is upon. Something the soul will have, which it looks upon as the best thing. Now Christ designs not to deprive us of our treasure, but to direct us in the choice of it.

1. A *good caution* against making *the things that are seen*, that *are temporal*, our best things, and placing our happiness in them. *Lay not up for yourselves treasures upon earth*. Christ's disciples had left all to follow him, let them still keep in the same good mind. Now we must *not lay up our treasures on earth*, that is, (1) We must not count these things the best things: we must not call them glory, but see and own that they have no glory in comparison with *the glory that excelleth*. (2) We must not covet an abundance of these things, nor be still grasping at more and more of them, as never knowing when we have enough. (3) We must not confide in them for futurity: must not say to the gold, *Thou art my hope*. (4) We must not content ourselves with them, as all we need or desire. It concerns thee to choose wisely, for thou art choosing for thyself, and shalt have as thou choosest. If we know and consider ourselves what we are, what we are made for, how large our capacities are, and how long our continuance, and that our souls are ourselves, we shall see it a foolish thing to *lay up* our *treasures on earth*.

2. Here is a *good reason* given why we should not look upon anything *on earth* as our *treasure*, because it is liable to loss and decay: (1) From corruption within. That which is treasure *upon earth moth and rust do corrupt*. Manna itself bred worms. The *rust* and the *moth* breed in the metal itself and in the garment itself. Worldly riches have in themselves a principle of corruption and decay. (2) From violence without. *Thieves break through and steal*. Every hand of violence will be aiming at the house where *treasure* is laid up; nor can anything be laid up so safe, but we may be spoiled of it. It is folly to make that our *treasure* which we may so easily be robbed of.

3. *Good counsel*, to make the joys and glories of the other world, those *things not seen* that *are eternal*, our best things, and to place our happiness in them. *Lay up for yourselves treasures in heaven*. There are *treasures in heaven*, as sure as there are on this earth; and those in heaven are the only true *treasures*. (1) It is our wisdom to *lay up* our *treasure in* those *treasures*; to give all diligence to make sure our title to eternal life through Jesus Christ, and to depend upon that as our happiness, and look upon all things here below with a holy contempt. If we thus make those *treasures* ours, they are laid up, and we may trust God to keep them safe for us. Let us not burthen ourselves with the cash of this world. The

JAMIESON, FAUSSET, BROWN

Verily I say unto you, They have their reward. 17. But thou, when thou fastest, anoint thine head, and wash thy face—as the Jews did, except when mourning (Dan. 10:3); so that the meaning is, "Appear as usual"—appear so as to attract no notice. **18. That thou appear not unto men to fast, but unto thy Father which is in secret: and thy Father, which seeth in secret, shall reward thee [openly]**—The "openly" seems evidently a later addition to the text of this verse from vss. 4, 7, though of course the idea is implied.

19-34. Concluding Illustrations of the Righteousness of the Kingdom—Heavenly-Mindedness and Filial Confidence. **19. Lay not up for ourselves [hoard not] treasures upon earth, where moth**—a "clothes-moth." Eastern treasures, consisting partly in costly dresses stored up (Job 27:16), were liable to be consumed by moths (Job 13:28; Isa. 50:9; 51:8). In James 5:2 there is an evident reference to our Lord's words here. **and rust**—any "eating into" or "consuming"; here, probably, "wear-and-tear." **doth corrupt**—cause to disappear. By this reference to moth and rust our Lord would teach how *perishable* are such earthly treasures. **and where thieves break through and steal**—Treasures these, how *precarious*! **20. But lay up for yourselves treasures in heaven**—The language in Luke (12:33) is very bold—"Sell that ye have, and give alms; provide yourselves bags which wax not old, a treasure in the heavens that faileth not . . . **where neither moth nor rust doth corrupt, and where thieves do not break through nor steal**—Treasures these, *imperishable* and *unassailable!* (Cf. Col. 3:2).

ADAM CLARKE

17. *Anoint thine head, and wash thy face*. These were forbidden in the Jewish canon on days of fasting and humiliation; and hypocrites availed themselves of this ordinance, that they might appear to fast.

18. *Thy Father which seeth in secret*. Let us not be afraid that our hearts can be concealed from God; but let us fear lest He perceive them to be more desirous of the praise of men than they are of that glory which comes from Him.

19. *Lay not up for yourselves treasures upon earth*. What blindness is it for a man to lay up that as a treasure which must necessarily perish! *Rust*. This word cannot be properly applied to *rust*, but to anything that consumes or cankers clothes or metals. *Where thieves do not break through*. Literally "dig through," i.e., the wall, in order to get into the house. This was not a difficult matter, as the house was generally made of mud and straw.

20. *Lay up . . . treasures in heaven*. It is certain we have not the smallest portion of temporal good but what we have received from the unmerited bounty of God; and if we give back to Him all we have received, yet still there is no merit that can fairly attach to the act, as the goods were the Lord's; **for I am not to suppose** that I can purchase anything from a man by his own property. On this ground the doctrine of human merit is one of the most absurd that ever was published among men or credited by sinners.

F. B. MEYER:

"Thy Father which is in secret, . . . which seeth in secret." How fondly Jesus repeats these words (vv. 4, 6, 18). Though compelled to live so much in the public gaze of men, his heart was always sighing for the secret place of fellowship with his Father, who waited for him there.

Of course, the main object of these paragraphs was to withdraw his disciples from the excessive outwardness of the age in which he spoke, and which necessarily detracted from the singleness, directness, and simplicity of the religious life. It is impossible to perform our religious duties before men, without insensibly considering what impression we are producing, and how far their estimation of us is being enhanced. And insofar as we seek these things, the stream is contaminated with mud and silt, and becomes turbid. We have just as much religious life as we show to God in secret—just that, no less, no more. Whatever is not wrought between thee and God, with no record but his eye, is chaff which the wind driveth away.

Here is a test for our alms, our prayers, and our fasting from sin and self-indulgence. If we do any of these to maintain or increase the consideration that men have of us, they count for nothing in the eye of God. But whatever is done for him alone will secure his inevitable notice and reward. Dwell on that very definite assurance: "Shall recompense thee." There is no doubt about it. For every petition breathed into his ear; for every sigh and tear; for every abstinence from sin and self—there will be a certain recompense, after the divine measure. Such seeds shall have a prolific harvest. Seek, then, the secret place, where prying eyes cannot follow and curious ears cannot overhear.

—Great Verses Through the Bible

MATTHEW HENRY

promises are bills of exchange, by which all true believers return their *treasure* to *heaven*, payable in the future state. (2) It is a great encouragement to us to *lay up* our *treasure in heaven*, for there it is safe; no *moth* nor *rust* will *corrupt* it; *thieves do not break through and steal.* It is a happiness above and beyond the changes and chances of time, *an inheritance incorruptible.*

4. A *good reason* why we should thus choose. *Where your treasure is*, on earth or in heaven, *there will your heart be.* The *heart* follows the *treasure*, as the needle follows the loadstone, or the sunflower the sun. *Where the treasure is there* the value and esteem are, *there* the love and affection are. *Where the treasure is there* our hope and trust are; *there* our joys and delights will be; and *there* our thoughts. The *heart* is God's due and that he may have it, our *treasure* must be laid up with him. Our *treasure* is our alms, prayers, and fastings, and the reward of them; if we have done these only to gain the applause of men, we have *laid up this treasure on earth.* Now it is folly to do this, for *the praise of men* we covet so much is liable to corrupt: a little folly, like a dead fly, will spoil it all, Eccles. x. 1. Slander and calumny are *thieves that break through and steal* it away. Hypocritical services lay up nothing in heaven (Isa. lviii. 3). But if we have prayed and fasted and given alms in truth and uprightness, with an eye to God, we have laid up that treasure *in heaven*; *a book of remembrance is written there* (Mal. iii. 16). Hypocrites are *written in the earth*, but God's faithful ones have their names *written in heaven*, Luke x. 20. His *well done* shall stand for ever; and if we have thus laid up our *treasure* with him, with him our *hearts* will be; and where can they be better?

II. We must take heed of hypocrisy and worldly-mindedness in choosing the *end we look at.* Our concern as to this is represented by two sorts of eyes which men have, a *single eye* and an *evil eye*, *v.* 22, 23.

1. *The eye*, that is, *the heart* (so some) if that *be single, free and bountiful*, if the heart be liberally affected and stand inclined to goodness and charity, it will direct the man to Christian actions, the whole conversation *will be full of light*, of good works, which are our *light shining before men*; but *if the heart be evil*, covetous, and hard, and envious, griping and grudging, *the body will be full of darkness*, the whole conversation will be heathenish and unchristian. *If the light that is in us be darkness*, if there be not so much as good nature in a man, not so much as a kind disposition, *how great is* the corruption of a man, and the *darkness* in which he sits! Luke xii. 33; 2 Cor. ix. 7.

2. *The eye*, that is, *the understanding* (so some); the practical judgment, the conscience, which is to the other faculties of the soul, as *the eye* is to the *body*, to guide and direct their motions; now *if this eye be single*, if it make a true and right judgment, it will rightly guide the affections and actions, which will all be *full of the light* of grace and comfort; *but if this be evil* and corrupt, the heart and life must needs be *full of darkness*, and the whole conversation corrupt. An error in the practical judgment is fatal, it is that which calls *evil good and good evil* (Isa. v. 20).

3. *The eye*, that is, *the aims* and *intentions*; by *the eye* we set our end before us. In everything we do in religion, there is something or other that we have in our *eye.* If we aim purely and only at the glory of God, seek his honour and favour, and direct all entirely to him, then *the eye is single, the whole body will be full of light*, all the actions will be regular and gracious, pleasing to God and comfortable to ourselves; *but if this eye be evil*, if, instead of aiming only at the glory of God, and our acceptance with him, we look aside at the applause of men, and while we profess to honour God, contrive to honour ourselves, and seek our own things under colour of *seeking the things of Christ*, this spoils all. It is of the last importance in religion, that we be right in our aims. The hypocrite is like the waterman, that looks one way and rows another; the true Christian like the traveller, that has his journey's end in his eye. The hypocrite soars like the kite, with his eye upon the prey below. The true Christian soars like the lark, higher and higher, forgetting the things that are beneath.

III. We must take heed of hypocrisy and worldly-mindedness in choosing the master we serve, *v.* 24. *No man can serve two masters.* Serving *two masters* is contrary to *the single eye*; for *the eye* will be to the master's hand, Ps. cxxiii. 1, 2. Our Lord Jesus here exposes the cheat which those put upon their own souls, who think to divide between God and the world, to have a *treasure on earth*, and a *treasure in heaven* too, to please God and please men too.

1. A general maxim laid down; *No man can serve two masters*, much less two gods; for their commands

JAMIESON, FAUSSET, BROWN

21. For where your treasure is [that which ye value most] **there will your heart be also**—"Thy treasure—thy heart" is probably the true reading here: "your," in Luke 12:34, from which it seems to have come in here. Obvious though this maxim be, by what multitudes who profess to bow to the teaching of Christ is it practically disregarded! "What a man loves," says LUTHER, quoted by THOLUCK, "that is his God. For he carries it in his heart, he goes about with it night and day, he sleeps and wakes with it; be it what it may—wealth or pelf, pleasure or renown." But because "laying up" is not in itself sinful, nay, in some cases enjoined (II Cor. 12:14), and honest industry and sagacious enterprise are usually rewarded with prosperity, many flatter themselves that all is right between them and God, while their closest attention, anxiety, zeal, and time are exhausted upon these earthly pursuits. To put this right, our Lord adds what follows, in which there is profound practical wisdom.

22. The light [the lamp] **of the body is the eye: if therefore thine eye be single**—simple, clear. As applied to the outward eye, this means general soundness; particularly, not looking two ways. Here, as also in classical Greek, it is used figuratively to denote the simplicity of the mind's eye, singleness of purpose, looking right at its object, as opposed to having two ends in view. (See Prov. 4:25-27.) **thy whole body shall be full of light**—illuminated. As with the bodily vision, the man who looks with a good, sound eye, walks in light, seeing every object clear; so a simple and persistent purpose to serve and please God in everything will make the whole character consistent and bright.

23. But if thine eye be evil—distempered, or, as we should say, If we have got a *bad* eye—**thy whole body shall be full of darkness**—darkened. As a vitiated eye, or an eye that looks not straight and full at its object, sees nothing as it is, so a mind and heart divided between heaven and earth is all dark. **If therefore the light that is in thee be darkness, how great is that darkness!**—As the conscience is the regulative faculty, and a man's inward purpose, scope, aim in life, determines his character—if these be not simple and heavenward, but distorted and double, what must all the other faculties and principles of our nature be which take their direction and character from these, and what must the whole man and the whole life be but a mass of darkness? In Luke (11: 36) the converse of this statement very strikingly expresses what pure, beautiful, broad perceptions the *clarity of the inward eye* imparts: "If thy whole body therefore be full of light, having no part dark, the whole shall be full of light, as when the bright shining of a candle doth give thee light." But now for the application of this. **24. No man can serve**—The word means to "belong wholly and be entirely under command to." **two masters: for either he will hate the one, and love the other; or else he will hold to the one, and despise the other**—Even if the two masters be of one character and have but one object, the servant must *take law* from one or the other: though he may do what is agreeable to both, he cannot, in the nature of the thing, be *servant* to

ADAM CLARKE

21. *Where your treasure is.* If God be the Treasure of our souls, our hearts—i.e., our affections and desires—will be placed on things above. An earthly-minded man proves that his treasure is below; a heavenly-minded man shows that his treasure is above.

22. *The light of the body is the eye.* That is, the eye is to the body what the sun is to the universe in the daytime, or a lamp or candle to a house at night. *If therefore thine eye be single.* "Simple, uncompounded," i.e., so perfect in its structure as to see objects distinctly and clearly.

23. *Evil*, i.e., "diseased or defective." An evil eye was a phrase in use among the ancient Jews to denote an envious, covetous man or disposition; a man who repined at his neighbor's prosperity, loved his own money, and would do nothing in the way of charity for God's sake. Our blessed Lord, however, extends and sublimes this meaning, and uses the sound eye as a metaphor to point out that simplicity of intention and purity of affection with which men should pursue the supreme good.

24. *No man can serve two masters.* The master of our heart may be fitly termed the *love* that reigns in it. We serve that only which we love supremely. *He will hate the one, and love the other.* The word *hate* has the same sense here as it has in many places of Scripture; it merely signifies to love less.

MATTHEW HENRY

will some time or other cross or contradict one another. While *two masters* go together, a servant may follow them both; but when they part, you will see to which he belongs. This truth is plain enough in common cases.

2. The application of it to the business in hand. *Ye cannot serve God and Mammon. Mammon* is a Syriac word, that signifies gain; so that whatever in this world is, or is accounted by us to be, *gain* (Phil. iii. 7), is *mammon. Whatever is in the world, the lust of the flesh, the lust of the eye, and the pride of life,* is *mammon.* Self, the unity in which the world's trinity centres, sensual, secular self, is the *mammon* which cannot be served in conjunction with *God.* He does not say, We *must* not or we *should* not, but we *cannot serve God and Mammon*; we *cannot* love both (1 John ii. 15; James iv. 4); or hold to both, or hold by both in observance, obedience, attendance, trust, and dependence, for they are contrary, the one to the other. Let us not then *halt between God and Baal, but choose ye this day whom ye will serve,* and abide by your choice.

Verses 25–34

There is scarcely any one sin against which our Lord Jesus more largely and earnestly warns his disciples, than the sin of disquieting, distracting, distrustful cares about the things of this life.

I. The prohibition laid down. It is the counsel and command of the Lord Jesus, that we *take no thought* about the things of this world; *I say unto you.* He says it as our Lawgiver, and the Sovereign of our hearts; he says it as our Comforter, and the Helper of our joy. What is it that he says? *Take no thought. Be not in care.* It is the repeated command of the Lord Jesus to his disciples, that they should not divide and pull in pieces their own minds which care about the world. There is a *thought* concerning the things of this life, which is not only lawful, but duty.

But the *thought* here forbidden is, 1. A disquieting, tormenting *thought,* which disturbs our joy in God, which breaks the sleep, and hinders our enjoyment of ourselves, of our friends, and of what God has given us. 2. A distrustful, unbelieving *thought.* God has promised to provide for those that are his all things needful for life as well as godliness, *the life that now is,* food and a covering: not dainties, but necessaries. He never said, "They shall be feasted," but, "*Verily, they shall be fed.*" Now an inordinate care for time to come, and fear of wanting those supplies, spring from a disbelief of these promises, and of the wisdom and goodness of Divine Providence. But for the future, we must *cast our care upon God,* and *take no thought,* because it looks like a jealousy of God, who knows how to give what we want when we know not how to get it. Let our souls dwell at ease in him! This gracious carelessness is the same with that sleep which God gives to his beloved.

Take no thought for your life. Life is our greatest concern for this world; *All that a man has will he give for his life*; yet take no thought about it. Refer it to God to *lengthen* or *shorten* it as he pleases; *my times are in thy hand,* and they are in a good hand. Refer it to God to embitter or sweeten it as he pleases. We must not be solicitous, no not about the necessary support of this life, *food* and *raiment*; these God has promised. Say not, *What shall we eat?* Though many good people have the prospect of little, yet there are few but have present support.

Take no thought for the morrow, for the time to come. Be not solicitous for the future. As we must not *boast of* tomorrow, so we must not *care for* tomorrow.

II. The reasons and arguments to enforce this prohibition. To show how much the heart of Christ is upon it, and what *pleasure he takes* in those that *hope in his mercy,* the command is backed with the most powerful arguments. To free us from anxious thoughts and to expel them, Christ here suggests to us *comforting* thoughts, that we may be filled with them. They may be weakened by right reason, but it is by an active faith only that they can be overcome.

1. *Is not the life more than meat, and the body than raiment? v.* 25. Yes, no doubt it is; the thing speaks for itself. Our *life* is a greater blessing than our *livelihood.* Meat and raiment are in order to life, and the *end* is more noble and excellent than the *means.* The daintiest food and finest raiment are from the *earth,* but life from the *breath of God.* This is an encouragement to us to trust God for *food* and *raiment,* and so to ease ourselves of all perplexing cares about them. God has given us life, and given us the body; what cannot he do for us, who did that? —what will he not? If we take care about our souls and eternity, which are more than the body, and its life, we may leave it to God to provide for us food and raiment, which are less. He that guards us

JAMIESON, FAUSSET, BROWN

more than one. Much less if, as in the present case, their interests are quite different, and even conflicting. In this case, if our affections be in the service of the one—if we "love the one"—we must of necessity "hate the other"; if we determine resolutely to "hold to the one," we must at the same time disregard, and (if he insist on his claims upon us) even "despise the other." **Ye cannot serve God and mammon**—The word "*mamon*"—better written with one *m*—is a foreign one, whose precise derivation cannot certainly be determined, though the most probable one gives it the sense of "what one trusts in." Here, there can be no doubt it is used for *riches,* considered as an idol master, or god of the heart. The service of this god and the true God together is here, with a kind of indignant curtness, pronounced impossible. But since the teaching of the preceding verses might seem to endanger our falling short of what is requisite for the present life, and so being left destitute, our Lord now comes to speak to that point.

25. Therefore I say unto you, Take no thought—"Be not solicitous." The English word "thought," when our version was made, expressed this idea of "solicitude," "anxious concern"—as may be seen in any old English classic; and in the same sense it is used in I Samuel 9:5, etc. But this sense of the word has now nearly gone out, and so the mere English reader is apt to be perplexed. *Thought* or forethought, for temporal things—in the sense of reflection, consideration—is required alike by Scripture and common sense. It is that anxious solicitude, that oppressive care, which springs from unbelieving doubts and misgivings, which alone is here condemned. (See Phil. 4:6).

for your life, what ye shall eat, or what ye shall drink; nor yet for your body, what ye shall put on—In Luke (12:29) our Lord adds, "neither be ye unsettled"—not "of doubtful mind," as in our version. When "careful (or 'full of care') about nothing," but committing all in prayer and supplication with thanksgiving unto God, the apostle assures us that "the peace of God, which passeth all understanding, shall keep our hearts and minds in Christ Jesus" (Phil. 4:6, 7); i.e., shall guard both our feelings and our thoughts from undue agitation, and keep them in a holy calm. But when we commit our whole temporal condition to the wit of our own minds, we get into that "unsettled" state against which our Lord exhorts His disciples.

Is not the life more than meat [food] and the body than raiment?—If God, then, gives and keeps up the greater—the life, the body—will He withhold the less, food to sustain life and raiment to clothe the body?

ADAM CLARKE

Mammon is used for *money.*

25. *Therefore.* "On this account," namely, that you may not serve mammon, but have unshaken confidence in God, *I say unto you. Take no thought.* Be not anxiously careful. Prudent care is never forbidden by our Lord, but only that anxious, distracting solicitude which, by dividing the mind and drawing it different ways, renders it utterly incapable of attending to any solemn or important concern. In this and the following verses our Lord lays down several reasons why men should not disquiet themselves about the wants of life or concerning the future. The *first* is the experience of greater benefits already received.

Is not the life more than meat, and the body than raiment? Can He who gave us our bodies, and breathed into them the breath of life, before we could ask them from Him, refuse us that which is necessary to preserve both, and when we ask it in humble confidence?

MATTHEW HENRY

against the evils we are exposed to, will supply us with the *good things* we are in need of.

2. *Behold the fowls of the air*, and *consider the lilies of the field.* Here is an argument taken from God's common providence toward the inferior creatures. A fine pass fallen man has come to, that he must be sent to school to the *fowls of the air*, and that they must *teach him*!

(1) Look upon the *fowls*, and learn to trust God *for food* (*v.* 26). Observe the providence of God concerning them. There are various sorts of fowls; they are numerous, some of them ravenous, but they are all fed, and fed with food convenient for them. The fowls, as they are least serviceable to man, so they are least within his care; men often feed upon them, but seldom feed them; yet they are fed, and it is *your heavenly Father that feeds them*; he *knows all the wild fowls of the mountains*, better than you know the tame ones at your own barn-door. But that which is especially observed here is, that they are fed without any care or project of their own; *they sow not, neither do they reap, nor gather into barns.* Every day, as duly as the day comes, provision is made for them, and their *eyes wait on God*, that great and good Housekeeper, who *provides food for all flesh.* Improve this for your encouragement to trust in God. *Are ye not much better than they?* Yes, certainly you are. The *heirs* of heaven are much better than the *fowls* of heaven; nobler and more excellent beings, and, by faith, they soar higher. He is their Maker and Lord, their Owner and Master; but besides all this, he is your Father; you are his children, his first-born; now he that feeds his birds surely will not starve his babes. They trust your Father's providence, and will not you trust it? In dependence upon that, they are careless for the morrow; and being so, they live the merriest lives of all creatures; they *sing among the branches.* If we were, by faith, as unconcerned about the morrow as they are, we should sing as cheerfully as they do.

(2) Look upon the *lilies*, and learn to trust God for *raiment.* That is another part of our care, *what we shall put on.* This care returns almost as often as that for our daily bread. *Consider the lilies of the field;* not only *look upon* them (every eye does that with pleasure), but *consider* them. There is a great deal of good to be learned from what we see every day, if we would but consider it. Consider how *frail* the lilies are; they are the *grass of the field.* Thus *all flesh is grass*: though some in the endowments of body and mind are as lilies, much admired, still they are grass. This grass *today is*, and *tomorrow is cast into the oven*; in a little while the place that *knows us* will *know us no more.* We should not take thought for the morrow, what we shall put on, because, perhaps, by tomorrow, we may have occasion for our grave-clothes. Consider how *free from care* the lilies are: they *toil not* as men do, to earn clothing; *neither do they spin*, as women do, to make clothing. It does not follow that we must therefore neglect, or do carelessly, the proper business of this life. Idleness *tempts* God, instead of *trusting* him. Consider how *fair*, how *fine* the lilies are; *how they grow*; what they *grow from.* The root of the lily is, in the winter, lost and buried under ground, yet, when spring returns, it appears, and starts up in a little time; hence it is promised to God's Israel, that they shall grow *as the lily.* Consider what they *grow to.* Out of that obscurity in a few weeks they come to be so very gay, that even *Solomon, in all his glory, was not arrayed like one of these.* Let him dress himself as fine as he could, he comes far short of the beauty of the lilies, and a bed of tulips outshines him. Let us, therefore, be ambitious of the *wisdom* of Solomon rather than the *glory* of Solomon, in which he was outdone by the lilies. Knowledge and grace are the perfection of man, not beauty, much less fine clothes. Now God is here said thus to *clothe the grass of the field.* All the excellences of the creature flow from God. It was he that gave the horse his strength, and the lily its beauty. Consider how instructive all this is to us, *v.* 30.

First, As to *fine* clothing; this teaches us not to care for it at all, not to covet it, nor to be proud of it, for after all our care in this the lilies will far outdo us; we cannot dress so fine as they do, why then should we attempt to vie with them? Their adorning will soon perish, and so will ours.

Secondly, As to *necessary* clothing; this teaches us to cast the care of it upon God. If he give such fine clothes to the grass, much more will he give fitting clothes to his own children. Observe the title he gives them (*v.* 30), *O ye of little faith.* This may be taken, 1. As an encouragement to true faith, though it be but weak. Great faith shall be commended, and shall procure great things, but little faith shall not be rejected. *Sound* believers shall be provided for, though they be not *strong* believers. The babes in the

JAMIESON, FAUSSET, BROWN

Behold the fowls of the air—in vs. 28, "observe well," and in Luke 12:24, "consider"—so as to learn wisdom from them. **for they sow not, neither do they reap, nor gather into barns; yet your heavenly Father feedeth them. Are ye not much better than they?**—nobler in yourselves and dearer to God. The argument here is from the greater to the less; but how rich in detail! The brute creation—void of reason—are incapable of sowing, reaping, and storing: yet your heavenly Father suffers them not helplessly to perish, but sustains them without any of those processes. Will He see, then, His own children using all the means which reason dictates for procuring the things needful for the body—looking up to Himself at every step—and yet leave them to starve?

ADAM CLARKE

26. *Behold the fowls of the air.* The *second* reason why we should not be anxiously concerned about the future is the example of the smaller animals, which the providence of God feeds without their own labor, though He be not their father.

G. CAMPBELL MORGAN:

Let us ponder His teaching, first about the birds. He says in effect: "These birds of the air neither sow nor reap nor gather into barns, but your Father feedeth them; you can sow and reap and gather, therefore much more does your Father care for you." The Lord's argument here is not that we are to cease our sowing and reaping and gathering, but that if He takes care of those who cannot do such things, much more will He take care of those who can. These birds of the air are without rational forethought. By comparison with men, there can be no toiling, no sowing, no reaping, no gathering. But Jesus says, "God has given you the power of rational forethought, and much more will he take care of you." It is not that we are to neglect the use of reason, or forethought, or preparation. It is not that we are to take no thought—unhappy mistranslation—but that we are to take thought for the morrow without anxiety, knowing that, as God cares for the birds, He will more perfectly take care of us.

So also with the flowers. "They toil not, neither do they spin; yet I shall say unto you that even Solomon in all his glory was not arrayed like one of these." Did you imagine that was figurative, an overstrained metaphor? Take that flower, that huleh lily, gorgeous and beautiful in its coloring, and put it by the side of Solomon in his magnificence, in his robes of gold and silver and jewels and splendor—the lily is more beautifully clothed than Solomon. Take the finest fabric that monarch ever wore and submit it to microscopic examination, and it is sackcloth. Take the lily and submit its garment of delicate velvet to microscopic examination and investigation, and the more perfect your lens the more exquisite the weaving of the robe of the lily will be seen to be. Christ is not indulging in hyperbole. He is stating cold fact. No garment loomed to the finest and softest texture is anything but rough sackcloth when placed by the side of the drapery with which He clothed the lily. Christ says, "Open your eyes, My children, and look at the lilies lying scattered over the valleys and mountains, growing among thorns, and know that when God makes the lily, kings desire and cannot obtain such a robing. Looking at the flower, and seeing all its decking, know this:

'He who clothes the lilies,
Will clothe His children too.' "

There is not a flower and not a petal which, in exquisite finish and delicate perfection, would not put all the robes of a king to shame.—*The Gospel According to Matthew*

JAMIESON, FAUSSET, BROWN

28. And why take ye thought for raiment? Consider [observe well] **the lilies of the field, how they grow: they toil not**—as men, planting and preparing the flax. **neither do they spin**—as women. **29. And yet I say unto you, That even Solomon in all his glory was not arrayed like one of these**—What incomparable teaching!—best left in its own transparent clearness and rich simplicity. **30. Wherefore, if God so clothe the grass**—the "herbage." **of the field, which to-day is, and to-morrow is cast into the oven**—wild flowers cut with the grass, withering by the heat, and used for fuel. (See Jas 1: 11). **shall He not much more clothe you, O ye of little faith?**—The argument here is something fresh. Gorgeous as is the array of the flowers that deck the fields, surpassing all artificial human grandeur, it is for but a brief moment; you are ravished with it to-day, and tomorrow it is gone; your own hands have seized and cast it into the oven: Shall, then, God's children, so dear to Him, and instinct with a life that cannot die, be left naked? He does not say, Shall they not be more beauteously arrayed? but, Shall He not much more *clothe* them? that being all He will have them regard as secured to them (cf. Heb. 13:5). The expression, "Little-faithed ones," which our Lord applies once and again to His disciples (ch. 8:26; 14:31; 16:8), can hardly be regarded as rebuking any actual manifestations of unbelief at that early period, and before such an audience. It is His way of gently chiding the *spirit* of unbelief, so natural even to the best, who are surrounded by a world of sense, and of kindling a generous desire to shake it off.

ADAM CLARKE

28. *And why take ye thought for raiment?* Or, "why are ye anxiously careful about raiment?" The *fourth* reason against such inquietudes is the example of inanimate creatures. The herbs and flowers of the field have their being, nourishment, exquisite flavors, and beautiful hues from God himself. They are not only without anxious care, but also without care or thought of every kind. *Consider.* Diligently consider this, "lay it earnestly to heart," and let your confidence be unshaken in the God of infinite bounty and love.

29. *Solomon in all his glory.* Some suppose that, as the robes of state worn by the Eastern kings were usually white, as were those of the nobles among the Jews, therefore the lily was chosen for the comparison.

30. *If God so clothe the grass of the field.* Christ confounds both the luxury of the rich in their superfluities and the distrust of the poor as to the necessaries of life. Let man, who is made for God and eternity, learn from a flower of the field how low the care of Providence stoops. All our inquietudes and distrusts proceed from lack of faith. *To morrow is cast into the oven.* The inhabitants of the East, to this day, make use of dry straw, withered herbs, and stubble, to heat their ovens.

MATTHEW HENRY

family are fed and clothed, as well as those that are grown up, and with a special care and tenderness. Or, 2. It is rather a rebuke to weak faith, though it be true. If we had but more faith, we should have less care.

3. *Which of you*, the wisest, the strongest of you, *by taking thought, can add one cubit to his stature?* We did not arrive at the stature we are by our own care and thought, but by the providence of God. An infant of a span long has grown up to be a man of six feet, he grew he knew not how, by the power and goodness of God. Now he that made our bodies, and made them of such a size, surely will take care to provide for them. The growing age is the thoughtless, careless age, yet we grow; and shall not he who reared us to this, provide for us now we are reared? We cannot alter the stature we are of, if we would. We are not all of a size, yet the difference in stature between one and another is not material, nor of any great account. Now as we do in reference to our bodily stature, so we should do in reference to our worldly estate. We should not covet an abundance of the wealth of this world, any more than we would covet the addition of a cubit to our stature, which is a great deal in a man's height; it is enough to grow by inches; such an addition would but make one unwieldy, and a burden to one's self. We must reconcile ourselves to our state, as we do to our stature; we must set the conveniences against the inconveniences, and so make a virtue of necessity. We cannot alter the disposals of Providence.

4. *After all these things do the Gentiles seek*, *v.* 32. The *Gentiles* seek *these things*, because they know not *better things*; they are eager for this world, because they are strangers to a better; they seek these things with care and anxiety, because they are *without God in the world*, and understand not his providence. They fear and worship their idols, but know not how to trust them. But it is a shame for Christians, who build upon nobler principles, to walk as Gentiles walk, and to fill their heads and hearts with these things.

5. *Your heavenly Father knows ye have need of all these things;* these necessary things, food and raiment; he knows our wants better than we do ourselves. You think, if such a good friend did but know your wants and straits, you would soon have relief: your God knows them; and he is your Father that loves you and pities you, and is ready to help you. Though he knows our wants, he will know them from us. Therefore, we should ease ourselves of the burthen of care, by casting it upon God, because it is he *that careth for us*. If he cares, why should we care?

6. *Seek first the kingdom of God, and his righteousness, and all these things shall be added unto you*, *v.* 33. Here is a double argument against the sin of *thoughtfulness*; *take no thought* for your life, the life of the body; for, (1) You have greater and better things to take thought about, the life of your soul, your eternal happiness; that is the *one thing needful* (Luke x. 42), about which you should employ your thoughts. (2) You have a surer and easier, a safer and a more compendious way to obtain the necessaries of this life, and that is, by *seeking first the kingdom of God*.

[1] The great duty required: it is the sum and substance of our whole duty: "*Seek first the kingdom of God*." Our duty is to seek; *though we have not attained*, but in many things fail and come short, sincere seeking is accepted. We must mind heaven as our end, and holiness as our way. We make nothing of our religion, if we do not make heaven of it. And with the *happiness* of this kingdom, seek the *righteousness* of it; *God's righteousness*. *Seek first the kingdom of God*. We must seek the things of Christ more than our own things. "Seek these things *first*; first in thy days: let the morning of youth be dedicated to God. Seek this first every day; let waking thoughts be of God." Let him that is the First, have the first.

[2] The gracious promise annexed; *all these things*, the necessary supports of life, *shall be added unto you*; shall be *given over and above*; as he that buys goods has paper and packthread given him into the bargain. *Godliness has the promise of the life that now is*, 1 Tim. iv. 8. We then begin at the right end of our work, when we begin with God. As to all the things of this life, Jehovah-jireh—the Lord will provide as much of them as he sees good for us, and more we would not wish for. God's Israel were not only brought to Canaan at last, but had their charges borne through the wilderness.

JAMIESON, FAUSSET, BROWN

27. Which of you, by taking thought [anxious solicitude]—**can add one cubit unto his stature?**—"Stature" can hardly be the thing intended here: first, because the subject is the *prolongation of life*, by the supply of its necessaries of food and clothing: and next, because no one would dream of adding a cubit—or a foot and a half—to his stature, while in the corresponding passage in Luke (12:25, 26) the thing intended is represented as "that thing which is *least*." But if we take the word in its primary sense of "*age*" (for "stature" is but a secondary sense) the idea will be this, "Which of you, however anxiously you vex yourselves about it, can add so much as a step to the length of your life's journey?" To compare the length of life to measures of this nature is not foreign to the language of Scripture (cf. Ps. 39:5; II Tim. 4:7, etc.). So understood, the meaning is clear and the connection natural. In this the best critics now agree.

Therefore take no thought [solicitude], **saying, What shall we eat? or, What shall we drink? or, Wherewithal shall we be clothed? 32. (For after all these things do the Gentiles seek)**—rather, "pursue." Knowing nothing definitely beyond the present life to kindle their aspirations and engage their supreme attention, the heathen naturally pursue present objects as their chief, their only good. To what an elevation above these does Jesus here lift His disciples! **for your heavenly Father knoweth that ye have need of all these things**—How precious this word! Food and raiment are pronounced *needful* to God's children; and He who could say, "No man knoweth the Father but the Son, and he to whomsoever the Son will reveal Him" (ch. 11:27), says with an authority which none but Himself could claim, "Your heavenly Father *knoweth* that ye have need of all these things." Will not that suffice you, O ye needy ones of the household of faith? **33. But seek ye first the kingdom of God, and his righteousness; and all these things shall be added unto you**—This is the great summing up. Strictly speaking, it has to do only with the subject of the present section—the right state of the heart with reference to heavenly and earthly things; but being couched in the form of a brief general directory, it is so comprehensive in its grasp as to embrace the whole subject of this discourse. And, as if to make this the more evident, the two keynotes of this great sermon seem purposely struck in it—"the KINGDOM" and "the RIGHTEOUSNESS" of the kingdom—as the grand objects, in the supreme pursuit of which all things needful for the present life will be added to us. The precise sense of every word in this golden verse should be carefully weighed. *"The kingdom of God"* is the primary subject of the Sermon on the Mount—that kingdom which the God of heaven is erecting in this fallen world, within which are all the spiritually recovered and inwardly subject portion of the family of Adam, under Messiah as its Divine Head and King. *"The righteousness thereof"* is the character of all such, so amply described and variously illustrated in the foregoing portions of this discourse. The *"seeking"* of these is the making them the object of supreme choice and pursuit; and the seeking of them *"first"* is the seeking of them before and above all else. The *"all these things"* which shall in that case be added to us are just the "all these things" which the last words of the preceding verse assured us "our heavenly Father knoweth that we have need of"; i.e., all we require for the present life. And when our Lord says they shall be *"added,"* it is implied, as a matter of course, that the seekers of the kingdom and its righteousness shall have these as their proper and primary portion: the rest being their gracious reward for *not* seeking them. (See an illustration of the principle of this in II Chron. 1:11, 12.) What follows is but a reduction of this great general direction into a practical and ready form for

ADAM CLARKE

27. *Which of you by taking thought can add one cubit unto his stature?* The *third* reason against these carking cares is the unprofitableness of human solicitude, unless God vouchsafe to bless it. What can our uneasiness do but render us still more unworthy of the divine care? *Add one cubit unto his stature*. I think ***helikian*** should be rendered "age" here, and so our translators have rendered the word in John ix. 21, "He is of age."

31. *What shall we eat? or, What shall we drink?* These three inquiries engross the whole attention of those who are living without God in the world. The belly and back of a worldling are his compound god; and these he worships in the lust of the flesh, in the lust of the eye, and in the pride of life.

32. *For after all these things do the Gentiles seek*. The *fifth* reason against solicitude about the future is that to concern ourselves about these wants with anxiety, as if there was no such thing as a providence in the world; with great affection towards earthly enjoyments, as if we expected no other; and without praying to God or consulting His will, as if we could do anything without Him—this is to imitate the worst kind of heathens, who live without hope, and without God in the world. *Seek*. "To seek intensely, earnestly, again and again." The true characteristic of the worldly man; his soul is never satisfied—Give! give! is the ceaseless language of his earth-born heart. *Your heavenly Father knoweth*. The *sixth* reason against this anxiety about the future is—because God, our Heavenly Father, is infinite in wisdom and knows all our wants.

33. *His righteousness*. That holiness of heart and purity of life which God requires of those who profess to be subjects of that spiritual Kingdom mentioned above. The *seventh* reason against these worldly cares and fears is—because the business of our salvation ought to engross us entirely; hither all our desires, cares, and inquiries ought to tend. Grace is the way to glory—holiness, the way to happiness.

MATTHEW HENRY

7. *The morrow shall take thought for the things of itself: sufficient unto the day is the evil thereof, v.* 34. Every day brings along with it its own burthen of cares and grievances. It brings along with it its own strength and supply too. *Let the morrow take thought for the things of itself.* If wants and troubles be renewed with the day, there are aids and provisions renewed likewise; *compassions,* that are *new every morning,* Lam. iii. 22, 23. Let us refer it therefore to the morrow's strength to do the morrow's work, and bear the morrow's burthen. This does not forbid a prudent foresight, and preparation accordingly, but a perplexing solicitude, and a prepossession of difficulties and calamities, which may perhaps never come. The meaning is, let us *mind present duty,* and then *leave events to God;* do the *work of the day in its day,* and then let *tomorrow bring its work along with it. Sufficient unto the day is the evil thereof.* This present day has trouble enough attending it, we need not *accumulate* burthens by *anticipating* our trouble, nor borrow perplexities from tomorrow's evils to add to those of this day. Let us not pull that upon ourselves all together at once, which Providence has wisely ordered to be borne by parcels. By our daily prayers we may procure strength to bear us up under our daily troubles, and to arm us against the temptations that attend them, and then let none of these things move us.

JAMIESON, FAUSSET, BROWN

daily use. **34. Take therefore no thought** [anxious care] **for the morrow: for the morrow shall take thought for the things of itself**—(or, according to other authorities, "for itself")—shall have its own causes of anxiety.

Sufficient unto the day is the evil thereof—An admirable practical maxim, and better rendered in our version than in almost any other, not excepting the preceding English ones. Every day brings its own cares; and to anticipate is only to double them.

ADAM CLARKE

34. *Take therefore no thought.* That is, "Be not therefore anxiously careful." The *eighth* and last reason against this preposterous conduct is that carking care is not only useless in itself, but renders us miserable beforehand.

Sufficient unto the day is the evil thereof. "Sufficient for each day is its own calamity." Each day has its peculiar trials; we should meet them with confidence in God. As we should live but a day at a time, so we should take care to suffer no more evils in one day than are necessary attached to it. He who neglects the present for the future is acting opposite to the order of God, his own interest, and to every dictate of sound wisdom. Let us live for eternity, and we shall secure all that is valuable in time.

MATTHEW HENRY — CHAPTER 7

Verses 1–6

Our Saviour is here directing us how to conduct ourselves in reference to the faults of others.

I. A caution *against judging, v.* 1, 2. The prohibition; *Judge not.* We must judge ourselves, and judge of our own acts, but we must not judge our brother. We must not sit in the judgment-seat, to make our word a law to everybody. We must not *despise him,* nor *set him at nought,* Rom. xiv. 10. We must not judge rashly. We must not judge uncharitably, unmercifully, nor with a spirit of revenge, and a desire to do mischief. We must not judge the hearts of others, nor their intentions, for it is God's prerogative to try the heart. Nor must we judge of their eternal state, nor call them *hypocrites, reprobates,* and *castaways;* that is stretching beyond our line; what have we to do, thus to judge another man's servant? Counsel him, and help him, but do not judge him. The reason to enforce this prohibition. *That ye be not judged.* This intimates, (1) That if we presume to judge others, we may expect to be ourselves judged. Commonly none are more censured, than those who are most censorious; and no mercy shall be shown to the reputation of those that show no mercy to the reputation of others. Yet that is not the worst of it; they shall be judged of God; from him they shall receive the *greater condemnation,* James iii. 1. Both parties must appear before him (Rom. xiv. 10), who, as he will relieve the *humble sufferer,* will also resist the *haughty scorner,* and give him enough of judging. (2) That if we be modest and charitable in our censures of others, and decline judging them, and judge ourselves rather, *we shall not be judged of the Lord.* As God will forgive those that forgive their brethren; so he will not judge those that will not judge their brethren; the *merciful shall find mercy.*

The judging of those that judge others is according to the law of retaliation; *With what judgment ye judge, ye shall be judged, v.* 2. The righteous God, in his judgments, often observes a rule of proportion. *With what measure ye mete, it shall be measured to you again;* perhaps in this world, so that men may read their sin in their punishment. What would become of us, if God should be as exact and severe in judging us, as we are in judging our brethren; if he should weigh us in the same balance? We may justly expect it, if we be extreme to mark what our brethren do amiss. In this, as in other things, the violent dealings of men return upon their own heads.

II. Some cautions *about reproving.* Because we must not judge others, which is a great sin, it does not therefore follow that we must not reprove others, which is a great duty, and may be a means of *saving a soul from death.*

1. It is not everyone who is fit to reprove. Those who are themselves guilty of the same faults of which they accuse others, or of worse, bring shame upon themselves, and are not likely to do good to those whom they reprove, *v.* 3–5. Here is,

(1) A just reproof to the censorious, who quarrel with their brother for small faults, while they allow themselves in great ones; who are quick-sighted to spy *a mote* in his eye, but are not sensible of *a beam in their own.* [1] There are degrees in sin: some sins are comparatively but as *motes,* others as *beams;*

JAMIESON, FAUSSET, BROWN — CHAPTER 7

VSS. 1-12. MISCELLANEOUS SUPPLEMENTARY COUNSELS. That these verses are entirely supplementary is the simplest and most natural view of them. All attempts to make out any evident con nection with the immediately preceding context are, in our judgment, forced. But, though supplementary, these counsels are far from being of subordinate importance. On the contrary, they involve some of the most delicate and vital duties of the Christian life. In the vivid form in which they are here presented, perhaps they could not have been introduced with the same effect under any of the foregoing heads; but they spring out of the same great principles, and are but other forms and manifestations of the same evangelical "righteousness."

Censorious Judgment (vss. 1-5). **1. Judge not, that ye be not judged**—To "judge" here does not exactly mean to pronounce condemnatory judgment, nor does it refer to simple judging at all, whether favorable or the reverse. The context makes it clear that the thing here condemned is that disposition to look unfavorably on the character and actions of others, which leads invariably to the pronouncing of rash, unjust, and unlovely judgments upon them. No doubt it is the judgments so pronounced which are here spoken of; but what our Lord aims at is the spirit out of which they spring. Provided we eschew this unlovely spirit, we are not only warranted to sit in judgment upon a brother's character and actions, but in the exercise of a necessary discrimination are often constrained to do so for our own guidance. It is the violation of the law of love involved in the exercise of a censorious disposition which alone is here condemned. And the argument against it—"that ye be not judged"—confirms this: "that your own character and actions be not pronounced upon with the like severity"; i.e., at the great day. **2. For with what judgments ye judge, ye shall be judged: and with what measure ye mete** [whatever standard of judgment ye apply to others] **it shall be measured to you again**—This proverbial maxim is used by our Lord in other connections—as in Mark 4:24, and with a slightly different application in Luke 6:38—as a great principle in the divine administration. Unkind judgment of others will be judicially returned upon ourselves, in the day when God shall judge the secrets of men by Jesus Christ. But, as in many other cases under the divine administration, such harsh judgment gets self-punished even here. For people shrink from contact with those who systematically deal out harsh judgment upon others—naturally concluding that they themselves may be the next victims—and feel impelled in self-defense, when exposed to it, to roll back upon the assailant his own censures. **3. And why beholdest thou the mote**—"splinter," here very well rendered "mote," denoting any small fault. **that is in thy brother's eye, but considerest not the beam that is in thine own eye?**—denoting the much greater fault which we overlook in ourselves.

ADAM CLARKE — CHAPTER 7

1. *Judge not, that ye be not judged.* These exhortations are pointed against rash, harsh, and uncharitable judgments, the thinking evil, where no evil seems, and speaking of it accordingly.

2. *For with what judgment.* He who is severe on others will naturally excite their severity against himself.

3. *And why beholdest thou the mote?* Might be translated the "splinter"; for "splinter" bears some analogy to *beam,* but *mote* does not. It often happens that the faults which we consider as of the first enormity in others are, to our own iniquities, as a chip is when compared to a large beam.

MATTHEW HENRY

some as a *gnat*, others as a *camel*: not that there is any sin little, for there is no little God to sin against. [2] Our own sins ought to appear greater to us than the same sins in others, for the sins of others must be extenuated, but our own aggravated. [3] There are many that have *beams in their own eyes*, and yet do not consider it. They are under the guilt and dominion of very great sins, and yet are not aware of it, but justify themselves, as if they needed no repentance nor reformation. With great assurance, they say, *We see*. [4] It is common for those who are most sinful themselves, and least sensible of it, to be most forward and free in judging and censuring others. Pride and uncharitableness are commonly *beams* in the eyes of those that pretend to be critical and nice in their censures of others. Nay, many are guilty of that in secret, which they have the face to punish in others when it is discovered. [5] Men's being so severe upon the faults of others, while they are indulgent of their own, is a mark of hypocrisy. *Thou hypocrite, v.* 5. Whatever such a one may pretend, it is certain that he is no enemy to sin (if he were, he would be an enemy to his own sin), and therefore he is not worthy of praise. This spiritual charity must begin at home; "*For how canst thou say*, how canst thou for shame say, to thy brother, *Let me help to reform thee*, when thou takest no care to reform thyself? [6] The consideration of what is amiss in ourselves, though it ought not to keep us from administering friendly reproof, ought to keep us from magisterial censuring.

(2) Here is a good rule for reprovers, *v.* 5. Go in the right method, *first cast the beam out of thine own eye*. Our own badness is so far from excusing us in not reproving, that our being by it rendered unfit to reprove is an aggravation of our badness. A man's *of*fence will never be his *de*fence: but I must first reform myself, that I may thereby help to reform my brother, and may qualify myself to reprove him. Those who blame others, ought to be blameless and harmless themselves. The snuffers of the sanctuary were to be of pure gold.

2. It is not everyone that is fit to be reproved; *Give not that which is holy unto the dogs, v.* 6. Our zeal against sin must be guided by discretion, and we must not go about to give instructions, counsels, and rebukes, much less comforts, to hardened scorners. Throw a pearl to a swine, and he will resent it, as if you threw a stone at him; therefore give not to dogs and swine (unclean creatures) holy things. Good counsel and reproof are a holy thing, and a pearl: they are ordinances of God, they are precious. Among the generation of the wicked, there are some that have so long *walked in the way of sinners*, that they have sat down *in the seat of the scornful*; they professedly hate and despise instruction, and set it at defiance. Reproofs of instruction are ill bestowed upon such, and expose the reprover to all the contempt and mischief that may be expected from dogs and swine. Those are to be reckoned such, who *hate reproofs* and reprovers, and fly in the face of those who, in kindness to their souls, show them their sin and danger. These sin against the remedy; who shall heal and help those that will not be healed and helped? *It is not meet to take the children's bread, and cast it to the dogs*. Yet we must be very cautious whom we condemn as dogs and swine. Many a patient is lost, by being thought to be so, who, if means had been used, might have been saved. Our Lord Jesus is very tender of the safety of his people, and would not have them needlessly to expose themselves to the fury of those that will *turn again and rend* them.

Verses 7–11

Our Saviour, in the foregoing chapter, had spoken of prayer as a commanded duty, by which God is honoured. Here he speaks of it as the appointed means of obtaining what we need.

I. Here is a precept in three words to the same purport, *Ask, Seek, Knock* (*v.* 7); that is, in one word, "Pray; pray, and pray again. *Ask*, as a beggar asks alms." Those that would be rich in grace, must betake themselves to the poor trade of begging, and they shall find it a thriving trade. "*Ask;* represent your wants and burthens to God. *Ask* as a traveller asks the way; to pray is to *enquire of God* (Ezek. xxxvi. 37). *Seek* as for a thing of value that we have lost. *Seek by prayer* (Dan. ix. 3). *Knock*, as he that desires to enter into the house knocks at the door." Sin has shut and barred the door against us; by prayer, we knock; *Lord, Lord, open to us*. Christ knocks at our door (Rev. iii. 20; Cant. v. 2); and allows us to knock at his, which is a favour we do not allow to common beggars. Seeking and knocking imply something more than asking and praying. We must not only *ask* but *seek*; we must second our prayers with our endeavours; we must, in the use

JAMIESON, FAUSSET, BROWN

Or how wilt thou say to thy brother, Let me pull out the mote out of thine eye; and, behold, a beam is in thine own eye? 5. Thou hypocrite [Hypocrite] **—first cast out the beam out of thine own eye; and then shalt thou see clearly to cast out the mote out of thy brother's eye**—Our Lord uses a most hyperbolical, but not unfamiliar figure, to express the monstrous inconsistency of this conduct. The "hypocrisy" which, not without indignation, He charges it with, consists in the pretense of a zealous and compassionate charity, which cannot possibly be real in one who suffers worse faults to lie uncorrected in himself. He only is fit to be a reprover of others who jealously and severely judges himself. Such persons will not only be slow to undertake the office of censor on their neighbors, but, when constrained in faithfulness to deal with them, will make it evident that they do it with *reluctance* and not satisfaction, with *moderation* and not exaggeration, with *love* and not harshness.

Prostitution of Holy Things (vs. 6): The opposite extreme to that of censoriousness is here condemned —want of discrimination of character. **6. Give not that which is holy unto the dogs**—savage or snarling haters of truth and righteousness. **neither cast ye your pearls before swine**—the impure or coarse, who are incapable of appreciating the priceless jewels of Christianity. In the East, dogs are wilder and more gregarious, and, feeding on carrion and garbage, are coarser and fiercer than the same animals in the West. Dogs and swine, besides being ceremonially unclean, were peculiarly repulsive to the Jews, and indeed to the ancients generally. **lest they trample them under their feet**—as swine do— **and turn again and rend you**—as dogs do. Religion is brought into contempt, and its professors insulted, when it is forced upon those who cannot value it and will not have it. But while the indiscriminately zealous have need of this caution, let us be on our guard against too readily setting our neighbors down as dogs and swine, and excusing ourselves from endeavoring to do them good on this poor plea.

Prayer (vss. 7-11). Enough, one might think, had been said on this subject in ch. 6:5-15. But the difficulty of the foregoing duties seems to have recalled the subject, and this gives it quite a new turn. "How shall we ever be able to carry out such precepts as these, of tender, holy, yet discriminating love?" might the humble disciple inquire. "Go to God with it," is our Lord's reply; but He expresses this with a fulness which leaves nothing to be desired, urging now not only confidence, but importunity in prayer. **7. Ask, and it shall be given you; seek, and ye shall find; knock, and it shall be opened unto you**—Though there seems evidently a climax here, expressive of more and more importunity, yet each of these terms used presents what we desire of God in a different light. We *ask* for what we *wish;* we *seek* for what we *miss;* we *knock* for that from which we feel ourselves *shut out*. Answering to this threefold representation is the triple assurance of success to our believing efforts. "But ah!" might some humble disciple say, "I cannot persuade myself that *I* have any interest with God." To meet this, our Lord repeats the triple

ADAM CLARKE

4. *Or how wilt thou say?* That man is utterly unfit to show the way of life to others who is himself walking in the way of death.

5. *Thou hypocrite*. A hypocrite, who professes to be what he is not (viz., a true Christian), is obliged, for the support of the character he has assumed, to imitate all the dispositions and actions of a Christian; consequently he must reprove sin, and endeavor to show an uncommon affection for the glory of God.

6. *Give not that which is holy*. "The holy or sacred thing"; i.e., anything, especially, of the sacrificial kind, which had been consecrated to God. As a general meaning of this passage, we may just say: The sacrament of the Lord's Supper, and other holy ordinances which are instituted only for the genuine followers of Christ, are not to be dispensed to those who are continually returning like the snarling, ill-natured dog to their easily predominant sins of rash judgment, barking at and tearing the characters of others by evil speaking, backbiting, and slandering; nor to him who, like the swine, is frequently returning to wallow in the mud of sensual gratifications and impurities.

7. *Ask . . . seek . . . knock*. These three words include the ideas of want, loss, and earnestness. *Ask*: turn beggar at the door of mercy. You are destitute of all spiritual good, and it is God alone who can give it to you; and you have no claim but what His mercy has given you on itself. *Seek*: You have lost your God, your paradise, your soul. Look about you—leave no stone unturned. There is no peace, no final salvation for you till you get your soul restored to the favor and image of God. *Knock*: Be in earnest—be importunate. Eternity is at hand! And, if you die in your sins, where God is you shall never come. *Ask* with confidence and humility. *Seek* with care and application. *Knock* with earnestness and perseverance.

MATTHEW HENRY

of the appointed means, *seek* for that which we *ask* for, else we tempt God. We must not only *ask*, but *knock*; we must come to God's door, must *ask* importunately; not only pray, but plead and wrestle with God.

II. Here is a promise annexed: *our labour* in prayer, if indeed we do labour in it, *shall not be in vain*: where God finds a praying heart, he will be found a prayer-hearing God; *he shall give thee an answer of peace*.

1. The promise is made, and made so as exactly to answer the precept, *v.* 7. God will meet those that attend on him; *Ask, and it shall be given you;* not lent you, not sold you, but *given you*; and what is more free than gift? It is but *ask* and have; *ye have not, because ye ask not*, or *ask not aright*; what is not worth asking, is not worth having, and then it is worth nothing. *Seek*, and *ye shall find*, and then you do not lose your labour; God is himself *found of those that seek* him, and if we find him we have enough. "*Knock, and it shall be opened*; the door of mercy and grace shall no longer be shut against you as enemies and intruders, but opened to you as friends and children. If the door be not *opened* at the first *knock*, *continue instant in prayer*; it is an affront to a friend to *knock* at his door, and then go away; though he tarry, yet wait."

2. It is repeated, *v.* 8. It is to the same purport, yet with some addition. It is made to extend to all that pray aright. *Everyone that asketh*, receiveth, whether Jew or Gentile, high or low, they are all alike welcome to *the throne of grace*, if they come in faith: *for God is no respecter of persons*. It is made in words of the present tense, which is more than a promise for the future. *Everyone that asketh*, not only *shall* receive, but *receiveth*; so sure and inviolable are the promises of God, that they do, in effect, give present possession. What we have in hope, according to the promise, is as sure, and should be as sweet, as what we have in hand. Conditional grants become absolute upon the performance of the condition; so here, *he that asketh, receiveth*.

3. It is illustrated, by a similitude taken from earthly parents, and their innate readiness to give their children what they ask, Christ appeals to his hearers, *What man is there of you*, though ever so morose and ill-humoured, *whom if his son ask bread, will he give him a stone? v.* 9, 10. Whence he infers (*v.* 11), *If ye then, being evil*, yet grant your children's requests, *much more will your heavenly Father give you the good things you ask*. Now this is of use,

(1) To *direct* our prayers and expectations. We must come to God, as children to a *Father in heaven.* How naturally does the child in want or distress run to the father with its complaints. We must come to him for *good things*, for those he *gives to them that ask him*. He knows what is good for us, we must therefore leave it with him; *Father, thy will be done.* We often ask that of God which would do us hurt if we had it; he knows this, and therefore does not give it to us. Denials in love are better than grants in anger; we should have been undone ere this if we had had all we desired.

(2) To *encourage* our prayers and expectations. We may hope that we shall not be denied and disappointed: we shall not have *a stone* for *bread*, to break our teeth (though we have a hard crust to employ our teeth), nor *a serpent* for *a fish*, to sting us. God has put into the hearts of parents a compassionate inclination to succour and supply their children, according to their need. No law was ever thought necessary to oblige parents to maintain their legitimate children. He has assumed the relation of a Father to us, and owns us for his children. He compares his concern for his people to that of a father for his children (Ps. ciii. 13), nay, to that of a mother, which is usually more tender, Isa. lxvi. 13; xlix. 14, 15. But here it is supposed, that his love, and tenderness, and goodness, far excel that of any earthly parent; and therefore it is argued with a *much more*. Our earthly fathers have taken care of us; we have taken care of our children; much more will God take care of his. And, *First*, God is more knowing; parents are often foolishly fond, but God is wise, infinitely so. *Secondly*, God is more kind. All the compassions of all the tender fathers in the world compared *with the tender mercies of our God*, would be but as a candle to the sun, or a drop to the ocean. God is more rich, and more ready to give to his children than the fathers of our flesh can be.

Verses 12–14

Our Lord Jesus here presses upon us that righteousness towards men which is an essential branch of true religion, and that religion towards God which is an essential branch of universal righteousness.

I. We must make righteousness our rule, and be ruled by it, *v.* 12. *Therefore*, lay this down for your

JAMIESON, FAUSSET, BROWN

assurance He had just given, but in such a form as to silence every such complaint.

8. For every one that asketh receiveth; and he that seeketh findeth; and to him that knocketh it shall be opened—Of course, it is presumed that he asks aright—i.e., in faith—and with an honest purpose to make use of what he receives. "If any of you lack wisdom, let him ask of God. But let him ask in faith, nothing wavering [undecided whether to be altogether on the Lord's side]. For he that wavereth is like a wave of the sea driven with the wind and tossed. For *let not that man think that he shall receive any thing of the Lord*" (Jas 1:5-7). Hence, "Ye ask, and receive not, because ye ask amiss, that ye may consume it upon your lusts" (Jas. 4:3).

9. Or what man is there of you, whom if his son ask bread [a loaf] **will he give him a stone?**—round and smooth like such a loaf or cake as was much in use, but only to mock him. **10. Or if he ask a fish, will he give him a serpent?**—like it, indeed, but only to sting him. **11. If ye then, being evil, know how to give good gifts unto your children, how much more shall your Father which is in heaven give good things to them that ask him!**—Bad as our fallen nature is, the *father* in us is not extinguished. What a heart, then, must the Father of all fathers have towards His pleading children! In the corresponding passage in Luke (see on 11:13), instead of "good things," our Lord asks whether He will not much more give *the Holy Spirit* to them that ask Him. At this early stage of His ministry, and before such an audience, He seems to avoid such sharp doctrinal teaching as was more accordant with His plan at the riper stage indicated in Luke, and in addressing His own disciples exclusively.

Golden Rule (vs. 12). **12. Therefore**—to say all in one word. **all things whatsoever ye would that men should do to you, do ye even so [the same thing and in the same way] to them: for this is the law and the prophets**—"This is the substance of all relative duty; all Scripture in a nutshell." In-

ADAM CLARKE

8. *For every one that asketh receiveth.* Prayer is always heard after one manner or other. No soul can pray in vain that prays as directed above.

9. *Or what man is there . . . whom if his son?* Men are exhorted to come unto God with the persuasion that He is a most gracious and compassionate Parent, who possesses all heavenly and earthly good, knows what is necessary for each of His creatures, and is infinitely ready to communicate that which they need most. *Will he give him a stone?* Will he not readily give him bread if he have it? This was a proverb in other countries; a benefit grudgingly given by an avaricious man is called by Seneca stony bread.

11. *If ye, then, being evil.* Who are radically and diabolically depraved, yet feel yourselves led, by natural affection, to give those things to your children which are necessary to support their lives, how much more will your Father who is in heaven, whose nature is infinite goodness, mercy, and grace, *give good things*—His grace and Spirit (the Holy Ghost, Luke xi. 13)—*to them that ask him?*

12. *Therefore all things whatsoever ye would that men.* The general meaning of it is this: "Guided by justice and mercy, do unto all men as you would have them to do to you, were your circumstances and theirs reversed."

MARTIN LUTHER:

After teaching His disciples and instituting the office of the ministry, telling them what they are expected to preach and how they are to live, Christ, the Lord, now adds an admonition to prayer. By this He intends to teach them that, second only to the office of preaching, prayer is the chief work of a Christian and an inseparable part of the sermon. He also wants to indicate that because of all the temptations and hindrances we face, nothing is more necessary in Christendom than continual and unceasing prayer that God would give His grace and His Spirit to make the doctrine powerful and efficacious among us and among others. That is why, in the words from the prophet Zechariah (Zech. 12:10), God promised that He would pour out upon the Christian a Spirit of grace and of supplication. In these two items He summarizes all Christian existence.—*Luther's Works*

MATTHEW HENRY

principle, to do as you would be done by; that you may have the benefit of the foregoing promises. Fitly is the law of justice subjoined to the law of prayer, for unless we be honest in our conversation, God will not hear our prayers, Isa. i. 15–17; lviii. 6, 9; Zech. vii. 9, 13. We cannot expect to receive *good things from God*, if we do not *fair things*, and that which is *honest*, and *lovely, and of good report* among men.

1. The rule of justice laid down; *Whatsoever ye would that men should do to you, do you even so to them.* Christ came to teach us, not only what we are to know and believe, but what we are to do; what we are to do, not only toward God, but toward men. The golden rule of equity is, to do to others as we would they should do to us. We must not do to others the evil they have done to us, nor the evil which they would do to us, if it were in their power; but what we desire should be done to us. This is grounded upon that great commandment, *Thou shalt love thy neighbour as thyself.* As we must bear the same affection to our neighbour that we would have borne to ourselves, so we must do the same good offices. We must do that to our neighbour which we ourselves acknowledge to be fit and reasonable. We may fear, lest God by his judgments should do to us as we have done to others, if we have not done as we would be done by.

2. A reason given to enforce this rule; *This is the law and the prophets.* It is the summary of that second great commandment, which is one of the two, *on which hang all the law and the prophets, ch.* xxii. 40. We have not this in so many words, either in *the law* or *the prophets*, but it is the concurring language of the whole. Christ has here adopted it into this law; so that both the Old Testament and the New agree in prescribing this to us, to do as we would be done by.

II. We must make religion our business, and be intent upon it. Observe here,

1. The account that is given of the bad way of sin, and the good way of holiness. There are but two ways, right and wrong, good and evil; the way to heaven, and the way to hell; in one of which we are all of us walking: no middle place hereafter, no middle way now.

Here is, (1) An account given us of the way of sin and sinners; both what is the best, and what is the worst of it. That which allures multitudes into it, and keeps them in it; *the gate is wide, and the way broad*, and there are many travellers in that way. *First*, "You will have abundance of liberty, in that way. You may go in at this gate with all your lusts about you; it gives no check to your appetites, to your passions: you may *walk in the way of your heart, and in the sight of your eyes.*" There is choice of sinful ways, contrary to each other, but all paths in this *broad way*. *Secondly*, "You will have abundance of company in that way: *many there be that go in* at this gate, and walk in this way." If we *follow the multitude*, it will be *to do evil*: if we go with the crowd, it will be the wrong way. It is natural for us to incline to go down the stream, and do as the most do. If many perish, we should be the more cautious. That which should affright us all from it, is that it *leads to destruction*. Whether it be the high way of open profaneness, or the back way of close hypocrisy, if it be the way of sin, it will be our ruin, if we repent not.

(2) Here is an account given us of the way of holiness. What there is in it that frightens many from it. Christ deals faithfully with us, and tells us,

First, That *the gate is strait*. Conversion and regeneration are *the gate*, by which we enter into this way. Out of a state of sin into a state of grace we must pass, by the new birth, John iii. 3, 5. This is a *strait gate*, hard to find, and hard to get through; like a passage between two rocks, 1 Sam. xiv. 4. There must be *a new heart, and a new spirit*, and *old things must pass away*. The bent of the soul must be changed. We must swim against the stream; much opposition must be struggled with, and broken through from without, and from within. It is easier to set a man against all the world than against himself, and yet this must be in conversion. It is a *strait gate*, for we must stoop, or we cannot go in at it; we must become as little children; we must deny ourselves, put off the world, *put off the old man*; we must be willing to forsake all for our interest in Christ. *The gate is strait* to all, but to some straiter than to others; as to the rich. *The gate is strait*; blessed be God, it is not shut up, nor locked against us, nor kept with a flaming sword, as it will be shortly, *ch.* xxv. 10.

Secondly, That *the way is narrow*. We are not in heaven as soon as we have got through *the strait gate*, no, we must go through a wilderness, must travel a *narrow way*, hedged in by the divine law, which *is exceedingly broad*, and that makes *the way narrow*;

JAMIESON, FAUSSET, BROWN

comparable summary! How well called "the royal law!" (Jas. 2:8; cf. Rom. 13:9). It is true that similar maxims are found floating in the writings of the cultivated Greeks and Romans, and naturally enough in the Rabbinical writings. But so expressed as it is here—in immediate connection with, and as the sum of *such* duties as has been just enjoined, and such principles as had been before taught—it is to be found nowhere else. And the best commentary upon this fact is, that never till our Lord came down thus to teach did men effectually and widely exemplify it in their practice. The precise sense of the maxim is best referred to common sense. It is not, of course, what—in our wayward, capricious, grasping moods—we should *wish* that men would do to us, that we are to hold ourselves bound to do to them; but only what—in the exercise of an impartial judgment, and putting ourselves in their place—we consider it reasonable that they should do to us, that we are to do to them.

G. CAMPBELL MORGAN:

What is this summarizing of our duty? Do unto your neighbor what you would that your neighbor should do to you. That is the whole thing. We are told sometimes that this is not peculiar to Jesus Christ. That the Golden Rule is not the peculiar property of Christianity. But you cannot find this rule anywhere else. Hillel, the great Hebrew master, said, "Do not do to thy neighbor what is hateful to thyself." That is very like it. He said that before Jesus came. Socrates, before Christ, wrote these words: "What stirs your anger when done to you by others, that do not to others." That is very much like it. Aristotle said, "We should bear ourselves toward others as we would desire they should bear themselves toward us." That seems even nearer, but it is not the same. Confucius, the great Chinese teacher, said, "What you do not want done to yourself, do not do to others." These things were said before Christ spoke, and we are told they are the same.

There is a radical difference—these are negative and passive; Christ's command is positive and active. These say to man, "Stand still, and do not do what you do not want anyone to do to you"; Christ says, "Go and do what you would that he should do to you. It is not merely that you are to refrain from harming him; you are to do him good. It is not that you are not to rob him; you are to give to him. It is not that you are not to murder him; you are to love him." And so the gleams of light which characterize the teaching of Gentiles, as well as the revelation which had come to Jews, He took up and fulfilled and made final. We might, out of a selfish self-respect, decline to harm our neighbor, but we cannot do this higher thing without power. We cannot do continuously what we would our neighbor should do to us save as we ask, seek, and knock, and know that our Father is pledged to us in power.—*The Gospel According to Matthew*

13-29. CONCLUSION AND EFFECT OF THE SERMON ON THE MOUNT. We have here the application of the whole preceding discourse. *Conclusion of the Sermon on the Mount* (vss. 13-27). "The righteousness of the kingdom," so amply described, both in principle and in detail, would be seen to involve *self-sacrifice* at every step. Multitudes would never face this. But it must be faced, else the consequences will be fatal. This would divide all within the sound of these truths into two classes: the many, who will follow the path of ease and self-indulgence —end where it might; and the few, who, bent on eternal safety above everything else, take the way that leads to it—at whatever cost. This gives occasion to the two opening verses of this application. **13. Enter ye in at the strait gate**—as if hardly wide enough to admit one at all. This expresses the difficulty of the first right step in religion, involving, as it does, a triumph over all our natural inclinations. Hence the still stronger expression in Luke (13:24), "Strive to enter in at the strait gate." **for wide is the gate** [easily entered] **and broad is the way** [easily trodden] **that leadeth to destruction, and** [thus lured] **many there be which go in thereat:**

ADAM CLARKE

13. *Enter ye in at the strait gate.* The words in the original are very emphatic: Enter in (to the kingdom of Heaven) through this strait gate, i.e., of doing to everyone as you would he should do unto you; for this alone seems to be the *strait gate* which our Lord alludes to. *For wide is the gate.* And very "broad"; a spacious, roomy place that leadeth forward into that *destruction*, meaning eternal misery.

MATTHEW HENRY

self must be denied; daily temptations must be resisted; duties must be done that are against our inclination. We must endure hardness, must wrestle and be in an agony, must watch in all things, and walk with care and circumspection. We must go *through much tribulation.* It is a way hedged about with thorns; blessed be God, it is not hedged up. But, as the understanding and will grow more and more sound, it will open and enlarge, and grow more and more pleasant.

Thirdly, The gate being so *strait and the way so narrow*, it is not strange that there are but *few that find it*, and choose it. Many pass it by, through carelessness; they will not be at the pains to find it; they are well as they are, and see no need to change their way. Others look upon it, but shun it; they like not to be so limited and restrained. Those that are going to heaven are but few. This discourages many: they are loth to be singular, to be solitary. However, instead of stumbling at this, say rather, If so few are going to heaven, there shall be more room for me. Let us see what there is in this way, which, notwithstanding this, should invite us all to it; it *leads to life*, to present comfort in the favour of God, which is the life of the soul; to eternal bliss, the hope of which, at the end of our way, should reconcile us to all the difficulties and inconveniences of the road. *The gate is strait and the way narrow* and uphill, but one hour in heaven will make amends for all.

2. The great concern and duty of every one of us, in consideration of all this; *Enter ye in at the strait gate.* The matter is fairly stated; life and death, good and evil, are set before us; both the ways, and both the ends. Choose you this day which you will walk in; nay, the matter determines itself, and will not admit of a debate. Delay not, therefore; deliberate not any longer, but *enter ye in at the strait gate*; *knock* at it by sincere and constant prayers and endeavours, *and it shall be opened.* It is true, we can neither go in, or go on, without the assistance of divine grace; but it is as true, that grace is freely offered, and shall not be wanting to those that seek it, and submit to it.

Verses 15–20

We have here a caution against *false prophets*, to take heed that we be not deceived and imposed upon by them. *Prophets* are properly such as foretell things to come; there are some mentioned in the Old Testament, who pretended to that without warrant, and the event disproved their pretensions. But *prophets* did also teach the people their duty, so that *false prophets* here are false teachers.

They are false teachers and *false prophets*, 1. Who produce false commissions, who pretend to have immediate warrant and direction from God to set up for *prophets*, and to be divinely inspired, when they are not so. 2. Who preach false doctrine in those things that are essential to religion; who teach that which is contrary to *the truth as it is in Jesus.* Beware of them, suspect them, try them, and when you have discovered their falsehood, avoid them, having nothing to do with them.

I. A good reason for this caution, *Beware of* them, for they are *wolves in sheep's clothing, v.* 15.

1. We have need to be very cautious, because their pretences are very fair and plausible, and such as will deceive us, if we be not upon our guard. They *come in sheep's clothing*, in the habit of *prophets.* We must take heed of being imposed upon by men's dress and garb. Or it may be taken figuratively; they pretend to be sheep, and outwardly appear so innocent, harmless, meek, useful, and all that is good, as to be excelled by none. They and their errors are gilded with the specious pretences of sanctity and devotion. Satan turns himself *into an angel of light*, 2 Cor. xi. 13, 14.

2. Because under these pretensions their designs are very malicious and mischievous; *inwardly they are ravening wolves.* Every *hypocrite* is a *goat* in sheep's clothing; but a *false prophet* is a *wolf* in sheep's clothing. Those that would cheat us of any truth, and possess us with error, whatever they pretend, design mischief to our souls. Paul calls them *grievous wolves*, Acts xx. 29. Now since it is so easy a thing, and withal so dangerous, to be cheated, *Beware of false prophets.*

II. Here is a good rule to go by in this caution; we must *prove all things* (1 Thess. v. 21); *ye shall know them by their fruits, v.* 16–20. Observe,

1. The illustration of this comparison, of the fruit's being the discovery of the tree. You cannot always distinguish them by their bark and leaves, nor by the spreading of their boughs, but *by their fruits ye shall know them.* The fruit is according to the tree. Christ insists upon this, the agreeableness between the fruit and the tree. If you know what the tree is, you may

JAMIESON, FAUSSET, BROWN

Because strait is the gate, and narrow is the way, which leadeth unto life—In other words, the whole course is as difficult as the first step; and (so it comes to pass that)—**few there be that find it.** The recommendation of the broad way is the ease with which it is trodden and the abundance of company to be found in it. It is sailing with a fair wind and a favorable tide. The natural inclinations are not crossed, and fears of the issue, if not easily hushed, are in the long run effectually subdued. The one disadvantage of this course is its end—it "leadeth to destruction." The great Teacher says it, and says it as "One having authority." To the supposed injustice or harshness of this He never once adverts. He leaves it to be inferred that such a course righteously, naturally, necessarily so ends. But whether men see this or no, here He lays down the law of the kingdom, and leaves it with us. As to the other way, the disadvantage of it lies in its narrowness and solicitude. Its very first step involves a revolution in all our purposes and plans for life, and a surrender of all that is dear to natural inclination, while all that follows is but a repetition of the first great act of self-sacrifice. No wonder, then, that few find and few are found in it. But it has one advantage—it "leadeth unto life." Some critics take "the gate" here, not for the first, but the last step in religion; since gates seldom open into roads, but roads usually terminate in a gate, leading straight to a mansion. But as this would make our Lord's words to have a very inverted and unnatural form as they stand, it is better, with the majority of critics, to view them as we have done. But since such teaching would be as unpopular as the way itself, our Lord next forewarns His hearers that preachers of smooth things—the true heirs and representatives of the false prophets of old—would be rife enough in the new kingdom.

15. Beware [But beware] **of false prophets**—i.e., of teachers coming as authorized expounders of the mind of God and guides to heaven. (See Acts 20:29, 30; II Pet. 2:1, 2). **which come to you in sheep's clothing**—with a bland, gentle, plausible exterior; persuading you that the gate is not strait nor the way narrow, and that to teach so is illiberal and bigoted—precisely what the old prophets did (Ezek. 13:1-10, 22). **but inwardly they are ravening wolves**—bent on devouring the flock for their own ends (II Cor. 11:2, 3, 13-15).

16. Ye shall know them by their fruits—not their doctrines—as many of the elder interpreters and some later ones explain it—for that corresponds to the tree itself; but the practical effect of their teaching, which is the proper fruit of the tree. **Do men gather grapes of thorns** [any kind of prickly plant] **or figs of thistles?**—a threepronged variety. The general sense is obvious—Every tree bears its own fruit.

ADAM CLARKE

14. *Because strait is the gate.* Instead of *because,* I should prefer "how," which reading is supported by a great majority of the best MSS., versions, and fathers. How strait is that gate! This mode of expression more forcibly points out the difficulty of the way to the Kingdom. *Few there be that find it.* The strait gate signifies literally what we call a wicket, i.e., a little door in a large gate. *Gate,* among the Jews, signifies, metaphorically, the entrance, introduction, or means of acquiring anything. So they talk of the gate of repentance, the gate of prayers and the gate of tears. When God, say they, shut the gate of paradise against Adam, He opened to him the gate of repentance.

15. *Beware of false prophets.* By false prophets we are to understand teachers of erroneous doctrines, who come professing a commission from God, but whose aim is not to bring the heavenly treasure to the people, but rather to rob them of their earthly good.

16. *Ye shall know them by their fruits.* Fruits, in the Scripture and Jewish phraseology, are taken for "works" of any kind.

MATTHEW HENRY

know what fruit to expect. Never look to gather *grapes from thorns, nor figs from thistles*; it is not in their nature to produce such fruits. [1] Corrupt, vicious, unsanctified hearts are like thorns and thistles, which came in with sin, are worthless, vexing, and for the fire at last. [2] Good works are *good fruit*, like grapes and figs, pleasing to God and profitable to men. [3] This *good fruit* is never to be expected from bad men, any more than *a clean thing out of an unclean*. On the other hand, if you know what the fruit is, you may, by that, perceive what the tree is. *A good tree cannot bring forth evil fruit*; and *a corrupt tree cannot bring forth good fruit*. But then that must be reckoned the fruit of the tree which it brings forth naturally, plentifully and constantly and which is its usual product. Men are known, not by particular acts, but by the course and tenor of their conversation, and by the more frequent acts.

2. The application of this to the false prophets.

(1) By way of terror and threatening (*v.* 19); *Every tree that brings not forth good fruit is hewn down*. This very saying John the Baptist had used, *ch.* iii. 10. Christ could have spoken the same sense in other words; but he thought it no disparagement to him to say the same that John had said before him. To write and speak the same things must not be grievous, for it is safe. Note the description of barren trees; they are trees that do *not bring forth good fruit*; though there be fruit, if it be not *good fruit*, the tree is accounted barren. Note also the doom of barren trees: *they are*, that is, certainly they shall be, *hewn down, and cast into the fire*; God will deal with them as men deal with dry trees that cumber the ground.

(2) By way of trial; *By their fruits ye shall know them*.

[1] *By the fruits* of their persons, their words and actions, and the course of their conversation. If you would know whether they be right or not, observe how they live; their works will testify for them or against them. Those are not taught nor sent of the holy God, whose lives evidence that they are led by the unclean spirit. God puts the treasure into earthen vessels, but not into such corrupt vessels.

[2] *By the fruits* of their doctrine; their fruits as prophets. What do they tend to? What affections and practices will they lead those into, that embrace them? If *the doctrine be of God*, it will tend to promote serious piety, humility, charity, holiness, and love, with other Christian graces; but if, on the contrary, the doctrines these prophets preach have a manifest tendency to make people proud, worldly, and contentious, unjust or uncharitable, and take people off from governing themselves and their families by the strict rules of *the narrow way*, we may conclude, that *this persuasion comes not of him that calleth us*, Gal. v. 8. *This wisdom is not from above*, James iii. 15. *Faith and a good conscience* are held together, 1 Tim. i. 19; iii. 9.

Verses 21–29

We have here the conclusion of this long and excellent sermon, the scope of which is to show the indispensable necessity of obedience to the commands of Christ.

I. He shows, by a plain remonstrance, that an outward profession of religion, however remarkable, will not bring us to heaven, unless there be a correspondent conversation, *v.* 21–23.

1. Christ's law laid down, *v.* 21. *Not every one that saith, Lord, Lord, shall enter into the kingdom of heaven, into the kingdom of* grace and glory. Christ here shows, It will not suffice to say, *Lord, Lord*; in word and tongue to own Christ for our Master, and to make address to him, and professions of him accordingly. But can we imagine that this is enough to bring us to heaven, or that he who knows and requires the heart should be so put off with shows for substance? Compliments among men are pieces of civility that are returned with compliments, but they are never paid as real services; and can they then be of any account with Christ? This is not to take us off from saying, *Lord, Lord*; from professing Christ's name, and being bold in professing it, but from resting in these, in the *form of godliness*, without *the power*. It is necessary to our happiness that we *do the will of* Christ, which is indeed *the will of* his *Father in heaven*. Now this is his will, that we believe in Christ, that we repent of sin, that we live a holy life, that we *love one another*. *This is his will, even our sanctification*. Saying and doing are two things, often parted in the conversation of men: he that said, *I go, sir*, stirred never a step (*ch.* xxi. 30); but these two things *God has joined* in his command.

2. The hypocrite's plea against the strictness of this law, offering other things in lieu of obedience, *v.* 22. They put in their plea with great importunity, *Lord, Lord*; and with great confidence, appealing to Christ

JAMIESON, FAUSSET, BROWN

17. Even so every good tree bringeth forth good fruit: but a corrupt tree bringeth forth evil fruit. 18. A good tree cannot bring forth evil fruit, neither can a corrupt tree bring forth good fruit—Obvious as is the truth here expressed in different forms—that the heart determines and is the only proper interpreter of the actions of our life—no one who knows how the Church of Rome makes a merit of actions, quite apart from the motives that prompt them, and how the same tendency manifests itself from time to time even among Protestant Christians, can think it too obvious to be insisted on by the teachers of divine truth. Here follows a wholesome digression. **19. Every tree that bringeth not forth good fruit is hewn down, and cast into the fire**—See on ch. 3:10.

20. Wherefore by their fruits ye shall know them—i.e., But the point I now press is not so much the end of such, as the means of detecting them; and this, as already said, is their fruits. The hypocrisy of teachers now leads to a solemn warning against religious hypocrisy in general.

21. Not every one that saith unto me, Lord, Lord—the reduplication of the title "Lord" denoting zeal in according it to Christ (see Mark 14:45). Yet our Lord claims and expects this of all His disciples, as when He washed their feet: "Ye call me Master and Lord: and ye say well; for so I am" (John 13:13). **shall enter into the kingdom of heaven; but he that doeth the will of my Father which is in heaven**—that will which it had been the great object of this discourse to set forth. Yet our Lord says warily, not "the will of *your* Father," but "of *My* Father"; thus claiming a relationship to His Father with which His disciples might not intermeddle, and which He never lets down. And He so speaks here to give authority to His asseverations. But now He rises higher still—not formally *announcing* Himself as the Judge, but intimating what men will say to Him, and He to them, *when* He sits as their final judge. **22. Many will say to me in that day**—What day? It is emphatically unnamed. But it is the day to which He had just referred, when men shall "enter" or not enter "into the kingdom of heaven." (See a similar way of speaking of "that day" in II Tim. 1:12; 4:8). **Lord, Lord**—The reiteration denotes surprise. "What, Lord? How is this? Are *we* to be disowned?" **have we not prophesied**—or, "publicly taught." As one of the special gifts of the Spirit in the early Church, it has the sense of "inspired and authoritative teaching," and is

ADAM CLARKE

17. *So every good tree*. As the *thorn* can produce only thorns, not grapes; and the thistle, not figs, but prickles, so an unregenerate heart will produce fruits of degeneracy. As we perfectly know that a good tree will not produce bad fruit, and the bad tree will not, cannot produce good fruit, so we know that the profession of godliness, while the life is ungodly, is imposture, hypocrisy, and deceit. A man cannot be a saint and a sinner at the same time.

18. *A good tree cannot bring forth evil fruit*. Love to God and man is the root of the good tree, and from this principle all its fruit is found.

19. *Every tree that bringeth not forth good fruit*. What a terrible sentence is this against Christless pastors and Christless hearers!

20. *Wherefore by their fruits*. This truth is often repeated, because our eternal interests depend so much upon it. Not to have good fruit is to have evil; there can be no innocent sterility in the invisible tree of the heart.

21. *Not every one*. The sense of this verse seems to be this: No person, by merely acknowledging My authority, believing in the divinity of My nature, professing faith in the perfection of My righteousness, and the infinite merit of My atonement, *shall enter into the kingdom of heaven*—shall have any part with God in glory; but *he that doeth the will of my Father*—he who gets the bad tree rooted up, the good tree planted, and continues to bring forth fruit to the glory and praise of God.

22. *Many will say to me in that day*. "In that very day," viz., the day of judgment—*Have we not prophesied*, taught, publicly preached, *in thy name;* acknowledging Thee to be the only Saviour, and proclaiming Thee as such to others; *cast out demons*, impure spirits, who had taken possession of the bodies of men; *done many wonderful works*, miracles, being assisted by supernatural agency to invert even the course of nature, and thus prove the truth of the doctrine we preached?

MARTIN LUTHER:

The words "You will know them by their fruits" are set down as a distinguishing mark and a standard for judging and recognizing these prophets. If we are taken in, that is no one's fault but our own. He has not left us in doubt but has portrayed them clearly and precisely. "If their sheep's clothing makes it impossible for you to judge them," He says, "then take note of their fruits and works, and see whether these are upright and good." You may say: "All right, but how do I recognize these? They may fool me too." Answer: You know what God's commandments are. See whether they agree with them. I will guarantee that no schismatic spirit will come without making his own special mark and leaving a stench behind so that you can tell that the devil has been there. No false teaching or heresy has ever arisen without bringing along the distinguishing mark He points to here: that it has set forth works different from the ones which God has commanded and ordained. The world is seduced simply because it follows insane reason and leaves the Word of God lying under the bench. It does not notice what He commands, and meanwhile it stares at the masks in the hope of seeing something special.—*Luther's Works*

MATTHEW HENRY

concerning it; *Lord*, dost not thou know, (1) That *we have prophesied in thy name?* Yes, it may be so; Balaam and Caiaphas were overruled to prophesy, and Saul was against his will *among the prophets*, yet that did not save them. These *prophesied* in his *name*, but he did not send them; they only made use of his name to serve a turn. (2) That *in thy name we have cast out devils?* That may be too; Judas *cast out devils*, and yet was a *son of perdition*. A man might *cast devils out* of others, and yet have a devil, nay, and be a devil himself. (3) That *in thy name we have done many wonderful works*. Gifts of tongues and healing would recommend men to the world, but it is real holiness or sanctification that is accepted of God. Grace and love are *a more excellent way* than *removing mountains*, or *speaking with the tongues of men and of angels*, 1 Cor. xiii. 1, 2. Grace will bring a man to heaven without working miracles, but working miracles will never bring a man to heaven without grace. They had not many good works to plead; they could not pretend to have done many gracious works of piety and charity; one such would have passed better in their account than *many wonderful works*. Miracles have now ceased, and with them this plea; but do not carnal hearts still encourage themselves in their groundless hopes, with the like vain supports? Let us take heed of resting in external privileges and performances, lest *we deceive ourselves*.

3. The rejection of this plea as frivolous. The same that is the Law-Maker (*v.* 21) is here the Judge according to that law (*v.* 23). *I never knew you*, and therefore *depart from me, ye that work iniquity*.—Observe, (1) Why, and upon what ground, he rejects them and their plea—because they were *workers of iniquity*. It is possible for men to have a great name for piety, and yet to be *workers of iniquity*; and those that are so will *receive the greater damnation*. (2) How it is expressed; *I never knew you*. This intimates, that if he had ever known them, as *the Lord knows them that are his*, had ever owned them and loved them as his, he would have known them, and owned them, and *loved them, to the end*; but he *never* did *know* them, for he always knew them to be hypocrites. Those that go no further in Christ's service than a bare profession, he does not accept, nor will he own them in the great day. See from what a height of hope men may fall into the depth of misery! How they may go to hell, by the gates of heaven! At God's bar, a profession of religion will not bear out any man in the practice and indulgence of sin; therefore *let every one that names the name of Christ, depart from all iniquity*.

II. He shows, by a parable, that hearing these sayings of Christ will not make us happy, if we do not make conscience of doing them; but that if we hear them and do them, we are *blessed in our deed*, *v.* 24–27.

1. The hearers of Christ's word are here divided into two sorts: some that hear, and do what they hear; others that hear and do not.

(1) Some that *hear his sayings and do them*: blessed be God that there are any such, though comparatively few. To hear Christ is not barely to give him the hearing, but to obey him. It is a mercy that we *hear* his *sayings*: *Blessed are those ears*, *ch.* xiii. 16, 17. But, if we practise not what we hear, we *receive* that *grace in vain*. All the *sayings* of Christ, not only the laws he has enacted, but the truths he has revealed, must be done by us. It is not enough to *hear* Christ's *sayings*, and understand them, *hear* them, and remember them, *hear* them, and talk of them, repeat them, dispute for them; but we must *hear, and do* them. *This do, and thou shalt live.* Those only *that hear, and do*, are *blessed* (Luke xi. 28; John xiii. 17), and are akin to Christ (*ch.* xii. 50).

(2) There are others who *hear* Christ's *sayings and do them not*; their religion rests in bare hearing, and goes no further. *They hear* God's *words*, as if they desired to *know his ways*, like a people *that did righteousness, but they will not do them*, Ezek. xxxiii. 30, 31; Isa. lviii. 2. The seed is sown, but it never comes up. Those who only *hear* Christ's *sayings, and do them not*, sit down in the midway to heaven, and that will never bring them to their journey's end.

2. These two sorts of hearers are here represented in their true characters, and the state of their case, under the comparison of two builders; one was *wise*, and *built upon a rock*, and his building stood in a storm; the other *foolish*, and *built upon the sand*, and his building fell. The general scope of this parable teaches us that the only way to make sure work for our souls and eternity, is to *hear and do the sayings of* the Lord Jesus. They make sure the *good part*, who, like Mary, when they hear the word of Christ, *sit at his feet* in subjection to it: *Speak, Lord, for thy servant heareth.* The particular parts of it teach us

JAMIESON, FAUSSET, BROWN

ranked next to the apostleship. (See I Cor. 12: 28; Eph. 4:11.) In this sense it is used here, as appears from what follows. **in thy name**—or, "to thy name," and so in the two following clauses—"having reference to Thy name as the sole power in which we did it." **and in thy name have cast out devils? and in thy name done many wonderful works**—or, miracles. These are selected as three examples of the highest services rendered to the Christian cause, and through the power of Christ's own name, invoked for that purpose; He Himself, too, responding to the call. And the threefold repetition of the question, each time in the same form, expresses in the liveliest manner the astonishment of the speakers at the view now taken of them.

23. And then will I profess unto them—or, openly proclaim—tearing off the mask. **I never knew you**—What they claimed intimacy with Christ, is just what He repudiates, and with a certain scornful dignity. "Our acquaintance was not broken off—there never was any." **depart from me**—(Cf. ch. 25:41). The connection here gives these words an awful significance. They claimed intimacy with Christ, and in the corresponding passage, Luke 13: 26, are represented as having gone out and in with Him on familiar terms. "So much the worse for you," He replies: "I bore with that long enough; but now—begone!" **ye that work iniquity**—not "that *wrought* iniquity"; for they are represented as fresh from the scenes and acts of it as they stand before the Judge. (See on the almost identical, but even more vivid and awful, description of the scene in Luke 13:24-27.) That the apostle alludes to these very words in II Tim. 2:19 there can hardly be any doubt—"Nevertheless the foundation of God standeth sure, having this seal, The Lord *knoweth* them that are His. And, Let every one that nameth the *name* of Christ depart from iniquity."

24. Therefore—to bring this discourse to a close. **whosoever heareth these sayings of mine, and doeth them**—see James 1:22, which seems a plain allusion to these words; also Luke 11:28; Romans 2:13; I John 3:7—

I will liken him unto a wise man—a shrewd, prudent, provident man. **which built his house upon a rock**—the rock of true discipleship, or genuine subjection to Christ.

ADAM CLARKE

23. *Will I profess.* I will fully and plainly tell them, *I never knew you*—I never "approved" of you; for so the word is used in many places, in both the Old and New Testaments. You held the truth in unrighteousness, while you preached My pure and holy doctrine; and for the sake of My own truth, and through My love to the souls of men, I blessed your preaching. But yourselves I could never esteem, because you were destitute of the spirit of My gospel, unholy in your hearts, and unrighteous in your conduct. *Depart from me.* What a terrible word! What a dreadful separation! Depart from Me, from the very Jesus whom you have proclaimed, in union with whom alone eternal life is to be found! For, united to Christ, all is heaven; separated from Him, all is hell.

24. *Therefore whosoever heareth these sayings of mine.* That is, the excellent doctrines laid down before in this and the preceding two chapters.

I will liken him unto a wise man. To a prudent man, a man of sense and understanding, who, foreseeing the evil, hideth himself, who proposes to himself the best end, and makes use of the proper means to accomplish it. True wisdom consists in getting the building of our salvation completed. To this end we must build on the Rock, Christ Jesus, and make the building firm, by keeping close to the maxims of His gospel, and having our tempers and lives conformed to its word and spirit; and when, in order to this, we lean on nothing but the grace of Christ, we then build upon a solid rock.

MATTHEW HENRY

divers good lessons. (1) That we have everyone a house to build, and that house is our hope for heaven. It ought to be our chief and constant care, to *make our calling and election sure*. Many never mind this: it is the furthest thing from their thoughts; they are building for this world, as if they were to be here always, but take no care to build for another world. All who take upon them a profession of religion, profess to enquire, what they shall *do to be saved*; how they may get to heaven at last, and may have a well-grounded hope of it in the meantime. (2) That there is *a rock* provided for us to build this house upon, *and that rock is Christ*. He *is our Hope*, 1 Tim. i, 1.

Christ in us is so; we must ground our hopes of heaven upon the fulness of Christ's merit, for the pardon of sin, the power of his Spirit, for the sanctification of our nature, and the prevalency of his intercession, for the conveyance of all that good which he has purchased for us. The church is *built upon his Rock*, and so is every believer. He is strong and immovable as a *rock*; we may venture our all upon him, and shall not be made *ashamed of our hope*. (3) That there is a remnant, who by hearing and doing the *sayings of* Christ, build their hopes *upon* this Rock. Those *build upon* Christ, who make it their constant care to conform to all the rules of his holy religion, and therein depend entirely upon him for assistance from God, and acceptance with him, *and count* every *thing but loss and dung that they may win Christ*, and be found in him. Building *upon a rock* requires care and pains: they that would make their *calling and election sure*, must *give diligence*. They are wise builders who *begin to build* so as they may be *able* to *finish* (Luke xiv. 30), and therefore lay a firm foundation. (4) That there are many who profess that they hope to go to heaven, but despise this *Rock*, and build their hopes *upon the sand*. Everything besides Christ is sand. Some build their hopes upon their worldly prosperity, as if that were a sure token of God's favour, Hos. xii. 8. Others upon their external profession of religion. They are called Christians, were baptized, go to church, hear Christ's word, say their prayers, and do nobody any harm; but it is all sand, too weak to bear such a fabric as our hopes of heaven. (5) That there is a storm coming, that will try what our hopes are bottomed on. *Rain, and floods, and wind, will beat upon the house;* the trial is sometimes in this world; *when tribulation and persecution arise because of the word*, then it will be seen, who only heard the word, and who heard and practised it. However, when death and judgment come, then the storm comes. Then everything else will fail us but these hopes, and then, if ever, they will be turned into everlasting fruition. (6) That those hopes which are built upon Christ the Rock will stand, and will stand the builder in stead when the storm comes. His comforts will not fail; they will be his strength and song, *as an anchor of the soul, sure and steadfast*. When he comes to the last encounter, those hopes will take off the terror of death and the grave; will be approved by the Judge; will stand the test of the great day; and will be crowned with endless glory, 2 Cor. i. 12; 2 Tim. iv. 7, 8. (7) That those hopes which foolish builders ground upon anything but Christ, will certainly fail them on a stormy day. He shall *lean upon his house, but it shall not stand*, Job. viii. 14, 15. It fell in the storm, when the builder had most need of it, and expected it would be a shelter to him. It was a great disappointment to the builder; the shame and loss were great. The higher men's hopes have been raised, the lower they fall. It is the sorest ruin of all that attends formal professors.

III. In the two last verses, we are told what impressions Christ's discourse made upon the auditory. *They were astonished at his doctrine;* it is to be feared that few of them were brought by it to follow him: but for the present, they were filled with wonder. It is possible for people to admire good preaching, and yet to remain in ignorance and unbelief; to be astonished, and yet not sanctified. The reason was because he taught them *as one having authority, and not as the scribes*. The scribes pretended to as much authority as any teachers whatsoever, and were supported by all the external advantages that could be obtained. They spake as those that were not themselves masters of what they preached: the word did not come from them with any life or force; they delivered it as a schoolboy says his lesson; but Christ delivered his discourse, as a judge gives his charge. His lessons were laws; his word a word of command. Christ, upon the mountain, showed more true authority than the scribes in Moses' seat. Thus when Christ teaches by his Spirit in the soul, he teaches with authority. He says, *Let there be light, and there is light.*

JAMIESON, FAUSSET, BROWN

MARTIN LUTHER:

Now He closes this with a beautiful analogy, showing the final outcome of both: "Everyone who hears and practices My teaching is a fine, smart builder, who does not build on sand but first finds a strong rock as a foundation. Once he has this, he builds on it so that his house may last and stand firm. Then when the storms and rains strike around it and above it, and when the floods and winds strike beneath it to wash away the ground and upset the house, it stands immovable against all of them though it were defying them. But everyone who erects his building on sand will discover that it will stand only until the rain and the floods wash it away and the wind upsets it, so that it lies in a heap or collapses by itself." With this analogy He intends to give us a faithful warning to be careful that we hold tight to His teaching and do not let go of Christ in our hearts, as our only sure foundation (1 Cor. 3:1) and the cornerstone of our salvation and blessedness (1 Pet. 2:6), as St. Paul and St. Peter call Him on the basis of Isaiah 28:16. If we stand grounded and built on that, we shall remain impregnable. We can let the world and the devil and all the false teachers and schismatic spirits send rain and hail and slush on us and storm and rage around us with every kind of danger and trouble.—*Luther's Works*

25. And the rain [from above] **descended, and the floods** [from below] **came, and the winds** [sweeping across] **blew, and** [thus from every direction] **beat upon that house; and it fell not; for it was founded upon a rock**—See I John 2:17.

26. And every one that heareth these sayings of mine—in the attitude of discipleship—**and doeth them not, shall be likened unto a foolish man, which built his house upon the sand**—denoting a loose foundation—that of an empty profession and mere external services.

27. And the rain descended, and the floods came, and the winds blew, and beat upon [struck against] **that house; and it fell: and great was the fall of it**—terrible the ruin! How lively must this imagery have been to an audience accustomed to the fierceness of an Eastern tempest, and the suddenness and completeness with which it sweeps everything unsteady before it!

Effect of the Sermon on the Mount. (vss. 28, 29). **28. And it came to pass, when Jesus had ended these sayings, the people were astonished at his doctrine**—rather, "His teaching," for the reference is to the manner of it quite as much as the matter, or rather more so.

29. For he taught them as [one] **having authority**—The word "one," which our translators have here inserted, only weakens the statement. **and not as the scribes**—The consciousness of divine authority, as Lawgiver, Expounder and Judge, so beamed through His teaching, that the scribes' teaching could not but appear drivelling in such a light.

ADAM CLARKE

25. *And the rain descended, and the floods came, and the winds blew.* There are three general kinds of trials to which the followers of God are exposed, and to which, some think, our Lord alludes here: *First,* those of temporal afflictions, coming in the course of divine providence; these may be likened to the torrents of *rain. Second,* those which come from the passions of men, and which may be likened to the impetuous *rivers. Third,* those which come from Satan and his angels, and which, like tempestuous *whirlwinds,* threaten to carry everything before them. He alone whose soul is built on the Rock of ages stands all these shocks; and not only stands in, but profits by them.

26. *And every one that heareth . . . and doeth them not.* Was there ever a stricter system of morality delivered by God to man than in this sermon? He who reads or hears it and does not look to God to conform his soul and life to it, and notwithstanding is hoping to enter into the kingdom of Heaven, is like the fool who *built his house upon the sand.* When the rain, the rivers, and the winds come, his building must fall, and his soul be crushed into the nethermost pit by its ruins.

27. *And the rain descended, and the floods came.* A fine illustration of this may be seen in the case of the fishermen in Bengal, who, in the dry season, build their huts on the beds of sand from which the river has retired. But when the rain sets in suddenly, as it often does, accompanied with violent northwest winds, and the waters pour down in torrents from the mountains, in one night multitudes of these buildings are swept away, and the place where they stood is on the next morning indiscoverable.

28. *The people were astonished.* "The multitudes," for vast crowds attended the ministry of this most popular and faithful of all preachers. They *were astonished at his doctrine.* They heard the law defined in such a manner as they had never thought of before, and this sacred system of morality urged home on their consciences with such clearness and authority as they had never felt under the teaching of their scribes and Pharisees.

29. *Having authority.* They felt a commanding power and authority in His word, i.e., His doctrine. His statements were perspicuous, His exhortations persuasive, His doctrine sound and rational, and His arguments irresistible.

MATTHEW HENRY

CHAPTER 8

The people that heard him were *astonished at his doctrine*; and the effect was, that *when he came down from the mountain, great multitudes followed him.* They to whom Christ has manifested himself, cannot but desire to be better acquainted with him. They who know much of Christ should covet to know more. It is pleasing to see people so well affected to Christ, as to think they can never hear enough of him. Yet they who gathered to him did not cleave to him. They who followed him closely and constantly were but few, compared with the multitudes that were but followers at large.

In these verses we have an account of Christ's *cleansing a leper*. This is fitly recorded with the first of Christ's miracles, 1. Because the leprosy was looked upon, among the Jews, as a particular mark of God's displeasure; and therefore Christ, to show that he came to turn away the wrath of God, by taking away sin, began with the cure of a leper. 2. Because this disease, as it was supposed to come immediately from the hand of God, so also it was supposed to be removed immediately by his hand, and therefore it was not attempted to be cured by physicians, but was put under the inspection of the priests, the Lord's ministers, who waited to see what God would do. Christ proved himself God, by recovering many from the leprosy, and authorizing his disciples, in his name, to do so too (*ch.* x. 8), and it is put among the proofs of his being, the Messiah, *ch.* xi. 5. He also showed himself to be the Saviour of his people from their sins; for though every disease is both the fruit of sin, and a figure of it, as the disorder of the soul, yet the leprosy was in a special manner so. It is treated, not as a sickness, but as an uncleanness; the priest was to pronounce the party clean or unclean, according to the indications: but the honour of making the lepers clean was reserved for Christ. The law discovered sin (for by the law is the knowledge of sin), and pronounced sinners unclean; but could go no further; it could not *make the comers thereunto perfect*. But Christ takes away sin; cleanses us from it.

I. The leper's address to Christ. We may suppose that the leper, though shut out by his disease from the cities of Israel, yet got within hearing of Christ's sermon, and was encouraged by it to make his application to him; for he that taught *as one having authority*, could heal so. His address is, *Lord, if thou wilt, thou canst make me clean.* The cleansing of him may be considered.

1. As a temporal mercy; a mercy to the body. And so it directs us, not only to apply ourselves to Christ, but it also teaches us in what manner to apply ourselves to him; with an assurance of his power, but with a submission to his will; *Lord,* if *thou wilt, thou canst.* His *promise* of them is limited by a regard to his glory and our good: when we cannot be sure of his will, we may be sure of his wisdom and mercy, to which we may cheerfully refer ourselves; *Thy will be done.*

2. As a typical mercy. Sin is the leprosy of the soul; it shuts us out from communion with God, it is necessary that we be cleansed from this leprosy. Now, observe, It is our comfort when we apply ourselves to Christ, as the great Physician, that if he will, he can make us clean; and we should, with an humble, believing boldness, go to him and tell him so. (1) We must rest ourselves upon his power; we must be confident of this, that Christ *can* make us clean. (2) We must recommend ourselves to his pity; we cannot demand it as a debt, but we must humbly request it as a favour; "*Lord, if thou wilt.* I throw myself at thy feet, and if I perish, I will perish there."

II. Christ's answer to this address, which was very kind, *v.* 3.

1. *He put forth his hand and touched him.* The leprosy was a noisome, loathsome disease, yet Christ touched him. There was a ceremonial pollution contracted by the touch of a leper; but Christ would show, that when he conversed with sinners, he was in no danger of being infected by them.

2. He said, *I will, be thou clean.* He did not put him upon a tedious, troublesome, chargeable course of physic, but spake the word and healed him. (1) Here is a word of kindness, *I will*; I am as willing to help thee, as thou art to be helped. Christ is a Physician, that does not need to be sought for, he is always in the way; does not need to be urged, while we are yet speaking, he hears; does not need to be paid, he heals, freely, not for price nor reward. He is as willing as he is able to save sinners. (2) A word of power, *Be thou clean.* Both a power of authority, and a power of energy, are exerted in this word. Christ heals by a word of command to us; *Be thou clean.* But there goes along with this a word of command concerning us, a word that does the work; *I will that thou be clean.* The Almighty grace which speaks it, shall not

JAMIESON, FAUSSET, BROWN

CHAPTER 8

Vss. 1-4. Healing of a Leper. (= Mark 1:40-45; Luke 5:12-16). The time of this miracle seems too definitely fixed here to admit of our placing it where it stands in Mark and Luke, in whose Gospels no such precise note of time is given. **1. When he was come down from the mountain, great multitudes followed him. 2. And, behold, there came a leper**—"a man full of leprosy," says Luke 5:12. Much has been written on this disease of leprosy, but certain points remain still doubtful. All that needs be said here is that it was a cutaneous disease, of a loathsome, diffusive, and, there is reason to believe, when thoroughly pronounced, incurable character; that though in its distinctive features it is still found in several countries—as Arabia, Egypt, and South Africa—it prevailed, in the form of what is called white leprosy, to an unusual extent, and from a very early period, among the Hebrews; and that it thus furnished to the whole nation a familiar and affecting symbol of sin, considered as (1) *loathsome,* (2) *spreading,* (3) *incurable.* And while the ceremonial ordinances for detection and cleansing prescribed in this case by the law of Moses (Lev. 13, 14) held forth a coming remedy "for sin and for uncleanness" (Ps. 51:7; II Kings 5:1, 7, 10, 13, 14), the numerous cases of leprosy with which our Lord came in contact, and the glorious cures of them which He wrought, were a fitting manifestation of the work which He came to accomplish. In this view, it deserves to be noticed that the first of our Lord's miracles of healing recorded by Matthew is this cure of a leper. **and worshipped him**—in what sense we shall presently see. Mark says (1:40), he came, "beseeching and kneeling to Him," and Luke says (5:12), "he fell on his face."

saying, Lord, if thou wilt, thou canst make me clean—As this is the only cure of leprosy recorded by all the three first Evangelists, it was probably the first case of the kind; and if so, this leper's faith in the power of Christ must have been formed in him by what he had heard of His other cures. And how striking a faith is it! He does not say he *believed* Him able, but with a brevity expressive of a confidence that knew no doubt, he says simply, "Thou canst." But of Christ's willingness to heal him he was not so sure. It needed more knowledge of Jesus than he could be supposed to have to assure him of that. But one thing he was sure of, that He had but to "will" it. This shows with what "worship" of Christ this leper fell on his face before Him. Clear theological knowledge of the Person of Christ was not then possessed even by those who were most with Him and nearest to Him. Much less could full insight into all that we know of the Only-begotten of the Father be expected of this leper. But he who at that moment felt and owned that to heal an incurable disease needed but the *fiat* of the Person who stood before him, had assuredly that very faith in the germ which now casts its crown before Him that loved us, and would at any time die for His blessed name. **3. And Jesus**—or "He," according to another reading,—"moved with compassion," says Mark (1:41); a precious addition. **put forth his hand, and touched him**—Such a touch occasioned ceremonial defilement (Lev. 5:3); even as the leper's coming near enough for contact was against the Levitical regulations (Lev. 13:46). But as the man's faith told him there would be no case for such regulations if the cure he hoped to experience should be accomplished, so He who had healing in His wings transcended all such statutes. **saying, I will; be thou clean**—How majestic those two words! By not assuring the man of His *power* to heal him, He delightfully sets His seal to the man's previous confession of that power; and by assuring him of the one thing of which he had any doubt, and for which he waited—His *will* to do it—He makes a claim as divine as the cure which immediately followed it.

ADAM CLARKE

CHAPTER 8

1. *From the mountain.* That mountain on which He had delivered the preceding inimitable sermon. *Great multitudes followed him.* Having been deeply impressed with the glorious doctrines which they had just heard.

2. *And, behold, there came a leper.* The leprosy was an inveterate cutaneous disease, appearing in dry, thin, white, scurfy scales or scabs, either on the whole body or on some part of it, usually attended with violent itching and often with great pain. The various symptoms of this dreadful disorder, which was a striking emblem of sin, may be seen in Leviticus xiii—xiv, where also may be read the legal ordinances concerning it.

Lord, if thou wilt, thou canst make me clean. As this leper may be considered as a fit emblem of the corruption of man by sin, so may his cure, of the redemption of the soul by Christ. A sinner, truly penitent, seeks God with a respectful faith; approaches Him in the spirit of adoration; humbles himself under His mighty hand, acknowledging the greatness of his fall and the vileness of his sin. His prayer, like that of the leper, should be humble, plain, and full of confidence in that God who can do all things, and of dependence upon His will or mercy, from which all good must be derived. It is peculiar to God that He need only *will* what He intends to perform. His power is His will.

3. *Jesus put forth his hand . . . I will; be thou clean.* The most sovereign authority is assumed in this speech of our blessed Lord—*I will.* There is here no supplication of any power superior to His own; and the event proved to the fullest conviction, and by the clearest demonstration, that His authority was absolute and His power unlimited.

MATTHEW HENRY

be wanting to those who truly desire it.

III. The happy change hereby wrought: *Immediately his leprosy was cleansed.* Nature works gradually, but the God of nature works immediately; he speaks, it is done.

IV. The after-directions Christ gave him. It is fit that they who are cured by Christ should ever after be ruled by him.

1. *See thou tell no man;* "Tell no man till thou hast shown thyself to the priest, and he has pronounced thee clean; and so thou hast a legal proof, both that thou wast before a leper, and art now thoroughly cleansed." Christ would have his miracles to appear in their full light and evidence, and not to be published till they could appear so.

2. *Go show thyself to the priest*, according to the law, Lev. xiv. 2. Christ took care to have the law observed, lest he should give offence, and to show that he will have order kept up, and good discipline and respect paid to those that are in office.

3. *Offer the gift that Moses commanded*, in token of thankfulness to God, and recompense to the priest for his pains; and this *for a testimony unto them.* It shall be a testimony, that there is one among them who does that which the high priest cannot do. Let it remain upon record as a witness of my power, and a testimony for me *to* them, if they will use it and improve it; but *against* them, if they will not.

Verses 5-13

We have here an account of Christ's curing the centurion's servant of a palsy. This was done at Capernaum, where Christ now dwelt, *ch.* iv. 13. Christ went about doing good, and came home to do good too; every place he came to was the better for him.

The persons Christ had now to do with were,

1. A *centurion*; he was a supplicant, a Gentile, a Roman, an officer of the army. Though he was a soldier (and a little piety commonly goes a great way with men of that profession), yet he was a godly man. God has his remnant among all sorts of people. No man's calling or place in the world will be an excuse for his unbelief and impiety. And sometimes where grace conquers the unlikely, it is more than a conqueror. Though he was a Roman soldier, and his very dwelling among the Jews was a badge of their subjection to the Roman yoke, yet Christ, who was *King of the Jews*, favoured him; and therein has taught us to do good to our enemies. Though he was a Gentile, yet Christ countenanced him. Now good old Simeon's word began to be fulfilled, that he should be *a light to lighten the Gentiles*, as well as *the glory of his people Israel*. The leprous Jews Christ touched and cured, for he preached personally to them; but the paralytic Gentiles he cured at a distance; for to them he did not go in person, but *sent his word and healed them*; yet in them he was more magnified.

2. *The centurion's servant.* He is as ready to heal the poorest servant, as the richest master; for himself *took upon him the form of a servant*, to show his regard to the meanest.

I. The grace of the centurion working towards Christ. Can any good thing come out of a Roman soldier? Come and see, and you will find abundance of good coming out of this centurion.

1. His affectionate address to Jesus Christ, which speaks,

(1) A pious regard to our great Master, as one able and willing to succour and relieve poor petitioners. He came to him *beseeching him* with cap in hand as a humble suitor. By this it seems that he saw more in Christ than appeared at first view; saw that which commanded respect. The greatest of men must turn beggars, when they have to do with Christ. He owns Christ's sovereignty, in calling him Lord, and referring the case to him, and to his will, and wisdom. He knew he had to do with a wise and gracious Physician, to whom the opening of the malady was equivalent to the most earnest request. A humble confession of our spiritual wants and diseases shall not fail of an answer of peace. Pour out thy complaint, and mercy shall be poured out.

(2) A charitable regard to his poor servant. We read of many that came to Christ for their children, but this is the only instance of one that came to him for a servant: *Lord, my servant lieth at home sick.* It is the duty of masters to concern themselves for their servants, when they are in affliction. The servant could not have done more for the master, than the master did here for the servant. The centurion's servants were very dutiful to him (*v.* 9), and here we see what made them so; he was very kind to them, and that made them the more cheerfully obedient to him. The palsy is a disease in which the physician's skill commonly fails; it was therefore a great evidence of his faith in the power of Christ, to come to him

JAMIESON, FAUSSET, BROWN

And immediately his leprosy was cleansed—Mark, more emphatic, says (1: 42), "And as soon as He had spoken, immediately the leprosy departed from him, and he was cleansed"—as perfectly as instantaneously. What a contrast this to modern pretended cures! **4. And Jesus** ["straitly charged him, and forthwith sent him away," Mark 1:43, and] **saith unto him, See thou tell no man**—A hard condition this would seem to a grateful heart, whose natural language, in such a case, is "Come, hear, all ye that fear God, and I will declare what He hath done for my soul" (Ps. 66:16). We shall presently see the reason for it. **but go thy way, show thyself to the priest, and offer the gift that Moses commanded** [Lev. 14] **for a testimony unto them**—a palpable witness that the Great Healer had indeed come, and that "God had visited His people." What the sequel was, our Evangelist Matthew does not say; but Mark thus gives it (1:45): "But he went out, and began to publish it much, and to blaze abroad the matter, insomuch that Jesus could no more openly enter into the city, but was without in desert places: and they came to Him from every quarter." Thus—by an over-zealous, though most natural and not very culpable, infringement of the injunction to keep the matter quiet—was our Lord, to some extent, thwarted in His movements. As His whole course was sublimely noiseless (ch. 12:19), so we find Him repeatedly taking steps to prevent matters prematurely coming to a crisis with Him. (But see on Mark 5:19, 20). "And He withdrew Himself," adds Luke (5:16), "into the wilderness, and prayed"; retreating from the popular excitement into the secret place of the Most High, and thus coming forth as dew upon the mown grass, and as showers that water the earth (Ps. 72:6). And this is the secret both of strength and of sweetness in the servants and followers of Christ in every age.

5-13. HEALING OF THE CENTURION'S SERVANT. (= Luke 7:1-10.) This incident belongs to a later stage. For the exposition, see on Luke 7:1-10.

These centurions were Roman officers, so called from being captains over a hundred soldiers. Though a heathen by birth and early training, he had become acquainted with the Jewish religion probably either while quartered at Capernaum or in some other Galilean town; although there were so many proselytes to the Jewish religion in all the principal Greek and Roman cities that he might have embraced the true faith even before his arrival in the Holy Land. The same may be said of Cornelius (Acts 10:1). His character appears here in the most beautiful light. The value which he set upon this dying servant and his anxiety for his recovery—as if he had been his own son—is the first feature in it; for, as Bp. Hall observes, he is unworthy to be well served who will not sometimes wait upon his followers. This servant was "sick of the palsy, grievously tormented."

How devoutly would this centurion, as he thought of the Providence that brought him into contact with the chosen people, and thus turned his heathen darkness into light, exclaim with the sweet Psalmist of Israel, "The lines are fallen unto me in pleasant places; yea, I have a goodly heritage"! (Ps. 16:6). And Cornelius also (Acts 10:1); and Lydia (Acts 16:14). And by what wonderful providences have hundreds and thousands since then been brought, as by accident and through circumstances the most trivial, into contact with the truth which has set them free! But, perhaps, if we knew all, it would be found that in every case it is in a way perfectly casual and all unexpected that the ear first hears effectually the loving voice which says, "Look unto me, and be saved." And if so, what materials will this afford for wonder in heaven, when the whole story of each one's life will stand up before his view distinct and vivid; and what a fund of blissful intercourse will be thus provided when the redeemed will, as we may reasonably believe, exchange with each other their past experience as each says to the other, "Come, all ye that fear God, and I will declare what he hath done for my soul!"

ADAM CLARKE

And immediately his leprosy was cleansed. What an astonishing sight! A man whose whole body was covered over with the most loathsome disease cleansed from it in a moment of time! Was it possible for any soul to resist the evidence of this fact?

4. *Jesus saith unto him, See thou tell no man.* Had our Lord, at this early period, fully manifested himself as the Messiah, the people in all likelihood would have proclaimed Him King. This, however, refused by Him, must have excited the hatred of the Jewish rulers and the jealousy of the Roman government; and, speaking after the manner of men, His further preachings and miracles must have been impeded. This alone seems to be the reason why He said to the leper, *See thou tell no man. Shew thyself to the priest.* This was to conform to the law instituted in this case, Lev. xiv. 1, etc. *Offer the gift.* This gift was two living, clean birds, some cedarwood, with scarlet and hyssop, Lev. xiv. 4, which were to be brought for his cleansing; and, when clean, two he lambs, one ewe lamb, three tenth deals of flour, and one log of oil, v. 10. But if the person were poor, then he was to bring one lamb, one tenth deal of flour, one log of oil, and two turtledoves or young pigeons, vv. 21-22.

Now all this was to be done *for a testimony unto them*, to prove that this leper, who was doubtless well-known in the land, had been thoroughly cleansed; and thus, in this private way, to give full proof to the priesthood that Jesus was the true Messiah. The Jewish rabbins allowed that curing the lepers should be a characteristic of the Messiah; therefore the obstinacy of the priests in rejecting Christ was utterly inexcusable.

5. *A centurion.* A Roman military officer who had the command of 100 men.

6. *Lord.* Rather, "Sir," for so the word should always be translated when a Roman is the speaker. *Lieth at home.* "Lieth all along"; intimating that the disease had reduced him to a state of the utmost impotence, through the grievous torments with which it was accompanied. *Sick of the palsy.* Or "paralytic."

MATTHEW HENRY

for a cure, which was above the power of natural means to effect. Observe, How pathetically he represents his servant's case as very sad; he is *sick of the palsy*, a disease which commonly makes the patient senseless of pain, but this person was *grievously tormented.* We should thus concern ourselves for the souls of our children, and servants, that are spiritually sick of the palsy, and bring them to Christ by faith and prayer, bring them to the means of healing and health.

2. Observe his great humility and self-abasement. After Christ had intimated his readiness to come and heal his servant (*v.* 7), he expressed himself with the more humbleness of mind. Humble souls are made more humble, by Christ's gracious condescensions to them. *Lord, I am not worthy that thou shouldst come under my roof* (*v.* 8), which speaks mean thoughts of himself, and high thoughts of our Lord Jesus. He does not say, "My servant is not worthy that thou shouldst come into his chamber, because it is in the garret"; But *I am not worthy that thou shouldst come into my house.* The centurion was a great man, yet he owned his unworthiness before God. Humility very well becomes persons of quality. Christ now made but a mean figure in the world, yet the centurion paid him this respect. We should have a value and veneration for what we see of God, even in those who, in outward condition, are every way our inferiors. In all our approaches to Christ, and to God through Christ, it becomes us to abase ourselves, and to lie low in the sense of our own unworthiness.

3. Observe his great faith. The more humility the more faith. He had an assurance of faith not only that Christ could cure his servant, but,

(1) That he could cure him at a distance. There needed not any physical contact, as in natural operations, not any application to the part affected. We read afterwards of those, who brought the *man sick of the palsy to Christ*, through much difficulty, and set him before him; and Christ commended their faith for a *working* faith. This centurion did not bring his man *sick of the palsy*, and Christ commended his faith for a *trusting* faith: true faith is accepted of Christ, though variously appearing: Christ puts the best construction upon the different methods of religion that people take. Nearness and distance are alike to him. Distance of place cannot obstruct either the knowing or working of him that *fills all places.*

(2) That he could cure him with a *word*, not send him a medicine, much less a charm; but *speak the word only*, and I do not question but *my servant shall be healed.* Herein he owns him to have a divine power. With men, saying and doing are two things; but not so with Christ.

The centurion's faith in the power of Christ he here illustrates by the dominion he had, as a centurion, over his soldiers, as a master over his servants; he says to one, *Go, and he goes, &c.* They were all at his beck and command, so that he could by them execute things at a distance. Thus could Christ speak, and it is done. The centurion had this command over his soldiers, though he was himself a *man under authority*; much more had Christ this power, who is the supreme and sovereign Lord of all. Such servants we all should be to God: we must go and come at his bidding, according to the directions of his word, and the disposals of his providence. When his will crosses our own, his must take place, and our own be set aside. Such servants bodily diseases are to Christ. It is a matter of comfort to all that belong to Christ, that every disease is made to serve the intentions of his grace. They need not fear sickness, nor what it can do, who see it in the hand of so good a Friend.

II. Here is the grace of Christ appearing towards this centurion; for to the gracious he will show himself gracious.

1. He complies with his address at the first word. *I will come and heal him* (*v.* 7); not *I will come and see him*—that had evinced him a kind Saviour; but, *I will come and heal him*—that shows him a mighty, an almighty Saviour. He has *healing under his wings*; his coming is healing. The centurion desired he would heal his servant; he says, *I will come and heal him*; thus expressing more favour than he did either ask or think of. Christ often outdoes the expectations of poor supplicants. He would not go down to see a nobleman's sick child, who insisted upon his coming down (John iv. 47–49), but he proffers to go down to see a sick servant. Christ's humility in being willing to come, gave an example to him, and occasioned his humility, in owning himself unworthy to have him come. Christ's gracious condescensions to us, should make us the more humble and self-abasing before him.

2. He commends his faith, and takes occasion from it to speak a kind word of the poor Gentiles, *v.* 10–12.

JAMIESON, FAUSSET, BROWN

Bright as was the radiance which shone from the Old Testament upon this mind that had been reared in pagan darkness, it rested not there, but was only guided by it to Him of whom Moses, in the law, and the prophets did write. Nor was his a hesitating or superficial faith. Capernaum being the place of Christ's stated residence while in Galilee, this devout officer seems to have not only heard His public addresses, but made himself sufficiently acquainted with the wonders of His gracious hand to have every doubt as to His claims removed, and a profound conviction implanted in his mind of His divine dignity. When, therefore, he has need of His interposition, he applies for it with undoubting confidence, "beseeching him to come and heal his servant." But he shrinks from a personal application as "unworthy to come to him"; and though he had petitioned Jesus to come and heal his servant, he sends again to say that it was too much honor to him that He should come under his roof, but that since one word of command from Him would suffice, he would be content with that. What wonderful faith is this for a convert from heathenism to reach! The arguments by which he illustrates the power of Jesus to order diseases to be gone—as servants in entire subjection to their Master and Lord—are singularly expressive of a faith in the sovereignty of Christ over the elements of nature and the forces of life to which nothing was impossible. And when we "see how faith wrought with his works [in loving God's nation and building them a synagogue], and by works his faith was made perfect"; and when we observe how all this anxiety of his was not like that of Jairus for the life of an only daughter (ch. 8: 42), nor like that of the nobleman for his son (John 4:27), but for a servant that was dear to him, can we wonder that Jesus should say, "I have not found so great faith, no, not in Israel"?

For I also am a man set under authority, having under me soldiers; and I say unto one, Go, and he goeth; and to another, Come, and he cometh; and to my servant, Do this, and he doeth it. "I know both to obey and command: though but a subaltern, my orders are implicitly obeyed: Shall not diseases, then, obey their Lord, and at His word be gone?"

ADAM CLARKE

F. B. MEYER:

Rewards of faith. The Lord can touch thy heart, leprous with impurity, and make its stain depart, so that, as in the case of Naaman, its foulness shall become "like unto the flesh of a little child" (see 2 Kings 5:14). The psalmist cried, "Purge me with hyssop, and I shall be clean," alluding to the rite for the cleansing of the leper (Ps. 51:7; Lev. 14:4). But one touch of Christ's hand is enough, for he is the Great High Priest.

He also can heal the paralysis which has limited thy service and pinned thee down in helplessness. As the centurion recognized, because Christ was obedient to the Father's Law, he was able to wield the Father's power. He humbled himself and became obedient to the death of the cross; therefore God hath highly exalted him, that he might send tides of living energy into the paralyzed will. The Apostle Paul testified, "I can do all things through Christ which strengtheneth me."—*Bible Commentary*

8. *But speak the word only.* Or, "Speak by word or command." Jesus can will away the palsy, and speak away the most grievous torments.

9. *For I am a man under authority.* That is, "under the authority of others." The argument of the centurion seems to run thus. If I, who am a person subject to the control of others, yet have some so completely subject to myself that I can say to one, *Come, and he cometh;* to another, *Go, and he goeth;* and to my slave, *Do this, and he doeth it;* how much more then canst Thou accomplish whatsoever Thou willest, being under no control, and having all things under Thy command!

7. *I will come and heal him.* "I am coming, and will heal him." Jesus did not positively say, *I will come and heal him;* this could not have been strictly true, because our Lord healed him without going to the house. Foreseeing the exercise of the centurion's faith, He promises that while He is coming, ere He arrives at the house, He will heal him, and this was literally done, v. 13.

MATTHEW HENRY

(1) As to the centurion himself; he not only approved him and accepted him (that honour have all true believers), but he admired him and applauded him: that honour great believers have.

[1] Christ admired him, not for his greatness, but for his graces. *When Jesus heard it, he marvelled;* not as if it were to him new and surprising, but it was great and excellent, rare and uncommon, and Christ spoke of it as wonderful, to teach us what to admire; not worldly pomp and decorations, but the beauty of holiness. The wonders of grace should affect us more than the wonders of nature or providence, and spiritual attainments more than any achievements in this world.

[2] He *applauded* him in what he said to *them that followed. Verily, I have not found so great faith, no, not in Israel.* Now this speaks, *First, Honour to the centurion*; who, though not a son of Abraham's loins, was an heir of Abraham's faith. The thing that Christ seeks is *faith*, and wherever it is, he *finds* it, though but *as a grain of mustard seed.* We must be forward, to give those their due praise, that are not within our denomination or pale. *Secondly*, It speaks *shame to Israel.* When *the Son of man comes*, he *finds* little *faith*, and, therefore, he finds so little *fruit.* Christ said this *to those that followed him.* They were Abraham's seed; in jealousy for that honour, let them not suffer themselves to be outstripped by a Gentile, especially in that grace for which Abraham was eminent.

(2) As to others. Christ tells them two things, which could not but be very surprising to them who had been taught that *salvation was of the Jews.*

[1] That *a great many of the Gentiles should be saved, v.* 11. The faith of the centurion was but a specimen of the conversion of the Gentiles. This was a topic our Lord Jesus touched often upon; he speaks with assurance; *I say unto you*, although an intimation of this kind enraged the Nazarenes against him, Luke iv. 27. Christ gives us here an *idea*, *First*, of the *persons* that shall be *saved*; many *from the east and the west*: he had said (*ch.* vii. 14), *Few there be that find the way to life*; and yet here *many shall come.* Few at one time, and in one place; yet, when they come altogether, they will be a great many. They shall come *from the east* and *from the west*; places far distant from each other; and yet they shall all meet at the right hand of Christ, the Centre of their unity. God has his remnant in all places. Though they were *strangers to the covenant of promise* now, and had been long, yet who knows what *hidden ones* God had among them then? When we come to heaven, as we shall miss a great many there, that we thought had been going thither, so we shall meet a great many there, that we did not expect. *Secondly*, Christ gives us an idea of the *salvation itself.* They shall come, shall come together, shall come together to Christ, 2 Thess. ii. 1. 1. They shall be admitted *into the kingdom of grace* on earth; they shall be *blessed with faithful Abraham.* This makes Zaccheus a son of Abraham, Luke xix. 9. 2. They shall be admitted into the *kingdom of glory in heaven.* They shall sit down to rest from their labours, as having done their day's work; sitting denotes *continuance*: while we *stand*, we are *going*; where we *sit*, we mean to *stay*; as *at a table*; that is the metaphor here; they shall sit down to be *feasted*; which denotes both *fulness* of *communication*, and *freedom* and familiarity of communion, Luke xxii. 30. They shall *sit down with Abraham.* They who in this world were ever so far distant from each other in time, place, or outward condition, shall all meet together in heaven. Holy society is a part of the felicity of heaven.

[2] That a great many of the Jews should perish, *v.* 12. Observe,

First, A strange sentence passed; *The children of the kingdom shall be cast out; the kingdom of God*, of which they boasted that they were *the children*, shall be taken from them. In the great day it will not avail men to have been *children of the kingdom*, either as Jews or as Christians; for men will then be judged, not by what they were *called*, but by what they *were.* Being born of professing parents denominates us *children of the kingdom*; but if we rest in that, and have nothing else to show for heaven but that, we shall be *cast out.*

Secondly, A strange punishment for *the workers of iniquity* described; *They shall be cast into outer darkness*, the darkness of those that are without. *They shall be cast out* from God, and all true comfort, and *cast into darkness.* It is *utter darkness*; without any remainder, or mixture, or hope, of light; not the least gleam or glimpse of it; it is darkness that results from their being shut out of heaven, the land of light.

3. He cures his servant. He grants him that for which he applied, which was a real answer, *v.* 13.

(1) What Christ said to him: he said that which

JAMIESON, FAUSSET, BROWN

When Jesus heard these things, he marvelled at him. As Bengel hints, Jesus marveled but at two things—*faith* (as here) and *unbelief* (Mark 6:6): at the one, considering the general blindness in spiritual things; at the other, considering the light that shone around all who were privileged to hear Him and behold His works. But the unprecedented faith of this heathen convert could not fail to fill His soul with peculiar admiration. **and turned him about, and said unto the people that followed him**—Jews, no doubt, **I have not found so great faith, no, not in Israel**—among the chosen people; this Gentile outstripping all the children of the covenant.

A most important addition to this statement is given by Matthew (8:11, 12), who wrote specially for the Jews: "And I say unto you, that many shall come from the east and west"—from all parts of the heathen world—"and shall sit down"—"shall recline," as at a feast, "with Abraham, and Isaac, and Jacob"—the fathers of the ancient covenant. Luke, reporting a solemn repetition of these words on a later occasion (ch. 13:28-30), adds, "and all the prophets," "in the kingdom of heaven": "but the children of the kingdom"—born to its privileges, but void of faith, "shall be cast out into outer darkness," the darkness outside the banqueting-house; "there [or in this outside region] shall be weeping and gnashing of teeth"—the one expressive of *anguish*, the other of *despair.*

When He says that this centurion was, after all, but one of a class which, from the most distant and unpromising spots, would occupy the highest places and be in the most favored company in the kingdom of heaven—while those that had been nursed in the arms and dandled upon the knees and had sucked the breasts of God's lawgivers and prophets, and basked in the sunshine of supernatural truth and divine ordinances, without any inward transformation, would be thrust out, and found weltering in anguish and despair—what a warning does it utter to the religiously favored, and what encouragement does it hold out to work hopefully among the heathen abroad and the outcasts at home, that "there are first which shall be last, and there are last which shall be first!"

ADAM CLARKE

10. *I have not found so great faith, no, not in Israel.* That is, I have not found so great an instance of confidence and faith in My power, even among the Jews, as this Roman, a Gentile, has shown himself to possess.

11. *Many shall come from the east and west.* Men of every description, of all countries, and of all professions; *and shall sit down*, that is, to meat, for this is the proper meaning. The rabbins represent the blessedness of the kingdom of God under the notion of a banquet.

***With Abraham, and Isaac, and Jacob.* In the closest communion with the most eminent followers of God. But if we desire to inherit the promises, we must be followers of them who through faith and patience enjoy them. Let us therefore imitate Abraham in his faith, Isaac in his obedience unto death, and Jacob in his hope and expectation of good things to come.**

12. *Shall be cast out into outer darkness.* As the enjoyment of that salvation which Jesus Christ calls the kingdom of Heaven is here represented under the notion of a nuptial festival, at which the guests sat down in a reclining posture with the master of the feast, so the state of those who were excluded from the banquet is represented as deep darkness, because the nuptial solemnities took place at night. And because they who were shut out were not only exposed to shame, but also to hunger and cold, therefore it is added, *There shall be weeping and gnashing of teeth.*

MATTHEW HENRY

made the cure as great a favour to him as it was to his servant, and much greater; *As thou hast believed, so be it done to thee.* The servant got a cure of his disease, but the master got the confirmation and approbation of his faith. Christ often gives encouraging answers to his praying people, when they are interceding for others. It is kindness to us, to be heard for others. *Be it done as thou believest.* What could he have more? Yet what was said to him is said to us all, *Believe, and ye shall receive; only believe.* See here the power of Christ, and the power of faith. As Christ can *do* what he will, so an active believer may *have* what he will from Christ.

(2) What was the effect of this saying: the prayer of faith was a prevailing prayer, it ever was so, and ever will be so; it appears, by the suddenness of the cure, that it was *miraculous*: *he spake, and it was done*; and this was a proof of his omnipotence, that he has a long arm.

Verses 14–17

I. A particular account of the cure of *Peter's wife's mother*, who was ill *of a fever*.

1. The *case* which was nothing extraordinary; it is recorded as an instance of Christ's peculiar care of, and kindness to, the families of his disciples. Here we find, (1) That Peter had a *wife*, and yet *was called to be an apostle of Christ*; and Christ countenanced the marriage state. (2) That Peter had a *house*, though Christ had not, *v.* 20. Thus was the disciple better provided for than his Lord. (3) That he had a house at Capernaum, though he was originally of Bethsaida; it is probable, he removed to Capernaum, when Christ removed thither, and made that his principal residence. It is worth while to change our quarters, that we may be near to Christ. (4) That he had his *wife's mother* with him in his family, which is an example to yoke-fellows to be kind to one another's relations as their own. Probably, this good woman was old, and yet was respected and taken care of, as old people ought to be, with all possible tenderness. (5) That she lay ill *of a fever*. The palsy was a chronic disease, the fever an acute disease, but both were brought to Christ.

2. The *cure*, *v.* 15. (1) How it was *effected*; *He touched her hand;* not to know the disease, as the physicians do, by the pulse, but to heal it. This was an intimation of his kindness and tenderness. The scripture *speaks the word*, the Spirit gives the touch, touches the heart, touches the hand. (2) How it was *evidenced*: this showed that the *fever left her, she arose, and ministered to them*. By this it appears, [1] That the mercy was perfected. They that recover from fevers by the power of nature are commonly weak and feeble. She was immediately so well as to go about the business of the house. [2] That the mercy was sanctified. Though she was thus dignified by a peculiar favour, yet she does not assume importance, but is as ready to wait at table, if there be occasion, as any servant. They must be humble whom Christ has honoured; being thus delivered, she studies what she shall render. It is very fit that they whom Christ hath healed should minister unto him, as his humble servants, all their days.

II. Here is a general account of the many cures that Christ wrought. This cure of Peter's mother-in-law brought him abundance of patients. "He healed such a one; why not me? Such a one's friend, why not mine?" Now we are here told,

1. What he did, *v.* 16. (1) *He cast out devils; cast out the* evil *spirits with his word.* About the time of Christ's being in the world, there seems to have been more than ordinary letting loose of the devil, to possess and vex the bodies of people; and God wisely ordered it so, that Christ might have the fairer and more frequent opportunities of showing his power over Satan. (2) *He healed all that were sick;* all without exception, though the patient was ever so mean, and the case ever so bad.

2. How the scripture was herein fulfilled, *v.* 17. Among other things, it was written of him (Isa. liii. 4), *Surely he hath borne our griefs, and carried our sorrows:* it is referred to, 1 Peter ii. 24, and there it is construed, *he hath borne our sins*; here it is referred to, and is construed, *he hath borne our sicknesses*; our sins make our sicknesses our griefs; Christ bore away sin by the merit of his death, and bore away sickness by the miracles of his life. Many are the diseases and calamities to which we are liable in the body: and there is more, in this one line of the gospels, to support and comfort us under them, than in all the writings of the philosophers. He bore them for us in his *passion*, and bears them with us in *compassion*, being *touched with the feeling of our infirmities*: and thus he bears them off from us. Observe how emphatically it is expressed here: *Himself took our infirmities, and bare our sicknesses;* he was both able

JAMIESON, FAUSSET, BROWN

"And Jesus said unto the centurion, Go thy way: and as thou hast believed, so be it done unto thee. And his servant was healed the self-same hour" (Matt. 8:13), teaching that, as in these bodily diseases, so in the salvation of the soul, all hinges on faith.

14-17. Healing of Peter's Mother-in-Law, and Many Others. (= Mark. 1:29-34; Luke 4: 38-41). For the exposition, see on Mark 1:29-34.

But Simon's wife's mother lay sick of a fever—Luke, as was natural in "the beloved *physician*" (Col. 4:14), describes it professionally; calling it a "great fever," and thus distinguishing it from that lighter kind which the Greek physicians were wont to call "small fevers," as Galen, quoted by Wetstein, tells us.

and immediately the fever left her, and she ministered unto them—preparing their sabbath-meal: in token both of the perfectness and immediateness of the cure, and of her gratitude to the glorious Healer.

And at even, when the sun did set—so Matthew 8:16. Luke (4:40) says it was setting. **they brought unto him all that were diseased, and them that were possessed with devils**—the demonized. From Luke 13:14 we see how unlawful they would have deemed it to bring their sick to Jesus for a cure during the sabbath hours. They waited, therefore, till these were over, and then brought them in crowds. Our Lord afterwards took repeated occasion to teach the people by example, even at the risk of His own life, how superstitious a straining of the sabbath-rest this was. **And all the city was gathered together at the door**—of Peter's house; i.e., the sick and those who brought them, and the wondering spectators. This bespeaks the presence of an eye-witness, and is one of those lively examples of word-painting so frequent in this Gospel. **And he healed many that were sick of divers diseases, and cast out many devils**—In Matthew 8:16 it is said, "He cast out the spirits with His word"; or rather, "with a word"—a word of command. **and suffered not the devils to speak, because they knew him**—Evidently they *would* have spoken, if permitted, proclaiming His Messiahship in such terms as in the synagogue; but once in one day, and that testimony immediately silenced, was enough. See on vs. 24. After this account of His miracles of healing, we have in Matthew 8:17 this pregnant quotation, "That it might be fulfilled which was spoken by Esaias the prophet, saying [53:4], Himself took our infirmities, and bare our sicknesses."

ADAM CLARKE

13. *As thou hast believed; so be it done.* "According to your faith be it done unto you," is a general measure of God's dealings with mankind. God is the same in the present time which He was in ancient days; and miracles of healing may be wrought on our own bodies and souls, and on those of others, by the instrumentality of our faith. But, alas! where is faith to be found! *And his servant was healed in the selfsame hour.* "In that very hour." Faith is never exercised in the power and goodness of God till it is needed; and, when its is exercised, God works the miracle of healing.

14. *Peter's house.* That Peter lived at Capernaum, and that Christ lodged with him, is fully evident from this verse compared with chap. xvii. 24. *Peter's . . . wife's mother.* Learn hence, says Theophylact, that marriage is no hindrance to virtue, since the chief of the apostles had his wife. Marriage is one of the first of divine institutions, and is a positive command of God. He says the state of celibacy is not good, Gen. ii. 18. Those who pretend to say that the single state is more holy than the other slander their Maker, and say in effect, "We are too holy to keep the commandments of God."

15. *He touched her hand.* Can anything on this side the unlimited power of God effect such a cure with only a touch? If the Scriptures had not spoken of the divinity of Christ, these proofs of His power must have demonstrated it to the common sense of every man whose creed had not previously blinded him.

16. *When the even was come.* The Jews kept their Sabbath from evening to evening, according to the law, Lev. xxiii. 32, "From even unto even, shall ye celebrate your sabbath." Hence it was that the sick were not brought out to our Lord till after sunset, because then the Sabbath was ended. *Many that were possessed with devils.* Dr. Lightfoot gives two sound reasons why Judea, in our Lord's time, abounded with demoniacs. First, because they were then advanced to the very height of impiety. See what Josephus, their own historian, says of them: There was not (said he) a nation under heaven more wicked than they were. Secondly, because they were then strongly addicted to magic, and so, as it were, invited evil spirits to be familiar with them. *And healed all that were sick.* Not a soul did the Lord Jesus ever reject who came to Him soliciting His aid. Need any sinner despair who comes to Him, conscious of his spiritual malady, to be healed by His merciful hand?

17. *Himself took our infirmities.* The quotation is taken from Isa. liii. 4, where the verb *nasa* signifies to "bear sin," so as to "make atonement for it." And the rabbins understand this place to speak of the sufferings of the Messiah for the sins of Israel; and say that all the diseases, all the griefs, and all the punishments due to Israel shall be borne by Him. Christ fulfills the prophecies in all respects, and is himself the completion and truth of them, as being the Lamb and Victim of God, which bears and takes away the sin of the world. The text in Isaiah refers properly to the taking away of sin; and this in the Evangelist, to the removal of corporeal afflictions. But as the diseases of the body are the emblems of the sin of the soul, Matthew, referring to the prediction of the prophet, con-

MATTHEW HENRY

and willing to interpose in that matter, and concerned to deal with *our infirmities and sicknesses*, as our Physician.

Verses 18–22

I. Christ's removing to *the other side of the sea of Tiberias*, and his ordering his disciples, whose boats attended him, to get their transport-vessels ready, in order to it, *v.* 18. He must go about to do good; the necessities of souls called to him, *Come over, and help us* (Acts xvi. 9); he removed *when he saw great multitudes about him*. Though by this it appeared that they were desirous to have him there, he knew there were others as desirous to have him with them, and they must have their share of him: his being acceptable and useful in one place was no objection against, but a reason for, his going to another. Many would be glad of such helps, if they could have them at next door, who will not be at pains to follow them to *the other side*.

II. Christ's communication with two, who, upon his remove to *the other side*, were loth to stay behind, and had a mind to follow him, not as others, who were his followers at large, but to come into close discipleship, which the most were shy of.

We have here Christ's managing of two different tempers, one quick and eager, the other dull and heavy; and his instructions are adapted to each of them, and designed for our use.

1. Here is one that was *too hasty in promising*; and he was *a certain scribe* (*v.* 19), a scholar, a learned man, one of those that studied and expounded the law; generally we find them in the gospels to be men of no good character. They were very seldom following Christ; yet here was one that bid pretty fair for discipleship.

(1) How he expressed his forwardness; *Master, I will follow thee, whithersoever thou goest*. I know not how any man could have spoken better. His profession of a self-dedication to Christ is, [1] Very ready *inclination*: he is not called to it by Christ, of his own accord, he proffers himself to be a close follower of Christ; he is not a pressed man, but a volunteer. [2] Very resolute; he seems to be at a point in this matter. "I am determined, *I will* do it." [3] It was unlimited and without reserve. "*I will follow thee whithersoever thou goest.*" Yet it appears, by Christ's answer, that his resolution was rash. There are many resolutions for religion, produced by some sudden pangs of conviction, and taken up without due consideration, that prove abortive, and come to nothing: soon ripe, soon rotten.

(2) How Christ tried his forwardness, whether it was sincere or not, *v.* 20. He let him know that this *Son of man*, whom he is so eager to follow, *has not where to lay his head*, *v.* 20. It is strange in itself, that the Son of God, when he came into the world, should put himself into such a very low condition, as to want the convenience of a certain resting-place. See here, *First*, How well provided for the inferior creatures are: *The foxes have holes;* their holes are their castles. *The birds of the air*, though they take no care for themselves, yet are taken care of, and *have nests* (Ps. civ. 17). *Secondly*, How poorly the Lord Jesus was provided for. He had not a settlement, had not a place of repose, not a house of his own, to put his head in, not a pillow of his own, to lay his head on. He and his disciples lived upon the charity of well-disposed people, that *ministered to him of their substance*, Luke viii. 2. Christ submitted to this that he might show us the vanity of worldly wealth, and teach us to look upon it with a holy contempt; that he might purchase better things for us, and so *make us rich*, 2 Cor. viii. 9. It is strange that such a declaration should be made on this occasion. One scribe might be capable of doing him more credit and service than twelve fishermen: but Christ saw his heart, and answered to the thoughts of that, and therein teaches us all how to come to Christ. *First*, The scribe's resolve seems to have been sudden; and Christ would have us, when we take upon us a profession of religion, to *sit down and count the cost* (Luke xiv. 28). It is no advantage to religion, to take men by surprise, ere they are aware. They that take up a profession *in a pang*, will throw it off again *in a fret*; let him that will follow Christ know the worst of it, and expect to lie hard, and fare hard. *Secondly*, His resolve seems to have been from a worldly, covetous principle. He saw what abundance of cures Christ wrought, and concluded that he had large fees, and would get an estate quickly. He is not for following Christ, unless he can *get by him*.

2. Here is another that was too *slow in performing*. Delay in execution is as bad, on the one hand, as precipitancy in resolution is on the other hand; let it never be said, we left that to be done tomorrow, which we could do today.

JAMIESON, FAUSSET, BROWN

18-22. INCIDENTS ILLUSTRATIVE OF DISCIPLESHIP: (= Luke 9:57-62). The incidents here are two: in the corresponding passage of Luke they are three. Here they are introduced before the mission of the Twelve: in Luke, when our Lord was making preparation for His final journey to Jerusalem. But to conclude from this, as some good critics do (as BENGEL, ELLICOTT, etc.) that one of these incidents at least occurred twice—which led to the mention of the others at the two different times—is too artificial. Taking them, then, as one set of occurrences, the question arises. Are they recorded by Matthew or by Luke in their proper place? NEANDER, SCHLEIERMACHER, and OLSHAUSEN adhere to Luke's order; while MEYER, DE WETTE, and LANGE prefer that of Matthew. Probably the first incident is here in its right place. But as the command, in the second incident, to preach the kingdom of God, would scarcely have been given at so early a period, it is likely that it and the third incident have their true place in Luke. Taking these three incidents up here then we have—

I. *The Rash or Precipitate Disciple* (vss. 19, 20). **19. And a certain scribe came, and said unto him, Master, I will follow thee whithersoever thou goest. 20. And Jesus saith unto him, The foxes have holes, and the birds of the air have nests; but the Son of man hath not where to lay his head**—Few as there were of the scribes who attached themselves to Jesus. it would appear, from his calling Him Teacher, that this one was a "disciple" in that looser sense of the word in which it is applied to the crowds who flocked after Him, with more or less conviction that His claims were well founded. But from the answer which he received we are led to infer that there was more of transient emotion—of temporary impulse—than of intelligent principle in the speech. The preaching of Christ had riveted and charmed him; his heart had swelled; his enthusiasm had been kindled; and in this state of mind he will go anywhere with Him, and feels impelled to tell Him so. "Wilt thou?" replies the Lord Jesus. "Knowest thou whom thou art pledging thyself to follow, and whither haply He may lead thee? No warm home, no downy pillow has He for thee: He has them not for Himself. The foxes are not without their holes, nor do the birds of the air lack their nests; but the Son of man has to depend on the hospitality of others, and borrow the pillow whereon He lays His head." How affecting is this reply! And yet He rejects not this man's offer, nor refuses him the liberty to follow Him. Only He will have him know what he is doing, and "count the cost." He will have him weigh well the real nature and the strength of his attachment, whether it be such as will abide in the day of trial. If so, he will be right welcome, for Christ puts none away. But it seems too plain that in this case that had not been done. And so we have called this the Rash or Precipitate Disciple.

II. *The Procrastinating or Entangled Disciple* (vss. 21, 22). As this is more fully given in Luke, we must take both together. "And He said unto another of His disciples, Follow Me. But he said, **"Lord, suffer me first to go and bury my father.**

ADAM CLARKE

sidered the miraculous healing of the body as an emblem of the soul's salvation by Christ Jesus.

18. *Unto the other side.* Viz., of the Lake of Genesareth, whence He proceeded to the country of the Gergesenes, v. 28.

19. *A certain scribe.* Few of this class came to the Lord Jesus for instruction or salvation. *Master.* Rather, "teacher," the person who shows or points out a particular way or science. *I will follow thee whithersoever thou goest.* Every teacher among the Jews had disciples, and some especially that followed or accompanied them wherever they went, that they might have some person at hand with whom they might converse concerning the divine law.

20. *The foxes have holes.* Reader! are you a poor man? and do you fear God? Then what comfort must you derive from the thought that you so nearly resemble the Lord Jesus! *Son of man.* A Hebrew phrase, expressive of humiliation and debasement; and, on that account, applied emphatically to himself by the meek and lowly Jesus. Besides, it seems here to be used to point out the incarnation of the Son of God, according to the predictions of the prophets, Ps. viii. 5; Dan. vii. 13. And as our Lord was now showing forth His eternal divinity in the miracles He wrought, He seems studious to prove to them the certainty of His incarnation, because on this depended the atonement for sin. Indeed our Lord seems more intent on giving the proofs of His *humanity* than of His *divinity,* the latter being necessarily manifested by the miracles which He was continually working.

21 *Another of his disciples.* This does not mean any of the twelve, but one of those who were constant hearers of our Lord's preaching, the name of *disciple* being common to all those who professed to believe in Him, John vi. 66. *Bury*

MATTHEW HENRY

(1) The excuse that this disciple made, to defer an immediate attendance on Christ (*v.* 21); "*Lord, suffer me first to go and bury my father.*" His father (some think) was now sick, or dying, or dead; others think, he was only aged, and not likely in a course of nature, to continue long. This seemed a reasonable request, and yet it was not right. He had not the zeal he should have had for the work, and therefore pleaded this, because it seemed a plausible plea. An unwilling mind never wants an excuse. The preference should have been given to Christ.

(2) Christ's disallowing of this excuse (*v.* 22); *Jesus said to him, Follow me;* and, no doubt, power accompanied this word to him, as to others, and he did *follow Christ.* We are brought to Christ by the force of his call to us, not of our promises to him. When Christ calls, he will overcome, and make the call effectual, 1 Sam. iii. 10. His excuse is laid aside as insufficient; *Let the dead bury their dead. Let the dead* spiritually *bury the dead* corporally; let worldly offices be left to worldly people; do not thou encumber thyself with them. Burying the dead, and especially a dead father, is a good work, but it is not thy work, at this time: thou hast something else to do, and must not defer that. Piety to God must be preferred before piety of parents, though that is a great and needful part of our religion. We must comparatively neglect and disesteem our nearest relations, when they come in competition with Christ, and either our doing for him, or our suffering for him.

Verses 23-27

Christ had given sailing orders to his disciples (*v.* 18), that they should *depart to the other side of the sea of Tiberias.* He chose to go by water. It had not been much about, if he had gone by land; but he chose to cross the lake. It is a comfort to those *who go down to the sea in ships,* and are often in perils there, to reflect that they have a Saviour to trust in and pray to, who knows what it is to be at sea, and to be in storms there. 2. *His disciples followed him;* the twelve kept close to him. They, and they only, will be found the true disciples of Christ, that are willing to go to sea with him, to follow him into dangers and difficulties. Many would be content to go the land-way to heaven, but those that would rest with Christ hereafter must follow him now wherever he leads them, into a ship or into a prison, as well as into a palace.

I. The peril and perplexity of the disciples in this voyage. Those who follow him must count upon difficulties, *v.* 20.

1. *There arose a very great storm, v.* 24. This storm was *for their sakes,* as John xi. 4. Christ would show that they who are passing with him over the ocean of this world to the other side, must expect storms by the way. It is only the upper region that enjoys a perpetual calm, this lower one is ever and anon disturbed and disturbing.

2. Jesus Christ *was asleep in this storm.* We never read of Christ's sleeping but at this time; this was a sleep, not of security, like Jonah's in a storm, but of holy serenity, and dependence upon his Father. He had no guilt, no fear within to disturb his repose. Those that can lay their heads upon the pillow of a clear conscience, may sleep quietly and sweetly in a storm (Ps. iv. 8), as Peter, Acts xii. 6. He slept at this time, to try the faith of his disciples, whether they could trust him when he seemed to slight them.

3. The poor disciples, though used to the sea, were in a great fright, and in their fear *came to* their Master,

JAMIESON, FAUSSET, BROWN

But Jesus said unto him, Follow me; and let the dead bury their dead—or, as more definitely in Luke, "Let the dead bury their dead: but go thou and preach the kingdom of God." This disciple did not, like the former, volunteer his services, but is called by the Lord Jesus, not only to follow, but to preach Him. And he is quite willing; only he is not ready just yet. "Lord, I *will;* but"—"There is a difficulty in the way just now; but that once removed, I am Thine." What now is this difficulty? Was his father actually dead—lying a corpse—having only to be buried? Impossible. As it was the practice, as noticed on Luke 7:12, to bury on the day of death, it is not very likely that this disciple would have been here at all if his father had just breathed his last; nor would the Lord, if He was there, have hindered him discharging the last duties of a son to a father. No doubt it was the common case of a son having a frail or aged father, not likely to live long, whose head he thinks it his duty to see under the ground ere he goes abroad. "This aged father of mine will soon be removed; and if I might but delay till I see him decently interred, I should then be free to preach the kingdom of God wherever duty might call me." This view of the case will explain the curt reply, "Let the dead bury their dead: but go thou and preach the kingdom of God." Like all the other paradoxical sayings of our Lord, the key to **it is the different senses—a higher and a lower—in which the same word "dead" is used: There are two kingdoms of God in existence upon earth; the kingdom of nature, and the kingdom of grace: To the one kingdom all the children of this world, even the most ungodly, are fully alive; to the other, only the children of light: The reigning irreligion consists not in indifference to the common humanities of social life, but to things spiritual and eternal: Fear not, therefore, that your father will in your absence be neglected, and that when he breathes his last there will not be relatives and friends ready enough to do to him the last offices of kindness. Your wish to discharge these yourself is natural, and to be allowed to do it a privilege not lightly to be foregone. But the kingdom of God lies now all neglected and needy: Its more exalted character few discern; to its paramount claims few are alive: and to "preach" it fewer still are qualified and called: But thou art: The Lord therefore hath need of thee: Leave, then, those claims of nature, high though they be, to those who are dead to the still higher claims of the kingdom of grace, which God is now erecting upon earth—Let the dead bury their dead; but go thou and preach the kingdom of God. And so have we here the genuine, but Procrastinating or Entangled Disciple.**

23-27. Jesus, Crossing the Sea of Galilee, Miraculously Stills a Tempest. (=Mark 4:35-41; Luke 8:22-25). For the exposition, see on Mark 4:35-41.

he saith unto them, Let us pass over unto the other side—to the east side of the lake, to grapple with a desperate case of possession, and set the captive free, and to give the Gadarenes an opportunity of hearing the message of salvation, amid the wonder which that marvellous cure was fitted to awaken and the awe which the subsequent events could not but strike into them. **And there arose a great storm of wind**—"a tempest of wind." To such sudden squalls the Sea of Galilee is very liable from its position, in a deep basin, skirted on the east by lofty mountain ranges, while on the west the hills are intersected by narrow gorges through which the wind sweeps across the lake, and raises its waters with great rapidity into a storm. **and the waves beat into the ship**—kept beating or pitching on the ship. **so that it was now full**—rather, "so that it was already filling." In Matthew (8:24), "insomuch that the ship was covered with the waves"; but this is too strong. It should be, "so that the ship was getting covered by the waves." So we must translate the word used in Luke (8:23)—not as in our version—"And there came down a storm on the lake, and they were filled [with water]"—but "they were getting filled," i.e., those who sailed; meaning, of course, that their ship was so. **And he was in the hinder**—or stern—**part of the ship, asleep on a pillow**—either a place in the vessel made to receive the head, or a cushion for the head to rest on. It was evening; and after the fatigues of a busy day of teaching under the hot sun, having nothing to do while crossing the lake, He sinks into a deep sleep, which even this tempest raging around and tossing the little

ADAM CLARKE

my father. Probably his father was old, and apparently near death; but it was a maxim among the Jews that, if a man had any duty to perform to the dead, he was, for that time, free from the observance of any other precept or duty.

22. *Let the dead bury their dead.* It was usual for the Jews to consider a man as *dead* who had departed from the precepts of the law; and, on this ground, every transgressor was reputed a dead man. Our Lord's saying, being in common use, had nothing difficult in it to a Jew. Natural death is the separation of the body and soul; spiritual death, the separation of God and the soul. Men who live in sin are dead to God. Leave the *spiritually* dead to bury their *natural* dead.

G. CAMPBELL MORGAN:

Then another man spoke to Him, and Luke tells us that it was in answer to something that Jesus said to him. Jesus said, "Follow me," and the man replied, "Lord, suffer me first to go and bury my father." Notice that Matthew calls this man a disciple, so that when Jesus called him to "follow," it was not a call to discipleship, but to service, for Luke again introduces something which Matthew omits. Jesus said to him, "Leave the dead to bury their own dead; but go thou and publish abroad the kingdom of God."

What was the trouble in this man's case? There was in his heart a conflicting affection—that for his father. We have hardly caught the real value of this story; we have treated it as though this man wanted to attend a funeral, and asked time to do so. Dr. George Adam Smith tells of how he was one day trying hard to persuade a young man to go with him as a guide into a district not frequented by travelers. Healthy and robust he stood by his tent, a genuine Arab; and there, sitting in the doorway of the tent, was his father, of patriarchal appearance, but well and healthy. The intended journey would have occupied some months at least, and the young man at last, with peculiar courtesy, said, "Sir, suffer me first to bury my father," thus using the very words of the Bible story, and revealing its true meaning. There was no immediate prospect of the death of the father; but the son said, "I cannot leave my father"—a most admirable thing, a beautiful thing, examined by all the canons of human conduct; a noble decision on the part of the young Arab, and right, if anybody else called other than the King. But here at once we see the claim of Jesus. He was perpetually setting up these superlative claims for himself. He had none of the humility of the human teacher. His claim was always the claim of an absolute supremacy. He never admitted that any other tie of affection could be allowed for a moment to interfere with the soul's loyalty to himself, and He crystalized this fact into one burning sentence when He said, "He that loveth father or mother more than me, is not worthy of me." That is the principle He applied when He said, "leave the dead to bury their own dead."

—*The Gospel According to Matthew*

MATTHEW HENRY

v. 25. Whither else should they go? It was well they had him so near them. They *awoke him* with their prayers; *Lord, save us, we perish.* They who would learn to pray must go to sea. Imminent and sensible dangers will drive people to him who alone can help in time of need. Their petition is, *Lord, save us.* They believed he *could* save them; they begged he *would.* Christ's errand into the world was *to save,* but those only *shall be saved that call on the name of the Lord,* Acts ii. 21. They call him, *Lord,* and then pray, *Save us.* Christ will save none but those that are willing to take him for their Lord. Their plea is, *We perish*; which was the language of their fear; they had received a sentence of death within themselves, and this they plead, "*We perish,* if thou dost not save us; look upon us therefore with pity." It was the language of their fervency. It becomes us thus to strive and wrestle in prayer; *therefore* Christ slept, that he might draw out this importunity.

II. The power and grace of Jesus Christ put forth for their succour. Christ may sleep when his church is in a storm, but he will not outsleep himself.

1. He rebuked the disciples (*v.* 26); *Why are ye fearful, O ye of little faith?* He does not chide them for disturbing him with their prayers, but for disturbing themselves with their fears. Christ reproved them first, and then delivered them. His dislike of their fears; "*Why are ye fearful?* Ye, my disciples?" His discovery of the cause and spring of their fears; *O ye of little faith.* Many that have true faith are weak in it, and it does but little. By faith we might see through the storm to the quiet shore, and encourage ourselves with hope that we shall weather our point.

2. *He rebukes the wind.* See, (1) How *easily* this was done, with a word's speaking. (2) How *effectually* it was done. *There was a great calm,* all of a sudden. Ordinarily, after a storm, there is such a fret of the waters, that it is a good while ere they can settle; but if Christ speak the word, not only the storm ceases, but all the effects of it, all the remains of it. Great storms of doubt, and fear in the soul sometimes end in a wonderful calm.

3. This excited their astonishment (*v.* 27); *The men marvelled.* They had been long acquainted with the sea, and never saw a storm so immediately turned into a perfect calm, in all their lives. Observe, (1) Their admiration of Christ; *What manner of man is this!* Christ is a Nonsuch; everything in him is admirable: none so wise, so mighty, so amiable, as he. (2) The reason of it; *Even the winds and the sea obey him.* Upon this account, Christ is to be admired, that he has a commanding power even over *winds and seas.* He that can do this, can do anything, can do enough to encourage our confidence and comfort in him, in the most stormy day, within or without, Isa. xxvi. 4.

Verses 28–34

We have here the story of Christ's casting the devils out of two men that were possessed. The scope of this chapter is to show the divine power of Christ. Christ has not only all *power in heaven and earth* and all deep places, but has the keys of hell too. It was observed in general (*v.* 16), that Christ *cast out the spirits with his word*; here we have a particular instance of it. Though Christ was sent chiefly *to the lost sheep of the house of Israel,* yet some sallies he made among the borderers, as here, to gain this victory over Satan. Observe, concerning this legion of devils, What work they made where they *were,* and where they *went.*

I. What work they made where they *were*; which appears in the miserable condition of these two that were possessed by them.

1. They dwelt among *the tombs*; thence they came when they met Christ. Conversing among the graves increased the melancholy and frenzy of the poor possessed creatures, and also made them more formidable to other people, who generally startle at anything that stirs among *the tombs.*

2. They were *exceeding fierce*; not only ungovernable themselves, but mischievous to others, frightening many, having hurt some; *so that no man durst pass that way.* The devil bears malice to mankind, and shows it by making men spiteful and malicious one to another. Mutual enmities, where there should be mutual endearments and assistances, those lusts that war in the members, pride, envy, malice, revenge, make him as unfit for human society, as unworthy of it, and as much an enemy to the comfort of it, as these poor possessed creatures were.

3. They bid defiance to Jesus Christ, and disclaimed all interest in him, *v.* 29. It is an instance of the power of God over the devils, that they could not keep them from meeting Jesus Christ. His chains could hold them, when the chains that men made for them could not. But being brought before him,

JAMIESON, FAUSSET, BROWN

vessel did not disturb. **and they awake him, and say unto him, Master**—or "Teacher." In Luke (8:24) this is doubled—in token of their life-and-death earnestness—"Master, Master." **carest thou not that we perish?**—Unbelief and fear made them sadly forget their place, to speak so. Luke has it, "Lord, save us, we perish." When those accustomed to fish upon that deep thus spake, the danger must have been imminent. They say nothing of what would become of *Him,* if they perished; nor think, whether, if He could not perish, it was likely He would let this happen to them; but they hardly knew what they said. **And he arose, and rebuked the wind**—"and the raging of the water" (Luke 8:24). **and said unto the sea, Peace, be still**—two sublime words of command, from a Master to His servants, the elements. **And the wind ceased, and there was a great calm**—The sudden hushing of the wind would not at once have calmed the sea, whose commotion would have settled only after a considerable time. But the word of command was given to both elements at once. **And he said unto them, Why are ye so fearful?**—There is a natural apprehension under danger; but there was unbelief in their fear. It is worthy of notice how considerately the Lord defers this rebuke till He had first removed the danger, in the midst of which they would not have been in a state to listen to anything. **how is it that ye have no faith?**—next to none, or none in present exercise. In Luke it is, "Why are ye fearful, O ye of little faith?" *Faith* they had, for they applied to Christ for relief: but *little,* for they were afraid, though Christ was in the ship. Faith dispels fear, but only in proportion to its strength. **And they feared exceedingly**—were struck with deep awe. **and said one to another, What manner of man is this, that even the wind and the sea obey him?**—'What is this? Israel has all along been singing of JEHOVAH, 'Thou rulest the raging of the sea: when the waves thereof arise, Thou stillest them!' 'The Lord on high is mightier than the noise of many waters, yea, than the mighty waves of the sea!' (Ps. 89:9; 93:4). But, lo, in this very boat of ours is One of our own flesh and blood, who with His word of command hath done the same! Exhausted with the fatigues of the day, He was but a moment ago in a deep sleep, undisturbed by the howling tempest, and we had to waken Him with the cry of our terror; but rising at our call, His majesty was felt by the raging elements, for they were instantly hushed—'WHAT MANNER OF MAN IS THIS?' "

28-34. JESUS HEALS THE GERGESENE DEMONIACS. (= Mark 5:1-20; Luke 8:26-39). For the exposition, see on Mark 5:1-20.

And they came over unto the other side of the sea, into the country of the Gadarenes. And when he was come out of the ship, immediately—(see vs. 6)—**there met him a man with an unclean spirit**—"which had devils [demons] long time" (Luke 8:27). In Matthew (8:28), "there met him two men possessed with devils." Though there be no discrepancy between these two statements—more than between two witnesses, one of whom testifies to something done by one person, while the other affirms that there were two—it is difficult to see how the principal details here given could apply to more than one case. **Who had his dwelling among the tombs**—Luke says, "He ware no clothes, neither abode in any house." These tombs were hewn out of the rocky caves of the locality, and served for shelters and lurking-places (Luke 8:26).

Because that he had been often bound with fetters and chains . . .—Luke says (8:29) that "oftentimes it [the unclean spirit] had caught him"; and after mentioning how they had vainly tried to bind him with chains and fetters, because, "he brake the bands," he adds, "and was driven of the devil [demon] into the wilderness." The dark tyrant-power by which he was held clothed him with superhuman strength and made him scorn restraint. Matthew (8:28) says he was "exceeding fierce, so that no man might pass by that way." He was the terror of the whole locality.

ADAM CLARKE

25. *Lord, save us: we perish.* One advantage of trials is to make us know our weakness, so as to oblige us to have recourse to God by faith in Christ. It is by faith alone that we may be said to approach Him; by love we are united to Him, and by prayer we awake Him.

26. *Why are ye fearful, O ye of little faith?* Faith is ever bold—incredulity always timid. When faith fails in temptation, there is the utmost danger of shipwreck. *Then he arose, and* rebuked the winds, as the agitation of the sea was only the effect of the wind, it was necessary to remove the cause of the disturbance, that the effect might cease. *There was a great calm.* One word of Christ can change the face of nature; one word of His can restore calm and peace to the most troubled and disconsolate soul.

27. *The men marvelled.* Every part of the creation (man excepted) hears and obeys the Creator's voice. *What manner of man is this?* "How great is this Person!" Here was God fully manifest; but it was in the flesh—there were the hidings of His power.

28. *The country of the Gergesenes.* This word is variously written in the MSS. and versions: Gergasenes, Gerasenes, Gadarenes. *Two possessed with devils.* Mark and Luke mention only one demoniac, probably the fiercer of the two.

MATTHEW HENRY

they protested against his jurisdiction, and broke out into a rage, *What have we to do with thee, Jesus, thou Son of God?* Here is,

(1) *One* word that the devil spoke like a *saint*; he addressed himself to Christ as *Jesus the Son of God*; a *good* word, and at this time, when it was a truth but in the proving, it was a *great* word too. Even the devils know, and believe, and confess Christ to be the *Son of God*, and yet they are devils still. It is not knowledge, but love, that distinguishes saints from devils.

(2) *Two* words that he said like a *devil*, like himself. [1] A word of defiance; *What have we to do with thee?* It is true that the devils have nothing to do with Christ as a Saviour. O the depth of this mystery of divine love, that fallen man hath so much *to do with Christ*, when fallen angels have nothing *to do with* him! It is possible for men to call Jesus *the Son of God*, and yet have nothing to do with him. It is as true, that the devils desire not to have anything *to do with Christ* as a Ruler; they hate him, they are filled with enmity against him. But it is not true, that the devils have nothing *to do with Christ* as a Judge, for they have, and they know it.

[2] A word of dread and deprecation; "*Art thou come hither to torment us*—to cast us out from these men, and to restrain us from doing the hurt we would do?" To be turned out, and tied up, from doing mischief, is a torment to the devil. Should not we then count it our heaven to be doing well, and reckon that our torment, whether within or without, that hinders us from well-doing?

II. Let us now see what work they made where they *went*, when they were turned out of the men possessed, and that was into *a herd of swine*, which *was a good way off*, *v.* 30. These Gergesenes, though living on the other side Jordan, were Jews. What had they to do with *swine*?

1. How the devils seized the *swine*. Though they were *a good way off*, yet the devils had an eye upon them.

(1) They *asked* leave to enter *into the swine* (*v.* 31); *they besought him*, with all earnestness, *If thou cast us out, suffer us to go away into the herd of swine*. Hereby, [1] They discover their own inclination to do mischief, and what a pleasure it is to them. If they might not be suffered to hurt men in their bodies, they would hurt them in their goods, and in that too they intend hurt to their souls, by making Christ a burthen to them. [2] They own Christ's power over them; that, without his sufferance and permission, they could not so much as hurt a *swine*. This is comfortable to all the Lord's people, that, though the devil's power be very great, yet it is limited, and not equal to his malice (what would become of us, if it were?) especially that it is under the control of our Lord Jesus.

(2) They *had* leave. Christ said unto them, *Go* (*v.* 32), as God did to Satan, when he desired leave to afflict Job. God does often, for wise and holy ends, permit the efforts of Satan's rage, and suffer him to do the mischief he would. Christ permitted this for the punishment of the Gadarenes, who perhaps, though Jews, took a liberty to eat *swine's* flesh, contrary to the law: however, their keeping *swine* bordered upon evil. The devils, in obedience to Christ's command, came out of the men, and having permission, *when they were come out, immediately they went into the herd of swine*. See what an industrious enemy Satan is, and how expeditious; he will lose no time in doing mischief.

2. *Whither they hurried them*, when they had seized them. They were made to *run violently down a steep place into the sea*, where they all perished, to the number of about *two thousand*, Mark v. 13. The possession which the devil gets is for destruction. Thus the devil hurries people to sin, hurries them to that which they have resolved against, and which they know will be shame and grief to them. Thus likewise, he hurries them to ruin.

3. *What effect this had upon the owners*. The report of it was soon brought them by the swine-herds, who seemed to be more concerned for the loss of the swine than anything else, for they went not to tell *what was befallen to the possessed of the devils*, till the swine were lost, *v.* 33. Christ went not *into the city*, but the news of his being there did.

Now, (1) Their curiosity brought them out to see Jesus. The *whole city came out to meet him*. Thus many go out, in profession, to meet Christ for company, that have no real affection for him, nor desire to know him.

(2) Their covetousness made them *willing to be rid of him*. Instead of inviting him into their city, or bringing their sick to him to be healed, they desired him to *depart out of their coasts*. And now the devils had what they aimed at in drowning the swine; *they*

JAMIESON, FAUSSET, BROWN

. What have I to do with thee, Jesus, Son of the most high God? I adjure thee by God, that thou torment me not—or, as in Matthew 8:29, "Art Thou come to torment us before the time?" (See on ch. 1:24.) Behold the *tormentor* anticipating, dreading, and entreating exemption from *torment!* In Christ they discern their destined Tormentor; the time, they know, is fixed, and they feel as if it were come already! (Jas. 2:19.)

Now there was there, nigh unto the mountains—rather, "to the mountain," according to what is clearly the true reading. In Matthew 8:30, they are said to have been "a good way off." But these expressions, far from being inconsistent, only confirm, by their precision, the minute accuracy of the narrative. **a great herd of swine feeding**—There can hardly be any doubt that the owners of these were Jews, since to them our Lord had now come to proffer His services. This will explain what follows. **And all the devils besought him, saying** —"if thou cast us out" (Matt. 8:31)—**Send us into the swine, that we may enter into them**—Had they spoken out all their mind, perhaps this would have been it: "If we must quit our hold of this man, suffer us to continue our work of mischief in another form, that by entering these swine, and thus destroying the people's property, we may steel their hearts against Thee!"

And forthwith Jesus gave them leave—In Matthew this is given with majestic brevity—"Go!" The owners, if Jews, drove an illegal trade; if heathens, they insulted the national religion: in either case the permission was just. **And the unclean spirits went out**—of the man **—and entered into the swine: and the herd ran violently**—rushed—**down a steep place**—down the hanging cliff—**into the sea (they were about two thousand)**—The number of them is given by this graphic Evangelist alone. **and were choked in the sea**—"perished in the waters" (Matt. 8:32).

And they that fed the swine fled, and told it—"told everything, and what was befallen to the possessed of the devils" (Matt. 8:33)—**in the city, and in the country. And they went out to see what it was that was done**—Thus had they the evidence, both of the herdsmen and of their own senses, to the reality of both miracles. **And they come to Jesus**—Matthew (8:34) says, "Behold, the whole city came out to meet Jesus."

And they began to pray him to depart out of their coasts—Was it the owners only of the valuable property now lost to them that did this? Alas, no! For Luke (8:37) says, "Then the whole multitude of the country of the Gadarenes round about besought Him to depart from them; for they were taken with great fear." The evil spirits had thus, alas! their

ADAM CLARKE

29. *What have we to do with thee?* The literal translation is, "What is it to us and to Thee?" which perhaps might be understood to imply their disclaiming any design to interfere with the work of Christ, and that He should not therefore meddle with them; for it appears they exceedingly dreaded His power. *What have we to do with thee?* is a Jewish phrase which often occurs in the Old Testament, signifying an abrupt refusal of some request, or a wish not to be troubled with the company or importunity of others. *Art thou come hither to torment us before the time?* From this it appears that a greater degree of punishment awaited these demons than they at that time endured; and that they knew there was a time determined by the divine Judge when they should be sent unto greater torments.

A. T. ROBERTSON:

29. "Thou Son of God" (*huie tou theou*). The recognition of Jesus by the demons is surprising. The whole subject of demonology is difficult. Some hold that it is merely the ancient way of describing disease. But that does not explain the situation here. Jesus is represented as treating the demons as real existences separate from the human personality. Missionaries in China today claim that they have seen demons cast out. The devil knew Jesus clearly, and it is not strange that Jesus was recognized by the devil's agents. They know that there is nothing in common between them and the Son of God (*hemin kai soi*, ethical dative) and they fear torment "before the time" (*pro kairou*). Usually *ta daimonia* is the word in the New Testament for demons, but in 8:31 we have *hoi daimones* (the only example in the N.T.). *Daimonion* is a diminutive of *daimon*. In Homer *daimon* is used synonymously with *theos* and *thea*. Hesiod employed *daimon* of men of the golden age as tutelary deities. Homer has the adjective *daimonios* usually in an evil sense. Empedocles considered the demons both bad and good. They were thus used to relieve the gods and goddesses of much rascality. Grote (*History of Greece*) notes that the Christians were thus by pagan usage justified in calling idolatry the worship of demons (see 1 Cor. 10-20 f.; 1 Tim. 4:1; Rev. 9:20; 16:13 f.). In the Gospels, demons are the same as unclean spirits (Mark 5:12, 15; 3:22, 30; Luke 4:33). The demons are disturbers (Vincent) of the whole life of man (Mark 5:2 f.; 7:25; Matt. 12:45; Luke 13:11, 16).

—*Word Pictures in the New Testament*

33. *And they that kept them fled.* Terrified at what had happened to the swine.

34. *The whole city came out.* Probably with the intention to destroy Jesus for having destroyed their swine; but, having seen Him, they were awed by His presence, and only besought Him to depart from their borders. Many rather choose to lose Jesus Christ than those temporal goods by which they gratify their passions at the expense of their souls. They love even their swine better than their salvation.

MATTHEW HENRY

did it, and then made the people believe that *Christ* had done it, and so prejudiced them against him. Thus the devil sows tares in God's fields. There are a great many who prefer their swine before their Saviour, and so come short of Christ, and salvation by him.

CHAPTER 9

Verses 1-8

The first words of this chapter oblige us to look back to the close of that which precedes it, where we find the Gadarenes so resenting the loss of their swine, that they were disgusted with Christ's company, and besought him to *depart out of their coasts.* Now here it follows, *He entered into a ship, and passed over.* They bid him begone, and he took them at their word. Christ will not tarry long where he is not welcome, but abides with those that covet and court his stay. He did not leave some destroying judgment behind him, to punish them, as they deserved, for their contempt and contumacy. He *entered into a ship, and passed over.* This was the day of his patience; he came not to *destroy men's lives,* but to save them; not to kill, but to cure.

He came *into his own city, Capernaum,* the principal place of his residence at present (Mark ii. 1), and therefore called *his own city.* When the Gadarenes desired Christ to depart, they of Capernaum received him. If Christ be affronted by some, there are others in whom he will be glorious; if one will not, another will.

Now the first occurrence was the cure of the man sick of the palsy.

I. The *faith of his friends* in bringing him to Christ. His distemper was such, that he could not come to Christ himself, but as he was carried. Even the halt and the lame may be brought to Christ, and they shall not be rejected by him. Little children cannot go to Christ themselves, but he will have an eye to the faith of those that bring them, and it shall not be in vain. *Jesus saw their faith,* the faith of the paralytic himself, as well as of them that brought him. Now their faith was, 1. A strong faith; they firmly believed that Jesus Christ both could and would heal him. 2. A humble faith; though the sick man was unable to stir a step, they would not ask Christ to make him a visit, but brought him to attend on Christ. It is fitter that we should wait on Christ, than he on us. 3. An active faith: in the belief of Christ's power and goodness, they brought the sick man to him, *lying on a bed,* which could not be done without a deal of pains. Note, a strong faith regards no obstacles in pressing after Christ.

II. The *favour of Christ,* in what he said to him; *Son, be of good cheer, thy sins be forgiven thee.* This was a sovereign cordial to a sick man. We read not of anything said to Christ. They set him before Christ; that was enough. It is not in vain to present ourselves and our friends to Christ, as the objects of his pity. Misery cries as well as sin, and mercy is no less quick of hearing than justice. Here is, in what Christ said, 1. A kind compellation; *Son.* 2. A gracious encouragement; "*Be of good cheer.*" Probably the poor man was afraid of a rebuke for being brought in so rudely: but Christ does not stand upon ceremony; he bids him *be of good cheer.* 3. A good reason for that encouragement; *Thy sins are forgiven thee.* Now this may be considered as an introduction to the cure of his bodily distemper; "Thy sins are *pardoned,* and therefore thou shalt be healed." If we have the comfort of our reconciliation to God, with the comfort of our recovery from sickness, this makes it a mercy indeed to us, as to Hezekiah, Isa. xxxviii. 17. As a reason of the command to *be of good cheer,* whether he were cured of his disease or not; "Though I should not heal thee, wilt thou not say thou hast not sought in vain, if I assure thee that *thy sins are pardoned.*" They who, through grace, have some evidence of the forgiveness of their sins, have reason to be of good cheer, whatever outward troubles or afflictions they are under.

III. The *cavil of the scribes* at that which Christ said (*v.* 3); They *said within themselves,* in their hearts, *among themselves,* in their secret whisperings, *This man blasphemeth.* See how the greatest instance of heaven's power and grace is branded with the blackest note of hell's enmity.

IV. The conviction which Christ gave them of the unreasonableness of this cavil, before he proceeded.

1. He *charged them with it.* Though they did but say it within themselves he *knew their thoughts.* Note, Our Lord Jesus has the perfect knowledge of all that we say within ourselves. Thoughts are secret and sudden, yet naked and open before Christ. The sins that begin and end in the heart, and go no further, are as dangerous as any other.

JAMIESON, FAUSSET, BROWN

object. Irritated, the people could not suffer His presence; yet awe-struck, they dared not order Him off: so they entreat Him to withdraw, and—He takes them at their word.

CHAPTER 9

Vss. 1-8. Healing of a Paralytic. (= Mark 2:1-12; Luke 5:17-26.) This incident appears to follow next in order of time to the cure of the leper (ch. 8:1-4). For the exposition, see on Mark 2:1-12.

And again he entered into Capernaum—"His own city" (Matt. 9:1). **and it was noised that he was in the house**—no doubt of Simon Peter (ch. 1:29).

And they come unto him—i.e., towards the house where He was. **bringing one sick of the palsy**—"lying on a bed" (Matt. 9: 2). **which was borne of four**—a graphic particular of Mark only.

When Jesus saw their faith—It is remarkable that all the three narratives call it "*their* faith" which Jesus saw. That the patient himself had faith, we know from the proclamation of his forgiveness, which Jesus made before all; and we should have been apt to conclude that his four friends bore him to Jesus merely out of benevolent compliance with the urgent entreaties of the poor sufferer. But here we learn, not only that his bearers had the same faith with himself, but that Jesus marked it as a faith which was not to be defeated—a faith victorious over all difficulties. This was the faith for which He was ever on the watch, and which He never saw without marking, and, in those who needed anything from Him, richly rewarding. **he said unto the sick of the palsy, Son**—"be of good cheer" (Matt. 9:2). **thy sins be forgiven thee**—By the word "be," our translators perhaps meant "are," as in Luke (5:20). For it is not a command to his sins to depart, but an authoritative proclamation of the man's pardoned state as a believer. And yet, as the Pharisees understood our Lord to be *dispensing* pardon by this saying, and Jesus not only acknowledges that they were right, but founds His whole argument upon the correctness of it, we must regard the saying as a royal proclamation of the man's forgiveness by Him to whom it belonged to dispense it; nor could such a style of address be justified on any lower supposition. (See on Luke 7:41, etc.).

Why doth this man thus speak blasphemies? who can forgive sins but God only?—In this second question they expressed a great truth. (See Isa. 43:25; Mic. 7:18; Ex. 34: 6, 7, etc.). Nor was their first question altogether unnatural, though in our Lord's sole case it was unfounded. That a man, to all appearances like one of themselves, should claim authority and power to forgive sins, they could not, on the first blush of it, but regard as in the last degree startling; nor were they entitled even to weigh such a claim, as worthy of a hearing, save on supposition of resistless evidence afforded by Him in support of the claim. Accordingly, our Lord deals with them as men entitled to such evidence, and supplies it; at the same time chiding them for rashness, in drawing harsh conclusions regarding Himself.

ADAM CLARKE

CHAPTER 9

1. *He . . . came into his own city.* Viz., Capernaum, where He seems to have had His common residence at the house of Peter. This verse properly belongs to the preceding chapter.

2. *Lying on a bed.* A "couch" or "sofa," such as they reclined on at meals. *Seeing their faith.* The faith of the paralytic person, and the faith of those who brought him.

Be of good cheer. "Son, take courage!" Probably he began to despond, and Christ spoke thus to support his faith. *Thy sins be forgiven thee.* Moral evil has been the cause of all the natural evil in the world. Christ goes to the source of the malady, which is sin. It is probable that this paralytic person had, in the earnest desires of his heart, entreated the cure of his soul, leaving his body to the care of others, as the first miracle of healing is wrought on his soul. It may be necessary to be observed that it was a maxim among the Jews that no diseased person could be healed till all his sins were blotted out. Hence our Lord first forgives the sins and then heals the body of the paralytic person. This appears to have been founded on Ps. ciii. 3. "Who forgiveth all thine iniquities; who healeth all thy diseases." See also Ps. xli. 3-4. It may be observed, also, that most people are more in earnest about their souls when in sickness than in health, and therefore are more earnest in prayer for salvation.

3. *This man blasphemeth.* Wherever it is used in reference to God, it simply signifies "to speak impiously" of His nature, or attributes, or works. "Injurious speaking" is its proper translation when referred to man.

4. *Jesus knowing their thoughts.* In telling them what the thoughts of their hearts were (for they had expressed nothing publicly), He gave them the fullest proof of His power to forgive sins; because only God can forgive sins, and only God can search and know the heart.

MATTHEW HENRY

2. He *argued them out of it, v.* 5, 6. Where observe, (1) How he *asserts* his authority in the *kingdom of grace.* He undertakes to make out, that the *Son of Man,* the Mediator, has *power on earth to forgive sins.* What an encouragement is this to poor sinners to repent, that the power of pardoning sin is put into the hands of the *Son of Man,* who is bone of our bone! And if he had this *power on earth,* much more now that he is exalted to the Father's right hand.

(2) How he *proves* it, by his power in the kingdom of nature. Is it not as easy to say, *Thy sins are forgiven thee,* as to say, *Arise and walk?* He that can cure the disease can, in like manner, forgive the sin. This is a general argument to prove that Christ had a divine mission. The *power* that appeared in his cures proved him *sent of God;* and the *pity* that appeared in them proved him sent of God *to heal and save.* The palsy was but a symptom of the disease of sin; now he made it to appear, that he could effectually cure the original disease, by the immediate removal of that symptom. He that had power to remove the punishment, no doubt, had power to remit the sin. His great errand to the world was, to *save his people from their sins.*

V. The immediate cure of the sick man. Christ turned from disputing with them, and spake healing to him. The most necessary arguings must not divert us from doing the good that our *hand finds to do.* He saith to *the sick of the palsy, Arise, take up thy bed, and go to thine house;* and a healing, quickening, strengthening power accompanied this word (*v.* 7): *he arose and departed to his house.* He sent him to *his house,* to be a blessing to his family, where he had been so long a burthen.

VI. The impression which this made upon the multitude (*v.* 8); they *marvelled,* and *glorified God.* They glorified God, for what he had done for this poor man. Others' mercies should be our praises, and we should give him thanks for them. They admired him, not as God, or the Son of God, but as a *man* to whom God *had given such power.* God must be glorified in all the power that is *given to men* to do good. For all power is originally his; it is in him, as the Fountain, in men, as the cisterns.

Verses 9–13

In these verses we have an account of the grace and favour of Christ to poor publicans, particularly to Matthew.

I. The call of Matthew, the penman, of this gospel. Mark and Luke call him Levi. Some think Christ gave him the name of Matthew when he called him to be an apostle; as Simon, he surnamed Peter. Matthew signifies, *the gift of God.*

1. The posture that Christ's call found Matthew in. He was *sitting at the receipt of custom,* for he was a publican, Luke v. 27. He was in his calling, as the rest of them whom Christ called, *ch.* iv. 18. As Satan chooses to come, with his temptations, to those that are idle, so Christ chooses to come, with his calls, to those that are employed. It was a calling of ill fame among serious people; because it was attended with so much corruption and temptation, and there were so few in that business that were honest men. God has his remnant among all sorts of people. None can justify themselves in their unbelief, by their calling in the world; for there is no *sinful* calling, but some have been saved *out of it,* and no *lawful calling,* but some have been saved *in it.*

2. The preventing power of his call. We find not that Matthew looked after Christ, or had any inclination to follow him. He is found of those that seek him not. Christ *spoke first;* we have not chosen him, but he hath chosen us. He said, *Follow me.* The call was effectual, for he came at the call; *he arose, and* followed him immediately; neither denied, nor deferred his obedience. The power of divine grace soon answers and overcomes all objections. He quitted his post, and his hopes of preferment in that way; and, though we find the disciples that were fishers occasionally fishing again afterwards, we never find Matthew at the receipt of custom again.

II. Christ's converse with publicans and sinners upon this occasion; *Jesus sat at meat in the house, v.* 10. The other evangelists tell us, that Matthew made a *great feast,* which the poor fishermen, when they were called, were not able to do. But when he comes to speak of this himself, he neither tells us that it was his own house, nor that it was a feast, but only that he *sat at meat in the house.* It well becomes us to speak sparingly of our own good deeds.

When Matthew invited Christ, he invited his disciples to *come along with him.* Note, They that welcome Christ, must welcome all that are his, for his sake, and let them have a room in their hearts. He invited many publicans and sinners to *meet him.*

JAMIESON, FAUSSET, BROWN

Why reason ye these things—or, as in Matthew, "Wherefore think ye evil." **in your hearts? Whether is it easier to say to the sick of the palsy, Thy sins be**—or "are"—**forgiven thee; or to say, Arise, and take up thy bed and walk?**—"Is it easier to command away disease than to bid away sin? If, then, I do the one which you can see, know thus that I have done the other, which you cannot see."
But that ye may know that the Son of man hath power on earth to forgive sins—that forgiving power dwells in the Person of this Man, and is exercised by Him while on this earth and going out and in with you. **(he saith to the sick of the palsy), I say unto thee, Arise, and take up thy bed, and go thy way into thine house**—This taking up the portable couch, and walking home with it, was designed to prove the completeness of the cure. **And immediately he arose, took up the bed**—"Sweet saying!" says BENGEL: "The bed had borne the man: now the man bore the bed." **and went forth before them all**—proclaiming by that act to the multitude, whose wondering eyes would follow him as he pressed through them, that He who could work such a glorious miracle of healing, must indeed "have power on earth to forgive sins." **We never saw it on this fashion**—"never saw it thus," or, as we say, "never saw the like." In Luke (5:26) it is, "We have seen strange [unexpected] things to-day"—referring both to the miracles wrought and the forgiveness of sins pronounced by Human Lips. In Matthew (9:8) it is, "They marvelled, and glorified God, which had given such power unto men." At forgiving power they wondered not, but that a man, to all appearance like one of themselves, should possess it!

9-13. MATTHEW'S CALL AND FEAST. (= Mark 2:14-17; Luke 5:27-32.) *The call of Matthew* (vs. 9). **9. And as Jesus passed forth from thence**—i.e., from the scene of the paralytic's cure in Capernaum, towards the shore of the Sea of Galilee, on which that town lay. Mark, as usual, pictures the scene more in detail, thus (2:13): "And He went forth again by the seaside; and all the multitude resorted unto Him, and He taught them"—or, "kept teaching them." "And as He passed by" **he saw a man, named Matthew**—the writer of this precious Gospel, who here, with singular modesty and brevity, relates the story of his own calling. In Mark and Luke he is called *Levi,* which seems to have been his family name. In their lists of the twelve apostles, however, Mark and Luke give him the name of Matthew, which seems to have been the name by which he was known as a disciple. While he himself sinks his family name, he is careful not to sink his occupation, the obnoxious associations with which he would place over against the grace that called him from it, and made him an apostle. (See on ch. 10:3.) Mark alone tells us (2:14) that he was "the son of Alphaeus"—the same, probably, with the father of James the Less. From this and other considerations it is pretty certain that he must at least have heard of our Lord before this meeting. Unnecessary doubts, even from an early period, have been raised about the identity of Levi and Matthew. No capable jury, with the evidence before them which we have in the Gospels, would hesitate in giving a unanimous verdict of identity. **sitting at the receipt of custom**—as a publican, which Luke (5:27) calls him. It means the place of receipt, the toll-house or booth in which the collector sat. Being in this case by the seaside, it might be the ferry tax for the transit of persons and goods across the lake, which he collected. (See on ch. 5:46.) **and he saith unto him, Follow me**—Witching words these, from the lips of Him who never employed them without giving them resistless efficacy in the hearts of those they were spoken to. **And he** ["left all" (Luke 5:28)] **arose and followed him.**

The Feast (vss. 10-13). **10. And it came to pass, as Jesus sat at meat in the house**—The modesty of our Evangelist signally appears here. Luke says (vs. 29) that "Levi made Him *a great feast,*" or "reception," while Matthew merely says, "He sat at meat"; and Mark and Luke say that it was in Levi's "own house," while Matthew merely says, "He sat at meat *in the house.*" Whether this feast was made now, or not till afterwards, is a point of some importance in the order of events, and not agreed among harmonists. The probability is that it did not take place till a considerable time afterwards. For Matthew, who ought surely to know what took place while his Lord was speaking at his own table,

ADAM CLARKE

5. *For whether is easier, to say, Thy sins be forgiven thee; or to say, Arise, and walk?* Both are equally easy, and equally difficult, for both require unlimited power to produce them. And everything is equally easy to that power which is unlimited. A universe can be as easily produced by a single act of the divine will as the smallest elementary part of matter.

6. *But that ye may know.* External miracles are the proofs of internal ones. Three miracles are wrought in this case: (1) The remission of the poor man's sins. (2) The discernment of the secret thoughts of the scribes. (3) The restoring of the paralytic, in an instant, to perfect soundness. Thus one miracle becomes the proof and establishment of another. Never was a clearer proof of omnipotent energy and mercy brought under the senses of man. Here is an absolutely perfect miracle wrought, and here are absolute incontestable proofs that the miracle *was* wrought; and the conclusion is the fullest demonstration of the divinity of the ever-blessed Jesus. *Arise, take up thy bed.* Being enabled to obey this command was the public proof that the man was made whole.

9. *Named Matthew.* Generally supposed to be the same who wrote this history of our blessed Lord. *Mathai* signifies a "gift" in Syriac; probably so named by his parents as implying a "gift from God."

The receipt of custom. The customhouse, the place where the taxes levied by the Romans of the Jews were collected. *Follow me.* That is, Become My disciple. *And he arose, and followed him.* How blessed it is to be obedient to the first call of Christ—how much happiness and glory are lost by delays, though conversion at last may have taken place!

10. *Sat at meat in the house.* Viz., of Matthew, who it appears, from Luke v. 29, made a great feast on the occasion, thus testifying his gratitude for the honor done him; and that his friends and acquaintances might profit by the teaching of his new Master, he invites them to the entertainment that was honored by the presence of Christ. His companions, it appears, were not of the most creditable kind. They were "taxgatherers and sinners."

MATTHEW HENRY

This was the chief thing Matthew aimed at in this treat, that he might have an opportunity of bringing his old associates acquainted with Christ. They who are effectually brought to Christ themselves, cannot but be desirous that others also may be brought to him, and ambitious of contributing something towards it. True grace will not contentedly eat its morsels alone, but will invite others. And surely some of them will *follow him*, as he *followed Christ*. Thus did Andrew and Philip, John i. 41, 45; iv. 29.

III. The displeasure of the Pharisees at this, *v.* 11. They cavilled at it; *why eateth your Master with publicans and sinners?* Christ was quarrelled with. It was not the least of his sufferings, that he *endured the contradiction of sinners against himself.* Though he never spoke or did anything amiss, everything he said and did was found fault with. Thus he taught us to expect and prepare for reproach, and to bear it patiently. They that quarrelled with him were the Pharisees. They were very strict in avoiding *sinners*, but not in avoiding *sin*; none greater zealots than they for the *form* of godliness, nor greater enemies to the *power* of it. They brought their cavil, not to Christ himself; they had not the courage to face him with it, but to his disciples. Being offended at the Master, they quarrel with the disciples. It concerns Christians to be able to vindicate and justify Christ, and his doctrines and laws, and to be *ready always to give an answer to those that ask them a reason of the hope that is in them*, 1 Peter iii. 15. While he is an Advocate for us in heaven, let us be advocates for him on earth, and make his reproach our own. The complaint was his *eating with publicans and sinners*: to be intimate with wicked people is against the law of God (Ps. cxix. 115; i. 1); and perhaps by accusing Christ of this to his disciples, they hoped to tempt them from him. To be intimate with publicans was against the *tradition of the elders*, and, therefore, they looked upon it as a heinous thing. They were angry with Christ for this, (1) Because they *wished ill to him.* It is an easy and very common thing to put the worst constructions upon the best words and actions. (2) Because they *wished no good to* publicans and sinners, but envied Christ's favour to them. It may justly be suspected, that they have not the grace of God themselves, who grudge others a share in that grace.

IV. The defence that Christ made for himself and his disciples, in justification of their converse with publicans and sinners. Let him alone to vindicate himself and to plead his own cause, to answer for himself, and for us too. Two things he urges in his defence,

1. The necessity and exigence of the case of the publicans, which called aloud for his help. It was the extreme necessity of poor, lost sinners, that brought Christ from the pure regions above, to these impure ones; and the same was it, that brought him into this company which was thought impure. He proves the necessity of the case of the publicans: *they that be whole need not a physician, but they that are sick.* The publicans are sick, and they need one to help and heal them, which the Pharisees think they do not. Note, Sin is the sickness of the soul. It is deforming, weakening, disquieting, wasting, killing, but, blessed be God, not incurable. Jesus Christ is the great Physician of souls. Wise and good men should be as physicians to all about them; Christ was so. Sin-sick souls have need of this Physician, for their disease is dangerous; nature will not help itself; no man can help us; such need have we of Christ, that we are undone, eternally undone, without him. There are multitudes who fancy themselves to be sound and whole, who think they have *no need of Christ*, but that they can shift for themselves well enough without him, as Laodicea, Rev. iii. 17. See John ix. 40, 41. He proves, that their necessity did sufficiently justify his conduct, for that necessity made it *an act of charity*, which ought always to be preferred before the formalities of a religious profession, in which *bene*ficence and *muni*ficence are far better than *magni*ficence, as much as substance is better than shows or shadows. If to do well ourselves is better than sacrifice, as Samuel shows (1 Sam. xv. 22, 23), much more to do good to others. To promote the conversion of souls is the greatest act of mercy imaginable; it is *saving a soul from death*, James v. 20. Observe how Christ quotes this, *Go ye and learn what that meaneth.* It is not enough to be acquainted with the letter of scripture, but we must learn to understand the meaning of it. And they have best learned the meaning of the scriptures, that have learned how to apply them as a reproof to their own faults, and a rule for their own practice. This scripture which Christ quoted, served not only to vindicate him, but, [1] To show wherein true religion consists; not in external observances: but in doing all the good we

JAMIESON, FAUSSET, BROWN

tells us that the visit of Jairus, the ruler of the synagogue, occurred at that moment (vs. 18). But we know from Mark and Luke that this visit of Jairus did not take place till after our Lord's return, at a later period from the country of the Gadarenes. (See Mark 5:21, etc., and Luke 8:40, etc.). We conclude, therefore, that the feast was not made in the novelty of his discipleship, but after Matthew had had time to be somewhat established in the faith; when returning to Capernaum, his compassion for old friends, of his own calling and character, led him to gather them together that they might have an opportunity of hearing the gracious words which proceeded out of His Master's mouth, if haply they might experience a like change. **behold, many publicans and sinners**—Luke says, "a great company" (vs. 29)—**came and sat down with him and his disciples.** In all such cases the word rendered "sat" is "reclined," in allusion to the ancient mode of lying on couches at meals. **11. And when the Pharisees**—"and scribes," add Mark and Luke. **saw it, they** "murmured" or "muttered," says Luke (5: 30). **said unto his disciples**—not venturing to put their question to Jesus Himself. **Why eateth your Master with publicans and sinners?**—(See on Luke 15:2.)

12. But when Jesus heard [that], he said unto them—to the Pharisees and scribes; addressing Himself to them, though they had shrunk from addressing Him. **They that be whole need not a physician, but they that are sick**—i.e., "Ye deem yourselves whole; My mission, therefore, is not to you: The physician's business is with the sick; therefore eat I with publicans and sinners." Oh, what myriads of broken hearts, of sin-sick souls, have been bound up by this matchless saying!

13. But go ye and learn what that meaneth (Hos. 6:6), **I will have mercy, and not sacrifice**—i.e., the one rather than the other. "Sacrifice," the chief part of the ceremonial law, is here put for a religion of literal adherence to mere rules; while "mercy" expresses such compassion for the fallen as seeks to lift them up. The duty of keeping aloof from the polluted, in the sense of "having no fellowship with the unfruitful works of darkness," is obvious enough; but to understand this as prohibiting such intercourse

ADAM CLARKE

11. *When the Pharisees saw it.* The self-righteous Pharisees considered it equal to legal defilement to sit in company with taxgatherers and heathens.

12. *They that be whole need not a physician.* A common proverb, which none could either misunderstand or misapply.

13. *I will have mercy, and not sacrifice.* Quoted from 1 Sam. xv. 22. These are remarkable words. We may understand them as implying: (1) That God prefers an act of mercy, shown to the necessitous, to any act of religious worship to which the person might be called at that time. (2) That the whole sacrificial system was intended only to point out the infinite mercy of God to fallen man, in his redemption by the Blood of the new covenant. (3) That we should

F. B. MEYER:

The friend of sinners. The name Levi indicates that Matthew sprang from a priestly line. He had lost all self-respect to become the abhorred instrument of the Roman government, collecting dues on the merchandise that crossed the lake. But our Lord sees veins of gold and precious gems in most unlikely places, and he detected the apostle and evangelist in this despised publican.

Wherever a man is found by Christ, he sets himself to find others, and the Lord is willing to cooperate in any efforts to bring others to know him. He will sit with perfect grace among publicans and sinners, lifting them to his own pure and holy level. He is always to be found where there are sin-sick souls; and where hearts are famished for love and joy, he is with them as their bridegroom.
—*Bible Commentary*

MATTHEW HENRY

can to the bodies and souls of others; in righteousness and peace. [2] To condemn the Pharisaical hypocrisy of those who place religion in rituals, more than in morals, *ch.* xxiii. 23.

2. The nature and end of his own commission. "*I am not come to call the righteous, but sinners to repentance*, and therefore must converse with publicans." (1) What his errand was; it was to *call to repentance*. A call to us to change our mind and to change our way. (2) With whom his errand lay; not with *the righteous*, but with *sinners*. If the children of men had not been *sinners*, there had been no occasion for Christ's coming among them. Therefore his *greatest business* lies with the *greatest sinners*; the more dangerous the sick man's case is, the more occasion there is for the physician's help. Christ came into the world to *save sinners*, but especially *the chief* (1 Tim. i. 15). Christ came not with an expectation of succeeding among *the righteous*, those who conceit themselves so, and therefore will sooner be sick of their Saviour, than sick of their sins, but among the convinced humble *sinners*; to them Christ will come, for to them he will be welcome.

Verses 14–17

The objections which were made against Christ and his disciples gave occasion to some of the most profitable of his discourses; and thus the wisdom of Christ brings good out of evil. So here, from a reflection upon the conduct of his family, arose a discourse concerning his tenderness for it.

I. The objection which the disciples of John made against Christ's disciples, for not fasting so often as they did; which they are charged with, as another instance of the looseness of their profession, besides that of eating with publicans and sinners. It appears by the other evangelists (Mark ii. 18 and Luke v. 33) that the disciples of the Pharisees joined with them because they, being more in favour with Christ and his disciples, could do it more plausibly. It is no new thing for bad men to set good men together by the ears: if the people of God differ in their sentiments, designing men will take that occasion to sow discord. Now the complaint is, *Why do we and the Pharisees fast often, but thy disciples fast not?* It is a pity the duties of religion, which ought to be the confirmations of holy love, should be made the occasions of strife and contention.

1. How they boasted of their own fasting. *We and the Pharisees fast often.* Fasting has in all ages of the church been consecrated, upon special occasions, to the service of religion; the Pharisees were much in it. The disciples of John *fasted often.* The severer part of religion is often most *minded* by those that are yet under the discipline of the Spirit, as a *Spirit of bondage*, whereas, though these are good in their place, we must pass through them to that life of delight in God and dependence on him, to which these should lead. There is a proneness in professors to brag of their own performances in religion, and not only to boast of them before men, but to plead them before God, and confide in them as a righteousness.

2. How they blamed Christ's disciples for not fasting so often as they did. *Thy disciples fast not.* They could not but know, that Christ had instructed his disciples to keep their fasts private, and to manage themselves so as that they might not *appear unto men to fast.* We must not judge of people's religion by that which falls under the eye and observation of the world. It is common for vain professors to make themselves a standard in religion as if all that did less than they, did too little, and all that did more than they, did too much.

3. How they brought this complaint to Christ. If Christ's disciples, either by omission or commission, give offence, Christ himself will be sure to hear of it, and be reflected upon for it. *O Jesus, are these thy Christians?* The quarrel with Christ was brought to the disciples (*v.* 11), the quarrel with the disciples was brought to Christ (*v.* 14), this is the way of sowing discord and killing love, to set people against ministers, ministers against people, and one friend against another.

II. The apology which Christ made for his disciples in this matter. When they had nothing to say for themselves, he had something ready to say for them. What we do according to the precept and pattern of Christ, he will be sure to bear us out in.

Two things Christ pleads in defence of their *not fasting*.

1. That it was not a season proper for that duty (*v.* 15): *Can the children of the bride-chamber mourn, as long as the bridegroom is with them?* Christ's answer is so framed, as that it might sufficiently justify the practice of his own disciples, and yet not condemn the institution of John, or the practice of his disciples.

JAMIESON, FAUSSET, BROWN

with them as is necessary to their recovery, is to abuse it. This was what these pharisaical religionists did, and this is what our Lord here exposes. **for I am not come to call the righteous, but sinners [to repentance]**—The words enclosed in brackets are of doubtful authority here, and more than doubtful authority in Mark 2:17; but in Luke 5:32 they are undisputed. We have here just the former statement stripped of its figure. "The righteous" are the whole; "sinners," the sick. When Christ "called" the latter, as He did Matthew, and probably some of those publicans and sinners whom he had invited to meet Him, it was to heal them of their spiritual maladies, or save their souls: "The righteous," like those miserable self-satisfied Pharisees, "He sent empty away."

14-17. DISCOURSE ON FASTING. See on Luke 5: 33-39.

As this discourse is recorded by the first three Evangelists immediately after their account of the feast which Matthew made to his Lord, there can be no doubt that it was delivered on that occasion.

Mark introduces the subject thus (2:18): "And the disciples of John and of the Pharisees used to fast." These disciples of John, who seem not to have statedly followed Jesus, occupied a position intermediate between the Pharisaic life and that to which Jesus trained His own disciples; further advanced than the one, not so far advanced as the other. "And they come and say unto him"—or, according to our Evangelist, to whose narrative we now come, they brought their difficulty to Him through our Lord's own disciples. **And they said unto him, Why do the disciples of John fast often, and make prayers, and likewise the disciples of the Pharisees?** These seem to have fasted twice in the week (Luke 18:12), besides the prescribed seasons, **but thine eat and drink**—or, as in Matthew and Mark, "thy disciples fast not?"

And he said unto them, Can ye make the children of the bride-chamber—the bridal attendants, **fast while the bridegroom is with them?** Glorious title for Jesus to take to himself! The Old Testament is full

ADAM CLARKE

not rest in the sacrifices, but look for the mercy and salvation prefigured by them. *Go ye and learn.* A form of speech in frequent use among the rabbins, when they referred to any fact or example in the Sacred Writings.

W. E. VINE:

The answers of Christ to the questions of the disciples of John and of the Pharisees reveal His whole purpose and method. No doubt He and His followers observed such a fast as that on the Day of Atonement, but He imposed no frequent fasts in addition. What He taught was suitable to the change of character and purpose which He designed for His disciples. His claim to be the Bridegroom (Matt. 9:15), and the reference there to the absence of fasting, virtually involved a claim to be the Messiah (cf. Zech. 8:19).

—Vine's Expository Dictionary

14. *Thy disciples fast not.* Probably meaning that they did not fast so frequently as the others did, or for the same purposes, which is very likely, for the Pharisees had many superstitious fasts. They fasted in order to have lucky dreams, to obtain the interpretation of a dream, or to avert the evil import of a dream. They also fasted often in order to obtain the things they wished for. The tract *taanith* is full of these fasts, and of the wonders performed thus by the Jewish doctors.

MATTHEW HENRY

When at any time we are unjustly censured, our care must be only to clear ourselves, not to recriminate, or throw dirt upon others.

Now his argument is taken from the common usage of joy and rejoicing during the continuance of marriage solemnities, when all instances of melancholy and sorrow are looked upon as improper and absurd. The disciples of Christ were the *children of the bride-chamber*, invited to the wedding-feast, and welcome there. The faithful followers of Christ, who have the Spirit of adoption, have a continual feast, while they who have the spirit of bondage and fear, cannot rejoice for joy, as other people. The disciples of Christ had *the bridegroom with them*, which the disciples of John had not; their master was now cast into prison and therefore it was seasonable for them to *fast often*. Such a day would come upon the disciples of Christ, when the bridegroom should be taken from them, and *then should they fast*. The thoughts of parting grieved them when he was going, John xvi. 6. Tribulation and affliction befell them when he was gone, and gave them occasion of *mourning* and *praying*, that is, of religious fasting. It is merry or melancholy with the children of the bride-chamber, according as they have more or less of the bridegroom's presence. The presence and nearness of the sun makes day and summer, his absence and distance, night and winter. Christ is all in all to the church's joy. Every duty is to be done in its proper season. See Eccles. vii. 14; James v. 13. There is a time to mourn and a time to laugh, to each of which we should accommodate ourselves, and bring forth fruit in due season.

2. That they had not strength sufficient for that duty. This is set forth in two similitudes, one of putting *new cloth into an old garment*, which does but pull the old to pieces (*v.* 16); the other of putting *new wine into old bottles*, which does but burst the bottles, *v.* 17. Christ's disciples were not able to bear these severe exercises so well as those of John and of the Pharisees. They, being taken immediately from their callings, had not been used to such religious austerities, and were unfit for them, and would by them be rather unfitted for their other work. Some duties of religion are harder and more difficult than others, such as religious fasting and the duties that attend it. The best of Christ's disciples pass through a state of infancy; all the trees in Christ's garden are not of a growth, nor all his scholars in the same form; there are *babes in Christ* and grown men. The weakness and infirmity of young Christians ought to be considered: as the food provided for them must be such as is proper for their age (1 Cor. iii. 2; Heb. v. 12), so must the work be that is cut out for them. Christ would not speak to his disciples that which they could not then bear, John xvi. 12. Young beginners in religion must not be put upon the hardest duties at first, lest they be discouraged. Such as was Jacob's care of his children and cattle, not to overdrive them (Gen. xxxiii. 13), such is Christ's care of the little ones of his family, and the lambs of his flock: he gently leads them. There may be *over*-doing even in *well*-doing, a being *righteous over-much*; and such an *over*-doing as may prove an *un*doing through the subtlety of Satan.

Verses 18–26

We have here two passages of history put together; that of the raising of Jairus's daughter to life, and that of the curing of the woman that had *the bloody issue*, as he was going to Jairus's house, which is introduced in a parenthesis, in the midst of the other; for Christ's miracles were thick sown, and interwoven. He was called to do these good works from speaking the things foregoing, in answer to the cavils of the Pharisees, *v.* 18: *While he spake these things;* and we may suppose it a pleasing interruption given to that unpleasant work of disputation, which, though sometimes needful, a good man will gladly leave, to go about a work of devotion or charity.

I. The ruler's address to Christ, *v.* 18. *A certain ruler*, a ruler of the synagogue, *came and worshipped him. Have any of the rulers believed on him?* Yes, here was one. This ruler had a little daughter, of twelve years old, just dead, and this breach made upon his family comforts was the occasion of his coming to Christ. In trouble we should visit God: the death of our relations should drive us to Christ, who is our life. Now observe,

1. His humility in this address to Christ. He came with his errand to Christ himself. It is no disparagement to the greatest rulers, personally to attend on the Lord Jesus. He *worshipped him*. They that would receive mercy from Christ must give honour to Christ.

2. His faith in this address; "*My daughter is even now dead*," and though any other physician would

JAMIESON, FAUSSET, BROWN

of this conjugal tie between Jehovah and His people, to be realized in Messiah. See Matt. 22:2 and compare John 3:29. **But the days will come**—rather, "But days will come," **when the bridegroom shall be taken away from them**—a delicate and affecting allusion to coming events, and the grief with which these would fill the disciples, **and then shall they fast in those days**—"In My presence such exercises were unseemly: when bereft of Me, they will have time enough and cause enough."

And he spake also a parable unto them; No man putteth a piece of a new garment upon an old. In Matthew and Mark the word employed signifies "uncarded," "unfulled," or "undressed" cloth, which, as it is apt to shrink when wetted, would rend the old cloth to which it was sewed: **if otherwise**—if he will do so unwise a thing, **then both the new maketh a rent, and the piece that was taken out of the new agreeth not with the old. And no man putteth new wine into old bottles**—"wine-skins." They were made usually of goat-skins, and of course would be liable to burst in the case supposed: **else,** if he do such a thing, **the new wine will burst the bottles, and be spilled, and the bottles shall perish. But new wine must be put into new bottles; and both are preserved.**

18-26. The Woman with the Issue of Blood Healed.—The Daughter of Jairus Raised to Life. (= Luke 8: 40-56; Mark 5:21-43.) For the exposition, see on Mark 5:21-43.

And, behold, there cometh one of the rulers of the synagogue—of which class there were but few who believed in Jesus (John 7:48). One would suppose from this that the ruler had been with the multitude on the shore, anxiously awaiting the return of Jesus, and immediately on His arrival had accosted Him as here related. But Matthew (9:18) tells us that the ruler came to Him while He was in the act of speaking at His own table on the subject of fasting; and as we must suppose that this converted publican ought to know what took place on that memorable occasion when he made a feast to his Lord, we conclude that here the right order is indicated by the First Evangelist alone. **Jairus by name**—or "Jaeirus." It is the same name as *Jair*, in the Old Testament (Num. 32:41; Judg. 10:3; Esther 2:5). **and when he saw him, he fell at his feet**—in Matthew (9:18), "worshipped Him." The meaning is the same in both. **And besought him greatly, saying, My little daughter**—Luke (8:42) says, "He

ADAM CLARKE

15. *Can the children of the bridechamber?* These persons were the companions of the bridegroom, who accompanied him to the house of his father-in-law when he went to bring the bride to his own home. The marriage feast among the Jews lasted seven days, but the new-married woman was considered to be a bride for thirty days.

16. *No man putteth a piece of new cloth.* "No man putteth a patch of unscoured cloth upon an old garment."

That which is put in . . . taketh from the garment. Instead of closing up the rent, it makes a larger, by tearing away with it the whole breadth of the cloth over which it was laid; "it taketh its fulness or whole breadth from the garment."

17. *New wine into old bottles.* It is still the custom, in the Eastern countries, to make their bottles of goatskins. If these happened to be old, and new wine were put into them, the violence of the fermentation must necessarily burst them; and therefore newly made bottles were employed for the purpose of putting that wine in which had not yet gone through its state of fermentation. The institutes of Christ, and those of the Pharisees, could never be brought to accord; an attempt to combine the two systems would be as absurd as it would be destructive. The old covenant made way for the new, which was its completion and its end; but with that old covenant the new cannot be incorporated.

18. *A certain ruler.* There were two officers in the synagogue: *chazan,* the bishop or overseer of the congregation; and *rosh,* the head or ruler of the congregation. The *chazan* takes the book of the law and gives it to the *rosh,* or ruler, and he appoints who shall read the different sections. Jairus, who is the person intended here, was, in this latter sense, the ruler or governor of one of the synagogues, probably at Capernaum.

My daughter is even now dead. Or, "My daughter was just now dying"; or "is

MATTHEW HENRY

now come too late, yet Christ comes not too late; he is a Physician after death, for he is *the resurrection and the life*; "*O come* then, *and lay thy hand upon her, and she shall live*." This was quite above the power of nature, yet within the power of Christ, who has *life in himself, and quickeneth whom he will*. We cannot in faith bring him such a request as this; while there is life, there is hope, and room for prayer; but when our friends are dead, the case is determined. But while Christ was here upon earth working miracles, such a confidence as this was not only allowable but very commendable.

II. The readiness of Christ to comply with his address, *v.* 19. *Jesus* immediately *arose*, left his company, *and followed him*; he was not only willing to grant him what he desired, in raising his daughter to life, but to gratify him so far as to come to his house to do it. Surely *he never said to the seed of Jacob, Seek ye me in vain*. And observe, when *Jesus followed him, so did his disciples*, whom he had chosen for his constant companions; it was not for state, or that he might come with observation, that he took his attendants with him, but that they might be the witnesses of his miracles, who were hereafter to be the preachers of his doctrine.

III. The healing of the poor woman's bloody issue. I call her a poor woman, not only because her case was piteous, but because, though she had had something in the world, she had *spent it all upon physicians*, for the cure of her distemper, and was never the better; which was a double aggravation of the misery of her condition, that she had impoverished herself for the recovery of her health, and yet had not her health either. This *woman was diseased with a constant issue of blood twelve years* (*v.* 20); a disease, which was not only weakening and wasting, but which also rendered her ceremonially unclean, and shut her *out from the courts of the Lord's house*; but it did not cut her off from approaching to Christ. She applied herself to Christ, and received mercy from him, by the way.

1. The woman's great faith in Christ, and in his power. Her disease was of such a nature, that her modesty would not suffer her to speak openly to Christ for a cure, as others did, but she believed him to have such an overflowing fulness of healing virtue, that the very *touch of his garment* would be her cure. This, perhaps, had something of fancy mixed with faith; for she had no precedent for this way of application to Christ. But what *weakness of understanding* there was in it, Christ was pleased to overlook, and to accept the sincerity and strength of her faith. She believed she should be healed if she did but *touch* the very *hem of his garment*, the very extremity of it. There is virtue in everything that belongs to Christ. Such a fulness of grace is there in Christ, that *from it we may all receive*, John i. 16.

2. Christ's great favour to this woman. He did not suspend his healing influences, but suffered this bashful patient to steal a cure unknown to any one else, though she could not think to do it unknown to him. And now she was well content to be gone, for she had what she came for, but Christ was not willing to let her go so: the triumphs of her faith must be to her praise and honour. He *turned about* to see her (*v.* 22), and soon discovered her. It is great encouragement to humble Christians, that they who hide themselves from men are known to Christ. who sees in secret their applications to heaven when most private.

(1) He *puts gladness into her heart*, by that word, *Daughter, be of good comfort*. She feared being chidden for coming clandestinely, but she is encouraged. He calls her *daughter*, for he spoke to her with the tenderness of a father, as he did *to the man sick of the palsy* (*v.* 2), whom he called *son*. He bids her *be of good comfort*. His bidding her *be comforted*, brought comfort with it, as his saying, *Be ye whole*, brought health with it.

(2) He puts honour upon her faith. That grace of all others gives most honour to Christ, and therefore he puts most honour upon it; *Thy faith has made thee whole*. This woman had more faith than she thought she had. She was spiritually healed; that cure was wrought in her which is the proper fruit and effect of faith, the pardon of sin and the work of grace. Her bodily cure was the fruit of faith, of her faith, and that made it a happy, comfortable cure indeed. They out of whom the devils were cast, were helped by Christ's sovereign power; some by the faith of others (as *v.* 2); but it is *thy faith that has made thee whole*.

IV. The posture in which he found the ruler's house, *v.* 23.—He *saw the people and the minstrels*, or musicians, *making a noise*. The house was in a hurry: such work does death make, when it comes into a family; and, perhaps, the necessary cares that arise

JAMIESON, FAUSSET, BROWN

had one only daughter, about twelve years of age." According to a well-known rabbin, quoted by LIGHTFOOT, a daughter. till she had completed her twelfth year, was called "little," or "a little maid"; after that, "a young woman." **lieth at the point of death**—Matthew gives it thus: "My daughter is even now dead"—"has just expired." The news of her death reached the father after the cure of the woman with the issue of blood: but Matthew's brief account gives only the *result*, as in the case of the centurion's servant (Matt. 8:5, etc.). **come and lay thy hands on her, that she may be healed; and she shall live**—or, "that she may be healed and live," according to a fully preferable reading. In one of the class to which this man belonged, so steeped in prejudice, such faith would imply more than in others.

The Woman with an Issue of Blood Healed

And Jesus went with him; and much people followed him, and thronged him—The word in Luke is stronger—"choked," "stifled Him." **And had suffered many things of many physicians**—The expression perhaps does not necessarily refer to the suffering she endured under medical treatment, but to the much varied treatment which she underwent. **and had spent all that she had, and was nothing bettered, but rather grew worse**—pitiable case, and affectingly aggravated; emblem of our natural state as fallen creatures (Ezek. 16:5, 6), and illustrating the worse than vanity of all human remedies for spiritual maladies (Hos. 5:13). The higher design of all our Lord's miracles of healing irresistibly suggests this way of viewing the present case, the propriety of which will still more appear as we proceed. **When she had heard of Jesus, came**—This was the right experiment at last. What had she "heard of Jesus?" No doubt it was His marvellous cures she had heard of; and the hearing of these, in connection with her bitter experience of the vanity of applying to any other, had been blessed to the kindling in her soul of a firm confidence that He who had so willingly wrought such cures on others was able and would not refuse to heal her also. **in the press behind**—shrinking, yet seeking. **touched his garment**—According to the ceremonial law, the touch of anyone having the disease which this woman had would have defiled the person touched. Some think that the recollection of this may account for her stealthily approaching Him in the crowd behind, and touching but the hem of His garment. But there was an instinct in the faith which brought her to Jesus, which taught her, that if that touch could set her free from the defiling disease itself, it was impossible to communicate defilement to Him, and that this wondrous Healer must be above such laws. **For she said**—"within herself" (Matt. 9:21). **If I may touch but his clothes, I shall be whole**—i.e., if I may but *come in contact* with this glorious Healer *at all*. Remarkable faith this!

And he said unto her, Daughter—"be of good comfort" (Luke 8:48). **thy faith hath made thee whole; go in peace, and be whole of thy plague**—Though healed as soon as she believed, it seemed to her a stolen cure—she feared to acknowledge it. Jesus therefore sets His royal seal upon it. But what a glorious dismissal from the lips of Him who is "our Peace" is that, "Go in peace!"

And he cometh—rather, "they come." **to the house of the ruler of the synagogue, and seeth the tumult, and them that wept and wailed greatly**—"the minstrels and the

ADAM CLARKE

by this time dead"; i.e., as Mr. Wakefield properly observes, She was so ill when I left home that she must be dead by this time. This turn of the expression reconciles the account given here with that in Mark and Luke. To be successful in our applications to God by prayer, four things are requisite; and this ruler teaches us what they are. *First,* A man should place himself in the presence of God—he came unto Him. *Secondly,* He should humble himself sincerely before God—*he fell* down before Him—*at his feet,* Mark v. 22. *Thirdly,* He should lay open his wants with a holy earnestness—he *besought him* greatly, Mark v. 23. *Fourthy,* He should have unbounded confidence in the power and goodness of Christ, that his request shall be granted —*lay thy hand upon her, and she shall live.* Imposition of hands was a rite anciently used by the servants of God, through which heavenly influences were conveyed to the bodies and souls of men.

19. *Jesus arose, and followed him.* Our blessed Lord could have acted as well at a distance as present; but He goes to the place, to teach His ministers not to spare either their steps or their pains when the salvation of a soul is in question.

20. *The hem of his garment.* The "fringes," which the Jews were commanded to wear on their garments. See Num. xv. 38.

21. *She said within herself, If I may but touch his garment.* Her disorder was of that delicate nature that modesty forbade her to make any public acknowledgment of it, and therefore she endeavored to transact the whole business in private.

22. *Daughter, be of good comfort.* "Take courage, Daughter." *Thy faith hath made thee whole.* "This thy faith hath saved thee"; i.e., your faith in My power has interested that power in your behalf, so that you are saved from your disorder, and from all its consequences.

23. *Saw the minstrels and the people making a noise.* "Pipers." That pipes were in use among the Jews, in times of calamity or death, is evident from Jer. xlviii. 36. And among the

MATTHEW HENRY

at such a time, when our dead is to be decently buried out of our sight, give some useful diversion to that grief which is apt to prevail and play the tyrant. The people in the neighbourhood came together to condole on account of the loss, to comfort the parents, to prepare for, and attend on, the funeral, which the Jews were not wont to defer long. The musicians were among them, according to the custom of the Gentiles, with their doleful, melancholy tunes, to increase the grief, and stir up the lamentations of those that attended on this occasion. Thus they indulged a passion that is apt enough of itself to grow intemperate, and affected to *sorrow as those that had no hope*. See how religion provides cordials, where irreligion administers corrosives. Heathenism aggravates that grief which Christianity studies to assuage. The parents, who were immediately touched with the affliction, were silent, while *the people and minstrels*, whose lamentations were forced, made such a noise. The loudest grief is not always the greatest; rivers are most noisy where they run shallow. *That grief is most sincere, which shuns observation.*

V. The rebuke that Christ gave to this hurry and noise, *v.* 24. He said, *Give place.* Note, Sometimes, when *the sorrow of the world* prevails, it is difficult for Christ and his comforts to enter. They that harden themselves in sorrow, and, like Rachel, *refuse to be comforted*, should think they hear Christ saying to their disquieting thoughts, *Give place.* He gives a good reason why they should not thus disquiet themselves and one another; *The maid is not dead but sleepeth.* 1. This was eminently true of this maid, that was immediately to be raised to life; she was really dead, but not so to Christ, who knew within himself what he would do, and could do. This death must be but of short continuance, and therefore is but a sleep, like one night's rest. 2. It is in a sense true of all that die, chiefly of them *that die in the Lord.* (1) Death is a sleep. All nations and languages, for the softening of that which is so dreadful, and withal so unavoidable, and the reconciling of themselves to it, have agreed to call it so. It is not the sleep of the soul; its activity ceases not; but the sleep of the body, which lies down in the grave, still and silent. Sleep is a short death, and death a long sleep. But *the death of the righteous* is in a special manner to be looked upon as a sleep, Isa. lvii. 2. They sleep in Jesus (1 Thess. iv. 14); they not only rest from the toils and labours of the day, but *rest in hope* of a joyful waking again in the morning of the resurrection, when they shall wake refreshed, wake to a new life, *wake to sleep no more.* (2) The consideration of this should moderate our grief at the death of our dear relations: say not, They *are* lost; no, they are but *gone before.* The apostle speaks of it as an absurd thing to imagine that *they that are fallen asleep in Christ are perished* (1 Cor. xv. 18).

Now could it be thought that such a comfortable word as this, from the mouth of our Lord Jesus, should be ridiculed as it was? *They laughed him to scorn.* The words and works of Christ which cannot be understood, yet are not therefore to be despised. We must adore the mystery of divine sayings, even when they seem to contradict what we think ourselves most confident of. Yet even this tended to the confirmation of the miracle: for it seems she was so apparently dead, that it was thought a very ridiculous thing to say otherwise.

VI. The raising of the damsel to life by the power of Christ, *v.* 25. *The people were put forth.* Scorners that laugh at what they see and hear that is above their capacity, are not proper witnesses of the wonderful works of Christ, the glory of which lies not in pomp, but in power.

Christ went in and *took her by the hand*, as it were to awake her, and to help her up. The high priest, that typified Christ, was not to come near the dead (Lev. xxi. 10, 11), but Christ *touched the dead.* Christ, having power to raise the dead, is above the infection, and therefore is not shy of touching them. He *took her by the hand, and the maid arose.* So easily, so effectually was the miracle wrought; by a touch. Dead souls are not raised to spiritual life, unless Christ *take them by the hand.* He helps us up, or we lie still.

VII. The general notice that was taken of this miracle, though it was wrought privately; *v.* 26, *the fame thereof went abroad into all that land:* it was the common subject of discourse. Christ's works are more talked of than considered and improved. Though we at this distance have not seen Christ's miracles, yet blessed *are they that have not seen, and yet have believed*, John xx. 29.

Verses 27-34

In these verses we have an account of two more miracles wrought together by our Saviour.

I. The giving of sight to two blind men, *v.* 27-31.

JAMIESON, FAUSSET, BROWN

people making a noise" (Matt. 9:23)—lamenting for the dead. (See II Chron. 35:25; Jer. 9:20; Amos 5:16.)

And when he was come in, he saith unto them, Why make ye this ado, and weep? the damsel is not dead, but sleepeth—so brief her state of death as to be more like a short sleep.

And they laughed him to scorn—rather, simply, "laughed at Him"—"knowing that she was dead" (Luke 8:53); an important testimony this to the reality of her death. **But when he had put them all out**—The word is strong—"turned them all out"; meaning all those who were making this noise, and any others that may have been there from sympathy, that only those might be present who were most nearly concerned, and those whom He had Himself brought as witnesses of the great act about to be done.

And straightway the damsel—The word here is different from that in vss. 39, 40, 41, and signifies "young maiden," or "little girl." **arose, and walked**—a vivid touch evidently from an eyewitness. **And they were astonished with a great astonishment**—The language here is the strongest.

27-34. Two Blind Men, and a Dumb Demoniac Healed. These two miracles are recorded by Matthew alone. *Two Blind Men Healed* (vss. 27-31).

ADAM CLARKE

Greeks and Romans, as well as among the Jews, persons were hired on purpose to follow the funeral processions with lamentations. See Jer. ix. 17-21; Amos v. 16. Even the poorest among the Jews were required to have two pipers and one mourning woman.

24. *The maid is not dead, but sleepeth.* That is, she is not dead so as to continue under the power of death; but shall be raised from it as a person is from natural sleep.

They laughed him to scorn. "They ridiculed Him"—"they grinned a ghastly smile," expressive of the contempt they felt for His person and knowledge.

25. *He . . . took her by the hand, and the maid arose.* The fountain of life thus communicating its vital energy to the dead body. Where death has already taken place, no power but that of the great God can restore to life; in such a case, vain is the help of man. So the soul that is dead in trespasses and sins—that is, sentenced to death because of transgression—and is thus dead in law, can be restored to spiritual life only by the mighty power of the Lord Jesus, because He alone has made the atonement, and He alone can pardon transgression.

26. *And the fame thereof went abroad.* In this business Jesus himself scarcely appears, but the work effected by His sovereign power is fully manifested; to teach us that it is the business of a successful preacher of the gospel to conceal himself as much as possible, that God alone may have the glory of His own grace.

G. CAMPBELL MORGAN:

Look at the King again, and mark His method. How the method varies! It is a great picture, this of Jesus coming to the house of Jairus. It is so exquisite in its beauty that we need the three Gospel stories to see it. He came in where the child was lying dead, and He said, "She is not dead, but sleepeth." And they laughed Him to scorn. What did He do? He put them all out. Do not imagine that this King is only capable of tenderness; He can do very drastic things. He was justified in His action. When He came in they were wailing; before He had been there two minutes they were laughing; but there are some people who must be put out before Jesus can do anything. "He could there do no mighty work . . . because of their unbelief." A critical, scorning, scoffing crowd must be put out before He can do anything. He himself was affected by it. Criticism was sterilizing in its effect upon Him. Faith was fertilizing.—*The Gospel According to Matthew*

MATTHEW HENRY

Christ is the Fountain of light as well as life.

1. The importunate address of the blind men to Christ. He was returning from the ruler's house to his own lodgings, and these *blind men followed him*, as beggars do, with their incessant cries, *v.* 27. He that cured diseases so easily, so effectually, and, withal, at so cheap a rate, shall have patients enough.

(1) The title which these blind men gave to Christ; *Thou Son of David, have mercy on us.* The promise made to David, that of his loins the Messiah should come, was well known. At this time there was a general expectation of his appearing; these blind men know, and own, and proclaim it in the streets of Capernaum, that he is come, and that this is he. They who, by the providence of God, are deprived of bodily sight, may yet, by the grace of God, have *the eyes of their understanding so enlightened*, as to discern those great things of God, *which are hid from the wise and prudent.*

(2) Their petition, *Have mercy on us.* Whatever our necessities and burthens are, we need no more for supply and support, than a share in the *mercy of our Lord Jesus.* Whether he heal us or no, if he *have mercy on us*, we have enough. They did not each of them say for himself, *Have mercy on me*, but both for one another, *Have mercy on us.* Fellow-sufferers should be joint-petitioners. In Christ there is enough for all.

(3) Their importunity in this request; they *followed him, crying.* It seems, he did not take notice of them at first, for he would try their faith, which he knew to be strong; would quicken their prayers, and make his cures the more valued, when they did not always come at the first word; and would teach us to *continue instant in prayer, always to pray, and not to faint. When he came into the house*, they *followed him* thither, and *came to him.* Christ's doors are always open to believing and importunate petitioners; it seemed rude in them to rush into the house after him, when he desired to retire; but, such is the tenderness of our Lord Jesus, that they were not more bold than welcome.

2. The confession of faith, which Christ drew from them upon this occasion. When they came to him for mercy, he asked them, *Believe ye that I am able to do this?* Faith is the great condition of Christ's favours. They who would receive the *mercy* of Christ, must firmly believe the *power* of Christ. What we would have him do for us, we must be fully assured that he is *able to do.* Nature may work fervency, but it is only grace that can work faith. They had intimated their faith in the office of Christ as *Son of David*, and in his mercy; but Christ demands likewise a profession of faith in his power. *Believe ye that I am able?* This will amount to their belief of his being not only *the Son of David*, but *the Son of God*; for it is God's prerogative to *open the eyes of the blind* (Ps. cxlvi. 8). Still it is put to us, *Believe we that Christ is able to do for us.* To believe the power of Christ is not only to assure ourselves of it, but to commit ourselves to it, and encourage ourselves in it.

To this question they give an immediate answer, without hesitation: they said, *Yea, Lord.*

3. The cure that Christ wrought on them; *he touched their eyes, v.* 29. He put the cure upon their faith, *According to your faith be it unto you.* When they begged for a cure, he enquired into their faith (*v.* 28), *Believe ye that I am able?* He did not enquire into their wealth, whether they were able to pay him for a cure; but into their faith; and now they had professed their faith he referred the matter to that: "The power you believe in shall be exerted for you; *According to your faith be it unto you.*" It is a great comfort to true believers that Jesus Christ knows their faith, and is well pleased with it. Though it be weak, though others do not discern it, though they themselves are ready to question it, it is known to him. They who apply themselves to Jesus Christ, shall be dealt with *according to their faith*; not according to their *fancies*, nor according to their *profession.* True believers may be sure to find all that favour which is offered in the gospel; and our comforts ebb or flow, according as our faith is stronger or weaker; we are not straitened in Christ, let us not then be straighted in ourselves.

4. The charge he gave them to keep it private (*v.* 30), *See that no man know it.* In the good we do, we must not seek our own praise, but only the glory of God. It must be more our care and endeavour to be useful, than to be known and observed to be so. Some think that Christ, in keeping it private, showed his displeasure against the people of Capernaum, who had seen so many miracles, and yet believed not. It is just in Christ to deny the means of conviction to those that are obstinate in their infidelity; and to shroud the light from those that shut their eyes against it. He did it in discretion, for his own preservation; because the more he was proclaimed, the more jealous

JAMIESON, FAUSSET, BROWN

27. And when Jesus departed thence, two blind men followed him [hearing, doubtless, as in a later case is expressed, "that Jesus passed by" (ch. 20:30)] **crying, and saying, Thou son of David, have mercy on us.** It is remarkable that in the only other recorded case in which the blind applied to Jesus for their sight, and obtained it, they addressed Him, over and over again, by this one Messianic title, so well known—"Son of David" (ch. 20:30). Can there be a doubt that their faith fastened on such great Messianic promises as this, "Then the eyes of the blind shall be opened . . ." (Isa. 35:5)? and if so, this appeal to Him, as the Consolation of Israel, to do His predicted office, would fall with great weight upon the ears of Jesus.

28. And when he was come into the house—To try their faith and patience, He seems to have made them no answer. But **the blind men came to Him** [which, no doubt, was what He desired] **and Jesus saith unto them, Believe ye that I am able to do this? they said unto him, Yea, Lord**—Doubtless our Lord's design was not only to put their faith to the test by this question, but to deepen it, to raise their expectation of a cure, and so prepare them to receive it; and the cordial acknowledgment, so touchingly simple, which they immediately made to Him of His power to heal them, shows how entirely that object was gained.

29. Then touched he their eyes, saying, According to your faith be it unto you—not, Receive a cure *proportioned* to your faith. but, Receive this cure as *granted to* your faith. Thus would they carry about with them, in their restored vision, a gracious seal of the faith which drew it from their compassionate Lord.

30. And their eyes were opened: and Jesus straitly charged them—The expression is very strong, denoting great earnestness.

ADAM CLARKE

27. *Son of David.* This was the same as if they had called Him "Messiah." Two things here are worthy of remark: (1) That it was a generally received opinion at this time in Judea that the Messiah should be Son of David, John vii. 42 (2) That Jesus Christ was generally and incontestably acknowledged as coming from this stock, Matt. xii. 23.

28. *When he was come into the house.* That is, the house of Peter at Capernaum, where He ordinarily lodged. *Believe ye that I am able to do this?* Without faith Jesus does nothing to men's souls now, no more than He did to their bodies in the days of His flesh. *They said unto him, Yea, Lord.* Under a sense of our spiritual blindness we should have: (1) A lively faith in the almighty grace of Christ. (2) A fervent, incessant cry for the communication of this grace. (3) A proper view of His incarnation, because it is through His union with our nature, and by His sufferings and death, we are to expect salvation.

29. *According to your faith.* See on chap. viii. 13.

30. *Straitly charged them.* He charged them severely; He charged them, on pain of His displeasure, not to make it as yet public. See the reasons, chap. viii. 4.

MATTHEW HENRY

would the rulers of the Jews be of his growing interest among the people.

But honour is like the shadow, which, as it flees from those that follow it, so it follows those that flee from it (*v.* 21); *They spread abroad his fame.* Though it may be excused as honestly meant for the honour of Christ, yet it cannot be justified, being done against a particular charge. Whenever we profess to direct our intention to the glory of God, we must see to it that the action be according to the will of God.

II. The healing of a *dumb man*, that was *possessed with a devil.*

1. His case, which was very sad. He was under the power of the devil in this particular instance, that he was disabled from speaking, *v.* 32. See the calamitous state of this world, and how various the afflictions of the afflicted are! We have no sooner dismissed *two blind men*, but we meet with a *dumb man.* How thankful should we be to God for our sight and speech! When the devil gets possession of a soul, it is made silent as to anything that is good; dumb in prayers and praises. This poor creature *they brought to Christ*, who entertained not only those that came of themselves in their own faith, but those that were *brought to him* by their friends in the faith of others. They brought him in just as *the blind man went out.* See how unwearied Christ was in doing good; how closely one good work followed another! Treasures of mercy, wondrous mercy, are hid in him; which may be continually communicated, but can never be exhausted.

2. His cure, which was very sudden (*v.* 33), *When the devil was cast out, the dumb spake.* Christ's cures strike at the root, and remove the effect by taking away the cause; they open the lips, by breaking Satan's power in the soul.

3. The consequences of this cure.

(1) *The multitudes marvelled;* and well they might; though *few believed, many wondered.* The admiration of the common people is sooner raised than any other affection.

(2) *The Pharisees* blasphemed, *v.* 34. When they could not gainsay the convincing evidence of these miracles, they fathered them upon the devil, as if they had been wrought by compact and collusion: *he casteth out devils* (say they) by *the prince of the devils.* This breathes nothing but malice and falsehood, and hellish enmity in the highest degree; it is diabolism all over. Because the people marvelled, they must say something to diminish the miracle, and this was all they could say.

Verses 35-38

I. A conclusion of the foregoing account of Christ's preaching and miracles (*v.* 35); *He went about all the cities teaching and healing.* This is the same we had before, iv. 23. There it ushers in the more particular record of Christ's preaching (*ch.* v. vi. and vii) and of his cures (*ch.* viii and ix), and here it is elegantly repeated in the close of these instances, as the *quod erat demonstrandum—the point to be proved*; as if the evangelist should say, "Now I hope I have made it out that Christ preached and healed."

Observe how Christ in his preaching had respect,

1. To the private towns. He visited not only the great and wealthy cities, but the poor, obscure villages; there he preached, there he healed. The souls of those that are meanest in the world are as precious to Christ, and should be to us, as the souls of those that make the greatest figure.

2. To the public worship. He taught *in their synagogues*, (1) That he might bear a testimony to solemn assemblies. (2) That he might have an opportunity of preaching there, where people were gathered together, with an expectation to hear.

II. A preface, or introduction, to the account in the following chapter, of his sending forth his apostles. *He* took notice of *the multitude* (*v.* 36); not only of the crowds that *followed him*, but of the vast numbers of people with whom (as he passed along) he observed the country to be replenished: so very populous was that nation now grown; and it was the effect of God's blessing on Abraham.

1. He pitied them, and was concerned for them (*v.* 36); *He was moved with compassion on them;* not upon a temporal account, as he pitied the blind, and lame, and sick; but upon a spiritual account; he was concerned to see them ignorant and careless, and ready to perish for lack of vision. It was pity to souls that brought him from heaven to earth, and there to the cross. Christ pities those most that pity themselves least; so should we.

See what moved this pity. (1) *They fainted*: they were destitute, vexed, wearied. They wanted help for their souls, and had none at hand that was good for anything. The scribes and Pharisees filled them with vain notions, therefore *they fainted*; for what

JAMIESON, FAUSSET, BROWN

31. But they, when they were departed, spread abroad his fame in all that country—(See on ch. 8:4.)

A Dumb Demoniac Healed (vss. 32-34). **32. As they went out, behold, they brought to him a dumb man possessed with a devil**—"demonized." The dumbness was not natural, but was the effect of the possession.

33. And when the devil [demon] **was cast out, the dumb spake**—The particulars in this case are not given; the object being simply to record the instantaneous restoration of the natural faculties on the removal of the malignant oppression of them, the form which the popular astonishment took, and the very different effect of it upon another class. **and the multitudes marvelled, saying, It was never so seen in Israel**—referring, probably, not to this case only, but to all those miraculous displays of healing power which seemed to promise a new era in the history of Israel. Probably they meant by this language to indicate, as far as they thought it safe to do so, their inclination to regard Him as the promised Messiah. **34. But the Pharisees said, He casteth out devils through the prince of the devils**—"the demons through the prince of the demons." This seems to be the first muttering of a theory of such miracles which soon became a fixed mode of calumniating them—a theory which would be ridiculous if it were not melancholy as an outburst of the darkest malignity. (See on ch. 12:24, etc.)

35-ch. 10:5. THIRD GALILEAN CIRCUIT—MISSION OF THE TWELVE APOSTLES. As the Mission of the Twelve supposes the previous choice of them—of which our Evangelist gives no account, and which did not take place till a later stage of our Lord's public life—it is introduced here out of its proper place, which is after what is recorded in Luke 6: 12-19.

Third Galilean Circuit (vs. 35)—and probably the last. **35. And Jesus went about all the cities and villages, teaching in their synagogues, and preaching the gospel of the kingdom, and healing every sickness and every disease** [**among the people**]—The bracketed words are of more than doubtful authority here, and were probably introduced here from ch. 4:23. The language here is so identical with that used in describing the first circuit (ch. 4:23), that we may presume the work done on both occasions was much the same. It was just a further preparation of the soil, and a fresh sowing of the precious seed. (See on ch. 4:23.) To these fruitful journeyings of the Redeemer, "with healing in His wings," Peter no doubt alludes, when, in his address to the household of Cornelius, he spoke of "How God anointed Jesus of Nazareth with the Holy Ghost and with power: who *went about* doing good, and healing all that were oppressed of the devil: for God was with Him" (Acts 10:38).

Jesus, Compassionating the Multitudes, Asks Prayer for Help (vss. 36-38). He had now returned from His preaching and healing circuit, and the result, as at the close of the first one, was the gathering of a vast and motley multitude around Him. After a whole night spent in prayer, He had called His more immediate disciples, and from them had solemnly chosen the twelve; then, coming down from the mountain, on which this was transacted, to the multitudes that waited for Him below, He had addressed to them—as we take it—that discourse which bears so strong a resemblance to the Sermon on the Mount that many critics take it to be the same. (See on Luke 6:12-49; and on ch. 5, Introductory Remarks.) Soon after this, it should seem, the multitudes still hanging on Him, Jesus is touched with their wretched and helpless condition, and acts as is now to be described. **36. But when he saw the multitudes, he was moved with compassion**

ADAM CLARKE

31. *But they . . . spread abroad his fame.* They should have held their peace, for "to *obey* is better than *sacrifice,*" 1 Sam. xv. 22; but man must always be wiser than God.

32. *A dumb man possessed with a devil.* Some demons rendered the persons they possessed paralytic, some blind, others dumb. It was the interest of Satan to hide his influences under the appearance of natural disorders.

33. *And when the devil was cast out, the dumb spake.* The very miracle which was now wrought was to be the demonstrative proof of the Messiah's being manifested in the flesh. See Isa. xxxv. 5-6. *It was never so seen in Israel.* The greatest of the prophets has never been able to do such miracles as these.

34. *He casteth out devils through the prince of the devils.* It is a consummate piece of malice to attribute the works of God to the devil. Envy cannot suffer the approbation which is given to the excellencies of others. Those whose hearts are possessed by this vice speak the very language of the devil.

35. *Jesus went about all the cities and villages.* Of Galilee. See on chap. iv. 23-24. A real minister of Jesus Christ, after His example, is neither detained in one place by a comfortable provision made by some nor discouraged from pursuing his work by the calumny and persecution of others.

36. *Moved with compassion.* From *splanchnon,* "a bowel." The Jews esteemed the bowels

MATTHEW HENRY

spiritual health, and life, and vigour can there be in those souls, that are fed with husks and ashes, instead of *the bread of life*? (2) *They were scattered abroad, as sheep having no shepherd.* No creature is more apt to go astray than a sheep, and when gone astray more helpless, shiftless, and exposed, or more unapt to find the way home again: sinful souls *are as lost sheep*; they need the care of shepherds to bring them back. The case of those people is very pitiable, who either have no ministers at all, or those that are as bad as none; that seek their own things, not *the things of Christ*.

2. He excited his disciples to pray for them. It appears (Luke vi. 12, 13) that upon this occasion, before he sent out his apostles, he did himself spend a great deal of time in prayer. Those we pity we should pray for.

(1) How the case stood; *The harvest truly is plenteous, but the labourers are few.* There was a great deal of work to be done, and a great deal of good likely to be done, but there wanted hands to do it. It was an encouragement, that *the harvest* was so *plenteous*. It was not strange, that there were multitudes that needed instruction, but it was what does not often happen, that they who needed it, desired it. It is a blessed thing, to see people in love with good preaching. The valleys are then covered over with corn, and there are hopes it may be well gathered in. A harvest-day should be a busy day. It was a pity when it was so that *the labourers* should be so *few*; that the corn should shed and spoil, and rot upon the ground for want of reapers; loiterers many, but *labourers* very *few*.

(2) What was their duty in this case (*v.* 38); *Pray ye therefore the Lord of the harvest.* When things look discouraging, we should pray more and then we should complain and fear less. [1] God is *the Lord of the harvest; my Father is the Husbandman*, John xv. 1. It is for him and to him, and to his service and honour that *the harvest* is gathered in. It is very comfortable to those who wish well to *the harvest-work*, that God himself presides in it, who will be sure to order all for the best. [2] Ministers are and should be *labourers* in God's *harvest*; the ministry is a *work* and must be attended to accordingly; it is *harvest-work*, which is needful work; work that requires everything to be done in its season, and diligence to do it thoroughly; but it is pleasant work; they *reap in joy*, and the joy of the preachers of the gospel is likened to the *joy of harvest* (Isa. ix. 2, 3); and *he that reapeth receiveth wages; the hire of the labourers* that reap down God's field, shall not be *kept back*, as theirs was, James v. 4. It is God's work to *send forth labourers*; Christ makes ministers (Eph. iv. 11); the office is of his appointing, the qualifications of his working, the call of his giving. All that love Christ and souls, should show it by their earnest prayers to God, especially when *the harvest is plenteous, that he would send forth* more skilful, faithful, wise, and industrious *labourers into his harvest*. Christ puts his friends upon praying this, just before he sends apostles forth to labour in *the harvest*. Further observe, that Christ said this to his disciples, who were to be employed as *labourers*. They must pray, First, That God *would send them forth. Here am I, send me*, Isa. vi. 8. Commissions, given in answer to prayer, are most likely to be successful; Paul is a chosen vessel, for *behold he prays*, Acts ix. 11, 15.

JAMIESON, FAUSSET, BROWN

on them, because they fainted—This reading, however, has hardly any authority at all. The true reading doubtless is, "were harassed." **and were scattered abroad**—rather, "lying about," "abandoned," or "neglected." **as sheep, having no shepherd**—their pitiable condition as wearied under bodily fatigue, a vast disorganized mass, being but a faint picture of their wretchedness as the victims of pharisaic guidance; their souls uncared for, yet drawn after and hanging upon Him. This moved the Redeemer's compassion.

37. Then saith he unto his disciples, The harvest truly is plenteous—His eye doubtless rested immediately on the Jewish field, but this he saw widening into the vast field of "the world" (ch. 13:38), teeming with souls having to be gathered to Him. **but the labourers**—men divinely qualified and called to gather them in.

38. Pray ye therefore the Lord of the harvest—the great Lord and Proprietor of all. Cf. John 15:1, "I am the true vine, and My Father is the husbandman."

that he will send forth labourers into his harvest—The word properly means "thrust forth"; but this emphatic sense disappears in some places, as in vs. 25, and John 10:4—"When He *putteth forth* His own sheep." (See on ch. 4:1.)

ADAM CLARKE

to be the seat of sympathy and the tender passions, and so applied the organ to the sense. *And were scattered abroad.* "Thrown down, or, all along." They were utterly neglected as to the interests of their souls, and rejected by the proud and disdainful Pharisees.

37. *The harvest.* The souls who are ready to receive the truth are very numerous, *but the labourers are few.* There are multitudes of scribes, Pharisees, and priests, of reverend and right reverend men; but there are few that work. Jesus wishes for laborers, not gentlemen who are either idle drones or slaves to pleasure and sin.

38. *That he will send forth labourers.* "That He would thrust forth laborers." It is God's province to thrust out such preachers as shall labor; and it is our duty to entreat Him to do so. A minister of Christ is represented as a day laborer. He comes into the harvest, not to become lord of it, not to live on the labor of others but to work, and to labor his day. Though the work may be very severe, yet, to use a familiar expression, there are good wages in the harvest home; and the day, though hot, is but a short one.

MATTHEW HENRY — CHAPTER 10

Verses 1–4

I. Who they were that Christ ordained to be his apostles or ambassadors; they were his disciples, *v.* 1. He had called them sometime before to be disciples, and he then told them that they should be made fishers of men, which promise he now performed. Christ commonly confers honours and graces by degrees. All this while Christ had kept these twelve,

1. In a state of probation. Though he knows what is in man, though he knew from the first what was in them (John vi. 70), yet he took this method to give an example to his church. The ministry being a great trust, it is fit that men should be tried for a time, before they are entrusted with it.

2. In a state of preparation. All this while he had been fitting them for this great work. He prepared them by *taking them to be with him.* The best preparative for the work of the ministry, is an acquaintance and communion with Jesus Christ. They that would *serve Christ*, must first be *with him* (John xii. 26). Paul had Christ revealed, not only *to him*, but *in him*, before he went to preach him among the Gentiles, Gal. i. 16. By *teaching them*; they were with him as scholars or pupils, he opened the scriptures

JAMIESON, FAUSSET, BROWN — CHAPTER 10

Vss. 1-5. Mission of the Twelve Apostles. (= Mark 6:7-13; Luke 9:1-6.) The last three verses of ch. 9 form the proper introduction to the Mission of the Twelve, as is evident from the remarkable fact that the Mission of the Seventy was prefaced by the very same words. (See on Luke 10:2.)

ADAM CLARKE — CHAPTER 10

1. *Twelve disciples.* Our Lord seems to have had the twelve patriarchs, heads of the congregation of Israel, in view in His choosing twelve disciples. That He had the plan of the ancient Jewish church in His eye is sufficiently evident from chap. xix. 28; and from Luke x. 1; xxii. 30; John xvii. 1, etc.; and Rev. xxi. 12-14.

MATTHEW HENRY

to them, and opened their understandings to understand the scriptures: to them it was given to *know the mysteries of the kingdom of heaven*, and to them they were *made plain*. They that design to be teachers must first be learners; they must receive, that they may give. Christ *taught his disciples* before he sent them forth (*ch.* v. 2), and afterwards, when he enlarged their commission, he gave them more ample instructions, Acts i. 3.

II. What the commission was that he gave them.

1. He *called them to him, v.* 1. He had called them to come *after* him before; now he calls them to come *to* him, admits them to a greater familiarity. The priests under the law were said to *draw near* and *approach* God, nearer than the people; the same may be said of gospel ministers; they are called to draw near to Christ. It is observable, that when the disciples were to be *instructed*, they *came unto* him of their own accord, *ch.* v. 1. But now they were to be *ordained*, he *called them*. It well becomes the disciples of Christ to be more forward to learn than to teach. We must *wait for a call*, a clear call, ere we take upon us to *teach others*.

2. He *gave them power*, *ἐξουσίαν*, *authority* in his name, to command men to obedience, and for the confirmation of that authority, to command devils too into a subjection. All rightful authority is derived from Jesus Christ. All power is given to him without limitation. Some of his honour he put on his ministers, as Moses put some of his on Joshua. He gave them *power over unclean spirits*, and over *all manner of sickness*. The design of the gospel was to *conquer the devil* and to *cure the world*.

(1) He gave them power *against unclean spirits, to cast them out*. The power that is committed to the ministers of Christ, is directly levelled against the devil and his kingdom. Christ gave them power to cast him out of the bodies of people; but that was to signify the destruction of his *spiritual kingdom*, and all the works of the devil; for which purpose the *Son of God* was *manifested*.

(2) He gave them power to *heal all manner of sickness*. He authorised them to work miracles for the confirmation of their doctrine, to prove that it was of God; to prove that it is not only faithful, but well *worthy of all acceptation*; that the design of the gospel is to heal and save; but the miracles Christ wrought, and appointed his apostles to work, evince him to be, not only the great Teacher and Ruler, but the Redeemer, of the world. *They were to heal all manner of sickness*, and *all manner of disease*, without exception even of those that are reckoned incurable, and the reproach of physicians. In the grace of the gospel there is a salve for every sore, a remedy for every malady. There is no spiritual disease so malignant, so inveterate, but there is a sufficiency of power in Christ for the cure of it. Let none therefore say there is no hope, or that the breach is wide as the sea, that cannot be healed.

III. The number and names of those that were commissioned; they are made apostles, that is, messengers. An angel, and an apostle, both signify the same thing—one *sent on an errand*, an ambassador. All faithful ministers are sent of Christ, but they that were first, and immediately, sent by him, are eminently called *apostles*, the prime ministers of state in his kingdom. Christ himself is called an apostle (Heb. iii. 1), for he was *sent by the Father*, and so sent them, John xx. 21. The prophets were called God's messengers.

1. Their number was twelve, referring to the number of the tribes of Israel. The gospel church must be the Israel of God; the Jews must be first invited into it; the apostles must be spiritual fathers, to beget a seed to Christ. Israel after the flesh is to be rejected for their infidelity; these twelve, therefore, are appointed to be the fathers of another Israel. These twelve, by their doctrine, were to judge the twelve tribes of Israel, Luke xxii. 30. This was that famous jury (and to make it a grand jury, Paul was added to it) that was impanelled to enquire between the King of kings, and the body of mankind.

2. Their names are here left upon record, and it is their honour; yet in this they had more reason to rejoice, that their names were *written in heaven* (Luke x. 20).

(1) There are some of these twelve apostles, of whom we know no more, from the scripture, than their names; as Bartholomew, and Simon the Canaanite. All the good ministers of Christ are not alike famous, nor their actions alike celebrated.

(2) They are named by couples; for at first they were sent forth *two and two*, because *two are better than one*; they would be serviceable to each other, and the more serviceable jointly to Christ and souls; what one forgot the other would remember. Three couples of them were brethren; Peter and Andrew,

W. E. VINE:

EXOUSIA denotes authority (from the impersonal verb *exesti*, "it is lawful"). From the meaning of leave or permission, or liberty of doing as one pleases, it passed to that of the ability or strength with which one is endued, then to that of the power of authority, the right to exercise power (Matt. 9:6; 21:23; 2 Cor. 10:8); or the power of rule or government, the power of one whose will and commands must be obeyed by others (Matt. 28:18; John 17:2; Jude 25; Rev. 12:10; 17:13); more specifically of apostolic authority (2 Cor. 10:8; 13:10); the power of judicial decision (John 19:10); of managing domestic affairs (Mark 13:34). By metonymy, or name-change (the substitution of a suggestive word for the name of the thing meant), it stands for that which is subject to authority or rule (Luke 4:6); or, as with the English "authority," one who possesses authority, a ruler, magistrate (Rom. 13:1-3; Luke 12:11; Titus 3:1); or a spiritual potentate (Eph. 3:10; 6:12; Col. 1:16; 2:10, 15; 1 Pet. 3:22). The R.V. usually translates it "authority."—*Vine's Expository Dictionary*

JAMIESON, FAUSSET, BROWN

And when he had called unto him his twelve disciples, he gave them power—The word signifies both "power," and "authority" or "right." Even if it were not evident that here both ideas are included, we find both words expressly used in the parallel passage of Luke (9:1)—"He gave them power and authority"—in other words, He both *qualified* and *authorized* them. **against**—or "over."

2. Now the names af the twelve apostles are these—The other Evangelists enumerate the twelve in immediate connection with their appointment (Mark 3:13-19; Luke 6:13-16). But our Evangelist, not intending to record the appointment, but only the Mission of the Twelve, gives their names here. And as in the Acts (1:13) we have a list of the Eleven who met daily in the upper room with the other disciples after their Master's ascension until the day of Pentecost, we have four catalogues in all for comparison. **The first, Simon, who is called Peter**—(See on John 1:42). **and Andrew his brother; James [the son] of Zebedee, and John his brother**—named after James, as the younger of the two. **3. Philip and Bartholomew**—That this person is the same with "Nathanael of Cana in Galilee" is justly concluded for the three following reasons: First, because Bartholomew is not so properly an individual's name as a family surname; next, because not only in this list, but in Mark's and Luke's, he follows the name of "Philip," who was the instrument of bringing Nathanael first to Jesus (John 1:45); and again, when our Lord, after His resurrection, appeared at the Sea of Tiberias, "Nathanael of Cana in Galilee" is mentioned along with six others, all of them apostles, as being present (John 21:2). **Matthew the publican**—In none of the four lists of the Twelve is this apostle so branded but in his own, as if he would have all to know how deep a debtor he had been to his Lord. (See on ch. 1:3, 5, 6; 9:9.) **James the son of Alphaeus**—the same person apparently who is called *Cleopas* or *Clopas* (Luke 24:18; John 19:25); and, as he was the husband of Mary, sister to the Virgin, James the Less must have been our Lord's cousin. **and Lebbaeus, whose surname was Thaddaeus**—the same, without doubt, as "Judas the brother of James," mentioned in both the lists of

ADAM CLARKE

He gave them power against unclean spirits. Here we find the first call to the Christian ministry, and the end proposed by the commission given. He whose ministry is not accompanied with healing to diseased souls was never called of God. But let it be observed that, though the spiritual gifts requisite for the ministry must be supplied by God himself, yet this does not preclude the importance of *human learning*. No man can have his mind too well cultivated, to whom a dispensation of the gospel is committed. The influence of the Spirit of God was no more designed to render human learning useless than that learning should be considered as superseding the necessity of divine inspiration.

2. *Apostles.* This is the first place where the word is used. *Apostolos*, an "apostle," comes from *apostello*, "I send a message." The word was anciently used to signify a person commissioned by a king to negotiate any affair between him and any other power or people. It is worthy of notice that those who were Christ's *apostles* were first His *disciples*; to intimate that men must be first *taught* of God before they be *sent* of God. These twelve apostles were chosen: (1) That they might be with our Lord, to see and witness His miracles, and hear His doctrine; (2) That they might bear testimony of the former, and preach His truth to mankind. *The first, Simon, who is called Peter, and Andrew his brother.* We are not to suppose that the word *first* refers to any kind of dignity, as some have imagined; it merely signifies the "first in order"—the person first mentioned.

3-4. *Bartholomew.* Many are of opinion that this was Nathanael, mentioned in John i. 46, whose name was probably *Nathanael bar Talmai*, Nathanael, the son of Talmai. Here his own name is repressed, and he is called *Bar Talmai*, or *Bartholomew*, from his father. *Matthew the publican.* The writer of this history. *James* the son *of Alphaeus.* This person was also called Cleopas, or Clopas, Luke xxiv. 18; John xix. 25. He had married Mary, sister to the blessed Virgin, John xix. 25.

MATTHEW HENRY

James and John, and the other James and Lebbeus. It is an excellent thing, when brethren by nature are brethren by grace, and those two bonds strengthen each other.

(3) Peter is named first, because he was first called; or because he was the most forward man among them, and upon all occasions made himself the mouth of the rest; but that gave him no power over the rest of the apostles, nor is there the least mark of any supremacy that was given to him, or ever claimed by him, in this sacred college.

(4) Matthew, the penman of this gospel, is here joined with Thomas (*v.* 3), but in two things there is a variation from the accounts of Mark and Luke, Mark iii. 18; Luke vi. 15. There, Matthew is put first, but here, in his own catalogue, Thomas is put first. It well becomes the disciples of Christ in honour to prefer one another. There he is only called Matthew, here Matthew the publican. It is good for those who are advanced to honour with Christ, to look *unto the rock whence they were hewn*; often to remember what they were before Christ called them, that thereby divine grace may be the more glorified. Matthew the apostle was Matthew the publican.

(5) Simon is called the Canaanite, or Simon the Zealot.

(6) Judas Iscariot is always named last, and with that black brand upon his name, *who also betrayed him*. Such spots there have been in our feasts of charity; tares among the wheat, wolves among the sheep; but there is a day of discovery and separation coming, when hypocrites shall be unmasked and discarded.

Verses 5-15

We have here the instructions that Christ gave to his disciples, when he gave them their commission. In this he *commanded them*. With these commands Christ commanded a blessing.

I. The people to whom he sent them.

1. Not to the Gentiles nor the Samaritans. They must not *go into the way of the Gentiles*. As to the Samaritans, their country lay between Judæa and Galilee, so that they could not avoid *going into the way* of the Samaritans, but they must *not enter into any of their cities*. This restraint was upon them only in their first mission, afterwards, they were appointed to go *into all the world*, and teach *all nations*.

2. But *to the lost sheep of the house of Israel*. The first offer of salvation must be made to the Jews, Acts iii. 26. Christ had a particular and very tender concern for the *house of Israel*. He looked with compassion upon them as *lost sheep*, whom he, as a shepherd, was to gather out of the by-paths of sin and error, into which they were gone astray, and in which, if not brought back, they would wander endlessly. Christ gives this description of those to whom they were sent, to quicken them to diligence in their work. They were sent to the house of Israel (of which number they themselves lately were), whom they could not but pity, and be desirous to help.

II. The preaching work which he appointed them. He did not send them forth without an errand; no, *As ye go, preach*, *v.* 7. They must proclaim the beginning of the gospel, saying, *The kingdom of heaven is at hand*. Not that they must say nothing else, but this must be their text; on this subject they must enlarge. It is said (Mark vi. 12), *they went out, and preached that men should repent*; which was the proper use and application of this doctrine concerning the approach of the *kingdom of heaven*. The preaching of this was like the morning light, to give notice of the approach of the rising sun. This proclaims salvation at hand, *nigh them that fear God; mercy and truth meet together* (Ps. lxxxv. 9, 10), that is, *the kingdom of heaven at hand*: not so much the personal presence of the king; that must not be doated upon; but a spiritual kingdom which is to be set up, when his bodily presence is removed, in the hearts of men.

Now this was the same that John the Baptist and Christ had preached before. People need to have good truths pressed again and again upon them, and if they be preached and heard with new affections, they are as if they were fresh to us. And there is a kingdom of glory yet to come, which we must speak of as at hand, and quicken people to diligence from the consideration of that.

III. The power he gave them to work miracles for the confirmation of their doctrine, *v.* 8. When he

JAMIESON, FAUSSET, BROWN

Luke (6:16; Acts 1:13), while no one of the name of Lebbaeus or Thaddaeus is so. It is he who in John (14:22) is sweetly called "Judas, not Iscariot." That he was the author of the Catholic Epistle of "Jude," and not "the Lord's brother" (ch. 13:55), unless these be the same, is most likely. **4. Simon the Canaanite;** rather "Kananite," but better still, "the Zealot," as he is called in Luke 6:15, where the original term should not have been retained as in our version ("Simon, called Zelotes"), but rendered "Simon, called the Zealot." The word "Kananite" is just the Aramaic, or Syro-Chaldaic, term for "Zealot." Probably before his acquaintance with Jesus, he belonged to the sect of the Zealots, who bound themselves, as a sort of voluntary ecclesiastical police, to see that the law was not broken with impunity. **and Judas Iscariot**—i.e., Judas of Kerioth, a town of Judah (Josh. 15:25); so called to distinguish him from "Judas the brother of James" (Luke 6:16). **who also betrayed him**—a note of infamy attached to his name in all the catalogues of the Twelve.

5-42. THE TWELVE RECEIVE THEIR INSTRUCTIONS. This directory divides itself into three distinct parts. The *first* part—extending from vs. 5 to vs. 15—contains directions for the brief and temporary mission on which they were now going forth, with respect to the places they were to go to, the works they were to do, the message they were to bear, and the manner in which they were to conduct themselves. The *second* part—extending from vs. 16 to vs. 23—contains directions of no such limited and temporary nature, but opens out into the permanent exercise of the Gospel ministry. The *third* part—extending from vs. 24 to vs. 42—is of wider application still, reaching not only to the ministry of the Gospel in every age, but to the service of Christ in the widest sense. *It is a strong confirmation of this threefold division, that each part closes with the words,* "VERILY I SAY UNTO YOU (vss. 15, 23, 42).

Directions for the Present Mission (vss. 5-15). **5. These twelve Jesus sent forth, and commanded them, saying, Go not into the way of the Gentiles, and into any city of the Samaritans enter ye not**—The Samaritans were Gentiles by blood; but being the descendants of those whom the king of Assyria had transported from the East to supply the place of the ten tribes carried captive, they had adopted the religion of the Jews, though with admixtures of their own: and, as the nearest neighbors of the Jews, they occupied a place intermediate between them and the Gentiles. Accordingly, when this prohibition was to be taken off, on the effusion of the Spirit at Pentecost, the apostles were told that they should be Christ's witnesses first "in Jerusalem, and in all Judea," then "in Samaria," and lastly, "unto the uttermost part of the earth" (Acts 1:8). **6. But go rather to the lost sheep of the house of Israel**—Until Christ's death, which broke down the middle wall of Partition (Eph. 2:14), the Gospel commission was to the Jews only, who, though the visible people of God, were "lost sheep," not merely in the sense which all sinners are (Isa. 53:6; I Pet. 2:25; cf. with Luke 19:10), but as abandoned and left to wander from the right way by faithless shepherds (Jer. 50:6, 17; Ezek. 34:2-6, etc.). **7. And as ye go, preach, saying, The kingdom of heaven is at hand**—(See on ch. 3:2).

ADAM CLARKE

Simon. He was third son of Alphaeus, and brother of James and Jude, or Judas, Matt. xiii. 55. *The Canaanite*. This word is not put here to signify a particular people, as it is elsewhere used in the Sacred Writings; but it is formed from the Hebrew *kana*, which signifies "zealous," literally translated by Luke, chap. vi. 15, *Zelotes*, or the "zealous," probably from his great fervency in preaching the gospel of his Master. But see Luke vi. 15. *Judas Iscariot*. Probably from the Hebrew *ish kerioth*, a "man of Kerioth," which was a city in the tribe of Judah, Josh. xv. 25, where it is likely this man was born. As *iscara* signifies "strangulation," and Judas hanged himself after he had betrayed our Lord, Dr. Lightfoot seems inclined to believe that he had his name from this circumstance, and that it was not given him till after his death. *Who also betrayed him*. Rather, "even he who betrayed Him, or delivered Him up."

5. *These twelve Jesus sent forth, and commanded*. To be properly qualified for a minister of Christ, a man must be, (1) filled with the Spirit of holiness; (2) called to this particular work; (3) instructed in its nature; and (4) commissioned to go forth and testify the gospel of the grace of God. These are four different gifts which a man must receive from God by Christ Jesus. To these let him add all the human qualifications he can possibly attain, as in his arduous work he will require every gift and every grace. *Go not into the way of the Gentiles*. Our Lord only intended that the *first* offers of salvation should be made to the Jewish people, and that the heathen should not be noticed in this first mission, that no stumbling block might be cast in the way of the Jews. *Into any city of the Samaritans enter ye not*. The Samaritans afterwards had the gospel preached to them by Christ himself, John iv. 4, etc., for the reason assigned above. Such as God seems at first to pass by are often those for whom He has designed His greatest benefits (witness the Samaritans, and the Gentiles in general), but He has His own proper time to discover and reveal them. The history of the *Samaritans* is sufficiently known from the Old Testament. Properly speaking, the inhabitants of the city of Samaria should be termed Samaritans; but this epithet belongs chiefly to the people sent into that part of the Promised Land by Shalmaneser, king of Assyria, when he carried the Israelites that dwelt there captives beyond the Euphrates, and sent a mixed people, principally Cuthites, to dwell in their place. These were altogether heathens at first, but they afterwards incorporated the worship of the true God with that of their idols. See the whole account, 2 Kings xvii. 5, etc. From this time they feared Jehovah, and served other gods till after the Babylonish captivity. From Alexander the Great, Sanballat, their governor, otained permission to build a temple upon Mount Gerizim. which the Jews conceiving to be in opposition to their temple at Jerusalem, hated them with a perfect hatred, and would have no fellowship with them. The Samaritans acknowledge the divine authority of the law of Moses, and carefully preserve it in their own characters, which are probably the genuine ancient Hebrew. The Samaritan Pentateuch is printed in the London Polyglott.

6. *But go rather to the lost sheep*. The Jewish church was the ancient fold of God; but the sheep had wandered from their Shepherd, and were lost. Our blessed Lord sends these under-shepherds to seek, find, and bring them back to the Shepherd and Overseer of their souls.

7. *And as ye go, preach*. "As you proceed, proclaim like heralds"—make this proclamation wherever you go, and while you are journeying. Preach and travel; and, as you travel, preach—proclaim salvation to all you meet. Wherever the ministers of Christ go, they find lost, ruined souls; and wherever they find them, they should proclaim Jesus, and His power to save. For an explanation of the word "proclaim" or *preach*, see on chap. iii. 1. From this commission we learn what the grand subject of apostolic preaching was—*The kingdom of heaven is at hand!*

MATTHEW HENRY

sent them to preach the same doctrine that he had preached, he empowered them to confirm it, by the same divine seals, which could never be set to a lie. This is not necessary now the kingdom of God is come; to call for miracles now is to lay again the foundation when the building is reared. They are directed here,

1. To use their power in doing good: *Heal the sick, cleanse the lepers.* They are sent abroad as public blessings, to intimate to the world, that love and goodness were the spirit and genius of that gospel which they came to preach, and of that kingdom which they were employed to set up. By this it would appear, that they were the servants of that God who is good and does good, and whose mercy is *over all his works.* We read not of their raising any to life before the *resurrection of Christ*, yet they were instrumental to raise many to *spiritual life.*

2. In *doing good freely*; *Freely ye have received, freely give.* They must cure *gratis*, further to exemplify the nature and complexion of the gospel kingdom, which is made up, not only of grace, but of free grace. And the reason is, because *freely you have received.* The consideration of Christ's freeness in doing good to us, should make us free in doing good to others.

IV. The provision that must be made for them in this expedition. As to that,

1. They must make no provision for it themselves, *v.* 9, 10. *Provide neither gold nor silver.* As, on the one hand, they shall not raise estates by their work, so, on the other hand, they shall not spend what little they have of their own upon it. Christ would teach them, (1) To act *under the conduct of human prudence.* They were now to make but a short excursion, therefore, why should they burthen themselves with that which they would have no occasion for? (2) To act in *dependence upon Divine Providence.* They must be taught to live, without *taking thought for life, ch.* vi. 25, &c. They who go upon Christ's errand, have, of all people, most reason to trust him for *food convenient.* Christ's hired servants shall have *bread enough and to spare*; while we abide faithful to God and our duty, and are in care to do our work well, we may cast all our other care upon God.

2. They might expect that those to whom they were sent would *provide for them* what was necessary, *v.* 10. They must not expect to be fed by miracles, as Elijah was: but they might depend upon God to incline the hearts of those they went among, to be kind to them, and provide for them. Ministers are, and must be, workmen, labourers, and they that are so are *worthy of their meat.* Christ would have his disciples, as not to distrust their God, so not to distrust their countrymen, so far as to doubt of a comfortable subsistence among them. If you preach to them, and endeavour to do good among them, surely they will give you meat and drink enough for your necessities; and if they do, never desire dainties; God will pay you your wages hereafter, and it will be running on in the mean time.

V. The proceedings they were to observe in dealing with any place, *v.* 11-15.

1. They are here directed how to conduct themselves toward those that were *strangers to them.*

(1) In *strange towns and cities*: when you come to a town, *enquire who* in it *is worthy.* It is supposed that there were some such in every place, as were better disposed than others to receive the gospel, and the preachers of it. In the worst of times and places, we may charitably hope that there are some who swim against the stream, and are as wheat among the chaff. There were saints in Nero's household. Enquire who is worthy, who there are that have some fear of God before their eyes. Previous dispositions to that which is good, are both directions and encouragements to ministers, in dealing with people. There is most hope of the word being profitable to those who are already so well inclined, as that it is acceptable to them; and there is here and there one such. They must enquire out such; not enquire for the best inns; public houses were no proper places for them that neither took money with them (*v.* 9), nor expected to receive any (*v.* 8); but they must look out for accommodations in private houses, with those that would entertain them well, and expect no other recompence for it but a prophet's reward, an apostle's reward, their praying and preaching. They that entertain the gospel, must neither grudge the expense of it, nor promise themselves to get by it in this world. Christ's disciples, wherever they come, should ask for the good people of the place, and be acquainted with them; when we took God for our God, we took his people for our people, and like will rejoice in its like. It is implied, that if they did enquire who was worthy, they might discover them. Anyone could tell them, there lives an honest,

JAMIESON, FAUSSET, BROWN

8. Heal the sick, cleanse the lepers, [raise the dead,] cast out devils—(The bracketed clause—"raise the dead"—is wanting in many MSS.). Here we have the first communication of supernatural power by Christ Himself to His followers—thus anticipating the gifts of Pentecost. And right royally does He dispense it.

freely ye have received, freely give—Divine saying, divinely said! (Cf. Deut. 15: 10, 11; Acts 3:6)—an apple of gold in a setting of silver (Prov. 25:11.) It reminds us of that other golden saying of our Lord, rescued from oblivion by Paul, "It is more blessed to give than to receive" (Acts 20:35). Who can estimate what the world owes to such sayings, and with what beautiful foliage and rich fruit such seeds have covered, and will yet cover, this earth! **9. Provide neither gold, nor silver, nor brass in**—for—**your purses**—lit., "your belts," in which they kept their money. **10. Nor scrip for your journey**—the bag used by travelers for holding provisions. **neither two coats**—or tunics, worn next the skin. The meaning is, Take no change of dress, no additional articles. **neither shoes**—i.e., change of them. **nor yet staves**—The received text here has "a staff," but our version follows another reading, "staves," which is found in the received text of Luke (9:3). The true reading, however, evidently is "a staff"—meaning, that they were not to procure even that much expressly for this missionary journey, but to go with what they had. No doubt it was the misunderstanding of this that gave rise to the reading "staves" in so many MSS. Even if this reading were genuine, it could not mean "more than one"; for who, as ALFORD well asks, would think of taking a spare staff? **for the workman is worthy of his meat**—his "food" or "maintenance"; a principle which, being universally recognized in secular affairs, is here authoritatively applied to the services of the Lord's workmen, and by Paul repeatedly and touchingly employed in his appeals to the churches (Rom. 15:27; I Cor. 9:11; Gal. 6:6), and once as "scripture" (I Tim. 5:18).

11. And into whatsoever city or town—town or village. **ye shall enter** [carefully] **inquire who in it is worthy**—or "meet" to entertain such messengers; not in point of rank, of course, but of congenial disposition. **and there abide till ye go thence**—not shifting about, as if discontented, but returning the welcome given with a courteous, contented, accommodating disposition.

ADAM CLARKE

8. *Raise the dead.* This is wanting in the MSS. marked EKLMS of *Griesbach,* and in those marked BHV of *Mathai,* and in upwards of *one hundred* others. It is also wanting in the *Syriac* (Vienna edition), latter *Persic, Sahidic, Armenian, Slavonic,* and in one copy of the *Itala;* also in *Athanasius, Basil,* and *Chrysostom.* There is no evidence that the disciples raised any dead person previously to the resurrection of Christ. The words should certainly be omitted, unless we could suppose that the authority now given respected not only their present mission, but comprehended also their future conduct. *Freely ye have received, freely give.* A rule very necessary, and of great extent. A minister or laborer in the gospel vineyard, though worthy of his comfortable support while in the work, should never preach for hire, or make a secular traffic of a spiritual work.

9. *Provide neither gold, nor silver, nor brass in your purses.* "In your girdles." It is supposed that the people of the East carry their money in a fold of their girdles. This is scarcely correct; they carry it in a purse in the bosom, under the girdles. This I have often observed. "Have no money in your purse" is a command, obedience to which was secured by the narrow circumstances of most of the primitive genuine preachers of the gospel.

10. *Nor scrip for your journey.* To carry provisions. It was a leathern pouch hung about their necks, in which they put their victuals. This was, properly, the shepherd's bag. *Neither two coats.* Nothing to encumber you. *The workman is worthy of his meat.* "Of his maintenance." It is a maintenance, and that only, which a minister of God is to expect, and that he has a divine right to; but not to make a fortune, or lay up wealth. Besides, it is the *workman,* he that labors in the Word and doctrine, that is to get even this.

11. *Into whatsoever city or town ye shall enter.* In the commencement of Christianity, Christ and His preachers were all itinerant. *Enquire who in it is worthy.* That is, of a good character; for a preacher of the gospel should be careful of his reputation, and lodge only with those who are of a regular life. *There abide till ye go thence.* "Go not from house to house," Luke x. 7. Acting contrary to this precept has often brought a great disgrace on the gospel of God. Stay in your own lodging as much as possible, that you may have time for prayer and study. Seldom frequent the tables of the rich and great; if you do, it will unavoidably prove a snare to you.

MATTHEW HENRY

sober, good man; for this is a character which, like the ointment of the right hand, betrays itself, and fills the house with its odours. In the house of those they found worthy, they must continue. They are justly suspected, as having no good design, that are often changing their quarters. It becomes the disciples of Christ to make the best of that which is, to abide by it, and not be for shifting upon every dislike or inconvenience.

(2) In strange houses. When they had found the house of one they thought worthy, they must at their entrance salute it. "In those common civilities, be beforehand with people. Salute the family, [1] To draw on further discourse, and so to introduce your message." (From matters of common conversation, we may insensibly pass into that communication which is good to the use of edifying.) [2] To try whether you are welcome or not. He that will not receive your salutation kindly, will not receive your message kindly. [3] To insinuate yourselves into their good opinion. *Salute the family*, that they may see that though you are serious, you are not morose. Religion teaches us to be courteous and civil, and obliging to all with whom we have to do. Their instructions were, when they came into a house, not to *command it*, but to *salute it*; for *love's sake rather to beseech*, is the evangelical way, Philemon 8, 9. Souls are first drawn to Christ with the *cords of a man*, and kept to him by the *bands of love*, Hos. xi. 4.

When they had saluted the family after a godly sort, they must, by the return, judge concerning the family; if *the house be worthy, let your peace come* and rest *upon it; if not, let it return to you, v.* 13. It seems then, that after they had enquired for the *most worthy* (*v.* 11), it was possible they might light upon those that were unworthy. Though it is wisdom to hearken to, yet it is folly to rely upon, common report and opinion; we ought to use a judgment of discretion, and to see with our own eyes. Now this rule is intended,

First, For satisfaction to the apostles. The common salutation was, *Peace be unto you*. Christ tells them that this gospel prayer (for so it was now become) should be put up for all, as the gospel proffer was made to all indefinitely, and that they should leave it to God to determine the issue of it. If the house be worthy, it will reap the benefit of your blessing; if not, there is no harm done, you will not lose the benefit of it; *it shall return to you*. It becomes us to judge charitably *of all*, to pray heartily *for all*, and to conduct ourselves courteously *to all*, for that is our part.

Secondly, For direction to them. "If, upon your salutation, it appear that they are indeed worthy, let them have more of your company, and so *let your peace come upon them*; preach the gospel to them, peace by Jesus Christ; but if otherwise, if they carry it rudely to you, and shut their doors against you, *let your peace*, as much as in you lies, *return to you.* Retract what you have said, and turn your backs upon them. Great blessings are often lost by a neglect seemingly small and inconsiderable.

2. They are here directed how to carry it towards those that were refusers of them. The case is put (*v.* 14) of those that *would not receive them, nor hear their words.* There would be those that would slight them, and put contempt on them and their message. The best and most powerful preachers of the gospel must expect to meet with some, that will not so much as give them the hearing, nor show them any token of respect. Many turn *a deaf ear*, even to the *joyful sound.* Contempt of the gospel, and contempt of gospel ministers, commonly go together, and they will either of them be construed into a contempt of Christ, and will be reckoned for accordingly. Note.

(1) The directions given to the apostles what to do. They must *depart out of that house or city*. The gospel will not tarry long with those that put it away from them. At their departure they must *shake off the dust of their feet* in detestation of their wickedness. The apostles must not so much as carry away the dust of their city with them, as a denunciation of wrath against them. It was to signify that God would *shake them off*. They who *despise* God and his gospel shall be *lightly esteemed.*

(2) The *doom passed* upon such *wilful recusants, v.* 15. It shall be *more tolerable, in the day of judgment, for the land of* Sodom, as wicked a place as it was. They that would not hear the doctrine that would save them, shall be made to hear the sentence that will ruin them. There are different degrees of punishment in that day. Sodom and Gomorrah were exceedingly wicked (Gen. xiii. 13), and that which filled up the measure of their iniquity, was that they *received not* the angels that were sent to them, but abused them (Gen. xix. 4, 5), and *hearkened not to their words, v.* 14. And yet it will be more tolerable for them than

JAMIESON, FAUSSET, BROWN

12. And when ye come into an house—or "the house," but it means not the worthy house, but the house ye first enter, to try if it be worthy.

salute it—show it the usual civilities.

13. And if the house be worthy—showing this by giving you a welcome—**let your peace come upon it**—This is best explained by the injunction to the Seventy, "And into whatsoever house ye enter, first say, Peace be to this house" (Luke 10:5). This was the ancient salutation of the East, and it prevails to this day. But from the lips of Christ and His messengers, it means something far higher, both in the gift and the giving of it, than in the current salutation. (See on John 14:27.)

but if it be not worthy, let your peace return to you—If your peace finds a shut, instead of an open, door in the heart of any household, take it back to yourselves, who know how to value it; and it will taste the sweeter to you for having been offered, even though rejected.

And whosoever shall not receive you, nor hear your words, when ye depart out of that house or city—for possibly a whole town might not furnish one "worthy." **shake off the dust of your feet**—"for a testimony against them," as Mark and Luke add. By this symbolical action they vividly shook themselves from all *connection* with such, and all *responsibility* for the guilt of rejecting them and their message. Such symbolical actions were common in ancient times, even among others than the Jews, as strikingly appears in Pilate (ch. 27:24). And even to this day it prevails in the East. **15. Verily I say unto you, It shall be more tolerable**—more bearable—**for Sodom and Gomorrah in the day of judgment, than for that city**—Those Cities of the Plain, which were given to the flames for their loathsome impurities, shall be treated as less criminal, we are here taught, than those places which, though morally respectable, reject the Gospel message and affront those that bear it.

ADAM CLARKE

12. *Salute it.* Saying, "Peace be to this house."

13. *If the house be worthy.* If that family be proper for a preacher to lodge in, and the master be ready to embrace the message of salvation. *Your peace.* The blessings you have prayed for shall come upon the family; God will prosper them in their bodies, souls, and substance. *Let your peace.* The blessings prayed for, return to you. "It shall turn back upon yourselves." They shall get nothing, and you shall have an increase.

14. *Shake off the dust of your feet.* The Jews considered themselves defiled by the dust of a heathen country, which was represented by the prophets as a polluted land, Amos vii. 17, when compared with the land of Israel, which was considered as a holy land, Ezek. xlv. 1. Therefore, to shake the dust of any city of Israel from off one's clothes or feet was an emblematical action, signifying a renunciation of all further connection with them, and placing them on a level with the cities of the heathen. See Amos ix. 7.

15. *In the day of judgment.* Or, "punishment." Perhaps not meaning the day of general judgment, nor the day of the destruction of the Jewish state by the Romans, but a day in which God should send punishment on that particular city, or on that person, for their crimes. So the day of judgment of Sodom and Gomorrah was the time in which the Lord destroyed them by fire and brimstone.

MATTHEW HENRY

for those who receive not Christ's ministers and hearken not to their words. *Son, remember!* will sound most dreadfully in the ears of such as had a fair offer made them of *eternal life*, and chose death rather.

Verses 16–42

All these verses relate to the sufferings of Christ's ministers in their work, which they are here taught to expect, and prepare for; they are directed also how to bear them, and how to go on with their work in the midst of them. This part of the sermon looks further than to their present mission. They are here forewarned of the troubles they should meet with, when, after Christ's resurrection, their commission should be *enlarged.* Christ tells them, they must expect greater sufferings than they were yet called to. It is good to be told what troubles we may hereafter meet with, that we may provide accordingly, and may not boast, as if we had put off the harness, when we are yet but girding it on.

We have here intermixed, I. Predictions of trouble: and, II. Prescriptions of counsel and comfort, with reference to it.

I. We have here predictions of trouble: which the disciples should meet with in their work: Christ foresaw *their* sufferings as well as his own, and yet will have them go on, as he went on himself; and he foretold them, not only that the troubles might not be a surprise to them, and so a shock to their faith, but that, being the accomplishment of a prediction, they might be a confirmation to their faith.

He tells them what they should suffer, and from whom.

1. *What they should suffer:* hard things to be sure; for, *Behold, I send you forth as sheep in the midst of wolves, v.* 16. And what may a flock of poor, helpless, unguarded sheep expect, in the midst of a herd of ravenous wolves, but to be worried and torn? They are as *sheep among wolves,* that is frightful; but Christ sends them forth, that is comfortable; for he that sends them forth will protect them, and bear them out.

(1) They must expect to be hated, *v.* 22. *Ye shall be hated for my name's sake:* that is the root of all the rest, and a bitter root it is. Those whom Christ loves, the world hates. *If the world hated Christ without a cause* (John xv. 25), no marvel if it hated those that bore his image and served his interests. It is grievous to be *hated,* and to be the object of so much ill-will, but it is *for thy name's sake;* which, as it speaks the true reason of the hatred, whatever is pretended, so it speaks comfort to them who are thus hated; it is for a good cause, and they have a good friend that shares with them in it, and takes it to himself.

(2) They must expect to be apprehended and arraigned as malefactors. Their restless malice is resistless malice, and they will not only attempt, but will prevail, to *deliver you up to the councils* (*v.* 17, 18). A deal of mischief is often done to good men, under colour of law and justice. They must look for trouble, not only from inferior magistrates in the councils, but from governors and kings, the supreme magistrates. We find this often fulfilled in the *acts of the apostles.*

(3) They must expect to be put to death (*v.* 21); *They shall deliver them to death.* The malice of the enemies rages so high as to inflict this; the faith and patience of the saints stand so firm as to expect this; the wisdom of Christ permits it, knowing how to make the blood of the martyrs *the seal of the truth,* and *the seed of the church.* By this noble army's not loving *their lives to the death,* Satan has been vanquished, and the kingdom of Christ and its interests greatly advanced.

(4) They must expect, in the midst of these sufferings, to be branded with the most odious and ignominious names and characters that could be. Persecutors would be ashamed in this world, if they did not first dress up those in bear-skins whom they thus bait, and represent them in such colours as may serve to justify such cruelties. The blackest of all the ill characters they give them is here stated; they call them Beelzebub, the name of the prince of the devils, *v.* 25. Since every one thinks he hates the devil, thus they endeavour to make them odious to all mankind. Satan's sworn enemies are represented as his friends; the apostles, who pulled down the devil's kingdom, were called devils. Satan's sworn servants would be thought to be his enemies, and they never more effectually do his work, than when they pretend to be fighting against him. Many times they who themselves are nearest akin to the devil, are most apt to father others upon him.

(5) These sufferings are here represented by a sword and division, *v.* 34, 35. *Think not that I am come to*

A. T. ROBERTSON:

16. "As sheep in the midst of wolves" (*hos probata en mesoi lukon*). The presence of wolves on every hand was a fact then and now. Some of these very sheep (10:6) at the end will turn out to be wolves and cry for Christ's crucifixion. The situation called for consummate wisdom and courage. The serpent was the emblem of wisdom or shrewdness, intellectual keenness (Gen. 3:1; Ps. 58:5), the dove of simplicity (Hos. 7:11). It was a proverb, this combination, but one difficult of realization.—*Word Pictures in the New Testament*

JAMIESON, FAUSSET, BROWN

Directions for the Future and Permanent Exercise of the Christian Ministry (vss. 16-23). **16. Behold, I send you forth**—The "I" here is emphatic, holding up Himself as the Fountain of the Gospel ministry, as He is also the Great Burden of it. **as sheep**—defenseless—**in the midst of wolves**—ready to make a prey of you (John 10:12). To be left exposed, as sheep to wolves, would have been startling enough; but that the sheep should be *sent* among the wolves would sound strange indeed. No wonder this announcement begins with the exclamation, "Behold."

18. And ye shall be brought before governors—provincial rulers—**and kings**—the highest tribunals—**for my sake, for a testimony against them**—rather, "to them," in order to bear testimony to the truth and its glorious effects. **and** [to] **the Gentiles**—a hint that their message would not long be confined to the lost sheep of the house of Israel. The Acts of the Apostles are the best commentary on these warnings.

ADAM CLARKE

16. *Behold, I send you forth as sheep in the midst of wolves.* He who is called to preach the gospel is called to embrace a state of constant labor and frequent suffering. He who gets ease and pleasure in consequence of embracing the ministerial office neither preaches the gospel nor is sent of God. If he did the work of an evangelist, wicked men and demons would both oppose him.

18. *Ye shall be brought before governors.* By governors and kings we may understand the Roman proconsuls, governors of provinces, and the kings who were tributary to the Roman government, and the emperors themselves, before whom many of the primitive Christians were brought. *For a testimony against them and*

CHARLES H. SPURGEON:

Some have refused to burn at the stake, and have been burned in their own beds; and many more have dreaded the pains of persecution, and so have plunged into the flames of hell by apostasy.

Should persecution rage and flame,
Still trust in thy Redeemer's name;
In fiery trials thou shalt see
That, "as thy days, thy strength shall be."

When call'd to bear the weighty cross,
Or sore affliction, pain, or loss,
Or deep distress, or poverty,
Still, "as thy days, thy strength shall be."

—*Spurgeon's Devotional Bible*

MATTHEW HENRY

send peace, temporal peace and outward prosperity. Christ came to give us *peace* with God, *peace* in our consciences, *peace* with our brethren, but *in the world ye shall have tribulation.* If all the world would receive Christ, there would then follow a universal *peace*, but while there are and will be so many that reject him, the children of God, that are called out of the world, must expect to feel the fruits of their enmity.

[1] Look not for *peace, but a sword.* Christ came to give *the sword of the word*, with which his disciples fight against the world, and *the sword of persecution*, with which the world fights against the disciples, being *cut to the heart* with *the sword of the word* (Acts vii. 54), and *cruel* work this sword made. Christ sent that gospel, which gives occasion for the drawing of this sword, and so may be said to send this sword.

[2] Look not for *peace*, but division (*v.* 35), *I am come to set men at variance.* This effect of the preaching of the gospel is not the fault of the gospel, but of those who do not receive it. The faith of those that believe condemns those that believe not, and, therefore, they have an enmity against them that believe. The most violent and implacable feuds have ever been those that have arisen from difference in religion; no enmity like that of the persecutors, no resolution like that of the persecuted. Christ has dealt fairly and faithfully with us, in telling us the worst we can meet with in his service; and he would have us deal so with ourselves, in sitting down and counting the cost.

2. We are here told from whom, and by whom, they should suffer these hard things. Surely hell itself must be let loose, and devils must become incarnate, ere such spiteful enemies could be found to a doctrine, the substance of which was *goodwill toward men.* No, would you think it? all this mischief arises to the preachers of the gospel from those to whom they came to preach salvation.

These hard things Christ's disciples must suffer,

(1) From men (*v.* 17). "*Beware of men;* you will have need to stand upon your guard." Persecuting rage and enmity turn men into brutes, into devils. It is a sad pass that the world is come to, when the best friends it has, have need to *beware of men.* It aggravates the troubles of Christ's suffering servants, that they arise from those who *are bone of their bone*, made of the same blood. The nature of man, if it be not sanctified, is the worst nature in the world next to that of devils.

(2) From professing men, men that *have a form of godliness*, and make a show of religion. *They will scourge you in their synagogues*, their places of meeting for the worship of God, and for the exercise of their church-discipline: so that they looked upon the scourging of Christ's ministers to be a branch of their religion. Paul was *five times scourged in the synagogues*, 2 Cor. xi. 24. Christ's disciples have suffered much from conscientious persecutors, that *scourge them in their synagogues*, cast them out and kill them, and *think they do God good service* (John xvi. 2).

(3) From great men, and men in authority. The Jews did not only scourge them, which was the utmost their remaining power extended to, but they delivered them up to the Roman powers, as they did Christ, John xviii. 30. *Ye shall be brought before governors and kings* (*v.* 18), who, having more power, are in a capacity of doing the more mischief.

(4) From all men (*v.* 22). *Ye shall be hated of all men*, of all wicked men, and these are the generality of men. So few are there that love, and own, and countenance Christ's righteous cause, that we may say, the friends of it are *hated of all men.* As far as the apostasy from God goes, so far the enmity against the saints goes; sometimes it appears more general than at other times, but there is something of this poison lurking in the hearts of all *the children of disobedience.*

(5) From those of their own kindred. *The brother shall deliver up the brother to death, v.* 21. *A man shall be*, upon this account, *at variance with his own father; the persecuting daughter will be against the believing mother*, where natural affection and filial duty, one would think, should prevent or soon extinguish the quarrel; and then, no marvel *if the daughter-in-law be against the mother-in-law.* In general, *a man's foes shall be they of his own household* (*v.* 36). They who should be his friends will be incensed against him for embracing Christianity, and especially for adhering to it when it comes to be persecuted, and will join with his persecutors against him. The strongest bonds of relative love and duty have often been broken through, by an enmity against Christ and his doctrine. Sufferings from such are more grievous; nothing cuts more than this, *It was thou, a man, mine equal* (Ps. lv. 12, 13); and the enmity of such is commonly most implacable; *a brother*

JAMIESON, FAUSSET, BROWN

34. Think not that I am come to send peace on earth: I came not to send peace, but a sword—strife, discord, conflict; deadly opposition between eternally hostile principles, penetrating into and rending asunder the dearest ties. **35. For I am come to set a man at variance against his father, and the daughter against her mother, and the daughter-in-law against her mother-in-law**—(See on Luke 12:51-53).

But beware of men; for they will deliver you up to the councils—the local courts, used here for civil magistrates in general.

and they will scourge you in their synagogues—By this is meant persecution at the hands of the ecclesiastics.

22. And ye shall be hated of all men for my name's sake—The universality of this hatred would make it evident to them, that since it would not be owing to any temporary excitement, local virulence, or personal prejudice, on the part of their enemies, so no amount of discretion on their part, consistent with entire fidelity to the truth, would avail to stifle that enmity—though it might soften its violence, and in some cases avert the outward manifestations of it. **21. And the brother shall deliver up the brother to death, and the father the child: and the children shall rise up against their parents, and cause them to be put to death**—for example, by lodging information against them with the authorities. The deep and virulent hostility of the old nature and life to the new—as of Belial to Christ—was to issue in awful wrenches of the dearest ties; and the disciples, in the prospect of their cause and themselves being launched upon society, are here prepared for the worst.

ADAM CLARKE

34. *Think not that I am come to send peace.* The meaning of this difficult passage will be plain when we consider the import of the word *peace*, and the expectation of the Jews. The word *shalom* was used among the Hebrews to express all possible blessings, temporal and spiritual, but especially the former. The import of our Lord's teaching here is this: Do not imagine, as the Jews in general vainly do, that I am come to *send forth*, by forcing out the Roman power, that temporal prosperity which they long for. I am not come for this purpose, but to send forth the Roman sword, to cut off a disobedient and rebellious nation, the cup of whose iniquity is already full, and whose crimes cry aloud for speedy vengeance.

35. *I am come to set a man at variance.* The spirit of Christ can have no union with the spirit of the world. Even a father, while unconverted, will oppose a godly child. Thus the spirit that is in those who sin against God is opposed to that spirit which is in the followers of the Most High.

17. *But beware of men.* Or, Be on your guard against men, these men; i.e. your countrymen; those from whom you might have reasonably expected comfort and support; and especially those in power, who will abuse that power to oppress you. *Councils* ("sanhedrins") and *synagogues.* See on chap. v. 22. "By *synagogues* we may understand here, not the places of public worship, but assemblies where *three* magistrates, chosen out of the principal members of the synagogue, presided to adjust differences among the people: these had power, in certain cases, to condemn to the *scourge*, but not to *death.* See Acts xxii. 19; 2 Cor. xi. 24, compared with Luke xii. 11." See Lightfoot.

22. *Ye shall be hated of all men for my name's sake.* Because ye are attached to Me, and saved from the corruption that is in the world, therefore the world will hate you. "The laws of Christ condemn a vicious world, and gall it to revenge."

21. *And the brother shall deliver up the brother.* What an astonishing enmity is there in the soul of man against God and goodness!

MATTHEW HENRY

offended is harder to be won than a strong city, Prov. xviii. 19.

II. With these predictions of trouble, we have here prescriptions of counsels and comforts for a time of trial. Let us gather up what he says,

1. By way of counsel and direction in several things.

(1) *Be ye wise as serpents, v.* 16. A precept, recommending to us that wisdom of the prudent, which is to understand his way, as useful at all times, but especially in suffering times. It is the will of Christ that his people and ministers, being so much exposed to troubles in this world, as they usually are, should not needlessly expose themselves, but use all fair and lawful means for their own preservation. In the cause of Christ we must sit loose to life and all its comforts, but must not be prodigal of them. We must *be wise*, not to pull trouble upon our own heads.

(2) *Be ye harmless as doves.* "Be mild, and meek, and dispassionate; not only do nobody any hurt, but bear nobody any ill will." We must *be wise*, not to wrong ourselves, but rather so than wrong anyone else; must use the harmlessness of the *dove* to bear twenty injuries, rather than the subtlety of the *serpent* to offer or to return one. *The Spirit descended on Christ as a dove*, and all believers partake of *the Spirit of Christ, a dove-like* spirit, made for love, not for war.

(3) *Beware of men, v.* 17. "Be always upon your guard, and avoid dangerous company; take heed what you say and do." It becomes those who are gracious to be cautious. We know not whom to trust. Ever since our Master was betrayed with a kiss, by one of his own disciples, we have need to *beware of men*.

(4) *Take no thought how or what ye shall speak, v.* 19. "When you are brought before magistrates, conduct yourselves decently, but afflict not yourselves with care how you shall come off. A prudent thought there must be, but not an anxious, perplexing, disquieting thought; let this *care be cast upon God*. Affect not quaint expressions, flourishes of wit, and laboured periods, which only serve to gild a bad cause; the gold of a good one needs it not." The disciples of Christ must be more thoughtful how to *do* well than how to *speak* well; how to *keep* their integrity than how to *vindicate* it. *Our lives, no boasting words*, form the best apology.

(5) *When they persecute you in this city, flee to another, v.* 23. "Thus reject them who reject you and your doctrine, and try whether others will not receive you and it. Thus shift for your own safety." In case of imminent peril, the disciples of Christ may and must secure themselves by flight, when God, in his providence, opens to *them a door of escape*. He that flies may fight again. It is no inglorious thing for Christ's soldiers to quit their ground, provided they do not quit their colours: they may go out of the way of *danger*, though they must not go out of the way of *duty*.

(6) *Fear them not* (*v.* 26), because *they can but kill the body* (*v.* 28). They who truly fear God, need not fear man; and they who are afraid of the least sin, need not be afraid of the greatest trouble. *Yet will we not fear, though the earth be removed*, while we have so good a God, so good a cause, and so *good a hope through grace*.

[1] A good reason against this fear, taken from the limited power of the enemies; they *kill the body*, that is the utmost their rage can extend to; *they are not able to kill the soul*, nor to do it any hurt, and the soul is the man. The soul is killed when it is separated from God and his love, which is its life; now this is out of the reach of their power. *Tribulation, distress, and persecution* may separate us from all the world, but cannot part between us and God, cannot make us either not to love him, or not to be loved by him, Rom. viii. 35, 37. If, therefore, we were more concerned about our souls, as our jewels, we should be less afraid of men. They can but crush the cabinet.

[2] A good remedy against it, and that is, to fear God. *Fear him who is able to destroy both soul and body in hell. Hell* is the destruction both of *soul and body*; not of the *being* of either, but the *well*-being of both. This destruction comes from the power of God: he is *able to destroy*. God *is therefore to be feared*, even by the best saints in this world. The fear of God, and of his power reigning in the soul, will be a sovereign antidote against the fear of man. It is better to fall under the frowns of all the world, than under God's frowns, and therefore, as it is most right in itself, so it is most safe for us, *to obey God rather than men*, Acts iv. 19.

(7) *What I tell you in darkness, that speak ye in light* (*v.* 27); "whatever hazards you run, go on with your work, publishing and proclaiming the everlasting gospel to all the world; that is your business, mind that. The design of the enemies is not merely to

JAMIESON, FAUSSET, BROWN

be ye therefore wise as serpents, and harmless as doves—Wonderful combination this! Alone, the wisdom of the serpent is mere cunning, and the harmlessness of the dove little better than weakness: but in combination, the wisdom of the serpent would save them from unnecessary exposure to danger; the harmlessness of the dove, from sinful expedients to escape it. In the apostolic age of Christianity, how harmoniously were these qualities displayed! Instead of the fanatical thirst for martyrdom, to which a later age gave birth, there was a manly combination of unflinching zeal and calm discretion, before which nothing was able to stand.

19. But when they deliver you up, take no thought—be not solicitous or anxious. (See on ch. 6:25.) **how or what ye shall speak**—i.e., either in what *manner* ye shall make your defense, or of what *matter* it shall consist—**for it shall be given you in that same hour what ye shall speak**—(See Exod. 4:12; Jer. 1:7).

23. But when they persecute you in this city, flee ye into another—"into the other." This, though applicable to all time, and exemplified by our Lord Himself once and again, had special reference to the brief opportunities which Israel was to have of "knowing the time of His visitations."

28. And fear not them which kill the body, but are not able to kill the soul—In Luke 12:4, "and after that have no more that they can do." **but rather fear him**—In Luke this is peculiarly solemn, "I will forewarn you whom ye shall fear," even Him—**which is able to destroy both soul and body in hell**—A decisive proof this that there is a hell for the body as well as the soul in the eternal world; in other words, that the torment that awaits the lost will have elements of suffering adapted to the *material* as well as the spiritual part of our nature, both of which, we are assured, will exist for ever. In the corresponding warning contained in Luke, Jesus calls His disciples "My friends," as if He had felt that such sufferings constituted a bond of peculiar tenderness between Him and them.

27. What I tell you in darkness—in the privacy of a teaching for which men are not yet ripe—**that speak ye in the light**—for when ye go forth all will be

ADAM CLARKE

Wise ("prudent") *as serpents, and harmless as doves.* This is a proverbial saying; so in *Shir hashirim Rabba*, fol. 16, "The holy blessed God said to the Israelites, Ye shall be towards me as upright as the doves; but, towards the Gentiles, as cunning as serpents."

19. *Take no thought how or what he shall speak.* Be not anxiously careful, because such anxiety argues distrust in God, and infallibly produces a confused mind. In such a state, no person is fit to proclaim or vindicate the truth. This promise, *It shall be given you,* banishes all distrust and inquietude on dangerous occasions; but without encouraging sloth and negligence, and without dispensing with the obligation we are under to prepare ourselves by the meditation of sacred truths, by the study of the Holy Scriptures, and by prayer.

23. *But when they persecute you.* It is prudence and humility (when charity or righteousness obliges us not to the contrary) to avoid persecution.

28. *Fear not them which kill the body.* Those who slay with acts of cruelty, alluding probably to the cruelties which persecutors should exercise on His followers in their martyrdom. *But are not able to kill the soul.* Hence we find that the body and the soul are distinct principles, for the body may be slain and the soul escape; and, secondly, that the soul is immaterial, for the murderers of the body are not able, have it not in their power, to injure it. *Fear him.* It is not hellfire we are to fear, but it is God, without the stroke of whose justice hell itself would be no punishment, and whose frown would render heaven itself insupportable.

27. *What I tell you in darkness.* A man ought to preach that only which he has learned from God's Spirit, and His testimonies; but let him not pretend to bring forth anything new or

MATTHEW HENRY

destroy *you*, but to suppress *that*, and, therefore, whatever be the consequence, publish *that*." *What I tell you, that speak ye. Many things Christ spake openly, and nothing in secret* varying from what he preached in public, John xviii. 20. But they must deliver their embassy publicly, *in the light*, and *upon the house-tops*; for the doctrine of the gospel is what all are concerned in. The first indication of the reception of the Gentiles into the church, was *upon a house-top*, Acts x. 9. There is no part of Christ's gospel that needs, upon any account, to be concealed; *the whole counsel of God must be revealed*. In never so mixed a multitude let it be plainly and fully delivered.

2. By way of comfort and encouragement. Here is very much said to that purpose, and all little enough, considering the many hardships they were to grapple with, throughout the course of their ministry, and their present weakness. Christ therefore shows them why they should be of good cheer.

(1) Here is one word peculiar to their present mission, *v.* 23. *Ye shall not have gone over the cities of Israel, till the Son of man be come.* It was a comfort, [1] That what they said should be made good: they said *the Son of man* is coming, and *behold, he comes. Christ will confirm the word of his messengers.* [2] That it should be made good quickly. It is matter of comfort to Christ's labourers, that their working time will be short, and soon over; the work and warfare will in a little time be accomplished. [3] That then they should be advanced to a higher station. *When the Son of man comes, they shall be endued with greater power from on high.*

(2) Here are many words that relate to their work in general, and the troubles they were to meet with in it; and *they are good words and comfortable words.*

[1] That their sufferings were *for a testimony against them and the Gentiles*, *v.* 18. When the Jewish consistories transfer you to the Roman governors, that they may have you put to death, your being hurried thus from one judgment-seat to another, will help to make your testimony the more public, and will give you an opportunity of bringing the gospel to the Gentiles, as well as to the Jews. God's people, and especially God's ministers, are his witnesses not only in their *doing* work, but in their *suffering* work. Hence they are called martyrs—*witnesses* for Christ. Now if their sufferings be a testimony, how cheerfully should they be borne!

[2] That upon all occasions they should have God's special presence with them, and the immediate assistance of his Holy Spirit, *it shall be given you* (said Christ) *in that same hour what ye shall speak.* Christ's disciples were chosen *from among the foolish of the world*, unlearned and ignorant men, and, therefore, might justly distrust their own abilities, especially when they were called before great men. First, they are here promised that *it should be given them*, not sometime before, but *in that same hour, what they should speak*. They shall speak *extempore*, and yet shall speak as much to the purpose, as if it had been never so well studied. When God calls us out to speak for him, we may depend upon him to teach us what to say. Secondly, They are here assured, that the blessed Spirit should draw up their plea for them. *It is not ye that speak, but the Spirit of your Father, which speaketh in you*, *v.* 20. They were not left to themselves upon such an occasion, but God undertook for them; his Spirit of wisdom spoke *in* them. God gave them an ability, not only to speak to the purpose, but what they did say, to say it with holy zeal. The same Spirit that assisted them in the pulpit, assisted them at the bar. They cannot but come off well, who have such an advocate.

[3] That *he that endures to the end shall be saved*, *v.* 22. Here it is very comfortable to consider, First, that there will be an *end* of these troubles; they may last long, but will not last always. Christ comforted himself with this, and so may his followers; *The things concerning me have an end*, Luke xxii. 37. The troubles may seem tedious, but, blessed be God, they are not everlasting. Secondly, That while they continue, they may be *endured*; they may be borne, and borne *to the end*, because the sufferers shall be borne up under them, in everlasting arms: *The strength shall be according to the day*, 1 Cor. x. 13. Thirdly, Salvation will be the eternal recompence of all those *that endure to the end*. The weather stormy, and the way foul, but the pleasure of home will make amends for all. They who *endure but awhile, and in time of temptation fall away*, have run in vain, and lose all that they have attained; but they who persevere, are sure of the prize, and they only. *Be faithful unto death*, and then thou shalt have *the crown of life*.

[4] That whatever hard usage the disciples of Christ meet with, it is no more than what their Master met with before (*v.* 24, 25). *The disciple is not above his*

JAMIESON, FAUSSET, BROWN

ready—**and what ye hear in the ear, that preach ye upon the housetops**—Give free and fearless utterance to all that I have taught you while yet with you. *Objection:* But this may cost us our life? *Answer:* It may, but there their power ends:

for verily I say unto you—what will startle you, but at the same time show you the solemnity of your mission, and the need of economizing the time for it. **Ye shall not have gone over**—Ye shall in nowise have completed—**the cities of Israel, till the Son of man be come**—To understand this—as LANGE and others do—in the first instance, of Christ's own peregrinations, as if He had said, "Waste not your time upon hostile places, for I Myself will be after you ere your work be over"—seems almost trifling. "The coming of the Son of man" has a fixed doctrinal sense, here referring immediately to the crisis of Israel's history as the visible kingdom of God, when Christ was to come and judge it; when "the wrath would come upon it to the uttermost"; and when, on the ruins of Jerusalem and the old economy, He would establish His own kingdom. This, in the uniform language of Scripture, is more immediately "the coming of the Son of man," "the day of vengeance of our God" (ch. 16:28; 24:27, 34; cf. with Heb. 10:25; Jas. 5:7-9)—but only as being such a lively anticipation of His second coming for vengeance and deliverance. So understood, it is parallel with ch. 24:14 (on which see).

For it is not ye that speak, but the Spirit of your Father which speaketh in you—How remarkably this has been verified, the whole history of persecution thrillingly proclaims—from the Acts of the Apostles to the latest martyrology.

but he that endureth to the end shall be saved—a great saying, repeated, in connection with similar warnings, in the prophecy of the destruction of Jerusalem (ch. 24:13); and often reiterated by the apostle as a warning against "drawing back unto perdition" (Heb. 3:6, 13; 6:4-6; 10:23, 26-29, 38, 39; etc.). As "drawing back unto perdition" is merely the palpable evidence of the want of "root" from the first in the Christian profession (Luke 8:13), so "enduring to the end" is just the proper evidence of its reality and solidity.

Directions for the Service of Christ in Its Widest Sense (vss. 24-42). **24. The disciple is not above his master**—teacher. **nor the servant above his lord**

ADAM CLARKE

mysterious. There is nothing that concerns our salvation that is newer than the new covenant; and in that there are, properly speaking, no mysteries. What was secret before is now made manifest in the gospel of the ever-blessed God. See Eph. iii. 1-12. *What ye hear in the ear.* The doctor who explained the law in Hebrew had an interpreter always by him, in whose ears he softly whispered what he said; this interpreter spoke aloud what had been thus whispered to him. The spirit of our Lord's direction appears to be this: Whatever I speak to you is for the benefit of mankind—keep nothing from them; declare explicitly the whole counsel of God; *preach ye* (proclaim) *upon the housetops.* The houses in Judea were flat-roofed, with ballustrades round about, which were used for the purpose of taking the air, prayer, meditation, and it seems, from this place, for announcing things in the most public manner.

Ye shall not have gone over ("ended" or finished," margin) *the cities.* The word here is generally understood as implying "to go over or through," intimating that there should not be time for the disciples to travel over the cities of Judea before the destruction predicted by Christ should take place. But this is very far from being the truth, as there were not less than forty years after this was spoken before Jerusalem was destroyed. Some contend that the passage should be translated, "Ye shall not have instructed, i.e., preached the gospel in the cities of Israel, till the Son of man be come." *Till the Son of man be come* may refer either to the outpouring of the Spirit on the Day of pentecost or to the subversion of the Jewish state.

20. *For it is . . . the Spirit of your Father.* This was an extraordinary promise, and was literally fulfilled to those first preachers of the gospel; and to them it was essentially necessary, because the New Testament dispensation was to be fully opened by their extraordinary inspiration. In a certain measure it may be truly said that the Holy Spirit animates the true disciples of Christ and enables them to *speak. Your Father.* This is added to excite and increase their confidence in God.

He that endureth to the end shall be saved. He who holds fast faith and a good conscience *to the end*, till the punishment threatened against this wicked people be poured out, he *shall be saved*, preserved from the destruction that shall fall upon the workers of iniquity.

24. *The disciple is not above his master* Or in plainer terms, "A scholar is not above his teacher." Jesus is the great Teacher; we pro-

MATTHEW HENRY

master. Here it is given as a reason, why they should not stumble at the hardest sufferings. They are reminded of this saying, John xv. 20. It is a proverbial expression, *The servant is not better than his master,* and, therefore, let him not expect to fare *better.* Jesus Christ our Lord and Master met with very hard usage from the world; they called him Beelzebub, the god of flies, the name of the chief of the devils, with whom they said he was in league. It is hard to say which is here more to be wondered at, the wickedness of men who thus abused Christ, or the patience of Christ, who suffered himself to be thus abused; that Satan's greatest Enemy and Destroyer should be run down as his confederate, and yet *endure such contradiction of sinners.* The consideration of the ill treatment which Christ met with in the world, should engage us to expect and prepare for the like, and to bear it patiently; nor think it hard if they who are shortly to be made *like him in glory,* be now made *like him in sufferings.* Christ began in the *bitter cup,* let us be willing to pledge him; his bearing the cross made it easy for us.

[5] That *there is nothing covered that shall not be revealed, v.* 26. We understand this, First, Of the revealing of the gospel to all the world. "Do you *publish it* (*v.* 27), for it shall be published. The truths which are now, as mysteries, hid from the children of men, shall all be made known, to all nations, in their own language," Acts ii. 11. The *ends of the earth must see this salvation.* It is a great encouragement to those who are doing Christ's work, that it is a work which shall certainly be done. It is a plough which God will speed. Or, Secondly, Of the clearing up of the innocency of Christ's suffering servants. However their innocency and excellency are now *covered,* they *shall be revealed.* All their reproach shall be rolled away, and their graces and services, that are now *covered, shall be revealed,* 1 Cor. iv. 5. Let Christ's ministers faithfully reveal his truths, and then leave it to him, in due time, to reveal their integrity.

[6] That the providence of God is in a special manner conversant about the saints, in their suffering, *v.* 29–31. It is good to have recourse to our first principles, and particularly to the doctrine of God's universal providence, extending itself to all the creatures, and all their actions, even the smallest and most minute.

First, The general extent of providence to all the creatures, even the least, and least considerable, to the *sparrows, v.* 29. These little animals are of so small account, that one of them is not valued; there must go two to be worth *a farthing* (nay, you shall have five for a halfpenny, Luke xii. 6), and yet they are not shut out of the divine care; *One of them shall not fall to the ground without your Father.* They do not light on *the ground* for food, to pick up a grain of corn, but *your* heavenly *Father,* by his providence, laid it ready for them. Now he that feeds the sparrows, will not starve the saints. They do *not fall to the ground* by death, either a natural or a violent death, without the notice of God. Even their death comes within the notice of the divine providence; much more does the death of his disciples. Now this God, who has such an eye to the sparrows, because they are his creatures, much more will have an eye to you, who are his children. If a sparrow die not *without your Father,* surely a man does not,—a Christian,—a minister,—my friend, my child. There is enough in the doctrine of God's providence to silence all the fears of God's people: *Ye are of more value than many sparrows.*

Secondly, The particular cognizance which providence takes of the disciples of Christ, especially in their sufferings (*v.* 30), *But the very hairs of your head are all numbered.* This is a proverbial expression, denoting the account which God takes and keeps of all the concernments of his people, even of those that are most minute, and least regarded. If God numbers their hairs, much more does he number their heads, and take care of their lives, their comforts, their souls. It intimates, that God takes more care of them, than they do of themselves. God *numbers the hairs of* his people, and *not a hair of their head shall perish* (Luke xxi. 18); not the least hurt shall be done them so precious to God are his saints, and their lives and deaths!

[7] That he will shortly, in the day of triumph, own those who now own him, in the day of trial, when those who deny him shall be for ever disowned and rejected by him, *v.* 32, 33. It is our duty, and if we do it, it will hereafter be our unspeakable honour and happiness, to *confess Christ before men.* It is our duty, not only to believe in Christ, but to profess that faith, in suffering for him, when we are called to it, as well as in serving him. However this may expose us to reproach and trouble now, we shall

JAMIESON, FAUSSET, BROWN

—another maxim which our Lord repeats in various connections (Luke 6:40; John 13:16; 15:20). **25. It is enough for the disciple that he be as his master, and the servant as his lord. If they have called the master of the house Beelzebub**—All the Greek MSS, write "Beelzebul," which undoubtedly is the right form of this word. The other reading came in no doubt from the Old Testament "Baalzebub," the god of Ekron (II Kings 1:2), which it was designed to express. As all idolatry was regarded as devil worship (Lev. 17:7; Deut. 32:17; Ps. 106:37; I Cor. 10:20), so there seems to have been something peculiarly satanic about the worship of this hateful god, which caused his name to be a synonym of Satan. Though we nowhere read that our Lord was actually called "Beelzebul," He was charged with being in league with Satan under that hateful name (ch. 12:24, 26), and more than once Himself was charged with "having a devil" or "demon" (Mark 3:30; John 7:20; 8:48). Here it is used to denote the most opprobrious language which could be applied by one to another. **how much more shall they call them of his household**—"the inmates." Three relations in which Christ stands to His people are here mentioned: He is their Teacher—they His disciples; He is their Lord—they His servants; He is the Master of the household—they its inmates. In all these relations, He says here, He and they are so bound up together that they cannot look to fare better than He, and should think it enough if they fare no worse. **26. Fear them not therefore: for there is nothing covered, that shall not be revealed; and hid, that shall not be known** i.e., There is no use, and no need, of concealing anything; right and wrong, truth and error, are about to come into open and deadly collision; and the day is coming when all hidden things shall be disclosed, everything seen as it is, and every one have his due (I Cor. 4:5).

29. Are not two sparrows sold for a farthing?—In Luke (12:6) it is "five sparrows for two farthings"; so that, if the purchaser took two farthings' worth, he got one in addition—of such small value were they. **and one of them shall not fall on the ground**—exhausted or killed—**without your Father**—"Not one of them is forgotten before God," as it is in Luke.

30. But the very hairs of your head are all numbered—See Luke 21:18 (and cf. for the language I Sam. 14:45; Acts 27:34). **31. Fear ye not therefore, ye are of more value than many sparrows**—Was ever language of such simplicity felt to carry such weight as this does? But here lies much of the charm and power of our Lord's teaching.

32. Whosoever therefore shall confess me before men—despising the shame—**him will I confess also before my Father which is in heaven**—I will not be ashamed of him, but will own him before the most august of all assemblies. **33. But**

ADAM CLARKE

fess to be His scholars. He who keeps the above saying in his heart will never complain of what he suffers.

25. *It is enough for the disciple that he be as his master.* Can any man who pretends to be a scholar or disciple of Jesus Christ expect to be treated well by the world? Will not the world love its own, and them only? Why, then, so much impatience under sufferings, such an excessive sense of injuries, such delicacy? Can you expect anything from the world better than you receive? *Beelzebub.* This name is variously written in the MSS. *Beelzeboul, Beelzeboun, Beelzebud,* but there is a vast majority in favor of the reading *Beelzebul,* which should, by all means, be inserted in the text instead of *Beelzebub.* It is supposed that this idol was the same with *Baalzebub* the *god fly,* worshipped at Ekron, 2 Kings i. 2, etc., who had his name changed afterwards by the Jews to *Baal zebul,* the *dung god,* a title expressive of the utmost contempt.

26. *Fear them not.* A general direction to all the persecuted followers of Christ. Fear them not, for they can make you suffer nothing worse than they have made Christ suffer; and under all trials He has promised the most ample support. *For there is nothing covered.* God sees everything; this is consolation to the upright, and dismay to the wicked. And He will bring into judgment every work, and every secret thing, whether good or bad, Eccles. xii. 14.

29. *Are not two sparrrows sold for a farthing?* The word *assarion,* which we translate *farthing,* is found among the rabbins in the word *aisar,* which is used among them to express a thing of the lowest or almost no value. The doctrine intended to be inculcated is this: The providence of God extends to the minutest things; everything is continually under the government and care of God, and nothing occurs without His will or permission. If then He regards *sparrows,* how much more man, and how much more still the soul that trusts in Him! *Without your Father.* Without the will of your Father. All things are ordered by the *counsel* of God. This is a great consolation to those who are tried and afflicted.

30. *But the very hairs of your head are all numbered.* Nothing is more astonishing than the care and concern of God for His followers. The least circumstances of their lives are regulated, not merely by that general providence which extends to all things, but by a particular providence which fits and directs all things to the design of their salvation, causing them all to cooperate for their present and eternal good.

31. *Fear ye not therefore, ye are of more value.* None can estimate the value of a soul, for which Christ has given His blood and life! Have confidence in His goodness, for He who so dearly purchased you will miraculously preserve and save you.

32. *Whosoever therefore shall confess me before men.* That is, whosoever shall acknowledge Me to be the Messiah, and have his heart and life regulated by My spirit and doctrine. It is not merely sufficient to have the heart right before

MATTHEW HENRY

be abundantly recompensed for that, *in the resurrection of the just*. "*I will confess him before my Father*, when it will do him the most service; I will present him, will represent him to *my Father*." Those who honour Christ he will thus honour. They honour him *before men*; that is a *poor* thing: he will honour them *before* his *Father*; that is a *great* thing. It is a dangerous thing for any to deny and disown *Christ before men*; for they who do so will be disowned by him *in the great day*, when they have most need of him: he will not own them for his servants who would not own him for their Master: *I tell you, I know you not*, *ch.* vii. 23.

[8] That the foundation of their discipleship was laid in such a temper and disposition, as would make sufferings very light and easy to them; and it was upon the condition of a preparedness for suffering, that Christ took them to be his followers, *v.* 37-39. He told them at first, that they were *not worthy of* him, if they were not willing to part with all for him. Now, in the Christian profession, they are reckoned unworthy the dignity and felicity of it, that put not such a value upon their interest in Christ, as to prefer that before any other interests. They cannot expect the gains of a bargain, who will not come up to the terms of it. If religion be worth *any*thing, it is worth *every*thing. They who like not Christ on these terms, may leave him at their peril. Whatever we part with for this pearl of price, we may comfort ourselves with this persuasion, that it is well worth what we give for it. The terms are, that we must prefer Christ.

(1) Before our nearest and dearest relations; *father or mother, son or daughter*. Children must love their parents, and parents must love their children; but if they love them better than Christ, they are unworthy of him. As we must not be *deterred* from Christ by the hatred of our relations which he spoke of (*v.* 21, 35, 36), so we must not be *drawn* from him, by their love.

(2) Before our ease and safety. We must *take up our cross* and *follow him*, else we are *not worthy* of him. Here observe, 1. They who would *follow Christ*, must expect *their cross* and *take it up*. 2. In taking *up the cross*, we must *follow Christ's* example, and bear it as he did. 3. It is a great encouragement to us, when we meet with crosses, that in bearing them we *follow Christ*, who has showed us the way, and that if we follow him faithfully, he will lead us through sufferings like him, to glory with him.

(3) Before life itself, *v.* 39. *He that findeth his life shall lose it;* he that thinks he has found it when he has saved it, and kept it, by denying Christ, *shall lose it* in an eternal death; but *he that loseth his life for Christ's sake*, that will part with it rather than deny Christ, *shall find it*, to his unspeakable advantage, an eternal life. They are best prepared for the life to come, that sit most loose to this present life.

[9] That Christ himself would so heartily espouse their cause, as to show himself a friend to all their friends, *v.* 40-42. *He that receiveth you, receiveth me.*

It is here implied, that though the generality would reject them, yet they should meet with some who would receive and entertain them, would bid the message welcome to their hearts, and the messengers to their houses, for the sake of it. Christ's ministers shall not *labour in vain*.

Jesus Christ takes what is done to his faithful ministers, whether in kindness or in unkindness, as done to himself, and reckons himself *treated* as they are *treated*. *He that receiveth you, receiveth me.* See how Christ may still be entertained by those who would testify their respects to him; his people and ministers we have always with us; and he is *with them always*, even to the end of the world. Nay, the honour rises higher, *He that receiveth me, receiveth him that sent me*. By entertaining Christ's ministers, they entertain not *angels unawares*, but Christ, nay, and God himself, and *unawares* too, as appears, *ch.* xxv. 37. *When saw we thee an hungered?*

Though the kindness done to Christ's disciples be never so small, yet if there be occasion for it, and ability to do no more, it shall be accepted, though it be *but a cup of cold water given to one of these little ones, v.* 42. Kindnesses shown to Christ's disciples are valued in Christs's books, not according to the cost of the gift, but according to the love and affection of the giver. On that score the widow's mite not only passed current, but was stamped high, Luke xxi. 3, 4. Thus they who are truly rich in graces may be rich in good works, though poor in the world.

Kindness to Christ's disciples which he will accept, must be done with an eye to Christ, and for his sake. A prophet must be received *in the name of a prophet*, and a *righteous man* in the name of a *righteous man*, and one of those *little ones* in *the name of a disciple*; because they are righteous, and so bear Christ's image. Christ does not interest himself in the matter,

JAMIESON, FAUSSET, BROWN

whosoever shall deny me before men, him will I also deny before my Father which is in heaven—before that same assembly: "He shall have from Me his own treatment of Me on the earth." (But see on ch. 16:27.)

36. And a man's foes shall be they of his own household—This saying, which is quoted, as is the whole verse, from Micah 7:6, is but an extension of the Psalmist's complaint (Ps. 41:9; 55: 12-14), which had its most affecting illustration in the treason of Judas against our Lord Himself (John 13:18; Matt. 26:48-50). Hence would arise the necessity of a choice between Christ and the nearest relations, which would put them to the severest test. **37. He that loveth father or mother more than me, is not worthy of me; and he that loveth son or daughter more than me, is not worthy of me**—(Cf. Deut. 33:9). As the preference of the one would, in the case supposed, necessitate the abandonment of the other, our Lord here, with a sublime, yet awful self-respect, asserts His own claims to supreme affection. **38. And he that taketh not his cross, and followeth after me, is not worthy of me**—a saying which our Lord once and again emphatically reiterates (ch. 16:24; Luke 9:23; 14:27). We have become so accustomed to this expression—"taking up one's cross"—in the sense of "being prepared for trials in general for Christ's sake," that we are apt to lose sight of its primary and proper sense here—"a preparedness to go forth even to crucifixion," as when our Lord had to bear His own cross on His way to Calvary—a saying the more remarkable as our Lord had not as yet given a hint that He would die this death, nor was crucifixion a Jewish mode of capital punishment. **39. He that findeth his life shall lose it: and he that loseth his life for my sake shall find it**—another of those pregnant sayings which our Lord so often reiterates (ch. 16:25; Luke 17:33; John 12:25). The pith of such paradoxical maxims depends on the double sense attached to the word "life"—a lower and a higher, the natural and the spiritual, the temporal and eternal. An entire sacrifice of the lower, with all its relationships and interests—or, a willingness to make it which is the same thing—is indispensable to the preservation of the higher life; and he who cannot bring himself to surrender the one for the sake of the other shall eventually lose both. **40. He that receiveth**—entertaineth—**you, receiveth me; and he that receiveth me, receiveth him that sent me**—As the treatment which an ambassador receives is understood and regarded as expressing the light in which he that sends him is viewed, so, says our Lord here, "Your authority is Mine, as Mine is My Father's."

41. He that receiveth a prophet—one divinely commissioned to deliver a message from heaven. Predicting future events was no necessary part of a prophet's office, especially as the word is used in the New Testament. **in the name of a prophet**—for his office' sake and love to his master. (See II Kings 4:9, 10.) **shall receive a prophet's reward**—What

ADAM CLARKE

God; there must be a firm, manly, and public profession of Christ before men.

33. *Whosoever shall deny me.* Whosoever prefers his worldly interest to his duty to God sets a greater value on earthly than on heavenly things, and prefers the friendship of men to the approbation of God. Let it be remembered that to be renounced by Christ is to have Him for neither Mediator nor Saviour. To appear before the tribunal of God without having Christ for our Advocate, and, on the contrary, to have Him there as our Judge, and a Witness against us—how can a man think of this and not die with horror!

36. *A man's foes shall be they of his own household.* Our Lord refers here to their own traditions. So *Sota*, fol. 49. "A little before the coming of the Messiah, the son shall insult the father, the daughter rebel against her mother, the daughter-in-law against her mother-in-law; and each man shall have his own household for his enemies."

37. *He that loveth father or mother more than me.* He whom we love the most is he whom we study most to please, and whose will and interests we prefer in all cases. If, in order to please a father or mother who is opposed to vital godliness, we abandon God's ordinances and followers, we are unworthy of anything but hell.

38. *He that taketh not his cross,* i.e., he who is not ready, after My example, to suffer death in the cause of My religion, *is not worthy of me*, does not deserve to be called My disciple.

39. *He that findeth his life,* i.e., he who, for the sake of his temporal interest, abandons his spiritual concerns, shall lose his soul; and he who, in order to avoid martyrdom, abjured the pure religion of Christ, shall lose his soul, and perhaps his life too.

40. *He that receiveth you,* treats you kindly, *receiveth me.* I will consider the kindness as shown to myself, for he who receiveth Me as the true Messiah receiveth that God by whose counsels and through whose love I am come.

41. *He that receiveth a prophet.* A "teacher," not a "foreteller of future events," for this is not always the meaning of the word, but one commissioned by God to teach the doctrines of eternal life. It is no small honor to receive into one's house a minister of Jesus Christ. Many sayings of this kind are found among the rab-

MATTHEW HENRY

unless we first interest him in it.

Kindnesses shown to Christ's people and ministers, shall not only be accepted, but richly and suitably rewarded. He does not say, that they *deserve* a reward; we cannot merit anything as wages, from the hand of God; but they shall *receive a reward* from the free gift of God; and they shall *in no wise lose it*. The reward may be deferred, but it shall in no wise be *lost*, nor shall they be any *losers* by the delay. 2. This is a *prophet's reward*, and a *righteous man's*. That is, either, (1) The reward that God gives to prophets and righteous men; the blessings conferred upon them shall distil upon their friends. Or, (2) The reward he gives by prophets and righteous men; in answer to their prayers (Gen. xx. 7), *He is a prophet, and he shall pray for thee*, that is a prophet's reward. Prophets' rewards are spiritual blessings in heavenly things, and if we know how to value them, we shall reckon them good payment.

JAMIESON, FAUSSET, BROWN

an encouragement to those who are not prophets! (See John 3:5-8.) **and he that receiveth a righteous man in the name of a righteous man**—from sympathy with his character and esteem for himself as such—**shall receive a righteous man's reward**—for he must himself have the seed of righteousness who has any real sympathy with it and complacency in him who possesses it. **42. And whosoever shall give to drink unto one of these little ones**—Beautiful epithet! Originally taken from Zechariah 13:7. The reference is to their lowliness in spirit, their littleness in the eyes of an undiscerning world, while high in Heaven's esteem. **a cup of cold water only**—meaning, the smallest service. **in the name of a disciple**—or, as it is in Mark (9:41), because ye are Christ's: from love to Me, and to him from his connection with Me. **verily I say unto you, he shall in no wise lose his reward**—There is here a descending climax—"a prophet," "a righteous man," "a little one"; signifying that however low we come down in our services to those that are Christ's, all that is done for His sake, and that bears the stamp of love to His blessed name, shall be divinely appreciated and owned and rewarded.

ADAM CLARKE

bins, and this one is common: "He who receives a learned man, or an elder, into his house, is the same as if he had received the *Shekinah*." And again: "He who speaks against a faithful pastor, it is the same as if he had spoken against God himself."

42. *Little ones.* My apparently mean and generally despised disciples. *Verily . . . he shall in no wise lose his reward.* The rabbins have a similar saying: "He that gives food to one that studies in the law, God will bless him in this world, and give him a lot in the world to come." Love heightens the smallest actions, and gives a worth to them which they cannot possess without it.

MATTHEW HENRY — CHAPTER 11

Verses 1–6

The first verse of this chapter some join to the foregoing chapter, and make it (not unfitly) the close of that.

1. The ordination sermon which Christ preached to his disciples in the foregoing chapter is here called his commanding them. Their preaching of the gospel was not only permitted them, but it was enjoined them. *Necessity was laid upon them*, 1 Cor. ix. 16.

2. When Christ had said what he had to say to his disciples, he *departed thence*. It should seem they were very loth to leave their Master, till *he departed* and separated himself from them; as the nurse withdraws the hand, that the child may learn to go by itself. Christ would now teach them how to live, and how to work, without his bodily presence. It was *expedient for them*, that Christ should thus go away for awhile.

3. Christ departed, *to teach and preach* in the cities whither he sent his disciples before him to *work miracles* (*ch.* x. 1–8), and so to raise people's expectations, and to make way for his entertainment. Thus was the *way of the Lord prepared*. When Christ empowered them to *work miracles*, he employed himself in *teaching* and *preaching*, as if that were the more honourable of the two. That was but in order to do this. Healing the sick was the *saving of bodies*, but preaching the gospel was to the *saving of souls*. Christ had directed his disciples to preach (*ch.* x. 7), yet he did not leave off preaching himself. How unlike are they to Christ, who yoke others only that they may themselves be idle! The increase and multitude of labourers in the Lord's work should be made not an excuse for our negligence, but an encouragement to our diligence. The more busy others are, the more busy we should be, and all little enough, so much work is there to be done. He went to preach *in their cities*, which were populous places; he cast the net of the gospel where there were most fish to be enclosed.

Here is next recorded a message which John Baptist sent to Christ, and his return to it, *v.* 2–6. We heard before that Jesus heard of John's sufferings, *ch.* iv. 12. Now we are told that John, in prison, hears of Christ's doings. He *heard in the prison the works of Christ*; and no doubt he was glad to hear of them. Nothing is more comfortable to God's people in distress, than to *hear of the works of Christ*; especially to experience them in their own souls. This turns a prison into a palace. Some way or other Christ will convey the notices of his love to those that are in trouble for conscience' sake.

Now John Baptist hearing of Christ's works, sent two of his disciples to him; and what passed between them and him we have here an account of.

I. The question they had to propose to him: *Art thou he that should come, or do we look for another?* This was a serious and important question. It is taken for granted that the Messiah should come. They intimate, that if this be not *he*, they would *look for another*. We must not be weary of looking for him that is to come. Though he tarry, wait for him, for he that shall come will come, though not in our time. They intimate likewise, that if they be convinced that this is he, they will not be sceptics, they will be satisfied, and will look *for no other*. They therefore ask, *Art thou he?* John had said for his part, *I am not the Christ*, John i. 20. Some think that John sent this question for his own satisfaction. It is true he had borne a noble testimony to Christ;

JAMIESON, FAUSSET, BROWN — CHAPTER 11

VSS. 1-19. THE IMPRISONED BAPTIST'S MESSAGE TO HIS MASTER—THE REPLY, AND DISCOURSE, ON THE DEPARTURE OF THE MESSENGERS, REGARDING JOHN AND HIS MISSION. (=Luke 7:18-35). **1. And it came to pass, when Jesus had made an end of commanding his**—rather, "the"—**twelve disciples, he departed thence to teach and to preach in their cities**—This was scarcely a fourth circuit—if we may judge from the less formal way in which it was expressed—but, perhaps, a set of visits paid to certain places, either not reached at all before, or too rapidly passed through, in order to fill up the time till the return of the Twelve. As to their labors, nothing is said of them by our Evangelist. But Luke (9:6) says, "They departed, and went through, the towns," or "villages," "preaching the Gospel, and healing everywhere." Mark (6:12, 13), as usual, is more explicit: "And they went out, and preached that men should repent. And they cast out many devils [demons], and anointed with oil many that were sick, and healed them." Though this "anointing with oil" was not mentioned in our Lord's instructions—at least in any of the records of them—we know it to have been practiced long after this in the apostolic Church (see Jas. 5:14, and cf. Mark 6:12, 13)—not *medicinally*, but as a sign of the healing virtue which was communicated by their hands, and a symbol of something still more precious. It was *unction*, indeed, but, as BENGEL remarks, it was something very different from what Romanists call *extreme* unction. He adds, what is very probable, that they do not appear to have carried the oil about with them, but, as the Jews used oil as a medicine, to have employed it just as they found it with the sick, in their own higher way. **2. Now when John had heard in the prison**—For the account of this imprisonment, see on Mark 6:17-20. **the works of Christ, he sent . . .**—On the whole passage, see on Luke 7:18-35.

He had now lain in prison probably a full year, far away from the scene of his Master's labors. But his faithful disciples appear from time to time to have kept him informed of them. At length the tidings they brought him, including no doubt those of the resurrection of the widow of Nain's son from the dead, appear to have determined the lonely prisoner to take a step which probably he had often thought of but till now shrunk from.

Art thou he that should come? or look we for another? Was this a question of doubt as to the messiahship of his Lord, as rationalists are fain to represent it? Impossible, from all we know of him. Was it then purely for the satisfaction of his disciples, as some expositors, more concerned for the Baptist's reputation than for simple and natural interpretation, take it? Obviously not. The whole strain of our Lord's reply shows that it was designed for John himself. Clearly it was a message of *impatience*, and almost of *desperation*. It seemed, no doubt, hard to him that his Master should let him lie so long in prison for his fidelity—useless to his Master's cause and a comparative stranger to His proceedings—after having been honored to announce and introduce Him to His work and

ADAM CLARKE — CHAPTER 11

1. This verse properly belongs to the preceding chapter, from which it should on no account be separated, as with that it has the strictest connection, but with this it has none. *Their cities.* The cities of the Jews.

2. *John had heard in the prison.* John was cast into prison by order of Herod Antipas, chap. xiv. 3, etc., a little after our Lord began His public ministry, chap. iv. 12; and after the first Passover, John iii. 24.

3. *Art thou he that should come?* "He that cometh" seems to have been a proper name of the Messiah; to save or deliver is necessarily implied. There is some difficulty in what is here spoken of John. Some have thought he was utterly ignorant of our Lord's divine mission, and that he sent merely for his own information; but this is certainly inconsistent with his own declaration, Luke iii. 15, etc.; John i. 15, 26, 33; iii. 28, etc. Others suppose he sent the message merely for the instruction of his disciples; that, as he saw his end approaching, he wished them to have the fullest conviction that Jesus was the Messiah, that they might attach themselves to Him. A third opinion takes

MATTHEW HENRY

he had declared him to be the *Son of God* (John i. 34), the Lamb of God (*v.* 29), and he that *should baptize with the Holy Ghost* (*v.* 33), and *sent of God* (John iii. 34), which were great things. But he desired to be further and more fully assured. In matters relating to Christ and our salvation by him, it is good to be sure. Christ appeared not in that external pomp and power in which it was expected he should appear; his own disciples stumbled at this, and perhaps John did so; Christ saw something of this at the bottom of this enquiry, when he said, *blessed is he who shall not be offended in me.* It is hard, even for good men, to bear up against vulgar errors. John's doubt might arise from his own present circumstances. He was a prisoner, and might be tempted to think, if Jesus be indeed the Messiah, whence is it that I, his friend and forerunner, am brought into this trouble, and am left to be so long in it. Doubtless there was a good reason why our Lord Jesus did not go to John in prison, but John construed it into a neglect, and it was perhaps a shock to his faith in Christ. [1] Where there is true faith, yet there may be a mixture of unbelief. The best are not always alike strong. [2] Troubles for Christ, especially when they continue long unrelieved, are such trials of faith as sometimes prove too hard to be borne up against. [3] The remaining unbelief of good men may sometimes, in an hour of temptation, strike at the root, and call in question the most fundamental truths which were thought to be well settled. The best saints have need of the best helps they can get for the strengthening of their faith, and the arming of themselves against temptations to infidelity. Others think that John sent his disciples to Christ with this question, not so much for his own satisfaction as for theirs. Though he was a prisoner they adhered to him, attended on him; they loved him, and would not leave him. They were weak in knowledge, and wavering in their faith, and needed instruction and confirmation; and in this matter they were somewhat prejudiced; being jealous *for their* master, they were jealous *of our* Master; they were loth to acknowledge Jesus to be the Messiah, because he eclipsed John. Good men are apt to have their judgments biassed by their interest. Now John would have their mistakes rectified, and wished them to be as well satisfied as he himself was. John was all along industrious to turn over his disciples to Christ, as from the grammar-school to the academy. Ministers' business is to direct everybody to Christ. And those who would know the certainty of the doctrine of Christ, must apply themselves to him, who is come to give an understanding. They who would grow in grace must be inquisitive.

II. Here is Christ's answer to this question, *v.* 4-6. It was a real answer, an answer in fact. Christ will have us to spell out the convincing evidences of gospel truths, and to take pains in digging for knowledge.

1. He points them to what they heard and saw, which they must tell John. Christ refers us to the things we *hear and see. Go and tell John.*

(1) *What you see* of the *power of Christ's miracles*; you see how, by the word of Jesus, *the blind receive their sight*, the *lame walk*, &c. Christ's miracles were done openly, and in the view of all. *Truth seeks not concealment.* They are to be considered, [1] As the *acts of a divine power.* None but the God of nature could thus overrule and outdo the power of nature. It is particularly spoken of as God's prerogative to *open the eyes of the blind*, Ps. cxlvi. 8. Miracles are therefore the broad seal of heaven, and the doctrine they are affixed to must be of God. However *lying wonders* may be vouched for in proof of *false doctrines*, *true miracles* evince a divine commission; such Christ's were, and they leave no room to doubt that he was sent of God. [2] As the *accomplishment of a divine prediction.* It was foretold (Isa. xxxv. 5, 6), that our God should come, and that then *the eyes of the blind should be opened.*

(2) Tell him *what you hear* of the *preaching of his gospel.* Faith, though confirmed by seeing, comes by hearing. That *the poor have the gospel preached to them.* The *Old Testament* prophets were sent mostly to kings and princes, but Christ preached to the *congregations of the poor.* Christ's gracious condescensions and compassions to *the poor*, are an evidence that it was he that should bring to the world the tender mercies of our God. Or we may understand it, not so much of the *poor of the world*, as the *poor in spirit*, and so that scripture is fulfilled, Isa. lxi. 1, *He hath anointed me to preach glad tidings to the meek.* It is a proof of Christ's divine mission that his doctrine is gospel indeed; good news to those who are truly humble in the denial of self; to them it is accommodated, for whom God always declared he had mercy in store. That the *poor receive the gospel*, and are wrought upon by it, they receive and entertain the

JAMIESON, FAUSSET, BROWN

to the people. And since the wonders of His hand seemed only to increase in glory as He advanced, and it could not but be easy for Him who preached deliverance to the captives, and the opening of the prison to them that were bound, to put it into the heart of Herod to set him at liberty, or to effect his liberation in spite of him, he at length determines to see if, through a message from the prison by his disciples, he cannot get Him to speak out His mind, and at least set his own at rest. This, we take it, was the real object of his message. The message itself, indeed, was far from a proper one. It was peevish; it was presumptuous; it was all but desperate. He had gone depressed; he was losing heart; his spirit was clouded; Heaven's sweet light had, to some extent, departed from him; and this message was the consequence. As it was announced that he should come in the spirit and power of Elijah, so we find him treading in that prophet's steps rather more than was desirable (1 Kings 19:1-4).

Then Jesus answering said unto them, Go your way, and tell John what things ye have seen and heard. No doubt along with the miracles which they "saw," they would "hear" those magic words with which He rolled away the maladies that came before Him. Nor would He fail to drop some other words of grace, fitted to impress the minds of the messengers, and, when reported, to cheer the spirit of their lonely master. **how that the blind see, the lame walk, the lepers are cleansed, the deaf hear, the dead are raised.** As the article is lacking in each of these clauses, the sense would be better perceived by the English reader thus, though scarcely tunable enough: "Blind persons are seeing, lame people are walking, leprous persons are getting cleansed, deaf people are hearing, dead persons are being raised."

To the poor the gospel is preached—or "is [in course of] being preached"; alluding to the great messianic prediction, as it was uttered and appropriated by himself at Nazareth, "The Spirit of the Lord is upon me, because he hath anointed me to preach the gospel to the poor."

ADAM CLARKE

a middle course between the two former, and states that, though John was at first perfectly convinced that Jesus was the Christ, yet, entertaining some hopes that He would erect a secular kingdom in Judea, wished to know whether this was likely to take place speedily. It is very probable that John now began, through the length of his confinement, to entertain doubts relative to His kingdom, which perplexed and harassed his mind; and he took the most reasonable way to get rid of them at once, viz., by applying to Christ himself.

4. *Go and shew John again those things which ye do hear and see.* Christ would have men to judge only of Him and of others by their works. This is the only safe way of judging. A man is not to be credited because he professes to know such and such things, but because he demonstrates by his conduct that his pretensions are not vain.

5. *The lame walk.* They "walk about," to give the fullest proof to the multitude that their cure was real. These miracles were not only the most convincing proofs of the supreme power of Christ, but were also emblematic of that work of salvation which He effects in the souls of men. (1) Sinners are *blind;* their understanding is so darkened by sin that they see not the way of truth and salvation. (2) They are *lame*—not able to walk in the path of righteousness. (3) They are *leprous*—their souls are defiled with sin, the most loathsome and inveterate disease. (4) They are *deaf* to the voice of God, His Word, and their own consciences. (5) They are *dead* in trespasses and sins, God, who is the Life of the soul, being separated from it by iniquity. Nothing less than the power of Christ can redeem from all this; and from all this, that power of Christ actually does redeem every penitent, believing soul. Giving sight to the blind and raising the dead are allowed by the ancient rabbins to be works which the Messiah should perform when He should manifest himself in Israel. *The poor have the gospel preached to them.* And what was this gospel? Why, the glad tidings that Jesus Christ came into the world to save sinners; that He opens the eyes of the blind; enables the lame to walk with an even, steady, and constant pace in the way of holiness; cleanses the lepers from all the de-

F. B. MEYER:

How doubts may be solved. The Baptist was languishing in a gloomy dungeon in the castle of Machaerus, on the farther shores of the Dead Sea—like a wild creature of the desert, suddenly entrapped. The darkness of his cell depressed his spirit; it seemed strange, too, if Jesus were the Messiah, that he did not overthrow the tyrant rule of Herod and release his captive friend.

When you are in doubt, go straight to Jesus and ask him to deal with it! Our Lord did not argue with the messengers sent by John, but pointed to the beneficent works that the Father had given him to do (cf. John 5:36; also Isa. 29:18; 35:5, 6). The influence of Christ on individuals and the world is the best testimony to the validity of his claims. The demonstration of Christianity is to be found in its acceptance and practice.

John's disciples had gone before our Lord uttered this great eulogy on his faithful friend, lest he should be exalted beyond measure and lest his faith should not have room to grow. Ah, downcast soul, who art writing hard things of thyself, it may be that thy merciful Lord is viewing thy life more accurately and estimating it more lovingly than thou knowest.—*Bible Commentary*

MATTHEW HENRY

gospel. The wonderful efficacy of the gospel is a proof of its divine original. The poor are *wrought upon* by it. The gospel of Christ made its way into their untutored minds.

2. He pronounces a *blessing* on those that *were not offended in him, v.* 6. They who are not wilfully prejudiced against him, and scandalized in him (so the word is), cannot but receive his doctrine, and so be *blessed in him.* There are many things in Christ which they who are ignorant and unthinking are apt to be offended at. The meanness of his appearance, his education at Nazareth, the poverty of his life, the despicableness of his followers, the slights which the great men put upon him, the strictness of his doctrine, the contradiction it gives to flesh and blood, and the sufferings that attend the profession of his name; these are things that keep many from him, who otherwise cannot but see much of God in him. Thus he is set *for the fall of many*, even in Israel. They are happy who get over these offences. *Blessed are they.* The expression intimates, that it is a difficult thing to conquer these prejudices, and a dangerous thing not to conquer them.

Verses 7–15

Some of Christ's disciples might perhaps take occasion from the question John sent, to reflect upon him, as weak and wavering, and inconsistent with himself, to prevent which Christ gives him this character. We must take all occasions, especially such as discover anything of infirmity, to speak well of those who are praiseworthy. John the Baptist, when he was upon the stage, and Christ in privacy and retirement, bore testimony to Christ; and now that Christ appeared publicly, and John was under a cloud, he bore testimony to John. John had abased himself to honour Christ (John iii. 29, 30, *ch.* iii. 11), had made himself nothing, that Christ might be All, and now Christ dignifies him with this character. They who humble themselves shall be exalted, and those that honour Christ he will honour. John had now *finished his testimony*, and now Christ commends him. Christ reserves honour for his servants when they *have done their work*, John xii. 26.

I. Christ spoke thus honourably of John, not in the hearing of John's disciples, but *as they departed*, just after they were gone, Luke vii. 24. He would not so much as seem to flatter John, nor have these praises of him reported to him. Though we must be forward to give to all their due praise for their encouragement, yet we must avoid everything that looks like flattery. Pride is a corrupt humour, which we must not feed either in others or in ourselves.

II. What Christ said concerning John, was intended not only for his praise, but for the people's profit, to revive the remembrance of John's ministry. "Now, consider, *what went ye out into the wilderness to see?* Put this question to yourselves." 1. John preached *in the wilderness.* If teachers be removed into corners, it is better to go on after them than to be without them. Now if his preaching was worth taking so much pains to hear it, surely it was worth taking some care to recollect it. The greater the difficulties we have broken through to hear the word, the more we are concerned to profit by it. 2. They went out to him to see him; rather for curiosity than for conscience. Many that attend on the word come rather to see and be seen, than to learn and be taught, to have something to talk of, than to be made wise to salvation. Christ puts it to them, *what went ye out to see?* We think when the sermon is done, the care is over; no, then the greatest of the care begins. *What brought you thither?* Was it custom or company, or was it a desire to honour God and get good? *What have you brought thence?* What knowledge, and grace, and comfort? *What went you to see?*

III. Let us see what the commendation of John was. Well, says Christ, "I will tell you what a man John the Baptist was."

1. "He was a firm, resolute man, and not *a reed shaken with the wind.* He was not wavering in his principles, nor uneven in his conversation." When the wind of popular applause on the one hand blew fresh and fair, when the storm of Herod's rage on the other hand grew fierce and blustering, John was still the same, the same in all weathers. The testimony he had borne to Christ was not the testimony of *a reed*; it was not a weather-cock testimony. The people flocked to him, because he was not as a reed. There is nothing lost in the long run by an unshaken resolution, to go on with our work, neither courting the smiles, nor fearing the frowns of men.

2. He was a *self-denying* man. "Was he a man *clothed in soft raiment*? If so, you would not have gone *into the wilderness* to see him, but to the *court.* You went to see one that had *his raiment of camel's*

JAMIESON, FAUSSET, BROWN

And blessed is he, whosoever shall not be offended in me. "Let these things convince him that My hand is not shortened that it cannot save; but blessed is he who can take Me with just as much light as to his future lot as is vouchsafed to him." This was all the reply that the messengers received. Not a ray of light is cast on his prospect, nor a word of commendation uttered while his disciples are present; he must die in simple faith, and as a martyr to his fidelity. But no sooner are they gone, than Jesus breaks forth into a glorious commendation of him.

When the three Hebrew youths were threatened with the burning fiery furnace if they would not worship Nebuchadnezzar's golden idol, they expressed their full conviction that the God they served both could and would deliver them; but even should they be mistaken in this expectation, they were still resolved rather to suffer than to sin. And they suffered not. But John did. He had indeed counted the cost, but he had it to pay. "Wilt thou be faithful even unto death?" was the question, and his spirit answered, "Yes." "Canst thou lie in prison unrescued, and even uncheered, save by the light thou already hast, and at length in a moment be despatched by those whom thy fidelity hath stung to the quick?" To this also his true heart doubtless bowed, though the trying question was never explicitly submitted to him. And such is what thousands of the martyrs of Jesus have undergone for His name. Nor can we doubt that this very record of the Lord's procedure toward the Baptist has soothed many a one when called to pass through a like dreary period of comfortless suffering, ending in death, for Jesus' sake.

And when the messengers of John were departed, he began to speak unto the people concerning John, What went ye out into the wilderness for to see? A reed shaken with the wind?—"a man driven about by every gust of popular opinion, and uttering an uncertain sound? Such is not John."

ADAM CLARKE

filement of their sins; opens the ears of the deaf to hear His pardoning words; and raises those who were dead in trespasses and sins to live in union with himself to all eternity.

6. *Blessed is he, whosoever shall not be offended in me.* Or, "Happy is he who will not be stumbled at Me."

TODAY'S DICTIONARY OF THE BIBLE:

John's special office ceased with the baptism of Jesus, who must now "increase" as the King came to his kingdom. He continued, however, for a while to bear testimony to the messiahship of Jesus. He pointed him out to his disciples, saying, "Behold the Lamb of God." His public ministry was suddenly (after about six months probably) brought to a close by his being cast into prison by Herod, whom he had reproved for the sin of having taken to himself the wife of his brother Philip (Luke 3:19). He was shut up in the castle of Machaerus, a fortress on the southern extremity of Peraea, 9 miles east of the Dead Sea, and here he was beheaded. His disciples, having consigned the headless body to the grave, went and told Jesus all that had occurred (Matt. 14:3-12). Our Lord himself testified regarding him that he was a "burning and a shining light" (John 5:35). John functions as the link between the Testaments, being both the last in the tradition of Old Testament prophecy and the herald of the New Covenant.

7. *What went ye out into the wilderness to see?* The purport of our Lord's design, in this and the following verses, is to convince the scribes and Pharisees of the inconsistency of their conduct in acknowledging John the Baptist for a divinely authorized teacher and not believing in the very Christ which he pointed out to them. He also shows, from the excellencies of John's character, that their confidence in him was not misplaced, and that this was a further argument why they should have believed in Him, whom the Baptist proclaimed as being far superior to himself.

A reed shaken with the wind? An emblem of an irresolute, unsteady mind, which believes and speaks one thing today and another tomorrow. Christ asks these Jews if they had ever found anything in John like this: Was he not ever steady and uniform in the testimony he bore to Me?

MATTHEW HENRY

hair, and a *leathern girdle about his loins*; his clothing agreed with the *wilderness* he lived in, and the doctrine he preached there, that of repentance. Now you cannot think that he who was such a stranger to the pleasures of a court, should be brought to change his mind by the terrors of a prison." They who have lived a life of mortification, are least likely to be driven off from their religion by persecution. He was not a man clothed in *soft raiment*; such *there are*, but they are *in kings' houses*. It becomes people in all their appearances to be consistent with their character and their situation. They who are preachers must not affect to look like courtiers. Prudence teaches us to be *of a piece*.

3. His greatest commendation of all was his office and ministry.

(1) He was *a prophet*, yea, and *more than a prophet* (*v.* 9). John said of himself, he was not *that prophet*, that great prophet, the Messiah himself; and now Christ (a very competent Judge) says of him, that he was *more than a prophet*. The forerunner of Christ was not a king, but a prophet, a *transcendent* prophet, more than an *Old Testament prophet*; they *saw Christ's day* at a distance; but John saw the day dawn, he saw the sun rise. They spake of Christ, but he pointed to him: he said, *Behold the Lamb of God!*

(2) He was the same that was predicted to be Christ's forerunner (*v.* 10); *This is he of whom it is written*. He was prophesied of by the other prophets, and therefore was greater than they. Malachi prophesied concerning John, *Behold, I send my messenger before thy face*. It was great preferment to John above all the prophets, that he was Christ's harbinger. He was a *messenger* sent on a great errand; he is *my messenger* sent *of God*, and sent before the *Son of God*. His business was to *prepare Christ's way*. This he had said of himself (John i. 23) and now Christ said it of him. Much of the beauty of God's dispensations lies in their mutual connection and coherence, and the reference they have one to another. That which advanced John above the *Old Testament* prophets was, that he went immediately before Christ. The nearer any are to Christ, the more truly honourable they are.

(3) There *was not a greater born of women* than John the Baptist, *v.* 11. Christ knew how to value persons according to the degrees of their worth, and he prefers John before all that went before him. Of all that God had raised up and called to any service in his church, John is the most eminent. Many had been born of women that made a great figure in the world, but Christ prefers John before them. Greatness is not to be measured by appearances and outward splendour, but they are the greatest men who are the greatest saints, and the greatest blessings, who are, as John was, *great in the sight of the Lord*, Luke i. 15.

Notwithstanding, he that is least in the kingdom of heaven is greater than he. There are degrees of glory in heaven, some that are less than others there; though every vessel is alike full, all are not alike large and capacious. The least saint in heaven is *greater*, and knows more, and loves more, and does more in praising God, and receives more from him, than the greatest in this world. By the *kingdom of heaven* here, is rather to be understood the *kingdom of grace*, the gospel dispensation in the perfection of its power and purity; and *ὁ μικρότερος—he that is less* in that is *greater than John*. So it agrees with what John the Baptist said (John i. 15), *He that cometh after me is preferred before me*. But it is rather to be understood of the apostles and ministers of the *New Testament*. John preached Christ coming, but they preached Christ not only come, but *crucified* and *glorified*. John came to the dawning of the gospel-day, but he was taken off before the noon of that day, before the rending of the veil, before Christ's death and resurrection, and the pouring out of the Spirit; so that the least of the apostles and evangelists, having greater discoveries made to them, and being employed in a greater embassy, is *greater than John*. All the true greatness of men is derived from, and denominated by, the gracious manifestation of Christ to them. What reason have we to be thankful that our lot is cast in the days of the *kingdom of heaven*, under such advantages of light and love! And the greater the advantages, the greater will the account be, if we *receive the grace of God in vain*.

(4) The great commendation of John the Baptist was, that God owned his ministry, and made it wonderfully successful for the breaking of the ice, and the preparing of people for the *kingdom of heaven*. *From the days of* the first appearing of *John the Baptist*, until now *the kingdom of heaven suffereth violence—Βιάζεται—vim patitur*, like the

JAMIESON, FAUSSET, BROWN

But what went ye out for to see? A man clothed in soft raiment?—"a self-indulgent, courtly preacher? Such was not John." **Behold, they which are gorgeously apparelled, and live delicately, are in king's courts.** "If that be the man ye wanted, ye must go in quest of him to royal palaces."

But what went ye out for to see? A prophet?—"a faithful straightforward utterer of the testimony given him to bear?" **Yea, I say unto you, and much more than a prophet.** "If that was what ye flocked to the wilderness to see in John, then ye have not been disappointed; for he is that, and much more than that."

This is he of whom it is written (Mal. 3:1), Behold, I send my messenger before thy face, which shall prepare thy way before thee. See Mark 1:3 and Luke 1:17. "There were many prophets, but only one Forerunner of the Lord's Christ; and this is he."

For I say unto you, Among those that are born of women there is not—"there hath not risen" (Matt. 11:11)—**a greater prophet than John the Baptist: but he that is least in the kingdom of God is greater than he.** The point of comparison is manifestly not personal character; for as it could hardly be said that in this respect he excelled every human being that preceded him, so it would be absurd to say that he was outstripped by the least advanced of the disciples of Christ. It is of his official *standing* or *position* in the economy of grace that our Lord is speaking. In that respect he was above all that ever went before him, inasmuch as he was the last and most honored of the Old Testament prophets, and stood on the very edge of the new economy, though belonging to the old: but for this very reason, the humblest member of the new economy was *in advance of him*.

ADAM CLARKE

8. *A man clothed in soft raiment?* A second excellency in John was his sober and mortified life. A preacher of the gospel should have nothing about him which savors of effeminacy and worldly pomp. *Are in kings' houses.* A third excellency in John was, he did not affect high things. He was contented to live in the desert, and to announce the solemn and severe truths of his doctrine to the simple inhabitants of the country.

9. *A prophet? yea . . . and more than a prophet.* That is, one more excellent than a prophet; one greatly beyond all who had come before him, being the immediate forerunner of Christ, and who was especially commissioned to prepare the way of the Lord. This was a fourth excellency.

10. *Behold, I send my messenger.* A fifth excellency of the Baptist was his preparing the way of the Lord, being the instrument, in God's hand, of preparing the people's hearts to receive the Lord Jesus; and it was probably through his preaching that so many thousands attached themselves to Christ immediately on His appearing as a public Teacher.

11. *A greater than John the Baptist.* A sixth excellency of the Baptist—he was greater than any prophet from the beginning of the world till that time: (1) Because he was prophesied of by them, Isa. xl. 3; Mal. iii. 1. (2) Because he had the privilege of showing the fulfilment of their predictions, by pointing out that Christ has now come, which they foretold should come. (3) Because he saw and enjoyed that salvation which they could only foretell. *Nothwithstanding he that is least in the kingdom of heaven.* By the kingdom of Heaven in this verse is meant the fullness of the blessings of the gospel of peace, which fullness was not known till after Christ had been crucified, and had risen from the dead. Now the least in this Kingdom, the meanest preacher of a crucified, risen, and glorified Saviour, was greater than John, who was not permitted to live to see the plenitude of gospel grace in the pouring out of the Holy Spirit.

JOHN WESLEY:

11. "But he that is least in the kingdom of heaven is greater than he." An ancient author says, "One perfect in the law, as John was, is inferior to one who is baptized unto the death of Christ. For this is the kingdom of heaven, even to be buried with Christ, and to be raised up together with him. John was greater than all who had been born of women; but he was cut off before the kingdom of heaven was given (he means that righteousness, peace, and joy, which constitute the present, inward kingdom of heaven). He was blameless, as to that righteousness which is by the law: but he fell short of those who are perfected by the spirit of life which is in Christ. Whoever therefore is least in the kingdom of heaven, by regeneration, is greater than any who has attained only the righteousness of the law, for the law maketh nothing perfect." It may also mean, the real believer has a more perfect knowledge of Jesus Christ, of his redemption and kingdom than John the Baptist had, who died before the full manifestation of the gospel.—*Wesley's Notes on the New Testament*

MATTHEW HENRY

violence of an army taking a city by storm, or of a crowd bursting into a house, so the *violent take it by force*. Multitudes are wrought upon by the ministry of John, and become his disciples. And it is,

[1] An *improbable* multitude. Those strove for a place in this kingdom, that one would think had no right nor title to it, and so seemed to be intruders. When the *children of the kingdom* are excluded out of it, and many come into it *from the east and the west*, then it *suffers violence*. The publicans and harlots believed John, whom the scribes and Pharisees rejected, and so went into the kingdom of God before them. It is no breach of good manners to go to heaven before our betters: and it is a great commendation of the gospel from the days of its infancy, that it has brought many to holiness that were very unlikely.

[2] An *importunate* multitude. This violence denotes a strength, and vigour, and earnestness of desire and endeavour, in those who followed John's ministry. It shows us also, what fervency and zeal are required of all those who design to make heaven of their religion. They who would *enter into the kingdom of heaven* must *strive to enter*; that kingdom suffers a holy violence; we must run, and wrestle, and fight, and be *in an agony*, and all little enough to win such a prize, and to get over such opposition from without and from within. *The violent take it by force*. They who will have an interest in the great salvation are carried out towards it with a strong desire, will have it *upon any terms*, and not think them hard, nor quit their hold without a blessing, Gen. xxxii. 26. The kingdom of heaven was never intended to indulge the ease of triflers, but to be the rest of them that labour. Oh that we could see a greater number with a *holy* contention thrusting themselves into it!

(5) The ministry of John was the *beginning of the gospel*.

[1] In John the Old Testament dispensation began to die, *v.* 13. The discoveries of the Old Testament began to be superseded by the more clear manifestation of the *kingdom of heaven* as *at hand*. When Christ says, *all the prophets and the law prophesied until John*, he shows us, First, How the light of the Old Testament was set up; it was set up in *the law and the prophets*, who spoke, though darkly, of Christ and his kingdom. Blessed be God that we have both the New Testament doctrine to explain the Old Testament prophecies, and the Old Testament prophecies to confirm and illustrate the New Testament doctrine (Heb. i. 1); like the two cherubim, they look at each other. The scripture is teaching to this day, though the penmen of it are gone. Moses and the prophets are dead; the apostles and evangelists are dead (Zech. i. 5), but the *word of the Lord endures for ever* (1 Pet. i. 25). Secondly, How this light was *laid aside*. Even before the sun rises, the morning light makes candles to shine dim. Their prophecies of a Christ to come became out of date, when John said, *He is come*.

[2] In him the New Testament day began to dawn; for (*v.* 14) *This is Elias, that was for to come*. John was as the loop that coupled the two Testaments. The concluding prophecy of the Old Testament was, *Behold, I will send you Elijah*, Mal. iv. 5, 6. Those words prophesied until John, and then, being turned into a history, they ceased to prophesy. Christ speaks of it as a great truth, that John the Baptist is the Elias of the New Testament; one that should come in the spirit and power of Elias (Luke i. 17), and especially as it is in the prophecy, that should *turn the hearts of the fathers to the children*. Christ suspects the welcome of it, *if ye will receive it*. Not but that it was true, whether they would receive it or not, but he upbraids them with their prejudices. Or, "If *you will receive him*, or if you will receive the ministry of John as that of the promised Elias, he will be an Elias to you, to turn you and prepare you for the Lord." Christ is a Saviour, and John an Elias, to those who will receive the truth concerning them.

Lastly, Our Lord Jesus closes this discourse with a solemn demand of attention (*v.* 15): *He that hath ears to hear, let him hear;* which intimates, that those things were dark and hard to be understood, and therefore needed attention, but of great concern and consequence, and therefore well deserved it. The things of God are of great and common concern: everyone that has *ears to hear* anything, is concerned to hear this. It intimates that God requires no more from us but the right use and improvement of the faculties he has already given us. He requires those to hear that have ears. They do not hear, because, like the deaf adder, they *stop their ears*.

Verses 16–24

Christ was going on in the praise of John the Baptist and his ministry, but here stops on a sudden,

JAMIESON, FAUSSET, BROWN

"And from the days of John the Baptist until now the kingdom of heaven suffereth violence, and the violent take it by force"; "is being forced, and violent persons are seizing it." The sense of these remarkable words is best seen in the form in which they were afterward repeated, as preserved by our Evangelist alone (Luke 16:16): "The law and the prophets were until John"—who stood midway between the old economy of the law and the prophets and the new; above the one, but below the other—"since that time the kingdom of God is preached, and every man presseth into it," or "is forcing his way into it." The idea is that of a *rush* for something unexpectedly and transportingly brought within their reach. In the one passage the *struggle* to obtain entrance is the prominent idea; in the other and later one it is the *multitude* that were thus pressing or forcing their way in.

What our Lord says of John in both places is that his ministry constituted the honorable point of transition from the one state of things to the other. "For," to continue Matthew's addition to this Discourse, "all the prophets and the law prophesied until John."

"And if ye will receive it, this is Elias, which was for to come. He that hath ears to hear, let him hear." They expected the literal Elijah the Tishbite to reappear before the coming of Messiah; misinterpreting the closing words of the prophet Malachi (4:5), and misled by the LXX which rendered it, "Behold, I send you Elijah *the Tishbite*." But our Lord here tells them plainly that this promised messenger was no other than John the Baptist of whom he had been speaking; although, knowing that this would be a startling and not very welcome announcement to those who confidently looked for the reappearance of the ancient prophet himself from heaven, He first says it was intended *for those who could take it in*, and then calls the attention of all who had ears to hear it to what he had said.

Is it not extraordinary that, after our Lord's most explicit declaration here, that John the Baptist was the Elias that prophecy taught the Church to look for before the coming of Messiah, there are Christian students of prophecy who affirm that the Jews were quite right in expecting the literal Elijah from heaven; and who, while admitting that John was an Elias, sent to announce the *first* coming of Christ, maintain that the prophecy will only be properly fulfilled in the coming of the Tishbite himself to prepare men for His *second* coming? The thing to be condemned here is not so much the extravagance of the expectation itself, which, the more one thinks of it, will appear the more extravagant, but the manifest distortion which it puts upon our Lord's words, and the violence which it does to the prophecy. But all this comes of an out-and-out literalism in the interpretation of prophecy, which in some cases brings out conclusions, not only very harsh, but scarcely consistent with the principle itself.

ADAM CLARKE

12. *The kingdom of heaven suffereth violence*. The taxgatherers and heathen, whom the scribes and Pharisees think have no right to the kingdom of the Messiah, filled with holy zeal and earnestness, seize at once on the proffered mercy of the gospel, and so take the Kingdom as by force from those learned doctors who claimed for themselves the chiefest places in that Kingdom. He that will take, get possession of, the Kingdom of righteousness, peace, and spiritual joy must be in earnest. All hell will oppose him in every step he takes; and if a man be not absolutely determined to give up his sins and evil companions, and have his soul saved at all hazards, and at every expense, he will surely perish everlastingly. This requires a violent earnestness.

14. *This is Elias, which was for to come*. This should always be written Elijah, that as strict a conformity as possible might be kept up between the names in the Old Testament and the New. The prophet Malachi, who predicted the coming of the Baptist in the spirit and power of Elijah, gave the *three* following distinct characteristics of him. First, That he should be the forerunner and messenger of the Messiah: "Behold, I will send my messenger . . . before me," Mal. iii. 1. Secondly, That he should appear before the destruction of the second Temple: "And the Lord, whom ye seek, shall suddenly come to his temple," *ibid*. Thirdly, That he should preach repentance to the Jews; and that, some time after, the great and terrible day of the Lord should come, and the Jewish land be smitten with a curse, chap. iv. 5-6. Now these three characters agree perfectly with the conduct of the Baptist and what shortly followed his preaching, and have not been found in anyone else, which is a convincing proof that Jesus was the promised Messiah.

15. *He that hath ears to hear, let him hear*. As if our Lord had said, These things are so clear and manifest that a man has only to hear them to be convinced and fully satisfied of their truth.

MATTHEW HENRY

and turns that to the reproach of those who enjoyed both that, and the ministry of Christ and his apostles, too, in vain. As to that generation, we may observe to whom he *compares them* (*v.* 16–19), and as to the particular places he instances, we may observe with whom he *compares them, v.* 20–24.

I. As to that *generation.* The generality continued in unbelief and obstinacy. John was a great and good man, but the generation in which his lot was cast was as barren and unprofitable as could be, and unworthy of him. The badness of the places where good ministers live serves for a foil to their beauty. Having commended John, he condemns those who had him among them, and did not profit by his ministry.

This our Lord Jesus here sets forth in a parable. *Whereunto shall I liken this generation?* The similitude is taken from some common custom among the Jewish children at their play, who, as is usual with children, imitated the fashions of grown people at their marriages and funerals, *rejoicing* and *lamenting;* but being all a jest, it made no impression; no more did the ministry either of John the Baptist or of Christ upon that generation.

The parable will be best explained by opening it and the illustration of it together in these five observations.

Note, 1. The God of heaven uses a variety of proper means and methods for the conversion and salvation of poor souls; he would *have all men to be saved,* and therefore leaves no stone unturned in order to it. In the parable, this is called his *piping* to us, and his *mourning* to us; he hath *piped to us* in the precious promises of the gospel, proper to work upon hope, and mourned to us in the dreadful threatenings of the law, proper to work upon fear. He has *piped to us* in gracious and merciful providences, *mourned to us* in calamitous, afflicting providences.

In the explanation of the parable is set forth the different temper of John's ministry and of Christ's. On the one hand, John came *mourning to them, neither eating nor drinking.* Now this, one would think, should work upon them; for such an austere, mortified life as this, was very agreeable to the doctrine he preached: and that minister is most likely to do good, whose conversation is according to his doctrine; and yet the preaching even of such a minister is not always effectual. On the other hand, *the Son of man came eating and drinking,* and so he *piped unto them.* Christ conversed familiarly with all sorts of people, not affecting any peculiar strictness or austerity. Those who were not awed by John's frowns, would be allured by Christ's smiles; from whom St. Paul learned to become *all things to all men,* 1 Cor. ix. 22. There may be a *great diversity of operations,* where *it is the same God that worketh all in all* (1 Cor. xii. 6), and this *various manifestation of the Spirit is given to every man to profit withal, v.* 7. Observe especially that God's ministers are variously gifted. Some are Boanerges—*sons of thunder;* others, Barnabases—*sons of consolation;* yet *all these worketh that one and the self-same Spirit* (1 Cor. xii. 11), and therefore we ought not to condemn either, but to praise both, and praise God for both.

Note, 2. The various methods which God takes for the conversion of sinners, are with many fruitless and ineffectual: *"Ye have not danced, ye have not lamented."* Now if people will neither be awakened by the *greatest* things, nor allured by the *sweetest* things, nor startled by the most *terrible* things, nor be made sensible by the *plainest* things; if they will hearken to the voice neither of scripture, nor reason, nor experience, nor providence, nor conscience, nor interest, what more can be done? It is some comfort to faithful ministers, when they see little success of their labours, that it is no new thing for the best preachers and the best preaching in the world to come short of the desired end. *Who has believed our report?*

Note, 3. That commonly those persons who do not profit by the means of grace, are perverse, they do all the hurt they can to others, by raising and propagating prejudices against the word, and the faithful preachers of it. So *this generation* did; because they were resolved not to believe Christ and John, they set themselves to abuse them, and to represent them as the worst. As for John the Baptist, they say, *He has a devil.* They imputed his strictness and reservedness to melancholy, and some kind or degree of a possession of Satan. As for Jesus Christ, they imputed his free and obliging conversation to the more vicious habit of luxury and flesh-pleasing: *Behold a gluttonous man and a wine-bibber.* No reflection could be more foul and invidious; yet none could be more false and unjust; for Christ *pleased not himself* (Rom. xv. 3), nor did ever any man live such a life of self-denial, mortification, and contempt of the world, as Christ lived. The most unspotted innocency,

JAMIESON, FAUSSET, BROWN

As when John the Baptist ushered in an era of new light and liberty in the kingdom of God, "every man pressed into it"; so there have been periods in the history of the Church ever since, in which a light and a freedom altogether unwonted have been infused into the Christian ministry, or men have been raised up outside the regular ministry, but gifted specially for special work, and particularly for rousing the impenitent to flee from the coming wrath and lay hold on eternal life, whose labors God designs to bless to the shaking of the dry bones and the turning of many to righteousness. Publicans and sinners—the most unlikely classes—are then to be seen flocking to Christ; while scribes and Pharisees—the respectably religious and the formal among the ministers of the Gospel—stand aloof, and cannot easily conceal their dislike at what they deem irregularities, and fanaticism, and dangers. At such a time it will be the part of the simplehearted and the wise to hail, on the one hand, the ingathering of souls to Christ, however it be effected, and, on the other hand, by prudent and kindly guidance of it, to keep so glorious a work from being marred by human folly.

When men want an excuse for rejecting or disregarding the grace of the Gospel, they easily find it. And there are none more ready and common than those arising out of something objectionable in the mode of presenting the truth. One preacher is too austere, another too free; one is too long, another too short; one is too sentimental, another too hard. Nothing pleases; nobody quite suits them. But oh, when the soul is hungry, how welcome is God's solid truth, Christ's precious Gospel, however it comes! And so, "Wisdom is justified of her children," who know her, hail her, clasp her to their bosom, however humbly clad; while those who do otherwise only show themselves to be "full souls," to whom even a honeycomb is distasteful—"the whole, who need not the Physician," and prize Him not.

ADAM CLARKE

16. *But whereunto shall I liken this generation?* That is, the Jewish people—"this race." *In the markets.* Or "places of concourse." *Calling unto their fellows.* Or "companions."

17. *We have piped unto you, and ye have not danced.* We have begun the music, which should have been followed by the dance, but you have not attended to it. *We have mourned . . . and ye have not lamented.* "You have not smote the breast."

18. *For John came neither eating nor drinking.* Leading a very austere and mortified life, and yet you did not receive him.

He hath a devil. He is a vile hypocrite, influenced by a demon to deceive and destroy the simple.

19. *The Son of man came eating and drinking.* That is, went wheresoever He was invited to eat a morsel of bread, and observed no rigid fasts. *They say, Behold a man gluttonous.* Whatever measures the followers of God may take, they will not escape the censure of the world; the best way is not to be concerned at them.

MATTHEW HENRY

and the most unparalleled excellency, will not always be a fence *against the reproach of tongues*; nay, a man's best gifts and best actions may be made the matter of his reproach. The best of our actions may become the worst of our accusations. It was true in some sense, that Christ was *a Friend to publicans and sinners*, the best Friend they ever had, for he *came into the world to save sinners*; but this is, and will be to eternity, Christ's praise, and they forfeited the benefit of it who thus turned it to his reproach.

Note, 4. They are *like children sitting in the markets*; they are foolish as children, froward as children, mindless and playful as children; would they but *show themselves men* in understanding, there would be some hopes of them. *The market-place they sit in* is to some a place of idleness (*ch.* xx. 3); to others a place of worldly business (James iv. 13); to all a place of noise or diversion. Their heads, and hands, and hearts are full of the world, the cares of which *choke the word*, and choke their souls at last. Thus *in the markets* they are, and there they *sit*; in these things their hearts rest, and by them they resolve to abide.

Note, 5. Though the means of grace be thus slighted and abused by many, by the most, yet there is a remnant that through grace do improve them. *But wisdom is justified of her children.* Christ is *Wisdom*; in him *are hid treasures of wisdom.* The gospel is *wisdom*, it is *the wisdom from above*: true believers are begotten again by it, and born from above too: they are wise *children.* These *children of wisdom justify wisdom*; they comply with the designs of Christ's grace. *The publicans justified God, being baptized with the baptism of John*, and afterwards embracing the gospel of Christ. Paul is *not ashamed of the gospel of Christ*, because, whatever it is to others, *to them that believe it is the power of God unto salvation*, Rom. i. 16. When *the cross of Christ*, which to others is *foolishness* and *a stumbling-block*, is *to them that are called the wisdom of God and the power of God* (1 Cor. i. 23, 24), here is *wisdom justified of her children.* If the unbelief of some reproach Christ by giving him the lie, the faith of others shall honour him by setting to its seal that he is true, and that *he also is wise*, 1 Cor. i. 25. Whether we do it or not, it will be done. That *generation is not passed away*, but remains in a succession of the like; for as it was then, it has been since and is still; *some believe the things which are spoken, and some believe not.*

II. As to the particular *places* in which Christ was most conversant. *Then began he to upbraid them*, *v.* 20. He began to preach to them long before (*ch.* iv. 17), but he did not *begin to upbraid* till now. Rough and unpleasing methods must not be taken, till gentler means have first been used. Christ is not apt *to upbraid. Wisdom* first invites, but when her invitations are slighted, then she *upbraids.* Those do not go in Christ's method, who begin with upbraidings.

1. The sin charged upon them; the most shameful, ungrateful thing that could be, that *they repented not.* Wilful impenitency is the great damning sin of multitudes that enjoy the gospel. The great doctrine that both John the Baptist and Christ, and the apostles preached, was repentance; the great thing designed, both in the *piping* and in the *mourning*, was to prevail with people to change their minds and ways, to leave their sins and turn to God; and this they would not be brought to. Christ reproved them for their other sins, that he might *lead them to repentance*; but when *they repented not, He upbraided them* with it, that they might upbraid themselves, and might at length see the folly of it, as that which alone makes the sad case a desperate one, and the wound incurable.

2. The aggravation of the sin; they were *the cities in which most of his mighty works were done.* By Christ's *mighty works* they should have been prevailed with, not only to receive his doctrine, but to obey his law; the curing of bodily diseases should have been the healing of their souls, but it had not that effect. The stronger inducements we have to repent, the more heinous is the impenitency and the severer will the reckoning be.

(1) Chorazin and Bethsaida are here instanced (*v.* 21, 22), they have each of them their woe: *Woe unto thee, Chorazin, woe unto thee, Bethsaida.* Christ came *into the world to bless us*; but if that blessing be slighted, he has woes in reserve, and his woes are of all others the most terrible. These two cities were rich and populous places; Bethsaida was lately advanced to a city by Philip the tetrarch; out of it Christ took at least three of his apostles: thus highly were these places favoured! Soon after this they decayed, and dwindled into mean, obscure villages. So fatally does sin ruin cities, and so certainly does the word of Christ take place!

Now Chorazin and Bethsaida are here compared with Tyre and Sidon. Christ, to convince and humble them, here shows,

JAMIESON, FAUSSET, BROWN

But Wisdom is justified of all her children. As cross, capricious children, invited by their playmates to join them in their amusements, will play with them neither at weddings nor at funerals (juvenile imitations of the joyous and mournful scenes of life), so that generation rejected both John and his Master: the one because he was too unsocial—as if under some dark demoniacal influence; the other, because he was too much the reverse, lax in his habits, and consorting with the lowest classes of society. But the children of Wisdom recognize and honor her whether in the austere garb of the Baptist or in the more attractive style of his Master, whether in the Law or in the Gospel, whether in rags or in royalty; as it is written, "The full soul loatheth an honeycomb: but to the hungry soul every bitter thing is sweet" (Prov. 27:7).

20-30. OUTBURST OF FEELING, SUGGESTED TO THE MIND OF JESUS BY THE RESULT OF HIS LABORS IN GALILEE. The connection of this with what goes before it and the similarity of its tone make it evident, we think, that it was delivered on the same occasion, and that it is but a new and more comprehensive series of reflections in the same strain. **20. Then began he to upbraid the cities wherein most of his mighty works were done, because they repented not.**

21. Woe unto thee, Chorazin!—not elsewhere mentioned, but it must have lain near Capernaum. **woe unto thee, Bethsaida**—"fishing-house," a fishing station—on the western side of the Sea of Galilee, and to the north of Capernaum; the birthplace of three of the apostles—the brothers Andrew and Peter, and Philip. These two cities appear to be singled out to denote the whole region in which they lay—a region favored with the Redeemer's presence, teaching, and works above every other. **for if the mighty works**—the miracles—**which were done in you had been done in Tyre and Sidon**—ancient and celebrated commercial cities, on the northeastern shores of the Mediterranean Sea, lying north of Palestine, and the

ADAM CLARKE

But wisdom is justified of her children. Of, here and in many places of our translation, ought to be written "by" in modern English. It is likely that by *children* our Lord simply means the fruits or effects of wisdom, according to the Hebrew idiom, which denominates the fruits or effects of a thing as its children.

20. *Then began he to upbraid the cities.* The more God has done to draw men unto himself, the less excusable are they if they continue in iniquity.

21. *Woe unto thee, Chorazin . . . Bethsaida!* It would be better to translate "alas for thee" than *woe unto thee.* The former is an exclamation of pity; the latter, a denunciation of wrath. *Tyre and Sidon* were two heathen cities situated on the shore of the Mediterranean Sea, into which it does not appear that Christ ever went, though He was often very nigh to them.

CHARLES H. SPURGEON:

They could not agree as to what they should play. Some of them proposed to imitate a wedding, and began to pipe, but the others would not dance. "Well, then," said they, "let us perform a funeral," and they commenced to mourn, but their wayward companions would not respond with lamentations. Even so, it is hard to find ministers to please men: one is too rambling, and another too logical; and if one preacher be condemned for being vulgar, another is censured for his flowery style. There is no satisfying fastidious tastes. If we are in a right state of heart, we shall remember George Herbert's words: "Judge not the preacher; he is thy judge." —*Spurgeon's Devotional Bible*

ALEXANDER MACLAREN:

Our Lord takes these two little fishing villages, and He parallels and contrasts them with the two great maritime cities of Tyre and Sidon, and says that these insignificant places have far more light than those had. Then He isolates Capernaum, a place of more importance, and His own usual settled residence; and, in like manner, He contrasts it with the long-buried Sodom, and proclaims the superiority of the illumination which fell on the more modern three. Why were they so superior? Because they had Moses? because they had the prophets, the law, the temple, the priesthood? By no means. Because they had *Him*. So He sets himself forth as being the highest and clearest of all the revelations that God has made to the world, and asserts that in Him, in His character, in His deeds, men ought to find motives that should bow them in penitence before God—motives sweeter, tenderer, stronger than any that the world knows besides. There is no such light of the knowledge of the glory of God anywhere else as there is in the face of Jesus Christ.
—*Expositions of Holy Scripture*

MATTHEW HENRY

[1] That Tyre and Sidon would not have been so bad as Chorazin and Bethsaida. If they had had the same word preached, and the same miracles wrought among them, *they would have repented,* and that *long ago,* as Nineveh did, in *sackcloth and ashes.* Christ, who knows the hearts of all, knew that if he had gone and lived among them, and preached among them, he should have done more good there than where he was; yet he continued where he was for some time, to encourage his ministers to do so, though they see not the success they desire. Our repentance is slow and delayed, but theirs would have been speedy; they would have repented long ago. Ours has been slight and superficial; theirs would have been deep and serious, in *sackcloth and ashes.*

[2] That therefore Tyre and Sidon shall not be so miserable as Chorazin and Bethsaida, but it shall be *more tolerable* for them in the *day of judgment, v.* 22. In that judgment, all the means of grace that were enjoyed in the state of probation will certainly come into the account, and it will be enquired, not only how bad we were, but how much better we might have been. If self-reproach be the torture of hell, it must needs be hell indeed to those who had such a fair opportunity of getting to heaven.

(2) Capernaum is here condemned with an emphasis (*v.* 23), *"And thou, Capernaum."* Christ's miracles here were *daily bread,* and therefore, as the manna of old, were despised and called light bread. Many a sweet and comfortable lecture of grace Christ had read them to little purpose, and therefore here he reads them a dreadful lecture of wrath.

We have here Capernaum's doom, Thou *which are exalted to heaven shalt be brought down to hell.* Those who enjoy the gospel in power and purity, are thereby *exalted to heaven*; they are lifted up *toward heaven*; but if, notwithstanding, they still *cleave to the earth,* they may thank themselves that they are not lifted up *into heaven.* Our external privileges will be so far from saving us, that if our hearts and lives be not agreeable to them, they will but inflame the reckoning: the higher the precipice is, the more fatal is the fall from it. We have it here put in comparison with the doom of Sodom. Christ here tells us, That Capernaum's means would have saved Sodom. If these miracles had been done among the Sodomites, as bad as they were, they would have repented, and *their city would have remained unto this day* a monument of sparing mercy. Upon true repentance through Christ, even the greatest sin shall be pardoned and the greatest ruin prevented. *It shall be more tolerable for the land of Sodom than for that city.*

Verses 25–30

I. Christ here returns thanks to God for his favour to those *babes* who had the mysteries of the gospel *revealed to them* (*v.* 25, 26). *Jesus answered and said.* It is called an answer because it is so comfortable a reply to the melancholy considerations preceding. With this thought therefore he refreshes himself; and to make it the more refreshing, he puts it into a thanksgiving. We may take great encouragement in looking upward to God, when round about us we see nothing but what is discouraging. *Jesus answered and said, I thank thee.* Thanksgiving is a proper answer to dark and disquieting thoughts, and may be an effectual means to silence them. Songs of praise are sovereign cordials to drooping souls. When we have no other answer ready to the suggestions of grief and fear, we may have recourse to this, *I thank thee, O Father*; let us bless God that it is not worse with us than it is.

1. The titles he gives to God: *O Father, Lord of heaven and earth.* In all our approaches to God, by praise as well as by prayer, it is good for us to eye him as a Father. Mercies are then doubly sweet, and powerful to enlarge the heart in praise, when they are received as tokens of a Father's love. It becomes children to be grateful and to say, *Thank you, father,* as readily as, *Pray, father.* When we come to God as a Father, we must withal remember, that he is *Lord of heaven and earth*; which obliges us to come to him with reverence, and yet with confidence, as one able to defend us from all evil and to supply us with all good.

2. The thing he gives thanks for: *Because thou hast hid these things from the wise and prudent, and* yet *revealed them to babes. These things; the things that belong to our peace,* Luke xix. 42. The great things of the everlasting gospel have been and are hid from many that were *wise and prudent,* that were eminent for learning and worldly policy. *The world by wisdom knew not God,* 1 Cor. i. 21. Men may dive deeply into the mysteries of nature and into the mysteries of state, and yet be ignorant of, and mistaken about, the mysteries of *the kingdom of heaven,* for want of an experience of the power of them. While *the wise and prudent men* of the world are in the dark about

JAMIESON, FAUSSET, BROWN

latter the northernmost. As their wealth and prosperity engendered luxury and its concomitant evils—irreligion and moral degeneracy—their overthrow was repeatedly foretold in ancient prophecy, and once and again fulfilled by victorious enemies. Yet they were rebuilt, and at this time were in a flourishing condition. **they would have repented long ago in sackcloth and ashes**—remarkable language, showing that they had done less violence to conscience, and so, in God's sight, were less criminal than the region here spoken of. **22. But I say unto you, It shall be more tolerable**—more endurable—**for Tyre and Sidon at the day of judgment, than for you.**

23. And thou, Capernaum—(see on ch. 4:13)—**which art exalted unto heaven**—Not even of Chorazin and Bethsaida is this said. For since at Capernaum Jesus had His stated abode during the whole period of His public life which He spent in Galilee, it was *the most favored spot upon earth,* the most exalted in privilege. **shall be brought down to hell: for if the mighty works, which have been done in thee, had been done in Sodom**—destroyed for its pollutions—**it would have remained until this day**—having done no such violence to conscience, and so incurred speakably less guilt. **24. But I say unto you, That it shall be more tolerable for the land of Sodom in the day of judgment, than for thee**—"It has been indeed," says Dr. STANLEY, "more tolerable, in one sense, in the day of its earthly judgment, for the land of Sodom than for Capernaum; for the name, and perhaps even the remains of Sodom are still to be found on the shores of the Dead Sea; while that of Capernaum has, on the Lake of Gennesareth, been utterly lost." But the judgment of which our Lord here speaks is still future; a judgment not on material cities, but their responsible inhabitants—a judgment final and irretrievable.

25. At that time Jesus answered and said—We are not to understand by this, that the previous discourse had been concluded, and that this is a record only of something said about the same period. For the connection is most close, and the word "answered"—which, when there is no one to answer, refers to something just before said, or rising in the mind of the speaker in consequence of something said—confirms this. What Jesus here "answered" evidently was the melancholy results of His ministry, lamented over in the foregoing verses. It is as if He had said, "Yes; but there is a brighter side to the picture; even in those who have rejected the message of eternal life, it is the pride of their own hearts only which has blinded them, and the glory of the truth does but the more appear in their inability to receive it. Nor have all rejected it even here; souls thirsting for salvation have drawn water with joy from the wells of salvation; the weary have found rest; the hungry have been filled with good things, while the rich have been sent empty away." **I thank thee**—rather, "I assent to thee." But this is not strong enough. The idea of *"full"* or "cordial" concurrence is conveyed by the preposition. The thing expressed is adoring acquiescence, holy satisfaction with that law of the divine procedure about to be mentioned. And as, when He afterwards uttered the same words, He "exulted in spirit" (see on Luke 10:21), probably He did the same now, though not recorded. **O Father, Lord of heaven and earth**—He so styles His Father here, to signify that from Him of right emanates all such high arrangements. **because thou hast hid these things**—the knowledge of these saving truths. **from the wise and prudent**—The former of these terms points to the men who pride themselves upon their speculative or philosophical attainments; the latter to the men of worldly shrewdness—the clever, the sharp-witted, the men of affairs. The distinction is a natural one, and was well understood. (See I Cor. 1: 19, etc.) But why had the Father hid from such the things that belonged to their peace, and why did Jesus so emphatically set His seal to this arrange-

ADAM CLARKE

23. ***Thou, Capernaum, which art exalted unto heaven.*** **A Hebrew metaphor expressive of the utmost prosperity and the enjoyment of the greatest privileges. This was properly spoken of this city because that in it our Lord dwelt, and wrought many of His miraculous works.** ***Shalt be brought down to hell.*** **Perhaps not meaning here the place of torment, but rather a state of desolation. The original word is** ***Hades*** **—the invisible receptacle or mansion of the dead, answering to** ***sheol,*** **in Hebrew; and implying, often, (1) the grave; (2) the state of separate souls, or unseen world of spirits, whether of torment, Luke xvi. 23, or in general, Rev. i. 18; vi. 8; xx. 13-14. The word** ***hell,*** **used in the common translation, conveys now an improper meaning of the original word, because** ***hell*** **is used only to signify the place of the damned.**

24. ***Day of judgment*** **may either refer to that particular time in which God visits for iniquity or to that great day in which He will judge the world by the Lord Jesus Christ.**

25. ***I thank thee.*** **"I fully agree with Thee"—I am perfectly of the same mind. Thou hast acted in all things according to the strictest holiness, justice, mercy, and truth.**

MATTHEW HENRY

gospel mysteries, even the *babes in Christ* have the sanctifying saving knowledge of them: *Thou hast revealed them unto babes.* The learned men of the world were not made choice of to be the preachers of the gospel, but *the foolish things of the world* (1 Cor. ii. 6, 8, 10). This difference between *the prudent* and the *babes* is of God's own making. It is he that has *hid these things from the wise and prudent*; he gave them parts, and learning, and much of human understanding above others, and they were proud of that, and rested in it, and looked no further. Had they honoured God with the wisdom and prudence they had, he would have given them the knowledge of these better things. It is he that has *revealed them unto babes.* Thus *he resists the proud*, and *gives grace to the humble*, James iv. 6. This dispensation must be resolved into the divine sovereignty. Christ himself referred it to that; *Even so, Father, for so it seemed good in thy sight.* Christ here subscribes to the will of his Father in this matter; *Even so.* Let God take what way he pleases to glorify himself. We can give no reason why Peter, a fisherman, should be made an apostle, and not Nicodemus, a Pharisee, and a ruler of the Jews, though he also believed in Christ; but *so it seemed good in God's sight.* This way of dispensing divine grace is to be acknowledged by us with all thankfulness. We must thank God, That *these things* are *revealed.* That they are *revealed to babes*; and this honour put upon those whom the world pours contempt upon. It magnifies the mercy to them, that *these things* are *hid from the wise and prudent*, and divine power and wisdom made to shine the more bright. See 1 Cor. i. 27, 31.

II. Christ here makes a gracious offer of the benefits of the gospel to all.

1. The solemn preface which ushers in this call or invitation. Christ prefixes his authority, produces his credentials.

Two things he here lays before us, *v.* 27.

(1) His commission from the Father: *All things are delivered unto me of my Father* He is authorised to settle a new covenant between God and man, and to offer peace and happiness to the apostate world, upon such terms as he should think fit. This encourages us to come to Christ, that he is commissioned to receive us, and to give us what we come for, and has *all things delivered to him* for that purpose, by him who is *Lord of all.* All powers, all treasures are in his hand. God has made him the great Referee, the blessed Daysman, to lay his hand upon us both; that which we have to do is to agree to the reference, to submit to the arbitration of the Lord Jesus, for the taking up of this unhappy controversy, and to enter into bonds to stand to his award.

(2) His intimacy with the Father: *No man knoweth the Son but the Father, neither knoweth any man the Father save the Son.* It must therefore be a great encouragement to us to be assured, that they understood one another very well in this affair; that the Father knew the Son, and the Son knew the Father, and both perfectly, so that there could be no mistake in the settling of this matter; as often there is among men, to the overthrow of contracts, and the breaking of the measures taken. *None knows the Father save the Son*, he adds, *and he to whom the Son will reveal him.* The happiness of men lies in an acquaintance with God; it *is life eternal.* Those who would have an acquaintance with God, must apply themselves to Jesus Christ; for the light of the knowledge of the glory of God shines in the face of Christ, 2 Cor. iv. 6.

2. Here is the offer itself that is made to us, and an invitation to accept of it. We are here invited to Christ, as our Priest, Prince, and Prophet, to be saved.

(1) We must come to Jesus Christ as our Rest, and repose ourselves in him (*v.* 28), *Come unto me all ye that labour.* The character of the persons invited; *all that labour, and are heavy laden.* This is a word in season to him that is weary. But it is rather to be understood of the burthen of sin, both the guilt and the power of it. All those, and those only, are invited to rest in Christ, that are sensible of sin as a burthen, and groan under it; that are not only convinced of the evil of sin, of their own sin, but are contrite in soul for it; that are really sick of their sins. This is a necessary preparative for pardon and peace. The Comforter must first convince (John xvi. 8). The invitation itself: *Come unto me.* See here how he holds out *the golden sceptre*, that we may touch the top of it and may live. It is the duty and interest of weary *and heavy laden* sinners to *come to Jesus Christ.* We must accept of him, as our Physician and Advocate, freely willing to be saved by him, in his own way, and upon his own terms. The blessing promised to those that do come: *I will give you rest.* Truly *rest is good*, especially to those *that labour and are heavy laden.* Jesus Christ will give assured rest to those

JAMIESON, FAUSSET, BROWN

ment? Because it is not for the offending and revolted to speak or to speculate, but to listen to Him from whom we have broken loose, that we may learn whether there be any recovery for us at all; and if there be, on what principles—of what nature—to what ends. To bring our own "wisdom and prudence" to such questions is impertinent and presumptuous; and if the truth regarding them, or the glory of it, be "hid" from us, it is but a fitting retribution, to which all the right-minded will set their seal along with Jesus. **hast revealed them unto babes**—to babelike men; men of unassuming docility, men who, conscious that they know nothing, and have no right to sit in judgment on the things that belong to their peace, determine simply to "hear what God the Lord will speak." Such are well called "babes." (See Heb. 5:13; I Cor. 13:11; 14:20, etc.) **26. Even so, Father; for so it seemed good**—the emphatic and chosen term for expressing any object of divine complacency; whether Christ Himself (see on ch. 3:17), or God's gracious eternal arrangements (see on Phil. 2:13)—**in thy sight**—This is just a sublime echo of the foregoing words; as if Jesus, when He uttered them, had paused to reflect on it, and as if the glory of it—not so much in the light of its own reasonableness as of God's absolute will that so it should be—had filled His soul.

27. All things are delivered unto me of my Father—He does not say, They are *revealed*—as to one who knew them not, and was an entire stranger to them save as they were discovered to Him—but, They are "delivered over," or "committed," to Me of My Father; meaning the whole administration of the kingdom of grace. So in John 3:35, "The Father loveth the Son, and hath given all things into His hand" (see on that verse). But though the "all things" in both these passages refer properly to the kingdom of grace, they of course include all things necessary to the full execution of that trust—that is, *unlimited* power. (So ch. 28:18; John 17:2; Eph. 1:22). **and no man knoweth the Son, but the Father; neither knoweth any man the Father, save the Son, and he to whomsoever the Son will**—willeth—**to reveal him**—What a saying is this, that "the Father and the Son are mutually and exclusively known to each other!" A higher claim to equality with the Father cannot be conceived. Either, then, we have here one of the revolting assumptions ever uttered, or the proper divinity of Christ should to Christians be beyond dispute. "But, alas for me!" may some burdened soul, sighing for relief, here exclaim. If it be thus with us, what can any poor creature do but lie down in passive despair, unless he could dare to hope that *he* may be one of the favored class "to whom the Son is willing to reveal the Father." But nay. This testimony to the sovereignty of that gracious "will," on which alone men's salvation depends, is designed but to reveal the source and enhance the glory of it when once imparted—not to paralyze or shut the soul up in despair. Hear, accordingly, what follows: **28. Come unto me, all ye that labour and are heavy laden, and I will give you rest**—Incomparable, ravishing sounds these—if ever such were heard in this weary, groaning world! What gentleness, what sweetness is there in the very style of the invitation—"Hither to Me"; and in the words, "All ye that toil and are burdened," the universal wretchedness of man is depicted, on both its sides—the *active* and the *passive* forms of it.

ADAM CLARKE

G. CAMPBELL MORGAN:

To what sort of people, then, does He reveal these things? To babes. And here the Greek word traced to its root means "not speaking," and in this use indicates the immature, which means that they are not indisposed to receive. Or again, to leave the figure of the infant, let the Master speak as He spoke on another occasion, and we see how His philosophy is always the same. "Except ye be converted"—turned back—"and become as little children"—believing that there is something you do not know, believing that the knowledge in your possession is not final—unless you get there, you cannot enter the Kingdom of God. "I thank thee, O Father, Lord of heaven and earth, that thou didst hide these things from the wise and understanding"—the men of acumen who put things together and imagine all God's truth can be expressed in the sequence of their reasoning—"and didst reveal them unto babes"—who do not know anything, but who are dreaming toward truth, in whom is the spirit of romance, the spirit that soars.

What a blessed thing it is that God has always revealed these things to the simplehearted and the simpleminded! One may have lost the priestism of ecclesiasticism, but there is a new priestism abroad today which says that we cannot interpret this Book unless we know original languages in all their ramifications. It is not true. The man who can put two and two together as to Semitic languages, and as to Greek dialect, may never see the flame of glory that any little child can see who takes up the Book and studies it with the simple heart of the babe.
—*The Gospel According to Matthew*

27. *No man knoweth the Son, but the Father; neither knoweth any man.* None can fully comprehend the nature and attributes of God but Christ; and none can fully comprehend the nature, incarnation, etc., of Christ but the Father.

28. *Come unto me.* This phrase in the new covenant implies, simply, believing in Christ and becoming His disciple or follower. *All ye that labour and are heavy laden.* The Jews, heavily laden with the burdensome rites of the Mosaic institution, rendered still more oppressive by the additions made by the scribes and Pharisees, who, our Lord says (chap. xxiii. 4), bound on "heavy burdens"; and laboring, by their observance of the law, to make themselves pleasing to God, are here invited to lay down their load, and receive the salvation procured for them by Christ. Sinners, wearied in the ways of iniquity, are also invited to come to this Christ and find speedy relief. Penitents, burdened with the guilt of their crimes, may come to this Sacrifice and find instant pardon. Believers, sorely tempted, and oppressed by the remains of the carnal mind, may come to this Blood that cleanseth from all unrighteousness; and, purified from all sin, and powerfully succored in every temptation, they shall find uninterrupted *rest* in this complete Saviour.

MATTHEW HENRY

weary souls, that by a lively faith come to him for it; a *rest* in God, in his love.

(2) We must come to Jesus Christ as our Ruler, and submit ourselves to him (*v.* 29). *Take my yoke upon you.* The *rest* he promises is a release from the drudgery of sin, not from the service of God. Christ has a *yoke* for our necks, as well as a *crown* for our heads. To call those who are weary *and heavy laden*, to *take a yoke upon* them, looks like adding *affliction to the afflicted*; but the pertinency of it lies in the word *my*: "You are under a *yoke* which makes you weary: shake that off and try mine, which will make you easy." It is Christ's *yoke*; the *yoke* he has appointed; a *yoke* he has himself drawn in before us, for *he learned obedience*, and which he does by his Spirit draw in with us, for *he helpeth our infirmities*, Rom. viii. 26. A *yoke* speaks some hardship, but if the beast must draw, the *yoke* helps him.

Now this is the hardest part of our lesson, and therefore it is qualified (*v.* 30). *My yoke is easy and my burden is light*; you need not be afraid of it. The *yoke* of Christ's commands is an *easy yoke*; there is nothing in it to gall the yielding neck, nothing to hurt us, but, on the contrary, much to refresh us. It is a *yoke* that is lined with love. Such is the nature of all Christ's commands, all summed up in one word, and that a sweet word, love. It may be a little hard at first, but it is easy afterwards; the love of God and the hope of heaven will make it *easy*. The *burden* of Christ's cross is a *light burden*, very light. This *burden* in itself is *not joyous, but grievous*; yet as it is Christ's, it is *light*. Paul knew as much of it as any man, and he calls it a *light affliction*, 2 Cor. iv. 17. As afflictions abound, and are prolonged, consolations abound, and are prolonged too.

(3) We must come to Jesus Christ as our Teacher, and set ourselves to learn of him, *v.* 29. Christ has erected a great school, and has invited us to be his scholars. We must enter ourselves, associate with his scholars, and daily attend the instructions he gives by his word and Spirit. We must so *learn of Christ* as to *learn Christ* (Eph. iv. 20), for he is both Teacher and Lesson, Guide and Way, and All in All.

Two reasons are given why we must *learn of Christ*. *I am meek and lowly in heart*. He is *meek*, and can have *compassion on the ignorant*. Many able teachers are hot and hasty, which is a great discouragement to those who are dull and slow; but Christ knows how to bear with such, and to open their understandings. *He is lowly in heart.* He condescends to teach poor scholars, to teach novices. He teaches the first principles, such things as are milk for babes; he stoops to the meanest capacities. It is an encouragement to us to put ourselves to school to such a Teacher. *You shall find rest to your souls.* Rest for the soul is the most desirable rest. The only way, and a sure way to find *rest for our souls*, is to sit at Christ's feet and hear his word. The *understanding* finds *rest* in the *knowledge of* God and Jesus Christ, and is there abundantly satisfied. The affections find rest in the love of God and Jesus Christ, and meet with that in them which gives them an abundant satisfaction; quietness and assurance for ever. This rest is to be had with Christ for all those who learn of him.

CHAPTER 12

Verses 1–13

The Jewish teachers had corrupted many of the commandments, by interpreting them more loosely than they were intended; but concerning the fourth commandment, they had erred in the other extreme, and interpreted it too strictly.

Now that which our Lord Jesus here lays down is, that the works of necessity and mercy are lawful on the sabbath day.

It is usual to settle the meaning of a law by judgments given upon cases that happen in fact, and in like manner is the meaning of this law settled.

I. Christ, by justifying his disciples in plucking the ears of corn on the sabbath day, shows that *works of necessity* are *lawful* on that day. Now here observe,

1. What it was that the disciples did. They were following their Master one sabbath day through a cornfield and *they were hungry*. Providence ordered it that they *went through the corn*, and there they were supplied. God has many ways of bringing suitable provision to his people when they need it. Being in the cornfields, they began to *pluck the ears of corn*; the law of God allowed this (Deut. xxiii. 25), to teach people to be neighbourly, and not to insist upon property in a small matter whereby another may be benefited. This was but slender provision for Christ and his disciples, but it was the best they had, and

JAMIESON, FAUSSET, BROWN

Take my yoke upon you—the yoke of subjection to Jesus—**and learn of me; for I am meek and lowly in heart: and ye shall find rest unto your souls**—As Christ's willingness to empty Himself to the uttermost of His Father's requirements was the spring of ineffable repose to His own Spirit, so in the same track does He invite all to follow Him, with the assurance of the same experience.

30. For my yoke is easy, and my burden is light—Matchless paradox, even among the paradoxically couched maxims in which our Lord delights! That rest which the soul experiences when once safe under Christ's wing makes all yokes easy, all burdens light.

CHAPTER 12

VSS. 1-8. PLUCKING CORN-EARS ON THE SABBATH DAY. (=Mark. 2:23-28; Luke 6:1-5.) The season of the year when this occurred is determined by the event itself. Ripe corn-ears are found in the fields only just before harvest. The barley harvest seems clearly intended here, at the close of our March and beginning of our April. It coincided with the Passover season, as the wheat harvest with Pentecost. But in Luke (6:1) we have a still more definite note of time, if we could be certain of the meaning of the peculiar term which he employs to express it. "It came to pass [he says] on the sabbath, which was the *first-second,*" for that is the proper rendering of the word, and not "the second sabbath after the first," as in our version.

1. At that time Jesus went on the sabbath day through the corn—"the cornfields" (Mark 2:23; Luke 6:1). **and his disciples were an hungered**—not as one may be before his regular meals; but evidently from shortness of provisions: for Jesus defends their plucking the corn-ears and eating them on the plea of *necessity*. **and began to pluck the ears of corn, and to eat**—"rubbing them in their hands" (Luke 6:1).

ADAM CLARKE

29. *Take my yoke upon you.* Strange paradox! that a man already weary and overloaded must take a new weight upon him, in order to be eased and find rest! *I am meek and lowly in heart.* Wherever pride and anger dwell, there is nothing but mental labor and agony; but where the meekness and humility of Christ dwell, all is smooth, even, peaceable, and quiet. For "the work of righteousness is peace; and the effect of righteousness quietness and assurance for ever," Isa. xxxii. 17.

30. *For my yoke is easy.* My gospel imposes nothing that is difficult; on the contrary, it provides for the complete removal of all that which oppresses and renders man miserable, viz., sin.

ALEXANDER MACLAREN:

This is a strange sort of King who cannot even feed His servants. What a glimpse into the penury of their usual condition the quiet statement that the disciples were hungry gives us, especially if we remember that it is not likely that the Master had fared better than they! Indeed, His reference to David and his band of hungry heroes suggests that "he [Christ] was an hungered" as well as "they that were with him." As they traversed some field path through the tall yellowing corn, they gathered a few ears, as the merciful provision of the law allowed, and hastily began to eat the rubbed-out grains. As soon as they "began," the eager Pharisees, who seem to have been at their heels, call Him to "behold" this dreadful crime, which, they think, requires His immediate remonstrance. If they had had as sharp eyes for men's necessities as for their faults, they might have given them food which it was "lawful" to eat, and so obviated this frightful iniquity. But that is not the way of the Pharisees. Moses had not forbidden such gleaning, but the casuistry which had spun its multitudinous webs over the law, hiding the gold beneath their dirty films, had decided that plucking the ears was of the nature of reaping, and reaping was work, and work was forbidden, which being settled, of course the inferential prohibition became more important than the law from which it was deduced. That is always the case with human conclusions from revelation; and the more questionable these are, the more they are loved by their authors.

—*Expositions of Holy Scripture*

MATTHEW HENRY

they were content with it.

2. What was the offence that the Pharisees took at this. It was but a dry breakfast, yet the Pharisees would not let them eat that in quietness. They did not quarrel with them for taking another man's corn, but for doing it *on the sabbath day*; for plucking and rubbing the ears of corn on that day was expressly forbidden, because it was *a kind of reaping*.

3. What was Christ's answer to this cavil of the Pharisees. The disciples could say little for themselves. But Christ has something to say for them, and justifies what they did.

(1) He justifies them by precedents, which were allowed to be good by the Pharisees themselves. He urges an ancient instance of David: "*Have ye not read* the story (1 Sam. xxi. 6) of David's eating the show-bread, which by the law was appropriated to the priest?" That which bore out David in eating the show-bread was not his dignity but his hunger. The greatest shall not have their lusts indulged, but the meanest shall have their wants considered. That may be done in a case of necessity which may not be done at another time; there are laws which necessity has not, but it is a law to itself. He urges a daily instance of the priests, which they likewise *read in the law. The priests in the temple* did a great deal of servile work on the sabbath day, which in a common case would *have been profaning the sabbath*, because the temple-service required and justified it. This intimates, that those labours are lawful on the sabbath day which are necessary, not only to the *support of life*, but to the *service of the day*; as tolling a bell to call the congregation together, travelling to church, and the like. Sabbath rest is to promote, not to hinder, sabbath worship.

(2) He justifies them by arguments, three cogent ones.

[1] *In this place is one greater than the temple*, v. 6. If the temple-service would justify what the priests did in their ministration, the service of Christ would much more justify the disciples in what they did in their attendance upon him. Christ, in a cornfield, was *greater than the temple*.

[2] *God will have mercy and not sacrifice*, v. 7. This is quoted from Hos. vi. 6. It was used before, *ch.* ix. 13, in vindication of mercy to the souls of men; here, of mercy to their bodies. The rest of the sabbath was ordained for man's good. *If you had known what this means*, had known what it is to be of a merciful disposition, you would have been sorry that they were forced to do this to satisfy their hunger, and would *not have condemned the guiltless*. It is not enough for us to know the scriptures, but we must labour to *know the meaning* of them. *Let him that readeth understand*. Ignorance of the meaning of the scripture is especially shameful in those who take upon them to teach others.

[3] *The Son of man is Lord even of the sabbath day*, v. 8. That law, as all the rest, is put into the hand of Christ, to be altered, enforced, or dispensed with, as he sees good. He was authorised to make such an alteration of that day, as that it should become the Lord's day, the Lord Christ's day.

Christ having thus silenced the Pharisees, and got clear of them (*v.* 9), *departed*, and *went into their synagogue*, the synagogue of these Pharisees, in which they presided, and toward which he was going, when they picked this quarrel with him. We must take heed lest anything that occurs in our way to holy ordinances unfit us for, or divert us from, our due attendance on them. We must not, for the sake of private feuds and personal piques, draw back from public worship. Satan gains this point, if, by sowing discord among brethren, he prevail to drive them, or any of them, from the synagogue, and the communion of the faithful.

II. Christ, by *healing the man that had the withered hand on the sabbath day*, shows that works of mercy are lawful and proper to be done on that day.

Here is, 1. The affliction that this poor man was in. This poor man was in the synagogue. Those who can do but little, or have but little to do for the world, must do so much the more for their souls; as the rich, the aged, and the infirm.

2. A spiteful question which the Pharisees put to Christ upon the sight of this man. *They asked him, saying, Is it lawful to heal?* We read not here of any address this poor man made to Christ for a cure, but they observed Christ began to take notice of him, and knew it was usual for him to be *found of those that sought him not*, and therefore with their badness they anticipated his goodness. Did ever any ask, whether it is lawful for God to heal, to send his word and heal? *Is it lawful to heal?* To enquire into the lawfulness and unlawfulness of actions is very good, and we cannot apply ourselves to any with such enquiring more fitly than to Christ; but they asked here, not that they might be instructed by him,

JAMIESON, FAUSSET, BROWN

2. But when the Pharisees saw it, they said unto him, Behold, thy disciples do that which is not lawful to do upon the sabbath day—The act itself was expressly permitted (Deut. 23:25). But as being "servile work," which was prohibited on the sabbath day, it was regarded as sinful. **3. But he said unto them, Have ye not read**—or, as Mark has it, "Have ye never read." **what David did** (1 Sam. 21:1-6)—**when he was an hungered, and they that were with him; 4. How he entered into the house of God, and did eat the showbread, which was not lawful for him to eat, neither for them which were with him, but only for the priests?**—No example could be more apposite than this. The man after God's own heart, of whom the Jews ever boasted, when suffering in God's cause and straitened for provisions, asked and obtained from the high priest what, according to the law, it was illegal for anyone save the priests to touch. Mark (2:26) says this occurred "in the days of Abiathar the high priest." But this means not during his high priesthood—for it was under that of his father Ahimelech—but simply, in his time. Ahimelech was soon succeeded by Abiathar, whose connection with David, and prominence during his reign, may account for his name, rather than his father's, being here introduced. Yet there is not a little confusion in what is said of these priests in different parts of the Old Testament. Thus he is called both the son of the father of Ahimelech (I Sam. 22:20; II Sam. 8:17); and Ahimelech is called Ahiah (I Sam. 14:3), and Abimelech (I Chron. 18:16). **5. Or have ye not read in the law, how that on the sabbath days the priests in the temple profane the sabbath**—by doing "servile work"—**and are blameless?**—The double offerings required on the sabbath day (Num. 28:9) could not be presented, and the new-baked showbread (Lev. 24:5; I Chron. 9:32) could not be prepared and presented every sabbath morning, without a good deal of servile work on the part of the priests; not to speak of circumcision, which, when the child's eighth day happened to fall on a sabbath, had to be performed by the priests on that day. (See on John 7:22, 23). **6. But I say unto you, That in this place is one greater than the temple**—or rather, according to the reading which is best supported, "something greater." The argument stands thus: "The ordinary rules for the observance of the sabbath give way before the requirements of the temple; but there are rights here before which the temple itself must give way." Thus indirectly, but not the less decidedly, does our Lord put in His own claims to consideration in this question—claims to be presently put in even more nakedly. **7. But if ye had known what this meaneth, I will have mercy, and not sacrifice**—(Hos. 6:6; Mic. 6:6-8, etc.). See on ch. 9:13. **ye would not have condemned the guiltless**—i.e., Had ye understood the great principle of all religion, which the Scripture everywhere recognizes—that ceremonial observances must give way before moral duties, and particularly the necessities of nature—ye would have refrained from these captious complaints against men who in this matter are blameless. But our Lord added a specific application of this great principle to the law of the sabbath, preserved only in Mark: "And he said unto them, the sabbath was made for man, and not man for the sabbath" (Mark 2:27). A glorious and far-reaching maxim, alike for the permanent establishment of the sabbath and the true freedom of its observance. **8. For the Son of man is Lord even of the sabbath day**—In what sense now is the Son of man Lord of the sabbath day? Not surely to abolish it—that surely were a strange lordship, especially just after saying that it was made or instituted for MAN—but to *own* it, to *interpret* it, to *preside over* it, and to *ennoble* it, by merging it in the "Lord's Day" (Rev. 1:10), breathing into it an air of liberty and love necessarily unknown before, and thus making it the nearest resemblance to the eternal sabbatism.

9-21. THE HEALING OF A WITHERED HAND ON THE SABBATH DAY, AND RETIREMENT OF JESUS TO AVOID DANGER. (=Mark 3:1-12; Luke 6:6-11). *Healing of a Withered Hand* (vss. 9-14). **9. And when he was departed thence**—but "on another sabbath" (Luke 6:6)—**he went into their synagogue**—and taught," He had now, no doubt, arrived in Galilee; but this, it would appear, did not occur at Capernaum, for after it was over, He "withdrew Himelf," it is said "*to the sea*" (Mark 3:7), whereas Capernaum was *at* the sea. **And, behold, there was a man which had his hand withered**—disabled by paralysis (as in I Kings 13:4). It was his right hand, as Luke graphically notes. **And they asked him, saying, Is it lawful to heal on the sabbath days? that they might accuse him**—Matthew and Luke say they "watched Him whether He would heal on the

ADAM CLARKE

3. *Have ye not read what David did?* The original history is in 1 Sam. xxi. 1-6.

4. *He entered into the house of God.* Viz., the house of Ahimelech, the priest, who dwelt at Nob, with whom the Tabernacle then was, in which the Divine Presence was manifested. *And did eat the shewbread.* "Bread of the presence," or faces, because this bread was to be set continually before the face of Jehovah. See the notes on Exod. xxv. 23 and 30.

5. *The priests . . . profane the sabbath.* Profane, i.e., put it to what might be called a common use, by slaying and offering up sacrifices, and by doing the services of the Temple.

6. *In this place is one greater than the temple.* Does not our Lord refer here to Mal. iii. 1? Compare this with Heb. iii. 3. The Jews esteemed nothing greater than the Temple, except God, who was worshipped in it. Christ, by asserting He is *greater than the temple,* asserts that He is God.

8. *The Son of man is Lord even of the sabbath day.* The change of the Jewish into the Christian Sabbath, called the "Lord's day," Rev. i. 10, shows that Christ is not only the Lord, but also the truth and completion of it. For it seems to have been by an especial providence that this change has been made and acknowledged all over the Christian world.

10. *A man which had his hand withered.* Probably through a partial paralysis. The man's hand was withered; but God's mercy had still preserved to him the use of his feet. He uses them to bring him to the public worship of God, and Jesus meets and heals him there.

MATTHEW HENRY

but *that they might accuse him.*

3. Christ's answer to this question, by way of appeal to themselves, and their own opinion and practice, *v.* 11, 12. In case a *sheep* should fall into a pit on the sabbath day, *would they not lift it out?* No doubt they might do it, the fourth commandment allows it; they must do it, for a *merciful man regardeth the life of his beast,* and for their parts they would do it, rather than lose a sheep; does Christ take care for sheep? Yes, he does; he preserves and provides for both man and beast. But here he says it for our sakes (1 Cor. ix. 9, 10), and hence argues, *How much then is a man better than a sheep?* Man, in respect of his being, is a great deal better, and more valuable, than the best of the brute creatures. They do not consider this, who are more solicitous for the education, preservation, and supply of their horses and dogs than of God's poor, or perhaps their own household.

Hence Christ infers a truth that *it is lawful to do well on the sabbath days;* they had asked, *Is it lawful to heal?* Christ proves it is lawful to *do well.* There are more ways of *doing well* upon sabbath days, than by the duties of God's immediate worship; this is *doing good;* and this must be done from a principle of love and charity, and this is *doing well,* and it *shall be accepted.*

4. Christ's curing of the man, notwithstanding the offence which he foresaw the Pharisees would take at it, *v.* 13. Duty is not to be left undone, nor opportunities of doing good neglected, for fear of giving offence. He said to the man, "*Stretch forth thy hand,* exert thyself as well as thou canst;" and he did so, *and it was restored whole.* In order to our cure, he commands us to *stretch forth our hands,* to improve our natural powers, and do as well as we can; to stretch them out in prayer to God, to stretch them out to lay hold on Christ by faith, to stretch them out in holy endeavours. Now this man could not stretch forth his withered hand of himself, yet Christ bid him do it. God's commands to us to do the duty which of ourselves we are not able to do are no more absurd or unjust, than this command to the man with the withered hand, *to stretch it forth;* for with the command, there is a promise of grace which is given by the word.

Verses 14–21

I. The cursed malice of the Pharisees against Christ (*v.* 14); being enraged at the convincing evidence of his miracles, they *went out, and held a council against him, how they might destroy him.* That which vexed them was, not only that by his miracles his honour eclipsed theirs, but that the doctrine he preached was directly opposite to their pride and hypocrisy, and worldly interest; but they pretended to be displeased at his breaking the sabbath day, which was by the law a capital crime. They took counsel, not to imprison nor banish him, but to destroy him, to be the death of him who came *that we might have life.* What an indignity was hereby put upon our Lord Jesus, to run him down as an outlaw, and the plague of his country, who was the greatest blessing of it, the Glory of his people Israel!

II. Christ's absconding upon this occasion, and the privacy he chose, to decline, not his work, but his danger; because *his hour was not yet come* (*v.* 15), *he withdrew himself from thence.* He could have secured himself by miracle, but chose to do it in the ordinary way of flight and retirement. Herein he humbled himself, that he was driven to the common shift of those who are most helpless; thus also he would give an example to his own rule, *When they persecute you in one city, flee to another.*

Christ did not retire for his own ease, nor seek an excuse to leave off his work. He was even then doing good, when he was forced to flee for the same. Thus he gave an example to his ministers, to do what they can, when they cannot do what they would. The common people crowded after him; *great multitudes followed him* and found him out. But it was really his honour, as it was also the honour of his grace, that the poor were evangelised; that when they received him, he received them and healed them all. Christ came into the world to be a Physician-general, as the sun to the lower world, *with healing under his wings.* Though the Pharisees persecuted Christ for doing good, yet he went on in it. He *healed them all,* and yet (*v.* 16), *charged them that they should not make him known;* which may be looked upon as an act of prudence. Christ though he would not omit doing good, yet would do it with as little noise as possible. Wise and good men, though they covet to do good, yet are far from coveting to have it talked of when it is done; because it is God's acceptance, not men's applause, that they aim at. His withdrawal was also an act of humility and self-denial, to set us an

JAMIESON, FAUSSET, BROWN

sabbath day." They were now come to the length of dogging His steps, to collect materials for a charge of impiety against Him. It is probable that it was to their *thoughts* rather than their words that Jesus addressed Himself in what follows. **11. And he said unto them, What man shall there be among you that shall have one sheep, and if it fall into a pit on the sabbath day, will he not lay hold on it, and lift it out? 12. How much then is a man better than a sheep?**—Resistless appeal! "A righteous man regardeth the life of his beast" (Prov. 12:10), and would instinctively rescue it from death or suffering on the sabbath day; how much more his nobler fellow man! But the reasoning, as given in the other two Gospels, is singularly striking: "But He knew their thoughts, and said to the man which had the withered hand, Rise up, and stand forth in the midst. And he arose and stood forth. Then said Jesus unto them, I will ask you one thing: Is it lawful on the sabbath days to do good, or to do evil? to save life or to destroy it?" (Luke 6:8, 9), or as in Mark (3:4), "to kill?" He thus shuts them up to this startling alternative: "Not to do good, when it is in the power of our hand to do it, is to do evil; not to save life, when we can, is to kill"—and must the letter of the sabbath rest be kept at this expense? This unexpected thrust shut their mouths. By this great ethical principle our Lord, we see, held Himself bound, as man. But here we must turn to Mark, whose graphic details make the second Gospel so exceedingly precious. "When He had looked round about on them with anger, being grieved for the hardness of their hearts, He saith unto the man" (Mark 3:5). This is one of the very few passages in the Gospel history which reveal our Lord's *feelings.* How holy this anger was appears from the "grief" which mingled with it at "the hardness of their hearts." **13. Then saith he to the man, Stretch forth thine hand. And he stretched it forth**—the power to obey going forth with the word of command. **and it was restored whole, like as the other**—The poor man, having faith in this wonderful Healer—which no doubt the whole scene would singularly help to strengthen—disregarded the proud and venomous Pharisees, and thus gloriously put them to shame.

14. Then the Pharisees went out, and held a council against him, how they might destroy him—This is the first explicit mention of their murderous designs against our Lord. Luke (6:11) says, they were filled with madness, and communed one with another what they might do to Jesus." But their doubt was not, *whether* to get rid of Him, but *how* to compass it. Mark (3:6), as usual, is more definite: "The Pharisees went forth, and straightway took counsel with the Herodians against Him, how they might destroy Him." These Herodians were supporters of Herod's dynasty, created by Cæsar—a political rather than religious party. The Pharisees regarded them as untrue to their religion and country. But here we see them combining together against Christ as a common enemy. So on a subsequent occasion (ch. 22:15, 16).

Jesus Retires to Avoid Danger (vss. 15-21). **15. But when Jesus knew it, he withdrew himself from thence**—whither, our Evangelist says not; but Mark (3:7) says "it was *to the sea*"—to some distance, no doubt, from the scene of the miracle, the madness, and the plotting just recorded. **and great multitudes followed him, and he healed them all**—Mark gives the following interesting details: "A great multitude from Galilee followed Him, and from Judea and from Jerusalem, and from Idumea, and from beyond Jordan; and they about Tyre and Sidon, a great multitude, when they had heard what great things He did, came unto Him. And He spake to His disciples, that a small ship should wait on Him because of the multitude, lest they should throng Him. For He had healed many; insomuch that they pressed upon Him for to touch Him, as many as had plagues. And unclean spirits, when they saw Him, fell down before Him, and cried, saying, Thou art the Son of God. And He straitly charged them that they should not make Him known" (Mark 3:7-12). How glorious this extorted homage to the Son of God! But as this was not the time, so neither were they the fitting preachers, as BENGEL says. (See on Mark 1:25, and cf. Jas. 2:19.) Coming back now to our Evangelist: after saying, "He healed them all," he continues: **16. And charged them**—the healed—**that they should not make him known**—(See on ch. 8:4).

ADAM CLARKE

12. *How much then is a man better than a sheep?* There are many persons who call themselves Christians who do more for a beast of burden or pleasure than they do for a man for whom Christ died!

13. *Stretch forth thine hand.* The bare command of God is a sufficient reason of obedience. Faith disregards apparent impossibilities, where there are a command and a promise of God. The effort to believe is often that faith by which the soul is healed. It is worthy of remark that as the man was healed with a word, without even a touch, the Sabbath was unbroken, even according to their most rigid interpretation of the letter of the law.

14. *Held a council against him.* Nothing sooner leads to utter blindness and hardness of heart than envy.

15. *Jesus . . . withdrew himself from thence.* It is the part of prudence and Christian charity not to provoke, if possible, the blind and the hardened. *Great multitudes followed him, and he healed them all.* The rejection of the gospel in one place has often been the means of sending it to and establishing it in another.

MATTHEW HENRY

example of humility, and to teach us not to proclaim our own goodness or usefulness, or to desire to have it proclaimed. Christ would have his disciples to be the reverse of those who did all their works *to be seen of men.*

III. The fulfilling of the scriptures in all this, *v.* 17. The scripture here said to be fulfilled is Isa. xlii. 1–4, which is quoted at large, *v.* 18–21. The scope of it is to show how mild and quiet, and yet how successful, our Lord Jesus should be in his undertaking.

1. The pleasure of the Father in Christ (*v.* 18); *Behold, my Servant whom I have chosen, my Beloved in whom my soul is well pleased.* Hence we may learn,

(1) That our Saviour was God's Servant in the great work of our redemption. As a *Servant,* he had a great work appointed him, and a great trust reposed in him. In the work of our salvation he took upon him the form of a servant. The motto of this Prince is, *Ich dien—I serve.*

(2) That Jesus Christ was chosen of God, as the only fit and proper person for the management of the great work of our redemption. He is *my Servant whom I have chosen.* None but he was able to do the Redeemer's work, or fit to wear the Redeemer's crown. Christ did not thrust himself upon this work, but was duly chosen into it.

(3) That Jesus Christ is God's Beloved, his beloved Son.

(4) That Jesus Christ is one in whom the Father is well pleased. And he is well pleased with us in him; for he has *made us accepted in the Beloved,* Eph. i. 6. All the interest which fallen man has or can have in God is grounded upon and owing to God's *well-pleasedness* in Jesus Christ.

2. The promise of the Father to him in two things.

(1) That he should be every way well qualified for his undertaking; *I will put my Spirit upon him,* as a Spirit of *wisdom and counsel,* Isa. xi. 2, 3. Those whom God calls to any service, he will be sure to fit and qualify for it. He received the Spirit, not by measure, but *without measure,* John iii. 34. Whoever they be that God has chosen, and in whom he is well pleased, he will be sure to *put his Spirit upon them.* Wherever he confers his love, he confers somewhat of his likeness.

(2) That he should be abundantly successful in his undertaking. Those whom God sends he will certainly own.

[1] He shall *show judgment to the Gentiles.* Christ in his own person preached to those who bordered upon the heathen nations (see Mark iii. 6–8), and by his apostle showed his gospel, called here his *judgment,* to the Gentile world. The gospel, which has a direct tendency to the reforming and bettering of men's hearts, and lives, shall be showed to the Gentiles.

[2] *In his name shall the Gentiles trust, v.* 21. He shall so show judgment to them, that they shall heed and observe what he shows them, and be influenced by it to depend upon him. The great design of the gospel, is to bring people to trust in the name of Jesus Christ; his name Jesus, a Saviour. The law we wait for is the law of faith, the law of trusting in his name. This is now his great commandment, that we *believe in Christ,* 1 John iii. 23.

3. The prediction concerning him, and his mild and quiet management of his undertaking, *v.* 19, 20.

(1) That he should carry on his undertaking without noise or ostentation. *He shall not strive, or make an outcry.* Christ and his kingdom *come not with observation,* Luke xvii. 20, 21. He *was in the world and the world knew him not.* He spake in a still small voice, which was alluring to all, but terrifying to none; he did not affect to make a noise, but came down silently like the dew.

(2) That he should carry on his undertaking without severity and rigour (*v.* 20). *A bruised reed shall he not break.* Some understand this of his patience in bearing with the wicked. Others rather understand it of his power and grace in bearing up the weak. In general, the design of his gospel is to establish such a method of salvation as encourages sincerity, though there be much infirmity; it does not insist upon a sinless obedience, but accepts an upright, willing mind. As to particular persons, that follow Christ, observe, How their case is here described—they are like *a bruised reed,* and *smoking flax.* Young beginners in religion are weak as a bruised reed, and their weakness offensive like smoking flax. Christ's disciples were as yet but weak, and many are so that have a place in his family. He will not discourage them, much less reject them or cast them off; the reed that is bruised shall not be broken and trodden down, but shall be supported, and made as strong as a cedar or flourishing palm-tree. The candle newly lighted, though it only smokes and does not flame, shall not be blown out, but blown up. The *day of*

JAMIESON, FAUSSET, BROWN

17. That it might be fulfilled which was spoken by Esaias the prophet, saying (Isa. 42:1). **18. Behold my servant, whom I have chosen; my beloved, in whom my soul is well pleased: I will put my Spirit upon him, and he shall show judgment to the Gentiles. 19. He shall not strive nor cry; neither shall any man hear his voice in the streets.**

21. And in his name shall the Gentiles trust—Part of His present audience were Gentiles—from Tyre and Sidon—first fruits of the great Gentile harvest contemplated in the prophecy.

20. A bruised reed shall he not break, and smoking flax shall he not quench, till he send forth judgment unto victory—"unto truth," says the Hebrew original, and the LXX also. But our Evangelist merely seizes the spirit, instead of the letter of the prediction in this point. The grandeur and completeness of Messiah's victories would prove, it seems, not more wonderful than the unobtrusive noiselessness with which they were to be achieved. And whereas one rough touch will break a bruised reed, and quench the flickering, smoking flax, His it should be, with matchless tenderness, love, and skill, to lift up the meek, to strengthen the weak hands and confirm the feeble knees, to comfort all that mourn, to say to them that are of a fearful heart, Be strong, fear not.

W. E. VINE:

AGAPETOS, from *agapao,* to love, is used of Christ as loved by God (Matt. 3:17); of believers (Rom. 1:7); of believers, one of another (1 Cor. 4:14); often as a form of address (1 Cor. 10:14). Wherever the A.V. has "dearly beloved," the R.V. has "beloved"; so, "well beloved" in 3 John 1; in 1 John 2:7, A.V., "brethren" (*adelphos*), the R.V. has "beloved," according to the mss. which have *agapetos.—Vine's Expository Dictionary*

ADAM CLARKE

18. *Behold my servant.* This title was given to our blessed Lord in several prophecies. See Isa. xlii. 1; liii. 2. Christ assumes it, Ps. xl. 7-9. Compare these with John xvii. 4 and Phil. ii. 7. God required an acceptable and perfect service from man; but man, being sinful, could not perform it. Jesus, taking upon Him the nature of man, fully performed the whole will of God.

And he shall shew judgment to the Gentiles. That is, He will publish the gospel to the heathen; for the word here answers to the word *mishpat* of the prophet, and it is used among the Hebrews to signify laws, precepts, and a whole system or body of doctrine.

21. *And in his name shall the Gentiles trust.* "They shall hope."

19. *He shall not strive, not cry.* The spirit of Christ is not a spirit of contention, murmuring, clamor, or litigiousness. He who loves these does not belong to Him. Christ therefore fulfilled a prophecy by withdrawing from this place, on account of the rage of the Pharisees.

20. *A bruised reed shall he not break.* A *reed* is, in Scripture, the emblem of weakness, Ezek. xxix. 6; and a *bruised* reed must signify that state of weakness that borders on dissolution and death. *And smoking flax shall he not quench. Linos* means the wick of a lamp, and *typhomenon* is intended to point out its expiring state, when the oil has been all burnt away from it, and nothing is left but a mere snuff, emitting smoke. Some suppose the Jewish state, as to ecclesiastical matters, is here intended, the prophecy declaring that Christ would not destroy it, but leave it to expire of itself, as it already contained the principles of its own destruction. Others have considered it as implying that great tenderness with which the blessed Jesus should treat the weak and the ignorant, whose good desires must not be stifled, but encouraged. The *bruised reed* may recover itself, it permitted to vegetate under the genial influences of heaven; and the life and light of

MATTHEW HENRY

small things is the day of *precious* things. The good issue and success of this, intimated in that, *till he send forth judgment unto victory*. Both the preaching of the gospel in the world, and the power of the gospel in the heart, shall prevail. Grace shall get the upper hand of corruption, and shall at length be perfected in glory. Truth and victory are much the same, for *great is the truth, and will prevail.*

Verses 22–37

I. Christ's glorious conquest of Satan, in the gracious cure of one under his power.

1. The man's case was very sad; he was *possessed with a devil*. This poor man that was possessed was blind and dumb; a miserable case! he could neither see to help himself, nor speak to others to help him. Satan blinds the eye of faith and seals up the lips of prayer.

2. His cure was very strange, and the more so, because sudden; *he healed him*. And the cause being removed, immediately the effect ceased; the *blind and dumb both spake and saw*. When Satan's power is broken in the soul, the eyes are opened to see God's glory, and the lips opened to speak his praise.

II. The conviction which this gave to the people, to *all the people*: they *were amazed*. They inferred from it, "*Is not this the Son of David?*" We may take this, 1. As an *enquiring* question. It was a good question that they started; but, it should seem, it was soon lost, and was not prosecuted. Such convictions as these should be brought to a head, and then they are likely to be brought to the heart. Or, 2. As an *affirming* question; *Is not this the Son of David?* "Yes, certainly it is, it can be no other." So plain and easy was the way made to this great truth of Christ being the Messiah and Saviour of the world, that the common people could not miss it; see the *wayfaring men, though fools, could not err therein*. See Isa. xxxv. 8. The world by wisdom knew not God, and by the foolish things the wise were confounded.

III. The blasphemous cavil of the Pharisees, *v.* 24. They were proud of the reputation they had among the people; *that* fed their pride, supported their power, and filled their purses. Those who bind up their happiness in the praise and applause of men, expose themselves to a perpetual uneasiness upon every favourable word that they hear said of any other. The shadow of honour followed Christ, who fled from it, and fled from the Pharisees, who were eager in the pursuit of it. Observe,

1. How scornfully they speak of Christ, *this fellow*. It is a bad thing to speak of good men with disdain because they are poor.

2. How blasphemously they speak of his miracles; they could not deny the matter of fact; it was as plain as the sun, that devils were cast out by the word of Christ. They had no other way to avoid the conclusion, that *this is the Son of David*, than by suggesting that *Christ cast out devils by Beelzebub*; that there was a compact between Christ and the devil; pursuant to that, the devil was not cast out, but did voluntarily retire.

IV. Christ's reply to this base insinuation, *v.* 25–30. *Jesus knew their thoughts*. Jesus Christ knows what we are thinking at any time, knows what is in man; he *understands our thoughts afar off*. Christ's reply is said to be to their thoughts, because he knew that they did not say it in their haste, but that it was the product of a rooted malignity.

Christ's reply to this imputation is copious and cogent.

1. It would be very strange, and highly improbable, that Satan should be cast out by such a compact, because then Satan's *kingdom would be divided against itself*, *v.* 25, 26.

(1) Here is a known rule laid down, that in all societies a common ruin is the consequence of mutual quarrels: *Every kingdom divided against itself is brought to desolation*. Divisions commonly end in desolations; if we clash, we break; if we divide one from another, we become an easy prey to a common enemy. Churches and nations have known this by sad experience.

(2) The application of it to the case in hand (*v.* 26), *If Satan cast out Satan;* if the prince of the devils should be at variance with the inferior devils, the whole kingdom and interest would soon be broken; nay, if Satan should come into a compact with Christ, it must be to his own ruin; for the manifest design and tendency of Christ's preaching and miracles was to overthrow the kingdom of Satan. If he should fall in with Christ, *how should then his kingdom stand?* He would himself contribute to the overthrow of it. This victory must be obtained by nobler methods. Let the prince of the devils

JAMIESON, FAUSSET, BROWN

22-37. A Blind and Dumb Demoniac Healed, and Reply to the Malignant Explanation Put upon It. (=Mark 3:20-30; Luke 11:14-23.) The precise time of this section is uncertain. Judging from the statements with which Mark introduces it, we should conclude that it was when our Lord's popularity was approaching its zenith, and so before the feeding of the five thousand. But, on the other hand, the advanced state of the charges brought against our Lord, and the plainness of His warnings and denunciations in reply, seem to favor the later period at which Luke introduces it. "And the multitude," says Mark (3:20, 21), "cometh together again," referring back to the immense gathering which Mark had before recorded (ch. 2:2)—"so that they could not so much as eat bread. And when His friends"—or rather, "relatives," as appears from vs. 31, and see on ch. 12:46—"heard of it, they went out to lay hold on Him; for they said, He is beside Himself." Cf. II Corinthians 5:13, "For whether we be beside ourselves, it is *to God*. **22. Then was brought unto him one possessed with a devil**—"a demonized person—**blind and dumb, and he healed him, insomuch that the blind and the dumb both spake and saw. 23. And all the people were amazed, and said, Is not this the son of David?**—The form of the interrogative requires this to be rendered, "Is this the Son of David?" And as questions put in this form (in *Greek*) suppose doubt, and expect rather a negative answer, the meaning is, "Can it possibly be?"—the people thus indicating their secret impression that this must be He; yet saving themselves from the wrath of the ecclesiastics, which a direct assertion of it would have brought upon them. (See on a similar question in John 4:29; and on the phrase, "Son of David," on ch. 9:27.) **24. But when the Pharisees heard it**—Mark (3:22) says, "the scribes which came down from Jerusalem"; so that this had been a hostile party of the ecclesiastics, who had come all the way from Jerusalem to collect materials for a charge against Him. (See on vs. 14.) **they said, This fellow**—an expression of contempt—**doth not cast out devils, but by Beelzebub**—rather, Beelzebul (see on ch. 10:25)—**the prince of the devils**—Two things are here implied—first, that the bitterest enemies of our Lord were unable to deny the reality of His miracles; and next, that they believed in an *organized internal kingdom of evil*, under one chief. This belief would be of small consequence, had not our Lord set His seal to it; but this He immediately does. Stung by the unsophisticated testimony of "all the people," they had no way of holding out against His claims but the desperate shift of ascribing His miracles to Satan. **25. And Jesus knew their thoughts**—"called them" (Mark 3:23). **and said unto them, Every kingdom divided against itself is brought to desolation; and every city or house**—household—**divided against itself shall not stand:**

26. And if Satan cast out Satan, he is divided against himself; how shall then his kingdom stand?—The argument here is irresistible. "No organized society can stand—whether kingdom, city, or household—when turned against itself; such intestine war is suicidal: But the works I do are destructive of Satan's kingdom: That I should be in league with Satan, therefore, is incredible and absurd."

ADAM CLARKE

the expiring lamp may be supported by the addition of fresh oil." Jesus therefore quenches not faint desires after salvation, even in the worst and most undeserving of men; for even such desires may lead to the fullness of the blessing of the gospel of peace. *Judgment unto victory*. See v. 18. By *judgment* understand the gospel, and by *victory* its complete triumph over Jewish opposition and Gentile impiety. He will continue by these mild and gentle means to work till the whole world is Christianized and the universe filled with His glory.

22. *One possessed with a devil, blind, and dumb*. A person from whom the indwelling demon took away both sight and hearing. Satan makes himself master of the heart, the eyes, and the tongue of the sinner. His heart he fills with the love of sin; his eyes he blinds that he may not see his guilt, and the perdition which awaits him; and his tongue he hinders from prayer and supplication, though he gives it increasing liberty in blasphemies, lies, slanders, etc. None but Jesus can redeem from this threefold captivity.

23. *Is not this the son of David?* Is not this the true Messiah? Do not these miracles sufficiently prove it?

24. ***Beelzebub*. See chap. x. 25.**

MATTHEW HENRY

muster up all his forces. Christ will be too hard for his united force, and his kingdom shall not stand.

2. It was not at all strange, or improbable, that devils should be cast out by the Spirit of God.

(1) *How* otherwise *do your children cast them out*? There were those among the Jews who, by invocation of the name of the most high God, or the God of Abraham, Isaac, and Jacob, did sometimes cast out devils. Josephus speaks of some in his time that did it; we read of *Jewish exorcists* (Acts xix. 13), and of some that *in Christ's name cast out devils*, though they did not follow him (Mark ix. 38). These the Pharisees condemned not, but imputed what they did to the Spirit of God. It was therefore merely from spite and envy to Christ, that they would own that others cast out devils by the Spirit of God, but suggest that he did it by compact with Beelzebub. The judgments of envy are made not by reason, but prejudice.

(2) This casting out of devils was a certain token and indication of the approach and appearance of the kingdom of God (*v.* 28); "But if it be indeed that *I cast out devils by the Spirit of God*, the kingdom of the Messiah is now about to be set up among you." Other miracles that Christ wrought proved him *sent of God*, but this proved him sent of God to destroy the devil's kingdom and his works. The destruction of the devil's power is wrought by the Spirit of God. If the devil's interest in a soul be sunk and broken by the Spirit of God, as a Sanctifier, no doubt but *the kingdom of God is come* to that soul, the kingdom of grace, a blessed earnest of the kingdom of the glory.

3. The comparing of Christ's miracles with his doctrine evidenced that he was so far from being in league with Satan, that he was at open enmity and hostility against him (*v.* 29); *How can one enter into a strong man's house, and plunder his goods*, and carry them away, *except he first bind the strong man? And then he* may do what he pleases with his goods. The world was in Satan's possession, and under his power, so is every unregenerate soul; there Satan resides, there he rules. The design of Christ's gospel was to spoil the devil's house, which, as a strong man, he kept in the world; *to turn the people from darkness to light*, from sin to holiness. Pursuant to this design, he bound the strong man, when he cast out unclean spirits by his word. When he showed how easily and effectually he could cast the devil out of people's bodies, he encouraged all believers to hope that, whatever power Satan might usurp and exercise in the souls of men, Christ by his grace would break it. When some of the worst of sinners were sanctified and justified, and became the best of saints, then Christ spoiled the devil's house, and will spoil it more and more.

4. This holy war, which Christ was carrying on with vigour against the devil and his kingdom, was such as would not admit of a neutrality (*v.* 30), *He that is not with me is against me.* In the little differences that may arise between the disciples of Christ among themselves, we are taught to seek peace, by accounting those who *are not against us, to be with us* (Luke ix. 50); but in the great quarrel between Christ and the devil, no peace is to be sought. He that is not hearty *for* Christ, will be reckoned with as really *against* him: he that is cold in the cause, is looked upon as an enemy. We must be entirely, faithfully, and immovably, on Christ's side: it is the *right* side, and will at last be the *rising* side.

The latter clause is to the same purport: *He that gathereth not with me scattereth.* Christ's errand into the world was to gather in his harvest, to gather in those whom the Father had given him, John xi. 52. Christ expects and requires from those who are with him, that they gather with him; gather others to him. If we *gather not with Christ, we scatter*; it is not enough, not to do hurt, but we must do good.

V. Here is a discourse of Christ's upon this occasion, concerning tongue-sins; *Wherefore I say unto you.* He warns the people concerning three sorts of tongue-sins.

1. Blasphemous words against the Holy Ghost are the worst kind of tongue-sins, and unpardonable, *v.* 31, 32.

(1) Here is a gracious assurance of the pardon of all sin upon gospel terms. The greatness of sin shall be no bar to our acceptance with God, if we truly repent and believe the gospel: *All manner of sin and blasphemy shall be forgiven unto men.* Though it *reach up to the heavens*, yet *with the Lord there is mercy, that reacheth beyond the heavens*; mercy will be extended even to blasphemy, a sin immediately touching God's name and honour. Paul obtained mercy, who had *been a blasphemer*, 1 Tim. i. 13. Well may we say, *Who is a God like unto thee, pardoning iniquity?* Micah vii. 18. Even *words spoken against the Son of man shall be forgiven*, as theirs

JAMIESON, FAUSSET, BROWN

27. And if I by Beelzebub cast out devils, by whom do your children—"your sons," meaning here the "disciples" or pupils of the Pharisees, who were so termed after the familiar language of the Old Testament in speaking of the sons of the prophets (I Kings 20:35; II Kings 2:3, etc.). Our Lord here seems to admit that such works were wrought by them; in which case the Pharisees stood self-condemned, as expressed in Luke (11:19), "Therefore shall they be your judges."

28. But if I cast out devils by the Spirit of God—In Luke (11:20) it is, "with [or 'by'] the finger of God." This latter expression is just a figurative way of representing the *power* of God, while the former tells us the *living Personal Agent* was made use of by the Lord Jesus in every exercise of that power. **then**—"no doubt" (Luke 11:20). **the kingdom of God is come unto you**—rather "upon you," as the same expression is rendered in Luke: —i.e., "If this expulsion of Satan is, and can be, by no other than the Spirit of God, then is his Destroyer already in the midst of you, and that kingdom which is destined to supplant his is already rising on its ruins." **29. Or else how can one enter into a**—or rather, "the"—**strong man's house, and spoil his goods, except he first bind the strong man? and then he will spoil his house.**

30. He that is not with me is against me; and he that gathereth not with me scattereth abroad—On this important parable, in connection with the corresponding one (vss. 43-45), see on Luke 11:21-26.

31. Wherefore I say unto you, All manner of sin and blasphemy shall be forgiven unto men—The word "blasphemy" properly signifies "detraction," or "slander." In the New Testament it is applied, as it is here, to vituperation directed against God as well as against men; and in this sense it is to be understood as an aggravated form of sin. Well, says our Lord, all sin—whether in its ordinary or its more aggravated forms—shall find forgiveness with God. Accordingly, in Mark (3:28) the language is still stronger: "All sin shall be forgiven unto the sons of men, and blasphemies wherewith soever they shall blaspheme." There is no sin whatever, it seems, of which it may be said. "That is not a pardonable sin." This glorious assurance is not to be limited by what follows; but, on the contrary, what follows is to be explained by this. **but the blasphemy against the Holy Ghost**

ADAM CLARKE

27. *By whom do your children cast them out? Children*, or sons, of the prophets means the disciples of the prophets; and children or sons of the Pharisees, disciples of the Pharisees. From Acts xix. 13-14, it is evident there were *exorcists* among the Jews, and from our Lord's saying here, it is also evident that the disciples of the Pharisees did cast out demons, or at least those who educated them wished to have it believed that they had such a power. Our Lord's argument here is extremely conclusive: If the man who casts our demons proves himself thereby to be in league with and influenced by Satan, then your disciples, and you who taught them, are all of you in league with the devil.

28. *But if I cast out devils by the Spirit of God.* Perhaps the *Spirit of God* is here mentioned by way of opposition to the magical incantations of the Jews; for it is well-known that by fumigations and magical washings they professed to cast out devils. *Then the kingdom of God.* For the destruction of the kingdom of Satan plainly implies the setting up of the kingdom of God. *Is come unto you.* Is come unexpectedly upon you.

29. *Else how can one enter into a strong man's house?* Men, through sin, are become the very house and dwelling place of Satan, having of their own accord surrendered themselves to this unjust possessor; for whoever gives up his soul to sin gives it up to the devil. It is Jesus, and Jesus alone, who can deliver from the power of this bondage. When Satan is cast out, Jesus purifies and dwells in the heart.

30. *He that is not with me is against me.* There is no medium between loving the Lord and being His enemy—between belonging to Christ or to Satan. If we be on the side of the devil, we must expect to go to the devil's hell; if we be on the side of Christ, we may expect to go to His heaven.

Scattereth abroad. This seems to have been a proverbial form of speech, and may be a metaphor taken from shepherds. He who does not help the true shepherd to gather his flock into the fold is, most likely, one who wishes to scatter them, that he may have the opportunity of stealing and destroying them.

31. *All manner of sin and blasphemy.* Injurious or impious speaking, mocking, and deriding speech.

MATTHEW HENRY

were who reviled him at his death, many of whom repented and found mercy.

(2) Here is an exception of *the blasphemy against the Holy Ghost*, which is here declared to be the only unpardonable sin. What is this sin; it is *speaking against the Holy Ghost.* See what malignity there is in tongue-sins, when the only unpardonable sin is so. *But Jesus knew their thoughts, v.* 25. It is not all speaking against the person or essence of the Holy Ghost, or merely the resisting of his internal working in the sinner himself, that is here meant; for *who then should be saved*? None are excepted by name, nor any by description, but those only *that blaspheme the Holy Ghost.* This blasphemy is excepted, not for any defect of mercy in God, or merit in Christ, but because it inevitably leaves the sinner in infidelity and impenitency. Those who fear they have committed this sin, give a good sign that they have not. Those therefore who blaspheme this dispensation of the Spirit, cannot possibly be brought to believe in Christ; those who shall impute them to a collusion with Satan, as the Pharisees did the miracles, what can convince them? This is such a stronghold of infidelity as a man can never be beaten out of, and is therefore unpardonable, because hereby repentance is hid from the sinner's eyes. See the sentence that is passed upon it: *It shall not be forgiven, neither in this world, nor in the world to come.* There is no cure for a sin so directly against the remedy.

2. Christ speaks here concerning other wicked words, the products of corruption reigning in the heart, and breaking out thence, *v.* 33–35. Our Lord Jesus therefore points to the springs and heals them; let the heart be sanctified and it will appear in our words.

(1) The heart is the *root*, the language is the *fruit* (*v.* 33); if the nature of the tree be good, it will bring forth fruit accordingly. Wherever lust reigns in the heart it will break out; diseased lungs make an offensive breath. Men's language discovers what country they are of. "*Either make the tree good, and then the fruit will be good;* get pure hearts and then you will have pure lips and pure lives; or else *the tree will be corrupt, and the fruit* accordingly." You may make a crab-stock to become a good tree, by grafting into it a shoot from a good tree, and then the fruit will be good; but if the tree be still the same, plant it where you will, and water it how you will, the fruit will be still corrupt. Unless the heart be *trans*formed, the life will never be thoroughly *re*formed. It should be more our care to be good really, than to seem good outwardly.

(2) The heart is the fountain, the words are the streams (*v.* 34); *Out of the abundance of the heart the mouth speaks*, as the streams are the overflowings of the spring. Evil words are the natural, genuine product of an evil heart. Nothing but the salt of grace, cast into the spring, will heal the waters, *season the speech*, and purify the *corrupt communication.* This they wanted, they were evil; *and how can ye, being evil, speak good things?* The people looked upon the Pharisees as a generation of saints, but Christ calls them *a generation of vipers.* Now what could be expected from a *generation of vipers*, but that which is poisonous and malignant? Can the viper be otherwise than venomous? Bad things may be expected from bad people. Christ would have his disciples know what sort of men they were to live among, that they might know what to look for. They are as Ezekiel *among scorpions* (Ezek. ii. 6), and must not think it strange if they be stung and bitten.

(3) The heart is the *treasury*, the words are the things brought out of that treasury (*v.* 35). It is the character of a *good man*, that he has a *good treasure in his heart*, and from thence *brings forth good things*, as there is occasion. Graces, comforts, experiences, good knowledge, good affections, good resolutions, these are a *good treasure in the heart*; the word of God hidden there, the law of God written there, divine truths dwelling and ruling there, are a treasure there, valuable and suitable, kept safe and kept secret, as the stores of the good householder, but ready for use upon all occasions. Some pretend to good expenses that have not a *good treasure*—such will soon be bankrupts: some hope they have it in them; thank God, whatever their words and actions are, they have good hearts; but *faith without works is dead*: and some have a *good treasure* of wisdom and knowledge, but they are not communicative: they have a talent, but know not how to trade with it. The complete Christian in *this* bears the image of God, that he both *is good, and does good.* It is the character of *an evil man*, that he has an *evil treasure in his heart*, and out of it *bringeth forth evil things.*

3. Christ speaks here concerning *idle words*, and shows what evil there is in them (*v.* 36, 37). *For every idle word*, or discourse, *that men speak, they shall give account.* God takes notice of every word we say,

JAMIESON, FAUSSET, BROWN

shall not be forgiven unto men. 32. And whosoever speaketh a word against the Son of man, it shall be forgiven him: but whosoever speaketh against the Holy Ghost, it shall not be forgiven him, neither in this world, neither in the world to come—In Mark the language is awfully strong, "hath never forgiveness, but is in danger of eternal damnation"—or rather, according to what appears to be the preferable though very unusual reading, "in danger of eternal guilt"—a guilt which he will underlie for ever. Mark has the important addition (vs. 30), "Because they said, He hath an unclean spirit." (See on ch. 10:25.) What, then, is this sin against the Holy Ghost—the unpardonable sin? One thing is clear: Its unpardonableness cannot arise from anything in the nature of sin itself; for that would be a naked contradiction to the emphatic declaration of vs. 31, that all manner of sin is pardonable. And what is this but the fundamental truth of the Gospel? (See Acts 13:38, 39; Rom. 3:22, 24; I John 1:7, etc.). Then, again when it is said (vs. 32), that to speak against or blaspheme the Son of man is pardonable, but the blasphemy against the Holy Ghost is not pardonable, it is not to be conceived that this arises from any greater sanctity in the one blessed Person than the other. These remarks so narrow the question that the true sense of our Lord's words seem to disclose themselves at once. It is a contrast between slandering "the Son of man" *in His veiled condition and unfinished work*—which might be done "ignorantly, in unbelief" (I Tim. 1:13), and slandering the same blessed Person after the blaze of glory which *the Holy Ghost* was soon to throw around His claims, and in the full knowledge of all that. This would be to slander Him with eyes open, or to do it "presumptuously." To blaspheme Christ in the former condition—when even the apostles stumbled at many things—left them still open to conviction on fuller light: but to blaspheme Him in the latter condition would be to hate the light the clearer it became, and resolutely to shut it out; which, of course, precludes salvation. (See on Heb. 10:26-29). The Pharisees had not as yet done this: but in charging Jesus with being in league with hell they were displaying beforehand a malignant determination to shut their eyes to all evidence, and so, *bordering upon*, and *in spirit* committing, the unpardonable sin. **33. Either make the tree good . . .**

34. O generation of vipers—(See on ch. 3:7). **how can ye, being evil, speak good things? for out of the abundance of the heart the mouth speaketh**—a principle obvious enough, yet of deepest significance and vast application. In Luke 6:45 we find it uttered as part of the discourse delivered after the choice of the apostles.

35. A good man, out of the good treasure of the heart, bringeth—or, putteth—**forth good things: and an evil man, out of the evil treasure, bringeth**—or putteth—**forth evil things**—The word "putteth" indicates the spontaneity of what comes from the heart; for it is out of the abundance of the heart that the mouth speaketh. We have here a new application of a former saying (see on ch. 7:16-20). Here, the sentiment is, "There are but two kingdoms, interests, parties—with the proper workings of each: If I promote the one, I cannot belong to the other; but they that set themselves in wilful opposition to the kingdom of light openly proclaim to what other kingdom they belong. As for you, in what ye have now uttered, ye have but revealed the venomous malignity of your hearts."

36. But I say unto you, That every idle word that men shall speak, they shall give account thereof in the day of judgment—They might say,

ADAM CLARKE

But the blasphemy against the Holy Ghost, i.e., when the person obstinately attributed those works to the devil which he had the fullest evidence could be wrought only by the Spirit of God. That this, and nothing else, is the sin against the Holy Spirit is evident from the connection in this place, and more particularly from Mark iii. 28-30. Here the matter is made clear beyond the smallest doubt—the "unpardonable sin," as some term it, is neither less nor more than ascribing the miracles Christ wrought, by the power of God, to the spirit of the devil. Many sincere people have been grievously troubled with apprehensions that they had committed the unpardonable sin; but let it be observed that no man who believes the divine mission of Jesus Christ ever can commit this sin.

32. *Neither in this world, neither in the world to come.* Neither in this dispensation, viz., the Jewish, nor in that which is to come, viz., the Christian. *The world to come* is a constant phrase for the times of the Messiah in the Jewish writers.

33. *Either make the tree good.* The works will resemble the heart. Nothing good can proceed from an evil spirit; no good fruit can proceed from a corrupt heart. Before the heart of man can produce any good, it must be renewed and influenced by the Spirit of God.

34. *O generation of vipers.* These are apparently severe words, but they were extremely proper in reference to that execrable people to whom they were addressed. The whole verse is an inference from what was spoken before. *Out of the abundance* (the overflowings) *of the heart.* Wicked words and sinful actions may be considered as the overflowings of a heart that is more than full of the spirit of wickedness; and holy words and righteous deeds may be considered as the overflowings of a heart that is filled with the Holy Spirit, and running over with love to God and man.

35. *A good man out of the good treasure of the heart.* The good heart is the good treasury, and the treasure that is in it is the love of God, and of all mankind. The bad heart is the bad treasury, and its treasure is the carnal mind, which is enmity against God, and ill will to man.

36. *Every idle word.* A word that does nothing, that neither ministers grace nor instruction to them who hear it. The word corresponds

MATTHEW HENRY

even that which we ourselves do not notice. Vain, idle, impertinent talk is displeasing to God; it is the product of a vain and trifling heart. We must shortly account for these idle words; they will prove us unprofitable servants, that have not improved the faculties of reason and speech, which are part of the talents we are entrusted with. *By thy words thou shalt be justified or condemned.* The constant tenor of our discourse, according as it is gracious or not gracious, will be an evidence for us, or against us.

Verses 38–45

It is probable that these Pharisees were not the same that cavilled at him (*v.* 24), and would not credit the signs he gave: but another set of them, who would not content themselves with the signs he gave, unless he would give them such further proof as they should demand.

I. Their address to him, *v.* 38. They compliment him with the title of *Master*, pretending respect for him, when they intended to abuse him; all are not indeed Christ's servants, who call him *Master*. Their request is, *We would see a sign from thee.* It was highly reasonable that they should see a sign, that he should by miracles prove his divine mission. But it was highly unreasonable to demand a sign now, when he had given so many signs already. It is natural to proud men to *pre*scribe to God, and then to make that an excuse for not *sub*scribing to him; but a man's *of*fence will never be his *de*fence.

II. His answer to this insolent demand.

1. He condemns the demand, as the language of *an evil and adulterous generation, v.* 39. He fastens the charge, not only on *the scribes and Pharisees*, but the whole nation of the Jews. They were an evil generation indeed, that not only hardened themselves against the conviction of Christ's miracles, but set themselves to abuse him, and put contempt on his miracles. They were *an adulterous generation.* As an adulterous brood; so they degenerated from the faith and obedience of their ancestors, that Abraham and Israel acknowledged them not. As an adulterous wife they departed from that God, to whom by covenant they had been espoused: they were guilty of infidelity, they did not look after gods of their own making, but they looked for signs of their own devising; and that was adultery.

2. He refuses to give them any other sign than he has already given them, but *that of the prophet Jonas.* Though Christ is always ready to hear and answer holy desires and prayers, yet he will not gratify corrupt lusts and humours. Those who *ask amiss, ask, and have not.* Signs were granted to those who desired them for the confirmation of their faith, as to Abraham and Gideon; but were denied to those who demanded them for the excuse of their unbelief.

Justly might Christ have said, They shall never see another miracle: but note his wonderful goodness. They shall have one sign of a different kind from all these, and that is, *the resurrection of Christ from the dead by his own power*, called here *the sign of the prophet Jonas.* That was such a sign as surpassed all the rest, completed and crowned them. And yet the unbelief of the Jews found out an evasion to shift off that too, by saying, *His disciples came and stole him away;* for none are so incurably blind as those who are resolved they will not see.

Now this sign of the prophet Jonas he further explains here: (*v.* 40) *As Jonas was three days and three nights in the whale's belly*, Christ shall be so long in the grave, and then shall rise again. As Jonah on the third day was discharged from his prison, and came to the land of the living again, so Christ on the third day should return to life, and rise out of his grave to send abroad the gospel to the Gentiles.

3. Christ takes this occasion to represent the sad character and condition of that generation in which he lived, a generation that would not be reformed. Persons and things now appear under false colours; characters and conditions are here changeable. Things are really, what they are eternally.

Now Christ represents the people of the Jews,

(1) As a generation that would be condemned by *the men of Nineveh*, whose *repenting at the preaching of Jonas* would *rise up in judgment* against them, *v.* 41. Christ's resurrection will be the sign of the prophet Jonas to them: but it will not have so happy an effect upon them, as that of Jonas had upon the Ninevites, for they were by it brought to such a repentance as prevented their ruin; but the Jews will be hardened in an unbelief that shall hasten their ruin. Christ renews his calls, sat and taught, taught in the synagogues. Christ, besides the warning given us of our danger, has shown wherein we must repent, and assured us of acceptance upon our repentance. Christ wrought abundance of miracles, and all

JAMIESON, FAUSSET, BROWN

"It was nothing: we meant no evil; we merely threw out a supposition, as one way of accounting for the miracle we witnessed; if it will not stand, let it go; why make so much of it, and bear down with such severity for it?" Jesus replies, "It was not nothing, and at the great day will not be treated as nothing: Words, as the index of the heart, however idle they may seem, will be taken account of, whether good or bad, in estimating character in the day of judgment."

38-50. A SIGN DEMANDED, AND THE REPLY—HIS MOTHER AND BRETHREN SEEK TO SPEAK WITH HIM, AND THE ANSWER. (=Luke 11:16, 24-36; Mark 3: 31-35; Luke 8:19-21.) *A Sign Demanded, and the Reply* (vss. 38-45). The occasion of this section was manifestly the same with that of the preceding. **38. Then certain of the scribes and of the Pharisees answered, saying, Master**—"Teacher," equivalent to "Rabbi." **we would see a sign from thee**—"a sign from heaven" (Luke 11:16); something of an immediate and decisive nature, to show, not that His miracles were *real*—that they seemed willing to concede—but that they were from above, not from beneath. These were not the same class with those who charged Him with being in league with Satan (as we see from Luke 11:15, 16); but as the spirit of both was similar, the tone of severe rebuke is continued. **39. But he answered and said unto them**—"when the people were gathered thick together" (Luke 11:29). **An evil and adulterous generation**—This latter expression is best explained by Jeremiah 3:20, "Surely as a wife treacherously departeth from her husband, so have ye dealt treacherously with Me, O house of Israel, saith the Lord." For this was the relationship in which He stood to the covenant people—"I am married unto you" (Jer. 3:14). **seeketh after a sign**—In the eye of Jesus this class were but the spokesmen of their generation, the exponents of the reigning spirit of unbelief. **and there shall no sign be given to it, but the sign of the prophet Jonas. 40. For as Jonas was**—"a sign unto the Ninevites, so shall also the Son of man be to this generation" (Luke 11:30). For as Jonas was **three days and three nights in the whale's belly**—(Jonah 1:17),—**so shall the Son of man be three days and three nights in the heart of the earth**—This was the second public announcement of His resurrection three days after His death. (For the first, see John 2:19.) Jonah's case was analogous to this, as being a signal judgment of God; reversed in three days; and followed by a glorious mission to the Gentiles. The expression "in the heart of the earth," suggested by the expression of Jonah with respect to the sea (2:3, in LXX), means simply the grave, but this considered as the most emphatic expression of real and total entombment. The period during which He was to lie in the grave is here expressed in round numbers, according to the Jewish way of speaking, which was to regard any part of a day, however small, included within a period of days, as a full day. (See I Sam. 30:12, 13; Esther 4:16; 5:1; ch. 27:63, 64, etc.). **41. The men of Nineveh shall rise in judgment with this generation, . . .**—The Ninevites, though heathens, repented at a man's preaching; while they, God's covenant people, repented not at the preaching of the Son of God—whose supreme dignity is rather implied here than expressed.

ADAM CLARKE

to the Hebrew *shave,* which signifies not only vain or empty, but also wicked and injurious, such as a false testimony against a neighbor.

37. *By thy words thou shalt be justified.* That is, the whole tenor of your conversation will be an evidence for or against you in the great day. "Lord, put a watch before the door of my lips!" is a prayer proper for all men.

39. *An evil and adulterous generation.* Or "race of people." Our Lord terms the Jews an adulterous race. Under the old covenant, the Jewish nation was represented as in a marriage contract with the Lord of hosts, as believers in the new covenant are represented as the spouse of Christ. All unfaithfulness and disobedience was considered as a breach of this marriage contract; hence the persons who were thus guilty are denominated adulterers and adulteresses.

40. *Three days and three nights.* Our Lord rose from the grave on the day but one after His crucifixion: so that, in the computation in this verse, the part of the day on which He was crucified, and the part of that on which He rose again, are severally estimated as an entire day; and this, no doubt, exactly corresponded to the time in which Jonah was in the belly of the fish. The very same quantity of time which is here termed three days and three nights, and which, in reality, was only one whole day, a part of two others, and two whole nights, is termed three days and three nights, in the Book of Esther: "Go . . . neither eat nor drink three days, night or day . . . and so will I go in unto the king," chap. iv. 16 Afterwards it follows, chap v. 1: "On the third day . . . Esther . . . stood in the inner court of the king's house." Thus, then, three days and three nights, according to this Jewish method of reckoning, included any part of the first day, the whole of the following night, the next day and its night, and any part of the succeeding or third day. *In the whale's belly.* A fish of the shark kind, and not a *whale,* is here meant. It is well-known that the throat of a *whale* is capable of admitting little more than the arm of an ordinary man; but many of the shark species can swallow a man whole, and men have been found whole in the stomachs of several.

41. *The men of Nineveh shall rise in judgment.* The voice of God, threatening temporal judgments, caused a whole people to repent who

MATTHEW HENRY

miracles of mercy: yet the Ninevites *repented at the preaching of Jonas*, but the Jews were not wrought upon by Christ's preaching. The goodness of some, who have less helps and advantages for their souls, will aggravate the badness of those who have much greater. Those who by the twilight discover *the things that belong to their peace*, will shame those who grope at noon-day.

(2) As a generation that would be condemned by the queen of the south, the queen of Sheba, *v.* 42. The Ninevites would shame them for not repenting, the queen of Sheba for not believing in Christ. She came from a far country to hear the wisdom of Solomon; yet people will not be persuaded to come and hear the wisdom of Christ. The queen of Sheba had no invitation to come to Solomon, nor any promise of being welcome; but we are invited to Christ, to sit at his feet and hear his word. She could not be sure that it would be worth her while to go so far on this errand; but we come not to Christ upon such uncertainties. *She came from the uttermost parts of the earth*, but we have Christ among us, and his word nigh us: *Behold he stands at the door, and knocks.* It should seem the wisdom the queen of Sheba came for was only philosophy and politics; but the wisdom that is to be had with Christ is wisdom to salvation. She could only *hear* Solomon's wisdom; he could not *give* her wisdom: but Christ will give wisdom to those who come to him.

(3) As a generation that were resolved to continue under the power of Satan. They are compared to one out of whom the devil is gone, but returns with double force, *v.* 43–45.

[1] The parable represents his possessing men's bodies: Christ having lately cast out a devil, and they having said *he had a devil*, gave occasion to show how much they were under the power of Satan. Christ's ejectment of him was final, and such as barred a re-entry: we find him charging the evil spirit to *go out, and enter no more*, Mark ix. 25.

[2] The application of the parable makes it to represent the case of the body of the Jewish church and nation: *So it shall be with this wicked generation*, that now resist, and will finally reject, the gospel of Christ. Let this be a warning to all nations and churches, to take heed of leaving their first love, of letting fall a good work of reformation begun among them, and returning to that wickedness which they seemed to have forsaken; *for the last state of such will be worse than the first.*

Verses 46–50

Observe, I. How Christ was interrupted in his preaching by *his mother and his brethren*, that *stood without, desiring to speak with him* (*v.* 46, 47); which desire of theirs was conveyed to him through the crowd.

1. He was as yet talking to the people. Christ's preaching was talking; it was plain, easy, and familiar, and suited to their capacity and case. The opposition we meet with in our work, must not drive us from it. He left off talking with the Pharisees, for he saw he could do no good with them; but continued to talk to the common people.

2. His mother and brethren stood without, desiring to speak with him, when they should have been standing within, desiring to hear him. They had the advantage of his daily converse in private, and therefore were less mindful to attend upon his public preaching. Familiarity and easiness of access breed some degree of contempt. There is too much truth in that common proverb, "The nearer the church, the further from God"; it is a pity it should be so.

3. They not only would not hear him themselves, but they interrupted others that *heard him gladly*. We often meet with hindrances and obstructions in our work, by our friends that are about us, and are taken off by civil respects from our spiritual concerns. Those who really wish well to us and to our work, may sometimes, by their indiscretion, prove our backfriends, and impediments to us in our duty. Christ once said to his mother, *How is it that ye sought me? Wist ye not, that I must be about my Father's business?* And it was then said, she *laid up that saying in her heart* (Luke ii. 49); but if she had remembered it now, she would not have given him this interruption when he was about his Father's business. There is many a good truth that we thought was well laid up when we heard it, which yet is out of the way when we have occasion to use it.

II. How he resented this interruption, *v.* 48–50.

1. He would not hearken to it. *Who is my mother and who are my brethren?* Not that natural affection is to be put off, but *everything is beautiful in its season*, and the less duty must stand by, while the greater is done. The nearest relations must be com-

JAMIESON, FAUSSET, BROWN

42. The queen of the south shall rise up in the judgment with this generation . . .—The queen of Sheba (a tract in Arabia, near the shores of the Red Sea) came from a remote country, "south" of Judea, to hear the wisdom of a mere man, though a gifted one, and was transported with wonder at what she saw and heard (I Kings 10:1-9). They, when a Greater than Solomon had come *to them*, despised and rejected, slighted and slandered Him.

43-45. When the unclean spirit is gone out of a man, . . .—On this important parable, in connection with the corresponding one (vs. 29) see on Luke 11:21-26. A charming little incident, given only in Luke 11:27, 28, seems to have its proper place here. "And it came to pass, as He spake these things, a certain woman of the company [out of the crowd] lifted up her voice and said unto Him, Blessed is the womb that bare Thee, and the paps which Thou hast sucked." With true womanly feeling she envies the mother of such a wonderful Teacher. And a higher and better than she had said as much before her (see on Luke 1:28). 42. How does our Lord, then, treat it? He is far from condemning it. He only holds up as "blessed rather" another class: "But he said, Yea rather, blessed are they that hear the word of God, and keep it"—in other words, the humblest real saint of God. How utterly alien is this sentiment from the teaching of the Church of Rome, which would doubtless excommunicate any one of its members that dared to talk in such a strain!

His Mother and Brethren Seek to Speak with Him, and the Answer (vss. 46-50). **46. While he yet talked to the people, behold, his mother and his brethren**—(see on ch. 13:55, 56)—**stood without, desiring to speak with him**—"and could not come at Him for the press" (Luke 8:19). For what purpose these came, we learn from Mark 3:20, 21. In His zeal and ardor He seemed indifferent both to food and repose, and "they went to lay hold of Him" as one "beside Himself." Mark says graphically, "And the multitude sat about Him"—or "around Him." **47. Then one said unto him, Behold, thy mother and thy brethren stand without, desiring to speak with thee, . . .**—Absorbed in the awful warnings He was pouring forth, He felt this to be an unseasonable interruption, fitted to dissipate the impression made upon the large audience—such an interruption as duty to the nearest relatives did not require Him to give way to. But instead of a direct rebuke, He seizes on the incident to convey a sublime lesson, expressed in a style of inimitable condescension.

ADAM CLARKE

had neither Moses nor Christ, neither the law nor the prophets, and who perhaps never had but this one preacher among them. What judgment may not we expect, if we continue impenitent, after all that God has bestowed upon us? *A greater than Jonas is here.* "Something more." The evidence offered by Jonah sufficed to convince and lead the Ninevites to repentance, but here was more evidence, and a greater Person; and yet so obstinate are the Jews that all is ineffectual. (1) Christ, who preached to the Jews, was infinitely greater than Jonah, in His nature, person, and mission. (2) Jonah preached repentance in Nineveh only forty days, and Christ preached among the Jews for several years. (3) Jonah wrought no miracles to authorize his preaching; but Christ wrought miracles every day, in every place where He went, and of every kind. And (4) Notwithstanding all this, the people of Judea did not repent, though the people of Nineveh did.

42. *The queen of the south.* In 1 Kings x. 1, this queen is said to be of Saba, which was a city and province of Arabia Felix, to the south, or southeast, of Judea. *Uttermost parts of the earth.* A form of speech which merely signifies "a great distance."

43. *When the unclean spirit.* If there had been no reality in demoniacal possessions, our Lord would have scarcely appealed to a case of this kind here to point out the real state of the Jewish people, and the desolation which was coming upon them.

44. *Into my house.* The soul of that person from whom he had been expelled by the power of Christ, and out of which he was to have been kept by continual prayer, faith, and watchfulness. *He findeth it empty.* "Unoccupied," empty of the former inhabitant, and ready to receive a new one, denoting a soul that has lost the life and power of godliness and the testimony of the Holy Spirit. *Swept, and garnished.* Idle, or unemployed, it may refer here to the person as well as to his state. His affections and desires are no longer busied with the things of God, but gad about, like an idle person, among the vanities of a perishing world. *Swept*, from love, meekness, and all the fruits of the Spirit; and *garnished*, "adorned, decorated," with the vain, showy trifles of folly and fashion.

45. *Seven other spirits more wicked. Seven* was a favorite number with the Jews, implying frequently, with them, something "perfect, completed, filled up," for such is the proper import of the Hebrew word *sheva* or *shevang*, nearly allied in sound to our *seven. The last state of that man is worse than the first.* His soul, before influenced by the Spirit of God, dilated and expanded under its heavenly influences, becomes more capable of refinement in iniquity, as its powers are more capacious than formerly. Evil habits are formed and strengthened by relapses; and relapses are multiplied, and become more incurable, through new habits. *So shall it be also unto this wicked generation.* And so it was, for they grew worse and worse, as if totally abandoned to diabolic influence, till at last the besom of destruction swept them and their privileges, national and religious, utterly away. What a terrible description of a state of apostasy is contained in these verses!

46. *His mother and his brethren.* These are supposed to have been the cousins of our Lord, as the word *brother* is frequently used among the Hebrews in this sense. But there are others who believe Mary had other children beside our Lord and that these were literally His brothers who are spoken of here. And although it be possible that these were the sons of Mary, the wife of Cleopas or Alpheus, his mother's sister, called his "relations," Mark iii. 21, yet it is as likely that they were the children of Joseph and Mary, and brethren of our Lord, in the strictest sense of the word.

48. *Who is my mother? and who are my brethren?* The reason of this seeming disregard of His relatives was this: They came to seize upon Him, for they thought He was distracted. See Mark iii. 21.

MATTHEW HENRY

paratively hated, that is, we must love them less than Christ (Luke xiv. 26), and our duty to God must have the preference. And we must not take it ill of our friends, nor put it upon the score of their wickedness, if they prefer the pleasing of God before the pleasing of us. Nay, we must deny ourselves and our own satisfaction, rather than do that which may any way divert our friends from, or distract them in, their duty to God.

2. He took that occasion to prefer his disciples, who were his spiritual kindred, before his natural relations as such. He would rather be profiting his disciples, than pleasing his relations.

(1) The description of Christ's disciples. They are such as *do the will of his Father*; not only hear it, and know it, and talk of it, but *do it*.

(2) The dignity of Christ's disciples: *The same is my brother, and sister, and mother*. His disciples, that had left all to follow him, and embraced his doctrine, were dearer to him than any that were akin to him according to the flesh. It was very endearing and very encouraging for Christ to say, *Behold my mother and my brethren*; yet it was not *their* privilege alone, *this honour have all the saints*. All obedient believers are near akin to Jesus Christ. He loves them, converses freely with them as his relations. He bids them welcome to his table, sees that they want nothing that is fit for them, nor will ever be ashamed of his poor relations, but will confess them before men, before the angels, and before his Father.

JAMIESON, FAUSSET, BROWN

49. And he stretched forth his hand toward his disciples—How graphic is this! It is the language evidently of an eye-witness. **and said, Behold my mother and my brethren! 50. For whosoever shall do the will of my Father which is in heaven, the same is my brother, and sister, and mother**—i.e., "There stand here the members of a family transcending and surviving this of earth: Filial subjection to the will of My Father in heaven is the indissoluble bond of union between Me and all its members; and whosoever enters this hallowed circle becomes to Me brother, and sister, and mother!"

ADAM CLARKE

50. *Whosoever shall do the will of my Father.* Those are the best-acknowledged relatives of Christ who are united to Him by spiritual ties, and who are become one with Him by the indwelling of His Spirit. We generally suppose that Christ's relatives must have shared much of His affectionate attention, and doubtless they did; but here we find that whosoever does the will of God is equally esteemed by Christ as His *brother, sister,* or even His *mother.* What an encouragement for fervent attachment to God!

MATTHEW HENRY

CHAPTER 13

Verses 1–23

1. *When* Christ preached this sermon; it was the same day that he preached the sermon in the foregoing chapter: so unwearied was he in doing good. Christ was for preaching both ends of the day. An afternoon sermon well heard, will be so far from driving out the morning sermon, that it will rather clench it, and fasten the nail in a sure place. Though Christ had been in the morning opposed, disturbed and interrupted, yet he went on with his work; and in the latter part of the day, we do not find that he met with such discouragements. Those who with courage and zeal break through difficulties in God's service, will perhaps find them not so apt to recur as they fear. Resist them, and they will flee.

2. *To whom* he preached; there were *great multitudes gathered together to him*, and they were the auditors. Sometimes there is most of the *power* of religion where there is least of the *pomp* of it. When Christ went to the *sea-side, multitudes* were presently *gathered together to him*. Where the king is, there is the court; where Christ is, there is the church, though it be by the sea-side. Those who would get good by the word, must be willing to follow it in all its removes; when the ark shifts, shift after it.

3. *Where* he preached this sermon. His meeting-place was the sea-side. He went out of the house (because there was no room for the auditory) into the open air. As he had not a house of his own to live in, so he had not a chapel of his own to preach in. By this he teaches us in the external circumstances of worship not to covet that which is stately, but to make the best of the conveniences which God in his providence allots to us. When Christ was born, he was crowded into the stable, and now to the sea-side, upon the strand, where all persons might come to him with freedom. His pulpit was a ship. No place amiss for such a Preacher, whose presence dignified and consecrated any place: let not those who preach Christ be ashamed, though they have mean and inconvenient places to preach in.

4. *What* and *how* he preached. *He spake many things unto them.* Many more it is likely than are here recorded. They were not trifles, but things of everlasting consequence, that Christ spoke of. What he spake was in parables. It was a way of teaching used very much, and it was found very profitable, and the more so from its being pleasant. Our Saviour used it much, and in it condescended to the capacities of people, and lisped to them in their own language.

I. We have here the general reason why Christ taught in parables. The disciples were a little surprised at it, for hitherto, in his preaching, he had not much used them, and therefore they ask, *Why speakest thou to them in parables?* Because they were truly desirous that the people might hear with understanding. They do not say, Why speakest thou to *us*? (they knew how to get the parables explained) but to *them*.

To this question Christ answers largely, *v.* 11–17, where he tells them, that *therefore* he preached by parables, because thereby the things of God were

JAMIESON, FAUSSET, BROWN

CHAPTER 13

VSS. 1-52. JESUS TEACHES BY PARABLES. (= Mark 4:1-34; Luke 8:4-18; 13:18-20.) *Introduction* (vss. 1-3). **1. The same day went Jesus out of the house, and sat by the seaside. 2. And great multitudes were gathered together unto him, so that he went into a ship**—the article in the received text lacks authority—**and sat; and the whole multitude stood on the shore**—How graphic this picture!—no doubt from the pen of an eyewitness, himself impressed with the scene. It was "the same day" on which the foregoing solemn discourse was delivered, when His kindred thought Him "beside Himself" for His indifference to food and repose—that same day retiring to the seashore of Galilee; and there seating Himself, perhaps for coolness and rest, the crowds again flock around Him, and He is fain to push off from them, in the boat usually kept in readiness for Him; yet only to begin, without waiting to rest, a new course of teaching by parables to the eager multitudes that lined the shore. To the parables of our Lord there is nothing in all language to be compared, for simplicity, grace, fulness, and variety of spiritual teaching. They are adapted to all classes and stages of advancement, being understood by each according to the measure of his spiritual capacity.

3. And he spake many things unto them in parables, saying, . . .—These parables are SEVEN in number; and it is not a little remarkable that while this is the *sacred number*, the first FOUR of them were spoken to the mixed multitude, while the remaining THREE were spoken to the Twelve in private—these divisions, *four* and *three*, being themselves notable in the symbolical arithmetic of Scripture. Another thing remarkable in the structure of these parables is, that while the first of the Seven—that of the Sower—is of the nature of an Introduction to the whole, the remaining Six consist of *three pairs*—the Second and Seventh, the Third and Fourth, and the Fifth and Sixth, corresponding to each other; each pair setting forth the same general truths, but with a certain diversity of aspect. All this can hardly be accidental.

Reason for Teaching in Parables (vss . 10-17). **10. And the disciples came, and said unto him**—"they that were with Him, when they were alone" (Mark 4:10). **Why speakest thou to them in parables?**—Though before this He had couched some

ADAM CLARKE

CHAPTER 13

1. *The same day.* Our Lord scarcely ever appears to take any rest. He is incessant in His labors, and instant in season and out of season; and in this He has left all His successors in the ministry an example, that they should follow His steps. *Went Jesus out of the house.* This was the house of Peter. *Sat by the sea side.* The Sea of Galilee, on the borders of which the city of Capernaum was situated.

2. *Into a ship.* It probably belonged to some of the fishermen (see chap. iv. 22).

3. *He spake many things unto them in parables.* A comparison or similitude, in which one thing is compared with another, especially spiritual things with natural, by which means these spiritual things are better understood, and make a deeper impression on an attentive mind.

MATTHEW HENRY

made more plain and easy to them who were willing to be taught, and at the same time more difficult and obscure to those who were willingly ignorant. A parable, like the pillar of cloud and fire, turns a dark side towards Egyptians, which confounds them, but a light side towards Israelites, which comforts them.

1. This reason is laid down (*v.* 11): *Because it is given unto you to know the mysteries of the kingdom of heaven, but to them it is not given.* That is, (1) The disciples had knowledge, but the people had not. The people are ignorant, are yet but babes, and must be taught as such by plain similitudes: for though they have eyes, they know not how to use them; so some. Or, (2) The disciples were well inclined to the knowledge of gospel mysteries, and would search into the parables, but the carnal hearers that rested in bare hearing, would be never the wiser, and so would justly suffer for their remissness. A parable is a shell that keeps good fruit *for* the diligent, but keeps it *from* the slothful. There are mysteries in the kingdom of heaven. It is graciously given to the disciples of Christ to be acquainted with these mysteries. Knowledge is the first gift of God, it was given to the apostles, because they were Christ's constant followers and attendants. The nearer we draw to Christ, and the more we converse with him, the better acquainted we shall be with gospel mysteries. It is given to all true believers, who have an experimental knowledge of the gospel mysteries, and that is without doubt the best knowledge.

2. This reason is further illustrated by the rule God observes in dispensing his gifts; he bestows them on those who improve them, but takes them away from those who bury them.

(1) Here is a promise to him that has and uses what he has; he shall have more abundance: God's favours are earnests of further favours: where he lays the foundation, he will build upon it.

(2) Here is a threatening to him that has not; that has, but uses not what he has; from him shall be *taken away* that which he has or seems to have. God will *call in* his talents out of their hands that are likely to become bankrupts quickly.

3. This reason is particularly explained, with reference to the two sorts of people Christ had to do with.

(1) Some were willingly ignorant; and such were amused by the parables (*v.* 13); *because they seeing, see not.* They had shut their eyes against the clear light of Christ's plainer preaching, and therefore were now left in the dark. It is just with God to take away the light from those who shut their eyes against it.

Now in this the scripture would be fulfilled, *v.* 14, 15. It is quoted from Isa. vi. 9, 10. It is referred to no less than six times in the New Testament. That which was spoken of the sinners in Isaiah's time was fulfilled in those in Christ's time, and it is still fulfilling every day. Here is,

First. A description of sinners' wilful blindness and darkness, which is their sin. *This people's heart is waxed gross;* it is *fattened,* so the word is; which denotes both sensuality and senselessness. And when the heart is thus heavy, no wonder that the ears are dull of hearing. They shut both the learning senses; for their eyes also they have closed, resolved that they would not see light come into the world, when the Sun of Righteousness arose.

Secondly, A description of that judicial blindness, which is the just punishment of this. "*By hearing, ye shall hear, and shall not understand;* what means of grace you have, shall be to no purpose to you; though in mercy to others, they are continued." The saddest condition a man can be in is to sit under the most lively ordinances with a dead, stupid, untouched heart.

Thirdly, The woeful effect and consequence of this; *Lest at any time they should see. Lest they should be converted, and I should heal them.*

Note, That seeing, hearing, and understanding, are necessary to conversion; for God, in working grace, deals with men as men, as rational agents; he draws with the cords of a man, changes the heart by opening the eyes, and turns *from the power of Satan unto God,* by turning first *from darkness to light,* Acts xxvi. 18. All those who are truly converted to God, shall certainly be healed by him. "If they be converted I shall heal them, I shall save them."

(2) Others were effectually called to be the disciples of Christ and were truly desirous to be taught of him. By these parables the things of God were made more plain and easy, more intelligible and familiar, and more apt to be remembered (*v.* 16, 17). *Your eyes see, your ears hear.* Now this Christ speaks of,

[1] As a blessing; "*Blessed are your eyes for they see, and your ears for they hear;* it is your happiness, and it is a happiness for which you are indebted to

JAMIESON, FAUSSET, BROWN

things in the parabolic form, for more vivid illustration, it would appear that He now, for the first time, formally employed this method of teaching. **11. He answered and said unto them, Because it is given unto you to know the mysteries of the kingdom of heaven**—The word "mysteries" in Scripture is not used in its classical sense—of religious secrets, nor yet of things incomprehensible, or in their own nature difficult to be understood—but in the sense of things of purely divine revelation, and, usually, things darkly announced under the ancient economy, and during all that period darkly understood, but fully published under the Gospel (I Cor. 2:6-10; Eph. 3:3-6, 8, 9). "The mysteries of the kingdom of heaven," then, mean those glorious Gospel truths which at that time only the more advanced disciples could appreciate, and they but partially. **but to them it is not given**—(See on ch. 11:25). Parables serve the double purpose of *revealing* and *concealing;* presenting "the mysteries of the kingdom" to those who know and relish them, though in never so small a degree, in a new and attractive light; but to those who are insensible to spiritual things yielding only, as so many tales, some temporary entertainment. **12. For whosoever hath**—i.e., keeps; as a thing which he values. **to him shall be given, and he shall have more abundance**—He will be rewarded by an increase of what he so much prizes. **but whosoever hath not**—who lets this go or lie unused, as a thing on which he sets no value. **from him shall be taken away even that he hath**—or as it is in Luke (8:18), "what he seemeth to have," or, thinketh he hath. This is a principle of immense importance, and, like other weighty sayings, appears to have been uttered by our Lord on more than one occasion, and in different connections. (See on ch. 25:9.) As a great ethical principle, we see it in operation everywhere, under the general law of *habit;* in virtue of which moral principles become stronger by exercise, while by disuse, or the exercise of their contraries, they wax weaker, and at length expire. The same principle reigns in the intellectual world, and even in the animal—if not in the vegetable also—as the facts of physiology sufficiently prove. Here, however, it is viewed as a divine ordination, as a judicial retribution in continual operation under the divine administration. **13. Therefore speak I to them in parables**—which our Lord, be it observed, did not begin to do till His miracles were malignantly ascribed to Satan. **because they seeing, see not**—They "saw," for the light shone on them as never light shone before; but they "saw not," for they closed their eyes.

and hearing, they hear not; neither do they understand—They "heard," for He taught them who "spake as never man spake"; but they "heard not," for they took nothing in, apprehending not the soul-penetrating, life-giving words addressed to them. In Mark and Luke, what is here expressed as a human fact is represented as the fulfilment of a divine purpose—"that seeing they may see, and not perceive . . ." The explanation of this lies in the statement of the foregoing verse—that, by a fixed law of the divine administration, the duty men voluntarily refuse to do, and in point of fact do not do, they at length become morally incapable of doing. **14. And in them is fulfilled**—rather, is fulfilling, or is receiving its fulfilment. **the prophecy of Esaias, which saith**—(Isa. 6:9, 10—here quoted according to the LXX). **By hearing ye shall hear, and shall not understand, . . .**—They were thus judicially sealed up under the darkness and obduracy which they deliberately preferred to the light and healing which Jesus brought nigh to them.

16. But blessed are your eyes, for they see; and your ears, for they hear—i.e., "Happy ye, whose eyes and ears, voluntarily and gladly opened, are drinking in the light divine."

ADAM CLARKE

11. *It is given unto you to know the mysteries.* By *mysteries,* here, we may understand not only things concerning the scheme of salvation, which had not yet been revealed, but also the prophetic declarations concerning the future state of the Christian Church, expressed in the ensuing parables. *To them it is not given* to know the purport and design of these things—they are gross of heart, earthly, and sensual, and do not improve the light they have received.

12. *Whosoever hath, to him shall be given.* This is an allusion to a common custom in all countries. He who possesses much or is rich, to such a person presents are ordinarily given. *Whosoever hath not, from him shall be taken away even that he hath.* That is, the poor man; he that has little may be easily made a prey of, and so lose his little.

13. *Therefore speak I to them in parables.* On this account, viz., to lead them into a proper knowledge of God. I speak to them in parables, natural representations of spiritual truths, that they may be allured to inquire, and to find out the spirit which is hidden under the letter; *because . . . seeing* the miracles which I have wrought, they *see not,* i.e., the end for which I have wrought them; *and hearing* My doctrines, *they hear not,* so as to profit by what is spoken. *Neither do they understand;* they do not lay their hearts to it.

14. *In them is fulfilled.* "Is again fulfilled"; this proper meaning of the Greek word has been generally overlooked. The Evangelist means that as these words were fulfilled in the Jews, in the time of the prophet Isaiah, so they are now *again* fulfilled in these their posterity, who exactly copy their fathers' example. These awful words may be *again* fulfilled in us if we take not warning by the things which these disobedient people have suffered. *By hearing ye shall hear.* Jesus Christ shall be sent to you; His miracles you shall fully see; and His doctrines you shall distinctly hear—but God will not force you to receive the salvation which is offered.

15. *Heart is waxed gross.* "Is become fat"—inattentive, stupid, insensible. They hear heavily with their ears—are half asleep while the salvation of God is preached unto them. *Their eyes they have closed.* Totally and obstinately resisted the truth of God, and shut their eyes against the light. *Lest . . . they should see.* Lest they should see their lost estate, and be obliged to turn unto God and seek His salvation. His state is truly deplorable who is sick unto death and yet is afraid of being cured. The fault is here totally in the people, and not at all in that God whose name is Mercy and whose nature is love.

16. *But blessed are your eyes.* You improve the light which God has given you, and you receive an increase of heavenly wisdom by every miracle and by every sermon.

MATTHEW HENRY

the peculiar favour and blessing of God." The hearing ear and the seeing eye are God's work. They are a blessed work, which shall be fulfilled with power, when those who *now see through a glass darkly, shall see face to face*. The apostles were to teach others, and therefore were themselves blessed with the clearest discoveries of divine truth.

[2] As a transcendent blessing, desired by, but not granted to, many prophets and righteous men, *v.* 17. The Old Testament saints, who had some glimpses, some glimmerings of gospel light, coveted earnestly further discoveries. Those who know something of Christ, cannot but covet to know more. There was then, as there is still, a *glory to be revealed*; something in reserve, *that they without us should not be made perfect*, Heb. xi. 40. It is good for us to consider what means we enjoy, and what discoveries are made to us, now under the gospel, above what they had, and enjoyed, who lived under the Old Testament dispensation.

II. One of the parables which our Saviour put forth; it is that of the *sower and the seed*. Christ's parables are borrowed from common, ordinary things, from the most obvious things, that are of every day's observation, and come within the reach of the meanest capacity. Christ chose to do thus, 1. That spiritual things might hereby be made more plain the more easy to slide into our understandings. 2. That we might take occasion from those things which fall so often under our view, to meditate with delight on the things of God; and thus, when our hands are busiest about the world, we may notwithstanding that, but even with the help of that, be led to have our hearts in heaven. Thus the word of God shall talk with us, talk familiarly with us.

The parable of the sower is plain enough, *v.* 3–9. The exposition of it we have from Christ himself, who knew best what was his own meaning. "*Hear ye therefore the parable of the sower* (*v.* 18); you have heard it, but let us go over it again." *Then* only we hear the word aright, and to good purpose, when we understand what we hear; it is no hearing at all, if it be not with understanding. It is God's grace indeed that gives the understanding, but it is our duty to give our minds to understand.

Let us therefore compare the parable and the exposition.

(1) The seed sown is the word of God, here called *the word of the kingdom* (*v.* 19): the kingdom of heaven. This word is the seed sown, which seems a dead, dry thing, but all the product is virtually in it. It is *incorruptible seed* (1 Pet. i. 23).

(2) The sower that scatters the seed is our Lord Jesus Christ, either by himself, or by his ministers; see *v.* 37. Preaching to a multitude is sowing the corn; we know not where it must light; only see that it be good, that it be clean, and be sure to give it seed enough.

(3) The ground in which this seed is sown is the hearts of the children of men, which are differently qualified and disposed. Man's heart is like soil, capable of improvement, of bearing good fruit; it is a pity it should lie fallow. As it is with the earth; some sort of ground, take ever so much pains with it, and throw ever so good seed into it, yet it brings forth no fruit to any purpose; while the good soil brings forth plentifully: so it is with the hearts of men, whose different characters are here represented by four sorts of ground, of which *three* are bad, and but *one* good. The number of fruitless hearers is very great, even of those who heard Christ himself.

[1] The highway ground, *v.* 4–19. They had pathways through their cornfields (*ch.* xii. 1), and the seed that fell on them never entered, and so the birds picked it up.

First, What kind of hearers are compared to *the highway ground*; such as *hear the word and understand it not*. They take no heed to it, take no hold of it; they do not come with any design to get good. They mind not what is said, it comes in at one ear and goes out at the other, and makes no impression.

Secondly, How they come to be unprofitable hearers. The *wicked one*, that is, the devil, *cometh and catcheth away that which was sown*.—Such mindless, careless, trifling hearers are an easy prey to Satan; who, as he is the great murderer of souls, so he is the great thief of sermons. If we break not up the fallow ground, by preparing our hearts for the word, and if we cover not the seed afterwards, by meditation and prayer; if we give not a *more earnest heed to the things which we have heard*, we are as the highway ground.

[2] The *stony ground. Some fell upon stony places* (*v.* 5, 6), which represents the case of hearers who receive some good impressions of the word, but they are not lasting, *v.* 20, 21. It is possible we may be a great deal better than some others, and yet not be

JAMIESON, FAUSSET, BROWN

17. For verily I say unto you, That many prophets and righteous men have desired—rather, 'coveted'—**to see those things which ye see, and have not seen them; and to hear those things which ye hear, and have not heard them**—Not only were the disciples blessed above the blinded just spoken of, but favored above the most honored and the best that lived under the old economy, who had but glimpses of the things of the new kingdom, just sufficient to kindle in them desires not to be fulfilled to any in their day. In Luke 10:23, 24, where the same saying is repeated on the return of the Seventy—the words, instead of "many prophets and righteous men," are "many prophets *and kings*"; for several of the Old Testament saints were kings.

First Parable: THE SOWER (vss. 3-9, 18-23). This parable may be entitled, THE EFFECT OF THE WORD DEPENDENT ON THE STATE OF THE HEART. For the exposition of this parable, see on Mark 4:1-9, 14-20.

THE SOWER, THE SEED, AND THE SOIL. **Hearken; Behold, there went out a sower to sow**—What means this? **The sower soweth the word**—or, as in Luke (8:11), "Now the parable is this: The seed is *the word of God*." But who is "the sower"? This is not expressed here because if "the word of God" be the seed, every scatterer of that precious seed must be regarded as a sower. It is true that in the parable of the tares it is said, "He that soweth the good seed is the Son of man," as "He that soweth the tares is the devil" (Matt. 13:37, 38). But these are only the great unseen parties, struggling in this world for the possession of man. Each of these has his agents among men themselves; and Christ's agents in the sowing of the good seed are the *preachers* of the word. Thus, as in all the cases about to be described, the sower is the same, and the seed is the same; while the result is entirely different, the whole difference must lie in the *soils*, which mean the *different states of the human heart*. And so, the great general lesson held forth in this parable of the sower is, that however faithful the preacher, and how pure soever his message, *the effect of the preaching of the word depends upon the state of the hearer's heart*. Now follow the cases.

First Case: THE WAYSIDE. **And it came to pass, as he sowed, some fell by the wayside**—by the side of the hard path through the field, where the soil was not broken up. **and the fowls [of the air] came and devoured it up**—Not only could the seed not get beneath the surface, but "it was trodden down" (Luke 8:5), and afterwards picked up and devoured by the fowls. What means this? **And these are they by the wayside, where the word is sown; but, when they have heard . . .**—or, more fully (Matt. 13:19), "When any one heareth the word of the kingdom, and understandeth it not, then cometh the wicked one, and catcheth away that which was sown in his heart." The great truth here taught is, that *hearts all unbroken and hard are no fit soil for saving truth*. They apprehend it not (Matt. 13:19) as God's means of restoring them to Himself; it penetrates not, makes no impression, but lies loosely on the surface of the heart, till the wicked one—afraid of losing a victim by his "believing to salvation" (Luke 8:12)—finds some frivolous subject by whose greater attractions to draw off the attention, and straightway it is gone. Of how many hearers of the word is this the graphic but painful history!

Second Case: THE STONY, or rather, ROCKY GROUND. **And some fell on stony ground, where it had not much earth**—"the rocky ground"; in Matthew (13:5), "the rocky places"; in Luke, "the rock." The thing intended is, not ground with

ADAM CLARKE

17. *Many prophets and righteous men.* These lived by and died in the faith of the promised Messiah; the fullness of the time was not then come for His manifestation in the flesh.

Under the parable of the *sower*, our Lord intimates (1) That of all the multitudes then attending His ministry, few would bring forth fruit to perfection; and (2) That this would be a general case in preaching the gospel among men.

19. *When any one heareth the word of the kingdom.* Viz., the preaching of the gospel of Christ. *And understandeth it not.* Perhaps more properly, "regardeth it not," does not lay his heart to it. *The wicked one.* He who distresses and torments the soul. Mark, chap. iv. 15, calls him *Satan*, the "adversary" or "opposer," because he resists men in all their purposes of amendment, and to the utmost of his power opposes, in order to frustrate, the influences of divine grace upon the heart. In the parallel place in Luke, viii. 12, he is called *the devil*. It is worthy of remark that the three Evangelists should use each a different appellative of this mortal enemy of mankind; probably to show that the devil, with all his powers and properties, opposes everything that tends to the salvation of the soul. *Catcheth away.* Makes the utmost haste to pick up the good seed, lest it should take root in the heart. A careless, inattentive hearer is compared to the *way side*—his heart is an open road, where evil affections and foolish and hurtful desires continually pass and repass without either notice or restraint.

4. *Some seeds fell by the way side.* The hard-beaten path, where no plough had broken up the ground.

5. *Stony places.* Where there was a thin surface of earth and a rock at the bottom.

MATTHEW HENRY

so good as we should be.

First, How far they went. 1. They *hear the word*; they turn neither their backs upon it, nor a deaf ear to it. Hearing the word will never bring us to heaven. 2. They are *quick in hearing, forthwith it sprung up* (*v.* 5), it sooner appeared above ground than that which was sown in the good soil. Hypocrites often get the start of true Christians in the shows of profession, and are often too hot to hold. He *receiveth it straightway*, without trying it; swallows it without chewing, and then there can never be a good digestion. 3. They receive it with joy. There are many that are very glad to hear a good sermon, that yet do not profit by it. Many *taste the good word of God* (Heb. vi. 5), and say they find sweetness in it, but some beloved lust is *rolled under the tongue*, which it would not agree with, and so they spit it out again. 4. They *endure for awhile*. Many endure for awhile, that do not endure to the end, they did run well, but something hindered them, Gal. v. 7.

Secondly, How they fell away, so that no fruit was brought to perfection. They have *no root in themselves*, no settled, fixed principles in their judgments, no firm resolution in their wills. It is possible there may be the green blade of a profession, where yet there is not the root of grace. Where there is not a principle, though there be a profession, we cannot expect perseverance. Those who have no root will endure but awhile.

Times of trial come, and then they come to nothing. *When tribulation and persecution arise because of the word, he is offended*. After a fair gale of opportunity usually follows a storm of persecution, to try who have received the word in sincerity, and who have not. It is wisdom to prepare for such a day. When trying times come, those who have no root are soon offended; they first quarrel with their profession, and then quit it. Persecution is represented in the parable by *the scorching sun* (*v.* 6); the same sun which warms and cherishes that which was well rooted, withers and burns up that which wanted root. Trials which shake some, confirm others, Phil. i. 12. Observe how soon they fall away; a profession taken up without consideration is commonly let fall without it: "Lightly come, lightly go."

[3] The thorny ground, *Some fell among thorns*. This went further than the former, for it had root. Prosperity destroys the word in the heart, as much as persecution does; and more dangerously, because more silently: the stones spoiled the root, the thorns spoil the fruit.

Now what are these choking thorns?

The cares of this world. Care for another world would quicken the springing of this seed, but care for this world chokes it. Worldly cares are fitly compared to thorns. They are entangling, vexing, scratching, and *their end is to be burned*, Heb. vi. 8. These thorns choke the good seed. Worldly cares are great hindrances to our profiting by the word of God. They eat up that vigour of soul which should be spent in divine things. Those who *are careful and cumbered about many things*, commonly neglect *the one thing needful*.

The deceitfulness of riches. Those who, by their care and industry, have raised estates, and from whom the danger that arises from care seems to be over are apt to promise themselves that in riches which is not in them; to rely upon them, and this chokes the word as much as care did. It is not so much riches, as *the deceitfulness of riches*, that does the mischief. We put our confidence in them, and raise our expectations from them, and then it is that they choke the good seed.

[4] The good ground (*v.* 18); *Others fell into good ground*, and it is pity but that good seed should always meet with good soil, and then there is no loss; such are *good hearers of the word*, *v.* 23.

Now that which distinguished this good ground from the rest, was, in one word, fruitfulness. He does not say that this good ground has no stones in it, or no thorns; but there were none that prevailed to hinder its fruitfulness. Saints, in this world, are not perfectly free from the remains of sin; but happily freed from the reign of it.

The hearers represented by the good ground are, *First*, Intelligent hearers; they *hear the word and understand it*; they understand not only the sense and meaning of the word, but their own concern in it; they understand it as a man of business understands his business.

Secondly, Fruitful hearers, which is an evidence of their good understanding: which *also beareth fruit*. We *then* bear fruit, when we practise according to the word, and we do as we are taught.

Thirdly, Not all alike fruitful; *some a hundredfold, some sixty, some thirty*. Among fruitful Christians, some are more fruitful than others: where there

JAMIESON, FAUSSET, BROWN

stones in it which would not prevent the roots striking downward, but ground where a quite thin surface of earth covers a rock. What means this?

And these are they likewise which are sown on stony ground . . .—"Immediately" the seed in such a case "springs up"—all the quicker from the shallowness of the soil—"because it has no depth of earth." But the sun, beating on it, as quickly scorches and withers it up, "because it has no root" (vs. 6), and "lacks moisture" (Luke 8:6). The great truth here taught is that *hearts superficially impressed are apt to receive the truth with readiness, and even with joy* (Luke 8:13); *but the* heat of tribulation or persecution because of the word, or *the trials which their new profession brings upon them quickly dries up their relish for the truth, and withers all the hasty promise of fruit which they showed*. Such disappointing issues of a faithful and awakening ministry—alas, how frequent are they!

Third Case: THE THORNY GROUND. **And some fell among thorns, and the thorns grew up, and choked it, and it yielded no fruit**—This case is that of ground not thoroughly cleaned of the thistles, etc.; which, rising above the good seed, "choke" or "smother" it, excluding light and air, and drawing away the moisture and richness of the soil. Hence it "becomes unfruitful" (Matt. 13:22); it grows, but its growth is checked, and it never ripens. The evil here is neither a hard nor a shallow soil—there is *softness* enough, and *depth* enough; but it is the existence in it of what draws all the moisture and richness of the soil away to itself, and so *starves the plant*. What now are these "thorns?" **And these are they which are sown among thorns; such as hear the word, And the cares of this world, and the deceitfulness of riches, and the lusts of other things entering in**—or "the pleasures of this life" (Luke 8:14)—**choke the word, and it becometh unfruitful.** First, "The cares of this world" —anxious, unrelaxing attention to the business of this present life; second, "The deceitfulness of riches"—of those riches which are the fruit of this worldly "care"; third, "The pleasures of this life," or "the lusts of other things entering in"—the enjoyments in themselves may be innocent, which worldly prosperity enables one to indulge. These "*choke*" or "*smother*" the word; drawing off so much of one's attention, absorbing so much of one's interest, and using up so much of one's time, that only the dregs of these remain for spiritual things, and a fagged, hurried, and heartless formalism is at length all the religion of such persons. What a vivid picture is this of the mournful condition of many, especially in great commercial countries, who once promised much fruit! "They bring no fruit *to perfection*" (Luke 8:14); indicating how much *growth* there may be, in the early stages of such a case, and *promise* of fruit—which after all never *ripens*.

Fourth Case: THE GOOD GROUND. **And other fell on good ground, and did yield fruit . . .**—The goodness of this last soil consists in its qualities being precisely the reverse of the other three soils: from its softness and tenderness, receiving and cherishing the seed; from its depth, allowing it to take firm root, and not quickly losing its moisture; and from its cleanness, giving its whole vigor and sap to the plant. In such a soil the seed "brings forth fruit," in all different degrees of profusion, according to the measure in which the soil possesses those qualities. **And these are they which are sown on good ground; such as hear the word, and receive it, and bring forth fruit, some thirtyfold, some sixty, and some an hundred**—A heart soft and tender, stirred to its depths on the great things of eternity, and jealously guarded from worldly engrossments, such only is the "honest and good heart" (Luke 8:15), which "keeps," i.e., "retains" the seed of the word, and bears fruit just in proportion as it is such a heart. Such "bring forth fruit with *patience*" (vs. 15), or continuance, "enduring to the end"; in contrast with those in whom the word is "choked" and brings no

ADAM CLARKE

20. *But he that received the seed into stony places, the same is he.* That is, is a fit emblem of that man who, hearing the gospel, is affected with its beauty and excellency, and immediately receiveth it *with joy*—is glad to hear what God has done to make man happy.

21. *Yet hath he not root in himself.* His soul is not deeply convinced of its guilt and depravity; the fallow ground is not properly ploughed up, nor the rock broken. *When tribulation or persecution ariseth,* which he did not expect, "he is soon stumbled"—seeks some pretext to abandon both the doctrine and the followers of Christ.

7. *Among thorns.* Where the earth was ploughed up, but the brambles and weeds had not been cleared away.

22. *He also that received seed among the thorns.* In land ploughed, but not properly cleared and weeded. *Is he*—represents that person *that heareth the word; and the care,* rather "the anxiety" the whole system of anxious, carking cares. *The deceitfulness of riches.* Which promise peace and pleasure, but can never give them. *Choke the word.* Or "together choke the word," meaning either that these grow up together with the word, overtop, and choke it, or that these united together, viz., carking, worldly cares, with the delusive hopes and promises of riches, cause the man to abandon the great concerns of his soul and seek, in their place, what he shall eat, drink, and wherewithal he shall be clothed. Dreadful stupidity of man, thus to barter spiritual for temporal good—a heavenly inheritance for an earthly portion! The seed of the Kingdom can never produce much fruit in any heart till the thorns and thistles of vicious affections and impure desires be plucked up by the roots and burned.

8. *Good ground.* Where the earth was deep, the field well-ploughed, and the brambles and weeds all removed.

23. *Good ground.* That which had depth of mold, was well-ploughed and well-weeded. *Is he that heareth.* Who diligently attends the ministry of *the word. And understandeth it.* Lays the subject to heart, deeply weighing its nature, design, and importance. *Which also beareth fruit.* His fruitfulness being an almost necessary consequence of his thus laying the divine message to heart. Let it be observed that to *hear,* to *understand,* and to *bring forth fruit* are the three grand evidences of a genuine believer. He who does not *hear* the word of wisdom cannot *understand* what makes for his peace; and he who does not *understand* what the gospel requires him to be and to perform cannot *bring forth fruit*; and he who is not fruitful, very fruitful, cannot be a disciple of Christ, see John xv. 8; and he who is not Christ's disciple cannot enter into the kingdom of God. From the different portions of fruit produced by the good ground, a

MATTHEW HENRY

is true grace, yet there are degrees of it; all Christ's scholars are not in the same form. But if the ground be good, and the fruit right, those who bring forth but thirtyfold shall be graciously accepted of God, and it will be fruit abounding to their account.

Lastly, He closes the parable with a solemn call to attention (*v.* 9), *Who hath ears to hear, let him hear.* The sense of hearing cannot be better employed than in hearing the word of God. Some are for hearing sweet melody: there is no melody like that of the word of God; others are for hearing *new things* (Acts xvii. 21): no news like that.

Verses 24-43

I. Another reason given why Christ preached by parables, *v.* 34, 35. *All these things he spoke in parables,* because the time was not yet come for the more clear and plain discoveries of the mysteries of the kingdom. Christ tries all ways and methods to do good to the souls of men. If men will not be instructed and influenced by plain preaching, he will try them with parables. 1. The matter of Christ's preaching. The mystery of the gospel had been *hid in God*, in his councils and decrees, *from the beginning of the world.* Eph. iii. 9. 2. The manner of Christ's preaching; he preached by parables; wise sayings, but figurative, and which help to engage attention and a diligent search.

II. The parable of the *tares*, and the exposition of it.

1. The disciples' request to their Master to have this parable expounded to them (*v.* 36); *Jesus sent the multitude away;* and it is to be feared many of them went away no wiser than they came. It is sad to think how many go away from sermons with the word of grace in their ears, but not the work of grace in their hearts. Christ *went into the house*, not so much for his own repose, as for particular converse with his disciples. The disciples laid hold on the opportunity, and *they came to him.* Those who would be wise for everything else, must be wise to discern and improve their opportunities, especially of converse with Christ. We lose the benefit of many a sermon by vain and unprofitable discourse after it. See Luke xxiv. 32. Private conference would contribute much to our profiting by public preaching.

The disciples' request to their Master was, *Declare unto us the parable of the tares.* This implied an acknowledgment of their ignorance, which they were not ashamed to make. Those are rightly disposed for Christ's teaching, that are sensible of their ignorance, and sincerely desirous to be taught. Christ had expounded the foregoing parable unasked, but for the exposition of this they ask him. The first light and the first grace are given further degrees of both which must be daily prayed for.

2. The exposition Christ gave of the parable. Now the drift of the parable is, to represent to us the present and future state of the kingdom of heaven, the gospel church: Christ's care of it, the devil's enmity against it, the mixture that there is in it of good and bad in this world, and the separation between them in the other world.

Let us go over the particulars of the exposition of the parable.

(1) *He that sows the good seed is the Son of man.* Jesus Christ is the Lord of the field, *the Lord of the harvest*, the Sower of good seed. Whatever good seed there is in the world, it all comes from the hand of Christ, and is of his sowing: truths preached, graces planted, souls sanctified, are good seed, and all owing to Christ. Ministers are instruments in Christ's hand to sow good seed.

(2) *The field is the world;* the world of mankind, a large field, capable of bringing forth good fruit; the more is it to be lamented that it brings forth so much bad fruit. It is his field, and because it is his he took care to sow it with good seed.

(3) *The good seed are the children of the kingdom,* true saints. Not in profession only, as the Jews were (*ch.* viii. 12), but in sincerity. They are the good seed, precious as seed, Ps. cxxvi. 6. The seed is scattered, so are the saints; dispersed, here one and there another, though in some places thicker sown than in others.

(4) *The tares are the children of the wicked one.* They are the children of the devil. They are tares in the field of this world; they do no good, they do hurt. They are weeds in the garden, have the same rain, and sunshine, and soil, with the good plants, but are good for nothing.

(5) *The enemy that sowed the tares is the devil.* He is an enemy to the field of the world, which he endeavours to make his own, by sowing his tares in it. They were sown *while men slept.* Satan watches all opportunities. We have therefore need to *be sober, and vigilant.* The enemy, when he had sown

JAMIESON, FAUSSET, BROWN

fruit *to perfection.* The "thirtyfold" is designed to express the *lowest* degree of fruitfulness; the "hundredfold" the *highest*; and the "sixtyfold" the *intermediate* degrees of fruitfulness. As a "hundredfold," though not unexampled (Gen. 26:12), is a rare return in the natural husbandry, so the highest degrees of spiritual fruitfulness are too seldom witnessed. The closing words of this introductory parable seem designed to call attention to the *fundamental* and *universal* character of it. **And he said unto them, He that hath ears to hear, let him hear.**

34. All these things spake Jesus unto the multitude in parables; and without a parable spake he not unto them—i.e., on this occasion; refraining not only from all naked discourse, but even from all interpretation of these parables to the mixed multitude. **35. That it might be fulfilled which was spoken by the prophet, saying**—(Ps. 78:2, nearly as in LXX)— **I will open my mouth in parables . . .**—Though the Psalm seems to contain only a summary of Israelitish *history*, the Psalmist himself calls it "a parable," and "dark sayings from of old"—as containing, *underneath the history*, truths for all time, not fully brought to light till the Gospel day.

Second and Seventh Parables, or *First Pair:* THE WHEAT AND THE TARES, and THE GOOD AND BAD FISH (vss. 24-30; vss. 36-43; and vss. 47-50). The subject of both these parables—which teach the same truth, with a slight diversity of aspect—is:

THE MIXED CHARACTER OF THE KINGDOM IN ITS PRESENT STATE, AND THE FINAL ABSOLUTE SEPARATION OF THE TWO CLASSES.

The Tares and the Wheat (vss. 24-30, 36-43). **24. Another parable put he forth unto them, saying, The kingdom of heaven is likened unto a man which sowed good seed in his field**—Happily for us, these exquisite parables are, with like charming simplicity and clearness, expounded to us by the Great Preacher Himself. Accordingly, we pass to: **36-38. Then Jesus sent the multitude away, and went into the house: and his disciples came unto him, saying, Declare unto us the parable of the tares of the field, . . .**—In the parable of the Sower, "the seed is the word of God" (Luke 8:11). But here that word has been received into the heart, and has converted him that received it into a new creature, a "child of the kingdom," according to that saying of James (1:18), "Of His own will begat He us with the word of truth, that we should be a kind of first fruits of His creatures." It is worthy of notice that this vast field of the world is here said to be *Christ's own*—"His field," says the parable. (See Psalm 2:8.)

25. But while men slept, his enemy came and sowed tares among the wheat, and went his way. 38. The tares are the children of the wicked one—As this sowing could only be "while men slept," no blame seems intended, and certainly none is charged upon "the servants"; it is probably just the dress of the parable. **39. The enemy that sowed them is the devil**—emphatically "*His* enemy" (vs. 25). (See Gen. 3:15; I John 3:8.) By "tares" is meant, not what in our husbandry is so called, but some noxious plant, probably *darnel.* "The tares are the children of the wicked one"; and by their being sown "among

ADAM CLARKE

hundred, sixty, and *thirty,* we may learn that all sound believers are not equally fruitful. All hear, understand, and bring forth fruit, but not in the same degrees—occasioned partly by their situation and circumstances not allowing them such extensive opportunities of receiving and doing good; and partly by lack of mental capacity—for every mind is not equally improvable. Let it be further observed that the unfruitfulness of the different lands was not owing to bad seed or an unskillful sower—the same sower sowed the same seed in all, and with the same gracious design—but it is unfruitful in many because they are careless, inattentive, and worldly-minded.

9. *Who hath ears to hear.* Let every person who feels the necessity of being instructed in the things which concern his soul's welfare pay attention to what is spoken, and he shall become wise unto salvation.

35. *By the prophet.* As the quotation is taken from Ps. lxxviii. 2, which is attributed to Asaph, he must be the *prophet* who is meant in the text; and, indeed, he is expressly called a prophet, 1 Chron. xx. v. 2.

36. *Jesus . . . went into the house: and his disciples came.* Those who attend only to the public preaching of the gospel of God are not likely to understand fully the mysteries of the kingdom of Heaven. To understand clearly the purport of the divine message, a man must come to God by frequent, fervent, secret prayer.

24. *The kingdom of heaven.* God's method of managing the affairs of the world and the concerns of His Church. *Is likened unto a man which sowed good seed in his field.* In general, the world may be termed the field of God; and in particular, those who profess to believe in God through Christ are His field or farm, among whom God sows nothing but the pure, unadulterated word of His truth.

25. *But while men slept.* When the professors were lukewarm and the pastors indolent, *his enemy came and sowed tares,* degenerate wheat. The righteous and the wicked are often mingled in the Visible Church.

CHARLES H. SPURGEON:

Our Saviour did not mean such tares as grow in our country, but a sort of mock wheat common in the East. The evil one could not prevent the springing up of the good seed, and therefore he tried to impede its growth, and spoil its harvest by throwing in among it noxious seed. The devil cannot destroy the church, and therefore he endeavors to mar its beauty by the introduction of hypocrites. These are in many respects so like to true Christians that it is not possible to remove them without expelling genuine believers with them by mistake. Open sinners we can easily remove from the church; but not those who have the outward manners of Christians; however wrong at heart they may be, we are unable to judge them, and must let them remain.—*Spurgeon's Devotional Bible*

MATTHEW HENRY

the tares, *went his way* (*v.* 25), that it might not be known who did it. When Satan is doing the greatest mischief, he studies most to conceal himself. If the enemy sow the tares, he may even go his way, they will spring up of themselves and do hurt; whereas, when good seed is sown, it must be tended, watered, and fenced, or it will come to nothing. The tares appeared not till *the blade sprung up, and brought forth fruit, v.* 26. There is a great deal of secret wickedness in the hearts of men, which is long hid under the cloak of a plausible profession, but breaks out at last. When a trying time comes, when fruit is to be brought forth, then you will return and discern between the sincere and the hypocrite: then you may say, This is wheat, and that is tares. The servants, when they were aware of it, complained to their master (*v.* 27); *Sir, didst thou not sow good seed in thy field?* No doubt he did; considering the seed which Christ sows, we may well ask, with wonder, *Whence* should *these tares come?* It is sad to see such tares, such weeds, in the garden of the Lord; to see the good soil wasted, the good seed choked, and such a reflection cast on the name and honour of Christ. The Master was soon aware whence it was (*v.* 28); *An enemy has done this.* He does not lay the blame upon the servants; they could not help it. The ministers of Christ, that are faithful and diligent, shall not be judged of Christ, for the mixture of bad with good, hypocrites with the sincere, in the field of the church. *It must needs be that such offences will come;* and they shall not be laid to our charge, if we do our duty. The servants were very forward to have these tares rooted up. "*Wilt thou that we go* and do it presently?" The Master very wisely prevented this (*v.* 29); *Nay, lest while ye gather up the tares, ye root up also the wheat with them.* It is not possible for any man infallibly to distinguish between tares and wheat. It is possible there may be a discipline, either so mistaken in its rules, or so overnice in the application of them, as may prove vexatious to many that are truly godly and conscientious. The tares, if continued under the means of grace, may become good corn; therefore have patience with them.

(6) *The harvest is the end of the world, v.* 39. This world will have an end. At harvest all is ripe and ready to be cut down: both good and bad are ripe at the great day. At harvest every man reaps as he sowed; every man's ground, and seed, and skill, and industry, will be manifested.

(7) *The reapers are the angels.* The angels are servants to Christ, holy enemies to the wicked, and faithful friends to all the saints, and therefore fit to be thus employed.

(8) The *fire*, into which the *tares* shall then be cast.

[1] The tares will then be gathered out: *The reapers* (whose primary work it is to gather in the corn) shall be charged first to *gather out the tares.* Though good and bad are together in this world undistinguished, yet at the great day they shall be parted.

[2] They will then be *bound in bundles, v.* 30. Those who have been associates in sin, will be so in shame and sorrow.

[3] They will *be cast into a furnace of fire*; they are fit for nothing but fire. *There shall be weeping, and gnashing of teeth;* comfortless sorrow, and an incurable indignation at God.

(9) Heaven is the *barn. But gather the wheat into my barn:* so it is in the parable, *v.* 30. All God's wheat shall be lodged together in God's barn. There will be sheaves of corn, as well as bundles of tares: they will then be secured, and no longer exposed to wind and weather, sin and sorrow: no longer afar off, and at a great distance, in the field, but near, in the barn.

In the explanation of the parable, this is gloriously represented (*v.* 43); *Then shall the righteous shine forth as the sun in the kingdom of their Father.* The honour in reserve for them is, that they *shall shine forth as the sun in that kingdom.* Here they are obscure and hidden (Col. iii. 3), their beauty is eclipsed by their poverty, and the meanness of their outward condition; but then they shall shine forth as the sun from behind a dark cloud. They shall shine as the sun, the most glorious of all visible beings. Those who shine as lights in this world, that God may be glorified, shall shine as the sun in the other world, that *they* may be glorified. Our Saviour concludes, as before, with a demand of attention; *Who hath ears to hear, let him hear.*

III. Here is the parable of the *grain of mustard-seed, v.* 31, 32. The scope of this parable is to show, that the beginnings of the gospel *would be small, but that its latter end would greatly increase.*

Now concerning the work of the gospel, observe,

1. That it is commonly very weak and small at first, *like a grain of mustard-seed, which is one of*

JAMIESON, FAUSSET, BROWN

the wheat" is meant their being deposited within the territory of the visible Church. As they resemble the children of the kingdom, so they are produced, it seems, by a similar process of "sowing"—the seeds of evil being scattered and lodging in the soil of those hearts upon which falls the seed of the world. The enemy, after sowing his "tares," "went his way"—his dark work soon done, but taking time to develop its true character. **26. But when the blade was sprung up, and brought forth fruit, then appeared the tares also**—the growth in both cases running parallel, as antagonistic principles are seen to do. **27. So the servants of the householder came**—i.e., Christ's ministers—**and said unto him, Sir, didst not thou sow good seed in thy field? from whence then hath it tares?**—This well expresses the surprise, disappointment, and anxiety of Christ's faithful servants and people at the discovery of "false brethren" among the members of the Church. **28. He said unto them, An enemy hath done this**—Kind words these from a good Husbandman, honorably clearing His faithful servants of the wrong done to his field. **The servants said unto him, Wilt thou then that we go and gather them up?**—Cf. with this the question of James and John (Luke 9:54), "Lord, wilt Thou that we command fire to come down from heaven and consume" those Samaritans? In this kind of zeal there is usually a large mixture of carnal heat. (See Jas. 1:20.) **29. But he said, Nay**—"It will be done in due time, but not now, nor is it your business." **lest, while ye gather up the tares, ye root up also the wheat with them**—Nothing could more clearly or forcibly teach the difficulty of distinguishing the two classes, and the high probability that in the attempt to do so these will be confounded. **30, 39. Let both grow together**—i.e., in the visible Church. **until the harvest**—till the one have ripened for full salvation, the other for destruction. **The harvest is the end of the world**—the period of Christ's second coming, and of the judicial separation of the righteous and the wicked. Till then, no attempt is to be made to effect such separation. But to stretch this so far as to justify allowing openly scandalous persons to remain in the communion of the Church, is to wrest the teaching of this parable to other than its proper design, and go in the teeth of apostolic injunctions (I Cor. 5). **and in the time of harvest I will say to the reapers. And the reapers are the angels**—But whose angels are they? "The Son of man shall send forth HIS angels (vs. 41). Cf. I Peter 3:22, "Who is gone into heaven, and is on the right hand of God; angels and authorities and powers being made subject unto him." **Gather ye together first the tares, and bind them in bundles to burn them**—"in the fire" (vs. 40)—**but gather the wheat into my barn**—Christ, as the Judge, will separate the two classes (as in ch. 25:32). It will be observed that the tares are burned *before* the wheat is housed; in the exposition of the parable (vss. 41, 43) the same order is observed: and the same in ch. 25:46—as if, in some literal sense, "with thine eyes shalt thou behold and see the reward of the wicked" (Ps. 91:8). **41. The Son of man shall send forth his angels, and they shall gather out of his kingdom**—to which they never really belonged. They usurped their place and name and outward privileges; but "the ungodly shall not stand in the judgment, nor sinners [abide] in the congregation of the righteous" (Ps. 1:5). **all things that offend**—all those who have proved a stumbling block to others—**and them which do iniquity**—The former class, as the worst, are mentioned first. **42. And shall cast them into a**—rather, "the"—**furnace of fire: there shall be wailing and gnashing of teeth**—What terrific strength of language—the "casting" or "flinging" expressive of indignation, abhorrence, contempt (cf. Ps. 9:17; Dan. 12:2): "the furnace of fire" denoting the fierceness of the torment: the "wailing" signifying the anguish this causes; while the "gnashing of teeth" is a graphic way of expressing the despair in which its remedilessness issues (see on ch. 8:12)! **43. Then shall the righteous shine forth as the sun in the kingdom of their Father**—as if they had been under a cloud during their present association with ungodly pretenders to their character, and claimants of their privileges, and obstructors of their course. **Who hath ears to hear, let him hear**—(See on Mark 4:9).

Third and Fourth Parables, or *Second Pair:* THE MUSTARD SEED and THE LEAVEN (vss. 31-33). The subject of both these parables, as of the first pair, is the same, but under a slight diversity of aspect, namely—

THE GROWTH OF THE KINGDOM FROM THE SMALLEST BEGINNINGS TO ULTIMATE UNIVERSALITY.

ADAM CLARKE

26. *When the blade was sprung up . . . then appeared the tares also.* Satan has a shoot of iniquity for every shoot of grace; and when God revives His work, Satan revives his also. No marvel, therefore, if we find scandals arising suddenly to discredit a work of grace where God has begun to pour out His Spirit.

27. *So the servants . . . said unto him, Sir, didst not thou sow good seed?* A faithful and vigilant minister of Christ fails not to discover the evil, to lament it, and to address himself to God by prayer, in order to find out the cause of it, and to receive from Him proper information how to behave on the occasion.

28. *An enemy hath done this.* It is the interest of Satan to introduce hypocrites and wicked persons into religious societies, in order to discredit the work of God, and to favor his own designs. *Wilt thou then that we go and gather them up?* A zeal which is rash and precipitate is as much to be feared as the total lack of strict discipline.

29. *But he said, Nay.* God judges quite otherwise than men of this mixture of good and evil in the world; He knows the good which He intends to produce from it, and how far His patience towards the wicked should extend in order to their conversion, or the further sanctification of the righteous.

30. *Let both grow together.* Though every minister of God should separate from the Church of Christ every incorrigible sinner, yet he should proceed no further. The man is not to be persecuted in his body or goods because he is not sound in the faith—God tolerates him; so should men.

31. *The kingdom of heaven is like to a grain of mustard seed.* This parable is a representation of the progress of the gospel in the world, and of the growth of grace in the soul. That grace which leads the soul to the fullness of glory may begin, and often does, in a single

MATTHEW HENRY

the least of all seeds. In particular places, the first breaking out of the gospel light is but as *the dawning of the day.* Young converts are like *lambs* that must be *carried in his arms,* Isa. xl. 11.

2. That yet it is growing and coming on. *A grain of mustard-seed* is small, but however, it is seed, and has in it a disposition to grow. Gracious habits confirmed, actings quickened, and knowledge more clear, faith more confirmed, love more inflamed; here is the seed growing.

3. That it will at last come to a great degree of strength and usefulness; *when it is grown to* some maturity, *it becomes a tree.* The church is like a great tree, in which the fowls of the air do lodge; God's people have recourse to it for food and rest, shade and shelter. In particular persons, growing grace will be strong grace, and will bring much to pass. Grown Christians must covet to be useful to others, as the mustard-seed when grown is to the birds.

IV. Here is the parable of the *leaven, v.* 33.

1. *A woman took* this *leaven*; it was her work. Ministers are employed in leavening places, in leavening souls, with the gospel.

2. The leaven was *hid in three measures of meal.* The heart is, as the meal, soft and pliable; it is the tender heart that is likely to profit by the word. It is *three measures of meal,* a great quantity, for *a little leaven leaveneth the whole lump.* The leaven must be *hid in the heart.* We must lay it up, as Mary laid up the sayings of Christ, Luke ii. 51.

3. The leaven thus hid in the dough, works there. The leaven works speedily, so does the word, and yet gradually. It works silently and insensibly (Mark iv. 26), yet strongly and irresistibly. Hide but the leaven in the dough, and all the world cannot hinder it from communicating its taste and relish to it, and yet none sees how it is done, but by degrees *the whole is leavened.* Thus it was in the world. The apostles, by their preaching, hid a handful of leaven in the great mass of mankind, and it had a strange effect; it put the world into a ferment, and in a sense turned it *upside down* (Acts xvii. 6). It was thus effectual, not by outward force, and therefore not by any such force resistible and conquerable, but by *the Spirit of the Lord of hosts, who works, and none can hinder.* Thus it is in the heart. It works a change, not in the substance; the dough is the same, but in the quality. It works a universal change; it diffuses itself into all the powers and faculties of the soul. This change is such as makes the soul to partake of the nature of the word, as the dough does of the leaven. It is a word of faith and repentance, holiness and love, and these are wrought in the soul by it. When the dough is leavened, then to the oven with it; trials and afflictions commonly attend this change; but thus saints are fitted to be bread for our Master's table.

Verses 44–52

I. That of the *treasure hid in the field.* Hitherto he had compared *the kingdom of heaven* to small things. In this parable and the next he represents it as of great value in itself. It is here likened *to a treasure hid in the field,* which, if we will, we may make our own.

1. Jesus Christ is the true Treasure; in him there is an abundance of all that which is rich and useful, and if we have an interest in him, it is all our own.

2. The gospel is the field in which this treasure is hid. It is hid, not *in a garden enclosed,* but *in a field,* an open field. Whatever royal mines we find, they are all our own, if we take the right course.

3. It is a great thing to discover the treasure hid in this field, and the unspeakable value of it. The richest mines are often in grounds that appear most barren. What is the Bible more than other good books? But those who have *searched the scriptures,* so as in them to find Christ and *eternal life* (John v. 39), have discovered such a treasure in this field as makes it infinitely more valuable.

4. Those who discern this treasure in the field, and value it aright, will never be easy till they have made it their own upon any terms. He rejoices in it, though as yet the bargain be not made; he is glad there is such a bargain to be had. He resolves to *buy this field*: they who embrace gospel offers, upon gospel terms, buy this field; they make it their own, for the sake of the unseen treasure in it. And so intent he is upon it, *that he sells all to buy this field*: they who would have saving benefit by Christ, must *count everything but loss, that they may win Christ, and be found in him.*

II. That of *the pearl of price* (*v.* 45, 46).

1. All the children of men are busy, *seeking goodly pearls*: one would be rich, another would be honourable, another would be learned; but the most are imposed upon, and take up with counterfeits for pearls.

2. Jesus Christ is a *Pearl of great price*; in having him, we have enough to make us happy here and

JAMIESON, FAUSSET, BROWN

The Mustard Seed (vss. 31, 32). **31. Another parable put he forth unto them, saying, The kingdom of heaven is like to a grain of mustard seed, which a man took, and sowed in his field; 32. Which indeed is the least of all seeds**—not absolutely, but popularly and proverbially, as in Luke 17:6, "If ye had faith as a grain of mustard seed," i.e., 'never so little faith.' **but when it is grown, it is the greatest among herbs**—not absolutely, but in relation to the small size of the seed, and in warm latitudes proverbially great. **and becometh a tree, so that the birds of the air come and lodge in the branches thereof**—This is added, no doubt, to express the *amplitude* of the tree. But as this seed has a hot, fiery vigor, gives out its best virtues when bruised, and is grateful to the taste of birds, which are accordingly attracted to its branches both for shelter and food, is it straining the parable, asks TRENCH, to suppose that, besides the wonderful *growth* of His kingdom, our Lord selected this seed to illustrate further the *shelter, repose* and *blessedness* it is destined to afford to the nations of the world?

The Leaven (vs. 33). **33. Another parable spake he unto them; The kingdom of heaven is like unto leaven, which a woman took and hid in three measures of meal, till the whole was leavened**—This parable, while it teaches the same general truth as the foregoing one, holds forth, perhaps, rather the *inward* growth of the kingdom, while "the Mustard Seed" seems to point chiefly to the *outward.* It being a woman's work to knead, it seems a refinement to say that "the woman" here represents *the Church,* as the instrument of depositing the leaven. Nor does it yield much satisfaction to understand the "three measures of meal" of that threefold division of our nature into "spirit, soul, and body," alluded to in 1 Thessalonians 5:23, or of the threefold partition of the world among the three sons of Noah (Gen. 10:32), as some do. It yields more real satisfaction to see in this brief parable just the *all-penetrating* and *assimilating* quality of the Gospel, by virtue of which it will yet mould all institutions and tribes of men, and exhibit over the whole earth one "kingdom of our Lord and of His Christ."

Fifth and Sixth Parables, or *Third Pair:* THE HIDDEN TREASURE and THE PEARL OF GREAT PRICE (vss. 44-46). The subject of this last pair, as of the two former, is the same, but also under a slight diversity of aspect: namely—

THE PRICELESS VALUE OF THE BLESSINGS OF THE KINGDOM. And while the one parable represents the Kingdom as *found without seeking,* the other holds forth the Kingdom as *sought and found.*

The Hidden Treasure (vs. 44). **44. Again, the kingdom of heaven is like unto treasure hid in a field**—no uncommon thing in unsettled and half-civilized countries, even now as well as in ancient times, when there was no other way of securing it from the rapacity of neighbors or marauders. (Jer. 41:8; Job 3:21; Prov. 2:4.) **the which when a man hath found**—i.e., unexpectedly found. **he hideth, and for joy thereof**—on perceiving what a treasure he had lighted on, surpassing the worth of all he possessed. **goeth and selleth all that he hath, and buyeth that field**—in which case, by Jewish law, the treasure would become his own.

The Pearl of Great Price (vss. 45, 46). **45. Again, the kingdom of heaven is like unto a merchantman, seeking goodly pearls. 46. Who, when he had found one pearl of great price, went and sold all that he had, and bought it**—The one pearl of great price, instead of being found by accident, as in the former case, is found by one whose *business* it is to seek for such, and who finds it just

ADAM CLARKE

good desire—a wish to escape hell, or a desire to enjoy God in heaven.

32. *Which indeed is the least of all seeds.* That is, of all those seeds which produce plants, whose stems and branches, according to the saying of the botanists, are apt *arborescere,* to grow into a ligneous or *woody* substance. *Becometh a tree.* That is, it is not only the largest of plants which are produced from such small seeds, but partakes, in its substance, the close, woody texture, especially in warm climates, where we are informed it grows to an almost incredible size.

33. *The kingdom of heaven is like unto leaven.* On the nature and effects of *leaven,* see the note on Exod. xii. 8. As the property of *leaven* is to change, or assimilate to its own nature, the meal or dough with which it is mixed, so the property of the grace of Christ is to change the whole soul into its own likeness; and God intends that this principle should continue in the soul till all is leavened—till the whole bear the image of the heavenly, as it before bore the image of the earthly. Both these parables are prophetic, and were intended to show principally how, from very small beginnings, the gospel of Christ should pervade all the nations of the world and fill them with righteousness and true holiness.

44. *The kingdom of heaven is like unto treasure hid in a field.* "To a hidden treasure." We are not to imagine that the *treasure* here mentioned, and to which the gospel salvation is likened, means a pot or chest of money hidden in the field, but rather a gold or silver mine, which he who found out could not get at, or work, without turning up the field, and for this purpose he bought it. *He hideth,* i.e., "he kept secret," told the discovery to no person, till he had bought the field.

Our Lord's meaning seems to be this: *The kingdom of heaven*—the salvation provided by the gospel—*is like unto treasure*—something of inestimable worth—*hid in a field.* It is a rich mine, the veins of which run in all directions in the sacred Scriptures; therefore the field must be dug up, the records of salvation diligently and carefully turned over, and searched. *Which when a man hath found*—when a sinner is convinced that the promise of life eternal is to him, "he kept secret"—pondered the matter deeply in his heart; he examines the preciousness of the treasure, and counts the cost of purchase. *For joy thereof*—finding that this salvation is just what his needy soul requires, and what will make him presently and eternally happy, *goeth and selleth all that he hath*—renounces his sins, abandons his evil companions, and relinquishes all hope of salvation through his own righteousness; *and buyeth that field*—not merely buys the Book for the sake of the salvation it describes, but, by the Blood of the covenant, buys gold tried in the fire, white raiment, etc.; in a word, pardon and purity, which he receives from God for the sake of Jesus.

45. *A merchant man, seeking goodly pearls.* The meaning of this parable is the same with

MATTHEW HENRY

for ever.

3. A true Christian is a spiritual *merchant,* that seeks and finds this pearl of price; and, as one that is resolved to be spiritually rich, trades high: *He went and bought that pearl;* did not only bid for it, but purchased it.

4. Those who would have a saving interest in Christ, must be willing to part with all for him, leave all to follow him. A man may buy gold too dear, but not this pearl of price.

III. That of the *net cast into the sea, v.* 47–49.

1. Here is the parable itself. The world is a vast sea. The preaching of the gospel is the casting of a net into this sea, to catch something out of it. This net gathers of every kind, as large dragnets do. In the visible church there is a deal of trash and rubbish, dirt and weeds and vermin, as well as fish. There is a time coming when this net will be full, and drawn to the shore. The net is now filling; sometimes it fills faster than at other times, but still it fills. When the net is full and drawn to the shore, there shall be a separation between the good and bad that were gathered in it. The good shall be gathered into vessels, as valuable, and therefore to be carefully kept, but the bad shall be cast away. While the net is in the sea, it is not known what is in it, the fishermen themselves cannot distinguish; but they carefully draw it, and all that is in it, to the shore, for the sake of the good that is in it.

2. Here is the explanation of the latter part of the parable, the former is obvious and plain enough: but the latter part refers to that which is yet to come, and is therefore more particularly explained, *v.* 49, 50. *So shall it be at the end of the world.* We must not look for the net full of all good fish; the vessels will be so, but in the net they are mixed. (1) The distinguishing of the wicked from the righteous. (2) The doom of the wicked when they are thus severed. They shall be *cast into the furnace.*

IV. Here is the parable of the *good householder,* which is intended to rivet all the rest.

1. The occasion of it was the good proficiency which the disciples had made in learning, and their profiting by this sermon in particular. He asked them, *Have ye understood all these things?* He was ready to explain what they did not understand. It is the will of Christ, that all those who read and hear the word should understand it; for otherwise how should they get good by it? They answered him, *Yea, Lord.* When they did not understand, they asked for an explication, *v.* 36. And the exposition of that parable was a key to the rest. Good truths mutually explain and illustrate one another.

2. The scope of the parable itself was to give his approbation and commendation of their proficiency. Christ is ready to encourage willing learners in his school, though they are but weak; and to say, *Well done, well said.*

(1) He commends them as *scribes instructed unto the kingdom of heaven.* They were now learning that they might teach. Those who are to instruct others, have need to be well instructed themselves. The instruction of a gospel minister must be in the *kingdom of heaven.* Not instructed to the kingdom of heaven, he will make but a bad minister.

(2) He compares them to a good householder, who *brings forth out of his treasure things new and old*; fruits of last year's growth and this year's gathering, abundance and variety. What should be a minister's furniture, *a treasure of things new and old.* Old experiences, and new observations, all have their use; and we must not content ourselves with old discoveries, but must be adding new. Live and learn. What use he should make of this furniture; he should *bring forth*: laying up is in order to laying out, for the benefit of others. Christ himself received that he might give; so must we, and we shall have more. In bringing forth, things new and old do best together; old truths, but new methods and expressions.

Verses 53–58

We have here Christ in his own country. His own countrymen had rejected him once, yet he came to them again. Christ does not take refusers at their first word, but repeats his offers to those who have often repulsed them. He had a natural affection to his own country. His treatment this time was much the same as before, scornful and spiteful.

I. How they expressed their contempt of him. When he *taught them in their synagogue, they were astonished* that it should be so; looking upon him as unlikely to be such a teacher. Two things they upbraided him with.

1. His want of academical education. They owned that he had wisdom, and did mighty works; but the question was, Whence he had them. Note, Mean and prejudiced spirits are apt to judge of men by

JAMIESON, FAUSSET, BROWN

in the way of *searching* for such treasures. But in both cases the surpassing value of the treasure is alike recognized, and in both all is parted with for it.

The Good and Bad Fish (vss. 47-50). The object of this brief parable is the same as that of the Tares and Wheat. But as its details are fewer, so its teaching is less rich and varied. **47. Again, the kingdom of heaven is like unto a net, that was cast into the sea, and gathered of every kind**—The word here rendered "net" signifies a large *drag-net,* which draws everything after it, suffering nothing to escape, as distinguished from a *casting-net* (Mark 1:16, 18). The far-reaching efficacy of the Gospel is thus denoted. This Gospel net "gathered of every kind," meaning every variety of character. **48. Which, when it was full, they drew to shore**—for the separation will not be made till the number of the elect is accomplished. **and sat down**—expressing the deliberateness with which the judicial separation will at length be made. **and gathered the good into vessels, but cast the bad away**—lit., 'the rotten,' but here meaning, 'the foul' or 'worthless' fish: corresponding to the "tares" of the other parable. **49. So shall it be at the end of the world . . .**—(See on vs. 42). We have said that each of these two parables holds forth the same truth under a slight diversity of aspect. What is that diversity? First, the *bad,* in the former parable, are represented as vile seed sown among the wheat by the enemy of souls; in the latter, as foul fish drawn forth out of the great sea of human beings by the Gospel net itself. Both are important truths—that the Gospel draws within its pale, and into the communion of the visible Church, multitudes who are Christians only in name; and that the injury thus done to the Church on earth is to be traced to the wicked one. But further, while the former parable gives chief prominence to the present mixture of good and bad, in the latter, the prominence is given to the future separation of the two classes.

51. Jesus saith unto them—i.e., to the Twelve. He had spoken the first *four* in the hearing of the mixed multitude: the last *three* He reserved till, on the dismissal of the mixed audience, He and the Twelve were alone (vs. 36, etc.). **Have ye understood all these things? They say unto him, Yea, Lord. 52. Then said he unto them, Therefore**—or as we should say, Well, then. **every scribe**—or Christian teacher: here so called from that well-known class among the Jews. (See ch. 23:34). **which is instructed unto the kingdom of heaven**—himself taught in the mysteries of the Gospel which he has to teach to others. **is like unto a man that is an householder which bringeth forth**—"turneth" or "dealeth out." **out of his treasure**—his store of divine truth. **things new and old**—old truths in ever new forms, aspects, applications, and with ever new illustrations.

53-58. HOW JESUS WAS REGARDED BY HIS RELATIVES. (= Mark 6:1-6; Luke 4:16-30.) **53. And it came to pass, that, when Jesus had finished these parables, he departed thence. 54. And when he was come into his own country**—i.e., Nazareth; as is plain from Mark 6:1. See on John 4:43, where also the same phrase occurs. This, according to the majority of Harmonists, was the *second* of *two* visits which our Lord paid to Nazareth during His public ministry; but in our view it was His *first* and *only* visit to it. See on ch. 4:13; and for the reasons, see on Luke 4:16-30. **Whence hath this man this wisdom, and these mighty works?**—"these miracles." These surely are not like the questions of people who had asked precisely the same questions before, who from astonishment had proceeded to rage, and

ADAM CLARKE

the other; and both were spoken to impress more forcibly this great truth on the souls of the people—eternal salvation from sin and its consequences is the supreme good of man, should be sought after above all things, and prized beyond all that God has made.

47. *Is like unto a net.* A "dragnet." As this is dragged along it keeps gathering all in its way, both good and bad, small and great; and when it is brought to the shore, those which are proper for use are preserved, and those which are not are either destroyed or thrown back into the water. By the *net* may be understood the preaching of the gospel of the Kingdom, which keeps drawing men into the profession of Christianity and into the fellowship of the Visible Church of Christ.

52. *Every scribe.* Minister of Christ; *which is instructed*—taught of God; *unto the kingdom of heaven*—in the mysteries of the gospel of Christ; *out of his treasure*—his granary or storehouse; *things new and old*—a Jewish phrase for "great plenty." A small degree of knowledge is not sufficient for a preacher of the gospel. The sacred writings should be his treasure, and he should properly understand them. Some have thought that old and new things here, which imply the produce of the past and the produce of the present year, may also refer to the *old* and *new* covenants—a proper knowledge of the Old Testament Scriptures and of the doctrines of Christ as contained in the New.

54. *And when he was come into his own country.* Probably Nazareth, where His parents lived, and where He had continued till His thirtieth year, though it appears He had a lodging in Peter's house at Capernaum.

MATTHEW HENRY

their education, and to enquire more into their rise than into their reasons. "*Whence has this man these mighty works?*" If they had not been wilfully blind, they must have concluded him to be divinely assisted and commissioned, who without the help of education gave such proofs of extraordinary wisdom and power.

2. The meanness and poverty of his relations, *v.* 55, 56. They upbraid him with his father. *Is not this the carpenter's son?* What harm in that? No disparagement to him to be the son of an honest tradesman. This carpenter was *of the house of David* (Luke i. 27), *a son of David* (*ch.* i. 20); though a carpenter, yet a person of honour. Some sordid spirits regard no branch, no not the Branch from the stem of Jesse (Isa. xi. 1), if it be not the top branch. They upbraid him with his mother. Why, truly, *his mother is called Mary*, and that was a very common name, and they all knew her, and knew her to be an ordinary person; and this is turned to his reproach, as if men had nothing to be valued by but splendid titles; poor things to measure worth by. They upbraid him with his brethren, whose names they knew, good men but poor men, and therefore despised; and Christ for their sakes. His sisters too are all with us; they should therefore have loved him and respected him the more, because he was one of themselves, but therefore they despised him. They were *offended in him.*

II. See how he resented this contempt, *v.* 57, 58.

1. It did not trouble his heart. He mildly imputes it to the common humour of the children of men, to undervalue excellences that are cheap, and common, and home-bred, It is usually so. *A prophet is not without honour, save in his own country.* Prophets should have honour paid them, and commonly have; men of God are great men, and men of honour, and challenge respect. Notwithstanding this, they are commonly least regarded and reverenced in their own country. Familiarity breeds contempt.

2. It did for the present (to speak with reverence), in effect, tie his hands: *He did not many mighty works there, because of their unbelief.* Unbelief is the great obstruction to Christ's favours. So that if mighty works be not wrought in us, it is not for want of power or grace in Christ, but for want of faith in us.

JAMIESON, FAUSSET, BROWN

in their rage had hurried Him out of the synagogue, and away to the brow of the hill whereon their city was built, to thrust Him down headlong, and who had been foiled even in that object by His passing through the midst of them, and going His way. But see on Luke 4:16, etc. **55. Is not this the carpenter's son?**—In Mark (6:3) the question is, "Is not this the carpenter?" In all likelihood, our Lord, during His stay under the roof of His earthly parents, wrought along with His legal father. **is not his mother called Mary?**—'Do we not know all about His parentage? Has He not grown up in the midst of us? Are not all His relatives our own townsfolk? Whence, then, such wisdom and such miracles?' These particulars of our Lord's *human* history constitute the most valuable testimony, first, to His true and real humanity—for they prove that during all His first thirty years His townsmen had discovered nothing about Him different from other men; secondly, to the divine character of His mission—for these Nazarenes proclaim both the unparalleled character of His teaching and the reality and glory of His miracles, as transcending human ability; and thirdly, to His wonderful humility and self-denial—in that when He was such as they now saw Him to be, He yet never gave any indications of it for thirty years, because "His hour was not yet come." **And his brethren, James, and Joses, and Simon, and Judas? 56. And his sisters, are they not all with us? Whence then hath this man all these things?** An exceedingly difficult question here arises—What were these "brethren" and "sisters" to Jesus? Were they, *First,* His full brothers and sisters? or, *Secondly,* Were they His step-brothers and step-sisters, children of Joseph by a former marriage? or, *Thirdly,* Were they His cousins, according to a common way of speaking among the Jews respecting persons of collateral descent? On this subject an immense deal has been written, nor are opinions yet by any means agreed. For the second opinion there is no ground but a vague tradition, arising probably from the wish for some such explanation. The first opinion undoubtedly suits the text best in all the places where the parties are certainly referred to (ch. 12:46; and its parallels, Mark 3:31, and Luke 8:19; our present passage, and its parallels, Mark 6:3; John 2:12; 7:3, 5, 10; Acts 1:14). But, in addition to other objections, many of the best interpreters, thinking it in the last degree improbable that our Lord, when hanging on the cross, would have committed His mother to John if He had had full brothers of His own then alive, prefer the third opinion; although, on the other hand, it is not to be doubted that our Lord might have good reasons for entrusting the guardianship of His doubly widowed mother to the beloved disciple in preference even to full brothers of His own. Thus dubiously we prefer to leave this vexed question, encompassed as it is with difficulties. As to the names here mentioned, the *first* of them, "JAMES," is afterwards called "the Lord's brother" (see on Galatians 1:19), but is perhaps not to be confounded with "James the son of Alpheus," one of the Twelve, though many think their identity beyond dispute. This question also is one of considerable difficulty, and not without importance; since the James who occupies so prominent a place in the Church of Jerusalem, in the latter part of the Acts, was apparently the apostle, but is by many regarded as "the Lord's brother," while others think their identity best suits all the statements. The *second* of those here named, "JOSES" (or Joseph), must not be confounded with "Joseph called Barsabas, who was surnamed Justus" (Acts 1:23); and the *third* here named, "SIMON," is not to be confounded with Simon the Kananite or Zealot (see on ch. 10:4). These three are nowhere else mentioned in the New Testament. The *fourth* and last-named, "JUDAS," can hardly be identical with the apostle of that name—though the brothers of both were of the name of "James"—nor (unless the two be identical, was this Judas) with the author of the catholic Epistle so called. **58. And he did not many mighty works there, because of their unbelief**—"save that He laid His hands on a few sick folk, and healed them" (Mark 6:5). See on Luke 4:16-30.

ADAM CLARKE

55. *Is not his mother called Mary? and his brethren, James . . . ?* This insulting question seems to intimate that our Lord's family was a very obscure one; and that they were of small repute among their neighbors, except for their piety. It is possible that *brethren* and *sisters* may mean here "near relations," as the words are used among the Hebrews in this latitude of meaning; but I confess it does not appear to me likely. Why should the children of another family be brought in here to share a reproach which it is evident was designed for Joseph, the carpenter; Mary, his wife; Jesus, their son; and their other children?

57. *And they were offended in him.* They took offense at Him, making the meanness of His family the reason why they would not receive Him as a prophet, though they were astonished at His wisdom and at His miracles, v. 54. *A prophet is not without honour.* This seems to have been a proverbial mode of speech, generally true, but not without some exceptions.

G. CAMPBELL MORGAN:

Let us look at the King himself. If we have noticed their familiarity with Him, what shall we say of His familiarity with them? He also knew them; He had lived in their midst and observed them. He had seen them in the process of their growth, as they had seen Him in the process of His growth; and from the human side, He was more familiar with these people than with any others. But He also knew them in their deepest life, as He knows the underlying secret in every life. "He needed not that any one should bear witness concerning man; for he himself knew what was in man." And yet, notwithstanding this, He went back to them once more. He taught them, and wrought among them, and gave them new manifestations of himself; things they never could have discovered, for they were not emblazoned upon His personality. He gave them manifestations of His power in great grace; but the final thing is this, "He did not many mighty works there because of their unbelief." The popular conception of a miracle or "mighty work" is that it is something which creates belief, and we should be inclined to say that was His opportunity for a miracle just because they did not believe. But there is a matter to bear in mind perpetually. Jesus never wrought miracles to create belief. Not in a single instance in the New Testament can we find that a miracle was wrought to create belief or faith. They were all beneficent. Unbelief was the atmosphere in which He could not perform a miracle, and there was lacking at Nazareth the atmosphere in which it was possible for Him to work a miracle, a wonder, a mighty power. Belief is not merely intellectual conviction. They had intellectual conviction. They knew His wisdom, they knew His power; they were perfectly convinced of the wisdom of His speech, of the might of His work. Belief is the abandoning of the will to conviction, the handing over of the life to the thing concerning which we are convinced. If we say we believe in God the Father Almighty, and live all the week as though there were no God, we may have an intellectual conviction of His existence, but we do not believe in God. They believed intellectually certain things concerning Him, but as belief is the abandonment to conviction, when that abandonment is withheld, there can be no progress; contact is not made.—*The Gospel According to Matthew*

MATTHEW HENRY

CHAPTER 14

We have here the story of John's martyrdom.

I. The occasion of relating this story here, *v.* 1, 2.

1. The account brought to Herod of the miracles which Christ wrought. Herod the tetrarch or chief governor of Galilee *heard of the fame of Jesus.* At that time, when his countrymen slighted him, upon the account of his meanness and obscurity, he began to be famous at court. The gospel, like the sea, gets in one place what it loses in another. It should seem, Herod had not heard of him till now, and now only heard the fame of him. It is the unhappiness of the great ones of the world, that they are most out of the way of hearing the best things (1 Cor. ii. 8).

2. The construction he puts upon this (*v.* 2); *He said to his servants this is John the Baptist; he is risen from the dead.* John, while he lived, *did no miracle* (John x. 41); but Herod concludes, that, being risen from the dead, he is clothed with a greater power than he had while he was living. Observe here concerning Herod,

(1) How he was disappointed in what he intended by beheading John. He thought if he could get that troublesome fellow out of the way, he might go on in his sins, undisturbed and uncontrolled; yet no sooner is that effected, than he hears of Jesus and his disciples preaching the same pure doctrine that John preached. Ministers may be silenced, and imprisoned, and banished, and slain, but the word of God cannot be run down. Sometimes God raises up many faithful ministers out of the ashes of one.

(2) How he was filled with causeless fears, merely from the guilt of his own conscience. A guilty conscience suggests everything that is frightful, and, like a whirlpool, gathers all to itself that comes near it. Thus *the wicked flee when none pursue* (Prov. xxviii. 1).

(3) How, notwithstanding this, he was hardened in his wickedness. He does not express the least remorse or sorrow for his sin in putting him to death. The devils believe and tremble, but they never believe and repent.

II. The story itself of the imprisonment and martyrdom of John. If Christ's forerunner was thus treated, let not his followers expect to be caressed by the world.

1. John's faithfulness in reproving Herod, *v.* 3, 4. Herod was one of John's hearers (Mark vi. 20), and therefore John might be the more bold with him.

The particular sin he reproved him for was, marrying his brother Philip's wife, not his widow (that had not been so criminal), but his wife. Philip was now living, and Herod inveigled his wife from him, and kept her for his own. For this sin John reproved him: *It is not lawful for thee to have her.* He charges it upon him as a sin: It is not *lawful.* That which by the law of God is unlawful to other people, is by the same law unlawful to princes and the greatest of men. There is no prerogative, no, not for the greatest and most arbitrary kings, to break the laws of God. If princes and great men break the law of God, it is very fit they should be told of it by proper persons, and in a proper manner.

2. The imprisonment of John for his faithfulness, *v.* 3. *Herod laid hold on John, bound him, and put him in prison;* partly to gratify his own revenge, and partly to please Herodias. Faithful reproofs, if they do not profit, usually provoke. It is no new thing for God's ministers to suffer ill for doing well. Troubles abide those most that are most diligent and faithful in doing their duty.

3. The restraint that Herod lay under from further venting of his rage against John, *v.* 5.

(1) He would have put him to death. Perhaps that was not intended at first when he imprisoned him, but his revenge by degrees boiled up to that height.

(2) That which hindered him was his *fear of the multitude, because they counted John as a prophet.* It was not because he feared God (if the fear of God had been before his eyes he would not have imprisoned him), nor because he feared John, but because he feared the people; he was afraid for himself, his own safety. Tyrants have their fears. Wicked men are restrained from the most wicked practices, merely by their secular interest, and not by any regard to God. The danger of sin that appears to sense, or to fancy only, influences men more than that which appears to faith. Men fear being hanged for that which they do not fear being damned for.

4. The contrivance of bringing John to his death. Now here we have an account of his release, not by any other discharge than death, the period of all a good man's troubles.

Herodias laid the plot; her implacable revenge thirsted after John's blood, and would be satisfied with nothing less. Cross the carnal appetites, and they turn into the most barbarous passions. Herodias

JAMIESON, FAUSSET, BROWN

CHAPTER 14

Vss. 1-12. Herod Thinks Jesus a Resurrection of the Murdered Baptist—Account of His Imprisonment and Death. (=Mark 6:14-29; Luke 9:7-9.) The time of this alarm of Herod Antipas appears to have been during the mission of the Twelve, and shortly after the Baptist—who had been in prison for probably more than a year—had been cruelly put to death.

Herod's Theory of the Works of Christ (vss. 1, 2). **1. At that time Herod the tetrarch**—Herod Antipas, one of the three sons of Herod the Great, and own brother of Archelaus (ch. 2:22), who ruled as *ethnarch* over Galilee and Perea. **heard of the fame of Jesus**—"for His name was spread abroad" (Mark 6:14). **2. And said unto his servants**—his counsellors or court-ministers. **This is John the Baptist: he is risen from the dead . . .**—The murdered prophet haunted his guilty breast like a specter and seemed to him alive again and clothed with unearthly powers in the person of Jesus.

Account of the Baptist's Imprisonment and Death (vss. 3-12). For the exposition of this portion, see on Mark 6:17-29.

For Herod himself had sent forth, and laid hold upon John, and bound him in prison—in the castle of Machærus, near the southern extremity of Herod's dominions, and adjoining the Dead Sea [Josephus, *Antiquities,* 18:5, 2]. **for Herodias' sake**—She was the granddaughter of Herod the Great. **his brother Philip's wife**—and therefore the niece of both brothers. This Philip, however, was not the tetrarch of that name mentioned in Luke 3:1 (see there), but one whose distinctive name was "Herod Philip," another son of Herod the Great—who was disinherited by his father. Herod Antipas' own wife was the daughter of Aretas, king of Arabia; but he prevailed on Herodias, his half-brother Philip's wife, to forsake her husband and live with him, on condition, says Josephus (*Antiquities,* 18:5, 1), that he should put away his own wife. This involved him afterwards in war with Aretas, who totally defeated him and destroyed his army, from the effects of which he was never able to recover himself. **For John had said unto Herod, It is not lawful for thee to have thy brother's wife**—Noble fidelity! It was not lawful because Herod's wife and Herodias husband were both living; and further, because the parties were within the forbidden degrees of consanguinity (see Lev. 20:21); Herodias being the daughter of Aristobulus, the brother of both Herod and Philip [Josephus, 18:5, 4].

ADAM CLARKE

CHAPTER 14

1. *Herod the tetrarch.* This was Herod Antipas, the son of Herod the Great. The word *tetrarch* properly signifies a person who rules over the fourth part of a country; but it is taken in a more general sense by the Jewish writers, meaning sometimes simply a governor, or a king; see v. 9. The estates of Herod the Great were not, at his death, divided into four tetrarchies, but only into three. One was given by the Emperor Augustus to Archelaus; the second to Herod Antipas, the person in the text; and the third to Philip: all three, sons of Herod the Great.

3. *For Herodias' sake.* This infamous woman was the daughter of Aristobulus and Berenice, and granddaughter of Herod the Great. Her first marriage was with Herod Philip, her uncle, by whom she had Salome. Some time after, she left her husband, and lived publicly with Herod Antipas, her brother-in-law, who had been before married to the daughter of Aretas, king of Arabia Petraea. As soon as Aretas understood that Herod had determined to put away his daughter, he prepared to make war on him. The two armies met, and that of Herod was cut to pieces by the Arabians; and this, Josephus says, was supposed to be a judgment of God on him for the murder of John the Baptist. See the account in Josephus, *Antiq.,* lib. xviii, c. 7.

4. *For John said unto him, It is not lawful for thee to have her.* Here is an instance of zeal, fidelity, and courage highly worthy of imitation.

5. *He feared the multitude.* Miserable prince, who fears more to offend his people than to sin against his God by shedding innocent blood!

A. B. SIMPSON:

The story of John's murder has many fine lessons in which our present space will not permit us to dwell at length, but we cannot refrain from noticing the length to which human unbelief and sin will dare to go. The vile woman and weak man had refused the message of God through John, convicting them of their sin, and perhaps they never thought that they would go farther. But now we find their rejection of God's word leading them on to malignant hate and bloody crime. So sin pursues its terrible progression in every age, and, when we disobey God, we never know where the last step of our downward course is to land us. And what a lesson this is on worldliness. Mr. Spurgeon might well say that whenever he saw a dance, he felt a little nervous about the throat, and remembered that the first Baptist preacher lost his head on account of one.—*Christ in the Bible*

MATTHEW HENRY

contrived how to bring about the murder of John so artificially as to save Herod's credit, and so to pacify the people.

(1) The humouring of Herod by the damsel's dancing upon a birthday. In honour of the day, there must needs be, as usual, a ball at court; and, to grace the solemnity, the daughter of Herodias danced before them; who being the queen's daughter, it was more than she ordinarily condescended to do. This young lady's dancing pleased Herod.

(2) The rash and foolish promise which Herod made to this wanton girl, to give her whatsoever she would ask: and this promise confirmed with an oath, *v.* 7. It was a very extravagant obligation which Herod here entered into, and no way becoming a prudent man.

(3) The bloody demand the young lady made of John the Baptist's head, *v.* 8. She was before instructed of her mother. The case of those children is very sad, whose parents are *their counsellors to do wickedly.*

Herod having given her her commission, and Herodias her instructions, she requires John the Baptist's head in a charger. John must be beheaded then; that is the death by which he must glorify God. Yet this is not enough, the thing must be humoured too, and not only a revenge, but a fancy must be gratified; it must be *given her here in a charger,* served up in blood. It must be given her, and she will reckon it a recompence for her dancing, and desire no more.

(4) Herod's grant of this demand (*v.* 9); *The king was sorry,* at least took on him to be so, but, *for the oath's sake, he commanded it to be given her. The king was sorry.* Many a man sins with regret, that never has any true regret for his sin; sins with reluctancy, and yet goes on to sin. Here is a pretended conscience of his oath, with a specious show of honour and honesty; he must needs do something, for the oath's sake. It is a great mistake to think that a wicked oath will justify a wicked action. No man can lay himself under an obligation to sin, because God has already so strongly obliged every man against sin. Here is a real baseness in compliance with wicked companions. Herod yielded, not so much for the sake of the oath, but because it was public, and in compliment to *them that sat at meat with him;* he granted the demand that he might not seem, before them, to have broken his engagement. A point of honour goes much further with many than a point of conscience. Here is a real malice to John at the bottom of this concession, or else he might have found out evasions enough to have got clear of his promise. *He commanded it to be given her.*

(5) The execution of John, pursuant to this grant (*v.* 10); *He sent and beheaded John in the prison.* He must be beheaded with expedition, to gratify Herodias. It was done in the night. It was done in the prison, not at the usual place of execution, for fear of an uproar. A great deal of innocent blood, of martyr's blood, has thus been huddled up in corners.

Thus was that voice silenced, that burning and shining light extinguished; thus did that prophet, that Elias, of the New Testament, fall a sacrifice to the resentments of an imperious, whorish woman.

5. The disposal of the poor remains of this blessed saint and martyr.

(1) The damsel brought the head in triumph to her mother, as a trophy of the victories of her malice and revenge, *v.* 11.

(2) The disciples *buried the body,* and brought the news in tears to our Lord Jesus.

[1] *They buried the body.* There is a respect owing to the servants of Christ, not only while they live, but in their bodies and memories when they are dead.

[2] *They went and told Jesus;* not so much that he might shift for his own safety as that they might receive comfort from him, and be taken in among his disciples. When anything ails us at any time, it is our duty and privilege to make Christ acquainted with it. It will be a relief to our burthened spirits to unbosom ourselves to a friend we may be free with. When the shepherds are smitten, the sheep need not be scattered while they have the great Shepherd of the sheep to go to, who is still the same, Heb. xiii. 8, 20. Comforts otherwise highly valuable, are sometimes *therefore* taken from us, because they come between us and Christ, and are apt to carry away that love and esteem which are due to him only. It is better to be drawn to Christ by want and loss, than not to come to him at all.

Verses 13-21

This passage of story, concerning Christ's feeding *five thousand men with five loves and two fishes,* is recorded by all the four Evangelists.

JAMIESON, FAUSSET, BROWN

And when the daughter of the said Herodias—i.e.,—her daughter by her proper husband, Herod Philip: Her name was Salome [JOSEPHUS, *ibid.*].

And she said, The head of John the Baptist—Abandoned women are more shameless and heartless than men. The Baptist's fidelity marred the pleasures of Herodias, and this was too good an opportunity of getting rid of him to let slip. **I will that thou give me by and by**—rather, "at once" —**in a charger**—large, flat trencher—**the head of John the Baptist.**

And the king was exceeding sorry—With his feelings regarding John, and the truths which so told upon his conscience from that preacher's lips, and after so often and carefully saving him from his paramour's rage, it must have been very galling to find himself at length entrapped by his own rash folly. **yet for his oath's sake**—See how men of no principle, but troublesome conscience, will stick at breaking a rash oath, while yielding to the commission of the worst crimes! **and for their sakes which sat with him**—under the influence of that false shame, which could not brook being thought to be troubled with religious or moral scruples. To how many has this proved a fatal snare!

beheaded him in the prison—after, it would seem, more than twelve months' imprisonment. Blessed martyr! Dark and cheerless was the end reserved for thee: but now thou hast thy Master's benediction, "Blessed is he whosoever shall not be offended in Me" (Matt. 11:6), and hast found the life thou gavest away (Matt. 10:39). But where are they in whose skirts is found thy blood? **And brought his head in a charger, and gave it to the damsel: and the damsel gave it to her mother**—Herodias did not shed the blood of the stern reprover; she only got it done, and then gloated over it, as it streamed from the trunkless head. **And when his disciples heard of it**—i.e., the Baptist's own disciples. **they came and took up his corpse, and laid it in a tomb** —"and went and told Jesus" (Matt. 14:12). If these disciples had, up to this time, stood apart from Him, as adherents of John (Matt. 11:2), perhaps they now came to Jesus, not without some secret reflection on Him for His seeming neglect of their master; but perhaps, too, as orphans, to cast in their lot henceforth with the Lord's disciples. How Jesus felt, or what He said, on receiving this intelligence, is not recorded; but He of whom it was said, as He stood by the grave of His friend Lazarus, "Jesus wept," was not likely to receive such intelligence without deep emotion. And one reason why He might not be unwilling that a small body of John's disciples should cling to him to the last, might be to provide some attached friends who should do for his precious body, on a small scale, what was afterwards to be done for His own.

ADAM CLARKE

6. *Herod's birthday.* Either the day in which he was born or the day on which he began to reign, for both were termed birthdays. See 1 Sam. xiii. 1; Hos. vii. 5. The kings of Persia were accustomed to reject no petition that was preferred to them during the entertainment. *The daughter.* This was Salome, mentioned before.

8. *Give me here John Baptist's head in a charger.* The word *charger* formerly signified a large dish, bowl, or drinking cup; anything is better than *charger,* which never conveyed much meaning, and now conveys none.

9. *The king was sorry.* He knew John to be a righteous man. *Nevertheless for the oath's sake.* "The oaths"—he had probably sworn again and again—one sin begets many.

11. *His head was . . . given to the damsel: and she brought it to her mother.* There is no person so revengeful as a lascivious woman when reproved and blamed. A preacher of the gospel has most to fear from this quarter.

MATTHEW HENRY

I. The great resort of people to Christ, when he was retired *into a desert place*, *v.* 13. He withdrew into privacy when he heard, not of John's death, but of the thoughts Herod had concerning him, that he was *John the Baptist risen from the dead*, he departed further off, to get out of Herod's jurisdiction. In times of peril, when God opens a door of escape, it is lawful to flee for our own preservation, unless we have some special call to expose ourselves. *He departed by ship. When the people heard it, they followed him on foot* from all parts. Such an interest Christ had in the affections of the multitude, that his withdrawing from them did but draw them after him with so much the more eagerness. It should seem, there was more crowding to Christ after John's martyrdom than before. Sometimes *the sufferings of the saints* are made to further the gospel (Phil. i. 12). When Christ and his word withdraw from us, it is best for us (whatever flesh and blood may object to the contrary) to follow it. The presence of Christ and his gospel makes a desert place not only tolerable, but desirable; it makes the wilderness an Eden.

II. The tender compassion of our Lord Jesus towards those who thus followed him, *v.* 14. He went forth, and appeared publicly among them. He went forth from his retirement, when he saw people desirous to hear him, as one willing both to toil himself, and to expose himself, for the good of souls. *When he saw the multitude, he had compassion on them.* The sight of a great multitude may justly move compassion. None like Christ for pity to souls; *his compassions fail not.* He did not only pity them, but he helped them; many of them were *sick, and he, in compassion to them, healed them.* After awhile, they were all hungry, *and he, in compassion to them, fed them.*

III. The motion which the disciples made for the dismissing of the congregation, and Christ's setting aside the motion. They thought there was a good day's work done, and it was time to disperse. Christ's disciples are often more careful to show their discretion, than to show their zeal. Christ would not dismiss them hungry as they were, but orders his disciples to provide for them. Christ all along expressed more tenderness toward the people than his disciples did. See how loth Christ is to part with those who are resolved to cleave to him! *They need not depart.*

But if they be hungry, they have need to depart, for that is a necessity which has no law, therefore *give you them to eat. The Lord is for the body;* it is *the work of his hands*, it is part of his purchase; he was himself clothed with a body, that he might encourage us to depend upon him for the supply of our bodily wants. If we *seek first the kingdom of God*, and make that our chief care, we may depend upon God to *add other things to* us, as far as he sees fit.

IV. The slender provision that was made for this great multitude; and here we must compare the number of invited guests with the bill of fare.

1. The number of the guests was *five thousand of men, besides women and children.* This was a vast auditory that Christ preached to, and we have reason to think an attentive auditory; and yet, it should seem, far the greater part came to nothing; they went off and followed him no more. We would rather perceive the acceptableness of the word by the conversion, than by the crowds, of its hearers; though that also is a good sight and a good sign.

2. The bill of fare was very disproportionable to the number of the guests, but *five loaves and two fishes.* This provision the disciples carried about with them for the use of the family, now they *were retired into the desert.* Here is neither plenty, nor variety, nor dainty; a dish of fish was no rarity to them that were fishermen, but it was food convenient for the twelve; here was no wine or strong drink; fair water from the rivers in the desert was the best they had to drink with their meat; and yet out of this Christ will have the multitude fed. Those who have but a little, yet when the necessity is urgent, must relieve others out of that little, and that is the way to make it more.

V. The liberal distribution of this provision among the multitude (*v.* 18, 19); *Bring them hither to me.* Note, The way to have our creature-comforts, comforts indeed to us, is to bring them to Christ. That is likely to prosper and do well with us, which we put into the hands of our Lord Jesus, that he may dispose of it as he pleases, and that we may take it back from his hand, and then it will be doubly sweet to us.

1. The seating of the guests (*v.* 19); *He commanded them to sit down.* But what shall we do for chairs for them all? Let them *sit down on the grass.* Here is not so much as a cloth spread, no plates or napkins laid, no knives or forks, nor so much as a bench to sit down on; but *he commanded them to sit down*

JAMIESON, FAUSSET, BROWN

12-21. HEARING OF THE BAPTIST'S DEATH, JESUS CROSSES THE LAKE WITH TWELVE AND MIRACULOUSLY FEEDS FIVE THOUSAND. (= Mark 6:30-44; Luke 9: 10-17; John 6:1-14.) For the exposition of this section—one of the very few where all the four Evangelists run parallel—see on Mark 6:30-44. Observe the various reasons He had for crossing to the other side. First, Matthew (14:13) says, that "when Jesus heard" of the murder of His faithful forerunner—from those attached disciples of his who had taken up his body and laid it in a sepulchre (see on vs. 29)—"He departed by ship into a desert place apart"; either to avoid some apprehended consequences to Himself, arising from the Baptist's death (Matt. 10:23), or more probably to be able to indulge in those feelings which that affecting event had doubtless awakened, and to which the bustle of the multitude around Him was very unfavorable. Next, since He must have heard the report of the Twelve with the deepest interest, and probably with something of the emotion which He experienced on the return of the Seventy (see on Luke 10:17-22), He sought privacy for undisturbed reflection on this begun preaching and progress of His kingdom. Once more, He was wearied with the multitude of "comers and goers"—depriving Him even of leisure enough to take His food—and wanted *rest:* "Come ye yourselves apart into a desert place, and rest a while . . . ." Under the combined influence of all these considerations, our Lord sought this change.

was moved with compassion toward them, because they were as sheep not having a shepherd—At the sight of the multitudes who had followed Him by land and even got before Him, He was so moved, as was His wont in such cases, with compassion, because they were like shepherdless sheep, as to forego both privacy and rest that He might minister to them. Here we have an important piece of information from the Fourth Evangelist (John 6:4), "And the passover, a feast of the Jews, was nigh"—rather, "Now the passover, the feast of the Jews, was nigh." This accounts for the multitudes that now crowded around Him. They were on their way to keep that festival at Jerusalem. But Jesus did not go up to this festival, as John expressly tells us, (ch. 7:1)—remaining in Galilee, because the ruling Jews sought to kill Him.

Send them away, that they may go into the country round about, and into the villages, and buy themselves bread: for they have nothing to eat—John tells us (6:5, 6) that "Jesus said to Philip, Whence shall we buy bread, that these may eat? (And this He said to prove him: for He Himself knew what He would do.)" The subject may have been introduced by some remark of the disciples; but the precise order and form of what was said by each can hardly be gathered with precision, nor is it of any importance. **He answered and said unto them**—"They need not depart" (Matt. 14:10). **Give ye them to eat**—doubtless said to prepare them for what was to follow.

Five, and two fishes—John is more precise and full: "One of His disciples, Andrew, Simon Peter's brother, saith unto Him, There is a lad here which hath five barley loaves and two small fishes: but what are they among so many?" (John 6:8, 9.) Probably this was the whole stock of provisions then at the command of the disciples —no more than enough for one meal to them—and entrusted for the time to this lad. "He said, Bring them hither to me" (Matthew 14:18).

And he commanded them to make all sit down by companies upon the green grass—or "green hay"; the rank grass of those bushy wastes. For, as John (6:10) notes, "there was much grass in the place."

ADAM CLARKE

13. *When Jesus heard of it, he departed thence.* Had the blessed Jesus continued in that place, it is probable the hand of this impure female murderer would have been stretched out against Him also. He withdrew therefore, not through fear, but to teach His messengers rather to yield to the storm than expose themselves to destruction, where, from circumstances, the case is evidently hopeless. *The people . . . followed him on foot.* Or "by land," which is a common acceptation of the word in the best Greek writers.

14. *Jesus . . . was moved with compassion.* He was moved with "tender compassion," so I think the word should in general be translated.

15. *Send the multitude away, that they may go . . . and buy.* The disciples of Christ are solicitous for the people's temporal as well as spiritual welfare; and he is not worthy to be called a minister of Christ who does not endeavor to promote both to the uttermost of his power.

16. *They need not depart.* He that seeks first the kingdom of Heaven is sure to have every temporal requisite.

17. *We have here but five loaves, and two fishes.* When we are deeply conscious of our own necessities, we shall be led to depend on Jesus with a firmer faith. God often permits His servants to be brought low, that they may have repeated opportunities of proving the kindness and mercy of their gracious Lord and Master.

MATTHEW HENRY

on the grass. By doing everything thus, without any pomp or splendour, he plainly showed *that his kingdom was not of this world.*

2. The craving of a blessing. He himself *looked up to heaven, and blessed, and gave thanks*; he praised God for the provision they had, and prayed to God to bless it to them. Herein he has taught us that good duty of craving a blessing and giving thanks at our meals: God's good creatures must be *received with thanksgiving.* When Christ *blessed, he looked up to heaven,* to teach us, in prayer, to eye God as a *Father in heaven*; and when we receive our creature-comforts to look thitherward, as taking them from God's hand, and depending on him for a blessing.

3. The carving of the meat. The Master of the feast was himself head-carver, for *he brake, and gave the loaves to the disciples, and the disciples to the multitude.* Ministers can never fill the people's hearts, unless Christ first fill their hands: and what he has given to the disciples, they must give to the multitude. And, blessed be God, be the multitude ever so great, there is enough for all, enough for each.

4. The increase of the meat. Here is no mention of any word that Christ spoke, by which the food was multiplied; the purposes and intentions of his mind and will shall take effect, though they be not spoken out: but this is observable, that the meat was multiplied, not in the heap at first, but in the distribution of it. Thus grace grows by being acted, and, while other things perish in the using, spiritual gifts increase in the using. Thus *there is that scattereth, and yet increaseth.*

VI. The plentiful satisfaction of all the guests with this provision.

1. There was enough: *They did all eat, and were filled.* Those whom Christ feeds, he fills. As there was enough for all, *they did all eat,* so there was enough for each, *they were filled*; though there was but a little, there was enough, and that is as good as a feast. The blessing of God can make a little go a great way.

2. There was to spare: *They took up of the fragments that remained, twelve baskets full,* one basket for each apostle: thus what they gave they had again, and a great deal more with it. This was to show that the provision Christ makes for those who are his is not bare and scanty, but rich and plenteous; an overflowing fulness.

It is the same divine power which multiplies *the seed sown in the ground* every year, and makes *the earth yield her increase*; so that what was brought out by handfuls, is brought home in sheaves. *This is the Lord's doing.*

Verses 22-33

We have here the story of another miracle which Christ wrought for the relief of his friends and followers, his *walking upon the water to his disciples.*

I. Christ's dismissing of his disciples and *the multitude,* after he had fed them miraculously. He *constrained his disciples to get into a ship, and to go before him unto the other side, v.* 22. St. John gives a particular reason for the hasty breaking up of this assembly, because the people were so affected with the miracle of the loaves, that they were about *to take him by force, and make him a king* (John vi. 15).

1. Christ sent the people away. He sent them away with a blessing, with some parting words of caution, counsel, and comfort.

2. He *constrained the disciples to go into a ship* first, for till they were gone the people would not stir. The disciples were loth to go, and would not have gone, if he had not *constrained* them.

II. Christ's retirement hereupon (*v.* 23); *He went up into a mountain apart to pray.* Observe here,

1. That he was alone; *he went apart into a solitary place, and was there all alone.* He chose sometimes to be alone, to set us an example. Those are not Christ's followers that do not care for being alone; that cannot enjoy themselves in solitude, when they have none else to converse with, none else to enjoy, but God and their own hearts.

2. That he was alone at prayer; that was his business in this solitude, to pray. Christ has herein set before us an example of secret prayer, and the performance of it secretly, according to the rule he gave, *ch.* vi. 6. When the disciples went to sea, their Master went to prayer.

3. That he was long alone; *there he was when the evening was come,* and, for aught that appears, there he was till towards morning, *the fourth watch of the night. The night* came on, and it was a stormy tempestuous night, yet he continued *instant in prayer.* It is good when we find our hearts enlarged, to continue long in secret prayer.

III. The condition that the poor disciples were in at this time: *Their ship was now in the midst of the*

JAMIESON, FAUSSET, BROWN

And when he had taken the five loaves and the two fishes, he looked up to heaven—Thus would the most distant of them see distinctly what He was doing. **and blessed**—John says, "And when he had given thanks." The sense is the same. This thanksgiving for the meal, and benediction of it as the food of thousands, was the crisis of the miracle. **and brake the loaves, and gave them to his disciples to set before them**—thus virtually holding forth these men as His future ministers.

And they did all eat, and were filled—All the four Evangelists mention this: and John (6:11) adds, "and likewise of the fishes, as much as they would"—to show that vast as was the multitude, and scanty the provisions, the meal to each and all of them was a plentiful one. "When they were filled, He said unto His disciples, Gather up the fragments that remain, that nothing be lost" (John 6:12). This was designed to bring out the whole extent of the miracle. **And they took up twelve baskets full of the fragments, and of the fishes**—"Therefore (says John 6:13), they gathered them together, and filled twelve baskets with the fragments of the five barley loaves, which remained over and above unto them that had eaten." The article here rendered "baskets" in all the four narratives was part of the luggage taken by Jews on a journey—to carry, it is said, both their provisions and hay to sleep on, that they might not have to depend on Gentiles, and so run the risk of ceremonial pollution. In this we have a striking corroboration of the truth of the four narratives. Internal evidence renders it clear, we think, that the first three Evangelists wrote independently of each other, though the fourth must have seen all the others. But here, each of the first three Evangelists uses the same word to express the apparently insignificant circumstance that the baskets employed to gather up the fragments were of the kind which even the Roman satirist, JUVENAL, knew by the name of *cophinus,* while in both the narratives of the feeding of the Four Thousand the baskets used are expressly said to have been of the kind called *spuris.* (See on ch. 8:19, 20.) **And they that did eat of the loaves were about five thousand men** —"besides women and children" (Matt. 14:21). Of these, however, there would probably not be many; as only the males were obliged to go to the approaching festival.

22-36. JESUS CROSSES TO THE WESTERN SIDE OF THE LAKE, WALKING ON THE SEA—INCIDENTS ON LANDING. (= Mark 6:45; John 6:15-24.) For the exposition, see on John 6:15-24.

And straightway he constrained his disciples to get into the ship, and to go to the other side before—Him—**unto Bethsaida** —Bethsaida of Galilee (John 12:21). John says they "went over the sea towards Capernaum"—the wind, probably, occasioning this slight deviation from the direction of Bethsaida. **while he sent away the people**—"the multitude." His object in this was to put an end to the misdirected excitement in His favor (John 6:15), into which the disciples themselves may have been somewhat drawn. The word "constrained" implies reluctance on their part, perhaps from unwillingness to part with their Master and embark at night, leaving Him alone on the mountain. **And when he had sent them away, he departed into a mountain to pray**—thus at length getting that privacy and rest which He had vainly sought during the earlier part of the day; opportunity also to pour out His soul in connection with the extraordinary excitement in His favor that evening—which appears to have marked the zenith of His reputation, for it began to decline the very next day; and a place whence He might watch the disciples on the lake, pray for them in their extremity, and observe the right time for coming to them, in a new manifestation of His glory, on the sea. **And when even was come**—the later evening (see on vs. 35). It had come even when the disciples embarked (Matt. 14:23; John 6:16). **the ship was in the midst of the sea, and he alone on the land**—John says (6:17), "It was now dark, and Jesus was not come to them." Perhaps they made no great effort to push across at first, having a lingering hope that their Master would yet join them, and so allowed the darkness to come on. "And the sea arose" (adds the beloved disciple, 6: 18), "by reason of a great wind that blew."

ADAM CLARKE

19. *And took the five loaves.* This was the act of the father of a family among the Jews—his business it was to take the bread into his hands, and render thanks to God, before any of the family was permitted to taste of it. *Looking up to heaven.* To teach us to acknowledge God as the Supreme Good, and Fountain of all excellence. *He blessed.* The word "God" should, I think, be rather inserted here than the word "them," because it does not appear that it was the loaves which Christ blessed, but that God who had provided them; and this indeed was the Jewish custom, not to bless the food, but the God who gave it. However, there are others who believe the loaves are meant, and that He blessed them in order to multiply them. *And brake.* The Jews made their bread broad and thin like cakes, and to divide such, being very brittle, there was no need of a knife.

20. *They did all eat, and were filled.* Here was an incontestable miracle—5,000 men, besides women and children, fed with 5 cakes and 2 fishes! But did not this creation of bread prove the unlimited power of Jesus? Undoubtedly; and nothing less than eternal power and Godhead could have effected it. *They took up . . . twelve baskets.* It was customary for many of the Jews to carry a basket with them at all times, and Wakefield's conjecture here is very reasonable: "By the number here particularized, it should seem that each apostle filled his own bread basket." The simple reason why the Jews carried baskets with them appears to be this: When they went into Gentile countries, they carried their own provision with them, as they were afraid of being polluted by partaking of the meat of heathens.

22. *Jesus constrained his disciples to get into a ship.* Either they were afraid to return into the jurisdiction of Herod or they were unwilling to embark without their Lord and Protector, and would not enter their boat till Christ had commanded them to embark. *Unto the other side.* Towards Capernaum, v. 34; John vi. 16-17; or Bethsaida—see on Mark vi. 45.

23. *He went up into a mountain apart, to pray.* Some make this part of our Lord's conduct emblematic of the spirit and practice of prayer, and observe that the proper dispositions and circumstances for praying well are: (1) retirement from the world, (2) elevation of the heart to God, (3) solitude, and (4) the silence and quiet of the night. It is certain in this also Christ has left us an example that we should follow His steps.

MATTHEW HENRY

sea, tossed with waves, v. 24.

1. They were got into the midst of the sea when the storm rose. We may have fair weather at the beginning of our voyage, and yet meet with storms before we arrive at the port we are bound for. After a long calm expect some storm or other.

2. The disciples were now where Christ sent them, and yet met with this storm. It is no new thing for Christ's disciples to meet with storms in the way of their duty, and to be sent to sea then when their Master foresees a storm; but let them not take it unkindly. Christ designs hereby to manifest himself with the more wonderful grace to them and for them.

3. It was a great discouragement to them now that they had not Christ with them, as they had formerly when they were in a storm. Thus Christ used his disciples first to less difficulties, and then to greater, and so trains them up by degrees to live *by faith*.

4. Though *the wind was contrary*, and they were tossed with waves, yet being ordered by their Master *to the other side*, they did not tack about and come back again, but made the best of their way forward. Though troubles and difficulties may disturb us in our duty, they must not drive us from it.

IV. Christ's approach to them in this condition (*v.* 25); and in this we have an instance,

1. Of his goodness, that he went unto them, as one that took cognizance of their case, and was under a concern about them. The extremity of the church and people of God is Christ's opportunity to visit them and appear for them.

2. Of his power, that he *went unto them, walking on the sea*. This is a great instance of Christ's sovereign dominion over all the creatures. We need not enquire how this was done. It is sufficient that it proves his divine power. Christ can take what way he pleases to save his people.

V. Here is an account of what passed between Christ and his distressed friends upon his approach.

1. Between him and all the disciples. We are here told,

(1) How their fears were raised (*v.* 26); *When they saw him walking on the sea, they were troubled, saying, It is a spirit. It is an apparition*; so it might much better be rendered. These disciples said, *It is a spirit;* when they should have said, *It is the Lord;* it can be no other. Even the appearances and approaches of deliverance are sometimes the occasions of trouble and perplexity to God's people, who are sometimes most frightened when they are least hurt. The appearance of a spirit, or the fancy of it, cannot but be frightful. The more acquaintance we have with God, the Father of spirits, and the more careful we are to keep ourselves in his love, the better able we shall be to deal with those fears. A little thing frightens us in a storm. Most of our danger from outward troubles arises from the occasion they give for inward trouble.

(2) How these fears were silenced, *v.* 27. He delayed his succour for some time; but he hastened his succour against their fright, as much the more dangerous; he straightway laid that storm with his word, *Be of good cheer; it is I; be not afraid.* He rectified their mistake, by making himself known to them, *It is I.* He does not name himself to these disciples, it was enough to say, *It is I;* they *knew his voice, as his sheep* (John x. 4), as Mary Magdalene, John xx. 16. It was enough to make them easy, to understand who it was they saw. A right knowledge opens the door to true comfort, especially the knowledge of Christ. He encouraged them against their fright; *It is I*, and therefore, *Be of good cheer*. If Christ's disciples be not cheerful in a storm, it is their own fault, he would have them so. *Be not afraid;* 1. "Be not afraid of me, now that you know it is I." Christ will not be a terror to those to whom he manifests himself; when they come to understand him aright, the terror will be over. 2. "*Be not afraid* of the tempest, of the winds and waves; fear them not, while I am so near you. I am he that concerns himself for you, and will not stand by and see you perish." Nothing needs be a terror to those that have Christ near them, and know he is theirs; no, not death itself.

2. Between him and Peter, *v.* 28–31.

(1) Peter's courage, and Christ's countenancing that.

[1] It was very bold in Peter, that he would venture to come to Christ *upon the water* (*v.* 28); *Lord, if it be thou, bid me come unto thee.* Courage was Peter's master grace; and that made him so forward above the rest to express his love to Christ, though others perhaps loved him as well.

It is an instance of Peter's affection to Christ, that he desired to come to him. When he sees Christ he is impatient to be with him. He does not say,

JAMIESON, FAUSSET, BROWN

And he saw them toiling in rowing; for the wind was contrary unto them—putting forth all their strength to buffet the waves and bear on against a head wind, but to little effect. He "saw" this from His mountain-top, and through the darkness of the night, for His heart was all with them: yet would He not go to their relief till His own time came. **and about the fourth watch of the night**—The Jews, who used to divide the night into three watches, latterly adopted the Roman division into four watches, as here. So that, at the rate of three hours to each, the fourth watch, reckoning from six P.M., would be three o'clock in the morning. "So when they had rowed about five and twenty or thirty furlongs" (John 6:19)—rather more than halfway across. The lake is about seven miles broad at its widest part. So that in eight or nine hours they had only made some three and a half miles. By this time, therefore, they must have been in a state of exhaustion and despondency bordering on despair; and now at length, having tried them long enough—

he cometh unto them, walking upon the sea—"and draweth nigh unto the ship" (John 6:19). **and would have passed by them**—but only in the sense of Luke 24:28; Genesis 32:26; cf. Genesis 18:3, 5; 42:7. **But when they saw him walking upon the sea, they supposed it had been a spirit, and cried out**—"for fear" (Matt. 14:26). He would appear to them at first like a dark moving speck upon the waters; then as a human figure; but in the dark tempestuous sky, and not dreaming that it could be their Lord, they take it for a spirit. Cf. Luke 24:37. **For they all saw him, and were troubled. And immediately he talked with them, and saith unto them, Be of good cheer: It is I; be not afraid**—There is something in these two little words—given by Matthew, Mark and John—"'Tis I," which from the mouth that spake it and the circumstances in which it was uttered, passes the power of language to express. Here were they in the midst of a raging sea, their little bark the sport of the elements, and with just enough of light to descry an object on the waters which only aggravated their fears. But Jesus deems it enough to dispel all apprehension to let them know that *He was there.* From other lips that "I am" would have merely meant that the person speaking was such a one and not another person. That, surely, would have done little to calm the fears of men expecting every minute, it may be, to go to the bottom. But spoken by One who at that moment was "treading upon the waves of the sea," and was about to hush the raging elements with His word, what was it but the Voice which cried of old in the ears of Israel, even from the days of Moses, "I AM"; "I, EVEN I, AM HE!" Cf. John 18:5, 6; 8:58. Now, that Word is "made flesh, and dwells among us," uttering itself from beside us in dear familiar tones—"It is the Voice of my Beloved!" How far was this apprehended by these frightened disciples? There was one, we know, in the boat who outstripped all the rest in susceptibility to such sublime appeals. It was not the deep-toned writer of the Fourth Gospel, who, though he lived to soar beyond all the apostles, was as yet too young for prominence, and all unripe. It was Simon-Barjonas. Here follows a very remarkable and instructive episode, recorded by Matthew alone:

Peter Ventures to Walk upon the Sea (Matt. 14:28-32). 28. "And Peter answered Him, and said, Lord, If it be Thou, bid me come unto Thee on the water"; not "*let* me," but "give me the word of *command*"—"command," or "order me to come unto Thee upon the waters."

ADAM CLARKE

24. *Tossed with waves.* "Grievously agitated."

25. *The fourth watch.* Anciently the Jews divided the night into three watches, consisting of four hours each. The first watch is mentioned, Lam. ii. 19; the second, Judg. vii. 19; and the third, Exod. xiv. 24; but a fourth watch is not mentioned in any part of the Old Testament. This division the Romans had introduced in Judea, as also the custom of dividing the day into twelve hours; see John xi. 9. The first watch began at six o'clock in the evening, and continued till nine; the second began at nine, and continued till twelve; the third began at twelve, and continued till three the next morning, and the fourth began at three, and continued till six. It was, therefore, between the hours of three and six in the morning that Jesus made His appearance to His disciples.

Walking on the sea. Thus suspending the laws of gravitation was a proper manifestation of unlimited power. Jesus did this by His own power; therefore Jesus showed forth His Godhead.

27. *It is I; be not afraid.* Nothing but this voice of Christ could, in such circumstances, have given courage and comfort to His disciples. Those who are grievously tossed with difficulties and temptations require a similar manifestation of His power and goodness. When He proclaims himself in the soul, all sorrow and fear and sin are at an end.

MATTHEW HENRY

Bid me walk on the waters, as desiring it for the miracle sake; but, *Bid me come to thee*, as desiring it for Christ's sake. True love will break through fire and water to come to Christ. Those that would have benefit by Christ as a Saviour, must thus by faith come to him. When, for a small moment, Christ has forsaken his people, his returns are welcome and most affectionately embraced.

It is an instance of Peter's caution and due observance of the will of Christ, that he would not come without a warrant. Not, "If it be thou, I will come"; but *If it be thou, bid me come*. The boldest spirits must wait for a call to hazardous enterprises, and we must not rashly and presumptuously thrust ourselves upon them.

It is an instance of Peter's faith and resolution, that he ventured upon the water when Christ bid him. What difficulty or danger could stand before such a faith and such a zeal?

[2] It was very kind in Christ, that he was pleased to own him in it, *v.* 29. Christ knew that it came from a sincere and zealous affection to him, and graciously accepted of it. Christ is well pleased with the expressions of his people's love, though mixed with manifold infirmities, and makes the best of them.

He bid him *come*. When Peter asked a sign, he had it, because he did it with a resolution to trust Christ.

He bore him out when he did come; *Peter walked upon the water*. The communion of true believers with Christ is represented by their being *quickened with him, raised up with him*. Now, methinks, it is represented in this story by their *walking with him on the water*. Through the strength of Christ we are borne up above the world, kept from sinking into it, from being overwhelmed by it, obtain a victory over it (1 John v. 4).

He walked upon the water, not for diversion or ostentation, but to go to Jesus. Nor can we ever come to Jesus, unless we be upheld by his power; which power we must depend upon, as Peter when he *walked upon the water*: and there is no danger of sinking while *underneath are the everlasting arms*.

(2) Here is Peter's cowardice, and Christ's reproving him and succouring him. Christ bid him come, not only that he might walk upon the water, and so know Christ's power, but that he might sink, and so know his own weakness. Peter's great fear (*v.* 30); *He was afraid.* The strongest faith and the greatest courage have a mixture of fear. Those that can say, *Lord, I believe*; must say, *Lord, help my unbelief.* Peter was very stout at first, but afterwards his heart failed him. The lengthening out of a trial discovers the weakness of faith.

The cause of this fear; *He saw the wind boisterous.* While Peter kept his eye fixed upon Christ, and upon his word and power, he *walked upon the water* well enough; but when he took notice withal of the danger he was in, then he feared. Looking at difficulties with an eye of sense more than at precepts and promises with an eye of faith is at the bottom of all our inordinate fears. Peter, *when he saw the wind boisterous*, should have remembered what he had seen (*ch.* viii. 27), when the winds and the sea obeyed Christ.

The effect of this fear; *He began to sink.* While faith kept up, he kept above water: but when faith staggered, *he began to sink*. The sinking of our spirits is owing to the weakness of our faith; we are upheld (but it is as we are saved) *through faith* (1 Pet. i. 5). It was Christ's great mercy to him, that, upon the failing of his faith, he did not leave him to sink outright, to sink to the *bottom as a stone* (Exod. xv. 5), but gave him time to cry, *Lord, save me.* Such is the care of Christ concerning true believers; though weak, they do but begin to sink!

The remedy he had recourse to in this distress, the old, tried, approved remedy, and that was prayer: he cried, *Lord, save me.* 1. The manner of his praying; it is fervent and importunate; *He cried.* When faith is weak, prayer should be strong. 2. The matter of his prayer was pertinent and to the purpose; *He cried, Lord, save me.* Those that would be saved, must not only *come* to him, but *cry* to him for salvation; but we are never brought to this, till we find ourselves sinking; sense of need will drive us to him.

Christ's great favour to Peter, in this fright.

He saved him. For immediately *he stretched forth his hand, and caught him.* Note, Christ's time to save is, when we sink: he helps at a dead lift. Christ's hand is still stretched out to all believers, to keep them from sinking. Never fear, he will hold his own.

He rebuked him; for as many as he loves and saves, he reproves and chides; *O thou of little faith, wherefore didst thou doubt?* Faith may be true, and yet

ALEXANDER MACLAREN:

Let us take the warning from this venturesomeness of a generous, impulsive, enthusiastic religious nature, and remember that the most genuine faith and religious emotion need to be sobered and steadied by reflection, and by searching into our own motives, before we venture upon the water, howsoever much we may wish to go there. Make very sure that your zeal for the Lord has an element of sober permanence in it, and that it is the result, not of a mere transitory feeling, but of a steady, settled purpose. And do not push yourself voluntarily into places of peril or of difficulty, where the fighting is hard and the fire heavy, unless you have reasonable grounds for believing that you can stand the strain. Bring quiet, sober reason into the loftiest and loveliest enthusiasm of your faith, and then there will be something in it that will live through storm, and walk the water with unwetted and unsinking foot.—*Expositions of Holy Scripture*

JAMIESON, FAUSSET, BROWN

29. "And He said, Come." Sublime word, issuing from One conscious of power over the raging element, to bid it serve both Himself and whomsoever else He pleased! "And when Peter was come down out of the ship, he walked upon the water"—"waters"—"to come to Jesus." "It was a bold spirit," says Bishop Hall, "that could wish it; more bold that could act it—not fearing either the softness or the roughness of that uncouth passage."

30. "But when he saw the wind boisterous, he was afraid; and beginning to sink, he cried, saying, Lord, save me." The wind was as boisterous before, but Peter "*saw*" it not, seeing only the power of Christ, in the lively exercise of faith. Now he "*sees*" the fury of the elements, and immediately the power of Christ to bear him up fades before his view, and this makes him "afraid"—as how could he be otherwise, without any *felt* power to keep him up? He then "begins to sink"; and finally, conscious that his experiment had failed, he casts himself, in a sort of desperate confidence, upon his "Lord" for deliverance!

31. "And immediately Jesus stretched forth His hand, and caught him, and said unto him, O thou of little faith, wherefore didst thou doubt?" *This rebuke was not administered while Peter was sinking, nor till Christ had him by the hand:* first reinvigorating his faith, and then with it enabling him again to walk upon the crested wave. Useless else had been this loving reproof, which owns the *faith* that had ventured on the deep upon the bare

ADAM CLARKE

29. *Peter . . . walked on the water.* However impossible the thing commanded by Christ may appear, it is certain He will give power to accomplish it to those who receive His word by faith; but we must take care never to put Christ's power to the proof for the gratification of a vain curiosity, or even for the strengthening of our faith, when the ordinary means for doing that are within our reach.

30. *When he saw the wind boisterous, he was afraid.* It was by faith in the power of Christ he was upheld; when that faith failed by which the laws of gravitation were suspended, no wonder that those laws returned to their wonted action, and that he began to sink. It was not the violence of the winds nor the raging of the waves which endangered his life, but his littleness of faith.

31. *Jesus stretched forth his hand.* Every moment we stand in need of Christ. While we stand, we are upheld by His power only; and when we are falling, or have fallen, we can be saved only by His mercy.

MATTHEW HENRY | JAMIESON, FAUSSET, BROWN | ADAM CLARKE

weak; at first, like a grain of mustard-seed. Peter had faith enough to bring him upon the water, yet, because not enough to carry him through, Christ tells him he had but *little*. Our discouraging doubts and fears are all owing to the weakness of our faith: *therefore* we *doubt*, because we are but *of little faith*. Could we but believe more, we should doubt less. It is true, he doth not cast off weak believers, but it is as true, that he is not pleased with weak faith, no, not in those that are nearest to him. *Wherefore didst thou doubt?* What reason was there for it? There is no good reason why Christ's disciples should be of a doubtful mind, no, not in a stormy day, because he is ready to them, *a very present Help*.

VI. The *ceasing of the storm*, *v.* 32. When Christ was come into the ship, they were presently at the shore. Christ *walked upon the water* till he came to the ship, and then went into that, when he could as easily have walked to the shore. When Christ came into the ship, Peter came in with him. Companions with Christ in his patience, shall be companions in his kingdom, Rev. i. 9. Those that walk with him shall reign with him.

When they were come into the ship, immediately the storm ceased. When Christ comes into a soul, he makes winds and storms to cease there, and commands peace. Welcome Christ, and *the noise of her waves will soon be quelled.* The way to be still is, to know that he is God, that he is the *Lord with us*.

VII. The adoration paid to Christ hereupon (*v.* 33); *They that were in the ship came and worshipped him, and said, Of a truth, thou art the Son of God.* Two good uses they made of this distress, and this deliverance.

1. It was a confirmation of their faith in Christ. They knew before that he was the Son of God, but now they know it better. Faith, after a conflict with unbelief, is sometimes the more active, and gets to greater degrees of strength by being exercised. Now they *know it of a truth*. Faith *then* grows, when it arrives at a full assurance, when it sees clearly, and saith, *Of a truth*.

2. They took occasion from it to *give him the glory due unto his name. They worshipped Christ*. When Christ manifests his glory for us, we ought to return it to him (Ps. l. 15). Their worship and adoration of Christ were thus expressed, *Of a truth thou art the Son of God*. The matter of our creed may and must be made the matter of our praise. Faith is the proper principle of worship, and worship the genuine product of faith.

Verses 34-36

We have here an account of miracles by wholesale, which Christ wrought on the other side of the water, in the land of Gennesaret. Whithersoever Christ went, he was doing good.

I. The forwardness and faith of *the men of that place*. These were more noble than the Gergesenes, their neighbours. Those *besought Christ to depart* from them, they had no occasion for him; these besought him to help them, they had need of him. Christ reckons it the greatest honour we can do him, to make use of him. Now here we are told,

1. How *the men of that place* were brought to Christ; they *had knowledge of him*. It is probable that his miraculous passage over the sea might help to make way for his entertainment in those parts; and perhaps it was one thing Christ intended in it, for he has great reaches in what he does. They that know Christ's name, will make their application to him: if Christ were better known, he would not be neglected as he is; he is trusted as far as he is known.

They *had knowledge of him*, that is, of his being among them. The discerning of the day of our opportunities is a good step toward the improvement of it. It is better to know that there *is* a prophet among us than that there *has been one*.

2. How they brought others to Christ; *They sent out into all that country*. Note, those that have got the knowledge of Christ themselves, should do all they can to bring others acquainted with him too. We must not eat these spiritual morsels alone; there is in Christ enough for us all, so that there is nothing got by monopolising. When we have opportunities of getting good to our souls, we should bring as many as we can to share with us. More than we think of would close with opportunities, if they were but called upon and invited to them. Neighbourhood is an advantage of doing good which must be improved.

3. What their business was with Christ; *They brought unto him all that were diseased*. If love to Christ and his doctrine will not bring them to him, yet self-love would. Did we but rightly seek our own things, the things of our own peace and welfare, we should seek the things of Christ.

4. How they made their application to him; *They*

word of Christ, but asks why that *distrust* which so quickly marred it. 32. "And when they [Jesus and Peter] were come into the ship, the wind ceased."

And he went up unto them into the ship—John (6:21) says, "Then they willingly received him into the ship"—or rather, "Then were they willing to receive Him" (with reference to their previous terror); but implying also a glad welcome, their first fears now converted into wonder and delight. "And immediately," adds the beloved disciple, "they were at the land whither they went," or "were bound." This additional miracle, for as such it is manifestly related, is recorded by the fourth Evangelist alone. As the storm was suddenly calmed, so the little bark—propelled by the secret power of the Lord of nature now sailing in it—glided through the now unruffled waters, and, while they were wrapt in wonder at what had happened, not heeding their rapid motion, *was found* at port, to their still further surprise.

Then are they glad, because at rest
And quiet now they be;
So to the haven He them brings
Which they desired to see.

Matthew (14:33) says, "Then they that were in the ship came [i.e., ere they got to land] and worshipped him, saying, Of a truth Thou art the Son of God." But our Evangelist is wonderfully striking. **and the wind ceased and they were sore amazed in themselves beyond measure, and wondered**—The Evangelist seems hardly to find language strong enough to express their astonishment.

And when they had passed over, they came into the land of Gennesaret—from which the lake sometimes takes its name, stretching along its western shore. Capernaum was their landing-place (John 6:24, 25).

—At this period of our Lord's ministry the popular enthusiasm in His favor was at its height.

32. *The wind ceased.* Jesus is the Prince of Peace, and all is peace and calm where He condescends to enter and abide.

34. *The land of Gennesaret.* It was from this country that the sea or lake of Gennesaret had its name.

35. *The men of that place had knowledge of him,* i.e., "They knew Him again." They had already seen His miracles; and now they collect all the diseased people they can find, that He may have the same opportunity of showing forth His marvellous power, and they of being the instruments of relieving their friends and neighbors.

MATTHEW HENRY

besought him that they might only touch the hem of his garment, v. 36. They applied themselves to him, (1) With great importunity; they besought him. The greatest favours and blessings are to be obtained from Christ by entreaty; *Ask, and it shall be given.* (2) With great humility. Their desiring to touch the hem of his garment, intimates that they thought themselves unworthy that he should so much as speak to their case, much less touch them for their cure; but they will look upon it as a great favour, if he will give them leave to *touch the hem of his garment.* (3) With great assurance of the all-sufficiency of his power, not doubting but that they should be healed, even by touching the hem of his garment. They were sure that there was in him such an overflowing fulness of healing virtue, that *they* could not fail of a cure, who were but admitted near him. It was in this country and neighbourhood that the woman with the bloody issue was cured by *touching the hem of his garment,* and was commended for her faith (*ch.* ix. 20–22); and thence, probably, they took occasion to ask this. It is good using those means and methods which others before us have sped well in the use of.

II. The fruit and success of this their application to Christ. It was not in vain for as *many as touched, were made perfectly whole.* Christ's cures are perfect cures. Those that he heals, he heals perfectly. He doth not do his work by halves. There is abundance of healing virtue in Christ for all that apply themselves to him, be they ever so many. The least of Christ's institutions, like the hem of his garment, is replenished with the overflowing fulness of his grace. The healing virtue that is in Christ, is put forth for the benefit of those that by a true and lively faith touch him. Christ is in heaven, but his word is nigh us, and he himself in that word. When we mix faith with the word, submit to its influences and commands, then we touch the hem of Christ's garment. It is but thus touching, and we are made whole.

JAMIESON, FAUSSET, BROWN

and besought him that they might touch if it were but the border of his garment—having heard, no doubt, of what the woman with the issue of blood experienced on doing so (ch. 5:25-29), and perhaps of other unrecorded cases of the same nature.

and as many as touched him—or "it"—the border of His garment—**were made whole**—All this they *continued* to do and to experience while our Lord was in that region. The *time* corresponds to that mentioned (John 7:1), when He "walked in Galilee," instead of appearing in Jerusalem at the passover, "because the Jews," i.e., *the rulers,* "sought to kill Him"—while *the people* sought to enthrone Him!

ADAM CLARKE

36. *That they might only touch the hem of his garment.* What mighty influence must the grace and Spirit of Christ have in the soul when even the border or *hem of his garment* produced such wonders in the bodies of those who touched it!

MATTHEW HENRY

CHAPTER 15

Verses 1–9

I. Here is the cavil of the scribes and Pharisees at Christ's disciples, for *eating with unwashen hands.* They were men of learning and men of business. These scribes and Pharisees here introduced were of Jerusalem; they should therefore have been better than others, but they were worse. External privileges, if they be not duly improved, commonly swell men up the more with pride and malignity.

Now if these great men be the accusers, pray what is the accusation? Nonconformity to the canons of their church (*v.* 2); *Why do thy disciples transgress the tradition of the elders?* This charge they make good in a particular instance; *They wash not their hands when they eat bread.*

Observe, 1. What was the *tradition of the elders*—That people should often wash their hands, and always at meat. This they placed a great deal of religion in, supposing that the meat they touched with unwashen hands would be defiling to them. The Pharisees practised this themselves, and with a great deal of strictness imposed it upon others. Nay, they would not eat meat with one that did not wash before meat.

2. What was the transgression of this tradition or injunction by the disciples; it seems, they did not wash their hands when they ate bread. The custom was innocent enough, and had a decency in its civil use. But when it came to be practised and imposed as a religious rite and ceremony, and such a stress laid upon it, the disciples, though weak in knowledge, yet were so well taught as not to comply with it, or observe it; no not when the scribes and Pharisees had their eye upon them. They had already learned St. Paul's lesson.

3. What was the complaint of the scribes and Pharisees against them. They quarrel with Christ about it, "*Why do thy disciples transgress* the canons of the church?" It was well that the complaint was made to Christ; for the disciples themselves were perhaps not so well able to give a reason for what they did as were to be wished.

II. Here is Christ's answer to this cavil, and his justification of the disciples.

Two ways Christ replies upon them;

1. By way of recrimination, *v.* 3–6. They were spying motes in the eyes of his disciples, but Christ shows them a beam in their own. It is such a censure of their tradition (and the authority of that was what they built their charge upon) as makes not only a non-compliance lawful, but an opposition a duty.

(1) The charge in general is, *You transgress the*

JAMIESON, FAUSSET, BROWN

CHAPTER 15

Vss. 1-20. DISCOURSE ON CEREMONIAL POLLUTION. (= Mark 7:1, 23.) The time of this section was after that Passover which was nigh at hand when our Lord fed the five thousand (John 6:4)—the third Passover, as we take it, since His public ministry began, but which He did not keep at Jerusalem for the reason mentioned in John 7:1. **1. Then came to Jesus scribes and Pharisees, which were of**—or "from"—**Jerusalem**—Mark says they "came from" it: a deputation probably sent from the capital expressly to watch Him. As He had not come to them at the last Passover, which they had reckoned on, they now come to Him. "And," says Mark, "when they saw some of His disciples eat bread with defiled, that is to say, with unwashen hands"—hands not ceremonially cleansed by washing—"they found fault. For the Pharisees, and all the Jews, except they wash their hands oft"—lit., "in" or "with the fist"; i.e., probably washing the one hand by the use of the other—though some understand it, with our version, in the sense of 'diligently,' 'sedulously'—"eat not, holding the tradition of the elders"; acting religiously according to the custom handed down to them. "And when they come from the market"—"And after market": after any common business, or attending a court of justice, where the Jews, as WEBSTER and WILKINSON remark, after their subjection to the Romans, were especially exposed to intercourse and contact with heathens—"except they wash, they eat not. And many other things there be, which they have received to hold, as the washing of cups and pots, brazen vessels and tables"—rather, "couches," such as were used at meals, which probably were merely *sprinkled* for ceremonial purposes. "Then the Pharisees and scribes asked Him," **saying, 2. Why do thy disciples transgress the tradition of the elders? for they wash not their hands when they eat bread. 3. But he answered and said unto them, Why do ye also transgress the commandment of God by your tradition?**—The charge is retorted with startling power: "The tradition they transgress is but *man's,* and is itself the occasion of heavy transgression, undermining the authority of *God's law.*"

ADAM CLARKE

CHAPTER 15

1. *Scribes and Pharisees . . . of Jerusalem.* Our Lord was now in Galilee, chap. xiv. 34.

2. *Elders.* Rulers and magistrates among the Jews. *The tradition of the elders.* The word tradition has occupied a most distinguished place, in both the Jewish and the Christian Church. Man is ever fond of mending the work of his Maker, and hence he has been led to put his finishing hand even to divine revelation! The Latin term, *tradition,* is from *trado,* to "deliver," especially "from one to another—to hand down." Among the Jews, *tradition* signifies what is also called the *oral* law, which they distinguish from the *written* law. This last contains the Mosaic precepts, as found in the Pentateuch; the former, the traditions of the elders, i.e., traditions, or doctrines, that had been successively handed down from Moses through every generation, but not committed to writing. The Jews feign that, when God gave Moses the written law, He gave him also the oral law, which is the interpretation of the former. This law Moses at first delivered to Aaron, then to his sons Eleazar and Ithamar, and after these to the seventy-two elders, who were six of the most eminent men chosen out of each of the twelve tribes. These seventy-two, with Moses and Aaron, delivered it again to all the heads of the people, and afterwards to the congregation at large. They say also that before Moses died he delivered his oral law, or system of traditions, to Joshua, and Joshua to the elders which succeeded him—they to the prophets, and the prophets to each other, till it came to Jeremiah, who delivered it to Baruch, his scribe, who repeated it to Ezra, who delivered it to the men of the great synagogue.

3. *Why do ye also transgress the commandment?* Ye accuse My disciples of transgressing the traditions of the elders—I accuse you of transgressing the commands of God and that too in favor of your own tradition, thus preferring the inventions of men to the positive

MATTHEW HENRY

commandment of God by your tradition. They call it the *tradition of the elders*, laying stress upon the antiquity of the usage, and the authority of them that imposed it. *You transgress the commandment of God.* Note, Those who are most zealous of their own impositions, are commonly most careless of God's commands.

(2) The proof of this charge is in a particular instance, that of their transgressing the fifth commandment.

[1] Let us see what the command of God is (*v.* 4), what the precept, and what the sanction of the law is.

The precept is, *Honour thy father and thy mother;* this is enjoined by the common Father of mankind. The whole of children's duty to their parents is included in this of honouring them, which is the spring and foundation of all the rest.

The sanction of this law in the fifth commandment, is, a promise, *that thy days may be long*; but our Saviour waives that, lest any should thence infer it to be only a thing commendable and profitable, and insists upon the penalty annexed to the breach of this commandment in another scripture, which denotes the duty to be highly and indispensably necessary; *He that curseth father or mother, let him die the death.* By our Saviour's application of this law, it appears, that denying service or relief to parents is included in cursing them. Though the language be respectful enough, and nothing abusive in it, yet what will that avail, if the deeds be not agreeable?

[2] Let us see what was the contradiction which the tradition of the elders gave to this command. It was not direct and downright, but implicit; their casuists gave them such rules as furnished them with an easy evasion from the obligation of this command, *v.* 5, 6. Observe,

First, What their tradition was; That a man could not in any case bestow his worldly estate better than to give it to the priests, and devote it to the service of the temple: and that when anything was so devoted, it was not only unlawful to alienate it, but all other obligations, though ever so just and sacred, were thereby superseded.

Secondly, How they allowed the application of this to the case of children. When their parents' necessities called for their assistance, they pleaded, that all they could spare from themselves and their children, they had devoted to the treasury of the temple; *It is a gift, by whatsoever thou mightest be profited by me*, and therefore their parents must expect nothing from them. This, they taught, was a good and valid plea, and many undutiful, unnatural children made use of it, and they justified them in it, and said, *He shall be free.* But the absurdity and impiety of this tradition were very evident: for revealed religion was intended to improve, not to overthrow, natural religion; one of the fundamental laws of which is this of honouring our parents. This was *making the command of God of no effect.* To break the law is bad, but to *teach men so*, as the scribes and Pharisees did, is much worse, *ch.* v. 19. To what purpose is the command given, if it be not obeyed?

2. The other part of Christ's answer is by way of reprehension; and that which he here charges them with, is hypocrisy; *Ye hypocrites, v.* 7. It is the prerogative of him who searcheth the heart, and knows what is in man, to pronounce who are hypocrites. The eye of man can perceive open profaneness, but it is only the eye of Christ that can discern hypocrisy, Luke xvi. 15. And as it is a sin which his eye discovers, so it is a sin which of all others his soul hates.

Now Christ fetches his reproof from Isa. xxix. 13. *Well did Esaias prophesy of you.* Isaiah spoke it of the men of that generation to which he prophesied, yet Christ applies it to these scribes and Pharisees. Threatenings directed against others, belong to us, if we be guilty of the same sins. Isaiah prophesied not of them only, but of all other hypocrites, against whom that word of his is still levelled, and stands in force. The prophecies of scripture are every day in the fulfilling.

(1) The description of hypocrites, in two things. In their own performances of religious worship, *v.* 8, when they *draw nigh to God with their mouth, and honour him with their lips, their heart is far from him.*

First, How far a hypocrite goes; he draws nigh to God, and honours him; he is, in profession a worshipper of God. The *Pharisee went up to the temple to pray*; he does not stand at that distance which those are at, who *live without God in the world.* They honour him; that is, they take on them to honour God, they join with those that do so. Some honour God has even from the services of hypocrites.

Secondly, Where he rests and takes up; this is done

JAMIESON, FAUSSET, BROWN

4. For God commanded, saying, Honour thy father and mother Deut. 5:16; **and, He that curseth father or mother, let him die the death**—(Exod. 21:17).

But ye say, Whosoever shall say to his father or his mother, It is a gift—or simply, "A gift!" In Mark it is, "*Corban!*" i.e., "An oblation!" meaning, any unbloody offering or gift dedicated to sacred uses. **by whatsoever thou mightest be profited by me; 6. And honour not his father or his mother, [he shall be free]**—i.e., It is true, father—mother—that by giving to thee this, which I now present, thou mightest be profited by me; but I have gifted it to pious uses, and therefore, at whatever cost to thee, I am not now at liberty to alienate any portion of it. "And," it is added in Mark, "ye suffer him no more to do aught for his father or his mother." To dedicate property to God is indeed lawful and laudable, but not at the expense of filial duty. **Thus have ye made the commandment of God of none effect**—cancelled or nullified it—**by your tradition. 7. Ye hypocrites, well did Esaias prophesy of you, saying**—(Isa. 29:13)—

8. This people draweth nigh unto me with their mouth, . . .—By putting the commandments of men on a level with the divine requirements, *their whole worship was rendered vain*—a principle of deep moment in the service of God. "For," it is added in Mark 7:8, "laying aside the commandment of God, ye hold the tradition of men, as the washing of pots and cups; and many other such like things ye do." The drivelling nature of their multitudinous observances is here pointedly exposed, in contrast with the manly observance of "the commandment of God"; and when our Lord says, "Many other such like things ye do,"

ADAM CLARKE

precepts of God. Pretenders to zeal often prefer superstitious usages to the divine law, and human inventions to the positive duties of Christianity.

4. *Honour thy father and mother.* This word was taken in great latitude of meaning among the Jews; it not only meant respect and submission, but also "to take care of a person, to nourish and support him, to enrich." See Num. xxii. 17; Judg. xiii. 17; 1 Tim. v. 17. And that this was the sense of the law, as it respected parents, see Deut. xxvii. 16, and see the note on Exod. xx. 12.

5. *It is a gift. Corban* (Mark vii. 11), an offering of approach; something consecrated to the service of God in the Temple, by which a man had the privilege of approaching his Maker.

7. *Hypocrites, well did Esaias prophesy of you.* In every place where the proper names of the Old Testament occur in the New, the same mode of orthography should be followed: I therefore write *Isaiah* with the Hebrew, not *Esaias*, with the Greek. This prophecy is found in chap. xxix. 13.

MATTHEW HENRY

but with his mouth and with his lips. It is piety but from the teeth outwards; he shows much love, and that is all, there is in his heart no true love. Hypocrites are those that only make a lip-labour of religion and religious worship.

Thirdly, What that is wherein he comes short; it is in the main matter; *Their heart is far from me*, habitually alienated and estranged (Eph. iv. 18), actually wandering and dwelling upon something else. A hypocrite says one thing, but thinks another. The great thing that God looks at and requires is the heart (Prov. xxiii. 26). In their prescriptions to others. This is an instance of their hypocrisy, that *they teach for doctrines the commandments of men*. When men's inventions are tacked to God's institutions, and imposed accordingly, this is hypocrisy, a mere human religion. God will have his own work done by his own rules, and accepts not that which he did not himself appoint. That only comes *to* him, that comes *from* him.

(2) The doom of hypocrites; it is put in a little compass; *In vain do they worship me*. Their worship does not attain the end for which it was appointed; it will neither please God, nor profit themselves. If it be not *in spirit*, it is not *in truth*, and so it is all nothing. Lip-labour is lost labour.

Verses 10-20

I. The solemn introduction to this discourse (*v.* 10); *He called the multitude*. Christ had a regard to the multitude. The humble Jesus embraced those whom the proud Pharisees looked upon with disdain. He turns from them as wilful and unteachable, and turns to the multitude, who, though weak, were humble, and willing to be taught. To them he said, *Hear and understand*. Note, What we hear from the mouth of Christ, we must give all diligence to understand. Not only scholars, but even the multitude, the ordinary people, must apply their minds to understand the words of Christ.

II. The truth itself laid down (*v.* 11), in two propositions.

1. *Not that which goes into the mouth defileth the man*. It is not the kind or quality of our food, nor the condition of our hands, that affects the soul with any moral polution or defilement. *The kingdom of God is not meat and drink*, Rom. xiv. 17. That defiles the man, by which guilt is contracted before God, and the man is rendered offensive to him, and disfitted for communion with him; now what we eat does not this. He was now beginning to teach his followers to *call nothing common or unclean*; and if Peter, when he was bid to *kill and eat*, had remembered this word, he would not have said, *Not so, Lord*, Acts x. 13-15, 28.

2. *But that which comes out of the mouth, this defiles a man*. We are polluted, not by the meat we eat with unwashen hands, but by the words we speak from an unsanctified heart. It is not the disciples that defile themselves with what they eat, but the Pharisees that defile themselves with what they speak spitefully and censoriously of them. Those who charge guilt upon others for transgressing the commandments of men, many times bring greater guilt upon themselves, by transgressing the law of God against rash judging.

III. The offence that was taken at this truth and the account brought to Christ of that offence (*v.* 12); *"The disciples said unto him, Knowest thou that the Pharisees were offended."*

1. It was not strange that the Pharisees should be offended at this plain truth. Sore eyes cannot bear clear light; and nothing is more provoking to proud imposers than the undeceiving of those whom they have first blindfolded and then enslaved, great contenders for the formalities of religion, being commonly as great contemners of the substantials of it.

2. The disciples thought it strange that their Master should say that which he knew would give so much offence; he did not use to do so. But he knew what he said, and to whom he said it, and would teach us, that though in indifferent things we must be tender of giving offence, yet we must not, for fear of that, evade any truth or duty. Truth must be owned, and duty done; and if any be offended, it is his own fault; it is scandal, not given, but taken.

Perhaps the disciples themselves stumbled at the word Christ said and therefore objected this to Christ, that they might themselves be better informed. They seem likewise to have a concern upon them for the Pharisees. They would not have the Pharisees go away displeased at anything Christ had said; and therefore, though they do not desire him to retract it, they hope he will explain, correct, and modify it. Weak hearers are sometimes more solicitous than they should be not to have wicked hearers offended.

JAMIESON, FAUSSET, BROWN

it is implied that He had but given a specimen of the hideous treatment which the divine law received, and the grasping disposition which, under the mask of piety, was manifested by the ecclesiastics of that day.

10. And he called the multitude, and said unto them—The foregoing dialogue, though in the people's hearing, was between Jesus and the pharisaic cavilliers, whose object was to disparage Him with the people. But Jesus, having put them down, turns to the multitude, who at this time were prepared to drink in everything He said, and with admirable plainness, strength, and brevity, lays down the great principle of real pollution, by which a world of bondage and uneasiness of conscience would be dissipated in a moment, and the sense of sin be reserved for deviations from the holy and eternal law of God. **Hear and understand: 11. Not that which geeth into the mouth defileth a man; but that which cometh out of the mouth, this defileth a man**—This is expressed even more emphatically in Mark (17:15, 16), and it is there added, "If any man have ears to hear, let him hear." As in ch. 13:9. this so oft-repeated saying seems designed to call attention to the *fundamental* and *universal* character of the truth it refers to.

12. Then came his disciples, and said unto him, Knowest thou that the Pharisees were offended, after they heard this saying?—They had given vent to their irritation, and perhaps threats, not to our Lord Himself, from whom they seem to have slunk away, but to some of the disciples, who report it to their Master.

ADAM CLARKE

8. *Their heart is far from me.* The true worship of God consists in the union of the heart to Him—where this exists not, a particle of the spirit of devotion cannot be found.

9. *In vain they do worship me.* By the traditions of the elders, not only the word of God was perverted, but His worship also was greatly corrupted. But the Jews were not the only people who have acted thus; whole Christian churches, as well as sects and parties, have acted in the same way.

10. *Hear, and understand. Hear*—make it a point of conscience to attend to the ministry of the Word. Understand—be not satisfied with attending places of public worship merely; see that the teaching be of God, and that you lay it to heart.

11. *Not that which goeth into the mouth defileth.* This is an answer to the carping question of the Pharisees mentioned in v. 2: "Why do Thy disciples eat with unwashed hands?"

That which cometh out of the mouth. That is, what springs from a corrupt, unregenerate heart —a perverse will and impure passions—these defile, i.e., make him a sinner.

12. *The Pharisees were offended.* None so liable to take offense as formalists and hypocrites, when you attempt to take away the false props from the one and question the sincerity of the other. Besides, Pharisees must never be suspected of ignorance, for they are the men, and wisdom must die with them!

MATTHEW HENRY

IV. The doom passed upon the Pharisees and their corrupt traditions. Two things Christ here foretells concerning them.

1. The rooting out of them and their traditions (*v.* 13); *Every plant which my heavenly Father hath not planted, shall be rooted up.* Their sect, and way, and constitution, were plants not of God's planting. The rules of their profession were no institutions of his, but owed their origin to pride and formality. In the visible church, it is no strange thing to find plants that our heavenly Father has not planted. Let the husbandman be ever so careful, his ground will cast forth weeds of itself, more or less, and there is an enemy busy sowing tares. What is corrupt, though of God's permitting, is not of his planting; he sows nothing but *good seed in his field.* Let us not therefore be deceived, as if all must needs be right that we find in the church, and all those persons and things our Father's plants that we find in our Father's garden. *By their fruit you shall know them.* Those plants that are not of God's planting, shall not be of his protecting, but shall undoubtedly be rooted up. What is not of God shall not stand, Acts v. 38. But the gospel of truth is great, and will remain. It cannot be rooted up.

2. The ruin of them; and their followers, *v.* 14.

(1) Christ bids his disciples *let them alone.* "Have no converse with them or concern for them; neither court their favour, nor dread their displeasure; they will take their course, and let them take the issue of it. They are wedded to their own fancies, and will have everything their own way; let them alone. Seek not to please a generation of men that please not God" (1 Thess. ii. 15). The case of those sinners is sad indeed, whom Christ orders his ministers to let alone.

(2) He gives them two reasons for it. *Let them alone;* for,

[1] They are proud and ignorant; two bad qualities that often meet, and render a man incurable in his folly, Prov. xxvi. 12. *They are blind leaders of the blind.* They are grossly ignorant in the things of God, and yet so proud, that they think they see better and further than any, and therefore undertake to be leaders of others, to show others the way to heaven, when they themselves know not one step of the way; and, accordingly, they prescribe to all, and proscribe those who will not follow them. Though they were blind, if they had owned it, and come to Christ for eye-salve, they might have seen. *Are we blind also?* They were confident that *they themselves were guides of the blind* (Rom. ii. 19, 20), were appointed to be so, and fit to be so; that everything they said was an oracle and a law.

[2] They are posting to destruction; *Both shall fall into the ditch.* This must needs be the end of it, if both be so blind, and yet both so bold, venturing forward, and yet not aware of danger. The blind leaders and the blind followers will perish together. Those that by their cunning craftiness draw others to sin and error, shall not, with all their craft and cunning, escape ruin themselves. If *both fall together into the ditch,* the blind leaders will fall undermost, and have the worst of it. They that have thus mutually increased each other's sin, will mutually exasperate each other's ruin.

V. Instruction given to the disciples concerning the truth Christ had laid down, *v.* 10. Though Christ rejects the wilfully ignorant who care not to be taught, he can have compassion on the ignorant who are willing to learn, Heb. v. 2.

1. Their desire to be better instructed in this matter (*v.* 15); in this request as in many others, Peter was their speaker; *Declare unto us this parable.* What Christ said was plain, yet they call it a parable, and cannot understand it. Weak understandings are apt to turn plain truths into parables, and to seek for a knot in a bulrush. Where a weak head doubts concerning any word of Christ, an upright heart and a willing mind will seek for instruction. The disciples, though offended, sought for satisfaction, imputing the offence, not to the doctrine delivered, but to the shallowness of their own capacity.

2. The reproof Christ gave them for their weakness and ignorance (*v.* 16); *Are ye also yet without understanding?* As many as Christ loves and teaches, he thus rebukes. Two things aggravate their dullness and darkness. That they were the disciples of Christ; "Are *ye* also without understanding? Ye whom I have admitted into so great a degree of familiarity with me, are ye so unskilful in the word of righteousness?" The ignorance and mistakes of those that profess religion, and enjoy the privileges of church-membership, are justly a grief to the Lord Jesus. That they had been a great while Christ's scholars; "Are ye *yet* so, after ye have been so long under my teaching?" Had they been but of yesterday in Christ's

JAMIESON, FAUSSET, BROWN

13. But he answered and said, Every plant, which my heavenly Father hath not planted, shall be rooted up—They are offended, are they? Heed it not: their corrupt teaching is already doomed: the garden of the Lord upon earth, too long cumbered with their presence, shall yet be purged of them and their accursed system: yea, and whatsoever is not of the planting of My heavenly Father, the great Husbandman (John 15:1), shall share the same fate.'

14. Let them alone: they be blind leaders of the blind. And if the blind lead the blind, both shall fall into the ditch—Striking expression of the ruinous effects of erroneous teaching!

15. Then answered Peter and said unto him—"when He was entered into the house from the people," says Mark. **Declare unto us this parable.**

16. And Jesus said, Are ye also yet without understanding?—Slowness of spiritual apprehension in His genuine disciples grieves the Saviour: from others He expects no better (ch. 13: 11).

ADAM CLARKE

13. *Every plant.* "Every plantation." The Pharisees, as a religious body, were now a plantation of trees which God did not plant, water, nor own; therefore, they should be *rooted up.*

14. *Let them alone.* "Give them up, or leave them." Our blessed Lord meant "give them up," have no kind of religious connection with them, and the strong reason for which He immediately adds, because they are *blind leaders.* Probably the words may be understood as a sort of proverbial expression for "Don't mind them: pay no regard to them. They are altogether unworthy of notice."

16. *Are ye also yet without understanding?* The word which we translate *yet* should be here rendered "still": Are ye still void of understanding? The word is used in this sense by several Greek writers.

A. T. ROBERTSON:

"They are blind guides" (*tuphloi eisin hodegoi*). What a graphic picture! Once in Cincinnati a blind man introduced me to his blind friend. He said that he was showing him the city. Jesus is not afraid of the Pharisees. Let them alone to do their worst. Blind leaders and blind victims will land in the ditch. A proverbial expression in the Old Testament.—*Word Pictures in the New Testament*

MATTHEW HENRY

school, it had been another matter. Christ expects from us some proportion of knowledge, and grace, and wisdom, according to the time and means we have had. See John xiv. 9.

3. The explication Christ gave them of this doctrine of pollutions. He here shows us,

(1) What little danger we are in of pollution from that which *entereth in at the mouth, v.* 17. An inordinate appetite, intemperance, and excess in eating, come out of the heart, and are defiling; but meat in itself is not so, as the Pharisees supposed. What there is of dregs and defilement in our meat, nature (or rather the God of nature) has provided a way to clear us of it; *it goes in at the belly, and is cast out into the draught*, and nothing remains to us but pure nourishment. By this means nothing defiles; if we eat with unwashen hands, and so anything unclean mix with our food, nature will separate it, and cast it out, and it will be no defilement to us. It may be a piece of cleanliness, but it is no point of conscience, to wash before meat.

(2) What great danger we are in of pollution from that which *proceeds out of the mouth* (*v.* 18). There is no defilement in the products of God's bounty; the defilement arises from the products of our corruption. Now here we have,

[1] The corrupt fountain of that which proceeds out of the mouth; it comes from the heart. It is the heart that is so desperately wicked (Jer. xvii. 9); for there is no sin in word or deed, which was not first in the heart. All evil speakings come forth from the heart, and are defiling.

[2] Some of the corrupt streams which flow from this fountain, specified,

First, *Evil thoughts*, sins against all the commandments. There is a great deal of sin that begins and ends in the heart, and goes no further.

Secondly, *Murders*, these come from a malice in the heart against our brother's life, or a contempt of it. Hence he *that hates his brother*, is said to be a *murderer*; he is so at God's bar, 1 John iii. 15.

Thirdly, *Adulteries* and *fornications*, these come from the wanton, unclean, carnal heart; and the lust that reigns there. There is adultery in the heart first, and then in the act, *ch.* v. 28.

Fourthly, *Thefts*, cheats, wrongs, rapines, and all injurious contracts. The fountain of all these is in the heart. *Achan coveted, and then took*, Joshua vii. 20, 21.

Fifthly, *False witness*. If truth, holiness, and love, which God *requires in the inward parts*, reigned as they ought, there would be no false witness bearing.

Sixthly, *Blasphemies*, speaking evil of God, speaking evil of our neighbour. These are the overflowing of the gall within.

Now *these are the things which defile a man, v.* 20. Sin is defiling to the soul, renders it unlovely and abominable in the eyes of the pure and holy God; unfit for communion with him.

These therefore are the things we must carefully avoid, and all approaches toward them, and not lay stress upon the washing of the hands. He concludes, *To eat with unwashen hands this defileth not a man.* If he wash, he is not the better before God; if he wash not, he is not the worse.

Verses 21-29

We have here that famous story of Christ's *casting the devil out of the woman of Canaan's daughter*; it has something in it singular and very surprising, and which looks favourably upon the poor Gentiles, and is an earnest of that mercy which Christ had in store for them. Here is a gleam of that *light* which was *to lighten the Gentiles*, Luke ii. 32.

I. *Jesus went thence.* Justly is the light taken from those that either play by it, or rebel against it. Though Christ endure long, he will not always *endure, the contradition of sinners against himself.* Wilful prejudices against the gospel, and cavils at it, often provoke Christ to withdraw.

II. When he went thence, he *departed into the coasts of Tyre and Sidon*; not to those cities, but into that part of the land of Israel which lay that way. While he went about doing good, he was never out of his way. The dark corners of the country, which lay most remote, shall have their share of his benign influences. Here it was, that this miracle was wrought, in the story of which we may observe,

1. The address of the woman of Canaan to Christ, *v.* 22. She was a Gentile, *a stranger to the commonwealth of Israel.* God will have his remnant out of all nations, chosen vessels in all coasts, even the most unlikely. If Christ had not now made a visit to these coasts, it is probable that she had never come to him. It is often an excitement to a dormant faith and zeal, to have opportunities of acquaintance with Christ brought to our doors.

JAMIESON, FAUSSET, BROWN

17, 18. Do not ye yet understand that whatsoever entereth in at the mouth, . . .—Familiar though these sayings have now become, what freedom from bondage to outward things do they proclaim, on the one hand; and on the other, how searching is the truth which they express—that nothing which enters from without can really defile us; and that only the evil that is in the heart, that is allowed to stir there, to rise up in thought and affection, and to flow forth in voluntary action, really defiles a man!

19. For out of the heart proceed evil thoughts—"evil reasonings"; referring here more immediately to those corrupt reasonings which had stealthily introduced and gradually reared up that hideous fabric of tradition which at length practically nullified the unchangeable principles of the moral law. But the statement is far broader than this; viz., that the first shape which the evil that is in the heart takes, when it begins actively to stir, is that of "considerations" or "reasonings" on certain suggested actions. **murders, adulteries, fornications, thefts, false witness, blasphemies**—detractions, whether directed against God or man; here the reference seems to be to the latter. Mark adds, "covetousnesses"—or desires after more; "wickednesses"—here meaning, perhaps, malignities of various forms; "deceit, lasciviousness"—meaning, excess or enormity of any kind, though by later writers restricted to lewdness; "an evil eye"—meaning, all looks or glances of envy, jealousy, or ill-will towards a neighbor; "pride, foolishness"—in the Old Testament sense of "folly"; i.e., criminal senselessness, the folly of the *heart*. How appalling is this black catalogue! **20. These are the things which defile a man: but to eat with unwashen hands defileth not a man**—Thus does our Lord sum up this whole searching discourse.

21-28. The Woman of Canaan and Her Daughter. For the exposition, see on Mark 7:24-30.

The first words of this narrative show that the incident followed, in point of time, immediately on what precedes it. **And from thence he arose, and went into**—or "unto". **borders of Tyre and Sidon**—the two great Phœnician seaports, but here denoting the territory generally, to the frontiers of which Jesus now came. But did Jesus actually enter this heathen territory? The whole narrative, we think, proceeds upon the supposition that He did. His immediate object seems to have been to avoid the wrath of the Pharisees at the withering exposure He had just made of their traditional religion.

The woman was a Greek—i.e., "a Gentile," as in the margin. **a Syrophœnician by nation**—so called as inhabiting the Phœnician tract of Syria. Juvenal uses the same term, as was remarked by Justin Martyr and Tertullian. Matthew calls her "a woman of Canaan"—a more intelligible description to his Jewish readers (cf. Judg. 1:30, 32, 33).

ADAM CLARKE

19. *Evil thoughts.* "Wicked dialogues"—for in all evil surmisings the heart holds a conversation, or dialogue, with itself. For *murders*, two MSS. have "envyings," and three others have both. Envy and murder are nearly allied; the former has often led to the latter.

20. *These . . . defile a man.* Our Lord's argument is very plain. What goes into the mouth descends into the stomach and other intestines; part is retained for the nourishment of the body, and part is ejected, as being improper to afford nourishment. Nothing of this kind defiles the soul, because it does not enter into it; but the evil principles that are in it, producing evil thoughts, murders, etc., these defile the soul, because they have their seat and operation in it.

21. *Departed into the coasts of Tyre and Sidon.* "Towards" the coasts, or confines. It is not clear that our Lord ever left the land of the Hebrews. Tyre and Sidon are usually joined together, principally because they are but a few miles distant from each other.

22. *A woman of Canaan.* Matthew gives her this name because of the people from whom she sprung—the descendants of Canaan, Judg. i. 31-32; but Mark calls her a "Syrophenician," because of the country where she dwelt. The Canaanites and Phoenicians have often been confounded. This is frequently the case in the Septuagint. Compare Gen. xlvi. 10 with Exod. vi. 15, where the same person is called a Phoenician in the one place and a Canaanite in the other.

MATTHEW HENRY | JAMIESON, FAUSSET, BROWN | ADAM CLARKE

MATTHEW HENRY

Her address was very importunate, she *cried* to Christ, as one in earnest.

(1) She relates her misery; *My daughter is grievously vexed with a devil.* The vexations of children are the trouble of parents. Tender parents very sensibly feel the miseries of those that are pieces of themselves. "Though vexed with the devil, yet she is my daughter still." The greatest afflictions of our relations do not dissolve our obligations to them, and therefore ought not to alienate our affections from them. It was the distress and trouble of her family, that now brought her to Christ. Because she came in faith, he did not reject her. Though it is need that drives us to Christ, yet we shall not therefore be driven from him.

(2) She requests for mercy; *Have mercy on me, O Lord, thou Son of David.*

Her petition is, *Have mercy on me.* She does not limit Christ, but mercy, mercy is the thing she begs: she pleads not merit, but depends upon mercy. Mercies to the children are mercies to the parents; favours to ours are favours to us. It is the duty of parents to pray for their children, and to be earnest in prayer for them. Bring them to Christ by faith and prayer, who alone is able to heal them.

2. The discouragement she met with in this address; in all the story of Christ's ministry we do not meet with the like. He was wont to countenance and encourage all that came to him, and either to *answer before they called,* or *to hear while they were yet speaking;* but here was one otherwise treated: and what could be the reason of it? Some think that Christ showed himself backward to gratify this poor woman, because he would not give offence to the Jews, by being as free and as forward in his favour to the Gentiles as to them. Or rather, Christ treated her thus, to try her; he knows what is in the heart, knew the strength of her faith, and how well able she was, by his grace, to break through such discouragements; he *therefore* met her with them, *that the trial of her faith might be found unto praise, and honour, and glory,* 1 Pet. i. 6, 7. Many of the methods of Christ's providence, and especially of his grace, in dealing with his people, which are dark and perplexing, may be explained with the key of this story. There may be love in Christ's heart while there are frowns in his face.

Observe the particular discouragements given her:

(1) When she cried after him, *he answered her not a word, v.* 23. His ear was wont to be always open and attentive to the cries of poor supplicants; but to this poor woman he turned a deaf ear, and she could get neither an alms nor an answer. But Christ knew what he did, and *therefore* did not answer, that she might be the more earnest in prayer. By seeming to draw away the desired mercy from her, he drew her on to be so much the more importunate for it. Every accepted prayer is not immediately an answered prayer. Sometimes God seems not to regard his people's prayers, but it is to prove, and so to *improve,* their faith.

(2) When the disciples spake a good word for her, he gave a reason why he refused her, which was yet more discouraging.

It was some little relief, that the disciples interposed on her behalf; they said, *Send her away, for she crieth after us.* The disciples, though wishing she might have what she came for, yet therein consulted rather their own ease than the poor woman's satisfaction; "*Send her away* with a cure, *she cries after us,* and is troublesome to us, and shames us." Continued importunity may be uneasy to men, even to good men; but Christ loves to be cried after.

Christ's answer to the disciples quite dashed her expectations; "*I am not sent, but to the lost sheep of the house of Israel.*" Importunity seldom conquers the settled reason of a wise man. He doth not only not answer her, but he argues against her, and stops her mouth with a reason. It is a great trial, when we have occasion given us to question whether we be of those to whom Christ was sent. But, blessed be God, no room is left for that doubt; the distinction between Jew and Gentile is taken away; we are sure that he *gave his life a ransom for many,* and if for many, why not for me?

When she continued her importunity, he insisted upon the unfitness of the thing, and gave her not only a repulse, but a seeming reproach too (*v.* 26); *It is not meet to take the children's bread and to cast it to dogs.* This seems to cut her off from all hope, and might have driven her to despair, if she had not had a very strong faith indeed. Gospel grace and miraculous cures (the appurtenances of it), were children's bread; and lay not upon the same level with that rain from heaven, and those fruitful seasons, which God gave to the nations whom he suffered *to walk in their own ways* (Acts xiv. 16, 17); no, these

JAMIESON, FAUSSET, BROWN

and she besought him that he would cast forth the devil out of her daughter—"She cried unto Him, saying, Have mercy on me, O Lord, Son of David: my daughter is grievously vexed with a devil" (Matt. 15:22). Thus, though no Israelite herself, she salutes Him as Israel's promised Messiah. Here we must go to Matthew 15:23-25 for some important links in the dialogue omitted by our Evangelist.

23. "But he answered her not a word." The design of this was first, perhaps, to show that He was not *sent* to such as she. He had said expressly to the Twelve, "Go not into the way of the Gentiles" (Matt. 10:5); and being now among them Himself, He would, for consistency's sake, let it be seen that He had not gone thither for *missionary* purposes. Therefore He not only kept silence, but had actually left the house, and—as will presently appear—was proceeding on His way back, when this woman accosted Him. But another reason for keeping silence plainly was to try and whet her faith, patience, and perseverance. And it had the desired effect: "She *cried after them,*" which shows that He was already on His way from the place. "And His disciples came and besought Him, saying, Send her away; for she crieth after us." They thought her troublesome with her importunate cries, just as they did the people who brought young children to be blessed of Him, and they ask their Lord to "send her away," i.e., to grant her request and be rid of her; for we gather from His reply that they meant to solicit favor for her, though not for her sake so much as their own. 24. "But He answered and said, I am not sent but unto the lost sheep of the house of Israel"—a speech evidently intended for the disciples themselves, to satisfy them that, though the grace He was about to show to this Gentile believer was *beyond His strict* commission, He had not gone *spontaneously* to dispense it. Yet did even this speech open a gleam of hope, could she have discerned it. For thus might she have spoken: "I am not SENT, did He say? Truth, Lord, Thou comest not hither in quest of *us,* but I come in quest of *Thee;* and must I go empty away? So did not the woman of Samaria, whom when Thou foundest her on Thy way to Galilee, Thou sentest away to make many rich!' But this our poor Syrophœnician could not attain to. What, then, can she answer to such a speech? Nothing.

ADAM CLARKE

Have mercy on me. How proper is this prayer for a penitent! There are many excellencies contained in it; (1) It is short, (2) humble, (3) full of faith, (4) fervent, (5) modest, (6) respectful, (7) rational, (8) relying only on the mercy of God, (9) persevering. *Son of David.* An essential character of the true Messiah.

23. *He answered her not a word.* Seemed to take time to consider her request, and to give her the opportunity of exercising her faith, and manifesting her fervor.

24. *I am not sent but unto the lost sheep.* By the divine appointment I am come to preach the gospel to the Jews only.

MATTHEW HENRY

were peculiar favours, appropriated to the peculiar people. The Gentiles were looked upon by the Jews with great contempt, were called and counted *dogs.* Christ here seems to allow it, and therefore thinks it not meet that the Gentiles should share in the favours bestowed on the Jews.

Now this Christ urgeth against this woman of Canaan; "How can she expect to eat of the children's bread, who is not of the family?" Those whom Christ intends most signally to honour, he first humbles and lays low in a sense of their own meanness and unworthiness. We must first see ourselves to be as dogs, *less than the least of all God's mercies,* before we are fit to be dignified and privileged with them. Christ delights to exercise great faith with great trials, and sometimes reserves the sharpest for the last, that, *being tried, we may come forth like gold.*

3. Many a one, thus tried, would either have sunk into silence, or broken out into passion. "Here is cold comfort," might she have said, "for a poor distressed creature; as good for me to have stayed at home. Not only to have a piteous case slighted, but to be called a *dog!" "Is this the Son of David?"* (might she have said): "Is this he that has such a reputation for kindness, tenderness, and compassion? I am not a dog, I am a woman, and an honest woman, and a woman in misery; and I am sure it is not meet to call me *dog.*" A humble, believing soul, that truly loves Christ, takes everything in good part that he saith and doeth, and puts the best construction upon it.

She breaks through all these discouragements, (1) With an earnestness of desire in prosecuting her petition. This appeared upon the former repulse (*v.* 25); *Then came she, and worshipped him, saying, Lord, help me.* She continued to pray. What Christ said, silenced the disciples; you hear no more of them; they took the answer, but the woman did not. The more sensibly we feel the burthen, the more resolutely we should pray for the removal of it. She improved in prayer. Instead of blaming Christ, or charging him with unkindness, she seems rather to suspect herself. She fears lest she had not been humble and reverent enough, and therefore now *she came, and worshipped him*; or she fears that she had not been earnest enough, and therefore now she cries, *Lord, help me.* When the answers of prayer are deferred, God is thereby teaching us to pray more, and pray better. Disappointments in the success of prayer, must be excitements to the duty of prayer. Christ, in his agony, *prayed more earnestly.* She waives the question, whether she was of those to whom Christ was sent or no; but, "Whether an Israelite or no, I come to the Son of David for mercy, and *I will not let him go, except he bless me.*" Many weak Christians perplex themselves with questions and doubts about their election; such had better mind their errand to God, and continue instant in prayer for mercy and grace; throw themselves by faith at the feet of Christ, and say, *If I perish, I will perish here.* If we cannot *reason* down our unbelief, let us *pray* it down. Her prayer is very short, but comprehensive and fervent, *Lord, help me.* Take this, *First,* As lamenting her case. It is not in vain for broken hearts to bemoan themselves; God looks upon them then. Or, *Secondly,* As begging grace to assist her in this hour of temptation. She found it hard to keep up her faith when it was thus frowned upon, and therefore prays, *"Lord, help me."* Or, *Thirdly,* As enforcing her original request, *"Lord, help me*; Lord, give me what I come for." She believed that Christ could and would help her. Still she keeps up good thoughts of Christ, and will not quit her hold. *Lord, help me,* is a good prayer, if well put up; and it is pity that it should be turned into a byword, and that we should take God's name in vain in it. (2) With a holy skilfulness of faith, suggesting a very surprising plea. Christ had placed the Jews with the children, *as olive plants round about* God's *table,* and had put the Gentiles with the dogs, under the table. There is nothing got by contradicting any word of Christ, though it bear ever so hard upon us. But this poor woman, since she cannot object against it, resolves to make the best of it (*v.* 27); *Truth, Lord; yet the dogs eat of the crumbs.* Her acknowledgment was very humble: *Truth, Lord.* You cannot speak so meanly and slightly of a humble believer, but he is ready to speak as meanly and slightly of himself. *"Truth, Lord;* I cannot deny it; I am a dog, and have no right to the children's bread." Her improvement of this into a plea was very ingenious; *Yet the dogs eat of the crumbs.* It was by a singular acumen, and spiritual quickness and sagacity, that she discerned matter of argument in that which looked like a slight. A lively, active faith will make that to be for us, which seems to be against us. Faith can find encouragement even in that which is discouraging, and get nearer to God by taking hold on

JAMIESON, FAUSSET, BROWN

for it is not meet to take the children's bread, and to cast it unto the dogs— Is this the death of her hopes? Nay, rather it is life from the dead. Out of the eater shall come forth meat (Judg. 14:14). "At evening-time, it shall be light" (Zech. 14:7). "Ah! I have it now. Had He kept silence, what could I have done but go unblest? but He hath spoken, and the victory is mine."

She has reached her lowest depth, her darkest moment: she will just utter her last cry: 25. "Then came she and worshipped Him, saying, Lord, help me!" This appeal, so artless, wrung from the depths of a believing heart, and reminding us of the publican's "God be merciful to me a sinner," moved the Redeemer at last to break silence—but in what style?

And she answered and said unto him, Yes, Lord—or, as the same word is rendered in Matthew 15:27. "Truth, Lord."

ADAM CLARKE

25. *Lord, help me.* Let me also share in the deliverance afforded to Israel.

26. *The children's bread.* The salvation provided for the Jews, who were termed "the children of the kingdom." And cast it to the "little dogs"; such the Gentiles were reputed by the Jewish people, and our Lord uses that form of speech which was common among His countrymen.

27. *Truth, Lord.* Yes Lord. This appears to be not so much an assent as a bold reply to our Lord's reason for apparently rejecting her suit. The little dogs share with the children, for they eat the crumbs which fall from their masters' table. I do not desire what is provided for these highly favored children, only what they leave. A single exertion of Thy almighty power, in the healing of my afflicted daughter, is all that I wish for; and this the highly favored Jews can well spare without lessening the provision made for themselves. Is not this the sense of this noble woman's reply?

G. CAMPBELL MORGAN:

The great truth taught by all this is that the benefits of the Kingdom are granted to simple faith. Look at this woman. In the background was her religion; in the foreground was her need. The worship of Astarte, perhaps, had sufficed for her till then. But when the dark day came, and the demon entered her child and she cried and wailed to the goddess Astarte, there was no answer. And so, as this woman came to Jesus Christ, we see her religious background fading away, because it could not help her. In the foreground there was her anguish. Mark how she came; how faith operated. She came first of all against prejudice, for the prejudice of the Gentile was as great against the Jew as that of the Jew against the Gentile. Here the prejudice was on both sides, and yet this woman, driven by her need, came to seek Him.

She persevered against silence. Sometimes we question the meaning of Christ's strange attitude toward this woman. In Mark's Gospel we read that when He came into this region, "he entered into a house, and would have no man know it." He went into the house for rest. How did the woman get to Him? Mark says, "He could not be hid." Why not? She was outside, and her need drew Him forth. He could not remain in hiding or in rest while that woman was outside in trouble. And when He came out of the house, she proffered her request, first calling Him Son of David; and He was silent. And the disciples came to Jesus and said to Him, "Send her away: for she crieth after us." We might misunderstand that request if it were not for Christ's reply to her, which shows that they meant, "Give her what she wants and let her go." They were not unkind; they did not mean to refuse her and send her away. Christ's answer was, "I was not sent but unto the lost sheep of the house of Israel." That was His reason for not giving her what she sought. She still pleaded; and dropped the title distinctive of Hebraism—"Son of David." She put the whole of her need into the one word, "Lord, help me." Then He turned toward her and spoke, and at the first moment His speech seemed almost more unkind than His silence. "It is not meet to take the children's bread and cast it to the dogs." Here again occurs a word we need to examine. There are two distinct words for dogs, and they mark two entirely different ideas. We all know how profound was the hatred of the Hebrew to the low, marauding, fierce, half-scavenger, half-wolf dog of that country. But then it is also true that dogs were found in Jewish households; they were the little dogs, the playthings of the children; and the word Christ used here was that for the little dogs. Probably there was a great welling of pity and tenderness in the voice of Jesus as He said to her, "It is not meet to take the children's bread and cast it to the [little] dogs." Now, on the basis of that distinction, let us see what she said: "Yea, Lord, for even the little dogs eat of the crumbs that fall from the masters' tables." Notice carefully the placing of the apostrophe. "Masters" is plural. It is as if she said, "It is true I am outside the covenant; they are masters, they have been for centuries. If you say you cannot take the bread of the children and give it to the little dogs under the table, the playthings of the children, it is quite true; but even the little dogs have the crumbs." It is not surprising that Jesus looked at her and said, "O woman, great is thy faith: be it done unto thee even as thou wilt." Against prejudice she came, against silence she persevered, against exclusion she proceeded, against rebuff she won. That is what He found outside the covenant. Her appeal was based on faith. When she said, "Son of David," it was the hope of faith. When she said, "Lord, help me," it was the appeal of faith. When she said, "True, Lord, yet the little dogs eat of the crumbs," it was what an old Puritan commentator called "the wit of faith," using the word wit in the true old Saxon sense, the tact of faith.—*The Gospel According to Matthew*

MATTHEW HENRY

that hand which is stretched out to push it away.

Her plea is, *Yet the dogs eat of the crumbs.* It is true, the full and regular provision is intended for the children only, but the small, casual, neglected crumbs are allowed to the dogs, and are not grudged them. Surely then some of the broken meat may fall to a poor Gentile; "I beg a cure by the by, which is but as a crumb, though of the same precious bread, yet but a small inconsiderable piece, compared with the loaves which they have." When we are ready to surfeit on the children's bread, we should remember how many there are, that would be glad of the crumbs. Our broken meat in spiritual privileges, would be a feast to many a soul.

Her humility and necessity made her glad of crumbs. Those who are conscious to themselves that they deserve nothing, will be thankful for anything. The least of Christ is precious to a believer, and the very crumbs of the bread of life.

Her faith encouraged her to expect these crumbs. Why should it not be at Christ's table, as at a great man's, where the dogs are fed as sure as the children? She calls it their *master's* table; if she were a dog, she was *his* dog. It is good lying in God's house, though we lie at the threshold there.

4. The happy issue and success of all this. She came off with credit and comfort from this struggle; and, though a Canaanite, approved herself a true daughter of Israel, who, *like a prince, had power with God, and prevailed. Then Jesus said, O woman, great is thy faith.* Now he begins to speak like himself, and to put on his own countenance. He commended her faith. *O woman, great is thy faith.* It is her faith that he commends. There were several other graces which shone bright in her conduct of this affair—wisdom, humility, meekness, patience, perseverance in prayer; but these were the product of her faith. Because of all graces faith honours Christ most, therefore of all graces Christ honours faith most. It is the greatness of her faith. Though the faith of all the saints is alike precious, yet it is not in all alike strong; all believers are not of the same size and stature.

The greatness of faith consists much in a resolute adherence to Jesus Christ, to love him, and trust him, as a Friend, even when he seems to come forth against us as an Enemy. Though weak faith, if true, shall not be rejected, yet great faith shall be commended. He cured her daughter; "*Be it unto thee even as thou wilt:* I can deny thee nothing, take what thou camest for." Great believers may have what they will for the asking. When our will conforms to the will of Christ's precept, his will concurs with the will of our desire. Those that will deny Christ nothing shall find that he will deny them nothing at last, though for a time he seems to hide his face from them.

The event was answerable to the word of Christ; *Her daughter was made whole from that very hour;* the mother's faith prevailed for the daughter's cure. *He spake, and it was done.*

Verses 29–39

I. A general account of Christ's cures, his curing by wholesale. The tokens of Christ's power and goodness are neither scarce nor scanty; for there is in him an overflowing fulness.

1. The place where these cures were wrought; it was *near the sea of Galilee.* We read not of anything he did in the coasts of Tyre and Sidon, but the casting of the devil out of the woman of Canaan's daughter, as if he took that journey on purpose, with that in prospect. Let not ministers grudge their pains to do good, though but to few. He that knows the worth of souls, would go a great way to help to save one from death and Satan's power.

But *Jesus departed thence.* Having let fall that crumb under the table, he here returns to make a full feast for the children. We may do that occasionally for one, which we may not make a constant practice of. Christ steps into the coast of Tyre and Sidon, but he *sits down by the sea of Galilee* (*v.* 29). He *sat down on a mountain,* that all might see him, and have free access to him; for he is an open Saviour. He sat down there as one waiting to be gracious. He settled himself to this good work.

2. The multitudes and maladies that were healed by him (*v.* 30); *Great multitudes came to him.* We are soon sensible of bodily pain and sickness, but few are concerned about their souls and their spiritual diseases. Such was the goodness of Christ, that he admitted all sorts of people; the poor as well as the rich are welcome to Christ. He never looked with contempt upon the vulgar, the *herd,* as they are called; for the souls of peasants are as precious with him as the souls of princes. Such was the power of Christ, that he healed all sorts of diseases; those that came to him, brought their sick relations and friends along with them, and *cast them down at Jesus' feet,*

JAMIESON, FAUSSET, BROWN

yet the dogs eat of the children's crumbs—which fall from their master's table" (Matt. 15:27). "I thank Thee, O blessed One, for that word! That's my whole case. Not of the children? True. A dog? True also: *Yet* the dogs under the table are allowed to eat of the children's crumbs—the droppings from their master's full table: Give me that, and I am content: One crumb of power and grace from Thy table shall cast the devil out of my daughter." Oh, what lightning-quickness, what reach of instinctive ingenuity, do we behold in this heathen woman!

And he said unto her—"O woman, great is thy faith" (Matt. 15:28). As BENGEL beautifully remarks, Jesus "marvelled" only at two things—*faith* and *unbelief* (see on Luke 7:9).

Matthew is more specific; "And her daughter was made whole from that very hour." The wonderfulness of this case in all its features has been felt in every age of the Church, and the balm it has administered, and will yet administer, to millions will be known only in that day that shall reveal the secrets of all hearts.

29-39. MIRACLES OF HEALING—FOUR THOUSAND MIRACULOUSLY FED. For the exposition, see on Mark 7:31; 8:10.

And again, departing from the coasts of Tyre and Sidon, he came unto the Sea of Galilee—or, according to what has very strong claims to be regarded as the true text here, "And again, departing from the coasts of Tyre, He came through Sidon to the Sea of Galilee." The MSS. in favor of this reading, though not the most numerous, are weighty, while the versions agreeing with it are among the most ancient; and all the best critical editors and commentators adopt it. In this case we must understand that our Lord, having once gone out of the Holy Land the length of Tyre, proceeded as far north as Sidon, though without ministering, so far as appears, in those parts, and then bent His steps in a southeasterly direction. There is certainly a difficulty in the supposition of so long a *detour* without any missionary object: and some may think this sufficient to cast the balance in favor of the received reading. Be this as it may, on returning from these coasts of Tyre, He passed **through the midst of the coasts**—frontiers—**of Decapolis**—crossing the Jordan, therefore, and approaching the lake on its east side. Here Matthew, who omits the details of the cure of this deaf and dumb man, introduces some particulars, from which we learn that it was only one of a great number. "And Jesus," says that Evangelist (15:29-31), "departed from thence, and came nigh unto the Sea of Galilee, and went up into a mountain"—the mountain range bounding the lake on the northeast, in Decapolis:

ADAM CLARKE

28. *O woman, great is thy faith.* The hindrances thrown in this woman's way only tended to increase her faith. Her faith resembles a river which becomes enlarged by the dykes opposed to it, till at last it sweeps them entirely away with it. *Her daughter was made whole.* Persevering faith and prayer are next to omnipotent.

29. *Went up into a mountain.* "The mountain." "Meaning," says Wakefield, "some particular mountain which he was accustomed to frequent."

MATTHEW HENRY

v. 30. We read not of anything they said to him, but they laid them down before him as objects of pity. Their calamities spake more for them than the tongue of the most eloquent orator could. Whatever our case is, the only way to find ease and relief is, to lay it at Christ's feet, and then submit it to him, and refer it to his disposal.

Here were *lame, blind, dumb, maimed, and many others*, brought to Christ. See what work sin has made! What various diseases are human bodies subject to! See what work the Saviour makes! He conquers those hosts of enemies to mankind. *He sent his word, and healed them.* This is an instance of Christ's power, which may comfort us in all our weaknesses; and of his pity, which may comfort us in all our miseries.

3. The influence that this had upon the people, *v.* 31.

(1) They *wondered*, and well they might. Christ's works should be our wonder.

(2) *They glorified the God of Israel.* Miracles, which are the matter of our wonder, must be the matter of our praise; and mercies, which are the matter of our rejoicing, must be the matter of our thanksgiving. If he heal our diseases, all that is within us must bless his holy name; and if we have been graciously preserved from blindness, and lameness, and dumbness, we have as much reason to bless God as if we had been cured. The standers-by glorified God. God must be acknowledged with praise and thankfulness in the mercies of others as in our own.

II. Here is a particular account of his feeding *four thousand men* with *seven loaves, and a few little fishes*, as he had lately fed *five thousand with five loaves.* The guests indeed were now not quite so many as then, and the provision a little more; he wrought his miracles as the occasion required. Both then and now he took as many as were to be fed, and made use of all that was at hand to feed them with. When once the utmost powers of nature are exceeded, we must say, *This is the finger of God;* and it is neither here nor there how far they are outdone.

1. Christ's pity (*v.* 32); *I have compassion on the multitude.* He tells his disciples this, both to try and to excite their compassion. In what he said to them, Observe,

(1) The case of the multitude; *They continue with me now three days, and have nothing to eat.* This is an instance of their zeal, and the strength of their affection to Christ and his word, that they not only left their callings, to attend upon him on weekdays, but underwent a deal of hardship, to continue with him; they wanted necessary food and had scarcely enough to keep life and soul together. They esteemed the words of Christ more than their necessary food. With what tenderness Christ spoke of it; *I have compassion on them.* It had become them to have compassion on him, who took so much pains with them for three days together, and yet for aught that appears he was fasting too. Our Lord Jesus keeps an account how long his followers continue their attendance on him, and takes notice of the difficulty they sustain in it.

Now the exigence the people were reduced to serves to magnify. The mercy of their supply: he fed them when they were hungry; and then food was doubly welcome. The miracle of their supply. If two hungry meals make the third a glutton, what would three hungry days do? And yet *they did all eat and were filled.* There are mercy and grace enough with Christ, to give the most earnest and enlarged desire an abundant satisfaction; *Open thy mouth wide, and I will fill it.*

(2) The care of our master concerning them; *I will not send them away fasting, lest they should faint by the way.* It is the unhappiness of our present state, that when our souls are in some measure elevated and enlarged, our bodies cannot keep pace with them in good duties. The weakness of the flesh is a great grievance to the willingness of the spirit.

2. Christ's power. His pity of their wants sets his power on work for their supply.

(1) How his power was distrusted by his disciples (*v.* 33); *whence should we have so much bread in the wilderness?* They had been not only the witnesses, but the ministers, of the former miracle; the multiplied bread went through their hands; so that it was an instance of great weakness for them to ask, *Whence shall we have bread?* Could they be at a loss, while they had their Master with them? Forgetting former experiences leaves us under present doubts.

Christ knew how slender the provision was, but he would know it from them (*v.* 34); *How many loaves have ye?* Before he would work, he would have it seen how little he had to work on, that his power might shine the brighter. What they had,

JAMIESON, FAUSSET, BROWN

"And great multitudes came unto Him, having with them lame, blind, dumb, maimed"—not "mutilated," which is but a secondary sense of the word, but "deformed"—"and many others, and cast them down at Jesus' feet; and He healed them: insomuch that the multitude [multitudes] wondered, when they saw the dumb to speak, the maimed to be whole, the lame to walk, and the blind to see; and they glorified the God of Israel"—who after so long and dreary an absence of visible manifestation, had returned to bless His people as of old (cf. Luke 7: 16). Beyond this it is not clear from the Evangelist's language that the people saw into the claims of Jesus.

And were beyond measure astonished, saying, He hath done all things well—reminding us, says TRENCH, of the words of the first creation (Gen. 1: 31, LXX), upon which we are thus not unsuitably thrown back, for Christ's work is in the truest sense "a new creation," **he maketh both the deaf to hear and the dumb to speak**—"and they glorified the God of Israel" (Matt. 15:31).

I have compassion on the multitude—an expression of that deep emotion in the Redeemer's heart which always preceded some remarkable interposition for relief. (See Matt. 14:14; 20:34; Mark 1: 41; Luke 7:13; also Matt. 9:36, before the mission of the Twelve; cf. Judg. 2:18; 10:16.) **because they have now been with me**—in constant attendance—**three days, and have nothing to eat:**

And if I send them away fasting to their own houses, they will faint by the way—In their eagerness they seem not to have thought of the need of provisions for such a length of time; but the Lord thought of it. In Matt. (15:32) it is, "I will not send them away fasting"—or rather, "To send them away fasting I am unwilling." **From whence can a man satisfy these men with bread here in the wilderness?**—Though the question here is the same as when He fed the five thousand, they evidently *now* meant no more by it than that *they* had not the means of feeding the multitude; modestly leaving the Lord to decide what was to be done. And this will the more appear from His not now trying them, as before, by saying, "They need not depart, give ye them to eat"; but simply asking what they had, and then giving His directions. **And he asked them. How many loaves have ye? And they said, Seven**—It was important in this case, as in the former, that the precise number of the loaves should be brought out. Thus also does the distinctness of the two miracles appear.

ADAM CLARKE

ALEXANDER MACLAREN:

Jesus is again on the shores of the lake, after a tour through the Tyrian and Sidonian territory, and then eastwards and southwards, to its eastern bank. There He, as on several former occasions, seeks seclusion and repose in the hills, which is broken in upon by the crowds. The old excitement and rush of people begin again. And large numbers of sick, "lame, blind, dumb, maimed and many others" are brought. They are cast "down at his feet" in hot haste, with small ceremony, and, as would appear, with little petitioning for His healing power. But the same grace, for which the Canaanite woman had needed to plead so hard, now seems to flow almost unasked. She had, as it were, wrung a drop out; now it gushes abundantly. She had not got her "crumb" without much pleading; these get the bread almost without asking. It is this contrast of scant and full supplies which the evangelist would have us observe. And he points his meaning plainly enough by that expression, "they glorified the God of Israel," which seems to be Matthew's own, and not his quotation of what the crowd said. This abundance of miracle witnesses to the preeminence of Israel over the Gentile nations, and to the special revelation of himself which God made to them in His Son. The crowd may have found in it only fuel for narrow national pride and contempt; but it was the divine method for the founding of the kingdom nonetheless; and these two scenes, set thus side by side, teach the same truth, that the King of men is first the King of Israel.

—*Expositions of Holy Scripture*

33. *Whence should we have so much bread in the wilderness?* This world is a desert, where nothing can be found to satisfy the soul of man but the salvation which Christ has procured.

MATTHEW HENRY

they had for themselves, and it was little enough, but Christ would have them bestow it all upon the multitude. It becomes Christ's disciples to be generous, their Master was so: what we have, we should be free of. Niggardliness to-day, out of thoughtfulness for tomorrow, is a complication of corrupt affection that ought to be mortified. The disciples asked, *Whence should we have bread?* Christ asked, *How many loaves have ye?* We must not think so much of our wants as of our havings.

(2) How his power was discovered to the multitude.

[1] The provision that was at hand; *seven loaves, and a few little fishes*. It is probable that the fish was such as they had themselves taken. It is comfortable to *eat the labour of our hands* (Ps. cxxviii. 2). And what we have got by God's blessing on our labour we should be free of; for *therefore* we must labour, *that we may have to give*, Eph. iv. 28.

[2] The putting of the people in a posture to receive it (*v.* 35); *He commanded the multitude to sit down on the ground*. They saw but very little provision, yet they must sit down, in faith that they should have a meal's meat out of it.

[3] The distributing of the provision among them. He first *gave thanks*. The word used in the former miracle was *he blessed*. It comes all to one; giving thanks to God is a proper way of craving a blessing from God. He then *broke the loaves and gave to his disciples, and they to the multitude*, Though the disciples had distrusted Christ's power, yet he made use of them now as before; he is not provoked, as he might be, by the weakness and infirmities of his ministers, to lay them aside; but still he gives to them, and they to his people, of the word of life.

[4] The plenty there was among them (*v.* 37). *They did all eat, and were filled*. Those whom Christ feeds, he fills. While we labour for the world, we labour for that which satisfieth not (Isa. lv. 2); but those that duly wait on Christ shall be *abundantly satisfied with the goodness of his house*.

To show that they had all enough, there was a great deal left—*seven baskets full of broken meat;* but enough to show that with Christ *there is bread enough, and to spare*; supplies of grace for more than seek it, and for those that seek more.

[5] The account taken of the guests; not that they might pay their share, but that they might be witnesses to the power and goodness of Christ.

[6] The dismission of the multitude, and Christ's departure to another place (*v.* 39). He *sent away* the people. Though he had fed them twice, they must not expect miracles to be their daily bread. Let them now go home to their callings, and to their own tables.

JAMIESON, FAUSSET, BROWN

And they that had eaten were about four thousand: and he sent them away—Had not our Lord distinctly referred, in this very chapter and in two successive sentences, to the feeding of the five thousand and of the four thousand as two distinct miracles, many critics would have insisted that they were but two different representations of one and the same miracle, as they do of the two expulsions of the buyers and sellers from the temple, at the beginning and end of our Lord's ministry. But even in spite of what our Lord says, it is painful to find such men as NEANDER endeavoring to identify the two miracles. The localities, though both on the eastern side of the lake, were different; the time was different; the preceding and following circumstances were different; the period during which the people continued fasting was different—in the one case not even one entire day, in the other three days; the number fed was different—five thousand in the one case, in the other four thousand; the number of the loaves was different—five in the one case, in the other seven; the number of the fishes in the one case is definitely stated by all the four Evangelists—two; in the other case both give them indefinitely—"a few small fishes"; in the one case the multitude were commanded to sit down "upon the green grass"; in the other "on the ground"; in the one case the number of the baskets taken up filled with the fragments was twelve, in the other seven; but more than all, perhaps, because apparently quite incidental, in the one case the name given to the kind of baskets used is the same in all the four narratives—the *cophinus* (see on ch. 6:43); in the other case the name given to the kind of baskets used, while it is the same in both the narratives, is quite different—the *spuris*, a basket large enough to hold a man's body, for Paul was let down in one of these from the wall of Damascus (Acts 9:25). It might be added, that in the one case the people, in a frenzy of enthusiasm, would have taken Him by force to make Him a king; in the other case no such excitement is recorded. In view of these things, who could have believed that these were one and the same miracle, even if the Lord Himself had not expressly distinguished them?

ADAM CLARKE

37. *They did all eat, and were filled*. "They were satisfied." The husks of worldly pleasures may *fill* the man, but cannot *satisfy* the soul.

38. *Four thousand*. Let the poor learn from these miracles to trust in God for support. Whatever His ordinary providence denies, His miraculous power will supply.

39. *He sent away the multitude*. But not before He had instructed their souls, and fed and healed their bodies. *The coasts of Magdala*. In the parallel place, Mark viii. 10, this place is called Dalmanutha. Either Magdala was formed by a transposition of letters from Dalman, to which the Syriac termination *atha* had been added, or the one of these names refers to the country and the other to a town in that neighborhood.

MATTHEW HENRY

CHAPTER 16

Verses 1–4

We have here Christ's discourse with the Pharisees and Sadducees, men at variance among themselves, and yet unanimous in their opposition to Christ. Christ and Christianity meet with opposition on all hands.

I. Their demand, and the design of it.

1. The demand was of a sign from heaven; this they desired him to show them; pretending they were very willing to be satisfied and convinced. That which they pretended to desire was,

(1) Some other sign than what they had yet had. They had great plenty of signs; every miracle Christ wrought was a sign. But this will not serve; they despised those signs which relieved the necessity of the sick and sorrowful, and insisted upon some sign which would gratify the curiosity of the proud. The evidence that is given is sufficient to satisfy an unprejudiced understanding, but was not intended to please a vain humour. And it is an instance of the deceitfulness of the heart, to think that we should be wrought upon by the means and advantages which we have not, while we slight those which we have.

(2) It must be a sign from heaven. They would have such miracles to prove his commission, as were wrought at the giving of the law upon mount Sinai: thunder, and lightning, and the voice of words were the sign from heaven they required.

2. The design was to tempt him; not to be taught by him, but to ensnare him. If he should show them a sign from heaven, they would attribute it to a confederacy with the *prince of the power of the air*. When they had signs from heaven, they tempted Christ, saying, *Can he furnish a table in the wilderness?* Now that he had furnished a table in the wilderness, they tempted him, saying, *Can he give us a sign from heaven?*

II. Christ's reply to this demand.

1. He condemns their overlooking of the signs

JAMIESON, FAUSSET, BROWN

CHAPTER 16

VSS. 1-12. A SIGN FROM HEAVEN SOUGHT AND REFUSED—CAUTION AGAINST THE LEAVEN OF THE PHARISEES AND SADDUCEES. For the exposition, see on Mark 8:11-21.

seeking of him a sign from heaven, tempting him—not in the least desiring evidence for their conviction, but hoping to entrap Him.

ADAM CLARKE

CHAPTER 16

1. *Shew them a sign*. These sects, however opposed among themselves, most cordially unite in their opposition to Christ and His truth. *Tempting . . . him*. Feigning a desire to have His doctrine fully proved to them, that they might credit it, and become His disciples, but having no other design than to betray and ruin Him.

A. T. ROBERTSON:

"The Pharisees and Sadducees" (*hoi Pharisaioi kai Saddoukaioi*). The first time that we have this combination of the two parties who disliked each other exceedingly. Hate makes strange bedfellows. They hated Jesus more than they did each other. Their hostility has not decreased during the absence of Jesus, but rather increased. "Tempting him" (*peirazontes*). Their motive was bad. "A sign from heaven" (*semeion ek tou ouranou*). The scribes and Pharisees had already asked for a sign (12:38). Now this new combination adds "from heaven." What did they have in mind? They may not have had any definite idea to embarrass Jesus. The Jewish apocalypses did speak of spectacular displays of power by the Son of Man (the Messiah).—*Word Pictures in the New Testament*

MATTHEW HENRY

they had, *v.* 2, 3. They were seeking for the signs of the kingdom of God, when it was already among them.

To expose this, he observes to them,

(1) Their skilfulness and sagacity in other things, particularly in natural prognostications of the weather. There are common rules drawn from observation and experience, by which it is easy to foretell very probably what weather it will be. We *know not the balancing of the clouds* (Job xxxvii. 16), but we may spell something from the faces of them.

(2) Their sottishness and stupidity in the concerns of their souls; *Can ye not discern the signs of the times?* "Do you not see that the Messiah is come?" The miracles Christ wrought, and the gathering of the people to him, were plain indications that the *kingdom of heaven was at hand*, that this was *the day of their visitation*. It is great hypocrisy, when we slight the signs of God's ordaining, to seek for signs of our own prescribing. "Do not you foresee your own ruin coming for rejecting him?" It is the undoing of multitudes, that they are not aware what will be the end of their refusing Christ.

2. He refuses to give them any other sign (*v.* 4). He calls them *an adulterous generation*; because, while they professed themselves of the true church and spouse of God, they treacherously departed from him, and brake their covenants with him. He refuses to gratify their desire. Christ will not be prescribed to; *we ask, and have not, because we ask amiss*. He refers them to the sign of the prophet Jonas, which should yet be given them; his resurrection from the dead, and his preaching by his apostles to the Gentiles. Though the fancies of proud men shall not be humoured, yet the faith of the humble shall be supported.

This discourse broke off abruptly; *he left them and departed*. Christ will not tarry long with those that tempt him, but justly withdraws from those that are disposed to quarrel with him.

Verses 5–12

We have here Christ's discourse with his disciples concerning bread, in which, as in many other discourses, he speaks to them of spiritual things under a similitude, and they misunderstand him of carnal things. The occasion of it was, their forgetting to victual their ship; usually they carried bread along with them. But now they forgot; we will hope it was because their minds and memories were filled with better things. Christ's disciples are often such as have no great forecast for the world.

I. Here is the caution Christ gave them, to *beware of the leaven of the Pharisees*. Disciples are in most danger from hypocrites; against those that are openly vicious they stand upon their guard, and therefore the caution is doubled, *Take heed, and beware*.

The corrupt principles and practices of the Pharisees and Sadducees are compared to leaven; they fermented wherever they came.

II. Their mistake concerning this caution, *v.* 7. They thought Christ hereby upbraided them with their improvidence and forgetfulness. Or, they took it for a caution, not to be familiar with the Pharisees and Sadducees, not to eat with them, whereas the danger was not in their bread (Christ himself did eat with them, Luke vii. 36; xi. 37; xiv. 1), but in their principles.

III. The reproof Christ gave them for this.

1. He reproves their distrust of his ability and readiness to supply them in this strait (*v.* 8); "*O ye of little faith*, why are ye in such perplexity because ye have *taken no bread*, that ye can mind nothing else?" He does not chide them for their little forecast, as they expected he would. Parents and masters must not be angry at the forgetfulness of their children and servants, more than is necessary to make them take more heed another time; we are all apt to be forgetful of our duty. See how easily Christ forgave his disciples' carelessness; and do likewise. But that which he chides them for is their little faith.

(1) He would have them to depend upon him for supply. Though Christ's disciples be brought into wants and straits, through their own carelessness and incogitancy, yet he encourages them to trust in him for relief. We must not therefore use this as an excuse for our want of charity to those who are really poor, that they should have minded their own affairs better, and then they would not have been in need. It may be so, but they must not therefore be left to starve when they are in need.

(2) He is displeased at their solicitude in this matter. The weakness and shiftlessness of good people in their worldly affairs is that for which men are apt to condemn them; but it is not such an offence to Christ as their inordinate care and anxiety about those things. We must endeavour to keep

JAMIESON, FAUSSET, BROWN

The first part of the answer is given in Matthew alone (16:2, 3): "He answered and said unto them, When it is evening, ye say, It will be fair weather; for the sky is red. And in the morning, It will be foul weather to-day: for the sky is red and lowering [sullen, gloomy]. Hypocrites! ye can discern the face of the sky; but can ye not discern the signs of the times?" The same simplicity of purpose and careful observation of the symptoms of approaching events which they showed in common things would enable them to "discern the signs of the times"—or rather "seasons," to which the prophets pointed for the manifestation of the Messiah. The scepter had departed from Judah; Daniel's seventy weeks were expiring, etc.; and many other significant indications of the close of the old economy, and preparations for a freer and more comprehensive one, might have been discerned. But all was lost upon them.

Why doth this generation—"this wicked and adulterous generation" (Matt. 16:4)—**seek after a sign?**—when they have had such abundant evidence already. **There shall no sign be given unto this generation**—lit., "If there shall be given to this generation a sign"; a Jewish way of expressing a solemn and peremptory determination to the contrary (cf. Heb. 4:5; Ps. 95:11, *Margin*). "A generation incapable of appreciating such demonstrations shall not be gratified with them." In Matthew 16:4 He added, "but the sign of the prophet Jonas." (See on Matthew 12:39, 40.) **And he left them**—no doubt with tokens of displeasure.

Now the disciples had forgotten to take bread, neither had they in the ship with them more than one loaf—This is another example of that graphic circumstantiality which gives such a charm to this briefest of the four Gospels. The circumstance of the "one loaf" only remaining, as WEBSTER and WILKINSON remark, was more suggestive of their Master's recent miracles than the entire absence of provisions. **And he charged them, saying, Take heed, beware of the leaven of the Pharisees**—"and of the Sadducees" (Matt. 16:6). **and of the leaven of Herod**—The teaching or "doctrine" (Matt. 16:12) of the Pharisees and of the Sadducees was quite different, but both were equally pernicious; and the Herodians, though rather a political party, were equally envenomed against our Lord's spiritual teaching. See on Matthew 12:14. The *penetrating* and *diffusive* quality of leaven, for good or bad, is the ground of the comparison. **And they reasoned among themselves, saying, It is because we have no bread**—But a little while ago He was tried with the obduracy of the Pharisees; now He is tried with the obtuseness of His own disciples. The *nine* questions following each other in rapid succession (vss. 17-21) show how deeply He was hurt at this want of spiritual apprehension, and worse still, their low thoughts of Him, as if He would utter so solemn a warning on so petty a subject. It will be seen, however, from the very form of their conjecture, "It is because *we* have no bread," and our Lord's astonishment that they should not by that time have known better with what He took up His attention—that He ever left *the whole care for His own temporal wants to the Twelve:* that He did this so entirely, that finding they were reduced to their last loaf they felt as if unworthy of such a trust, and could not think but that the same thought was in their Lord's mind which was pressing upon their own; but that in this they were so far wrong that it hurt His feelings—sharp just in proportion to His love—that such a thought of Him should have entered their minds! Who that, like angels, "desire to look into these things" will not prize such glimpses above gold?

ADAM CLARKE

2. *When it is evening.* There are certain signs of fair and foul weather, which you are in the constant habit of observing, and which do not fail.

3. *The sky is red and lowering.* The signs of fair and foul weather were observed in a similar manner among the Romans, and indeed among most other people.

4. *Wicked and adulterous generation.* The Jewish people are represented in the Sacred Writings as married to the Most High; but, like a disloyal wife, forsaking their true Husband, and uniting themselves to Satan and sin. *Seeketh after a sign,* "seeketh sign upon sign," or still "another sign." Our blessed Lord had already wrought miracles sufficient to demonstrate both His divine mission and His divinity; only one was further necessary to take away the scandal of His cross and death, to fulfill the Scriptures, and to establish the Christian religion; and that was His resurrection from the dead, which, He here states, was typified in the case of Jonah.

5. *Come to the other side.* Viz., the coast of Bethsaida, by which our Lord passed, going to Caesarea, for He was now on His journey thither. See v. 13, and Mark viii. 22, 27.

6. *Beware of the leaven.* Bad doctrines act in the soul as leaven does in meal; they assimilate the whole spirit to their own nature. A man's particular creed has a greater influence on his tempers and conduct than most are aware of. Pride, hypocrisy, and worldly-mindedness, which constituted *the leaven of the Pharisees* and Sadducees, ruin the major part of the world.

7. *They reasoned.* For, as Lightfoot observes, the term leaven was very rarely used among the Jews to signify doctrine, and therefore the disciples did not immediately apprehend His meaning.

MATTHEW HENRY

the mean between the extremes of carelessness and carefulness; but of the two, the excess of thoughtfulness about the world worst becomes Christ's disciples.

(3) The aggravation of their distrust was the experience they had so lately had of the power and goodness of Christ in providing for them, *v.* 9, 10. They had him with them who could provide bread for them. If they had not the cistern, they had the Fountain. *Do ye not yet understand, neither remember?* Christ's disciples are often to be blamed for the shallowness of their understandings, and the slipperiness of their memories. "Remember *how many baskets ye took up.*" These baskets were intended for memorials, by which to keep the mercy in remembrance. He that could furnish them with such an overplus then, surely could furnish them with what was necessary now. We are *therefore* perplexed with present cares and distrusts, because we do not duly remember our former experiences of divine power and goodness.

2. He reproves their misunderstanding of the caution he gave them (*v.* 11); *How is it that you do not understand?* Christ's disciples may well be ashamed of the slowness and dullness of their apprehensions in divine things. *I spake it not unto you concerning bread.* He took it ill, (1) That they should think him as thoughtful about bread as they were; whereas his *meat and drink were to do his Father's will.* (2) That they should be so little acquainted with his way of preaching, as to take that literally which he spoke by way of parable.

IV. The rectifying of the mistake by this reproof (*v.* 12); *Then understood they* what he meant. He did not tell them expressly what he meant, but repeated what he had said; and so obliged them to arrive at the sense of it in their own thoughts. Thus Christ teaches by the Spirit of wisdom in the heart, opening the understanding to the Spirit of revelation in the word. And those truths are most precious, which we have thus digged for.

Verses 13–20

We have here a private conference which Christ had with his disciples concerning himself. It was in the coasts of Cæsarea Philippi, there in that remote corner, perhaps, there was less flocking after him than in other places, which gave him leisure for this private conversation with his disciples.

I. He enquires what the opinions of others were concerning him; *Who do men say that I, the Son of man, am?*

1. He calls himself the *Son of man*; which may be taken either, (1) As a title common to him with others. He was called, and justly, *the Son of God*, for so he was (Luke i. 35); but he called himself the Son of man; for he is really and truly "Man, made of a woman." Or, (2) As a title peculiar to him as Mediator.

2. He enquires what people's sentiments were concerning him: "*Who do men say that I am? The Son of man?*" (So I think it might better be read.) "Do they own me for the Messiah?" He asks not, "Who do the *scribes* and *Pharisees* say that I am?" But, "Who do *men* say that I am?" He referred to the common people, whom the Pharisees despised. The common people conversed more familiarly with the disciples than they did with their Master, and therefore from them he might better know what they said. Christ had not plainly said who he was, but left people to infer it from his works, John x. 24, 25. Now he would know what inferences the people drew from *them.*

3. To this question the disciples gave him an answer (*v.* 14). *Some say, thou art John the Baptist, &c.* They are different opinions; some say one thing, and others another. Truth is one; but those who vary from that commonly vary one from another. Being so noted a Person, everyone would be ready to pass his verdict upon him, and, "Many men, many minds." They are honourable opinions. It is possible for men to have good thoughts of Christ, and yet not right ones, a high opinion of him, and yet not high enough. They all suppose him to be *one risen from the dead*; which perhaps arose from a confused notion they had of the resurrection of the Messiah. They are all false opinions, built upon mistakes.

(1) *Some say, thou art John the Baptist.* Herod said so (*ch.* xiv. 2), and those about him would be apt to say as he said.

(2) *Some Elias;* taking occasion, no doubt, from the prophecy of Malachi (*ch.* iv. 5), *Behold, I will send you Elijah.*

(3) *Others Jeremias.*

(4) *Or, one of the prophets.* This shows what an honourable idea they entertained of the prophets. Rather than they would allow Jesus of Nazareth, one of their own country, to be such an extraordinary

JAMIESON, FAUSSET, BROWN

How is it that ye do not understand?—"do not understand that the warning I gave you could not have been prompted by any such petty consideration as the want of loaves in your scrip." Profuse as were our Lord's miracles, we see from this that they were not wrought at random, but that He carefully noted their minutest details, and desired that this should be done by those who witnessed, as doubtless by all who read the record of them. Even the different kind of baskets used at the two miraculous feedings, so carefully noted in the two narratives, are here also referred to; the one smaller, of which there were twelve, the other much larger, of which there were seven.

13-28. Peter's Noble Confession of Christ, and the Benediction Pronounced upon Him—Christ's First Explicit Announcement of His Approaching Sufferings, Death, and Resurrection—His Rebuke of Peter and Warning to All the Twelve. (= Mark 8:27; 9:1; Luke 9:18-27.) The time of this section—which is beyond doubt, and will presently be mentioned—is of immense importance, and throws a touching interest around the incidents which it records. *Peter's Confession, and the Benediction Pronounced upon Him* (vss. 13-20). **13. When Jesus came into the coasts**—"the parts," i.e., the territory or region. In Mark (8:27) it is "the towns" or "villages." **of Caesarea Philippi**—It lay at the foot of Mount Lebanon, near the sources of the Jordan, in the territory of Dan, and at the northeast extremity of Palestine. It was originally called *Panium* (from a cavern in its neighborhood dedicated to the god *Pan*) and *Paneas.* Philip, the tetrarch, the only good son of Herod the Great, in whose dominions Paneas lay, having beautified and enlarged it, changed its name to *Caesarea,* in honor of the Roman emperor, and added *Philippi* after his own name, to distinguish it from the other *Caesarea* (Acts 10:1) on the northeast coast of the Mediterranean Sea. (Josephus, *Antiquities,* 15:10, 3; 18:2, 1.) This quiet and distant retreat Jesus appears to have sought with the view of talking over with the Twelve the fruit of His past labors, and breaking to them for the first time the sad intelligence of His approaching death. **he asked his disciples**—"by the way," says Mark (8: 27), and "as He was alone praying," says Luke (9: 18). **saying, Whom**—or more grammatically, "Who"—**do men say that I the Son of man am?**—(or, "that the Son of man is"—the recent editors omitting here the *me* of Mark and Luke; though the evidence seems pretty nearly balanced)—i.e., 'What are the views generally entertained of Me, the Son of man, after going up and down among them so long?' He had now closed the first great stage of His ministry, and was just entering on the last dark one. His spirit, burdened, sought relief in retirement, not only from the multitude, but even for a season from the Twelve. He retreated into "the secret place of the Most High," pouring out His soul "in supplications and prayers, with strong crying and tears" (Heb. 5:7). On rejoining His disciples, and as they were pursuing their quiet journey, He asked them this question. **14. And they said, Some say that thou art John the Baptist**—risen from the dead. So that Herod Antipas was not singular in his surmise (ch. 14:1, 2). **some, Elias**—(Cf. Mark 6:15). **and others, Jeremias**—Was this theory suggested by a supposed resemblance between the "Man of Sorrows" and "the weeping prophet"? **or one of the prophets**—or, as Luke (9: 8) expresses it, "that one of the old prophets is risen again." In another report of the popular opinions which Mark (6:15) gives us, it is thus expressed, "That it is a prophet [or], as one of the prophets":

ADAM CLARKE

9-10. *Do ye not yet understand . . . the five loaves . . . Neither the seven?* How astonishing is it that these men should have any fear of lacking bread, after having seen the two miracles which our blessed Lord alludes to above!

12. They now perceived that He warned them. against the superstition of the Pharisees, which produced hypocrisy, pride, envy, etc., and the false doctrine of the Sadducees, which denied the existence of a spiritual world, the immortality of the soul, the resurrection of the body, and the providence of God.

13. *Caesarea Philippi.* A city, in the tribe of Naphtali, near to Mount Libanus, in the province of Iturea. Its ancient name was *Dan*, Gen. xiv. 14; afterwards it was called *Lais*, Judg. xviii. 7. But Philip the tetrarch, having rebuilt and beautified it, gave it the name of Caesarea, in honor of Tiberius Caesar, the reigning emperor; but to distinguish it from another Caesarea, which was on the coast of the Mediterranean Sea, and to perpetuate the fame of him who rebuilt it, it was called Caesarea Philippi, or Caesarea of Philip.

Whom do men say? He asked His disciples this question, not because He was ignorant what the people thought and spoke of Him, but to have the opportunity, in getting an express declaration of their faith from themselves, to confirm and strengthen them in it; but see on Luke ix.

Some . . . John the Baptist. By this and other passages we learn that the Pharisaic doctrine of the transmigration of souls was pretty general; for it was upon this ground that they believed that the soul of the Baptist, or of Elijah, Jeremiah, or some of the prophets, had come to a new life in the body of Jesus.

MATTHEW HENRY

Person as his works bespoke him to be, they would say, "It was not he, but *one of the old prophets*."

II. He enquires what *their* thoughts were concerning him; "*But who say ye that I am?*" *v.* 15. The disciples had themselves been better taught than others; had, by their intimacy with Christ, greater advantages of getting knowledge than others had. Those who have more acquaintance with Christ than others, should have truer sentiments concerning him, and be able to give a better account of him than others. The disciples were trained up to teach others, and therefore it was highly requisite that they should understand the truth themselves. This is a question we should every one of us be frequently putting to ourselves, "*Who* do we say, *what* kind of one do we say, that *the Lord Jesus is*?" It is well or ill with us, according as our thoughts are right or wrong concerning Jesus Christ.

Well, this is the question. Peter's answer to this question, *v.* 16. Peter answers in the name of all the rest, they all consenting to it, and concurring in it. Peter's temper led him to be forward in speaking upon all such occasions, and sometimes he spoke well, sometimes amiss; in all companies there are found some warm, bold men, to whom a precedency of speech falls of course; Peter was such a one.

Peter's answer is short, but it is full, and true, and to the purpose; *Thou art the Christ, the Son of the living God.* This is the conclusion of the whole matter. The people called him *a Prophet*, *that Prophet* (John vi. 14); but the disciples own him to be the Christ, the anointed One. It was a great thing to believe this concerning one whose outward appearance was so contrary to the general idea the Jews had of the Messiah. He called himself the *Son of Man*; but they owned him to be *the Son of the living God. They* know and believe him to be *the Son of the living God*, and to be the *Life of the world.* Let us then go to Christ; Lord Jesus, *thou art the Christ, the Son of the living God.* Note: Christ's approbation of his answer (*v.* 17-19).

1. As a believer, *v.* 17. Christ shows himself well pleased with Peter's confession, that it was so clear and express. Christ shows him whence he received the knowledge of this truth. At the first discovery of this truth in the dawning of the gospel day, it was a mighty thing to believe it.

Peter had the happiness of it; *Blessed art thou, Simon Bar-jona.* He reminds him of his rise and original; he was *Bar-jonas—The son of a dove.* Let him remember *the rock out of which he was hewn*, that he may see he was not born to this dignity, but preferred to it by the divine favour; it was free grace that made him to differ. Having reminded him of this, he makes him sensible of his great happiness as a believer; *Blessed art thou.* True believers are truly blessed, and those are blessed indeed whom Christ pronounces blessed. All happiness attends the right knowledge of Christ.

God must have the glory of it; "*For flesh and blood have not revealed it to thee.* This light sprang neither from nature nor from education, but from my Father who is in heaven." Saving faith is the gift of God, and, wherever it is, is wrought by him. *Therefore* thou art blessed, because *my Father has revealed it to thee.* Blessed are they that are thus highly favoured.

2. Christ replies to him as an apostle or minister, *v.* 18, 19. There is nothing lost by being forward to confess Christ; for those who thus honour him, he will honour.

Upon occasion of this great confession made of Christ, which is the church's homage and allegiance, he signed and published this royal, this divine charter, by which that body politic is incorporated.

Now the purport of this charter is,

First, To establish the being of the church; *I say also unto thee.* It is Christ that makes the grant, he who is the church's Head. The grant is put into Peter's hand; "I say it to *thee*." The New Testament charter is here delivered to Peter as an agent, but to the use and behoof of the church in all ages, according to the purposes therein specified and contained. Now it is here promised, that Christ would build his church upon a rock. This body politic is incorporated by the style and title of *Christ's church.* It is a number of the children of men called out of the world. and set apart from it, and dedicated to Christ. The Builder and Maker of the church is Christ himself; *I will build it. Ye are God's building;* and building is a progressive work; the church in this world is like a house in the building. It is a comfort that Christ, who has divine wisdom and power, undertakes to build it. The foundation on which it is built is, *this Rock.* Let the architect do his part ever so well, if the foundation be rotten, the building will not stand; let us therefore see what the foundation is. The church is built upon a *rock*; a firm, strong,

JAMIESON, FAUSSET, BROWN

in other words, That He was a prophetical person, resembling those of old. **15. He saith unto them, But whom**—rather, "who"—**say ye that I am?**—He had never put this question before, but the crisis He was reaching made it fitting that He should now have it from them. We may suppose this to be one of those moments of which the prophet says, in His name, "Then I said, I have labored in vain; I have spent my strength for naught, and in vain" (Isa. 49:4): Lo, these three years I come seeking fruit on this fig tree; and what is it? As the result of all, I am taken for John the Baptist, for Elias, for Jeremias, for one of the prophets. Yet some there are that have beheld My glory, the glory as of the Only-begotten of the Father, and I shall hear their voice, for it is sweet.

16. And Simon Peter answered and said, Thou art the Christ, the Son of the living God—He does not say, "Scribes and Pharisees, rulers and people, are all perplexed; and shall we, unlettered fishermen, presume to decide?" But feeling the light of his Master's glory shining in his soul, he breaks forth—not in a tame, prosaic acknowledgment, "*I believe that Thou art . . .*"—but in the language of adoration—such as one uses in worship, "Thou art the Christ, the Son of the Living God!" He first owns Him the promised *Messiah* (see on ch. 1:16); then he rises higher, echoing the voice from heaven—"This is My beloved Son, in whom I am well pleased"; and in the important addition—"Son of the Living God"—he recognizes the essential and eternal life of God as in this His Son—though doubtless without that distinct perception afterwards vouchsafed. **17. And Jesus answered and said unto him, Blessed art thou**—Though it is not to be doubted that Peter, in this noble testimony to Christ, only expressed the conviction of all the Twelve, yet since he alone seems to have had clear enough apprehensions to put that conviction in proper and suitable words, and courage enough to speak them out, and readiness enough to do this at the right time—so he only, of all the Twelve, seems to have met the present want, and communicated to the saddened soul of the Redeemer at the critical moment that balm which was needed to cheer and refresh it. Nor is Jesus above giving indication of the deep satisfaction which this speech yielded Him, and hastening to respond to it by a signal acknowledgment of Peter in return. **Simon-Barjona**—or, "son of Jona" (John 1:42), or "Jonas" (John 21:15). This name, denoting his humble fleshly extraction, seems to have been purposely here mentioned, to contrast the more vividly with the spiritual elevation to which divine illumination had raised him. **for flesh and blood hath not revealed it unto thee**—"This is not the fruit of human teaching." **but my Father which is in heaven**—In speaking of God, Jesus, it is to be observed, never calls Him, "our Father" (see on John 20:17), but either "your Father"—when He would encourage His timid believing ones with the assurance that He was theirs, and teach themselves to call Him so—or, as here, "My Father," to signify some peculiar action or aspect of Him as "the God and Father of our Lord Jesus Christ."

ADAM CLARKE

16. *Thou art the Christ, the Son of the living God.* Every word here is emphatic—a most concise, and yet comprehensive, confession of faith. *The Christ*, or "Messiah," points out His divinity, and shows His office; *the Son* designates His person. On this account it is that both are joined together so frequently in the new covenant. *Of the living God*—literally, of God the Living One. *Living.* A character applied to the Supreme Being, not only to distinguish Him from the dead idols of paganism, but also to point Him out as the Source of life, present, spiritual, and eternal. Probably there is an allusion here to the great name *Yehovah*, which properly signifies being or existence.

17. *Blessed art thou, Simon Bar-jona.* Or "Simon, son of Jonah." *Flesh and blood. I.e.*, "Man"; no human being hath revealed this.

G. CAMPBELL MORGAN:

Jesus did not pronounce a reward upon Peter, for the discovery he had made, when He said, "Blessed art thou, Simon Bar-Jonah." On the contrary, He was rather describing the condition into which Peter had come by the gain of this new knowledge which he had confessed. Such confession, that He was the Christ, and the Son of the living God, was in itself the result of divine illumination. Not in the confession, but in the consciousness out of which the confession was born was Peter blessed. Probably he spoke for the rest as well as for himself, but one man at least had made contact with the purposes and power of God. He said, "Thou art the Christ, the Son of the living God." Jesus said, "Blessed art thou, Simon Bar-Jonah." That is the key to the situation. That is the discovery upon which the human soul is remade. That is the discovery upon which human society is to be remade. That is the discovery upon which the city of God is to be built, and the everlasting Kingdom established.

How did Peter learn this fact? Let the Lord continue, "Flesh and blood hath not revealed it unto thee, but my Father who is in heaven." He took hold of a common colloquialism of His times and used it. The man in the street would say, "Flesh and blood cannot endure this; flesh and blood cannot see through this." Christ said, "That confession you have made is not something that another man told you; you have not discovered it; my Father hath revealed it unto thee."

—The Gospel According to Matthew

MATTHEW HENRY

and lasting foundation, which time will not waste, nor will it sink under the weight of the building. Christ would not build his house upon the sand, for he knew that storms would arise. It is built upon *this* rock; thou art *Peter*, which signifies *a stone* or *rock*; Christ gave him that name when he first called him (John i. 42), and here he confirms it. From the mention of this significant name, occasion is taken for this metaphor of *building upon a rock*.

Some by this rock understand Peter himself as an apostle. The church is built upon the foundation of the apostles, Eph. ii. 20. The first stones of that building were laid in and by their ministry. Now Peter being that apostle by whose hand the first stones of the church were laid, both in Jewish converts (Acts ii), and in the Gentile converts (Acts x), he might in some sense be said to be the rock on which it was built.

Others, by this *rock*, understand *Christ*; "*Thou art Peter*, thou hast the name of a *stone*, but *upon this rock*, pointing to himself, *I will build my church*." He took occasion from Peter, to speak of himself as the Rock. Christ is both its Founder and its Foundation; he draws souls, and draws them to himself; to him they are united, and on him they rest and have a constant dependence.

Others, by this *rock* understand this confession which Peter made of Christ, and this comes all to one with understanding it of Christ himself. "Now," saith Christ, "this is that great truth *upon which I will build my church*." Take away this truth itself, and the universal church falls to the ground. If Christ be not the Son of God, Christianity is a cheat. Take away the faith and confession of this truth from any particular church, and it ceases to be a part of Christ's church. This is *articulus stantis et cadentis ecclesiae*—that article, with the admission or the denial of which the church either rises or falls; "the main hinge on which the door of salvation turns"; those who let go this, do not hold the foundation.

Christ here promises to preserve and secure his church, when it is built; *The gates of hell shall not prevail against it*. This implies that the church has enemies that fight against it, and endeavour its ruin and overthrow, here represented by *the gates of hell, that is*, the city of hell; (which is directly opposite to this heavenly city, this *city of the living God*), the devil's interest among the children of men. This assures us that the enemies of the church shall not gain their point. While the world stands, Christ will have a church in it. Somewhere or other the Christian religion shall have a being, though not always in the same degree of purity and splendour, yet so as that the entail of it shall never be quite cut off. The church may be foiled in particular encounters, but in the main battle it shall come off *more than a conqueror*.

The other part of this charter is, to settle the *Second*, Government of the church, *v.* 19. A city without government is a chaos. Now this constituting of the government of the church, is here expressed by the delivering of the keys, and, with them, a power to bind and loose. This invests all the apostles and their successors with a ministerial power to guide and govern the church of Christ, as it exists in particular congregations or churches, according to the rules of the gospel. The keys were first put into Peter's hand, because he was the first *that opened the door of faith to the Gentiles*, Acts. x. 28. Christ, having incorporated his church, hath appointed the office of the ministry for the keeping up of order and government, and to see that his laws be duly served. He doth not say, The keys *shall* be given, but, *I will give* them; for ministers derive their authority from Christ, and all their power is to be used in his name. The power here delegated is a spiritual power; it is a power *pertaining to the kingdom of heaven*, that is, to the church, to the gospel dispensation. It is the *power* of the keys that is given, alluding to the custom of investing men with authority in such a place, by delivering to them the keys of the place. Or as the master of the house gives the keys to the steward, the keys of the stores where the provisions are kept. It is a power to *bind and loose*, that is (following the metaphor of the keys), to shut and open. It is a power which Christ has promised to own the due administration of; *It shall be bound in heaven, and loosed in heaven*. The word of the gospel, in the mouth of faithful ministers, is to be looked upon, not as the word of man, but as the word of God, and to be received accordingly.

Now *the keys of the kingdom of heaven are*,

(1) The key of *doctrine*, called the key of *knowledge*. Now the apostles had an extraordinary power of this kind; some things forbidden by the law of Moses were now to be allowed; some things allowed there were now to be forbidden; and the apostles were

JAMIESON, FAUSSET, BROWN

18. And I say also unto thee—i.e., "As thou hast borne such testimony to Me, even so in return do I to thee." **That thou art Peter**—At his first calling, this new name was announced to him as an honor afterwards to be conferred on him (John 1:43). Now he gets it, with an explanation of what it was meant to convey. **and upon this rock**—As "Peter" and "Rock" are one word in the dialect familiarly spoken by our Lord—the Aramaic or Syro-Chaldaic, which was the mother tongue of the country—this exalted *play upon the word* can be fully seen only in languages which have one word for both. Even in the Greek it is imperfectly represented. In French, as WEBSTER and WILKINSON remark, it is perfect, *Pierre —pierre*. **I will build my Church**—not on the man Simon Barjona; but on him as the heavenly-taught confessor of a faith. "My Church," says our Lord, calling the Church HIS OWN; a magnificent expression regarding Himself, remarks BENGEL—nowhere else occurring in the Gospel.

and the gates of hell—"of Hades," or, the unseen world; meaning, the gates of Death: in other words, "It shall never perish." Some explain it of "the assaults of the powers of darkness"; but though that expresses a glorious truth, probably the former is the sense here.

19. And I will give unto thee the keys of the kingdom of heaven—the kingdom of God about to be set up on earth—**and whatsoever thou shalt bind on earth shall be bound in heaven: and whatsoever thou shalt loose on earth shall be loosed in heaven**—Whatever this mean, it was soon expressly *extended to all the apostles* (ch. 18:18); so that the claim of supreme authority in the Church, made for Peter by the Church of Rome, and then arrogated to themselves by the popes as the legitimate successors of St. Peter, is baseless and impudent. As first in confessing Christ, Peter got this commission before the rest; and with these "keys," on the day of Pentecost, he first "opened the door of faith" to the *Jews*, and then, in the person of Cornelius, he was honored to do the same to the *Gentiles*. Hence, in the lists of the apostles, Peter is always first named. See on ch. 18:18. One thing is clear, that not in all the New Testament is there the vestige of any authority either claimed or exercised by Peter, or conceded to him, above the rest of the apostles—a thing conclusive against the Romish claims in behalf of that apostle.

ADAM CLARKE

18. *Thou art Peter*. This was the same as if He had said "I acknowledge you for one of My disciples"—for this name was given him by our Lord when He first called him to the apostleship. *Peter* signifies a stone, or fragment of a "rock"; and our Lord, whose constant custom it was to rise to heavenly things through the medium of earthly, takes occasion from the name, the metaphorical meaning of which was "strength" and "stability," to point out the solidity of the confession, and the stability of that cause which should be founded on "the Christ, the Son of the living God."

"Upon this very rock," this true confession of yours—that I am the Messiah, that am come to reveal and communicate the living God, that the dead, lost world may be saved—upon this very Rock, myself, thus confessed, will I build My Church, "my assembly, or congregation," i.e., of persons who are made partakers of this precious faith. That Peter is not designed in our Lord's words must be evident to all who are not blinded by prejudice. Peter was only one of the builders in this sacred edifice, who himself tells us was built on this living Foundation Stone: 1 Pet. ii. 4-5. Therefore Jesus Christ did not say, "On you, Peter, will I build My Church," but changes immediately the expression and says, "Upon that very rock," to show that He addressed neither Peter nor any other of the apostles. So the supremacy of Peter and the infallibility of the Church of Rome must be sought in some other scripture, for they certainly are not to be found in this. *The gates of hell*, i.e., the "machinations and powers" of the invisible world. In ancient times the gates of fortified cities were used to hold councils in, and were usually places of great strength. Our Lord's expression means that neither the plots, stratagems, nor strength of Satan and his angels should ever so far prevail as to destroy the sacred truths in the above confession.

19. *The keys of the kingdom*. By the *kingdom of heaven* we may consider the true Church, that house of God, to be meant; and by the *keys*, the power of admitting into that house, or of preventing any improper person from coming in. In other words, the doctrine of salvation and the full declaration of the way in which God will save sinners, and who they are that shall be finally excluded from heaven, and on what account. When the Jews made a man a doctor of the law, they put into his hand the key of the closet in the Temple where the sacred books were kept, and also tablets to write upon, signifying by this that they gave him authority to teach, and to explain the Scriptures to the people. This prophetic declaration of our Lord was literally fulfilled to Peter, as he was made the first instrument of opening, i.e., preaching the doctrines of the kingdom of Heaven to the Jews, Acts ii. 41; and to the Gentiles, Acts x. 44-47; xi. 1; xv. 7. *Whatsoever thou shalt bind on earth*. This mode of expression was frequent among the Jews; they considered that everything that was done upon earth, according to the order of

MATTHEW HENRY

empowered to declare this to the world. When Peter was first taught himself, and then taught others, *to call nothing common or unclean,* this power was exercised. There is also an ordinary power hereby conveyed to all ministers, to tell people, in God's name, and according to the scriptures, *what is good, and what the Lord requires of them.* Christ gives his apostles power to shut or open the book of the gospel to people, as the case required. When ministers preach pardon and peace to the penitent, wrath and the curse to the impenitent, in Christ's name, they act then pursuant to this authority of binding and loosing.

(2) The key of *discipline,* which is but the application of the former to particular persons, upon a right estimate of their characters and actions. The judge doth not make the law, but only declares what is law, and gives sentence accordingly. Christ's ministers have a power to admit into the church; "*Go, disciple all nations, baptising them;* those who profess faith in Christ, and obedience to him, admit them by baptism." Ministers are to let in to *the wedding-feast those that are bidden*; and to keep out such as are apparently unfit for so holy a communion. They have a power to expel and cast out such as have forfeited their church-membership. They have a power to restore and to receive in again, upon their repentance, such as had been thrown out; to loose those whom they had bound. The apostles had a miraculous gift of *discerning spirits*; yet even *they* went by the rule of outward appearances, which ministers may still make a judgment upon, if they be skilful and faithful.

Here is the charge which Christ gave his disciples, to keep this private for the present (*v.* 20); *They must tell no man that he was Jesus the Christ.* What they had professed to him, they must not yet publish to the world, for several reasons: Because this was the time of preparation for his kingdom: the great thing now preached, was, that *the kingdom of heaven was at hand.* Everything is beautiful in its season, and it is good advice, *Prepare thy work, and afterwards build,* Prov. xxiv. 27. Christ would have his Messiahship proved by his works. He was so secure of the demonstration of his miracles that he waived other witnesses. Christ would not have the apostles preach this, till they had the most convincing evidence ready to allege in confirmation of it. Great truths may suffer damage by being asserted before they can be sufficiently proved. Now the great proof of Jesus being the Christ was his resurrection. It was requisite that the preachers of so great a truth should be furnished with greater measures of the Spirit than the apostles as yet had. When Christ was glorified and the Spirit poured out, we find Peter proclaiming upon the house-tops what was here spoken in a corner. As there is a time to keep silence, so there is a time to speak.

Verses 21-23

I. Christ's foretelling of his sufferings. Some hints he had already given of his sufferings, but now he *began* to show it, to speak plainly and expressly of it. Hitherto he had not touched upon this, because the disciples were weak, but now that they were more ripe in knowledge, and strong in faith, he began to tell them this. Christ reveals his mind to his people gradually, and lets in light as they can bear it, and are fit to receive it.

From that time, when they had made that full confession of Christ, when he found them knowing in one truth, he taught them another. If they had not been well grounded in the belief of Christ's being the Son of God, it would have been a great shaking to their faith. All truths are not to be spoken to all persons at all times, but such as are proper and suitable to their present state. Now observe,

1. What he foretold concerning his sufferings, the particulars and circumstances of them, and all surprising. The place where he should suffer. He must go to Jerusalem, the head city, the holy city, and suffer there. There all the sacrifices were offered, there therefore *he* must die, *who is the great sacrifice.* The persons by whom he should suffer; *the elders, and chief priests, and scribes.* Those that should have been most forward in owning and admiring Christ, were the most bitter in persecuting him. What he should suffer; *he must suffer many things, and be killed.* His enemies' insatiable malice, and his own invincible patience, appear in the variety and multiplicity of his sufferings (he suffered many things) and in the extremity of them; nothing less than his death would satisfy them, he must be killed. What should be the happy issue of all his sufferings; he shall *be raised again the third day.* His rising again the third day proved him to be the Son of God, notwithstanding his sufferings; and therefore he

JAMIESON, FAUSSET, BROWN

20. Then charged he his disciples that they should tell no man that he was Jesus the Christ—Now that He had been so explicit, they might naturally think the time come for giving it out openly; but here they are told it had not.

Announcement of His Approaching Death, and Rebuke of Peter (vss. 21-28). The occasion here is evidently the same. **21. From that time forth began Jesus to show unto his disciples**—i.e., with an *explicitness and frequency* He had never observed before—**how that he must go unto Jerusalem and suffer many things** "and be rejected," (Matthew and Mark)—**of the elders and chief priests and scribes**—not as before, merely by not receiving Him, but by formal deeds. **and be killed, and be raised again the third day**—Mark (8:32) adds, that "He spake that saying openly"—"explicitly," or "without disguise."

ADAM CLARKE

God, was at the same time done in heaven. Hence they were accustomed to say that when the priest, on the Day of Atonement, offered the two goats upon earth, the same were offered in heaven. As one goat, therefore, is permitted to escape on earth, one is permitted to escape in heaven; and when the priests cast the lots on earth, the priest also casts the lots in heaven. The disciples of our Lord, from having the *keys,* i.e., the true knowledge of the doctrine of the kingdom of Heaven, should be able at all times to distinguish between the clean and the unclean, and pronounce infallible judgment; and this "binding" and "loosing," or pronouncing fit or unfit for fellowship with the members of Christ, being always according to the doctrine of the gospel of God, should be considered as proceeding immediately from heaven, and consequently as divinely ratified. "Binding" and "loosing" were terms in frequent use among the Jews, and they meant bidding and forbidding, granting and refusing, declaring lawful or unlawful.

20. *Then charged he his disciples.* "He strictly charged them."

21. *From that time forth began Jesus.* Before this time our Lord had spoken of His death only in a vague and obscure manner (see chap. xii. 40) because He would not afflict His disciples with this matter sooner than necessity required. But now, as the time of His crucifixion drew nigh, He spoke of His sufferings and death in the most express and clear terms. Three sorts of persons, our Lord intimates, should be the cause of His death and passion: the *elders,* the *chief priests,* and the *scribes.*

A. T. ROBERTSON:

20. "That they should tell no man" (*hina medeni eiposin*). Why? For the very reason that he had himself avoided this claim in public. He was the Messiah (*ho Christos*), but the people would inevitably take it in a political sense. Jesus was plainly profoundly moved by Peter's great confession on behalf of the disciples. He was grateful and confident of the final outcome. But he foresaw peril to all. Peter had confessed him as the Messiah and on this rock of faith thus confessed he would build his church or kingdom. They will all have and use the keys to this greatest of all buildings, but for the present they must be silent.—*Word Pictures in the New Testament*

MATTHEW HENRY

mentions that, to keep up their faith. Thus we must look upon Christ's suffering for us, trace in it the way to his glory; and thus we must look upon our suffering for Christ, look through it to the recompence of reward. *If we suffer with him, we shall reign with him.*

2. Why he foretold his sufferings. His sufferings were no surprise to him, did not come upon him as a snare, but he had a distinct and certain foresight of them, which greatly magnifies his love. To rectify the mistakes which his disciples had imbibed concerning the external pomp and power of his kingdom, here Christ reads them another lesson, tells them of the cross and sufferings. Those that follow Christ must be dealt plainly with, and warned not to expect great things in this world. It was to prepare them for the share, at least, of sorrow and fear, which they must have in his sufferings. When he suffered many things, the disciples could not but suffer some; let them know it before, and, being fore-*warned*, may be fore-*armed*.

II. The offence which Peter took at this: he said, *Be it far from thee, Lord. He took him, and began to rebuke him.*

1. It did not become Peter to contradict his Master, or take upon him to advise him. When God's dispensations are either intricate or cross to us, it becomes us silently to acquiesce in, and not to prescribe to, the divine will; God knows what he has to do, without our teaching.

2. It savoured much of fleshly wisdom. It is the corrupt part of us, that is thus solicitous to sleep in a whole skin. We are apt to look upon sufferings as they relate to this present life, to which they are uneasy; but there are other rules to measure them by. He would have Christ to dread suffering as much as he did; but we mistake, if we measure Christ's love and patience by our own.

III. Christ's displeasure against Peter for this suggestion of his, *v.* 23. We do not read of anything said or done by any of his disciples, at any time, that he resented so much as this. How he expressed his displeasure: *Get thee behind me, Satan.* Just now, he had said, *Blessed art thou, Simon;* but here, *Get thee behind me, Satan;* and there was cause for both. A good man may by a surprise of temptation soon grow very unlike himself. It is the subtlety of Satan, to send temptations to us by the unsuspected hands of our best and dearest friends. Even the kindnesses of our friends are often abused by Satan, and made use of as temptations to us. We should learn to know the devil's voice when he speaks in a saint as well as when he speaks in a serpent. We must be free and faithful in reproving the dearest friend we have. We must not compliment, but rebuke, mistaken courtesies. Why did Christ thus resent a motion that seemed not only harmless, but kind? Two reasons are given:

1. *Thou art my hindrance* (so it may be read); "thou standest in my way." Christ was hastening on in the work of our salvation, and his heart was so much upon it, that he took it ill to be hindered. Peter was not so sharply reproved for disowning and denying his Master in his sufferings as he was for dissuading him from them. Our Lord Jesus preferred our salvation before his own ease and safety; he came into the world, not to spare himself, as Peter advised, but to spend himself. *Thou art an offence to me.* Those that engage in any great and good work must expect to meet with hindrance and opposition from friends and foes, from within and from without. Those that hinder us from doing or suffering for God, when we are called to it, whatever they are in other things in that they are *Satans, adversaries* to us.

2. *Thou savourest not the things that are of God, but those that are of men. The things that are of God* often clash and interfere with *the things that are of men*, that is, with our own wealth, pleasure, and reputation.

Verses 24–28

Christ, having shown his disciples that *he* must suffer, here shows them that *they* must suffer too.

I. Here is the law of discipleship laid down, and the terms fixed, upon which we may have the honour and benefit of it, *v.* 24.

1. What it is to be a disciple of Christ; it is to come after him. A true disciple of Christ is one that doth follow him in duty, and shall follow him to glory. He is one that comes after Christ, not one that prescribes to him, as Peter now undertook to do. A disciple of Christ comes after him, as the sheep after the shepherd, one that walks in the same way that he walked in, treads in his steps, and *follows the Lamb, whithersoever he goes.*

2. What are the great things required of those that will be Christ's disciples; *If any man will come.*

F. B. MEYER:

"Have mercy on thee, Lord! this shall never be unto thee." Throughout his life, these words were perpetually flung at the heart of Christ. Spare thyself this hunger, the devil said in the wilderness, on the threshold of Christ's public ministry; spare thyself this agonizing death, he said again in the garden, on the eve of the crucifixion.

It is noticeable that the cross was surrounded by voices that repeated the same words. They that passed by it wagged their heads, and said, "Thou that destroyest the temple and buildest it in three days, save thyself." The chief priests mocked Him, with the scribes and elders, and said, "Can he not save himself?" The soldiers also mocked him, coming to him, offering him vinegar, and saying, "If thou art the King of the Jews, save thyself." And one of the malefactors which were hanged railed on him, saying, "Art not thou the Christ? save thyself and us." All these voices spoke after the methods of human wisdom.—*Great Verses Through the Bible*

JAMIESON, FAUSSET, BROWN

22. Then Peter took him—aside, apart from the rest; presuming on the distinction just conferred on him; showing how *unexpected* and *distasteful* to them all was the announcement. **and began to rebuke him**—affectionately, yet with a certain generous indignation, to chide Him. **saying, Be it far from thee: this shall not be unto thee**—i.e., 'If I can help it': the same spirit that prompted him in the garden to draw the sword in His behalf (John 18:10).

23. But he turned, and said—in the hearing of the rest; for Mark (8:33) expressly says, "When He had turned about and looked on His disciples, He rebuked Peter"; perceiving that he had but boldly uttered what others felt, and that the check was needed by them also. **Get thee behind me, Satan**—the same words as He had addressed to the Tempter (Luke 4:8); for He felt in it a satanic lure, a whisper from hell, to move Him from His purpose to suffer. So He shook off the Serpent, then coiling around Him, and "felt no harm" (Acts 28:5). How quickly has the "rock" turned to a devil! The fruit of divine teaching the Lord delighted to honor in Peter; but the mouthpiece of hell, which he had in a moment of forgetfulness become, the Lord shook off with horror. **thou art an offence**—a stumbling block—**unto me:** 'Thou playest the Tempter, casting a stumbling block in My way to the Cross. Could it succeed, where wert thou? and how should the Serpent's head be bruised?'

for thou savourest not—thou thinkest not—**the things that be of God, but those that be of men**—"Thou art carried away by human views of the way of setting up Messiah's kingdom, quite contrary to those of God." This was kindly said, not to take off the sharp edge of the rebuke, but to explain and justify it, as it was evident Peter knew not what was in the bosom of his rash speech.

24. Then said Jesus unto his disciples—Mark (8:34) says, "When He had called the people unto Him, with His disciples also, He said unto them"—turning the rebuke of one into a warning to all. **If any man will come after me, let him deny himself, and take up his cross, and follow me.**

ADAM CLARKE

22. *Then Peter took him.* "Took Him up"—suddenly interrupted Him, as it were calling Him to order. *Be it far from thee, Lord.* "Be merciful to thyself, Lord." Peter knew that Christ had power sufficient to preserve himself from all the power and malice of the Jews, and wished Him to exert that in His own behalf which He had often exerted in the behalf of others.

23. *Get thee behind me, Satan.* "Get behind Me, you adversary." This is the proper translation of the Hebrew word *Satan*, from which the Greek word is taken. Our blessed Lord certainly never designed that men should believe He called Peter "devil" because he, through erring affection, had wished Him to avoid that death which He predicted to himself. This translation, which is literal, takes away that harshness which before appeared in our Lord's words. *Thou art an offence unto me.* You are a stumbling block in My way, to impede Me in the accomplishment of the great design.

Thou savourest not. That is, "do not relish," or, do not "understand or discern" the things of God—you are wholly taken up with the vain thought that My kingdom is of this world. He who opposes the doctrine of the atonement is an adversary and offense to Christ, though he be as sincere in his profession as Peter himself was.

MATTHEW HENRY

It denotes a deliberate choice, and cheerfulness and resolution in that choice. Christ will have his people volunteers.

Let him deny himself. Peter had advised Christ to spare himself, but Christ tells them all, they must be so far from *sparing* themselves, that they must *deny* themselves. If self-denial be a hard lesson, and against the grain to flesh and blood it is no more than what our Master learned and practised before us and for us. All the disciples and followers of Jesus Christ must deny themselves. It is the fundamental law of admission into Christ's school; it is both the *strait* gate, and the *narrow* way. We must deny ourselves absolutely, we must not admire our own shadow, nor gratify our own humour; nor seek our own things, nor be our own end. We must deny ourselves comparatively; we must deny ourselves for Christ; we must deny ourselves for our brethren, and for their good; and we must deny ourselves for ourselves, deny the appetites of the body for the benefit of the soul.

Let him take up his cross. The cross is here put for all sufferings, as men or Christians; providential afflictions, persecutions for righteousness' sake, every trouble that befalls us, either for doing well or for not doing ill. It should reconcile us to troubles, and take off the terror of them, that they are what we bear in common with Christ, and such as he hath borne before us. Every disciple of Christ hath his cross, and must count upon it, and everyone feels most from his own burthen. Crosses are the common lot of God's children, but of this common lot each hath his particular share. It is good for us to call the cross we are under *our own,* and entertain it accordingly. We are apt to think we could bear such a one's cross better than our own; but that is best which is, and we ought to make the best of it. Every disciple of Christ must take up that which the wise God hath made his cross. We must not make crosses to ourselves, but must accommodate ourselves to those which God has made for us. Our rule is, not to go a step out of the way of duty, either to meet a cross, or to miss one. We must not by our rashness and indiscretion pull crosses down upon our own heads, but must take them up when they are laid in our way. We must take it up out of our way, and we must then go on with it in our way, though it lie heavy. That which we have to do, is, not only to bear the cross, but we must *take up* the cross, must improve it to some good advantage. We should not say, "This is an evil, and I must bear it, because I cannot help it"; but, "This is an evil, and I will bear it, because it shall work for my good." When we *rejoice in our afflictions, and glory in them,* then we take up the cross.

Let him follow me, in this particular of taking up the cross. Do we bear the cross? We therein follow Christ, who bears it *before* us, bears it *for* us, and so bears it *from* us. He bore the heavy end of the cross, the end that had the curse upon it, that was a heavy end, and so made the other light and easy for us. Or, we may take it in general, we must follow Christ in all instances of holiness and obedience. To do well and to suffer ill, is to follow Christ. Those that come after Christ, must follow after him.

II. Self-denial, and patient suffering, are hard lessons, which will never be learned if we consult with flesh and blood; let us therefore consult with our Lord Jesus, about some considerations proper to these duties of self-denial and suffering for Christ. 1. The weight of that eternity which depends upon our present choice (*v.* 25); *Whosoever will save his life,* by denying Christ, *shall lose it*; and whosoever is content to *lose his life,* for owning Christ, *shall find it.* Here are *life and death, good and evil, the blessing and the curse, set before us.* Observe, The misery that attends the most plausible apostasy. *Whosoever will save his life* in this world, if it be by sin, he *shall lose it* in another; he that forsakes Christ, to preserve a temporal life and avoid a temporal death, will certainly come short of eternal life, and will be hurt of the second death, and eternally held by it. The life saved is but for a moment, the death shunned is but as a sleep; but the life lost is everlasting, and the death run upon is an endless separation from all good. 2. The advantage that attends the most perilous and expensive constancy; *Whosoever will lose his life for Christ's sake* in this world, *shall find it* in a better. Many a life is lost, for Christ's sake. Christ's holy religion is handed down to us, sealed with the blood of thousands. Though many have been losers for Christ, even of life itself, yet never anyone was, or will be, a loser by him in the end. An assurance of the life they should find, in lieu of the life they hazarded, hath enabled them to triumph over death in all its terrors; to go smiling to a scaffold, and stand singing at a stake. 3. The worth

JAMIESON, FAUSSET, BROWN

25. For whosoever will save—is minded to save, or bent on saving—**his life shall lose it, and whosoever will lose his life for my sake shall find it**—See on ch. 10:38, 39. "A suffering and dying Messiah liketh you ill; but what if His servants shall meet the same fate? They may not; but who follows Me must be prepared for the worst."

ADAM CLARKE

24. *Will come after me.* I.e., to be My disciple. *Let him deny himself.* "Let him deny, or renounce, himself fully—in all respects—perseveringly." A man's *self* is to him the prime cause of most of his miseries.

25. *For whosoever will save his life.* That is, "shall wish to save his life"—at the expense of his conscience, and casting aside the cross, he, *shall lose it*—the very evil he wishes to avoid shall overtake him; and he shall lose his soul in the bargain. See then how necessary it is to renounce oneself!

G. CAMPBELL MORGAN:

In view of that mistake of Peter, our Lord restated the terms of His discipleship, "If any man would come after me." They all wanted to, they all loved Him, they all had affection for Him. He said, "If this is so, if any man desires to come after me, let him first deny himself; and secondly, take up his cross." Let us consider those conditions carefully. Denying of self is far more than self-denial in our usual sense of that term. Perhaps we may best illustrate it by declaring that we have no right to make any sacrifice for Jesus Christ which He does not appoint. When a man takes on him some effort of sacrifice simply because he thinks sacrifice is the right thing, and does not wait for orders, he is as surely a skandalon to his Lord as when he does not deny himself and take up his cross at the command of the Master. The true disciple chooses neither song nor dirge, neither sunshine nor shadow; has no choice but to know his Master's will and to do it. If He appoints for us the blue waters of the lake and all the sunshine of the summer, then let us rejoice therein, and not vex our souls because we know no suffering and pain. If He appoint a sunless sky, then God make us willing to take the way, because the way is His appointment. We must be in His will if we are to cooperate with Him.

The program of the disciple is expressed in these words, "Follow me." That is, make the "must" of My life the "must" of your life. I must. Does not that mean suffering? It may, or it may not. Suffering is not the deepest thing in the "must." The deepest thing is this: I must cooperate with the purpose of God, whatsoever it may be. I must cooperate with Him toward that resurrection that means ransom and redemption. On the way, there may be the suffering and the killing—there surely will be some measure of it—but the suffering and the killing are not the deepest things. The deepest thing is that we get into touch with God and do His will; and whether it be laughter or crying, sorrowing or sighing, the secret of life is to follow Him on the pathway of loyalty to the divine will.

He explained this in gracious terms when He said, "Whosoever would save his life shall lose it; and whosoever shall lose his life for my sake shall find it." This is the commonplace philosophy of true life. It is always so. Find any man who is always saving his life, and he will lose it. The way to lose our physical life is always to be saving it. The way to lose our mental life is to be careful that it never feels the storms and bruises of passion. The way to lose our spiritual life is to be so perpetually anxious to get into heaven that we never move into line with God in His work for the building of His Kingdom here on earth.—*The Gospel According to Matthew*

MATTHEW HENRY

of the soul which lies at stake, and the worthlessness of the world in comparison of it (*v.* 26). *What is a man profited, if he gain the whole world and lose his own soul?* This alludes to that common principle, that, whatever a man gets, if he lose his life, it will do him no good, he cannot enjoy his gains. But it looks higher, and speaks of the soul as immortal, and a loss of it beyond death, which cannot be compensated by the gain of the whole world. Our souls are our own not in respect of dominion and property, but in respect of nearness and concern; our souls are our own, for they are ourselves. It is possible for the soul to be lost, and there is danger of it. The soul is lost when it is eternally separated from all the good, to all the evil that a soul is capable of; when it is separated from the favour of God. If the soul be lost, it is of the sinner's own losing. The *man loses his own soul,* for he does that which is certainly destroying to it, and neglects that which alone would be saving. One soul is worth more than all the world; our own souls are of greater value to us than all the wealth, honour, and pleasures of this present time, if we had them. The winning of the world is often the losing of the soul. Many a one has ruined his eternal interests by his preposterous and inordinate care to secure and advance his temporal ones. The loss of the soul is so great a loss, that the gain of the whole world will not countervail it, or make it up. He that loses his soul, though it be to gain the world, makes a very bad bargain for himself. When he comes to balance the account, and to compare profit and loss, he will find that he is ruined to all intents and purposes, is irreparably broken.

What shall a man give in exchange for his soul? If once the soul be lost, it is lost for ever. It is a loss that can never be repaired, never be retrieved. Therefore it is good to be wise in time, and do well for ourselves. Here are some considerations proper to encourage us in self-denial and suffering for Christ.

(1) The assurance we have of Christ's glory, at his second coming to judge the world, *v.* 27. If we see things as they *will* appear then, we shall see them as they *should* appear now.

The great encouragement to steadfastness in religion is taken from the second coming of Christ, considering it,

[1] As his honour; *The Son of man shall come in the glory of his Father, with his angels.* To look upon Christ in his state of humiliation would discourage his followers from taking any pains, or running any hazards for him; but with an eye of faith to see the Captain of our salvation coming in his glory, will animate us, and make us think nothing too much to do, or too hard to suffer, for him. [2] As our concern; *Then he shall reward every man according to his works.* Jesus Christ will come as a Judge, to dispense rewards and punishments. Men will then be rewarded, not according to their gains in this world, but according to their works, according to what they were and did, and the constancy of faithful souls recompensed with a crown of life. The best preparative for that day is to *deny ourselves, and to take up our cross, and follow Christ*; for so we shall make the Judge our Friend. The rewarding of men according to their works is deferred till that day. Here good and evil seem to be dispensed promiscuously; but in that day all will be set to rights.

(2) The near approach of his kingdom in this world, *v.* 28. It was so near, that there were some attending him who should live to see it. At the end of time, he shall come in his Father's glory; but now, in the fulness of time, he was to come in his own kingdom, his mediatorial kingdom. Some little specimen was given of his glory a few days after this, in his transfiguration (*ch.* xvii. 1). The apostles were employed in setting up Christ's kingdom; let them know, for their comfort, that whatever opposition they meet with, yet they shall carry their point. It is a great encouragement to suffering saints to be assured, not only of the safety, but of the advancement of Christ's kingdom among men; not only *notwithstanding* their sufferings, but *by* their sufferings. This shall be done shortly, in the present age. The nearer the church's deliverances are, the more cheerful should we be in our sufferings for Christ. It is spoken as a favour to those that should survive the present cloudy time, that they should see better days.

JAMIESON, FAUSSET, BROWN

26. For what is a man profited, if he shall gain the whole world, and lose—or forfeit—**his own soul? or what shall a man give in exchange for his soul?**—Instead of these weighty words, which we find in Mark also, it is thus expressed in Luke: "If he gain the whole world, and lose himself, or be cast away," or better, "If he gain the whole world, and destroy or forfeit himself." How awful is the stake as here set forth! If a man makes the present world—in its various forms of riches, honors, pleasures, and such like—the object of supreme pursuit, be it that he gains the world; yet along with it he forfeits his own soul. Not that any ever did, or ever will gain the whole world—a very small portion of it, indeed, falls to the lot of the most successful of the world's votaries—but to make the extravagant concession, that by giving himself entirely up to it, a man gains the whole world; yet, setting over against this gain the forfeiture of his soul—necessarily following the surrender of his whole heart to the world—what is he profited? But, if not the whole world, yet possibly something else may be conceived as an equivalent for the soul. Well, what is it?—"Or what shall a man give in exchange for his soul?" Thus, in language the weightiest, because the simplest, does our Lord shut up His hearers, and all who shall read these words to the end of the world, to the priceless value to every man of his own soul. In Mark and Luke the following words are added: "Whosoever therefore shall be ashamed of Me and of My words [shall be ashamed of belonging to Me, and ashamed of My Gospel] in this adulterous and sinful generation" (see on ch. 12:39), "of him shall the Son of man be ashamed when He cometh in the glory of His Father, with the holy angels" (Mark 8:38; Luke 9:26). He will render back to that man his own treatment, disowning him before the most august of all assemblies, and putting him to "*shame* and everlasting *contempt*" (Dan. 12:2). "O shame," exclaims BENGEL, "to be put to shame before God, Christ, and angels!" The sense of *shame* is founded on our love of *reputation,* which causes instinctive aversion to what is fitted to lower it, and was given us as a preservative from all that is properly *shameful.* To be *lost to shame* is to be nearly past hope. (Zeph. 3:5; Jer. 6:15; 3:3.) But when Christ and "His words" are unpopular, the same instinctive desire to *stand well with others* begets that temptation to be ashamed of Him which only the expulsive power of a higher affection can effectually counteract. **27. For the Son of man shall come in the glory of his Father with his angels**—in the splendor of His Father's authority and with all His angelic ministers, ready to execute His pleasure. **and then he shall reward . . .**

28. Verily I say unto you, There be some standing here—"some of those standing here." **which shall not taste of death, till they see the Son of man coming in his kingdom**—or, as in Mark (9:1), "till they see the kingdom of God come with power"; or, as in Luke (9:27), more simply still, "till they see the kingdom of God." The reference, beyond doubt, is to the firm establishment and victorious progress, in the lifetime of some then present, of that new kingdom of Christ, which was destined to work the greatest of all changes on this earth, and be the grand pledge of His final coming in glory.

ADAM CLARKE

26. *Lose his own soul.* Or "lose his life." On what authority many have translated the word *psyche* in the twenty-fifth verse "life," and in this verse *soul,* I know not, but am certain it means "life" in both places. If a man should gain the whole world, its riches, honors, and pleasures, and lose his life, what would all these profit him, seeing they can be enjoyed only during life?

27. *For the Son of man shall come in the glory of his Father.* This seems to refer to Dan. vii. 13-14. "Behold, one like the Son of man came . . . to the Ancient of days . . . And there was given him dominion, and glory, and a kingdom, that all people, nations, and languages, should serve him." This was the glorious mediatorial Kingdom which Jesus Christ was now about to set up, by the destruction of the Jewish nation and polity, and the diffusion of His gospel through the whole world. If the words be taken in this sense, the *angels* or messengers may signify the apostles and their successors in the sacred ministry, preaching the gospel in the power of the Holy Ghost. It is very likely that the words do not apply to the final judgment, to which they are generally referred, but to the wonderful display of God's grace and power after the Day of Pentecost.

28. *There be some . . . which shall not taste of death.* This verse seems to confirm the above explanation, as our Lord evidently speaks of the establishment of the Christian Church after the Day of Pentecost, and its final triumph after the destruction of the Jewish polity; as if He had said, "Some of you, My disciples, shall continue to live until these things take place." The destruction of Jerusalem and the Jewish economy, which our Lord here predicts, took place about forty years after this; and some of the persons now with Him doubtless survived that period, and witnessed the extension of the Messiah's kingdom. Our Lord told them these things before, that when they came to pass they might be confirmed in the faith, and expect an exact fulfillment of all the other promises and prophecies which concerned the extension and support of the kingdom of Christ.

MATTHEW HENRY

CHAPTER 17

We have here the story of Christ's transfiguration; he had said that the *Son of man should* shortly *come in his kingdom*, with which promise all the three evangelists industriously connect this story.

When Christ was here in his humiliation, though his state, in the main, was a state of abasement and afflictions, there were some glimpses of his glory intermixed. But the series of his public ministry being a continued humiliation, here, just in the midst of that, comes in this discovery of his glory.

Now concerning Christ's transfiguration, observe,

I. The circumstances of it, which are here noted, *v.* 1.

1. The time; *six days* after he had the solemn conference with his disciples, *ch.* xvi. 21. Nothing is recorded to be said or done by our Lord Jesus for six days before his transfiguration. *Then* when Christ seems to be doing nothing for his church, expect, ere long, something more than ordinary.

2. The place; it was *on the top of a high mountain apart.* Christ chose a mountain, (1) As a secret place. He went apart; Christ chose a retired place to be transfigured in, because his appearing publicly in his glory was not agreeable to his present state; and thus he would teach us that privacy much befriends our communion with God. (2). Those that would maintain intercourse with Heaven, must frequently withdraw, and they will find themselves never less alone than when alone, for the Father is with them. Those that would have a transforming fellowship with God, must not only retire, but ascend; lift up their hearts, and *seek things above.*

3. The witnesses of it. He took with him Peter and James and John. He took three, a competent number to testify what they should see. Christ makes his appearances certain enough, but not too common that they might be blessed, who have not seen, and yet have believed. He took these three because they were the chief of his disciples. They were afterward to be the witnesses of his agony, and this was to prepare them for that. A sight of Christ's glory, while we are here in this world, is a good preparative for our sufferings with him, as these are preparatives for the sight of his glory in the other world.

II. The manner of it (*v.* 2); *He was transfigured before them.* The substance of his body remained the same; he was not turned into a spirit, but his body, which had appeared in weakness and dishonour, now appeared in power and glory. Now, in his transfiguration, he gave his disciples a glimpse of his glory, which could not but change his form.

Now his transfiguration appeared in two things:

1. *His face did shine as the sun.* The face is the principal part of the body, by which we are known; therefore such a brightness was put on Christ's face. It shone as the sun when he goes forth in his strength, so clear, so bright; the more sensibly glorious, because it suddenly broke out, as it were, from behind a black cloud.

2. *His raiment was white as the light.* The shining of the face of Moses was so weak, that it could easily be concealed by a thin veil; but such was the glory of Christ's body, that his clothes were enlightened by it.

III. The companions of it. There now *appeared unto them Moses and Elias talking with him, v.* 3. There were glorified saints attending him, that, when there were *three to bear record on earth,* Peter, James, and John, these might be some to bear record from heaven too. We see here, that they who are fallen asleep in Christ are not perished. These two were Moses and Elias. The Jews had great respect for the memory of Moses and Elias, and therefore they came to witness of him. In them the law and the prophets honoured Christ, and bore testimony to him. Moses and Elias appeared to the disciples; they saw them, and heard them talk, and they knew them to be Moses and Elias; glorified saints shall know one another in heaven. They talked with Christ. Christ has communion with the blessed.

IV. The great pleasure and satisfaction that the disciples took in the sight of Christ's glory. Peter, as usual, spoke for the rest; *Lord, it is good for us to be here.* Peter here expresses,

1. The delight they had in this converse; *Lord, it is good to be here.* He speaks the sense of his fellow-disciples; It is good not only for *me,* but for *us.* He did not covet to monopolise this favour, but gladly takes them in. He saith this to Christ. The soul that loves Christ, and loves to be with him, loves to go and tell him so; *Lord, it is good for us to be here.* All the disciples of the Lord Jesus reckon it is good for them to be with him in the holy mount. It is good to be here where Christ is; it is good to be here, retired and alone with Christ; to be here, where we may behold the beauty of the Lord Jesus.

JAMIESON, FAUSSET, BROWN

CHAPTER 17

Vss. 1-13. JESUS IS TRANSFIGURED—CONVERSATION ABOUT ELIAS. (=Mark 9:2-13; Luke 9:28-36.) For the exposition, see on Luke 9:28-36.

JESUS TRANSFIGURED. **an eight days after these sayings**—including the day on which this was spoken and that of the Transfiguration. Matthew and Mark say "after six days," *excluding* these two days. As the "sayings" so definitely connected with the transfiguration scene are those announcing His *death*—at which Peter and all the Twelve were so startled and scandalized—so this scene was designed to show to the eyes as well as the heart how *glorious* that death was in the view of Heaven. **Peter, James, and John**—partners before in secular business; now sole witnesses of the resurrection of Jairus' daughter (Mark 5:37), the transfiguration, and the agony in the garden (Mark 14:33). **a mountain**—not *Tabor,* according to long tradition, with which the facts ill comport, but some one near the lake. **to pray**—for the period He had now reached was a critical and anxious one. (See on Matt. 16:13.) But who can adequately translate those "strong cryings and tears?" Methinks, as I steal by His side, I hear from Him these plaintive sounds, Lord, who hath believed Our report? I am come unto Mine own and Mine own receive Me not; I am become a stranger unto My brethren, an alien to My mother's children: Consider Mine enemies, for they are many, and they hate Me with cruel hatred. Arise, O Lord, let not man prevail. Thou that dwellest between the cherubim, shine forth: Show Me a token for good: Father, glorify Thy name." **as he prayed, the fashion . . .**—Before He cried He was answered, and while He was yet speaking He was heard. Blessed interruption to prayer this! Thanks to God, transfiguring manifestations are not quite strangers here. Ofttimes in the deepest depths, out of groanings which cannot be uttered, God's dear children are suddenly transported to a kind of heaven upon earth, and their soul is made as the chariots of Amminadab. Their prayers fetch down such light, strength, holy gladness, as make their face to shine, putting a kind of celestial radiance upon it (II Corinthians 3:18, with Exod. 34:29-35). **raiment white . . .**—Matthew says, "His face did shine as the sun" (17:2), and Mark says "His raiment became shining, exceeding white as snow, so as no fuller on earth can white them" (9:2). The light, then, it would seem, shone not *upon* Him *from without,* but *out of* Him *from within;* He was all irradiated, was in one blaze of celestial glory. What a contrast to that "visage more marred than men, and His form than the sons of men!" (Isa. 52:14). **there talked with him two men . . . Moses and Elias . . . appeared in glory**—"Who would have believed these were not *angels* had not their *human* names been subjoined?" [BENGEL]. (Cf. Acts 1:10; Mark 16:5.) Moses represented "the law," Elijah "the prophets," and both together the whole testimony of the Old Testament Scriptures, and the Old Testament saints, to Christ; now not borne in a *book,* but by *living men,* not to a *coming,* but a *come* Messiah, *visibly,* for they "appeared," and *audibly,* for they "spake." **spake**—"were speaking."

ADAM CLARKE

CHAPTER 17

1. *After six days.* Mark ix. 2 has the same number; but Luke says, ix. 28, after "eight" days. The reason of this difference seems to be the following: Matthew and Mark reckon the days from that mentioned in the preceding chapter to that mentioned in this; Luke includes both days, as well as the six intermediate. Hence the one makes eight, the other six, without any contradiction. *Peter, James, and John.* He chose those that they might be witnesses of His transfiguration, two or three witnesses being required by the Scripture to substantiate any fact. The same three were made witnesses of His agony in the garden, chap. xxvi. 37. *An high mountain.* This was one of the mountains of Galilee, but whether Mount Tabor or not is uncertain. Some think it was Mount Hermon. St. Luke says Christ and His disciples went up into the mountain to pray, chap. ix. 28.

2. *Was transfigured.* That fullness of the Godhead which dwelt bodily in Christ now shone forth through the human nature, and manifested to His disciples not only that divinity which Peter had before confessed, chap. xvi. 16, but also the glorious resurrection body, in which they should exist in the presence of God to eternity.

3. *Moses and Elias.* Elijah came from heaven in the same body which he had upon earth, for he was translated, and did not see death, 2 Kings ii. 11. And the body of Moses was probably raised again as a pledge of the resurrection. It was a constant and prevalent tradition among the Jews that both Moses and Elijah should appear in the times of the Messiah, and to this very tradition the disciples refer, v. 10. We may conceive that the law in the person of Moses, the great Jewish legislator, and the prophets in the person of Elijah, the chief of the prophets, came now to do homage to Jesus Christ, and to render up their authority into His hands, as He was the End of the law and the grand Subject of the predictions of the prophets. This appears more particularly from what Luke says, chap. ix. 31, that Moses and Elijah conversed with our Lord on His death, which He was about to accomplish, because in it all the rites, ceremonies, and sacrifices of the law, as well as the predictions of the prophets, were fulfilled.

MATTHEW HENRY

2. The desire they had of the continuance of it; *Let us make here three tabernacles.* There was in this, as in many other of Peter's sayings, more zeal than discretion.

(1) Here was a zeal for this converse with heavenly things. Those that by faith *behold the beauty of the Lord* in his house, cannot but desire to *dwell there all the days of their life.* It is good to be in holy ordinances as a man at home, not as a wayfaring man.

(2) Yet in this zeal he betrayed a great deal of weakness and ignorance. What need had Moses and Elias of tabernacles? Christ had lately foretold his sufferings; Peter forgets this, or, to prevent it, will needs be building tabernacles in the mount of glory, out of the way of trouble. There is a proneness in good men to expect the crown without the cross. We are out in our aim, if we look for a heaven here upon earth. It is not for strangers and pilgrims to talk of building, or to expect a continuing city.

Yet it is some excuse for the incongruity of Peter's proposal, not only that *he knew not what he said* (Luke ix. 33), but also that he submitted the proposal to the wisdom of Christ; *If thou wilt, let us make tabernacles.*

Now to this which Peter said, there was no reply made; the disappearing of the glory would soon answer it.

V. The glorious testimony which God the Father gave to our Lord Jesus.

Now concerning this testimony from heaven to Christ, observe.

1. How it came, and in what manner it was introduced. There was a cloud. We find often in the Old Testament, that a cloud was the visible token of God's presence. He took possession of the tabernacle in a cloud, and afterwards of the temple; where Christ was in his glory, the temple was, and there God showed himself present. It was a bright cloud. Under the law it was commonly a thick and dark cloud that God made the token of his presence. But *we are now come* to the mount that is crowned with a bright cloud. That was a dispensation of darkness, and terror, and bondage, this of light, love, and liberty. It overshadowed them. God, in manifesting himself to his people, considers their frame. This cloud was to their eyes as parables to their understandings, to convey spiritual things by things sensible, as they were able to bear them. *There came a voice out of the cloud,* and it was the voice of God. Here was no thunder, or lightning, or voice of a trumpet, as there was when the law was given by Moses, but only a voice, a still small voice.

2. What this testimony from heaven was; *This is my beloved Son, hear ye him.*

(1) The great gospel mystery revealed; *This is my beloved Son, in whom I am well pleased.* This was the very same that was spoken from heaven at his baptism (*ch.* iii. 17). Moses and Elias were great men, and favourites of Heaven, yet they were but servants; but Christ is *a Son,* and in him God was always well pleased. Moses was a great intercessor, and Elias a great reformer; but in Christ God is reconciling the world; his intercession is more prevalent than that of Moses, and his reformation more effectual than that of Elias.

This repetition of the same voice that came from heaven at his baptism was to show the thing was established. What God hath thus spoken once, yea twice, no doubt he will stand to. Now it was repeated, because he was entering upon his sufferings, to arm him against the terror, and his disciples against the offence, of the cross. When sufferings begin to abound, consolations are given more abundantly.

(2) The great gospel duty required, *Hear ye him.* God is well pleased with none in Christ but those that hear him. It is not enough to give him the hearing (what will that avail us?) but we must hear him, and heed him. Whoever would know the mind of God, must hearken to Jesus Christ; for by him God has in these last days spoken to us. God does here, as it were, turn us over to Christ for all the revelations of his mind.

Christ now appeared in glory; and the more we see of Christ's glory, the more cause we shall see to hearken to him.

Moses and Elias were now with him; the law and the prophets; hitherto it was said, *Hear them,* Luke xvi. 29. No, saith God, *hear him,* and that is enough; him, and not Moses and Elias, hear Christ, and you will not want them.

VI. The fright which the disciples were put into by this voice, and the encouragement Christ gave them.

1. The disciples *fell on their faces, and were sore afraid.* The greatness of the light, and the surprise of it, might have a natural influence upon them, to dispirit them. But that was not all, extraordinary

JAMIESON, FAUSSET, BROWN

cloud—not one of our watery clouds, but the Shekinah-cloud (see on Matt. 23:39), the pavilion of the manifested presence of God with His people, what Peter calls "the excellent" of "magnificent glory" (II Pet. 1:17). **a voice**—"*such* a voice," says Peter emphatically; "and this voice [he adds] we heard, when we were with Him in the holy mount" (II Pet. 1:17, 18).

my beloved Son... hear him—*reverentially, implicitly, alone.* **Jesus was found alone**—Moses and Elias are gone. Their work is done, and they have disappeared from the scene, feeling no doubt with their fellow servant the Baptist, "He must increase, but I must decrease." The cloud too is gone, and the naked majestic Christ, braced in spirit, and enshrined in the reverent affection of His disciples, is left—to suffer!

ADAM CLARKE

4. *Then answered Peter . . . let us make here three tabernacles.* That is, when he saw Moses and Elijah ready to depart from the mount, Luke ix. 33, he wished to detain them, that he might always enjoy their company with that of his Lord and Master, still supposing that Christ would set up a temporal kingdom upon earth.

5. *A bright cloud overshadowed them.* A *cloud* was frequently the symbol of the Divine Presence.

This is my beloved Son. "This is My Son, the beloved One, in whom I have delighted," or "been well pleased." God adds His testimony of approbation to what was spoken of the sufferings of Christ by Moses and Elijah, thus showing that the sacrificial economy of the old covenant was in itself of no worth, but as it referred to the grand atonement which Jesus was about to make. Therefore He says, "In Him have I delighted," intimating that it was in Him alone, as typified by those sacrifices, that He had delighted through the whole course of the legal administration; and that it was only in reference to the death of His Son that He accepted the offerings and oblations made to Him under the old covenant.

Hear . . . him. The disciples wished to detain Moses and Elijah that they might hear them, but God shows that the law which had been in force, and the prophets which had prophesied, until now, must all give place to Jesus; and He alone must now be attended to, as "the way, the truth, and the life," for no man could now come unto the Father but through Him.

6. *Fell on their face.* Dismayed by the voice, and dazzled by the glory of the cloud. So Daniel, chap. viii. 17, and Saul of Tarsus, Acts ix. 4.

MATTHEW HENRY

appearances of God have ever been terrible to man, who has been afraid to hear anything immediately from God. It is well for us that God speaks to us by men like ourselves, whose terror shall not make us afraid.

2. Christ graciously raised them up with abundance of tenderness. Observe here, (1) What he did; *he came, and touched them.* His approaches banished their fears. Christ's touches were often healing, and here they were strengthening and comforting. (2) What he said; *Arise, and be not afraid.* It is Christ by his word, and the power of his grace going along with it, that raises up good men from their dejections, and silences their fears; and none but Christ can do it; *Arise, be not afraid.* Causeless fears would soon vanish, if we would not yield to them. Considering what they had seen and heard, they had more reason to rejoice than to fear. Through the infirmity of the flesh, we often frighten ourselves with that wherewith we should encourage ourselves. After they had an express command from heaven to hear Christ, the first word they had from him was, *Be not afraid.*

VII. The disappearing of the vision (*v.* 8); *They* lift up themselves, and then *lift up their eyes,* and *saw no man, save Jesus only.* It is not wisdom to raise our expectations high in this world, for the most valuable of our glories and joys here are vanishing, even those of near communion with God are so, not a continual feast, but a running banquet. Two heavens are too much for those to expect that never deserve one. Now *they saw no man, save Jesus only.* Christ will tarry with us when Moses and Elias are gone.

VIII. The discourse between Christ and his disciples as they came down from the mountain, *v.* 9–13. *They came down from the mountain.* We must come down from the holy mountains, where we have communion with God; even there we have no continuing city. When the disciples came down, Jesus came with them. When we return to the world again after an ordinance, it must be our care to take Christ with us. As they came down, they talked of Christ. Note, When we are returning from holy ordinances, it is good to entertain ourselves and one another with discourse suitable to the work we have been about.

Here is, (1) The charge that Christ gave the disciples to keep the vision very private for the present (*v.* 9); *Tell it to no man till the Son of man is risen.* If they had proclaimed it, the credibility of it would have been shocked by his sufferings, which were now hastening on. But let the publication of it be adjourned till after his resurrection, and then that and his subsequent glory will be a great confirmation of it. Everything is beautiful in its season. Christ's time is the best and fittest for the manifesting of himself and must be attended to by us.

(2) An objection which the disciples made against something Christ had said (*v.* 10); "*Why then say the scribes that Elias must first come?*" When the disciples could not reconcile what Christ said with what they had heard out of the Old Testament, they desired him to explain it to them. When we are puzzled with scripture difficulties, we must apply ourselves to Christ by prayer for his Spirit to open our understandings and to lead us into all truth.

(3) The solving of this objection. *Ask, and it shall be given*; ask instruction, and it shall be given. Christ allows the prediction (*v.* 11); "*Elias truly shall first come, and restore all things;* so far you are in the right." Christ did not come to alter or invalidate anything foretold in the Old Testament. John Baptist came to restore things spiritually, to revive the decays of religion, which means the same with this, *he shall restore all things.* John preached repentance, and that restores all things. He asserts the accomplishment. The scribes say true, that *Elias shall come; but I say unto you,* what the scribes could not say, that *Elias is come, v.* 12. God's promises are often fulfilled, and men perceive it not, but enquire, *Where is the promise?* when it is already performed. The scribes busied themselves in criticising upon the scripture, but understood not by the signs of the times the fulfilling of the scripture. It is easier to explain the word of God than to apply it and make a right use of it.

Because they knew him not, *they have done to him whatsoever they listed*; if they had known, they would not have crucified Christ, or beheaded John. He adds, *Likewise also shall the Son of man suffer of them.* When they had imbrued their hands in the blood of John Baptist, they were ready to do the like to Christ. As men deal with Christ's servants, so they would deal with him himself.

(4) The disciples' satisfaction in Christ's reply to their objection (*v.* 13); *They understood that he spake unto them of John the Baptist.* He did not name John,

JAMIESON, FAUSSET, BROWN

ALEXANDER MACLAREN:

Then comes the articulate witness to the Son. The solemnity and force of the attestation are increased, if we conceive of the disciples as outside the cloud and parted from Jesus. This word is meant for them only, and so is distinguished from the similar voice at the baptism, and has added the imperative "Hear him." The voice bears witness to the mystery of our Lord's person. It points to the contrast between His two attendants and Him. They are servants, "this is the Son." It sets forth His supernaturally born humanity, and, deeper still, His true and proper divinity, which John unfolds, in his Gospel, as the deepest meaning of the name. It testifies to the unbroken union of love between the Father and Him, and therein to the absolute perfection of our Lord's character. He is the adequate object of the eternal divine love. As He has been from the timeless depths of old, He is, in His human life, the object of the ever-unruffled divine complacency, in whom the Father can see himself as in a pure mirror. It enjoins obedient listening. God's voice bids us hear Christ's voice. If He is the beloved Son, listening to Him is listening to God. This is the purpose of the whole, so far as we are concerned. We are to hear Him when He declares God; when He witnesses of himself, of His love, His work, His death, His judgeship; when He invites us to come to Him, and find rest; when He commands and when He promises. Amid the Babel of this day, let us listen to that voice, low and gentle, pleading and soft, authoritative, majestic, and sovereign. It will one day shake "not the earth only, but also the heaven." But, as yet, it calls us with strange sweetness, and the music of love in every tone. Well for us if our hearts answer, "Speak, Lord; for thy servant heareth."

Matthew tells us that this voice from the cloud completely unmanned the disciples, who fell on their faces and lay there, we know not how long, till Jesus came and laid a loving hand on them, bidding them arise and not fear. So when they staggered to their feet and looked around, they saw nothing but the grey stones of the hillside and the blue sky. "That dread voice was past," and the silence was broken only by the hum of insects or the twitter of a far-off bird. The strange guests have gone; the radiance has faded from the Master's face, and all is as it used to be. "They saw no one, save Jesus only." It is the summing up of revelation; all others vanish, He abides. It is the summing up of the world's history. Thickening folds of oblivion wrap the past, and all its mighty names become forgotten; but His figure stands out, solitary against the background of the past, as some great mountain, which travelers see long after the lower summits are sunk beneath the horizon. Let us make this the summing up of our lives. We can venture to take Him for our sole helper, pattern, love, and aim, because He, in His singleness, is enough for our hearts. There are many fragmentary precious things, but there is only one pearl of great price. And then this will be a prophecy of our deaths—a brief darkness, a passing dread, and then His touch and His voice saying, "Arise, be not afraid." So we shall lift up our eyes, and find earth faded, and its voices fallen dim, and see "no one any more, save Jesus only."

—*Expositions of Holy Scripture*

ADAM CLARKE

7. *Jesus came and touched them.* Exactly parallel to this account is Dan. viii. 18, "I was in a deep sleep [i.e., a trance] on my face toward the ground: but he touched me, and set me upright." It is very likely that this transfiguration took place in the night, which was a more proper season to show forth its glory than the daytime. Luke, chap. ix. 37, expressly says that it was on the next day after the Transfiguration that our Lord came down from the mount.

9. *Tell the vision to no man.* See the note on chap. xvi. 20; and further observe that, as this Transfiguration was intended to show forth the final abolition of the whole ceremonial law, it was necessary that a matter which could not fail to irritate the Jewish rulers and people should be kept secret till Jesus had accomplished vision and prophecy by His death and resurrection.

10. *Why then say the scribes that Elias must first come?* As the disciples saw that Elijah returned to heaven, knowing the tradition of the elders, and the prophecy on which the tradition was founded, Mal. iv. 5-6, "Behold, I will send you Elijah the prophet before . . . the great and dreadful day of the Lord [shall come]: and he shall turn the hearts," it was natural enough for them to inquire what the meaning of the tradition and the intention of the prophecy were.

11. *Elias truly shall first come, and restore all things.* Or "will reform." No fanciful restoration of all men, devils, and damned spirits is spoken of as either being done or begun by the ministry of John, but merely that he should preach a doctrine tending to universal reformation of manners, and should be greatly successful. See Matt. iii. 1-7 and especially Luke iii. 3-15, where we find that a general reformation had taken place: (1) among the common people; (2) among the taxgatherers, and (3) among the soldiers. And as John announced the coming Christ, who was to baptize with the Holy Ghost, i.e., to enlighten, change, and purify the heart, that the reform might be complete, both outward and inward, he may be said, in the strictest sense of the word, to have fulfilled the prophecy. And that he was the Elijah mentioned by Malachi, the words of Gabriel to the Virgin Mary prove, Luke i. 17—"And he [John] shall go before him [Christ] in the spirit and power of Elias, to turn the hearts of the fathers to the children, and the disobedient to the wisdom of the just."

12. *Knew him not.* "They have not acknowledged him." That is, the Jewish rulers have not acknowledged him, did not receive him as the forerunner of the Messiah.

MATTHEW HENRY | JAMIESON, FAUSSET, BROWN | ADAM CLARKE

but gives them such a description of him as would put them in mind of what he had said to them formerly concerning him; *This is Elias.* When we diligently use the means of knowledge, how strangely are mists scattered and mistakes rectified!

Verses 14-21

I. A melancholy representation of the case of this child, made to Christ by the afflicted father. This was immediately upon his coming down from the mountain where he was transfigured. Christ's glories do not make him unmindful of us and of our wants and miseries. This poor man's address was very importunate; he came kneeling to Christ. Sense of misery will bring people to their knees. He delights to be thus wrestled with.

Two things the father of the child complains of.

1. The distress of his child (*v.* 15); *Lord, have mercy on my son.* Parents are doubly concerned to pray for their children, not only that are weak and cannot, but much more that are wicked and will not, pray for themselves. (1) The nature of this child's disease was very sad; *He was lunatic and sore vexed.* A lunatic is properly one whose distemper lies in the brain. The child had the falling-sickness, and the hand of Satan was in it. Those whom Satan got possession of, he afflicted by those diseases of the body which do most affect the mind; for it is the soul that he aims to do mischief to. The father, in his complaint, saith, *He is lunatic,* taking notice of the effect; but Christ, in the cure, rebuked the devil, and so struck at the cause. Thus he doth in spiritual cures. (2) The effects of the disease were very deplorable; *He oft falls into the fire, and into the water.*

2. The disappointment of his expectation from the disciples (*v.* 16); *I brought him to thy disciples, and they could not cure him.* Christ gave his disciples power to cast out devils (*ch.* x. 1, 8), and therein they were successful (Luke x. 17); yet at this time they failed in the operation, though there were nine of them together. It is for the honour of Christ to come in with help at a dead-lift, when other helpers cannot help. Sometimes he keeps the cistern empty, that he may bring us to himself, the Fountain. But the failures of instruments shall not hinder the operations of his grace, which will work, if not *by* them, yet *without* them.

II. The rebukes that Christ gave.

1. He chid those about him (*v.* 17); *O faithless and perverse generation!* This is not spoken to the disciples, but to the people, and perhaps especially to the scribes. Christ himself could not do many mighty works among a people in whom unbelief reigned. It was here owing to the faithlessness of this generation, that they could not obtain those blessings from God, which otherwise they might have had; as it was owing to the weakness of the disciples' faith, that they could not do those works for God, which otherwise they might have done.

Two things he upbraids them with. (1) His presence with them so long; "*How long shall I be with you?* Will you always need my bodily presence, and never come to such maturity as to be fit to be left? Must the child be always carried, and will it never learn to go alone?" (2) His patience with them so long; *How long shall I suffer you?* The faithlessness and perverseness of those who enjoy the means of grace are a great grief to the Lord Jesus. He is God, and not man, else he would not suffer so long, nor bear so much, as he doth.

2. He cured the child, and set him to rights again. He called, *Bring him hither to me.* Though the people were perverse, and Christ was provoked, yet care was taken of the child. Though Christ may be angry, he is never unkind. *Bring him to me.* When all other helps and succours fail, we are welcome to Christ.

See here an emblem of Christ's undertaking as our Redeemer.

(1) He breaks the power of Satan (*v.* 18); *Jesus rebuked the devil,* as one having authority. Christ's victories over Satan are obtained by the power of his word. Satan cannot stand before the rebukes of Christ, though his possession has been ever so long.

(2) He redresses the grievances of the children of men; *The child was cured from that very hour.* It was an immediate cure, and a perfect one. This is an encouragement to parents to bring their children to Christ. Not only bring them to Christ by prayer, but bring them to the word of Christ. Christ's rebukes, brought home to the heart, will ruin Satan's power there.

III. Christ's discourse with his disciples hereupon.

1. They ask the reason why they could not cast out the devil at this time (*v.* 19); *They came to Jesus apart.* Ministers, who are to deal for Christ in public, have need to keep up a private communion with him. We should make use of the liberty of access we have

14-23. Healing of a Demoniac Boy—Second Explicit Announcement by Our Lord of His Approaching Death and Resurrection. (=Mark 9:14-32; Luke 9:37-45.) The time of this section is sufficiently denoted by the events which all the narratives show to have immediately preceded it—the first explicit announcement of His death, and the transfiguration—both being between His third and His fourth and last Passover.

Healing of the Demoniac and Lunatic Boy (vss. 14-21). For the exposition of this portion, see on Mark 9:14-32.

Master, I have brought unto thee my son—"mine only child" (Luke 9:38). **which hath a dumb spirit**—a spirit whose operation had the effect of rendering his victim speechless, and deaf also (vs. 25). In Matthew's report of the speech (17:15), the father says "he is lunatic"; this being another and most distressing effect of the possession.

and I spake to thy disciples that they should cast him out; and they could not—Our Lord replies to the father by a severe rebuke to the disciples. As if wounded at the exposure before such a multitude, of the weakness of His disciples' faith, which doubtless He felt as a reflection on Himself, He puts them to the blush before all, but in language fitted only to raise expectation of what He Himself would do.

He answereth him, and saith, O faithless generation—"and perverse," or "perverted" (Matt. 17:17; Luke 9:41). **how long shall I be with you? how long shall I suffer you?**—language implying that it was a shame to them to want the faith necessary to perform this cure, and that it needed some patience to put up with them. It is to us surprising that some interpreters, as Chrysostom and Calvin, should represent this rebuke as addressed, not to the disciples at all, but to the scribes who disputed with them. Nor does it much, if at all, mend the matter to view it as addressed to both, as most expositors seem to do. With Bengel, De Wette, and Meyer, we regard it as addressed directly to the nine apostles who were unable to expel this evil spirit. And though, in ascribing this inability to their "want of faith" and the "perverted turn of mind" which they had drunk in with their early training, the rebuke would undoubtedly apply, with vastly greater force, to those who twitted the poor disciples with their inability, it would be to change the whole nature of the rebuke to suppose it addressed to those who had *no faith at all,* and were *wholly perverted.* It was because faith sufficient for curing this youth was to be expected of the disciples, and because they should by that time have got rid of the perversity in which they had been reared, that Jesus exposes them thus before the rest. And who does not see that this was fitted, more than anything else, to impress upon the bystanders the severe loftiness of the training He was giving to the Twelve, and the unsophisticated footing He was on with them? **Bring him unto me**—The order to bring the patient to Him was instantly obeyed; when, lo! as if conscious of the presence of his Divine Tormentor, and expecting to be made to quit, the foul spirit rages and is furious, determined to die hard, doing all the mischief he can to this poor child while yet within his grasp.

14. *When they were come to the multitude.* It appears that a congregation had been collected during our Lord's stay on the mount. *Kneeling down to him.* Or falling at His knees.

15. *My son . . . is lunatick.* One who was most affected with this disorder at the change and full of the moon. But this lunacy was occasioned by a demon. *Ofttimes he falleth into the fire, and oft into the water.* Those who are under the influence of the devil are often driven to extremes in everything. Such are often driven into the *fire* of presumption or the *waters* of despair. Satan takes advantage of our natural temper, state of health, and outward circumstances to plague and ruin our souls.

17. *O faithless and perverse generation.* These and the following words may be considered as spoken: (1) To the disciples, because of their unbelief, v. 20. (2) To the father of the possessed, who should have brought his son to Christ. (3) To the whole multitude, who were slow of heart to believe in Him as the Messiah, notwithstanding the miracles which He wrought.

MATTHEW HENRY

to Jesus apart, where we may be free and particular with him. That which is amiss may, when found out, be amended.

2. Christ gives them two reasons why they failed.

(1) It was *because of their unbelief, v.* 20. When he spake to the father of the child and to the people, he charged it upon their unbelief; when he spake to his disciples, he charged it upon theirs; for the truth was, there were faults on both sides. When the preaching of the word seems not to be so successful as sometimes it has been, the people are apt to lay all the fault upon the ministers, and the ministers upon the people; whereas, it is more becoming for each to own his own faultiness, and to say, "It is owing to me." Though they had faith, yet that faith was weak and ineffectual. As far as faith falls short of its due strength, vigour, and activity, it may truly be said, "There is unbelief." Many are chargeable with unbelief, who yet are not to be called *unbelievers.* It is because of our unbelief, that we bring so little to pass in religion, and come short, in that which is good.

Our Lord Jesus takes this occasion to show them the power of faith, *If ye have faith as a grain of mustard-seed,* ye shall do wonders, *v.* 20. Some make the comparison to refer to the quality of the mustard-seed, which is, when bruised, sharp and penetrating; "If you have an active growing faith, not dead, flat, or insipid, you will not be baffled thus." But it rather refers to the quantity; "If you had but a grain of true faith, though so little that it were like that which is the least of all seeds, you would do wonders." The faith here required, is that which had for its object that particular revelation by which Christ gave his disciples power to work miracles in his name. It was a faith in this revelation that they were defective in. Perhaps their Master's absence with the three chief of his disciples might occasion some doubts concerning their power to do this. It is good for us to be diffident of ourselves and of our own strength; but it is displeasing to Christ, when we distrust any power derived from him or granted by him.

If ye have ever so little of this faith in sincerity *ye shall say to this mountain, Remove.* This is a proverbial expression, denoting that which follows, and no more, *Nothing shall be impossible to you.* They distrusted the power they had received, and so failed. To convince them of this, Christ shows them what they might have done. An active faith can remove mountains, not of itself, but in the virtue of a divine power engaged by a divine promise.

(2) Because there was something in the kind of the malady, which rendered the cure more than ordinarily difficult (*v.* 21); *"This kind goes not out but by prayer and fasting."* The extraordinary power of Satan must not discourage our faith, but quicken us to a greater intenseness in the acting of it, and more earnestness in praying to God for the increase of it. Fasting and prayer are proper means for the fetching in of divine power to our assistance. Fasting is of use to put an edge upon prayer; it is an evidence and instance of humiliation which is necessary in prayer. Fasting must be joined with prayer, to keep under the body.

Verses 22–23

Christ here foretells his own sufferings; he began to do it before (*ch.* xvi. 21); and, finding that it was to his disciples a hard saying, he saw it necessary to repeat it.

1. What he foretold concerning himself—that he should be betrayed and killed.

(1) He tells them that he should *be betrayed into the hands of men.* Men to whom he was allied by nature, and from whom therefore he might expect pity and tenderness; these are his persecutors and murderers.

(2) That *they should kill him*; nothing less than that would satisfy their rage; it was his blood, his precious blood, that they thirsted after. If he be a Sacrifice of atonement, he must be killed; without blood no remission.

(3) That *he shall be raised again the third day.* Still, when he spoke of his death, he gave a hint of his resurrection. This was an encouragement, not only to him, but to his disciples; for if he rise the third day, his absence from them will not be long, and his return to them will be glorious.

2. How the disciples received this; *They were exceedingly sorry.* Herein appeared their love to their Master's person, but with all their ignorance and mistake concerning his undertaking.

JAMIESON, FAUSSET, BROWN

And he said unto them, This kind can come forth by nothing but by prayer and fasting—i.e., as nearly all good interpreters are agreed, "this kind of evil spirits cannot be expelled," or "so desperate a case of demoniacal possession cannot be cured, but by prayer and fasting." But since the Lord Himself says that His disciples could not fast while He was with them, perhaps this was designed, as ALFORD hints, for their after-guidance—unless we take it as but a definite way of expressing the general truth, that great and difficult duties require special preparation and self-denial. But the answer to their question, as given in Matthew 17 is fuller: "And Jesus said unto them, Because of your unbelief. For verily I say unto you, If ye have faith as a grain of mustard seed, ye shall say unto this mountain, Remove hence to yonder place, and it shall remove; and nothing shall be impossible unto you" (vs. 20). See on ch. 11:23. "Howbeit this kind goeth not out but by prayer and fasting" (vs. 21). i.e., though nothing is impossible to faith, yet such a height of faith as is requisite for such triumphs is not to be reached either in a moment or without effort—either with God in prayer or with ourselves in self-denying exercises. Luke (9:43) adds, "And they were all amazed at the mighty power of God"—"at the majesty" or "mightiness of God," in this last miracle, in the Transfiguration, etc.; or, at the *divine grandeur* of Christ rising upon them daily.

Second Announcement of His Death (vss. 22, 23).

22. And while they abode in Galilee, Jesus said unto them—Mark (9:30), as usual, is very precise here: "And they departed thence"—i.e., from the scene of the last miracle—"and passed through Galilee; and He would not that any man should know it." So this was not a preaching, but a private, journey through Galilee. Indeed, His public ministry in Galilee was now all but concluded. Though He sent out the Seventy after this to preach and heal, He Himself was little more in public there, and He was soon to bid it a final adieu. Till this hour arrived, He was chiefly occupied with the Twelve, preparing them for the coming events. **The Son of man shall be betrayed into the hands of men . . . And they were exceeding sorry**—Though the shock would not be so great as at the first announcement (ch. 16:21, 22), their "sorrow" would not be the less, but probably the greater, the deeper the intelligence went down into their hearts, and a new wave dashing upon them by this repetition of the heavy tidings. Accordingly, Luke (9:43, 44), connecting it with the scene of the miracle just recorded, and the teaching which arose out of it—or possibly with all His recent teaching—says our Lord forewarned the Twelve that they would soon stand in need of all that teaching: "But while they wondered every one at all things which Jesus did, He said unto His disciples, Let these sayings sink down into your ears; for the Son of man shall be delivered . . . ": 'Be not carried off your feet by the grandeur you have lately seen in Me, but remember what I have told you, and now tell you again, that that Sun in whose beams ye now rejoice is soon to set in midnight gloom.' Remarkable is the antithesis in those words of our Lord preserved in all the three narratives—"The son of *man* shall be betrayed into the hands of *men.*" Luke adds (vs. 45) that "they understood not this saying, and it was hid from them, that they perceived it not"—for the plainest statements, when they encounter long-continued and obstinate prejudices, are seen through a distorting and dulling medium—"and were afraid to ask Him"; deterred partly by the air of lofty sadness with which doubtless these sayings were uttered, and on which they would be reluctant to break in, and partly by the fear of laying themselves open to rebuke for their shallowness and timidity. How artless is all this!

ADAM CLARKE

20. *As a grain of mustard seed.* Our Lord means a thriving and increasing faith; which like the grain of mustard seed, from being the least of seeds, becomes the greatest of all herbs, even a tree in whose branches the fowls of the air take shelter.

21. *This kind goeth not out but by prayer.* The whole verse is wanting in the famous Vatican MS., one of the most ancient and most authentic perhaps in the world. It is wanting also in the Coptic, Ethiopic, Syriac, Hieros., and one copy of the Itala. But all the MSS. acknowledge it in the parallel place, Mark ix. 29, only the Vatican MS. leaves out *fasting.* I strongly suspect it to be an interpolation; but, if it be, it is very ancient, as Origen, Chrysostom, and others of the primitive fathers acknowledged it.

23. *They were exceeding sorry.* Since the conversation on the mount with Moses and Elijah, Peter, James, and John could have no doubt that their Lord and Master must suffer, and that it was for this end He came into the world. But while they submitted to the counsel of God, their affection for Him caused them to feel exquisite distress.

MATTHEW HENRY

Verses 24-27

We have here an account of Christ's paying tribute.

I. Observe how it was demanded, *v.* 24. Christ was now at Capernaum.

1. The tribute demanded was not any civil payment to the Roman powers, but the church-duties, which were required from every person for the service of the temple, and the defraying of the expenses of the worship there.

2. The demand was very modest. Their question is, *Doth not your master pay tribute?* Some think that they sought an occasion against him. It should rather seem, they asked this with respect, intimating, that if he had any privilege to exempt him from this payment, they would not insist upon it.

Peter passed his word for his Master; "*Yes,* certainly; my *Master pays tribute." He was made under the law,* therefore under this law he was paid for at forty days old (Luke ii. 22), and now he paid for himself. Now this tax paid to the temple is called *an atonement for the soul,* Exod. xxx. 15. Christ, that in everything he might *appear in the likeness of sinners,* paid it though he had no sin to atone for. He did this to set us an example: Of *rendering to all their due tribute to whom tribute is due.* Of contributing to the support of the public worship of God in the places where we are. If we reap spiritual things, it is fit that we should return carnal things. If Christ pay tribute, who can pretend an exemption?

II. How it was disputed (*v.* 25), not with the collectors themselves, but with Peter, that he might be satisfied in the reason why Christ paid tribute. He brought the collectors into the house; but Christ anticipated him. The disciples of Christ are never attacked without his knowledge. He appeals to the way of the kings of the earth, which is, to take tribute of strangers. He applies this to himself; *Then are the children free.* Christ is the Son of God, and Heir of all things; and therefore not obliged to pay this tax for the service of the temple. Thus Christ asserts his right. God's children are freed by grace and adoption from the slavery of sin and Satan, but not from their subjection to civil magistrates in civil things; here the law of Christ is express. *Render to Caesar the things that are Caesar's.*

III. How it was paid, notwithstanding, *v.* 27.

1. For what reason Christ waived his privilege, and paid this tribute—*Lest we should offend them.* Christ considers that if he should refuse this payment, it would increase people's prejudice against him and his doctrine, and alienate their affections from him, and therefore he resolves to pay it. Christian prudence and humility teach us, in many cases, to recede from our right, rather than give offence by insisting upon it. We must never decline our duty for fear of giving offence, but we must sometimes deny ourselves in that which is our secular interest, rather than give offence.

2. What course he took for the payment of this tax (*v.* 27).

(1) The poverty of Christ; though he cured so many that were diseased; it seems, he did all gratis.

(2) The power of Christ, in fetching money out of a fish's mouth for this purpose. It was an evidence of his divinity, and that he is Lord of hosts. Those creatures that are most remote from man are at the command of Christ, even the fishes of the sea are under his feet (Ps. viii. 5). Now observe,

[1] Peter must catch the fish by angling. Peter has something to do, and it is in the way of his own calling too; to teach us diligence in the employment we are called *to,* and called *in.* Do we expect that Christ should give to us? Let us be ready to work for him.

[2] The fish came up, with money in the mouth of it. What work we do at Christ's command brings its own pay along with it.

[3] The piece of money was just enough to pay the tax for Christ and Peter. He would teach us not to covet superfluities, but, having enough for our present occasions, therewith to be content, and not to distrust God, though we live but from hand to mouth. Peter fished for this money, and therefore part of it went for his use. Those that are *workers together with Christ* in winning souls shall be sharers with him in his glory. *Give it for thee and me.* What Christ paid for himself was looked upon as a debt; what he paid for Peter was a courtesy to him. It is a desirable thing, if God so please, to have wherewithal of this world's goods, not only to be just, but to be kind; not only to be charitable to the poor, but obliging to our friends.

JAMIESON, FAUSSET, BROWN

24-27. THE TRIBUTE MONEY. The time of this section is evidently in immediate succession to that of the preceding one. The brief but most pregnant incident which it records is given by Matthew alone—for whom, no doubt, it would have a peculiar interest, from its relation to his own town and his own familiar lake. **24. And when they were come to Capernaum, they that received tribute money**—the double drachma; a sum equal to two Attic drachmas, and corresponding to the Jewish "half-shekel," payable, towards the maintenance of the temple and its services, by every male Jew of twenty years old and upward. For the origin of this annual tax, see Exodus 30:13, 14; II Chronicles 24:6, 9. Thus, it will be observed, it was not a civil, but an ecclesiastical tax. The tax mentioned in the next verse was a civil one. The whole teaching of this very remarkable scene depends upon this distinction. **came to Peter**—at whose house Jesus probably resided while at Capernaum. This explains several things in the narrative. **and said, Doth not your master pay tribute?**—The question seems to imply that the payment of this tax was *voluntary,* but *expected;* or what, in modern phrase, would be called a 'voluntary assessment.' **25. He saith, yes**—i.e., "To be sure He does"; as if eager to remove even the suspicion of the contrary. If Peter knew—as surely he did—that there was at this time no money in the bag, this reply must be regarded as a great act of faith in his Master. **And when he was come into the house**—Peter's—**Jesus prevented him**—anticipated him; according to the old sense of the word "prevent." **saying, What thinkest thou, Simon?**—using his family name for familiarity. **of whom do the kings of the earth take custom**—meaning custom on goods exported or imported—**or tribute**—meaning the poll-tax, payable to the Romans by everyone whose name was in the census. This, therefore, it will be observed, was strictly a *civil* tax. **of their own children, or of strangers**—This cannot mean 'foreigners,' from whom sovereigns certainly do not raise taxes, but those who are not of their own family, i.e., their subjects. **26. Peter saith unto him, Of strangers**—"of those not their children." **Jesus saith unto him, Then are the children free**—By "the children" our Lord cannot here mean Himself and the Twelve together, in some loose sense of their near relationship to God as their common Father. For besides that our Lord never once mixes Himself up with His disciples in speaking of their relation to God, but ever studiously keeps His relation and theirs apart (see, for example, on the last words of this chapter)—this would be to teach the right of believers to exemption from the dues required for sacred services, in the teeth of all that Paul teaches and that He Himself indicates throughout. He can refer here, then, only to Himself; using the word "children" evidently in order to express the general principle observed by sovereigns, who do not draw taxes from their own children, and thus convey the truth respecting His own exemption the more strikingly:—viz., "If the sovereign's own family be exempt, you know the inference in My case"; or to express it more nakedly than Jesus thought needful and fitting: "This is a tax for upholding My Father's House. As His Son, then, that tax is not due by Me—I AM FREE." **27. Notwithstanding, lest we should offend**—stumble—**them** all ignorant as they are of My relation to the Lord of the Temple, and should misconstrue a claim to exemption into indifference to His honor who dwells in it. **go thou to the sea**—Capernaum, it will be remembered, lay on the Sea of Galilee. **and cast an hook, and take up the fish that first cometh up; and when thou hast opened his mouth, thou shalt find a piece of money**—a stater. So it should have been rendered, and not indefinitely, as in our version, for the coin was an Attic silver coin equal to two of the afore-mentioned "didrachms" of half a shekel's value, and so, was the exact sum required for both. Accordingly, the Lord adds—**that take, and give unto them for me and thee**—lit., "instead of Me and thee"; perhaps because the payment was a *redemption of the person* paid for (Exod. 30:12)—in which view Jesus certainly was "free." If the house was Peter's, this will account for payment being provided on this occasion, not for all the Twelve, but only for him and His Lord. Observe, our Lord does not say "for us," but "for Me and thee"; thus distinguishing the Exempted One and His non-exempted disciple.

ADAM CLARKE

24. *They that received tribute.* This was not a tax to be paid to the Roman government, but a tax for the support of the Temple. The law, Exod. xxx. 13, obliged every male among the Jews to pay half a shekel yearly for the support of the Temple.

25. *He saith, Yes.* From this reply of Peter it is evident that our Lord customarily paid all taxes, tributes, etc., which were common among the people wherever He came. The children of God are subject to all civil laws in the places where they live—and should pay the taxes levied on them by public authority.

26. *Then are the children free.* As this money is levied for the support of that Temple of which I am the Lord, then I am not obliged to pay the tax; and My disciples, like the priests that minister, should be exempted from the necessity of paying.

JOHN WESLEY:

27. "Yet that we may not offend them"—Even those unreasonable men, who claim what they have no right to: do not contest it with them, but rather yield to their demand that violate peace or live. Oh, what would not one of a loving spirit do for peace! Anything which is not expressly forbidden in the Word of God. "A piece of money"—The original word is a stater, which was in value two shillings and sixpence; just the sum that was wanted. "Give for me and thee"—Peter had a family of his own; the other apostles were the family of Jesus.

What knowledge and power did our Lord here discover! Knowledge, penetrating into this animal, though beneath the waters; and power in directing this very fish to Peter's hook, though he himself was at a distance! How must this have encouraged both him and his brethren in a firm dependance on Divine Providence!
—*Wesley's Notes on the New Testament*

MATTHEW HENRY

CHAPTER 18

There never was a greater pattern of humility than Christ; he took all occasions to command it, to commend it, to his disciples and followers.

I. The occasion of this discourse concerning humility was an unbecoming contest among the disciples for precedency; *Who is the greatest in the kingdom of heaven?* They mean not, *who* by character but *who* by name. They had heard much, and preached much, of the kingdom of heaven; but as yet they were so far from having any clear notion of it, that they dreamt of a temporal kingdom, and the external pomp and power of it. They expected his kingdom would commence; and now they thought it was time to put in for their places in it; it is good, in such cases, to speak early. Instead of asking how they might have strength and grace to suffer with him, they ask him, "Who shall be highest in reigning with him." Many love to hear and speak of privileges and glory, who are willing to pass by the thoughts of work and trouble.

1. They suppose that all who have a place in that kingdom are great. Those are truly great who are truly good.

2. They suppose that there are degrees in this greatness. All the saints are honourable, but not all alike so.

3. They suppose it must be some of them, that must be prime ministers of state.

4. They strive who it should be, each having some pretence or other to it. We are very apt to amuse and humour ourselves with foolish fancies of things that will never be.

II. The discourse itself, which is a just rebuke to the question, *Who shall be greatest?*

Christ here teacheth them to be humble,

1. By a sign (*v.* 2); *He called a little child to him, and set him in the midst of them.* Humility is a lesson so hardly learned, that we have need by all ways and means to be taught it. When we look upon a little child, we should be put in mind of the use Christ made of this child. *He set him in the midst of them;* not that they might play with him, but that they might learn by him. Grown men, and great men, should not disdain the company of little children. They may either speak to them, and give instruction to them; or look upon them, and receive instruction from them.

2. By a sermon upon this sign; in which he shows them and us,

(1) The necessity of humility, *v.* 3. *Verily I say unto you, Except ye be converted, and become as little children, ye shall not enter into the kingdom of heaven.*

What it is that he requires and insists upon. *First,* "You must be converted, you must be of another mind." Besides the first conversion of a soul there are after-conversions from particular paths of back-sliding. Every step out of the way by sin, must be a step into it again by repentance. *Secondly,* You must *become as little children.* Converting grace makes us like little children. As children, we must be careful for nothing, but leave it to our heavenly Father to care for us (*ch.* vi. 31). We must be humble as little children; the child of a gentleman will play with the child of a beggar (Rom. xii. 16). The age of childhood is the learning age. What stress he lays upon this; Without this, *you shall not enter into the kingdom of heaven.* The disciples, when they put that question (*v.* 1), thought themselves sure of the kingdom of heaven. They were ambitious of being *greatest in the kingdom of heaven*; Christ tells them, that except they came to a better temper, they should never come thither. Our Lord designs here to show the great danger of pride and ambition. Pride threw the angels that sinned out of heaven, and will keep us out, if we be not converted from it.

(2) He shows the honour and advancement that attend humility (*v.* 4). He that humbles himself as a little child *the same is greatest in the kingdom of heaven.* The humblest Christians are the best Christians and most like to Christ, and highest in his favour, and fittest to serve God in this world, and enjoy him in another.

(3) The special care Christ takes for those that are humble.

Those that thus humble themselves will be afraid,

[1] That nobody will receive them; but (*v.* 5), *Whoso shall receive one such little child in my name, receiveth me.* Whatever kindnesses are done to such, Christ takes as done to himself. Though it be but one such little child that is received in Christ's name, it shall be accepted. The less they are in themselves, to whom we show kindness, the more there is of good will in it to Christ; the less it is for their sakes, the more it is for his; and he takes it accordingly.

[2] They will be afraid that everybody will abuse them. This objection he obviates (*v.* 6), where he warns

JAMIESON, FAUSSET, BROWN

CHAPTER 18

Vss. 1-9. Strife among the Twelve Who Should Be Greatest in the Kingdom of Heaven, with Relative Teaching. (=Mark 9:33-50; Luke 9:46-50.) For the exposition, see on Mark 9:33-50.

who should be the greatest—From Matthew 18:1 we should infer that the subject was introduced, not by our Lord, but by the disciples themselves, who came and asked Jesus who should be greatest. Perhaps one or two of them first referred the matter to Jesus, who put them off till they should all be assembled together at Capernaum. He had all the while "perceived the thought of their heart" (Luke 9:47); but now that they were all together "in the house," He questions them about it, and they are put to the blush, conscious of the *temper* towards each other which it had kindled. This raised the whole question afresh, and at this point our Evangelist takes it up. The subject was suggested by the recent announcement of the Kingdom (Matt. 16:19-28), the transfiguration of their Master, and especially the preference given to three of them at that scene.

And he took a child—"a little child" (Matt. 18:2); but the word is the same in both places, as also in Luke 9:47. **and set him in the midst of them:**

he said unto them—Here we must go to Matthew (18:3, 4) for the first of this answer: "Verily I say unto you, except ye be converted, and become as little children, ye shall not enter into the kingdom of Heaven:" i.e., "Conversion must be thorough; not only must the heart be turned to God in general, and from earthly to heavenly things, but in particular, except ye be converted from that carnal ambition which still rankles within you, into that freedom from all such feelings which ye see in this child, ye have neither part nor lot in the kingdom at all; and he who in this feature has most of the child, is highest there." Whosoever, therefore, shall "humble himself as this little child, the same is greatest in the kingdom of heaven": "for he that is [willing to be] least among you all, the same shall be great" (Luke 9:48).

37. **Whosoever shall receive one of such children**—so manifesting the spirit unconsciously displayed by this child. **in my name**—from love to Me. **receiveth me; and whosoever shall receive me, receiveth not me, but Him that sent me**—See on Matthew 10:40.

ADAM CLARKE

CHAPTER 18

1. *Who is the greatest?* Could these disciples have viewed the kingdom of Christ in any other light than that of a temporal one? Hence they wished to know whom He would make His prime minister—whom His general—whom His chief chancellor—whom supreme judge. The disciples having lately seen the keys delivered to Peter, and found that he, with James and John, had been privileged with being present at the Transfiguration, it is no wonder if a measure of jealousy and suspicion began to work in their minds. From this inquiry we may also learn that the disciples had no notion of Peter's supremacy.

3. *Except ye be converted.* Unless you are saved from those prejudices which are at present so baneful to your nation (seeking a temporal and not a spiritual kingdom), unless you are clothed with the spirit of humility, you cannot enter into the spirit, design, and privileges of My spiritual and eternal kingdom. *And become as little children.* I.e., be as truly without worldly ambition, and the lust of power, as little children are, who act among themselves as if all were equal.

5. *One such little child.* As our Lord in the preceding verses considers a little child an emblem of a genuine disciple, so by the term in this verse He means a disciple only. *Whoso shall receive,* i.e., show unto such a childlike, unambitious disciple of Mine any act of kindness for My sake, I will consider it as done to myself.

MATTHEW HENRY

all people not to offer any injury to one of Christ's little ones. This word makes a wall of fire about them; he that touches them, touches the apple of God's eye.

The crime supposed; *offending one of these little ones that believe in Christ.* Their believing in Christ unites them to him, so that, as they partake of the benefit of his sufferings, he also partakes in the wrong of theirs. Even the little ones that believe have the same privileges with the great ones. The best men have often met with the worst treatment in this world.

The punishment of this crime; intimated in that word, *Better for him that he were drowned in the depth of the sea.* The sin is so heinous, and the ruin proportionably so great, that he had better undergo the sorest punishments inflicted on the worst of malefactors, which can only kill the body.

Verses 7–14

Our Saviour here speaks of offences, or scandals,

I. In general, *v.* 7. That is an offence, 1. Which occasions guilt. 2. Which occasions grief. Christ here tells them,

(1) That they were certain things; *It must needs be, that offences come.* When we are sure there is danger, we should be the better armed. Not that Christ's word necessitates any man to offend, but it is a prediction upon a view of the causes. It is morally impossible but that there should be offences. Let us stand upon our guard.

(2) That they would be woeful things.

[1] A woe to the careless and unguarded, to whom the offence is given; *Woe to the world because of offences.* This present world is an evil world, it is so full of offences, of sins, and snares, and sorrows; a dangerous road we travel, full of stumbling-blocks, precipices, and false guides. Woe to the world. As for those whom God hath chosen they are preserved by the power of God, are helped over all these stones of stumbling.

[2] A woe to the wicked, who wilfully give the offence; *But woe to that man by whom the offence comes.* Though it must needs be, that the offence will come, that will be no excuse for the offenders. The guilt will be laid at the door of those who give the offence, though they also fall under a woe who take it. The righteous God will reckon with those who ruin the eternal interests of precious souls, and the temporal interests of precious saints. Men will be reckoned with, not only for their doings, but for the fruit of their doings.

II. In particular, Christ here speaks of offences given,

1. By us to ourselves, which is expressed by our hand or foot offending us; in such a case, it must be *cut off, v.* 8, 9. This Christ had said before (*ch.* v. 29, 30). Those hard sayings of Christ need to be repeated to us again and again, and all little enough. What it is that is here enjoined. We must part with an *eye*, or a *hand*, or a *foot*, whatever it is, which is dear to us, when it proves unavoidably an occasion of sin to us. Many prevailing temptations to sin arise from within ourselves; if there were never a devil to tempt us, we should be drawn away of our own lust. We must, as far as lawfully we may, part with that which we cannot keep without being entangled in sin by it. It is certain, the inward lust must be mortified. Corrupt inclinations and appetites must be checked and crossed. The outward occasions of sin must be avoided, though we thereby put as great a violence upon ourselves as it would be to cut off a hand, or pluck out an eye. We must think nothing too dear to part with, for the keeping of a good conscience. Upon what inducement this is required; *It is better for thee to enter into life maimed, than, having two hands, to be cast into hell.* The argument is the same with that of the apostle, Rom. viii. 13. *If we live after the flesh, we shall die. If we through the Spirit mortify the deeds of the body, we shall live;* that is meant by our *entering into life maimed*, that is, the body of sin maimed. They that are Christ's have nailed the flesh to the cross, but it is not yet dead; its life is prolonged, but its *dominion taken away.*

2. Concerning offences given by us to others.

(1) The caution itself; *Take heed that ye despise not one of these little ones.* He will be displeased with the great ones of the church, if they despise the little ones of it. We may understand it literally of little children; of them Christ was speaking, *v.* 2, 4. Or, figuratively; true but weak believers are these little ones, who are like little children, the lambs of Christ's flock. We must not despise them, not think meanly of them. We must not make a jest of their infirmities, not conduct ourselves scornfully or disdainfully toward them, as if we cared not what became of them. We must not impose upon the

JAMIESON, FAUSSET, BROWN

For whosoever shall offend one of these little ones that believe in me—or, shall cause them to stumble; referring probably to the effect which such unsavory disputes as they had held would have upon the inquiring and hopeful who came in contact with them, leading to the belief that after all they were no better than others. **it is better for him that a millstone were hanged about his neck**—The word here is simply "millstone," without expressing of which kind. But in Matthew 18:6 it is the "ass-turned" kind, far heavier than the small hand-mill turned by female slaves, as in Luke 17:35. It is of course the same which is meant here. **and he were cast into the sea**—meaning, that if by such a death that stumbling were prevented, and so its eternal consequences averted, it would be a happy thing for them. Here follows a striking verse in Matthew 18:7, "Woe unto the world because of offences!" (There will be stumblings and falls and loss of souls enough from the world's treatment of disciples, without any addition from you: dreadful will be its doom in consequence; see that ye share not in it.) "For it must needs be that offences come; but woe to that man by whom the offence cometh!" (The struggle between light and darkness will inevitably cause stumblings, but not less guilty is he who wilfully makes any to stumble.)

And if thy hand offend thee, cut it off: it is better for thee to enter into life maimed, than having two hands to go into hell—See Matthew 5:29, 30. The only difference between the words there and here is that there they refer to impure inclinations; here, to an ambitious disposition, an irascible or quarrelsome temper, and the like: and the injunction is to strike at the root of such dispositions and cut off the occasions of them. **And if thine eye offend thee, pluck it out: it is better for thee to enter into the kingdom of God with one eye, than having two eyes to be cast into hell-fire; Where their worm dieth not, and the fire is not quenched**—See on Matthew 5:30; and on the words "hell" and "hell-fire," or "the hell of fire," see on Matthew 5:22. The "unquenchableness" of this fire has already been brought before us (see on Matt. 3:12); and the awfully vivid idea of an undying worm, everlastingly consuming an unconsumable body, is taken from the closing words of the evangelical prophet (Isa. 66: 24), which seem to have furnished the later Jewish Church with its current phraseology on the subject of future punishment (see LIGHTFOOT).

ADAM CLARKE

6. *But whoso shall offend one of these little ones.* But, on the contrary, whosoever shall cause one of the least of those who believe in Me to be stumbled—to go into the spirit of the world, or give way to sin—such a one shall meet with the most exemplary punishment. *A millstone.* "An ass's millstone," because in ancient times, before the invention of wind and water mills, the stones were turned sometimes by slaves, but commonly by asses or mules.

7. *Woe!* or "Alas!" It is the opinion of some eminent critics that this word is ever used by our Lord to express sympathy and concern. *Because of offences.* Scandals, stumbling blocks, persecutions, etc.

F. B. MEYER:

An offense is anything that makes the path of a holy and useful life more difficult for others. Be sure, in all your actions, to consider the weaker ones who are watching and following you. "Father," said a boy, "take the safe path; I am coming." A man whose arm was caught in a machine saved his boy from being drawn in by severing the arm with a hatchet. All that hurts us or others, however precious, must be severed.—*Bible Commentary*

10. *One of these little ones.* One of My simple, loving, humble disciples.

MATTHEW HENRY

consciences of others. There is a respect owing to the conscience of every man who appears to be conscientious. We must take heed that we do not despise them; and be very cautious what we say and do, lest we should through inadvertency give offence to Christ's little ones.

(2) The reasons to enforce the caution. We must not look upon these little ones as contemptible. Let not those be looked upon by us with disdain, whom God has put honour upon. To prove that the little ones which believe in Christ are worthy to be respected, consider,

[1] The ministration of the good angels about them; *In heaven their angels always behold the face of my Father.* Two things he lets us know concerning them.

First, That they are the little ones' angels. God's angels are theirs. They can look by faith on the heavenly hosts, and call them theirs. It is bad being enemies to those who are so guarded; and it is good having God for our God, for then we have his angels for our angels.

Secondly, That *they always behold the face of the Father in heaven.* This bespeaks, 1. The angels' continual felicity and honour. The happiness of heaven consists in the vision of God, beholding his beauty. 2. It bespeaks their continual readiness to minister to the saints. They behold the face of God, expecting to receive orders from him what to do for the good of the saints. If we would behold the face of God in glory hereafter, we must behold the face of God now, in readiness to our duty.

[2] The gracious design of Christ concerning them (*v.* 11); *For the Son of man is come to save that which was lost.* This is a reason, *First,* Why the little ones' angels have such a charge concerning them, and attend upon them; it is in pursuance of Christ's design to save them. *Secondly,* Why they are not to be despised; because Christ came to save them, to save them that are lost. Our souls by nature are lost souls; as a traveller is lost, that is out of his way. Christ's errand into the world was to *save that which was lost,* to put us into the right way that leads to our great end. This is a good reason why the least and weakest believers should not be despised or offended. If Christ put such a value upon them, let us not undervalue them.

[3] The tender regard which our heavenly Father has to these little ones, and his concern for their welfare. This is illustrated by a comparison, *v.* 12–14.

Here is, *First,* The comparison, *v.* 12, 13. The owner that had lost one sheep out of a hundred diligently enquires after it, is greatly pleased when he has found it, and has in that a sensible and affecting joy, more than in the ninety and nine that wandered not. Now this is applicable, 1. To the state of fallen man in general; he is strayed like a lost sheep. Wandering man is sought upon the mountains, which Christ, in great fatigue, traversed in pursuit of him, and he is found; which is matter of joy. Greater joy there is in heaven for returning sinners than for remaining angels. 2. To particular believers, God is graciously concerned, not only for his flock in general, but for every lamb, or sheep, that belongs to it. Though they are many, yet out of those many he can easily miss one, for he is a *great* Shepherd, but not so easily lose it, for he is a *good* Shepherd.

Secondly, The application of this comparison (*v.* 14); *It is not the will of your Father, that one of these little ones should perish.* It is his will, that these little ones should be saved; it is the will of his design and delight. This care extends itself to every particular member of the flock, even the meanest.

Observe, Christ called God, *v.* 19, *my Father which is in heaven*; he calls him, *v.* 14, *your Father which is in heaven*; intimating that he is not ashamed to call his poor disciples *brethren.* This intimates likewise the ground of the safety of his little ones; that God is their Father. A father takes care of all his children, but is particularly tender of the little ones.

Verses 15–20

Christ, having cautioned his disciples not to give offence, comes next to direct them what they must do in case of offences given them.

I. Let us apply it to the quarrels that happen, upon any account, among Christians.

1. *Go, and tell him his fault between thee and him alone.* Do not suffer thy resentments to ripen into a secret malice (like a wound, which is most dangerous when it bleeds inwardly), but give vent to them in a mild and grave admonition, let them so spend themselves, and they will expire the sooner. If he has indeed done thee a considerable wrong, endeavour to make him sensible of it, but let the rebuke be private, between thee and him alone; if thou wouldest convince him, do not expose him, for that will but

JAMIESON, FAUSSET, BROWN

10-35. FURTHER TEACHING ON THE SAME SUBJECT, INCLUDING THE PARABLE OF THE UNMERCIFUL DEBTOR.

Same Subject (vss. 10-20). **10. Take heed that ye despise**—stumble—**not one of these little ones; for I say unto you, That in heaven their angels do always behold the face of my Father which is in heaven**—A difficult verse; but perhaps the following may be more than an illustration:—Among men, those who nurse and rear the royal children, however humble in themselves, are allowed free entrance with their charge, and a degree of familiarity which even the highest state ministers dare not assume. Probably our Lord means that, in virtue of their charge over His disciples (Heb. 1:13; John 1:51), the angels have *errands* to the throne, a *welcome* there, and a *dear familiarity* in dealing with "His Father which is in heaven," which on their own matters they could not assume.

For the Son of man is come to save that which was—or "is"—**lost**—A golden saying, once and again repeated in different forms. Here the connection seems to be, "Since the whole object and errand of the Son of man into the world is to save the lost, take heed lest, by causing offenses, ye lose the saved." That this is the idea intended we may gather from vs. 14. **12, 13. How think ye? If a man have an hundred sheep, and one of them be gone astray, . . .**—This is another of those pregnant sayings which our Lord uttered more than once. See on the delightful parable of the lost sheep in Luke 15:4-7. Only the object *there* is to show what the good Shepherd will do, when even one of His sheep is lost, to *find* it; *here* the object is to show, when found, how reluctant He is to *lose* it. Accordingly, it is added—vs.

14. Even so it is not the will of your Father which is in heaven that one of these little ones should perish—How, then, can He but visit for those "offenses" which endanger the souls of these little ones?

ADAM CLARKE

Their angels . . . always behold. Our Lord here not only alludes to, but in my opinion establishes, the notion received by almost all nations, viz., that every person has a guardian angel; and that these have always access to God, to receive orders relative to the management of their charge. See Ps. xxxiv. 7; Heb. i. 14. *Always behold the face.* Hence, among the Jews, the angels were styled "angels of the face," and Michael is said to be "the prince of the face." This is an allusion to the privilege granted by Eastern monarchs to their chief favorites and privy counsellors of Ahasuerus, are said to see the king's face. Esther i. 14.

11. *For the Son of man.* This is added as a second reason why no injury should be done to His followers. The Son of Man has so loved them as to come into the world to lay down His life for them.

14. *It is not the will of your Father.* If any soul be finally lost, it is not because God's will or counsel was against its salvation, or that a proper provision had not been made for it; but that, though light came into the world, it preferred darkness to light, because of its attachment to its evil deeds.

MATTHEW HENRY

exasperate him. "*If he shall hear thee*, well and good, *thou hast gained thy brother*, there is an end of the controversy, and it is a happy end; let no more be said of it, but let the falling out of friends be the renewing of friendship."

2. "*If he will not hear thee*, if he will not own himself in a fault, yet do not despair, but try what he will say to it, if thou take *one or two more*, not only to be witnesses of what passes, but to reason the case further with him."

3. "If *he shall neglect to hear them*, and will not refer the matter to their arbitration, then *tell it to the church*, and do not presently appeal to the magistrate, or fetch a writ for him." This is fully explained by the apostle (1 Cor. vi), where he reproves those that went to law before the unjust, and not before the saints (*v.* 1). This rule was then in a special manner requisite, when the civil government was in the hands of such as were not only aliens, but enemies.

4. "If he will not *hear the church* but persists in the wrong he has done thee *let him be to thee as a heathen man, and a publican*. Thou mayest, if thou wilt, break off thy friendship and familiarity with him; though thou must by no means study revenge, yet thou mayest choose whether thou wilt have any dealings with him. Thou wouldest have preserved his friendship, but he would not, and so has forfeited it." If a man cheat and abuse me once, it is his fault; if twice, it is my own.

II. Let us apply it to scandalous sins. Christ, designing to erect a church for himself in the world, here took care of the preservation, 1. Of its purity. 2. Of its peace and order.

(1) What is the case supposed? *If thy brother trespass against thee*. Church discipline is for church members. *Them that are without God judges*. Christ and believers have twisted interests; what is done against them Christ takes as done against himself, and what is done against him they cannot but take as done against themselves.

(2) What is to be done in this case.

[1] The rules prescribed, *v.* 15–17.

First, "*Go and tell him his fault between thee and him alone*. Do not stay till he comes to thee, but go to him, as the physician visits the patient. *Tell him his fault*, remind him of what he has done, and of the evil of it." People are loth to see their faults, and have need to be told of them. Great sins often amuse conscience, and for the present stupefy and silence it; and there is need of help to awaken it.

"*Tell him his fault*, ἔλεγξον αὐτὸν—*argue the case with him*" (so the word signifies). Where the fault is plain and great, and the person proper to deal with, we must with meekness and faithfulness tell people of what is amiss in them. Christian reproof is an ordinance of Christ for the bringing of sinners to repentance. "Let the reproof be private that it may appear you seek not his reproach, but his repentance." It is a good rule not to speak of our brethren's faults to others, till we have first spoken of them to themselves; this would make less reproaching and more reproving. It will be likely to work upon an offender, when he sees his reprover concerned not only for his salvation, in telling him his fault, but for his reputation in telling him of it privately.

"*If he shall hear thee, thou hast gained thy brother;* thou hast helped to save him from sin and ruin, and it will be thy credit and comfort," James *v.* 19, 20. If the loss of a soul be a great loss, the gain of a soul is sure no small gain.

Secondly, If that doth not prevail, *then take with thee one or two more*, *v.* 16. We must not be weary of well-doing, though we see not presently the good success of it. "If he will not hear thee, yet do not give him up as in a desperate case; but go on in the use of other means."

"*Take with thee one or two more;* 1. To assist thee; they may speak some pertinent convincing word which thou didst not think of, and may manage the matter with more prudence than thou didst." Christians should see their need of help in doing good, as in other things, so in giving reproofs. 2. "To affect him; he will be the more likely to be humbled for his fault, when he sees it witnessed against by *two or three*." Though in such a world as this it is rare to find one good whom *all men speak well of*, yet it is more rare to find one good whom *all men speak ill of*. 3. "To be witnesses of his conduct, in case the matter should afterward be brought before the church."

Thirdly, *If he neglect to hear them*, and will not be humbled, *then tell it to the church*, *v.* 17. There are some stubborn spirits to whom the likeliest means of conviction prove ineffectual; yet such must not be given over as incurable. Private admonitions must always go before public censures; if gentler

JAMIESON, FAUSSET, BROWN

A. B. SIMPSON:

The Lord Jesus has provided for the government and purity of His Church, and He has given authority to His servants to remove from this fellowship everything in opposition with its holy character. He has invested this discipline with the most sacred and binding authority, and He tells us in this passage that what we bind on earth He will bind in heaven, and what we loose on earth He will loose in heaven. When the willful and disobedient disciple refuses to yield to loving admonition and persists in some sinful and unchristian course, the Master has given to His people the right and power to remove that member and hand him over to the divine chastening until he shall truly repent and He tells us here that such an act on the part of the Church of God will be followed by the Lord's effectual dealing with all such cases. It will not be merely a matter of outward excommunication or public censure, but God's hand will deal with the offender through temporal judgment with a view to bringing the guilty one to repentance, or, as the apostle expressed it in another place, "for the destruction of the flesh that the spirit may be saved in the day of the Lord Jesus Christ."

Here we learn that our Christian attitude with the erring brother is always to deal with him personally and alone. We have no right to speak even to another of our brother's faults and offenses, until we have first dealt with him ourselves in loving faithfulness. It is only when this course has failed that we are permitted to resort to more rigid discipline. The Lord Jesus has made this the law of the Christian Church. Oh, how better it would be if His people would really live up to it! What a certain preventive it would be to the slander, the evil speaking, the strife and often the falling away of brethren who might have been saved by true obedience to the loving and wise commandment of the Master. Shall we take His message to us, here and henceforth thus deal with our erring brethren and prove to the world that the resources of the Church of Jesus Christ are adequate for her preservation, purity and power?—*Christ in the Bible*

15. Moreover, if thy brother shall trespass against thee, go and tell him his fault between thee and him alone: if he shall hear thee, thou hast gained thy brother, . . .—Probably our Lord had reference still to the late dispute, Who should be the greatest? After the rebuke—so gentle and captivating, yet so dignified and divine—under which they would doubtless be smarting, perhaps each would be saying, It was not *I* that began it, it was not I that threw out unworthy and irritating insinuations against my brethren. Be it so, says our Lord; but as such things will often arise, I will direct you how to proceed. *First*, Neither harbor a grudge against your offending brother, nor break forth upon him in presence of the unbelieving; but take him aside, show him his fault, and if he own and make reparation for it, you have done more service to him than even justice to yourself.

Next, If this fail, take two or three to witness how just your complaint is, and how brotherly your spirit in dealing with him.

Again, If this fail, bring him before the Church or congregation to which both belong.

ADAM CLARKE

15. *If thy brother*—any who is a member of the same religious society—*trespass against thee*, (1) *Go and* reprove him *alone*—it may be in person; if that cannot be so well done, by your messenger, or in writing (which in many cases is likely to be the most effectual). Observe, our Lord gives no liberty to omit this, or to exchange it for either of the following steps. If this do not succeed,

16. (2) *Take with thee one or two more*. Men whom he esteems, who may then confirm and enforce what you say; and afterwards, if need require, bear witness of what was spoken. If even this do not succeed, then, and not before,

MATTHEW HENRY

methods will do the work, those that are more rough and severe must not be used. Those that will be reasoned out of their sins, need not be shamed out of them. Let God's work be done effectually, but with as little noise as may be. Where private admonition does not prevail, there public censure must take place.

Tell it to the church. What church must be told—is the great question. By what follows, *v.* 18, it is plain that he means a Christian church, which, though not yet formed, was now in the embryo. "*Tell it to the church,* that particular church in the communion of which the offender lives. Tell it to the guides and governors of the church; let them examine the matter and, if they find the complaint frivolous and groundless, let them rebuke the complainant; if they find it just, let them rebuke the offender, and call him to repentance."

Fourthly, "*If he neglect to hear the church, let him be unto thee as a heathen man and a publican;* let him be cast out of the communion of the church." Those who put contempt on the orders and rules of a society, and bring reproach upon it, forfeit the honours and privileges of it. But observe, he doth not say, "Let him be to thee as a devil," but "as a heathen and a publican, as one in a capacity of being restored and received in again." But when by this he is humbled and reclaimed, he must be welcomed into communion again, and all shall be well.

[2] Here is a warrant signed for the ratification of all the church's proceedings according to these rules, *v.* 18. What was said before to Peter is here said to all the disciples. While ministers preach the word of Christ faithfully, and in their government of the church strictly adhere to his laws, they may be assured that he will own them, and stand by them. He will own them,

First, In their sentence of suspension; *Whatsoever ye shall bind on earth shall be bound in heaven.* If the censures of the church duly follow the institution of Christ, his judgments will follow the censures of the church, for Christ will not suffer his own ordinances to be trampled upon. Christ will not own those as his, nor receive them to himself, whom the church has duly delivered to Satan; but, if through error or envy the censures of the church be unjust, Christ will graciously find those who are so cast out, John ix. 34, 35.

Secondly, In their sentence of absolution; *Whatsoever ye shall lose on earth shall be loosed in heaven.* No church censures bind so fast, but that, upon the sinner's repentance and reformation, they may and must be loosed again. Sufficient is the punishment which has attained its end, and the offender must then be forgiven and comforted. Those who, upon their repentance, are received by the church into communion again may take the comfort of their absolution in heaven, if their hearts be upright with God.

Now it is a great honour which Christ here puts upon the church.

(1) God's readiness to answer the church's prayers (*v.* 19); *If two of you shall agree* harmoniously, *touching any thing that they shall ask, it shall be done for them.* Apply this,

[1] In general, to all the requests of the faithful praying seed of Jacob; they shall not *seek God's face in vain.* Many promises we have in scripture of a gracious answer to the prayers of faith, but this gives a particular encouragement to joint-prayer. No law of heaven limits the number of petitioners. If they join in the same prayer, or, though at a distance, agree in some particular matter of prayer, they shall speed well.

[2] In particular, to those requests that are put up to God about binding and loosing. The power of church discipline is not here lodged in the hand of a single person, but two, at least, are supposed to be concerned in it. Heats and animosities, among those whose work it is to remove offences, will be the greatest offence of all. Prayer must evermore go along with church discipline. Pass no sentence, which you cannot in faith ask God to confirm. Prayer must go along with all our endeavours for the conversion of sinners; see James v. 16. The unanimous petitions of the church of God, for the ratification of their just censures, shall be heard in heaven. God will set his fiat to the appeals and applications you make to him. God doth especially own and accept us, when we are praying for those that have offended him and us. *The Lord turned the captivity of Job,* not when he prayed for himself, but when he prayed for his friends who had trespassed against him.

(2) The presence of Christ in the assemblies of Christians, *v.* 20. Assemblies of Christians for holy purposes are hereby appointed, directed, and encouraged. They are hereby appointed; the church

JAMIESON, FAUSSET, BROWN

Lastly, If even this fail, regard him as no longer a brother Christian, but as one "without"—as the Jews did Gentiles and publicans.

18. Verily I say unto you, Whatsoever ye shall bind on earth shall be bound in heaven; and whatsoever ye shall loose on earth shall be loosed in heaven—Here, what had been granted but a short time before to Peter only (see on ch. 16:19) is plainly extended to all the Twelve; so that whatever it means, it means nothing peculiar to Peter, far less to his pretended successors at Rome. It has to do with admission to and rejection from the membership of the Church. But see on John 20:23.

19. Again I say unto you, That if two of you shall agree on earth as touching anything that they shall ask, it shall be done for them of my Father which is in heaven. 20. For where two or three are gathered together in—or "unto"—**my name, there am I in the midst of them**—On this passage—so full of sublime encouragement to Christian union in action and prayer—observe, first, the connection in which it stands. Our Lord had been speaking of church meetings before which the obstinate perversity of a brother was in the last resort to be brought, and whose decision was to be final—such honor does the Lord of the Church put upon its lawful assemblies. But not these assemblies only does He deign to countenance and honor. For even two uniting to bring any matter before Him shall find that they are not alone, for My Father is with them, says Jesus. Next, observe the *premium here put upon union in prayer.* As this cannot exist with fewer than two, so by letting it down so low as that number, He gives the utmost conceivable encouragement to union in this exercise. But what kind of union? Not an agreement merely to pray in concert, but to pray *for some definite thing.* "As touching anything which they shall ask," says our Lord—anything they shall agree to ask in concert. At the same time, it is plain He had certain things at that moment in His eye, as most fitting and needful subjects for such concerted prayer. The Twelve had been "falling out by the way" about the miserable question of precedence in their Master's kingdom, and this, as it stirred their corruptions, had given rise—or at least was in danger of giving rise—to "offenses" perilous to their souls. The Lord Himself had been directing them how to

ADAM CLARKE

17. (3) *Tell it unto the church.* Lay the whole matter before the congregation of Christian believers in that place of which he is a member, or before the minister and elders, as the representatives of the church or assembly.

If all this avail not, then, *Let him be unto thee as an heathen man and a publican.* To whom you are, as a Christian, to owe earnest and persevering goodwill and acts of kindness; but have no religious communions with him till, if he have been convicted, he acknowledge his fault. Whosoever follows this threefold rule will seldom offend others, and never be offended himself (Rev. J. Wesley). Reproving a brother who had sinned was a positive command under the law. See Lev. xix. 17. And the Jews have a saying that one of the causes of the ruin of their nation was, "No man reproved another."

18. *Whatsoever ye shall bind.* Whatever determinations you make, in conformity to these directions for your conduct to an offending brother, will be accounted just, and ratified by the Lord. Binding signified, and was commonly understood by the Jews at that time to be, a declaration that anything was unlawful to be done; and loosing signified, on the contrary, a declaration that anything may be lawfully done. The words *bind* and *loose* are used in a declaratory sense, of things, not of persons.

19. *If two of you shall agree.* "Symphonize, or harmonize." It is a metaphor taken from a number of musical instruments set to the same key and playing the same tune. Here it means a perfect agreement of the hearts, desires, wishes, and voices of two or more persons praying to God.

MATTHEW HENRY

of Christ in the world exists most visibly in religious assemblies; it is the will of Christ that these should be set up, and kept up. If there be no liberty and opportunity for large and numerous assemblies, yet then it is the will of God that two or three should gather together. When we cannot do what we would in religion, we must do as we can, and God will accept us. They are hereby directed to gather together in Christ's name. In the exercise of church discipline, they must *come together in the name of Christ*. In meeting for worship, we must have an eye to Christ; and in communion with all that in every place call upon him. When we come together to worship God in a dependence upon the Spirit and grace of Christ, having an actual regard to him as our Way to the Father, and our Advocate with the Father, then we are met together in his name. They are hereby encouraged with an assurance of the presence of Christ; *There am I in the midst of them.* Where his saints are, his sanctuary is, and there he will dwell. He is in the midst of them, that is, in their hearts; it is a spiritual presence, the presence of Christ's Spirit with their spirits, that is here intended. *There am I*, not only *I will be* there, but *I am there*; as if he came first, is ready before them, they shall find him there.

Though but two or three are met together, Christ is among them; this is an encouragement to the meeting of a few, when it is either, *First*, Of choice. There may be occasion sometimes for two or three to come together, either for mutual assistance in conference or joint assistance in prayer; there Christ will be present. Or, *Secondly*, By constraint; when there are not more than two or three to come together, or, if there be, they dare not. It is not the multitude, but the faith and sincere devotion, of the worshippers, that invites the presence of Christ; and though there be but two or three, the smallest number that can be, yet, if Christ make one among them, who is the principal one, their meeting is as honourable and comfortable as if they were two or three thousand.

Verses 21–35

I. Peter's question concerning this matter (*v.* 21); *Lord, how oft shall my brother trespass against me, and I forgive him?* Will it suffice to do it *seven times*?

1. He takes it for granted that he must forgive. He knows that he must not only not bear a grudge against his brother, or meditate revenge, but be as good a friend as ever, and forget the injury.

2. He thinks it a great matter to forgive till seven times; he means not *seven times a day*, as Christ said (Luke xvii. 4), but seven times in his life. There is a proneness in our corrupt nature to stint ourselves in that which is good, and to be afraid of doing too much in religion, particularly of forgiving too much, though we have so much forgiven us.

II. Christ's direct answer to Peter's question; *I say not unto thee, Until seven times*, but *Until seventy times seven*; a certain number for an indefinite one, but a great one. It does not look well for us to keep count of the offences done against us by our brethren. There is something of ill-nature in scoring up the injuries we forgive, as if we would allow ourselves to be revenged when the measure is full. It is necessary to pass by injuries, without reckoning how often; to forgive, and forget. God multiplies his pardons, and so should we. We should make it our constant practice to forgive injuries, and should accustom ourselves to it till it becomes habitual.

III. A further discourse of our Saviour's, by way of parable, to show the necessity of forgiving the injuries that are done to us. The parable is a comment upon the fifth petition of the Lord's prayer, *Forgive us our trespasses, as we forgive them that trespass against us.* Those, and those only, may expect to be forgiven of God, who forgive their brethren.

There are three things in the parable.

1. The master's wonderful clemency to his servant who was indebted to him; he forgave him ten thousand talents, out of pure compassion to him, *v.* 23–27. Where observe,

(1) Every sin we commit is a debt to God; not like a debt to an equal, contracted by buying or borrowing, but to a superior; like a debt to a prince when a recognizance is forfeited, or a penalty incurred by a breach of the law. We are all debtors; we owe satisfaction, and are liable to the process of the law.

(2) There is an account kept of these debts. This king *would take account of his servants.* God now reckons with us by our own consciences; conscience is an auditor for God in the soul, to call us to account, and to account with us. One of the first questions that an awakened Christian asks, is, *How much owest thou unto my Lord?* And unless it be bribed, it will tell the truth, and not write fifty for a hundred.

JAMIESON, FAUSSET, BROWN

deal with one another about such matters. "But now shows He unto them a more excellent way." Let them bring all such matters—yea, and everything whatsoever by which either their own loving relationship to each other, or the good of His kingdom at large, might be affected—to their Father in heaven; and if they be but agreed in petitioning Him about that thing, it shall be done for them of His Father which is in heaven. But further, it is not merely union in prayer for the same thing—for that might be with very jarring ideas of the thing to be desired—but it is to symphonious prayer, the prayer by kindred spirits, members of one family, servants of one Lord, constrained by the same love, fighting under one banner, cheered by assurances of the same victory; a living and loving union, whose voice in the divine ear is as the sound of many waters. Accordingly, what they ask *"on earth"* is done for them, says Jesus, "of My Father which is *in heaven."* Not for nothing does He say, "of MY FATHER"—not "YOUR FATHER"; as is evident from what follows: "For where two or three are gathered together *unto My name*"—the "My" is emphatic, *"there am I* in the midst of them." As His name would prove a spell to draw together many clusters of His dear disciples, so if there should be but two or three, that will attract Himself down into the midst of them; and related as He is to both the parties, the petitioners and the Petitioned—to the one on earth by the tie of His assumed flesh, and to the other in heaven by the tie of His eternal Spirit—their symphonious prayers on earth would thrill upward through Him to heaven, be carried by Him into the holiest of all, and so reach the Throne. Thus will He be the living Conductor of the prayer upward, and the answer downward.

Parable of the Unmerciful Debtor (vss. 21-35).

21. Then came Peter to him, and said, Lord, how oft shall my brother sin against me, and I forgive him?—In the recent dispute, Peter had probably been an object of special envy, and his forwardness in continually answering for all the rest would likely be cast up to him—and if so, probably by Judas—notwithstanding his Masters' commendations. And as such insinuations were perhaps made once and again, he wished to know how often and how long he was to stand it. **till seven times?**—This being the sacred and complete number, perhaps his meaning was, Is there to be a limit at which the needful forbearance will be *full*? **22. Jesus saith unto him, I say not unto thee, Until seven times; but, Until seventy times seven**—i.e., so long as it shall be needed and sought: you are never to come to the point of refusing forgiveness sincerely asked. (See on Luke 17:3, 4).

23. Therefore—'with reference to this matter'—**is the kingdom of heaven likened unto a certain king, which would take account of his servants**—or, would scrutinize the accounts of his revenue-collectors.

ADAM CLARKE

20. *For where two or three are gathered together.* There are many sayings among the Jews almost exactly similar to this, such as, "Wherever even two persons are sitting in discourse concerning the law, the Divine Presence is among them." *In my name* seems to refer particularly to a public profession of Christ and His gospel. *There am I in the midst.* None but God could say these words, to say them with truth, because God alone is everywhere present, and these words refer to His omnipresence.

21. *Till seven times?* Though *seven* was a number of perfection among the Hebrews, and often meant much more than the units in it imply, yet it is evident that Peter uses it here in its plain literal sense, as our Lord's words sufficiently testify. It was a maxim among the Jews never to forgive more than thrice. Peter enlarges this charity more than one-half, and our Lord makes even his enlargement septuple; see v. 22. Revenge is natural to man; i.e., man is naturally a vindictive being, and, in consequequence, nothing is more difficult to him than forgiveness of injuries.

22. *Seventy times seven.* There is something very remarkable in these words, especially if collated with Gen. iv. 24, where the very same words are used—If any man kill Lamech, he shall be avenged seventy times seven. The just God punishes sin in an exemplary manner. Sinful man, who is exposed to the stroke of divine justice, should be abundant in forgiveness, especially as only the merciful shall find mercy.

MATTHEW HENRY

(3) The debt of sin is a very great debt; and some are more in debt, by reason of sin, than others. When he *began to reckon*, one of the first defaulters appeared to owe *ten thousand talents*. The debt was ten thousand talents, a vast sum, a king's ransom or a kingdom's subsidy. See what our sins are, [1] For the heinousness of their nature; they are talents, the greatest denomination that ever was used in the account of money or weight. [2] For the vastness of their number; they are ten thousand, a myriad.

(4) The debt of sin is so great, that we are not able to pay it; *He had not to pay*. Sinners are insolvent debtors.

(5) If God should deal with us in strict justice, we should be condemned as insolvent debtors. Justice demands satisfaction. The servant had contracted this debt by his wastefulness and wilfulness, and therefore might justly be left to lie by it. *His lord commanded him to be sold; his wife and children to be sold, and all that he had, and payment to be made*. See here what every sin deserves; this is *the wages of sin*. Thus he would have *payment to be made*, that is, something done towards it; though it is impossible that the sale of one so worthless should amount to the payment of so great a debt.

(6) *The servant fell down* at the feet of his royal master, *and worshipped him*; or, as some copies read it, *he besought him*; his address was very submissive and very importunate; *Have patience with me, and I will pay thee all, v.* 26. The servant knew before that he was so much in debt, and yet was under no concern about it, till he was called to an account. Sinners are commonly careless about the pardon of their sins, till they come under the arrests of some awakening word, some startling providence, or approaching death. The stoutest heart will fail, when God sets the sins in order before it. He begs time; *Have patience with me*. Patience and forbearance are a great favour, but it is folly to think that these alone will save us; reprieves are not pardons. He promises payment; *Have patience* awhile, *and I will pay thee all*. He that *had nothing to pay* with (*v.* 25) fancied he could pay *all*. See how close pride sticks, even to awakened sinners; they are convinced, but not humbled.

(7) The God of infinite mercy is very ready, out of pure compassion, to forgive the sins of those that humble themselves before him (*v.* 27); *The lord of that servant*, since he could not be satisfied by the payment of the debt, would be glorified by the pardon of it. The servant's prayer was, *Have patience with me;* the master's grant is a discharge in full. The pardon of sin is owing to the mercy of God, to his tender mercy (Luke i. 77, 78); *He was moved with compassion*. There is forgiveness with God for the greatest sins, if they be repented of. Though the debt was vastly great, he *forgave it all, v.* 32. The forgiving of the debt is the loosing of the debtor; *He loosed him*. The obligation is cancelled, the judgment vacated. Though he discharged him from the penalty as a debtor, he did not discharge him from his duty as a servant. The pardon of sin doth not slacken, but strengthen, our obligations to obedience.

2. The servant's unreasonable severity toward his fellow-servant, notwithstanding his lord's clemency toward him, *v.* 28-30. This represents the sin of those who are rigorous and unmerciful in demanding that which is their own, to the utmost of right, which sometimes proves a real wrong. To exact satisfaction for debts of injury purely for revenge, though the law may allow it, savours not of a Christian spirit.

See here, (1) How small the debt was, how very small, compared with the *ten thousand talents* which his lord forgave him; *He owed him a hundred pence*. Offences done to men are nothing to those which are committed against God. Not that *therefore* we may make light of wronging our neighbour, for that is also a sin against God; but *therefore* we should make light of our neighbour's wronging us, and not aggravate it, or study revenge.

(2) How severe the demand was; *He laid hands on him, and took him by the throat*. What needed all this violence? The debt might have been demanded without taking the debtor by the throat. How lordly is this man's carriage, and yet how base and servile is his spirit! If he had been himself going to prison for his debt he might have had some pretence for going to this extremity in requiring his own; but frequently pride and malice prevail more to make men severe than the most urgent necessity would do.

(3) How submissive the debtor was; *His fellow servant fell down at his feet*, and humbled himself to him for this trifling debt, as much as he did to his lord for that great debt. The poor man's request is, *Have patience with me;* he honestly confesses the debt, only begs time. Forbearance, though it be no

JAMIESON, FAUSSET, BROWN

24. And when he had begun to reckon, one was brought unto him, which owed him ten thousand talents—If *Attic* talents are here meant, 10,000 of them would amount to above $ 7,500,000; if Jewish talents, to a much larger sum.

25. But forasmuch as he had not to pay, his lord commanded him to be sold, and his wife and children, and all that he had, and payment to be made—(See II Kings 4:1; Neh. 5:8; Lev. 25:39). **26. The servant therefore fell down, and worshipped him**—or did humble obeisance to him—**saying, Lord, have patience with me, and I will pay thee all**—This was just an acknowledgment of the justice of the claim made against him, and a piteous imploration of mercy.

27. Then the lord of that servant was moved with compassion, and loosed him, and forgave him the debt—Payment being hopeless, the master is first moved with compassion; next, liberates his debtor from prison; and then cancels the debt freely.

28. But the same servant went out, and found one of his fellow servants—Mark the difference here. The first case is that of master and servant; in this case, both are on a footing of equality. (See vs. 33, below.) **which owed him an hundred pence**—If Jewish money is intended, this debt was to the other less than *one to a million*. **and he laid hands on him, and took him by the throat**—he seized and throttled him. **saying, Pay me that thou owest**—Mark the mercilessness even of the tone.

29. And his fellow servant fell down at his feet, and besought him, saying, Have patience with me, and I will pay thee all—The same attitude, and the same words which

ADAM CLARKE

24. *Ten thousand talents*. "A myriad of talents," the highest number known in Greek arithmetical notation.

25. *He had not to pay*. That is "not being able to pay." *Commanded him to be sold . . . his wife and children*. Our Lord here alludes to an ancient custom among the Hebrews of selling a man and his family to make payment of contracted debts. See Exod. xxii. 3; Lev. xxv. 39, 47; 2 Kings iv. 1.

26. *Fell down, and worshipped him*. "Crouched as a dog before him," with the greatest deference, submission, and anxiety. *Have patience with me*. "Be long-minded towards me—give me longer space."

27. *Moved with compassion*. Or with "tender pity." This is the source of salvation to a lost world, the tender pity, the eternal mercy of God.

ALEXANDER MACLAREN:

Could a man have done like that? Ah! brethren, the things that would be monstrous in our relations to one another are common in our relations to God. Every day we see, and, alas! do, the very same thing in our measure and degree. Do you never treasure up somebody's slights? Do you never put away in a pigeonhole for safekeeping, endorsed with the doer's name on the back of it, the record of some trivial offense against you? It is but as a penny against a talent, for the worst that any of us can do to another is nothing as compared with what many of us have been doing all our lives toward God.

—*Expositions of Holy Scripture*

MATTHEW HENRY

acquittance, is sometimes a piece of needful and laudable charity. As we must not be hard, so we must not be hasty, in our demands, but think how long God bears with us.

(4) How implacable and furious the creditor was (*v.* 30); *He would not have patience with him,* but without mercy *cast him into prison.* How insolently did he trample upon one as good as himself, that submitted to him!

(5) How much concerned the rest of the servants were; *They were very sorry* (*v.* 31). The sins and sufferings of our fellow-servants should be matter of grief and trouble to us. To see a fellow-servant, either raging like a bear or trampled on like a worm, cannot but occasion great regret to all that have any jealousy for the honour either of their nature or of their religion.

(6) How notice of it was brought to the master; *They came, and told their lord.* They durst not reprove their fellow-servant for it, he was so unreasonable and outrageous; but they went to their lord. Let our complaints both of the wickedness of the wicked and of the afflictions of the afflicted, be brought to God, and left with him.

3. The master's just resentment of the cruelty his servant was guilty of.

(1) How he reproved his servant's cruelty (*v.* 32, 33); *O thou wicked servant.* Note, Unmercifulness is wickedness, it is great wickedness. He upbraids him with the mercy he had found with his master; *I forgave thee all that debt.* Those that will use God's favours, shall never be upbraided with them, but those that abuse them, may expect it. The greatness of sin magnifies the riches of pardoning mercy: we should think *how much has been forgiven us,* Luke vii. 47. He thence shows him the obligation he was under to be merciful to his fellow-servant; *Shouldst not thou also have had compassion on thy fellow-servant, even as I had pity on thee?* It is justly expected, that such as have received mercy, should show mercy. He shows him, *First,* That he should have been more compassionate to the distress of his fellow servant, because he had himself experienced the same distress. What we have had the feeling of ourselves, we can the better have the fellow feeling of with our brethren. *Secondly,* That he should have been more conformable to the example of his master's tenderness. The comfortable sense of pardoning mercy tends much to the disposing of our hearts to forgive our brethren. We must have compassion on our brethren, as God has on us.

(2) How he revoked his pardon (*v.* 34); *He delivered him to the tormentors, till he should pay all that was due unto him.* Though the wickedness was very great, his lord laid upon him no other punishment than the payment of his own debt. See how the punishment answers the sin; he that would not forgive shall not be forgiven. Our debts to God are never compounded; either all is forgiven or all is exacted; glorified Saints in heaven are pardoned all, through Christ's complete satisfaction.

Lastly, Here is the application of the whole parable (*v.* 35); *So likewise shall my heavenly Father do also unto you.* If God's governing be fatherly, it follows thence, that it is righteous, but it does not therefore follow that it is not rigorous. When we pray to God as *our Father in heaven,* we are taught to ask for *the forgiveness of sins, as we forgive our debtors.* We must *from our hearts* forgive. We do not forgive our offending brother aright, nor acceptably, if we do not forgive from the heart; for that is it that God looks at. No malice must be harboured there, nor ill will to any person. Yet this is not enough; we must from the heart desire and seek the welfare even of those that have offended us. The danger of not forgiving; *So shall your heavenly Father do.* This is not intended to teach us that God reverses his pardons to any, but that he denies them to those that are unqualified for them. Intimations enough we have in scripture of the forfeiture of pardons, for caution to the presumptuous; and yet we have security enough of the continuance of them, for comfort to those that are sincere, but timorous; that the one may fear, and the other may hope. Those that do not *forgive their brother's trespasses,* did never truly repent of their own, and therefore that which is *taken away* is only what *they seemed to have.* This is intended to teach us, that *they shall have judgment without mercy, that have showed no mercy,* James ii. 13. It is indispensably necessary to pardon and peace, that we not only *do justly,* but *love mercy.*

JAMIESON, FAUSSET, BROWN

drew compassion from his master, are here employed towards himself by his fellow servant. **30. And he would not; but went and cast him into prison, till he should pay the debt, . . .**—Jesus here vividly conveys the intolerable injustice and impudence which even the servants saw in this act on the part of one so recently laid under the heaviest obligation to their common master.

32, 33. Then his lord, after that he had called him, said unto him, O thou wicked servant, . . .—Before bringing down his vengeance upon him, he calmly points out to him how shamefully unreasonable and heartless his conduct was; which would give the punishment inflicted on him a double sting.

34. And his lord was wroth, and delivered him to the tormentors—more than *jailers;* denoting the severity of the treatment which he thought such a case demanded. **till he should pay all that was due unto him.**

35. So likewise—in this *spirit,* or on this principle—**shall my heavenly Father do also unto you, if ye from your hearts forgive not every one his brother their trespasses.**

ADAM CLARKE

30. *And he would not.* To the unmerciful, God will show no mercy; this is an eternal purpose of the Lord, which never can be changed. God teaches us what to do to a fellow sinner by what He does to us. Our fellowservant's debt to us, and ours to God, are as 100 denarii to 10,000 talents! When we humble ourselves before Him, God freely forgives us all this mighty sum! And shall we exact from our brother recompense for the most trifling faults?

34. *Delivered him to the tormentors.* Not only continued captivity is here intended, but the tortures to be endured in it.

35. *So likewise shall my heavenly Father do also unto you.* The goodness and indulgence of God towards us are the pattern we should follow in our dealings with others.

CHARLES H. SPURGEON:

God will deal with each of us upon the principle which sways our own life, and if we adopt a stern and severe mode of action, we must expect the same rule to be carried out in our case.—*Spurgeon's Devotional Bible*

JOHN WESLEY:

Imprisonment is a much severer punishment in the Eastern countries than in ours. State criminals are not only confined to a mean and scanty allowance, but are frequently loaded with clogs, or heavy yokes, so that they can neither lie nor sit at ease: and by frequent scourgings, and sometimes rackings, are brought to an untimely end. "Till he shall pay all that was due to him"—that is, without all hope of release; for this he could never do.

How observable is this account, and the great inference our Lord draws from it! (1) The debtor was freely and fully forgiven. (2) He willfully and grievously offended. (3) His pardon was retracted, the whole debt required, and the offender delivered to the tormentors forever. And shall we still say, But when *we* are once freely and fully forgiven, *our* pardon can never be retracted? Verily, verily, I say unto you, "So likewise will my heavenly Father do to you, if ye from your hearts forgive not everyone his brother their trespasses." Learn that the offenses which others commit against us are trivial compared with our offenses against God.—*Wesley's Notes on the New Testament*

MATTHEW HENRY

CHAPTER 19

1. He left Galilee. There he had been brought up, and had spent the greatest part of his life in that remote despicable part of the country. In this, as in other things, he appeared in a mean state, that he would go under the character of a Galilean, a north-countryman, the least polite and refined part of the nation. Now, having *finished these sayings, he departed from Galilee,* and it was his final farewell; for he never came to Galilee again till after his resurrection.

2. *He came into the coasts of Judæa, beyond Jordan,* that *they* might have their day of visitation as well as Galilee, for they also belonged *to the lost sheep of the house of Israel.*

3. *Great multitudes followed him.* When Christ departs, it is best for us to follow him. He *went about doing good*; for so it follows, *he healed them there.* This shows what they followed him for, to have their sick healed; and they found him as able and ready to help here, as he had been in Galilee.

Verses 3–12

We have here the law of Christ in the case of divorce, occasioned, as some other declarations of his will, by a dispute with *the Pharisees.*

I. The case proposed by the Pharisees (*v.* 3); *Is it lawful for a man to put away his wife?* This they asked, tempting him, not desiring to be taught by him. If he would declare himself now against divorce, they would make use of it for the prejudicing and incensing of the people of this country against him, who would look with a jealous eye upon one that attempted to cut them short in a liberty they were fond of. If he should say that divorces were not lawful, they would reflect upon him as an enemy to the law of Moses, which allowed them; if he should say that they were, they would represent his doctrine as not having that perfection in it which was expected in the doctrine of the Messiah, since though divorces were tolerated, they were looked upon by the stricter sort of people as not of good report.

Their question is, *Whether a man may put away his wife for every cause.* That it might be done for some cause, even for that of fornication, was granted; but may it be done, as now it commonly was done, by the looser sort of people, for any cause that a man shall think fit to assign, though ever so frivolous?

II. Christ's answer to this question; though it was proposed to tempt him, was a full one, not a direct one, but an effectual one. Now his argument is this: "If husband and wife are by the will and appointment of God joined together in the strictest and closest union, then they are not to be lightly, and upon every occasion, separated." He urges three things.

1. The creation of Adam and Eve, concerning which he appeals to their own knowledge of the scriptures; *Have ye not read? Ye have read* (but have not considered) *that he which made them at the beginning, made them male and female,* Gen. i. 27; v. 2. *He made them male and female,* one female for one male; so that Adam could not divorce his wife, and take another, for there was no other to take. It likewise intimated an inseparable union between them; Eve was a rib out of Adam's side, so that he could not put her away, but he must put away a piece of himself.

2. The fundamental law of marriage, which is, that *a man shall leave father and mother, and shall cleave to his wife, v.* 5. The relation between husband and wife is nearer than that between parents and children; now, if the filial relation may not easily be violated, much less may the marriage union be broken. May a child desert his parents, or may a parent abandon his children, for any cause, for every cause? No, by no means.

3. The nature of the marriage contract; it is a union of persons; *They twain shall be one flesh,* so that (*v.* 6) *they are no more twain, but one flesh.* A man's children are pieces of himself, but his wife is himself. As the conjugal union is closer than that between parents and children, so it is in a manner equivalent to that between one member and another in the natural body.

From hence he infers, *What God hath joined together, let not man put asunder.* Husband and wife are of God's joining together; *συνέζευξεν—he hath yoked them together,* so the word is. God himself instituted the relation between husband and wife. Though marriage be not peculiar to the church, but common to the world, yet it ought to be managed *after a godly sort, and sanctified by the word of God, and prayer.* A conscientious regard to God in this ordinance would have a good influence upon the duty, and consequently upon the comfort, of the relation. Husband and wife, being joined together

JAMIESON, FAUSSET, BROWN

CHAPTER 19

Vss. 1-12. Final Departure from Galilee—Divorce. (=Mark 10:1-12; Luke 9:51.)

Farewell to Galilee. **1. And it came to pass, that when Jesus had finished these sayings, he departed from Galilee**—This marks a very solemn period in our Lord's public ministry. So slightly is it touched here, and in the corresponding passage of Mark (10:1), that few readers probably note it as the Redeemer's *Farewell to Galilee,* which however it was. See on the sublime statement of Luke (9:51), which relates to the same transition stage in the progress of our Lord's work. **and came into the coasts**—or, boundaries—**of Judea beyond Jordan**—i.e., to the further, or east side of the Jordan, into Perea, the dominions of Herod Antipas. But though one might conclude from our Evangelist that our Lord went straight from the one region to the other, we know from the other Gospels that a considerable time elapsed between the departure from the one and the arrival at the other, during which many of the most important events in our Lord's public life occurred—probably a large part of what is recorded in Luke 9:51, onward to ch. 18:15, and part of John 7:2-11, 54. **2. And great multitudes followed him; and he healed them there**—Mark says further (10:1), that "as He was wont, He taught them there." What we now have on the subject of divorce is some of that teaching.

Divorce (vss. 3-12). **3. Is it lawful for a man to put away his wife for every cause?**—Two rival schools (as we saw on ch. 5:31) were divided on this question—a delicate one, as De Wette pertinently remarks, in the dominions of Herod Antipas.

4. And he answered and said unto them, Have ye not read, that he which made them at the beginning made them male and female—or better, perhaps, "He that made them made them from the beginning a male and a female."

5. And said, For this cause—to follow out this divine appointment. **shall a man leave father and mother, and shall cleave to his wife: and they twain shall be one flesh?**—Jesus here sends them back to the original constitution of man as one pair, a male and a female; to their marriage, as such, by divine appointment; and to the purpose of God, expressed by the sacred historian, that in all time one man and one woman should by marriage become one flesh—so to continue as long as both are in the flesh. This being *God's* constitution, let not *man* break it up by causeless divorces.

ADAM CLARKE

CHAPTER 19

1. *Beyond Jordan.* Or "by the side of Jordan." Matthew begins here to give an account of Christ's journey (the only one he mentions) to Jerusalem, a little before the Passover, at which He was crucified. See Mark x. 1; Luke ix. 51.

3. *Tempting him.* "Trying" what answer He would give to a question which, however decided by Him, would expose Him to censure. *Is it lawful . . . for every cause?* What made our Lord's situation at present so critical in respect to this question was: At this time there were two famous divinity and philosophical schools among the Jews, that of Shammai, and that of Hillel. On the question of divorce, the school of Shammai maintained that a man could not legally put away his wife except for whoredom. The school of Hillel taught that a man might put away his wife for a multitude of other causes, and when she did not "find grace in his sight"; i.e., when he saw any other woman that pleased him better.

5. *For this cause.* Being created for this very purpose, that they might glorify their Maker in a matrimonial connection. *Shall a man leave* (wholly give up) *father and mother*—the matrimonial union being more intimate and binding than even paternal or filial affection—and shall be "closely united, shall be firmly cemented" to his wife. A beautiful metaphor, which most forcibly intimates that nothing but death can separate them, as a well-glued board will break sooner in the whole wood than in the glued joint. *And they twain shall be one flesh.* Not only meaning that they should be considered as one body, but also as two souls in one body, with a complete union of interests, and an indissoluble partnership of life and fortune, comfort and support, desires and inclinations, joys and sorrows.

6. *What therefore God hath joined together.* "Yoked together," as oxen in the plough, where each must pull equally, in order to bring it on. Among the ancients, when persons were newly married, they put a yoke upon their necks or chains upon their arms to show that they were to be one, closely united, and pulling equally together in all the concerns of life.

MATTHEW HENRY

by the ordinance of God, are not to be put asunder by any ordinance of man.

III. An objection started by the Pharisees against this (*v.* 7); "*Why did Moses command to give a writing of divorcement*, in case a man did put away his wife?" He urged scripture reason against divorce; they allege scripture authority for it. The seeming contradictions that are in the word of God are great stumbling-blocks to men of corrupt minds.

IV. Christ's answer to this objection.

1. He rectifies their mistake concerning the law of Moses; they called it a *command*, Christ calls it but a *permission*, a *toleration*. Carnal hearts will take an ell if but an inch be given them.

But Christ tells them there was a reason for this toleration, not at all for their credit; *It was because of the hardness of your hearts*, that you were permitted to *put away your wives*. Moses complained of the people of Israel in his time, that *their hearts were hardened*, hardened against God; this is here meant of their being hardened against their relations. There is not a greater piece of hard-heartedness in the world than for a man to be harsh, and severe with his own wife. The Jews, it seems, were infamous for this, and therefore were allowed to put them away; better divorce them than do worse. A little compliance, to humour a madman, or a man in a frenzy, may prevent a greater mischief. The law of Moses considered the hardness of men's hearts, but the gospel of Christ cures it. By the law was the knowledge of sin, but by the gospel was the conquest of it.

2. He reduces them to the original institution; *But from the beginning it was not so*. Corruptions that are crept into any ordinance of God must be purged out by having recourse to the primitive institution. If the copy be vicious, it must be examined and corrected by the original.

3. He settles the point by an express law; *I say unto you* (*v.* 9); and it agrees with what he said before (*ch.* v. 32). Now, in both these places he allows divorce, in case of adultery; the reason of the law against divorce being this, *They two shall be one flesh*. If the wife play the harlot, and make herself one flesh with an adulterer, the reason of the law ceases, and so does the law. He disallows it in all other cases; *Whosoever puts away his wife, except for fornication, and marries another, commits adultery*. This is a direct answer to their query, that it is not lawful. There will be no occasion for divorces, if we *forbear one another, and forgive one another, in love*, as those that are, and hope to be, forgiven. No need of divorces, if *husbands love their wives, and wives be obedient to their husbands*, and they live together as heirs of the grace of life.

V. Here is a suggestion of the disciples against this law of Christ (*v.* 10); *If the case of the man be so with his wife, it is better not to marry*. It seems, the disciples themselves were loth to give up the liberty of divorce, thinking it a good expedient for preserving comfort in the married state. Unless they may have a liberty of divorce, they think it is good for a man not to marry. Corrupt nature is impatient of restraint. It is a foolish, peevish thing for men to abandon the comforts of this life, because of the crosses that are commonly woven in with them. No, whatever our condition is, we must bring our minds to it, be thankful for its comforts, submissive to its crosses, and make the best of that which is. If the yoke of marriage may not be thrown off at pleasure, it does not follow that *therefore* we must not come under it; but *therefore*, when we do come under it, we must resolve to comport with it, by love, and meekness, and patience, which will make divorce the most unnecessary undesirable thing that can be.

VI. Christ's answer to this suggestion (*v.* 11, 12). He allows it good for some not to marry; *He that is able to receive it, let him receive it*. Christ allowed what the disciples said, *It is good not to marry*, as giving them a rule that they who have the gift of continence do best if they continue single. The increase of grace is better than the increase of the family, and fellowship with the Father and with his Son Jesus Christ is to be preferred before any other fellowship. He disallows it, as utterly mischievous, to forbid marriage, because *all men cannot receive this saying*.

Christ here speaks of a twofold unaptness to marriage.

1. That which is a calamity by the providence of God; such as those labour under who are born eunuchs, or made so by men.

2. That which is a virtue by the grace of God; such is theirs who *have made themselves eunuchs for the kingdom of heaven's sake*. This is meant of an unaptness for marriage, not in body but in mind. Those have thus made themselves eunuchs who have attained a holy indifference to all the delights of the

JAMIESON, FAUSSET, BROWN

7. They say unto him, Why did Moses then command to give a writing of divorcement, and to put her away? 8. He saith unto them, Moses—as a civil lawgiver. **because of**—or "having respect to." **the hardness of your hearts**—looking to your low moral state, and your inability to endure the strictness of the original law. **suffered you to put away your wives**—tolerated a relaxation of the strictness of the marriage bond—not as approving of it, but to prevent still greater evils.

But from the beginning it was not so—This is repeated, in order to impress upon His audience the temporary and purely civil character of this Mosaic relaxation. **9. And I say unto you, Whosoever shall put away his wife, except . . .**—See on ch. 5:31.

10. His disciples say unto him, If the case of the man be so with his wife, it is not good to marry—i.e., "In this view of marriage, surely it must prove a snare rather than a blessing, and had better be avoided altogether."

11. But he said unto them, All men cannot receive this saying, save they to whom it is given—i.e., "That the unmarried state is better, is a saying not for everyone, and indeed only for such as it is divinely intended for." But who are these? they would naturally ask; and this our Lord proceeds to tell them in three particulars.

12. For there are some eunuchs which were so born from their mother's womb—persons constitutionally either incapable of or indisposed to marriage. **and there are some eunuchs which were made eunuchs of men**—persons rendered incapable by

ADAM CLARKE

7. *Why did Moses then command to give a writing of divorcement?* It is not an unusual case for the impure and unholy to seek for a justification of their conduct from the law of God itself, and to wrest scripture to their own destruction.

8. *Moses because of the hardness of your hearts.* Moses perceived that if divorce were not permitted, in many cases, the women would be exposed to great hardships through the "cruelty" of their husbands.

9. *Except it be for fornication.* The grand subject of dispute between the two schools mentioned above was the word in Deut. xxiv. 1, "When a man hath taken a wife, and she find no grace in his sight, because of some uncleanness." This the school of Shammai held to mean whoredom or adultery; but the school of Hillel maintained that it signified any corporeal defect which rendered the person deformed, or any bad temper which made the husband's life uncomfortable.

10. *If the case of the man.* "Of a husband," so I think the word should be translated here. Our word "husband" comes from the Anglo-Saxon *hus* and *band*: the "bond" of the house, anciently spelled "housebond"—so in my old MS. Bible. It is a lamentable case when the husband, instead of being the bond and union of the family, scatters and ruins it by dissipation, riot, and excess. *It is not good to marry.* That is, if a man have not the liberty to put away his wife when she is displeasing to him. God had said, Gen. ii. 18, It is not good for man to be alone, i.e., unmarried. The disciples seem to say that, if the husband have not the power to divorce his wife when she is displeasing to him, it *is not good for him to marry.* Here was a flat contradiction to the decision of the Creator.

12. *Eunuchs.* "To have the care of the bed or bedchamber," this being the principal employment of *eunuchs* in the Eastern countries, particularly in the apartments of queens and princesses. These are they whom our Lord says

MATTHEW HENRY

married state, have a fixed resolution, in the strength of God's grace, wholly to abstain from them. These are they that *can receive* this saying. This affection to the single state must be given of God; for none can receive it, *save they to whom it is given.* Continence is a special gift of God to some, and not to others. The single state must be chosen for the kingdom of heaven's sake. When it is for religion's sake, then it is approved and accepted of God. That condition is best for us, and to be chosen and stuck to accordingly, which is best for our souls, and tends most to the preparing of us for, and the preserving of us to, the kingdom of heaven.

Verses 13-15

I. The faith of those that brought them. The account here given of it, is, that *there were brought unto him little children, that he should put his hands on them, and pray, v.* 13. They testified their respect to Christ, and the value they had for his favour and blessing. They did a kindness to their children. Others brought their children to Christ, to be healed when they were sick; but these children were under no present malady, only they desired a blessing for them. It is a good thing when we come to Christ ourselves, and bring our children to him, before we are driven to him (as we say) by woe-need.

They desired that he would put his hands on them, and pray. Imposition of hands was a ceremony used especially in paternal blessings. It intimates something of love and familiarity mixed with power and authority and bespeaks an efficacy in the blessing. We cannot do better for our children than to commit them to the Lord Jesus, to be wrought upon, and prayed for, by him. We can but beg a blessing for them, it is Christ only that can command the blessing.

II. The fault of the disciples in rebuking them. They discountenanced the address as vain and frivolous, and reproved them that made it as impertinent and troublesome. It is well for us, that Christ has more love and tenderness in him than the best of his disciples have. And let us learn of him not to discountenance any willing well-meaning souls in their enquiries after Christ, though they are but weak. If *he* do not break the bruised reed, *we* should not.

III. The favour of our Lord Jesus.

1. He rebuked the disciples (*v.* 14); *Suffer little children, and forbid them not;* and he rectifies the mistake they went upon, *Of such is the kingdom of heaven.* The children of believing parents belong to the kingdom of heaven, and are members of the visible church. For this reason they are welcome to Christ, who is ready to entertain those who, when they cannot come themselves, are brought to him. And this, (1) In respect to the little children themselves, whom he had upon all occasions expressed a concern for. (2) With an eye to the faith of the parents who brought them. Parents are trustees of their children's wills. Therefore Christ accepts their dedication of them as their act and deed. (3) Therefore he takes it ill of those who forbid them, and exclude those whom he has received.

2. *He received the little children,* and did as he was desired; *he laid his hands on them,* that is, *he blessed them.* The strongest believer lives not so much by apprehending Christ as by being apprehended of him (Phil. iii. 12), and this the least child is capable of. If they cannot stretch out their hands to Christ, yet he can lay his hands on them, and so make them his own, and own them for his own.

Verses 16-22

Here is an account of what passed between Christ and a hopeful young gentleman; he is said to be a *young man* (*v.* 20); and I called him a *gentleman,* not only because he had great possessions, but because he was a ruler (Luke xviii. 18).

Now concerning this young gentleman, we are told how fair he bid for heaven and came short.

I. How fair he bid for heaven, and how kindly and tenderly Christ treated him.

1. The gentleman's serious address to Jesus Christ (*v.* 16); *Good Master, what good thing shall I do, that I may have eternal life?* Not a better question could be asked, nor more gravely.

(1) He gives Christ an honourable title, *Good Master.* It signifies not a ruling, but a teaching Master. His calling him *Master,* bespeaks his submissiveness, and willingness to be taught; and *good Master,* his affection and peculiar respect to the Teacher. It is a good thing when men's quality and dignity increase their civility and courtesy. It was gentleman-like to give this title of respect to Christ. It was not usual among the Jews to accost their teachers with the title of *good;* and therefore this bespeaks the uncommon respect he had for Christ.

JAMIESON, FAUSSET, BROWN

others. **and there be eunuchs which have made themselves eunuchs for the kingdom of heaven's sake**—persons who, to do God's work better, deliberately choose this state. Such was Paul (I Cor. 7:7). **He that is able to receive it, let him receive it**—"He who feels this to be his proper vocation, let him embrace it"; which, of course, is as much as to say—"he only." Thus, all are left free in this matter.

13-15. LITTLE CHILDREN BROUGHT TO CHRIST. (=Mark 10:13-16; Luke 18:15-17.) For the exposition, see on Luke 18:15-17.

infants—showing that some, at least, of those called in Matthew (19:13) and Mark (10:13) simply "little" or "young children," were literally "*babes.*" **touch them**—or, as more fully in Matthew, "put His hands on them and *pray,*" or invoke a "blessing" on them (Mark 10:16), according to venerable custom (Gen. 48:14, 15). **rebuked them**—Repeatedly the disciples thus interposed to save annoyance and interruption to their Master; but, as the result showed, *always against the mind of Christ* (Matt. 15:23; ch. 18:39, 40). Here, it is plain from our Lord's reply, that they thought the intrusion a useless one, as *infants* were not capable of receiving anything from Him. His ministrations were for *grown people.* **But Jesus**—*much displeased,"* says Mark (10:14); and invaluable addition. **said**—"SUFFER THE LITTLE CHILDREN TO COME UNTO ME"—"AND FORBID THEM NOT," is the important addition of Matthew (19:14) and Mark (10:14). What words are these from the lips of Christ! The price of them is above rubies. But the *reason* assigned, "FOR OF SUCH IS THE KINGDOM OF GOD," or "of heaven," as in Matthew 19:14, completes the previous information here conveyed; especially as interpreted by what immediately follows: "AND HE TOOK THEM UP IN HIS ARMS, PUT HIS HANDS UPON THEM, AND BLESSED THEM" (Mark 10:16). It is surely not to be conceived that all our Lord meant was to inform us, that seeing *grown people* must become childlike in order to be capable of the Kingdom of God, therefore they should not hinder *infants* from coming to Him, and therefore He took up and blessed *the infants themselves.* Was it not just the grave mistake of the disciples that infants should not be brought to Christ, because only grown people could profit by Him, which "much displeased" our Lord? And though He took the irresistible opportunity of lowering their pride of reason, by informing them that, in order to enter the Kingdom, "*instead of the children first becoming like them, they must themselves become like the children*" [RICHTER in STIER], this was but by the way; and, returning to the *children themselves,* He took them up in His gracious arms, put His hands upon them and blessed them, for no conceivable reason but to show that *they were thereby made capable,* AS INFANTS, *of the Kingdom of God.* And if so, then "*Can any man forbid water that these should not be baptized which have received the Holy Ghost as well as we?*" (Acts 10:47). But such application of the baptismal water can have no warrant here, save where the infants have been *previously brought to Christ Himself* for His benediction, and only as the *sign and seal* of that benediction.

16-30. THE RICH YOUNG RULER. (=Mark 10: 17-31; Luke 18:18-30.) For the exposition, see on Luke 18:18-30.

This case presents some remarkable points. (1) The man was of irreproachable moral character; and this amidst all the temptations of *youth,* for he was a "young man" (Matt. 19:22), and *wealth,* for "he was very rich" (vs. 23; Mark 10:22). (2) But restless notwithstanding, his heart craves eternal life. (3) Unlike the "rulers," to whose class he belonged (vs. 18), he so far believed in Jesus as to be persuaded He could authoritatively direct him on this vital point. (4) So earnest is he that he comes "running" and even "kneeling before Him," and that when He was gone forth *into the war* (Mark 10:17)—the high-road, by this time crowded with travellers to the passover; undeterred by the virulent opposition of the class he belonged to as a "ruler" and by the shame he might be expected to feel at broaching such a question in the hearing of a crowd and on the open road.

ADAM CLARKE

are *made eunuchs of men,* merely for the above purpose. *So born from their mother's womb.* Such as are naturally incapable of marriage, and consequently should not contract any. *For the kingdom of heaven's sake.* I believe our Lord here alludes to the case of the Essenes, one of the most holy and pure sects among the Jews. These abstained from all commerce with women, hoping thereby to acquire a greater degree of purity, and be better fitted for the kingdom of God. They had no children of their own, but constantly adopted those of poor people, and brought them up in their own way. *He that is able to receive.* These words are variously translated: he who can "take, let him take it"; "comprehend, let him comprehend it"; "admit, let him admit it." The meaning seems to be, Let the man who feels himself capable of embracing this way of life embrace it; but none can do it but he to whom it is given, who has it as a gift from his mother's womb.

13. *Then were there brought unto him little children.* These are termed by Luke, chap. xviii. 15, "infants," very young children; and it was on this account, probably, that the disciples rebuked the parents, thinking them too young to receive good. *That he should put his hands.* It was a common custom among the Jews to lay their hands on the heads of those whom they blessed or for whom they prayed. This seems to have been done by way of dedication or consecration to God—the person being considered as the sacred property of God ever after.

14. *Of such is the kingdom of heaven.* Or, "The kingdom of heaven is composed of such." A great part of God's kingdom is composed of such literally, and those only who resemble little children shall be received into it; see on chap. xviii. 3. Christ loves little children because He loves simplicity and innocence; He has sanctified their very age by passing through it himself—the holy Jesus was once a little child.

MATTHEW HENRY

(2) He comes to him upon an errand of importance (none could be more so), and he came not to tempt him, but sincerely desiring to be taught by him. His question is, *What good thing shall I do, that I may have eternal life?* He was convinced that there is a happiness prepared for those in the other world, who are prepared for it in this world. It was a rare thing for one of his age and quality to appear so much in care about another world. The rich are apt to think it below them to make such an enquiry as this; and young people think it time enough yet; but here was a young man, and a rich man, solicitous about his soul and eternity. He was sensible something must be done, some good thing, for the attainment of this happiness. We must be doing, and doing that which is good. The blood of Christ is the only purchase of eternal life (he merited it for us), but obedience to Christ is the appointed way to it, Heb. v. 9. Those that know what it is to have eternal life, and what it is to come short of it, will be glad to accept of it upon any terms. Such a holy violence does the kingdom of heaven suffer. Our great enquiry should be, *What shall we do, that we may have eternal life?* For this world has not that in it that will make us happy.

2. The encouragement that Jesus Christ gave to this address. It is not his manner to send any away without an answer, that come to him on such an errand, for nothing pleases him more, *v.* 17.

(1) He tenderly assists his faith; for, doubtless, he did not mean it for a reproof, when he said, *Why callest thou me good?* He intended no more than to own and honour him as a good man, but Christ would lead him to own and honour him as a good God; for *there is none good but one, that is God.* As Christ is graciously ready to make the best that he can of what is said or done amiss; so he is ready to make the most that can be of what is well said and well done. His constructions are often better than our intentions. All crowns must lie before his throne. God only is good. We in our language call him *God,* because he is good.

(2) He plainly directs his practice. Now Christ's answer is, in short, this, *If thou wilt enter into life, keep the commandments.* The end proposed is, entering into life. The young man, in his question, spoke of eternal life. Christ, in his answer, speaks of *life;* to teach us, that eternal life is the only true life. He desired to know how he might *have* eternal life; Christ tells him how he might *enter into it.* The way of *entering into it,* is, by obedience, and Christ directs us in that. Christ, who is our Life, is the Way to the Father. He is the only Way, but duty, and the obedience of faith, are the way to Christ. The way prescribed is, keeping the commandments. Keeping the commandments of God, according as they are revealed and made known to us, is the only way to life and salvation. *Keeping the commandments* includes *faith in Jesus Christ,* for that is the great commandment (1 John iii. 23). It is not enough for us to *know* the commandments of God, but we must *keep* them, keep in them as our way, keep to them as our rule. At his further instance and request, he mentions some particular commandments which he must keep (*v.* 18, 19); *The young man saith unto him, Which?*

In answer to this, Christ specifies several, especially the commandments of the second table. *First,* That which concerns our own and our neighbour's life; *Thou shalt do no murder. Secondly,* Our own and our neighbour's chastity, *Thou shalt not commit adultery. Thirdly,* Our own and our neighbour's wealth and outward estate, *Thou shalt not steal. Fourthly,* That which concerns truth, and our own and our neighbour's good name; *Thou shalt not bear false witness. Fifthly,* That which concerns the duties of particular relations; *Honour thy father and mother. Sixthly,* That comprehensive law of love in which they are all fulfilled, *Thou shalt love thy neighbour as thyself* (Gal. v. 14; Rom. xiii. 9), that *royal* law, James ii. 8.

Our Saviour here specifies second-table duties only; not as if the first were of less account, but, 1. Because they that now sat in Moses's seat, either wholly neglected, or greatly corrupted, these precepts in their preaching. While they pressed the tithing of *mint, anise, and cummin—judgment, and mercy, and faith*—the summary of second-table duties, were overlooked, *ch.* xxiii. 23. Their preaching ran out all in rituals and nothing in morals. 2. Because he would teach him, and us all, that moral honesty is a necessary branch of true Christianity. Though a mere moral man comes short of being a complete Christian, yet an immoral man is certainly no true Christian. Nay, though first-table duties have in them more of the essence of religion, yet second-table duties have in them more of the evidence of it. Our light *burns* in love to God, but it *shines* in love to

JAMIESON, FAUSSET, BROWN

Why . . .—Did our Lord mean then to teach that God only ought to be called "good"? Impossible, for that had been to contradict all Scripture teaching, and His own, too (Ps. 112:5; Matt. 25:21; Titus 1:8). Unless therefore we are to ascribe captiousness to our Lord, He could have had but one object – *to raise the youth's ideas of Himself,* as not to be classed merely with other "good masters," and declining to receive this title *apart from* the "One" who is essentially and only "good." This indeed is but distantly hinted; but unless this is seen in *the background* of our Lord's words, nothing worthy of Him can be made out of them. (Hence, *Socinianism,* instead of having any support here, is only baffled by it.)

Thou knowest . . .—Matthew is more complete here: "but if thou wilt enter into life, keep the commandments. He saith unto him, Which?"—as if he had said, Point me out one of them which I have not kept?—"Jesus said, Thou shalt . . ." (Matt. 19: 17, 18). Our Lord purposely confines Himself to the *second* table, which He would consider easy to keep, enumerating them all—for in Mark (10:19), "Defraud not" stands for the *tenth* (else the eighth is twice repeated). In Matthew the *sum* of this second table of the law is added, "Thou shalt love thy neighbor as thyself," as if to see if he would venture to say he had kept *that.*

ADAM CLARKE

16. *One came.* Much instruction may be had from seriously attending to the conduct, spirit, and question of this person. (1) He came running, Mark x. 17, and he was deeply convinced of the importance of his business, and seriously determined to seek so as to find. (2) He kneeled, or caught Him by the knees, thus evidencing his humility, and addressing himself only to mercy. (3) He came in the spirit of a disciple, or scholar, desiring to be taught a matter of the utmost importance to him—Good teacher. (4) He came in the spirit of obedience; he had worked hard to no purpose, and he is still willing to work, provided he can have a prospect of succeeding—*What good thing shall I do?* (5) His question was the most interesting and important that any soul can ask of God—How shall I be saved?

17. *Why callest thou me good?* Or, "Why do you question Me concerning that good thing?" The whole passage therefore may be read thus: "O Teacher! what good thing shall I do that I may have eternal life? And He said unto him, Why do you question Me concerning that good thing? There is One that is good." *Keep the commandments.* From this we may learn that God's great design in giving His law to the Jews was to lead them to the expectation and enjoyment of eternal life. But as all the law referred to Christ, and He became "the end of the law for righteousness" (justification) to all that believe, so He is to be received, in order to have the end accomplished which the law proposed.

A. B. SIMPSON:

The Lord quotes the second table of the law covering our duties to our neighbor, all summed up in one closing command: "Thou shalt love thy neighbor as thyself." This is familiar ground to the young man, and he confidently declares: "All these things have I kept from my youth up; what lack I yet?" Then the Lord presses the keen edge of the sword of truth into his hypocrisy that had so long deceived him. It was as if He had said, "You think you have obeyed the second table of the law and loved your neighbor as yourself, for that is the real spirit of the law. Well, I am going to apply a simple test. If you love your neighbor as yourself, it will not be difficult for you to share with him your wealth; and if you love the Lord with all your heart, it will be no sacrifice for you to give up all and follow Him. Therefore, as a simple test of your love to your neighbor and your love to God, Go, sell that thou hast and give to the poor, and thou shalt have treasure in heaven, and come and follow me." And lo, that young man's castle of self-righteousness crumbled into dust. In a moment he saw himself in his true selfishness.—*Christ in the Bible*

19. *Thou shalt love thy neighbour as thyself.* Self-love, as it is generally called, has been grievously declaimed against, even by religious people, as a most pernicious and dreadful evil. But they have not understood the subject on which they spoke. They have denominated that intense propensity which unregenerate men feel to gratify their carnal appetites and vicious passions self-love, whereas it might be more properly termed self-hatred or self-murder. If I am to love my neighbor as myself, and this "love worketh no ill to his neighbour," then self-love, in the sense in which our Lord uses it, is something excellent.

MATTHEW HENRY

our neighbour.

II. See here how he came short and wherein he failed.

1. By pride, and a vain conceit of his own merit and strength. When Christ told him what commandments he must keep, he answered very scornfully, *All these things have I kept from my youth up, v.* 20. Christ knew it, for he did not contradict him; nay, it is said in Mark, *He loved him*; and so far he was very good and pleasing to Christ. His observance of these commands was universal; *All these have I kept*: it was early and constant; *from my youth up.* A man may be free from gross sin, and yet come short of grace and glory.

It was commendable also, that he desired to know further what his duty was; *What lack I yet?* He was convinced that he wanted something to fill up his works before God, and was therefore desirous to know it, because, if he was not mistaken in himself, he was willing to do it. Having not yet attained, he thus seemed to press forward. And he applied himself to Christ. Who could bid fairer? Even in this that he said, he discovered his ignorance and folly. Had he been acquainted with the extent and spiritual meaning of the law, instead of saying, *All these have I kept; what lack I yet?* he would have said, with shame and sorrow, "All these have I broken, what shall I do to get my sins pardoned?" Take it how you will, what he said savoured of pride and vain-glory, and had in it too much of that boasting which is excluded by the law of faith (Rom. iii. 27). That word, *What lack I yet?* perhaps was not so much a desire of further instruction as a demand of the praise of his present fancied perfection.

2. He came short by an inordinate love of the world, and his enjoyments in it. This was the fatal rock on which he split. Observe,

(1) How he was tried in this matter (*v.* 21); *Jesus said unto him, If thou wilt be perfect, go and sell that thou hast.* Christ waived the matter of his boasted obedience to the law, and let that drop, because this would be a more effectual way of discovering him than a dispute of the extent of the law. What Christ said to him, he thus far said to us all, that, if we would approve ourselves Christians indeed, and would be found at last the heirs of eternal life, we must do these two things:

[1] We must practically prefer the heavenly treasures before all the wealth and riches in this world. Now, as an evidence of this, *First,* We must dispose of what we have in this world, for the honour of God, and in his service: "*Sell that thou hast, and give to the poor.* Sell what thou canst spare for pious uses, all thy superfluities; if thou canst not otherwise do good with it, sell it. Sit loose to it, be willing to part with it for the honour of God, and the relief of the poor." In those that have wherewithal, giving of alms is as necessary an evidence of that contempt of the world, and compassion to our brethren. When we embrace Christ, we must let go the world, for we cannot serve God and mammon. Christ knew that covetousness was the sin that did most easily beset this young man, that, though what he had he had got honestly, yet he could not cheerfully part with it, and by this he discovered his insincerity. *Secondly,* We must depend upon what we hope for in the other world as an abundant recompence for all we have left, or lost, or laid out, for God in this world; *Thou shalt have treasure in heaven.* Trust God for a happiness out of sight, which will make us rich amends for all our expenses in God's service. Christ immediately annexes this assurance of a treasure in heaven. Christ's promises make his precepts easy, and his yoke not only tolerable, but pleasant, and sweet, and very comfortable.

[2] We must devote ourselves entirely to the conduct and government of our Lord Jesus; *Come, and follow me.* It seems here to be meant of a close and constant attendance upon his person, but of us it is required that we follow Christ, strictly conform to his pattern, and keep his laws, and all this from a principle of love to him, and dependence on him, and with a holy contempt of everything else in comparison of him. This is to *follow Christ fully.* To sell all, and give to the poor, will not serve, unless we come, and follow Christ. If I give all my goods to feed the poor, and have not love, it profits me nothing.

(2) See how he was discovered. This touched him in a tender part (*v.* 22); *When he heard that saying, he went away sorrowful, for he had great possessions.* He was a rich man, and loved his riches, and therefore went away. Those who have much in the world are in the greatest temptation to love it. Such is the bewitching nature of worldly wealth, that those who want it least desire it most. The reigning love of this world keeps many from Christ, who seem to have some good desires toward him. A great estate, as

JAMIESON, FAUSSET, BROWN

All these . . . —"what lack I yet?" adds Matthew. Ah! this gives us a glimpse of his heart. Doubtless he was perfectly sincere; but something within whispered to him that *his* keeping of the commandments was *too easy* a way of getting to heaven. He felt something beyond this to be necessary; after keeping all the commandments he was at a loss to know what that could be; and he came to Jesus just upon that point. "Then," says Mark (10:21), "Jesus beholding him loved him," or "looked lovingly upon him." His sincerity, frankness, and nearness to the kingdom of God, in themselves most winning qualities, won our Lord's regard even though he turned his back upon Him—a lesson to those who can see nothing lovable save in the regenerate.

lackest . . . one thing—Ah! but that a fundamental, fatal lack. **sell . . .**—As riches were his idol, our Lord, who knew if from the first, lays His great authoritative grasp at once upon it, saying, "Now give Me up that, and all is right." No general direction about the disposal of riches, then, is here given, save that we are to sit loose to them and lay them at the feet of Him who gave them. He who does this with all he has, whether rich or poor, is a true heir of the kingdom of heaven.

was very sorrowful—Matthew more fully, "*went away* sorrowful"; Mark still more, "was sad" or "sullen" at that saying, and "went away grieved." Sorry he was, very sorry, to part with Christ; but to part with his riches would have cost him a pang more. When Riches or Heaven, on Christ's terms, were the alternative, the result showed to which side the balance inclined. Thus was he shown to lack the one all-

ADAM CLARKE

20. *All these things have I kept.* I have made these precepts the rule of my life. There is a difference worthy of notice between this and our Lord's word. He says, v. 17, *keep*, earnestly, diligently, as with watch and ward, probably referring not only to the letter but to the spirit. The young man modestly says, All these have I "observed"; I have paid attention to, and endeavored to regulate my conduct by them. I have "kept them in custody." *What lack I yet?* He felt a troubled conscience, and a mind unassured of the approbation of God; and he clearly perceived that something was wanting to make him truly happy.

21. *If thou wilt be perfect.* "Be complete," have the business "finished," and all hindrances to your salvation removed, *go and sell that thou hast*—go and dispose of your possessions, to which it is evident his heart was too much attached, *and give to the poor*—for your goods will be a continual snare to you if you keep them; *and thou shalt have treasure in heaven*—the loss, if it can be called such, shall be made amply up to you in that eternal life about which you inquired; *and come and follow me*—be My disciple, and I will appoint you to preach the kingdom of God to others.

22. *Went away sorrowful.* Men undergo great agony of mind while they are in suspense between the love of the world and the love of their souls. *He had great possessions.* And what were these in comparison of peace of conscience and mental rest?

F. B. MEYER:

How to enter the kingdom. Youth, with all its fervor and impetuosity, is very beautiful in itself and very dear to Christ. Here youth was combined with station, wealth, and noble character. It is not necessary that *all* should sell their goods and distribute the proceeds. It is a harder task to retain wealth and administer it for God. But it was necessary that the Master should prove to this young man that he was not fulfilling the Commandments quite so perfectly as he had supposed.

How few would wed poverty today if they had to choose! Yet great riches must lie hidden beneath her rustic dress. Christ chose her as his companion during his human life, and St. Francis of Assisi said that he took her for his bride. In Matthew the beatitude is phrased, "Blessed are the poor in spirit," but in Luke it states "Blessed be ye poor."—*Bible Commentary*

ALEXANDER MACLAREN:

What has become of the eagerness which brought him running to Jesus, and of the willingness to do any hard task to which he was set? It was real, but shallow. It deceived himself. But Christ's words cut down to the inner man, and laid bare for his own inspection the hard core of selfish worldliness which lay beneath. How many radiant enthusiasms, which cheat their subjects quite as much as their beholders, disappear like tinted mist when the hard facts of self-sacrifice strike against them! How much sheer worldliness disguises itself from itself and from others in glistering garments of noble sentiments, which fall at a touch when real giving up is called for, and show the ugly thing below! How much "religion" goes about the world, and gets made "a ruler" of the synagogue in recognition of its excellence, which needs but this Ithuriel's spear to start up in its own shape! The completeness and immediateness of the collapse are noticeable. The young man seems to speak no word, and to take no time for reflection. He stands for a moment, as if stunned, and then silently turns away. What a moment! His fate hung on it. Once more we see the awful mystery enacted before our eyes, of a soul gathering up its power to put away life. Who will say that the decision of a moment, which is the outcome of all the past, may not fix the whole future? This man had never before been consciously brought to the fork in the road; but now the two ways are before him, and, knowingly, he chooses the worse. Christ did not desire him to do so; but He did desire that he should choose, and should know that he did. It was the truest kindness to tear away the veil of surface goodness which hid him from himself, and to force him to a conscious decision.

—*Expositions of Holy Scripture*

MATTHEW HENRY

to those who are got above it, is a great furtherance, so to those who are entangled in the love of it, it is a great hindrance, in the way of heaven.

Yet something of honesty there was in it. He went away, and would not pretend to that, which he could not find in his heart to come up to the strictness of. Since he could not be a complete Christian, he would not be a hypocrite. Yet he was a thinking man, and well-inclined, and therefore *went away sorrowful.* He had a leaning toward Christ, and was loth to part with him. Many a one is ruined by the sin he commits with reluctance; leaves Christ sorrowfully, and yet is never truly sorry for leaving him, for, if he were, he would return to him.

Verses 23–30

We have here Christ's discourse with his disciples upon occasion of the rich man's breaking with Christ.

I. Christ took occasion from thence to show the difficulty of the salvation of rich people, *v.* 23–26.

1. That it is a very hard thing for a rich man to get to heaven. From the harms and falls of others it is good for us to infer that which will be of caution to us. This is vehemently asserted by our Saviour, *v.* 23, 24. He said this to his disciples, who were poor. The less they had of worldly wealth, the less hindrance they had in the way to heaven. This saying is ratified, *v.* 23. *Verily I say unto you.* It is repeated, *v.* 24. *Again I say unto you.* Thus he speaks once, yea, twice, that which man is loth to perceive and more loth to believe. He saith that it is a hard thing for a rich man to enter into the kingdom of heaven, either here or hereafter. The way to heaven is to all a narrow way, and the gate that leads into it, a strait gate, but it is particularly so to rich people. Rich people have great temptations to resist, and such as are very insinuating; it is hard not to be charmed with a smiling world. It must be a great measure of divine grace that will enable a man to break through these difficulties. He saith that the conversion and salvation of a rich man is so extremely difficult, that *it is easier for a camel to go through the eye of a needle, v.* 24. Nothing less than the almighty grace of God will enable a rich man to get over this difficulty. It is very rare for a man to be rich, and not to set his heart upon his riches; and it is utterly impossible for a man that sets his heart upon his riches, to get to heaven. The way to heaven is very fitly compared to a *needle's eye,* which is hard to hit and hard to get through. A rich man is fitly compared to a *camel,* a beast of burthen, for he has riches, as a camel has his load. This truth is very much wondered at, and scarcely credited by the disciples (*v.* 25); *They were exceedingly amazed, saying, Who then can be saved?* Many surprising truths Christ told them, which they were astonished at, and knew not what to make of. It was not on contradiction to Christ, but for awakening to themselves, that they said, *Who then can be saved?* When we think how good God is, it may seem a wonder that so *few* are his; but when we think how bad man is, it is a more wonder that so *many* are. *Who then can be saved?* Since so many are rich, and have great possessions, and so many more would be rich, and are well affected, to great possessions; who can be saved? This is a good reason why rich people should strive against the stream.

2. That, though it be hard, yet it is not impossible for the rich to be saved (*v.* 26); *Jesus beheld them,* turned and looked wistfully upon his disciples, *and he said unto them, with men this is impossible, but with God all things are possible.* This is a great truth in general. Nothing is too hard for God. When men are at a loss, God is not; but this truth is here applied, (1) To the salvation of any. *Who can be saved?* say the disciples. None, saith Christ, by any created power. *With men this is impossible.* It is a creation, it is a resurrection, and with men this is impossible; but *with God all things are possible.* (2) To the salvation of rich people especially; it is impossible with men that such should be saved, but with God even this is possible. The sanctification and salvation of such as are surrounded with the temptations of this world are not to be despaired of; it is possible. In this word of Christ there is an intimation of mercy Christ had yet in store for this young gentleman, who was now gone away sorrowful; it was not impossible to God yet to recover him.

II. Peter took occasion from hence to enquire what *they* should get by it, who had left all to follow him, *v.* 27, &c.

1. We have their expectations from Christ; *Behold, we have forsaken all, and have followed thee; what shall we have therefore?* Peter desires to know,

(1) Whether they had sufficiently come up to those terms: they had not sold all (for they had many of

JAMIESON, FAUSSET, BROWN

comprehensive requirement of the law—the *absolute subjection of the heart to God,* and this want vitiated all his other obediences.

—Mark says, He "looked round about"—as if first following the departing youth with His eye—"and saith unto His disciples." **how hardly . . .**—with what difficulty. In Mark an explanation is added, "How hard is it for them that *trust* in riches . . ."—i.e., with what difficulty is this idolatrous trust conquered, without which they cannot enter; and this is introduced by the word "children"—sweet diminutive of affection and pity (John 21:5). **easier for a camel . . .**—a proverbial expression denoting literally a thing impossible, but figuratively, very difficult.

For . . .—"At that rate none can be saved": "Well, it does pass *human* power, but not *divine.*

ADAM CLARKE

23. *A rich man shall hardly enter.* That is, into the spirit and privileges of the gospel in this world, and through them into the Kingdom of glory.

24. *A camel.* It was a mode of expression common among the Jews, and signified a thing impossible. Hence this proverb: "No man sees a palm tree of gold, nor an elephant passing through the eye of a needle."

26. *With men this is impossible.* God alone can take the love of the world out of human heart. Therefore the salvation of the rich is represented as possible only to Him.

G. CAMPBELL MORGAN:

"It is hard for a rich man to enter into the kingdom of heaven." That was a severe word, but there were tears in it, there was pity in it, there was love in it. We shall do no violence to this text if we change it slightly, and read, "It is very difficult for a rich man to enter into the kingdom of heaven." And when He repeated the same thing with a new emphasis, there was still the same tone and the same spirit, the tone and spirit of regret, and sorrow, and love, "And again I say unto you, It is easier for a camel to go through a needle's eye, than for a rich man to enter into the kingdom of God."

Why is it difficult for a rich man to enter into the kingdom of heaven? Here again we need not indulge in speculation. Let us go back to the King's own wonderful Manifesto—the Sermon on the Mount. In His first sentence He set the door open, and revealed how men may enter into all the blessedness which He described. "Blessed are the poor in spirit; for theirs is the kingdom of heaven." Now over against that fundamental assertion put those tender, regretful words of Jesus, "It is hard work for a rich man to enter in." Why? Because wealth means power, and power is far more likely to create pride than to create poverty of spirit. It is very difficult for a wealthy man to be poor in spirit; not impossible in the economy of God; but very, very difficult. Jesus had seen the going away of that rich young ruler, and the cry of His heart was full of sorrow, for He loved him.

—The Gospel According to Matthew

A. T. ROBERTSON:

24. "It is easier for a camel to go through a needle's eye" (*eukopoteron estin kamelon dia trematos rhaphidos eiselthein*). Jesus, of course, means by this comparison, whether an Eastern proverb or not, to express the impossible. The efforts to explain it away are jejune, like a ship's cable, *kamilon* or *rhaphis* as a narrow gorge or gate of entrance for camels which recognized stooping, etc. All these are hopeless, for Jesus pointedly calls the thing "impossible" (v. 26). The Jews in the Babylonian Talmud did have a proverb that a man even in his dreams did not see an elephant pass through the eye of a needle (Vincent). The Koran speaks of the wicked finding the gates of heaven shut "till a camel shall pass through the eye of a needle." But the Koran may have got this figure from the New Testament. The word for an ordinary needle is *rhaphis,* but, Luke (18:25) employs *belone,* the medical term for the surgical needle not elsewhere in the New Testament.

—Word Pictures in the New Testament

MATTHEW HENRY

them wives and families to provide for), but they had *forsaken all*. When we hear what are the characters of those that shall be saved, it concerns us to enquire whether we, through grace, answer those characters.

Lord, saith Peter, *we have forsaken all*. Alas! it was but a poor *all* that they had forsaken; and yet observe how Peter there speaks of it, as if it had been some mighty thing; *Behold, we have forsaken all*. We are too apt to make the most of our services and sufferings, our expenses and losses, for Christ, and to think we have made him much our debtor. However, Christ does not upbraid them with this. It was their *all*, like the widow's two mites, and was as dear to them as if it had been more, and therefore Christ took it kindly that they left it to follow him.

(2) Whether therefore they might expect *that treasure* which the young man shall have if he will sell all. All people are for what they can get; and Christ's followers are allowed to consult their own true interest, and to ask, *What shall we have?* Christ encourages us to ask what we shall gain by leaving all to follow him; that we may see he doth not call us to our prejudice, but unspeakably to our advantage. It is of a hoping, trusting faith, to ask, "What shall we *have*?" The disciples had never till now asked, *What shall we have?* They were so well assured of his goodness, that they knew they should not lose by him at last, and therefore minded their work, and asked not what should be their wages. It honours Christ, to trust him and serve him, and not to bargain with him.

2. We have here Christ's promises to them, and to all others that tread in the steps of their faith and obedience.

(1) To his immediate followers, *v.* 28. To them he promises not only *treasure*, but *honour*. *Ye which have followed me in the regeneration shall sit upon twelve thrones*. Observe, The *preamble* to the patent, or the *consideration* of the grant, which, as usual, is a recital of their services; "You have followed me in the regeneration, and therefore this will I do for you." The disciples had followed Christ when the gospel temple was but in the framing. Now they followed Christ with constant fatigue, when few did; and therefore on them he will put particular marks of honour. Christ hath special favour for those who begin early with him, who trust him further than they can see him. Peter spoke of their forsaking *all*, to follow him, Christ only speaks of their *following* him, which was the main matter. The *date* of their honour, *when the Son of man shall sit in the throne of his glory*. All that partake of the regeneration in grace shall partake of the regeneration in glory.

Now their honour being adjourned till the Son of man's sitting in the throne of his glory, intimates, *First*, That they must stay for their advancement till then. As long as our Master's glory is delayed, it is fit that ours should be so too. We must live, and work, and suffer, in faith, and hope, and patience. *Secondly*, That they must share with Christ in his advancement. They having suffered with a suffering Jesus, must reign with a reigning Jesus. The longest voyages make the richest returns. The honour itself hereby granted; *Ye also shall sit upon twelve thrones, judging the twelve tribes of Israel*.

The general intendment of this promise is, to show the glory and dignity reserved for the saints in heaven, which will be abundant recompence for the disgrace they suffered here in Christ's cause. There are higher degrees of glory for those that have done and suffered most. Here *bonds, and afflictions, and deaths, did abide them*, but there they *shall sit on thrones of glory*. And will not this be recompence enough to make up all their losses and expenses for Christ? The ratification of this grant; it is firm, it is inviolably immutably sure; for Christ hath said, "*Verily I say unto you*."

(2) Here is a promise to all others that should in like manner leave all to follow Christ. *This honour have all his saints*. Christ will take care they shall none of them lose by him (*v.* 29). Losses for Christ are here supposed. Christ had told them that his disciples must deny themselves. Now here he specifies particulars; for it is good to count upon the worst. If they have not forsaken all, yet they have forsaken a great deal, houses suppose, or dear relations, that would not go with them, to follow Christ; these are particularly mentioned, as hardest for a tender gracious spirit to part with; *brethren, or sisters, or father, or mother, or wife, or children*; and *lands* are added in the close, the profits of which were the support of the family.

The loss of these things is supposed to be *for Christ's name's sake*; else he doth not oblige himself to make it up. Many forsake brethren, and wife, and children, in humour and passion; that is a sinful desertion. But if we forsake them *for Christ's sake*, because we must either quit them, or quit our interest

JAMIESON, FAUSSET, BROWN

Lo . . .—in the simplicity of his heart (as is evident from the reply), conscious that the required surrender had been made, and generously taking in his brethren with him—"*we*"; not in the spirit of the young ruler. "All these have I kept," **left all**—"The workmen's little is as much his 'all' as the prince's much [BENGEL]. In Matthew (19:27) he adds, "What shall we have therefore?" How shall it fare with us?

There is no man . . .—graciously acknowledging at once the completeness and the acceptableness of the surrender as a thing already made. **house . . .**—The specification is still more minute in Matthew and Mark, to take in *every* form of self-sacrifice.

"Verily I say unto you, That ye which have followed Me in the Regeneration, when the Son of man shall sit in the throne of His glory, ye also shall sit on twelve thrones judging the twelve tribes of Israel." Ye who have now adhered to Me shall, in the new kingdom, rule, or give law to, the great Christian world, here set forth in Jewish dress as the twelve tribes, presided over by the twelve apostles on so many judicial thrones. In this sense certainly the promise has been illustriously fulfilled [CALVIN, GROTIUS, LIGHTFOOT, etc.]. But if the promise refers to the yet future glory (as may be thought from ch. 22:28-30, and as most take it), it points to the highest personal distinction of the first founders of the Christian Church.

for the kingdom of God's sake—in Mark, "for MY sake and the Gospel's."

ADAM CLARKE

27. *What shall we have therefore?* "What reward shall we get?"

28. *The regeneration*. Some refer this to the time in which the new heavens and the new earth shall be created, and the soul and body united.

Judging the twelve tribes. From the parallel place, Luke xxii. 28-30, it is evident that sitting on thrones and judging the twelve tribes means simply obtaining eternal salvation, and the distinguishing privileges of the Kingdom of glory, by those who continued faithful to Christ in His sufferings and death. *Judging*. "Governing, presiding, holding the first or most distinguished place."

MATTHEW HENRY

in Christ; if we do not quit our concern for them, or our duty to them, but our comfort in them, and will do it rather than deny Christ, this is that which shall be thus recompenced. It is not the suffering, but the cause, that makes both the martyr and the confessor.

It is supposed to be a great loss; and yet Christ undertakes to make it up. A recompence of these losses is here secured. Thousands have dealt with Christ, and have trusted him far; but never anyone lost by him, never anyone but was an unspeakable gainer by him.

A hundred-fold in this life; sometimes in *kind,* in the things themselves which they have parted with. God will raise up for his suffering servants more friends, that will be so to them for Christ's sake, than they have left that were so for their own sakes. The apostles, wherever they came, met with those that were kind to them, and entertained them, and opened their hearts and doors to them. However, they *shall receive a hundred-fold,* in *kindness.* Their graces shall increase, their comforts abound, they shall have tokens of God's love, and then they may truly say they have received a hundred times more comfort in God and Christ than they could have in *wife, or children.*

Eternal life at last. The former is reward enough, if there were no more. But this comes in over and above, as it were, into the bargain. Now, if we could but mix faith with the promise, and trust Christ for the performance of it, surely we should think nothing too much to do, nothing too hard to suffer, nothing too dear to part with, for him. *Many that are first, shall be last, and the last, first, v.* 30. God will cross his hands. The heavenly inheritance is not given as earthly inheritances commonly are, by seniority of age, and priority of birth, but according to God's pleasure. This is the text of another sermon, which we shall meet with in the next chapter.

CHAPTER 20

Verses 1–16

This parable of the labourers in the vineyard is intended,

I. To represent to us *the kingdom of heaven* (*v.* **1**). The laws of that kingdom are not wrapt up in parables, but plainly set down, as in the sermon upon the mount. The notions of it are more necessary to be illustrated than the duties of it; which is that which parables are designed for.

II. In particular, to represent to us that concerning the kingdom of heaven, which he had said in the close of the foregoing chapter, that *many that are first shall be last, and the last, first.*

The parable shows us, 1. That God is debtor to no man; a great truth. 2. That many who begin last, and promise little in religion, sometimes, by the blessing of God, arrive at greater attainments in knowledge, grace, and usefulness, than others whose entrance was more early, and who promised fairer. John is swifter of foot, and comes *first to the sepulchre*: but Peter has more courage, and goes *first into it.* Thus *many that are last, shall be first.* Some make it a caution to the disciples. Let them look to it, that they keep up their zeal; else their good beginnings will avail them little; they that seemed to be *first,* would be *last.* Sometimes those that are converted later in their lives, outstrip those that are converted earlier. 3. That *the recompence of reward* will be given to the saints, not according to the time of their conversion; not according to the seniority, but *according to the measure of the stature of the fulness of Christ.* Sufferers for Christ in the latter days, shall have the same reward with the martyrs and confessors of the primitive times, though they are more celebrated; and faithful ministers now, the same with the first fathers.

We have two things in the parable; the *agreement* with the labourers, and the *account* with them.

(1) Here is the agreement made with the labourers (*v.* 1–7); and here it will be asked, as usual, Who hires them? *A man that is a householder.* God is the great Householder; as a householder, he has work that he will have to be done, and servants that he will have to be doing. God hires labourers in kindness to them, to save them from idleness and poverty, and pay them for working for themselves. Whence are they hired? Out of *the market-place,* where, till they are hired into God's service, they *stand idle* (*v.* 3), *all the day idle* (*v.* 6). The soul of man stands ready to be hired into some service or other; it was (as all the creatures were) created to work, and is either a *servant to iniquity,* or a *servant to righteousness.* The devil, by his temptations, is *hiring labourers* into his field, to *feed swine.* God, by his gospel, is *hiring labourers into his vineyard, to dress it, and keep it,* paradise-work. We are put to our choice. Till we

JAMIESON, FAUSSET, BROWN

manifold more in this present time—in Matthew (19:29) "an hundredfold," to which Mark (10:30) gives this most interesting addition, "Now in this present time, houses, and brethren, and sisters, and mothers, and children, and lands, with persecutions." We have here the blessed promise of a *reconstruction of all human relationships and affections on a Christian basis and in a Christian state, after being sacrificed, in their natural form, on the altar of love to Christ.* This He calls "manifold more"—"an hundredfold more"—than what they sacrificed. Our Lord was Himself the first to exemplify this *new adjustment of His own relationships.* (See on Matt. 12:49, 50; and on II Cor. 6:14-18.) But this "with persecutions"; for how could such a transfer take place without the most cruel wrenches to flesh and blood? but the persecution would haply follow them into their new and higher circle, breaking that up too! But best of all, "in the world to come life everlasting." And

When the shore is won at last
Who will count the billows past?
KEBLE

These promises are for *every one* who forsakes his all for Christ.

CHAPTER 20

Vss. 1-16. PARABLE OF THE LABORERS IN THE VINEYARD. This parable, recorded only by Matthew, is closely connected with the end of ch. 19, being spoken with reference to Peter's question as to how it should fare with those who, like himself, had left all for Christ. It is designed to show that while *they* would be richly rewarded, a certain equity would still be observed towards *later* converts and workmen in His service. **1. For the kingdom of heaven is like unto a man that is an householder, . . .**—The figure of a vineyard, to represent the rearing of souls for heaven, the culture required and provided for that purpose, and the care and pains which God takes in that whole matter, is familiar to every reader of the Bible. (Ps. 80:8-16; Isa. 5:1-7; Jer. 2:21; Luke 20:9-16; John 15:1-8.) At vintage-time, as WEBSTER and WILKINSON remark, labor was scarce, and masters were obliged to be early in the market to secure it. Perhaps the pressing nature of the work of the Gospel, and the comparative paucity of laborers, may be incidentally suggested, ch. 9:37, 38. The "laborers," as in ch. 9:38, are first, the *official* servants of the Church, but after them and along with them *all* the servants of Christ, whom He has laid under the weightiest obligation to work in His service.

ADAM CLARKE

29. *Shall receive an hundredfold.* Viz., in this life, in value, though perhaps not in kind; and in the world to come *everlasting life.*

30. *But many that are first.* The Jews, who have been the first and most distinguished people of God, will in general reject the gospel of My grace, and be consequently rejected by Me. The Gentiles, who have had no name among the living, shall be brought to the knowledge of the truth, and become the first, the chief, and most exalted people of God.

CHAPTER 20

1. *For the kingdom of heaven is like unto a man . . . an householder.* The manner of God's proceeding under the gospel dispensation resembles a householder who went out at "daybreak," "together with the morning." This was what was called, among the Jews and Romans, the first hour, answering to six o'clock in the morning. *To hire labourers.* "Some workmen," for he had not got all that was necessary, because we find him going out at other hours to hire more.

G. CAMPBELL MORGAN:

This parable is intended to teach one simple truth, that a man's reward will be, not according to the length of his service, not according to the notoriety of his service, but according to his fidelity to the opportunity which is given him. The men at the beginning of the day entered into a covenant and an agreement. The Master of the vineyard went out later in the day, saw others standing idle, and sent them in. When He said, "Why stand ye here all the day idle?" their answer was, "Because no man hath hired us." That is why they had not been at work before, they had not had their opportunity. When He created opportunity by sending them in, then in that last hour they were true to the only opportunity they had, and therefore their reward was as great as the reward of the men that had been at work twelve hours. It is as though He said to Peter, to revert to our illustration, "If that young man comes now, though he has been long delayed, his reward will be as great as yours, if he is faithful."—*The Gospel According to Matthew*

MATTHEW HENRY

are hired into the service of God, we are standing all the day idle. The gospel call is given to those that *stand idle in the market-place*. The market-place is *a place of concourse*; it is a place of sport, there the *children are playing* (*ch.* xi. 16); it is a place of business, of noise and hurry. "Come, come from this market-place." What are they hired to do? To labour in his vineyard. The church is God's vineyard; it is of his planting, watering, and fencing. We are all called upon to be labourers in this vineyard. We have each of us our own vineyard to keep, our own soul; and it is God's, and to be kept and dressed for him. In this work we must not be slothful, not loiterers, but *labourers*, working. Work for God will not admit of trifling. A man may go idle to hell; but he that will go to heaven, must be busy. What shall be their wages? He promises, *First, A penny, v.* 2. A day's wages for a day's work, and the wages sufficient for a day's maintenance. This doth not prove that the reward of our obedience to God is *of works*, or *of debt*. It is to signify that there is a reward set before us, and a sufficient one. *Secondly, Whatsoever is right, v.* 4–7. God will be sure not to be behind-hand with any for the service they do him: never any lost by working for God. For what term are they hired? For *a day*. It is but a day's work that is here done. The time of life is the day. It is a short time; the reward is for eternity, the work is but for *a day*. This should quicken us to expedition and diligence in our work, that we have but a little time to work in. It should also encourage us in reference to the hardships and difficulties of our work, that it is but for *a day*; the approaching *shadow* will bring with it both rest, and *the reward of our work*. Hold out, faith, and patience, yet a little while. Notice is taken of the several hours of the day, at which the labourers were hired.

This may be, and commonly is, applied to the several ages of life, in which souls are converted to Christ. The effectual call is particular, and it is *then* effectual when we come to the call.

First, Some are effectually called, and begin to work in the vineyard when they are very young; are sent in early in the morning. Those that have such a journey to go, had need set out betimes, the sooner the better.

Secondly, Others are savingly wrought upon in middle age; *Go work in the vineyard, at the third, sixth, or ninth hour*. The power of divine grace is magnified in the conversion of some, when they are in the midst of their pleasures and worldly pursuits, as Paul. God has work for all ages; no time amiss to turn to God. The time past of our life may suffice that we have served sin; *Go ye also into the vineyard*. God turns away none that are willing to be hired.

Thirdly, Others are hired into the vineyard in old age, at *the eleventh hour*, when *the day of life is far spent*, and there is but *one hour* of the twelve remaining. "While there is life, there is hope." There is hope *for* old sinners; true repentance is never too late. There is hope *of old sinners*, that they may be brought to true repentance; nothing is too hard for Almighty grace to do, it can set those to work, who have contracted a habit of idleness. Nicodemus may *be born again when he is old*.

Yet let none, upon this presumption, put off their repentance till they are old. These were *sent into the vineyard*, it is true, *at the eleventh hour*; but nobody had hired them, or offered to hire them, before.

(2) Here is the account with the labourers. When the account was taken; *when the evening was come*, then, as usual, the day-labourers were called and paid. Evening time is the reckoning time. Faithful labourers shall receive their reward when they die; it is deferred till then, that they may wait with patience for it. Ministers call them into the vineyard, to do their work; death calls them out of the vineyard, to receive their penny: and those to whom the call into the vineyard is effectual, the call out of it will be joyful. They did not come for their pay till they were called; we must with patience wait God's time for our rest and recompence; go by our master's clock. What the account was; and in that observe, The general pay (*v.* 9, 10); *They received every man a penny*. Though there be degrees of glory in heaven, yet it will be to all a complete happiness. In heaven, every vessel will be full, brimful, though every vessel is not alike large and capacious.

The giving of a whole day's wages to those that had not done the tenth part of a day's work, is designed to show that God distributes his rewards by *grace* and *sovereignty*, and not of *debt*. Because *we are under grace*, and *not under the law*, even such defective services, done in sincerity, shall not only be accepted, but by free grace richly rewarded. Note the particular pleading with those that were offended with this distribution in gavelkind.

JAMIESON, FAUSSET, BROWN

2. And when he had agreed with the labourers for a penny—a usual day's hire. **he sent them into his vineyard.**

3. And he went out about the third hour—about nine o'clock, or after a fourth of the working day had expired: the day of twelve hours was reckoned from six to six. **and saw others standing idle**—unemployed. **in the market-place. 4. And said unto them, Go ye also into the vineyard; and whatsoever is right**—just, equitable, in proportion to their time. **I will give you. And they went their way. 5. Again he went out about the sixth and ninth hour**—about noon, and about three o'clock in the afternoon. **and did likewise**—hiring and sending into his vineyard fresh laborers each time. **6. And about the eleventh hour**—but one hour before the close of the working day; a most unusual hour both for offering and engaging **and found others standing idle, and saith, Why stand ye here all the day idle?**—Of course they had not been there, or not been disposed to offer themselves at the proper time; but as they were now willing, and the day was not over, and "yet there was room," they also are engaged, and on similar terms with all the rest. **8. So when even was come**—i.e., the reckoning time between masters and laborers (see Deut. 24:15); pointing to the day of final account—**the lord of the vineyard saith unto his steward**—answering to Christ Himself, represented "as a Son over His own house" (Heb. 3:6; see ch. 11:27; John 3:35; 5: 27). **Call the labourers and give them their hire, beginning from the last unto the first**—Remarkable direction this—last hired, first paid.

9. And when they came that were hired about the eleventh hour, they received every man a penny—a full day's wages. **10. But when the first came, they supposed that they should have received more**—This is that calculating, mercenary spirit which had peeped out—though perhaps very slightly—in Peter's question (ch. 19:27), and which this parable was designed once for all to put down among the servants of Christ.

ADAM CLARKE

3. *The third hour.* Nine o'clock in the morning. *Marketplace.* Where laborers usually stood till they were hired.

5. *The sixth hour.* "Twelve o'clock." *Ninth hour.* Three o'clock in the afternoon.

6. *Eleventh.* Five o'clock in the evening, when there was only one hour before the end of the Jewish day, which, in matters of labor, closed at six.

8. *When even was come.* Six o'clock, the time they ceased from labor, and the workmen came to receive their wages. *Steward.* "A manager of the household concerns" under the master.

A. B. SIMPSON:

The picture is a very graphic one. The Master comes to His vineyard in the morning at six o'clock and finds a lot of idle men around. He engages a number of laborers under a special contract at a penny a day, equal to about 15 cents in our money. This would be fair wages in the East today. Later, at nine o'clock, and again at noon, and again at three o'clock in the afternoon, He went to the vineyard and found others standing idle, and He sent them to work, but on a different contract. There was no stipulation of a penny a day, but simply the promise, "Whatsoever is right, I will give you." It was work for wages, but there was a degree of trust about it. But at five o'clock when the day was almost gone and only one hour was left for work, He found still others standing idle, and He sent them into the vineyard to work, but said nothing to them about wages. The reading in our old version of verse 7 is wrong. The Revised Version has given it correctly by leaving out the clause about wages. He simply sent these men to work without any promise or agreement whatever. When the evening came and all received their wages, these last laborers received the same as the men that had toiled all day long, practically twelve times as much as the first workmen.

When we come to inquire into the reason of this, we cannot forget that these last laborers worked in simple faith without any agreement at all, while the other labored under a law and contract. Truly, this represents the highest spirit of service, "all for love and nothing for reward." The first represents work done under the law; the second, perhaps, for that class of Christians that try to get through as cheaply as possible; the third for those who go purely under the principle of grace, who give their lives to God in simple faith and trust Him for everything. Their reward will be the largest of all. It is quite possible for us to be working for a reward rather than for the Master with love, and this form of selfishness, even though it be spiritual selfishness, will vitiate much of our best service.—*Christ in the Bible*

MATTHEW HENRY

1. The offence taken (*v.* 11, 12); *They murmured at the good man of the house;* not that there is, or can be, any discontent or murmuring in heaven, but there may be, and often are, discontent and murmuring concerning heaven and heavenly things, while they are in prospect and promise in this world. These labourers quarrelled with their master, and found fault, not because they had not enough, so much as because others were made *equal* with them. They boast of their good services; *We have borne the burthen and heat of the day.* Now *these last have worked but one hour,* and that too in the cool of the day; and yet *thou hast made them equal with us.* There is a great proneness in us to think that we have too little, and others too much, of the tokens of God's favour. Very apt we all are to undervalue the deserts of others, and to overvalue our own. Perhaps, Christ here gives an intimation to Peter, not to boast too much, as if, because he and the rest of them had borne the burthen and heat of the day thus, they must have a heaven by themselves. It is hard for those that do or suffer more than ordinary for God, not to be elevated too much with the thought of it.

2. The offence removed. Three things the master of the house urges.

(1) That the complainant had no reason at all to say he had any wrong done to him, *v.* 13, 14. *Friend, I do thee no wrong.* He calls him *friend,* for in reasoning with others we should use soft words and hard arguments. It is incontestably true, that God can do no wrong. Whatever God does to us, or withholds from us, he does us no wrong. If God gives that grace to others, which he denies to us, it is kindness to them, but no injustice to us; and bounty to another, while it is no injustice to us, we ought not to find fault with.

To convince the murmurer that he did no wrong, he refers him to the bargain: "*Didst not thou agree with me for a penny?* Thou shalt have that we agreed for." It is good for us often to consider what it was that we agreed with God for. Worldlings agree with God for their penny in this world; they chose *their portion in this life* (Ps. xvii. 14). Believers agree with God for their penny in the other world, and they must remember that they have so agreed.

He therefore ties him to his bargain (*v.* 14); *Take that thine is, and go thy way.* If we understand it of that which is ours by *gift,* the free gift of God, it teaches us *to be content with such things as we have.* If God be better in any respect to others than to us, yet we have no reason to complain while he is so much better to us than we deserve. He tells him that those he envied should fare as well as he did; "*I will give unto this last, even as unto thee.*"

(2) He had no reason to quarrel with the master; for what he gave was absolutely his own, *v.* 15. As before he asserted his justice, so here his sovereignty; *Is it not lawful for me to do what I will with my own?* He may therefore give or withhold his blessings, as he pleases. What God has, is his own; and this will justify him, in all the disposals of his providence; when God takes from us that which was dear to us we must silence our discontents with this; *May he not do what he will with his own? Absutlit, sed et dedit.—He hath taken away; but he originally gave.* We are in his hand, as clay in the hands of a potter; and it is not for us to prescribe to him, or strive with him.

(3) He had no reason to be angry that he came into the vineyard no sooner; for he was not sooner called; he had no reason to be angry that the master had given him wages for the whole day. *Is thine eye evil, because I am good?* The nature of envy; It is an evil eye. The eye is often both the inlet and the outlet of this sin. It is an evil eye, which is displeased at the good of others, and desires their hurt, and see the aggravation of it; "It is because I am good." Envy is unlikeness to God, who is good, and doeth good, and delighteth in doing good. It is a direct violation of both the two great commandments at once; both that of love to God, in whose will we should acquiesce, and love to our neighbour, in whose welfare we should rejoice.

Lastly, Here is the application of the parable (*v.* 16), in that observation which occasioned it (*ch.* xix. 30); *So the first shall be last, and the last first.* Christ, to obviate and silence their boasting, here tells them,

1. That they might possibly be outstripped by their successors in profession, and, might be found inferior to them in knowledge, grace, and holiness. Who knows but that the church, in its old age, may be more fat and flourishing than ever. What *labourers* may be *sent into the vineyard in the eleventh hour,* and what plentiful effusions of the Spirit may then be, above what has been yet, who can tell?

2. That they had reason to fear, lest they themselves should be found hypocrites at last; for *many*

JAMIESON, FAUSSET, BROWN

11. And when they had received it, they murmured against the goodman of the house—rather, "the householder," the word being the same as in vs. 1. **12. Saying, These last have wrought but one hour, and thou hast made them equal unto us, which have borne the burden and heat**—the burning heat—**of the day**—who have wrought not only longer but during a more trying period of the day.

13. But he answered one of them—doubtless the spokesman of the complaining party. **and said, Friend, I do thee no wrong: didst not thou agree with me for a penny? . . .**

15. Is it not lawful for me to do what I will with mine own? Is thine eye evil, because I am good?—i.e., "You appeal to *justice,* and by that your mouth is shut; for the sum you agreed for is paid you. Your case being disposed of, with the terms I make with other laborers you have nothing to do; and to grudge the benevolence shown to others, when by your own admission you have been honorably dealt with, is both unworthy envy of your neighbor, and discontent with the goodness that engaged and rewarded you in his service at all."

16. So the last shall be first, and the first last—i.e., "Take heed lest by indulging the spirit of these murmurers at the penny given to the last hired, ye miss your own penny, though first in the vineyard; while the consciousness of having come in so late may inspire these last with such a humble frame, and such admiration of the grace that has hired and rewarded them at all, as will put them into the foremost place in the end." **for many be called, but few chosen**—This is another of our Lord's terse and pregnant sayings, more than once uttered in different connections. (See ch. 19:30; 22:14.) The "calling" of which the New Testament almost invariably speaks is what divines call *effectual* calling, carrying with it a supernatural operation on the will to secure its consent. But that cannot be the meaning of it here; the "called" being emphatically distinguished from the "chosen." It can only mean here the "invited." And so the sense is, Many receive the invitations of the Gospel whom God has never "chosen to salvation through sanctification of the Spirit and belief of the truth" (II Thess. 2:13). But what, it may be asked, has this to do with the subject of our parable? Probably this—to teach us that men who have wrought in Christ's

ADAM CLARKE

13. *Friend, I do thee no wrong.* The salvation of the Gentiles can in itself become no impediment to the Jews; there is the same Jesus both for the Jew and for the Greek. Eternal life is offered to both through the Blood of the Cross, and there is room enough in heaven for all.

15. *Is it not lawful for me?* As eternal life is the free gift of God, He has a right to give it in whatever proportions, at whatever times, and on whatever conditions He pleases. *Is thine eye evil?* An evil eye among the Jews meant a malicious, covetous, or envious person.

MATTHEW HENRY

are called but few chosen. As to the outward call; *many are called,* and yet refuse (Prov. i. 24). There are but few *chosen* Christians, in comparison with the many that are only *called* Christians.

Verses 17–19

This is the third time that Christ gave his disciples notice of his approaching sufferings.

I. The privacy of this prediction; *He took the twelve disciples apart in the way.* His secret was with them, as his friends. It was a hard saying, and if any could bear it, they could. It was requisite that they should know of it, that, being fore-warned, they might be fore-armed. It was not fit to be spoken publicly as yet, because many that were cool toward him, would hereby have been driven to turn their backs upon him; because many that were hot for him, would hereby be driven to take up arms in his defence, and it might have occasioned *an uproar among the people* (*ch.* xxvi. 5). He never countenanced anything which had a tendency to prevent his sufferings.

II. The prediction itself, *v.* 18, 19.

1. It is but a repetition of what he had once and again said before, *ch.* xvi. 21; xvii. 22, 23. This intimates that he not only saw clearly what troubles lay before him, but that his heart was upon his suffering-work; it filled him, not with fear but with desire and expectation; he spoke thus frequently of his sufferings, because through them he was to enter into his glory.

2. He is more particular here in foretelling his sufferings than any time before. He had said (*ch.* xvi. 21), that he *should suffer many things, and be killed;* here he adds, that he shall be *condemned, and delivered to the Gentiles,* that *they shall mock him, and scourge him, and crucify him.* The more clearly he foresaw his sufferings, the more cheerfully he went forth to meet them. He foretells by whom he should suffer, by *the chief priests and the scribes;* so he had said before, but here he adds, *They shall deliver him to the Gentiles.* He was to suffer for the salvation both of Jews and Gentiles; both had a hand in his death, because he was to reconcile both by his cross, Eph. ii. 16.

3. Here, as before, he annexes the mention of his resurrection and his glory to that of his death and sufferings; *The third day he shall rise again.* He still brings this in to encourage himself in his sufferings, and to carry him cheerfully through them. *He endured the cross for the joy set before him;* he foresaw he should rise again, and rise quickly, the third day. The reward is not only sure, but very near. It was also to encourage his disciples, and comfort them, and to direct us, under all *the sufferings of this present time* to look at *the things that are not seen, that are eternal,* which will enable us to call the present afflictions light, and but for a moment.

Here is, first, the request of the two disciples to Christ, *v.* 20–23. The sons of Zebedee were James and John, two of the first three of Christ's disciples; Peter and they were his favourites; John was the disciple whom Jesus loved; yet none were so often reproved as they; whom Christ loves best he reproves most, Rev. iii. 19.

I. Here is the ambitious address they made to Christ, *v.* 20, 21. It was a great degree of faith, that they were confident of his kingdom, but a great degree of ignorance, that they still expected a temporal kingdom, with worldly pomp and power. In this they expected to be grandees. They ask not for employment in this kingdom, but for honour only. It is probable that the last word in Christ's foregoing discourse gave occasion to this request, that *the third day he should rise again.* What Christ said to comfort them, they thus abused. Some cannot bear comforts, but they turn them to a wrong purpose; as sweetmeats in a foul stomach produce bile. There was policy in the management of this address, that they put their mother on to present it, that it might be looked upon as her request, and not theirs. She was one of those women that attended Christ, and ministered to him; and they thought that he could deny her nothing, and therefore they made her their advocate. It was their mother's weakness thus to become the tool of their ambition. Those that are wise and good, would not be seen in an ill-favoured thing. In gracious requests, we should learn this wisdom, to desire the prayers of those that have an interest at the throne of grace; we should beg of our praying friends to pray for us, and reckon it a real kindness. There was pride at the bottom of it. Pride is a sin that most easily besets us, and which it is hard to get clear of. It is a holy ambition to strive to excel others in grace and holiness; but it is a sinful ambition to covet to exceed others in pomp and grandeur.

JAMIESON, FAUSSET, BROWN

service all their days may, by the spirit which they manifest at the last, make it too evident that, as between God and their own souls, they never were chosen workmen at all.

17-28. Third Explicit Announcement of His Approaching Sufferings, Death, and Resurrection—The Ambitious Request of James and John, and the Reply. (=Mark 10:32-45; Luke 18:31-34.) For the exposition, see on Mark 10:32-45.

And they were in the way—on the road. **going up to Jerusalem**—in Perea, and probably somewhere between Ephraim and Jericho, on the farther side of the Jordan, and to the northeast of Jerusalem.

Saying, Behold, we go up to Jerusalem—for the last time, and—"all things that are written by the prophets concerning the Son of man shall be accomplished" (Luke 18:31). **the Son of man shall be delivered unto the chief priests and unto the scribes; and they shall condemn him to death, and shall deliver him to the Gentiles**—This is the first express statement that the Gentiles would combine with the Jews in His death; the two grand divisions of the human race for whom He died thus taking part in crucifying the Lord of Glory, as Webster and Wilkinson observe. **And they shall mock him, and shall scourge him, and shall spit upon him, and shall kill him: and the third day he shall rise again**—Singularly explicit as this announcement was, Luke (18:34) says "they understood none of these things; and this saying was hid from them, neither knew they the things which were spoken." The meaning of the words they could be at no loss to understand, but their import in relation to His Messianic kingdom they could not penetrate; the whole prediction being right in the teeth of their preconceived notions. That they should have clung so tenaciously to the popular notion of an *un*suffering Messiah, may surprise us; but it gives inexpressible weight to their after-testimony to a suffering and dying Saviour.

Matthew (20:20) says their "mother came to Him with her sons, worshipping Him and desiring . . ." (Cf. Matt. 27:56, with ch. 15:40.) Salome was her name (ch. 16:1). We cannot be sure with which of the parties the movement originated; but as our Lord, even in Matthew's account, addresses Himself to James and John, taking no account of the mother, it is likely the mother was merely set on by them. The thought was doubtless suggested to her sons by the recent promise to the Twelve of "thrones to sit on, when the Son of man should sit on the throne of His glory" (Matt. 19:28); but after the reproof so lately given them (ch. 9:33, etc.) they get their mother to speak for them.

And he said unto them, What would ye that I should do for you?—Though well aware what was in their mind and their mother's, our Lord will have the unseemly petition uttered before all. **Grant unto us that we may sit, one on thy right hand, and the other on thy left hand, in thy glory**—i.e.,Assign to us the two places of highest honor in the coming kingdom. The semblance of a plea for so presumptuous a request might possibly have been drawn from the fact that one of the two usually leaned on the breast of Jesus, or sat next Him at meals, while the other was one of the favored three.

ADAM CLARKE

17. *And Jesus going up.* From Jericho to Jerusalem, chap. xix. 15.

18. *The Son of man shall be betrayed.* Or "will be delivered up." This is the third time that our Lord informed His disciples of His approaching sufferings and death. This was a subject of the utmost importance, and it was necessary they should be well prepared for such an awful event.

19. *Deliver him to the Gentiles to mock.* This was done by Herod and his Roman soldiers. See Luke xxiii. 11. *To scourge, and to crucify.* This was done by Pilate, the Roman governor. The punishment of the cross was Roman, not Jewish; but the chief priests condemned Him to it, and the Romans executed the sentence.

20. *The mother of Zebedee's children.* This was Salome.

21. *Grant that these my two sons.* James and John. See Mark xv. 40. In the preceding chapter, v. 28, our Lord had promised His disciples that they should sit on twelve thrones, judging the twelve tribes. Salome, probably hearing of this, and understanding it literally, came to request the chief dignities in this new government for her sons. And it appears it was at their instigation that she made this request, for Mark, chap. x. 35, informs us that these brethren themselves made the request, i.e., they made it through the medium of their mother.

MATTHEW HENRY

II. Christ's answer to this address (*v.* 22, 23), directed not to the mother, but to the sons that set her on. He reproved the ignorance and error of their petition; *Ye know not what ye ask.* They were much in the dark concerning the kingdom they had their eye upon. They knew not what it was to sit on his right hand, and on his left; they talked of it as blind men do of colours. Our apprehensions of that glory which is yet to be revealed, are like the apprehensions which a child has of the preferments of grown men. What it will be in the performance, eye has not seen, nor ear heard. They were much in the dark concerning the way to that kingdom. *They* know not what they ask, who ask for the end, but overlook the means. The disciples thought, when they had left what little *all* they had for Christ, all their service and sufferings were over, and it was now time to ask, *What shall we have?* They imagined their warfare was accomplished when it was scarcely begun, and they had yet but run with the footman. We know not what we ask, when we ask for the glory of wearing the crown, and ask not for grace to bear the cross in our way to it. See how he repressed the vanity and ambition of their request.

(1) He leads them to the thoughts of their sufferings, which they were not so mindful of as they ought to have been. Therefore he thinks it necessary to put them in mind of the hardships that were before them, that they might be no surprise or terror to them.

Observe, [1] How fairly he puts the matter to them. *Are you able to drink of the cup that I shall drink of?* Are you able to hold out to the end of it? Put the matter seriously to yourselves. They were not aware what was amiss in their spirits when they were lifted up with ambition. Christ sees that pride in us which we discern not in ourselves.

Note, That to suffer for Christ is *to drink of a cup,* and *to be baptised with a baptism.* It is supposed to be a bitter cup, those waters of a full cup, that are wrung out to God's people (Ps. lxxiii. 10). It is supposed to be a baptism, a washing with the waters of affliction; some are dipped in them; others have but a sprinkling of them; both are baptisms, some are overwhelmed in them, as in a deluge, others ill wet, as in a sharp shower. Even in this, *consolation doth more abound.* It is but a cup, bitter perhaps, but we shall see the bottom of it; it is a cup in the hand of a Father (John xviii. 11). It is but a baptism; if dipped, that is the worst of it, not drowned; perplexed, but not in despair. It is to drink of the same cup that Christ drank of, and to be baptised with the same baptism that he was baptised with. Christ is beforehand with us in suffering. 1. It bespeaks the condescension of a suffering Christ, that he would drink of such a cup (John xviii. 11); that he would be baptised with such a baptism. 2. It bespeaks the consolation of suffering Christians, that they do but pledge Christ in the bitter cup. It is good for us to be often putting it to ourselves, whether we are able to drink of this cup, and to be baptised with this baptism. We must expect suffering. Are we able to suffer cheerfully. What can we afford to part with for Christ? The truth is, Religion, if it be worth anything, is worth everything; but it is worth little, if it be not worth suffering for. Now let us sit down, and count the cost of dying for Christ rather than denying him, and ask, Can we take him upon these terms?

[2] See how boldly they engage for themselves; they said, *We are able;* but at the same time they fondly hoped that they should never be tried. As before they knew not what they asked, so now they knew not what they answered. But those are commonly most confident that are least acquainted with the cross.

[3] See how plainly and positively their sufferings are here foretold (*v.* 23); *Ye shall drink of my cup.* Sufferings foreseen will be the more easily borne. Christ will have us know the worst, that we may make the best of our way to heaven; *Ye shall drink;* that is, ye shall suffer.

(2) He leaves them in the dark about the degrees of their glory. To carry them cheerfully through their sufferings, it was enough to be assured that they should have *a place in his kingdom.* The lowest seat in heaven is an abundant recompence for the greatest sufferings on earth. *"To sit on my right hand and on my left is not mine to give,* and therefore it is not for you to ask it or to know it; *but it shall be given to them for whom it is prepared of my Father."* It is not mine to give to those that seek and are ambitious of it, but to those that by great humility and self-denial are prepared for it.

III. Here are the reproof and instruction which Christ gave to the other ten disciples for their displeasure at the request of James and John.

1. The fret that the ten disciples were in (*v.* 24).

JAMIESON, FAUSSET, BROWN

But Jesus said unto them, Ye know not what ye ask—How gentle the reply to such a request, preferred at such a time, after the sad announcement just made!

can ye drink of the cup that I drink of?—To "drink of a cup" is in Scripture a figure for getting one's fill either of good (Ps. 16:5; 23:5; 116:13; Jer. 16:7) or of ill (Ps. 75:8; John 18:11; Rev. 14:10). Here it is the cup of suffering. **and be baptized with the baptism that I am baptized with**—(Cf. for the language, Ps. 42:7). The object of this question seems to have been to try how far those two men were *capable* of the dignity to which they aspired and this on the principle that he who is able to suffer most for His sake will be the nearest to Him in His kingdom.

And they said unto him, We can—Here we see them owning their mother's petition for them as their own; and doubtless they were perfectly sincere in professing their willingness to follow their Master to any suffering He might have to endure. As for James, he was the first of the apostles who was honored, and showed himself able to be baptized with his Master's baptism of blood (Acts 12:1, 2); while *John,* after going through all the persecutions to which the infant Church was exposed from the Jews, and sharing in the struggles and sufferings occasioned by the first triumphs of the Gospel among the Gentiles, lived to be the victim, after all the rest had got to glory, of a bitter persecution in the evening of his days, for the word of God and for the testimony of Jesus Christ. Yes, they were dear believers and blessed men, in spite of this unworthy ambition, and their Lord knew it; and perhaps the foresight of what they would have to pass through, and the courageous testimony He would yet receive from them, was the cause of that gentleness which we cannot but wonder at in His reproof. **And Jesus said unto them, Ye shall indeed drink of the cup that I drink of; and with the baptism that I am baptized withal shall ye be baptized**—No doubt this prediction, when their sufferings at length came upon them, cheered them with the assurance, not that they would sit on His right and left hand—for of that thought they would be heartily ashamed—but that "if they suffered with Him, they should be also glorified together." **But to sit on my right hand and on my left hand in not mine to give; but it shall be given to them for whom it is prepared**—"of My Father" (Matt. 20:23). The supplement which our translators have inserted is approved by some good interpreters, and the proper sense of the word rendered "but" is certainly in favor of it. But besides that it makes the statement too elliptical—leaving too many words to be supplied—it seems to make our Lord repudiate the right to assign to each of His people his place in the kingdom of glory; a thing

ADAM CLARKE

22. *Ye know not what ye ask.* How strange is the infatuation in some parents which leads them to desire worldly or ecclesiastical honors for their children! He must be much in love with the Cross who wishes to have his child a minister of the gospel; for, if he be such as God approves of in the work, his life will be a life of toil and suffering.

F. B. MEYER:

22. "We are able." This is the cry of youth—ardent, impulsive, self-confident. It does not wait to calculate the ridges and hummocks that lie between it and its goal, but supposes that it will be able to skate the entire distance over the glistening azure-blue ice. Without hesitation it counts on being able to brave all difficulty, surmount all hardship, drink the cup, and be baptized with the baptism.

But these men slept in Gethsemane, forsook the Master when He was arrested, and one of them at least failed Him at the cross. Creature-might cannot carry us in the hour of our greatest peril. We can vaunt ourselves as we may; but we have to learn that we can follow Christ in his cup and baptism only after we have been endued with the Spirit of Pentecost. I once knew two who said these words to God, when He presented them with the cup of suffering and death. They did not know all it involved; and they confessed afterward that they could never have stood to their choice had they not been graciously and repeatedly enabled. But at the end they could not wish it to have been otherwise.

How different were the experiences of these two men! To one, the cup and baptism came swiftly, when he fell beneath the beheading axe of Herod (Acts 12:2); to the other, they came in long, long years of sharing in the patience of Jesus Christ. These are different aspects of the same fellowship of suffering—swift death or long waiting; but in both, nearness to Jesus. We have no right to cherish the assurance of sitting right and left of the throne if that only means our own power, authority, glory. But if it means nearness to Jesus, we may count on it with the utmost assurance.

—*Great Verses Through the Bible*

23. *Is not mine to give, but it shall be given to them for whom it is prepared of my Father.* The true construction of the words is this: "To sit on My right hand and on My left is not mine to give, except to them for whom it is prepared of My Father." According to the prediction of Christ, these brethren did partake of His afflictions. James was martyred by Herod, Acts xii. 2; and John was banished to Patmos for the testimony of Christ, Rev. i. 9.

MATTHEW HENRY

They were moved with indignation against the two brethren; not because they were desirous to be preferred, but because they were desirous to be preferred *before them.* Many seem to have indignation at sin; but it is not because it is sin, but because it touches them. These disciples were angry at their brethren's ambition, though they themselves, nay *because* they themselves, were as ambitious. It is common for people to be angry at those sins in others which they allow of and indulge in themselves. Nothing makes more mischief among brethren, or is the cause of more indignation and contention, than ambition.

2. The check that Christ gave them. He had reproved this very sin before (*ch.* xviii. 3), and told them they must be humble as little children; yet they relapsed into it, and yet he reproved them for it thus mildly.

He called them unto him, which intimates great tenderness and familiarity. He did not, in anger, bid them get out of his presence, but called them, in love, to come into his presence.

(1) They must not be *like the princes of the Gentiles.* Christ's disciples must not be like Gentiles, no not like princes of the Gentiles.

Observe, What is the way of the princes of the Gentiles (*v.* 25); to *exercise dominion and authority* over their subjects. That which bears them up in it is, that they are great, and great men think they may do anything. What is the will of Christ in this matter. "*It shall not be so among you.* You are to teach the subjects of this kingdom, to take pains with them, and suffer with them; you are not to *lord it over God's heritage* (1 Pet. v. 3), but to labour in it." The pomp and grandeur of the princes of the Gentiles ill become Christ's disciples. How then shall it be among the disciples of Christ? Something of greatness among them Christ himself had intimated, and here he explains it; "*He that will be great among you,* that *will be chief, let him be your minister, your servant,*" *v.* 26, 27. It is the duty of Christ's disciples to serve one another, for mutual edification. This includes both humility and usefulness. It is the dignity of Christ's disciples faithfully to discharge this duty. The way to be great and chief is to be humble and serviceable. Those are to be best accounted of, and most respected, that are most humble and self-denying, and lay out themselves most to do good. These honour God most, and those he will honour. As he must become a fool that would be wise, so he must become a servant that would be chief.

(2) They must be like the Master himself. The *Son of man came not to be ministered to, but to minister, and to give his life a ransom for many, v.* 28. Our Lord Jesus here sets himself before his disciples as a pattern of those two things before recommended, humility, and usefulness.

[1] Never was there such an example of humility and condescension as there was in the life of Christ, who came not to be *ministered unto, but to minister.* He was indeed ministered to as a poor man, but he was never ministered to as a great man. He once washed his disciples' feet, but we never read that they washed his feet. He came to minister help to all that were in distress; he made himself a servant to the sick and diseased; was as ready to their requests as ever any servant was at the beck of his master, and took as much pains to serve them.

[2] Never was there such an example of beneficence and usefulness as there was in the death of Christ, who *gave his life a ransom for many.* He lived as a servant, and went about doing good; but he died as a sacrifice, and in that he did the greatest good of all. He came into the world on purpose to give his life a ransom. He gives his honour and life too a ransom for his subjects. It was a ransom for many, sufficient for all, effectual for many; and, if for many, then, saith the poor doubting soul, "Why not for me?"

Now this is a good reason why we should not strive for precedency, because the cross is our banner, and our Master's death is our life. It is a good reason why we should study to do good. The nearer we are all concerned in, and the more we are advantaged by, the humility and humiliation of Christ, the more ready and careful we should be to imitate it.

Verses 29–34

I. Their address to Christ, *v.* 29, 30.

1. The circumstances of it are observable. It was as Christ and his disciples departed from Jericho; of that devoted place, which was rebuilt under a curse, Christ took his leave with this blessing. It was in the presence of *a great multitude that followed him;* Christ had a numerous attendance, and did good to them. This multitude that followed Christ was a mixed multitude. Some followed him for loaves,

JAMIESON, FAUSSET, BROWN

which He nowhere else does, but rather the contrary. It is true that He says their place is "prepared for them by His Father." But that is true of their admission to heaven at all; and yet from His great white throne Jesus will Himself adjudicate the kingdom, and authoritatively invite into it those on His right hand, calling them the "blessed of His Father"; so little inconsistency is there between the eternal choice of them by His Father, and that public adjudication of them, not only to heaven in general, but each to his own position in it, which all Scripture assigns to Christ. The true rendering, then, of this clause, we take it, is this: "But to sit on My right hand and on My left hand is not Mine to give, save to them for whom it is prepared." When therefore He says, "It is not Mine to give," the meaning is, "I cannot give it as a *favor* to whomsoever I *please,* or on a principle of *favoritism;* it belongs exclusively to those for whom it is prepared," etc. And if this be His meaning, it will be seen how far our Lord is from disclaiming the right to assign to each his proper place in His Kingdom; that on the contrary, He expressly asserts it, merely announcing that the principle of distribution is quite different from what these petitioners supposed. Our Lord, it will be observed, does not *deny* the petition of James and John, or say they shall *not* occupy the place in His kingdom which they now improperly sought:—for aught we know, *that may be their true place.* All we are sure of is, that their asking it was displeasing to Him "to whom all judgment is committed," and so was not fitted to gain their object, but just the reverse. (See what is taught in Luke 14:8-11.) One at least of these brethren, as ALFORD strikingly remarks, saw on the right and on the left hand of their Lord, as He hung upon the tree, the crucified thieves; and bitter indeed must have been the remembrance of this ambitious prayer at that moment. **And when the ten heard it, they began to be much displeased with James and John**—or "were moved with indignation," as the same word is rendered in Matthew 20:24. The expression "*began* to be," which is of frequent occurrence in the Gospels, means that more passed than is expressed, and that we have but the result. And can we blame the ten for the indignation which they felt? Yet there was probably a spice of the old spirit of rivalry in it, which in spite of our Lord's recent lengthened, diversified, and most solemn warnings against it, had not ceased to stir in their breasts. **But Jesus called them to him, and saith unto them, Ye know that they which are accounted to rule**—are recognized or acknowledged as rulers. **over the Gentiles exercise lordship over them: and their great ones exercise authority upon them**—as superiors exercising an acknowledged authority over inferiors. **But so shall it not be among you: but whosoever will be great among you, shall be your minister**—a subordinate servant. **And whosoever of you will be the chiefest**—or "first." **shall be**—i.e., "let him be, or "shall be he who is prepared to be." **servant of all**—one in the lowest condition of service. **For even the Son of man came not to be ministered unto, but to minister, and to give his life a ransom for.** instead of—**many**—i.e., "In the kingdom about to be set up, this principle shall have no place. All My servants shall there be equal; and the only greatness known to it shall be the greatness of humility and devotedness to the service of others. He that goes down the deepest in these services of self-denying humility shall rise the highest and hold the chiefest place in that kingdom; even as the Son of man, whose abasement and self-sacrifice for others, transcending all, gives Him of right a place above all!" As "the Word in the beginning with God," He *was* ministered unto; and as the risen Redeemer in our nature He now *is* ministered unto, "angels and authorities and powers being made subject unto Him" (I Pet. 3:22); but not for this came He hither. The Served of all came to be the Servant of all; and His last act was the grandest Service ever beheld by the universe of God—"HE GAVE HIS LIFE A RANSOM FOR MANY!" "Many" is here to be taken, not in contrast with *few* or with *all,* but in opposition to *one*—the one Son of man for the many sinners.

29-34. TWO BLIND MEN HEALED. (=Mark 10:46-52; Luke 18:35-43). For the exposition, see on Luke 18:35-43.

ADAM CLARKE

25. *Exercise dominion . . . and . . . authority upon them.* They "tyrannized" and "exercised arbitrary power" over the people.

26. *It shall not be so among you.* Every kind of lordship and spiritual domination over the Church of Christ, like that exercised by the Church of Rome, is destructive and antichristian. *Your minister.* Or "deacon." I know no other word which could at once convey the meaning of the original and make a proper distinction between it and *servant,* in v. 27. The office of a deacon, in the primitive Church, was to serve in the love feasts, to distribute the bread and wine to the communicants; to proclaim different parts and times of worship in the churches; and to take care of the widows, orphans, prisoners, and sick, who were provided for out of the revenues of the Church. Thus we find it was the very lowest ecclesiastical office.

27. *Your servant.* The lowest secular office, as deacon was the lowest ecclesiastical office.

28. *A ransom for many.* Or "a ransom instead of many,"—one Ransom, or Atonement, instead of the many prescribed in the Jewish law.

MATTHEW HENRY

and some for love, some for curiosity, very few with desire to be taught their duty; yet, for the sake of those few, he confirmed his doctrine by miracles wrought in the presence of great multitudes. Two blind men concurred in their request; for joint-prayer is pleasing to Christ, *ch.* xviii. 19. Being companions in the same tribulation, they were partners in the same supplication. It is good for those that are labouring under the same calamity, or infirmity of body or mind, to join together in the same prayer to God for relief, that they may quicken one another's fervency, and encourage one another's faith. There is mercy enough in Christ for all the petitioners. These blind men were *sitting by the way-side.* It is good thus to way-lay Christ, to be in his road.

They heard that Jesus passed by. Though they were blind, they were not deaf. Seeing and hearing are the learning senses. These blind men had heard of Christ by the hearing of the ear, but they desired that their eyes might see him. *When they heard that Jesus passed by,* they asked no further questions, but immediately *cried out.* It is good to improve the present opportunity. These blind men did so, and did wisely; for we do not find that Christ ever came to Jericho again. *Now is the accepted time.*

2. The address itself is more observable; *Have mercy on us, O Lord, thou Son of David,* repeated again, *v.* 31. Four things are recommended to us for an example in this address.

(1) Here is an example of importunity in prayer. They cried out as men in earnest; men in want are earnest, of course. Cold desires do but beg denials. When they were discountenanced in it, they cried the more. The stream of fervency, if it be stopped, will rise and swell the higher. This is wrestling with God in prayer, and makes us the fitter to receive mercy; for the more it is striven for, the more it will be prized and thankfully acknowledged.

(2) Of humility in prayer; in that word, *Have mercy on us,* not specifying the favour, or prescribing what; "Only have mercy." They ask not for silver and gold, though they were poor, but mercy, mercy. This is that which our hearts must be upon.

(3) Of faith in prayer; in the title they gave to Christ, which was in the nature of a plea; *O Lord, thou Son of David;* they confess that *Jesus Christ is Lord.* Thus they take their encouragement in prayer from his power, as in calling him the Son of David they take encouragement from his goodness, as Messiah, of whom so many kind and tender things had been foretold. It is of excellent use, in prayer, to eye Christ in the grace and glory of his Messiahship; to remember that he is the Son of David, whose office it is to help, and save.

(4) Of perseverance in prayer, notwithstanding discouragement. *The multitude rebuked them* and bid them *hold their peace.* In following Christ with our prayers, we must expect to meet with hindrances and manifold discouragements. Such rebukes are permitted, that faith and fervency, patience and perseverance, may be tried. These poor blind men were rebuked by the multitude that followed Christ. But they would not be beaten off so; when they were in pursuit of such a mercy. *They cried the more. Men ought always to pray, and not to faint;* to *pray with all perseverance* (Luke xviii. 1).

II. The answer of Christ to this address of theirs. The multitude rebuked them; but Christ encouraged them. It were sad for us, if the Master were not more kind and tender than the multitude. He will not suffer his humble supplicants to be run down, and put out of countenance.

1. *He stood still, and called them, v.* 32. He was now going up to Jerusalem, and yet he stood still to cure these blind men. When we are ever so much in haste about any business, yet we should be willing to stand still to do good. *He called them.* Christ not only enjoins us to pray, but invites us; holds out the golden sceptre to us, and bids us come touch the top of it.

2. He enquired further into their case; *What will ye that I shall do unto you?* "Here I am; let me know what you would have, and you shall have it." What would we more? *Ask, and it shall be given you.* One would think this a strange question, anyone might tell what they would have. Christ knew well enough; but he would know it from them, whether they begged only for an alms, as from a common person, or for a cure, as from the Messiah. The waterman in the boat, who with his hook takes hold of the shore, does not thereby pull the shore to the boat, but the boat to the shore. So in prayer we do not draw the mercy to ourselves, but ourselves to the mercy.

They soon made known their request to him; *Lord, that our eyes may be opened.* The wants and burthens of the body we are soon sensible of, and can readily relate. O that we were but as apprehensive of our

JAMIESON, FAUSSET, BROWN

In Mark the name is given—"blind Bartimaeus, the son of Timaeus." But there and in Matthew it was "as they departed from," or "went out of Jericho"; and in Matthew it is not one but "two blind men," beggars, that on this occasion received their sight. Several critics—as Greswell, Ebrard, Ellicott, Neander, Wieseler, with some of the Fathers—suppose one to have been healed on *entering,* the other on *leaving* Jericho. Others to whom this seems farfetched would leave the facts as recorded to speak independently for themselves. One thing seems clear, that these three narratives must have been written quite apart from each other; and another, that these divergences in the circumstantial details strongly corroborate the historical truth of the facts. Perhaps, *if we knew all the particulars,* we should see no difficulty; but that we have been left so far in the dark shows that the thing is of no moment anyway. Had there been any collusion among the authors of these Gospels, they would certainly have taken care to remove these "spots on the sun"—as Chrysostom, of the Fathers, with Olshausen van Osterzee and Alford fail not to observe.

And he cried, saying, Jesus, son of David, in other words, "Thou promised Messiah." That this was the understood sense of the phrase is evident from the acclamation with which the multitude greeted Him on His triumphal entry into Jerusalem (Matt. 21:9; 12:23). **have mercy on me!**

"The multitude" (Matt. 20:31), **rebuked him, that he should hold his peace**—and not annoy, or impede the progress of Jesus; very much in the spirit of the Twelve themselves but a little before, when infants were brought to Him and when the Syrophenician woman "cried after him" (Mark 7:26). But oh how differently from them did Jesus feel! **but he cried so much the more, Son of David, have mercy on me!** This is that *importunity,* so highly commended and richly rewarded in the Syrophenician woman, and so often enjoined (ch. 11:5); **And Jesus stood**—or "stood still," as rendered in Matthew and Mark, **and commanded him to be brought unto him.** Mark (10:49-45) has this interesting addition: "And they call the blind man, saying unto him, Be of good comfort: rise, he calleth thee." Is it just as one earnestly desiring an interview with some exalted person, but told by one official after another that it is vain to wait, for he will not succeed—they know it—yet persists in waiting for some answer to his suit, and at length the door opens, and a servant appears, saying, "You are to be admitted—He has called you." No doubt those who thus encouraged the poor man knew well the cure that would follow. "And he, casting away his garment, rose, and came to Jesus." How lively is this touch about the casting away of his garment! It is evidently the remark of an eyewitness, expressive of the exhilarating hope with which he was immediately filled. **And when he was come near, he asked him, saying, What wilt thou that I shall do unto thee?** It was plain enough to all present what the poor blind man wanted: but Jesus, by this question, would try him; would deepen his present consciousness of need; and would draw out his faith in Him, **and he said, Lord.** In Mark the term rendered "Lord" is "*Rabboni*"—an emphatic and confiding exclamation. **that I may receive my sight.**

ADAM CLARKE

30. *Two blind men.* Mark x. 46 and Luke xviii. 35 mention only one blind man, Bartimaeus. Probably he was mentioned by the other Evangelists as being a person well-known before and after his cure. *Sitting by the way side.* In the likeliest place to receive alms, because of the multitudes going and coming between Jerusalem and Jericho. *Cried out.* Though God had deprived them, for wise reasons, of their eyes, He left them the use of their speech. It is never so ill with us but it might be much worse; let us therefore be submissive and thankful.

JAMIESON, FAUSSET, BROWN:

This gracious cure was quite casual. Blind Bartimaeus sat that day, as usual, by the way-side begging; not dreaming that ere its shadows fell he should see the light of heaven. But, like other blind people, his ears had doubtless been all the quicker to hear whatever was flying about. And there can be no doubt that the tidings sent to the imprisoned Baptist—"The blind receive their sight"—had flown to him, with, very possibly, the details of some of the cures. And just, as in the case of the Syrophenician woman, and in that of the woman with the issue of blood, these tidings had wrought in his heart the conviction that He was the promised Messiah, and such a confidence in His power and grace, that he would say within himself, "O if He would but pass this way, how should I cry to Him as He that cometh in the name of the Lord; and, poor beggar though I be, the Son of David would not shut His ear against me—*for they tell me He never yet did that to any suppliant.* And who knows but He will come? They say He is even now in this region, and if He goes up to Jerusalem to keep the approaching Passover, He likely *will* come this way. But He may not come when I am here; and yet there is hope—but what is that stir I hear? What is it?" "Jesus of Nazareth passeth by!" "O transport! He comes, He comes! Now is my time." So, ere He comes up, the loud cry is heard, "Jesus, Son of David, have mercy on me!" In a moving crowd, accompanying some great person on a progress, there are always some who keep ahead of the main body. These, catching the sound first, officiously try to silence him, that there may be no commotion, no interruption. But the earnest suppliant is not to be moved by that. His opportunity has come, for which he had longed but scarce dared to hope; and he shall not be silenced. Nay, "so much the more" did he cry, "Son of David, have mercy on me!" At length the glorious Healer comes up to the spot, and the whole crowd must halt, while He cures this believing beggar. And first, He commands him to be called. They hasten through the crowd to the roadside, and bid the poor man be of good cheer, for the Lord has sent for him. This gives his faith time to ripen. "I thought it would come to that: Long looked for—come at last: my hopes refused to be damped: they could not silence me; my soul went forth to Him in yet louder cries, and not in vain: I'm to succeed; I shall, I shall!" Thus he comes into the presence of Jesus. "What wilt thou that I shall do unto thee?" As he could not *see* Him, the Lord takes this way of awakening through his *ears,* the expectation of relief, and gives him an opportunity of presenting in explicit terms the desire of his heart. "Lord," is his ready answer, "that I may receive my sight." It is enough. The Redeemer's heart yearns with compassion; He touches his eyes, and immediately he sees as other men.

33. *That our eyes may be opened.* He who feels his own sore, and the plague of his heart, has no great need of a prompter in prayer. A hungry man can easily ask bread; he has no

MATTHEW HENRY

spiritual maladies, and could as feelingly complain of them, especially our spiritual blindness! Lord, that the eyes of our mind may be opened! Were we but sensible of our darkness, we should soon apply ourselves to him. *Lord, that our eyes may be opened.*

3. He cured them. What he did was an instance,

(1) Of his pity; *He had compassion on them.* Misery is the object of mercy. It was the tender mercy of our God, that gave light and sight to them that sat in darkness, Luke i. 78, 79.

(2) Of his power. He did it easily, he touched their eyes; he did it effectually, *Immediately their eyes received sight.* These blind men, when they had received sight, *followed him.* None follow Christ blindfold. He first by his grace opens men's eyes, and so draws their hearts after him.

JAMIESON, FAUSSET, BROWN

Jesus—"had compassion on them, and touched their eyes," says Matthew, "and" said unto him, **Receive thy sight, thy faith hath saved thee. And immediately he received his sight, and**—now as a grateful disciple, **followed him, glorifying God.**

ADAM CLARKE

need to go to a book to get expressions to state his wants in. His hunger tells him he wants food, and he tells this to the person from whom he expects relief.

34. *So Jesus had compassion on them.* "He was moved with tender pity." The tender pity of Christ met the earnest cry of the blind men, and their immediate cure was the result. *They followed him.* As a proof of the miracle that was wrought, and of the gratitude which they felt to their Benefactor.

MATTHEW HENRY

CHAPTER 21

Verses 1-11

All the four evangelists take notice of this passage of Christ's *riding in triumph into Jerusalem,* five days before his death. He had lodged at Bethany, a village not far from Jerusalem, for some time; at a supper there the night before Mary had *anointed his feet,* John xii. 3. Our Lord Jesus travelled much, and his custom was to travel on foot from Galilee to Jerusalem; many a dirty weary step he had when *he went about doing good.* How ill does it become Christians to be inordinately solicitous about their own ease and state. Yet once in his life he rode in triumph, and it was now when he went into Jerusalem, to suffer and die.

I. The provision that was made for this solemnity; and it was very poor and ordinary.

1. The preparation was sudden and off-hand. For his glory in the other world was the glory his heart was upon; his glory in this world he was dead to. They were come to Bethphage, a long scattering street that lay toward the mount of Olives; when he entered upon that *he sent two of his disciples* to fetch him an ass.

2. It was very mean. He sent only for an ass and her colt, *v.* 2. Asses were much used in that country for travel; horses were kept only by great men, and for war. In his state of humiliation, he *rides upon an ass.*

3. It was not his own, but borrowed. He had nothing of this world's goods but what was given him or lent him.

The disciples who were sent to borrow this ass are directed to say, *The Lord has need of him.* In the borrowing of this ass,

(1) We have an instance of Christ's knowledge. Christ could tell his disciples where they should find an ass tied, and a colt with her.

(2) We have an instance of his power over the spirits of men. Christ asserts his right to use the ass, in bidding them bring it to him; but he foresees some hindrance which the disciples might meet with in this service; *If any man say aught to you, ye shall say, The Lord hath need of him.* What Christ sets us to do, he will bear us out in the doing of; *Straightway he will send them.*

(3) We have an example of justice and honesty, in not using the ass without the owner's consent.

II. The prediction that was fulfilled in this, *v.* 4, 5. Our Lord Jesus, in all that he did and suffered, had very much his eye upon this, *That the scriptures might be fulfilled.* This particularly which was written of him, Zech. ix. 9, where it ushers in a large prediction of the kingdom of the Messiah, *Tell ye the daughter of Sion, Behold, thy King cometh,* must be accomplished.

1. How the coming of Christ is foretold; *Tell ye the daughter of Sion, Behold, thy King cometh unto thee.* Jesus Christ is the church's King. Christ, the King of his church, came to his church, even in this lower world. Notice was given to the church beforehand of the coming of her King; *Tell the daughter of Sion.* Christ will have his coming looked for, and waited for, and his subjects big with expectation of it.

2. How his coming is described. When a king comes, something great and magnificent is expected. But there is nothing of that here; *Behold, he cometh to thee, meek, and sitting upon an ass.* When Christ would appear in his glory, it is in his meekness, not in his majesty. His temper is very mild. He is meek to suffer the greatest injuries and indignities for Sion's cause. He is easy of access, easy to be entreated. His government is mild and gentle, and his laws not written in the blood of his subjects, but in his own. His yoke is easy. As an evidence of this, his appearance is very mean, sitting upon an ass, a creature made not for state, but service, not for battles, but for burthens; slow in its motions, but sure, and

JAMIESON, FAUSSET, BROWN

CHAPTER 21

Vss. 1-9. CHRIST'S TRIUMPHAL ENTRY INTO JERUSALEM ON THE FIRST DAY OF THE WEEK. (=Mark 11:1-11; Luke 19:29-40; John 12:12-19). For the exposition of this majestic scene—recorded, as will be seen, by all the Evangelists—see on Luke 19:29-40.

And it came to pass, when he was come nigh to Bethphage and Bethany, at the mount called [the mount] of Olives. Our Evangelist alludes thus generally to Bethany, as if our Lord had merely passed by it, on His way to Jerusalem, because He was not to relate anything about His stay there, but only that He took it on His route to the capital. The word "Bethphage" means "*Fighouse,*" no doubt from the profusion of that fruit which this spot produced. That it lay, as Bethany did, on the eastern side of the mount of Olives, or the side farthest from the capital, is certain: but no traces of it are now to be found, and whether it was east or west, north or south, of Bethany, is not agreed. The small village of Bethany, meaning "*Datehouse,*" yet remains, "pleasantly situated," says Thomson, "near the southeastern base of the mount, and having many fine trees about and above it." **he sent two of his disciples, saying, Go ye into the village over against you**—that is, Bethphage; **in the which at your entering ye shall find a colt tied, whereon yet never man sat.** This last remarkable particular is mentioned both by Matthew and Mark. On its significance, see John 19:41. **Loose him, and bring him hither. And if any man ask you, Why do ye loose him? thus shall ye say unto him, Because the Lord hath need of him**—"and straightway he will send him hither" (Mark 11:3). Remarkable words! But the glorious Speaker knew all, and had the key of the human heart. It is possible the owner was a disciple; but whether or not, the Lord knew full well what the result would be. A remarkable parallel to it will be found in the case of Samuel (see 1 Sam. 10:2-7); but with this noteworthy difference, that it is impossible to read the narrative of Samuel's directions without observing that he knew himself all the while to be but a servant of the Lord, whereas the Lord himself is in every utterance and act of Jesus on this occasion.

Matthew here notes the well-known prophecy which was fulfilled in all this, on which we must pause for a little: "All this was done, that it might be fulfilled which was spoken by the prophet [Zech. 9:9], saying, Tell ye the daughter of Zion"—quoting here another bright messianic prophecy (Isa. 62:11) in place of Zechariah's opening words, "Rejoice greatly, O daughter of Zion; shout, O daughter of Jerusalem: Behold, thy King cometh unto thee." Here the prophet adds, "He is just, and having salvation" or "helped"; but the Evangelist omits these, passing on to what relates to the *lowly* character of His royalty: "meek, and sitting upon an ass, and a colt, the foal of an ass." It was upon the foal that our Lord sat, as Mark and Luke expressly state. While the horse was an animal of war, the ass was used for purposes of peace. In the times of the Judges, and for a considerable time afterward, horses were not used at all by the Israelites, and so even distinguished persons rode on asses (Judg. 5:10; 10:4; 12:14)—but not from any nobleness in that animal, or its being an emblem of royalty, as some say. "Nor," to use the words of Hengstenberg, "in all our accounts of the asses of the East, of which we have a great abundance, is there a single example of an ass being ridden by a king, or even a distinguished officer, on any state occasion; whereas here it is expressly *in His royal capacity* that the prophet says Jerusalem's King is to ride upon an ass." And there are not lacking proofs, adduced by this able critic, that in the East the ass was and is regarded with a measure of *contempt.* And does not the fulfillment of the prophecy which we behold here itself show that *lowliness* was stamped upon the act, royal though it was?

ADAM CLARKE

CHAPTER 21

1. *Bethphage.* A place on the west declivity of Mount Olivet, from which it is thought the whole declivity and part of the valley took their name. It is supposed to have derived its name from the fig trees which grew there.

2. *Ye shall find an ass tied, and a colt.* Asses and mules were in common use in Palestine; horses were seldom to be met with.

5. *Tell ye the daughter of Sion.* The quotation is taken from Zech. ix. 9, but not in the precise words of the prophet. This entry into Jerusalem has been termed the triumph of Christ. It was indeed the triumph of humility over pride and worldly grandeur, of poverty over affluence, and of meekness and gentleness over rage and malice. He is coming now meek, full of kindness and compassion to those who were plotting His destruction! He comes to deliver up himself into their hands; their King comes to be murdered by His subjects, and to make His death a ransom price for their souls!

MATTHEW HENRY

safe and constant. Sion's King comes riding, not on a prancing horse, which the timorous petitioner dares not come near, or a running horse, which the slow-footed petitioner cannot keep pace with, but on a quiet ass, that the poorest of his subjects may not be discouraged in their access to him.

III. The procession itself. His equipage; *The disciples did as Jesus commanded them* (*v.* 6). Christ's commands must not be disputed, but obeyed; and those that sincerely obey them, shall not be baulked or baffled in it; *They brought the ass and the colt.* They had not so much as a saddle for the ass, but the disciples threw some of their clothes upon it, and that must serve for want of better accommodations. We ought not to be nice or curious, or to affect exactness in outward conveniences. A holy indifference or neglect well becomes us in these things. The disciples furnished him with the best they had, and did not object the spoiling of their clothes when *the Lord had need of them.* We must not think the clothes on our backs too dear to part with for the service of Christ, for the clothing of his poor destitute and afflicted members. Christ stripped himself for us. His retinue; there was nothing in this stately or magnificent. He has his attendants, *a very great multitude*; they were only the common people, the mob (the *rabble* we should have been apt to call them), that graced the solemnity of Christ's triumph, and none but such. Christ is honoured by the multitude, more than by the magnificence, of his followers; for he values men by their souls, not by their preferments, names, or titles of honour.

Now, concerning this great multitude, we are here told, what they did; according to the best of their capacity, they studied to do honour to Christ. *They spread their garments in the way*, that he might ride upon them. When Jehu was proclaimed king, the captains put their garments under him, in token of their subjection to him. Those that take Christ for their King must lay their all under his feet; the clothes, in token of the heart. How shall we express our respects to Christ? What honour and what dignity shall be done to him? *Others cut down branches from the trees, and strewed them in the way*, as they used to do at the feast of tabernacles, in token of liberty, victory, and joy. What they said; *They that went before, and they that followed, cried, saying, Hosanna to the Son of David*, *v.* 9. When they carried branches about at the feast of tabernacles, they were wont to cry *Hosanna*, and from thence to call their bundles of branches their *hosannas*. *Hosanna* signifies, *Save now, we beseech thee*; referring to Ps. cxviii. 25, 26.

The hosannas with which Christ was attended bespeak two things: Their welcoming his kingdom. *Hosanna* bespeaks the same with, *Blessed is he that cometh in the name of the Lord*. *All nations shall call him blessed* (Ps. lxxii. 17); these here began, and all true believers in all ages concur in it, and call him blessed: it is the genuine language of faith. Well may we say, *Blessed is he*; for it is in him that we are blessed. Well may we follow *him* with our blessings, who meets us with his. Their wishing well to his kingdom was intimated in their *Hosannas*; earnestly desiring that it might be a victorious kingdom. If they understood it of a temporal kingdom it was their mistake, which a little time would rectify; however, their good-will was accepted. It is our duty earnestly to desire and pray for the prosperity and success of Christ's kingdom in the world. This we mean when we pray, *Thy kingdom come*. They add, *Hosanna in the highest*. Let him have a name above every name, a throne above every throne. We have here his entertainment in Jerusalem (*v.* 10); *When he was come into Jerusalem, all the city was moved;* everyone took notice of him, some were moved with wonder at the novelty of the thing, others with laughter at the meanness of it; some perhaps were moved with joy; others, of the Pharisaical class, were moved with envy and indignation. So various are the motions in the minds of men upon the approach of Christ's kingdom!

Upon this commotion we are further told,

1. What the citizens said; *Who is this?* They were, it seems, ignorant concerning Christ. The Holy One unknown in the holy city! In places where the clearest light shines, and the greatest profession of religion is made, there is more ignorance than we are aware of. Yet they were inquisitive concerning him. *Who is this King of glory?*

2. How the multitude answered them; *This is Jesus*, *v.* 11. In the account they give of him they were right in calling him *the Prophet, that great Prophet*. Yet they missed it, in saying he was *of Nazareth*: and it helped to confirm some in their prejudices against him. Some that are willing to honour Christ, and bear their testimony to him, yet labour under mistakes concerning him.

JAMIESON, FAUSSET, BROWN

And they that were sent went their way, and found even as he had said unto them. Mark is so singularly precise here that it is impossible to doubt that the description is fresh from one of the two disciples sent on this errand; and in that case, who can it be but Peter, of whose hand in this Gospel all antiquity testifies and internal evidence is so strong? Probably John was the other (cf. Mark 14:13 with Luke 22:8). "And they went their way [says Mark], and found the colt tied by the door without in a place where two ways met; and they loose him." Had not the minutest particulars of this grand entry into Jerusalem burned themselves into the memory of those dear disciples that were honored to take part in the preparations for it, such unimportant details had never been recorded.

They cast their garments upon the colt, and they set Jesus thereon—He allowing them to act this part of attendants on royalty, as befitting the state He was now, for the first and only time, assuming.

And as he went—or proceeded onward toward the city, **they spread their clothes in the way**—that is, the gathering crowds did so; attracted, probably, in the first instance, by the novelty of the spectacle, but a higher view of it by and by flashing across them. Matthew says, "And a very great multitude"—or, "the immense multitude spread their garments in the way; others cut down branches from the trees, and strawed them in the way." This casting of their garments beneath His feet was an ancient Oriental way of expressing the homage of a people toward their sovereign, or one whom they wished to welcome as such—as we see in the case of Jehu (2 Kings 9:13). And spreading a gorgeous cloth over the pathway that is to be trodden by a monarch on any great occasion is our modern way of doing the same thing.

Saying, "Hosanna" (Matt., Mark, and John); that is, "Save now" (Ps 128:25). **Blessed** [be]—or "is," as rendered in Matthew and John. Either way, it is their glad welcome **to the King that cometh in the name of the Lord**—in John (12:13), "the King of Israel"; in Matthew (21:9), "the Son of David"; in Mark (11:9, 10), after "Blessed is he that cometh in the name of the Lord," another exclamation is added, "Blessed be the kingdom of our father David, that cometh in the name of the Lord." In all likelihood, the exclamation was variously uttered by the multitude, and the same voices may have varied their acclaim, as they repeated it over and over again, **peace in heaven, and glory in the highest.**

10-22. Stir about Him in the City—Second Cleansing of the Temple, and Miracles There—Glorious Vindication of the Children's Testimony—The Barren Fig Tree Cursed, with Lessons from It. (=Mark 11:11-26; Luke 19:45-48.) For the exposition, see Luke 19 after vs. 44; and on Mark 11:12-26.

And when he was come into Jerusalem, all the city was moved—as the cavalcade advanced—**"saying, Who is this? 11. And the multitude"**—rather "the multitudes" from the procession itself—**said, This is Jesus, the prophet of,"** or, "from **Nazareth of Galilee."** By this they evidently meant something more than a mere prophet; and from John 6:14, 15, and this whole scene, it seems plain that they meant by this exclamation that it was the expected Messiah.

ADAM CLARKE

7. ***And put on them their clothes.*** Thus acknowledging Him to be their King, for this was a custom observed by the people when they found that God had appointed a man to the kingdom.

8. ***Cut down branches from the trees.*** Carrying palm and other branches was emblematical of victory and success, Rev. vii. 9.

9. ***Hosanna to the son of David.*** When persons applied to the king for help, or for a redress of grievances, they used the word *hosanna.* "Save now!" or "Save, we beseech thee!" ***Son of David.*** A well-known epithet of the Messiah. ***He that cometh in the name.*** He who comes in the name and authority of the Most High. ***Hosanna in the highest.*** Either meaning, Let the heavenly hosts join with us in magnifying this august Being!—or, let the utmost degrees of hosanna, of salvation, and deliverance, be communicated to Thy people! Probably there is an allusion here to the custom of the Jews in the Feast of Tabernacles. During the first seven days of that feast they went once round the altar, each day, with palm and other branches in their hands, singing hosanna. But on the eighth day of that feast they walked seven times round the altar, singing the hosanna; and this was termed the "great hosanna"; i.e., "Assist with the greatest succor."

10. ***All the city was moved.*** Or, "The whole city was in motion." Was in a tumult—they saw and heard plainly that the multitude had proclaimed Christ as King and Messiah. ***Who is this?*** Who is accounted worthy of this honor?

11. ***This is Jesus the prophet.*** That Prophet of whom Moses spoke in Deut. xviii. 18.

MATTHEW HENRY

Verses 12–17

It is in holy things that he rules, in the temple of God that he exercises authority. Now, what did he do there?

I. Thence he drove the buyers and sellers. Abuses must first be purged out before that which is right can be established. Here we are told,

1. What he did (*v.* 12); *He cast out all them that sold and bought;* he had done this once before (John ii. 14, 15). Buyers and sellers driven out of the temple, will return and nestle there again. The abuse was, buying and selling, and changing money, in the temple. Lawful things, ill timed, and ill placed, may become sinful things. They sold beasts for sacrifice, for the convenience of those that could more easily bring their money with them than their beast; and they changed money for those that wanted the half shekel. This might pass for the outward business of the house of God; and yet Christ will not allow of it. Great corruptions and abuses come into the church by the practices of those whose *gain is godliness*, that is, who make worldly gain the end of their godliness, and counterfeit godliness their way to worldly gain (1 Tim. vi. 5). The purging out of this abuse. Christ *cast them out that sold.* He did it before *with a scourge of small cords* (John ii. 15); now he did it with a look, with a frown, with a word of command. Some reckon this none of the least of Christ's miracles, that he should himself thus clear the temple. It is an instance of his power over the spirits of men, and the hold he has of them by their own consciences. *He overthrew the tables of the money-changers;* he did not take the money to himself, but scattered it, threw it to the ground, the fittest place for it.

2. What he said, to justify himself, and to convict them (*v.* 13); *It is written.* The eye must be upon the scripture, and that must be adhered to as the rule, the pattern in the mount.

(1) He shows, from a scripture prophecy, what the temple should be, and was designed to be; *My house shall be called the house of prayer;* which is quoted from Isa. lvi. 7. All the ceremonial institutions were intended to be subservient to moral duties; the house of sacrifices was to be a house of prayer, for that was the substance and soul of all those services.

(2) He shows how they had abused the temple, and perverted the intention of it; *Ye have made it a den of thieves.* Markets are too often dens of thieves, so many are the corrupt and cheating practices in buying and selling; but markets in the temple are certainly so, for they rob God of his honour, the worst of thieves.

II. There, in the temple, *he healed the blind and the lame*, *v.* 14. When he had driven the buyers and sellers out of the temple, he invited the blind and lame into it. It is good coming to the temple, when Christ is there, who, as he shows himself jealous for the honour of his temple, in expelling those who profane it, so he shows himself gracious to those who humbly seek him. *The blind and the lame* were debarred David's palace, but were admitted into God's house. The temple was profaned and abused when it was made a market-place, but it was graced and honoured when it was made an hospital; to be doing good in God's house, is more honourable, and better becomes it, than to be getting money there. Christ's healing was a real answer to that question, *Who is this?* His works testified of him more than the *hosannas.*

There also he silenced the offence which the chief priests and scribes took at the acclamations with which he was attended, *v.* 15, 16. They that should have been most forward to give him honour, were his worst enemies. They were inwardly vexed at the wonderful things that he did. If they had any sense, they could not but own the miracle of them; and if any good nature, could not but be in love with the mercy of them: yet, because they were resolved to oppose him, for these they envied him, and bore him a grudge. They openly quarrelled at the children's hosannas; they thought that hereby an honour was given him, which did not belong to him. Proud men cannot bear that honour should be done to any but to themselves, and are uneasy at nothing more than at the just praises of deserving men. When Christ is most honoured, his enemies are most displeased.

Here we have him (*v.* 16), taking part with the children against priests and scribes.

(1) The children were in the temple. It is good to bring children betimes to the house of prayer, *for of such is the kingdom of heaven.* Let children be taught to keep up the form of godliness, it will help to lead them to the power of it. Christ has a tenderness for the lambs of his flock.

(2) They were there *crying Hosannas to the Son of David.* This they learned from those that were

JAMIESON, FAUSSET, BROWN

And he went into the temple and began—or proceeded **to cast out**—but no mention is here made of the "whip of small cords" with which this was done the first time (John 2:15). It is simply said now, **He cast out them that sold therein, and them that bought**—"and overthrew the tables of the money-changers, and the seats of them that sold doves, and would not suffer that any man should carry any vessel through the temple"—that is, the temple-court. "There was always," says Lightfoot, "a constant market in the temple, in that place which was called 'The Shops,' where every day was sold wine, salt, oil, and other requisites to sacrifices; as also oxen and sheep, in the spacious court of the Gentiles." The "money-changers" were those who, for the convenience of the people, converted the current Greek and Roman money into Jewish coins, in which all temple dues had to be paid. The "doves" being required for sacrifice, as well as young pigeons on several prescribed occasions, could not conveniently be brought from great distances at the annual festivals, and so were naturally provided for them by dealers, as a matter of merchandise (Deut. 14:24-26). Thus the whole of these transactions were, in themselves, not only harmless, but nearly indispensable. The one thing about them which kindled the indignation of the Lord of the temple, now traversing its sacred precincts in the flesh, was the place where they were carried on—the profanation involved in such things being done within an inclosure sacred to the worship and service of God—and the effect of this in destroying in the minds of the worshipers the sanctity that should attach to everything on which that worship cast its shadow.

14. **And the blind and the lame came to him in the temple**—in the large sense of that word—**and he healed them.** If these miracles were wrought after the cleansing of the temple—as one would gather from Matthew—since they were wrought in the very temple-court from which the money-changers had been cleared out—they would set a divine seal on that act of mysterious authority. But as the second Gospel is peculiarly precise as to the order of these events, we incline to follow it, in placing the cleansing of the temple on the second day. Yet these miracles wrought in the temple on the lame and the blind are most touching, as the *last* recorded miraculous displays of His glory—with the single exception of the majestic cleansing of the temple—which He gave in public.

15. **And when the chief priests and the scribes saw the wonderful things which he did, and the children crying in the temple, and saying, Hosanna to the Son of David**—which was just the prolonged echo of the popular acclamations on His triumphal entry, but drawn forth anew from these children, on witnessing what doubtless filled their unsophisticated minds with wonder and admiration—**they were sore displeased.** 16. **And said unto him, Hearest thou what these say?**—stung most of all by this novel testimony to Jesus, as showing to what depths His popularity was reaching down, and from the mysterious effect of *such* voices upon the human spirit. "And Jesus saith unto them, Have ye never read [Ps. 8:2], Out of the mouth of babes and sucklings thou hast perfected praise?" This beautiful psalm is repeatedly referred to as prophetic of Christ, and this is the view of it which a sound interpretation of it will be found to yield. The testimony which it predicts that Messiah would receive from "babes"—a very remarkable feature of this prophetic psalm—was indeed here literally fulfilled, as was that of His being "numbered with the transgressors" (Isa. 53:12) and "pierced" (Zech. 12:10); but like those and similar predictions, it reaches deeper

ADAM CLARKE

12. *Moneychangers.* Persons who furnished the Jews and proselytes who came from other countries with the current coin of Judea, in exchange for their own.

13. *My house shall be called the house of prayer.* This is taken from Isa. lvi. 7. *But ye have made it a den of thieves.* This is taken from Jer. vii. 11. Our Lord alludes here to those dens and caves in Judea in which the public robbers either hid or kept themselves fortified.

14. *The blind and the lame came.* Having condemned the profane use of the Temple, He now shows the proper use of it. It is a house of prayer, where God is to manifest His goodness and power in giving sight to the spiritually blind, and feet to the lame.

15. *The chief priests . . . were sore displeased.* Or "were incensed." Incensed at what? At the purification of the profaned Temple! This was a work they should have done themselves, but for which they had neither grace nor influence; and their pride and jealousy will not suffer them to permit others to do it. Strange as it may appear, the priesthood itself, in all corrupt times, has been ever the most forward to prevent a reform in the Church.

MATTHEW HENRY

grown up. Little children say and do as they hear others say, and see others do; so easily do they imitate; and therefore great care must be taken to set them good examples, and no bad ones. Children will learn of those that are with them, either to curse and swear, or to pray and praise.

(3) Our Lord Jesus not only allowed it, but was very well pleased with it, and quoted a scripture which was fulfilled in it (Ps. viii. 2), or, at least, may be accommodated to it; *Out of the mouth of babes and sucklings thou hast perfected praise.* Christ is so far from being ashamed of the services of little children, that he takes particular notice of them (and children love to be taken notice of), and is well pleased with them. Praise is perfected out of the mouth of such; it has a peculiar tendency to the honour and glory of God for little children to join in his praises; the praise would be accounted defective and imperfect, if they had not their share in it; which is an encouragement for children to be good betimes, and to parents to teach them to be so. In the psalm it is, *Thou hast ordained strength. God perfecteth praise*, by *ordaining strength out of the mouths of babes and sucklings.* When great things are brought about by weak and unlikely instruments, God is thereby much honoured, for his *strength is perfected in weakness.* Christ, having thus silenced them, forsook them, *v.* 17. By repining at Christ's praises we drive him from us. *He left them* and he *went out of the city to Bethany*, which was a more quiet retired place; not so much that he might *sleep* undisturbed as that he might *pray* undisturbed.

Verses 18–22

I. Christ *returned in the morning to Jerusalem*, *v.* 18. Having work to do there, he returned.

II. *As he went, he hungered.* He was a man, and submitted to the infirmities of nature. He was a poor man, and had no present supply.

Christ *therefore* hungered, that he might have occasion to work this miracle and therein might give us an instance of his justice and his power.

1. See his *justice*, *v.* 19. He went to it, expecting fruit, because it had leaves; but, finding none, he sentenced it to a perpetual barrenness. All Christ's miracles hitherto were wrought for the good of men, and proved the power of his grace and blessing. Now, at last he would give a specimen of the power of his wrath and curse; yet this not on any man, woman or child, but on an inanimate tree; that is set forth for an example. This cursing of the barren fig-tree, represents the state of hypocrites in general; and so it teaches us, (1) That the fruit of fig-trees may justly be expected from those that have the leaves. Christ looks for the power of religion from those that make profession of it. (2) Christ's just expectations from flourishing professors are often frustrated and disappointed. Many have a name to live, and are not alive indeed. (3) The sin of barrenness is justly punished with the curse and plague of barrenness; *Let no fruit grow on thee henceforward for ever.* As one of the chiefest blessings, and which was the first, is, *Be fruitful*; so one of the saddest curses is, *Be no more fruitful.* (4) A false and hypocritical profession commonly withers in this world; the fig-tree that had no fruit, soon lost its leaves. Hypocrites may look plausible for a time, but, their profession will soon come to nothing; the gifts wither, common graces decay, and the falseness and folly of the pretender are manifested to all men. It represents the state of the nation and people of the Jews in particular; they were a fig-tree planted in Christ's way. They gave disappointment to our Lord Jesus. He came among them, expecting to find some fruit, something that would be pleasing to him. But his expectations were frustrated; he found nothing but leaves. They professed themselves expectant of the promised Messiah, but, when he came, they did not receive and entertain him. So we see the doom he passed upon them, *that never any fruit should grow upon them from henceforward for ever.* Never any good came from them (except the particular persons among them that believed), after they rejected Christ; they became worse and worse; blindness and hardness happened to them, and grew upon them. How soon did their fig-tree wither away, after they said, *His blood be on us, and on our children!*

2. See the *power* of Christ.

(1) The disciples admired the effect of Christ's curse (*v.* 20); *They marvelled.* They marvelled at the suddenness of the thing; *How soon is the fig-tree withered away!*

(2) Christ empowered them by faith to do the like (*v.* 21, 22). The description of this wonder-working faith; *If ye have faith, and doubt not.* Doubting of the power and promise of God is the great thing that spoils the efficacy and success of faith.

JAMIESON, FAUSSET, BROWN

than literal babes, even the "babes" to whom are revealed the mysteries of the Gospel.

Thus, it would seem, ended the first memorable day of the Redeemer's last week in Jerusalem. Of the close of it the following is the brief account of the First and Second Gospels, which we combine into one: "And he left them; and when now the eventide was come, he went out of the city into Bethany, with the twelve, and he lodged there" (Matt 21:17; Mark 11:11).

And on the morrow—The Triumphal Entry being on the first day of the week, this following day was Monday.

when they were come from Bethany—"in the morning" (Matt. 21:18). **he was hungry**—How was that? Had he stolen forth from that dear roof at Bethany to the "mountain to pray, and continued all night in prayer to God?" (Luke 6:12); or, "in the morning," as on a former occasion, "risen up a great while before day, and departed into a solitary place, and there prayed" (ch. 1:35); not breaking His fast thereafter, but bending His steps straight for the city, that He might "work the works of Him that sent Him while it was day"? (John 9:4). We know not, though one lingers upon and loves to trace out the every movement of that life of wonders. One thing, however we are sure of—it was *real bodily hunger* which He now sought to allay by the fruit of this fig tree, "if haply He might find any thing thereon"; not a mere *scene* for the purpose of teaching a lesson, as some early heretics maintained, and some still seem virtually to hold.

And seeing a fig tree—(In Matt. 21:19, it is "one fig tree," but the sense is the same as here, "a certain fig tree," as in Matt. 8:19, etc.) Bethphage, which adjoined Bethany, derives his name from its being a *fig region*—"House of figs."

he found nothing but leaves; for the time of figs was not yet—What the precise import of this explanation is, interpreters are not agreed. Perhaps all that is meant is, that as the proper fig season had not arrived, no fruit would have been expected even of this tree but for the leaves which it had, which were in this case prematurely and unnaturally developed. **And Jesus answered and said unto it, No man eat fruit of thee hereafter for ever**—That word did not *make* the tree barren, but sealed it up in its own barrenness. See on Matthew 13:13-15.

they saw the fig tree dried up from the roots—no partial blight, leaving life in the root; but it was now dead, root and branch. In Matthew 21:19 it is said it withered away as soon as it was cursed. But the full blight had not appeared probably at once; and in the dusk perhaps, as they returned to Bethany, they had not observed it. The precision with which Mark distinguishes the days is not observed by Matthew, intent only on holding up the truths which the incident was designed to teach. In Matthew the whole is represented as taking place at once, just as the two stages of Jairus' daughter—dying and dead—are represented by him as one. The only difference is between a mere summary and a more detailed narrative, each of which only confirms the other.

ADAM CLARKE

16. *Out of the mouth of babes.* The eighth psalm, out of which these words are quoted, is applied to Jeuss Christ in three other places in the new covenant, 1 Cor. xv. 27; Eph. i. 22; Heb. ii. 6. It was a common thing among the Jews for the children to be employed in public acclamations, and thus they were accustomed to hail their celebrated rabbins. This shouting of the children was therefore no strange thing in the land; only they were exasperated because a Person was celebrated against whom they had a rooted hatred.

17. *And he left them* (finally leaving them), *and went . . . into Bethany; and he lodged there.* Bethany was a village about two miles distant from Jerusalem, by Mount Olivet, John xi. 18; and it is remarkable that from this day till His death, which happened about six days after, He spent not one night in Jerusalem, but went every evening to Bethany, and returned to the city each morning. See Luke xxi. 37; xxii, 39; John viii. 1-2. They were about to murder the Lord of glory; and the true Light, which they had rejected, is now departing from them.

18. *Now in the morning as he returned into the city.* Which was His custom from the time He wholly left Jerusalem, spending only the daytime teaching in the Temple; see v. 17. This was probably on Thursday, the twelfth day of the month *Nisan. He hungered.* Probably neither He nor His disciples had anything but what they got from public charity, and the hand of that seems to have been cold at this time.

19. *He saw a fig tree in the way.* "By the roadside." As this fig tree was by the wayside, it was no private property; and on this account our Lord, or any other traveller, had a right to take of its fruit. For a full explanation of this difficult passage, relative to this emblematic fig tree, see on Mark xi. 13.

W. E. VINE:

SUKE, or *SUKEA*, a fig tree, is found in Matt. 21:19, 20, 21; 24:32; Mark 11:13, 20, 21; 13:28; Luke 13:6, 7; 21:29; John 1:48, 50; James 3:12; Rev. 6:13.

Note: A fig tree with leaves must have young fruits already, or it will be barren for the season. The first figs ripen in late May or early June. The tree in Mark 11:13 should have had fruit, unripe indeed, but existing. In some lands fig trees bear the early fruit under the leaves and the later fruit above the leaves. In that case the leaves were a sign that there should have been fruit, unseen from a distance, underneath the leaves. The condemnation of this fig tree lay in the absence of any sign of fruit.

—*Vine's Expository Dictionary*

MATTHEW HENRY

As certain as the promise is, so confident our faith should be. The power and prevalence of it expressed figuratively; *If ye shall say to this mountain, Be thou removed, it shall be done.* This is a proverbial expression; intimating that we are to believe that nothing is impossible with God, and therefore that what he has promised shall certainly be performed, though to us it seem impossible. The ways and means of exercising this faith; *All things whatsover ye shall ask in prayer, believing ye shall receive.* Faith is the soul, prayer is the body; both together make a complete man for any service. Faith, if it be right, will excite prayer; and prayer is not right, if it do not spring from faith. This is the condition of our receiving—we must *ask in prayer, believing.* The requests of prayer shall not be denied; the expectations of faith shall not be frustrated. It is but ask and have, believe and receive; and what would we more? Observe, How comprehensive the promise is—*all things whatsoever ye shall ask. All things,* in general; *whatsoever,* brings it to particulars. Such is the folly of our unbelief, that, though we think we assent to promises in the general, yet we fly off when it comes to particulars, and therefore, it is thus copiously expressed, *All things whatsoever.*

Verses 23-27

Our Lord Jesus (like St. Paul after him) preached his gospel *with much contention*; and here, just before he died, we have him engaged in controversy. The great contenders with him, were, *the chief priests and the elders,* the judges of two distinct courts, the chief priests presided in the ecclesiastical court, the elders of the people were judges of the civil courts. These joined to attack Christ, thinking they should find or make him obnoxious either to the one or to the other. Here we have them disturbing him when he was preaching, *v.* 23. They would neither receive his instructions themselves, nor let others receive them.

I. As soon as he came into Jerusalem, he went to the temple, though he had been affronted there the day before, was there in the midst of enemies and in the mouth of danger.

II. In the temple he was teaching; he had called it *a house of prayer* (*v.* 13), and here we have him preaching there. Praying and preaching must go together, and neither must encroach upon, or jostle out, the other. To make up communion with God, we must not only speak to him in prayer, but hear what he has to say to us by his word; ministers must *give themselves both to the word and to prayer.*

III. When Christ was teaching the people, the priests and elders came upon him, and challenged him to produce his orders. Yet good was brought out of the evil, for hereby occasion was given to Christ to dispel the objections that were advanced against him; and, while his adversaries thought by their power to have silenced him, he by his wisdom silenced them.

1. How he was assaulted by their insolent demand; *By what authority doest thou these things, and who gave thee this authority?* Had they duly considered his miracles, and the power by which he wrought them, they needed not to have asked this question. It is good for all that take upon them to act with authority, to put this question to themselves, "Who gave us that authority?" They who run before their warrant, run without their blessing.

Christ had often said it, and proved it beyond contradiction, that he was *a teacher sent of God* (John iii. 2); yet, at this time of day, when that point had been so fully cleared and settled, they come to him with this question. (1) In the ostentation of their own power. How haughtily do they ask, *Who gave thee this authority?* Intimating that he could have no authority, because he had none from them. It is common for the greatest abusers of their power to be the most rigorous assertors of it, and to take a pride and pleasure in any thing that looks like the exercise of it. (2) It was to ensnare and entangle him. Should he refuse to answer this question, they would insinuate to the people, that his silence was a tacit confessing of himself to be a usurper: should he plead an authority from God, they would, as formerly, demand a sign from heaven, or accuse him of blasphemy for it.

2. How he answered this demand with another, which would help them to answer it themselves (*v.* 24, 25); *I also will ask you one thing.* He declined giving them a direct answer, lest they should take advantage against him; but answers them with a question.

How this question is concerning John's baptism, here put for his whole ministry; "Was this *from heaven, or of men*? One of the two it must be." This question was not at all shuffling, to evade theirs; but,

JAMIESON, FAUSSET, BROWN

For verily I say unto you, That whosoever shall say unto this mountain, Be thou removed . . . he shall have whatsoever he saith—Here is the lesson now. From the nature of the case supposed—that they might wish a mountain removed and cast into the sea, a thing far removed from anything which they could be thought actually to desire—it is plain that not physical but moral obstacles to the progress of His kingdom were in the Redeemer's view, and that what He designed to teach was the great lesson, that *no obstacle should be able to stand before a confiding faith in God.* **Therefore I say unto you, What things soever ye desire, when ye pray, believe that ye receive them, and ye shall have them**—This verse only *generalizes* the assurance of the former verse; which seems to show that it was designed for the special encouragement of *evangelistic* and *missionary* efforts, while this is a directory for prevailing *prayer in general.*

23-46. THE AUTHORITY OF JESUS QUESTIONED, AND THE REPLY—THE PARABLES OF THE TWO SONS, AND OF THE WICKED HUSBANDMAN. (=Mark 11: 27-12; 12; Luke 20:1-19.) Now commences, as ALFORD remarks, that series of parables and discourses of our Lord with His enemies, in which He develops, more completely than ever before, His hostility to their hypocrisy and iniquity: and so they are stirred up to compass His death.

The Authority of Jesus Questioned, and the Reply (vss. 23-27). **23. By what authority doest thou these things!**—referring particularly to the expulsion of the buyers and sellers from the temple. **and who gave thee this authority?**

24. And Jesus answered and said unto them, I also will ask you one thing . . . 25. The baptism of John—meaning his whole mission and ministry, of which baptism was the proper character. **whence was it? from heaven, or of men?**—What wisdom there was in this way of meeting their question will best appear by their reply.

ADAM CLARKE

21. *If ye have faith, and doubt not.* "Removing mountains," and "rooting up of mountains" are phrases very generally used to signify the removing or conquering great difficulties—getting through perplexities. So, many of the rabbins were termed "rooters up of mountains," because they were dexterous in removing difficulties, solving cases of conscience. In this sense our Lord's words are to be understood. He that has faith will get through every difficulty and perplexity; mountains shall become molehills or plains before him.

F. B. MEYER:

Authority which silenced and condemned. Our Lord always refused to gratify idle curiosity. When an earnest seeker for truth, like Nicodemus, approached him to know the way of life, he was willing to give time and thought without stint. But of what use was it to endeavor to satisfy these men who had refused to acknowledge the divine mission of the forerunner! They would not speak out their inner convictions because of the effect it would have on their worldly prospects. For such as these, Christ has nothing. At all costs, we must be true to the inner light—that is, to God's Spirit within us.
—*Bible Commentary*

23. *By what authority doest thou these things?* The things which the chief priests allude to were His receiving the acclamations of the people as the promised Messiah, His casting the traders out of the Temple, and His teaching the people publicly in it.

25. *The baptism of John.* Had John a divine commission or not for his baptism and preaching? Our Lord here takes the wise in their own cunning. He knew the estimation John was in among the people, and He plainly saw that if they gave any answer at all they must convict themselves; and so they saw, when they came to examine the question.

MATTHEW HENRY

if they answered this question, it would answer theirs: should they say, against their consciences, that John's baptism was of men, yet it would be easy to answer, *John did no miracle* (John x. 41), Christ did many; but should they say, as they could not but own, that John's baptism was from heaven then their demand was answered, for he bare testimony to Christ. If they refused to answer it, that would be a good reason why he should not offer proofs of his authority to men that were obstinately prejudiced against the strongest conviction.

3. How they were hereby baffled and run aground. (1) How *they reasoned with themselves*, not concerning the merits of the cause; no, their care was, how to make their part good against Christ. Two things they considered and consulted—their credit, and their safety; the same things which *they* principally aim at, who *seek their own things*.

[1] They consider their own credit, which they would endanger if they should own John's baptism to be of God; for then Christ would ask them, before all the people, *Why did ye not believe him?*

[2] They consider their own safety, if they should say that John's baptism was of men; *We fear the people, for all hold John as a prophet*. It seems, then, *First*, That the people had truer sentiments of John than the chief priests and the elders had. This people, of whom they said in their pride that they *knew not the law, and were cursed* (John vii. 49), it seems, knew the gospel, and were blessed. *Secondly*, That the chief priests and elders stood in awe of the common people, which is an evidence that things were in disorder among them. If they had kept their integrity, and done their duty, they had kept up their authority, and needed not to fear the people. *Thirdly*, That it is usually the temper even of common people, to be zealous for the honour of that which they account sacred and divine. Hence the hottest contests have been about holy things. *Fourthly*, That the chief priests and elders were kept from an open denial of the truth, not by the fear of God, but purely by the fear of the people. Many bad people would be much worse than they are, if they durst.

(2) How they replied to our Saviour, and so dropped the question. They fairly confessed *We cannot tell*; that is, "We will not"; The more shame for them. When they would not confess their knowledge, they were constrained to confess their ignorance. And observe, by the way, when they said, *We cannot tell*, they told a lie, for they knew that John's baptism was of God. There are many who are more afraid of the *shame* of lying than of the *sin*, and therefore scruple not to speak that which they knew to be false concerning their own thoughts and apprehensions, because in those things they know nobody can disprove them.

Thus Christ avoided the snare they laid for him, and justified himself in refusing to gratify them; *Neither tell I you by what authority I do these things*. They were not fit to be discoursed with concerning Christ's authority; for men of such a disposition could not be convinced of the truth. Those that imprison the truths they know, in unrighteousness are justly denied the further truths they enquire after. Take away the talent from him that buried it; those that *will not* see, *shall not* see.

Verses 28–32

As Christ instructed his disciples by parables, so sometimes he convinced his adversaries by parables, which bring reproofs more close, and make men, or ever they are aware, to reprove themselves. This Christ designs here, as appears by the first words (*v.* 28), *But what think you?*

I. The parable itself, which represents two sorts of persons; some that prove better than they promise; others that promise better than they prove.

1. They had both one and the same father. There are favours which all alike receive from him, and obligations which all alike lie under to him. Yes, and yet there is a vast difference between men's characters.

2. They had both the same command given them; *Son, go work today in my vineyard.* God sets his children to work, though they are all heirs. (1) The work of religion, which we are called to engage in, is vineyard work, creditable, profitable, and pleasant. By the sin of Adam we were turned out to work upon the common, and to eat the herb of the field; but by the grace of our Lord Jesus we are called to work again in the vineyard. (2) The gospel call to work in the vineyard, requires present obedience; *Son, go work* today. We were not sent into the world to be idle, nor had we daylight given us to play by. (3) The exhortation speaketh unto us *as unto children, Son, go work*. It is the command of a Father, which carries with it both authority and affection, a Father

JAMIESON, FAUSSET, BROWN

If we shall say, From heaven; he will say unto us, Why did ye not then believe him?—"Why did ye not believe the testimony which he bore to Me, as the promised and expected Messiah?" for that was the burden of John's whole testimony. **26. But if we shall say, Of men; we fear the people**—rather the multitude. In Luke (20:6) it is, "all the people will stone us." **for all hold John as a prophet**—Crooked, cringing hypocrites! No wonder Jesus gave you no answer.

27. And they answered Jesus, and said, We cannot tell—Evidently their difficulty was, how to answer, so as neither to shake their determination to reject the claims of Christ nor damage their reputation with the people. For the truth itself they cared nothing whatever.

Neither tell I you by what authority I do these things—What composure and dignity of wisdom does our Lord here display, as He turns their question upon themselves, and, while revealing His knowledge of their hypocrisy, closes their mouths! Taking advantage of the surprise, silence, and awe produced by this reply, our Lord followed it up immediately by the two following parables.

Parable of the Two Sons (vss. 28-32.) **28. But what think ye? A certain man had two sons; and he came to the first and said, Son, go work to-day in my vineyard**—for true religion is a practical thing, a "bringing forth fruit unto God."

ADAM CLARKE

G. CAMPBELL MORGAN:

He said, in effect, "You are challenging Me as to whether I have any right to come into the house of God, and assume authority in the house of God. Am I a teacher answering the authority of God, or am I here as a man craving the popular acclaim of the people? I will ask you one question, The baptism of John, was it from heaven or from men?" Before He could reveal to them what they asked, He took them back to the last revelation which they had received; for readiness to receive a new revelation always depends upon the attitude to the previous one. That is always the principle of God's dealing with men. Thus we see that there was more in Christ's question than appears upon the surface. Supposing these men had admitted that the baptism of John was from heaven, then their question concerning Christ was immediately answered, because John had been His herald. John discontinued his ministry when Jesus began. John had said, "He must increase, but I must decrease." If they had accepted that testimony as from heaven, they would not have asked Him this question about His authority. They knew full well what John's testimony to Him had been. Thus there was an intimate connection between His question and their answer. The prime meaning of Jesus' question was this: "What did you do with the last light that fell upon your pathway? If you tell Me that, I shall know whether you are ready to receive more light or not!"

—The Gospel According to Matthew

27. *We cannot tell,* said they; which, in the words of truth, should have been, "We will not tell," for we will not have this man for the Messiah; because, if we acknowledge John as His forerunner, we must, of necessity, receive Jesus as the Christ.

28. *A certain man had two sons.* Under the emblem of these two sons—one of whom was a libertine, disobedient, and insolent, but who afterwards thought on his ways, and returned to his duty; and the second, a hypocrite, who promised all, and did nothing;—our Lord points out, on the one hand, the taxgatherers and sinners of all descriptions, who, convicted by the preaching of John and that of Christ, turned away from their iniquities and embraced the gospel; and, on the other hand, the scribes, Pharisees, and self-righteous people, who, pretending a zeal for the law, would not receive the salvation of the gospel.

MATTHEW HENRY

that is very tender of *his Son that serves him.*

3. Their conduct was very different. One of the sons did better than he said, proved better than he promised. His answer was bad, but his actions were good. Here is the untoward answer that he gave to his father; he said, flat and plain, *I will not.* Excuses are bad, but downright denials are worse; yet such peremptory refusals do the calls of the gospel often meet with. Some love their ease, and will not work. Their hearts are so much upon their own fields, that they are not for working in God's vineyard. They love the business of the world better than the business of their religion. Here is the happy change of his mind, and of his way, upon second thoughts; *Afterward he repented, and went. Afterward he repented.* Repentance is μετανοία—*an after-wit*: and μεταμέλεια—*an after-care.* Better late than never. When he repented, he went; that was the *fruit meet for repentance.* The only evidence of our repentance for our former resistance, is, immediately to comply, and set to work; and then what is past, shall be pardoned, and all shall be well. Our God *waits to be gracious,* and, notwithstanding our former follies, if we repent and mend, will favourably accept of us; blessed be God, we are under a covenant that leaves room for such a repentance. The other son said better than he did; his answer was good but his actions bad. To him the father *said likewise, v.* 30. The gospel call, though very different, is, in effect, the same to all. Observe,

(1) How fairly this other son promised; *He said, I go, sir.* He gives his father a title of respect, *sir.* He professes a ready obedience, *I go*; not, "I will go by and by," but, "Ready, sir, you may depend upon it, I go just now."

(2) How he failed in the performance; *He went not.* Saying and doing are two things; and many there are that say, and do not. Many with their mouth show much love, but their heart goes another way. Buds and blossoms are not fruit.

II. A general appeal upon the parable; *Whether of the twain did the will of his father? v.* 31. They both had their faults, one was rude, and the other was false. But the question is, Which was the better of the two, and the less faulty? And it was soon resolved; the first, because his actions were better than his words, and his latter end than his beginning. The tenor of the whole scripture gives us to understand that those are accepted as doing their Father's will, who, wherein they have missed it, are sorry for it, and do better.

III. A particular application of it to the matter in hand, *v.* 31, 32. The primary scope of the parable is, to show how the publicans and harlots entertained the doctrine, and submitted to the discipline, of John the Baptist, his forerunner, when the priests and elders slighted John the Baptist, and ran counter to the designs of his mission.

In Christ's application of this parable, observe,

1. How he proves that John's baptism was *from heaven, and not of men.* "If you *cannot* tell," saith Christ, "you *might* tell."

(1) By the scope of his ministry; *John came unto you in the way of righteousness.* Remember the rule of trial, *By their fruits ye shall know them*; the fruits of their doctrines, the fruits of their doings. Now it was evident that John came *in the way of righteousness.* In his ministry, he taught people to repent, and to work the works of righteousness.

(2) By the success of his ministry; *The publicans and the harlots believed him.* If God had not sent John the Baptist, he would not have crowned his labours with such wonderful success. The people's profiting is the minister's best testimonial.

2. How he reproves them for their contempt of John's baptism. To shame them for it, he sets before them the faith, repentance, and obedience, of the publicans and harlots, which aggravated their unbelief and impenitence.

(1) The publicans and harlots were like the first son in the parable, from whom little of religion was expected. They promised little good, and those that knew them promised themselves little good from them. And yet many of them were wrought upon by the ministry of John.

(2) The scribes and Pharisees, the chief priests and elders, and indeed the Jewish nation in general, were like the other son that gave good works. A hypocrite is more hardly convinced and converted than a gross sinner. It was an aggravation of their unbelief, [1] That John was such an excellent person. The better the means are, the greater will the account be, if not improved. [2] That, when they saw the publicans and harlots go before them into the kingdom of heaven, they did not afterward repent and believe. Through the pride of their countenance, they would not seek after God, after Christ.

JAMIESON, FAUSSET, BROWN

29. He answered and said, I will not—TRENCH notices the rudeness of this answer, and the total absence of any attempt to excuse such disobedience, both characteristic; representing careless, reckless sinners resisting God to His face.

30. And he came to the second, and said likewise. And he answered and said, I [go], sir—"I, sir." The emphatic "I," here, denotes the self-righteous complacency which says, "God, I thank thee that *I* am not as other men" (Luke 18:11). **and went not**—*He* did not "afterward repent" and refuse to go; for there was here no *intention* to go. It is the class that "say and do not" (ch. 23:3)—a falseness more abominable to God, says STIER, than any "I will not." **31. Whether of them twain did the will of his Father? They say unto him, The first**—Now comes the application. **Jesus saith unto them, Verily I say unto you, That the publicans and the harlots go**—or, "are going"; even now entering, while ye hold back—**into the kingdom of God before you**—The publicans and the harlots were the first son, who, when told to work in the Lord's vineyard, said, I will not; but afterwards repented and went. Their early life was a flat and flagrant refusal to do what they were commanded; it was one continued rebellion against the authority of God. The chief priests and the elders of the people, with whom our Lord was now speaking, were the second son, who said, I go, sir, but went not. They were early called, and all their life long professed obedience to God, but never rendered it; their life was one of continued disobedience. **32. For John came unto you in the way of righteousness**—i.e., calling you to repentance; as Noah is styled "a preacher of righteousness" (II Pet. 2:5), when like the Baptist he warned the old world to "flee from the wrath to come." **and ye believed him not**—They did not reject him; nay, they "were willing for a season to rejoice in his light" (John 5:35); but they would not receive his testimony to Jesus. **but the publicans and the harlots believed him**—Of the publicans this is twice expressly recorded, Luke 3:12; 7:29. Of the harlots, then, the same may be taken for granted, though the fact is not expressly recorded. These outcasts gladly believed the testimony of John to the coming Saviour, and so hastened to Jesus when He came. See Luke 7:37; 15:1, etc. **and ye, when ye had seen it, repented not afterward, that ye might believe him**—Instead of being "provoked to jealousy" by their example, ye have seen them flocking to the Saviour and getting to heaven, unmoved.

ADAM CLARKE

29. *I will not.* **This is the general reply of every sinner to the invitations of God, and in it the Most High is treated without ceremony or respect.**

30. *I go, sir.* **This is all respect, complaisance, and professed obedience. But he *went not;* he promised well, but did not perform. What a multitude of such are in the world, professing to know God but denying Him in their works! Alas! what will such professions avail, when God comes to take away the soul?**

31. *The publicans and the harlots.* **In all their former conduct they had said no. Now they yield to the voice of truth when they hear it, and enter into the Kingdom, embracing the salvation brought to them in the gospel. The others, who had always been professing the most ready and willing obedience, and who pretended to be waiting for the kingdom of God, did not receive it when it came, but rather chose, while making the best professions, to continue members of the synagogue of Satan.**

32. *John came unto you in the way of righteousness.* **Proclaiming the truth, and living agreeably to it. Or, "John came unto you, who are in the way of righteousness." This seems rather to be the true meaning and construction of this passage. The Jews are here distinguished from the Gentiles. The former were in *the way of righteousness,* had the revelation of God, and the ordinances of justice established among them.**

MATTHEW HENRY

Verses 33–46

This parable plainly sets forth the sin and ruin of the Jewish nation.

I. We have here the privileges of the Jewish church, represented by the letting out of a vineyard to the husbandmen. Observe,

1. How God established a church for himself in the world. The kingdom of God upon earth is here compared to a vineyard, furnished with all things requisite to an advantageous management and improvement of it. (1) He planted this vineyard. The church is *the planting of the Lord*. The earth of itself produces thorns and briars; but vines must be planted. (2) He hedged it round about. God's church in the world is taken under his special protection. It is *a hedge round about*. He will not have his vineyard to lie in common, that those who are without, may thrust in at pleasure; not to lie at large that those who are within, may lash out at pleasure. (3) He *digged a wine-press and built a tower*. God instituted ordinances in his church, for the due oversight of it, and for the promoting of its fruitfulness.

2. How he entrusted these visible church-privileges with the nation and people of the Jews; he let it out to them as husbandmen, because he would try them, and be honoured by them. And then he *went into a far country*. When God had in a visible appearance settled the Jewish church at mount Sinai, he did in a manner withdraw; they had no more such open vision, but were left to the written word.

II. God's expectation of rent from these husbandmen, *v.* 34. It was a reasonable expectation. 1. His expectations were not hasty, but staid *till the time of the fruit drew near*. God waits to be gracious, that he may give us time. 2. They were not high. He sent his *servants to them*, to remind them of their duty, and of the rent-day, and to help them in gathering in the fruit, and making return of it. 3. They were not hard; it was only to *receive the fruits*. He did not demand more than they could make of it, but some fruit of that which he himself planted—an observance of the laws and statutes he gave them.

III. The husbandmen's baseness in abusing the messengers that were sent to them.

1. When he sent them his servants, they abused them. The calls and reproofs of the word, if they do not engage, will but exasperate. See here what hath all along been the lot of God's faithful messengers, more or less; (1) To suffer; *so persecuted they the prophets*. They not only despised and reproached them, but treated them as the worst of malefactors. If they that *live godly in Christ Jesus* themselves shall *suffer persecution*, much more they that press others to it. (2) It has been their lot to suffer from their Master's own tenants; they were the husbandmen that treated them thus.

Now see, [1] How God persevered in his goodness to them. He sent other servants, more than the first; though the first sped not, but were abused. [2] How they persisted in their wickedness. They *did unto them likewise*. One sin makes way for another of the same kind.

2. At length, he sent them his Son; we have seen God's goodness in sending, and their badness in abusing, the servants; but in the latter instance both these exceed themselves.

(1) Never did grace appear more gracious than in *sending the Son*. This was done *last of all*. He was sent last; for if nothing else would work upon them, surely this would. *Surely they will reverence my Son*, and therefore I will send him. If they will but reverence the Son, the point is gained. *Surely they will reverence my Son*, for he comes with more authority than the servants could.

(2) Never did sin appear more sinful than in the abusing of him.

[1] How it was plotted (*v.* 38); *When they saw the Son*. This touched their copyhold, and they were resolved to make one bold push for it, and to preserve their wealth and grandeur by taking *him* out of the way. *This is the heir, come, let us kill him*. Pilate and Herod, the princes of this world, *knew not*. But the *chief priests and elders* knew that *this was the heir*, and therefore, *Come, let us kill him*. Many are killed for what they have. The chief thing they envied him, and for which they hated and feared him, was his interest in the people. Therefore *let us kill him*; and then, as if the premises must of course go to the occupant, *let us seize on his inheritance*. They thought, if they could but get rid of this Jesus, they should carry all before them. While they thought to kill him, and so to seize on his inheritance, he went by his cross to his crown.

[2] How this plot was executed, *v.* 39. No wonder they soon *caught him, and slew him*. Nay, looking upon him to be as unworthy to live, as they were

JAMIESON, FAUSSET, BROWN

Parable of the Wicked Husbandmen (vss. 33-46). **33. Hear another parable: There was a certain householder, which planted a vineyard**—See on Luke 13:6. **and hedged it round about, and digged a winepress in it, and built a tower**—These details are taken, as is the basis of the parable itself, from that beautiful parable of Isaiah 5:1-7, in order to fix down the application and sustain it by Old Testament authority. **and let it out to husbandmen**—These are just the ordinary spiritual guides of the people, under whose care and culture the fruits of righteousness are expected to spring up. **and went into a far country**—"for a long time" (Luke 20:9), leaving the vineyard to the laws of the spiritual husbandry during the whole time of the Jewish economy. On this phraseology, see on Mark 4:26. **34. And when the time of the fruit drew near, he sent his servants to the husbandmen**—By these "servants" are meant the prophets and other extraordinary messengers, raised up from time to time. See on ch. 23:37. **that they might receive the fruits of it**—See again on Luke 13:6. **35. And the husbandmen took his servants, and beat one**—see Jeremiah 37:15; 38:6. **and killed another**—see Jeremiah 26:20-23. **and stoned another**—see II Chronicles 24:21. Compare with this whole verse ch. 23:37, where our Lord reiterates these charges in the most melting strain. **36. Again, he sent other servants more than the first; and they did unto them likewise**—see II Kings 17:13; II Chronicles 36:16, 18; Nehemiah 9:26.

37. But last of all he sent unto them his son, saying, They will reverence my son—In Mark (12:6) this is most touchingly expressed: "Having yet therefore one son, His well-beloved, He sent Him also last unto them, saying, They will reverence My Son." Luke's version of it too (20:13) is striking: "Then said the lord of the vineyard, What shall I do? I will send My beloved Son: it may be they will reverence Him when they see Him." Who does not see that our Lord here severs Himself, by the sharpest line of demarkation, from all merely *human* messengers, and claims for Himself *Sonship* in its loftiest sense? (Cf. Heb. 3:3-6.) The expression, "*It may be* they will reverence My Son," is designed to teach the almost unimaginable guilt of *not* reverentially welcoming God's Son. **38. But when the husbandmen saw the son, they said among themselves**—Cf. Genesis 37:18-20; John 11:47-53. **This is the heir**—Sublime expression this of the great truth, that God's inheritance was destined for, and in due time is to come into the possession of, His own Son *in our nature* (Heb. 1:2). **come, let us kill him, and let us seize on his inheritance**—that so, from mere *servants*, we may become *lords*. This is the deep aim of the depraved heart; this is emphatically "the root of all evil." **39. And they caught him, and cast him out of the vineyard**—cf. Hebrews 13:11-13 ("without the gate—without the camp"); I Kings 21:13; John 19:17. **and slew him.**

ADAM CLARKE

33. *There was a certain householder*. Let us endeavor to find out a general and practical meaning for this parable. A *householder*—the Supreme Being. The *family*—the Jewish nation. The *vineyard*—the city of Jerusalem. The *fence*—the divine protection. The *winepress*—the law and sacrificial rites. The *tower*—the Temple, in which the Divine Presence was manifested. The *husbandmen*—the priests and doctors of the law. *Went from home*—entrusted the cultivation of the vineyard to the priests, with the utmost confidence, as a man would do who had the most trusty servants, and was obliged to absent himself from home for a certain time. Our Lord takes this parable from Isa. v. 1. *Digged a winepress*. Mark has the pit under the press, into which the liquor ran, when squeezed out of the fruit by the press.

34. *He sent his servants*. Prophets, which, from time to time, He sent to the Jewish nation to call both priests and people back to the purity of His holy religion. *Receive the fruits of it*. Alluding to the ancient custom of paying the rent of a farm in kind; that is, by a part of the produce of the farm.

35. *Beat one*. "Took his skin off, flayed him," probably alluding to some who had been excessively scourged.

36. *Other servants*. There is not a moment in which God does not shower down His gifts upon men, and require the fruit of them. *More than the first*. Or more honorable.

37. *Last of all he sent . . . his son*. This requires no comment. Our Lord plainly means himself. *They will reverence*. They will reflect upon their conduct and blush for shame because of it, when they see my son.

38. *Said among themselves*. Alluding to the conspiracies which were then forming against the life of our blessed Lord, in the councils of the Jewish elders and chief priests. See chap. xxvii. 1.

39. *Cast him out of the vineyard*. Utterly rejected the counsel of God against themselves, and would neither acknowledge the authority of Christ nor submit to His teaching.

MATTHEW HENRY

unwilling he should, *they cast him out of the vineyard*, and out of the holy city, for he was crucified *without the gate*, Heb. xiii. 12. As if *He* had been the shame and reproach, who was the greatest glory, of his people Israel.

IV. Here is their doom read out of their own mouths, *v.* 40, 41. He puts it to them, *When the Lord of the vineyard cometh, what will he do unto these husbandmen?* He puts it to themselves, for their stronger conviction. God's proceedings are so unexceptionable, that there needs but an appeal to sinners themselves concerning the equity of them. They could readily answer, *He will miserably destroy those wicked men.* Many can easily prognosticate the dismal consequences of other people's sins, that see not what will be the end of their own.

1. Our Saviour, in his question, supposes that *the lord of the vineyard will come*, and reckon with them. Persecutors say in their hearts, He *delays his coming*. Though he bear long with them, he will not bear always.

2. They, in their answer, suppose that it will be a terrible reckoning.

(1) That he will *miserably destroy those wicked men.* Let men never expect to do ill, and fare well. This was fulfilled upon the Jews, in that miserable destruction which was brought upon them by the Romans.

(2) That he will *let out his vineyard to other husbandmen.* God will have a church in the world. The unbelief and frowardness of man shall not make the word of God of no effect.

V. The further illustration and application of this by Christ himself, telling them, in effect, that they had rightly judged.

1. He illustrates it by referring to a scripture fulfilled in this (*v.* 42); *Did ye never read in the scriptures?* The scripture he quotes is Ps. cxviii. 22, 23, the same context out of which the children fetched their hosannas. The same word yields matter of praise and comfort to Christ's friends and followers, which speaks conviction and terror to his enemies. Such a two-edged sword is the word of God.

(1) The builders' rejecting of the stone is the same with the husbandmen's abusing of the son that was sent to them. They would not allow Christ a place in their building; they threw him aside as a despised broken vessel, a stone that would serve only for a stepping-stone, to be trampled upon.

(2) The advancing of this stone to be the head of the corner is the same with *letting out the vineyard to other husbandmen.* He who was rejected by the Jews was embraced by the Gentiles; and to that church, *Christ is all, and in all.*

(3) The hand of God was in all this; *This is the Lord's doing. It is marvellous in our eyes.* The wickedness of the Jews that rejected him is marvellous. The honour done him by the Gentile world is marvellous; that he whom men despised and abhorred, should be adored by kings! But *it is the Lord's doing*.

2. He applies it to them, and application is the life of preaching. He applies the sentence which they had passed (*v.* 41), and turns it upon themselves; not the former part of it, concerning the miserable destruction of the husbandmen (he could not bear to speak of that), but the latter part, of *letting out the vineyard to others.* Know then,

(1) That the Jews shall be unchurched; *The kingdom of God shall be taken from you.* To the Jews had long pertained *the adoption and the glory* (Rom. ix. 4); and the sacred trust of revealed religion, and bearing up of God's name in the world; but now it shall be so no longer. They were not only unfruitful in the use of their privileges, but opposed the gospel of Christ, and so forfeited them.

(2) That the Gentiles shall be taken in. Though his vine be plucked up in one place, he will find another to plant it in. The fall of Israel was the riches of the Gentiles. They shall bring forth the fruits better than the Jews had done. When he changes, it shall not be to his loss. He applies the scripture which he had quoted (*v.* 42), to their terror, *v.* 44. We have here the doom of two sorts of people. Some, through ignorance, stumble at Christ in his estate of humiliation; they, through their blindness and carelessness, fall on it, fall over it, and *they shall be broken.* The unbelief of sinners will be their ruin. Others oppose Christ, and bid defiance to him in his estate of exaltation, when this Stone is advanced to the head of the corner; and on them *it shall fall*, for they pull it on their own heads, and *it will grind them to powder.* Christ's kingdom will be a burthensome stone to all those that attempt to overthrow it, or heave it out of its place. None ever hardened his heart against God and prospered.

1. *They perceived that he spake of them* (*v.* 45), and that in what they said (*v.* 41) they had but read their

JAMIESON, FAUSSET, BROWN

40. When the lord therefore of the vineyard cometh—This represents 'the settling time,' which, in the case of the Jewish ecclesiastics, was that judicial trial of the nation and its leaders which issued in the destruction of their whole state. **what will he do unto those husbandmen? 41. They say unto him, He will miserably destroy those wicked men**—an emphatic alliteration not easily conveyed in English: "He will badly destroy those bad men," or "miserably destroy those miserable men," is something like it. **and will let out his vineyard unto other husbandmen, which shall render him the fruits in their seasons**—If this answer was given by the Pharisees, to whom our Lord addressed the parable, they thus unwittingly pronounced their own condemnation: as did David to Nathan the prophet (II Sam. 12:5-7), and Simon the Pharisee to our Lord (Luke 7:43, etc.). But if it was given, as the two other Evangelists agree in representing it, by our Lord Himself, and the explicitness of the answer would seem to favor that supposition, then we can better explain the exclamation of the Pharisees which followed it, in Luke's report—"And when they heard it, they said, God forbid"—His whole meaning now bursting upon them.

42. Jesus saith unto them. Did ye never read in the scriptures,—(Ps. 118:22, 23)—**The stone which the builders rejected . . .** A bright Messianic prophecy, which reappears in various forms (Isa. 28:16, etc), and was made glorious use of by Peter before the Sanhedrim (Acts 4:11). He recurs to it in his first epistle (I Pet. 2:4-6).

43. Therefore say I unto you, The kingdom of God—God's visible Kingdom, or Church, upon earth, which up to this time stood in the seed of Abraham. **shall be taken from you, and given to a nation bringing forth the fruits thereof**—i.e., the great evangelical community of the faithful, which, after the extrusion of the Jewish nation, would consist chiefly of Gentiles, until "all Israel should be saved" (Rom. 11:25, 26). This vastly important statement is given by Matthew only. **44. And whosoever shall fall on this stone shall be broken: but on whomsoever it shall fall, it will grind him to powder**—The Kingdom of God is here a Temple, in the erection of which a *certain stone,* rejected as unsuitable by the spiritual builders, is, by the great Lord of the House, made the keystone of the whole. On that Stone the builders were now "falling" and being "broken" (Isa. 8:15). They were sustaining great spiritual hurt; but soon that Stone should "fall upon *them*" and "grind them to powder" (Dan. 2:34, 35; Zech. 12:2)—in their *corporate* capacity, in the tremendous destruction of Jerusalem, but *personally,* as unbelievers, in a more awful sense still. **45. And when the chief priests and Pharisees had heard his parables**—referring to that of the Two Sons and this one of the Wicked Husbandmen—**they perceived that he spake of them.**

ADAM CLARKE

41. *He will miserably destroy those wicked men.* So, according to this Evangelist, our Lord caused them to pass that sentence of destruction upon themselves which was literally executed about forty years after.

42. *The stone.* R. Solom. Jarchi, on Micah v, says this *stone* means the Messiah. This seems to have been originally spoken of David, who was at first rejected by the Jewish rulers, but was afterwards chosen by the Lord to be the great ruler of His people, Israel. The quotation is taken from Ps. cxviii. 22. *The builders.* The chief priests and elders of the people, with the doctors of the law. *Rejected.* An expression borrowed from masons, who, finding a stone, which being tried in a particular place, and appearing improper for it, is thrown aside, and another taken; however, at last, it may happen that the very stone which had been before rejected may be found the most suitable as the headstone of the corner.

43. *Therefore say I.* Thus showing them that to them alone the parable belonged. *The kingdom of God shall be taken from you*—the gospel shall be taken from you, and given to the Gentiles, who will receive it, and bring forth fruit to the glory of God. *Bringing forth the fruits.* As in verse 34 an allusion is made to paying the landlord in kind, so here the Gentiles are represented as paying God thus. The returns which He expects for His grace are the fruits of grace; nothing can ever be acceptable in the sight of God that does not spring from himself.

44. The forty-fourth verse should certainly come before v. 43; otherwise the narration is not consecutive. This is an allusion to the punishment of stoning among the Jews. The place of stoning was twice as high as a man. While standing on this, one of the witnesses struck the culprit on the loins, so that he fell over this scaffold; if he died by the stroke and fall, well; if not, the other witness threw a stone upon his heart, and dispatched him. The stone thrown on the culprit was, in some cases, as much as two men could lift up.

45. *The chief priests . . . perceived that he spake of them.* The most wholesome advice passes for an affront with those who have shut their hearts against the truth. When that which should lead to repentance only kindles the flame of malice and revenge, there is but little hope of the salvation of such persons.

MATTHEW HENRY

own doom. A guilty conscience needs no accuser.

2. *They sought to lay hands on him.* When those who hear the reproofs of the word, perceive that it speaks of them, if it do not do them a great deal of good, it will certainly do them a great deal of hurt.

3. They durst not do it, *for fear of the multitude, who took him for a prophet.* God has many ways of restraining the remainders of wrath, as he has of making that which breaks out redound to his praise.

CHAPTER 22

Verses 1-14

We have here the parable of the guests invited to *the wedding-feast.* In this it is said (*v.* 1), *Jesus answered,* not to what his opposers *said,* but to what they *thought.* Christ knows how to answer men's thoughts, for he is a discerner of them. This parable represents the gospel offer, and the entertainment it meets with.

I. Gospel preparations are here represented by a feast which a king made *at the marriage of his son.*

1. Here is *a marriage made for his son.* Christ is the Bridegroom, the church is the bride. The gospel covenant is a marriage covenant betwixt Christ and believers.

2. Here is *a dinner prepared for this marriage, v.* 4. All the blessings of the new covenant, pardon of sin, the favour of God, peace of conscience, the promises of the gospel, the comforts of the Spirit, and a well-grounded hope of eternal life. These are the preparations for this feast, a heaven upon earth now, and a heaven in heaven shortly.

(1) It is *a feast. Oxen and fatlings are killed* for this feast; no niceties, but substantial food; enough, and enough of the best. A feast was made for love, it is a reconciliation feast. It was made *for laughter,* it is a rejoicing feast. It was made for fulness; the design of the gospel was to fill every *hungry soul with good things.* It was made for fellowship.

(2) It is a *wedding feast.* Wedding feasts are usually rich, free, and joyful. The first miracle Christ wrought, was, to make plentiful provision for a wedding feast (John ii. 7); and surely then he will not be wanting in provision for his own wedding feast.

(3) It is a *royal wedding feast;* it is *the feast of a king,* at the marriage, not of a servant, but of a son. The provision made for believers in the covenant of grace, is such as it becomes *the King of glory* to give. He gives like himself; for he gives himself, a feast indeed for a soul.

II. Gospel calls and offers are represented by an invitation to this feast. Those that make a feast will have guests to grace the feast with. God's guests are the children of men. *Lord, what is man,* that he should be thus dignified!

Now, 1. The guests *are called, bidden* to the wedding. All that are within hearing of the joyful sound of the gospel, to them is the word of this invitation sent. None are excluded but those that exclude themselves.

2. The guests are called upon; for in the gospel there are not only gracious proposals made, but gracious persuasives. See how much Christ's heart is set upon the happiness of poor souls! He not only provides for them, in consideration of their want, but sends to them, in consideration of their weakness and forgetfulness. When the invited guests were slack in coming, the king *sent forth other servants, v.* 4. One would think it had been enough to give men an intimation that they had leave to come, and should be welcome; that, during the solemnity of the wedding, the king kept open house. *Behold, the dinner is prepared, the oxen and fatlings are killed, and all things are ready;* pardon is ready, peace is ready, comfort is ready; the promises are ready, and heaven, at last, is ready to receive us. Is all this ready; and shall we be unready? Is all this preparation made for us; and is there any room to doubt of our welcome?

III. The cold treatment which the gospel of Christ often meets with among the children of men, represented by the cold treatment that this message met with and the hot treatment that the messengers met with.

1. The message was basely slighted (*v.* 3); *They would not come.* The reason why sinners come not to Christ and salvation by him is, not because they *cannot,* but because *they will not.* But this was not all (*v.* 5); *they made light of it;* they thought it not worth coming for; they could feast as well at home. Multitudes perish eternally through mere carelessness, who have not any direct aversion, but a prevailing indifference, to the matters of their souls.

And the reason why *they made light of the marriage feast* was, because they had other things that they minded more, and had more mind to; *they went*

JAMIESON, FAUSSET, BROWN

46. But when they sought to lay hands on him—which Luke (20:19) says they did "the same hour," hardly able to restrain their rage. **they feared the multitude**—rather, 'the multitudes'—**because they took him for a prophet**—just as they feared to say John's baptism was of men, because the masses took him for a prophet (vs. 26). Miserable creatures! So, for this time, "they left Him and went their way" (Mark 12:12).

CHAPTER 22

VSS. 1-14. PARABLE OF THE MARRIAGE OF THE KING'S SON. This is a different parable from that of the Great Supper, in Luke 14:15, etc., and is recorded by Matthew alone. **2. The kingdom of heaven is like unto a certain king, which made a marriage for his son**—"In this parable," as TRENCH admirably remarks, "we see how the Lord is revealing Himself in ever clearer light as the central Person of the kingdom, giving here a far plainer hint than in the last parable of the nobility of His descent. There He was indeed the Son, the only and beloved one (Mark 12:6), of the Householder; but here His race is royal, and He appears as Himself at once the King and the King's Son (Ps. 72:1). The last was a parable of the Old Testament history; and Christ is rather the last and greatest of the line of its prophets and teachers than the founder of a new kingdom. In that, God appears *demanding* something *from* men; in this, a parable of grace, God appears more as *giving* something *to* them. Thus, as often, the two complete each other: this taking up the matter where the other left it." The "marriage" of Jehovah to His people Israel was familiar to Jewish ears; and in Psalm 45 this marriage is seen consummated in the Person of Messiah "THE KING," Himself addressed as "GOD" and yet as anointed by "HIS GOD" with the oil of gladness above His fellows. These apparent contradictions (see on Luke 20:41-44) are resolved in this parable; and Jesus, in claiming to be this King's Son, *serves Himself Heir to all that the prophets and sweet singers of Israel held forth as to Jehovah's ineffably near and endearing union to His people.* But observe carefully, that THE BRIDE does not come into view in this parable; its design being to teach certain truths under the figure of *guests* at a wedding *feast,* and the want of a wedding *garment,* which would not have harmonized with the introduction of the Bride. **3. and sent forth his servants**—representing all preachers of the Gospel. **to call them that were bidden**—here meaning the Jews, who were "bidden," from the first choice of them onwards through every summons addressed to them by the prophets to hold themselves in readiness for the appearing of their King. **to the wedding**—or the marriage festivities, when the preparations were all concluded.

4. my oxen and my fatlings are killed, and all things are ready; come unto the marriage—This points to those Gospel calls *after* Christ's death, resurrection, ascension, and effusion of the Spirit, to which the parable could not directly allude, but when only it could be said, with strict propriety, "that all things were ready." Cf. I Corinthians 5:7, 8, "Christ our Passover is sacrificed for us; therefore, let us keep the feast"; also John 6:51, "I am the living bread which came down from heaven: if any man eat of this bread, he shall live for ever: and the bread which I will give is My flesh, which I will give for the life of the world." **and they would not come**—as the issue of the whole ministry of the Baptist, our Lord Himself, and His apostles thereafter, too sadly showed.

5. But they made light of it, and went their ways, one to his farm, another to his merchandise: 6. And the remnant took his servants, and entreated them

ADAM CLARKE

CHAPTER 22

2. *The kingdom of heaven.* It appears from Luke xiv. 15 that it was at an entertainment that this parable was originally spoken. It was a constant practice of our Lord to take the subjects of His discourses from the persons present, or from the circumstances of times, persons, and places. See chap. xvi. 6; John iv. 7-10; vi. 26-27; vii. 37. A preacher that can do so can never be at a loss for text or sermon. *A marriage for his son.* "A marriage feast." Or a feast of inauguration, when his son was put in possession of the government, and thus he and his new subjects became married together. See 1 Kings i. 5-9, 19, 25, where such a feast is mentioned. From this parable it appears plain that: (1) the king means the great God; (2) his son, the Lord Jesus; (3) the marriage, His incarnation, or espousing human nature, by taking it into union with himself; (4) the marriage feast, the economy of the gospel, during which men are invited to partake of the blessings purchased by, and consequent on, the incarnation and death of our blessed Lord; (5) by those who had been bidden, or "invited," v. 3, are meant the Jews in general, who had this union of Christ with human nature, and His sacrifice for sin, pointed out by various rites, ceremonies, and sacrifices under the law, and who by all the prophets had been constantly invited to believe in and receive the promised Messiah; (6) by the servants, we are to understand the first preachers of the gospel, proclaiming salvation to the Jews—John the Baptist and the seventy disciples, Luke x. 1 may be here particularly intended; (7) by the other servants, v. 4, the apostles seem to be meant, who, though they were to preach the gospel to the whole world, yet were to begin at Jerusalem, Luke xxiv. 47, with the first offers of mercy; (8) by their making light of it, v. 5, is pointed out their neglect of this salvation, and their preferring secular enjoyments to the kingdom of Christ; (9) by injuriously using some and slaying others of his servants, v. 6, is pointed out the persecution raised against the apostles by the Jews, in which some of them were martyred; (10) by sending forth his troops, v. 7, is meant the commission given to the Romans against Judea; and by the burning of their city, the total destruction of Jerusalem by Titus, the son of Vespasian, which happened about forty years after.

4. *Fatlings.* Properly, "fatted rams," 2 Sam. vi. 13; 1 Chron. xv. 26.

MATTHEW HENRY

their ways, one to his farm, and another to his merchandise. None turn their back on the feast, but given some plausible excuse or other, Luke xiv. 18. The country people have their farms to look after, about which there is always something or other to do; the town's people must tend their shops, and be constant upon the exchange. It is true, that both farmers and merchants must be diligent in their business, but not so as to keep them from making religion their main business. Both the city and the country have their temptations, the merchandise in the one, and the farms in the other; so that, whatever we have of the world in our hands, our care must be to keep it out of our hearts, lest it come between us and Christ.

2. The messengers were basely abused; *The remnant, the scribes and Pharisees, and chief priests;* these were the persecutors, these *took the servants, and treated them spitefully, and slew them.* In the application of the parable, it was matter of fact. The prophets and John the Baptist had been thus abused already, and the apostles and ministers of Christ must count upon the same.

IV. The utter ruin that was coming upon the Jewish church and nation is here represented by the revenge which the king, in wrath, took on these insolent recusants (*v.* 7); *He was wroth.*

1. What was the crying sin that brought the ruin; it was their being *murderers.* He does not say, he destroyed those *despisers of his call,* but *those murderers of his servants*; as if God were more jealous for the lives of his ministers than for the honour of his gospel. Persecution of Christ's faithful ministers fills the measure of guilt more than anything.

2. What was the ruin itself, that was coming; *He sent forth his armies.* The Roman armies were his armies, of his raising. God is the Lord of men's hosts, and makes what use he pleases of them, to serve his own purposes. It is set forth for an example to all that should oppose Christ and his gospel.

V. The bringing in of the Gentiles, is here represented by the furnishing of the feast with guests *out of the highways, v.* 8–10.

Here is, 1. The complaint of the master of the feast concerning those that were first bidden (*v.* 8), *The wedding is ready, but they which were bidden,* that is, the Jews, *were not worthy,* they were utterly unworthy, and had forfeited all the privileges they were invited to. It is not owing to God, that sinners perish, but to themselves.

2. The commission he gave to the servants, to invite other guests. The inhabitants of the *city* (*v.* 7) had refused; *Go into the highways* then; into *the way of the Gentiles,* which at first they were to decline, *ch.* x. 5. Thus by the fall of the Jews salvation is come to the Gentiles. Christ will have a *kingdom in the world,* though many reject the grace, and resist the power, of that kingdom. The offer of Christ and salvation to the Gentiles was, (1) Unlooked for and unexpected; such a surprise as it would be to wayfaring men upon the road to be met with an invitation to a wedding feast. To the Gentiles it was all new, what they had never heard of before (Acts xvii. 19, 20), and, consequently, what they could not conceive of as belonging to them. (2) It was universal and undistinguishing; *Go, and bid as many as you find.* The highways are public places. "Ask them that go by the way, ask anybody, tell them all, that they shall be welcome, whoever will, let him come, without exception."

3. The success of this second invitation (*v.* 10); *They gathered together all, as many as they found.* The design of the gospel is, (1) To gather souls together; not the nation of the Jews only, but *all the children of God* who were *scattered abroad* (John xi. 52), *the other sheep that were not of that fold,* John x. 16. (2) To gather them together to the wedding-feast to partake of the privileges of the new covenant. Where the dole is, there will the poor be gathered together.

Now the guests that were gathered were a multitude, *all, as many as they found*; so many, that the guest-chamber was filled. A mixed multitude, *both bad and good*; some that before their conversion were sober and well-inclined; others that had run to an excess of riot; *Such were some of you;* or, some that after their conversion proved bad; others that were upright and sincere, and proved of the right class. Ministers, in casting the net of the gospel, enclose *both good* fish *and bad.*

VI. The case of hypocrites, who are *in* the church, but not *of* it, is represented by *the guest that had not on a wedding garment*; one of the bad that were gathered in. Concerning this hypocrite observe,

1. His discovery, how he was found out, *v.* 11.

(1) *The king came in to see the guests,* to bid those welcome who came prepared, and to turn those out

JAMIESON, FAUSSET, BROWN

spitefully—insulted them—**and slew them**—These are two different classes of unbelievers: the one simply *indifferent;* the other absolutely *hostile*—the one, contemptuous *scorners;* the other, bitter *persecutors.*

7. But when the king—the Great God, who is the Father of our Lord Jesus Christ. **heard thereof, he was wroth**—at the affront put both on His Son, and on Himself who had deigned to invite them. **and he sent forth his armies**—The *Romans* are here styled God's armies, just as the Assyrian is styled "the rod of His anger" (Isa. 10:5), as being the executors of His judicial vengeance. **and destroyed those murderers**—and in what vast numbers did they do it! **and burned up their city**—Ah! Jerusalem, once "the city of the Great King" (Ps. 48:2), and even up almost to this time (ch. 5:35); but now it is "*their* city"—just as our Lord, a day or two after this, said of the temple, where God had so long dwelt, "Behold *your* house is left unto you desolate" (ch. 23:38)! Cf. Luke 19:43, 44.

8. The wedding is ready, but they which were bidden were not worthy—for how should those be deemed worthy to sit down at His table who had affronted Him by their treatment of His gracious invitation?

9. Go ye therefore into the highways—the great outlets and thoroughfares, whether of town or country, where human beings are to be found. **and as many as ye shall find, bid to the marriage**—i.e., just as they are.

10. So those servants went out into the highways, and gathered together all as many as they found, both bad and good—i.e., without making any distinction between open sinners and the morally correct. The Gospel call fetched in Jews, Samaritans, and outlying heathen alike. Thus far the parable answers to that of 'the Great Supper' (Luke 14:16, etc.). But the distinguishing feature of our parable is what follows:

ADAM CLARKE

ALEXANDER MACLAREN:

Why should they kill men whose only fault was bringing them a hospitable invitation? The incongruity of the representation has given offense to some interpreters, who are not slow to point out how Christ could have improved His parable. But the reality is more incongruous still, and the unmotived outburst of wrath against the innocent bearers of a kindly invitation is only too true to life. Mark the distinction drawn by our Lord between the bulk of the people who simply neglected, and the few who violently opposed. He does not charge the guilt on all. The murderers of Him and of His first followers were not the mass of the nation, who, left to themselves, would not have so acted, but the few who stirred up the many. But, though He does not lay the guilt at the door of all, yet the punishment falls on all, and, when the city is burned, the houses of the negligent and of the slayers are equally consumed; for simple refusal of the message and slaying the messengers were but the positive and superlative degrees of the same crime—rebellion against the king, whose invitation was a command.

—*Expositions of Holy Scripture*

8. *Were not worthy.* Among the Mohammedans, refusal to come to a marriage feast, when invited, is considered a breach of the law of God. Anyone that shall be invited to a dinner and does not accept the invitation disobeys God and His messenger; and anyone who comes uninvited, you may say is a thief, and returns a plunderer. It was probably considered in this light among all the Oriental nations. This observation is necessary in order to point out more forcibly the iniquity of the refusal mentioned in the text.

9. *Go ye therefore into the highways.* "Cross- or by-paths"; the places where two or more roads met in one, leading into the city, where people were coming together from various quarters of the country. Luke adds "hedges," to point out the people to whom the apostles were sent, as either miserable vagabonds or the most indigent poor, who were wandering about the country, or sitting by the sides of the ways and hedges, imploring relief. This verse points out the final rejection of the Jews and the calling of the Gentiles. It was a custom among the Jews, when a rich man made a feast, to go out and invite in all destitute travellers. *As many as ye shall find, bid to the marriage.* God sends His salvation to every soul, that all may believe and be saved.

10. *Gathered together all . . . both bad and good.* By the preaching of the gospel, multitudes of souls are gathered into what is generally termed the visible Church of Christ.

MATTHEW HENRY

who came otherwise. Let this be a warning to us against hypocrisy, that disguises will shortly be stripped off, and an encouragement to us in our sincerity, that God is a witness to it. This hypocrite was never discovered to be without *a wedding garment*, till *the king himself came in to see the guests*. It is God's prerogative to know who are sound at heart in their profession, and who are not. We may be deceived in men, either one way or other; but He cannot.

(2) As soon as he came in, *He saw there a man which had not on a wedding garment;* he soon had his eye upon him; there is no hope of being hid in a crowd from the arrests of divine justice; he had not on a wedding garment; he had not his best clothes on. If the gospel be the wedding feast, then the wedding garment is a frame of heart, and a course of life agreeable to the gospel. This man was not naked, or in rags; some raiment he had, but not a wedding garment. Those, and those only, who *put on the Lord Jesus*, and to whom he is all in all, have the wedding garment.

2. His trial (*v.* 12). How he was arraigned (*v.* 12); *Friend, how camest thou in hither, not having a wedding garment?* A startling question to one that was priding himself in the place he securely possessed at the feast. *Friend!* That was a cutting word; a seeming friend, under manifold ties and obligations to be a friend. *How camest thou in hither?* He does not chide the servants for letting him in, but he checks his presumption in crowding in, when he knew that his heart was not upright. Despised sabbaths and abused sacraments must be reckoned for. "How camest thou to the Lord's table, at such a time, unhumbled and unsanctified? *How camest thou in?* Not by the door, but *some other way, as a thief and a robber*." It is good for those that have a place in the church, often to put it to themselves, "How came I in hither? Have I a wedding-garment?" If we would thus *judge ourselves, we should not be judged*. How he was convicted; *he was speechless*: the man stood mute, upon his arraignment, being convicted and condemned by his own conscience. They who never heard a word of this wedding feast will have more to say for themselves; their sin will be more excusable than theirs who came to the feast without the wedding garment, and so sin against the clearest light and dearest love.

3. His sentence (*v.* 13); *Bind him hand and foot*, &c.

(1) He is ordered to be pinioned, as condemned malefactors are, to be manacled and shackled. Those that will not work and walk as they should, may expect to be bound hand and foot. They can neither resist nor outrun their punishment.

(2) He is ordered to be carried off from the wedding feast; *Take him away*. This bespeaks the punishment of loss in the other world; they shall be taken away from the king, from the kingdom, from the wedding feast. Those that walk unworthy of their christianity, forfeit all the happiness they presumptuously laid claim to.

(3) He is ordered into a doleful dungeon; *Cast him into utter darkness*. Hell is utter darkness, it is darkness out of heaven, the land of light; or it is extreme darkness, darkness to the last degree, without the least ray or spark of light, or hope of it. *There shall be weeping, and gnashing of teeth. Weeping*, an expression of great sorrow and anguish; and the *gnashing of teeth* is an expression of the greatest rage and indignation.

Lastly, The parable is concluded with that remarkable saying which we had before (*ch.* xx. 16), *Many are called, but few are chosen*, *v.* 14. Many called to the wedding feast, but few chosen to the wedding garment.

Verses 15–22

In these verses, we have him attacked by the Pharisees and Herodians with a question about paying tribute to Cæsar.

I. What the design was; *They took counsel to entangle him in his talk*. Now he is set upon from another quarter; the Pharisees will try whether they can deal with him by their learning in the law. It is in vain for the best and wisest of men to think that, by their ingenuity, or interest, or industry, or even by their innocence and integrity, they can escape the hatred and ill will of bad men, or screen themselves from *the strife of tongues*. See how unwearied the enemies of Christ and his kingdom are in their opposition!

1. *They took counsel*. The more there is of contrivance and consultation about sin, the worse it is. The more there is of the wicked wit in the contrivance of a sin, the more there is of the wicked will in the commission of it.

JAMIESON, FAUSSET, BROWN

11. And when the king came in to see the guests—Solemn expression this, of that *omniscient inspection of every professed disciple of the Lord Jesus* from age to age, in virtue of which his true character will hereafter be judicially proclaimed! **he saw there a man**—This shows that it is the judgment of *individuals* which is intended in this latter part of the parable: the first part represents rather *national* judgment. **which had not on a wedding garment**—The language here is drawn from the following remarkable passage in Zephaniah 1:7, 8:—"Hold thy peace at the presence of the Lord God; for the day of the Lord is at hand: for the Lord hath prepared a sacrifice, He hath bid His guests. And it shall come to pass in the day of the Lord's sacrifice, that I will punish the princes, and the king's children, and all such as are clothed with strange apparel." The custom in the East of presenting festival garments (see Gen. 45:22; II Kings 5:22), even though not clearly proved, is certainly presupposed here. It undoubtedly means something which they bring not of their own—for how could they have any such dress who were gathered in from the highways indiscriminately?—but which they *receive* as their appropriate dress. And what can that be but what is meant by "putting on the Lord Jesus," as "THE LORD OUR RIGHTEOUSNESS?" (See Ps. 45:13, 14.) Nor could such language be strange to those in whose ears had so long resounded those words of prophetic joy: "I will greatly rejoice in the Lord, my soul shall be joyful in my God; for He hath clothed me with the garments of salvation, He hath covered me with the robe of righteousness, as a bridegroom decketh himself with ornaments, and as a bride adorneth herself with her jewels" (Isa. 61:10). **12. Friend, how camest thou in hither, not having a wedding garment? And he was speechless**—being self-condemned.

13. Then said the king to the servants—the angelic ministers of divine vengeance (as in ch. 13:41)—**Bind him hand and foot**—putting it out of his power to resist. **and take him away, and cast him into outer darkness**—So ch. 8:12; 25:30. The expression is emphatic—"the darkness which is outside." To be "*outside*" at all—or, in the language of Revelation 22:15, to be "*without*" the heavenly city, excluded from its joyous nuptials and gladsome festivities—is sad enough of itself, without anything else. But to find themselves not only excluded from the brightness and glory and joy and felicity of the kingdom above, but thrust into a region of "darkness," with all its horrors, this is the dismal retribution here announced, that awaits the unworthy at the great day. **there**—in that region and condition. **shall be weeping and gnashing of teeth.** See on ch. 13:42. **14. For many are called, but few are chosen**—So ch. 19:30. See on ch. 20:16.

15-40. ENTANGLING QUESTIONS ABOUT TRIBUTE, THE RESURRECTION, AND THE GREAT COMMANDMENT, WITH THE REPLIES. (= Mark 12:13-34; Luke 20: 20-40.) For the exposition, see on Mark 12:13-34.

The time of this section appears to be still the third day (Tuesday) of Christ's last week. Matthew introduces the subject by saying (22:15), "Then went the Pharisees and took counsel how they might entangle Him in His talk." **And they send unto him certain of the Pharisees**—"their disciples," says Matthew; probably young and zealous scholars in that hardening school. **and of the Herodians**—See on Matthew 22:16. In Luke 20:20 these willing tools are called "spies, which should feign themselves just [righteous] men, that they might take hold of His words, that so they might deliver Him unto the power and authority of the governor." Their plan, then, was to entrap Him into some ex-

ADAM CLARKE

11. *When the king came.* When God shall come to judge the world. *Wedding garment.* Among the Orientals, long white robes were worn at public festivals; and those who appeared on such occasions with any other garments were esteemed, not only highly culpable, but worthy of punishment. This marriage feast or dinner (the communication of the graces of the gospel in this life) prepares for the marriage supper of the Lamb, Rev. xix. 7-9, the enjoyment of eternal blessedness in the Kingdom of glory. Now as without holiness no man can see the Lord, we may at once perceive what our Lord means by the *wedding garment*—it is holiness of heart and life. The text last quoted asserts that the fine, white, and clean linen (alluding to the marriage garment above mentioned) was an emblem of the righteousness of the saints.

12. *He saith unto him, Friend.* Rather, "companion." As this man represents the state of a person in the visible Church who neglects to come unto the Master of the feast for a marriage garment, for the salvation which Christ has procured, he cannot be with any propriety called a *friend*, but may well be termed a "companion," as being a member of the Visible Church. *He was speechless.* He was "muzzled" or "gagged." He had nothing to say in vindication of his neglect. There was a garment provided, but he neither put it on nor applied for it. His conduct, therefore, was in the highest degree insulting and indecorous.

13. *Cast him into outer darkness.* The Jewish marriages were performed in the night season, and the hall where the feast was made was superbly illuminated.

The *outer darkness* means, therefore, the darkness on the outside of this festal hall, rendered still more gloomy to the person who was suddenly thrust out into it from such a profusion of light.

MATTHEW HENRY

2. That which they aimed at was *to entangle him in his talk.* They saw him free and bold in speaking his mind, and hoped by that to get an advantage against him. It has been the old practice of Satan's agents and emissaries, to make a man an offender for a word, a word misplaced, or mistaken, or misunderstood; a word, though innocently designed, yet perverted by strained innuendos.

There are two ways by which the enemies of Christ might be revenged on him, and be rid of him; either by law or by force. By law they could not do it, unless they could make him obnoxious to the civil government. By force they could not do it, unless they could make him obnoxious to the people, but the people took Christ for a Prophet, and therefore his enemies could not raise the mob against him. The design was, to bring him into such a dilemma, that he must make himself liable to the displeasure either of the Jewish multitude, or of the Roman magistrates; let him take which side of the question he will. So they will gain their point, and make his own tongue to fall upon him.

II. The question which they put to him, *v.* 16, 17.

1. The persons they employed; they did not go themselves, but they sent their disciples, who would look less like tempters, and more like learners. Wicked men will never want wicked instruments to be employed in carrying on their wicked counsels.

With them they sent the Herodians, a party among the Jews, who made it their business to reconcile people to that government, and pressed all to pay their tribute. They went with the Pharisees to Christ, with this blind upon their plot, that while the Herodians demanded the tax, and the Pharisees denied it, they were both willing to refer it to Christ, as a proper Judge to decide the quarrel. Now, if he should countenance the paying of tribute, the Pharisees would incense the people against him; if he should discountenance or disallow it, the Herodians would incense the government against him. It is common for those that oppose one another, to continue in an opposition to Christ and his kingdom. Samson's foxes looked several ways, but met in one firebrand.

2. The preface; it was highly complimentary to our Sàviour (*v.* 16); *Master, we know that thou art true, and teachest the way of God in truth.* Note, It is a common thing for the most spiteful projects to be covered with the most specious pretences. Had they come to Christ with the most serious enquiry, and the most sincere intention, they could not have expressed themselves better. What they said of Christ was right that Jesus Christ was a faithful Teacher; *Thou art true, and teachest the way of God in truth.* He is the Truth itself. As for his doctrine, the matter of his teaching was the way of God that leads to happiness. The manner of it was in truth; he showed people *the right way.* That he was a bold Reprover. In preaching, he *cared not for any*; he valued no man's frowns or smiles, he did not court, he did not dread, either the great or the many. He *reproved with equity*, and never with partiality. Though what they said was true for the matter of it, yet there was nothing but flattery and treachery in the intention of it. They called him *Master*, when they were contriving to treat him as the worst of malefactors; they pretended respect for him, when they intended mischief against him; and they affronted his wisdom when they imagined that they could impose upon him with these pretences.

3. The proposal of the case; *What thinkest thou?* As if they had said, "Many men are of many minds in this matter; it is a case which relates to practice, and occurs daily; let us have thy thoughts freely in the matter, *Is it lawful to give tribute to Cæsar, or not?"* This implies a further question; Has Cæsar a right to demand it?

Now the question was, Whether it was lawful to pay these taxes voluntarily or, Whether they should not insist upon the ancient liberty of their nation, and rather suffer themselves to be distrained upon?

However, by this question they hoped to entangle Christ, and, which way soever he resolved it, to expose him to the fury either of the jealous Jews, or of the jealous Romans.

III. The breaking of this snare by the wisdom of the Lord Jesus.

1. He discovered it (*v.* 18); *He perceived their wickedness.* A temptation perceived is half conquered, for our greatest danger lies from snakes under the green grass; *and he said, Why tempt ye me, ye hypocrites?* Whatever vizard the hypocrite puts on, our Lord Jesus sees through it. He cannot be imposed upon, as we often are, by flatteries and fair pretences. *Why tempt ye me, ye hypocrites?* Those that presume to tempt Christ will certainly find him too hard for them, and that he is of more piercing eyes than not

JAMIESON, FAUSSET, BROWN

pression which might be construed into disaffection to the Roman government; the Pharisees themselves being notoriously discontented with the Roman yoke.

And when they were come, they say unto him, Master—Teacher—**we know that thou art true, and carest for no man; for thou regardest not the person of men, but teachest the way of God in truth**—By such flattery—though they said only the truth—they hoped to throw Him off His guard.

Is it lawful to give tribute to Cæsar, or not?—It was the civil poll-tax paid by all enrolled in the "census." See on Matthew 17:25.

But he, knowing their hypocrisy—"their wickedness" (Matt. 22:18); "their craftiness" (Luke 20:23). The malignity of their hearts took the form of craft, pretending what they did not feel—an anxious desire to be guided aright in a matter which to a scrupulous few might seem a question of some difficulty. Seeing perfectly through this, He **said unto them, Why tempt ye me?**—hypocrites!"

TODAY'S DICTIONARY OF THE BIBLE:

Herodians, a Jewish political party who sympathized with (Matt. 22:16; Mark 3:6; 12:13; Luke 20:20) the Herodian rulers in their general policy of government, and in the social customs which they introduced from Rome. They were at one with the Sadducees in holding the duty of submission of Rome, and of supporting the Herods on the throne. (Comp. Matt. 16:6; Mark 8:15.)

ADAM CLARKE

15. *In his talk.* "By discourse," intending to ask Him subtle and ensnaring questions, His answers to which might involve Him either with the Roman government or with the great Sanhedrin.

16. *The Herodians.* The preceding parable had covered the Pharisees with confusion. When it was ended they went out, not to humble themselves before God and deprecate the judgments with which they were threatened, but to plot afresh the destruction of their Teacher. The depth of their malice appears (1) in their mode of attack. They had often questioned our Lord on matters concerning religion, and His answers only served to increase His reputation and their confusion. They now shift their ground, and question Him concerning state affairs, and the question is such as must be answered; and yet the answer, to all human appearance, can be none other than what may be construed into a crime against the people or against the Roman government. (2) Their profound malice appears further in the choice of their companions in this business, viz., the Herodians. Herod himself was extremely attached to the Roman emperor, and made a public profession of it. All these considerations engaged the Pharisees to unite with the Herodians, who, as the Syriac intimates, were the domestics of Herod, in this infernal plot. (3) Their profound malice appears further in the praises they gave our Lord. "Teacher, *we know that thou art true, and teachest the way of God.*" This was indeed the real character of our blessed Lord; and now they bear testimony to the truth, merely with the design to make it subserve their bloody purposes. (4) Their malice appears still further in the question they propose.

Is it lawful to give tribute unto Caesar, or not?—v. 17. The constitution of the Jewish republic rendered an answer to this question extremely difficult: (1) In the presence of the people, who professed to have no other king but God, and looked on their independence as an essential point of their religion; (2) In the presence of the Pharisees, who were ready to stir up the people against Him if His decision could be at all construed to be contrary to their prejudices or to their religious rights. (3) In the presence of the Herodians, who, if the answer should appear to be against Caesar's rights, were ready to inflame their master to avenge, by the death of our Lord, the affront offered to his master, the emperor.

MATTHEW HENRY

to see, and more pure eyes than not to hate the disguised wickedness of hypocrites, that dig deep to hide their counsel from him.

2. He evaded it. (Such captious malicious questions deserve a reproof, not a reply): but our Lord Jesus gave a full answer to their question, and introduced it by an argument sufficient to support it.

(1) He forced them, ere they were aware, to confess Cæsar's authority over them, *v.* 19, 20. In dealing with those that are captious, it is good to give our reasons, and, if possible, reasons of confessed cogency, before we give our resolutions. Thus the evidence of truth may silence gainsayers by surprise, while they only stood upon their guard against the truth itself, not against the reason of it; *Show me the tribute-money.* The Romans demanded their tribute in their own money, which was current among the Jews at that time: that therefore is called the *tribute-money. A penny,* a Roman penny in silver, the most common piece then in use: it was stamped with the emperor's image and superscription, which was the warrant of the public faith for the value of the pieces so stamped.

Christ asked them, *Whose image is this?* They owned it to be Cæsar's.

(2) From thence he inferred the lawfulness of paying tribute to Cæsar (*v.* 21); *Render therefore to Cæsar the things that are Cæsar's;* not, "*Give* it him" (as they expressed it, *v.* 17), but, "Restore it; if Cæsar fill the purses, let Cæsar command them. When once a relation is admitted, the duty of it must be performed. *Render to all their due,* and particularly *tribute to whom tribute is due.*" Now by this answer, No offence was given. He did not interpose as a Judge or a Divider in matters of this nature. Christ discusses not the emperor's title, but enjoins a peaceable subjection to *the powers that be.* The government therefore had no reason to take offence at his determination, but to thank him, for it would strengthen Cæsar's interest with the people, who held him for a Prophet. As to the people, the Pharisees could not accuse him to them, because they themselves had, before they were aware, yielded the premises. Though truth seeks not a fraudulent concealment, yet it sometimes needs a prudent management, to prevent the offence which may be taken at it. His adversaries were reproved. Many excuse themselves from that which they must do, by arguing whether they may do it or no. They all withheld from God his dues, and are reproved for that. His disciples were instructed.

First, That the Christian religion is no enemy to civil government, but a friend to it.

Secondly, It is the duty of subjects to tender to magistrates that which, according to the laws of their country, is their due. The higher powers, being entrusted with the public welfare, are entitled, in consideration thereof, to a just proportion of the public wealth. It is doubtless a greater sin to cheat the government than to cheat a private person. My coat is my coat, by the law of man; but he is a thief, by the law of God, that takes it from me.

Thirdly, We must remember withal to render to God the things that are God's. If our purses be Cæsar's, our consciences are God's; we must render to God that which is his due, out of our time and out of our estates; from them he must have his share as well as Cæsar his; and if Cæsar's commands interfere with God's *we must obey God rather than men.*

Lastly, Observe how they were nonplussed by this answer; they *marvelled, and left him, and went their way, v.* 22. They admired his sagacity in discovering and evading a snare which they thought so craftily laid. One would think they should have marvelled and followed him; no, they marvelled and left him. There are many in whose eyes Christ is marvellous, and yet not precious. They admire his wisdom, but will not be guided by it. *They went their way,* as persons ashamed, and made an inglorious retreat. They quitted the field. There is nothing got by contending with Christ.

Verses 23-33

We have here Christ's dispute with the Sadducees concerning the resurrection.

I. The opposition which the Sadducees made to a very great truth of religion; they say, *There is no resurrection.* They lie under heavy censures among the writers of their own nation, as men of base and debauched conversations. They were the fewest in number of all the sects among the Jews, but generally persons of some rank. They said, There is no future state, no life after this; that, when the body dies, the soul is annihilated, and dies with it. They maintained, that, except God, there is no spirit (Acts xxiii. 8). The Pharisees and Sadducees were contrary

JAMIESON, FAUSSET, BROWN

bring me a penny that I may see it—"the tribute money" (Matt. 22:19). **And they brought it.**

And he saith unto them, Whose is this image—stamped upon the coin. **and superscription?**—the words encircling it on the obverse side. **And they said unto him, Cæsar's. And Jesus answering said unto them, Render to Cæsar the things that are Cæsar's**—Putting it in this general form, it was impossible for sedition itself to dispute it, and yet it dissolved the snare.

and to God the things that are God's—How much is there in this profound but to them startling addition to the maxim, and how incomparable is the whole for fulness, brevity, clearness, weight!

and they marvelled at him—"at His answer, and held their peace" (Luke 20:26), "and left Him, and went their way" (Matt. 22:22).

Then come unto him the Sadducees, which say there is no resurrection—"neither angel nor spirit" (Acts 23:7). They were the materialists of the day. See on Acts 23:7.

ADAM CLARKE

20. *Whose is this image and superscription?* He knew well enough whose they were, but He showed the excellency of His wisdom in making them answer to their own confusion. They came to ensnare our Lord in His discourse, and now they are ensnared in their own. He who digs a pit for his neighbor ordinarily falls into it himself.

21. *They say unto him, Caesar's.* The *image* was the head of the emperor; the *superscription,* his titles. Tiberius was emperor at this time. *Render therefore unto Caesar.* The conclusion is drawn from their own premises. You acknowledge this to be Caesar's coin; this coin is current in your land; the currency of this coin shows the country to be under the Roman government; and your acknowledgment that it is Caesar's proves you have submitted. Do not, therefore, be unjust; but render to Caesar the things which you acknowledge to be his; at the same time, be not impious, but render unto God the things which belong to God. The image of princes stamped on their coin denotes that temporal things belong all to their government. The image of God stamped on the soul denotes that all its faculties and powers belong to the Most High, and should be employed in His service.

22. *When they had heard these words, they marvelled.* And well they might—"Never man spake like this man." By this decision Caesar is satisfied—he gets his own to the uttermost farthing. God is glorified—His honor is in every respect secured. And the people are edified—one of the most difficult questions that could possibly come before them is answered in such a way as to relieve their consciences and direct their conduct.

MATTHEW HENRY

to each other, and yet confederates against Christ.

II. The objection they made against the truth, which was taken from a supposed case of a woman that had seven husbands successively; now they take it for granted, that, if there be a resurrection, it must be a return to such a state as this we are now in; and if so, it is an invincible absurdity for this woman, in the future state to have seven husbands, or else an insuperable difficulty which of them should have her, he whom she had first, or he whom she had last, or he whom she loved best, or he whom she lived longest with.

1. They suggest the law of Moses in this matter (*v.* 24), that the next of kin should marry the widow of him that died childless (Deut. xxv. 5). It was a political law to preserve the distinction of families and inheritances.

2. They put a case upon this statute. If it had not really occurred, yet possibly it might. Now this case supposes,

(1) The desolations that death sometimes makes in families. It often sweeps away a whole fraternity in a little time.

(2) The obedience of these seven brothers to the law. The seventh, who ventured last to marry the widow (many a one would say) was a *bold* man. I would say, if he did it purely in obedience to God, he was a *good* man, and one that made conscience of his duty.

But, *last of all, the woman died also.* Survivorship is but a reprieve. Death's bitter cup goes round, and, sooner or later, we must all pledge in it.

3. They propose a doubt upon this case (*v.* 28); "*In the resurrection, whose wife shall she be of the seven?* You cannot tell whose; and therefore we must conclude *there is no resurrection.*" The Pharisees, who professed to believe a resurrection, had very gross and carnal notions concerning the future state; expecting to find there the delights and pleasures of the animal life, which perhaps drove the Sadducees to deny the thing itself. While those that are erroneous deny the truth, those that are superstitious betray it to them. Let truth be set in a clear light, and then it appears in its full strength.

III. Christ's answer to this objection.

1. He reproves their ignorance (*v.* 29); *Ye do err.* Those do greatly err, in the judgment of Christ, who deny the resurrection and a future state. Here Christ reproved with the meekness of wisdom, and is not so sharp upon them (whatever was the reason) as sometimes he was upon the chief priests and elders; *Ye do err, not knowing.* Ignorance is the cause of error; those that are in the dark, miss their way. Ingorance is the cause of error about the resurrection and the future state. *What* it is in its particular instances, the wisest and best know not; it doth not yet appear what we shall be, it is a glory that is to be revealed. But that *is* a thing about which we are not left in the dark, blessed be God, we are not. *They know not the power of God;* which would lead men to infer that there *may be a* resurrection and a future state. The ignorance, disbelief, or weak belief, of God's power, is at the bottom of many errors, particularly theirs who deny the resurrection. When we are told of the soul's existence and agency in a state of separation from the body, we are ready to say, *How can these things be?* If a man die, shall he live again? And vain men, because they cannot comprehend the *way* of it, question the *truth* of it. This therefore we must fasten upon, in the first place, that God is omnipotent, and can do what he will; and then no room is left for doubting but that he will do what he has promised. His power far exceeds the power of nature. *They know not the scriptures,* which decidedly affirm that there shall be a resurrection and a future state. Now the scriptures speak plainly, that the soul is immortal, and there is another life after this. Christ rose again *according to the scriptures* (1 Cor. xv. 3); and so shall we. Ignorance of the scripture is the rise of abundance of mischief.

2. He rectifies their mistake and (*v.* 30) corrects those gross ideas which they had of the resurrection and a future state. It is not like the state we are now in upon earth; *They neither marry, nor are given in marriage.* In our present state marriage is necessary. All civilised nations have had a sense of the obligation of the marriage covenant. But, in the resurrection, there is no occasion for marriage. In heaven, *where there shall be no more deaths* (Rev. xxi. 4), there need be no more births.

It is like the state angels are now in, in heaven; *They are as the angels of God in heaven.* Man in his creation was *made a little lower than the angels* (Ps. viii. 5); but in his complete redemption and renovation will be as the angels; pure and spiritual as the angels, knowing and loving, ever praising God like them and with them. We should *therefore* desire and

JAMIESON, FAUSSET, BROWN

Do ye not therefore err, because ye know not the scriptures—regarding the future state. **neither the power of God?**—before which a thousand such difficulties vanish.

For when they shall rise from the dead, they neither marry, nor are given in marriage—"neither can they die any more" (Luke 20:36). Marriage is ordained to perpetuate the human family; but as there will be no breaches by death in the future state, this ordinance will cease.

are as the angels which are in heaven—In Luke it is "equal unto the angels." But as the subject is death and resurrection, we are not warranted to extend the equality here taught beyond the one point—the *immortality* of their nature. A beautiful clause is added in Luke—"and are the children

ADAM CLARKE

24. *Raise up seed unto his brother.* This law is mentioned in Deut. xxv. 5. The meaning of the expression is that the children produced by this marriage should be reckoned in the genealogy of the deceased brother and enjoy his estates. The word *seed* should be always translated "children" or "posterity."

25. *Seven brethren.* It is very likely that the Sadducees increased the number, merely to make the question the more difficult.

29. *Ye do err.* Or, "Ye are deceived"—by your impure passions, *not knowing the scriptures,* which assert the resurrection, *nor the* miraculous *power of God* by which it is to be effected.

A. B. SIMPSON:

It was a rather coarse story about a woman who had been married in succession to seven different brothers as they had successively died and she had married the next according to the Levitical law. At last she herself died, and now the absorbing question arises in their earnest and inquiring minds: "What are they all to do in the resurrection? What a perplexing time they will have, and which of them is to be her true husband then?"

It was a taking question, and for a moment there must have been many in the crowd that caught the ludicrousness of the idea, and nothing but infinite wisdom could have turned aside the force of the blow. But again the Lord was equal to it. The "greater than Solomon" was there. With quiet dignity He turns upon them with their own words: "Ye do err, not knowing the scriptures, nor the power of God." And then He proceeds to explain the true doctrine of the resurrection and to show them that it is not a resumption of the coarser material forms of our earthly life, but a higher existence in which we shall have passed beyond the laws of reproduction and shall dwell in a loftier fellowship with one another, even as the angels now, and all mere human relations shall pass into divine relations.—*Christ in the Bible*

G. CAMPBELL MORGAN:

This answer of Jesus was a most remarkable one. He went beneath the surface to the underlying fact of God. "God is not the God of the dead." The difficulty as to the bodily resurrection of a man is no difficulty at all when the question concerning God is settled. When a man understands the truth that the Bible reveals concerning God, the difficulties that the Bible presents concerning man, and what we call the supernatural, melt into thin air. He said to these rationalists in effect, "You are building your view of the impossibility of resurrection upon a misconception of God. Ye neither know the Scriptures, nor the power of God; which does not merely mean God's power to do this one thing, but God's essential power, the truth concerning God. God is the God of the living.
—*The Gospel According to Matthew*

MATTHEW HENRY

endeavour to do the will of God now as the angels do it in heaven, because we hope shortly to be like the angels who always behold our Father's face.

IV. Christ's argument to confirm this great truth; the matters being of great concern, he did not think it enough to discover the fallacy and sophistry of the objections, but backed the truth with a solid argument.

1. Whence he fetched his argument—from the scripture. *It is written* is Goliath's sword. *Have ye not read that which was spoken to you by God?* What the scripture speaks God speaks. What was spoken to Moses was spoken to us. It concerns us to read and hear what God hath spoken, because it is spoken to us. The latter prophets have more express proofs of a future state than the law of Moses has. No express revelation of it is made by the law of Moses; because so much of that law was peculiar to that people; but our Saviour finds a very solid argument for the resurrection even in the writings of Moses. Much scripture treasure lies underground, that must be digged for.

2. What his argument was (*v.* 32); *I am the God of Abraham.* This was not an express proof, and yet it was really a conclusive argument. Consequences from scripture, if rightly deduced, must be received as scripture,; for it was written for those that have the use of reason.

Now the drift of the argument is to prove,

(1) That there is a future state, another life after this. This is proved from what God said; *I am the God of Abraham.* For God to be anyone's God supposes some very extraordinary privileges and happiness. The God *of* Israel is a God *to* Israel, a spiritual Benefactor; an all-sufficient Benefactor, a God that is enough, a complete Good, and an eternal Benefactor; for he is himself an everlasting God, and will be to those that are in covenant with him an everlasting Good. It is manifest that these good men had no such extraordinary happiness, in *this* life, as might look anything like the accomplishments of so great a word as that. They were strangers in the land of promise; they had not a foot of ground of their own but a burying-place, which directed them to look for something beyond this life. In present enjoyments they came far short of their neighbours that were strangers to this covenant. What was there in this world to distinguish them from other people, any whit proportionable to the dignity and distinction of this covenant? Therefore there must certainly be a future state, in which, as God will ever live to be eternally rewarding, so Abraham, Isaac, and Jacob, will ever live to be eternally rewarded.

(2) That the soul is immortal, and the body shall rise again, to be united; if the former point be gained, these will follow; but they are likewise proved by considering the time when God spoke this; it was to Moses at the bush, long after Abraham, Isaac, and Jacob were dead and buried; and yet God saith, not, "*I was,*" or "*have been,*" but, *I am the God of Abraham.* Now *God is not the God of the dead, but of the living.* Which proves the immortality of the soul in a state of bliss; and that, by consequence, infers the resurrection of the body.

Lastly, We have the issue of this dispute. The Sadducees were *put to silence* (*v.* 34), and so put to shame. But the multitude *were astonished at his doctrine, v.* 33. 1. Because it was new to them. They had sorry scribes, or this had been no news to them. 2. Because it had something in it very good and great. Truth often shows the brighter, and is the more admired, for its being opposed.

Verses 34–40

I. The combination of the Pharisees against Christ, *v.* 34. They heard *that he had put the Sadducees to silence*; and they were *gathered together,* not to return him the thanks of their party, for his effectually asserting and confirming of the truth against the Sadducees, but to *tempt him,* in hopes to get the reputation of puzzling him who had puzzled the Sadducees. They were more vexed that Christ was honoured, than pleased that the Sadducees were silenced. It is an instance of Pharisaical envy and malice, to be displeased at the maintaining of a confessed truth, when it is done by those we do not like.

II. The lawyer's question, which he put to Christ. The lawyers were students in, and teachers of the law of Moses, as the scribes were. This lawyer *asked him a question, tempting him*; not with any design to ensnare him, as appears by St. Mark's relation of the story, where we find that this was he to whom Christ said, *Thou art not far from the kingdom of God,* Mark xii. 34, but only to see what he would say, and to draw on discourse with him, to satisfy his own and his friend's curiosity.

JAMIESON, FAUSSET, BROWN

of God"—not in respect of *character,* which is not here spoken of, but of *nature*—"being the children of the resurrection," as rising to an undecaying existence (Rom. 8:21, 23), and so being the children of their Father's immortality (I Tim. 6:16).

saying—(Exod. 3:6)—**I am the God of Abraham, and the God of Isaac, and the God of Jacob? He is not the God of the dead, but the God of the living**—not "the God of dead but [the God] of living persons." The word in brackets is almost certainly an addition to the genuine text, and critical editors exclude it. "For all live unto Him" Luke 20:28—"in His view," or "in His estimation." This last statement—found only in Luke—though adding nothing to the argument, is an important additional illustration. It is true, indeed, that to God no human being is dead or ever will be, but all mankind sustain an abiding conscious relation to Him; but the "all" here means "those who shall be accounted worthy to obtain that world." These sustain a gracious covenant relation to God which cannot be dissolved. (Cf. Rom. 6:10, 11.) In this sense our Lord affirms that for Moses to call the Lord the "GOD" of His patriarchal servants, if at that moment they had no existence, would be unworthy of Him. He "would be *ashamed* to be called their God, if He had not prepared for them a city" (Heb. 11:16). It was concluded by some of the early Fathers, from our Lord's resting His proof of the Resurrection on such a passage as this, instead of quoting some much clearer testimonies of the Old Testament, that the Sadducees, to whom this was addressed, acknowledged the authority of no part of the Old Testament but the Pentateuch; and this opinion has held its ground even till now. But as there is no ground for it in the New Testament, so JOSEPHUS is silent upon it; merely saying that they rejected the Pharisaic traditions. It was because the Pentateuch was regarded by all classes as the fundamental source of the Hebrew religion, and all the succeeding books of the Old Testament but as developments of it, that our Lord would show that even there the doctrine of the Resurrection was taught. And all the rather does He select this passage, as being not a bare annunciation of the doctrine in question, but as expressive of that glorious truth *out of which the Resurrection springs.* "And when the multitude heard this" (says Matt. 22:23), "they were astonished at His doctrine." "Then," adds Luke 20:39, 40, "certain of the scribes answering said, Master, thou hast well said"—enjoying His victory over the Sadducees. "And after that they durst not ask Him any [question at all]"—neither party could; both being for the time utterly foiled.

The Great Commandment "But when the Pharisees had heard that He had put the Sadducees to silence, they were gathered together" (Matthew 22:34). **And one of the scribes**—"a lawyer," says Matthew (22:35); i.e., teacher of the law. **came, and having heard them reasoning together, and perceiving that he had answered them well, asked him**—manifestly in no bad spirit. When Matthew therefore says he came "tempting," or "trying him," as one of the Pharisaic party who seemed to enjoy the defeat He had given to the Sadducees, we may suppose that though somewhat priding himself upon his insight into the law, and not indisposed to measure his knowledge with One in whom he had not yet learned to believe, he was nevertheless an honest-hearted, fair disputant.

Which is the first commandment of all?—first in importance; the primary, leading commandment, the most fundamental one. This was a question which, with some others, divided the Jewish teachers into rival schools.

ADAM CLARKE

31. *Have ye not read?* This quotation is taken from Exod. iii. 6, 16; and as the five books of Moses were the only part of Scripture which the Sadducees acknowledged as divine, our Lord, by confuting them from those books, proved the second part of His assertion, "You are ignorant of those very Scriptures which you profess to hold sacred."

32. *I am the God of Abraham.* Let it be observed that Abraham was dead upwards of three hundred years before these words were spoken to Moses; yet still God calls himself the *God of Abraham.* Now Christ properly observes that God *is not the God of the dead* (that word being equal, in the sense of the Sadducees, to an eternal annihilation), *but of the living.* It therefore follows that, if He be the *God of Abraham . . . Isaac, and . . . Jacob,* these are not dead, but alive; alive with God, though they had ceased, for some hundreds of years, to exist among mortals.

33. *The multitude . . . were astonished at his doctrine.* God uses the infidelity of some for the edification of others. Truth always gains by being opposed.

34. *They were gathered together.* "They came together with one accord," or, "for the same purpose"; i.e., of ensnaring Him in His discourse, as the Sadducees had done, v. 23.

35. *A lawyer.* "A teacher of the law." What is called *lawyer* in the common translation conveys a wrong idea to most readers. These teachers of the law were the same as the scribes.

MATTHEW HENRY

1. The question was, *Master*, which is the greatest commandment of the law? It is true, there are some commands that are the principles of the oracles of God, more extensive and inclusive than others.

2. The design was to try him not so much his knowledge as his judgment. It was a question disputed among the critics in the law. Now they would try what Christ said to this question; and if he should magnify one commandment, they would reflecton him as vilifying the rest. The question was harmless enough; and it appears by comparing Luke x. 27, 28, that it was an adjudged point among the lawyers, that the *love of God* and our *neighbour* is the great commandment, and the sum of all the rest.

III. Christ's answer to this question. Now Christ recommends to us as the great commandments, not those which are so exclusive of others, but, which are *therefore* great because inclusive of others. Observe,

1. Which these great commandments are (*v.* 37-39); the love of God and our neighbour, which are the spring and foundation of all the rest, which (these being supposed) will follow of course.

(1) All the law is fulfilled in one word, and that is, *love*. See Rom. xiii. 10. All obedience begins in the affections, and nothing in religion is done right, that is not done there first. Love is the leading affection, and therefore that, as the main fort, is to be first secured and garrisoned for God. Man is a creature cut out for love; thus therefore is the law written in the heart, that it is a *law of love*. Love is a short and sweet word; and, if that be *the fulfilling of the law*, surely the yoke of the command is very easy. Love is the rest and satisfaction of the soul; if we walk in this good old way, we shall find rest.

(2) The *love of God* is the first and great commandment of all. Now God, being good infinitely, originally, and eternally, is to be loved in the first place, and nothing loved beside him, but what is loved for him. *Love* is the first and great thing that God demands from us, and therefore the first and great thing that we should devote to him.

Now here we are directed,

[1] To love God as ours; *Thou shalt love the Lord thy God* as thine. To love God as ours is to love him because he is ours, and to conduct ourselves to him as ours, with obedience to him, and dependence on him.

[2] To love him *with all our heart, and soul, and mind.* Some make these to signify one and the same thing, to love him with all our powers; others distinguish them; the heart, soul, and mind, are the will, affections, and understanding. Our love of God must be a sincere love, and not in word and tongue only. It must be a strong love, we must love him in the most intense degree. It must be a singular and superlative love, we must love him more than anything else; this way the stream of our affections must entirely run. The heart must be united to love God, in opposition to a divided heart. All our love is too little to bestow upon him, and therefore all the powers of the soul must be engaged for him, and carried out toward him. *This is the first and great commandment;* for obedience to this is the spring of obedience to all the rest; which is only acceptable, when it flows from love.

(3) *To love our neighbour as ourselves* is the *second* great commandment (*v.* 39); *It is like unto that first;* it is inclusive of all the precepts of the second table, as that is of the first. It is *like* it, for it is founded upon it, and flows from it. It is implied, that we do, and should, love ourselves. There is a self-love which is corrupt, and it must be put off and mortified: but there is a self-love which is natural, and the rule of the greatest duty, and it must be preserved and sanctified. We must love ourselves, that is, we must have a due regard to the dignity of our own natures, and a due concern for the welfare of our own souls and bodies. It is prescribed, that we *love our neighbour as ourselves.* We must honour and esteem all men, and must wrong and injure none; and, as we have opportunity, must do good to all. We must love our neighbour as ourselves, as truly and sincerely as we love ourselves, and in the same instances; nay, in many cases we must deny ourselves for the good of our neighbour.

2. Observe what the weight and greatness of these commandments is (*v.* 40); *On these two commandments hang all the law and the prophets.* All hang upon the law of love; take away this, and all falls to the ground, and comes to nothing. Love is the more excellent way. This is the spirit of the law, which animates it; it is the root and spring of all other duties, the compendium of the whole Bible, not only of the law and the prophets, but of the gospel too. All hangs on these two commandments. *Love never faileth.* Into these two great commandments therefore let our hearts be delivered as into a mould; in the defence and evidence of these let us spend our zeal, and not in

JAMIESON, FAUSSET, BROWN

Hear, O Israel; the Lord our God is one Lord—This every devout Jew recited twice every day, and the Jews do it to this day; thus keeping up the great ancient national protest against the polytheisms and pantheisms of the heathen world: it is the great utterance of the national faith in One Living and Personal God—"ONE JEHOVAH!" **And thou shalt**—We have here the language of *law,* expressive of God's *claims.* What then are we here bound down to do? One word is made to express it. And what a word! Had the essence of the divine law consisted in *deeds,* it could not possibly have been expressed in a single word; for no one deed is comprehensive of all others embraced in the law. But as it consists in *an affection of the soul,* one word suffices to express it—but only one. *Fear,* though due to God and enjoined by Him, is *limited* in its sphere and *distant* in character. *Trust, hope,* and the like, though essential features of a right state of heart towards God, are called into action only by *personal necessity,* and so are—in a good sense, it is true, but still are properly—*selfish* affections; that is to say, they have respect to *our own well-being.* But LOVE is an *all-inclusive* affection, embracing not only every other affection proper to its object, but all that is proper to be *done* to its object; for as love spontaneously seeks to please its object, so, in the case of men to God, it is the native well-spring of a voluntary obedience.

Thou shalt love **the Lord, thy God**—i.e., Jehovah, the Self-Existent One, who has revealed Himself as the "I AM," and there is "*none else*"; who, though by His name JEHOVAH apparently at an unapproachable distance from His finite creatures, yet bears to *thee* a real and definite relationship, out of which arises *His claim* and *thy duty*—of LOVE. But with what are we to love Him? Four things are here specified. First, "Thou shalt love the Lord thy God" **with thy heart**—This sometimes means "the whole inner man"(as Prov. 4:23); but that cannot be meant here; for then the other three particulars would be superfluous. Very often it means "our emotional nature"—the seat of *feeling* as distinguished from our intellectual nature or the seat of *thought,* commonly called the "mind" (as in Phil. 4:7). But neither can this be the sense of it here; for here the heart is distinguished both from the "mind" and the "soul." The "heart," then, must here mean the *sincerity* of both the thoughts and the feelings; in other words, *uprightness* or *trueheartedness,* as opposed to a *hypocritical* or *divided* affection. But next, "Thou shalt love the Lord thy God" with thy soul. This is designed to command our emotional nature: Thou shalt put *feeling* or *warmth* into thine affection. Further, "Thou shalt love the Lord thy God" **with thy mind**—This commands our intellectual nature: Thou shalt put *intelligence* into thine affection—in opposition to a blind devotion, or mere devoteeism.

Taking these four things together, the command of the Law is, "Thou shalt love the Lord thy God *with all thy powers*—with a *sincere,* a *fervid,* an *intelligent,* an *energetic* love." But this is not all that the Law demands. God will have all these qualities in their most perfect exercise.

the second is like—"unto it" (Matt. 22:39); as demanding the same affection, and only the extension of it, in its proper measure, to the creatures of Him whom we thus love—our *brethren* in the participation of the same nature, and *neighbors,* as connected with us by ties that render each dependent upon and necessary to the other. **Thou shalt love thy neighbour as thyself**—Now, as we are not to love ourselves supremely, this is virtually a command, in the first place, *not* to love our neighbor with all our heart and soul and mind and strength. And thus it is a condemnation of the idolatry of the creature. Our supreme and uttermost affection is to be reserved for God. But as *sincerely* as ourselves we are to love all mankind, and with *the same readiness to do and suffer for them* as we should reasonably desire them to show to us. The golden rule (Matt. 7:12) is here our best interpreter of the nature and extent of these claims.

Matthew 22:40, "On these two commandments hang all the law and the prophets" (see on Matt. 5:17). It is as if He had said, "This is all Scripture in a nutshell; the whole law of human

ADAM CLARKE

36. *Which is the great commandment?* We see here three kinds of enemies and false accusers of Christ and His disciples, and three sorts of accusations brought against them: (1) The Herodians, or politicians and courtiers, who formed their questions and accusations on the rights of the prince, and matters of state, v. 16; (2) The Sadducees, or libertines, who founded theirs upon matters of religion, and articles of faith, which they did not credit, v. 23. (3) The Pharisees, lawyers, scribes, hypocritical pretenders to devotion, who founded theirs on that vital and practical godliness (the love of God and man) of which they wished themselves to be thought the sole proprietors.

37. What is implied in loving God with all the heart, soul, mind, strength, and when may a man be said to do this? (1) He loves God *with all* his *heart* who loves nothing in comparison of Him and nothing but in reference to Him, who is ready to give up, do, or suffer anything in order to please and glorify Him. (2) He loves God *with all* his *soul*, or rather, "with all his life," who is ready to give up life for His sake—to endure all sorts of torments, and to be deprived of all kinds of comforts, rather than dishonor God—who employs life with all its comforts and conveniences to glorify God in, by, and through all. (3) He loves God with all his strength, Mark xii. 30; Luke x. 27, who exerts all the powers of his body and soul in the service of God; who, for the glory of his Maker, spares neither labor nor cost; who sacrifices his time, body, health, ease, for the honor of God, his divine Master; who employs in His service all his goods, his talents, his power, credit, authority, and influence. (4) He loves God *with all* his *mind* (intellect) who applies himself only to know God and His holy will; who receives with submission, gratitude, and pleasure the sacred truths which God has revealed to man.

39. *Thou shalt love thy neighbour.* The love of our neighbor springs from the love of God as its Source; is found in the love of God as its principle, pattern, and end; and the love of God is found in the love of our neighbor as its effect, representation, and infallible mark.

40. *On these two commandments hang all the law and the prophets.* They are like the first and last links of a chain; all the intermediate ones depend on them. True religion begins and ends in love to God and man. These are the two grand links that unite God to man, man to his fellows, and men again to God.

MATTHEW HENRY

notions, names, and strifes of words. To the commanding power of these let everything else be made to bow.

Verses 41–46

Many questions the Pharisees had asked Christ, but now let him ask them a question; and he will do it when they are gathered together, *v.* 41. He took them all together, when they were in confederacy and consulting against him. God delights to baffle his enemies when they most strengthen themselves; he gives them all the advantages they can wish for, and yet conquers them.

I. Christ proposes a question to them, which they could easily answer; it was a question in their own catechism; "*What think ye of Christ? Whose Son is he?*" This they could easily answer, *The Son of David.* It was the common periphrasis of the Messiah; they called him *the Son of David.*

What think ye of Christ? They had put questions to him, one after another, out of the law; but he comes and puts a question to them upon the promise. Many are so full of the law, that they forget Christ, as if their duties would save them without his merit and grace. It concerns each of us seriously to ask ourselves, What think we of Christ? Some think not of him at all, some think meanly, and some think hardly, of him; but *to them that believe he is precious*; and *how precious then are the thoughts of him!*

II. He starts a difficulty upon their answer, which they could not so easily solve, *v.* 43–45. Many can so readily affirm the truth, that they think they have knowledge enough to be proud of, who, when they are called to confirm the truth, show they have ignorance enough to be ashamed of. The objection Christ raised was, *If Christ be David's son, how then doth David, in spirit, call him Lord?* He did not hereby design to ensnare them, as they did him, but to instruct them.

1. It is easy to see that David calls Christ *Lord.* Now, to prove that David, in spirit, called Christ *Lord*, he quotes Ps. cx. 1, which psalm the scribes themselves understood of Christ. It is a prophetical summary of the doctrine of Christ, it describes him executing the offices of a Prophet, Priest, and King.

Christ quotes the whole verse, which shows the Redeemer in his exaltation; (1) *Sitting at the right hand of God.* His sitting denotes both rest and rule; his sitting at God's right hand denotes superlative honour and sovereign power. (2) Subduing his enemies. There he shall sit, till they be all made either his friends or his footstool.

But that which this verse is quoted for is, that David calls the Messiah *his Lord*; *the Lord*, Jehovah, *said unto my Lord.*

2. It is not so easy for those who believe not the Godhead of the Messiah, to clear this from an absurdity, if Christ be David's son. If David call him *Lord*, that is laid down (*v.* 45) as the *more evident truth.* We must hold this fast, that he is David's Lord, and by that explain his being David's son.

III. We have here the success of this gentle trial which Christ made of the Pharisees' knowledge, in two things.

1. It puzzled them (*v.* 46); *No man was able to answer him a word.* Either it was their ignorance that they did not know, or their impiety that they would not own, the Messiah to be God; which truth was the only key to unlock this difficulty. Christ, as God, was David's *Lord*; and Christ, as Man, was David's *son.* This he did not now himself explain, but reserved it till the proof of it was completed by his resurrection.

2. It silenced them, and all others that sought occasion against him, *Neither durst any man, from that day forth, ask him any more questions.* Many are convinced, that are not converted, by the word. Had these been converted, they would have asked him more questions, especially that great question, *What must we do to be saved?* But since they could not gain their point, they would have no more to do with him.

CHAPTER 23

Verses 1–12

We find not Christ, in all his preaching, so severe upon any sort of people as upon these *scribes and Pharisees.* Yet these were the idols and darlings of the people, who thought, if but two men went to heaven, one would be a Pharisee. Now Christ directs his discourse here *to the multitude, and to his disciples* (*v.* 1), to rectify their mistakes concerning these scribes and Pharisees, by painting them out in their true colours. It is good to know the true characters of men, that we may not be imposed upon by great and mighty names, titles, and pretensions to power.

JAMIESON, FAUSSET, BROWN

duty in a portable, pocket form." Indeed, it is so *simple* that a child may understand it, so *brief* that all may remember it, so *comprehensive* as to embrace all possible cases. And from its very nature it is *unchangeable.*

41-46. CHRIST BAFFLES THE PHARISEES BY A QUESTION ABOUT DAVID AND MESSIAH. (= Mark 12:35-37; Luke 20:41-44.) For the exposition, see on Mark 12:35-37.

How say the scribes that Christ is the son of David?—How come they to give it out that Messiah is to be the son of David? In Matthew, Jesus asks them, "What think ye of Christ?" or of the promised and expected Messiah? "Whose son is He [to be]? They say unto Him, The son of David." The sense is the same. "He saith unto them, How then doth David in spirit call Him Lord?" (Matt. 22:42, 43.)

For David himself said by the Holy Ghost, The Lord said to my Lord, Sit thou on my right hand, till I make thine enemies thy footstool—(Ps. 110:1). **37. David therefore himself calleth him Lord; and whence is he then his son?**—There is but one solution of this difficulty. Messiah is at once inferior to David as his son according to the flesh, and superior to him as the Lord of a kingdom of which David is himself a subject, not the sovereign. The human and divine natures of Christ, and the spirituality of His kingdom—of which the highest earthly sovereigns are honored if they be counted worthy to be its subjects—furnish the only key to this puzzle.

And no man after that durst ask any question—all feeling that they were no match for Him, and that it was vain to enter the lists with Him.

CHAPTER 23

VSS. 1-39. DENUNCIATION OF THE SCRIBES AND PHARISEES—LAMENTATION OVER JERUSALEM, AND FAREWELL TO THE TEMPLE. (= Mark 12:38-40; Luke 20:45-47.) For this long and terrible discourse we are indebted, with the exception of a few verses in Mark and Luke, to Matthew alone. But as it is only an extended repetition of denunciations uttered not long before at the table of a Pharisee, and recorded by Luke (11:37-54), we may take both together in the exposition.

Denunciation of the Scribes and Pharisees (vss. 1-

ADAM CLARKE

41. *While the Pharisees were gathered together.* Jesus asks a question in His turn, utterly to confound them, and to show the people that the source of all the captious questions of his opponents was their ignorance of the prophecies relative to the Messiah.

42. *What think ye of Christ?* Or, What are your thoughts concerning "the Christ"—the Messiah? For to this title the emphatic article should always be added. *Whose son is he?* From what family is He to spring? *They say unto him, The son of David.* This was a thing well-known among the Jews, and universally acknowledged; see John vii. 42; and is a most powerful proof against them that the Messiah is come. Is it not evident that God designed that the Messiah should come at a time when the public genealogies might be inspected, to prove that it was He who was prophesied of, and that no other was to be expected? The Evangelists, Matthew and Luke, were so fully convinced of the conclusiveness of this proof that they had recourse to the public registers; and thus proved to the Jews, from their own records, that Jesus was born of the family mentioned by the prophets. Nor do we find that a scribe, Pharisee, or any other ever attempted to invalidate this proof, though it would have essentially subserved their cause, could they have done it.

43. *How then doth David in spirit* (or by the Spirit—by the inspiration of the Spirit of God) *call him Lord? saying,*

44. *The Lord* (Jehovah) *said unto my Lord.* (*Adonai*, my Prop, Stay, Master, Support), *Sit thou on my right hand.* Take the place of the greatest eminence and authority. *Till I make thine enemies thy footstool.* Till I subdue both Jews and Gentiles under Thee, and cause them to acknowledge Thee as their Sovereign and Lord. This quotation is taken from Ps. cx. 1; and from it these two points are clear: (1) That David wrote it by the inspiration of God; and (2) That it is a prophetic declaration of the Messiah.

45. *How is he his son?* As the Jews did not attempt to deny the conclusion of our Lord's question—which was, The Messiah is not only the Son of David according to the flesh, but He is the Lord of David according to His divine nature—then it is evident they could not. Indeed there was no other way of invalidating the argument but by denying that the prophecy in question related to Christ. But it seems the prophecy was so fully and so generally understood to belong to the Messiah that they did not attempt to do this; for it is immediately added, "No man was able to answer him a word." They were completely nonplussed and confounded.

46. *Neither durst any . . . ask him any more questions.* The Pharisees and Herodians were defeated, vv. 15-22. The Sadducees were confounded, vv. 29-33; the lawyers, nonplussed, vv. 37-40; and the Pharisees, finally routed, vv. 41-46. Thus did the wisdom of God triumph over the cunning of men.

CHAPTER 23

MATTHEW HENRY

Even the disciples need these cautions; for good men are apt to have their eyes dazzled with worldly pomp.

I. Christ allows their office as expositors of the law; *The scribes and Pharisees sit in Moses' seat* (*v.* 2), as public teachers and interpreters of the law. They were as judges, or a bench of justices; teaching and judging seem to be equivalent. Or, we may apply it, not to the Sanhedrim, but to the other Pharisees and scribes, that expounded the law, and taught the people how to apply it to particular cases. Moses had those in every city (so the expression is, Acts xv. 21), who preached him; this was their office, and it was just and honourable; it was requisite that there should be some at whose mouth the people might *enquire the law*. Many a good place is filled with bad men. The men are not so much honoured by the seat as the seat is dishonoured by the men. Good and useful offices and powers are not *therefore* to be condemned and abolished, because they fall sometimes into the hands of bad men, who abuse them.

Hence he infers (*v.* 3), "*Whatsoever they bid you observe, that observe and do.* As far as they *sit in Moses' seat*, that is, read and preach the law that was given by Moses, so far you must hearken to them." Now Christ would have the people to make use of the helps they gave them for the understanding of the scripture, and do accordingly. As long as their comments did illustrate the text, did make plain, and not *make void, the commandment of God*; so far they must be observed and obeyed. We must not think the worse of good truths for their being preached by bad ministers; nor of good laws for their being executed by bad magistrates. Though it is most desirable to have our food brought by angels, yet, if God send it to us by ravens, if it be good and wholesome, we must take it, and thank God for it.

II. He condemns the men. He had ordered the multitude to do as they taught; not to do as they did, to beware of their leaven; *Do not ye after their works.* As we must not swallow corrupt doctrines for the sake of any laudable practices of those that teach them, so we must not imitate any bad examples for the sake of the plausible doctrines of those that set them.

Our Saviour here, and in the following verses, specifies divers particulars of their works, wherein we must not imitate them. In general, they are charged with hypocrisy, dissimulation, or double-dealing in religion.

Four things are in these verses charged upon them.

1. Their saying and doing were two things. *They say, and do not;* they teach out of the law that which is good, but their conversation gives them the lie. Those are of all sinners most inexcusable that allow themselves in the sins they condemn in others, or in worse. This doth especially touch wicked ministers; for what greater hypocrisy can there be, than to press that upon others, which they themselves disbelieve and disobey; pulling down in their practice what they build up in their preaching; when in the pulpit, preaching so well that it is a pity they should ever come out; but, when out of the pulpit, living so ill that it is a pity they should ever come in; like bells, that call others to church, but hang out of it themselves.

It is applicable to all others that say, and do not; that make a plausible profession of religion, but do not live up to that profession. Great talkers, but little doers.

2. They were very severe in imposing upon others those things which they were not themselves willing to submit to the burthen of (*v.* 4); *They bind heavy burthens, and grievous to be borne;* not only insisting upon the minute circumstances of the law, but by imposing their own inventions and traditions, under the highest penalties. They loved to show their authority and to exercise their domineering faculty.

But see their hypocrisy; *They themselves will not move them with one of their fingers.* They pressed upon the people a strictness in religion which they themselves would not be bound by. They indulged their pride in giving law to others; but consulted their ease in their own practice. They would not ease the people in these things, nor put a finger to lighten their burthen, when they saw it pinched them.

3. They were all for show, and nothing for substance, in religion (*v.* 5); *All their works they do, to be seen of men.* We must do such good works, that they who see them may glorify God; but we must not proclaim our good works, with design that others may see them, and glorify us. All their end was to be praised of men, and therefore all their endeavour was to be seen of men. The *form* of godliness will get them a name to live, which is all they aim at, and therefore they trouble not themselves with the *power* of it, which is essential to a life indeed. He that does all to be seen does nothing to the purpose.

JAMIESON, FAUSSET, BROWN

36). The first twelve verses were addressed more immediately to the disciples, the rest to the scribes and Pharisees. **1. Then spake Jesus to the multitude**—to the multitudes. **and to his disciples. 2. Saying, The scribes and the Pharisees sit**—The Jewish teachers *stood* to read, but *sat* to expound the Scriptures, as will be seen by comparing Luke 4:16 with vs. 20—**in Moses' seat**—i.e., as interpreters of the law given by Moses.

3. All therefore—i.e., all which, as *sitting in that seat* and teaching *out of that law*. **they bid you observe, that observe and do**—The word "therefore" is thus, it will be seen, of great importance, as limiting those injunctions which He would have them obey to what they fetched from the law itself. In requiring implicit obedience to such injunctions, He would have them to recognize the authority with which they taught over and above the obligations of the law itself—an important principle truly; but He who denounced the traditions of such teachers (ch. 15:3) cannot have meant here to throw His shield over these. It is remarked by WEBSTER and WILKINSON that the warning to *beware* of the scribes is given by Mark and Luke without any qualification: the charge to *respect* and *obey* them being reported by Matthew alone, indicating for whom this Gospel was especially written, and the writer's desire to conciliate the Jews.

4. For they bind heavy burdens and grievous to be borne, and lay them on men's shoulders; but they themselves will not move them—"touch them not" (Luke 11:46)—**with one of their fingers**—referring not so much to the irksomeness of the legal rites, though they were irksome enough (Acts 15:10), as to the heartless rigor with which they were enforced, and by men of shameless inconsistency.

5. But all their works they do for to be seen of men—Whatever good they do, or zeal they show, has but one motive—human applause.

ADAM CLARKE

2. *The scribes and the Pharisees sit in Moses' seat.* They "sat" there formerly by divine appointment; they *sit* there now by divine permission. What our Lord says here refers to their expounding the Scriptures, for it was the custom of the Jewish doctors to *sit* while they expounded the law and prophets, chap. v. 1; Luke iv. 20-22, and to stand up when they read them. By the *seat* of Moses we are to understand authority to teach the law. Moses was the great teacher of the Jewish people, and the scribes are here represented as his successors.

3. *All therefore whatsoever.* That is, all those things which they read out of the law and prophets, and all things which they teach consistently with them. This must be our Lord's meaning. He could not have desired them to do everything without restriction which the Jewish doctors taught, because himself warns His disciples against their false teaching, and testifies that they had made the word of God of none effect by their traditions. See chap. xv. 6.

4. *They bind heavy burdens.* They are now so corrupt that they have added to the ceremonies of the law others of their own invention, which are not only burdensome and oppressive, but have neither reason, expediency, nor revelation, to countenance them. In a word, like all their successors in spirit to the present day, they were severe to others but very indulgent to themselves.

G. CAMPBELL MORGAN:

Said He, "The scribes and Pharisees have seated themselves on Moses' seat." That is not to say that Christ was saying their position was a false one, although there was a remarkably fine indication of the fact that they were never appointed by God. He was not saying their position was out of harmony with the thought and purpose and intention of God, because immediately afterward He said to the people, "All things therefore whatsoever they bid you, these do and observe." He recognized that a certain authority belonged to scribes and Pharisees. Bearing these two things in mind, we must be careful to see what He really meant. First of all, He said that they had seated themselves on Moses' seat. This was not a reference merely to the men of His own age. This was His definition of the position occupied by the whole order of the scribes. In all likelihood the order was instituted in the days of Ezra; and the scribe was the interpreter of the law, the man who taught the people its meaning. Now there was nothing wrong in such a position, and yet Christ was very careful to indicate in the way He stated the case, that they were self-appointed teachers. They seated themselves on Moses' seat. The expression "Moses' seat" demands our attention. It is peculiarly the word that indicates authority. The Greek word here is *cathedra*. These people sat on Moses' seat, the seat of the teachers, of authority, the seat from which they spoke in interpretation of the law with final authority. Their position was authoritative so far. It is impossible, however, to imagine that Christ meant here that men were to obey all the things that the Pharisees were telling them to do. We must not omit the "therefore" from the text, because He himself resolutely broke the traditions of the elders, treated with disdain the thousand and one things which they had superadded to the Mosaic economy, ignored their multitudinous technicalities, sat down with unwashed hands to eat as a protest against the externality of their religious ideals. So that He certainly did not mean to say that everything the scribes and Pharisees said to men, they were to do. We shall understand Him by putting emphasis on the "*therefore.*" They have seated themselves on Moses' chair. Therefore—that is, in so far as their interpretation is indeed true to the Mosaic economy—you must obey them; so far as they fulfill the function of the position they have taken, they have authority, and their teaching is binding upon men.—*The Gospel According to Matthew*

MATTHEW HENRY

He specifies two things which they did to be seen of men.

(1) *They made broad their phylacteries.* Those were little scrolls of paper or parchment, wherein were written, with great niceness, these four paragraphs of the law, Exod. xiii. 2–11; xiii. 11–16; Deut. vi. 4–9; xi. 13–21. These were sewn up in leather, and worn upon their foreheads and left arms. Now the Pharisees made broad these phylacteries, that they might be thought more holy, and strict, and zealous for the law, than others. It is a gracious ambition to covet to be really more holy than others, but it is a proud ambition to covet to appear so. It is good to excel in real piety, but not to exceed in outward shows.

(2) *They enlarged the borders of their garments.* God appointed the Jews to make borders or fringes upon their garments (Num. xv. 38), to be a memorandum to them of their being a peculiar people; but the Pharisees were not content to have these borders like other people's; they must be larger than ordinary, to answer their design of making themselves to be taken notice of; as if they were more religious than others.

4. They much affected pre-eminence and superiority. Pride was the darling reigning sin of the Pharisees. He describes their pride, *v.* 6, 7. They courted, and coveted places of honour and respect. In all public appearances, as *at feasts, and in the synagogues,* they expected, and had, to their hearts' delight, *the uppermost rooms and the chief seats.* They took place of all others, and precedency was adjudged to them, as persons of the greatest note and merit. It is not possessing the uppermost rooms, nor sitting in the chief seats, that is condemned (somebody must sit uppermost), but *loving* them. What is that but making an idol of ourselves, and then falling down and worshipping it—the worst kind of idolatry! It is bad anywhere, but especially in the synagogues. *There* to seek honour to ourselves, where we appear in order to give glory to God, and to humble ourselves before him, is indeed to mock God instead of serving him. It savours much of pride and hypocrisy, when people do not care for going to church, unless they can look fine and make a figure there.

Titles of honour and respect. They *loved greetings in the markets,* loved to have people put off their hats to them, and show them respect when they met them in the streets. This was meat and drink and dainties to them. The *greetings* would not have done them half so much good, if they had not been in the markets, where everybody might see how much they were respected, and how high they stood in the opinion of the people. For him that is taught in the word to give respect to him that teaches is commendable enough in him that gives it; but for him that teaches to love it, and demand it, is sinful and abominable; and, instead of teaching he has need to learn the first lesson in the school of Christ, which is humility. He cautions his disciples against being herein like them; "But be not ye called so, for ye shall not be of such a spirit," *v.* 8, &c.

Here is, A prohibition of pride. They are here forbidden to challenge titles of honour and dominion to themselves, *v.* 8–10. It is repeated twice; *Be not called Rabbi, neither be ye called Master* or *Guide.* Christ's ministers must not affect the name of *Rabbi* or *Master,* by way of distinction from other people; it is not agreeable to the simplicity of the gospel. They must not assume the authority and dominion implied in those names. The reasons for this prohibition are,

(1) *One is your Master, even Christ, v.* 8, and again, *v.* 10. Christ only is our Master, ministers are but ushers in the school.

(2) *All ye are brethren.* Ye are brethren, as ye are all disciples of the same Master. School-fellows are brethren, and, as such, should help one another in getting their lesson; but it will by no means be allowed that one of the scholars step into the master's seat, and give law to the school. They are forbidden to ascribe such titles to others (*v.* 9); "*Call no man your father upon the earth;* constitute no man the father of your religion." God only must be allowed as *the Father of our spirits,* Heb. xii. 9. Our religion must not be derived from, or made to depend upon, any man. We must not pin our faith on any man's sleeve, because we know not whither he will carry it. St. Paul calls himself *a Father* (1 Cor. iv. 15; Phil. 10); but he uses that title to denote, not authority, but affection: therefore he calls them not his *obliged,* but his *beloved,* sons, 1 Cor. iv. 14.

The reason given is, *One is your Father, who is in heaven.* He is the Fountain of it, and its Founder; the Life of it, and its Lord; from whom alone, as the Original, our spiritual life is derived, and on whom it depends. Christ having taught us to say, *Our Father, who art in heaven;* let us *call no man Father upon*

JAMIESON, FAUSSET, BROWN

they make broad their phylacteries—strips of parchment with Scripture-texts on them, worn on the forehead, arm, and side, in time of prayer.

and enlarge the borders of their garments—fringes of their upper garments (Num. 15: 37-40).

6. And love the uppermost rooms—The word "room" is now obsolete in the sense here intended. It should be "the uppermost place," i.e., the place of highest honor. **at feasts, and the chief seats in the synagogues.** See on Luke 14:7, 8.

And greetings in the markets, and to be called of men, Rabbi, Rabbi—It is the spirit rather than the *letter* of this that must be pressed; though the violation of the letter, springing from spiritual pride, has done incalculable evil in the Church of Christ. The reiteration of the word "Rabbi" shows how it tickled the ear and fed the spiritual pride of those ecclesiastics.

8. But be not ye called Rabbi; for one is your Master—your Guide, your Teacher.

And call no man your father upon the earth: for one is your Father, which is in heaven, . . .—To construe these injunctions into a condemnation of every title by which Church rulers may be distinguished from the flock which they rule, is virtually to condemn that rule itself; and accordingly the same persons do both—but against the whole strain of the New Testament and sound Christian judgment. But when we have guarded ourselves against these extremes, let us see to it that we retain the full spirit of this warning against that itch for ecclesiastical superiority which has been the bane and the scandal of Christ's ministers in every age. (On the use of the word "Christ" here, see on ch. 1:1.)

ADAM CLARKE

5. *Phylacteries.* These were small slips of parchment or vellum on which certain portions of the law were written. The Jews tied these about their foreheads and arms, for three different purposes: (1) To put them in mind of those precepts which they should constantly observe; (2) To procure their reverence and respect in the sight of the heathen; And (3) To act as amulets or charms to drive away evil spirits. An original phylactery lies now before me. It is a piece of fine vellum, about eighteen inches long, and an inch and a quarter broad. It is divided into four unequal compartments. In the first is written, in a very fair character, with many *apices,* after the mode of the German Jews, the first ten verses of Exodus xiii; in the second compartment is written from the eleventh to the sixteenth verse of the same chapter, inclusive; in the third, from the fourth to the ninth verse, inclusive, of Deuteronomy vi, beginning with *Hear, O Israel;* in the fourth, from the thirteenth to the twenty-first verse, inclusive, of Deuteronomy xi.

7. *To be called of men, Rabbi, Rabbi.* "My teacher! My teacher!" The second *rabbi* is omitted by several excellent MSS., by most of the ancient versions, and by some of the fathers. There are three words used among the Jews as titles of dignity which they apply to their doctors —Rabh, Rabbi, and Rabban. They may be considered as three degrees of comparison: *Rabh,* great; *Rabbi,* greater; and *Rabban,* greatest.

8. *But be not ye called Rabbi.* None of the prophets had ever received this title, nor any of the Jewish doctors before the time of Hillel and Shammai, which was about the time of our Lord.

9. *Call no man your father.* Our Lord probably alludes to the AB, or father of the Sanhedrin, who was the next after the *nasi,* or president. By which He gives His disciples to understand that He would have no second, after himself, established in His Church, of which He alone was the Head; and that perfect equality must subsist among them.

MATTHEW HENRY

earth. Here is a precept of humility and mutual subjection (*v*. 11); *He that is greatest among you shall be your servant*. Take it as a promise; "*He* shall stand highest in the favour of God, that is most submissive and serviceable": or as a precept; "He that is advanced to any place of dignity, *let him be your servant*." *He that is greatest* is not a lord, but a minister. Here is a good reason for all this, *v*. 12. Consider,

First, The punishment intended for the proud; *Whosoever shall exalt himself shall be abased*. If God give them repentance, they will be abased in their own eyes, and will abhor themselves for it; if they repent not, sooner or later they will be abased before the world.

Secondly, The preferment intended for the humble; *He that shall humble himself shall be exalted*. In this world the humble have the honour of being accepted with the holy God, and respected by all wise and good men; of being qualified for, and often called out to, the most honourable services; for honour is like the shadow, which flees from those that pursue it, and grasp at it, but follows those that flee from it. However, in the other world, they that have humbled themselves in contrition for their sin, shall be exalted to inherit the throne of glory.

Verses 13–33

In these verses we have eight woes levelled directly against the scribes and Pharisees by our Lord Jesus Christ, like so many claps of thunder, or flashes of lightning, from mount Sinai. Here are *eight* woes, in opposition to the eight beatitudes, Matt. v. 3. These woes are the more remarkable because of the meekness and gentleness of him that denounced them. He came to bless, and loved to bless; but, if his wrath be kindled, there is surely cause for it.

This is here the burthen of the song, and it is a heavy burthen; *Woe unto you, scribes and Pharisees*, hypocrites. The scribes and Pharisees were hypocrites; that is it in which all the rest of their bad characters are summed up. A hypocrite is a stage-player in religion (that is the primary signification of the word); he personates or acts the part of one that he neither is nor may be, or perhaps that he neither is nor would be.

Now each of these woes against the scribes and Pharisees has a reason annexed to it, justifying the judgment of Christ upon them; for his woes, his curses, are never causeless.

I. They were sworn enemies to the gospel of Christ, and consequently to the salvation of the souls of men (*v*. 13); *They shut up the kingdom of heaven, against men*. Christ came to *open the kingdom of heaven* to bring men to be subjects of that kingdom. Now the scribes and Pharisees, who sat in Moses's seat, and pretended to the key of knowledge, ought to have contributed their assistance herein. They that undertook to expound Moses and the prophets should have showed the people how they testified of Christ. Thus they might have facilitated that great work, and have helped thousands to heaven; but, instead of this, they shut up the kingdom of heaven; they made it their business to beget and nourish up in the minds of the people prejudices against Christ and his doctrine.

1. They would not go in themselves; *Have any of the rulers*, or *of the Pharisees, believed on him?* John vii. 48. No; they were too proud to stoop to his meanness; they did not like a religion which insisted so much on humility. Repentance was the door of admission into this kingdom, and nothing could be more disagreeable to the Pharisees than to repent. Therefore they *went not in themselves*; but that was not all.

2. They would not *suffer them that were entering to go in*. It is bad to keep away from Christ ourselves, but it is worse to keep others from him. Their not going in themselves was a hindrance to many; multitudes rejected the gospel only because their leaders did. They opposed both Christ's entertaining of sinners (Luke vii. 39), and sinners' entertaining of Christ; and used all their wit and power to serve their malice against him; and thus they *shut up the kingdom of heaven*, so that *they who would enter* into it must *suffer violence* (*ch*. xi. 12), and *press into it* (Luke xvi. 16).

II. They made religion and the form of godliness a cloak and stalking-horse to their covetous practices and desires, *v*. 14. Observe here,

1. What their wicked practices were; they *devoured widows' houses*, either by quartering themselves and their attendants upon them for entertainment; or by insinuating themselves into their affections, and so getting to be the trustees of their estates, which they could make an easy prey of. The thing they aimed at was to enrich themselves. And doubtless they did all this under colour of law; for they did it so art-

JAMIESON, FAUSSET, BROWN

11. But he that is greatest among you shall be your servant—This plainly means, "shall show that he is so by becoming your servant"; as in ch. 20:27, compared with Mark 10:44. **12. And whosoever shall exalt himself shall be abased**—See on Luke 18:14. What follows was addressed more immediately to the scribes and Pharisees.

13. But woe unto you, scribes and Pharisees, hypocrites! for ye shut up the kingdom of heaven against men—Here they are charged with *shutting heaven* against men: in Luke 11:52 they are charged with what was worse, *taking away the key*—"the key of knowledge"—which means, not the key to open knowledge, but knowledge as the only key to open heaven. A right knowledge of God's revealed word is eternal life, as our Lord says (John 17:3 and 5:39); but this they took away from the people, substituting for it their wretched traditions.

14. Woe unto you, scribes and Pharisees, hypocrites! for ye devour widows' houses . . .—Taking advantage of the helpless condition and confiding character of "widows," they contrived to obtain possession of their property, while by their "long prayers" they made them believe they were raised far above "filthy lucre." So much "the greater damnation" awaits them. What a lifelike description of the Romish clergy, the true successors of those scribes!

ADAM CLARKE

10. *Neither be ye called masters*. "Leaders." God is in all these respects jealous of His honor. To Him alone it belongs to guide and "lead" His Church, as well as to govern and defend it.

12. *Whosoever shall exalt himself*. The way to arrive at the highest degree of dignity, in the sight of God, is by being willing to become the servant of all. Nothing is more hateful in His sight than pride.

13-14. *Woe unto you, scribes!* I think these two verses should be transposed. This transposition is authorized by some of the best MSS., versions, and fathers. The fifteenth reads best after the thirteenth.

13. *Ye shut up the kingdom*. As a key by opening a lock gives entrance into a house, so knowledge of the sacred testimonies, manifested in expounding them to the people, may be said to open the way into the kingdom of Heaven. But where men who are termed teachers are destitute of this knowledge themselves, they may be said to *shut* this Kingdom, because they occupy the place of those who should teach, and thus prevent the people from acquiring heavenly knowledge. *The kingdom of heaven* here means the gospel of Christ; the Pharisees would not receive it themselves, and hindered the common people as far as they could.

W. E. VINE:

DIAKONOS is translated "servant" or "servants" in Matt. 22:13 (R.V. marg., "ministers"); 23:11 (R.V. marg., ditto); Mark 9:35, A.V. (R.V., "minister"); John 2:5, 9; 12:26; Rom. 16:1.
—Vine's Expository Dictionary

MATTHEW HENRY

fully that it passed uncensured.

2. What was the cloak with which they covered this wicked practice; *For a pretence they made long prayers;* very long indeed, if it be true which some of the Jewish writers tell us, that they spent three hours at a time in the formalities of meditation and prayer, and did it thrice every day. By this craft they got their wealth, and maintained their grandeur. Christ doth not here condemn long prayers, as in themselves hypocritical. Christ himself *continued all night in prayer to God.* Where there are many sins to be confessed, and many wants to pray for the supply of, and many mercies to give thanks for, there is occasion for long prayers. But the Pharisees' long prayers were for a *pretence*; by them they got the reputation of pious devout men, that loved prayer, and were the favourites of Heaven; and by this means people were made to believe it was not possible that such men as they should cheat them. Thus, while they seemed to soar heaven-ward, upon the wings of prayer, their eye, like the kite's, was all the while upon their prey on the earth, some widow's house or other that lay convenient for them. It is no new thing for the show and form of godliness to be made a cloak to the greatest enormities.

3. The doom passed upon them for this; *Therefore ye shall receive the greater damnation.* The pretences of religion, with which hypocrites disguise or excuse their sin now, will aggravate their condemnation shortly.

III. They shut up the kingdom of heaven against those that would turn to Christ, but at the same time *compassed sea and land to make proselytes* to themselves, *v.* 15.

1. Their commendable industry in making proselytes to the Jewish religion; for this, for one such, though but one, they compass sea and land. And what did they aim at? Not the glory of God, and the good of souls; but that they might have the credit of making them proselytes. The making of proselytes, if it be to the truth and serious godliness, and be done with a good design, is a good work. Such is the value of souls, that nothing must be thought too much to do, to save a soul from death. The industry of the Pharisees herein may show the negligence of many who would be thought to act from better principles, but will be at no pains or cost to propagate the gospel.

2. Their cursed impiety in abusing their proselytes when they were made. "*Ye make him twofold more the child of hell than yourselves.*" They are called *children of hell,* because of their rooted enmity to the kingdom of heaven, which was the principle and genius of Pharisaism. Perverted proselytes are commonly the greatest bigots; the scholars outdid their masters, (1) In fondness of ceremony. Weak heads commonly admire those shows and ceremonies which wise men cannot but think meanly of. (2) In fury against Christianity. Paul, a disciple of the Pharisees, was *exceedingly mad against the Christians* (Acts xxvi. 11), when his master, Gamaliel, seems to have been more moderate.

IV. They led the people into dangerous mistakes, particularly in the matter of oaths; which have been by all nations accounted sacred (*v.* 16); *Ye blind guides.* Christ denounces a woe to the blind guides that have the blood of so many souls to answer for.

(1) He lays down the doctrine they taught. They distinguished between an oath by *the temple* and an oath by the *gold of the temple*; an oath by *the altar* and an oath by *the gift upon the altar*; making the latter binding, but not the former. Here was a double wickedness; *First,* That there were some oaths which they dispensed with, and made light of, and reckoned a man was not bound by to assert the truth, or perform a promise. That doctrine cannot be of the God of truth which gives countenance to the breach of faith in any case whatsoever. Oaths are edge-tools and are not to be jested with. *Secondly,* That they preferred the gold before the temple, and the gift before the altar, to encourage people to bring gifts to the altar, and gold to the treasures of the temple, which they hoped to be gainers by.

(2) He shows the folly and absurdity of this distinction (*v.* 17–19); *Ye fools, and blind.*

To convict them of folly, he appeals to themselves, *Whether is greater, the gold or the temple that sanctifies the gold; the gift, or the altar that sanctifies the gift?* They that sware by the gold of the temple had an eye to it as holy; but what was it that made it holy but the holiness of the temple, to the service of which it was appropriated? And therefore the temple cannot be less holy than the gold, but must be more so.

(3) He rectifies the mistake (*v.* 20–22), by reducing all the oaths they had invented to the true intent of an oath, which is, By the name of the Lord: so

JAMIESON, FAUSSET, BROWN

15. Woe unto you, scribes and Pharisees, hypocrites! for ye compass sea and land to make one proselyte—from heathenism. We have evidence of this in JOSEPHUS.

and when he is made, ye make him twofold more the child of hell than yourselves—condemned, for the hypocrisy he would learn to practice, both by the religion he left and that he embraced.

16. Woe unto you, ye blind guides—Striking expression this of the ruinous effects of erroneous teaching. Our Lord, here and in some following verses, condemns the subtle distinctions they made as to the sanctity of oaths—distinctions invented only to promote their own avaricious purposes. **which say, Whosoever shall swear by the temple, it is nothing**—He has incurred no debt. **but whosoever shall swear by the gold of the temple**—meaning not the gold that adorned the temple itself, but the *Corban,* set apart for sacred uses (see on ch. 15:5). **he is a debtor!**—i.e., it is no longer his own, even though the necessities of the parent might require it. We know who the successors of these men are. **but whosoever sweareth by the gift that is upon it, he is guilty**—It should have been rendered, "he is a debtor," as in vs. 16. **19. Ye fools, and blind! for whether is greater, the gift, or the altar that sanctifieth the gift?**—(See Exod. 29:37.)

20-22. Whose therefore shall swear by the altar . . .—See on ch. 5:33-37.

ADAM CLARKE

15. *Compass sea and land.* A proverbial expression, similar to ours, "You leave no stone unturned"; intimating that they did all in their power to gain converts, not to God. but to their sect. *Proselyte.* "A stranger" or "foreigner"; one who is come from his own people and country to sojourn with another. *Twofold more.* The Greek word which has generally been translated "twofold," *kypke,* has been demonstrated to mean "more deceitful." *The child of hell.* A Hebraism for an excessively wicked person, such as might claim hell for his mother and the devil for his father.

G. CAMPBELL MORGAN:

The severity of Jesus is discovered in the words He made use of; in the repetition of the word "hypocrites," in the use of the words "fools and blind," in the one terrible sentence that appalls as we read it, in which He called them "serpents" and "offsprings of vipers," in that most fearful illustration suggested by His use of the term the "judgment of Gehenna." All these are terms which indicate the severity of Christ. We cannot cancel these terms; they are as surely here as anything else in the passage.

And yet, not to discover the other tone is to miss much. There were tears in His voice; there was sorrow in His heart. These things are not merely manifest in the last lamentation, "O Jerusalem, Jerusalem," but in all the woes. We do violence to the spirit of the Christ, and to the genius of the whole passage, if we put into the reading of the word "woe" nothing but thunder. It was a wail of compassion as well as a message of strong and severe denunciation. Yet even this compassion was denunciatory, for in every case He declared that the woe was unto these men.

—*The Gospel According to Matthew*

A. T. ROBERTSON:

15. "Twofold more a son of hell than yourselves" (*huion geennes diploteron humon*). It is a convert to Pharisaism rather than Judaism that is meant by "one proselyte" (*hena proseluton*), from *proserchomai,* newcomers, aliens. There were two kinds of proselytes: of the gate (not actual Jews, but God-fearers and well-wishers of Judaism, like Cornelius), of righteousness who received circumcision and became actual Jews. But a very small percent of the latter became Pharisees. There was a Hellenistic Jewish literature (Philo, Sibylline Oracles, etc.) designed to attract Gentiles to Judaism. But the Pharisaic missionary zeal (compass, *periagete,* go around) was a comparative failure. And success was even worse, Jesus says with pitiless plainness. The "son of Gehenna" means one fitted for and so destined for Gehenna. "The more converted the more perverted" (H. J. Holtzmann).

—*Word Pictures in the New Testament*

MATTHEW HENRY

that though an oath by the temple, or the altar, or heaven, be formally bad, yet it is binding. He that swears by the altar shall be interpreted by it and by all things thereon. And, the things thereon being offered up to God, to swear by it and them was, in effect, to call God himself to witness: for it was the altar of God; and he that went to that, went to God. He that swears by the temple, if he understand what he does, cannot but apprehend that the ground of such a respect to it is because it is the house of God, the place which he has chosen to put his name there; and therefore he swears *by it, and by him that dwells therein.* If a man swears by heaven, he sins (*ch.* v. 34); yet he shall not therefore be discharged from the obligation of his oath; no, God will make him know that the heaven he swears by, is his throne (Isa. lxvi. 1); and he that swears by the throne, appeals to him that sits upon it.

V. They were very strict and precise in the smaller matters of the law, but as careless and loose in the weightier matters, *v.* 23, 24. They were *partial in the law.* Sincere obedience is universal, and he that from a right principle obeys any of God's precepts, will have respect to them all. The partiality of the scribes and Pharisees appears here, in two instances.

1. They observed smaller duties, but omitted greater; they were very exact in paying tithes, when it came to *mint, anise,* and *cummin,* their exactness in tithing of which would not cost them much, but would be cried up, and they should buy reputation cheap. The Pharisee boasted of this, *I give tithes of all that I possess,* Luke xviii. 12. Paying tithes was their duty; Christ tells them they ought not to leave it undone. All ought in their places to contribute to the support and maintenance of a standing ministry. They that *are taught in the word,* and do not *communicate to them that teach them,* that love a cheap gospel, come short of the Pharisees.

But that which Christ here condemns them for, is, that they *omitted the weightier matters of the law, judgment, mercy, and faith.* All the things of God's law are weighty, but those are most weighty, which are most expressive of inward holiness in the heart. Judgment and mercy toward men, and faith toward God, are the weightier matters of the law, the *good things* which the *Lord our God requires* (Mic. vi. 8), to do justly, and love mercy, and humble ourselves by faith to walk with God. This is the obedience which is better than sacrifice or tithe. Mercy also is preferred before sacrifice, Hos. vi. 6. Nor will judgment and mercy serve without faith in divine revelation; for God will be honoured in his truths as well as in his laws.

2. They avoided lesser sins, but committed greater (*v.* 24); *Ye blind guides;* so he had called them before (*v.* 16), for their corrupt teaching; here he calls them so for their corrupt living. They were blind and partial; they *strained at a gnat, and swallowed a camel.* In their doctrine they strained at gnats, warned people against every least violation of the tradition of the elders. In their practice they strained at gnats, heaved at them, with a seeming dread, as if they had a great abhorrence of sin, and were afraid of it in the least instance; but they made no difficulty of those sins which, in comparison with them, were as a camel to a gnat. It is not the scrupling of a little sin that Christ here reproves, if it be a sin, though but a gnat, it must be strained at, but the doing of that, and then swallowing a camel.

VI. They were all for the outside, and not at all for the inside, of religion. This is illustrated by two similitudes.

1. They are compared to a vessel that is clean washed on the outside, but all dirt within, *v.* 25, 26. Now what a foolish thing would it be for a man to wash only the outside of a cup, which is to be looked at, and to leave the inside dirty, which is to be used; so they do who only avoid scandalous sins, that would spoil their reputation with men, but allow themselves in heart-wickedness, which renders them odious to the pure and holy God. In reference to this, observe,

(1) The practice of the Pharisees; they made clean the outside. In those things which fell under the observation of their neighbours, they seemed very exact; people generally took them for very good men. But within they were *full of extortion and excess.* While they would seem to be godly, they were neither sober nor righteous. And that we are really, which we are inwardly.

(2) The rule Christ gives, in opposition to this practice, *v.* 26. Those are blind, in Christ's account, who are strangers, and no enemies, to the wickedness of their own hearts; who see not, and hate not, the secret sin that lodgeth there. Self-ignorance is the most shameful and hurtful ignorance. The rule is, *Cleanse first that which is within.* The main business

F. B. MEYER:

Woes for the false-hearted. These repeated woes may be translated, "Alas for you!" Our Lord with unfailing accuracy indicates the inevitable doom which such conduct as that of the Pharisees and scribes must incur. He forewarned them that they could expect nothing in the dread future but the judgment of Gehenna—the metaphor being taken from the valley of Hinnom, south of Jerusalem, where fires were kept burning to consume rubbish and refuse.

Hypocrisy hides under a cloak of religion the sins which the ordinary moralist and worldling would condemn. It is very injurious, because it hinders men from entering the kingdom (v. 13). It is punctilious in its exactions, because while it strains out gnats, it swallows camels (vv. 23, 24). It expends itself on outward ritual. The Pharisees would not enter Pilate's hall on the day before the Passover, but they murdered the holy Savior. Above all things, let us be true, professing to be no more than we are!—*Bible Commentary*

JAMIESON, FAUSSET, BROWN

23. Woe unto you, scribes and Pharisees, hypocrites! for ye pay tithe of mint and anise—rather, "dill," as in margin—**and cummin**—In Luke (11:42) it is "and rue, and all manner of herbs." They grounded this practice on Leviticus 27:30, which they interpreted rigidly. Our Lord purposely names the most trifling products of the earth as examples of what they punctiliously exacted the tenth of. **and have omitted the weightier matters of the law, judgment, mercy, and faith**—In Luke (11:42) it is "judgment, mercy, and the love of God"—the expression being probably varied by our Lord Himself on the two different occasions. In both His reference is to Micah 6:6-8, where the prophet makes all acceptable religion to consist of three elements—"doing justly, loving mercy, and walking humbly with our God"; which third element presupposes and comprehends both the "faith" of Matthew and the "love" of Luke. See on Mark 12:29, 32, 33. The same tendency to merge greater duties in less besets even the children of God; but *it is the characteristic of hypocrites.* **these ought ye to have done, and not to leave the other undone**—There is no need for one set of duties to jostle out another; but it is to be carefully noted that of the *greater* duties our Lord says, "Ye ought to have done" them, while of the *lesser* He merely says, "Ye ought not to leave them undone." **24. Ye blind guides, which strain at a gnat**—The proper rendering—as in the older English translations, and perhaps our own as it came from the translators' hands—evidently is, "strain out." It was the custom, says TRENCH, of the stricter Jews to strain their wine, vinegar, and other potables through linen or gauze, lest unawares they should drink down some little unclean insect therein and thus transgress (Lev. 11:20, 23, 41, 42)—just as the Buddhists do now in Ceylon and Hindustan—and to this custom of theirs our Lord here refers. **and swallow a camel**—the largest animal the Jews knew, as the "gnat" was the smallest; both were by the law *unclean.*

25. within they are full of extortion—In Luke (11:39) the same word is rendered "ravening," i.e., "rapacity." **26. Thou blind Pharisee, cleanse first that which is within the cup and platter, that the outside of them may be clean also**—In Luke (11:40) it is, "Ye fools, did not He that made that which is without make that which is within also?"—"He to whom belongs the outer life, and of right demands its subjection to Himself, is the inner man less His?" A remarkable example this of our Lord's power of drawing the most striking illustrations of great truths from the most fa-

ADAM CLARKE

23. *Ye pay tithe of mint.* They were remarkably scrupulous in the performance of all the rites and ceremonies of religion, but totally neglected the soul, spirit, and practice of godliness. *Judgment.* Acting according to justice and equity towards all mankind. *Mercy*—to the distressed and miserable. And *faith* in God as the Fountain of all righteousness, mercy, and truth. *These ought ye to have done.* Our Lord did not object to their paying tithe even of common potherbs—this did not affect the spirit of religion. But while they did this and suchlike, to the utter neglect of justice, mercy, and faith, they showed that they had no religion, and knew nothing of its nature.

24. *Blind guides, which strain at a gnat, and swallow a camel.* This clause should be thus translated: "You strain out the gnat, but you swallow down the camel." In the common translation, *strain at a gnat* conveys no sense. Indeed it is likely to have been at first an error of the press, "at" for "out," which, on examination, I find escaped in the edition of 1611, and has been regularly continued since.

25. *Ye make clean the outside.* The Pharisees were exceedingly exact in observing all the washings and purifications prescribed by the law, but paid no attention to that inward purity which was typified by them. A man may appear clean without who is unclean within; but outward purity will not avail in the sight of God, where inward holiness is wanting. *Extortion and excess.* "Rapine and intemperance."

MATTHEW HENRY

of a Christian lies within, to get cleansed from the *filthiness of the spirit.*' Those sins must be conscientiously abstained from, which the eye of God only is a witness to, who searcheth the heart. *Cleanse first that which is within;* not that *only*, but that *first*; because, if due care be taken concerning that, the outside will be clean also. If renewing, sanctifying grace make clean the inside, that will have an influence upon the outside, for the commanding principle is within. If the heart be well kept, all is well, for *out of it are the issues of life.* First cleanse that which is within; we then make sure work, when this is our first work.

2. They are compared to *whited sepulchres, v.* 27, 28.

(1) They were fair without, like sepulchres, *which appear beautiful outward.* Some make it to refer to the custom of the Jews to whiten graves, that people might avoid them, because of the ceremonial pollution contracted by the touch of a grave. The formality of hypocrites doth but make all wise and good men the more careful to avoid them. It rather alludes to the custom of whitening the sepulchres of eminent persons, for the beautifying of them. It is said here (*v.* 29), that they *garnished the sepulchres of the righteous.* Now the righteousness of the scribes and Pharisees was like the ornaments of a grave, only for show. The top of their ambition was to *appear righteous before men*, and to be applauded and had in admiration by them.

(2) They were *foul* within, like sepulchres, *full of dead men's bones, and all uncleanness.* Thus were they full of hypocrisy and iniquity. It is possible for those that have their hearts full of sin, to have their lives free from blame, and to appear very good. But what will it avail us, to have the good work of our fellow-servants, if our Master doth not say, *Well done?*

VII. They pretended a deal of kindness for the memory of the prophets that were dead and gone, while they hated and persecuted those that were present with them. God is jealous for his honour in his laws and ordinances; but he has often expressed an equal jealousy for his honour in his prophets and ministers. Therefore, when our Lord Jesus comes to this head, he speaks more fully than upon any of the other (*v.* 29–37).

1. The respect which the scribes and Pharisees pretended for the prophets that were gone, *v.* 29, 30.

(1) They honoured the relics of the prophets, they built their tombs, and garnished their sepulchres. *The memory of the just is blessed*, when the names of those that hated and persecuted them shall be covered with shame. This is an instance of the hypocrisy of the scribes and Pharisees, who paid their respect to them. They can pay respect to the writings of the dead prophets, which tell them what they *should be*; but not the reproofs of the living prophets, which tell them what they *are*.

(2) They protested against the murder of them (*v.* 30); *If we had been in the days of our fathers, we would not have been partakers with them.* No, not they, they would sooner have lost their right hands than have done any such thing. And yet they were at this time plotting to murder Christ, *to whom all the prophets bore witness.* The deceitfulness of sinners' hearts appears very much in this, that, while they go down the stream of the sins of their own day, they fancy they should have swum against the stream of the sins of the former days; that, if they had had other people's opportunities, they should have improved them more faithfully. We are sometimes thinking, if we had lived when Christ was upon earth, how constantly we would have followed him; we would not have despised and rejected him, as they then did; and yet Christ in his Spirit, in his word, in his ministers, is still no better treated.

2. Their enmity and opposition to Christ and his gospel, notwithstanding, and the ruin they were bringing upon themselves and upon that generation thereby, *v.* 31–33. Observe here,

(1) The indictment proved; *Ye are witnesses against yourselves.* Sinners cannot hope to escape the judgment of Christ for want of proof against them, when it is easy to find them witnesses against themselves. By their own confession, it was the great wickedness of their forefathers, to kill the prophets. They who condemn sin in others, and yet allow the same or worse in themselves, are of all others most inexcusable, Rom. i. 32–ii. 1. By their own confession, these notorious persecutors were their ancestors; *Ye are the children of them.* Christ turns it upon them, that they were so by spirit and disposition. They are, as you say, *your* fathers, and you *take after your fathers*; it is the sin that runs in the blood among you.

(2) The sentence passed upon them. Christ here proceeds,

JAMIESON, FAUSSET, BROWN

miliar objects and incidents in life. To these words, recorded by Luke, He adds the following, involving a principle of immense value: "But rather give alms of such things as ye have, and behold, all things are clean unto you" (Luke 11:41). As the greed of these hypocrites was one of the most prominent features of their character (Luke 16:14), our Lord bids them exemplify the opposite character, and then their *outside*, ruled by this, would be beautiful in the eye of God, and their meals would be eaten with clean hands, though much fouled with the business of this everyday world. (See Eccles. 9:7.) **27. Woe unto you, scribes and Pharisees, hypocrites! for ye are like whited**—or, white-washed—**sepulchres**—(cf. Acts 23:3). The process of white-washing the sepulchres, as LIGHTFOOT says, was performed on a certain day every year, not for ceremonial cleansing, but, as the following words seem rather to imply, to beautify them. **which indeed appear beautiful outward, but are within full of dead men's bones, and of all uncleanness**—What a powerful way of conveying the charge, that with all their fair show their hearts were full of corruption! (Cf. Ps. 5:9; Rom. 3:13.) But our Lord, stripping off the figure, next holds up their iniquity in naked colors.

Wherefore ye be witnesses unto yourselves, that ye are the children of them which killed the prophets—i.e., "ye be witnesses that ye have inherited, and voluntarily served yourselves heirs to, the truth-hating, prophet-killing, spirit of your fathers." Out of pretended respect and honor, they repaired and beautified the sepulchres of the prophets, and with whining hypocrisy said, "If we had been in their days, how differently should we have treated these prophets?" While all the time they were witnesses to themselves that they were the children of them that killed the prophets, convicting themselves daily of as exact a resemblance in spirit and character to the very classes over whose deeds they pretended to mourn, as child to parent. In Luke 11:44 our Lord gives another turn to this figure of a grave: "Ye are as graves which appear not, and the men that walk

ADAM CLARKE

27. *For ye are like.* "Ye exactly resemble"—the parallel is complete. *Whited sepulchres.* "Whitewashed tombs." As the law considered those unclean who had touched anything belonging to the dead, the Jews took care to have their tombs whitewashed each year, that, being easily discovered, they might be consequently avoided.

30. *We would not have been partakers.* They imagined themselves much better than their ancestors; but our Lord, who knew what they would do, uncovers their hearts, and shows them that they are about to be more abundantly vile than all who had ever preceded them.

31. *Ye be witnesses.* There are many who think that, had they lived in the time of our Lord, they would not have acted towards Him as the Jews did. But we can scarcely believe that they who reject His gospel, trample underfoot His precepts, do despite to the Spirit of His grace, love sin and hate His followers, would have acted otherwise to Him than the murdering Jews, had they lived in the same times.

ALEXANDER MACLAREN:

If the Talmudical practice is as old as our Lord's time, the annual whitewashing was lately over. Its purpose was not to adorn the tombs, but to make them conspicuous, so that they might be avoided for fear of defilement. So He would say, with terrible irony, that the apparent holiness of the rulers was really a sign of corruption and a warning to keep away from them. What a blow at their self-complacency! And how profoundly true it is that the more punctiliously white the hypocrite's outside, the more foul is he within, and the wider berth will all discerning people give him! The terrible force of the figure needs no dwelling on. In Christ's estimate, such a soul was the very dwelling place of death; and foul odors and worms and corruption filled its sickening recesses. Terrible words to come from His lips into which grace was poured, and bold words to be flashed at listeners who held the life of the Speaker in their hands! There are two sorts of hypocrites, the conscious and the unconscious; and there are ten of the latter for one of the former, and each ten times more dangerous. Established religion breeds them, and they are especially likely to be found among those whose business is to study the documents in which it is embodied. These woes are not like thunder peals rolling above our heads, while the lightning strikes the earth miles away. A religion which is mostly whitewash is as common among us as ever it was in Jerusalem; and its foul accompaniments of corruption becoming more rotten every year, as the whitewash is laid on thicker, may be smelled among us, and its fatal end is as sure.—*Expositions of Holy Scripture*

MATTHEW HENRY

[1] To give them up to sin as irreclaimable (*v.* 32); *Fill ye up then the measure of your fathers.* Christ knew they were now contriving his death, and in a few days would accomplish it; "Well," saith he, "go on with your plot, walk in the way of your heart and in the sight of your eyes, and see what will come of it. You will but fill up the measure of guilt. *First,* There is a measure of sin to be filled up. God will bear long, but the time will come when he can *no longer forbear. Secondly,* Children fill up the measure of their father's sins when they are gone, if they persist in the same or the like. That national guilt which brings national ruin is made up of the sin of many in several ages. God justly visits the iniquity of the fathers upon the children that tread in the steps of it. *Thirdly,* Persecuting Christ, and his people and ministers, is a sin that fills the measure of a nation's guilt sooner than any other. *Fourthly,* It is just with God to give those up to their own heart's lusts, who obstinately persist in the gratification of them.

[2] He proceeds to give them up to ruin as irrecoverable, to a personal ruin in the other world (*v.* 33); *Ye serpents, ye generation of vipers, how can ye escape the damnation of hell?* These are strange words to come from the mouth of Christ, into whose lips grace was poured. But he can and will speak terror.

Here is, *First,* Their description; *Ye serpents.* Doth Christ call names? Yes, but this doth not warrant us to do so. He infallibly knew what was in man. They were a *generation of vipers;* they and those that joined with them, were a generation of envenomed, enraged, spiteful adversaries to Christ and his gospel. Christ calls them *serpents* and *vipers;* for he gives men their true characters, and delights to put contempt upon the proud.

Secondly, Their doom. *How can ye escape the damnation of hell?* Christ himself preached hell and damnation, for which his ministers have often been reproached by those that care not to hear of it. This doom coming from Christ, was more terrible than coming from all the prophets and ministers that ever were, for he is the Judge, into whose hands the keys of hell and death are put. There is a way of escaping this damnation. Repentance and faith are necessary to that escape; and how will *they* be brought to these, who are so conceited of themselves, and so prejudiced against Christ and his gospel, as they were? Publicans and harlots, who were sensible of their disease and applied themselves to the Physician, were more likely to escape the damnation of hell than those who, though they were in the high road to it, were confident they were in the way to heaven.

Verses 34-39

We have left the blind leaders fallen into the ditch; let us see what will become of the blind followers, and particularly Jerusalem.

I. Jesus Christ designs yet to try them with the means of grace; *I send unto you prophets, and wise men, and scribes.* One would think it should follow, "Therefore you shall never have a prophet sent to you any more;" but no, "*Therefore I will send unto you prophets,* to see if you will yet at length be wrought upon, or else to leave you inexcusable."

1. It is Christ that sends them; *I send.* By this he avows himself to be God, having power to gift and commission prophets. It is an act of kingly office. After his resurrection, he made this word good, when he said, *So send I you,* John xx. 21.

2. He sends them to the Jews first; "I send them to *you.*" They began at Jerusalem; and, wherever they went, they observed this rule, to make the first tender of gospel grace *to the Jews,* Acts xiii. 46.

3. Those he sends are called *prophets, wise men,* and *scribes,* Old Testament names for New Testament officers. We may take the apostles and evangelists for the prophets and wise men, and the pastors and teachers for the scribes, *instructed to the kingdom of heaven* (*ch.* xiii. 52); for the office of a scribe was honourable till the men dishonoured it.

II. He foresees and foretells the ill usage that his messengers would meet with among them; "*Some of them ye shall kill and crucify,* and yet I will send them." Christ knows beforehand how ill his servants will be treated, and yet sends them; yet he loves them never the less, for he designs to glorify himself by their sufferings, and them after them; he will counter-balance them, though not prevent them.

1. The cruelty of these persecutors; *Ye shall kill and crucify them.* It is no less than the blood, the life-blood, that they thirst after. Thus did the members partake of the sufferings of the Head, he was killed and crucified, and so were they. Christians must expect to resist unto blood.

2. Their unwearied industry; *Ye shall persecute*

JAMIESON, FAUSSET, BROWN

over them are not aware of them." As one might unconsciously walk over a grave concealed from view, and thus contract ceremonial defilement, so the plausible exterior of the Pharisees kept people from perceiving the pollution they contracted from coming in contact with such corrupt characters.

33. Ye serpents, ye generation of vipers, how can ye escape the damnation of hell?—In thus, at the end of His ministry, recalling the words of the Baptist at the outset of his, our Lord would seem to intimate that the only difference between their condemnation now and then was, that now they were ripe for their doom, which they were not then.

34. Wherefore, behold, I send unto you prophets, and wise men, and scribes—The *I* here is emphatic: "I am sending," i.e., "am about to send." In Luke 11:49 the variation is remarkable: "Therefore also, said the wisdom of God, I will send them . . . ." What precisely is meant by "the wisdom of God" here, is somewhat difficult to determine. To us it appears to be simply an announcement of a purpose of the Divine Wisdom, in the high style of ancient prophecy, to send a last set of messengers whom the people would reject, and rejecting, would fill up the cup of their iniquity. But, whereas in Luke it is "I, the Wisdom of God, will send them," in Matthew it is "I, Jesus, am sending them"; language only befitting the one sender of all the prophets, the Lord God of Israel now in the flesh. They are evidently evangelical messengers, but called by the familiar Jewish names of "prophets, wise men, and scribes," whose counterparts were the inspired and gifted servants of the Lord Jesus; for in Luke (11:49) it is "prophets and apostles."

ADAM CLARKE

32. *Fill ye up then.* Notwithstanding the profession you make, you will fill up the measure of your fathers—will continue to walk in their way, accomplish the fullness of every evil purpose by murdering Me; and then, when the measure of your iniquity is full, vengeance shall come upon you to the uttermost, as it did on your rebellious ancestors. The thirty-first verse should be read in a parenthesis, and then the thirty-second will appear to be, what it is, an inference from the thirtieth. You will fill up, or *fill ye up.* But it is manifest that the imperative is put here for the future, a thing quite consistent with the Hebrew idiom, and frequent in the Scriptures.

34. *Wherefore.* To show how My prediction, "You will fill up the measure of your fathers," shall be verified, *Behold, I send* (I am just going to commission them) *prophets . . . and some of them ye shall kill* (with legal process) and some you will crucify, pretend to try and find guilty, and deliver them into the hands of the Romans, who shall, through you, thus put them to death. By *prophets, wise men, and scribes,* our Lord intends the Evangelists, apostles, deacons, who should be employed in proclaiming His gospel—men who should equal the ancient prophets, their wise men, and scribes, in all the gifts and graces of the Holy Spirit.

W. E. VINE:

OPHIS, serpent. The characteristics of the serpent as alluded to in Scripture are mostly evil (though Matt. 10:16 refers to its caution in avoiding danger); its treachery (Gen. 49:17; 2 Cor. 11:3); its venom (Ps. 58:4; 1 Cor. 10:9; Rev. 9:19); its skulking (Job 26:13); its murderous proclivities (Ps. 58:4; Prov. 23:32; Eccles. 10:8, 11; Amos 5:19; Mark 16:18; Luke 10:19); the Lord used the word metaphorically of the scribes and Pharisees (Matt. 23:33). The general aspects of its evil character are intimated in the Lord's rhetorical question in Matt. 7:10 and Luke 11:11. Its characteristics are concentrated in the arch-adversary of God and man, the devil, metaphorically described as the serpent (2 Cor. 11:3; Rev. 12:9, 14, 15; 20:2).—*Vine's Expository Dictionary*

MATTHEW HENRY

them from city to city. As the apostles went from city to city, to preach the gospel, the Jews dodged them, and haunted them, and stirred up persecution against them, Acts xiv. 19; xvii. 13.

3. The pretence of religion in this; they scourged them in their synagogues, so that they did it as a piece of service to the church.

III. He imputes the sin of their fathers to them, because they imitated it; *That upon you may come all the righteous blood shed upon the earth, v.* 35, 36. Though God bear long with a persecuting generation, he will not bear always; and patience abused, turns into the greatest wrath.

Observe, 1. The extent of this imputation; it takes in *all the righteous blood shed upon the earth,* that is, the blood shed for righteousness' sake. He dates the account *from the blood of righteous Abel.* How early did martyrdom come into the world! He extends it *to the blood of Zacharias, the son of Barachias* (*v.* 36), as is most probable, *Zechariah the son of Jehoiada,* who was *slain in the court of the Lord's house,* 2 Chron. xxiv. 20, 21. His father is called *Barachias,* which signifies much the same with Jehoiada; and it was usual among the Jews for the same person to have two names; *whom ye slew,* ye of this nation, though not of this generation.

2. The effect of it; *All these things shall come;* all the guilt of this blood, all the punishment of it, it shall *all come upon this generation.* The destruction shall be so dreadful, as if God had once for all arraigned them for all the righteous blood shed in the world. It shall *come upon this generation;* which intimates, that it shall come quickly; some here shall live to see it. The sorer and nearer the punishment of sin is, the louder is the call to repentance and reformation.

IV. He laments the wickedness of Jerusalem, and justly upbraids them with the many kind offers he had made them, *v.* 37. See with what concern he speaks of that city; *O Jerusalem, Jerusalem!* The repetition is emphatic, and bespeaks abundance of commiseration. A day or two before Christ had wept over Jerusalem, now he sighed and groaned over it. Jerusalem, *the vision of peace* (so it signifies), must now be the seat of war and confusion. But wherefore will the Lord do all this to Jerusalem? Why? *Jerusalem hath grievously sinned.*

1. She persecuted God's messengers; *Thou that killest the prophets, and stonest them that are sent unto thee.* This sin is especially charged upon Jerusalem; because there the Sanhedrim, or great council, sat, who took cognizance of church matters, and therefore a prophet could not perish but in Jerusalem, Luke xiii. 33. They killed the prophets in popular tumults, mobbed them, as Stephen, and put the Roman powers on to kill them. At Jerusalem, where the gospel was first preached, it was first persecuted (Acts viii. 1), and that place was the headquarters of the persecutors; and thither the saints were brought bound, Acts ix. 2. *Thou stonest them.* There was abundance of other wickedness in Jerusalem; but this was the sin that made the loudest cry, and which God had an eye to more than any other.

2. She refused and rejected Christ, and gospel offers. The former was a sin *without* remedy, this *against* the remedy. The wonderful grace and favour of Jesus Christ toward them; *How often would I have gathered thy children together, as a hen gathers her chickens under her wings!* The favour proposed was the gathering of them. Christ's design is to gather poor souls, gather them in from their wanderings, gather them home to himself. It is here illustrated by a humble similitude; *as a hen* clucks *her chickens together.* Christ would have gathered them, *First,* With such a tenderness of affection as the hen does, which has, by instinct, a peculiar concern for her young ones. Christ's gathering of souls, comes from his love, Jer. xxxi. 3. *Secondly, For the same end. The hen gathered her chickens under her wings,* for protection and safety, and for warmth and comfort. The chickens naturally run to the hen for shelter, when they are threatened by the birds of prey; perhaps Christ refers to that promise (Ps. xci. 4), *He shall cover thee with his feathers.* There is *healing under Christ's wings;* that is more than the hen has for her chickens. The forwardness of Christ to confer this favour. His offers are, *First,* Very free; *I would have done it. Secondly,* Very frequent; *How often!* Christ often came up to Jerusalem, preached, and wrought miracles there. As often as we have heard the sound of the gospel, as often as we have felt the strivings of the Spirit, so often Christ would have gathered us. Their wilful refusal of this grace and favour; *Ye would not.* I would, and *ye would not.* He was willing to save them, but they were not willing to be saved by him.

V. He reads Jerusalem's doom (*v.* 38, 39); *Therefore*

JAMIESON, FAUSSET, BROWN

unto the blood of Zacharias son of Barachias, whom ye slew between the temple and the altar—As there is no record of any fresh murder answering to this description, probably the allusion is not to any recent murder, but to II Chronicles 24: 20-22, as the *last recorded* and most suitable case for illustration. And as Zacharias' last words were, "The Lord *require it,*" so they are here warned that of that generation it should be *required.* **36. Verily I say unto you, All these things shall come upon this generation**—As it was only in the last generation of them that "the iniquity of the Amorites was full" (Gen. 15:16), and then the abominations of ages were at once completely and awfully avenged, so the iniquity of Israel was allowed to accumulate from age to age till in that generation it came to the full, and the whole collected vengeance of heaven broke at once over its devoted head. In the first French Revolution the same awful principle was exemplified, and *Christendom has not done with it yet.*

Lamentation over Jerusalem, and Farewell to the Temple (vss. 37-39). **37. O Jerusalem, Jerusalem, thou that killest the prophets, and stonest them which are sent unto thee, . . .**—How ineffably grand and melting is this apostrophe! It is the very heart of God pouring itself forth through human flesh and speech. It is this incarnation of the innermost life and love of Deity, pleading with men, bleeding for them, and ascending only to open His arms to them and win them back by the power of this story of matchless love, that has conquered the world, that will yet "draw all men unto Him," and beautify and ennoble Humanity itself! "Jerusalem" here does not mean the mere city or its inhabitants; nor is it to be viewed merely as the metropolis of the *nation,* but as the *center of their religious life*—"the city of their solemnities, whither the tribes went up, to give thanks unto the name of the Lord"; and at this moment it was full of them. It is the whole family of God, then, which is here apostrophized by a name dear to every Jew, recalling to him all that was distinctive and precious in his religion. The intense feeling that sought vent in this utterance comes out first in the redoubling of the opening word—"Jerusalem, Jerusalem!" but, next, in the picture of it which He draws—"that killest the prophets, and stonest them which are sent unto thee!"—not content with spurning God's messages of mercy, that canst not suffer even the messengers to live! When He adds, "How often would I have gathered thee!" He refers surely to something beyond the six or seven times that He visited and taught in Jerusalem while on earth. No doubt it points to "the prophets," whom they "killed," to "them that were sent unto her," whom they "stoned." But whom would He have gathered so often? "Thee," truth-hating, mercy-spurning, prophet-killing Jerusalem—how often would I have gathered *thee!* Compare with this that affecting clause in the great ministerial commission, "that repentance and remission of sins should be preached in His name among all nations, *beginning at Jerusalem!"* (Luke 24:47). What encouragement to the heartbroken at their own long-continued and obstinate rebellion! But we have not yet got at the whole heart of this outburst. I would have gathered thee, He says, "even as a hen gathereth her chickens under her wings." Was ever imagery so homely invested with such grace and such sublimity as this, at our Lord's touch? And yet how exquisite the figure itself—of protection, rest, warmth, and all manner of conscious well-being in those poor, defenseless, dependent little creatures, as they creep under and feel themselves overshadowed by the capacious and kindly wing of the mother-bird! If, wandering beyond hearing of her peculiar call, they are overtaken by a storm or attacked by an enemy, what can they do but in the one case droop and die, and in the other submit to be torn in pieces? But if they can reach in time their

ADAM CLARKE

35. *Upon the earth.* "Upon this land," meaning probably the land of Judea, for thus the word is often to be understood. The national punishment of all the innocent *blood* which had been shed in the land shall speedily come upon you, *from the blood of . . . Abel,* the just, the first prophet and preacher of righteousness, Heb. xi. 4; 2 Pet. ii. 5, *unto the blood of Zacharias son of Barachias.* It is likely that our Lord refers to the murder of Zechariah, mentioned in 2 Chron. xxiv. 20-22, who said to the people, "Why transgress ye the commandments of the Lord, [so] that ye cannot prosper? because ye have forsaken the Lord, he hath also forsaken you. And they conspired against him, and stoned him . . . at the commandment of the king in the court of the house of the Lord. . . . And when he died, he said, The Lord look upon it, and require it." But it is objected that this Zechariah was called the son of Jehoiada, and our Lord calls this one the son of Barachiah. Let it be observed: (1) that double names were frequent among the Jews, and sometimes the person was called by one, sometimes by the other; (2) that Jerome says that in the Gospel of the Nazarenes it was Jehoiada, instead of Barachiah; (3) that Jehoiada and Barachiah have the very same meaning, the "praise or blessing of Jehovah"; (4) that as the Lord required the blood of Zechariah so fully that in a year all the princes of Judah and Jerusalem were destroyed by the Syrians, and Joash, who commanded the murder, was slain by his own servants, 2 Chron. xxiv. 23-25, and their state grew worse and worse, till at last the Temple was burned, and the people carried into captivity by Nebuzaradan—so it should also be with the present race. The Lord would, after the crucifixion of Christ, visit upon them the murder of all those righteous men, that their state should grow worse and worse, till at last the Temple should be destroyed, and they finally ruined by the Romans. *Between the temple and the altar.* That is, between the sanctuary and the altar of burnt offerings.

36. *Shall come upon this generation.* "Upon this race of men," viz., the Jews. This phrase often occurs in this sense in the Evangelists.

ALEXANDER MACLAREN:

The parting wail of rejected love. The lightning flashes of the sevenfold woes end in a rain of pity and tears. His full heart overflows in that sad cry of lamentation over the long-continued foiling of the efforts of a love that would fain have fondled and defended. What intensity of feeling is in the redoubled naming of the city! How yearningly and wistfully He calls, as if He might still win the faithless one, and how lingeringly unwilling He is to give up hope! How mournfully, rather than accusingly, He reiterates the acts which had run through the whole history, using a form of the verbs which suggests continuance. Mark, too, the matter-of-course way in which Christ assumes that He sent all the prophets whom, through the generations, Jerusalem had stoned.

So the lament passes into the solemn final leave-taking, with which our Lord closes His ministry among the Jews, and departs from the temple. As, in the parable of the marriage feast, the city was emphatically called "their city," so here the temple, in whose courts He was standing, and which in a moment He was to quit forever, is called "your house," because His departure is the withdrawing of the true Shechinah. It had been the house of God; now He casts it off and leaves it to them to do as they will with it. The saddest punishment of long-continued rejection of His pleading love is that it ceases at last to plead. The bitterest woe for those who refuse to render to Him the fruits of the vineyard is to get the vineyard for their own, undisturbed. Christ's utmost retribution for obstinate blindness is to withdraw from our sight.

—*Expositions of Holy Scripture*

MATTHEW HENRY

behold your house is left unto you desolate. Both the city and the temple, God's house and their own, all shall be laid waste. But it is especially meant of the temple, which they boasted of, and trusted to.

1. Their house shall be *deserted; It is left unto you.* Christ was now departing from the temple, and never came into it again. They doated on it, would have it to themselves; Christ must have no room or interest there. "Well," saith Christ, "it is left to you; take it, and made your best of it; I will never have anything more to do with it." Their city also was left to them, destitute of God's presence and grace.

2. It shall be *desolate; It is left unto you desolate.* It was immediately, when Christ left it, in the eyes of all that understood themselves, a very dismal melancholy place. Christ's departure makes the best furnished, best replenished place a wilderness. For what comfort can there be where Christ is not? This comes of men's rejecting Christ, and driving him away from them. It was, not long after, destroyed and ruined, and *not one stone left upon another.* The temple, that holy and beautiful house, became desolate. When God goes out, all enemies break in.

Lastly, Here is the final farewell that Christ took of them and their temple; *Ye shall not see me henceforth, till ye shall say, Blessed is he that cometh.* This bespeaks,

3. His departure from them. The time was at hand, when *he should leave the world, to go to his Father,* and be seen no more. *After his resurrection, he was seen only by a few chosen witnesses,* and they saw him not long, but he soon removed to the invisible world, and there will be *till the time of the restitution of all things,* when his welcome at his first coming will be repeated with loud acclamations; *Blessed is he that cometh in the name of the Lord.* Would we have our lot in that day with those that say, *Blessed is he that cometh?* let us be with them now, with them that truly worship, and truly welcome, Jesus Christ.

4. Their continued blindness and obstinacy; *Ye shall not see me,* that is, not see the light of the truth concerning me, nor *the things that belong to your peace, till ye shall say, Blessed is he that cometh.* Wilful blindness is often punished with judicial blindness. If they *will* not see, they *shall* not see. With this word he concludes his public preaching. When *the Lord comes with ten thousand of his saints,* he will convince all. They who now reproach and ridicule the hosannas of the saints will be of another mind shortly; it were therefore better to be of that mind now.

JAMIESON, FAUSSET, BROWN

place of safety, under the mother's wing, in vain will any enemy try to drag them thence. For rising into strength, kindling into fury, and forgetting herself entirely in her young, she will let the last drop of her blood be shed out and perish in defense of her precious charge, rather than yield them to an enemy's talons. How significant all this of what Jesus is and does for men! Under His great Mediatorial wing would He have "gathered" Israel. For the figure, see Deuteronomy 32:10-12; Ruth 2:12; Psalm 17:8; 36:7; 61:4; 63:7; 91:4; Isaiah 31:5; Malachi 4:2. The ancient rabbins had a beautiful expression for proselytes from the heathen—that they had "come under the wings of the Shekinah." For this last word, see on vs. 38. But what was the result of all this tender and mighty love? The answer is, "And ye would not." O mysterious word! mysterious the resistance of such patient Love-mysterious the liberty of self-undoing! The awful dignity of the *will,* as here expressed, might make the ears to tingle. **38. Behold, your house**—the temple, beyond all doubt; but *their* house now, not *the Lord's.* See on ch. 22:7. **is left unto you desolate**—deserted, i.e., of its Divine Inhabitant. But who is that? Hear the next words: **39. For I say unto you**—and these were *His last words* to the impenitent nation, see opening remarks on Mark 13.—**Ye shall not see me henceforth**—What? Does Jesus mean that He was Himself the Lord of the temple, and that it became "deserted" when HE finally left it? It is even so. Now is thy fate sealed, O Jerusalem, for the glory is departed from thee! That glory, once visible in the holy of holies, over the mercy seat, when on the day of atonement the blood of typical expiation was sprinkled on it and in front of it—called by the Jews the *Shekinah,* or the *Dwelling,* as being the visible pavilion of Jehovah—that glory, which Isaiah (ch. 6) saw in vision, the beloved disciple says was *the glory of Christ* (John 12:41). Though it was never visible in the second temple, Haggai foretold that *"the glory of that latter house should be greater than of the former"* (ch. 2:9) because "the Lord whom they sought was suddenly to come to His temple" (Mal. 3:1), not in a mere bright cloud, but enshrined in living humanity! Yet brief as well as "sudden" was the manifestation to be: for the words He was now uttering were to be HIS VERY LAST within its precincts. **till ye shall say, Blessed is he that cometh in the name of the Lord**—i.e., till those "Hosannas to the Son of David" with which the multitude had welcomed Him into the city—instead of "sore displeasing the chief priests and scribes" (ch. 21:15)—should break forth from the whole nation, as their glad acclaim to their once pierced, but now acknowledged, Messiah. That such a time will come is clear from Zechariah 12:10; Romans 11:26; II Corinthians 3:15, 16, etc. In what sense they shall then "see Him" may be gathered from Zechariah 2:10-13; Ezekiel 37:23-28; 39:28, 29, etc.

ADAM CLARKE

38. *Behold, your house.* "The Temple"; this is certainly what is meant.

39. *Ye shall not see me.* I will remove My gospel from you, and withdraw My protection.

Till ye shall say, Blessed. Till after the fullness of the Gentiles is brought in, when the word of life shall again be sent unto you; then will you rejoice, and bless, and praise Him *that cometh in the name of the Lord,* with full and final salvation for the lost sheep of the house of Israel. See Rom. xi. 26-27.

MATTHEW HENRY

CHAPTER 24

Verses 1–3

I. Christ's quitting *the temple,* and his public work there. He had said, in the close of the foregoing chapter, *Your house is left unto you desolate;* and here he made his words good; *He went out, and departed from the temple.* He departed from it, never to return to it any more; and then immediately follows a prediction of its ruin. That house is left desolate indeed, which Christ leaves. But Christ departed not till they drove him away; did not reject them, till they first rejected him.

II. His private discourse with his disciples; he left the temple, but he did not leave the twelve. When he left the temple, his disciples left it too, and came to him. It is good being where Christ is, and leaving that which he leaves.

1. *His disciples came to him, to show him the buildings of the temple.* It was a stately and beautiful structure. It was richly furnished with gifts and offerings. They showed Christ these things, and desired him to take notice of them, either,

(1) As being greatly pleased with them themselves, and expecting he should be so too. They had lived mostly in Galilee, at a distance from the temple, had seldom seen it, and therefore were the more struck with admiration at it, and thought he should admire as much as they did *all this glory.* Even good men are apt to be too much enamoured with outward pomp and gaiety, and to overvalue it, even in the things of God. The temple was indeed glorious, but, [1] Its glory was sullied and stained with the sin of the priests and people. [2] Its glory was eclipsed and outdone by the presence of Christ in it.

JAMIESON, FAUSSET, BROWN

CHAPTER 24

Vss. 1-51. CHRIST'S PROPHECY OF THE DESTRUCTION OF JERUSALEM, AND WARNINGS SUGGESTED BY IT TO PREPARE FOR HIS SECOND COMING. (= Mark 13:1-37; Luke 21:5-36.) For the exposition, see on Mark 13:1-37.

Jesus had uttered all His mind against the Jewish ecclesiastics, exposing their character with withering plainness, and denouncing, in language of awful severity, the judgments of God against them for that unfaithfulness to their trust which was bringing ruin upon the nation. He had closed this His last public discourse (Matt. 23) by a passionate lamentation over Jerusalem, and a solemn farewell to the temple. "And," says Matt. 24:1, "Jesus went out and departed from the temple"—never more to re-enter its precincts, or open His mouth in public teaching. *With this act ended His public ministry.* As He withdrew, says OLSHAUSEN, the gracious presence of God left the sanctuary; and the temple, with all its service, and the whole theocratic constitution, was given over to destruction. What immediately followed is, as usual, most minutely and graphically described by our Evangelist. **1. And as he went out of the temple, one of his disciples saith unto him**—The other Evangelists are less definite. "As some spake," says Luke; "His disciples came to Him," says Matthew. Doubtless it was the speech of one, the mouthpiece, likely, of others. **Master**—Teacher—**see what manner of stones and what buildings are here**—wondering probably, how so massive a pile could be overthrown, as seemed implied in our Lord's last words regarding it. JOSEPHUS, who gives

ADAM CLARKE

CHAPTER 24

This chapter contains a prediction of the utter destruction of the city and Temple of Jerusalem, and the subversion of the whole political constitution of the Jews; and is one of the most valuable portions of the new covenant Scriptures, with respect to the evidence which it furnishes of the truth of Christianity. Everything which our Lord foretold should come on the Temple, city, and people of the Jews has been fulfilled in the most correct and astonishing manner; and witnessed by a writer who was present during the whole, who was himself a Jew, and is acknowledged to be a historian of indisputable veracity in all those transactions which concern the destruction of Jerusalem. Without having designed it, he has written a commentary on our Lord's words, and shown how every tittle was punctually fulfilled, though he knew nothing of the scripture which contained this remarkable prophecy.

1. *And Jesus went out, and departed from the temple.* Or, "And Jesus, going out of the Temple, was going away." This is the arrangement of the words in several eminent manuscripts, versions, and fathers, and is much clearer than that in the common translation. The Jews say the Temple was built of white and green-spotted marble. Josephus says the stones were white and strong; fifty feet long, twenty-four broad, and sixteen thick. *Antiq,* b. 15, c. xi.

MATTHEW HENRY

Or, (2) As grieving that this house should be left desolate; they showed him the buildings, as if they would move him to reverse the sentence. Christ had lately looked upon *the precious souls, and wept for them,* Luke xix. 41. The disciples look upon the pompous buildings, and are ready to weep for them. In this, as in other things, *his thoughts are not like ours.*

2. Christ, hereupon, foretells the utter ruin and destruction that were coming upon this place, *v.* 2. A believing foresight of the defacing of all worldly glory will help to take us off from overvaluing it. *See ye not all these things?* They would have Christ look upon them, and be as much in love with them as they were. There is such a sight of these things as will do us good; so to see them as to see through them and see to the end of them.

Christ, instead of reversing the decree, ratifies it; *Verily, I say unto you, there shall not be left one stone upon another.* He speaks of it as a certain ruin; "*I say unto you.*" *I,* that know what I say. He speaks of it as an utter ruin. The temple shall not only be stripped, and plundered, and defaced, but utterly demolished and laid waste; *Not one stone shall be left unto another.* Though Titus, when he took the city, did all he could to preserve the temple, yet he could not restrain the enraged soldiers from destroying it utterly; and it was done to that degree, that Turnus Rufus ploughed up the ground on which it had stood.

3. The disciples enquire more particularly of the time when it should come to pass, and the signs of its approach, *v.* 3.

(1) Where they made this enquiry; privately, *as he sat upon the mount of Olives;* probably, he was returning to Bethany, and there sat down by the way, to rest him; the mount of Olives directly faced the temple, and from thence he might have a full prospect of it at some distance.

(2) What the enquiry itself was; *When shall these things be; and what shall be the sign of thy coming, and of the end of the world?* Here are three questions.

[1] Some think these questions do all point at one and the same thing—the destruction of the temple. Or, they thought the destruction of the temple must needs be the end of the world.

[2] Others think their question, *When shall these things be?* refers to the destruction of Jerusalem, and the other two to the end of the world. They had very confused thoughts of future events; so that perhaps it is not possible to put any certain construction upon this question of theirs.

Verses 4–31

The disciples had asked concerning the times, *When shall these things be?* Christ gives them no answer to that. But they had asked, *What shall be the sign?* That question he answers fully. Now the prophecy primarily respects the events near at hand; but as the prophecies of the Old Testament, which have an immediate reference to the affairs of the Jews, do certainly look further, to the gospel church and the kingdom of the Messiah, and are so expounded in the New Testament, so this prophecy, under the type of Jerusalem's destruction, looks as far forward as the general judgment. What Christ here saith to his disciples tends more to engage their caution than to satisfy their curiosity; more to prepare them for the events that should happen than to give them a distinct idea of the events themselves.

I. Christ begins with a caution, *Take heed that no man deceive you.* They expected to be told when these things should be, to be let into that secret; but this caution is a check to their curiosity, "*What is that to you?* Mind you your duty, follow me, and be not seduced from following me." Seducers are more dangerous enemies to the church than persecutors.

Three times in this discourse he mentions the appearing of *false prophets,* which was, 1. A presage of Jerusalem's ruin. Justly were they who killed the true prophets, left to be ensnared by false prophets; and they who crucified the true Messiah, left to be deceived and broken by false Christs and pretended Messiahs. 2. It was a trial to the disciples of Christ, and therefore agreeable to their state of probation, *that they which are perfect, may be made manifest.*

Now concerning these deceivers, observe here,

(1) The pretences they should come under. Satan acts most mischievously, when he appears as an angel of light: the colour of the greatest good is often the cover of the greatest evil. There should appear *false prophets* (*v.* 11–24); the deceivers would pretend to divine inspiration, when it was all a lie. Some think, the seducers here pointed to were such as had been settled teachers in the church, and revolted to error; and from such the danger is the greater, be-

JAMIESON, FAUSSET, BROWN

a minute account of the wonderful structure, speaks of stones forty cubits long (*Jewish War,* v. 5. 1.) and says the pillars supporting the porches were twenty-five cubits high, all of one stone, and that of the whitest marble (*ibid.,* v. 5.2). Six days' battering at the walls, during the siege, made no impression upon them (*ibid.,* vi. 4. 1). Some of the under-building, yet remaining, and other works, are probably as old as the first temple.

And Jesus answering said unto him, Seest thou these great buildings?—"Ye call My attention to these things? I have seen them. Ye point to their massive and durable appearance: now listen to their fate." **there shall not be left**—"left here" (Matt. 24:2). **one stone upon another, that shall not be thrown down**—Titus ordered the whole city and temple to be demolished [JOSEPHUS, *J. W.,* vii. 1. 1]; Eleazar wished they had all died before seeing that holy city destroyed by enemies' hands, and before the temple was so profanely *dug up* (*ibid.,* vii. 8. 7).

And as he sat upon the Mount of Olives, over against the temple—On their way from Jerusalem to Bethany they would cross Mount Olivet; on its summit He seats Himself, over against the temple, having the city all spread out under His eye. How graphically is this set before us by our Evangelist! **Peter and James and John and Andrew asked him privately**—The other Evangelists tell us merely that "the disciples" did so. But Mark not only says that it was four of them, but names them; and they were the first *quarternion* of the Twelve. **Tell us, when shall these things be? and what shall be the sign when all these things shall be fulfilled?**—"and what shall be the sign of Thy coming, and of the end of the world?" They no doubt looked upon the date of all these things as one and the same, and their notions of the things themselves were as confused as of the times of them. Our Lord takes His own way of meeting their questions.

And Jesus answering them began to say, Take heed lest any man deceive you: For many shall come in my name, saying, I am Christ—(see Matt. 24:5)—"and the time draweth nigh" (Luke 21:8); that is, the time of the kingdom in its full splendor.

ADAM CLARKE

2. *There shall not be left here one stone.* These seem to have been the last words He spoke as He left the Temple, into which He never afterwards entered; and when He got to the Mount of Olives, He renewed the discourse. From this mount, on which our Lord and His disciples now sat, the whole of the city and particularly the Temple were clearly seen. This part of our Lord's prediction was fulfilled in the most literal manner. Josephus says, *War,* b. vii, c. 1; "Caesar gave orders that they should now demolish the whole city and temple, except the three towers, Phaselus, Hippicus, and Mariamne, and a part of the western wall, and these were spared; but, for all the rest of the wall, it was laid so completely even with the ground, by those who dug it up to the foundation, that there was left nothing to make those that came thither believe it had ever been inhabited."

3. *Tell us, when shall these things be?* There appear to be three questions asked here by the disciples. (1) *"When shall these things be?"* viz., the destruction of the city, Temple, and Jewish state. (2) *"What shall be the sign of thy coming?"* viz., to execute these judgments upon them, and to establish Thy own Church. (3) *When shall this world end?* When wilt Thou come to judge the quick and the dead? But there are some who maintain that these are but three parts of the same question, and that our Lord's answers refer only to the destruction of the Jewish state, and that nothing is spoken here concerning the last or judgment day. *End of the world.* Or "of the age," viz., the Jewish economy, which is a frequent accommodated meaning of the word.

4. *Take heed that no man deceive you.* The world is full of deceivers, and it is only by taking heed to the counsel of Christ that even His followers can escape being ruined by them. From this to v. 31, our Lord mentions the signs which should precede His coming. The *first* sign is false christs.

MATTHEW HENRY

cause least suspected. One false traitor in the garrison may do more mischief than a thousand avowed enemies without. There should appear *false Christs, coming in Christ's name* (*v.* 5), assuming to themselves the name peculiar to him, and saying, *I am Christ, pseudo-christs, v.* 24. There was at that time a general expectation of the appearing of the Messias; they spoke of him; as *he that should come*; but when he did come, the body of the nation rejected him; which those who were ambitious of making themselves a name, took advantage of, and set up for Christs. These false Christs and false prophets would have their agents and emissaries busy in all places to draw people unto them, *v.* 23. *Then* when public troubles are great and threatening, and people will be catching at anything that looks like deliverance, then Satan will take the advantage of imposing on them; then they will say, *Lo, here is a Christ, or there* is one. The true Christ did not strive, nor cry; nor was it said of him, *Lo, here! or Lo, there!* (Luke xvii. 21). Christ is All in all, not here or there, but meets his people with a blessing *in every place where he records his name.*

(2) The proof they should offer for the making good of these pretences; *They shall show great signs and wonders* (*v.* 24), not true miracles, those are a divine seal, and with those the doctrine of Christ stands confirmed. It is not said, *They shall work miracles*, but, *They shall show great signs*; they are but a show.

(3) The success they should have in these attempts, *They shall deceive many* (*v.* 5), and again, *v.* 11. The devil and his instruments may prevail far in deceiving poor souls; few find the strait gate, but many are drawn into the broad way. *They shall deceive, if it were possible, the very elect, v.* 24. This bespeaks, *First*, The strength of the delusion; it is such as many shall be carried away by (so strong shall the stream be), even those that were thought to stand fast. Nothing but the almighty grace of God, pursuant to his eternal purpose, will be a protection. *Secondly*, The safety of the elect in the midst of this danger, which is taken for granted in that parenthesis, *If it were possible*, plainly implying that it is not possible, for they are *kept by the power of God.* Used proverbially by Galen; when he would express a thing very difficult and morally impossible, he saith, "You may sooner draw away a Christian from Christ."

(4) The repeated cautions which our Saviour gives; *therefore* he gave them warning, that they might watch (*v.* 25); *Behold, I have told you before.* He that is told before where he will be assaulted, may save himself. Christ's warnings are designed to engage our watchfulness. We are kept through faith, faith in Christ's word, which he has told us before. We must not believe those who say, *Lo, here is Christ;* or, *Lo, he is there, v.* 23. We believe that the true Christ is at the right hand of God, and that his spiritual presence is *where two or three are gathered together in his name.* There is not a greater enemy to true faith than vain credulity. The simple believeth every word, and runs after every cry. We must not go forth after those that say, *He is in the desert*, or, *He is in the secret chambers, v.* 26. We must not follow everyone that puts up the finger to point us to a new Christ, and a new gospel. Many a man's vain curiosity to go forth hath led him into a fatal apostasy.

II. He foretells wars and great commotions among the nations, *v.* 6, 7. When Christ was born, there was a universal peace in the empire, the temple of Janus was shut; but *think not that Christ came to send*, or continue such a *peace* (Luke xii. 51); no, his city and his wall are to be built even in troublesome times, and even wars shall forward his work.

1. A prediction of the event of the day; You will now shortly *hear of wars, and rumours of wars.* When wars are, they will be heard. See how terrible it is. Even the quiet in the land cannot but hear the rumours of war. See what comes of refusing the gospel! Those that will not hear the messengers of peace, shall be made to hear the messengers of war.

2. A prescription of the duty of the day; *See that ye be not troubled.* Is it possible to hear such sad news, and not be troubled? Yet, where the heart is fixed, trusting in God, it is kept in peace, and is not afraid. It is against the mind of Christ, that his people should have troubled hearts even in troublous times.

We must not be troubled, for two reasons.

(1) Because we are bid to expect this: the Jews must be punished; by this the justice of God and the honour of the Redeemer must be asserted; and therefore *all those things must come to pass.* God is but performing the thing that is appointed for us. Let us therefore acquiesce. The old house must be taken down (though it cannot be done without noise, and dust, and danger), ere the new fabric can be

JAMIESON, FAUSSET, BROWN

and shall deceive many—"Go ye not therefore after them" (Luke 21:8). The reference here seems not to be to pretended Messiahs, deceiving those who rejected the claims of Jesus, of whom indeed there were plenty—for our Lord is addressing His own genuine disciples—but to persons pretending to be Jesus Himself, returned in glory to take possession of His kingdom. This gives peculiar force to the words, "Go ye not therefore after them."

26. *If they shall say unto you, Behold, he is in the desert.* Is it not worthy of remark that our Lord not only foretold the appearance of these impostors, but also the manner and circumstances of their conduct? Some He mentions as appearing in the desert. Josephus says (*Ant.* b. xx, c. 7, and *War*, b. ii, c. 13): That many impostors and cheats persuaded the people to follow them to the desert, promising to show them signs and wonders done by the providence of God, is well-attested. An Egyptian false prophet, mentioned by Josephus, *Ant.* b. xx, c. 7, and in the Acts, chap. xxi. 38, "leddest out into the wilderness four thousand men that were murderers," but these were all taken or destroyed by Felix. Another promised salvation to the people if they would follow him to the desert, and he was destroyed by Festus, *Ant.* b. xx, c. 7. Also, one Jonathan, a weaver, persuaded a number to follow him to the desert, but he was taken and burnt alive by Vespasian. See *War*, b. vii, c. 11. As some conducted their deluded followers to the desert, so did others to the *secret chambers.* Josephus mentions a false prophet, *War*, b. vi, c. 5, who declared to the people in the city that God commanded them to go up into the Temple and there they should receive the signs of deliverance. A multitude of men, women, and children went up accordingly; but, instead of deliverance, the place was set on fire by the Romans, and 6,000 perished miserably in the flames, or in attempting to escape them.

And when ye shall hear of wars and rumours of wars, be ye not troubled—see on vs. 13, and compare Isaiah 8:11-14.

ADAM CLARKE

5. *For many shall come in my name.* Josephus says (*War*, b. ii, c. 13) that there were many who, pretending to divine inspiration, deceived the people, leading out numbers of them to the desert, pretending that God would there show them the signs of liberty, meaning redemption from the Roman power, and that an Egyptian false prophet led 30,000 men into the desert, who were almost all cut off by Felix. See Acts xxi. 38. It was a just judgment for God to deliver up that people into the hands of false christs who had rejected the true one. About twelve years after the death of our Lord, when Cuspius Fadus was procurator of Judea, arose an impostor of the name of Theudas, who said he was a prophet, and persuaded a great multitude to follow him with their best effects to the river Jordan, which he promised to divide for their passage; and saying these things, says Josephus, "he deceived many"—almost the very words of our Lord. A few years afterwards, under the reign of Nero, while Felix was procurator of Judea, impostors of this stamp were so frequent that some were taken and killed almost every day (Josephus *Ant.*, b. xx, cc. 4 and 7).

23-24. *Then if any man shall say unto you, Lo, here is Christ.* Our Lord had cautioned His disciples against false Christs and prophets before, v. 11; but He seems here to intimate that there would be especial need to attend to this caution about the time of the siege. And in fact many such impostors did arise about that time, promising deliverance from God; and the lower the Jews were reduced, the more disposed they were to listen to such deceivers. Like a man drowning, they were willing to catch even at a straw, while there was any prospect of being saved. But as it was to little purpose for a man to take upon him the character of the Christ, without miracles to avouch his divine mission, so it was the common artifice of these impostors to show *signs* and *wonders*—the very words used by Christ in this prophecy, and by Josephus in his history, *Ant.* b. xx, c. 7.

6. The *second* sign given by our Lord is *wars and rumours of wars.* These may be seen in Josephus (*Ant.*, b. xviii, c. 9; *War*, b. ii, c. 10), especially as to the *rumours of wars,* when Caligula ordered his statue to be set up in the Temple of God, which the Jews having refused, had every reason to expect a war with the Romans, and were in such consternation on the occasion that they even neglected to till their land.

7. *Nation shall rise against nation.* This portended the dissensions, insurrections, and mutual slaughter of the Jews and those of other nations who dwelt in the same cities together; as particularly at Caesarea, where the Jews and Syrians contended about the right of the city, which ended there in the total expulsion of the Jews, above 20,000 of whom were slain. The whole Jewish nation, being exasperated at this, flew to arms, and burned and plundered the neighboring cities and villages of the Syrians, making an immense slaughter of the people. The Syrians, in return, destroyed not a less number of the Jews. At Scythopolis they murdered upwards of 13,000. At Ascalon they killed 2,500. At Ptolemais they slew 2,000, and made many prisoners. The Tyrians also put many Jews to death, and imprisoned more. The people of Gadara did likewise; and all the other cities

MATTHEW HENRY

erected: the things that are shaken (and ill shaken they were) *must be removed, that the things which cannot be shaken may remain,* Heb. xii. 27.

(2) Because we are still to expect worse; *The end is not yet;* the end of time is not, and, while time lasts, we must expect trouble, or, "The end of these troubles is not yet. Do not give way to fear and trouble, sink not under the present burthen, but rather gather in all the strength and spirit you have, to encounter what is yet before you." If running with the footmen weary us, how shall we contend with horses? And if we be frightened at a little brook in our way, what shall we do in the swellings of Jordan? Jer. xii. 5.

III. He foretells other judgments more immediately sent of God—*famines, pestilences, and earthquakes.* These were the three judgments which David was to choose one out of; and he was in a great strait, for he knew not which was the worst. Beside war (and that is enough), there shall be, *Famine,* signified by the *black horse* under the *third seal,* Rev. vi. 5, 6. The sorest famine was in Jerusalem during the siege. *Pestilences,* signified by the *pale horse, and death upon him,* and *the grave at his heels,* under the *fourth seal,* Rev. vi. 7, 8. *Earthquakes in divers places.* Great desolations have sometimes been made by earthquakes, they have been the death of many, and the terror of more. But here they are spoken of as dreadful judgments, and yet but *the beginning of sorrows.*

IV. He foretells the persecution of his own people and ministers, and a general apostasy and decay in religion thereupon, *v.* 9, 10, 12.

1. The *cross* itself foretold, *v.* 9. Of all future events we are as much concerned, though commonly as little desirous, to know of our own sufferings as of anything else. Christ had told his disciples what hard things they should suffer; but they had hitherto experienced little of it, and therefore he reminds them again.

(1) They shall be *afflicted* with bonds and imprisonments.

(2) They shall be *killed.*

(3) They shall be *hated of all nations for Christ's name's sake,* as he had told them before, *ch.* x. 22. The world was generally leavened with enmity and malignity to Christians. What shall we think of this world, when the best men had the worst usage in it? It is the cause that makes the martyr, and comforts him; it was for Christ's sake that they were thus hated.

2. *The offence of the cross, v.* 10–12. Three ill effects of persecution are here foretold.

(1) The *apostasy* of some. When the profession of Christianity begins to cost men dear, *then shall many be offended,* shall first fall out with, and then fall off from, their profession. It is no new thing (though it is a strange thing) for those that have known the way of righteousness, to turn aside out of it. Suffering times are shaking times; and those fall in the storm, that stood in fair weather. Many will follow Christ in the sunshine, who will shift for themselves, and leave him to do so too, in the cloudy dark day.

(2) The *malignity* of others. Then *they shall betray one another,* that is, "Those that have treacherously deserted their religion, shall hate and betray those who adhere to it." Apostates have commonly been the most bitter and violent persecutors. Persecuting times are discovering times. Wolves in sheep's clothing will then throw off their disguise, and appear wolves: they shall *betray one another, and hate one another.*

(3) The general *declining* and *cooling* of most, *v.* 12. Expect these two things,

[1] The *abounding* of iniquity; though the world always lies in wickedness, yet there are some times in which it may be said, that *iniquity doth* in a special manner abound.

[2] The *abating* of love; this is the consequence of the former; *Because iniquity shall abound the love of many shall wax cold.* Understand it in general of true serious godliness, which is all summed up in *love;* it is too common for professors of religion to grow cool in their profession, when the wicked are hot in their wickedness. Or, it may be understood more particularly of brotherly love. When iniquity abounds, seducing iniquity, persecuting iniquity, this grace commonly waxes cold. Christians begin to be shy and suspicious one of another, and so love comes to nothing.

This gives a melancholy prospect of the times, that there shall be such a great decay of love; but, *First,* It is of the love of *many,* not of *all.* In the worst of times, God has his remnant that hold fast their integrity, and retain their zeal, as in Elijah's days, when he thought himself left alone. *Secondly,* This

JAMIESON, FAUSSET, BROWN

for such things must needs be; but the end shall not be yet—In Luke (21: 9), "the end is not by and by," or "immediately." Worse must come before all is over.

These are the beginnings of sorrows—"of travail-pangs," to which heavy calamities are compared. (See Jer. 4: 31, etc.). The annals of TACITUS tell us how the Roman world was convulsed, before the destruction of Jerusalem, by rival claimants of the imperial purple.

they shall deliver you up to councils; and in the synagogues ye shall be beaten—These refer to *ecclesiastical* proceedings against them. **and ye shall be brought before rulers and kings**—before *civil* tribunals next. **for my sake, for a testimony against them**—rather "unto them"—to give you an opportunity of bearing testimony to Me before them. In the Acts of the Apostles we have the best commentary on this announcement. (Cf. Matt. 10:17, 18.)

And ye shall be hated of all men for my name's sake—Matthew (24:12) adds this important intimation: "And because iniquity shall abound, the love of many"—'of the many,' or 'of the most', i.e., of the generality of professed disciples—"shall wax cold." Sad illustrations of the effect of abounding iniquity in cooling the love even of faithful disciples we have in the *Epistle of James,* written about the period here referred to, and too frequently ever since.

ADAM CLARKE

of Syria, in proportion as they hated or feared the Jews. At Alexandria the Jews and heathens fought, and 50,000 of the former were slain. The people of Damascus conspired against the Jews of that city, and assaulting them unarmed, killed 10,000 of them. *Kingdom against kingdom.* This portended the open wars of different tetrarchies and provinces against each other. The *third* sign, pestilence and famine—*There shall be famines, and pestilences.* There was a famine foretold by Agabus, Acts xi. 28, which is mentioned by Suetonius, Tacitus, and Eusebius, "which came to pass in the days of Claudius Caesar," and was so severe at Jerusalem that Josephus says (*Ant.,* b. xx, c. 2) many died for lack of food. *Pestilences* are the usual attendants of famines, as the scarcity and badness of provisions generally produce epidemic disorders. The *fourth* sign, *earthquakes, in divers places.* It means particularly those popular commotions and insurrections which have already been noted; but if we confine it to *earthquakes,* there were several in those times to which our Lord refers. The *fifth* sign, fearful portents. To these Luke adds that there shall be "fearful sights and great signs . . . from heaven," chap. xxi. 11.

8. *All these are the beginning of sorrows.* "Travailing pains." The whole land of Judea is represented under the notion of a woman in grievous travail; but our Lord intimates that all that had already been mentioned were only the first pangs and throes, and nothing in comparison of that hard and death-bringing labor which should afterwards take place. From the calamities of the nation in general, our Lord passes to those of the Christians; and, indeed, the sufferings of His followers were often occasioned by the judgments sent upon the land, as the poor Christians were charged with being the cause of these national calamities and were cruelly persecuted on that account.

9. *Then shall they deliver you up to be afflicted.* Rather, "Then they will deliver you up to affliction."

10. *Then shall many be offended, and shall betray one another.* To illustrate this point, one sentence out of Tacitus (*Annal.* l. xv) will be sufficient, who, speaking of the persecution under Nero, says, "At first several were seized, who confessed, and then by their discovery a great multitude of others were convicted and executed."

12. *The love of many shall wax cold.* By reason of these trials and persecutions from without, and those apostasies and false prophets from within, the love of many to Christ and His doctrine, and to one another, shall grow cold. Some openly deserting the faith, as v. 10; others corrupting it, as v. 11; and others growing indifferent about it, as v. 12. Even at this early period there seems to have been a very considerable defection in several Christian churches; see Gal. iii. 1-4; 2 Thess. iii. 1; 2 Tim. i. 15.

MATTHEW HENRY

love is grown cold, but not dead. There is life in the root, which will show itself when the winter is past.

3. Comfort administered in reference to this offence of the cross. for the support of the Lord's people under it (*v.* 13); *He that endures to the end, shall be saved.* It is comfortable to those who wish well to the cause of Christ in general, that, though many are offended, yet some shall endure to the end. It is comfortable to those who do thus endure to the end, and suffer for their constancy, that they shall be saved. Perseverance wins the crown, through free grace, and shall wear it. *They shall be saved.* The crown of glory will make amends for all. Choose rather to die at a stake with the persecuted, than to live in a palace with the persecutors.

V. He foretells the preaching of the gospel in all the world (*v.* 14); *This gospel shall be preached, and then shall the end come.* It is called *the gospel of the kingdom,* because it reveals the kingdom of grace, which leads to the kingdom of glory. This gospel, sooner or later, is to be preached in all the world, to every creature. The gospel is preached *for a witness to all nations,* that is, a faithful declaration of the mind and will of God.

1. It is intimated that the gospel should be, if not heard, yet at least heard of, throughout the then known world, before the destruction of Jerusalem. Within forty years after Christ's death, the *sound* of the gospel was *gone forth to the ends of the earth,* Rom. x. 18. St. Paul *fully preached the gospel from Jerusalem, and round about unto Illyricum*; and the other apostles were not idle. The persecuting of the saints at Jerusalem helped to disperse them, so that they *went everywhere, preaching the word,* Acts viii. 1-4.

2. It is likewise intimated that even in times of temptation, trouble, and persecution, the gospel of the kingdom shall force its way through the greatest opposition. Though the enemies of the church grow very hot, and many of her friends very *cool,* yet the gospel shall be preached. Then the people that do know their God, shall be strengthened to do the greatest exploits of all.

3. That which seems chiefly intended here, is, that the end of the world shall be *then,* and not till then, when the gospel has done its work in the world. When the mystery of God shall be finished, the mystical body completed, *then shall the end come,* of which he had said before (*v.* 6, 7), *not yet.*

VI. He foretells more particularly the ruin that was coming upon the people of the Jews, their city, temple, and nation, *v.* 15, &c. What he said here, would be of use to his disciples, both for their conduct and for their comfort, in reference to that great event.

1. The Romans *setting up the abomination of desolation in the holy place, v.* 15. Some understand by this an image, or statue, set up in the temple by some of the Roman governors, which was very offensive to the Jews. Since the captivity in Babylon, nothing was, nor could be, more distasteful to the Jews than an image in the holy place. Others choose to expound it by the parallel place (Luke xxi. 20), *when ye shall see Jerusalem compassed with armies.* Jerusalem was the holy city, Canaan the holy land, the Mount Moriah, which lay about Jerusalem, for its nearness to the temple was, they thought, in a particular manner holy ground; on the country lying round about Jerusalem the Roman army was encamped, that was the abomination that made desolate. Now this is said to be *spoken of by Daniel, the prophet,* who spoke more plainly of the Messiah and his kingdom than any of the Old Testament prophets did. Christ refers them to that prophecy of Daniel, that they might see how the ruin of their city and temple was spoken of in the Old Testament, which would confirm his prediction. As Christ by his precepts confirmed the law, so by his predictions he confirmed the prophecies of the Old Testament, and it will be of good use to compare both together.

Reference being here had to a prophecy, which is commonly dark and obscure, Christ inserts this memorandum, "*Whoso readeth, let him understand.*" Those that read the scriptures, should labour to understand the scriptures, else their reading is to little purpose; we cannot use that which we do not understand. And we must not despair of understanding even dark prophecies; the great New-Testament prophecy is called a *revelation,* not a *secret.* Now *things revealed belong to us,* and therefore must be humbly and diligently searched into.

2. The means of preservation which thinking men should betake themselves to (*v.* 16, 20); *Then let them which are in Judœa, flee.* We may take this, as a prediction of the ruin itself; that it should be irresistible; that it would be impossible for the stoutest hearts to make head against it, but they

JAMIESON, FAUSSET, BROWN

but he that shall endure unto the end, the same shall be saved—See on Matthew 10:21, 22; and cf. Hebrews 10:38, 39, which is a manifest allusion to these words of Christ; also Revelation 2:10. Luke adds these reassuring words: "But there shall not an hair of your heads perish" (21:18). Our Lord had just said (Luke 21:16) that they should be *put to death;* showing that this precious promise is far above immunity from mere bodily harm, and furnishing a key to the right interpretation of Psalm 91 and such like.

And the gospel must first be published among all nations—"for a witness, and then shall the end come" (Matt. 24:14). God never sends judgment without previous warning; and there can be no doubt that the Jews, already dispersed over most known countries, had nearly all heard the Gospel "as a witness," before the end of the Jewish state. The same principle was repeated and will repeat itself to "*the* end."

But when ye shall see—"Jerusalem compassed by armies"—by encamped armies; in other words, when ye shall see it *besieged,* and—**the abomination of desolation, spoken of by Daniel the prophet, standing where it ought not**—i.e., as explained in Matthew (24:15), "standing in the holy place." **(let him that readeth**—readeth that prophecy—**understand.)** That "the abomination of desolation" here alluded to was intended to point to the Roman ensigns, as the symbols of an idolatrous, and so unclean pagan power, may be gathered by comparing what Luke says in the corresponding verse (21:20); and commentators are agreed on it. It is worthy of notice, as confirming this interpretation, that in I Maccabees 1:54—which, though aprocryphal *Scripture,* is authentic *history*—the expression of Daniel is applied to the idolatrous profanation of the Jewish altar by Antiochus Epiphanes.

then let them that be in Judea flee to the mountains—The ecclesiastical historian, EUSEBIUS, early in the fourth century, tells us that the Christians fled to *Pella,* at the northern extremity of Perea, being "prophetically

ADAM CLARKE

13. *But he that shall endure* the persecutions that shall come—*unto the end,* to the destruction of the Jewish polity, without growing cold or apostatizing—*shall be saved,* shall be delivered in all imminent dangers, and have his soul at last brought to an eternal glory. It is very remarkable that not a single Christian perished in the destruction of Jerusalem, though there were many there when Cestius Gallus invested the city; and had he persevered in the siege, he would soon have rendered himself master of it. But when he unexpectedly and unaccountably raised the siege, the Christians took that opportunity to escape. See Eusebius, *Hist. Eccles.,* lib. iii, c. 5.

14. *And this gospel of the kingdom shall be preached in all the world.* But, notwithstanding these persecutions, there should be a universal publication of the glad tidings of the Kingdom *for a witness* [*testimony*] *to all nations.* God would have the iniquity of the Jews published everywhere before the heavy stroke of His judgments should fall upon them, that all mankind, as it were, might be brought as witnesses against their cruelty and obstinacy in crucifying and rejecting the Lord Jesus. *In all the world.* Perhaps no more is meant here than the Roman empire. Tacitus informs us (*Annal.* l. xv) that, as early as the reign of Nero, the Christians were grown so numerous at Rome as to excite the jealousy of the government, and in other parts they were in proportion. *Then shall the end come.* When this general publication of the gospel shall have taken place, then a period shall be put to the whole Jewish economy, by the utter destruction of their city and Temple.

15. *The abomination of desolation, spoken of by Daniel.* This *abomination of desolation* (Luke xxi. 20-21) refers to the Roman army; and this abomination standing *in the holy place* is the Roman army besieging Jerusalem. This, our Lord says, is what was spoken of by Daniel the prophet, in the ninth and eleventh chapters of his prophecy, and so let everyone who reads these prophecies understand them; and in reference to this very event they are understood by the rabbins. The Roman army is called an *abomination* for its ensigns and images, which were so to the Jews. Josephus says (*War,* b. vi, c. 6) the Romans brought their ensigns into the Temple, and placed them over against the eastern gate, and sacrificed to them there. The Roman army is therefore fitly called the *abomination,* and "the abomination that maketh desolate," as it was to desolate and lay waste Jerusalem; and this army besieging Jerusalem is called by Mark (chap. xiii. 14) "standing where it ought not," that is, as in the text here, *the holy place,* as not only the city, but a considerable compass of ground about it, was deemed holy, and consequently no profane persons should stand on it.

16. *Then let them which be in Judea flee into the mountains.* This counsel was remembered and wisely followed by the Christians afterwards. Eusebius and Epiphanius say that at this juncture, after Cestius Gallus had raised

MATTHEW HENRY

must have recourse to the last shift, getting out of the way. Christ here, to show how fruitless it would be to stand it out, bids everyone make the best of his way. We may take it as a direction to the followers of Christ what to do. Let them acquiesce in the decree that was gone forth, and with all speed quit the city and country, as they would quit a falling house or a sinking ship, as Lot quitted Sodom. He shows them, whither they must flee—from Judæa *to the mountains.* In times of imminent peril and danger, it is not only lawful, but our duty, to seek our own preservation by all good and honest means; and if God opens a door of escape, we ought to make our escape, otherwise we do not trust God but tempt him. While we only go out of the way of danger, not out of the way of duty, we may trust God to provide. He that flees, may fight again. See what haste they must make, *v.* 17, 18. The life will be in danger; and therefore he *that is on the house-top,* when the alarm comes, let him not *come down into the house,* but go the nearest way down, to make his escape; and so he that shall be *in the field,* will find it his wisest course to run immediately, for two reasons, *First,* Because the time which would be taken up in packing up his things, would delay his flight. When death is at the door, delays are dangerous. *Secondly,* Because the carrying of his clothes, and his other moveables and valuables with him, would but burthen him, and clog his flight. The Syrians, in their flight, *cast away their garments,* 2 Kings vii. 15. Those who carried off least, were safest in their flight. He that has grace in his heart carries his all along with him, when stripped of all.

Now those to whom Christ said this immediately, did not live to see this dismal day, none of all the twelve but John only; but they left the direction to their successors in profession, who pursued it, and it was of use to them; for when the Christians in Jerusalem and Judæa saw the ruin coming on, they all retired to a town called *Pella,* on the other side Jordan, where they were safe, so that of the thousands that perished in the destruction of Jerusalem, there was not so much as one Christian. Note, whom it would go hard with at that time (*v.* 19); *Woe to them that are with child, and to them that give suck.* To this same event that saying of Christ at his death refers (Luke xxiii. 29), They shall say, *Blessed are the wombs that never bare, and the paps that never gave suck.* To them the famine would be most grievous. To them the sword would be most terrible, when in the hand of worse than brutal rage. To them also the flight would be most afflictive; the women with child cannot make haste, or go far; the sucking child cannot be left behind, or, if it should, *can a woman forget it, that she should not have compassion on it?* If it be carried along, it retards the mother's flight, and so exposes her life. What they should pray against at that time—*that your flight be not in the winter, nor on the sabbath day, v.* 20. In general, it becomes Christ's disciples, in times of public trouble and calamity, to be much in prayer; that is a salve for every sore, never out of season. There is no remedy but you must flee, the decree is gone forth. Labour to make the best of that which is; and when you cannot in faith pray that you may not be forced to flee, yet pray that the circumstances of it may be graciously ordered, that, though the cup may not pass from you, yet the extremity of the judgment may be prevented. God has the disposing of the circumstances of events, which sometimes makes a great alteration one way or other; and therefore in those our eyes must be ever toward him. Christ's bidding them pray for this favour, intimates his purpose of granting it to them; and in a general calamity we must see and own wherein it might have been worse. When trouble is in prospect, at a great distance, it is good to lay in a stock of prayers beforehand; they must pray, *First, That their flight,* if it were the will of God, *might not be in the winter,* when the days are short, the weather cold, the ways dirty, and therefore travelling very uncomfortable, especially for whole families. Though the ease of the body is not to be *mainly* consulted, it ought to be *duly* considered; though we must take what God sends, and when he sends it, yet we may pray against bodily inconveniences, and are encouraged to do so. *Secondly,* That it might not be *on the sabbath day.* For the sabbath he often showed a concern. It intimates likewise that the sabbath is ordinarily to be observed as a day of rest from travel and worldly labour; but that works of necessity were lawful on the sabbath day, as this of fleeing from an enemy to save our lives. But it intimates, likewise, that it is very uneasy and uncomfortable to a good man, to be taken off by any work of necessity from the solemn service and worship of God on the sabbath day. We should pray that we may have

JAMIESON, FAUSSET, BROWN

directed"—perhaps by some prophetic intimation more explicit than this, which would be their chart —and that thus they escaped the predicted calamities by which the nation was overwhelmed.

And let him that is on the housetop not get down into the house, neither enter therein, to take any thing out of his house—i.e., let him take the outside flight of steps from the roof to the ground; a graphic way of denoting the extreme urgency of the case, and the danger of being tempted, by the desire to save his property, to delay till escape should become impossible.

But woe to them—or, "alas for them"—**that are with child, and to them that give suck in those days**—in consequence of the aggravated suffering which those conditions would involve. **And pray ye that your flight be not in the winter**—making escape perilous, or tempting you to delay your flight. Matthew (24:20) adds, "neither on the sabbath day," when, from fear of a breach of its sacred rest, they might be induced to remain.

ADAM CLARKE

the siege and Vespasian was approaching with his army, all who believed in Christ left Jerusalem and fled to Pella, and other places beyond the river Jordan; and so they all marvellously escaped the general shipwreck of their country—not one of them perished. See on v. 13.

17. *Let him which is on the house top.* The houses of the Jews, as well as those of the ancient Greeks and Romans, were flat-roofed, and had stairs on the outside, by which persons might ascend and descend without coming into the house. In the Eastern walled cities, these flat-roofed houses usually formed continued terraces from one end of the city to the other, which terraces terminated at the gates. He therefore who is walking on the housetop, let him *not come down to take any thing out of his house;* but let him instantly pursue his course along the tops of the houses, and escape out at the city gate as fast as he can.

18. *Neither let him which is in the field return back.* Because when once the army of the Romans sits down before the city, there shall be no more any possibility of escape, as they shall never remove till Jerusalem be destroyed.

19. *And woe unto them* (alas! for them) *that are with child!* For such persons are not in a condition to make their escape; neither can they bear the miseries of the siege. Josephus says the houses were full of women and children that perished by the famine, and that the mothers snatched the food even out of their own children's mouths. See *War,* b. v, c. 10.

20. *But pray ye that your flight be not in the winter.* For the hardness of the season, the badness of the roads, the shortness of the days, and the length of the nights will all be great impediments to your flight. *Neither on the sabbath day.* That you may not raise the indignation of the Jews by travelling on that day, and so suffer that death out of the city which you had endeavored to escape from within. Besides, on the Sabbath days the Jews not only kept within doors, but the gates of all the cities and towns in every place were kept shut and barred; so that if their flight should be on a Sabbath, they could not expect admission into any place of security in the land. Our Lord had ordered His followers to make their escape from Jerusalem when they should see it encompassed with armies; but how could this be done? God took care to provide amply for this. In the twelfth year of Nero, Cestius Gallus, the president of Syria, came against Jerusalem with a powerful army. He might, says Josephus, *War,* b. ii, c. 19, have assaulted and taken the city, and thereby put an end to the war; but without any just reason, and contrary to the expectation of all, he raised the siege and departed. Josephus remarks that, after Cestius Gallus had raised the siege, "many of the principal Jewish people, forsook the city, as men do a sinking ship." Vespasian was deputed in the room of Cestius Gallus, who, having subdued all the country, prepared to besiege Jerusalem, and invested it on every side. But the news of Nero's death, and soon after that of Galba, and the disturbances that followed, and the civil wars between Otho and Vitellius, held Vespasian and his son Titus in suspense. Thus the city was not actually besieged in form till after Vespasian was confirmed in the empire and Titus was appointed to command the forces in Judæa. It was in those incidental delays that the Christians, and indeed several others, provided for their own safety, by flight.

MATTHEW HENRY

quiet undisturbed sabbaths, and may have no other work than sabbath work to do on sabbath days; that we may attend upon the Lord without distraction. To flee in the winter is uncomfortable to the body; but to flee on the sabbath day is so to the soul.

3. The greatness of the troubles which should immediately ensue (*v.* 21); *Then shall be great tribulation;* when the measure of iniquity is full, then come the troubles. *There shall be great tribulation.* Great, indeed, when within the city plague and famine raged, and (worse than either) faction and division, so that every man's sword was against his fellow; then and there it was that the hands of the pitiful women flayed their own children. Josephus's *History of the Wars of the Jews*, has in it more tragical passages than perhaps any history whatsoever.

(1) It was a desolation unparalleled, such as *was not since the beginning of the world, nor ever shall be.* Many a city and kingdom has been made desolate, but never any with a desolation like this. No wonder that the ruin of Jerusalem was an unparalleled ruin, when the sin of Jerusalem was an unparalleled sin—even their crucifying Christ. The nearer any people are to God in profession and privileges, the greater and heavier will his judgments be upon them.

(2) It was a desolation which, if it should continue long, would be intolerable, so that *no flesh should be saved*, *v.* 22. *No flesh shall be saved;* he doth not say, "No *soul* shall be saved," for the destruction of the flesh may be for *the saving of the spirit in the day of the Lord Jesus.*"

But here is one word of comfort in the midst of all this terror—that *for the elects' sake these days shall be shortened*, not made shorter than what God had determined, but shorter than what he might have decreed, if he had dealt with them according to their sins. In times of common calamity God manifests his favour to the elect remnant; his peculiar treasure, which he will secure when the lumber is abandoned to the spoiler. The shortening of calamities is a kindness God often grants. Instead of complaining that our afflictions last so long, if we consider our defects, we shall see reason to be thankful that they do not last always; when it is bad with us, it becomes us to say, "Blessed be God that it is no worse."

And now comes in the repeated caution to take heed of being ensnared by false Christs, and false prophets (*v.* 23, &c.). Times of great trouble are times of great temptation and therefore we have need to double our guard then. Do not heed them, it is all but talk.

VII. He foretells the sudden spreading of the gospel in the world, about the time of these great events (*v.* 27, 28); *As the lightning comes out of the east, so shall the coming of the Son of man be.*

1. It seems primarily to be meant of his coming to set up his spiritual kingdom in the world. The gospel would be remarkable for two things.

(1) Its swift spreading; it shall fly as the lightning. The gospel is light (John iii. 19); and it is not in this as the lightning, that it is a sudden flash, and away, for it is sunlight, and daylight. It is as lightning in these respects:

[1] It is light from heaven, as the lightning. It is God, and not man, that sends the lightnings, and summons them.

[2] It is visible and conspicuous as the lightning. Truth seeks no corners, however it may sometimes be forced into them. Christ preached his gospel openly (John xviii. 20), and his apostles on *the housetop* (*ch.* x. 27).

[3] It was sudden and surprising to the world as the lightning. The powers of darkness were dispersed and vanquished by the gospel lightning.

[4] It spread far and wide, and that quickly and irresistibly, like the lightning, which comes, suppose, out of the east (Christ is said to ascend *from the east*), and lighteneth to the west. Gospel light rose with the sun, and went with the same, so that the beams of it reached to the ends of the earth. Though it was fought against, it could never be cooped up in a desert, or in a secret place, as the seducers were; but by this, according to Gamaliel's rule, proved itself to be *of God*, that it *could not be overthrown*, Acts v. 38, 39. How soon did the gospel lightning reach this island of Great Britain! Tertullian, who wrote in the second century, takes notice of it, *The fastnesses of Britain, though inaccessible to the Romans, were occupied by Jesus Christ.* This was the Lord's doing.

(2) Another thing remarkable concerning the gospel, was, its strange success in those places to which it was spread; it gathered in multitudes. The *lifting up of Christ from the earth*, that is, the preaching of Christ crucified, which, one would think, should drive all men from him, will *draw all men to him*

JAMIESON, FAUSSET, BROWN

For in those days shall be affliction, such as was not from the beginning of the creation which God created unto this time, neither shall be—Such language is not unusual in the Old Testament with reference to tremendous calamities. But it is matter of literal fact that there was crowded into the period of the Jewish war an amount and complication of suffering perhaps unparalleled; as the narrative of JOSEPHUS, examined closely and arranged under different heads, would show. **And except that the Lord had shortened those days, no flesh**—i.e., no human life—**should be saved: but for the elect's sake, whom he hath chosen, he hath shortened the days**—But for this merciful "shortening," brought about by a remarkable concurrence of causes, the whole nation would have perished, in which there yet remained a remnant to be afterwards gathered out. This portion of the prophecy closes, in Luke, with the following vivid and important glance at the subsequent fortunes of the chosen people: "And they shall fall by the sword, and shall be led away captive into all nations: and Jerusalem shall be trodden down of the Gentiles, until the times of the Gentiles be fulfilled" (Luke 21:24). The language as well as the idea of this remarkable statement is taken from Daniel 8: 10, 13. What, then, is its import here? It implies, first, that a time is coming when Jerusalem shall cease to be "trodden down of the Gentiles"; which it was then by pagan, and since and till now is by Mohammedan unbelievers: and next, it implies that the period when this treading down of Jerusalem by the Gentiles is to cease will be when "the times of the Gentiles are fulfilled" or "completed." But what does this mean? We may gather the meaning of it from Romans 11 in which the divine purposes and procedure towards the chosen people from first to last are treated in detail. In vs. 25 of that chapter these words of our Lord are thus reproduced: "For I would not, brethren, that ye should be ignorant of this mystery, lest ye should be wise in your own conceits; that blindness in part is happened to Israel, until the fulness of the Gentiles be come in." See the exposition of that verse, from which it will appear that "till the fulness of the Gentiles be come in"—or, in our Lord's phraseology, "till the times of the Gentiles be fulfilled"—does not mean "till the general conversion of the world to Christ," but "till the Gentiles have had their *full time* of that place in the Church which the Jews had before them." After that period of *Gentilism*, as before of *Judaism*, "Jerusalem" and Israel, no longer "trodden down by the Gentiles," but "grafted into their own olive tree," shall constitute, with the believing Gentiles, one Church of God, and fill the whole earth. What a bright vista does this open up!

ADAM CLARKE

21. *For then shall be great tribulation.* No history can furnish us with a parallel to the calamities and miseries of the Jews: rapine, murder, famine, and pestilence within; fire and sword, and all the horrors of war, without. Our Lord wept at the foresight of these calamities, and it is almost impossible for any humane person to read the relation of them in Josephus without weeping also. Luke, chap. xxi. 22, calls these the "days of vengeance, that all things which are written may be fulfilled."

22. *Except those days should be shortened.* Josephus computes the number of those who perished in the siege at eleven hundred thousand, besides those who were slain in other places, *War*, b. vi, c. 9; and if the Romans had gone on destroying in this manner, the whole nation of the Jews would, in a short time, have been entirely extirpated. But, for the sake of the elect, the Jews, that they might not be utterly destroyed, and for the Christians particularly, the days were shortened. These, partly through the fury of the zealots on one hand and the hatred of the Romans on the other, and partly through the difficulty of subsisting in the mountains, without houses or provisions, would in all probability have all been destroyed, by either the sword or famine, if the days had not been shortened. The besieged themselves helped to shorten those days by their divisions and mutual slaughters, and by fatally deserting their strongholds, where they never could have been subdued but by famine alone. So well-fortified was Jerusalem, and so well-provided to stand a siege, that the enemy without could not have prevailed had it not been for the factions and seditions within. When Titus was viewing the fortifications after the taking of the city, he could not help ascribing his success to God. "We have fought," said he, "with God on our side; and it is God who pulled the Jews out of these strong holds: for what could machines or the hands of men avail against such towers as these?" (*War*, b. vi, c. 9.)

27. *For as the lightning cometh out of the east, and shineth even unto the west.* It is worthy of remark that our Lord, in the most particular manner, points out the very march of the Roman army. They entered into Judea on the east, and carried on their conquest westward, as if not only the extensiveness of the ruin, but the very route which the army would take, were intended in the comparison of the lightning issuing from the east and shining to the west.

W. E. VINE:

PAROUSIA, lit., a presence, *para*, with, and *ousia*, being (from *eimi*, to be), denotes both an arrival and a consequent presence with. For instance, in a papyrus letter a lady speaks of the necessity of her *parousia* in a place in order to attend matters relating to her property there. Paul speaks of his *parousia* in Philippi (Phil. 2:12) (in contrast to his *apousia*, his absence). *Parousia* is used to describe the presence of Christ with His disciples on the Mount of Transfiguration (2 Pet. 1:16). When used of the return of Christ, at the rapture of the Church, it signifies, not merely His momentary coming for His saints, but His presence with them from that moment until His revelation and manifestation to the world. In some passages the word gives prominence to the beginning of that period, the course of the period being implied (1 Cor. 15:23; 1 Thess. 4:15; 5:23; 2 Thess. 2:1; James 5:7, 8; 2 Pet. 3:4). In some, the course is prominent (Matt. 24:3, 37; 1 Thess. 3:13; 1 John 2:28); in others the conclusion of the period (Matt. 24:27; 2 Thess. 2:8).—*Vine's Expository Dictionary*

MATTHEW HENRY

(John xii. 32). Whither should the soul go but to Jesus Christ, who *has the words of eternal life*? Those who have spiritual senses exercised, will know the voice of the good Shepherd from that of a thief and a robber. Saints will be where the true Christ is, not the false Christs. A living principle of grace is a kind of natural instinct in all the saints, drawing them to Christ to live upon him.

2. Some understand these verses of the coming of the Son of man *to destroy Jerusalem*.

Now here are two things intimated concerning it.

(1) That to the most it would be as unexpected as a flash of lightning, which indeed gives warning of the clap of thunder which follows, but is itself surprising.

(2) That it might be as justly expected as that the eagle should fly to the carcases. The desolation will come as certainly as the birds of prey to a dead carcase. The Jews were so corrupt and degenerate that they were become a carcase, obnoxious to the righteous judgment of God. The Romans were as an eagle, and the ensign of their armies was an eagle. The destruction shall find out the Jews wherever they are, as the eagle scents the prey.

3. It is very applicable to the day of judgment, the coming of our Lord Jesus Christ in that day. Now see here,

(1) How he shall come; *as the lightning*. Therefore those that enquire after Christ must not go into the desert or the secret places, nor listen to everyone that will put up the finger to invite them to a sight of Christ; but let them look upward, for the heavens must contain him, and thence *we look for the Saviour*.

(2) How the saints shall be gathered to him with the greatest swiftness and alacrity imaginable.

VIII. He foretells his second coming at the *end of time, v.* 29–31. *The sun shall be darkened,* &c.

1. Some think this is to be understood only of the destruction of Jerusalem and the Jewish nation; the darkening of the sun, moon, and stars, denotes the eclipse of the glory of that state. The *sign of the Son of man* (*v.* 30) means a signal appearance of the power and justice of the Lord Jesus in it, and the gathering *of his elect* (*v.* 31) signifies the delivering of a remnant from this sin and ruin.

2. It seems rather to refer to Christ's second coming. The only objection against this, is, that it is said to be *immediately after the tribulation of those days*; but as to that, (1) It is usual in the prophetical style to speak of things great and certain as near and just at hand, only to express the greatness and certainty of them. (2) *A thousand years are* in God's sight *but as one day*, 2 Pet. iii. 8. It is there urged, with reference to this very thing, and so it might be said to be immediately after.

Now concerning Christ's second coming, it is here foretold,

[1] That there shall be then a great and amazing change of the creatures, and particularly the *heavenly bodies* (*v.* 29). *The sun shall be darkened, and the moon shall not give her light. The stars shall fall;* and *the powers of heaven shall be shaken*. This intimates,

First, That there shall be a great change, in order to the making of all things new.

Secondly, It shall be a visible change, and such as all the world must take notice of; for such the darkening of the sun and moon cannot but be: and it would be an amazing change. The days of heaven, and the continuance of the sun and moon, are used to express that which is lasting and unchangeable, yet they shall thus be shaken.

Thirdly, It shall be a universal change. Nature shall sustain a general shock and convulsion, which yet shall be no hindrance to the joy and rejoicing of heaven and earth *before the Lord, when he cometh to judge the world*.

Fourthly, The sun was darkened at the death of Christ, for then was in one sense *the judgment of this world* (John xii. 31).

Fifthly, The glorious appearance of our Lord Jesus, will darken the sun and moon, as a candle is darkened in the beams of the noon-day sun.

Sixthly, The sun and moon shall be then darkened, because there will be no more occasion for them. To the saints that had their treasure above, such light of joy and comfort will be given as shall supersede that of the sun and moon, and render it useless.

[2] That *then shall appear the sign of the Son of man in heaven* (*v.* 30), the Son of man himself, as it follows here, *They shall see the Son of man coming in the clouds*. At his first coming, he was *set for a Sign that should be spoken against* (Luke ii. 34), but at his second coming, a sign that should be admired.

[3] That *then all the tribes of the earth shall mourn*, *v.* 30. Some of all the tribes and kindreds of the earth shall mourn, while the chosen remnant shall lift up their heads with joy, knowing that their re-

JAMIESON, FAUSSET, BROWN

For as the lightning cometh out of the east, and shineth even unto the west; so shall also the coming of the Son of man be." See on Luke 17:23, 24. "For wheresoever the carcass is, there will the eagles be gathered together." See on Luke 17:37.

But in those days, after that tribulation—"Immediately after the tribulation of those days" (Matt. 24:29). **the sun shall be darkened, and the moon shall not give her light. And the stars of heaven shall fall**—"and upon the earth distress of nations, with perplexity; the sea and the waves roaring; men's hearts failing them for fear, and for looking after those things which are coming on the earth" (Luke 21:25, 26). **and the powers that are in heaven shall be shaken**—Though the grandeur of this language carries the mind over the head of all periods but that of Christ's Second Coming, nearly every expression will be found used of the Lord's coming in terrible national judgments: as of Babylon (Isa. 13:9-13); of Idumea (Isa. 34:1, 2, 4, 8-10); of Egypt (Ezek. 32:7, 8); compare also Psalm 18:7-15; Isaiah 24:1, 17-19; Joel 2:10, 11, etc. We cannot therefore consider the mere strength of this language a proof that it refers exclusively or primarily to the precursors of the final day, though of course in "*that day*" it will have its most awful fulfilment. **And then shall they see the Son of man coming in the clouds with great power and glory**—In Matthew 24:30, this is given most fully: "And then shall appear the sign of the Son of man in heaven; and then shall all the tribes of the earth mourn, and they shall see the Son of man . . ." That this language finds its highest interpretation in the Second Personal Coming of Christ, is most certain. But the question is, whether that be the primary sense of it as it stands here? Now if the reader will turn to Daniel 7:13, 14, and connect with it the preceding verses, he will find, we think, the true key to our Lord's meaning here. There the powers that oppressed the Church —symbolized by rapacious wild beasts—are summoned to the bar of the Great God, who as the Ancient of days seats Himself, with His assessors, on a burning Throne: thousand thousands ministering to Him, and ten thousand times ten thousand standing before Him. "The judgment is set, and the books are opened." Who that is guided by the *mere words* would doubt that this is a description of the Final Judgment? And yet nothing is clearer than that it is *not,* but a description of a vast *temporal* judgment, upon organized bodies of men, for their incurable hostility to the kingdom of God upon earth. Well, after the doom of these has been pronounced and executed, and room thus prepared for the unobstructed development of the kingdom of God over the earth, what follows? "I saw in the night visions, and behold, one like THE SON OF MAN came with the clouds of heaven, and came to the Ancient of days, and they (the angelic attendants) brought Him near before Him." For what purpose? To receive investiture in the kingdom, which, as Messiah, of right belonged to Him. Accordingly, it is added, "And there was given Him dominion, and glory, and a kingdom, that all peoples, nations, and languages should serve Him: His dominion is an everlasting dominion, which shall not pass away, and His kingdom that which shall not be destroyed." Comparing this with our Lord's words, He seems to us, by "the Son of man [on which phrase, see on John 1:51] coming in the clouds with great power and glory," to mean, that when judicial vengeance shall once have been executed upon Jerusalem, and the ground thus cleared for the unobstructed establishment of His

ADAM CLARKE

28. *For wheresoever the carcase is.* "The dead carcass." The Jewish nation, which was morally and judicially dead. *There will the eagles.* The Roman armies, called so partly from their strength and fierceness and partly from the figure of these animals which was always wrought on their ensigns, or even in brass, placed on the tops of their ensign-staves. It is remarkable that the Roman fury pursued these wretched men wheresoever they were found. They were a dead carcass doomed to be devoured, and the Roman eagles were the commissioned devourers. See the pitiful account in Josephus, *War*, b. vii, cc. 2—3, 6, 9—11.

29. *Immediately after the tribulation.* Commentators generally understand this, and what follows, of the end of the world and Christ's coming to judgment; but the word *immediately* shows that our Lord is not speaking of any distant event, but of something immediately consequent on calamities already predicted—and that must be the destruction of Jerusalem.

30. *Then shall appear the sign of the Son of man.* The plain meaning of this is that the destruction of Jerusalem will be such a remarkable instance of divine vengeance and such a signal manifestation of Christ's power and glory that all the Jewish *tribes* shall mourn, and many will, in consequence of this manifestation of God, be led to acknowledge Christ and His religion. By "of the land," in the text, is evidently meant here, as in several other places, the land of Judea and its tribes, either its then inhabitants or the Jewish people wherever found.

MATTHEW HENRY

demption draws nigh, and their Redeemer. Penitent sinners look to Christ, and mourn after a godly sort; and they who sow in those tears, shall shortly reap in joy.

[4] That *then they shall see the Son of man coming in the clouds of heaven, with power and great glory. First,* The judgment of the great day will be committed to the Son of man. *Secondly,* The Son of man will at that day come in the clouds of heaven. Much of the intercourse between heaven and earth is by the clouds; drawn by heaven from the earth, distilled by heaven upon the earth. Christ went to heaven in a cloud, and *will in like manner come again,* Acts i. 9, 11. *Thirdly,* He will *come with power and great glory*: his first coming was in weakness and great meanness (2 Cor. xiii. 4). *Fourthly, Therefore* the Son of man will be the Judge, that he may be seen, that sinners thereby may be the more confounded. "Is this he whom we have slighted, and rejected, and rebelled against; whom we have crucified to ourselves afresh; who might have been our Saviour, but is our Judge?"

[5] That *he shall send his angels with a great sound of a trumpet, v.* 31. The angels shall be attendants upon Christ at his second coming; they shall be obliged to wait upon him. They are now ministering Spirits sent forth by him (Heb. i. 14), and will be so then. Their ministration will be ushered in with a great sound of a trumpet. Very fitly therefore shall there be the sound of a trumpet at the last day, when the saints shall enter upon their eternal jubilee.

[6] That *they shall gather together his elect from the four winds.* At the second coming of Jesus Christ, there will be a general meeting of all the saints. The gifts of love to eternity follow the thoughts of love from eternity; and *the Lord knows them that are his.* The angels shall be employed to bring them together, as Christ's servants, and as the saints' friends. They *shall be gathered from one end of heaven to the other*; the elect of God are scattered abroad (John xi. 52), but when that great gathering day comes, there shall not one of them be missing; distance of place shall keep none out of heaven, if distance of affection do not.

Verses 32–51

We have here the practical application of the foregoing prediction; in general, we must expect and prepare for the events here foretold.

I. We must expect them; "*Now learn a parable of the fig-tree, v.* 32, 33. Now learn what use to make of the things you have heard; that you may provide accordingly." The parable of the fig-tree is no more than this, that its budding and blossoming are a presage of summer. Thus when God begins to fulfil prophecies, he will make an end. After *the branch grows tender,* we expect the March winds, and the April showers, before the summer comes; however, we are sure it is coming; "so likewise ye, when the gospel day shall dawn, the perfect day will come. *Know that it is near.*" When the trees of righteousness begin to bud and blossom, when God's people promise faithfulness, it is a happy presage of good times. In them God begins his work, first prepares their heart, and then he will go on with it.

Now touching the events foretold here, which we are to expect,

1. Christ here assures us of the certainty of them (*v.* 35); *Heaven and earth shall pass away; but my words shall not pass away.* The word of Christ is more sure and lasting than heaven and earth. We may build with more assurance upon the word of Christ than we can upon the pillars of heaven, or the strong foundations of the earth; for, when they shall be no more, the word of Christ shall remain. In God's time, which is the best time, and in God's way, which is the best way, it shall certainly be fulfilled. Every word of Christ is very pure, and therefore very sure.

2. He here instructs us as to the time of them, *v.* 34, 36.

(1) As to *these things,* especially the ruin of the Jewish nation; "*This generation shall not pass away, till all these things be fulfilled* (*v.* 34); there are those now alive, that shall see Jerusalem destroyed. Because it might seem strange, he backs it with a solemn asseveration; "*Verily, I say unto you.* You may take my word for it, these things are at the door."

(2) But as to *that day and hour* which will put a period to time, *that knoweth no man, v.* 36. There is a certain day and hour fixed for the judgment to come; it is called *the day of the Lord.* That day and hour are a great secret. *No man knows it;* not the wisest by their sagacity, not the best by any divine discovery. None *knows but my Father only.* The uncertainty of the time of Christ's coming, is, to those who are watchful, *a savour of life unto life,* and makes them

JAMIESON, FAUSSET, BROWN

own kingdom, His true regal claims and rights would be visibly and gloriously asserted and manifested. See on Luke 9:28 (with its parallels in Matthew and Mark), in which nearly the same language is employed, and where it can hardly be understood of anything else than *the full and free estabishment of the kingdom of Christ on the destruction of Jerusalem.* But what is that "sign of the Son of man in heaven?" Interpreters are not agreed. But as before Christ came to destroy Jerusalem some appalling portents were seen in the air, so before His Personal appearing it is likely that something *analogous* will be witnessed, though of what nature it would be vain to conjecture. **And then shall he send his angels**—"with a great sound of a trumpet" (Matt. 24:31). **and shall gather together his elect . . .**—As the tribes of Israel were anciently gathered together by sound of trumpet (Exod. 19:13, 16, 19; Lev. 23: 24; Ps. 81:3-5), so any mighty gathering of God's people, by divine command, is represented as collected by sound of trumpet (Isa. 27:13; cf. Rev. 11: 15); and the ministry of angels, employed in all the great operations of Providence, is here held forth as the agency by which the present assembling of the elect is to be accomplished. LIGHTFOOT thus explains it: "When Jerusalem shall be reduced to ashes, and that wicked nation cut off and rejected, then shall the Son of man send His ministers with the trumpet of the Gospel, and they shall gather His elect of the several nations, from the four corners of heaven: so that God shall not want a Church, although that ancient people of His be rejected and cast off: but that ancient Jewish Church being destroyed, a new Church shall be called out of the Gentiles." But though something like this appears to be the primary sense of the verse, in relation to the destruction of Jerusalem, no one can fail to see that the language swells beyond any gathering of a human family into a Church upon earth, and forces the thoughts onward to that gathering of the Church "at the last trump," to meet the Lord in the air, which is to wind up the present scene. Still, this is not, in our judgment, the *direct* subject of the prediction; for the next verse limits the whole prediction to the generation then existing.

Now learn a parable of the fig tree—"Now from the fig tree learn the parable," or the high lesson which this teaches. **When her branch is yet tender, and putteth forth leaves**—"its leaves." **So ye, in like manner, when ye shall see these things come to pass**—rather, 'coming to pass'—**know that it**—"the kingdom of God" (Luke 21:31)—**is nigh, even at the doors**—that is, the full manifestation of it; for till then it admitted of no full development. In Luke (21:28) the following words precede these: "And when these things begin to come to pass, then look up, and lift up your heads; for your redemption draweth nigh"—their redemption, in the first instance certainly, from Jewish oppression (I Thess. 2:14-16; Luke 11:52): but in the highest sense of these words, redemption from all the oppressions and miseries of the present state at the second appearing of the Lord Jesus.

Heaven and earth shall pass away; but my words shall not pass away—the strongest possible expression of the divine authority by which He spake; not as Moses or Paul might have said of their own inspiration, for such language would be unsuitable in any merely human mouth.

Verily I say unto you, that this generation shall not pass till all these things be done—or "fulfilled" (Matt. 24:34; Luke 21: 32). Whether we take this to mean that the whole would be fulfilled within the limits of the generation then current, or, according to a usual way of speaking, that the generation then existing would not pass away without seeing a *begun* fulfilment of this prediction, the facts entirely correspond. For either the whole was fulfilled in the destruction accomplished by Titus, as many think; or, if we stretch it out, according to others, till the thorough dispersion of the Jews a little later, under Adrian, every requirement of our Lord's words seems to be met.

But of that day and that hour—i.e., the precise time. **knoweth no man**—lit., no one—**no, not the angels which are in heaven, neither the Son, but the Father**—This very remarkable statement regarding "the Son" is peculiar to Mark. Whether it

ADAM CLARKE

31. *He shall send his angels.* "His messengers," the apostles, and their successors in the Christian ministry. *With a great sound of a trumpet.* Or "a loud-sounding trumpet"—the earnest, affectionate call of the gospel of peace, life, and salvation. *Shall gather together his elect.* The Gentiles, who were now chosen or elected, in place of the rebellious, obstinate Jews, according to our Lord's prediction, Matt. viii. 11-12 and Luke xiii. 28-29. To Matthew's account, Luke adds, chap. xxi. 24, "They shall fall by the edge of the sword, and shall be led away captive into all nations: and Jerusalem shall be trodden down of the Gentiles, until the times of the Gentiles be fulfilled." The number of those who fell by the sword was very great. Eleven hundred thousand perished during the siege. Many were slain at other places and at other times. Many also were led away captives into all nations. Josephus says the number of the captives taken in the whole war amounted to 97,000. Those above seventeen years of age were sent to the works in Egypt; but most were distributed through the Roman provinces, to be destroyed in their theaters by the sword and by the wild beasts; and those under seventeen years of age were sold for slaves. Jerusalem also was, according to the prediction of our Lord, to be "trodden down of the Gentiles." Accordingly it has never since been in the possession of the Jews.

32. *Learn a parable of the fig tree.* That is, These signs which I have given you will be as infallible a proof of the approaching ruin of the Jewish state as the budding of the trees is a proof of the coming summer.

34. *This generation shall not pass.* "This race"; i.e., the Jews shall not cease from being a distinct people till all the counsels of God relative to them and the Gentiles be fulfilled. Some translate *this generation* as meaning the persons who were then living, that they should not die before these signs took place. But though this was true as to the calamities that fell upon the Jews, and the destruction of their government and Temple, yet as our Lord mentions Jerusalem's continuing to be under the power of the Gentiles till the fulness of the Gentiles should come in, i.e., till all the nations of the world should receive the gospel of Christ, after which the Jews themselves should be converted unto God, Rom. xi. 25. I think it more proper not to restrain its meaning to the few years which preceded the destruction of Jerusalem, but to understand it of the care taken by divine providence to preserve them as a distinct people, and yet to keep them out of their own land and from their Temple service. See on Mark xiii. 30. But still it is literally true in reference to the destruction of Jerusalem. John probably lived to see these things come to pass. The war began, as Josephus says, *Ant.* b. xx, c. 11, s. 1, in May, A.D. 66. The Temple was burnt August 10, A.D. 70, the same day and month on which it had been burnt by the king of Babylon, Josephus, *Ant.* b. xx, c. 11, s. 8. The city was taken September 8, in the second year of the reign of Vespasian, or the year of Christ 70, *Ant.* b. vi, c. 10.

36. *But of that day and hour. Hora* here is translated "season" by many eminent critics, and is used in this sense by both sacred and profane authors. As the *day* was not known in which Jerusalem should be invested by the Romans, therefore our Lord advised His disciples to pray that it might not be on a Sabbath; and as the "season" was not known, therefore they were to pray that it might not be in the winter, v. 20. See on Mark xiii. 32.

MATTHEW HENRY

more watchful; but to those who are careless, it is *a savour of death unto death,* and makes them more careless.

II. To this end we must expect these events, that we may prepare for them, *v.* 37–41. In these verses we have such an idea given us of the judgment day, as may serve to startle and awaken us.

It will be a surprising day, and a separating day.

1. It will be a surprising day, as the deluge was to the old world, *v.* 37–39. Besides his first coming, to save, he has other comings to judge. He saith (John ix. 39), *For judgment I am come;* and for judgment he will come.

Now this here is applicable,

(1) To *temporal judgments,* particularly that which was now hastening upon the nation and people of the Jews; though they had fair warning given them of it, yet it found them secure, crying, *Peace and safety.* Men's unbelief shall not make God's threatenings of no effect.

(2) To *the eternal judgment*; so the judgment of the great day is called, Heb. vi. 2. Now Christ here shows what were the temper and posture of the old world when the deluge came.

[1] They were sensual and worldly; *they were eating and drinking, marrying and giving in marriage.* They were all of them, except Noah, over head and ears in the world, and regardless of the word of God, and this ruined them. Universal neglect of religion is a more dangerous symptom to any people than particular instances here and there of daring irreligion. *Eating and drinking* are necessary to the preservation of man's life; *marrying and giving in marriage* are necessary to the preservation of mankind. They were unreasonable in it, inordinate and entire in the pursuit of the delights of sense. They were in these things as in their element, as if they had their being for no other end than to *eat and drink.* They were unreasonable in it; they were entire and intent upon the world and the flesh. They were eating and drinking, when they should have been repenting and praying.

[2] They were secure and careless; *they knew not, until the flood came, v.* 39. *Knew not!* Surely they could not but know. Did he not call them to repentance while his long-suffering waited? Their *not knowing* is joined with their *eating, and drinking, and marrying*; for, *First, Therefore* they were sensual, because they were secure. *Secondly, Therefore* they were secure, because they were sensual; were so taken up with things seen and present, that they had neither time nor heart to mind the things not seen as yet, which they were warned of. *They knew not, until the flood came.* The flood did come, though they would not foresee it. The evil day is never the further off for men's putting it far off from them. They did not know it till it was too late to prevent it. Judgments are most terrible and amazing to the secure, and those that have made a jest of them.

The application of this, concerning the old world, we have in these words; *So shall the coming of the Son of man be.* Security and sensuality are likely to be the epidemical diseases of the latter days. All are off their watch, and at their ease. As the flood took away the sinners of the old world, irresistibly and irrecoverably; so shall secure sinners, that mocked at Christ and his coming, be taken away.

2. It will be a separating day (*v.* 40, 41); *Then shall two be in the field.*

(1) We may apply it to the success of the gospel, especially at the first preaching of it; it divided the world; *some believed the things which were spoken,* and were taken to Christ; *others believed not,* and were left to perish in their unbelief.

When ruin came upon Jerusalem, a distinction was made by Divine Providence, according to that which had been before made by divine grace; for all the Christians among them were saved from perishing in that calamity. If we are safe when thousands fall on our right hand and our left, are not consumed when others are consumed round about us, so that we are as brands plucked out of the fire, we have reason to say, *It is of the Lord's mercies,* and it is a great mercy.

(2) We may apply it to the second coming of Jesus Christ, and the separation which will be made in that day. He had said before (*v.* 31), that the elect will be *gathered together.* Here it is applied to them who shall be found alive. Christ will come unlooked for, will find people busy at their usual occupations, *in the field, at the mill.* And it speaks abundance of comfort to the Lord's people. Are they mean and despised in the world, as the man-servant in the field, or the maid at the mill (Exod. xi. 5)? Yet they shall not be forgotten or overlooked in that day. Are they dispersed in distant and unlikely places, where one would not expect to find the heirs of glory, *in the*

JAMIESON, FAUSSET, BROWN

means that the Son was *not at that time in possession of the knowledge* referred to, or simply that it was not *among the things which He had received to communicate*—has been matter of much controversy even among the firmest believers in the proper Divinity of Christ. In the latter sense it was taken by some of the most eminent of the ancient Fathers, and by LUTHER, MELANCTHON, and most of the older Lutherans; and it is so taken by BENGEL, LANGE, WEBSTER and WILKINSON. CHRYSOSTOM and others understood it to mean that *as man* our Lord was ignorant of this. It is taken literally by CALVIN, GROTIUS, DE WETTE, MEYER, FRITZSCHE, STIER, ALFORD, and ALEXANDER. **Take ye heed, watch and pray; for ye know not when the time is.**

A. B. SIMPSON:

His advent. Our postmillennial friends are fond of telling us of the gradual progress of Christian influences and the improvement of the world and that, after a little while, things will be about right and we can expect the Lord to come down to congratulate us on the good work we have been able to do without Him.

The picture Jesus gives us is entirely different: "As the days of Noah were, so shall also the days of the coming of the Son of man be." We know that the days of Noah were marked by wickedness and crime, and it would seem as if the two crimes most rampant in Noah's time, namely violence and lust, are coming to the front again in our own day in the increasing prevalence of murder, divorce, and social corruption. While it is true that the elements of righteousness and spiritual power are making progress and the good are better than they ever were before, there can be no doubt that the bad are worse and the shadow grows as dark as the light grows bright.

His coming a surprise. These verses tell us that the Lord's coming will be a shock to this self-complacent world. It will also be a surprise to the modern prophets who have told us all about it so often and still persist in knowing the very schedule of events and the time which the Father hath put in His own power.

It will not be a surprise to His waiting people. "That day shall not overtake you as a thief." They may not know the day or hour, but they shall know enough to be ready. But to the world it will be a terrific and startling blow. "When they shall say peace and safety, then sudden destruction cometh upon them as travail upon a woman with child, and they shall not escape." Even for us, the followers of Christ, the only safety is to be always ready.

—*Christ in the Bible*

ADAM CLARKE

37-38. *As the days of Noe . . . they were eating and drinking.* The design of these verses seems to be that the desolation should be as general as it should be unexpected.

39. *And knew not.* "They considered not"—did not lay Noah's warning to heart, till it was too late to profit by it: *so shall it be*—and so it was in this coming of the Son of Man.

40-41. *Then shall two men . . . two women . . . one shall be taken, and the other left.* The meaning seems to be that so general should these calamities be that no two persons, wheresoever found, or about whatsoever employed, should be both able to effect their escape; and that captivity and the sword should have a complete triumph over this unhappy people. *Two women shall be grinding.* Women alone are still employed in grinding the corn in the East; and it is only when dispatch is required, or the uppermost millstone is heavy, that a second woman is added.

MATTHEW HENRY

field, at the mill? Yet the angels will find them there. A very great change it will be, to go to heaven from ploughing and grinding. Are they weak, and unable of themselves to move heavenward? They shall be taken. Those whom Christ has once apprehended and laid hold on, he will never lose his hold of. Are they intermixed with others, linked with them in the same habitations, societies, employments? Let not that discourage any true Christian; God knows how to separate the wheat and chaff in the same floor.

III. Here is a general exhortation to us, *to watch, and be ready, v.* 42, &c.

1. The duty required; *Watch, and be ready, v.* 42, 44.

(1) *Watch therefore, v.* 42. It is the great duty and interest of all the disciples of Christ to watch, to be awake and keep awake. As a sinful state or way is compared to *sleep*, senseless and inactive, so a gracious state or way is compared to *watching* and *waking*. We must watch for our Lord's coming. To watch implies not only to believe that our Lord will come, but to desire that he would come, to be often thinking of his coming. To watch for Christ's coming, is to maintain that gracious temper and disposition of mind which we should be willing that our Lord, when he comes, should find us in. Watching is supposed to be in the night, which is sleeping time; while we are in this world, it is *night* with us, and we must take pains to keep ourselves awake.

(2) *Be ye also ready,* We wake in vain, if we do not get ready. It is not enough to *look* for such things; but we must therefore *give diligence*. There is an inheritance which we then hope to enter upon, and we must have ourselves ready, made meet to partake of it.

2. The reasons to induce us to this watchfulness; which are two.

(1) Because the time of our Lord's coming is very uncertain. Let us consider then,

[1] That *we know not what hour he will come, v.* 42. We cannot know that we have a long time to live; nor can we know how little a time we have to live, for it may prove less than we expect.

[2] That he may *come at such an hour as we think not, v.* 44. Though we know not *when* he will come, we are sure he *will* come. *In such an hour as you think not*, that is, such an hour as they who are unready and unprepared, think not (*v.* 50); nay, such an hour as the most lively expectants perhaps thought least likely.

[3] That the children of this world are thus wise in their generation. This he shows in a particular instance, *v.* 43. If the master of a house had notice that a thief would come such a night, and such a watch of the night, though it were the midnight-watch, when he was most sleepy, yet he would be up, and listen to every noise in every corner, and he ready to give him a warm reception. Though we know not *just when* our Lord will come, yet, knowing that he *will* come, it concerns us to watch always. The day of the Lord comes *by surprise, as a thief in the night*. If Christ, when he comes, finds us asleep and unready, our house will be broken up, and we shall lose all we are worth. *Be ye also ready;* as ready at all times as the good man of the house would be at the hour when he expected the thief.

(2) Because the issue of our Lord's coming will be very happy and comfortable to those that shall be found ready, but very dismal and dreadful to those that shall not, *v.* 45, &c. This is represented by the different state of good and bad servants, when their lord comes to reckon with them. Now this parable seems especially intended as a warning to ministers; for the servant spoken of is a *steward*. Now observe what Christ here saith,

[1] Concerning the *good servant*; he shows here what he is—*a ruler of the household*; what, being so, he should be—*faithful* and *wise*; and what, if he be so, he shall be eternally—*blessed*.

First, We have here his place and office. He is one *whom his Lord has made ruler over his household, to give them meat in due season*. The church of Christ is his household, or family, standing in relation to him as the Father and Master of it. Gospel ministers are appointed *rulers* in this household; not as princes but as stewards, or other subordinate officers; not as lords, but as guides. They are rulers by Christ; what power they have is derived from him. The work of gospel ministers is to give to Christ's household their meat in due season, as stewards. Their work is *to give*, not take to themselves, but give to the family what the Master has bought, to *dispense* what Christ has *purchased*. It is to give *meat*; not to give *law* (that is Christ's work), but to deliver those doctrines to the church which, if duly digested, will be nourishment to souls. They must give the meat that is *sound* and *wholesome*. It must be given *in due season*, that is, whenever any opportunity offers itself; or time after time, according as the duty of every day

JAMIESON, FAUSSET, BROWN

The closing words of the Discourse, as given by Luke (21:34-36), are remarkable. "And take heed to yourselves, lest at any time your hearts be overcharged" or "weighted down with surfeiting"—"debauchery," or its effects; "and drunkenness" —meaning all animal excesses, which quench spirituality; "and cares of this life"—engrossing the interest, absorbing the attention, and so choking spirituality: "and so that day come upon you unawares. For as a snare"—a trap catching them when least expecting it—"shall it come on all them that dwell on the face of the whole earth. Watch ye therefore, and pray always"—the two great duties which, in prospect of trial, are always enjoined—"that ye may be accounted worthy to escape all these things that shall come to pass, and to stand before the Son of man." These warnings, though suggested by the need of preparedness for the tremendous calamities approaching, and the total wreck of the existing state of things, have reference to a coming of another kind, for judicial vengeance of another nature and on a grander and more awful scale—not ecclesiastical or political but *personal*; not temporal but *eternal*—when all safety and blessedness will be found to lie in being able to "stand before the Son of man" in the glory of His personal appearing.

ADAM CLARKE

42. *Watch therefore*. Be always on your guard, that you may not be taken unawares, and that you may be properly prepared to meet God in the way of either judgment or mercy, whensoever He may come.

45. *Who then is a faithful and wise servant?* All should live in the same expectation of the coming of Christ which a servant has with respect to the return of his master, who, in departing for a season, left the management of his affairs to him, and of which management he is to give an exact account on his master's return.

F. B. MEYER:

Watch and work. There are many comings of the Son of man before the final one to judgment. We may derive the full benefit of our Lord's words, even though we have arrived at no settled opinion as to the precise order of future events. The hour of our death is as uncertain as that of his coming in the clouds. For each, we should be ready!

Watchfulness is keeping awake! We are beset by temptations to sleep. Bunyan said that we are traveling over the Enchanted Ground, the air of which is very heavy and sleep-producing. How dull we are to perceive the unseen, or to meet the great opportunities of life! "Broken up" alludes to the mud or clay house which could not keep out the thief. Death breaks in and carries us away from all of our treasures (1 Thess. 5:2, 4).

We had best wait for our Lord while engaged in carefully discharging our appointed tasks. The Church is a big household in which each has his niche. To labor is to pray; to serve is to be ready.
—Bible Commentary

MATTHEW HENRY	JAMIESON, FAUSSET, BROWN	ADAM CLARKE

requires.

Secondly, His right discharge of this office. The good servant will be a good *steward*.

1. He is *faithful*; stewards must be so. He that is *trusted*, must be trusty; and the greater the trust is, the more is expected from them. It is a great good thing that is committed to *ministers*; and they must be faithful. Christ counts those ministers, and those only, that are *faithful*. A faithful minister of Jesus Christ is one that sincerely designs his master's honour, not his own; regards the meanest, reproves the greatest, and doth not respect persons.

2. He is wise to understand his duty. In guiding of the flock there is need, not only of the integrity of the heart, but the skilfulness of the hands. Honesty may suffice for a good *servant*, but wisdom is necessary to a *good steward*.

3. He is doing. The ministry is a good work, and they whose office it is, have always something to do; they must not indulge themselves in ease, but be doing, and doing to the purpose; not *talking*, but *doing*.

4. He is *found doing* when his Master comes; which intimates, (1) Constancy at his work. At what hour soever his Master comes, he is found busy at the work of the day. As with a good God the end of one mercy is the beginning of another, so with a good man, a good minister, the end of one duty is the beginning of another. (2) Perseverance in his work till the Lord come.

Thirdly, The recompence of reward intended him for this.

1. He shall be taken notice of. This is intimated in these words, Who then is that *faithful and wise servant*? Which supposes that there are but few who answer this character. Those who thus distinguish themselves now, Christ will in the great day both dignify and distinguish by the glory conferred on them.

2. He shall be blessed? *Blessed is that servant*. All the dead that die in the Lord are blessed, Rev. xiv. 13. But there is a peculiar blessedness secured to them that approve themselves faithful stewards, and are found so doing. Next to the honour of those who die in the field of battle, suffering for Christ as the martyrs, is the honour of those that die in the field of service, ploughing, and sowing, and reaping, for Christ.

3. He shall be preferred (*v.* 47); *He shall make him ruler over all his goods*. Great men, if the stewards of their house conduct themselves well in that place, commonly prefer them to be the managers of their estates. But the greatest honour which the kindest master ever did to his most tried servants in this world, is nothing to that weight of glory which the Lord Jesus will confer upon his faithful watchful servants in the world to come.

[2] Concerning the *evil* servant. Here we have, *First*, His description given (*v.* 48, 49). The vilest of creatures is a wicked man, the vilest of men is a wicked Christian, and the vilest of them a wicked minister.

1. The cause of his wickedness; He hath *said in his heart, My Lord delays his coming*; and therefore he begins to think he will never come. The delay of Christ's coming, though it is a gracious instance of his patience, is greatly abused by wicked people. They that walk by sense, are ready to say of the unseen Jesus, as the people did of Moses when he tarried in the mount upon their errand, *We wot not what is become of him*, and therefore *up, make us gods*, the world a god, the belly a god, anything but him that should be.

2. The particulars of his wickedness; he is a slave to his passions and his appetites.

(1) Persecution is here charged upon him. He begins to *smite his fellow servants*. It is no new thing to see evil servants smiting their fellow servants; both private Christians and faithful ministers. He smites them, either because they reprove him, or because they will not bow, and do him reverence. The steward, when he smites his fellow servants, does it under colour of his Master's authority, and in his name; but he shall know that he could not put a greater affront upon his Master.

(2) Profaneness and immorality; *He begins to eat and drink with the drunken*. He associates with the worst of sinners. The drunken are the merry and jovial company, and those he is for, and thus he hardens them in their wickedness. He does like them; *eats, and drinks, and is drunken*. This is an inlet to all manner of sin. Drunkenness is a leading wickedness; they who are slaves to that, are never masters of themselves in anything else. Well, this is the description of a wicked minister, who yet may have the common gifts of learning and utterance above others; and, as hath been said of some, may preach so well in the pulpit, that it is a pity he should ever

G. CAMPBELL MORGAN:

In the parable of the household, the word itself is suggestive. Jesus said: "Who then is the faithful and wise servant, whom his lord hath set over his *household*?" The Greek word here translated household is only once again used. In Revelation we read that "the leaves of the tree were for the *healing* of the nations." What relation can there be between *healing* and *household*? This question can be answered only by an understanding of what this word household really signifies. It is the word from which we derive our word therapeutic, and the basal idea of it is healing. The word household refers to all such in the house as serve.

That first word, "Who then is the faithful and wise *servant*?" is the word bond-slave; but the word household comes from another term for servant, which is other than the word bond-slave. It is a word that signifies a loving service, a purpose of healing in service. This is a case of metonymy, where one word is put for another, which the other suggests, as when we say a man keeps a good table, when we refer really to his food. This word in the parable, then, suggests the picture of a great house, and one Lord; and of all those in the house under His control, as thinking of His interests, while serving under His command. He used the word that indicated the love principle in service, the tender healing ministry that only grows out of love. Thus in a word, flaming and flashing with meaning, we discover our Lord's conception of His Church during the time of His absence. His household all serve, but all serve by love, and the ministry is a healing ministry.

Now let us very carefully notice His word: "Who then is the faithful and wise servant, whom his lord hath set over his household?" This word must be interpreted by the consistent teaching of the Lord, that service is the condition of greatness. The servant is "set over." Why "set over"? Because he is a servant. This is not a picture of the priesthood, or of the ministry according to many modern conceptions of these. There is no sense in which any priesthood or ministry is set over the Church of God, save by their ministry. "Whosoever would be first among you, shall be servant of all." Here is Christ's picture of one servant set over the rest, because he serves all the rest. It is not a picture of any man in the household, a picture of one in official authority; it is the picture of each one in the exercise of the ministry of healing and of love.

Now, in the parable we see two attitudes. First that of the faithful and wise servant. His attitude is simply that of bringing forth meat in due season, and feeding the rest; the attitude of caring for all the other members of the household during the Lord's absence, for the sake of the absent Lord. But there is another servant here, and Jesus speaks of him as "that evil servant." He says, "My lord tarrieth," He is not returning yet; and with that sense of the Master's absence, he turns to evil courses within the household, beating his fellow servants instead of feeding and caring for them; turning aside to the companionship of drunken men instead of standing in the place of loyalty to the absent Lord.

In the parable we have two results. When the lord returns, the servant who has been loyal to the service of his fellow servants, for the sake of his absent lord, is promoted and put into the place of a new authority; while the evil servant is cut asunder and cast out.

We must not attempt to carry these parables further than they go. This is a picture first of all of a household, and the relation of all within it to the absent Lord. To gather it up we may state it thus. We shall prove our loyalty in the Church of God to the absent Lord by the measure in which we serve one another; and we shall prove our disloyalty by the measure in which we beat and slay our brethren. —*The Gospel According to Matthew*

MATTHEW HENRY

come out, and yet live so ill out of the pulpit, that it is a pity he should ever come in.

Secondly, His doom read, *v.* 50, 51. Observe,

1. The surprise that will accompany his doom (*v.* 50); *The Lord of that servant will come.* Our putting off the thoughts of Christ's coming will not put off his coming. Whatever fancy he deludes himself with, his Lord will come. The coming of Christ will be a most dreadful surprise to secure and careless sinners, especially to wicked ministers; *He shall come in a day when he looketh not for him.* Behold, he has told us before.

2. The severity of his doom, *v.* 51. It is not more severe than righteous, but it is a doom that carries in it utter ruin.

(1) Death. His Lord shall *cut him asunder*, "he shall cut him off from the land of the living," from the congregation of the righteous, shall separate him unto evil. Death cuts off a good man, as a choice imp is cut off to be grafted in a better stock; but it cuts off a wicked man, as a withered branch is cut off for the fire. Or, as we read it, *shall cut him asunder*, that is, part body and soul. The soul and body of a godly man at death part fairly, the one cheerfully lifted up to God, the other left to the dust; but the soul and body of a wicked man at death are cut asunder, torn asunder.

(2) Damnation. He *shall appoint him his portion with the hypocrites*, and a miserable portion it will be, for *there shall be weeping*. There is a place and state where there is nothing but *weeping and gnashing of teeth*; which speaks the soul's tribulation and anguish under God's indignation and wrath. The divine sentence will appoint this place and state as the portion of those who by their own sin were fitted for it. He that is now *the Saviour*, will then be *the Judge*, and the everlasting state of the children of men will be as he appoints. When Christ would express the most severe punishment in the other world, he calls it *the portion of hypocrites.* Wicked ministers will have their portion in the other world with the worst of sinners, even with the hypocrites, and justly, for they are the worst of hypocrites. *Son, remember*, will be as cutting a word to a minister if he perish as to any other sinner whatsoever. Let them therefore who preach to others, fear, lest they themselves should be castaways.

JAMIESON, FAUSSET, BROWN

ALEXANDER MACLAREN:

The dreadful doom of the unwatchful servant is couched in terms of awful severity. The cruel punishment of sawing asunder, which, tradition says, was suffered by Isaiah and was not unfamiliar in old times, is his. What concealed terror of retribution it signifies we do not know. Perhaps it points to a fate in which a man shall be, as it were, parted into two, each at enmity with the other. Perhaps it implies a retribution in kind for his sin, which consisted, as the next clause implies, in hypocrisy, which is the sundering in twain of inward conviction and practice, and is to be avenged by a like but worse rending apart of conscience and will. At all events, it shadows a fearful retribution, which is not extinction, inasmuch as, in the next clause, we read that his portion—his lot, or that condition which belongs to him by virtue of his character—is with "the hypocrites." He was one of them, because, while he said "my lord," he had ceased to love and obey, having ceased to desire and expect; and therefore whatever is their fate shall be his, even to the "dividing asunder of soul and spirit," and setting eternal discord among the thoughts and intents of the heart. That is not the punishment of unwatchfulness, but of what unwatchfulness leads to, if unawakened. Let these words of the King ring an alarm for us all, and rouse our sleepy souls to watch, as becomes the children of the day.
—*Expositions of Holy Scripture*

ADAM CLARKE

51. *Cut him asunder.* This refers to an ancient mode of punishment used in several countries. Isaiah is reported to have been sawed asunder. That it was an ancient mode of punishment is evident from what Herodotus says: that Sabacus, king of Ethiopia, had a vision in which he was commanded to cut in two all the Egyptian priests.

MATTHEW HENRY — CHAPTER 25

Verses 1–13

I. That in general which is to be illustrated is, *the kingdom of heaven.* Some of Christ's parables had shown us what it is like now in the present reception of it, as *ch.* xiii. This tells us what it shall be like, when the mystery of God shall be finished, and that kingdom delivered up to the Father.

II. That by which it is illustrated, is, a marriage solemnity. It was a custom sometimes used among the Jews on that occasion, that the bridegroom came, attended with his friends, late in the night, to the house of the bride, where she expected him, attended with her bride-maids; who, upon notice given of the bridegroom's approach, were to go out with lamps in their hands, to light him into the house with ceremony and formality, in order to the celebrating of the nuptials with great mirth.

1. The *Bridegroom* is our Lord Jesus Christ. It bespeaks his singular and superlative love to, and his faithful and inviolable covenant with, his spouse the church.

2. The virgins are the professors of religion, members of the church; but here represented as *her companions.*

3. The office of these virgins is to meet the bridegroom, which is as much their happiness as their duty. They come to wait *upon* the bridegroom when he appears, and in the meantime to wait *for* him. As Christians, we profess ourselves to be, (1) Attendants upon Christ, to do him honour. Hold up the name, and hold forth the praise of the exalted Jesus; this is our business. (2) Expectants of Christ, and of his second coming. The second coming of Christ is the centre in which all the lines of our religion meet, and to which the whole of the divine life hath a constant reference and tendency.

4. Their chief concern is to have lights in their hands, when they attend the bridegroom, thus to do him honour and do him service. Christians are children of light.

Now concerning these ten virgins, we may observe, (1) Their different character, with the proof and evidence of it. Their character was, that *five were wise, and five foolish* (*v.* 2). Those of the same profession and denomination among men, may yet be of characters vastly different in the sight of God.

JAMIESON, FAUSSET, BROWN — CHAPTER 25

Vss. 1-13. PARABLE OF THE TEN VIRGINS. This and the following parable are in Matthew alone. **1. Then**—at the time referred to at the close of the preceding chapter, the time of the Lord's Second Coming to reward His faithful servants and take vengeance on the faithless. *Then* **shall the kingdom of heaven be likened unto ten virgins, which took their lamps, and went forth to meet the bridegroom**—This supplies a key to the parable, whose object is, in the main, the same as that of the last parable—to illustrate *the vigilant and expectant attitude of faith*, in respect of which believers are described as "they that look for Him" (Heb. 9:28), and "love His appearing" (II Tim. 4:8). In the last parable it was that of servants waiting for their absent Lord; in this it is that of virgin attendants on a Bride, whose duty it was to go forth at night with lamps, and be ready on the appearance of the Bridegroom to conduct the Bride to his house, and go in with him to the marriage. This entire and beautiful change of figure brings out the lesson of the former parable in quite a new light. But let it be observed that, just as in the parable of the Marriage Supper, so in this—the *Bride* does not come into view at all in this parable; the *Virgins* and the *Bridegroom* holding forth all the intended instruction: nor could believers be represented both as Bride and Bridal Attendants without incongruity. **2. And five of them were wise, and five were foolish**—They are not distinguished into good and bad, as TRENCH observes, but into "wise" and "foolish"—just as in ch. 7:25-27 those who reared their house for eternity are distinguished into "wise" and "foolish builders"; because in both cases a certain degree of goodwill towards the truth is assumed. To make anything of the equal number of both classes would, we think, be precarious, save to warn us how large a portion of those who, up to the last, so nearly resemble those that love Christ's appearing will be disowned by Him when He comes.

ADAM CLARKE — CHAPTER 25

1. *Then shall the kingdom of heaven.* The state of Jews and professing Christians—or the state of the Visible Church at the time of the destruction of Jerusalem, and in the day of judgment, for the parable appears to relate to both those periods. And particularly at the time in which Christ shall come to judge the world, it shall appear what kind of reception His gospel has met with. *Virgins.* Denoting the purity of the Christian doctrine and character. In this parable the *bridegroom* is generally understood to mean Jesus Christ. The *feast*, that state of felicity to which He has promised to raise His genuine followers. The *wise*, or "prudent," and *foolish virgins*, those who truly enjoy, and those who only profess, the purity and holiness of His religion. The *oil*, the grace and salvation of God, or that faith which works by love. The *vessel*, the heart in which this oil is contained. The *lamp*, the profession of enjoying the burning and shining light of the gospel of Christ. *Going forth*, the whole of their sojourning upon earth.

2. *Five of them were wise.* Or "provident"—they took care to make a proper provision beforehand, and left nothing to be done in the last moment. *Five were foolish.* "Careless." *Moros* is thus defined, "he who sees not what is proper or necessary." These did not see that it was necessary to have "oil in their vessels" (the salvation of God in their souls), as well as a burning lamp of religious profession, vv. 3-4.

MATTHEW HENRY

Those are wise or foolish indeed, that are so in the affairs of their souls. True religion is true wisdom; sin is folly. The evidence of this character was in the very thing which they were to attend to.

First, It was the folly of the foolish virgins, that they *took their lamps, and took no oil with them, v.* 3. They had just oil enough to make their lamps burn for the present, to make a show with, as if they intended to meet the bridegroom; but no cruse or bottle of oil with them for a recruit if the bridegroom tarried; thus hypocrites.

[1] They have no principle within. They have a lamp of profession in their hands, but have not in their hearts that stock which is necessary to carry them through the services and trials of the present state.

[2] They have no prospect of, nor make provision for, what is to come. They took lamps for a present show, but not oil for after use. They do not provide for hereafter, as the ant does, nor *lay up for the time to come*, 1 Tim. vi. 19.

Secondly, It was the wisdom of the wise virgins, that *they took oil in their vessels with their lamps, v.* 4. They had a good principle within, which would maintain and keep up their profession. The heart is the vessel, which it is our wisdom to get furnished; for, out of a good treasure there, good things must be brought; but if that root be rottenness, the blossom will be dust. Grace is the *oil* which we must have in this *vessel*. Our light must shine before men, in good works, but this cannot be, or not long, unless there be a fixed active principle in the heart, of faith in Christ, and love to God and our brethren. They that took oil in their vessels, did it upon supposition that perhaps the bridegroom might tarry. In looking forward it is good to prepare for the worst, to lay in for a long siege.

(2) Their common fault, during the bridegroom's delay; *They all slumbered and slept, v.* 5. The bridegroom tarried, that is, he did not come out so soon as they expected. What we look for as certain, we are apt to think is very near. Christ, as to us, *seems* to tarry, and yet really *does not*. But though Christ tarry past *our* time, he will not tarry past the *due* time. While he tarried, those that waited for him, grew careless, and forgot what they were attending; *They all slumbered and slept;* as if they had given over looking for him. Those that inferred the suddenness of it from its certainty, when that answered not their expectation, were apt from the delay to infer its uncertainty. The wise virgins kept their lamps burning, but did not keep themselves awake. Too many good Christians, when they have been long in profession, grow remiss, their graces are not lively, nor their works found perfect before God; and though all *love* be not lost, yet the *first* love is left.

(3) The surprising summons given them, to attend the bridegroom (*v.* 6); *At midnight there was a cry made, Behold, the bridegroom cometh.* Though Christ tarry long, he will come at last; though he seem slow, he is sure. His friends shall find, to their comfort, that *the vision is for an appointed time.* The year of the redeemed is fixed, and it will come. Christ's coming will be at our midnight, when we least look for him. His coming for the relief and comfort of his people, often is when the good intended seems to be at the greatest distance. Christ will come when he pleases, to show his sovereignty, and will not let us know when, to teach us our duty. When Christ comes, we must *go forth to meet him. Go ye forth to meet him,* is a call to those who are habitually prepared, to be actually ready. The notice given of Christ's approach, and the call to meet him, will be awakening; *There was a cry made.* His first coming was not with any observation at all, nor did they say, *Lo, here is Christ*, or *Lo, he is there; he was in the world, and the world knew him not;* but his second coming will be with the observation of all the world.

(4) The address they all made to answer this summons (*v.* 7); *They all arose, and trimmed their lamps,* snuffed them and supplied them with oil, and went about with all expedition to receive the bridegroom. This, in the wise virgins, bespeaks an actual preparation for the Bridegroom's coming. Even those that are best prepared for death, have work to do, to get themselves actually ready, that they may be *found in peace* (2 Pet. iii. 14), *found doing* (*ch.* xxiv. 46), and not *found naked*, 2 Cor. v. 3. It will be a day of search and enquiry; and it concerns us to think how we shall then be found. In the foolish virgins, it denotes a vain confidence, and conceit of the goodness of their state, and their readiness for another world.

(5) The distress which the foolish virgins were in, for want of *oil, v.* 8, 9. This bespeaks, [1] The apprehensions which some hypocrites have of the misery of their state, even on this side death, when God opens

JAMIESON, FAUSSET, BROWN

3. They that were foolish took their lamps, and took no oil with them: 4. But the wise took oil in their vessels with their lamps—What are these "lamps" and this "oil"? Many answers have been given. But since the foolish as well as the wise took their lamps and went forth with them to meet the Bridegroom, these lighted lamps and this advance a certain way in company with the wise, must denote that Christian profession which is common to all who bear the Christian name; while the insufficiency of this without something else, of which they never possessed themselves, shows that "the foolish" mean those who, with all that is common to them with real Christians, *lack the essential preparation for meeting Christ.* Then, since the wisdom of "the wise" consisted in their taking with their lamps a supply of oil in their vessels, keeping their lamps burning till the Bridegroom came, and so fitting them to go in with Him to the marriage, this supply of oil must mean that *inward reality of grace* which alone will stand when He appears whose eyes are as a flame of fire. But this is too general; for it cannot be for nothing that this inward grace is here set forth by the familiar symbol of *oil*, by which *the Spirit of all grace* is so constantly represented in Scripture. Beyond all doubt, this was what was symbolized by that precious anointing oil with which Aaron and his sons were consecrated to the priestly office (Exod. 30:23-25, 30); by "the oil of gladness above His fellows" with which Messiah was to be anointed (Ps. 45:7; Heb. 1:9), even as it is expressly said, that "God giveth not the Spirit by measure unto Him" (John 3:34); and by the bowl full of golden oil, in Zechariah's vision, which, receiving its supplies from the two olive trees on either side of it, poured it through seven golden pipes into the golden lampstand to keep it continually burning bright (Zech. 4)—for the prophet is expressly told that it was to proclaim the great truth, "Not by might, nor by power, but by MY SPIRIT, saith the Lord of hosts [shall this temple be built]. Who art thou, O great mountain [of opposition to this issue]? Before Zerubbabel thou shalt become a plain [or, be swept out of the way], and he shall bring forth the head-stone [of the temple], with shoutings [crying], GRACE, GRACE unto it." This supply of oil, then, representing that inward grace which distinguishes the wise, must denote, more particularly, that "supply of the Spirit of Jesus Christ," which, as it is the source of the new spiritual life at the first, is the secret of its *enduring* character. Everything *short of this* may be possessed by "the foolish"; while it is the possession of this that makes "the wise" to be "ready" when the Bridegroom appears, and fit to "go in with Him to the marriage." Just so in the parable of the Sower, the stony-ground hearers, "having no deepness of earth" and "no root in themselves," though they spring up and get even into ear, never ripen, while they in the good ground bear the precious grain. **5. While the bridegroom tarried**—So in ch. 24:48, "My Lord delayeth His coming"; and so Peter says sublimely of the ascended Saviour, "Whom the heaven must receive until the times of restitution of all things" (Acts 3:21, and cf. Luke 19:11, 12). Christ "tarries," among other reasons, to try the faith and patience of His people. **they all slumbered and slept**—the wise as well as the foolish. The world "slumbered" signifies, simply, "nodded," or, "became drowsy"; while the world "slept" is the usual word for lying down to sleep, denoting two stages of spiritual declension—first, that half-involuntary lethargy or drowsiness which is apt to steal over one who falls into inactivity; and then a conscious, deliberate yielding to it, after a little vain resistance. Such was the state alike of the wise and the foolish virgins, even till the cry of the Bridegroom's approach awoke them. So likewise in the parable of the Importunate Widow: "When the Son of man cometh, shall He find faith on the earth?" (Luke 18:8). **6. And at midnight**—i.e., the time when the Bridegroom will be least expected; for "the day of the Lord so cometh as a thief in the night" (I Thess. 5:2). **there was a cry made, Behold, the Bridegroom cometh; go ye out to meet him**—i.e., Be ready to welcome Him. **7. Then all those virgins arose, and trimmed their lamps**—the foolish virgins as well as the wise. How very long do both parties seem the same—almost to the moment of decision! Looking at the mere form of the parable, it is evident that the folly of "the foolish" consisted not in having no oil at all; for they must have had oil enough in their lamps to keep them burning up to this moment: their folly consisted in not making provision against its *exhaustion,* by taking with their lamp an *oil-vessel*

ADAM CLARKE

4. *Took oil in their vessels.* They not only had a sufficiency of oil in their lamps, but they carried a vessel with oil to recruit their lamps, when it should be found expedient. This the foolish or improvident neglected to do; hence, when the oil that was in their lamps burned out, they had none to pour into the lamps to maintain the flame.

5. *The bridegroom tarried.* The coming of the bridegroom to an individual may imply his death, His coming to the world—the final judgment. The delay—the time from a man's birth till his death, in the first case; in the second, the time from the beginning to the end of the world. *Slumbered and slept.* Or, "They became drowsy and fell asleep." As sleep is frequently used in the sacred writings for death, so drowsiness, which precedes sleep, may be considered as pointing out the decays of the constitution, and the sicknesses which precede death.

6. *At midnight there was a cry.* The Jewish weddings were generally celebrated in the night, yet they usually began at the rising of the evening star; but in this case there was a more than ordinary delay.

MATTHEW HENRY

their eyes to see their folly. Or, however, [2] The real misery of their state on the other side death, and in the judgment.

First, Their lamps are gone out. The lamps of hypocrites often go out in this life; when they who have begun in the spirit, end in the flesh. The profession withers, and the credit of it is lost; the hopes fail, and the comfort of them is gone. The gains of a hypocritical profession will not follow a man to judgment, *ch.* vii. 22, 23.

Secondly, They wanted oil to supply them when they were going out. An external profession well humoured may carry a man far, it may light him along this world, but the dams of the valley of the shadow of death will put it out.

Thirdly, They would gladly be beholden to the wise virgins for a supply out of their vessels; *Give us of your oil.* Those who now hate the strictness of religion, will, at death and judgment, wish for the solid comforts of it. Those who care not to live the life, yet would die the death, of the righteous. *Give us of your oil;* that is, "Speak a good word for us"; so some; but there is no occasion for vouchers in the great day, the Judge knows what is every man's true character. Those will see their need of grace hereafter, when it should save them, who will not see their need of grace now, when it should sanctify and rule them. It comes too late. There is no buying when the market is over, no bidding when the inch of candle is dropped.

Fourthly, They were denied a share in their companions' oil. *The wise answered, Not so;* that peremptory denial is not in the original, but supplied by the translators: these wise virgins would rather give a reason without a positive refusal, than (as many do) give a positive refusal without a reason. They were well inclined to help their neighbours in distress; but, We must not, we cannot, we dare not, do it, *lest there be not enough for us and you*; charity begins at home; but *go, and buy for yourselves.* Those that would be saved, must have grace of their own. Though we have benefit by the communion of saints, and the faith and prayers of others, yet our own sanctification is indispensably necessary to our own salvation. Every man shall give account of himself; for he cannot get another to muster for him in that day. Those that have most grace, have none to spare; all we have, is little enough for ourselves to appear before God in. The best have need to borrow from Christ, but they have none to lend to any of their neighbours. These wise virgins do not upbraid the foolish with their neglect, but give them the best advice the case will bear, *Go ye rather to them that sell.* When ministers attend such as have been mindless of God and their souls all their days, but are under death-bed convictions; and direct them to repent, and turn to God, and close with Christ; they do but as these wise virgins did by the foolish, even make the best of bad. They can but tell them what is to be done. It is good advice now, if it be taken in time, *Go to them that sell, and buy for yourselves.*

(6) The coming of the bridegroom, and the issue of all this.

[1] *While they went out to buy, the bridegroom came.* With regard to those that put off their great work to the last, it is a thousand to one, that they have not time to do it then. Getting grace is a work of time, and cannot be done in a hurry. While the poor awakened soul addresses itself, upon a sick bed, to repentance and prayer, in awful confusion, it scarcely knows which end to begin at. This comes of having oil to buy when we should burn it, and grace to get when we should use it.

The bridegroom came. Our Lord Jesus will come to his people, at the great day, as a Bridegroom; will come in pomp and rich attire, attended with his friends.

[2] *They that were ready, went in with him to the marriage.* To be eternally glorified is to be in his immediate presence, and in the most intimate fellowship and communion with him. Those, and those only, shall go to heaven hereafter, that are made ready for heaven here.

[3] *The door was shut,* as is usual when all the company is come. The door was shut, *First,* To secure those that were within. Adam was put into paradise, but the door was left open and so he went out again; but when glorified saints are put into the heavenly paradise, they are shut in. *Secondly,* To exclude those that were out. Now the gate is strait, yet it is open; but then it will be shut and bolted, and *a great gulf fixed.*

[4] The foolish virgins came when it was *too late* (*v.* 11); *Afterward came also the other virgins.* There are many that will seek admission into heaven when it is too late; as profane Esau, who *afterward would have inherited the blessing.* The vain confidence of hypocrites will carry them very far in their expectations

JAMIESON, FAUSSET, BROWN

wherewith to replenish their lamp from time to time, and so have it burning until the Bridegroom should come. Are we, then—with some even superior expositors—to conclude that the foolish virgins must represent true Christians as well as do the wise, since only true Christians have the Spirit, and that the difference between the two classes consists only in the one having the necessary watchfulness which the other wants? Certainly not. Since the parable was designed to hold forth the prepared and the unprepared to meet Christ at His coming, and how the unprepared might, up to the very last, be confounded with the prepared—the structure of the parable behooved to accommodate itself to this, by making the lamps of the foolish to burn, as well as those of the wise, up to a certain point of time, and only then to discover their inability to burn on for want of a fresh supply of oil. But this is evidently just a *structural device;* and the real difference between the two classes who profess to love the Lord's appearing is a *radical one*—the possession by the one class of *an enduring principle of spiritual life,* and the want of it by the other. **8. And the foolish said unto the wise, Give us of your oil; for our lamps are gone out**—rather, as in the margin, "are going out"; for oil will not light an extinguished lamp, though it will keep a burning one from going out. Ah! now at length they have discovered not only their own folly, but the wisdom of the other class, and they do homage to it. They did not perhaps despise them before, but they thought them righteous overmuch; now they are forced, with bitter mortification, to wish they were like them. **9. But the wise answered, Not so; lest there be not enough for us and you**—The words "Not so," it will be seen, are not in the original, where the reply is very elliptical—"In case there be not enough for us and you." A truly wise answer this. "And what, then, if we shall share it with you? Why, both will be undone." **but go ye rather to them that sell, and buy for yourselves**—Here again it would be straining the parable beyond its legitimate design to make it teach that men may get salvation even after they are supposed and required to have it already gotten. It is merely a friendly way of reminding them of the proper way of obtaining the needed and precious article, with a certain reflection on them for having it now to seek. Also, when the parable speaks of "selling" and "buying" that valuable article, it means simply, "Go, get it in the only legitimate way." And yet the word "buy" is significant; for we are elsewhere bidden, "buy wine and milk without money and without price," and "buy of Christ gold tried in the fire," (Isa. 55:1; Rev. 3:18). Now, since what we pay the demanded price for becomes thereby *our own property,* the salvation which we thus take gratuitously at God's hands, being bought in His own sense of that word, becomes ours thereby in inalienable possession. (Cf. for the language, Prov. 23:23; ch. 13:44.) **10. And while they went to buy, the Bridegroom came; and they that were ready went in with him to the marriage: and the door was shut**—They are sensible of their past folly; they have taken good advice: they are in the act of getting what alone they lacked: a very little more, and they also are ready. But the Bridegroom comes; the ready are admitted; "the door is shut," and they are undone. How graphic and appalling this picture of one *almost saved—but lost!* **11. Afterward came also the other virgins, saying, Lord, Lord, open to us**—In ch. 7:22 this reiteration of the name was an exclamation rather of surprise; here it is a piteous cry of urgency, bordering on despair. Ah! now at length their eyes are wide open, and they realize all the consequences of their past folly. **12. But he answered and said, Verily I say unto you, I know you not**—The attempt to establish a difference between "I know you not" here, and "I never knew you" in ch. 7:23—as if this were gentler, and so implied a milder fate, reserved for "the foolish" of this parable—is to be resisted, though advocated by such critics as OLSHAUSEN, STIER, and ALFORD. Besides being inconsistent with the general tenor of such language, and particularly the solemn moral of the whole (vs. 13), it is a *kind* of criticism which tampers with some of the most awful warnings regarding the future. If it be asked why unworthy guests were admitted to the marriage of the King's Son, in a former parable, and the foolish virgins are excluded in this one, we may answer, in the admirable words of GERHARD, quoted by TRENCH, that those festivities are celebrated in this life, in the Church militant; these at the last day, in the Church triumphant; to those, even they are admitted who are not adorned with the wedding garment; but to these, only they to whom it is granted to be arrayed in fine linen clean and white,

ADAM CLARKE

8. *Our lamps are gone out.* "Are going out." So then it is evident that they were once lighted. They had once hearts illuminated and warmed by faith and love; but they had backslidden from the salvation of God, and now they are excluded from heaven, because, through their carelessness, they have let the light that was in them become darkness, and have not applied in time for a fresh supply of the salvation of God.

9. *Lest there be not enough for us and you.* These had all been companions in the Christian course, and there was a time when they might have been helpful to each other; but that time is now past forever—none has a particle of grace to spare, not even to help the soul of the dearest relative! The grace which every man receives is just enough to save his own soul; he has no merits to bequeath to the church, no work of supererogation which can be placed to the account of another. *Go ye rather to them that sell, and buy.* "Rather go to them that sell, and buy for yourselves, lest there be not enough for us and you."

10. *While they went to buy, the bridegroom came.* What a dismal thing it is not to discover the emptiness of one's heart of all that is good till it is too late to make any successful application for relief! God alone knows how many are thus deceived. *And they that were ready.* "They who were prepared"—who had not only a burning *lamp* of an evangelical profession, but had *oil* in their *vessels,* the faith that works by love in their hearts, and their lives adorned with all the fruits of the Spirit. *The door was shut.* Dreadful and fatal words! No hope remains. Nothing but death can shut this door; but death may surprise us in our sins, and then despair is our only portion.

11. *Afterwards came also the other virgins, saying, Lord, Lord.* Earnest prayer when used in time may do much good; but it appears, from this parable, that there may come a time when prayer even to Jesus may be too late!—viz., when the door is shut—when death has separated the body and the soul.

MATTHEW HENRY

of happiness. They go to heaven-gate, and demand entrance, and yet are shut out.

[5] They were *rejected*, as Esau was (*v.* 12); *I know you not*. We are all concerned to *seek the Lord while he may be found*. Time was, when, *Lord, Lord, open to us*, would have sped well, by virtue of that promise, *Knock, and it shall be opened to you*; but now it comes too late.

Lastly, Here is a practical inference drawn from this parable (*v.* 13); *Watch therefore*. We had it before (*ch.* xxiv. 42), and here it is repeated as the most needful caution. Our great duty is to watch. Be awake, and be wakeful. It is a good reason for our watching, that the time of our Lord's coming is very uncertain; *we know neither the day nor the hour*.

Verses 14–30

We have here the parable of the *talents* committed to three servants; this implies that we are in a state of work and business, as the former implies that we are in a state of expectancy. *That* showed the necessity of habitual preparation, *this* of actual diligence in our present work and service. 1. The *Master* is Christ. 2. The *servants* are Christians, his own servants, so they are called.

We have three things, in general, in this parable.

I. The trust committed to these servants; Their master *delivered to them his goods*: having appointed them to work (for Christ keeps no servants to be idle), he left them something to work upon. 1. Christ's servants have and receive their all from him; nor have anything they can call their own but sin. 2. Our receiving from Christ is in order to our working for him. 3. Whatever we receive to be made use of for Christ, still the property is vested in him.

(1) On what occasion this trust was committed to these servants; The master was *travelling into a far country*. *When he ascended on high, he gave gifts unto men*. When Christ went to heaven, he was as a man *travelling into a far country*. When he went, he took care to furnish his church with all things necessary for it during his personal absence. Thus Christ, at his ascension, left his goods to his church.

(2) In what proportion this trust was committed. He gave *talents*. Christ's gifts are rich and valuable, the purchases of his blood inestimable, and none of them mean. He gave to some more, to others less; to everyone according to his several ability. When Divine Providence has made a difference in men's ability, grace dispenses spiritual gifts accordingly, but still the ability itself is from him. Everyone had some one talent at least, and that is not a despicable stock for a poor servant to begin with. A *soul* of our own is the *one* talent we are every one of us entrusted with, and it will find us with work. *It is the duty of a man to render himself beneficial to those around him. He that is useful to others, may be reckoned a common good*. All had not alike, for they had not all alike abilities and opportunities. Some are cut out for service in one kind, others in another, as the members of the natural body.

II. The different management and improvement of this trust, *v.* 16–18.

1. Two of the servants did well.

(1) They were diligent and faithful; *They went, and traded*; as soon as ever their master was gone, they immediately applied themselves to their business. Those that have so much work to do, as every Christian has, need to set about it quickly, and lose no time. *They went, and traded*. A true Christian is a spiritual tradesmen. A tradesman is one who, having made his trade his choice, and taken pains to learn it, makes it his business to follow it, makes all other affairs bend to it, and lives upon the gain of it. We have no stock of our *own* to trade with, but trade as factors with our master's stock. The endowments of the mind—the enjoyments of the world—must be improved for the honour of Christ. The ordinances of the gospel, and our opportunities of attending them, must be improved for the end for which they were instituted, and communion with God kept up by them, and the gifts and graces of the Spirit must be exercised.

(2) They were successful; they doubled their stock. The hand of the diligent makes rich in graces, and comforts, and treasures of good works. There is a great deal to be got by industry in religion. The returns were in proportion to the receivings. The greater gifts any have, the more pains they ought to take, as those must that have a large stock to manage. From those to whom he has given but two talents, he expects only the improvement of two; if they lay out themselves to do good according to the best of their capacity and opportunity, they shall be accepted, though they do not so much good as others.

2. The third did ill (*v.* 18); *He that had received one talent, went, and hid his lord's money*. The un-

JAMIESON, FAUSSET, BROWN

which is the righteousness of saints (Rev. 19:8); to those, men are called by the trumpet of the Gospel; to these by the trumpet of the Archangel; to those, who enters may go out from them, or be cast out; who is once introduced to these never goes out, nor is cast out, from them any more: wherefore it is said, "The door is shut." **13. Watch therefore; for ye know neither the day nor the hour wherein the Son of man cometh**—This, the moral or practical lesson of the whole parable, needs no comment.

14-30. Parable of the Talents. This parable, while closely resembling it, is yet a different one from that of The Pounds, in Luke 19:11-27; though Calvin, Olshausen, Meyer, and others identify them—but not De Wette and Neander. For the difference between the two parables, see the opening remarks on that of The Pounds. While, as Trench observes with his usual felicity, "the virgins were represented as *waiting* for their Lord, we have the servants *working* for Him; there the *inward spiritual life* of the faithful was described; here his *external activity*. It is not, therefore, without good reason that they appear in their actual order—that of the Virgins first, and of the Talents following—since it is the sole condition of a profitable outward activity for the kingdom of God, that the life of God be diligently maintained within the heart." **14. For [the kingdom of heaven is] as a man**—The ellipsis is better supplied by our translators in the corresponding passage of Mark (13:34), "[For the Son of man is] as a man . . . **travelling into a far country**—or more simply, "going abroad." The idea of long "tarrying" is certainly implied here, since it is expressed in vs. 19. **who called his own servants, and delivered unto them his goods**—Between master and slaves this was not uncommon in ancient times. Christ's "servants" here mean all who, by their Christian profession, stand in the relation to Him of entire subjection. His "goods" mean all their gifts and endowments, whether original or acquired, natural or spiritual. As all that slaves have belongs to their master, so Christ has a claim to everything which belongs to His people, everything which may be turned to good, and He demands its appropriation to His service, or, viewing it otherwise, they first offer it up to Him; as being "not their own, but bought with a price" (I Cor. 6:19, 20), and He "delivers it to them" again to be put to use in His service. **15. And unto one he gave five talents, to another two, and to another one**—While the *proportion of gifts* is different in each, the same *fidelity is* required of all, and equally rewarded. And thus there is perfect equity. **to every man according to his several ability**—his natural capacity as enlisted in Christ's service, and his opportunities in providence for employing the gifts bestowed on him. **and straightway took his journey**—Cf. ch. 21:33, where the same departure is ascribed to God, after setting up the ancient economy. In both cases, it denotes the leaving of men to the action of all those spiritual laws and influences of Heaven under which they have been graciously placed for their own salvation and the advancement of their Lord's kingdom. **16. Then he that had received the five talents went and traded with the same**—expressive of the activity which he put forth and the labor he bestowed. **and made them other five talents. 17. And likewise he that had received two he also gained other two**—each doubling what he received, and therefore *both equally faithful*.

ADAM CLARKE

13. *Watch therefore*. If to *watch* be to employ ourselves chiefly about the business of our salvation, alas! how few of those who are called Christians are there who do *watch!*

15. *He gave . . . to every man according to his several ability*. The talent which each man has suits his own state best, and it is only pride and insanity which lead him to desire and envy the graces and talents of another. The man who improves the grace he has received, however small, will as surely get to the kingdom of God as he who has received most from his Master and improved all.

In this parable of our Lord, four things may be considered:

I. *The master who distributes the talents*. (1) The master's *kindness*. The servants have nothing—deserve nothing—have no claim on their master; yet he, in his kindness, delivers unto them his goods, not for his advantage, but for their comfort and salvation. (2) The master distributes these goods *diversely*—giving to one five, to another two, and to another one. No person can complain that he has been forgotten; the master gives to each. (3) The master distributes his talents with *wisdom*. He gave to each *according to his several ability*, i.e., to the power he had to improve what was given.

II. *The servants who improved their talents*. These persons are termed slaves, such as were the property of the master, who might dispose of them as he pleased. *Then he that had received the five talents went and traded*, v. 16. (1) The work was *speedily* begun—as soon as the master gave the talents and departed, so soon they began to labor. There is not a moment to be lost—every moment has its grace, and every grace has its employment, and everything is to be done for eternity. (2) The work was *perseveringly* carried on; *after a long time the Lord of those servants cometh*, v. 19. The master was long before he returned, but they did not relax. Many begin well, and continue faithful for a time—but how few persevere to the end! (3) Their work was crowned with *success*. They doubled the sum which they had received. Every grace of God is capable of great improvement. (4) They were ready to give in a *joyful* account when their master came and called for them. (5) Their *recompense* from their gracious master. (*a*) They receive *praise*. *Well done, thou good and faithful servant* v. 21. What a glorious thing to have the approbation of God, and the testimony of a good conscience! They were good, pure, and upright within—*faithful*, using to God's glory the blessings He had given. (*b*) They receive gracious promises. "You have been faithful over a little; I will set you over much." These promises refer not only to a future here; for the more faithfully a man

MATTHEW HENRY

faithful servant was he that had but *one talent*: doubtless there are many that have five talents, and bury them all; great abilities, great advantages, and yet do no good with them: but Christ would hint to us, (1) That if he that had but one talent, be reckoned with thus for burying that one, much more will they be accounted offenders, that have more, that have many, and bury them. (2) That those who have least to do for God, frequently do least of what they have to do. Some make it an excuse, because they have not wherewithal to do what they say they would, they will not do what we are sure they can, and so sit down and do nothing; it is really an aggravation of their sloth, that when they have but one talent to take care about, they neglect that one.

He digged in the earth, and hid the talent, for fear it should be stolen. Money is like manure (so my Lord Bacon used to say), good for nothing in the heap, but it must be spread; and so it is in spiritual gifts; many have them, and make no use of them for the end for which they were given them.

He hid his *lord's money*; had it been his *own*, he might have done as he pleased. His fellow-servants were busy and successful in trading, and their zeal should have provoked his. Are others active, and shall we be idle?

III. The account of this improvement, *v.* 19. The account is deferred; it is not *till after a long time* that they are reckoned with. Yet the day of account comes at last; *The lord of those servants reckoneth with them.* We must all be reckoned with—what good we have got to our own souls, and what good we have done to others.

1. The good account of the faithful servants. The servants *giving up the account* (*v.* 20, 22); "*Lord, thou deliveredst to me five talents*, and to me *two*; behold, *I have gained five talents*, and I *two* talents *more*."

Christ's faithful servants acknowledge with thankfulness his vouchsafements to them; *Lord, thou deliveredst to me* such and such things. It is good to remember what we have received, that we may know what is expected from us, and may render according to the benefit. We must never look upon our improvements but with a general mention of God's favour to us, of the honour he has put upon us, in entrusting us with his goods. For the truth is, the more we do for God, the more we are indebted to him for making use of us.

They produce, as an evidence of their faithfulness, what they have gained. God's good stewards have something to show for their diligence; *Show me thy faith by thy works.* He that is a good man, *let him show it*, James iii. 13. And it is observable that he who had but *two* talents, gave up his account as cheerfully as he who had *five*; for our comfort, in the day of account, will be according to our faithfulness, our sincerity, not our success; according to the uprightness of our hearts, not according to the degree of our opportunities.

The master's acceptance and approbation of their account, *v.* 21, 23.

First, He commended them; *Well done, good and faithful servant.* Those that own and honour God now, he will own and honour shortly. Christ will give them their just characters, of *good and faithful*. Their performances will be accepted; *Well done.* Christ will call those, and those only, *good servants*, that have done well. If we do that which is good, and do it well, we shall have *praise of the same.* Some masters are so morose, that they will not commend their servants; it is thought enough not to chide: but Christ will commend his servants that do well; whether their praise be of men or no, it is of him. If he saith, *Well done*, we are happy.

Secondly, He rewards them. All their work and labour of love shall be rewarded.

Now this reward is here expressed two ways.

(1) In one expression agreeable to the parable; *Thou hast been faithful over a few things, I will make thee ruler over many things.* It is usual in the courts of princes, and families of great men, to advance those to higher offices, that have been faithful in lower. Christ is a master that will prefer his servants who acquit themselves well. Christ has honour in store for those that honour him. Here they are beggars; in heaven they shall be rulers.

Observe the disproportion between the work and the reward; there are but few things in which the saints are serviceable to the glory of God, but there are many things wherein they shall be glorified with God. What charge we receive from God, what work we do for God in this world, is but little, very little, compared with *the joy set before us.*

(2) In another expression, which slips out of the parable into the thing signified by it; *Enter thou into the joy of thy Lord.* The state of the blessed is a state of joy. Where there are the vision and fruition of

JAMIESON, FAUSSET, BROWN

18. But he that had received one went and digged in the earth, and hid his lord's money—not misspending, but simply making no use of it. Nay, his action seems that of one anxious that the gift should not be misused or lost, but ready to be returned, just as he got it.

19. After a long time the lord of those servants cometh and reckoneth with them—That any one—within the lifetime of the apostles at least—with such words before them, should think that Jesus had given any reason to expect His Second Appearing within that period, would seem strange, did we not know the tendency of enthusiastic, ill-regulated love of His appearing ever to take this turn. **20. Lord, thou deliveredst unto me five talents; behold, I have gained besides them five talents more**—How beautifully does this illustrate what the beloved disciple says of "boldness in the day of judgment," and his desire that "when He shall appear we may have confidence, and not be ashamed before Him at His coming!" (I John 4:17; 2:28).

21. His lord said unto him, Well done—a single word, not of bare satisfaction, but of warm and delighted commendation. And from what Lips!—**thou hast been faithful over a few things, I will make thee ruler over many things... 22. He also that had received two talents came... good and faithful servant: thou hast been faithful over a few things, I will make thee ruler over many things**—*Both are commended in the same terms, and the reward of both is precisely the same.* (See on vs. 15.) Observe also the contrasts: "Thou hast been faithful as a *servant;* now be a *ruler*—thou hast been *entrusted* with a *few* things; now have *dominion* over *many* things." **enter thou into the joy of thy lord**—thy Lord's own joy. (See John 15:11; Heb. 12:2.)

ADAM CLARKE

improves what God has already given him, the more he shall have from his gracious Master. For He giveth more grace, till He fills the faithful soul with His own fullness. (c) They receive glory. *Enter thou into the joy of thy Lord.* As you were partakers of My nature on earth, be sharers of My glory in heaven. The joy, the happiness wherewith I am happy, shall be your eternal portion!

III. *The servant who buried his talent. He that had received one went and digged in the earth, and hid his Lord's money*, v. 18. (1) See the *ingratitude* of this servant. His master gave him a talent, capable of being improved to his own present and eternal advantage; but he slights the mercy of his lord. (2) See his *idleness.* Rather than exert himself to improve what he has received, he goes and hides it. (3) See his gross *error.* He digs to hide it—puts himself to more trouble to render the mercy of God to him of none effect than he would have had in combating and conquering the world, the devil, and the flesh. (4) See his *injustice.* He takes his master's money, and neither improves nor designs to improve it, even while he is living on and consuming that bounty which would have been sufficient for a faithful servant. (5) Hear the *absurdity* of his *reasoning. Lord, I knew thee that thou art an hard* (or avaricious) *man, reaping where thou hast not sown*, v. 24. The wicked excuse of this faithless servant confuted itself and condemned him.

A. B. SIMPSON:

The endowment of these talents stands for everything in our natural, spiritual, and providential conditions which God has given us for the purpose of fitting us for service and usefulness—everything, in a word, which may tell in your life for the glory of God and the good of others. These talents, he says, were given according to "their several ability." God has put each one of us in the very best position to accomplish our own work for Him. There is something you can do that no one else can do; there is someone you can reach that no one else can reach. Your talent may consist of natural ability, social influence, financial resources, position in the church or the world, or special opportunities brought to you in connection with your life work. It is the sum of all the possibilities of usefulness in your life. God expects you to make the most of it for Him and others and is going to call you to account at the coming of Christ for the use you have made of your life.

The principle of which He will judge you will not be the amount of your talent, but the measure in which you have improved it. The man who had but two talents was rewarded as much as the man who had five, if it was found that he had made a proportionate improvement of his little endowment. The reward that the Master is to give at His coming will be a higher form of service. The coming age and the future kingdom is not to be a luxurious sinecure, but a magnificent opportunity for higher work and holy activity.—*Christ in the Bible*

MATTHEW HENRY	JAMIESON, FAUSSET, BROWN	ADAM CLARKE

God, a perfection of holiness, and the society of the blessed, there cannot but be a fulness of joy. This joy is the *joy of their Lord*; the joy which he himself has purchased and provided for them; the joy of the redeemed, bought with the sorrow of the Redeemer. Christ admits his faithful stewards into his own joy, to be joint-heirs with him. Glorified saints shall enter into this joy, shall have a full and complete possession of it, as they that were ready, *went* in to the marriage feast. Shortly they shall enter into it, shall be in it to eternity, as in their element.

2. The bad account of the slothful servant.

(1) His apology for himself, *v.* 24, 25. Though he had received but *one* talent, for that one he is called to account. None shall be called to an account for more than they have received; but for what we have, we must all account.

First, What he confides in. "*Lo, there thou hast that is thine;* if I have not made it more, as the others have done, yet this I can say, I have not made it less." This, he thinks, may serve to bring him off, if not with praise, yet with safety. Slothful professors, that are afraid of doing too much for God, yet hope to come off as well as those that take so much pains in religion. This servant thought that this account would pass well enough, because he could say, *There thou hast that is thine.* Many that are called Christians, build great hopes for heaven upon their being able to make such an account; as if no more were required, or could be expected.

Secondly, What he confesses. He owns the burying of his talent; *I hid thy talent in the earth.* He speaks as if that were no great fault; nay, as if he deserved praise for his prudence in putting it in a safe place, and running no hazards with it.

Thirdly, What he makes his excuse; *I knew that thou wert a hard man, and I was afraid.* Good thoughts of God would beget love, and that love would make us diligent and faithful; but hard thoughts of God beget fear, and that fear makes us slothful and unfaithful. His excuse bespeaks,

[1] The sentiments of an enemy; *I knew thee, that thou art a hard man.* Thus his *de*fence is his *of*fence. Observe how confidently he speaks; *I knew thee to be so.* How could he know him to be so? Does not all the world know the contrary, that he is so far from being a hard master, that *the earth is full of his goodness*, so far from reaping where he sowed not, that he sows a great deal where he reaps nothing? For he *causes the sun to shine, and his rain to fall, upon the evil and unthankful, and fills their hearts with food and gladness* who say to the Almighty, *Depart from us.* This suggestion bespeaks the common reproach which wicked people cast upon God, as if all the blame of their sin and ruin lay at his door, for denying them his grace. But if we perish, it is owing to ourselves.

[2] The spirit of a slave; *I was afraid.* This ill affection toward God arose from his false notions of him. Hard thoughts of God drive us from, and cramp us in his service. Those who think it impossible to please him, and in vain to serve him, will do nothing to purpose in religion.

(2) His Lord's answer to this apology. His plea is made to turn against him, and he is struck speechless with it.

First, His conviction, *v.* 26, 27. Two things he is convicted of.

[1] Slothfulness; *Thou wicked and slothful servant.* Slothful servants are wicked servants. He that is careless in God's work, is near akin to him that is busy in the devil's work. Omissions are sins, and must come into judgment; slothfulness makes way for wickedness. When the house is empty, the unclean spirit takes possession. When men sleep, the enemy sows tares.

[2] Self-contradiction (*v.* 26, 27); *Thou knewest that I reap where I sowed not: thou oughtest therefore to have put my money to the exchangers.* Three ways this may be taken; *a.* "Suppose I had been so hard a master, shouldest not thou therefore have been the more diligent and careful to please me, if not for *love*, yet for *fear*?" *b.* "If thou didst think me to be a hard master, and therefore durst not trade with the money thyself, for fear of losing by it, yet thou mightest have brought it to the bank, and then at my coming I should have received *my own with usury*." If we could not find in our hearts to venture upon more difficult and hazardous services, yet will that justify us in shrinking from those that were more safe and easy? Something is better than nothing; if we fail of showing our courage in bold enterprises, yet we must not fail to testify our goodwill in honest endeavours. *c.* "Suppose I did reap *where I sowed not*, yet that is nothing to thee, for I had sowed upon thee, and the talent was my money which thou wast entrusted with, not only to keep, but to improve."

CHARLES H. SPURGEON:

Deep down in all unregenerate hearts there lurks the idea that God is too severe upon poor erring mortals, expecting more of them than is reasonable. Yet, if they think so they ought to be roused to greater carefulness to render to the Lord full obedience; their knowledge of what the Lord demands will make their disobedience the more criminal.

He probably thought that as he could not do much, he would not do anything, and there are thousands of his opinion; they fancy that their little is not needed and will never be missed, and therefore they make no attempt to serve their Lord. Are we of that kind?

We all have some talent. It may be only one, but we are responsible for it. Are we acting up to the measure of our ability? Many wish they had more talents, but this is wrong, for the Lord has entrusted us with quite as many gifts as we shall be able to give a good account of. Our great concern should be to be found faithful stewards of such things as we have.—*Spurgeon's Devotional Bible*

24. Then he which had received the one talent came and said, Lord, I knew thee that thou art an hard man—harsh. The word in Luke (19:21) is "austere."—**reaping where thou hast not sown, and gathering where thou hast not strawed**—The sense is obvious: "I knew thou wast one whom it was impossible to serve, one whom nothing would please: exacting what was impracticable, and dissatisfied with what was attainable." Thus do men secretly think of God as a hard Master, and virtually throw on Him the blame of their fruitlessness.

25. And I was afraid—of making matters worse by meddling with it at all. **and went and hid thy talent in the earth**—This depicts the conduct of all those who shut up their gifts from the active service of Christ, without actually prostituting them to unworthy uses. Fitly, therefore, may it, at least, comprehend those, to whom TRENCH refers, who, in the early Church, pleaded that they had enough to do with their own souls, and were afraid of losing them in trying to save others; and so, instead of being the salt of the earth, thought rather of keeping their own saltness by withdrawing sometimes into caves and wildernesses, from all those active ministries of love by which they might have served their brethren. **Thou wicked and slothful servant**—"Wicked" or "bad" means "falsehearted," as opposed to the others, who are emphatically styled "*good* servants." The addition of "slothful" is to mark the precise nature of his wickedness: it consisted, it seems, not in his doing anything *against*, but simply *nothing for* his master.

Thou knewest that I reap where I sowed not, and gather where I have not strawed—He takes the servant's own account of his demands, as expressing graphically enough, not the *hardness* which he had basely imputed to him, but simply his demand of *a profitable return for the gift entrusted.* **27. thou oughtest therefore to have put my money to the exchangers**—the banker. **and then at my coming I should have received mine own with usury**—interest.

IV. *The awful punishment of this faithless servant.* (1) He is *reproached. Thou wicked and slothful servant! Wicked*—in your heart; *slothful*—in your work. *Thou knewest that I reap where I sowed not.* You are condemned by your own mouth—whose is the unemployed talent? Did I not give you this? And did I require the improvement of two when I gave you but one? You know I did not.

27. *With usury.* "With its produce," not *usury;* for that is unlawful interest, more than the money can properly produce.

MATTHEW HENRY

Secondly, His condemnation. The slothful servant is sentenced,

[1] To be deprived of his talent (*v.* 28, 29); *Take therefore the talent from him.* And the meaning of this part of the parable we have in the reason of the sentence (*v.* 29), *To every one that hath shall be given.* This may be applied, *a.* To the blessings of this life —worldly wealth and possessions. These we are entrusted with, to be used for the glory of God, and the good of those about us. But *from him that hath not*, that is, that hath these things as if he had them not, they *shall be taken away. b.* We may apply it to the means of grace. They who are diligent in improving the opportunities they have, God will enlarge them. *c.* We may apply it to the common gifts of the Spirit. He that hath these, and doeth good with them, shall have abundance; these gifts improve by exercise, and brighten by being used; the more we do, the more we may do, in religion; but those who stir not up the gift that is in them their gifts rust, and decay, and go out like a neglected fire.

[2] He is sentenced to be *cast into outer darkness*, *v.* 30.

(1) His character is that of an *unprofitable servant.* Slothful servants will be reckoned with as unprofitable servants. A slothful servant is a withered member in the body, he is good for nothing. In one sense, we are all *unprofitable servants* (Luke xvii. 10); we cannot *profit God.* It is not enough not to do hurt, but we must do good, must bring forth fruit, and though thereby God is not profited, yet he is glorified, John xv. 8.

(2) His doom is, to be *cast into outer darkness.* Their state is, [1] Very dismal; it is outer darkness. In the dark *no man can work*, a fit punishment for a slothful servant. It is *outer* darkness, *out* from the light of heaven, *out* from the joy of their Lord, into which the faithful servants were admitted; *out* from the feast. [2] Very doleful; there is weeping and gnashing of teeth. This will be the portion of the slothful servant.

Verses 31–46

We have here a description of the process of the last judgment in the great day. It is, as it were, the explanation of the former parables.

I. The placing of the judge upon the judgment-seat (*v.* 31); *When the Son of man shall come.*

1. That there is a judgment to come, in which every man shall be sentenced according to what he did in this world of trial and probation.

2. The administration of the judgment of the great day is committed to the Son of man. Here, as elsewhere, when the last judgment is spoken of, Christ is called *the son of man*, because he is to judge the sons of men (and, being himself of the same nature, he is the more unexceptionable).

3. Christ's appearing to judge the world will be splendid and glorious. Christ will come to the judgment-seat in real glory; and all the world shall see what the saints only do now believe—that he is the brightness of his Father's glory. His first coming was under a black cloud of obscurity; his second will be in a bright cloud of glory.

4. When Christ comes in his glory to judge the world, he will bring all his holy angels with him. This glorious person will have a glorious retinue, his holy myriads.

5. He will then sit upon the throne of his glory. He is *now* set down with the Father upon his throne; and it is a throne of grace, to which we may come boldly; but *then* he will sit upon the throne of glory, the throne of judgment. Christ, in the days of his flesh, was arraigned as a prisoner at the bar; but at his second coming, he will sit as a judge upon the bench.

II. The appearing of all the children of men before him (*v.* 32); *Before him shall be gathered all nations.* The judgment of the great day will be a general judgment. All must be summoned before Christ's tribunal; all nations, all those nations of men that are made of one blood, to dwell on all the face of the earth.

III. The distinction that will then be made; *He shall separate them one from another*, as the tares and wheat are separated at the harvest, the good fish and the bad at the shore, the corn and chaff in the floor. Wicked and godly here dwell together and are not certainly distinguishable one from another: but in that day they will be separated, and parted for ever. They cannot separate themselves one from another in this world (1 Cor. v. 10), nor can anyone else separate them (*ch.* xiii. 29); but the Lord knows them that are his, and he can separate them. This is compared to a shepherd's dividing between the sheep and the goats. 1. Jesus Christ is the great Shepherd;

JAMIESON, FAUSSET, BROWN

29. For unto every one that hath shall be given . . .—See on ch. 13:12. **30. And cast ye**—cast ye out. **the unprofitable servant**—the useless servant, that does his Master no service. **into outer darkness**—the darkness which is outside. On this expression see on ch. 22:13. **there shall be weeping and gnashing of teeth**—See on ch. 13:42.

31-46. THE LAST JUDGMENT. The close connection between this sublime scene—peculiar to Matthew—and the two preceding parables is too obvious to need pointing out. **31. When the Son of man shall come in his glory**—His *personal* glory-- **and all the holy angels with him**—See Deuteronomy 33:2; Daniel 7:9, 10; Jude 14; with Hebrews 1:6; I Peter 3:22—**then shall he sit upon the throne of his glory**—the glory of His *judicial authority.*

32. And before him shall be gathered all nations—or, "all the nations." That this should be understood to mean the *heathen nations,* or all *except* believers in Christ, will seem amazing to any simple reader. Yet this is the exposition of OLSHAUSEN, STIER, KEIL, ALFORD (though latterly with some diffidence), and of a number, though not all, of those who hold that Christ will come the second time before the millennium, and that the saints will be caught up to meet Him in the air before His appearing. Their chief argument is, the impossibility of any that ever knew the Lord Jesus wondering, at the Judgment Day, that they should be thought to have done—or left undone—anything "unto Christ." To that we shall advert when we come to it. But here we may just say, that if this scene does not describe a personal, public, final judgment on men, according to the treatment they have given to Christ—and consequently men within the Christian pale—we shall have to consider again whether our Lord's teaching on the greatest themes of human interest does indeed possess that incomparable simplicity and transparency of meaning which, by universal consent, has been ascribed to it. If it be said, But how can this be the general judgment, if only those within the Christian pale be embraced by it?—we answer, What is here described, as it certainly does not meet the case of all the family

ADAM CLARKE

(2) He is *stripped* of what he *possessed. Take therefore the talent from him.* Oh, terrible word! Remove the candlestick from that slothful, worldly-minded church; take away the inspirations of the Holy Spirit from that lukewarm, Christless Christian, who lives only to resist them and render them of none effect.

(3) He is *punished* with an everlasting *separation* from God and the glory of His power. *Cast* forth *the unprofitable servant*, v. 30. Let him have nothing but darkness who refused to walk in the light; let him have nothing but misery—*weeping and gnashing of teeth,* who has refused the happiness which God provided for him.

31. *When the Son of man shall come.* This must be understood of Christ's coming at the last day, to judge mankind, though all the preceding part of the chapter may be applied also to the destruction of Jerusalem.

32. *All nations.* Literally, "all the nations"—all the Gentile world; the Jews are necessarily included, but they were spoken of in a particular manner in the preceding chapter. *He shall separate them.* Set each kind apart by themselves. *As a shepherd divideth.* It does not appear that *sheep* and *goats* were ever penned or housed together, though they might feed in the same pasture; yet even this was not done but in separate flocks; so Virgil, *Eclog.* vii. v. 2.

MATTHEW HENRY

he now feeds his flock like a shepherd, and will shortly distinguish between those that are his, and those that are not. 2. The godly are like sheep—innocent, mild, patient, useful: the wicked are like goats, a baser kind of animal, unsavoury and unruly. The sheep and goats are here feeding all day in the same pasture, but will be coted at night in different folds. Being thus divided, he will set the *sheep on his right hand*, and the *goats on his left*, *v.* 33. Christ puts honour upon the godly, as we show respect to those we set on our right hand. All other divisions and subdivisions will then be abolished; but the great distinction of men into saints and sinners, sanctified and unsanctified, will remain for ever.

IV. The process of the judgment concerning each of these.

1. Concerning the godly, on the right hand. Observe here,

(1) The *glory* conferred upon them (*v.* 34); *The king shall say unto them.* He that was the Shepherd (which bespeaks the care and tenderness wherewith he will make this disquisition), is here the King. Where the word of this King is, there is power. Here are two things in this sentence:

[1] The acknowledging of the saints to be the blessed of the Lord; *Come, ye blessed of my Father.* He pronounces them *blessed*; and his saying they are blessed, makes them so. *Blessed of his Father*; reproached and cursed by the world, but blessed of God. All our blessings in heavenly things flow to us from God, as the Father of our Lord Jesus Christ, Eph. i. 3. He calls them *to come*: this *come* is, in effect, "*Welcome*, ten thousand welcomes, to the blessings of my Father; come to me, come to be for ever with me; you that followed me bearing the cross, now come along with me wearing the crown." We now come boldly to the throne of grace, but we shall then come boldly to the throne of glory.

[2] The admission of the saints into the blessedness and kingdom of the Father; *Inherit the kingdom prepared for you.*

First, The happiness they shall be possessed of is very rich.

a. It is a *kingdom*; which is reckoned the most valuable possession on earth, and includes the greatest wealth and honour. They that here are beggars, prisoners, accounted as the off-scouring of all things, shall then inherit a kingdom.

b. It is a kingdom *prepared*: the happiness must needs be great, for it is the product of the divine counsels.

c. It is prepared *for them.* This bespeaks, (*a*) The suitableness of this happiness. (*b*) Their property and interest in it. It is prepared on purpose for them; not only for such as you, but for you, you by name.

d. It is prepared *from the foundation of the world.* This happiness was designed for the saints, and they for it, before time began, from all eternity, Eph. i. 4.

Secondly, The tenure by which they shall hold and possess it is very good, they shall come and *inherit it.* It is God that makes heirs, heirs of heaven. We come to an inheritance by virtue of our sonship, our adoption; *if children, then heirs.* A title by inheritance is the sweetest and surest title. Saints, in this world, are as heirs under age, tutored and governed till the time appointed of the Father (Gal. iv. 1, 2); and then they shall be put in full possession of that which now through grace they have a title to; *Come*, and inherit it.

(2) The ground of this (*v.* 35, 36), *For I was an hungered, and ye gave me meat.* We cannot hence infer that any good works of ours merit the happiness of heaven; but it is plain that Jesus Christ will judge the world by the same rule by which he governs it, and therefore will reward those that have been obedient to that law. This happiness will be adjudged to obedient believers, upon the promise of God purchased by Jesus Christ. It is the purchase and promise that give the title, the obedience is only the qualification of the person designed.

Now the good works here mentioned are such as we commonly call works of charity to the poor, and it teaches us this in general, that faith working by love is all in all in Christianity; *Show me thy faith by thy works.* The good works here described imply three things, which must be found in all that are saved.

[1] Self-denial, and contempt of the world; reckoning the things of the world no further good things, than as we are enabled to do good with them: and those who have not wherewithal to do good, must show the same disposition, by being contentedly and cheerfully poor.

[2] Love to our brethren; which is the second great commandment. We must give proof of this love by our readiness to do good, and to communicate; good

JAMIESON, FAUSSET, BROWN

of Adam, is of course *so far* not general. But we have no right to conclude that the whole "judgment of the great day" will be limited to the point of view here presented. Other explanations will come up in the course of our exposition. **and he shall separate them**—now for the first time; the two classes having been mingled all along up to this awful moment. **as a shepherd divideth his sheep from the goats**—(see Ezek. 34:17). **33. And he shall set the sheep on his right hand**—the side of honor (I Kings 2:19; Ps. 45:9; 110:1, etc.). **but the goats on the left**—the side consequently of dishonor.

34. Then shall the King—Magnificent title, here for the first and only time, save in parabolical language, given to Himself by the Lord Jesus, and that on the eve of His deepest humiliation! It is to intimate that in then addressing the heirs of the kingdom, *He will put on all His regal majesty.* **say unto them on his right hand, Come**—the same sweet word with which He had so long invited all the weary and heavy laden to come unto Him for rest. Now it is addressed exclusively to such as *have* come and found rest. It is still, "Come," and to "rest" too; but to rest in a higher style, and in another region. **ye blessed of my Father, inherit the kingdom prepared for you from the foundation of the world**—The whole story of this their blessedness is given by the apostle, in words which seem but an expression of these: "Blessed be the God and Father of our Lord Jesus Christ, who hath blessed us with all spiritual blessings in heavenly places in Christ; according as He hath chosen us in Him before the foundation of the world, that we should be holy and without blame before Him in love." They were chosen from everlasting to the possession and enjoyment of all spiritual blessings in Christ, and so chosen in order to be holy and blameless in love. This is the holy love whose practical manifestations the King is about to recount in detail; and thus we see that their whole life of love to Christ is the fruit of an eternal purpose of love to them in Christ.

35. For I was an hungered . . thirsty . . . a stranger . . . 36. Naked . . . sick . . . prison, and ye came unto me. 37-39. Then shall the righteous answer him . . . 40. And the King shall answer and say unto them, Verily I say unto you, . . .—Astonishing dialogue this between the King, from the Throne of His glory, and His wondering people! "I was an hungered, and ye gave Me meat . . ."—"Not we," they reply. "We never did that, Lord: We were born out of due time, and enjoyed not the privilege of ministering unto Thee." "But ye did it to these My brethren, now beside you, when cast upon your love." "Truth, Lord, but was that doing it to Thee? Thy name was indeed dear to us, and we thought it a great honor to suffer shame for it. When among the destitute and distressed we discerned any of the household of faith, we will not deny that our hearts leapt within us at the discovery, and when their knock came to our dwelling, our bowels were moved, as though 'our Beloved Himself had put in His hand by the hole of the door.' Sweet was the fellowship we had with them, as if we had 'entertained angels unawares'; all difference between giver and receiver somehow melted away under the beams of that love of Thine which knit us together; nay, rather, as they left us with gratitude for our poor givings, we seemed the debtors—not

ADAM CLARKE

33. *He shall set the sheep.* The *right hand* signifies, among the rabbins, approbation and eminence; the *left hand*, rejection, and disapprobation. *Sheep*, which have ever been considered as the emblems of mildness, simplicity, patience, and usefulness, represent here the genuine disciples of Christ. *Goats*, which are naturally quarrelsome, lascivious, and excessively ill-scented, were considered as the symbols of riotous, profane, and impure men. They here represent all who have lived and died in their sins. See Ezek. xxxiv. 17 and Zech. x. 3.

34. *Ye blessed of my Father.* This is the King's address to his followers, and contains the reason why they were found in the practice of all righteousness, and were now brought to this state of glory—they were blessed—came as children, and received the benediction of the *Father*, and became, and continued to be, members of the heavenly family. *Inherit.* The inheritance is only for the children of the family—"if sons, then heirs," Gal. iv. 7, but not otherwise. *Prepared for you.* That is, The Kingdom of glory is designed for such as you. *From the foundation of the world.* It was God's purpose and determination to admit none into His heaven but those who were made partakers of His holiness, Heb. xii. 14.

35. *I was an hungred, and ye gave me meat.* Everything which is done to a follower of Christ, whether it be good or evil, He considers as done to himself; see v. 40; Acts ix. 4-5; Heb. vi. 10. Of all the fruits of the Spirit, none are mentioned here but those that spring from love, or mercy, because these give men the nearest conformity to God. Jesus had said, "Blessed are the merciful: for they shall obtain mercy"; and He here shows how this promise shall be fulfilled. The rabbins say: "As often as a poor man presents himself at thy door, the holy blessed God stands at his right hand: if thou give him alms, know that he who stands at his right hand will give thee a reward. But if thou give him not alms, he who stands at his right hand will punish thee." A *stranger, and ye took me in.* "You entertained Me."

MATTHEW HENRY

wishes are but mockeries without good works. Those that have not to give, must show the same disposition some other way.

[3] A believing regard to Jesus Christ. That which is here rewarded is the relieving of the poor for Christ's sake, out of love to him. Those good works shall then be accepted which are done in the name of the Lord Jesus, Col. iii. 17.

I was hungry, and *you gave them meat*. It is no new thing for those that are feasted with the dainties of heaven to be hungry and thirsty, and to want daily food; for those that are at home in God, to be strangers in a strange land; for those that have put on Christ, to want clothes to keep them warm; for those that have healthful souls, to have sickly bodies, and for those to be in prison, that Christ has made free. Works of charity and beneficence, according as our ability is, are necessary to salvation. These must be the proofs of our love, and of our professed subjection to the gospel of Christ. But they that show no mercy, shall have judgment without mercy.

Now this reason is modestly excepted against by the righteous, but is explained by the Judge himself.

a. It is questioned by the righteous, *v*. 37-39. Not as if they were loth to inherit the kingdom, or were ashamed of their good deeds. Christ has a mighty regard to works of charity, and is especially pleased with kindnesses done to his people for his sake. They bespeak the humble admiration which glorified saints will be filled with, to find such poor and worthless services, as theirs are, so highly celebrated, and richly rewarded: *Lord, when saw we thee an hungered, and fed thee?* Gracious souls are apt to think meanly of their own good deeds; especially as unworthy to be compared with the glory that shall be revealed. Saints in heaven will wonder what brought them thither, and that God should so regard them and their services. "*When saw we thee an hungered?* We have seen the poor in distress many a time; but when saw we thee?" Christ is more among us than we think he is.

b. It is explained by the Judge himself (*v*. 40); *Inasmuch as ye have done it to these my brethren*, to the least, to one of the least of them, *ye have done it unto me*. The good works of the saints, when they are produced in the great day, (*a*) Shall all be remembered; and not the least overlooked, no not a cup of cold water. (*b*) They shall be interpreted most to their advantage. As Christ makes the best of their infirmities, so he makes the most of their services.

But what will become of the godly poor, that had not wherewithal to do so? Must they be shut out? No, Christ will own them, even the least of them, as his brethren; he will not be ashamed, nor think it any disparagement to him, *to call them brethren*. In the height of his glory, he will not disown his poor relations. He will take the kindness done to them, as done to himself; *Ye have done it unto me*; which shows a respect to the poor that were relieved, as well as to the rich that did relieve them.

2. Here is the process concerning the wicked, those on the left hand. And in that we have,

(1) The sentence passed upon them, *v*. 41. He shall say to them, *Depart from me, ye cursed*.

[1] To be so near to Christ was some satisfaction, though under his frowns; but that will not be allowed, *Depart from me*. In this world they were often called to come to Christ, to come for life and rest, but they turned a deaf ear to his calls. Here they said to the Almighty, *Depart from us*; then he will say to them, *Depart from me*.

[2] If they must depart, and depart from Christ, might they not be dismissed with a blessing, with one kind and compassionate word at least? No, *Depart, ye cursed*. They that would not come to Christ, to inherit a blessing, must depart from him under the burthen of a curse. The righteous are called *the blessed of my Father*; for their blessedness is owing purely to the grace of God and his blessing, but the wicked are called only *ye cursed*, for their damnation is of themselves.

[3] If they must depart may they not go into some place of ease and rest? Will it not be misery enough for them to bewail their loss? They must depart into *fire*. This fire is the wrath of the eternal God.

[4] If into fire, prepared fire, O let it be but of short continuance, let them but pass *through* fire. No for the streams of mercy and grace being for ever excluded, there is nothing to extinguish it.

[5] If they must be doomed to such a state of endless misery yet may they not have some good company there? No, none but *the devil and his angels*. They served the devil while they lived, and therefore are justly sentenced to be where he is, as those that served Christ, are taken to be with him where

JAMIESON, FAUSSET, BROWN

they. But, Lord, were we all that time in company with Thee?" "Yes, that scene was all with Me," replies the King—"Me in the disguise of My poor ones. The door shut against Me by others was opened by you—'Ye took Me in.' Apprehended and imprisoned by the enemies of the truth, ye whom the truth had made free sought Me out diligently and found Me; visiting Me in My lonely cell at the risk of your own lives, and cheering My solitude; ye gave Me a coat, for I shivered; and then I felt warm. With cups of cold water ye moistened My parched lips; when famished with hunger ye supplied Me with crusts, and my spirit revived—"YE DID IT UNTO ME." What thoughts crowd upon us as we listen to such a description of the scenes of the Last Judgment! And in the light of this view of the heavenly dialogue, how bald and wretched, not to say unscriptural, is that view of it to which we referred at the outset, which makes it a dialogue between Christ and *heathens* who never heard of His name, and of course never felt any stirrings of His love in their hearts! To us it seems a poor, superficial objection to the *Christian* view of this scene, that Christians could never be supposed to ask such questions as the "blessed of Christ's Father" are made to ask here. If there were any difficulty in explaining this, the difficulty of the other view is such as to make *it*, at least, insufferable. But there is no real difficulty. The surprise expressed is not at their being told that they acted from love to Christ, but that *Christ Himself* was the *Personal Object* of all their deeds: that they found *Him* hungry, and supplied Him with food: that they brought water to *Him*, and slaked His thirst; that seeing *Him* naked and shivering, they put warm clothing upon Him, paid *Him* visits when lying in prison for the truth, and sat by *His* bedside when laid down with sickness. This is the astonishing interpretation which Jesus says "the King" will give to them of their own actions here below. And will any Christian reply, "How could this astonish them? Does not every Christian know that He does these very things, when He does them at all, just as they are here represented?" Nay, rather, is it conceivable that they should *not* be astonished, and almost doubt their own ears, to hear such an account of their own actions upon earth from the lips of the Judge? And remember, that Judge has come in His glory, and now sits upon the throne of His glory, and all the holy angels are with Him; and that it is from those glorified Lips that the words come forth, "Ye did all this unto ME." Oh, can we imagine such a word addressed to *ourselves*, and then fancy ourselves replying, "Of course we did—To whom else did we anything? It must be others than we that are addressed, who never knew, in all their good deeds, what they were about?" Rather, can we imagine ourselves not overpowered with astonishment, and scarcely able to credit the testimony borne to us by the King? **41. Then shall he say also unto them on the left hand, Depart from me, ye cursed . . .**—As for you on the left hand, ye did nothing for Me. I came to you also, but ye knew Me not: ye had neither warm affections nor kind deeds to bestow upon Me: I was as one despised in your eyes." "In *our* eyes, Lord? We never saw Thee before, and never, sure, behaved we so to Thee." "But thus ye treated these little ones that believe in Me and now stand on My right hand. In the disguise of these poor members of Mine I came soliciting your pity, but ye shut up your bowels of compassion from Me: I asked relief, but ye had none to give Me. Take back therefore your own coldness, your own contemptuous distance: Ye bid Me away from your presence, and now I bid you from Mine—*Depart from Me, ye cursed!*"

ADAM CLARKE

36. *I was sick, and ye visited me*. Relieving the strangers and visiting the sick were in high estimation among the Jews. One of their sayings on this head is worthy of notice: "He who neglects to visit the sick is like him who has shed blood." That is, as he has neglected, when it was in his power, to preserve life, he is as guilty in the sight of the Lord as he is who has committed murder.

37. *Lord, when saw we thee an hungred*. This barbarous expression, *an hungred*, should be banished out of the text, wheresoever it occurs, and the simple word "hungry" substituted for it. Whatever is done for Christ's sake is done through Christ's grace; and he who does the work attributes to Jesus both the will and the power by which the work was done, and seeks and expects the kingdom of Heaven, not as a reward, but as a gift of pure, unmerited mercy.

40. *Inasmuch as ye have done it unto one of the least of these my brethren*. The meanest follower of Christ is acknowledged by Him as His *brother!*

41. *Depart from me, ye cursed*. Or, "Ye cursed! depart." These words are the address of the King to the sinners, and contain the reason why they are to be separated from blessedness: You are cursed, because you have sinned, and would not come unto Me that you might have life. *Into everlasting fire*. This is the punishment of sense. You shall not only be separated from Me, but you shall be tormented—awfully, everlastingly tormented in that place of separation. *Prepared for the devil and his angels*. The devil and his angels sinned before the creation of the world, and the place of torment was *then* prepared for them. It never was designed for human souls; but as the wicked are partakers with the devil and his angels in their iniquities, in their rebellion against God, so it is right that they should be sharers with them in their punishment.

MATTHEW HENRY

he is.

The reason of this sentence assigned.

[1] All that is charged upon them, on which the sentence is grounded, is, omission; as, before, the servant was condemned, not for wasting his talent, but for burying it. "When I was in these distresses, you were so selfish that you did not *minister* as you might have done to my relief and succour." Omissions are the ruin of thousands.

[2] It is the omission of works of charity to the poor; for omitting the weightier matters of the law, *judgment, mercy, and faith.* Uncharitableness to the poor is a damning sin. *They shall have judgment without mercy, that have showed no mercy.* Sinners will be condemned, at the great day, for the omission of that good which it was in the power of their hand to do. Now this reason of the sentence is,

First, Objected against by the prisoners (*v.* 44); *Lord, when saw we thee an hungered, or athirst?* Condemned sinners, though they have no plea that will bear them out, will yet in vain offer excuses. *When saw we thee hungry, or thirsty, or naked?* They care not to repeat the full charge, as conscious to themselves of their own guilt. The matter of their plea bespeaks their former inconsideration of that which they might have known, but would not till now that it was too late. They imagined it was only a company of poor, weak, silly, and contemptible people that they put those slights upon; but they who do so, will be made to know that it was *Jesus whom they persecuted.*

Secondly, Justified by the Judge. He goes by this rule (*v.* 45); *Inasmuch as ye did it not to one of the least of these, ye did it not to me.* What is done against the faithful disciples and followers of Christ, even the least of them, he takes as done against himself. *In all their afflictions he is afflicted.* He that touches them, touches him in a part no less tender than the apple of his eye.

Lastly, Here is the execution of both these sentences, *v.* 46.

a. The wicked shall go away into everlasting punishment. Sentence will then be executed speedily. It can neither be thought that sinners should change their own natures, nor that God should give his grace to change them, when in this world the day of grace was misspent.

b. The righteous shall go away into life eternal; that is, they shall *inherit the kingdom, v.* 34. Heaven is life, it is all happiness. It is *eternal* life. There is no death to put a period to the life itself, nor old age to put a period to the comfort of it, or any sorrow to embitter it. Thus life and death, good and evil, the blessing and the curse, are set before us, that we may choose our way; and so shall our end be.

JAMIESON, FAUSSET, BROWN

46. And these shall go away—these "cursed" ones. Sentence, it should seem, was first *pronounced*—in the hearing of the wicked—upon the *righteous,* who thereupon sit as assessors in the judgment upon the wicked (I Cor. 6:2); but sentence is first *executed,* it should seem, upon the *wicked,* in the sight of the righteous—whose glory will thus not be beheld by the wicked, while *their* descent into "their own place" will be witnessed by the righteous, as BENGEL notes. **into everlasting punishment**—or, as in vs. 41, "everlasting fire, prepared for the devil and his angels." Cf. ch. 13:42; II Thessalonians 1:9, etc. This is said to be "prepared for the devil and his angels," because they were "first in transgression." But both have one doom, because one unholy character. **but the righteous into life eternal**—i.e., "life everlasting." The word in both clauses, being in the original the same, should have been the same in the translation also. Thus the decisions of this awful day will be final, irreversible, unending.

ADAM CLARKE

42. *I was an hungred, and ye gave me no meat.* I put it in your power to do good, and you would not. A variety of occasions offered themselves to you, but you neglected them all, so that My blessings in your hands, not being improved, according to My order, became a curse to you.

43. *I was a stranger.* If men were sure that Jesus Christ was actually somewhere in the land, in great personal distress, hungry, thirsty, naked, and confined, they would doubtless run unto and relieve Him. Now Christ assures us that a man who is hungry, thirsty, naked is His representative, and that whatever we do to such a one He will consider as done to himself.

44. *Lord, when saw we thee an hungred?* It is want of faith which in general produces hardheartedness to the poor. The man who sees only with eyes of flesh is never likely to discover Christ in the person of a man destitute of the necessaries of life.

46. *And these shall go away into everlasting punishment.* No appeal, no remedy, to all eternity! No end to the punishment of those whose final impenitence manifests in them an eternal will and desire to sin. By dying in a settled opposition to God, they cast themselves into a necessity of continuing in an eternal aversion from Him. But some are of the opinion that this punishment shall have an end. This is as likely as that the glory of the righteous shall have an end, for the same word is used to express the duration of the punishment as is used to express the duration of the state of glory. I have seen the best things that have been written in favor of the final redemption of damned spirits, but I never saw an answer to the argument against that doctrine drawn from this verse but what sound learning and criticism should be ashamed to acknowledge. Some have gone a middle way, and think that the wicked shall be annihilated. This, I think, is contrary to the text; if they *go into . . . punishment,* they continue to exist; for that which ceases to be ceases to suffer.

MATTHEW HENRY

CHAPTER 26

Verses 1–5

Here is, 1. The notice Christ gave his disciples of the near approach of his sufferings, *v.* 1, 2. He had often told them of his sufferings at a distance, now he speaks of them as at the door; *after two days.* Observe,

(1) The *time* when he gave this alarm; *when he had finished all these sayings.* Christ's witnesses die not till they have finished their testimony. He had bid his disciples to expect sad times, bonds and afflictions, and then tells them, *The Son of man is betrayed*; to intimate that they should fare no worse than he should, and that his sufferings should take the sting out of theirs.

(2) The thing itself he gave them notice of; *The Son of man is betrayed.* The thing was not only so sure, but so near, that it was as good as done. It is good to make sufferings that are yet to come, as present to us.

2. The plot of the chief priests, and scribes, and elders of the people, against the life of our Lord Jesus, *v.* 3–5. Many consultations had been held against the life of Christ; but this plot was laid deeper than any yet, for the grandees were all engaged in it. (1) The *place* where they met; *in the palace of the high priest.* (2) The plot itself; to *take Jesus by subtlety, and kill him*; nothing less than his blood, his lifeblood, would serve their turn. (3) The policy of the plotters; *Not on the feastday. Lest there should be an uproar among the people.* They were awed, not by the fear of God, but by the fear of the people; all their concern was for their own safety, not God's honour.

Verses 6–13

I. The singular kindness of a good woman to our Lord Jesus in anointing his head, *v.* 6, 7. It was *in Bethany*, a village hard by Jerusalem, and *in the*

JAMIESON, FAUSSET, BROWN

CHAPTER 26

VSS. 1-16. CHRIST'S FINAL ANNOUNCEMENT OF HIS DEATH, AS NOW WITHIN TWO DAYS, AND THE SIMULTANEOUS CONSPIRACY OF THE JEWISH AUTHORITIES TO COMPASS IT—THE ANOINTING AT BETHANY—JUDAS AGREES WITH THE CHIEF PRIESTS TO BETRAY HIS LORD. (=Mark 14:1-11; Luke 22:1-6; John 12:1-11.) For the exposition, see on Mark 14:1-11.

After two days was the feast of the passover, and of unleavened bread—The meaning is, that two days after what is about to be mentioned the passover would arrive; in other words, what follows occurred two days *before* the feast. **and the chief priests and the scribes sought how they might take him by craft, and put him to death**—From Matthew's fuller account (ch. 26) we learn that our Lord announced this to the Twelve as follows, being the first announcement to them of the precise time: "And it came to pass, when Jesus had finished all these sayings"—referring to the contents of chs. 24, 25, which He delivered to His disciples; His public ministry being now closed: from His *prophetical* He is now passing into His *priestly* office, although all along He Himself took our infirmities and bare our sicknesses—"He said unto His disciples, Ye know that after two days is [the feast of] the passover, and the Son of man is betrayed to be crucified."The *first* and the *last* steps of His final sufferings are brought together in this brief announcement of all that was to take place. The *passover* was the first and the chief of the three great annual festivals, commemorative of the redemption of God's people from Egypt, through the sprinkling of the blood of a lamb divinely appointed to be slain for that end; the destroying angel, "when he saw the blood, *passing over*" the Israelitish houses, on which that blood was seen,

ADAM CLARKE

CHAPTER 26

1. *When Jesus had finished all these sayings.* He began these sayings on Mount Olivet, chap. xxiv. 1, and continued them till He entered into Bethany, whither He was going.

2. *The passover.* A feast instituted in Egypt to commemorate the destroying angel's passing over the houses of the Israelites, when he slew the firstborn of the Egyptians. See the whole of this business largely explained in the notes on Exod. xii. 1-27. This feast began on the fourteenth day of the first moon, in the first month, Nisan, and it lasted only one day; but it was immediately followed by the days of unleavened bread, which were seven, so that the whole lasted eight days, and all the eight days are sometimes called the feast of *the passover,* and sometimes the "feast or days of unleavened bread." See Luke xxii. 1-7. *The Son of man is betrayed* (rather "delivered up") *to be crucified.* With what amazing calmness and precision does our blessed Lord speak of this awful event! What a proof does He here give of His prescience in so correctly predicting it, and of His love in so cheerfully undergoing it! These two verses have no proper connection with this chapter, and should be joined to the preceding.

3. *Then assembled together the chief priests.* That is, during the two days that preceded the Passover.

4. *And consulted that they might take Jesus by subtilty.* The providence of God frustrated their artful machinations; and that event which they wished to conduct with the greatest privacy and silence was transacted with all possible

MATTHEW HENRY

house of Simon the leper. Probably he was one who had been miraculously cleansed from his leprosy by our Lord Jesus, and he would express his gratitude to Christ by entertaining him; nor did Christ disdain to come in to him, and sup with him. The woman that did this, is supposed to have been Mary, the sister of Martha and Lazarus. She had a *box of ointment very precious*, which she *poured upon the head* of Christ as he sat at meat. This, among us, would be a strange sort of compliment. But it was then accounted the highest piece of respect. Now this may be looked upon,

1. As an act of faith in our Lord Jesus, the Christ, the Messiah, the anointed.

2. As an act of love and respect to him. Some think that this was she who *loved much* at first, and *washed Christ's feet with her tears* (Luke vii. 38, 47). Where there is true love in the heart to Jesus Christ, nothing will be thought too good, no, nor good enough, to bestow upon him.

II. The offence which the disciples took at this. They *had indignation* (*v.* 8, 9).

1. See how they expressed their offence at it. They said, *To what purpose is this waste?* Now this bespeaks,

(1) Want of tenderness toward this good woman, in interpreting her over-kindness (suppose it was so) to be wastefulness. Charity teaches us to put the best construction upon everything that it will bear. It is true, there may be over-doing in well-doing; but thence we must learn not to be censorious of others; because that which we may impute to the want of prudence, God may accept as an instance of abundant love. We must not say, Those do too much in religion, that do more than we do, but rather aim to do as much as they.

(2) Want of respect to their Master. It did not become them to call it *waste*, when they perceived that he admitted and accepted it as a token of his friend's love. We must take heed of thinking anything waste, which is bestowed upon the Lord Jesus, either by others or by ourselves.

2. See how they excused their offence at it; *This ointment might have been sold for much, and given to the poor.*

III. The reproof Christ gave to his disciples for the offence at this good woman (*v.* 10, 11); *Why trouble ye the woman?* Note, It is a great trouble to good people to have their good works censured and misconstrued; and it is a thing that Jesus Christ takes very ill. He here took part against all his disciples: so heartily does he espouse the cause of the *offended little ones, ch.* xviii. 10.

Observe his reason; *You have the poor always with you.*

1. There are some opportunities of doing and getting good which are constant, and which we must give constant attendance to the improvement of. Those who have a heart to do good, never need complain for want of opportunity.

2. There are other opportunities of doing and getting good, which come but seldom, and which ought to be preferred before the other; "*Me ye have not always*, therefore use me while ye have me." Sometimes special works of piety and devotion should take place of common works of charity.

IV. Christ's approbation and commendation of the kindness of this good woman. He calls it a *good work* (*v.* 10), and says more in praise of it than could have been imagined; particularly,

1. That the meaning of it was mystical (*v.* 12); *She did it for my burial.* Some think that she *intended* it so, and that the woman better understood Christ's frequent predictions of his death and sufferings than the apostles did. Christ interpreted it so; and he is always willing to make the best, to make the most of his people's well-meant words and actions.

2. That the memorial of it should be honourable (*v.* 13); *This shall be told for a memorial.* This act of faith and love was so remarkable, that the preachers of Christ crucified, and the inspired writers of the history of his passion, could not choose but take notice of this passage. None of all the trumpets of fame sound so loud and so long as the everlasting gospel. Though the honour of Christ is principally designed in the gospel, yet the honour of his saints and servants is not altogether overlooked. The memorial of this woman was to be preserved by mentioning her faith and piety in the preaching of the gospel, for example to others.

Verses 14–16

Immediately after an instance of the greatest kindness done to Christ, follows an instance of the greatest unkindness; such mixture is there of good and bad among the followers of Christ.

I. The traitor was Judas Iscariot; he is said to be *one of the twelve*, as an aggravation of his villainy.

JAMIESON, FAUSSET, BROWN

when he came to destroy all the first-born in the land of Egypt (Exod. 12)—bright typical foreshadowing of the great Sacrifice, and the Redemption effected thereby. Accordingly, "by the determinate counsel and foreknowledge of God, who is wonderful in counsel and excellent in working," it was so ordered that precisely at the passover season, "Christ our Passover should be sacrificed for us." On the day following the passover commenced "the feast of unleavened bread," so called because for seven days only unleavened bread was to be eaten (Exod. 12:18-20). See on I Corinthians 5:6-8. We are further told by Matthew (26:3) that the consultation was held in the palace of Caiaphas the high priest, between the chief priests, [the scribes], and the elders of the people, how "they might take Jesus by subtlety and kill Him." **But they said, Not on the feast day**—rather, not during the feast; not until the seven days of unleavened bread should be over—**lest there be an uproar of the people**—In consequence of the vast influx of strangers, embracing all the male population of the land who had reached a certain age, there were within the walls of Jerusalem at this festival some two million people; and in their excited state, the danger of tumult and bloodshed among "the people," who for the most part took Jesus for a prophet, was extreme. (See JOSEPHUS, *Antiquities*, xx. 5. 3.) What plan, if any, these ecclesiastics fixed upon for seizing our Lord, does not appear. But the proposal of Judas being at once and eagerly gone into, it is probable they were till then at some loss for a plan sufficiently quiet and yet effectual. So, just at the feast-time shall it be done; the unexpected offer of Judas relieving them of their fears. Thus, as BENGEL remarks, did the divine counsel take effect.

The Supper and the Anointing at Bethany Six Days before the Passover The time of this part of the narrative is *four days before* what has just been related. Had it been part of the regular train of events which our Evangelist designed to record, he would probably have inserted it in its proper place, before the conspiracy of the Jewish authorities. But having come to the treason of Judas, he seems to have gone back upon this scene as what probably gave immediate occasion to the awful deed. **And being in Bethany, in the house of Simon the leper, as he sat at meat, there came a woman**—It was "Mary," as we learn from John 12:3. **having an alabaster box of ointment of spikenard**—pure *nard*, a celebrated aromatic—(See Song of Sol. 1:12). **very precious**—"very costly" (John 12:3). **and she brake the box, and poured it on his head**—"and anointed," adds John, "the feet of Jesus, and wiped His feet with her hair: and the house was filled with the odor of the ointment." The only use of this was to refresh and exhilarate—a grateful compliment in the East, amid the closeness of a heated atmosphere, with many guests at a feast. Such was the form in which Mary's love to Christ, at so much cost to herself, poured itself out. **And there were some that had indignation within themselves and said**—Matthew says (26:8), "But when His disciples saw it, they had indignation, saying . . ." The spokesman, however, was none of the true-hearted Eleven—as we learn from John (12:4): "Then saith one of His disciples, Judas Iscariot, Simon's son, which should betray Him." Doubtless the thought stirred first in his breast, and issued from his base lips; and some of the rest, ignorant of his true character and feelings, and carried away by his plausible speech, might for the moment feel some chagrin at the apparent waste. **Why was this waste of the ointment made?**

For it might have been sold for more than three hundred pence—about $50 in our currency. **and have been given to the poor. And they murmured against her**—"This he said," remarks John, and the remark is of exceeding importance, "not that he cared for the poor but because he was a thief, and had the bag"—the scrip or treasure-chest—"and bare what was put therein"—not 'bare it off' by theft, as some understand it. It is true that he did this; but the expression means simply that he had charge of it and its contents, or was treasurer to Jesus and the Twelve. What a remarkable arrangement was this, by which an avaricious and dishonest person was not only taken into the number of the Twelve, but entrusted with the custody of their little property! The purposes which this served are obvious enough; but it is further noticeable, that the remotest hint was never given to the Eleven of his true character, nor did the disciples most favored with the intimacy of Jesus ever suspect him, till a few minutes before he voluntarily separated himself from their company—for ever! **And Jesus**

ADAM CLARKE

celebrity, amidst the thousands who resorted to Jerusalem at this season for the keeping of the Passover.

5. *Not on the feast day, lest there be an uproar.* It was usual for the Jews to punish criminals at the public festivals; but in this case they were afraid of an insurrection, as our Lord had become very popular. The providence of God directed it thus, for the reason given in the preceding note.

6. *Simon the leper.* This was probably no more than a surname, as Simon the Canaanite, chap. x. 4, and Barsabas Justus, Acts i. 23, and several others. Yet it might have been some person that Christ had healed of this disease.

7. *There came unto him a woman.* There is much contention among commentators about the transaction mentioned here and in John xii. 14, some supposing them to be different, others to be the same. Some think that the *woman* mentioned here was Mary, the sister of Lazarus; others, Mary Magdalene; but against the former opinion it is argued that it is not likely, had this been Mary the sister of Lazarus, that Matthew and Mark would have suppressed her name. Besides, say they, we should not confound the repast which is mentioned here with that mentioned by John, chap. xii. 3. This one was made only *two* days before the Passover, and that one *six* days before; the one was made at the house of Simon the leper, the other at the house of Lazarus, John xii. 1-2. At this, the woman poured the oil on the *head* of Christ; at the other, Mary anointed Christ's *feet* with it.

9. *And given to the poor.* How often does charity serve as a cloak for covetousness! God is sometimes robbed of His right under the pretense of devoting what is withheld to some charitable purpose, to which there was no intention ever to give it.

MATTHEW HENRY

When the *number of the disciples was multiplied* (Acts vi. 1), no marvel if there were some among them that were a shame and trouble to them; but when there were but twelve, and one of them was *a devil*, surely we must never expect any society perfectly pure on this side heaven. The twelve were Christ's chosen friends, and yet one of them betrayed him. No bonds of duty or gratitude will hold those that have a devil.

II. Here is the proffer which he made to the chief priests; he *went to them, and said, What will ye give me? v.* 15. They did not send for him, nor make the proposal to him; they could not have thought that one of Christ's own disciples should be false to him.

1. What Judas promised; "*I will deliver him unto you*; that you may seize him without noise, or danger of an uproar." In their conspiracy against Christ, this was it they were at a loss about, *v.* 4, 5. They durst not meddle with him in public, and knew not where to find him in private. Here the matter rested, and the difficulty was insuperable, till Judas came, and offered them his services. Those that give up themselves to be led by the devil, find him readier than they imagine to help them at a dead lift. Though the rulers, by their power and interest, could kill him when they had him in their hands, yet none but a disciple could betray him.

I will deliver him unto you. He did not offer himself to be a witness against Christ, though they wanted evidence, *v.* 59. This is an evidence of the innocency of our Lord Jesus, that his own disciple, who was false to him, could not charge him with anything criminal, though it would have served to justify his treachery.

2. What he asked in consideration of this undertaking; *What will ye give me?* This was the only thing that made Judas betray his Master; he hoped to get money by it. It was not the hatred of his Master, nor any quarrel with him, but purely the love of money; that, and nothing else, made Judas a traitor.

What will ye give me? Why, what did he want? Neither bread to eat, nor raiment to put on; neither necessaries nor conveniences. This covetous wretch could not be content, but comes basely cringing to the priests with, *What will ye give me?* It is not the *lack* of money, but the *love* of money, that is the root of all evil.

III. Here is the bargain which the chief priests made with him; *they covenanted with him for thirty pieces of silver.* By the law (Exod. xxi. 32), thirty pieces of silver was the price of a slave—a goodly price, at which Christ was valued! They *covenanted with him—they paid it down*, so some; gave him his wages in hand, to secure him and to encourage him.

IV. Here is the industry of Judas, in pursuance of his bargain (*v.* 16); *he sought opportunity to betray him*, his head was still working to find out how he might do it effectually. It is a very wicked thing to seek opportunity to sin, and to devise mischief; for it argues the heart fully set in men to do evil. He had time to repent; but now by his covenant the devil tells him that he must be true to his word, though ever so false to his Master.

Verses 17–25

We have here an account of Christ's keeping the passover.

I. The time when Christ ate the passover, was the usual time appointed by God, and observed by the Jews (*v.* 17); *the first day of the feast of unleavened bread.*

II. The place was particularly appointed by himself to the disciples, upon their enquiry (*v.* 17): they asked, *Where wilt thou that we prepare the passover?*

1. They took it for granted that their Master would eat the passover, though he was at this time persecuted by the chief priests, and his life sought; they knew that he would not be put by his duty, either by frightenings without or fears within.

2. They knew very well that there must be preparation made for it, and that it was their business; *Where wilt thou that we prepare?* Before solemn ordinances there must be solemn preparation.

3. They knew that he had no house of his own wherein to eat the passover.

4. They would not pitch upon a place without direction from him, and from him they had direction; he sent them to *such a man* (*v.* 18), who probably was a friend and follower of his, and to his house he invited himself and his disciples.

(1) Tell him, *My time is at hand*; he means the time of his death. He knew when it was at hand, and was busy accordingly; we *know not our time* (Eccles. ix. 12), and therefore must never be off our

JAMIESON, FAUSSET, BROWN

said, Let her alone; why trouble ye her? she hath wrought a good work on me—It was good in itself, and so was acceptable to Christ; it was eminently seasonable, and so more acceptable still; and it was "what she could," and so most acceptable of all. **For ye have the poor with you always**—referring to Deuteronomy 15:11. **and whensoever ye will ye may do them good: but me ye have not always**—a gentle hint of His approaching departure, by One who knew the worth of His own presence. **She hath done what she could**—a noble testimony, embodying a principle of immense importance. **she is come aforehand to anoint my body to the burying**—or, as in John (12:7), "Against the day of my burying hath she kept this." Not that she, dear heart, thought of His burial, much less reserved any of her nard to anoint her dead Lord. But as the time was so near at hand when that office would have to be performed, *and she was not to have that privilege even after the spices were brought for the purpose* (ch. 16:1), He lovingly *regards it as done now*. "In the act of love done to Him," says OLSHAUSEN beautifully, "she has erected to herself an eternal monument, as lasting as the Gospel, the eternal Word of God. From generation to generation this remarkable prophecy of the Lord has been fulfilled; and even we, in explaining this saying of the Redeemer, of necessity contribute to its accomplishment." "Who but Himself, asks STIER, "had the power to ensure to any work of man, even if resounding in His own time through the whole earth, an imperishable remembrance in the stream of history? Behold once more here the majesty of His royal judicial supremacy in the government of the world, in this, 'Verily I say unto you.' "

And Judas Iscariot, one of the twelve, went unto the chief priests, to betray him unto them—i.e., to make his proposals, and to bargain with them, as appears from. Matthew's fuller statement (ch. 26: 14, 15) which says, he "went unto the chief priests, and said, What will ye give me, and I will deliver Him unto you? And they covenanted with him for thirty pieces of silver." The thirty pieces of silver were thirty shekels, the fine paid for man-or maid-servant acidentally killed (Exod. 21:32), and equal to about $25 in our currency—"a *goodly* price that I was prized at of them!" (Zech. 11:13). **And when they heard it, they were glad, and promised to give him money**—Matthew alone records the precise sum, because a remarkable and complicated prophecy, which he was afterwards to refer to, was fulfilled by it. **And he sought how he might conveniently betray him**—or, as more fully given in Luke (22:6), "And he promised, and sought opportunity to betray Him unto them in the absence of the multitude." That he should avoid an "uproar" or "riot" among the people, which probably was made an essential condition by the Jewish authorities, was thus assented to by the traitor; into whom, says Luke (22:3), "Satan entered," to put him upon this hellish deed.

17-30. PREPARATION FOR AND LAST CELEBRATION OF THE PASSOVER, ANNOUNCEMENT OF THE TRAITOR, AND INSTITUTION OF THE SUPPER. (=Mark 14:12-26; Luke 22:7-23; John 13:1-3, 10, 11, 18-30.) For the exposition, see on Luke 22:7-23.

Then came the day of unleavened bread, when the passover must be killed. The day here alluded to—"the first day of unleavened bread"—was the 14th Nisan, when, about midday, labor was intermitted, and all leaven removed from the houses (Ex. 12:15-17). Then, "between the two evenings" (Ex. 12:6)—or between three and six o'clock—the paschal lamb was killed, and in the evening, when the 15th Nisan began, was eaten. And though "the days of unleavened bread" properly began with the 15th, the preparations for the festival being made on the 14th, it was popularly called, as here, the "first" day of unleavened bread—as we learn from Josephus, whose way of speaking agrees with that here employed. The two disciples being sent from Bethany to make the necessary preparations on the Thursday, our Lord and the other disciples followed them to the city later in the day, and probably as evening drew near.

ADAM CLARKE

10. *Why trouble ye the woman?* Or, "Why do you put the woman to pain?" A generous mind is ever pained when it is denied the opportunity of doing good, or when its proffered kindness is refused.

11. *Ye have the poor always with you.* And, consequently, have the opportunity of doing them good at any time. *But me ye have not always;* My bodily presence is about to be removed from you forever. The woman, under a presentiment of My death, is preparing Me for My burial.

12. *She did it for my burial.* Or, "She hath done it to embalm Me." Our Lord took this opportunity to tell them once more that He was shortly to die.

13. *Wheresoever this gospel shall be preached.* Another remarkable proof of the prescience of Christ. *For a memorial of her.* As embalming preserves the body from corruption, and she has done this good work to embalm and preserve this body, so will I order everything concerning this transaction to be carefully recorded, to preserve her memory to the latest ages. The actions which the world blames, through the spirit of envy, covetousness, or malice, God takes delight to distinguish and record.

14. *Then . . . Judas.* After this supper at Bethany, Judas returned to Jerusalem and made his contract with the chief priests.

16. *He sought opportunity.* "A convenient or fit opportunity." Men seldom leave a crime imperfect. When once sin is conceived, it meets, in general, with few obstacles, till it brings forth death. How deceitful, how deeply damning, is the love of money!

17. *Now the first day of the feast of unleavened bread.* As the Feast of Unleavened Bread did not begin till the day after the Passover, the fifteenth day of the month (Lev. xxiii. 5-6; Num. xxviii. 16-17), this could not have been, properly, the first day of that feast. But as the Jews began to eat unleavened bread on the fourteenth (Exod. xii. 18), this day was often termed the first of unleavened bread. The Evangelists use it in this sense, and call even the paschal day by this name. See Mark xiv. 12; Luke xxii. 7. *Where wilt thou that we prepare?* How astonishing is this, that He who created all things, whether visible or invisible, and by whom all things were upheld, should so empty himself as not to be Proprietor of a single house in His whole creation, to eat the last Passover with His disciples! It is worthy of note what the Talmudists say, that the inhabitants of Jerusalem did not let out their houses to those who came to the annual feasts, but afforded all accommodations of this kind gratis. A man might, therefore, go and request the use of any room, on such an occasion, which was as yet unoccupied.

18. *Go . . . to such a man.* It is probable that this means some person with whom Christ was well-acquainted, and who was known to the disciples. Grotius observes that the Greeks use

MATTHEW HENRY

watch; *our time is always ready* (John vii. 6), and therefore we must be always ready. When our Lord Jesus invited himself to this good man's house, he sent him this intelligence, that his time was at hand. Christ's secret is with them that entertain him in their hearts.

(2) Tell him, *I will keep the passover at thy house.* This was an instance of his authority, as *the Master*; he did not beg, but command, the use of his house for this purpose. Thus, when Christ by his Spirit comes into the heart, he demands admission, as one whose own the heart is and cannot be denied. His people shall be willing, for he makes them so. *I will keep the passover with my disciples.* Wherever Christ is welcome, he expects that his disciples should be welcome too. When we take God for our God, we take his people for our people.

III. The preparation was made by the disciples (*v.* 19); *They did as Jesus had appointed. They made ready the passover*; they got the lamb killed, and everything set in readiness for such a sacred solemn feast.

IV. They ate the passover according to the law (*v.* 20); *He sat down.* His sitting down, denotes the composedness of his mind, when he addressed himself to this solemnity; *He sat down with the twelve*, Judas not excepted. By the law, they were to *take a lamb for a household*; Christ's disciples were his household. They whom God has charged with families, must have their houses with them in serving the Lord.

V. We have here Christ's discourse with his disciples at the passover-supper. The usual subject was the deliverance of Israel out of Egypt (Exod. xii. 26, 27); but the great Passover is now ready to be offered, and the discourse of that swallows up all talk of the other.

1. The general notice Christ gives his disciples of the treachery that should be among them (*v.* 21); *One of you shall betray me.* Christ knew it. We know not what troubles will befall us, nor whence they will arise: but Christ knew all his. It magnifies his love, that he knew all things that should befall him, and yet did not draw back. When there was occasion, he let those about him know it. He had often told them that the Son of man should be betrayed; now he tells them that one of them should do it.

2. The disciples' feelings on this occasion, *v.* 22.

(1) *They were exceedingly sorrowful.* It troubled them much to hear that their Master should be betrayed. When Peter was first told of it, he said, *Be it far from thee.* It troubled them more to hear that one of them should do it. Gracious souls grieve for the sins of others, especially of those that have made a more than ordinary profession of religion. It troubled them most of all, that they were left at uncertainty which of them it was.

(2) *They began every one of them to say, Lord, is it I?* They were not apt to suspect Judas. Though he was *a thief*, yet, it seems, he had carried it so plausibly, that none of them so much as looked upon him, much less said, *Lord, is it Judas?* It is possible for a hypocrite to go through the world, not only undiscovered, but unsuspected; like bad money so ingeniously counterfeited that nobody questions it.

They were apt to suspect themselves; *Lord, is it I?* They feared the worst, and asked Him who knows us better than we know ourselves, *Lord is it I?* We know not how strongly we may be tempted, nor how far God may leave us to ourselves, and therefore have reason, *not to be high-minded, but fear*.

3. Further information given them concerning this matter (*v.* 23, 24), where Christ tells them, (1) That the traitor was a familiar friend; *He that dippeth his hand with me in the dish*, that is, One of you that are now with me at the table. It is base ingratitude to dip with Christ in the dish, and yet betray him. (2) That this was according to the scripture, which would take off the offence at it. The more we see of the fulfilling of the scripture in our troubles, the better we may bear them. (3) That it would prove a very dear bargain to the traitor; *Woe to that man by whom the Son of man is betrayed.* Though God can serve his own purposes by the sins of men, that doth not make the sinner's condition the less woeful; *It had been good for that man, if he had not been born.*

4. The conviction of Judas, *v.* 25. He asked, *Is it I?* to avoid coming under the suspicion of guilt by his silence. He knew very well that it was he, and yet wished to appear a stranger to such a plot. Note, Many whose consciences condemn them are very industrious to justify themselves before men, and put a good face on it, with, *Lord, is it I?* Christ soon answered this question; *Thou hast said.* It was enough to convict him, and, if his heart had not been wretchedly hardened, to have broken the neck of his plot, when he saw it discovered to his Master, and discovered by him.

JAMIESON, FAUSSET, BROWN

And when the hour was come—about six o'clock, **he sat down, and the twelve apostles with him**—the whole twelve, Judas included.

verily, I say unto you, One of you shall betray me—The announcement of vs. 18 seems not to have been plain enough to be quite apprehended, save by the traitor himself. He will therefore speak it out in terms not to be misunderstood. But how much it cost Him to do this, appears from the "trouble" that came over His "spirit"—visible emotion, no doubt—before He got it uttered. What wounded susceptibility does this disclose, and what exquisite delicacy in His social intercourse with the Twelve, to whom He cannot, without an effort, break the subject!

"They were exceeding sorrowful" (Matt. 26:22). (2) "They began to inquire among themselves which of them it was that should do this thing" (Luke 22:23). (3) "They began to say unto Him one by one, Is it I, and another, Is it I?" (Mark 14:19). Generous, simple hearts! They abhorred the thought, but, instead of putting it on others, each was only anxious to purge *himself*, and know if *he* could be the wretch. Their putting it at once to Jesus Himself, as knowing doubtless who was to do it, was the best, as it certainly was the most spontaneous and artless evidence of their innocence. (4) Jesus, apparently while this questioning was going on, added, "The Son of man goeth as it is written of Him, but woe unto that man by whom the Son of man is betrayed! It had been good for that man if he had not been born" (Matt. 26:24). (5) "Judas," *last of all*, "answered and said, *Lord, is it I?*" evidently feeling that when all were saying this, if he held his peace, that of itself would draw suspicion upon him. To prevent this the question is wrung out of him, but perhaps, amidst the stir and excitement at the table, in a half-suppressed tone as we are inclined to think the answer also was—"Thou hast said" (Matt. 26:25), or possibly by little more than a sign; for from vs. 28 it is evident that till the moment when he went out, he was not openly discovered.

ADAM CLARKE

this form when they mean some particular person who is so well-known that there is no need to specify him by name. *My time is at hand.* That is, the time of My crucifixion.

19. *And the disciples did.* The disciples that were sent on this errand were Peter and John. See Luke xxii. 9. *They made ready the passover.* That is, they provided the lamb, etc., which were appointed by the law for this solemnity.

20. *Now when the even was come, he sat down with the twelve.* It is a common opinion that our Lord ate the Passover some hours before the Jews ate it; for the Jews, according to custom, ate theirs at the end of the fourteenth day, but Christ ate His the preceding even, which was the beginning of the same sixth day, or Friday. The Jews begin their day at sunsetting, we at midnight. Thus Christ ate the Passover on the same day with the Jews, but not on the same hour. Christ kept this Passover the beginning of the fourteenth day, the precise day and hour in which the Jews had eaten their first Passover in Egypt. See Exod. xii. 6-12. And in the same part of the same day in which the Jews had sarcificed their first paschal lamb, viz., "between the two evenings," about the ninth hour, or three o'clock, Jesus Christ, our Passover, was sacrificed for us. For it was at this hour that He yielded up His last breath; and then it was that, the sacrifice being completed, Jesus said, "It is finished."

21. *One of you shall betray me.* Or "will deliver Me up." Judas had already *betrayed* Him, v. 15, and he was now about to deliver Him into the hands of the chief priests, according to the agreement he had made with them.

22. *They were exceeding sorrowful.* That is, the eleven who were innocent; and the hypocritical traitor, Judas, endeavored to put on the appearance of sorrow.

23. *He that dippeth his hand.* As the Jews ate the Passover a whole family together, it was not convenient for them all to dip their bread in the same dish. They therefore had several little dishes or plates, in which was the juice of the bitter herbs, mentioned Exod. xii. 8, on different parts of the table; and those who were nigh one of these dipped their bread in it. As Judas is represented as dipping in the same dish with Christ, it shows that he was either near or opposite to Him. If this man's heart had not been hardened, and his conscience seared beyond all precedent, by the deceitfulness of his sin, would he have showed his face in this sacred assembly, or have thus put the seal to his own perdition by eating of this sacrificial lamb?

24. *The Son of man goeth.* That is, is about to die. "Going, going away, departing" are frequently used in the best Greek and Latin writers for "death" or "dying." The same words are often used in the Scriptures in the same sense. *It had been good for that man.* Can this be said of any sinner, in the common sense in which it is understood, if there be any redemption from hell's torments? Can the doctrine of the non-eternity of hell's torments stand in the presence of this saying? Or can the doctrine of the annihilation of the wicked consist with this declaration? It was common for the Jews to say of any flagrant transgressor, "It would have been better for him had he never been born."

25. *Judas . . . said, Master, is it I?* What excessive impudence! He knew, in his conscience, that he had already betrayed his Master, and was waiting now for the servants of the chief priests, that he might deliver Him into their hands; and yet he says (hoping that he had transacted his business so privately that it had not yet transpired), *Master, is it I?* It is worthy of remark that each of the other disciples said, *Lord, is it I?* But Judas dares not, or will not, use this august title, but simpy say, "Teacher, is it I?" *Thou hast said.* "Ye have said" was a common form of expression for "Yes. It is so."

MATTHEW HENRY

Verses 26–30

We have here the institution of the great gospel ordinance of the Lord's supper.

I. The time when it was instituted—*as they were eating.* At the latter end of the passover-supper, before the table was drawn, because it was to come in the room of that ordinance. Christ is to us the Passover-sacrifice by which atonement is made (1 Cor. v. 7); *Christ our Passover is sacrificed for us.*

II. The institution itself. A sacrament must be instituted; it has both its being and significancy from the institution, from a divine institution. Hence the apostle (1. Cor. xi. 23, &c.), in that discourse of his concerning this ordinance, all along calls Jesus Christ *the Lord,* because, as *Lord,* he appointed this ordinance.

1. The body of Christ is signified and represented by bread; he had said formerly (John vi. 35), *I am the bread of life.* As the life of the body is supported by bread, so the life of the soul is supported and maintained by Christ's mediation.

(1) *He took bread—the loaf;* some loaf that lay ready at hand, fit for the purpose. His taking the bread was a solemn action, and was, probably, done in such a manner as to be observed by them that sat with him.

(2) *He blessed it;* set it apart for this use by prayer and thanksgiving. We do not find any set form of words used by him upon this occasion. Christ could command the blessing, and we, in his name, are emboldened to beg the blessing.

(3) *He brake it;* which denotes, [1] The breaking of Christ's body for us, that it might be fitted for our use; *He was bruised for our iniquities.* [2] The breaking of Christ's body to us, as the father of the family breaks the bread to the children.

(4) *He gave it to his disciples,* as the Master of the family, and the Master of this feast. *To the disciples,* because all the disciples of Christ have a right to this ordinance; and those shall have the benefit of it who are his disciples indeed; yet he gave it to them as he did the multiplied loaves, by them to be handed to all his other followers.

(5) *He said, Take, eat; this is my body, v.* 26. He here tells them,

[1] What they should do with it; *"Take, eat;* accept of Christ as he is offered to you, receive the atonement, approve of it, consent to it." Believing on Christ is expressed by *receiving him* (John i. 12), and *feeding upon him,* John vi. 57, 58. Meat looked upon, or the dish ever so well garnished, will not nourish us; it must be fed upon: so must the doctrine of Christ.

[2] What they should have with it; *This is my body,* not *οὗτος—this bread,* but *τοῦτο—this eating and drinking.* Believing carries all the efficacy of Christ's death to our souls. *This is my body,* spiritually and sacramentally; this signifies and represents my body. He employs sacramental language. We partake of the sun, not by having the bulk and body of the sun put into our hands, but the beams of it darted down upon us; so we partake of Christ by partaking of his grace, and the blessed fruits of the breaking of his body.

2. The blood of Christ is signified and represented by the wine (*v.* 27, 28); *He took the cup,* the grace-cup, which was set ready to be drank, after thanks returned, according to the custom of the Jews at the passover. *He gave thanks,* to teach us, not only in every ordinance, but in every part of the ordinance, to have our eyes up to God.

This cup he gave to the disciples,

(1) With a command; *Drink ye all of it.* Thus he welcomes his guests to his table, obliges them all to drink of his cup.

(2) With an explication; *For this is my blood of the New Testament.* Hitherto the blood of Christ had been represented by the blood of beasts, real blood: but, after it was actually shed, it was represented by the blood of grapes, metaphorical blood.

[1] *It is my blood of the New Testament.* The

JAMIESON, FAUSSET, BROWN

And he took bread, and gave thanks. In Matthew and Mark it is "and blessed it." The one act includes the other. He "gave thanks," not so much here for the literal bread as for that higher food which was couched under it; and He "blessed" it as the ordained channel of spiritual nourishment.

and brake it, and gave unto them, saying, This is my body, which is given for you: this do in remembrance of me. "The expression, 'This is my body,'" says Alexander most truly, "which is common to all the accounts, appears so unambiguous and simple an expression, that it is hard to recognize in it the occasion and the subject of the most protracted and exciting controversy that has rent the Church within the last thousand years. That controversy is so purely theological that it has scarcely any basis in the exposition of the text; the only word upon which it could fasten (the verb *is*) being one which in Aramaic (or Syro-Chaldaic), would not be expressed, and therefore belongs merely to the Greek translation of our Savior's language. Until the strong unguarded figures of the early Fathers had been petrified into a dogma, at first by popular misapprehension, and at last by theological perversion, these words suggested no idea but the one which they still convey to every plain unbiased reader, that our Savior calls the bread His body in the same sense that He calls himself a door (John 10:9), a vine (John 15:11), a root (Rev. 22:16), a star, and is described by many other metaphors in Scripture. The bread was an emblem of His flesh, as wounded for the sins of men, and as administered for their spiritual nourishment and growth in grace."

Likewise also the cup after supper—not after the Lord's Supper, as if the taking of the bread and of the cup in it were separated so far as that; but after the *paschal* supper, and consequently immediately after the distribution of the bread. The accounts of Matthew and of Mark would seem to imply that He gave thanks on taking the cup, as well as with the bread; but here, at any rate, and in the most authoritative account, perhaps, which we have, in 1 Cor 11:23, that is not said. **saying, This cup is the new testament in my blood, which is shed for you.** In Matthew (26:28), "This is my blood of the new testament, which is shed for many for the remission of sins." In 1 Cor. (11:25) "This cup is the new testament in my blood: this do ye, as oft as ye drink it, in remembrance of me." Most critics now maintain that the word here rendered "testament" should be rendered covenant, not only

ADAM CLARKE

26. *As they were eating.* Either an ordinary supper, or the paschal lamb, as some think. This is the first institution of what is termed the Lord's Supper. *Jesus took bread.* Of what kind? Unleavened bread, certainly, because there was no other kind to be had in all Judea at this time; for this was the first day of unleavened bread (v. 17), i.e., the fourteenth of the month Nisan, when the Jews, according to the command of God (Exod. xii. 15-20; xxiii. 15; and xxxiv. 25), were to purge away all leaven from their houses. For he who sacrified the Passover, having leaven in his dwelling, was considered to be such a transgressor of the divine law as could no longer be tolerated among the people of God, and therefore was to be cut off from the congregation of Israel. Now if any respect should be paid to the primitive institution, in the celebration of this divine ordinance, then unleavened, unyeasted bread should be used. *And blessed it.* Both Matthew and Mark use the word *blessed* instead of "gave thanks," which is the word used by Luke and Paul. The terms, in this case, are nearly of the same import, as both blessing and giving thanks were used on these occasions. But what was it that our Lord blessed? Not the bread, though many think the contrary, being deceived by the word *it,* which is improperly supplied in our version. In all the four places referred to above, whether the word *blessed* or *gave thanks* is used, it refers not to the bread, but to God, the Dispenser of every good. Our Lord here conforms himself to that constant Jewish custom, viz., of acknowledging God as the Author of every good and perfect gift, by giving thanks or taking the bread and taking the cup at their ordinary meals. The Jewish form of blessing, probably that which our Lord used on this occasion is: "Blessed be thou, our God, King of the universe who bringest forth bread out of the earth!" "Likewise, on taking the cup, they say: "Blessed be our God, the King of the universe, the Creator of the fruit of the vine!"

And brake it. We often read in the Scriptures of breaking bread, but never of cutting it. The breaking of the bread I consider essential to the proper performance of this solemn and significant ceremony, because this act was designed by our Lord to shadow forth the wounding, piercing, and breaking of His body upon the Cross. *And gave it to the disciples.* Not only the breaking, but also the distribution, of the bread are necessary parts of this rite. *This is my body.* Here it must be observed that Christ had nothing in His hands at this time but part of that unleavened bread which He and His disciples had been eating at supper, and therefore He could mean no more than this, viz., that the bread which He was now breaking *represented* His body, which in the course of a few hours was to be crucified for them. The truth is, there is scarcely a more common form of speech in any language than "This is" for "This represents or signifies." And as our Lord refers in the whole of this transaction to the ordinance of the Passover, we may consider Him as saying: "This bread is now My body in that sense in which the paschal lamb has been My body hitherto; and this cup is My blood of the New Testament in the same sense as the blood of bulls and goats has been My blood under the Old (Exodus xxiv; Hebrews ix). That is, the paschal lamb and the sprinkling of blood represented My sacrifice to the present time; this bread and this wine shall represent My body and blood through all future ages. Therefore, "Do this in remembrance of Me."

28. *For this is my blood of the new testament.* This is the reading both here and in Mark; but Luke and Paul say, "This cup is the new testament in my blood." This passage has been strangely mistaken. By *new testament,* many understand nothing more than the Book commonly known by this name, containing the four Gospels, Acts of the Apostles, apostolical Epistles, and Book of the Revelation; and they think that the cup of the new testament means no more than merely that cup which the Book called the New Testament enjoins in the sacrament of the Lord's Supper. The original which we translate *the new testament* and which is general title of all the contents of the Book already described simply means "the new covenant." *Covenant* signifies an agreement, con-

MATTHEW HENRY

covenant God is pleased to make with us, and all the benefits and privileges of it, are owing to the merits of Christ's death.

[2] *It is shed;* it was not shed till next day, but it was now upon the point of being shed, it is as good as done.

[3] *It is shed for many.* Christ came to confirm *a covenant with many.* The blood of the Old Testament was shed for a few. But Jesus Christ is a propitiation *for the sins of the whole world,* 1 John ii. 2.

[4] *It is shed for the remission of sins,* that is, to purchase remission of sins for us. The new covenant which is procured and ratified by the blood of Christ, is a charter of pardon, an act of indemnity, in order to a reconciliation between God and man. The pardon of sin is that great blessing which is, in the Lord's supper, conferred upon all true believers; it is the foundation of all other blessings, and the spring of everlasting comfort, *ch.* ix. 2, 3. A farewell is now bidden to the fruit of the vine, *v.* 29. How good to be here! Never such a heaven upon earth as was at this table; but it was not intended for a perpetuity.

First, He takes leave of such communion; *I will not drink henceforth of this fruit of the vine. Farewell this fruit of the vine,* this passover-cup, this sacramental wine. Dying saints take their leave of sacraments, and the other ordinances of communion which they enjoy in this world, with comfort, for the joy and glory they enter into supersede them all; when the sun rises, farewell the candles.

Secondly, He assures them of a happy meeting again at last. *Until that day when I drink it new with you.* Some understand it of the interviews he had with them after his resurrection. Others understand it of the joys and glories of the future state, which the saints shall partake of in everlasting communion with the Lord Jesus. Christ will himself partake of those pleasures; it was *the joy set before him,* which he had in his eye, and all his faithful friends and followers shall partake with him.

Lastly, Here is the close of the solemnity with a hymn (*v.* 30); *They sang a hymn* or psalm. Singing of psalms is a gospel-ordinance. It is very proper after the Lord's supper, as an expression of our joy in God through Jesus Christ, and a thankful acknowledgment of that great love wherewith God has loved us in him. It is not unseasonable, no, not in times of sorrow and suffering. Our spiritual joy should not be interrupted by outward afflictions.

When this was done, they *went out into the mount of Olives.* He would not stay in the house to be apprehended, lest he should bring the master of the house into trouble; but he retired into the adjacent country, the mount of Olives. They had the benefit of moonlight for this walk, for the passover was always at the full moon. After we have received the Lord's supper, it is good for us to retire for prayer and meditation, and to be alone with God.

JAMIESON, FAUSSET, BROWN

here but wherever else it occurs in the New Testament; being used in the Old Testament constantly by the LXX translators for the well-known Hebrew word signifying "covenant," which never signifies "testament." Here, in particular, there is a manifest allusion to Ex. 24:8, "Behold, the blood of the covenant which the Lord hath made with you concerning all these words." Now it is beyond doubt that "covenant" is the fundamental idea, and that in the Old Testament the word is correctly rendered "covenant." But let it be observed, first, that "testament" or "will" is the proper classical sense of the Greek word, and "disposition" or "covenant" but a secondary sense; and next, that in Heb. 9:15 the sense of "testament" appears to be so obviously what the apostle reasons on that to exclude it there, and restrict the meaning to "covenant," can only be made to yield the harshest sense. But the true harmony of both senses of the word, and how, in the case of Christ's death, the one runs into the other, will be seen, not by any criticism on the *word,* but by reflection on the *thing.* If it be true that by "covenant," or eternal divine arrangement, all the blessings of salvation become the rightful possession of believers solely *in virtue of Christ's death,* does not this almost irresistibly suggest to every reflecting mind the idea of a *testator's* death as a most true and exalted conception of the virtue of it? What can be a more natural view of the *principle* on which the fruits of Christ's death become ours than that of a testamentary disposition? Then, observe how near to this idea of His death our Lord himself came in what He said, when the Greeks sought to "see Jesus" on the eve of His last Passover. "The hour is come when the Son of man should be glorified: except a corn of wheat fall into the ground and die, it abideth alone; but if it die, it bringeth forth much fruit" (John 12:23, 24). Observe, too, His mode of expression twice over at the Supper table. "I *appoint* unto you, as my Father appointed unto me, a kingdom" (Luke 22:29); "Peace I *leave* with you; my peace I *give* unto you": and it will be seen, we think, how each idea suggests the other. While that of "covenant" is confessedly the fundamental one, that of "testament" is accessory or illustrative only. Yet the one is as real as the other, and presents a phase of the truth exceedingly precious. In this view Bengel substantially concurs, and Stier entirely.

"I will not drink henceforth of this fruit of the vine, until that day when I drink it new with you in my Father's kingdom," or, "in the kingdom of God" (Mark 14:25). The primary application of this, no doubt, is to the new Gospel kingdom to be fully erected when the old economy, with its Passover and temple rites, should disappear. But the best interpreters agree that its only full and proper application is to that celestial kingdom of which He speaks so beautifully in verse 30—"that ye may eat and drink at my table in my kingdom."

ADAM CLARKE

tract, or compact between two parties by which both are mutually bound to do certain things on certain conditions and penalties. It answers to the Hebrew *berith,* which often signifies, not only the covenant or agreement, but also the sacrifice which was slain on the occasion, by the blood of which the covenant was ratified; and the contracting parties professed to subject themselves to such a death as that of the victim in case of violating their engagements. In this place our Lord terms His blood "the blood of the new covenant"; by which He means that grand plan of agreement, or reconciliation, which God was now establishing between himself and mankind, by the passion and death of His Son, through whom alone men could draw nigh to God. *Which is shed* (poured out) *for many.* Often used in a sacrificial sense in the Septuagint, to "pour out" or "sprinkle" the blood of the sacrifices before the altar of the Lord, by way of atonement. See 2 Kings xvi. 15; Lev. viii. 15; ix. 9; Exod. xxix. 12; Lev. iv. 7, 14, 17, 30, 34; and in various other places. Our Lord, by this very remarkable mode of expression, teaches us that, as His body was to be broken or crucified, "in our stead," so here the Blood was to be poured out to make an atonement, as the words *remission of sins* sufficiently prove; for "without shedding of blood [there] is no remission," Heb. ix. 22. The whole of this passage will receive additional light when collated with Isa. liii. 11-12. "By his knowledge shall my righteous servant justify many; for he shall bear their iniquities . . . because he hath poured out his soul unto death . . . and he bare the sin of many." The pouring out of the soul unto death in the prophet answers to "This is the blood of the new covenant which is poured out for you," in the Evangelists. *For the remission of sins.* "For [or in reference to] the taking away of sins." For although the Blood is shed and the atonement made, no man's sins are taken away until as a true penitent he returns to God and, feeling his utter incapacity to save himself, believes in Christ Jesus, who is the Justifier of the ungodly. The phrase *remission of sins* (frequently used by the Septuagint), being thus explained by our Lord, is often used by the Evangelists and the apostles, and does not mean merely the pardon of sins, as it is generally understood, but the removal or taking away of sins—not only the guilt, but also the very nature of sin, and the pollution of the soul through it; and comprehends all that is generally understood by the terms justification and sanctification. Both Luke and Paul add that, after giving the bread, our Lord said, "This do in remembrance of me." And after giving the cup, Paul alone adds, "This do ye, as oft as ye drink it, in remembrance of me." The account as given by Paul should be carefully followed, being fuller, and received, according to his own declaration, by especial revelation from God. See 1 Cor. xi. 23. *For I have received of the Lord that which also I delivered unto you.*

29. *I will not drink henceforth of this fruit of the vine.* These words seem to intimate no more than this: We shall not have another opportunity of eating this bread and drinking this wine together, as in a few hours My crucifixion shall take place. *Until that day when I drink it new with you.* That is, I shall no more drink of the produce of the vine with you; but shall drink *new* wine—wine of a widely different nature from this—a wine which the kingdom of God alone can afford. The term *new* in Scripture is often taken in this sense. So the "new heaven," and "new earth," the "new covenant," the "new man" mean a heaven, earth, covenant, man of a very different nature from the former. From what our Lord says here, we learn that the sacrament of His supper is a type and a pledge to genuine Christians of the felicity they shall enjoy with Christ in the Kingdom of glory.

30. *And when they had sung an hymn.* Probably no more than a kind of recitative reading or chanting. As to the hymn itself, we know, from the universal consent of Jewish antiquity, that it was composed of Psalms 113—118, termed by the Jews *halel,* from *halelu-yah,* the first word in Psalm 113. These six psalms were always sung at every paschal solemnity. They sung this great hallel on account of the five great benefits referred to in it; viz., (1) The Exodus from Egypt, Ps. cxiv. 1, "When Israel

MATTHEW HENRY

Verses 31-35

We have here Christ's discourse with his disciples upon the way.

I. A prediction of the trial which both he and his disciples were now to go through. He here foretells,

1. A dismal scattering storm just arising, *v.* 31. (1) That they should *all be offended because of Christ that very night*; they would not have the courage to cleave to him but would all basely desert him. Offences will come among the disciples of Christ in an hour of trial and temptation; it cannot be but they should, for they are weak. Even they whose hearts are upright may sometimes be overtaken with an offence. There are some temptations and offences, the effects of which are general, *All you shall be offended.* Though there will be but one traitor, they will be all deserters. We have need to prepare for sudden trials, which may come to extremity in a very little time. How soon may a storm arise! The cross of Christ is the great stumbling-block to many that pass for his disciples.

(2) That herein the scripture would be fulfilled; *I will smite the Shepherd.* It is quoted from Zech. xiii. 7. Here is the smiting of the Shepherd in the sufferings of Christ, and the scattering of the sheep, thereupon, in the flight of the disciples. It was each one's care to shift for himself, and happy he that could get furthest from the cross.

2. He gives them the prospect of a comfortable gathering together again after this storm (*v.* 32); "*After I am risen again, I will go before you.* Though you will forsake me, I will not forsake you; though you fall I will take care you shall not fall finally: we shall have a meeting again in Galilee, *I will go before you*, as the shepherd before the sheep." The captain of our salvation knows how to rally his troops, when, through their cowardice, they have been put into disorder.

II. The presumption of Peter (*v.* 33); *Though all men be offended, yet will I never be offended.* Peter had a great stock of confidence, and was upon all occasions forward to speak; sometimes it did him a kindness, but at other times it betrayed him, as it did here.

1. How he bound himself with a promise, that he would never be offended in Christ. Before the Lord's supper, Christ's discourse led his disciples to *examine* themselves with, *Lord, is it I?* For that is our preparatory duty; after the ordinance, his discourse leads them to an *engaging* of themselves to close walking, for that is the subsequent duty.

2. How he fancied himself better armed against temptation than anyone else, *Though all men shall be offended yet will not I.* Peter supposes it possible that *some*, nay that *all*, might be offended, and yet he escape better than any. We should rather say, If it be possible that others may be offended, there is danger that I may be so.

III. The particular warning Christ gave Peter of what he would do, *v.* 34. He imagined that in the hour of temptation he should come off better than any of them, and Christ tells him that he should come off worse. "*Verily, I say unto thee;* take my word for it, who know thee better than thou knowest thyself." He tells him,

1. That he should deny him. He said, "Though all men, yet not I"; and he did it sooner than any.

2. How quickly he should do it; *this night*, before to-morrow, nay, *before cock-crowing.* As we know not how near we may be to trouble, so we know not how near we may be to sin; if God leave us to ourselves, we are always in danger.

3. How often he should do it; *thrice.* Christ tells him that he would do it again and again; for, when once our feet begin to slip, it is hard to recover our standing again.

IV. Peter's repeated assurances of his fidelity (*v.* 35); *Though I should die with thee.* He knew what he *should* do—rather die with Christ than deny him; and he thought what he *would* do—never be false to his Master, whatever it cost him; yet, it proved, he was. It is easy to talk boldly and carelessly of death at a distance; but it is not so soon done as said, when it comes to the setting-to, and death shows itself in its own colours.

What Peter said the rest subscribed to; *likewise also said all the disciples.* There is a proneness in good men to be over-confident of their own strength and stability. Those often fall soonest and foulest that are most confident of themselves. Those are least safe that are most secure.

Verses 36-46

In these verses we have the story of his agony in the garden. The clouds had been gathering a good while, and looked black. But now the storm began

JAMIESON, FAUSSET, BROWN

31-35. THE DESERTION OF JESUS BY HIS DISCIPLES, AND THE DENIAL OF PETER FORETOLD. (= Mark 14:27-31; Luke 22:31-38; John 13:36-38.) For the exposition, see on Luke 22:31-38.

Then saith Jesus unto them, All ye shall be offended because of me this night—"shall be stumbled in me"; temporarily staggered on seeing their Master apprehended. In the expression, "All ye," there may be a reference to the one who had just "gone out." Great as was the relief, now for the first time experienced by the Savior himself, on the traitor's voluntary separation from a fellowship to which He never in heart belonged (John 13:31), even in those who remained there was something which burdened the spirit and wounded the heart of the Man of Sorrows. It saddened Him to think that, within one brief hour or two of the time when their hearts had warmed toward Him more than ever at the Paschal and Communion table, they should every one of them be "stumbled" because of Him: **for it is written** [Zech. 13:7], **I will smite the Shepherd, and the sheep of the flock shall be scattered abroad.** 32. **But after I am risen again, I will go before you into Galilee.** He falls back upon this striking prophecy, partly to confirm their faith in what they would otherwise hardly think credible; and partly to console himself with the reflection that it was but one of "the things concerning him" which "would have an end"—that they would be but links in the chain, "doing what God's hand and purpose determined before to be done."

In Matthew and Mark it was when our Lord told them they should all be stumbled in Him that night that Peter said, "Though all men"—or rather, "all," meaning all that sat with him at the table—"shall be offended in thee, yet will I never be offended" (Matt. 26:33; Mark 14:29). But as the answer there given by our Lord is the same as that recorded by our Evangelist, he probably uttered both protestations in his vehemence at one time; his feeling being roused by our Lord singling him out from all the rest. Poor Peter, thou shalt yet pay dearly for that unlovely elevation of thyself above the rest of thy brethren, when thy risen Lord shall wring thy heart by asking thee, in presence of these very brethren, "Simon, son of Jonas, lovest thou me *more than these*?" (John 21:15-17). Yet no vain-glorious vaunt was this of Peter. It was just the outcoming of conscious attachment: insomuch that all the rest, feeling a cord touched in their own hearts by this protestation, immediately repeated it for themselves. For, add our two first Evangelists, "*Likewise also said all the disciples.*" Dear disciples! Ye spoke out but the feelings of your heart then; your Lord knew that, and doubtless was comforted by it, as a spontaneous utterance of your hearts' affection. But little thought ye how soon it was to be seen—in all of you, but in Peter preeminently—that "he that trusteth in his own heart is a fool" (Prov. 28:26). 34. **And he said, I tell thee, Peter, the cock shall not crow this day, before that thou shalt thrice deny that thou knoweth me.** Most interesting and touching is the fact, that whereas in the first, third, and fourth Gospels only *one* crowing of the cock is mentioned as sounding the note of Peter's fall; in the second Gospel—which all ancient tradition proclaims, and internal evidence suggests, to have been drawn up under the immediate eye of Peter—it is said that *two* crowings of the cock would sound his fall. And as it is Mark alone who records the fact that the cock did crow twice—the first time after one denial of his Lord, and the second immediately after the last—we have thus an affecting announcement, almost from his own pen, that warning after warning passed unheeded till the second knell rang in his ears and bitterly revealed how much wiser his Lord was than he.

36-46. THE AGONY IN THE GARDEN. (=Mark 14:32-42; Luke 22:39-46.) For the exposition, see on Luke 22:39-46.

ADAM CLARKE

went out of Egypt." (2) The miraculous division of the Red Sea, v. 3, "The sea saw it, and fled." (3) The promulgation of the law, v. 4, "The mountains skipped like . . . lambs." (4) The resurrection of the dead, Ps. cxvi. 9, "I will walk before the Lord in the land of the living." (5) The passion of the Messiah, Ps. cxv. 1, "Not unto us, O Lord, not unto us."

31. *All ye shall be offended.* Or rather, "You will all be stumbled"—you will all forsake Me, and lose in a great measure your confidence in Me. *This night.* The time of trial is just at hand.

I will smite the shepherd. It will happen to you as to a flock of sheep whose shepherd has been slain—the leader and guardian being removed, the whole flock shall be scattered, and be on the point of becoming a prey to ravenous beasts.

32. *But after I am risen again.* Do not lose your confidence; for though I shall appear for a time to be wholly left to wicked men, and be brought under the power of death, yet I will rise again, and triumph over all your enemies and mine. *I will go before you.* Still alluding to the case of the shepherd and his sheep. Though the shepherd have been smitten and the sheep scattered, the shepherd shall revive again, collect the scattered flock, and *go before* them, and lead them to peace, security, and happiness.

33. *Peter . . . said unto him, Though all men shall be offended . . . yet will I never.* The presumptuous person imagines he can do everything, and can do nothing; thinks he can excel all, and excels in nothing; promises everything, and performs nothing. The humble man acts a quite contrary part. There is nothing we know so little of as ourselves—nothing we see less of than our own weakness and poverty.

34. *Jesus said.* Our Lord's answer to Peter is very emphatic and impressive. *Verily*—I speak a solemn, weighty truth, you will not only be stumbled, fall off and forsake your Master, but you will even *deny* that you have, or ever had, any knowledge of or connection with Me; and this you will do, not by little and little, through a long process of time, till the apostasy, daily gathering strength, shall be complete; but you will do it *this* very *night*, and that not once only, but *thrice.*

35. *Though I should die with thee, yet will I not deny thee.* He does not take the warning which his Lord gave him—he trusts in the warm, sincere attachment to Christ which he now feels, not considering that this must speedily fail unless supported by the power of God.

MATTHEW HENRY

in good earnest.

I. The place where he underwent this mighty agony; it was *in a place called Gethsemane.* The name signifies *an olive-mill,* a press for olives, like a winepress, where they *trod the olives.* There our Lord Jesus began his passion; there it pleased the Lord to bruise him, and crush him, that fresh oil might flow to all believers from him.

II. The company he had with him, when he was in this agony.

1. He took all the twelve disciples with him to the garden, except Judas, who was at this time otherwise employed.

2. He took only Peter, and James, and John, with him into that corner of the garden where he suffered his agony. He left the rest at some distance, with this charge, *Sit ye here, while I go and pray yonder.* Christ went to pray alone, though he had lately prayed with his disciples, John xvii. 1. He took these three with him, because they had been the witnesses of his glory in his transfiguration (*ch.* xvii. 1, 2), and that would prepare them to be the witnesses of his agony. Those are best prepared to suffer with Christ, that have by faith beheld his glory. If we hope to reign with him, why should we not expect to suffer with him?

III. The agony itself that he was in; *He began to be sorrowful, and very heavy.* It is called an agony (Luke xxii. 44), a conflict. It was not any bodily pain or torment that he was in, it was from within; he troubled himself, John xi. 33. The words here used are very emphatical; he began *to be sorrowful, and in a consternation.* He had like a weight of lead upon his spirits.

But what was the cause of all this? What was it that put him into this agony? *Why art thou cast down,* blessed Jesus, and *why disquieted?* Certainly, it was nothing of despair or distrust of his Father, much less any conflict or struggle with him. As the Father loved him because he laid down his life for the sheep, so he was entirely subject to his Father's will in it. But,

1. He engaged in an encounter with the powers of darkness; so he intimates (Luke xxii. 53). *As the Father gave me commandment, so I do;* however it be, I must have a struggle with him, therefore *arise, let us go hence,* let us hasten to the field of battle, and meet the enemy. Christ, when he works salvation, is described like a champion taking the field, Isa. lix. 16–18.

2. He was now *bearing the iniquities* which the Father laid upon him, and, by his sorrow and amazement, he accommodated himself to his undertaking. The sufferings he was entering upon were for our sins; they were all made to meet upon him, and he knew it. As we are obliged to be sorry for our particular sins, so was he grieved for the sins of us all.

3. He had a full and clear prospect of all the sufferings that were before him. He foresaw the treachery of Judas, the unkindness of Peter, the malice of the Jews, and their base ingratitude. Death in its most dreadful appearances, death in pomp, attended with all its terrors, looked him in the face; and this made him sorrowful, especially because it was the wages of our sin, which he had undertaken to satisfy for. It is true, the martyrs have suffered for Christ without any such sorrow and consternation. But then, (1) Christ was now denied the supports and comforts which they had; that is, he denied them to himself. Their cheerfulness under the cross was owing to the divine favour, which, for the present, was suspended from the Lord Jesus. (2) His sufferings were of another nature from theirs. On the saints' cross there is a blessing pronounced, which enables them to rejoice under it (*ch.* v. 10, 12); but to Christ's cross there was a curse annexed, which made him sorrowful and very heavy under it. And his sorrow under the cross was the foundation of their joy under it.

IV. His complaint of this agony. He goes to his disciples (*v.* 38), and,

1. He acquaints them with his condition; *My soul is exceedingly sorrowful, even unto death.* It gives some little ease to a troubled spirit, to have a friend ready to unbosom itself to, and give vent to its sorrows. Christ here tells them, (1) What was the seat of his sorrow; it was his soul that was now in an agony. Christ suffered in soul as well as in body. (2) What was the degree of his sorrow. He was *exceedingly sorrowful.* It was sorrow in the highest degree, even unto death; it was a killing sorrow, such sorrow as no mortal man could bear and live. (3) The duration of it; it will continue even unto death. He now *began* to be sorrowful, and never ceased to be so till he said, *It is finished.* It was prophesied of Christ, that he should be *a Man of sorrows* (Isa. liii. 3).

2. He bespeaks their company and attendance;

JAMIESON, FAUSSET, BROWN

The walk to Gethsemane, we incline to think, was taken in silence. But no sooner was He on the spot than, having said to the whole of them, "Pray that ye enter not into temptation" (Luke 22:40), the internal commotion—which may have begun as soon as the "hymn" that closed the proceedings of the upper room died away in silence—would no longer conceal. As soon as He was "at the place," having said to eight out of the eleven, "Sit ye here while I go and pray yonder," He took Peter and James and John aside by themselves, or a little in advance of the rest, and "saith unto them, My soul is exceeding sorrowful, even unto death: tarry ye here and watch with me" (Matt. 26:38; Mark 14:34). Not, "Come and *see* Me, to be My witnesses"; but "Come and *watch with Me,* to bear Me company." It did Him good, it seems, to have them by Him. For He had a true humanity, only all the more tender and susceptible than ours that it was not blunted and dulled by sin. You may say, indeed, if company was what He wanted, He got little of it. True enough. They fell asleep. "I looked for some to take pity, but there was none; and for comforters, but I found none" (Ps. 69:20). It would have soothed His burdened spirit to have had their sympathy, but He did not get it. They were broken reeds. And so He had to tread the winepress alone. Yet was their presence, even while asleep, not quite in vain. Perhaps the spectacle would only touch His sensibilities the more, and rouse into quickened action His greathearted compassions. In fact, He did not want even them *too near* Him. For it is said, "He went forward a little"; or, as Luke (22:41) more precisely expresses it, "was withdrawn from them about a stone's cast." Yes, company is good, but there are times when even the best company can hardly be borne.

But now let us reverently draw near and see this great sight, the Son of God in a tempest of mysterious internal commotion—"the bush burning, and the bush not consumed." Every word of the threefold record is weighty, every line of the picture awfully bright. "Let us put off the shoes from off our feet, for the place whereon we stand is holy ground." "He began," says Matthew, "to be sorrowful and very heavy," or, "to be sorrowful and oppressed" (Matt. 26:37). Mark uses the last of these words, but places before it one more remarkable: "He began to be sore amazed, and to be very heavy"; or better, perhaps, "to be appalled and to be oppressed" (Mark 14:33). Although through life He had been "a man of sorrows, and acquainted with grief," there is no ground to think that even the select-est circle of His followers was made privy to them, save on one occasion before this, after His final entry into Jerusalem, when, upon the Greeks "desiring to see Jesus"—which seems to have brought the hour of His "uplifting" overwhelmingly before Him—He exclaimed, "Now is my soul troubled, and what shall I say? Father, save me from this hour? But for this cause came I unto this hour. Father, glorify thy name" (John 12:27, 28). This was just *Gethsemane anticipated.* But now the tempest rose as never before. "He *began* to be sorrowful," as if till this moment unacquainted with grief. So new to Him, indeed, was the feeling, that Mark, using a singularly bold word, says, He was "appalled" at it; and under the joint action of this "sorrow" and "amazement," He was "very heavy," oppressed, weighed down—so much so that He was fain to tell it to the three He had taken aside, and most affectingly gave this as His reason for wishing their company: "My soul is exceeding sorrowful, even unto death: tarry ye here and watch with me." "I feel as if nature were sinking under this load—as if life were ebbing out—as if death were coming before its time—as if I could not survive this." It is usual to compare here such passages as that of Jonah (4:4), "I do well to be angry even unto death," and even some classical passages of similar import; but these are all too low. In dealing with such scenes as this, one feels as if even the most ordinary phraseology must be interpreted with reference to the unique circumstances of the case.

ADAM CLARKE

36. *A place called Gethsemane.* A garden at the foot of the Mount of Olives. The name seems to be formed from *gath,* "a press," and *shemen,* "oil"; probably the place where the produce of the mount of Olives was prepared for use. The garden of the oil press, or olive press.

37. *And he took with him Peter and the two sons of Zebedee.* That is, James and John, the same persons who had beheld His transfiguration on the mount—that they might contemplate this agony in the light of that glory which they had there seen, and so be kept from being stumbled by a view of His present humiliation. *And very heavy.* "Overwhelmed with anguish." This word is used by the Greeks to denote the most extreme anguish which the soul can feel—excruciating anxiety and torture of spirit.

ALEXANDER MACLAREN:

Is it permitted us to ask what were the fountains of these bitter floods that swept over Christ's sinless soul? Was the mere physical shrinking from death all? If so, we may reverently say that many a maiden and old man, who drew all their fortitude from Jesus, have gone to stake or gibbet for His sake, with a calm which contrasts strangely with His agitation. Gethsemane is robbed of its pathos and nobleness if that be all. But it was not all. Rather, it was the least bitter of the components of the cup. What lay before Him was not merely death, but the death which was to atone for a world's sin, and in which, therefore, the whole weight of sin's consequences was concentrated. "The Lord hath made to meet on Him the iniquities of us all"; that is the one sufficient explanation of this infinitely solemn and tender scene. Unless we believe that, we shall find it hard to reconcile His agitation in Gethsemane with the perfection of His character as the captain of "the noble army of martyrs."—*Expositions of Holy Scripture*

38. *My soul is exceeding sorrowful* (or "is surrounded with exceeding sorrow"), *even unto death.* This latter word explains the two former: My soul is so dissolved in sorrow, My spirit is filled with such agony and anguish, that, if speedy succor be not given to My body, death must be the speedy consequence.

MATTHEW HENRY

Tarry ye here, and watch with me. Surely he was destitute indeed of help, when he entreated theirs, who, he knew, would be but miserable comforters. It is good to have, and therefore good to seek, the assistance of our brethren, when at any time we are in an agony.

V. What passed between him and his Father when he was in this agony; *Being in an agony, he prayed.* Prayer is never out of season, but it is especially seasonable in an agony.

1. The place where he prayed; *He went a little further*, withdrew from them. He retired for prayer; a troubled soul finds most ease when it is alone with God, who understands the broken language of sighs and groans. Christ has hereby taught us that secret prayer must be made secretly.

2. His posture in prayer; *He fell on his face;* his lying prostrate denotes, (1) The agony he was in, and the extremity of his sorrow. (2) His humility in prayer.

3. The prayer itself; wherein we may observe three things.

(1) The title he gives to God; *O my Father*. Thick as the cloud was, he could see God as a Father through it. It is a pleasing string to harp upon at such a time, *My Father*; whither should the child go, when anything grieves him, but to his father?

(2) The favour he begs; *If it be possible, let this cup pass from me.* He calls his sufferings a *cup*; not a river, not a sea, but a cup, which we shall soon see the bottom of. When we are under troubles, we should make the best, the least, of them, and not aggravate them. He begs that this cup might *pass from him*, that is, that he might avoid the sufferings now at hand; or, at least, that they might be shortened. This intimates no more than that he was really and truly Man, and as a Man he could not but be averse to pain and suffering. A prayer of faith against an affliction, may very well consist with the patience of hope under affliction. But observe the proviso; *If it be possible.* If God may be glorified, man saved, and the ends of his undertaking answered, without his drinking of this bitter cup, he desires to be excused; otherwise not. What we cannot do with the securing of our great end, we must reckon to be in effect impossible; Christ did so.

(3) His entire submission to, and acquiescence in, the will of God; *Nevertheless, not as I will, but as thou wilt.* Our Lord Jesus, though he had a quick sense of the extreme bitterness of the sufferings he was to undergo, yet was freely willing to submit to them for our redemption and salvation. The reason of Christ's submission to his sufferings, was, his Father's will; *as thou wilt, v.* 39. He grounds his own willingness upon the Father's will. He did what he did, and did it with delight, because it was the will of God. This he had often referred to, as that which put him upon, and carried him through, his whole undertaking. In conformity to this example of Christ, we must drink of the bitter cup which God puts into our hands, be it ever so bitter; though nature struggle, grace must submit.

4. The repetition of the prayer; *He went away again the second time, and prayed* (*v.* 42), and again the third time (*v.* 44). Though we may pray to God to prevent and remove an affliction, yet our chief errand must be, that he will give us grace to bear it well. It should be more our care to get our troubles sanctified, and our hearts satisfied under them, than to get them taken away. *He prayed, saying, Thy will be done.* Prayer is the offering up, not only of our desires, but of our resignations, to God. The third time he *said the same words.* It should seem by *v.* 40 that he continued *an hour* in his agony and prayer; but, whatever more he said, it was to this effect, deprecating his approaching sufferings, and yet resigning himself to God's will in them.

But what answer had he to this prayer? Certainly it was not made in vain; he that heard him *always*, did not deny him *now.* It is true, the cup did not pass from him, but he had an answer to his prayer; for, *He was strengthened with strength in his soul*; and that was a real answer, Luke xxii. 43. In answer to his prayer, God provided that he should not fail or be discouraged.

VI. What passed between him and his three disciples at this time.

1. The fault they were guilty of; that when he was in his agony, they were so little concerned, that they could not keep awake; he comes, and *finds them asleep, v.* 40. Much more should their love to their Master, and their care concerning him, have obliged them to a more close and vigilant attendance on him; yet they were so dull, that they could not keep their eyes open. What had become of us, if Christ had been now as sleepy as his disciples were? Christ engaged them to watch with him, as if he expected

JAMIESON, FAUSSET, BROWN

What next? He "kneeled down," says Luke; He "fell on his face," says Matthew; or "fell on the ground," as Mark expresses it. Perhaps the kneeling posture was tried for a moment, but quickly became intolerable: and unable to bear up under a pressure of spirit which felt like the ebbing out of life itself, He was compelled to seek the dust! And now went up a cry such as never before ascended from this earth; no, not from those lips which dropped as a honeycomb; "O my Father, if it be possible, let this cup pass from me; nevertheless not as I will, but as thou wilt" (Matt. 26:39). The variations in Mark 14:36 and Luke 22:42 are worthy of note. Mark's double form of the invocation, "Abba, Father," we may pretty confidently conjecture was the very one our Lord used—the hallowed, endeared form of the mother tongue "Abba," followed emphatically by the term "Father," that of educated life (Rom. 8:15). Then Mark breaks up the one expression of Matthew, "If it be possible, let this cup pass," into these two, identical in meaning, "All things are possible unto thee; take away this cup"; while Luke's expression, "If thou be *willing* to remove this cup" (as in the Greek), shows that the "possibility" of the other two Evangelists was understood to be one purely of divine *will* or arrangement, insomuch that the one word came naturally to be interchanged with the other. (To suppose that our Lord used the identical words of all the three accounts is absurd.)

That *tears* accompanied this piercing cry is not reported by any of the Evangelists—who appear to give rigidly what was *seen* by the three favored disciples in the clear moonlight, and *heard* by them in the unbroken stillness of the night air of Gethsemane, ere sleep overpowered their exhausted frames. But those remarkable words in the Epistle to the Hebrews—which, though they seem to express what often took place, have, beyond all doubt, a special reference to this night of nights—leave no doubt of it, as a fact well known in the Christian churches, that on this occasion the tears of the Son of God fell fast upon the earth, while His cries rent the heavens: "Who in the days of his flesh, when he had offered up prayers and supplications, *with strong crying and tears*" (Heb. 5:7). Exquisite here are the words of old Traill, which, though before quoted, are peculiarly appropriate here: "He filled the silent night with His crying, and watered the cold earth with His tears, more precious than the dew of Hermon, or any moisture, next unto His own blood, that ever fell on God's earth since the creation."

But now let us listen to the cry itself. "The cup" to which the Son of God was so averse—"the cup," the very prospect of drinking which so appalled and oppressed Him—"the cup," for the removal of which, if it were possible, He prayed so affectingly—that cup was assuredly no other than the death He was about to die. When He says, "If it be possible, let this cup pass from me," He tells me He didn't like it, and couldn't like it; its ingredients were too bitter, too revolting; but when He says, "Nevertheless, not my will, but thine be done," He proclaims in my ear His absolute obedient subjection to the Father. This view of the cup quite changed its character, and by the expulsive power of a new affection—I will not say, turned its bitterness into sweetness, for I see no signs of sweetness even in that sense, but—absorbed and dissolved His natural repugnance to drink it up.

But to return to the conflict, whose crisis is yet to come. Getting a momentary relief—for the agitation of His spirit seems to have come upon Him by surges—He returns to the three disciples, and finding them sleeping, He chides them, particularly Peter, in terms deeply affecting: "He saith unto Peter, What! could ye not watch with me one hour?" In Mark (which may almost be called Peter's own Gospel) this is particularly affecting, "He saith unto Peter, Simon, sleepest thou? Couldest not thou watch one hour? Watch ye and pray, lest ye enter into temptation. The spirit truly is ready, but the flesh is weak." How considerate

ADAM CLARKE

39. *This cup.* The word *cup* is frequently used in the Sacred Writings to point out sorrow, anguish, terror, death. It seems to be an allusion to a very ancient method of punishing criminals. A cup of poison was put into their hands, and they were obliged to drink it. Socrates was killed thus, being obliged by the magistrates of Athens to drink a cup of the juice of hemlock.

42. *O my Father, if this cup may not pass away from me.* If it be not possible to redeem fallen man unless I drink this cup, unless I suffer death for them; *thy will be done*—I am content to suffer whatever may be requisite to accomplish the great design. In this address the humanity of Christ most evidently appears, for it was His humanity alone that could suffer.

44. *Prayed the third time.* So Paul wrote: "I besought the Lord thrice, that it might depart from me" (2 Cor. xii. 8). This *thrice* repeating the same petition argues deep earnestness of soul.

MATTHEW HENRY

some succour from them, and yet they slept; surely it was the unkindest thing that could be. His enemies, who watched for him, were wakeful enough (Mark xiv. 43); but his disciples, who should have watched with him, were asleep.

2. Christ's favour to them, notwithstanding. Persons in sorrow are too apt to be cross and peevish with those about them, but Christ in his agony is as meek as ever and is not apt to take things ill.

When Christ's disciples put this slight upon him,

(1) *He came to them*, as if he expected to receive some comfort from them. They added grief to his sorrow; and yet he came to them, more careful for them than they were for themselves; when he was most engaged, yet he came to look after them; for those that were given him, were upon his heart, living and dying.

(2) He gave them a gentle reproof; he directed it to Peter, who used to *speak* for them; let him now *hear* for them. *What! could ye not watch with me one hour?* He speaks as one amazed to see them so stupid. Consider, [1] Who *they* were; "Could not *ye* watch—ye, my disciples and followers? From you I expected better things." [2] Who *he* was; "Watch with *me*." He awoke out of his sleep, to help them when they were in distress (*ch.* viii. 36); and could not they keep awake, at least to show their goodwill to him? [3] How small a thing it was that he expected from them—only to *watch with him*. If he had bid them do some great thing, or die with him, they thought they could have done it; and yet they could not do it, when he only desired them to *watch with him*. [4] How short a time it was that he expected it—but *one hour*; they were not set upon the guard whole nights, only *one hour*.

(3) He gave them good counsel; *Watch and pray, that ye enter not into temptation, v.* 41. There was an hour of temptation drawing on, and very near; the troubles of Christ were temptations to his followers to disbelieve and distrust him, to deny and desert him, and renounce all relation to him. There was danger of their entering into the temptation, as into a snare or trap. He therefore exhorts them to watch and pray; *Watch with me, and pray with me.* While they were sleeping, they lost the benefit of joining in Christ's prayer. "Watch *yourselves*, and pray *yourselves. Pray* that you may *watch*; beg of God by his grace to keep you awake, now that there is occasion."

(4) He kindly excused for them; *The spirit indeed is willing, but the flesh is weak.* We do not read of one word they had to say for themselves; but then he had a tender word to say on their behalf; in this he sets us an example of that love *which covers a multitude of sins.* He considered their frame, and did not chide them, for he remembered that they were but flesh; *and the flesh is weak, though the spirit be willing.* It is the unhappiness and burthen of Christ's disciples, that their bodies cannot keep pace with their souls in works of piety and devotion, but are many a time a cloud and clog to them; that, when the spirit is free and disposed to that which is good, the flesh is averse and indisposed. Yet it is our comfort, that our Master graciously considers this, and accepts the willingness of the spirit, and pities and pardons the weakness and infirmity of the flesh; for *we are under grace, and not under the law.*

(5) Though they continued dull and sleepy, he did not any further rebuke them for it; for, though we daily offend, yet he will not always chide. When he came to them the second time, we do not find that he said anything to them (*v.* 43); *he findeth them asleep again.* One would have thought that he had said enough to them to keep them awake; but it is hard to recover from a spirit of slumber. *Their eyes were heavy*, which intimates that they strove against it as much as they could, but were overcome by it, and therefore their Master looked upon them with compassion. When he came the third time, he left them to be alarmed with the approaching danger (*v.* 45, 46); *Sleep on now, and take your rest.* See here how Christ deals with those that suffer themselves to be overcome by security, and will not be awakened out of it. Sometimes he gives them up to the power of it; *Sleep on now.* He that will sleep, let him sleep still. The curse of spiritual slumber is the just punishment of the sin of it. Many times he sends some startling judgment. Those who will not be alarmed by reasons and arguments, had better be alarmed by swords and spears than left to perish in their security. Let those that would not believe, be made to feel.

As to the disciples here, their Master gave them notice of the near approach of his enemies. *The Son of man is betrayed into the hands of sinners.* And again, *He is at hand that doth betray me.* Christ's sufferings were no surprise to him. He called them to rise, and be going: not, "Rise, and let us flee

JAMIESON, FAUSSET, BROWN

and compassionate this allusion to the weakness of the flesh was at that moment, appears by the explanation which Luke gives of the cause of it—an explanation beautifully in accordance with his profession as "the beloved physician" (Col. 4:4)—"that he found them sleeping for sorrow" (Luke 22:45). What now? "Again he went away, and prayed, and spake the same words" (Mark 14:39). He had nothing more, it seems, and nothing else to say. But now the surges rise higher, beat more tempestuously, and threaten to overwhelm Him. To fortify Him against this, "there appeared an angel unto him from heaven, strengthening him": not to minister to Him spiritually, by supplies of heavenly light or comfort—of that He was to have none during this awful scene; nor if it had been otherwise, would it seem competent for an angel to convey it—but simply to sustain and brace up sinking nature for a yet hotter and fiercer struggle.

But again there is a lull; and returning to the three, "He found them asleep again (for their eyes were heavy), neither wist they what to answer him" (Mark 14:40) when He scolded them, perhaps in nearly the same terms. And now, once more, returning to His solitary spot, He "prayed the third time," saying the same words; but this time slightly varied. It is not now, "O my Father, if it be possible, let this cup pass from me"; but, "O my Father, *if this cup may not pass from me*, except I drink it, thy will be done." Had only one of these two forms of the petition occurred in the same Gospel, we might have thought that they were but verbal differences in the different reports of one and the same petition. But as they both occur in the same Gospel of Matthew, we are warranted in regarding the second as an intentional, and in that case momentous, modification of the first. The worst is over. The bitterness of death is past. He has *anticipated and rehearsed* His final conflict. The victory has now been won on the theater of an *invincible will*—to "give his life a ransom for many." He shall win it next on the arena of *the cross*, where it is to become an accomplished fact. "I *will* suffer" is the result of Gethsemane: "It is finished," bursts from the cross. Without the *deed*, the *will* had been all in vain. But His work was then consummated when into the palpable deed He carried the now manifested will—"by the which *will* we are sanctified through the offering of the body of Jesus Christ once for all" (Heb. 10:10).

At the close of the whole scene, returning once more to His three disciples, and finding them still sleeping, worn out with continued sorrow and racking anxiety, He says to them, with an irony of tender but deep emotion, "Sleep on now, and take your rest: behold, the hour is at hand, and the Son of man is betrayed into the hands of sinners. Rise, let us be going: behold, he is at hand that doth betray me" (Matt. 26:45, 46). While He yet spake, Judas appeared with his armed band, and so they proved miserable comforters, broken reeds. But thus in His whole work He was alone, and "of the people there was none with him."

ADAM CLARKE

40. ***He . . . saith unto Peter.*** **He addressed himself more particularly to this apostle because of the profession he had made, v. 33; as if He had said: "Is this the way you testify your affectionate attachment to Me? You all said you were ready to die with Me; *what*, then, cannot you *watch . . . one hour?*"**

41. ***That ye enter not into temptation. Watch*** **—that you be not taken unawares; *and pray*— that when it comes you may be enabled to bear it.**

45. ***Sleep on now, and take your rest.*** **Perhaps it might be better to read these words interrogatively, and paraphrase them thus: "Do you sleep on still?" My *hour*—in which I am to be delivered up, *is at hand;* therefore, now think of your own personal safety. *The Son of man is betrayed into the hands of sinners.* Viz., the Gentiles or heathens, who were generally distinguished by this appellation from the Jews.**

MATTHEW HENRY	JAMIESON, FAUSSET, BROWN	ADAM CLARKE

MATTHEW HENRY

from the danger"; but, "Rise, and let us go meet it". He intimates to them their folly, in sleeping away the time which they should have spent in preparation; now the event found them unready, and was a terror to them.

Verses 47-56

We are here told how the blessed Jesus was seized, and taken into custody; this followed immediately upon his agony, *while he yet spake*; for from the beginning to the close of his passion he had not the least intermission or breathing-time.

Now concerning the apprehension of the Lord Jesus,

I. Who the persons were, that were employed in it. Here was *Judas, one of the twelve*, at the head of this infamous guard: *he was guide to them that took Jesus* (Acts i. 16); without his help they could not have found him in this retirement. Here was *with him a great multitude*. This multitude was made up partly of a detachment out of the guards, these were Gentiles, *sinners*, as Christ calls them, *v.* 45. The rest were the servants and officers of the High Priest, and they were Jews; they that were at variance with each other, agreed against Christ.

II. How they were armed for this enterprise.

1. What weapons they were armed with; They came *with swords and staves*. They were not regular troops, but a tumultuous rabble. But wherefore is this ado? His hour being come for him to give up himself, all this force was needless. When a butcher goes into the field to take out a lamb for the slaughter, does he raise the militia, and come armed? No, he needs not; yet is there all this force used to seize the Lamb of God.

2. What warrant they were armed with; *They came from the chief priests, and elders of the people*. He was taken up by a warrant from the great sanhedrim, as a person obnoxious to them. Pilate, the Roman governor, gave them no warrant; but they were men who pretended to religion, and presided in the affairs of the church, that were active in this prosecution, and were the most spiteful enemies Christ had. Pilate upbraided him with it; *Thine own nation and the chief priests delivered thee to me*, John xviii. 35.

III. The manner how it was done, and what passed at that time.

1. How Judas betrayed him; he did his business effectually, and his resolution in this wickedness may shame us who fail in that which is good.

(1) The instructions he gave to the soldiers (*v.* 48). He *gave them a sign*, lest by mistake they should seize one of the disciples instead of him. *That same is he;* and when they had him in their hands, not to lose him—*Hold him fast*; for he had sometimes escaped from those who thought to secure him; as Luke iv. 30. And Judas by his kiss intended not only to distinguish him, but to detain him, while they came behind him, and laid hands on him.

(2) The dissembling compliment he gave his Master. He came close up to Jesus; surely when he comes to look him in the face, he will either be awed by its majesty, or charmed by its beauty. Dares he to come into his very sight and presence, to betray him? Peter denied Christ, but when *the Lord turned and looked* upon him, he relented presently; but Judas comes up to his Master's face, and betrays him. He said, *Hail, Master; and kissed him.* A kiss is a token of allegiance and friendship. But Judas, when he broke all the laws of love and duty, profaned this sacred sign to serve his purpose.

(3) The entertainment his Master gave him, *v.* 50. He calls him *friend*. He would teach us under the greatest provocation to forbear bitterness. He calls him *friend*, because he furthered his sufferings, and so *befriended* him; whereas, he called Peter *Satan* for attempting to hinder them. He asks him, "*Wherefore art thou come?* Is it peace, Judas? Explain thyself; if thou come as an enemy, what means this kiss? If as a friend, what mean these swords and staves? *Wherefore art thou present?* Why hadst thou not so much shame left thee, as to keep out of sight, which thou mightest have done, and yet have given the officers notice where I was?"

2. How the officers and soldiers secured him; *Then came they, and laid hands on Jesus, and took him;* they made him their prisoner. We may well imagine what rude and cruel hands they were, which this barbarous multitude laid on Christ; and now, it is probable, they handled him the more roughly for their being so often disappointed when they sought to lay hands on him. They could not have taken him, if he had not surrendered himself, and been *delivered by the determinate counsel and foreknowledge of God*, Acts ii. 23.

Our Lord Jesus was made a prisoner, because he

JAMIESON, FAUSSET, BROWN

47-56. BETRAYAL AND APPREHENSION OF JESUS—FLIGHT OF HIS DISCIPLES. (=Mark 14:43-52; Luke 22:47-54; John 18:1-12). For the exposition, see on John 18:1-12.

Judas . . . knew the place, for Jesus ofttimes—see ch. 8:1; Luke 21:37—**resorted thither with his disciples**—The baseness of this abuse of knowledge in Judas, derived from admission to the closest privacies of his Master, is most touchingly conveyed here, though nothing beyond bare narrative is expressed. Jesus, however, knowing that in this spot Judas would expect to find Him, instead of avoiding it, hies Him thither, as a Lamb to the slaughter. "No man taketh My life from Me, but I lay it down of Myself" (ch. 10:18). Besides, the scene which was to fill up the little breathing-time, the awful interval, between the Supper and the Apprehension—like the "silence in heaven for about the space of half an hour" between the breaking of the Apocalyptic Seals and the peal of the Trumpets of war (Rev. 8:1)—the AGONY—would have been too terrible for the upper room; nor would He cloud the delightful associations of the *last Passover* and the *first Supper* by pouring out the anguish of His soul there. The garden, however, with its amplitude, its shady olives, its endeared associations, would be congenial to His heart. Here He had room enough to retire—first, from eight of them, and then from the more favored three; and here, when that mysterious scene was over, the stillness would only be broken by the tread of the traitor.

Judas then—"He that was called Judas, one of the Twelve," says Luke, in language which brands him with peculiar infamy, as *in* the sacred circle while in no sense *of* it. **a band of men**—"the *detachment* of the Roman cohort on duty at the festival for the purpose of maintaining order" [WEBSTER and WILKINSON]. **officers from the chief priests and Pharisees**—captains of the temple and armed Levites. **lanterns and torches**—It was full moon, but in case He should have secreted Himself somewhere in the dark ravine, they bring the means of exploring its hiding-places—little knowing whom they had to do with. "Now he that betrayed Him had given them a sign, saying, Whomsoever I shall kiss, that same is He, hold Him fast" (Matt. 26:48). The cold-bloodedness of this speech was only exceeded by the deed itself. "And Judas went before them [Luke 22:47], and forthwith he came to Jesus, and said, Hail, Master, and kissed Him" (Matt. 26:49; cf. Exod. 4:27; 18:7; Luke 7:45). The impudence of this atrocious deed shows how thoroughly he had by this time mastered all his scruples. If the dialogue between our Lord and His captors was *before* this, as some interpreters think it was, the kiss of Judas was purely gratuitous, and probably to make good his right to the money; our Lord having presented Himself unexpectedly before them, and rendered it unnecessary for any one to point Him out. But a comparison of the narratives seems to show that our Lord's "coming forth" to the band was *subsequent* to the interview of Judas. "And Jesus said unto him, Friend"—not the endearing term "friend" (in ch. 15:15), but "companion," a word used on occasions of remonstrance or rebuke (as in Matt. 20:13; 22:12)—"Wherefore art thou come?" (Matt. 26:50). "Betrayest thou the Son of man with a kiss"—imprinting upon the foulest act the mark of tenderest affection? What *wounded feeling* does this express! Of this Jesus showed Himself on various occasions keenly susceptible—as all generous and beautiful natures do.

ADAM CLARKE

46. *Rise, let us be going.* That is, to meet them, giving thereby the fullest proof that I know all their designs and might have, by flight or otherwise, provided for My own safety. But I go willingly to meet that death which their malice designs Me, and through it provide for the life of the world.

47. *Judas, one of the twelve.* More deeply to mark his base ingratitude and desperate wickedness. *A great multitude with swords and staves.* They did not come as officers of justice but as a desperate mob.

48. *Gave them a sign.* How coolly deliberate is this dire apostate! The man whom *I shall kiss*—how deeply hypocritical! That is He; *hold him fast,* "seize Him"—how diabolically malicious!

49. *Hail, master.* A usual compliment among the Jews. Judas pretends to wish our Lord continued health while he is meditating His destruction! *And kissed him.* "And tenderly kissed Him"—this is the proper meaning of the original word. He kissed Him again and again—still pretending the most affectionate attachment to Him, though our Lord had before unmasked him.

50. *Jesus said unto him, Friend* (rather, "companion"), *wherefore art thou come?* How must these words have cut his very soul, if he had any sensibility left! Surely you, who have so long been My companion, are not come against Me, your Lord, Teacher, and Friend! What is the human heart not capable of, when abandoned by God, and influenced by Satan and the love of money!

MATTHEW HENRY

would in all things be treated as a malefactor, punished for our crime. He became a prisoner, that he might set us at liberty; for he said, *If ye seek me, let these go their way* (John xviii. 8); and those are free indeed, whom he makes so.

3. How Peter fought for Christ, and was checked for his pains. It is here only said to be *one of them that were with Jesus in the garden*; but in John xviii. 10, we are told that it was Peter who signalized himself upon this occasion.

(1) Peter's rashness (*v.* 51); He *drew his sword.* They had but two swords among them all (Luke xxii. 38), and one of them, it seems, fell to Peter's share; and now he thought it was time to draw it. But all the execution he did was the cutting off an ear from a servant of the High Priest; designing, it is likely, to cleave him down the head, he missed his blow. Peter had talked much of what he would do for his Master, he would *lay down his life for him*; yea, that he would; and now he would be as good as his word, and venture his life to rescue his Master. He had a great *zeal* for Christ, and his honour and safety; but it was not *according to knowledge*, nor guided by discretion; he did it without warrant. We must see not only our cause good, but our call clear, before we draw the sword. He indiscreetly exposed himself and his fellow-disciples to the rage of the multitude; for what could they with two swords do against a band of men?

(2) The rebuke which our Lord Jesus gave him (*v.* 52); *Put up again thy sword into its place.* He commands Peter to put up his sword, does not chide him indeed for what he had done, because done out of goodwill, but stops the progress of his arms. Christ's errand into the world was to make peace. As Christ forbade his disciples the sword of justice (*ch.* xx. 25, 26), so here the sword of war. Christ bade Peter put up his sword, and never bade him draw it again.

Three reasons Christ gives to Peter for this rebuke:

[1] His drawing the sword would be dangerous to himself and to his fellow-disciples; *They that take the sword, shall perish with the sword;* they that use violence, fall by violence; and men hasten and increase their own troubles by blustering bloody methods of self-defence. Grotius gives another, and a probable sense of this blow, making those that take the sword to be, not Peter, but the officers and soldiers that come with swords *to take Christ*; They shall *perish with the sword.* They took the Roman sword to seize Christ with, and by the Roman sword, not long after, they and their place and nation were destroyed.

[2] It was needless for him to draw his sword in defence of his Master, who, if he pleased, could summon into his service all the hosts of heaven (*v.* 53); *"Thinkest thou that I cannot now pray to my Father, and he shall send* from heaven effectual succours? Peter, if I would put by these sufferings, I could easily do it without thy hand or thy sword." Note, God has no need of us, of our services, much less of our sins, to bring about his purposes. God can do his work without us. Though Christ was crucified through weakness, it was a voluntary weakness; he submitted to death, not because he could not, but because he would not contend with it. Christ here lets us know,

First, What a great interest he had in his Father; *I can pray to my Father, and he will send me help.* It is a great comfort to God's people, when they are surrounded with enemies on all hands, that they have a way open heavenward; if they can do nothing else, they can pray to him that can do everything. And they who are much in prayer at other times, have most comfort in praying when troublesome times come. Christ saith, not only that God could, but that, if he insisted upon it, he would do it. He might yet have gone out free from the service, but he loved it, and would not; so that it was only with the cords of his own love that he was bound to the altar.

Secondly, What a great interest he had in the heavenly hosts; *He shall presently give me more than twelve legions of angels. a.* There is an *innumerable company of angels*, Heb. xii. 22. *b.* This innumerable company of angels are all at the disposal of our heavenly Father, and do his pleasure, Ps. ciii. 20, 21. *c.* These angelic hosts were ready to come in to the assistance of our Lord Jesus in his sufferings, if he had needed or desired it. *He shall give them me;* therefore angels are not to be prayed to, but the Lord of the angels. He shall *presently* give them me. See how ready his Father was to hear his prayer.

[3] It was no time to make any defence at all, or to offer to put by the stroke; *For how then shall the scriptures be fulfilled, that thus it must be? v.* 54. It was written, that Christ should be *led as a lamb*

JAMIESON, FAUSSET, BROWN

10, 11. Then Simon Peter, having a sword, drew it, and smote the high priest's servant, and cut off his right ear. The servant's name was Malchus–None of the other Evangelists mention the name either of the ardent disciple or of his victim. John being "known to the high priest" (vs. 15), the mention of the servant's name by *him* is quite natural, and an interesting mark of truth in a small matter. As to the *right* ear, specified both here and in Luke, the man was "likely foremost of those who advanced to seize Jesus, and presented himself in the attitude of a combatant; hence his right side would be exposed to attack. The blow of Peter was evidently aimed vertically at his head" [WESTER and WILKINSON].

Matthew adds to the address to Peter the following:–"For all they that take the sword shall perish by the sword" (Matt. 26:52)–i.e., 'Those who take the sword must run all the risks of human warfare; but Mine is a warfare whose weapons, as they are not carnal, are attended with no such hazards, but carry certain victory.'

"Thinkest thou that I cannot now"–even after things have proceeded so far–"pray to My Father, and He shall presently give Me"–rather, 'place at My disposal'–"more than twelve legions of angels"; with allusion, possibly, to the one angel who had, in His agony, "appeared to Him from heaven strengthening Him" (Luke 22:43); and in the precise number, alluding to the *twelve* who needed the help, Himself and His eleven disciples. (The full complement of a legion of Roman soldiers was six thousand.)

"But how then shall the scripture be fulfilled that thus it must be?" (Matt. 26:53, 54.) He could not suffer, according to the Scripture, if

ADAM CLARKE

51. *One of them which were with Jesus.* This was Peter—*struck a servant of the high priest's* (the servant's name was Malchus, John xviii. 10), *and smote off his ear.* In Luke xxii. 51 it is said, Jesus touched and healed it. Here was another miracle, and striking proof of the divinity of Christ.

52. *Put up again thy sword into his place.* Neither Christ nor His religion is to be defended by the secular arm. *Shall perish with the sword.* The general meaning of this verse is, they who contend in battle are likely, on both sides, to become the sacrifices of their mutual animosities. But it is probably a prophetic declaration of the Jewish and Roman states. The Jews put our Lord to death under the sanction of the Romans—both took the sword against Christ, and both perished by it. But how came Peter to have a sword? Judea was at this time so infested with robbers and cutthroats that it was not deemed safe for any person to go unarmed. He probably carried one for his mere personal safety.

53. *More than twelve legions of angels.* As if He had said, Instead of you twelve, one of whom is a traitor, My Father can give me *more than twelve legions of angels* to defend Me. A legion, at different times, contained different numbers; 4,200, 5,000, and frequently 6,000 men.

MATTHEW HENRY

to the slaughter, Isa. liii. 7. In all difficult cases, the word of God must be conclusive against our own counsels, and nothing must be done, nothing attempted, against the fulfilling of the scripture. We ought to say, "Let God's word and will take place, let his law be magnified and made honourable, whatever becomes of us." Thus Christ checked Peter, when he set up for his champion, and captain of his life-guard.

4. We are next told how Christ argued the case with them that came to take him (*v.* 55); though he did not resist them, yet he did reason with them. It will consist with Christian patience under our sufferings, calmly to expostulate with our enemies and persecutors. *Are ye come out*, (1) With rage and enmity, *as against a thief*, as if I were an enemy to the public safety, and deservedly suffered this? If he had been the plague of his country, he could not have been prosecuted with more heat and violence. (2) With all this power and force, as against the worst of thieves, that dare the law, bid defiance to public justice, and add rebellion to their sin?

He further expostulates with them, by reminding them how he had behaved himself hitherto toward them, and they toward him. *I sat daily with you in the temple teaching. Ye laid no hold on me.* How comes then this change? They were very unreasonable, in treating him as they did. He had given them no occasion to look upon him as a thief, for he had taught in the temple. Such gracious words as came from his mouth, were not the words of a thief, nor of one that had a devil. Nor had he given them occasion to look upon him as one that absconded, or fled from justice, that they should come in the night to seize him. They might find him every day in the temple, and there they might do as they pleased with him; for the chief priests had the custody of the temple. To come upon him thus clandestinely, in the place of his retirement, was base and cowardly. Thus the greatest hero may be villainously assassinated in a corner, by one that in open field would tremble to look him in the face.

But all this was done (so it follows, *v.* 56) *that the scriptures of the prophets might be fulfilled.* It is hard to say, whether these are the words of the sacred historian, as a comment upon this story, or, whether they are the words of Christ himself, that the scriptures of the prophets might be fulfilled, to which he had just now referred himself, *v.* 54.

5. How he was, in the midst of this distress, shamefully deserted by his disciples; *They all forsook him, and fled, v.* 56.

(1) This was their sin; and it was a great sin for them who had left all to follow him, now to leave him for they knew not what. There was unkindness in it. There was unfaithfulness in it, for they had solemnly promised to adhere to him, and never to forsake him.

(2) It was a part of Christ's suffering, it added affliction to his bonds, to be thus deserted. They should have stayed with him, to minister to him, and, if need were, to be witnesses for him at his trial. Christ, as a sacrifice for sins, stood thus abandoned. The deer that by the keeper's arrow is marked out to be hunted and run down, is immediately deserted by the whole herd. Christ, as the Saviour of souls, stood thus alone. He bore all, and did all himself.

Verses 57-68

We have here the arraignment of our Lord Jesus in the ecclesiastical court, before the great sanhedrim. Observe,

I. The sitting of the court; the scribes and the elders were assembled, though it was in the dead time of the night; yet, to gratify their malice against Christ, they sat up all night, to be ready to fall upon the prey.

1. Who they were, that were assembled; the *scribes*, the principal teachers, and *elders*, the principal rulers, of the Jewish church: these were the most bitter enemies to Christ our great teacher and ruler. 2. Where they were assembled; *in the palace of Caiaphas the High Priest*; there they assembled two days before, to lay the plot (*v.* 3), and there they now convened again, to prosecute it. His house should have been the sanctuary of oppressed innocency, but it is become the throne of iniquity; and no wonder, when even God's house of prayer was made a den of thieves.

II. The setting of the prisoner to the bar; they that had *laid hold on Jesus, led him away*, hurried him, no doubt, with violence. He was brought into Jerusalem through that which was called the *sheep-gate*, for that was the way into town from the mount of Olives; and it was so called because the sheep appointed for sacrifice were brought that way to the temple; very fitly therefore is Christ led that way.

III. The cowardice and faint-heartedness of Peter (*v.* 58).

JAMIESON, FAUSSET, BROWN

He allowed Himself to be delivered from the predicted death. "And He touched his ear and healed him" (Luke 22:51); for "the Son of man came not to destroy men's lives, but to save them" (Luke 9. 56), and, even while they were destroying His, to save theirs.

"In that hour," says Matthew (26:55, 56), and probably now, on the way to judgment. when the crowds were pressing upon Him, "said Jesus to the multitudes, Are ye come out as against a thief, with swords and staves, for to take Me"—expressive of the indignity which He felt to be thus done to Him—"I sat daily with you in the temple, and ye laid no hold on Me. But this" (adds Luke 22:53) "is your hour and the power of darkness." Matthew continues—"But all this was done that the scriptures of the prophets might be fulfilled. Then all the disciples forsook Him and fled" (Matt. 26:56)—thus fulfilling His prediction (Mark 14:27; ch. 16:32).

57-75. Jesus Arraigned before the Sanhedrim, Condemned to Die, and Shamefully Entreated—The Denial of Peter. (=Mark 14:53-72; Luke 22:54-71; John 18:13-18, 24-27.) For the exposition, see on Mark 14:53-72.

And they led Jesus away to the high priest: and with him were assembled—or rather, "there gathered together unto him"—**all the chief priests and the elders and the scribes**—it was then a full and formal meeting of the Sanhedrim. Now, as the first three Evangelists place all Peter's denials of his Lord after this, we should naturally conclude that they took place *while our Lord stood before the Sanhedrim.* But besides that the natural impression is that the scene around the fire took place *overnight*, the *second crowing of the cock*, if we are to credit ancient writers, would occur about the beginning of the fourth watch, or between three and four in the morning. By that time, however, the Council had probably convened, being warned, perhaps, that they were to prepare for being called at any hour of the morning, should the Prisoner be successfully secured. If this be correct, it is fairly certain that only the *last* of Peter's three denials would take place while our Lord was under trial before the Sanhedrim. One thing more may require explanation. If our Lord had to be transferred from the residence of Annas to that of Caiaphas, one is apt to wonder that there

ADAM CLARKE

54. *But how then*—had I such a defense—*shall the scriptures be fulfilled*, which say *that thus it must be?* That is, that I am to suffer and die for the sin of the world. Probably the scriptures to which our Lord principally refers are Psalms xxii; lxix; and especially Isaiah liii and Dan. ix. 24-27. Christ shows that they had no power against Him but what He permitted, and that He willingly gave up himself into their hands.

56. *But all this was done.* This is probably the observation of the Evangelist. *Then all the disciples forsook him, and fled.* He had but twelve who professed inviolable attachment to Him. One of these betrayed Him; another denied Him with oaths; and the rest ran away and utterly abandoned Him to His implacable enemies!

57. *They . . . led him away to Caiaphas.* John says, chap. xviii. 13, that they led him first to Annas; but this appears to have been done merely to do him honor as the father-in-law of Caiaphas, and his colleague in the high priesthood. But as the Sanhedrin was assembled at the house of Caiaphas, it was there He must be brought to undergo His mock trial.

MATTHEW HENRY

1. He followed him, but it was *afar off*. Some sparks of love and concern for his Master there were in his breast, and therefore he followed him; but fear and concern for his own safety prevailed, and therefore he followed afar off. It looks ill, and bodes worse, when those that are willing to be Christ's disciples, are not willing to be known to be so. To follow him afar off, is by little and little to go back from him. There is danger in drawing back, nay, in looking back.

2. He followed him, but he *went in, and sat with the servants*. He went in where there was a good fire, and sat with the servants, not to silence their reproaches, but to screen himself. It was presumption in Peter thus to thrust himself into temptation; he that does so, throws himself out of God's protection.

3. He followed him, but it was only to *see the end*, led more by his curiosity than by his conscience; he attended as an idle spectator rather than as a disciple. He went in, only to look about him; it is not unlikely that Peter went in, expecting that Christ would have made his escape miraculously out of the hands of his persecutors; having so lately struck them down, who came to seize him; and this he had a mind to see: if so, it was folly for him to think of seeing any other end than what Christ had foretold, that he should be put to death. It is more our concern to prepare for the end, whatever it may be, than curiously to enquire what the end will be. The event is God's, but the duty is ours.

IV. The trial of our Lord Jesus in this court.

1. They examined witnesses against him. The crimes properly cognizable in their court, were, false doctrine and blasphemy; these they endeavoured to prove upon him.

(1) Their search for proof; *They sought false witness against him*; they had seized him, bound him, abused him, and after all have to seek for something to lay to his charge, and can show no cause for his commitment. They made proclamation, that, if anyone could give information against the prisoner at the bar, they were ready to receive it, and presently many bore false witness against him (*v.* 60).

(2) Their success in this search; in several attempts they were baffled, they sought false testimonies among themselves, others came in to help them, and yet they found none.

But at last they met with *two* witnesses, who, it seems, agreed in their evidence, and therefore were hearkened to, in hopes that now the point was gained. The words they swore against him, were, that he should say, *I am able to destroy the temple of God, and to build it in three days, v.* 61. Now by this they designed to accuse him, [1] As an enemy to the temple, and one that sought for the destruction of it. [2] As one that dealt in witchcraft, or some such unlawful arts, by the help of which he could rear such a building in three days. Now, as to this, *First*, The words were mis-recited; he said, *Destroy ye this temple* (John ii. 19); they come, and swear that he said, *I am able to destroy* this temple, as if the design against it were his. He said, *In three days I will raise it up*, a word properly used of a living temple; *I will raise it to life*. They come, and swear that he said, *I am able to build it*; which is properly used of a house temple. *Secondly*, The words were misunderstood; *he spoke of the temple of his body* (John ii. 21), but they swore that he said the *temple of God*, meaning this holy place. There have been, and still are, such as *wrest* the sayings of Christ *to their own destruction*. He was accused, that we might not be condemned; and if at any time we suffer thus, have all manner of evil, not only said, but *sworn, against us falsely*, let us remember that we cannot expect to fare better than our Master.

(3) Christ's silence under all these accusations, to the amazement of the court, *v.* 62. The High Priest, the judge of the court, arose in some heat, and said, "*Answerest thou nothing?* Come, you the prisoner at the bar; you hear what is sworn against you, what have you now to say for yourself?" *But Jesus held his peace* (*v.* 63), not because he wanted something to say, or knew not how to say it, but that the scripture might be fulfilled (Isa. liii. 7); *As the sheep is dumb before the shearer*, and before the butcher, *so he opened not his mouth*. He was silent, because *his hour was come*; he would not deny the charge, because he was willing to submit to the sentence. He stood mute at this bar, that we might have something to say at God's bar.

2. They examined our Lord Jesus himself upon an oath. They will try, contrary to the law of equity, to make him accuse himself.

Here is the interrogatory put to him by the High Priest. The question itself; *Whether thou be the Christ, the Son of God?* That is, Whether thou pretend to be so? For they will by no means admit it into

JAMIESON, FAUSSET, BROWN

is no mention of His being marched from the one to the other. But the building, in all likelihood, was one and the same; in which case He would merely have to be taken perhaps across the court, from one chamber to another. **And Peter followed him afar off, even into**—or "from afar, even to the interior of"—**the palace of the high priest**—"An Oriental house," says ROBINSON, "is usually built around a quadrangular interior court; into which there is a passage (sometimes arched) through the front part of the house, closed next the street by a heavy folding gate, with a smaller wicket for single persons, kept by a porter. The interior court, often paved or flagged, and open to the sky, is the *hall*, which our translators have rendered 'palace,' where the attendants made a fire; and the passage beneath the front of the house, from the street to this court, is the *porch*. The place where Jesus stood before the high priest may have been an open room, or place of audience on the groundfloor, in the rear or on one side of the court; such rooms, open in front, being customary. It was close upon the court, for Jesus heard all that was going on around the fire, and turned and looked upon Peter (Luke 22:61).

"And Peter stood with them and warmed himself." "He went in," says Matthew (26:58), "and sat with the servants *to see the end*." These two minute statements throw an interesting light on each other. His wishing to "see the end," or issue of these proceedings, was what led him into the palace, for he evidently feared the worst. But once in, the serpent-coil is drawn closer; it is a cold night, and why should not he take advantage of the fire as well as others? Besides, in the talk of the crowd about the all-engrossing topic he may pick up something which he would like to hear. Poor Peter! But now, let us leave him warming himself at the fire, and listening to the hum of talk about this strange case by which the subordinate officials, passing to and fro and crowding around the fire in this open court, would while away the time; and, following what appears the order of the Evangelical Narrative, let us turn to Peter's Lord.

And the chief priests and all the council sought for witness against Jesus to put him to death—Matthew (26:59) says they "sought *false* witness." They knew they could find nothing valid; but having their Prisoner to bring before Pilate, they behooved to *make a case*. **and found none**—none that would suit their purpose, or make a decent ground of charge before Pilate. **For many bare false witness against him**—From their debasing themselves to "*seek*" them, we are led to infer that they were *bribed* to bear false witness; though there are never wanting sycophants enough, ready to sell themselves for naught, if they may but get a smile from those above them: see a similar scene in Acts 6:11-14. How is one reminded here of that complaint, "False witnesses did rise up: they laid to my charge things that I knew not" (Ps. 31:11)! "*At the last* came two false witnesses." As no two had before agreed in anything, they felt it necessary to secure a duplicate testimony to something, but they were long of succeeding. And what was it, when at length it was brought forward? **saying, We heard him say, I will destroy this temple that is made with hands, and within three days I will build another made without hands**—On this charge, observe, first, that eager as His enemies were to find criminal matter against our Lord, they had to go back to the outset of His ministry, His first visit to Jerusalem, more than three years before this. In all that He said and did after that, though ever increasing in boldness, they could find nothing. Next, that even then, they fix only on one speech, of two or three words, which they dared to adduce against Him. Further, they most manifestly pervert the speech of our Lord.

Answerest thou nothing? what is it which these witness against thee?—Clearly, they felt that *their case had failed*, and by this artful question the high priest hoped to get *from His own mouth* what they had in vain tried to obtain from their false and contradictory witnesses. But in this, too, they failed. **But he held his peace, and answered nothing**—This must have nonplussed them. But they were not to be easily baulked of their object. **Again the high priest**—arose (Matt. 26:62), matters having now come to a crisis. **asked him, and said unto him, Art thou the Christ, the Son of the Blessed?**—Why our Lord should have answered this question, when He was silent as to the former, we might not have quite seen, but for Matthew,

ADAM CLARKE

58. *Peter followed him afar off*. Poor Peter! This is the beginning of his dreadful fall. His fear kept him from joining the company and publicly acknowledging his Lord, and his affection obliged him to follow at a distance that he might see the end. *And sat with the servants, to see the end*. When a man is weak in faith and can as yet only follow Christ at a distance, he should avoid all dangerous places and the company of those who are most likely to prove a snare to him.

59. *All the council, sought false witness*. What a prostitution of justice! They first resolve to ruin Him, and then seek the proper means of effecting it; they declare Him criminal, and after that do all they can to fix some crime upon Him, that they may appear to have some shadow of justice on their side when they put Him to death.

61. *I am able to destroy the temple of God*. (1) These words were not fairly quoted. Jesus had said, John ii. 19, "Destroy this temple, and in three days I will raise it up." (2) The innuendo which they produce, applying these words to a pretended design to destroy the temple at Jerusalem, was utterly unfair; for these words He spoke of the temple of His body.

MATTHEW HENRY

consideration, whether he be really so or no. They only wished him to confess that he called himself so, that they might on that indict him as a deceiver. What will not pride and malice carry men to? The solemnity of the proposal of it; *I adjure thee by the living God, that thou tell us.* Not that he had any regard to the living God, but took his name in vain; only thus he hoped to gain his point with our Lord Jesus. If he should refuse to answer when he was thus adjured, they would charge him with contempt of the blessed name of God.

Christ's answer to this interrogatory (*v.* 64), in which,

(1) He owns himself to be *the Christ the Son of God. Thou hast said;* that is, "It is as thou hast said"; for in St. Mark it is, *I am.* Hitherto, he seldom professed himself expressly to be the Christ, the Son of God; but now he would not omit to make a confession of it, *First,* Because that would have looked like a disowning of that truth which he came into the world to bear witness to. *Secondly,* It would have looked like declining his sufferings. He thus confessed himself, for example and encouragement to his followers, when they are called to it, to *confess him before men,* whatever hazards they run by it.

(2) He refers himself, for the proof of this, to his second coming. It is probable that they looked upon him with a scornful disdainful smile, when he said, *I am.* To that this *nevertheless* refers. "Though now you see me in this low and abject state, *nevertheless* the day is coming when I shall appear otherwise." *Hereafter ye shall see the Son of man sitting on the right hand of power, to judge the world;* of which his coming shortly to judge and destroy the Jewish nation would be a type and earnest. *First,* Whom they should see; *the Son of man.* Having owned himself the Son of God, even now in his estate of humiliation, he speaks of himself as the Son of man, even in his estate of exaltation; for he had these two distinct natures in one person. He is *Immanuel,* God with us. *Secondly,* In what posture they should see him; *Sitting on the right hand of power.* Though now he stood at the bar, they should shortly see him sit on the throne. *Coming in the clouds of heaven.* He had spoken of this day to his disciples, a while ago, for their comfort, and had bid them *lift up their heads* for joy in the prospect of it, Luke xxi. 27, 28. Now he speaks of it to his enemies, for their terror.

V. His conviction upon this trial; *The High Priest rent his clothes,* according to the custom of the Jews, when they heard or saw anything done or said which they looked upon to be a reproach to God.

1. The crime he was found guilty of; *blasphemy. He hath spoken blasphemy.* Christ, when *he was made Sin for us,* was condemned as a blasphemer for the truth he told them.

2. The evidence upon which they found him guilty; *Ye have heard the blasphemy;* why should we trouble ourselves to examine *witnesses* any further? Thus was he *judged out of his own mouth* at their bar, because we were liable to be so judged at God's bar. There is no need of witnesses against us; our own consciences are against us instead of a thousand witnesses.

VI. His sentence passed, upon this conviction, *v.* 66.

Here is, 1. Caiaphas's appeal to the bench; *What think ye?* When he had already prejudged the cause, and pronounced him a blasphemer, then, as if he were willing to be advised, he asks the judgment of his brethren. He knew that by the authority of his place he could sway the rest, and therefore declares his judgment, and presumes they are all of his mind.

2. Their concurrence with him; they said, *He is guilty of death;* perhaps they did not all concur: it is certain that Joseph of Arimathea, if he was present, dissented (Luke xxiii. 51); so did Nicodemus, and, it is likely, others with them; however, the majority carried it that way. The judgment was, "*He is guilty of death;* by the law he deserves to die." Though they had not power now to put any man to death, yet by such a judgment as this they made a man an *outlaw* among his people, and so exposed him to the fury either of a popular tumult, as Stephen was, or to be clamoured against before the governor, as Christ was.

VII. The abuses and indignities done to him after sentence passed (*v.* 67, 68); *Then,* when he was found guilty, they *spat in his face.* Because they had not power to put him to death, and could not be sure that they should prevail with the governor to be their executioner, they would do him all the mischief they could, now that they had him in their hands. When they had passed sentence upon our Lord Jesus, he was treated as if he were not only *worthy of death,* but as if that were too good for him. See how they

JAMIESON, FAUSSET, BROWN

who says (26:63) that the high priest *put Him upon solemn oath,* saying, "I adjure Thee by the living God, that Thou tell us whether Thou be the Christ, the Son of God." Such an adjuration was understood to render an answer legally necessary (Lev. 5:1). **And Jesus said, I am**—or, as in Matthew 26:64, "Thou hast said [it]." In Luke, however (22:70), the answer, "Ye say that I am," should be rendered—as DE WETTE, MEYER, ELLICOTT, and the best critics agree that the preposition requires—"Ye say [it], for I am [so]." Some words, however, were spoken by our Lord before giving His answer to this solemn question. These are recorded by Luke alone (22:67, 68): "Art Thou the Christ [they asked]? tell us. And He said unto them, If I tell you, ye will not believe: and if I also ask [interrogate] "you, ye will not answer Me, nor let Me go." This seems to have been uttered before giving His direct answer, as a calm remonstrance and dignified protest against the prejudgment of His case and the unfairness of their mode of procedure. But now let us hear the rest of the answer, in which the conscious majesty of Jesus breaks forth from behind the dark cloud which overhung Him as He stood before the Council. **and**—in that character—**ye shall see the Son of man sitting on the right hand of power, and coming in the clouds of heaven**—In Matthew (26:64) a slightly different but interesting turn is given to it by one word: "Thou hast said [it]: nevertheless"—We prefer this sense of the word to "besides," which some recent critics decide for—"I say unto you, Hereafter shall ye see the Son of man sit on the right hand of power, and coming in the clouds of heaven." The word rendered "hereafter" means, not "at some future time" (as today "hereafter commonly does), but what the English word originally signified, "after here," "after now," or "from this time." Accordingly, in Luke 22:69, the words used mean "from now." So that though the reference we have given it to the day of His glorious Second Appearing is too obvious to admit of doubt, He would, by using the expression, "From this time," convey the important thought which He had before expressed, immediately after the traitor left the supper-table to do his dark work, "*Now* is the Son of man glorified" (John 13:31). At this moment, and by this speech, did He "witness *the* good confession" emphatically and properly, as the apostle says in I Timothy 6:13.

Then the high priest rent his clothes—On this expression of *horror of blasphemy,* see II Kings 18:37—**and saith, What need we any further witnesses? Ye have heard the blasphemy**—(See John 10:33). In Luke (22:71), "For we ourselves have heard of His own mouth"—an affectation of religious horror. **what think ye?**—'Say what the verdict is to be.' **they all condemned him to be guilty of death**—or of a capital crime, which *blasphemy* against God was according to the Jewish law (Lev. 24:16). Yet *not absolutely all;* for *Joseph* of Arimathea, "a good man and a just," was one of that Council, and "*he was not a consenting party* to the counsel and deed of them," for that is the strict sense of the words of Luke 23:50, 51. Probably he absented himself, and *Nicodemus* also, from this meeting of the Council, the temper of which they would know too well to expect their voice to be listened to; and in that case, the words of our Evangelist are to be taken strictly, that, without one dissentient voice, "all [present] condemned him to be guilty of death."

ADAM CLARKE

63. ***I adjure thee by the living God.*** **I put Thee to Thy oath. To this solemn adjuration Christ immediately replies, because He is now called on, in the name of God, to bear another testimony to the truth.**

64. ***Thou hast said.*** **That is, I am the Christ, the promised Messiah (see on v. 25) and you and this whole nation shall shortly have the fullest proof of it. For *hereafter,* in a few years, *shall ye see the Son of man sitting on the right hand of power,* fully invested with absolute dominion, *and coming in the clouds of heaven,* to execute judgment upon this wicked race. Our Lord appears to refer to Dan. vii. 13: "One like the Son of man came with the clouds of heaven." This may also refer to the final judgment.**

65. ***The high priest rent his clothes.*** **This rending of the high priest's garments was expressly contrary to the law, Lev. x. 6 and xxi. 10. But it was a common method of expressing violent grief, Gen. xxxvii. 29, 34; Job i. 20, and horror at what was deemed blasphemous or impious, 2 Kings xviii. 37; xix. 1; Acts xiv. 14. All that heard a blasphemous speech were obliged to rend their clothes, and never to sew them up again.**

66. ***He is guilty of death.*** **"He is liable to death." All the forms of justice are here violated. The judge becomes a party and accuser, and proceeds to the verdict without examining whether all the prophecies concerning the Messiah and the innumerable miracles which He wrought did not justify Him.**

MATTHEW HENRY

abused him.

1. *They spat in his face.* It is an expression of the greatest contempt and indignation possible; looking upon him as more despicable than the very ground they spit upon. Yet Christ submitted to it. Thus was confusion poured upon his face, that ours might not be filled with everlasting shame and contempt.

2. *They buffeted him, and smote him with the palms of their hands.* This added pain to the shame, for both came in with sin. Here the margin reads it, *They smote him with rods;* for so ἐῤῥάπισαν signifies, and this he submitted to.

3. They challenged him to tell who struck him, having first blindfolded him; *Prophesy unto us, thou Christ, who is he that smote thee?* They made sport of him, as the Philistines did with Samson; it is grievous to those that are in misery, for people to make merry *about* them, but much more to make merry *with* them and their misery. They had heard him called a *prophet*; this they upbraided him with, and pretended to make a trial of; as if the divine omniscience must stoop to a piece of children's play.

Verses 69–75

We have here the story of Peter's denying his Master, and it comes in as a part of Christ's sufferings. Observe how he fell, and how he got up again by repentance.

I. His sin. The immediate occasion of Peter's sin. He sat without in the palace, among the servants of the High Priest. Bad company is to many an occasion of sin; and those who needlessly thrust themselves into it, go upon the devil's ground; they scarcely can come out of such company, without guilt or grief, or both. The temptation came, when he was challenged as a retainer to Jesus of Galilee. First one maid, and then another, and then the rest of the servants, charged it upon him; *Thou also wert with Jesus of Galilee, v.* 69. And again, *This fellow was with Jesus of Nazareth, v.* 71. And again (*v.* 73), *Thou also art one of them, for thy speech betrayeth thee* to be a Galilean. Happy he whose speech betrays him to be a disciple of Christ. Observe how scornfully they speak of Christ—Jesus *of Galilee*, and *of Nazareth*, upbraiding him with the country he was of: and how disdainfully they speak of Peter—*This fellow;* as if they thought it a reproach to them to have such a man in their company. The sin itself. When he was charged as one of Christ's disciples, he denied it, was ashamed and afraid to own himself so. Upon the first mention of it, he said, *I know not what thou sayest*. This was a shuffling answer; he pretended that he did not understand the charge. It is a fault to pretend that we do not understand, or did not think of, or remember, that which yet we do apprehend, and did think of, and remember; this is a species of lying which we are more prone to than any other, because in this a man is not easily disproved. It is yet a greater fault to be shy of Christ, to dissemble our knowledge of him; it is, in effect, to *deny* him. Upon the next attack, he said, flat and plain, *I know not the man*, and backed it with an oath, *v.* 72. This was, in effect, to say, I will not own him. Why, Peter? Canst thou look upon yonder Prisoner at the bar, and say thou dost not know him? Hast thou forgotten all the kind and tender looks thou hast had from him, and all the intimate fellowship thou hast had with him? Canst thou look him in the face, and say that thou dost not know him? Upon the third assault, *he began to curse and to swear, saying, I know not the man, v.* 74. This was worst of all, for the way of sin is downhill. He cursed and swore, 1. To back what he said, and to gain credit to it, and yet what he said, was false. We have reason to suspect the truth of that which is backed with rash oaths and imprecations. None but the devil's sayings need the devil's proofs. 2. He designed it to be an evidence for him, that he was none of Christ's disciples, for this was none of their language.

This is written for warning to us, that we sin not after the similitude of Peter's transgression; that we never, either directly or indirectly, deny Christ the Lord, dissembling our knowledge of him, and being ashamed of him and his words. This sin was aggravated considering who he was; an apostle, one of the first three. The greater profession we make of religion, the greater is our sin if in anything we walk unworthily. What fair warning his Master had given him of his danger. How solemnly he had promised to adhere to Christ in this night of trial; he had said again and again, "*I will never deny thee.*" How soon he fell into this sin after the Lord's supper. There to receive such an inestimable pledge of redeeming love, and yet the same night, before morning, to disown his Redeemer, was indeed *turning aside quickly*. How weak comparatively the temptation was; it

JAMIESON, FAUSSET, BROWN

The Blessed One Is Now Shamefully Entreated

Every word here must be carefully observed, and the several accounts put together, that we may lose none of the awful indignities about to be described. **some began to spit on him**—or, as in Matthew 26:67, "to spit in [into] His face." Luke (22:63) says in addition, "And the men that held Jesus mocked him"—or cast their jeers at Him. **to cover his face**—or "to blindfold him" (as in Luke 22:64). **to buffet him**—Luke's word, which is rendered "smote Him" (22:63), is a stronger one, conveying an idea for which we have an exact equivalent in English, but one too colloquial to be inserted here—**began to say unto him, Prophesy**—In Matthew 26:68 this is given more fully: "Prophesy unto us, thou Christ, Who is he that smote Thee?" The sarcastic fling at Him as "*the Christ,*" and the demand of Him in this character to name the unseen perpetrator of the blows inflicted on Him, was in them as infamous as to Him it must have been, and was intended to be, stinging.

And as Peter was beneath in the palace—This little word "*beneath*"—one of our Evangelist's graphic touches—is most important for the right understanding of what we may call the topography of the scene. We must take it in connection with Matthew's word (26:69): "Now Peter sat *without* in the palace"—or quadrangular court, in the center of which the fire would be burning; and crowding around and buzzing about it would be the menials and others who had been admitted within the court. At the upper end of this court, probably, would be the memorable chamber in which the trial was held—*open to the court,* likely, and *not far from the fire* (as we gather from Luke 22:61), but *on a higher level*; for (as our verse says) the court, with Peter in it, was "beneath" it. The ascent to the Council chamber was perhaps by a short flight of steps. If the reader will bear this explanation in mind, he will find the intensely interesting details which follow more intelligible. **there cometh one of the maids of the high priest**—"the damsel that kept the door" (John 18:17). The Jews seem to have employed women as porters of their doors (Acts 12:13). **And when she saw Peter warming himself, she looked upon him**—Luke (22:56) is here more graphic; "But a certain maid beheld him as he sat by the fire"—lit., 'by the *light,*' which, shining full upon him, revealed him to the girl—"and earnestly looked upon him"—or, 'fixed her gaze upon him.' His demeanor and timidity, which must have attracted notice, as so generally happens, leading," says OLSHAUSEN, "to the recognition of him." **and said, And thou also wast with Jesus of Nazareth**—"with Jesus the Nazarene," or, "with Jesus of Galilee" (Matthew 26:69). The *sense* of this is given in John's report of it (18:17), "Art not thou also one of this man's disciples?" i.e., thou as well as "that other disciple," whom she knew to be one, but did not challenge, perceiving that he was a privileged person. In Luke (22:56) it is given as a remark made by the maid to one of the bystanders—this man was also with Him." If so expressed in Peter's hearing—drawing upon him the eyes of every one that heard it (as we know it did, Matt. 26:70), and compelling him to answer to it—that would explain the different forms of the report naturally enough. But in such a case this is of no real importance. **But he denied**—"before all" (Matt. 26:70). **saying, I know not, neither understand I what thou sayest**—in Luke, "I know Him not." **And he went out into the porch**—the vestibule leading to the street—no doubt finding the fire-place too *hot* for him; possibly also with the hope of escaping—but that was not to be, and perhaps he dreaded that, too. Doubtless by this time his mind would be getting into a sea of commotion, and would fluctuate every moment in its resolves. **And a maid saw him again**—or, "a girl." It might be rendered "the girl"; but this would not necessarily mean the same one as before, but might, and probably does, mean just the female who had charge of the door or gate near which Peter now was. Accordingly, in Matthew 26:71, she is expressly called "another [maid]." But in Luke it is a *male* servant: "And after a little while (from the time of the first denial) another"—i.e., as the word signifies, "another male" servant. But there is no real difficulty, as the challenge, probably, after being made by one was reiterated by another. Accordingly, in John, it is, "*They* said therefore unto him . . .," as if more than one challenged him at once. **and began to say to them that stood by, This is**

ADAM CLARKE

67. *Then did they spit in his face.* This was done as a mark of the most profound contempt. See Job xvi. 10 and xxx. 10; Isa. l. 6; Mic. v. 1. The judges now delivered Him into the hands of the mob. *And buffeted him.* Smote Him with their fists. "Beat with the hand, the fingers being clenched." *Smote him with the palms of their hands.* "Smite the cheek with the open hand."

68. *Prophesy unto us, thou Christ.* Their conduct toward Him now was expressly prophesied of, by a man whose divine mission they did not pretend to deny; see Isa. l. 6. It appears that, before they buffeted Him, they bound up His eyes; see Mark xiv. 65.

69. *A damsel came unto him.* "A maidservant." *Thou also wast with Jesus.* What a noble opportunity had Peter now to show his zeal for the insulted cause of truth and his attachment to his Master!

72. *And again he denied with an oath.* He has told a lie, and he swears to support it. A liar has always some suspicion that his testimony is not credited, for he is conscious of his own falsity, and is therefore naturally led to support his assertions by oaths.

73. *Thy speech.* "Your manner of speech," "that dialect of yours"—his accent being different from that of Jerusalem. *Bewrayeth thee.* "Makes you manifest."

74. *Then began he to curse and to swear.* Rather, "Then he began positively to affirm."

MATTHEW HENRY

was not the judge, nor any of the officers of the court, that charged him with being a disciple of Jesus, but a silly maid or two. How often he repeated it; even after the cock had crowed once he continued in the temptation, and a second and third time relapsed into the sin.

Thus was his sin aggravated; but on the other hand there is this to extenuate it, that, what he said he said *in his haste*. He fell into the sin by surprise, not as Judas, with design; his heart was against it.

II. Peter's repentance for this sin, *v.* 75.

1. What it was, that brought Peter to repentance.

(1) *The cock crew* (*v.* 74). The word of Christ can put a significancy upon whatever sign he shall please to choose. The crowing of a cock is to Peter instead of a John Baptist, the voice of one calling to repentance. Conscience should be to us as the crowing of the cock, to put us in mind of what we had forgotten. Where there is a living principle of grace in the soul, though for the present overpowered by temptation, a little hint will serve, when God sets in with it, to recover it from a by-path. Here was the crowing of a cock made a happy occasion of the conversion of a soul. Christ comes sometimes in mercy *at cock-crowing*.

(2) *He remembered the words of the Lord;* this was it that brought him to himself, a sense of his ingratitude to Christ. Nothing grieves a penitent more than that he has sinned against the grace of the Lord Jesus and the tokens of his love.

2. How his repentance was expressed; *He went out, and wept bitterly*.

(1) His sorrow was secret; he went out, out of the High Priest's hall, vexed at himself that ever he came into it. He went out into the porch before (*v.* 71); and if he had gone quite off then, his second and third denial had been prevented; but then he came in again, now he went out and came in no more.

(2) His sorrow was serious; *He wept bitterly*. Sorrow for sin must not be slight, but great and deep. Those that have sinned sweetly, must weep bitterly; for, sooner or later, sin will be bitterness. This deep sorrow is requisite to evidence that there is a real change of mind. Peter, who wept so bitterly for denying Christ, never denied him again, but *confessed* him often and openly, and in the mouth of danger. True repentance for any sin will be best evidenced by our abounding in the contrary grace and duty. Some of the ancients say, that as long as Peter lived, he never heard a cock crow but it set him a weeping. Those that have truly sorrowed for sin, will sorrow upon every remembrance of it; yet not so as to hinder, but rather to increase, their joy in God and in his mercy and grace.

JAMIESON, FAUSSET, BROWN

one of them—or, as in Matthew 26:71—"This [fellow] was also with Jesus the Nazarene." **And he denied it again**—In Luke, "Man, I am not." But worst of all in Matthew—"And again he denied with an oath, I do not know the man" (26:72). This was the Second Denial, more vehement, alas! than the first.

Peter's THIRD DENIAL *of His Lord.*

And a little after—"about the space of one hour after" (Luke 22:59). **they that stood by said again to Peter, Surely thou art one of them: for thou art a Galilean, and thy speech agreeth thereto**—"bewrayeth (or "discovereth") thee" (Matt. 26:73). In Luke it is, "Another confidently affirmed, saying, Of a truth this [fellow] also was with him: for he is a Galilean." The Galilean dialect had a more *Syrian* cast than that of Judea. *If Peter had held his peace,* this peculiarity had not been observed; but hoping, probably, to put them off the scent by joining in the *fireside talk,* he was thus discovered. The Fourth Gospel is particularly interesting here: "One of the servants of the high priest, being his kinsman (or kinsman to him) whose ear Peter cut off, saith, Did not I see thee in the garden with Him?" (John 18:26.) No doubt his relationship to Malchus drew his attention to the man who had smitten him, and this enabled him to identify Peter. "Sad reprisals!" exclaims BENGEL. Poor Peter! Thou art caught in thine own toils; but like a wild bull in a net, thou wilt toss and rage, filling up the measure of thy terrible declension by one more denial of thy Lord, and that the foulest of all.

But he began to curse—'anathematize,' or wish himself accursed if what he was now to say was not true. **and to swear**—or to take a solemn oath. **saying, I know not this man of whom ye speak. And Peter called to mind the word that Jesus said unto him, Before the cock crow twice, thou shalt deny me thrice. And when he thought thereon, he wept**—To the same effect is the statement of the First Evangelist (Matt. 26:75), save that like "the beloved physician," he notices the "bitterness" of the weeping. The most precious link, however, in the whole chain of circumstances in this scene is beyond doubt that "look" of deepest, tenderest import reported by Luke alone. Who can tell what lightning flashes of wounded love and piercing reproach shot from that "look" through the eye of Peter into his heart! "And Peter remembered the word of the Lord, how He had said unto him, Before the cock crow, thou shalt deny Me thrice. And Peter went out and wept bitterly." How different from the sequel of Judas' act!

ADAM CLARKE

The cock crew. This animal becomes, in the hand of God, the instrument of awaking the fallen apostle at last to a sense of his fall, danger, and duty.

75. *Peter remembered the word of Jesus*. Luke says, chap. xxii. 61, "The Lord turned, and looked upon Peter." *And wept bitterly*. Felt bitter anguish of soul, which evidenced itself by the tears of contrition which flowed plentifully from his eyes. "Let him that standeth take heed lest he fall." Where the mighty have been slain, what shall support the feeble? Only the grace of the almighty God. This transaction is recorded by the inspired penmen: (1) That all may watch unto prayer, and shun the occasions of sin. (2) That if a man be unhappily overtaken in a fault, he may not despair, but cast himself immediately with a contrite heart on the infinite tenderness and compassion of God.

MATTHEW HENRY

CHAPTER 27

Verses 1-10

We left Christ in the hands of the chief priests and elders, condemned to die, but they could only show their teeth. The Romans had taken from the Jews the power of capital punishment; they could put no man to death, and therefore early in the morning another council is held, to consider what is to be done.

I. Christ is delivered up to Pilate, that he might execute the sentence they had passed upon him. Pilate is characterized by the Roman writers of that time, as a man of a rough and haughty spirit; the Jews had a great enmity to his person, and were weary of his government, and yet they made use of him as the tool of their malice against Christ.

1. They *bound* Jesus. Having found him guilty, they tied his hands behind him, as they usually do with convicted criminals. He was already bound with the bonds of love to man, and of his own undertaking, else he had soon broken these bonds, as Samson did his.

2. *They led him away* in a sort of triumph, led him *as a lamb to the slaughter*. It was nearly a mile from Caiaphas's house to Pilate's. All that way they led him through the streets of Jerusalem, when in the morning they began to fill, to make him a spectacle to the world.

3. They *delivered him to Pontius Pilate*; according to that which Christ had often said, that he should be *delivered to the Gentiles*. Christ was to be the Saviour both of Jews and Gentiles; and therefore Christ was brought into the judgment both of Jews and Gentiles, and both had a hand in his death.

II. The money which they had paid to Judas for betraying Christ, is by him delivered back to them, and Judas, in despair, hangs himself. The chief priests and elders supported themselves with *this*, in prosecuting Christ, that his own disciple betrayed him to them; but now, in the midst of the prosecution,

JAMIESON, FAUSSET, BROWN

CHAPTER 27

Vss. 1-10. JESUS LED AWAY TO PILATE—REMORSE AND SUICIDE OF JUDAS. (= Mark 15:1; Luke 23:1; John 18:28).

Jesus Led Away to Pilate (vss. 1, 2). For the exposition of this portion, see on John 18:28, etc.

Then led they Jesus from Caiaphas to the hall of judgment—but not till "in the morning the chief priests held a consultation with the elders and scribes and the whole council against Him to put Him to death, and bound Him" (Matt. 27:1; and see on Mark 15:1). The word here rendered "hall of judgment" is from the Latin, and denotes 'the palace of the governor of a Roman province.' **they themselves went not into the judgment hall lest they should be defiled**—by contact with ceremonially unclean Gentiles. **but that they might eat the passover**—If this refer to the principal part of the festival, the eating of the lamb, the question is, how our Lord and His disciples came to eat it the night before; and, as it was an *evening* meal, how ceremonial defilement contracted in the *morning* would unfit them for partaking of it, as after 6 o'clock it was reckoned a new day. These are questions which have occasioned immense research and learned treatises. But as the usages of the Jews appear to have somewhat varied at different times, and our present knowledge of them is not sufficient to clear up all difficulties, they are among the not very important questions which probably will never be entirely solved.

ADAM CLARKE

CHAPTER 27

1. *When the morning was come*. As soon as it was light. *Took counsel against Jesus*. They had begun this counsel the preceding evening; see chap. xxvi. 59. But as it was contrary to all forms of law to proceed against a person's life by night, they seem to have separated for a few hours, and then, at the break of day, came together again, pretending to conduct the business according to the forms of law. *To put him to death*. They had already determined His death, and pronounced the sentence of death on Him; chap. xxvi. 66. And now they assemble under the pretense of reconsidering the evidence and deliberating on it, to give the greater appearance of justice to their conduct.

MATTHEW HENRY

that string failed them, and even *he* is made to them a *witness* of Christ's innocency, which served, 1. For glory to Christ in the midst of his sufferings, and a specimen of his victory over Satan who had entered into Judas. 2. For warning to his persecutors, and to leave them the more inexcusable.

(1) See here how Judas *repented*: not like Peter, who repented, believed, and was pardoned: no, he repented, despaired, and was ruined.

[1] What induced him to repent. It was *when he saw that he was condemned.* Judas, it is probable, expected that Christ would have made his escape out of their hands, and then Christ would have had the honour, the Jews the shame, and he the money, and no harm done. This he had no reason to expect, because he had so often heard his Master say that he must be *crucified.* Those who measure actions by the consequences of them rather than by the divine law, will find themselves mistaken in their measures. The way of sin is down-hill; and if we cannot easily stop ourselves, much less can we stop others whom we have set going in a sinful way. He *repented himself.* When he was tempted to betray his Master, the thirty pieces of silver looked very fine and glittering. But when the thing was done, and the money paid, the silver was become dross. Now his conscience flew in his face; "What have I done! What a fool, what a wretch, am I, to sell my Master for such a trifle! It is owing to me, that he is bound and condemned, spat upon and buffeted. I little thought it would have come to this, when I made that wicked bargain." The remembrance of his Master's goodness to him, steeled his convictions, and made them the more piercing. Now he found his Master's words true; *It were better for that man, that he had never been born.* Sin will soon change its taste.

[2] What were the indications of his repentance. *First,* He made restitution; *He brought again the thirty pieces of silver to the chief priests.* Now the money burned in his conscience, and he was as sick of it as ever he had been fond of it. That which is ill gotten, will never do good to those that get it. If he had repented, and brought the money back before he had betrayed Christ, he might have done it with comfort; but now it was too late, now he cannot do it without horror. What is unjustly gotten, must not be kept; for that is a continuance in the sin by which it was got. He brought it to those from whom he had it, to let them know that he repented his bargain.

Secondly, He made confession (*v.* 4); *I have sinned, in that I have betrayed innocent blood.* 1. To the *honour of Christ,* he pronounces his blood *innocent.* He, freely and without being urged to it, pronounces him innocent, to the face of those who had pronounced him *guilty.* 2. To *his own shame,* he confesses that he had sinned, in betraying this blood. He does not lay the blame on anyone else, but takes it all to himself; "I have sinned, in doing it." Thus far Judas went toward his repentance, yet it was *not to salvation.* He confessed, but not to God, did not go to him, and say, *I have sinned, Father, against heaven.*

(2) See here how the chief priests and elders entertained Judas's penitential confession; they said, *What is that to us? See thou to that.*

[1] See here how carelessly they speak of the betraying of Christ. *What is that to us?* Was it nothing to them that they had thirsted after this blood, and hired Judas to betray it, and had now condemned it to be shed unjustly?

[2] See here how carelessly they speak the sin of Judas; he said, *I have sinned,* and they said, "*What is that to us?* What are we concerned in thy sin, that thou tellest us of it?" It is folly for us to think that the sins of others are nothing to us, especially those sins that we are any way accessory to, or partakers in. The guilt of sin is not so easily transferred as some people think it is. If there were guilt in the matter, they tell Judas that he must *look to it,* he must *bear it. First,* Because he had betrayed him to them. His was indeed *the greater sin* (John xix. 11); but it did not therefore follow, that theirs was no sin. *Secondly,* Because he knew and believed him to be innocent. "If he be innocent, see thou to it. We have adjudged him *guilty,* and therefore may justly prosecute him as such." Wicked practices are buoyed up by wicked principles, and particularly by this, That sin is sin only to those that think it to be so; that it is no harm to persecute a good man, if we take him to be a bad man.

[3] See how carelessly they speak of the conviction, terror, and remorse, that Judas was under. They were glad to make use of him in the sin, and were then very fond of him. But now they slighted him, had nothing to say to him, but turned him over to his own terrors. Those that are resolvedly impenitent, look with disdain upon the penitent. When

JAMIESON, FAUSSET, BROWN

Remorse and Suicide of Judas (vss. 3-10). This portion is peculiar to Matthew. On the progress of guilt in the traitor, see on Mark 14:1-11; and on John 13:21-30. **3. Then Judas, which had betrayed him, when he saw that he was condemned**—The condemnation, even though not unexpected, might well fill him with horror. But perhaps this unhappy man expected, that, while he got the bribe, the Lord would miraculously escape, as He had once and again done before, out of His enemies' power: and if so, his remorse would come upon him with all the greater keenness. **repented himself**—but, as the issue too sadly showed, it was "the sorrow of the world, which worketh death" (II Cor. 7:10)

—and brought again the thirty pieces of silver to the chief priests and elders—A remarkable illustration of the power of an awakened conscience. A short time before, the promise of this sordid pelf was temptation enough to his covetous heart to outweigh the most overwhelming obligations of duty and love; now, the possession of it so lashes him that he cannot use it, cannot even keep it! **4. Saying, I have sinned in that I have betrayed the innocent blood**—What a testimony this to Jesus! Judas had been with Him in all circumstances for three years; his post, as treasurer to Him and the Twelve (John 12:6), gave him peculiar opportunity of watching the spirit, disposition, and habits of his Master; while his covetous nature and thievish practices would incline him to dark and suspicious, rather than frank and generous, interpretations of all that He said and did. If, then, he could have fastened on one questionable feature in all that he had so long witnessed, we may be sure that no such speech as this would ever have escaped his lips, nor would he have been so stung with remorse as not to be able to keep the money and survive his crime. **And they said, What is that to us? see thou to that**—"Guilty or innocent is nothing to us: We have Him now—begone!" Was ever speech more hellish uttered?

ADAM CLARKE

3. *Judas . . . when he saw that he was condemned, repented.* **There is much of the wisdom and goodness of God to be seen in this part of Judas' conduct. Had our Lord been condemned to death on the evidence of one of His own disciples, it would have furnished infidels with a strong argument against Christ and the Christian religion.**

4. *Innocent blood.* A Hebraism for an "innocent man." *What is that to us?* What is it? A great deal. You should immediately go and reverse the sentence you have pronounced, and liberate the innocent Person.

G. CAMPBELL MORGAN:

This is the final picture of Judas. What are the things that are impressed upon our mind as we look at him? First, a too-late repentance; secondly, a too-late restitution, the flinging back of the thirty pieces of silver; and finally, an appalling retribution coming upon him by his own hand. Judas appears in this trial scene as one of the band of Christ's own disciples, one of the inner circle. In following this Gospel, we have seen vast multitudes crowding about Him, the rulers and those in authority deeply interested in Him. We have also seen how they gradually fell away, the rulers first, and then the multitudes, until He slowly and solemnly proceeded to the place He occupied in the awful hour of His passion, absolutely alone so far as human friendship was concerned. Judas had been His companion along the highway of His public ministry. He had sat at the table with Him, and had heard those intimate and private conversations. He had been one of the inner circle of souls, loyal to Him, at least by confession and profession. This man was the traitor in the camp, the betrayer of our Lord from the inner circle to the outer circle; as in turn, they of His own nationality became His betrayers to that yet wider circle of Roman power. So by a process of betrayal from the inner circle outward, our Lord was handed over by a member of His own disciples to the foes plotting for His own life and by the members of His own nation to the nation without, which cared nothing for Him, but wholly for themselves.

Many brilliant and interesting attempts have been made to redeem Judas from obloquy, but let us be content to abide by his own conception of what he had done—"I have sinned." Not, I have blundered, or have been mistaken, or foolish, or wrong; not, I have attempted to hurry this Messiah to declare himself, but, "I have sinned." As we look at Judas in that terrible picture, we see a man filled with terror, the terror of a lost soul; the sense of sin, and the dread of its issue. Not regret, not the sense of sin with desire to escape it, but the sense of sin with desire to escape the issue of it. That is not the repentance that brings man to God. If a man simply repents of sin, by attempting to escape its issue, he knows nothing of repentance in the true sense of the word. Repentance which would be glad to bear the fire of hell if it would purge from sin is the repentance that works salvation.—*The Gospel According to Matthew*

MATTHEW HENRY

they had brought him into the snare, they not only left him, but laughed at him. Sinners, under convictions, will find their old companions in sin, but miserable comforters. It is usual for those that love the treason, to hate the traitor.

(3) Here is the utter despair that Judas was hereby driven into. He grew desperate, *v.* 5.

[1] *He cast down the pieces of silver in the temple.* The chief priests would not take the money, for fear of taking thereby the whole guilt to themselves. Judas would not keep it, it was too hot for him to hold, he therefore threw it down in the temple, that, whether they would or no, it might fall into the hands of the chief priests.

[2] *He went, and hanged himself. First, He retired*; he withdrew into some solitary place. Woe to him that is in despair, and is alone. If Judas had gone to Christ, or to some of the disciples, perhaps he might have had relief, bad as the case was. *Secondly*, He became his own executioner; *He hanged himself.* Judas had a *sight* and *sense* of sin, but no apprehension of the mercy of God in Christ. His sin, we may suppose, was not in its own nature unpardonable: but he concluded, as Cain, that his iniquity was greater than could be forgiven. And some have said, that Judas sinned more in *despairing* of the mercy of God, than in *betraying* his Master's blood. He throws himself into the fire, to avoid the flame; but miserable is the case when a man must go to hell for ease. 1. We have an instance of the wretched end of those into whom Satan enters, and particularly those that are given up to the love of money. 2. We have an instance of the wrath of God. As in the story of Peter we behold the goodness of God, and the triumphs of Christ's grace in the conversion of some sinners; so in the story of Judas we behold the severity of God. 3. We have an instance of the direful effects of despair; it often ends in self-murder. Let us think as bad as we can of sin, provided we do not think it unpardonable; let us despair of help in ourselves, but not of help in God. And self-murder, though prescribed by some of the heathen moralists, is certainly a remedy worse than the disease, how bad soever the disease may be.

(4) The disposal of the money which Judas brought back, *v.* 6–10. It was laid out in the purchase of a field, called *the potter's field.* And this field was to be a burying-place for strangers. It looks like an instance of their humanity, that they took care for the *burying of strangers.* It was no instance of their humility that they would bury strangers in a place by themselves. Strangers must keep their distance, alive and dead, and that principle must go down to the grave.

This buying of the potter's field took place not long after; for Peter speaks of it soon after Christ's ascension: yet it is here recorded.

First, To show the hypocrisy of the chief priests and elders. They scruple to put that money into the treasury, or *corban*, of the temple, with which they had hired the traitor. They would not put that money into it, which was the price of blood. The hire of a traitor they thought parallel to the hire of a whore, and the price of a malefactor (such a one they made Christ to be) equivalent to the price of a dog, neither of which was to be *brought into the house of the Lord.* Thus they that *swallowed a camel, strained at a gnat.* They think to *atone* for what they had done, by this public good act of providing a burying-place for strangers, though not at their own charge.

Secondly, To signify the favour intended by the blood of Christ to *strangers*, and sinners of the Gentiles. Through the price of his blood, a resting place is provided for them after death. The *grave* is the potter's field, but Christ by his blood *purchased* it. He has altered the property of it (as a purchaser doth), so that now death is ours, the grave is ours, a bed of rest for us.

Thirdly, To perpetuate the infamy of those that bought and sold the blood of Christ. This field was commonly called *Aceldama—the field of blood*; not by the chief priests, they hoped in this burying-place to bury the remembrance of their own crime; but by the people. They fastened this name upon the field *in perpetuam rei memoriam—for a perpetual memorial.*

Fourthly, That we may see how the scripture was fulfilled (*v.* 9, 10); *Then was fulfilled that which was spoken by Jeremy the prophet.* The words quoted are found in the prophecy of Zechariah, *ch.* xi. 12. How they are here said to be spoken by Jeremy is a difficult question. The Syriac version, which is ancient, reads only, *It was spoken by the prophet*, not naming any. The Jews used to say, *The spirit of Jeremiah was in Zechariah.* Here that is really acted, which was there but figuratively expressed. The sum of money is the same—*thirty pieces of silver*; this they *weighed for his price*, and this was *cast to the potter in the house*

JAMIESON, FAUSSET, BROWN

5. And he cast down the pieces of silver—The sarcastic, diabolical reply which he had got, in place of the sympathy which perhaps he expected, would deepen his remorse into an agony —**in the temple**—the temple proper, commonly called "the sanctuary," or "the holy place," into which only the priests might enter. How is this to be explained? Perhaps he flung the money in after them. But thus were fulfilled the words of the prophet—"I cast them to the potter in the house of the Lord" (Zech. 11:13)—**and departed, and went and hanged himself**—See, for the details, on Acts 1:18.

ADAM CLARKE

5. *In the temple* signifies, properly, the Temple itself, into which none but the priests were permitted to enter. "Near the Temple," by the Temple door, where the boxes stood to receive the freewill offerings of the people, for the support and repairs of the sacred edifice. *Hanged himself.* Or was "strangled." Some eminent critics believe that he was only suffocated by excessive grief, and thus they think the account here given will agree with that in Acts i. 18. I have my doubts. The old method of reconciling the two accounts appears to me quite plausible—he went and strangled himself, and the rope breaking, he fell down; and by the violence of the fall his body was burst, and "his bowels gushed out."

ALEXANDER MACLAREN:

Universally, this is true, that sooner or later, when the delirium of passion and the rush of temptation are over and we wake to consciousness, we find that we are none the richer for the thing gained, and oh! so infinitely the poorer for the means by which we gained it. It is that old story of the Veiled Prophet that wooed and won the hearts of foolish maidens, and, when he had them in his power in the inner chamber, removed the silver veil which they had thought hid dazzling glory and showed hideous features that struck despair into their hearts. Every man's sin does that for him. And to you I come now with this message: every wrong thing that you do, great or small, will be like some of those hollow images of the gods that one hears of in barbarian temples—looked at in front, fair, but when you get behind them you find a hollow, full of dust and spiders' webs and unclean things.

That is the first lesson that lies in these words of this wretched traitor; but again, here is an awful picture for us of the hell upon earth, of a conscience which has no hope of pardon. I do not suppose that Judas was lost, if he were lost, because he betrayed Jesus Christ, but because, having betrayed Jesus Christ, he never asked to be forgiven. And I suppose that the difference between the traitor who betrayed Him and the other traitor who denied Him was this, that the one, when "he went out and wept bitterly," had the thought of a loving Master with him, and the other, when "he went out and hanged himself," had the thought of nothing but that foul deed glaring before him. I pray you to learn this lesson: you cannot think too much, too blackly, of your own sins, but you may think too exclusively of them, and if you do, they will drive you to madness of despair.

—*Expositions of Holy Scripture*

JAMIESON, FAUSSET, BROWN

6. And the chief priests took the silver pieces, and said, It is not lawful for to put them into the treasury—"the *Corban,*" or chest containing the money dedicated to sacred purposes (see on ch. 15:5).

because it is the price of blood—How scrupulous now! But those punctilious scruples made them unconsciously fulfil the Scripture.

Then was fulfilled that which was spoken by Jeremy the prophet, saying—(Zech. 11:12, 13). Never was a complicated prophecy, otherwise hopelessly dark, more marvellously fulfilled. Various conjectures have been formed to account for Matthew's ascribing to Jeremiah a prophecy found in the book of Zechariah. But since with this book he was plainly familiar, having quoted one of its most remarkable prophecies of Christ but a few chapters before (ch. 21:4, 5), the question is one more of critical interest than real importance. Perhaps the true explanation is the following, from

ADAM CLARKE

6. *The treasury.* The place whither the people brought their freewill offerings for the service of the Temple.

7. *To bury strangers in.* "The strangers," probably meaning, as some learned men conjecture, the Jewish strangers who might have come to Jerusalem, either to worship or on some other business, and died there during their stay.

8. *The field of blood.* In vain do the wicked attempt to conceal themselves; God makes them instrumental in discovering their own wickedness. Judas, by returning the money, and the priests, by laying it out, raise to themselves an eternal monument—the one of his treachery, the others of their perfidiousness, and both of the innocence of Jesus Christ.

9. *Jeremy the prophet.* The words quoted here are not found in the prophet Jeremiah, but in Zech. xi. 13. It was ancient custom among the Jews, says Dr. Lightfoot, to divide the Old Testament into three parts. The first beginning with the law was called The Law; the second beginning with the Psalms was called The Psalms; the third beginning with the prophet in question was called Jeremiah. Thus, then, the writings of Zechariah and the other prophets being included in that division that began with Jeremiah, all quotations from it would go under

MATTHEW HENRY

of the Lord; which was here literally accomplished. The giving of the price of him that was valued, not for him, but for the *potter's field*, bespeaks, 1. The high value that ought to be put upon Christ. He cannot be *valued with the gold of Ophir*, nor this unspeakable Gift *bought with money*. 2. The low value that was put upon him. *They of the children of Israel* did strangely undervalue him, when his price did but reach to buy a potter's field, a pitiful sorry spot of ground, not worth looking upon. *Cast it to the potter*, so it is in Zechariah; a contemptible petty chapman, not the merchant that deals in things of value. He gave kings' ransoms for them, but they gave a slave's ransom for him (see Exod. xxi. 32), and valued him but at the rate of a potter's field. But all this was *as the Lord appointed*.

Verses 11-25

We have here an account of what passed in Pilate's judgment-hall.

I. The trial Christ had before Pilate.

1. His arraignment; *Jesus stood before the governor*, as the prisoner before the judge. We could not stand before God because of our sins, if Christ had not been thus made sin for us. He was arraigned that we might be discharged.

2. His indictment; *Art thou the king of the Jews?* Now they thought that whoever was the Christ, must be the *king of the Jews*, and must deliver them from the Roman power, and restore to them a temporal dominion. They accused our Lord Jesus, as making himself king of the Jews, in opposition to the Roman yoke. They assuring the governor that, if he made himself Christ, he made himself king of the Jews, the governor takes it for granted, that he goes about to pervert the nation, and subvert the government. *Art thou a king?*

3. His plea; *Jesus said unto him*, "*Thou sayest*. It is as thou sayest, though not as thou meanest; I am a king, but not such a king as thou dost suspect me to be."

4. The evidence (*v.* 12); He was *accused of the chief priests*. Pilate found *no fault in him*; whatever was said, nothing was proved, and therefore what was wanting in matter they made up in noise and violence.

5. The prisoner's silence as to the prosecutors' accusations; *He answered nothing*. Because there was no occasion; nothing was alleged but what carried its own confutation along with it. His hour was come, and he submitted to his Father's will; *Not as I will, but as thou wilt*. Pilate pressed him to make some reply (*v.* 13); *Hearest thou not how many things they witness against thee?* Pilate, having no malice at all against him, was desirous he should clear himself, urges him to it. He wondered at his silence. Pilate is not said to be angry at it, but to have *marvelled greatly* at it, as a thing very unusual. He thought it strange that he had not one word to say for himself.

II. The outrage and violence of the people, in pressing the governor to crucify Christ. The chief priests by the power of the mob gained the point which they could not otherwise carry. Now here are two instances of their outrage.

1. Their preferring Barabbas before him, and choosing to have him released rather than Jesus.

(1) It seems it was grown into a custom with the Roman governors, for the humouring of the Jews, to grace the feast of the passover with the release of a prisoner, (*v.* 15).

(2) The prisoner put in competition with our Lord Jesus was Barabbas; he is here called a *notable* prisoner (*v.* 16). *Treason*, *murder*, and *felony*, are the three most enormous crimes that are usually punished by the sword of justice; and Barabbas was guilty of all three, Luke xxiii. 19; John xviii. 40. A *notable prisoner* indeed, whose crimes were so complicated.

(3) The proposal was made by Pilate the governor (*v.* 17); *Whom will ye that I release unto you?* Pilate proposed to them to have Jesus *released*; he was convinced of his innocency, and that the prosecution was malicious; yet had not the courage to acquit him, as he ought to have done, by his own power, but would have him released by the people's election, and so he hoped to satisfy both his own *conscience*, and the *people* too. But such little tricks and artifices as these are the common practice of those that seek more to please men than God. *What shall I do then*, saith Pilate, *with Jesus, who is called Christ?* He puts the people in mind of this, that this *Jesus*, whose release he proposed, was looked upon by some among them as the Messiah.

The reason why Pilate *laboured* thus to get Jesus *discharged* was because he knew that *for envy the chief priests had delivered him up* (*v.* 18); that it was not his *guilt*, but his goodness, that they were pro-

JAMIESON, FAUSSET, BROWN

LIGHTFOOT: "Jeremiah of old had the first place among the prophets, and hereby he comes to be mentioned above all the rest in ch. 16:14; because he stood first in the volume of the prophets [as he proves from the learned DAVID KIMCHI] therefore he is first named. When, therefore, Matthew produceth a text of Zechariah under the name of Jeremy, he only cites the words of the volume of the prophets under his name who stood first in the volume of the prophets. Of which sort is that also of our Saviour (Luke 24:41), "All things must be fulfilled which are written of Me in the Law, and the Prophets, and the Psalms," or the Book of Hagiographa, in which the Psalms were placed first."

11-26. JESUS AGAIN BEFORE PILATE—HE SEEKS TO RELEASE HIM, BUT AT LENGTH DELIVERS HIM TO BE CRUCIFIED. (=Mark 15:1-15; Luke 23:1-25; John 18:28-40). For the exposition, see on Luke 23:1-25, and on John 18:28-40.

Art thou the King of the Jews?—In Luke 23:2 they charge our Lord before Pilate with "perverting the nation, and forbidding to give tribute to Cæsar, saying that He Himself is Christ a king." Perhaps this was what occasioned Pilate's question. **Jesus answered . . . , Sayest thou this of thyself, or did others tell it thee of me?**—an important question for our Lord's case, to bring out whether the word "*King*" were meant in a *political* sense, with which Pilate had a right to deal, or whether he were merely *put up* to it by His accusers, who had no claims to charge Him but such as were of a purely *religious* nature, with which Pilate had nothing to do.

I find in him no fault—no crime. This so exasperated "the chief priests and elders" that, afraid of losing their prey, they poured forth a volley of charges against Him, as appears from Luke 23:4, 5: on Pilate's affirming His innocence, "they were *the more fierce*, saying, He stirreth up the people, teaching throughout all Jewry, beginning from Galilee to this place." They see no hope of getting Pilate's sanction to His death unless they can fasten upon Him a charge of conspiracy against the government; and as *Galilee* was noted for its turbulence (Luke 13:1; Acts 5:37), and our Lord's ministry lay chiefly there, they artfully introduce it to give color to their charge. "And the chief priests accused Him of *many things*, but He answered nothing (Mark 15.3). Then said Pilate unto Him, Hearest Thou not how many things they witness against Thee? And He answered him to never a word, insomuch that the governor marvelled greatly" (Matt. 27:13, 14). See on Mark 15:3-5. In his perplexity, Pilate, hearing of Galilee, bethinks himself of the expedient of sending Him to Herod, in the hope of thereby further shaking off responsibility in the case. See on Mark 15:6, and on Luke 23:6-12. The return of the prisoner only deepened the perplexity of Pilate, who, "calling together the chief priests, rulers, and people," tells them plainly that not one of their charges against "this man" had been made good, while even Herod, to whose jurisdiction he more naturally belonged, had done nothing to Him: He "will therefore chastise and release him" (Luke 23:13-16). **But ye have a custom that I should release one unto you at the passover . . .**—See on Mark 15:7-11. "On the typical import of the choice of Christ to suffer, by which Barabbas was set free, see Leviticus 16, particularly vss. 5-10, where the subject is the *sin offering* on the great day of atonement" [KRAFFT in LUTHARDT].

ADAM CLARKE

the name of this prophet. If this be admitted, it solves the difficulty at once.

12. *He answered nothing*. An answer to such accusations was not necessary; they sufficiently confuted themselves.

14. *Marvelled greatly*. Silence under calumny manifests the utmost magnanimity. The chief priests did not admire this because it confounded them; but Pilate, who had no interest to serve by it, was deeply affected. This very silence was predicted, Isa. liii. 7.

15. *The governor was wont to release*. Whence this custom originated among the Jews is not known; probably it was introduced by the Romans themselves, or by Pilate, merely to oblige the Jews, by showing them this public token of respect.

16. *A notable prisoner called Barabbas*. This person had, a short time before, raised an insurrection in Jerusalem, in which it appears, from Mark xv. 7, some lives were lost. In some MSS. this man has the surname of *Jesus*.

18. *For envy*. "Through malice." Then it was his business, as an upright judge, to disperse this mob, and immediately release Jesus. Seeing malice is capable of putting even Christ himself to death, how careful should we be not to let the least spark of it harbor in our breasts! Let it be remembered that malice as often originates from *envy* as it does from anger.

MATTHEW HENRY

voked at. Anyone that heard the *hosannas* with which Christ was but a few days ago brought into Jerusalem, would have thought that Pilate might safely have referred this matter to the commonalty. But it proved otherwise.

(4) While Pilate was thus labouring the matter, he was confirmed in his unwillingness to condemn Jesus, by a message sent him from his wife (*v.* 19), by way of caution; *Have thou nothing to do with that just man, for I have suffered many things this day in a dream because of him.* Observe, The special providence of God, in sending this dream to Pilate's wife; it is not likely that she had heard anything, before, concerning Christ. Perhaps she was one of the *devout and honourable women*, and had some sense of religion. She *suffered many things* in this dream. It seems that it was a frightful dream, and her thoughts *troubled her.* See the tenderness and care of Pilate's wife, in sending this caution, thereupon, to her husband; *Have nothing to do with that just man.* This was an honourable testimony to our Lord Jesus, witnessing for him that he was a *just man.* When his friends were afraid to appear in defence of him, God made even those that were strangers and enemies, to speak in his favour; when Peter denied him, Judas confessed him; when the chief priests pronounced him guilty of death, Pilate declared he *found no fault* in him; when the women that loved him stood afar off, Pilate's wife, who knew little of him, showed a concern for him. It was a fair warning to Pilate; *Have nothing to do with him.* God has many ways of giving checks to sinners in their sinful pursuits, and it is a great mercy to have such checks. It is also our great duty to hearken to them. Pilate's lady sent him this warning, out of the love she had to him; let him take it how he would, she would give him the caution. It is an instance of true love to our friends and relations, to do what we can to keep them from sin; and the nearer any are to us, and the greater affection we have for them, the more solicitous we should be. The best friendship is friendship to the soul.

(5) The chief priests and the elders were busy, all this while, to influence the people in favour of Barabbas, *v.* 20. They *persuaded the multitude that they should ask Barabbas, and destroy Jesus.* Thus they managed the mob, which otherwise were well affected to Jesus, and, if they had not been so much at the beck of their priests, would never have done such a preposterous thing as to prefer Barabbas before Jesus. We cannot but look upon these wicked priests with indignation. Great power put into their hands they wretchedly abused, and the leaders of the people caused them to err. We cannot but look upon the deluded people with pity; *I have compassion on the multitude*, to see them hurried thus violently to so great wickedness.

(6) Being thus over-ruled by the priests, at length they made their choice, *v.* 21. *Whether of the twain* (saith Pilate) *will ye that I release unto you?* He hoped that he had gained his point, to have Jesus released. But, to his great surprise, they said *Barabbas.* Were ever men that pretended to reason or religion, guilty of such prodigious madness, such horrid wickedness! This was it that Peter charged so home upon them (Acts iii. 14); *Ye desired a murderer to be granted to you.*

2. Their pressing earnestly to have Jesus crucified, *v.* 22, 23. Pilate, being amazed at their choice of Barabbas puts it to them, "*What shall I do then with Jesus?*" *They all said, Let him be crucified.* That death they desired he might die, because it was looked upon as the most scandalous and ignominious; and they hoped thereby to make his followers ashamed to own him, and their relation to him. Malice and rage made them forget all rules of order and decency, and turned a court of justice into a *riotous, tumultuous,* and *seditious assembly.* See what a change was made upon the mind of the populace in a little time: when he *rode in triumph* into Jerusalem, so *general* were the *acclamations of praise*, that one would have thought he had *no enemies*; but now when he was *led in triumph* to Pilate's judgment-seat, so *general* were the *outcries* of enmity, that one would think he had *no friends.* Such revolutions are there in this changeable world, through which our way to heaven lies, as our Master's did, *by honour and dishonour, by evil report, and good report.*

Now, as to this demand, we are further told,

(1) How Pilate objected against it; *Why, what evil hath he done?* A proper question for a judge to ask before he pass a sentence of death. It is much for the honour of the Lord Jesus, that, though he suffered as an evil-doer, yet neither his judge nor his prosecutors could find that he had done any evil. This repeated assertion of his unspotted innocency, plainly intimates that he died to satisfy for the sins of others;

JAMIESON, FAUSSET, BROWN

ALEXANDER MACLAREN:

Pilate takes his place on his official seat to wait for, and then to ratify, their vote. In that pause, he perhaps felt some compunction at paltering with justice, which it was Rome's one virtue to administer. How his wife's message would increase his doubt! Was her dream a divine warning, or a mere reflection in sleep of waking thoughts? It is noticeable that Matthew records several dreams which conveyed God's will—for example, to Joseph and to the Magi, and here may be another instance; or some tidings as to Jesus may have reached the lady, though not her husband, and her womanly sense of right may have shaped the dream and given her vivid impressions of the danger of abetting a judicial murder. But Matthew seems to tell of her intervention mainly in order to preserve her testimony to Jesus' innocence, and to point out one more of the fences which Pilate trampled down in his dread of offending the rulers. A wife's message, conveying what both he and she probably regarded as a supernatural warning, was powerless to keep him back from his disgraceful failure of duty.

While he was fighting against the impression of that message, the rulers were busy in the crowd, suggesting the choice of Barabbas. It was perhaps his wife's words that stung him to act at once and have done with his inner conflict. So he calls for the decision of the alternative which he had already submitted. His dignity would suffer if he had to wait longer for an answer. He got it at once, and the unanimous vote was for Barabbas. Probably the rulers had skillfully manipulated the people. The multitude is easily led by demagogues, but, left to itself, its instincts are usually right, though its perception of character is often mistaken. Why was Barabbas preferred? Probably just because he had been cast into prison for sedition, and so was thought to be a good patriot. Popular heroes often win their reputation by very questionable acts, and Barabbas was forgiven his being a murderer for the sake of his being a rebel.

But it was not so much that Barabbas was loved as that Jesus was hated, and it was not the multitude so much as the rulers that hated him. Many of those now shrieking, "Crucify Him!" had shouted "Hosanna!" a day or two before till they were hoarse. The populace was guilty of fickleness, blindness, rashness, too easy credence of the crafty calumnies of the rulers. But a far deeper stain rests on these rulers who had resisted the light, and were now animated by the basest self-interest in the garb of keen regard for the honor of God. There were very different degrees of guilt in the many voices that roared "Barabbas!"

Pilate made one more feeble attempt to save Jesus by asking what was to be done with Him. The question was an ignoble abdication of his judicial office, and perhaps was meant as a salve for his own conscience, and an excuse to his wife, enabling him to say, "I did not crucify Him; they did"—a miserable pretext, the last resort of a weak man, who knew that he was doing a wrong and cowardly thing.

—*Expositions of Holy Scripture*

ADAM CLARKE

19. *I have suffered many things . . . in a dream.* **There is no doubt that God had appeared unto this woman, testifying the innocence of Christ, and showing the evils which should pursue Pilate if this innocent blood should be shed by his authority.**

20. *Ask Barabbas.* **Who had raised an insurrection and committed murder—and to** *destroy Jesus,* **who had, during the space of three years and a half, gone about unweariedly, from village to village, instructing the ignorant, healing the diseased, and raising the dead.**

22. *What shall I do then with Jesus?* **Showing, hereby, that it was his wish to release Him.**

23. *What evil hath he done?* **Pilate plainly saw that there was nothing laid to His charge for which, consistently with the Roman laws, he could condemn Him.** *But they cried out the more.* **What strange fury and injustice! They could not answer Pilate's question,** *What evil hath he done?* **He had done none, and they knew He had done none; but they were determined on His death.**

MATTHEW HENRY

for if it had not been for our transgressions that he was thus wounded, and for our offences that he was delivered up, and that upon his own voluntary undertaking to atone for them, I see not how these extraordinary sufferings of a person that had never thought, said, or done, anything amiss, could be reconciled with the justice and equity of that providence that governs the world, and at least *permitted* this to be done in it.

(2) How they *insisted* upon it; *They cried out the more, Let him be crucified.* They do not go about to show any evil he had done, but, right or wrong, he must be *crucified.* This unjust judge was wearied by importunity into an unjust sentence, as he in the parable into a just one (Luke xviii. 4, 5), and the cause carried purely by noise.

III. Here is the *devolving* of the *guilt* of Christ's blood upon the *people* and *priests.*

1. Pilate endeavours to transfer it from himself, *v.* 24. He sees it *to no purpose to contend.* What he said, (1) Would do no good; *he could prevail nothing.* See how strong the stream of lust and rage sometimes is; neither authority nor reason will prevail to give check to it. Nay, (2) It was more likely to *do hurt;* he saw that rather a *tumult was made.* This rude and brutish people fell to high words, and began to threaten Pilate what they would do if he did not gratify them. Now this turbulent tumultuous temper of the Jews contributed more than anything to the ruin of that nation not long after; for their frequent insurrections provoked the Romans to destroy them, and their inveterate quarrels among themselves made them an easy prey to the common enemy. Thus their sin was their ruin.

The priests were apprehensive that their endeavours to *seize* Christ would have caused an uproar, especially *on the feast day;* but it proved that Pilate's endeavour to *save* him, caused an uproar, and that on the feast day; so uncertain are the sentiments of the crowd. This puts him into a *great strait,* betwixt the peace of his own mind, and the peace of the city. Had he steadily and resolutely adhered to the sacred laws of justice, he had not been in any perplexity. A man in whom was found *no fault,* ought not to be crucified, upon any pretence whatsoever, nor must an unjust thing be done, to gratify any man or company of men in the world. Pilate thinks to trim the matter, and to pacify both the people and his own conscience too, by *doing it,* and yet *disowning it.*

Now Pilate endeavours to clear himself from the guilt,

[1] By a *sign;* He *took water, and washed his hands before the multitude;* not as if he thought thereby to cleanse himself from any guilt contracted before God, but to acquit himself before the people. He *borrowed* the ceremony from that law which appointed it to be used for the clearing of the country from the guilt of an undiscovered murder (Deut. xxi. 6, 7); and he used it the more to affect the people with the conviction he was under of the prisoner's innocency.

[2] By a *saying;* in which, *First,* He *clears* himself; *I am innocent of the blood of this just person.* What nonsense was this, to condemn him, and yet protest that he was innocent of his blood! For men to protest against a thing, and yet to practise it, is only to proclaim that they sin against their consciences. *Secondly,* He casts it upon the priests and people; "*See ye to it*"; do you answer it before God and the world. Sin is a brat that nobody is willing to own; and many deceive themselves with this, that they shall bear no blame if they can but find any to lay the blame upon; but it is not so easy a thing to transfer the guilt of sin as many think it is. The priests threw it upon Judas; *See thou to it;* and now Pilate throws it upon them; *See ye to it.*

2. The priests and people *consented* to take the guilt *upon themselves;* they all said, "*His blood be on us, and on our children*". They, in the heat of their rage, agreed to it, rather than lose the prey they had in their hands, and cried, *His blood be upon us.* By this they designed to indemnify Pilate. But those that are themselves bankrupts and beggars will never be admitted security for others. None could bear the sin of others, except him that had none of his own to answer for; it is a bold undertaking, and too big for any creature, to become bound for a sinner to Almighty God. But they did really imprecate wrath and vengeance upon themselves and their posterity. Christ had lately told them, that upon them would come *all the righteous blood shed upon the earth,* from that of the righteous Abel; but as if that were too little, they here imprecate upon themselves the guilt of that blood which was more precious than all the rest, and the guilt of which would lie heavier. Observe, How *cruel* they were in their *imprecation.* They imprecated the punishment of this sin, not only upon themselves, but upon *their*

JAMIESON, FAUSSET, BROWN

G. CAMPBELL MORGAN:

The story of Pilate is a story of conscience; and there are these distinct movements in the process: first conscience startled; then conscience struggling; then conscience compromising; and, finally, conscience drugged, silenced! The final revelation of the study is that the man who governs his life simply by conscience is likely to ruin his life.

His conscience was startled by the very presence of Jesus. There would seem to be no other explanation. Pilate was a man never popular, even among his own friends; hard, cold, dispassionate, used to scenes of blood; a man who in all likelihood had risen from the rank of a slave, not immediately, but by succession. The man who rises without the grace of God always becomes the greatest despot when he is given power. But when the priests came to Pilate, bearing that Prisoner, he was a startled man. No such prisoner had stood before him up to that moment. Pilate embodied Roman authority; but here was a Prisoner at the bar, who immediately became the Judge, while the judge became the prisoner. Pilate felt the influence of His stately and quiet affirmation of Kingship. "Art thou the King of the Jews?" which meant to say, "Thou art claiming to be the King of the Jews; it is an absurd position; settle it at once by saying that Thou art not!" But instead of a denial, there was an affirmation. Pilate expected the Prisoner would wish to escape; he found the Prisoner had no desire to escape. Pilate himself would have given anything to escape. His conscience was aroused.

Then we see a man struggling with his conscience. His arguments for Jesus as against the priests, and that last suggestion supposed to be by himself a master-stroke of cleverness, prove this. It was his custom to release a notable prisoner. Barabbas was a man guilty of robbery and murder, and yet a man making claims to free his people. Barabbas means "son of the father" and is a title rather than a name. Some of the ancient manuscripts give the name as Jesus Barabbas. In all probability he had set up messianic claims, on the low level of a material fight and robbery. Pilate saw the difference, and thought that surely these religious men, if driven to choice, would be bound to accept Jesus. So little did Pilate know of priestism! "Which will you have, Jesus which is called Christ, or Barabbas?"

Then there occurred an interval in which the priests persuaded the people to ask for Barabbas; and, as John tells us, in the loneliness of an inner chamber, face to face with Christ, Pilate asked, "What is truth?"

The hidden interview over, the people were ready to answer; and Pilate came with his question, "Which of the two will ye that I release unto you?" They replied, "Barabbas." Then, perplexed, struggling with his conscience, Pilate said, "What then shall I do unto Jesus who is called Christ?" Again the answer came, quick and ready, priest-inspired, "Let him be crucified." And again Pilate asked, "Why, what evil hath he done?" We see how now his conscience was struggling between obedience and expedience; struggling as to whether it would obey the deep conviction concerning the Man in front of him or listen to the clamor of these men, and secure his own position. He knew the subtlety of the priests, he knew full well if he handed Jesus over to freedom, they would complain against him at Rome, that he had committed high treason against Caesar.

Then followed the washing of his hands in water. Judas, a frenzied soul, went back and faced the high priests and said, "I have betrayed innocent blood." Now Pilate said, "I am innocent of the blood of this righteous man; see ye to it."

What next? Conscience drugged. "Then . . . Jesus he scourged and delivered to be crucified."
—The Gospel According to Matthew

ADAM CLARKE

24. *Pilate . . . took water, and washed his hands.* Thus signifying his innocence. It was a custom among the Hebrews, Greeks, and Latins to wash the hands in token of innocence, and to show that they were pure from any imputed guilt. In case of an undiscovered murder, the elders of that city which was nearest to the place where the dead body was found were required by the law, Deut. xxi. 1-10, to wash their hands over the victim which was offered to expiate the crime, and thus make public protestation of their own innocence.

25. *His blood be on us, and on our children.* If this Man be innocent, and we put Him to death as a guilty person, may the punishment due to such a crime be visited upon us, and upon our children after us! What a dreadful imprecation! and how literally fulfilled! They were visited with the same kind of punishment; for the Romans crucified them in such numbers when Jerusalem was taken that there was found a deficiency of crosses for the condemned and of places for the crosses.

MATTHEW HENRY

children too. It was madness to pull it upon themselves, but the height of barbarity to entail it on their posterity. See what enemies wicked men are to their own children and families. From the time they imprecated this blood upon them, they were followed with one judgment after another. Yet on some of them, and some of theirs, this blood came, not to *condemn* them, but to *save* them; divine mercy, upon their repenting and believing, cut off this entail, and then *the promise* was again *to them, and to their children.* God is better to us and ours than we are.

Verses 26-32

I. The sentence passed, and the warrant signed for his execution; and this *immediately*, the same hour.

1. Barabbas was released; to intimate that Christ was condemned for this purpose, that sinners, even the chief of sinners, might be *released*; he was *delivered up*, that we might be delivered. In this *unparalleled instance* of divine grace, the *upright* is a *ransom for the transgressors*, the just for the unjust.

2. Jesus was *scourged*; this was an ignominious cruel punishment, especially as it was inflicted by the Romans, who were not under the moderation of the Jewish law, which forbade scourgings, above forty stripes.

3. He was then *delivered to be crucified*; a kind of death used only among the Romans; the manner of it is such, that it seems to be the result of wit and cruelty in combination, to make death in the highest degree terrible and miserable. A cross was set up in the ground, to which the hands and feet were nailed, on which nails the weight of the body hung, till it died of the pain. It was a bloody death, a painful, shameful, cursed death; it was so miserable a death, that merciful princes appointed those who were condemned to it by the law, to be strangled first, and then nailed to the cross.

II. The barbarous treatment which the soldiers gave him. When he was condemned, he ought to have had some time allowed him to prepare for death. There was a law made by the Roman senate that the execution of criminals should be deferred at least *ten days* after sentence. But there were scarcely allowed so many minutes to our Lord Jesus. The storm continued without any intermission.

When he was *delivered* to be *crucified*, that was enough; they that *kill the body*, yield that there is no more that they *can do*, but Christ's enemies will *do more*. His guards set themselves to abuse him. Perhaps it was not so much in spite to him, as to make *sport* for themselves, that they thus abused him. They understood that he *pretended to a crown*; to *taunt* him with that gave them some diversion, and an opportunity to make themselves and one another merry.

Observe, 1. *Where* this was done—in the *common hall*. The *governor's house*, which should have been a shelter to the wronged and abused, is made the theatre of this barbarity. Those in authority will be accountable, not only for the wickedness which they *do*, or *appoint*, but for that which they do not restrain.

2. *Who* were concerned in it. They gathered the *whole band*, the soldiers that were to attend the execution.

3. What particular indignities were done him.

(1) They *stripped him, v.* 28. The shame of nakedness came in with sin (Gen. iii. 7).

(2) They *put on him a scarlet robe*, some old red cloak, such as the Roman soldiers wore, in imitation of the *scarlet robes* which kings and emperors wore; thus upbraiding him with his being called *a King*. This *sham* of majesty they put upon him in his dress, only to expose him to the spectators, as the more *ridiculous*.

(3) They *platted a crown of thorns, and put it upon his head, v,* 29. This was to carry on the humour of making him a *mock-king*; yet, had they intended it only for a *reproach*, they might have *platted a crown of straw*, or *rushes*, but they designed it to be painful to him. Thorns signify afflictions. These Christ put into a *crown*; so much did he alter the property of them to them that are his, giving them cause to *glory in tribulation*, and making it to work for them a weight of glory. Christ was crowned with thorns, to show that *his kingdom was not of this world*, nor the glory of it worldly glory, but is attended here with bonds and afflictions, while the glory of it is *to be revealed.*

(4) They *put a reed in his right hand*; this was intended for a *mock-sceptre*, another of the *insignia* of the majesty they jeered him with; as if this were a sceptre good enough for such a King. Like sceptre, like kingdom, both weak and wavering, and withering and worthless; but they were quite mistaken, for his throne is *for ever and ever*.

JAMIESON, FAUSSET, BROWN

Pilate took Jesus and scourged him—in hope of appeasing them. (See on Mark 15:15.) "And the soldiers led Him away into the palace, and they call the whole band" (Mark 15:16)—the body of the military cohort stationed there—to take part in the mock coronation now to be enacted.

27-33. JESUS, SCORNFULLY AND CRUELLY ENTREATED OF THE SOLDIERS, IS LED AWAY TO BE CRUCIFIED. (=Mark 15:16-22; Luke 23:26-31; John 19:2, 17.) For the exposition, see on Mark 15:16-22.

and they put on him a purple robe—in mockery of the *imperial purple;* first "stripping him" (Matt. 27:28) of His own outer garment. The robe may have been the "gorgeous" one in which Herod arrayed and sent Him back to Pilate (Luke 23:11). "And they put a reed into His right hand" (Matt. 27:29)—in mockery of the regal *scepter*. "And they bowed the knee before Him" (Matt. 27:29).

. **the soldiers platted a crown of thorns, and put it on his head**—in mockery of a regal *crown*.

ADAM CLARKE

26. *Scourged Jesus.* This is allowed to have been a very severe punishment of itself among the Romans, the flesh being generally cut by the whips used for this purpose. It has been thought that Pilate might have spared this additional cruelty of whipping, but it appears that it was a common custom to scourge those criminals which were to be crucified (see Josephus De Bello, lib. ii, c. 25), and lenity in Christ's case is not to be allowed; He must take all the misery in full tale. *Delivered him to be crucified.* Tacitus, the Roman historian, mentions the death of Christ in very remarkable terms: "Nero put those who commonly went by the name of Christians to the most exquisite tortures. The author of this name was Christ, who was capitally punished in the reign of Tiberius, by Pontius Pilate the Procurator."

27. *The common hall.* Or *praetorium.* Called so from the *praetor*, a principal magistrate among the Romans, whose business it was to administer justice in the absence of the consul.

28. *Stripped him.* Took off His mantle, or upper garment. *A scarlet robe.* Or, according to Mark and John, a purple robe, such as emperors and kings wore.

29. *A crown of thorns.* It does not appear that this crown was intended to be an instrument of punishment or torture to His head, but rather to render Him ridiculous; for which cause also they put a *reed* in His hand, by way of sceptre, and bowed their knees, pretending to do Him homage. The crown was not probably of thorns in our sense of the word; there are eminently learned men who think that the crown was formed of the herb *acanthus*. This, however, is a prickly plant, though nothing like *thorns* in the common meaning of that word. Painters, the worst of all commentators, frequently represent Christ with a crown of long thorns, which one standing by is striking into His head with a stick. These representations engender ideas both false and absurd.

MATTHEW HENRY

(5) They *bowed the knee before him, and mocked him, saying, Hail, King of the Jews!* Having made him a sham King, they thus make a jest of doing homage to him, thus ridiculing his pretensions to sovereignty.

(6) They *spit upon him*; thus he had been abused in the High Priest's hall, *ch.* xxvi. 67. In doing homage, the subject kissed the sovereign, in token of his allegiance; but they, in this mock-homage, instead of kissing him, spit in his face. It is strange that the sons of men should ever do such a piece of *villainy*, and that the Son of God should ever *suffer* such a piece of *ignominy*.

(7) They *took the reed, and smote him on the head.* That which they had made the *mock-ensign* of his royalty, they now make the real instrument of *their* cruelty, and *his pain.* They smote him, it is probable, upon the *crown of thorns*, and so struck them into his head, which made the most sport for them, to whom his pain was the greatest pleasure. All this misery and shame he underwent, that he might purchase for us everlasting life, and joy, and glory.

III. The conveying of him to the place of execution. After they had mocked and abused him, as long as they thought fit, they then *took the robe off from him*; and they put his own raiment on him, because that was to fall to the soldiers' share, that were employed in the execution. No mention is made of their taking off the *crown of thorns*, whence it is commonly supposed (though there is no certainty of it) that he was crucified with that on his head.

1. They *led him away* to be *crucified*; he was led *as a lamb to the slaughter*, as a sacrifice to the altar. We may well imagine how they hurried him on, and dragged him along, with all the speed possible. They led him away *out of the city*; for Christ, that he might sanctify the people with his own blood, *suffered without the gate* (Heb. xiii. 12).

2. They compelled Simon of Cyrene *to bear his cross, v.* 32. It seems, at first he *carried the cross* himself. And this was intended, as other things, both for pain and shame to him. But after a while they *took the cross* off from him, either, (1) In compassion to him, because they saw it was too great a load for him. We can hardly think that they had any consideration of that. But, (2) Perhaps it was because he could not, with the cross on his back, go forward so fast as they would have him. Or, (3) They were afraid, lest he should faint away under the load of his cross, and die, and so prevent what their malice further intended to do against him. Taking the cross off from him, they *compelled* one Simon of Cyrene to bear it. It was a reproach, and none would do it but by compulsion. Some think that this Simon was a disciple of Christ, at least a well-wisher to him, and that they knew it, and therefore put this upon him. All that will approve themselves disciples indeed, must follow Christ, *bearing his cross.*

Verses 33–49

We have here the crucifixion of our Lord Jesus.

I. The place where our Lord Jesus was put to death.

1. They came to a place called *Golgotha*, near adjoining to Jerusalem, probably the common place of execution. But now in the same place where criminals were sacrificed to the justice of the government, was our Lord Jesus sacrificed to the justice of God. Some think that it was called *the place of a skull*, because it was the common charnel-house, where the bones and skulls of dead men were laid together out of the way, lest people should touch them, and be defiled thereby. When by dying Christ would destroy death, he added this circumstance of honour to his victory, that he triumphed over death upon his own dunghill.

2. There they *crucified* him (*v.* 35), nailed his hands and feet to the cross, and then reared it up, and him hanging on it; for so the manner of the Romans was to crucify. Let our hearts be touched with the feeling of that exquisite pain which our blessed Saviour now endured. And when we behold what manner of death he died, let us in that behold with *what manner of love he loved us.*

II. The barbarous and abusive treatment they gave him. As if death, so great a death, were not bad enough, they contrived to add to the bitterness and terror of it.

1. By the drink they provided for him before he was nailed to the cross, *v.* 34. It was usual to have a cup of spiced wine for those to drink of, that were to be put to death. But with that cup which Christ was to drink of, they mingled *vinegar and gall*, to make it sour and bitter. He *tasted thereof*, and so had the *worst* of it, took the bitter taste into his mouth; now he was *tasting* death in its full bitterness.

JAMIESON, FAUSSET, BROWN

And said, Hail, King of the Jews!—doing Him derisive homage, in the form used on approaching the emperors. "And they spit upon Him, and took the reed and smote Him on the head" (Matt. 27:30). The best comment on these affecting details is to *cover the face.*

Cyrenian—of Cyrene, in Libya, on the north coast of Africa, where were many Jews who had a synagogue at Jerusalem (Acts 6:9, and see 2:10). He was "the father of Alexander and Rufus" (Mark 15:21), probably better known afterwards than himself, as disciples. (See Rom. 16:13.) **out of the country**—and casually drawn into that part of the crowd. **laid the cross**—"Him they compel to bear His cross," (Matt. 27:32)—sweet compulsion, if it issued in him or his sons *voluntarily* "taking up *their* cross!" It would appear that our Lord had first to bear His own cross (John 19:17), but being from exhaustion unable to proceed, it was laid on another to bear it "after Him."

34-50. Crucifixion and Death of the Lord Jesus. (=Mark 15:25-37; Luke 23:33-46; John 19:18-30). For the exposition, see on John 19: 18-30.

And he bearing his cross—(See on Luke 23:26). **went forth**—Cf. Hebrews 13:11-13, "without the camp"; "without the gate." On arriving at the place, "they gave Him vinegar to drink mingled with gall [wine mingled with myrrh, Mark 15:23], and when He had tasted thereof, He would not drink" (Matt. 27:34). This potion was stupefying, and given to criminals just before execution, to deaden the sense of pain.

> Fill high the bowl, and spice it well, and pour
> The dews oblivious: for the Cross is sharp,
> The Cross is sharp, and He
> Is tenderer than a lamb.
> [Keble]

But *our Lord would die with every faculty clear, and in full sensibility to all His sufferings.*

> Thou wilt feel all, that Thou may'st pity all;
> And rather would'st Thou wrestle with strong pain
> Than overcloud Thy soul,
> So clear in agony,
> Or lose one glimpse of Heaven before the time,
> O most entire and perfect Sacrifice,
> Renewed in every pulse.
> [Keble]

ADAM CLARKE

32. *A man of Cyrene . . . him they compelled to bear his cross.* In John, chap. xix. 16-17, we are told Christ himself bore the Cross, and this it is likely He did for a part of the way; but, being exhausted with the scourging and other cruel usage which He had received, He was found incapable of bearing it alone. Therefore they obliged Simon, not, **I** think, to bear it entirely, but to assist Christ, by bearing a part of it. It was a constant practice among the Romans to oblige criminals to bear their crosses to the place of execution, insomuch that Plutarch makes use of it as an illustration of the misery of vice. "Every kind of wickedness produces its own particular torment, just as every malefactor, when he is brought forth to execution, carries his own cross."

33. *A place called Golgotha.* From the Hebrew *golgoleth*, "a skull," probably so called from the many skulls of those who had suffered crucificion and other capital punishments scattered up and down in the place. It is the same as Calvary, *Calvaria*, i.e., *calvi capitis area*, the place of bare skulls. Some think the place was thus called because it was in the form of a human skull. It is likely that it was the place of public execution.

34. *They gave him vinegar to drink mingled with gall.* Perhaps *gall* signifies no more than bitters of any kind. It was a common custom to administer a stupefying potion compounded of sour wine, which is the same as vinegar, frankincense, and myrrh to condemned persons to help to alleviate their sufferings or so disturb their intellect that they might not be sensible

CHARLES H. SPURGEON:

Even as Isaiah had prophesied: "I gave my back to the smiters, and my cheeks to them that plucked off the hair; I hid not my face from shame and spitting." An old writer says concerning this shameful spitting, "What couldest thou have found on earth more vile and loathsome in order to thy abasement than that man should spit on thee? and this, moreover, with such railing and insult, as though thou wert the pest of mankind, a blasphemer and an outcast unworthy of the merest decencies of life! What, Lord, was there in thee to be loathed? Why, then, do they thus contemn and spit upon thee? Oh, my God, it is my due, not thine! Truly do I, Lord, deserve to be spitted on by every creature, as a vile and harmful thing, a wretched sinner, unworthy to live; but thou, Infinite Mercy, dost promote me to honor, dost spare me, and, for my sake, dost yield up the majesty of thy person and thy divine countenance to be humbled by such loathsome affronts and insults!"
—*Spurgeon's Devotional Bible*

MATTHEW HENRY

He *would not drink it*, because he would not have the *best of it*; would have nothing like an opiate to lessen his sense of pain, for he would die so as to *feel himself die*.

2. By the dividing of his garments, *v.* 35. When they nailed him to the cross, they *stripped* him of his garments. If we be at any time stripped of our comforts for Christ, let us bear it patiently; he was stripped for us. Enemies may strip us of our *clothes*, but cannot strip us of our *best comforts*; cannot take from us the *garments of praise*. The clothes of those that are executed are the executioner's fee: four soldiers were employed in crucifying Christ, and they must each of them have a share; his upper garment, if it were divided, would be of no use to any of them, and therefore they agreed to *cast lots* for it. Perhaps they had heard of those that had been cured by touching the hem of his garment, and they thought it valuable for some magic virtue in it. Or, It was for diversion; to pass away the time while they waited for his death, they would play a game at dice for the clothes. but, whatever they designed, the word of God is herein accomplished. In that famous *psalm*, the first words of which Christ made use of upon the cross, it was said, *They parted my garment among them, and cast lots upon my vesture*, Ps. xxii. 18. Christ stripped himself of his glories, to divide them among us.

They now *sat down, and watched him, v.* 36. But Providence so ordered it, that those who were appointed to *watch* him, thereby became unexceptionable witnesses for him; having the opportunity to see and hear that which extorted from them that noble confession (*v.* 54), *Truly this was the Son of God.*

3. By the *title* set up over his head, *v.* 37. It was usual not only by a crier to proclaim before them, but by a writing also over their heads to notify what was the crime for which they suffered; so they set up over Christ's head his accusation written, *This is Jesus the King of the Jews.* Here was no crime alleged against him. It is not said that he was a pretended Saviour, or a usurping King, but, *This is Jesus, a Saviour*; surely that was no crime; and, *This is the King of the Jews*; nor was that a crime; for they expected that the Messiah should be so. Here was a very glorious truth asserted concerning him—that he is *Jesus the King of the Jews*, that King whom the Jews expected and ought to have submitted to. Pilate, instead of accusing Christ as a Criminal, proclaimed him a *King*, and that *three times*, in three inscriptions. Thus God makes men to serve *his* purposes, quite beyond *their own.*

4. By his companions with him in suffering, *v.* 38. There were *two thieves crucified with him* at the same time, in the same place, under the same guard; two highway-men, or robbers upon the road, as the word properly signifies. It is probable that this was appointed to be *execution-day.* However it was, the scripture was fulfilled in it (Isa. liii. 12), *He was numbered with the transgressors.*

(1) It was a reproach to him, that he was *crucified with them.* He was made to partake with the vilest malefactors in their plagues, as if he had been a partaker with them in their sins. He was, at his death, numbered among the transgressors, that we, at our death, might be *numbered among the saints.*

(2) It was an additional reproach, that he was crucified *in the midst, between them*, as if he had been the worst of the three, the principal malefactor; for among *three* the *middle* is the place for the chief. Every circumstance was contrived to his dishonour, as if the great Saviour were of all others the *greatest sinner.* It was also intended to ruffle and discompose him, in his last moments, with the shrieks, and groans, and blasphemies, of these malefactors. But thus would Christ affect himself with the miseries of sinners, when he was suffering for their salvation.

5. By the blasphemies and revilings with which they loaded him when he was hanging upon the cross. One would have thought that, when they had nailed him to the cross, they had done their worst. A dying man, though an infamous man, should be treated with compassion. For aught that appears, not one of his friends, who the other day cried *Hosanna* to him, durst be seen to show him any respect.

(1) The common *people, that passed by, reviled him.* His extreme misery and exemplary patience under it, did not make them to relent; but they who by their outcries brought him to this, now think to justify themselves in it by their reproaches, as if they *did well* to *condemn* him. They *reviled* him.

[1] The persons that reviled him; *they that passed by*, the travellers that went along the road; they were possessed with prejudices against him by the reports and clamours of the High Priest's creatures. It is a hard thing to keep up a good opinion of persons and things that are *everywhere* run down,

JAMIESON, FAUSSET, BROWN

Then the soldiers, when they had crucified Jesus, took his garments, and made four parts; to every soldier—the four who nailed Him to the cross, and whose perquisite they were. **a part, and also his coat**—the Roman *tunic*, or close-fitting vest. **without seam, woven from the top throughout**—"perhaps denoting considerable skill and labor as necessary to produce such a garment, the work probably of one or more of the women who ministered in such things unto Him, Luke 8:3" [WEBSTER and WILKINSON]. **Let us not rend it, but cast lots . . ., whose it shall be, that the scripture might be fulfilled which saith, They parted my raiment among them; and for my vesture they did cast lots . . .** (Psalm 22:18). That a prediction so exceedingly specific—distinguishing one piece of dress from others, and announcing that while *those* should be parted amongst several, *that* should be given by lot to one person—that such a prediction should not only be fulfilled to the letter, but by a party of heathen military, without interference from either the friends of the enemies of the Crucified One, is surely worthy to be ranked among the wonders of this all-wonderful scene.

Pilate wrote a title, and put it on the cross . . . Jesus of Nazareth, the King of the Jews . . . and it was written in Hebrew—or Syro-Chaldaic, the language of the country—**and Greek**—the current language—**and Latin**—the official language. These were the chief languages of the earth, and this secured that all spectators should be able to read it. Stung by this, the Jewish ecclesiastics entreat that it may be so altered as to express, not His real dignity, but His false claim to it. But Pilate thought he had yielded quite enough to them; and having intended expressly to spite and insult them by this title, for having got him to act against his own sense of justice, he peremptorily refused them. And thus, amidst the conflicting passions of men, was proclaimed, in the chief tongues of mankind, from the Cross itself and in circumstances which threw upon it a lurid yet grand light, the truth which drew the Magi to His manger, and will yet be owned by all the world!

they crucified him, and two others with him—"malefactors" (Luke 23:33), "thieves" (rather "robbers," Matt. 27:38; Mark 15:27). **on either side one and Jesus in the midst**—a hellish expedient, to hold Him up as the worst of the three. But in this, as in many other of their doings, "the scripture was fulfilled, which saith (Isa. 53:12), *And he was numbered with the transgressors*"—(Mark 15: 28)—though the prediction reaches deeper.

ADAM CLARKE

of them. Some person, out of kindness, appears to have administered this to our blessed Lord; but He, as in all other cases, determining to endure the fullness of pain, refused to take what was thus offered to Him, choosing to tread the winepress alone.

35. *And they crucified him.* Crucifixion properly means the act of nailing or tying to a cross. The cross was made of two beams, either crossing at the top at right angles, like a *T*, or in the middle of their length, like an *X*. There was, besides, a piece on the center of the transverse beam, to which the accusation or statement of the crime of the culprit was attached, and a piece of wood which projected from the middle, on which the person sat, as on a sort of saddle, and by which the whole body was supported. It was probably the Romans who introduced it among the Jews. Before they became subject to the Romans, they used hanging or gibbeting, but not the cross. This punishment was the most dreadful of all others, for both the shame and the pain of it; and so scandalous that it was inflicted as the last mark of detestation upon the vilest of people. It was the punishment of robbers and murderers, provided they were slaves; but if they were free, it was thought too infamous a punishment for such, let their crimes be what they might. The body of the criminal was fastened to the upright beam, by nailing or tying the feet to it, and on the transverse piece by nailing, and sometimes tying the hands to it. The anguish occasioned by crucifixion was so intense that *crucio*, among the Romans, was the common word by which they expressed suffering and torment in general. *And parted his garments, casting lots.* These were the Roman soldiers who had crucified Him; and it appears from this circumstance that in those ancient times the spoils of the criminal were claimed by the executioners, as they are to the present day. It appears that they divided a part, and cast lots for the rest; viz., for His seamless coat, John xix. 23-24. *That it might be fulfilled which was spoken by the prophet,* [*saying*], *They parted my garments among them, and upon my vesture did they cast lots.* The whole of this quotation should be omitted, as making no part originally of the genuine text of this Evangelist. It is omitted by almost every MS. of worth and importance, by almost all the versions, and the most reputable of the primitive fathers, who have written or commented on the place. The words are plainly an interpolation, borrowed from John xix. 24, in which place they will be properly noticed.

36. *They watched him.* To prevent His disciples or relatives from taking away the body or affording any relief to the Sufferer.

37. *His accusation.* It was a common custom to affix a label to the cross, giving a statement of the crime for which the person suffered. It is with much propriety that Matthew calls this *accusation*, for it was false that Christ ever pretended to be King of the Jews in the sense the inscription held forth. He was accused of this, but there was no proof of the accusation; however it was affixed to the Cross. From John xix. 21 we find that the Jews wished this to be a little altered: "Write," said they, "that he said, I am King of the Jews," thus endeavoring by the addition of a vile lie to countenance their own conduct in putting Him to death. But this Pilate refused to do. Both Luke, chap. xxiii. 38, and John, chap. xix. 20, say that this accusation was written in Greek, Latin, and Hebrew.

38. *Two thieves.* "Robbers," or cutthroats, men who had committed robbery and murder; for it does not appear that persons were crucified for robbery only. Thus was our Lord "numbered" (His name enrolled, placed as it were in the death warrant) "with the transgressors," according to the prophetic declaration, Isa. liii. 12, and the Jews placed Him between these two, perhaps to intimate that He was the worst felon of the three.

MATTHEW HENRY

and spoken against. Every one is apt to say as the most say, and to throw a stone at that which is put into an ill name.

[2] The gesture they used, in contempt of him—*wagging their heads*; which signifies their triumph in his fall, and their insulting over him.

[3] The taunts and jeers they uttered. These are here recorded.

First, They upbraided him with his *destroying of the temple*. They industriously spread it among the people, to bring an *odium* upon him, that he had a design to destroy the temple; than which nothing would more *incense* the people against him. *"Thou that destroyest the temple*, that vast and strong fabric, try thy strength now in plucking up that *cross*, and drawing those *nails*, and so *save thyself*; if thou hast the power thou hast boasted of, this is a proper time to exert it, and give proof of it." He was *crucified in weakness* (2 Cor. xiii. 4), so it seemed to them; but indeed Christ crucified is the *Power of God*.

Secondly, They upbraided him with his saying that he was *the Son of God*; If thou be so, say they, *come down from the cross*. Now they take the devil's words out of his mouth, with which he tempted him in the wilderness (*ch.* iv. 3, 6), and renew the same assault; *If thou be the Son of God*. They think that now, or never, he must prove himself to be the *Son of God*; forgetting that he had proved it by the miracles he wrought; and unwilling to wait for the complete proof of it by his own resurrection, to which he had so often referred. This comes of judging things by the present aspect of them, without a due remembrance of what is *past*, and a patient expectation of *what may further be produced*.

(2) The *chief priests and scribes*, *v.* 41. They did not think it enough to invite the rabble to do it. They should have been in the temple at their devotion, for it was the first day of the feast of unleavened bread. but they were here at the place of execution, spitting their venom at the Lord Jesus. Did they disparage themselves thus, to do despite to Christ, and shall we be afraid of disparaging ourselves, by joining with the multitude to *do him honour*?

Two things the priests and elders upbraided him with.

[1] That he could not *save himself*, *v.* 42. *First*, They take it for granted that he *could not* save himself, and therefore had not the power he pretended to, when really he *would not* save himself, because he would die to *save us*. *Secondly*, They would insinuate that, because he did not now save himself, therefore all his pretence to save others was but sham and delusion. *Thirdly*, They upbraid him with being *the King of Israel*. Many people would like the *King of Israel* well enough, if he would but *come down from the cross*. But the matter is settled; if no cross, then no Christ, no crown. Those that would reign with him, must be willing to suffer with him, for Christ and his cross are *nailed together* in this world. *Fourthly*, They challenged him to *come down from the cross*. But his unchangeable love and resolution set him above, and fortified him against, this temptation, so that he did not *fail*, nor was *discouraged*. *Fifthly*, They promised that, if he would *come down from the cross, they would believe him*. When they had formerly demanded a sign, he told them that the sign he would give them, should be not his *coming down from the cross*, but, which was a greater instance of his power, his *coming up from the grave*. But to promise ourselves that we would believe, if we had such and such means and motives of faith as we ourselves would prescribe, is not only a gross instance of the deceitfulness of our hearts, but the sorry *refuge*, or *subterfuge* rather, of an obstinate destroying infidelity.

[2] That God, *his Father*, would *not save him* (*v.* 43); *He trusted in God*, for he said, *I am the Son of God*. Those who call God *Father*, and themselves *his children*, thereby profess to put a confidence in him, Ps. ix. 10. Now they suggest, that he did but deceive himself and others; for, if he had been the Son of God he would not have been *abandoned to* all this misery, much less *abandoned in* it. It was intended, *First*, To *vilify* him, and to make the standers-by think him a deceiver and an imposter. *Secondly*, To *terrify* him, and drive him to distrust and despair of his Father's power and love.

(3) To complete the reproach, the *thieves also that were crucified with him* were not only not reviled as he was, as if they had been saints compared with him, but *cast the same in his teeth*; that is, one of them did, who said, *If thou be the Christ, save thyself and us*, Luke xxiii. 39. One would think that of all people this thief had *least cause*, and should have had *least mind*, to banter Christ.

Well, thus our Lord Jesus having undertaken to satisfy the justice of God for the wrong done him in

JAMIESON, FAUSSET, BROWN

Now come the *mockeries*, and from four different quarters:—(1) "And *they that passed by* reviled Him, wagging their heads" in ridicule (Ps. 22:7; 109:25; cf. Jer. 18:16; Lam. 2:15). "Ah!"—'Ha,' an exclamation here of derision. "Thou that destroyest the temple, and buildest it in three days, save Thyself and come down from the cross" (Matt. 27:39, 40; Mark 15:29, 30). "It is evident that our Lord's saying, or rather this *perversion* of it (for He claimed not to *destroy*, but to *rebuild* the temple destroyed by them) had greatly exasperated the feeling which the priests and Pharisees had contrived to excite against Him. It is referred to as the principal fact brought out in evidence against Him on the trial (cf. Acts 6:13, 14), as an offense for which He deserved to suffer. And it is very remarkable that now *while it was receiving its real fulfilment*, it should be made more public and more impressive by the insulting proclamation of His enemies. Hence the importance attached to it after the resurrection, ch. 2:22" [WEBSTER and WILKINSON].

(2) "Likewise also the *chief priests*, mocking Him, *with the scribes and elders*, said, He saved others, Himself He cannot save." There was a deep truth in this, as in other taunts; for *both* He could not do, having "come to give *His* life a ransom for *many*." No doubt this added an unknown sting to the reproach. "If He be the king of Israel, let Him now come down from the cross, and we will believe Him." *No, they would not;* for those who resisted the evidence from the resurrection of Lazarus, and from His own resurrection, were beyond the reach of any amount of merely *external* evidence. "He trusted in God that He would deliver him; let Him deliver Him now if He will have Him [or 'delight in Him,] cf. Ps. 18:19; Deut. 21:14]; for He said, I am the Son of God" (Matthew 27:41-43). We thank you, O ye chief priests, scribes, and elders, for this triple testimony, unconsciously borne by you, to our Christ: first to *His habitual trust in God*, as a feature in His character so marked and palpable that even ye found upon it your impotent taunt; next, *to His identity with the Sufferer of the 22d Psalm*, whose very words (vs. 8) ye unwittingly appropriate, thus *serving yourselves heirs* to the dark office and impotent malignity of Messiah's enemies; and again, to the true sense of that august title which He took to Himself, "THE SON OF GOD," which He rightly interpreted at the very first (see on ch. 5:18) as a claim to that *oneness of nature* with Him, and *dearness to Him*, which a son has to his father. (3) "And *the soldiers* also mocked Him, coming to Him and offering Him vinegar, and saying, If thou be the king of the Jews, save Thyself" (Luke 23:36, 37). They insultingly offer to share with Him their own vinegar, or sour wine, the usual drink of Roman soldiers, it being about the time of their midday meal. In the taunt of the soldiers we have one of those *undesigned coincidences* which so strikingly verify these historical records. While the ecclesiastics deride Him for calling Himself, "the *Christ*, the *King of Israel*, the *Chosen*, the *Son of God*," the soldiers, to whom all such phraseology was mere Jewish jargon, make sport of Him as a pretender to *royalty* ("KING of the Jews"), an office and dignity which it belonged to them to comprehend. *"The thieves* also, which were crucified with Him, cast the same in His teeth" (Matt. 27:44; Mark 15:32). Not *both* of them, however, as some commentators unnaturally think we must understand these words; as if some sudden change came over the *penitent* one, which turned him from an unfeeling railer into a trembling petitioner. The plural "thieves" need not denote more than the *quarter* or *class* whence came this last and cruelest taunt—i.e., 'Not only did scoffs proceed from the *passers-by*, the *ecclesiastics*, the *soldiery*, but even from His *fellow sufferers*,' a mode of speaking which no one would think necessarily meant both of them. Cf. Matthew 2:20, "*They* are dead which sought the child's life," meaning *Herod;* and Mark 9:1, "There be *some* standing here," where it is next to certain that only John, the youngest and last survivor of

ADAM CLARKE

39. *Wagging their heads.* In token of contempt.

40. *Thou that destroyest.* Who pretended that you could have destroyed the Temple, and built it up again in three days. Cruelty is obliged to take refuge in lies in order to vindicate its infamous proceedings. *If thou be the Son of God.* Or rather, "a son of God," i.e., a peculiar favorite of the Most High.

42. *He saved others; himself he cannot save.* Or, "Cannot He save himself?"

43. *If he will have him.* Or "if He delight in Him."

44. *The thieves also . . . cast the same in his teeth.* That is, one of the robbers; for one, we find, was a penitent, Luke xxiii. 39-40.

MATTHEW HENRY

his honour by sin, he did it by suffering *in his honour*; by submitting to the utmost indignity that could be done to the worst of men; because he was made sin for us, he was thus made a curse for us.

III. We have here the frowns of heaven, which our Lord Jesus was under, in the midst of all these injuries and indignities from men. Concerning which, observe,

1. How this was signified—by an extraordinary and miraculous eclipse of the sun, which continued for *three hours, v.* 45. An extraordinary light gave intelligence of the birth of Christ (*ch.* ii. 2), and therefore it was proper that an extraordinary darkness should notify his death, for he is the *Light of the world.* This surprising, amazing, darkness was designed to stop the mouths of those blasphemers, who were reviling Christ as he hung on the cross. Though their hearts were not changed, yet they were silent, and stood doubting what this should mean, till after *three hours* the darkness *scattered*, and then (as appears by *v.* 47), like Pharaoh when the plague was over, they hardened their hearts. But that which was principally intended in this darkness, was, (1) Christ's present *conflict* with the *powers of darkness.* He fights them on their own ground; gives them all the advantage they could have against him by this darkness, lets them take the *wind* and *sun*, and yet baffles them, and so becomes more than a conqueror. (2) His present want of heavenly comforts. This darkness signified that dark cloud which the human soul of our Lord Jesus was now under. God makes his sun to shine upon the just and upon the unjust; but even the light of the sun was withheld from our Saviour, when he was *made sin for us.* When earth denied him a drop of cold water, heaven denied him a beam of light; having to deliver us from *utter darkness*, he did himself, in the depth of his sufferings, walk in darkness, and had no light. During the *three hours* that this darkness continued, we do not find that he said *one word*, but passed this time in a silent retirement into his own soul. Never were there three such hours since the day that God created man upon the earth, never such a dark and awful scene; the *crisis* of that great affair of man's redemption and salvation.

2. How he complained of it (*v.* 46); *About the ninth hour*, when it began to clear up, after a long and silent conflict. *Jesus cried, Eli, Eli, lama sabachthani?* The words are related in the Syriac tongue, in which they were spoken, for the sake of the perverse construction which his enemies put upon them, in putting *Elias*, for *Eli.* Now observe here,

(1) Whence he borrowed this complaint—from Ps. xxii. 1. This, and that other word, *Into thy hands I commit my spirit*, he fetched from David's psalms to teach us of what use the word of God is to us, to direct us in prayer, which will *help our infirmities.*

(2) How he uttered it—*with a loud voice*; which bespeaks the extremity of his pain and anguish, the strength of nature remaining in him, and the great earnestness of his spirit in this expostulation.

(3) What the complaint was—*My God, My God, why hast thou forsaken me?* A strange complaint to come from the mouth of our Lord Jesus, who, we are sure, was one in whom he was always *well pleased.* The Father now loved him, nay, he knew that *therefore he loved him, because he laid down his life for the sheep*; what, and yet forsaken of him, and in the midst of his sufferings too! Surely never sorrow was like unto that sorrow which extorted such a complaint as this. No wonder that such a complaint as this made the earth to quake, and rent the rocks.

Note, [1] That our Lord Jesus was, in his sufferings, for a time, *forsaken by his Father.* So he saith himself, who we are sure was under no mistake concerning his own case. Not as if there were any abatement of his Father's love to him, or his to his Father; but his Father forsook him. He delivered him up into the hands of his enemies, and did not appear to deliver him out of their hands. No angel is sent from heaven to deliver him, no friend on earth raised up to appear for him. When *his soul* was first *troubled*, he had a *voice from heaven* to comfort him (John xii. 27, 28); when he was in his agony in the garden, there appeared an angel from heaven strengthening him; but now he had neither the one nor the other. God hid his face from him. Christ was made *Sin* for us, a *Curse* for us; and therefore, though God loved him as a Son, he frowned upon him as a Surety.

[2] That Christ's being *forsaken* of his Father was the most grievous of his sufferings. Here he laid the most doleful accents. When his Father stood at a distance, he cried out thus; for this was it that *put wormwood and gall* into the affliction and misery.

[3] That our Lord Jesus, even when he was thus forsaken of his Father, kept hold of him as his God,

JAMIESON, FAUSSET, BROWN

the apostles, is meant. And is it conceivable that this penitent thief should have first himself reviled the Saviour, and then, on his views of Christ suddenly changing, he should have turned upon his fellow sufferer and fellow reviler, and rebuked him not only with dignified sharpness, but in the language of *astonishment* that he should be capable of such conduct? Besides, there is a deep calmness in all that he utters, extremely unlike what we should expect from one who was the subject of a mental revolution so sudden and total. On the scene itself, see on Luke 23:29-43.

Now occurred the supernatural *darkness*, recorded by all the other Evangelists, but not here. "Now from the sixth hour (12, noon) there was darkness over all the land unto the ninth hour" (Matt. 27: 45). No ordinary eclipse of the sun could have occurred at this time, it being then *full moon*, and this obscuration lasted about *twelve times* the length of any ordinary eclipse. (Cf. Exod. 10:21, 23). Beyond doubt, the divine intention of the portent was to invest this darkest of all tragedies with a gloom expressive of its real character.

"And about the ninth hour Jesus cried, ELI, ELI, LAMA SABACTHANI . . . *My God, My God, why hast Thou forsaken Me?*" (Matt. 27:46). As the darkness commenced at the sixth hour, the second of the Jewish hours of prayer, so it continued till the ninth hour, *the hour of the evening sacrifice*, increasing probably in depth, and *reaching its deepest gloom at the moment of this mysterious cry*, when the flame of the one great "Evening Sacrifice" was burning fiercest. The words were made to His hand. They are the opening words of a Psalm (the 22d) full of the last "sufferings of Christ and the following glories" (I Pet. 1:11). "FATHER," was the cry in the first prayer which He uttered on the cross, for matters had not then come to the worst. "Father" was the cry of His last prayer, for matters had then passed their worst. But at this crisis of His sufferings, "Father" does not issue from His lips, for the light of a Father's countenance was then mysteriously eclipsed. He falls back, however, on a title expressive of His *official* relation, which, though lower and more distant in itself, yet when grasped in pure and naked faith was mighty in its claims, and rich in psalmodic associations. And what deep earnestness is conveyed by the redoubling of this title! But as for the cry itself, it will never be fully comprehended. An absolute desertion is not indeed to be thought of; but a total eclipse of the *felt* sense of God's presence it certainly expresses. It expresses *surprise*, as under the experience of something not only *never before known*, but *inexplicable* on the footing which had till then subsisted between Him and God. *It is a question which the lost cannot utter.* They are forsaken, *but they know why.* Jesus is forsaken, but *does not know and demands to know why.* It is thus *the cry of conscious innocence*, but of innocence unavailing to draw down, at that moment, the least token of approval from the unseen Judge—innocence whose only recognition at that moment lay in the thick surrounding gloom which but reflected the horror of great darkness that invested His own spirit. *There was indeed a cause for it*, and He knew it too—the "why" must not be pressed so far as to exclude this. *He must taste this bitterest of the wages of sin* "*who did no sin.*" But that is not the point now. In Him there was no cause at all (ch. 14:30) and He takes refuge in the glorious fact. When no ray from above shines in upon Him, He strikes a light out of His own breast. If God will not own Him, He shall own Himself. On the rock of His unsullied allegiance to Heaven He will stand, till the light of Heaven returns to His spirit. And it is near to come. While He is yet speaking, the fierceness of the flame is beginning to abate. One incident and insult more, and the experience of one other predicted element of suffering, and the victory is His. The incident, and the insult springing out of it, is the misunderstanding of the cry, for we can hardly suppose that it was anything else. "Some of them that stood there, when they heard that, said, This man calleth for Elias" (Matthew 27:47).

ADAM CLARKE

45. *There was darkness over all the land.* I am of opinion that does not mean all the world but only the land of Judea. So the word is used chap. xxiv. 30; Luke ix. 25, and in other places.

46. *My God, my God, why hast thou forsaken me?* These words are quoted by our Lord from Ps. xxii. 1; they are of very great importance, and should be carefully considered. Some suppose "that the divinity had now departed from Christ, and that his human nature was left unsupported to bear the punishment due to men for their sins." But this is by no means to be admitted, as it would deprive His sacrifice of its infinite merit, and consequently leave the sin of the world without an atonement. Take deity away from any redeeming act of Christ and redemption is ruined. Others imagine that our Lord spoke these words to the Jews only, to prove to them that He was the Messiah. "The Jews," say they, "believed this psalm to speak of the Messiah. They quoted the eighth verse of it against Christ—'He trusted on the Lord that he would deliver him: let him deliver him, seeing he delighted in him.' (See this chap., v. 43.) To which our Lord immediately answers, *My God, my God*, thus showing that He was the Person of whom the Psalmist prophesied." I have doubts concerning the propriety of this interpretation. The words might be thus translated: "My God! My God! to what sort of persons hast Thou left Me?" The words thus understood are rather to be referred to the wicked Jews than to our Lord, and are an exclamation indicative of the obstinate wickedness of His crucifiers, who steeled their hearts against every operation of the Spirit and power of God. Through the whole of the Sacred Writings, God is represented as *doing* those things which, in the course of His providence, he only *permits to be done.* Therefore the words, "To whom hast Thou left or given Me up?" are only a form of expression for "How astonishing is the wickedness of those persons into whose hands I am fallen!" If this interpretation be admitted, it will free this celebrated passage from much embarrassment, and make it speak a sense consistent with itself, and with the dignity of the Son of God. The words of Mark, chap. xv. 34, agree pretty nearly with this translation of the Hebrew: "To what [sort of persons, understood] has Thou left me?" But whatever may be thought of the above mode of interpretation, one thing is certain, viz., that the words could not be used by our Lord in the sense in which they are generally understood. This is sufficiently evident, for He well knew why He was come *unto that hour;* nor could He be forsaken of God, in whom dwelt all the fullness of the Godhead bodily. The Deity, however, might restrain so much of its consolatory support as to leave the human nature fully sensible of all its sufferings, so that the consolations might not take off any part of the keen edge of His passion; and this was necessary to make His sufferings meritorious. And it is probable that this is all that is intended by our Lord's quotation from the twenty-second psalm. Taken in this view, the words convey an unexceptionable sense, even in the common translation.

MATTHEW HENRY

notwithstanding; *My God, my God*; though forsaking me, yet *mine*. This supported him, and bore him up, that even in the depth of his sufferings God was his God, and this he resolves to keep fast hold of.

(4) See how his enemies impiously bantered and ridiculed this complaint (*v.* 47); *They said, This man calleth for Elias.* Some think that this was the ignorant mistake of the Roman soldiers, who knew not the signification of *Eli, Eli*, and so made this blundering comment upon these words of Christ. Many of the reproaches cast upon the word of God and the people of God, take rise from gross mistakes. Those that hear by the halves, pervert what they hear. But others think that it was the wilful mistake of some of the Jews, who knew very well what he said, but were disposed to abuse him, and to misrepresent him as one who, being forsaken of God, was driven to trust in creatures. It is no new thing for the most pious devotions of the best men to be ridiculed and abused by profane scoffers. Christ's words were so, though he spoke as never man spoke.

IV. The cold comfort which his enemies ministered to him in this agony.

1. Some *gave him vinegar to drink* (*v.* 48); instead of some cordial-water to revive and refresh him under this heavy burthen. *One of them ran* to fetch it.

2. Others, with the same purpose of disturbing and abusing him, refer him to Elias (*v.* 49); "*Let be, let us see whether Elias will come to save him.* Come, let him alone, he has appealed to Elias, and *to Elias let him go.*"

Verses 50-56

We have here, at length, an account of the death of Christ.

I. The *manner* how he breathed his last (*v.* 50); between the third and the sixth hour, that is, between nine and twelve o'clock, as we reckon, he was nailed to the cross, and soon after the ninth hour, that is, between three and four o'clock, in the afternoon, he *died.* That was the time of the offering of the evening sacrifice, and the time when the paschal lamb was killed; and Christ our Passover was sacrificed for us.

Two things are here noted concerning the manner of Christ's dying.

1. That he *cried with a loud voice*, as before, *v.* 46. Now,

(1) This was a sign, that, after all his pains and fatigues, his life was *whole* in him, and nature *strong.* The voice of dying men is one of the first things that fails; with a panting breath and a faltering tongue, a few broken words are hardly spoken, and more hardly heard. But Christ, just before he expired, spoke like a man *in his full strength*, to show that his life was not forced from him, but was freely *delivered* by him into his Father's hands.

(2) It was significant. His crying with a loud voice when he died, signified that his death should be published and proclaimed to all the world. Christ's loud cry was like a trumpet blown over the sacrifices.

2. That then he *yielded up the ghost.* This is the usual periphrasis of dying; to show that the Son of God upon the cross did truly and properly die by the violence of the pain he was put to. His *soul* was separated from his *body*, and so his body was left really and truly dead. He had undertaken to make his soul an *offering for sin.*

II. The miracles that attended his death. So many miracles being wrought *by him* in his life, we might well expect some to be wrought concerning him at his death.

1. *Behold, the veil of the temple was rent in twain.* Just as our Lord Jesus expired, at the time of the offering of the evening sacrifice, *the veil of the temple was rent* by an invisible power; that veil which parted between the *holy place* and the *most holy.* In this, as in others of Christ's miracles, there was a mystery.

(1) It was in correspondence with the temple of Christ's body, which was now in the dissolving. Death is the rending of the veil of flesh which interposes between us and the holy of holies; the death of Christ was so, the death of true Christians is so.

(2) It signified the revealing and unfolding of the mysteries of the Old Testament. The veil of the temple was for concealment, for it was highly penal for any person to see the furniture of the most holy place, except the High Priest, and he but once a year, with great ceremony and through a cloud of smoke. But now, at the death of Christ, all was laid open, the mysteries were unveiled, so that now he that runs may read the meaning of them.

(3) It signified the uniting of Jew and Gentile, by the removing of the partition wall between them, which was the ceremonial law. Christ, in his death, repealed the ceremonial law, took it out of the way, nailed it to his cross. Christ died, to rend all dividing veils, and to make all his one, John xvii. 21.

JAMIESON, FAUSSET, BROWN

filled a sponge with vinegar, and put it upon—a stalk of—**hyssop, and put it to his mouth**—Though a stalk of this plant does not exceed eigtheen inches in length, it would suffice, as the feet of crucified persons were not raised high. "The rest said, Let be"—[i.e., as would seem, 'Stop that officious service'] "let us see whether Elias will come to save Him" (Matt. 27:49). This was the last cruelty He was to suffer, but it was one of the most unfeeling. "And when Jesus had cried with a loud voice" (Luke 23:46). This "*loud voice,*" noticed by three of the Evangelists, does not imply, as some able interpreters contend, that our Lord's strength was so far from being exhausted that He needed not to die then, and surrendered up His life sooner than Nature required, merely because it was the appointed time. It was indeed the appointed time, but time that He should be "crucified *through weakness*" (I Cor. 13:4), and Nature was now reaching its utmost exhaustion. But just as even His own dying saints, particularly the martyrs of Jesus, have sometimes had such gleams of coming glory immediately before breathing their last, as to impart to them a strength to utter their feelings which has amazed the bystanders, so this *mighty voice* of the expiring Redeemer was nothing else but the exultant spirit of the Dying Victor, receiving the fruit of His travail just about to be embraced, and nerving the organs of utterance to an ecstatic expression of its sublime feelings (not so much in the *immediately* following words of tranquil surrender, in Luke, as in the *final* shout, recorded only by John): "FATHER, INTO THY HANDS I COMMEND MY SPIRIT!" (Luke 23:46). Yes, the darkness is past, and the true light now shineth. His soul has emerged from its mysterious horrors; "*My God*" is heard no more, but in unclouded light He yields sublime into His *Father's* hands the infinitely precious spirit—using here also the words of those matchless Psalms (31:5) which were ever on His lips. "As the Father receives the spirit of Jesus, so Jesus receives those of the faithful" (Acts 7:59) [BENGEL]. And now comes the expiring mighty shout— **It is finished! and he bowed his head and gave up the ghost.** What is finished? The Law is fulfilled as never before, nor since, in His "obedience unto death, even the death of the cross"; Messianic prophecy is accomplished; Redemption is completed; "He hath finished the transgression, and made reconciliation for iniquity, and brought in everlasting righteousness, and sealed up the vision and prophecy, and anointed a holy of holies"; He has inaugurated the kingdom of God and given birth to a new world.

51-66. SIGNS AND CIRCUMSTANCES FOLLOWING THE DEATH OF THE LORD JESUS—HE IS TAKEN DOWN FROM THE CROSS, AND BURIED—THE SEPULCHRE IS GUARDED. (=Mark 15:38-47; Luke 23:47-56; John 19:31-42).

The Veil Rent (vs. 51). **51. And, behold, the veil of the temple was rent in twain from the top to the bottom**—This was the thick and gorgeously wrought veil which was hung between the "holy place" and the "holiest of all," shutting out all access to the presence of God as manifested "from above the mercy seat and from between the cherubim"—"the Holy Ghost this signifying, that the way into the holiest of all was *not yet* made manifest" (Heb. 9:8). Into this holiest of all none might enter, not even the high priest, save once a year, on the great day of atonement, and then only with the blood of atonement in his hands, which he sprinkled "upon and before the mercy seat seven times" (Lev. 16:14)—to signify that *access for sinners to a holy God is only through atoning blood.* But as they had only the blood of bulls and of goats, which could not take away sins (Heb. 10:4), during all the long ages that preceded the death of Christ the thick veil remained; the blood of bulls and of goats continued to be shed and sprinkled; and once a year access to God through an atoning sacrifice was vouchsafed—*in a picture*, or rather, was *dramatically represented*, in those symbolical actions—nothing more. But *now*, the one atoning Sacrifice being provided in the precious blood of Christ, access to this holy God could no longer be

ADAM CLARKE

47. *This man calleth for Elias.* Probably these were Hellenistic Jews, who did not fully understand the meaning of our Lord's words. Elijah was daily expected to appear as the forerunner of the Messiah, whose arrival, under the character of a mighty prince, was generally supposed to be at hand throughout the East. See Mal. iii. 23; Matt. ii. 2-4; xvii. 10-12.

48. *Took a spunge.* This being the most convenient way to reach a liquid to His mouth; tied it *on a reed*, that they might be able to reach His lips with it. This reed, as we learn from John, was a stalk of hyssop, which in that country must have grown to a considerable magnitude. This appears also to have been done in mercy, to alleviate His sufferings. See v. 34.

50. *Yielded up the ghost.* "He dismissed the spirit." He himself willingly gave up that life which it was impossible for man to take away. It is not said that He hung on the Cross till He died through pain and agony; nor is it said that His bones were broken, the sooner to put Him out of pain, and to hasten His death. But that He himself "dismissed the soul," that He might thus become, not a forced sacrifice, but a freewill Offering for sin. Now, as our English word *ghost*, from the Anglo-Saxon *gast*, an "inmate, inhabitant, guest" (a casual visitant), also a "spirit," is now restricted among us to the latter meaning, always signifying the immortal spirit or soul of man, the guest of the body; and as giving up the spirit, ghost, or soul, is an act not proper to man, though commending it to God, in our last moments, is both an act of faith and piety; and as giving up the ghost, i.e., dismissing His spirit from His body, is attributed to Jesus Christ, to whom alone it is proper. I therefore object against its use in every other case. Every man, since the Fall, has not only been liable to death, but has deserved it, as all have forfeited their lives because of sin. Jesus Christ, as born immaculate, and having never sinned, had not forfeited His life, and therefore may be considered as naturally and properly immortal. "No man," says He, "taketh it," My life, "from me, but I lay it down of myself. I have power to lay it down, and I have power to take it again . . . Therefore doth my Father love me, because I lay down my life, that I might take it again," John x. 18, 17. Hence we rightly translate Matt. xxvii. 50. "He gave up the ghost"; i.e., He "dismissed His spirit," that He might die for the sin of the world. The Evangelist John, xix. 30, makes use of an expression to the same import, which we translate in the same way: "He delivered up His spirit." We translate Mark xv. 37 and Luke xxiii. 46, "He gave up the ghost," but not correctly, because the word in both these places is very different—"He breathed His last," or "expired"; though in the latter place, Luke xxiii. 46, there is an equivalent expression —"Father, into thy hands I commend my spirit"; i.e., "I place My soul in Thy hand," proving that the act was His own, that no man could take His life away from Him, that He did not die by the perfidy of His disciple or the malice of the Jews, but by His own free act. Thus He laid down his life for the sheep. Of Ananias and Sapphira, Acts v. 5, 10, and of Herod, Acts xii. 23, our translation says, they "gave up the ghost"; but the word in both places is simply to "breathe out," to "expire," or "die." But in no case, either by the Septuagint in the Old, or any of the sacred writers in the New Testament, is "He dismissed his spirit," or "delivered up his spirit," spoken of any person but Christ. Abraham, Isaac, Ishmael, Jacob, and others "breathed their last"; Ananias, Sapphira, and Herod "expired"; but none, Jesus Christ excepted, "gave

MATTHEW HENRY

(4) It signified the consecrating and laying open of *a new and living way* to God. The veil kept people off from drawing near to the most holy place, where the *Shechinah* was. But the rending of it signified that Christ by his death opened a way to God, [1] *For himself.* Having offered his sacrifice in the outer court, the blood of it was now to be sprinkled upon the mercy-seat within the veil. Though he did not personally ascend into the holy place not made with hands till above forty days after, yet he immediately acquired a right to enter, and had a virtual admission. [2] *For us in him:* so the apostle applies it, Heb. x. 19, 20. He died, to *bring us to God*, and, in order thereunto, to rend that veil of guilt and wrath which interposed between us and him. We have free access through Christ to the throne of grace, or mercy-seat, now, and to the throne of glory hereafter, Heb. iv. 16. *When Christ had overcome the sharpness of death, he opened the kingdom of heaven to all believers.* Nothing can obstruct or discourage our access to heaven.

2. The *earth did quake.* This earthquake signified two things.

(1) The *horrible* wickedness of *Christ's crucifiers.* The earth, by trembling under such a load, bore its testimony to the innocency of him that was persecuted, and against the impiety of those that persecuted him.

(2) The *glorious* achievements of *Christ's cross.* This *earthquake* signified the mighty shock, nay, the fatal blow, now given to the devil's kingdom. God shakes all nations, when the Desire of all nations is to come.

3. The *rocks rent*; the hardest and firmest part of the earth was made to feel this mighty shock. Christ had said, that if the children should cease to cry *Hosanna, the stones would immediately cry out*; and now, in effect, they did so, proclaiming the glory of the suffering Jesus. Jesus Christ is *the Rock*; and the rending of *these* rocks, signified the rending of *that* rock, (1) That in the clefts of it we may be *hid*, as Moses in the cleft of the rock at Horeb, that there we may *behold the glory of the Lord*, as he did. (2) That from the cleft of it rivers of living water may flow, and follow us in this wilderness. When we celebrate the memorial of Christ's death, our hard and rocky hearts must be *rent*—the heart, and not the garments. That heart is harder than a rock, that will not *yield*, that will not *melt*, where Jesus Christ is *evidently set forth crucified*.

4. The *graves were opened.* It should seem, the same earthquake that rent the rocks, *opened the graves*, and many bodies of *saints which slept, arose.* Death to the saints is but the *sleep* of the body, and the *grave* the bed it *sleeps in*; they awoke by the power of the Lord Jesus, and (*v.* 53) came *out of the graves after his resurrection, and went into Jerusalem, the holy city, and appeared unto many.* We may raise many enquiries concerning it, which we cannot resolve: as, [1] *Who* these *saints* were, that *did arise.* Some think, the *ancient patriarchs*, that were in such care to be buried in the land of Canaan. Others think, these that arose were *modern saints.* such as had seen Christ in the flesh, but died before him. What if we should suppose that they were the *martyrs*, who in the Old Testament times had sealed the truths of God with their blood. Sufferers with Christ shall *first* reign with him. [2] It is uncertain whether (as some think) they arose to life, now at the death of Christ, but did not *go into the city* till after his resurrection; or whether they did not *revive* and *rise* till after the resurrection; only, for brevity-sake, it is mentioned here, upon the mention of the *opening of the graves.* [3] Some think that they arose only to bear witness of Christ's resurrection to those to whom they appeared, and, having finished their testimony, retired to their graves again. But it is more agreeable, both to Christ's honour and theirs, to *suppose* that they arose as Christ did, to *die no more.* Surely on them who did partake of his first resurrection, a *second* death had no power. [4] To whom they appeared, whether enemies or friends, in what manner they appeared, how often, what they said and did, are secret things which belong not to us. The relating of this matter so briefly, is a plain intimation to us, that we must not look that way for a confirmation of our faith; we have a more sure word of prophecy.

Yet we may learn many good lessons from it. [1] That even those who lived and died before the death and resurrection of Christ, had saving benefit thereby, as well as those who have lived since. [2] That Jesus Christ, by dying, conquered, disarmed, and disabled, death. These saints that arose, were the present trophies of the victory of Christ's cross over the powers of *death.* [3] That, in virtue of Christ's resurrection, the bodies of all the saints shall, in

JAMIESON, FAUSSET, BROWN

denied; and so the moment the Victim expired on the altar, that thick veil which for so many ages had been the dread symbol of *separation between God and guilty men* was, without a hand touching it, mysteriously "rent in twain from top to bottom" —"the Holy Ghost this signifying, that the way into the holiest of all was NOW made manifest!" How emphatic the statement, "*from top to bottom*"; as if to say, Come boldly now to the Throne of Grace; *the veil is clean gone*; the mercy seat stands open to the gaze of sinners, and the way to it is sprinkled with the blood of Him—"who through the eternal Spirit hath offered Himself without spot to God!" Before, it was death *to go in*, now it is *death to stay out.* See more on this glorious subject on Hebrews 10:19-22.

An Earthquake—The Rocks Rent—The Graves Opened, that the Saints Which Slept in Them Might Come Forth after Their Lord's Resurrection (vss. 51-53). **51. and the earth did quake**—From what follows it would seem that this earthquake was local, having for its object the rending of the rocks and the opening of the graves—**and the rocks rent**—"were rent"—the physical creation thus sublimely proclaiming, at the bidding of its Maker, the *concusssion* which at that moment was taking place in the moral world at the most critical moment of its history. Extraordinary rents and fissures have been observed in the rocks near this spot.

52. And the graves were opened; and many bodies of the saints which slept arose—These sleeping saints (see on I Thess. 4:14) were Old Testament believers, who—according to the usual punctuation in our version—were quickened into resurrection-life at the moment of their Lord's death, but lay in their graves till His resurrection, when they came forth. But it is far more natural, as we think, and consonant with other Scriptures, to understand that only the graves were opened, probably by the earthquake, at our Lord's death, and this only in preparation for the subsequent exit of those who slept in them, when the Spirit of life should enter into them from their risen Lord, and along with Him they should come forth, trophies of His victory over the grave. Thus, in the opening of the graves at the moment of the Redeemer's expiring, there was a glorious symbolical proclamation that the death which had just taken place had "swallowed up death in victory"; and whereas the saints that slept in them were awakened only by their risen Lord, to accompany Him out of the tomb, it was fitting that "the Prince of Life" "should be *the First* that should rise from the dead" (Acts 26:23; I Cor. 15:20, 23; Col. 1:18; Rev. 1:5). **and went into the holy city**—that city where He, in virtue of whose resurrection they were now alive, had been condemned. **and appeared unto many**—that there might be undeniable evidence of their own resurrection first, and through it of their Lord's. Thus, while it was not deemed fitting that He Himself should appear again in Jerusalem, save to the disciples, provision was made that the fact of His resurrection should be left in no doubt. It must be observed, however, that the resurrection of these sleeping saints was not like those of the widow of Nain's son, of Jairus' daughter, of Lazarus, and of the man who "revived and stood upon his feet," on his dead body touching the bones of Elisha (II Kings 13:21)—which were mere temporary recallings of the departed spirit to the *mortal* body, to be followed by a final departure of it "till the trumpet shall sound." But this was a resurrection *once for all, to life everlasting;* and so there is no room to doubt that they went to glory with their Lord, as bright trophies of His victory over death.

ADAM CLARKE

up the ghost, dismissed, or delivered up his own spirit."

51. *The veil of the temple was rent.* That is, the veil which separated the holy place, where the priests ministered, from the holy of holies, into which the high priest only entered, and that once a year, to make a general expiation for the sins of the people. This rending of the veil was emblematical, and pointed out that the separation between Jews and Gentiles was now abolished, and that the privilege of the high priest was now communicated to all mankind. All might henceforth have access to the throne of grace, through the one great Atonement and Mediator, the Lord Jesus. See this beautifully illustrated in Heb. x. 19-22.

52. *And the graves were opened.* By the earthquake; *and many bodies of saints which slept*, i.e., were dead, sleep being a common expression for death in the Scriptures.

53. *And came out of the graves after his resurrection.* Not before, as some have thought, for Christ was himself the Firstfruits of them, who slept, 1 Cor. xv. 20. The *graves* were opened at His death by the earthquake, and the bodies came out at His *resurrection. And appeared unto many.* Thus establishing the truth of our Lord's resurrection in particular, and of the resurrection of the body in general, by many witnesses.

MATTHEW HENRY

the fulness of time, *rise again*. This was an earnest of the general resurrection at the last day.

III. The conviction of his enemies that were employed in the execution, *v.* 54.

1. The persons convinced; *the centurion, and they that were with him watching Jesus.* (1) They were *soldiers*, whose profession is commonly hardening, and whose breasts are commonly not so susceptible as some others of the impressions either of fear or pity. But there is no spirit too big, too bold, for the power of Christ to break and humble. (2) They were *Romans, Gentiles,* yet they only were convinced. Here were the Gentiles *softened*, and the Jews *hardened*. (3) They were the persecutors of Christ, and those that but just before had reviled him, as appears Luke xxiii. 36. How soon can God, by the power he has over men's consciences, alter their language.

2. The means of their conviction; they perceived *the earthquake*, which frightened them, and saw the other *things that were done*. These had their end on these soldiers, whatever they had on others.

3. The expressions of this conviction, in two things.

(1) The *terror* that was *struck* upon them; they *feared greatly*; feared lest they should have been buried in the darkness, or swallowed up in the earthquake. God can easily frighten the most daring of his adversaries. Guilt puts men into fear. Whereas there are those who will not fear, *though the earth be removed*, Ps. xlvi. 1, 2.

(2) The *testimony* that was *extorted* from them; they said, *Truly this was the Son of God*. It was the great matter now in dispute, the point upon which he and his enemies had *joined issue, ch.* xxvi. 63, 64. His disciples believed it, but at this time durst not confess it; our Saviour himself was tempted to question it, when he said, *Why hast thou forsaken me?* The Jews, now that he was dying upon the cross, looked upon it as plainly determined against him. And yet now this centurion and the soldiers make this voluntary confession of the Christian faith, *Truly this was the Son of God*. The best of his disciples could not have said more at any time, and at this time they had not faith and courage enough to say thus much.

IV. The attendance of his friends, that were witnesses of his death, *v.* 55, 56.

1. Who they were; *many women who followed him from Galilee*. Not his apostles (only elsewhere we find John by the cross, John xix. 26), their hearts failed them, they durst not appear. But here were a company of women, some would have called them *silly* women, that *boldly* stuck to Christ, when the rest of his disciples had basely deserted him. Even those of the weaker sex are often, by the grace of God, made strong in faith. There have been women martyrs, famous for courage and resolution in Christ's cause. Now of these women it is said, (1) That they had *followed Jesus from Galilee*, out of the great love they had to him. The males only were obliged to come up, to worship at the feast. Now having followed him such a long journey they resolved not to forsake him now. Our former services and sufferings for Christ should be an argument with us, faithfully to persevere to the end in our attendance on him. (2) That they *ministered to him* of their substance. How gladly would they have ministered to him now, if they might have been admitted! When we are restrained from doing what we *would*, we must do what we can, in the service of Christ. (3) Some of them are particularly named. They were such as we have several times met with *before*, and it was their praise, that we meet with them *to the last*.

2. What they did; they were *beholding afar off*.

(1) They stood *afar off*. It was an aggravation of the sufferings of Christ, that his *lovers and friends stood aloof from his sore*. Perhaps they might have come nearer, if they would; but good people, when they are in sufferings, must not think it strange, if some of their best friends be shy of them. If we be thus looked strangely upon, remember, our Master was so before us.

(2) They were there *beholding*; when they were debarred from doing any other office of love to him, they looked a look of love toward him. It was a *sorrowful* look. We may well imagine how it cut them to the heart, to see him in this torment. Let us with an eye of faith behold Christ and him crucified, and be affected with that great love wherewith he loved us. It was no more than a look; they beheld him, but they could not *help him*. When Christ was in his sufferings, the best of his friends were but spectators and lookers on.

Verses 57-66

We have here an account of Christ's *burial*. 1. The *kindness* and *goodwill* of his friends that *laid him in the grave*. 2. The *malice* and *ill will* of his enemies

JAMIESON, FAUSSET, BROWN

The Centurion's Testimony (vs. 54). **Now when the centurion**—the military superintendent of the execution.

and they that were with him watching Jesus, saw the earthquake—or felt it and witnessed its effects. **and those things that were done**—reflecting upon the entire transaction. **they feared greatly**—convinced of the presence of a Divine Hand.

saying, Truly this was the Son of God—There cannot be a reasonable doubt that this expression was used in the Jewish sense, and that it points to the claim which Jesus made to be the Son of God, and on which His condemnation expressly turned. The meaning, then, clearly is that He must have been what He professed to be; in other words, that He was no impostor. There was no medium between those two. See, on the similar testimony of the penitent thief—"This man hath done nothing amiss"—on Luke 23:41.

The Galilean Women (vss. 55, 56). **55. And many women were there beholding afar off, which followed Jesus**—The sense here would be better brought out by the use of the pluperfect, "which had followed Jesus." **from Galilee, ministering unto him**—As these dear women had ministered to Him during His glorious missionary tours *in* Galilee (see on Luke 8:1-3), so from this statement it should seem that they accompanied him and ministered to His wants *from* Galilee on His final journey to Jerusalem. **56. Among which was Mary Magdalene**—(see on Luke 8:2). **and Mary the mother of James and Joses**—the wife of Cleophas, or rather Clopas, and sister of the Virgin (John 19:25). See on ch. 13:55, 56. **and the mother of Zebedee's children**—i.e., Salome: cf. Mark 15:40. All this about the women is mentioned for the sake of what is afterwards to be related of their purchasing spices to anoint their Lord's body.

The Taking Down from the Cross and the Burial (vss 57-60). For the exposition of this portion, see on John 19:38-42.

ADAM CLARKE

54. *The centurion.* The Roman officer who superintended the execution, called *centurio,* from *centum,* a hundred, because he had the command of 100 men.

Truly this was the Son of God. An innocent, holy, and divine Person; and God thus shows His disapprobation of this bloody tragedy. It is not likely that this centurion had any knowledge of the expectation of the Jews relative to the Messiah, and did not use the words in this sense. "A son of God," as the Romans used the term, would signify no more than a very eminent or divine person, a hero.

55. *Many women.* To their everlasting honor, these women evidenced more courage and affectionate attachment to their Lord and Master than the disciples did, who had promised to die with Him rather than forsake Him. *Beholding afar off.* "At a distance."

56. *Mary Magdalene.* She probably had her name from Magdala, a village or district in Lower Galilee. See chap. xv. 39. *Mary the mother of James.* She was mother of him called James the lesser, or junior, who was son of Alphaeus or Cleopas; see chap. x. 3; Mark xv. 40; John xix. 25; and she was sister to the Holy Virgin. Thus it appears that there were four remarkable Marys mentioned in the Gospels: (1) Mary the Virgin, wife of Joseph. (2) Mary Salome, her sister, wife of Cleopas, John xix. 25. (3) Mary Magdalene, or Mary of Magdala; and (4) Mary, the sister of Martha and Lazarus, John xi. 1.

MATTHEW HENRY

that were very solicitous to keep him there.

I. His friends gave him a *decent burial.*

1. Jesus Christ was *buried*; when his precious soul was gone to paradise, his blessed body was deposited in the chambers of the grave. He was buried, to make his death the more certain, and his resurrection the more illustrious. Pilate would not deliver his body to be buried, till he was well assured that he was really dead. He was *buried*, that he might take off the terror of the grave, and make it easy to us, might warm and perfume that cold noisome bed for us, and that we might be *buried with him.*

2. The particular circumstances of his burial here related.

(1) The time *when* he was buried; *when the evening was come*; the same evening that he died, before sunset, as is usual in burying malefactors. It was not deferred till the next day, because it was *the sabbath.*

(2) The person that took care of the funeral was Joseph of Arimathea. The apostles had all fled. The women that followed him durst not move in it; then did God stir up this good man to do it; for what work God has to do, he will find out instruments to do it. Joseph was a fit man, for, [1] He had wherewithal to do it, being a *rich man.* Most of Christ's disciples were poor men; but here was one that was a *rich man*, ready to be employed in a piece of service which required *a man of estate.* Worldly wealth in some services to be done for Christ is an advantage and an opportunity, and it is well for those who have it, if withal they have a heart to use it for God's glory. [2] He was well affected to our Lord Jesus, for he was himself *his disciple*, though he did not openly profess it. Christ has more secret disciples than we are aware of.

(3) The grant of the dead body procured from Pilate, *v.* 58. Joseph *went to* Pilate, the proper person to be applied to on this occasion. Pilate was willing to give the body to one that would inter it decently. In Joseph's petition, and Pilate's ready grant of it, *honour* was done to Christ, and a testimony borne to his *integrity.*

(4) The dressing of the body in its graveclothes (*v.* 59); though he was an honourable counsellor, yet he himself *took the body*, as it should seem, into his own arms, from the infamous and accursed tree (Acts xiii. 29); for where there is true love to Christ, no service will be thought too mean to stoop to for him. Having taken it, he wrapped it in a *clean linen cloth*; for burying in linen was then the common usage. This common act of humanity, if done after a *godly sort*, may be made an acceptable piece of Christianity.

(5) The depositing of it in the sepulchre, *v.* 60. A private funeral did best befit him whose kingdom came not with observation. He was laid in a *borrowed* tomb, in Joseph's burying place; as he had not a house of his own, wherein to *lay his head* while he lived, so he had not a grave of his own, wherein to *lay his body* when he was dead. The grave is the peculiar heritage of a *sinner.* There is nothing we can truly call our own but our sins and our graves. When we go to the grave, we go to our own place; but our Lord Jesus, who had no sin of his own, had no grave of his own; dying under imputed sin, it was fit that he should be buried in a *borrowed* grave. He was laid in a *new tomb*, which Joseph, it is likely, designed *for himself*; it would, however, be *never the worse* for *his* lying in it, who was to rise so quickly, but a *great deal the better* for *his* lying in it, who has altered the property of the grave. It was a tomb *hewn out of a rock.* Christ's sepulchre should be in a solid entire rock, that no room might be left to suspect his disciples had access to it to steal the body; for there was no access to it but by the door, which was watched. A *great stone was rolled to the door of his sepulchre*; this also was according to the custom of the Jews in burying their dead, as appears by the description of the grave of Lazarus (John xi. 38). If the grave were his prison, now was the prison-door locked and bolted. The rolling of the stone to the grave's mouth, was with them as filling up the grave is with us, it completed the funeral. It is the most melancholy circumstance in the funerals of our Christian friends, when we have laid their bodies in the dark and silent grave to go home, and leave them behind; but alas, it is not we that *go home*, and *leave them behind*, no, it is they that are gone to the better home, and have left us behind.

(6) The company that attended the funeral; and that were very *small* and *mean.* Some good women that were true mourners—*Mary Magdalene, and the other Mary, v.* 56. These, as they had attended him *to the cross*, so they followed him to *the grave.* True love to Christ will carry us through to the utmost, in following him. Death itself cannot quench that divine fire.

JAMIESON, FAUSSET, BROWN

Joseph of Arimathea—"a rich man" (Matt. 27:57), thus fulfilling Isaiah 53:9; "an honorable counsellor," a member of the Sanhedrim, and of good condition, "which also waited for the kingdom of God" (Mark 15:43), a devout expectant of Messiah's kingdom; "a good man and a just, the same had not consented to the counsel and deed of them" (Luke 23:50, 51—he had gone the length, perhaps, of dissenting and protesting in open council against the condemnation of our Lord); "who also himself was Jesus' disciple" (Matt. 27:57). **being a disciple of Jesus, but secretly, for fear of the Jews**—"He went in boldly unto Pilate" (Mark 15:43)—lit., "having taken courage went in," or "had the boldness to go in." Mark alone, as his manner is, notices the *boldness* which this required. The act would without doubt identify him *for the first time* with the disciples of Christ. Marvellous it certainly is, that one who while Jesus was yet alive merely refrained from condemning Him, not having the courage to espouse His cause by one positive act, should, now that He was dead, and His cause apparently dead with Him, summon up courage to go in personally to the Roman governor and ask permission to take down and inter the body. But if this be the first instance, it is not the last, that *a seemingly dead Christ has wakened a sympathy which a living one had failed to evoke. The heroism of faith is usually kindled by desperate circumstances, and is not seldom displayed by those who before were the most timid, and scarce known as disciples at all.*

Then took they the body of Jesus, and wound it in linen clothes with the spices, as the manner of the Jews is to bury—the mixed and pulverized myrrh and aloes shaken into the folds, and the entire body, thus swathed, wrapt in an outer covering of "clean linen cloth" (Matt. 27:59). Had the Lord's own friends had the least reason to think that the spark of life was still in Him, would *they* have done this? But even if one could conceive them mistaken, could anyone have lain thus enveloped for the period during which He was in the grave, and life still remained? Impossible. When, therefore, He walked forth from the tomb, we can say with the most absolute certainty, "Now is Christ *risen from the dead*, and become the first fruits of them that slept" (I Cor. 15:20). No wonder that the learned and the barbarians alike were prepared to die for the name of the Lord Jesus; for such evidence was to the unsophisticated resistless. (No mention is made of *anointing* in this operation. No doubt it was a hurried proceeding, for fear of interruption, and because it was close on the sabbath, the women seem to have set this as their proper task "as soon as the sabbath should be past" (Mark 16:1). But as the Lord graciously held it as undesignedly anticipated by Mary at Bethany (Mark 14:8), so this was probably all the anointing, in the strict sense of it, which He received. **Now in the place where he was crucified there was a garden, and in the garden a new sepulchre**—The choice of this tomb was, on *their* part, dictated by the double circumstance that it was so near at hand, and by its belonging to a friend of the Lord; and as there was need of haste, even they would be struck with the providence which thus supplied it. "There laid they Jesus therefore, because of the Jew's preparation-day, for the sepulchre was nigh at hand." But there was one recommendation of it which probably would not strike them; but God had it in view. Not its being "hewn out of a rock" (Mark 15:46), accessible only at the entrance, which doubtless would impress them with its security and suitableness.

The Women Mark the Sacred Spot, that They Might Recognize It on Coming Thither to Anoint the Body (vs. 61). **61. And there was Mary Magdalene, and the other Mary**—"the mother of James and Joses," mentioned before (vs. 56)—**sitting over against the sepulchre**—See on Mark 16:1.

ADAM CLARKE

57. *When the even.* This must have been about three o'clock or a little after; for our Lord having expired about three o'clock, v. 46, and the Jewish Passover beginning about four, it was necessary that Joseph, who would not fail to eat the Passover at the usual time, should have obtained and buried the body of Christ some time before four o'clock. But such was the general consternation, occasioned by the prodigies that took place on this most awful occasion, that we may safely conjecture that nothing was done in order, and perhaps the Passover itself was not eaten at the usual hour, if at all, that day. *A rich man.* He was a counsellor of the great Sanhedrin, Luke xxiii. 50; and, from the accounts given of him by the Evangelists, we learn that he was a man of the greatest respectability. He now acted a more honorable part than all the disciples of our Lord. He was of Arimathaea, or Rama, in the tribe of Benjamin, Matt. ii. 17, but lived ordinarily in Jerusalem as being a member of the great council.

58. *Begged the body.* That he might bury it honorably; otherwise, by the Jewish customs, He would have either been burned, or buried in the common place appointed for executed criminals.

59. *Wrapped it in a clean linen cloth.* The Jews, as well as the Egyptians, added spices to keep the body from putrefaction, and the linen was wrapped about every part to keep the aromatics in contact with the flesh. From John xix. 39-40 we learn that a mixture of myrrh and aloes of 100 pounds' weight had been applied to the body of Jesus when He was buried. And that a second embalmment was intended, we learn from Luke xxiii. 56 and xxiv. 1, as the hurry to get the body interred before the Sabbath did not permit them to complete the embalming in the first instance.

60. *Laid it in his own new tomb.* To all human appearance the body of Christ must have had the same burial place with those of the two robbers, as "he was numbered with the transgressors," and suffered with them; for then He was a Sacrifice, bearing the sin of the world in His own body on the tree. But now the Sacrifice is offered, the atonement made and accepted; He is no longer to be enrolled with the transgressors, and, according to a prophecy delivered nearly seven hundred years before that time, He is to have the burying place of a rich man. See Isa. liii. 9-10. Had our Lord been buried in the common burial ground of the malefactors, His resurrection could not have been so distinctly remarked, as the chief priests would never have thought of sealing the stone there or setting a watch. But now that the body is given into the hands of a friend, they judge it necessary to make use of these precautions, in order, as they said, to prevent imposture; and from this very circumstance the resurrection of Christ had its fullest evidence, and was put beyond the power of successful contradiction.

61. *Mary Magdalene, and the other Mary.* The mother of James and Joses, v. 56. The mother of our Lord had probably, by this time, been taken home to the house of John. See John xix. 26-27. *Sitting over against the sepulchre.* These holy women, filled with that love to their Lord which death cannot destroy, cleaved to Him in life, and in death were not divided. They came to the grave to see the end, and overwhelmed with sorrow and anguish, sat down to mourn.

MATTHEW HENRY

II. His enemies did what they could to prevent his resurrection; what they did herein was *the next day that followed the day of the preparation*, *v.* 62. That was the seventh day of the week, the Jewish *sabbath*. All that day, Christ lay dead in the grave. On that day, the *chief priests and Pharisees*, when they should have been at their devotions, asking pardon for the sins of the week past, were dealing with Pilate about securing the sepulchre.

(1) Their address to *Pilate*. They desire a guard may be set on the sepulchre.

[1] Their petition sets forth, that *that deceiver had said, After three days I will rise again*. He had said so, and his disciples *remembered* those very words for the confirmation of their faith, but his persecutors remember them for the provocation of their rage and malice. Thus the same word of Christ to the one was a savour of life unto life, to the other of death unto death.

[2] It further sets forth their jealousy; *lest his disciples come by night, and steal him away, and say, He is risen*.

First, That which *really* they were afraid of, was, his *resurrection*; that which is most Christ's honour and his people's joy, is most the terror of his enemies. So the chief priests and Pharisees laboured to defeat the predictions of Christ's resurrection; if he should rise, that would break all their measures. Christ's enemies, even when they have gained their point, are still in fear of losing it again. Perhaps the priests were surprised at the respect shown to Christ's dead body by Joseph and Nicodemus, two honourable counsellors, nor can they forget his raising Lazarus from *the dead*, which so confounded them.

Secondly, That which they took on them to be afraid of, was, lest *his disciples should come by night, and steal him away*, which was a very improbable thing. They had not the courage to own him while he lived, and it was not likely that his death should put courage into such cowards. What could they promise themselves by stealing away his body, and making people believe he was risen. What good would it do them, to carry on a cheat upon themselves, to steal away his body, and say, *He is risen*? The chief priests apprehend that if the doctrine of Christ's resurrection be once preached and believed, the *last error will be worse than the first*. Those that oppose Christ and his kingdom, will see not only their attempts baffled, but themselves miserably *plunged* and *embarrassed*, their errors each worse than other, and the last worst of all.

[3] In consideration hereof, they humbly move to have a guard set upon the sepulchre till the third day; *Command that the sepulchre be made sure*. One would think that death's prisoners needed no other guard, and that the grave were *security* enough to itself.

(2) Pilate's answer to this address (*v.* 65); *Ye have a watch, make it sure, as sure as you can*. He was ready to gratify Christ's friends, in allowing them the body, and his enemies, in setting a guard upon it, being desirous to please all sides, looking upon the hopes of one side and the fears of the other to be alike ridiculous. *Ye have a watch*; but, as if ashamed to be himself seen in such a thing, he leaves the management of it wholly to them. Methinks that word, *Make it as sure as you can*, looks like a banter, either, [1] Of their *fears*; "Be sure to set a strong guard upon the dead man"; or rather, [2] Of their *hopes*; "Do your worst, but if he be of God, he will rise, in spite of you and all your guards." Tertullian, speaking of Pilate, saith, *In his conscience he was a Christian*; and it is possible that he might be under such convictions, yet never be thoroughly persuaded, any more than Agrippa or Felix was, to be a Christian.

(3) The wonderful care they took, hereupon, to secure the sepulchre (*v.* 66); *They sealed the stone*. But not trusting too much to that, withal they *set a watch*, to keep *his disciples* from coming to *steal him away*. God brought this good out of it, that they who were set to *oppose* his resurrection, thereby had an opportunity to observe it, and did so, and told the chief priests what they observed. To guard the sepulchre against the poor weak disciples, was folly, because *needless*; but to think to guard it against the power of God was folly, because *fruitless* and to no purpose.

JAMIESON, FAUSSET, BROWN

The Sepulchre Guarded (vss. 62-66). **62. Now the next day, that followed the day of the preparation**—i.e., after six o'clock of our *Saturday* evening. The crucifixion took place on the *Friday* and all was not over till shortly before sunset, when the Jewish sabbath commenced; and "that sabbath day was an high day" (John 19:31), being the first day of the feast of unleavened bread. That day being over at six on Saturday evening, they hastened to take their measures. **63. Saying, Sir, we remember that that deceiver**—Never, remarks BENGEL, will you find the heads of the people calling Jesus by His own name. And yet here there is betrayed a certain uneasiness, which one almost fancies they only tried to stifle in their own minds, as well as crush in Pilate's, in case he should have any lurking suspicion that he had done wrong in yielding to them. **said, while he was yet alive**—Important testimony this, from the lips of His bitterest enemies, to *the reality of Christ's death*; the cornerstone of the whole Christian religion. **After three days**—which, according to the customary Jewish way of reckoning, need signify no more than "after the commencement of the third day." **I will rise again**—"I rise," in the present tense, thus reporting not only the *fact* that this prediction of His had reached their ears, but that they understood Him to look forward *confidently* to its occurring on the very day named.

and say unto the people, he is risen from the dead.—Did they really fear this? **so the last error shall be worse than the first**—the imposture of His pretended resurrection worse than that of His pretended Messiahship.

64. Command therefore that the sepulchre be made sure—by a Roman guard. **until the third day**—after which, if He still lay in the grave, the imposture of His claims would be manifest to all.

65. Pilate said unto them, Ye have a watch—The guards had already acted under orders of the Sanhedrim, with Pilate's consent; but probably they were not clear about employing them as a night-watch without Pilate's express authority. **go your way, make it as sure as ye can**—as ye know how, or in the way ye deem securest. Though there may be no irony in this speech, it evidently insinuated that *if* the event should be contrary to their wish, it would not be for want of sufficient human appliances to prevent it. **66. So they went, and made the sepulchre sure, sealing the stone**—which Mark (16:4) says was "very great." **and setting a watch**—to guard it. What more could man do? But while they are trying to prevent the resurrection of the Prince of Life, God makes use of their precautions for His own ends. Their stone-covered, sealsecured sepulchre shall preserve the sleeping dust of the Son of God free from all indignities, in undisturbed, sublime repose; while their watch shall be His guard of honor until the angels shall come to take their place.

ADAM CLARKE

62. *The next day*. This was the seventh, or Saturday, and might be what we should term the evening of the sixth, or Friday, because the Jews always ended their day when the sun set, and then began the next. *That followed the day of the preparation*. That is, of the Sabbath. The victuals which were to be used on the Sabbath by the Jews were always prepared the preceding evening before the sun set. It is of this *preparation* that the Evangelist speaks here, and it is the same which is mentioned by Mark, chap. xv. 42; by Luke, chap. xxiii. 54; and by John, chap. xix. 31. But there was another preparation which happened in the same day, viz., the preparation of the Passover. This began about twelve o'clock, and continued till four, the time in which they ate the paschal lamb. See John xix. 14.

63. *Sir, we remember*. While these wicked men are fulfilling their own vicious counsels, they are subserving the great cause of Christianity. Everything depended on the resurrection of Christ. If it did not appear that He rose from the dead, then the whole system was false, and no atonement was made. It was necessary, therefore, that the chief priests should make use of every precaution to prevent an imposture, that the resurrection of Christ might have the fullest evidence to support it. See on v. 60. The word *kyrie* is here very properly translated "Sir," which, in many other places, is as improperly translated *Lord*. When a Roman is the speaker or the person addressed, *kyrie* should always be translated "sir"; when strangers address our Lord, the word is a title of civil respect, and should, in general, be translated in the same way. *After three days I will rise again*. This they probably took from His saying, "Destroy this temple, and in three days I will raise it up." If so, they destroyed, by their own words, the false accusation they brought against Him to put Him to death. Then they perverted the meaning; now they declare it. Thus the wise are taken in their own craftiness.

65. *Ye have a watch*. The Jews had a corps of Roman troops, consisting of several companies, as a guard for the Temple, Acts iv. 1. These companies mounted guard by turns; see Luke xxii. 4. Some of these companies, which were not then on duty, Pilate gave them leave to employ to watch the tomb.

66. *Made the sepulchre sure, sealing the stone, and setting a watch*. Or rather, "made the tomb secure by the guard, and by sealing the stone." The guard was to take care that the disciples should not steal him away; and the seal, which was probably the seal of the governor, was to prevent the guards from being corrupted so as to permit the theft. So everything was done which human policy and prudence could to prevent a resurrection, which these very precautions had the most direct tendency to authenticate and establish. How wonderful are the wisdom and goodness of God!

MATTHEW HENRY

CHAPTER 28

For the proof of Christ's resurrection, we have here the testimony of *the angel*, and of *Christ* himself. Let us not prescribe to Infinite Wisdom, which ordered that the witnesses of his resurrection should see him *risen*, but not see him *rise*. His incarnation was a mystery; so was this *second incarnation*.

I. The *coming* of the *good women* to the *sepulchre*.

1. *When* they came; *in the end of the sabbath, as it began to dawn toward the first day of the week, v.* 1. This fixes the time of Christ's resurrection.

(1) He arose the *third day* after his death. He was buried in the evening of the sixth day of the week, and arose in the morning of the first day of the following week.

(2) He arose *after the Jewish sabbath*, and it was the passover-sabbath. Christ on *the sixth day finished* his work; he said, *It is finished*; on the seventh day he rested, and then on the first day of the next week did as it were begin a new world, and enter upon new work. The time of the saints' lying in the grave, is a sabbath to them for there they *rest from their labours* (Job iii. 17).

(3) He arose upon the *first day of the week*; on the first day of the first week God *commanded the light to shine out of darkness*; on this day therefore did he who was to be the Light of the world, shine out of the darkness of the grave. It arose again in the first-day sabbath, called the *Lord's day* (Rev. i. 10), and no other day of the week is from henceforward mentioned in all the New Testament than this. The sabbath was instituted in remembrance of the *perfecting* of the work of creation, Gen. ii. 1. Man by his revolt made a breach upon that *perfect work*, which was never perfectly repaired till Christ arose from the dead. He who on that day arose from the dead, is the same by whom, and for whom, all things were at first created, and now anew created.

(4) He arose *as it began to dawn* toward that day; as soon as it could be said that the *third day* was come, he *arose*. Christ arose *when the day began to dawn*, because then the day-spring from on high did again visit us, Luke i. 78. His passion began in the night; when he hung on the cross the sun was darkened; he was laid in the grave in the dusk of the evening; but he arose from the grave when the sun was near rising, for he is the *bright and morning Star* (Rev. xxii. 16), the *true Light*.

2. Who they were, that came to the sepulchre; *Mary Magdalene and the other Mary*, the same that attended the funeral, and *sat over against the sepulchre*, as before they *sat over against the cross*; still they studied to express their love to Christ. Their attendance on Christ not only *to* the grave, but *in* the grave, represents his like care for those that are his. As Christ in the grave was beloved of the *saints*, so the saints in the grave are beloved of Christ; for death and the grave cannot slacken that bond of love which is between them.

3. What they *came to do*: the other evangelists say that they came to anoint the body; Matthew saith that they came to *see the sepulchre*. They went, to show their goodwill in another visit to the dear remains of their beloved Master. Visits to the grave are of great use to Christians, especially visits to the grave of our Lord Jesus, where we may see sin buried out of sight, and the great proof of redeeming love shining illustriously even in that *land of darkness*.

II. The appearance of an angel of the Lord to them, *v.* 2-4. We have here an account of the manner of the resurrection of Christ.

1. There was a *great earthquake*. When he died, the earth that *received him*, shook for fear; now that he arose, the earth that *resigned him*, leaped for joy in his exaltation. It was the *signal* of Christ's victory. Those who are sanctified, and thereby raised to a spiritual life, while it is in the doing find an earthquake in their own bosoms, as Paul, who *trembled* and was *astonished*.

2. The *angel of the Lord descended from heaven*. The angels frequently attended our Lord Jesus, but upon the cross we find no angel attending him: when his Father *forsook him*, the angels withdrew from him; but now that he is resuming the glory, behold, the *angels of God worship him*.

3. He came, and rolled back the stone from the door, and sat upon it. The *stone* of our sins was *rolled* to the door of the grave of our Lord Jesus, but to demonstrate that divine justice was satisfied, an angel was commissioned to roll back the stone. All the powers of death and darkness are under the control of the God of light and life. An angel from heaven has power to *break the seal*, though it were the *great seal of Israel*, and is able to *roll away the stone*, though ever so great. The angel's *sitting* upon the *stone*, when he had *rolled it away*, is very observable. There he sat, defying all the powers of hell to roll

JAMIESON, FAUSSET, BROWN

CHAPTER 28

VSS. 1-15. GLORIOUS ANGELIC ANNOUNCEMENT ON THE FIRST DAY OF THE WEEK, THAT CHRIST IS RISEN—HIS APPEARANCE TO THE WOMEN—THE GUARDS BRIBED TO GIVE A FALSE ACCOUNT OF THE RESURRECTION. (=Mark 16:1-8; Luke 24:1-8; John 20:1).

The Resurrection Announced to the Women (vss. 1-8). **1. In the end of the sabbath, as it began to dawn**—after the Sabbath, as it grew toward daylight. **toward the first day of the week**—Luke (24:1) has it, "very early in the morning"—properly, "at the first appearance of daybreak"; and corresponding with this, John (20:1) says, "when it was yet dark." See on Mark 16:2. Not an hour, it would seem, was lost by those dear lovers of the Lord Jesus. **came Mary Magdalene, and the other Mary**—"the mother of James and Joses" (see on ch. 27:56, 61). **to see the sepulchre**—with a view to the anointing of the body, for which they had made all their preparations. (See on Mark 16:1, 2).

And, behold, there was—i.e., there had been, before the arrival of the women. **a great earthquake; for the angel of the Lord descended from heaven . . .**—And this was the state of things when the women drew near. Some judicious critics think all this was transacted while the women were approaching; but the view we have given, which is the prevalent one, seems the more natural. All this august preparation—recorded by Matthew alone—bespoke the grandeur of the exit which was to follow. The angel sat upon the huge stone, to overawe, with the lightning-luster that darted from him, the Roman guard, and do honor to his rising Lord.

ADAM CLARKE

CHAPTER 28

1. *In the end of the sabbath.* "After the end of the week." In general the Jews divided their natural day, which consisted of twenty-four hours, into day and night. Their artificial day began at the rising and ended at the setting of the sun; all the rest of the time, from the setting to the rising of the sun, they termed night. Hence the same word, in Hebrew, signifies both evening and night, Gen. i. 5; Mark vi. 47. Matthew has employed the word in this extensive sense here, pointing out the latter part of the Jewish night, that which immediately preceded the rising of the sun, and not that first part which we call the evening. The transaction mentioned here evidently took place early on the morning of the third day after our Lord's crucifixion; what is called our Sunday morning, or first day of the next week.

Came . . . to see the sepulchre. That is, they set out at this time in order to visit the tomb of our Lord, and also to weep there, John xi. 31, and to embalm the body of our Lord, Luke xxiv. 1. Matthew omits Mary Salome, mentioned by Mark; and Joanna, the wife of Chuza, Herod's steward, mentioned by Luke. The other Mary was the wife of Cleopas, and mother of James and Joses, mentioned before, chap. xxvii. 56. Were not Mary and Salome two distinct persons?

2. *A great earthquake.* A "shaking" or "commotion" of any kind; probably the word means no more than the confusion caused among the guards by the angel's appearance. All this had taken place before the women reached the sepulchre. *The angel of the Lord descended from heaven.* Matthew is very particular in this to show that the word *angel* is not to be taken in the sense of an ordinary messenger, who might have come from Joseph of Arimathaea, or from any other; but in the sense of an extraordinary messenger, who descended from God out of heaven for this very purpose. It is likely that the angel had descended, rolled away the stone, and was sitting on it, before the women reached the tomb.

MATTHEW HENRY

the stone to the grave again. The angel sat as a guard to the grave, having frightened away the enemies' *black* guard; he sat, expecting the women, and ready to give them an account of his resurrection.

4. That his *countenance was like lightning, and his raiment white as snow*, *v.* 3. His look upon the keeper was like flashes of lightning. The *whiteness* of his raiment was an emblem, not only of purity, but of joy and triumph. When Christ died, the court of heaven *went into deep mourning*, signified by the *darkening of the sun*; but when he arose, they again put on the *garments of praise*. The glory of this angel represented the glory of Christ, to which he was now risen, for it is the same description that was given of him in his transfiguration (*ch.* xvii. 2); but when he conversed with his disciples after his resurrection, he drew a veil over it.

5. That *for fear of him the keepers did shake, and became as dead men*, *v.* 4. They were *soldiers*, that thought themselves hardened against fear, yet the very sight of an angel struck them with terror. The resurrection of Christ, as it is the joy of his friends, so it is the terror and confusion of his enemies. *They did shake;* the word is the same with that which was used for the earthquake, *v.* 2. When the *earth* shook, these *children of the earth*, that had their portion in it, *shook too*; whereas, those that have their happiness in things above, *though the earth be removed, yet are without fear*. They were posted here, to *keep a dead man in his grave*—as easy a piece of service surely as was ever assigned them, and yet it proves too hard for them.

III. The message which this angel delivered to the women, *v.* 5-7.

1. He *encourages them against their fears*, *v.* 5. To come near to graves and tombs, especially in silence and solitude, has something in it *frightful*, much more was it so to those women, to find an angel at the sepulchre; but he soon makes them easy with the word, *Fear not ye*. The keepers shook, and became as dead men, but, *Fear not ye*. "Let not the news I have to tell you, be any surprise to you; let it be no terror to you, for his resurrection will be your consolation. *Fear not ye, for I know that ye seek Jesus*. I do not come to frighten you, but to encourage you." Those that *seek Jesus*, have no reason to be *afraid*; for, if they seek him diligently they shall *find him*. *Ye seek Jesus that was crucified*. He mentions his being crucified, the more to commend their love to him; "You seek him still, though *he was crucified*." True believers love and seek Christ, not only *though* he was crucified, but *because* he was so.

2. He *assures them of the resurrection of Christ*; and there was enough in that to silence their fears, *v.* 6. To be told *He is not here*, would have been no welcome news to those who sought him, if it had not been added, *He is risen*. We must not hearken to those who say, *Lo, here is Christ*, *or*, *Lo, he is there*, for he is not *here*, he is not *there*, he is *risen*. We must seek him as one *risen*. They that make pictures and images of Christ, forget that *he is not here, he is risen*; our communion with him must be spiritual, by faith in his word. We must seek him with great *reverence* and *humility*, and an awful regard to his glory, for *he is risen*. We must seek him with a *heavenly mind*; when we are ready to make this world our home, and to say, *It is good to be here*, let us remember our Lord Jesus *is not here, he is risen*, and therefore let not our *hearts* be *here*, but let them *rise* too.

Two things the angel refers these women to, for the confirmation of their faith.

(1) To his *word* now *fulfilled*, which they might *remember*; *He is risen, as he said*. "He said that he *would rise*, why should you be backward to *believe* that which he told you would be?" Let us never think that strange, of which the word of Christ has raised our expectations. If we remember what Christ hath said *to us*, we shall be the less surprised at what he does *with us*.

(2) To his *grave* now *empty*, which they might *look into*; "*Come, see the place where the Lord lay*. Compare what you have *heard*, with what you *see*, and, putting both together, you will *believe*." It may have a good influence upon us, to come, and with an eye of faith *see the place where the Lord lay*. When we look into the grave, where we expect we must lie, to take off the terror of it, let us look into the grave where the Lord lay; the place where *our Lord* lay.

3. He *directs them* to go *carry the tidings* of it to his disciples (*v.* 7); Go *quickly, and tell his disciples*. It was good to be here, but they have other work appointed them. They must not have the *monopoly* of it, must not hold their peace. They must go *tell the disciples*. Public usefulness to others must be preferred before the pleasure of secret communion

JAMIESON, FAUSSET, BROWN

3. His countenance—appearance—**was like lightning, and his raiment white as snow**—the one expressing the *glory*, the other the *purity* of the celestial abode from which he came.

4. And for fear of him the keepers did shake, and became as dead men—Is the sepulchre "sure" now, O ye chief priests? He that sitteth in the heavens doth laugh at you.

5. And the angel answered and said unto the women, Fear not ye—The "ye" here is emphatic, to contrast their case with that of the guards. "Let those puny creatures, sent to keep the Living One among the dead, for fear of Me shake and become as dead men (vs. 4); but ye that have come hither on another errand, fear not ye." **for I know that ye seek Jesus, which was crucified**—Jesus the Crucified.

6. He is not here; for he is risen, as he said—See on Luke 24:5-7. **Come**—as in ch. 11:28. **see the place where the Lord lay.** Charming invitation! "Come, see the spot where the Lord of glory lay: now it is an empty grave: He lies not here, but He *lay* there. Come, feast your eyes on it!" But see on John 20:12.

7. And go quickly, and tell his disciples—For a precious addition to this, see on Mark 16:7. **that he is risen from the dead; and, behold, he goeth before you into Galilee**—to which those women belonged (ch. 27:55).

ADAM CLARKE

3. *His countenance.* "His appearance" or "his face," for so the word is used in some of the best Greek writers. It seems, from Mark xvi. 5, that this angel had assumed the appearance of a young man. *Like lightning.* Coruscations of glory continually flaming from his face. This might produce the confusion mentioned in v. 2. *His raiment white as snow.* He was clothed in garments emblematical of the glad tidings which he came to announce. It would have been inconsistent with the message he brought had the angel appeared in black robes, such as those preposterously wear who call themselves his successors in the ministry of a once suffering, but now risen and highly exalted, Saviour.

4. *The keepers . . became as dead men.* God can, by one and the same means, comfort His servants and terrify His enemies. The resurrection of Christ is a subject of terror to the servants of sin and a subject of consolation to the sons of God, because it is proof of the resurrection of both—the one to shame and everlasting contempt—the other to eternal glory and joy.

5. *I know that ye seek Jesus.* Speaking after the manner of men, these women deserved to be the first witnesses of the resurrection of Christ. During life they ministered to Him, and in death they were not divided. They attended Him to the Cross, notwithstanding their attachment to Him exposed them to the most imminent danger; and now they come to watch and weep at His tomb. The common opinion is that women are more fickle and less courageous than men. The reverse of this I believe to be the truth in those who are thoroughly converted to God; and who, previously to conversion, whether man or woman, can be trusted in any case?

6. *Come, see the place.* The tomb in which our Lord was laid was no doubt like the rest of the Jewish burying places, a receptacle for the several dead of a whole family, divided into separate niches, where each had his place. *Come, see the place* was tantamount to, Come and see the niche in which He was laid—it is now empty. Nor was there any other body in the place, for the tomb was a *new* one, in which no man had ever been laid, John xix. 41; so there could be no deception in the case.

7. *Go quickly, and tell his disciples.* Thus these faithful women proclaim the gospel to those who were afterwards to be the teachers of the whole human race! *That he is risen from the dead.* There is a remarkable saying of

A. B. SIMPSON:

Christ's resurrection was witnessed by the angels of God. Not often do these mighty beings interpose in human affairs. Certainly they do not come down from heaven to play a farce such as the enemies of Christ's resurrection would imply. Their presence on this occasion intimates that some stupendous event had occurred. There were apparently two angelic parties, the one that rolled away the stone and two others that afterward were found sitting where the body of Jesus had lain. So mighty was this glorious being that "his countenance was like lightning and his raiment white as snow, and for fear of him the keepers did shake and became as dead men." But as the women drew near with their loving offerings for the body of Jesus, He answered and said unto them, "Fear not."

The voice of heaven proclaims the resurrection of Jesus Christ. The mighty angels, who came down at Sinai and at the Savior's birth and who are to come once more when the Lord returns, were there to herald His victory over the grave and the ushering in of the great redemption which His death assured. Joyfully we listen to their message and echo back the glad refrain, "The Lord is risen indeed!"—*Christ in the Bible*

MATTHEW HENRY

with God ourselves.

(1) The *disciples* of Christ must first be *told the news*; not, Go, tell the *chief priests* and the *Pharisees*, that they may be *confounded*; but, Tell the disciples, that they may be *comforted*. God anticipates the joy of his friends more than the *shame* of his enemies. *Tell his disciples;* [1] That they may encourage themselves under their present sorrows and dispersions. It was a dismal time with them, between grief and fear; what a cordial would this be to them now, to hear, *their Master is risen!* [2] That they may enquire further into it themselves. This was to set them on seeking him, and to prepare them for his appearance to them. General hints excite to closer searches. They shall now hear of him, but shall very shortly see him.

(2) The *women* are sent to tell it to them. This was a recompence for their constant affectionate adherence to him, at the cross, and in the grave, and a rebuke to the disciples who forsook him. As *the woman was first in the transgression*, so these women were first in the belief of the redemption from transgression by Christ's resurrection.

(3) They were bid to *go quickly* upon this errand. Why, what haste was there? Would not the news keep cold, and be welcome to them at any time? Yes, but they were now overwhelmed with grief, and Christ would have this cordial hastened to them. We must always be ready and forward to do good to our brethren, and to carry comfort to them, now, quickly.

(4) They were directed to appoint the disciples to *meet him in Galilee*. Now this general rendezvous was appointed in Galilee, eighty or a hundred miles from Jerusalem; [1] *In kindness* to those of his disciples that remained in Galilee, and *did not* (perhaps they *could not*) come up to Jerusalem. Christ knows where his disciples dwell, and will visit there. Even to them that are at a distance from the plenty of the means of grace he will graciously *manifest himself*. [2] In consideration of the weakness of his disciples that were now at Jerusalem, who as yet were *afraid of the Jews*, and durst not appear publicly. Christ knows our fears, and considers our frame, and made his appointment where there was least danger of disturbance.

Lastly, The angel solemnly affirms upon his word the truth of what he had related to them; "*Lo, I have told you*, you may be assured of it." This angel was *now* sent to certify the resurrection of Christ to the disciples, and so leave it in their hands to be published to the world. "*I have done my errand*, I have faithfully delivered my message, *I have told you*." Those messengers from God, that discharge their trust faithfully, may take the comfort of that, whatever the success be.

IV. The women's *departure* from the *sepulchre*, to bring notice to the disciples, *v.* 8.

1. What frame and temper of spirit they were in; They *departed with fear and great joy*; a strange mixture, fear and joy at the same time, in the same soul. To hear that Christ was risen, was matter of joy; but to be led into his grave, and to see an angel, and talk with him about it, could not but cause fear. It was good news, but they were *afraid* that it was too *good* to be true. It is said of their *joy*, it was *great* joy; it is not said so of their fear. Holy fear has joy attending it. It is only perfect love and joy that will cast out all fear.

2. What haste they made; *They did run*. The fear and joy together quickened their pace, and added wings to their motion. Those that are sent on God's errand must not loiter, or lose time.

3. What errand they went upon; They ran, to *bring his disciples word*. They ran, to comfort them with the same comforts wherewith they themselves were comforted of God. The disciples of Christ should be forward to communicate to each other their experiences, should tell others what God has *done for their souls*, and spoken to them. Joy in Christ Jesus will betray itself.

V. Christ's appearing to the women, to confirm the testimony of the angel, *v.* 9, 10. These zealous good women, not only heard the first tidings of him, but had the first sight of him, after his resurrection. Jesus Christ is often better than his word, but never worse; often anticipates, but never frustrates, the believing expectations of his people.

1. Christ's surprising appearance to the women; *As they went to tell his disciples, behold, Jesus met them*. God's gracious visits usually meet us in the way of duty, and to those who use what they have for others' benefit, more shall be given. This interview with Christ was unexpected. Christ is nearer to his people than they imagine. Christ was *nigh them*, and still in *the word is nigh us*.

2. The salutation wherewith he accosted them;

JAMIESON, FAUSSET, BROWN

there shall ye see him—This must refer to those more public manifestations of Himself to large numbers of disciples at once, which He vouchsafed only in Galilee; for individually He was seen of some of those very women almost immediately after this (vss. 9, 10).

Lo, I have told you—Behold, ye have this word from the world of light!

8. And they departed quickly—Mark (16:8) says "they fled." **from the sepulchre with fear and great joy**—How natural this combination of feelings! See on a similar statement of Mark 16:11.

and did run to bring his disciples word—"Neither said they anything to any man [by the way]; for they were afraid" (Mark 16:8).

ADAM CLARKE

R. Judah Hakkodesh, which some critics quote on this subject: "After three days the soul of the Messiah shall return to its body, and he shall go out of that stone in which he shall be buried."

Goeth before you into Galilee. As himself promised, chap. xxvi. 32.

8. *They departed quickly from the sepulchre*. At the desire of the angel they went into the tomb, to have the fullest certainty of the Resurrection. *Fear and great joy. Fear* produced by the appearance of this glorious messenger of God, and *great joy* occasioned by the glad tidings of the resurrection of their Lord and Master. At the mention of unexpected good news, fear and joy are generally intermingled.

F. B. MEYER:

The open and empty tomb. Ere the sun had risen and while the glory of the dawn was faint in the eastern sky, the women were well on their way. But he whom they sought had gone. How often we look down into the grave of the dead past, or we peer for help into the diaries, prayers, and rites of departed saints or a moribund church—but we do not find the Lord. The divine Leader of souls is not behind us, but before; not in the grave of the dead past, but in the vanguard of the world's march. Lo, he beckons us on to follow the ascension mountain and the opened Heaven!

The Lord engaged women as messengers of his resurrection (Ps. 68:11). How eagerly they caught his idea, and with what alacrity they endeavored to fulfill it. And as they went, he for whom they went met them! It is ever thus. We go on his errands, but we do not leave him as we go. On the contrary, he meets us (Isa. 64:5).—*Bible Commentary*

A. T. ROBERTSON:

8. "With fear and great joy" (*meta phobou kai charas megales*). A touch of life was this as the excited women ran quickly (*tachu edramon*) as they had been told "to bring his disciples word" (*apaggeilai tois mathetais autou*). They had the greatest piece of news that it was possible to have. Mark calls it fear and ecstasy. Anything seemed possible now. Mark even says that at first they told no one anything, for they were afraid (Mark 16:9), the tragic close of the text of Mark in Aleph and B, our two oldest manuscripts. But these mingled emotions of ecstasy and dread need cause no surprise when all things are considered.—*Word Pictures in the New Testament*

MATTHEW HENRY

All hail—χαίρετε. We use the old *English form of salutation,* wishing *all health* to those we meet; for so *All hail* signifies. And it bespeaks, (1) The goodwill of Christ to us and our happiness. (2) The freedom and holy familiarity which he used in his fellowship with his disciples; for he called them *friends.* But the Greek word signifies, *Rejoice ye.* They were affected both with *fear* and *joy;* what he said to them tended to encourage their joy (*v.* 9), *Rejoice ye,* and to silence their fear (*v.* 10), *Be not afraid.* It is the will of Christ that his people should be a cheerful joyful people, and his resurrection furnishes them with abundant matter for joy.

3. The affectionate respect they paid him; *They came, and held him by the feet, and worshipped him.* Thus they expressed, (1) The *reverence* and *honour* they had *for* him. (2) The *love* and *affection* they had *to* him; they *held him, and would not let him go.* (3) The *transport of joy* they were in, now that they had this further assurance of his resurrection.

4. The encouraging words Christ said to them, *v.* 10. We do not find that they said anything to him, their affectionate embraces and adorations spoke plainly enough; and what he said to them was no more than what the angel had said (*v.* 5, 7). Now observe here,

(1) How he rebukes their fear; *Be not afraid.* The news, though strange, was both *true* and *good.* Christ arose from the dead, to silence his people's fears, and there is enough in that to silence them.

(2) How he repeats their message; "*Go, tell my brethren,* that they must prepare for a journey into Galilee, and there *they shall see me.*" If there be any communion between our souls and Christ, it is he that *appoints the meeting,* and he will observe the appointment. But that which is especially observable here, is, that he calls his disciples *his brethren.* He never called them so till after his resurrection, here and John xx. 17. Christ did not now converse so constantly and familiarly with his disciples as he had done before his death; but he gives them this endearing title, *Go to my brethren.* They had shamefully *deserted* him in his sufferings; but he not only continues his purpose to *meet* them, but calls them *brethren.*

Verses 11-15

We have here the confession of the adversaries that were upon the guard; and there are two things which strengthen this testimony—that they were *eye-witnesses*—and that they were *enemies,* set there to oppose and obstruct his resurrection.

I. How this testimony was *given in* to the chief priests (*v.* 11). *Some of the watch came into the city,* and brought to those who employed them, the report of their disappointment. *They showed to the chief priests all the things that were done;* told them of the earthquake, the descent of the angel, the rolling of the stone away, and the coming of the body of Jesus alive out of the grave. So the utmost means of conviction were afforded them. It might justly have been expected that they should now have believed in Christ, but they were obstinate in their infidelity, and therefore sealed up under it.

II. How it was baffled and stifled by them. They called an assembly, and considered what was to be done. For their own parts, they were resolved not to believe that Jesus was risen; but their care was, to keep others from believing.

The result of their debate was, that those soldiers must by all means be bribed off, and hired not to tell tales. They *put money into their hands.* They *gave large money* unto *the soldiers.* These chief priests loved their money as well as most people did, and were as loth to part with it; and yet, to carry on a malicious design against the gospel of Christ, they were very prodigal of it. Here was *large money* given for the advancing of that which they knew to be a lie, yet many grudge a little money for the advancement of that which they know to be the truth. Let us never starve a good cause, when we see a bad one so liberally supported. They *put a lie into their mouths* (*v.* 13); *Say ye, His disciples came by night, and stole him away while we slept;* a sorry shift is better than none, but this is a sorry one indeed. (1) The sham was *ridiculous,* and carried along with it its own confutation. If *they slept,* how could they know anything of the matter, or say who came? But had it been ever so plausible, (2) It was a wicked thing for these priests and elders to hire those soldiers to tell a deliberate lie.

But lest the soldiers should object the penalty they incurred by the Roman law for *sleeping upon the guard,* which was very severe (Acts xii. 19), they promised to interpose with the governor; "*We will persuade him, and secure you.*" If really these soldiers had slept, and so suffered the disciples to steal him

JAMIESON, FAUSSET, BROWN

Appearance to the Women (vss. 9, 10). This appearance is recorded only by Matthew. **9. And as they went to tell his disciples, behold, Jesus met them, saying, All hail!**—the usual salute, but from the lips of Jesus bearing a higher signification. **And they came and held him by the feet**—How truly womanly!

10. Then said Jesus unto them, Be not afraid—What dear associations would these familiar words—now uttered in a higher style, but by the same Lips—bring rushing back to their recollection! **go tell my brethren that they go into Galilee, and there shall they see me**—The brethren here meant must have been His brethren after the flesh (cf. 13:55); for His brethren in the higher sense (see on John 20:17) had several meetings with Him at Jerusalem *before* He went to Galilee, which they would have missed if they had been the persons ordered to Galilee to meet Him.

The Guards Bribed (vss. 11-15). The whole of this important portion is peculiar to Matthew. **11. Now when they were going**—while the women were on their way to deliver to His brethren the message of their risen Lord. **some of the watch came into the city, and showed unto the chief priests all the things that were done**—Simple, unsophisticated soldiers! How could ye imagine that such a tale as ye had to tell would not at once commend itself to your scared employers? Had they doubted this for a moment, would they have ventured to go near them, knowing it was death to a Roman soldier to be proved asleep when on guard? and of course that was the only other explanation of the case. **12. And when they were assembled with the elders**—But Joseph at least was absent: Gamaliel probably also; and perhaps others.

and had taken counsel, they gave large money unto the soldiers—It would need a good deal; but the whole case of the Jewish authorities was now at stake. With what contempt must these soldiers have regarded the Jewish ecclesiastics! **13. Saying, Say ye, His disciples came by night, and stole him away while we slept**—which, as we have observed, was a capital offense for soldiers on guard.

14. And if this come to the governor's ears—rather, "If this come before the governor"; i.e., not in the way of mere report, but for judicial investigation—**we will persuade him, and secure you**—The "we" and the "you" are emphatic here—"we shall [take care to]. persuade him

ADAM CLARKE

9. *All hail.* "Be safe, rejoice."

10. *Be not afraid.* They were seized with fear at the sight of the angel, and this was now renewed by this unexpected appearance of Christ. *Go tell my brethren.* This is the first time our Lord called His disciples by this endearing name. They no doubt thought that their Lord would reproach them with their past cowardice and infidelity; but, in speaking thus, He gives them a full assurance, in the most tender terms, that all that was past was as buried forever.

11. *Some of the watch.* Or "guards." Probably the rest still remained at the tomb, waiting for orders to depart, and had sent these to intimate to their employers the things that had taken place.

12. *With the elders.* That is, the "senators" of the great Sanhedrin or Jewish council of state, elsewhere called "the elders of the people"; they could now meet, as the Sabbath was over.

13. *His disciples came by night.* This was as absurd as it was false. On one hand, the terror of the disciples, the smallness of their number (only eleven), and their almost total want of faith; on the other, the great danger of such a bold enterprise, the number of armed men who guarded the tomb, the authority of Pilate and of the Sanhedrin, must render such an imposture as this utterly devoid of credit. *Stole him away while we slept.* Here is a whole heap of absurdities. (1) Is it likely that so many men would all fall asleep, in the open air, at once? (2) Is it at all probable that a Roman guard should be found off their watch, much less asleep, when it was instant death, according to the Roman military laws, to be found in this state? (3) Could they be so sound asleep as not to awake with all the noise which must be necessarily made by removing the great stone and taking away the body? (4) Is it at all likely that these disciples could have had sufficient time to do all this, and to come and return, without being perceived by any person? And (5), If they were asleep, how could they possibly know that it was the *disciples* that stole Him, or indeed that any person or persons stole Him? For, being asleep, they could see no person.

14. *If this come to the governor's ears.* Pilate. *We will persuade him* that it is for his own interest and honor to join in the deception; and we will render you *secure*—we will take care that you shall not suffer that punishment for this pretended breach of duty which otherwise you might expect.

MATTHEW HENRY

away, the priests and elders would certainly have been the forwardest to solicit the governor to punish them for their treachery; so that *their* care for the soldiers' safety plainly gives the lie to the story.

Well, thus was the plot laid; now what success had it?

[1] Those that were *willing to deceive*, took the money, and did as they were taught. They *took the money*; that was it they aimed at, and nothing else. Money is a bait for the blackest temptation; mercenary tongues will sell the truth for it.

The great argument to prove Christ to be the Son of God, is, his resurrection and none could have more convincing proofs of the truth of that than these soldiers had; they saw the angel descend from heaven, saw the stone rolled away, saw the body of Christ come out of the grave, and yet they were so far from being convinced by it themselves, that they were hired to belie him, and to hinder others from believing in him. The most sensible evidence will not convince men, without the concurring operation of the Holy Spirit.

[2] Those that were willing to be deceived, not only credited, but propagated, the story; This *saying is commonly reported among the Jews until this day*. The sham took well enough, and answered the end. The Jews, when they were pressed with the argument of Christ's resurrection, had this still ready to reply, *His disciples came, and stole him away*. When once a lie is raised, none knows how far it will spread, nor how long it will last, nor what mischief it will do.

Verses 16–20

This evangelist passes over several other appearances of Christ, recorded by Luke and John, and hastens to this, which was of all other the most solemn, as being promised and appointed again and again before his death, and after his resurrection.

I. How the disciples attended his appearance, according to the appointment (*v.* 16); *They went into Galilee*, a long journey to go for one sight of Christ, but it was worth while.

1. Because he appointed them to do so. Though it seemed a needless thing to go into Galilee, yet they had learned to obey Christ's commands and not object against them. Those who would maintain communion with Christ, must attend him there where he has appointed.

2. Because that was to be a public and general meeting. The place was a *mountain in Galilee*, probably the same mountain on which he was transfigured. There they met, for privacy, and perhaps to signify the exalted state into which he was entered.

II. How they were affected with the appearance of Christ to them, *v.* 17. We are told,

1. That they *worshipped him*; many of them did so, nay, it should seem, they all did that, they gave divine honour to him. All that see the Lord Jesus with an eye of faith are obliged to *worship him*.

2. But *some doubted*. Even among those that *worship* there are some that *doubt*. The faith of those that are sincere, may yet be very weak and wavering. *They hung in suspense*, as the scales of the balance, when it is hard to say which preponderates. It tended much to the honour of Christ, that the disciples *doubted* before they *believed*; so that they cannot be said to be credulous, and willing to be imposed upon; for they first *questioned*, and *proved all things*, and then *held fast* that which was *true*, and which they found to be so.

III. What Jesus Christ said to them (*v.* 18–20); *Jesus came, and spoke unto them*. He did not stand at a distance, but *came near*, and gave them such convincing proofs of his resurrection, as turned the wavering scale, and made their faith to triumph over their doubts. *He came, and spoke* familiarly *to them*, as one friend speaks to another. Christ now delivered to his apostles the great charter of his kingdom in the world, was sending them out as his ambassadors, and here gives them their credentials.

In opening this great chapter, we may observe two things.

1. The commission which our Lord Jesus received himself from the Father. Being about to *authorize* his apostles, here he tells us, *All power is given unto me in heaven and in earth*. Hereby he asserts his universal dominion as Mediator. He has *all power*. (1) *Whence* he hath this power. It was *given* him, by a grant from him who is the Fountain of all being, and consequently of all power. As God, equal with the Father, all power was originally and essentially *his*; but as Mediator, as God-man, *all power was given him*. He had this *power* given him *over all flesh*, that he might *give eternal life to as many as were given him* (John xvii. 2). This power he was now more signally invested in, upon his

JAMIESON, FAUSSET, BROWN

and keep you from trouble," or "save you harmless." The grammatical form of this clause implies that the thing supposed was expected to happen. The meaning then is, "If this come before the governor—as it likely will—we shall see to it that. . . ." The "persuasion" of Pilate meant, doubtless, quieting him by a bribe, which we know otherwise he was by no means above taking (like Felix afterwards, Acts 24:26). **15. So they took the money, and did as they were taught**—thus consenting to brand themselves with infamy.

and this saying is commonly reported among the Jews until this day—to the date of the publication of this Gospel. The wonder is that so clumsy and incredible a story lasted so long. But those who are resolved *not* to come to the light will catch at straws. JUSTIN MARTYR, who flourished about A.D. 170, says, in his *Dialogue with Trypho the Jew*, that the Jews dispersed the story by means of special messengers sent to every country.

16-20. JESUS MEETS WITH THE DISCIPLES ON A MOUNTAIN IN GALILEE, AND GIVES FORTH THE GREAT COMMISSION. **16. Then the eleven disciples went away into Galilee**—but certainly not before the second week after the resurrection, and probably somewhat later. **into a mountain where Jesus had appointed them**—It should have been rendered "the mountain," meaning some certain mountain which He had named to them—probably the night before He suffered, when He said, "After I am risen, I will go before you into Galilee" (ch. 26:32; Mark 14:28). What it was can only be conjectured; but of the two between which opinions are divided—the Mount of the Beatitudes or Mount Tabor—the former is much the more probable, from its nearness to the Sea of Tiberias, where last before this the Narrative tells us that He met and dined with seven of them. (John 21:1, etc.). That the interview here recorded was the same as that referred to in one place only—I Corinthians 15:6—when "He was seen of above five hundred brethren at once; of whom the greater part remained unto that day, though some were fallen asleep," is now the opinion of the ablest students of the evangelical history. Nothing can account for such a number as five hundred assembling at one spot but the expectation of some promised manifestation of their risen Lord: and the promise before His resurrection, twice repeated after it, best explains this immense gathering. **17. And when they saw him, they worshipped him; but some doubted**—certainly none of "the Eleven," after what took place at previous interviews in Jerusalem. But if the five hundred were now present, we may well believe this of some of them.

ADAM CLARKE

15. *Until this day.* That is to say, the time in which Matthew wrote his Gospel.

16. *Then the eleven disciples went.* When the women went and told them that they had seen the Lord, and that He had promised to meet them in Galilee. From the eleventh to the fifteenth verse inclusive should be read in a parenthesis, as the sixteenth verse is the continuation of the subject mentioned in the tenth.

17. *But some doubted.* That is, Thomas only at first doubted. The expression simply intimates that they did not all believe at that time.

18. *And Jesus came and spake unto them.* It is supposed by some that the reason why any doubted was that, when they saw Jesus at first, He was at a distance; but when He came up, drew near to them, they were fully persuaded of the identity of His person. *All power is given unto me.* Or, "All authority in heaven and upon earth is given unto Me." One fruit of the sufferings and resurrection of Christ is represented to be His having authority or right *in heaven* to send down the Holy Spirit—to raise up His followers thither—and to crown them in the Kingdom of an endless glory; *in earth*, to convert sinners; to sanctify, protect, and perfect His Church; to subdue all nations to himself;

MATTHEW HENRY

resurrection. (2) *Where* he has this power; in *heaven and earth*, comprehending the universe. He is *Lord of all*. He has all *power in heaven*. He has power of dominion over the angels. He has power of intercession with his Father, he intercedes not as a suppliant, but as a demandant; *Father, I will*. He has *all power on earth* too; he prevails with men, and deals with them as one having authority, by the ministry of reconciliation. All souls are his, and to him *every* heart and *knee must bow*, and *every tongue confess* him to be the *Lord*. This our Lord Jesus tells them to take off the offence of the cross; they had no reason to be ashamed of *Christ crucified*, when they saw him *thus glorified*.

2. The commission he gives to those whom he sent forth; *Go ye therefore*. This commission is given, (1) To the *apostles* primarily, the architects that laid the foundation of the church. It is not only a word of command, like that, *Son, go work*, but a word of encouragement, *Go*, and *fear not, have I not sent you?* They must go, and bring the gospel to their doors, *Go ye*. *As an eagle stirs up her nest, flutters over her young*, to excite them to fly (Deut. xxxii. 11), so Christ stirs up his disciples, to disperse themselves over all the world. (2) It is given to their successors, the ministers of the gospel, whose business it is to transmit the gospel from age to age, to the end of the world in time. Christ, at his ascension, gave not only apostles and prophets, but *pastors and teachers*, Eph. iv. 11. Now observe,

How far his commission is extended; to *all nations*. Go, and disciple *all nations*. Now this plainly signifies it to be the will of Christ, *First*, That the covenant of peculiarity, made with the Jews, should now be cancelled and disannulled. Whereas the apostles, when first sent out, were forbidden to go into the way of the Gentiles, now they were sent to *all nations*. *Secondly*, That salvation by Christ should be offered to all, and none excluded that did not by their unbelief and impenitence exclude themselves. The salvation they were to preach is a *common salvation*. *Thirdly*, That Christianity should be twisted in with national constitutions, that the kingdoms of the world should become Christ's kingdoms, and their kings the church's nursing-fathers.

What is the principal intention of this commission; to *disciple* all nations. "*Admit them disciples;* do your utmost to make the nations Christian nations"; Christ the Mediator is setting up a kingdom in the world, bring the nations to be his subjects; setting up a school, bring the nations to be his scholars; raising an army, enlist the nations of the earth under his banner. The work which the apostles had to do, was, to set up the Christian religion in all places, and it was honourable work; the achievements of the mighty heroes of the world were nothing to it. They conquered the nations for themselves, and made them miserable; the apostles conquered them for Christ, and made them happy.

Their instructions for executing this commission. *First*, They must *admit disciples* by the *sacred rite of baptism*; "Go into all nations, preach the gospel to them, work miracles among them, and persuade them to come in themselves, and bring their children with them, into the church of Christ, and then admit them and theirs into the church, by washing them with water." *Secondly*, This baptism must be administered *in the name of the Father, and of the Son, and of the Holy Ghost*. That is, 1. *By authority from heaven*, and not *of man*; for his ministers act by authority from the three persons in the Godhead. 2. *Calling upon the name* of the Father, Son, and Holy Ghost. Everything is sanctified by prayer, and particularly the waters of baptism. But, 3. It is *into the name* (εἰς το ὄνομα) of *Father, Son, and Holy Ghost*; this was intended as the *summary* of the first principles of the Christian religion. By our being baptized, we solemnly profess, (1) Our *assent* to the scripture-revelation concerning *God, the Father, Son, and Holy Ghost*. (2) Our *consent* to a covenant-relation to God, *the Father, Son, and Holy Ghost*. Baptism is a *sacrament*, that is, it is *an oath*. It is an oath of *abjuration*, by which we renounce the world and the flesh, as rivals with God for the throne in our hearts; and an oath of *allegiance*, by which we resign and give up *ourselves* to God, to be *his, body, soul, and spirit*, to be governed by his will, and made happy in his favour; *we become his men*, so the form of homage in our law runs. [1] It is into the name of *the Father*, believing him to be the *Father of our Lord Jesus Christ*, and *our Father*, as our Creator, Preserver, and Benefactor, to whom therefore we resign ourselves, to rule us, as free agents, by his law; and as our *chief good*, and *highest* end. [2] It is into the name of *the Son*, the *Lord Jesus Christ*, the *Son of God*. In baptism we *assent*, as Peter did, *Thou art Christ, the Son of the living God*

JAMIESON, FAUSSET, BROWN

A. B. SIMPSON:

The word *power* here more exactly means "dominion, authority," and has reference to the sceptre and sovereignty of a king. The Lord Jesus means that He has been appointed to administer the government, both of heaven and earth, until the consummation of redemption. It is, indeed, a glorious and transcendent claim.

He has all power to settle the standing and destiny of every sinner, and to control all our future prospects and our relations to God. He himself could say, "Thou hast given him power over all flesh, that he should give eternal life to as many as thou hast given him." Through His name and the acceptance of His words all sins are forgiven, and the guilty soul in a moment translated out of the kingdom of Satan and from the curse of sin and hell to the glorious liberty of the children of God and heirship of His everlasting kingdom. He has power, in a moment, to arrest the sentence of judgment and condemnation, and to proclaim the guilty acquitted, justified, and joint-heirs with himself of all the hopes of the Gospel.

The power of salvation is in His hands. The Son of God has received from the Father the right to emancipate every criminal under the sun from every curse of the law of God if he will accept His mighty clemency. Well may we rejoice in the power of Jesus—His power to save. Well may the prophet cry in wonder and admiration, "Who is this that cometh from Edom, with dyed garments from Bozrah? I that speak in righteousness, mighty to save."

—*Christ in the Bible*

19. Go ye therefore, and teach all nations—rather, "make disciples of all nations"; for "teaching," in the more usual sense of that word, comes in afterwards, and is expressed by a different term.

baptizing them in the name—It should be, "into the name"; as in I Corinthians 10: 2, "And were all baptized unto (or rather '*into*') Moses"; and Galatians 3:27, "For as many of you as have been baptized *into* Christ." **of the Father, and of the Son, and of the Holy Ghost;**

ADAM CLARKE

and, finally, to judge all mankind. If Jesus Christ were not equal with the Father, could He have claimed this equality of power without being guilty of impiety and blasphemy? Surely not; and does He not, in the fullest manner, assert His Godhead, and His equality with the Father, by claiming and possessing all the authority in heaven and earth?—i.e., all the power and authority by which both empires are governed?

19. *Go ye therefore*. Because I have the authority aforesaid, and can send whomsoever I will to do whatsoever I please.

***Teach*, "make disciples of all nations," bring them to an acquaintance with God who bought them, and then baptize *them in the name of the Father*. It is natural to suppose that adults were the first subjects of baptism; for as the gospel was, in a peculiar manner, sent to the Gentiles, they must hear and receive it before they could be expected to renounce their old prejudices and idolatries and come into the bonds of the Christian covenant. But certainly no argument can be drawn from this concession against the baptism of children. When the Gentiles and Jews had received the faith and blessings of the gospel, it is natural enough to suppose they should wish to get their children incorporated with the Visible Church of Christ; especially if, as many pious and learned men have believed, baptism succeeded to circumcision, which I think has never yet been disproved. The apostles knew well that the Jews not only circumcised the children of proselytes, but also baptized them; and as they now received a commission to teach and proselyte all the nations, and baptize them in the name of the Holy Trinity, they must necessarily understand that infants were included. Nor could they, the custom of their country being considered, have understood our Lord differently unless He had, in the most express terms, said that they were not to baptize children, which neither He nor His apostles ever did. And as to the objection that the baptized were obliged to profess their faith, and that, therefore, only adults should be baptized, there is no weight at all in it; because what is spoken of such refers to those who, only at that period of life, heard the gospel, and were not born of parents who had been Christians; therefore they could not have been baptized into the Christian faith, forasmuch as no such faith was at their infancy preached in the world. *In the name of the Father*. Baptism, properly speaking, whether administered by dipping or sprinkling, signifies a full and eternal consecration of the person to the service and honor of that Being in whose name it is administered. But this consecration can never be made to a creature; therefore the *Father*, and the *Son*, and the *Holy Spirit* are not creatures. Again, baptism is not made in the name of a quality or attribute of the divine nature; therefore the *Father*, and the *Son*, and**

MATTHEW HENRY

(*ch.* xvi. 16), and *consent*, as Thomas did, *My Lord, and my God*, John xx. 28. We take Christ to be our Prophet, Priest, and King, and give up ourselves to be taught, and saved, and ruled, by him. [3] It is into the name of *the Holy Ghost*. We give up ourselves to his conduct and operation, as our sanctifier, teacher, guide and comforter. *Thirdly*, Those that are thus baptized, and enrolled among the disciples of Christ, must be taught (*v.* 20); *Teaching them to observe all things, whatsoever I have commanded you.* This denotes two things. The duty of *disciples*, of all *baptized Christians*; they must observe all things whatsoever Christ has commanded, and, in order to that, must submit to the teaching of those whom he sends. He *enlists* soldiers that he may *train them* up for his service.

All that are baptized, are thereby obliged, (1) To make the command of Christ their rule. We are by baptism *bound*, and must *obey*. (2) To *observe* what Christ has commanded. Due *obedience* to the commands of Christ requires a diligent observation. (3) To observe *all things*, that he has commanded, without exception; all the *moral* duties, and all the *instituted* ordinances. (4) To confine themselves to the commands of Christ, and as not to *diminish* from them, so not to *add* to them. (5) To learn their duty according to the law of Christ, from those whom he has appointed to be teachers in his school. The duty of the apostles of Christ, and his ministers; and that is, to *teach* the commands of Christ. They must teach *them*, and in the knowledge of *them* Christians must be *trained up*. The heirs of heaven, till they come to age, must be *under tutors and governors*. Here is the assurance he gives them of his spiritual presence with them in the execution of this commission; *And lo, I am with you always, even unto the end of the world.* Observe,

(1) The favour promised them; *I am with you*. Not, *I will be* with you, but *I am*. He was now about to leave them; his bodily presence was now to be removed from them, and this grieved them; but he assures them of his *spiritual* presence, *I am with you*; that is, "My Spirit is with you, the Comforter shall *abide with you*, John xvi. 7. I am *with you*, and not *against* you: with you to take your part, to be on your side. I am *with you*, and not *absent from you*, not at a distance; I am a very *present help*," Ps. xlvi. 1. Christ was now sending them to set up his kingdom in the world. And then doth he seasonably promise them his presence with them, [1] To *carry them* on through the difficulties they were likely to meet with. "I am with you, to *bear you up*, to plead your cause; with you in all your services, in all your sufferings." [2] To *succeed* this great undertaking; "Lo, *I am with you*, to make your ministry effectual for the discipling of the nations." It was an unlikely thing that they should persuade people to become the disciples of a *crucified* Jesus; but *lo, I am with you*, and therefore you shall *gain your point*.

(2) The continuance of the favour, *always, even unto the end of the world*.

[1] They shall have his *constant* presence; *always*, πάσας τὰς ἡμέρας—*all days*, every day. "I will be with you on sabbath days and week days, fair days and foul days, winter days and summer days." Since his resurrection he had appeared to them *now and then*. But he assures them that they shall have his spiritual presence continued to them without intermission. The *God of Israel*, the *Saviour*, is sometimes *a God that hideth himself* (Isa. xlv. 15), but never a God that absenteth himself; sometimes *in the dark*, but never *at a distance*.

[2] They shall have his perpetual presence, even to *the end of the world*. This is hastening towards its period; and even till then the Christian religion shall, in one part of the world or other, he *kept up*, and the presence of Christ continued with his ministers. I am with you *to the end of the world, First*, With *you and your writings*. There is a divine power going along with the scriptures of the New Testament, not only preserving them in being, but producing strange effects by them, which will continue to the end of time. *Secondly*, With you and *your successors*; with all who thus *baptize* and thus *teach*. This is an encouraging word to all the faithful ministers of Christ, that what was said to the apostles, was said to them all, *I will never leave thee, nor forsake thee.*

Two solemn farewells we find our Lord Jesus giving to his church, and his parting word at both of them is very encouraging; one was here, "*Lo, I am with you always;* I leave you, and yet still I am with you"; the other was, "*Surely, I come quickly*. I leave you for awhile, but I will be with you again shortly," Rev. xxii. 20. By this it appears that he did not part in anger, but in love, and that it is his will we should keep up both our communion with him and our expectation of him.

JAMIESON, FAUSSET, BROWN

Teaching them—This is teaching in the more usual sense of the term; or instructing the converted and baptized disciples. **to observe all things whatsoever I have commanded you: and, lo, I**—The "I" here is emphatic. It is enough that *I*—**am with you alway**—"all the days"; i.e., till making converts, baptizing, and building them up by Christian instruction, shall be no more. **even unto the end of the world. Amen**—This glorious Commission embraces two primary departments, the *Missionary* and the *Pastoral*, with two sublime and comprehensive *Encouragements* to undertake and go through with them.

First, The MISSIONARY department (vs. 18): "Go, make disciples of all nations." In the corresponding passage of Mark (16:15) it is, "Go ye into all the world, and preach the Gospel to every creature." The only difference is, that in this passage the *sphere*, in its worldwide compass and its universality of *objects*, is more fully and definitely expressed; while in the former the great *aim* and certain *result* is delightfully expressed in the command to "make disciples of all nations." "Go, conquer the world for Me; carry the glad tidings into all lands and to every ear, and deem not this work at an end till all nations shall have embraced the Gospel and enrolled themselves My disciples." Now, Was all this meant to be done by the Eleven men nearest to Him of the multitude then crowding around the risen Redeemer? Impossible. Was it to be done even in their lifetime? Surely not. In that little band Jesus virtually addressed Himself to all who, in every age, should take up from them the same work. Before the eyes of the Church's risen Head were spread out, in those Eleven men, all His servants of every age; and one and all of them received His commission at that moment. Well, what next? Set the seal of visible discipleship upon the converts, by "baptizing them into the name," i.e., into the whole fulness of the grace "of the Father, and of the Son, and of the Holy Ghost," as belonging to them who believe. (See on II Cor. 13:14.) This done, the Missionary department of your work, which in its own nature is temporary, must merge in another, which is permanent. This is—

Second, The PASTORAL department (vs. 20): "Teach them"—teach these baptized members of the Church visible—"to observe all things whatsoever I have commanded you," My apostles, during the three years ye have been with Me.

What must have been the feelings which such a Commission awakened? "WE who have scarce conquered our own misgivings—we, fishermen of Galilee, with no letters, no means, no influence over the humblest creature, conquer the world for Thee, Lord? Nay, Lord, do not mock us." "I mock you not, nor send you a warfare on your own charges. For"—Here we are brought to—

Third, The ENCOURAGEMENTS to undertake and go through with this work. These are two; one in the van, the other in the rear of the Commission itself.

First Encouragement: "All power in *heaven*"—the whole power of Heaven's love and wisdom and strength, "and all power in *earth*"—power over all persons, all passions, all principles, all movements—to bend them to this one high object, the evangelization of the world: All this "is *given unto Me*." as the risen Lord of all, to be *by Me placed at your command*—"Go ye therefore." But there remains a—

ADAM CLARKE

the *Holy Spirit* are not qualities or attributes of the divine nature. The orthodox, as they are termed, have generally considered this text as a decisive proof of the doctrine of the Holy Trinity, and what else can they draw from it? Is it possible for words to convey a plainer sense than do these? And do they not direct every reader to consider the *Father*, the *Son*, and the *Holy Spirit* as three distinct Persons?

20. *Teaching them to observe all things.* Men are ignorant of divine things and must be taught. Only those can be considered as proper teachers of the ignorant who are thoroughly instructed in whatsoever Christ has commanded. Persons who are entrusted with the public ministry of the Word should take care that they teach not human creeds and confessions of faith in place of the Sacred Writings but those things, and those only, which Jesus has commanded.

ALEXANDER MACLAREN:

There is another step still. Making disciples and bringing into communion with the Godhead is not all that is to flow from, and correspond to, and realize in the individual, the absolute authority of Jesus Christ—"teaching them to observe all things whatsoever I have commanded you." We hear a great deal in these days about the worthlessness of mere dogmatic Christianity. Jesus Christ anticipated all that talk, and guarded it from exaggeration. For what He tells us here that we are to train ourselves and others in is not creed but conduct; not things to be believed or credenda but things to be done or agenda—"teaching them to observe all things whatsoever I have commanded you." A creed that is not wrought out in actions is empty; conduct that is not informed, penetrated, regulated by creed is unworthy of a man, not to say of a Christian. What we are to know we are to know in order that we may do, and so inherit the benediction, which is never bestowed upon them that know, but upon them that, knowing these things, are blessed in, as well as for, the doing of them.

That training is to be continuous, educating to new views of duty; new applications of old truths, new sensitiveness of conscience, unveiling to us, ever as we climb, new heights to which we aspire. The Christian Church has not yet learned—thank God it is learning, though by slow degrees—all the moral and practical implications and applications of "the truth as it is in Jesus." And so these are the three things by which the Church recognizes and corresponds to the universal dominion of Christ, the making disciples universally; the bringing them into the communion of the Father, the Son, and the Holy Spirit; and the training of them to conduct ever approximating more and more to the divine ideal of humanity in the glorified Christ.

The great promise. "I am with you alway, even unto the end of the world," or, as it might be read, "with you all the days, even to the accomplishment of the age." Note that emphatic "I am," which does not only denote certainty, but is the speech of Him who is lifted above the lower regions where Time rolls and the succession of events occurs. That "I am" covers all the varieties of was, is, will be. Notice the long vista of variously tinted days which opens here. Howsoever many they be, howsoever different their complexion, days of summer and days of winter, days of sunshine and days of storm, days of buoyant youth and days of stagnant, stereotyped old age, days of apparent failure and days of apparent prosperity, He is with us in them all. They change, He is "the same yesterday, and to-day, and for ever."

—*Expositions of Holy Scripture*

MATTHEW HENRY

There is one word more remaining, which must not be overlooked, and that is *Amen*; which is not a cipher, intended only for a concluding word, like *finis* at the end of a book. It bespeaks Christ's confirmation of this promise, *Lo, I am with you*. It is his *Amen*, in whom all the promises are *Yea and Amen*. It bespeaks the church's concurrence with it, in their desire, and prayer, and expectation. It is the evangelist's *Amen—So be it*, blessed Lord. Our *Amen* to Christ's promises turns them into prayers.

JAMIESON, FAUSSET, BROWN

Second Encouragement: "And lo! I am with you all the days"—not only to perpetuity, but without one day's interruption, "even to the end of the world," The "Amen" is of doubtful genuineness in this place. If, however, it belongs to the text, it is the Evangelist's own closing word.

ADAM CLARKE

And, lo, I am with you alway. Literally, "Behold, I am with you every day." *Unto the end of the world.* Some translate, "to the end of this age," meaning the apostolic age, or Jewish dispensation; and then they refer the promise of Christ's presence to the working of miracles, and explain this by Mark xvi. 17-19, "In my name shall they cast out devils." But though the words are used in this sense in several places, see chap. xiii. 39-40, 49 and xxiv. 3, yet it is certain they were repeatedly used among the primitive ecclesiastical writers to denote the "consummation of all things"; and it is likely that this is the sense in which they are used here.

THE GOSPEL ACCORDING TO MARK

I. Sanctification (1:1-13)
- *A. "John came" (1:1-8)*
  - 1. According to prophecy (1:1-3)
  - 2. Prophesying (1:4-8)
- *B. "Jesus came" (1:9-13)*
  - 1. Obedience (1:9)
  - 2. Anointing (1:10, 11)
  - 3. Testing (1:12, 13)

II. Service (1:14-8:30)
- *A. First disciples and first work (1:14-3:12)*
  - 1. Works (1:14-2:12)
  - 2. Words (2:13-28)
  - 3. Works and words (3:1-12)
- *B. Appointment of twelve, and advance in toil (3:13-6:6)*
  - 1. Twelve appointed (3:13-19a)
  - 2. Continued toil and teaching (3:19b-6:6)
- *C. Commission of twelve and cooperation in service (6:7-8:30)*
  - 1. The apostles' departure (6:7-13)
  - 2. Herod and Jesus (6:14-29)
  - 3. The apostles' return (6:30-32)
  - 4. The feeding of the multitudes (6:33-44)
  - 5. The disciples and the storm (6:45-52)
  - 6. Healing the multitudes (6:53-56)
  - 7. The scribes and Pharisees (7:1-23)
  - 8. Journeying (7:24-8:30)

III. Sacrifice (8:31-16:20)
- *A. Anticipated (8:31-10:52)*
  - 1. New terms (8:31-9:1)
  - 2. New manifestations (9:2-27)
  - 3. Teaching (9:28-10:45)
  - 4. The healing of Bartimaeus (10:46-52)
- *B. Approached (11:1-14:42)*
  - 1. Jesus and the city (11:1-26)
  - 2. Jesus and the rulers (11:27-12:34)
  - 3. Jesus and the multitudes (12:35-40)
  - 4. Jesus and disciples (12:41-14:42)
- *C. Accomplished (14:43-15:47)*
  - 1. Disciples (14:43-72)
    - a. Betray (14:43-49)
    - b. Forsake (14:50-53)
    - c. Deny (14:54-72)
  - 2. The people (15:1-15)
    - a. Yield to priests (15:1-12)
    - b. Clamor for blood (15:13-15)
  - 3. The rulers (15:16-47)
    - a. Slay (15:16-41)
    - b. Bury (15:42-47)
- *D. Conclusion (16:1-20)*
  - 1. The risen one (16:1-13)
  - 2. The commission (16:14-18)
  - 3. The ascension (16:19, 20)

We have heard the evidence given by the first witness to the doctrine and miracles of our Lord Jesus; and now here is another witness produced, who calls for our attention.

Concerning *this witness.* His name is *Mark. Marcus* was a Roman name, and a very common one, and yet we have no reason to think but that he was by birth a Jew; but as Saul took the Roman name of *Paul,* so he of *Mark.* We read of John whose surname was *Mark,* sister's son to Barnabas, whom Paul was displeased with (Acts 15:37, 38), but afterward had a great kindness for, and not only ordered the churches to receive him (Col. 4:10), but sent for him to be his assistant, with this encomium, "He is profitable to me for the ministry" (2 Tim. 4:11); and he reckons him among his fellow laborers (Philem. 24). We read of Marcus whom Peter calls his *son* (1 Pet. 5:13); whether that was the same with the other is altogether uncertain. It is a tradition very current among the ancients, that St. Mark wrote this gospel under the direction of St. Peter, and that it was confirmed by his authority. Thus wrote Hieron, "Mark, the disciple and interpreter of Peter, being sent from Rome by the brethren, wrote a concise gospel"; and Tertullian said, "Mark, the interpreter of Peter, delivered in writing the things which had been preached by Peter." It is true Mark was no apostle, yet we think that both he and Luke were of the number of the seventy disciples. St. Jerome said that, after the writing of this gospel, he went into Egypt, and was the first that preached the gospel at Alexandria, where he founded a church, to which he was a great example of holy living.

Concerning *this testimony.* Mark's gospel is but short, much shorter than Matthew's, not giving so full an account of Christ's sermons as that did, but insisting chiefly on his miracles. It is very much a repetition of what we had in Matthew; many remarkable circumstances being added to the stories there related, but not many new matters. It was fit that such great things as these should be spoken and written, once, yea twice, because man is so unapt to perceive them, and so apt to forget them. Though it was written at Rome it was written in Greek, as was St. Paul's epistle to the Romans, the Greek being the more universal language.

CHAPTER 1

Verses 1–8

I. What the New Testament is. It is *the gospel of Jesus Christ the Son of God, v.* 1. 1. It is *gospel.* It is a *good word,* and well *worthy of all acceptation;* it brings us glad tidings. 2. It is the *gospel of Jesus Christ.* The foregoing gospel began with the *generation of Jesus Christ*—that was but preliminary, this comes immediately to the business—*the gospel of Christ.* 3. This Jesus is the *Son of God.* That truth is the foundation on which the gospel is built, and which it is written to demonstrate.

II. What the *reference* of the New Testament is to the Old. The gospel of Jesus Christ *begins,* and so we shall find it *goes on,* just *as it is written in the prophets, v.* 2. which was most proper and powerful for the conviction of the Jews, who believed the Old Testament prophets to be sent of God, but it is of use to us all, for the confirmation of our faith both in the Old Testament and in the New.

Quotations are here borrowed from two prophecies —that of Isaiah, and that of Malachi, both of whom spoke to the same purport concerning *the beginning of the gospel of Jesus Christ,* in the ministry of John.

CHAPTER 1

Vss. 1-8. The Preaching and Baptism of John. (=Matthew 3:1-12; Luke 3:1-18.) **1. The beginning of the gospel of Jesus Christ, the Son of God** —By the "Gospel" of Jesus Christ here is evidently meant the blessed Story which our Evangelist is about to tell of His Life, Ministry, Death, Resurrection, and Glorification, and of the begun Gathering of Believers in His Name. The abruptness with which he announces his subject, and the energetic brevity with which, passing by all preceding events, he hastens over the ministry of John and records the Baptism and Temptation of Jesus—as if impatient to come to the Public Life of the Lord of glory—have often been noticed as characteristic of this Gospel—a Gospel whose direct, practical, and singularly vivid setting imparts to it a preciousness peculiar to itself. What strikes every one is, that though the briefest of all the Gospels, this is in some of the principal scenes of our Lord's history the fullest. But what is not so obvious is, that wherever the finer and subtler feelings of humanity, or the deeper and more peculiar hues of our Lord's character were brought

CHAPTER 1

1. *The beginning of the gospel.* With utmost propriety Mark begins the Gospel dispensation by the preaching of John the Baptist, the forerunner of Jesus Christ and the first proclaimer of the incarnated Messiah. *Son of God.* Mark thus points out Jesus' divine origin, and thus glances at His miraculous conception. This was an essential character of the Messiah. See Matt. xvi. 16; xxvi. 63; Luke xxii. 67, etc.

MATTHEW HENRY

1. Malachi spoke very plainly (*ch.* iii. 1) concerning John Baptist. *Behold, I send my messenger before thy face, v.* 2. Christ himself had taken notice of this, and applied it to John (Matt. xi. 10), who was God's *messenger*, sent to *prepare Christ's way.*

2. Isaiah, the most evangelical of all the prophets, *begins* the evangelical part of his prophecy with this, which points to the *beginning of the gospel of Christ*, (Isa. xl. 3); *The voice of him that crieth in the wilderness, v.* 3. Matthew had taken notice of this, and applied it to John, *ch.* iii. 3. Such is the corruption of the world, that there is something to do to *make room* for him. When God sent his Son into the world, he *took care*, and when he sends him into the heart, he *takes care*, effectual care, to *prepare his way before him.* The mistakes of the judgment are rectified, and the *crooked ways* of the affections; then way is made for Christ's comforts. It is in a *wilderness*, for such this world is, that *Christ's way* is prepared, and theirs that follow him, like that which Israel passed through to Canaan. They that are sent to *prepare the way of the Lord*, in such a vast howling wilderness as this is, have need to cry *aloud.*

III. What the *beginning* of the New Testament was. The gospel began in John Baptist. His baptism was the dawning of the *gospel day.*

1. In John's way of *living* there was the beginning of a *gospel spirit*; for it bespoke great self-denial, mortification of the flesh, a holy contempt of the world, and nonconformity to it. The more we sit loose to the body, and live above the world, the better we are prepared for Jesus Christ.

2. In John's *preaching* and *baptizing* there was the *beginning* of the *gospel doctrines and ordinances.* (1) He preached the *remission of sins,* which is the great gospel privilege. (2) He preached *repentance*, in order to it; he told people that there must be a renovation of their hearts and a reformation of their lives. (3) He preached Christ, and directed his hearers to *expect him* speedily to appear, and to *expect great things* from him. He preached, [1] The great *pre-eminence* Christ is *advanced to*; so high, so great, is Christ, that John thinks himself unworthy to be employed in the meanest office about him, even to *stoop down*, and *untie his shoes.* [2] The great *power* Christ is *invested with*; He *comes after me* in time, but he is *mightier than I*, for he is able to *baptize with the Holy Ghost.* [3] The great *promise* Christ makes in his gospel to those who have *repented*, and have had their sins forgiven them; They shall be *baptized with* the Holy Ghost. And, *lastly*, All those who received his doctrine, and submitted to his institution, he *baptized with water*, as the manner of the Jews was to admit proselytes, in token of their *cleansing themselves* by repentance and reformation, and of God's *cleansing them* both by remission and by sanctification.

3. In the success of John's preaching, and the disciples he admitted by baptism, there was the *beginning of a gospel church.* He baptized *in the wilderness*, but *there went out unto him all the land of Judæa, and they of Jerusalem*, and *were all baptized of him.* They entered themselves his disciples, and bound themselves to his discipline; in token of which, they *confessed their sins*; he admitted them his disciples, in token of which, he *baptized* them. Many of these afterward became followers of Christ, and preachers of his gospel, and this grain of mustard-seed became a *tree.*

Verses 9–13

We have here a brief account of Christ's baptism and temptation.

I. His *baptism*, which was his first public appearance, after he had long lived obscurely *in Nazareth.*

1. See how *humbly* he *owned* God, by coming to be *baptized of John.* Though he was perfectly pure and unspotted, yet he was *washed* as if he had been *polluted.*

2. See how *honourably* God owned him, when he submitted to John's *baptism.*

(1) He *saw the heavens opened*; thus he was owned to be the Lord from heaven. Matthew saith, *The heavens were opened to him.* Mark saith, *He saw them opened.* Many have the heavens opened to receive them, but they do not see it.

(2) He *saw the Spirit like a dove descending upon him.* It is an ancient tradition, that *a great light shone round the place.*

(3) He heard a voice which was intended for his encouragement to proceed in his undertaking, and therefore it is here expressed as directed *to him, Thou art my beloved Son.* God is *well pleased* in him, and so well pleased in him, as to be well pleased *with us* in him.

II. His *temptation.* The *good Spirit* that descended upon him, *led him into the wilderness, v.* 12. Retire-

JAMIESON, FAUSSET, BROWN

out, these, though they should be lightly passed over by all the other Evangelists, are sure to be found here, and in touches of such quiet delicacy and power, that though scarce observed by the cursory reader, they leave indelible impressions upon all the thoughtful and furnish a key to much that is in the other Gospels. These few opening words of the Second Gospel are enough to show, that though it was the purpose of this Evangelist to record chiefly the outward and palpable facts of our Lord's public life, he recognized in Him, in common with the Fourth Evangelist, the glory of the Only-begotten of the Father. **2. As it is written in the prophets,**—(Mal. 3:1; Isa. 40:3)—**Behold, I send my messenger before thy face, which shall prepare thy way before thee. 3. The voice of one crying in the wilderness, Prepare ye the way of the Lord, make his paths straight**—The second of these quotations is given by Matthew and Luke in the same connection, but they reserve the former quotation till they have occasion to return to the Baptist, after his imprisonment (Matt. 11:10; Luke 7: 27). (Instead of the words, "as it is written in the Prophets," there is weighty evidence in favor of the following reading: "As it is written in Isaiah the prophet." This reading is adopted by all the latest critical editors. If it be the true one, it is to be explained thus—that of the two quotations, the one from Malachi is but a later development of the great primary one in Isaiah, from which the whole prophetical matter here quoted takes its name. But the received text is quoted by IRENAEUS, before the end of the second century, and the evidence in its favor is greater in *amount*, if not in weight. The chief objection to it is, that if this was the true reading, it is difficult to see how the other one could have got in at all; whereas, if it be not the true reading, it is very easy to see how it found its way into the text, as it removes the startling difficulty of a prophecy beginning with the words of Malachi being ascribed to Isaiah). For the exposition, see on Matthew 3:1-6, 11.

9-11. BAPTISM OF CHRIST, AND DESCENT OF THE SPIRIT UPON HIM IMMEDIATELY THEREAFTER. (= Matt. 3:13-17; Luke 3:21, 22.) See on Matthew 3:13-17.

12, 13. TEMPTATION OF CHRIST. (=Matt. 4:1-11; Luke 4:1-13.) See on Matthew 4:1-11.

1. Then—an indefinite note of sequence. But Mark's word (1:12) fixes what we should have presumed was meant, that it was "immediately" after His baptism; and with this agrees the statement of Luke (4:1). **was Jesus led up**—i.e., from the low Jordan valley to some more elevated spot. **of the Spirit**—that blessed Spirit immediately before spoken of as descending upon Him at His baptism, and abiding upon Him. Luke, connecting these two scenes, as if the one were but the sequel of the other, says, "Jesus, being full of the Holy Ghost, returned from Jordan, and was led . . . ." Mark's expression has a startling sharpness about it—"Immediately the Spirit driveth Him," "putteth," or "hurrieth Him forth," or "impelleth Him." (See the same word in Mark 1:43; 5:40; Matt. 9:25; 13:52; John 10:4.) The thought thus strongly expressed is the mighty constraining impulse of the Spirit under which He went; while

ADAM CLARKE

2. *As it is written in the prophets.* Rather, "As it is written by Isaiah the prophet." I think this reading should be adopted, instead of that in the common text. It is the reading of several MSS. and versions of great repute, and in several of the Fathers. As this prophecy is found both in Isaiah and Malachi, early scribes probably changed the reading to *the prophets*, that it might comprehend both.

3. *The voice of one crying.* See on Matt. iii. 1-3.

4. *John.* The original name is *Yehochanan*, compounded of *Yehovah chanan*, the "grace or mercy of Jehovah"—a most proper and significant name for the forerunner of the "God of all grace." It was John's business to proclaim the gospel of the grace of God, and to point out that Lamb or sacrifice of God which takes away the sin of the world. *For the remission of sins.* Or "toward the remission." They were to repent, and be baptized with reference to the remission of sins. Repentance prepared the soul for it, and baptism was the type or pledge of it.

5. *All the land.* See on Matt. iii. 4-6. *Confessing their sins.* It was an invariable custom among the Jews to admit no proselyte to baptism till he had in the most solemn manner declared that he had renounced forever all idolatrous worship, all heathen superstitions, and promised an entire and unreserved submission to the law of Moses.

6. *John was clothed . . .* See the note on Matt. iii. 4.

7. *The latchet of whose shoes.* The shoe of the ancients was properly only a sole tied round the foot and ankle with strings or thongs.

8. *I indeed have baptized you with water.* As if he had said: This baptism is not to be rested in; it is only an emblem of that which you must receive from Him who is mightier than I. It is He only who can communicate the Holy Spirit; and water baptism is nothing, but as it points out, and leads to, the baptism of the Holy Ghost.

12. *The spirit driveth him.* "Pulleth Him forth." Matthew says, chap. iv. 1, "was . . . led up."

MATTHEW HENRY

ment from the world is an opportunity of more free converse with God, and therefore must sometimes be chosen. Mark observes this circumstance of his being *in the wilderness*—that he was *with the wild beasts.* It was an instance of his Father's care of him, that he was preserved from being torn in pieces by the wild beasts. Special protections are earnests of seasonable supplies. In that wilderness,

1. The *evil spirits* were *busy with him*; he *was tempted of Satan.* Christ himself was tempted, not only to teach us, that *it is no sin to be tempted,* but to direct us whither to go for succour when we are tempted, even to him that *suffered,* being *tempted.*

2. The *good spirits* were *busy about him*; the *angels ministered to him.* The ministration of the good angels about us, is matter of great comfort in reference to the malicious designs of the evil angels against us.

Verses 14–22

I. A general account of Christ's preaching in Galilee.

1. When Jesus began to preach in Galilee; *After that John was put in prison.* When he had *finished* his testimony, then Jesus *began* his.

2. What he preached; *The gospel of the kingdom of God.* Christ came to set up the kingdom of God among men, and he set it up by the preaching of his gospel, and a power going along with it.

(1) The great *truths* Christ preached; *The time is fulfilled, and the kingdom of God is at hand.* Christ gives them notice of it; "The time prefixed is now *at hand*; glorious discoveries of divine light, life, and love, are now to be made." God keeps time; when *the time is fulfilled*, the *kingdom of God is at hand.*

(2) The great *duties* inferred from thence. Christ gave them to *understand the times,* that they might know *what Israel ought to do*; they fondly expected the Messiah to appear in external pomp and power, and therefore thought, when that *kingdom of God* was *at hand,* they must prepare for war, and for victory. Christ tells them, in the prospect of that kingdom approaching, they must *repent, and believe the gospel.* By repentance we must lament and forsake our sins, and by faith we must receive the forgiveness of them. Both these must go together: we must not think either that reforming our lives will save us without trusting in the righteousness and grace of Christ, or that trusting in Christ will save us without the reformation of our hearts and lives. Christ hath joined these two together, and let no man think to put them asunder. Thus the preaching of the gospel began, and thus it continues; still the call is, Repent, and believe, and live a *life of repentance* and *a life of faith.*

II. Christ appearing as a teacher, here is next his *calling of disciples, v.* 16–20. Observe, 1. Christ will have followers. If he set up a school, he will have scholars; if he set up his standard, he will have soldiers; if he preach, he will have hearers. 2. The instruments Christ chose to employ in setting up his kingdom, were the *weak* and *foolish things of the world*; not called from the great sanhedrim, or the schools of the rabbin, but picked up from among the tarpaulins *by the sea-side.* 3. Though Christ needs not the help of man, yet he is pleased to make use of it in setting up his kingdom. 4. Christ puts honour upon those who are *diligent in their business,* and *loving to one another*; so those were, whom Christ called. He found them *employed,* and employed *together. Industry* and unity are *good* and *pleasant,* and there the Lord Jesus commands the blessing. 5. The business of ministers is to *fish for souls,* and *win them to Christ.* Ministers, in preaching the gospel, *cast the net* into the waters, Matt. xiii. 47. Some are enclosed and brought to shore, but far the greater number escape. If many a draught brings home nothing, yet they must go on. 6. Those whom Christ calls, must *leave all,* to follow him; and by his grace he inclines them to do so. We must sit loose to the world, and forsake everything that is inconsistent with our duty to Christ. Mark takes notice of James and John, that they left not only *their father* (which we had in Matthew), but *the hired servants,* being their *fellow-labourers* and pleasant comrades; not only relations, but companions, must be left for Christ, and old acquaintance.

III. Here is a particular account of his preaching in Capernaum. 1. When Christ *came into Capernaum,* he *straightaway* applied himself to his work there, and took the *first* opportunity of preaching the gospel. Those will think themselves concerned not to *lose time,* who consider what a deal of work they have to do, and what a little time to do it in. 2. Christ religiously observed the sabbath day. 3. Sabbaths are to be sanctified in *religious assemblies,* if we have opportunity; it is a *holy day.* 4. In *religious assemblies*

JAMIESON, FAUSSET, BROWN

Matthew's more gentle expression, "was led up," intimates how purely voluntary on His own part this action was. **into the wilderness**—probably the wild Judean desert. The particular spot which tradition has fixed upon has hence got the name of *Quarantana* or *Quarantaria,* from the forty days, —"an almost perpendicular wall of rock twelve or fifteen hundred feet above the plain" [ROBINSON'S *Palestine*]. The supposition of those who incline to place the temptation amongst the mountains of Moab is, we think, very improbable. **to be tempted** —The *Greek* word (*peirazein*) means simply to *try* or make proof of; and when ascribed to God in His dealings with men, it means, and can mean no more than this. Thus, Genesis 22:1, "It came to pass that God did tempt Abraham," or put his faith to a severe proof. (See Deut. 8:2.) But for the most part in Scripture the word is used in a bad sense, and means to entice, solicit, or provoke to sin. Hence the name here given to the wicked one—"the tempter" (vs. 3). Accordingly "to be tempted" here is to be understood both ways. The Spirit conducted Him into the wilderness simply to have His faith *tried;* but as the agent in this trial was to be the wicked one, whose whole object would be to seduce Him from His allegiance to God, it was a *temptation* in the bad sense of the term. The unworthy inference which some would draw from this is energetically repelled by an apostle (Jas. 1:13-17). **of the devil.** The word signifies a slanderer—one who casts imputations upon another. Hence that other name given him (Rev. 12:10), "The accuser of the brethren, who accuseth them before our God day and night." Mark (1:13) says, "He was forty days tempted of *Satan,*" a word signifying an *adversary,* one who lies in wait for, or sets himself in opposition to another. These and other names of the same fallen spirit point to different features in his character or operations. What was the high design of this? First, as we judge, to give our Lord a taste of what lay before Him in the work He had undertaken; next, to make trial of the glorious equipment for it which He had just received; further, to give Him encouragement, by the victory now to be won, to go forward spoiling principalities and powers, until at length He should make a show of them openly, triumphing over them in His cross: that the tempter, too, might get a taste, at the very outset, of the new kind of material in *man* which he would find he had here to deal with; finally, that He might acquire experimental ability "to succor them that are tempted" (Heb. 2:18). The temptation evidently embraced two stages: the one continuing throughout the forty days' fast; the other, at the conclusion of that period.

14-20. CHRIST BEGINS HIS GALILEAN MINISTRY —CALLING OF SIMON AND ANDREW, JAMES AND JOHN. See on Matthew 4:12-22.

21-39. HEALING OF A DEMONIAC IN THE SYNAGOGUE OF CAPERNAUM, AND THEREAFTER OF SIMON'S MOTHER-IN-LAW AND MANY OTHERS—JESUS, NEXT DAY, IS FOUND IN A SOLITARY PLACE AT MORNING PRAYERS, AND IS ENTREATED TO RETURN, BUT DECLINES, AND GOES FORTH ON HIS FIRST MISSIONARY CIRCUIT. (=Luke 4:31-44; Matt. 8:14-17; 4:23-25.) **21. And they went into Capernaum**—(See on Matthew 4:13). **and straightway on the sabbath day he entered into the synagogue, and taught—** This should have been rendered, "straightway on the sabbaths He entered into the synagogue and taught," or "continued to teach." The meaning is, that as He began this practice on the very first sabbath after coming to settle at Capernaum, so He continued it regularly thereafter.

ADAM CLARKE

13. *With the wild beasts.* This is a curious circumstance, which is mentioned by none of the other Evangelists, and seems to intimate that He was in the most remote, unfrequented, and savage part of the desert; which, together with the diabolic influence, tended to render the whole scene the more horrid.

15. *The time is fulfilled.* That is, the time appointed for sending the Messiah; and particularly the time specified by Daniel, chap. ix. 24-27.

16. *Andrew his brother.* Instead of the common reading, *his brother,* the best MSS. and versions have "the brother of Simon," which should be received into the text.

A. T. ROBERTSON:

20. "With the hired servants" (*meta ton misthoton*). One hired for wages (*misthos*), a very old Greek word. Zebedee and his two sons evidently had an extensive business in co-operation with Andrew and Simon (Luke 5:7, 10). Mark alone has this detail of the hired servants left with Zebedee. They left the boat and their father (Matt. 4:22) with the hired servants. The business would go on while they left all (Luke 5:11) and became permanent followers of Jesus. Many a young man has faced precisely this problem when he entered the ministry. Could he leave father and mother, brothers and sisters, while he went forth to college and seminary to become a fisher of men? Not the least of the sacrifices made in the education of young preachers is that made by the home folks who have additional burdens to bear because the young preacher is no longer a breadwinner at home. Most young preachers joyfully carry on such burdens after entering the ministry.—*Word Pictures in the New Testament*

MATTHEW HENRY

on sabbath-days, the gospel is to be preached. 5. Christ was a non-such preacher; he did not preach *as the scribes*, who expounded the law of Moses by rote; it came not *from the heart*, and therefore came not *with authority*. But Christ taught *as one that had authority*.

Verses 23–28

As soon as Christ began to preach, he began to work miracles for the confirmation of his doctrine.

I. Christ's *casting the devil* out of a man that was possessed, in the synagogue at Capernaum. *There was in the synagogue a man with an unclean spirit*, *ἐν πνεύματι ἀκαθάρτῳ—in an unclean spirit;* for the spirit had the man in his possession, and led him captive at his will. This man *was in the synagogue*; he did not come either to be taught or to be healed.

1. The rage which the unclean spirit expressed at Christ; *He cried out*, as one in an agony, at the presence of Christ. We are told what he said, *v.* 24, where he doth not *make terms*, but speaks as one that knew his doom. (1) He calls him *Jesus of Nazareth*; for aught that appears, he was the first that called him so. (2) Yet a confession is extorted from him—that he is *the holy One of God*. Those who have only a *notion* of Christ, and have no faith in him, or love to him, go no further than the devil doth. (3) He in effect acknowledgeth that he could not stand before the power of Christ; "*Let us alone;* for if thou take us to task, we are undone, thou canst *destroy us*." (4) He desires to have *nothing to do* with Jesus Christ; for he *despairs* of being *saved* by him, and *dreads* being *destroyed* by him.

2. The victory which Jesus Christ obtained over the unclean spirit. It is in vain for Satan to beg and pray, *Let us alone*; his power must be broken, and the poor man must be relieved. (1) Jesus *commands*. As he taught, so he healed, *with authority*. Jesus *rebuked him*; *Hold thy peace; φιμώθητι—be muzzled*. Christ has a muzzle for that unclean spirit when he *fawns* as well as when he *barks*. But this is not all, he must not only *hold his peace*, but he must *come out of the man*. (2) The unclean spirit *yields*, for there is no remedy (*v.* 26); He *tore him*, put him into a *strong convulsion*. When he would not *touch* Christ, in fury at him he grievously disturbed this poor creature. Thus, when Christ by his grace delivers poor souls out of the hands of Satan, it is not without a grievous toss and tumult in the soul. He *cried with a loud voice*, to frighten the spectators, and make himself seem terrible.

II. The impression which this miracle made upon the minds of the people, *v.* 27, 28.

1. It astonished them that saw it; *They were all amazed*. This was surprising to them, and put them upon considering with themselves, and enquiring of one another, "*What is this new doctrine?* For it must certainly be of God, which is thus confirmed." The Jewish exorcists pretended by charm or invocation to drive away evil spirits; but this was quite another thing, *with authority he commands them*. Surely it is our interest to make *him* our Friend, who has the control of infernal spirits.

2. It raised his reputation among all that heard it; *Immediately his fame spread abroad into the whole adjacent region of Galilee*. The story was presently got into everyone's mouth, together with the remark made upon it, *What new doctrine is this?* So that it was universally concluded, that he was a *Teacher come from God*. Thus he *prepared his own way*, now that John, who was his harbinger, was clapped up.

Verses 29–39

In these verses, we have,

I. A particular account of one miracle that Christ wrought, in the cure of Peter's wife's mother.

1. When Christ had done that which *spread his fame* throughout all parts, he did not then sit still, as some think that they may *lie in bed* when their *name is up*. No, he continued to *do good*. Those who are in reputation, had need be busy and careful to keep it up.

2. When he *came out of the synagogue*, where he had taught and healed with a divine authority, yet he conversed familiarly with the poor fishermen that attended him.

3. He went into Peter's house, probably invited thither to such entertainment as a poor fisherman could give him, and he accepted of it.

4. He cured his mother-in-law, who was sick. Wherever Christ comes, he comes to do good, and will be sure to pay richly for his entertainment. The same hand that *healed* her, *strengthened* her, so that she was able to *minister* to them; the cure is in order to that, to fit for action.

JAMIESON, FAUSSET, BROWN

22. And they were astonished at his doctrine—or "teaching"—referring quite as much to the manner as the matter of it. **for he taught them as one that had authority, and not as the scribes**—See on Matthew 7:28, 29. **23. And there was in their synagogue a man with**—lit., "in"—**an unclean spirit**—i.e., so entirely under demoniacal power that his personality was sunk for the time in that of the spirit. The frequency with which this character of "impurity" is ascribed to evil spirits—some twenty times in the Gospels—is not to be overlooked. **and he cried out, 24. Saying, Let us alone**—or rather, perhaps, "ah!" expressive of mingled *astonishment* and *terror*. **what have we to do with thee**—an expression of frequent occurrence in the Old Testament (I Kings 17:18; II Kings 3:13; II Chron. 35:21, etc.). It denotes *entire separation of interests:*—i.e., "Thou and we have nothing in common; we want not Thee; what wouldst Thou with us?" For the analogous application of it by our Lord to His mother, see on John 2:4. **thou Jesus of Nazareth**—"Jesus, Nazarene!" an epithet originally given to express contempt, but soon adopted as the current designation by those who held our Lord in honor (Luke 18:37; ch. 16:6; Acts 2:22). **art thou come to destroy us?**—In the case of the Gadarene demoniac the question was, "Art Thou come hither to torment us before the time?" (Matt. 8:29). Themselves tormentors and destroyers of their victims, they discern in Jesus their own destined tormentor and destroyer, anticipating and dreading what they know and feel to be awaiting them! Conscious, too, that their power was but permitted and temporary, and perceiving in Him, perhaps, the woman's Seed that was to bruise the head and destroy the works of the devil, they regard His approach to them on this occasion as a signal to let go their grasp of this miserable victim. **I know thee who thou art, the Holy One of God**—This and other even more glorious testimonies to our Lord were given, as we know, with no good will, but in hope that, by the acceptance of them, He might appear to the people to be in league with evil spirits—a calumny which His enemies were ready enough to throw out against Him. But a Wiser than either was here, who invariably rejected and silenced the testimonies that came to Him from beneath, and thus was able to rebut the imputations of His enemies against Him (Matt. 12:24-30). The expression, "Holy One of God," seems evidently taken from that Messianic Psalm (16:10), in which He is styled "Thine Holy One." **25. And Jesus rebuked him, saying, Hold thy peace, and come out of him**—A glorious word of command. BENGEL remarks that it was only the testimony borne to Himself which our Lord meant to silence. That he should afterwards cry out for fear or rage (vs. 26) He would right willingly permit. **26. And when the unclean spirit had torn him**—Luke (4:35) says, "When he had thrown him in the midst." Malignant cruelty—just showing what he *would* have done, if permitted to go farther: it was a last fling! **and cried with a loud voice**—the voice of enforced submission and despair. **he came out of him**—Luke (4:35) adds, "and hurt him not." Thus impotent were the malignity and rage of the impure spirit when under the restraint of "the Stronger than the strong one armed" (Luke 11:21, 22). **27. What thing is this? what new doctrine**—teaching—**is this?**—The audience, rightly apprehending that the miracle was wrought to illustrate the teaching and display the character and glory of the Teacher, begin by asking what novel kind of teaching this could be, which was so marvellously attested. **28. And immediately his fame spread abroad throughout all the region round about Galilee**—rather, "the whole region of Galilee"; though some, as MEYER and ELLICOTT, explain it of the country surrounding Galilee. **29. And forthwith, when they were come out of the synagogue**—so also in Luke 4:38. **they entered into the house of Simon and Andrew, with James and John**—The mention of these four—which is peculiar to Mark—is the first of those traces of Peter's hand in this Gospel, of which we shall find many more. The house being his, and the illness and cure so nearly affecting himself, it is interesting to observe this minute specification of the number and names of the witnesses; interesting also as the first occasion on which the sacred triumvirate of Peter and James and John are selected from among the rest, to be a threefold cord of testimony to certain events in their Lord's life (see on ch. 5:37)—Andrew being present on this occasion, as the occurrence took place in his own house. **30. But Simon's wife's mother lay sick of a fever**—Luke, as was natural in "the beloved *physician*" (Col. 4:14), describes it professionally; calling it a "great fever," and thus

ADAM CLARKE

22. *As one that had authority.* From God, to do what He was doing, and to teach a pure and beneficent system of truth. *And not as the scribes.* Who had no such authority, and whose teaching was not accompanied by the power of God to the souls of the people: (1) because the matter of the teaching did not come from God, and (2) because the teachers themselves were not commissioned by the Most High.

23. *A man with an unclean spirit.* This demoniac is mentioned only by Mark and Luke, chap. iv. 31. It seems the man had lucid intervals; else he could not have been admitted into the synagogue. *Unclean [or impure] spirit*—a common epithet for those fallen spirits; but here it may mean one who filled the heart of him he possessed with lascivious thoughts, images, desires, and propensities.

24. *What have we to do with thee?* Or, "What is it to us and to Thee?" or, What business hast Thou with us? There is a phrase exactly like it in 2 Sam. xvi. 10, "What have I to do with you, ye sons of Zeruiah?" The Septuagint translate the Hebrew just as the Evangelist does here; it is the same idiom in both places. *Art thou come to destroy us?* We may suppose this spirit to have felt and spoken thus: "Is this the time of which it hath been predicted that in it the Messiah should destroy all that power which we have usurped and exercised over the bodies and souls of men? Alas! it is so: I now plainly see *who thou art, the Holy One of God*, who art come to destroy unholiness, in which we have our residence, and through which we have our reign in the souls of men." An unholy spirit is the only place where Satan can have his full operation, and show forth the fullness of his destroying power.

25. *And Jesus rebuked him.* A spirit of this cast will yield only to the sovereign power of the Son of God.

26. *And when the unclean spirit had torn him.* "And . . . had thrown him [down] in the midst," Luke iv. 35, and "convulsed" him.

27. *For with authority.* They had never heard such a gracious doctrine, and had never seen any teaching supported by miracles before. How much must this Person be superior to men! They are brought into subjection by unclean spirits; this Person subjects unclean spirits to himself.

28. *And immediately his fame spread abroad.* The word *immediately* is used more frequently by this Evangelist than by any other writer of the new covenant. It is very often superfluous, and may often be omitted in the translation without any prejudice to the sense of the passage in which it is found.

29. See this account of the healing of Peter's mother-in-law explained at large, Matt. viii. 14-17.

Peter's house. That Peter lived at Capernaum, and that Christ lodged with him, is fully evident from this verse compared with chap. xvii. 24. *Peter's . . . wife's mother.* Learn hence, says Theophylact, that marriage is no hindrance to virtue, since the chief of the apostles had his wife. Marriage is one of the first of divine institutions, and is a positive command of God. He says the state of celibacy is not good, Gen. ii. 18. Those who pretend to say that the single state is more holy than the other slander their

MATTHEW HENRY

II. A general account of many cures he wrought—diseases healed, devils expelled. It was on the *evening of the sabbath*, when the *sun did set*, or *was set*; perhaps many scrupled bringing their sick to him, till the sabbath was over.

1. How *numerous* the patients were; *All the city was gathered at the door*, as beggars for a dole. That *one cure* in the synagogue occasioned this crowding after him. Others speeding well with Christ should quicken us in our enquiries after him. Christ was flocked after in a *private house*, as well as in the *synagogue*; wherever he is, there let his servants, his patients, be.

2. How *powerful* the Physician was; he *healed all* that were brought to him, though ever so many. Nor was it some one particular disease, that Christ set up for the cure of, but he healed those that were *sick of divers* diseases. And that miracle particularly which he wrought in the synagogue, he *repeated in the house* at night; for he *cast out many devils*, and *suffered not the devils to speak.*

III. His *retirement* to his *private devotion* (*v.* 35); *He prayed*, prayed alone; to set us an example of secret prayer. Though as God he was *prayed to*, as man he *prayed*. He found time to be alone with his Father.

1. The time *when* Christ prayed. (1) It was *in the morning*, the morning after the *sabbath day*. We must go to the *throne of grace*, every day in the week. This *morning* was the morning of the *first day of the week*, which afterward he sanctified, and made remarkable, by another sort of *rising early*. (2) It was early, *a great while before day*. When others were asleep in their beds, he was *praying*. When our spirits are most fresh and lively, then we should take time for *devout* exercises.

2. The place *where* he prayed; He *departed into a solitary place*. Secret prayer must be made secretly. Those that have the most business in public, and of the best kind, must sometimes be *alone with God.*

IV. His *return* to his *public* work. The disciples thought they were *up early*, but found their Master was up *before them*, *followed him* to his *solitary place*, and there *found him* at prayer, *v.* 36, 37. They told him that he was much wanted, *All men seek for thee*. They were proud that their Master was become so popular already, and would have him appear *in public*, yet more in that place, because it was *their own city*. "No," saith Christ, "*Let us go into the next towns*, the *villages, that I may preach there also, for therefore came I forth*, to *go about doing good*." He *preached in their synagogues throughout all Galilee*, and, to illustrate and confirm his doctrine, *he cast out devils.*

JAMIESON, FAUSSET, BROWN

distinguishing it from that lighter kind which the Greek physicians were wont to call "small fevers," as GALEN, quoted by WETSTEIN, tells us. **and anon**—immediately. **they tell him of her**—naturally hoping that His compassion and power towards one of His own disciples would not be less signally displayed than towards the demonized stranger in the synagogue. **31. And he came and took her by the hand**—rather, "And advancing, He took her . . ." The beloved physician again is very specific: "And He stood over her." **and lifted her up**—This act of condescension, most felt doubtless by Peter, is recorded only by Mark. **and immediately the fever left her, and she ministered unto them**—preparing their sabbath-meal: in token both of the perfectness and immediateness of the cure, and of her gratitude to the glorious Healer. **32. And at even, when the sun did set**—so Matthew 8:16. Luke (4:40) says it was setting. **they brought unto him all that were diseased, and them that were possessed with devils**—the demonized. From Luke 13:14 we see how unlawful they would have deemed it to bring their sick to Jesus for a cure during the sabbath hours. They waited, therefore, till these were over, and then brought them in crowds. Our Lord afterwards took repeated occasion to teach the people by example, even at the risk of His own life, how superstitious a straining of the sabbath-rest this was. **33. And all the city was gathered together at the door**—of Peter's house; i.e., the sick and those who brought them, and the wondering spectators. This bespeaks the presence of an eye-witness, and is one of those lively examples of word-painting so frequent in this Gospel. **34. And he healed many that were sick of divers diseases, and cast out many devils**—In Matthew 8:16 it is said, "He cast out the spirits with His word"; or rather, "with a word"—a word of command. **and suffered not the devils to speak, because they knew him**—Evidently they *would* have spoken, if permitted, proclaiming His Messiahship in such terms as in the synagogue; but once in one day, and that testimony immediately silenced, was enough. See on vs. 24. After this account of His miracles of healing, we have in Matthew 8:17 this pregnant quotation, "That it might be fulfilled which was spoken by Esaias the prophet, saying [53:4], Himself took our infirmities, and bare our sicknesses." **35. And in the morning**—i.e., of the day after this remarkable sabbath; or, *on the first day of the week*. His choosing this day to inaugurate a new and glorious stage of His public work, should be noted by the reader. **rising up a great while before day**—"while it was yet night," or long before daybreak. **he went out**—all unperceived from Peter's house, where He slept. **and departed into a solitary place, and there prayed**—or, "continued in prayer." He was about to begin His first preaching and healing circuit; and as on similar solemn occasions (Luke 5:16; 6:12; 9:18, 28, 29; ch. 6:46), He spent some time in special prayer, doubtless with a view to it. What would one not give to have been, during the stillness of those grey morning-hours, within hearing—not of His "strong crying and tears," for He had scarce arrived at the stage for that—but of His calm, exalted anticipations of the work which lay immediately before Him, and the outpourings of His soul about it into the bosom of Him that sent Him! He had doubtless enjoyed some uninterrupted hours of such communings with His heavenly Father ere His friends from Capernaum arrived in search of Him. As for them, they doubtless expected, after such a day of miracles, that the next day would witness similar manifestations. When morning came, Peter, loath to break in upon the repose of his glorious Guest, would await His appearance beyond the usual hour; but at length, wondering at the stillness, and gently coming to see where the Lord lay, he finds it—like the sepulchre afterwards—empty! Speedily a party is made up to go in search of Him, Peter naturally leading the way. **36. And Simon and they that were with him followed after him**—rather, "pressed after Him." Luke (4:42) says, "The multitudes sought after Him"; but this would be a party from the town. Mark, having his information from Peter himself, speaks only of what related directly to him. "They that were with him" would probably be Andrew his brother, James and John, with a few other choice brethren. **37. And when they had found him**—evidently after some search. **they said unto him, All men seek for thee**—By this time, "the multitudes" who, according to Luke, "sought after Him"—and who, on going to Peter's house, and there learning that Peter and a few more were gone in search of Him, had set out on the same errand—

ADAM CLARKE

Maker, and say in effect, "We are too holy to keep the commandments of God."

He touched her hand. Can anything on this side the unlimited power of God effect such a cure with only a touch? If the Scriptures had not spoken of the divinity of Christ, these proofs of His power must have demonstrated it to the common sense of every man whose creed had not previously blinded him.

32. *When the sun did set.* See on Matt. viii. 16.

When the even was come. The Jews kept their Sabbath from evening to evening, according to the law, Lev. xxiii. 32, "From even unto even, shall ye celebrate your sabbath." Hence it was that the sick were not brought out to our Lord till after sunset, because then the Sabbath was ended. *Many that were possessed with devils.* Dr. Lightfoot gives two sound reasons why Judea, in our Lord's time, abounded with demoniacs. First, because they were then advanced to the very height of impiety. See what Josephus, their own historian, says of them: There was not (said he) a nation under heaven more wicked than they were. Secondly, because they were then strongly addicted to magic, and so, as it were, invited evil spirits to be familiar with them. *And healed all that were sick.* Not a soul did the Lord Jesus ever reject who came to Him soliciting His aid. Need any sinner despair who comes to Him, conscious of his spiritual malady, to be healed by His merciful hand?

35. *In the morning . . . a great while before day.* By *the morning* is to be understood the whole space of three hours which finished the fourth watch of the night. *And there prayed.* Not that He needed anything, for in Him dwelt "all the fulness of the Godhead bodily," but that He might be a Pattern to us. Everything that our blessed Lord did He performed either as our Pattern or as our Sacrifice.

36. *And Simon . . . followed after him.* "Followed Him eagerly."

37. *All men seek for thee.* Some to hear; some to be healed; some to be saved; and some, perhaps, through no good motive.

MATTHEW HENRY

Verses 40–45

We have here the story of Christ's *cleansing a leper.* It teaches us,

1. *How to apply ourselves to Christ;* come as this leper did, (1) With great *humility*; this leper came *beseeching him, and kneeling down to him* (*v.* 40); it teaches us that those who would receive grace and mercy from Christ, must approach to him with humility and reverence. (2) With a firm belief of *his power*; *Thou canst make me clean.* He believes it with application, not only in general, *Thou canst do everything* (as John xi. 22), but, *Thou canst make me clean.* What we believe of the power of Christ we must bring home to our particular case; *Thou canst do this for me.* (3) With submission to the will of Christ; *Lord, if thou wilt.* With the modesty that became a poor petitioner, he refers his own particular case to him.

2. *What to expect from Christ;* that according to our faith it shall be to us. His address is not in the form of prayer, yet Christ answered it as a request. (1) Christ was *moved with compassion.* This is added here, in Mark, to show that Christ's power is employed by his pity for the relief of poor souls. Our *misery* makes us the objects of his *mercy.* And what he does for us he does with all possible tenderness. (2) He *put forth his hand, and touched him.* In healing souls, Christ *toucheth them.* Christ *toucheth and healeth too.* (3) He said, *I will, be thou clean.* The poor leper put an *if* upon the will of Christ; *If thou wilt;* but that *doubt* is soon put *out of doubt*; *I will.* Christ most readily *wills* favours to those that most readily *refer themselves* to his will. He was confident of Christ's *power*; Thou *canst make me clean*; and Christ will show how much his power is drawn out into act by the faith of his people, *Be thou clean.* And power accompanied this word, and the cure was perfect in an instant; *Immediately his leprosy* vanished, and there remained no more sign of it, *v.* 42.

3. *What to do when we have received mercy from Christ.* We must with his favours receive his commands. When Christ had cured him, *he strictly charged him.* I am apt to think that this refers not to the directions he gave him to conceal it (*v.* 44), for those are mentioned by themselves; but that this was such a charge as he gave to the impotent man whom he cured, John v. 14, *Sin no more, lest a worse thing come unto thee.* He also appointed him, (1) To *show himself to the priest.* (2) Till he had done that, not to *say anything* of it *to any man.* He must not *proclaim* it, because that would much increase the crowd that followed Christ, which he thought was too great already; not as if he were unwilling to *do good to all*, to as many as came; but he would do it with as little *noise* as might be. What to think of the leper's *publishing* it, and *blazing it abroad,* I know not. The leper ought to have observed his orders; yet, no doubt, it was with a good design that he *proclaimed* the cure, and it had no other ill effect than that it increased the multitudes which followed Christ, to that degree, that he *could no more openly enter into the city*, which obliged him to go into *desert places.* This shows how *expedient* it was for us, that Christ should go *away*, for his bodily presence could be but in one place at a time. By his spiritual presence he is with his people wherever they are, and comes to them to *every quarter.*

CHAPTER 2

Verses 1–12

Christ having been for some time preaching about in the country, here returns to Capernaum, his headquarters.

I. The great resort there was to him. Though he was *in the house* yet people came to him as soon as it was *noised* that he was in town. *Straightway many were gathered together to him.* Where the king is, there is the court. *There was no room to receive them,* they were so numerous, *no not so much as about the door.* A blessed sight, to see people thus flying like a cloud to Christ's house.

II. The good entertainment Christ gave them; he *preached the word unto them, v.* 2. Many of them perhaps came only for cures, and many perhaps only for curiosity, to get a sight of him; but when he had them together he *preached to them.* He thought it not at all amiss to preach in a house, on a week day; though some might reckon it both an improper place and an improper time.

JAMIESON, FAUSSET, BROWN

would have arrived, and "came unto Him and stayed Him, that He should not depart from them" (Luke 4:42); all now urging His return to their impatient townsmen. **38. And he said unto them, Let us go**—or, according to another reading, "Let us go elsewhere." **into the next towns**—rather, "unto the neighboring village-towns"; meaning those places intermediate between towns and villages, with which the western side of the Sea of Galilee was studded. **that I may preach there also; for therefore came I forth**—not from Capernaum, as DE WETTE miserably interprets, nor from His privacy in the desert place, as MEYER, no better; but from the Father. Cf. John 16:28, "I came forth from the Father, and am come into the world . . ."—another proof, by the way, that the lofty phraseology of the Fourth Gospel was not unknown to the authors of the others, though their design and point of view are different. The language in which our Lord's reply is given by Luke (4:43) expresses the high necessity under which, in this as in every other step of His work, He acted—"I must preach the kingdom of God to other cities also; for therefore"—or, "to this end"—"am I sent." An act of self-denial it doubtless was, to resist such pleadings to return to Capernaum. But there were overmastering considerations on the other side.

40-45. HEALING OF A LEPER. (=Matt. 8:1-4; Luke 5:12-16.) See on Matthew 8:1-4.

Jesus ["straitly charged him, and forthwith sent him away," Mark 1:43, and] **saith unto him, See thou tell no man**—A hard condition this would seem to a grateful heart, whose natural language, in such a case, is "Come, hear, all ye that fear God, and I will declare what He hath done for my soul" (Ps. 66:16). We shall presently see the reason for it. **but go thy way, show thyself to the priest, and offer the gift that Moses commanded** [Lev. 14] **for a testimony unto them**—a palpable witness that the Great Healer had indeed come, and that "God had visited His people." What the sequel was, our Evangelist Matthew does not say; but Mark thus gives it (1:45): "But he went out, and began to publish it much, and to blaze abroad the matter, insomuch that Jesus could no more openly enter into the city, but was without in desert places: and they came to Him from every quarter." Thus—by an over-zealous, though most natural and not very culpable, infringement of the injunction to keep the matter quiet—was our Lord, to some extent, thwarted in His movements. As His whole course was sublimely noiseless (ch. 12:19), so we find Him repeatedly taking steps to prevent matters prematurely coming to a crisis with Him. (But see on Mark 5:19, 20). "And He withdrew Himself," adds Luke (5:16), "into the wilderness, and prayed"; retreating from the popular excitement into the secret place of the Most High, and thus coming forth as dew upon the mown grass, and as showers that water the earth (Ps. 72:6). And this is the secret both of strength and of sweetness in the servants and followers of Christ in every age.

CHAPTER 2

Vss. 1-12. HEALING OF A PARALYTIC. (=Matt. 9:1-8; Luke 5:17-26.) This incident, as remarked on Matthew 9:1, appears to follow next in order of time after the cure of the leper (ch. 1:40-45). **1. And again he entered into Capernaum**—"His own city" (Matt. 9:1). **and it was noised that he was in the house**—no doubt of Simon Peter (ch. 1:29). **2. And straightway many were gathered together, insomuch that there was no room to receive them, no, not so much as about the door**—This is one of Mark's graphic touches. No doubt in this case, as the scene occured at his informant's own door, these details are the vivid recollections of that honored disciple. **and he preached the word unto them**—i.e., indoors; but in the hearing, doubtless, of the multitude that pressed around. Had He gone forth, as He naturally would, the paralytic's faith would have had no such opportunity to display itself. Luke (5:17) furnishes an additional and very important incident in the scene—as follows: "And it came to pass on a certain day, as He was teaching, that there were Pharisees and doctors of the law sitting by, which were come out of every town," or village, "of Galilee, and Judea, and Jerusalem." This was the highest testimony yet borne to our Lord's growing influence, and the necessity increasingly felt by the ecclesiastics through-

ADAM CLARKE

38. *The next towns.* Properly signifies such towns as resembled cities for magnitude and number of inhabitants, but which were not walled, as were cities. *For therefore came I forth.* For this purpose am I come forth—to preach the gospel to every creature, that all might hear, and fear, and return unto the Lord. The towns and the villages will not come to the preacher—the preacher must go to them, if he desires their salvation.

39. *And he preached.* "He continued preaching." This is the proper meaning of the words. He never slackened His pace—He continued proclaiming the glad tidings of salvation to all. There was no time to be lost—immortal souls were perishing for lack of knowledge; and the grand adversary was prowling about, seeking whom he might devour.

40. *There came a leper.* See the notes on Matt. vii. 2, etc. Should any be inclined to preach on this cleansing of the leper, Mark is the best Evangelist to take the account from, because he is more circumstantial than either Matthew or Luke.

45. *Began to publish it much.* Began to publish "many things"; probably all that he had heard about our Lord's miraculous works. *Jesus could no more openly enter into the city.* A city of Galilee, probably Chorazin or Bethsaida, in which He did not appear, for fear of exciting the jealousy of the secular government or the envy and malice of the Jewish rulers.

CHAPTER 2

1. *In the house.* The house of Peter, with whom Christ lodged when at Capernaum.

2. *So much as about the door.* Meaning the yard or court before the house. *Preached the word.* The doctrine of the kingdom of God.

MATTHEW HENRY

III. The presenting of a poor cripple to him, to be helped by him. The patient was one *sick of the palsy*, but perfectly disabled, so that he was *borne of four*, was carried upon *a bed*, as if he had been upon *a bier*. It was his misery, that he needed to be so carried, it was their charity, who did so carry him. These kind relations or neighbours thought, if they could but carry this poor man once to Christ, they should not need to carry him any more; and therefore made hard shift to get him to him, they *uncovered the roof where he was, v.* 4. It had no *upper room*, but the *ground-floor* was open to the roof: and these petitioners for the poor paralytic, when they could not get through the crowd at the door, got their friend by some means or other to the roof of the house, took off some of the tiles, and so let him down upon his bed with cords into the house where Christ was preaching. This bespoke both their *faith* and their *fervency*. Hereby it appeared that they were in earnest, and would not go away, nor *let Christ go without a blessing*, Gen. xxxii. 26.

IV. The kind word Christ said to this poor patient; *He saw their faith*; *theirs* that brought him. He commended *their faith*, because they did bring their friend through so much difficulty. True faith and strong faith may work variously, conquering sometimes the objections of reason, sometimes those of sense; but, however manifested, it shall be accepted and approved by Jesus Christ. Christ said, *Son, thy sins be forgiven thee*. The *compellation* is very *tender—Son*. Christ owns true believers as his sons: *a son*, and yet sick of the palsy. The *cordial* is very rich; *Thy sins are forgiven thee*. The word of Christ was to take his thoughts off from the disease, which was the effect, and to lead them to the sin, the cause, that he might be more concerned about that, to get that pardoned. Recovery from sickness is *then* a mercy indeed, when way is made for it by the pardon of sin. The way to remove the effect, is, to take away the cause. Pardon of sin strikes at the root of all diseases, and either cures them, or alters their property.

V. The cavil of the scribes at that which Christ said. They were expositors of the law, and their doctrine was *true*. But their application was *false*. It is *true, None can forgive sins but God only*; but it is false that therefore Christ cannot. But Christ *perceived in his spirit that they so reasoned within themselves*; this proves him to be God.

JAMIESON, FAUSSET, BROWN

out the country of coming to some definite judgment regarding Him. "And the power of the Lord was [present] to heal them"—or, "was [efficacious] to heal them," i.e., the sick that were brought before Him. So that the miracle that is now to be described was among the most glorious and worthy to be recorded of many then performed; and what made it so was doubtless the faith which was manifested in connection with it, and the proclamation of the forgiveness of the patient's sins that immediately preceded it. **3. And they come unto him**—i.e., towards the house where He was. **bringing one sick of the palsy**—"lying on a bed" (Matt. 9: 2). **which was borne of four**—a graphic particular of Mark only. **4. And when they could not come nigh unto him for the press**—or, as in Luke, "when they could not find by what way they might bring him in because of the multitude," they "went upon the housetop"—the flat or terrace-roof, universal in Eastern houses. **they uncovered the roof where he was: and when they had broken it up, they let down the bed**—or portable couch—**wherein the sick of the palsy lay**—Luke says, they "let him down through the tilling with his couch into the midst before Jesus." Their whole object was to *bring the patient into the presence of Jesus;* and this not being possible in the ordinary way, because of the multitude that surrounded Him, they took the very unusual method here described of accomplishing their object, and succeeded. Several explanations have been given of the way in which this was done; but unless we knew the precise plan of the house, and the part of it from which Jesus taught—which may have been a quadrangle or open court, within the buildings of which Peter's house was one, or a gallery covered by a veranda—it is impossible to determine precisely how the thing was done. One thing, however, is clear, that we have both the accounts from an eye-witness. **5. When Jesus saw their faith**—It is remarkable that all the three narratives call it "*their* faith" which Jesus saw. That the patient himself had faith, we know from the proclamation of his forgiveness, which Jesus made before all; and we should have been apt to conclude that his four friends bore him to Jesus merely out of benevolent compliance with the urgent entreaties of the poor sufferer. But here we learn, not only that his bearers had the same faith with himself, but that Jesus marked it as a faith which was not to be defeated—a faith victorious over all difficulties. This was the faith for which He was ever on the watch, and which He never saw without marking, and, in those who needed anything from Him, richly rewarding. **he said unto the sick of the palsy, Son**—"be of good cheer" (Matt. 9:2). **thy sins be forgiven thee**—By the word "be," our translators perhaps meant "are," as in Luke (5:20). For it is not a command to his sins to depart, but an authoritative proclamation of the man's pardoned state as a believer. And yet, as the Pharisees understood our Lord to be *dispensing* pardon by this saying, and Jesus not only acknowledges that they were right, but founds His whole argument upon the correctness of it, we must regard the saying as a royal proclamation of the man's forgiveness by Him to whom it belonged to dispense it; nor could such a style of address be justified on any lower supposition. (See on Luke 7:41, etc.). **6. But there were certain of the scribes**—"and the Pharisees" (Luke 5:21)—**sitting there**—those Jewish ecclesiastics who, as Luke told us, "were come out of every village of Galilee, and Judea, and Jerusalem," to make their observations upon this wonderful Person, in anything but a teachable spirit, though as yet their venomous and murderous feeling had not showed itself. **and reasoning in their hearts. 7. Why doth this man thus speak blasphemies? who can forgive sins but God only?**—In this second question they expressed a great truth. (See Isa. 43:25; Mic. 7:18; Ex. 34: 6, 7, etc.). Nor was their first question altogether unnatural, though in our Lord's sole case it was unfounded. That a man, to all appearances like one of themselves, should claim authority and power to forgive sins, they could not, on the first blush of it, but regard as in the last degree startling; nor were they entitled even to weigh such a claim, as worthy of a hearing, save on supposition of resistless evidence afforded by Him in support of the claim. Accordingly, our Lord deals with them as men entitled to such evidence, and supplies it; at the same time chiding them for rashness, in drawing harsh conclusions regarding Himself. **8. Why reason ye these things**—or, as in Matthew, "Wherefore think ye evil." **in your hearts? 9. Whether is it easier to say to the sick of the palsy, Thy sins be**—or "are"—**forgiven thee; or to say, Arise, and**

ADAM CLARKE

3. *One sick of the palsy.* "A paralytic person." See Matt. ix. 1. *Borne of four.* Four men, one at each corner of the sofa or couch on which he lay. This sick man appears to have been too feeble to come himself, and too weak to be carried in any other way.

4. *They uncovered the roof.* The houses in the East are generally made flat-roofed, that the inhabitants may have the benefit of taking the air on them. They are also furnished with battlements round about, Deut. xxii. 8; Judg. xvi. 27; and 2 Sam. xi. 2, to prevent persons from falling off; and have a trapdoor by which to descend into the house. This door, it appears, was too narrow to let down the sick man and his couch; so *they uncovered the roof*, removed a part of the tiles, and having *broken it up*, taken away the laths or timber to which the tiles had been attached, they then had room to let down the afflicted man.

ALEXANDER MACLAREN:

Faith, if worth anything, comes to the surface in act. Was it the faith of the bearers, or of the sick man, which Christ rewarded? Both. As Abraham's intercession delivered Lot, as Paul in the shipwreck was the occasion of safety to all the crew, so one man's faith may bring blessings on another. But if the sick man, too, had not had faith, he would not have let himself be brought at all, and would certainly not have consented to reach Christ's presence by so strange and, to him, dangerous a way—being painfully hoisted up some narrow stair, and then perilously let down, at the risk of cords snapping, or hands letting go, or bed giving way. His faith, apparently, was deeper than theirs; for Christ's answer, though it went far beyond his or their expectations, must have been molded to meet his deepest sense of need. His heart speaks in the tender greeting "son," or, as the margin has it, "child"—possibly pointing to the man's youth, but more probably an appellation revealing the mingled love and dignity of Jesus, and taking this man into the arms of His sympathy.

—*Exposition of Holy Scriptures*

7. *Why doth this man thus speak blasphemies?* See this explained, Matt. ix. 3.

This man blasphemeth. Wherever it is used in reference to God, it simply signifies "to speak impiously" of His nature, or attributes, or works. "Injurious speaking" is its proper translation when referred to man.

MATTHEW HENRY

God's royalties are inseparable, and he that could *know thoughts*, could *forgive sins*. Now he proves his power to *forgive sin*, by demonstrating his power to cure the *man sick of the palsy*, *v.* 9–11. He would not have pretended to do *the one*, if he could not have done *the other*; *that ye may know that the Son of man has power on earth to forgive sin, Thou that art* sick of the palsy, *arise, take up thy bed*. He could not have cured the disease, which was the effect, if he could not have taken away the sin, which was the cause. He that could by a word accomplish the sign, could doubtless perform the thing signified. It was proper enough to appeal, whether it is easier to say, *Thy sins are forgiven thee*, or to say, *Arise, and walk*? The removing of the punishment as such, was the remitting of the sin; he that could go so far in the cure, no doubt could perfect it.

VI. The cure of the sick man, and the impression it made upon the people, *v.* 12. He not only *arose* out of his bed, perfectly well, but *he took up his bed and went forth before them all*; and *they were all amazed*, and *glorified God* saying, "*We never saw it on this fashion*." Christ's works were without precedent. When we see what he does in healing souls, we must own that we *never saw the like*.

Verses 13–17

I. Christ preaching by the *sea-side* (*v.* 13), whither he went *for room*. Upon the strand there might come as many as would. It should seem by this, that our Lord Jesus had a strong voice, and could and did speak loud.

II. His calling Levi; the same with Matthew, who had a place in the custom-house at Capernaum, from which he was denominated a *publican*; his place fixed him by the waterside, and thither Christ went to meet with him. It is probable that Matthew was but a loose extravagant young man, or else, being a Jew, he would never have been a publican. Christ called him to *follow him*. With God, through Christ, there is mercy to pardon the greatest sins, and grace to sanctify the greatest sinners. Matthew, that had been a publican, became an evangelist. Great sin and scandal before conversion, are no bar to great gifts, graces, and advancements, after; nay, God may be the more glorified. In bodily cures, ordinarily, he was *sought unto*, but in these spiritual cures, he was *found of them that sought him not*. For this is the great evil and peril of the disease of sin, that those who are under it, desire not to be *made whole*.

III. His familiar converse with *publicans and sinners*, *v.* 15. We are here told, 1. That Christ *sat at meat in Levi's house*, who invited *him and his disciples* to the farewell feast he made to his friends, when he left all to attend on Christ. 2. That *many publicans and sinners* sat with Christ in Levi's house, and *they followed him*. They followed Levi; so some understand it. I rather take it, that they *followed Jesus* because of the report they had heard of him. They did not *for conscience-sake* leave all to follow him, but *for curiosity-sake* they came to Levi's feast, to see him. The publicans are here and elsewhere ranked with *sinners*, the worst of *sinners*. (1) Because commonly they *were such*; so general were the corruptions in the execution of that office, oppressing, exacting, and taking bribes or fees to extortion, and *accusing falsely*. (2) Because the Jews had a particular antipathy to them and their office, as an affront to the liberty of their nation, and thought it scandalous to be seen in their company. Such as these our blessed Lord was pleased to converse with, when he appeared *in the likeness of sinful flesh*.

IV. The *offence* which the scribes and Pharisees took at this, *v.* 16. They would not come to hear him preach, which they might have been convinced and edified by; but they would come themselves to *see him* sit with publicans and sinners, which they would be provoked by. They endeavoured to put the disciples out of conceit with their Master, and therefore put the question to them. *How is it, that he eateth and drinketh with publicans and sinners?*

V. Christ's justification of himself in it, *v.* 17. He stood to what he did, and would not withdraw. Those are too tender of their own *good name*, who, to preserve it with some nice people, will decline a *good work*. Christ would not do so. They thought the publicans were to be *hated*. "No," saith Christ, "they are to be *pitied*, they are *sick* and *need a physician*; they are sinners, and need a Saviour." They thought Christ's character should separate him from them; "No," saith Christ, "*I came not to call the righteous, but sinners to repentance*. It is to a *sinful world* that I am sent, and therefore my business lies most with those that are the greatest sinners in it." Or thus; "*I am not come to call the righteous*, the

JAMIESON, FAUSSET, BROWN

take up thy bed and walk?—"Is it easier to command away disease than to bid away sin? If, then, I do the one which you can see, know thus that I have done the other, which you cannot see." **10. But that ye may know that the Son of man hath power on earth to forgive sins**—that forgiving power dwells in the Person of this Man, and is exercised by Him while on this earth and going out and in with you. **(he saith to the sick of the palsy), 11. I say unto thee, Arise, and take up thy bed, and go thy way into thine house**—This taking up the portable couch, and walking home with it, was designed to prove the completeness of the cure. **12. And immediately he arose, took up the bed**—"Sweet saying!" says BENGEL: "The bed had borne the man: now the man bore the bed." **and went forth before them all**—proclaiming by that act to the multitude, whose wondering eyes would follow him as he pressed through them, that He who could work such a glorious miracle of healing, must indeed "have power on earth to forgive sins." **We never saw it on this fashion**—"never saw it thus," or, as we say, "never saw the like." In Luke (5:26) it is, "We have seen strange [unexpected] things to-day"—referring both to the miracles wrought and the forgiveness of sins pronounced by Human Lips. In Matthew (9:8) it is, "They marvelled, and glorified God, which had given such power unto men." At forgiving power they wondered not, but that a man, to all appearance like one of themselves, should possess it!

13-17. LEVI'S (OR MATTHEW'S) CALL AND FEAST. (=Mat. 9:9-13; Luke 5:27-32). See on Matthew 9:9-13.

And as Jesus passed forth from thence—i.e., from the scene of the paralytic's cure in Capernaum, towards the shore of the Sea of Galilee, on which that town lay. Mark, as usual, pictures the scene more in detail, thus (2:13): "And He went forth again by the seaside; and all the multitude resorted unto Him, and He taught them"—or, "kept teaching them." "And as He passed by" he saw a man, named Matthew—the writer of this precious Gospel, who here, with singular modesty and brevity, relates the story of his own calling. In Mark and Luke he is called *Levi,* which seems to have been his family name. In their lists of the twelve apostles, however, Mark and Luke give him the name of Matthew, which seems to have been the name by which he was known as a disciple. While he himself sinks his family name, he is careful not to sink his occupation, the obnoxious associations with which he would place over against the grace that called him from it, and made him an apostle. (See on ch. 10:3.) Mark alone tells us (2:14) that he was "the son of Alphaeus"—the same, probably, with the father of James the Less. From this and other considerations it is pretty certain that he must at least have heard of our Lord before this meeting. Unnecessary doubts, even from an early period, have been raised about the identity of Levi and Matthew. No capable jury, with the evidence before them which we have in the Gospels, would hesitate in giving a unanimous verdict of identity. **sitting at the receipt of custom**—as a publican, which Luke (5:27) calls him. It means the place of receipt, the toll-house or booth in which the collector sat. Being in this case by the seaside, it might be the ferry tax for the transit of persons and goods across the lake, which he collected. (See on ch. 5:46.) **and he saith unto him, Follow me**—Witching words these, from the lips of Him who never employed them without giving them resistless efficacy in the hearts of those they were spoken to.

And when the Pharisees—"and scribes," add Mark and Luke. **saw it, they** "murmured" or "muttered," says Luke (5:30). **said unto his disciples**—not venturing to put their question to Jesus Himself. **Why eateth your Master with publicans and sinners?**—(See on Luke 15:2.) **But when Jesus heard [that], he said unto them**—to the Pharisees and scribes; addressing Himself to them, though they had shrunk from addressing Him. **They that be whole need not a physician, but they that are sick**—i.e., "Ye deem yourselves whole; My mission, therefore, is not to you: The physician's business is with the sick; therefore eat I with publicans and sinners." Oh, what myriads of broken hearts, of sin-sick souls, have been bound up by this matchless saying!

for I am not come to call the righteous, but sinners [to repentance]—The words enclosed in brackets are of more than doubtful authority here, and more than doubtful authority in Mark 2:17; but in Luke 5:32 they are undisputed. We have here just the former statement stripped of its figure. "The righteous" are the

ADAM CLARKE

Jesus knowing their thoughts. In telling them what the thoughts of their hearts were (for they had expressed nothing publicly), He gave them the fullest proof of His power to forgive sins; because only God can forgive sins, and only God can search and know the heart.

For whether is easier, to say, Thy sins be forgiven thee; or to say, Arise, and walk? Both are equally easy, and equally difficult, for both require unlimited power to produce them. And everything is equally easy to that power which is unlimited. A universe can be as easily produced by a single act of the divine will as the smallest elementary part of matter.

But that ye may know. External miracles are the proofs of internal ones. Three miracles are wrought in this case: (1) The remission of the poor man's sins. (2) The discernment of the secret thoughts of the scribes. (3) The restoring of the paralytic, in an instant, to perfect soundness. Thus one miracle becomes the proof and establishment of another. Never was a clearer proof of omnipotent energy and mercy brought under the senses of man. Here is an absolutely perfect miracle wrought, and here are absolute incontestable proofs that the miracle *was* wrought; and the conclusion is the fullest demonstration of the divinity of the ever-blessed Jesus. *Arise, take up thy bed.* Being enabled to obey this command was the public proof that the man was made whole.

14. *Levi.* The same as Matthew; he appears to have been a Jew, though employed in the odious office of a taxgatherer. For an account of his call, see his Gospel, chap. ix. 9.

Named Matthew. Generally supposed to be the same who wrote this history of our blessed Lord. *Mathai* signifies a "gift" in Syriac; probably so named by his parents as implying a "gift from God." *The receipt of custom.* The customhouse, the place where the taxes levied by the Romans of the Jews were collected. *Follow me.* That is, Become My disciple. *And he arose, and followed him.* How blessed it is to be obedient to the first call of Christ—how much happiness and glory are lost by delays, though conversion at last may have taken place!

16. *Sinners.* The Gentiles or heathens are generally to be understood in the Gospels, for this was a term the Jews never applied to any of themselves. See the note on Matt. ix. 10.

Sat at meat in the house. Viz., of Matthew, who it appears, from Luke v. 29, made a great feast on the occasion, thus testifying his gratitude for the honor done him; and that his friends and acquaintances might profit by the teaching of his new Master, he invites them to the entertainment that was honored by the presence of Christ. His companions, it appears, were not of the most creditable kind. They were "taxgatherers and sinners."

17. *To repentance.* This is omitted by many manuscripts and versions, and many authorities approve of the omission.

MATTHEW HENRY

proud Pharisees that think themselves righteous, but poor publicans, that own themselves to be sinners, and are glad to be invited and encouraged to repent." It is good dealing with those that there is hope of.

Verses 18–28

Here he is put to justify his disciples; and in what they do according to his will he will justify them, and bear them out.

I. He justifies them in their *not fasting*. Why do the Pharisees and the disciples of John fast? They *used to fast*, the Pharisees fasted *twice in the week* (Luke xviii. 12), and probably the disciples of John did so too. Thus apt are strict professors to make their own practice a standard, and to censure and condemn all that do not fully come up to it. They invidiously suggest that if Christ went among sinners to do them *good*, yet the disciples went to indulge their appetites, for they never knew what it was to fast. Ill-will always suspects the worst.

Two things Christ pleads in excuse of his disciples *not fasting*.

1. That these were *easy days* with them, and fasting was not so *seasonable* now as it would be hereafter, *v.* 19, 20. There is a time for all things.

2. That these were *early days* with them, and they were not so able for the severe exercises of religion as hereafter they would be. The Pharisees had long accustomed themselves to such austerities; and John Baptist himself came neither eating nor drinking. But it was not so with Christ's disciples; their Master came *eating and drinking*, and had not bred them up to the difficult services of religion as yet. To put them upon such frequent fasting at first, would be a discouragement to them, it would be of as ill consequence as *putting new wine into old casks*, or sewing *new cloth* to that which is worn thin and threadbare, *v.* 21, 22. God graciously *considers the frame* of young Christians, that are *weak* and *tender*, and so must we; nor must we expect more than the *work of the day in its day*, and that day according to the strength. Weak Christians must take heed of *overtasking* themselves, and of making the yoke of Christ otherwise than it is, easy, and sweet, and pleasant.

II. He justifies them in *plucking the ears of corn on the sabbath day*, which, I will warrant you, a disciple of the Pharisees would not dare to have done; for it was contrary to an express tradition of their elders. They reflect upon the discipline of Christ's school, as too easy, so common it is for those who deny the *power of godliness*, to be jealous for the *form*, and censorious of those who affect not *their* form.

Observe, 1. What a poor breakfast Christ's disciples had on a sabbath-day morning, when they were going to church (*v.* 23); they *plucked the ears of corn*, and that was the best they had. They were so intent upon spiritual dainties, that they forget even their *necessary food*.

2. How even this was *grudged them* by the Pharisees, upon supposition that it was not lawful to *pluck the ears of corn* on the sabbath day, that that was as much a servile work as *reaping* (*v.* 24); *Why do they on the sabbath day that which is not lawful?* If Christ's disciples do that which is unlawful, Christ will be reflected upon. It is observable, that when the Pharisees thought Christ did amiss, they told the disciples (*v.* 16); and now when they thought the disciples did amiss, they spoke to Christ.

3. How Christ defended them.

(1) By example. They had a good precedent for it in David's eating the *showbread* (*v.* 25, 26); *Have ye never read?* Ritual observances must give way to moral obligations; and that may be done in a case of necessity, which otherwise may not be done.

(2) By argument. To reconcile them to the disciples' *plucking the ears of corn*, let them consider whom the sabbath was *made for* (*v.* 27); *it was made for man, and not man for the sabbath.* The sabbath is a sacred and divine institution; but we must receive and embrace it as a privilege and a benefit, not as a task and a drudgery. God never designed it to be an *imposition* upon us, and therefore we must not make it so to ourselves. Man was made *for God*, and for his honour and service, but he was not *made for the sabbath*. God did design it to be an *advantage* to us. He made it *for man*. He had *some* regard to our *bodies* in the institution, that they might rest, and not be tired out with the constant business of this world. He had *much more* regard to our *souls*. The *sabbath* was made a day of rest, only in order to its being a day of holy work, a day of communion with God, a day of praise and thanksgiving; and the rest from worldly business is *therefore* necessary, that we may closely apply ourselves to this work. See here, [1] What a *good Master* we serve, all whose institutions are for our own benefit. It is not he, but we,

JAMIESON, FAUSSET, BROWN

whole; "sinners," the sick. When Christ "called" the latter, as He did Matthew, and probably some of those publicans and sinners whom he had invited to meet Him, it was to heal them of their spiritual maladies, or save their souls: "The righteous," like those miserable self-satisfied Pharisees, "He sent empty away."

18-22. Discourse on Fasting. (=Matt. 9:14-17; Luke 5:33-39). See on Luke 5:33-39.

There may seem to be some inconsistency between the freedom and joy which our Lord here indirectly teaches to be characteristic of the new economy, and that sadness at His departure in person from the Church which He intimates would be the proper feeling of all that love Him during the present state. But the two are quite consistent. We may sorrow for one thing and rejoice for another, even at the same time. The one, indeed, will necessarily chasten the other; and so it is here. The liberty wherewith Christ hath made us free is a well-spring of resistless and commanded joy; nor is this a jot abated, but only chastened and refined, by the widowed feeling of Christ's absence. But neither is this sense of Christ's absence the less real and sad that we are taught to "rejoice in the Lord alway," "whom having not seen we love, in whom believing we rejoice with joy unspeakable and full of glory," in the assurance that "when he who is our life shall appear, we also shall appear with him in glory."

23-28. Plucking Corn-ears on the Sabbath day. (=Matt. 12:1-8; Luke 6:1-5.) See on Matthew 12: 1-8.

At that time Jesus went on the sabbath day through the corn—"the cornfields" (Mark 2:23; Luke 6:1). **and his disciples were an hungered**—not as one may be before his regular meals; but evidently from shortness of provisions: for Jesus defends their plucking the corn-ears and eating them on the plea of *necessity*. **and began to pluck the ears of corn, and to eat**—"rubbing them in their hands" (Luke 6:1). **But when the Pharisees saw it, they said unto him, Behold, thy disciples do that which is not lawful to do upon the sabbath day**—The act itself was expressly permitted (Deut. 23:25). But as being "servile work," which was prohibited on the sabbath day, it was regarded as sinful. **But he said unto them, Have ye not read**—or, as Mark has it, "Have ye never read." **what David did** (1 Sam. 21:1-6)—**when he was an hungered, and they that were with him; How he entered into the house of God, and did eat the showbread, which was not lawful for him to eat, neither for them which were with him, but only for the priests?**—No example could be more apposite than this. The man after God's own heart, of whom the Jews ever boasted, when suffering in God's cause and straitened for provisions, asked and obtained from the high priest what, according to the law, it was illegal for anyone save the priests to touch. Mark (2:26) says this occurred "in the days of Abiathar the high priest." But this means not during his high priesthood—for it was under that of his father Ahimelech—but simply, in his time. Ahimelech was soon succeeded by Abiathar, whose connection with David, and prominence during his reign, may account for his name, rather than his father's, being here introduced. Yet there is not a little confusion in what is said of these priests in different parts of the Old Testament. Thus he is called both the son of the father of Ahimelech (I Sam. 22:20; II Sam. 8:17); and Ahimelech is called Ahiah (I Sam. 14:3), and Abimelech (I Chron. 18:16).

"And he said unto them, the sabbath was made for man, and not man for the sabbath" (Mark 2:27). A glorious and far-reaching maxim, alike for the permanent establishment of the sabbath and the true freedom of its observance.

ADAM CLARKE

Thy disciples fast not. Probably meaning that they did not fast so frequently as the others did, or for the same purposes, which is very likely, for the Pharisees had many superstitious fasts. They fasted in order to have lucky dreams, to obtain the interpretation of a dream, or to avert the evil import of a dream. They also fasted often in order to obtain the things they wished for. The tract *taanith* is full of these fasts, and of the wonders performed thus by the Jewish doctors.

Can the children of the bridechamber? These persons were the companions of the bridegroom, who accompanied him to the house of his father-in-law when he went to bring the bride to his own home. The marriage feast among the Jews lasted seven days, but the new-married woman was considered to be a bride for thirty days.

21. *No man . . . seweth.* See Matt. ix. 16. "No man seweth a piece of unscoured cloth upon an old garment."

That which is put in . . . taketh from the garment. Instead of closing up the rent, it makes a larger, by tearing away with it the whole breadth of the cloth over which it was laid; "it taketh its fulness or whole breadth from the garment."

New wine into old bottles. It is still the custom, in the Eastern countries, to make their bottles of goatskins. If these happened to be old, and new wine were put into them, the violence of the fermentation must necessarily burst them; and therefore newly made bottles were employed for the purpose of putting that wine in which had not yet gone through its state of fermentation. The institutes of Christ, and those of the Pharisees, could never be brought to accord; an attempt to combine the two systems would be as absurd as it would be destructive. The old covenant made way for the new, which was its completion and its end; but with that old covenant the new cannot be incorporated.

26. *The days of Abiathar the high priest.* It appears from 1 Sam. xxi. 1, which is the place referred to here, that Ahimelech was then high priest at Nob. And from 1 Sam. xxii. 20; xxiii. 6; and 1 Chron. xviii. 16, it appears that Abiathar was the son of Ahimelech. Some suggest that Abiathar was the *priest*, and Ahimelech or Abimelech the *high priest*, and thus endeavor to reconcile both the sacred historians. Others reconcile the accounts thus: Ahimelech was called *Ahimelech Abiathar, ab*, "father," understood; and Abiathar was called *Abiathar Ahimelech, ben*, "son," understood. Probably they both officiated in the high priesthood, and the name of the office was indifferently applied to either. *Shewbread.* See Matt. xii. 4.

27. *The Sabbath was made for man.* That he might have the seventh part of his whole time to devote to the purposes of bodily rest and spiritual exercises. And in these respects it is of infinite use to mankind. Where no Sabbath is observed, there disease, poverty, and profligacy generally prevail. Had we no Sabbath, we should soon have no religion.

MATTHEW HENRY

that are gainers by our service. [2] What we should aim at in our *sabbath work.* If the sabbath was made for man, we should then ask ourselves at night, "What am I the better for this sabbath day?" [3] What care we ought to take not to make those exercises of religion burthens to ourselves or others, which God ordained to be blessings. Consider whom the sabbath was *made by* (*v.* 28); "*The Son of man is Lord also of the sabbath.*" The sabbath days are *days of the Son of man*; he is the Lord of the day, and to his honour it must be observed. The shifting of it one day forward to the first day of the week, was to be in remembrance of *his* resurrection, and therefore the Christian sabbath was to be called *the Lord's day.*

JAMIESON, FAUSSET, BROWN

For the Son of man is Lord even of the sabbath day—In what sense now is the Son of man Lord of the sabbath day? Not surely to abolish it—that surely were a strange lordship, especially just after saying that it was made or instituted for MAN—but to *own* it, to *interpret* it, to *preside over* it, and to *ennoble* it, by merging it in the "Lord's Day" (Rev. 1:10), breathing into it an air of liberty and love necessarily unknown before, and thus making it the nearest resemblance to the eternal sabbatism.

ADAM CLARKE

28. *The Son of man is Lord.* See on Matt. xii. 7-8. Some have understood this as applying to men in general, and not to Christ. It was made for man, for his ease, comfort, and use, and to these purposes he is to apply it. But this is a very harsh, and at the same time a very lax, mode of interpretation; for it seems to say that a man may make what use he pleases of the Sabbath; and were this true, the moral obligation of the Sabbath would soon be annihilated. God ordained the Sabbath not only to be a type of that rest which remains for the people of God, but also to be a means of promoting the welfare of men in general.

MATTHEW HENRY — CHAPTER 3

Verses 1–12

Here, as before, we have our Lord Jesus busy at work *in the synagogue* first, and then by *the seaside*; to teach us that his presence should not be confined either to the one or to the other, but, wherever any are gathered together in his name there is he in the midst of them.

I. When he *entered again into the synagogue*, he improved the opportunity he had there, of doing good.

1. The patient's case was piteous; he had a *withered hand*, by which he was disabled to work for his living; let those be helped that cannot help themselves.

2. The spectators were very unkind, both to the patient and to the Physician; instead of interceding for a poor neighbour, they did what they could to hinder his cure: for they intimated that if Christ cured him now on the sabbath day, they would accuse him as a *Sabbath breaker.*

3. Christ dealt very fairly with the spectators, and dealt with them *first*, if possible to *prevent* the offence.

(1) He laboured to convince their judgment. He bade the man *stand forth* (*v.* 3), that by the sight of him they might be moved with compassion. And then he appeals to their own consciences; "*Is it lawful to do good on the sabbath days, or to do evil?* Whether is better to *save life* or to *kill*?" What fairer question could be put? And yet, because they saw it would turn against them, *they held their peace.*

(2) When they rebelled against the light, he *lamented their stubbornness* (*v.* 5); *He looked round about on them with anger, being grieved for the hardness of their hearts.* The *sin* he had an eye to, was, the *hardness of their hearts.* We hear what is said amiss, and see what is done amiss; but Christ looks at the *root of bitterness* in the heart, the blindness and hardness of *that.* [1] How he was *provoked* by the sin; he looked *round upon them*; and he looked *with anger*; his anger, it is probable, appeared in his countenance. The sin of sinners is very displeasing to Jesus Christ; and the way to be angry, and not to sin, is to be angry, as Christ was, at nothing but sin. [2] How he *pitied* the sinners; he was *grieved for the hardness of their hearts.* It is a great grief to our Lord Jesus, to see sinners bent upon their own ruin, for he would not that any should perish. This is a good reason why the hardness of our own hearts and of the hearts of others, should be a grief to us.

4. Christ dealt very kindly with the patient; he bade him *stretch forth his hand*, and it was immediately *restored.* Christ has hereby taught us to go on with resolution in the way of our duty, how violent soever the opposition is, that we meet with in it. We must not deny ourselves the satisfaction of serving God, and doing good, though offence may unjustly be taken at it. None could be more tender of giving offence than Christ; yet, rather than send this poor man away uncured, he would venture offending all the scribes and Pharisees that compassed him about. He hath hereby given us a *specimen* of the cures wrought by his grace upon *poor souls*; our hands are spiritually *withered*, the powers of our souls weakened by sin. Though our hands are withered, and we cannot of ourselves *stretch them forth*, we must attempt it, must, as well as we can, *lift them up* to God in prayer, *lay hold* on Christ and eternal life, and employ them in good works; and if we do our endeavour, power goes along with the word of Christ, he effects the cure. If we will not offer to *stretch them out*, it is our own fault that we are not healed.

5. The enemies of Christ dealt very barbarously with him. Such a work of *mercy* should have engaged their love *to him*, and such a work of *wonder* their faith *in him.* But, instead of that, the Pharisees and the Herodians, *took counsel together against him, how they might destroy him.*

II. When he withdrew *to the sea*, he did good there.

JAMIESON, FAUSSET, BROWN — CHAPTER 3

VSS. 1-12. THE HEALING OF A WITHERED HAND ON THE SABBATH DAY, AND RETIREMENT OF JESUS TO AVOID DANGER. (=Matt. 12:9-21; Luke 6:6-11.) See on Matthew 12:9-21.

he went into their synagogue—and taught," He had now, no doubt, arrived in Galilee; but this, it would appear, did not occur at Capernaum, for after it was over, He "withdrew Himelf," it is said "*to the sea*" (Mark 3:7), whereas Capernaum was *at* the sea. **And, behold, there was a man which had his hand withered**—disabled by paralysis (as in I Kings 13:4). It was his right hand, as Luke graphically notes.

Matthew and Luke say they "watched Him whether He would heal on the sabbath day." They were now come to the length of dogging His steps, to collect materials for a charge of impiety against Him. It is probable that it was to their *thoughts* rather than their words that Jesus addressed Himself in what follows.

Resistless appeal! "A righteous man regardeth the life of his beast" (Prov. 12:10), and would instinctively rescue it from death or suffering on the sabbath day; how much more his nobler fellow man! But the reasoning, as given in the other two Gospels, is singularly striking: "But He knew their thoughts, and said to the man which had the withered hand, Rise up, and stand forth in the midst. And he arose and stood forth. Then said Jesus unto them, I will ask you one thing: Is it lawful on the sabbath days to do good, or to do evil? to save life or to destroy it?" (Luke 6:8, 9), or as in Mark (3:4), "to kill?" He thus shuts them up to this startling alternative: "Not to do good, when it is in the power of our hand to do it, is to do evil; not to save life, when we can, is to kill"—and must the letter of the sabbath rest be kept at this expense? This unexpected thrust shut their mouths. By this great ethical principle our Lord, we see, held Himself bound, as man. But here we must turn to Mark, whose graphic details make the second Gospel so exceedingly precious. "When He had looked round about on them with anger, being grieved for the hardness of their hearts, He saith unto the man" (Mark 3:5). This is one of the very few passages in the Gospel history which reveal our Lord's *feelings.* How holy this anger was appears from the "grief" which mingled with it at "the hardness of their hearts." **Then saith he to the man, Stretch forth thine hand. And he stretched it forth**—the power to obey going forth with the word of command. **and it was restored whole, like as the other**—The poor man, having faith in this wonderful Healer—which no doubt the whole scene would singularly help to strengthen—disregarded the proud and venomous Pharisees, and thus gloriously put them to shame.

Then the Pharisees went out, and held a council against him, how they might destroy him—This is the first explicit mention of their murderous designs against our Lord. Luke (6:11) says, they were filled with madness, and communed one with another what they might do to Jesus." But their doubt was not, *whether* to get rid of Him, but *how* to compass it. Mark (3:6), as usual, is more definite: "The Pharisees went forth, and straightway took counsel with the Herodians against Him, how they might destroy Him." These Herodians were supporters of Herod's dynasty, created by Cæsar—a political rather than religious party. The Pharisees regarded them as untrue to their religion and country. But here we see them combining together against Christ as a common enemy. So on a subsequent occasion (ch. 22:15, 16).

ADAM CLARKE — CHAPTER 3

1. *A man there which had a withered hand.* See this explained on Matt. xii. 10, etc., and on Luke vi. 6, 10.

2. *They watched him.* "They maliciously watched Him." See on Luke xiv. 1.

4. *To do good . . . or . . . evil? to save life, or to kill?* It was a maxim with the Jews, as it should be with all men, that he who neglects to preserve life when it is in his power is to be reputed a murderer.

5. *With anger, being grieved for the hardness of their hearts.* These words are not found in any of the other Evangelists. For *hardness,* some manuscripts read "deadness"; and others, "blindness." Join all these together, and they will scarcely express the fullness of this people's wretchedness. By a long resistance to the *grace* and Spirit of God, their hearts had become *callous;* they were past feeling. By a long opposition to the light of God, they became dark in their understanding, were *blinded* by the deceitfulness of sin, and thus were past seeing. By a long continuance in the practice of every evil work, they were cut off from all union with God, the Fountain of spiritual life; and, becoming *dead* in trespasses and sins, they were incapable of any resurrection but through a miraculous power of God. *With anger.* The anger which our Lord felt proceeded from excessive grief, which was occasioned by their obstinate stupidity and blindness. *Whole as the other.* This is omitted by the best MSS. and versions.

6. *Herodians.* For an account of these, see the note on Matt. xvi. 1; xxii. 16.

MATTHEW HENRY

He quitted the place; to teach us in troublous times to shift for our own safety.

1. How he was followed into his retirement. When some had such an enmity to him, that they drove him out of their country, others had such a value for him, that they followed him wherever he went. *Great multitudes* followed him from all parts of the nation. (1) What induced them to follow him; it was the report they heard of the *great things he did.* Some wished to *see* one that had done such *great things,* and others hoped he would do great things *for them.* The consideration of the *great things* Christ has done, should engage us to *come to him.* (2) What they followed him for (*v.* 10); They *pressed upon him, to touch him, as many as had plagues.* Diseases are here called *plagues,* corrections, chastisements. Those that were under these *scourgings* came to Jesus; this is the errand on which sickness is sent, to quicken us to enquire after Christ, and apply ourselves to him as our Physician. They *pressed upon him,* each striving which should get *nearest to him,* and which should be *first served.* They desired leave but to *touch him,* having faith to be healed, not only by *his* touching *them,* but by *their* touching him. (3) What provision he made to be ready to attend them (*v.* 9); He *spoke to his disciples,* that a *small ship should wait on him,* to carry him from place to place on the same coast; without pressing through the crowds of people that followed him for curiosity. Wise men, as much as they can, decline a crowd.

2. What abundance of good he did in his retirement. He did not withdraw to be idle, nor did he send back those who rudely crowded after him when he withdrew, but took it kindly, and gave them what they came for; for he never said to any that sought him diligently, *Seek ye me in vain.* (1) Diseases were effectually cured. He *healed many.* (2) *Devils* were effectually *conquered;* those whom unclean spirits had got possession of, *when they saw him,* trembled at his presence, and they also *fell down before him,* not to supplicate his favour, but to deprecate his wrath. (3) Christ sought not applause to himself in doing those great things, for *he strictly charged* those for whom he did them, *that they should not make him known* (*v.* 12); that they should not be *industrious* to spread the notice of his cures, as it were by advertisements in the newspapers, but let them leave *his own works to praise him,* and let the report of them *diffuse itself,* and make its own way. Let the *standers-by* carry away the intelligence of it.

Verses 13–21

I. The choice Christ made of the *twelve apostles* to be his constant followers and attendants.

1. The introduction to this *call* or *promotion* of disciples; He *goes up into a mountain,* and his errand thither was *to pray.*

2. The rule he went by in his choice, and that was his own good pleasure; *He called unto him whom he would.* Not such as we should have thought *fittest to be called;* but such as he *thought fit* to call, and determined to *make fit* for the service to which he called them. Christ calls *whom he will.*

3. The efficacy of the call; He *called them* to separate themselves from the crowd, and stand by him, and they *came unto him.* Those whom it was his *will* to call, he made *willing to come.*

4. The end and intention of this call; He *ordained them that they should be with him* constantly, to be witnesses of *his doctrine, manner of life, and patience,* that they might *fully know it;* they must be *with him,* to receive instructions *from him,* that they might be qualified to give instructions *to others.* It would *require time* to fit them for that which he designed them for. Christ's ministers must be much *with him.*

5. The power he gave them to work miracles. He ordained them to *heal sicknesses and to cast out devils.* This showed that the power which Christ has to work these miracles was an *original* power; that he had it not *as a Servant,* but *as a Son in his own house.* Our Lord Jesus had *life in himself,* and the Spirit without measure; for he could give this power even to the *weak* and *foolish things* of the world.

6. Their number and names; He *ordained twelve,* according to the number of the twelve tribes of Israel. They are here named not just in the same order as they were in Matthew, but as there, so here, Peter is put first and Judas last. Here Matthew is put before Thomas; but in that catalogue which Matthew himself drew up, he puts himself after Thomas. But that which Mark only takes notice of in this list of the apostles, is, that Christ called James and John *Boanerges,* which is, *The sons of thunder;* perhaps they were remarkable for a loud commanding voice, they were thundering preachers; or, rather, it denotes the zeal and fervency of their spirits. Yet John, one

JAMIESON, FAUSSET, BROWN

But when Jesus knew it, he withdrew himself from thence—whither, our Evangelist says not; but Mark (3:7) says "it was *to the sea*"—to some distance, no doubt, from the scene of the miracle, the madness, and the plotting just recorded. **and great multitudes followed him, and he healed them all**—Mark gives the following interesting details: "A great multitude from Galilee followed Him, and from Judea and from Jerusalem, and from Idumea, and from beyond Jordan; and they about Tyre and Sidon, a great multitude, when they had heard what great things He did, came unto Him. And He spake to His disciples, that a small ship should wait on Him because of the multitude, lest they should throng Him. For He had healed many; insomuch that they pressed upon Him for to touch Him, as many as had plagues. And unclean spirits, when they saw Him, fell down before Him, and cried, saying, Thou art the Son of God. And He straitly charged them that they should not make Him known" (Mark 3:7-12). How glorious this extorted homage to the Son of God! But as this was not the time, so neither were they the fitting preachers, as BENGEL says. (See on Mark 1:25, and cf. Jas. 2:19.) Coming back now to our Evangelist: after saying, "He healed them all," he continues: **And charged them**—the healed—**that they should not make him known**—(See on ch. 8:4).

13-19. THE TWELVE APOSTLES CHOSEN. See on Luke 6:12-19.

went out—probably from Capernaum. **all night in prayer . . . and when . . . day, he called . . .**—The work with which the next *day* began shows what had been the burden of this *night's* devotions. As He directed His disciples to pray for "laborers" just before sending themselves forth (see on Matt. 9:37; 10:1), so here we find the Lord Himself in prolonged communion with His Father in preparation for the solemn appointment of those men who were to give birth to His Church, and from whom the world in all time was to take a new mould. How instructive is this!

And when he had called unto him his twelve disciples, he gave them power—The word signifies both "power," and "authority" or "right." Even if it were not evident that here both ideas are included, we find both words expressly used in the parallel passage of Luke (9:1)—"He gave them power and authority"—in other words, He both *qualified* and *authorized* them. **against**—or "over." **Now the names af the twelve apostles are these**—The other Evangelists enumerate the twelve in immediate connection with their appointment (Mark 3:13-19; Luke 6:13-16). But our Evangelist, not intending to record the appointment, but only the Mission of the Twelve, gives their names here. And as in the Acts (1:13) we have a list of the Eleven who met daily in the upper room with the other disciples after their Master's ascension until the day of Pentecost, we have four catalogues in all for comparison. **The first, Simon, who is called Peter**—(See on John 1:42). **and Andrew his brother; James [the son] of Zebedee, and John his brother**—named after James, as the younger of the two. **Philip and Bartholomew**—That this person is the same with "Nathanael of Cana in Galilee" is justly concluded for the three following reasons: First, because Bartholomew is not so properly an individual's name as a family surname; next, because not only in this list, but in Mark's and Luke's, he follows the name of "Philip," who was the instrument of bringing Nathanael first to Jesus (John 1:45); and again, when our Lord, after His resurrection, appeared at

ADAM CLARKE

7. *Galilee.* See Matt. iv. 13, 15.

8. *Tyre and Sidon.* See Matt. xi. 21. *When they had heard what great things he did, came unto him.* So if Christ be persecuted and abandoned by the wicked, there are a multitude of pious souls who earnestly seek and follow Him. He who labors for God will always find more than he loses, in the midst of all his contradictions and persecutions.

9. *A small ship.* It was doubtless a boat, which probably belonged to some of the disciples. Our Lord was at this time teaching by the Sea of Galilee. The word *ship* is utterly improper in many places of our translation, and tends to mislead the people.

10. *They pressed upon him.* "Rushed upon Him," through eagerness to have their spiritual and bodily maladies immediately removed. *Plagues.* Properly such "disorders" as were inflicted by the Lord. The word *plague* tends to mislead.

A. T. ROBERTSON:

11. "Whensoever they beheld him" (*hotan auton etheoroun*). Imperfect indicative with *hotan* of repeated action. They kept falling down before him (*prosepipton*) and crying, (*ekrazon*) and he kept charging or rebuking (*epitima*) them, all imperfects. The unclean spirits (demons) recognize Jesus as the Son of God, as before. Jesus charged them not to make him known as he had also done before. He did not wish this testimony. It was a most exciting ordeal and is given only by Mark.
—*Word Pictures in the New Testament*

14. *He ordained twelve.* He "made" twelve. Here is nothing of what we call *ordaining.* Christ simply appointed them to be with Him, and that He might send them occasionally to preach.

15. *To have power to heal . . . and to cast out devils.* The business of a minister of Christ is: (1) to preach the gospel, (2) to be the physician of souls, and (3) to wage war with the devil and destroy his kingdom.

16. *Simon.* See on Matt. x. 2, etc.

17. *Sons of thunder.* Probably so named because of their zeal and power in preaching the gospel. Some think that our Lord gave this appellative to the sons of Zebedee because of

MATTHEW HENRY

of those *sons of thunder*, was full of love and tenderness, as appears by his epistles, and was the beloved disciple.

7. Their retirement with their Master, and close adherence to him; *They went into a house.* Now that this jury was impanelled, they *stood together, to hearken to their evidence.*

II. The continual crowds that attended Christ's motions (*v.* 20); The *multitude cometh together again*, unsent for, and unseasonably pressing upon him, so that he and his disciples could not get time *so much as to eat bread.* Yet he did not shut his doors against the petitioners, but bade them welcome. They whose hearts are enlarged in the work of God, can easily bear with great inconveniences to themselves, in the prosecution of it. It is happy when zealous *hearers* and zealous *preachers* thus *meet*, and encourage one another. This was a gale of opportunity worth improving. It is good striking while the iron is hot.

III. The care of his relations concerning him (*v.* 21); *When his friends* in Capernaum heard how he was followed they *went out, to lay hold on him*, and fetch him home, for they said, *He is beside himself.* 1. Some understand it of an absurd preposterous care, which had more in it of reproach to him than of respect; and so we must take it as we read it, *He is beside himself.* His kindred were willing to hearken to this ill construction which some put upon his great zeal, and to conclude him crazed in his intellects. 2. Others understand it of a *well-meaning* care; and then they read ἐξέστη—"*He fainteth*, he has no time to *eat bread*, and therefore his strength will fail him; he will be stifled with the crowd of people. Therefore let us use a friendly violence with him, and get him a little *breathing-time.*" They who go on with vigour and zeal in the work of God, must expect to meet with hindrances, both from the groundless disaffection of their enemies, and the mistaken affections of their friends.

Verses 22–30

Here is, I. The impudent impious brand which the scribes fastened upon Christ's casting out devils. These *scribes came down from Jerusalem, v.* 22. It should seem they came this long journey on purpose to hinder the progress of the doctrine of Christ. Coming from Jerusalem, where were the most polite and learned scribes, they were in the greater capacity to do mischief; the reputation of scribes from Jerusalem would have an influence not only upon the *country people*, but upon the *country scribes.* They could not deny but that he cast out devils, but they insinuated that *he had Beelzebub* on his side, and by *the prince of the devils cast out devils.* There is a trick in the case; Satan is not *cast out*, he only *goes out* by consent.

II. The rational answer which Christ gave to this objection.

1. Satan is so *subtle*, that he will never voluntarily quit his possession; *If Satan cast out Satan, his kingdom is divided against itself*, and it *cannot stand, v.* 23–26. He *called them to him*, he vouchsafed to reason the case with them, *that every mouth may be stopped.* It was plain that the doctrine of Christ *made war* upon the devil's kingdom, and had a direct tendency to break his power, and it was as plain that the casting of him out of the bodies of people confirmed that doctrine. Everyone knows that Satan is no *fool*, nor will act so directly against his own interest.

2. Christ is so *wise*, that, being engaged in war with him, he will attack his forces wherever he meets them, whether in the bodies or souls of people, *v.* 27. It is plain, Christ's design is to *enter into the strong man's house*, and to *spoil his goods.* Therefore it is natural to suppose that he will thus *bind the strong man*, and thus show that he has gained a victory over him.

III. The awful warning Christ gave them to take heed how they spoke such dangerous words as these; however they might make light of them, as only conjectures, and the language of *free-thinking*, if they persisted in it, it would be of fatal consequence to them; it would be found a sin against the last remedy, and consequently *unpardonable.* It is true, the gospel *promiseth*, because Christ hath *purchased*, forgiveness for the greatest sins and sinners, *v.* 28. Many of those who reviled Christ on the cross found mercy, and Christ himself prayed, *Father, forgive them*; but this was *blaspheming the Holy Ghost*, for it was by the Holy Spirit that he *cast out* devils, and they said, It was *by the unclean spirit, v.* 30.

Verses 31–33

Here is, 1. The *disrespect* which Christ's *kindred, according to the flesh*, showed to him when he was preaching; they not only *stood without*, but they sent in a message to *call him out to them* (*v.* 31, 32).

JAMIESON, FAUSSET, BROWN

the Sea of Tiberias, "Nathanael of Cana in Galilee" is mentioned along with six others, all of them apostles, as being present (John 21:2). **Matthew the publican**—In none of the four lists of the Twelve is this apostle so branded but in his own, as if he would have all to know how deep a debtor he had been to his Lord. (See on ch. 1:3, 5, 6; 9:9.) **James the son of Alphaeus**—the same person apparently who is called *Cleopas* or *Clopas* (Luke 24:18; John 19:25); and, as he was the husband of Mary, sister to the Virgin, James the Less must have been our Lord's cousin. **and Lebbaeus, whose surname was Thaddaeus**—the same, without doubt, as "Judas the brother of James," mentioned in both the lists of Luke (6:16; Acts 1:13), while no one of the name of Lebbaeus or Thaddaeus is so. It is he who in John (14:22) is sweetly called "Judas, not Iscariot." That he was the author of the Catholic Epistle of "Jude," and not "the Lord's brother" (ch. 13:55), unless these be the same, is most likely. **Simon the Canaanite;** rather "Kananite," but better still, "the Zealot," as he is called in Luke 6:15, where the original term should not have been retained as in our version ("Simon, called Zelotes"), but rendered "Simon, called the Zealot." The word "Kananite" is just the Aramaic, or Syro-Chaldaic, term for "Zealot." Probably before his acquaintance with Jesus, he belonged to the sect of the Zealots, who bound themselves, as a sort of voluntary ecclesiastical police, to see that the law was not broken with impunity. **and Judas Iscariot**—i.e., Judas of Kerioth, a town of Judah (Josh. 15:25); so called to distinguish him from "Judas the brother of James" (Luke 6:16). **who also betrayed him**—a note of infamy attached to his name in all the catalogues of the Twelve.

20-30. JESUS IS CHARGED WITH MADNESS AND DEMONIACAL POSSESSION—HIS REPLY. (=Matt. 12:22-37; Luke 11:14-26.) See on Matthew 12:22-37, and on Luke 11:21-26.

In Mark the language is awfully strong, "hath never forgiveness, but is in danger of eternal damnation"—or rather, according to what appears to be the preferable though very unusual reading, "in danger of eternal guilt"—a guilt which he will underlie for ever. Mark has the important addition (vs. 30), "Because they said, He hath an unclean spirit." (See on ch. 10:25.) What, then, is this sin against the Holy Ghost—the unpardonable sin? One thing is clear: Its unpardonableness cannot arise from anything in the nature of sin itself; for that would be a naked contradiction to the emphatic declaration of vs. 31, that all manner of sin is pardonable. And what is this but the fundamental truth of the Gospel? (See Acts 13:38, 39; Rom. 3:22, 24; I John 1:7, etc.). Then, again when it is said (vs. 32), that to speak against or blaspheme the Son of man is pardonable, but the blasphemy against the Holy Ghost is not pardonable, it is not to be conceived that this arises from any greater sanctity in the one blessed Person than the other. These remarks so narrow the question that the true sense of our Lord's words seem to disclose themselves at once. It is a contrast between slandering "the Son of man" *in His veiled condition and unfinished work*—which might be done "ignorantly, in unbelief" (I Tim. 1:13), and slandering the same blessed Person after the blaze of glory which *the Holy Ghost* was soon to throw around His claims, and in the full knowledge of all that. This would be to slander Him with eyes open, or to do it "presumptuously." To blaspheme Christ in the former condition—when even the apostles stumbled at many things—left them still open to conviction on fuller light: but to blaspheme Him in the latter condition would be to hate the light the clearer it became, and resolutely to shut it out; which, of course, precludes salvation. (See on Heb. 10:26-29). The Pharisees had not as yet done this; but in charging Jesus with being in league with hell they were displaying beforehand a malignant determination to shut their eyes to all evidence, and so, *bordering upon*, and *in spirit* committing, the unpardonable sin.

31-35. HIS MOTHER AND BRETHREN SEEK TO SPEAK WITH HIM, AND THE REPLY. (=Matt. 12:46-50; Luke 8:19-21.) See on Matthew 12:46-50.

ADAM CLARKE

their desire to bring fire down from heaven, i.e., a storm of thunder and lightning, to overturn and consume a certain Samaritan village, the inhabitants of which would not receive their Master. See the account in Luke ix. 53-54. It was a very usual thing among the Jews to give to their rabbins surnames which signified some particular quality or excellence.

19. *Into an house.* As Christ was now returned to Capernaum, this was probably the house of Peter, mentioned in chap. ii. 1.

20. *Eat bread.* Had no time to take any necessary refreshment.

21. *His friends.* Or "relations." *They said, He is beside himself.* The enemies of Christ raised this report; and His relatives, probably thinking that it was true, went to confine Him. Let a Christian but neglect the care of his body for a time, in striving to enter in at the strait gate; let a minister of Christ but impair his health by his pastoral labors—presently "he is distracted"; he has "not the least conduct nor discretion." But let a man forget his soul, let him destroy his health by debaucheries, let him expose his life through ambition, and he may, notwithstanding, pass for a very prudent and sensible man!

22. *He hath Beelzebub.* See on Matt. xii. 24-26.

Beelzebub. This name is variously written in the MSS. *Beelzeboul, Beelzeboun, Beelzebud*, but there is a vast majority in favor of the reading *Beelzebul*, which should, by all means, be inserted in the text instead of *Beelzebub.* It is supposed that this idol was the same with *Baalzebub* the *god fly*, worshipped at Ekron, 2 Kings i. 2, etc., who had his name changed afterwards by the Jews to *Baal zebul*, the *dung god*, a title expressive of the utmost contempt.

27-30. *No man.* For an explanation of these verses, and a definition of the sin against the Holy Ghost, see Matt. xii. 29-33.

29. *Eternal damnation.* Or "everlasting judgment." But instead, BL and two others read *hamartematos*, "sin." The *Codex Bezae*, two others, and some of the fathers read *hamartias*, a word of the same import. Grotius, Mill, and Bengel prefer this latter reading. *Sin* or *trespass* is the reading of the Coptic, Armenian, Gothic, Vulgate, and all the Itala but two. *Everlastinge trespas* is the translation in my old MSS. English Bible.

MATTHEW HENRY

2. The *respect* which Christ showed to his spiritual kindred upon this occasion. Now, as at other times, he put a *comparative neglect* upon his mother. He looked upon those that *sat about* him, and pronounced those of them that not only heard, but did, the will of God, to be to him as *his brother, and sister, and mother*; as much esteemed, loved, and cared for, as his nearest relations, *v.* 33–35. This is a good reason why we should *honour those that fear the Lord*, that we may share with the saints in this honour.

CHAPTER 4

Verses 1–20

The foregoing chapter began with Christ's *entering into the synagogue* (*v.* 1); this chapter begins with Christ's *teaching again by the seaside*. Thus he changed his method, that if possible all might be reached and wrought upon.

Here seems to be a new convenience found out, which had not been used before, and that was—his standing *in a ship*, while his hearers *stood upon the land*.

I. The *way of teaching* that Christ used with the *multitude* (*v.* 2); He *taught them many things*, but it was *by parables*, which would *tempt them to hear*; for people love to be spoken to in their own language, and careless hearers will catch at a plain comparison borrowed from common things. Unless they would take pains to search into it, it would but amuse them; *seeing they would see, and not perceive* (*v.* 12). They wilfully shut their eyes against the light, and therefore justly did Christ put it into the dark lantern of a parable, which had a bright side toward those who applied it to themselves, but to those who were only *willing for a season to play with it*, it only gave a flash of light now and then, but sent them away in the dark.

II. The way of *expounding* that he used with his *disciples*; *When he was alone* by himself, not only the *twelve*, but others that were *about him with the twelve*, took the opportunity to *ask him* the meaning of the parables, *v.* 10. And he told them what a distinguishing favour it was to them, that they were made acquainted with the *mystery of the kingdom of God*, *v.* 11. That *instructed* them, which others were only *amused* with. Those who know the *mystery* of the *kingdom of heaven*, must acknowledge that it is *given to them*; they receive both the light and the sight from Jesus Christ.

1. The parable of the sower, as we had it, Matt. xiii. 3, &c. He begins (*v.* 3), with, *Hearken*, and concludes (*v.* 9) with, *He that hath ears to hear, let him hear*. The words of Christ demand attention; even that which as yet we do not *thoroughly* understand, or not *rightly*, we must carefully attend to. We shall find more in Christ's sayings than at first there seemed to be.

2. The exposition of it to the disciples. Here is a question Christ put to them before he expounded it, which we had not in Matthew (*v.* 13); "*Know ye not this parable?* Know ye not the meaning of it? *How then will ye know all parables?*" "If ye know not this, which is so plain, how will ye understand other parables, which will be more dark and obscure?" This should quicken us both to prayer and pains that we may get knowledge. If we understand not the plain truths of the gospel, how shall we master those that are more difficult? This parable is to teach you to be attentive to the word, and affected with it, that you may *understand* it. "If ye receive not this, ye will not know how to use the key by which ye must be let into all the rest." Before Christ expounds the parable, (1) He shows them how sad *their* case was, who were not let into the meaning of the doctrine of Christ; *To you it is given, but not to them*. It will help us to put a value upon the privileges we enjoy as disciples of Christ, to consider the deplorable state of those who want such privileges, *lest they should be converted, and their sins should be forgiven them*, *v.* 12. Those only who are *converted*, have *their sins forgiven them*. (2) He shows them what a shame it was, that they needed such particular explanations of the word they heard, and did not apprehend it at first. Those that would improve in knowledge, must be made sensible of their ignorance.

He gives them the interpretation of the parable of the sower, as we had it before in Matthew. Let us only observe here,

First, That in the great field of the church, the word of God is dispensed to all promiscuously; *The sower soweth the word* (*v.* 14), sows it at a venture, not knowing where it will light, or what fruit it will bring forth. He *scatters* it, in order to the *increase* of it. Christ was awhile *sowing* himself, when he

JAMIESON, FAUSSET, BROWN

—Absorbed in the awful warnings He was pouring forth, He felt this to be an unseasonable interruption, fitted to dissipate the impression made upon the large audience—such an interruption as duty to the nearest relatives did not require Him to give way to. But instead of a direct rebuke, He seizes on the incident to convey a sublime lesson, expressed in a style of inimitable condescension.

CHAPTER 4

VSS. 1-34. PARABLE OF THE SOWER—REASON FOR TEACHING IN PARABLES—PARABLES OF THE SEED GROWING WE KNOW NOT HOW, AND OF THE MUSTARD SEED. (=Matt. 13:1-23, 31, 32; Luke 8:4-18.) **1. And he began again to teach by the seaside: and there was gathered unto him a great multitude**—or, according to another well-supported reading, "a mighty" or "immense multitude." **so that he entered into a ship**—rather, "the ship," meaning the one mentioned in ch. 3:9. (See on Matt. 12:15). **and sat in the sea; and the whole multitude was by the sea on the land**—crowded on the seashore to listen to Him. (See on Matt. 13:1,2.) **2. And he taught them many things by parables, and said unto them in his doctrine**—or "teaching."

Parable of the Sower (vss. 3-9, 13-20). After this parable is recorded, the Evangelist says: **vs. 10. And when he was alone, they that were about him with the twelve**—probably those who followed Him most closely and were firmest in discipleship, next to the Twelve. **asked of him the parable**—The reply would seem to intimate that this parable of the sower was of that fundamental, comprehensive, and introductory character which we have assigned to it (see on Matt. 13:1).

13. Know ye not this parable? and how then will ye know all parables?—Probably this was said not so much in the spirit of rebuke, as to call their attention to the exposition of it which He was about to give, and so train them to the right apprehension of His future parables. As in the parables which we have endeavored to explain in Matthew 13, we shall take this parable and the Lord's own exposition of the different parts of it together.

THE SOWER, THE SEED, AND THE SOIL. **3. Hearken; Behold, there went out a sower to sow**—What means this? **14. The sower soweth the word**—or, as in Luke (8:11), "Now the parable is this: The seed is *the word of God*." But who is "the sower"? This is not expressed here because if "the word of God" be the seed, every scatterer of that precious

ADAM CLARKE

31. *His brethren and his mother.* Or rather, "his mother and his brethren." This is the arrangement of the best and most ancient MSS.; and this clause, *and thy sisters*, should be added to verse 32 on the authority of numerous manuscripts and some editions and marginal renderings. Griesbach has received this reading into the text.

CHAPTER 4

2. *He taught them many things by parables.* See every part of this parable of the sower explained on Matt. xiii. 1.

10. *They that were about him.* None of the other Evangelists intimate that there were any besides the twelve with Him: but it appears there were several others present; and though they were not styled disciples, yet they appear to have seriously attended to His public and private instructions.

13. *Know ye not this parable?* The scope and design of which is so very obvious. *How then will ye know all parables?* Of which mode of teaching you should be perfect masters, in order that you may be able successfully to teach others. This verse is not found in any of the other Evangelists.

MATTHEW HENRY

went about teaching and preaching; now he sends his ministers and sows by their hand.

Secondly, That of the many that hear the word of the gospel, there are, comparatively, but few that receive it, so as to bring forth the fruits of it; here is but one in four, that comes to good. It is sad to think, how much of the precious seed of the word of God is lost, and *sown in vain*; but there is a day coming when *lost sermons* must be accounted for.

Fourthly, The reason why the word doth not leave commanding, abiding, impressions upon the minds of the people. The fault is in themselves, not in the word; some are careless forgetful hearers, and these get *no good at all* by the word; it comes in at one ear, and goes out at the other; others have their convictions overpowered by their corruptions, and they lose the good impressions the word has made upon them, so that they get no *abiding* good by it.

Fifthly, The devil is very busy about loose, careless hearers, as the fowls of the air go about the seed that lies above ground. *Like the fowls*, he comes swiftly, and carries away the word ere we are aware. Though we cannot keep them from hovering over our heads we may not let them nestle in our hearts.

Thirdly, Many are much affected with the word for the present, who yet receive no abiding benefit by it. The motions of soul they have, answerable to what they hear, are but a mere flash, like the crackling of thorns under a pot. Those represented here by the stony ground, received the word *with gladness*, and yet came to nothing.

Seventhly, Impressions that are not *deep*, will not be *durable*. Many that keep their profession in fair days, lose it in a storm; and as those that go to sea only for pleasure, come back again when the wind arises. It is the ruin of hypocrites, that they *have no root*; they do not act from a living fixed principle. He is the Christian, that is *one inwardly*.

Sixthly, Many that are not openly *scandalized*, so as to throw off their profession, as they on the stony ground did, yet have the efficacy of it secretly *choked* and stifled, so that it comes to nothing.

Eighthly, Many are hindered from profiting by the word of God, by their abundance of the world. Many a good lesson is choked and lost by that prevailing complacency in the world, which *they* are apt to have, on whom it smiles.

Ninthly, Those that are not encumbered with the cares of the world, and the deceitfulness of riches, may yet lose the benefit of their profession by the *lusts of other things*; this is added here in Mark; an inordinate appetite toward those things that are pleasing to sense or to the fancy. Those that have but little of the world, may yet be ruined by an indulgence of the body.

JAMIESON, FAUSSET, BROWN

seed must be regarded as a sower. It is true that in the parable of the tares it is said, "He that soweth the good seed is the Son of man," as "He that soweth the tares is the devil" (Matt. 13:37, 38). But these are only the great unseen parties, struggling in this world for the possession of man. Each of these has his agents among men themselves; and Christ's agents in the sowing of the good seed are the *preachers* of the word. Thus, as in all the cases about to be described, the sower is the same, and the seed is the same; while the result is entirely different, the whole difference must lie in the *soils*, which mean the *different states of the human heart*. And so, the great general lesson held forth in this parable of the sower is, that however faithful the preacher, and how pure soever his message, *the effect of the preaching of the word depends upon the state of the hearer's heart*. Now follow the cases.

First Case: THE WAYSIDE. **4. And it came to pass, as he sowed, some fell by the wayside**—by the side of the hard path through the field, where the soil was not broken up. **and the fowls [of the air] came and devoured it up**—Not only could the seed not get beneath the surface, but "it was trodden down" (Luke 8:5), and afterwards picked up and devoured by the fowls. What means this? **15. And these are they by the wayside, where the word is sown; but, when they have heard . . .**—or, more fully (Matt. 13:19), "When any one heareth the word of the kingdom, and understandeth it not, then cometh the wicked one, and catcheth away that which was sown in his heart." The great truth here taught is, that *hearts all unbroken and hard are no fit soil for saving truth*. They apprehend it not (Matt. 13:19) as God's means of restoring them to Himself; it penetrates not, makes no impression, but lies loosely on the surface of the heart, till the wicked one—afraid of losing a victim by his "believing to salvation" (Luke 8:12)—finds some frivolous subject by whose greater attractions to draw off the attention, and straightway it is gone. Of how many hearers of the word is this the graphic but painful history!

Second Case: THE STONY, or rather, ROCKY GROUND. **5. And some fell on stony ground, where it had not much earth**—"the rocky ground"; in Matthew (13:5), "the rocky places"; in Luke, "the rock." The thing intended is, not ground with stones in it which would not prevent the roots striking downward, but ground where a quite thin surface of earth covers a rock. What means this? **16. And these are they likewise which are sown on stony ground . . .**—"Immediately" the seed in such a case "springs up"—all the quicker from the shallowness of the soil—"because it has no depth of earth." But the sun, beating on it, as quickly scorches and withers it up, "because it has no root" (vs. 6), and "lacks moisture" (Luke 8:6). The great truth here taught is that *hearts superficially impressed are apt to receive the truth with readiness, and even with joy* (Luke 8:13); *but the* heat of tribulation or persecution because of the word, or *the trials which their new profession brings upon them quickly dries up their relish for the truth, and withers all the hasty promise of fruit which they showed*. Such disappointing issues of a faithful and awakening ministry—alas, how frequent are they!

Third Case: THE THORNY GROUND. **7. And some fell among thorns, and the thorns grew up, and choked it, and it yielded no fruit**—This case is that of ground not thoroughly cleaned of the thistles, etc.; which, rising above the good seed, "choke" or "smother" it, excluding light and air, and drawing away the moisture and richness of the soil. Hence it "becomes unfruitful" (Matt. 13:22); it grows, but its growth is checked, and it never ripens. The evil here is neither a hard nor a shallow soil—there is *softness* enough, and *depth* enough; but it is the existence in it of what draws all the moisture and richness of the soil away to itself, and so *starves the plant*. What now are these "thorns?" **18. And these are they which are sown among thorns; such as hear the word, 19. And the cares of this world, and the deceitfulness of riches, and the lusts of other things entering in**—or "the pleasures of this life" (Luke 8:14)—**choke the word, and it becometh unfruitful.** First, "The cares of this world"—anxious, unrelaxing attention to the business of this present life; second, "The deceitfulness of riches"—of those riches which are the fruit of this worldly "care"; third, "The pleasures of this life," or "the lusts of other things entering in"—the enjoyments in themselves may be innocent, which worldly prosperity enables one to indulge. These "*choke*" or "*smother*" the word; drawing off so

ADAM CLARKE

4. *The fowls.* "Of the air" is the common reading; but it should be omitted, on the authority of many MSS. and almost all the versions. Bengel and Griesbach have left it out of the text. It seems to have been inserted in Mark from Luke viii. 5.

When any one heareth the word of the kingdom. Viz., the preaching of the gospel of Christ. *And understandeth it not.* Perhaps more properly, "regardeth it not," does not lay his heart to it. *The wicked one.* He who distresses and torments the soul. Mark, chap. iv. 15, calls him *Satan*, the "adversary" or "opposer," because he resists men in all their purposes of amendment, and to the utmost of his power opposes, in order to frustrate, the influences of divine grace upon the heart. In the parallel place in Luke, viii. 12, he is called *the devil*. It is worthy of remark that the three Evangelists should use each a different appellative of this mortal enemy of mankind; probably to show that the devil, with all his powers and properties, opposes everything that tends to the salvation of the soul. *Catcheth away.* Makes the utmost haste to pick up the good seed, lest it should take root in the heart. A careless, inattentive hearer is compared to the *way side*—his heart is an open road, where evil affections and foolish and hurtful desires continually pass and repass without either notice or restraint.

He also that received seed among the thorns. In land ploughed, but not properly cleared and weeded. *Is he*—represents that person *that heareth the word; and the care*, rather "the anxiety" the whole system of anxious, carking cares. *The deceitfulness of riches.* Which promise peace and pleasure, but can never give them. *Choke the word.* Or "together choke the word," meaning either that these grow up together with the word, overtop, and choke it, or that these united together, viz., carking, worldly cares, with the delusive hopes and promises of riches, cause the man to abandon the great concerns of his soul and seek, in their place, what he shall eat, drink, and wherewithal he shall be clothed. Dreadful stupidity of man, thus to barter spiritual for temporal good—a heavenly inheritance for an earthly portion! The seed of the Kingdom can never produce much fruit in any heart till the thorns and thistles of vicious affections and impure desires be plucked up by the roots and burned.

MATTHEW HENRY

Tenthly, Fruit is the thing that God expects and requires from those that enjoy the gospel: fruit according to the *seed*; a temper of mind, and a course of life, agreeable to the gospel. This is *fruit,* and it will abound to our account.

Lastly, No good fruit is to be expected but from good seed. If the seed be sown on *good ground,* if the heart be humble, and holy, and heavenly, there will be *good fruit,* and it will *abound* sometimes even to a *hundredfold.*

Verses 21-34

I. Those who *are good* ought to *do good*; that is to *bring forth fruit.* God expects a grateful return of his gifts to us, and a useful improvement of his gifts in us; for (*v.* 21), *Is a candle brought to be put under a bushel, or under a bed?* No, but that it may be *set on a candlestick.* All Christians, as they have *received the gift,* must *minister the same.* Gifts and graces make a man *as a candle*; the most eminent are but candles, poor lights, compared with the *Sun of righteousness.* A candle gives light but a *little way,* and but a *little while,* and is easily blown out, and continually burning down and wasting. Many who are *lighted* as candles, put themselves *under a bed, or under a bushel*: they do not *manifest* grace themselves, nor *minister* grace to others. Like a taper in an urn, they burn to themselves. Those who are lighted as candles, should set themselves *on a candlestick*; that is, should improve all opportunities of doing good. We are not born for ourselves.

The reason given for this, is, because *there is nothing hid, which shall not be manifested, v.* 22. There is no treasure of gifts and graces lodged in any but with design to be communicated; nor was the gospel made a *secret* to the apostles. It should *come abroad,* and be divulged to all the world. Though Christ expounded the parables to his disciples privately, yet it was with design to make them the more publicly useful; they were *taught,* that they might teach.

II. It concerns those who hear the word of the gospel, to *mark* what they hear, and to *make a good use* of it, *If any man have ears to hear, let him hear, v.* 23. It is added (*v.* 24), *Take heed what ye hear,* and give a due regard to that which ye do hear; *Consider what ye hear.* What we hear, doth us no good, unless we consider it; those especially that are to teach others must themselves be very observant of the things of God. We must likewise *take heed what we hear,* by *proving* all things, that we may *hold fast that which is good.* As we deal with God, God will deal with us, "*With what measure ye mete, it shall be measured to you.*" As we improve the talents we are entrusted with, we shall increase them; if we make use of the knowledge we have, it shall sensibly grow, as stock in trade both by being turned; *Unto you that hear, shall more be given; to you that have, it shall be given, v.* 25. Gifts and graces multiply by being exercised.

If we do not *use,* we *lose,* what we have; *From him that hath not shall be taken even that which he hath.* Burying a talent is the betraying of a trust, and amounts to a forfeiture; and gifts and graces *rust* for want of *wearing.*

III. The good seed of the gospel sown in the world, and sown in the heart, doth by degrees produce wonderful effects, but without noise (*v.* 26, &c.); *So is the kingdom of God.*

1. It will *come up;* though it seem lost and buried under the clods, it will find or make its way through them. The seed *cast into the ground will spring.* After a field is sown with corn, how soon is the sur-

JAMIESON, FAUSSET, BROWN

much of one's attention, absorbing so much of one's interest, and using up so much of one's time, that only the dregs of these remain for spiritual things, and a fagged, hurried, and heartless formalism is at length all the religion of such persons. What a vivid picture is this of the mournful condition of many, especially in great commercial countries, who once promised much fruit! "They bring no fruit *to perfection*" (Luke 8:14); indicating how much *growth* there may be, in the early stages of such a case, and *promise* of fruit—which after all never *ripens.*

Fourth Case: The GOOD GROUND. **8. And other fell on good ground, and did yield fruit . . .**—The goodness of this last soil consists in its qualities being precisely the reverse of the other three soils: from its softness and tenderness, receiving and cherishing the seed; from its depth, allowing it to take firm root, and not quickly losing its moisture; and from its cleanness, giving its whole vigor and sap to the plant. In such a soil the seed "brings forth fruit," in all different degrees of profusion, according to the measure in which the soil possesses those qualities. **20. And these are they which are sown on good ground; such as hear the word, and receive it, and bring forth fruit, some thirtyfold, some sixty, and some an hundred**—A heart soft and tender, stirred to its depths on the great things of eternity, and jealously guarded from worldly engrossments, such only is the "honest and good heart" (Luke 8:15), which "keeps," i.e., "retains" the seed of the word, and bears fruit just in proportion as it is such a heart. Such "bring forth fruit with *patience*" (vs. 15), or continuance, "enduring to the end"; in contrast with those in whom the word is "choked" and brings no fruit *to perfection.* The "thirtyfold" is designed to express the *lowest* degree of fruitfulness; the "hundredfold" the *highest*; and the "sixtyfold" the *intermediate* degrees of fruitfulness. As a hundredfold," though not unexampled (Gen. 26:12), is a rare return in the natural husbandry, so the highest degrees of spiritual fruitfulness are too seldom witnessed. The closing words of this introductory parable seem designed to call attention to the *fundamental* and *universal* character of it. **9. And he said unto them, He that hath ears to hear, let him hear.**

Reason for Teaching in Parables (vss. 11, 12). **11, 12. And he said unto them, Unto you it is given to know the mystery of the kingdom of God: but unto them . . .**—See on Matthew 13:10-17. **21. And he said unto them, Is a candle**—or "lamp"—**brought to be put under a bushel, or under a bed? and not to be set on a candlestick?**—"that they which enter in may see the light" (Luke 8:16). See on Matthew 5:15, of which this is nearly a repetition. **22. For there is nothing hid which shall not be manifested . . .**—See on Matthew 10:26, 27; but the connection there and here is slightly different. Here the idea seems to be this—'I have privately expounded to you these great truths, but only that ye may proclaim them publicly; and if ye will not, others will. For these are not designed for secrecy. They are imparted to be diffused abroad, and they shall be so; yea, a time is coming when the most hidden things shall be brought to light.' **23. If any man have ears to hear, let him hear**—This for the second time on the same subject (see on vs. 9). **24. And he saith unto them, Take heed what ye hear**—In Luke (8:18) it is, "Take heed how ye hear." The one implies the other, but both precepts are very weighty. **with what measure ye mete, it shall be measured to you**—See on Matthew 7:2. **and unto you that hear**—i.e., thankfully, teachably, profitably. **shall more be given. 25. For he that hath, to him shall be given; and he that hath not, from him shall be taken even that which he hath**—or "seemeth to have," or "thinketh he hath." (See on Matt. 13:12.) This "having" and "thinking he hath" are not different; for when it hangs loosely upon him, and is not appropriated to its proper ends and uses, it both *is* and *is not* his.

Parable of the Seed Growing We Know not How (vss. 26-29). This beautiful parable is peculiar to Mark. Its design is to teach the *Imperceptible Growth* of the word sown in the heart, from its earliest stage of development to the ripest fruits of practical righteousness. **26. So is the kingdom of God, as if a man should cast seed into the ground;**

ADAM CLARKE

Good ground. That which had depth of mold, was well-ploughed and well-weeded. *Is he that heareth.* Who diligently attends the ministry of *the word. And understandeth it.* Lays the subject to heart, deeply weighing its nature, design, and importance. *Which also beareth fruit.* His fruitfulness being an almost necessary consequence of his thus laying the divine message to heart. Let it be observed that to *hear,* to *understand,* and to *bring forth fruit* are the three grand evidences of a genuine believer. He who does not *hear* the word of wisdom cannot *understand* what makes for his peace; and he who does not *understand* what the gospel requires him to be and to perform cannot *bring forth fruit*; and he who is not fruitful, very fruitful, cannot be a disciple of Christ, see John xv. 8; and he who is not Christ's disciple cannot enter into the kingdom of God. From the different portions of fruit produced by the good ground, a *hundred, sixty,* and *thirty,* we may learn that all sound believers are not equally fruitful. All hear, understand, and bring forth fruit, but not in the same degrees—occasioned partly by their situation and circumstances not allowing them such extensive opportunities of receiving and doing good; and partly by lack of mental capacity—for every mind is not equally improvable. Let it be further observed that the unfruitfulness of the different lands was not owing to bad seed or an unskillful sower—the same sower sowed the same seed in all, and with the same gracious design—but it is unfruitful in many because they are careless, inattentive, and worldly-minded.

21. *Is a candle . . . put under a bushel?* The design of My preaching is to enlighten men; My parables are not designed to hide the truth, but to make it more manifest.

22. *For there is nothing hid.* Probably our Lord means that all that had hitherto been secret relative to the salvation of a lost world, or only obscurely pointed out by types and sacrifices, shall now be uncovered and made plain by the everlasting gospel. See on Matt. v. 15; x. 26.

25. *He that hath.* See on Matt. xiii. 12.

Whosoever hath, to him shall be given. This is an allusion to a common custom in all countries. He who possesses much or is rich, to such a person presents are ordinarily given. *Whosoever hath not, from him shall be taken away even that he hath.* That is, the poor man; he that has little may be easily made a prey of, and so lose his little.

26. *So is the kingdom of God.* This parable is mentioned only by Mark, a proof that Mark did not abridge Matthew.

MATTHEW HENRY

face of it altered! How gay and pleasant doth it look, when it is covered with green!

2. The husbandman cannot describe how it comes up; it is one of the mysteries of nature; It *springs and grows up, he knows not how, v.* 27. Thus we know not how the Spirit by the word makes a change in the heart, any more than we can account for the blowing of the wind, which we hear the sound of, but cannot tell whence it comes, or whither it goes.

3. The husbandman, when he hath sown the seed, doth nothing toward the springing of it up; *He sleeps, and rises, night and day,* and perhaps never so much as thinks of the corn he hath sown, and yet *the earth brings forth fruit of itself,* according to the ordinary course of nature. Thus the *word of grace,* when it is received in faith, is in the heart a *work of grace.*

4. It grows gradually; *first the blade, then the ear, after that the full corn in the ear, v.* 28. When it is sprung up, it will go forward; nature will have its course, and so will grace. Christ's interest, is, and will be, a *growing* interest; and though *the beginning be small, the latter end will greatly increase.* Though at first it is but a tender *blade,* which the frost may nip, or the foot may crush, yet it will increase to *the ear,* to the *full corn in the ear.* God carries on his work insensibly and without noise, but insuperably and without fail.

5. It comes to perfection at last (*v.* 29); *When the fruit is brought forth,* then he *puts in the sickle.* From the fruit of the gospel taking place and working in the soul, Christ *gathers in* a harvest. When those that receive the gospel aright, have finished their course, the harvest comes, when they shall be gathered as *wheat into God's barn* (Matt. xiii. 30).

IV. The work of grace is small in its beginnings, but comes to be great and considerable at last (*v.* 30–32); "*Whereunto shall I liken the kingdom of God?* How shall I make you to understand the designed method of it?" It is *like a grain of mustard-seed;* he had compared it before to *seed sown,* here to *that seed,* intending thereby to show,

1. That the beginnings of the *gospel kingdom* would be very small, like that which is *one of the least of all seeds.* The work of grace in the soul, is, at first, but the *day of small things;* a *cloud* no *bigger than a man's hand.* Never were there such great things undertaken by such an inconsiderable handful, as that of the discipling of the nations by the ministry of the apostles.

2. That the perfection of it will be very great; *When it grows up, it becomes greater than all herbs.* The gospel kingdom in the world, shall increase and spread to the remotest nations of the earth. The difference between a *grain of mustard seed* and a *great tree,* is nothing to that between a *young convert* on earth and a *glorified saint* in heaven.

With many such parables he spoke the word unto them (*v.* 33). He spoke in parables, *as they were able to hear them;* he fetched his comparisons from those things that were familiar to them. His manner of expression was easy, and such as they might hereafter recollect to their edification. But, for the present, *without a parable spoke he not unto them, v.* 34. The disciples themselves understood those sayings of Christ afterward, which at first they did not rightly take the sense of. But these parables *he expounded to them, when they were alone.* We cannot but wish we had had that exposition, as we had of the parable of the sower.

Verses 35–41

This miracle which Christ wrought for the relief of his disciples, in stilling the storm, we had before (Matt. viii. 23, &c.); but it is here more fully related.

1. It was *the same day, when the even was come, v.* 35. When he had been *labouring in the world and doctrine* all day, instead of *reposing* himself, he *exposeth* himself. The end of a toil may perhaps be but the beginning of a toss.

2. He himself proposed putting to sea at night, because he would lose no time; *Let us pass over to the other side;* he has work to do there. Christ went about doing good, and no difficulties in his way should hinder him.

3. They did not put to sea, till *they had sent away the multitude,* that is, answered all their requests; for he sent none home complaining that they had attended him *in vain.*

4. They took him *even as he was,* without any cloak to throw over him, which he ought to have had, to keep him *warm,* when he went to sea at night. We may learn hence not to be over nice and solicitous about the body.

5. The storm was so great, that the ship was *full of water* (*v.* 37). The ship being little, the waves beat into it so that *it was full.*

JAMIESON, FAUSSET, BROWN

27. And should sleep, and rise night and day—go about his other ordinary occupations, leaving it to the wellknown laws of vegetation under the genial influences of heaven. This is the sense of "the earth bringing forth fruit *of herself,*" in the next verse. **28. For the earth bringeth forth fruit of herself; first the blade, then the ear, after that the full corn in the ear**—beautiful allusion to the succession of similar stages, though not definitely marked periods, in the Christian life, and generally in the kingdom of God.

29. But when the fruit is brought forth—to maturity—**immediately he putteth in the sickle, because the harvest is come**—This charmingly points to the transition from the earthly to the heavenly condition of the Christian and the Church.

Parable of the Mustard Seed (vss. 30-32). For the exposition of this portion, see on Matthew 13: 31, 32.

33. And with many such parables spake he the word unto them, as they were able to hear it—Had this been said in the corresponding passage of Matthew, we should have concluded that what that Evangelist recorded was but a specimen of other parables spoken on the same occasion. But Matthew (13:34) says, "All *these* things spake Jesus unto the multitude in parables"; and as Mark records only some of the parables which Matthew gives, we are warranted to infer that the "many such parables" alluded to here mean no more than the full complement of them which we find in Matthew. **34. But without a parable spake he not unto them**—See on Matthew 13:34. **and when they were alone, he expounded all things to his disciples**—See on vs. 22.

35-ch. 5:20. Jesus, Crossing the Sea of Galilee, Miraculously Stills a Tempest—He Cures the Demoniac of Gadara. (=Matt. 8:23-34: Luke 8:22-39.) The time of this section is very definitely marked by our Evangelist, and by him alone, in the opening words.

Jesus Stills a Tempest on the Sea of Galilee (vss. 35-41). **35. And the same day**—on which He spoke the memorable parables of the preceding section, and of Matthew 13. **when the even was come**—See on ch. 6:35. This must have been the earlier evening—what we should call the afternoon—since after all that passed on the other side, when He returned to the west side, the people were waiting for Him in great numbers (vs. 21; Luke 8:40). **he saith unto them, Let us pass over unto the other side**—to the east side of the lake, to grapple with a desperate case of possession, and set the captive free, and to give the Gadarenes an opportunity of hearing the message of salvation, amid the wonder which that marvellous cure was fitted to awaken and the awe which the subsequent events could not but strike into them. **36. And when they had sent away the multitude, they took him even as he was in the ship**—i.e., without any preparation, and without so much as leaving the vessel, out of which He had been all day teaching. **And there were also**

ADAM CLARKE

27. *And should sleep, and rise night and day.* That is, he should sleep by night and rise by day, for so the words are obviously to be understood. *He knoweth not how.* How a plant grows is a mystery in nature which the wisest philosopher in the universe cannot fully explain.

28. *Bringeth forth . . . of herself.* By its own energy, without either the influence or industry of man. *The full corn.* "Full wheat"; the perfect, full-grown, or ripe head of grain. The kingdom of God, which is generated in the soul by the word of life, under the influence of the Holy Spirit, is first very small; there is only a *blade,* but this is full of promise, for a good blade shows there is a good seed at bottom, and that the soil in which it is sown is good also. *Then the ear*—the strong stalk grows up, and the ear is formed at the top. The faith and love of the believing soul increase abundantly; it is justified freely through the redemption that is in Christ. It has the *ear* which is shortly to be filled with the ripe grain, the outlines of the whole image of God. *Then the full corn.* The soul is purified from all unrighteousness; and, having escaped the corruption that is in the world, it is made a partaker of the divine nature, and is filled with all the fullness of God.

29. *He putteth in the sickle.* "He sendeth out the sickle," i.e., the reapers—the instrument, by a metonomy, being put for the persons who use it. This is a common figure. It has been supposed that our Lord intimates here that, as soon as a soul is made completely holy, it is taken into the kingdom of God. But certainly the parable does not say so. When the corn is ripe, it is reaped for the benefit of him who sowed it, for it can be of little or no use till it be ripe. So when a soul is saved from all sin, it is capable of being fully employed in the work of the Lord; it is then, and not till then, fully fitted for the Master's use. God saves men to the uttermost, that they may here perfectly love Him and worthily magnify His name. To take them away the moment they are capable of doing this would be, so far, to deprive the world and the Church of the manifestation of the glory of His grace.

31. *A grain of mustard seed.* See on Matt. xiii. 31-32.

33. *With many such parables. Many* is omitted by L, sixteen others; the Syriac, both the Persic, one Arabic, Coptic, Armenian, Aethiopic, and two of the Itala. Mill approves of the omission, and Griesbach leaves it doubtful. It is probably an interpolation. The text reads better without it. *As they were able to hear.* Or to "understand," always suiting His teaching to the capacities of His hearers. I have always found that preacher most useful who could adapt his phrase to that of the people to whom he preached.

34. *He expounded all things to his disciples.* That they might be capable of instructing others. Outside hearers, those who do not come into close fellowship with the true disciples of Christ, have seldom more than a superficial knowledge of divine things. In the fellowship of the saints, where Jesus the Teacher is always to be found, everything is made plain—for the secret of the Lord is with them who fear Him.

35. *Let us pass over unto the other side.* Our Lord was now by the Sea of Galilee.

36. *They took him even as he was in the ship.* The construction of this verse is exceedingly difficult. The meaning appears to be this: The disciples sailed off with Him just as He was in the boat out of which He had been teaching the people, and they did not wait to provide any accommodations for the passage. This I believe to be the meaning of the inspired penman.

MATTHEW HENRY

6. There were *with him other little ships*, which, no doubt, shared in the distress and danger. The *multitude went away* when he put to sea, but some there were, that would venture upon the water with him. One may boldly and cheerfully put to sea in Christ's company, yea though we foresee a storm.

7. Christ was asleep in this storm. It was *in the hinder part of the ship*, the pilot's place: he lay at the helm.

He had a *pillow* there. And he *slept*, to try the faith of his disciples and to stir up prayer: upon the trial, their faith appeared *weak*, and their prayers *strong*. Sometimes when the church is in a storm, Christ seems as if he were asleep, unconcerned in the troubles of his people, and regardless of their prayers. When he sleeps he doth not sleep; the keeper of Israel doth not so much as slumber (Ps. cxxi. 3, 4); he slept, but his heart was awake.

8. His disciples encouraged themselves with their having his presence, and thought it the best way to improve that, and appeal to that, and ply the oar of prayer rather than their other oars. Their confidence lay in this, that they had their Master with them; and the ship that has Christ in it, though it may be *tossed*, cannot *sink*. They *awoke Christ*. When Christ seems as if he slept in a storm, he is awakened by the prayers of his people; we may be at our wits' end, but not at our faith's end, while we have such a Saviour to go to. Their address to Christ is here expressed very emphatically; *Master, carest thou not that we perish?* I confess this sounds somewhat harsh, rather like chiding him for sleeping than begging him to awake. I know no excuse for it, but the present distress they were in, which put them into such a fright, that they knew not what they said. They do Christ a deal of wrong, who suspect him to be *careless* of his people in distress.

9. The word of command with which Christ rebuked the storm, we have here, and had not in Matthew, *v.* 39. He says, *Peace, be still—be silent, be dumb*. Let not the wind any longer roar, nor the sea rage. The noise is threatening and terrifying; let us hear no more of it. This is, (1) A word of command to us; when our wicked hearts are *like the troubled sea which cannot rest* (Isa. lvii. 20); let us think we hear the law of Christ, saying, *Be silent, be dumb*. Think not confusedly, speak not unadvisedly; but *be still*. (2) A word of comfort to us, that, be the storm of trouble ever so loud, ever so strong, Jesus Christ can lay it with a word's speaking. He that made the seas, can make them *quiet*.

10. The reproof Christ gave them for their fears, is here carried further than in Matthew. There it is, *Why are ye fearful?* Here, *Why are ye so fearful?* There it is, *O ye of little faith*. Here it is, *How is it that ye have no faith?* Not that the disciples were without faith. But at this time their fears prevailed so that they seemed to *have no faith* at all. It was out of the way, when they had occasion for it, and so it was as if they had not had it. Those may suspect their faith, who can entertain such a thought as that Christ *careth not* though his *people perish*.

Lastly, The impression this miracle made upon the disciples, is here differently expressed. In Matthew it is said, *The men marvelled;* here it is said, *They feared greatly*. Now their fear was rectified by their faith. When they feared the winds and the seas, it was for want of the reverence they ought to have had for Christ. But now that they saw a demonstration of his power over them, they feared *them* less, and *him* more. They had *feared* the power and wrath of the Creator in the storm, and that fear had torment and amazement in it; but now they feared the power and grace of the Redeemer in the calm; and it had pleasure and satisfaction in it. They said, *What manner of man is this?* Surely more than a man, *for even the winds and the seas obey him*.

JAMIESON, FAUSSET, BROWN

with him other little ships—with passengers, probably, wishing to accompany Him. **37. And there arose a great storm of wind**—"a tempest of wind." To such sudden squalls the Sea of Galilee is very liable from its position, in a deep basin, skirted on the east by lofty mountain ranges, while on the west the hills are intersected by narrow gorges through which the wind sweeps across the lake, and raises its waters with great rapidity into a storm. **and the waves beat into the ship**—kept beating or pitching on the ship. **so that it was now full**—rather, "so that it was already filling." In Matthew (8:24), "insomuch that the ship was covered with the waves"; but this is too strong. It should be, "so that the ship was getting covered by the waves." So we must translate the word used in Luke (8:23)—not as in our version—"And there came down a storm on the lake, and they were filled [with water]"—but "they were getting filled," i.e., those who sailed; meaning, of course, that their ship was so. **38. And he was in the hinder**—or stern—**part of the ship, asleep on a pillow**—either a place in the vessel made to receive the head, or a cushion for the head to rest on. It was evening; and after the fatigues of a busy day of teaching under the hot sun, having nothing to do while crossing the lake, He sinks into a deep sleep, which even this tempest raging around and tossing the little vessel did not disturb. **and they awake him, and say unto him, Master**—or "Teacher." In Luke (8: 24) this is doubled—in token of their life-and-death earnestness—"Master, Master." **carest thou not that we perish?**—Unbelief and fear made them sadly forget their place, to speak so. Luke has it, "Lord, save us, we perish." When those accustomed to fish upon that deep thus spake, the danger must have been imminent. They say nothing of what would become of *Him*, if they perished; nor think, whether, if He could not perish, it was likely He would let this happen to them; but they hardly knew what they said. **39. And he arose, and rebuked the wind**—"and the raging of the water" (Luke 8:24). **and said unto the sea, Peace, be still**—two sublime words of command, from a Master to His servants, the elements. **And the wind ceased, and there was a great calm**—The sudden hushing of the wind would not at once have calmed the sea, whose commotion would have settled only after a considerable time. But the word of command was given to both elements at once. **40. And he said unto them, Why are ye so fearful?**—There is a natural apprehension under danger; but there was unbelief in their fear. It is worthy of notice how considerately the Lord defers this rebuke till He had first removed the danger, in the midst of which they would not have been in a state to listen to anything. **how is it that ye have no faith?**—next to none, or none in present exercise. In Luke it is, "Why are ye fearful, O ye of little faith?" *Faith* they had, for they applied to Christ for relief: but *little*, for they were afraid, though Christ was in the ship. Faith dispels fear, but only in proportion to its strength. **41. And they feared exceedingly**—were struck with deep awe. **and said one to another, What manner of man is this, that even the wind and the sea obey him?**—'What is this? Israel has all along been singing of JEHOVAH, 'Thou rulest the raging of the sea: when the waves thereof arise, Thou stillest them!' 'The Lord on high is mightier than the noise of many waters, yea, than the mighty waves of the sea!' (Ps. 89:9; 93:4). But, lo, in this very boat of ours is One of our own flesh and blood, who with His word of command hath done the same! Exhausted with the fatigues of the day, He was but a moment ago in a deep sleep, undisturbed by the howling tempest, and we had to waken Him with the cry of our terror; but rising at our call, His majesty was felt by the raging elements, for they were instantly hushed—'WHAT MANNER OF MAN IS THIS?' "

ADAM CLARKE

CHARLES H. SPURGEON:

The day had been a very illustrious one. Our Lord had remarkably displayed His teaching and healing powers. Great crowds had been attracted and He had both delivered to them most precious parables and wrought among them most marvelous cures. Grand as the day was, it could not come to a close without a storm. After the same manner you will find it in the history of the Church of God, that intermingled with great successes will be great afflictions. Pentecost is followed by persecution: Peter's sermon by Peter's imprisonment. Though today a church may flourish abundantly, in a very short time it may be visited with stern adversities; it may be tried nonetheless, but all the more, because God is in its midst and is blessing it. When our Lord took ship, the weather appears to have been very fair, and many little boats, which scarce would have tempted the sea had its surface been ruffled, put out upon the lake under the convoy of the great teacher's vessel. His was the admiral's flag ship, and they were the happy fleet. They made a gay flotilla sailing softly like seabirds when the ocean is in a gentle mood. All hearts were happy, all spirits were serene, and the sleep of the Master was but a type of the general peace. Nature reposed; the lake was as a molten looking-glass, everything was quiet; and yet all of a sudden, as is the custom with these deep-lying inland seas, the storm fiend rushed from his haunt among the mountains, sweeping everything before it; the little vessel was hard put to it, she was well-nigh filled with water, and ready to sink through the force of the driving hurricane. Thus may our loveliest calms be succeeded by overwhelming storms. A Christian man is seldom long at ease.

—*The Treasury of the New Testament*

39. *Peace, be still.* "Be silent! Be still!" There is uncommon majesty and authority in these words. Who but God could act thus? Perhaps this saving of His disciples in the boat might be designed to show forth that protection and deliverance which Christ will give to His followers, however violently they may be persecuted by earth or hell.

40. *Why are ye so fearful?* Having Me with you. *How is it that ye have no faith?* Having already had such proofs of My unlimited power and goodness.

41. *What manner of man is this?* They were astonished at such power proceeding from a Person who appeared to be only like one of themselves.

MATTHEW HENRY — CHAPTER 5

Verses 1–20

We have here an instance of Christ's dispossessing the strong man armed. This he did when he was come *to the other side*, whither he went through a storm; his business there was to rescue this poor creature out of the hands of Satan.

I. The miserable condition that this poor creature was in; he was under the power of an *unclean spirit*; he was raving mad; his condition seems to have been worse than any of the possessed, that were Christ's patients.

1. He had *his dwelling among the tombs*, among the graves of dead people. Their tombs were out of

JAMIESON, FAUSSET, BROWN — CHAPTER 5

Glorious Cure of the Gadarene Demoniac (vss. 1-20). **1. And they came over unto the other side of the sea, into the country of the Gadarenes. 2. And when he was come out of the ship, immediately**—(see vs. 6)—**there met him a man with an unclean spirit**—"which had devils [demons] long time" (Luke 8:27). In Matthew (8:28), "there met him two men possessed with devils." Though there be no discrepancy between these two statements—more than between two witnesses, one of whom testifies to something done by one person, while the other affirms that there were two—it is difficult to

ADAM CLARKE — CHAPTER 5

1. *The Gadarenes.* Some of the MSS. have *Gergasenes*, and some of them *Gerasenes*. The Gadarenes were included within the limits of the Gergasenes. Dr. Lightfoot supposes that, of the two demoniacs mentioned here, one was of Gadara, and consequently a heathen, the other was a Gergesenian, and consequently a Jew; and he thinks that Mark and Luke mention the Gadarene demoniac because his case was a singular one, being the only heathen cured by our Lord except the daughter of the Syro-phoenician woman.

MATTHEW HENRY

the cities, in *desolate places*. Perhaps the devil drove him to *the tombs*. The touch of a grave was polluting. The *unclean spirit* drives people into that company that is *defiling*, and so keeps possession of them. Christ, by rescuing souls out of Satan's power, *saves the living from among the dead*.

2. He was very strong and ungovernable; *No man could bind him*. Not only cords would not hold him, but *chains* and *fetters of iron* would not, *v*. 3, 4. This sets forth the sad condition of those souls in which the devil has dominion. Some notoriously wilful sinners are like this madman. The commands and curses of the law are as *chains* and *fetters*, to restrain sinners from their wicked courses; but they *break those bonds in sunder*.

3. He was a terror and torment to himself and to all about him, *v*. 5. The devil is a *cruel* master. This wretched creature was *night and day in the mountains and in the tombs, crying, and cutting himself with stones*. What is a man, when reason is *de*throned and Satan *en*throned?

II. His application to Christ (*v*. 6); *When he saw Jesus afar off*, coming ashore, he *ran, and worshipped him*. He usually *ran upon* others with *rage*, but he *ran to* Christ with *reverence*. That was done by an invisible hand of Christ, which could not be done with chains and fetters; his fury was all on a sudden curbed. The poor man came, and *worshipped Christ*, in a sense of the need he had of his help, the power of Satan in and over him being, for this instant, suspended.

III. The word of command Christ gave (*v*. 8); *Come out of him, thou unclean spirit*. He made the man desirous to be relieved, when he enabled him to *run, and worship him*, and then put forth his power for his relief. If Christ *work in us* heartily to pray for a deliverance from Satan, he will work for us that deliverance.

IV. The dread which the devil had of Christ. The *man ran*, and *worshipped Christ*; but it was the devil in the man, that *cried with a loud voice* (making use of the poor man's tongue), *What have I to do with thee? v*. 7. 1. He calls God the *most high God*, above all other gods. 2. He owns Jesus to be the *Son of God*. It is no strange thing to hear the best words drop from the worst mouths. Piety from the teeth outward is an easy thing. The most fair-spoken hypocrite cannot say better than to call Jesus the Son of God and yet that the devil did. 3. He disowns any design against Christ; "*What have I to do with thee?*" 4. He deprecates his wrath; I *adjure thee*, that, though those drive me out hence, yet that thou *torment me not*.

V. The account Christ took from this unclean spirit of his name. This we had not in Matthew. Christ asked him, *What is thy name? My name is Legion, for we are many*. Now this intimates that the devils are, 1. *Military* powers. The devils war against God and his glory, Christ and his gospel, men and their holiness and happiness. 2. That they are *numerous*; he *owns*, or rather he *boasts—We are many*; as if he hoped to be *too many* for Christ himself to deal with. 3. That they are *unanimous*; they are *many* devils, and yet but *one legion* engaged in the same wicked cause. 4. That they are very *powerful*; Who can stand before a *legion?* We are not a match for our spiritual enemies, in our own strength; but *in the Lord, and in the power of his might*, we shall be able to *stand against them*.

VI. The request of this legion, that Christ would suffer them to go into a herd of swine that was *feeding nigh unto the mountains* (*v*. 11). Their request was, 1. That he *would not send them away out of the country* (*v*. 10); not only that he would not *torment them before the time*; but that he would not *banish* them *that country*. They seem to have had a particular affection for *that country*; or, rather, a particular spite to it. 2. That he would suffer them to *enter into the swine*.

VII. The permission Christ gave them to enter into the swine, and the immediate destruction of the swine thereby; *He gave them leave* (*v*. 13). Immediately the *unclean spirits entered into the swine*, which by the law were unclean creatures. Those that, like the swine, delight in *the mire* of sensual lusts, are fit habitations for Satan. The consequence of the devils entering into the swine, was, that they all *ran mad* presently, and ran headlong into the adjoining sea, where they were all drowned, to the number of *two thousand*.

VIII. The report of all this dispersed through the country immediately. They that *fed the swine*, hastened to the owners, to give an account of their charge, *v*. 14. This drew the people together, to see what was done.

JAMIESON, FAUSSET, BROWN

see how the principal details here given could apply to more than one case. **3. Who had his dwelling among the tombs**—Luke says, "He ware no clothes, neither abode in any house." These tombs were hewn out of the rocky caves of the locality, and served for shelters and lurking-places (Luke 8:26). **4. Because that he had been often bound with fetters and chains . . .**—Luke says (8:29) that "oftentimes it [the unclean spirit] had caught him"; and after mentioning how they had vainly tried to bind him with chains and fetters, because, "he brake the bands," he adds, "and was driven of the devil [demon] into the wilderness." The dark tyrant-power by which he was held clothed him with superhuman strength and made him scorn restraint. Matthew (8:28) says he was "exceeding fierce, so that no man might pass by that way." He was the terror of the whole locality. **5. And always, night and day, he was in the mountains, and in the tombs, crying, and cutting himself with stones**—Terrible as he was to others, he himself endured untold misery, which sought relief in tears and self-inflicted torture. **6. But when he saw Jesus afar off, he ran and worshipped him**—not with the spontaneous alacrity which says to Jesus, "Draw me, we will *run* after thee," but inwardly compelled, with terrific rapidity, before the Judge, to receive sentence of expulsion. **7. What have I to do with thee, Jesus, Son of the most high God? I adjure thee by God, that thou torment me not**—or, as in Matthew 8:29, "Art Thou come to torment us before the time?" (See on ch. 1:24.) Behold the *tormentor* anticipating, dreading, and entreating exemption from *torment!* In Christ they discern their destined Tormentor; the time, they know, is fixed, and they feel as if it were come already! (Jas. 2:19.) **8. For he said unto him**—i.e., before the unclean spirit cried out. **Come out of the man, unclean spirit!**—Ordinarily, obedience to a command of this nature was immediate. But here, a certain delay is permitted, the more signally to manifest the power of Christ and accomplish His purposes. **9. And he asked him, What is thy name?**—The object of this question was to extort an acknowledgment of the virulence of demoniacal power by which this victim was enthralled. **And he answered, saying, My name is Legion: for we are many**—or, as in Luke, "because many devils [demons] were entered into him." A legion, in the Roman army, amounted, at its full complement, to six thousand; but here the word is used, as such words with us, and even this one, for an indefinitely large number—large enough however to rush, as soon as permission was given, into two thousand swine and destroy them. **10. And he besought him much that he would not send them away out of the country**—The entreaty, it will be observed, was made by *one spirit*, but in behalf of *many*—"*he* besought Him not to send *them* . . ."—just as in the former verse, "*he* answered *we* are many." But what do they mean by entreating so earnestly not to be ordered out of the country? Their next petition (vs. 12) will make that clear enough. **11. Now there was there, nigh unto the mountains**—rather, "to the mountain," according to what is clearly the true reading. In Matthew 8:30, they are said to have been "a good way off." But these expressions, far from being inconsistent, only confirm, by their precision, the minute accuracy of the narrative. **a great herd of swine feeding**—There can hardly be any doubt that the owners of these were Jews, since to them our Lord had now come to proffer His services. This will explain what follows. **12. And all the devils besought him, saying**—"if thou cast us out" (Matt. 8:31)—**Send us into the swine, that we may enter into them**—Had they spoken out all their mind, perhaps this would have been it: "If we must quit our hold of this man, suffer us to continue our work of mischief in another form, that by entering these swine, and thus destroying the people's property, we may steel their hearts against Thee!" **13. And forthwith Jesus gave them leave**—In Matthew this is given with majestic brevity—"Go!" The owners, if Jews, drove an illegal trade; if heathens, they insulted the national religion: in either case the permission was just. **And the unclean spirits went out**—of the man—**and entered into the swine: and the herd ran violently**—rushed—**down a steep place**—down the hanging cliff—**into the sea (they were about two thousand)**—The number of them is given by this graphic Evangelist alone. **and were choked in the sea**—"perished in the waters" (Matt. 8:32). **14. And they that fed the swine fled, and told it**—"told everything, and what was befallen to the possessed of the devils" (Matt. 8:33)—**in the city, and in the country. And they went out to see what it was that**

ADAM CLARKE

2. *A man with an unclean spirit*. There are two mentioned by Matthew, who are termed "demoniacs."

3. *Who had his dwelling among the tombs*. See Matt. viii. 28.

4. *With fetters and chains*. His strength, it appears, was supernatural, no kind of chains being strong enough to confine him.

5. *Crying, and cutting himself with stones*. In this person's case we see a specimen of what Satan could do in all the wicked if God should permit him. But even the devil himself has his chain, and he who often binds others is always bound himself.

6. *Worshipped him*. "Did Him homage," compelled thereto by the power of God. How humiliating to Satan thus to be obliged to acknowledge the superiority of Christ!

7. *What have I to do with thee?* Or, "What is it to Thee and me?" or, "Why dost Thou trouble thyself with me?" See on chap. i. 24 and Matt. viii. 29, where the idiom and meaning are explained.

10. *Out of the country*. Strange that these accursed spirits should find it any mitigation of their misery to be permitted to exercise their malevolence in a particular district! But as this is supposed to have been a heathen district, therefore the demons might consider themselves in their own territories; and probably they could act there with less restraint than they could do in a country where the worship of God was established.

G. CAMPBELL MORGAN:

I am not going to enter into any discussion of the old-time difficulty, the controversy between Huxley and Gladstone, about that herd of swine. Suffice it to say that our Lord was exercising His ministry in Jewish territory, and even if Josephus is right, that this was a Greek city, it is nevertheless true that our Lord was dealing with the children of Israel, and in the destruction of the swine He was rebuking their indulgence in a traffic absolutely forbidden.

—The Gospel According to Mark

MATTHEW HENRY

When they saw how wonderfully the poor man was cured, they hence conceived a *veneration for Christ, v.* 15. They saw him that was *possessed with the devil sitting clothed and in his right mind*; when Satan was cast out, he came to himself, and was his own man presently. Those who are grave and sober, and live by rule and with consideration, thereby make it appear that by the power of Christ the devil's power is broken in their souls.

The sight of this *made them afraid*; it astonished them, and forced them to own the power of Christ, and that he is *worthy to be feared.* When they found that their swine were lost, they thence conceived a *dislike of Christ*, they prayed him to *depart out of their coasts*, for they think not any good he can do them sufficient to make them amends for the loss of so many swine, fat swine, it may be, and ready for the market. Now the devils had what they would have; for by no handle do these evil spirits more effectually manage sinful souls than by that of the love of the world. If they would but part with their sins, he had life and happiness for them; but, being loth to quit either their sins or their swine, they chose rather to abandon their Saviour. Thus they do, who, rather than let go a base lust, will throw away their interest in Christ. They wished him further off.

IX. An account of the conduct of the poor man after his deliverance. 1. He *desired that he might go along with Christ* (*v.* 18). 2. Christ *would not suffer him* to go with him. He had other work for him to do; he must go home to his friends, and tell them what *great things the Lord had done for him*, and his neighbours and friends might be edified, and invited to believe in Christ. He must take particular notice rather of Christ's *pity* than of his *power*; he must tell them what *compassion* the Lord had had on him in his misery. 3. The man, in a transport of joy, proclaimed, all the country over, what *great things Jesus had done for him, v.* 20. And see what was the effect of it; *All men did marvel*, but few went any further. Many that cannot but wonder at the works of Christ, yet do not, as they ought, *wonder after him.*

Verses 21–34

The Gadarenes having desired Christ to leave their country, he did not stay to trouble them long, but presently went by water, back *to the other side* (*v.* 21), and there *much people gathered to him.* If there be some that reject Christ, yet there are others that receive him, and bid him welcome.

I. Here is one, that comes *openly* to *beg* a cure for a sick child; and it is no less a person than one of the *rulers of the synagogue.* He was not named in Matthew, he is here, *Jairus*, or *Jair*, Judges x. 3.

JAMIESON, FAUSSET, BROWN

was done—Thus had they the evidence, both of the herdsmen and of their own senses, to the reality of both miracles. **15. And they come to Jesus**—Matthew (8:34) says, "Behold, the whole city came out to meet Jesus." **and see him that was possessed with the devil**—the demonized person—**and had the legion, sitting**—"at the feet of Jesus," adds Luke (8:35); in contrast with his former *wild* and *wandering* habits. **and clothed**—As our Evangelist had not told us that he "ware no clothes," the meaning of this statement could only have been conjectured but for "the beloved physician" (Luke 8:27), who supplies the missing piece of information here. This is a striking case of what are called *Undesigned Coincidences* amongst the different Evangelists; one of them taking a thing for granted, as familiarly known at the time, but which we should never have known but for one or more of the others, and without the knowledge of which some of their statements would be unintelligible. The clothing which the poor man would feel the want of the moment his consciousness returned to him, was doubtless supplied to him by some of the Twelve. **and in his right mind**—but now, oh, in what a lofty sense! (Cf. an analogous, though a different kind of case, Dan. 4:34-37.) **and they were afraid**—Had this been *awe* only, it had been natural enough; but other feelings, alas! of a darker kind, soon showed themselves. **16. And they that saw it told them how it befell to him that was possessed with the devil** ('the demonized person') **and also concerning the swine**—Thus had they the double testimony of the herdsmen and their own senses. **17. And they began to pray him to depart out of their coasts**—Was it the owners only of the valuable property now lost to them that did this? Alas, no! For Luke (8:37) says, "Then the whole multitude of the country of the Gadarenes round about besought Him to depart from them; for they were taken with great fear." The evil spirits had thus, alas! their object. Irritated, the people could not suffer His presence; yet awe-struck, they dared not order Him off: so they entreat Him to withdraw, and—He takes them at their word. **18. he that had been possessed with the devil prayed him that he might be with him**—the grateful heart, fresh from the hand of demons, clinging to its wondrous Benefactor. How exquisitely natural! **19. Howbeit, Jesus suffered him not, . . .**—To be a missionary for Christ, in the region where he was so well known and so long dreaded, was a far nobler calling than to follow Him where nobody had ever heard of him, and where other trophies not less illustrious could be raised by the same power and grace. **20. And he departed, and began to publish**—not only among his friends, to whom Jesus immediately sent him, but—**in Decapolis**—so called, as being a region of ten cities. (See on Matt. 4:25.) **how great things Jesus had done for him: and all men did marvel**—Throughout that considerable region did this monument of mercy proclaim his new-found Lord; and some, it is to be hoped, did more than "marvel."

21-43. The Daughter of Jairus Raised to Life—The Woman with an Issue of Blood Healed. (= Matt. 9:18-26; Luke 8:41-56.) The occasion of this scene will appear presently.

Jairus' Daughter (vss. 21-24). **21. And when Jesus was passed over again by ship unto the other side**—from the Gadarene side of the lake, where He had parted with the healed demoniac, to the west side, at Capernaum. **much people gathered unto him**—who "gladly received Him; for they were all waiting for Him" (Luke 8:40). The abundant teaching earlier that day (ch. 4:1, etc., and Matthew 13) had only whetted the people's appetite: and disappointed, as would seem, that He had left them in the evening to cross the lake, they remain hanging about the beach, having got a hint, probably through some of His disciples, that He would be back the same evening. Perhaps they witnessed at a distance the sudden calming of the tempest. The tide of our Lord's popularity was now fast rising. **and he was nigh unto the sea. 22. And, behold, there cometh one of the rulers of the synagogue**—of which class there were but few who believed in Jesus (John 7:48). One would suppose from this that the ruler had been with the multitude on the shore, anxiously awaiting the return of Jesus, and immediately on His arrival had accosted Him as here related. But Matthew (9:18) tells us that the ruler came to Him while He was in the act of speaking at His own table on the subject of fasting; and as we must suppose that this converted publican ought to know what took place on that memorable occasion when he made a feast to his Lord, we conclude that here the right order is indicated by the First Evangelist alone. **Jairus by name**—or

ADAM CLARKE

ALEXANDER MACLAREN:

The terrified Gerasenes beseech Jesus to leave them. They had rather have their swine than their Savior, and so, though they saw the demoniac sitting, "clothed, and in his right mind," at the feet of Jesus, they in turn beseech that He should take himself away. Fear and selfishness prompted the prayer. The communities on the eastern side of the lake were largely Gentile; and, no doubt, these people knew that they did many worse things than swine-keeping, and may have been afraid that some more of their wealth would have to go the same road as the herd. They did not want instruction, nor feel that they needed a healer. Were their prayers so very unlike the wishes of many of us? Is there nobody nowadays unwilling to let the thought of Christ into his life, because he feels an uneasy suspicion that, if Christ comes, a good deal will have to go? How many trades and schemes of life really beseech Jesus to go away and leave them in peace!

And He goes away. The tradegy of life is that we have the awful power of severing ourselves from His influence. Christ commands unclean spirits, but He can only plead with hearts. And if we bid Him depart, He is fain to leave us for the time to the indulgence of our foolish and wicked schemes. If any man open, He comes in—oh, how gladly! but if any man slam the door in His face, He can but tarry without and knock. Sometimes His withdrawing does more than His loudest knocking; and sometimes they who repelled Him as He stood on the beach call Him back as He moves away to the boat. It is in the hope that they may that He goes.

—*Expositions of Holy Scripture*

20. *Decapolis.* See on Matt. iv. 25.

G. CAMPBELL MORGAN:

Jarius employed a phrase which had at its very heart a sense of proprietorship: "my little daughter!" Ah! we may love all children, all the bairns may seem to us the special messengers of God to mortals; but there is a difference. Parental love has within itself an almost terrifying, and yet most exquisitely tender sense of responsibility. If a man shall say to me, "It is your duty to do thus or so," I shall challenge him for his reason; and if he shall reply, "For your own sake," I may answer, "Stand out of my sunlight, and do not interfere with me!" But if he shall say, "For the sake of that boy in your home," he has conquered me, he has mastered me! Oh! that strange agony in the love of parent for child that makes the parent ever tremble! "My little daughter." That is a picture in itself.

Luke records the fact that she was an only daughter, and that she was twelve years of age. Twelve years of sunshine, twelve years of music in the home! She had come to that wonderful age which today we are describing as the period of adolescence, when will is becoming supreme, and choices and elections are being made alone, when all life seems to be breaking from bud into larger blossom with the potentiality of fruitage. Twelve years of age!

—*The Gospel According to Mark*

MATTHEW HENRY

He addressed himself to Christ with great humility and reverence; *When he saw him, he fell at his feet,* and with great importunity, he *besought him greatly,* as one in earnest. He has a *little daughter,* about twelve years old, the darling of the family, and she *lies a-dying*; but he believes that if Christ will but come, and *lay his hands upon her,* she will return even from the gates of the grave. He said, at first, when he came, *She lies a-dying* (so Mark); but afterward, *She is even now dead* (so Matthew); but he still prosecutes his suit. Christ readily agreed, and went with him, *v.* 24.

II. Here is another, that comes *clandestinely* to *steal* a cure (if I may so say) for herself; and she got the relief she came for. This cure was wrought by *the way,* as he was going to raise the ruler's daughter. Many of his discourses, and some of his miracles, are dated *by the way-side*; we should be doing good, not only when we *sit in the house,* but when we *walk by the way.*

1. The piteous case of this poor woman. She had a constant *issue of blood* upon her, for *twelve years.* She had had the best advice of physicians, that she could get, and had made use of the many medicines and methods they prescribed; but now that she had spent all she had among them, they gave her up as incurable. It is usual with people not to apply themselves to Christ, till they have tried in vain all other helpers, and find them, as certainly they will, *physicians of no value.* And he will be found a *sure refuge,* even to those who make him their *last refuge.*

2. The strong faith that she had in the power of Christ to heal her; *If I may but touch his clothes, I shall be whole, v.* 28. A private cure was what she wished for, and her faith was suited to her case.

3. The wonderful effect produced by it; *She came in the* crowd *behind* him, and with much ado got to *touch his garment,* and immediately she felt the cure wrought, *v.* 29. The flux of blood was *dried up,* and she felt herself perfectly well all over her in an instant. Those whom Christ heals of the disease of sin, that bloody issue, cannot but experience in themselves a universal change for the better.

4. Christ's enquiry after his concealed patient, and the encouragement he gave her; Christ *knew in himself that virtue had gone out of him, v.* 30. Being desirous to see his patient, he asked, not in displeasure, as one affronted, but in tenderness, as one concerned, *Who touched my clothes?* The disciples almost ridiculed his question (*v.* 31); *The multitudes throng thee, and sayest thou, Who touched me?*

JAMIESON, FAUSSET, BROWN

"Jaeirus." It is the same name as *Jair,* in the Old Testament (Num. 32:41; Judg. 10:3; Esther 2:5). **and when he saw him, he fell at his feet**—in Matthew (9:18), "worshipped Him." The meaning is the same in both. **23. And besought him greatly, saying, My little daughter**—Luke (8:42) says, "He had one only daughter, about twelve years of age." According to a well-known rabbin, quoted by LIGHTFOOT, a daughter. till she had completed her twelfth year, was called "little," or "a little maid"; after that, "a young woman." **lieth at the point of death**—Matthew gives it thus: "My daughter is even now dead"—"has just expired." The news of her death reached the father after the cure of the woman with the issue of blood: but Matthew's brief account gives only the *result,* as in the case of the centurion's servant (Matt. 8:5, etc.). **come and lay thy hands on her, that she may be healed; and she shall live**—or, "that she may be healed and live," according to a fully preferable reading. In one of the class to which this man belonged, so steeped in prejudice, such faith would imply more than in others.

The Woman with an Issue of Blood Healed (vss. 23-34). **24. And Jesus went with him; and much people followed him, and thronged him**—The word in Luke is stronger—"choked," "stifled Him." **26. And had suffered many things of many physicians**—The expression perhaps does not necessarily refer to the suffering she endured under medical treatment, but to the much varied treatment which she underwent. **and had spent all that she had, and was nothing bettered, but rather grew worse**—pitiable case, and affectingly aggravated; emblem of our natural state as fallen creatures (Ezek. 16:5, 6), and illustrating the worse than vanity of all human remedies for spiritual maladies (Hos. 5:13). The higher design of all our Lord's miracles of healing irresistibly suggests this way of viewing the present case, the propriety of which will still more appear as we proceed. **27. When she had heard of Jesus, came**—This was the right experiment at last. What had she "heard of Jesus?" No doubt it was His marvellous cures she had heard of; and the hearing of these, in connection with her bitter experience of the vanity of applying to any other, had been blessed to the kindling in her soul of a firm confidence that He who had so willingly wrought such cures on others was able and would not refuse to heal her also. **in the press behind**—shrinking, yet seeking. **touched his garment**—According to the ceremonial law, the touch of anyone having the disease which this woman had would have defiled the person touched. Some think that the recollection of this may account for her stealthily approaching Him in the crowd behind, and touching but the hem of His garment. But there was an instinct in the faith which brought her to Jesus, which taught her, that if that touch could set her free from the defiling disease itself, it was impossible to communicate defilement to Him, and that this wondrous Healer must be above such laws. **28. For she said**—"within herself" (Matt. 9:21). **If I may touch but his clothes, I shall be whole**—i.e., if I may but *come in contact* with this glorious Healer *at all.* Remarkable faith this! **29. And straightway the fountain of her blood was dried up**—Not only was her issue of blood stanched (Luke 8:44), but the cause of it was thoroughly removed, insomuch that by her bodily sensations she immediately knew herself perfectly cured. **30. And Jesus immediately knowing in himself that virtue**—or "efficacy." **had gone out of him**—He was conscious of the forthgoing of His healing power, which was not—as in prophets and apostles—something *foreign to Himself* and imparted merely, but what He had *dwelling within Him* as "His own fulness." **turned him about in the press**—crowd. **and said, Who touched my clothes? 31. And his disciples said unto him**—Luke says (8:45), "When all denied, Peter and they that were with Him said, Master"—**Thou seest the multitude thronging thee, and sayest thou, Who touched me?**—"Askest thou, Lord, who touched Thee? Rather ask who touched Thee *not* in such a throng." "And Jesus said, Somebody hath touched Me"—a certain person has touched Me"—"for I perceive that virtue is gone out of Me" (Luke 8:46). Yes, the multitude "*thronged* and *pressed* Him"—they *jostled against* Him, but all *involuntarily;* they were merely *carried along;* but one, one only—"a certain person—TOUCHED HIM," with the conscious, voluntary, dependent touch of faith, reaching forth its hand expressly to have contact with Him. This and this only Jesus acknowledges and seeks out. Even so, as AUGUSTINE long ago said, *multitudes still come*

ADAM CLARKE

23. *My little daughter.* "That little daughter of mine." The words express much tenderness and concern. Luke observes, chap. viii. 42, that she was his "only daughter," and was about "twelve years of age." *At the point of death.* "In the last extremity, the last gasp." See on Matt. ix. 18.

25. *A certain woman.* See Matt. ix. 20.

26. *Had suffered many things of many physicians . . . and was nothing bettered, but rather grew worse.* No person will wonder at this account when he considers the therapeutics of the Jewish physicians in reference to hemorrhages, especially of the kind with which this woman was afflicted. From some of these nostrums it is evident the woman could not be *bettered,* and from some others it is as evident that she must be made *worse;* and from all together it is indubitably certain that she must have *suffered many things*—and from the persons employed, the expense of the medicaments, and the number of years she was afflicted, as she was not a person of great opulence, it is most perfectly credible that she *spent all that she had.* She was therefore a fit patient for the Great Physician. It has been said, and the saying is a good one, "Man's extremity is God's opportunity." Never could the power and goodness of God be shown in a more difficult and distressful case. And now Jesus comes, and she is healed.

27. *Came in the press behind.* She had formed her resolution in faith; she executes it, notwithstanding her weakness, with courage; and now she finds it crowned with success.

31. *Thou seest the multitude thronging thee.* Many touch Jesus who are not healed by Him; the reason is, they do it not by faith, through a sense of their wants, and a conviction of His ability and willingness to save them. Faith conveys the virtue of Christ into the soul, and spiritual health is the immediate consequence of this received virtue.

MATTHEW HENRY

Christ passed by the affront, and *looks around* to *see her that had done this thing*; not that he might *blame* her for her presumption, but that he might *commend* and *encourage* her faith, and by his own act and deed might *warrant* and *confirm* the cure. As secret acts of sin, so secret acts of faith, are known to the Lord Jesus, and are under his eye. The poor woman, hereupon, presented herself to the Lord Jesus (*v.* 33), *fearing and trembling*, not knowing how he would take it. Christ's patients are often trembling, when they have reason to be triumphing. She might have come boldly, *knowing what was done in her*; yet, *knowing that*, she *fears* and *trembles.* It was a *surprise*, and was not yet, as it should have been, a *pleasing* surprise. However, she *fell down before him.* There is nothing better for those that fear and tremble, than to throw themselves at the feet of the Lord Jesus. And she *told him all the truth.* We must not be ashamed to own the secret transactions between Christ and our souls; but, when called to it, mention what he has done for our souls, and the experience we have had of *healing virtue* derived from him. What an encouraging word he gave her (*v.* 34); *Daughter, thy faith hath made thee whole.* God's grace will set the seal of its *amen* to the prayers and hopes of faith, saying, "So be it, and so it shall be, to thee." And therefore, "*Go in peace.*"

Verses 35–43

Christ, having healed an incurable disease, here goes on to triumph over death.

I. The melancholy news is brought to Jairus, that his *daughter is dead.* While there is life, there is hope, and room for the use of means; but when life is gone, it is past recall; *Why troublest thou the Master any further? v.* 35. Ordinarily, the proper thought in this case, is, "The matter is determined, the will of God is done, and I submit, I acquiesce; *The Lord gave, and the Lord hath taken away.*" But here the case was extraordinary; the death of the child doth not, as usually, put an end to the narrative.

II. Christ encourageth the afflicted father yet to hope. Christ had stayed to work a cure by the way, but he shall be no sufferer by that, nor loser by the gain of others; *Be not afraid, only believe.* We may suppose Jairus at a pause, whether he should ask Christ to go on or no; but have we not as much occasion for the grace of God, and his consolations, when death is in the house, as when sickness is? Christ therefore soon determines this matter; "*Be not afraid* that my coming will be to no purpose, only believe that I will make it turn to a good account." *Only believe.* Keep up a confidence in Christ, and a dependence upon him, and he will do what is for the best. Believe the resurrection, and then be not afraid.

III. He went with a select company to the house where the dead child was. Now he shook off the crowd, and *suffered no man to follow him* but his three bosom-disciples, Peter, and James, and John.

IV. He raised the dead child to life. Here we may observe,

1. That the child was extremely well beloved, for the relations and neighbours *wept and wailed greatly.*

2. That it was evident beyond dispute, that the child was really and truly dead. Their *laughing* Christ to *scorn*, for saying, *She is not dead, but sleepeth*, serves for the proof of this.

3. That Christ put those out as unworthy to be witnesses of the miracle, who were so ignorant in the things of God, as not to understand him when he spoke of death as a *sleep*, or so scornful, as to ridicule him for it.

4. That he took the parents of the child to be witnesses of the miracle, and designed it for *their* comfort, who were the *true*, for they were the *silent* mourners.

5. That Christ raised the child to life by a word of power, which is recorded here, and recorded in Syriac, the language in which Christ spoke, for the greater certainty of the thing; *Talitha, cumi; Damsel, I say unto thee, Arise.* Christ said, *Arise from the dead;* meaning, *I command* that thou arise; nay, there is more in it—the dead have not power to arise, therefore power goes along with this word, to make it effectual. Christ works while he commands, and works by the command, and therefore may command what he pleaseth, even the dead to arise. Such is the gospel call to those that are by nature dead in trespasses and sins, and can no more rise from that death by their own power, than this child could.

6. That the damsel, as soon as life returned, *arose, and walked, v.* 42. Spiritual life will appear by our *rising* from the bed of sloth and carelessness, our

JAMIESON, FAUSSET, BROWN

similarly close to Christ in the means of grace, but all to no purpose, being only sucked into the crowd. The voluntary, living contact of faith is that electric conductor which alone draws virtue out of Him. **32. And he looked round about to see her that had done this thing**—not for the purpose of summoning forth a culprit, but, as we shall presently see, to obtain from the healed one a testimony to what He had done for her. **33. But the woman, fearing and trembling, knowing what was done in her**—alarmed, as a humble, shrinking female would naturally be, at the necessity of so public an exposure of herself, yet conscious that she had a tale to tell which would speak for her. **came and fell down before him, and told him all the truth**—In Luke (8:47) it is, "When the woman saw that she was not hid, she came trembling, and falling down before Him, she declared unto Him before all the people for what cause she had touched Him, and how she was healed immediately." This, though it tried the modesty of the believing woman, was just what Christ wanted in dragging her forth, her public testimony to the facts of her case—the disease, with her abortive efforts at a cure, and the instantaneous and perfect relief which her touching the Great Healer had brought her. **34. And he said unto her, Daughter**—"be of good comfort" (Luke 8:48). **thy faith hath made thee whole; go in peace, and be whole of thy plague**—Though healed as soon as she believed, it seemed to her a stolen cure—she feared to acknowledge it. Jesus therefore sets His royal seal upon it. But what a glorious dismissal from the lips of Him who is "our Peace" is that, "Go in peace!"

Jairus' Daughter Raised to Life (vss. 35-43). **35. Thy daughter is dead; why troublest thou the Master**—the Teacher—**any further? 36. he saith unto the ruler of the synagogue, Be not afraid, only believe**—Jesus, knowing how the heart of the agonized father would sink at the tidings, and the reflections at the *delay* which would be apt to rise in his mind, hastens to reassure him, and in His accustomed style: "Be not afraid, only believe"—words of unchanging preciousness and power! How vividly do such incidents bring out Christ's knowledge of the human heart and tender sympathy! (Heb. 4:15.) **37. And he suffered no man to follow him, save Peter, and James, and John the brother of James**—See on ch. 1:29. **38. And he cometh**—rather, "they come." **to the house of the ruler of the synagogue, and seeth the tumult, and them that wept and wailed greatly**—"the minstrels and the people making a noise" (Matt. 9:23)—lamenting for the dead. (See II Chron. 35:25; Jer. 9:20; Amos 5:16.) **39. And when he was come in, he saith unto them, Why make ye this ado, and weep? the damsel is not dead, but sleepeth**—so brief her state of death as to be more like a short sleep. **40. And they laughed him to scorn**—rather, simply, "laughed at Him"—"knowing that she was dead" (Luke 8:53); an important testimony this to the reality of her death. **But when he had put them all out**—The word is strong—"turned them all out"; meaning all those who were making this noise, and any others that may have been there from sympathy, that only those might be present who were most nearly concerned, and those whom He had Himself brought as witnesses of the great act about to be done. **he taketh the father and the mother of the damsel, and them that were with him**—Peter, and James, and John. **and entereth in where the damsel was lying.**

41. And he took the damsel by the hand—as He did Peter's mother-in-law (ch. 1:31). **and said unto her, Talitha cumi**—The words are Aramaic, or Syro-Chaldaic, the then language of Palestine. Mark loves to give such wonderful words just as they were spoken. See ch. 7:34; 14:36.

42. And straightway the damsel—The word here is different from that in vss. 39, 40, 41, and signifies "young maiden," or "little girl." **arose, and walked**—a vivid touch evidently from an eyewitness.

ADAM CLARKE

CHARLES H. SPURGEON:

She trembled as Jesus looked for her. Those blessed eyes looked around, and by and by they lighted upon her, and as she gazed upon them, she did not feel so much alarmed as before; but, still afraid and trembling, she came and fell down before Him, and told Him all the truth. Then He gently raised her up, and said, "Daughter, thy faith hath made thee whole; go in peace, and be whole of thy plague." Now she knew her cure from Christ's lips as well as from her own consciousness. She had now the divine witness bearing witness with her spirit that she was indeed a healed one.

—*The Treasury of the New Testament*

34. *Be whole of thy plague.* Rather, "Continue whole," not, *Be whole,* for she was already healed. But this contains a promise, necessary to her encouragement, that her disorder should afflict her no more.

35. *Why troublest thou the Master?* These people seem to have had no other notion of our Lord than that of an eminent physician, who might be useful while there was life, but afterwards could do nothing.

36. *Jesus . . . saith.* These words were spoken by our Lord to the afflicted father, immediately on his hearing of the death of his child, to prevent that distress which he otherwise must have felt on finding that the case was now, humanly speaking, hopeless.

38. *He cometh.* But *they come* is the reading of a number of MSS. and several versions.

40. *The father and the mother.* Prudence required that they should be present, and be witnesses of the miracle. *And them that were with him.* That is, Peter, James, and John, v. 37. It is remarkable that our Lord gave a particular preference to these three disciples, beyond all the rest, on three very important occasions. They were present (1) at the Transfiguration, (2) at the raising of Jairus' daughter, and (3) at His agony in the Garden of Gethsemane.

MATTHEW HENRY

walking *up and down* in Christ's name and strength.

7. That all who saw it, and heard of it, admired the miracle, and him that wrought it; *They were astonished with a great astonishment.* They could not but acknowledge that there was something in it extraordinary and very great, and yet they knew not what to make of it, or to infer from it.

8. That Christ endeavoured to conceal it; *He charged them straitly, that no man should know it.* It was sufficiently known to a competent number, but he would not have it as yet *proclaimed* any further.

9. That Christ took care something should be *given her to eat.* By this it appeared that she was raised not only to life, but to a good state of health, that she had an appetite to her meat. Where Christ hath given *spiritual life,* he will provide food for the support and nourishment of it unto life eternal, for he will *never forsake,* or be wanting to, the *work of his own hands.*

JAMIESON, FAUSSET, BROWN

And they were astonished with a great astonishment—The language here is the strongest.

43. And he charged them straitly—strictly—**that no man should know it**—The only reason we can assign for this is His desire not to let the public feeling regarding Him come too precipitately to a crisis. **and commanded that something should be given her to eat**—in token of perfect restoration.

ADAM CLARKE

43. *Something should be given her to eat.* For though He had employed an extraordinary power to bring her to life, He wills that she should be continued in existence by the use of ordinary means. "When the miraculous power of God is necessary, let it be resorted to; when it is not necessary, let the ordinary means be used." To act otherwise would be to tempt God.

MATTHEW HENRY

CHAPTER 6

Verses 1–6

I. Christ makes a visit to *his own country,* that was *Nazareth;* where his relations were. He had been in danger of his life among them (Luke iv. 29), and yet he came among them again; so strangely doth he wait to be gracious.

II. There he *preached* in their *synagogue,* on the *sabbath day, v.* 2. On sabbath days, the word of God is to be preached according to Christ's example.

III. They could not but own that which was very honourable concerning him. 1. That he spoke with great *wisdom.* 2. That he did *mighty works.* They acknowledged the two great proofs of the divine original of his gospel—the *divine wisdom,* and the *divine power,* and yet, though they could not deny the premises, they would not admit the conclusion.

IV. They studied to disparage him. All this *wisdom,* and all these *mighty works,* shall be of no account. *Is not this the Carpenter?* In Matthew, they upbraid him with being the carpenter's son. But, it seems, they could say further, *Is not this the Carpenter?* 1. He would thus *humble himself* as one that had taken upon him the form of a servant. 2. He would thus teach us to *abhor idleness,* and to find *ourselves something to do* in this world. Nothing is more pernicious for young people than to get a *habit of sauntering.* The Jews had a good rule for this—that their young men who were designed for scholars, were yet bred up to some trade, as Paul was a tent-maker, that they might have some business to fill up their time with. 3. He would thus put an honour upon despised mechanics, and encourage those who eat the labour of their hands, though great men look upon them with contempt.

Another thing they upbraided him with, was, the meanness of his relations; "*He is the son of Mary;* his *brethren* and *sisters* are here *with us;* we know his family and kindred;" and therefore, though they were *astonished* at his doctrine (*v.* 2), yet they were *offended* at his person (*v.* 3), and for that reason would not receive his doctrine.

V. Let us see how Christ bore this contempt.

1. He partly *excused it* (*v.* 4); *A prophet is not despised anywhere but in his own country.* Doubtless many have got over this prejudice, but ordinarily it holds good, that ministers are seldom so acceptable and successful in their own country as among strangers; *familiarity* in the younger years breeds a contempt, the advancement of one that was an inferior begets *envy,* and men will hardly set those among the guides of their souls whose fathers they were ready to set with the dogs of their flock.

2. He did *some good* among them, notwithstanding the slights they put upon him, for he is kind even to the evil and unthankful; *He laid his hands upon a few sick folks, and healed them.*

3. Yet he *could there do* no such mighty works as in other places, because of the unbelief that prevailed among the people, *v.* 5. It is a strange expression, as if unbelief tied the hands of omnipotence itself; he *would have done* as many miracles there as he had done elsewhere, but he could not. They forfeited the honour of having them wrought for them. By unbelief and contempt of Christ men stop the current of his favours to them, and put a bar in their own door.

4. He *marvelled because of their unbelief, v.* 6. We never find Christ wondering but at the *faith* of the Gentiles that were strangers, as the *centurion* (Matt. viii. 10), and the woman of Samaria, and at the unbelief of Jews that were his own countrymen.

5. He *went round about the villages, teaching.* If we cannot do good where we would, we must do it

JAMIESON, FAUSSET, BROWN

CHAPTER 6

VSS. 1-6. CHRIST REJECTED AT NAZARETH. (= Matt. 13:54-58; Luke 4:16-30.) See on Luke 4: 16-30.

A large gap here occurs, embracing the important transactions in Galilee and Jerusalem which are recorded in John 1:29 to 4:54, and which occurred *before* John's imprisonment (John 3:24); whereas the transactions here recorded occurred (as appears from Matt. 4:12, 13) *after* that event. The visit to Nazareth recorded in Matthew 13:54-58 (and Mark 6:1-6) we take to be not a later visit, but the same with this first one; because we cannot think that the Nazarenes, after being so enraged at His *first* display of wisdom as to attempt His destruction, should, on a *second* display of the same, wonder at it and ask how He came by it, as if they had never witnessed it before.

Is not this the carpenter's son? Is not his mother called Mary? And his brothers—James and Joses and Simon and Judas—"don't we all know them? Haven't we done business with them? Haven't they been in our houses? And this Jesus himself, have we not seen Him in boyhood and youth moving about among us? Can this be He of whom Moses and all the prophets wrote? Can this be He who is sent to heal the brokenhearted, and comfort all that mourn? Incredible!" Nor can it be doubted that a nearer view of Him than even ordinary Nazarenes could have was the very thing that stumbled His own "brethren," who for a while, we are told, "did not believe in him," and that made even the whole family think He was "beside himself" (Mark 3:21).

And he said . . .—Her replies to the one proverb by another, equally familiar, which we express in a rougher form—"Too much familiarity breeds contempt." Our Lord's long residence in Nazareth merely as a townsman had made Him *too common,* incapacitating them for appreciating Him as others did who were *less familiar with His everyday demeanor in private life.* A most important principle, to which the wise will pay due regard. (See also Matt. 7:6, on which our Lord Himself ever acted.)

ADAM CLARKE

CHAPTER 6

1. *And he went out from thence.* That is, from Capernaum.

3. *Is not this the carpenter?* Among the ancient Jews, every father was bound to do four things for his son: (1) to circumcise him, (2) to redeem him, (3) to teach him the law, (4) to teach him a trade. And this was founded on the following just maxim: "He who teaches not his son to do some work is as if he taught him robbery!" It is therefore likely that Joseph brought up our Lord to his own trade.

F. B. MEYER:

In the opening paragraph of this chapter, we learn of hatred and rejection of those who had enjoyed the rich privileges of being the neighbors and associates of our Lord from his earliest days. They could not discern the divine in the human, the heavenly under the earthly veil. The Savior, therefore, driven from their towns, goes about the villages, depriving himself of the companionship of His disciples in order to spread the Good News as far as possible. The Lord is still in his Church through the Holy Spirit, but his power is limited and neutralized by our unbelief. It is useless to ask him to put forth his great power and save us so long as we have made it practically impossible for him to do as we ask. The old-time cry was: "Why shouldst thou be as a mighty man that cannot save?" The answer is supplied here: "He could do no mighty work . . . and he marvelled because of their unbelief." Faith is our capacity for God, and there are several conditions for its nurture and growth.—*Bible Commentary*

MATTHEW HENRY

where we can, though but in the villages. Sometimes the gospel of Christ finds better entertainment in the country villages, than in the populous cities.

Verses 7-13

I. The commission given to the twelve apostles, to preach and work miracles. Hitherto they had been conversant with Christ, and had sat at his feet, had heard his doctrine, and seen his miracles. They had *received*, that they might *give*, had *learned*, that they might *teach*; and therefore now he *began to send them forth*. They must not always be studying in the academy, to get knowledge. Though they were not as yet so well accomplished as they were to be, yet, according to their present ability and capacity, they must be set to work, and make further improvements afterward. Now observe here,

1. That Christ sent them forth *by two and two*; this Mark takes notice of. They went two and two to a place that they might be company for one another when they were among strangers, and might strengthen the hands, and encourage the hearts, one of another; might help one another. It is an approved maxim, *Two are better than one*. Christ would thus teach his ministers to associate, and both lend and borrow help.

2. That he *gave them power over unclean spirits*. He commissioned them to attack the devil's kingdom, and empowered them to cast him out of the bodies of those that were possessed.

3. That he *commanded them* not to take provisions along with them, neither *victuals* nor *money*, that they might appear, wherever they came, to be poor men. When afterward he bid them *take purse and scrip* (Luke xxii. 36), that did not intimate that his care of them was abated from what it had been; but, that they should meet with worse times and worse entertainment than they met with at their first mission. In Matthew and Luke they are forbidden to *take staves* with them, that is, fighting staves; but here in Mark they are bid to take nothing save a *staff only*, that is, a walking staff, such as pilgrims carried. They must not put on *shoes*, but *sandals* only; they must go in the readiest plainest dress they could, and must not so much as have *two coats*. What they wanted, those they preached to would cheerfully accommodate them with.

4. He directed them, whatever city they came to, to make that house their headquarters, which happened to be their first quarters (*v.* 10); "*There abide till ye depart from that place.* And since ye know ye come on an errand sufficient to make you welcome, have such charity for your friends that first invited you, as to believe they do not think you burthensome."

5. He pronounces a very heavy doom upon those that rejected the gospel they preached (*v.* 11); "*Whosoever shall not receive you*, or will not so much as *hear you, depart thence*, and *shake off the dust under your feet, for a testimony against them.*" That dust, like the dust of Egypt (Exod. ix. 9), shall turn into a plague to them; and their condemnation in the great day, will be more intolerable than *that of Sodom.*

II. The apostles' conduct in pursuance of their commission. Though they were conscious to themselves of great weakness, yet, in obedience to their Master's order, and in dependence upon his strength, they *went out* as Abraham, not knowing whither they went.

1. The doctrine they preached; *They preached that men should repent* (*v.* 12); that they should change their minds, and reform their lives. The great design of gospel preachers, and the great tendency of gospel preaching, should be, to bring people to repentance, to a *new heart* and a *new way*. They did not amuse people with curious speculations, but told them that they must repent of their sins, and turn to God.

2. The miracles they wrought. The power Christ gave them *over unclean spirits*, was not ineffectual, nor did they receive it in vain, but used it, for they *cast out many devils* (*v.* 13); and they *anointed with oil many that were sick, and healed them.*

Verses 14-29

I. The wild notions that the people had concerning our Lord Jesus, *v.* 15. His own countrymen could believe nothing great concerning him, because they knew his poor kindred; but others were yet willing to believe anything rather than the truth. They said, He is Elias, whom they expected; or, *He is the prophet*, one of the Old Testament prophets raised to life; or *as one of the prophets*, a prophet now newly raised up.

II. The opinion of Herod concerning him. He said, "It is certainly John Baptist, *v.* 14. *It is John whom I beheaded*, *v.* 16. He is *risen from the dead*;

JAMIESON, FAUSSET, BROWN

7-13. MISSION OF THE TWELVE APOSTLES. (= Matt. 10:1, 5-15; Luke 9:1-6.) See on Matthew 10:1, 5-15.

And when he had called unto him his twelve disciples, he gave them power—The word signifies both "power," and "authority" or "right." Even if it were not evident that here both ideas are included, we find both words expressly used in the parallel passage of Luke (9:1)—"He gave them power and authority"—in other words, He both *qualified* and *authorized* them. **against**—or "over." **Provide neither gold, nor silver, nor brass in**—for—**your purses**—lit., "your belts," in which they kept their money. **Nor scrip for your journey**—the bag used by travelers for holding provisions. **neither two coats**—or tunics, worn next the skin. The meaning is, Take no change of dress, no additional articles. **neither shoes**—i.e., change of them.

And whosoever shall not receive you, nor hear your words, when ye depart out of that house or city—for possibly a whole town might not furnish one "worthy." **shake off the dust of your feet**—"for a testimony against them," as Mark and Luke add. By this symbolical action they vividly shook themselves from all *connection* with such, and all *responsibility* for the guilt of rejecting them and their message. Such symbolical actions were common in ancient times, even among others than the Jews, as strikingly appears in Pilate (ch. 27:24). And even to this day it prevails in the East. **Verily I say unto you, It shall be more tolerable**—more bearable—**for Sodom and Gomorrah in the day of judgment, than for that city**—Those Cities of the Plain, which were given to the flames for their loathsome impurities, shall be treated as less criminal, we are here taught, than those places which, though morally respectable, reject the Gospel message and affront those that bear it.

14-29. HEROD THINKS JESUS A RESURRECTION OF THE MURDERED BAPTIST—ACCOUNT OF HIS DEATH. (= Matt. 14:1-12; Luke 9:7-9.)

Herod's View of Christ (vss. 14-16). **14. And King Herod**—i.e., Herod Antipas, one of the three sons of Herod the Great, and own brother of Archelaus (Matt. 2:22), who ruled as *ethnarch* over Galilee and Perea. **heard of him; (for his name was spread abroad); and he said**—"unto his servants" (Matt. 14:2), his councillors or courtministers. **That John the Baptist was risen from the dead**—The murdered prophet haunted his guilty breast

ADAM CLARKE

7. *By two and two.* That they might encourage and support each other, and to show that union among the ministers of the gospel is essential to the promotion of the cause of truth.

8. *A staff only.* It is likely He desired them to take only one with every two, merely for the purpose of carrying any part of their clothes on, when they should be obliged to strip them off by reason of the heat; for walking staves, or things of this kind, were forbidden—see Matt. x. 10. But probably no more is designed than simply to state that they must not wait to make any provision for the journey, but go off just as they were, leaving the provision necessary in the present case to the care of Divine Providence.

9. *Shod with sandals.* The sandal seems to have been similar to the Roman *solea*, which covered only the sole of the foot, and was fastened about the foot and ankle with straps. *Sandals* were originally a part of the woman's dress; ancient authors represent them as worn only by women. In Matt. x. 10 the disciples are commanded to take no *shoes*, which word is nearly of the same import with *sandals;* but, as our Lord intimates to them that they should be free from all useless incumbrances, that they might fulfill His orders with the utmost diligence and dispatch, so we may suppose that the sandal was a lighter kind of wear than the shoe; and indeed the word *sandal* might be properly translated a "light shoe."

11. *And whosoever shall not receive you.* "Whatsoever place will not receive you" is the reading of some versions. *Verily.* All this clause is omitted in several MSS. and versions. Mill and Beza approve of the omission, and Griesbach leaves it out of the text. It has probably been transferred here from Matt. x. 15.

13. *Anointed with oil many that were sick.* This is spoken of only here and in Jas. v. 14. This ceremony was in great use among the Jews, and in certain cases it might be profitable. But in the cases mentioned here, which were merely miraculous, it could avail no more of itself than the imposition of hands. It was used symbolically, as an emblem of that ease, comfort, and joy which they prayed God to impart to the sick.

MATTHEW HENRY

he is come again with greater power, and *now mighty works do show forth themselves in him.*"

1. Where there is an *idle faith*, there is commonly a *working fancy.* The people said, It is a prophet risen from the dead; Herod said, *It is John Baptist risen from the dead.* It seems by this, that the *rising of a prophet from the dead*, to do *mighty works*, was thought neither impossible nor improbable, and it was now readily suspected when it was *not true*; but afterward, when *it was true* concerning Christ, it as obstinately gainsaid and denied. Those who most wilfully disbelieve the truth, are commonly most credulous of errors and fancies.

2. They who fight against the cause of God, will find themselves baffled, even when they think themselves conquerors.

3. A guilty conscience needs no accuser or tormentor but itself. *I beheaded him;* and the terror of it made him imagine that Christ was John risen. He feared John while he lived, and now, fears him ten times worse when he is dead. One might as well be haunted with ghosts and furies, as with the horrors of an accusing conscience.

4. There may be the terrors of strong conviction, where there is not the truth of a saving conversion.

III. A narrative of Herod's putting John Baptist to death.

1. The great value and veneration which Herod had some time had for John Baptist, which is related only by this evangelist, *v.* 20.

(1) He *feared John, knowing that he was a just man, and a holy.* It is possible that a man may have a great reverence for good men, and especially for good ministers, yea, and for that in them that is good, and yet himself be a bad man. [1] John was a *just man, and a holy*; to make a complete good man, both justice and holiness are necessary; holiness toward God, and justice toward men. [2] Herod knew this by personal acquaintance with him. Those that have but little justice and holiness themselves, may yet discern it with respect in others. [3] He therefore *feared* him, he honoured him. Many that are not good themselves, have respect for those that are.

(2) He *observed* him; he took notice of that in him that was praiseworthy, and commended it in the hearing of those about him; he made it appear that he observed what John said and did.

(3) He *heard him* preach; which was great condescension.

(4) He *did many of those things* which John in his preaching taught him. He was not only a *hearer of the word*, but in part a *doer of the work.* But it will not suffice to do *many* things, unless we have *respect to all* the commandments.

(5) He *heard him gladly.* There is a flashy joy, which a hypocrite may have in hearing the word. The *stony ground received the word with joy*, Luke viii. 13.

2. John's faithfulness to Herod, in telling him of his faults. Herod had married his brother Philip's wife, *v.* 17. John *reproved* him, told him plainly, *It is not lawful for thee to have thy brother's wife.* This was Herod's own iniquity, which he could not leave, when he did many things that John taught him. Though he were a king, he would not spare him, any more than Elijah did Ahab. Though it was dangerous to offend Herod, and much more to offend Herodias, yet John would run the hazard rather than be wanting in his duty. Those ministers that would be found faithful in the work of God, must not be afraid of the face of man.

3. The malice which Herodias bore to John for this (*v.* 19); She *has a quarrel with him, and would have him killed*; but when she could not obtain that, she got him committed to prison, *v.* 17. Many that pretend to honour prophesying, are for smooth things only, and love good preaching, if it keep far enough from their beloved sin. But it is better that sinners persecute ministers now for their faithfulness, than curse them eternally for their unfaithfulness.

4. The plot laid to take off John's head. *When a convenient day was come* (*v.* 21). There must be a ball at court, upon the king's birthday. To grace the solemnity, the daughter of Herodias must *dance* publicly, and Herod must take on him to be wonderfully charmed with her dancing. The king hereupon must make her an extravagant promise, to give her *whatever she would ask*, even to the *half of the kingdom.* This promise is bound with an oath; *He sware unto her, Whatsoever thou shalt ask, I will give.* She, being instructed by Herodias her mother, asked the *head of John Baptist*; and she must have it brought her *in a charger*, as a pretty thing for her to play with (*v.* 24, 25); and there must be no delay, no time lost, she must have it *by and by.* Herod granted it, and the execution was done im-

JAMIESON, FAUSSET, BROWN

like a specter, and seemed to him alive again and clothed with unearthly powers, in the person of Jesus. **15. Others said, That it is Elias. And others, That it is a prophet, or as one of the prophets**—See on Matthew 16:14. **16. But when Herod heard thereof, he said, It is John, whom I beheaded; he is risen from the dead**—"himself has risen"; as if the innocence and sanctity of his faithful reprover had not suffered that he should lie long dead.

Account of the Baptist's Imprisonment and Death (vss. 17-29). **17. For Herod himself had sent forth, and laid hold upon John, and bound him in prison**—in the castle of Machærus, near the southern extremity of Herod's dominions, and adjoining the Dead Sea [JOSEPHUS, *Antiquities*, 18:5, 2]. **for Herodias' sake**—She was the granddaughter of Herod the Great. **his brother Philip's wife**—and therefore the niece of both brothers. This Philip, however, was not the tetrarch of that name mentioned in Luke 3:1 (see there), but one whose distinctive name was "Herod Philip," another son of Herod the Great—who was disinherited by his father. Herod Antipas' own wife was the daughter of Aretas, king of Arabia; but he prevailed on Herodias, his half-brother Philip's wife, to forsake her husband and live with him, on condition, says JOSEPHUS (*Antiquities*, 18:5, 1), that he should put away his own wife. This involved him afterwards in war with Aretas, who totally defeated him and destroyed his army, from the effects of which he was never able to recover himself.

20. For Herod feared John—but, as BENGEL notes, John feared not Herod. **knowing that he was a just man and an holy**—Cf. the ease of Elijah with Ahab, after the murder of Naboth (I Kings 21:20). **and observed him**—rather, as in the margin, "kept" or "saved him"; i.e., from the wicked designs of Herodias, who had been watching for some pretext to get Herod entangled and committed to despatch him. **and when he heard him, he did many things**—many good things under the influence of the Baptist on his conscience. **and heard him gladly**—a striking statement this, for which we are indebted to our graphic Evangelist alone, illustrating the working of contrary principles in the slaves of passion. But this only shows how far Herodias must have wrought upon him, as Jezebel upon Ahab, that he should at length agree to what his awakened conscience kept him long from executing.

18. For John had said unto Herod, It is not lawful for thee to have thy brother's wife—Noble fidelity! It was not lawful because Herod's wife and Herodias husband were both living; and further, because the parties were within the forbidden degrees of consanguinity (see Lev. 20:21); Herodias being the daughter of Aristobulus, the brother of both Herod and Philip [JOSEPHUS, 18:5, 4]. **19. Therefore Herodias had a quarrel against him**—rather, as in the margin, "had a grudge against him." Probably she was too proud to speak to him; still less would she quarrel with him. **and would have killed him; but she could not.**

21. And when a convenient day—for the purposes of Herodias—**was come, that Herod**—rather, A convenient day being come, when Herod—**on his birthday, made a supper to his lords, high captains, and chief** [**estates**] **of Galilee**—This graphic minuteness of detail adds much to the interest of the tragic narrative. **22. And when the daughter of the said Herodias**—i.e.,—her daughter by her proper husband, Herod Philip: Her name was Salome [JOSEPHUS, *ibid.*]. **came in and danced, and pleased Herod and them that sat with him, the king said unto the damsel**—"the girl" (See on ch. 5:42). **Ask of me whatsoever thou wilt, and I will give it thee. 23. And he**—the king, so called, but only by courtesy (see on vs. 14). **sware unto her Whatsoever thou shalt ask of me, unto the half of my kingdom**—Those in whom passion and luxury have destroyed self-command will in a capricious moment say and do what in their cool moments they bitterly regret. **24. And she said, The head of John the Baptist**—Abandoned women are more shameless and heartless than men. The Baptist's fidelity marred the pleasures of Herodias, and this was too good an

ADAM CLARKE

15. *Or as one of the prophets. Or* is omitted by many MSS. Bengel, Wetstein, and Griesbach leave it out of the text. The omission of it mends the sense much.

ALEXANDER MACLAREN:

He "feared John"—the jailer afraid of his prisoner—"knowing that he was a righteous man and an holy." Goodness is awful. The worst men know it when they see it, and pay it the homage of dread, if not of love. "And kept him safe" (not ob- but pre-served him); that is, from Herodias' revenge. "And when he heard him, he was much perplexed." The reading thus translated differs from that in the Authorized Version by two letters only, and obviously is preferable. Herod was a weak-willed man, drawn by two stronger natures pulling in opposite directions.

So he alternated between lust and purity, between the foul kisses of the temptress at his side and the warnings of the prophet in his dungeon. But in all his vacillation he could not help listening to John, but "heard him gladly," and mind and conscience approved the nobler voice. Thus he staggered along, with religion enough to spoil some of his sinful delights, but not enough to make him give them up.

In such a condition one is liable to unrest and frequent inner conflict. Truly, he is "much perplexed" whose conscience pulls him one way and his inclinations another. There is no more miserable condition than that of the man whose will is cleft in twain, and who has a continual battle raging within. Conscience may be bound and thrust down into a dungeon, like John, and lust and pride may be carousing overhead, but their mirth is hollow, and every now and then the stern voice comes up through the gratings, and the noisy revelry is hushed, while it speaks doom. Such a state of inner strife comes often from unwillingness to give up one special evil.

—*Expositions of Holy Scripture*

19. *Would have killed.* "Sought to kill him." See the whole of this account, from v. 17 to v. 29, explained on Matt. xiv. 2-12.

21. *Lords.* Probably governors of particular districts. *High captains.* Literally, "chiefs" or "captains" over 1,000 men, military chiefs. *Chief estates.* Probably such as might be called nobles by title only, having no office civil or military; probably magistrates.

23. *Unto the half of my kingdom.* A noble price for a dance! This extravagance in favor of female dancers has the fullest scope in the East, even to the present day.

MATTHEW HENRY

mediately while the company were together. But he takes on him, (1) To be very backward to it, and that he would not for all the world have done it, if he had not been surprised into such a promise; The *king was exceeding sorry*. He could not do it but with great regret and reluctancy; natural conscience will not suffer men to sin easily. (2) He takes on him to be very sensible of the obligation of his oath. The promise was rashly made, and could not bind him to do an unrighteous thing. Sinful oaths must be repented of, and therefore not performed. He was hurried into the doing of it by those about him, only to carry on the humour; for he did it *for their sakes who sat with him.* **Thus do princes make themselves slaves to those whose respect they covet. The king sent an** *executioner*, **a soldier of his guard. Bloody tyrants have executioners ready to obey their most cruel and unrighteous decrees.**

5. The effect of this is, that Herod's wicked court is *all in triumph*, the head is made a present of *to the damsel*, and by her to her *mother*, *v.* 28. And John Baptist's sacred college is *all in tears*. When they *heard of it*, they came, and took up the neglected *corpse*, and *laid it in a tomb*.

Verses 30–44

I. The return to Christ of the apostles whom he had sent forth (*v.* 7). They *gathered themselves together*, and came to Jesus to give him an account of what they had done. They *told him all things*, both *what they had done, and what they had taught*. Ministers are accountable both for what they *do*, and for what they *teach*. Let them not either *do* anything, or *teach* anything, but what they are willing should be related and repeated to the Lord Jesus.

II. The tender care Christ took for their repose, after the fatigue they had (*v.* 31); *He said unto them, Come ye yourselves apart into a desert place, and rest awhile*. It should seem that John's disciples came to Christ with the mournful tidings of their master's death, much about the same time that his own disciples came to him. Christ takes cognizance of the *frights* of some, and the *toils* of others, of his disciples, and provides suitable relief for both, rest for those that are tired, and refuge for those that are terrified. With what kindness and compassion doth Christ say to them, *Come, and rest!* The most active servants of Christ cannot be always upon the stretch of business, but have bodies that require some relaxation, some breathing-time. And the Lord is for the body, considers its frame, and not only allows it time for rest, but puts it in mind of resting. Those that work diligently and faithfully, may cheerfully retire to rest. 1. Christ calls them to come *themselves apart*; if they must *rest*, they must be *alone*. 2. He invites them not to some pleasant country-seat, but *into a desert place*. No wonder that he who had but a ship for his preaching place, had but a desert for his resting place. 3. He calls them only to rest *awhile*; only to *get breath*, and then to go to work again. 4. The reason given for this, is, *for there were many coming and going, and they had no leisure so much as to eat*. Let but proper time be set, and kept for everything, and a great deal of work may be done with a great deal of ease; but if people be continually coming and going, a little work will not be done without a deal of trouble.

JAMIESON, FAUSSET, BROWN

opportunity of getting rid of him to let slip. **25. I will that thou give me by and by**—rather, "at once" —**in a charger**—large, flat trencher—**the head of John the Baptist. 26. And the king was exceeding sorry**--With his feelings regarding John, and the truths which so told upon his conscience from that preacher's lips, and after so often and carefully saving him from his paramour's rage, it must have been very galling to find himself at length entrapped by his own rash folly. **yet for his oath's sake**—See how men of no principle, but troublesome conscience, will stick at breaking a rash oath, while yielding to the commission of the worst crimes! **and for their sakes which sat with him**—under the influence of that false shame, which could not brook being thought to be troubled with religious or moral scruples. To how many has this proved a fatal snare! **he would not reject her. 27. And immediately the king sent an executioner**—one of the guards in attendance. The word is Roman, denoting one of the Imperial Guard. **and commanded his head to be brought: and he went and beheaded him in the prison**—after, it would seem, more than twelve months' imprisonment. Blessed martyr! Dark and cheerless was the end reserved for thee: but now thou hast thy Master's benediction, "Blessed is he whosoever shall not be offended in Me" (Matt. 11:6), and hast found the life thou gavest away (Matt. 10:39). But where are they in whose skirts is found thy blood? **28. And brought his head in a charger, and gave it to the damsel: and the damsel gave it to her mother**—Herodias did not shed the blood of the stern reprover; she only got it done, and then gloated over it, as it streamed from the trunkless head. **29. And when his disciples heard of it**—i.e., the Baptist's own disciples. **they came and took up his corpse, and laid it in a tomb** —"and went and told Jesus" (Matt. 14:12). If these disciples had, up to this time, stood apart from Him, as adherents of John (Matt. 11:2), perhaps they now came to Jesus, not without some secret reflection on Him for His seeming neglect of their master; but perhaps, too, as orphans, to cast in their lot henceforth with the Lord's disciples. How Jesus felt, or what He said, on receiving this intelligence, is not recorded; but He of whom it was said, as He stood by the grave of His friend Lazarus, "Jesus wept," was not likely to receive such intelligence without deep emotion. And one reason why He might not be unwilling that a small body of John's disciples should cling to him to the last, might be to provide some attached friends who should do for his precious body, on a small scale, what was afterwards to be done for His own.

30-56. The Twelve, on Their Return, Having Reported the Success of Their Mission, Jesus Crosses the Sea of Galilee with Them, Teaches the People, and Miraculously Feeds Them to the Number of Five Thousand—He Sends His Disciples by Ship Again to the Western Side, while He Himself Returns Afterwards Walking on the Sea—Incidents on Landing. (= Matt. 14:13-36; Luke 9:10-17; John 6:1-24.) Here, for the first time, all the four streams of sacred text run parallel. The occasion and all the circumstances of this grand section are thus brought before us with a vividness quite remarkable.

Five Thousand Miraculously Fed (vss. 30-44). **30. And the apostles gathered themselves together**—probably at Capernaum, on returning from their mission (vss. 7-13). **and told him all things, both what they had done, and what they had taught**—Observe the various reasons He had for crossing to the other side. First, Matthew (14:13) says, that "when Jesus heard" of the murder of His faithful forerunner—from those attached disciples of his who had taken up his body and laid it in a sepulchre (see on vs. 29)—"He departed by ship into a desert place apart"; either to avoid some apprehended consequences to Himself, arising from the Baptist's death (Matt. 10:23), or more probably to be able to indulge in those feelings which that affecting event had doubtless awakened, and to which the bustle of the multitude around Him was very unfavorable. Next, since He must have heard the report of the Twelve with the deepest interest, and probably with something of the emotion which He experienced on the return of the Seventy (see on Luke 10:17-22), He sought privacy for undisturbed reflection on this begun preaching and progress of His kingdom. Once more, He was wearied with the multitude of "comers and goers"—depriving Him even of leisure enough to take His food—and wanted *rest:* "Come ye yourselves apart into a desert place, and rest a while . . . ." Under the combined influence of all these considerations, our Lord sought this change. **32. And they departed**

ADAM CLARKE

26. *For their sakes which sat with him.* Probably these persons joined in with the request, and were glad of this opportunity to get this light of Israel extinguished, he being a public reprover of all their vices.

30. *The apostles gathered themselves together.* For they went different ways before, by two and two, v. 7; and now they return and meet Christ at Capernaum.

31. *Rest a while.* Rest is necessary for those who labor, and a zealous preacher of the gospel will as often stand in need of it as a galley slave.

A. T. ROBERTSON:

27. "A soldier of his guard" (*spekoulatora*). Latin word speculator. A spy, scout, lookout, and often executioner. It was used of the bodyguard of the Roman emperor and so for one of Herod's spies. He was used to do errands of this sort and it was soon done. It was a gruesome job, but he soon brought John's head to the damsel, apparently in the presence of all, and she took it to her mother. This miserable tetrarch, the slave of Herodias, was now the slave of his fears. He is haunted by the ghost of John and shudders at the reports of the work of Jesus.

29. "His corpse" (*to ptoma autou*). See Matt. 24:28. It was a mournful time for the disciples of John. "They went and told Jesus" (Matt. 14:12). What else could they do?

—*Word Pictures in the New Testament*

MATTHEW HENRY

5. They withdrew, accordingly, *by ship*, *v.* 32. Going *by water* was much less toilsome than going *by land* would have been. They went away *privately*. The most public persons cannot but wish to be private sometimes.

III. The diligence of the people to follow him. They are not blamed for it, nor bid to go back, but bid welcome. A failure in good manners will easily be excused in those who follow Christ, if it be but made up in a fulness of good affections. They followed him *out of the cities*, quitted their houses and shops, their callings and affairs. They followed him *afoot*, though he was gone by sea. They stuck to him. They *ran* afoot, and made such haste, that they *out-went* the disciples. Nay they followed him, though it was into a *desert place*. The presence of Christ will turn a wilderness into a paradise.

IV. The entertainment Christ gave them (*v.* 34); *When he saw much people*, instead of being moved with displeasure, he was *moved with compassion toward them*, because *they were as sheep having no shepherd*, they seemed to be well-inclined, and manageable as sheep. But they had *no shepherd*, none to lead and guide them in the right way, and therefore, in compassion to them, he not only *healed their sick*, as it is in Matthew, but he *taught them many things*.

V. The provision he made for them all; all his hearers he generously made his guests, and treated them at a *splendid* entertainment: so it might truly be called, because a *miraculous* one.

1. The disciples moved that they should be *sent home*. When *the day was now far spent* they said, *This is a desert place*, and *much time is now past*; *send them away to buy bread*, *v.* 35, 36. This the disciples suggested to Christ; but we do not find that the multitude themselves did. The disciples thought it would be a kindness to them to dismiss them. Willing minds will do more, and hold out longer, in that which is good, than one would expect from them.

2. Christ ordered that they should all be fed (*v.* 37); *Give ye them to eat*. To teach us to be kind to those who are rude to us, he ordered provision to be made for them; that bread which Christ and his disciples took with them into the desert, that they might make a quiet meal of it for themselves, he will have them to partake of. Thus was he given to hospitality. They attended on the spiritual food of his word, and then he took care that they should not want corporal food. The way of duty, as it is the way of safety, so it is the way to supply. Providence, not *tempted*, but duly *trusted*, never yet failed any of God's faithful servants, but has refreshed many with seasonable and surprising relief.

3. The disciples objected against it as impracticable; *Shall we go, and buy two hundred penny-worth of bread, and give them to eat?* Instead of waiting for directions from Christ, they perplex the cause with projects of their own. Christ would let them see their folly in forecasting for themselves, that they might put the greater value upon his provision for them.

4. Christ effected it, to universal satisfaction. They had brought with them *five loaves*, and *two fishes*, and that is the bill of fare. This was but a little for Christ and his disciples, and yet this they must give away. We often find Christ entertained at other people's tables, but here we have him supping a great many at his own charge.

(1) The provision was *ordinary*. Here were no rarities. If we have for necessity, it is no matter though we have not for delicacy and curiosity. The promise to them that fear the Lord, is, that verily they shall be fed; he doth not say, They shall be *feasted*.

(2) The guests were *orderly*; for they *sat down by companies on the green grass* (*v.* 39), they *sat down in ranks by hundreds and by fifties* (*v.* 40), for God is the God of order, and not of confusion.

(3) A blessing was craved upon the meat; *He looked up to heaven, and blessed*. Christ did not call one of

JAMIESON, FAUSSET, BROWN

into a desert place by ship privately—"over the Sea of Galilee, which is the Sea of Tiberias," says John (6:1), the only one of the Evangelists who so fully describes it; the others having written when their readers were supposed to know something of it, while the last wrote for those at a greater distance of time and place. This "desert place" is more definitely described by Luke (9:10) as "belonging to the city called Bethsaida." This must not be confounded with the town so called on the western side of the lake (see on Matt. 11:21). This town lay on its northeastern side, near where the Jordan empties itself into it: in Gaulonitis, out of the dominions of Herod Antipas, and within the dominions of Philip the Tetrarch (Luke 3:1), who raised it from a village to a city, and called it *Julias*, in honor of Julia, the daughter of Augustus [JOSEPHUS, *Antiquities*, 18:2, 1]. **33. And the people**—the multitudes—**saw them departing, and many knew him**—The true reading would seem to be: "And many saw them departing, and knew or recognized [them]." **and ran afoot**—Here, perhaps, it should be rendered "by land"—running round by the head of the lake, and taking one of the fords of the river, so as to meet Jesus, who was crossing with the Twelve by ship. **thither out of all cities, and outwent them**—got before them—**and came together unto him**—How exceedingly graphic is this! every touch of it betokening the presence of an eye-witness. John (6:3) says, that "Jesus went up into a mountain"—somewhere in that hilly range, the green tableland which skirts the eastern side of the lake. **34. And Jesus, when he came out of the ship**—having gone on shore—**saw much people**—a great multitude—**and was moved with compassion toward them, because they were as sheep not having a shepherd**—At the sight of the multitudes who had followed Him by land and even got before Him, He was so moved, as was His wont in such cases, with compassion, because they were like shepherdless sheep, as to forego both privacy and rest that He might minister to them. Here we have an important piece of information from the Fourth Evangelist (John 6:4), "And the passover, a feast of the Jews, was nigh"—rather, "Now the passover, the feast of the Jews, was nigh." This accounts for the multitudes that now crowded around Him. They were on their way to keep that festival at Jerusalem. But Jesus did not go up to this festival, as John expressly tells us, (ch. 7:1)—remaining in Galilee, because the ruling Jews sought to kill Him. **35. And when the day was now far spent**—"began to wear away" or "decline," says Luke (9:12). Matthew (14:15) says, "when it was evening"; and yet he mentions a later evening of the same day (vs. 23). This earlier evening began at three P.M.; the latter began at sunset. **36. Send them away, that they may go into the country round about, and into the villages, and buy themselves bread: for they have nothing to eat**—John tells us (6:5, 6) that "Jesus said to Philip, Whence shall we buy bread, that these may eat? (And this He said to prove him: for He Himself knew what He would do.)" The subject may have been introduced by some remark of the disciples; but the precise order and form of what was said by each can hardly be gathered with precision, nor is it of any importance. **37. He answered and said unto them**—"They need not depart" (Matt. 14:10). **Give ye them to eat**—doubtless said to prepare them for what was to follow. **And they say unto him, Shall we go and buy two hundred pennyworth of bread, and give them to eat?**—"Philip answered Him, Two hundred pennyworth of bread is not sufficient for them, that every one of them may take a little" (John 6:7). **38. He saith unto them, How many loaves have ye? go and see. And when they knew, they say, Five, and two fishes**—John is more precise and full: "One of His disciples, Andrew, Simon Peter's brother, saith unto Him, There is a lad here which hath five barley loaves and two small fishes: but what are they among so many?" (John 6:8, 9.) Probably this was the whole stock of provisions then at the command of the disciples—no more than enough for one meal to them—and entrusted for the time to this lad. "He said, Bring them hither to me" (Matthew 14:18). **39. And he commanded them to make all sit down by companies upon the green grass**—or "green hay"; the rank grass of those bushy wastes. For, as John (6:10) notes, "there was much grass in the place." **40. And they sat down in ranks, by hundreds, and by fifties**—Doubtless this was to show at a glance the number fed, and to enable all to witness in an orderly manner this glorious miracle. **41. And when he had taken the five loaves and the two fishes, he looked up to heaven**—Thus would the

ADAM CLARKE

33. *The people*. Or "the multitudes." This is wanting in many MSS., but it seems necessary to make the sense clear. There is scarcely a verse in the whole New Testament that has suffered so much from transcribers as this verse. Amidst the abundance of various readings, one can scarcely tell what its original state was.

34. *Much people*. See this miracle explained on Matt. xiv. 14, etc.

Jesus . . . was moved with compassion. He was moved with "tender compassion," so I think the word should in general be translated.

Send the multitude away, that they may go . . . and buy. The disciples of Christ are solicitous for the people's temporal as well as spiritual welfare; and he is not worthy to be called a minister of Christ who does not endeavor to promote both to the uttermost of his power.

They need not depart. He that seeks first the kingdom of Heaven is sure to have every temporal requisite.

We have here but five loaves, and two fishes. When we are deeply conscious of our own necessities, we shall be led to depend on Jesus with a firmer faith. God often permits His servants to be brought low, that they may have repeated opportunities of proving the kindness and mercy of their gracious Lord and Master.

And took the five loaves. This was the act of the father of a family among the Jews—his business it was to take the bread into his hands, and render thanks to God, before any of the family was permitted to taste of it. *Looking up to heaven*. To teach us to acknowledge God as the Supreme Good, and Fountain of all excellence.

MATTHEW HENRY

his disciples to crave a blessing, but did it himself (*v.* 41); and by virtue of this blessing the bread strangely multiplied, and so did the fishes, for they did *all eat, and were filled*, though they were to the number of *five thousand*, *v.* 42–44. Christ came into the world, to be the great feeder as well as the great healer; and in him there is enough for all that come to him. None are sent empty away from Christ, but those that come to him full of themselves.

(4) Care was taken of the fragments that remained, with which they filled *twelve baskets*. Though Christ had bread enough at command, he would hereby teach us, not to make waste.

Verses 45–56

I. The dispersing of the assembly; Christ *constrained his disciples* to go before by ship to Bethsaida. The people were loth to scatter. For now that they had got a good supper, they were in no haste to leave him.

II. Christ departed *into a mountain, to pray*. He *prayed*; he was much in prayer; he prayed often, and prayed long. He went *alone*, to pray, to set us an example, and to encourage us in our *secret* addresses to God, he prayed *alone*. A good man is never less alone than when alone with God.

III. The disciples were in distress at sea; *The wind was contrary* (*v.* 48), so that they *toiled in rowing*. This was a specimen of the hardships they were to expect, when hereafter he should send them abroad to preach the gospel. The church is often like a ship at sea, *tossed with tempests, and not comforted*; we may have Christ for us, and yet wind and tide against us; but it is a comfort to Christ's disciples in a storm, that their Master is in the heavenly mount, interceding for them.

JAMIESON, FAUSSET, BROWN

most distant of them see distinctly what He was doing. **and blessed**—John says, "And when he had given thanks." The sense is the same. This thanksgiving for the meal, and benediction of it as the food of thousands, was the crisis of the miracle. **and brake the loaves, and gave them to his disciples to set before them**—thus virtually holding forth these men as His future ministers. **and the two fishes divided he among them all. 42. And they did all eat, and were filled**—All the four Evangelists mention this: and John (6:11) adds, "and likewise of the fishes, as much as they would"—to show that vast as was the multitude, and scanty the provisions, the meal to each and all of them was a plentiful one. "When they were filled, He said unto His disciples, Gather up the fragments that remain, that nothing be lost" (John 6:12). This was designed to bring out the whole extent of the miracle. **43. And they took up twelve baskets full of the fragments, and of the fishes**—"Therefore (says John 6:13), they gathered them together, and filled twelve baskets with the fragments of the five barley loaves, which remained over and above unto them that had eaten." The article here rendered "baskets" in all the four narratives was part of the luggage taken by Jews on a journey—to carry, it is said, both their provisions and hay to sleep on, that they might not have to depend on Gentiles, and so run the risk of ceremonial pollution. In this we have a striking corroboration of the truth of the four narratives. Internal evidence renders it clear, we think, that the first three Evangelists wrote independently of each other, though the fourth must have seen all the others. But here, each of the first three Evangelists uses the same word to express the apparently insignificant circumstance that the baskets employed to gather up the fragments were of the kind which even the Roman satirist, JUVENAL, knew by the name of *cophinus*, while in both the narratives of the feeding of the Four Thousand the baskets used are expressly said to have been of the kind called *spuris*. (See on ch. 8:19, 20.) **44. And they that did eat of the loaves were about five thousand men**—"besides women and children" (Matt. 14:21). Of these, however, there would probably not be many; as only the males were obliged to go to the approaching festival.

Jesus Recrosses to the Western side of the Lake, Walking on the Sea (vss. 45-56). One very important particular given by John alone (6:15) introduces this portion: "When Jesus therefore perceived that they would take Him by force, to make Him a king, He departed again into a mountain Himself alone." **45. And straightway he constrained his disciples to get into the ship, and to go to the other side before**—Him—**unto Bethsaida**—Bethsaida of Galilee (John 12:21). John says they "went over the sea towards Capernaum"—the wind, probably, occasioning this slight deviation from the direction of Bethsaida. **while he sent away the people**—"the multitude." His object in this was to put an end to the misdirected excitement in His favor (John 6:15), into which the disciples themselves may have been somewhat drawn. The word "constrained" implies reluctance on their part, perhaps from unwillingness to part with their Master and embark at night, leaving Him alone on the mountain. **46. And when he had sent them away, he departed into a mountain to pray**—thus at length getting that privacy and rest which He had vainly sought during the earlier part of the day; opportunity also to pour out His soul in connection with the extraordinary excitement in His favor that evening—which appears to have marked the zenith of His reputation, for it began to decline the very next day; and a place whence He might watch the disciples on the lake, pray for them in their extremity, and observe the right time for coming to them, in a new manifestation of His glory, on the sea. **47. And when even was come**—the later evening (see on vs. 35). It had come even when the disciples embarked (Matt. 14:23; John 6:16). **the ship was in the midst of the sea, and he alone on the land**—John says (6:17), "It was now dark, and Jesus was not come to them." Perhaps they made no great effort to push across at first, having a lingering hope that their Master would yet join them, and so allowed the darkness to come on. "And the sea arose" (adds the beloved disciple, 6:18), "by reason of a great wind that blew." **48. And he saw them toiling in rowing; for the wind was contrary unto them**—putting forth all their strength to buffet the waves and bear on against a head wind, but to little effect. He "saw" this from His mountain-top, and through the darkness of the night, for His heart was all with them: yet would He not go to their relief till His own time

ADAM CLARKE

41. *And blessed.* I think the word *God* should be inserted here, as in Matt. xiv. 19. See the note there. The food we receive from God is already blessed, and does not stand in need of being blessed by man; but God, who gives it, deserves our warmest thanksgivings, as frequently as we are called to partake of His bounty.

43. *Twelve baskets.* These were either the baskets used by the disciples, see Matt. xiv. 20, or baskets belonging to some of the multitude, who might have brought some with them to carry provisions, or other things necessary for the sick, whom they brought to Christ to be healed.

44. *Were about five thousand.* This miracle is mentioned by all the four Evangelists. It is one of the most astonishing that Christ has wrought. It is a miracle whch could not be counterfeited, and a full proof of the divinity of Christ.

45. *To the other side before unto Bethsaida.* John says, chap. vi. 17, to "Capernaum." It is probable our Lord ordered them to steer to one or other of these two places, which were about four miles distant, and on the same side of the Sea of Galilee.

He went up into a mountain apart, to pray. Some make this part of our Lord's conduct emblematic of the spirit and practice of prayer, and observe that the proper dispositions and circumstances for praying well are: (1) retirement from the world, (2) elevation of the heart to God, (3) solitude, and (4) the silence and quiet of the night. It is certain in this also Christ has left us an example that we should follow His steps.

47. *The ship was in the midst of the sea.* See all the parts of this wonderful transaction considered on Matt. xiv. 22-33.

MATTHEW HENRY

IV. Christ made them a kind visit upon the water. He chose to help them in the most endearing manner possible, and therefore came to them himself.

1. He did not come till the *fourth watch of the night*, not till after three o'clock in the morning; but then he came. If Christ's visits to his people be deferred long, yet at length he will come.

2. He came, walking upon the waters. The sea was now tossed with waves, and yet Christ came, walking upon it. No difficulties can obstruct Christ's gracious appearances for his people. He will either find, or force, a way through the most tempestuous sea, for their deliverance.

3. He *would have passed by them*. Providence, when it is acting designedly and directly for the succour of God's people, yet sometimes seems as if it were *giving them the go-by*. They thought that *he would*, but we may be sure that he would not, *have passed by them*.

4. They were frightened at the sight of him, supposing him to have been an apparition; *They all saw him, and were troubled* (*v.* 50). We often perplex and frighten ourselves with phantasms, the creatures of our own fancy and imagination.

5. He encouraged them, and silenced their fears, by making himself known to them; *Be of good cheer, it is I; be not afraid*. We know not Christ till he is pleased to reveal himself to us. "*It is I;* I your Master, I your friend." The knowledge of Christ, as he is in himself, and near to us, is enough to make the disciples of Christ cheerful even in a storm, and no longer fearful. Christ's presence with us in a stormy day, is enough to make us of good cheer, though clouds and darkness be round about us. He doth not tell them who he was, they knew his voice, as the sheep know the voice of their own shepherd. When Christ said to those that came to apprehend him by force, *I am he*, they were struck down by it, John xviii. 6. When he saith to those that come to apprehend him by faith, *I am he*, they are raised up by it, and comforted.

6. He *went up to them into the ship*. Let them but have their Master with them, and all is well. And as soon as he was come into the ship, *the wind ceased*. The wind ceased all of a sudden. Though we hear not the command given, yet, if thus the wind cease, and we have the comfort of a calm, say, It is because Christ is in the ship.

7. They were more surprised and astonished at this miracle than did become them, *They were sore amazed in themselves*. But why all this confusion about it? It was because they *considered not the miracle of the loaves*; had they given that its due weight they would not have been so much surprised at this; for his multiplying the bread was as great an instance

JAMIESON, FAUSSET, BROWN

came. **and about the fourth watch of the night**—The Jews, who used to divide the night into three watches, latterly adopted the Roman division into four watches, as here. So that, at the rate of three hours to each, the fourth watch, reckoning from six P.M., would be three o'clock in the morning. "So when they had rowed about five and twenty or thirty furlongs" (John 6:19)—rather more than halfway across. The lake is about seven miles broad at its widest part. So that in eight or nine hours they had only made some three and a half miles. By this time, therefore, they must have been in a state of exhaustion and despondency bordering on despair; and now at length, having tried them long enough—**he cometh unto them, walking upon the sea**—"and draweth nigh unto the ship" (John 6:19). **and would have passed by them**—but only in the sense of Luke 24:28; Genesis 32:26; cf. Genesis 18:3, 5; 42:7. **49. But when they saw him walking upon the sea, they supposed it had been a spirit, and cried out**—"for fear" (Matt. 14:26). He would appear to them at first like a dark moving speck upon the waters; then as a human figure; but in the dark tempestuous sky, and not dreaming that it could be their Lord, they take it for a spirit. Cf. Luke 24:37. **50. For they all saw him, and were troubled. And immediately he talked with them, and saith unto them, Be of good cheer: It is I; be not afraid**—There is something in these two little words—given by Matthew, Mark and John—"'Tis I," which from the mouth that spake it and the circumstances in which it was uttered, passes the power of language to express. Here were they in the midst of a raging sea, their little bark the sport of the elements, and with just enough of light to descry an object on the waters which only aggravated their fears. But Jesus deems it enough to dispel all apprehension to let them know that *He was there*. From other lips that "I am" would have merely meant that the person speaking was such a one and not another person. That, surely, would have done little to calm the fears of men expecting every minute, it may be, to go to the bottom. But spoken by One who at that moment was "treading upon the waves of the sea," and was about to hush the raging elements with His word, what was it but the Voice which cried of old in the ears of Israel, even from the days of Moses, "I AM"; "I, EVEN I, AM HE!" Cf. John 18:5, 6; 8:58. Now, that Word is "made flesh, and dwells among us," uttering itself from beside us in dear familiar tones—"It is the Voice of my Beloved!" How far was this apprehended by these frightened disciples? There was one, we know, in the boat who outstripped all the rest in susceptibility to such sublime appeals. It was not the deep-toned writer of the Fourth Gospel, who, though he lived to soar beyond all the apostles, was as yet too young for prominence, and all unripe. It was Simon-Barjonas. Here follows a very remarkable and instructive episode, recorded by Matthew alone:

51. And he went up unto them into the ship—John (6:21) says, "Then they willingly received him into the ship"—or rather, "Then were they willing to receive Him" (with reference to their previous terror); but implying also a glad welcome, their first fears now converted into wonder and delight. "And immediately," adds the beloved disciple, "they were at the land whither they went," or "were bound." This additional miracle, for as such it is manifestly related, is recorded by the fourth Evangelist alone. As the storm was suddenly calmed, so the little bark—propelled by the secret power of the Lord of nature now sailing in it—glided through the now unruffled waters, and, while they were wrapt in wonder at what had happened, not heeding their rapid motion, *was found* at port, to their still further surprise.

Then are they glad, because at rest
And quiet now they be;
So to the haven He them brings
Which they desired to see.

Matthew (14:33) says, "Then they that were in the ship came [i.e., ere they got to land] and worshipped him, saying, Of a truth Thou art the Son of God." But our Evangelist is wonderfully striking. **and the wind ceased and they were sore amazed in themselves beyond measure, and wondered**—The Evangelist seems hardly to find language strong enough to express their astonishment. **52. For they considered not the miracle of the loaves; for their heart was hardened**—What a singular statement! The meaning seems to be that if they had

ADAM CLARKE

The fourth watch. Anciently the Jews divided the night into three watches, consisting of four hours each. The first watch is mentioned, Lam. ii. 19; the second, Judg. vii. 19; and the third, Exod. xiv. 24; but a fourth watch is not mentioned in any part of the Old Testament. This division the Romans had introduced in Judea, as also the custom of dividing the day into twelve hours; see John xi. 9. The first watch began at six o'clock in the evening, and continued till nine; the second began at nine, and the fourth began at three, and continued twelve, and continued till three next morning; and the fourth began at three, and continued till six. It was, therefore, between the hours of three and six in the morning that Jesus made His appearance to His disciples. *Walking on the sea.* Thus suspending the laws of gravitation was a proper manifestation of unlimited power. Jesus did this by His own power; therefore Jesus showed forth His Godhead.

49. *They supposed it had been a spirit.* That is, by whom the storm had been raised.

It is I; be not afraid. Nothing but this voice of Christ could, in such circumstances, have given courage and comfort to His disciples. Those who are grievously tossed with difficulties and temptations require a similar manifestation of His power and goodness. When He proclaims himself in the soul, all sorrow and fear and sin are at an end.

G. CAMPBELL MORGAN:

The story of the storm is one concerning these men, in the way of His will. He asked them to enter the boat and cross back again to the other shore. They went. Remember that the way of His will was the way of the storm. He sent them into the storm, and there is a strong word used here concerning that storm. We have translated it "distressed." Far more literally we may render, "They were tormented in rowing." Why did they not turn back to the other shore? The wind was contrary. There was the difficulty. The wind was blowing off the shore to which He had commanded them to go. It would have been the simplest thing to tack, to put about, and run before the wind. But no! they must not do that. Why not? He sent them in that direction! They were tormented in the very path of obedience. But it was also the way of His power. He came after them. The wind was contrary to Him also, but did not hinder Him. The waters were storm-tossed for Him also, but they constituted the pavement of His victorious footsteps. When presently He was in the boat, the storm ceased.—*The Gospel According to Mark*

MATTHEW HENRY

of his power as his walking on the water. It is for want of a right understanding of Christ's former works, that we are transported at the thought of his present works, as if there never were the like before.

V. When they came to the land of Gennesaret the people bid them very welcome; *The men of that place knew Jesus* (*v.* 53), and knew what mighty works he did wherever he came, they knew likewise that he used to stay but a little while at a place, and therefore, *They ran through that whole region round about*, with all possible expedition, and *began to carry about in beds those that were sick*, there was no danger of their getting cold when they hoped to get a cure, *v.* 55. Let him go where he would, he was crowded with patients, they *laid the sick in the streets*, to be in his way, and begged leave for them to touch if it were but *the border of his garment, and as many as touched, were made whole*. We do not find that they were desirous to be taught by him, only to be healed. If ministers could now cure people's bodily diseases, what multitudes would attend them! But it is sad to think how much more concerned the most of men are about their bodies than about their souls.

JAMIESON, FAUSSET, BROWN

but "considered [reflected upon] the miracle of the loaves," wrought but a few hours before, they would have *wondered at nothing* which He might do within the whole circle of power and grace.

Incidents on Landing (vss. 53-56). The details here are given with a rich vividness quite peculiar to this charming Gospel. **53. And when they had passed over, they came into the land of Gennesaret**—from which the lake sometimes takes its name, stretching along its western shore. Capernaum was their landing-place (John 6:24, 25). **and drew to the shore**—a nautical phrase, nowhere else used in the New Testament. **54. And when they were come out of the ship, straightway they knew him**—"immediately they recognized Him"; i.e., the people did. **55. and began to carry about in beds those that were sick, where they heard he was**—At this period of our Lord's ministry the popular enthusiasm in His favor was at its height. **56. and besought him that they might touch if it were but the border of his garment**—having heard, no doubt, of what the woman with the issue of blood experienced on doing so (ch. 5:25-29), and perhaps of other unrecorded cases of the same nature. **and as many as touched him**—or "it"—the border of His garment—**were made whole**—All this they *continued* to do and to experience while our Lord was in that region. The *time* corresponds to that mentioned (John 7:1), when He "walked in Galilee," instead of appearing in Jerusalem at the passover, "because the Jews," i.e., *the rulers*, "sought to kill Him"—while *the people* sought to enthrone Him!

ADAM CLARKE

53. *The land of Gennesaret*. This country lay on the coast of the Sea of Galilee: it is described by Josephus as being exceedingly pleasant and fertile. It had its name of Gennesaret from *gen*, a "garden," and *sar*, a "prince," either because the king had a garden there or because of its great fertility.

54. *They knew him*. "They recollected Him," for He had before preached and wrought miracles in different places of the same country.

56. *Villages*. Probably small towns near cities. *Country*. Villages at a distance from cities and large public towns.

MATTHEW HENRY — CHAPTER 7

Verses 1–23

One great design of Christ's coming, was, to set aside the ceremonial law which God made, and to put an end to it; to make way for which he begins with the ceremonial law which men had made, and added to the law of God's making. These Pharisees and scribes with whom he had this argument, are said to *come from Jerusalem* down to Galilee—fourscore or a hundred miles, to pick quarrels with our Saviour there.

I. What the tradition of the elders was: by it all were enjoined to *wash their hands* before meat; a cleanly custom, and no harm in it; but they placed religion in it. They interposed their authority, and commanded all to do it upon pain of excommunication; this they kept up as a *tradition of the elders*.

We have here an account of the practice of the Pharisees and *all the Jews*, *v.* 3, 4. 1. They *washed their hands oft*. 2. They particularly washed before they *ate bread*; for that was the rule; they must be sure to wash before they ate the bread on which they begged a blessing, else he was thought to be defiled. 3. They took special care, when they came in *from the markets*, to wash their hands. It signifies any place of concourse where there were people of all sorts, and, it might be supposed, some heathen or Jews under a ceremonial pollution, by coming near to whom they thought themselves polluted. They say, The rule of the rabbis was—That, if they washed their hands well in the morning, the first thing they did, it would serve for all day, provided they kept alone; but, if they went into company, they must not, at their return, either eat or pray till they had washed their hands. 4. They added to this the washing of *cups* and *pots*, and *brazen vessels*, nay, and the very *tables* on which they ate their meat. There were many cases in which, by the law of Moses, washings were appointed; but they *added* to them, and enforced the observation of their own impositions as much as of God's institutions.

II. What the practice of Christ's disciples was; they knew what the law was, and the common usage; but they would not be bound up by it: they ate bread with *defiled*, that is, with *unwashen hands*, *v.* 2. The disciples knew (it is probable) that the Pharisees had their eye upon them, and yet they would not humour them by a compliance with their traditions, and ate bread with *unwashen* hands; and herein *their righteousness*, however it might seem to come short, did really *exceed, that of the scribes and Pharisees*, Matt. v. 20.

III. The offence which the Pharisees took at this; They *found fault* (*v.* 3). They brought a complaint against them to their Master, expecting that he should check them, and order them to conform. They do not ask, Why do not thy disciples *do as we do*? But, Why do not they *walk according to the tradition of the elders*? *v.* 5.

IV. Christ's vindication of them; in which,

1. He argues with the Pharisees concerning the

JAMIESON, FAUSSET, BROWN — CHAPTER 7

Vss. 1-23. DISCOURSE ON CEREMONIAL POLLUTION. (=Matt. 15:1-20). See on Matthew 15:1-20.

The time of this section was after that Passover which was nigh at hand when our Lord fed the five thousand (John 6:4)—the third Passover, as we take it, since His public ministry began, but which He did not keep at Jerusalem for the reason mentioned in John 7:1.

Then came to Jesus scribes and Pharisees, which were of—or "from"—**Jerusalem**—Mark says they "came from" it: a deputation probably sent from the capital expressly to watch Him. As He had not come to them at the last Passover, which they had reckoned on, they now come to Him. "And," says Mark, "when they saw some of His disciples eat bread with defiled, that is to say, with unwashen hands"—hands not ceremonially cleansed by washing—"they found fault. For the Pharisees, and all the Jews, except they wash their hands oft"—lit., "in" or "with the fist"; i.e., probably washing the one hand by the use of the other—though some understand it, with our version, in the sense of 'diligently,' 'sedulously'—"eat not, holding the tradition of the elders"; acting religiously according to the custom handed down to them. "And when they come from the market"—"And after market": after any common business, or attending a court of justice, where the Jews, as WEBSTER and WILKINSON remark, after their subjection to the Romans, were especially exposed to intercourse and contact with heathens—"except they wash, they eat not. And many other things there be, which they have received to hold, as the washing of cups and pots, brazen vessels and tables"—rather, "couches," such as were used at meals, which probably were merely *sprinkled* for ceremonial purposes. "Then the Pharisees and scribes asked Him," **saying, Why do thy disciples transgress the tradition of the elders? for they wash not their hands when they eat bread.**

ADAM CLARKE — CHAPTER 7

1. *Came from Jerusalem*. Probably for the express purpose of disputing with Christ, that they might entangle Him in His talk.

3. *Except they wash their hands*. The hand to the wrist—"Unless they wash the hand up to the wrist, *eat not*." This sort of washing was, and still continues to be, an act of religion in the Eastern countries. It is particularly commanded in the Koran, Surat, v, v. 7, "O believers, when ye wish to pray, wash your faces, and your hands up to the elbows—and your feet up to the ankles," which custom it is likely Mohammed borrowed from the Jews. The Jewish doctrine is this: "If a man neglect the washing, he shall be eradicated from this world."

4. *Except they wash*. Or "dip." But instead of the word in the text, the famous Codex Vaticanus (B), eight others, and Euthymius have *sprinkle*. However the Jews sometimes washed their hands previously to their eating; at other times they simply dipped or plunged them into the water. *Of cups*. Any kind of earthen vessels. *Pots*. "Of measures," a measure for liquids, formed from the Latin *sextarius*, equal to a pint and a half English. *Of brasen vessels*. These, if polluted, were only to be washed or passed through the fire, whereas the earthen vessels were to be broken. *And of tables*. "Beds, couches." This is wanting in some MSS.

2. *They found fault*. This is wanting in many MSS. and several versions; Mill and Bengel approve the omission, and Griesbach rejects the word. If the third and fourth verses be read in a parenthesis, the second and fifth verses will appear to be properly connected, without the above clause.

MATTHEW HENRY

authority by which this ceremony was imposed; but this he did not speak of publicly to the multitude (as appears by his *calling the people* to him, *v.* 14) lest he should have seemed to stir them up to faction; but addressed it as a reproof to the persons concerned.

(1) He reproves them for their hypocrisy in pretending to honour God, when really they had no such design in their religious observances (*v.* 6, 7); *They honour me with their lips*, they pretend it is for the glory of God, but really *their heart is far from God.* They rested in the outside of all their religious exercises, and their hearts were not right with God in them, and this was worshipping God in vain; for neither was he pleased with such sham-devotions, nor were they profited by them.

(2) He reproves them for placing religion in the inventions and injunctions of their elders and rulers; They *taught for doctrines the traditions of men.* They were enforcing the canons of their church, and judged of people's being Jews or no, according as they did, or did not, conform to them, without any consideration had, whether they lived in obedience to God's laws or no. Instead of providing the substance, they presumptuously added to the ceremony, and were very nice in *washing pots and cups*; and observe, he adds, *Many other suchlike things ye do, v.* 8. Superstition is an endless thing.

(3) He reproves them for *laying aside the commandment of God*, and overlooking that, and in their discipline conniving at the violation of that, as if that were no longer of force, *v.* 8. It is the mischief of impositions, that too often they who are zealous for them, have little zeal for the essential duties of religion. Nay, they *rejected the commandment of God, v.* 9. *Ye do fairly disannul and abolish the commandment of God;* and even *by* your traditions *make the word of God of no effect*, *v.* 13. They were entrusted to expound the law, and to enforce it; and, under pretence of using that power, they violated the law, and dissolved the bonds of it.

This he gives them a particular instance of, and a flagrant one—God commanded children to *honour their parents*, not only by the law of Moses, but by the law of nature; and whoso *reviletlh*, or *speaketh evil of*, father or mother, *let him die the death*, *v.* 10. It is the duty of children, if their parents be poor, to relieve them, according to their ability; and if those children are worthy to die, that curse their parents, much more those that starve them. But they will find him out an expedient by which he may be discharged from this obligation, *v.* 11. If his parents be in want, and he has wherewithal to help them, but has no mind to do it, let him swear by the *Corban* that is, by the *gold of the temple*, and the *gift upon the altar*, that his parents shall not be profited by him, and, if they ask anything of him, let him tell them this, and it is enough; as if by the obligation of this wicked vow he had discharged himself from the obligation. He concludes, *And many such things do ye.* Where will men stop, when once they have made the word of God give way to their tradition? These eager imposers of such ceremonies, at first only *made light* of God's commandments *in comparison* with their traditions, but afterward *made void* God's commandments, if they stood *in competition* with them.

2. He instructs the people concerning the principles upon which this ceremony was grounded. It was requisite that this part of his discourse should be public, he therefore *called the people unto him* (*v.* 14), and bid them *hear and understand.* It is not enough for the common people to *hear*, but they must *understand* what they hear. Corrupt customs are best cured by rectifying corrupt notions.

Now that which he goes about to set them right in, is, what the pollution is, which we are in danger of being damaged by, *v.* 15. (1) Not by the *meat we eat*, that is but from without, and goes through a man. But, (2) It is by the breaking out of the corruption that is in our hearts. We become odious in the sight of God by that which *comes out* of us; our wicked thoughts and affections, words and actions, these defile us, and these only. Our care must therefore be, to *wash our heart from wickedness.*

3. He gives his disciples, in private, an explication of the instructions he gave the people. They *asked him concerning the parable* (*v.* 17). (1) He reproves their dulness; "*Are ye so without understanding also?*" He doth not expect they should understand everything; "But are ye so weak as not to understand *this*?" (2) He explains this truth to them, that they might *perceive* it, and then they would *believe* it. [1] That that which we eat and drink cannot defile us, so as to call for any religious washing; it *goes into the stomach*, and what there may be in it that is defiling is voided and gone. But, [2] It is that which

JAMIESON, FAUSSET, BROWN

Ye hypocrites, well did Esaias prophesy of you, saying—(Isa. 29:13)— **This people draweth nigh unto me with their mouth, . . .**—By putting the commandments of men on a level with the divine requirements, *their whole worship was rendered vain*—a principle of deep moment in the service of God. "For," it is added in Mark 7:8, "laying aside the commandment of God, ye hold the tradition of men, as the washing of pots and cups; and many other such like things ye do." The drivelling nature of their multitudinous observances is here pointedly exposed, in contrast with the manly observance of "the commandment of God"; and when our Lord says, "Many other such like things ye do," it is implied that He had but given a specimen of the hideous treatment which the divine law received, and the grasping disposition which, under the mask of piety, was manifested by the ecclesiastics of that day.

Thus have ye made the commandment of God of none effect—cancelled or nullified it—**by your tradition.**

But he answered and said unto them, Why do ye also transgress the commandment of God by your tradition?—The charge is retorted with startling power: "The tradition they transgress is but *man's*, and is itself the occasion of heavy transgression, undermining the authority of *God's law*."

For God commanded, saying, Honour thy father and mother Deut. 5:16; **and, He that curseth father or mother, let him die the death**—(Exod. 21:17). **But ye say, Whosoever shall say to his father or his mother, It is a gift**—or simply, "A gift!" In Mark it is, "*Corban*!" i.e., "An oblation!" meaning, any unbloody offering or gift dedicated to sacred uses. **by whatsoever thou mightest be profited by me; And honour not his father or his mother, [he shall be free]**—i.e., It is true, father—mother—that by giving to thee this, which I now present, thou mightest be profited by me; but I have gifted it to pious uses, and therefore, at whatever cost to thee, I am not now at liberty to alienate any portion of it. "And," it is added in Mark, "ye suffer him no more to do aught for his father or his mother." To dedicate property to God is indeed lawful and laudable, but not at the expense of filial duty.

And he called the multitude, and said unto them—The foregoing dialogue, though in the people's hearing, was between Jesus and the pharisaic cavilliers, whose object was to disparage Him with the people. But Jesus, having put them down, turns to the multitude, who at this time were prepared to drink in everything He said, and with admirable plainness, strength, and brevity, lays down the great principle of real pollution, by which a world of bondage and uneasiness of conscience would be dissipated in a moment, and the sense of sin be reserved for deviations from the holy and eternal law of God. **Hear and understand: Not that which geeth into the mouth defileth a man; but that which cometh out of the mouth, this defileth a man**—This is expressed even more emphatically in Mark (17:15, 16), and it is there added, "If any man have ears to hear, let him hear." As in ch. 13:9, this so oft-repeated saying seems designed to call attention to the *fundamental* and *universal* character of the truth it refers to.

Are ye also yet without understanding?—Slowness of spiritual apprehension in His genuine disciples grieves the Saviour: from others He expects no better (ch. 13: 11). **Do not ye yet understand that whatsoever entereth in at the mouth, . . .**—Familiar though these sayings have now become, what freedom from bondage to outward things do they proclaim, on the one hand; and on the other, how searching is the truth which they express—that nothing which enters from without can really defile us; and that only the evil that is in the heart, that is

ADAM CLARKE

W. E. VINE:

HUPOKRITES, primarily denotes one who answers; then, a stage actor; it was a custom for Greek and Roman actors to speak in large masks with mechanical devices for augmenting the force of the voice; hence the word became used metaphorically of a dissembler, a hypocrite. It is found only in the Synoptists, and always used by the Lord, fifteen times in Matthew; elsewhere, Mark 7:6; Luke 6:42; 11:44 (in some mss.); 12:56; 13:15.

—Vine's Expository Dictionary

8. *Washing of pots and cups.* This whole clause is wanting in some MSS. and versions.

9. *Full well.* A strong irony. How noble is your conduct! From conscientious attachment to your own traditions you have annihilated the commandments of God! *That ye may keep.* God's law was nothing to these men in comparison of their own; hear a case in point. "Rabba said, How foolish are most men! They observe the precepts of the divine law, and neglect the statutes of the rabbins!"

10. *For Moses said.* See all these verses, from this to the twenty-third, explained on Matt. xv. 3-20.

14. *When he had called all the people.* But instead of *all*, "again" is the reading of some MSS. and versions. Mill and Griesbach approve of this reading.

Are ye also yet without understanding? The word which we translate *yet* should be here rendered "still": Are ye still void of understanding? The word is used in this sense by several Greek writers.

MATTHEW HENRY

comes out from the heart, the corrupt heart, that defiles us. What comes out from the *mind* of a man is that which defiles him before God, and calls for a religious washing (*v.* 21); *From within, out of the heart of men,* thence that which defiles proceeds, thence comes all the mischief. As a corrupt fountain sends forth corrupt streams, so doth a corrupt heart. Divers particulars are specified, as in Matthew; we had one there, which is not here, and that is, *false witness-bearing*; but *seven* are mentioned here, to be added to those we had there. *First, Covetousnesses,* for it is plural; *immoderate desires* of more of the wealth of the world, and the gratifications of sense, and still more, still crying, *Give, give. Secondly, Wickedness,* malice, hatred, and ill-will, a desire to do mischief, and a delight in mischief done. *Thirdly, Deceit;* which is wickedness covered and disguised, that it may be the more securely and effectually committed. *Fourthly, Lasciviousness;* that filthiness and foolish talking which the apostle condemns; the eye full of adultery, and all wanton dalliances. *Fifthly,* The *evil eye*; the envious eye, and the covetous eye, grudging others the good we give them, or grieving at the good they do or enjoy. *Sixthly, Pride*; exalting ourselves in our own conceit above others, and looking down with scorn and contempt upon others. *Seventhly, Foolishness;* imprudence, inconsideration; some understand it especially of vainglorious boasting. *Ill-thinking* is put first, as that which is the spring of our own *com*missions, and *unthinking* put last, as that which is the spring of all our *o*missions. Of all these he concludes (*v.* 23), 1. That they *come from within,* from the corrupt nature. 2. That they *defile the man*; they render a man unfit for communion with God, they bring a stain upon the conscience.

Verses 24–30

I. How *humbly* Christ was pleased to *conceal himself.* Never man was so cried up as he was in Galilee, and therefore, to teach us not to be fond of popular applause, he arose from thence, and *went into the borders* of Tyre and Sidon, where he was little known; and there he entered *into a* private *house*, and he *would have no man to know it.* As there is a time to *appear*, so there is a time to *retire.* Or, he would not be known, because he was among Gentiles, to whom he would not be so forward to show himself as to the tribes of Israel.

II. How *graciously* he was pleased to *manifest himself,* notwithstanding. Though he would not carry a harvest of miraculous cures into those parts, he let fall this one which we have here an account of. *He could not be hid;* for, though a candle may be put under a bushel, the sun cannot. Christ was too well known to be long *hid*, anywhere.

1. The application made to him by a poor woman in distress and trouble. She was a Gentile, a Greek, *an alien to the covenant of promise*; she was by extraction a Syrophenician; she had a *daughter*, a *young* daughter, that was possessed *with the devil.* Her address was, (1) Very humble, pressing, and importunate; *She heard of him,* and *came, and fell at his feet.* Christ never put any from him, that fell at his feet, which a poor trembling soul may do, that has not boldness and confidence to throw itself into his arms. (2) It was very particular; she tells him what she wanted. She besought him that he would *cast forth the devil out of her daughter*, *v.* 26. The greatest blessing we can ask of Christ for our children is, that he would break the power of Satan, that is, the power of sin, in their souls.

2. The discouragement he gave to this address (*v.* 27); He said unto her, "*Let the children first be filled;* let the Jews have all the miracles wrought for them, that they have occasion for, and let not that which was intended for them, be thrown to those who are not of God's family, and who are as *dogs in comparison of them,* and who are as *dogs to them,* snarling at them, and ready to worry them." Where Christ knows the faith of poor supplicants to be strong, he sometimes delights to try it, and put it to the stretch. But his saying, *Let the children first be filled,* intimates that there was mercy in reserve for the Gentiles, and not far off; for the Jews began already to be surfeited with the gospel of Christ, and some of them had desired him to *depart out of their coasts.* The children begin to play with their meat, and their leavings would be a feast for the Gentiles.

3. The turn she gave to this word of Christ, which made against her, and her improvement of it, to make it for her, *v.* 28. She said, "*Yes, Lord,* I own it is true that the *children's bread* ought not to be cast to the dogs, but they were never denied the *crumbs,*

JAMIESON, FAUSSET, BROWN

allowed to stir there, to rise up in thought and affection, and to flow forth in voluntary action, really defiles a man! **For out of the heart proceed evil thoughts**—"evil reasonings"; referring here more immediately to those corrupt reasonings which had stealthily introduced and gradually reared up that hideous fabric of tradition which at length practically nullified the unchangeable principles of the moral law. But the statement is far broader than this; viz., that the first shape which the evil that is in the heart takes, when it begins actively to stir, is that of "considerations" or "reasonings" on certain suggested actions. **murders, adulteries, fornications, thefts, false witness, blasphemies**—detractions, whether directed against God or man; here the reference seems to be to the latter. Mark adds, "covetousnesses"—or desires after more: "wickednesses"—here meaning, perhaps, malignities of various forms; "deceit, lasciviousness"—meaning, excess or enormity of any kind, though by later writers restricted to lewdness; "an evil eye"—meaning, all looks or glances of envy, jealousy, or ill-will towards a neighbor; "pride, foolishness"—in the Old Testament sense of "folly"; i.e., criminal senselessness, the folly of the *heart.* How appalling is this black catalogue! **These are the things which defile a man: but to eat with unwashen hands defileth not a man**—Thus does our Lord sum up this whole searching discourse.

24-37. THE SYROPHOENICIAN WOMAN AND HER DAUGHTER—A DEAF AND DUMB MAN HEALED. (= Matt. 15:21-31).

The Syrophoenician Woman and Her Daughter (vss. 24-30). The first words of this narrative show that the incident followed, in point of time, immediately on what precedes it. **24. And from thence he arose, and went into**—or "unto". **borders of Tyre and Sidon**—the two great Phœnician seaports, but here denoting the territory generally, to the frontiers of which Jesus now came. But did Jesus actually enter this heathen territory? The whole narrative, we think, proceeds upon the supposition that He did. His immediate object seems to have been to avoid the wrath of the Pharisees at the withering exposure He had just made of their traditional religion. **and entered into an house, and would have no man know it**—because He had not come there to minister to heathens. But though not "*sent* but to the lost sheep of the house of Israel" (Matt. 15:24), He hindered not the lost sheep of the vast Gentile world from coming to Him, nor put them away when they did come—as this incident was designed to show. **but he could not be hid**—Christ's fame had early spread from Galilee to this very region (ch. 3:8; Luke 6:17). **25. For a certain woman, whose young daughter had an unclean spirit**—or, as in Matthew, "was badly demonized." **heard of him**—One wonders how; but distress is quick of hearing. **26. The woman was a Greek**—i.e., "a Gentile," as in the margin. **a Syrophœnician by nation**—so called as inhabiting the Phœnician tract of Syria. JUVENAL uses the same term, as was remarked by JUSTIN MARTYR and TERTULLIAN. Matthew calls her "a woman of Canaan"—a more intelligible description to his Jewish readers (cf. Judg. 1:30, 32, 33). **and she besought him that he would cast forth the devil out of her daughter**—"She cried unto Him, saying, Have mercy on me, O Lord, Son of David: my daughter is grievously vexed with a devil" (Matt. 15:22). Thus, though no Israelite herself, she salutes Him as Israel's promised Messiah. Here we must go to Matthew 15:23-25 for some important links in the dialogue omitted by our Evangelist. **27. But Jesus said unto her, Let the children first be filled**—"Is there hope for me here?" "Filled FIRST?" "Then my turn, it seems, *is* coming!"—but then, "The CHILDREN first?" "Ah! when, on that rule, shall my turn ever come!" But ere she has time for these ponderings of His word, another word comes to supplement it. **for it is not meet to take the children's bread, and to cast it unto the dogs**—Is this the death of her hopes? Nay, rather it is life from the dead. Out of the eater shall come forth meat (Judg. 14:14). "At evening-time, it shall be light" (Zech. 14:7). "Ah! I have it now. Had He kept silence, what could I have done but go unblest? but He hath spoken, and the victory is mine." **28. And she answered and said unto him, Yes, Lord**—or, as the same word is rendered in Matthew 15:27. "Truth, Lord." **yet the dogs eat of the children's crumbs**—which fall from their

ADAM CLARKE

19. *Purging all meats.* For what is separated from the different aliments taken into the stomach, and thrown out of the body, is the innutritious parts of all the meats that are eaten; and thus they are purged, nothing being left behind but what is proper for the support of the body.

Evil thoughts. "Wicked dialogues"—for in all evil surmisings the heart holds a conversation, or dialogue, with itself. For *murders,* two MSS. have "envyings," and three others have both. Envy and murder are nearly allied; the former has often led to the latter.

These . . . defile a man. Our Lord's argument is very plain. What goes into the mouth descends into the stomach and other intestines; part is retained for the nourishment of the body, and part is ejected, as being improper to afford nourishment. Nothing of this kind defiles the soul, because it does not enter into it; but the evil principles that are in it, producing evil thoughts, murders, etc., these defile the soul, because they have their seat and operation in it.

24. *Into the borders of Tyre and Sidon.* Or "into the country between Tyre and Sidon."

25. *A certain woman.* See this account of the Syrophoenician woman explained at large, Matt. xv. 21-28.

26. *The woman was a Greek.* All heathen or idolaters were called *Greeks* by the Jews. Jews and Greeks divided the whole world at this period.

The children's bread. The salvation provided for the Jews, who were termed "the children of the kingdom." And cast it to the "little dogs"; such the Gentiles were reputed by the Jewish people, and our Lord uses that form of speech which was common among His countrymen.

Truth, Lord. Yes Lord. This appears to be not so much an assent as a bold reply to our Lord's reason for apparently rejecting her suit.

MATTHEW HENRY

and they are allowed a place *under the table*, that they may be ready to receive them. I ask not for a *loaf*, no, nor for a *morsel*, only for a *crumb*; do not refuse me that." This she speaks, magnifying the abundance of miraculous cures with which she heard the Jews were feasted, in comparison with which a single cure was but as a crumb. Perhaps she had heard of Christ's feeding five thousand lately at once, after which, there could not but be some crumbs left for the dogs.

4. The grant Christ thereupon made of her request. For *this saying, Go thy way*, thou shalt have what thou camest for, *the devil is gone out of thy daughter, v.* 29. This encourages us to *pray* and not to *faint*, not doubting but to prevail at last. Christ's saying that it *was done*, did it effectually, for (*v.* 30) she *came to her house*, depending upon the word of Christ, and so she *found it*, the *devil was gone out*. Christ can conquer Satan at a distance. She found her daughter not in any toss or agitation, but very quietly *laid on the bed*, and reposing herself; waiting for her mother's return, to rejoice with her, that she was so *finely well*.

Verses 31–37

Our Lord Jesus seldom stayed long in a place. When he had cured the woman of Canaan's daughter, he had done what he had to do in that place, and returned *to the sea of Galilee*. He did not come directly thither, but fetched a compass *through the midst of the coasts of Decapolis*, which lay mostly on the other side Jordan.

Now here we have the story of a cure that Christ wrought, which is not recorded by any other of the evangelists; it is of one that was *deaf* and *dumb*.

I. His case was sad, *v.* 32. There were those that brought to him one that was *deaf*; and he had an *impediment in his speech*. He was perfectly unfit for conversation, and deprived both of the pleasure and of the profit of it; he had not the satisfaction either of hearing other people talk, or of telling his own mind. Let us take occasion from hence to give thanks to God for preserving to us the sense of hearing, especially that we may be capable of hearing the word of God; and the faculty of speech, especially that we may be capable of speaking God's praises. They that brought this poor man to Christ, besought him that he would *put his hand upon him*. It is not said, They besought him to *cure him*, but to *put his hand upon him*, to take cognizance of his case, and put forth his power to do to him as he pleased.

II. His cure was solemn, and some of the circumstances of it were singular.

1. Christ *took him aside from the multitude, v.* 33. Ordinarily, he wrought his miracles publicly, but this he did privately. Let us learn of Christ to do good where no eye sees, but his.

2. He used more significant actions, in the doing of this cure, than usual. (1) He *put his fingers into his ears*. (2) He spit upon his own finger, and then *touched his tongue*, and so loosened that with which his tongue was tied; these were no causes that could in the least contribute to his cure, but only signs for the encouraging of his faith and theirs that brought him.

JAMIESON, FAUSSET, BROWN

master's table" (Matt. 15:27). "I thank Thee, O blessed One, for that word! That's my whole case. Not of the children? True. A dog? True also: *Yet* the dogs under the table are allowed to eat of the children's crumbs—the droppings from their master's full table: Give me that, and I am content: One crumb of power and grace from Thy table shall cast the devil out of my daughter." Oh, what lightning-quickness, what reach of instinctive ingenuity, do we behold in this heathen woman! **29. And he said unto her**—"O woman, great is thy faith" (Matt. 15:28). As BENGEL beautifully remarks, Jesus "marvelled" only at two things—*faith* and *unbelief* (see on Luke 7:9). **For this saying go thy way; the devil is gone out of thy daughter**—That moment the deed was done. **30. And when she was come to her house, she found the devil gone out, and her daughter laid upon the bed**—But Matthew is more specific; "And her daughter was made whole from that very hour." The wonderfulness of this case in all its features has been felt in every age of the Church, and the balm it has administered, and will yet administer, to millions will be known only in that day that shall reveal the secrets of all hearts.

Deaf and Dumb Man Healed (vss. 31-37). **31. And again, departing from the coasts of Tyre and Sidon, he came unto the Sea of Galilee**—or, according to what has very strong claims to be regarded as the true text here, "And again, departing from the coasts of Tyre, He came through Sidon to the Sea of Galilee." The MSS. in favor of this reading, though not the most numerous, are weighty, while the versions agreeing with it are among the most ancient; and all the best critical editors and commentators adopt it. In this case we must understand that our Lord, having once gone out of the Holy Land the length of Tyre, proceeded as far north as Sidon, though without ministering, so far as appears, in those parts, and then bent His steps in a southeasterly direction. There is certainly a difficulty in the supposition of so long a *detour* without any missionary object: and some may think this sufficient to cast the balance in favor of the received reading. Be this as it may, on returning from these coasts of Tyre, He passed **through the midst of the coasts**—frontiers—**of Decapolis**—crossing the Jordan, therefore, and approaching the lake on its east side. Here Matthew, who omits the details of the cure of this deaf and dumb man, introduces some particulars, from which we learn that it was only one of a great number. "And Jesus," says that Evangelist (15:29-31), "departed from thence, and came nigh unto the Sea of Galilee, and went up into a mountain"—the mountain range bounding the lake on the northeast, in Decapolis: "And great multitudes came unto Him, having with them lame, blind, dumb, maimed"—not "mutilated," which is but a secondary sense of the word, but "deformed"—"and many others, and cast them down at Jesus' feet; and He healed them: insomuch that the multitude [multitudes] wondered, when they saw the dumb to speak, the maimed to be whole, the lame to walk, and the blind to see; and they glorified the God of Israel"—who after so long and dreary an absence of visible manifestation, had returned to bless His people as of old (cf. Luke 7: 16). Beyond this it is not clear from the Evangelist's language that the people saw into the claims of Jesus. Well, of these cases Mark here singles out one, whose cure had something peculiar in it. **32. And they bring unto him one that was deaf ... and they beseech him to put his hand upon him**—In their eagerness they appear to have been somewhat too officious. Though usually doing as here suggested, He will deal with this case in His own way. **33. And he took him aside from the multitude**—As in another case He "took the blind man by the hand and led him out of the town" (ch. 8: 23), probably to fix his undistracted attention on Himself, and, by means of certain actions He was about to do, to awaken and direct his attention to the proper source of relief. **and put his fingers into his ears**—As his indistinct articulation arose from his deafness, our Lord addresses Himself to this first. To the impotent man He said, "Wilt thou be made whole?" to the blind men, "What will ye that I shall do unto you?" and "Believe ye that I am able to do this?" (John 5:6; Matt. 20:32; 9: 28.) But as this patient could *hear* nothing, our Lord substitutes symbolical actions upon each of the organs affected. **and he spit and touched his tongue**—moistening the man's parched tongue with saliva from His own mouth, as if to lubricate the organ or facilitate its free motion; thus indicating the source of the healing virtue to be His own person. (For similar actions, see ch. 8:23; John

ADAM CLARKE

The little dogs share with the children, for they eat the crumbs which fall from their masters' table. I do not desire what is provided for these highly favored children, only what they leave. A single exertion of Thy almighty power, in the healing of my afflicted daughter, is all that I wish for; and this the highly favored Jews can well spare without lessening the provision made for themselves. Is not this the sense of this noble woman's reply?

30. *Laid upon the bed.* The demon having tormented her so that her bodily strength was exhausted, and she was now laid upon the couch to take a little rest.

G. CAMPBELL MORGAN:

The next picture that Mark gives is that of a man deaf and having an impediment in his speech. This is a picture of personal disability. The whole point of the picture, however, as it occurs here in the Gospel, is not that of the man's personal disability. It is rather that of the fact that this man in this Gentile region was brought to Jesus by his friends. It is never safe to base too much upon the argument of silence, but at least it is an interesting fact to note that the man made no appeal to Christ. He did not come to Christ on his own initiative. His friends brought him and besought Jesus that He would touch him. So while the man stands central in the picture, in some senses, I look again, and in the sympathy of these men for their friend, men outside the company of Israel, outside that racial relationship which was religious in its function, I see something human. I am again impressed by the elemental superiority over racial disadvantage. Oh, yes, these men were Gentiles, but they were men. Oh! yes, these people also probably were of the Canaanite race, but they had sympathy in their heart; witness their effort to bring their friend to Jesus.—*The Gospel According to Mark*

32. *They bring unto him one that was deaf, and had an impediment in his speech.* Though from the *letter* of the text, it does not appear that this man was absolutely deprived of speech (for *mogilalos* literally signifies one that cannot speak plainly, a stammerer), yet it is certain also that the word means a dumb person; and it is likely that the person in question was dumb, because he was deaf; and it is generally found that he who is totally deaf is dumb also.

33. *And he spit, and touched his tongue.* This place is exceedingly difficult. There is scarcely an action of our Lord's life but one can see an evident reason for, except this. Various interpretations are given of it—none of them satisfies my mind. After all, it is possible that what is attributed here to Christ belongs to the person who was cured. I will give my sense of the place in a short paraphrase: And Jesus *took him aside from the multitude: and* (the deaf man) *put his fingers into his ears*, intimating thereby to Christ that they were so stopped that he could not hear; *and having spat out*, that there might be nothing remaining in his mouth to offend the sight when Christ should look at his tongue, *he touched his tongue*, showing to Christ that it was so bound that he could not speak;

MATTHEW HENRY

3. He *looked up to heaven.* Thus he signified that it was by a divine power. He also hereby directed his patient who could *see,* though he could not *hear,* to look up to heaven for relief.

4. He sighed; not as if he found any difficulty in working this miracle; thus he expressed his pity for the miseries of human life, and his sympathy with the afflicted in their afflictions, as one that was himself *touched with the feeling of their infirmities.*

5. He said, *Ephphatha;* that is, *Be opened. Be opened,* served both parts of the cure; "Let the *ears* be *opened,* let the *lips* be *opened,* let him hear and speak freely," and the effect was answerable (*v.* 35); *Straightway his ears were opened, and the string of his tongue was loosed.* Happy he who, as soon as he had his hearing and speech, had the blessed Jesus so near him, to converse with.

Now this cure was, (1) A proof of Christ's being the Messiah; for it was foretold that by his power the *ears of the deaf should be unstopped,* and the *tongue of the dumb* should be made to *sing,* Isa. xxxv. 5, 6. (2) It was a specimen of the operations of his gospel upon the minds of men. The great command of the gospel, and grace of Christ to poor sinners, is *Ephphatha—Be opened.* He *opens the heart,* and thereby opens the ear to receive the word of God, and opens the mouth in prayer and praises.

6. He ordered it to be kept very private, but it was made very public. It was his humility, that he *charged them they should tell no man, v.* 36. Most men will proclaim their own goodness, or, at least, desire that others should proclaim it. We should take pleasure in doing good, but not in its being known. It was their zeal, that they published it, before Christ would have had it published. But they meant honestly, and therefore it is to be reckoned rather an act of indiscretion than an act of disobedience, *v.* 36. But they that told it, and they that heard it, were *beyond measure astonished.* This was said by everybody, it was the common verdict, *He hath done all things well* (*v.* 37). They are ready to witness for him, not only that he has done no evil, but that he has done a great deal of good, and has done it well, and all gratis, *without money and without price.* He *maketh both the deaf to hear, and the dumb to speak;* and that is *well,* and therefore *they* are inexcusable who will speak ill of him.

JAMIESON, FAUSSET, BROWN

9:6.) **34. And looking up to heaven**—ever acknowledging His Father, even while the healing was seen to flow from Himself (see on John 5:19). **he sighed**—"over the wreck," says TRENCH, "which sin had brought about, and the malice of the devil in deforming the fair features of God's original creation." But, we take it, there was a yet more painful impression of that "evil thing and bitter" whence all our ills have sprung, and which, when "Himself took our infirmities and bare our sicknesses" (Matt. 8:17), became mysteriously His own.

In thought of these his brows benign,
Not even in healing, cloudless shine.
KEBLE

and saith unto him, Ephphatha, that is, Be opened—Our Evangelist, as remarked on ch. 5:41, loves to give such wonderful words just as they were spoken. **35. And straightway his ears were opened**—This is mentioned first as the source of the other derangement. **and the string of his tongue was loosed, and he spake plain**—The cure was thus alike instantaneous and perfect. **36. And he charged them that they should tell no man**—Into this very region He had sent the man out of whom had been cast the legion of devils, to proclaim "what the Lord had done for him" (ch. 5:19). Now He will have them "tell no man." But in the former case there was no danger of obstructing His ministry by "blazing the matter" (ch. 1:45), as He Himself had left the region; whereas now He was sojourning in it. **but the more he charged them, so much the more a great deal they published it**—They could not be restrained; nay, the prohibition seemed only to whet their determination to publish His fame. **37. And were beyond measure astonished, saying, He hath done all things well**—reminding us, says TRENCH, of the words of the first creation (Gen. 1: 31, LXX), upon which we are thus not unsuitably thrown back, for Christ's work is in the truest sense "a new creation," **he maketh both the deaf to hear and the dumb to speak**—"and they glorified the God of Israel" (Matt. 15:31). See on vs. 31 of this chapter.

ADAM CLARKE

and he looked up to heaven, as if to implore assistance from above; *and he groaned,* being distressed because of his present affliction, and thus implored relief. For, not being able to *speak,* he could only *groan* and *look up,* expressing by these signs, as well as he could, his afflicted state, and the desire he had to be relieved. Then Jesus, having compassion upon him, *said, Be opened: and immediately his ears were opened,* so that he could hear distinctly; and the impediment to his speaking was removed, so that *he spake properly.* The original will admit of this interpretation; and this, I am inclined to believe, is the true meaning of this otherwise (to me and many others) unaccountable passage.

35. *He spake plain.* "Distinctly, without stammering."

36. *Tell no man.* See on Matt. viii. 4. This miracle is not mentioned by any other of the Evangelists—another proof that Mark did not abridge Matthew.

37. *He hath done all things well.* This has been, and ever will be, true of every part of our Lord's conduct. In creation, providence, and redemption He hath done all things well.

MATTHEW HENRY

CHAPTER 8

Verses 1–9

We had the story of a miracle very like this before, in this gospel (*ch.* vi. 35), and of this same miracle (Matt. xv. 32).

1. Our Lord Jesus was greatly followed; *The multitude was very great* (*v.* 1); the common people, who had more honesty, and therefore more true wisdom, than their leaders, kept up their high thoughts of him. With such Christ conversed, and was familiar; this encouraged the meanest to come to him for life and grace.

2. *They were with him three days, and had nothing to eat;* that was hard service. Never let the Pharisee say, that *Christ's disciples fast not.* Yet they *continued* with Christ, and did not speak of leaving him till he spoke of dismissing them. True zeal makes nothing of hardships in the way of duty. It was an old saying among the Puritans, *Brown bread and the gospel are good fare.*

3. Christ said, *I have compassion on the multitude.* Whom the proud Pharisees looked upon with disdain, the humble Jesus looked upon with pity and tenderness. But that which he chiefly considers, is, *They have been with me three days, and have nothing to eat.* Whatever losses we sustain, or hardships we go through, for Christ's sake, and in love to him, he will take care that they shall be made up to us one way or other. Observe with what sympathy Christ saith (*v.* 3), *If I send them away fasting to their own houses, they will faint by the way.* He considered that *many of them came from afar,* and had a great way home. When we see *multitudes* attending upon the word preached, it is comfortable to think that Christ knows whence they all come, though we do not. Christ would by no means have them go home fasting, for it is not his manner to send those *empty* away from him, that in a right manner attend on him.

4. The doubts of Christians are sometimes made to work for the magnifying of the power of Christ. The disciples could not imagine whence so many men should be *satisfied with bread* here in this wilderness, *v.* 4. That therefore must needs be *wonderful,* which the disciples looked upon as *impossible.*

5. Christ's time to act for the relief of his people, is, when things are brought to the last extremity. That he might not invite them to follow him for the *loaves,* he did not supply them but when they were

JAMIESON, FAUSSET, BROWN

CHAPTER 8

VSS. 1-26. FOUR THOUSAND MIRACULOUSLY FED—A SIGN FROM HEAVEN SOUGHT AND REFUSED—THE LEAVEN OF THE PHARISEES AND SADDUCEES—A BLIND MAN AT BETHSAIDA RESTORED TO SIGHT. (= Matt. 15:32 to 16:12.) This section of miscellaneous matter evidently follows the preceding one in point of time, as will be seen by observing how it is introduced by Matthew.

Feeding of the Four Thousand (vss. 1-9). **1. In those days the multitude being very great . . .**

2. I have compassion on the multitude—an expression of that deep emotion in the Redeemer's heart which always preceded some remarkable interposition for relief. (See Matt. 14:14; 20:34; Mark 1: 41; Luke 7:13; also Matt. 9:36, before the mission of the Twelve; cf. Judg. 2:18; 10:16.) **because they have now been with me**—in constant attendance—**three days, and have nothing to eat: 3. And if I send them away fasting to their own houses, they will faint by the way**—In their eagerness they seem not to have thought of the need of provisions for such a length of time; but the Lord thought of it. In Matt. (15:32) it is, "I will not send them away fasting"—or rather, "To send them away fasting I am unwilling." **4. From whence can a man satisfy these men with bread here in the wilderness?**—Though the question here is the same as when He fed the five thousand, they evidently *now* meant no more by it than that *they* had not the means of feeding the multitude; modestly leaving the Lord to decide what was to be done. And this will the more appear from His not now trying them, as before, by saying, "They need not depart, give ye them to eat"; but simply asking what they had, and then giving His directions. **5. And he asked them. How many loaves have ye? And they said, Seven**—It was important in this case, as in the former, that the precise number of the loaves should be brought out. Thus also does the distinctness of the two miracles appear.

ADAM CLARKE

CHAPTER 8

1. *The multitude being very great.* Or rather, "There was again a great multitude." Instead of *very great,* I read *again a great,* which is the reading of many MSS. and versions. There had been such a multitude gathered together once before, who were fed in the same way. See chap. vi. 34, etc.

2. *Have nothing to eat.* If they had brought any provisions with them, they were now entirely expended, and they stood in immediate need of a supply.

3. *For divers of them came from far.* And they could not possibly reach their respective homes without perishing, unless they got food.

MATTHEW HENRY

utterly reduced, and then he *sent them away*.

6. The bounty of Christ is inexhaustible. Christ *repeated* this miracle. His favours are renewed, as our wants and necessities are. In the former miracle, Christ used all the bread he had, which was *five loaves*, and fed all the guests he had, which were *five thousand*. **He might have said, "If five loaves would feed five thousand, four may feed four thousand"**; he took all the seven loaves, and fed with them the four thousand; for he would teach us to use what we have, and make the best of that which is.

7. In our Father's house *there is bread enough, and to spare*. Those need not fear wanting, that have Christ to live upon.

8. It is good for those that follow Christ, *to keep together*. Christ fed them all. Christ's sheep must abide by the flock, and verily they shall be fed.

Verses 10–21

Still Christ is upon motion; now he visits the parts of Dalmanutha. Meeting with occasions of dispute, there, and not with opportunities of doing good, he *entered into the ship again* (*v*. 13), and came back.

I. How he refused to gratify the Pharisees, who challenged him to give them a *sign from heaven*. They *came forth* on purpose to *question with him*, that they might ensnare him.

1. They demanded of him a *sign from heaven*, as if the signs he gave them on earth were not sufficient. They demanded this sign, *tempting him;* not in hopes that he would give it them, that they might imagine themselves to have a pretence for their infidelity.

2. He denied them their demand; He *sighed deeply in his spirit, v*. 12. He *groaned* (so some), being grieved for the *hardness of their hearts*. It troubles him, that sinners should thus stand in their own light, and put a bar in their own door. He expostulates with them upon this demand; "*Why doth this generation seek after a sign;* this generation, that is so unworthy to have the gospel brought to it, and to have any sign accompanying it; *this generation*, that has had such plenty of sensible and merciful signs given them in the cure of their sick? What an absurdity is it for them to desire a sign!" (2) He refuses to answer their demand; *Verily, I say unto you, there shall no sign be given to this generation*. He denied them, and then *left them*, as men not fit to be talked with; if they will not be convinced, they shall not; leave them to their strong delusions.

JAMIESON, FAUSSET, BROWN

9. And they that had eaten were about four thousand: and he sent them away—Had not our Lord distinctly referred, in this very chapter and in two successive sentences, to the feeding of the five thousand and of the four thousand as two distinct miracles, many critics would have insisted that they were but two different representations of one and the same miracle, as they do of the two expulsions of the buyers and sellers from the temple, at the beginning and end of our Lord's ministry. But even in spite of what our Lord says, it is painful to find such men as NEANDER endeavoring to identify the two miracles. The localities, though both on the eastern side of the lake, were different; the time was different; the preceding and following circumstances were different; the period during which the people continued fasting was different—in the one case not even one entire day, in the other three days; the number fed was different—five thousand in the one case, in the other four thousand; the number of the loaves was different—five in the one case, in the other seven; the number of the fishes in the one case is definitely stated by all the four Evangelists—two; in the other case both give them indefinitely—"a few small fishes"; in the one case the multitude were commanded to sit down "upon the green grass"; in the other "on the ground"; in the one case the number of the baskets taken up filled with the fragments was twelve, in the other seven; but more than all, perhaps, because apparently quite incidental, in the one case the name given to the kind of baskets used is the same in all the four narratives—the *cophinus* (see on ch. 6:43); in the other case the name given to the kind of baskets used, while it is the same in both the narratives, is quite different—the *spuris*, a basket large enough to hold a man's body, for Paul was let down in one of these from the wall of Damascus (Acts 9:25). It might be added, that in the one case the people, in a frenzy of enthusiasm, would have taken Him by force to make Him a king; in the other case no such excitement is recorded. In view of these things, who could have believed that these were one and the same miracle, even if the Lord Himself had not expressly distinguished them?

Sign from Heaven Sought (vss. 10-13). **10. And straightway he entered into a ship**—"into the ship," or "embarked." **with his disciples, and came into the parts of Dalmanutha**—In Matthew (15:39) it is "the coasts of Magdala." Magdala and Dalmanutha were both on the western shore of the lake, and probably not far apart. From the former the surname "Magdalene" was probably taken, to denote the residence of Mary Magdalene. Dalmanutha may have been a village, but it cannot now be identified with certainty. **11. seeking of him a sign from heaven, tempting him**—not in the least desiring evidence for their conviction, but hoping to entrap Him. The first part of the answer is given in Matthew alone (16:2, 3): "He answered and said unto them, When it is evening, ye say, It will be fair weather: for the sky is red. And in the morning, It will be foul weather to-day: for the sky is red and lowering [sullen, gloomy]. Hypocrites! ye can discern the face of the sky; but can ye not discern the signs of the times?" The same simplicity of purpose and careful observation of the symptoms of approaching events which they showed in common things would enable them to "discern the signs of the times"—or rather "seasons," to which the prophets pointed for the manifestation of the Messiah. The scepter had departed from Judah; Daniel's seventy weeks were expiring, etc.; and many other significant indications of the close of the old economy, and preparations for a freer and more comprehensive one, might have been discerned. But all was lost upon them. **12. And he sighed deeply in his spirit**—The language is very strong. These glimpses into the interior of the Redeemer's heart, in which our Evangelist abounds, are more precious than rubies. The state of the Pharisaic heart, which prompted this desire for a fresh sign, went to His very soul. **and saith, Why doth this generation**—"this wicked and adulterous generation" (Matt. 16:4)—**seek after a sign?**—when they have had such abundant evidence already. **There shall no sign be given unto this generation**—lit., "If there shall be given to this generation a sign"; a Jewish way of expressing a solemn and peremptory determination to the contrary (cf. Heb. 4:5; Ps. 95:11, *Margin*). "A generation incapable of appreciating such demonstrations shall not be gratified with them." In Matthew 16:4 He added, "but the sign of the prophet Jonas." (See on Matthew 12:39, 40.) **13. And he left them**—no doubt with tokens of displeasure.

The Leaven of the Pharisees and Sadducees (vss.

ADAM CLARKE

7. *And they had a few small fishes*. This is not noticed in the parallel place, Matt. xv. 36.

They did all eat, and were filled. "They were satisfied." The husks of worldly pleasures may *fill* the man, but cannot *satisfy* the soul.

Four thousand. Let the poor learn from these miracles to trust in God for support. Whatever His ordinary providence denies, His miraculous power will supply.

He sent away the multitude. But not before He had instructed their souls, and fed and healed their bodies.

CHARLES H. SPURGEON:

Brethren, who knows what may come out of seven loaves and a few small fishes? Yea, the enemies may do what they like; they may preach what they please; they may take away one pulpit after another from the orthodox; they may bury us under the rubbish of evolution and false philosophy; but we shall rise again. These small clouds will soon blow over. There may not remain one single sound expounder of the gospel; but as long as God lives, the gospel will not die. Its power may slumber, but ere long it shall awake out of sleep, and cry like a mighty man who shouteth by reason of wine. As long as we have one match left, we can yet set the world on fire. As long as one Bible remains, the empire of Satan is in danger. Only barley loaves and a few small fishes were in the possession of the apostolic company; but Jesus found them and began to work with them.—*The Treasury of the New Testament*

10. *Dalmanutha*. See the note on Matt. xv. 39.

The coasts of Magdala. In the parallel place, Mark viii. 10, this place is called Dalmanutha. Either Magdala was formed by a transposition of letters from Dalman, to which the Syriac termination *atha* had been added, or the one of these names refers to the country and the other to a town in that neighborhood.

Shew them a sign. These sects, however opposed among themselves, most cordially unite in their opposition to Christ and His truth. *Tempting . . . him*. Feigning a desire to have His doctrine fully proved to them, that they might credit it, and become His disciples, but having no other design than to betray and ruin Him.

12. *And he sighed deeply in his spirit*. Or "having deeply groaned"—so the word properly means. He was exceedingly affected at their obstinacy and hardness of heart. See Matt. xvi. 1-4.

Wicked and adulterous generation. The Jewish people are represented in the Sacred Writings as married to the Most High; but, like a disloyal wife, forsaking their true Husband, and uniting themselves to Satan and sin. *Seeketh after a sign*, "seeketh sign upon sign," or still "another sign." Our blessed Lord had already wrought miracles sufficient to demonstrate both His divine mission and His divinity; only one was further necessary to take away the scandal of His cross and death, to fulfill the Scriptures, and to establish the Christian religion; and that was His resurrection from the dead, which, He here states, was typified in the case of Jonah.

MATTHEW HENRY

II. How he warned his disciples against the leaven of the Pharisees and of Herod. Observe here,

1. What the caution was (*v.* 15); "*Take heed, beware,* lest ye partake of the *leaven of the Pharisees.*" Matthew adds, *and of the Sadducees*; Mark adds, *and of Herod.* The leaven of both was the same; they were unsatisfied with the signs they had, and would have others of their own devising; "Take heed of *this leaven*" (saith Christ), "be convinced by the miracles ye have seen."

2. How they misunderstood this caution. It seems, at their putting to sea this time, they had *forgotten to take bread,* and *had not in their ship more than one loaf, v.* 14. They *reasoned among themselves,* what should be the meaning of this caution, and concluded "*It is because we have no bread.*" They *reasoned it,* they *disputed* about it; one said, "It was owing to you"; and the other said, "It was owing to you, that we are so ill provided for this voyage." Thus distrust of God makes Christ's disciples quarrel among themselves.

3. The reproof Christ gave them for their uneasiness in this matter. The reproof is given with some warmth, for he knew their hearts, and knew they needed to be thus soundly chidden; "*Perceive ye not yet, neither understand? Have ye your hearts yet hardened? Having eyes, see ye not? Having ears, hear ye not?* How strangely stupid and senseless are ye! *Do ye not remember when I broke the five loaves among the five thousand,* and soon after, the *seven loaves among the four thousand?* Do ye not remember *how many baskets full ye took up* of the fragments?" Yes, they did remember. and could tell that they took up *twelve* baskets full one time, and *seven* another; "Why, then," saith he, "*how is it that ye do not understand?* As if he that multiplied *five* loaves, and *seven,* could not multiply one." They seemed to suspect that that one was not matter enough to work upon. As if it were not all alike to the Lord, to save by many or few, and as easy to make one loaf to feed five thousand as five. It was therefore proper to remind them, not only of the sufficiency, but of the overplus, of the former meals. The experiences we have had of God's goodness to us in the way of duty, greatly aggravate our distrust of him. Our *not understanding* of the true intent and meaning of God's favours to us, is equivalent to our not remembering of them. We are *therefore* overwhelmed with present cares and distrusts, because we do not *understand,* and remember, what we have known and seen of the power and goodness of our Lord Jesus. When we thus *forget the works of God,* and distrust him, we should chide ourselves severely for it, as Christ doth his disciples here.

Verses 22–26

This cure is related only by this evangelist.

I. Here is a *blind man* brought to Christ by his friends, with a desire that he would *touch him, v.* 22. Here appears the faith of those that brought him; but the man himself showed not that earnestness for, or expectation of, a cure that other blind men did. If those that are spiritually blind, do not pray for themselves, yet let their friends and relations pray for them, that Christ would be pleased to *touch them.*

II. Here is Christ *leading* this blind man, *v.* 23. He did not bid his friends lead him, he himself *took him by the hand, and led him.* Never had poor blind man such a Leader. He led him *out of the town.* Had he herein only designed privacy, he might have led him into a house, into an inner chamber, and have cured him there. Perhaps Christ took the blind man *out of the town,* that he might have a larger prospect in the *open fields,* to try his sight with, than he could have in the *close streets.*

III. Here is the cure of the blind man. In this cure we may observe, 1. That Christ used a *sign*; he *spat on his eyes,* and *put his hand upon him.* He could have cured him, as he did others, with a word, but thus he was pleased to assist his faith which was very weak, and to help him against his *unbelief.* 2. That the cure was wrought *gradually,* which was not usual in Christ's miracles. He *asked him if he saw aught, v.* 23. And he *looked up*; and he said, *I see men as trees walking;* he could not distinguish men from trees, otherwise than that he could discern them to move. He had some glimmerings of sight, and betwixt him and the sky could perceive a man erect like a tree. 3. It was soon completed;

JAMIESON, FAUSSET, BROWN

14-21). **14. Now the disciples had forgotten to take bread, neither had they in the ship with them more than one loaf**—This is another example of that graphic circumstantiality which gives such a charm to this briefest of the four Gospels. The circumstance of the "one loaf" only remaining, as WEBSTER and WILKINSON remark, was more suggestive of their Master's recent miracles than the entire absence of provisions. **15. And he charged them, saying, Take heed, beware of the leaven of the Pharisees**—"and of the Sadducees" (Matt. 16:6). **and of the leaven of Herod**—The teaching or "doctrine" (Matt. 16:12) of the Pharisees and of the Sadducees was quite different, but both were equally pernicious; and the Herodians, though rather a political party, were equally envenomed against our Lord's spiritual teaching. See on Matthew 12:14. The *penetrating* and *diffusive* quality of leaven, for good or bad, is the ground of the comparison. **16. And they reasoned among themselves, saying, It is because we have no bread**—But a little while ago He was tried with the obduracy of the Pharisees; now He is tried with the obtuseness of His own disciples. The *nine* questions following each other in rapid succession (vss. 17-21) show how deeply He was hurt at this want of spiritual apprehension, and worse still, their low thoughts of Him, as if He would utter so solemn a warning on so petty a subject. It will be seen, however, from the very form of their conjecture, "It is because *we* have no bread," and our Lord's astonishment that they should not by that time have known better with what He took up His attention—that He ever left *the whole care for His own temporal wants to the Twelve:* that He did this so entirely, that finding they were reduced to their last loaf they felt as if unworthy of such a trust, and could not think but that the same thought was in their Lord's mind which was pressing upon their own; but that in this they were so far wrong that it hurt His feelings—sharp just in proportion to His love—that such a thought of Him should have entered their minds! Who that, like angels, "desire to look into these things" will not prize such glimpses above gold? **17. have ye your heart yet hardened?**—How strong an expression to use of true-hearted disciples! See on ch. 6:52. **18. Having eyes, see ye not? and having ears, hear ye not?**—See on Matthew 13:13. **and do ye not remember? 19. When I brake the five loaves among**—the—**five thousand, how many baskets full of fragments took ye up? . . . 21. How is it that ye do not understand?**—"do not understand that the warning I gave you could not have been prompted by any such petty consideration as the want of loaves in your scrip." Profuse as were our Lord's miracles, we see from this that they were not wrought at random, but that He carefully noted their minutest details, and desired that this should be done by those who witnessed, as doubtless by all who read the record of them. Even the different kind of baskets used at the two miraculous feedings, so carefully noted in the two narratives, are here also referred to; the one smaller, of which there were twelve, the other much larger, of which there were seven.

Blind Man at Bethsaida Restored to Sight (vss. 22-26). **22. And he cometh to Bethsaida**—Bethsaida-Julias, on the northeast side of the lake, whence after this He proceeded to Cæsarea Philippi (vs. 27). **and they bring a blind man unto him, and besought him to touch him**—See on ch. 7:32. **23. And he took the blind man by the hand, and led him out of the town**—Of the deaf and dumb man it is merely said that "He took him aside" (ch. 7:33); but this blind man He *led by the hand* out of the town, doing it Himself rather than employing another—great humility, exclaims BENGEL—that He might gain his confidence and raise his expectation. **and when be had spit on his eyes**—the organ affected—see on ch. 7:33. **and put his hands upon him, he asked him if he saw aught. 24. And he looked up, and said, I see men as trees, walking**—This is one of the cases in which one edition of what is called the received text differs from another. That which is decidedly the best supported, and has also internal evidence on its side is this: "I see men; for I see [them] as trees walking"—i.e., he could distinguish them from trees only by their motion; a minute mark of truth in the narrative, as ALFORD observes, describing how human objects had appeared to him during that gradual failing of sight which had ended in blindness.

ADAM CLARKE

14. *Now the disciples had forgotten to take bread.* See all this, to v. 21, explained at large on Matt. xvi. 4-12.

Beware of the leaven. Bad doctrines act in the soul as leaven does in meal; they assimilate the whole spirit to their own nature. A man's particular creed has a greater influence on his tempers and conduct than most are aware of. Pride, hypocrisy, and worldly-mindedness, which constituted *the leaven of the Pharisees* and Sadducees, ruin the major part of the world.

They reasoned. For, as Lightfoot observes, the term leaven was very rarely used among the Jews to signify doctrine, and therefore the disciples did not immediately apprehend His meaning.

Do ye not yet understand . . . the five loaves . . . Neither the seven? How astonishing is it that these men should have any fear of lacking bread, after having seen the two miracles which our blessed Lord alludes to above!

They now perceived that He warned them. against the superstition of the Pharisees, which produced hypocrisy, pride, envy, etc., and the false doctrine of the Sadducees, which denied the existence of a spiritual world, the immortality of the soul, the resurrection of the body, and the providence of God.

23. *And he took the blind man by the hand.* Giving him proof of His readiness to help him, and thus preparing him for the cure which He was about to work. *Led him out of the town.* Thus showing the inhabitants that He considered them unworthy of having another miracle wrought among them. *When he had spit on his eyes.* There is a similar transaction to this mentioned in John ix. 6. It is likely this was done merely to separate the eyelids, as in certain cases of blindness they are found always gummed together. It required a miracle to restore the sight, and this was done in consequence of Christ having laid His hands upon the blind man. It required no miracle to separate the eyelids, and therefore natural means only were employed—this was done by rubbing them with spittle, but whether by Christ or by the blind man is not absolutely certain. See on chap. vii. 33.

24. *I see men as trees, walking.* His sight was so imperfect that he could not distinguish between men and trees, only by the motion of the former.

MATTHEW HENRY

Christ never doeth *his work* by the halves. He *put his hands again upon his eyes*, to disperse the remaining darkness, and then bade him look up again, and he *saw every man clearly*, *v.* 25. Now Christ took this way, (1) Because he would not *tie himself to a method*. He did not cure by *rote*. Providence gains the same end in different ways, that men may attend its motions with an *implicit faith*. (2) Because it should be to the patient *according to his faith*; and perhaps this man's faith was at first very weak, but afterward gathered strength, and accordingly his cure was. (3) Thus Christ would show how, and in what method, those are healed by his grace, who by nature are *spiritually blind*; at first, their knowledge is confused, they see *men as trees walking*; but like the light of the morning, it *shines more and more to the perfect day*, and then they *see all things clearly*.

IV. The directions Christ gave the man he had cured, not to *tell it to any in the town of Bethsaida*, nor so much as to *go into the town*. Christ doth not forbid him to tell it to others, but he must not tell it to *any in the town*. Slighting Christ's favours is forfeiting them; and Christ will make those know the worth of their privileges by the want of them, that would not know them otherwise. They will not see, and therefore shall not see.

Verses 27–38

We have read a great deal of the doctrine Christ preached, and the miracles he wrought. It is now time for us to pause a little, and to consider what these things mean. What shall we think of them? Is the record of these things designed only for an amusement, or to furnish us with matter for discourse? No, certainly *these things are written, that we may believe that Jesus is the Christ the Son of God* (John xx. 31). Three things we are here taught to infer from the miracles Christ wrought.

I. They *prove* that he is the Son of God, and Saviour of the world. This his disciples, who were the eye-witnesses of those works, here profess their belief of.

1. Christ enquired of them: *Who do men say that I am? v.* 27. Though it is a small thing for us to be judged of men, yet it may sometimes do us good to know what people say of us, not that we may seek our own glory, but that we may hear of our faults.

2. The account they gave him, was such as plainly intimated the *high opinion* the people had of him. Though they came short of the truth, yet they were convinced by his miracles that he was an extraordinary person, with a divine commission. None of the people said that he was a Deceiver, but some said that *he was John Baptist*, others *Elias*, others *one of the prophets*, *v.* 28. All agreed that he was one *risen from the dead*.

3. The account they gave him of their own sentiments concerning him. *But whom say ye that I am?* To this they have an answer ready, *Thou art the Christ*, the Messiah often promised, and long expected, *v.* 29. This they knew, and must shortly publish and maintain; but for the present they must keep it secret (*v.* 30), till the proof of it was completed, and they were completely qualified to maintain it.

II. These miracles of Christ *take off the offence of the cross*, and assure us that Christ was, in it, not conquered, but a Conqueror. Now that the disciples are convinced that Jesus is the Christ, they may bear to hear of his sufferings, *v.* 31.

1. Christ *taught* his disciples that he must *suffer many things*, Though they had got over the vulgar error of the Messiah's being a temporal Prince, yet still they retained it, so far as to expect that he would *shortly restore the kingdom to Israel*. Christ here gives them a prospect of the contrary, that he must be *rejected of the elders, and the chief priests*, and *the scribes*; that, instead of being crowned, *he must be killed*, he must be crucified, and *after three days he must rise again* to a heavenly life, and to be *no more in this world*. This he spoke *openly* (*v.* 32). He said it freely and plainly, and did not wrap it up in ambiguous expressions. He spoke it cheerfully and without any terror, and would have them to hear it so: he spoke that saying *boldly*, as one that not only knew he *must* suffer and die, but made it his own act and deed.

2. Peter opposed it; *He took him, and began to rebuke him*. Here Peter showed more love than discretion, a zeal for Christ, and his safety, but not according to knowledge. He took hold of him, as it were to stop and hinder him, took him in his arms, and embraced him (so some understand it); or he took him aside privately, and *began to rebuke* him. **This was not the language of the least authority, but** of the greatest affection. Our Lord Jesus allowed his disciples to be free with him, but Peter here took too

JAMIESON, FAUSSET, BROWN

25. After that he put his hands again upon his eyes, and made him look up; and he was restored, and saw every man clearly—Perhaps the one operation perfectly restored the *eyes*, while the other imparted immediately the *faculty of using them*. It is the only recorded example of a *progressive* cure, and it certainly illustrates similar methods in the spiritual kingdom. Of the four recorded cases of sight restored, all the patients save one either *came* or *were brought* to the Physician. In the case of the man born blind, *the Physician came* to the patient. So some seek and find Christ; of others He is found who seek Him not.

26. Neither go into the town, nor tell it to any in the town—Besides the usual reasons against going about "blazing the matter," retirement in this case would be salutary to himself.

27-38. Peter's Noble Confession of Christ—Our Lord's First Explicit Announcement of His Approaching Sufferings, Death, and Resurrection—His Rebuke of Peter, and Warning to All the Twelve. (= Matt. 16:13-27; Luke 9:18-26.) For the exposition, see on Matthew 16:13-28.

he asked his disciples—"by the way," says Mark (8:27), and "as He was alone praying," says Luke (9:18). **saying, Whom**—or more grammatically, "Who"—**do men say that I the Son of man am?**—(or, "that the Son of man is"—the recent editors omitting here the *me* of Mark and Luke; though the evidence seems pretty nearly balanced)—i.e., 'What are the views generally entertained of Me, the Son of man, after going up and down among them so long?' He had now closed the first great stage of His ministry, and was just entering on the last dark one. His spirit, burdened, sought relief in retirement, not only from the multitude, but even for a season from the Twelve. He retreated into "the secret place of the Most High," pouring out His soul "in supplications and prayers, with strong crying and tears" (Heb. 5:7). On rejoining His disciples, and as they were pursuing their quiet journey, He asked them this question. **And they said, Some say that thou art John the Baptist**—risen from the dead. So that Herod Antipas was not singular in his surmise (ch. 14:1, 2). **some, Elias**—(Cf. Mark 6:15). **and others, Jeremias**—Was this theory suggested by a supposed resemblance between the "Man of Sorrows" and "the weeping prophet"? **or one of the prophets**—or, as Luke (9:8) expresses it, "that one of the old prophets is risen again." In another report of the popular opinions which Mark (6:15) gives us, it is thus expressed, "That it is a prophet [or], as one of the prophets": in other words, That He was a prophetical person, resembling those of old.

From that time forth began Jesus to show unto his disciples—i.e., with an *explicitness and frequency* He had never observed before—**how that he must go unto Jerusalem and suffer many things** "and be rejected," (Matthew and Mark)—**of the elders and chief priests and scribes**—not as before, merely by not receiving Him, but by formal deeds. **and be killed, and be raised again the third day**—Mark (8:32) adds, that "He spake that saying openly"—"explicitly," or "without disguise."

Then Peter took him—aside, apart from the rest; presuming on the distinction just conferred on him; showing how *unexpected* and *distasteful* to them all was the announcement. **and began to rebuke him**—affectionately, yet with a certain generous indignation, to chide Him.

ADAM CLARKE

25. *And saw every man clearly*. Our Lord could have restored this man to sight in a moment; but He chose to do it in the way mentioned in the text, to show that He is a Sovereign of His own graces; and to point out that, however insignificant means may appear when He chooses to work by them; and that, however small the first manifestations of mercy may be, they are nevertheless the beginnings of the fullness of the blessings of the gospel of peace.

26. *He sent him away to his house*. So it appears that this person did not belong to Bethsaida, for in going to his house he was not to enter into the village. This miracle is not mentioned by any other of the Evangelists. It affords another proof that Mark did not abridge Matthew's Gospel.

27. *And Jesus went out*. See on Matt. xvi. 13-20.

And he spake that saying. Concerning the certainty and necessity of His sufferings—*openly*: "with great plainness, confidence, or emphasis," so that the disciples now began fully to understand Him. This is an additional observation of Mark. For Peter's reproof, see on Matt. xvi. 22, etc.

Then Peter took him. "Took Him up"—suddenly interrupted Him, as it were calling Him to order. *Be it far from thee, Lord*. "Be merciful to thyself, Lord." Peter knew that Christ had power sufficient to preserve himself from all the power and malice of the Jews, and wished Him to exert that in His own behalf which He had often exerted in the behalf of others.

MATTHEW HENRY

great a liberty.

3. Christ checked him for his opposition (*v.* 33); He *turned about*, and *looked on his disciples*, to see if the rest of them were of the same mind, and he said, *Get thee behind me, Satan.* Peter little thought to have had such a sharp rebuke, but perhaps expected as much commendation now for his love as he had lately had for his faith. Christ knows what manner of spirit we are of, when we ourselves do not. (1) Peter spoke as one that did not rightly understand the purposes and counsels of God. The most potent enemies could not overpower him whom diseases and deaths, whom winds and waves and devils themselves, were forced to obey and yield to. He looked upon his death only as a *martyrdom* which he thought might be prevented. He knew not that the thing was necessary for the glory of God, the destruction of Satan, and the salvation of man, that the Captain of our salvation must be *made perfect through sufferings.* The wisdom of man is perfect folly, when it pretends to give measures to the divine counsels. The cross of Christ was to some a stumbling-block, and to others foolishness. (2) Peter spoke as one that did not rightly understand the nature of Christ's kingdom; he took it to be *temporal* and *human*, whereas it is *spiritual* and *divine. Thou savourest not the things that are of God, but those that are of men.* Peter seemed to mind more the things that relate to the lower world, than those which relate to the upper world, and the life to come. Minding the *things of men* more than the *things of God*, and his glory and kingdom, is a very great sin, and the root of much sin, and very common among Christ's disciples. *Thou art not wise* (so it may be read) *in the things of God*, but in the *things of men.* It seems policy to shun trouble, but if with that we shun duty it will be folly in the end.

III. These miracles of Christ should engage us all to *follow him*, whatever it cost us, not only as they were *confirmations* of his *mission*, but as they were *explications* of his *design*; plainly intimating that by his Spirit he would do that for our blind, deaf, lame, leprous, diseased, possessed *souls*, which he did for the *bodies* of those many who in those distresses applied themselves to him. This is written, that we may believe that he is the great Physician of souls, and may become his patients. He *called all the people to him*, to hear this. This is that which all are concerned to know, and consider, if they expect Christ should heal *their souls.*

1. They must not be *indulgent* of the *ease of the body*; for (*v.* 34), "*Whosoever will come after me, let him deny himself*, and live a life of self-denial; let him not pretend to be his own physician, and let him *take up his cross*, and thus let him continue to *follow me.*" Those that will be Christ's patients must attend on him, converse with him, receive instruction and reproof from him, and must resolve they will never forsake him.

2. They must not be *solicitous*, no, not for *the life of the body*, when they cannot keep it without quitting Christ, *v.* 35. Are we invited by the words and works of Christ to follow him? Let us sit down, and count the cost, whether we can prefer our advantages by Christ before life itself. When the devil is drawing away disciples and servants after him, he conceals the worst of it. What there is of trouble and danger in the service of Christ, he tells us of it before, and is not afraid that we should know the worst; because the *advantages* of his service abundantly suffice to *balance* the *discouragements*, if we will but impartially set the one over against the other.

(1) We must *not dread the loss of our lives in the cause of Christ* (*v* 35); *Whosoever will save his life*, by declining Christ, or by disowning him after he has in profession come to Christ, he shall *lose it*, and all his hopes of eternal life; such a bad bargain will he make for himself. But whosoever *shall lose his life*, shall be truly willing to lose it, when he cannot keep it without denying Christ, he shall *save it*, he shall be an unspeakable gainer. It is looked upon to be some kind of recompence to those who lose their lives in the service of their prince and country, to have their memories honoured and their families provided for; but what is that to the recompence which Christ makes in eternal life to all that die for him?

(2) We must *dread the loss of our souls* (*v.* 36, 37); *For what shall it profit a man, if he should gain the whole world*, by denying Christ, and *lose his own soul?* **"True it is,"** said Bishop Hooper, the night before he suffered martyrdom, "that *life is sweet*, and *death is bitter*, but *eternal death is more bitter*, and *eternal life is more sweet.*" The gain of all the world *in sin*, is not sufficient to countervail the ruin of the soul *by sin.*

What that is that men do, to *save their lives*, and

JAMIESON, FAUSSET, BROWN

But he turned, and said—in the hearing of the rest; for Mark (8:33) expressly says, "When He had turned about and looked on His disciples, He rebuked Peter"; perceiving that he had but boldly uttered what others felt, and that the check was needed by them also. **Get thee behind me, Satan**—the same words as He had addressed to the Tempter (Luke 4:8); for He felt in it a satanic lure, a whisper from hell, to move Him from His purpose to suffer. So He shook off the Serpent, then coiling around Him, and "felt no harm" (Acts 28:5). How quickly has the "rock" turned to a devil! The fruit of divine teaching the Lord delighted to honor in Peter; but the mouthpiece of hell, which he had in a moment of forgetfulness become, the Lord shook off with horror. **thou art an offence**—a stumbling block—**unto me:** 'Thou playest the Tempter, casting a stumbling block in My way to the Cross. Could it succeed, where wert thou? and how should the Serpent's head be bruised?' **for thou savourest not**—thou thinkest not—**the things that be of God, but those that be of men**—"Thou art carried away by human views of the way of setting up Messiah's kingdom, quite contrary to those of God." This was kindly said, not to take off the sharp edge of the rebuke. but to explain and justify it, as it was evident Peter knew not what was in the bosom of his rash speech.

Then said Jesus unto his disciples—Mark (8:34) says, "When He had called the people unto Him, with His disciples also, He said unto them"—turning the rebuke of one into a warning to all.

If any man will come after me, let him deny himself, and take up his cross, and follow me. For whosoever will save—is minded to save, or bent on saving—**his life shall lose it, and whosoever will lose his life for my sake shall find it**—See on ch. 10:38, 39. "A suffering and dying Messiah liketh you ill; but what if His servants shall meet the same fate? They may not; but who follows Me must be prepared for the worst." **For what is a man profited, if he shall gain the whole world, and lose**—or forfeit—**his own soul? or what shall a man give in exchange for his soul?**—Instead of these weighty words, which we find in Mark also, it is thus expressed in Luke: "If he gain the whole world, and lose himself, or be cast away," or better, "If he gain the whole world, and destroy or forfeit himself." How awful is the stake as here set forth! If a man makes the present world—in its various forms of riches, honors, pleasures, and such like -the object of supreme pursuit, be it that he gains the world; yet along with it he forfeits his own soul. Not that any ever did, or ever will gain the whole world—a very small portion of it, indeed, falls to the lot of the most successful of the world's votaries—but to make the extravagant concession, that by giving himself entirely up to it, a man gains the whole world; yet, setting over against this gain the forfeiture of his soul—necessarily following the surrender of his whole heart to the world—what is he profited? But, if not the whole world, yet possibly something else may be conceived as an equivalent for the soul. Well, what is it?—"Or what shall a man give in exchange for his soul?" Thus, in language the weightiest, because the simplest, does our Lord shut up His hearers, and all who shall read these words to the end of the world, to the priceless value to every man of his own soul. In Mark and Luke the following words are added: "Whosoever therefore shall be ashamed of Me and of My words [shall be ashamed of belonging to Me, and ashamed of My Gospel] in this adulterous and sinful generation" (see on ch. 12:39), "of him shall the Son of man be ashamed when He cometh in the

ADAM CLARKE

Get thee behind me, Satan. "Get behind Me, you adversary." This is the proper translation of the Hebrew word *Satan*, from which the Greek word is taken. Our blessed Lord certainly never designed that men should believe He called Peter "devil" because he, through erring affection, had wished Him to avoid that death which He predicted to himself. This translation, which is literal, takes away that harshness which before appeared in our Lord's words. *Thou art an offence unto me.* You are a stumbling block in My way, to impede Me in the accomplishment of the great design. *Thou savourest not.* That is, "do not relish," or, do not "understand or discern" the things of God—you are wholly taken up with the vain thought that My kingdom is of this world. He who opposes the doctrine of the atonement is an adversary and offense to Christ, though he be as sincere in his profession as Peter himself was.

34. *Whosoever will come after me.* It seems that Christ formed, on the proselytism of the Jews, the principal qualities which He required in the proselytes of His covenant. The *first* condition of proselytism among the Jews was that he that came to embrace their religion should come voluntarily and that neither force nor influence should be employed in this business. This is also the first condition required by Jesus Christ, and which He considers as the foundation of all the rest: "If a man be willing to come after Me." The *second* condition required in the Jewish proselyte was that he should perfectly renounce all his prejudices, his errors, his idolatry, and everything that concerned his false religion; and that he should entirely separate himself from his most intimate friends and acquaintances. It was on this ground that the Jews called proselytism a "new birth," and proselytes "newborn" and "new men"; and our Lord requires men to be born again, not only of water, but by the Holy Ghost. See John iii. 5. All this our Lord includes in this word, *Let him deny himself.* To this the following scriptures refer: Matt. x. 33; John iii. 3, 5; 2 Cor. v. 17. The *third* condition on which a person was admitted into the Jewish church as a proselyte was that he should submit to the yoke of the Jewish law and bear patiently the inconveniences and sufferings with which a profession of the Mosiac religion might be accompanied. Christ requires the same condition; but, instead of the yoke of the law, He brings in His own doctrine, which He calls His yoke, Matt. xi. 29; and His *cross*, the *taking up* of which not only implies a bold profession of Christ crucified, but also a cheerful submitting to all the sufferings and persecutions to which He might be exposed, and even to death itself. The *fourth* condition was that he should solemnly engage to continue in the Jewish religion, faithful even unto death. This condition Christ also requires; and it is comprised in this word, *Let him . . . follow me.*

35. *For whosoever will save his life.* On this and the following verses, see Matt. xvi. 24, etc.

MATTHEW HENRY

gain the world, he tells us (*v.* 38), *Whosoever therefore shall be ashamed of me, and of my words, in his adulterous and sinful generation, of him shall the Son of man be ashamed.* The disadvantage that the cause of Christ labours under in this world, is, that it is to be owned and professed in an *adulterous and sinful generation.* Some ages, some places, are more especially sinful, as that was in which Christ lived; in such a *generation* the cause of Christ is opposed and run down, and those that own it, are exposed to reproach and contempt, and everywhere ridiculed and *spoken against.* There are many, who, though they cannot but own that the cause of Christ is a righteous cause, are *ashamed* of it. They are *ashamed* of their relation to Christ. They cannot bear to be frowned upon and despised, and therefore throw off their profession. There is a day coming, when the cause of Christ will appear as bright and illustrious as now it appears mean and contemptible. *They* shall not share with him in his glory then, that were not willing to share with him in his disgrace now.

JAMIESON, FAUSSET, BROWN

glory of His Father, with the holy angels" (Mark 8: 38; Luke 9:26). He will render back to that man his own treatment, disowning him before the most august of all assemblies, and putting him to "*shame* and everlasting *contempt*" (Dan. 12:2). "O shame," exclaims BENGEL, "to be put to shame before God, Christ, and angels!" The sense of *shame* is founded on our love of *reputation*, which causes instinctive aversion to what is fitted to lower it, and was given us as a preservative from all that is properly *shameful.* To be *lost to shame* is to be nearly past hope. (Zeph. 3:5; Jer. 6:15; 3:3.) But when Christ and "His words" are unpopular, the same instinctive desire to *stand well with others* begets that temptation to be ashamed of Him which only the expulsive power of a higher affection can effectually counteract. **For the Son of man shall come in the glory of his Father with his angels**—in the splendor of His Father's authority and with all His angelic ministers, ready to execute His pleasure.

ADAM CLARKE

38. *Whosoever therefore shall be ashamed of me.* Our Lord hints here at one of the principal reasons of the incredulity of the Jews—they saw nothing in the person of Jesus Christ which corresponded to the pompous notions which they had formed of the Messiah. *And of my words.* This was another subject of offense to the Jews: the doctrine of the Cross must be believed; a suffering Messiah must be acknowledged; and poverty and affliction must be borne; and death, perhaps, suffered in consequence of becoming His disciples.

MATTHEW HENRY

CHAPTER 9

Verses 1–13

I. A prediction of Christ's kingdom now near approaching, *v.* 1. That which is foretold is, 1. That the *kingdom of God* would *come*, and would come so as to be *seen.* 2. That it would come *with power*, and bear down the opposition that was given to it. 3. That it would come while some now *present were alive*; There are some *standing here, that shall not taste of death*, till they *see* it.

II. A specimen of that kingdom in the transfiguration of Christ, *six days* after Christ spoke that prediction. He gives them this glimpse of his glory, to show that his sufferings were voluntary, and to prevent the *offence of the cross.*

1. It was on the top of a *high mountain.* Tradition saith, It was on the top of Mount Tabor that Christ was transfigured.

2. The witnesses of it were Peter, James, and John; these were the *three* that were to *bear record on earth*, answering to Moses, Elias, and the *voice from heaven.* As there are distinguishing favours which are given to disciples and not to the world, so there are to some disciples and not to others. All the saints are a people *near to Christ*, but some lie in his bosom. James was the first of all the twelve that died for Christ, and John survived them all, to be the last eye-witness of this glory; he bore record (John i. 14); *We saw his glory:* and so did Peter, 2 Pet. i. 16–18.

3. The manner of it; *He was transfigured before them.* See what a great change human bodies are capable of, when God is pleased to put an honour upon them. His *raiment became shining, exceeding white as snow*, beyond what the fuller's art could do toward whitening it.

4. His companions in this glory were Moses and Elias (*v.* 4); They appeared *talking with him*, to *testify* to him. Moses and Elias lived at a great distance of time one from another, but that breaks no squares in heaven, where the *first shall be last, and the last first*, that is, all one in Christ.

5. The great delight that the disciples took in seeing this sight, and hearing this discourse, is expressed by Peter; *He said, Master, it is good for us to be here, v.* 5. Though Christ was transfigured, and was in discourse with Moses and Elias, yet he gave Peter leave to speak to him. Many, when they are in their greatness, oblige their friends to keep their distance; but even to the glorified Jesus true believers have access with boldness. Even in this heavenly discourse there was room for Peter to put in a word; and this is it, "*Lord, it is good to be here, for let us make tabernacles.*" Gracious souls reckon it *good to be* in communion with Christ, good to be *in the mount* with him. If it is good to be with Christ transfigured only upon a mountain with Moses and Elias, how good will it be to be with Christ glorified in heaven with all the saints! But observe, While Peter was for staying here, he forgot what need there was of the presence of Christ among the people. At this very time, the other disciples wanted them greatly, *v.* 14. When it is well with us, we are apt to be mindless of others. It was a weakness in Peter to prefer private communion with God before public usefulness. Peter talked of making three distinct tabernacles for Moses, Elias, and Christ, which was not well-contrived. One tabernacle will hold them all; they dwell together in unity. But whatever was incongruous in what he said, he may be excused, for they were all *sore afraid*; and he, for his part, *wist not what to say* (*v.* 6).

6. The voice that came from heaven, was an attestation of Christ's mediatorship, *v.* 7. *There was a cloud*

JAMIESON, FAUSSET, BROWN

CHAPTER 9

VSS. 1-13. JESUS IS TRANSFIGURED—CONVERSATION ABOUT ELIAS. (= Matt. 16:28-17:13; Luke 9: 27-36.) See Luke 9:27-36.

not taste of death till they see the kingdom of God—"see it come with power" (Mark 9:1); or see "the Son of man coming in His kingdom" (Matt. 16:28). The reference, beyond doubt, is to the firm establishment and victorious progress, in the lifetime of some then present, of that new Kingdom of Christ, which was destined to work the greatest of all changes on this earth, and be the grand pledge of His final coming in glory.

Peter, James, and John—partners before in secular business; now sole witnesses of the resurrection of Jairus' daughter (Mark 5:37), the transfiguration, and the agony in the garden (Mark 14:33). **a mountain**—not *Tabor*, according to long tradition, with which the facts ill comport, but some one near the lake.

-Before He cried He was answered, and while He was yet speaking He was heard. Blessed interruption to prayer this! Thanks to God, transfiguring manifestations are not quite strangers here. Ofttimes in the deepest depths, out of groanings which cannot be uttered, God's dear children are suddenly transported to a kind of heaven upon earth, and their soul is made as the chariots of Amminadab. Their prayers fetch down such light, strength, holy gladness, as make their face to shine, putting a kind of celestial radiance upon it (II Corinthians 3:18, with Exod. 34:29-35). **raiment white . . .**—Matthew says, "His face did shine as the sun" (17:2), and Mark says "His raiment became shining, exceeding white as snow, so as no fuller on earth can white them" (9:2). The light, then, it would seem, shone not *upon* Him *from without*, but *out of* Him *from within;* He was all irradiated, was in one blaze of celestial glory. What a contrast to that "visage more marred than men, and His form than the sons of men!" (Isa. 52:14). **there talked with him two men . . . Moses and Elias . . . appeared in glory**—"Who would have believed these were not *angels* had not their *human* names been subjoined?" [BENGEL]. (Cf. Acts 1:10; Mark 16:5.) Moses represented "the law," Elijah "the prophets," and both together the whole testimony of the Old Testament Scriptures, and the Old Testament saints, to Christ; now not borne in a *book*, but by *living men*, not to a *coming*, but a *come* Messiah, *visibly*, for they "appeared," and *audibly*, for they "spake." **spake**—"were speaking."

ADAM CLARKE

CHAPTER 9

1. *There be some.* This verse properly belongs to the preceding chapter, and to the preceding discourse. It is in this connection in Matt. xvi. 27-28. See the notes there.

2. *And after six days Jesus taketh with him Peter.* For a full account of the nature and design of the Transfiguration, see on Matt. xvii. 1, etc. *An high mountain.* I have conjectured, Matt. xvii. 1, that this was one of the mountains of Galilee; some say Hermon, some Tabor.

Peter, James, and John. He chose those that they might be witnesses of His transfiguration, two or three witnesses being required by the Scripture to substantiate any fact. The same three were made witnesses of His agony in the garden, chap. xxvi. 37. *An high mountain.* This was one of the mountains of Galilee, but whether Mount Tabor or not is uncertain. Some think it was Mount Hermon. St. Luke says Christ and His disciples went up into the mountain to pray, chap. ix. 28.

Was transfigured. That fullness of the Godhead which dwelt bodily in Christ now shone forth through the human nature, and manifested to His disciples not only that divinity which Peter had before confessed, chap. xvi. 16, but also the glorious resurrection body, in which they should exist in the presence of God to eternity.

Moses and Elias. Elijah came from heaven in the same body which he had upon earth, for he was translated, and did not see death, 2 Kings ii. 11. And the body of Moses was probably raised again as a pledge of the resurrection. It was a constant and prevalent tradition among the Jews that both Moses and Elijah should appear in the times of the Messiah, and to this very tradition the disciples refer, v. 10. We may conceive that the law in the person of Moses, the great Jewish legislator, and the prophets in the person of Elijah, the chief of the prophets, came now to do homage to Jesus Christ, and to render up their authority into His hands, as He was the End of the law and the grand Subject of the predictions of the prophets. This appears more particularly from what Luke says, chap. ix. 31, that Moses and Elijah conversed with our Lord on His death, which He was about to accomplish, because in it all the rites, ceremonies, and sacrifices of the law, as well as the predictions of the prophets, were fulfilled.

Then answered Peter . . . let us make here three tabernacles. That is, when he saw Moses and Elijah ready to depart from the mount, Luke ix. 33, he wished to detain them, that he might always enjoy their company with that of his Lord and Master, still supposing that Christ would set up a temporal kingdom upon earth.

A bright cloud overshadowed them. A *cloud* was frequently the symbol of the Divine Presence. *This is my beloved Son.* "This is My Son, the beloved One, in whom I have delighted," or "been well pleased." God adds His

MATTHEW HENRY

that overshadowed them. Peter had talked of making tabernacles for Christ and his friends; but *while he yet spoke* God created his tabernacle *not made with hands.* Now out of this cloud it was said, *This is my beloved Son, hear him.* God owns him, and accepts him, as his beloved Son.

7. The vision disappeared (*v.* 8); *Suddenly when they had looked round about* all was gone, *they saw no man any more.* Jesus only remained with them, and he not transfigured, but as he used to be. Christ doth not leave the soul, when extraordinary joys and comforts leave it. Christ's disciples have, and shall have, his ordinary presence with them always, even to the end of the world. Let us thank God for *daily bread,* and not expect a continual feast on this side heaven.

8. The discourse between Christ and his disciples, as they came down from the mount.

(1) He charged them to keep this matter very private, till he was *risen from the dead, v.* 9. He, being now in a state of humiliation, would have nothing publicly taken notice of, that might seem disagreeable to such a state. This enjoining of silence to the disciples, would likewise be of use to them, to prevent their boasting. It is a mortification to a man, to be tied up from telling of his advancements, and may help to hide pride from him.

(2) The disciples were at a loss what the *rising from the dead* should mean. Here is another thing that embarrasses them (*v.* 11). *Why say the Scribes, Elias must first come?* But Elias was gone, and Moses too. The scribes taught them to expect the person of Elias, whereas the prophecy intended one *in the spirit and power of Elias.*

(3) Christ gave them a key to the prophecy concerning Elias (*v.* 12, 13); "It is indeed prophesied that Elias will come, and will *restore all things.* It is also prophesied of the *Son of man* that he must *suffer many things,* and be *set at nought.* Though the scribes do not tell you so, the *scriptures* do, and you have as much reason to expect that as the other. But as to Elias, I tell you *he is come*; and if you consider a little, you will understand whom I mean, it is one to whom they have *done whatsoever they listed.*" The true Elias, as well as the true Messiah promised, is come, and we are to look for *no other.* He is come, and hath been, and done, according as was *written of him.*

Verses 14-29

We have here the story of Christ's casting the devil out of a child.

I. Christ's return to his disciples, and the perplexity he found them in. Christ's glory above does not make him forget the concerns of his church below, *v.* 14. And he came very seasonably, when the disciples were embarrassed and run a-ground. A child possessed with a devil was brought to them, and they could not cast out the devil, whereupon the scribes triumphed as if the day were their own. He *found the scribes questioning with them.* Christ's return was very welcome, no doubt, to the disciples, and *un*welcome to the scribes. But particular notice is taken of its being very surprising to the people.

When they *beheld him* coming to them again, they were *greatly amazed*; and *running to him,* they saluted him. It is easy to give a reason why they should be glad to see him; but why were they *amazed, greatly amazed,* when they beheld him? Probably, there might remain something unusual in his countenance. Instead of seeming *fatigued,* there appeared a wonderful briskness and sprightliness in his looks, which *amazed* them.

II. The case which perplexed the disciples, brought before him. He asked the scribes, "*What question ye with them?* What is the quarrel now?" The scribes made no answer, for they were confounded at his presence; the disciples made none, for they were comforted, and now left all to him. But the father of the child opened the case, *v.* 17, 18. 1. His child is

JAMIESON, FAUSSET, BROWN

cloud—not one of our watery clouds, but the Shekinah-cloud (see on Matt. 23:39), the pavilion of the manifested presence of God with His people, what Peter calls "the excellent" of "magnificent glory" (II Pet. 1:17). **a voice**—"*such* a voice," says Peter emphatically; "and this voice [he adds] we heard, when we were with Him in the holy mount" (II Pet. 1:17, 18). **my beloved Son . . . hear him**—*reverentially, implicitly, alone.* **Jesus was found alone**—Moses and Elias are gone. Their work is done, and they have disappeared from the scene, feeling no doubt with their fellow servant the Baptist, "He must increase, but I must decrease." The cloud too is gone, and the naked majestic Christ, braced in spirit, and enshrined in the reverent affection of His disciples, is left—to suffer! **kept it close**—feeling, for once at least, that such things were unmeet as yet for the general gaze.

14-32. Healing of a Demoniac Boy—Second Explicit Announcement of His Approaching Death and Resurrection. (= Matt. 17:14-23; Luke 9:37-45.)

Healing of the Demoniac Boy (vss. 14-29). **14. And when he came to his disciples, he saw a great multitude about them, and the scribes questioning with them**—This was "on the next day, when they were come down from the hill" (Luke 9:37). The Transfiguration appears to have taken place at night. In the morning, as He came down from the hill on which it took place—with Peter, and James, and John—on approaching the other nine, He found them surrounded by a great multitude, and the scribes disputing or discussing with them. No doubt these cavillers were twitting the apostles of Jesus with their inability to cure the demoniac boy of whom we are presently to hear, and insinuating doubts even of their Master's ability to do it; while they, zealous for their Master's honor, would no doubt refer to His past miracles in proof of the contrary. **15. And straightway all the people**—the multitude. **when they beheld him, were greatly amazed**—were astounded. **and running to him saluted him**—The singularly strong expression of surprise, the sudden arrest of the discussion,and the rush of the multitude towards Him, can be accounted for by nothing less than something amazing in His appearance. There can hardly be any doubt that *His countenance still retained traces of His transfiguration-glory.* (See Exod. 34:29, 30.) So Bengel, De Wette, Meyer, Trench, Alford. No wonder, if this was the case, that they not only ran to Him, but saluted Him. Our Lord, however, takes no notice of what had attracted them, and probably it gradually faded away as He drew near; but addressing Himself to the scribes, He demands the subject of their discussion, ready to meet them where they had pressed hard upon His half-instructed and as yet timid apostles. **16. And he asked the scribes, What question ye with them?**—Ere they had time to reply, the father of the boy, whose case had occasioned the dispute, himself steps forward and answers the question; telling a piteous tale of deafness, and dumbness, and fits of epilepsy—ending with this, that the disciples, though entreated, could not perform the cure. **17. And one of the multitude answered, and said, Master, I have brought**

ADAM CLARKE

testimony of approbation to what was spoken of the sufferings of Christ by Moses and Elijah, thus showing that the sacrificial economy of the old covenant was in itself of no worth, but as it referred to the grand atonement which Jesus was about to make. Therefore He says, "In Him have I delighted," intimating that it was in Him alone, as typified by those sacrifices, that He had delighted through the whole course of the legal administration; and that it was only in reference to the death of His Son that He accepted the offerings and oblations made to Him under the old covenant. *Hear . . . him.* The disciples wished to detain Moses and Elijah that they might hear them, but God shows that the law which had been in force, and the prophets which had prophesied, until now, must all give place to Jesus; and He alone must now be attended to, as "the way, the truth, and the life," for no man could now come unto the Father but through Him.

Tell the vision to no man. See the note on chap. xvi. 20; and further observe that, as this Transfiguration was intended to show forth the final abolition of the whole ceremonial law, it was necessary that a matter which could not fail to irritate the Jewish rulers and people should be kept secret till Jesus had accomplished vision and prophecy by His death and resurrection.

Why then say the scribes that Elias must first come? As the disciples saw that Elijah returned to heaven, knowing the tradition of the elders, and the prophecy on which the tradition was founded, Mal. iv. 5-6, "Behold, I will send you Elijah the prophet before . . . the great and dreadful day of the Lord [shall come]: and he shall turn the hearts," it was natural enough for them to inquire what the meaning of the tradition and the intention of the prophecy were.

12. *And how it is written.* Rather, "as also it is written."

15. *Were greatly amazed.* Probably because He came so unexpectedly.

MATTHEW HENRY

possessed with a *dumb spirit*, and in his fits *is speechless*; wheresoever the fit takes him, the spirit *tears* him, throws him into such violent convulsions as almost pull him to pieces; and, *he foams* at the mouth, and *gnashes with his teeth.* Though the fits go off presently, yet they leave him so weak, that he *pines away*, is worn to a skeleton.

2. The disciples cannot give him any relief; "I *desired they would cast him out*, but *they could not*; and therefore thou couldest never have come in better time; *Master, I have brought him to thee.*"

III. The rebuke he gave to them all (*v.* 19); *O faithless generation, how long shall I be with you? How long shall I suffer you?* Them he calls a *faithless generation*, and speaks as one weary of *being with them*, and of *bearing with* them. "How long shall I be among these *faithless people*, and suffer them?"

ALEXANDER MACLAREN:

Dear friends, here is "a little window through which we may see a great matter," if we will only think of how all that solitude, and all that sorrow of uncomprehended aims, was borne lovingly and patiently, right away on to the very end, for every one of us. I know that there are many of the aspects of Christ's life in which Christ's griefs tell more on the popular apprehension; but I do not know that there is one in which the title of "The Man of Sorrows" is to all deeper thinking more pathetically vindicated than in this—the solitude of the uncomprehended and the unaccepted Christ and His pain at His disciples' faithlessness.

—*Expositions of Holy Scripture*

IV. The deplorable condition that the child was actually in, when he was brought to Christ, and the doleful representation which the father made of it. When the child saw Christ, he fell into a fit; *The spirit straightway tore him,* as if the devil would set Christ at defiance, and hoped to be too hard for him too, and to keep possession in spite of him. The child *fell* on the *ground, and wallowed foaming.*

Christ asked, *How long since this came to him?* And, it seems, the disease was of long standing; it came to him *of a child* (*v.* 21), which made the case the more sad, and the cure the more difficult.

V. The pressing instances which the father of the child makes with Christ for a cure (*v.* 22); *Oft-times it hath cast him into the fire, and into the waters, to destroy him.* But *if thou canst do anything, have compassion on us, and help us.* The leper was confident of Christ's power, but put an *if* upon his will (Matt. viii. 2); *If thou wilt, thou canst.* This poor man referred himself to his goodwill, but put an *if* upon his power.

JAMIESON, FAUSSET, BROWN

unto thee my son—"mine only child" (Luke 9:38). **which hath a dumb spirit**—a spirit whose operation had the effect of rendering his victim speechless, and deaf also (vs. 25). In Matthew's report of the speech (17:15), the father says "he is lunatic"; this being another and most distressing effect of the possession. **18. And wheresoever he taketh him, he teareth him; and he foameth, and gnasheth with his teeth, and pineth away**—rather, "becomes withered," "dried up," or "paralyzed"; as the same word is everywhere else rendered in the New Testament. Some additional particulars are given by Luke, and by our Evangelist below. "Lo," says he in Luke 9:39, "a spirit taketh him, and he suddenly crieth out; and it teareth him that he foameth again, and bruising him hardly [or with difficulty] departeth from him." **and I spake to thy disciples that they should cast him out; and they could not**—Our Lord replies to the father by a severe rebuke to the disciples. As if wounded at the exposure before such a multitude, of the weakness of His disciples' faith, which doubtless He felt as a reflection on Himself, He puts them to the blush before all, but in language fitted only to raise expectation of what He Himself would do. **19. He answereth him, and saith, O faithless generation**—"and perverse," or "perverted" (Matt. 17:17; Luke 9:41). **how long shall I be with you? how long shall I suffer you?**—language implying that it was a shame to them to want the faith necessary to perform this cure, and that it needed some patience to put up with them. It is to us surprising that some interpreters, as CHRYSOSTOM and CALVIN, should represent this rebuke as addressed, not to the disciples at all, but to the scribes who disputed with them. Nor does it much, if at all, mend the matter to view it as addressed to both, as most expositors seem to do. With BENGEL, DE WETTE, and MEYER, we regard it as addressed directly to the nine apostles who were unable to expel this evil spirit. And though, in ascribing this inability to their "want of faith" and the "perverted turn of mind" which they had drunk in with their early training, the rebuke would undoubtedly apply, with vastly greater force, to those who twitted the poor disciples with their inability, it would be to change the whole nature of the rebuke to suppose it addressed to those who had *no faith at all,* and were *wholly perverted.* It was because faith sufficient for curing this youth was to be expected of the disciples, and because they should by that time have got rid of the perversity in which they had been reared, that Jesus exposes them thus before the rest. And who does not see that this was fitted, more than anything else, to impress upon the bystanders the severe loftiness of the training He was giving to the Twelve, and the unsophisticated footing He was on with them? **Bring him unto me**—The order to bring the patient to Him was instantly obeyed; when, lo! as if conscious of the presence of his Divine Tormentor, and expecting to be made to quit, the foul spirit rages and is furious, determined to die hard, doing all the mischief he can to this poor child while yet within his grasp. **20. And they brought him unto him: and when he saw him, straightway the spirit tare him**—Just as the man with the legion of demons, "when he *saw* Jesus, ran and worshipped Him" (ch. 5:6), so this demon, *when he saw Him,* immediately "tare him." The feeling of terror and rage was the same in both cases. **and he fell on the ground, and wallowed foaming**—Still Jesus does nothing, but keeps conversing with the father about the case—partly to have its desperate features told out by him who knew them best, in the hearing of the spectators; partly to let its virulence have time to show itself; and partly to deepen the exercise of the father's soul, to draw out his faith, and thus to prepare both him and the bystanders for what He was to do. **21. And he asked his father, How long is it ago since this came unto him? And he said, Of a child . . .**—Having told briefly the affecting features of the case, the poor father, half dispirited by the failure of the disciples and the aggravated virulence of the malady itself in presence of their Master, yet encouraged too by what he had heard of Christ, by the severe rebuke He had given to His disciples for not having faith enough to cure the boy, and by the dignity with which He had ordered him to be brought to Him—in this mixed state of mind, he closes his description of the case with these touching words: **but if thou canst do anything, have compassion on us, and help us**—"us," says the father; for it was a sore family affliction. Cf. the language of the Syrophœnician woman regarding her daughter, "Lord, help *me.*" Still nothing is done: the man is but *struggling into faith:* it must come a step farther. But he had to do with Him

ADAM CLARKE

17. *A dumb spirit.* That is, a demon who afflicted those in whom it dwelt with an incapacity of speaking.

18. *Pineth away.* By these continual torments; so he was not only deaf and dumb, but sorely tortured besides.

O faithless and perverse generation. These and the following words may be considered as spoken: (1) To the disciples, because of their unbelief, v. 20. (2) To the father of the possessed, who should have brought his son to Christ. (3) To the whole multitude, who were slow of heart to believe in Him as the Messiah, notwithstanding the miracles which He wrought.

ALEXANDER MACLAREN:

Do not let us forget that in this short, sharp cry of anguish—for it is that—there may be detected by the listening ear not only the tone of personal hurt, but the tone of disappointed and thwarted love. Because of their unbelief He knew that they could not receive what He desired to give them. We find Him more than once in His life hemmed in, hindered, balked of His purpose, thwarted, as I may say, in His design, simply because there was no one with a heart open to receive the rich treasure that He was ready to pour out. He had to keep it locked up in His own spirit, else it would have been wasted and spilled upon the ground.

—*Expositions of Holy Scripture*

20. *When he saw him . . . the spirit tare him; and he fell on the ground,* etc. When this demon saw Jesus, he had great rage, knowing that his time was short; and hence the extraordinary convulsions mentioned above.

22. *If thou canst do any thing.* I have already tried Thy disciples, and find they can do nothing in this case; but if *thou* hast any power, in mercy use it in our behalf.

MATTHEW HENRY

VI. The answer Christ gave to his address (*v.* 23); *If thou canst believe, all things are possible to him that believeth.* He tacitly checks the weakness of his faith. The sufferer put it upon Christ's power, *If thou canst do anything*; but Christ turns it upon him, and puts him upon questioning his own faith, and will have him impute the disappointment to the want of that; *If thou canst believe.* He graciously encourages the strength of his desire; "*All things are possible to him that believes* the almighty power of God, to which all things are possible." In dealing with Christ, very much is put upon our believing, and very much promised to it. *Canst thou believe?* Darest thou believe? *If thou canst believe,* it is possible that thy hard heart may be softened, thy spiritual diseases may be cured; and that, weak as thou art, thou mayest be able to hold out to the end.

VII. The *profession of faith* which the poor man made hereupon (*v.* 24); He cried out, "*Lord, I believe;* my cure shall not be prevented by the want of faith; *Lord, I believe.*" He adds a prayer for grace to enable him more firmly to rely upon Christ to save; *Help thou my unbelief.* Those that complain of unbelief, must look up to Christ for grace to *help* them against it, *and his grace* shall be *sufficient for them.* "*Help mine unbelief*; help out what is wanting in my faith with thy grace, the strength of which is perfected in our weakness."

VIII. The cure of the child. Christ *saw the people come running together,* and therefore kept them in suspense no longer, but *rebuked the foul spirit.* 1. What the charge was which Christ gave to this unclean spirit; "*Thou dumb and deaf spirit come out of him* immediately, and *enter no more into him.* Let him not only be brought out of this fit, but let his fits never return." Whom Christ cures, he cures effectually. Satan may *go out himself,* and yet recover possession; but if Christ *cast* him out, he will *keep* him out. 2. How the unclean spirit took it; he grew yet more outrageous, he *cried,* and *rent him sore,* gave him such a twitch at parting, that he was *as one dead. Many said, He is dead.* 3. How the child was perfectly restored (*v.* 27); *Jesus took him by the hand, took fast hold of him,* and strongly bore him up, and he arose and recovered, and all was well.

IX. The reason he gave to the disciples why they could not cast out this devil. They *enquired* of him privately *why they could not,* and he told them (*v.* 29), *This kind can come forth by nothing* but *prayer and fasting.* The disciples must not think to do their work always with a like ease; but Christ can do that with a word's speaking, which they must prevail for the doing of by *prayer and fasting.*

Verses 30–40

I. Christ foretells his own approaching sufferings. He *passed through Galilee,* and *would not that any man should know it* (*v.* 30). The time of his sufferings drew nigh, and therefore he was willing to converse only with his disciples, to prepare them for the approaching trial, *v.* 31.

JAMIESON, FAUSSET, BROWN

who breaks not the bruised reed, and who knew how to inspire what He demanded. The man had said to Him, "*If Thou canst do.*" **23. Jesus said unto him, If thou canst believe**—The man had said, "If Thou canst do *anything.*" Jesus replies. **all things are possible to him that believeth**—"My doing all depends on thy believing." To impress this still more, He redoubles upon the believing: "If thou canst believe, all things are possible to him that believeth." Thus the Lord helps the birth of faith in that struggling soul; and now, though with pain and sore travail, it comes to the birth, as TRENCH, borrowing from OLSHAUSEN, expresses it. Seeing the case stood still, waiting not upon the Lord's power but his own faith, the man becomes immediately conscious of conflicting principles, and rises into one of the noblest utterances on record. **24. And straightway the father of the child cried out, and said with tears, Lord, I believe: help thou mine unbelief**—i.e., " 'Tis useless concealing from Thee, O Thou mysterious, mighty Healer, the unbelief that still struggles in this heart of mine; but that heart bears me witness that I do believe in Thee; and if distrust still remains, I disown it, I wrestle with it, I seek help from Thee against it." Two things are very remarkable here: First, *The felt and owned presence of unbelief,* which only the strength of the man's faith could have so revealed to his own consciousness. Second, *His appeal to Christ for help against his felt unbelief*—a feature in the case quite unparalleled, and showing, more than all protestations could have done, the insight he had attained into the existence of *a power in Christ more glorious than any he had besought for his poor child.* The work was done; and as the commotion and confusion in the crowd was now increasing, Jesus at once, as Lord of spirits, gives the word of command to the dumb and deaf spirit to be gone, never again to return to his victim. **26. And the spirit cried, and rent him sore, and came out of him; and he was as one dead; insomuch that many said, He is dead**—The malignant, cruel spirit, now conscious that his time was come, gathers up his whole strength, with intent by a last stroke to kill his victim, and had nearly succeeded. But the Lord of life was there; the Healer of all maladies, the Friend of sinners, the Seed of the woman, "the Stronger than the strong man armed," was there. The very faith which Christ declared to be enough for everything being now found, it was not possible that the serpent should prevail. Fearfully is he permitted to bruise the *heel,* as in this case; but his own *head* shall go for it—his works shall be destroyed (I John 3:8). **27. But Jesus took him by the hand, and lifted him up; and he arose. 28. Why could not we cast him out? 29. And he said unto them, This kind can come forth by nothing but by prayer and fasting**—i.e., as nearly all good interpreters are agreed, "this kind of evil spirits cannot be expelled," or "so desperate a case of demoniacal possession cannot be cured, but by prayer and fasting." But since the Lord Himself says that His disciples could not fast while He was with them, perhaps this was designed, as ALFORD hints, for their after-guidance—unless we take it as but a definite way of expressing the general truth, that great and difficult duties require special preparation and self-denial. But the answer to their question, as given in Matthew 17 is fuller: "And Jesus said unto them, Because of your unbelief. For verily I say unto you, If ye have faith as a grain of mustard seed, ye shall say unto this mountain, Remove hence to yonder place, and it shall remove; and nothing shall be impossible unto you" (vs. 20). See on ch. 11:23. "Howbeit this kind goeth not out but by prayer and fasting" (vs. 21). i.e., though nothing is impossible to faith, yet such a height of faith as is requisite for such triumphs is not to be reached either in a moment or without effort—either with God in prayer or with ourselves in self-denying exercises. Luke (9:43) adds, "And they were all amazed at the mighty power of God" —"at the majesty" or "mightiness of God," in this last miracle, in the Transfiguration, etc.; or, at the *divine grandeur* of Christ rising upon them daily.

Second Explicit Announcement of His Approaching Death and Resurrection (vss. 30-32). **30. And they departed thence, and passed**—were passing along. **through Galilee; and he would not that any man should know it**—By comparing Matthew 17:22, 23 and Luke 9:43, 44 with this, we gather, that as our Lord's reason for going through Galilee more privately than usual on this occasion was to reiterate to them the announcement which had so shocked them at the first mention of it, and thus familiarize them with it by little and little, so this was His reason for enjoining silence upon them as

ADAM CLARKE

23. *If thou canst believe.* This was an answer to the inquiry above. I can furnish a sufficiency of power, if *you* can but bring faith to receive it. Why are not our souls completely healed? Why is not every demon cast out? Why are not pride, self-will, love of the world, lust, anger, peevishness, with all the other bad tempers and dispositions which constitute the mind of Satan, entirely destroyed? Alas! it is because we do not *believe.* Jesus is able; more, Jesus is willing; but we are not willing to give up our idols; we give not credence to His word; therefore has sin a being in us, and dominion over us.

24. *Lord, I believe.* The word *Lord* is omitted by many MSS. and versions. Griesbach leaves it out. The omission, I think, is proper, because it is evident the man did not know our Lord, and therefore could not be expected to accost Him with a title expressive of that authority which he doubted whether He possessed, unless we grant that he used the word *kyrie* after the Roman custom, for "Sir." *Help thou mine unbelief.* That is, assist me against it. Give me a power to believe.

25. *I charge thee.* Considerable emphasis should be laid on the pronoun: You resisted the command of My disciples; now *I* command you to come out.

29. *Prayer and Fasting.* See on Matt. xvii. 21. This case is related by both Matthew and Luke, but it is greatly amplified in Mark's account, and many new circumstances related—another proof that Mark did not abridge Matthew.

30. *They . . . passed through Galilee.* See on Matt. xvii. 22-27.

MATTHEW HENRY

He said to them, *The Son of man is delivered into the hands of men* (*v.* 31), and *they shall kill him.* That *men,* who have *reason,* and should have *love,* that they should be thus spiteful to the *Son of man,* who came to redeem and save them, is unaccountable. But still it is observable that when Christ spoke of his death, he always spoke of his resurrection.

But they *understood not that saying, v.* 32. The words were plain enough, but they could not be reconciled to the thing, and they were *afraid to ask him.* Many remain ignorant because they are ashamed to enquire.

II. He rebukes his disciples for magnifying themselves. When he came to Capernaum, he privately asked his disciples what it was that they *disputed among themselves by the way, v.* 33. As our other discourses among ourselves by the way, so especially our disputes, will be all called over again, and we shall be called to an account about them. Of all disputes, Christ will be sure to reckon with his disciples for their disputes about precedency and superiority: that was the subject of the debate here, *who should be the greatest, v.* 34. Nothing could be more contrary to the two great laws of Christ's kingdom, which are *humility* and *love,* than *desiring* preferment in the world, and *disputing* about it. This ill temper he took all occasions to check. They were willing to *cover this fault* (*v.* 34); they *held their peace.* As they would not *ask* (*v.* 32), because they were ashamed to own their ignorance, so here they would not *answer* because they were ashamed to own their pride. He was willing to *amend this fault* in them, and therefore *sat down,* that he might have a solemn and full discourse with them.

He *called the twelve to him,* and told them, 1. That ambition, instead of gaining them preferment in his kingdom, would but postpone their preferment; *If any man desire* and aim *to be first,* he shall *be last;* he that exalteth himself, shall be abased. 2. That there is no preferment to be had under him, but an opportunity for, and an obligation to, so much the more labour and condescension. 3. That those who are most humble and self-denying, do most resemble Christ, and shall be most tenderly owned by him. *He took a child in his arms.* "Look you," saith he; "*whosoever shall receive* one like this child, *receives me.* Those of a humble, meek, mild disposition are such as I will own and countenance, and so will my *Father* too, for he who thus *receiveth me, receiveth him that sent me.*"

JAMIESON, FAUSSET, BROWN

to their present movements. **31. For he taught his disciples, and said unto them**—"Let these sayings sink down into your ears" (Luke 9:44); not what had been passing between them as to His grandeur, but what He was now to utter. **The Son of man is delivered**—The use of the present tense expresses how near at hand He would have them to consider it. As BENGEL says, steps were already in course of being taken to bring it about. **into the hands of men**—This remarkable antithesis, "the Son of *man* shall be delivered into the hands of *men,*" it is worthy of notice, is in all the three Evangelists. **and they shall kill him**—i.e., "Be not carried off your feet by all that grandeur of Mine which ye have lately witnessed, but bear in mind what I have already told you and now distinctly repeat, that that Sun in whose beams ye now rejoice is soon to set in midnight gloom." **and after he is killed, he shall rise the third day. 32. But they understood not that saying**—"and it was hid from them, [so] that they preceived it not" (Luke 9:45). **and were afraid to ask him**—Their most cherished ideas were so completely dashed by such announcements, that they were afraid of laying themselves open to rebuke by asking Him any questions. But "they were exceeding sorry" (Matt. 17:23). While the other Evangelists, as WEBSTER and WILKINSON remark, notice their ignorance and their fear, Matthew, who was one of them, retains a vivid recollection of their sorrow.

33-50. STRIFE AMONG THE TWELVE WHO SHOULD BE GREATEST IN THE KINGDOM OF HEAVEN, WITH RELATIVE TEACHING—INCIDENTAL REBUKE OF JOHN FOR EXCLUSIVENESS. (= Matt. 18:1-9; Luke 9:46-50.)

Strife among the Twelve, with Relative Teaching (vss. 33-37). **33. What was it that ye disputed among yourselves by the way?**—From this we gather that after the painful communication He had made to them, the Redeemer had allowed them to travel so much of the way by themselves; partly, no doubt, that He might have privacy for Himself to dwell on what lay before Him, and partly that they might be induced to weigh together and prepare themselves for the terrible events which He had announced to them. But if so, how different was their occupation! **34. But they held their peace: for by the way they had disputed among themselves, who should be the greatest**—From Matthew 18:1 we should infer that the subject was introduced, not by our Lord, but by the disciples themselves, who came and asked Jesus who should be greatest. Perhaps one or two of them first referred the matter to Jesus, who put them off till they should all be assembled together at Capernaum. He had all the while "perceived the thought of their heart" (Luke 9:47); but now that they were all together "in the house," He questions them about it, and they are put to the blush, conscious of the *temper* towards each other which it had kindled. This raised the whole question afresh, and at this point our Evangelist takes it up. The subject was suggested by the recent announcement of the Kingdom (Matt. 16:19-28), the transfiguration of their Master, and especially the preference given to three of them at that scene. **35. If any man desire to be first, the same shall be last of all, and servant of all**—i.e., "let him be" such: he must be prepared to take the last and lowest place. See on ch. 10:42-45. **36. And he took a child**—"a little child" (Matt. 18:2); but the word is the same in both places, as also in Luke 9:47. **and set him in the midst of them: and when he had taken him in his arms**—This beautiful trait is mentioned by our Evangelist alone. **he said unto them**—Here we must go to Matthew (18:3, 4) for the first of this answer: "Verily I say unto you, except ye be converted, and become as little children, ye shall not enter into the kingdom of Heaven:" i.e., "Conversion must be thorough; not only must the heart be turned to God in general, and from earthly to heavenly things, but in particular, except ye be converted from that carnal ambition which still rankles within you, into that freedom from all such feelings which ye see in this child, ye have neither part nor lot in the kingdom at all; and he who in this feature has most of the child, is highest there." Whosoever, therefore, shall "humble himself as this little child, the same is greatest in the kingdom of heaven": "for he that is [willing to be] least among you all, the same shall be great" (Luke 9:48). **37. Whosoever shall receive one of such children**—so manifesting the spirit unconsciously displayed by this child. **in my name**—from love to Me. **receiveth me; and whosoever shall receive me, receiveth not me, but Him that sent me**—See on Matthew 10:40.

ADAM CLARKE

32. *But they understood not.* It does not appear likely, from Matthew's account, that three of the disciples, Peter, James, and John, could be ignorant of the reasons of Christ's death and resurrection, after the Transfiguration. On the contrary, from that time they must have had at least a general understanding of this important subject. But the other nine might have been ignorant of this matter, who were not present at the Transfiguration; probably it is of these that the Evangelist speaks here.

33. *And being in the house.* That is, Peter's house, where He ordinarily lodged.

34. *Who should be the greatest.* See on Matt. xviii. 1-5.

Who is the greatest? Could these disciples have viewed the kingdom of Christ in any other light than that of a temporal one? Hence they wished to know whom He would make His prime minister—whom His general—whom His chief chancellor—whom supreme judge. The disciples having lately seen the keys delivered to Peter, and found that he, with James and John, had been privileged with being present at the Transfiguration, it is no wonder if a measure of jealousy and suspicion began to work in their minds. From this inquiry we may also learn that the disciples had no notion of Peter's supremacy.

One such little child. As our Lord in the preceding verses considers a little child an emblem of a genuine disciple, so by the term in this verse He means a disciple only. *Whoso shall receive,* i.e., show unto such a childlike, unambitious disciple of Mine any act of kindness for My sake, I will consider it as done to myself.

MATTHEW HENRY

III. While they are striving which of them should be greatest, they will not allow those who are not in communion with them to be anything.

1. The account which John gave him, of the restraint they had laid upon one from making use of the name of Christ, because he was not of their society. *Master*, saith John, *we saw one casting out devils in thy name, but he followeth not us, v.* 38. (1) It was strange that one who was not a professed disciple and follower of Christ, should yet have power to *cast out devils*, in his name, for that seemed to be peculiar to those whom he called. And why might not he receive that power from Christ, whose *Spirit*, like the wind, *blows where it listeth*, without such an outward call as the apostles had? And perhaps there were many more such. Christ's grace is not tied to the visible church. (2) It was strange that one who *cast out devils* in the name of Christ, did not join himself to the apostles, and follow Christ with them, but should continue to act in *separation* from them. I know of nothing that could hinder him from following them, unless because he was loth to leave all to follow them. The thing did not look well, and therefore the disciples *forbade him* to make use of Christ's name as they did, unless he would follow him as they did. Thus apt are we to imagine that those do not follow Christ at all, who do not follow him *with us*, and that those do nothing well, who do not just as we do. But the *Lord knows them that are his*, however they are dispersed.

2. The rebuke he gave to them for this (*v.* 39); *Jesus said, "Forbid him not."* That which is good, and doeth good, must not be prohibited, though there may be some defect or irregularity in the manner of doing it. If Christ be preached, Paul therein doth, and will rejoice, though he be eclipsed by it, Phil. i. 18. Two reasons Christ gives why such should not be forbidden. (1) Because we cannot suppose that any man who makes use of Christ's name in working miracles, should blaspheme his name, as the scribes and Pharisees did. (2) Because those that differed in communion, while they agreed to fight against Satan under the banner of Christ, ought to look upon one another as on the same side. *He that is not against us is on our part.* As to the great controversy between Christ and Beelzebub, he had said, *He that is not with me is against me*, Matt. xii. 30. He that will not own Christ, owns Satan. But as to those that own Christ, that follow him, though *not with us*, we must reckon that they are not against us, and therefore are *on our part.*

Verses 41-50

I. Christ promiseth a reward to all those that are any way kind to his disciples (*v.* 41); "*Whosoever shall give you a cup of water because you belong to Christ, he shall not lose his reward.*" It is the honour and happiness of Christians, that they *belong to Christ*; they wear his livery as retainers to his family; nay, they are more nearly related, they are *members of his body.* The relieving of Christ's poor in their distresses, is a good deed; he accepts it, and will reward it. What kindness is done to Christ's poor, must be done them *for his sake*, and *because they belong to him*; for that is it that sanctifies the kindness. This is a reason why we must not discountenance and discourage those who are serving the interests of Christ's kingdom, though they are not in everything of our mind and way. If Christ reckons *kindnesses to us* services to *him*, we ought to reckon *services to him* kindnesses to us, and to encourage them, though done by those that follow not with us.

II. He threatens those that *offend* his *little ones*, *v.* 42. Whosoever shall grieve any true Christians, though they be of the weakest, shall either restrain them from doing good, or draw them in to commit sin, it were *better for him that a millstone were hanged about his neck, and he were cast into the sea*: his punishment will be very great.

III. He warns all his followers to take heed of ruining their own souls. This charity must begin at home; if we must take heed of doing anything to hinder others from good, much more careful must we be to avoid everything that will take us off from our duty, or lead us to sin; and that which doth so we must part with, though it be ever so dear to us. Observe,

1. The case supposed, that our own *hand*, or *eye*, or *foot*, *offends us*; that the impure *corruption* we indulge is as dear to us as an eye or a hand. Suppose the beloved is become a sin, or the sin a beloved. Suppose we must part with it, or part with Christ and a good conscience.

2. The duty prescribed in that case; *Pluck out the eye, cut off the hand and foot*, mortify the darling lust, crucify it. Let the idols that have been *delectable*

JAMIESON, FAUSSET, BROWN

Incidental Rebuke of John for Exclusiveness (vss. 38-41). **38. And John aswered him, saying, Master, we saw one casting out devils in thy name, and he followeth not us: and we forbade him, because he followeth not us**—The link of connection here with the foregoing context lies, we apprehend, in the emphatic words which our Lord had just uttered, "in My name." "Oh," interposes John—young, warm, but not sufficiently apprehending Christ's teaching in these matters—"that reminds me of something that we have just done, and we should like to know if we did right. We saw one casting out devils "in *Thy name*," and we forbade him, because he followeth not us. Were we right, or were we wrong?" Answer—"Ye were wrong." "But we did it because he followeth not us." "No matter."

39. But Jesus said, Forbid him not: for there is no man which shall do a miracle in my name, that can lightly—soon, i.e., readily—**speak evil of me. 40. For he that is not against us is on our part**—Two principles of immense importance are here laid down: "First, No one will readily speak evil of Me who has the faith to do a miracle in My name; and second, If such a person cannot be supposed to be *against* us, ye are to consider him *for* us." Let it be carefully observed that our Lord does not say this man should *not* have "followed them," nor yet that it was indifferent whether he did or not; but simply teaches how such a person was to be regarded, *although he did not*—viz., as a reverer of His name and a promotor of His cause.

41. For whosoever shall give you a cup of water to drink in my name, because ye belong to Christ, verily I say unto you, he shall not lose his reward—See on Matthew 10:42.

Continuation of Teaching Suggested by the Disciple's Strife (vss. 42-50). What follows appears to have no connection with the incidental reproof of John immediately preceding. As that had interrupted some important teaching, our Lord hastens back from it, as if no such interruption had occurred. **42. For whosoever shall offend one of these little ones that believe in me**—or, shall cause them to stumble; referring probably to the effect which such unsavory disputes as they had held would have upon the inquiring and hopeful who came in contact with them, leading to the belief that after all they were no better than others. **it is better for him that a millstone were hanged about his neck**—The word here is simply "millstone," without expressing of which kind. But in Matthew 18:6 it is the "ass-turned" kind, far heavier than the small hand-mill turned by female slaves, as in Luke 17:35. It is of course the same which is meant here. **and he were cast into the sea**—meaning, that if by such a death that stumbling were prevented, and so its eternal consequences averted, it would be a happy thing for them. Here follows a striking verse in Matthew 18:7, "Woe unto the world because of offences!" (There will be stumblings and falls and loss of souls enough from the world's treatment of disciples, without any addition from you: dreadful will be its doom in consequence; see that ye share not in it.) "For it must needs be that offences come; but woe to that man by whom the offence cometh!" (The struggle between light and darkness will inevitably cause stumblings, but not less guilty is he who wilfully makes any to stumble.) **43. And if thy hand offend thee, cut it off: it is better for thee to enter into life maimed, than having two hands to go into hell**—See Matthew 5:29, 30. The only difference between the words there and here is that there they refer to impure inclinations; here, to an ambitious disposition, an irascible or quarrelsome temper, and the like: and the injunction is to strike at the root of such dispositions and cut off the occasions of them. **47. And if thine eye offend thee, pluck it out: it is better for thee to enter into the kingdom of God with one eye, than having two eyes to be cast into hell-fire;**

ADAM CLARKE

38. *We saw one casting out devils in thy name.* It can scarcely be supposed that a man who knew nothing of Christ, or who was only a common exorcist, could be able to work a miracle in Christ's name. We may therefore safely imagine that this was either one of John the Baptist's disciples, who, at his master's command, had believed in Jesus, or one of the seventy whom Christ had sent out, Luke x. 1-7, who, after he had fulfilled his commission, had retired from accompanying the other disciples. But as he still held fast his faith in Christ and walked in good conscience, the influence of his Master still continued with him, so that he could cast out demons as well as the other disciples. *We forbad him.* I do not see that we have any right to attribute any other motive to John than that which he himself owns—*because he followeth not us*—because he did not attach himself constantly to Thee, as we do, we thought he could not be in a proper spirit.

39. *Forbid him not.* If you meet him again, let him go on quietly in the work in which God owns him. If he were not of God, the demons would not be subject to him, and his work could not prosper. A spirit of bigotry has little countenance from these passages. There are some who are so outrageously wedded to their own creed and religious system that they would rather let sinners perish than suffer those who differ from them to become the instruments of their salvation.

40. *He that is not against us is on our part.* Or rather, "Whosoever is not against you is for you."

There is a parallel case to this mentioned in Num. xi. 26-29. The reader will easily observe that Joshua and John were of the same bigoted spirit, and that Jesus and Moses acted from the spirit of candor and benevolence.

But whoso shall offend one of these little ones. But, on the contrary, whosoever shall cause one of the least of those who believe in Me to be stumbled—to go into the spirit of the world, or give way to sin—such a one shall meet with the most exemplary punishment. *A millstone.* "An ass's millstone," because in ancient times, before the invention of wind and water mills, the stones were turned sometimes by slaves, but commonly by asses or mules.

MATTHEW HENRY

things, be cast away as *detestable* things. It is necessary that the part which is gangrened should be taken off for the preservation of the whole. Self must be denied, that it may not be destroyed.

3. The necessity of doing this. The flesh must be mortified, that we may *enter into life* (*v.* 43, 45), into the kingdom of God, *v.* 47. Though, by abandoning sin, we may, for the present, feel ourselves as if we were *halt* and *maimed*, yet it is for *life*; and all that men have, they will give for their lives. These *halts* and *maims* will be the *marks of the Lord Jesus*, will be in that kingdom *scars of honour*.

4. The danger of not doing this. The matter is brought to this issue, that either sin must die, or we must die. If we be *ruled* by sin, we shall inevitably be *ruined* by it. With what an emphasis of terror are those words repeated three times here, *Where their worm dieth not, and the fire is not quenched!* The reflections and reproaches of the sinner's own conscience are the *worm that dieth not*. The wrath of God fastening upon a guilty and polluted conscience, is the *fire* that is *not quenched*; for it is the wrath of the living God, into whose hands it is a fearful thing to fall. Philo saith, The punishment of the wicked is *to live for ever dying*.

The last two verses are somewhat difficult, and interpreters agree not in the sense of them; *for every-one* shall be *salted with fire, and every sacrifice shall be salted with salt*. Therefore *have salt in yourselves*. It was appointed by the law of Moses, that every sacrifice should be *salted with salt*, not to *preserve* it but because it was the food of God's table. The nature of man, being *corrupt*, and as such being called *flesh*, some way or other must be *salted*, in order to its being a sacrifice to God. Our chief concern is, to present ourselves *living sacrifices* to the grace of God (Rom. xii. 1), and, in order to our acceptableness, we must be *salted with salt*. We must have in our souls a savour of grace. Those that have the salt of grace, must make it appear that they have it; that they *have salt in themselves*, a living principle of grace in their hearts, which works out all corrupt dispositions. Our *speech* must be *always with grace seasoned with* this salt, that no *corrupt communication* may *proceed out of our mouth*, but we may loathe it as much as we would to put putrid meat into our mouths. As this gracious salt will keep our own consciences void of offence, so it will keep our conversation with others so, that we may not offend any of Christ's little ones. We must not only have this salt of grace, but we must always retain the relish and savour of it; for if this *salt lose its saltness, wherewith will ye season it?* They who will not be *salted with the salt* of divine grace, will be *salted with fire*. The pleasures they have lived in, *shall eat their flesh, as it were fire*. Now since this will certainly be the doom of those that do not crucify the flesh with its affections and lusts, let us, knowing this *terror of the Lord*, be *persuaded* to do it.

JAMIESON, FAUSSET, BROWN

48. Where their worm dieth not, and the fire is not quenched—See on Matthew 5:30; and on the words "hell" and "hell-fire," or "the hell of fire," see on Matthew 5:22. The "unquenchableness" of this fire has already been brought before us (see on Matt. 3:12); and the awfully vivid idea of an undying worm, everlastingly consuming an unconsumable body, is taken from the closing words of the evangelical prophet (Isa. 66: 24), which seem to have furnished the later Jewish Church with its current phraseology on the subject of future punishment (see LIGHTFOOT). **49. For every one shall be salted with fire, and every sacrifice shall be salted with salt**—A difficult verse, on which much has been written—some of it to little purpose. "Every one" probably means "Every follower of mine"; and the "fire" with which he "must be salted" probably means "a fiery trial" to season him. (Cf. Mal. 3:2, etc.) The reference to salting the sacrifice is of course to that maxim of the Levitical law, that every acceptable sacrifice must be sprinkled with salt, to express symbolically its soundness, sweetness, wholesomeness, acceptability. But as it had to be *roasted* first, we have here the further idea of a salting with fire. In this case, "every sacrifice," in the next clause, will mean, "Every one who would be found an acceptable offering to God"; and thus the whole verse may perhaps be paraphrased as follows: "Every disciple of Mine shall have a fiery trial to undergo, and everyone who would be found an odor of a sweet smell, a sacrifice acceptable and well-pleasing to God, must have such a *salting*, like the Levitical sacrifices." Another, but, as it seems to us, far-fetched as well as harsh, interpretation—suggested first, we believe, by MICHAELIS, and adopted by ALEXANDER—takes the "every sacrifice which must be salted with fire" to mean those who are "cast into hell," and the *preservative* effect of this salting to refer to the preservation of the lost not only *in* but *by means of* the fire of hell. Their reason for this is that the other interpretation changes the meaning of the "fire," and the characters too, from the lost to the saved, in these verses. But as our Lord confessedly ends His discourse with the case of His own true disciples, the transition to them in the preceding verse is perfectly natural; whereas to apply the preservative salt of the sacrifice to the preserving quality of hell-fire, is equally contrary to the symbolical sense of salt and the Scripture representations of future torment. Our Lord has still in His eye the unseemly jarrings which had arisen among the Twelve, the peril to themselves of allowing any indulgence to such passions, and the severe self-sacrifice which salvation would cost them. **50. Salt is good; but if the salt have lost his saltness**—its power to season what it is brought into contact with. **wherewith will ye season it?**—How is this property to be restored? See on Matthew 5: 13. **Have salt in yourselves**—See to it that ye retain in yourselves those precious qualities that will make you a blessing to one another, and to all around you. **and**—with respect to the miserable strife out of which all this discourse has sprung, in one concluding word—**have peace one with another**—This is repeated in I Thessalonians 5:13.

ADAM CLARKE

43. *The fire that never shall be quenched.* That is, "the inextinguishable fire." The same clause in v. 45 is omitted in BCL, seven others, Syriac, later Persic, Coptic, and one Itala. "Eternal fire" is the expression of Matthew.

44. *Where their worm dieth not.* The bitter reflection, "I might have avoided sin, but I did not; I might have been saved, but I would not," must be equal to ten thousand tormentors. What intolerable anguish must this produce in a damned soul! *Their worm.* It seems everyone has his *worm*, his peculiar remorse for the evils he did, and for the grace he rejected; while the *fire*, the state of excruciating torment, is common to all. Reader! may the living God save you from this *worm* and from this *fire! The fire is not quenched.* The state of punishment is continual; there is no respite, alleviation, nor end!

49. *For every one shall be salted with fire.* Every one of those who shall live and die in sin; but there is great difficulty in this verse. The Codex Bezae and some other MSS. have omitted the first clause; and several MSS. keep the first and omit the last clause—*and every sacrifice shall be salted with salt.* Some take the whole in a good sense, as referring to the influence of the Spirit of God in the hearts of believers, which shall answer the same end to the soul, in preserving it from the contagion that is in the world, as salt did in the sacrifices offered to God to preserve them from putrefaction. Old Trapp's note on the place pleases me as much as any I have seen: "The *Spirit*, as *salt*, must dry up those bad *humors* in us which breed the never-dying worm; and, as fire, must waste our corruptions, which else will carry us on to the unquenchable fire." Perhaps the whole is an allusion to the purification of vessels, and especially such metallic vessels as were employed in the service of the sanctuary. Probably the following may be considered as a parallel text: "Every thing that may abide the fire, ye shall make it go through the fire, and it shall be clean . . . and all that abideth not the fire ye shall make go through the water," Num. xxxi. 23. You disciples are the Lord's sacrifice; you shall go through much tribulation, in order to enter into My kingdom. But you are salted, you are influenced by the Spirit of God, and are immortal till your work is done; and should you be offered up, martyred, this shall be a means of establishing more fully the glad tidings of the Kingdom. And this Spirit shall preserve all who believe on Me from the corruption of sin, and from eternal perdition. That converts to God are represented as His offering, see Isa. lxvi. 20, the very place which our Lord appears to have here in view.

50. *Have salt in yourselves.* See that you have at all times the preserving principle of divine grace in your hearts, and give that proof of it which will satisfy your own minds and convince or silence the world. Live in brotherly kindness and peace with each other.

MATTHEW HENRY

CHAPTER 10

Verses 1–12

Our Lord Jesus did not continue long in a place, for the whole land of Canaan was his parish, and therefore he would visit every part of it. Here we have him in the *coasts* of Judæa, eastward, as we found him, not long since, in the utmost borders westward, near Tyre and Sidon. Thus was his circuit like that of the sun, from whose light and heat nothing is hid.

I. *Resorted to* by the *people*, *v.* 1. They came to him *again*, and, *as he was wont, he taught them again.* He did *as he was wont*. In Matthew it is said, *He healed them*; here it is said, *He taught them.* His *teaching* was *healing* to poor souls. He *taught them again.* Such is the fulness of the Christian doctrine, that there is still more to be learned; and such our forgetfulness, that we need to be reminded of what we do know.

II. *Disputed with* by the Pharisees.

1. A question they started concerning divorce (*v.* 2); *Is it lawful for a man to put away his wife?* They proposed it, *tempting him*, seeking an occasion against him, which side soever he should take of the question. Ministers must stand upon their guard, lest, under pretence of being advised with, they be ensnared.

JAMIESON, FAUSSET, BROWN

CHAPTER 10

Vss. 1-12. FINAL DEPARTURE FROM GALILEE—DIVORCE. (=Matt. 19:1-12; Luke 9:51.) See on Matthew 19:1-12.

and came into the coasts—or, boundaries—**of Judea beyond Jordan**—i.e., to the further, or east side of the Jordan, into Perea, the dominions of Herod Antipas. But though one might conclude from our Evangelist that our Lord went straight from the one region to the other, we know from the other Gospels that a considerable time elapsed between the departure from the one and the arrival at the other, during which many of the most important events in our Lord's public life occurred—probably a large part of what is recorded in Luke 9:51, onward to ch. 18:15, and part of John 7:2-11, 54.

Is it lawful for a man to put away his wife for every cause?—Two rival schools (as we saw on ch. 5:31) were divided on this question—a delicate one, as DE WETTE pertinently remarks, in the dominions of Herod Antipas.

ADAM CLARKE

CHAPTER 10

1. *He arose.* "He departed thence." Many transactions took place between those mentioned in the preceding chapter and these that follow, which are omitted by Matthew and Mark; but they are related by both Luke and John.

2. *Is it lawful for a man to put away his wife?* See this question about divorce largely explained on Matt. xix. 3-12.

MATTHEW HENRY

2. Christ's reply to them with a question (*v.* 3); *What did Moses command you?* This he asked them, to testify his respect to the law of Moses, and to show that he came not to destroy it.

3. The fair account they gave of the law of Moses, expressly concerning divorce, *v.* 4. Christ asked, *What did Moses command you?* They own that Moses only *suffered*, or *permitted*, a man to write his wife a *bill of divorce*, and to put *her away*, Deut. xxiv. 1.

4. The answer that Christ gave to their question, in which he abides by the doctrine he had formerly laid down in this case (Matt. v. 32), *That whosoever puts away his wife, except for fornication, causeth her to commit adultery*. He here shows,

(1) That the reason why Moses, in his *law*, permitted divorce, was only *for the hardness of their hearts* (*v.* 5).

(2) That the account which Moses, in this *history*, *gives* of the institution of marriage, affords such a reason against divorce, as amounts to a prohibition of it.

Moses tells us, God made man *male and female*, *one* male, and *one* female; so that *Adam could not* put away his wife and take another. The law was, That a man must *leave his father and mother, and cleave to his wife* (*v.* 7); which intimates not only the nearness of the relation, but the perpetuity of it. The result of the relation is, that, though they are *two*, yet they are *one*, they are *one flesh*, *v.* 8. The union between them is a sacred thing that must not be violated. God himself has *joined them together*; he has in wisdom and goodness appointed them who are thus joined together, to live together in love till death parts them. Marriage is not an invention of men, but a divine institution. The bond which God himself has tied, is not to be lightly untied.

5. Christ's discourse with his disciples, in private, about this matter, *v.* 10-12. It was an advantage to them, that they had opportunity of personal converse with Christ, not only about gospel mysteries, but about moral duties. No more is here related of this private conference, than the law Christ laid down in this case—That it is adultery for a man to put away his wife, and marry another; it is adultery *against the wife* he puts away, *v.* 11. He adds, *If a woman shall put away her husband*, and *be married to another*, she *commits adultery* (*v.* 12). Wisdom and grace, holiness and love, reigning in the heart, will make those commands easy which to the carnal mind may be as a heavy yoke.

Verses 13-16

It is looked upon as the indication of a kind and tender disposition to take notice of little children, and this was remarkable in our Lord Jesus, which is an encouragement not only to little children to apply themselves to Christ, but to grown people, who are conscious to themselves of weakness and childishness, and of being helpless and useless, like little children.

I Little children brought to Christ, *v.* 13. It doth not appear that they needed any bodily *cure*, nor were they capable of being *taught*. They that had the care of them were mostly concerned *about their souls*, their better part. They believed that Christ's blessing would do their souls good; and therefore to him they brought them, that he might *touch* them, knowing that he could reach their hearts, when nothing their parents could say to them, or do for them, would reach them. We may present our children to Christ, now that he is in heaven, and therein we may act faith upon the fulness and extent of his grace, and the promise *to us and to our children*.

II. The *dis*couragement which the disciples gave to the bringing of children to Christ; *They rebuked them that brought them.*

III. The *en*couragement Christ gave to it. He took it very ill that his disciples should keep them off; *When he saw it, he was much displeased*, *v.* 14. Christ is very angry with his own disciples, if they discountenance any in coming to him themselves, or in bringing their children to him. He ordered that they should be *brought to him*; suffer *little children* to *come to me.* Little children are welcome betimes to the throne of grace with their Hosannas. He came to set up the *kingdom of God* among men, and took this occasion to declare that that kingdom admitted *little children* to be the subjects of it. There must be something of the temper and disposition of little children found in all that Christ will own and bless. We must *receive the kingdom of God as little children* (*v.* 15); that is, we must stand affected to Christ and his grace as little children do to their parents, nurses, and teachers. We must be *inquisitive*. as children, must learn as children and in learning must *believe*. The mind of a child is white paper, you may

JAMIESON, FAUSSET, BROWN

suffered you to put away your wives—tolerated a relaxation of the strictness of the marriage bond—not as approving of it, but to prevent still greater evils.

He saith unto them, Moses—as a civil lawgiver. **because of**—or "having respect to." **the hardness of your hearts**—looking to your low moral state, and your inability to endure the strictness of the original law.

"He that made them made them from the beginning a male and a female." **And said, For this cause**—to follow out this divine appointment. **shall a man leave father and mother, and shall cleave to his wife: and they twain shall be one flesh?**—Jesus here sends them back to the original constitution of man as one pair, a male and a female; to their marriage, as such, by divine appointment; and to the purpose of God, expressed by the sacred historian, that in all time one man and one woman should by marriage become one flesh—so to continue as long as both are in the flesh. This being *God's* constitution, let not *man* break it up by causeless divorces.

13-19. Little Children Brought to Christ. (=Matt. 19:13-15; Luke 18:15-17.) See on Luke 18:15-17.

infants—showing that some, at least, of those called in Matthew (19:13) and Mark (10:13) simply "little" or "young children," were literally "*babes.*" **touch them**—or, as more fully in Matthew, "put His hands on them and *pray*," or invoke a "blessing" on them (Mark 10:16), according to venerable custom (Gen. 48:14, 15). **rebuked them**—Repeatedly the disciples thus interposed to save annoyance and interruption to their Master; but, as the result showed, *always against the mind of Christ* (Matt. 15:23; ch. 18:39, 40). Here, it is plain from our Lord's reply, that they thought the intrusion a useless one, as *infants* were not capable of receiving anything from Him. His ministrations were for *grown people.* **But Jesus**—*much displeased,"* says Mark (10:14); and invaluable addition. **said**—"Suffer the little children to come unto Me"—"and forbid them not," is the important addition of Matthew (19:14) and Mark (10:14). What words are these from the lips of Christ! The price of them is above rubies. But the *reason* assigned, "For of such is the Kingdom of God," or "of heaven," as in Matthew 19:14, completes the previous information here conveyed; especially as interpreted by what immediately follows: "And He took them up in His arms, put His hands upon them, and blessed them" (Mark 10:16). It is surely not to be conceived that all our Lord meant was to inform us, that seeing *grown people* must become childlike in order to be capable of the Kingdom of God, therefore they should not hinder *infants* from coming to Him, and therefore He took up and blessed *the infants themselves.* Was it not just the grave mistake of the disciples that infants should not be brought to Christ, be-

ADAM CLARKE

Except it be for fornication. The grand subject of dispute between the two schools mentioned above was the word in Deut. xxiv. 1, "When a man hath taken a wife, and she find no grace in his sight, because of some uncleanness." This the school of Shammai held to mean whoredom or adultery; but the school of Hillel maintained that it signified any corporeal defect which rendered the person deformed, or any bad temper which made the husband's life uncomfortable.

Moses because of the hardness of your hearts. Moses perceived that if divorce were not permitted, in many cases, the women would be exposed to great hardships through the "cruelty" of their husbands.

For this cause. Being created for this very purpose, that they might glorify their Maker in a matrimonial connection. *Shall a man leave* (wholly give up) *father and mother*—the matrimonial union being more intimate and binding than even paternal or filial affection—and shall be "closely united, shall be firmly cemented" to his wife. A beautiful metaphor, which most forcibly intimates that nothing but death can separate them, as a well-glued board will break sooner in the whole wood than in the glued joint. *And they twain shall be one flesh.* Not only meaning that they should be considered as one body, but also as two souls in one body, with a complete union of interests, and an indissoluble partnership of life and fortune, comfort and support, desires and inclinations, joys and sorrows.

12. *And if a woman shall put away her husband.* From this it appears that in some cases the wife assumed the very same right of divorcing her husband that the husband had of divorcing his wife; and yet this is not recorded anywhere in the Jewish laws, as far as I can find, that the women had such a right.

13. *And they brought young children.* See on Matt. xix. 13-15.

Then were there brought unto him little children. These are termed by Luke, chap. xviii. 15, "infants," very young children; and it was on this account, probably, that the disciples rebuked the parents, thinking them too young to receive good. *That he should put his hands.* It was a common custom among the Jews to lay their hands on the heads of those whom they blessed or for whom they prayed. This seems to have been done by way of dedication or consecration to God—the person being considered as the sacred property of God ever after.

Of such is the kingdom of heaven. Or, "The kingdom of heaven is composed of such." A great part of God's kingdom is composed of such literally, and those only who resemble little children shall be received into it; see on chap. xviii. 3. Christ loves little children because He loves simplicity and innocence; He has sanctified their very age by passing through it himself—the holy Jesus was once a little child.

MATTHEW HENRY

write upon it what you will; such must our minds be to the pen of the blessed Spirit. Children are under government; so must we be. Little children depend upon their parents' wisdom and care, are carried in their arms, and take what they provide for them; and thus must we receive the *kingdom of God*, with a humble resignation of ourselves to Jesus Christ, and an easy dependence upon him. He received the children, and gave them what was desired (*v.* 16); *He took them up in his arms, put his hands upon them,* and *blessed them.* They begged he would touch them, but he did more. He *took them in his arms. He shall gather the lambs in his arms, and carry them in his bosom.* Time was, when Christ himself was taken up in old Simeon's arms, Luke ii. 28. And now he took up these children, not complaining of the burthen, but pleased with it. He *put his hands upon them.* He *blessed* them. Our children are happy, if they have but the *Mediator's blessing* for their portion.

Verses 17–31

I. Here is a *hopeful meeting* between Christ and a *young man*; such he is said to be (Matt. xix. 20, 22), and a *ruler* (Luke xviii. 18).

1. He came *running* to Christ; he laid aside the gravity and grandeur of a ruler; he manifested his earnestness and importunity; he *ran* as one *in haste*. He had now an opportunity of consulting this great Prophet, and he would not let slip the opportunity.

2. He came to him when he was *in the way*, in the midst of company.

3. He *kneeled to him,* in token of the great value and veneration he had for him, and his earnest desire to be taught by him. He *bowed the knee*, as one that meant to *bow the soul* to him.

4. His address to him was serious and weighty; *Good Master, what shall I do, that I may inherit eternal life?* He thinks it a thing possible, that he may *inherit eternal life,* looking upon it not only as set before us, but as offered to us. Most men enquire for good to be *had* in this world, he asks for *good to be done* in this world; not, Who will make us to *see good*? But, "Who will make us to *do good*?" He enquires for *happiness* in the way of *duty*. Now this was, (1) A very serious question. *Then* there begins to be some hope of people, when they begin to enquire solicitously, what they shall do to get to heaven. (2) It was proposed to a right person, one that was every way fit to answer it, being himself *the Way, the Truth,* and *the Life*; who came *from heaven* on purpose, first to make, and then to make known, the way *to heaven.* It is peculiar to the Christian religion, both to show eternal life, and to show the way to it. (3) It was proposed with a good design—to be instructed. We find this same question put by a lawyer (Luke x. 25), with a bad design; he *tempted him, saying, Master, what shall I do?* It is not so much the good *words* as the good *intention* of them that Christ looks at.

5. Christ encouraged this address by *assisting his faith, v.* 18. He called him *good Master*; Christ would have him mean thereby, that he looked upon him to be *God*, since there is none good but *one*, that is *God.* Our English word *God* doubtless hath affinity with *good*. Further, he directed his practice (*v.* 19); *Keep the commandments.* He mentions the six commandments of the second table, which prescribe our duty to our neighbour. The fifth commandment is here put last, as that which should especially be remembered and observed, to keep us to all the rest.

6. The young man bid fair for heaven, having been free from any open gross violations of the divine commands. *Master, all these have I observed from my youth.* He thought he had, and his neighbours thought so too. He that could say he was free from scandalous sin, went further than many in the way to eternal life.

7. Christ had a kindness for him; *Jesus, beholding him, loved him, v.* 21. Christ particularly *loves* to see young people, and rich people, *asking the way to heaven, with their faces thitherward.*

II. Here is a *sorrowful parting* between Christ and this young man.

1. Christ gave him a command of trial. Has he indeed his heart upon it? Bring him to the touchstone. Can he find in his heart to *part with his riches* for the service of Christ? Let him know the worst now; if he will not come up to these terms, let him quit his pretensions; as good at first as at last. "*Sell whatsoever thou hast;* and be a *father to the poor.*" Every man, according to his ability, must relieve the poor. Worldly wealth is given us as a *talent*, to be used and employed for the glory of our great Master in the world, who hath so ordered it, that the poor we should have always with us as his receivers. Can he find in his heart to go through the hardest, costliest

JAMIESON, FAUSSET, BROWN

cause only grown people could profit by Him, which "much displeased" our Lord? And though He took the irresistible opportunity of lowering their pride of reason, by informing them that, in order to enter the Kingdom, *"instead of the children first becoming like them, they must themselves become like the children"* [RICHTER in STIER], this was but by the way; and, returning to the *children themselves,* He took them up in His gracious arms, put His hands upon them and blessed them, for no conceivable reason but to show that *they were thereby made capable,* AS INFANTS, *of the Kingdom of God.*

17-31. THE RICH YOUNG RULER. (=Matt. 19: 16-30; Luke 18:18-30.) See on Luke 18:18-30.

This case presents some remarkable points. (1) The man was of irreproachable moral character; and this amidst all the temptations of *youth,* for he was a "young man" (Matt. 19:22), and *wealth,* for "he was very rich" (vs. 23; Mark 10:22). (2) But restless notwithstanding, his heart craves eternal life. (3) Unlike the "rulers," to whose class he belonged (vs. 18), he so far believed in Jesus as to be persuaded He could authoritatively direct him on this vital point. (4) So earnest is he that he comes "running" and even "kneeling before Him," and that when He was gone forth *into the war* (Mark 10:17)—the high-road, by this time crowded with travellers to the passover; undeterred by the virulent opposition of the class he belonged to as a "ruler" and by the shame he might be expected to feel at broaching such a question in the hearing of a crowd and on the open road. **Why . . .**—Did our Lord mean then to teach that God only ought to be called "good"? Impossible, for that had been to contradict all Scripture teaching, and His own, too (Ps. 112:5; Matt. 25:21; Titus 1:8). Unless therefore we are to ascribe captiousness to our Lord, He could have had but one object — *to raise the youth's ideas of Himself,* as not to be classed merely with other "good masters," and declining to receive this title *apart from* the "One" who is essentially and only "good." This indeed is but distantly hinted; but unless this is seen in *the background* of our Lord's words, nothing worthy of Him can be made out of them. (Hence, *Socinianism,* instead of having any support here, is only baffled by it.) **Thou knowest . . .**—Matthew is more complete here: "but if thou wilt enter into life, keep the commandments. He saith unto him, Which?"—as if he had said, Point me out one of them which I have not kept?—"Jesus said, Thou shalt . . ." (Matt. 19: 17, 18). Our Lord purposely confines Himself to the *second* table, which He would consider easy to keep, enumerating them all—for in Mark (10:19), "Defraud not" stands for the *tenth* (else the eighth is twice repeated). In Matthew the *sum* of this second table of the law is added, "Thou shalt love thy neighbor as thyself," as if to see if he would venture to say he had kept *that.* **All these . . .**—"what lack I yet?" adds Matthew. Ah! this gives us a glimpse of his heart. Doubtless he was perfectly sincere; but something within whispered to him that *his* keeping of the commandments was *too easy* a way of getting to heaven. He felt something beyond this to be necessary; after keeping all the commandments he was at a loss to know what that could be; and he came to Jesus just upon that point. "Then," says Mark (10:21), "Jesus beholding him loved him," or "looked lovingly upon him." His sincerity, frankness, and nearness to the kingdom of God, in themselves most winning qualities, won our Lord's regard even though he turned his back upon Him—a lesson to those who can see nothing lovable save in the regenerate. **lackest . . . one thing**—Ah! but that a fundamental, fatal lack. **sell . . .**—As riches were his idol, our Lord, who knew if from the first, lays His great authoritative grasp at once upon it, saying, "Now give Me up that, and all is right." No general direction about the disposal of riches, then, is here given, save that we are to sit loose to them and lay them at the feet of Him who gave them. He who does this with all he has, whether rich or poor, is a true heir of the kingdom of heaven.

ADAM CLARKE

16. ***And he took them up in his arms.*** **Jesus Christ loves little children, and they are objects of His most peculiar care.** ***And blessed them.*** **Then, though little children, they were capable of receiving Christ's blessing. If Christ embraced them, why should not His Church embrace them?**

17. ***There came one running.*** **See the case of this rich young man largely explained on Matt. xix. 16, etc.**

One came. Much instruction may be had from seriously attending to the conduct, spirit, and question of this person. (1) He came running, Mark x. 17, and he was deeply convinced of the importance of his business, and seriously determined to seek so as to find. (2) He kneeled, or caught Him by the knees, thus evidencing his humility, and addressing himself only to mercy. (3) He came in the spirit of a disciple, or scholar, desiring to be taught a matter of the utmost importance to him—Good teacher. (4) He came in the spirit of obedience; he had worked hard to no purpose, and he is still willing to work, provided he can have a prospect of succeeding—*What good thing shall I do?* (5) His question was the most interesting and important that any soul can ask of God—How shall I be saved?

Why callest thou me good? Or, "Why do you question Me concerning that good thing?" The whole passage therefore may be read thus: "O Teacher! what good thing shall I do that I may have eternal life? And He said unto him, Why do you question Me concerning that good thing? There is One that is good." *Keep the commandments.* From this we may learn that God's great design in giving His law to the Jews was to lead them to the expectation and enjoyment of eternal life. But as all the law referred to Christ, and He became "the end of the law for righteousness" (justification) to all that believe, so He is to be received, in order to have the end accomplished which the law proposed.

All these things have I kept. I have made these precepts the rule of my life. There is a difference worthy of notice between this and our Lord's word. He says, v. 17, *keep,* earnestly, diligently, as with watch and ward, probably referring not only to the letter but to the spirit. The young man modestly says, All these have I "observed"; I have paid attention to, and endeavored to regulate my conduct by them. I have "kept them in custody." *What lack I yet?* He felt a troubled conscience, and a mind unassured of the approbation of God; and he clearly perceived that something was wanting to make him truly happy.

21. ***Then Jesus beholding him.*** **"Looking earnestly" or "affectionately upon him,"** ***loved him,*** **because of his youth, his earnestness, and his sincerity.** ***One thing thou lackest.*** **What was that? A heart disengaged from the world, and a complete renunciation of it and its concerns, that he might become a proper and successful laborer in the Lord's vineyard.**

If thou wilt be perfect. "Be complete," have the business "finished," and all hindrances to your salvation removed, *go and sell that thou hast*—go and dispose of your possessions, to which it is evident his heart was too much attached, *and give to the poor*—for your goods will be a continual snare to you if you keep them; *and thou shalt have treasure in heaven*—the loss, if it can be called such, shall be made amply up to you in that eternal life about which

MATTHEW HENRY

services he may be called to as a disciple of Christ, and depend upon him for a recompence *in heaven*? Doth he really believe there is a treasure in heaven sufficient to make up all he can leave, or lose, or lay out, for Christ? Is he willing to deal with Christ *upon trust*? Can he give him credit for all he is worth; and be willing to bear a present cross, in expectation of a future crown?

2. Upon this he flew off (*v.* 22); *He was sad at that saying;* was sorry that he could not be a follower of Christ upon any easier terms, that he could not *lay hold* on eternal life, and *keep hold* of his temporal possessions too. But since he could not come up to the terms of discipleship, he was so fair as not to pretend to it; *He went away grieved.* Here appeared the truth of that (Matt. vi. 24), *Ye cannot serve God and mammon*; while he held to mammon he did in effect *despise* Christ. He bids for what he has a mind for in the market, yet goes away grieved, and leaves it, because he cannot have it at his own price.

III. Here is Christ's discourse with his disciples. We are tempted to wish that Christ had *mollified* that saying and taken off the hardness of it: but he knew all men's hearts; he would not court him to be his follower, because he was a *rich man* and a ruler; but, if he will go, let him go. Christ will keep no man against his will.

1. The difficulty of the salvation of those who have an abundance of this world; because there are few who have *a deal to leave*, that can be *persuaded to leave it* for Christ.

(1) Christ asserts this here; *He looked about* upon his *disciples*; *How hardly shall they who have riches enter into the kingdom of God!* v. 23. They have many temptations to grapple with, and many difficulties to get over, which lie not in the way of poor people. But he explains himself, *v.* 24, where he calls the disciples *children*, because as such they should be *taught* by him. Whereas he had said, *How hardly will those who have riches get to heaven;* here he tells them, that the danger arose not so much from their *having* riches as from their *trusting to them.* They that have such a value as this for the wealth of the world, will never be brought to put a right value upon Christ and his grace. They that *have* ever so much riches, but do not *trust in them*, have got over the difficulty, and can easily part with them for Christ: but they that have ever so little, if they set their hearts upon that little, it will keep them from Christ. He enforces this assertion with, *v.* 25, *It is easier for a camel to go through the eye of a needle, than for a rich man to enter into the kingdom of God.* [1] Some imagine there might be some wicket-gate, or door, to Jerusalem, commonly known by the name of *the needle's eye*, for its straitness, through which a camel could not be got, unless he were unloaded. So a rich man cannot get to heaven, unless he be willing to part with the burthen of his worldly wealth, and stoop to the duties of a humble religion. [2] Others suggest that the word we translate a *camel*, sometimes signifies a *cable-rope*. A rich man, compared with the poor, is as a cable to a single thread, and it will not go through the *needle's eye*, unless it be untwisted. So the rich man must be loosed and disentangled from his riches, that thread by thread he may be got through the eye of the needle, otherwise he is good for nothing but to cast anchor in the earth.

(2) This truth was very surprising to the disciples; *They were astonished at his words, v.* 24. *They were astonished out of measure, and said among themselves, Who then can be saved?* They knew what abundance of promises there were, in the Old Testament, of temporal good things; they knew likewise that they who are rich have so much the larger opportunities of doing good, and therefore were amazed to hear that it should be so hard for rich people to go to heaven.

(3) Christ reconciled them to it, by referring it to the almighty power of God, to help even rich people over the difficulties that lie in the way of their salvation (*v.* 27); He *looked upon them:* "*With men it is impossible*, but the grace of God can do it, for *with him all things are possible.*"

2. The greatness of the salvation of those that have but a little of this world, and leave it for Christ. This he speaks of, upon occasion of Peter's mentioning what he and the rest of the disciples had left to follow him; *Behold* (saith he), *we have left all to follow thee, v.* 28. "You have *done well,*" saith Christ, "you shall be abundantly recompensed, and not only you shall be *reimbursed*, who have left but a little, but those that have ever so much, though it were so much as this young man had." (1) The loss is supposed to be very great; he specifies, Worldly wealth; *houses* are here put first, and *lands* last: a man may

JAMIESON, FAUSSET, BROWN

was very sorrowful—Matthew more fully, "*went away* sorrowful"; Mark still more, "was sad" or "sullen" at that saying, and "went away grieved." Sorry he was, very sorry, to part with Christ; but to part with his riches would have cost him a pang more. When Riches or Heaven, on Christ's terms, were the alternative, the result showed to which side the balance inclined. Thus was he shown to lack the one all-comprehensive requirement of the law—the *absolute subjection of the heart to God,* and this want vitiated all his other obediences.

when Jesus saw—Mark says, He "looked round about"—as if first following the departing youth with His eye—"and saith unto His disciples." **how hardly . . .**—with what difficulty. In Mark an explanation is added, "How hard is it for them that *trust* in riches . . ."—i.e., with what difficulty is this idolatrous trust conquered, without which they cannot enter; and this is introduced by the word "children"—sweet diminutive of affection and pity (John 21:5).

easier for a camel . . .—a proverbial expression denoting literally a thing impossible, but figuratively, very difficult.

For . . .—"At that rate none can be saved": "Well, it does pass *human* power, but not *divine.*

Lo . . .—in the simplicity of his heart (as is evident from the reply), conscious that the required surrender had been made, and generously taking in his brethren with him—"*we*"; not in the spirit of the young ruler. "All these have I kept," **left all**—"The workmen's little is as much his 'all' as the prince's much [BENGEL]. In Matthew (19:27) he adds, "What shall we have therefore?" How shall it fare with us? **There**

ADAM CLARKE

you inquired; *and come and follow me*—be My disciple, and I will appoint you to preach the kingdom of God to others.

22. *And he was sad at that saying.* This young man had perhaps been a saint, and an eminent apostle, had he been poor! From this, and a multitude of other cases, we may learn that it is oftentimes a misfortune to be rich. But who is aware of this?—and who believes it?

Went away sorrowful. Men undergo great agony of mind while they are in suspense between the love of the world and the love of their souls. *He had great possessions.* And what were these in comparison of peace of conscience and mental rest?

A rich man shall hardly enter. That is, into the spirit and privileges of the gospel in this world, and through them into the Kingdom of glory.

A camel. It was a mode of expression common among the Jews, and signified a thing impossible. Hence this proverb: "No man sees a palm tree of gold, nor an elephant passing through the eye of a needle."

With men this is impossible. God alone can take the love of the world out of human heart. Therefore the salvation of the rich is represented as possible only to Him.

MATTHEW HENRY

quit his *house*, which should be for his habitation, and his *land*, which should be for his maintenance; or his dear relations. *Father and mother, wife and children, brethren and sisters.* Without these the world would be a wilderness; yet, when we must either forsake these or Christ, we must remember that we stand in nearer relation to Christ than we do to any creature. The greatest trial of a good man's constancy is, when his love to Christ comes to stand in competition with a love that is lawful, nay, that is his duty. It is easy to such a one to forsake a *lust* for Christ; but to forsake a *father*, a *brother*, a *wife*, for Christ, that is, to forsake those whom he knows he must love, is hard. And yet he must do so, rather than deny or disown Christ. It is not the *suffering*, but the *cause*, that makes the *martyr*. And therefore, (2) The advantage will be great. *They shall receive a hundred-fold in this time, houses, and brethren, and sisters.* He shall have abundance of comfort while he lives, sufficient to make up all his losses. Suffering Christians shall have a *hundred-fold* in the comforts of the Spirit sweetening their creature comforts. It is added here in Mark, *with persecutions.* Even when they are gainers by Christ, let them still expect to be sufferers for him. They shall have *eternal life in the world to come.* If they receive a hundred-fold in this world, one would think they should not be encouraged to expect any more. Yet, as if that were a small matter, they shall have *life eternal* into the bargain. But because they talked so much, and really more than became them, of *leaving all* for Christ, he tells them, though they were *first called*, that there should be disciples called after them, that should be preferred before them. Then the *first* were *last*, and the last *first.*

Verses 32–45

I. Christ's prediction of his own sufferings.

1. See here how bold he was; when they were going up to Jerusalem, *Jesus went before them, v.* 32. Now that the time was at hand, more than ever, he *pressed forward. Jesus went before them, and they were amazed.* They began now to consider what imminent danger they ran themselves into, when they went to Jerusalem; and they were ready to tremble at the thought of it. To hearten them, therefore, Christ *went before them.* When we see ourselves entering upon sufferings, it is encouraging to see our Master go before us. Or, *He went before them,* and *therefore* they were *amazed*; they admired to see with what cheerfulness and alacrity he went on. Christ's courage and constancy are, and will be, the wonder of all his disciples.

2. See here how timorous and faint-hearted his disciples were; *As they followed, they were afraid.* Their Master's courage should have put spirit into them.

3. See here what method he took to silence their fears. He did not go about to make the matter better than it was, but told them *again* the *things that should happen to him.* He knew the worst of it, and therefore went on thus boldly, and he will let them know the worst of it. Come, *be not afraid.* He *shall rise again*; the issue of his sufferings will be glorious to himself, and advantageous to all that are his, *v.* 33, 34. The method and particulars of Christ's sufferings are more largely foretold here than in any other of the predictions. Christ had a perfect foresight, not only of his own death, but of all the aggravating circumstances of it; and yet he thus went forth to meet it.

JAMIESON, FAUSSET, BROWN

is no man . . .—graciously acknowledging at once the completeness and the acceptableness of the surrender as a thing already made. **house . . .**—The specification is still more minute in Matthew and Mark, to take in *every* form of self-sacrifice. **for the kingdom of God's sake**—in Mark, "for MY sake and the Gospel's." See on ch. 6:22. **manifold more in this present time**—in Matthew (19:29) "an hundredfold," to which Mark (10:30) gives this most interesting addition, "Now in this present time, houses, and brethren, and sisters, and mothers, and children, and lands, with persecutions." We have here the blessed promise of a *reconstruction of all human relationships and affections on a Christian basis and in a Christian state, after being sacrificed, in their natural form, on the altar of love to Christ.* This He calls "manifold more"—"an hundredfold more"—than what they sacrificed. Our Lord was Himself the first to exemplify this *new adjustment of His own relationships.* (See on Matt. 12:49, 50; and on II Cor. 6:14-18.) But this "with persecutions"; for how could such a transfer take place without the most cruel wrenches to flesh and blood? but the persecution would haply follow them into their new and higher circle, breaking that up too! But best of all, "in the world to come life everlasting." And

When the shore is won at last
Who will count the billows past?
KEBLE

These promises are for *every one* who forsakes his all for Christ.

32-45. THIRD EXPLICIT AND STILL FULLER ANNOUNCEMENT OF HIS APPROACHING SUFFERINGS, DEATH, AND RESURRECTION—THE AMBITIOUS REQUEST OF JAMES AND JOHN, AND THE REPLY. (= Matt. 20:17-28; Luke 18:31-34.)

Third Announcement of His approaching Sufferings, Death, and Resurrection (vss. 32-34). **32. And they were in the way**—on the road. **going up to Jerusalem**—in Perea, and probably somewhere between Ephraim and Jericho, on the farther side of the Jordan, and to the northeast of Jerusalem. **and Jesus went before them**—as GROTIUS says, in the style of an intrepid Leader. **and they were amazed**—or "struck with astonishment" at His courage in advancing to certain death. **and as they followed, they were afraid**—for their own safety. These artless, lifelike touches—not only from an eye-witness, but one whom the noble carriage of the Master struck with wonder and awe—are peculiar to Mark, and give the second Gospel a charm all its own; making us feel as if we ourselves were in the midst of the scenes it describes. Well might the poet exclaim—

The Saviour, what a noble flame
Was kindled in His breast,
When, hasting to Jerusalem,
He march'd before the rest!
COWPER

And he took again the twelve—referring to His previous announcements on this sad subject. **and began to tell them what things should happen unto him**—were going to befall Him." The word expresses something already begun but not brought to a head, rather than something wholly future. **33. Saying, Behold, we go up to Jerusalem**—for the last time, and—"all things that are written by the prophets concerning the Son of man shall be accomplished" (Luke 18:31). **the Son of man shall be delivered unto the chief priests and unto the scribes; and they shall condemn him to death, and shall deliver him to the Gentiles**—This is the first express statement that the Gentiles would combine with the Jews in His death; the two grand divisions of the human race for whom He died thus taking part in crucifying the Lord of Glory, as WEBSTER and WILKINSON observe. **34. And they shall mock him, and shall scourge him, and shall spit upon him, and shall kill him: and the third day he shall rise again**—Singularly explicit as this announcement was, Luke (18:34) says "they understood none of these things; and this saying was hid from them, neither knew they the things which were spoken." The meaning of the words they could be at no loss to understand, but their import in relation to His Messianic kingdom they could not penetrate; the whole prediction being right in the teeth of their preconceived notions. That they should have clung so tenaciously to the popular notion of an *un*suffering Messiah, may surprise us; but it gives

ADAM CLARKE

29. *And the gospel's.* Read, "for the sake of the gospel," on the authority of most MSS. and almost all the versions.

30. *In this time.* "In this very time." Though Jews and Gentiles have conspired together to destroy both Me and you, My providence shall so work that nothing shall be lacking while anything is necessary. Those who have left all for the sake of Christ do find, among genuine Christians, spiritual relatives, which are as dear to them as fathers, mothers, etc. Yet they have the promise of *receiving an hundredfold* often literally fulfilled; for wherever a Christian travels among Christians, the shelter of their houses and the product of their lands are at his service as far as they are requisite. *With persecutions.* For while you meet with nothing but kindness from true Christians, you shall be despised, and often afflicted, by those who are enemies to God and goodness. But, for your comfort, you shall have *in the world to come,* "the coming world" (that world which is on its way to meet you), *eternal life.*

And Jesus going up. From Jericho to Jerusalem,

32. *And he took again the twelve.* Or thus: "For having again taken the twelve." I translate *kai* "for," which signification it often bears; see Luke i. 22; John xii. 35, and elsewhere. This gives the reason of the wonder and fear of the disciples, for He *began to tell them,* on the way, what was to befall Him.

The Son of man shall be betrayed. Or "will be delivered up." This is the third time that our Lord informed His disciples of His approaching sufferings and death. This was a subject of the utmost importance, and it was necessary they should be well prepared for such an awful event.

Deliver him to the Gentiles to mock. This was done by Herod and his Roman soldiers. See Luke xxiii. 11. *To scourge, and to crucify.* This was done by Pilate, the Roman governor. The punishment of the cross was Roman, not Jewish; but the chief priests condemned Him to it, and the Romans executed the sentence.

MATTHEW HENRY

II. The check he gave to two of his disciples for their ambitious request. This story is much the same here as we had it Matt. xx. 20. Only there they are said to have made their request by their mother, here they are said to make it themselves. As, on the one hand, there are some that do not *use*, so, on the other hand, there are some that *abuse*, the great encouragements Christ has given us in prayer. It was a culpable presumption in these disciples to make such a boundless demand upon their Master;

We would that thou shouldst do for us whatsoever we shall desire. We had much better leave it to him to do for us what he sees fit, and he will do more than we can desire, Eph. iii. 20. We must be cautious how we make general promises. *What would ye that I should do for you?* He would have them go on with their suit, that they might be made ashamed of it. James and John conclude, If Christ *rise again*, he must be a king, and if he be a king, his apostles must be peers, and one of these would willingly be the *first peer of the realm*, and the other next him. To *be good* should be more our care than to *look great*, or to have the pre-eminence. Our weakness and short-sightedness appear as much in our prayers as in any thing. It is folly to *pre*scribe to God, and wisdom to *sub*scribe. It is the will of Christ that we should prepare for sufferings, and leave it to him to recompense us for them. Our care must be, that we may have wisdom and grace to know how to suffer with him, and then we may trust him to provide in the best manner how we shall reign with him.

ALEXANDER MACLAREN:

How lonely Jesus was! While He strode before the Twelve, absorbed in thoughts of the cross to which He was pressing, they, as they followed, "amazed" and "afraid," were thinking not of what He would suffer, but of what they might gain. He saw the cross. They understood little of it, but supposed that somehow it would bring in the kingdom, and they dimly saw thrones for themselves. Hence James and John try to secure the foremost places, and hence the others' anger at what they thought an unfair attempt to push in front of them. What a contrast between Jesus, striding on ahead with "set" face, and the Twelve unsympathetic and self-seeking, lagging behind to squabble about preeminence! We have in this incident two parts: the request and its answer, the indignation of the Ten and its rebuke. The one sets forth the qualifications for the highest place in the kingdom; the other, the paradox that preeminence there is service.

James and John were members of the group of original disciples who stood nearest to Jesus, and of the group of three whom He kept specially at His side. Their present place might well lead them to expect preeminence in the kingdom, but their trick was mean, as being an underhanded attempt to forestall Peter, the remaining one of the three, as putting forward their mother as spokeswoman, and as endeavoring to entrap Jesus into promising before the disclosure of what was desired. Matthew tells that the mother was brought in order to make the request, and that Jesus brushed her aside by directing His answer to her sons ("Ye know not what ye ask"). The attempt to get Jesus' promise without telling what was desired betrayed the consciousness that the wish was wrong. His guarded counter-question would chill them and make their disclosure somewhat hesitating.

Note the strangely blended good and evil of the request. The gold was mingled with clay; selfishness and love delighting in being near Him both had place in it. We may well recog-

JAMIESON, FAUSSET, BROWN

inexpressible weight to their after-testimony to a suffering and dying Saviour.

Ambitious Request of James and John—The Reply (vss. 35-45). **35. And James and John, the sons of Zebedee, come unto him, saying**—Matthew (20:20) says their "mother came to Him with her sons, worshipping Him and desiring . . ." (Cf. Matt. 27:56, with ch. 15:40.) Salome was her name (ch. 16:1). We cannot be sure with which of the parties the movement originated; but as our Lord, even in Matthew's account, addresses Himself to James and John, taking no account of the mother, it is likely the mother was merely set on by them. The thought was doubtless suggested to her sons by the recent promise to the Twelve of "thrones to sit on, when the Son of man should sit on the throne of His glory" (Matt. 19:28); but after the reproof so lately given them (ch. 9:33, etc.) they get their mother to speak for them. **Master, we would that thou shouldest do for us whatsoever we shall desire**—thus cautiously approaching the subject. **36. And he said unto them, What would ye that I should do for you?**—Though well aware what was in their mind and their mother's, our Lord will have the unseemly petition uttered before all. **37. Grant unto us that we may sit, one on thy right hand, and the other on thy left hand, in thy glory**—i.e.,Assign to us the two places of highest honor in the coming kingdom. The semblance of a plea for so presumptuous a request might possibly have been drawn from the fact that one of the two usually leaned on the breast of Jesus, or sat next Him at meals, while the other was one of the favored three. **38. But Jesus said unto them, Ye know not what ye ask**—How gentle the reply to such a request, preferred at such a time, after the sad announcement just made! **can ye drink of the cup that I drink of?**—To "drink of a cup" is in Scripture a figure for getting one's fill either of good (Ps. 16:5; 23:5; 116:13; Jer. 16:7) or of ill (Ps. 75:8; John 18:11; Rev. 14:10). Here it is the cup of suffering. **and be baptized with the baptism that I am baptized with**—(Cf. for the language, Ps. 42:7). The object of this question seems to have been to try how far those two men were *capable* of the dignity to which they aspired and this on the principle that he who is able to suffer most for His sake will be the nearest to Him in His kingdom. **39. And they said unto him, We can**—Here we see them owning their mother's petition for them as their own; and doubtless they were perfectly sincere in professing their willingness to follow their Master to any suffering He might have to endure. As for James, he was the first of the apostles who was honored, and showed himself able to be baptized with his Master's baptism of blood (Acts 12:1, 2); while *John*, after going through all the persecutions to which the infant Church was exposed from the Jews, and sharing in the struggles and sufferings occasioned by the first triumphs of the Gospel among the Gentiles, lived to be the victim, after all the rest had got to glory, of a bitter persecution in the evening of his days, for the word of God and for the testimony of Jesus Christ. Yes, they were dear believers and blessed men, in spite of this unworthy ambition, and their Lord knew it; and perhaps the foresight of what they would have to pass through, and the courageous testimony He would yet receive from them, was the cause of that gentleness which we cannot but wonder at in His reproof. **And Jesus said unto them, Ye shall indeed drink of the cup that I drink of; and with the baptism that I am baptized withal shall ye be baptized**—No doubt this prediction, when their sufferings at length came upon them, cheered them with the assurance, not that they would sit on His right and left hand—for of that thought they would be heartily ashamed—but that "if they suffered with Him, they should be also glorified together." **40. But to sit on my right hand and on my left hand in not mine to give; but it shall be given to them for whom it is prepared**—"of My Father" (Matt. 20:23). The supplement which our translators have inserted is approved by some good interpreters, and the proper sense of the word rendered "but" is certainly in favor of it. But besides that it makes the statement too elliptical—leaving too many words to be supplied—it seems to make our Lord repudiate the right to assign to each of His people his place in the kingdom of glory; a thing which He nowhere else does, but rather the contrary. It is true that He says their place is "prepared for them by His Father." But that is true of their admission to heaven at all; and yet from His great white throne Jesus will Himself adjudicate the kingdom, and authoritatively invite into it those on His right hand, calling them the "blessed of His

ADAM CLARKE

35. *And James and John . . . come unto him.* The request here mentioned, Matthew says, chap. xx. 20, was made by Salome, their mother. The two places may be easily reconciled thus: The mother introduced them, and made the request as if from herself; Jesus, knowing whence it had come, immediately addressed himself to James and John, who were standing by; and the mother is no further concerned in the business.

Ye know not what ye ask. How strange is the infatuation in some parents which leads them to desire worldly or ecclesiastical honors for their children! He must be much in love with the Cross who wishes to have his child a minister of the gospel; for, if he be such as God approves of in the work, his life will be a life of toil and suffering.

38. *And be baptized.* "Or be baptized." Instead of *and*, "or" is the reading of many versions and MSS.

W. E. VINE:

BAPTISMA, baptism, consisting of the processes of immersion, submersion and emergence (from *bapto*, to dip), is used (a) of John's baptism; (b) of Christian baptism; (c) of the overwhelming afflictions and judgments to which the Lord voluntarily submitted on the cross, e.g., Luke 12:50; (d) of the sufferings His followers would experience, not of a vicarious character, but in fellowship with the sufferings of their Master. Some mss. have the word in Matt. 20:22, 23; it is used in Mark 10:38, 39, with this meaning.

—Vine's Expository Dictionary

Is not mine to give, but it shall be given to them for whom it is prepared of my Father. The true construction of the words is this: "To sit on My right hand and on My left is not mine to give, except to them for whom it is prepared of My Father." According to the prediction of Christ, these brethren did partake of His afflictions. James was martyred by Herod, Acts xii. 2; and John was banished to Patmos for the testimony of Christ, Rev. i. 9.

MATTHEW HENRY

nize our own likenesses in these two with their love spotted with self-regard, and be grateful for the gentle answer which did not blame the desire for preeminence, but sought to test the love. It was not only to teach them that He brought them back to think of the cross which must precede the glory, but because His own mind was so filled with it that He saw that glory only as through the darkness which had to be traversed to reach it. But for us all, the question is solemn and heart-searching.

Was not the answer, "We are able," too bold? They knew neither what they asked nor what they promised; but just as their ignorant question was partly redeemed by its love, their ignorant vow was ennobled by its very rashness, as well as by the unfaltering love in it. They did not know what they were promising, but they knew that they loved Him so well that to share anything with Him would be blessed. So it was not in their own strength that the swift answer rushed to their lips, but in the strength of a love that makes heroes out of cowards. And they nobly redeemed their pledge. We, too, if we are Christ's, have the same question put to us, and, weak and timid as we are, may venture to give the same answer, trusting to His strength.

—*Expositions of Holy Scripture*

III. The check he gave to the rest of the disciples, for their uneasiness at it. *They began to be much displeased*, to have *indignation about James and John, v.* 41. They were angry at them for affecting precedency, because each of them hoped to have it himself. So these discovered their own ambition, in their displeasure at the ambition of James and John; and Christ took this occasion to warn them against it, *v.* 42–44. He *called them to him* in a familiar way, to give them an example of condescension. He shows them,

1. That dominion was generally *abused in the world* (*v.* 42); *They that seem to rule over the* Gentiles, *they exercise lordship over them*, that is all they study and aim at. Their care is, what they shall get by their subjects to support their own pomp and grandeur, not what they shall do for them.

2. That therefore it ought not to be *admitted into the church*; "*It shall not so be among you;* those that shall be put under your charge, must be as sheep under the charge of the *shepherd*, who is to tend them and feed them, and be a servant to them, not as horses under the command of the driver, that works them and beats them, and gets his pennyworths out of them. He that affects to be great and chief, *he shall be servant of all*. He that would be *truly* great and chief, he must lay out himself to do good to all. Those not only shall be most *honoured* hereafter, but are most *honourable* now, who are most useful." To convince them of this, he sets before them his own example (*v.* 45). He takes upon him *the form of a servant*, comes not to be *ministered to*, and waited upon, but *to minister*. He becomes *obedient to death*, for he *gives his life a ransom for many*.

Verses 46–52

This passage of story agrees with that in Matt. xx. 29, &c. Only that there we were told of *two* blind men; here, and Luke xviii. 35, only of *one*: but if there were *two*, there was *one*. This one is named here; he was called *Bartimæus*, that is, the *son of Timæus*.

I. This blind man sat *begging*. Those who are disabled to get a livelihood by their own labour, are the most proper objects of charity; and particular care ought to be taken of them.

II. He cried out; *Have mercy on me, O Lord, thou Son of David*. Misery is the object of mercy.

III. Christ encouraged him, for he *stood still, and commanded him to be called*. We must never reckon it a hindrance to us in our way, to *stand still*, when it is to do a good work. Those about him, who had

JAMIESON, FAUSSET, BROWN

Father"; so little inconsistency is there between the eternal choice of them by His Father, and that public adjudication of them, not only to heaven in general, but each to his own position in it, which all Scripture assigns to Christ. The true rendering, then, of this clause, we take it, is this: "But to sit on My right hand and on My left hand is not Mine to give, save to them for whom it is prepared." When therefore He says, "It is not Mine to give," the meaning is, "I cannot give it as a *favor* to whomsoever I *please*, or on a principle of *favoritism;* it belongs exclusively to those for whom it is prepared," etc. And if this be His meaning, it will be seen how far our Lord is from disclaiming the right to assign to each his proper place in His Kingdom; that on the contrary, He expressly asserts it, merely announcing that the principle of distribution is quite different from what these petitioners supposed. Our Lord, it will be observed, does not *deny* the petition of James and John, or say they shall *not* occupy the place in His kingdom which they now improperly sought:—for aught we know, *that may be their true place*. All we are sure of is, that their asking it was displeasing to Him "to whom all judgment is committed," and so was not fitted to gain their object, but just the reverse. (See what is taught in Luke 14:8-11.) One at least of these brethren, as ALFORD strikingly remarks, saw on the right and on the left hand of their Lord, as He hung upon the tree, the crucified thieves; and bitter indeed must have been the remembrance of this ambitious prayer at that moment. **41. And when the ten heard it, they began to be much displeased with James and John**—or "were moved with indignation," as the same word is rendered in Matthew 20:24. The expression "*began* to be," which is of frequent occurrence in the Gospels, means that more passed than is expressed, and that we have but the result. And can we blame the ten for the indignation which they felt? Yet there was probably a spice of the old spirit of rivalry in it, which in spite of our Lord's recent lengthened, diversified, and most solemn warnings against it, had not ceased to stir in their breasts. **42. But Jesus called them to him, and saith unto them, Ye know that they which are accounted to rule**—are recognized or acknowledged as rulers. **over the Gentiles exercise lordship over them: and their great ones exercise authority upon them**—as superiors exercising an acknowledged authority over inferiors. **43. But so shall it not be among you: but whosoever will be great among you, shall be your minister**—a subordinate servant. **44. And whosoever of you will be the chiefest**—or "first." **shall be**—i.e., "let him be, or "shall be he who is prepared to be." **servant of all**—one in the lowest condition of service. **45. For even the Son of man came not to be ministered unto, but to minister, and to give his life a ransom for.** instead of—**many**—i.e., "In the kingdom about to be set up, this principle shall have no place. All My servants shall there be equal; and the only greatness known to it shall be the greatness of humility and devotedness to the service of others. He that goes down the deepest in these services of self-denying humility shall rise the highest and hold the chiefest place in that kingdom; even as the Son of man, whose abasement and self-sacrifice for others, transcending all, gives Him of right a place above all!" As "the Word in the beginning with God," He *was* ministered unto; and as the risen Redeemer in our nature He now *is* ministered unto, "angels and authorities and powers being made subject unto Him" (I Pet. 3:22); but not for this came He hither. The Served of all came to be the Servant of all; and His last act was the grandest Service ever beheld by the universe of God—"HE GAVE HIS LIFE A RANSOM FOR MANY!" "Many" is here to be taken, not in contrast with *few* or with *all*, but in opposition to *one*—the one Son of man for the many sinners.

46-52. BLIND BARTIMEUS HEALED. (=Matt. 20:29-34; Luke 18:35-43.) See on Luke 18:35-43.

In Matthew 20: 29-34, they are *two*, as in the case of the Demoniac of Gadara. In Matthew and Mark (10:46-52) the occurrence is connected with Christ's *departure from* Jericho; in Luke with His *approach to it*. Many ways of accounting for these slight divergences of detail have been proposed. Perhaps, *if we knew all the facts*, we should see no difficulty; but that we have been left so far in the dark shows that the thing is of no moment any way. One thing is plain, there could have been no collusion among the authors of these Gospels, else they would have taken care to remove these "spots on the sun."

ADAM CLARKE

W. E. VINE:

AGANAKTEO, to be indignant, to be moved with indignation (from *agan*, much, *achomai*, to grieve), is translated "were moved with indignation" of the ten disciples against James and John, Matt. 20:24; in Mark 10: 41, R.V. (A.V., "they began to be much displeased"); in Matt. 21:15, of the chief priests and scribes, against Christ and the children, R.V., "they were moved with indignation" (A.V., "they were sore displeased"); in 26:8, of the disciples against the woman who anointed Christ's feet, "they had indignation"; so Mark 14:4; in Mark 10:14, of Christ, against the disciples, for rebuking the children, "He was moved with indignation," R.V. (A.V., "he was much displeased"); in Luke 13:14, of the ruler of the synagogue against Christ for healing on the Sabbath, "being moved with indignation," R.V., A.V., "[answered] with indignation."

—*Vine's Expository Dictionary*

41. *When the ten heard it.* See Matt. xx. 24-28.

Exercise dominion . . . and . . . authority upon them. They "tyrannized" and "exercised arbitrary power" over the people.

It shall not be so among you. Every kind of lordship and spiritual domination over the Church of Christ, like that exercised by the Church of Rome, is destructive and antichristian. *Your minister.* Or "deacon." I know no other word which could at once convey the meaning of the original and make a proper distinction between it and *servant*, in v. 27. The office of a deacon, in the primitive Church, was to serve in the love feasts, to distribute the bread and wine to the communicants; to proclaim different parts and times of worship in the churches; and to take care of the widows, orphans, prisoners, and sick, who were provided for out of the revenues of the Church. Thus we find it was the very lowest ecclesiastical office.

Your servant. The lowest secular office, as deacon was the lowest ecclesiastical office.

A ransom for many. Or "a ransom instead of many,"—one Ransom, or Atonement, instead of the many prescribed in the Jewish law.

46. *Blind Bartimaeus. Bar* in Syriac signifies "son." It appears that he was thus named because Timeus, *Talmeus* or *Talmai*, was the name of his father, and thus the son would be called Bar-talmeus, or *Bartholomew*. It was because he was the most remarkable that this Evangelist mentions him by name, as a person probably well-known in those parts.

MATTHEW HENRY

discouraged him at first, perhaps were now the persons that signified to him the gracious call of Christ; "*Be of good comfort, rise, he calls thee*." The gracious invitations Christ gives us to come to him, are great encouragements to our hope, that we shall have what we come for.

IV. The poor man, hereupon, *cast away his* loose upper *garment*, and came to Jesus (*v.* 50); he cast away everything that might be in danger of throwing him down, or might any way hinder him. Those who would come to Jesus must cast away the garment of their own sufficiency, and the sin that, like long garments, doth *most easily beset them*, Heb. xii. 1.

V. The particular favour he begged, was, that his *eyes might be opened*; that so he might be able to work for his living, and might be no longer burthensome to others.

VI. This favour he received; his eyes were opened (*v.* 52). "*Thy faith hath made thee whole;* not thy importunity, but *thy faith*, setting Christ on work, or rather Christ setting thy faith on work." Those supplies are most comfortable, that are fetched in by our faith. When he had *received his sight*, he *followed Jesus by the way*. By this he made it appear that he was thoroughly cured, that he no more needed one to lead him. When he had his sight, he made this use of it. It is not enough to *come to Christ* for spiritual healing, but, when we are healed, we must continue to follow him. Those that have spiritual eye-sight, see that beauty in Christ, that will effectually draw them to *run after him*.

JAMIESON, FAUSSET, BROWN

commanded . . .—Mark has this interesting addition: "And they call the blind man, saying unto him, Be of good comfort, rise, He calleth thee"—just as one earnestly desiring an interview with some exalted person, but told by one official after another that it is vain to wait, as he will not succeed (they know it), yet persists in waiting for some answer to his suit, and at length the door opens, and a servant appears, saying, "You will be admitted—he has called you." *And are there no other suitors to Jesus who sometimes fare thus?* "And he, casting away his garment"—how lively is this touch, evidently of an eye-witness, expressive of his earnestness and joy—"came to Jesus" (Mark 10:49, 50). **What wilt thou . . .**—to try them; to deepen their present consciousness of need; and to draw out their faith in Him. **Lord** "*Rabboni*" (Mark 10:51); an emphatic and confiding exclamation. (See on John 9.)

ADAM CLARKE

50. *And he, casting away his garment.* He cast off his outward covering, a blanket, or loose piece of cloth, the usual upper garment of an Asiatic mendicant, which kept him from the inclemency of the weather, that he might have nothing to hinder him from getting speedily to Christ. If every penitent were as ready to throw aside his self-righteousness and sinful encumbrances as this blind man was to throw aside his garment, we should have fewer delays in conversions than we now have.

52. *Followed Jesus in the way.* Instead of *Jesus*, several eminent critics read *him*.

MATTHEW HENRY — CHAPTER 11

Verses 1–11

We have here the story of the public entry Christ made into Jerusalem. And he came into town thus remarkably, 1. To show that he was not afraid of the power and malice of his enemies in Jerusalem. He did not steal into the city *incognito*, as one that durst not show his face. 2. To show that he was not cast down or disquieted at the thoughts of his approaching sufferings. He came, not only publicly, but cheerfully.

I. The *outside* of this triumph was very *mean*; he rode upon an ass's *colt*. This *colt* was borrowed too. Christ went upon the water in a *borrowed* boat, ate the passover in a *borrowed* chamber, was buried in a *borrowed* sepulchre, and here rode on *borrowed* ass. Let not Christians scorn to be beholden one to another, and, when need is, to go borrowing, for our Master did not. He had no rich trappings; they threw their clothes upon the colt, and so he *sat upon him*, *v.* 7. All the show they could make was, by *spreading their garments in the way*, and *strewing branches of trees in the way* (*v.* 8), as they used to do at the feast of tabernacles. They are instructions to us, not to *mind high things*, but to *condescend to them of low estate*. How ill doth it become Christians to *take state*, when Christ was so far from affecting it!

II. The *inside* of this triumph was very *great*. **Christ showed his knowledge of things distant, and his power over the wills of men, when he sent his disciples for the colt, *v.* 1–3. He showed his dominion** over the *creatures* in riding on *a colt that was never backed*. Perhaps Christ, in riding the ass's colt, would give a shadow of his power over the spirit of man, who is born as *the wild ass's colt*, Job xi. 12. The colt was brought from a place *where two ways met* (*v.* 4), as if Christ would show that he came to direct those into the right way, who had *two ways* before them, and were in danger of taking the wrong. Christ received the joyful *hosannas* of the people. It was God that put it into the hearts of these people to cry *Hosanna*.

(1) They *welcomed* his *person* (*v.* 9); *Blessed is he that cometh*, so often promised, so long expected; he comes *in the name of the Lord*; *Blessed be he:* let him have our applauses, and best affections; he is a *blessed* Saviour, and brings blessings to us, and blessed be he that sent him.

(2) They *wished well* to his *interest*, *v.* 10. They believed that he had a *kingdom*, that it was the kingdom of *their father David*; a kingdom that came *in the name of the Lord*. *Blessed be this kingdom;* let it come in the power of it. Let it go on *conquering*, *and to conquer*. *Hosanna* to this kingdom; all happines attend it.

Christ, thus *attended*, thus *applauded*, came into the city, and went directly *to the temple*. He came to the temple, and took a view of the present state of it, *v.* 11. He *looked round about upon all things*, but as yet said nothing. He let things be as they were for this night, intending the next morning to apply himself to the necessary reformation. We may be

JAMIESON, FAUSSET, BROWN — CHAPTER 11

Vss. 1-11. Christ's Triumphal Entry into Jerusalem, on the First Day of the Week. (= Matt. 21:1-9; Luke 19:29-40; John 12:12, 19.) See on Luke 19:29-40.

Bethphage—"house of figs," a village which with Bethany lay along the further side of Mount Olivet, east of Jerusalem.

set Jesus on—He allowing this, as befitting the *state* He was for the first and only time assuming.

the Lord hath need . . .—He both knew all and had the key of the human heart. (See on vs. 5.) Perhaps the owner was a disciple.

whole multitude . . .—The language here is very grand, intended to express a burst of admiration far wider and deeper than ever had been witnessed before. **Blessed be the King . . .**—Mark more fully, "Hosanna," i.e., "*Save now*," the words of Psalm 118:25, which were understood to refer to Messiah; and so they add, "to the Son of David, blessed is He that cometh in the name of the Lord (Ps. 118:26), Hosanna in the highest." This was the very loftiest style in which He could be saluted as the promised Deliverer.

11-26. The Barren Fig Tree Cursed, with Lessons from It—Second Cleansing of the Temple, on the Second and Third Days of the Week. (=Matt. 21:12-22; Luke 19:45-48). **11. And Jesus entered into Jerusalem, and into the temple: and when he had looked round about upon**—surveyed—**all things, and now the eventide was come, he went out into Bethany with the twelve**—Thus briefly does

ADAM CLARKE — CHAPTER 11

1. *He sendeth forth two of his disciples.* This was done but a few days before the Passover. See our Lord's entry into Jerusalem illustrated, on Matt. xxi. 1-17.

2. *Whereon never man sat.* No animal was allowed to be employed in sacred uses, even among the heathen, that had previously been used for any domestic or agricultural purpose; and those which had never been yoked were considered as sacred.

3. *And straightway he will send him hither.* From the text I think it is exceedingly plain that our Lord did not beg, but borrow, the colt; therefore the latter clause of this verse should be understood as the promise of *returning* him. Is not the proper translation the following? "And if anyone say to you, Why do ye this? Say, The Lord hath need of him, and will speedily send him back hither."

6. *And they let them go.* Having a full assurance that the beast should be safely and speedily restored.

10. *In the name of the Lord.* Omitted by some MSS. and several versions. *Hosanna in the highest.* See on Matt. xxi. 9.

11. *When he had looked round about upon all things.* He examined everything, to see if the matters pertaining to the divine worship were properly conducted, to see that nothing was wanting, nothing superfluous. *And now the eventide was come.* The time in which He usually left Jerusalem to go to Bethany.

MATTHEW HENRY

confident that God sees all the wickedness that is in the world, though he do not presently reckon for it, nor cast it out. Christ, having made his remarks upon what he saw in the temple, retired in the evening to a friend's house at Bethany.

Verses 12–26

I. Christ's cursing the fruitless fig-tree. He returned in the morning, at working-time; and so intent was he upon his work, that he went out from Bethany without breakfast, and *was hungry* (*v.* 12). He went to a *fig-tree*, being well *adorned* with green leaves which he hoped to find *enriched* with some fruit. But he *found nothing but leaves*; he hoped to find some fruit, *for* though *the time of* gathering in *figs* was near, it *was not yet*. There was not so much as one fig to be found upon it, though it was so full of leaves. However, Christ was willing to make an example of it, not to the *trees*, but to the *men*, of that generation, and therefore cursed it. He said unto it, *Never let any man eat fruit of thee hereafter for ever*, *v.* 14. This was intended to be a type and figure of the doom passed upon the Jewish church, to which he came, *seeking fruit, but found none* (Luke xiii. 6, 7). The *disciples heard* what sentence Christ passed on this tree, and took notice of it. Woes from Christ's mouth are to be observed and kept in mind, as well as blessings.

II. His clearing the temple of the market people that frequented it, and of those that made it a thoroughfare. He came, hungry as he was, to Jerusalem, and went straight to the temple, and began to reform those abuses which the day before he had marked out. He came not, as he was falsely accused, to *destroy* the temple, but to purify and refine it.

1. He cast out the *buyers* and *sellers*, *overthrew the tables of the money-changers* (and threw the money to the ground, the fitter place for it), and threw down the *seats of them that sold doves.* And he did it without opposition; for what he did, was manifested to be right and good, even in the consciences of those that had connived at it, and countenanced it, because they got money by it. It may be some encouragement to zealous reformers, that frequently the purging out of corruptions, and the correcting of abuses, prove an easier piece of work than was apprehended. Prudent attempts sometimes prove successful beyond expectation.

2. He *would not suffer that any man should carry any vessel through the temple*, *v.* 16. The Jews owned that it was one of the instances of honour due to the temple, not to make the mountain of the house, or the court of the Gentiles, a road, or common passage, or to come into it with any bundle.

3. He gave a good reason for this; because it was written, *My house shall be called of all nations, The house of prayer*, *v.* 17. It shall pass among all people under that character. *It shall be the house of prayer to all nations;* it was so in the first institution of it. Christ will have the temple to be, (1) A *house of prayer*. After he had turned out the oxen and doves, which were things for sacrifice, he revived the appointment of it as a *house of prayer.* (2) That it should be so *to all nations*, and not to the people of the Jews only; for *whosoever shall call on the name of the Lord, shall be saved.* When Christ drove out the buyers and sellers at the beginning of his ministry, he only charged them with making the temple *a house of merchandise* (John ii. 16); but now he chargeth them with making it a *den of thieves.* Those that suffer vain worldly thoughts to lodge within them when they are at their devotions, turn the *house of prayer* into a *house of merchandise*; but they that make long prayers for a pretence to devour widows' houses, turn it into a *den of thieves*.

4. The scribes and the chief priests were extremely nettled at this, *v.* 18. They hated him, and yet they *feared him*, lest he should next overthrow *their* seats, and expel *them*. They found that *all the people were astonished at his doctrine*, and that everything he said was an oracle and a law to them; and what durst *he* not attempt, being thus supported? They therefore sought, not how they might make their peace with him, but *how they might destroy him.* They care not what they do, to support their own power and grandeur.

III. His discourse with his disciples, upon occasion of the fig-tree's withering away. At *even*, as usual, he *went out of the city* (*v.* 19), to Bethany. The next morning, as they *passed by*, they observed the *fig-tree dried up from the roots*, *v.* 20. The curse was no more than that it should never bear fruit again, but the effect goes further, *it is dried up from the roots.* If it bear no fruit, it shall bear no leaves to cheat people.

1. How the disciples were affected with it. Peter remembered Christ's words, and said, with surprise, *Master, behold, the fig-tree which thou cursedst is*

JAMIESON, FAUSSET, BROWN

our Evangelist dispose of this His first day in Jerusalem, after the triumphal entry. Nor do the Third and Fourth Gospels give us more light. But from Matthew (21:10, 11, 14-16) we learn some additional and precious particulars, for which see on Luke 19:45-48. It was not now safe for the Lord to sleep in the city, nor, from the day of His Triumphal Entry, did He pass one night in it, save the last fatal one.

The Barren Fig Tree Cursed (vss. 12-14). **12. And on the morrow**—The Triumphal Entry being on the first day of the week, this following day was Monday. **when they were come from Bethany**—"in the morning" (Matt. 21:18). **he was hungry**—How was that? Had he stolen forth from that dear roof at Bethany to the "mountain to pray, and continued all night in prayer to God?" (Luke 6:12); or, "in the morning," as on a former occasion, "risen up a great while before day, and departed into a solitary place, and there prayed" (ch. 1:35); not breaking His fast thereafter, but bending His steps straight for the city, that He might "work the works of Him that sent Him while it was day"? (John 9:4). We know not, though one lingers upon and loves to trace out the every movement of that life of wonders. One thing, however we are sure of—it was *real bodily hunger* which He now sought to allay by the fruit of this fig tree, "if haply He might find any thing thereon"; not a mere *scene* for the purpose of teaching a lesson, as some early heretics maintained, and some still seem virtually to hold. **13. And seeing a fig tree**—(In Matt. 21:19, it is "one fig tree," but the sense is the same as here, "a certain fig tree," as in Matt. 8:19, etc.) Bethphage, which adjoined Bethany, derives his name from its being a *fig region*—"House of figs." **afar off having leaves**—and therefore promising fruit, which in the case of figs come before the leaves. **he came, if haply he might find any thing thereon: and when he came to it, he found nothing but leaves; for the time of figs was not yet**—What the precise import of this explanation is, interpreters are not agreed. Perhaps all that is meant is, that as the proper fig season had not arrived, no fruit would have been expected even of this tree but for the leaves which it had, which were in this case prematurely and unnaturally developed. **14. And Jesus answered and said unto it, No man eat fruit of thee hereafter for ever**—That word did not *make* the tree barren, but sealed it up in its own barrenness. See on Matthew 13:13-15. **And his disciples heard it**—and marked the saying. This is introduced as a connecting link, to explain what was afterwards to be said on the subject, as the narrative has to proceed to the other transactions of this day.

Second Cleansing of the Temple (vss. 15-18). For the exposition of this portion, see on Luke 19: 45-48.

As the first cleansing was on His *first* visit to Jerusalem (John 2:13-22), so this second cleansing was on His last. **den of thieves**—banded together for plunder, reckless of principle. The mild term "house of merchandise,' used on the former occasion, was now unsuitable. **sought**—continued seeking, i.e., daily, as He taught.

Lessons from the Cursing of the Fig Tree (vss. 20-26). **20. And in the morning**—of Tuesday, the third day of the week: He had slept, as during all this week, at Bethany. **as they passed by**—going into Jerusalem again. **they saw the fig tree dried up from the roots**—no partial blight, leaving life in the root; but it was now dead, root and branch. In Matthew 21:19 it is said it withered away as soon as it was cursed. But the full blight had not appeared probably at once; and in the dusk perhaps, as they returned to Bethany, they had not

ADAM CLARKE

13. *For the time of figs was not yet.* Rather, "For it was not the season of gathering figs yet." When our Lord saw this fig tree by the wayside, apparently flourishing, he went to it to gather some of the figs. Being on the wayside, it was not private but public property, and any traveller had an equal right to its fruit. As it was not as yet the time for gathering in the fruits, and yet about the time when they were ready to be gathered, our Lord with propriety expected to find some. This tree was intended to point out the state of the Jewish people. (1) They made a profession of the true religion. (2) They considered themselves the peculiar people of God, and despised and reprobated all others. (3) They were only hypocrites, having nothing of religion but the profession—*leaves*, and no *fruit*. Our Lord's conduct towards this tree is to be considered as emblematical of the treatment and final perdition which was to come upon this hypocritical and ungodly nation. (1) It was a proper time for them to have borne fruit. Jesus had been preaching the doctrine of repentance and salvation among them for more than three years; the choicest influences of Heaven had descended upon them; and everything was done in this vineyard that ought to be done, in order to make it fruitful. (2) The time was now at hand in which God would require fruit, good fruit; and, if it did not produce such, the tree should be hewn down by the Roman axe. Therefore (1) The *tree* is properly the Jewish nation; (2) Christ's *curse*, the sentence of destruction which had now gone out against it; and (3) *Its withering away*, the final and total ruin of the Jewish state by the Romans. His cursing the fig tree was not occasioned by any resentment at being disappointed at not finding fruit on it, but to point out unto His disciples the wrath which was coming upon a people who had now nearly filled up the measure of their iniquity.

15. *And they come.* This was the next day after our Lord's triumphant entry into Jerusalem; for on the evening of that day He went to Bethany and lodged there, v. 11, and returned the next morning to Jerusalem.

19. *He went out of the city.* To go to Bethany.

MATTHEW HENRY

withered away, *v.* 21. Christ's curses have wonderful effects, and make those to wither that flourished like the green bay-tree. And this seemed very strange to the disciples. They could not imagine how that *fig-tree* should *so soon wither away*: but this comes of rejecting Christ, and being rejected by him.

2. The good instructions Christ gave them from it; for of *those* even this *withered* tree was *fruitful*.

(1) Christ teacheth them from hence to *pray in faith* (*v.* 22); *Have faith in God*. They admired the power of Christ's word of command; "Why," saith Christ, "a lively active faith would put as great a power into your prayers, *v.* 23, 24. *Whosoever shall say to this mountain, Be removed, and be cast into the sea;* and if he *shall not doubt in his heart, but shall believe that those things which he saith shall come to pass, he shall have whatsoever he saith*." Through the strength and power of God in Christ, the greatest difficulty shall be got over, and the thing shall be effected. And therefore (*v.* 24), "*What things soever ye desire, when ye pray believe that ye shall* receive them; nay, believe that ye *do receive them*, and he that has power to give them, saith, *Ye shall have them. I say unto you*, Ye shall, *v.* 24. *Verily* I say unto you, Ye shall," *v.* 23. Now this is to be applied, [1] To that *faith of miracles* which the apostles and first preachers of the gospel were endued with. [2] It may be applied to that *miracle of faith*, which all true Christians are endued with. *It justifies* us (Rom. v. 1), and so removes mountains of guilt, and casts them into the *depths of the sea*. It *purifies* the heart (Acts xv. 9), and so removes mountains of corruption. It is by faith that the world is conquered, Satan's fiery darts are quenched, a soul is crucified with Christ, and yet lives.

(2) To this is added here that necessary qualification of the prevailing prayer, that we freely forgive, and be in charity with all men (*v.* 25, 26); *When ye stand praying*, forgive. When we are at prayer, we must remember to pray for others, particularly for our enemies, and those that have wronged us. If we have injured others before we pray, we must go and *be reconciled to them*, Matt. v. 23, 24. But if they have injured us, we go a nearer way to work, and must immediately from our hearts *forgive* them; because this is a *good step* towards obtaining the *pardon* of our own sins: *Forgive*, that *your Father may forgive you*; because the want of this is a certain bar to the obtaining of the pardon of our sins; "*If ye do not forgive, neither will your Father forgive your trespasses*." This ought to be remembered in prayer, because one great errand we have to the throne of grace, is, to pray for the pardon of our sins. Our Saviour often insists on this, for it was his great design to engage his disciples to love one another.

Verses 27-33

We have here Christ examined by the great Sanhedrim concerning his authority. They came to him when he was *walking in the temple, teaching* the people. The cloisters, in the courts of the temple, were fitted for this purpose. The great men *came to him*, and did as it were arraign him at the bar with this question, *By what authority doest thou these things? v.* 28.

I. How they designed hereby to run him aground, and embarrass him. If they could make it out before the people, that he had not a *legal mission*, that he was not duly *ordained*, they would tell the people that they *ought not to hear him*. This they made the last refuge of an obstinate unbelief; they were resolved to find some flaw or other in his commission. This is indeed a question, which all that act either as magistrates or as ministers, ought to be furnished with a good answer to, *By what authority do I these things?* For *how can men preach except they be sent?*

II. How he effectually ran them aground, and embarrassed them, with this question, "What are your thoughts concerning *the baptism of John*? *Was it from heaven, or of men? Answer me*," *v.* 30. By the resolving of *their* question into *this*, our Saviour intimates how near akin his doctrine and baptism were to John's; they had the same design and tendency—to introduce the gospel kingdom.

They knew what they *thought* of this question; they could not but think that *John Baptist* was a man sent of God. But the difficulty was, what they should *say to it* now.

1. If they own the baptism of John to be *from heaven*, they *shame themselves*; for Christ will presently turn it upon them, *Why did ye not then believe him?* They could not bear that Christ should say this, but they could bear it that their own consciences should say so.

2. If they say, "*It is of men*, he was not sent of God," they *expose themselves*; the people will be ready to do them a mischief; for *all men counted John that he*

JAMIESON, FAUSSET, BROWN

observed it. The precision with which Mark distinguishes the days is not observed by Matthew, intent only on holding up the truths which the incident was designed to teach. In Matthew the whole is represented as taking place at once, just as the two stages of Jairus' daughter—dying and dead—are represented by him as one. The only difference is between a mere summary and a more detailed narrative, each of which only confirms the other. **21. And Peter calling to remembrance saith unto him**—satisfied that a miracle so very peculiar—a miracle, not of *blessing*, as all His other miracles, but of *cursing*—could not have been wrought but with some higher reference, and fully expecting to hear something weighty on the subject. **Master, behold, the fig tree which thou cursedst is withered away**—so connecting the two things as to show that he traced the death of the tree entirely to the curse of his Lord. Matthew (21:20) gives this simply as a general exclamation of surprise by the disciples "how soon" the blight had taken effect. **22. And Jesus answering saith unto them, Have faith in God. 23. For verily I say unto you, That whosoever shall say unto this mountain, Be thou removed . . . he shall have whatsoever he saith**—Here is the lesson now. From the nature of the case supposed—that they might wish a mountain removed and cast into the sea, a thing far removed from anything which they could be thought actually to desire—it is plain that not physical but moral obstacles to the progress of His kingdom were in the Redeemer's view, and that what He designed to teach was the great lesson, that *no obstacle should be able to stand before a confiding faith in God*. **24. Therefore I say unto you, What things soever ye desire, when ye pray, believe that ye receive them, and ye shall have them**—This verse only *generalizes* the assurance of the former verse; which seems to show that it was designed for the special encouragement of *evangelistic* and *missionary* efforts, while this is a directory for prevailing *prayer in general*. **25. And when ye stand praying, forgive, if ye have aught against any; that your Father also which is in heaven may forgive you your trespasses . . .**—This is repeated from the Sermon on the Mount (see on Matt. 6:14, 15); to remind them that if this was necessary to the acceptableness of *all* prayer, much more *when great things were to be asked and confidently expected*.

27-33. THE AUTHORITY OF JESUS QUESTIONED—HIS REPLY. (=Matt. 21:23-27; Luke 20:1-8.) See on Matthew 21:23-27.

By what authority doest thou these things!—referring particularly to the expulsion of the buyers and sellers from the temple. **and who gave thee this authority? And Jesus answered and said unto them, I also will ask you one thing . . .**

The baptism of John—meaning his whole mission and ministry, of which baptism was the proper character. **whence was it? from heaven, or of men?**—What wisdom there was in this way of meeting their question will best appear by their reply.

If we shall say, From heaven; he will say unto us, Why did ye not then believe him?—"Why did ye not believe the testimony which he bore to Me, as the promised and expected Messiah?" for that was the burden of John's whole testimony. **But if we shall say, Of men; we fear the people**—rather the multitude. In Luke (20:6) it is, "all the people will stone us." **for all hold John as a prophet**—Crooked, cringing hypo-

ADAM CLARKE

22. *Have faith in God.* "Have the faith of God," i.e., Have strong faith, or the strongest faith, for thus the Hebrews expressed the superlative degree.

25. *When ye stand praying.* This expression may mean no more than, "When ye are disposed or have a mind, to pray," i.e., whenever you perform that duty. But the Pharisees loved to pray standing, that they might be seen of men.

26. The verse is wanting in some MSS. and editions.

27-33. See on Matt. xxi. 23-27.

By what authority doest thou these things? The things which the chief priests allude to were His receiving the acclamations of the people as the promised Messiah, His casting the traders out of the Temple, and His teaching the people publicly in it.

The baptism of John. Had John a divine commission or not for his baptism and preaching? Our Lord here takes the wise in their own cunning. He knew the estimation John was in among the people, and He plainly saw that if they gave any answer at all they must convict themselves; and so they saw, when they came to examine the question.

32. *They feared the people.* Or rather, "We fear," etc.

MATTHEW HENRY

was a prophet indeed. There is a carnal slavish fear, which not only wicked subjects but wicked rulers likewise are liable to. (1) They were confounded and forced to make a dishonourable retreat; to pretend ignorance—*We cannot tell.* What Christ did by his wisdom we must labour to do by our well doing—*put to silence the ignorance of foolish men,* 1 Pet. ii. 15. (2) Christ justified himself in refusing to give them an answer to their imperious demand; *Neither tell I you by what authority I do these things.* They did not deserve to be told; nor did *he* need to *tell them,* since no man could do those miracles which he did unless God were with him.

JAMIESON, FAUSSET, BROWN

crites! No wonder Jesus gave you no answer. **27. And they answered Jesus, and said, We cannot tell**—Evidently their difficulty was, how to answer, so as neither to shake their determination to reject the claims of Christ nor damage their reputation with the people. For the truth itself they cared nothing whatever. **Neither tell I you by what authority I do these things**—What composure and dignity of wisdom does our Lord here display, as He turns their question upon themselves, and, while revealing His knowledge of their hypocrisy, closes their mouths! Taking advantage of the surprise, silence, and awe produced by this reply, our Lord followed it up immediately by the two following parables.

ADAM CLARKE

We cannot tell, said they; which, in the words of truth, should have been, "We will not tell," for we will not have this man for the Messiah; because, if we acknowledge John as His forerunner, we must, of necessity, receive Jesus as the Christ.

MATTHEW HENRY

CHAPTER 12

Verses 1–12

Christ had formerly in parables showed how he designed to set up the gospel church; now he begins in parables to show how he would lay aside the Jewish church.

I. They that enjoy the privileges of the visible church, have a vineyard let out to them, from the occupiers of which rent is justly expected. Members of the church are God's tenants, and they have both a good Landlord and a good bargain, and may live well upon it, if it be not their own fault.

II. Those whom God lets out his vineyard to, he sends his servants to, to put them in mind of his just expectations from them, *v.* 2.

III. It is sad to think what base usage God's faithful ministers have met with, in all ages. The Old Testament prophets were persecuted. They *beat them,* and *sent them empty away* (*v.* 3); that was bad: they *wounded them,* and *sent them away shamefully entreated* (*v.* 4); that was worse: nay, at length, they came to such a pitch of wickedness, that they *killed* them, *v.* 5.

IV. It was no wonder if those who abused the prophets, abused Christ himself. God did at length send them his Son, his *well-beloved.* And it might be expected that he whom their Master *loved,* they also should respect and love (*v.* 6); "*They will reverence my son.*" But, instead of *reverencing* him because he was the son and heir, they *therefore* hated him, *v.* 7. They were the more enraged against him, and determined to put him to death, that all the respect might be paid to them only; "*The inheritance shall be ours.*" There is an *inheritance,* which, if they had duly *reverenced the Son,* might have been theirs, a heavenly inheritance. So they *took him, and killed him*; and they *cast him out of the vineyard.*

V. For such sinful and shameful doings nothing can be expected but a fearful doom (*v.* 9); *What shall therefore the Lord of the vineyard do?*

1. He will *come, and destroy the husbandmen.* When they killed his servants, and his Son, he determined to *destroy* them; and this was fulfilled when Jerusalem was laid waste.

2. He will *give the vineyard to others.* This was fulfilled in the taking in of the Gentiles, and the abundance of fruit which the *gospel brought forth in all the world,* Col. i. 6. If some from whom we expected well, prove bad, it doth not follow but that others will be better.

3. Their opposition to Christ's exaltation shall be no obstruction to it (*v.* 10, 11); *The stone which the builders rejected,* is *become the Head of the corner.* God will set Christ as *his King,* upon his *holy hill of Zion.* And all the world shall see and own this to be *the Lord's doing.*

Now what effect had this parable upon the chief priests and scribes? They knew *he spoke this parable against them, v.* 12. They could not but see their own faces in the glass of it. (1) They *sought to lay hold on him,* and make him their prisoner immediately, and so to fulfil what he had just now said they would do to him, *v.* 8. (2) Nothing restrained them from it but the awe they stood in of the people; they did not *reverence* Christ, nor had any *fear of* God before their eyes. (3) They *left him, and went their way*; if they could not do hurt to him, they resolved he should not do good to them, and therefore they got out of the hearing of his powerful preaching. If men's prejudices be not conquered by the evidence of truth, they are but confirmed. If the gospel be not a *savour of life unto life,* it will be a *savour of death unto death.*

Verses 13–17

Here we have him tempted, or *at*tempted rather, with a question about the lawfulness of paying tribute to Caesar.

I. The persons they employed were the *Pharisees*

JAMIESON, FAUSSET, BROWN

CHAPTER 12

VSS. 1-12. PARABLE OF THE WICKED HUSBANDMEN. (=Matt. 21:33-46; Luke 20:9-18.) See on Matthew 21:33-46.

There was a certain householder, which planted a vineyard—See on Luke 13:6. **and hedged it round about, and digged a winepress in it, and built a tower**—These details are taken, as is the basis of the parable itself, from that beautiful parable of Isaiah 5:1-7, in order to fix down the application and sustain it by Old Testament authority. **and let it out to husbandmen**—These are just the ordinary spiritual guides of the people, under whose care and culture the fruits of righteousness are expected to spring up. **and went into a far country**—"for a long time" (Luke 20:9), leaving the vineyard to the laws of the spiritual husbandry during the whole time of the Jewish economy. On this phraseology, see on Mark 4:26. **And when the time of the fruit drew near, he sent his servants to the husbandmen**—By these "servants" are meant the prophets and other extraordinary messengers, raised up from time to time. See on ch. 23:37. **that they might receive the fruits of it**—See again on Luke 13:6.

They will reverence my son—In Mark (12:6) this is most touchingly expressed: "Having yet therefore one son, His well-beloved, He sent Him also last unto them, saying, They will reverence My Son." Luke's version of it too (20:13) is striking: "Then said the lord of the vineyard, What shall I do? I will send My beloved Son: it may be they will reverence Him when they see Him." Who does not see that our Lord here severs Himself, by the sharpest line of demarkation, from all merely *human* messengers, and claims for Himself *Sonship* in its loftiest sense? (Cf. Heb. 3:3-6.) The expression, "*It may be* they will reverence My Son," is designed to teach the almost unimaginable guilt of *not* reverentially welcoming God's Son. **But when the husbandmen saw the son, they said among themselves**—Cf. Genesis 37:18-20; John 11:47-53. **This is the heir**—Sublime expression this of the great truth, that God's inheritance was destined for, and in due time is to come into the possession of, His own Son *in our nature* (Heb. 1:2). **come, let us kill him, and let us seize on his inheritance**—that so, from mere *servants,* we may become *lords.* This is the deep aim of the depraved heart; this is emphatically "the root of all evil." **And they caught him, and cast him out of the vineyard**—cf. Hebrews 13:11-13 ("without the gate—without the camp"); I Kings 21:13; John 19:17. **and slew him.**

And when the chief priests and Pharisees had heard his parables—referring to that of the Two Sons and this one of the Wicked Husbandmen—**they perceived that he spake of them. But when they sought to lay hands on him**—which Luke (20:19) says they did "the same hour," hardly able to restrain their rage. **they feared the multitude**—rather, 'the multitudes'—**because they took him for a prophet**—just as they feared to say John's baptism was of men, because the masses took him for a prophet (vs. 26). Miserable creatures! So, for this time, "they left Him and went their way" (Mark 12:12).

13-40. ENTANGLING QUESTIONS ABOUT TRIBUTE, THE RESURRECTION, AND THE GREAT COMMANDMENT, WITH THE REPLIES—CHRIST BAFFLES THE PHARISEES BY A QUESTION ABOUT DAVID, AND DENOUNCES THE SCRIBES. (=Matt. 22:15-46; Luke 20:20-47). The time of this section appears to be still the third

ADAM CLARKE

CHAPTER 12

1. *A certain man planted a vineyard.* See this parable explained, Matt. xxi. 33-41.

4. *At him they cast stones, and wounded him in the head.* Or rather, "they made short work of it." We have followed the Vulgate in translating the original, *wounded him in the head,* in which signification, I believe, the word is found in no Greek writer. [It] signifies to "sum up, to comprise," and is used in this sense by Paul, Rom. xiii. 9.

9. *And will give the vineyard unto others.* I will give it into the care of new vinedressers, the Evangelists and apostles. And under their ministry, multitudes were brought to God before the destruction of Jerusalem.

A. T. ROBERTSON:

12. "Against them" (*pros autous*). So in Luke. It was a straight shot, this parable of the Rejected Stone (12:10 f.) and the longer one of the Wicked Husbandmen. There was no mistaking the application, for he had specifically explained the application (Matt. 21:43-45). The Sanhedrin were so angry that they actually started or sought to seize him, but fear of the populace now more enthusiastic for Jesus than ever held them back. They went off in disgust, but they had to listen to the parable of the King's Son before going (Matt. 22:1-14).

—*Word Pictures in the New Testament*

MATTHEW HENRY

and the *Herodians*, *v.* 13. The Pharisees were great sticklers for the liberty of the Jews, and, if he should say, It is lawful to give tribute to Caesar, they would incense the common people against him. The Herodians were great sticklers for the Roman power, and, if he should discountenance the paying of tribute to Caesar, they would incense the governor against him. It is no new thing for those that are at variance in other things, to join in a confederacy against Christ.

II. The pretence they made was, that they desired him to resolve them a case of conscience, *v.* 14. They complimented him at a high rate, called him *Master*, owned him for a Teacher of the *way of God*, a Teacher of it *in truth*, who would not be brought by smiles or frowns to depart a step from the rules of equity and goodness; "*Thou carest for no man*, nor *regardest the person of men; thou art right*, and dost in a right manner declare good and evil, truth and falsehood." They knew that he taught the way of God in truth, and yet rejected the counsel of God against themselves.

III. The question they put was, *Is it lawful to give tribute to Caesar, or not?* They would be thought desirous to know their duty. Really they desired nothing but to know what he would say, in hopes that, which side soever he took of the question, they might take occasion from it to accuse him. They seemed to refer the determining of this matter to Christ; they put the question fairly, *Shall we give, or shall we not give?* They seemed resolved to stand to his award. Many seem desirous to know their duty, who are no ways disposed to do it.

IV. Christ determined the question, and evaded the snare, *v.* 15–17. He *knew their hypocrisy*. Hypocrisy, though ever so artfully managed, cannot be concealed from the Lord Jesus. He sees the *potsherd* that is *covered* with the *silver dross*. He knew they intended to ensnare him, and therefore contrived the matter so as to ensnare them. He made them acknowledge that the current money of their nation was Roman money, had the emperor's image on one side, and his *superscription* on the reverse; and if so, 1. *Caesar* might command their money for the public benefit. *Render to Caesar the things that are Caesar's*. The circulation of the money is from him as the fountain, and therefore it must return to him. 2. Caesar might not command their consciences, nor did he pretend to it. "Pay your tribute, therefore, without murmuring or disputing, but be sure to *render to God the things that are God's*." Many that seem careful to give to men their due, are in no care to give to God *the glory due to his name*. All that heard Christ, *marvelled* at the discretion of his answer, but I doubt none were brought by it, as they ought to be, to render to God themselves and their devotions. Many will commend the wit of a sermon, that will not be commanded by the divine laws of a sermon.

Verses 18–27

The Sadducees, who were the deists of that age, here attack our Lord Jesus. They were not bigots and persecutors, but sceptics and infidels, and their design was upon his doctrine. They denied that there was any resurrection, any world of spirits, any state of rewards and punishments on the other side of death; now those great and fundamental truths which they denied, Christ had made it his business to establish and prove, and therefore they set themselves to perplex his doctrine.

I. See here the method they take to entangle it; they quote the ancient law, by which, if a man died without issue, his brother was obliged to marry his widow, *v.* 19. They suppose a case to happen that, according to that law, seven brothers were, successively, the husbands of one woman, *v.* 20. Probably, these Sadducees intended hereby to ridicule that law. Those who deny divine truths, commonly set themselves to disparage divine laws and ordinances. Their design was to expose the doctrine of the resurrection; for they suppose that if there be a future state, it must be such a one as this, and then the doctrine, they think, is clogged either with this invincible absurdity, that a woman in that state must have seven husbands, or else with this insolvable difficulty, whose wife she must be. See with what subtlety these heretics *undermine* the truth; they do not *deny* it, they do not seem to doubt of it. They pretend to own the truth, as if they were not Sadducees. They take it for granted that there is a resurrection, and would be thought to desire instruction concerning it, when really they are designing to give it a fatal stab, and think that they shall do it. It is the common artifice of heretics and Sadducees to perplex and entangle the truth, which they have not the impudence to deny.

II. See here the method Christ takes to clear and establish this truth. This was a matter of moment,

JAMIESON, FAUSSET, BROWN

day (Tuesday) of Christ's last week. Matthew introduces the subject by saying (22:15), "Then went the Pharisees and took counsel how they might entangle Him in His talk." **13. And they send unto him certain of the Pharisees**—"their disciples," says Matthew; probably young and zealous scholars in that hardening school. **and of the Herodians** —See on Matthew 22:16. In Luke 20:20 these willing tools are called "spies, which should feign themselves just [righteous] men, that they might take hold of His words, that so they might deliver Him unto the power and authority of the governor." Their plan, then, was to entrap Him into some expression which might be construed into disaffection to the Roman government; the Pharisees themselves being notoriously discontented with the Roman yoke.

Tribute to Cæsar (vss. 14-17). **14. And when they were come, they say unto him, Master**—Teacher—**we know that thou art true, and carest for no man; for thou regardest not the person of men, but teachest the way of God in truth**—By such flattery—though they said only the truth—they hoped to throw Him off His guard. **Is it lawful to give tribute to Cæsar, or not?**—It was the civil poll-tax paid by all enrolled in the "census." See on Matthew 17:25. **15. Shall we give, or shall we not give? But he, knowing their hypocrisy**—"their wickedness" (Matt. 22:18); "their craftiness" (Luke 20:23). The malignity of their hearts took the form of craft, pretending what they did not feel—an anxious desire to be guided aright in a matter which to a scrupulous few might seem a question of some difficulty. Seeing perfectly through this, He **said unto them, Why tempt ye me?**—hypocrites!" **bring me a penny that I may see it**—"the tribute money" (Matt. 22:19). **16. And they brought it. And he saith unto them, Whose is this image**—stamped upon the coin. **and superscription?**—the words encircling it on the obverse side. **And they said unto him, Cæsar's. 17. And Jesus answering said unto them, Render to Cæsar the things that are Cæsar's**—Putting it in this general form, it was impossible for sedition itself to dispute it, and yet it dissolved the snare. **and to God the things that are God's**—How much is there in this profound but to them startling addition to the maxim, and how incomparable is the whole for fulness, brevity, clearness, weight! **and they marvelled at him**—"at His answer, and held their peace" (Luke 20:26), "and left Him, and went their way" (Matt. 22:22).

The Resurrection (vss. 18-27). **18. Then come unto him the Sadducees, which say there is no resurrection**—"neither angel nor spirit" (Acts 23:7). They were the materialists of the day. See on Acts 23:7. **and they asked him, saying, 19-22. Master, Moses wrote unto us**—(Deut. 25:5)—**If a man's brother die, and leave his wife behind him . . . And the seven had her, and left no seed: last of all the woman died also. 23. In the resurrection therefore when they shall rise . . .**

ADAM CLARKE

13. *And they send unto him.* See this, and to v. 17, largely explained on Matt. xxii. 15-22.

The Herodians. The preceding parable had covered the Pharisees with confusion. When it was ended they went out, not to humble themselves before God and deprecate the judgments with which they were threatened, but to plot afresh the destruction of their Teacher. The depth of their malice appears (1) in their mode of attack. They had often questioned our Lord on matters concerning religion, and His answers only served to increase His reputation and their confusion. They now shift their ground, and question Him concerning state affairs, and the question is such as must be answered; and yet the answer, to all human appearance, can be none other than what may be construed into a crime against the people or against the Roman government. (2) Their profound malice appears further in the choice of their companions in this business, viz., the Herodians. Herod himself was extremely attached to the Roman emperor, and made a public profession of it. All these considerations engaged the Pharisees to unite with the Herodians, who, as the Syriac intimates, were the domestics of Herod, in this infernal plot. (3) Their profound malice appears further in the praises they gave our Lord. "Teacher, *we know that thou art true, and teachest the way of God.*" This was indeed the real character of our blessed Lord; and now they bear testimony to the truth, merely with the design to make it subserve their bloody purposes. (4) Their malice appears still further in the question they propose. *Is it lawful to give tribute unto Caesar, or not?* The constitution of the Jewish republic rendered an answer to this question extremely difficult: (1) In the presence of the people, who professed to have no other king but God, and looked on their independence as an essential point of their religion; (2) In the presence of the Pharisees, who were ready to stir up the people against Him if His decision could be at all construed to be contrary to their prejudices or to their religious rights. (3) In the presence of the Herodians, who, if the answer should appear to be against Caesar's rights, were ready to inflame their master to avenge, by the death of our Lord, the affront offered to his master, the emperor.

18. See this question, concerning the resurrection, explained in detail on Matt. xxii. 23-32.

Raise up seed unto his brother. This law is mentioned in Deut. xxv. 5. The meaning of the expression is that the children produced by this marriage should be reckoned in the genealogy of the deceased brother and enjoy his estates. The word *seed* should be always translated "children" or "posterity."

Seven brethren. It is very likely that the Sadducees increased the number, merely to make the question the more difficult.

23. *When they shall rise.* This clause is wanting in several MSS.

MATTHEW HENRY

and therefore Christ does not pass it over lightly, but enlarges upon it.

1. He charges the Sadducees with *error*, and charges that upon their *ignorance. Do ye not therefore err?* Ye cannot but be sensible of it yourselves, and that the cause of your error is, (1) Because ye do not *know the scriptures.* Not but that the Sadducees had read the scriptures, and perhaps were ready in them; yet they might be truly said not to *know the scriptures,* because they did not know the sense and meaning of them, but put false constructions upon them. A right knowledge of the scripture, as the fountain whence all revealed religion now flows, and the foundation on which it is built, is the best preservative against error. Keep the truth, the scripture-truth, and it shall keep thee. (2) Because ye *know not the power of God.* They could not but know that God is almighty, but they would not apply that doctrine to this matter, but gave up the truth to the objections of the impossibility of it. The power of God, seen in the return of the spring (Ps. civ. 30), in the reviving of the corn (John xii. 24), in the restoring of an abject people to their prosperity (Ezek. xxxvii. 12–14), in the raising of so many to life, miraculously, both in the Old Testament and in the New, and especially, in the resurrection of Christ (Eph. i. 19, 20), are all earnests of our resurrection by the same power (Phil. iii. 21); *according to the mighty working whereby he is able to subdue all things to himself.*

2. He sets aside all the force of their objection, by setting the doctrine of the future state in a true light (*v.* 25); *When they shall rise from the dead, they neither marry, nor are given in marriage.* It is a folly to ask, *Whose wife shall she be of the seven?* It is no wonder if we confound ourselves with endless absurdities, when we measure our ideas of the world of spirits by the affairs of this world of sense.

III. He builds the doctrine of the future state, and of the blessedness of the righteous in that state, upon the covenant of God with Abraham, which God was pleased to own, after Abraham's death, *v.* 26, 27. He appeals to the scriptures; *Have ye not read in the book of Moses?* Now that which he refers them to is, what God said to Moses at the bush, I *am the God of Abraham*; not only, I *was* so, but I *am* so. It is absurd to think that God's relation to Abraham should be continued, and thus solemnly recognized, if Abraham was annihilated, or that the *living God* should be the portion and happiness of a man that is dead, and must be for ever so. You must conclude, 1. That Abraham's soul exists and acts in a state of separation from the body. 2. That therefore, some time or other, the body must rise again. Upon the whole matter, he concludes, *Ye therefore do greatly err.* Those that deny the resurrection, greatly err, and ought to be told so.

Verses 28–34

Only we have here an account of *one* of them, a scribe, who had so much civility in him as to take notice of Christ's answer to the Sadducees, and to own that he had *answered well*, and much to the purpose (*v.* 28). We have his application to Christ for instruction, and it was such as became him; not tempting Christ, but desiring to improve his acquaintance with him.

JAMIESON, FAUSSET, BROWN

24. Do ye not therefore err, because ye know not the scriptures—regarding the future state. **neither the power of God?**—before which a thousand such difficulties vanish. **25. For when they shall rise from the dead, they neither marry, nor are given in marriage**—"neither can they die any more" (Luke 20:36). Marriage is ordained to perpetuate the human family; but as there will be no breaches by death in the future state, this ordinance will cease. **but are as the angels which are in heaven**—In Luke it is "equal unto the angels." But as the subject is death and resurrection, we are not warranted to extend the equality here taught beyond the one point—the *immortality* of their nature. A beautiful clause is added in Luke—"and are the children of God"—not in respect of *character,* which is not here spoken of, but of *nature*—"being the children of the resurrection," as rising to an undecaying existence (Rom. 8:21, 23), and so being the children of their Father's immortality (I Tim. 6:16). **26. And as touching the dead, that they rise: have ye not read in the book of Moses**—"even Moses" (Luke 20:37), whom they had just quoted for the purpose of entangling Him. **how in the bush God spake unto him**—either "at the bush," as the same expression is rendered in Luke 20:37, i.e., when he was there; or "in the (section of his history regarding the) bush." The structure of our verse suggests the latter sense, which is not unusual. **saying**—(Exod. 3:6)—**I am the God of Abraham, and the God of Isaac, and the God of Jacob? 27. He is not the God of the dead, but the God of the living**—not "the God of dead but [the God] of living persons." The word in brackets is almost certainly an addition to the genuine text, and critical editors exclude it. "For all live unto Him" Luke 20:28—"in His view," or "in His estimation." This last statement—found only in Luke—though adding nothing to the argument, is an important additional illustration. It is true, indeed, that to God no human being is dead or ever will be, but all mankind sustain an abiding conscious relation to Him; but the "all" here means "those who shall be accounted worthy to obtain that world." These sustain a gracious covenant relation to God which cannot be dissolved. (Cf. Rom. 6:10, 11.) In this sense our Lord affirms that for Moses to call the Lord the "GOD" of His patriarchal servants, if at that moment they had no existence, would be unworthy of Him. He "would be *ashamed* to be called their God, if He had not prepared for them a city" (Heb. 11:16). It was concluded by some of the early Fathers, from our Lord's resting His proof of the Resurrection on such a passage as this, instead of quoting some much clearer testimonies of the Old Testament, that the Sadducees, to whom this was addressed, acknowledged the authority of no part of the Old Testament but the Pentateuch; and this opinion has held its ground even till now. But as there is no ground for it in the New Testament, so JOSEPHUS is silent upon it; merely saying that they rejected the Pharisaic traditions. It was because the Pentateuch was regarded by all classes as the fundamental source of the Hebrew religion, and all the succeeding books of the Old Testament but as developments of it, that our Lord would show that even there the doctrine of the Resurrection was taught. And all the rather does He select this passage, as being not a bare annunciation of the doctrine in question, but as expressive of that glorious truth *out of which the Resurrection springs.* "And when the multitude heard this" (says Matt. 22:23), "they were astonished at His doctrine." "Then," adds Luke 20:39, 40, "certain of the scribes answering said, Master, thou hast well said"—enjoying His victory over the Sadducees. "And after that they durst not ask Him any [question at all]"—neither party could; both being for the time utterly foiled.

The Great Commandment (vss. 28-34). "But when the Pharisees had heard that He had put the Sadducees to silence, they were gathered together" (Matthew 22:34). **28. And one of the scribes**—"a lawyer," says Matthew (22:35); i.e., teacher of the law. **came, and having heard them reasoning together, and perceiving that he had answered them well, asked him**—manifestly in no bad spirit. When Matthew therefore says he came "tempting," or "trying him," as one of the Pharisaic party who seemed to enjoy the defeat He had given to the Sadducees, we may suppose that though somewhat priding himself upon his insight into the law, and not indisposed to measure his knowledge with One in whom he had not yet learned to believe, he was nevertheless an honest-hearted, fair disputant. **Which is the first commandment of all?**—first in

ADAM CLARKE

Ye do err. Or, "Ye are deceived"—by your impure passions, *not knowing the scriptures,* which assert the resurrection, *nor the* miraculous *power of God* by which it is to be effected.

Have ye not read? This quotation is taken from Exod. iii. 6, 16; and as the five books of Moses were the only part of Scripture which the Sadducees acknowledged as divine, our Lord, by confuting them from those books, proved the second part of His assertion, "You are ignorant of those very Scriptures which you profess to hold sacred."

I am the God of Abraham. Let it be observed that Abraham was dead upwards of three hundred years before these words were spoken to Moses; yet still God calls himself the *God of Abraham.* Now Christ properly observes that God *is not the God of the dead* (that word being equal, in the sense of the Sadducees, to an eternal annihilation), *but of the living.* It therefore follows that, if He be the *God of Abraham . . . Isaac, and . . . Jacob,* these are not dead, but alive; alive with God, though they had ceased, for some hundreds of years, to exist among mortals.

The multitude . . . were astonished at his doctrine. God uses the infidelity of some for the edification of others. Truth always gains by being opposed.

A lawyer. "A teacher of the law." What is called *lawyer* in the common translation conveys a wrong idea to most readers. These teachers of the law were the same as the scribes.

MATTHEW HENRY

I. He enquired, *Which is the first commandment of all? v.* 28. He doth not mean the first in *order*, but the first in *weight* and *dignity*. Not that any commandment of God is little, but some are greater than others, moral precepts than rituals, and of some we may say, They are the *greatest of all*.

II. Christ gave him a direct answer to this enquiry, *v.* 29–31. Those that sincerely desire to be instructed concerning their duty, Christ will *guide in judgment*, and *teach his way*. He tells him,

1. That the great commandment of all, which is indeed inclusive of all, is, that of *loving God with all our hearts*. Where this is the commanding principle in the soul, there is a disposition to every other duty. Love is the leading affection of the soul; the love of God is the leading grace in the renewed soul. Where this is not, nothing else that is good is done. Loving God with all our heart, will effectually take us off from all those things that are rivals with him for the throne in our souls. No commandment will be grievous where this principle commands, and has the ascendant. Now here in Mark, our Saviour prefixes to this command the great doctrinal truth upon which it is built (*v.* 29); *Hear, O Israel, The Lord our God is one Lord;* if we firmly believe this, it will follow, that we shall love him *with all our heart*. If he be one, our hearts must be one with him, and since there is no God besides, no rival must be admitted with him upon the throne.

CHARLES H. SPURGEON:

We may deduce that a man is bound to love God heartily: that is plain enough, for it says, "Thou shalt love the Lord thy God with all thy heart." Yes, there is to be in our love to God a heartliness. We are to throw our whole selves into the love that we give to Him. Not the kind of love that some people give to their fellows when they say, "Be ye warmed and filled," and nothing more. No: our heart is to have its whole being absorbed into God, so that God is the hearty object of its pursuit and its most mighty love. See how the word *all* is repeated again and again. The whole going forth of the being, the whole stirring up of the soul, is to be for God, and for God only. "With all thy heart."

Again: as we are to love God heartily, we are to love Him with all our souls. Then we are to love Him with all our life; for that is the meaning of it. If we are called to die for God, we are to prefer God before our own life. We shall never reach the fullness of this commandment till we get as far as the martyrs, who rather than disobey God would be cast into the furnace, or devoured by wild beasts. We must be ready to give up house, home, liberty, friends, comfort, joy, and life at the command of God, or else we have not carried out this commandment, "Thou shalt love Him with all thy heart and with all thy life."

And, next we are to love God with all our mind. That is, the intellect is to love God. Now, many men believe in the existence of a God, but they do not love that belief. They know there is a God, but they greatly wish there were none. But the Christian never wishes such a thing as that. The thought that there is a God is the sunshine of his existence. His intellect bows before the Most High; not like a slave who bends his body because he must, but like the angel who prostrates himself because he loves to adore his Maker. His intellect is as fond of God as his imagination. "Oh!" he saith, "my God, I bless Thee that Thou art; for Thou art my highest treasure, my richest and my rarest delight. I love Thee with all my intellect; I have neither thought, nor judgment, nor conviction, nor reason, which I do not lay at Thy feet, and consecrate to Thine honor."

And, once again, this love to God is to be characterized by activity; for we are to love Him with all our heart, heartily—with all our soul, that is, to the laying down of our life—with all our mind, that is mentally; and we are to love

JAMIESON, FAUSSET, BROWN

importance; the primary, leading commandment, the most fundamental one. This was a question which, with some others, divided the Jewish teachers into rival schools. Our Lord's answer is in a strain of respect very different from what He showed to cavillers—ever observing His own direction, "Give not that which is holy to the dogs, neither cast ye your pearls before swine; lest they trample them under their feet, and turn again and rend you" (Matt. 7:6). **29. And Jesus answered him, The first of all the commandments is**—The readings here vary considerably. TISCHENDORF and TREGELLES read simply, "the first is"; and they are followed by MEYER and ALFORD. But though the authority for the precise form of the received text is slender, a form almost identical with it seems to have most weight of authority. Our Lord here gives His explicit sanction to the distinction between commandments of a more *fundamental* and *primary* character, and commandments of a more *dependent* and *subordinate* nature; a distinction of which it is confidently asserted by a certain class of critics that the Jews knew nothing, that our Lord and His apostles nowhere lay down, and which has been invented by Christian divines. (Cf. Matt. 23: 23.) **Hear, O Israel; the Lord our God is one Lord**—This every devout Jew recited twice every day, and the Jews do it to this day; thus keeping up the great ancient national protest against the polytheisms and pantheisms of the heathen world: it is the great utterance of the national faith in One Living and Personal God—"ONE JEHOVAH!" **30. And thou shalt**—We have here the language of *law*, expressive of God's *claims*. What then are we here bound down to do? One word is made to express it. And what a word! Had the essence of the divine law consisted in *deeds*, it could not possibly have been expressed in a single word; for no one deed is comprehensive of all others embraced in the law. But as it consists in *an affection of the soul*, one word suffices to express it—but only one. *Fear*, though due to God and enjoined by Him, is *limited* in its sphere and *distant* in character. *Trust, hope*, and the like, though essential features of a right state of heart towards God, are called into action only by *personal necessity*, and so are—in a good sense, it is true, but still are properly—*selfish* affections; that is to say, they have respect to *our own well-being*. But LOVE is an *all-inclusive* affection, embracing not only every other affection proper to its object, but all that is proper to be *done* to its object; for as love spontaneously seeks to please its object, so, in the case of men to God, it is the native well-spring of a voluntary obedience. It is, besides, the most *personal* of all affections. One may fear an *event*, one may hope for an *event*, one may rejoice in an *event;* but one can love only a *Person*. It is the *tenderest*, the most *unselfish*, the most *divine* of all affections. Such, then, is the affection in which the essence of the divine law is declared to consist. **Thou shalt love**—We now come to the glorious Object of that demanded affection. Thou shalt love **the Lord, thy God**—i.e., Jehovah, the Self-Existent One, who has revealed Himself as the "I AM," and there is "*none else*"; who, though by His name JEHOVAH apparently at an unapproachable distance from His finite creatures, yet bears to *thee* a real and definite relationship, out of which arises *His claim* and *thy duty*—of LOVE. But with what are we to love Him? Four things are here specified. First, "Thou shalt love the Lord thy God" **with thy heart**—This sometimes means "the whole inner man"(as Prov. 4:23); but that cannot be meant here; for then the other three particulars would be superfluous. Very often it means "our emotional nature"—the seat of *feeling* as distinguished from our intellectual nature or the seat of *thought*, commonly called the "mind" (as in Phil. 4:7). But neither can this be the sense of it here; for here the heart is distinguished both from the "mind" and the "soul." The "heart," then, must here mean the *sincerity* of both the thoughts and the feelings; in other words, *uprightness* or *trueheartedness*, as opposed to a *hypocritical* or *divided* affection. But next, "Thou shalt love the Lord thy God" with thy soul. This is designed to command our emotional nature: Thou shalt put *feeling* or *warmth* into thine affection. Further, "Thou shalt love the Lord thy God" **with thy mind**—This commands our intellectual nature: Thou shalt put *intelligence* into thine affection—in opposition to a blind devotion, or mere devoteeism. Lastly, "Thou shalt love the Lord thy God" **with thy strength**—This commands our energies: Thou shalt put *intensity* into thine affection—"Do it with thy might" (Eccles. 9:10). Taking these four

ADAM CLARKE

Which is the great commandment? We see here three kinds of enemies and false accusers of Christ and His disciples, and three sorts of accusations brought against them: (1) The Herodians, or politicians and courtiers, who formed their questions and accusations on the rights of the prince, and matters of state, v. 16; (2) The Sadducees, or libertines, who founded theirs upon matters of religion, and articles of faith, which they did not credit, v. 23. (3) The Pharisees, lawyers, scribes, hypocritical pretenders to devotion, who founded theirs on that vital and practical godliness (the love of God and man) of which they wished themselves to be thought the sole proprietors.

30. *Thou shalt love the Lord.* On the nature and properties of the love of God and man, and the way in which this commandment is fulfilled, see the notes on Matt. xxii. 37, etc.

What is implied in loving God with all the heart, soul, mind, strength, and when may a man be said to do this? (1) He loves God *with all* his *heart* who loves nothing in comparison of Him and nothing but in reference to Him, who is ready to give up, do, or suffer anything in order to please and glorify Him. (2) He loves God *with all* his *soul*, or rather, "with all his life," who is ready to give up life for His sake—to endure all sorts of torments, and to be deprived of all kinds of comforts, rather than dishonor God—who employs life with all its comforts and conveniences to glorify God in, by, and through all. (3) He loves God with all his strength, Mark xii. 30; Luke x. 27, who exerts all the powers of his body and soul in the service of God; who, for the glory of his Maker, spares neither labor nor cost; who sacrifices his time, body, health, ease, for the honor of God, his divine Master; who employs in His service all his goods, his talents, his power, credit, authority, and influence. (4) He loves God *with all* his *mind* (intellect) who applies himself only to know God and His holy will; who receives with submission, gratitude, and pleasure the sacred truths which God has revealed to man.

MATTHEW HENRY

Him with all our strength, that is, actively. I am to throw my whole soul into the worship and adoration of God. I am not to keep back a single hour, or a single farthing of my wealth, or a single talent that I have, or a single atom of strength, bodily or mentally, from the worship of God. I am to love Him with all my strength.

—*The Treasury of the New Testament*

2. That the second great commandment is, to *love our neighbour as ourselves* (*v.* 31), and we must show it by *doing as we would be done by.* As we must therefore love God better than ourselves, so we must *love our neighbour as ourselves,* because he is of the same nature with ourselves; and if a fellow-Christian, and of the same sacred society, the obligation is the stronger. *Hath not one God created us?* Has not one Christ redeemed us? Well might Christ say, *There is no other commandment greater than these;* for in these all the law is fulfilled, and if we make conscience of obedience to these, all other instances of obedience will follow of course.

III. The scribe consented to what Christ said, *v.* 32, 33. 1. He commends Christ's decision of this question; *Well, Master, thou hast said the truth.* It shall be brought in evidence against those who persecuted Christ, as a deceiver, that one of themselves confessed that he *said the truth,* and said it *well.* And thus must we subscribe to Christ's sayings, must set to our seal that they are true. 2. He comments upon it. Christ had quoted that great doctrine, that *the Lord our God is one Lord*; and this he not only assented to, but added, "*There is none other but he.*" This excludes all rivals with him, and secures the throne in the heart entire for him. Christ had laid down that great law, of loving God *with all our heart*; and this also he explains—that it is loving him *with the understanding.* Our love to God, as it must be an *entire,* so it must be an *intelligent,* love; we must love him with *all* the understanding; our rational powers and faculties must all be set on work to lead out the affections of our souls toward God. Christ had said, "To love God and our neighbour is the greatest commandment of all"; "Yea," saith the scribe, "it is *more than all whole-burnt offerings and sacrifices,* more acceptable to God." There were those who held, that the law of *sacrifices* was the *greatest commandment* of all; but this scribe readily agreed with our Saviour in this—that the law of love to God and our neighbour is greater than that of *sacrifice,* even than that of *whole-burnt-offerings.*

IV. Christ approved of what he said, and encouraged him to proceed in his enquiries of him, *v.* 34. 1. He owned that he understood well, as far as he went; so far, so good. *Jesus saw that he answered discreetly,* and was the more pleased with it, because he had of late met with so many that answered *indiscreetly.* He answered as *one that had a mind*; as one that had his wits about him; whose judgment was not biassed. He answered as one that allowed himself liberty and leisure to consider, and as one that had considered. 2. He owned that he stood fair for a further advance; "*Thou art not far from the kingdom of God,* the kingdom of grace and glory." There is hope of those who make a good use of the light they have, and go as far as that will carry them, that by the grace of God they will be led further. What became of this scribe we are not told, but would willingly hope that he took the hint Christ hereby gave him, and that he proceeded to enquire of him what was the great commandment of the gospel too. Yet, if he did not, we are not to think it strange; for there are many who are *not far from the kingdom of God,* and yet never come thither. *No man, after that, durst ask him any question;* those that desired to *learn,* were *ashamed* to ask, and those that designed to *cavil,* were *afraid* to ask.

Verses 35–40

I. Christ shows the people how weak and defective the scribes were in their preaching, and how unable to solve the difficulties that occurred in the scriptures of the Old Testament. Of this he gives an instance, which is not so fully related here as it was in Matthew.

1. They told the people that the Messiah was to be the *Son of David* (*v.* 35), and they were in the right. The people took it as what the scribes said; whereas the truths of God should rather be quoted from our

JAMIESON, FAUSSET, BROWN

things together, the command of the Law is, "Thou shalt love the Lord thy God *with all thy powers*—with a *sincere,* a *fervid,* an *intelligent,* an *energetic* love." But this is not all that the Law demands. God will have all these qualities in their most perfect exercise. "Thou shalt love the Lord thy God," says the Law, "with *all* thy heart," or, with perfect sincerity; "Thou shalt love the Lord thy God with *all* thy soul," or, with the utmost fervor; "Thou shalt love the Lord thy God with *all* thy mind," or, in the fullest exercise of an enlightened reason; and "Thou shalt love the Lord thy God with *all* thy strength," or, with the whole energy of our being! So much for the First Commandment. **31. And the second is like**—"unto it" (Matt. 22:39); as demanding the same affection, and only the extension of it, in its proper measure, to the creatures of Him whom we thus love—our *brethren* in the participation of the same nature, and *neighbors,* as connected with us by ties that render each dependent upon and necessary to the other. **Thou shalt love thy neighbour as thyself**—Now, as we are not to love ourselves supremely, this is virtually a command, in the first place, *not* to love our neighbor with all our heart and soul and mind and strength. And thus it is a condemnation of the idolatry of the creature. Our supreme and uttermost affection is to be reserved for God. But as *sincerely* as ourselves we are to love all mankind, and with *the same readiness to do and suffer for them* as we should reasonably desire them to show to us. The golden rule (Matt. 7:12) is here our best interpreter of the nature and extent of these claims. **There is none other commandment greater than these**—or, as in Matthew 22:40, "On these two commandments hang all the law and the prophets" (see on Matt. 5:17). It is as if He had said, "This is all Scripture in a nutshell; the whole law of human duty in a portable, pocket form." Indeed, it is so *simple* that a child may understand it, so *brief* that all may remember it, so *comprehensive* as to embrace all possible cases. And from its very nature it is *unchangeable.* It is inconceivable that God should require from his rational creatures anything *less,* or in substance anything *else,* under any *dispensation,* in any *world,* at any *period* throughout eternal duration. He cannot but claim this—all this—alike in *heaven,* in *earth,* and in *hell!* And this incomparable summary of the divine law belonged to the *Jewish religion!* As it shines in its own self-evidencing splendor, so it reveals its own true source. The religion from which the world has received it could be none other than a *Godgiven religion!* **32. And the scribe said unto him, Well, Master**—Teacher—**thou hast said the truth: for there is one God; and there is none other but he**—The genuine text here seems clearly to have been, "There is one," without the word "God"; and so nearly all critical editors and expositors read. **33. And to love him with all the heart . . . and to love his neighbour as himself, is more than all whole burnt offerings and sacrifices**—more, i.e., than all positive institutions; thereby showing insight into the essential difference between what is *moral* and in its own nature *unchangeable,* and what is obligatory only *because enjoined,* and only *so long as enjoined.* **34. And when Jesus saw that he answered discreetly**—rather, "intelligently," or "sensibly"; not only in a good spirit, but with a promising measure of insight into spiritual things. **he said unto him, Thou art not far from the kingdom of God**—for he had but *to follow out a little further* what he seemed sincerely to own, to find his way into the kingdom. He needed only the experience of another eminent scribe who at a later period said, "We know that *the law is spiritual,* but *I am carnal,* sold under sin": who exclaimed, "O wretched man that I am! Who shall deliver me?" but who added, "I thank God through Jesus Christ!" (Rom. 7:14, 24, 25). Perhaps among the "great company of the priests" and other Jewish ecclesiastics who "were obedient to the faith," almost immediately after the day of Pentecost (Acts 6:7), this upright lawyer was one. But for all his nearness to the Kingdom of God, it may be he never entered it. **And no man after that durst ask any question**—all feeling that they were no match for Him, and that it was vain to enter the lists with Him.

Christ Baffles the Pharisees regarding David (vss. 35-37). **35. And Jesus answered and said, while he taught in the temple**—and "while the Pharisees were gathered together" (Matt. 22:41). **How say the scribes that Christ is the son of David?**—How come they to give it out that Messiah is to be the son of David? In Matthew, Jesus asks them, "What think ye of Christ?" or of the promised and expected Messiah? "Whose son is He [to be]?" They

ADAM CLARKE

Thou shalt love thy neighbour. The love of our neighbor springs from the love of God as its Source; is found in the love of God as its principle, pattern, and end; and the love of God is found in the love of our neighbor as its effect, representation, and infallible mark.

On these two commandments hang all the law and the prophets. They are like the first and last links of a chain; all the intermediate ones depend on them. True religion begins and ends in love to God and man. These are the two grand links that unite God to man, man to his fellows, and men again to God.

32. *And the scribe said.* The answer of the scribe, contained in verses 32-34, is not found in either Matthew or Luke. This is another proof against Mark's supposed abridgment.

34. *Thou art not far from the kingdom of God.* This scribe appears to have been a prudent, sensible, and pious man; almost a Christian—so near the kingdom of God that he might have easily stepped in.

35. *How say the scribes?* See Matt. xxii. 41, etc.

MATTHEW HENRY

Bibles than from our ministers, for there is the original of them.

2. Yet they could not tell them how to call him *his Lord*, as he doth, Ps. cx. 1. They had taught the people that concerning the Messiah, which would be for the honour of their nation—that he should be a branch of their royal family; but they had not taken care to teach them that he should be the Son of God, and, as such, and not otherwise, *David's Lord.* If any should object, *How then doth David himself call him Lord?* they would not know how to avoid the force of the objection. Note, Those are unworthy to sit in Moses's seat, who, though they are able to preach the truth, are not in some measure able to defend it when they have preached it, and to convince gainsayers.

Now this galled the scribes, to have their ignorance thus exposed; but the *common people heard him gladly, v.* 37. What he preached was surprising and affecting, and they had never heard such preaching. Probably there was something more than ordinarily commanding and charming in his voice and way of delivery which recommended him to the affections of the common people; for we do not find that any were wrought upon to *believe* in him, and to *follow* him. And perhaps some of these cried, *Crucify him*, as Herod heard John Baptist gladly, and yet cut off his head.

II. He cautions the people to take heed of suffering themselves to be imposed upon by the scribes; *He said unto them in his doctrine*, "*Beware of the scribes*" (*v.* 38).

1. They affect to appear *very great*; for they go in *long clothing*, as princes, or judges. Their going in such clothing was not sinful, but their *loving* to go in it, this was a product of pride. Christ would have his disciples go with *their loins girt*.

2. They affect to appear *very good*; for they pray, they make *long prayers*. They took care it should be known that they prayed, that they prayed long. This they did *for a pretence*, that they might seem to love prayer.

3. They coveted applause, and were fond of it; they loved *salutations in the market-places*, and the *chief seats in the synagogues, and the uppermost rooms at feasts*. To have these given them, they thought, expressed the value *they* had for them, who did know them, and gained them respect for those who did not.

4. They herein aimed to *enrich* themselves. They *devoured widows' houses*; it was to screen themselves from the suspicion of dishonesty, that they put on the mask of piety; and that they might not be thought as bad as the worst, they were studious to seem as good as the best. Let not prayers, no nor *long prayers*, be thought the worse of, if made in humility and sincerity, for their having been by some thus abused. Iniquity, thus disguised with a show of piety, is *double* iniquity, so its doom will be doubly heavy; *These shall receive greater damnation.*

Verses 41-44

This passage of story was not in Matthew, but is here and in Luke; it is Christ's commendation of the poor widow, that cast *two mites* into the treasury.

I. There was a *public fund* for charity, a poor's-box, and this in *the temple*; for works of charity and works of piety very fitly go together. We often find *prayers* and *alms* in conjunction, as Acts x. 2, 4. It is good for those to *lay by as God has prospered them* (1 Cor. xvi. 2), that they may have something ready to give when an object of charity offers itself.

II. Jesus Christ has *an eye* upon it; *He sat over against the treasury, and beheld how the people cast money into it.* Our Lord Jesus takes notice of what we contribute to pious and charitable uses; whether we give liberally or sparingly; whether we do it as unto the Lord, or only to be seen of men.

III. He saw *many that were rich cast in much*: and it was a good sight to see rich people charitable, to see *many* rich people so, and to see them cast in *much.* Those that are rich, ought to give richly; if God give abundantly to us, he expects we should give abundantly.

IV. There was a *poor widow that cast in two mites, which make a farthing* (*v.* 42); and our Lord Jesus highly commended her; *called his disciples* to him, and bid them take notice of it (*v.* 43); told them that she could very ill spare that which she gave, it was *all her living.* He reckoned it more than all that put together, which the rich people threw in; for they did *cast in of their abundance, but she of her want, v.* 44. Now many would have been ready to censure this *poor widow*; why should she give to others, when she had little enough for herself? Charity begins at home. It is so rare a thing to find any that would not blame this widow, that we cannot expect to find

JAMIESON, FAUSSET, BROWN

say unto Him, The son of David." The sense is the same. "He saith unto them, How then doth David in spirit call Him Lord?" (Matt. 22:42, 43.) **36. For David himself said by the Holy Ghost, The Lord said to my Lord, Sit thou on my right hand, till I make thine enemies thy footstool**—(Ps. 110:1). **37. David therefore himself calleth him Lord; and whence is he then his son?**—There is but one solution of this difficulty. Messiah is at once inferior to David as his son according to the flesh, and superior to him as the Lord of a kingdom of which David is himself a subject, not the sovereign. The human and divine natures of Christ, and the spirituality of His kingdom—of which the highest earthly sovereigns are honored if they be counted worthy to be its subjects—furnish the only key to this puzzle. **And the common people**—the immense crowd. **heard him gladly** "And no man was able to answer Him a word; neither durst any man from that day forth ask Him any more questions" (Matthew 22: 46).

The Scribes Denounced (vss. 38-40). **38. And he said unto them in his doctrine**—rather, "in His teaching"; implying that this was but a specimen of an extended discourse, which Matthew gives in full (ch. 23). Luke says (20:45) this was "in the audience of all the people said unto His disciples." **Beware of the scribes, which love**—or like—**to go in long clothing**—(see on Matt. 23:5). **and [love] salutations in the market-places, 39. And the chief seats in the synagogues, and the uppermost rooms**—or positions—**at feasts**—See on this love of distinction, Luke 14:7; and on Matthew 6:5.

40. Which devour widows' houses, and for a pretence make long prayers: these shall receive greater damnation—They took advantage of their helpless condition and confiding character to obtain possession of their property, while by their "long prayers" they made them believe they were raised far above "filthy lucre." So much the "greater damnation" awaited them. (Cf. Matt. 23:33.) A lifelike description this of the Romish clergy, the true successors of "the scribes."

41-44. THE WIDOW'S TWO MITES. (=Luke 21: 1-4.) See on Luke 21:1-4.

He had "sat down over against the treasury" (Mark 12:41), probably to rest, for He had continued long standing as he taught in the temple-court (Mark 11:27), and "looking up He saw"—as in Zaccheus' case, not quite casually. **the rich . . .** —"the people," says Mark 12:41 "cast money into the treasury, and many cast in much"; i.e., into chests deposited in one of the courts of the temple to receive the offerings of the people towards its maintenance (II Kings 12:9; John 8:20).

two mites—"which make a farthing" (Mark 12:42), the smallest Jewish coin. "She might have kept one" [BENGEL]. **And he said**—"to His disciples," whom He "called to Him" (Mark 12:43), to teach from it a great future lesson. **more than . . . all**—in proportion to her means, which is God's standard (II Cor. 8:12). **of their abundance**—their *superfluity;* what they had to spare," or beyond what they needed. **of her penury**—or "want" (Mark 12:44)—her *deficiency*, of what was *less* than her own wants required, "all the living she had." Mark still more emphatically, "all that she had—

ADAM CLARKE

How is he his son? As the Jews did not attempt to deny the conclusion of our Lord's question—which was, The Messiah is not only the Son of David according to the flesh, but He is the Lord of David according to His divine nature—then it is evident they could not. Indeed there was no other way of invalidating the argument but by denying that the prophecy in question related to Christ. But it seems the prophecy was so fully and so generally understood to belong to the Messiah that they did not attempt to do this; for it is immediately added, "No man was able to answer him a word." They were completely nonplussed and confounded.

37. *The common people heard him gladly.* And doubtless many of them were brought to believe and receive the truth. By the comparatively poor the gospel is still best received.

38. *Beware of the scribes.* See on Matt. xxiii. 1, etc.

The scribes and the Pharisees sit in Moses' seat. They "sat" there formerly by divine appointment; they *sit* there now by divine permission. What our Lord says here refers to their expounding the Scriptures, for it was the custom of the Jewish doctors to *sit* while they expounded the law and prophets, chap. v. 1; Luke iv. 20-22, and to stand up when they read them. By the *seat* of Moses we are to understand authority to teach the law. Moses was the great teacher of the Jewish people, and the scribes are here represented as his successors.

41. *Cast money into the treasury.* It is worthy of observation that the money put into the treasury, even by the rich, is termed by the Evangelist "brass money," probably that species of small brass coin which was called *prutah* among the Jews, two of which make a farthing. We call this *mite,* from the French, *miete,* which signifies a crumb or very small morsel. The *prutah* was the smallest coin in use among the Jews, and there is a canon among the rabbins that no person shall put less than two *prutahs* into the treasury. This poor widow would not give less, and her poverty prevented her from giving more. And whereas it is said that *many . . . rich* persons *cast in much* (many), this may only refer to the number of the *prutahs* which they threw in, and not to the value. What opinion should we form of a rich man who, in a collection for a public charity, threw in only a handful of halfpence? The whole of this account is lacking in Matthew —another proof that Mark did not abridge him.

MATTHEW HENRY

any that will imitate her; and yet our Saviour commends her. We must hence learn, 1. That *giving alms*, is an excellent good thing, and highly pleasing to the Lord Jesus; he will graciously accept of it, though in some circumstances there may not be all the discretion in the world. 2. Those that have but a *little*, ought to give alms out of *their little*. We should in many cases pinch ourselves, that we may supply the necessities of others; this is loving our neighbours as ourselves. 3. Public charities should be encouraged, and though there may be some mismanagement of them, yet that is not a good reason why we should not bring in our *quota* to them. 4. Though we can give but *a little* in charity, it shall be accepted of Christ, who requires *according to what a man has, and not according to what he has not*; two mites shall be put upon the score, and brought to account, if given in a right manner, as if they had been two pounds. 5. It is much to the praise of charity, when we give not only *to our power*, but *beyond our power*, as the Macedonian churches, whose *deep poverty abounded to the riches of their liberality*, 2 Cor. viii. 2, 3, and trust God to provide for us some other way, *this is thank-worthy.*

CHAPTER 13

F. B. MEYER:

Our Lord departed from the temple, never again to enter its sacred precincts or to open his mouth in public teaching. When he withdrew, the whole system of Judaism was given over to desolation, and the predictions spoken at this time were minutely fulfilled in the fall of Jerusalem under Titus. The temple was blotted out. Indeed, a plowshare passed over its site; the people were sold into slavery or butchered in the gladiatorial shows; their nationality was obliterated, and their land given to strangers.
—*Bible Commentary*

Verses 1–4

I. How apt many of Christ's own disciples are to idolize things that look *great*, and have been long looked upon as *sacred*. One of them said to him, "Look, Master, *what manner of stones, and what buildings are here* (*v.* 1). We never saw the like in Galilee; O do not leave this fine place."

II. How little Christ values external pomp, where there is not real purity; "*Seest thou these great buildings*" (saith Christ)? "I tell thee, the time is at hand when *there shall not be left one stone upon another, that shall not be thrown down*," *v.* 2. He looks with *pity* upon the ruin of precious souls, and weeps over them, for on them he has put a great value; but we do not find him look with any pity upon the ruin of a magnificent house, when he is driven out of it by sin. With what little concern doth he say, *Not one stone shall be left on another!* While any part remained standing, there might be some hopes of the repair of it; but what hope is there, when not one stone is *left upon another*?

III. How natural it is to us to desire to know things to come, and the times of them; more inquisitive we are apt to be about that than about our duty. His disciples knew not how to *digest* this doctrine, and therefore they were in pain till they got him alone, and got more out of him concerning this matter. As he was returning to Bethany therefore, he *sat upon the mount of Olives, over against the temple*; and there four of them agreed to *ask him privately*, what he meant by the destroying of the temple. Probably, Christ's discourse, in answer to it, was in the hearing of the rest of the disciples, yet *privately*, that is, apart from the multitude. Their enquiry is, *When shall these things be?* They will not question whether they shall be or no, but are willing to hope it is a great way off. "Tell us *what shall be the sign, when all these things shall be fulfilled?*"

JAMIESON, FAUSSET, BROWN

her whole subsistence." Note: (1) *As temple offerings are needed still for the service of Christ at home and abroad, so "looking down" now, as then "up," Me "sees" who "cast in," and how much.* (2) *Christ's standard of commendable offering is not our superfluity, but our deficiency*—not what will never be missed, but what costs us some real sacrifice, and just in proportion to the relative amount of that sacrifice. (See II Cor. 8:1-3.)

CHAPTER 13

Vss. 1-37. Christ's Prophecy of the Destruction of Jerusalem, and Warnings Suggested by It to Prepare for His Second Coming. (=Matt. 24:1-51; Luke 21:5-36.) Jesus had uttered all His mind against the Jewish ecclesiastics, exposing their character with withering plainness, and denouncing, in language of awful severity, the judgments of God against them for that unfaithfulness to their trust which was bringing ruin upon the nation. He had closed this His last public discourse (Matt. 23) by a passionate lamentation over Jerusalem, and a solemn farewell to the temple. "And," says Matt. 24:1, "Jesus went out and departed from the temple"—never more to re-enter its precincts, or open His mouth in public teaching. *With this act ended His public ministry.* As He withdrew, says Olshausen, the gracious presence of God left the sanctuary; and the temple, with all its service, and the whole theocratic constitution, was given over to destruction. What immediately followed is, as usual, most minutely and graphically described by our Evangelist. **1. And as he went out of the temple, one of his disciples saith unto him**—The other Evangelists are less definite. "As some spake," says Luke; "His disciples came to Him," says Matthew. Doubtless it was the speech of one, the mouthpiece, likely, of others. **Master**—Teacher —**see what manner of stones and what buildings are here**—wondering probably, how so massive a pile could be overthrown, as seemed implied in our Lord's last words regarding it. Josephus, who gives a minute account of the wonderful structure, speaks of stones forty cubits long (*Jewish War*, v. 5. 1.) and says the pillars supporting the porches were twenty-five cubits high, all of one stone, and that of the whitest marble (*ibid.*, v. 5.2). Six days' battering at the walls, during the siege, made no impression upon them (*ibid.*, vi. 4. 1). Some of the underbuilding, yet remaining, and other works, are probably as old as the first temple. **2. And Jesus answering said unto him, Seest thou these great buildings?**—"Ye call My attention to these things? I have seen them. Ye point to their massive and durable appearance: now listen to their fate." **there shall not be left**—"left here" (Matt. 24:2). **one stone upon another, that shall not be thrown down**—Titus ordered the whole city and temple to be demolished [Josephus, *J. W.*, vii. 1. 1]; Eleazar wished they had all died before seeing that holy city destroyed by enemies' hands, and before the temple was so profanely *dug up* (*ibid.*, vii. 8. 7). **3. And as he sat upon the Mount of Olives, over against the temple**—On their way from Jerusalem to Bethany they would cross Mount Olivet; on its summit He seats Himself, over against the temple, having the city all spread out under His eye. How graphically is this set before us by our Evangelist! **Peter and James and John and Andrew asked him privately**—The other Evangelists tell us merely that "the disciples" did so. But Mark not only says that it was four of them, but names them; and they were the first *quarternion* of the Twelve. **4. Tell us, when shall these things be? and what shall be the sign when all these things shall be fulfilled?**—"and what shall be the sign of Thy coming, and of the end of the world?" They no doubt looked upon the date of all these things as one and the same, and their notions of the things themselves were as confused as of the times of them. Our

ADAM CLARKE

F. B. MEYER:

In terrible words (vv. 38-40), Christ denounced the moral and religious leaders of the time. They made a pretense and a gain of their religion. How great the contrast between them and this poor widow, who cast into God's treasury all that she had to provide for her day's living! Our Lord is quick to notice acts like these, which give evidence of the true heart.
—*Bible Commentary*

CHAPTER 13

And Jesus went out, and departed from the temple. Or, "And Jesus, going out of the Temple, was going away." This is the arrangement of the words in several eminent manuscripts, versions, and fathers, and is much clearer than that in the common translation.

1. *See what manner of stones.* Josephus says (*Ant.* b. xv, c. xi) "that these stones were white and strong, fifty feet long, twenty-four broad, and sixteen in thickness." If this account can be relied on, well might the disciples be struck with wonder at such a superb edifice, and formed by such immense stones! The principal contents of this chapter are largely explained in the notes on Matthew xxiv.

There shall not be left here one stone. These seem to have been the last words He spoke as He left the Temple, into which He never afterwards entered; and when He got to the Mount of Olives, He renewed the discourse. From this mount, on which our Lord and His disciples now sat, the whole of the city and particularly the Temple were clearly seen. This part of our Lord's prediction was fulfilled in the most literal manner. Josephus says, *War*, b. vii, c. 1; "Caesar gave orders that they should now demolish the whole city and temple, except the three towers, Phaselus, Hippicus, and Mariamne, and a part of the western wall, and these were spared; but, for all the rest of the wall, it was laid so completely even with the ground, by those who dug it up to the foundation, that there was left nothing to make those that came thither believe it had ever been inhabited."

MATTHEW HENRY

Verses 5–13

Our Lord Jesus, in reply to their question, sets himself, not so much to satisfy their curiosity as to direct their consciences; but gives them the cautions which were needful, with reference to the events that should now shortly come to pass.

I. They must take heed that they be not *deceived* by the *seducers* and *impostors* that should now shortly arise (*v.* 5, 6); "*Take heed lest any man deceive you.* Many shall come *in my name,* saying, *I am Christ.*" After the Jews had rejected the true Christ, they were imposed upon by many false Christs. Those false Christs *deceived many;* Therefore *take heed lest they deceive you.* When many are deceived, we should thereby be awakened to look to ourselves.

II. They must take heed that they be not *disturbed* at the noise of wars, which they should be alarmed with, *v.* 7, 8. At some times the nations are more distracted and wasted with wars than at other times; so it shall be now; Christ was born into the world when there was a general peace, but soon after he went out of the world there were general wars; *Nation shall rise against nation, and kingdom against kingdom.* "But *be not troubled at it.* Let it be no *surprise* to you; *such things must needs be.* Let it be no *terror* to you, you have no concern in them, and therefore need not be apprehensive of any damage by them." Those that despise the smiles of the world, and do not court and covet them, may despise the frowns of the world, and need not fear them. "Let it not be looked upon as an omen of the approaching period of the world, for the *end is not yet* (*v.* 7). Think not that these *wars* will bring the world to a period. Let it not be looked upon as if in them God had done his worst. Be not troubled at the wars you shall hear of, for they are but *the beginnings of sorrows,* and therefore, you ought to *prepare for worse;* for there shall also be *earthquakes in divers places,* and there *shall be famines* and *troubles.* The world shall be full of *troubles,* but *be not ye troubled;* but *fear not ye their fear.*" The disciples of Christ may enjoy a holy security and serenity of mind, when all about them is in the greatest disorder.

III. They must take heed that they be not *drawn away* from Christ by the sufferings they should meet with for Christ's sake. Again, he saith, "*Take heed to yourselves, v.* 9. Though you may escape the *sword of war,* better than some of your neighbours, yet be not secure; you will be exposed to the *sword of justice* more than others. *Take heed* therefore lest you *deceive* yourselves with the hopes of outward prosperity, when it is *through many tribulations* that *you must enter into the kingdom of God. Take heed* what you say and do, for you will have many eyes upon you."

1. What the trouble is which they must expect. They shall be *hated of all men;* trouble enough! The thoughts of *being hated* are grievous to a tender spirit. Those that are *malicious,* will be *mischievous.* It was not for anything amiss in them, or done amiss by them, that they were *hated,* but for Christ's name's sake. The world hated them because he loved them. Their own *relations* shall *betray them,* those to whom they were most nearly allied, and on whom therefore they depended for protection. Their *church-rulers* shall inflict *their censures* upon them; "You shall be *delivered up,* and shall be *beaten in the synagogues* with forty stripes at a time, as offenders against the law." It is no new thing for the church's artillery, through the treachery of its officers, to be turned against some of its best friends. *Governors* and *kings* shall use their power against them. They shall *cause you to be put to death,* as enemies to the empire. They must resist unto blood and still resist.

2. What they shall have to comfort themselves with.

(1) That the work they were called to should be carried on and prosper (*v.* 10); "*The gospel* shall, for all this, be *published among all nations,* and the *sound* of it shall *go forth into all the earth.*" It is comfort to those who suffer for the gospel, that, though they may be crushed and borne down, the gospel cannot; it shall keep its ground, and carry the day.

(2) That their sufferings, instead of obstructing their work, should forward it; "Your being *brought before governors and kings* shall be for *a testimony of them* (so some read it, *v.* 9); it shall give you an opportunity of preaching the gospel to those before whom you are brought as criminals." Or, as we read it, It shall be for a testimony *against them,* against both the judges and the prosecutors. The gospel is a testimony to us concerning Christ and heaven. If we receive it, it will be a testimony for us: it will justify and save us; if not, it will be a testimony *against* us in the great day.

(3) That, when they were brought before kings

JAMIESON, FAUSSET, BROWN

Lord takes His own way of meeting their questions.

Prophecies of the Destruction of Jerusalem (vss. 5-31). **5. And Jesus answering them began to say, Take heed lest any man deceive you: 6. For many shall come in my name, saying, I am Christ**—(see Matt. 24:5)—"and the time draweth nigh" (Luke 21:8); that is, the time of the kingdom in its full splendor. **and shall deceive many**—"Go ye not therefore after them" (Luke 21:8). The reference here seems not to be to pretended Messiahs, deceiving those who rejected the claims of Jesus, of whom indeed there were plenty—for our Lord is addressing His own genuine disciples—but to persons pretending to be Jesus Himself, returned in glory to take possession of His kingdom. This gives peculiar force to the words, "Go ye not therefore after them." **7. And when ye shall hear of wars and rumours of wars, be ye not troubled**—see on vs. 13, and compare Isaiah 8:11-14. **for such things must needs be; but the end shall not be yet**—In Luke (21: 9), "the end is not by and by," or "immediately." Worse must come before all is over.

8. These are the beginnings of sorrows—"of travail-pangs," to which heavy calamities are compared. (See Jer. 4: 31, etc.). The annals of TACITUS tell us how the Roman world was convulsed, before the destruction of Jerusalem, by rival claimants of the imperial purple.

9. But take heed to yourselves: for—"before all these things" (Luke 21:12); i.e., before these public calamities come. **they shall deliver you up to councils; and in the synagogues ye shall be beaten**—These refer to *ecclesiastical* proceedings against them.

10. And the gospel must first be published among all nations—"for a witness, and then shall the end come" (Matt. 24:14). God never sends judgment without previous warning; and there can be no doubt that the Jews, already dispersed over most known countries, had nearly all heard the Gospel "as a witness," before the end of the Jewish state. The same principle was repeated and will repeat itself to "*the* end."

and ye shall be brought before rulers and kings—before *civil* tribunals next. **for my sake, for a testimony against them**—rather "unto them"—to give you an opportunity of bearing testimony to Me before them. In the Acts of the Apostles we have the best commentary on this announcement. (Cf. Matt. 10:17, 18.)

ADAM CLARKE

Take heed that no man deceive you. The world is full of deceivers, and it is only by taking heed to the counsel of Christ that even His followers can escape being ruined by them. From this to v. 31, our Lord mentions the signs which should precede His coming. The *first* sign is false christs.

For many shall come in my name. Josephus says (*War,* b. ii, c. 13) that there were many who, pretending to divine inspiration, deceived the people, leading out numbers of them to the desert, pretending that God would there show them the signs of liberty, meaning redemption from the Roman power, and that an Egyptian false prophet led 30,000 men into the desert, who were almost all cut off by Felix. See Acts xxi. 38. It was a just judgment for God to deliver up that people into the hands of false christs who had rejected the true one. About twelve years after the death of our Lord, when Cuspius Fadus was procurator of Judea, arose an impostor of the name of Theudas, who said he was a prophet, and persuaded a great multitude to follow him with their best effects to the river Jordan, which he promised to divide for their passage; and saying these things, says Josephus, "he deceived many"—almost the very words of our Lord. A few years afterwards, under the reign of Nero, while Felix was procurator of Judea, impostors of this stamp were so frequent that some were taken and killed almost every day (Josephus *Ant.,* b. xx, cc. 4 and 7).

The *second* sign given by our Lord is *wars and rumours of wars.* These may be seen in Josephus (*Ant.,* b. xviii, c. 9; *War,* b. ii, c. 10), especially as to the *rumours of wars,* when Caligula ordered his statue to be set up in the Temple of God, which the Jews having refused, had every reason to expect a war with the Romans, and were in such consternation on the occasion that they even neglected to till their land.

9. *Councils.* "Sanhedrins." The grand Sanhedrin consisted of seventy-two elders (this was the national council of state), and the small Sanhedrins, which were composed of twenty-three counsellors. *Synagogues.* Courts of justice for villages, etc., consisting of three magistrates, chosen out of the principal directors of the synagogue in that place.

And this gospel of the kingdom shall be preached in all the world. But, notwithstanding these persecutions, there should be a universal publication of the glad tidings of the Kingdom *for a witness [testimony] to all nations.* God would have the iniquity of the Jews published everywhere before the heavy stroke of His judgments should fall upon them, that all mankind, as it were, might be brought as witnesses against their cruelty and obstinacy in crucifying and rejecting the Lord Jesus. *In all the world.* Perhaps no more is meant here than the Roman empire. Tacitus informs us (*Annal.* l. xv) that, as early as the reign of Nero, the Christians were grown so numerous at Rome as to excite the jealousy of the government, and in other parts they were in proportion. *Then shall the end come.* When this general publication of the gospel shall have taken place, then a period shall be put to the whole Jewish economy, by the utter destruction of their city and Temple.

Rulers. Or "governors." The Roman deputies, such as Pontius Pilate. *Kings.* The tetrarchs of Judea and Galilee, who bore this name.

MATTHEW HENRY

and governors for Christ's sake, they should have special assistance from heaven (*v.* 11); "*Take no thought beforehand what ye shall speak*, but *whatsoever shall be given you in that hour* that *speak ye*, and fear not the success of it, because it is *offhand*, for *it is not ye that speak*, but it is *the Holy Ghost*." When we are engaged in the service of Christ, we may depend upon the aids of the Spirit of Christ.

(4) That heaven at last would *make amends for all*; *he that shall endure to the end, the same shall be saved*," *v.* 13. Perseverance gains the crown. The salvation here promised is more than a deliverance from evil, it is an everlasting blessedness.

Verses 14–23

The Jews, in rebelling against the Romans, and in persecuting the Christians, were setting both God and man against them. Now here we have a prediction of that ruin which came upon them within less than forty years after this.

I. What is here foretold concerning it.

1. That the Roman *armies* should make a descent upon Judæa, and invest Jerusalem, the holy city. These were the *abomination* of *desolation*. They had rejected Christ as an *abomination*, who would have been their *salvation*; and now God brought upon them an abomination that would be their *desolation*. This army stood *where it ought not*, in and about the *holy city*, which the heathen ought not to have approached. Sin made the breach, at which the glory went out, and the abomination of desolation broke in, *and stood where it ought not*.

2. That when the Roman *army* should come into the country, there would be no safety anywhere but by quitting the country, and that with all possible expedition. A man cannot have so much as his life given him for a prey, but by *fleeing to the mountains* out of Judæa; and let him take the first alarm, and make the best of his way. If he be *on the house-top*, and spies them coming, let him not *go down to take anything out of the house*, for it will occasion his losing of time. If he be in the field, let him get away as he is, and not *turn back again, to take up his garment*, *v.* 16. If he can save his life, let him reckon it a good bargain, though he can save nothing else, and be thankful to God, that, though he is cut short, he is not cut off.

3. That it would go very hard at that time with poor mothers and nurses (*v.* 17); "*Woe to them that are with child*, that cannot shift for themselves, nor make haste as others can. And *woe to them that give suck*, that know not how either to leave the tender infants behind them, or to carry them along with them." The time may often be, when the greatest comforts may prove the greatest burthens. It would likewise be very uncomfortable, if they should be forced to flee *in the winter* (*v.* 18). If there be no remedy but that trouble must come, yet we may desire and pray that the circumstances of it may be so ordered as to be a mitigation of the trouble; and when things are bad, we ought to consider they might have been worse

4. There should be such destruction and desolation made, as could not be paralleled in any history (*v.* 19); *In those days shall be affliction, such as was not from the beginning of the creation which God created unto this day, neither shall be*. It threatened a universal slaughter of all the people of the Jews; so barbarously did they devour one another, and the Romans devour them all, that, if their wars had continued a little longer, *no flesh could have been saved*. But in the midst of wrath God remembered mercy. He *shortened the days*. Many particular persons had their lives given them for a prey, by the storm's subsiding when it did. It was *for the elects' sake* that those days were shortened; *many* among them fared the better for the sake of the *few* among them that believed in Christ. There was a promise, that *a remnant* should be saved (Isa. x. 22). God's own *elect cry day and night to him*, and their prayers must be answered, Luke xviii. 7.

JAMIESON, FAUSSET, BROWN

11. But when they shall lead you, and deliver you up, take no thought beforehand—"Be not anxious beforehand." **what ye shall speak, neither do ye premeditate**—"Be not filled with apprehension, in the prospect of such public appearances for Me, lest ye should bring discredit upon My name, nor think it necessary to prepare beforehand what ye are to say." **but whatsoever shall be given you in that hour, that speak ye: for it is not ye that speak, but the Holy Ghost**—(See on Matt. 10:19, 20). **13. And ye shall be hated of all men for my name's sake**—Matthew (24:12) adds this important intimation: "And because iniquity shall abound, the love of many"—'of the many,' or 'of the most', i.e., of the generality of professed disciples—"shall wax cold." Sad illustrations of the effect of abounding iniquity in cooling the love even of faithful disciples we have in the *Epistle of James*, written about the period here referred to, and too frequently ever since. **but he that shall endure unto the end, the same shall be saved**—See on Matthew 10:21, 22; and cf. Hebrews 10:38, 39, which is a manifest allusion to these words of Christ; also Revelation 2:10. Luke adds these reassuring words: "But there shall not an hair of your heads perish" (21:18). Our Lord had just said (Luke 21:16) that they should be *put to death;* showing that this precious promise is far above immunity from mere bodily harm, and furnishing a key to the right interpretation of Psalm 91 and such like. **14. But when ye shall see**—"Jerusalem compassed by armies"—by encamped armies; in other words, when ye shall see it *besieged*, and—**the abomination of desolation, spoken of by Daniel the prophet, standing where it ought not**—i.e., as explained in Matthew (24:15), "standing in the holy place." **(let him that readeth**—readeth that prophecy—**understand.)** That "the abomination of desolation" here alluded to was intended to point to the Roman ensigns, as the symbols of an idolatrous, and so unclean pagan power, may be gathered by comparing what Luke says in the corresponding verse (21:20); and commentators are agreed on it. It is worthy of notice, as confirming this interpretation, that in I Maccabees 1:54—which, though aprocryphal *Scripture*, is authentic *history*—the expression of Daniel is applied to the idolatrous profanation of the Jewish altar by Antiochus Epiphanes. **then let them that be in Judea flee to the mountains**—The ecclesiastical historian, EUSEBIUS, early in the fourth century, tells us that the Christians fled to *Pella*, at the northern extremity of Perea, being "prophetically directed"—perhaps by some prophetic intimation more explicit than this, which would be their chart—and that thus they escaped the predicted calamities by which the nation was overwhelmed. **15. And let him that is on the housetop not get down into the house, neither enter therein, to take any thing out of his house**—i.e., let him take the outside flight of steps from the roof to the ground; a graphic way of denoting the extreme urgency of the case, and the danger of being tempted, by the desire to save his property, to delay till escape should become impossible. **16. And let him that is in the field not turn back again for to take up his garment. 17. But woe to them**—or, "alas for them"—**that are with child, and to them that give suck in those days**—in consequence of the aggravated suffering which those conditions would involve. **18. And pray ye that your flight be not in the winter**—making escape perilous, or tempting you to delay your flight. Matthew (24:20) adds, "neither on the sabbath day," when, from fear of a breach of its sacred rest, they might be induced to remain. **19. For in those days shall be affliction, such as was not from the beginning of the creation which God created unto this time, neither shall be**—Such language is not unusual in the Old Testament with reference to tremendous calamities. But it is matter of literal fact that there was crowded into the period of the Jewish war an amount and complication of suffering perhaps unparalleled; as the narrative of JOSEPHUS, examined closely and arranged under different heads, would show. **20. And except that the Lord had shortened those days, no flesh**—i.e., no human life—**should be saved: but for the elect's sake, whom he hath chosen, he hath shortened the days**—But for this merciful "shortening," brought about by a remarkable concurrence of causes, the whole nation would have perished, in which there yet remained a remnant to be afterwards gathered out. This portion of the prophecy closes, in Luke, with the following vivid and important glance at the subsequent fortunes of the chosen people: "And they shall fall by the sword, and shall be led away captive into all nations: and Jerusalem shall be trodden down of the Gentiles, until the times of the Gentiles be fulfilled"

ADAM CLARKE

11. *Neither do ye premeditate*. This is wanting in some MSS. and versions. On this verse see Matt. x. 19.

But he that shall endure the persecutions that shall come—*unto the end*, to the destruction of the Jewish polity, without growing cold or apostatizing—*shall be saved*, shall be delivered in all imminent dangers, and have his soul at last brought to an eternal glory. It is very remarkable that not a single Christian perished in the destruction of Jerusalem, though there were many there when Cestius Gallus invested the city; and had he persevered in the siege, he would soon have rendered himself master of it. But when he unexpectedly and unaccountably raised the siege, the Christians took that opportunity to escape. See Eusebius, *Hist. Eccles.*, lib. iii, c. 5.

The abomination of desolation, spoken of by Daniel. This *abomination of desolation* (Luke xxi. 20-21) refers to the Roman army; and this abomination standing *in the holy place* is the Roman army besieging Jerusalem. This, our Lord says, is what was spoken of by Daniel the prophet, in the ninth and eleventh chapters of his prophecy, and so let everyone who reads these prophecies understand them; and in reference to this very event they are understood by the rabbins. The Roman army is called an *abomination* for its ensigns and images, which were so to the Jews. Josephus says (*War*, b. vi, c. 6) the Romans brought their ensigns into the Temple, and placed them over against the eastern gate, and sacrificed to them there. The Roman army is therefore fitly called the *abomination*, and "the abomination that maketh desolate," as it was to desolate and lay waste Jerusalem; and this army besieging Jerusalem is called by Mark (chap. xiii. 14) "standing where it ought not," that is, as in the text here, *the holy place*, as not only the city, but a considerable compass of ground about it, was deemed holy, and consequently no profane persons should stand on it.

Then let them which be in Judea flee into the mountains. This counsel was remembered and wisely followed by the Christians afterwards. Eusebius and Epiphanius say that at this juncture, after Cestius Gallus had raised the siege and Vespasian was approaching with his army, all who believed in Christ left Jerusalem and fled to Pella, and other places beyond the river Jordan; and so they all marvellously escaped the general shipwreck of their country—not one of them perished. See on v. 13.

Let him which is on the house top. The houses of the Jews, as well as those of the ancient Greeks and Romans, were flat-roofed, and had stairs on the outside, by which persons might ascend and descend without coming into the house. In the Eastern walled cities, these flat-roofed houses usually formed continued terraces from one end of the city to the other, which terraces terminated at the gates. He therefore who is walking on the housetop, let him *not come down to take any thing out of his house;* but let him instantly pursue his course along the tops of the houses, and escape out at the city gate as fast as he can.

Except those days should be shortened. Josephus computes the number of those who perished in the siege at eleven hundred thousand, besides those who were slain in other places, *War*, b. vi, c. 9; and if the Romans had gone on destroying in this manner, the whole nation of the Jews would, in a short time, have been entirely extirpated. But, for the sake of the elect, the Jews, that they might not be utterly destroyed, and for the Christians particularly, the days were shortened. These, partly through the fury of the zealots on one hand and the hatred of the Romans on the other, and

MATTHEW HENRY

II. What directions are given to the disciples with reference to it.

1. They must shift for the safety of *their lives*; "When you see the country invaded, and the city invested, without further deliberation or delay, *let them that are in Judæa, flee to the mountains, v.* 14. Do you go out of the ship when you see it sinking"

2. They must provide for the safety of *their souls. Then, if any man shall* say unto you, *Lo, here is Christ*, or, *Lo, he is there, believe them not*; for *false christs*, and *false prophets, shall arise*, v. 22. *False christs* shall *rise*, and false prophets that shall preach them up; or such, as set up for *prophets*, and they shall *show signs* and lying *wonders*. They *shall seduce, if it were possible, the very elect*; so plausible shall their pretences be, that they shall draw away many that were forward and zealous professors of religion, many that were very likely to have persevered. They *shall seduce, if it were possible, the very elect*. In consideration hereof, let the disciples be cautious whom they give credit to (*v.* 23); But *take ye heed.* Christ knew that they were of the *elect*, and yet he said to them, *Take heed.* An assurance of persevering, and cautions against apostasy, will very well consist with each other. God will keep them, but they must keep themselves. "*I have foretold you all things*; that, being *forewarned*, you may be *fore-armed*."

Verses 24-27

These verses seem to point at Christ's second coming, to judge the world; the disciples, in their question, had confounded the *destruction* of Jerusalem and the *end of the world* (Matt. xxiv. 3), which was built upon a mistake, as if the temple must needs stand as long as the world stands; this mistake Christ rectifies. And here he foretells,

1. The final dissolution of the present frame and fabric of the world; *The sun shall be darkened*, and the *moon* shall no more *give her light*. The *stars of heaven* shall fall as leaves in autumn; and the *powers that are in heaven shall be shaken.*

2. The visible appearance of the Lord Jesus, to whom the judgment of that day shall be committed (*v.* 26); *Then shall they see the Son of man coming in the clouds.* He shall come with *great power and glory. Every eye shall then see him.*

JAMIESON, FAUSSET, BROWN

(Luke 21:24). The language as well as the idea of this remarkable statement is taken from Daniel 8: 10, 13. What, then, is its import here? It implies, first, that a time is coming when Jerusalem shall cease to be "trodden down of the Gentiles"; which it was then by pagan, and since and till now is by Mohammedan unbelievers: and next, it implies that the period when this treading down of Jerusalem by the Gentiles is to cease will be when "the times of the Gentiles are fulfilled" or "completed." But what does this mean? We may gather the meaning of it from Romans 11 in which the divine purposes and procedure towards the chosen people from first to last are treated in detail. In vs. 25 of that chapter these words of our Lord are thus reproduced: "For I would not, brethren, that ye should be ignorant of this mystery, lest ye should be wise in your own conceits; that blindness in part is happened to Israel, until the fulness of the Gentiles be come in." See the exposition of that verse, from which it will appear that "till the fulness of the Gentiles be come in"—or, in our Lord's phraseology, "till the times of the Gentiles be fulfilled"—does not mean "till the general conversion of the world to Christ," but "till the Gentiles have had their *full time* of that place in the Church which the Jews had before them." After that period of *Gentilism*, as before of *Judaism*, "Jerusalem" and Israel, no longer "trodden down by the Gentiles," but "grafted into their own olive tree," shall constitute, with the believing Gentiles, one Church of God, and fill the whole earth. What a bright vista does this open up! **21. And then, if any man shall say to you, Lo, here is Christ; or, lo he is there; believe him not**—So Luke 17:23. No one can read JOSEPHUS' account of what took place before the destruction of Jerusalem without seeing how strikingly this was fulfilled. **to seduce, if it were possible, even the elect**—implying that this, though all *but* done, will prove impossible. What a precious assurance! (Cf. II Thess. 2:9-12.) **23. But take ye heed; behold, I have foretold you all things**—He had just told them that the seduction of the elect would prove impossible; but since this would be all but accomplished, He bids them be on their guard, as the proper means of averting that catastrophe. In Matthew (24:26-28) we have some additional particulars: "Wherefore, if they shall say unto you, Behold, He is in the desert; go not forth: behold, He is in the secret chambers; believe it not. For as the lightning cometh out of the east, and shineth even unto the west; so shall also the coming of the Son of man be." See on Luke 17:23, 24. "For wheresoever the carcass is, there will the eagles be gathered together." See on Luke 17:37. **24. But in those days, after that tribulation**—"Immediately after the tribulation of those days" (Matt. 24:29). **the sun shall be darkened, and the moon shall not give her light. 25. And the stars of heaven shall fall**—"and upon the earth distress of nations, with perplexity; the sea and the waves roaring; men's hearts failing them for fear, and for looking after those things which are coming on the earth" (Luke 21:25, 26). **and the powers that are in heaven shall be shaken**—Though the grandeur of this language carries the mind over the head of all periods but that of Christ's Second Coming, nearly every expression will be found used of the Lord's coming in terrible national judgments: as of Babylon (Isa. 13:9-13); of Idumea (Isa. 34:1, 2, 4, 8-10); of Egypt (Ezek. 32:7, 8); compare also Psalm 18:7-15; Isaiah 24:1, 17-19; Joel 2:10, 11, etc. We cannot therefore consider the mere strength of this language a proof that it refers exclusively or primarily to the precursors of the final day, though of course in "*that day*" it will have its most awful fulfilment. **26. And then shall they see the Son of man coming in the clouds with great power and glory**—In Matthew 24:30, this is given most fully: "And then shall appear the sign of the Son of man in heaven; and then shall all the tribes of the earth mourn, and they shall see the Son of man . . ." That this language finds its highest interpretation in the Second Personal Coming of Christ, is most certain. But the question is, whether that be the primary sense of it as it stands here? Now if the reader will turn to Daniel 7:13, 14, and connect with it the preceding verses, he will find, we think, the true key to our Lord's meaning here. There the powers that oppressed the Church —symbolized by rapacious wild beasts—are summoned to the bar of the Great God, who as the Ancient of days seats Himself, with His assessors, on a burning Throne: thousand thousands ministering to Him, and ten thousand times ten thousand standing before Him. "The judgment is set, and the books are opened." Who that is guided by the *mere words* would doubt that this is a description of

ADAM CLARKE

partly through the difficulty of subsisting in the mountains, without houses or provisions, would in all probability have all been destroyed, by either the sword or famine, if the days had not been shortened. The besieged themselves helped to shorten those days by their divisions and mutual slaughters, and by fatally deserting their strongholds, where they never could have been subdued but by famine alone. So well-fortified was Jerusalem, and so well-provided to stand a siege, that the enemy without could not have prevailed had it not been for the factions and seditions within. When Titus was viewing the fortifications after the taking of the city, he could not help ascribing his success to God. "We have fought," said he, "with God on our side; and it is God who pulled the Jews out of these strong holds: for what could machines or the hands of men avail against such towers as these?" (*War*, b. vi, c. 9.)

Then if any man shall say unto you, Lo, here is Christ. Our Lord had cautioned His disciples against false Christs and prophets before, v. 11; but He seems here to intimate that there would be especial need to attend to this caution about the time of the siege. And in fact many such impostors did arise about that time, promising deliverance from God; and the lower the Jews were reduced, the more disposed they were to listen to such deceivers. Like a man drowning, they were willing to catch even at a straw, while there was any prospect of being saved. But as it was to little purpose for a man to take upon him the character of the Christ, without miracles to avouch his divine mission, so it was the common artifice of these impostors to show *signs* and *wonders*—the very words used by Christ in this prophecy, and by Josephus in his history, *Ant.* b. xx, c. 7.

Immediately after the tribulation. Commentators generally understand this, and what follows, of the end of the world and Christ's coming to judgment; but the word *immediately* shows that our Lord is not speaking of any distant event, but of something immediately consequent on calamities already predicted—and that must be the destruction of Jerusalem.

Then shall appear the sign of the Son of man. The plain meaning of this is that the destruction of Jerusalem will be such a remarkable instance of divine vengeance and such a signal manifestation of Christ's power and glory that all the Jewish *tribes* shall mourn, and many will, in consequence of this manifestation of God, be led to acknowledge Christ and His religion. By "of the land," in the text, is evidently meant here, as in several other places, the land of Judea and its tribes, either its then inhabitants or the Jewish people wherever found.

MATTHEW HENRY

TODAY'S DICTIONARY OF THE BIBLE:

The functions of angels are manifold. (a) In the widest sense they are agents of God's providence (Ex. 12:23; 2 Sam. 24:16; 2 Kings 19:35; 1 Chron. 21:16; Ps. 104:4; Acts 12:23; 1 Cor. 10:10; Heb. 11:28). (b) They are specially God's agents in carrying on his great work of redemption. There is no notice of angelic appearances to man till after the call of Abraham. From that time onward there are frequent references to their ministry on earth (Gen. 18:19; 24:7, 40; 28:12; 32:1). They appear to rebuke idolatry (Judg. 2:1-4), to call Gideon (Judg. 6:11, 12), and to consecrate Samson (13:3). In the days of the prophets, from Samuel onward, the angels appear only in their behalf (1 Kings 19:5; 2 Kings 6:17; Dan. 4:13, 23; 10:10, 13, 20, 21; Zech. 1-6).

The Incarnation introduces a new era in the ministrations of angels. They come with their Lord to earth to do him service while here. Predicting his advent (Matt. 1:20; Luke 1:26-38), they minister to him after his temptation and agony (Matt 4:11; Luke 22:43), and declare his resurrection and ascension (Matt. 28:2-8; John 20:12, 13; Acts 1:10, 11). They are now ministering spirits to the people of God (Ps. 34:7; 91:11; Matt. 18:10; Acts 5:19; 8:26; 10:3; 12:7; 27:23; Heb. 1:14). Rejoicing over a penitent sinner (Luke 15:10), they bear the souls of the redeemed to paradise (Luke 16:22); and they will be the ministers of judgment hereafter on the great day (Matt. 13:39, 41, 49; 16:27; 24:31).

3. The gathering together of all the elect to him (*v.* 27); He shall *send his angels,* and *gather together his elect* to him. They shall be fetched *from the uttermost parts of the earth,* most remote from the place where Christ's tribunal shall be set, and shall be brought to the *uttermost part of heaven.* A faithful Israelite shall be carried safely, though it were from the utmost border of the land of bondage to the utmost border of the land of promise.

Verses 28–37

We have here the application of this prophetical sermon.

I. "As to the *destruction* of Jerusalem, *expect* it to come very *shortly*; as when the *branch of the fig-tree becomes soft,* and the *leaves sprout forth,* ye expect that summer will come shortly, *v,* 28. So when *ye see these things come to pass,* when ye see the Jewish nation embroiled in wars, distracted by false christs and prophets, and drawing upon them the displeasure of the Romans, then say that their *ruin is nigh, even at the door.*" The disciples themselves were indeed all of them, except John, taken away from the evil to come, but the next generation would live to see it. "*This generation* that is now rising up, shall not all be worn off before *all these things* come to pass. And as this destruction is near and within ken, so it is sure."

JAMIESON, FAUSSET, BROWN

the Final Judgment? And yet nothing is clearer than that it is *not,* but a description of a vast *temporal* judgment, upon organized bodies of men, for their incurable hostility to the kingdom of God upon earth. Well, after the doom of these has been pronounced and executed, and room thus prepared for the unobstructed development of the kingdom of God over the earth, what follows? "I saw in the night visions, and behold, one like THE SON OF MAN came with the clouds of heaven, and came to the Ancient of days, and they (the angelic attendants) brought Him near before Him." For what purpose? To receive investiture in the kingdom, which, as Messiah, of right belonged to Him. Accordingly, it is added, "And there was given Him dominion, and glory, and a kingdom, that all peoples, nations, and languages should serve Him: His dominion is an everlasting dominion, which shall not pass away, and His kingdom that which shall not be destroyed." Comparing this with our Lord's words, He seems to us, by "the Son of man [on which phrase, see on John 1:51] coming in the clouds with great power and glory," to mean, that when judicial vengeance shall once have been executed upon Jerusalem, and the ground thus cleared for the unobstructed establishment of His own kingdom, His true regal claims and rights would be visibly and gloriously asserted and manifested. See on Luke 9:28 (with its parallels in Matthew and Mark), in which nearly the same language is employed, and where it can hardly be understood of anything else than *the full and free estabishment of the kingdom of Christ on the destruction of Jerusalem.* But what is that "sign of the Son of man in heaven?" Interpreters are not agreed. But as before Christ came to destroy Jerusalem some appalling portents were seen in the air, so before His Personal appearing it is likely that something *analogous* will be witnessed, though of what nature it would be vain to conjecture. **27. And then shall he send his angels**—"with a great sound of a trumpet" (Matt. 24:31). **and shall gather together his elect . . .**—As the tribes of Israel were anciently gathered together by sound of trumpet (Exod. 19:13, 16, 19; Lev. 23: 24; Ps. 81:3-5), so any mighty gathering of God's people, by divine command, is represented as collected by sound of trumpet (Isa. 27:13; cf. Rev. 11: 15); and the ministry of angels, employed in all the great operations of Providence, is here held forth as the agency by which the present assembling of the elect is to be accomplished. LIGHTFOOT thus explains it: "When Jerusalem shall be reduced to ashes, and that wicked nation cut off and rejected, then shall the Son of man send His ministers with the trumpet of the Gospel, and they shall gather His elect of the several nations, from the four corners of heaven: so that God shall not want a Church, although that ancient people of His be rejected and cast off: but that ancient Jewish Church being destroyed, a new Church shall be called out of the Gentiles." But though something like this appears to be the primary sense of the verse, in relation to the destruction of Jerusalem, no one can fail to see that the language swells beyond any gathering of a human family into a Church upon earth, and forces the thoughts onward to that gathering of the Church "at the last trump," to meet the Lord in the air, which is to wind up the present scene. Still, this is not, in our judgment, the *direct* subject of the prediction; for the next verse limits the whole prediction to the generation then existing. **28. Now learn a parable of the fig tree**—"Now from the fig tree learn the parable," or the high lesson which this teaches. **When her branch is yet tender, and putteth forth leaves**—"its leaves." **29. So ye, in like manner, when ye shall see these things come to pass**—rather, 'coming to pass'—**know that it**—"the kingdom of God" (Luke 21:31)—**is nigh, even at the doors**—that is, the full manifestation of it; for till then it admitted of no full development. In Luke (21:28) the following words precede these: "And when these things begin to come to pass, then look up, and lift up your heads; for your redemption draweth nigh"—their redemption, in the first instance certainly, from Jewish oppression (I Thess. 2:14-16; Luke 11:52): but in the highest sense of these words, redemption from all the oppressions and miseries of the present state at the second appearing of the Lord Jesus. **30. Verily I say unto you, that this generation shall not pass till all these things be done**—or "fulfilled" (Matt. 24:34; Luke 21: 32). Whether we take this to mean that the whole would be fulfilled within the limits of the generation then current, or, according to a usual way of speaking, that the generation then existing would not pass away without seeing a *begun* fulfilment of this prediction, the facts entirely correspond. For

ADAM CLARKE

W. E. VINE:

EKLEKTOS lit. signifies picked out, chosen (*ek,* from, *lego,* to gather, pick out), and is used of (a) Christ, the chosen of God, the Messiah (Luke 23:35), and metaphorically as a "living stone," "a chief corner stone" (1 Pet. 2:4, 6); (b) angels (1 Tim. 5:21), as chosen to be of especially high rank in administrative association with God, or as His messengers to human beings, doubtless in contrast to fallen angels (see 2 Pet. 2:4 and Jude 6); (c) believers (Jews or Gentiles), Matt. 24:22, 24, 31; Mark 13:20, 22, 27; Luke 18:7; Rom. 8:33; Col. 3:12; 2 Tim. 2:10; Tit. 1:1; 1 Pet. 1:1; 2:9 (as a spiritual race); Matt. 20:16; 22:14 and Rev. 17:14, "chosen"; individual believers are so mentioned in Rom. 16:13; 2 John 1, 13.

Believers were chosen "before the foundation of the world" (cf. "before times eternal," 2 Tim. 1:9), in Christ (Eph. 1:4); to adoption (Eph. 1:5); good works (Eph. 2:10); conformity to Christ (Rom. 8:29); salvation from the delusions of the Antichrist and the doom of the deluded (2 Thess. 2:13); eternal glory (Rom. 9:23).—*Vine's Expository Dictionary*

He shall send his angels. "His messengers," the apostles, and their successors in the Christian ministry. *With a great sound of a trumpet.* Or "a loud-sounding trumpet"—the earnest, affectionate call of the gospel of peace, life, and salvation. *Shall gather together his elect.* The Gentiles, who were now chosen or elected, in place of the rebellious, obstinate Jews, according to our Lord's prediction, Matt. viii. 11-12 and Luke xiii. 28-29. To Matthew's account, Luke adds, chap. xxi. 24, "They shall fall by the edge of the sword, and shall be led away captive into all nations: and Jerusalem shall be trodden down of the Gentiles, until the times of the Gentiles be fulfilled." The number of those who fell by the sword was very great. Eleven hundred thousand perished during the siege. Many were slain at other places and at other times. Many also were led away captives into all nations. Josephus says the number of the captives taken in the whole war amounted to 97,000. Those above seventeen years of age were sent to the works in Egypt; but most were distributed through the Roman provinces, to be destroyed in their theaters by the sword and by the wild beasts; and those under seventeen years of age were sold for slaves. Jerusalem also was, according to the prediction of our Lord, to be "trodden down of the Gentiles." Accordingly it has never since been in the possession of the Jews.

Learn a parable of the fig tree. That is, These signs which I have given you will be as infallible a proof of the approaching ruin of the Jewish state as the budding of the trees is a proof of the coming summer.

30. *This generation.* "This very race of men." It is certain that this word has two meanings in the Scriptures: that given in the text, and that above. *Generation* signifies a period of a certain number of years, sometimes more, sometimes less. In Deut. i. 35 and ii. 14, Moses uses the word to point out a term of thirty-eight years, which was precisely the number in the

MATTHEW HENRY

Christ doth not speak these things, merely to frighten them; no, they are the declarations of God's fixed purpose; "*Heaven and earth shall pass away*; but *my words shall not pass away*" (*v.* 31).

II. "As to the *end of the world*, do not enquire when it will come, for of *that day*, and *that hour*, *knoweth no man*; it is not revealed by any word of God, either to *men* on earth, or to *angels in heaven*." But it follows, *neither the Son*; but is there anything which the Son is ignorant of? There were those in the primitive times, who taught from this text, that there were some things that Christ, as man, was *ignorant* of; they said, "It was no more absurd to say so, than to say that his human soul suffered grief and fear." Christ, as God, could not be ignorant of anything; but the divine wisdom which dwelt in our Saviour, did communicate itself to his human soul, according to the divine pleasure, so that his human nature might sometimes not know some things; therefore Christ is said to grow in wisdom (Luke ii. 52).

III. "As to both, your duty is to *watch and pray* (*v.* 33); *Take ye heed* of everything that would indispose you for your Master's coming; *watch* for his coming, that it may not at any time be a surprise to you, and *pray* for that grace which is necessary to qualify you for it, for *ye know not what the time is*; and you are concerned to be ready for that *every day*, which may come *any day*." This he illustrates, in the close, by a parable.

1. Our Master is gone away, and left us something which we must give account of, *v.* 34. He is *as a man taking a far journey*; he has *left his house on earth*, and left his servants in their offices, given *authority* to some, and *work* to others. They that have *authority* given them, in that had *work* assigned them, for those that have the greatest *power* have the most *business*; and to them to whom he gave *work*, he gave *authority*, to do that work. And when he took his last leave, he *appointed the porter to watch*, to be sure to be ready to open to him at his return. Thus our Lord Jesus, when he *ascended on high*, left something for all his servants to do. *All* are appointed to work, and some authorized to rule.

2. We ought to be always upon our watch, in expectation of his return, *v.* 35–37. Our Lord *will come*, and will come as the *Master of the house*, to take account of his servants. We know not *when he will come*. This is applicable to his coming to us in particular, at our death, as well as to the general judgment. Our present life is a *night*, a dark night, compared with the other life; we know not in which watch of the night our Master will come, whether in the days of youth, or middle age, or old age; but as soon as we are born, we begin to die, and therefore, as soon as we are capable of expecting anything, we must expect death. Our great care must be, that, whenever our Lord comes, he does not *find us sleeping*, secure in ourselves, off our guard, *ready* to say, He will not come, and *unready* to meet him. His coming will indeed be *coming suddenly*. It is therefore the indispensable duty of all Christ's disciples, to *watch*, to be awake, and keep awake; "*What I say unto you* four (*v.* 37), I *say unto all*, what I say to you of this generation, I say to all that shall believe in me, in every age, *Watch*, *watch*, expect my second coming, prepare for it, that you may be found in peace, without spot, and blameless."

JAMIESON, FAUSSET, BROWN

either the whole was fulfilled in the destruction accomplished by Titus, as many think; or, if we stretch it out, according to others, till the thorough dispersion of the Jews a little later, under Adrian, every requirement of our Lord's words seems to be met. **31. Heaven and earth shall pass away; but my words shall not pass away**—the strongest possible expression of the divine authority by which He spake; not as Moses or Paul might have said of their own inspiration, for such language would be unsuitable in any merely human mouth.

Warnings to Prepare for the Coming of Christ Suggested by the Foregoing Prophecy (vss. 32-37). It will be observed that, in the foregoing prophecy, as our Lord approaches the crisis of the day of vengeance on Jerusalem and redemption for the Church—at which stage the analogy between that and the day of final vengeance and redemption waxes more striking—His language rises and swells beyond all temporal and partial vengeance, beyond all earthly deliverances and enlargements, and ushers us resistlessly into the scenes of the final day. Accordingly, in these six concluding verses it is manifest that preparation for "THAT DAY" is what our Lord designs to inculcate. **32. But of that day and that hour**—i.e., the precise time. **knoweth no man**—lit., no one—**no, not the angels which are in heaven, neither the Son, but the Father**—This very remarkable statement regarding "the Son" is peculiar to Mark. Whether it means that the Son was *not at that time in possession of the knowledge* referred to, or simply that it was not *among the things which He had received to communicate*—has been matter of much controversy even among the firmest believers in the proper Divinity of Christ. In the latter sense it was taken by some of the most eminent of the ancient Fathers, and by LUTHER, MELANCTHON, and most of the older Lutherans; and it is so taken by BENGEL, LANGE, WEBSTER and WILKINSON. CHRYSOSTOM and others understood it to mean that *as man* our Lord was ignorant of this. It is taken literally by CALVIN, GROTIUS, DE WETTE, MEYER, FRITZSCHE, STIER, ALFORD, and ALEXANDER. **33. Take ye heed, watch and pray; for ye know not when the time is. 34. For the Son of man is as a man taking a far journey . . .**—The idea thus far is similar to that in the opening part of the parable of the talents (Matt. 25:14, 15). **and commanded the porter**—the gatekeeper—**to watch**—pointing to the official duty of the ministers of religion to give warning of approaching danger to the people. **35. Watch ye therefore; for ye know not when the master of the house cometh, at even, or at midnight, or at the cock-crowing, or in the morning**—an allusion to the four Roman watches of the night. **36. Lest, coming suddenly, he find you sleeping**—See on Luke 12:35-40, 42-46. **37. And what I say unto you**—this discourse, it will be remembered, was delivered in private. **I say unto all, Watch**—anticipating and requiring the diffusion of His teaching by them among all His disciples, and its perpetuation through all time.

ADAM CLARKE

present case; for Jerusalem was destroyed about thirty-eight years after our Lord delivered this prediction. But as there are other events in this chapter which certainly look beyond the destruction of Jerusalem, and which were to take place before the Jews should cease to be a distinct people, I should therefore prefer the translation given above. See Matt. xxiv. 34.

But of that day and hour. *Hora* here is translated "season" by many eminent critics, and is used in this sense by both sacred and profane authors. As the *day* was not known in which Jerusalem should be invested by the Romans, therefore our Lord advised His disciples to pray that it might not be on a Sabbath; and as the "season" was not known, therefore they were to pray that it might not be in the winter, v. 20. See on Mark xiii. 32.

34. *Left his house*. "Family." Our blessed Lord and Master, when He ascended to heaven, commanded His servants to be faithful and watchful.

35. *Watch ye therefore*. The more the master is expected, the more diligent ought the servants to be in working, watching, and keeping themselves in readiness.

36. *He find you sleeping*. A porter asleep exposes the house to be robbed, and well deserves punishment.

MATTHEW HENRY

CHAPTER 14

II. Of the *malice of Christ's enemies*.

1. The chief priests consulted how they might *put him to death*, *v.* 1, 2. The feast of the *passover* was now at hand, and at *that* feast he must be crucified, (1) That his death and sufferings might be the more public. (2) That the anti-type might answer to the type. Christ, our Passover, was sacrificed for us, at the same time that the paschal lamb was sacrificed, and Israel's deliverance out of Egypt was *commemorated*.

JAMIESON, FAUSSET, BROWN

CHAPTER 14

VSS. 1-11. THE CONSPIRACY OF THE JEWISH AUTHORITIES TO PUT JESUS TO DEATH—THE SUPPER AND THE ANOINTING AT BETHANY—JUDAS AGREES WITH THE CHIEF PRIESTS TO BETRAY HIS LORD. (=Matt. 26:1-16; Luke 22:1-6; John 12:1-11.) The events of this section appeared to have occurred on the fourth day (*Wednesday*) of the Redeemer's Last Week.

Conspiracy of the Jewish Authorities to Put Jesus to Death (vss. 1, 2). **1. After two days was the feast of the passover, and of unleavened bread**—The meaning is, that two days after what is about to be mentioned the passover would arrive; in other words, what follows occurred two days *before* the feast. **and the chief priests and the scribes sought how they might take him by craft, and put him to death**—From Matthew's fuller account (ch. 26) we learn that our Lord announced this to the Twelve as follows, being the first announcement to them of the precise time: "And it came to pass, when Jesus had finished all these sayings"—referring to the contents of chs. 24, 25, which He delivered to His disciples; His public ministry being now closed: from His *prophetical* He is now passing into His *priestly* office, although all along He Himself took

ADAM CLARKE

CHAPTER 14

1. *Unleavened bread*. After they began to eat unleavened bread; see on Matt. xxvi. 2.

The passover. A feast instituted in Egypt to commemorate the destroying angel's passing over the houses of the Israelites, when he slew the firstborn of the Egyptians. See the whole of this business largely explained in the notes on Exod. xii. 1-27. This feast began on the fourteenth day of the first moon, in the first month, Nisan, and it lasted only one day; but it was immediately followed by the days of unleavened bread, which were seven, so that the whole lasted eight days, and all the eight days are sometimes called the feast of *the passover*, and sometimes the "feast or days of unleavened bread." See Luke xxii. 1-7.

And consulted that they might take Jesus by subtilty. The providence of God frustrated their artful machinations; and that event which they wished to conduct with the greatest privacy and silence was transacted with all possible celebrity, amidst the thousands who resorted to Jerusalem at this season for the keeping of the Passover.

MATTHEW HENRY

G. CAMPBELL MORGAN:

For what reason were these men conscious of hatred of Jesus? He had rebuked their ideals through the whole course of His public ministry. Ideals are always closely related to conduct; consequently the whole tenor of His teaching had been to rebuke their conduct.

During the latter days of His ministry He had rebuked their failures as shepherds of the people. Functional failure is always related to organic failure. Sometimes the physicians tell us that there is a functional trouble, and not an organic one, and we are always comforted. Yet the physician would admit that functional failure is at least an organic peril. Where functional failure is as pronounced as it was in the case of these men, it is demonstration of organic failure. These men had been compelled, in the whole course of the ministry of Jesus Christ, and superlatively in these closing days, to stand disclosed; unwillingly, but definitely self-confessed as corrupt, as having failed. Their hatred of Jesus was consequently of One who had revealed their failure.

—*The Gospel According to Mark*

Now see, How *spiteful* Christ's enemies were, for they aimed not only to *silence* him, but to be revenged on him for all the good he had done. How *subtle* they were; *Not on the feast-day, Lest there should be an uproar* (*v.* 2); lest they should rise, and rescue him. They who *desired* nothing more than the *praise* of men, dreaded nothing more than the rage and displeasure of men.

Verses 1–11

We have here instances,

I. Of the *kindness of Christ's friends.* Some friends he had, even in and about Jerusalem, that loved him, and never thought they could do enough for him.

1. Here was *one friend,* that was so kind as to *invite him to sup with him, v.* 3. Though he had a prospect of his death approaching, yet he did not abandon himself to a melancholy retirement from all company.

2. Here was *another friend,* that was so kind as to *anoint his head* with very precious ointment as he *sat at meat.* This was an extraordinary piece of respect paid him by a good woman that thought nothing too good to bestow upon Christ. Did he pour out his soul unto death for us, and shall we think any box of ointment too precious to pour out upon him? It is observable that she took care to pour it all out upon Christ's head; she *broke the box.* Christ must be honoured with *all we* have. Do we give him the *precious ointment* of our best affections? Let him have them *all*; love him *with all the heart.*

(1) There were those that put a *worse construction* upon this than it *deserved.* They called it a *waste of the ointment, v.* 4. The *liberal* and *bountiful* ought not to be called *wasteful.* They pretended it might have been *sold,* and *given to the poor, v.* 5. A common charity to the poor will not excuse from a particular act of piety to the Lord Jesus.

JAMIESON, FAUSSET, BROWN

our infirmities and bare our sicknesses—"He said unto His disciples, Ye know that after two days is [the feast of] the passover, and the Son of man is betrayed to be crucified."The *first* and the *last* steps of His final sufferings are brought together in this brief announcement of all that was to take place. The *passover* was the first and the chief of the three great annual festivals, commemorative of the redemption of God's people from Egypt, through the sprinkling of the blood of a lamb divinely appointed to be slain for that end; the destroying angel, "when he saw the blood, *passing over*" the Israelitish houses, on which that blood was seen, when he came to destroy all the first-born in the land of Egypt (Exod. 12)—bright typical foreshadowing of the great Sacrifice, and the Redemption effected thereby. Accordingly, "by the determinate counsel and foreknowledge of God, who is wonderful in counsel and excellent in working," it was so ordered that precisely at the passover season, "Christ our Passover should be sacrificed for us." On the day following the passover commenced "the feast of unleavened bread," so called because for seven days only unleavened bread was to be eaten (Exod. 12:18-20). See on I Corinthians 5:6-8. We are further told by Matthew (26:3) that the consultation was held in the palace of Caiaphas the high priest, between the chief priests, [the scribes], and the elders of the people, how "they might take Jesus by subtlety and kill Him." **2. But they said, Not on the feast day**—rather, not during the feast; not until the seven days of unleavened bread should be over—**lest there be an uproar of the people**—In consequence of the vast influx of strangers, embracing all the male population of the land who had reached a certain age, there were within the walls of Jerusalem at this festival some two million people; and in their excited state, the danger of tumult and bloodshed among "the people," who for the most part took Jesus for a prophet, was extreme. (See JOSEPHUS, *Antiquities,* xx. 5. 3.) What plan, if any, these ecclesiastics fixed upon for seizing our Lord, does not appear. But the proposal of Judas being at once and eagerly gone into, it is probable they were till then at some loss for a plan sufficiently quiet and yet effectual. So, just at the feast-time shall it be done; the unexpected offer of Judas relieving them of their fears. Thus, as BENGEL remarks, did the divine counsel take effect.

The Supper and the Anointing at Bethany Six Days before the Passover (vss. 3-9). The time of this part of the narrative is *four days before* what has just been related. Had it been part of the regular train of events which our Evangelist designed to record, he would probably have inserted it in its proper place, before the conspiracy of the Jewish authorities. But having come to the treason of Judas, he seems to have gone back upon this scene as what probably gave immediate occasion to the awful deed. **3. And being in Bethany, in the house of Simon the leper, as he sat at meat, there came a woman**—It was "Mary," as we learn from John 12:3. **having an alabaster box of ointment of spikenard**—pure *nard,* a celebrated aromatic—(See Song of Sol. 1:12). **very precious**—"very costly" (John 12:3). **and she brake the box, and poured it on his head**—"and anointed," adds John, "the feet of Jesus, and wiped His feet with her hair: and the house was filled with the odor of the ointment." The only use of this was to refresh and exhilarate—a grateful compliment in the East, amid the closeness of a heated atmosphere, with many guests at a feast. Such was the form in which Mary's love to Christ, at so much cost to herself, poured itself out. **4. And there were some that had indignation within themselves and said**—Matthew says (26:8), "But when His disciples saw it, they had indignation, saying . . ." The spokesman, however, was none of the true-hearted Eleven—as we learn from John (12:4): "Then saith one of His disciples, Judas Iscariot, Simon's son, which should betray Him." Doubtless the thought stirred first in his breast, and issued from his base lips; and some of the rest, ignorant of his true character and feelings, and carried away by his plausible speech, might for the moment feel some chagrin at the apparent waste. **Why was this waste of the ointment made? 5. For it might have been sold for more than three hundred pence**—about $50 in our currency. **and have been given to the poor. And they murmured against her**—"This he said," remarks John, and the remark is of exceeding importance, "not that he cared for the poor but because he was a thief, and had the bag"—the scrip or treasure-chest—"and bare what was put therein"—not 'bare it off' by theft, as some understand it. It is true that he did this; but the expression means simply that he had charge

ADAM CLARKE

G. CAMPBELL MORGAN:

They were strangely moved by fear, afraid to do the thing that was in their heart. Read again the statement: "Not during the feast, lest haply there shall be a tumult of the people." Why should they fear a tumult among the people? They were perfectly acquainted with the fact that the great human conscience, as expressed in the life of the multitude, agreed with the ideals of Jesus, agreed with His condemnation of their own failure. They feared a tumult. And why should there not be a tumult? What is there necessarily evil in a tumult of the people? Their fear was purely selfish; behind their fear of the people in tumult, there lurked a craven fear of Rome, and of the possible loss of favor, and position. Again, what a high tribute to Jesus, that these men in this hour were afraid of the tumult, which would be inspired by popular love of, and belief in, all that for which He had stood.—*The Gospel According to Mark*

Not on the feast day, lest there be an uproar. It was usual for the Jews to punish criminals at the public festivals; but in this case they were afraid of an insurrection, as our Lord had become very popular. The providence of God directed it thus, for the reason given in the preceding note.

Simon the leper. This was probably no more than a surname, as Simon the Canaanite, chap. x. 4, and Barsabas Justus, Acts i. 23, and several others. Yet it might have been some person that Christ had healed of this disease.

3. *Spikenard.* Or "nard." An Indian plant, whose root is very small and slender. It puts forth a long and small stalk, and has several ears or spikes even with the ground, which has given it the name of spikenard. *Very precious.* Or rather, "unadulterated." Theophylact gives this interpretation of the passage: "Unadulterated nard, and prepared with fidelity."

There came unto him a woman. There is much contention among commentators about the transaction mentioned here and in John xii. 14, some supposing them to be different, others to be the same. Some think that the *woman* mentioned here was Mary, the sister of Lazarus; others, Mary Magdalene; but against the former opinion it is argued that it is not likely, had this been Mary the sister of Lazarus, that Matthew and Mark would have suppressed her name. Besides, say they, we should not confound the repast which is mentioned here with that mentioned by John, chap. xii. 3. This one was made only *two* days before the Passover, and that one *six* days before; the one was made at the house of Simon the leper, the other at the house of Lazarus, John xii. 1-2. At this, the woman poured the oil on the *head* of Christ; at the other, Mary anointed Christ's *feet* with it.

And given to the poor. How often does charity serve as a cloak for covetousness! God is sometimes robbed of His right under the pretense of devoting what is withheld to some

MATTHEW HENRY

(2) Our Lord Jesus put a *better construction* upon it than, for aught that appears, was *designed.* Christ makes it to be an act of *great faith,* as well as *great* love (*v.* 8); "*She is come aforehand, to anoint my body to the burying.*" See how Christ's heart was filled with the thoughts of his death, how familiarly he spoke of it upon all occasions. It is usual for those who are *condemned to die,* to have their coffins prepared, and other provision made for their funerals, while they are yet alive; and *so* Christ accepted *this.* Christ never rode in triumph into Jerusalem, but when he came thither to suffer; nor had ever his head anointed, but for *his burial.*

(3) He recommended this piece of heroic piety to all ages; *Wherever this gospel shall be preached, it shall be spoken of, for a memorial of her, v.* 9. Thus was this good woman repaid for her box of ointment. *She lost neither her oil nor her labour.* She got by it that good name which is *better than precious ointment,* Those that *honour* Christ *he will honour.*

2. Judas, his *disguised enemy,* contracted with them for the betraying of him, *v.* 10, 11. He *went to the chief priests,* to tender his service in this affair.

(1) That which he proposed to them, was, to *betray Christ* to them without making an *uproar among the people,* which they were afraid of. Did they know that he had a mind to serve them, and make court to him? No, they could not imagine that any of his intimates should be so base. The spirit that works in all the children of disobedience, knows how to bring them in to the assistance one of another in a wicked project.

(2) That which he proposed to himself, was, to *get money* by the bargain; *they promised to give him money.* Covetousness was Judas's master-lust. They promised him *money.* Perhaps it was Judas's covetousness that brought him at first to *follow Christ,* having a promise that he should be cash-keeper, or purser, to the society, and he loved in his heart to be fingering money; and now that there was money to be got on the other side, he was as ready to betray him as ever he had been to follow him.

(3) Having secured the money, he set himself to make good his bargain; he sought *how he might conveniently betray him.* See what need we have to be careful that we do not ensnare ourselves in sinful engagements. It is a rule in our law, as well as in our religion, that an *obligation* to do an *evil thing* is *null* and *void;* it binds to repentance, not to performance. See how the way of sin is down-hill—when men are *in,* they must *on.*

Verses 12-31

I. Christ's eating the passover with his disciples, the night before he died. No apprehension of trouble, come or coming, should put us out of frame for our attendance on holy ordinances.

1. Christ ate the passover at the *usual time,* when the other Jews did. It was on the first day of that feast, which was called, *The feast of unleavened bread,* even that day when they *killed the passover, v.* 12.

2. He directed his disciples how to find the place where he intended to eat the passover. "*Go into the city* and *there shall meet you a man bearing a pitcher of water; follow him, go in* where he *goes,* enquire for his master, *the good man of the house* (*v.* 14), and desire him to show you a room." No doubt, the inhabitants of Jerusalem had rooms fitted up to be *let out,* for this occasion, to those that came out of the country to keep the passover and one of those Christ made use of. Probably he went where he was not known, that he might be *undisturbed* with his disciples. Perhaps he notified it by *a sign,* and by *such a sign* to intimate that he will dwell in the *clean heart,* that is, *washed* as with *pure water.* Where he designs to come, a pitcher of water must go before him.

JAMIESON, FAUSSET, BROWN

of it and its contents, or was treasurer to Jesus and the Twelve. What a remarkable arrangement was this, by which an avaricious and dishonest person was not only taken into the number of the Twelve, but entrusted with the custody of their little property! The purposes which this served are obvious enough; but it is further noticeable, that the remotest hint was never given to the Eleven of his true character, nor did the disciples most favored with the intimacy of Jesus ever suspect him, till a few minutes before he voluntarily separated himself from their company—for ever! **6. And Jesus said, Let her alone; why trouble ye her? she hath wrought a good work on me**—It was good in itself, and so was acceptable to Christ; it was eminently seasonable, and so more acceptable still; and it was "what she could," and so most acceptable of all. **7. For ye have the poor with you always**—referring to Deuteronomy 15:11. **and whensoever ye will ye may do them good: but me ye have not always**—a gentle hint of His approaching departure, by One who knew the worth of His own presence. **8. She hath done what she could**—a noble testimony, embodying a principle of immense importance. **she is come aforehand to anoint my body to the burying**—or, as in John (12:7), "Against the day of my burying hath she kept this." Not that she, dear heart, thought of His burial, much less reserved any of her nard to anoint her dead Lord. But as the time was so near at hand when that office would have to be performed, *and she was not to have that privilege even after the spices were brought for the purpose* (ch. 16:1), He lovingly *regards it as done now.* "In the act of love done to Him," says OLSHAUSEN beautifully, "she has erected to herself an eternal monument, as lasting as the Gospel, the eternal Word of God. From generation to generation this remarkable prophecy of the Lord has been fulfilled; and even we, in explaining this saying of the Redeemer, of necessity contribute to its accomplishment." "Who but Himself, asks STIER, "had the power to ensure to any work of man, even if resounding in His own time through the whole earth, an imperishable remembrance in the stream of history? Behold once more here the majesty of His royal judicial supremacy in the government of the world, in this, 'Verily I say unto you.'" **10. And Judas Iscariot, one of the twelve, went unto the chief priests, to betray him unto them**—i.e., to make his proposals, and to bargain with them, as appears from. Matthew's fuller statement (ch. 26: 14, 15) which says, he "went unto the chief priests, and said, What will ye give me, and I will deliver Him unto you? And they covenanted with him for thirty pieces of silver." The thirty pieces of silver were thirty shekels, the fine paid for man-or maid-servant acidentally killed (Exod. 21:32), and equal to about $25 in our currency—"a *goodly* price that I was prized at of them!" (Zech. 11:13). **11. And when they heard it, they were glad, and promised to give him money**—Matthew alone records the precise sum, because a remarkable and complicated prophecy, which he was afterwards to refer to, was fulfilled by it. **And he sought how he might conveniently betray him**—or, as more fully given in Luke (22:6), "And he promised, and sought opportunity to betray Him unto them in the absence of the multitude." That he should avoid an "uproar" or "riot" among the people, which probably was made an essential condition by the Jewish authorities, was thus assented to by the traitor; into whom, says Luke (22:3), "Satan entered," to put him upon this hellish deed.

12-26. PREPARATION FOR, AND LAST CELEBRATION OF, THE PASSOVER—ANNOUNCEMENT OF THE TRAITOR—INSTITUTION OF THE SUPPER. (=Matt. 26: 17-30; Luke 22:7-23, 39; John 13:21-30.) See on Luke 22:7-23, 39; and on John 13:10, 11, 18, 19, 21-30.

the day of unleavened bread—strictly the 15th Nisan (part of our March and April) *after* the paschal lamb was killed; but here, the 14th (Thursday). Into the difficult questions raised on this we cannot here enter. **when ye are entered the city**—He Himself probably stayed at Bethany during the day. **there shall a man . . .**

ADAM CLARKE

charitable purpose, to which there was no intention ever to give it.

Why trouble ye the woman? Or, "Why do you put the woman to pain?" A generous mind is ever pained when it is denied the opportunity of doing good, or when its proffered kindness is refused.

Ye have the poor always with you. And, consequently, have the opportunity of doing them good at any time. *But me ye have not always;* My bodily presence is about to be removed from you forever. The woman, under a presentiment of My death, is preparing Me for My burial.

8. *To anoint my body to the burying.* "Against," or "in reference to," its embalmment, thus pointing out My death and the embalmment of My body, for the bodies of persons of distinction were wrapped up in aromatics to preserve them from putrefaction.

9. *For a memorial of her.* See on Matt. xxvi. 13.

As embalming preserves the body from corruption, and she has done this good work to embalm and preserve this body, so will I order everything concerning this transaction to be carefully recorded, to preserve her memory to the latest ages. The actions which the world blames, through the spirit of envy, covetousness, or malice, God takes delight to distinguish and record.

Then . . . Judas. After this supper at Bethany, Judas returned to Jerusalem and made his contract with the chief priests.

11. *They were glad.* The joy that arises from the opportunity of murdering an innocent person must be completely infernal.

He sought opportunity. "A convenient or fit opportunity." Men seldom leave a crime imperfect. When once sin is conceived, it meets, in general, with few obstacles, till it brings forth death. How deceitful, how deeply damning, is the love of money!

Now the first day of the feast of unleavened bread. As the Feast of Unleavened Bread did not begin till the day after the Passover, the fifteenth day of the month (Lev. xxiii. 5-6; Num. xxviii. 16-17), this could not have been, properly, the first day of that feast. But as the Jews began to eat unleavened bread on the fourteenth (Exod. xii. 18), this day was often termed the first of unleavened bread. The Evangelists use it in this sense, and call even the paschal day by this name. See Mark xiv. 12; Luke xxii. 7. *Where wilt thou that we prepare?* How astonishing is this, that He who created all things, whether visible or invisible, and by whom all things were upheld, should so empty himself as not to be Proprietor of a single house in His whole creation, to eat the last Passover with His disciples! It is worthy of note what the Talmudists say, that the inhabitants of Jerusalem did not let out their houses to those who came to the annual feasts, but afforded all accommodations of this kind gratis. A man might, therefore, go and request the use of any room, on such an occasion, which was as yet unoccupied.

MATTHEW HENRY

3. He ate the passover in an *upper room furnished.* In eating his common meals he chose that which was homely, sat down on the grass: but, when he was to keep a sacred feast, in honour of that he would be at the expense of as good a room as he could get.

4. He ate it *with the twelve.* If Christ came *with the twelve,* then Judas was with them, though he was at this time contriving to betray his Master; and it is plain by what follows (*v.* 20), that he was there: he did not absent himself, lest he should have been suspected. Christ did not *exclude* him from the feast, though he *knew* his wickedness, for it was not as yet become public.

II. Christ's discourse with his disciples, as they were *eating* the passover.

1. They were *pleasing* themselves with the society of *their Master*; but he tells them that they must now presently lose him; *The Son of man is betrayed.* If he be *betrayed,* the next news you will hear of him, is, that he is *crucified* and *slain*; *The Son of man goes, as it is written of him, v.* 21.

2. They were *pleasing* themselves with the society *one of another,* but Christ casts a damp upon the joy of that, by telling them, *One of you that eateth with me shall betray me, v.* 18. Christ said this, if it might be, to startle the conscience of Judas, and to awaken him to repent of his wickedness, and to draw back from the brink of the pit. But for aught that appears, he who was *most concerned in* the warning, was *least concerned at* it. All the rest were affected with it. They began to be *sorrowful.* Here were the *bitter herbs,* with which this *passover-feast* was taken. They began to be *suspicious* of themselves; they said *one by one, Is it I? And another said, Is it I?* They were more jealous of themselves than of *one another.* It is the law of charity, to *hope the best* (1 Cor. xiii. 5–7), because we assuredly *know,* therefore we may justly *suspect,* more evil by ourselves than by our brethren. They trusted more to *his words* than to *their own hearts*; and therefore do not say, "I am sure *it is not I*", but, "*Lord, is it I?*"

Now, in answer to their enquiry, Christ saith that, [1] Which would make them easy; "It is not *you,* nor *you*; it is this that now *dips with me in the dish.*" [2] Which, one would think, should make Judas very *uneasy.* If he go on in his undertaking, it is upon the sword's point, for *woe to that man by whom the Son of man is betrayed*; it were *better for him that he had never been born.* It is very probable that Judas encouraged himself in it with *this* thought, that his Master had often said he must be betrayed; "And if it must be done, surely God *will not find fault* with him that doth it." But Christ tells him that this will be no shelter or excuse to him; *The Son of man indeed goes, as it is written of him,* but *woe to that man by whom he is betrayed.* Christ was delivered indeed by *the determinate counsel and fore-knowledge of God*; but, notwithstanding that, it is *with wicked hands that he is crucified and slain,* Acts ii. 23.

III. The institution of the Lord's supper.

1. It was instituted in the close of a *supper.* In the Lord's supper there is no *bodily repast* intended. It is food for *the soul* only, and therefore a very little of that which is for the body, as much as will serve for a *sign,* is enough.

2. It was instituted by the *example* of Christ himself; by the practice of our Master himself, because intended for those who are already his disciples.

3. It was instituted with *blessing* and *giving of thanks*; the gifts of common providence are to be so received much more the gifts of special grace. He *blessed* (*v.* 22), and *gave thanks, v.* 23.

4. It was instituted to be a *memorial* of his *death*; and therefore he *broke* the bread, to show how it pleased the Lord to *bruise him*; and he called the *wine,* which is the blood of the grape, the *blood of the New Testament.* Frequent mention is made of the *blood,* the *precious blood,* as the price of our redemption. It is called the *blood of the New Testament*; for the covenant of grace became a *testament,* and of force by the death of Christ, the testator. It is said to be *shed for many,* to bring *many* sons to glory, Heb. ii. 10. It was sufficient for *many,* being of infinite value; we read of a great multitude which no man could number, that had all *washed their robes, and made them white in the blood of the Lamb* (Rev. vii. 9–14); and still it is a *fountain opened.* How comfortable is this that the blood of Christ is *shed for many*! And if for *many,* why not for *me*? If for sinners, sinners of the Gentiles, the chief of sinners, then *why not for me*?

5. It was a sign of the conveyance of those benefits to us, which were purchased for us by his death; and therefore he broke the bread *to them* (*v.* 22), and said, *Take eat* of it: he gave the cup *to them,* and ordered them to *drink of it, v.* 23.

6. It was instituted with an eye to the happiness

JAMIESON, FAUSSET, BROWN

And he shall show you a large upper room furnished, or "spread" with tables, and couches, and covering, all ready for supper. Such large apartments were set apart by the inhabitants of the city for the accommodation of parties from the country.

Verily, verily, I say unto you, One of you shall betray me—The announcement of vs. 18 seems not to have been plain enough to be quite apprehended, save by the traitor himself. He will therefore speak it out in terms not to be misunderstood. But how much it cost Him to do this, appears from the "trouble" that came over His "spirit"—visible emotion, no doubt—before He got it uttered. What wounded susceptibility does this disclose, and what exquisite delicacy in His social intercourse with the Twelve, to whom He cannot, without an effort, break the subject! **the disciples looked one on another, doubting of whom he spake**—Further intensely interesting particulars are given in the other Gospels: (1) "They were exceeding sorrowful" (Matt. 26:22). (2) "They began to inquire among themselves which of them it was that should do this thing" (Luke 22:23). (3) "They began to say unto Him one by one, Is it I, and another, Is it I?" (Mark 14:19). Generous, simple hearts! They abhorred the thought, but, instead of putting it on others, each was only anxious to purge *himself,* and know if *he* could be the wretch. Their putting it at once to Jesus Himself, as knowing doubtless who was to do it, was the best, as it certainly was the most spontaneous and artless evidence of their innocence. (4) Jesus, apparently while this questioning was going on, added, "The Son of man goeth as it is written of Him, but woe unto that man by whom the Son of man is betrayed! It had been good for that man if he had not been born" (Matt. 26:24). (5) "Judas," *last of all,* "answered and said, *Lord, is it I?*" evidently feeling that when all were saying this, if he held his peace, that of itself would draw suspicion upon him. To prevent this the question is wrung out of him, but perhaps, amidst the stir and excitement at the table, in a half-suppressed tone as we are inclined to think the answer also was—"Thou hast said" (Matt. 26:25), or possibly by little more than a sign; for from vs. 28 it is evident that till the moment when he went out, he was not openly discovered.

This cup is the new testament in my blood, which is shed for you. In Matthew (26:28), "This is my blood of the new testament, which is shed for many for the remission of sins." In 1 Cor. (11:25) "This cup is the new testament in my blood: this do ye, as oft as ye drink it, in remembrance of me." Most critics now maintain that the word here rendered "testament" should be rendered covenant, not only here but wherever else it occurs in the New Testament; being used in the Old Testament constantly by the LXX translators for the well-known Hebrew word signifying "covenant," which never signifies "testament." Here, in particular, there is a manifest allusion to Ex. 24:8, "Behold, the blood of the covenant, which the Lord hath made with you concerning all these words." Now it is beyond doubt that "covenant" is the fundamental idea, and that in the Old Testament the word is correctly rendered "covenant." But let it be observed, first, that "testament" or "will" is the proper classical sense of the Greek work, and "disposition" or "covenant" but a secondary sense; and next, that in Heb. 9:15, the sense of "testament" appears to be so obviously what the apostle reasons on that to exclude it there, and restrict the meaning to "covenant," can only be made to yield the harshest sense.

ADAM CLARKE

15. *Furnished.* "Spread" with carpets—so this word is often used. But it may also signify the couches on which the guests reclined when eating. It does not appear that the Jews ate the Passover now, as their fathers did formerly, standing, with their shoes on and their staves in their hands.

One of you shall betray me. Or "will deliver Me up." Judas had already *betrayed* Him, v. 15, and he was now about to deliver Him into the hands of the chief priests, according to the agreement he had made with them.

They were exceeding sorrowful. That is, the eleven who were innocent; and the hypocritical traitor, Judas, endeavored to put on the appearance of sorrow.

19. *And another said, Is it I?* This clause is wanting in several MSS. and versions.

20. *That dippeth with me in the dish.* In the East persons never eat together from one dish, except when a strong attachment subsists between two or more persons of the same caste; in such a case one invites another to come and sit by him and eat from the same dish. This custom seems to have existed among the Jews; and the sacred historian mentions this notice of our Lord's, *It is one of the twelve, that dippeth with me in the dish,* to mark more strongly the perfidy of the character of Judas.

21. *Goeth.* That is, to die.

Jesus took bread. Of what kind? Unleavened bread, certainly, because there was no other kind to be had in all Judea at this time; for this was the first day of unleavened bread (v. 17), i.e., the fourteenth of the month Nisan, when the Jews, according to the command of God (Exod. xii. 15-20; xxiii. 15; and xxxiv. 25), were to purge away all leaven from their houses. For he who sacrified the Passover, having leaven in his dwelling, was considered to be such a transgressor of the divine law as could no longer be tolerated among the people of God, and therefore was to be cut off from the congregation of Israel. Now if any respect should be paid to the primitive institution, in the celebration of this divine ordinance, then unleavened, unyeasted bread should be used. *And blessed it.* Both Matthew and Mark use the word *blessed* instead of "gave thanks," which is the word used by Luke and Paul. The terms, in this case, are nearly of the same import, as both blessing and giving thanks were used on these occasions. But what was it that our Lord blessed? Not the bread, though many think the contrary, being deceived by the word *it,* which is improperly supplied in our version. In all the four places referred to above, whether the word *blessed* or *gave thanks* is used, it refers not to the bread, but to God, the Dispenser of every good. Our Lord here conforms himself to that constant Jewish custom, viz., of acknowledging God as the Author of every good and perfect gift, by giving thanks or taking the bread and taking the cup at their ordinary meals. The Jewish form of blessing, probably that which our Lord used on this occasion is: "Blessed be thou, our God, King of the universe who bringest forth bread out of the earth!" "Likewise, on taking the cup, they say: "Blessed be our God, the King of the universe, the Creator of the fruit of the vine!"

MATTHEW HENRY

of heaven, and to be an earnest and foretaste of that, and thereby to put our mouths out of taste for all the pleasures and delights of sense (*v.* 25); *I will drink no more of the fruit of the wine.* Lord, hasten the day, when I shall *drink* it *in the kingdom of God.*

7. It was closed with a *hymn, v.* 26. This was Christ's *swan-like* song, which he sung just before he entered upon his agony; probably, that which was usually sung, Ps. cxiii to cxviii.

IV. Christ's discourse with his disciples, as they were returning to Bethany by moonlight. When they had *sung the hymn,* presently they *went out.* The Israelites were forbidden to go out of their houses the night that they ate the passover, for fear of the sword of the destroying angel. But because Christ, the *great shepherd,* was to be *smitten,* he *went out* purposely to expose himself to the sword, as a champion; they *evaded* the destroyer, but Christ *conquered* him.

1. Christ here foretells that in his sufferings he should be *deserted* by all his disciples; "*You will all be offended because of me, this night.*" Christ knew this before, and yet welcomed them at his table. Nor should we be discouraged from coming to the Lord's supper, by the fear of relapsing into sin afterward; but, the greater our danger is, the more need we have to fortify ourselves by the diligent conscientious use of holy ordinances. Christ tells them that they would be *offended in him.* Hitherto, they had *continued with him in his temptations*; though they had sometimes offended him, yet they had not been *offended in him*; but now the storm would be so great, that they would all *slip their anchors,* and be in danger of *shipwreck.* The *smiting* of the shepherd is often the *scattering* of the sheep: the whole flock suffers for it, and is endangered by it.

But Christ encourages them with a promise that they shall rally again, shall return both to their duty and to their comfort (*v.* 28); "*After I am risen* I will *go before you into Galilee.*"

2. He foretells that he should be *denied* particularly by Peter. When they *went out* to go to the mount of Olives, we may suppose that they dropped Judas (he stole away from them). But Christ tells them that they would have no reason to boast of their constancy. Though God keeps us from being as bad as the worst, yet we may well be ashamed to think that we are not better than we are.

(1) Peter is confident that he should not *do so ill* as the rest of the disciples (*v.* 29); *Though all should be offended, yet will not I.* He supposes himself to be able to receive the shock of a temptation, and bear up against it, *all alone*; to *stand,* though nobody stood *by him.* It is bred in the bone with us, to *think well* of ourselves, and *trust* to *our own hearts.*

(2) Christ tells him that he will *do worse* than any of them. They will all *desert* him, but he will *deny* him; not once, but *thrice*; and that presently; "*This day, even this night before the cock crow twice,* thou wilt *deny* that ever thou hadst any knowledge of me."

(3) He stands to his promise; "*If I should die with thee, I will not deny thee*": and, no doubt, he thought as he said. Judas said nothing like this, when Christ told him he would betray him. He sinned by contrivance, Peter by surprise; Peter was *overtaken in this fault.* It was ill done of Peter, to contradict his Master. If he had said, with fear and trembling, "Lord, give me grace to keep me from denying thee," it might have been prevented: but they were all thus confident; they who said, *Lord, is it I?* now said, *It shall never be me.* Being acquitted from their fear of betraying Christ, they were now secure. But he that thinks he stands, must learn to take heed lest he fall.

Verses 32–42

Christ is here entering upon his sufferings, and begins with those which were the sorest of all his sufferings, those in his *soul.* Here we have him in his *agony.*

I. He retired for prayer; *Sit ye here* (saith he to his disciples), while I go a little further, and *pray.* He had lately prayed *with them* (John xvii); and now he appoints them to withdraw while he goes to his Father upon an errand peculiar to himself.

II. Even into that retirement he took with him *Peter, and James, and John* (*v.* 33), three competent witnesses of this part of his humiliation. These three had boasted most of their ability and willingness to suffer with him; Peter here, in this chapter, and James and John (*ch.* x. 39); and therefore Christ takes them to stand by, and see what a struggle he had, to convince them that they knew not what they said. It is fit that they who are most confident, should be *first* tried, that they may be made sensible of their folly and weakness.

III. There he was in a tremendous agitation (*v.* 33); *He began to be sore amazed*—a word not used in

JAMIESON, FAUSSET, BROWN

27-31. THE DESERTION OF JESUS BY HIS DISCIPLES, AND THE FALL OF PETER, FORETOLD. (=Matt. 26:31-35; Luke 22:31-38; John 13:36-38.) See on Luke 22:31-46.

In Matthew and Mark it was when our Lord told them they should all be stumbled in Him that night, that Peter said, "Though all men"—or rather, "all," meaning all that sat with him at the table—"shall be offended in Thee, yet will I never be offended" (Matt. 26:33; Mark 14:29). But as the answer there given by our Lord is the same as that recorded by our Evangelist, he probably uttered both protestations in his vehemence at one time; his feeling being roused by our Lord singling him out from all the rest. Poor Peter, thou shalt yet pay dear for that unlovely elevation of thyself above the rest of thy brethren, when thy risen Lord shall wring thy heart by asking thee, in presence of these very brethren, "Simon, son of Jonas, lovest thou Me more than these?" (John 21:15-17). Yet no vain-glorious vaunt was this of Peter. it was just the outcoming of conscious attachment; insomuch that all the rest, feeling a cord touched in their own hearts by this protestation, immediately repeated it for themselves. For, add our two first Evangelists, "Likewise also said all the disciples." Dear disciples! Ye spoke out but the feelings of your heart then; your Lord knew that, and doubtless was comforted by it, as a spontaneous utterance of your hearts' affection. But little thought ye how soon it was to be seen—in all of you, but in Peter pre-eminently—that "he that trusteth in his own heart is a fool" (Prov. 23:26). **And he said, I tell thee, Peter, the cock shall not crow this day, before that thou shalt thrice deny that thou knowest me.** Most interesting and touching is the fact, that whereas in the first, third, and fourth Gospels only *one* crowing of the cock is mentioned as sounding the note of Peter's fall, in the second Gospel—which all ancient tradition proclaims, and internal evidence suggests, to have been drawn up under the immediate eye of Peter—it is said that *two* crowings of the cock would sound his fall. And as it is Mark alone who records the fact that the cock did crow twice—the first time after one denial of his Lord, and the second immediately after the last—we have thus an affecting announcement, almost from his own pen, that warning after warning passed unheeded, till the second knell rung in his ears and bitterly revealed how much wiser his Lord was than he.

32-42. THE AGONY IN THE GARDEN. (=Matt. 26:36-46; Luke 22:39-46). See on Luke 22:39-46.

the place—the Garden of Gethsemane, on the west or city side of the mount. Comparing all the accounts of this mysterious scene, the facts appear to be these: (1) He bade nine of the Twelve remain "here" while He went and prayed "yonder."

ADAM CLARKE

And when they had sung an hymn. Probably no more than a kind of recitative reading or chanting. As to the hymn itself, we know, from the universal consent of Jewish antiquity, that it was composed of Psalms 113—118, termed by the Jews *halel,* from *halelu-yah,* the first word in Psalm 113. These six psalms were always sung at every paschal solemnity. They sung this great hallel on account of the five great benefits referred to in it; viz., (1) The Exodus from Egypt, Ps. cxiv. 1, "When Israel went out of Egypt." (2) The miraculous division of the Red Sea, v. 3, "The sea saw it, and fled." (3) The promulgation of the law, v. 4, "The mountains skipped like . . . lambs." (4) The resurrection of the dead, Ps. cxvi. 9, "I will walk before the Lord in the land of the living." (5) The passion of the Messiah, Ps. cxv. 1, "Not unto us, O Lord, not unto us."

All ye shall be offended. Or rather, "You will all be stumbled"—you will all forsake Me, and lose in a great measure your confidence in Me. *This night.* The time of trial is just at hand. *I will smite the shepherd.* It will happen to you as to a flock of sheep whose shepherd has been slain—the leader and guardian being removed, the whole flock shall be scattered, and be on the point of becoming a prey to ravenous beasts.

But after I am risen again. Do not lose your confidence; for though I shall appear for a time to be wholly left to wicked men, and be brought under the power of death, yet I will rise again, and triumph over all your enemies and mine. *I will go before you.* Still alluding to the case of the shepherd and his sheep. Though the shepherd have been smitten and the sheep scattered, the shepherd shall revive again, collect the scattered flock, and *go before* them, and lead them to peace, security, and happiness.

Peter . . . said unto him, Though all men shall be offended . . . yet will I never. The presumptuous person imagines he can do everything, and can do nothing; thinks he can excel all, and excels in nothing; promises everything, and performs nothing. The humble man acts a quite contrary part. There is nothing we know so little of as ourselves—nothing we see less of than our own weakness and poverty.

30. *That . . . thou. Su* is added by most MSS. and versions. It adds much to the energy of the passage, every word of which is deeply emphatical. "Verily I say unto you that you, this day, in this very night, before the cock shall crow twice, you will deny Me."

Though I should die with thee, yet will I not deny thee. He does not take the warning which his Lord gave him—he trusts in the warm, sincere attachment to Christ which he now feels, not considering that this must speedily fail unless supported by the power of God.

A place called Gethsemane. A garden at the foot of the Mount of Olives. The name seems to be formed from *gath,* "a press," and *shemen,* "oil"; probably the place where the produce of the mount of Olives was prepared for use. The garden of the oil press, or olive press.

And he took with him Peter and the two sons of Zebedee. That is, James and John, the same persons who had beheld His transfiguration on the mount—that they might contemplate this agony in the light of that glory which they had there seen, and so be kept from being stumbled by a view of His present humiliation. *And very heavy.* "Overwhelmed with anguish." This word is used by the Greeks to denote the most extreme anguish which the soul can feel—excruciating anxiety and torture of spirit.

MATTHEW HENRY

Matthew, but very significant; it bespeaks something like that *horror of great darkness*, which *fell upon Abraham* (Gen. xv. 12). Never was *sorrow* like unto *his* at that time. Yet there was not the least disorder or irregularity in this commotion of his spirits; for he had no corrupt nature to mix with them, as we have. If water have a sediment at the bottom, though it may be clear while it stands still, yet, when shaken, it grows muddy; so it is with our affections: but pure water in a clean glass, though ever so much stirred, continues clear; and so it was with Christ.

IV. He made a sad complaint of this agitation. He said, *My soul is exceeding sorrowful*. He was *made sin for us*, and therefore was thus *sorrowful*; he fully knew the *malignity* of the *sins* he was to *suffer for*; and having the highest degrees of love to God, who was *offended* by them, and of love to *man*, who was damaged and endangered by them, no marvel that *his soul* was *exceeding sorrowful*. He was *made a curse* for us; the curses of the law were transferred to him as our surety and representative. He now *tasted death* (as he is said to do, Heb. ii. 9), he *drank up* even the dregs of the cup; he *tasted* all the bitterness of it.

Now the consideration of Christ's sufferings in *his soul*, and his *sorrows* for us, should be of use to us,

(1) To *embitter our sins*. Can we ever entertain a *favourable* or so much as a *slight* thought of sin, when we see what impression sin made upon the Lord Jesus? Shall that *sit light* upon our souls, which sat *so heavy* upon his? Was Christ in such an agony for our sins, and shall we never be in an agony about them? If Christ thus suffered for sin, let us *arm ourselves with the same mind*.

(2) To *sweeten our sorrows*; if our souls be at any time *exceeding sorrowful*, let us remember that our Master was so before us, and the *disciple is not greater than his Lord*. Why should we affect to *drive away* sorrow, when Christ for our sakes, submitted to it, and thereby not only took out the *sting* of it, but put *virtue* into it, and made it *profitable*, nay, and put *sweetness* into it, and made it comfortable. Blessed Paul was *sorrowful*, and yet *always rejoicing*.

V. He ordered his disciples to keep with him; he said to them, *Tarry ye here and watch*. He had said to the other disciples nothing but, Sit ye here (*v.* 32); but these three he bids to tarry *and watch*, as expecting more from them than from the rest.

VI. He addressed himself to God by prayer (*v.* 35); He *fell on the ground, and prayed*. It was but a little before this, that in prayer he *lifted up his eyes* (John xvii. 1); but here, being in an agony, he *fell upon his face*. As *Man*, he *deprecated* his sufferings, that, *if it were possible, the hour might pass from him* (*v.* 35). We have his very words (*v.* 36), *Abba, Father*. The Syriac word is here retained, which Christ used, and which signifies *Father*, to intimate what an emphasis our Lord Jesus, in his *sorrows*, laid upon it, and would have us to lay. Father, *all things are possible to thee*. Even that which we cannot expect to be done for us, we ought yet to believe that God is *able to do*: and when we submit to his will, it must be with a believing acknowledgment of his power, that *all things are possible to him*. As *Mediator*, he *acquiesced* in the will of God concerning them; "*Nevertheless, not what I will, but what thou wilt*."

VII. He roused his disciples, who were dropped asleep while he was at prayer, *v.* 37, 38. He comes to look after them, since they did not look after him; and he *finds them asleep*. This carelessness of theirs was a presage of their further offence in deserting him. He had so lately commended them for *continuing with him in his temptations*, though they had not been without their faults. They had lately promised not to be *offended in him*; what! and yet mind him so little? He particularly upbraided Peter with his drowsiness; *Simon, sleepest thou? Couldest thou not watch one hour?* He did not require him to watch *all night* with him, only for *one hour*. He doth not over-task us, nor weary us.

As those whom Christ *loves* he *rebukes* when they do amiss, so those whom he *rebukes* he counsels and comforts. It was a very wise and faithful word of advice which Christ here gave to his disciples; *Watch and pray, lest ye enter into temptation, v.* 38. It was bad to *sleep* when Christ was in his agony, but if they did not stir up themselves, and fetch in grace and strength from God by prayer, they would *do worse*; and so they did, when they all forsook him, and fled. It was a very kind and tender excuse that Christ made for them; "*The spirit truly is willing*; you would willingly *keep awake*, but you cannot." *The flesh is weak*, and if you do not *watch* and *pray*, you may be overcome, notwithstanding. The consideration of the *weakness* and infirmity *of our flesh* should engage and quicken us to *prayer* and *watchfulness*.

JAMIESON, FAUSSET, BROWN

(2) He "took the other three, Peter, James, and John, and began to be sore amazed [appalled], sorrowful, and very heavy [oppressed], and said, My soul is exceeding sorrowful even unto death"—'I feel as if nature would sink under this load, as if life were ebbing out, and death coming before its time'-

-"tarry ye here, and watch with Me"; not, 'Witness for Me,' but, 'Bear Me company.' It did Him good, it seems, to have them beside Him. (3) But soon even they were too much for Him: He must be alone. "He was withdrawn from them about a stone's-cast"—though near enough for them to be competent witnesses—and kneeled down, uttering that most affecting prayer (Mark 14:36), that if possible "the cup," of His approaching *death*, "might pass from Him, but if not, His Father's will be done": implying that *in itself* it was so purely revolting that only its being the Father's will would induce Him to taste it, but that *in that view* of it He was perfectly prepared to drink it. It is no struggle between a reluctant and a compliant will, but between two views of one event—an *abstract* and a *relative* view of it, in the one of which it was *revolting*, in the other *welcome*. By signifying how it felt in the *one* view, He shows His beautiful oneness with ourselves in nature and feeling; by expressing how He regarded it in the other light, He reveals His absolute obediential subjection to His Father. (4) On this, having a momentary relief, for it came upon Him, we imagine, by surges, He returns to the three, and finding them sleeping, He addresses them affectingly, particularly *Peter*, as in Mark 14:37, 38. He then (5) goes back, not now to kneel, but fell on His face on the ground, saying the same words, but with this turn, "If this cup *may not pass* . . ." (Matt. 26:42)—i.e., 'Yes, I understand this mysterious silence (Ps. 22:1-6); it may not pass; I am to drink it, and I will'—"Thy will be done!" (6) Again, for a moment relieved, He returns and finds them "sleeping for sorrow," warns them as before, but puts a loving construction upon it, separating between the "willing spirit" and the **"weak flesh."** (7) Once more, returning to His solitary spot, the surges rise higher, beat more tempestuously, and seem ready to overwhelm Him. To fortify Him for this, "there appeared an angel unto Him from heaven strengthening Him"—not to minister light or comfort (He was to have none of that, and they were not needed nor fitted to convey it), but purely to sustain and brace up sinking nature for a yet hotter and fiercer struggle. And now, He is "in an agony, and prays more earnestly"—even Christ's prayer, it seems, admitted of and now demanded such increase—"and His sweat was as it were great drops [literally clots] of blood falling down to the

ADAM CLARKE

My soul is exceeding sorrowful (or "is surrounded with exceeding sorrow"), *even unto death*. This latter word explains the two former: My soul is so dissolved in sorrow, My spirit is filled with such agony and anguish, that, if speedy succor be not given to My body, death must be the speedy consequence.

36. *Abba, Father*. This Syriac word, which intimates filial affection and respect and parental tenderness, seems to have been used by our blessed Lord, merely considered as man, to show His complete submission to His Father's will, and the tender affection which He was conscious His Father had for Him. *Abba*, Syriac, is here joined to *pater*, Greek, both signifying "father"; so Paul, Rom. viii. 15; Gal. iv. 6. The reason is that from the time in which the Jews became conversant with the Greek language, by means of the Septuagint version and their commerce with the Roman and Greek provinces, they often intermingled Greek and Roman words with their own language.

O my Father, if this cup may not pass away from me. If it be not possible to redeem fallen man unless I drink this cup, unless I suffer death for them; *thy will be done*—I am content to suffer whatever may be requisite to accomplish the great design. In this address the humanity of Christ most evidently appears, for it was His humanity alone that could suffer.

He . . . saith unto Peter. He addressed himself more particularly to this apostle because of the profession he had made, v. 33; as if He had said: "Is this the way you testify your affectionate attachment to Me? You all said you were ready to die with Me; *what*, then, cannot you *watch . . . one hour?*"

That ye enter not into temptation. Watch—that you be not taken unawares; *and pray*—that when it comes you may be enabled to bear it.

A. T. ROBERTSON:

33. "Greatly amazed and sore troubled" (*ekthambeisthai kai ademonein*). Matt. 26:37 has "sorrowful and sore troubled." Mark alone uses *exthambeisthai* (here and in 9:15). There is a papyrus example given by Moulton and Milligan's *Vocabulary*. The verb *thambeo* occurs in Mark 10:32 for the amazement of the disciples at the look of Jesus as he went toward Jerusalem. Now Jesus himself feels amazement as he directly faces the struggle in the Garden of Gethsemane. He wins the victory over himself in Gethsemane and then he can endure the loss, despising the shame. For the moment he is rather amazed and homesick for heaven. "Long as He had foreseen the Passion, when it came clearly into view its terror exceeded His anticipations" (Swete). "He learned from what he suffered" (Heb. 5:8), and this new experience enriched the human soul of Jesus.

—Word Pictures in the New Testament

MATTHEW HENRY

VIII. *He repeated* his address to his Father (*v.* 39); *He went again, and prayed,* saying *the same word*; he spoke to the same purport, and again *the third time.* This teaches us, that *men ought always to pray, and not to faint,* Luke xviii. 1. Though the answers to our prayers do not come quickly, yet we must renew our requests. Paul, when he was *buffeted by a messenger of Satan, besought the Lord thrice,* as Christ did here, before he obtained an answer of peace, 2 Cor. xii. 7, 8. He must come a second and a third time, for the visits of God's grace, in answer to prayer, come sooner or later, according to the pleasure of his will.

IX. He *repeated* his visits to his disciples. Thus he gave a specimen of his continued care for his church on earth, even when it is *half asleep.* He came the *second time* to his disciples, and *found them asleep again, v.* 40. See how the infirmities of Christ's disciples *return* upon them, and *overpower* them, and what clogs those bodies of ours are to our souls. This second time he spoke to them as before, but *they wist not what to answer him.* Like men between sleeping and waking, they knew not where they were, or what they said. But, the *third time,* they were bid to *sleep* if they would (*v.* 41); "*Sleep on now, and take your rest.*" *It is enough;* we had not that word in Matthew. "You have had warning enough to keep awake, and would not take it. Now *the hour is come,* in which I knew you would all forsake me." The *Son of man* is now *betrayed into the hands of sinners.* "Come, *rise up. Let us go,* for *lo, he that betrayeth me is at hand.*"

Verses 43–52

We have here the *seizing* of our Lord Jesus by the officers of the chief priests. He began first to suffer *in his soul,* but afterward suffered in his body.

I. Here is a band of rude miscreants employed to *take* our Lord Jesus; *a great multitude with swords and staves.* At the head of this rabble is Judas, *one of the twelve.* It is no new thing for a very fair and plausible profession to end in a shameful and fatal apostasy.

II. Men of no less figure than the *chief priests, and the scribes,* and *the elders,* sent them, and set them on work, who pretended to expect the Messiah, and to be ready to welcome him; and yet, when he *is come,* they set themselves against him, and resolve to run him down.

III. Judas betrayed him *with a kiss.* He called him, *Master, Master, and kissed him.* It is enough to put one for ever out of conceit with being called of men *Rabbi, Rabbi* (Matt. xxiii. 7), since it was with this compliment that Christ was betrayed.

IV. They arrested him, and made him their prisoner (*v.* 46); *They laid their hands on him,* rude and violent hands, and *took him* into custody.

V. Peter laid about him in defence of his Master, and wounded one of the assailants. He was *one of them that stood by,* of them that *were with him* (so the word signifies). He *drew a sword,* and aimed, it is likely, to cut off the head, but missed his blow, and only *cut off the ear,* of a servant of the high priest, *v.* 47. It is easier to *fight* for Christ, than to *die* for him; but Christ's good soldiers overcome, not by taking away other people lives, but by laying down their own.

VI. Christ shows them the absurdity of their proceedings against him. 1. That they came out *against him,* as against a *thief,* whereas he was *innocent* of any crime; he *taught daily in the temple,* and if he had any wicked design, there it would some time or other have been discovered. By his fruits he was known to be a good tree; why then did they come out against him *as a thief*? 2. That they came to take him thus *privately,* whereas he was neither *ashamed* nor *afraid* to appear *publicly* in the temple. He was none of those *evil-doers* that *hate the light,* neither come *to the light,* John iii. 20. To come upon him thus at midnight, and in the place of his retirement, was base and cowardly. But this was not all. 3. They came *with swords and staves,* as if he had been in arms against the government. There was no occasion for those weapons; but they made this ado, (1) To secure themselves from the rage of some; they came armed, because they *feared the people.* (2) To expose him to the rage of others. By coming *with swords and staves to take him,* they represented him to the people as a dangerous turbulent man.

VII. He reconciled himself to all this injurious, ignominious treatment, by referring himself to the Old Testament predictions of the Messiah. I am hardly used, *but* I submit, for *the scriptures must be fulfilled, v.* 49. See here what a regard Christ had to the *scriptures*; he would bear anything rather than that the least jot or tittle of the word of God should

JAMIESON, FAUSSET, BROWN

ground." What was this? *Not His proper sacrificial offering,* though essential to it. It was just the internal struggle, apparently hushing itself before, but now swelling up again, convulsing His whole inner man, and this so affecting His animal nature that the sweat oozed out from every pore in thick drops of blood, falling to the ground. It was just *shuddering nature* and *indomitable will* struggling together. But again the cry, If it must be, *Thy will be done,* issues from His lips, and all is over. "The bitterness of death is past." He has anticipated and rehearsed His final conflict, and won the victory—now on the theater of an *invincible will,* as then on the arena of the Cross. 'I *will* suffer,' is the grand result of Gethsemane: "It is finished" is the shout that bursts from the Cross. The Will without the Deed had been all in vain; but His work was consummated when He carried the now manifested Will into the palpable Deed, "*by the which* WILL *we are sanctified* THROUGH THE OFFERING OF THE BODY OF JESUS CHRIST ONCE FOR ALL" (Heb. 10:10). (8) At the close of the whole scene, finding them still sleeping (worn out with continued sorrow and racking anxiety), He bids them, with an irony of deep emotion, "sleep on now and take their rest, the hour is come, the Son of man is betrayed into the hands of sinners, rise, let us be going, the traitor is at hand." And while He spoke, Judas approached with his armed band. Thus they proved "miserable comforters," broken reeds; and thus in His whole work He was *alone,* and "of the people there was none with Him."

43-52. BETRAYAL AND APPREHENSION OF JESUS—FLIGHT OF HIS DISCIPLES. (=Matt. 26:47-56; Luke 22:47-53; John 18:1-12.) See on John 18: 1-12.

Judas then—"He that was called Judas, one of the Twelve," says Luke, in language which brands him with peculiar infamy, as *in* the sacred circle while in no sense *of* it. **a band of men**—"the *detachment* of the Roman cohort on duty at the festival for the purpose of maintaining order" [WEBSTER and WILKINSON]. **officers from the chief priests and Pharisees**—captains of the temple and armed Levites. **lanterns and torches**—It was full moon, but in case He should have secreted Himself somewhere in the dark ravine, they bring the means of exploring its hiding-places—little knowing whom they had to do with. "Now he that betrayed Him had given them a sign, saying, Whomsoever I shall kiss, that same is He, hold Him fast" (Matt. 26:48). The cold-bloodedness of this speech was only exceeded by the deed itself. "And Judas went before them [Luke 22:47], and forthwith he came to Jesus, and said, Hail, Master, and kissed Him" (Matt. 26:49; cf. Exod. 4:27; 18:7; Luke 7:45). The impudence of this atrocious deed shows how thoroughly he had by this time mastered all his scruples. If the dialogue between our Lord and His captors was *before* this, as some interpreters think it was, the kiss of Judas was purely gratuitous, and probably to make good his right to the money; our Lord having presented Himself unexpectedly before them, and rendered it unnecessary for any one to point Him out. But a comparison of the narratives seems to show that our Lord's "coming forth" to the band was *subsequent* to the interview of Judas. "And Jesus said unto him, Friend"—not the endearing term "friend" (in ch. 15:15), but "companion," a word used on occasions of remonstrance or rebuke (as in Matt. 20:13; 22: 12)—"Wherefore art thou come?" (Matt. 26:50). "Betrayest thou the Son of man with a kiss"—imprinting upon the foulest act the mark of tenderest affection? What *wounded feeling* does this express! Of this Jesus showed Himself on various occasions keenly susceptible—as all generous and beautiful natures do.

Then Simon Peter, having a sword, drew it, and smote the high priest's servant, and cut off his right ear. The servant's name was Malchus—None of the other Evangelists mention the name either of the ardent disciple or of his victim. John being "known to the high priest" (vs. 15), the mention of the servant's name by *him* is quite natural, and an interesting mark of truth in a small matter. As to the *right* ear, specified both here and in Luke, the man was "likely foremost of those who advanced to seize Jesus, and presented himself in the attitude of a combatant; hence his right side would be exposed to attack. The blow of Peter was evidently aimed vertically at his head" [WESTER and WILKINSON].

ADAM CLARKE

Prayed the third time. So Paul wrote: "I besought the Lord thrice, that it might depart from me" (2 Cor. xii. 8). This *thrice* repeating the same petition argues deep earnestness of soul.

My hour—in which I am to be delivered up, *is at hand;* therefore, now think of your own personal safety. *The Son of man is betrayed into the hands of sinners.* Viz., the Gentiles or heathens, who were generally distinguished by this appellation from the Jews.

Rise, let us be going. That is, to meet them, giving thereby the fullest proof that I know all their designs and might have, by flight or otherwise, provided for My own safety. But I go willingly to meet that death which their malice designs Me, and through it provide for the life of the world.

Judas, one of the twelve. More deeply to mark his base ingratitude and desperate wickedness. *A great multitude with swords and staves.* They did not come as officers of justice but as a desperate mob.

Gave them a sign. How coolly deliberate is this dire apostate! The man whom *I shall kiss*—how deeply hypocritical! That is He; *hold him fast,* "seize Him"—how diabolically malicious!

Hail, master. A usual compliment among the Jews. Judas pretends to wish our Lord continued health while he is meditating His destruction! *And kissed him.* "And tenderly kissed Him"—this is the proper meaning of the original word. He kissed Him again and again—still pretending the most affectionate attachment to Him, though our Lord had before unmasked him.

One of them which were with Jesus. This was Peter—*struck a servant of the high priest's* (the servant's name was Malchus, John xviii. 10), *and smote off his ear.* In Luke xxii. 51 it is said, Jesus touched and healed it. Here was another miracle, and striking proof of the divinity of Christ.

But how then—had I such a defense—*shall the scriptures be fulfilled,* which say *that thus it must be?* That is, that I am to suffer and die for the sin of the world. Probably the

MATTHEW HENRY

fall to the ground. See what use we are to make of the Old Testament; we must search for Christ, the true *treasure hid in that field.*

VIII. All Christ's disciples, hereupon, deserted him (*v.* 50); *They all forsook him, and fled.* They were very confident that they should adhere to him; but even good men know not what they will do, till they are tried. If it was such a comfort to him as he had lately intimated, that they had hitherto *continued with him* in his lesser trials (Luke xxii. 28), we may well imagine what a grief it was to him, that they deserted him now in the greatest. Let not those that suffer for Christ, think it strange, if they be thus deserted, and if all the herd shun the wounded deer. When St. Paul was in peril, none *stood by him,* but *all men forsook him,* 2 Tim. iv. 16.

IX. The noise disturbed the neighbourhood, *v.* 51, 52. This passage of story we have not in any other of the evangelists. Here is an account of a *certain young man,* who, as it should seem, was no disciple of Christ, who *followed him* to see what would become of him. Now observe concerning him,

1. How he was *frightened out of his bed,* to be a *spectator* of Christ's sufferings. Such a *multitude,* so armed, could not but produce a great stir; this alarmed our *young man,* who had the curiosity to go, and see what the matter was, and was in such haste to inform himself, that he could not stay to dress himself, but threw a sheet about him. When all his disciples had quitted him, he continued to *follow him,* desirous to *hear* what he would say, and *see* what he would do.

2. See how he was *frightened into his bed* again, when he was in danger of being made a *sharer* in Christ's sufferings. His own disciples had run away from him; but this young man thought he might securely attend him, especially being so far from being armed, that he was not so much as clothed; but *the young men,* the Roman soldiers, who were called to assist, *laid hold of him.* Finding himself in danger, he *left the linen cloth* by which they had *caught hold of him,* and *fled away naked.* This passage is recorded to show what a narrow escape the disciples had of falling into their hands, out of which nothing could have kept them but their Master's care of them; *If ye seek me, let these go their way,* John xviii. 8. It also intimates that there is *no hold* of those who are led by curiosity only, and not by faith and conscience, to follow Christ.

Verses 53–65

We have here Christ's arraignment, trial, conviction, and condemnation, before the great sanhedrim, of which the *high priest* was president, the same Caiaphas that had lately adjudged it expedient he should be put to death, guilty or not guilty (John xi. 50), and who therefore might justly be excepted against as partial.

I. Christ is hurried away to his *house.* And there though in the dead of the night, *all the chief priests, and elders, and scribes,* that were in the secret, were *assembled,* ready to receive the prey; so sure were they of it.

W. E. VINE:

In the Gospels the term denotes the official residence in Jerusalem of the Roman governor, and the various translations of it in our versions arose from a desire either to indicate the special purpose for which that residence was used on the occasion in question, or to explain what particular building was intended. But whatever building the governor occupied was the Praetorium. It is most probable that in Jerusalem he resided in the well-known palace of Herod.... Pilate's residence has been identified with the castle of Antonia, which was occupied by the regular garrison. The probability is that it was the same as Herod's palace. Herod's palace in Caesarea was used as the Praetorium there, and the expression in Acts 23:35, marg., "Herod's praetorium," is abbreviated from "the praetorium of Herod's palace."
—*Vine's Expository Dictionary*

JAMIESON, FAUSSET, BROWN

53-72. Jesus Arraigned before the Sanhedrim, Condemned to Die, and Shamefully Entreated—The Fall of Peter. (=Matt. 26:57-75; Luke 22:54-71; John 18:13-18, 24-27.) Had we only the first three Gospels, we should have concluded that our Lord was led immediately to Caiaphas, and had before the Council. But as the Sanhedrim could hardly have been brought together at the dead hour of night—by which time our Lord was in the hands of the officers sent to take Him—and as it was only "as soon as it was day" that the Council met (Luke 22:66), we should have had some difficulty in knowing what was done with Him during those intervening hours. In the Fourth Gospel, however, all this is cleared up, and a very important addition to our information is made (John 18:13, 14, 19-24).

Peter Obtains Access within the Quadrangle of the High Priest's Residence, and Warms Himself at the Fire (vss. 53,54). **53. And they led Jesus away to the high priest: and with him were assembled**—or rather, "there gathered together unto him"—**all the chief priests and the elders and the scribes**—it was then a full and formal meeting of the Sanhedrim. Now, as the first three Evangelists place all Peter's denials of his Lord after this, we should naturally conclude that they took place *while our Lord stood before the Sanhedrim.* But besides that the natural impression is that the scene around the fire took place *overnight,* the *second crowing of the cock,* if we are to credit ancient writers, would occur about the beginning of the fourth watch, or between three and four in the morning. By that time, however, the Council had probably convened, being warned, perhaps, that they were to prepare for being called at any hour of the morning, should the Prisoner be successfully secured. If this be correct, it is fairly certain that only the *last* of Peter's three denials would take place while our Lord was under trial before the Sanhedrim. One thing more may require explanation. If our Lord had to be transferred from the residence of Annas to that of Caiaphas, one is apt to wonder that there is no mention of His being marched from the one to the other. But the building, in all likelihood, was one and the same; in which case He would merely have to be taken perhaps across the court, from one chamber to another. **54. And Peter followed him afar off, even into**—or "from afar, even to the interior of"—**the palace of the high priest**—"An Oriental house," says Robinson, "is usually built around a quadrangular interior court; into which there is a passage (sometimes arched) through the front part of the house, closed next the street by a heavy folding gate, with a smaller wicket for single persons, kept by a porter. The interior court, often paved or flagged, and open to the sky, is the *hall,* which our translators have rendered 'palace,' where the attendants made a fire; and the passage beneath the front of the house, from the street to this court, is the *porch.* The place where Jesus stood before the high priest may have been an open room, or place of audience on the ground-floor, in the rear or on one side of the court; such rooms, open in front, being customary. It was close upon the court, for Jesus heard all that was

ADAM CLARKE

scriptures to which our Lord principally refers are Psalms xxii; lxix; and especially Isaiah liii and Dan. ix. 24-27. Christ shows that they had no power against Him but what He permitted, and that He willingly gave up himself into their hands.

Then all the disciples forsook him, and fled. **He had but twelve who professed inviolable attachment to Him. One of these betrayed Him; another denied Him with oaths; and the rest ran away and utterly abandoned Him to His implacable enemies!**

A. T. ROBERTSON:

51. "A certain young man" (*neaniskos tis*). This incident alone in Mark. It is usually supposed that Mark himself, son of Mary (Acts 12:12), in whose house they probably had observed the passover meal, had followed Jesus and the apostles to the Garden. It is a lifelike touch quite in keeping with such a situation. Here after the arrest he was following with Jesus.
—*Word Pictures in the New Testament*

51. ***A certain young man.*** **Probably raised from his sleep by the noise which the rabble made who came to apprehend Jesus, having wrapped the sheet or some of the bedclothing about him, became thereby the more conspicuous. On his appearing, he was seized; but as they had no way of holding him but only by the cloth which was wrapped round him, he disengaged himself from that, and so escaped out of their hands. This circumstance is not related by any other of the Evangelists.**

They . . . led him away to Caiaphas. **John says, chap. xviii. 13, that they led him first to Annas; but this appears to have been done merely to do him honor as the father-in-law of Caiaphas, and his colleague in the high priesthood. But as the Sanhedrin was assembled at the house of Caiaphas, it was there He must be brought to undergo His mock trial.**

Peter followed him afar off. **Poor Peter! This is the beginning of his dreadful fall. His fear kept him from joining the company and publicly acknowledging his Lord, and his affection obliged him to follow at a distance that he might see the end.**

MATTHEW HENRY

II. *Peter followed* at a distance, *v.* 54. But when he came to the high priest's palace, he *sat with the servants.* The high priest's fire side was no proper place, nor his servants proper company for Peter, but it was his *entrance into a temptation.*

ALEXANDER MACLAREN:

His love pushed him into a dangerous place. He was in bad company among the inferior sort of servants huddled around the fire that cold morning, at the lower end of the hall; and as its light flickered on his face, he was sure to be recognized. But we have not now to do with his denial. Rather, he is the type of a true disciple, coercing his human weakness and cowardice to yield to the attraction which draws him to his Lord, and restful in the humblest place where he can catch a glimpse of His face, and so be, as he long after alleged it as his chief title to authority to have been, "a witness of the sufferings of Christ."—*Expositions of Holy Scripture*

III. Great diligence was used to procure, for love or money, false witnesses against Christ. They had seized him as a malefactor, and now they had him they had no indictment to prefer against him, but they *sought for witnesses against him,* if they *would accuse him, v.* 55, 56. The chief priests and elders were by the law entrusted with the prosecuting and punishing of *false witnesses* (Deut. xix. 16, 17). It is time to cry, *Help, Lord,* when the physicians of a land are its troublers, and those that should be the conservators of peace and equity, are the corrupters of both.

G. CAMPBELL MORGAN:

The fundamental wrong, so far as the rulers were concerned, was that the whole case was prejudged. That is perfectly patent. "The chief priests and the whole council sought witness against Jesus"—by no means to discover the truth concerning Him but "to put him to death." The revelation of some intellectual obscurity or wickedness is obvious. They were gathered together ostensibly for the purpose of investigation; but really they were mastered by one determination; the death of the Man who was arraigned before them. The inevitable issue of such a gathering would be that of ignorance. Light could not penetrate their minds. They were predetermined to encompass, at all costs, the destruction of the Prisoner at the bar. Ignorance must be the result of that attitude of mind. There was no room for light. What was said by one and another was contorted, twisted, to the one purpose of putting Him to death.

Let us watch the proceedings, for they reveal some striking facts. These men, mastered by this unholy passion, set upon realizing and encompassing the death of this Prisoner at the bar, were nevertheless compelled to a recognition of the rights of truth. Else why should they look for witnesses at all? Why not dispense with a trial, and at once lay violent hands upon Him? No, that even they dare not do. They must seek some accusation which will appear to be true. They must find witnesses; they must have some reason for the thing they do. This was the unconscious compliment which devilish falsehood paid to the ascendancy of truth.

JAMIESON, FAUSSET, BROWN

going on around the fire, and turned and looked upon Peter (Luke 22:61). **and he sat with the servants, and warmed himself at the fire**—The graphic details, here omitted, are supplied in the other Gospels. John 18:18, "And the servants and officers stood there" that is, in the hall, within the quadrangle, open to the sky, "who had made a fire of coals," or charcoal (in a brazier probably), "for it was cold." John alone of all the Evangelists mentions the *material,* and the *coldness* of the night, as WEBSTER and WILKINSON remark. The elevated situation of Jerusalem, observes THOLUCK, renders it so cold about Easter as to make a watch fire at night indispensable. "And Peter stood with them and warmed himself." "He went in," says Matthew (26:58), "and sat with the servants *to see the end."* These two minute statements throw an interesting light on each other. His wishing to "see the end," or issue of these proceedings, was what led him into the palace, for he evidently feared the worst. But once in, the serpent-coil is drawn closer; it is a cold night, and why should not he take advantage of the fire as well as others? Besides, in the talk of the crowd about the all-engrossing topic he may pick up something which he would like to hear. Poor Peter! But now, let us leave him warming himself at the fire, and listening to the hum of talk about this strange case by which the subordinate officials, passing to and fro and crowding around the fire in this open court, would while away the time; and, following what appears the order of the Evangelical Narrative, let us turn to Peter's Lord.

The Judicial Trial and Condemnation of the Lord Jesus by the Sanhedrim (vss. 55-64). But let the reader observe, that though this is introduced by the Evangelist before any of the denials of Peter are recorded, we have given reasons for concluding that probably the *first two denials* took place while our Lord was with Annas, and the last only during the trial before the Sanhedrim. **55. And the chief priests and all the council sought for witness against Jesus to put him to death**—Matthew (26:59) says they "sought *false* witness." They knew they could find nothing valid; but having their Prisoner to bring before Pilate, they behooved to *make a case.* **and found none**—none that would suit their purpose, or make a decent ground of charge before Pilate. **56. For many bare false witness against him**—From their debasing themselves to *"seek"* them, we are led to infer that they were *bribed* to bear false witness; though there are never wanting sycophants enough, ready to sell themselves for naught, if they may but get a smile from those above them: see a similar scene in Acts 6:11-14. How is one reminded here of that complaint, "False witnesses did rise up: they laid to my charge things that I knew not" (Ps. 31:11)!—**but their witness agreed not together**—If even *two* of them had been agreed, it would have been greedily enough laid hold of, as all that the law insisted upon even in capital cases (Deut. 17:6). But even in this they failed. One cannot but admire the providence which secured this result; since, on the one hand, it seems astonishing that those unscrupulous prosecutors and their ready tools should so bungle a business in which they felt their whole interests bound up; and, on the other hand, if they *had* succeeded in making even a plausible case, the effect on the progress of the Gospel might for a time have been injurious. But at the very time when His enemies were saying, "God hath forsaken Him; persecute and take Him; for there is none to deliver Him" (Ps. 71:11), He whose Witness He was and whose work He was doing was keeping Him as the apple of His eye, and while He was making the wrath of man to praise Him, was restraining the remainder of that wrath (Ps. 76:10). **57. And there arose certain, and bare false witness against him**—Matthew (26:60) is more precise here: *"At the last* came two false witnesses." As no two had before agreed in anything, they felt it necessary to secure a duplicate testimony to something, but they were long of succeeding. And what was it, when at length it was brought forward? **saying, 58. We heard him say, I will destroy this temple that is made with hands, and within three days I will build another made without hands**—On this charge, observe, first, that eager as His enemies were to find criminal matter against our Lord, they had to go back to the outset of His ministry, His first visit to Jerusalem, more than three years before this. In all that He said and did after that, though ever increasing in boldness, they could find nothing. Next, that even then, they fix only on one speech, of two or three words, which they dared to adduce against Him. Further, they most manifestly pervert the

ADAM CLARKE

54. *Peter followed.* On Peter's denial, see Matt. xxvi. 57, etc. *At the fire.* Literally, "at the light," i.e., a fire that cast considerable light, in consequence of which the maidservant was the better able to distinguish him; see v. 67.

And sat with the servants, to see the end. When a man is weak in faith and can as yet only follow Christ at a distance, he should avoid all dangerous places and the company of those who are most likely to prove a snare to him.

All the council, sought false witness. What a prostitution of justice! They first resolve to ruin Him, and then seek the proper means of effecting it; they declare Him criminal, and after that do all they can to fix some crime upon Him, that they may appear to have some shadow of justice on their side when they put Him to death.

I am able to destroy the temple of God. (1) These words were not fairly quoted. Jesus had said, John ii. 19, "Destroy this temple, and in three days I will raise it up." (2) The innuendo which they produce, applying these words to a pretended design to destroy the temple at Jerusalem, was utterly unfair; for these words He spoke of the temple of His body.

MATTHEW HENRY

True, there was a ghastly readiness to compromise, to accept as true the basest falsehood, if only it might be made to serve their purpose of having an appearance of truth. Oh! it was an unholy business; it is a terrible picture. Yet it is a wonderful illustration of that marvelous and inherent consciousness of right and wrong, from which humanity never has, and never can escape. Whenever humanity forgets to make its bow to truth, then humanity is entirely and absolutely hopeless.

—The Gospel According to Mark

IV. He was at length charged with words which, as they were represented, seemed to threaten *the temple* (*v.* 57, 58), but the witnesses to this matter did not agree (*v.* 59). *Their testimony was not sufficient*, nor equal to the charge of a capital crime; they did not accuse him of that upon which a *sentence of death* might be founded.

V. He was urged to be his own accuser (*v.* 60); The *high priest stood up* and said, *Answerest thou nothing?* This he said under pretence of justice and fair dealing, but really with a design to ensnare him, that they might *accuse him.* We may well imagine with what an air of haughtiness and disdain this proud high priest brought our Lord Jesus to this question. Pleased to think that *he* seemed silent, who had so often silenced those that picked quarrels with him. Still Christ *answered nothing*, that he might set us an example, 1. Of *patience* under calumnies and false accusations. 2. Of *prudence*, when a man shall be made an *offender for a word*, and our *de*fence made our *of*fence.

VI. When he was asked *whether he was the Christ*, he confessed, and denied not, that *he was*, *v.* 61, 62. He asked, *Art thou the Son of the Blessed?* that is, the Son of *God*?

And for the proof of his being the *Son of God*, he binds them over to his second coming; "*Ye shall see the Son of man sitting on the right hand of power*; that *Son of man* that now appears so mean you shall shortly see and *tremble before*." Now, one would think that such a word as this should have startled the court, and at least, in the opinion of some of them, should have amounted to a *demurrer*, or *arrest of judgment*. When Paul at the bar reasoned of the *judgment to come*, the judge *trembled*, and adjourned the trial, Acts. xxiv. 25.

JAMIESON, FAUSSET, BROWN

speech of our Lord. We say not this because in Mark's form of it, it differs from the report of the words given by the Fourth Evangelist (John 2:18-22)—the only one of the Evangelists who reports it all, or mentions even any visit paid by our Lord to Jerusalem before His last—but because the one report bears truth, and the other falsehood, on its face. When our Lord said on that occasion, "Destroy this temple, and in three days I will raise it up," they *might*, for a moment, have understood Him to refer to the temple out of whose courts He had swept the buyers and sellers. But *after* they had expressed their astonishment at His words, in that sense of them, and reasoned upon the time it had taken to rear the temple as it then stood, since *no answer* to this appears to have been given by our Lord, it is hardly conceivable that they should continue in the persuasion that this was really His meaning. But finally, even if the more ignorant among them had done so, it is next to certain that *the ecclesiastics*, who were *the prosecutors* in this case, *did not believe that this was His meaning.* For in less than three days after this they went to Pilate, saying, "Sir, we remember that that deceiver said, while he was yet alive, *after three days I will rise again*" (Matt. 27:63). Now what utterance of Christ known to His enemies, *could* this refer to, if not to this very saying about destroying and rearing up the temple? And if so, it puts it beyond a doubt that by this time, at least, they were perfectly aware that our Lord's words referred to *His death by their hands and His resurrection by His own.* But this is confirmed by the next verse. **59. But neither so did their witness agree together**—i.e., not even as to so brief a speech, consisting of but a few words, was there such a concurrence in their mode of reporting it as to make out a decent case. In such a charge *everything depended on the very terms alleged to have been used.* For every one must see that a very slight turn, either way, given to such words, would make them either something like *indictable matter,* or else a *ridiculous ground for a criminal charge*—would either give them a colorable pretext for the charge of impiety which they were bent on making out, or else make the whole saying appear, on the worst view that could be taken of it, as merely some mystical or empty boast. **60. Answerest thou nothing? what is it which these witness against thee?**—Clearly, they felt that *their case had failed,* and by this artful question the high priest hoped to get *from His own mouth* what they had in vain tried to obtain from their false and contradictory witnesses. But in this, too, they failed. **61. But he held his peace, and answered nothing**—This must have nonplussed them. But they were not to be easily baulked of their object. **Again the high priest**—arose (Matt. 26:62), matters having now come to a crisis. **asked him, and said unto him, Art thou the Christ, the Son of the Blessed?**—Why our Lord should have answered this question, when He was silent as to the former, we might not have quite seen, but for Matthew, who says (26:63) that the high priest *put Him upon solemn oath,* saying, "I adjure Thee by the living God, that Thou tell us whether Thou be the Christ, the Son of God." Such an adjuration was understood to render an answer legally necessary (Lev. 5:1). **62. And Jesus said, I am**—or, as in Matthew 26:64, "Thou hast said [it]." In Luke, however (22:70), the answer, "Ye say that I am," should be rendered—as DE WETTE, MEYER, ELLICOTT, and the best critics agree that the preposition requires—"Ye say [it], for I am [so]." Some words, however, were spoken by our Lord before giving His answer to this solemn question. These are recorded by Luke alone (22:67, 68): "Art Thou the Christ [they asked]? tell us. And He said unto them, If I tell you, ye will not believe: and if I also ask [interrogate] "you, ye will not answer Me, nor let Me go." This seems to have been uttered before giving His direct answer, as a calm remonstrance and dignified protest against the prejudgment of His case and the unfairness of their mode of procedure. But now let us hear the rest of the answer, in which the conscious majesty of Jesus breaks forth from behind the dark cloud which overhung Him as He stood before the Council. **and**—in that character—**ye shall see the Son of man sitting on the right hand of power, and coming in the clouds of heaven**—In Matthew (26:64) a slightly different but interesting turn is given to it by one word: "Thou hast said [it]: nevertheless"—We prefer this sense of the word to "besides," which some recent critics decide for—"I say unto you, Hereafter shall ye see the Son of man sit on the right hand of power, and coming in the clouds of heaven." The word rendered "hereafter" means, not

ADAM CLARKE

ALEXANDER MACLAREN:

The single specimen of the worthless evidence given may be either a piece of misunderstanding or of malicious twisting of innocent words; nor can we decide whether the witnesses contradicted one another or each himself. The former is the more probable, as the fundamental principle of the Jewish law of evidence ("two or three witnesses") would, in that case, rule out the testimony. The saying which they garble meant the very opposite of what they made it mean. It represented Jesus as the restorer of that which Israel should destroy. It referred to His body which is the true Temple; but the symbolic temple "made with hands" is so inseparably connected with the real, that the fate of the one determines that of the other. Strangely significant, therefore, is it, that the rulers heard again, though distorted, at that moment when they were on their trial, the far-reaching sentence, which might have taught them that in slaying Jesus they were throwing down the temple and all which centered in it, and that by His resurrection, His own act, He would build up again a new polity, which yet was but the old transfigured, even "the church, which is his body." His work destroys nothing but "the works of the devil." He is the restorer of the divine ordinances and gifts which men destroy, and His death and resurrection bring back in nobler form all the good things lost by sin, "the desolations of many generations." The history of all subsequent attacks on Christ is mirrored here. The foregone conclusion, the evidence sought as an after-thought to give a colorable pretext, the material found by twisting His teaching, the blindness which accuses Him of destroying what He restores, and fancies itself as preserving what it is destroying, have all reappeared over and over again.

—Expositions of Holy Scripture

I adjure thee by the living God. I put Thee to Thy oath. To this solemn adjuration Christ immediately replies, because He is now called on, in the name of God, to bear another testimony to the truth.

Thou hast said. That is, I am the Christ, the promised Messiah (see on v. 25) and you and this whole nation shall shortly have the fullest proof of it.

For *hereafter,* in a few years, *shall ye see the Son of man sitting on the right hand of power,* fully invested with absolute dominion, *and coming in the clouds of heaven,* to execute judgment upon this wicked race. Our Lord appears to refer to Dan. vii. 13: "One like the Son of man came with the clouds of heaven." This may also refer to the final judgment.

MATTHEW HENRY

TODAY'S DICTIONARY OF THE BIBLE:

Son of Man. (1.) Denotes mankind generally, with special reference to their weakness and frailty (Job 25:6; Ps. 8:4; 144:3; 146:3; Isa. 51:12, etc.).

(2.) It is a title frequently given to the prophet Ezekiel, probably to remind him of his human weakness.

(3.) In the New Testament it is used forty-three times as a distinctive title of the Savior. In the Old Testament it is used only in Ps. 80:17 and Dan. 7:13 with this application. While there is much debate over the meaning of this title, it is almost certain that it does not denote Christ's humanity but rather is a title with far-reaching messianic implications.

VII. The high priest, upon this confession of his, convicted him as *a blasphemer* (*v.* 63); He *rent his clothes.* If Saul's rending Samuel's mantle was made to signify the rending of the kingdom from him (1 Sam. xv. 27, 28), much more did Caiaphas's rending his own clothes signify the rending of the priesthood from him, as the rending of the veil, at Christ's death, signified the throwing of all open.

VIII. They agreed that he was a blasphemer, and, as such, was guilty of a capital crime, *v.* 64. So they *all condemned him* to be *guilty of death*; what friends he had in the great sanhedrim, did not appear, it is probable that they had not notice.

IX. They set themselves to abuse him and to make sport with him, *v.* 65. It should seem that some of the priests themselves so far forgot the dignity, and the gravity which became them, that they helped their servants in playing the fool with a condemned prisoner. This they made their diversion, while they *waited for the morning.* If they did not think it below them to abuse Christ, shall we think anything below us, by which we may do him honour.

Verses 66–72

We have here the story of Peter's denying Christ.

1. It began in *keeping at a distance* from him. Peter had followed *afar off* (*v.* 54). Those that are *shy* of Christ, are in a fair way to *deny* him.

JAMIESON, FAUSSET, BROWN

"at some future time" (as today "hereafter commonly does), but what the English word originally signified, "after here," "after now," or "from this time." Accordingly, in Luke 22:69, the words used mean "from now." So that though the reference we have given it to the day of His glorious Second Appearing is too obvious to admit of doubt, He would, by using the expression, "From this time," convey the important thought which He had before expressed, immediately after the traitor left the supper-table to do his dark work, "*Now* is the Son of man glorified" (John 13:31). At this moment, and by this speech, did He "witness *the* good confession" emphatically and properly, as the apostle says in I Timothy 6:13. Our translators render the words there, "Who *before* Pontius Pilate witnessed"; referring it to the admission of His being a *King,* in the presence of Cæsar's own chief representative. But it should be rendered, as LUTHER renders it, and as the best interpreters now understand it, "Who *under* Pontius Pilate witnessed . . . In this view of it, the apostle is referring not to what our Lord confessed *before* Pilate—which, though noble, was not of such primary importance—but to that sublime confession which, under Pilate's administration, He witnessed before the only competent tribunal on such occasions, the Supreme Ecclesiastical Council of God's chosen nation, that He was THE MESSIAH, and THE SON OF THE BLESSED ONE; in the former word owning His Supreme *Official,* in the latter His Supreme *Personal,* Dignity. **63. Then the high priest rent his clothes**—On this expression of *horror of blasphemy,* see II Kings 18: 37—**and saith, What need we any further witnesses? 64. Ye have heard the blasphemy**—(See John 10: 33). In Luke (22:71), "For we ourselves have heard of His own mouth"—an affectation of religious horror. **what think ye?**—'Say what the verdict is to be.' **they all condemned him to be guilty of death**—or of a capital crime, which *blasphemy* against God was according to the Jewish law (Lev. 24:16). Yet *not absolutely all;* for *Joseph* of Arimathea, "a good man and a just," was one of that Council, and "*he was not a consenting party* to the counsel and deed of them," for that is the strict sense of the words of Luke 23:50, 51. Probably he absented himself, and *Nicodemus* also, from this meeting of the Council, the temper of which they would know too well to expect their voice to be listened to; and in that case, the words of our Evangelist are to be taken strictly, that, without one dissentient voice, "all [present] condemned him to be guilty of death."

The Blessed One Is Now Shamefully Entreated (vs. 65). Every word here must be carefully observed, and the several accounts put together, that we may lose none of the awful indignities about to be described. **65. some began to spit on him**—or, as in Matthew 26:67, "to spit in [into] His face." Luke (22:63) says in addition, "And the men that held Jesus mocked him"—or cast their jeers at Him. **to cover his face**—or "to blindfold him" (as in Luke 22:64). **to buffet him**—Luke's word, which is rendered "smote Him" (22:63), is a stronger one, conveying an idea for which we have an exact equivalent in English, but one too colloquial to be inserted here—**began to say unto him, Prophesy**—In Matthew 26:68 this is given more fully: "Prophesy unto us, thou Christ, Who is he that smote Thee?" The sarcastic fling at Him as "*the Christ,*" and the demand of Him in this character to name the unseen perpetrator of the blows inflicted on Him, was in them as infamous as to Him it must have been, and was intended to be, stinging. **and the servants did strike him with the palms of their hands**—or "struck Him on the face" (Luke 22:64). Ah! Well did He say prophetically, in that Messianic prediction which we have often referred to, "I gave My back to the smiters, and My cheeks to them that plucked off the hair: I hid not My face from shame and spitting!" (Isa. 50:6). "And many other things blasphemously spake they against Him" (Luke 22:65). This general statement is important, as showing that virulent and varied as were the *recorded* affronts put upon Him, they are but a *small specimen* of what He endured on that dark occasion.

Peter's FIRST DENIAL *of His Lord* (vss. 66-68). **66. And as Peter was beneath in the palace**—This little word "*beneath*"—one of our Evangelist's graphic touches—is most important for the right understanding of what we may call the topography of the scene. We must take it in connection with Matthew's word (26:69): "Now Peter sat *without* in the palace"—or quadrangular court, in the center of which the fire would be burning; and crowding around and buzzing about it would be the menials

ADAM CLARKE

TODAY'S DICTIONARY OF THE BIBLE:

Blasphemy. In the sense of speaking evil of God, this word is found in Ps. 74:18; Isa. 52:5; Rom. 2:24; Rev. 13:1, 6; 16:9, 11, 21. It denotes also any kind of calumny, or evil-speaking, or abuse (1 Kings 21:10; Acts 13:45; 18:6, etc.). Our Lord was accused of blasphemy when he claimed to be the Son of God (Matt. 26:65; comp. Matt. 9:3; Mark 2:7). They who deny his messiahship blaspheme Jesus (Luke 22:65; John 10:36).

The high priest rent his clothes. This rending of the high priest's garments was expressly contrary to the law, Lev. x. 6 and xxi. 10. But it was a common method of expressing violent grief, Gen. xxxvii. 29, 34; Job i. 20, and horror at what was deemed blasphemous or impious, 2 Kings xviii. 37; xix. 1; Acts xiv. 14. All that heard a blasphemous speech were obliged to rend their clothes, and never to sew them up again.

He is guilty of death. "He is liable to death." All the forms of justice are here violated. The judge becomes a party and accuser, and proceeds to the verdict without examining whether all the prophecies concerning the Messiah and the innumerable miracles which He wrought did not justify Him.

Then did they spit in his face. This was done as a mark of the most profound contempt. See Job xvi. 10 and xxx. 10; Isa. l. 6; Mic. v. 1. The judges now delivered Him into the hands of the mob. _And buffeted him._ Smote Him with their fists. "Beat with the hand, the fingers being clenched." _Smote him with the palms of their hands._ "Smite the cheek with the open hand."

Prophesy unto us, thou Christ. Their conduct toward Him now was expressly prophesied of, by a man whose divine mission they did not pretend to deny; see Isa. l. 6. It appears that, before they buffeted Him, they bound up His eyes; see Mark xiv. 65.

MATTHEW HENRY

2. It was occasioned by his associating with the high priest's servants. They that think it dangerous to be in company with Christ's disciples, because thence they may be drawn in to *suffer for him,* will find it much more dangerous to be in company with his enemies, because there they may be drawn into *sin against him.*

3. The temptation was, his being charged as a disciple of Christ; *Thou also wert with Jesus of Nazareth, v.* 67.

G. CAMPBELL MORGAN:

Let us try to put the doings of these two places side by side. Probably the court where Jesus stood in the midst of the priests and elders was somewhat elevated, by a few steps perhaps, from "the court beneath," as Mark says, where the officers and the maid-servants were, and Peter also. In the first false witness after false witness arose; the high priest put Jesus on oath; Jesus took the oath that the confession that Peter made several months ago was true. In the second, there was the clamor of the gossip of the officers, the saucy laugh of a servant maid, as she said to Peter, "You belong to them." The great soul of Peter stumbled and fell at the laugh of that serving-maid, and presently he took an oath that he did not know Jesus; Jesus on oath, within; Peter on oath, without. Peter outside, taking his oath that he did not know Him; Jesus inside, taking His oath that what Peter had said in the better hour of his life was true. The contrast is vivid.
—*The Gospel According to Mark*

This is one of them (*v.* 69), *for thou art a Galilean,* one may know that by thy speaking broad, *v.* 70. It doth not appear that he was *challenged* upon it, but only *bantered* upon it, and in danger of being ridiculed as a fool for it. Sometimes the cause of Christ seems to fall so much on the losing side, that everybody has a stone to throw at it. Yet, all things considered, the temptation could not be called *formidable*; it was only a *maid* that casually cast her eye upon him, and said, *Thou art one of them,* to which he needed not to have made any reply.

JAMIESON, FAUSSET, BROWN

and others who had been admitted within the court. At the upper end of this court, probably, would be the memorable chamber in which the trial was held —*open to the court,* likely, and *not far from the fire* (as we gather from Luke 22:61), but *on a higher level*; for (as our verse says) the court, with Peter in it, was "beneath" it. The ascent to the Council chamber was perhaps by a short flight of steps. If the reader will bear this explanation in mind, he will find the intensely interesting details which follow more intelligible. **there cometh one of the maids of the high priest**—"the damsel that kept the door" (John 18:17). The Jews seem to have employed women as porters of their doors (Acts 12:13). **67. And when she saw Peter warming himself, she looked upon him**—Luke (22:56) is here more graphic; "But a certain maid beheld him as he sat by the fire"—lit., 'by the *light,*' which, shining full upon him, revealed him to the girl—"and earnestly looked upon him"—or, 'fixed her gaze upon him.' His demeanor and timidity, which must have attracted notice, as so generally happens, leading," says OLSHAUSEN, "to the recognition of him." **and said, And thou also wast with Jesus of Nazareth**—"with Jesus the Nazarene," or, "with Jesus of Galilee" (Matthew 26:69). The *sense* of this is given in John's report of it (18:17), "Art not thou also one of this man's disciples?" i.e., thou as well as "that other disciple," whom she knew to be one, but did not challenge, perceiving that he was a privileged person. In Luke (22:56) it is given as a remark made by the maid to one of the bystanders—this man was also with Him." If so expressed in Peter's hearing—drawing upon him the eyes of every one that heard it (as we know it did, Matt. 26:70), and compelling him to answer to it—that would explain the different forms of the report naturally enough. But in such a case this is of no real importance. **68. But he denied**—"before all" (Matt. 26:70). **saying, I know not, neither understand I what thou sayest**—in Luke, "I know Him not." **And he went out into the porch**—the vestibule leading to the street—no doubt finding the fire-place too *hot* for him; possibly also with the hope of escaping—but that was not to be, and perhaps he dreaded that, too. Doubtless by this time his mind would be getting into a sea of commotion, and would fluctuate every moment in its resolves. AND THE COCK CREW. See on Luke 22:34. This, then, was the First Denial.

Peter's SECOND DENIAL *of His Lord* (vss. 69, 70). There is here a verbal difference among the Evangelists, which without some information which has been withheld, cannot be quite extricated. **69. And a maid saw him again**—or, "a girl." It might be rendered "the girl"; but this would not necessarily mean the same one as before, but might, and probably does, mean just the female who had charge of the door or gate near which Peter now was. Accordingly, in Matthew 26:71, she is expressly called "another [maid]." But in Luke it is a *male* servant: "And after a little while (from the time of the first denial) another"—i.e., as the word signifies, "another male" servant. But there is no real difficulty, as the challenge, probably, after being made by one was reiterated by another. Accordingly, in John, it is, "*They* said therefore unto him . . .," as if more than one challenged him at once. **and began to say to them that stood by, This is one of them**—or, as in Matthew 26:71—"This [fellow] was also with Jesus the Nazarene." **70. And he denied it again**—In Luke, "Man, I am not." But worst of all in Matthew—"And again he denied with an oath, I do not know the man" (26:72). This was the Second Denial, more vehement, alas! than the first.

Peter's THIRD DENIAL *of His Lord.* (vss. 70-72). **70. And a little after**—"about the space of one hour after" (Luke 22:59). **they that stood by said again to Peter, Surely thou art one of them: for thou art a Galilean, and thy speech agreeth thereto**—"bewrayeth (or "discovereth") thee" (Matt. 26:73). In Luke it is, "Another confidently affirmed, saying, Of a truth this [fellow] also was with him: for he is a Galilean." The Galilean dialect had a more *Syrian* cast than that of Judea. *If Peter had held his peace,* this peculiarity had not been observed; but hoping, probably, to put them off the scent by joining in the *fireside talk,* he was thus discovered. The Fourth Gospel is particularly interesting here: "One of the servants of the high priest, being his kinsman (or kinsman to him) whose ear Peter cut off, saith, Did not I see thee in the garden with Him?" (John 18:26.) No doubt his relationship to Malchus drew his attention to the man who had smitten him, and this enabled him to identify Peter. "Sad reprisals!" exclaims BENGEL. Poor Peter!

ADAM CLARKE

A damsel came unto him. "A maidservant." *Thou also wast with Jesus.* What a noble opportunity had Peter now to show his zeal for the insulted cause of truth and his attachment to his Master!

G. CAMPBELL MORGAN:

Peter was lying about his faith. He did know Him; more, he wonderfully understood Him. He was also violating his own love. Here was an instance of the contradiction of sinners against themselves. He was wounding his own soul. This must be borne in mind. Peter's love for Jesus never failed; his faith in Jesus never failed. Christ had said to him, "I have prayed for thee that thy faith fail not," and his faith never failed. His hope failed, the light of hope went out; his courage failed; but never his faith, nor his love. Here, then, was a man who believed in Jesus, who loved Him with a great heart, or he never would have followed Him to that court; denying his faith, and the denial was a lie; denying his love, and the denial was a lie. His own intelligence was insulted; the truth that was in him, and never really destroyed, was flung in the mire.—*The Gospel According to Mark*

And again he denied with an oath. He has told a lie, and he swears to support it. A liar has always some suspicion that his testimony is not credited, for he is conscious of his own falsity, and is therefore naturally led to support his assertions by oaths.

Thy speech. "Your manner of speech," "that dialect of yours"—his accent being different from that of Jerusalem. *Bewrayeth thee.* "Makes you manifest."

MATTHEW HENRY

4. The sin was very great; he *denied Christ before men*, at a time when he ought to have confessed and owned him. Christ had often given notice to his disciples of his own sufferings; yet, when they came, they were to Peter as great a surprise and terror as if he had never heard of them before. When Christ was admired and flocked after, he could readily own him; but now that he is deserted, and despised, and run down, he is ashamed of him, and will own no relation to him.

5. His repentance was very speedy. He repeated his denial thrice, and the third was worst of all, for then he *cursed* and *swore*, to confirm his denial.

Then the *cock crew* the second time, which put him in mind of his Master's words, the warning he had given him, with that particular circumstance of the *cock crowing twice*; and when he thought thereon, he wept. Some observe that this evangelist, who wrote, as some have thought, by St. Peter's direction, speaks as fully of Peter's sin as any of them, but more briefly of his *sorrow*, which Peter, in modesty, would not have to be magnified, and because he thought he could never sorrow enough for so great a sin. *Fixing his mind upon it*, he wept. It is not a transient thought of that which is humbling, that will suffice, but we must dwell upon it.

JAMIESON, FAUSSET, BROWN

Thou art caught in thine own toils; but like a wild bull in a net, thou wilt toss and rage, filling up the measure of thy terrible declension by one more denial of thy Lord, and that the foulest of all. **71. But he began to curse**—'anathematize,' or wish himself accursed if what he was now to say was not true. **and to swear**—or to take a solemn oath. **saying, I know not this man of whom ye speak. 72. And the second time the cock crew.** The other three Evangelists, who mention but one crowing of the cock—and that not the first, but the second and last one of Mark—all say the cock crew "immediately," but Luke says, "Immediately, while he yet spake, the cock crew" (22:60). Alas!—But now comes the wonderful sequel.

The Redeemer's Look upon Peter, and Peter's Bitter Tears (vs. 72; Luke 22:61, 62). It has been observed that while the beloved disciple is the only one of the four Evangelists who does not record the repentance of Peter, he is the only one of the four who records the affecting and most beautiful scene of his complete restoration (John 21:15-17). Luke 22:61: "And the Lord turned and looked upon Peter." How? it will be asked. We answer, From the chamber in which the trial was going on, in the direction of the court where Peter then stood —in the way already explained. See on vs. 66. Our Second Evangelist makes no mention of this look, but dwells on the warning of his Lord about the double crowing of the cock, which would announce his triple fall, as what rushed stingingly to his recollection and made him dissolve in tears. **And Peter called to mind the word that Jesus said unto him, Before the cock crow twice, thou shalt deny me thrice. And when he thought thereon, he wept**—To the same effect is the statement of the First Evangelist (Matt. 26:75), save that like "the beloved physician," he notices the "bitterness" of the weeping. The most precious link, however, in the whole chain of circumstances in this scene is beyond doubt that "look" of deepest, tenderest import reported by Luke alone. Who can tell what lightning flashes of wounded love and piercing reproach shot from that "look" through the eye of Peter into his heart! "And Peter remembered the word of the Lord, how He had said unto him, Before the cock crow, thou shalt deny Me thrice. And Peter went out and wept bitterly." How different from the sequel of Judas' act! Doubtless the hearts of the two men towards the Saviour were perfectly different from the first; and the treason of Judas was but the consummation of the wretched man's resistance of the blaze of light in the midst of which he had lived for three years, while Peter's denial was but a momentary obscuration of the heavenly light and love to his Master which ruled his life. But the immediate cause of the blessed revulsion which made Peter "weep bitterly" was, beyond all doubt, this heart-piercing "look" which his Lord gave him. And remembering the Saviour's own words at the table, "Simon, Simon, Satan hath desired to have you, that he may sift you as wheat; *but I prayed for thee, that thy faith fail not,*" may we not say that *this prayer fetched down all that there was in that "look"* to pierce and break the heart of Peter, to keep it from despair, to work in it "repentance unto salvation not to be repented of," and at length, under other healing touches, to "restore his soul?" (See on Mark 16:7.)

ADAM CLARKE

Then began he to curse and to swear. Rather, "Then he began positively to affirm." *The cock crew.* This animal becomes, in the hand of God, the instrument of awaking the fallen apostle at last to a sense of his fall, danger, and duty.

Peter remembered the word of Jesus. Luke says, chap. xxii. 61, "The Lord turned, and looked upon Peter." *And wept bitterly.* Felt bitter anguish of soul, which evidenced itself by the tears of contrition which flowed plentifully from his eyes. "Let him that standeth take heed lest he fall." Where the mighty have been slain, what shall support the feeble? Only the grace of the almighty God. This transaction is recorded by the inspired penmen: (1) That all may watch unto prayer, and shun the occasions of sin. (2) That if a man be unhappily overtaken in a fault, he may not despair, but cast himself immediately with a contrite heart on the infinite tenderness and compassion of God.

MATTHEW HENRY

CHAPTER 15

Verses 1–14

I. A *consultation* held by the great Sanhedrim for the effectual prosecution of our Lord Jesus. They met *early in the morning* about it; they lost no time, but followed their blow in good earnest. The unwearied industry of wicked people in doing that which is evil, should shame us for our backwardness and slothfulness in that which is good.

II. The delivering of him up a prisoner to Pilate; they *bound him*. Christ was bound, to make bonds easy to us, and enable us, as Paul and Silas, to sing in bonds. It is good for us often to *remember the bonds* of the Lord Jesus, as bound with him who was *bound for us*. They led him through the streets of Jerusalem, to expose *him* to contempt, and we may well imagine how miserably he looked after such a night's usage as he had had. They voluntarily betrayed him that was *Israel's crown*, to them that were *Israel's yoke*.

III. The examining of him by Pilate upon interrogatories (*v.* 2); "*Art thou the king of the Jews?*" "Yea," saith Christ, "it is as *thou sayest*, I am that Messiah."

IV. The articles of impeachment exhibited against him, and his silence under the charge and accusation.

JAMIESON, FAUSSET, BROWN

CHAPTER 15

Vss. 1-20. Jesus Is Brought before Pilate—At a Second Hearing, Pilate, after Seeking to Release Him, Delivers Him Up—After Being Cruelly Entreated, He Is Led Away to Be Crucified. (=Matt.26:1, 2, 11-31; Luke 23:1-6, 13-25; John 18:28-19:16.) See on John 18:28-19; 16. **Then led they Jesus from Caiaphas to the hall of judgment**—but not till "in the morning the chief priests held a consultation with the elders and scribes and the whole council against Him to put Him to death, and bound Him" (Matt. 27:1; and see on Mark 15:1). The word here rendered "hall of judgment" is from the Latin, and denotes 'the palace of the governor of a Roman province.'

Pilate . . . called Jesus, and said . . . , Art thou the King of the Jews?—In Luke 23:2 they charge our Lord before Pilate with "perverting the nation, and forbidding to give tribute to Cæsar, saying that He Himself is Christ a king." Perhaps this was what occasioned Pilate's question.

ADAM CLARKE

CHAPTER 15

1. *In the morning.* See Matt. xxvii. 1, etc.

When the morning was come. As soon as it was light. *Took counsel against Jesus.* They had begun this counsel the preceding evening; see chap. xxvi. 59. But as it was contrary to all forms of law to proceed against a person's life by night, they seem to have separated for a few hours, and then, at the break of day, came together again, pretending to conduct the business according to the forms of law.

MATTHEW HENRY

The chief priests turned informers, and did in person *accuse Christ of many things* (*v*. 3), and witness against him, *v*. 4. Wicked priests are generally the worst of men. The better anything is, the worse it is when it is corrupted. These priests were very eager and noisy in their accusation; but Christ *answered nothing*, *v*. 3. While Pilate urged him to clear himself, and was desirous he should (*v*. 4), yet still he stood mute (*v*. 5), he *answered nothing*, which Pilate thought very strange. He gave Pilate a direct answer (*v*. 2), but would not answer the prosecutors and witnesses, because the things they alleged, were notoriously false, and he knew Pilate himself was convinced they were so. As Christ *spoke* to admiration, so he *kept silence* to admiration.

V. The proposal Pilate made to the people, to have Jesus released to them, since it was the custom of the feast to grace the solemnity with the release of one prisoner. The people expected and demanded that he should do *as he had ever done to them* (*v*. 8). Now Pilate perceived that the chief priests delivered up Jesus *for envy*, *v*. 10. It was easy to see that it was not his *guilt*, but his *goodness*, that they were provoked at. He thought that he might safely appeal from the priests to the people. Let them demand him to be *released*, and Pilate will readily do it. There was indeed another prisoner, *one Barabbas*, that had an interest, and would have some votes; but he questioned not but Jesus would out-poll him.

VI. The unanimous outrageous clamours of the people to have *Christ put to death*, and particularly to have him *crucified*. It was a great surprise to Pilate, when he found that they all agreed to desire that Barabbas might be *released*, *v*. 11. Pilate opposed it all he could; "*What will ye that I shall do to him whom ye call the King of the Jews?*" *v*. 12. They say, *Crucify him*. When Pilate objected, *Why, what evil has he done?* they did not pretend to answer it, but *cried out the more exceedingly*, *Crucify him, crucify him*. Now the priests promised themselves that it would influence Pilate two ways to condemn him. 1. It might incline him to believe Christ *guilty*, when there was so general an out-cry against him. "Surely," might Pilate think, "he must needs be a bad man, whom all the world is weary of." It has been the common artifice of Satan, to put Christ and his religion into an ill name, and so to run them down. But let us *judge* of persons and things by their merits, and not prejudge by common fame and the cry of the country. 2. It might induce him to condemn Christ, to *please* the people, and indeed for *fear* of *displeasing* them. Though he was not so *weak* as to be governed by their opinion, to believe him guilty, yet he was so *wicked* as to be swayed by their outrage, to condemn him, though he believed him innocent. Our Lord Jesus dying as a *sacrifice* for the *sins of many*, he fell a sacrifice to the *rage of many*.

Verses 15–21

I. Pilate, to gratify the Jews' malice, delivers Christ to be *crucified*, *v*. 15. *Willing to content the people*, he *released Barabbas unto them*, and *delivered Jesus* to be *crucified*. Though he *had scourged him* before, hoping that would *content* them, and then not designing to crucify him, yet he went on to that. He who could persuade himself to *chastise* one that was innocent (Luke xxiii. 16), could by degrees persuade himself to *crucify* him.

Christ was *crucified*, for that was, 1. A *bloody* death, and *without blood no remission*, Heb. ix. 22. Christ was to lay down *his life* for us, and therefore shed *his blood*. 2. It was a *painful* death. Christ died, so as that he might *feel himself die*. Christ would meet death in its greatest terror, and so conquer it. 3. It was a *shameful* death, the death of slaves, and the vilest malefactors. The *cross* and the *shame* are put together. Christ makes *satisfaction* by submitting to the greatest reproach and ignominy. Yet this was not the worst. 4. It was a *cursed* death; thus it was branded by the Jewish law (Deut. xxi. 23). Now that Christ has submitted to be *hanged upon a tree*, the reproach and curse of that kind of death are quite rolled away.

II. Pilate, to gratify the gay humour of the Roman soldiers, delivered him to them, to be abused and spitefully treated. They called together *the whole regiment* that was then in waiting, and they went into an inner hall, where they ignominiously abused our Lord Jesus, as a king. 1. Do kings wear robes of purple or scarlet? They *clothed him with purple*. 2. Do kings wear *crowns*? They *platted a crown of thorns*, and *put it on his head*. A crown of straw, or rushes, would have been banter enough; but this was pain also. He wore the crown of thorns which we had deserved, that we might wear the crown of glory which he merited. 3. Are kings attended with the acclamations of their subjects, *O king, live for ever?*

JAMIESON, FAUSSET, BROWN

"And the chief priests accused Him of *many things*, but He answered nothing (Mark 15.3). Then said Pilate unto Him, Hearest Thou not how many things they witness against Thee? And He answered him to never a word, insomuch that the governor marvelled greatly" (Matt. 27:13, 14). See on Mark 15:3-5. In his perplexity, Pilate, hearing of Galilee, bethinks himself of the expedient of sending Him to Herod, in the hope of thereby further shaking off responsibility in the case. See on Mark 15:6, and on Luke 23:6-12. The return of the prisoner only deepened the perplexity of Pilate, who, "calling together the chief priests, rulers, and people," tells them plainly that not one of their charges against "this man" had been made good, while even Herod, to whose jurisdiction he more naturally belonged, had done nothing to Him: He "will therefore chastise and release him" (Luke 23:13-16). **But ye have a custom that I should release one unto you at the passover . . .**—See on Mark 15:7-11. "On the typical import of the choice of Christ to suffer, by which Barabbas was set free, see Leviticus 16, particularly vss. 5-10, where the subject is the *sin offering* on the great day of atonement" [KRAFFT in LUTHARDT].

they cried out—their fiendish rage kindling afresh at the sight of Him—**Crucify him, crucify him**—

Pilate took Jesus and scourged him—in hope of appeasing them. (See on Mark 15:15.) "And the soldiers led Him away into the palace, and they call the whole band" (Mark 15:16)—the body of the military cohort stationed there—to take part in the mock coronation now to be enacted.

the soldiers platted a crown of thorns, and put it on his head—in mockery of a regal *crown*. **and they put on him a purple robe**—in mockery of the *imperial purple;* first "stripping him" (Matt. 27:28) of His own outer garment. The robe may have been the "gorgeous" one in which Herod arrayed and sent Him back to Pilate (Luke 23:11). "And they put a reed into His right hand" (Matt. 27:29)—in mockery of the regal *scepter*. "And they bowed the knee before Him" (Matt. 27:29).

ADAM CLARKE

He answered nothing. An answer to such accusations was not necessary; they sufficiently confuted themselves.

Marvelled greatly. Silence under calumny manifests the utmost magnanimity. The chief priests did not admire this because it confounded them; but Pilate, who had no interest to serve by it, was deeply affected. This very silence was predicted, Isa. liii. 7.

The governor was wont to release. Whence this custom originated among the Jews is not known; probably it was introduced by the Romans themselves, or by Pilate, merely to oblige the Jews, by showing them this public token of respect.

8. *The multitude crying aloud.* The word itself strongly marks the vociferations or, to come nearer the original word, the bellowing of the multitude. It signifies, properly, a loud and long cry, such as Christ emitted on the Cross. See the whole history of these proceedings against our Lord treated at large on Matthew xxvii.

A notable prisoner called Barabbas. This person had, a short time before, raised an insurrection in Jerusalem, in which it appears, from Mark xv. 7, some lives were lost. In some MSS. this man has the surname of *Jesus*.

For envy. "Through malice." Then it was his business, as an upright judge, to disperse this mob, and immediately release Jesus. Seeing malice is capable of putting even Christ himself to death, how careful should we be not to let the least spark of it harbor in our breasts! Let it be remembered that malice as often originates from *envy* as it does from anger.

What shall I do then with Jesus? Showing, hereby, that it was his wish to release Him.

Scourged Jesus. This is allowed to have been a very severe punishment of itself among the Romans, the flesh being generally cut by the whips used for this purpose. It has been thought that Pilate might have spared this additional cruelty of whipping, but it appears that it was a common custom to scourge those criminals which were to be crucified (see Josephus De Bello, lib. ii, c. 25), and lenity in Christ's case is not to be allowed; He must take all the misery in full tale. *Delivered him to be crucified.* Tacitus, the Roman historian, mentions the death of Christ in very remarkable terms: "Nero put those who commonly went by the name of Christians to the most exquisite tortures. The author of this name was Christ, who was capitally punished in the reign of Tiberius, by Pontius Pilate the Procurator."

17. *And platted a crown of thorns.* In the note on Matt. xxvii. 29, I have ventured to express a doubt whether our Lord was crowned with *thorns*, in our sense of the word, this crown being designed as an instrument of torture. I am still of the same opinion, having considered the subject more closely since writing that note.

MATTHEW HENRY

That also is mimicked; they saluted him with "*Hail, King of the Jews*." 4. Kings have *sceptres* put into their hand, marks of dominion; to imitate this, they put a *reed in his right hand*. Those who despise the authority of the Lord Jesus do, in effect, *put a reed in his hand*; nay, and, as these here, *smite him on the head* with it. 5. Subjects, when they swear allegiance, were wont to *kiss* their sovereign; but, instead of that, *spit upon him*. 6. Kings used to be addressed upon the *knee*; and this also they brought into the jest, they *bowed the knee, and worshipped him*; this they did in scorn, to make themselves and one another laugh. He was thus mocked, not in *his own clothes*, but in another's, to signify that he suffered not for his own sin; the crime was ours, the shame his. Those that bow the knee to Christ, but do not bow the soul, put the same affront upon him that these here did.

III. The soldiers, at the hour appointed, led him away from Pilate's judgment-hall to the place of execution (*v.* 20). They compelled one Simon of Cyrene to carry his cross for him. He *passed by, coming out of the country*, not thinking of any such matter. We must not think it strange, if crosses come upon us suddenly, and we be surprised by them. The cross was a very troublesome unwieldy load: but he that carried it a few minutes, had the honour to have his name upon record in the book of God. Wherever this gospel is preached, there shall this be told for a memorial of him.

Verses 22–32

We have here the *crucifixion* of our Lord Jesus.

I. The *place where* he was crucified; it was called *Golgotha—the place of a skull*: it was the common place of execution, for he was in all respects numbered with the transgressors.

II. The *time when* he was crucified; it was the *third* hour, *v.* 25. At the *third hour*, according to the Jews' way of reckoning, that is, about nine of the clock in the morning, or soon after, they nailed him to the cross.

III. The indignities that were done him, when he was nailed to the cross.

1. It being the custom to give *wine* to persons that were to be *put to death*, they *mingled* his with *myrrh*, which was *bitter*; he *tasted* it, but would not drink it; was willing to admit the bitterness of it, but not the benefit of it.

2. The garments of those that were crucified, being, as with us, the executioners' fee, the soldiers *cast lots* upon his garments (*v.* 24), so making themselves merry with his misery.

3. They set a superscription over his head, *The king of the Jews*, *v.* 26. Here was no crime alleged, but his sovereignty owned. Perhaps Pilate meant to cast disgrace upon Christ as a baffled king, or upon the Jews, as a people that deserved no better a king: however, God intended it to be the proclaiming even of Christ upon the cross, the *king of Israel*; though Pilate knew not what he wrote, any more than Caiaphas what he said, John xi. 51. Whenever we look unto Christ crucified, we must remember the inscription over his head, that he is a king.

4. They crucified *two thieves* with him, *one on his right hand, the other on his left*, and him in the midst as the worst of the three (*v.* 27). While he lived he has *associated* with sinners, to do them good; and now when he died, he was for the same purpose joined with them, for he *came into the world*, and went out of it, to *save sinners*. But this evangelist takes particular notice of the fulfilling of the scriptures in it, *v.* 28. In that famous prediction of Christ's sufferings (Isa. liii. 12), it was foretold that he should be numbered with the *transgressors*.

5. The spectators instead of condoling with him in his misery, added to it by insulting over him.

(1) Even they that *passed by railed on him*, *v.* 29. They taunted him, and expressed themselves with the utmost detestation of him, and indignation at him. The chief priests, no doubt, put these sarcasms into their mouths, *Thou that destroyest the temple, and buildest it in three days, now*, if thou canst, *save thyself*, and *come down from the cross*.

(2) Even the chief priests, who, being *taken from among men* and ordained for men, should be tender of those that are suffering and dying (Heb. v. 1, 2), yet they *mocked him, they said, He saved others, himself he cannot save*. They challenged him to *come down from the cross*, if he could, *v.* 22. Let them but *see* that, and they would *believe*.

(3) Even they that were crucified with him, reviled him (*v.* 32).

Verses 33–41

Here we have an account of Christ's dying.

I. There was a thick *darkness* over *the whole land* for three hours. The Jews had often demanded of Christ a *sign from heaven*; and now they had one,

JAMIESON, FAUSSET, BROWN

And said, Hail, King of the Jews!—doing Him derisive homage, in the form used on approaching the emperors. "And they spit upon Him, and took the reed and smote Him on the head" (Matt. 27:30). The best comment on these affecting details is to *cover the face*.

21-37. CRUCIFIXION AND DEATH OF THE LORD JESUS. (=Matt. 27:32-50; Luke 23:26-46; John 19:17-30.) See on John 19:17-30.

And he bearing his cross—(See on Luke 23:26). **went forth**—Cf. Hebrews 13:11-13, "without the camp"; "without the gate." On arriving at the place, "they gave Him vinegar to drink mingled with gall [wine mingled with myrrh, Mark 15:23], and when He had tasted thereof, He would not drink" (Matt. 27:34). This potion was stupefying, and given to criminals just before execution, to deaden the sense of pain.

they crucified him, and two others with him—"malefactors" (Luke 23:33), "thieves" (rather "robbers," Matt. 27:38; Mark 15:27). **on either side one and Jesus in the midst**—a hellish expedient, to hold Him up as the worst of the three. But in this, as in many other of their doings, "the scripture was fulfilled, which saith (Isa. 53:12), *And he was numbered with the transgressors*"—(Mark 15: 28)—though the prediction reaches deeper. "Then said Jesus"—['probably while being nailed to the CROSS'] [OLSHAUSEN], "FATHER, FORGIVE THEM, FOR THEY KNOW NOT WHAT THEY DO" (Luke 23:34)—and again the Scripture was fulfilled which said, "And He made intercession for the transgressors" (Isa. 53:12), though this also reaches deeper. (See Acts 3:17; 13:27; and cf. I Tim. 1:13).

"And *they that passed by* reviled Him, wagging their heads" in ridicule (Ps. 22:7; 109:25; cf. Jer. 18:16; Lam. 2:15). "Ah!"—'Ha,' an exclamation here of derision. "Thou that destroyest the temple, and buildest it in three days, save Thyself and come down from the cross" (Matt. 27:39, 40; Mark 15:29, 30). "It is evident that our Lord's saying, or rather this *perversion* of it (for He claimed not to *destroy*, but to *rebuild* the temple destroyed by them) had greatly exasperated the feeling which the priests and Pharisees had contrived to excite against Him. It is referred to as the principal fact brought out in evidence against Him on the trial (cf. Acts 6:13, 14), as an offense for which He deserved to suffer. And it is very remarkable that now *while it was receiving its real fulfilment*, it should be made more public and more impressive by the insulting proclamation of His enemies. Hence the importance attached to it after the resurrection, ch. 2:22" [WEBSTER and WILKINSON].

"Now from the sixth hour (12, noon) there was darkness over all the land unto the ninth hour" (Matt. 27: 45). No ordinary eclipse of the sun could have occurred at this time, it being then *full moon*, and

ADAM CLARKE

21. *A Cyrenian.* One of Cyrene, a celebrated city in Libya. *The father of Alexander and Rufus.* It appears that these two persons were well-known among the first disciples of our Lord. It is not unlikely that this is the same *Alexander* who is mentioned, Acts xix. 33, and that the other is the *Rufus* spoken of by Paul, Rom. xvi. 13.

A place called Golgotha. From the Hebrew *golgoleth*, "a skull," probably so called from the many skulls of those who had suffered crucificion and other capital punishments scattered up and down in the place. It is the same as Calvary, *Calvaria*, i.e., *calvi capitis area*, the place of bare skulls. Some think the place was thus called because it was in the form of a human skull. It is likely that it was the place of public execution.

25. *The third hour.* It has been before observed that the Jews divided their night into four watches, of three hours each. They also divided the day into four general parts. The first began at sunrise; the second, three hours after; the third, at midday; the fourth, three hours after, and continued till sunset. Christ having been nailed to the Cross a little after midday, John xix. 14-17, and having expired about three o'clock, Mark xv. 33, the whole business of the Crucifixion was finished within the space of this third division of the day, which Mark calls here the *third hour.* Commentators and critics have found it very difficult to reconcile this *third* hour of Mark, with the *sixth* hour of John, chap. xix. 14. It is supposed that the true reading, in John xix. 14, should be the *third* instead of the *sixth.*

They gave him vinegar to drink mingled with gall. Perhaps *gall* signifies no more than bitters of any kind. It was a common custom to administer a stupefying potion compounded of sour wine, which is the same as vinegar, frankincense, and myrrh to condemned persons to help to alleviate their sufferings or so disturb their intellect that they might not be sensible of them. Some person, out of kindness, appears to have administered this to our blessed Lord; but He, as in all other cases, determining to endure the fullness of pain, refused to take what was thus offered to Him, choosing to tread the winepress alone.

28. *The scripture was fulfilled.* All this verse is wanting in many MSS., some versions, and several of the fathers.

Wagging their heads. In token of contempt.

Thou that destroyest. Who pretended that you could have destroyed the Temple, and built it up again in three days. Cruelty is obliged to take refuge in lies in order to vindicate its infamous proceedings. *If thou be the Son of God.* Or rather, "a son of God," i.e., a peculiar favorite of the Most High.

He saved others; himself he cannot save. Or, "Cannot He save himself?"

MATTHEW HENRY

but such a one as signified the blinding of their eyes. It was a sign of the darkness that was come, and coming, upon the nation. This intimated to them, that the things which belonged to their peace, were now *hid from their eyes*. It was the power of darkness that they were now under, the works of darkness that they were now doing.

II. Toward the close of this darkness, our Lord Jesus, in the agony of his soul, cried out, *My God, my God, why hast thou forsaken me? v.* 34. The darkness signified the present cloud which the human soul of Christ was under, when he was making it an *offering for sin*. Our Lord Jesus was denied the light of the sun, when he was in his sufferings, to signify the withdrawing of the light of God's countenance. And this he complained of more than anything; he did not complain of his disciples' forsaking him, but of his Father's, 1. Because this *wounded his spirit*; and that is a thing *hard to bear*. 2. Because in this especially he was *made sin for us*. These symptoms of divine wrath were like that fire from heaven which had been sent sometimes, to consume the sacrifices; and it was always a token of God's acceptance. The fire that should have fallen upon the *sinner*, if God had not been pacified, fell upon the *sacrifice*, as a token that he was so; therefore it now fell upon Christ. When Paul was to be *offered* as a sacrifice for *the service of saints*, he could *joy* and *rejoice* (Phil. ii. 17); but it is another thing to be offered as a sacrifice for *the sin of sinners*.

III. Christ's prayer was bantered by them that stood by (*v.* 35, 36); because he cried, *Eli, Eli*, or (as Mark has it, according to the Syriac dialect) *Eloi, Eloi*, they said, *He calls for Elias*, though they knew very well what he said, and what it signified, *My God, My God*. One of them *filled a sponge with vinegar*, and reached it up to him upon a reed, *v.* 36. This was intended for a further affront and abuse to him: and whoever it was that checked him who did it, did but add to the reproach; "*Let him alone; let us see whether Elias will come to take him down*; and if not, we may conclude that he also hath abandoned him."

IV. Christ did again *cry with a loud voice*, and so *gave up the ghost*, *v.* 37. He was now commanding his soul into his Father's hand. Though speech fails, that we cannot *cry with a loud voice*, as Christ did, yet if God be the *strength of the heart*, that will not fail. Christ was really and truly *dead*, for he *gave up the ghost*; his human soul departed to the world of spirits, and left his body a breathless clod of clay.

V. Just at that instant that Christ died upon *mount Calvary*, the veil of the *temple* was *rent in twain from the top to the bottom*, *v.* 38. This bespoke a great deal, 1. Of terror to the unbelieving Jews; for it was a presage of the utter destruction of their church and nation, which followed not long after. 2. It bespeaks a great deal of comfort to all believing Christians, for it signifies the consecrating and laying open to us of a *new and living way into the holiest* by the *blood of Jesus*.

VI. The centurion who commanded the detachment which had the oversight of the execution was convinced, and confessed that this Jesus was the *Son of God*, *v.* 39. One thing that satisfied him, was, that he *so cried out, and gave up the ghost*. He said, to the honour of Christ, and the shame of those that abused him, *Truly this man was the Son of God*. But what reason had he to say so? 1. He had reason to say that he suffered *unjustly*. He suffered for saying that he was *the Son of God*; so that if he suffered unjustly, then what he said was true, and he was indeed the *Son of God*. 2. He had reason to say that he was a *favourite of heaven*, seeing how Heaven did him honour at his death. "Surely," thinks he, "this must be some divine person, highly beloved of God." Our Lord Jesus, even in the depth of his sufferings and humiliation, was the Son of God, and was declared to be so *with power*.

VII. There were some of his friends, the good women especially, that attended him (*v.* 40, 41); *There were women looking on afar off*: the *men* durst not be seen at all. The women durst not come near, but stood at a distance, overwhelmed with grief. Some of these women are here named. *Mary Magdalene* was one; she owed all her comfort to his power and goodness, which rescued her out of the possession of seven devils, in gratitude for which she thought she could never do enough for him. *Mary* also was there, *the mother of James the little*. This Mary was the wife of Cleophas or Alpheus, sister to the virgin Mary. These women had followed Christ *from Galilee*, though they were not required to attend the feast, as the males were. Now to see *him* upon a cross, whom they thought to have seen upon a throne, could not but be a great disappointment to them. Those that follow Christ, in expectation

JAMIESON, FAUSSET, BROWN

this obscuration lasted about *twelve times* the length of any ordinary eclipse. (Cf. Exod. 10:21, 23). Beyond doubt, the divine intention of the portent was to invest this darkest of all tragedies with a gloom expressive of its real character.

"And about the ninth hour Jesus cried, ELI, ELI, LAMA SABACTHANI . . . *My God, My God, why hast Thou forsaken Me*?" (Matt. 27:46). As the darkness commenced at the sixth hour, the second of the Jewish hours of prayer, so it continued till the ninth hour, *the hour of the evening sacrifice*, increasing probably in depth, and *reaching its deepest gloom at the moment of this mysterious cry*, when the flame of the one great "Evening Sacrifice" was burning fiercest. The words were made to His hand. They are the opening words of a Psalm (the 22d) full of the last "sufferings of Christ and the following glories" (I Pet. 1:11). "FATHER," was the cry in the first prayer which He uttered on the cross, for matters had not then come to the worst. "Father" was the cry of His last prayer, for matters had then passed their worst. But at this crisis of His sufferings, "Father" does not issue from His lips, for the light of a Father's countenance was then mysteriously eclipsed. He falls back, however, on a title expressive of His *official* relation, which, though lower and more distant in itself, yet when grasped in pure and naked faith was mighty in its claims, and rich in psalmodic associations. And what deep earnestness is conveyed by the redoubling of this title! But as for the cry itself, it will never be fully comprehended. An absolute desertion is not indeed to be thought of; but a total eclipse of the *felt* sense of God's presence it certainly expresses. It expresses *surprise*, as under the experience of something not only *never before known*, but *inexplicable* on the footing which had till then subsisted between Him and God. *It is a question which the lost cannot utter*. They are forsaken, *but they know why*. Jesus is forsaken, but *does not know and demands to know why*. It is thus *the cry of conscious innocence*, but of innocence unavailing to draw down, at that moment, the least token of approval from the unseen Judge—innocence whose only recognition at that moment lay in the thick surrounding gloom which but reflected the horror of great darkness that invested His own spirit.

38-47. SIGNS AND CIRCUMSTANCES FOLLOWING THE DEATH OF THE LORD JESUS.—HE IS TAKEN DOWN FROM THE CROSS AND BURIED—THE SEPULCHRE IS GUARDED. (=Matt. 27:51-66; Luke 23:45, 47-56; John 19:31-42). See on Matthew 27:51-56; and on John 19:31-42.

Truly this was the Son of God—There cannot be a reasonable doubt that this expression was used in the Jewish sense, and that it points to the claim which Jesus made to be the Son of God, and on which His condemnation expressly turned. The meaning, then, clearly is that He must have been what He professed to be; in other words, that He was no impostor. There was no medium between those two. See, on the similar testimony of the penitent thief—"This man hath done nothing amiss"—on Luke 23:41.

many women were there beholding afar off, which followed Jesus—The sense here would be better brought out by the use of the pluperfect, "which had followed Jesus." **from Galilee, ministering unto him**—As these dear women had ministered to Him during His glorious missionary tours *in* Galilee (see on Luke 8:1-3), so from this statement it should seem that they accompanied him and ministered to His wants *from* Galilee on His final journey to Jerusalem. **Among which was Mary Magdalene**—(see on Luke 8:2). **and Mary the mother of James and Joses**—the wife of Cleophas, or rather Clopas, and sister of the Virgin (John 19:25). See on ch. 13:55, 56. **and the mother of Zebedee's children**—i.e., Salome: cf. Mark 15:40. All this about the women is mentioned for the sake of what is afterwards to be related of their purchasing spices to anoint their Lord's body.

ADAM CLARKE

"My God! My God! to what sort of persons hast Thou left Me?" The words thus understood are rather to be referred to the wicked Jews than to our Lord, and are an exclamation indicative of the obstinate wickedness of His crucifiers, who steeled their hearts against every operation of the Spirit and power of God. Through the whole of the Sacred Writings, God is represented as *doing* those things which, in the course of His providence, he only *permits to be done*. Therefore the words, "To whom hast Thou left or given Me up?" are only a form of expression for "How astonishing is the wickedness of those persons into whose hands I am fallen!" If this interpretation be admitted, it will free this celebrated passage from much embarrassment, and make it speak a sense consistent with itself, and with the dignity of the Son of God. The words of Mark, chap. xv. 34, agree pretty nearly with this translation of the Hebrew: "To what [sort of persons, understood] has Thou left me?" But whatever may be thought of the above mode of interpretation, one thing is certain, viz., that the words could not be used by our Lord in the sense in which they are generally understood. This is sufficiently evident, for He well knew why He was come *unto that hour;* nor could He be forsaken of God, in whom dwelt all the fullness of the Godhead bodily. The Deity, however, might restrain so much of its consolatory support as to leave the human nature fully sensible of all its sufferings, so that the consolations might not take off any part of the keen edge of His passion; and this was necessary to make His sufferings meritorious. And it is probable that this is all that is intended by our Lord's quotation from the twenty-second psalm. Taken in this view, the words convey an unexceptionable sense, even in the common translation.

37. *Gave up the ghost.* This was about three o'clock, or what was termed by the Jews the ninth hour, about the time that the paschal lamb was usually sacrificed. The darkness mentioned here must have endured about two hours and a half.

The veil of the temple was rent. That is, the veil which separated the holy place, where the priests ministered, from the holy of holies, into which the high priest only entered, and that once a year, to make a general expiation for the sins of the people. This rending of the veil was emblematical, and pointed out that the separation between Jews and Gentiles was now abolished, and that the privilege of the high priest was now communicated to all mankind. All might henceforth have access to the throne of grace, through the one great Atonement and Mediator, the Lord Jesus. See this beautifully illustrated in Heb. x. 19-22.

The centurion. The Roman officer who superintended the execution, called *centurio*, from *centum*, a hundred, because he had the command of 100 men. *Truly this was the Son of God.* An innocent, holy, and divine Person; and God thus shows His disapprobation of this bloody tragedy. It is not likely that this centurion had any knowledge of the expectation of the Jews relative to the Messiah, and did not use the words in this sense. "A son of God," as the Romans used the term, would signify no more than a very eminent or divine person, a hero.

Many women. To their everlasting honor, these women evidenced more courage and affectionate attachment to their Lord and Master than the disciples did, who had promised to die with Him rather than forsake Him. *Beholding afar off.* "At a distance."

Mary Magdalene. She probably had her name from Magdala, a village or district in Lower Galilee. See chap. xv. 39. *Mary the mother of James.* She was mother of him called James the lesser, or junior, who was son of Alphaeus or Cleopas; see chap. x. 3; Mark xv. 40; John xix. 25; and she was sister to the Holy Virgin.

MATTHEW HENRY

of great things in this world by him, may probably live to see themselves sadly disappointed.

Verses 42–47

We are here attending the funeral of our Lord Jesus.

I. How the body of Christ was *begged.* It was at the disposal of the government. We are here told,

1. When the body of Christ was begged, and why such haste was made with the funeral; *The even was come*, and it was *the preparation*, that is, *the day before the sabbath, v.* 42. The Jews were more strict in the observation of the sabbath than of any other feast; and therefore, though this day was itself a *feast-day*, yet they observed it more religiously as the *eve* of the *sabbath.* The day before the sabbath should be a day of preparation for the sabbath. We should get ready for it a day before; nay, the whole week should be divided between the improvement of the foregoing sabbath and the preparation for the following sabbath.

2. Who it was that begged the body; it was *Joseph of Arimathea*, who is here called an *honourable counsellor* (*v.* 43), a person of character and distinction; he was one of the *great Sanhedrim.* But here is a more shining character put upon him; he was one that *waited for the kingdom of God.* Those who *wait for the kingdom of God*, and hope for an interest in the privileges of it, must show it by their forwardness to own Christ's cause. This man God raised up for this necessary service, when none of Christ's disciples could, or durst, undertake it. *Joseph went in boldly to Pilate;* though he knew how much it would affront the chief priests, yet he *put on courage*; perhaps at first he was a little afraid.

3. What a surprise it was to Pilate, to hear that he was *dead*, especially that he was *already dead.* Pilate doubted whether he was yet dead or no, fearing lest he should be imposed upon, and the body should be *taken down alive.* He therefore called the centurion, his own officer, and asked him *whether he had been any while dead* (*v.* 44). The centurion could assure him of this, for he had particularly observed how he *gave up the ghost, v.* 39. There was a special providence in it, that there might be no pretence to say that he was buried alive, and so to take away the truth of his resurrection. Thus the truth of Christ gains confirmation, sometimes, even from its enemies.

II. How the body of Christ was *buried.* Pilate gave Joseph leave to take down the body, and do what he pleased with it.

1. Joseph bought *fine linen* to wrap the body in, though in such a case old linen might have been thought sufficient.

2. He *took down* the body, mangled and macerated as it was, and *wrapt it in the linen* as a treasure of great worth.

3. He *laid it in a sepulchre* of his own, in a private place. This sepulchre belonged to Joseph. Abraham when he had no other possession in the land of Canaan, yet had a burying-place, but Christ had not so much as that. This sepulchre was *hewn out of a rock*, for Christ died to make the grave a *refuge* and shelter to the saints.

4. He *rolled a stone to the door of the sepulchre*, for so the manner of the Jews was to bury.

5. Some of the good women attended the funeral, and *beheld where he was laid*, that they might come after the sabbath to anoint the dead body, because they had not time to do it now. When our great Mediator and Lawgiver was buried, special notice was taken of his sepulchre, because he was to *rise again*: and the care taken of his body, bespeaks the care which he himself will take concerning his body the church. Our meditations on Christ's burial should lead us to think of our own, and should help to make the grave familiar to us, and so to render that bed easy which we must shortly make in the darkness.

JAMIESON, FAUSSET, BROWN

the preparation—sabbath eve. **that the bodies should not remain**—over night, against the Mosaic law (Deut. 21:22, 23). **on the sabbath day, for that sabbath day was an high**—or 'great'—**day**—the first day of unleavened bread, and, as concurring with an ordinary sabbath, the most solemn season of the ecclesiastical year. Hence their peculiar jealousy lest the law should be infringed.

Joseph of Arimathea—"a rich man" (Matt. 27:57), thus fulfilling Isaiah 53:9; "an honorable counsellor," a member of the Sanhedrim, and of good condition, "which also waited for the kingdom of God" (Mark 15:43), a devout expectant of Messiah's kingdom; "a good man and a just, the same had not consented to the counsel and deed of them" (Luke 23:50, 51—he had gone the length, perhaps, of dissenting and protesting in open council against the condemnation of our Lord); "who also himself was Jesus' disciple" (Matt. 27:57). **being a disciple of Jesus, but secretly, for fear of the Jews**—"He went in boldly unto Pilate" (Mark 15:43)—lit., "having taken courage went in," or "had the boldness to go in." Mark alone, as his manner is, notices the *boldness* which this required. The act would without doubt identify him *for the first time* with the disciples of Christ. Marvellous it certainly is, that one who while Jesus was yet alive merely refrained from condemning Him, not having the courage to espouse His cause by one positive act, should, now that He was dead, and His cause apparently dead with Him, summon up courage to go in personally to the Roman governor and ask permission to take down and inter the body. But if this be the first instance, it is not the last, that *a seemingly dead Christ has wakened a sympathy which a living one had failed to evoke. The heroism of faith is usually kindled by desperate circumstances, and is not seldom displayed by those who before were the most timid, and scarce known as disciples at all.* "And Pilate marvelled if he were"—rather "wondered that he was" "already dead." "And calling the centurion, he asked him whether He had been any while dead"—Pilate could hardly credit what Joseph had told him, that He had been dead "some time," and, before giving up the body to His friends, would learn how the fact stood from the centurion, whose business it was to oversee the execution. "And when he knew it of the centurion," that it was as Joseph had said, "he gave"—rather 'made a gift of'—"the body to Joseph"; struck, possibly, with the rank of the petitioner and the dignified boldness of the petition, in contrast with the spirit of the other party and the low rank to which he had been led to believe all the followers of Christ belonged. Nor would he be unwilling to show that he was not going to carry this black affair any farther.

ADAM CLARKE

42. *The day before the sabbath.* What we would call Friday evening. As the law of Moses had ordered that no criminal should continue hanging on a tree or gibbet till the setting of the sun, Joseph, fearing that the body of our Lord might be taken down and thrown into the common grave with the two robbers, came and earnestly entreated Pilate to deliver it to him, that he might bury it in his own new tomb.

43. *Went in boldly unto Pilate.* It needed no small measure of courage to declare now for Jesus, who had been a few hours ago condemned as a blasphemer by the Jews and as a seditious person by the Romans; and this was the more remarkable in Joseph because hitherto, for fear of the Jews, he had been only a secret disciple of our Lord. See John xix. 38.

Wrapped it in a clean linen cloth. The Jews, as well as the Egyptians, added spices to keep the body from putrefaction, and the linen was wrapped about every part to keep the aromatics in contact with the flesh. From John xix. 39-40 we learn that a mixture of myrrh and aloes of 100 pounds' weight had been applied to the body of Jesus when He was buried. And that a second embalmment was intended, we learn from Luke xxiii. 56 and xxiv. 1, as the hurry to get the body interred before the Sabbath did not permit them to complete the embalming in the first instance.

47. *Beheld where he was laid.* The courage and affection of these holy women cannot be too much admired. The strength of the Lord is perfected in weakness; for here a timid man and a few weak women acknowledge Jesus in death, when the strong and the mighty utterly forsook Him.

MATTHEW HENRY

CHAPTER 16

Verses 1–8

Never was there such a *sabbath* since the sabbath was first instituted as this was; during all this sabbath our Lord Jesus lay in the grave. It was *to him* a sabbath of *rest*, but a *silent* sabbath; it was to his disciples a melancholy sabbath, spent in tears and fears. Well, this sabbath is over, and the first day of the week is the first day of a new world.

I. The affectionate visit which the good women that had attended Christ, now made to his sepulchre. They set out from their lodgings *very early in the morning*, so that it was *sun-rising* by the time they got to the sepulchre. They had *bought sweet spices* too, and came not only to *bedew* the dead body with their tears, but to *perfume* it with their *spices, v.* 1.

JAMIESON, FAUSSET, BROWN

CHAPTER 16

Vss. 1-20. Angelic Announcement to the Women on the First Day of the Week, that Christ Is Risen—His Appearances after His Resurrection—His Ascension—Triumphant Proclamation of His Gospel. (=Matt. 28:1-10, 16-20; Luke 24:1-51; John 20:1, 2, 11-29.)

The Resurrection Announced to the Women (vss. 1-8). **1. when the sabbath was past**—that is, at sunset of our Saturday. **Mary Magdalene**—see on Luke 8:2. **Mary the mother of James**—James the Less (see on ch. 15:40). **and Salome**—the mother of Zebedee's sons (cf. ch. 15:40 with Matt. 27:56). **had bought sweet spices, that they might come and anoint him**—The word is simply "bought." But

ADAM CLARKE

1. *And anoint him.* Rather "to embalm Him." This is a proof that they had not properly understood what Christ had so frequently spoken, viz., that He would rise again the third day. And this inattention or unbelief of theirs is a proof of the truth of the Resurrection.

MATTHEW HENRY

Nicodemus had bought a very large quantity of *dry spices, myrrh* and *aloes*, John xix. 39. But these good women did not think that enough; they bought spices, some perfumed oils, to *anoint him*. The respect which others have showed to Christ's name, should not hinder us from showing our respect to it.

II. The care they were in about the rolling away of the stone, and the superseding of that care (*v.* 3, 4); *They said among themselves*, as they were coming along, and now drew near the sepulchre, *Who shall roll us away the stone from the door of the sepulchre? For it was very great*, more than they with their united strength could move. And there was another difficulty much greater than this, to be got over, which they knew nothing of, to wit, a guard of soldiers set to *keep* the sepulchre; who, had they come before they were frightened away, would have frightened them away. But their gracious love to Christ carried them to the sepulchre; and see how by the time they came thither, both these difficulties were removed, both the *stone* which they *knew of*, and the *guard* which they *knew not of*. They saw *that the stone was rolled away*. They who seek Christ diligently, will find the difficulties that lie in their way strangely to vanish, and themselves helped over them beyond their expectation.

III. The assurance that was given them by an angel, that the Lord Jesus was risen from the dead, and had left him there to tell those so who came thither to enquire after him.

1. They *entered into the sepulchre*, and saw that the body of Jesus was not there. He, who by his death undertook to pay our debt, in his resurrection took out our acquittance, and the matter in dispute was determined by an incontestable evidence that he was the Son of God.

2. They saw a *young man sitting on the right side* of the sepulchre. The angel appeared in the likeness of *a man*, of a *young man*; for angels grow not *old*. This angel was *sitting* on *the right hand* as they went into the sepulchre, *clothed with a long white garment*, a garment down to the feet. The sight of him might justly have encouraged them, but they were *affrighted*. Thus many times that which should be matter of comfort to us, through our own mistakes and misapprehensions proves a terror to us.

3. He silences their fears by assuring them that here was cause enough for triumph, but none for trembling (*v.* 6); *He saith to them, Be not affrighted*. Be not affrighted, for, (1) "Ye are faithful lovers of Jesus Christ, and therefore, instead of being *confounded*, ought to be *comforted*. *Ye seek Jesus of Nazareth, which was crucified*." He speaks of Jesus as one that *was crucified*; "The thing is *past*, that scene is over, ye must not dwell so much upon the sad circumstances of his crucifixion as to be unapt to believe the joyful news of his resurrection." He *was* crucified, but he *is* glorified. After his entrance upon his glory, he never drew any veil over his sufferings, nor was shy of having his cross spoken of. (2) "It will therefore be good news to you, to hear that, instead of anointing him dead, you may rejoice in him living. *He is risen, he is not here*, not dead, but alive again. And you may here see *the place where they laid him*. You see he is gone hence, not stolen either by his enemies or by his friends, but *risen*."

4. He orders them to give speedy notice of this to his disciples. Thus they were made the apostles of the apostles, which was a recompence of their affection in attending him on the cross, to the grave, and in the grave. They first came, and were first served; no other of the disciples durst come near his sepulchre. None came near him but a few women, who were not able so much as to *roll away the stone*.

(1) They must tell the *disciples*, that *he is risen*. It is a dismal time with them, their dear Master is dead, and all their hopes and joys are buried in his grave; so that there remains no more spirit in them, they are perfectly at their wits' end. "O, go quickly to them," saith the angel, "tell them that *their Master is risen*; this will keep them from sinking into despair." Christ is not ashamed to own his poor disciples; his preferment doth not make him shy of them, for he took early care to have it *notified* to them. Christ is not extreme to mark what *they* do amiss, whose hearts are upright with him.

(2) They must be sure to tell Peter. This is particularly taken notice of by this evangelist, who is supposed to have written by Peter's direction. He is particularly named: *Tell Peter*, for, [1] It will be good news to him, more welcome to him than to any of them; for he is in sorrow for sin. [2] He will be afraid, lest the joy of this good news do not belong to him. Had the angel said only, *Go, tell his disciples*, poor Peter would have been ready to sigh, and say, "But I doubt I cannot look upon myself as one of them, for I disowned him, and deserve to be disowned by him"; to obviate that, "Go to Peter

JAMIESON, FAUSSET, BROWN

our translators are perhaps right in rendering it here "had bought," since it would appear, from Luke 23:56, that they had purchased them immediately after the Crucifixion, on the *Friday* evening, during the short interval that remained to them before sunset, when the sabbath rest began; and that they had only deferred using them to anoint the body till the sabbath rest should be over. On this "anointing," see on John 19:40. **2. very early in the morning**—see on Matthew 28:1. **the first day of the week, they came unto the sepulchre at the rising of the sun**—not quite literally, but "at earliest dawn"; according to a way of speaking not uncommon, and occurring sometimes in the Old Testament. Thus our Lord rose on the third day; having lain in the grave part of Friday, the whole of Saturday, and part of the following First day. **3. they said among themselves**—as they were approaching the sacred spot. **Who shall roll us away the stone from the door of the sepulchre? . . . for it was very great**—On reaching it they find their difficulty gone—the stone already rolled away by an unseen hand. *And are there no others who, when advancing to duty in the face of appalling difficulties, find their stone also rolled away?* **5. entering into the sepulchre, they saw a young man**—In Matthew 28:2 he is called "the angel of the Lord"; but here he is described as he appeared to the eye, in the bloom of a life that knows no decay. In Matthew he is represented as sitting on the stone *outside* the sepulchre; but since even there he says, "*Come*, see the place where the Lord lay" (28:6), he seems, as ALFORD says, to have gone in with them from without; only awaiting their arrival to accompany them into the hallowed spot, and instruct them about it. **sitting on the right side**—having respect to the position in which His Lord had lain there. This trait is peculiar to Mark; but cf. Luke 1:11. **clothed in a long white garment**—On its *length*, see Isaiah 6:1; and on its *whiteness*, see on Matthew 28:3. **and they were affrighted.**

6. he saith unto them, Be not affrighted—a stronger word than "Fear not" in Matthew. **Ye seek Jesus of Nazareth, which was crucified**—"the Nazarene, the Crucified," **he is risen; he is not here**—See on Luke 24:5, 6. **behold the place where they laid him**—See on Matthew 28:6.

7. But go your way, tell his disciples and Peter—This Second Gospel, being drawn up—as all the earliest tradition states—*under the eye of Peter*, or from materials chiefly furnished by him, there is something deeply affecting in the preservation of this little phrase by Mark alone. **that he goeth before you into Galilee; there shall ye see him, as he said unto you**—See on Matthew 28:7.

ADAM CLARKE

2. *Very early in the morning.* This was the time they left their own houses, and by the rising of the sun they got to the tomb. As the preceding day was the Sabbath, they could not, consistently with the observances of that day, approach the tomb.

In the end of the sabbath. "After the end of the week." In general the Jews divided their natural day, which consisted of twenty-four hours, into day and night. Their artificial day began at the rising and ended at the setting of the sun; all the rest of the time, from the setting to the rising of the sun, they termed night. Hence the same word, in Hebrew, signifies both evening and night, Gen. i. 5; Mark vi. 47. Matthew has employed the word in this extensive sense here, pointing out the latter part of the Jewish night, that which immediately preceded the rising of the sun, and not that first part which we call the evening. The transaction mentioned here evidently took place early on the morning of the third day after our Lord's crucifixion; what is called our Sunday morning, or first day of the next week. *Came . . . to see the sepulchre.* That is, they set out at this time in order to visit the tomb of our Lord, and also to weep there, John xi. 31, and to embalm the body of our Lord, Luke xxiv. 1. Matthew omits Mary Salome, mentioned by Mark; and Joanna, the wife of Chuza, Herod's steward, mentioned by Luke. The other Mary was the wife of Cleopas, and mother of James and Joses, mentioned before, chap. xxvii. 56. Were not Mary and Salome two distinct persons?

6. *Jesus of Nazareth.* The Jews had given this name to Christ by way of reproach, Matt. ii. 23; but as it was under this name that He was crucified, John xix. 19, the angel here, and the apostles after, have given Him the same name, Acts iv. 10, etc. Names which the world in derision fixes on the followers of God often become the general appellatives of religious bodies; thus *Quakers, Puritans, Pietists,* and *Methodists* have in their respective times been the *nicknames* given in derision by the world to those who separated themselves from its corruptions.

7. *Tell his disciples and Peter.* Why is not Peter included among the disciples? For this plain reason—he had forfeited his discipleship, and all right to the honor and privileges of an apostle, by denying his Lord and Master. However he is now a penitent; tell him that Jesus is risen from the dead, and is ready to heal his backsliding, and love him freely; so that, after being converted, he may strengthen his brethren.

MATTHEW HENRY

by name, and tell him, he shall be as welcome as any of the rest to *see* him in Galilee." A sight of Christ will be very welcome to a true penitent, and a true penitent shall be very welcome to a sight of Christ, for there is joy in heaven concerning him.

(3) They must appoint them all, and Peter by name, to give him the meeting in Galilee, as *he said unto you*, Matt. xxvi. 32. All the meetings between Christ and his disciples are of his own appointing. Christ never forgets his appointment. In all meetings between Christ and his disciples, he is the most forward. *He goes before you.*

IV. The account which the women did bring of this to the disciples (*v.* 8); They *went out quickly*, and *ran from the sepulchre, trembling* and *amazed*. Christ had often told them, that *the third day he would rise again*; had they given that its due notice and credit, they would have come to the sepulchre, expecting to have found him risen, and would have received the news of it with a joyful assurance, and not with all this terror and amazement. They showed not anything of it to any man that they *met by the way*, for *they were afraid*, afraid it was too good news to be true.

Verses 9-13

We have here a very short account of two of Christ's appearances.

I. He appeared to Mary Magdalene, to her first in the garden, which we have a particular narrative of, John xx. 14. It was she *out of whom he had cast seven devils*; and she *loved much*; and this honour Christ did her, that she was the first that saw him after his resurrection. The closer we cleave to Christ, the sooner we may expect to see him, and the more to see of him.

1. She brings notice of what she had seen, to the disciples; not only to the *eleven*, but to the rest that followed him, *as they mourned and wept*, *v.* 10. And it was an evidence of their great love to Christ. But when their *weeping* had *endured a night* or two, comfort returned, as Christ had promised them; *I will see you again, and your heart shall rejoice.* Better news cannot be brought to disciples in tears, than to tell them of Christ's resurrection.

2. They could not give credit to the report she brought them. They heard that *he was alive*, and had been seen of her. Yet *they believed not*. They fear that she is *imposed upon*, and that it was but a fancy that she *saw him*. Had they believed the *frequent* predictions of it from his own mouth, they would not have been now so incredulous of the report of it.

II. He appeared to two of the disciples, *as they went into the country*, *v.* 12. This refers, no doubt, to that which is largely related (Luke xxiv. 13, &c.), of what passed between Christ and the two disciples *going to Emmaus*. He is here said to have appeared to them in *another form*, in another dress than what he usually wore.

1. These *two* witnesses gave in their *testimony* to this proof of Christ's resurrection; *They went and told it to the residue*, *v.* 13. Being *satisfied* themselves, they were desirous to give their brethren the *satisfaction* they had, that they might be comforted as they were.

2. This did not gain credit with all; *Neither believed they them.* Now there was a wise providence in it, that the proofs of Christ's resurrection were given in thus *gradually*, and admitted thus *cautiously*. We have the more reason to believe those who did themselves believe so slowly: had they swallowed it presently, they might have been thought *credulous*, and their testimony the less to be *regarded*; but their *disbelieving* at first, shows that they did not believe it afterward but upon a full conviction.

Verses 14-18

I. The *conviction* which Christ gave his apostles of the truth of his resurrection (*v.* 14); He *appeared to them* himself, when they were all together, *as they sat at meat*, which gave him an opportunity to *eat and drink with them*, for their full satisfaction; see Acts x. 41. And still, when he appeared to them, he *upbraided them with their unbelief and hardness of heart.* The evidences of the truth of the gospel are so full, that those who receive it not, may justly be *upbraided* with their unbelief; and it is owing to the *hardness of their heart*, its senselessness and stupidity. Though they had not till now seen him themselves, they are justly blamed *because they believed not them who had seen him after he was risen.* It will not suffice for an excuse of our infidelity in the great day, to say, "*We did not see him* after he was risen," for we ought to have believed the testimony of those who did see him.

II. The *commission* which he gave them to set up his kingdom among men by the preaching of his *gospel.*

1. *To whom* they were to preach *the gospel.* Hitherto they had been sent only to *the lost sheep of the house of Israel*, and were forbidden to go into the *way of the Gentiles*, or into any city of the Samaritans;

JAMIESON, FAUSSET, BROWN

8. And they went out quickly, and fled from the sepulchre: for they trembled and were amazed—"for tremor and amazement seized them." **neither said they anything to any man; for they were afraid**—How intensely natural and simple is this!

Appearances of Jesus after His Resurrection (vss. 9-18). **9. Now when Jesus was risen early the first day of the week, he appeared first to Mary Magdalene, out of whom he had cast seven devils**—There is some difficulty here, and different ways of removing it have been adopted. She had gone with the other women to the sepulchre (vs. 1), parting from them, perhaps, before their interview with the angel, and on finding Peter and John she had come with them back to the spot; and it was at this second visit, it would seem, that Jesus appeared to this Mary, as detailed in John 20:11-18. *To a woman was this honor given to be the first that saw the risen Redeemer, and that woman was* NOT *his virgin-mother.* **11. they, when they had heard that he was alive, and had been seen of her, believed not**—This, which is once and again repeated of them all, is most important in its bearing on their subsequent testimony to His resurrection at the risk of life itself.

12. After that he appeared in another form—(cf. Luke 24:16). **unto two of them as they walked, and went into the country**—The reference here, of course, is to His manifestation to the two disciples going to Emmaus, so exquisitely told by the Third Evangelist (see on Luke 24:13, etc.). **13. they went and told it unto the residue: neither believed they them.**

ADAM CLARKE

8. *They departed quickly from the sepulchre.* At the desire of the angel they went into the tomb, to have the fullest certainty of the Resurrection. *Fear and great joy. Fear* produced by the appearance of this glorious messenger of God, and *great joy* occasioned by the glad tidings of the resurrection of their Lord and Master. At the mention of unexpected good news, fear and joy are generally intermingled.

9. *Now when Jesus was risen*, etc.—This, to the conclusion of the Gospel, is wanting in the famous Codex Vaticanus, and has anciently been wanting in many others. In the margin of the later Syriac version there is a remarkable addition after this verse; it is as follows: "And they declared briefly all that was commanded, to them that were with Peter. Afterward Jesus himself published by them, from east to west, the holy and incorruptible preaching of eternal salvation. Amen." *Mary Magdalene.* It seems likely that, after this woman had carried the news of Christ's resurrection to the disciples, she returned alone to the tomb; and that it was then that Christ appeared to her, John xx. 1-12; and a little after, He appeared to all the women together, Matt. xxviii. 9; Luke xxiv. 10.

10. *Them that had been with him.* Not only the eleven disciples, but several others who had been the occasional companions of Christ and the apostles. *Mourned and wept.* Because they had lost their Lord and Master, and had basely abandoned Him in His extremity.

12. *He appeared . . . unto two of them.* These were the two who were going to Emmaus. The whole account is given by Luke, chap. xxiv. 13-34, where see the notes.

14. *And upbraided them with their unbelief.* Never were there people so difficult to be persuaded of the truth of spiritual things as the disciples. It may be justly asserted that people of so skeptical a turn of mind would never credit anything till they had the fullest evidence of its truth. The unbelief of the disciples is a strong proof of the truth of the gospel of God.

MATTHEW HENRY

but now they are authorized to *go into all the world*, and to *preach the gospel* of Christ to *every creature*, to the Gentiles as well as to the Jews; to every human creature that is capable of receiving it. These eleven men could not themselves preach it to all the world, much less to *every creature* in it; but they and the other disciples, with those who should afterward be added to them, must *disperse* themselves several ways, and, wherever they went, carry the gospel along with them. They must make it the business of their lives to send those glad tidings *up and down the world* with all possible fidelity and care, not as an amusement or entertainment, but as a solemn message from God to men, and an appointed means of making men happy.

2. What is the *summary of the gospel* they are to preach (*v.* 16); "Set before the world life and death, good and evil. Now go and tell them," (1) "That if they *believe the gospel*, and give up themselves to be Christ's disciples; if they *renounce* the devil, the world, and the flesh, and be *devoted* to Christ, they *shall be saved* from the guilt and power of sin, it shall not *rule* them, it shall not *ruin* them. He that is a true Christian, shall be saved through Christ." *Baptism* was appointed to be the *inaugurating* rite, by which those that embraced Christ owned him. (2) "*If they believe not they shall be damned*, by the sentence of a *despised* gospel, added to that of a broken law." And even this is *gospel*, it is good news, that nothing else but unbelief shall damn men, which is a sin against the remedy.

3. What power they should be endowed with, for the confirmation of the doctrine they were to preach (*v.* 17); *These signs shall follow them that believe*. They shall do wonders *in Christ's name*, the same name into which they were baptized, in the virtue of power derived from him, and fetched in by prayer. Some particular signs are mentioned; (1) They shall *cast out devils*; this power was more common among Christians than any other. (2) They shall *speak with new tongues*, which they had never learned, or been acquainted with; and this was both a *miracle* for the confirming of the truth of the gospel, and a *means* of spreading the gospel among those nations that had not heard it. (3) They shall *take up serpents*. This was fulfilled in Paul, who was not hurt by the *viper* that *fastened on his hand*, which was acknowledged a great miracle by the barbarous people, Acts xxviii. 5, 6. (4) If they be compelled by their persecutors to *drink any deadly* poisonous thing, *it shall not hurt them*. (5) They shall not only be preserved from hurt themselves, but they shall be enabled to do good to others; *They shall lay hands on the sick*, and they *shall recover*. Many of the elders of the church had this power, as appears by James v. 14, where they are said to *anoint* the sick *with oil in the name of the Lord*. With what assurance of success might they go about the executing of their commission, when they had such credentials as these to produce!

Verses 19–20

1. Christ *welcomed* into the *upper world* (*v.* 19): *After the Lord had spoken* what he had to say to his disciples, he *went up into heaven*, in a cloud; which we have a particular account of (Acts i. 9); he was *received up*, and he *sat on the right hand of God*. Now he is glorified with the glory he had before the world.

2. Christ *welcomed* in this *lower world*. (1) We have here the apostles working diligently for him; they *went forth, and preached everywhere* far and near. Though the doctrine they preached was directly contrary to the *spirit* and *genius* of the world, though it met with abundance of opposition, yet the preachers of it were neither *afraid* nor *ashamed*. (2) We have here God *working* effectually *with them*, to make their labours successful, by *confirming the word with signs following*, partly by the miracles that were wrought upon the *bodies* of people, and partly by the influence it had upon the *minds* of people. These were properly *signs following* the word—the reformation of the world, the destruction of idolatry, the conversion of sinners, the comfort of saints; and these signs still follow it, and that they may do so more and more, for the honour of Christ and the good of mankind, the evangelist prays, and teaches us to say *Amen*. Father in heaven, thus let thy name be hallowed, and let thy kingdom come.

JAMIESON, FAUSSET, BROWN

... **15. he said unto them, Go ye into all the world, and preach the Gospel to every creature**—See on John 20:19-23; and on Luke 24: 36-49.

16. He that believeth and is baptized—Baptism is here put for the external signature of the inner faith of the heart, just as "confessing with the mouth" is in Romans 10:10; and there also as here this *outward* manifestation, once mentioned as the proper fruit of faith, is not repeated in what follows (Romans 10:11)—**shall be saved; but he that believeth not shall be damned**—These awful issues of the reception or rejection of the Gospel, though often recorded in other connections, are given in this connection only by Mark.

17. these signs shall follow them that believe ... 18. They shall take up serpents ...—These two verses also are peculiar to Mark.

The Ascension and Triumphant Proclamation of the Gospel Thereafter (vss. 19-20). **19. So then after the Lord**—an epithet applied to Jesus by this Evangelist only in the two concluding verses, when He comes to His glorious Ascension and its subsequent fruits. It is most frequent in Luke. **had spoken unto them, he was received up into heaven**—See on Luke 24:50, 51. **and sat on the right hand of God**—This great truth is here only related as a fact in the Gospel history. In that exalted attitude He appeared to Stephen (Acts 7:55, 56); and it is thereafter perpetually referred to as His proper condition in glory. **20. they went forth, and preached everywhere, the Lord working with them, and confirming the word with signs following. Amen.**—We have in this closing verse a most important link of connection with the Acts of the Apostles, where He who directed all the movements of the infant Church is perpetually styled "THE LORD"; thus illustrating His own promise for the founding and building up of the Church, "Lo, I AM WITH YOU alway!"

ADAM CLARKE

15. *Go ye into all the world.* See on Matt. xxviii. 19. *And preach the gospel to every creature.* "Proclaim the glad tidings"—of Christ crucified, and raised from the dead—"to all the creation"—to the Gentile world.

16. *He that believeth.* He that credits this gospel as a revelation from God; *and is baptized*—takes upon him the profession of it, obliging himself to walk according to its precepts; *shall be saved*—redeemed from sin here, and brought at last to the enjoyment of My eternal glory. *But he that believeth not shall be damned*—because he rejects the only provision that could be effectual to his soul's salvation.

17. *These signs shall follow.* Or rather, "accompany." *Them that believe.* "The believers," as we express it; i.e., the apostles, and all those who in those primitive times were endued with miraculous powers, for the confirmation of the doctrines they preached. *In my name.* That is, by the authority and influence of the almighty Jesus. *Cast out devils.* Whose kingdom Jesus Christ was manifested to destroy. *Speak with new tongues.* This was most literally fulfilled on the Day of Pentecost, Acts ii. 4-12.

18. *Take up serpents.* This also was literally fulfilled in the case of Paul, Acts xxviii. 5. *If they drink any deadly thing.* Being understood —if they should through mistake or accident drink any poisonous matter, their constant Preserver will take care that it shall not injure them. See a similar promise, Isa. xliii. 2. *They shall lay hands on the sick.* And I will convey a healing power by their hands, so that the sick shall recover, and men shall see that these are sent and acknowledged by the Most High. Several instances of this kind are found in the Acts of the Apostles.

19. *After the Lord had spoken* these things, and conversed with them for forty days, *he was received up into heaven*, there to appear in the presence of God for us.

20. *The Lord working with them.* This cooperation was twofold, internal and external. Internal, illuminating their minds, convincing them of the truth, and establishing them in it. External, conveying their word to the souls that heard it, by the demonstration of the Holy Ghost; convincing them of sin, righteousness, and judgment; justifying them by His blood, and sanctifying them by His Spirit. Though miraculous powers are not now requisite, because the truth of the gospel has been sufficiently confirmed, yet this cooperation of God is indispensably necessary, without which no man can be a successful preacher, and without which no soul can be saved. *With signs following.* "The accompanying signs"; viz., those mentioned in the seventeenth and eighteenth verses, and those others just now spoken of, which still continue to be produced by the energy of God, accompanying the faithful preaching of His unadulterated Word. *Amen.* This is added here by many MSS. and versions, but is supposed not to have made a part of the text originally.

THE GOSPEL ACCORDING TO LUKE

I. Perfect (1:1-3:38)
- *A. Prologue (1:1-4)*
- *B. Being and birth (1:5-2:39)*
  1. Angelic annunciations (1:5-38)
  2. The two mothers (1:39-56)
  3. The births (1:57-2:39)
- *C. Childhood and confirmation (2:40-52)*
  1. Growth (2:40)
  2. Confirmation (2:41-51)
  3. Advancement (2:52)
- *D. Development and anointing (3:1-22)*
  1. The ministry of John (3:1-20)
  2. Anointing and attestation (3:21, 22)
- *E. Genealogy (3:23-38)*

II. Perfected (4:1-9:36)
- *A. Temptation: first process and issue—the devil (4:1-14)*
  1. The challenge (4:1, 2)
  2. The process (4:3-12)
  3. The issue (4:13, 14)
- *B. Teaching: second process and issue—man (4:15-9:27)*
  1. Induction and things following (4:15-6:11)
  2. The twelve (6:12-8:56)
  3. The issue (9:1-27)
- *C. Transfiguration: third process and issue—God (9:28-36)*
  1. The process is in the perfecting already considered
  2. The issue (9:28-36)

III. Perfecting (9:37-24:53)
- *A. Prelude (9:37-50)*
  1. Symbolic miracle (9:37-45)
  2. The disciples (9:46-50)
- *B. Purpose and preparation (9:51-18:30)*
  1. Purpose—the key to all that follows (9:51)
  2. Preparation (9:52-18:30)
- *C. Approach and accomplishment (18:31-24:12)*
  1. Approach—the key to all that follows (18:31-34)
  2. Accomplishment—the priest making atonement alone (18:35-24:12)
     a. "Up to Jerusalem" (18:35-19:44)
     b. "Delivered to Gentiles" (19:45-23:56)
     c. "The third day" (24:1-12)
- *D. Administration (24:13-53)*
  1. The new interpretation creating passion (24:13-35)
  2. The new comradeship creating confidence (24:36-43)
  3. The new commission creating responsibility (24:44-49)
  4. The new benediction creating worship (24:50-53)

We are now entering into the labors of another evangelist, *Luke.* Some think he was the only one of all the penmen of the Scripture who was not of the seed of Israel. He was a Jewish proselyte, and, as some conjecture, converted to Christianity by the ministry of St. Paul; and after his coming into Macedonia (Acts 26:10), he was his constant companion. He had employed himself in the study and practice of physics; hence, Paul calls him "Luke, the beloved physician" (Col. 4:14). Some of the pretended ancients tell you that he was a painter, and drew a picture of the Virgin Mary. He is supposed to have written this gospel when he was associated with St. Paul. Some think this is "the brother" whom Paul speaks of (2 Cor. 8:18), "whose praise is in the gospel throughout all the churches of Christ."

His way and manner of writing are accurate and exact, his style polite and elegant, yet perspicuous. He expresses himself in a vein of purer Greek than is to be found in the other writers of the holy story. Thus he relates divers things more copiously than the other evangelists; and thus he especially treats of those things which relate to the priestly office of Christ. It is uncertain when, or about what time, this gospel was written. Some think it was written at Rome, a little before he wrote his history of the *Acts of the Apostles* (which is a continuation of this), when he was there with Paul, while he was a prisoner, and preaching in "his own hired house," with which the history of the Acts concludes; and then Paul says that "only Luke is with me" (2 Tim. 4:11). When he was under that voluntary confinement with Paul, he had leisure to compile these two histories (and many excellent writings the church has been indebted to a prison for). Jerome says Luke died when he was eighty-four years of age, and was never married.

MATTHEW HENRY

CHAPTER 1

Verses 1–4

Complimental prefaces and dedications, the language of flattery and the food and fuel of pride, are justly condemned by the wise and good; but it doth not therefore follow, that such as are useful and instructive are to be run down; such is this. It is not certain who this Theophilus was; the name signifies a *friend of God*; some think that it does not mean any particular person, but everyone that is a *lover of God.* But it is rather to be understood of some particular person, probably a magistrate; because Luke gives him here the same title of respect which St. Paul gave to Festus the governor, Acts xxvi. 25. Religion does not destroy civility and good manners, but teaches us, according to the usages of our country, to *give honour to them to whom honour is due.*

I. Why St. Luke wrote this gospel. It is certain that he was moved by the Holy Ghost, not only *to* the writing, but *in* the writing of it; but in both he was moved as a reasonable creature, and not as a mere machine; and he was made to consider,

1. That the things he wrote of were things that were *most surely believed among all Christians,* and therefore things which they ought to be instructed in. He will not write about things of *doubtful disputation,* but the things which are, and ought to be, most *surely believed.* Though it is not the foundation of our faith, yet it is a support to it, that the articles of our creed are things that have been long *most surely believed.* The doctrine of Christ is what thousands of the wisest and best of men have *ventured their souls upon.*

JAMIESON, FAUSSET, BROWN

CHAPTER 1

Vss. 1-4. It appears from the Acts of the Apostles, and the Apostolic Epistles, that the earliest preaching of the Gospel consisted of a brief summary of the facts of our Lord's earthly history, with a few words of pointed application to the parties addressed. Of these astonishing facts, notes would naturally be taken and *digests* put into circulation. It is to such that Luke here refers; and in terms of studied respect, as narratives of what was "believed surely," or "on sure grounds" among Christians, and drawn up from the testimony of "eye-witnesses and ministering servants of the word." But when he adds that "it seemed good to him also to write in order, having traced down all things with exactness from their first rise," it is a virtual claim for his own Gospel to supersede these "many" narratives. Accordingly, while not one of them has survived the wreck of time, this and the other canonical Gospels live, and shall live, the only fitting vehicles of those life-bringing facts which have made all things new. Apocryphal or spurious gospels, upheld by parties unfriendly to the truths exhibited in the canonical Gospels, have *not* perished; but those well-meant and substantially correct narratives here referred to, used only while better were not to be had, were by tacit consent allowed to merge in the four peerless documents which from age to age, and with astonishing unanimity, have been accepted as the written charter of all Christianity.

ADAM CLARKE

CHAPTER 1

1. *Many have taken in hand.* Great and remarkable characters always have many biographers. So it appears it was with our Lord. But as most of these accounts were inaccurate, recording as facts things which had not happened, and through ignorance or design mistaking others, especially in the place where Luke wrote, it seemed good to the Holy Spirit to inspire this holy man with the most correct knowledge of the whole history of our Lord's birth, preaching, miracles, sufferings, death, resurrection, and ascension, that the sincere, upright followers of God might have a sure foundation on which they might safely build their faith. *Most surely believed among us.* "Facts confirmed by the fullest evidence." Everything that had been done or said by Jesus Christ was so public, so plain, and so accredited by thousands of witnesses, who could have had no interest in supporting an imposture, as to carry the fullest conviction to the hearts of those who heard and saw Him of the divinity of His doctrine and the truth of His miracles.

MATTHEW HENRY

2. That it was requisite there should be a *declaration made in order* of those things; that the history of the life of Christ should be *methodized*. When things are *put in order*, we know the better where to *find them* for *our own* use, and how to *keep* them for the benefit of *others*.

3. That there were *many who had undertaken* to *publish* narratives of the *life of Christ*. Others' services to Christ must not be reckoned to supersede ours, but rather to quicken them.

4. That the truth of the things he had to write was *confirmed* by the *concurring testimony* of those who were competent and unexceptionable witnesses of them. What he was now about to publish, agreed with that which had been delivered by word of mouth, over and over, by those who from the beginning were *eye-witnesses and ministers of the word*, v. 2. (1) The apostles were *ministers of the word* of Christ, or of the doctrine of Christ; they, having received it themselves, ministered it to others, 1 John i. 1. They had not a gospel to make as masters, but a gospel to preach as ministers. (2) The *ministers of the word* were *eye-witnesses*. They did themselves *hear* the doctrine of Christ, and *see* his miracles, and had them not by report, at second hand. (3) They were so *from the beginning* of Christ's ministry, *v*. 2. He had his disciples with him when he wrought his *first miracle*, John ii. 11. They *companied with him all the time that he went in and out among them*, Acts i. 21. (4) The *written* gospel, which we have to *this day*, exactly agrees with the gospel which was *preached* in the *first days* of the church. (5) That he himself had a *perfect understanding* of the *things* he wrote of, *from the first*, *v*. 3. He asserts his own ability for this undertaking: "It seemed good to me, having attained to the exact knowledge of all things." He had diligently *searched* into these things. He had made it his business to inform himself concerning particulars. He had received his intelligence, not only by tradition, but by revelation. He wrote his history of things *reported* by tradition, but *ratified* by inspiration. He could therefore say that he had a *perfect understanding* of these things. He knew them, *accurately*, exactly.

II. Observe why he sent it to *Theophilus*: "I wrote unto thee these things *in order, that thou mightest know the certainty of those things wherein thou hast been instructed*." It is implied that he had been *instructed* in these things either before his baptism, or since, or both, according to the rule, Matt. xxviii. 19, 20. *Concerning which thou hast been catechized;* so the word is; the most knowing Christians began with being catechized. It was intended that he should *know the certainty of those things*. There is a *certainty* in the gospel of Christ, there is that therein which we may build upon; and those who have been well instructed in the things of God should give diligence to *know the certainty* of those things, to know not only what we believe, but why we believe it, that we may be able to give a *reason of the hope that is in us*.

Verses 5–25

The two preceding evangelists begin the gospel with the baptism of John and his ministry. This evangelist, designing to give a more particular account than had been given of our Saviour's conception and birth, determines to do so of John Baptist.

I. The account given of *his parents* (*v*. 5): They lived *in the days of Herod the king*, who was a foreigner, and a deputy for the Romans, who had lately made Judæa a province of the empire. This is taken notice of to show that the sceptre was quite departed from Judah. Israel is enslaved, yet then comes the glory of Israel.

Now the father of John Baptist was a priest, a son of Aaron; his name *Zacharias*. No families in the world were ever so honoured of God as those of Aaron and David; with one was made the covenant of priesthood, with the other that of royalty. Christ was of David's house, his forerunner of Aaron's. This Zacharias was *of the course of Abia*. When in David's time the family of Aaron was multiplied, he divided them into twenty-four courses, for the more regular performance of their office. The eighth of those was that of *Abia* (1 Chron. xxiv. 10), who was descended from Eleazar, Aaron's eldest son.

JAMIESON, FAUSSET, BROWN

1. set forth in order—more simply, to draw up a narrative.

2. from the beginning—that is, of His public ministry, as is plain from what follows.

3. from the very first—that is, from the very earliest events; referring to those precious details of the birth and early life, not only of our Lord, but of His forerunner, which we owe to Luke alone. **in order**—or "consecutively"—in contrast, probably, with the disjointed productions to which he had referred. But this must not be pressed too far; for, on comparing it with the other Gospels, we see that in some particulars the strict chronological order is not observed in this Gospel. **most excellent**—or "most noble"—a title of rank applied by this same writer twice to Felix and once to Festus (Acts 22:26; 24:3; 26:25). It is likely, therefore, that "Theophilus" was chief magistrate of some city in Greece or Asia Minor [WEBSTER and WILKINSON].

4. that thou mightest know—"know thoroughly." **hast been instructed**—orally instructed—lit., "catechized" or "catechetically taught," at first as a catechumen or candidate for Christian baptism.

5-25. ANNOUNCEMENT OF THE FORERUNNER. **5. Herod**—(See on Matt. 2:1). **course of Abia**—or Abijah; the eighth of the twenty-four orders of courses into which David divided the priests (see I Chron. 24:1, 4, 10). Of these courses only four returned after the captivity (Ezra 2:34-39), which were again subdivided into twenty-four—retaining the ancient name and order of each. They took the whole temple service for a week each.

ADAM CLARKE

2. *Even as they delivered them unto us which from the beginning were eyewitnesses.* Probably this alludes to the Gospels of Matthew and Mark, which it is likely were written before Luke wrote his, and on the models of which he professes to write his own; and *from the beginning* must mean from the time that Christ first began to proclaim the glad tidings of the Kingdom. *Eyewitnesses* must necessarily signify those who had been with Him from the beginning, and consequently had the best opportunities of knowing the truth of every fact.

3. *Having had perfect understanding.* "Having accurately traced up"—entered into the very spirit of the work, and examined everything to the bottom; in consequence of which investigation I am completely convinced of the truth of the whole. Though God gives His Holy Spirit to all them who ask Him, yet this Gift was never designed to set aside the use of those faculties with which He has already endued the soul, and which are as truly His gifts as the Holy Spirit itself is. The nature of inspiration, in the case of Luke, we at once discover: he set himself by impartial inquiry and diligent investigation to find the whole truth and to relate nothing but the truth; and the Spirit of God presided over and directed his inquiries, so that he discovered the whole truth and was preserved from every particle of error. *From the very first.* "From their origin." Some think *anothen* should, in this place, be translated "from above"; and that it refers to the inspiration by which Luke wrote. I prefer our translation, or "from the origin," which several good critics contend for, and which meaning it has in some of the best Greek writers. *Theophilus.* As the literal import of this word is "friend of God," some have supposed that under this name Luke comprised all the followers of Christ, to whom, as "friends of God," he dedicated this faithful history of the life, doctrine, death, and resurrection of our Lord. But this interpretation appears to have little solidity in it; for if all the followers of Christ are addressed, why is the singular number used? and what good end could there be accomplished by using a feigned name? Besides, *most excellent* could never be applied in this way, for it evidently designates a particular person, and one probably distinguished by his situation in life; though this does not necessarily follow from the title, which was often given in the way of friendship. *Theophilus* appears to have been some very reputable Greek or Roman who was one of Luke's disciples.

4. *Wherein thou hast been instructed.* In which you have been "catechized." It appears that Theophilus had already received the first elements of the Christian doctrine, but had not as yet been completely grounded in them. That he might know the certainty of the things in which he had been thus catechized, by having all the facts and their proofs brought before him *in order*, the Evangelist sent him this faithful and divinely inspired narrative.

5. *In the days of Herod, the king.* This was Herod, surnamed the Great, the son of Antipater, an Idumean by birth, who had professed himself a proselyte to the Jewish religion, but regarded no religion further than it promoted his secular interests and ambition. Thus, for the first time, the throne of Judah was filled by a person not of Jewish extraction, who had been forced upon the people by the Roman government. Hence it appears plain that the prophecy of Jacob, Gen. xlix. 10, was now fulfilled, for the sceptre had departed from Judah; and now was the time, according to another prophecy, to look for the Governor from Bethlehem, who should rule and feed the people of Israel, Mic. v. 1-2. *The course of Abia.* When the sacerdotal families grew very numerous, so that all could not officiate together at the Tabernacle, David divided them into twenty-four classes, that they might minister by turns, 1 Chron. xxiv. 1, etc., each family serving a whole week, 2 Kings xi. 7; 2 Chron. xxiii. 8. *Abia* was the eighth in the order in which they had been originally established, 1 Chron. xxiv. 10. These dates and persons are particularly mentioned as a full confirmation of the truth of the facts themselves; because any person, at the time this Gospel was written, might have satisfied himself by applying to the family of John the Baptist, the family

MATTHEW HENRY | JAMIESON, FAUSSET, BROWN | ADAM CLARKE

The wife of this Zacharias was of the daughters of Aaron too, and her name was *Elisabeth*, the very same name with *Elisheba*, the wife of Aaron, Exod. vi. 23. The priests were very careful to marry within their own family.

Now that which is observed concerning Zacharias and Elisabeth is,

1. That they were a very religious couple (*v.* 6): *They were both righteous before God;* they were sincerely and really so. They *approved* themselves *to him.* It is a happy thing when those who are joined to each other in marriage are both *joined to the Lord. They walked in all the commandments and ordinances of the Lord, blameless.* They showed it, not by their talk, but by their *works*; by the way they walked in and the rule they walked by. They walked not only in the *ordinances* of the Lord, which related to divine worship, but in the *commandments* of the Lord, which have reference to all the instances of a good conversation. Not that they never did in anything *come short* of their duty, but it was their constant care and endeavour to *come up* to it. Though they were not *sinless*, yet they were *blameless*; nobody could charge them with any open scandalous sin; they lived *honestly* and *inoffensively*.

2. That they had been long *childless*, *v.* 7. Children are a *heritage of the Lord.* They are valuable desirable blessings; yet many there are, who are *righteous before God*, who yet are not thus blessed. Elisabeth was *barren*, and they began to despair of ever having children, for they were both now *well stricken in years.* Many eminent persons were born of mothers that had been long childless, as Isaac, Jacob, Joseph, Samson, Samuel, and so here John Baptist, to make their birth the more remarkable and the blessing of it the more valuable to their parents.

II. The appearing of an angel to his father Zacharias, as he was ministering in the temple, *v.* 8–11. Observe,

1. How Zacharias was employed in the service of God (*v.* 8): He *executed the priest's office, before God, in the order of his course*; it was his *week of waiting*, and he was *upon duty.* Now it fell to Zacharias's lot to burn incense morning and evening for that week of his waiting, as other services fell to other priests *by lot* likewise. It was the burning of the daily incense at the *altar of incense* (*v.* 11), which was *in the temple* (*v.* 9), not in the most holy place, into which the high priest entered. The Jews say that one and the same priest burned not incense twice in all his days (there were such a multitude of them), at least never more than one week.

While Zacharias was burning incense in the temple, *the whole multitude of the people were praying without, v.* 10. These all addressed themselves to their devotions (in mental prayer, for their voice was not heard), when by the tinkling of a bell they had notice that the priest was gone in to burn incense. Now observe here, (1) That the true Israel of God always were a *praying* people. (2) That *then*, when ritual and ceremonial appointments were in full force, as this of *burning incense*, yet moral and spiritual duties were required to go along with them. David knew that when he was at a distance from the altar his prayer might be heard *without incense.* But, when he was *compassing the altar*, the incense could not be accepted *without prayer*, any more than the shell without the kernel. (3) That it is not enough for us to be where God is worshipped, if our hearts do not join in the worship. (4) All the prayers we offer up to God here in his courts are acceptable and successful only in virtue of the incense of Christ's intercession in the temple of God above. We cannot expect an interest in Christ's intercession if we do not *pray*, and pray *with our spirits*, and continue instant in prayer.

2. How, when he was thus employed, he was *honoured* with a messenger sent from heaven to him (*v.* 11): *There appeared unto him an angel of the Lord.*

his wife was of the daughters of Aaron—The priests might marry into any tribe, but "it was most commendable of all to marry one of the priests' line" [LIGHTFOOT].

6. commandments and ordinances—The one expressing their *moral*—the other their *ceremonial*—obedience [CALVIN and BENGEL], (Cf. Ezek. 11:20; Heb. 9:1). It has been denied that any such distinction was known to the Jews and New Testament writers. But Mark 12:33, and other passages, put this beyond all reasonable doubt.

7. So with Abraham and Sarah, Isaac and Rebekah, Elkanah and Hannah, Manoah and his wife.

9. his lot was to burn incense—The part assigned to each priest in his week of service was decided by lot. Three were employed at the offering of incense—to remove the ashes of the former service; to bring in and place on the golden altar the pan filled with hot burning coals taken from the altar of burnt offering; and to sprinkle the incense on the hot coals; and, while the smoke of it ascended, to make intercession for the people. This was the most distinguished part of the service (Rev. 8:3), and this was what fell to the lot of Zacharias at this time [LIGHTFOOT]. **10. praying without**—outside the court in front of the temple, where stood the altar of burnt offering; the men and women in separate courts, but the altar visible to all. **the time of incense**—which was offered along with the morning and evening sacrifice of every day; a beautiful symbol of the acceptableness of the *sacrifice* offered on the altar of burnt offering, with coals from whose altar the incense was burnt (Lev. 16:12, 13). This again was a symbol of the "living sacrifice" of themselves and their services offered daily to God by the worshippers. Hence the language of Psalm 141:2; Revelation 8:3. But that the acceptance of this daily offering depended on the *expiatory virtue* presupposed in the burnt offering, and pointing to the one "sacrifice of a sweet-smelling savor" (Eph. 5:2), is evident from Isaiah 6:6, 7.

of our Lord, or the surrounding neighbors. What a full proof of the Gospel history! It was published immediately after the time in which these facts took place; and among the very people, thousands of whom had been eyewitnesses of them; and among those, too, whose essential interest it was to have discredited them if they could. And yet, in all that age, in which only they could have been contradicted with advantage, no man ever arose to call them in question! What an absolute proof was this that the thing was impossible, and that the truth of the Gospel history was acknowledged by all who paid any attention to the evidences it produced! *Of the daughter of Aaron.* That is, she was of one of the sacerdotal families. This shows that John was most nobly descended. His father was a priest, and his mother the daughter of a priest; and thus by both father and mother he descended from the family of Amram, of whom came Moses, Aaron, and Miriam, the most illustrious characters in the whole Jewish history.

6. *They were both righteous.* Upright and holy in all their outward conduct in civil life. *Before God.* Possessing the spirit of the religion they professed; exercising themselves constantly in the presence of their Maker, whose eye they knew was upon all their conduct, and who examined all their motives. *Walking in all the commandments and ordinances of the Lord blameless.* None being able to lay any evil to their charge. They were as exemplary and conscientious in the discharge of their religious duties as they were in the discharge of the offices of civil life. Perhaps *commandments* may here mean the Decalogue; and *ordinances,* the ceremonial and judicial laws which were delivered after the Decalogue, as all the precepts delivered from Exodus xxi to xxiv are termed *ordinances.*

7. *Both were now well stricken in years.* By the order of God, sterility and old age both met in the person of Elisabeth to render the birth of a son (humanly speaking) impossible. This was an exact parallel to the case of Sarah and Abraham, Gen. xi. 30; xvii. 17. Christ must (by the miraculous power of God) be born of a virgin; whatever was connected with or referred to His incarnation must be miraculous and impressive. Isaac was his grand type, and therefore must be born miraculously—contrary to the common course and rule of nature. John the Baptist was to be the forerunner of Christ; his birth, like that of Isaac, must be miraculous, because, like the other, it was to be a representation of the birth of Christ. Therefore his parents were both far advanced in years, and besides, Elisabeth was naturally barren. The birth of these three extraordinary persons was announced nearly in the same way. God himself foretells the birth of Isaac, Gen. xvii. 16. The angel of the Lord announces the birth of John the Baptist, Luke i. 13; and six months after, the angel Gabriel, the same angel, proclaims to Mary the birth of Christ!

8. *Before God.* In the Temple, where God used to manifest His presence, though long before this time He had forsaken it; yet on this important occasion the angel of His presence had visited it.

9. *His lot was.* We are informed in the Talmud that it was the custom of the priests to divide the different functions of the sacerdotal office among themselves by *lot*; and in this case the decision of the lot was that Zacharias should at that time burn the incense before the Lord in the holy place.

10. *The whole multitude . . . were praying.* The incense was itself an emblem of the prayers and praises of the people of God; see Ps. cxli. 2; Rev. viii. 1. While therefore the rite is being performed by the priest, the people are employed in the thing signified. Happy the people who attend to the spirit as well as the letter of every divine institution! Incense was burnt twice a day in the Temple, in the morning and in the evening, Exod. xxx. 7-8; but the Evangelist does not specify the time of the day in which this transaction took place. It was probably in the morning.

11. *There appeared unto him an angel of the Lord.* There had been neither prophecy nor

MATTHEW HENRY

This angel stood *on the right side of the altar of incense*, on Zacharias's right hand. Zacharias had a good angel standing *at his right hand*, to encourage him.

3. What impression this made upon Zacharias (*v.* 12): *When Zacharias saw him* he was *troubled*, and *fear fell upon him*, *v.* 12. Though he was *righteous before God*, and *blameless* in his conversation, yet he could not be without some apprehensions. Ever since man sinned, his mind has been unable to bear the glory of such revelations and his conscience afraid of evil tidings brought by them. And for this reason God chooses to speak to us by men like ourselves, whose *terror* shall *not make us afraid*.

III. The message which the angel had to deliver to him, *v.* 13. He began his message, as angels generally did, with, *Fear not*. Perhaps when he saw the angel he was afraid lest he came to rebuke him for some mistake or miscarriage; "No," saith the angel, "*Fear not*, but compose thyself, that thou mayest with a sedate and even spirit receive the message I have to deliver to thee." Let us see what that is.

1. The *prayers* he has often made shall now receive an *answer of peace*: *Fear not, Zacharias, for thy prayer is heard*. If he means his particular prayer *for a son*, it must be the prayers he had formerly made for that mercy, when he was likely to have children. God will now, in giving this mercy, look a great way back to the prayers that he had made long since for and with his wife. Prayers of faith are *filed* in heaven, and are not *forgotten*, though the thing prayed for is not presently *given* in. If he means the prayers he was *now making*, we may suppose that those were according to the duty of his place, for the Israel of God and their welfare, and the performance of the promises made to them concerning the Messiah and the coming of his kingdom: "This prayer of thine is now *heard*; for thy wife shall shortly conceive him that is to be the Messiah's forerunner." Some of the Jewish writers themselves say that the priest, when he burnt incense, prayed for the *salvation of the whole world*; and now that prayer shall be heard. In general, "The prayers thou *now* makest, and all thy prayers, are accepted of God, and this shall be the sign that thou art accepted of God, Elisabeth shall *bear thee a son*."

2. He shall have a son in his old age, by Elisabeth his wife, who had been long barren. He is directed what name to give his son: *Call him John*, in Hebrew *Johanan*, a name we often meet with in the Old Testament: it signifies *gracious*.

3. This son shall be the joy of his family and of all his relations, *v.* 14. He shall be a *welcome child. Thou* for thy part *shalt have joy and gladness*. Mercies that have been long *waited for*, when they *come at last*, are the more acceptable. "He shall be such a son as thou shalt have reason to rejoice in; many parents, if they could foresee what their children will prove, instead of *rejoicing* at their birth, would wish they had *never been*; but I will tell thee what thy son will be, and then thou wilt not need to *rejoice with trembling* at his birth, as the best must do, but mayest rejoice with triumph at it. Nay, and *many shall rejoice at his birth*; all the relations of the family will rejoice in it, and all its well-wishers, because it is for the honour and comfort of the family," *v.* 58.

4. This son shall be a distinguished *favourite of Heaven*, and a distinguished *blessing to the earth*. The honour of having *a son* is nothing to the honour of having *such a son*.

(1) He shall be *great in the sight of the Lord*. God will *set him before his face* continually. He shall be a prophet, yea *more than a prophet*. He shall be *much*, he shall be *great, in the sight of the Lord*.

(2) He shall be a Nazarite, set apart to God from everything that is *polluting*; in token of this, according to the law of Nazariteship, he *shall drink neither wine nor strong drink*. He shall be a Nazar te for life. Which intimates that those that would be *eminent* servants of God, and employed in *eminent* services, must learn to live a life of self-denial and mortification, must be dead to the pleasures of sense, and keep their minds from everything that is darkening and disturbing to them.

(3) He shall be abundantly fitted and qualified for those great and eminent services. *He shall be filled with the Holy Ghost, even from his mother's womb*. [1.] Those that would be filled with the Holy Ghost must be sober and temperate, and very moderate in the use of wine and strong drink. *Be not drunk with wine*, but *be filled with the Spirit*, Eph. v. 18. [2.] It is possible that infants may be wrought upon by the *Holy Ghost*, even from their *mother's womb*; for John Baptist even then was *filled with the Holy Ghost*. God has promised to *pour out his Spirit* upon the *seed* of believers, Isa. xliv. 3.

JAMIESON, FAUSSET, BROWN

11. right side—the south side, between the altar and the candlestick, Zacharias being on the north side, in front of the altar, while offering incense [WEBSTER and WILKINSON]. But why there? The right was the favorable side (Matt. 25:33) [SCHOTTGEN and WETSTEIN in MEYER]; cf. Mark 16:5.

13. thy prayer is heard—doubtless for *offspring*, which by some presentiment he even yet had not despaired of. **John**—the same as "Johanan," so frequent in the Old Testament, meaning "Jehovah's gracious gift."

14. shall rejoice—so they did (vss. 58, 66); but the meaning rather is, "shall have cause to rejoice"—it would prove to many a joyful event.

15. great in the sight of the Lord—nearer to Him in official standing than all the prophets. (See on Matt. 11: 10, 11.) **drink neither wine . . .**—i.e., shall be a *Nazarite*, or "a separated one" (Num. 6:2, etc.). As the leper was the living symbol of *sin*, so was the Nazarite of *holiness;* nothing inflaming was to cross his lips; no razor to come on his head; no ceremonial defilement to be contracted. Thus was he to be "holy to the Lord [ceremonially] all the days of his separation." This separation was in ordinary cases temporary and voluntary: only *Samson* (Judg. 13:7), *Samuel* (I Sam. 1:11), and *John Baptist* were Nazarites from the womb. It was fitting that the utmost severity of legal consecration should be seen in Christ's forerunner. HE was the REALITY and PERFECTION of the Nazarite without the symbol, which perished in that living realization of it: "Such an High Priest became us, who was SEPARATE FROM SINNERS" (Heb. 7:26). **filled with the Holy Ghost, from . . . womb**—a holy vessel for future service.

ADAM CLARKE

angelic ministry vouchsafed to this people for about four hundred years. But now, as the Sun of Righteousness is about to arise upon them, the dayspring from on high visits them, that they may be prepared for that kingdom of God which was at hand.

12. *Zacharias . . . was troubled*. Or "confounded" at his sudden and unexpected appearance; *and fear fell upon him*, lest this heavenly messenger were come to denounce the judgments of God against a faithless and disobedient people, who had too long and too well merited them.

13. *Thy prayer is heard*. This probably refers, first, to the frequent prayers which he had offered to God for a son; and second, to those which he had offered for the deliverance and consolation of Israel. They are all heard—you shall have a son, and Israel shall be saved. If fervent, faithful prayers be not immediately answered, they should not be considered as lost; all such are heard by the Lord, are registered in heaven, and shall be answered in the most effectual way and in the best time. Answers to prayer are to be received by faith; but faith should not only accompany prayer while offered on earth, but follow it all its way to the throne of grace, and stay with it before the throne till dismissed with its answer to the waiting soul. *Thou shalt call his name John*. For the proper exposition of this name, see on Mark i. 4.

14. *Thou shalt have joy*. "He will be joy and gladness to you." A child of prayer and faith is likely to be a source of comfort to his parents. *Many shall rejoice at his birth*. He shall be the minister of God for good to multitudes, who shall, through his preaching, be turned from the error of their ways and converted to God, their Saviour.

15. *He shall be great in the sight of the Lord*. That is, before Jesus Christ, whose forerunner he shall be; or he shall be a "truly great person," for so this form of speech may imply. *Neither wine nor strong drink*. I.e., all fermented liquors which have the property of intoxicating, or producing drunkenness. The original word, *sikera*, comes from the Hebrew, *shakar*, "to inebriate." "Any inebriating liquor," says Jerome, "is called *sicera*, whether made of *corn, apples, honey, dates*, or any other fruits." *Shall be filled with the Holy Ghost*. Shall be divinely designated to this particular office, and qualified for it, *from his mother's womb*—from the instant of his birth.

MATTHEW HENRY	JAMIESON, FAUSSET, BROWN	ADAM CLARKE

MATTHEW HENRY

(4) He shall be instrumental for the conversion of many souls to God, and the preparing of them to receive and entertain the gospel of Christ, *v.* 16, 17. He shall be sent to the *children of Israel*, and not to the Gentiles; to the *whole* nation, and not to the family of *the priests only*. He shall go before *the Lord their God*, that is, before the Messiah. John shall *go before him*, a little before him, to give notice of his approach, and to prepare people to receive him. He shall go *in the spirit and power of Elias*. That is, *First*, He shall be such a man as Elias was, and do such works as Elias did—shall, like him, preach the necessity of repentance and reformation to a very corrupt and degenerate age—shall like him, be bold and zealous in reproving sin and witnessing against it even in the greatest, and be hated and persecuted for it. He shall be carried on in his work, as Elijah was, by a divine *spirit* and *power*, which shall crown his ministry with wonderful success. John Baptist went before Christ and his apostles, and introduced the gospel dispensation by preaching the substance of the gospel doctrine and duty, *Repent, with an eye to the kingdom of heaven. Secondly*, He shall be that very person who was prophesied of by Malachi under the name of Elijah (Mal. iv. 5), who should be *sent before the coming of the day of the Lord.* He shall *turn many of the children of Israel to the Lord their God.* Whatever has a tendency to *turn us from iniquity*, will turn us to Christ as *our Lord and our God*; for those who through grace are wrought upon to shake off the yoke of sin, will soon be persuaded to take upon them the yoke of the *Lord Jesus.* Hereby he shall *turn the hearts of the fathers to the children*, that is, of the Jews to the Gentiles; shall help to conquer the rooted prejudices which the Jews have against the Gentiles, which was begun to be done by John Baptist, who baptized and taught Roman soldiers as well as Jewish Pharisees, and who cured the pride and confidence of those Jews who gloried in their having Abraham to their father, and told them that God would *out of stones raise up children unto Israel*, Matt. iii. 9. When the Jews that embraced the faith of Christ were brought to join in communion with the Gentiles that did so too, then the heart of the fathers was turned to the children. And the effect of this will be, that enmities will be slain and discord made to cease; and they that are at variance, being united in his baptism, will be better reconciled one to another. This agrees with the account Josephus gives of John Baptist, *Antiq. lib.* 18. *cap*, 7. "That he was a good man, and taught the Jews the exercise of virtue, in piety towards God, and righteousness towards one another." And he saith, "The people flocked after him, and were exceedingly delighted in his doctrine." Thus he turned the hearts of fathers and children to God and one another, by *turning the disobedient to the wisdom of the just. First*, True religion is *the wisdom of just men.* It is both our wisdom and our duty to be religious; there is both equity and prudence in it. *Secondly*, It is not impossible but that those who have been unbelieving and *disobedient* may be turned to the *wisdom of the just*; divine grace can conquer the greatest ignorance and prejudice. *Thirdly*, The great design of the gospel is to bring people *home* to God, and to bring them nearer to *one another.* Hereby he shall *make ready a people prepared for the Lord.* All that are to be *devoted* to the Lord, and *made happy* in him, must first be *prepared* and *made ready* for him. Nothing has a more direct tendency to prepare people for Christ than the doctrine of repentance. When sin is thereby made grievous, Christ will become very precious.

IV. Zacharias's unbelief of the angel's prediction, and the rebuke he was laid under. We are here told,

1. What his unbelief spoke, *v.* 18. *Whereby shall I know this?* There are many instances in the Old Testament of those that had children when they were old, yet he cannot believe that he shall have this child of promise: *"For I am an old man*, and my wife is now well *stricken in years.* Therefore he must have *a sign* given him, or he will not believe." Though he had this notice given him in the temple, though it was given him when he was praying, and burning incense, and though a firm belief that God has an almighty power, and with him *nothing is impossible*, was enough to silence all objections, yet considering his own body and his wife's too much, unlike a son of Abraham, he *staggered at the promise.*

2. How his unbelief was *silenced*, and he *silenced* for it.

(1) The angel *stops his mouth.* Doth he ask, *Whereby shall I know this?* Let him know it by this, *I am Gabriel*, *v.* 19. He puts his name to his prophecy. This angel readily saith, *I am Gabriel*, which signifies *the power of God*, or, the *mighty one of God.* He is Gabriel, who *stands in the presence of God.* "Though

JAMIESON, FAUSSET, BROWN

16, 17. A religious and moral *reformer*, Elijah-like, he should be (Mal. 4:6, where the "turning of the people's heart to the Lord" is borrowed from I Kings 18:37). In both cases their success, though *great*, was *partial*—the *nation* was not gained. **17. before him**—before "the Lord their God" (vs. 16). By comparing this with Malachi 3:1 and Isaiah 40:3, it is plainly "Jehovah" in the flesh of Messiah [CALVIN and OLSHAUSEN] before whom John was to go as a *herald* to announce His approach, and a *pioneer* to prepare His way. **in the spirit**—after the model. **and power of Elias**—not his miraculous power, for "John did no miracle" (John 10:41), but his power in "turning the heart," or with like success in his ministry. Both fell on degenerate times; both witnessed fearlessly for God; neither appeared much save in the direct exercise of their ministry; both were at the head of schools of disciples; the success of both was similar.

fathers to the children—taken *literally*, this denotes the *restoration of parental fidelity* [MEYER and others], the decay of which is the beginning of religious and social corruption—one prominent feature of the coming revival being put for the whole. But what follows, explanatory of this, rather suggests a *figurative* sense. If "the disobedient" be "the children," and to "the fathers" belongs "the wisdom of the just" [BENGEL], the meaning will be, "he shall bring back the ancient spirit of the nation into their degenerate children" [CALVIN, etc.]. So Elijah invoked *"the God of Abraham, Isaac, and Israel,"* when seeking to "turn their heart back again" (I Kings 18:36, 37).

to make ready . . .—more clearly, "to make ready for the Lord a prepared people," to have in readiness a people prepared to welcome Him. Such preparation requires, in every age *and every soul*, an operation corresponding to the Baptist's ministry.

18. whereby . . .—Mary believed what was far harder without a sign. Abraham, though older, and doubtless Sarah, too, when the same promise was made to him, "staggered not at the promise of God through unbelief, but was strong in faith, giving glory to God." This was that in which Zacharias failed.

19. Gabriel—signifying "man of God," the same who appeared to Daniel at the time of incense (Dan. 9:21) and to Mary (vs. 26). **stand, . . .**—as his attendant (cf. I Kings 17:1).

ADAM CLARKE

16. *Many of the children of Israel shall he turn.* See this prediction fulfilled, chap. iii. 10-18.

17. *He shall go before him.* Jesus Christ, *in the spirit and power of Elias;* he shall resemble Elijah in his retired and austere manner of life, and in his zeal for the truth, reproving even princes for their crimes; compare 1 Kings xxi. 17-24 with Matt. xiv. 4. It was on these accounts that the Prophet Malachi, chap. iv. 6, had likened John to this prophet. See also Isa. xl. 3 and Mal. iv. 5-6.

To turn the hearts of the fathers. By a very expressive figure of speech Abraham, Isaac, and Jacob, and the rest of the patriarchs are represented here as having their hearts alienated from the Jews, their children, because of their unbelief and disobedience; but that the Baptist should so far succeed in converting them to the Lord their God that these holy men should again look upon them with delight and acknowledge them for their children.

The disobedient. Or "unbelieving," the persons who would no longer credit the predictions of the prophets relative to the manifestation of the Messiah. Unbelief and disobedience are so intimately connected that the same word in the sacred writings often serves for both.

19. *I am Gabriel.* This angel is mentioned in Dan. viii. 16; ix. 21. The original is exceedingly expressive; it is compounded of *geburah* and *el*, "the might of the strong God." An angel

MATTHEW HENRY

I am now talking with thee here, yet *I stand in the presence of God. I am sent to speak to thee,* sent on purpose to *show thee these glad tidings,* which, being so well worthy of all acceptation, thou oughtest to have received cheerfully."

(2) The angel *stops his mouth* indeed. "That thou mayest object no more, *behold thou shalt be dumb, v.* 20. If thou wilt have a sign for the support of thy faith, it shall be such a one as shall be also the punishment of thine unbelief; thou *shult not be able to speak till the day that these things shall be performed," v.* 20. Thou shalt be both *dumb* and *deaf;* the same word signifies both, and it is plain that he lost his hearing as well as his speech, for his friends *made signs* to him (*v.* 62) as well as he to them, *v.* 22. God dealt *justly* with him, because he had objected against God's word. God dealt *kindly* with him, and very tenderly and graciously. For, *First,* Thus he prevented his speaking any more such distrustful unbelieving words. It is better not to speak at all than to *speak wickedly. Secondly,* Thus he *confirmed* his faith; and, by his being disabled to *speak,* he is enabled to *think* the better. *Thirdly,* Thus he was kept from divulging the vision, and boasting of it. *Fourthly,* It was a great mercy that God's words should be fulfilled in their season, notwithstanding his sinful distrust. He shall not be for ever *dumb,* but only *till the day that these things shall be performed,* and then thy *lips* shall be *opened,* that thy *mouth* may *show forth God's praise.*

V. The return of Zacharias to the people, and at length to his family, and the conception of this child of promise.

1. The people staid, expecting Zacharias to come out of the temple, because he was to pronounce the blessing upon them in the name of the Lord. Though he staid beyond the usual time, yet they did not hurry away without the blessing, but *waited* for him, marvelling that he *tarried so long in the temple,* and afraid lest something was amiss, *v.* 21.

2. When he came out, he was *speechless, v.* 22. He was now to have dismissed the congregation with a blessing, but was dumb and not able to do it.

3. He made a shift to give them to understand that he had *seen a vision,* for he *beckoned to them,* and *remained speechless, v.* 22. The Old Testament speaks by signs; it *beckons to us,* but *remains speechless.* It is the gospel that speaks to us articulately, and gives us a clear view of that which in the Old Testament was seen *through a glass darkly.*

4. He staid out the *days of his ministration;* for, his lot being to *burn incense,* he could do that, though he was *dumb* and *deaf.* When we cannot perform the service of God so well as we would, yet, if we perform it as well as we can, God will accept of us in it.

5. He then returned to his family, and his *wife conceived, v.* 23, 24. *She hid herself five months,* and kept in private. (1) Lest she should do herself any prejudice. (2) Lest she should contract any ceremonial pollution which might intrench upon the Nazariteship of her child. (3) Some think it was in an excess of modesty that she *hid herself.* Or, it was in token of her humility, that she might not seem to boast of the honour God had put upon her. (4) She *hid herself* for devotion. She gives this reason for her retirement, "*For thus hath the Lord dealt with me;* he hath *taken away my reproach among men.*" Fruitfulness was looked upon to be so great a blessing among the Jews that it was a great reproach to be barren; and those who were so were concluded to be guilty of some great sin *unknown.* Now Elisabeth triumphs, that not only this reproach is taken away, but great glory is put upon her instead of it: *Thus hath the Lord dealt with me in the days wherein he looked on me.*

Verses 26–38

We have here notice given us of all that it was fit we should know concerning the incarnation and conception of our blessed Saviour. The same angel, Gabriel, that was employed in making known to Zacharias God's purpose concerning *his son,* is employed in this also; for in this, the same glorious work of redemption, which was *begun* in that, is *carried on.*

I. We have here an account given of the mother of our Lord.

1. Her name was *Mary,* the same name with *Miriam,* the sister of Moses and Aaron; the name signifies *exalted.*

2. She was a daughter of the royal family, lineally descended from David, and she herself and all her friends knew it, for she went under the title and character of the *house of David.* She was enabled by God's providence, and the care of the Jews, to pre-

JAMIESON, FAUSSET, BROWN

20. dumb—speechless. **not able**—deprived of the power of speech (vs. 64). He asked a *sign,* and now he got it. **until the day . . .**—See on vs. 64.

21. waited—to receive from him the usual benediction (Num. 6:23-27). **tarried so long**—It was not usual to tarry long, lest it should be thought vengeance had stricken the people's representative for something wrong [LIGHTFOOT]. **22. speechless**—dumb, and deaf also (see vs. 62).

24. hid five months—till the event was put beyond doubt and became apparent.

26-38. ANNUNCIATION OF CHRIST. (See on Matt. 1:18-21.) **26. sixth month**—of Elisabeth's time.

ADAM CLARKE

with such a name was exceedingly proper for the occasion, as it pointed out that all-prevalent power by which the strong God could accomplish every purpose and subdue all things to himself. *That stand in the presence of God.* This is an allusion to the case of the prime minister of an Eastern monarch, who alone has access to his master at all times and is therefore said, in the Eastern phrase, "to see the presence," or "to be in the presence." From the allusion we may conceive the angel Gabriel to be in a state of high favor and trust before God.

20. *Thou shalt be dumb.* "Silent"; this translation is literal; the angel immediately explains it, You shall not be *able to speak.* Dumbness ordinarily proceeds from a natural imperfection or debility of the organs of speech. In this case there was no natural weakness or unfitness in those organs; but for his rash and unbelieving speech, silence is imposed upon him by the Lord, and he shall not be able to break it till the Power that has silenced him gives him again the permission to speak! Let those who are intemperate in the use of their tongues behold here the severity and mercy of the Lord: nine months' silence for one intemperate speech! Many, by giving way to the language of unbelief, have lost the language of praise and thanksgiving for months, if not years!

21. *The people waited.* The time spent in burning the incense was probably about half an hour, during which there was a profound silence as the people stood without engaged in mental prayer. To this there is an allusion in Rev. viii. 1-5. Zacharias had spent not only the time necessary for burning the incense, but also that which the discourse between him and the angel took up.

22. *They perceived that he had seen a vision.* As the sanctuary was separated from the court by a great veil, the people could not see what passed; but they understood this from Zacharias himself, who "made signs," or "nodded" unto them to that purpose. Signs are the only means by which a dumb man can convey his ideas to others.

23. *As soon as the days of his ministration were accomplished.* Each family of the priesthood officiated one whole week, 2 Kings xi. 17.

24. *Hid herself five months.* That she might have the fullest proof of the accomplishment of God's promise before she appeared in public, or spoke of her mercies.

25. *To take away my reproach.* As fruitfulness was a part of the promise of God to His people, Gen. xvii. 6, and children, on this account, being considered as a particular blessing from Heaven, Exod. xxiii. 26; Lev. xxvi. 9; Ps. cxxvii. 3, so barrenness was considered among the Jews as a reproach, and a token of the disapprobation of the Lord, 1 Sam. i. 6.

MATTHEW HENRY

serve their genealogies, to *make it out*, and as long as the promise of the Messiah was to be fulfilled it was *worth keeping*; but for those now, who are brought low in the world, to have descended from persons of honour, is not worth mentioning.

3. She was *a virgin*, but *espoused* to one of the same royal stock, like her, however, of low estate. His name was Joseph; he also was *of the house of David*, Matt. i. 20. Christ's mother was a *virgin*. But he was born of a *virgin espoused*, made up to be married, and contracted, to put honour upon the married state.

4. She lived in Nazareth, a *city of Galilee*, a remote corner of the country, and in no reputation for religion or learning, but which bordered upon the heathen, and therefore was called *Galilee of the Gentiles*. The angel was sent to her from Nazareth. No distance or disadvantage of place shall be a prejudice to those for whom God has favours in store.

II. The *address* of the angel to her, *v.* 28. He surprised her with this salutation, *Hail, thou that art highly favoured*. This was intended to raise in her, 1. A value for *herself*. In some, who like Mary pore only on their *low estate*, there is occasion for it. 2. An expectation of great news, not from abroad, but from above. *Hail, thou, χαῖρε—rejoice thou*; it was the usual form of salutation.

(1) She is dignified: "Thou art *highly favoured*. God, in his choice of thee to be the mother of the Messiah, has put an honour upon thee peculiar to thyself."

(2) She has the presence of God with her: "*The Lord is with thee*." Nothing is to be despaired of, not the performance of any service, not the obtaining of any favour, though ever so great, if we have *God with us*.

(3) She has the blessing of God upon her: "*Blessed art thou among women*; not only thou shalt be accounted so by men, but thou shalt be so. Thou that art so *highly favoured* in this instance mayest expect in other things to be *blessed*." She explains this herself (*v.* 48), *All generations shall call me blessed*.

III. The consternation she was in, upon this address, *v.* 29. *When she saw him* she is *confounded* at it, as not conscious to herself of anything that either *merited* or *promised* such great things; and she *cast in her mind what manner of salutation this should be*. Was it from heaven or of men? Her thoughtfulness upon this occasion gives a very useful intimation to young people of her sex, when addresses are made to them, to consider and *cast in their minds* what manner of *salutations* they are.

IV. The message itself which the angel had to deliver to her. He went on with his errand, *v.* 30. To what he had said she made no reply; he therefore confirms it: "*Fear not, Mary, thou hast found favour with God* more than thou thinkest of, as there are many who think they are more favoured of God than really they are." Doth God favour thee? Is he for thee? No matter who is against thee.

1. Though she is a *virgin*, she shall have the honour of being a *mother*: "*Thou shalt conceive in thy womb, and bring forth a son*, thou shalt *call his name Jesus*," *v.* 31.

2. Though she lives in *poverty* and *obscurity*, yet she shall have the honour to be the mother of the Messiah; her son shall be named *Jesus—a Saviour*. He will be very *nearly allied* to the *upper world*. He *shall be great*, truly great, for he shall be called *the Son of the Highest*. He shall be *called*, and not *miscalled*, the *Son of the Highest*. Those who are the children of God, are *truly great*, and therefore are concerned to be *very good*, 1 John iii. 1, 2. He will be very *highly preferred* in the *lower world*; for, though appearing in the form of a servant, yet *the Lord God shall give unto him the throne of his father David*, *v.* 32. His people will not *give him that throne*, but the *Lord God* shall give him a right to *rule them*, and set him as *his king* upon the *holy hill of Zion*. He assures her, (1) That his kingdom shall be *spiritual*: he shall *reign over the house of Jacob*. It must therefore be a *spiritual* kingdom, the house of Israel *according to promise*, that he must *rule over*. (2) That it shall be eternal: he shall reign *for ever*, and *of his kingdom there shall be no end*. Other crowns endure not *to every generation*, but Christ's doth.

V. The further information given her, upon her enquiry.

1. It is a just enquiry which she makes: "*How shall this be?*" *v.* 34. She knew that the Messiah must be born of *a virgin*; and, if she must be his mother, she desires to know how. This was not the language of her distrust, but of a desire to be further instructed.

2. It is a satisfactory answer that is given to it, *v.* 25. (1) She shall conceive by *the power of the Holy Ghost*. A divine power will undertake it, the

JAMIESON, FAUSSET, BROWN

Joseph, of the house of David—(See on Matthew 1: 16).

28. highly favoured—a word only once used elsewhere (Eph. 1:6, "made accepted"): cf. vs. 30, "Thou hast found favour with God." The mistake of the *Vulgate's* rendering, "full of grace," has been taken abundant advantage of by the Romish Church. As the mother of our Lord, she was the most "blessed among women" in external distinction; but let them listen to the Lord's own words. "Nay, rather blessed are they that hear the word of God and keep it." (See on ch. 11:27.)

A. T. ROBERTSON:

30. "Favor" (*charin*). Grace. Same root as *chairo* (rejoice) and *charitoo* in verse 28. To find favor is a common Old Testament phrase. *Charis* is a very ancient and common word with a variety of applied meanings. They all come from the notion of sweetness, charm, loveliness, joy, delight, like words of grace (Luke 4:22), growing grace (Eph. 4:29), with grace (Col. 4:6). The notion of kindness is in it also, especially of God toward men as here. It is a favorite word for Christianity, the Gospel of the grace of God (Acts 20:24) in contrast with law or works (John 1:16). Gratitude is expressed also (Luke 6:32), especially to God (Rom. 6:17). "With God" (*para toi theoi*). Beside God.

—*Word Pictures in the New Testament*

31. The angel purposely conforms his language to Isaiah's famous prophecy (ch. 7:14) [CALVIN]. **32, 33.** This is but an echo of the sublime prediction in Isaiah 9:6, 7.

34. How . . .—not the unbelief of Zacharias, "Whereby shall I know this?" but, taking the fact for granted, "*How is it to be*, so contrary to the unbroken law of human birth?" Instead of reproof, therefore, her question is answered in mysterious detail. **35. Holy Ghost**—(See on Matthew 1:18). **power of the highest**—the immediate energy of the Godhead conveyed by the Holy Ghost.

ADAM CLARKE

26. *A city of Galilee*. As Joseph and Mary were both of the family of David, the patrimonial estate of which lay in Bethlehem, it seems as if the family residence should have been in that city, and not in Nazareth; for we find that, even after the return from the Captivity, the several families went to reside in these cities to which they originally belonged. See Neh. xi. 3. But it is probable that the Holy Family removed to Galilee for fear of exciting the jealousy of Herod, who had usurped that throne to which they had an indisputable right.

28. *And the angel came in unto her*. Some think that all this business was transacted in a vision, and that there was no personal appearance of the angel. When divine visions were given, they are announced as such in the sacred writings; nor can we with safety attribute anything to a vision where a divine communication is made, unless it be specified as such in the text. *Hail*. Analogous to, "Peace be to you"—May you enjoy all possible blessings! *Highly favoured*. As being chosen in preference to all the women upon earth to be the mother of the Messiah. Not the "mother of God," for that is blasphemy. *The Lord is with thee*. You are about to receive the most convincing proofs of God's peculiar favor toward you. *Blessed art thou among women*. That is, you are favored beyond all others.

29. *She was troubled at his saying*. The glorious appearance of the heavenly messenger filled her with amazement, and she was puzzled to find out the purport of his speech.

31. *Thou . . . shalt call his name JESUS*. See on Matt. i. 20-21; here; chap. ii. 21; and John i. 29.

33. *The house of Jacob*. All who belong to the twelve tribes, the whole Israelitish people.

34. *Seeing I know not a man*. Or "husband." As she was only contracted to Joseph, and not as yet married, she knew that this conception could not have yet taken place; and she modestly inquires by what means the promise of the angel is to be fulfilled in order to regulate her conduct accordingly.

35. *The Holy Ghost shall come upon thee*. This conception shall take place suddenly, and the Holy Spirit himself shall be the grand Operator. *The power*, the miracle-working power, *of the Highest shall overshadow thee*, to accomplish this purpose, and to protect you from danger. As there is a plain allusion to the Spirit of God brooding over the face of the waters, to render them prolific, Gen. i. 2, I am the more firmly established in the opinion advanced on Matt. i. 20, that the rudiments of the human nature of Christ were a real creation in the womb of the Virgin, by the energy of the Spirit of God. *Therefore also that holy thing* (or Person) . . . *shall be called the Son of God*. We may plainly perceive here that the angel does not give the appellation of *Son of God* to the divine nature of Christ, but to that holy person or thing which was to be born of the Virgin by the energy of the Holy Spirit. The divine nature could not be born of the Virgin; the human nature was born of her. The divine nature had no beginning; it was God manifested in the flesh, 1 Tim. iii. 16; it was that Word which, being in the beginning (from eternity) with God, John i. 2, was afterwards made flesh (became manifest in human nature), and tabernacled among us, John i. 14. Of this divine nature the angel does not particularly speak here, but of the tabernacle or shrine which God was now preparing for it, viz., the *holy thing* that was to be born of the Virgin. Two natures must ever be distinguished in Christ: the human nature, in reference to which He is the Son of God and inferior to Him, Mark xiii. 32; John v. 19; xiv. 28; and the divine nature,

MATTHEW HENRY

power of *the Holy Ghost* himself.

(2) She must *ask no questions* concerning the way and manner how it shall be wrought; for the Holy Ghost, as the *power of the Highest*, shall *overshadow* her. The formation of every babe in the womb, and the entrance of the spirit of life into it, is a mystery in nature. We were *made in secret*. Much more was the formation of the child Jesus a *mystery*.

(3) The child she shall conceive is a *holy thing*, and therefore must not be conceived by *ordinary generation*. He is spoken of emphatically, *That Holy Thing*, such as never was; and he shall be called *the Son of God*. His human nature must be so produced, as it was fit that should be which was to be taken into union with the divine nature.

3. It was a further encouragement to her faith to be told that *her cousin Elisabeth*, though stricken in years, was *with child*, *v.* 36. Here is an age of wonders beginning. *This is the sixth month with her that was called barren*. The angel assures Mary of this, to encourage her faith, and concludes with that great truth, of undoubted certainty and universal use, *For with God nothing shall be impossible* (*v.* 37), and, if nothing, then not this. No *word* of God must be *incredible to us*, as long as no *work* of God is *impossible to him*.

VI. Her acquiescence in the will of God concerning her, *v.* 38. She owns herself, 1. A believing subject to the divine authority: "*Behold, the handmaid of the Lord*. Lord, I am at thy service." She leaves the issue with God, and submits entirely to his will. 2. A believing expectant of the divine favour. She is not only content that it should be so, but humbly desires that it may be so: *Be it unto me according to thy word*. We must, as Mary here, *guide* our desires by the word of God, and *ground* our hopes *upon* it. Be it unto me *according to thy word*; just so, and no otherwise.

Hereupon, *the angel departed from her*; having completed the errand he was sent upon, he returned.

Verses 39–56

We have here an interview between the two happy mothers, Elisabeth and Mary. Sometimes it may prove a better piece of service than we think to bring good people together, to compare notes.

I. The visit which Mary made to Elisabeth, *v.* 39. She *arose*, and left her affairs, to attend this greater matter: *in those days, at that time*. She went *with care, diligence*, and *expedition*. She went *to a city of Judah in the hill-country*; thither Mary hastened, though it was a long journey, some scores of miles.

It is generally supposed that she went thither for the confirming of her faith, and to rejoice with her sister-favourite. And, besides, she went thither, perhaps, that she might be more retired from company, or else might have more agreeable company than she could have in Nazareth. We may suppose that she did not acquaint any of her neighbours at Nazareth with the message she had received from heaven, yet longed to *talk over* a thing she had a thousand times *thought over*, and knew no person in the world with whom she could *freely* converse concerning it but her cousin Elisabeth. It is very beneficial and comfortable for those that have a good work of grace begun in their souls, to consult those who are in the same case. They will find that, as in water face answers to face, so doth the heart of man to man, of Christian to Christian.

II. The meeting between Mary and Elisabeth. Mary entered into the house of Zacharias. She *saluted Elisabeth* (*v.* 40), told her that she was come to make her visit, and *rejoice with her* in her joy.

1. The babe *leaped in her womb*, *v.* 41. It is very probable that she had often felt the child stir; but this was a more than ordinary motion of the child, which alarmed her to expect something very extraordinary. The *babe leaped* as it were to give a signal to his mother that *he* was now at hand whose forerunner he was to be.

2. Elisabeth was herself *filled with the Holy Ghost*, or a Spirit of prophecy, by which she was given to understand that the Messiah was at hand. The uncommon motion of the babe in her womb was a token of the extraordinary emotion of her spirit under a divine impulse.

III. The welcome which Elisabeth, by the Spirit of prophecy, gave to Mary, the mother of our Lord.

1. She congratulates her on her honour. She *spoke with a loud voice*. She said, *Blessed art thou among women*, the same word that the angel had said, *v.* 28. But Elisabeth adds a reason, *Therefore blessed art thou* because *blessed is the fruit of thy womb*. Elisabeth was the wife of a priest, and in years, yet she *grudges* not that her kinswoman, who was many years younger than she, should have the honour of conceiving in her virginity, and being the mother of the Messiah,

JAMIESON, FAUSSET, BROWN

overshadow—a word suggesting how gentle, while yet efficacious, would be this Power [BENGEL]; and its mysterious secrecy, withdrawn, as if by a cloud, from human scrutiny [CALVIN]. **that holy thing born of thee**—that holy Offspring of thine. **therefore . . . Son of God**—That Christ is the Son of God in His divine and eternal nature is clear from all the New Testament; yet here we see that Sonship efflorescing into human and palpable manifestation by His being born, through "the power of the Highest," an Infant of days. We must neither think of a *double* Sonship, as some do, harshly and without all ground, nor deny what is here plainly expressed, the connection between His human birth and His proper personal Sonship. **36. thy cousin**—"relative," but how near the word says not. **conceived . . .**—This was to Mary an *unsought* sign, in reward of her faith. **37. For . . .**—referring to what was said by the angel to Abraham in like case (Gen. 18:14), to strengthen her faith. **38.** Marvellous faith in *such* circumstances!

39-56. VISIT OF MARY TO ELISABETH. **39. hill country**—the mountainous tract running along the middle of Judea, from north to south [WEBSTER and WILKINSON]. **with haste**—transported with the announcement to herself and with the tidings, now first made known to her, of Elisabeth's condition. **a city of Juda**—probably Hebron (see Josh. 20:7; 21:11).

40. saluted Elisabeth—now returned from her seclusion (vs. 24). **41. babe leaped**—From vs. 44 it is plain that this maternal sensation was something extraordinary—a sympathetic emotion of the unconscious babe, at the presence of the mother of his Lord.

ADAM CLARKE

which was from eternity, and equal to God, John i. 1; x. 30; Rom. ix. 5; Col. i. 16-18. It is true that to Jesus the Christ, as He appeared among men, every characteristic of the divine nature is sometimes attributed without appearing to make any distinction between the divine and human natures. But is there any part of the Scriptures in which it is plainly said that the divine nature of Jesus was *the Son of God?* Here, I trust, I may be permitted to say, with all due respect for those who differ from me, that the doctrine of the eternal sonship of Christ is in my opinion anti-scriptural and highly dangerous.

36. *Thy cousin Elisabeth.* "Thy kinswoman." As Elisabeth was of the tribe of Levi, v. 5, and Mary of the tribe of Judah, they could not be relatives but by the mother's side. *She hath also conceived.* And this is wrought by the same power and energy through which you shall conceive. Thus God has given you a proof and pledge, in what He has done for Elisabeth, of what He will do for you; therefore, have faith in God. *Who was called barren.* It is probable that Elisabeth got this appellative by way of reproach; or to distinguish her from some other Elisabeth, also well-known, who had been blessed with children. Perhaps this is the reproach which Elisabeth speaks of in v. 25, her common name among men, among the people who knew her, being "Elisabeth the barren."

37. *For with God nothing shall be impossible.* Words of the very same import with those spoken by the Lord to Sarah, when He foretold the birth of Isaac, Gen. xviii. 14, "Is any thing too hard for the Lord?" As there can be no doubt that Mary perceived this allusion to the promise and birth of Isaac, so she must have had her faith considerably strengthened by reflecting on the intervention of God in that case.

38. *Behold the handmaid of the Lord.* I fully credit what thou sayest, and am perfectly ready to obey thy commands, and to accomplish all the purposes of thy grace concerning me. It appears that at the instant of this act of faith, and purposed obedience, the conception of the immaculate humanity of Jesus took place; and it was done unto her according to his word.

39. *In those days.* As soon as she could conveniently fit herself out for the journey. *With haste.* This probably refers to nothing else than the earnestness of her mind to visit her relative Elisabeth, and to see what the Lord had wrought for her.

41. *Elisabeth was filled with the Holy Ghost.* This seems to have been the accomplishment of the promise made by the angel, v. 15, "He shall be filled with the Holy Ghost, even from his mother's womb." The mother is filled with the Holy Spirit, and the child in her womb becomes sensible of the divine influence.

42. *Blessed art thou among women.* Repeating the words of the angel, v. 28, of which she had probably been informed by the holy Virgin, in the present interview.

MATTHEW HENRY

whereas the honour put upon her was *much less*; she *rejoices* in it. While we cannot but own that we are more *favoured* of God than we deserve, let us by no means envy that others are *more highly* favoured than we are.

2. She acknowledges her condescension, in making her this visit (*v.* 43): *Whence is this to me, that the mother of my Lord should come to me?* She calls the virgin Mary the *mother of her Lord.* She not only bids her welcome to her house, but reckons this visit a great favour, which she thought herself unworthy of. *Whence is this to me?* Those that are filled with the Holy Ghost have *low thoughts* of their own merits, and high thoughts of God's favours.

3. She acquaints her with the concurrence of the babe in her womb, in this welcome to her (*v.* 44): "*As soon as the voice of thy salutation sounded in my ears*, not only my heart *leaped for joy*, but the *babe in my womb did so* too." He *leaped* as it were *for joy* that the Messiah, whose harbinger he was to be, would himself come so soon after him. This would serve very much to strengthen the faith of the virgin, that there were such assurances as these given to others.

4. She commends her faith, and encourages it (*v.* 45): *Blessed is she that believed.* Believing souls are blessed souls. They are *blessed* who *believe* the word of God, for that word will not fail them; *there shall*, without doubt, *be a performance of those things which are told her from the Lord.* The faithfulness of God is the blessedness of the faith of the saints. Those that have experienced the performance of God's promises themselves should encourage others to hope that he will be as good as his word to them also.

IV. Mary's song of praise, upon this occasion. Elisabeth's prophecy was an echo to the virgin Mary's salutation, and this song is yet a stronger *echo* to that prophecy. We may suppose the blessed virgin to come in, very much *fatigued* with her journey; yet she forgets that, and is inspired with new life, and vigour, and joy, upon the confirmation she here meets with of her faith.

1. Here are the expressions of joy and praise, and God alone the object of the praise and centre of the joy. Observe how Mary here speaks of God.

(1) With great reverence of him, as *the Lord*: "*My soul doth magnify the Lord.*" Those, and those only, are *advanced* in mercy, who are thereby brought to think the more *highly* and *honourably* of God. The more honour God has any way put upon us, the more honour we must study to give to him; and *then* only are we accepted in magnifying the Lord, when our *souls* magnify him, and *all that is within us.* Praising work must be soul work.

(2) With great complacency in him as *her Saviour*: *My spirit rejoiceth in God my Saviour.* This seems to have reference to the Messiah, whom she was to be the mother of. She calls him *God her Saviour*; for the angel had told her that he should be the *Son of the Highest*, and that his name should be *Jesus, a Saviour*; this she fastened upon, with application to herself: *He is God my Saviour.* Even the mother of our Lord had need of an interest in him as her Saviour, and would have been undone without it.

2. Here are just causes assigned for this joy and praise.

(1) Upon *her own* account, *v.* 48, 49. Her *spirit rejoiced in the Lord*, because of the *kind* things he had done for her. *He has regarded the low estate of his handmaiden.* "He has chosen me to this honour, notwithstanding my great meanness, poverty, and obscurity." And, if God *regards her low estate*, he not only thereby gives a specimen of his favour to the whole race of mankind, whom he *remembers in their low estate*, but secures a lasting honour to her (for such the honour is that God bestows, honour that fades not away): "*From henceforth all generations shall call me blessed.*" Elisabeth had once and again called her *blessed*: "But that is not all," saith she, "all generations of Gentiles as well as Jews shall call me so." Her *soul magnifies* the Lord (*v.* 49): *He that is mighty has done to me great things.* A *great* thing indeed, that a *virgin* should *conceive.* A *great* thing indeed, that Messiah should now at length be born. It is the *power of the Highest* that appears in this. She adds, *and holy is his name.* He that is *mighty*, even he *whose name is holy*, has *done to me great things.* Glorious things may be expected from him that is both *mighty* and *holy*; who *can do everything*, and *will* do everything *well* and *for the best.*

(2) Upon the account of *others.* The virgin Mary, as the mother of the Messiah, is become a kind of public person, and therefore *looks abroad*, looks *about her*, looks *before her*, and takes notice of God's various dealings with the children of men, *v.* 50, &c. It is a certain truth that *God has mercy in store*,

JAMIESON, FAUSSET, BROWN

42-44. What beautiful superiority to *envy* have we here! High as was the distinction conferred upon herself, Elisabeth loses sight of it altogether, in presence of one more honored still; upon whom, with her unborn Babe, in an ecstasy of inspiration, she pronounces a benediction, feeling it to be a wonder unaccountable that the mother of her Lord should come to *her*." "Turn this as we will, we shall never be able to see the propriety of calling an unborn child "Lord," but by supposing Elisabeth, like the prophets of old, enlightened to perceive the Messiah's *Divine nature*" [OLSHAUSEN]. "The mother of *my Lord*"—but not "*My Lady*" (cf. ch. 20:42; John 20:28) [BENGEL]. **45.** An additional benediction on the Virgin for her implicit faith, in tacit and delicate contrast with her own husband. **for . . .**—rather, as in the margin, "that." **46-55.** A magnificent canticle, in which the strain of Hannah's ancient song, in like circumstances, is caught up, and just slightly modified and sublimed. Is it unnatural to suppose that the spirit of the blessed Virgin had been drawn beforehand into mysterious sympathy with the ideas and the tone of this hymn, so that when the life and fire of inspiration penetrated her whole soul it spontaneously swept the chorus of this song, enriching the Hymnal of the Church with that spirit-stirring canticle which has resounded ever since from its temple walls? In both songs, those holy women, filled with wonder to behold "the proud, the mighty, the rich," passed by, and, in their persons the lowliest chosen to usher in the greatest events, sing of this as no capricious movement, but *a great law of the kingdom of God,* by which He delights to "*put down the mighty from their seats and exalt them of low degree.*" In both songs the strain dies away on CHRIST; in Hannah's under the name of "Jehovah's King"—to whom, through all His line, from David onwards to Himself, He will "give strength"; His "Anointed," whose horn He will exalt (I Sam. 2:10); in the Virgin's song, it is as the "Help" promised to Israel by all the prophets. **My soul . . . my spirit**—"all that is within me" (Ps. 103:1). **47. my Saviour**—Mary, poor heart, never dreamt, we see, of her own "immaculate conception"—in the offensive language of the Romanists—any more than of her own immaculate life.

ALEXANDER MACLAREN:

There is a deep truth there. God's voice is made more sure to our weakness when it is echoed by human lips, and our inmost hopes attain substance when they are shared and spoken by another. We need not attribute to the maiden from Nazareth philosophical accuracy when she speaks of her "soul" and "spirit." Her first words are a burst of rapturous and wondering praise, in which the full heart runs over. Silence is impossible, and speech a relief. They are not to be construed with the microscopic accuracy fit to be applied to a treatise on psychology. "All that is within" her praises and is glad. She does not think so much of the stupendous fact as of her own meekly exultant heart, and of God, to whom its outgoings turn. There are moods in which the devout soul dwells on its own calm blessedness and on God, its source, more directly than on the gift which brings it.

Note the twofold act—magnifying and rejoicing. We magnify God when we take into our vision some fragment more of the complete circle of His essential greatness, or when, by our means, our fellows are helped to do so. The intended effect of all His dealings is that we should think more nobly—that is, more worthily—of Him. The fuller knowledge of His friendly greatness leads to joy in Him which makes the spirit bound as in a dance—for such is the meaning of the word "rejoice"—and which yet is calm and deep. Note the double name of God—Lord and Savior. Mary bows in lowly obedience, and looks up in as lowly, conscious need of deliverance, and beholding in God both His majesty and His grace, magnifies and exults at once.—*Expositions of Holy Scripture*

ADAM CLARKE

43. *The mother of my Lord.* The prophetic spirit, which appears to have overshadowed Elisabeth, gave her a clear understanding in the mystery of the birth of the promised Messiah.

45. *Blessed is she that believed; for there shall be.* Or, "Blessed is she who hath believed that there shall be." This I believe to be the proper arrangement of the passage, and is thus noticed in the marginal reading. Faith is here represented as the foundation of true happiness, because it receives the fulfillment of God's promises.

46. *And Mary said.* Two copies of the Itala, and some books mentioned by Origen, give this song to Elisabeth. It is a counterpart of the song of Hannah, as related in 1 Sam. ii. 1-10. *My soul doth magnify the Lord.* The verb signifies "to celebrate with words, to extol with praises." This is the only way in which God can be magnified, or made great; for, strictly speaking, nothing can be added to God, for He is infinite and eternal. Therefore the way to magnify Him is to show forth and celebrate those acts in which He has manifested His greatness.

47. *My spirit hath rejoiced.* "Exulted." These words are uncommonly emphatical—they show that Mary's whole soul was filled with the divine influence, and wrapped up in God.

48. *He hath regarded.* "Looked favorably." In the most tender and compassionate manner He has visited me in my humiliation, drawing the reasons of His conduct, not from any excellence in me, but from His own eternal kindness and love. *All generations shall call me blessed.* This was the character by which alone she wished to be known, viz., "The blessed or happy virgin." What dishonor do those do to this holy woman who give her names and characters which her pure soul would abhor, and which properly belong to God, her *Saviour!* By her votaries she is addressed as "Queen of Heaven," "Mother of God," titles both absurd and blasphemous.

49. *He that is mighty hath done to me great things!* Or "miracles." *Holy is his name.* Probably the word which Mary used was *chesed,* which though we sometimes translate *holy,* see Ps. lxxxvi. 2; cxlv. 17, yet the proper meaning is "abundant goodness, exuberant kindness"; and this well agrees with the following clause.

MATTHEW HENRY

mercy in reserve. But never did this appear so as in sending his Son into the world to save us (*v.* 50): *His mercy is on them that fear him;* it has always been so. But he hath manifested this *mercy*, so as never before, in sending his Son to bring in an everlasting righteousness, and work out an everlasting salvation, for them that fear him, and this *from generation to generation*; for there are gospel privileges transmitted by entail, and intended for perpetuity. In him *mercy* is settled upon all that *fear God*, pardoning mercy, healing mercy, accepting mercy, crowning mercy, *from generation to generation*, while the world stands. It has been a common observation that God in his providence puts *contempt* upon the *haughty* and *honour* upon the *humble*. As God had, with his *mercy* to her, shown himself *mighty* also (*v.* 48, 49), so he had, with his *mercy on them that fear him, shown strength* likewise *with his arm*. In the course of his providence, it is his usual method to *cross the expectations of men. Proud men* expect to carry all before them, but he *scatters them in the imagination of their hearts*, and brings them low. The *mighty* think to secure themselves by might *in their seats*, but he *puts them down*, while, on the other hand, those of *low degree* are wonderfully *exalted*. This observation concerning *honour* holds likewise concerning *riches*; many who were so poor that they had not bread for themselves and their families, by some surprising turn of Providence in favour of them, come to be *filled with good things*; while, on the other hand, those who were rich, are strangely impoverished, and *sent away empty*. God takes a pleasure in *disappointing* their expectations who promise themselves *great things* in the world, and in *out-doing* the expectations of those who promise themselves but *a little*. As a *good* God, it is his glory to exalt those who humble themselves, and to speak comfort to those who fear before him. The gospel grace is shown

1. In the *spiritual honours* it dispenses. When the proud Pharisees were rejected, and Publicans and sinners went *into the kingdom of heaven* before them,—when the Jews, who *followed after the law of righteousness*, did not attain it, and the Gentiles, who never thought of it, attained to righteousness (Rom. ix. 30, 31),—when God chose not the *wise men after the flesh*, not the *mighty*, or the *noble*, to preach the gospel, and plant Christianity in the world, but the *foolish* and *weak* things of the world, and things that were despised (1 Cor. i. 26, 27)—then he *scattered the proud*, and *put down the mighty*, but *exalted them of low degree*.

2. In the *spiritual riches* it dispenses, *v.* 53. (1) Those who see their need of Christ, he *fills* with *good things*, with the *best things*; he gives liberally to them, and they are *abundantly satisfied*. Those who are weary and heavy-laden shall find rest with Christ, and those who thirst are called to *come to him and drink*. (2) Those who are rich, who, like Laodicea, think they have *need of nothing*, are full of themselves, and think they have a sufficiency in themselves, those he *sends away* from his door; he sends them *empty* away; they come *full of self*, and are sent away *empty of Christ*.

It was always expected that the Messiah should be the strength and glory of his people Israel, and so he is in a peculiar manner (*v.* 54): *He hath helped his servant Israel*. He hath taken them by the hand, and *helped them up* that were fallen and could not help themselves. The sending of the Messiah, on whom *help* was *laid* for poor sinners, was the greatest kindness that could be done and that which magnifies it is,

First, That it is *in remembrance of his mercy*. While this blessing was deferred, his people were often ready to ask, *Has God forgotten to be gracious?* But now he made it appear that he had not forgotten, but *remembered, his mercy. He remembered the days of old*.

Secondly, That it is *in performance of his promise*. It is a mercy not only designed, but declared (*v.* 55); it was *what he spoke to our fathers*, and particularly to Abraham, that *in his seed all the families of the earth shall be blessed* with the blessings that are *for ever*. What God hath spoken he will perform; what he hath spoken to the fathers will be performed to their seed.

Lastly, Mary's return to Nazareth (*v.* 56), after she had continued with Elisabeth about *three months*. Those in whose hearts Christ is formed take more delight than they used to do in *sitting alone* and *keeping silence*.

Verses 57–66

I. The birth of John Baptist, *v.* 57. *Elisabeth's full time came, that she should be delivered*, and then *she brought forth a son*. Promised mercies are to be

JAMIESON, FAUSSET, BROWN

ALBERT BARNES:

51. "Hath showed strength with his arm." The "arm" is the symbol of strength. The expression in this and the subsequent verses has no particular reference to his mercy to Mary. From a contemplation of his goodness to her, she enlarges her views to a contemplation of his goodness and power in general, and to a celebration of the praises to God for all that he has done to all men. This is the nature of true piety. It does not terminate in thinking of God's mercy toward ourselves. It thinks of others, and praises God that others also are made partakers of His mercy, and that His goodness is manifested to all His works. "He scattereth the proud." He hath often done it in time of battle and war. When the proud Assyrian, Egyptian, or Babylonian had come against the people of God, He had often scattered them and driven away their armies. "In the imagination of their hearts." Those who were lifted up or exalted in their own view. Those who thought themselves to be superior to other men.

52. "Hath put down the mighty." The "mighty" here denotes princes, kings, or conquerors (see Isa. 14:2-14). Their "seats." Their "thrones," or the places where they sat in pomp and power. "Exalted them." Raised them up, or placed them in the seats of those who had been removed. "Low degree." Low or humble birth and condition in life. This probably has reference to the case of her ancestor David. Mary was celebrating the mercies of God to herself, to her family, and of course to her ancestors. It was natural to allude to that great event in their history when Saul was overcome in battle, and when David was taken from the sheepfold and placed on the throne. The origin of illustrious families is often obscure. Men are often raised by industry, talent, and the favor of God, from very humble stations—from the farm or mechanic's shop—to places of great trust in the church and state. They who are thus elevated, if imbued with right feelings, will not despise their former employments nor their former companions, nor will they esteem their parents or friends the less because they still remain in the same rank in life. No conduct is more odious and unchristian than to be ashamed of our birth or the humble circumstances of our friends. —*Popular Commentary*

54. holpen—Cf. Psalm 89:19, "I have laid *help* on One that is mighty." **55. As he spake to our fathers**—*The sense requires this clause to be read as a parenthesis.* (Cf. Mic. 7:20; Ps. 98:3.) **for ever**—the perpetuity of Messiah's kingdom, as expressly promised by the angel (vs. 33). **56. abode with her about three months**—What an honored roof was that which, for such a period, overarched these cousins! and yet not a trace of it is now to be seen, while the progeny of those two women—the one but the honored pioneer of the other—have made the world new. **returned to her own house**—at Nazareth, *after which took place what is recorded in* Matthew 1:18-25.

57-80. Birth and Circumcision of John—Song of Zacharias, and Progress of the Child.

ADAM CLARKE

50. *His mercy is on them that fear him.* His exuberant kindness manifests itself in acts of mercy to all those who fear or reverence His name; and this is continued *from generation to generation*, because He is abundant in goodness, and because He delights in mercy. This is a noble, becoming, and just character of the God of the Christians; a Being who delights in the salvation and happiness of all His creatures, because His name is mercy, and His nature love.

51. *He hath shewed strength.* Or, "He hath gained the victory." The word is used for "victory," by Homer, Hesiod, Sophocles, Euripides, and others. *With his arm.* Grotius has well observed that God's efficacy is represented by His finger, His great power by His hand, and His omnipotence by His arm. The plague of lice was the "finger" of God, Exod. vii. 18. The plagues in general were wrought by His "hand," Exod. iii. 20. And the destruction of Pharaoh's host in the Red Sea, which was effected by the omnipotence of God, is called the act of His "arm," Exod. xv. 16. *He hath scattered.* "Hath scattered abroad"; as a whirlwind scatters dust and chaff. *The proud.* Or "haughty"—the haughty men, who wish to be noticed in preference to all others, and feel sovereign contempt for all but themselves. These God scatters abroad—instead of being in His sight, as in their own, the most excellent of the earth, He treats them as straw, stubble, chaff, and dust. *In the imagination of their hearts.* While they are forming their insolent, proud, and oppressive projects—laying their plans, and imagining that accomplishment and success are waiting at their right hand—the whirlwind of God's displeasure blows, and they and their machinations are dissipated together.

52. *He hath put down the mighty from their seats.* Or, "He hath taken down potentates from their thrones." This probably alludes to the removal of Saul from the throne of Israel, and the establishment of the kingdom in the person and family of David. And as Mary spoke prophetically, this saying may also allude to the destruction of the kingdom of Satan and his allies, and the final prevalence of the kingdom of Christ.

53. *Filled the hungry . . . the rich he hath sent empty away.* God is here represented under the notion of a Person of unbounded benevolence, who is daily feeding multitudes at His gates. The poor man comes through a sense of his want to get his daily support, and God feeds him; the rich man comes through the lust of gain, to get more added to his abundance, and God sends him away empty—not only gives him nothing more, but often deprives him of that which he has, because he has not improved it to the honor of the Giver.

54. *He hath holpen* [*supported*] *his servant Israel.* Israel is here represented as falling, and the Lord comes speedily in and props him up. The house of David was now ready to fall and rise no more; Jesus, being born of the very last branch of the regal line, revived the family, and restored the dominion. *In remembrance of his mercy.* By *mercy*, the covenant which God made with Abraham, Gen. xv. 18, as intended; which covenant proceeded from God's eternal mercy, as in it salvation was promised to all the nations of the earth. See Gen. xvii. 19 and xxii. 18; and this promise was, one form or other, given to all the fathers, v. 55. This song properly consists of three parts. (1) In the *first* part Mary praises God for what He had done for *herself*, vv. 46-50. (2) In the *second*, she praises Him for what He had done, and would do, against the oppressors of *His people*, vv. 51-53. (3) In the *third*, she praises Him for what He had done, and would do, for His *Church*, vv. 53-56.

56. *And Mary abode with her about three months.* According to some, the departure of Mary from Hebron must have been but a few days before the birth of John, as nine months had now elapsed since Elisabeth's conception; see v. 36.

57. *Now Elisabeth's full time came.* But, according to others, we are to understand the three months of Mary's visit as preceding the

MATTHEW HENRY

expected when the *full time* for them is come, and not before.

II. The great joy that was among all the relations of the family, upon this extraordinary occasion (*v.* 58): *Her neighbours and her cousins heard of it.* Now these here discovered, 1. A *pious* regard to God. They acknowledged that *the Lord had magnified his mercy to her*, so the word is. Many things concurred to make the mercy *great*—that she had been long barren, was now old, but especially that the child should be *great in the sight of the Lord.* 2. A *friendly* regard to Elisabeth. When she rejoiced, they *rejoiced with her.* We ought to take *pleasure* in the prosperity of our neighbours and friends, and to be thankful to God for *their* comforts as for our own.

III. The dispute that was among them concerning the naming him (*v.* 59): *On the eighth day* they *came together, to circumcise the child.* They that rejoiced in the birth of the child came together to the circumcising of him. The greatest comfort we can take in our children is in *giving them up to God.* The baptism of our children should be more our joy than their birth.

Now it was the custom, when they circumcised their children, to *name them*, and it is not unfit that they should be left *nameless* till they are by name *given up to God.*

1. *Some* proposed that he should be called by his father's name, *Zacharias.* They intended hereby to do honour to the father, who was not likely to have another child.

2. The *mother* opposed it, and would have him called *John*; having learned that God appointed this to be his name (*v.* 60): *He shall be called Johanan—Gracious*, because he shall introduce the gospel of Christ, wherein God's grace shines more brightly than ever.

3. The *relations* objected against that (*v.* 61): "*There is none of thy kindred that is called by that name;* and therefore let him have the name of some of his kindred."

4. They appealed to the *father*, for it was his office to *name the child*, *v.* 62. They *made signs* to him, by which it appears that he was *deaf* as well as *dumb.* However, they gave him to understand what the dispute was which he only could determine; whereupon he made signs to them to give him a *table-book.* He wrote these words, *His name is John*, *v.* 63. Not, "It shall be so," or, "I would have it so," but, "It is so." The matter is determined already. When Zacharias could not *speak*, he *wrote.* When ministers have their mouths stopped, that they cannot preach, yet they may be doing good as long as they have not their hands tied, that they cannot write. Zacharias's pitching upon the same name that Elisabeth had chosen was a great surprise to the company: *They marvelled all.*

5. He thereupon recovered the use of his speech (*v.* 64): *His mouth was opened immediately.* The time prefixed for his being silenced was *till the day that these things shall be fulfilled*, *v.* 20. That time was now expired, whereupon the restraint was taken off, and God gave him the *opening of the mouth again.* Infidelity closed his mouth, and now believing opens it again. *His mouth was opened, and he spake, and praised God.* When God opens our lips, our mouths must *show forth his praise.* As good be without our speech as not use it in *praising God.*

6. These things were told all the country over, to the great amazement of all that heard them, *v.* 65, 66. We are here told, (1) That *these sayings were discoursed of*, and were the common talk all about the *hill-country of Judæa.* (2) That most people who heard of these things were put into consternation by them: *Fear came on all them that dwelt round about* there. (3) It raised the expectations of people concerning this child. They *laid up these* presages *in their hearts.* What we hear, that may be of use to us, we should *treasure* up, that we may be able to bring forth, for the benefit of others, things new and old, and may be able to look back and to say, "It was what we might expect." They said *within* themselves, and said *among* themselves, "*What manner of child shall this be?* What will be the fruit when these are the buds?"

Lastly, It is said, *The hand of the Lord was with him*; that is, he was taken under the special protection of the Almighty, from his birth, as one designed for something great. God has ways of operating upon children in their infancy, which we cannot account for. God never made a soul but he knew how to sanctify it.

Verses 67–80

We have here the song wherewith Zacharias *praised God* when his *mouth was opened*; in it he is said to *prophesy*, *v.* 67.

I. How he was qualified for this: *He was filled with*

JAMIESON, FAUSSET, BROWN

59. eighth day—The law (Gen. 17:12) was observed, even though the eighth day after birth should be a sabbath (John 7:23; and see Phil. 3:5). **called him**—lit., "were calling"—i.e., (as we should say) "were for calling." The *naming* of children at baptism has its origin in the Jewish custom at circumcision (Gen. 21:3, 4); and the names of Abram and Sarai were changed at its first performance (Gen. 17:5, 15).

62. made signs—showing he was deaf, as well as dumb.

63. marvelled all—at his giving the same name, not knowing of any communication between them on the subject. **64. mouth opened immediately**—on thus palpably showing his full faith in the vision, for disbelieving which he had been struck dumb (vss. 13, 20).

65. fear—religious awe; under the impression that God's hand was specially in these events (cf. ch. 5:26; 7:16; 8:37).

66. hand of the Lord was with him—by special tokens marking him out as one destined to some great work (I Kings 18:46; II Kings 3:15; Acts 11:21).

ADAM CLARKE

birth of John, which would complete the time of Elisabeth's pregnancy, according to v. 36, and the only difficulty is to ascertain whether Mary went immediately to Hebron after her salutation or whether she tarried nearly three months before she took the journey.

58. *And her neighbours and her cousins . . . rejoiced with her.* Because sterility was a reproach; and they now rejoiced with their relative, from whom that reproach was now rolled away.

59. *On the eighth day they came to circumcise.* See an account of this institution in the note on Gen. xvii. 10-14. Had circumcision been essential to an infant's salvation, God would not have ordered it to be delayed to the eighth day, because in all countries multitudes die before they arrive at that age. Baptism, which is generally allowed to have been substituted for circumcision, is no more necessary to the salvation of an infant than circumcision was. Both are signs of the covenant—circumcision, of the putting away the impurity of the flesh; and baptism, of the "washing of regeneration, and renewing of the Holy Ghost." *They called him Zacharias.* Among the Jews, the child was named when it was circumcised, and ordinarily the name of the father was given to the firstborn son.

60. *Not so; but he shall be called John.* This is the name which the angel desired should be given him, v. 13, and of which Zacharias by writing had informed his wife. There is something very remarkable in the names of this family: *Zacharias,* the "memory or memorial of Jehovah"; *Elisabeth,* the "Sabbath or rest of my strong God"—names probably given them by their parents, to point out some remarkable circumstance in their conception or birth; and *John,* which should always be written *Jehochanan* or *Yehochanan,* the "grace or mercy of Jehovah"—so named because he was to go before and proclaim the "God of all grace," and the mercy granted through Him to a lost world.

61. *None of thy kindred.* As the Jewish tribes and families were kept sacredly distinct, it appears the very names of the ancestors were continued among their descendants, partly through reverence for them and partly to avoid confusion in the genealogical tables, which, for the sake of distinguishing the inheritances, were carefully preserved in each of the families.

62. *They made signs to his father.* Who, it appears from this, was deaf as well as dumb; otherwise they might have asked him and obtained his answer in this way.

63. *A writing table.* "A "tablet," diminutive of a "table."

64. The latter clause of the preceding verse should be joined with the beginning of this, as follows: *And they marvelled all, for his mouth was opened.* The people did not wonder because Zacharias said, *He shall be called John,* but because he himself was that instant restored to the use of his speech. *And he spake, and praised God.* In his nine months' silence he had learned the proper use of his tongue; and God, whose power was discredited by it, is now magnified.

65. *And fear came.* Seeing what they might have thought a paralytic affection so suddenly and effectually healed. This word certainly means in several places "religious fear or reverence"; and in this sense it is used in Acts ix. 31; Rom. iii. 18; xiii. 7; 1 Pet. i. 17; ii. 18; iii. 2.

66. *What manner of child shall this be!* As there have been so many extraordinary things in his conception and birth, surely God has designed him for some extraordinary purpose. These things they *laid . . . up in their hearts,* patiently waiting to see what God would work. *The hand of the Lord was with him.* God defended and prospered him in all things, and the prophetic spirit began to rest upon him.

67. *Zacharias . . . prophesied.* The word *prophesy* is to be taken here in its proper acceptation, for the "predicting or foretelling future events." Zacharias spoke not only of what God had already done, but also of what He was about to do in order to save a lost world.

MATTHEW HENRY

the Holy Ghost; he was divinely inspired. God not only *forgave* him his unbelief and distrust, he *filled him* with the *Holy Ghost*.

II. What the matter of his song was. Here is nothing said of the private concerns of his own family, the rolling away of the reproach from it, but in this song he is wholly taken up with the kingdom of the Messiah. The Old Testament prophecies are often expressed in *praises* and *new songs*, so is this beginning of New Testament prophecy: *Blessed be the Lord God of Israel*. Zacharias, speaking of the work of redemption, called him the *Lord God of Israel*, because to Israel the prophecies, promises, and types, of the redemption had hitherto been given, and to them the first proffers and proposals of it were now to be made.

Now Zacharias here blesses God,

1. For the work of *salvation* that was to be wrought out by the Messiah himself, *v.* 68–75.

(1) In sending the Messiah, God has *made a gracious visit* to his people; he hath *visited them* as a friend, to take cognizance of their case.

(2) He has *wrought out redemption* for them: *He has redeemed his people*. This was the errand on which Christ *came into the world*, to redeem those that were sold *for* sin, and sold *under* sin. Christ redeems them by *price* out of the hands of God's justice, and redeems them by *power* out of the hands of Satan's tyranny.

(3) He has fulfilled the *covenant of royalty* made with the most famous *Old Testament prince*, that is, David. Glorious things had been said of his family, that on him, as a *mighty one*, *help* should be *laid*. But that family had been long in a manner *cast off*. Now here it is gloried in, that, according to the promise, the *horn* of David should again be *made to bud*; he *hath raised up a horn of salvation for us in the house of his servant David* (*v.* 69), there, where it was promised and expected to arise. There is in Christ, and in him only, *salvation for us*, and it is a *horn of salvation*. It is an *honourable* salvation. It is *raised up* above all other salvations, none of which are to be compared with it. It is a *plentiful salvation*. It is a *cornucopia—a horn of plenty*. It is a *powerful salvation*. He has raised up such a salvation as shall *pull down* our spiritual enemies, and *protect* us from them.

(4) He has fulfilled all the precious promises made to the church by the most famous *Old Testament prophets* (*v.* 70): *As he spoke by the mouth of his holy prophets*. His doctrine of salvation by the Messiah is confirmed by an appeal to the prophets. God is now *doing* that which he has long ago *spoken of*. See, [1] How *sacred* the prophecies of this salvation were. The prophets who delivered them were *holy prophets*, and it was the *holy God* himself that *spoke by* them. [2] How *ancient* they were: ever *since the world began*. God having promised, when the world began, that the *Seed of the woman should break the serpent's head*. [3] What a wonderful *harmony* and *concert* we perceive among them. God spoke the same thing by them all.

Now what is this *salvation* which was prophesied of?

First, It is a *rescue* from the malice of *our enemies*; *a salvation out of our enemies*, from among them, and *out of the power of them that hate us* (*v.* 71); it is a salvation from sin. He shall *save his people from their sins*, that they may not have dominion over them, Matt. i. 21.

Secondly, It is a *restoration* to the *favour of God*; it is to *perform the mercy promised to our forefathers*, *v.* 72. The Redeemer shall *reinstate* us in the *mercy of God* and *re-establish* us in *his covenant*; which was signified by the *promises* made to the patriarchs, and the *holy covenant* made with them, *the oath which he swore to our Father Abraham*, *v.* 73. That which was promised to the fathers, and is performed to us, is *mercy*, pure mercy; nothing in it is owing to our *merit*. He loved us because he would love us. God herein had an eye to his *holy* covenant, that covenant with Abraham: *I will be a God to thee and thy seed*. This his seed had *really forfeited* by their transgressions; this he *seemed to have forgotten* in the calamities brought upon them; but he will now *remember* it.

Thirdly, It is a qualification for, and an encouragement to, the service of God. Thus was *the oath he sware to our Father Abraham*, That he would *give us* power and grace to *serve him*, in an acceptable manner to him and a comfortable manner to ourselves, *v.* 74, 75. The great design of gospel grace is not to discharge us from, but to engage us to, and encourage us in, the service of God. We are *therefore* delivered from the iron yoke of sin, that our necks may be put under the sweet and easy yoke of the Lord Jesus. *The very bonds which he has loosed do bind*

JAMIESON, FAUSSET, BROWN

68-79.
There is not a word in this noble burst of divine song about his own child; like Elisabeth losing sight entirely of self, in the glory of a Greater than both. **Lord God of Israel**—the ancient covenant God of the peculiar people. **visited and redeemed**—i.e., in order to redeem: returned after long absence, and broken His long silence (see on Matt. 15:31). In the Old Testament, God is said to "visit" chiefly for *judgment*, in the New Testament for *mercy*. Zacharias would, as yet, have but imperfect views of such "visiting and redeeming," "saving from and delivering out of the hand of enemies" (vss. 71, 74). But this Old Testament phraseology, used at first with a *lower* reference, is, when viewed in the light of a loftier and more comprehensive kingdom of God, equally adapted to express the most spiritual conceptions of the redemption that is in Christ Jesus.

69. horn of salvation—i.e., "strength of salvation," or "mighty Salvation," meaning the Saviour Himself, whom Simeon calls "Thy Salvation" (ch. 2:30). The metaphor is taken from those animals whose *strength* is in their *horns* (Ps. 18:2; 75:10; 132:17). **house of . . . David**—*This shows that Mary must have been known to be of the royal line*, independent of Joseph; of whom Zacharias, if he knew anything, could not know that after this he would recognize Mary. **70. since the world began**—or, "from the earliest period."

72. the mercy promised . . . his holy covenant . . . 73. the oath . . . to . . . Abraham—The whole work and kingdom of Messiah is represented as a mercy pledged on oath to Abraham and his seed, to be realized at an appointed period; and at length, in "the fulness of the time," gloriously made good. Hence, not only "*grace*," or the *thing* promised; but "*truth*," or *fidelity* to the promise, are said to "come by Jesus Christ" (John 1:17).

ADAM CLARKE

68. *Blessed be the Lord God of Israel; for.* Zacharias praises God for two grand benefits which He had granted to His people. (1) He has *visited* them. (2) He has *ransomed* them. God visits His people in the incarnation of Jesus Christ; therefore this Christ is called by Him "Jehovah the God of Israel." Here the highest and most glorious character of the Supreme Being is given to Christ. *He hath . . . redeemed.* "He hath made a ransom"—laid down the ransom price. *Lytroo* signifies particularly to "ransom a captive from the enemy, by paying a price." The following remarkable passage from Josephus, *Ant.*, b. xiv, c. 14, sect. 1, fully illustrates this meaning of the original. "Herod, not knowing what had happened to his brother, hastened to ransom him from the enemy, and was willing to pay a ransom for him, to the amount of three hundred talents." Sinners are fallen into the hands of their enemies, and are captives to sin and death. Jesus ransoms them by His own blood, and restores them to life, liberty, and happiness.

69. *And hath raised up an horn of salvation.* That is, a "mighty and glorious Saviour," a quotation from Ps. xviii. 2. Horns are the well-known emblems of strength, glory, and power, in both sacred and profane writers, because the strength and beauty of horned animals consist in their horns. It is likely that the allusion is here made to the horns of the altar; and as the altar was a place of refuge and safety, and those who laid hold on its horns were considered to be under the protection of the Lord, so, according to the expression of Zacharias, Jesus Christ is a new Altar, to which whosoever flees shall find refuge. *In the house of his servant David.* Or "in the family"; so the word *house* is often used in the Sacred Writings. In v. 32 the angel states that Mary was of the family of David; and Zacharias, who from the nature of his office must have been well acquainted with the public genealogical tables, attests the same thing. This is a matter of considerable importance, because it shows forth the truth of all the prophetic declarations, which uniformly state that the Messiah should come from the family and sit on the throne of David.

71. *That we should be saved* (literally, *a salvation*) *from our enemies.* As Zacharias spoke by the inspiration of the Holy Spirit, the salvation which he mentions here must necessarily be understood in a spiritual sense. Satan, death, and sin are the enemies from whom Jesus came to deliver us. Sin is the most dangerous of all, and is properly the only enemy we have to fear.

MATTHEW HENRY

us faster unto him. We are hereby enabled, 1. To serve God *without fear*—ἀφόβως. We are *therefore* put into a state of *holy safety* that we might serve God with a *holy security* and *serenity of mind*, as those that are *quiet from the fears of evil.* God must be served with a *filial fear*, a reverent obedient fear, an awakening quickening fear, but not with a *slavish fear*, like that of the slothful servant, who represented him to himself as a *hard master*, and unreasonable. 2. To serve him in *holiness and righteousness*, which includes the whole duty of man towards God and our neighbour. 3. To serve him, *before him*, in the duties of his *immediate* worship, to serve him as those that have an eye always upon him, and see his eye always upon us, upon our inward man. 4. To serve him *all the days of our life.* Christ *loved us to the end*, and thereby engaged us to *love him to the end.*

2. He *blessed God* for the work of *preparation* for this salvation, which was to be done by John Baptist (*v.* 76): *Thou child* shalt be called *the prophet of the Highest.* Jesus Christ is *the Highest.* John Baptist was *his prophet.* Prophecy had now long ceased, but in John it *revived.* John's business was,

(1) To prepare people for the salvation: *Thou shalt go before the face of the Lord* to *prepare his ways.* Let everything that may obstruct his progress, or embarrass it, or hinder people from coming to him, be taken away: see Isa. xl. 3, 4.

(2) To give people a general idea of the salvation, for the doctrine he preached was that the *kingdom of heaven* is at hand. There are two things in which you must know that this salvation consists:—

[1] The *forgiveness* of what we have *done amiss.* It is salvation *by the remission of sins, v.* 77. John Baptist gave people to understand that, though their case was sad, it was not desperate, for pardon might be obtained *through the tender mercy of our God*: there was nothing in us but a *piteous case* to recommend us to the divine compassion.

[2] *Direction* to *do better* for the time to come. The gospel salvation sets up a clear and true light, by which we may order our steps aright. In it *the day-spring hath visited us from on high* (*v.* 78); and this also is owing to the *tender mercy of our God.* Christ is *the morning Light*, the *rising Sun.* The gospel brings *light* with it, leaves us not to wander in the darkness of Pagan ignorance, or in the moonlight of the Old Testament types or figures, but in it the day dawns; in John Baptist it began to break, but increased apace, and *shone more and more to the perfect day.* We have as much reason to welcome the gospel day as those have to welcome the morning who had long waited for it. *First*, The gospel is *discovering*; it is to *give light to them that sit in darkness*, the *light of the knowledge of the glory of God in the face of Jesus Christ. Secondly*, It is *reviving*; it brings light to them that sit *in the shadow of death*, as condemned prisoners in the dungeon, to bring them the tidings of a *pardon*, at least of a *reprieve* and opportunity of producing a pardon. How pleasant is that light! *Thirdly*, It is *directing*; it is to *guide our feet in the way of peace.* It guides us into the way of making our peace with God; that *way of peace* which as sinners we have wandered from and *have not known*, nor could ever have known of ourselves.

In the last verse, we have a short account of the younger years of John Baptist. We are here told,

1. Of his *eminence* as to the *inward man*: The *child grew* in the capacities of his mind, so that he *waxed strong in spirit*, had a strong judgment and strong resolution. Those that are strong in the Lord are *strong in spirit.*

2. Of his *obscurity* as to the *outward man*: *He was in the deserts.* There he spent most of his time, in contemplation and devotion, and had not his education in the schools, or at the feet of the rabbin. Many a one is qualified for great usefulness, who yet is buried alive; and many are long so buried who are designed, and are thereby in the fitting, for so much greater usefulness at last; as John Baptist, who was *in the desert* only *till the day of his showing to Israel.* There is a time fixed for the *showing* of those favours to Israel which are reserved.

JAMIESON, FAUSSET, BROWN

74. that he would grant us . . . How comprehensive is the view here given! (1) The *purpose* of all redemption—"that we should *serve* Him"—i.e., "the Lord God of Israel" (vs. 68). The word signifies *religious* service distinctively—"the *priesthood* of the New Testament" [BENGEL]. (2) The *nature* of this service—"in holiness and righteousness before Him"—or, as in His presence (cf. Ps. 56:13). (3) Its *freedom*—"being delivered out of the hand of our enemies." (4) Its *fearlessness*—"might serve Him without fear." (5) Its *duration*—"all the days of our life." **76-79.** Here are the dying echoes of this song; and very beautiful are these closing notes—like the setting sun, shorn indeed of its noontide radiance, but skirting the horizon with a wavy and quivering light—as of molten gold—on which the eye delights to gaze, till it disappears from the view. The song passes not here from Christ to John, but only from Christ direct to Christ as heralded by His forerunner. **76. thou child**—not "my son"—this child's relation to himself being lost in his relation to a Greater than either. **prophet of the Highest; for thou shalt go before him**—i.e., "the Highest." As "the Most High" is an epithet in Scripture only of *the supreme God*, it is inconceivable that inspiration should apply this term, as here undeniably, to Christ, unless He were "God over all blessed for ever" (Rom. 9:5). **77. to give knowledge of salvation**—To sound the note of a *needed* and *provided* "salvation" was the noble office of John, above all that preceded him; as it is that of all subsequent ministers of Christ; but infinitely loftier was it to be the "Salvation" itself (vs. 69 and ch. 2:30). **by the remission of . . . sins**—This stamps at once the *spiritual* nature of the salvation here intended, and explains vss. 71, 74. **78. Through the tender mercy . . .**—the sole spring, necessarily, of all salvation *for sinners.*

dayspring from on high . . .—either *Christ Himself*, as the "Sun of righteousness" (Mal. 4:2), arising on a dark world [BEZA, GROTIUS, CALVIN, DE WETTE, OLSHAUSEN, etc.], or the light which He sheds. The sense, of course, is one.

79. (Cf. Isa. 9:2; Matt. 4:13-17.) "That St. Luke, of all the Evangelists, should have obtained and recorded these inspired utterances of Zacharias and Mary—is in accordance with his character and habits, as indicated in vss. 1-4" [WEBSTER and WILKINSON].

80. And the child . . .—"a concluding paragraph, indicating, in strokes full of grandeur, the bodily and mental development of the Baptist; and bringing his life up to the period of his public appearance" [OLSHAUSEN]. **in the deserts**—probably "the wilderness of Judea" (Matt. 3:1), whither he had retired early in life, in the *Nazarite* spirit, and where, free from rabbinical influences and alone with God, his spirit would be educated, like Moses in the desert, for his future high vocation. **his showing unto Israel**—the presentation of himself before his nation, as Messiah's forerunner.

ADAM CLARKE

74-75. *Being delivered.* The salvation brought by Jesus Christ consists in the following things: (1) We are to be *delivered out of the hand of our enemies,* so that sin shall neither have dominion over us nor existence in us. (2) We are to *serve* (worship) God, to render Him that service and adoration which the letter and spirit of His religion require. (3) We are to live *in holiness,* a strict inward conformity to the mind of Christ—*and righteousness,* a full outward conformity to the precepts of the gospel. (4) This is to be done *before* God, under the continual influence and support of His grace, and with a constant evidence of His presence and approbation. (5) This state is a state of true happiness—it is *without fear.* Sin is all cast out; holiness is brought in. God's power upholds and His approbation cheers and comforts the believing heart. (6) This blessedness is to continue as long as we exist—*all the days of our life,* in all ages, in all situations, and in all circumstances.

76-79. *And thou, child, etc.* Zacharias proclaims the dignity, employment, doctrine, and success of his son, and the ruin and recovery of the Jews and the Gentiles. (1) His dignity. *Thou . . . shalt be called* (constituted) *the prophet of the Highest. Prophet* has two acceptations: first, a person who foretells future events; and, second, a teacher of men in the things of God, 1 Cor. xiv. 3. John was a prophet in both senses. He had the honor of being the last and clearest prophet of the old covenant and the first of the new. (2) His employment. *Thou shalt go before the face of the Lord to prepare his ways.* He should be the immediate forerunner of Jesus Christ, none being capable of succeeding him in his ministry but Christ himself. He was to *prepare his ways,* to be the honored instrument, in the hands of God, of disposing the hearts of multitudes of the Israelites to believe in and follow the Lord Jesus. (3) Zacharias points out the doctrine or teaching of John. It should be the science of *salvation.* (4) Zacharias predicts the success of his son's ministry. Under his preaching the people should be directed to that *tender mercy* of God through which they might obtain *the remission of their sins,* vv. 77-78. (5) Zacharias points out the wretched state in which the inhabitants of Judea and the Gentile world were then found. Their *feet* had wandered out of *the way of peace* (v. 79), of temporal and spiritual prosperity. They had got into a state of *darkness*—they were blind concerning the things of God, and the things which belonged to their salvation. They had become contented inhabitants of this land of intellectual darkness—they had sat down in it, and were not concerned to get out of it. They were about to perish in it—*death* had his dominion there; and his swift approaches to them were now manifested to the prophet by seeing his *shadow* cast upon them. Ignorance of God and salvation is *the shadow of death;* and the substance, eternal ruin, is essentially connected with the projected shadow. See these phrases explained at large on Matt. iv. 16. (6) Zacharias proclaims the recovery of a lost world. As the removal of this darkness and redemption from this death were now at hand, John is represented as being a *dayspring from on high,* a "morning star," that foretold the speedy approach of the day, for the rising of the Sun of Righteousness. That these words should be applied to John, and not to Christ, I am fully satisfied.

80. *The child grew.* Increased in stature and bodily vigor. *And waxed strong in spirit*—had his understanding divinely illuminated and confirmed in the truths of God. *And was in the deserts*—the city of Hebron, the circumjacent hill country, and in or near Nazareth. *Till the day of his shewing,* or "manifestation"—till he was thirty years of age, before which time the law did not permit a man to enter into the public ministry, Num. iv. 3.

MATTHEW HENRY

CHAPTER 2

The *fulness of time* was now come, when God would send forth his Son, and it was foretold that he should be born at Bethlehem. Now here we have an account of the time, place, and manner of it.

I. The time when our Lord Jesus was born.

1. He was born at the time when the *fourth monarchy* was in its height. He was born *in the days* of Augustus Cæsar, when the Roman empire extended itself further than ever before or since, including Parthia one way, and Britain another way; so that it was then called *Terrarum orbis imperium—The empire of the whole earth*; and here that empire is called *all the world* (*v.* 1), for there was scarcely any part of the civilized world, but what was dependent on it.

2. He was born when Judæa was become a province of the empire, and tributary to it; as appears evidently by this, that when all the Roman empire was taxed, the Jews were taxed among the rest. Jerusalem was taken by Pompey the Roman general, about sixty years before this. Judæa was ruled by Cyrenius the Roman governor of Syria (*v.* 2). This was the *first taxing* that was made in Judæa, the first badge of their servitude.

3. There is another circumstance, as to the time, which is, that there was now universal peace in the empire. The temple of Janus was now shut, which it never used to be if any wars were on foot; and now it was fit for the Prince of peace to be born.

II. The place where our Lord Jesus was born is very observable. He was born at *Bethlehem*; so it was foretold (Mic. v. 2), the scribes so understood it (Matt. ii. 5, 6), so did the common people, John vii. 42. The name of the place was significant. Bethlehem signifies *the house of bread*; a proper place for him to be born in who is the Bread of life, the Bread that *came down from heaven*. Bethlehem was the city of David, where he was born, and therefore there *he* must be born who was the *Son of David*. Zion was also called *the city of David*, yet Christ was not born there; for Bethlehem was that city of David where he was born in meanness, to be a *shepherd*; and this our Saviour chose for the place of his birth; not Zion, where he ruled in power and prosperity. Now when the virgin Mary was with child, and near her time, Providence so ordered it that, by order from the emperor, all the subjects of the *Roman empire* were to be *taxed*; that is, they were to be *registered* and *enrolled*, according to their families, which is the proper signification of the word here used.

That which Augustus designed was either to gratify his *pride* in knowing the numbers of his people, and proclaiming it to the world, or he did it in *policy*, to make his government appear the more formidable; but Providence had another reach in it. All the world shall be at the trouble of being *enrolled*, only that Joseph and Mary may. This brought them up from Nazareth in Galilee to Bethlehem in Judæa, because they were *of the stock and lineage of David*, *v.* 4, 5. Divers ends of Providence were served by this.

1. Hereby the virgin Mary was brought, *great with child*, to Bethlehem, to be *delivered* there, according to the prediction. See how *man purposes and God disposes*.

2. Hereby it appeared that Jesus Christ was of the *seed* of David; for what brings his mother to Bethlehem, now, but because she *was of the stock and lineage of David*?

3. Hereby it appeared that he was *made under the law*; for he became a subject of the Roman empire as soon as he was born. Instead of having kings tributaries to him, when he came into the world he was himself a tributary.

III. The circumstances of his birth, which were very mean. He was indeed a *first-born son*; but it was poor honour to be the first-born of such a poor woman as Mary was, who had no inheritance but what was *in nativity*.

1. He was under some abasements in common with other children; he was *wrapped in swaddling clothes*, as other children are when they are new-born, as if he could be bound, or needed to be kept straight. The Ancient of days became an infant of a span long.

2. He was under some abasements peculiar to himself.

(1) He was born *at an inn*. Christ was born *in an inn*, to intimate that he came into the world but to sojourn here for awhile, as in an inn. An inn receives all comers, and so does Christ. He hangs out the banner of love for his sign, and whoever comes to him, he will in no wise cast out; only, unlike other inns, he welcomes those that come *without money and without price*.

(2) He was born *in a stable*; so some think the word signifies which we translate *a manger*. Because

JAMIESON, FAUSSET, BROWN

CHAPTER 2

Vss. 1-7. Birth of Christ. **1. Cæsar Augustus**—the first of the Roman emperors. **all the world**—so the vast Roman Empire was termed. **taxed**—enrolled, or register themselves. **2. first . . . when Cyrenius . . .**—a very perplexing verse, inasmuch as Cyrenius, or Quirinus, appears not to have been governor of Syria for about ten years after the birth of Christ, and the "taxing" under his administration was what led to the insurrection mentioned in Acts 5:37. That there *was* a taxing, however, of the whole Roman Empire under Augustus, is now admitted by all; and candid critics, even of skeptical tendency, are ready to allow that there is not likely to be any real inaccuracy in the statement of our Evangelist. Many superior scholars would render the words thus, "This registration was *previous* to Cyrenius being governor of Syria"—as the word "first" is rendered in John 1:15; 15:18. In this case, of course, the difficulty vanishes. But it is perhaps better to suppose, with others, that the registration may have been ordered with a view to the taxation, about the time of our Lord's birth, though the taxing itself—an obnoxious measure in Palestine—was not carried out till the time of Quirinus. **3. went . . to his own city**—the city of his *extraction*, according to the Jewish custom, not of his *abode*, which was the usual Roman method. **4, 5.** Not only does Joseph, who was of the royal line, go to Bethlehem (I Samuel 16:1), but Mary too—not from choice surely in her condition, but, probably, for personal enrolment, as herself an heiress. **5. espoused wife**—now, without doubt, taken home to him, as related in Matthew 1:18; 25: 6.

6. while . . . there . . .—Mary had up to this time been living at the wrong place for Messiah's birth. A little longer stay at Nazareth, and the prophecy would have failed. But lo! with no intention certainly on her part, much less of Cæsar Augustus, to fulfil the prophecy, she is brought from Nazareth to Bethlehem, and at that nick of time her period arrives, and her Babe is born (Ps. 118:23). "Every creature walks blindfold; only He that dwells in light knows whether they go" [Bishop Hall]. **7. first-born**—So Matthew 1:25, 26; yet the law, in speaking of the first-born, regardeth not whether any were born *after* or no, but only that none were born *before* [Lightfoot]. **wrapt him . . . laid him**—The mother herself did so. Had she then none to help her? It would seem so (II Cor. 8:9). **a manger**—the manger, the bench to which the horses' heads were tied, on which their food could rest [Webster and Wilkinson]. **no room in the inn**—a square erection, open inside, where travellers put up, and whose rear parts were used as stables. The ancient tradition, that our Lord was born in a grotto or cave, is quite consistent with this, the country being rocky. In Mary's condition the journey would be a slow one, and ere they arrived, the inn would be fully occupied—affecting anticipation of the reception He was throughout to meet with (John 1:11).

ADAM CLARKE

CHAPTER 2

1. ***Caesar Augustus.*** **This was Caius Caesar Octavianus Augustus, who was proclaimed emperor of Rome in the twenty-ninth year before our Lord, and died** A.D. **14.** ***That all the world should be taxed.*** **"The whole of that empire." It is agreed, on all hands, that this cannot mean the** ***whole world,*** **as in the common translation, for this very sufficient reason, that the Romans had not the dominion of the whole earth, and therefore could have no right to raise levies or taxes in those places to which their dominion did not extend.**

7. ***Laid him in a manger.*** **Many have thought that this was a full proof of the meanness and poverty of the Holy Family, that they were obliged to take up their lodging in a stable; but such people overlook the reason given by the inspired penman,** ***because there was no room for them in the inn.*** **As multitudes were going now to be enrolled, all the lodgings in the inn had been occupied before Joseph and Mary arrived.**

G. CAMPBELL MORGAN:

"In those days"--a "decree from Caesar Augustus." Caesar Augustus was the first Roman emperor. His real name was Caius Octavius. He was a great-nephew of Julius Caesar. The word "Augustus" is significant. That was his title. He took the name "Caesar" by courtesy and by adoption. In process of time the title "Augustus" was dropped, and the title became "Caesar." When this man became Imperator, and the matter was under discussion as to what title he should assume, he declined to be called "Dictator," which suggests a temporary office. He declined also to be called "King," as it did not signify enough. In consultation with the Roman Senate, this name was created for him, "Augustus," derivable from the word "Augur"; and consequently indicating a religious sanction. He was moving toward that which happened subsequently, the claim of deity on the part of the supreme ruler of the Roman Empire. Gradually the power of government had been taken from the people, and vested in military governors; and at last this man, a singularly able man, a singularly astute man, gained the supreme power. He became the first emperor, the first Imperator, with a capital "I." "Imperator" is a military title. The generals of the Roman republic had all been called "Imperators"; but at last the plural ended, and the singular marked despotism, autocracy. The Roman republic had passed away, and in its place had emerged the Roman Empire, under Augustus Caesar.

—*The Gospel According to Luke*

MATTHEW HENRY

there was *no room in the inn*, and for want of conveniences, nay for want of necessaries, he was laid *in the manger*, instead of a cradle. His being born in a stable and laid in a manger was an instance, [1] Of the poverty of his parents. Had they been rich, room would have been made for them. [2] Of the corruption and degeneracy of manners in that age. If there had been any common humanity among them, they would not have turned a woman in travail into a stable. [3] It was an instance of the humiliation of our Lord Jesus. We were become by sin like an outcast infant, helpless and forlorn; and such a one Christ was.

Verses 8–20

The meanest circumstances of Christ's humiliation were all along attended with some discoveries of his glory, to balance them. When we saw him *wrapped in swaddling clothes* and *laid in a manger*, we were tempted to say, "Surely this cannot be the *Son of God*." But see his birth attended with a choir of angels, and we shall say, "Surely it can be no other than the *Son of God*."

We had in Matthew an account of the notice given to the wise men, who were Gentiles, by a star; here we are told of the notice given of it to the shepherds who were Jews, by an angel: to each God chose to speak in the language they were most conversant with.

I. How the shepherds were employed; they were *abiding in the fields* and *keeping watch over their flocks by night*, *v.* 8. The angel was not sent to the chief priests or the elders, but to a company of poor shepherds. The patriarchs were shepherds and by this instance God would show that he had still a favour for those of that innocent employment. They were not *sleeping* in their beds, when this news was brought them, but *abiding in the fields*, and *watching*. They were broad awake, and therefore could not be deceived in what they saw and heard, so as those may be who are half asleep. They were employed now, not in acts of devotion, but in the business of their calling; they were *keeping watch over their flock*. We are not out of the way of divine visits when we are sensibly employed in an honest calling, and abide with God in it.

II. How they were surprised with the appearance of an angel (*v.* 9): *Behold, an angel of the Lord came upon them*, of a sudden. The angel's *coming upon them* intimates that they little thought of such a thing, or expected it. Gracious visits are made us from heaven, *or ever we are aware*. They saw and heard the *glory of the Lord round about them*; such as made the night as bright as day. This made them *sore afraid*, as fearing some evil tidings. While we are conscious to ourselves of so much guilt, we have reason to fear lest every express from heaven should be a messenger of wrath.

III. What the message was which the angel had to deliver to the shepherds, *v.* 10–12. "*Fear not*, you *need not* fear your enemies, and *should not* fear your friends." He furnishes them with abundant matter for joy: "Behold, I *evangelize to you great joy*. It shall bring *joy to all people*; that *unto you is born this day a Saviour which is Christ the Lord, in the city of David*," *v.* 11. "The Saviour *is born this day*; and, since it is matter of *great joy to all people*, you may proclaim it. He is born in the place where it was foretold he should be born, in the *city of David*; and he is born *to you*; to you Jews he is sent in the first place, to *bless you*, to you *shepherds*, though poor and mean in the world." This refers to Isa. ix. 6. *Unto us a child is born, unto us a son is given*. This is matter of *joy* indeed to all people, great joy. Long-looked for is come at last. He gives them a sign for the confirming of their faith in this matter. "You will find him by this token: he is lying in a *manger*, where surely never any new-born infant was laid before. You will find him wrapped in *swaddling clothes*, and *laid in a manger*.

IV. The angels' *doxology* to God, and *congratulations* of men, upon this solemn occasion, *v.* 13, 14. The message was no sooner delivered by one angel than suddenly there was with that angel *a multitude of the heavenly hosts praising God*. Let God have the honour of this work: *Glory to God in the highest*; *Glory to God*, whose kindness and love designed this favour, and whose wisdom contrived it. Other works of God are for his glory, but the redemption of the world is for his *glory in the highest*. Let men have the joy of it: *On earth peace, goodwill toward men*. If God be at peace with us, all peace results from it. Peace is here put for *all good*. All the *good* we have, or hope, is owing to God's *goodwill*; and, if we have the comfort of it, he must have the glory of it. Here was the *peace proclaimed* with great solemnity; whoever will, let them come and take the benefit of it.

JAMIESON, FAUSSET, BROWN

Wrapt in His swaddling-bands,
And in His manger laid,
The hope and glory of all lands
Is come to the world's aid.
No peaceful home upon His cradle smiled,
Guests rudely went and came where slept the royal Child.
KEBLE

But some "guests went and came" *not* "rudely," but reverently. God sent visitors of His own to pay court to the newborn King.

8-20. ANGELIC ANNUNCIATION TO THE SHEPHERDS—THEIR VISIT TO THE NEWBORN BABE. **8. abiding in the fields**—staying there, probably in huts or tents. **watch . . . by night**—or, night watches, taking their turn of watching. From about passover-time in April until autumn, the flocks pastured constantly in the open fields, the shepherds lodging there all that time. (From this it seems plain that the period of the year usually assigned to our Lord's birth is too late.) Were these shepherds chosen to have the first sight of the blessed Babe without any respect of their own state of mind? That, at least, is not God's way. "No doubt, like Simeon (vs. 25), they were among the waiters for the Consolation of Israel" [OLSHAUSEN]; and, if the simplicity of their rustic minds, their quiet occupation, the stillness of the midnight hours, and the amplitude of the deep blue vault above them for the heavenly music which was to fill their ear, pointed them out as fit recipients for the first tidings of an Infant Saviour, the congenial meditations and conversations by which, we may suppose, they would beguile the tedious hours would perfect their preparation for the unexpected visit. Thus was Nathanael engaged, all alone but not unseen, under the fig tree, in unconscious preparation for his first interview with Jesus. (See on John 1:48.) So was the rapt seer on his lonely rock "in the spirit on the Lord's Day," little thinking that this was his preparation for hearing behind him the trumpet-voice of the Son of man (Rev. 1:10, etc.). But if the shepherds in His immediate neighborhood had the *first*, the sages from afar had the *next* sight of the newborn King. Even so still, simplicity first, science next, finds its way to Christ, whom

In quiet ever and in shade
Shepherds and Sage may find—
They, who have bowed untaught to Nature's sway,
And they, who follow Truth along her star-pav'd way.
KEBLE

9. glory of the Lord—"the brightness or glory which is represented as encompassing all heavenly visions" [OLSHAUSEN]. **sore afraid**—So it ever was (Dan. 10:7, 8; Luke 1:12; Rev. 1:17). Men have never felt easy with the invisible world laid suddenly open to their gaze. It was never meant to be permanent; a momentary purpose was all it was intended to serve. **10. to all people**—"to the whole people," i.e., of Israel; to be by them afterwards opened up to the whole world. (See on vs. 14.) **11. unto you is born . . .**—you shepherds, Israel, mankind [BENGEL]. Cf. Isaiah 9:6, "Unto us a Child is born." It is a *birth*—"The Word is *made flesh*." When? "*This day*." Where? "*In the city of David*"—in the right *line* and at the right *spot;* where prophecy bade us look for Him, and faith accordingly expected Him. How dear to us should be these *historic moorings* of our faith! With the loss of them, all substantial Christianity is lost. By means of them how many have been kept from making shipwreck, and attained to a certain external admiration of Him, ere yet they have fully "beheld His glory." **a Saviour**—not One who *shall* be a Saviour, but "*born a Saviour*." **Christ the Lord**—"magnificent appellation!" [BENGEL]. "This is the only place where these words come together; and I see no way of understanding this "Lord" but as corresponding to the Hebrew JEHOVAH" [ALFORD]. **12. a sign**—"the sign." **the babe**—"a Babe." **a manger**—"the manger." The sign was to consist, it seems, solely in the overpowering *contrast* between the things just said of Him and the lowly condition in which they would find Him—Him whose goings forth have been from of old, from everlasting, "ye shall find a Babe"; whom the heaven of heavens cannot contain, "wrapt in swaddling-bands"; the "Saviour, Christ the Lord," lying in a manger! Thus early were these amazing contrasts, which are His chosen style, held forth. (See II Cor. 8:9.) **13. suddenly**—as if only waiting till their fellow had done. **with the angel**—who retires not, but is joined by others, come to seal

ADAM CLARKE

8. *There were . . . shepherds abiding in the field.* It was a custom among the Jews to send out their sheep to the deserts, about the Passover, and bring them home at the commencement of the first rain; during the time they were out, the shepherds watched them night and day. As the Passover occurred in the spring, and the first rain began early in the month of *Marchesvan,* which answers to part of our October and November, we find that the sheep were kept out in the open country during the whole of the summer. And as these shepherds had not yet brought home their flocks, it is a presumptive argument that October had not yet commenced, and that, consequently, our Lord was not born on the twenty-fifth of December, when no flocks were out in the fields.

9. *The angel of the Lord came upon them.* Or "stood over them." It is likely that the angel appeared in the air at some little distance above them, and that from him the rays of *the glory of the Lord shone round about them,* as the rays of light are projected from the sun. *They were sore afraid.* Terrified with the appearance of so glorious a being, and probably fearing that he was a messenger of justice, coming to announce divine judgments or punish them immediately for sins with which their consciences would not fail, on such an occasion, to reproach them.

10. *Behold, I bring you good tidings.* I am not come to declare the judgments of the Lord, but His merciful loving-kindness, the subject being a matter of *great joy.* He then declares his message. *Unto you*—to the Jews first, and then to the human race.

11. *A Saviour, which is Christ the Lord. A Saviour,* the same as *Jesus,* from to "make safe, to deliver, preserve, to make alive." *Which is Christ.* "The anointed," the same as Messiah. This name points out the Saviour of the world in His prophetic, regal, and sacerdotal offices, as in ancient times prophets, kings, and priests were anointed with oil when installed into their respective offices. Anointing was the same with them as consecration is with us. It appears from Isa. lxi. 1 that anointing with oil in consecrating a person to any important office, whether civil or religious, was considered as an emblem of the communication of the gifts and graces of the Holy Spirit. *The Lord.* The supreme, eternal Being, the Ruler of the heavens and the earth. The Septuagint generally translate *Yehovah* by *Kyrios.* This Hebrew word, from *hayah, he was,* properly points out the eternity and self-existence of the Supreme Being. Jesus is a *Prophet,* to reveal the will of God, and instruct men in it. He is a *Priest,* to offer up sacrifice, and make atonement for the sin of the world. He is *Lord,* to rule over and rule in the souls of the children of men.

12. *This shall be a sign* (or token) *unto you; Ye shall find* this glorious Person, however strange it may appear, *wrapped in swaddling clothes, lying in a manger.* It is by humility that Christ comes to reign; and this is the only way into His kingdom! Pride is the character of all the children of Adam; humility, the mark of the Son of God, and of all His followers. Christ came in the way of humility to destroy that pride which is the root of evil in the souls of men.

13. *Suddenly there was with the angel.* This multitude of the heavenly host had just now descended from on high, to honor the newborn Prince of Peace, to give His parents the fullest conviction of His glory and excellence, and to teach the shepherds, who were about to be the first proclaimers of the gospel, what to think and what to speak of Him who, while He appeared as a helpless Infant, was the Object of worship to the angels of God.

MATTHEW HENRY

It is on earth peace, to *men of goodwill* (so some copies read it), ἀνθρώποις εὐδοκίας; to men who have a *goodwill to God*; or to men whom God has a *goodwill to*. This is a *faithful saying*, and well *worthy of all acceptation, That the goodwill of God toward men is glory to God in the highest, and peace on the earth.*

V. The visit which the shepherds made to the newborn Saviour. 1. They consulted about it, *v.* 15. While the angels were singing their hymn, they could attend to that only; but, *when they were gone away from them into heaven, the shepherds said one to another, Let us go to Bethlehem.* And it is no reflection upon the testimony of angels, no nor upon a divine testimony itself, to get it corroborated by observation and experience. These shepherds do not speak doubtfully, "Let us go see whether it be so or no"; but with assurance, *Let us go see this thing which is come to pass*; for what room was left to doubt of it, when *the Lord had* thus *made it known to them*? 2. They immediately made the visit, *v.* 16. They lost no time, but *came with haste* to the place, and there *they found Mary and Joseph*, and *the babe lying in the manger.* The poverty and meanness in which they found *Christ the Lord* were no shock to their faith, who themselves knew what it was to live a life of comfortable communion with God in very poor and mean circumstances. We have reason to think that the shepherds told Joseph and Mary of the vision of the angels they had seen, and the song of the angels they had heard, which was a great encouragement to them, more than if a visit had been made them by the best ladies in the town.

VI. The care which the shepherds took to spread the report of this (*v.* 17): *When they had seen it* they made *known abroad* the whole story of what was *told them*, both by the *angels*, and by Joseph and Mary, *concerning this child*, that he was the Saviour, even *Christ the Lord*, that in him there is *peace on earth.* This they told everybody, and agreed in their testimony concerning it. What impression did it make upon people? Why truly, *All they that heard it wondered at those things which were told them by the shepherds, v.* 18. They wondered, but never *enquired any further* about the Saviour, but let the thing drop as a *nine days' wonder*.

VII. The use which those made of these things, who did believe them. 1. The virgin Mary made them the matter of her *private meditation.* She said little, but *kept all these things*, and *pondered them in her heart, v.* 19. As she had silently left it to God to clear up her virtue, when that was suspected, so she silently leaves it to him to publish her honour, now when it was veiled; and it is satisfaction enough to find that, if no one else takes notice of the birth of her child, angels do. The truths of Christ are worth keeping; and the way to keep them safe is to *ponder them.* Meditation is the best help to memory. 2. The shepherds made them the matter of their more *public praises.* If others were not affected with those things, yet they themselves were (*v.* 20): They *returned, glorifying and praising God.* God would accept the thanksgivings they offered to him. They praised God for what *they had heard* from the angel, and for what *they had seen*, the babe *in the manger*, as it had been spoken to them. They thanked God that they had seen Christ. As afterwards the cross of Christ, so now his *manger*, was to some *foolishness* and a *stumbling-block*, but others saw in it, and admired, and praised, the wisdom *of God* and the *power of God.*

Verses 21–24

Our Lord Jesus, being *made of a woman*, was *made under the law*, Gal. iv. 4. As the son of a daughter of Abraham he was made under the law of *Moses.*

Now here we have two instances of his being *made under* that *law*, and submitting to it.

I. He was *circumcised* on the very day that the law appointed (*v.* 21): *When eight days were accomplished* they *circumcised* him. Though it was a *painful* operation, yet Christ would undergo it for us. Though it supposed him a *stranger*, that was by that ceremony to be admitted into covenant with God, though it supposed him a *sinner*, *yet* he submitted to it; nay, *therefore* he submitted to it, because he would be made in the likeness, not only of *flesh*, but of *sinful flesh*, Rom. viii. 3. Though thereby he made himself a *debtor to the whole law* (Gal. v. 3), yet he submitted to it. Christ was circumcised, that he might own himself of the seed of Abraham; that he might own himself a surety for our sins, and an undertaker for our safety; that he might justify the dedication of the infant seed of the church to God, by that ordinance which is the instituted seal of the covenant, as circumcision was (Rom. iv. 11), and baptism is.

At his circumcision he had his name given him; he was called *Jesus* or *Joshua*, for he was *so named*

JAMIESON, FAUSSET, BROWN

and to celebrate the tidings he has brought. **heavenly host**—or "army," an *army* celebrating *peace*! [BENGEL] "transferring the occupation of their exalted station to this poor earth, which so seldom resounds with the pure praise of God" [OLSHAUSEN]; to let it be known how this event is regarded in *heaven* and should be regarded on *earth.* **14. Glory . . .**—brief but transporting hymn—not only in articulate human speech, for our benefit, but in tunable measure, in the form of a Hebrew parallelism of two complete clauses, and a third one only amplifying the second, and so without a connecting "and." The "*glory to God,*" which the newborn "Saviour" was to bring, is the first note of this sublime hymn: to this answers, in the second clause, the "*peace on earth,*" of which He was to be "the Prince" (Isa. 9:6)—probably sung responsively by the celestial choir; while quickly follows the glad echo of this note, probably by a third detachment of the angelic choristers—"*good will to men.*" "They say not, glory to God in *heaven*, where angels are, but, using a rare expression, "*in the highest* [heavens]," whither angels aspire not," (Heb. 1:3, 4) [BENGEL]. "Peace" with God is the grand necessity of a fallen world. To bring in this, and all other peace in its train, was the prime errand of the Saviour to this earth, and, along with it, Heaven's whole "good will to men"—the divine complacency on a new footing—descends to rest upon men, as upon the Son Himself, in whom God is "well-pleased." (Matt. 3:17, the same word as here.) **15. Let us go . . .**—lovely simplicity of devoutness and faith this! They are not taken up with the angels, the glory that invested them, and the lofty strains with which they filled the air. Nor do they say, Let us go and see *if this be true*—they have no misgivings. But "Let us go and see this thing *which is come to pass,* which *the Lord hath made known unto us.*" Does not this confirm the view given on vs. 8 of the spirit of these humble men? **16. with haste**—Cf. ch. 1:39; Matthew 28:8 ("did *run*"); John 4:28 ("left her water-pot," as they do their flocks, in a transport). **found Mary . . .**—"mysteriously guided by the Spirit to the right place through the obscurity of the night" [OLSHAUSEN]. **a manger**—"*the* manger," as before. **17. made known abroad**—before their return (vs. 20), and thus were the first evangelists [BENGEL]. **20. glorifying and praising God . . .**—The latter word, used of the song of the angels (vs. 13), and in ch. 19:37, and ch. 24:53, leads us to suppose that theirs was a song too, probably some canticle from the Psalter—meet vehicle for the swelling emotions of their simple hearts at what "they had *heard* and *seen.*"

21. CIRCUMCISION OF CHRIST—Here only recorded, and even here merely alluded to, for the sake of the name then given to the holy Babe, "JESUS," or SAVIOUR (Matt. 1:21; Acts 13:23). Yet in this naming of Him "Saviour," in the act of circumcising Him, which was a symbolical and bloody removal of the body of sin, we have a tacit intimation that they "had need"—as John said of His Baptism—rather to be circumcised by Him "with the circumcision made without hands, in the putting off of the body [of the sins] of the flesh by the circumcision of Christ" (Col. 2:11), and that He only "suffered it to be so, because thus it became Him to fulfil all righteousness" (Matt. 3:15). Still the circumcision of Christ had a profound bearing on His own work—by few rightly apprehended. For since "he that is circumcised is a *debtor to do the whole law*" (Gal. 5:3), Jesus thus bore about with Him in His very flesh the seal of a voluntary obligation to do the whole law—by Him only possible in the flesh since the fall. And as He was "made under the law" for no ends of His own, but only "*to redeem them that were under the law,* that we might receive the adoption of sons" (Gal. 4:4, 5), the obedience to which His circumcision pledged Him was a *redeeming obedience*—that of a "Saviour." And, finally, as "Christ hath redeemed us from the curse of the law" by "being made *a curse for us*" (Gal. 3:13), we must regard Him, in His circumcision, as brought under a palpable pledge to be "*obedient unto death, even the death of the cross*" (Phil. 2:8).

22-40. PURIFICATION OF THE VIRGIN—PRESENTATION OF THE BABE IN THE TEMPLE—SCENE THERE WITH SIMEON AND ANNA. **22, 24 her purification**—Though the most and best copies read "their," it was the mother only who needed purifying from the legal uncleanness of child-bearing. "The days" of this purification for a male child were forty in all (Lev. 12:2, 4), on the expiry of which the mother was required to offer a lamb for a burnt offering, and a turtledove or a young pigeon for a sin offering. If she could not afford a lamb, the mother had to bring another turtledove or young pigeon;

ADAM CLARKE

14. *Glory to God in the highest.* The design of God, in the Incarnation, was to manifest the hidden glories of His nature, and to reconcile men to each other and to himself. The angels therefore declare that this Incarnation shall manifest and promote the *glory* of *God,* not only in the *highest* heavens, among the *highest* orders of beings, but in the *highest* and most exalted degrees. *Peace, good will toward men.* Men are in a state of hostility with Heaven and with each other. The carnal mind is enmity against God. He who sins wars against his Maker. When men become reconciled to God, through the death of His Son, they love one another. They have *peace* with God, *peace* in their own consciences, and *peace* with their neighbors; *good will* dwells among them, speaks in them, and works by them.

15. *Let us now go even unto Bethlehem.* Let us go across the country at the nearest, that we may lose no time, that we may speedily see this glorious Reconciler of God and man.

17. *They made known abroad the saying.* These shepherds were the first preachers of the gospel of Christ; and what was their text? Why, *Glory to God in the highest heavens,* and *on earth peace and goodwill among men.*

19. *And pondered them in her heart.* "Weighing them in her heart." "Weighing" is an English translation of our word "pondering," from the Latin *ponderare.* Every circumstance relative to her Son's birth, Mary treasured up in her memory; and every new circumstance she weighed, or compared with those which had already taken place, in order to acquire the fullest information concerning the nature and mission of her Son.

20. *The shepherds returned, glorifying and praising*—These simple men, having satisfactory evidence of the truth of the good tidings, and feeling a divine influence upon their own minds, returned to the care of their flocks, glorifying God for what He had shown them, and for the blessedness which they felt.

21. *When eight days were accomplished.* The law had appointed that every male should be circumcised at eight days old, or on the eighth day after its birth, Gen. xvii. 12; and our blessed Lord received circumcision in token of His subjection to the law, Gal. iv. 4; v. 3.

22. *Days of her purification.* That is, thirty-three days after what was termed the seven days of her uncleanness—forty days in all; for that was the time appointed by the law, after the birth of a male child. See Lev. xii. 2, 6. The MSS. and versions differ much in the pronoun in this place: some reading *her purification;* others, *his purification;* others, *their purification.* Two versions and two of the fathers omit the pronoun. *Their* and *his* have the greatest authorities in their support, and the former is received into most of the modern editions. The purification of every mother and

MATTHEW HENRY

of the angel to his mother Mary *before he was conceived in the womb* (Luke i. 31) and to his supposed father Joseph after, Matt. i. 21. It was a *common name* among the Jews, and in this he would be made *like unto his brethren.* It was the name of two eminent types of him in the Old Testament, Joshua, the successor of Moses; and Joshua, the high priest, Zech. vi. 11, 13. It was very significant of his undertaking. Jesus signifies a *Saviour.* He *brings salvation.*

II. He was *presented* in the temple. This was done at the time appointed by the law, when he was forty days old, *when the days of her purification were accomplished, v.* 22. Now, according to the law,

1. The child Jesus, being a first-born son, was *presented to the Lord.* The law is here recited (*v.* 23): *Every male that opens the womb shall be called holy to the Lord.* Christ was the *first-born* among many brethren, and was *called holy to the Lord,* so as never any other was; yet he was *presented to the Lord* as other first-born were, and no otherwise. But, according to the law, he was *redeemed,* Num. xviii. 15. *The first-born of man shalt thou redeem,* and *five shekels* was the value, Lev. xxvii. 6; Num. xviii. 16. But probably in case of poverty the priest was allowed to take less, or perhaps nothing; for no mention is made of it here.

2. The mother brought her offerings, *v.* 24. So *it is said in the law of the Lord,* that law which was yet in force, she must offer *a pair of turtle-doves,* or *two young pigeons*; had she been of ability, she must have brought a *lamb for a burnt-offering,* and a *dove for a sin-offering*; but, being poor, and not able to reach the price of a lamb, she brings *two doves,* one for *a burnt-offering and the other for a sin-offering* (see Lev. xii. 6, 8). Christ was not *conceived* and *born* in sin, as others are, yet, because he was made under the law, he complied with it. *Thus it became him to fulfil all righteousness.*

Verses 25–40

Even when he humbles himself, still Christ has honour done him. Simeon and Anna now do him honour, by the inspiration of the Holy Ghost.

I. A very honourable testimony is born to him by Simeon. Now observe here,

1. The account that is given us concerning this Simeon, or Simon. He dwelt now in Jerusalem, and was eminent for his piety and communion with God. Some learned men, who have been conversant with the Jewish writers, find that there was at this time one Simeon, a man of great note in Jerusalem. The Jews say that he was endued with a *prophetical* spirit. One thing objected against this conjecture is that at this time his father Hillel was living, and that he himself lived many years after this; but, as to that, he is not here said to be old; and his saying *Now let thy servant depart* intimates that he was willing to die *now,* but does not conclude that therefore he did die quickly. Another thing objected is that the son of Simeon was Gamaliel, a Pharisee, and an enemy to Christianity; but, as to that, it is no new thing for a faithful lover of Christ to have a son a bigoted Pharisee.

The account given of him here is, (1) That he was *just* and *devout, just* towards men and *devout* towards God; these two must always go together, and each will befriend the other, but neither will atone for the defect of the other. (2) That he *waited for the consolation of Israel,* that is, for the coming of the Messiah. Christ is not only the author of his people's comfort, but the matter and ground of it. He was long coming, and they who believed he would come continued *waiting, desiring* his coming, and *hoping* for it with *patience*; I had almost said, with some degree of *impatience* waiting till it came. The consolation of Israel is to be waited for, and it is worth waiting for, and it will be very welcome to those who have *waited* for it, and continue waiting. (3) That the *Holy Ghost* was upon him, not only as a Spirit of holiness, but as a Spirit of prophecy; he was *filled with the Holy Ghost.* (4) That he had a gracious promise made him, that before he died he should have a sight of the Messiah, *v.* 26. He received *this oracle* (for so the word signifies), *that he should not see death before he had seen* the Messiah, *the Lord's Anointed.* Those, and those only, can with courage *see death,* and look it in the face without terror, that have had by faith a sight of Christ.

2. The seasonable coming of Simeon into the temple, at the time when Christ was presented there, *v.* 27. Just then, when Joseph and Mary brought in the child, Simeon came, by direction of *the Spirit,* into the temple. The same Spirit that had provided for the support of his hope now provided for the transport of his joy. Those that would see Christ must go to his temple; for there *the Lord, whom ye seek,* shall suddenly come to *meet you,* and there you

JAMIESON, FAUSSET, BROWN

and, if even this was beyond her means, then a portion of fine flour, but without the usual fragrant accompaniments of oil and frankincense, as it represented a sin offering (Lev. 12:6-8; 5:7-11). From the intermediate offering of "a pair of turtledoves or two young pigeons," we gather that Joseph and the Virgin were in poor circumstances (II Cor. 8:9), though not in abject poverty. Being a first-born male, they "bring him to Jerusalem, to present him to the Lord." All such had been claimed as "holy to the Lord," or set apart to sacred uses, in memory of the deliverance of the first-born of Israel from destruction in Egypt, through the sprinkling of blood (Exod. 13:2). In lieu of these, however, one whole tribe, that of Levi, was accepted, and set apart to occupations exclusively sacred (Num. 3:11-38); and whereas there were 273 fewer Levites than first-born of all Israel on the first reckoning, each of these first-born was to be redeemed by the payment of five shekels, yet not without being *"presented* (or brought) *unto the Lord,"* in token of His rightful claim to them and their service (Num. 3:44-47; 18:15, 16). It was in obedience to this "law of Moses," that the Virgin presented her babe unto the Lord, "in the east gate of the court called Nicanor's Gate, where she herself would be sprinkled by the priest with the blood of her sacrifice [LIGHTFOOT]. By that Babe, in due time, we were to be redeemed, "not with corruptible things as silver and gold, but with the precious blood of Christ" (I Pet. 1:18, 19), and the consuming of the mother's burnt offering, and the sprinkling of her with the blood of her sin offering, were to find their abiding realization in the "living sacrifice" of the Christian mother herself, in the fulness of a "heart sprinkled from an evil conscience," by "the blood which cleanseth from all sin."

just—upright in his moral character. **devout**—of a religious frame of spirit. **waiting for the consolation of Israel**—a beautiful title of the coming Messiah, here intended.

the Holy Ghost was—supernaturally—**upon him**—Thus was the Spirit, after a dreary absence of nearly 400 years, returning to the Church, to quicken expectation, and prepare for coming events. **26. revealed by the Holy Ghost**—implying, beyond all doubt, the personality of the Spirit. **should see not death till he had seen**—"sweet antithesis!" [BENGEL]. How would the one sight gild the gloom of the other! He was, probably, by this time, advanced in years. **27, 28.** The Spirit guided him to the temple at the very moment when the Virgin was about to present Him to the Lord.

ADAM CLARKE

child, which the law enjoined, is a powerful argument in proof of that original corruption and depravity which every human being brings into the world. The woman to be purified was placed in the east gate of the court, called Nicanor's gate, and was there sprinkled with blood; thus she received the atonement.

24. *And to offer a sacrifice.* Neither mother nor child was considered as in the Lord's covenant or under the divine protection till these ceremonies prescribed by the law had been performed. *A pair of turtledoves.* One was for a burnt offering and the other for a sin offering; see Lev. xii. 8. The rich were required to bring a lamb; but the poor and middling classes were required to bring either two *turtledoves* or two *pigeons.* This is a proof that the Holy Family were not in affluence. Jesus sanctified the state of poverty, which is the general state of man, by passing through it. Therefore the poor have the gospel preached unto them, and the poor are they who principally receive it.

25. *And, behold, there was a man in Jerusalem.* This man is distinguished because of his singular piety. There can be no doubt that there were many persons in Jerusalem named *Simeon,* besides this man; but there was none of the name who merited the attention of God so much as he in the text.

The same man was just. He steadily regulated all his conduct by the law of his God; *and devout*—he had fully consecrated himself to God, so that he added a pious heart to a righteous conduct. The original word signifies also a person of good report—one well received among the people, or one cautious and circumspect in matters of religion. *Waiting for the consolation of Israel.* That is, the Messiah, who was known among the pious Jews by this character; He was to be the *consolation of Israel* because He was to be its Redemption. *The Holy Ghost was upon him.* He was a man divinely inspired, overshadowed, and protected by the power and influence of the Most High.

26. *It was revealed unto him.* He was "divinely informed"—he had an express communication from God concerning the subject. "The secret of the Lord is with them that fear him." The soul of a righteous and devout man is a proper habitation for the Holy Spirit. *The Lord's Christ.* Rather, "the Lord's anointed": that Prophet, Priest, and King who was typified by so many anointed persons under the old covenant.

27. *He came by the Spirit into the temple.* Probably he had in view the prophecy of Malachi, chap. iii. 1, "The Lord, whom ye seek, shall suddenly come to his temple." Now the prophecy was just going to be fulfilled; and the Holy Spirit, who dwelt in the soul of this

MATTHEW HENRY

must be ready to *meet him*.

3. The abundant satisfaction wherewith he welcomed this sight: *He took him up in his arms* (*v.* 28), he *embraced* him, laid him in his bosom, as near his heart as he could, which was as full of joy as it could hold. He *took him up in his arms*, to present him to the Lord. When we receive the record which the gospel gives us of Christ with a lively faith, and the offer it makes us of Christ with love and resignation, then we *take Christ in our arms*. It was promised him that he should have a sight of Christ; but more is *performed* than was *promised*: he has him in his arms.

4. The solemn declaration he made hereupon: *He blessed God*, and said, *Lord, now let thou thy servant depart in peace*, *v.* 29-32.

(1) He has a pleasant prospect *concerning himself*, he is arrived at a holy contempt of life, and desire of death: "*Lord, now let thou thy servant depart*, for mine eyes have seen the salvation I was promised a sight of before I died." Here is, [1] An acknowledgment that God had been *as good as his word*. Never any that hoped in God's word were made ashamed of their hope. [2] A thanksgiving for it. He *blessed God* that he saw that salvation in his arms. [3] A confession of his faith, that this child in his arms was the *Saviour*, the *Salvation* itself; *thy salvation*, the salvation of thine appointing, the salvation *which thou hast prepared*. [4] It is a farewell to this world: "*Now let thy servant depart*." The eye is not satisfied with seeing till it hath *seen Christ*, and then it is. What a poor thing doth this world look to one that hath Christ in his arms and salvation in his eye! [5] It is a welcome to death: *Now let thy servant depart*. Simeon is promised that he should not *see death* till he had *seen Christ*; and he is willing to construe what was expressed, as an intimation that, when he had seen Christ, he should die: *Lord, be it so*, saith he, *now let me depart*. See here, *First*, How *comfortable* the death of a good man is; he departs *as God's servant* from the place of his toil to that of his rest. He departs *in peace*, peace with God, peace with his own conscience; in *peace* with death. *Secondly*, What is the ground of this comfort? *For mine eyes have seen thy salvation*. It bespeaks a believing expectation of a happy state on the other side death, through this salvation he now had a sight of, which not only takes off the terror of death, but makes in *gain*, Phil. i. 21. Those that have welcomed Christ may welcome death.

(2) He has a pleasant prospect concerning the world, and concerning the church. This salvation shall be a blessing to the world. It is *prepared before the face of all people*, to be a *light to lighten the Gentiles* that now sit in darkness. This has reference to Isa. xlix. 6, *I will give thee for a light to the Gentiles*; for Christ came to be the light of the world, not a candle in the Jewish candlestick, but the *Sun of righteousness*; a blessing to the church: *the glory of thy people Israel*. Of those who were Israelites indeed, of the spiritual Israel, he was indeed *the glory*, and will be so to eternity. They shall *glory* in him. When Christ ordered his apostles to preach the gospel to all nations, therein he made himself a *light to lighten the Gentiles*; and when he added, *beginning at Jerusalem*, he made himself *the glory of his* people Israel.

5. The prediction concerning this child, which he delivered to Joseph and Mary. They *marvelled at those things* which were still more and more fully and plainly spoken concerning this child, *v.* 33. And because they were affected with, and had their faith strengthened by, that which was said to them, here is more said to them.

(1) Simeon shows them what reason they had to *rejoice*; for he *blessed them* (*v.* 34). He *prayed* for them that God would *bless* them, and would have others do so too. He is set *for the rising again of many in Israel*, that is, for the conversion of many to God that are dead and buried in sin, and for the consolation of many in God that are sunk and lost in sorrow and despair. Those whom he is set *for the fall of* may be the same with those whom he is set for the *rising again of*; *For their fall, in order to their rising again*. He wounds and then heals, Paul *falls*, and rises again.

(2) He shows them likewise what reason they had to *rejoice with trembling*. Lest Joseph and Mary especially, should be *lifted up* with the abundance of the revelations, here is a *thorn in the flesh* for them, and it is what we sometimes need. It is true, Christ shall be a blessing to Israel; but there are those in Israel whom he is *set for the fall of*, who will be prejudiced and enraged against him, and offended. As it is pleasant to think how many there are to whom Christ and his gospel are a savour of life unto life, so it is sad to think how many there are to

JAMIESON, FAUSSET, BROWN

28. took him up in his arms—immediately recognizing in the child, with unhesitating certainty, the promised Messiah, without needing Mary to inform him of what had happened to her. [OLSHAUSEN]. The remarkable act of taking the babe in his arms must not be overlooked. It was as if he said, "This is all my salvation and all my desire" (II Sam. 23:5).

29. Lord—"Master," a word rarely used in the New Testament, and selected here with peculiar propriety, when the aged saint, feeling that his last object in wishing to live had now been attained, only awaited his Master's word of command to "depart." **now lettest ...**—more clearly, "now Thou art releasing Thy servant"; a patient yet reverential mode of expressing a desire to depart. **30. seen thy salvation**—Many saw this child, nay, the full-grown "man, Christ Jesus," who never saw in Him "God's Salvation." This estimate of an object of sight, an unconscious, helpless babe, was pure faith. He "beheld His glory" (John 1:14). In another view it was *prior faith* rewarded by *present sight*.

32. all people—all the peoples, mankind at large. **a light to the Gentiles**—then in thick darkness. **glory of thy people Israel**—already Thine, and now, in the believing portion of it, to be so more gloriously than ever. It will be observed that this "swan-like song, bidding an eternal farewell to this terrestrial life" [OLSHAUSEN], takes a more comprehensive view of the kingdom of Christ than that of Zacharias, though the kingdom they sing of is one.

34, 35. set—appointed. **fall and rising again of many in Israel, and for a sign spoken against**—Perhaps the former of these phrases expresses the two stages of temporary "fall of many in Israel" through unbelief, during our Lord's earthly career, and the subsequent "rising again" of *the same persons* after the effusion of the Spirit at pentecost threw a new light to them on the whole subject; while the latter clause describes the determined enemies of the Lord Jesus. Such opposite views of Christ are taken from age to age. **35. Yea, ...**—"Blessed as thou art among women, thou shalt have thine own deep share of the struggles and sufferings which this Babe is to occasion"—pointing not only to the continued obloquy and rejection of this Child of hers, those agonies of His which she was to witness at the cross, and her desolate condition thereafter, but to dreadful alternations of faith and unbelief, of hope and fear regarding Him, which she would have to pass through.

ADAM CLARKE

righteous man, directed him to go and see its accomplishment. Those who come, under the influence of God's Spirit, to places of public worship will undoubtedly meet with Him who is the Comfort and Salvation of Israel. *After the custom of the law*. To present Him to the Lord, and then redeem Him by paying five shekels, Num. xviii. 15-16, and to offer those sacrifices appointed by the law.

28. *Then took he him up in his arms*. What must the holy soul of this man have felt in this moment!

29. *Lord, now lettest thou thy servant depart in peace*. "Now Thou dismissest," "loosest" him from life, having lived long enough to have the grand end of life accomplished. *According to thy word*. It was promised to him that he should not die till he had seen the Lord's Anointed, v. 26; and now, having seen Him, he expects to be immediately dismissed in peace into the eternal world, having a full assurance and enjoyment of the salvation of God.

30. *Thy salvation*. That Saviour which it became the goodness of God to bestow upon man, and which the necessities of the human race required. Christ is called our *salvation*, as He is called our Life, our Peace, our Hope; i.e., He is the Author of all these to them who believe.

31. *Which thou hast prepared*. Which Thou hast "made ready" *before the face*, in the presence, *of all people*. Here salvation is represented under the notion of a feast which God himself has provided for the whole world, and to partake of which He has invited all the nations of the earth. There seems a direct allusion here to Isa. xxv. 6, "In this mountain shall the Lord of hosts make unto all people a feast of fat things." Salvation is properly the food of the soul, by which it is nourished unto eternal life; he that receiveth not this must perish forever.

32. *A light to lighten the Gentiles*. "A light of the Gentiles, for revelation." By Moses and the prophets, a "light of revelation" was given to the Jews, in the blessedness of which the Gentiles did not partake. By Christ and His apostles a luminous revelation is about to be given unto the Gentiles, from the blessedness of which the Jews in general, by their obstinacy and unbelief, shall be long excluded. But to all true Israelites it shall be a *glory*, an evident fulfillment of all the predictions of the prophets, relative to the salvation of a lost world; and the first offers of it shall be made to the Jewish people, who may see in it the truth of their own Scriptures indisputably evinced.

33. *Joseph and his mother marvelled*. For they did not as yet fully know the counsels of God relative to the salvation which Christ was to procure, nor the way in which the purchase was to be made.

34. *This child is set for the fall*. This seems an allusion to Isa. viii. 14-15: Jehovah, God of hosts, shall be "for a stone of stumbling and for a rock of offence to both the houses of Israel ..; And many among them shall stumble, and fall." As Christ did not come as a temporal deliverer, in which character alone the Jews expected Him, the consequence should be, they would reject Him, and so fall by the Romans. See Rom. xi. 11-12 and Matthew xxiv. But in the fullness of time there shall be a *rising again of many in Israel*. See Rom. xi. 26. *And for a sign*. A "mark" to shoot at—a metaphor taken from archers. Or perhaps Simeon refers to Isa. xi. 10-12. "There shall be a root of Jesse, which shall stand for an ensign of the people; to it shall the Gentiles seek"—intimating that the Jews would reject it, while the Gentiles should flock to it as their ensign of honor, under which they were to enjoy a glorious rest.

35. *Yea, a sword shall pierce through thy*

MATTHEW HENRY

whom he is a savour of death unto death. He is set for *a sign*, to be admired by some, but by others, by many, spoken against. He had many *eyes upon him*, he was a *sign*, but he had many *tongues against* him. The effects of this will be that the *thoughts of many hearts will be revealed* (v. 35). The secret good affections and dispositions in the minds of some will be revealed by their embracing Christ, and closing with him; the secret corruptions and vicious dispositions of others will be revealed by their enmity to Christ and their rage against him. Men will be judged of by the thoughts of their hearts, their thoughts concerning Christ. The *word of God* is a discerner of the *thoughts* and *intents of the heart*. It is true, Christ shall be a comfort to his mother; but be not thou too proud of it, for *a sword shall pass through thine own soul also*. He shall be a suffering Jesus. "Thou *shalt suffer with him*, by sympathy, because of the nearness of thy relation, and strength of affection, to him." When he was abused, it was *a sword in her bones*. When she stood by his cross, and saw him dying, we may well think her inward grief was such that it might truly be said, *A sword pierced through her soul*, it cut her to the heart. Thou shalt *suffer for him*. Many understand it as a prediction of her martyrdom.

II. He is taken notice of by one *Anna*, a *prophetess*.

1. The account here given of this Anna, who she was. She was *A prophetess*. Perhaps no more is meant than that she was one who had understanding in the scriptures above other women, and made it her business to instruct the *younger women* in the things of God. God *left not himself without witness*. She was *the daughter of Phanuel* and her name signifies *gracious*. She was of *the tribe of Asher*, which was in Galilee. She was of *a great age*, a widow of about eighty-four years. She never married again, but continued a widow to her dying day, which is mentioned to her praise. She was a constant resident *in* or at least attendant *on* the temple. Some think she had lodgings in the courts of the temple; others think her not *departing from the temple* means no more, than that she was constantly there at the time of divine service; when any good work was to be done, she was ready to join in it. She *served God with fastings and prayers night and day*; she gave up herself wholly to her devotions, and spent that time in religious exercises which others spent in eating and drinking and sleeping. And in these she *served* God; that was it that put a value upon them and an excellency into them. She *served God*, and aimed at his honour, in *fasting and praying*. Other duties are in season now and then, but we must *pray always*. It is a pleasant sight to see aged Christians abounding in acts of devotion, as those that are not *weary of well-doing*, but that take more and more pleasure in them. Anna is now at length abundantly recompensed for her attendance so many years in the temple.

2. The testimony she bore to our Lord Jesus (*v*. 38): *She came in at that instant*, she, who was so *constant* to the temple, could not miss the opportunity. She *gave thanks likewise to the Lord*, just as Simeon, perhaps like him, wishing now to depart in peace. We should be excited to our duty by the praises and thanksgiving of others; why should not we *give thanks likewise*, as well as they? She, as a prophetess, instructed others concerning him: She *spoke of him to all them* that believed the Messiah would come, and with him *looked for redemption in Jerusalem*. Some there were in Jerusalem that *looked for redemption*; yet but a few, for Anna, it should seem, had acquaintance with all. She knew where to find them, or they where to find her, and she told them all the good news, that she had seen the Lord. Those that have an acquaintance with Christ *themselves* should do all they can to bring *others* acquainted with him.

Lastly, Here is a short account of the infancy and childhood of our Lord Jesus. *Where* he spent it, *v*. 39. They *returned into Galilee*. Luke relates no more concerning them, till they were returned into Galilee; but it appears by St. Matthew's gospel (*ch*. ii) that from Jerusalem they returned to Bethlehem, and there they continued till they were directed to flee into Egypt, and, returning thence when Herod was dead, they were directed to go to their old quarters in Nazareth. It is here called *their own city*. *How* he spent it, *v*. 40. In all things *it behoved him to be made like unto his brethren*, and therefore he passed through infancy and childhood as other children did. As other children, he *grew* in stature of body, and the improvement of understanding in his human soul. Whereas other children are weak in understanding and resolution, he was *strong in spirit*. By the Spirit of God his human soul was endued with extraordinary vigour. Whereas other children have *foolishness bound in their hearts*, he was *filled with*

JAMIESON, FAUSSET, BROWN

that the thoughts . . .—Men's views and decisions regarding Christ are a mirror in which the very "thoughts of their hearts" are seen.

37. Anna—or, Hannah. **a prophetess**—another evidence that "the last times" in which God was to "pour out His Spirit upon all flesh" were at hand. **of the tribe of Aser**—one of the ten tribes, of whom many were not carried captive, and not a few reunited themselves to Judah after the return from Babylon. The distinction of tribes, though practically destroyed by the captivity, was well enough known up to their final dispersion (Rom. 11:1; Heb. 7:14); nor is it now entirely lost. **lived . . .**—she had lived seven years with her husband, and been a widow eighty-four years; so that if she married at the earliest marriageable age, twelve years, she could not at this time be less than 103 years old. **37. departed not from the temple**—was found there at all stated hours of the day, and even during the night services of the temple watchmen (Ps. 134:1, 2), "serving God with fastings and prayer." (See I Tim. 5:5, suggested by this.)

38. coming in—"presenting herself." She had been there already but now is found "standing by," as Simeon's testimony to the blessed Babe died away, ready to take it up "in turn" (as the word rendered "likewise" here means). **to all them . . .**—the sense is, "to all them in Jerusalem that were looking for redemption"—saying in effect, In that Babe are wrapt up all your expectations. If this was at the hour of prayer, when numbers flocked to the temple, it would account for her having such an audience as the words imply [ALFORD].

39. Nothing is more difficult than to fix the precise order in which the visit of the Magi, with the flight into and return from Egypt (Matt. 2), are to be taken, in relation to the circumcision and presentation of Christ in the temple, here recorded. It is perhaps best to leave this in the obscurity in which we find it, as the result of two independent, though if we knew all, easily reconcilable narratives. **40.** His mental development kept pace with His bodily, and "the grace of God," the divine favor, rested manifestly and increasingly upon Him. See vs. 52.

ADAM CLARKE

own soul also. Probably meaning, You *also*, as well as your Son, shall die a martyr for the truth. But as this is a metaphor used by the most respectable Greek writers to express the most pungent sorrow, it may here refer to the anguish Mary must have felt when standing beside the cross of her tortured Son, John xix. 25.

36. *Anna, a prophetess*. It does not appear that this person was a *prophetess* in the strict sense of the word, i.e., one who could foretell future events, but rather a holy woman who, from her extensive knowledge and deep experience in divine things, was capable of instructing others—according to the use of the word *propheteuo*, 1 Cor. xiv. 3: "He that prophesieth, speaketh unto men to edification, and exhortation, and comfort." So we find this holy widow proclaiming Jesus to all who looked "for redemption in Jerusalem," v. 38. *The tribe of Aser*. This was one of the ten tribes of the kingdom of Israel, several families of which had returned from their idolatry unto God, in the time that Hezekiah proclaimed the Passover in Jerusalem, which is mentioned in 2 Chron. xxx. 1-11. *Seven years*. She was a pure virgin when married, was favored with her husband but *seven* years, and was now in all, taking in the time of her virginity, marriage, and widowhood, eighty-four years of age. At such an age it might be supposed she was reasonably exempted from performing the severer duties of religion, but her spirit of piety continued still to burn with a steady and undiminished flame.

37. *Departed not from the temple*. Attended constantly at the hours of prayer, which were nine in the morning and three in the afternoon. See Acts ii. 15; iii. 1. It does not appear that women had any other functions to perform in that holy place. *With fastings*. She accompanied her devotion with frequent fastings, probably not oftener than twice in the week, for this was the custom of the most rigid Pharisees; see chap. xviii. 12.

38. *Coming in that instant*. "At that very time"—while Simeon held the blessed Redeemer in his arms, and was singing his departing and triumphal song. *Gave thanks likewise*. She, as well as Simeon, returned God public thanks for having sent this Saviour to Israel. *Spake of him*. Of the nature and design of His mission, and the glory that should take place in the land. *To all them that looked for redemption*. As Daniel's seventy weeks were known to be now completed, the more pious Jews were in constant expectation of the promised Messiah. *In Jerusalem*. It is probable she went about from house to house, testifying the grace of God.

40. *The child grew*. As to His body—being in perfect health. *Waxed strong in spirit*. His rational soul became strong and vigorous. *Filled with wisdom*. The divinity continuing to communicate itself more and more in proportion to the increase of the rational principle. The reader should never forget that Jesus was perfect man as well as God. *And the grace of God was upon him*. The word not only means *grace* in the common acceptation of the word (some blessing granted by God's mercy to those who are sinners, or have no merit), but it means also "favor" or "approbation"; and this sense I think most proper for it here when applied to the human nature of our blessed Lord; and thus our translators render the same word, v. 52. Even Christ himself, who knew no sin, grew in the favor of God, and as to His human nature, increased in the graces of the Holy Spirit.

MATTHEW HENRY

wisdom. Everything he said and did was wisely said, and wisely done, above his years. Whereas other children show that the corruption of nature is in them, and *the tares of sin* grow up with the *wheat of reason*, he made it appear that nothing but *the grace of God was upon him.* He was *greatly beloved*, and high in the favour of God.

Verses 41–52

We have here the only story recorded concerning our blessed Saviour, from his infancy to the day of his showing to Israel, and therefore we are concerned to make much of this, for it is in vain to wish we had more.

I. Christ's *going up with his parents* to Jerusalem, at the feast of the passover, *v.* 41, 42. It was their constant practice to attend there, according to the law, though it was a long journey, and they were poor. Public ordinances must be frequented, and we must not *forsake the assembling of ourselves together.* They *went up* thither, *after the custom of the feast.* The child Jesus, at *twelve years old*, went up with them. The Jewish doctors say that at twelve years old children must begin to fast from time to time, and that at thirteen years old a child begins to be *a son of the commandment*, having been from his infancy, by virtue of his circumcision, *a son of the covenant.* Those children that are forward in other things should be put forward in religion. Those children that were in their infancy dedicated to God should be called upon, when they are grown up, to come to the *gospel passover*, to the Lord's supper, that they may make it their own act and deed to join themselves to the Lord.

II. Christ's *tarrying behind his parents at Jerusalem*, unknown to them.

1. His parents did not return till they had *fulfilled the days*; they had stayed there all the seven days at the feast, though it was not absolutely necessary that they should stay longer than the two first days. It is good to stay to the conclusion of an ordinance, as becomes those who say, *It is good to be here*, and not to hasten away.

2. The child *tarried behind in Jerusalem*, not because he was loth to go home, or shy of his parents' company, but because he had business to do there, and would let his parents know that he had a *Father in heaven*, whom he was to be *observant* of more than of *them*; and respect to *him* must not be construed disrespect *to them.* It is good to see young people willing to *dwell in the house of the Lord*; they are then like Christ.

3. His parents went the *first day's journey* without any suspicion that he was left behind, for they *supposed him to have been in the company*, *v.* 44. On these occasions, the crowd was very great, and they concluded that he came along with some of their neighbours, and they *sought him among their kindred and acquaintance.* Pray did *you* see our Son? or, Did *you* see him? They *found him not*, *v.* 45. There are many, too, many who are our kinsfolk and acquaintance, that we cannot avoid conversing with, among whom we find little or nothing of Christ: When they could not hear of him, yet they hoped they should meet with him at the place where they lodged that night; but *there* they could learn no tidings of him.

4. When they found him not at their quarters at night, they *turned back again*, next morning, to *Jerusalem, seeking him.* Those that would find Christ must *seek till they find*; for he will at length be found of those that seek him. Those that have lost their comforts in Christ, must bethink themselves where, and when, and how, they lost them, and must *turn back again* to the place where they last had them.

5. The *third day* they found him *in the temple.* There they found him *sitting in the midst of them* (*v.* 46), not standing as a *catechumen* to be examined or instructed by them. This is an instance, not only that he was *filled with wisdom* (*v.* 40), but that he had both a desire to increase it and a readiness to communicate it; and herein he is an example to children and young people, who should learn of Christ to delight in the company of those they may get good by, and choose to *sit in the midst of* the doctors rather than in the midst of the players. Many a youth at Christ's age now would have been playing with the *children in the temple*, but he was sitting with the *doctors in the temple.* He *heard* them. Those that would *learn* must be *swift to hear.* He *asked them questions*; whether, as a teacher (he had authority so to ask) or as a learner (he had humility so to ask) I know not. He returned *answers* to them, which were very surprising and satisfactory, *v.* 47. And his wisdom and *understanding* appeared as much in the questions he asked as in the answers he gave, so that all who heard him *were astonished*:

JAMIESON, FAUSSET, BROWN

41-52. FIRST CONSCIOUS VISIT TO JERUSALEM. "Solitary flowered out of the wonderful enclosed garden of the thirty years, plucked precisely there where the swollen bud, at a *distinctive crisis* (at twelve years of age), bursts into flower. To mark that is assuredly the design and the meaning of this record" [STIER]. **42. went up**—"were wont to go." Though males only were required to go up to Jerusalem at the three annual festivals (Exod. 23:14-17), devout women, when family duties permitted, went also, as did Hannah (I Sam. 1:7), and, as we here see, the mother of Jesus. **when twelve years old**—At this age every Jewish boy was styled "a son of the law," being put under a course of instruction and trained to fasting and attendance on public worship, besides being set to learn a trade. At this age accordingly our Lord is taken up for the first time to Jerusalem, at the passover season, the chief of the three annual festivals. But oh, with what thoughts and feelings must this Youth have gone up! Long ere He beheld it, He had doubtless "loved the habitation of God's house and the place where His honor dwelt" (Ps. 26:8), a love nourished, we may be sure, by that "word hid in His heart," with which in afterlife He showed so perfect a familiarity. As the time for His first visit approached, could one's ear have caught the breathings of His young soul, he might have heard Him whispering, "As the hart panteth after the water brooks, so panteth my soul after Thee, O God. The Lord loveth the gates of Zion more than all the dwellings of Jacob. I was glad when they said unto me, Let us go unto the house of the Lord. Our feet shall stand within thy gates, O Jerusalem!" (Ps. 42:1; 87:2; 122:1, 2). On catching the first view of "the city of their solemnities," and high above all in it, "the place of God's rest," we hear Him saying to Himself, "Beautiful for situation, the joy of the whole earth is Mount Zion, on the sides of the north, the city of the great King: Out of Zion, the perfection of beauty, God doth shine" (Ps. 48:2; 50:2). Of His feelings or actions during all the eight days of the feast not a word is said. As a devout child, in company with its parents, He would go through the services, keeping His thoughts to Himself. But methinks I hear Him, after the sublime services of that feast, saying to Himself, "He brought me to the banqueting-house, and his banner over me was love. I sat down under his shadow with great delight, and his fruit was sweet to my taste" (Song of Sol. 2:3, 4). **43. as they returned**—If the duties of life must give place to worship, worship, in its turn, must give place to them. *Jerusalem* is good, but *Nazareth* is good, too; let him who neglects the one, on pretext of attending to the other, ponder this scene. **tarried behind . . . Joseph and his mother knew not**—Accustomed to the discretion and obedience of the lad [OLSHAUSEN], they might be thrown off their guard. **44. sought him among their kinsfolk and acquaintances**—On these sacred journeys, whole villages and districts travelled in groups together, partly for protection, partly for company; and as the well-disposed would beguile the tediousness of the way by good discourse, to which the child Jesus would be no silent listener, they expect to find Him in such a group. **45, 46.** After three sorrowing days, they find Him still in Jerusalem, not gazing on its architecture, or surveying its forms of busy life, but in the temple—not the "sanctuary" (as in ch. 1:9), to which only the priests had access, but in some one of the enclosures around it, where the rabbins, or "doctors," taught their scholars. **46. hearing . . . asking**—The method of question and answer was the customary form of rabbinical teaching; teacher and learner becoming by turns questioner and answerer, as may be seen from their extant works. This would give full scope for all that "astonished them in His understanding and answers." Not that He assumed the office of *teaching*—"His hour" for that "was not yet come," and His equipment for that was not complete; for He had yet to "increase in wisdom" as well as "stature" (vs. 52). In fact, the beauty of Christ's example lies very much in His never at one stage of His life anticipating the duties of another. All would be in the style and manner of a learner, "opening His mouth and panting." "His soul breaking for the longing that it had unto God's judgments at all times" (Ps. 119:20), and now more than ever before, when finding Himself for the first time in His Father's house. Still there would be in *His questions* far more than in *their answers*; and if we may take the frivolous interrogatories with which they afterwards plied Him, about the woman that had seven husbands and such like, as a specimen of their present drivelling questions, perhaps we shall not greatly err, if we

ADAM CLARKE

41. *His parents went . . . every year.* This was their constant custom, because positively enjoined by the law, Exod. xxiii. 17. But it does not appear that infants were obliged to be present; and yet all the men-children are positively ordered to make their appearance at Jerusalem thrice in the year, Exod. xxxiv. 23. And our Lord, being now *twelve years old*, v. 42, accompanies His parents to the feast. Probably this was the very age at which the male children were obliged to appear before the Lord at the three public festivals—the Feast of Unleavened Bread, of Weeks, and of Tabernacles. According to the Jewish canons, it was the age at which they were obliged to begin to learn a trade.

43. *Had fulfilled the days.* Eight days in the whole: one was the Passover, and the other seven the days of unleavened bread.

44. *Supposing him to have been in the company.* Some have supposed that the men and women marched in separate companies on these occasions, which is very likely; and that sometimes the children kept company with the men, sometimes with the women. This might have led to what otherwise seems to have been inexcusable carelessness in Joseph and Mary. Joseph, not seeing Jesus in the men's company, might suppose He was with His mother in the women's company; and Mary, not seeing Him with her, might imagine He was with Joseph. *And they sought him.* "They earnestly sought Him." They are now both duly affected with a sense of their great loss and great negligence. *Kinsfolk and acquaintance.* Those of the same family and neighborhood went up to Jerusalem together on such occasions.

45. *Seeking him.* Or rather, "seeking Him diligently." This is the reading of several MSS., Vulgate, and nine copies of the Itala.

46. *Sitting in the midst of the doctors.* The rabbins, who were explaining the law and the ceremonies of the Jewish religion to their disciples. *Asking them questions.* Not as a scholar asks his teacher, to be informed; but as a teacher, who proposes questions to his scholars in order to take an occasion to instruct them.

47. *Answers.* The word seems not to mean *answers* only, but what Jesus said by way of question to the doctors, v. 46.

MATTHEW HENRY

they never heard one so young, nor indeed any of their greatest doctors, talk sense at the rate that he did. He *gave them a taste* (says Calvin) of his divine wisdom and knowledge. *They understood not;* they were only *astonished.*

6. His mother talked with him privately about it. *v.* 48. Joseph and Mary were both *amazed* to find him there, and to find that he had so much respect showed him as to be admitted to *sit among the doctors.* His mother told him how ill they took it: "*Son, why hast thou thus dealt with us?* Why didst thou put us into such a fright?" *Thy father and I have sought thee, sorrowing.* Those may have leave to complain of their losses that think they have lost Christ. They did not sorrow and sit down in despair, but sorrowed and *sought.* They that thus seek him in sorrow shall find him, at length, with so much the greater joy. He gently reproved their inordinate solicitude about him (*v.* 49): "*How is it that you sought me?* Wist ye not that I *ought* to be, *ἐν τοῖς τοῦ πατρός μου;—in my Father's house?*" so some read it. "*Under my Father's care* and protection." "*At my Father's work*" (so we take it): I must be *about my Father's business,* and therefore could not go home as soon as you might. *Wist ye not?* It was his errand into the world, and his meat and drink in the world, to do his Father's will, and finish his work: and yet at that time his parents *understood not this saying, v.* 50.

Lastly, Here is their return to Nazareth. He did not urge his parents either to come and settle at Jerusalem, but very willingly retired into his obscurity at Nazareth, where for many years he was, as it were, buried alive. But here we are told,

1. That he was *subject to his parents;* as it should seem, worked with his father at the trade of a carpenter. Herein he hath given an example to children to be dutiful and obedient to their parents in the Lord. Though his parents were poor and mean, though he was *strong in spirit,* and *filled with wisdom,* yet he was subject to his parents; how then will *they* answer it who, though foolish and weak, yet are disobedient to their parents?

2. That his mother, though she did not perfectly understand her son's sayings, yet *kept them in her heart.* However we may neglect men's sayings because they are obscure, yet we must not think so of God's sayings. That which at first is dark, so that we know not what to make of it, may afterwards become plain and easy. We may find use for that another time which now we see not how to make useful to us.

3. That he improved, and came on, to admiration (*v.* 52): *He increased in wisdom and stature.* This is meant of his human nature, his body increased in *stature* and bulk, he grew in the growing age; and his soul increased *in wisdom,* and in all the endowments of a human soul. As the faculties of his human soul grew more and more capable, the gifts it received from the divine nature were more and more communicated. And he increased in *favour with God and man.* The image of God shone brighter in him, when he grew up to be a youth, than it did, or could, while he was an *infant* and a *child.*

JAMIESON, FAUSSET, BROWN

suppose that "the questions" which He now "asked them" in return were just the germs of those pregnant questions with which He astonished and silenced them in after years: "*What think ye of Christ? Whose Son is He? If David call Him Lord, how is He then his Son?*" "*Which is the first and great commandment?*" "*Who is my neighbour?*" **49. about my Father's businesss**—lit., "in" or "at My Fathers," i.e., either "about My Father's *affairs,*" or "in My Father's *courts*"—where He dwells and is to be found—*about His hand,* so to speak. This latter shade of meaning, which includes the former, is perhaps the true one, Here He felt Himself *at home,* breathing His own proper air. His words convey a gentle rebuke of their obtuseness in requiring Him to *explain this.* "Once here, thought ye I should so readily hasten away? Let ordinary worshippers be content to keep the feast and be gone; but is this all ye have learnt of Me?" Methinks we are here let into the holy privacies of Nazareth; for what He says they *should* have known, He must have given them *ground* to know. She tells Him of the sorrow with which *His father* and she had sought Him. He speaks of *no Father but one,* saying, in effect, My Father has *not* been seeking Me; I have been with Him all this time; "the King hath brought me into His chambers . . . His left hand is under my head, and His right hand doth embrace me" (Song of Sol. 1:4; 2:6). How is it that ye do not understand? (Mark 8:21.) **50, 51. understood not**—probably He had never expressly *said* as much, and so confounded them, though it was but the true interpretation of many things which they had seen and heard from Him at home. (See on John 14:4, 5). But lest it should be thought that now He threw off the filial yoke, and became His own Master henceforth, and theirs too, it is purposely added, "And He went down *with them,* and was *subject unto them.*" The marvel of this condescension lies in its coming after such a scene, and such an assertion of His higher Sonship; and the words are evidently meant to convey this. "From this time we have *no more mention of Joseph.* The next we hear is of his "mother and brethren" (John 2:12); whence it is inferred, that between this time and the commencement of our Lord's public life, *Joseph died*" [ALFORD], having now served the double end of being the protector of our Lord's Virgin-mother, and affording Himself the opportunity of presenting a matchless pattern of subjection to both parents. **52.** See on vs. 40. **stature**—or better, perhaps, as in the margin, "age," which implies the other. This is all the record we have of the next eighteen years of that wondrous life. What seasons of tranquil meditation over the lively oracles, and holy fellowship with His Father; what inlettings, on the one hand, of light, and love, and power from on high, and outgoings of filial supplication, freedom, love, and joy on the other, would these eighteen years contain! And would they not seem "but a few days" if they were so passed, however ardently He might long to be more directly "about His Father's business?"

ADAM CLARKE

48. *Why hast thou thus dealt with us?* It certainly was not His fault, but theirs. Men are very apt to lay on others the blame of their own misconduct.

49. *How is it that ye sought me?* Is not this intended as a gentle reproof? *My Father's business.* "My Father's concerns." Some think that these words should be translated, "In My Father's house," which was a reason that they should have sought Him in the Temple only. As if He had said, Where should a child be found, but in his father's house?

51. *Was subject unto them.* Behaved towards them with all dutiful submission. Probably His working with His hands at His reputed father's business is here also implied; see on v. 41. No child among the Jews was ever brought up in idleness.

52. *Jesus increased in wisdom.* See on v. 40.

MATTHEW HENRY

CHAPTER 3

Verses 1-14

John's baptism introducing a new dispensation, it was requisite that we should have a particular account of it. Glorious things were said of John (*ch.* i. 15, 17); but we lost him in the deserts, and there he remains until *the day of his showing unto Israel, ch.* i. 80.

I. The date of the beginning of John's baptism; this is here taken notice of, which was not by the other evangelists, that the truth of the thing might be confirmed by the exact fixing of the time. And it is dated,

1. By the government of the heathen, which the Jews were under.

(1) It is dated by the reign of the Roman emperor; it was in the fifteenth year of Tiberius Cæsar, the third of the twelve Cæsars, a very bad man. The people of the Jews, after a long struggle, were of late made a province of the empire, and were under the dominion of this Tiberius; an inconsiderable despicable part of the Roman empire.

(2) It is dated by the governments of the viceroys that ruled in the several parts of the Holy Land under the Roman emperor, which was another badge of their servitude, for they were all foreigners. Pilate is here said to be the governor, president, or procurator, of Judæa. This character is given of him by some other writers, that he was a wicked man, and one that made no conscience of a lie. He reigned ill,

JAMIESON, FAUSSET, BROWN

CHAPTER 3

Vss. 1-20. PREACHING, BAPTISM, AND IMPRISONMENT OF JOHN. See on Matthew 3:1-12; Mark 6:17, etc. **1, 2.** Here the curtain of the New Testament is, as it were, drawn up, and the greatest of all epochs of the Church commences. Even our Lord's own age (vs. 23) is determined by it [BENGEL]. No such elaborate chronological precision is to be found elsewhere in the New Testament, and it comes fitly from him who claims it as the peculiar recommendation of his Gospel, that he had "accurately traced down all things from the first" (ch. 1:3). Here, evidently, commences his proper narrative. **the fifteenth year of Tiberius**—reckoning from the period when he was admitted, three years before Augustus' death, to a share of the empire [WEBSTER and WILKINSON], about the end of the year of Rome 779, or about four years before the usual reckoning. **Pilate . . . governor of Judea**—His proper title was *Procurator,* but with more than the usual powers of that office. After holding it about ten years he was ordered to Rome, to answer to charges brought against him, but ere he arrived Tiberius died (A.D. 35), and soon after Pilate committed suicide. **Herod**—(See on Mark 6:14). **Philip**—a different and very superior Philip to the one whose wife Herodias went to live with Herod Antipas. (See Mark 6:17.) **Iturea**—to the northeast of Palestine; so called from Ishmael's son

ADAM CLARKE

CHAPTER 3

1. *Fifteenth year.* This was the fifteenth of his principality and thirteenth of his monarchy; for he was two years joint emperor, previously to the death of Augustus. *Tiberius Caesar.* This emperor succeeded Augustus, in whose reign Christ was born. He began his reign August 19, A.D. 14, reigned twenty-three years, and died March 16, A.D. 37, aged seventy-eight years. He was a most infamous character. During the latter part of his reign especially, he did all the mischief he possibly could; and that his tyranny might not end with his life, he chose Caius Caligula for his successor, merely on account of his bad qualities. *Herod.* This was Herod Antipas, the son of Herod the Great, who murdered the innocents. It was the same Herod who beheaded John Baptist, and to whom our Lord was sent by Pilate. *Ituraea and . . . Trachonitis.* Two provinces of Syria, on the confines of Judea. *Abilene.* Another province of Syria, which had its name from Abila, its chief city. These estates were left to Herod Antipas and his brother *Philip* by the will of their father, Herod the Great, and were confirmed to them by the decree of Augustus.

That Philip was tetrarch of *Trachonitis* in the fifteenth year of Tiberius we are assured by Josephus, who says that Philip the brother of

MATTHEW HENRY

and at last was displaced and sent to Rome, to answer for his maladministrations. The other three are called *tetrarchs*, some think from the countries which they had the command of, each of them being over a *fourth part* of that which had been entirely under the government of Herod the Great.

2. By the government of the Jews among themselves, *v.* 2. Annas and Caiaphas were the high priests. God had appointed that there should be but one high priest at a time, but here were two, to serve some ill turn or other.

II. The origin and tendency of John's baptism.

1. The origin of it was *from heaven*: *The word of God came unto John*, *v.* 2. It is the same expression that is used concerning the Old Testament prophets (Jer. i. 2); for John was a prophet, yea, more than a prophet. John is here called *the son of Zacharias*, to refer us to what the angel said to his father. The word of the Lord came to him *in the wilderness*; for those whom God *fits* he will find out, wherever they are. As the word of the Lord is not *bound* in a *prison*, so it is not *lost* in a *wilderness*. John was the *son of a priest*, now entering upon the thirtieth year of his age; and therefore, according to the custom of the temple, he was now to be admitted into the temple-service. But God had called him to a more honourable ministry.

2. The scope and design of it were to bring all the people of his country off from their sins and home to their God, *v.* 3. *He came* first *into all the country about Jordan*, that part of the country which Israel took possession of first; there was the banner of the gospel first displayed. John resided in the most solitary part of the country; but, when the word of the Lord came to him, he quitted his deserts, and came into the inhabited country. Those that are *best pleased* in their retirements must cheerfully *exchange* them, when God calls them into places of concourse. *He came into all the country, preaching* a new *baptism.* The sign or ceremony, was such as was ordinarily used among the Jews, *washing with water*, by which proselytes were sometimes admitted, but the meaning of it was, *repentance for the remission of sins.*

(1) They were thereby obliged to *repent of their sins*, to be *sorry* for what they had done amiss, and to *do so no more.* The former they *professed*, and were concerned to be *sincere* in their professions; the latter they *promised*, and were concerned to *make good* what they promised. He bound them to change their mind, and change their way, and to *make them new hearts* and to live new lives.

(2) They were thereby assured of the pardon of their sins, upon their repentance. As the baptism he administered bound them not to submit to the power of sin, so it sealed to them a gracious and pleadable discharge from the guilt of sin.

III. The fulfilling of the scriptures in the ministry of John. The other evangelists had referred us to the same text that is here referred to, that of Esaias, *ch.* xl. 3. It is *written in the book of the words of Esaias the prophet.* Among them it is found that there should be *the voice of one crying in the wilderness*; and John is that voice; he cries, *Prepare ye the way of the Lord, and make his paths straight.* Luke goes further on with the quotation than Matthew and Mark had done, and applies the following words likewise to John's ministry (*v.* 5, 6), *Every valley shall be filled.* 1. The humble shall by it be *enriched* with grace. 2. The proud shall by it be humbled; *Every mountain and hill shall be brought low.* 3. Sinners shall be converted to God; *The crooked ways* and the *crooked* spirits shall be *made straight.* God by his grace can make that straight which sin hath made crooked. 4. Difficulties that were hindering and discouraging in the way to heaven shall be removed: *The rough ways shall be made smooth.* The gospel has made the way to heaven *plain* and easy to be *found, smooth* and easy to be *walked in.* 5. The great salvation shall be more fully discovered than ever, and the discovery of it shall spread further (*v.* 6): *All flesh shall see the salvation of God;* not the Jews only, but the Gentiles. All shall *see* it, and some of all sorts shall *see* it, enjoy it, and have the benefit of it.

IV. The general warnings and exhortations which he gave to those who submitted to his baptism, *v.* 7–9. In Matthew he is said to have preached these same things to *many of the Pharisees and Sadducees*, that *came to his baptism* (Matt. iii. 7–10); but here he is said to have spoken them *to the multitude, that came forth to be baptized of him*, *v.* 7. This was the purport of his preaching to all that came to him. As he did not flatter the *great*, so neither did he compliment the *many*, but gave the same reproofs of sin and warnings of wrath to the *multitude* that he did to the Sadducees and Pharisees; for, if they had not the same faults, they had others as bad. Now observe here,

JAMIESON, FAUSSET, BROWN

Itur or *Jetur* (I Chron. 1:31), and anciently belonging to the half tribe of Manasseh. **Trachonitis**—farther to the northeast, between Iturea and Damascus; a rocky district, infested by robbers, and committed by Augustus to Herod the Great to keep in order. **Abilene**—still more to the northeast, so called from *Abila*, eighteen miles from Damascus [ROBINSON]. **Annas and Caiaphas . . . high priests**—the former, though deposed, retained much of his influence, and, probably, as *sagan* or deputy, exercised much of the power of the high priesthood along with Caiaphas (John 18:13; Acts 4:6). Both Zadok and Abiathar acted as high priests in David's time (II Sam. 15:35), and it seems to have become the fixed practice to have two (II Kings 25: 18). **word of God came unto John**—*Such formulas,* of course, *are never used when speaking of Jesus,* because the divine nature manifested itself in Him not at certain isolated moments of His life. *He was the one everlasting manifestation of the Godhead*—THE WORD [OLSHAUSEN].

And were baptized of him in Jordan, confessing [probably confessing aloud] **their sins**—This baptism was at once a public seal of their felt need of deliverance from sin, of their expectation of the coming Deliverer, and of their readiness to welcome Him when He appeared. The baptism itself startled, and was intended to startle, them. They were familiar enough with the *baptism of proselytes* from heathenism; but this *baptism of Jews* themselves was quite new and strange to them.

Prepare ye the way of the Lord, make his paths straight—This prediction is quoted in all the four Gospels, showing that it was regarded as a great outstanding one, and the predicted forerunner as the connecting link between the old and the new economies. Like the great ones of the earth, the Prince of peace was to have His immediate approach proclaimed and His way prepared; and the call here—taking it generally—is a call to put out of the way whatever would obstruct His progress and hinder His complete triumph, whether those hindrances were public or personal, outward or inward. In Luke (3:5, 6) the quotation is thus continued: "Every valley shall be filled, and every mountain and hill shall be brought low; and the crooked shall be made straight, and the rough ways shall be made smooth; and all flesh shall see the salvation of God." **5. every valley . . .**—*levelling* and *smoothing,* obvious figures, the sense of which is in the first words of the proclamation, *"Prepare ye the way of the Lord."*

6. all flesh . . .—(quoted literally from the Septuagint of Isa. 40:5). The idea is that every obstruction shall be so removed as to reveal to the whole world the Salvation of God in Him whose name is the "Saviour" (cf. Ps. 98:3; Isa. 11:10; 49:6; 52:10; Luke 2:31, 32; Acts 13:47).

ADAM CLARKE

Herod died in the twentieth year of Tiberius, after he had governed Trachonitis, Batanea, and Gaulonitis thirty-seven years, *Antiq.*, b. xviii, c. 5, s. 6. And Herod continued tetrarch of Galilee till he was removed by Caligula, the successor of Tiberius, *Antiq.*, b. xviii, c. 8, s. 2. That *Lysanias* was tetrarch of *Abilene* is also evident from Josephus. He continued in this government till the Emperor Claudius took it from him, A.D. 42, and made a present of it to Agrippa. See *Antiq.*, b. xix, c. 5, s. 1. *Tetrarch* signifies the "ruler of the fourth part of a country." See the note on Matt. xiv. 1.

2. *Annas and Caiaphas being the high priests.* Caiaphas was the son-in-law of Annas or Ananias, and it is supposed that they exercised the high priest's office by turns. *The word of God came unto John.* That is, the Holy Spirit revealed to him this doctrine of salvation. This *came* upon him in the desert, where he was living in such a state of austerity as gave him full right to preach all the rigors of penitence to others.

3. *The baptism of repentance.* See on Matt. iii. 4-6, and Mark i. 1 and xvi at the end.

Were baptized. Were the people dipped or sprinkled? Those who are dipped or immersed in water, in the name of the Holy Trinity, I believe to be evangelically baptized; those who are washed or sprinkled with water in the name of the Father, and of the Son, and of the Holy Ghost, I believe to be equally so. *Confessing their sins.* Earnestly acknowledging that their sins were their own, thus taking the whole blame upon themselves, and laying nothing to the charge of God or man. This is essential to true repentance; and till a man take the whole blame on himself, he cannot feel the absolute need he has of casting his soul on the mercy of God, that he may be saved.

4. *Prepare ye the way.* It was customary for the Hindoo kings, when on journeys, to send a certain class of the people two or three days before them, to command the inhabitants to clear the ways—a very necessary precaution where there are no public roads.

5. *Every valley shall be filled.* All hindrances shall be taken out of the way. A quotation from the Greek version of Isa. xl. 4, containing an allusion to the preparations made in rough countries to facilitate the march of mighty kings and conquerors.

7-9. On this account of the Baptist's mode of preaching, see the notes on Matt. iii. 7-11.

Pharisees. A very numerous sect among the Jews, who, in their origin, were very probably a pure and holy people. It is likely that they got the name of Pharisees, i.e., Separatists (from *pharash,* "to separate"), from their separating themselves from the pollution of the Jewish national worship. But in process of time, like all religious sects and parties, they degenerated; they lost the spirit of their institu-

MATTHEW HENRY

1. That the guilty corrupted race of mankind is become a *generation of vipers*; not only poisoned, but poisonous; hateful to God, hating one another.

2. This generation of vipers is fairly warned to *flee from the wrath to come*, which is certainly before them if they continue such. We are not only warned of this wrath, but are put into a way to escape it, if we look about us in time.

3. There is no way of *fleeing from the wrath to come*, but by *repentance*.

4. Those that profess repentance are highly concerned to live like penitents (*v.* 8): *Bring forth therefore fruits meet for repentance*, else you cannot escape *the wrath to come*. By the change of our way must be evidenced the change of our mind.

5. If we be not really holy, both in heart and life, our profession of religion will stand us in no stead at all: *Begin not* now to frame excuses from this great duty of repentance, by *saying within yourselves, We have Abraham to our father*.

6. We have therefore no reason to depend upon our external privileges and professions of religion, because God can effectually secure his own honour and interest without us. If we were cut off and ruined, he could raise up to himself a church out of the most unlikely,—*children to Abraham* even *out of stones*.

7. The greater professions we make of repentance, and the greater assistances and encouragements are given us to repentance, the nearer and the sorer will our destruction be if we do not *bring forth fruits meet for repentance*. Now that the kingdom of heaven is at hand, *now* that the *axe is laid to the root of the tree*, threatenings to the wicked and impenitent are now more terrible than before, as encouragements to the penitent are now more comfortable.

8. Barren trees will be cast into the fire at length; it is the fittest place for them: *Every tree* that doth not bring forth fruit, *good fruit*, is *hewn down*, and *cast into the fire*.

V. The particular instructions he gave to several sorts of persons, that enquired of him concerning their duty: the *people*, the *publicans*, and the *soldiers*. Some of the Pharisees and Sadducees came to his baptism; but we do not find them asking, *What shall we do?* They thought they knew. But the *people*, the *publicans*, and the *soldiers*, who knew that they had done amiss, and were conscious to themselves of great ignorance and unacquaintedness with the divine law, were particularly inquisitive: *What shall we do?* Those that are *baptized* must be *taught*. Those that profess and promise repentance in general must evidence it by particular instances of reformation. They that would do their duty must desire to know their duty. These here enquire, not, *What shall this man do?* but, What shall *we* do? What *fruits meet for repentance* shall we *bring forth?* Now John gives answer to each, according to their place and station.

(1) He tells the *people* their duty, and that is to be charitable (*v* 11): *He that has two coats*, let him *give*, or *lend* at least, *to him that has none*, to keep him warm. The gospel requires *mercy*, and not sacrifice; and the design of it is to engage us to do all the good we can. *Food and raiment* are the two supports of life; he that hath *meat* to spare, let him give to him that is destitute of *daily food*. What we have we are but stewards of, and must use it, accordingly, as our Master directs.

(2) He tells the *publicans* their duty, the collectors of the emperor's revenue (*v.* 13): *Exact no more than that which is appointed you.* They must do justice between the government and the merchant, and not oppress the people in levying the taxes. They must not think that because it was their office to take care that the people did not defraud the prince they might therefore, by the power they had, bear hard upon the people, as those that have ever so little a branch of power are apt to abuse it: "Collect for Cæsar the things that are Cæsar's, and do not enrich yourselves by taking more." The public revenues must be applied to the public service, and not to gratify the avarice of private persons. He does not direct the publicans to quit their places, the employment is in itself lawful and necessary, but let them be just and honest in it.

(3) He tells the *soldiers* their duty, *v.* 14. Some think that these soldiers were Romans; and then it is an early instance of Gentiles embracing the gospel and submitting to it. Military men seldom seem inclined to religion; yet these submitted even to the Baptist's strict profession, and desired to receive the *word of command* from him: *What must we do?* In answer to this enquiry, John does not bid them lay down their arms, but cautions them against the sins that soldiers were commonly guilty of. They must not be injurious to *the people* among whom they were

JAMIESON, FAUSSET, BROWN

O generation of vipers—"Viper-brood," expressing the deadly influence of both sects alike upon the community. Mutually and entirely antagonistic as were their religious principles and spirit, the stern prophet charges both alike with being the poisoners of the nation's religious principles. In ch. 12:34, and 23:33, this strong language of the Baptist is anew applied by the faithful and true Witness to the Pharisees specifically—the only party that had zeal enough actively to diffuse this poison. **who hath warned you** [given you the hint, as the idea is] **to flee from the wrath to come?**—"What can have brought *you* hither?" John more than suspected it was not so much their own spiritual anxieties as the popularity of his movement that had drawn them thither. What an expression is this, "The wrath to come!" God's "wrath," in Scripture, is His righteous displeasure against sin, and consequently against all in whose skirts sin is found, arising out of the essential and eternal opposition of His nature to all moral evil. This is called "the *coming* wrath," not as being wholly future—for as a merited sentence it lies on the sinner already, and its effects, both inward and outward, are to some extent experienced even now—but because the impenitent sinner will not, until "the judgment of the great day," be concluded under it, will not have sentence publicly and irrevocably passed upon him, will not have it discharged upon him and experience its effects without mixture and without hope. In this view of it, it is a wrath *wholly* to come, as is implied in the noticeably different form of the expression employed by the apostle in I Thessalonians 1:10. Not that even true penitents came to John's baptism with all these views of "the wrath to come." But what he says is that this was the *real import of the step itself*. In this view of it, how striking is the word he employs to express that step—*fleeing* from it—as of one who, beholding a tide of fiery wrath rolling rapidly towards him, sees in instant flight his only escape! **Bring forth therefore fruits** [the true reading clearly is "fruit" **meet for repentance**—that is, such fruit as *befits* a true penitent. John now being gifted with a knowledge of the human heart, like a true minister of righteousness and lover of souls here directs them how to evidence and carry out their repentance, supposing it genuine; and in the following verses warns them of their danger in case it were not.

10-14. What shall we do then?—to show the sincerity of our repentance.

11. two coats . . .—directed against the reigning *avarice*.

12. publicans . . . 13. Exact no more . . .—directed against that *extortion* which made the publicans a byword. (See on ch. 19:2, 8.)

ADAM CLARKE

tion. They ceased to recur to first principles, and had only the form of godliness, when Jesus Christ preached in Judea; for He bore witness that they did make the outside of the cup and platter clean—they observed the rules of their institution but the spirit was gone. *Sadducees.* A sect who denied the existence of angels and spirits, consequently all divine influence and inspiration, and also the resurrection of the dead. The Sadducees of that time were the materialists and deists of the Jewish nation. When the sect of the Pharisees arose cannot be distinctly ascertained, but it is supposed to have been some time after the Babylonish captivity. The sect of the Sadducees were the followers of one Sadok, a disciple of Antigonus Sochaeus, who flourished about three centuries before Christ. *O generation of vipers.* A terribly expressive speech. A serpentine brood, from a serpentine stock. As their fathers were, so were they, children of the wicked one. This is God's estimate of a sinner, whether he wade in wealth or soar in fame. *The wrath to come.* The desolation which was about to fall on the Jewish nation for their wickedness, and threatened in the last words of their own Scriptures. See Mal. iv. 6. "Lest I come and smite the earth with a curse." This wrath or curse was coming; they did not prevent it by turning to God, and receiving the Messiah, and therefore the wrath of God came upon them to the uttermost.

And now also the ax is laid. Or, Even now the ax lieth. As if he had said, There is not a moment to spare—God is about to cut off every impenitent soul—you must therefore either turn to God immediately or be utterly and finally ruined. It was customary with the prophets to represent the kingdoms, nations, and individuals, whose ruin they predicted, under the notion of forests and trees doomed to be cut down. See Jer. xlvi. 22-23; Ezek. xxxi. 3, 11-12. The Baptist follows the metaphor; the Jewish nation is the tree, and the Romans the ax which, by the just judgment of God, was speedily to cut it down.

10. *What shall we do then?* The preaching of the Baptist had been accompanied with an uncommon effusion of that Spirit which convinces of sin, righteousness, and judgment. The people who heard him now earnestly begin to inquire what they must do to be saved. They are conscious that they are exposed to the judgments of the Lord, and they wish to escape from the coming wrath.

11. *He that hath two coats.* He first teaches the great mass of the people their duty to each other. They were uncharitable and oppressive, and he taught them not to expect any mercy from the hand of God while they acted towards others in opposition to its dictates. If men be unkind and uncharitable towards each other, how can they expect the mercy of the Lord to be extended towards themselves?

12. *Then came also publicans.* He next instructs the taxgatherers in the proper discharge of their duty, though it was an office detested by the Jews at large, yet the Baptist does not condemn it. It is only the abuse of it that he speaks against. If taxes be necessary for the support of a state, there must be collectors of them; and the collector, if he properly discharge his duty, is not only a useful, but also a respectable, officer. But it seems the Jewish taxgatherers exacted much more from the people than government authorized them to do, v. 13, and the surplus they pocketed. For an account of the *publicans,* see the note on Matt. v. 46.

MATTHEW HENRY

quartered: "*Do violence to no man.* Your business is to keep the peace, do not you *do violence* to any. *Shake no man*" (so the word signifies); "do not put people into fear; the sword of war, as well as that of justice, is to be a terror only to evil doers, but a protection to those that do well." Nor must they *accuse any falsely* to the government, thereby to make themselves formidable, and get bribes. They must not be injurious to their *fellow-soldiers*; for some think that caution, not to *accuse falsely*, has special reference to them: "Be not forward to complain one of another to your superior officers, that you may be revenged on those whom you have a pique against." They must not be given to mutiny, or contend with their generals about their pay: "*Be content with your wages.* While you have what you agreed for, do not murmur that it is not more." It is discontent with what they have that makes men oppressive and injurious. It is wisdom to make the best of that which is.

Verses 15–20

I. How the people took occasion, from the ministry and baptism of John, to think of the Messiah, and to think of him as at the door. Thus the way of the Lord was *prepared.* When men's expectations are raised, that which they are in expectation of becomes doubly acceptable. Now when they observed what an excellent doctrine John Baptist preached, 1. They began presently to consider that now was the time for the Messiah to appear. Never did the corrupt state of the Jews more need a reformation, nor their distressed state more need a deliverance, than now. 2. Their next thought was, "Is not this he that should come?" *All* thinking *men mused*, or reasoned, *in their hearts*, concerning John, *whether he were the Christ or not.* His life was holy and strict, his preaching powerful and with authority, and therefore "why may we not think that he is the Messiah?" That which puts people upon considering, reasoning with themselves, prepares the way for Christ.

II. How John disowned all pretensions to the honour of being himself the Messiah, but confirmed them in their expectations of him that really was the Messiah, *v.* 16, 17. John's office, as a crier or herald, was to give notice that the *kingdom of God was at hand*; and therefore, when he had told all manner of people severally what they must do, he tells them one thing more which they must all do: they must expect the Messiah now shortly to appear. And this serves as an *answer* to their *musings* and debates concerning himself.

1. He declares that the utmost he could do was to *baptize* them *with water.* He could only exhort them to *repent*, and assure them of forgiveness, upon repentance.

2. He consigns them, and turns them over, as it were, to Jesus Christ, for whom he was sent to *prepare the way*, and would have them no longer to *debate* whether John was the Messiah or no, but to look for him that was really so.

(1) John owns the Messiah to have a greater *excellency* than he had; he is one the *latchet of whose shoe* he does not think himself *worthy to loose.* John was *a prophet*, yea *more than a prophet*, more so than any of the Old Testament prophets; but Christ was a prophet more than John. This was a great truth which John came to preach; but the manner of his expressing it bespeaks his humility, and in it he not only *does justice* to the Lord Jesus, but *does him honour* too. Thus highly does it become us to speak of Christ, and thus humbly of ourselves.

(2) He owns him to have a greater *energy* than he had: "He is *mightier than I.*" They thought that a wonderful power went along with John; but what was that compared with the power which Jesus would come clothed with? John can do no more than *baptize with water*, in token of this, that they ought to purify and cleanse themselves; but Christ can, and will, *baptize with the Holy Ghost*; he can give the *Spirit* to cleanse and purify the heart. John can only preach a *distinguishing* doctrine. and by word and sign *separate between the precious and the vile*; but Christ hath his *fan in his hand*, with which he can, and will, perfectly separate between the wheat and the chaff. He *will thoroughly purge his floor.* John can only *speak comfort* to those that receive the gospel, but Jesus Christ will *give them comfort.* John can only promise them that they shall be safe; but Christ will make them so. John can only *threaten* hypocrites, and tell the *barren trees* that they shall be *hewn down* and *cast into the fire*; but Christ can execute that threatening; those that are as *chaff*, light, and vain, and worthless, *he will burn with fire unquenchable.*

The evangelist concludes his account of John's preaching with an *et cetera* (*v.* 18): *Many other things in his exhortation preached he unto the people. First,*

JAMIESON, FAUSSET, BROWN

soldiers . . . Do violence to none—The word signifies to "shake thoroughly," and so to "intimidate," probably in order to extort money or other property. **accuse . . . falsely**—acting as informers vexatiously, on frivolous or false grounds. **content with your wages**—"rations." We may take this as a warning against mutiny, which the officers attempted to suppress by largesses and donations [WEBSTER and WILKINSON]. And thus the "fruits" which would evidence their repentance were just resistance to the reigning sins, particularly of the *class* to which the penitent belonged, and the manifestation of an opposite spirit.

15-17. whether he were the Christ—showing both how successful he had been in awakening the expectation of Messiah's immediate appearing, and the high estimation, and even reverence, which his own character commanded.

16. John answered . . .—either to the deputation from Jerusalem (see John 1:19, etc.), or on some other occasion, simply to remove impressions derogatory to his blessed Master which he knew to be taking hold of the popular mind. **saying unto them all, . . .**—in solemn protestation. So far from entertaining such a thought as laying claim to the honors of Messiahship, the meanest services I can render to that "Mightier than I that is coming after me," are too high an honor for me. Beautiful spirit, distinguishing this servant of Christ throughout! **one mightier than I**—"the Mighter than I."

18. many other things, . . .—such as we read in John 1:29, 33, 34; 3:27-36.

ADAM CLARKE

14. *The soldiers likewise demanded of him.* He, thirdly, instructs those among the military. They were either Roman soldiers or the soldiers of Herod or Philip. Use no violence to any; do not extort money or goods by force or violence from any. *Neither accuse any falsely.* Or "on a frivolous pretense"—"be not sycophants," like those who are base flatterers of their masters, who to ingratiate themselves into their esteem, malign, accuse, and impeach the innocent. *Be content with your wages.* The word signifies not only the money which was allotted to a Roman soldier, which was two *oboli*, about three halfpence per day, but also the necessary supply of wheat, barley, etc.

15. *Whether he were the Christ.* So general was the reformation which was produced by the Baptist's preaching that the people were ready to consider him as the promised Messiah. Thus John came in the spirit and power of Elijah, and reformed all things; showed the people, the taxgatherers, and the soldiers their respective duties, and persuaded them to put away the evil of their doings. See the note on Matt. xvii. 11.

16-17. On these verses see Matt. iii. 11-12 and Mark i. 7-8, and particularly the note on John iii. 5.

But he that cometh after me, or, is coming after me, who is now on His way, and will shortly make His appearance. Jesus Christ began His ministry when He was thirty years of age, Luke 3:23, which was the age appointed by the law, Num. iv. 3. John the Baptist was born about six months before Christ; and as he began his public ministry when thirty years of age, then this coming after refers to six months after the commencement of John's public preaching, at which time Christ entered upon His. *Whose shoes I am not worthy to bear.* This saying is expressive of the most profound humility and reverence. To put on, take off, and carry the shoes of their masters was not only among the Jews but also among the Greeks and Romans the work of the vilest slaves. *With the Holy Ghost, and with fire.* That the influences of the Spirit of God are here designed needs but little proof. Christ's religion was to be a spiritual religion, and was to have its seat in the heart. Outward precepts, however well they might describe, could not produce inward spirituality. This was the province of the Spirit of God, and of Him alone; therefore He is represented here under the similitude of fire, because He was to illuminate and invigorate the soul, penetrate every part, and assimilate the whole to the image of the God of glory.

Whose fan is in his hand. The Romans are here termed God's fan, as in v. 10 they were called His ax, and as in 12:7, they are termed His troops or armies. *His floor.* Does not this mean the land of Judea, which had been long, as it were, the threshing floor of the Lord? God says He will now, by the winnowing fan (viz., the Romans), throughly cleanse this floor. The *wheat*, those who believe in the Lord Jesus, He *will gather* into His *garner*, either take to heaven from the evil to come, or put in a place of safety, as He did the Christians by sending them to Pella previously to the destruction of Jerusalem. *But he will burn up the chaff*—the disobedient and rebellious Jews, who

MATTHEW HENRY

John was an *affectionate* preacher. He was *exhorting*, beseeching; he pressed things home upon his hearers, as one in earnest. *Secondly*, He was a *practical* preacher. Much of his preaching was *exhortation*, quickening them to their duty, directing them in it, and not amusing them with matters of nice speculation. *Thirdly*, He was a *popular* preacher. He addressed himself *to the people, to the laity*, and accommodated himself to their capacity, as promising himself best success among them. *Fourthly*, He was an *evangelical* preacher, *he preached the gospel* to the people; in all his *exhortations*, he directed people to Christ, and excited and encouraged their expectations of *him*. *Fifthly*, He was a *copious* preacher: *Many other things he preached, many things, and different*. He *varied* in his preaching, that those who were not reached, and touched, and wrought upon by one truth, might be by another.

III. How full a stop was put to John's preaching. When he was in the midst of his usefulness he was imprisoned by the malice of Herod (*v*. 19, 20): *Herod the tetrarch being reproved by him*, not only for living in incest with his brother Philip's wife, but for the many other *evils which Herod had done* (for those that are wicked in one instance are commonly so in many others), he could not *bear it*, and *added* this wickedness to all the rest, that he *shut up John in prison*. Because he could not bear his reproofs, others should be deprived of the benefit of his instructions and counsels. Must he be silenced who is the *voice of one crying in the wilderness*? But thus the faith of his disciples must be tried; thus the unbelief of those who rejected him must be punished; thus he must be Christ's forerunner in suffering as well as preaching. He must now give way to him, and, the Sun being risen, the morning-star must of course disappear.

Verses 21-38

The evangelist mentioned John's imprisonment before Christ's being baptized, though it was nearly a year after it, because he would finish the story of John's ministry, and then introduce that of Christ.

I. A short account of Christ's baptism. Jesus came, to be baptized of John, and he was so, *v*. 21, 22.

1. It is here said that, *when all the people were baptized*, then *Jesus was baptized*. Christ would be baptized last, among the common people, and in the rear of them. He saw what multitudes were hereby prepared to receive him, and then he appeared.

2. Notice is here taken of Christ's *praying* when he was *baptized*, which was not in Matthew: being baptized, and *praying*. He *prayed*, as others did, for he would thus keep up communion with his Father. He prayed for the discovery of his Father's favour to him, and the descent of the Spirit. What was promised to Christ, he must obtain by prayer: *Ask of me and I will give thee*, &c.

3. When he prayed, *the heaven was opened*. Sin had shut up heaven, but Christ's prayer opened it again. Prayer is an ordinance that *opens heaven*: *Knock, and it shall be opened unto you*.

4. *The Holy Ghost descended in a bodily shape like a dove upon him*. When he begins to preach, *the Spirit of the Lord is upon him*. Now this is here expressed by a sensible evidence for his encouragement in his work, and for the satisfaction of John the Baptist; for he was told before that by this sign it should be notified to him which was the Christ.

5. There came *a voice from heaven* from the *excellent glory* (so it is expressed, 2 Pet. i. 17), *Thou art my beloved Son*. Here, and in Mark, it is expressed as spoken *to* Christ; in Matthew as spoken *of* him: *This is my beloved Son*. It comes all to one. It was foretold concerning the Messiah, *I will be his Father, and he shall be my Son*, 2 Sam. vii. 14. It was also foretold that he should be God's *elect, in whom his soul delighted* (Isa. xlii. 1); and, accordingly, it is here declared, *Thou art my beloved Son, in whom I am well pleased*.

II. A long account of Christ's pedigree, which had been more briefly related by St. Matthew.

1. His age: *He now began to be about thirty years of age*. At this age the priests were to enter upon the full execution of their office, Num. iv. 3.

2. His pedigree, *v*. 23, &c. Matthew had given us somewhat of this. He goes no higher than Abraham, but Luke brings it as high as Adam. Matthew designed to show that Christ was the son of Abraham, in whom *all the families of the earth are blessed*, and that he was heir to the throne of David; and therefore he begins with Abraham, and brings the genealogy down to Jacob, who was the father of Joseph, an heir-male of the house of David: but Luke, designing to show that Christ was the *seed of the woman*, that should break the serpent's head, traces his pedigree upward as high as Adam, and begins it with Eli, or Heli, who was the father, not of Joseph,

JAMIESON, FAUSSET, BROWN

19, 20. but Herod . . .—See on Mark 6:14, etc. **and for all the evils which Herod had done**—important fact here only mentioned, showing how *thoroughgoing* was the fidelity of the Baptist to his royal hearer, and how strong must have been the workings of conscience in that slave of passion when, notwithstanding such plainness, he "did many things and heard John gladly" (Mark 6:20, 26).

21, 22. BAPTISM OF AND DESCENT OF THE SPIRIT UPON JESUS. See on Matthew 3:13-17. **21. when all the people were baptized**—that He might not seem to be merely one of the crowd. Thus, as He rode into Jerusalem upon an ass, "*whereon yet never man sat*" (ch. 19:30), and lay in a sepulchre "*wherein was never man yet laid*" (John 19:41), so in His baptism He would be "*separate from sinners*."

23-38. GENEALOGY OF JESUS. **23. he began to be about thirty**—i.e., "was about entering on His thirtieth year." So our translators have taken the word [and so CALVIN, BEZA, BLOOMFIELD, WEBSTER and WILKINSON, etc.]: but "was about thirty years of age when He began (His ministry)," makes better Greek, and is probably the true sense [BENGEL, OLSHAUSEN, DE WETTE, MEYER, ALFORD, etc.]. At this age the priests entered on their office (Num. 4: 3). **being, as was supposed, the son of Joseph . . .**—Have we in this genealogy, as well as in Matthew's, the line of *Joseph?* or is this the line of *Mary?*—a point on which there has been great difference of opinion and much acute discussion. Those who take the *former* opinion contend that it is the natural sense of this verse, and that no other would have been thought of but for its supposed improbability and the uncertainty which it seems to throw over our Lord's real descent. But it is liable to another difficulty; viz., that in this case Matthew makes "*Jacob*," while Luke makes "*Heli*," to be Joseph's father; and though the same man had often more than one name, we ought not to resort to that supposition, in such a case as this, without necessity. And then, though the descent of Mary from David would be liable to no real doubt, even though we had no table of her line preserved to us (see, for example, ch. 1:2-32, and on ch. 2:5), still it does seem unlikely—we say not incredible—that two genealogies of our Lord should be preserved to us, neither of which gives his *real* descent. Those who take the *latter* opinion, that we have here the line of *Mary*, as in Matthew that of *Joseph*—here His *real*, there His *reputed* line—explain the statement about Joseph, that he was "*the son of* Heli," to mean that he was his *son-in-law*, as the husband of his daughter Mary (as in Ruth 1:11, 12), and believe that Joseph's name is only introduced instead of Mary's, in conformity with the Jewish custom in such tables. Perhaps this view is attended with fewest difficulties, as it certainly is the best supported. However we decide, it is a satisfaction to know that not a doubt was thrown out by the bitterest of the early enemies of Christianity as to *our Lord's real descent from David*. On comparing the two genealogies, it will be found that Matthew, writing more immediately for *Jews*, deemed it enough to show that the Saviour was sprung from Abraham and David; whereas Luke, writing more immediately for *Gentiles*, traces the descent back to Adam, the parent stock of the whole human family, thus showing Him to be the promised "Seed of the woman." "The possibility of constructing such a table, comprising a period of thousands of years, in an uninterrupted line from father to son, of a family that dwelt for a long time in the utmost retirement, would be inexplicable, had not the members of this line been endowed with *a thread* by which they could extricate them-

ADAM CLARKE

would not come unto Christ, that they might have life. *Unquenchable fire*. That cannot be extinguished by man.

19. *Herod the tetrarch*. See this subject explained at large, Matt. xiv. 1, etc., and Mark vi. 21, 23.

Herod the tetrarch. This was Herod Antipas, the son of Herod the Great. The word *tetrarch* properly signifies a person who rules over the fourth part of a country; but it is taken in a more general sense by the Jewish writers, meaning sometimes simply a governor, or a king; see v. 9. The estates of Herod the Great were not, at his death, divided into four tetrarchies, but only into three. One was given by the Emperor Augustus to Archelaus; the second to Herod Antipas, the person in the text; and the third to Philip: all three, sons of Herod the Great.

21. *Jesus also being baptized*. See on Matt. iii. 16-17.

23, etc. *Thirty years of age*. This was the age required by the law, to which the priests must arrive before they could be installed in their office; see Num. iv. 3. *Being (as was supposed) the son of Joseph*. This same phrase is used by Herodotus to signify one who was only reputed to be the son of a particular person. Much learned labor has been used to reconcile this genealogy with that in Matthew, chap. i, and there are several ways of doing it; the following, which appears to me to be the best, is also the most simple and easy. Matthew, in *descending* from Abraham to Joseph, the spouse of the blessed Virgin, speaks of sons properly such, by way of natural generation: *Abraham begat Isaac, and Isaac begat Jacob*, etc. But Luke, in *ascending* from the Saviour of the world to God himself, speaks of *sons* either properly or improperly such; on this account he uses an indeterminate mode of expression. *And Jesus himself began to be about thirty years of age, being (as was supposed) the son of Joseph . . . of Heli . . . of Matthat, etc.* After this observation it is next necessary to consider that, in the genealogy described by Luke, there are two sons improperly such: i.e., two sons-in-law instead of two sons. The two sons-in-law who are to be noticed in this genealogy are Joseph, the son-in-law of Heli, whose own father was Jacob, Matt. i. 16; and Salathiel, the son-in-law of Neri, whose own father was Jechonias, 1 Chron. iii. 17 and Matt. i. 12. This remark alone is sufficient to remove every difficulty. Thus it appears that Joseph, son of Jacob, according to Matthew, was son-in-law of Heli, according to Luke. And Salathiel, son of Jechonias, according to the former, was son-in-law of Neri, according to the latter. Mary therefore appears to have been the daughter of Heli, so called by abbreviation for *Heliachim*, which is

MATTHEW HENRY

but of the virgin Mary. Matthew draws the pedigree from Solomon, whose natural line ending in Jechonias, the legal right was transferred to Salathiel, who was of the house of Nathan, another son of David, which line Luke here pursues, and so leaves out all the kings of Judah. It is well for us that our salvation doth not depend upon our being able to solve all these difficulties. It is further worthy of observation, that, when those records of the Jewish genealogies had continued thirty or forty years after these extracts out of them, they were all lost and destroyed with the Jewish state and nation; for now there was no more occasion for them.

The genealogy concludes with this, *who was the son of Adam, the son of God.* He was both the ***Son of Adam*** and the ***Son of God,*** **that he might be a proper** Mediator between God and the sons of Adam, and might bring the sons of Adam to be, through him, the *sons of God.*

JAMIESON, FAUSSET, BROWN

selves from the many families into which every tribe and branch was again subdivided, and thus hold fast and know *the* member that was destined to continue the lineage. This thread was the hope that Messiah would be born of the race of Abraham and David. The ardent desire to behold Him and be partakers of His mercy and glory suffered not the attention to be exhausted through a period embracing thousands of years. Thus the member destined to continue the lineage, whenever doubtful, became easily distinguishable, awakening the hope of a final fulfilment, and keeping it alive until it was consummated" [OLSHAUSEN]. **24-30. son of Matthat, . . .**—(See on Matt. 1:13-15). In vs. 27, Salathiel is called the *son,* while in Matthew 1:12, he is called the *father* of Zerubbabel. But they are probably different persons. **38. son of God**—Cf. Acts 17:28.

ADAM CLARKE

the same in Hebrew with *Joachim.* Joseph, son of Jacob, and Mary, daughter of Heli, were of the same family. Both came from Zerubbabel: Joseph from Abiud, his eldest son, Matt. i. 13; and Mary by Rhesa, the youngest. See v. 27. It is worthy of being remarked that Matthew, who wrote principally for the Jews, extends his genealogy to Abraham, through whom the promise of the Messiah was given to the Jews; but Luke, who wrote his history for the instruction of the Gentiles, extends his genealogy to Adam, to whom the promise of the Redeemer was given in behalf of himself and of all his posterity.

36. *Of Cainan.* This *Cainan,* the son of *Arphaxad,* and father of *Sala,* is not found in any other Scripture genealogy.

MATTHEW HENRY — CHAPTER 4

Verses 1–13

In this story of Christ's temptation, observe,

I. How he was *prepared* and *fitted* for it.

1. He was *full of the Holy Ghost,* who had *descended* on him *like a dove.* Those are well armed against the strongest temptations that are *full of the Holy Ghost.*

2. He was newly *returned from Jordan,* where he was baptized, and owned by a voice from heaven to be the beloved Son of God. When we have had the most comfortable communion with God, and the clearest discoveries of his favour to us, we may expect that Satan will set upon us (the richest ship is the pirate's prize), and that God will suffer him to do so, that the power of his grace may be manifested and magnified.

3. He was *led by the Spirit into the wilderness.* His being *led into the wilderness gave* some advantage to the tempter; for there he had him alone. *Woe to him that is alone! He might* give Satan advantage, who knew his own strength; *we may not,* who know our own weakness. He *gained* some advantage to himself, during his forty days, fasting in the wilderness. We may suppose that he was wholly taken up in proper meditation, that he spent all his time in immediate, intimate converse with his Father, as Moses in the mount. And this prepared him for Satan's assaults, and hereby he was fortified against them.

4. He continued fasting (*v.* 2): *In those days he did eat nothing.* As by retiring into the *wilderness* he showed himself perfectly indifferent to the *world,* so by his *fasting* he showed himself perfectly indifferent to the *body;* and Satan cannot easily take hold of those who are thus loosened from, and dead to, the *world* and the *flesh.*

II. How he was assaulted by one temptation after another, and how he defeated the design of the tempter in every assault. During the *forty days,* he was *tempted of the devil* (*v.* 2). But at the end of the forty days he did as it were close with him, when he perceived *that he was hungry, v.* 2.

1. He tempted him to *distrust his Father's* care of him, and to *set up for himself* (*v.* 3): *If thou be the Son of God, command this stone to be made bread.* (1) "I counsel thee to do it; for God, if he be thy Father, has forgotten thee." If we begin to think of living by our own forecast, without depending upon divine Providence, we must look upon it as a temptation of Satan's, and reject it accordingly; it is Satan's counsel to think of an independence upon God. (2) "I *challenge* thee to do it, if thou canst; if thou dost not do it, I will say thou art *not the Son of God.*" Christ yielded not to the temptation. *First,* Because he would not do what Satan bade him do. We must not do anything that looks like *giving place to the devil.* Miracles were wrought for the confirming of faith, and the devil had no faith to be confirmed. *Secondly,* He wrought miracles for the ratification of his doctrine, and therefore till he began to *preach* he would not begin to work miracles. *Thirdly,* He would not work miracles *for himself* and his own supply. He would rather turn *water into wine,* for the credit and convenience of his friends, than *stones into bread,* for his own *necessary supply. Fourthly,* He would reserve the proof of his being the Son of God for hereafter. *Fifthly,* He would not do anything that looked like distrust of his Father. He would, like the other children of God, live in a dependence upon the divine Providence and promise. He returned a scripture-answer to it (*v.* 4): *It is written.* This is the first word recorded as spoken by Christ after his instalment in his prophetical office; and it is a quotation out of the Old Testament.

JAMIESON, FAUSSET, BROWN — CHAPTER 4

Vss. 1-13. TEMPTATION OF CHRIST.—See on Matthew 4:1-11.

Then—an indefinite note of sequence. But Mark's word (1:12) fixes what we should have presumed was meant, that it was "immediately" after His baptism; and with this agrees the statement of Luke (4:1). **was Jesus led up**—i.e., from the low Jordan valley to some more elevated spot. **of the Spirit**—that blessed Spirit immediately before spoken of as descending upon Him at His baptism, and abiding upon Him. Luke, connecting these two scenes, as if the one were but the sequel of the other, says, "Jesus, being full of the Holy Ghost, returned from Jordan, and was led . . . ." Mark's expression has a startling sharpness about it—"Immediately the Spirit driveth Him," "putteth," or "hurrieth Him forth," or "impelleth Him." (See the same word in Mark 1:43; 5:40; Matt. 9:25; 13:52; John 10:4.) The thought thus strongly expressed is the mighty constraining impulse of the Spirit under which He went; while Matthew's more gentle expression, "was led up," intimates how purely voluntary on His own part this action was. **into the wilderness**—probably the wild Judean desert. The particular spot which tradition has fixed upon has hence got the name of *Quarantana* or *Quarantaria,* from the forty days, —"an almost perpendicular wall of rock twelve or fifteen hundred feet above the plain" [ROBINSON'S *Palestine*]. The supposition of those who incline to place the temptation amongst the mountains of Moab is, we think, very improbable. **to be tempted** —The *Greek* word (*peirazein*) means simply to *try* or make proof of; and when ascribed to God in His dealings with men, it means, and can mean no more than this. Thus, Genesis 22:1, "It came to pass that God did tempt Abraham," or put his faith to a severe proof. (See Deut. 8:2.) But for the most part in Scripture the word is used in a bad sense, and means to entice, solicit, or provoke to sin. Hence the name here given to the wicked one—"the tempter" (vs. 3). Accordingly "to be tempted" here is to be understood both ways. The Spirit conducted Him into the wilderness simply to have His faith *tried;* but as the agent in this trial was to be the wicked one, whose whole object would be to seduce Him from His allegiance to God, it was a *temptation* in the bad sense of the term. The unworthy inference which some would draw from this is energetically repelled by an apostle (Jas. 1:13-17). **of the devil.** The word signifies a slanderer—one who casts imputations upon another. Hence that other name given him (Rev. 12:10), "The accuser of the brethren, who accuseth them before our God day and night." Mark (1:13) says, "He was forty days tempted of *Satan,*" a word signifying an *adversary,* one who lies in wait for, or sets himself in opposition to another. These and other names of the same fallen spirit point to different features in his character or operations. What was the high design of this? First, as we judge, to give our Lord a taste of what lay before Him in the work He had undertaken; next, to make trial of the glorious equipment for it which He had just received; further, to give Him encouragement, by the victory now to be won, to go forward spoiling principalities and powers, until at length He should make a show of them openly, triumphing over them in His cross: that the tempter, too, might get a taste, at the very outset, of the new kind of material in *man* which he would find he had here to deal with; finally, that He might acquire experimental ability "to succor them that are tempted" (Heb. 2:18).

ADAM CLARKE — CHAPTER 4

1. *Was led by the Spirit.* Or, "And was carried about." Matthew says, "he was brought up." Mark says, "the Spirit driveth him"—"putteth Him forth." But each of the Evangelists attributes this to the Holy Ghost, not to Satan.

To be tempted. The first act of the ministry of Jesus Christ was a combat with Satan. Does not this receive light from Gen. iii. 15: "I will put enmity between" the woman's Seed and thy seed; "it shall bruise thy head, and thou shalt bruise his heel."

And when he had fasted forty days. It is remarkable that Moses, the great lawgiver of the Jews, previous to his receiving the law from God, fasted forty days in the mount; that Elijah, the chief of the prophets, fasted also forty days; and that Christ, the Giver of the new covenant, should act in the same way. Was not all this intended to show that God's kingdom on earth was to be spiritual and living? That it should not consist "in meat and drink; but righteousness, and peace, and joy in the Holy Ghost," Rom. xiv. 17?

And when the tempter. This onset of Satan was made (speaking after the manner of men) judiciously; he came when Jesus, after having fasted forty days and forty nights, was hungry. Now as hunger naturally diminishes the strength of the body, the mind gets enfeebled, and becomes easily irritated; and if much watching and prayer be not employed, the uneasiness which is occasioned by a lack of food may soon produce impatience, and in this state of mind the tempter has great advantages. *Command that these stones.* The meaning of this temptation is: "Distrust the divine providence and support, and make use of illicit means to supply Thy necessities."

MATTHEW HENRY

The word of God is our *sword*, and faith in that word is our *shield*; we should therefore be *mighty in the scriptures*. The text of scripture he makes use of is quoted from Deut. viii. 3: "*Man shall not live by bread alone*. I need not turn the stone into bread; man can live *by every word of God*, by whatever God will appoint that he shall live by." God has many ways of providing for his people, without the ordinary means of subsistence; and therefore he is not at any time to be distrusted, but at all times to be depended upon, in the way of duty. She was an active believer who said that she had made many a meal's meat of the promises when she wanted bread.

2. He tempted him to *accept from him* the kingdom and to *do him homage*, *v.* 5–7. This evangelist puts this temptation second, which Matthew had put last, and which, it should seem, was really the last. Now observe,

(1) How Satan *managed* this temptation.

[1] He gave him a prospect of *all the kingdoms of the world in a moment of time*. He *took him up* for this purpose *into a high mountain*. It was done *in a moment of time*; whereas, if a man take a prospect of but one country, he must do it successively. Thus the devil thought to impose upon our Saviour with a fallacy; and, by making him believe that he could *show him all the kingdoms of* the world, would draw him into an opinion that he could *give him* all those kingdoms.

[2] He boldly alleged that these kingdoms were *all delivered to him*, that he had power to dispose of them and all their *glory*, and to give them to *whomsoever he would* (*v.* 6), but clogged with this condition, that he should *fall down and worship him*.

[3] He demanded of him homage and adoration: *If thou wilt worship me, all shall be thine*, *v.* 7. He would have him worship him himself. He would indent with him, that, when he had got possession of the kingdoms of this world, he should make no alteration of religions in them. Then let him take all the power and glory of the kingdoms if he pleased. Let who will take the wealth and grandeur of this earth, Satan has all he would have if he can but have men's hearts and adorations.

(2) How our Lord Jesus *triumphed* over this temptation. He gave it a peremptory repulse, rejected it with abhorrence (*v.* 8): "*Get thee behind me, Satan*." Such a temptation as this was not to be *reasoned with*, but immediately refused; it was presently knocked on the head with one word, *It is written, Thou shalt worship the Lord thy God*; and not only so, but *him only*, him and *no other*. Men must be *turned from the power of Satan unto God*, from the worship of devils to the worship of the only living and true God. This is the great divine law that Christ will re-establish among men, and reduce men to the obedience of, *That God only is to be served and worshipped*.

3. He tempted him to a presumptuous confidence of his Father's protection.

(1) What he designed in this temptation: *If thou be the Son of God, cast thyself down*, *v.* 9. He would have him seek for a new proof of his being the *Son of God*, as if that which his Father had given him by the voice from heaven, and the descent of the Spirit upon him, were not sufficient. He would have him seek a new method of proclaiming and publishing this to the world. If he would now declare from *the pinnacle of the temple*, among all the great people who attend the temple service, that he was the Son of God, and then, for proof of it, throw himself down unhurt, he would presently be received by everybody as a messenger sent from heaven. Or the fall might be his death, and then he should have got him finely out of the way.

(2) How he backed and enforced this temptation. He suggested, *It is written*, *v.* 10. Christ had quoted scripture against him; and he thought he would be quits with him, and would show that he could quote scripture as well as he. *He shall give his angels charge over thee*, and *in their hands they shall bear thee up*. It is true, God has promised the protection of angels, to encourage us to trust him, not to tempt him; as far as the promise of God's presence with us, so far the promise of the angels' ministration goes, but no further.

(3) How he was baffled and defeated in the temptation, *v.* 12. Christ quoted Deut. vi. 16, where it is said, *Thou shalt not tempt the Lord thy God*, by desiring a sign for the proof of divine revelation, when he has already given that which is sufficient.

III. What was the result and issue of this combat, *v.* 13. Our victorious Redeemer kept his ground, and came off a conqueror, not for himself only, but for us also.

1. The devil emptied his quiver: *He ended all the temptation*. Did Christ suffer, being tempted, till

JAMIESON, FAUSSET, BROWN

It is written—(Deut. 8:3). **Man shall not live by bread alone**—more emphatically, as in the *Greek*, "Not by bread alone shall man live." **but by every word that proceedeth out of the mouth of God**—Of all passages in Old Testament Scripture, none could have been pitched upon more apposite, perhaps not one so apposite, to our Lord's purpose. "The Lord . . . led thee [said Moses to Israel, at the close of their journeyings] these forty years in the wilderness, to humble thee, and to prove thee, to know what was in thine heart, whether thou wouldest keep His commandments, or no. And He humbled thee, and suffered thee to hunger, and fed thee with manna, which thou knewest not, neither did thy fathers know; that He might make thee know that man doth not live by bread only . . .", "Now, if Israel spent, not forty days, but forty years in a waste, howling wilderness, where there were no means of human subsistence, not starving, but divinely provided for, on purpose to prove to every age that human support depends not upon bread, but upon God's unfailing word of promise and pledge of all needful providential care, am I, distrusting this word of God, and despairing of relief, to take the law into My own hand? True, the Son of God is able enough to turn stones into bread: but what the Son of God is able to do is not the present question, but what is *man's duty* under want of the necessaries of life. And as Israel's condition in the wilderness did not justify their unbelieving murmurings and frequent desperation, so neither would Mine warrant the exercise of the power of the Son of God in snatching despairingly at unwarranted relief. As man, therefore, I will await divine supply, nothing doubting that at the fitting time it will arrive." The *second* temptation in this Gospel is in Luke's the *third*.

Then saith Jesus unto him, Get thee hence, Satan—Since the tempter has now thrown off the mask, and stands forth in his true character, our Lord no longer deals with him as a pretended friend and pious counsellor, but calls him by his right name—His knowledge of which from the outset He had carefully concealed till now—and orders him off. This is the final and conclusive evidence, as we think, that Matthew's must be the right order of the temptations. For who can well conceive of the tempter's returning to the assault after this, in the pious character again, and hoping still to dislodge the consciousness of His Sonship, while our Lord must in that case be supposed to quote Scripture to one He had called the devil to his face—thus throwing His pearls before worse than swine? **for it is written**—(Deut. 6:13). Thus does our Lord part with Satan on the rock of Scripture. **Thou shalt worship**—In the *Hebrew* and LXX it is, "Thou shalt *fear*"; but as the sense is the same, so "worship" is here used to show emphatically that what the tempter claimed was precisely what God had forbidden. **the Lord thy God, and him only shalt thou serve**—The word "serve" in the second clause, is one never used by the LXX of any but *religious* service; and in this sense exclusively is it used in the New Testament, as we find it here. Once more the word "only," in the second clause—not expressed in the *Hebrew* and LXX—is here added to bring out emphatically the *negative* and *prohibitory* feature of the command.

He shall give his angels charge concerning thee: and in [rather, on] **their hands they shall bear thee up, lest at any time thou dash thy foot against a stone**—The quotation is precisely as it stands in the *Hebrew* and LXX, save that after the first clause the words, "to keep thee in all thy ways," are here omitted. Not a few good expositors have thought that this omission was intentional, to conceal the fact that this would *not* have been one of "His ways," i.e., of duty. But as our Lord's reply makes no allusion to this, but seizes on the great principle involved in the promise quoted, so when we look at the promise itself, it is plain that the sense of it is precisely the same whether the clause in question be inserted or not. **Jesus said unto him, It is written again**—(Deut. 6:16), q.d., "True, it is so written, and on that promise I implicitly rely; but in using it there is another Scripture which must not be forgotten. **Thou shalt not tempt the Lord thy God**—Preservation in danger is divinely pledged: shall I then *create* danger, either to put the promised security skeptically to the proof, or wantonly to demand a display of it? That were "to tempt the Lord my God," which, being expressly forbidden, would forfeit the right to expect preservation."

ADAM CLARKE

But by (or upon,) *every word. Rhema* in Greek answers to *dabar* in Hebrew, which means not only "a word spoken" but also "thing, purpose, appointment." Our Lord's meaning seems to be this: God purposes the welfare of His creatures—all His appointments are calculated to promote this end. Some of them may appear to man to have a contrary tendency; but even *fasting* itself, when used in consequence of a divine injunction, becomes a means of supporting that life which it seems naturally calculated to impair or destroy.

An exceeding high mountain, and sheweth him. If the words *all the kingdoms of the world* be taken in a literal sense, then this must have been a visionary representation, as the highest mountain on the face of the globe could not suffice to make evident even one hemisphere of the earth, and the other must of necessity be in darkness. But if we take *the world* to mean only the land of Judea and some of the surrounding nations, as it appears sometimes to signify, then the mountain described by the Abbe Mariti (*Travels Through Cyprus*, etc.) could have afforded the **prospect in question**. Speaking of it, he says, "Here we enjoyed the most beautiful prospect imaginable. This part of the mountain overlooks the mountains of Arabia, the country of Gilead, the country of the Amorites, the plains of Moab, the plains of Jericho, the river Jordan, and the whole extent of the Dead Sea. It was here that the devil said to the Son of God, 'All these kingdoms will I give thee, if thou wilt fall down and worship me.'"

7. *If thou therefore wilt worship me.* This temptation is the last in order, as related by Matthew; and it is not reasonable to suppose that any other succeeded to it. Luke has here told the particulars, but not in the order in which they took place. See every circumstance of this temptation considered and explained in the notes on Matt. iv. 1-11.

Pinnacle of the temple. It is very likely that this was what was called the king's gallery; which, as Josephus says, "deserves to be mentioned among the most magnificent things under the sun: for upon a stupendous depth of a valley, scarcely to be fathomed by the eye of him that stands above, Herod erected a gallery of a vast height, from the top of which if any looked down, he would grow dizzy, his eyes not being able to reach so vast a depth."

Cast thyself down. Our Lord had repelled the first temptation by an act of confidence in the power and goodness of God, and now Satan solicits Him to make trial of it. Through the unparalleled subtlety of Satan, the very means we made use of to repel one temptation may be used by him as the groundwork of another. *He shall give his angels charge.* This is a mutilated quotation of Ps. xci. 11. The clause "to keep thee in all thy ways," Satan chose to leave out, as quite unsuitable to his design. That God has promised to protect and support His servants admits of no dispute; but as the path of duty is the way of safety, they are entitled to no good when they walk out of it. *In their hands they shall bear thee up.* This quotation from Ps. xci. 11 is a metaphor taken from a nurse's management of her child. In teaching it to walk, she guides it along plain ground; but when stones or other obstacles occur, she lifts up the child and carries it over them, and then sets it down to walk again.

Thou shalt not tempt. To expose myself to any danger naturally destructive, with the vain presumption that God will protect and defend me from the ruinous consequences of my imprudent conduct, is to tempt God.

MATTHEW HENRY

all the temptation was ended? And must not we expect also to pass all our trials, to go through the *hour of temptation* assigned us?

2. He then quitted the field: He *departed from him.* He saw it was to no purpose to attack him, he had no blind side, no weak or unguarded part in his wall. If we resist the devil, he will flee from us.

3. Yet he continued his malice against him; he departed but *for a season,* till the season when he was again to be let loose upon him, but as a *persecutor,* to bring him to *suffer.* He *departed now* till that season came which Christ calls the *power of darkness* (*ch.* xxii. 53), and when the prince of this world would again *come,* John xiv. 30.

Verses 14–30

Having defended himself against the devil's assaults, he now begins to act *offensively,* and to make those attacks upon him, by his preaching and miracles, which he could not resist or repel.

I. What is here said in general of his preaching, and the entertainment it met with *in Galilee.* Thither he came *in the power of the Spirit.* He was not to wait for a call from men, for he had light and life in himself. There he *taught in their synagogues,* their places of public worship, where they met, not, as in the temple, for ceremonial services, but for devotion. These came to be more frequent since the captivity, when the ceremonial worship was near expiring. This he did so as that he gained a great reputation. *A fame of him went through all that region* (*v.* 14), and it was a good fame; for (*v.* 15) he *was glorified of all.* Now, at first, he met with no contempt or contradiction; all *glorified* him, and there were none as yet that vilified him.

II. Of his preaching at Nazareth, the city where he was brought up. And here we are told how he *preached* there, and how he was *persecuted.*

1. How he preached there.

(1) The opportunity he had for it: *He came to Nazareth* when he had gained a reputation in other places. There he took occasion to preach, [1] In the *synagogue,* where it had been *his custom* to attend when he was a private person, *v.* 16. But, now that he was entered upon his public ministry, there he preached. [2] On the sabbath day, the proper time which the pious Jews spent, not in a mere ceremonial rest from worldly labour, but in the duties of God's worship.

(2) The call he had to it. He *stood up to read.* They had in their synagogues seven readers every sabbath, the first a priest, the second a Levite, and the other five Israelites of that synagogue. We often find Christ *preaching* in other synagogues, but never *reading,* except in this synagogue at Nazareth, of which he had been many years a member. The *book of the prophet Esaias* was *delivered to him.* The second lesson for *that* day being in the prophecy of Esaias, they gave him that volume to read in.

(3) The text he preached upon. He *stood up to read.* Now the book being *delivered to him,* [1] He *opened* it. The books of the Old Testament were in a manner *shut up* till Christ opened them, Isa. xxix. 11. [2] He *found* the place which was appointed to be read *that day.* Now his text was taken out of Isa. lxi. 1, 2, which is here quoted at large, *v.* 18, 19. There was a providence in it that that portion of scripture should be read that day, which speaks so very plainly of the Messiah. This text gives a full account of Christ's undertaking, and the work he came into the world to do.

First, How he was qualified for the work: *The Spirit of the Lord is upon me.* All the gifts and graces of the Spirit were conferred upon him, not by measure, as upon other prophets, but without measure, John iii. 34.

Secondly, How he was commissioned: *Because he has anointed me, and sent me.* His being *anointed* signifies both his being fitted for the undertaking and called to it.

Thirdly, What his work was. He was qualified and commissioned.

(*a*). To be a great *prophet.* He was *anointed to preach;* that is three times mentioned here. To *whom* he was to preach: to the *poor;* to those that were *poor in the world;* to those that were *poor in spirit,* to the meek and humble, and to those that were truly sorrowful for sin. *What* he was to *preach.* In general, he must preach *the gospel.* He is sent to *evangelize* them; not only to preach to them, but to make that preaching effectual; to bring it, not only to their ears, but to their hearts. Three things he is to preach:

(*i*) *Deliverance to the captives.* The gospel is a proclamation of liberty, like that to Israel in Egypt and in Babylon. It is a deliverance from the worst of thraldoms, which all those shall have the benefit of that are willing to make Christ their Head.

JAMIESON, FAUSSET, BROWN

Then the devil leaveth him—Luke says, "And when the devil had exhausted"—or "quite ended," as in Luke 4:2—"every [mode of] temptation, he departed from him till a season." The definite "season" here indicated is expressly referred to by our Lord in John 14:36 and Luke 22:52, 53.

14-32. JESUS, ENTERING ON HIS PUBLIC MINISTRY, MAKES A CIRCUIT OF GALILEE—REJECTION AT NAZARETH. *N.B.*—A large gap here occurs, embracing the important transactions in Galilee and Jerusalem which are recorded in John 1:29 to 4:54, and which occurred *before* John's imprisonment (John 3:24); whereas the transactions here recorded occurred (as appears from Matt. 4:12, 13) *after* that event. The visit to Nazareth recorded in Matthew 13:54-58 (and Mark 6:1-6) we take to be not a later visit, but the same with this first one; because we cannot think that the Nazarenes, after being so enraged at His *first* display of wisdom as to attempt His destruction, should, on a *second* display of the same, wonder at it and ask how He came by it, as if they had never witnessed it before.

16. as his custom was—Cf. Acts 17:2.

stood up for to read—Others besides rabbins were allowed to address the congregation. (See Acts 13:15.)

18, 19. To have fixed on any passage announcing His *sufferings* (as Isaiah 53), would have been unsuitable at that early stage of His ministry. But He selects a passage announcing the sublime object of His whole mission, its divine character, and His special endowments for it; expressed in the first person, and so singularly adapted to *the first opening of the mouth* in His prophetic capacity, that it seems as if made expressly for this occasion. It is from the well-known section of Isaiah's prophecies whose burden is that mysterious "SERVANT OF THE LORD," despised of man, abhorred of the nation, but before whom kings on seeing Him are to arise, and princes to worship; in visage more marred than any man and His form than the sons of men, yet sprinkling many nations; laboring seemingly in vain, and spending His strength for naught and in vain, yet Jehovah's Servant to raise up the tribes of Jacob and be His Salvation to the ends of the earth (Isa. 49, etc.). The quotation is chiefly from the Septuagint version, used in the synagogues.

ADAM CLARKE

14. *Returned in the power of the Spirit.* "In the mighty power of the Spirit." Having now conquered the grand adversary, he comes in the miracle-working energy of the Spirit to show forth His power, Godhead, and love to the people, that they might believe and be saved. He who, through the grace of God, resists and overcomes temptation is always bettered by it. This is one of the wonders of God's grace, that those very things which are designed for our utter ruin He makes the instruments of our greatest good.

15. *And he taught in their synagogues.* We do not find even the persecuting Jews ever hindered Christ or His disciples from preaching in their synagogues. *Glorified of all.* All felt the power of His preaching, and acknowledged the divinity of His mission. The scandal of the Cross had not yet taken place.

16. *To Nazareth, where he had been brought up.* It is likely that our Lord lived principally in this city till the thirtieth year of His age; but after He entered on His public ministry, His usual place of residence was at the house of Peter, in Capernaum. *As his custom was.* Our Lord regularly attended the public worship of God in the synagogues, for there the Scriptures were read. To worship God publicly is the duty of every man, and no man can be guiltless who neglects it. If a person cannot get such public worship as he likes, let him frequent such as he can get. Better to attend the most indifferent than to stay at home, especially on the Lord's day.

Stood up for to read. The Jews, in general, sat while they taught or commented on the Sacred Writings or the traditions of the elders; but when they *read* either the law or the prophets, they invariably *stood up;* it was not lawful for them even to lean against anything while employed in reading.

17. *And when he had opened the book.* "When He had unrolled it." The Sacred Writings used to this day, in all the Jewish synagogues, are written on skins of parchment or vellum, sewed end to end, and rolled on two rollers, beginning at each end; so that, in reading from right to left, they roll off with the left, while they roll on with the right. Probably the place in the Prophet Isaiah here referred to was the lesson for that day; and Jesus unrolled the manuscript till He came to the place. Then, after having read, He rolled it up again, and returned it to the officer, v. 20, the ruler of the synagogue, or his servant, whose business it was to take care of it.

18. *The Spirit of the Lord.* This is found in Isa. lxi. 1; but our Lord immediately adds to it v. 7 of chap. xlii. The proclaiming of liberty to the captives and the acceptable year (or year of acceptance) of the Lord is a manifest allusion to the proclaiming of the year of jubilee by sound of trumpet; see Lev. xxv. 9, etc., and the notes there. This was a year of general release of debts and obligations, of bond men and women, of lands and possessions which had been sold from the families and tribes to which they belonged. Our Saviour, by applying this text to himself, a text so manifestly relating to the institution above mentioned, plainly declares the typical design of that institution. *He hath*

MATTHEW HENRY

(*ii*) *Recovering of sight to the blind.* He came not only by the word of his gospel to bring *light* to them that sat *in the dark*, but by the power of his grace to give sight to them that were *blind*. Christ came to tell us that he has *eye-salve* for us, which we may have for the asking: that, if our prayer be, *Lord, that our eyes may be opened*, his answer shall be, *Receive your sight*.

(*iii*) *The acceptable year of the Lord*, *v.* 19. He came to let the world know that the God whom they had offended was willing to be reconciled to them, and to *accept* of them upon new terms. It alludes to the year of *release*, or that of *jubilee*, which was an *acceptable year*. It was an acceptable time, for it was a day of salvation.

(*b*) Christ came to be a great *Physician*; for he was sent to *heal the broken-hearted*, to give peace to those that were troubled and humbled for sins, and to bring them to rest who were weary and heavy-laden, under the burden of guilt and corruption.

(*c*) To be a great *Redeemer*. He not only proclaims liberty to the captives, but he sets at liberty them that are bruised. The prophets could but *proclaim liberty*, but Christ, as one having authority, as one that had *power on earth to forgive sins*, came to *set at liberty*; and therefore this clause is added here.

(4) Here is Christ's *application* of this text to himself (*v.* 21): When he had read it, he *rolled up the book*, and gave it again *to the minister*, or *clerk*, that attended, and *sat down*, according to the custom of the Jewish teachers. Now he *began* his discourse thus, "*This day is this scripture fulfilled in your ears.*" It now began to be fulfilled in Christ's entrance upon his public ministry; *now*, in the report they heard of his preaching and miracles in other places; *now*, in his preaching to them in their own synagogue. Many other gracious words proceeded out of his mouth, which these were but the *beginning* of; for Christ often preached long sermons, which we have but a short account of. This was enough to introduce a great deal: *This day is this scripture fulfilled.* The works of God are the accomplishment not only of his secret word, but of his word revealed; and it will help us to understand both the scriptures and the providences of God to compare them one with another.

(5) Here is the *attention* and *admiration* of the auditors.

[1] Their *attention* (*v.* 20): *The eyes of all them that were in the synagogue were fastened on him.* It is good, in hearing the word, to keep the eye fixed upon the minister by whom God is speaking to us; for, as the eye affects the heart, so, usually, the heart follows the eye, and is wandering, or fixed, as that is.

[2] Their *admiration* (*v.* 22): *They all bore him witness* and *wondered at the gracious words that proceeded out of his mouth*; and yet, as appears by what follows, they did not *believe in him.* They admired the *gracious words which proceeded out of his mouth.* Christ's words are *words of grace.* And these words of grace are to be *wondered at*; Christ's name was Wonderful, and in nothing was he more so than in his grace, in the words of his grace, and the power that went along with those words. Their wonder increased as they *said, Is not this Joseph's son?* Some from this suggestion took occasion perhaps so much the more to admire his *gracious words*, concluding he must needs be *taught of God*, while others perhaps with this consideration corrected their wonder at his gracious words, and concluded there could be nothing *really* admirable in them, whatever appeared, because he was the *Son of Joseph.*

(6) Christ's anticipating an objection which he knew to be in the minds of many of his hearers. Observe,

[1] What the objection was (*v.* 23): "*You will surely say to me, Physician, heal thyself.* You will expect that I should work miracles among you, as I have done in other places." Most of Christ's miracles were *cures*;—"Now why should not the sick in thine own city be *healed* as well as those in other cities?" They were designed to cure people of their unbelief:—"Now why should not the disease of unbelief be cured in those of thine own city as well as in those of others? *Whatsoever we have heard done in Capernaum, do here also in thine own country.*" They were pleased with *Christ's gracious words*, only because they hoped they were but the introduction to some *wondrous works* of his. They thought their own town as worthy to be the stage of miracles as any other. And why should not his neighbours and acquaintance have the benefit of his preaching and miracles, rather than any other?

[2] How he answers this objection against the course he took.

First, By a plain and positive reason why he would not make Nazareth his headquarters (*v.* 24), because it generally holds true *that no prophet is accepted in*

JAMIESON, FAUSSET, BROWN

19. acceptable year—an allusion to the jubilee year (Lev. 25:10), a year of universal *release* for person and property. (See also Isa. 49:8; II Cor. 6:2.) As the maladies under which humanity groans are here set forth under the names of *poverty, broken-heartedness, bondage, blindness, bruisedness* (or *crushedness*), so, as the glorious HEALER of all these maladies, Christ announces Himself in the act of reading it, stopping the quotation just before it comes to "the day of vengeance," which was only to come on the rejecters of His message (John 3: 17). The first words, "THE SPIRIT of the LORD is upon ME," have been noted since the days of the Church Fathers, as an illustrious example of *Father, Son, and Holy Ghost* being exhibited as in distinct yet harmonious action in the scheme of salvation. **20. the minister**—the *chazan* or synagogue-officer. **all eyes . . . fastened on Him**—astounded at His putting in such claims. **21. began to say . . .**—His whole address was just a detailed application to Himself of this and perhaps other like prophecies.

22. gracious words—"the words of grace," referring both to the richness of His matter and the sweetness of His manner (Ps. 45:2).

Is not this . . .—(See on Matt. 13:54-56). They knew He had received no rabbinical education, and anything *supernatural* they seemed incapable of conceiving.

23. this proverb—like our "Charity begins at home." **whatsoever . . .**—"Strange rumors have reached our ears of Thy doings at Capernaum; but if such power resides in Thee to cure the ills of humanity, why has none of it yet come nearer home, and why is all this alleged power reserved for strangers?" His choice of Capernaum as a place of residence since entering on public life was, it seems, already well known at Nazareth; and when He did come thither, to give no displays of His power when distant places were ringing with His fame, wounded their pride. He had indeed "laid his hands on a few sick folk and healed them" (Mark 6:5); but this seems to have been done quite privately the general unbelief precluding anything more open. **24. And he said . . .**—Her replies to the one proverb by another, equally familiar, which we express in a rougher form—"Too much familiarity breeds contempt." Our Lord's long residence in

ADAM CLARKE

anointed me. I have been designed and set apart for this very purpose; My sole business among men is to proclaim glad tidings *to the poor.* All the functions of this new Prophet are exercised on the hearts of men; and the grace by which He works in the heart is a grace of healing, deliverance, and illumination.

A. B. SIMPSON:

The first note and the supreme note in it is joyfulness. It is a message of hope to a sorrowing, despairing world. It has been well called "the Gospel of the Jubilee." Its undertone and its echo is gladness, victory, deliverance for all the evils that oppress humanity. It is the "sovereign balm for every wound." It is the remedy for the ills of humanity. Back of it stands the splendid figure of the Year of Jubilee. This is just the meaning of the closing clause to "proclaim the acceptable year of the Lord."

Every fifty years there came to ancient Israel a great festival that lasted a whole year long. All labor ceased and the earth abundantly supplied, the preceding year, enough for two. Nature rested, man rested and every home and synagogue and sanctuary and spot became the scene of festival and gladness. With its early dawn, the jubilee trumpets rang out upon every mountaintop and summoned the people to a year of rejoicing, and, as the year wore on, you might have seen many a family moving back to the vine-clad cottage which they had been compelled to lose years before for some mortgage debt. You might have seen sons and daughters traveling home and welcomed by rejoicing fathers and mothers as they came back from the slavery to which they had been consigned as hostages for some family debt. You might have seen bonds and mortgages, promissory notes and liens torn up or burned to ashes while every debt was cancelled, every slave set free, every prison opened and every lost heritage restored. All this Jesus Christ came to fulfill in a higher and grander sense by proclaiming an everlasting jubilee for all who accept His grace. Surely, such a gospel is indeed humanity's greatest boon and the announcement of such a message a fitting and glorious inauguration of the Gospel of the Son of Man.

—Christ in the Bible

20. *Were fastened on him.* Were "attentively fixed on Him."

22. *At the gracious words.* "To the words of grace," or the doctrines of grace, which He then preached.

23. *Physician, heal thyself.* That is, heal the brokenhearted in Thine own country, as the latter clause of the verse explains it; but they were far from being in a proper spirit to receive the salvation which He was ready to communicate, and therefore they were not healed.

MATTHEW HENRY

his own country. Experience seals this. Familiarity breeds contempt; and we are apt to think meanly of those whose conversation we have been accustomed to. That is most esteemed that is *far-fetched* and *dear-bought*, above what is *home-bred*, though really more excellent. Christ declined working miracles, or doing anything extraordinary, at Nazareth, because of the rooted prejudices they had against him there.

Secondly, By pertinent examples of two of the most famous prophets of the Old Testament. Elijah maintained a *widow of Sarepta*, a *city of Sidon*, one that was a stranger to the commonwealth of Israel, when there was a *famine in the land*, *v.* 25, 26. As God would hereby show himself a *Father of the fatherless*, and a *Judge of the widows*, so he would show that he was rich in mercy to all, even to the Gentiles. Elisha cleansed Naaman the Syrian of his leprosy, though he was a Syrian, and not only a foreigner, but an enemy to Israel (*v.* 27): *Many lepers were in Israel in the days of Eliseus*. And yet we do not find that Elisha cleansed them, but only this Syrian; for none besides had faith to apply himself to the prophet for a cure. Christ himself often met with greater faith among Gentiles than in Israel. Christ wrought his miracles, though not among his townsmen, yet among Israelites, whereas these great prophets wrought theirs among Gentiles.

2. How he was *persecuted* at Nazareth.

(1) That which provoked them was his taking notice of the favour which God by Elijah and Elisha showed to the Gentiles: *When they heard these things, they were filled with wrath* (*v.* 28), a great change since *v.* 22, when they *wondered at the gracious words that proceeded out of his mouth*; thus uncertain are the opinions and affections of the multitude, and so very fickle. If they had mixed faith with those gracious words of Christ which they wondered at, they would have been awakened by these latter words of his. Those only *pleased the ear*, and went no further, and therefore these *grated on the ear*. But that which especially exasperated them was that he intimated some kindness God had in reserve for the Gentiles. Their pious ancestors pleased themselves with the hopes of adding the Gentiles to the church; but this degenerate race hated to think that any others should be taken in.

(2) They were provoked to that degree that they made an attempt upon his life. They *rose up* in a tumultuous manner against him. They *thrust him out of the city*. They thrust from them the Saviour and the salvation. They *led him to the brow of the hill*, with a purpose to *throw him down headlong*. Though they had heard such a fame of him and had but just now themselves *admired his gracious words*, yet they hurried him away in a popular fury, or frenzy rather, to put him to death in a most barbarous manner.

(3) Yet he escaped, because his hour was not yet come: He *passed through the midst of them*, unhurt. They *drove* him from them, and he *went his way*. He would have gathered Nazareth, but they *would not*, and therefore their house is *left to them desolate*. But now, though they *received him not*, there were those that did.

Verses 31–44

When Christ was expelled from Nazareth, he came to Capernaum, another city of Galilee.

I. His preaching: *He taught them on the sabbath days*, *v.* 31. Christ's preaching much affected the people (*v.* 32); they were *astonished at his doctrine*, there was weight in every word he said, and admirable discoveries were made to them by it. *His word was with power;* there was a commanding force in it, and a working power went along with it to the consciences of men.

II. His miracles.

1. Two particularly specified, showing Christ to be,

(1) A *controller* and *conqueror* of *Satan* by his power to cast him out of the bodies of those he had taken possession of. [1] The devil is an *unclean spirit*, his nature directly contrary to that of the pure and *holy* God. [2] This unclean spirit works in the children of men. [3] It is possible that those who are very much under the power and working of Satan may yet be found *in the synagogue*. [4] Even the devils *know and believe* that *Jesus Christ is the Holy One of God*. [5] They believe and *tremble*. This unclean spirit *cried out with a loud voice*, apprehensive that Christ was now come to destroy him. [6] The devils have *nothing to do with Jesus Christ*, nor desire to have anything to do with him. [7] Christ has the devil under check: *He rebuked him*, saying, *Hold thy peace;* and this word he spoke *with power*; *Be muzzled*. Christ did not only enjoin him silence, but stopped his mouth. [8] In the breaking of Satan's power, both the enemy that is conquered shows his malice, and Christ, the conqueror, shows his over-

JAMIESON, FAUSSET, BROWN

Nazareth merely as a townsman had made Him *too common*, incapacitating them for appreciating Him as others did who were *less familiar with His everyday demeanor in private life*. A most important principle, to which the wise will pay due regard. (See also Matt. 7:6, on which our Lord Himself ever acted.) **25-27. But I tell you . . .**—falling back for support on the well-known examples of Elijah and Elisha (Eliseus), whose miraculous power, passing by those who were *near*, expended itself on those *at a distance*, yea on *heathens*, "the two great prophets who stand at the commencement of prophetic antiquity, and whose miracles strikingly prefigured those of our Lord. As He intended like them to feed the poor and cleanse the lepers, He *points to these miracles of mercy*, and not to the *fire* from heaven and the *bears* that tore the mockers" [STIER]. **three years and six months**—So James 5:17, including perhaps the six months *after the last fall of rain*, when there would be little or none at any rate; whereas in I Kings 18:1, which says the rain returned "in the third year," that period is probably not reckoned. **26, 27. save . . . saving**—"but only." (Cf. Mark 13:32, *Greek*.) **Sarepta**—"Zarephath" (I Kings 17:9), a heathen village between Tyre and Sidon. (See Mark 7:24.)

28, 29. when they heard these things—these allusions to the *heathen*, just as afterwards with Paul (Acts 22:21, 22). **rose up**—broke up the service irreverently and rushed forth. **thrust him**—with violence, as a prisoner in their hands. **brow . . .**—Nazareth, though not built on the ridge of a hill, is in part surrounded by one to the west, having several such precipices. (See II Chron. 25:12; II Kings 9:33.) It was a mode of capital punishment not unusual among the Romans and others. This was the first insult which the Son of God received, and it came from "them of His own household!" (Matt. 10:36.) **30. passing through the midst . . .**—evidently in a miraculous way, though perhaps quite noiselessly, leading them to wonder afterwards what spell could have come over them, that they allowed Him to escape. (Similar escapes, however, in times of persecution, are not unexampled.) **31. down to Capernaum**—It lay on the Sea of Galilee (Matt. 4:13), whereas Nazareth lay high.

33-37. DEMONIAC HEALED. **unclean**—The frequency with which this character of *impurity* is applied to evil spirits is worthy of notice. **cried out . . .**—(See on Matt. 8:29; Mark 3:11).

35. rebuked them . . .—(see on vs. 41). **thrown him . . .**—see on Mark 9:20.

ADAM CLARKE

24. *No prophet is accepted*. See on Matt. xiii. 55-57.

25. *In the days of Elias*. See this history, 1 Kings xvii. 1-9, compared with chap. xviii. 1-45. This was evidently a miraculous interference, as no rain fell for three years and six months, even in the rainy seasons.

26. *Unto none of them was Elias sent, save unto Sarepta*. The sentence is elliptical, and means this: To *none of them* was Elias sent; he was not sent except to *Sarepta;* for the widow at Sarepta was a Sidonian, not a widow of Israel.

27. *None of them was cleansed*. This verse is to be understood as the twenty-sixth; for Naaman, being a Syrian, was no leper in Israel.

28. *Were filled with wrath*. They seem to have drawn the following conclusion from what our Lord spoke: "The Gentiles are more precious in the sight of God than the Jews; and to them His miracles of mercy and kindness shall be principally confined." This was pretty near the truth, as the event proved. Those who profit not by the light of God, while it is among them, shall have their candle extinguished.

30. *Passing through the midst of them*. Either He shut their eyes so that they could not see Him or He so overawed them by His power as to leave them no strength to perform their murderous purpose. The man Christ Jesus was immortal till His time came, and all His messengers are immortal till their work is done.

31. *Came down to Capernaum*. Which it is likely He made His ordinary place of residence from this time.

32. *His word was with power*. "With authority." He assumed the tone and manner of a new Lawgiver; and uttered all His doctrines, not in the way of exhortation or advice, but in the form of precepts and commands, the unction of the Holy Spirit accompanying all He said.

33. *A spirit of an unclean devil*. As "demon" was used in both a good and a bad sense before and after the time of the Evangelists, the word *unclean* may have been added here by Luke merely to express the quality of *this* spirit. But it is worthy of remark that the inspired writers never use the word *demon* in a good sense.

MATTHEW HENRY

ruling grace. The devil showed what he would have done, when he *threw the man in the midst*, as if he would have dashed him to pieces. Christ showed what a power he had over him, in that he not only forced him to leave him, but to leave him without so much as *hurting* him. Whom Satan cannot *destroy*, he will do all the *hurt* he can to; but this is a comfort, he can harm them no further than Christ permits; nay, he shall not do them any real harm. He *came out*, and *hurt him not*. [9] Christ's power over devils was universally acknowledged and adored, *v.* 36. They were *all amazed, saying, What a word is this!* They that pretended to cast out devils did it with abundance of charms and spells, but Christ commanded them *with authority and power*. [10] This, as much as anything, gained Christ a reputation, and spread his fame. This instance of his power, magnified, and was looked upon as greatly magnifying him (*v.* 37); upon the account of this, *the fame of him went out*, more than ever, *into every place of the country round about*. Our Lord Jesus, when he set out at first in his public ministry, was greatly talked of, more than afterwards, when people's admiration wore off with the novelty of the thing.

(2) Christ showed himself to be *a healer of diseases*. In the former, he struck at the root of man's misery, which was Satan's enmity: in this, he strikes at one of the most spreading branches of it, one of the most common calamities of human life, and that is bodily diseases. These our Lord Jesus came to take away the sting of. Of all bodily diseases none are more common or fatal to grown people than *fevers*. Now here we have Christ's curing a fever with a word's speaking; the place was in Simon's house, his patient was Simon's wife's mother, *v.* 38, 39. [1] Christ is a guest that will pay well for his entertainment; those that bid him welcome into their hearts and houses shall be no losers by him; he comes with healing. [2] Even families that Christ visits may be visited with sickness. Houses that are blessed with his *distinguishing favours* are liable to the *common calamities* of this life. Simon's wife's mother was *ill* of a *fever*. [3] Even good people may sometimes be exercised with the sharpest afflictions. She was *taken with a great fever*, very acute, and high, and threatening. [4] No age can exempt from diseases. [5] When our relations are sick, we ought to apply ourselves to Christ, by faith and prayer, on their account: *They besought him for her*. [6] Christ has a tender concern for his people when they are in sickness and distress: *He stood over her*, as one concerned for her. [7] Christ had, and still has, a sovereign power over bodily diseases: *He rebuked the fever*, and *it left her*. [8] This proves Christ's cures to be miraculous, that they were done in an instant: *Immediately she arose*. [9] Where Christ gives a new life he designs and expects that it should be a new life indeed, spent more than ever in his service. If distempers be rebuked, and we arise from a bed of sickness, we must set ourselves to minister to Jesus Christ. [10] Those that minister to Christ must be ready to minister to all that are his for his sake: She *ministered to them*, not only to *him* that had cured her, but to them that had *besought him for her*.

2. A general account of many other miracles which Christ did. He *cured many that were diseased*, and it was *when the sun was setting* (*v.* 40); in the evening of that sabbath day which he had spent in the synagogue. It is good to abound in the work of the day, in some good work or other, even till sunset; as those that call the sabbath, and the business of it, *a delight*. He cured *all that were sick* of *divers diseases*. He had a remedy for every malady. The sign he used in healing was *laying his hands* on the sick. He healed by his own power. He cast the devil out of many that were possessed, *v.* 41. They said, *Thou art Christ the Son of God*. Christ *rebuked them*, and did not *suffer them to say that they knew him to be the Christ*.

3. Here is his removal from Capernaum, *v.* 42, 43.

(1) He *retired* for awhile into a place of *solitude*. It was but a little while that he allowed himself for sleep. *When it was day*, he went *into a desert place* to be sometimes *alone with God*, as even those should be, and contrive to be, that are most engaged in public work. They will find themselves never *less alone* than when *thus alone*.

(2) He *returned* again to the places of *concourse* and to the work he had to do there. Though a *desert place* may be a convenient *retreat*, yet it is not a *convenient residence*, because we were not sent into this world to *live to ourselves*. He was earnestly solicited to stay at Capernaum. *The people* were exceedingly fond of him. *They sought him*, and, though it was in a *desert place*, they *came unto him*. A desert is no desert if we be *with Christ* there. They

JAMIESON, FAUSSET, BROWN

36. What a word—a word from the *Lord of spirits.*

38-41. PETER'S MOTHER-IN-LAW, AND MANY OTHERS, HEALED. See on Matt. 8:14-17.

And forthwith, when they were come out of the synagogue—so also in Luke 4:38. **they entered into the house of Simon and Andrew, with James and John**—The mention of these four—which is peculiar to Mark—is the first of those traces of Peter's hand in this Gospel, of which we shall find many more. The house being his, and the illness and cure so nearly affecting himself, it is interesting to observe this minute specification of the number and names of the witnesses; interesting also as the first occasion on which the sacred triumvirate of Peter and James and John are selected from among the rest, to be a threefold cord of testimony to certain events in their Lord's life (see on ch. 5:37)—Andrew being present on this occasion, as the occurrence took place in his own house. **But Simon's wife's mother lay sick of a fever**—Luke, as was natural in "the beloved *physician*" (Col. 4:14), describes it professionally; calling it a "great fever," and thus distinguishing it from that lighter kind which the Greek physicians were wont to call "small fevers," as GALEN, quoted by WETSTEIN, tells us. **and anon**—immediately. **they tell him of her**—naturally hoping that His compassion and power towards one of His own disciples would not be less signally displayed than towards the demonized stranger in the synagogue.

And he healed many that were sick of divers diseases, and cast out many devils—In Matthew 8:16 it is said, "He cast out the spirits with His word"; or rather, "with a word"—a word of command.

41. suffered them not to speak—The marginal reading here is wrong. Our Lord ever refused testimony from devils, *for the very reason why they were eager to give it*, because He and they would thus seem to be one interest, as His enemies actually alleged. (See on Matt. 12:24, etc.; see also Acts 16:16-18.)

42-44. JESUS, SOUGHT OUT AT MORNING PRAYER, AND ENTREATED TO STAY, DECLINES FROM THE URGENCY OF HIS WORK. See on Mark 1:35-39, where we learn how early He retired, and how He was engaged in solitude when they came seeking Him.

ADAM CLARKE

35. *And hurt him not*. Though he "convulsed" him, Mark i. 26, and threw him down in the midst of them, probably with the design to take away his life, yet our Lord permitted it not; and this appears to be the meaning of the place. The spirit was not permitted essentially to injure him at that time.

37. *The fame*. The "sound." This is a very elegant metaphor. The people are represented as struck with astonishment, and the "sound" goes out through all the coasts, in allusion to the propagation of sound by a smart stroke upon any substance, by which the air is suddenly agitated and conveys the report made by the stroke to distant places.

38. *Simon's wife's mother*. See on Matt. viii. 14-17. As soon as Peter began to follow Christ, his family began to benefit by it.

Peter's house. That Peter lived at Capernaum, and that Christ lodged with him, is fully evident from this verse compared with chap. xvii. 24. *Peter's . . . wife's mother*. Learn hence, says Theophylact, that marriage is no hindrance to virtue, since the chief of the apostles had his wife. Marriage is one of the first of divine institutions, and is a positive command of God. He says the state of celibacy is not good, Gen. ii. 18. Those who pretend to say that the single state is more holy than the other slander their Maker, and say in effect, "We are too holy to keep the commandments of God."

40. *When the sun was setting*. And consequently the Sabbath ended, for before this it would have been unlawful to bring their sick to be healed.

42. *And the people sought him*. Rather "Sought Him earnestly." This reading is supported by many MSS. The people had tasted

MATTHEW HENRY

detained him that he should not depart from them. It ought not to discourage the ministers of Christ that some reject them, for they will meet with others that will welcome them and their message. He chose rather to *diffuse* the light of his gospel to *many* places than to fix it to *one.* Though he was welcome at Capernaum, yet he is *sent to preach the gospel to other cities also.* They that enjoy the benefit of the gospel must be willing that others also should share in that benefit, and not covet the *monopoly* of it. Christ, though he preached not in vain in the synagogue at Capernaum, yet would not be tied to that, but *preached in the synagogues of Galilee, v.* 44. It is well for us that our Lord Jesus has not tied himself to any one place or people, but, wherever two or three are gathered in his name, he will be in the midst of them.

CHAPTER 5

Verses 1–11

This passage of story is the same with that which was more briefly related by Matthew and Mark, of Christ's calling Peter and Andrew to be *fishers of men,* Matt. iv. 18, and Mark i. 16. They had not related this miraculous draught of fishes at that time, having only in view the calling of his disciples; but Luke gives us that story as one of the many signs which Jesus did, which *had not been written* in the foregoing books.

I. What vast *crowds* attended Christ's preaching: *The people pressed upon him to hear the word of God* (*v.* 1). The people *flocked about him* (so the word signifies); they showed respect to his preaching, though not without some rudeness to his person, which was very excusable, for they *pressed upon him.* Some would reckon this a discredit to him when none of the *rulers* or of *the Pharisees believed in him.* Their souls were as precious as the souls of the grandees, and it is his aim to bring not so much the mighty as the *many sons* to God. See how the people relished *good preaching*: they pressed to *hear the word of God*; they could perceive it to be the *word of God,* and therefore they coveted to hear it.

II. What poor *conveniences* Christ had for preaching: *He stood by the lake of Gennesaret* (*v.* 1), upon a level with the crowd, so that they could neither see him nor hear him; he was lost among them, he was crowded, and in danger of being crowded into the water: what must he do? *There were two ships,* or *fishing boats* brought to shore, one belonging to Simon and Andrew, the other to Zebedee and *his sons, v.* 2. At first, Christ saw Peter and Andrew fishing at some distance (so Matthew tells us, *ch.* iv. 18); but he waited till they came to land, and till the *fishermen,* that is, the servants, were *gone out of them.* Christ *entered* into that *ship* that belonged to Simon, and begged of him that he would lend it him for a pulpit; and *prayed him* that he would *thrust out a little from the land,* which would be the worse for his being *heard,* but Christ would have it so, that he might the better be *seen*; and it is his being *lifted up* that *draws men to him.* It intimates that Christ had a strong voice (strong indeed, for he made the *dead* to hear it). There he *sat down,* and *taught the people* the good knowledge of the Lord.

III. What a particular acquaintance Christ, hereupon, fell into with these fishermen, They had had some conversation with him before, which began at John's baptism (John i. 40, 41); they were with him at *Cana of Galilee* (John ii. 2), and in Judæa (John iv. 3); but as yet they were not called to attend him constantly. Now it was that they were called into a more intimate fellowship with Christ.

1. When Christ had done preaching, he ordered Peter to apply himself to the business of his calling again: *Launch out into the deep, and let down your nets, v.* 4. It was not the sabbath day, and therefore, as soon as the lecture was over, he set them to work. With what cheerfulness may we go about the duties of our calling when we have been *in the mount* with God. It is our wisdom and duty so to manage our religious exercises as that they may befriend our worldly business, and so to manage our worldly business as that it may be no enemy to our religious exercises.

2. Peter having *attended* upon Christ in his *preaching,* Christ will *accompany* him in his *fishing.* He stayed with Christ at the shore, and now Christ will *launch out* with him *into the deep.*

3. Christ ordered Peter and his ship's crew to *cast their nets into the sea,* which they did, in obedience to him, though they had been hard at it all night, and had *caught nothing, v.* 4, 5. We may observe here,

(1) How melancholy their business had now been: "*Master, we have toiled all the night and have taken nothing.*" One would have thought that this should

JAMIESON, FAUSSET, BROWN

stayed him—"were staying Him," or sought to do it. What a contrast to the Gadarenes! The nature of His mission required Him to keep moving, that all might hear the glad tidings (Matt. 8:34). **43. I must . . .**—but duty only could move Him to deny entreaties so grateful to His spirit.

CHAPTER 5

Vss. 1-11. Miraculous Draught of Fishes—Call of Peter, James, and John. Not their *first* call, however, recorded in John 1:35-42; nor their *second,* recorded in Matthew 4:18-22; but their *third* and last before their appointment to the apostleship. That these calls were all distinct and *progressive,* seems quite plain. (Similar stages are observable in other eminent servants of Christ.)

3. taught . . . out of the ship—See on Matthew 13: 2).

4. for a draught—munificent recompense for the use of his boat.

5. Master—betokening not surely a first acquaintance, but a relationship already formed. **all night**—the usual time of fishing

ADAM CLARKE

the good word of God, and now they cleave to Christ with their whole hearts. Hearing the words of Christ and feeling the influence of His Spirit upon the soul will attract and influence the heart; and indeed nothing else can do it. *And stayed him.* Strove "to detain Him"; "they caught hold of Him," thus showing their great earnestness to be further instructed.

43. *I must preach the kingdom of God to other cities.* To proclaim the kingdom of God was the Messiah's great work; healing the diseases of the people was only an emblematical and secondary work, a work that was to be the proof of His goodness, and the demonstration of His authority to preach the gospel, and open the kingdom of Heaven to all believers.

CHAPTER 5

1. *The people pressed upon him.* There was a glorious prospect of a plentiful harvest, but how few of these blades came to full corn in the ear! To hear with diligence and affection is well; but a preacher of the gospel may expect that, out of crowds of hearers, only a few, comparatively, will fully receive the truth and hold out to the end.

The lake of Gennesaret. Called also the "sea of Galilee," Matt. iv. 18 and Mark i. 16; and the "sea of Tiberias," John vi. 1. No synagogue could have contained the multitudes who attended our Lord's ministry, and therefore He was obliged to preach in the open air.

2. *Two ships.* "Two vessels." It is highly improper to term these *ships.* They appear to have been only such small boats as are used to manage nets on flat, smooth beaches.

3. *And taught . . . out of the ship.* They pressed so much upon Him on the land, through their eagerness to hear the doctrine of life, that He could not conveniently speak to them, and so was obliged to get into one of the boats; and, having pushed a little out from the land, He taught them. The smooth, still water of the lake must have served excellently to convey the sounds to those who stood on the shore.

5. *Simon . . . said unto him, Master. Epistota.* This is the first place where this word occurs; it is used by none of the inspired penmen but

MATTHEW HENRY

have excused them from hearing the sermon; but it was more refreshing and reviving to them than the softest slumbers. But they mention it to Christ, when he bids them go a fishing again. Some *callings* are much more *toilsome* than others are, and more perilous; yet Providence has so ordered it for the common good that there is no useful calling so discouraging but some or other have a genius for it. Those who follow their business, and get abundance by it with a great deal of ease, should think with compassion of those who cannot follow theirs but with a great fatigue, and hardly get a bare livelihood by it. Be the calling ever so laborious, it is good to see people diligent in it. These fishermen, that were thus *industrious*, Christ singled out for his favourites. Even those who are most diligent in their business often meet with disappointments; they who *toiled all night* yet *caught nothing*. We must do our duty, and then leave the event to God. When we are tired with our worldly business, and crossed in our worldly affairs, we are welcome to come to Christ, and spread our case before him.

(2) How ready their obedience was to the command of Christ: *Nevertheless, at thy word, I will let down the net*. Though they had *toiled all night*, yet, if Christ bid them, they will renew their toil. For every fresh service they shall have a fresh supply of *grace sufficient*. Though they have *taken nothing*, yet, if Christ bid them *let down for a draught*, they will hope to take *something*. We must not abruptly quit the callings wherein we are called because we have not the success in them we promised ourselves. The ministers of the gospel must continue to *let down* that *net*, though they have perhaps *toiled long* and *caught nothing*; and this is thankworthy, to continue unwearied in our labours, though we see not the success of them. In this they have an eye to the *word of Christ*: "*At thy word, I will let down the net*.' We are *then* likely to speed well when we follow the guidance of Christ's word.

4. The draught of fish they caught was so much beyond what was ever known that it amounted to a miracle (*v.* 6): They *enclosed a great multitude of fishes*, so that *their net broke*. It was so great a *draught* that they had not hands sufficient to draw it up; but they were obliged to beckon to their partners to come and help them, *v.* 7. But the greatest evidence of the vastness of the draught was that they filled both the ships with fish, to such a degree that they overloaded them, and they *began to sink*.

Now by this vast draught of fishes, Christ intended to show his *dominion* in the *seas* as well as on the *dry land*, over its *wealth* as over its *waves*. He intended hereby to confirm the doctrine he had just now preached out of Peter's ship. We may suppose that the people on shore stayed halting about there, to see what he would do next; and this miracle immediately following would be a confirmation to their faith, of his being at least *a teacher come from God*. He intended hereby to repay Peter for the loan of his boat. Christ's recompences for services done to his name are abundant, they are superabundant. He intended hereby to give a specimen, to those who were to be his ambassadors to the world, of the success of their embassy, that though they might for a time, and in one particular place, *toil* and *catch nothing*, yet they should be instrumental to bring in many to Christ, and enclose many in the gospel net.

5. The impression made upon Peter was very remarkable.

(1) All *concerned* were *astonished*, and the more *astonished* for their being *concerned*. All the boat's crew were *astonished at the draught of fishes which they had taken* (*v.* 9); they were all surprised. *So were also James and John, who were partners with Simon* (*v.* 10). Now they were the more *affected* with it, because they *understood* it better than others did. They that were well acquainted with this sea had never seen such a draught of fishes fetched out of it, and therefore they could not be tempted to diminish it, by suggesting that it was what might as well have happened at *any time*. It greatly corroborates the evidence of Christ's miracles that those who were best *acquainted* with them most *admired* them. Because they were most *interested* in it, and *benefited* by it. Peter and his part-owners were gainers by this great draught of fishes; their *joy* was a *helper* to their *faith*. When Christ's works of wonder are to us, in particular, works of grace, then especially they command our faith in his doctrine.

(2) Peter was astonished to such a degree that he *fell down at Jesus's knees*, as he sat in the stern of his boat, and said, *Depart from me, for I am a sinful man, O Lord*, *v.* 8. He thought himself unworthy of the favour of Christ's presence in his boat. It was the language of Peter's humility and self-denial,

JAMIESON, FAUSSET, BROWN

then (John 21:3), and even now Peter, as a fisherman, knew how hopeless it was to "let down his net" again, save as a mere act of faith, "at His word" of command, which carried in it, as it ever does, assurance of success. (This shows he must have been already and for some time a follower of Christ.)

CHARLES H. SPURGEON:

The way in which to serve God is to do it at His word. I pray that none of us may sink into serving the Lord as a matter of routine. May we never fall to serving Him in our own strength. We must preach, teach, and labor in His name, because we hear Him bidding us do it. We must act at His word. If this were the case we should work with much more faith, with much more earnestness, and with much more likelihood of success. It is a blessed thing to see Christ sitting in the boat while you cast out the net. If you catch a glimpse of His approving smile as He watches you, you will work right heartily. We must labor in entire dependence upon Him, not preaching or teaching because in our judgment it is the right thing to do—Peter did not think so—but because Jesus gives the word, and His word is law. You must not work because you have any expectation of success from the excellence of your work, or from the nature of the people among whom you labor, but because Jesus has given you the word. You stand there doing a thing which critics sneer at as absurd, but you do it in all confidence, believing that it must be wise, because Jesus bids you do it.

I remember well how some of our brethren used to talk to us. They said, "You preach the gospel to dead sinners: you bid them repent and believe. You might as well shake a handkerchief over a grave and bid the corpse come out of it." Exactly so. They spoke the truth, but then I would delight to go and shake a handkerchief over graves and bid the dead live if Jesus bade me do so. I should expect to see the cemetery crack and heave from end to end if I were sent on such an errand by the Lord. I would accept the duty joyfully. The more absurd the wise men of our age make the gospel out to be, and the more they show that it is powerless to produce the end designed, the more will we persevere in our old method of preaching Jesus crucified. Our resolves are not to be shaken by that mode of reasoning. We never did draw our argument for preaching the gospel from the work itself, but from the orders given us to do it, and we would rather be acting upon the responsibility of Christ than upon our own. I would rather be a fool and do what Christ tells me than be the wisest man of the modern school and despise the word of the Lord. I would rather lay the responsibility of my life at the feet of Him who bids me live according to His word than seek out an object in life for myself, and feel that the responsibility rested on my own shoulders. Let us be willing to be under orders to Christ, willing to persevere under difficulties, willing to begin anew in His service from this very hour.

—*The Treasury of the New Testament*

6. net brake—rather "was breaking," or "beginning to break," as in vs. 7, "beginning to sink."

8. Depart . . .—Did Peter then wish Christ to leave him? Verily no. His all was wrapt up in Him (John 6:68). "Twas rather, Woe is me, Lord! How shall I abide this blaze of glory? A sinner such as I am is not fit company for Thee." (Cf. Isa. 6:5.)

ADAM CLARKE

Luke, and he applies it only to our blessed Lord. It properly signifies a *praefect*, or one who is *set over* certain affairs or persons; it is used also for an instructor or teacher. Peter considered Christ, from what he had heard, as Teacher of a divine doctrine, and as having authority to command. He seems to comprise both ideas in this appellation; he listened attentively to His teaching, and readily obeyed His orders.

We have toiled all the night. They had cast the net several times in the course of the night, and drew it to shore without success, and were now greatly disheartened. *At thy word I will let down the net.* He who assumes the character of a fisher of men, under any authority that does not proceed from Christ, is sure to catch nothing; but he who labors by the order and under the direction of the great Shepherd and Bishop of souls cannot labor in vain.

6. *Their net brake.* Or "began to break," or was "likely to be broken." Had it broken, as our version states, they could have caught no fish.

7. *They beckoned unto their partners.* Had not these been called in to assist, the net must have been broken and all the fish lost. What a pity there should be such envious separation among the different sects that profess to believe in Christ Jesus! Did they help each other in the spirit of Christian fellowship, more souls would be brought to the knowledge of the truth. Some will rather leave souls to perish than admit of partners in the sacred work. It is an intolerable pride to think nothing well done but what we do ourselves, and a diabolic envy to be afraid lest others should be more successful than we are. *They . . . filled both the ships.* Both the boats had as many as they could carry, and were so heavily laden that they were ready to sink. As one justly observes, "There are fish plenty to be taken, were there skillful hands to take, and vessels to contain them. Many are disputing about the size, capacity, and goodness of their nets and their vessels, while the fish are permitted to make their escape."

8. *Depart from me; for I am a sinful man.* "Go out from" me, i.e., from my boat. Peter was fully convinced that this draught of fish was a miraculous one; and that God himself had particularly interfered in this matter, whose presence and power he reverenced in the person

MATTHEW HENRY

and had not the least tincture of the devils' dialect, *What have we to do with thee, Jesus, thou Son of God?* His acknowledgment was very just, and what it becomes us all to make: *I am a sinful man,* O *Lord.* Even the *best men* are *sinful men,* and should be ready upon all occasions to own it, and especially to own it to Jesus Christ. His inference from it was what *might have been* just, though really it was not so. If I be a *sinful man,* as indeed I am, I ought to say, "*Come to me, O Lord,* or let me come to thee, or I am undone, *for ever undone.*" Peter may well be excused, if, in a sense of his own sinfulness and vileness, he cried out on a sudden, *Depart from me.* Those whom Christ designs to admit to the most *intimate acquaintance* with him he first makes sensible that they deserve to be set at the *greatest distance* from him. We must all own ourselves *sinful men,* and that therefore Jesus Christ might justly *depart from us;* but we must *therefore fall down at his knees,* to pray him that he would not depart.

6. The occasion which Christ took from this to intimate to Peter (*v.* 10), and soon after to James and John (Matt. iv. 21), his purpose to make them his apostles. He *said unto Simon,* "Thou shalt both see and do greater things than these; *fear not, henceforth thou shalt catch men.* That shall be a more *astonishing* miracle, and infinitely more *advantageous* than this."

Lastly, The fishermen's farewell to their calling, in order to their constant attendance on Christ (*v.* 11): *When they had brought their ships to land* they *forsook all and followed him.* It is observable that they *left all to follow Christ,* when their calling prospered in their hands more than ever it had done. When *riches increase,* and we are therefore most in temptation to *set our hearts* upon them, then to quit them for the service of Christ, this is *thankworthy.*

Verses 12–16

I. The cleansing of a leper, *v.* 12–14. This narrative we had both in Matthew and Mark. It is here said to have been *in a certain city* (*v.* 12); it was in Capernaum. This man is said to be *full of leprosy;* he had that distemper in a high degree. Let us learn here,

1. What we must do in the sense of our spiritual leprosy. We must *seek Jesus.* We must humble ourselves before him, as this leper, seeing Jesus, *fell on his face.* We must be *ashamed* of our pollution, and blush to lift up our faces before the *holy Jesus.* We must earnestly desire to be *cleansed.* We must firmly believe Christ's ability and sufficiency to cleanse us: Lord, *thou canst make me clean,* though I be *full of leprosy.* No doubt is to be made of the merit and grace of Christ. We must be importunate in prayer: *He fell on his face and besought him;* they that would be cleansed must reckon it a favour worth wrestling for. We must refer ourselves to the goodwill of Christ: *Lord, if thou wilt, thou canst.* This is not so much the language of his *diffidence,* or *distrust* of the goodwill of Christ, as of his submission to the goodwill of Jesus Christ.

2. What we may expect from Christ, if we thus apply ourselves to him. We shall find him very forward to take cognizance of our case (*v.* 13): *He put forth his hand and touched him.* His *touching the leper* was wonderful condescension; but it is much greater to us when he is himself *touched with the feeling of our infirmities.* We shall find him very *compassionate,* and ready to relieve us; he said, "*I will,* whosoever comes to me to be healed, *I will in no wise cast him out.*" We shall find him all-sufficient, and able to heal and cleanse us, though we be ever so full of this loathsome leprosy. One word, one touch, from Christ, did the business: *Immediately the leprosy departed from him.*

3. What he requires from those that are cleansed, *v.* 14. We must be very *humble* (*v.* 14): *He charged him to tell no man.* He must not tell it to his own honour. Those whom Christ hath healed and cleansed must know that he hath done it in such a way as for ever excludes boasting. We must be very *thankful: Go, and offer for thy cleansing.* Christ did not require him to give him a fee, but to bring the sacrifice of praise to God. We must *keep close to our duty; go to the priest.* The man whom Christ had made whole he *found in the temple,* John v. 14. Those who by any affliction have been detained from public ordinances should, when the affliction is removed, attend on them the more diligently.

4. Christ's *public serviceableness* to men and his *private communion* with God.

(1) Though never any had so much *pleasure* in his *retirements* as Christ had, yet he was *much in a crowd,* to do good, *v.* 15. Though the leper should altogether hold his peace, yet the thing could not be hid, *so much the more went there a fame abroad of him.* For honour is like a shadow, which flees from those

JAMIESON, FAUSSET, BROWN

10. Simon, fear not—This shows how the Lord read Peter's speech. *The more highly they deemed Him, ever the more grateful it was to the Redeemer's spirit. Never did they pain Him by manifesting too lofty conceptions of Him.* **from henceforth**—marking a new stage of their connection with Christ. The last was simply, "I will make you fishers." **fishers of men**—"What wilt thou think, Simon, overwhelmed by this draught of fishes, when I shall bring to thy net what will beggar all this glory?" (See on Matt. 4:18.) **11. forsook all**—They did this before (Matt. 4:20); now they do it again; and yet after the Crucifixion they are at their boats once more (John 21:3). In such a business this is easily conceivable. After pentecost, however, they appear to have finally abandoned their secular calling.

12-16. LEPER HEALED. (See on Matt. 8:2-4.)

And, behold, there came a leper—"a man full of leprosy," says Luke 5:12. Much has been written on this disease of leprosy, but certain points remain still doubtful. All that needs be said here is that it was a cutaneous disease, of a loathsome, diffusive, and, there is reason to believe, when thoroughly pronounced, incurable character; that though in its distinctive features it is still found in several countries—as Arabia, Egypt, and South Africa—it prevailed, in the form of what is called white leprosy, to an unusual extent, and from a very early period, among the Hebrews; and that it thus furnished to the whole nation a familiar and affecting symbol of SIN, considered as (1) *loathsome,* (2) *spreading,* (3) *incurable.*

And Jesus—or "He," according to another reading,—"moved with compassion," says Mark (1:41); a precious addition. **put forth his hand, and touched him**—Such a touch occasioned ceremonial defilement (Lev. 5:3); even as the leper's coming near enough for contact was against the Levitical regulations (Lev. 13:46). But as the man's faith told him there would be no case for such regulations if the cure he hoped to experience should be accomplished, so He who had healing in His wings transcended all such statutes. **saying, I will; be thou clean**—How majestic those two words! By not assuring the man of His *power* to heal him, He delightfully sets His seal to the man's previous confession of that power; and by assuring him of the one thing of which he had any doubt, and for which he waited—His *will* to do it—He makes a claim as divine as the cure which immediately followed it. **And immediately his leprosy was cleansed**—Mark, more emphatic, says (1:42), "And as soon as He had spoken, immediately the leprosy departed from him, and he was cleansed"—as perfectly as instantaneously. What a contrast this to modern pretended cures! **And Jesus** ["straitly charged him, and forthwith sent him away," Mark 1:43, and] **saith unto him, See thou tell no man**—A hard condition this would seem to a grateful heart, whose natural language, in such a case, is "Come, hear, all ye that fear God, and I will declare what He hath done for my soul" (Ps. 66:16). We shall presently see the reason for it. **but go thy way, show thyself to the priest, and offer the gift that Moses commanded** [Lev. 14] **for a testimony unto them**—a palpable witness that the Great Healer had indeed come, and that "God had visited His people." What the sequel was, our

ADAM CLARKE

of Jesus. But as he felt himself a sinner, he was afraid the divine purity of Christ could not possibly endure him; therefore he wished for a separation from that power, which he was afraid might break forth and consume him. It seems to have been a received maxim among the Jews that whoever had seen a particular manifestation of God should speedily die.

10. *Thou shalt catch men.* "You shall catch men alive"; this is the proper signification of the word. *Fear not.* These discoveries of God tend to life, not to death; and you shall become the instruments of life and salvation to a lost world.

11. *They forsook all, and followed him.* God expects this from every person, and especially from those in whose hearts, or in whose behalf, He has wrought a miracle of grace or of providence.

12. *A certain city.* This was some city of Galilee, probably Chorazin or Bethsaida.

And, behold, there came a leper. The leprosy was an inveterate cutaneous disease, appearing in dry, thin, white, scurfy scales or scabs, either on the whole body or on some part of it, usually attended with violent itching and often with great pain. The various symptoms of this dreadful disorder, which was a striking emblem of sin, may be seen in Leviticus xiii—xiv, where also may be read the legal ordinances concerning it. *Lord, if thou wilt, thou canst make me clean.* As this leper may be considered as a fit emblem of the corruption of man by sin, so may his cure, of the redemption of the soul by Christ. A sinner, truly penitent, seeks God with a respectful faith; approaches Him in the spirit of adoration; humbles himself under His mighty hand, acknowledging the greatness of his fall and the vileness of his sin. His prayer, like that of the leper, should be humble, plain, and full of confidence in that God who can do all things, and of dependence upon His will or mercy, from which all good must be derived. It is peculiar to God that He need only *will* what He intends to perform. His power is His will.

Jesus put forth his hand . . . I will; be thou clean. The most sovereign authority is assumed in this speech of our blessed Lord—*I will.* There is here no supplication of any power superior to His own; and the event proved to the fullest conviction, and by the clearest demonstration, that His authority was absolute and His power unlimited. *And immediately his leprosy was cleansed.* What an astonishing sight! A man whose whole body was covered over with the most loathsome disease cleansed from it in a moment of time! Was it possible for any soul to resist the evidence of this fact?

Jesus saith unto him, See thou tell no man. Had our Lord, at this early period, fully manifested himself as the Messiah, the people in all likelihood would have proclaimed Him King. This, however, refused by Him, must have excited the hatred of the Jewish rulers and the jealousy of the Roman government; and, speaking after the manner of men, His further preachings and miracles must have been impeded. This alone seems to be the reason why He said to the leper, *See thou tell no man. Shew thyself to the priest.* This was to conform to the law instituted in this case, Lev. xiv. 1, etc. *Offer the gift.* This gift was two living, clean birds, some cedarwood, with scarlet and hyssop,

MATTHEW HENRY

that pursue it, but follows those that decline it. The less good men say of themselves, the more will others say of them. But Christ reckoned it a small honour to him that his *fame went abroad*; it was much more so that hereby multitudes were brought to receive benefit by him. By his preaching. They came together to *hear* him. By his miracles. They came *to be healed by him of their infirmities*.

(2) Though never any did so much *good in public*, yet he found time for *pious* and *devout retirements* (*v.* 16): *He withdrew himself into the wilderness, and prayed.* It is likewise our wisdom so to order our affairs as that our public work and our secret work may not interfere with one another. Secret prayer must be performed secretly; and those that have ever so much to do of the best business in this world must keep up constant stated times for it.

Verses 17–26

I. A general account of Christ's preaching and miracles, *v.* 17. He was *teaching on a certain day*, not on the sabbath day, but on a *week-day*. Preaching and hearing the word of *God* are *good works*, if they be *done well*, any day in the *week*. It was in a *private house*; for even there where we ordinarily converse with our friends it is not improper to give and receive good instruction. *And the power of the Lord was to heal them.* It was *mighty* to heal them; to heal their souls, to give them a new life, a new nature. It may be meant (and so it is generally taken) of the healing of those who were *diseased in body*, who came to him for cures. Whenever there was occasion, Christ had not *to seek* for his power, it was *present to heal. There were Pharisees, and doctors of the law, sitting by;* not sitting *at his feet*, to learn of him. But, by what follows (*v.* 21), it appears that they were *not healed*, but cavilled at Christ. They sat by as spectators, censors, and spies, to pick up something on which to ground a reproach or accusation. How many are there in the midst of our assemblies that do not *sit under* the word, but *sit by*! It is to them as a *tale* that is *told them*, not as a *message* that is *sent them*; they are willing that we should preach *before them*, not that we should preach *to them.* These Pharisees and scribes *came out of every town of Galilee, and Judæa, and Jerusalem*; they came from all parts of the nation. Christ went on with his work of *preaching* and *healing*, though he saw these Pharisees *sitting by*, who, he knew, *despised* him, and watched to *ensnare him*.

II. A particular account of the cure of the man *sick of the palsy*.

1. The doctrines that are taught us and confirmed to us by the story of this cure. (1) That sin is the fountain of all sickness, and the forgiveness of sin is the only foundation upon which a recovery from sickness can comfortably be built. They presented the *sick man* to Christ, and he said, "*Man, thy sins are forgiven thee* (*v.* 20), that is the blessing thou art most to prize and seek." The cords of our iniquity are the bands of our affliction. (2) That Jesus Christ has power on earth to *forgive sins*. This was the thing intended to be proved (*v.* 24): *That ye may know* and believe *that the Son of man hath power to forgive sins*, he *saith to the sick of the palsy, Arise, and walk*; and he is cured immediately. Christ claims one of the prerogatives of the King of kings when he undertakes to *forgive sin*, and it is justly expected that he should produce a good proof of it. "Well," saith he, "I will put it upon this issue: here is a man struck with a palsy, and *for his sin*; if I do not with a word's speaking cure his disease, then say that I am not entitled to the prerogative of forgiving sin: but, if I do, you must own that *I have power to forgive sins*." Thus it was put upon a fair trial, and one word of Christ determined it. He did but say, *Arise, take up thy couch*, and that *chronical* disease had an *instantaneous* cure; *immediately he arose before them.* They must all own that there could be no cheat or fallacy in it. (3) That Jesus Christ is God. He appears to be so, [1] By *knowing the thoughts* of the scribes and Pharisees (*v.* 22). [2] By doing that which their thoughts owned none could do but God only (*v.* 21): *Who can forgive sins*, say they, *but only God?* "I will prove," saith Christ, "that I can forgive sins"; and what follows then but that *he is God*?

2. The duties that are taught us, and recommended to us, by this story. (1) In our applications to Christ, we must be very *pressing* and *urgent*. They that were the friends of this sick man *sought means to bring him in before Christ* (*v.* 18); and, when they were baffled in their endeavour, they did not give up their cause; but when they could not get in by *the door*, it was so crowded, they untiled the house, and let the poor patient down through the roof, *into the midst before Jesus*, *v.* 19. In this Jesus Christ *saw their faith*, *v.* 20. When the centurion and the woman

JAMIESON, FAUSSET, BROWN

Evangelist Matthew does not say; but Mark thus gives it (1:45): "But he went out, and began to publish it much, and to blaze abroad the matter, insomuch that Jesus could no more openly enter into the city, but was without in desert places: and they came to Him from every quarter." Thus—by an over-zealous, though most natural and not very culpable, infringement of the injunction to keep the matter quiet—was our Lord, to some extent, thwarted in His movements. As His whole course was sublimely noiseless (ch. 12:19), so we find Him repeatedly taking steps to prevent matters prematurely coming to a crisis with Him. (But see on Mark 5:19, 20). "And He withdrew Himself," adds Luke (5:16), "into the wilderness, and prayed"; retreating from the popular excitement into the secret place of the Most High, and thus coming forth as dew upon the mown grass, and as showers that water the earth (Ps. 72:6). And this is the secret both of strength and of sweetness in the servants and followers of Christ in every age.

17-26. PARALYTIC HEALED. (See on Matt. 9: 1-8.)

17. Pharisees and doctors . . . sitting by—the highest testimony yet borne to our Lord's growing influence, and the necessity increasingly felt by the ecclesiastics throughout the country of coming to some definite judgment regarding Him. **power of the Lord . . . present**—with Jesus. **to heal them**—the sick people.

19. housetop—the flat roof. **through the tiling . . . before Jesus**—(See on Mark 2:2).

thy sins be forgiven thee—By the word "be," our translators perhaps meant "are," as in Luke (5:20). For it is not a command to his sins to depart, but an authoritative proclamation of the man's pardoned state as a believer. And yet, as the Pharisees understood our Lord to be *dispensing* pardon by this saying, and Jesus not only acknowledges that they were right, but founds His whole argument upon the correctness of it, we must regard the saying as a royal proclamation of the man's forgiveness by Him to whom it belonged to dispense it; nor could such a style of address be justified on any lower supposition. (See on Luke 7:41, etc.).

24. take up thy couch—"sweet saying! The bed had borne the man; now the man shall bear the bed!" [BENGEL].

Why doth this man thus speak blasphemies? who can forgive sins but God only?—In this second question they expressed a great truth. (See Isa. 43:25; Mic. 7:18; Ex. 34: 6, 7, etc.). Nor was their first question altogether unnatural, though in our Lord's sole case it was unfounded. That a man, to all appearances like one of themselves, should claim authority and power to forgive sins, they could not, on the first blush of it, but regard as in the last degree startling; nor were they entitled even to weigh such a claim, as worthy of a hearing, save on supposition of resistless evidence afforded by Him in support of the claim. Accordingly, our Lord deals with them as men entitled to such evidence, and supplies it; at the same time chiding them for rashness, in drawing harsh conclusions regarding Himself.

When Jesus saw their faith—It is remarkable that all the three nar-

ADAM CLARKE

Lev. xiv. 4, which were to be brought for his cleansing; and, when clean, two he lambs, one ewe lamb, three tenth deals of flour, and one log of oil, v. 10. But if the person were poor, then he was to bring one lamb, one tenth deal of flour, one log of oil, and two turtledoves or young pigeons, vv. 21-22.

Now all this was to be done *for a testimony unto them*, to prove that this leper, who was doubtless well-known in the land, had been thoroughly cleansed; and thus, in this private way, to give full proof to the priesthood that Jesus was the true Messiah. The Jewish rabbins allowed that curing the lepers should be a characteristic of the Messiah; therefore the obstinacy of the priests in rejecting Christ was utterly inexcusable.

16. *And he withdrew himself into the wilderness.* Or rather, "He frequently withdrew into the desert." He made it a frequent custom to withdraw from the multitudes for a time, and pray, teaching hereby the ministers of the gospel that they are to receive fresh supplies of light and power from God by prayer, that they may be the more successful in their work; and that they ought to seek frequent opportunities of being in private with God and their books. A man can give nothing unless he first receive it; and no man can be successful in the ministry who does not constantly depend upon God, for the excellence of the power is all from Him. Why is there so much preaching, and so little good done? Is it not because the preachers mix too much with the world, keep too long in the crowd, and are so seldom in private with God?

17. *On a certain day.* This was when He was at Capernaum. See Mark ii. 1. *The power of the Lord.* The "mighty" or "miraculous" power of the Lord, i.e., of Jesus, was there *to heal them*—as many as were diseased in either body or soul. Where the teaching of Christ is, there also is the power of Christ to redeem and save.

18. *A man which was taken with a palsy.* See this case described on Matt. ix. 1, etc., and Mark ii. 1, etc.

Lying on a bed. A "couch" or "sofa," such as they reclined on at meals. *Seeing their faith.* The faith of the paralytic person, and the faith of those who brought him. *Be of good cheer.* "Son, take courage!" Probably he began to despond, and Christ spoke thus to support his faith. *Thy sins be forgiven thee.* Moral evil has been the cause of all the natural evil in the world. Christ goes to the source of the malady, which is sin. It is probable that this paralytic person had, in the earnest desires of his heart, entreated the cure of his soul, leaving his body to the care of others, as the first miracle of healing is wrought on his soul. It may be necessary to be observed that it was a maxim among the Jews that no diseased person could be healed till all his sins were blotted out. Hence our Lord first forgives the sins and then heals the body of the paralytic person.

21. *Who can forgive sins, but God alone?* If Jesus were not God, He could not forgive sins; and His arrogating this authority would have been blasphemy against God, in the most proper sense of the word. That these scribes and Pharisees might have the fullest proof of His Godhead, He works in their presence three miracles, which from their nature could be effected only by an omniscient and omnipotent Being. The miracles are: (1) the remission of the poor man's sins, (2) the discernment of the secret thoughts of the scribes, (3) the restoration of the paralytic in an instant to perfect soundness.

MATTHEW HENRY

of Canaan were in no care at all to bring the patients they interceded for into Christ's presence, but believed that he could cure them *at a distance*, he commended *their faith*. In *these* there seemed to be an apprehension that it was requisite the *patient* should be *brought into his presence*, yet he did not *censure* and *condemn* their weakness, did not ask them, "Are you under such a degree of infidelity as to think I could not have cured him, though he had been out of doors?" But he made the best of it, and even in *this* he saw *their faith*. It is a comfort to us that we serve a Master that is willing to *make the best* of us. (2) When we are sick, we should be more in care to get our sins pardoned than to get our sickness removed. (3) The mercies which we have the comfort of, God must have the praise of. The man *departed to his own house, glorifying God, v.* 25. (4) The miracles which Christ wrought were *amazing* to those that saw them, and we ought to *glorify* God in them, *v.* 26. They said, "*We have seen strange things today.*" They *glorified* God, who had sent into their country such a benefactor to it; and were *filled with fear*, with a reverence of God.

Verses 27–35

All this, except the last verse, we had before in Matthew and Mark; it is not the story of any *miracle in nature* wrought by our Lord Jesus, but it is an account of some of the *wonders of his grace*.

I. It was a wonder of his grace that he would call a *publican*, from the *receipt of custom*, to be his disciple and follower, *v.* 27. By this he *exposed himself*, and got the invidious character of a *friend of publicans and sinners*.

II. It was a wonder of his grace that the call was made *effectual*, *v.* 28. This publican, though those of that employment commonly had little inclination to religion, *rose up, and followed Christ*. There is no heart too hard for the Spirit and grace of Christ to work upon, nor any difficulties in the way of a sinner's conversion insuperable to his power.

III. It was a wonder of his grace that he would not only admit a converted publican into his family, but would keep company with unconverted publicans. Here is a wonder of grace indeed, that Christ undertakes to be the Physician of souls *distempered* by sin, and ready to *die* of the distemper (he is a Healer by office, *v.* 31)—that he came to call *sinners*, the worst of sinners, to repentance, and to assure them of pardon, upon repentance, *v.* 32. These are glad tidings of great joy indeed.

IV. It was a wonder of his grace that he did so patiently bear the *contradiction of sinners* against himself and his disciples, *v.* 30. He did not express his resentment of the cavils of the scribes and Pharisees, but answered them with reason and meekness.

V. It was a wonder of his grace that, in the discipline under which he trained up his disciples, he *considered their frame*, and proportioned their services to their strength. It was objected that he did not make *his disciples* to *fast* so often as those of the *Pharisees* and John Baptist did, *v.* 33. He insisted most upon that which is the *soul of* fasting, the living of a life of self-denial, which is as much better than fasting and corporal penances as *mercy* is better than *sacrifice*.

VI. It was a wonder of his grace that Christ reserved the trials of his disciples for their latter times, when by his grace they were in some good measure better prepared and fitted for them. Now they were as the *children of the bride-chamber*, when the *bridegroom is with them*, when they have plenty and joy, and every day is a festival. But this will not last always. *The days will come* when the *bridegroom shall be taken away from them, v.* 35. When Christ shall leave them with their hearts full of sorrow, their hands full of work, and the world full of enmity and rage against them, *then shall they fast*.

VII. It was a wonder of his grace that he proportioned their exercises to their strength. He would not put *new cloth upon an old garment* (*v.* 36), nor *new wine into old bottles* (*v.* 37, 38); he would not, as soon as ever he had called them out of the world, put them upon the strictnesses and austerities of discipleship, lest they should be tempted to *fly off*. Christ would train up his followers gradually to the discipline of his family; for no man, having *drank old wine*, will *of a sudden*, straightway, *desire new*, or relish it, but will say, *The old is better*, because he has been *used to it*, *v.* 39. The disciples will be tempted to think their old way of living better, till they are by degrees trained up to this way whereunto they are called. Christ's disciples, though they had not so much of the *form of godliness*, had more of the *power of it*.

JAMIESON, FAUSSET, BROWN

ratives call it "*their* faith" which Jesus saw. That the patient himself had faith, we know from the proclamation of his forgiveness, which Jesus made before all; and we should have been apt to conclude that his four friends bore him to Jesus merely out of benevolent compliance with the urgent entreaties of the poor sufferer. But here we learn, not only that his bearers had the same faith with himself, but that Jesus marked it as a faith which was not to be defeated—a faith victorious over all difficulties. This was the faith for which He was ever on the watch, and which He never saw without marking, and, in those who needed anything from Him, richly rewarding.

"We have seen strange [unexpected] things to-day"—referring both to the miracles wrought and the forgiveness of sins pronounced by Human Lips. In Matthew (9:8) it is, "They marvelled, and glorified God, which had given such power unto men." At forgiving power they wondered not, but that a man, to all appearance like one of themselves, should possess it!

27-32. LEVI'S CALL AND FEAST. (See on Matt. 9:9-13; and Mark 2:14.)

sitting at the receipt of custom—as a publican, which Luke (5:27) calls him. It means the place of receipt, the toll-house or booth in which the collector sat. Being in this case by the seaside, it might be the ferry tax for the transit of persons and goods across the lake, which he collected. (See on ch. 5:46.) **and he saith unto him, Follow me**—Witching words these, from the lips of Him who never employed them without giving them resistless efficacy in the hearts of those they were spoken to. **And he** ["left all" (Luke 5:28)] **arose and followed him.**

30. their scribes—a mode of expression showing that Luke was writing for *Gentiles*.

33-39. FASTING. (See on Matt. 9:14-17.) The *incongruities* mentioned in vss. 36-38 were intended to illustrate the difference between the *genius* of the old and new economies, and the danger of *mixing up* the one with the other. As in the one case supposed, "the rent is made worse," and in the other, "the new wine is spilled," *so by a mongrel mixture of the ascetic ritualism of the old with the spiritual freedom of the new economy, both are disfigured and destroyed*. The additional parable in vs. 39, which is peculiar to Luke, has been variously interpreted. But the "new wine" seems plainly to be the evangelical freedom which Christ was introducing; and the old, the opposite spirit of Judaism: men long accustomed to the latter could not be expected "straightway"—all at once—to take a liking for the former; i.e., "These inquiries about the difference between My disciples and the Pharisees," and even John's, are not surprising; they are the effect of *a natural revulsion against sudden change*, which time will cure; *the new wine will itself in time become old, and so acquire all the added charms of antiquity*. What lessons does this teach, on the one hand, to those who unreasonably cling to what is getting antiquated; and, on the other, to hasty reformers who have no patience with the timidity of their weaker brethren!

ADAM CLARKE

26. *Strange things.* "Paradoxes." A paradox is something that appears false and absurd, but is not really so, or something contrary to the commonly received opinion.

27. *Levi.* See on Matt. ix. 9; Mark ii. 14.

28. *And he left all.* "Completely abandoning" his office, and everything connected with it. He who wishes to preach the gospel, like the disciples of Christ, must have no earthly entanglement.

29. *A great feast.* "A splendid entertainment." The word refers more properly to the number of the guests, and the manner in which they were received, than to the quality or quantity of the fare. A great number of his friends and acquaintance were collected on the occasion, that they might be convinced of the propriety of the change he had made, when they had the opportunity of seeing and hearing his heavenly Teacher.

37. *The new wine will burst the bottles.* These old bottles would not be able to stand the fermentation of the new wine, as the old sewing would be apt to give way. It is scarcely necessary to remark that the Eastern bottles are made of skins, generally those of goats.

39. *The old is better.* Is more "agreeable to the taste or palate." The "old wine," among the rabbins, was "the wine of three leaves"—that is, wine three years old—because, from the time that the vine had produced that wine, it had put forth its leaves three times.

MATTHEW HENRY

CHAPTER 6

I. Christ justifies his disciples in a *work of necessity* for themselves on that day, and that was *plucking the ears of corn*, when they were hungry on that day. This story here has a date, which we had not in the other evangelists; it was *on the second sabbath after the first* (*v.* 1), that is, the *first sabbath after the second day of unleavened bread*, from which day they reckoned the *seven weeks* to the feast of pentecost. We may observe, 1. Christ's disciples ought not to be nice and curious in their diet, but take up with what is easiest got, and be thankful. These disciples *plucked the ears of corn, and did eat* (*v.* 1); a little served them, and that which had no delicacy in it. 2. Many are forward to censure others for the most innocent and inoffensive actions, *v.* 2. The Pharisees quarrelled with them as doing that which it *was not lawful to do on the sabbath days*, when it was their own practice to feed deliciously on sabbath days. 3. Jesus Christ will justify his disciples, and will own and accept of them in many a thing which men tell them *it is not lawful for them to do*. 4. Ceremonial appointments may be dispensed with, in cases of necessity, *v.* 3, 4. And, if God's own appointments might be thus set aside for a greater good, much more may the traditions of men. 5. Works of necessity are particularly allowable on the sabbath day. 6. Jesus Christ, though he allowed works of necessity on the sabbath day, will notwithstanding have us to know and remember that it is his day (*v.* 5): *The Son of man is Lord also of the sabbath*. In the kingdom of the Redeemer, the sabbath day is to be turned into a *Lord's day*. In token of this, it shall not only have a new name, the *Lord's day*, but shall be transferred to a new day, the first day of the week.

II. He justifies himself in doing *works of mercy* for others on the sabbath day. 1. Christ on the sabbath day *entered into the synagogue*. It is our duty, as we have opportunity, to sanctify sabbaths in religious assemblies. Our place must not be empty without very good reason. 2. In the synagogue, on the sabbath day, *he taught*. Christ took all opportunities to teach, not only his disciples, but the multitude. 3. Christ's patient was one of his hearers. *A man whose right hand was withered* came. Those that would be *cured* by the grace of Christ must be willing to *learn* the doctrine of Christ. 4. Among those who were the hearers and the eye-witnesses, there were some who came with no other design than to pick quarrels with him, *v.* 7. The scribes and Pharisees *watched him*, as the lion does his prey, whether he would *heal on the sabbath day, that they might find an accusation against him*. 5. Jesus Christ was neither *ashamed* nor *afraid* to own the purposes of his grace, *v.* 8. He bade the man *rise, and stand forth*, hereby to try the patient's faith and boldness. 6. He appealed to his adversaries themselves, whether it was the design of the fourth commandment to restrain men from doing good on the sabbath day, that good which their hand finds to do, and which cannot so well be put off to another time (*v.* 9): *Is it lawful to do good, or evil, on the sabbath days?* 7. He healed the poor man, though he knew that his enemies would not only take offence at it, but take advantage against him for it, *v.* 10. 8. His adversaries were hereby enraged so much the more against him, *v.* 11. Instead of being brought to be in love with him as a benefactor to mankind,—they were *filled with madness*, vexed that they could not frighten him from doing good. They were *mad* at Christ, *mad* at the people, *mad* at themselves. When they could not prevent his working this miracle, they *communed one with another what they might do to Jesus*, what other way they might take to run him down.

Verses 12–19

In these verses, we have our Lord Jesus in *secret*, in *his family*, and in *public*; and in all three acting like himself.

I. In *secret* we have him *praying to God*, *v.* 12. This evangelist takes frequent notice of Christ's retirements, to give us an example of secret prayer, without which it is impossible that the soul should prosper. *In those days*, when his enemies were filled with madness against him, he went out to *pray*. He was *alone* with God; he *went out into a mountain, to pray*, where he might have no disturbance or interruption given him. He was *long* alone with God: *He continued all night in prayer*. We think one half hour a great deal, but Christ continued a *whole night* in meditation and secret prayer. We have a great deal of *business* at the throne of grace, and we should take a great *delight* in communion with God, and by both these we may be kept sometimes long at prayer.

II. We have him nominating his immediate attendants, that should be the constant auditors of his

JAMIESON, FAUSSET, BROWN

CHAPTER 6

Vss. 1-5. PLUCKING CORN EARS ON THE SABBATH. (See on Matt. 12:1-8; and Mark 2:23-28.) **1. second sabbath after the first**—an obscure expression, occurring here only, generally understood to mean, the first sabbath after the second day of unleavened bread. The reasons cannot be stated here, nor is the opinion itself quite free from difficulty.

Lord also—rather "even" (as in Matt. 12:8). **of the sabbath**—as naked a claim to *all the authority of Him who gave the law at Mount Sinai* as could possibly be made; i.e., "I have said enough to vindicate the men ye carp at on My account: *but in this place is the Lord of the law, and they have* HIS *sanction."* (See on Mark 2:28.)

6-11. WITHERED HAND HEALED. (See on Matthew 12:9-15; and Mark 3:1-7). **7. watched whether . . .**—In Matthew this is put as an ensnaring question of theirs to our Lord, who accordingly speaks to *the state of their hearts* (vs. 9), just as if they had spoken it out.

9. good, or . . . evil, save . . . or destroy—By this novel way of putting His case, our Lord teaches the great ethical principle, that *to neglect any opportunity of doing good is to incur the guilt of doing evil;* and by this law He bound His own spirit. (See on Mark 3:4.) **11. filled with madness**—The word denotes senseless rage at the confusion to which our Lord had put them, both by word and deed. **what . . . do to Jesus**—not so much *whether* to get rid of Him, but *how* to compass it. (See on Matt. 3:6.)

12-19. THE TWELVE APOSTLES CHOSEN—GATHERING MULTITUDES—GLORIOUS HEALING. **12, 13. went out**—probably from Capernaum. **all night in prayer . . . and when . . . day, he called . . .**—The work with which the next *day* began shows what had been the burden of this *night's* devotions. As He directed His disciples to pray for "laborers" just before sending themselves forth (see on Matt. 9:37; 10:1), so here we find the Lord Himself in prolonged communion with His Father in preparation for the solemn appointment of those men who were to give birth to His Church, and from whom the world in all time was to take a new mould. How instructive is this! **13-16.** (See on Matt. 10:2-4.)

ADAM CLARKE

CHAPTER 6

1. *On the second sabbath after the first.* "In the first Sabbath after the second." What does this mean? In answering this question, commentators are greatly divided. By this Sabbath seems meant that which immediately followed the two great feasts, the first and last day of the Passover, and was, therefore, the *second* after the proper Passover day. The words in the Greek seem to signify the "second first Sabbath"; and, in the opinion of some, the Jews had three first Sabbaths: viz., the first Sabbath after the Passover, that after the Feast of Pentecost, and that after the Feast of Tabernacles. According to this opinion, this "second first Sabbath" must have been the first Sabbath after Pentecost. This was the second day after the Passover, the day in which they were forbidden to labor, Lev. xxiii. 6, and for this reason was termed *sabbath,* Lev. xxiii. 15. But here it is marked by the name "second first Sabbath," because, being the day after the Passover, it was in this respect the *second;* and it was also the *first,* because it was the first day of unleavened bread, Exod. xii. 15-16. I think, with many commentators, that this transaction happened on the first Sabbath of the month Nisan; that is, after the second day of the Feast of Unleavened Bread. We may well suppose that our Lord and His disciples were on their way from Jerusalem to Galilee, after having kept the Passover. The word "the second first," is omitted by some MSS. and versions and the verse is read thus: "It came to pass, that he walked through the corn fields on a Sabbath day." I suppose they omitted the above word because they found it difficult to fix the meaning, which has been too much the case in other instances.

2. *Which is not lawful.* See on Matt. xii. 2-8.

3. *What David did.* See on Mark ii. 26-27.

4. After this verse, the Codex Bezae and two ancient MSS. have the following extraordinary addition: *On the same day, seeing one working on the Sabbath, he said unto him, Man, if indeed thou knowest what thou dost, blessed art thou; but if thou knowest not, thou art cursed, and art a transgressor of the law.* Whence this strange addition proceeded, it is hard to tell. The meaning seems to be this: If you now work on the Jewish Sabbath, from a conviction that that Sabbath is abolished, and a new one instituted in its place, then happy are you, for you have received divine instruction in the nature of the Messiah's kingdom; but if you do this through a contempt for the law of God, then you are accursed, forasmuch as you are a transgressor of the law.

6. *Whose right hand was withered.* See on Matt. xii. 10, etc.

7. *Watched him.* "They maliciously watched Him." This is the import of the word, chap. xiv. 1; xx. 20, and in the parallel place, Mark iii. 2.

9. *I will ask you one thing.* I will put a question to you. See on Mark iii. 4-5.

12. *In prayer to God.* Or "in the prayer of God"; i.e., "very fervent and earnest prayer."

MATTHEW HENRY

doctrine and eye-witnesses of his miracles, that hereafter they might be sent forth as *apostles*, his *messengers* to the world, *v.* 13. After he had *continued all night in prayer*, one would have thought that, *when it was day*, he should have reposed himself. No, as soon as anybody was stirring, he *called unto him his disciples*. In serving God, our great care should be, not to *lose time*, but to make the end of one good duty the beginning of another. Ministers are to be ordained with *prayer* more than ordinarily *solemn*. The number of the apostles was *twelve*. Their names are here recorded; it is the *third time* that we have met with them, and in each of the *three* places the *order* of them differs. Never were men so privileged, and yet one of them had a devil, and proved a traitor (*v.* 16); yet Christ, when he chose him, was not deceived in him.

III. In *public* we have him *preaching* and *healing*, the two great works between which he divided his time, *v.* 17. He came down with the twelve from the mountain, and *stood in the plain*, and there were presently gathered about him, not only the *company of his disciples*, but also a great *multitude of people*, a mixed multitude *out of all Judæa and Jerusalem*. They came also from the *sea-coast of Tyre and Sidon*. Though they bordered upon Canaanites, yet there were some well affected to Christ; such there were dispersed in all parts, here and there one. They *came to hear him*, and he *preached* to them. It is worthwhile to go a great way to hear the word of Christ, and to go out of the way of other business for it. They came to be *cured* by him, and he *healed* them. Some were troubled *in body*, and some *in mind*; some had *diseases*, some had *devils*; but both the one and the other, were *healed*, for he has power over *diseases* and *devils* (*v.* 17, 18). Nay, it should seem, those who had no *particular diseases* to complain of yet found it a great confirmation and renovation to their bodily *health* and *vigour* to partake of the *virtue that went out of him*; for (*v.* 19) *the whole multitude sought to touch him*, and they were all, one way or other, the better for him: he *healed them all*; and who is there that doth not need, upon some account or other, to be *healed*? There is a *fulness of grace* in Christ, that is enough for all, enough for each.

Verses 20–26

Here begins a practical discourse of Christ, most of which is found in the *sermon upon the mount*, Matt. v. and vii.

I. Blessings pronounced upon *suffering saints* (*v.* 20): He *lifted up his eyes upon his disciples*, not only the *twelve*, but the whole *company of them* (*v.* 17), and directed his discourse to them. There he *sat*, as one having authority; thither *they come to him* (Matt. v. 1).

1. "You are *poor*, you have *left all to follow me*. But you are blessed in your poverty, nay, you are blessed *for* it, for *yours is the kingdom of God*, all the comforts and graces of his kingdom here and all the glories and joys of his kingdom hereafter; yours it *shall be*, nay, yours *it is*."

2. "You *hunger now* (*v.* 21), you are not *fed to the full* as others are, you are glad of a few *ears of corn* for a meal's meat; thus you hunger now in this world, but in the other world *you shall be filled*."

3. "You *weep now*. But *blessed are you*; your present sorrows are no *prejudices* to your future joy, but *preparatories* for it: *You shall laugh*. You are but *sowing in tears*, and shall shortly *reap in joy*," Ps. cxxvi. 5, 6. God is treasuring up comforts for them; and the day is coming when their *mouth shall be filled with laughing and their lips with rejoicing*, Job. viii. 21.

4. "You now undergo *the world's ill will*. You must expect all the base treatment that a spiteful world can give you for Christ's sake, because you serve him and his interests. Wicked men will *hate you*, because your doctrine and life convict and condemn them. *They will reproach you*, will charge you with the blackest crimes, which you are perfectly innocent of, will fasten upon you the blackest characters, which you do not deserve; they will *cast out your name as evil*. *Blessed are you* when you are so used. It is an honour to you, as it is to a brave hero to be employed in the wars, in the service of his prince; and therefore *rejoice you in that day, and leap for joy*, *v.* 23. Do not only *bear it*, but *triumph* in it. You are treated as the prophets were before you, and therefore not only need not be ashamed of it, but may justly rejoice in it. You will for this be abundantly *recompensed*. *Your reward is great in heaven*. Though you may be losers for Christ, you shall not be losers by him in the end."

II. *Woes* denounced against *prospering sinners as miserable people*, though the world *envies them*. These we had not in Matthew. It should seem, the best exposition of *these woes*, compared with the

JAMIESON, FAUSSET, BROWN

17. in the plain—by some rendered "on a level place," i.e., a piece of high tableland, by which they understand the same thing, as "on the mountain," where our Lord delivered the sermon recorded by Matthew (5:1), of which they take this following discourse of Luke to be but an abridged form. But as the sense given in our version is the more accurate, so there are weighty reasons for considering the discourses different. This one contains little more than a fourth of the other; it has *woes* of its own, as well as the beatitudes common to both; but above all, that of Matthew was plainly delivered a good while *before*, while this was spoken *after* the choice of the twelve; and as we know that our Lord delivered some of His weightiest sayings more than once, there is no difficulty in supposing this to be one of His more extended repetitions; nor could anything be more worthy of it. **19. healed**—kept healing, denoting successive acts of mercy till it went over "*all*" that needed. There is something unusually grand and pictorial in this touch of description.

20, 21. In the Sermon on the Mount the benediction is pronounced upon the "poor *in spirit*" and those who "hunger and thirst *after righteousness*" (Matt. 5:3, 6). Here it is simply on the "poor" and the "hungry now." In this form of the discourse, then, our Lord seems to have had in view "*the poor of this world*, rich in faith, and heirs of the kingdom which God hath promised to them that love Him," as these very beatitudes are paraphrased by James (2:5).

21. laugh—How charming is the liveliness of this word, to express what in Matthew is called being "comforted!"

22. separate you—whether from their *Church*, by excommunication, or from their society; both hard to flesh and blood. **for the Son of man's sake**—Cf. Matthew 5:11, "for MY SAKE"; and immediately before, "for *righteousness'* sake" (vs. 10). Christ thus *binds up the cause of righteousness in the world with the reception of Himself*. **23. leap for joy**—a livelier word than "be exceeding glad" of "exult" (Matt. 5:12).

ADAM CLARKE

13. *He chose twelve*. "He chose twelve out of them." Our Lord at this time had several disciples, persons who were converted to God under His ministry; and out of these converts He chose twelve, whom He appointed to the work of the ministry; and called them *apostles*, i.e., persons "sent" or commissioned by himself to preach that gospel to others by which they had themselves been saved.

15. *Called Zelotes*. Some Jews gave this name to themselves according to Josephus (*War*, b. iv, c. iii, s. 9 and vii, c. vii, s. 1), "because they pretended to be more than ordinarily *zealous* for religion, and yet practiced the very worst of actions." It is very probable that this name was first given to certain persons who were *more zealous* for the cause of pure and undefiled religion than the rest of their neighbors.

17. *And stood in the plain*. In Matt. v. 1, which is supposed to be the parallel place, our Lord is represented as delivering this sermon on the mountain; and this has induced some to think that the sermon mentioned here by Luke, though the same in substance with that in Matthew, was delivered in a different place, and at another time. But, as Dr. Priestly justly observes, Matthew's saying that Jesus was "sat down" after He had gone up to the mountain, and Luke's saying that He *stood on the plain* when He healed the sick, before the discourse, are no inconsistencies. Jesus ascends a mountain, employs the night in prayer; and, having thus solemnly invoked the divine blessing, authoritatively separates the twelve apostles from the mass of His disciples. He then descends, and heals in the plain all the diseased among a great multitude, collected from various parts by the fame of His miraculous power. Having thus created attention, He likewise satisfied the desire of the people to hear His doctrine, retiring first to the mountain whence He came, that His attentive hearers might follow Him and might better arrange themselves before Him.

20. *Blessed be ye poor*. See the Sermon on the Mount paraphrased and explained, Matthew v; vi; vii.

22. *They shall separate you*. Meaning, They will excommunicate you, or "separate you from their communion." Luke, having spoken of their separating or excommunicating them, continues the same idea in saying that they would *cast out* their *name* likewise, as a thing evil in itself. By *your name* is meant their name as His disciples. As such, they were sometimes called "Nazarenes," and sometimes "Christians"; and both these names were matter of reproach in the mouths of their enemies. So James (ii. 7) says to the converts, "Do not they blaspheme that worthy name by the which ye are called"? So when Paul (in Acts xxiv. 5) is called "a ringleader of the sect of the Nazarenes," the character of "a pestilent fellow" and that of "a mover of sedition" are joined to it; and in Acts xxviii. 22 the Jews say to Paul, "As concerning this sect, we know that every where it is spoken against"; and this is implied in 1 Pet. iv. 14, when he says, "If ye be reproached for the name of Christ," i.e., as "Christians," agreeably to what follows there in v. 16, "If any man suffer as a Christian." In after times we find Pliny, *Epist.* x. 97, consulting the Emperor Trajan whether or not he should "punish the name itself (of Christian), though no evil should be found in it."

23. *Did their fathers unto the prophets*. See 1 Kings xviii. 4; xix. 20; 2 Chron. xxiv. 21; xxxvi. 16; Neh. ix. 26.

MATTHEW HENRY

foregoing *blessings*, is the parable of the rich *man* and Lazarus. Here is a *woe* to them that are *rich*, that is, that *trust in riches*; woe to them, for *they have received their consolation*, that which they placed their happiness in, *v.* 24. They in their lifetime received *their good things*, which, in their account, were the *best things*. "You that are *rich* are in temptation to *set your hearts* upon a *smiling* world, and to say, *Soul, take thine ease* in the embraces of it." It is the *folly* of carnal worldlings that they make the things of this world *their consolation*, which were intended only for their *convenience*. They please themselves with them; and to them the *consolations of God* are small, and of no account. It is their misery that they are *put off* with them as *their consolation*. Here is a *woe* to them that are *full* (*v.* 25), and have *more than heart could wish*. They are *full of themselves*, without God and Christ. Woe to such, for *they shall hunger*, they shall shortly be *stripped* and *emptied* of all the things they are so proud of. Here is a *woe* to them that *laugh now*, that have always a *disposition to be merry*, and always something to *make merry with*, and are always entertaining themselves with the laughter of the fool. *Woe unto such*, for it is but *now*, for a little time, that they *laugh*; they shall *mourn and weep* shortly. Here is a *woe* to them *whom all men speak well of*, that is, who make it their great and only care to gain the praise and applause of men (*v.* 26): "*Woe unto you;* it would be a bad sign that you were not faithful to your trust, and to the souls of men, if you preached so as that nobody would be disgusted; for your business is to tell people of their faults. The false prophets indeed, that flattered your fathers in their wicked ways, were caressed and spoken well of. We should desire to have the approbation of those that are wise and good; but, as we should despise the reproaches, so we should also despise the praises, of the fools in Israel.

Verses 27–36

These verses agree with Matt. v. 38, to the end of that chapter: *I say unto you that hear* (*v.* 27), to all you that hear, for these are lessons of universal concern. *He that has an ear, let him hear.* Now the lessons Christ here teaches us are,

I. That we must render to all their due, and be honest and just in all our dealings (*v.* 31): *As ye would that men should do to you, do ye also to them likewise;* for this is *loving your neighbour as yourselves*. We must *put our souls into their souls' stead*, and then pity and succour them, as we should desire and justly expect to be ourselves pitied and succoured.

II. That we must be free in *giving* to them that *need* (*v.* 30): "*Give to every man that asketh of thee*, that wants necessaries, which thou hast wherewithal to supply out of thy superfluities. Give to those that are not able to help themselves." Christ would have his disciples ready to distribute, and willing to communicate, *to their power* in ordinary cases, and beyond their power in extraordinary.

III. That we must be generous in *forgiving* those that have been any way injurious to us.

1. We must not be *extreme* in *demanding* our right, when it is denied us: "*Him that taketh away thy cloak, forbid him not to take thy coat also* (*v.* 29). Let him have that too, rather than fight for it. And (*v.* 30) *of him that taketh thy goods*, of such do not *exact them*; if Providence have made such insolvent, do not take the advantage of the law against them, but rather lose it than *take them by the throat*," Matt. xviii. 28.

2. We must not be rigorous in revenging a wrong when it is done us: "*Unto him that smiteth thee on the one cheek, offer also the other*. If anyone *smite thee on the cheek*, rather than give another blow to him, be ready to receive another from him"; that is, "leave it to God to plead thy cause, and do thou sit down silent under the affront."

3. Nay, we must *do good to them that do evil to us.* This is that which our Saviour chiefly designs to teach us, as a law peculiar to his religion, and a branch of the perfection of it. We must be kind to those from whom we have *received injuries*. We must not only *love our enemies*, and bear a good will to them, but we must *do good* to them. We must study to make it appear, by positive acts, that we bear them no malice, nor seek revenge. Do they *curse* us, speak ill of us, and wish ill to us? Do they *despitefully use us*, in word or deed? Do they endeavour to make us contemptible or odious? Let us *bless them*, and *pray for them*, speak well of them, the best we can, wish well to them, and be intercessors with God for them. This is repeated, *v.* 35: *Love your enemies*, and *do them good.* To recommend this difficult duty to us, it is represented as a generous thing, and an attainment few arrive at. *To love those that love us* has nothing

JAMIESON, FAUSSET, BROWN

24, 25. rich . . . full . . . laugh—who have all their good things and joyous feelings *here and now*, in perishable objects.

received your consolation—(see on ch. 16:25). **shall hunger**—their inward craving strong as ever, but the materials of satisfaction forever gone.

26. all . . . speak well of you—alluding to the court paid to the false prophets of old (Mic. 2:11). For the principle of this woe, and its proper limits, see John 15:19.

27-36. (See on Matt. 5:44-48; 7:12; and 14:12-14.)

Give to him that asketh thee—The sense of *unreasonable* asking is here implied (cf. Luke 6:30). **and from him that would borrow of thee turn not thou away**—Though the word signifies classically "to have money lent to one on security," or "with interest," yet as this was not the original sense of the word, and as usury was forbidden among the Jews (Exod. 22:25, etc.), it is doubtless simple borrowing which our Lord here means, as indeed the whole strain of the exhortation implies. This shows that such counsels as "Owe no man anything" (Rom. 13:8), are not to be taken absolutely; else the Scripture commendations of the righteous for "lending" to his necessitous brother (Ps. 37:36; 112:5; Luke 6: 37) would have no application. **turn not thou away**—a graphic expression of unfeeling refusal to relieve a brother in extremity.

And if any man will sue thee at the law, and take way thy coat—the inner garment; in pledge for a debt (Exod. 22:26, 27). **let him have thy cloak also**—the outer and more costly garment. This overcoat was not allowed to be retained over night as a pledge from the poor because they used it for a bed-covering.

But I say unto you, That ye resist not evil; but whosoever shall smite thee on thy right check, turn to him the other also—Our Lord's own meek, yet dignified bearing, when smitten rudely on the cheek (John 18:22, 23), and *not* literally presenting the other, is the best comment on these words. It is the preparedness, after one indignity, not to invite but to submit meekly to another, without retaliation, which this strong language is meant to convey.

But I say unto you, Love your enemies—The word here used denotes *moral* love, as distinguished from the other word, which expresses *personal* affection. Usually, the former denotes "complacency in the character" of the person loved; but here it denotes the benignant, compassionate outgoings of desire for anothers' good. **bless them that curse you, do good to them that hate you, and pray for them which despitefully use you, and persecute you**—The best commentary on these matchless counsels is the bright example of Him who gave them. (See I Pet. 2:21-24; and cf. Rom. 12:20, 21; I Cor. 4:12; I Pet. 3:9). But though such

ADAM CLARKE

24-26. *But woe unto you that are rich!* The Pharisees, who were laden with the spoils of the people which they received in gifts. These three verses are not found in the sermon as recorded by Matthew. They seem to be spoken chiefly to the scribes and Pharisees, who, in order to be pleasing to all, spoke to everyone what he liked best; and by finesse, flattery, and lies found out the method of gaining and keeping the good opinion of the multitude.

ALBERT BARNES:

26. "When all men shall speak well of you." When they shall praise or applaud you. The men of the world will not praise or applaud *my* doctrine; they are opposed to it, and therefore, if they speak well of *you* and *your* teaching, it is proof that you do not teach the true doctrine. If you do not do this, then there will be woe upon you. If men teach false doctrines for true; if they declare that God has spoken that which he has not spoken, and if they oppose what he has delivered, then heavy punishments will await them. "For so did their fathers." The "fathers" or "ancestors" of this people; the ancient Jews. "To the false prophets." Men who pretended to be of God—who delivered their *own* doctrines as the truth of God, and who accommodated themselves to the desires of the people. Of this number were the prophets of Baal and the false prophets who appeared in the time of Jeremiah.—*Popular Commentary*

Give to him that asketh thee, and from him that would borrow. To give and lend freely to all who are in need is a general precept from which we are excused only by our inability to perform it.

29. *Thy cloak . . . thy coat. Coat, chiton,* signifies "undergarment"; and *cloak, himation,* means "upper garment."

30. *Ask them not again.* Or, "Do not beg them off." It is probable that what is here spoken relates to requiring a thing speedily that had been lent, while the reason for borrowing it still continues. In Ecclus. xx. 15, it is a part of the character of a very bad men "that to-day he lendeth, and to-morrow will he ask it again."

34. *Of whom ye hope to receive.* Or "whom ye expect to return it."

35. *Love ye your enemies.* This is the most sublime precept ever delivered to man. A false religion durst not give a precept of this nature, because, without supernatural influence, it must be forever impracticable. In these words of our blessed Lord we see the tenderness, sincerity, extent, disinterestedness, pattern, and issue of the love of God dwelling in man.

MATTHEW HENRY

uncommon in it, nothing peculiar to Christ's disciples, for *sinners* will *love those that love them.* It is but following nature and puts no force at all upon it (*v.* 32). "And (*v.* 33) *if you do good to them that do good to you, what thanks have you?* What credit are you to the name of Christ, or what reputation do you bring to it? for *sinners also do even the same.* But it becomes you to do something more excellent and eminent, to do that which sinners will not do: you must *render good for evil*"; *then* we are to our God *for a name and a praise*, and he will have the thanks. We must be kind to those from whom we expect no manner of advantage (*v.* 35): *Lend, hoping for nothing again.* We must *lend* though we have reason to suspect that what we *lend* we *lose*, lend to those who are so poor that it is not probable they will be able to pay us again. Here are two motives to this generous charity. It will redound to our profit; for our *reward shall be great, v.* 35. What is lent and lost on earth, from a true principle of charity, will be made up to us. "You shall not only be *repaid*, but *rewarded*, greatly rewarded; it will be said to you, *Come, ye blessed, inherit the kingdom.*" It will redound to our honour; for herein we shall resemble God in his goodness, which is the greatest glory: "*Ye shall be the children of the Highest.*" It is the glory of God that he is *kind to the unthankful and to the evil.* Hence he infers (*v.* 36), *Be merciful*, as *your Father is merciful*; this explains Matt. v. 48, "*Be perfect, as your Father is perfect.* Imitate your Father in those things that are his brightest perfections." Those that are *merciful* as God is *merciful*, even *to the evil and the unthankful*, are *perfect* as God is *perfect.* This should strongly engage us to be merciful to our brethren, not only that God is so to others, but that he is so to us, though we have been, and are, evil and unthankful; it is of his mercies that *we* are not consumed.

Verses 37–49

All these sayings of Christ we had before in Matthew. They were sayings that Christ often used. We need not be critical here in seeking for the coherence: they are golden sentences, like Solomon's proverbs or parables.

I. We ought to be very candid in our censures of others, because we need grains of allowance ourselves: "Therefore *judge not* others, because then *you* yourselves *shall not be judged*; therefore *condemn not* others, because then *you* yourselves *shall not be condemned, v.* 37. God will not *judge* and *condemn* you, men will not." They that are merciful to other people's names shall find others merciful to theirs.

II. If we are of a *giving* and a *forgiving* spirit, we shall ourselves reap the benefit of it: *Forgive and you shall be forgiven.* If we forgive the injuries done to us by others, others will forgive our inadvertencies. If we forgive others' trespasses against *us*, God will forgive our trespasses against *him.* And he will be no less mindful of the *liberal* that *devise liberal things* (*v.* 38): *Give, and it shall be given to you. Men* shall *return it into your bosom;* for God often makes use of *men* as instruments, not only of his *avenging*, but of his *rewarding* justice. God will incline the hearts of others to give to us when we need, and to give liberally, *good measure pressed down and shaken together.* Whom God recompenses he recompenses *abundantly.*

III. We must expect to be dealt with ourselves as we deal with others: *With the same measure that ye mete it shall be measured to you again.* Those that deal *hardly* with others may expect to be paid in their own coin; but they that deal *kindly* with others have reason to hope that God will raise them up friends who will deal kindly with them.

IV. Those who put themselves under the guidance of the ignorant and erroneous are likely to perish with them (*v.* 39): *Can the blind lead the blind? Shall not both fall* together *into the ditch?* How can they expect any other? Those that are led by the common opinion, course, and custom, of this world, are themselves blind, and are led by the blind.

V. Christ's followers cannot expect better treatment in the world than their Master had, *v.* 40. Let them not promise themselves more honour or pleasure in the world than Christ had. Let each live a life of labour and self-denial as his Master doth, and make himself a servant of all; let him stoop, and let him toil, and do all the good he can, and then he will be a complete disciple.

VI. Those who take upon them to rebuke and reform others are concerned to look to it that they be themselves without rebuke, *v.* 41, 42. It is very absurd for any to pretend to be so quick-sighted as to spy small faults in others, like a mote in the eye, when they are themselves so perfectly past feeling as not to perceive *a beam in their own eye.* How canst

JAMIESON, FAUSSET, BROWN

precepts were never before expressed—perhaps not even conceived—with such breadth, precision, and sharpness as here, our Lord is here only the incomparable Interpreter of the law in force from the beginning; and this is the only satisfactory view of the entire strain of this discourse.

For if ye love them which love you, what reward have ye? do not even the publicans the same?—The publicans, as collectors of taxes due to the Roman government, were ever on this account obnoxious to the Jews, who sat uneasy under a foreign yoke, and disliked whatever brought this unpleasantly before them. But the extortion practiced by this class made them hateful to the community, who in their current speech ranked them with "harlots." Nor does our Lord scruple to speak of them as others did, which we may be sure He never would have done if it had been calumnious. The meaning, then, is, "In loving those who love you, there is no evidence of superior principle; the worst of men will do this: even a publican will go that length." **And if ye salute your brethren only**—of the same nation and religion with yourselves. **what do ye more [than others]?**—what do ye uncommon or extraordinary? i.e, wherein do ye *excel*? **do not even the publicans so?**—The true reading here appears to be, "Do not even the heathens the same?" Cf. ch. 18:17, where the excommunicated person is said to be "as an heathen man and a publican."

37, 38. See on Matt. 7:1, 2; but this is much fuller and more graphic. **Judge not, that ye be not judged**—To "judge" here does not exactly mean to pronounce condemnatory judgment, nor does it refer to simple judging at all, whether favorable or the reverse. The context makes it clear that the thing here condemned is that disposition to look unfavorably on the character and actions of others, which leads invariably to the pronouncing of rash, unjust, and unlovely judgments upon them. No doubt it is the judgments so pronounced which are here spoken of; but what our Lord aims at is the spirit out of which they spring. Provided we eschew this unlovely spirit, we are not only warranted to sit in judgment upon a brother's character and actions, but in the exercise of a necessary discrimination are often constrained to do so for our own guidance. It is the violation of the law of love involved in the exercise of a censorious disposition which alone is here condemned. And the argument against it—"that ye be not judged"—confirms this: "that your own character and actions be not pronounced upon with the like severity"; i.e., at the great day. **For with what judgments ye judge, ye shall be judged: and with what measure ye mete** [whatever standard of judgment ye apply to others] **it shall be measured to you again**—This proverbial maxim is used by our Lord in other connections—as in Mark 4:24, and with a slightly different application in Luke 6:38—as a great principle in the divine administration. Unkind judgment of others will be judicially returned upon ourselves, in the day when God shall judge the secrets of men by Jesus Christ.

39. Can the blind . . .—not in the Sermon on the Mount, but recorded by Matthew in another and very striking connection (ch. 15:14). **40. The disciple . . .** i.e., "The disciple aims to come up to his master, and he thinks himself complete when he does so: if you then be blind leaders of the blind, the perfection of one's training under you will only land him the more certainly in one common ruin with yourselves." **41-49.** (See on Matt. 7:3-5, 16-27.)

why beholdest thou the mote—"splinter," here very well rendered "mote," denoting any small fault. **that is in thy brother's eye, but considerest not the beam that is in thine own eye?**—denoting the much greater fault which we overlook in ourselves.

ADAM CLARKE

32. *For sinners also love those that love them.* I believe the word is used by Luke in the same sense in which "taxgatherers" is used by Matthew, chap. v. 46-47, and signifies "heathens"; not only men who have no religion, but men who acknowledge none.

Lend, hoping for nothing again. The rabbins say that he who lends without usury, God shall consider him as having observed every precept.

36. *Be ye therefore merciful.* Or "compassionate." A merciful or compassionate man easily forgets injuries; pardons them without being solicited; and does not permit repeated returns of ingratitude to deter him from doing good, even to the unthankful and the unholy. See on Matt. v. 7.

37. *Judge not.* See on Matt. vii. 1. *Forgive.* The mercy and compassion which God recommends extend to the forgiving of all the injuries we have received, or can receive.

38. *Bosom.* Or "lap." Almost all ancient nations wore long, wide, and loose garments; and when about to carry anything which their hands could not contain, they used a fold of their robe in nearly the same way as women here use their aprons. The phrase is continually occurring in the best and purest Greek writers. See also Ps. cxxix. 7; Prov. vi. 27; xvii. 23. *The same measure that ye mete withal it shall be measured to you again.* The same words we find in the Jerusalem Targum on Gen. xxxviii. 26. Our Lord, therefore, lays down a maxim which themselves allowed.

39. *Can the blind lead the blind?* This appears to have been a general proverb, and to signify that a man cannot teach what he does not understand. This is strictly true in spiritual matters. A man who is not illuminated from above is utterly incapable of judging concerning spiritual things, and wholly unfit to be a guide to others.

40. *Every one that is perfect.* Or "thoroughly instructed." The noun is used by the Greek medical writers to signify the reducing a disjointed limb. It sometimes signifies to "repair" or "mend," and in this sense it is applied to broken nets, Matt. iv. 21; Mark i. 19; but in this place, and in Heb. xiii. 21; 2 Tim. iii. 17, it means "complete instruction and information." Everyone who is "thoroughly instructed" in divine things, who has his heart united to God, whose disordered tempers and passions are purified and "restored to harmony and order"; everyone who has in him the mind that was in Christ, though he cannot be above, yet will be *as*, his Teacher—"holy, harmless, undefiled, separate from sinners."

MATTHEW HENRY

thou offer thy service to thy brother, to *pull out the mote from his eye*, which requires a good eye as well as a good hand, when thou thyself hast a *beam in thine own eye*. To help to pull the mote out of our brother's eye is a good work, but then we must qualify ourselves for it by beginning with ourselves; reforming our own lives.

VII. We may expect that men's words and actions will be according as *they* are.

1. The heart is the *tree*, and the words and actions are fruit according to the nature of the tree, *v.* 43, 44. If a man be really a *good man*, though perhaps he may not abound in fruit, and though he may be sometimes like a tree in winter, yet he does not *bring forth corrupt fruit*; though he may not do you all the good he should, yet he will not do you hurt. If he cannot reform ill manners, he will not *corrupt good manners*. If the fruit that a man brings forth be *corrupt* you may be sure that he is not a *good tree*. On the other hand, a *corrupt tree doth not bring forth good fruit*, though it may bring forth green leaves. So neither can you expect any *good conduct* from those who have justly a *bad character*. If the fruit be good, you may conclude that the tree is so; for *every tree is known by its fruit*.

2. The heart is the *treasure*, and the words and actions are the produce from that treasure, *v.* 45. The reigning love of God and Christ in the heart is *a good treasure in the heart*: it enriches a man, it furnishes him with a good stock to spend upon, for the benefit of others. Out of such a *good treasure* a man may bring forth that which is good. But where the love of the world and the flesh reign there is an *evil treasure* in the heart, out of which an *evil man* is continually bringing forth *that which is evil*. *Of the abundance of the heart the mouth speaks;* what the mouth ordinarily speaks generally agrees with what is innermost and uppermost in the heart. Not but that a good man may possibly drop a bad word, and a wicked man make use of a good word to serve a bad turn; but, for the most part, the heart is as the words are, *vain* or *serious*; it therefore concerns us to get our hearts filled, not only with *good*, but with *abundance* of it.

VIII. It is not enough to *hear* the sayings of Christ, but we must *do* them.

1. It is putting an *affront upon him* to call him *Lord, Lord*, if we do not make conscience of conforming to his will. We do but mock Christ, as they that in scorn said, *Hail, King of the Jews*, if we call him ever so often *Lord, Lord*, and yet walk in the way of our own hearts.

2. It is *putting a cheat* upon ourselves if we think that *hearing* the sayings of Christ will bring us to heaven, without *doing* them. This he illustrates by a similitude (*v.* 47-49), which shows,

(1) That those only make sure work for their souls and eternity who do not only *come* to Christ as his scholars, and *hear his sayings*, but do them. They are like a *house built on a rock*. These are they that *take pains* in religion, as they do that *build on a rock*,—that *begin low*, as they do,—that *dig deep*, that found their hope upon Christ, who is the Rock of ages (and other foundation can no man lay). They who do thus do well for themselves; for, [1] They shall keep their integrity, in times of temptation and persecution; when others fall from their own steadfastness they shall *stand fast in the Lord*. [2] They shall keep their comfort, and peace, and hope, and joy, in the midst of the greatest distresses. The *storms* and *streams* of affliction shall not shock them, for their feet are *set upon a rock*. [3] Their everlasting welfare is secured. Obedient believers are *kept by the power of Christ, through faith, unto salvation*, and shall never perish.

(2) That those who rest in a bare hearing of the sayings of Christ, and do not live up to them, are but preparing for a fatal disappointment: *He that heareth and doeth not*, he is like a man that *built a house without a foundation*. His hopes will fail him when he most needs the *comfort* of them. When the *stream beats vehemently* upon his house, it is gone, the sand it is built upon is washed away, and *immediately it falls*.

JAMIESON, FAUSSET, BROWN

Or how wilt thou say to thy brother, Let me pull out the mote out of thine eye; and, behold, a beam is in thine own eye? Thou hypocrite [Hypocrite]—**first cast out the beam out of thine own eye; and then shalt thou see clearly to cast out the mote out of thy brother's eye**—Our Lord uses a most hyperbolical, but not unfamiliar figure, to express the monstrous inconsistency of this conduct. The "hypocrisy" which, not without indignation, He charges it with, consists in the pretense of a zealous and compassionate charity, which cannot possibly be real in one who suffers worse faults to lie uncorrected in himself. He only is fit to be a reprover of others who jealously and severely judges himself. Such persons will not only be slow to undertake the office of censor on their neighbors, but, when constrained in faithfulness to deal with them, will make it evident that they do it with *reluctance* and not satisfaction, with *moderation* and not exaggeration, with *love* and not harshness.

A good tree cannot bring forth evil fruit, neither can a corrupt tree bring forth good fruit—Obvious as is the truth here expressed in different forms—that the heart determines and is the only proper interpreter of the actions of our life—no one who knows how the Church of Rome makes a merit of actions, quite apart from the motives that prompt them, and how the same tendency manifests itself from time to time even among Protestant Christians, can think it too obvious to be insisted on by the teachers of divine truth.

Not every one that saith unto me, Lord, Lord—the reduplication of the title "Lord" denoting zeal in according it to Christ (see Mark 14:45). Yet our Lord claims and expects this of all His disciples, as when He washed their feet: "Ye call me Master and Lord: and ye say well; for so I am" (John 13:13). **shall enter into the kingdom of heaven; but he that doeth the will of my Father which is in heaven**—that will which it had been the great object of this discourse to set forth. Yet our Lord says warily, not "the will of *your* Father," but "of *My* Father"; thus claiming a relationship to His Father with which His disciples might not intermeddle, and which He never lets down. And He so speaks here to give authority to His asseverations. But now He rises higher still—not formally *announcing* Himself as the Judge, but intimating what men will say to Him, and He to them, *when* He sits as their final judge.

Therefore—to bring this discourse to a close. **whosoever heareth these sayings of mine, and doeth them**—see James 1:22, which seems a plain allusion to these words; also Luke 11:28; Romans 2:13; I John 3:7—**I will liken him unto a wise man**—a shrewd, prudent, provident man. **which built his house upon a rock**—the rock of true discipleship, or genuine subjection to Christ. **And the rain** [from above] **descended, and the floods** [from below] **came, and the winds** [sweeping across] **blew, and** [thus from every direction] **beat upon that house; and it fell not; for it was founded upon a rock**—See I John 2:17. **And every one that heareth these sayings of mine**—in the attitude of discipleship—**and doeth them not, shall be likened unto a foolish man, which built his house upon the sand**—denoting a loose foundation—that of an empty profession and mere external services. **And the rain descended, and the floods came, and the winds blew, and beat upon** [struck against] **that house; and it fell: and great was the fall of it**—terrible the ruin! How lively must this imagery have been to an audience accustomed to the fierceness of an Eastern tempest, and the suddenness and completeness with which it sweeps everything unsteady before it!

ADAM CLARKE

41. *And why beholdest thou the mote?* See this explained on Matt. vii. 3-5.

43. *Corrupt fruit.* Literally, *rotten fruit;* but here it means such fruit as is unfit for use. See on Matt. vii. 17-20.

45. *A good man.* See on Matt. xii. 35.

46. *Lord, Lord.* God judges of the heart, not by *words*, but by *works*.

47. *I will shew you.* "I will show you plainly." I will enable you fully to comprehend My meaning on this subject by the following parable.

48. *He is like a man.* See on Matt. vii. 24-27.

And the rain descended, and the floods came. A fine illustration of this may be seen in the case of the fishermen in Bengal, who, in the dry season, build their huts on the beds of sand from which the river has retired. But when the rain sets in suddenly, as it often does, accompanied with violent northwest winds, and the waters pour down in torrents from the mountains, in one night multitudes of these buildings are swept away, and the place where they stood is on the next morning indiscoverable.

MATTHEW HENRY

CHAPTER 7

Some difference there is between this story of the cure of the centurion's servant as it is related here and as we had it in Matt. viii. 5, &c. There it was said that the centurion came to Christ; here it is said that he sent to him first some of the *elders of the Jews* (*v.* 3), and afterwards some other *friends*, *v.* 6.

This miracle is here said to have been wrought by our Lord Jesus *when he had ended all his sayings in the audience of the people*, *v.* 1. What Christ said he said *publicly*; *In secret have I said nothing*, John xviii. 20.

I. The centurion's servant that was sick was *dear to his master*, *v.* 2. It was the praise of the servant that by his diligence and faithfulness, he recommended himself to his master's esteem and love. Servants should study to *endear* themselves to their masters. It was likewise the praise of the master that, when he had a good servant, he knew how to value him. Many masters think it favour enough to the best servants they have not to rate them, whereas they ought to be kind to them, and tender of them, and solicitous for their welfare and comfort.

II. The master, *when he heard of Jesus*, *v.* 3, begged that *Christ would come and heal his servant*.

III. He sent some of the *elders of the Jews* to Christ, thinking that a greater piece of respect to Christ than if he had come himself. For that reason he sent Jews. And not ordinary Jews either, but *elders of the Jews*, that the dignity of the messengers might give honour to him to whom they were sent.

IV. The elders of the Jews were hearty intercessors for the centurion: *They besought him instantly* (*v.* 4), pleading for the centurion that which he would never have pleaded for himself, *that he was worthy for whom he should do this.* The centurion said, *I am not* so much as *worthy* of a visit (Matt. viii. 8), but the elders of the Jews thought him worthy of the cure. But that which they insisted upon in particular was, that, though he was a Gentile, yet he was a hearty well-wisher to the Jewish nation and religion, *v.* 5. *He loveth our nation* (which few of the Gentiles did). Even conquerors, and those *in power*, ought to keep up an affection for the conquered, and those they have *power over.* He was well-affected to their worship: *He built them a* new *synagogue* at Capernaum. Hereby he testified his veneration for the God of Israel, and his desire to have an interest in the prayers of God's Israel. Building places of meeting for religious worship is a very *good work*, and those who do good works of that kind are *worthy of double honour*.

V. Jesus Christ was very ready to show kindness to the centurion. He presently *went with them* (*v.* 6), though he was a Gentile. The centurion did not think himself worthy to visit Christ (*v.* 7), yet Christ thought him worthy to be visited by him.

VI. The centurion gave further proofs both of his humility and of his faith. *When he was now not far from the house* he *sends friends* to meet him with fresh expressions, 1. Of his *humility*: "*Lord, trouble not thyself*, for I am unworthy of such an honour." This bespeaks not only his low thoughts of himself, notwithstanding the greatness of his figure; but his high thoughts of Christ, notwithstanding the meanness of his figure in the world. 2. Of his *faith*: "Lord, *trouble not thyself*; thou canst *cure* my servant without coming *under my roof. Say in a word, and my servant shall be healed.*" He illustrates this faith of his by a comparison taken from his own profession, and is confident that Christ can as easily command away the distemper as he can command any of his soldiers, as he can send a soldier on an errand, *v.* 8.

VII. Our Lord Jesus was wonderfully well pleased with the faith of the centurion, and the more surprised at it because he was a Gentile; and, the centurion's faith having thus honoured Christ, see how he honoured it (*v.* 9): *He turned him about* and *said to the people that followed him, I have not found so great faith, no not in Israel.* Christ will have those that follow him to observe and take notice of the great examples of faith—especially when any such are found among those that do not follow Christ so closely as they do in profession—that we may be shamed by the strength of their faith out of the weakness and waverings of ours.

VIII. The cure was *presently* and *perfectly* wrought (*v.* 10): *They that were sent* went back, and found the servant well. Christ will take cognizance of the distressed case of poor servants, for there *is no respect of persons with him.* Nor are the Gentiles excluded from the benefit of his grace.

Verses 11-18

We have here the story of Christ's raising to life a widow's son at Nain, which Matthew and Mark had made no mention of.

JAMIESON, FAUSSET, BROWN

CHAPTER 7

Vss. 1-10. Centurion's Servant Healed. (See on Matt. 8:5-13.)

2. And a certain centurion's servant, who was dear unto him, was sick, and ready to die. These centurions were Roman officers, so called from being captains over a hundred soldiers. Though a heathen by birth and early training, he had become acquainted with the Jewish religion probably either while quartered at Capernaum or in some other Galilean town; although there were so many proselytes to the Jewish religion in all the principal Greek and Roman cities that he might have embraced the true faith even before his arrival in the Holy Land. The same may be said of Cornelius (Acts 10:1). His character appears here in the most beautiful light. The value which he set upon this dying servant and his anxiety for his recovery—as if he had been his own son—is the first feature in it; for, as Bishop Hall observes, he is unworthy to be well served who will not sometimes wait upon his followers.

4. he was worthy . . .—a testimony most precious, coming from those who probably were strangers to the principle from which he acted (Eccles. 7:1).

5. loved our nation—Having found that "salvation was of the Jews," he loved them for it. **built . . .**—His love took this practical and appropriate form.

These elders content not themselves with delivering the humble petition of the centurion himself, but urge their own arguments in support of it. And how precious is the testimony they bear to this devout soldier; all the more so as coming from persons who were themselves probably strangers to the principle from which he acted. "He loveth our nation," they say; for he had found, in his happy experience, as our Lord said to the woman of Samaria, that "Salvation is of the Jews" (John 4:22); "and [they add] he hath built us a synagogue"—rebuilding the synagogue of the place at his own sole expense. His love to the Jews took this appropriate and somewhat costly form. He would leave a monument in Capernaum of the debt he owed to the God of Israel by providing for His worship and the comfort of His worshipers. **Lord, trouble not thyself; for I am not worthy that thou shouldest enter under my roof.** What deep humility! **7. Wherefore neither thought I myself worthy to come unto thee: but say in a word.** In Matthew it is "but speak the word only"—or more expressively, "but speak only a word." **and my servant shall be healed.** No such faith as this had been before displayed. **8. For I also am a man set under authority, having under me soldiers; and I say unto one, Go, and he goeth; and to another, Come, and he cometh; and to my servant, Do this, and he doeth it**—"I know both to obey and command: though but a subaltern, my orders are implicitly obeyed: Shall not diseases, then, obey their Lord, and at His word be gone?" **9. When Jesus heard these things, he marvelled at him.** As Bengel hints, Jesus marveled but at two things—*faith* (as here) and *unbelief* (Mark 6:6): at the one, considering the general blindness in spiritual things; at the other, considering the light that shone around all who were privileged to hear Him and behold His works. But the unprecedented faith of this heathen convert could not fail to fill His soul with peculiar admiration. **and turned him about, and said unto the people that followed him**—Jews, no doubt, **I have not found so great faith, no, not in Israel**—among the chosen people; this Gentile outstripping all the children of the covenant.

ADAM CLARKE

CHAPTER 7

2. *A certain centurion's servant.* See this miracle explained on Matt. viii. 5-13.

A centurion. A Roman military officer who had the command of 100 men.

3. *Elders of the Jews.* These were either "magistrates" in the place, or the *elders* of the synagogue which the centurion had built, v. 5. He sent these, probably, because he was afraid to come to Christ himself, not being a Jew, by either nation or religion. In the parallel place in Matthew he is represented as coming to Christ himself; but it is a usual form of speech in all nations to attribute the act to a person which is done, not by himself, but by his authority.

But speak the word only. Or, "Speak by word or command." Jesus can will away the palsy, and speak away the most grievous torments.

For I am a man under authority. That is, "under the authority of others." The argument of the centurion seems to run thus. If I, who am a person subject to the control of others, yet have some so completely subject to myself that I can say to one, *Come, and he cometh;* to another, *Go, and he goeth;* and to my slave, *Do this, and he doeth it;* how much more then canst Thou accomplish whatsoever Thou willest, being under no control, and having all things under Thy command!

I have not found so great faith, no, not in Israel. That is, I have not found so great an instance of confidence and faith in My power, even among the Jews, as this Roman, a Gentile, has shown himself to possess.

10. *Found the servant whole.* This cure was the effect of the faith, prayer, and humility of the centurion, through which the almighty energy of Jesus Christ was conveyed to the sick man. But these very graces in the centurion were the products of grace. It is God himself who, by the gifts of His mercy, disposes the soul to receive its cure; and nothing can contribute to the reception of His grace but what is the fruit of grace itself. The apostle says, "The grace of God that bringeth salvation hath appeared to all men," Titus ii. 11. It should therefore be our concern, not to resist the operations of this grace: for though we cannot endue ourselves with any gracious disposition, yet we can quench the Spirit, by whose agency these are produced in the soul. The centurion had not received the grace of God in vain.

MATTHEW HENRY

I. Where, and when, this miracle was wrought. It was the *next day after* he had cured the centurion's servant, *v.* 11. It was done at the gate of a small city, or town, called *Nain*, not far from Capernaum.

II. Who were the witnesses of it. It was done in the sight of two crowds that met in or near the gate of the city. There was a crowd of *disciples* and other *people* attending Christ (*v.* 11), and a crowd of relations and neighbours attending the funeral of the young man, *v.* 12.

III. How it was wrought by our Lord Jesus. The person raised to life was a *young man.* This young man was the *only son of his mother*, and *she a widow.* She depended upon him to be the staff of her old age, but he proves a broken reed; every man at his best estate is so. We may well think how deep the *sorrow* of this poor mother was for her *only son*, and it was the deeper in that she was a *widow. Much people of the city was with her*, *condoling* with her loss, to *comfort* her. Christ showed both his *pity* and his *power* in raising him to life. See how *tender* his *compassions* are towards the afflicted (*v.* 13): *When the Lord saw* the poor widow following her son to the grave, *he had compassion on her.* Here was no application made to him for her. *Purely from the goodness of his nature*, he was troubled for her. The case was piteous, and he looked upon it with pity. He *said unto her, Weep not.* What a pleasing idea does this give us of the compassions of the Lord Jesus, and the multitude of his *tender mercies.* Christ said, *Weep not;* and he could give her a reason for it which no one else could: "Weep not for a *dead son*, for he shall presently become a *living one.*" This was a reason peculiar to her case; yet there is a reason common to all that sleep in Jesus, that they shall rise again, shall rise in glory; and therefore we must *not sorrow as those that have no hope*, 1 Thess. iv. 13. Let our *passion* at such a time be checked and calmed by the consideration of Christ's *compassion.* See how *triumphant* his *commands* are over even death itself (*v.* 14): *He came, and touched the bier.* Hereby he intimated to the bearers that they should not proceed. Hereupon *they that bore him stood still*, and then with solemnity, as one that had authority, he said, *Young man, I say unto thee, Arise.* Power went along with that word to *put life* into him. Christ's dominion over death was evidenced by the immediate effect of his word (*v.* 15): *He that was dead sat up.* Have we grace from Christ? Let us show it. Another evidence of life was that he *began to speak;* for whenever Christ gives us spiritual life he *opens the lips* in prayer and praise. He *delivered him to his mother*, to attend her as became a dutiful son. Now she was *comforted*, according to the time in which she had been afflicted.

IV. What influence it had upon the people (*v.* 16): *There came a fear on all;* they were all struck with wonder at this miracle, and *glorified God.* The Lord and his goodness, as well as the Lord and his greatness, are to be feared. The inference they drew from it was, "*A great prophet is risen up among us*, and in him *God hath visited his people.*" This would be *life from the dead* indeed to all them that waited for the consolation of Israel. The report of this miracle was carried, in general, all the country over (*v.* 17): *This rumour of him went forth through all Judæa*, which lay a great way off, and throughout all Galilee, which was the *region round about.* Many have the *rumour* of Christ's gospel in their ears that have not the *savour* and *relish* of it in their souls. In particular, it was carefully brought to John Baptist, who was now in prison (*v.* 18): *His disciples came*, and gave him an account of all things, that he might know that though *he* was bound yet *the word of the Lord was not bound*; God's work was going on, though he was laid aside.

Verses 19–35

I. We have here the message John Baptist sent to Christ, and the return he made to it. The great thing we are to enquire concerning Christ is whether he be he that should come, or whether we are to look for another, *v.* 19, 20. We are sure that God has promised that a Saviour shall come; we are as sure that what he has promised he will perform. If this Jesus be that promised Messiah, we will receive him; but, if not, we will continue our expectations, and will wait for him. The faith of John Baptist himself wanted to be *confirmed* in this matter. The great men of the Jewish church had not owned him. Nothing of that power and grandeur was to be seen about him in which it was expected that the Messiah would appear; and therefore it is not strange that they should ask, *Art thou the Messiah?* Christ left it to his own works to praise him. While John's messengers were with him, he wrought many miraculous cures, *in that same hour, v.* 21. *He cured*

JAMIESON, FAUSSET, BROWN

11-17. WIDOW OF NAIN'S SON RAISED TO LIFE. (In Luke only.) **11. Nain**—a small village not elsewhere mentioned in Scripture, and only this once probably visited by our Lord; it lay a little to the south of Mount Tabor, about twelve miles from Capernaum. **12. carried out**—"was being carried out." Dead bodies, being ceremonially unclean, were not allowed to be buried within the cities (though the kings of David's house were buried in the city of David), and the funeral was usually on the same day as the death. **only son . . .**—affecting particulars, told with delightful simplicity.

13, 14. the Lord—"This sublime appellation is more usual with Luke and John than Matthew; Mark holds the mean" [BENGEL]. **saw her, he had compassion . . .**—What consolation to thousands of the bereaved has this single verse carried from age to age!

14, 15. What mingled majesty and grace shines in this scene! The Resurrection and the Life in human flesh, with a word of command, bringing back life to the dead body; Incarnate Compassion summoning its absolute power to dry a widow's tears!

16. visited his people—more than bringing back the days of Elijah and Elisha (I Kings 17:17-24; II Kings 4:32-37; and see on Matt. 15:31).

18-35. THE BAPTIST'S MESSAGE, THE REPLY, AND CONSEQUENT DISCOURSE.

20. When the men were come unto him, they said, John Baptist hath sent us unto thee, saying, Art thou he that should come? or look we for another? Was this a question of doubt as to the messiahship of his Lord, as rationalists are fain to represent it? Impossible, from all we know of him. Was it then purely for the satisfaction of his disciples, as some expositors, more concerned for the Baptist's reputation than for simple and natural interpretation, take it? Obviously not. The whole strain of our Lord's reply shows that it was designed for John himself. Clearly it was a message of impatience, and almost of desperation. It seemed, no doubt, hard to him that his Master should let him lie so long in prison for his fidelity—useless to his Master's cause and a comparative stranger to His proceedings—after having been honored to announce and introduce Him to His work and

ADAM CLARKE

11. *Nain.* A small city of Galilee, in the tribe of Issachar. According to Eusebius, it was two miles from Mount Tabor, southward; and near to Endor.

12. *Carried out.* The Jews always buried their dead without the city, except those of the family of David.

CHARLES H. SPURGEON:

It was a remarkable incident, this meeting of the two processions at the gates of Nain. If someone with a fine imagination could picture it, what an opportunity he would have for developing his poetical genius! I venture on no such effort. Yonder a procession descends from the city. Our spiritual eyes see death upon the pale horse coming forth from the city gate with great exultation. He has taken another captive. Upon that bier behold the spoils of the dread conqueror! Mourners by their tears confess the victory of death. Like a general riding in triumph to the Roman capital, death bears his spoils to the tomb. What shall hinder him?

Suddenly the procession is arrested by another: a company of disciples and much people are coming up the hill. We need not look at the company, but we may fix our eyes upon One who stands in the center, a Man in whom lowliness was always evident, and yet majesty was never wanting. It is the living Lord, even He who only hath immortality, and in Him death has now met his destroyer. The battle is short and decisive; no blows are struck, for death has already done his utmost. With a finger the chariot of death is arrested; with a word the spoil is taken from the mighty, and the lawful captive is delivered. Death flies defeated from the gates of the city, while Tabor and Hermon, which both looked down upon the scene, rejoice in the name of the Lord. This was a rehearsal upon a small scale of that which shall happen by and by, when those who are in their graves shall hear the voice of the Son of God and live: "then shall the last enemy be destroyed." Only let death come into contact with Him who is our life, and it is compelled to relax its hold, whatever may be the spoil which it has captured. Soon shall our Lord come in His glory, and then before the gates of the New Jerusalem we shall see the miracle at the gates of Nain multiplied a myriad times.

—The Treasury of the New Testament

18. *The disciples of John shewed him.* It is very likely that John's disciples attended the ministry of our Lord at particular times.

19. *Art thou he that should come?* Are you the promised Messiah? See on Matt. xi. 3. Some have thought that this character of our Lord, "he who cometh," refers to the prophecy

MATTHEW HENRY

many of their infirmities and plagues in body, and of *evil spirits*, and *unto many that were blind he gave sight*. He multiplied the cures, that there might be no ground left to suspect a fraud; and then (*v.* 22) he bade them *go and tell John what they had seen*. And he and they might easily argue, as even the common people did (John vii. 31), *When Christ cometh, will he do more miracles than these which this man hath done?* You see that Jesus does this to the bodies of people, and therefore must conclude this is he that should come to do it to the souls of people, and you are to *look for no other*. To his miracles in the kingdom of nature he adds this in the kingdom of grace (*v.* 22), *To the poor the gospel is preached*, which they knew was to be done by the Messiah. Judge, therefore, whether you can look for any other that will more fully answer the characters of the Messiah. He gave them an intimation of the danger people were in of being prejudiced against him (*v.* 23): *Blessed is he whosoever shall not be offended in me*, or *scandalized* at me. Christ's education at Nazareth, his residence at Galilee, the meanness of his family and relations, his poverty, and the despicableness of his followers—these and the like were stumbling-blocks to many. He is *blessed*, for he is wise, humble, and well disposed, that is not overcome by these prejudices. It is a sign that God has *blessed* him, *and he shall be blessed* indeed, blessed in Christ.

II. We have here the high encomium which Christ gave of John Baptist; *when they were departed* (*v.* 24). Let them now consider *what they went out into the wilderness to see*. "Come," saith Christ, "I will tell you."

1. He was a man of steadiness and constancy. He was not a *reed shaken with the wind*; he was *firm* as a *rock*, not *fickle* as a *reed*.

2. He was a man of unparalleled *self-denial*. He was not *a man clothed in soft raiment*, nor did he *live delicately* (*v.* 25); but, on the contrary, he lived in a wilderness and was clad and fed accordingly.

3. He was *a prophet*. Nay, he was *more*, he was *much more than a prophet* (*v.* 26), than any of the prophets of the Old Testament; for they spoke of Christ as at a distance, he spoke of him as at the door.

4. He was the harbinger and forerunner of the Messiah, and was himself prophesied of in the Old Testament (*v.* 27): *This is he of whom it is written* (Mal. iii. 1), *Behold, I send my messenger before thy face*. Before he sent the Master himself, he sent a messenger, to give notice of his coming. It was a *previous* indication, plain enough, of the *spiritual* nature of Christ's kingdom, that the messenger he sent before him to *prepare his way* did it by preaching repentance and reformation. Certainly that kingdom was not of this world which was thus ushered in.

5. He was so great that really there was not a *greater prophet* than he. *Prophets* were the *greatest* that were *born of women*, and John was the *greatest* of all the *prophets*. And yet *he that is least in the kingdom of God is greater than he*. The meanest of those that *follow the Lamb* far excel the greatest of those that went before him. Those therefore who live under the gospel dispensation have so much the more to answer for.

III. We have here the just censure of the men of that generation.

1. Christ here shows what contempt was put upon John Baptist, while he was preaching and baptizing. Those who did show him any respect were but the common ordinary sort of people, *v.* 29. *The people* indeed, the vulgar herd, of whom it was said, *This people, who know not the law, are cursed* (John vii. 49), and the publicans, these were *baptized with his baptism*, and became his disciples. By their repentance and reformation they *justified God* in appointing such a one as John Baptist to be the forerunner of the Messiah: they hereby made it to appear that it was the best method that could be taken, for it was not in vain to *them*, whatever it was to others. The great men of their church and nation heard him indeed, but they were not *baptized of him*, *v.* 30. The Pharisees and the lawyers *rejected the counsel of God against themselves*; if they had closed with the counsel of God, it had been *for themselves*; but they *rejected it*, and it was *against themselves*, it was to their own ruin.

2. He here shows the strange perverseness of the men of that generation, and the prejudices they conceived. They made but a jesting matter of the methods God took to do them good (*v.* 31): "*Whereunto shall I liken the men of this generation?* They are, then, *like children sitting in the market-place*, that mind nothing that is serious, but are as full of play as they can hold. As if God were but in jest with them, as children are with one another in the

JAMIESON, FAUSSET, BROWN

to the people. And since the wonders of His hand seemed only to increase in glory as He advanced, and it could not but be easy for Him who preached deliverance to the captives, and the opening of the prison to them that were bound, to put it into the heart of Herod to set him at liberty, or to effect his liberation in spite of him, he at length determines to see if, through a message from the prison by his disciples, he cannot get Him to speak out His mind, and at least set his own at rest. This, we take it, was the real object of his message. The message itself, indeed, was far from a proper one. It was peevish; it was presumptuous; it was all but desperate. He had gotten depressed; he was losing heart; his spirit was clouded; heaven's sweet light had, to some extent, departed from him; and this message was the consequence. As it was announced that he should come in the spirit and power of Elijah, so we find him treading in that prophet's steps rather more than was desirable (1 Kings 14:1-4).

24. And when the messengers of John were departed, he began to speak unto the people concerning John. What went ye out into the wilderness for to see? A reed shaken with the wind?—"a man driven about by every gust of popular opinion, and uttering an uncertain sound? Such is not John." **25. But what went ye out for to see? A man clothed in soft raiment?**—"a self-indulgent courtly preacher? Such was not John." **Behold, they which are gorgeously apparelled, and live delicately, are in kings' courts.** "If that be the man ye wanted, ye must go in quest of him to royal palaces." **26. But what went ye out for to see? A prophet?**—"a faithful straightforward utterer of the testimony given him to bear?" **Yea, I say unto you, and much more than a prophet.** "If that was what ye flocked to the wilderness to see in John, then ye have not been disappointed; for he is that, and much more than that." **27. This is he of whom it is written** (Mal. 3:1), **Behold, I send my messenger before thy face, which shall prepare thy way before thee.** (See Mark 1:3; Luke 1:17.) "There were many prophets, but only one Forerunner of the Lord's Christ; and this is he." **28. For I say unto you, Among those that are born of women there is not**—"there hath not risen" (Matt. 11:11) **a greater prophet than John the Baptist: but he that is least in the kingdom of God is greater than he.** The point of comparison is manifestly not personal character; for as it could hardly be said that in this respect he excelled every human being that preceded him, so it would be absurd to say that he was outstripped by the least advanced of the disciples of Christ. It is of his official standing or position in the economy of grace that our Lord is speaking. In that respect he was above all that ever went before him, inasmuch as he was the last and most honored of the Old Testament prophets, and stood on the very edge of the new economy, though belonging to the old: but for this very reason, the humblest member of the new economy was in advance of him.

29, 30. And all the people that heard—"on hearing (this)." These are the observations of *the Evangelist*, not of our Lord. **and the publicans**—a striking clause. **justified God, being baptized . . .** —rather, "having been baptized." The meaning is, They acknowledged the divine wisdom of such a preparatory ministry as John's, in leading them to Him who now spake to them (see ch. 1:16, 17); whereas the Pharisees and lawyers, true to themselves in refusing the baptism of John, set at naught also the merciful design of God in the Saviour Himself, to their own destruction.

31-35. the Lord said . . .—As cross, capricious children, invited by

ADAM CLARKE

of Jacob, Gen. xlix. 10, where He is called *Shiloh*, which Grotius and others derive from *shalach*, "he sent." Hence, as the time of the fulfillment of the prophecy drew nigh, He was termed, "He who cometh," i.e., He who is just now ready to make His appearance in Judea. In Zech. ix. 9, a similar phrase is used, "Behold, thy King cometh unto thee . . . having salvation." This is meant of the Messiah only; therefore I think the words "to save" are necessarily implied.

21. *Unto many that were blind he gave sight*. Rather, "He kindly gave sight"; or, "He graciously gave sight." This is the proper meaning of the original words. In all His miracles, Jesus showed the tenderest mercy and kindness; not only the cure, but the manner in which He performed it, endeared Him to those who were objects of His compassionate regards.

22-28. See these verses explained at large on Matt. xi. 4-15.

A prophet? yea . . . and more than a prophet. That is, one more excellent than a prophet; one greatly beyond all who had come before him, being the immediate forerunner of Christ, and who was especially commissioned to prepare the way of the Lord. This was a fourth excellency.

Behold, I send my messenger. A fifth excellency of the Baptist was his preparing the way of the Lord, being the instrument, in God's hand, of preparing the people's hearts to receive the Lord Jesus; and it was probably through his preaching that so many thousands attached themselves to Christ immediately on His appearing as a public Teacher.

A greater than John the Baptist. A sixth excellency of the Baptist—he was greater than any prophet from the beginning of the world till that time: (1) Because he was prophesied of by them, Isa. xl. 3; Mal. iii. 1. (2) Because he had the privilege of showing the fulfilment of their predictions, by pointing out that Christ has now come, which they foretold should come. (3) Because he saw and enjoyed that salvation which they could only foretell. *Nothwithstanding he that is least in the kingdom of heaven*. By the kingdom of Heaven in this verse is meant the fullness of the blessings of the gospel of peace, which fullness was not known till after Christ had been crucified, and had risen from the dead. Now the least in this Kingdom, the meanest preacher of a crucified, risen, and glorified Saviour, was greater than John, who was not permitted to live to see the plenitude of gospel grace in the pouring out of the Holy Spirit.

29. *Justified God*. Or "declared God to be just." The sense is this: John preached that the divine wrath was coming upon the Jews, from which they might flee by repentance, chap. iii. 7. The Jews, therefore, who were baptized by Him, with the baptism of repentance, did thereby acknowledge that it is but *justice* in God to punish them for their wickedness unless they repented, and were baptized in token of it. This is the sense in which the word is used here and in Ps. li. 4, compared with Job xxxii. 2, and by this Evangelist again in chap. x. 29 and xvi. 15.

30. *Rejected the counsel of God*. Or "frustrated the will of God." Kypke says the verb has two meanings: (1) to "disbelieve"; (2) "despise, or disobey," and that both senses may be properly conjoined here. The will of God was that all the inhabitants of Judea should repent at the preaching of John, be baptized, and believe in Christ Jesus. Now as they did not repent at John's preaching, so they did not believe his testimony concerning Christ. Thus the will, gracious counsel, or design of God relative to their salvation was annulled or frustrated. They *disbelieved* His promises, *despised* the Messiah, and *disobeyed* His precepts.

31. *And the Lord said*. Almost every MS. of

MATTHEW HENRY

market-place (*v.* 32), they turn it all off with a banter." This is the ruin of multitudes, they can never persuade themselves to be *serious* in the concerns of their souls. O the amazing stupidity and vanity of the blind and ungodly world! The Lord awaken them out of their security. They still found something or other to carp at. John Baptist was a reserved austere man, lived much in solitude, and ought to have been hearkened to as a man of thought and contemplation; but this, which was his praise, was turned to his reproach. Because he came *neither eating nor drinking you say*, "*He has a devil;* he is a melancholy man, he is possessed." Our Lord Jesus was of a more free and open conversation; he *came eating and drinking*, *v.* 34. He would go and dine with Pharisees, and with publicans. In hopes of doing good both to the one and the other, he conversed familiarly with them. By this it appears that the ministers of Christ may be of very different tempers and dispositions, very different ways of preaching and living, and yet all good and useful. Therefore none must make themselves a standard to all others, nor judge hardly of those that do not do just as they do. John Baptist bore witness to Christ, and Christ applauded John Baptist, though they were the reverse of each other in their way of living. But the common enemies of them both reproached them both. The very same men that had represented John as *crazed in his intellects*, represented our Lord Jesus as *corrupt in his morals*; *he is a gluttonous man, and a wine-bibber*. Ill-will never speaks well.

3. He shows that, notwithstanding this, God will be glorified in the salvation of a chosen remnant (*v.* 35): *Wisdom is justified of all her children.* Wisdom's children are herein unanimous, one and all, they have all a complacency in the methods of grace which divine wisdom takes, and think never the worse of them for their being ridiculed by some.

Verses 36–49

When and where this passage of story happened does not appear, but it comes in here, upon occasion of Christ's being reproached as *a friend to publicans and sinners*. Who this woman was that here testified so great an affection to Christ does not appear.

I. The civil entertainment which a Pharisee gave to Christ (*v.* 36): *One of the Pharisees desired him that he would eat with him.* It appears that this Pharisee did not believe in Christ, for he will not own him to be a *prophet* (*v.* 39), and yet our Lord Jesus accepted his invitation, *went into his house, and sat down to meat.* And those may venture further into the society of such as are prejudiced against Christ, who have wisdom and grace sufficient to instruct and argue with them, than others may.

II. The great respect which a poor penitent sinner showed him. It was a woman in the city *that was a sinner*, a *harlot*, and infamous. She *knew that Jesus sat at meat in the Pharisee's house*, and she came to acknowledge her obligations to him, having no opportunity of doing it in any other way than by *washing* his feet, and anointing them with some sweet ointment that she brought with her for that purpose. Now this woman did not look Christ in the face, but came *behind him*, and did the part of a *maid-servant*.

Now in what this good woman did, we may observe,

1. Her *deep humiliation* for sin. She stood behind him *weeping*; her eyes had been the inlets and outlets of sin, and now she makes them fountains of tears. Her face is now foul with weeping, which perhaps used to be covered with paints. Her hair now made a towel of, which before had been plaited and adorned. We have reason to think that she had before sorrowed for sin; but now that she had an opportunity of coming into the presence of Christ, her sorrow was renewed.

2. Her *strong affection* to the Lord Jesus. This was what our Lord Jesus took special notice of, that she *loved much*, *v.* 42, 47. She *washed his feet*, she washed them with *her tears*, tears of joy; she was in a transport, to find herself so near her Saviour, whom her soul loved. She *kissed his feet*. It was a kiss of adoration as well as affection. *She wiped them with her hair.* Her eyes shall yield water to wash them, and her hair be a towel to wipe them; and she *anointed* his feet *with the ointment*. All true penitents have a dear love to the Lord Jesus.

III. The offence which the Pharisee took at Christ, for admitting the respect which this poor penitent paid him (*v.* 39): *He said within himself, This man, if he were a prophet*, would then have so much *knowledge* as to perceive that *this woman is a sinner*, and so much *sanctity* as *therefore* not to suffer her to come so near him. See how apt proud and narrow souls are to think that others should be as haughty

JAMIESON, FAUSSET, BROWN

their playmates to join them in their amusements, will play with them neither at weddings nor funerals (juvenile imitations of the joyous and mournful scenes of life), so that generation rejected both John and his Master: the one because he was too unsocial—more like a demoniac than a rational man; the other, because He was too much the reverse, given to animal indulgences, and consorting with the lowest classes of society. But the children of Wisdom recognize and honor her, whether in the austere garb of the Baptist or in the more attractive style of his Master, whether in the Law or in the Gospel, whether in rags or in royalty, for *"the full soul loatheth an honeycomb, but to the hungry soul every bitter thing is sweet"* (Prov. 27:7).

36-50. CHRIST'S FEET WASHED WITH TEARS. **37, 38. a sinner**—one who had led a profligate life. *N.B.—There is no ground whatever for the popular notion that this woman was Mary Magdalene*, nor do we know what her name was. (See on ch. 8:2.)

an alabaster box of ointment—a perfume-vessel, in some cases very costly (John 12:5). "The ointment has here a peculiar interest, as the offering by a penitent of what had been an accessory in her unhallowed work of sin" [ALFORD]. **38. at his feet behind him**—the posture at meals being a reclining one, with the feet out behind. **began to wash . . .**—to "water with a shower." The tears, which were quite *involuntary*, poured down in a flood upon His naked feet, as she bent down to kiss them; and deeming them rather fouled than washed by this, she hastened to wipe them off with the only towel she had, the long tresses of her own hair, "with which slaves were wont to wash their masters' feet" [STIER]. **kissed**—The word signifies "to kiss fondly, to caress," or to "kiss again and again," which vs. 45 shows is meant here. What prompted this? *Much love, springing from a sense of much forgiveness.* So says He who knew her heart (vs. 47). Where she had met with Christ before, or what words of His had brought life to her dead heart and a sense of divine pardon to her guilty soul, we know not. But probably she was of the crowd of "publicans and *sinners*" whom Incarnate Compassion drew so often around Him, and heard from His lips some of those words such as never man spake, "Come unto Me, all ye that labour . . . . No personal interview had up to this time taken place between them; but she could keep her feelings no longer to herself, and having found her way to Him (and entered along with him, vs. 45), they burst forth in this surpassing yet most artless style, as if her whole soul would go out to Him. **39. the Pharisee**—who had formed no definite opinion of our Lord, and invited Him apparently to obtain materials for a judgment. **spake within himself . . .**—"Ha! I have Him now; He plainly knows nothing of the person He allows to touch Him; and so, He can be no prophet." Not so fast, Simon; thou hast not seen through thy Guest yet, but He hath seen through thee.

ADAM CLARKE

authority and importance, with most of the versions, omits these words. As the *Evangelistaria* (the books which contained those portions of the Gospels which were read in the churches) began at this verse, the words were probably at first used by them to introduce the following parable. There is the fullest proof that they never made a part of Luke's text.

32. *They are like unto children.* See on Matt. xi. 16-19. It is probable that our Lord alludes here to some play or game among the Jewish children, no account of which is now on record.

For John came neither eating nor drinking. Leading a very austere and mortified life, and yet you did not receive him. *He hath a devil.* He is a vile hypocrite, influenced by a demon to deceive and destroy the simple.

The Son of man came eating and drinking. That is, went wheresoever He was invited to eat a morsel of bread, and observed no rigid fasts. *They say, Behold a man gluttonous.* Whatever measures the followers of God may take, they will not escape the censure of the world; the best way is not to be concerned at them.

35. *Wisdom is justified.* Probably the *children of wisdom* is a mere Hebraism here for the "products or fruits of wisdom"; hence the Vatican MS., one other, and some versions have "works," instead of "sons," in the parallel place, Matt. xi. 19.

36. *One of the Pharisees.* Called Simon, v. 40. This account is considered by many critics and commentators to be the same with that in Matt. xxvi. 6, etc.; Mark xiv. 3; and John xii. 3. This subject is considered pretty much at large in the notes on Matt. xxvi. 6, etc., to which the reader is requested to refer.

37. *A woman . . . which was a sinner.* Many suppose that this woman had been a notorious public prostitute. My own opinion is that she had been a mere heathen who dwelt in this city (probably Capernaum) who, through the ministry of Christ, had been before this converted to God, and came now to give this public testimony of her gratitude to her gracious Deliverer from the darkness and guilt of sin. I am inclined to think that the original word is used for "heathen" or "Gentile" in several places of the sacred writings. I am fully persuaded that this is its meaning in Matt. ix. 10-11, 13; xi. 19; and xxvi. 45—*The Son of man is betrayed into the hands of sinners,* i.e., is delivered into the hands of the "heathens," viz., the Romans, who alone could put Him to death. I think also it has this meaning in Luke vi. 32-34; xv. 1-2, 7, 10; xix. 7; John ix. 31. I think no other sense can be justly assigned to it in Gal. ii. 15: "We who are Jews by nature, and not sinners of the Gentiles." It is, I think, likely that the grand subject of the self-righteous Pharisee's complaint was her being a "heathen." As those who were touched by such contracted a legal defilment, he could not believe that Christ was a conscientious Observer of the law, seeing He permitted her to touch Him, knowing who she was; or, if He did not know that she was a heathen, it was a proof that He was no prophet, v. 39, and consequently had not the discernment of spirits which prophets were supposed to possess. Many suppose this person to be the same as Mary Magdalene, but of this there is no solid proof.

38. *Stood at his feet behind him.* In taking their meals the Eastern people reclined on one side; the loins and knees being bent to make the more room, the feet of each person were turned outwards behind him. This is the meaning of standing behind at His feet. *Began to wash his feet with tears.* She began to water His feet—to

MATTHEW HENRY

and censorious as themselves.

IV. Christ's justification of the woman in what she did to him, and of himself in admitting it. Christ knew what the Pharisee spoke *within himself*, and made answer to it: *Simon, I have something to say unto thee, v.* 40. Simon is willing to give him the hearing: *He saith, Master, say on.* Now Christ, in his answer to the Pharisee, reasons thus:—It is true this woman has been a sinner: he knows it; but she is a *pardoned* sinner, which supposes her to be a *penitent* sinner. What she did to him was an expression of her *great love* to her Saviour. If she was pardoned, who had been *so great a sinner*, it might reasonably be expected that she should love her Saviour more than others, and if this was the fruit of her love, and flowing from a sense of the pardon of her sins, it became him to accept of it, and it ill became the Pharisee to be offended at it.

1. He by a parable forces Simon to acknowledge that the greater sinner this woman had been the greater love she ought to show to Jesus Christ when her *sins* were *pardoned, v.* 41–43. A man had *two debtors* that were both insolvent, but one of them owed him *ten times* more than the other. He very freely *forgave them both*, and did not take the advantage of the law against them. Now they were both sensible of the great kindness they had received; but *which of them will love him most?* Certainly, saith the Pharisee, he to *whom he forgave most*. Hence learn the duty between debtor and creditor.

(1) The *debtor*, if he have *anything to pay*, ought to make satisfaction to his *creditor*.

(2) If God in his providence have disabled the debtor to pay his debt, the creditor ought not to be severe with him, but *freely to forgive him*.

(3) The debtor that has found his creditors merciful ought to be very grateful to them; and ought to love them. Some insolvent debtors, instead of being *grateful*, are *spiteful*, to their creditors that lose by them, and cannot give them a good word. But this parable speaks of God (or rather of the Lord Jesus himself, for he it is that forgives) and sinners are the debtors: and so we may learn here, [1] That *sin is a debt*, and *sinners are debtors* to God Almighty. As creatures, we owe a debt, a debt of obedience. We have not paid our rent; nay, we have wasted our Lord's goods, and so we become debtors. [2] That some are deeper in debt to God, by reason of sin, than others are: *One owed five hundred pence and the other fifty*. The Pharisee was the less debtor, yet he a debtor too, which was more than he thought himself. This woman was the *greater debtor*. Some sinners are in themselves greater debtors than others. [3] That, whether our debt be more or less, it is *more* than we are able to pay: *They had nothing to pay*, nothing at all to make a composition with. No righteousness of our own will pay it, no, not our repentance and obedience for the future; for it is what we are already bound to. [4] That the God of heaven is *ready* to forgive, *frankly* to *forgive*, poor sinners. If we repent, and believe in Christ, our iniquity shall not be laid to our charge. God has proclaimed his name gracious and merciful, and ready to forgive sin. [5] That those who have their sins *pardoned* are obliged to *love him* that pardoned them; and the more is forgiven them, the more they should love him. The *greater sinners* any have been before their conversion, the *greater saints* they should be after. When a *persecuting Saul* became a preaching Paul he *laboured more abundantly*.

2. He applies this parable to the different temper and conduct of the Pharisee and the sinner. Christ seems rea ly to allow that he was one *forgiven*, though to him *less was forgiven*. He did indeed show some love to Christ, but nothing to what this poor woman showed. "Observe," saith Christ to him, "she is one that has much forgiven her, and therefore, she should love much more than thou dost, and so it appears. *Seest thou this woman?* (*v.* 44). Consider how much kinder a friend she is to me than thou art; should I then accept thy kindness, and refuse hers? Thou didst not so much as order a basin of water to be brought, to wash my feet in, but she has done much more: *she has washed my feet with tears*, and has *wiped them with the hairs of her head*, in token of her great love to me. Thou didst not so much as kiss my cheek, but *this woman has not ceased to kiss my feet* (*v.* 45). Thou didst not provide me a little common oil, as usual, to anoint my head with; but she has bestowed a box of precious *ointment* upon *my feet* (*v.* 46)." The reason why some people blame the pains and expense of zealous Christians, in religion, is because they are not willing themselves to come up to it, but resolve to rest in a *cheap* and *easy* religion.

3. He silenced the Pharisee's cavil: *I say unto thee*, Simon, *her sins, which are many, are forgiven, v.* 47. He owns that she had been guilty of *many sins*:

JAMIESON, FAUSSET, BROWN

40-43. Like Nathan with David, our Lord conceals His home-thrust under the veil of a parable, and makes His host himself pronounce upon the case. The two debtors are the woman and Simon; the criminality of the one was *ten times* that of the other (in the proportion of "500" to "50"); but both being equally insolvent, both are with equal frankness forgiven; and Simon is made to own that the greatest debtor to forgiving mercy will cling to her Divine Benefactor with the deepest gratitude. Does our Lord then admit that Simon was a forgiving man? Let us see.

ALEXANDER MACLAREN:

When you begin to talk about the guilt of actions in God's sight, you have to go far below the mere surface. If we could see the infinite complexity of motives—aggravations on the one side and excuses on the other—which go to the doing of a single deed, we should not be so quick to pronounce that the publican and the harlot are worse than the Pharisee. It is quite possible that an action which passes muster in regard to the morality of the world may, if regard be had (which God only can exercise) to the motive for which it is done, be as bad as, if not worse than, the lust and the animalism, drunkenness and debauchery, crime and murder, which the vulgar scales of the world consider to be the heavier. If you once begin to try to measure guilt, you will have to pass under the surface appearance, and will find that many a white and dazzling act has a very rotten inside, and that many a very corrupt and foul one does not come from so corrupt a source as at first sight might seem to be its origin. Let us be very modest in our estimate of the varying guilt of actions, and remember that, deep down below all diversities, there lies a fundamental identity in which there is no difference, that all of us respectable people that never broke a law of the nation, and scarcely ever a law of propriety, in our lives, and the outcasts, if there are any here now, the drunkards, the sensualists, all of us stand in this respect in the same class. We are all debtors, for we have "all sinned and come short of the glory of God." A viper an inch long and the thickness of whipcord has a sting and poison in it, and is a viper. And if the question is whether a man has got smallpox or not, one spot is as good evidence as if he was spotted all over. So, remember, he who owes five hundred and he who owes the tenth part of it, which is fifty, are both debtors.

—*Expositions of Holy Scripture*

44-47. I entered . . . no water—a compliment to guests. Was this "much love?" Was it *any*? **45. no kiss** —of salutation. How much love was here? *Any at all?* **46. with oil . . . not anoint**—even common *olive oil* in contrast with the woman's "ointment" or *aromatic balsam*. What evidence was thus afforded of any feeling which forgiveness prompts? Our Lord speaks this with delicate politeness, as if *hurt* at these inattentions of His host, which though not *invariably* shown to guests, were the customary marks of studied respect and regard. The inference is plain—*only one of the debtors was really forgiven*, though in the first instance, to give room for the play of withheld feelings, the forgiveness of both is supposed in the parable. **47. Her sins which are many**—"Those many sins of hers," our Lord, who admitted how much more she owed than the Pharisee, now proclaims in naked terms the forgiveness of her guilt. **for**—not *because*, as if love were the cause of forgiveness, but "inasmuch as," or "in proof of which." The latter clause of the verse, and the whole structure of the parable, plainly show this to be the meaning. **little forgiven . . . loveth little**—delicately ironical intimation of *no love* and *no forgiveness* in the present case. **48. said unto her . . .**—an unsought assurance, usually springing up unexpected in the midst of active duty and warm affections, while

ADAM CLARKE

let a shower of tears fall on them. As the Jews wore nothing like our shoes (theirs being a mere sole, bound about the foot and ankle with thongs), their feet being so much exposed had frequent need of washing, and this they ordinarily did before taking their meals. *Kissed his feet.* With affectionate tenderness, or "kissed them again and again." See on Matt. xxvi. 49. The kiss was used in ancient times as the emblem of love, religious reverence, subjection, and supplication. It has the meaning of supplication, in the way of adoration, accompanied with subjection. See 1 Kings xix. 18, "Every mouth which hath not kissed him [Baal]"; and Job xxxi. 27, "My mouth hath [not] kissed my hand"—I have paid no sort of adoration to false gods; and Ps. ii. 12, "Kiss the Son, lest he be angry"—close in with Him, embrace affectionately, the offers of mercy made unto you through Christ Jesus, "lest he [the Lord] be angry [with you], and ye perish"—which commandment this woman seems to have obeyed, in both the literal and the spiritual sense. Kissing the feet was practiced also among the heathens to express subjection of spirit and earnest supplication. Kissing the feet is a further proof that this person had been educated a heathen. This was no part of a Jew's practice.

41. *A certain creditor*. It is plain that in this parable our Lord means, by the *creditor*, God; and, by the *two debtors*, Simon and the woman who was present. Simon, who had the light of the law, and who in consequence of his profession as a Pharisee was obliged to abstain from outward iniquity, might be considered as the debtor who owed only *fifty* pence, or *denarii*. The woman, whom I have supposed to be a heathen, not having these advantages, having no rule to regulate her actions, and no curb on her evil propensities, may be considered as the debtor who owed *five hundred pence*, or *denarii*. And when both were compared, Simon's debt to God might be considered, in reference to hers, as *fifty* to *five hundred*. However we find, notwithstanding this great disparity, both were insolvent. Simon, the religious Pharisee, could no more pay his *fifty* to God than this poor heathen her *five hundred;* and if both be not freely forgiven by the divine mercy, both must finally perish. Having *nothing to pay, he* kindly *forgave them both*.

42. *Which of them will love him most?* Which is under the greater obligation and should love him most?

43. *He to whom he forgave most*. By this acknowledgment he was, unknowingly to himself, prepared to receive our Lord's reproof.

44. *Thou gavest me no water*. In this respect Simon was sadly deficient in civil respect, whether this proceeded from forgetfulness or contempt. The custom of giving water to wash the guest's feet was very ancient. See instances in Gen. xviii. 4; xxiv. 32; Judg. xix. 21; 1 Sam. xxv. 41.

46. *My head with oil thou didst not anoint*. Anointing the head with oil was as common among the Jews as washing the face with water is among us. See Ruth iii. 3; 2 Sam. xii. 20; xiv. 2; 2 Kings iv. 2; and Ps. xxiii. 5, where the author alludes to the Jewish manner of receiving and entertaining a guest.

47. *For she loved much*. Or, "Therefore she loved much." It appears to have been a consciousness of God's forgiving love that brought her at this time to the Pharisee's house. In the common translation her forgiveness is represented to be the consequence of her loving much, which is causing the tree to produce the root, and not the root the tree. I have considered *hoti* here as having the sense of *dioti*, "there-

MATTHEW HENRY

"But they are *forgiven* her, *for she loved much.*" It should be rendered, *therefore she loved much*; for it is plain that her loving much was not the *cause*, but the *effect*, of her pardon. *We love God* because *he first loved us;* he did not forgive us because we first loved him. "But to *whom little is forgiven*, as is to thee, *the same loveth little*, as thou dost." Instead of grudging greater sinners the mercy they find with Christ we should be stirred up by their example to examine ourselves whether we be indeed forgiven, and do love Christ.

4. He silenced her fears. Christ said unto her, *Thy sins are forgiven, v.* 48. She was dismissed with this word from Christ, *Thy sins are forgiven!* and what an effectual prevention would this be of her return to sin again! Though there were those present who quarrelled with Christ, in their own minds, for presuming to forgive sin, and to pronounce sinners absolved (*v.* 49), yet he *stood to what he had said.* He would now show that he had *pleasure in forgiving sin*; he loves to speak pardon and peace to penitents: *He said to the woman, Thy faith hath saved thee, v.* 50. All these expressions of sorrow for sin, and love to Christ, were the effects and products of faith. As faith of all graces doth most honour God, so Christ doth of all graces put most honour upon faith.

CHAPTER 8

Verses 1–3

I. *What* Christ *made* the *constant business* of his *life*—it was *preaching*; in that work he was indefatigable, and went about doing good (*v.* 1). 1. *Where* he preached: *He went about.* He was an *itinerant* preacher, did not confine himself to one place, but diffused the beams of his light. He went about *through every city*, that none might plead ignorance. Hereby he set an example to his disciples; they must traverse the nations of the earth, as he did the cities of Israel. Nor did he confine himself to the *cities*, but went into the *villages*, among the plain country-people. 2. What he preached: *He showed the glad tidings of the kingdom of God.* Tidings of the *kingdom of God* are *glad tidings*, and those Jesus Christ came to bring. It was *glad tidings* to the world that there was hope of its being *reformed* and *reconciled.* 3. Who were his attendants: *The twelve were with him* to learn from him what and how to preach hereafter.

II. *Whence* he *had* the *necessary supports* of life: He lived upon the kindness of his friends. There were *certain women* that *ministered to him of their substance, v.* 2, 3. Some of them are named; but there were *many others.*

1. They were such, for the most part, as were the monuments of his power and mercy; they had been *healed by him of evil spirits and infirmities.* We are bound in *interest* to attend him, that we may be ready to apply ourselves to him for help in case of a relapse; and we are bound in *gratitude* to serve him and his gospel, who hath *saved* us, and saved us *by it.*

2. One of them was Mary Magdalene, out of whom had been *cast seven devils.* Some think that she was one that had been *very wicked*, and then we may suppose her to be the woman that *was a sinner* mentioned just before, *ch.* vii. 37. Upon her repentance and reformation she found mercy, and became a zealous disciple of Christ. The worse any have been before their conversion the more they should study to do for Christ after. This Mary Magdalene was attending on Christ's cross and his sepulchre.

3. Another of them was *Joanna the wife of Chuza, Herod's steward.* Her *husband*, though preferred in Herod's court, had received the gospel, and was very willing that his wife should be both a hearer of Christ and a contributor to him.

4. There were many of them that *ministered to Christ of their substance.* Though he was rich, yet for our sakes *he became poor*, and lived upon alms. Christ would rather be beholden to his known friends for a maintenance for himself and his disciples than be burdensome to strangers. It is the duty of those who are taught in the word to *communicate to them who teach them in all good things.*

Verses 4–21

The former paragraph began with an account of Christ's industry in *preaching* (*v.* 1); this begins with an account of the people's industry in hearing, *v.* 4. *He went into every city*, to preach; but there were those here that came *to him out of every city*, would not stay till he came to *them*, nor think that they had enough when he left *them*, but *met him* when he was coming towards them, and *followed him* when he was going from them.

Much people were gathered together, abundance of

JAMIESON, FAUSSET, BROWN

often it flies from those who mope and are paralyzed for want of it. **49, 50. they that sat . . . Who is this . . . ?**—No wonder they were startled to hear One who was reclining at the same couch, and partaking of the same hospitalities with themselves, assume the awful prerogative of "even forgiving sins." But so far from receding from this claim, or softening it down, our Lord only repeats it, with two precious additions: one, announcing what was the one secret of the "forgiveness" she had experienced, and which carried "salvation" in its bosom; the other, a glorious dismissal of her in that "peace" which she had already felt, but is now assured she has His full warrant to enjoy! This wonderful scene teaches two very weighty truths: (1) *Though there be degrees of guilt, insolvency, or inability to wipe out the dishonor done to God, is common to all sinners.* (2) *As Christ is the Great Creditor to whom all debt, whether great or small, contracted by sinners is owing, so to Him belongs the prerogative of forgiving it.* This latter truth is brought out in the structure and application of the present parable as it is nowhere else. Either then Jesus was a blaspheming deceiver, or He is God manifest in the flesh.

CHAPTER 8

Vss. 1-3. A Galilean Circuit, with the Twelve and Certain Ministering Women. (In Luke only.) **went**—travelled, made a progress. **throughout every city and village**—through town and village. **preaching . . .**—the Prince of itinerant preachers scattering far and wide the seed of the Kingdom. **2. certain women . . . healed . . .**—on whom He had the double claim of having brought healing to their bodies and new life to their souls. Drawn to Him by an attraction more than magnetic, they accompany Him on this tour as His *almoners*—ministering unto Him of their substance. Blessed Saviour! It melts us to see Thee living upon the love of Thy ransomed people. That they bring Thee their poor offerings we wonder not. Thou hast sown unto them spiritual things, and they think it, as well they might, a small thing that Thou shouldst reap their material things (I Cor. 9: 11). But dost Thou take it at their hand, and subsist upon it? "Oh, the depth of the riches"—of this poverty of His! **Mary Magdalene**—i.e., probably, of *Magdala* (on which see Matt. 15:39). **went**—rather "had gone." **seven devils**—(Mark 16:9). It is a great wrong to this honored woman to identify her with the once profligate woman of ch. 7:37, and to call all such penitents *Magdalenes.* The mistake has arisen from confounding unhappy demoniacal possession with the conscious entertainment of diabolic impurity, or supposing the one to have been afflicted as a punishment for the other —for which there is not the least scriptural ground. **3. Joanna, wife of Chuza, Herod's steward**—If the steward of such a godless, cruel, and licentious wretch as Herod Antipas (see on Mark 6:14, etc.) differed greatly from himself, his post would be no easy or enviable one. That he was a disciple of Christ is very improbable, though he might be favorably disposed towards Him. But what we know not of him, and may fear he lacked, we are sure his wife possessed. Healed either of "evil spirits" or of some one of the "infirmities" here referred to—the ordinary diseases of humanity—she joins in the Saviour's train of grateful, clinging followers. Of "Susanna," next mentioned, we know nothing but the name, and that here only. But her services on this memorable occasion have immortalized her name. "Wheresoever this gospel shall be preached throughout the whole world, this also that she hath done," in ministering to the Lord of her substance on His Galilean tour, "shall be spoken of as a memorial of her" (Mark 14:9). **many others**—i.e., many other *healed women.* What a train! and all ministering unto Him of their substance, and He allowing them to do it and subsisting upon it! "He who was the support of the spiritual life of His people disdained not to be supported by them in the body. He was not ashamed to penetrate so far into the depths of poverty as to live upon the alms of love. He only fed others miraculously; for Himself, He lived upon the love of His people. He gave all things to men, His brethren, and received all things from them, enjoying thereby the pure blessing of love: which is then only perfect when it is at the same time both giving and receiving. Who could invent such things as these? *"It was necessary to live in this*

ADAM CLARKE

fore"; because, to make this sentence suit with the foregoing parable, vv. 42-43, and with what immediately follows here, *but to whom little is forgiven, the same loveth little*, we must suppose her love was the *effect* of her being pardoned, not the *cause* of it. *Hoti* seems to have the sense of "therefore" in Matt. xiii. 13; John viii. 44; 1 Cor. x. 17; and in the Septuagint, in Deut. xxxiii. 52; Isa. xlix. 19; Hos. ix. 15; and Eccles. v. 6. Both these particles are often interchanged in the New Testament.

48. *Thy sins are forgiven.* He gave her the fullest assurance of what He had said before to Simon (v. 47). While the Pharisee murmured, the poor penitent rejoiced.

50. *Thy faith hath saved thee. Thy faith* hath been the instrument of receiving the salvation which is promised to those who repent. *Go in peace.* Though peace of conscience be the inseparable consequence of the pardon of sin, yet here it seems to be used as a valediction or farewell; as if He had said, May goodness and mercy continue to follow you! In this sense it is certainly used in Judg. xviii. 6; 1 Sam. i. 17; xx. 42; xxix. 7; 2 Sam. xv. 9; Jas. ii. 16.

CHAPTER 8

1. *Throughout every city and village.* That is, of Galilee.

2. *Out of whom went seven devils.* Who had been possessed in a most extraordinary manner; probably a case of inveterate lunacy, brought on by the influence of evil spirits. The number *seven* may here express the superlative degree. Mary Magdalene is commonly thought to have been a prostitute before she came to the knowledge of Christ, and then to have been a remarkable penitent. So historians and painters represent her: but neither from this passage nor from any other of the New Testament can such a supposition be legitimately drawn. I conclude, therefore, that the common opinion is a vile slander on the character of one of the best women mentioned in the gospel of God, and a reproach cast on the character and conduct of Christ and His disciples. From the whole account of Mary Magdalene it is highly probable that she was a person of great respectability in that place; such a person as the wife of Chuza, Herod's steward, could associate with, and a person on whose conduct or character the calumniating Jews could cast no aspersions.

3. *Herod's steward.* Though the original word signifies sometimes the "inspector" or "overseer" of a province, and sometimes a "tutor of children," yet here it seems to signify the "overseer of Herod's domestic affairs," the "steward of his household." *Unto him.* Instead of *unto him*, meaning Christ, many of the best MSS. and versions have *to them*, meaning both our Lord and the twelve apostles; see v. 1. This is unquestionably the true meaning.

MATTHEW HENRY

fish to cast his net among; and he was as ready and willing to *teach* as they were to be *taught*.

I. Necessary and excellent rules and cautions for hearing the word, in the parable of *the sower.* When Christ had put forth this parable, the disciples were *inquisitive* concerning the meaning of it, *v.* 9. They asked him, *What might this parable be?* We should covet earnestly to know the true *in*tent, and full *ex*tent, of the word we hear. They had opportunity of acquainting themselves with the mystery and meaning of his word, which others had not: *Unto you it is given, v.* 10. Happy are we, and for ever indebted to free grace, if the same thing that is a *parable* to others, with which they are only *amused,* is a *plain truth* to us.

Now from the parable itself, and the explication of it, observe,

1. The *heart of man* is as *soil* to the *seed of God's word*; it is capable of receiving it, and bringing forth the fruits of it; but, unless that seed be sown in it, it will bring forth nothing valuable. Our care therefore must be to bring the *seed* and the *soil* together.

2. The *success* of the *seeding* is very much according to the nature and temper of the *soil.* The word of God *is to us,* as *we are, a savour of life unto life,* or *of death unto death.*

3. The devil is a subtle and spiteful enemy. He takes the word out of the hearts of *careless* hearers, *lest they should believe and be saved, v.* 12. This is added here to teach us that we cannot be *saved* unless we *believe.* That therefore the devil does all he can to keep us from *believing,* to make us not believe the word when we read and hear it; or, if we heed it for the present, to make us forget it again, and let it slip (Heb. ii. 1); or, if we remember it, to create prejudices in our minds against it, or *divert* our minds from it to something else; and all is *lest we should believe and be saved.*

4. Where the word of God is heard *carelessly* there is commonly a *contempt* put upon it too. It is added here in the parable that the seed which fell by the wayside was *trodden down, v.* 5.

5. Those on whom the word makes *some* impressions, but they are not *deep* and *durable* ones; as the seed sown upon the rock, where it gains no root, *v.* 13. These *for awhile believe,* their profession promises something, but in *time of temptation they fall away* from their good beginnings.

6. The *pleasures of this life* are as dangerous and mischievous thorns to choke the good seed of the word. This is added here (*v.* 14), which was not in the other evangelists. The delights of sense may ruin the soul, even lawful delights, indulged, and too much delighted in.

7. It is not enough that the fruit be brought forth, but it must be *brought to perfection,* it must be fully ripened. If it be not, it is as if there was no fruit at all brought forth; for that which in Matthew and Mark is said to be *unfruitful* is the same that here is said to *bring forth none to perfection.*

8. The good ground, which brings forth *good fruit,* is an *honest* and *good heart* (*v.* 15); a heart firmly fixed for God and duty, an upright heart, a tender heart, is an honest and good heart, which, having heard the word, *understands* it (so it is in Matthew), *receives* it (so it is in Mark), and *keeps* it (so it is here), as the soil not only *receives,* but keeps, the seed.

9. Where the word is well kept there is fruit brought forth *with patience.* This also is added here; Patience to continue to the end in well-doing.

10. In consideration of all this, we ought to take *heed how we hear* (*v.* 18); take heed of those things that will hinder our profiting by the word we hear; take heed *lest* we hear carelessly and slightly; and take heed after we have heard the word, lest we lose what we have gained.

II. Needful instructions given to those that are appointed to preach the word, and to those also that have heard it. Those that have *received the gift* must *minister the same.* People that have profited by the word must look upon themselves as *lighted candles.* A *candle* must not be *covered with a vessel* nor *put under a bed, v.* 16. Ministers and Christians are to be lights in the world. Their light must shine before men; they must not only *be good,* but *do good.* What is now done *in secret* will shortly be *manifested* and *made known, v.* 17. What is committed to you *in secret* should be made manifest *by you*; for your Master did not give you talents to be buried, but to be traded with. The gifts we have will either be continued to us, or taken from us, according as we do, or do not, make use of them for the glory of God: *Whosoever hath, to him shall be given, v.* 18. He that hath gifts, and does good with them, shall have more; he that *buries his talent* shall lose it. From him that hath not shall be taken away even *that which he hath,* so it is in Mark; that which he *seemeth*

JAMIESON, FAUSSET, BROWN

manner that it might be so recorded" [OLSHAUSEN].

4-18. PARABLE OF THE SOWER. (See on Mark 4:3-9, 14-20.)

Behold, there went out a sower to sow—What means this? **The sower soweth the word**—or, as in Luke (8:11), "Now the parable is this: The seed is *the word of God.*" But who is "the sower"? This is not expressed here because if "the word of God" be the seed, every scatterer of that precious seed must be regarded as a sower. It is true that in the parable of the tares it is said, "He that soweth the good seed is the Son of man," as "He that soweth the tares is the devil" (Matt. 13:37, 38). But these are only the great unseen parties, struggling in this world for the possession of man. Each of these has his agents among men themselves; and Christ's agents in the sowing of the good seed are the *preachers* of the word. Thus, as in all the cases about to be described, the sower is the same, and the seed is the same; while the result is entirely different, the whole difference must lie in the *soils,* which mean the *different states of the human heart.* And so, the great general lesson held forth in this parable of the sower is, that however faithful the preacher, and how pure soever his message, *the effect of the preaching of the word depends upon the state of the hearer's heart.* Now follow the cases.

"When any one heareth the word of the kingdom, and understandeth it not, then cometh the wicked one, and catcheth away that which was sown in his heart." The great truth here taught is, that *hearts all unbroken and hard are no fit soil for saving truth.* They apprehend it not (Matt. 13:19) as God's means of restoring them to Himself; it penetrates not, makes no impression, but lies loosely on the surface of the heart, till the wicked one—afraid of losing a victim by his "believing to salvation" (Luke 8:12) —finds some frivolous subject by whose greater attractions to draw off the attention, and straightway it is gone. Of how many hearers of the word is this the graphic but painful history!

"The pleasures of this life," or "the lusts of other things entering in"—the enjoyments in themselves may be innocent, which worldly prosperity enables one to indulge. These "*choke*" or "*smother*" the word; drawing off so much of one's attention, absorbing so much of one's interest, and using up so much of one's time, that only the dregs of these remain for spiritual things, and a fagged, hurried, and heartless formalism is at length all the religion of such persons.

A heart soft and tender, stirred to its depths on the great things of eternity, and jealously guarded from worldly engrossments, such only is the "honest and good heart" (Luke 8:15), which "keeps," i.e., "retains" the seed of the word, and bears fruit just in proportion as it is such a heart. Such "bring forth fruit with *patience*" (vs. 15), or continuance, "enduring to the end"; in contrast with those in whom the word is "choked" and brings no fruit *to perfection.* The "thirtyfold" is designed to express the *lowest* degree of fruitfulness; the "hundredfold" the *highest*; and the "sixtyfold" the *intermediate* degrees of fruitfulness. As a hundredfold," though not unexampled (Gen. 26:12), is a rare return in the natural husbandry, so the highest degrees of spiritual fruitfulness are too seldom witnessed. The closing words of this introductory parable seem designed to call attention to the *fundamental* and *universal* character of it.

16. No man . . .—(see on Matt. 5:15, of which this is nearly a repetition). **17. For nothing . . .**—(see on ch. 12:2.

18. how ye—in Mark 4: 24, "*what ye* hear." The one implies the other. The precept is very weighty. **seemeth to have**—or

ADAM CLARKE

5. *A sower went out to sow.* See all this parable largely explained on Matt. xiii. 1-23.

When any one heareth the word of the kingdom. Viz., the preaching of the gospel of Christ. *And understandeth it not.* Perhaps more properly, "regardeth it not," does not lay his heart to it. *The wicked one.* He who distresses and torments the soul. Mark, chap. iv. 15, calls him *Satan,* the "adversary" or "opposer," because he resists men in all their purposes of amendment, and to the utmost of his power opposes, in order to frustrate, the influences of divine grace upon the heart. In the parallel place in Luke, viii. 12, he is called *the devil.* It is worthy of remark that the three Evangelists should use each a different appellative of this mortal enemy of mankind; probably to show that the devil, with all his powers and properties, opposes everything that tends to the salvation of the soul. *Catcheth away.* Makes the utmost haste to pick up the good seed, lest it should take root in the heart. A careless, inattentive hearer is compared to the *way side*—his heart is an open road, where evil affections and foolish and hurtful desires continually pass and repass without either notice or restraint.

But he that received the seed into stony places, the same is he. That is, is a fit emblem of that man who, hearing the gospel, is affected with its beauty and excellency, and immediately receiveth it *with joy*—is glad to hear what God has done to make man happy.

Yet hath he not root in himself. His soul is not deeply convinced of its guilt and depravity; the fallow ground is not properly ploughed up, nor the rock broken. *When tribulation or persecution ariseth,* which he did not expect, "he is soon stumbled"—seeks some pretext to abandon both the doctrine and the followers of Christ.

He also that received seed among the thorns. In land ploughed, but not properly cleared and weeded. *Is he*—represents that person *that heareth the word; and the care,* rather "the anxiety" the whole system of anxious, carking cares. *The deceitfulness of riches.* Which promise peace and pleasure, but can never give them. *Choke the word.* Or "together choke the word," meaning either that these grow up together with the word, overtop, and choke it, or that these united together, viz., carking, worldly cares, with the delusive hopes and promises of riches, cause the man to abandon the great concerns of his soul and seek, in their place, what he shall eat, drink, and wherewithal he shall be clothed. Dreadful stupidity of man, thus to barter spiritual for temporal good—a heavenly inheritance for an earthly portion! The seed of the Kingdom can never produce much fruit in any heart till the thorns and thistles of vicious affections and impure desires be plucked up by the roots and burned.

15. *With patience.* Rather, "with perseverance." The Greek word which our translators render *patience* properly signifies here, and in Rom. ii. 7, "perseverance." The *good ground,* because it is *good,* strong and vigorous, continues to bear; bad or poor ground cannot produce a good crop, and besides it is very soon exhausted. The persons called the *good ground* in the text are filled with the power and influence of God and therefore continue to bring forth fruit; i.e., they persevere in righteousness. From this we may learn that the "perseverance of the saints," as it is termed, necessarily implies that they continue to bring forth fruit to the glory of God. Those who are not fruitful are not in a state of perseverance.

16. *Lighted a candle.* This is a repetition of a part of our Lord's Sermon on the Mount. See the notes on Matt. v. 15; x. 26; and on Mark iv. 21-22.

17. *For nothing is secret.* Whatever I teach you in private, you shall teach publicly; and you shall illustrate and explain every parable now delivered to the people.

18. *Even that which he seemeth to have.*

MATTHEW HENRY

to have, so it is in Luke. The grace that is lost was but *seeming* grace, was never *true*. Men do but *seem* to have what they do not *use*.

III. Great encouragement given to those that prove themselves faithful *hearers of the word*, by being *doers of the work*, in a particular instance of Christ's respect to his disciples, in preferring them even before his nearest relations (*v.* 19–21). Observe what crowding there was after Christ. There was no coming near for the throng of people that attended him. Some of his nearest kindred were least solicitous to hear him preach. Instead of getting *within*, desiring to *hear him*, they stood *without*, desiring to *see him*. Jesus Christ would rather be busy at his work than conversing with his friends. Christ is pleased to own those as his nearest and dearest relations that *hear the word of God and do it*.

Verses 22–39

We have here two illustrious proofs of the power of our Lord Jesus—his power over the *winds*, and his power over the *devils*. See Mark iv. and v.

I. His power over the winds.

1. Christ ordered his disciples to put to sea: *He went into a ship with his disciples*, *v.* 22. If Christ sends his disciples, he goes *with them*. And those may safely and boldly venture anywhere that have Christ accompanying them. *He said, Let us go over unto the other side*.

2. Those that put to sea in a calm, yea, and at Christ's word, must yet *prepare for a storm*. There *came down a storm of wind on the lake* (*v.* 23), and presently their ship was so tossed that it was filled with water, and they were in jeopardy of their lives.

3. Christ was *asleep* in the storm, *v.* 23. Some bodily refreshment he must have. The disciples of Christ may really have his gracious presence with them at sea, and in a storm, and yet he may seem as if he were *asleep*; he may not immediately appear for their relief. Thus he will try their faith and patience and make their deliverance the more welcome when it comes at last.

4. A complaint to Christ of our danger is enough to engage him to awake, and appear for us, *v.* 24. They cried, *Master, master, we perish!* The way to have our fears silenced is to bring them to Christ. Those that in sincerity call upon him as *their Master*, may be sure that he will not let them *perish*.

5. Christ's business is to *lay storms*, as it is Satan's business to *raise* them. He delights to do it: for he came to *proclaim peace on earth*. He *rebuked the wind and the raging of the water*, and immediately *they ceased* (*v.* 24); all of a sudden, *there was a great calm*.

6. When our dangers are over, it becomes us to take to ourselves the shame of our own fears and to give to Christ the glory of his power. Christ gives them a rebuke for their inordinate fear: *Where is your faith? v.* 25. Many that have *true faith* have it to seek when they have occasion to use it. A little thing disheartens them; and *where is their faith* then? They give him the glory of his power: *They, being afraid, wondered*. Those that had feared the storm feared him that had stilled it, and *said one to another, What manner of man is this!*

II. His power over *the devil*. Presently after the winds were stilled they were brought to their desired haven, and *arrived at the country of the Gadarenes*, and there went ashore (*v.* 26, 27).

1. These *malignant* spirits are very *numerous*. They that had taken possession of this one man called themselves *Legion* (*v.* 30), because *many devils were entered into him*: he had *had devils a long time*, *v.* 27. They either were, or at least would be thought to be, a *legion*.

2. They have an *inveterate enmity* to man. This man in whom the devils had got possession *wore no clothes, neither abode in any house* (*v.* 27). They forced this man to *abide in the tombs*, to make him so much the more a terror to himself and to all about him.

3. They are very *strong, fierce*, and unruly, and hate and scorn to be restrained: *He was kept bound with chains and in fetters*, but he *broke the bands*, *v.* 29. Those that are *ungovernable* by any other thereby show that they are under Satan's government. *He was driven of the devil*. Those that are under Christ's government are *sweetly led* with the bands of love; those that are under the devil's government are *furiously driven*.

4. They are much enraged against our Lord Jesus, and have a great dread and horror of him: *When the man saw Jesus*, he *roared out* and *fell down before him*, and owned him to be *the Son of God most high*, that was infinitely above him and too hard for him; but protested against having any league or confederacy with him: *What have I to do with thee?* The devils have neither inclination to do service to Christ nor

JAMIESON, FAUSSET, BROWN

"thinketh that he hath" (*Margin*). The "having" of Matthew 13:12 (on which see), and this "thinking he hath," are not different. Hanging loosely on him, and not appropriated, it *is* and *is not* his.

19-21. HIS MOTHER AND BRETHREN DESIRE TO SPEAK WITH HIM. (See on Mark 12:46-50.)

22-25. JESUS, CROSSING THE LAKE, STILLS THE STORM. (See on Matt. 8:23-27, and Mark 4:35-41.) **23. filled**—lit., "were getting filled," i.e., those who sailed; meaning that their ship was so.

Let us pass over unto the other side—to the east side of the lake, to grapple with a desperate case of possession, and set the captive free, and to give the Gadarenes an opportunity of hearing the message of salvation, amid the wonder which that marvellous cure was fitted to awaken and the awe which the subsequent events could not but strike into them.

Master—or "Teacher." In Luke (8:24) this is doubled—in token of their life-and-death earnestness—"Master, Master." **carest thou not that we perish?**—Unbelief and fear made them sadly forget their place, to speak so. Luke has it, "Lord, save us, we perish." When those accustomed to fish upon that deep thus spake, the danger must have been imminent. They say nothing of what would become of *Him*, if they perished; nor think, whether, if He could not perish, it was likely He would let this happen to them; but they hardly knew what they said. **And he arose, and rebuked the wind**—"and the raging of the water" (Luke 8:24).

And the wind ceased, and there was a great calm—The sudden hushing of the wind would not at once have calmed the sea, whose commotion would have settled only after a considerable time. But the word of command was given to both elements at once.

how is it that ye have no faith?—next to none, or none in present exercise. In Luke it is, "Why are ye fearful, O ye of little faith?" *Faith* they had, for they applied to Christ for relief: but *little*, for they were afraid, though Christ was in the ship. Faith dispels fear, but only in proportion to its strength. **And they feared exceedingly**—were struck with deep awe.

26-39. DEMONIAC OF GADARA HEALED. (See on Matt. 8:28-34; and Mark 5:1-20.)

there met him a man with an unclean spirit—"which had devils [demons] long time" (Luke 8:27). In Matthew (8:28), "there met him two men possessed with devils." Though there be no discrepancy between these two statements—more than between two witnesses, one of whom testifies to something done by one person, while the other affirms that there were two—it is difficult to see how the principal details here given could apply to more than one case. **Who had his dwelling among the tombs**—Luke says, "He ware no clothes, neither abode in any house." These tombs were hewn out of the rocky caves of the locality, and served for shelters and lurking-places (Luke 8:26).

Because that he had been often bound with fetters and chains . . .—Luke says (8:29) that "oftentimes it [the unclean spirit] had caught him"; and after mentioning how they had vainly tried to bind him with chains and fetters, because, "he brake the bands," he adds, "and was driven of the devil [demon] into the wilderness." The dark tyrant-power by which he was held clothed him with superhuman strength and made him scorn restraint. Matthew (8:28) says he was "exceeding fierce, so that no man might pass by that way." He was the terror of the whole locality.

What have I to do with thee, Jesus, Son of the most high God? I adjure thee by God, that thou torment me not—or, as in Matthew

ADAM CLARKE

Or rather, "even what he hath." *What he seemeth to have* seems to me to contradict itself. Let us examine this subject a little. (1) To *seem* to have a thing is only to have it in appearance and not in reality; but what is possessed in appearance only can only be taken away in appearance; therefore on the one side there is no gain, and on the other side no loss. On this ground, the text speaks just nothing. (2) It is evident that *what he seemeth to have*, here, is equivalent to *what he hath*, in the parallel places, Mark iv. 25; Matt. xiii. 12; xxv. 29; and in Luke xix. 26. (3) It is evident also that these persons had something which might be taken away from them. (4) The word *dokein* is often an expletive; so Xenophon in *Hellen*, vi. "Because he seemed to be" (i.e., was) "their father's friend." So in his *Oecon*, "Among the cities that seemed to be" (actually were) "at war." So *Athenaeus*, lib. vi, ch. 4, "They who seemed to be" (who really were) "the most opulent, drank out of brazen cups." (5) It often *strengthens* the sense, and is thus used by the very best Greek writers.

19. *His mother and his brethren*. See the notes on Matt. xii. 46, etc., and on Mark iii. 31, etc.

22. *Let us go over*. See on Matt. viii. 24, etc., and Mark iv. 36-41.

23. *There came down a storm of wind . . . and they . . . were in jeopardy*. This is a parallel passage to that in Jon. i. 4, "There was a mighty tempest in the sea, so that the ship was like to be broken." The word *jeopardy*, an inexpressive French term, is properly the exclamation of a disappointed gamester, *Jeu perdu!* "The game is lost!"

25. *Where is your faith?* You have a power to believe, and yet do not exercise it! You have "little faith" (Matt. viii. 26) because you do not use the grace which I have already given you. Many are looking for *more* faith without using that which they have.

26. *The country of the Gadarenes*. Or, according to several MSS., *Gerasenes* or *Gergasenes*. See on Matt. viii. 28 and Mark v. 1.

27. *A certain man*. See the case of this demoniac considered at large on the parallel places, Matt. viii. 28-34; Mark v. 1-20.

What have we to do with thee? The literal translation is, "What is it to us and to Thee?" which perhaps might be understood to imply their disclaiming any design to interfere with the work of Christ, and that He should not therefore meddle with them; for it appears they

MATTHEW HENRY

expectation to receive benefit by him. But they dreaded his power and wrath: *I beseech thee, torment me not.* They do not say, *I beseech thee, save me,* but only, *Torment me not.* See whose language *they* speak that have only a dread of hell but no desire of heaven as a place of holiness and love.

5. They are perfectly *at the command,* and under *the power,* of our Lord Jesus; and they knew it, for they *besought him that he would not command them to go into the deep.* O what a comfort is this to the Lord's people, that all the powers of darkness are under the check and control of the Lord Jesus! He can send them to *their own place,* when he pleaseth.

6. They delight in *doing mischief.* When they found there was no remedy, but they must quit their hold of this poor man, they begged they might have leave to take possession of a *herd of swine, v.* 32. When he could not destroy the man, he would destroy the swine. If he could not hurt them in their bodies, he would hurt them in their goods, which sometimes prove a great temptation to men to draw them from Christ, as here. Christ *suffered them to enter into the swine.* They entered into the *swine;* and no sooner had they entered into them than the herd ran violently *down a steep place into the lake,* and were *drowned.*

7. When the devil's power is broken in any soul that soul recovers itself: *The man out of whom the devils were departed sat at the feet of Jesus, v.* 35. While he was under the devil's power he was ready to *fly in the face* of Jesus; but now he *sits at his feet.* If God has possession of us, he preserves to us the government and enjoyment of ourselves; but, if Satan has possession of us, he robs us of both. We are never more our own than when we are Christ's.

Let us now see what was the effect of this miracle.

(1) What effect it had upon the people of that country: *The swineherds went and told it* both *in city and country* (*v.* 34). They told *by what means he that was possessed of the devils was healed* (*v.* 36), that it was by sending the devils into the swine, as if Christ could not have delivered the man out of their hands, but by delivering the swine into them. *The people came out, to see what was done,* and *they were afraid* (*v.* 35); they were *taken with great fear* (*v.* 37). They thought more of the destruction of the swine than of the deliverance of their poor afflicted neighbour, and therefore *the whole multitude besought Christ to depart from them.* None need to be afraid of Christ that are willing to forsake their sins and give up themselves to him. But Christ took them at their word: *He went up into the ship, and returned back again.* Those lose their Saviour, and their hopes in him, that love their swine better.

(2) What effect it had upon the poor man. He *desired* Christ's company as much as others *dreaded* it: he besought Christ that *he might be with him,* as others were *that have been healed by him of evil spirits and infirmities* (*v.* 2). He was loth to stay among those rude and brutish Gadarenes that desired Christ to depart from them. But Christ sent him home, to publish among those that knew him the great things God had done for him, that so he might be a blessing to his country, as he had been a burden to it. We must sometimes deny ourselves the satisfaction even of spiritual benefits and comforts, to gain an opportunity of being serviceable to the souls of others.

Verses 40-56

Christ was driven away by the *Gadarenes.* But when he returned to the *Galileans,* they *gladly received him, wished* and *waited* for his return, and *welcomed* him with all their hearts, *v.* 40. He returned, and found work to do in the place whence he came, fresh work. The needy you have always with you.

We have here two miracles interwoven, as they were in Matthew and Mark.

I. A *public address* made to Christ by *a ruler of the synagogue,* whose name was *Jairus,* on the behalf of a little daughter of his, that was very ill. Jairus, though a *ruler, fell down at Jesus's feet.* He *besought him* that he would *come into his house;* not having the *faith* of the centurion, who desired Christ only to *speak the* healing *word* at a distance. But Christ complied with his request; *he went along* with him. Strong faith shall be applauded, and yet weak faith shall not be rejected. When Christ was going *the people thronged him.* Let us not complain of a crowd, and a throng, and a hurry, as long as we are in the way of our duty, and *doing good;* but otherwise it is what every wise man will keep himself out of as much as he can.

II. Here is a *secret application* made to Christ by a woman ill of a *bloody issue,* which had been the consumption of her body and the consumption of her purse too; for *she had spent all her living upon physicians,* and was never the better, *v.* 43. The nature of

JAMIESON, FAUSSET, BROWN

8:29, "Art Thou come to torment us before the time?" (See on ch. 1:24.) Behold the *tormentor* anticipating, dreading, and entreating exemption from *torment!* In Christ they discern their destined Tormentor; the time, they know, is fixed, and they feel as if it were come already! (Jas. 2:19.) **For he said unto him**—i.e., before the unclean spirit cried out. **Come out of the man, unclean spirit!** —Ordinarily, obedience to a command of this nature was immediate. But here, a certain delay is permitted, the more signally to manifest the power of Christ and accomplish His purposes.

And the unclean spirits went out—of the man —**and entered into the swine: and the herd ran violently**—rushed—**down a steep place**—down the hanging cliff—**into the sea (they were about two thousand)**—The number of them is given by this graphic Evangelist alone. **and were choked in the sea**—"perished in the waters" (Matt. 8:32).

And they come to Jesus—Matthew (8:34) says, "Behold, the whole city came out to meet Jesus." **and see him that was possessed with the devil**—the demonized person—**and had the legion, sitting**—"at the feet of Jesus," adds Luke (8:35); in contrast with his former *wild* and *wandering* habits. **and clothed**—As our Evangelist had not told us that he "ware no clothes," the meaning of this statement could only have been conjectured but for "the beloved physician" (Luke 8:27), who supplies the missing piece of information here. This is a striking case of what are called *Undesigned Coincidences* amongst the different Evangelists; one of them taking a thing for granted, as familiarly known at the time, but which we should never have known but for one or more of the others, and without the knowledge of which some of their statements would be unintelligible. The clothing which the poor man would feel the want of the moment his consciousness returned to him, was doubtless supplied to him by some of the Twelve. **and in his right mind**—but now, oh, in what a lofty sense! (Cf. an analogous, though a different kind of case, Dan. 4:34-37.) **and they were afraid**—Had this been *awe* only, it had been natural enough; but other feelings, alas! of a darker kind, soon showed themselves. **And they that saw it told them how it befell to him that was possessed with the devil** ('the demonized person') **and also concerning the swine**—Thus had they the double testimony of the herdsmen and their own senses. **And they began to pray him to depart out of their coasts**— Was it the owners only of the valuable property now lost to them that did this? Alas, no! For Luke (8:37) says, "Then the whole multitude of the country of the Gadarenes round about besought Him to depart from them; for they were taken with great fear." The evil spirits had thus, alas! their object. Irritated, the people could not suffer His presence; yet awe-struck, they dared not order Him off: so they entreat Him to withdraw, and—He takes them at their word.

40-56. Jairus' Daughter Raised, and Issue of Blood Healed. (See on Matthew 9:18-26; and Mark 5:21-43.) **40. gladly received him, for . . . all waiting for him**—The abundant teaching of that day (in Matt. 13: and see Mark 4:36), had only whetted the people's appetite; and disappointed, as would seem, that He had left them in the evening to cross the lake, they remain hanging about the beach, having got a hint, probably through some of His disciples, that He would be back the same evening. Perhaps they witnessed at a distance the sudden calming of the tempest. Here at least they are, watching for His return, and welcoming Him to the shore. The tide of His popularity was now fast rising.

ADAM CLARKE

exceedingly dreaded His power. *What have we to do with thee?* is a Jewish phrase which often occurs in the Old Testament, signifying an abrupt refusal of some request, or a wish not to be troubled with the company or importunity of others. *Art thou come hither to torment us before the time?* From this it appears that a greater degree of punishment awaited these demons than they at that time endured; and that they knew there was a time determined by the divine Judge when they should be sent unto greater torments.

33. *Then went the devils out of the man, and entered into the swine.* Some critics and commentators would have us to understand all this of the man himself, who, they say, was a most outrageous maniac; and that, being permitted by our Lord, he ran after the swine, and drove them all down a precipice into the sea! This is solemn trifling indeed; or, at least, trifling with solemn things. It is impossible to read over the account, as given here by Luke, and admit this mode of explanation.

34. *They fled, and went and told it. They . . . went* is omitted by almost every MS. of repute and by the best of the ancient versions.

The whole city came out. Probably with the intention to destroy Jesus for having destroyed their swine; but, having seen Him, they were awed by His presence, and only besought Him to depart from their borders. Many rather choose to lose Jesus Christ than those temporal goods by which they gratify their passions at the expense of their souls. They love even their swine better than their salvation.

40. *Gladly received him.* This is the proper import of the word; therefore our translators needed not to have put *gladly* in italics, as though it were not expressed in the text.

41. *A man named Jairus.* See these two miracles—the raising of Jairus' daughter and the cure of the afflicted woman—considered and explained at large on Matt. ix. 18-26 and Mark v. 22-43.

42. *The people thronged him.* Almost "suffocated Him"—so great was the throng about Him.

43. *Spent all her living upon physicians.* See the note on Mark v. 26.

MATTHEW HENRY

her disease was such that she did not care to make a public complaint of it and therefore she took this opportunity of coming to Christ *in a crowd.* Her *faith* was very *strong*; for she doubted not but that by the *touch* of the *hem of his garment* she should derive from him healing virtue, looking upon him to be such a full fountain of mercies that she should *steal* a cure and he not *miss it.* Thus many a poor soul is *healed,* and *helped,* and *saved,* by Christ, that is *lost in a crowd.* The woman found an immediate change for the better in herself, and that her disease was cured, *v.* 44. Believers have comfortable communion with Christ *incognito.*

III. Here is a *discovery* of this secret cure.

1. Christ takes notice that there is a cure wrought: *Virtue is gone out of me, v.* 46. Those that have been healed by virtue derived from Christ must *own* it, for he *knows it.* It was his delight that *virtue* was gone out of him to do any good, and he did not grudge it to the meanest; they were as welcome to it as to the light and heat of the sun.

2. The poor patient owns her case, and the benefit she had received: *When she saw that she was not hid, she came, and fell down before him, v.* 47. *She came trembling,* and yet *her faith saved her, v.* 48. There may be *trembling* where yet there is saving faith. She *declared before all the people for what cause she had touched him,* because she believed that a touch would cure her, and it did so.

3. The great physician confirms her cure, and sends her away with the comfort of it: *Be of good comfort: thy faith hath made thee whole, v.* 48. It was obtained *surreptitiously* and *underhand,* but it was secured and seconded *aboveboard.* She *is* healed, and she *shall be* healed.

IV. Here is an *encouragement* to Jairus not to distrust the power of Christ, *though his daughter was now dead,* and they that brought him the tidings advised him not to give *the Master any further trouble* about her: *Fear not,* saith Christ, *only believe.* Our *faith in Christ* should be bold and daring. Though the child is dead, yet *believe,* and all shall be well.

V. The *preparatives* for the raising of her to life again. 1. The *choice* Christ made of witnesses that should see the miracle wrought. A *crowd* followed him, but perhaps they were rude and noisy; however, it was not fit to let such a multitude come into a gentleman's house, especially now that the family was all in sorrow; *therefore* he sent them back. He took none with him but Peter, and James, and John, designing these three, with the parents, to be the only spectators of the miracle. 2. The *check* he gave to the mourners. *They all wept, and bewailed her.* But Christ bids them *not weep*; *for she is not dead, but sleepeth.* He means, as to her peculiar case, that she was not dead for good and all; it would be to her friends as if she had been but a few hours asleep. But it is applicable to all that die in the Lord; therefore we should not sorrow for them as those that have *no hope,* because death is but a *sleep.* This was a comfortable word which Christ said to these mourners, yet they wickedly ridiculed it, and *laughed him to scorn* for it. They *knew that she was dead,* they were certain of it, and therefore nothing less than a *divine power* could restore her to life. But he *put them all out, v.* 54. They were unworthy to be the witnesses of this work of wonder.

VI. Her return to life: *He took her by the hand* (as we do by one that we would awake out of sleep, and help up), and he called, saying, *Maid, arise, v.* 55. Here that is expressed which was only implied in the other evangelists, that *her spirit came again.* Where the soul of this child was in this interval we are not told; it was in the hand of the *Father of spirits.* When *her spirit came again* she arose, and made it appear that she was alive by her motion, as she did also by her appetite; for Christ *commanded to give her meat.* In the last verse, we need not wonder to find *her parents astonished.*

JAMIESON, FAUSSET, BROWN

45. Who touched me?—"Askest Thou, Lord, who touched Thee? Rather ask who touched Thee *not* in such a throng." **46. Somebody hath touched**—yes, the multitude *"thronged* and *pressed* Him—"they *jostled against* Him," but all *involuntarily;* they were merely *carried along; but one, one only*—"Somebody TOUCHED" HIM, with the conscious, voluntary, dependent touch of faith, reaching forth its hands expressly to have contact with Him. This and this only Jesus acknowledges and seeks out. Even so, as the Church Father AUGUSTINE long ago said, *multitudes still come similarly close to Christ in the means of grace, but all to no purpose, being only sucked into the crowd.* The voluntary, living contact of faith is that electric conductor which alone draws virtue out of Him. **47. declared . . . before all**—This, though a great trial to the shrinking modesty of the believing woman, was just what Christ wanted in dragging her forth, her public testimony to the facts of her case—both her disease, with her abortive efforts at a cure, and the instantaneous and perfect relief which her touch of the Great Healer had brought her.

ALEXANDER MACLAREN:

Notice that our Lord never forbids weeping unless He takes away its cause. "Weep not" is another of the futile forms of words with which men try to encourage and comfort one another. There is nothing more cruel than to forbid tears to the sad heart. Jesus Christ never did that except when He was able to bring that which took away occasion for weeping. He lets grief have its way. He means us to run rivers of waters down our cheeks when He sends us sorrows. We shall never get the blessing of these till we have felt the bitterness of them. We shall never profit by them if we stoically choke back the manifestations of our grief, and think that it is submissive to be dumb. Let sorrow have way. Tears purge the heart from which their streams come. But Jesus Christ says to us all, "Weep not," because He comes to us all with that which, if I may so say, puts a rainbow into the teardrops, and makes it possible that the great paradox should be fulfilled in our hearts, "As sorrowful yet always rejoicing." Weep not; or if you weep, let the tears have thankfulness as well as grief in them. It is a difficult commandment, but it is possible when His lips tell us not to weep, and we have obeyed the central exhortation, "Only believe."

—*Expositions of Holy Scripture*

give her meat—(see on Mark 5:43).

ADAM CLARKE

Came in the press behind. She had formed her resolution in faith; she executes it, notwithstanding her weakness, with courage; and now she finds it crowned with success.

Thou seest the multitude thronging thee. Many touch Jesus who are not healed by Him; the reason is, they do it not by faith, through a sense of their wants, and a conviction of His ability and willingness to save them. Faith conveys the virtue of Christ into the soul, and spiritual health is the immediate consequence of this received virtue.

46. *I perceive that virtue. Dynamin,* divine or miraculous power.

Why troublest thou the Master? These people seem to have had no other notion of our Lord than that of an eminent physician, who might be useful while there was life, but afterwards could do nothing.

Jesus . . . saith. These words were spoken by our Lord to the afflicted father, immediately on his hearing of the death of his child, to prevent that distress which he otherwise must have felt on finding that the case was now, humanly speaking, hopeless.

The father and the mother. Prudence required that they should be present, and be witnesses of the miracle. *And them that were with him.* That is, Peter, James, and John, v. 37. It is remarkable that our Lord gave a particular preference to these three disciples, beyond all the rest, on three very important occasions. They were present (1) at the Transfiguration, (2) at the raising of Jairus' daughter, and (3) at His agony in the Garden of Gethsemane.

54. *He put them all out.* That is, the pipers and those who made a noise, weeping and lamenting. See Matt. ix. 23; Mark v. 38.

55. *And he commanded to give her meat.* Though she was raised to life by a miracle, she was not to be preserved by a miracle. Nature is God's great instrument, and He delights to work by it; nor will He do anything by His sovereign power, in the way of miracle, that can be effected by His ordinary providence.

MATTHEW HENRY

CHAPTER 9

Verses 1–9

I. The method Christ took to spread his gospel. He had *himself* travelled about; but he could be only in one place at a time, and therefore now he *sent* his twelve disciples abroad. Let them disperse themselves, some one way and some another, to *preach the kingdom of God.* For the confirming of their doctrine he empowered them to work miracles (*v.* 1, 2): He *gave them authority over all devils,* to dispossess them, and cast them out. He authorized and appointed them likewise to *cure diseases,* and to *heal the sick,* which would not only convince people's judgments, but gain their affections. This was their commission.

JAMIESON, FAUSSET, BROWN

CHAPTER 9

Vss. 1-6. MISSION OF THE TWELVE APOSTLES. (See on Matt. 10:1-15.) **1. power and authority**—He both *qualified* and *authorized* them.

ADAM CLARKE

CHAPTER 9

1. *Power and authority.* The words properly mean here the power to work miracles, and that authority by which the whole demoniac system was to be subjected to them. The reader will please to observe: (1) Luke mentions both *devils* (demons) and *diseases;* therefore he was either mistaken or demons and diseases are not the same. (2) The treatment of these two was not the same; the demons were to be cast out, the diseases to be healed. See Matt. x. 1.

2. *To preach the kingdom of God.* For an explication of this phrase, see on Matt. iii. 2.

MATTHEW HENRY

1. What Christ directed them to do, in prosecution of this commission. (1) They must not be solicitous to recommend themselves to people's esteem by their outward appearance. They must *go as they were*, and not change their clothes, or so much as put on a pair of new shoes. (2) They must depend upon Providence, and the kindness of their friends. They must not take with them *either bread or money*. Christ would not have his disciples *shy* of receiving the kindnesses of their friends, but rather to *expect* them. (3) They must not change their lodgings, as suspecting that those who entertained them were *weary* of them; "*Whatsoever house ye enter into there abide* (*v.* 4), that people may know where to find you; *there abide* till you *depart* out of that city; stay with those you are used to." (4) They must put on authority, and speak *warning* to those who *refused* them as well as comfort to those that *received* them, *v.* 5. "If there be any place that will not entertain you, bind them over to the judgment of God for it; *shake off the dust of your feet* for a *testimony against them*."

2. What they did, in prosecution of this commission (*v.* 6): *They departed* from their Master's presence; they *went through the towns, preaching the gospel, and healing everywhere*. Their work was the same with their Master's, doing good both to souls and bodies.

II. We have here Herod's perplexity and vexation at this. The communicating of Christ's power to those who were sent forth in his name was an *amazing* and *convincing* proof of his being the Messiah. That he could not only work miracles *himself*, but empower others to work miracles too, this spread his fame more than anything. *They had been with Jesus*, Acts iv. 13. When the country sees such as these *healing the sick* in the name of Jesus it gives it an alarm.

1. The *various speculations* it *raised* among the *people*, who, though they thought not *rightly*, yet could not but think *honourably*, of our Lord Jesus, and that he was one come from the other world; that either John Baptist or *one of the old prophets* was *risen again*; or that Elias *had appeared*, *v.* 7, 8.

2. The *great perplexity* it *created* in the mind of Herod: *When he had heard of all that was done* by Christ, he was ready to conclude with them that *John was risen from the dead*. "What shall I do now?" saith Herod. "John *have I beheaded, but who is this*? Is he carrying on John's work, or is he come to avenge John's death?" Those who oppose God will find themselves more and more *embarrassed*. He *desired to see him*; and why did he not go and see him? He desired to see him, but we do not find that ever he did, till he saw him at his bar.

Verses 10–17

I. The account which the twelve gave their Master of the success of their ministry. *When they returned, they told him all that they had done*.

II. Their *retirement*, for a little *breathing*: He *took them, and went aside privately into a desert place*. He that hath appointed our man-servant and maid-servant to rest would have his servants to rest too. Those in the most public stations, must sometimes go aside privately, both for the repose of their bodies, and for the furnishing of their minds by meditation for further public work.

III. The *resort* of the people to him, and the kind *reception* he gave them. They *followed* him, though it was into a *desert place*. He *welcomed* them, *v.* 11. Pious zeal may excuse a little rudeness; it did with Christ, and should with us. Though they came unseasonably, yet Christ gave them what they came for. He *spoke unto them of the kingdom of God*. He *healed them that had need of healing*. Christ hath still a power over bodily diseases, and heals his people that *need healing*. Sometimes he sees that we need the *sickness* for the good of our souls, more than the *healing* for the ease of our bodies. Death is the servant, to heal the saints of *all diseases*.

IV. The plentiful provision Christ made for the multitude that attended him. With *five loaves* of bread, and *two fishes*, he fed *five thousand men*. This narrative we had twice before, and shall meet with it again; it is the only miracle of our Saviour's that is recorded by all the four evangelists. Let us only observe out of it, 1. Those who diligently attend upon Christ in the way of duty, and therein deny or expose themselves, are taken under his particular care. He will not see those that fear him, and serve him faithfully, want any good thing. 2. Our Lord Jesus was of a free and generous spirit. His disciples said, *Send them away, that they may get victuals;* but Christ said, "No, *give ye them to eat;* let what we have go as far as it will reach, and they are welcome to it." Thus he has taught both ministers and Christians to *use hospitality without grudging*. Those

JAMIESON, FAUSSET, BROWN

Nor scrip for your journey—the bag used by travelers for holding provisions. **neither two coats**—or tunics, worn next the skin. The meaning is, Take no change of dress, no additional articles. **neither shoes**—i.e., change of them. **nor yet staves**—The received text here has "a staff," but our version follows another reading, "staves," which is found in the received text of Luke (9:3). The true reading, however, evidently is "a staff"—meaning, that they were not to procure even that much expressly for this missionary journey, but to go with what they had.

And whosoever shall not receive you, nor hear your words, when ye depart out of that house or city—for possibly a whole town might not furnish one "worthy." **shake off the dust of your feet**—"for a testimony against them," as Mark and Luke add. By this symbolical action they vividly shook themselves from all *connection* with such, and all *responsibility* for the guilt of rejecting them and their message. Such symbolical actions were common in ancient times, even among others than the Jews, as strikingly appears in Pilate (ch. 27:24). And even to this day it prevails in the East.

7-9. HEROD TROUBLED AT WHAT HE HEARS OF CHRIST, DESIRES TO SEE HIM. (See on Mark 6:14-30.)

7. **perplexed**—at a loss, embarrassed. **said of some, that John was risen**—Among many opinions, this was the one which Herod himself adopted, for the reason, no doubt, mentioned on Mark 6:14.

9. **desired to see him**—but did not, till as a prisoner He was sent to him by Pilate just before His death, as we learn from ch. 23:8.

10-17. ON THE RETURN OF THE TWELVE, JESUS RETIRES WITH THEM TO BETHSAIDA, AND THERE MIRACULOUSLY FEEDS FIVE THOUSAND. (See on Mark 6:31-44.)

And they departed into a desert place by ship privately—"over the Sea of Galilee, which is the Sea of Tiberias," says John (6:1), the only one of the Evangelists who so fully describes it; the others having written when their readers were supposed to know something of it, while the last wrote for those at a greater distance of time and place. This "desert place" is more definitely described by Luke (9:10) as "belonging to the city called Bethsaida." This must not be confounded with the town so called on the western side of the lake (see on Matt. 11:21). This town lay on its northeastern side, near where the Jordan empties itself into it: in Gaulonitis, out of the dominions of Herod Antipas, and within the dominions of Philip the Tetrarch (Luke 3:1), who raised it from a village to a city, and called it *Julias*, in honor of Julia, the daughter of Augustus [JOSEPHUS, *Antiquities*, 18:2, 1].

And when the day was now far spent—"began to wear away" or "decline," says Luke (9:12). Matthew (14:15) says, "when it was evening"; and yet he mentions a later evening of the same day (vs. 23). This earlier evening began at three P.M.; the latter began at sunset. **Send them away, that they may go into the country round about, and into the villages, and buy themselves bread: for they have nothing to eat**—John tells us (6:5, 6) that "Jesus said to Philip, Whence shall we buy bread, that these may eat? (And this He said to prove him: for He Himself knew what He would do.)"

Give ye them to eat—doubtless said to prepare them for what was to follow.

ADAM CLARKE

3. *Take nothing.* See on Mark vi. 7-8. *Neither money.* See on Matt. x. 9.

Provide neither gold, nor silver, nor brass in your purses. "In your girdles." It is supposed that the people of the East carry their money in a fold of their girdles. This is scarcely correct; they carry it in a purse in the bosom, under the girdles. This I have often observed. "Have no money in your purse" is a command, obedience to which was secured by the narrow circumstances of most of the primitive genuine preachers of the gospel.

7. *Herod the tetrarch.* See on Matt. xiv. 1. *By him.* This is omitted by some MSS. and versions. It is probable that Luke might have written, "Herod, hearing of all the things that were done"; but Matthew says particularly that it was the fame of Jesus of which he heard, chap. xiv. 1.

He was perplexed. "He was greatly perplexed." It is a metaphor taken from a traveller who in his journey meets with several paths, only one of which leads to the place whither he would go; and, not knowing which to take, he is distressed with perplexity and doubt.

10. *Told him all.* "Related distinctly."

11. *The people . . . followed him.* Observe here five grand effects of divine grace. (1) The people are drawn to *follow* Him. (2) He kindly *receives* them. (3) He *instructs* them in the things of God. (4) He *heals* all their diseases. (5) He *feeds* their bodies and their souls.

12. *Send the multitude away.* See this miracle explained at large on the parallel places, Matt. xiv. 15-21; Mark vi. 36-44.

***Send the multitude away, that they may go . . . and buy.* The disciples of Christ are solicitous for the people's temporal as well as spiritual welfare; and he is not worthy to be called a minister of Christ who does not endeavor to promote both to the uttermost of his power.**

MATTHEW HENRY

that have but a little, let them do what they can with that little, and that is the way to make it more. 3. Jesus Christ has not only physic, but food. He not only *heals them that need healing*, but feeds them too that need feeding. Christ has provided not only to save the soul from perishing by its diseases, but to nourish the soul unto life eternal. 4. All the gifts of Christ are to be received in a regular orderly manner: *Make them sit down by fifties in a company*, *v.* 14. 5. When we are receiving our creature-comforts, we must *look up to heaven.* Christ did so, to teach us to do so. We receive them from God, we depend upon God's blessing upon them to make them serviceable to us, and desire that blessing. 6. The blessing of Christ will make a little go a great way. 7. Those whom Christ *feeds* he *fills*; as there is in him enough for *all*, so there is enough for *each*. Here were *fragments taken up*, to assure us that in our Father's house there is *bread enough, and to spare.* We are not straitened or stinted, in him.

Verses 18-27

One circumstance of this discourse is taken notice of here which we had not in the other evangelists—that Christ was *alone praying*, and his *disciples with him*, when he entered into this discourse, *v.* 18. He found some time to be *alone* in private, for converse with himself, with his Father, and with his disciples. When Christ was alone he was *praying*. It is good for us to improve our solitude for devotion, that, *when we are alone*, we may *not be alone*, but may have *the Father with us.* When Christ was alone, praying, his *disciples were with him*, to join with him in his prayer. Christ *prayed* with them before he *examined* them. Those we give instructions to we should put up prayers for and with. He discourses with them,

I. Concerning himself; and enquires,

1. What *the people* said of him: *Who say the people that I am?* They tell him what conjectures concerning him they had heard in their converse with the common people. Ministers would know better how to suit their instructions, reproofs, and counsels, to the case of ordinary people, if they did but converse more frequently and familiarly with them. The more conversant the physician is with his patient, the better he knows what to do for him. Some said that he was John Baptist, who was beheaded but the other day; others Elias, or *one of the old prophets*; anything but what he was.

2. What *they* said of him. Saith Peter, "We know that thou art *the Christ of God*, the *Anointed* of God." Now one would have expected that Christ should have charged his disciples to publish it to everyone they met with; but no, he *strictly charged them to tell no man that thing* as yet. After his resurrection, which completed the proof of it, Peter made the temple ring of it, that *God had made this same Jesus both Lord and Christ* (Acts ii. 36); but as yet the evidence was not ready to be summed up, and therefore it must be concealed.

II. Concerning his own *sufferings* and *death.* Now that his disciples were well established in the belief of his being the Christ, and able to bear it, he speaks of them expressly, *v.* 22. They must not yet preach that he was *the Christ*, because the wonders that would attend his death and resurrection would be the most convincing proof of his being *the Christ of God.*

III. Concerning their sufferings for him.

1. We must *accustom* ourselves to all instances of *self-denial* and *patience*, *v.* 23. We must not indulge our ease and appetite, for then it will be hard to bear toil, and weariness, and want, for Christ. We frequently meet with crosses in the way of duty; and, though we must not pull them upon our own heads, yet, when they are laid for us, we must *take them up*, carry them after Christ, and make the best of them.

2. We must *prefer the salvation and happiness of our souls* before any *secular concern* whatsoever. Reckon upon it, (1) That he who to preserve his liberty or estate, nay, or to save his life, denies Christ and his truths, will be, not only not a *saver*, but an unspeakable *loser*, in the issue. *He that will save his life upon these terms will lose it*, will lose that which is of infinitely more value, his precious soul. (2) We must firmly believe also that, if we lose our life for cleaving to Christ, we shall *save* it to our unspeakable advantage. We shall have it again a new and an eternal life. (3) That the gain of all the world, if we should forsake Christ, would be so far from countervailing the eternal loss and ruin of the soul that it would bear no manner of proportion to it, *v.* 25. If we could be supposed to gain all the wealth, honour, and pleasure, in the world, by denying Christ, yet when, by *so doing*, we *lose ourselves* to all eternity, and are *cast away* at last, what good will our worldly gain do us? In Matthew and Mark the dreadful

JAMIESON, FAUSSET, BROWN

And they did all eat, and were filled—All the four Evangelists mention this: and John (6:11) adds, "and likewise of the fishes, as much as they would"—to show that vast as was the multitude, and scanty the provisions, the meal to each and all of them was a plentiful one. "When they were filled, He said unto His disciples, Gather up the fragments that remain, that nothing be lost" (John 6:12). This was designed to bring out the whole extent of the miracle. **And they took up twelve baskets full of the fragments, and of the fishes**—"Therefore (says John 6:13), they gathered them together, and filled twelve baskets with the fragments of the five barley loaves, which remained over and above unto them that had eaten." The article here rendered "baskets" in all the four narratives was part of the luggage taken by Jews on a journey—to carry, it is said, both their provisions and hay to sleep on, that they might not have to depend on Gentiles, and so run the risk of ceremonial pollution.

18-27. PETER'S CONFESSION OF CHRIST—OUR LORD'S FIRST EXPLICIT ANNOUNCEMENT OF HIS APPROACHING DEATH, AND WARNINGS ARISING OUT OF IT. (See on Matt. 16:13-28; and Mark 8:34.)

Whom—or more grammatically, "Who"—**do men say that I the Son of man am?**—(or, "that the Son of man is"—the recent editors omitting here the *me* of Mark and Luke; though the evidence seems pretty nearly balanced)—i.e., 'What are the views generally entertained of Me, the Son of man, after going up and down among them so long?' He had now closed the first great stage of His ministry, and was just entering on the last dark one. His spirit, burdened, sought relief in retirement, not only from the multitude, but even for a season from the Twelve. He retreated into "the secret place of the Most High," pouring out His soul "in supplications and prayers, with strong crying and tears" (Heb. 5:7). On rejoining His disciples, and as they were pursuing their quiet journey, He asked them this question.

And Simon Peter answered and said, Thou art the Christ, the Son of the living God—He does not say, "Scribes and Pharisees, rulers and people, are all perplexed; and shall we, unlettered fishermen, presume to decide?" But feeling the light of his Master's glory shining in his soul, he breaks forth—not in a tame, prosaic acknowledgment, "*I believe that Thou art* . . ."—but in the language of adoration—such as one uses in worship, "THOU ART THE CHRIST, THE SON OF THE LIVING GOD!" He first owns Him the promised *Messiah* (see on ch. 1:16); then he rises higher, echoing the voice from heaven—"This is My beloved Son, in whom I am well pleased"; and in the important addition—"Son of the LIVING GOD"—he recognizes the essential and eternal life of God as in this His Son—though doubtless without that distinct perception afterwards vouchsafed.

From that time forth began Jesus to show unto his disciples—i.e., with an *explicitness and frequency* He had never observed before—**how that he must go unto Jerusalem and suffer many things** "and be rejected," (Matthew and Mark)—**of the elders and chief priests and scribes**—not as before, merely by not receiving Him, but by formal deeds. **and be killed, and be raised again the third day**—Mark (8:32) adds, that "He spake that saying openly"—"explicitly," or "without disguise."

24. will save—"is minded to save," bent on saving. The pith of this maxim depends—as often in such weighty sayings (for example, "Let the *dead* bury the *dead*," Matt. 8:22)—on the double sense attached to the word "life," a lower and a higher, the natural and the spiritual, temporal and eternal. An entire sacrifice of the lower, or a willingness to make it, is indispensable to the preservation of the higher life; and he who cannot bring himself to surrender the one for the sake of the other shall eventually lose both.

ADAM CLARKE

We have here but five loaves, and two fishes. When we are deeply conscious of our own necessities, we shall be led to depend on Jesus with a firmer faith. God often permits His servants to be brought low, that they may have repeated opportunities of proving the kindness and mercy of their gracious Lord and Master.

And took the five loaves. This was the act of the father of a family among the Jews—his business it was to take the bread into his hands, and render thanks to God, before any of the family was permitted to taste of it. *Looking up to heaven.* To teach us to acknowledge God as the Supreme Good, and Fountain of all excellence. *He blessed.* The word "God" should, I think, be rather inserted here than the word "them," because it does not appear that it was the loaves which Christ blessed, but that God who had provided them; and this indeed was the Jewish custom, not to bless the food, but the God who gave it. However, there are others who believe the loaves are meant, and that He blessed them in order to multiply them. *And brake.* The Jews made their bread broad and thin like cakes, and to divide such, being very brittle, there was no need of a knife.

18. *Whom say the people?* "The common people," i.e., the mass of people.

Whom do men say? He asked His disciples this question, not because He was ignorant what the people thought and spoke of Him, but to have the opportunity, in getting an express declaration of their faith from themselves, to confirm and strengthen them in it; but see on Luke ix. 20. *Some . . . John the Baptist.* By this and other passages we learn that the Pharisaic doctrine of the transmigration of souls was pretty general; for it was upon this ground that they believed that the soul of the Baptist, or of Elijah, Jeremiah, or some of the prophets, had come to a new life in the body of Jesus.

Thou art the Christ, the Son of the living God. Every word here is emphatic—a most concise, and yet comprehensive, confession of faith. *The Christ*, or "Messiah," points out His divinity, and shows His office; *the Son* designates His person. On this account it is that both are joined together so frequently in the new covenant. *Of the living God*—literally, of God the Living One. *Living.* A character applied to the Supreme Being, not only to distinguish Him from the dead idols of paganism, but also to point Him out as the Source of life, present, spiritual, and eternal. Probably there is an allusion here to the great name *Yehovah*, which properly signifies being or existence.

23. *If any man will come after me.* See on Matt. xvi. 24 and on Mark viii. 34, where the nature of proselytism among the Jews is explained.

24. *Will save his life.* See on Matt. xvi. 24, etc.

25. *Lose himself.* That is, his "life" or "soul." See the parallel places, Matt. xvi. 25; Mark viii. 35, and especially the note on the former. *Or be cast away.* "Or receive [spiritual] damage." I have added the word "spiritual" here, which I conceive to be necessarily implied. Because if a man received only temporal damage in some respect or other, yet gaining the whole world must amply compensate him. But if he should receive spiritual damage—hurt to his soul in the smallest degree—the possession of the universe could not indemnify him.

MATTHEW HENRY

issue is a man's *losing his own soul*, here it is *losing himself*, which plainly intimates that *our souls* are *ourselves. The soul is the man;* and it is well or ill with us according as it is well or ill with our souls. The body cannot be happy if the soul be miserable in the other world; but the soul may be happy though the body be greatly afflicted and oppressed in this world.

3. We must therefore *never be ashamed* of Christ and his gospel, *v.* 26. *For whosoever shall be ashamed of me and of my words, of him shall the Son of man be ashamed*, and justly. He can expect no other than that in the great day, when his case calls for Christ's appearance on his behalf, Christ will be ashamed to own such a cowardly, worldly, sneaking spirit, and will say, "He is none of mine; he belongs not to me." As Christ had a state of *humiliation* and of *exaltation*, so likewise has his cause. They, and they only, that are willing to suffer with it when it suffers, shall reign with it when it reigns. Observe here, How Christ, to support himself and his followers under present disgraces, speaks *magnificently* of the lustre of his second coming. He shall come *in his own glory*. This was not mentioned in Matthew and Mark. He shall come *in his Father's glory*. He shall come in *the glory of the holy angels*. What a figure will the blessed Jesus make in that day! Did we believe it, we should never be ashamed of him or his words now.

Lastly, To encourage them in suffering for him, he assures them that *the kingdom of God* would now *shortly be set up*, *v.* 27. "The kingdom of God shall come in its power in the present age, while some here present are alive." They *saw the kingdom of God* when the Spirit was poured out, when the gospel was preached to all the world and nations were brought to Christ by it.

Verses 28–36

We have here the narrative of Christ's transfiguration which was designed for a specimen of that glory of his of which he had lately been speaking, and, consequently, an encouragement to his disciples to suffer for him, and never to be ashamed of him. We had this account before in Matthew and Mark.

I. Here is one circumstance of the narrative that seems to differ from the other two evangelists. They said that it was *six days* after the foregoing sayings; Luke says that it was *about eight days after*, that is, it was that day sevennight, six whole days intervening, and it was the eighth day.

II. Here are divers circumstances added and explained.

1. We are *here* told that Christ had this honour put upon him when he was *praying*: He *went up into a mountain to pray* (*v.* 28), and *as he prayed* he was *transfigured*. When Christ *humbled* himself to pray, he was thus *exalted*. Christ himself must *sue out* the favours that were purposed for him, and promised to him. And thus he intended to put an *honour* upon the duty of prayer, and to *recommend* it to us. It is a transfiguring, transforming duty. By prayer we fetch in the wisdom, grace, and joy, which *make the face to shine*.

2. Luke does not use the word *transfigured* (which Matthew and Mark used), but makes use of a phrase equivalent, *the fashion of his countenance was another thing from what it had been*; and *his raiment* was *white and glistening*; it was *bright like lightning* (a word used only here), so that he seemed to be arrayed all with light, to *cover himself with light as with a garment*.

3. It was said in Matthew and Mark that Moses and Elias *appeared to them*; here it is said that they *appeared in glory*. He being in glory, they *appeared with him in glory*.

4. We are here told what was the subject of the discourse between Christ and the two great prophets of the Old Testament: *They spoke of his decease, which he should accomplish at Jerusalem. His departure;* that is, *his death*. (1) The death of Christ is here called his *exit*, his *going out*, his *leaving the world*. The death of the saints is their *exodus*, their departure out of the Egypt of this world, their release out of a *house of bondage*. (2) This departure of his he *must accomplish*; for thus it was determined in the counsel of God, and could not be altered. (3) He must accomplish it at Jerusalem. (4) Moses and Elias spoke of this, to intimate that the *sufferings* of Christ, and his *entrance into his glory*, were what Moses and *the prophets* had *spoken of*; see Luke xxiv. 26, 27. (5) Our Lord Jesus, even in his transfiguration, was willing to enter into a discourse concerning his death and sufferings. In our greatest glories on earth, let us remember that here *we have no continuing city*.

JAMIESON, FAUSSET, BROWN

26. ashamed of me, and of my words—The sense of *shame* is one of the strongest in our nature, one of the social affections founded on our love of *reputation*, which causes instinctive aversion to what is fitted to lower it, and was given us as a preservative from all that is properly *shameful*. When one is, in this sense of it, *lost to shame*, he is nearly past hope (Zech. 3:5; Jer. 6:15; 3:3). But when Christ and "His words"—Christianity, especially in its more spiritual and uncompromising features—are unpopular, the same instinctive desire to *stand well with others* begets the temptation to be ashamed of Him, which only the 'expulsive power' of a higher affection can effectually counteract. **Son of man be ashamed when he cometh . . .**—He will render to that man his own treatment; He will disown him before the most august of all assemblies, and put him to "*shame* and everlasting *contempt*" (Dan. 12:2). "Oh shame, to be put to shame before God, Christ, and angels!" [BENGEL]. **27. not taste of death till they see the kingdom of God**—"see it come with power" (Mark 9:1); or see "the Son of man coming in His kingdom" (Matt. 16:28). The reference, beyond doubt, is to the firm establishment and victorious progress, in the lifetime of some then present, of that new Kingdom of Christ, which was destined to work the greatest of all changes on this earth, and be the grand pledge of His final coming in glory.

28-36. JESUS TRANSFIGURED. **28. an eight days after these sayings**—including the day on which this was spoken and that of the Transfiguration. Matthew and Mark say "after six days," *excluding* these two days. As the "sayings" so definitely connected with the transfiguration scene are those announcing His *death*—at which Peter and all the Twelve were so startled and scandalized—so this scene was designed to show to the eyes as well as the heart how *glorious* that death was in the view of Heaven. **Peter, James, and John**—partners before in secular business; now sole witnesses of the resurrection of Jairus' daughter (Mark 5:37), the transfiguration, and the agony in the garden (Mark 14:33). **a mountain**—not *Tabor*, according to long tradition, with which the facts ill comport, but some one near the lake. **to pray**—for the period He had now reached was a critical and anxious one. (See on Matt. 16:13.) But who can adequately translate those "strong cryings and tears?" Methinks, as I steal by His side, I hear from Him these plaintive sounds, Lord, who hath believed Our report? I am come unto Mine own and Mine own receive Me not; I am become a stranger unto My brethren, an alien to My mother's children: Consider Mine enemies, for they are many, and they hate Me with cruel hatred. Arise, O Lord, let not man prevail. Thou that dwellest between the cherubim, shine forth: Show Me a token for good: Father, glorify Thy name." **29. as he prayed, the fashion . . .**—Before He cried He was answered, and while He was yet speaking He was heard. Blessed interruption to prayer this! Thanks to God, transfiguring manifestations are not quite strangers here. Ofttimes in the deepest depths, out of groanings which cannot be uttered, God's dear children are suddenly transported to a kind of heaven upon earth, and their soul is made as the chariots of Amminadab. Their prayers fetch down such light, strength, holy gladness, as make their face to shine, putting a kind of celestial radiance upon it (II Corinthians 3:18, with Exod. 34:29-35). **raiment white . . .**—Matthew says, "His face did shine as the sun" (17:2), and Mark says "His raiment became shining, exceeding white as snow, so as no fuller on earth can white them" (9:2). The light, then, it would seem, shone not *upon* Him *from without*, but *out of* Him *from within;* He was all irradiated, was in one blaze of celestial glory. What a contrast to that "visage more marred than men, and His form than the sons of men!" (Isa. 52:14). **30, 31. there talked with him two men . . . Moses and Elias . . . appeared in glory**—"Who would have believed these were not *angels* had not their *human* names been subjoined?" [BENGEL]. (Cf. Acts 1:10; Mark 16:5.) Moses represented "the law," Elijah "the prophets," and both together the whole testimony of the Old Testament Scriptures, and the Old Testament saints, to Christ; now not borne in a *book*, but by *living men*, not to a *coming*, but a *come* Messiah, *visibly*, for they "appeared," and *audibly*, for they "spake." **spake**—"were speaking." **of his decease**—"departure"; beautiful euphemism (softened term) for *death*, which Peter, who witnessed the scene, uses to express his own expected death, and the use of which single term seems to have recalled the whole by a sudden rush of recollection,

ADAM CLARKE

26. *Ashamed of me.* See on Mark viii. 38.

Whosoever therefore shall be ashamed of me. Our Lord hints here at one of the principal reasons of the incredulity of the Jews—they saw nothing in the person of Jesus Christ which corresponded to the pompous notions which they had formed of the Messiah. *And of my words.* This was another subject of offense to the Jews: the doctrine of the Cross must be believed; a suffering Messiah must be acknowledged; and poverty and affliction must be borne; and death, perhaps, suffered in consequence of becoming His disciples.

28. *About an eight days after.* See the whole of this important transaction explained at large on Matt. xvii. 1-13.

After six days. Mark ix. 2 has the same number; but Luke says, ix. 28, after "eight" days. The reason of this difference seems to be the following: Matthew and Mark reckon the days from that mentioned in the preceding chapter to that mentioned in this; Luke includes both days, as well as the six intermediate. Hence the one makes eight, the other six, without any contradiction. *Peter, James, and John.* He chose those that they might be witnesses of His transfiguration, two or three witnesses being required by the Scripture to substantiate any fact. The same three were made witnesses of His agony in the garden, chap. xxvi. 37. *An high mountain.* This was one of the mountains of Galilee, but whether Mount Tabor or not is uncertain. Some think it was Mount Hermon. St. Luke says Christ and His disciples went up into the mountain to pray, chap. ix. 28.

Was transfigured. That fullness of the Godhead which dwelt bodily in Christ now shone forth through the human nature, and manifested to His disciples not only that divinity which Peter had before confessed, chap. xvi. 16, but also the glorious resurrection body, in which they should exist in the presence of God to eternity.

Moses and Elias. Elijah came from heaven in the same body which he had upon earth, for he was translated, and did not see death, 2 Kings ii. 11. And the body of Moses was probably raised again as a pledge of the resurrection. It was a constant and prevalent tradition among the Jews that both Moses and Elijah should appear in the times of the Messiah, and to this very tradition the disciples refer, v. 10. We may conceive that the law in the person of Moses, the great Jewish legislator, and the prophets in the person of Elijah, the chief of the prophets, came now to do homage to Jesus Christ, and to render up their authority into His hands, as He was the End of the law and the grand Subject of the predictions of the prophets. This appears more particularly from what Luke says, chap. ix. 31, that Moses and Elijah conversed with our Lord on His death, which He was about to accomplish, because in it all the rites, ceremonies, and sacrifices of the law, as well as the predictions of the prophets, were fulfilled.

31. *His decease.* "That going out [or death] of His." That peculiar kind of death—its nature, circumstances, and necessity being considered.

MATTHEW HENRY

CHARLES H. SPURGEON:

It is worthy of note that He was transfigured while He was praying. Every blessing comes to the great Head of the Church, and to all the members of His mystical body, through prayer. There is nothing promised to us without prayer; but, with prayer, everything is provided for us, and by prayer we shall ascend into glory.
—*The Treasury of the New Testament*

5. We are here told, which we were not before, that the disciples were *heavy with sleep*, *v.* 32. Perhaps it was owing to a sinful carelessness: when Christ was at prayer with them, they did not regard his prayer as they should have done, and, to punish them for that, they were left to *sleep on now*, and so lost an opportunity of seeing how that work of wonder was wrought. These three were now asleep, when Christ was in *his glory*, as afterwards they were, when he was in *his agony*. Nothing could be more affecting to these disciples, one would think, than the *glories* and the *agonies* of their Master, and both in the highest degree; and yet neither the one nor the other would serve to *keep them awake*. What need have we to pray to God for quickening grace, to make us not only *alive*, but *lively*! After awhile they *recovered themselves*, and then they took an exact view of all those glories, so that they were able to give a particular account, as we find one of them does, of all that passed when they were with Christ *in the holy mount*, 2 Pet. i. 18.

6. It is here observed that it was when Moses and Elias were now about to *depart* that Peter said, *Lord, it is good to be here, let us make three tabernacles.* Thus we are often not sensible of the worth of our mercies till we are about to lose them; nor do we covet and court their continuance till they are upon the departure. Peter said this, *not knowing what he said.*

7. It is here added, concerning the *cloud* that *overshadowed them*, that they *feared as they entered into the cloud.* This cloud was a token of God's more peculiar presence. Then no wonder that the disciples were *afraid to enter into it.* But never let any be afraid to enter into a cloud with Jesus Christ; for he will be sure to bring them safely through it.

8. The *voice* which came from heaven is here, and in Mark, related not so fully as in Matthew: *This is my beloved Son, hear him*: though those words, *in whom I am well pleased*, which we have both in Matthew and Peter, are not expressed, they are implied in that, *This is my beloved Son.*

Lastly, The apostles are here said to have kept this vision private. They *told no man in those days.* As there is a time *to speak*, so there is a time to *keep silence.* Everything is beautiful and useful in its season.

Verses 37–42

This passage of story in Matthew and Mark follows immediately upon that of Christ's transfiguration, and his discourse with his disciples after it; but here it is said to be *on the next day, as they were coming down from the hill.* It was not till next day that they *came down from the hill*, and then he found things in some disorder among his disciples. 1. How forward the people were to receive Christ at his return to them. *Much people met him*, as, at other times, much people *followed* him. 2. How importunate the father of the lunatic child was with Christ for help for him (*v.* 38): *I beseech thee, look upon my son;* this is his request; one compassionate look from Christ is enough to set everything to rights. Let us bring ourselves and our children to Christ, to be *looked upon.* His plea is, *He is my only child.* They that have many children may balance their affliction in one with their comfort in the rest. 3. How *deplorable* the case of the *child* was, *v.* 39. He was under the power of an evil spirit, that *took him*; when the fit seized him, he suddenly *cried out*, and many a time his shrieks had pierced the heart of his tender father. This malicious

JAMIESON, FAUSSET, BROWN

and occasioned that delightful allusion to this scene which we find in II Peter 1:15-18. **which he should accomplish**—"was to fulfil." **at Jerusalem**—Mark the *historical character* and *local features* which Christ's death assumed to these glorified men—as important as it is charming—and see on ch. 2:11. What now may be gathered from this statement? (1) *That a dying Messiah is the great article of the true Jewish theology.* For a long time the Church had fallen clean away from the faith of this article, and even from a preparedness to receive it. But here we have that jewel raked out of the dunghill of Jewish traditions, and by the true representatives of the Church of old made the one subject of talk with Christ Himself. (2) *The adoring gratitude of glorified men for His undertaking to accomplish such a decease; their felt dependence upon it for the glory in which they appeared; their profound interest in the progress of it, their humble solaces and encouragements to go through with it; and their sense of its peerless and overwhelming glory.* "Go, matchless, adored One, a Lamb to the slaughter! rejected of men, but chosen of God and precious; dishonored, abhorred, and soon to be slain by men, but worshipped by cherubim, ready to be greeted by all heaven. In virtue of that decease we are here; our all is suspended on it and wrapped up in it. Thine every step is watched by us with ineffable interest; and though it were too high an honor to us to be permitted to drop a word of cheer into that precious but now clouded spirit, yet, as the first fruits of harvest; the very joy set before Him, we cannot choose but tell Him that what is the depth of shame to Him is covered with glory in the eyes of Heaven, that the Cross to Him is the Crown to us, that that 'decease' is all our salvation and all our desire." And who can doubt that such a scene *did* minister deep cheer to that spirit? 'Tis said they "talked" not *to Him*, but "*with Him*"; and if they told *Him* how glorious His decease was, might He not fitly reply, "I know it, but your voice, as messengers from heaven come down to tell it Me, is music in Mine ears." **32. and when they were awake**—so, certainly, the most commentators: but if we translate literally, it should be "*but having kept awake*" [MEYER, ALFORD]. Perhaps "*having roused themselves up*" [OLSHAUSEN] may come near enough to the literal sense; but from the word used we can gather no more than that they *shook off their drowsiness.* It was night, and the Lord seems to have spent the whole night on the mountain (vs. 37). **saw his glory . . .**—The emphasis lies on "*saw,*" qualifying them to become "*eye-witnesses* of His majesty" (II Pet. 1:16). **33. they departed**—Ah! bright manifestations in this vale of tears are always "departing" manifestations. **34, 35. a cloud**—not one of our watery clouds, but the Shekinah-cloud (see on Matt. 23:39), the pavilion of the manifested presence of God with His people, what Peter calls "the excellent" of "magnificent glory" (II Pet. 1:17). **a voice**—"*such* a voice," says Peter emphatically; "and this voice [he adds] we heard, when we were with Him in the holy mount" (II Pet. 1:17, 18). **35. my beloved Son . . . hear him**—*reverentially, implicitly, alone.* **36. Jesus was found alone**—Moses and Elias are gone. Their work is done, and they have disappeared from the scene, feeling no doubt with their fellow servant the Baptist, "He must increase, but I must decrease." The cloud too is gone, and the naked majestic Christ, braced in spirit, and enshrined in the reverent affection of His disciples, is left—to suffer! **kept it close**—feeling, for once at least, that such things were unmeet as yet for the general gaze.

37-45. DEMONIAC AND LUNATIC BOY HEALED—CHRIST'S SECOND EXPLICIT ANNOUNCEMENT OF HIS DEATH AND RESURRECTION. (See on Mark 9:14-32). **And one of the multitude answered, and said, Master, I have brought unto thee my son**—"mine only child" (Luke 9:38). **which hath a dumb spirit**—a spirit whose operation had the effect of rendering his victim speechless, and deaf also (vs. 25). In Matthew's report of the speech (17:15), the father says "he is lunatic"; this being another and most distressing effect of the possession. **And wheresoever he taketh him, he teareth him; and he foameth, and gnasheth with his teeth, and pineth away**—rather, "becomes withered," "dried up," or "paralyzed"; as the same word is everywhere else rendered in the New Testament. Some additional particulars are given by Luke, and by our Evangelist below. "Lo," says he in Luke 9:39, "a spirit taketh him, and he suddenly crieth out; and it teareth him that he foameth again, and bruising him hardly [or with difficulty] departeth from him."

ADAM CLARKE

ALBERT BARNES:

32. "Heavy with sleep." Borne down with sleep—oppressed, overcome with sleep. It may seem remarkable that they should fall asleep on such an occasion; but we are to bear in mind that this may have been in the night, and that they were weary with the toils of the day. Besides, they did not fall asleep while the transfiguration lasted. While Jesus was praying, or perhaps after he closed, they fell asleep. While they were sleeping his countenance was changed, and Moses and Elias appeared. The first that they saw of it was after they awoke, having been probably awakened by the shining of the light around them.
—*Popular Commentary*

A bright cloud overshadowed them. A *cloud* was frequently the symbol of the Divine Presence. *This is my beloved Son.* "This is My Son, the beloved One, in whom I have delighted," or "been well pleased." God adds His testimony of approbation to what was spoken of the sufferings of Christ by Moses and Elijah, thus showing that the sacrificial economy of the old covenant was in itself of no worth, but as it referred to the grand atonement which Jesus was about to make. Therefore He says, "In Him have I delighted," intimating that it was in Him alone, as typified by those sacrifices, that He had delighted through the whole course of the legal administration; and that it was only in reference to the death of His Son that He accepted the offerings and oblations made to Him under the old covenant. *Hear . . . him.* The disciples wished to detain Moses and Elijah that they might hear them, but God shows that the law which had been in force, and the prophets which had prophesied, until now, must all give place to Jesus; and He alone must now be attended to, as "the way, the truth, and the life," for no man could now come unto the Father but through Him.

35. *This is my beloved Son.* Instead of "the beloved One," some MSS. and versions have "the chosen One"; and the Aethiopic translator, as in several other cases, to be sure of the true reading, retains both.

39. *A spirit taketh him.* This very phrase is used by heathen writers when they speak of supernatural influence.

MATTHEW HENRY

spirit *tore him*, and *bruised* him, and *departed not from him* but with great difficulty. What mischief doth Satan do where he gets possession! But happy they that have access to Christ! 4. How defective the disciples were in their faith. Though Christ had given them *power over unclean spirits*, yet they *could not* cast out this *evil spirit*, *v.* 40. Either they distrusted the power they were to fetch in strength from, or they did not exert themselves in prayer as they ought; for this Christ reproved them. 5. How effectual the cure was, which Christ wrought upon this child, *v.* 42. Christ can do that for us which his disciples cannot: *Jesus rebuked the unclean spirit*. The devil *threw the child down, and tore him*, as if he would have pulled him to pieces. But one word from Christ *healed the child*, and made good the damage the devil had done him. He *delivered him again to his father*. When our children are recovered from sickness, we must receive them as delivered to us again, receive them as life from the dead. It is comfortable to receive them from the hand of Christ: "Here, take this child, and be thankful; take it, and bring it up for me, for thou hast it again from me." With such cautions as these, parents should receive their children *from Christ's hands*, and then with comfort put them again *into his hands*.

Verses 43–50

I. The impression which Christ's miracles made upon all that beheld them (*v.* 43): *They were all amazed at the mighty power of God*. Their wonder was universal: they wondered *every one*. The causes of it were universal: they wondered at *all things which Jesus did*; all his actions had something uncommon and surprising in them.

II. The notice Christ gave to his disciples of his approaching sufferings: *The Son of man shall be delivered into the hands of men*. That is here *implied* which is *expressed* by the other evangelists: *They shall kill him*. But that which is peculiar here is, 1. The connection of this with what goes next before, of the admiration with which the people were struck at beholding Christ's miracles (*v.* 43): *While they all wondered at all things which Jesus did, he said this to his disciples*. They had a fond conceit of his temporal kingdom, and that he should reign, in secular pomp and power; and now they thought that this *mighty power* of his would easily effect the thing. Therefore Christ takes this occasion to tell them again that he was so far from having men *delivered into his hands* that he must be *delivered into the hands of men*. 2. The solemn preface with which it is introduced: "*Let these sayings sink down into your ears*. Admit what I say, and submit to it." *Let it sink down into your hearts*; so the Syriac and Arabic read it. The word of Christ does us no good, unless we let it sink down into our heads and hearts. 3. The unaccountable stupidity of the disciples. It was said in Mark, *They understood not that saying*. It was plain enough, but they *would not understand it in the literal* sense; and they *could not* understand it in any other, *and were afraid to ask him* lest they should be undeceived and awaked out of their pleasing dream. But it is here added that *it was hidden from them, that they perceived it not*. We cannot think that it was *in mercy* hidden from them, lest they should be swallowed up with overmuch sorrow at the prospect of it; but that it was a paradox, because they *made it so* to themselves.

III. The rebuke Christ gave to his disciples for their disputing among themselves which should be greatest, *v.* 46–48. This passage we had before, and, the more is the pity, we shall meet with the like again.

1. Ambition of honour, and strife for superiority and precedency, are sins that most easily beset the disciples of our Lord Jesus. They flow from corruptions which they are highly concerned to subdue and mortify, *v.* 46. They that expect to be *great* in this world commonly aim high, and nothing will serve them short of being *greatest*; this exposes them to a great deal of temptation and trouble, which they are safe from that are content to be *little*, to be *least*, to be *less than the least*.

2. Jesus Christ is perfectly acquainted with the thoughts and intents of our hearts: He *perceived their thoughts*, *v.* 47. Thoughts are *words* to him, and *whispers* are loud cries.

3. Christ will have his disciples to aim at that honour which is to be obtained by a quiet humility, and not at that which is to be obtained by a restless and aspiring ambition. Christ *took a child, and set him by him*, *v.* 47 (for he always expressed a tenderness and kindness for little children). (1) Let them be of the *temper* of this child, *humble* and *quiet*, and *easy* to itself. Let them be willing to be *the least*, if that would contribute anything to their usefulness. (2) Let them assure themselves that this was the way

JAMIESON, FAUSSET, BROWN

Bring him unto me–The order to bring the patient to Him was instantly obeyed; when, lo! as if conscious of the presence of his Divine Tormentor, and expecting to be made to quit, the foul spirit rages and is furious, determined to die hard, doing all the mischief he can to this poor child while yet within his grasp. **And they brought him unto him: and when he saw him, straightway the spirit tare him**–Just as the man with the legion of demons, "when he *saw* Jesus, ran and worshipped Him" (ch. 5:6), so this demon, *when he saw Him*, immediately "tare him." The feeling of terror and rage was the same in both cases.

43-45. the mighty power of God–"the majesty" or "mightiness" of God in this last miracle, the transfiguration, etc.: the *divine grandeur* of Christ rising upon them daily. By comparing Matthew 17:22, and Mark 9:30, we gather that this had been the subject of conversation between the Twelve and their Master as they journeyed along.

44. these sayings–not what was passing between them about His grandeur [MEYER, etc.], but what He was now to repeat for the second time about His sufferings [DE WETTE, STIER, ALFORD, etc.]; i.e., "Be not carried off your feet by all this grandeur of Mine, but bear in mind what I have already told you, and now distinctly repeat, that that Sun in whose beams ye now rejoice is soon to set in midnight gloom." "The Son of *man*," says Christ, "into the hands of *men*"–a remarkable antithesis (also in Matt. 17:22, and Mark 9:31). **45. and they feared**–"insomuch that they feared." Their most cherished ideas were so completely dashed by such announcements, that they were afraid of laying themselves open to rebuke by asking Him any questions.

46-48. STRIFE AMONG THE TWELVE, WHO SHOULD BE GREATEST–JOHN REBUKED FOR EXCLUSIVENESS. **46-48.** (See on Matt. 18:1-5.)

And he took a child–"a little child" (Matt. 18:2); but the word is the same in both places, as also in Luke 9:47. **and set him in the midst of them: and when he had taken him in his arms**–This beautiful trait is mentioned by our Evangelist alone. **he said unto them**–Here we must go to Matthew (18:3, 4) for the first of this answer: "Verily I say unto you, except ye be converted, and become as little children, ye shall not enter into the kingdom of Heaven:" i.e., "Conversion must be thorough; not only must the heart be turned to God in general, and from earthly to heavenly things, but in particular, except ye be converted from that carnal ambition which still rankles within you, into that freedom from all such feelings which ye see in this child, ye have neither part nor lot in the kingdom at all; and he who in this feature has most of the child, is highest there." Whosoever, therefore, shall "humble himself as this little child, the same is greatest in the kingdom of heaven": "for he that is [willing to be] least among you all, the same shall be great" (Luke 9:48).

ADAM CLARKE

42. *The devil threw him down, and tare him.* See this case considered at large on Matt. xvii. 15-18 and on Mark ix. 14-27.

43. *The mighty power.* This "majesty" of God. They plainly saw that it was a case in which any power inferior to that of God could be of no avail, and they were deeply struck with the majesty of God manifested in the conduct of the blessed Jesus.

44. *Let these sayings sink down into your ears.* Or "put these words into your ears." To other words you may lend occasional attention—but to what concerns My sufferings and death you must ever listen. Let them constantly occupy a place in your most serious meditations and reflections.

45. *But they understood not.* See the note on Mark ix. 32.

46. *There arose a reasoning.* "A dialogue took place"—one inquired, and another answered, and so on.

MATTHEW HENRY

to preferment. They that loved Christ would *therefore receive* them *in his name*, because they did most resemble him. Christ would take the kindnesses done to them as done to himself: *Whosoever shall receive one such child receiveth me;* and *whosoever receiveth me, receiveth him that sent me;* and what greater honour can any man attain to in this world than to have God and Christ own themselves received and welcomed in him?

IV. The rebuke Christ gave to his disciples for discouraging one that honoured him and served him, but was not of their communion, but, upon occasional hearing of Christ, believed in him, and made use of his name with faith and prayer in a serious manner, for the casting out of devils. This man they *rebuked and restrained*; they would not let him pray and preach, though it was to the honour of Christ. He did not *follow Christ with them.* Jesus Christ chid them for what they did: "*Forbid him not* (*v.* 50), but rather encourage him, for he is carrying on the same design that you are. He will meet you in *the same end*, though he does not accompany you in *the same way. He that is not against us is for us*, and therefore ought to be countenanced by us." We need not lose any of our friends, while we have so few, and so many enemies. Those may be found faithful followers of Christ, and, as such, may be accepted of him, though they do not follow *with us.*

Verses 51-56

This passage of story we have not in any other of the evangelists. Here they were for putting infidels to death. Christ reprimanded them, for a spirit of bigotry and persecution is directly contrary to the spirit of Christ.

I. The *readiness* and *resolution* of our Lord **Jesus**, in prosecuting his great undertaking for our redemption and salvation. Of this we have an instance, *v.* 51: *When the time was come that he should be received up, he steadfastly set his face to go to Jerusalem.* There was a time fixed for the sufferings and death of our Lord Jesus, and he knew well enough when it was. Then he appeared most publicly of all, and was most busy, knowing that his time was short. When he saw his death and sufferings approaching, he looked through them and beyond them, to the glory that should follow, when he should be *received up into glory* (1 Tim. iii. 16). All good Christians may frame to themselves the same notion of death, and may call it their being *received up*, to be with Christ where he is. On this prospect of the joy set before him, he *steadfastly set his face to go to Jerusalem.* He was fully *determined* to go, and would not be dissuaded; he went *directly* to Jerusalem. He went cheerfully and courageously thither. He *did not fail nor was discouraged, knowing* that he should be not only *justified*, but glorified, not only not *run down*, but *received up.* How should this shame us *for*, and shame *us out of*, our backwardness to do and suffer for Christ!

II. The *rudeness* of the Samaritans in a *certain village* who would not *receive him.* 1. How *civil* he was to them: *He sent messengers before his face*, that went to take up lodgings, and to know whether he might have leave to accommodate himself and his company among them. He sent some to *make ready* for him that his coming might be no surprise. 2. How *uncivil* they were to him, *v.* 53. They did not *receive him*, would not suffer him to come into their village. He would have been the greatest blessing that ever came to their village, and yet they forbid him entrance. Now the reason was *because his face was as though he would go to Jerusalem.* The great controversy between the Jews and the Samaritans was about the place of worship—whether Jerusalem or mount Gerizim near Sychar; see John iv. 20. And so hot was the controversy between them that the *Jews would have no dealings with the Samaritans*, nor they with them, John iv. 9. They were particularly incensed against Christ, who was a celebrated teacher, for owning and adhering to the temple at Jerusalem. They would not show him the common civility which probably they used formerly to show him in his journey thither.

III. The *resentment* which James and John expressed of this affront, *v.* 54. When these two heard this message brought, they were all in a flame presently, and nothing will serve them but Sodom's doom upon this village.

1. Here indeed was something commendable, for they showed, (1) A great confidence in the power they had received from Jesus Christ. They could with a word's speaking fetch *fire from heaven. Wilt thou that we speak the word*, and the thing will be done. (2) A great zeal for the honour of their Master. They took it very ill that he who did good wherever he came and found a hearty welcome should be denied

JAMIESON, FAUSSET, BROWN

49, 50. John answered . . .—The link of connection here with the foregoing context lies in the words "in My name" (vs. 48). "Oh, as to that," said John, young, warm, but not sufficiently apprehending Christ's teaching in these things, "we saw one casting out devils in Thy name, and we forbade him: Were we wrong?" "Ye were wrong." "But we did because he followeth not us,'" "No matter. For (1) There is no man which shall do a miracle in My name that can lightly [soon] speak evil of Me' [Mark 9:39]. And (2) If such a person cannot be supposed to be '*against* us,' you are to consider him '*for* us.'" Two principles of immense importance. Christ does not say this man should *not* have followed "with them," but simply teaches how he was to be regarded *though he did not*—as a reverer of His name and a promoter of His cause. Surely this condemns not only those horrible attempts *by force* to shut up all within one visible pale of discipleship, which have deluged Christendom with blood in Christ's name, but the same spirit in its milder form of proud ecclesiastic scowl upon all who "after the form which they call *a sect* (as the word signifies, Acts 24:14), do so worship the God of their fathers." Visible unity in Christ's Church is devoutly to be sought, but this is not the way to it. *See the noble spirit of Moses* (Num. 11:24-29).

51-56. The Period of His Assumption Approaching, Christ Takes His Last Leave of Galilee—The Samaritans Refuse to Receive Him.

51. the time was come—rather, "the days were being fulfilled," or approaching their fulfilment—**that he should be received up**—"of His assumption," meaning His exaltation to the Father; a sublime expression, taking the sweep of His whole career, as if at one bound He was about to vault into glory. The work of Christ in the flesh is here divided into *two great stages;* all that preceded this belonging to the one, and all that follows it to the other. During the one, He formally "*came to His own,*" and "*would have gathered them*"; during the other, the awful consequences of "*His own receiving Him not*" rapidly revealed themselves. **he steadfastly set his face**—the "He" here is emphatic—"He Himself then." See His own prophetic language, "I have set my face like a flint" (Isa. 50:7). **go to Jerusalem**—as His *goal*, but including His preparatory visits to it at the feasts of tabernacles and of dedication (John 7:2, 10; and 10:22, 23), and all the intermediate movements and events. **52. messengers before his face . . . to make ready for him**—He had not done this before; but now, instead of avoiding, He seems to court publicity—all now hastening to maturity. **53. did not receive him, because . . .**—The Galileans, in going to the festivals at Jerusalem, usually took the Samaritan route [Josephus, *Antiquities*, 20. 6. 1], and yet seem to have met with no such inhospitality. But if they were asked to prepare quarters *for the Messiah*, in the person of one whose "face was as though He would go *to Jerusalem*," their national prejudices would be raised at so marked a slight upon their claims. (See on John 4:20.)

54. James and John not *Peter*, as we should have expected, but those "*sons of thunder*" (Mark 3:17), who afterwards wanted to have all the highest honors of the Kingdom to themselves, and the younger of whom had been rebuked already for his exclusiveness (vss. 49, 50). Yet this was "the disciple whom Jesus loved," while the other willingly drank of His Lord's bitter cup. (See on Mark 10:38-40 and Acts 12:2.) That same fiery zeal, in a mellowed and hallowed form, in the beloved disciple, we find in II John 5: 10 and III John 10.

ADAM CLARKE

49. *We forbad him.* See this subject considered on Mark ix. 38, etc.

We saw one casting out devils in thy name. It can scarcely be supposed that a man who knew nothing of Christ, or who was only a common exorcist, could be able to work a miracle in Christ's name. We may therefore safely imagine that this was either one of John the Baptist's disciples, who, at his master's command, had believed in Jesus, or one of the seventy whom Christ had sent out, Luke x. 1-7, who, after he had fulfilled his commission, had retired from accompanying the other disciples. But as he still held fast his faith in Christ and walked in good conscience, the influence of his Master still continued with him, so that he could cast out demons as well as the other disciples. *We forbad him.* I do not see that we have any right to attribute any other motive to John than that which he himself owns—*because he followeth not us*—because he did not attach himself constantly to Thee, as we do, we thought he could not be in a proper spirit.

Forbid him not. If you meet him again, let him go on quietly in the work in which God owns him. If he were not of God, the demons would not be subject to him, and his work could not prosper. A spirit of bigotry has little countenance from these passages. There are some who are so outrageously wedded to their own creed and religious system that they would rather let sinners perish than suffer those who differ from them to become the instruments of their salvation.

52. *Sent messengers.* "Angels," literally; but this proves that the word "angel" signifies a messenger of any kind, whether divine or human. The messengers in this case were probably James and John.

53. *His face was.* They saw He was going up to Jerusalem to keep the feast (it was the Feast of Tabernacles, John vii. 2); and knowing Him thereby to be a Jew, they would afford nothing for His entertainment; for in religious matters the Samaritans and Jews had no dealings; see John iv. 9. The Samaritans were a kind of mongrel heathens; they feared Jehovah, and served other gods, 2 Kings xvii. 34.

54. *That we command fire.* Vengeance belongs to the Lord. What we suffer for His sake should be left to himself to reprove or punish. The insult is offered to Him, not to us.

MATTHEW HENRY

the liberty of the road by a parcel of paltry Samaritans. (3) A submission, notwithstanding, to their Master's goodwill and pleasure. They will not offer to do such a thing, unless Christ give leave: *Wilt thou* that we do it? (4) A regard to the examples of the prophets that were before them. It is doing *as Elias did.* They thought that this *precedent* would be their *warrant*; so apt are we to misapply the examples of good men.

2. But though there was something right in what they said, yet there was much more amiss for (1) This was not the first time, by a great many, that our Lord Jesus had been thus affronted, yet he never called for any judgment upon them, but patiently put up with the injury. (2) These were Samaritans, from whom better was not to be expected, and perhaps they had heard that Christ had forbidden his disciples to *enter into any of the cities of the Samaritans* (Matt. x. 5), and therefore it was not so bad in them as in others who knew more of Christ. (3) Perhaps it was only some few of the town that sent that rude message to him, while, for aught they knew, there were many in the town who would have gone to meet him and welcomed him. (4) Their Master had never yet upon any occasion called for *fire from heaven.* James and John were the two disciples whom Christ had called *Boanerges*—sons of thunder (Mark iii. 17); and will not that serve them, but they must be *sons of lightning* too? (5) The example of Elias did not reach the case. Elijah was sent to display the terrors of the law, but it is a dispensation of grace that is now to be introduced, to which such a terrible display of divine justice will not be at all agreeable.

IV. The *reproof* he gave to James and John (*v.* 55): He *turned* and *rebuked them*; for *as many as he loves he rebukes and chastens*, particularly for what they do, that is irregular and unbecoming them, under colour of zeal for him.

1. He shows them in particular their mistake: *Ye know not what manner of spirit ye are of.* (1) "You *are not aware* how much there is of pride, and passion, and personal revenge, covered under this pretence of zeal for your Master." There may be much corruption lurking, nay, and stirring too, in the hearts of good people, and they themselves not be sensible of it. (2) "You *do not consider* what a *good spirit* you *should be of.* Surely you have yet to learn what the spirit of Christ is. Have you not been taught to *love your enemies*, and to *bless them that curse you*, and to call for grace from heaven, not fire from heaven, upon them? You are under the dispensation of love, and liberty, and grace, which was ushered in with a proclamation of *peace on earth* and *goodwill toward men.*"

2. He shows them the general design and tendency of his religion (*v.* 56): *The Son of man* is not himself come *to destroy men's lives, but to save them.* He designed to propagate his holy religion by love and sweetness, and everything that is inviting and endearing, not by fire and sword, by miracles of healing, not by plagues and miracles of destruction, as Israel was brought out of Egypt. Christ came to *slay* all *enmities*, not to foster them. Christ came, not only to save men's *souls*, but to save their *lives* too. Christ would have his disciples do good to all, but hurt to none, to draw men into his church with the *cords of a man and the bands of love*, but not think to drive men into it.

V. His *retreat* from this village. Christ would not only not punish them for their rudeness but quietly and peaceably *went to another village*, where they were not so stingy. If some be very rude, instead of revenging it, we should try whether others will not be more civil.

Verses 57–62

We have here an account of three several persons that offered themselves to follow Christ.

I. Here is one that is extremely forward to follow Christ immediately, but seems to have been too rash and not to have set down and counted the cost.

1. He makes Christ a very large promise (*v.* 57): *As they went in the way* one said to him, *Lord*, I will *follow thee whithersoever thou goest.* This must be the resolution of all that will be found Christ's disciples indeed; they *follow the Lamb whithersoever he goes.*

2. Christ gives him a necessary caution, not to promise himself great things in the world, in following him; for *the Son of man has not where to lay his head.*

We may look upon this, (1) As *setting forth* the *very low condition* that our Lord Jesus was in, in this world. He not only wanted the delights and ornaments that great princes usually have, but even such accommodations for mere necessity as the *foxes* have, and the *birds of the air.* He that made all did not make

JAMIESON, FAUSSET, BROWN

fire . . . as Elias—a plausible case, occurring also in *Samaria* (II Kings 1:10-12).

55, 56. know not what . . . spirit The thing ye demand, though in keeping with the *legal,* is unsuited to the genius of the *evangelical* dispensation. The sparks of *un*holy indignation would seize readily enough on this example of Elias, though our Lord's rebuke (as is plain from vs. 56) is directed to the *principle* involved rather than the animal heat which doubtless prompted the reference. "It is a golden sentence of Tillotson, Let us never do anything for religion which is contrary to religion" [WEBSTER and WILKINSON].

56. for the Son of man . . .—a saying truly divine, of which all His miracles—for salvation, never destruction—were one continued illustration. **went to another**—illustrating His own precept (Matt. 10:23).

57-62. INCIDENTS ILLUSTRATIVE OF DISCIPLESHIP. **57, 58.** The PRECIPITATE disciple. (See on Matt. 8:19, 20.) **59, 60.** The PROCRASTINATING disciple. (See on Matt. 8:21, 22.)

ADAM CLARKE

55. *Ye know not what manner of spirit ye are of.* Ye do not consider that the present is a dispensation of infinite mercy and love, and that the design of God is not to destroy sinners, but to give them space to repent, that He may save them unto eternal life. And ye do not consider that the zeal which you feel springs from an evil principle, being more concerned for your own honor than for the honor of God. The disciples of that Christ who died for His enemies should never think of avenging themselves on their persecutors. The words, *Ye know not what manner of spirit ye are of. For the Son of man is not come to destroy men's lives, but to save them,* are wanting in many MSS.

57. *A certain man.* He was a scribe. See on Matt. viii. 19-22. It is probable that this took place when Christ was at Capernaum, as Mathew represents it, and not on the way to Jerusalem through Samaria.

A certain scribe. Few of this class came to the Lord Jesus for instruction or salvation. *Master.* Rather, "teacher," the person who shows or points out a particular way or science. *I will follow thee whithersoever thou goest.* Every teacher among the Jews had disciples, and some especially that followed or accompanied them wherever they went, that they might have some person at hand with whom they might converse concerning the divine law.

The foxes have holes. Reader! are you a poor man? and do you fear God? Then what comfort must you derive from the thought that you so nearly resemble the Lord Jesus! *Son of*

G. CAMPBELL MORGAN:

His disciples in loyalty went to a Samaritan village; and in loyalty, when the Samaritans would not receive Him, would have destroyed the Samaritans by fire. It was loyalty, but it was loyalty out of harmony with the spirit of the Master, and out of harmony with the method of the Master. It is possible to be zealous for the honor of God in a spirit which puts us out of fellowship with God. That is what kept Moses out of the promised land. Loyalty in a wrong spirit. He spake inadvisedly with his lips when he went to the people clamoring for water and grumbling against God. He smote the rock, and he showed an angry spirit; and God excluded him from the promised land.

Well, what is the true spirit? What did Jesus do?

"They went to another village."

To destroy by fire in loyalty to Him would manifest a spirit contrary to the Cross. His face was toward Jerusalem. That revealed His spirit. That revealed His attitude. He was led as a lamb to the slaughter, as a sheep before her shearers is dumb, so He opened not His mouth. When He was reviled, He reviled not again. That is the spirit of the Cross. The spirit that wants to call down fire upon those that are refusing Jesus Christ is not Christ's spirit in that it lacks the principle of the Cross. Are we with James and John—loyal, passionately devoted, wanting to destroy men by fire? Our loyalty, because it is in a wrong spirit, puts us out of fellowship with Jesus Christ. Fellowship with Christ means going all the way to Calvary, bearing shame and scoffing rude, with no anger, and no desire to call down fire.—*The Gospel According to Luke*

MATTHEW HENRY

a dwelling-place for himself, not a house of his own to put his head in. He here calls himself the *Son of man*, a Son of Adam, partaker of flesh and blood. He glories in his condescension towards us, to testify his love to us, and to teach us a holy contempt of the world, and a continual regard to another world. Christ was thus poor, to sanctify and sweeten poverty to his people. We may well be content to fare as Christ did. (2) As proposing this to the consideration of those who intend to be his disciples. If we mean to follow Christ, we must not reckon upon making anything *more than heaven* of our religion. Christ tells this man what he must count upon if he followed him, to lie cold and uneasy, to fare hard, and live in contempt; if he could not submit to this, let him not pretend to follow Christ. This word sent him back, for aught that appears; but it will be no discouragement to any that know what there is in Christ and heaven to set in the scale against this.

II. Here is another, that seems *resolved* to follow Christ, but he *begs a day*, *v.* 59. To this man Christ first gave the call; he said to him, *Follow me*. This man to whom Christ gave a call, though he hesitated at first, yet, as it should seem, afterwards yielded. It is not of *him that willeth*, nor *of him that runneth* (as that forward spark in the foregoing verses), but of God that showeth mercy, that *gives* the call.

1. The excuse he made: "*Lord, suffer me first to go and bury my father*. I have an aged father at home, who cannot live long, and will need me while he does live; let me go and attend on him until he is dead, and then I will do anything." We may here see three temptations. (1) We are tempted to *rest* in a *discipleship at large*, in which we may be *at a loose end*, and not to come *close*. (2) We are tempted to *defer* the doing of that which we know to be our duty, and to put it off to some other time. When we have got clear of such a care and difficulty, then we will begin to think of being religious; and so we are cozened out of all our time, by being cozened out of the present time. (3) We are tempted to think that our duty to our relations will excuse us from our duty to Christ. The *kingdom of God and the righteousness thereof* must be sought and minded *in the first place*.

2. Christ's answer to it (*v.* 60): "*Let the dead bury their dead*. Thou hast other work to do; *go thou, and preach the kingdom of God*." Not that Christ would have his followers or his ministers to be *unnatural*; our religion teaches us to be kind and good in every relation. But we must not make these offices an excuse from our duty to God. If the nearest and dearest relation we have in the world stand in our way to keep us from Christ, it is necessary that we have a zeal that will make us forget *father and mother*. No excuses must be admitted against a present obedience to the call of Christ.

III. Here is another that is willing to follow Christ, but he must have a *little time* to *talk with his friends* about it.

1. His request for a dispensation, *v.* 61. He said, "*Lord, I will follow thee*; but *let me first go bid them farewell that are at home*." *Let me go and set in order my household affairs*, so some understand it. Now that which was amiss in this is, (1) That he looked upon his following Christ as a melancholy, troublesome, dangerous thing; it was to him as if he were *going to die*, and therefore he must take *leave* of all his friends; whereas in following Christ, he might be more a comfort and blessing to them than if he had continued with them. (2) That he seemed to have his worldly concerns more upon his heart than would consist with a close attendance to his duty as a follower of Christ. He seemed to hanker after his relations and family concerns; they stuck to him. It may be he had bidden them *farewell* once, but *Loth to depart bids oft farewell*, and therefore he must bid them *farewell* once more, for they are *at home at his house*. (3) That he was willing to enter into a temptation from his purpose of following Christ. To go and bid them *farewell* that were *at home at his house* would be to expose himself to the strongest solicitations imaginable to alter his resolution; for they would all *beg* and *pray* that he would not *leave them*. Those that resolve to follow their Redeemer, must resolve that they will not so much as parley with their tempter.

2. The rebuke which Christ gave him for this request (*v.* 62): "*No man, having put his hand to the plough*, will *look back*, or look behind him, for then he makes balks with his plough, and the ground he ploughs is *not fit* to be sown; so thou, if thou hast a design to follow me, yet if thou *lookest back* to a worldly life again and hankerest after that, *thou art not fit for the kingdom of God*. Thou art not a *sower* fit to *scatter* the good seed of the kingdom if thou canst *hold the plough* no better." Ploughing

JAMIESON, FAUSSET, BROWN

III. *The Irresolute or Wavering Disciple* (Luke 9: 61, 62). Vs. 61: "And another also said, Lord, I will follow thee; but let me first go bid them farewell which are at home at my house. Vs. 62: And Jesus said unto him, No man, having put his hand to the plough, and looking back, is fit for the kingdom of God." But for the very different replies given, we should hardly have discerned the difference between this and the second case: the one man called, indeed, and the other volunteering, as did the first; but both seemingly alike willing, and only having a difficulty in their way just at that moment. But, by help of what is said respectively to each, we perceive the great difference between the two cases. From the warning given against "looking back," it is evident that this man's discipleship was not yet *thorough*, his separation from the world not entire. It is not a case of *going* back, but of *looking* back; and as there is here a manifest reference to the case of "Lot's wife" (Gen. 19:26; and see on Luke 17:32), we see that it is not *actual return* to the world that we have here to deal with, but a *reluctance to break with it*. The figure of putting one's hand to the plough and looking back is an exceedingly vivid one, and to an agricultural people most impressive. As ploughing requires an eye intent on the furrow to be made, and is marred the instant one turns about, so will they come short of salvation who prosecute the work of God with a distracted attention, a divided heart. The reference may be chiefly to ministers; but the application at least is general. As the image seems plainly to have been suggested by the case of Elijah and Elisha, a difficulty may be raised, requiring a moment's attention. When Elijah cast his mantle about Elisha, which the youth quite understood to mean appointing him his successor, he was ploughing with twelve yoke of oxen, the last pair held by himself. Leaving his oxen, he ran after the prophet, and said, "Let me, I pray thee, kiss my father and my mother, and [then] I will follow thee." Was this said *in the same spirit* with the same speech uttered by our disciple? Let us see. "And Elijah said unto him, Go back again: for what have I done to thee." Commentators take this to mean that Elijah had really done nothing to hinder him from going on with all his ordinary duties. But to us it seems clear that Elijah's intention was to try what manner of spirit the youth was of:—"Kiss thy father and mother? And why not? By all means, go home and stay with them; for what have I done to thee? I did but throw a mantle about thee; but what of that?" If this was his meaning, Elisha thoroughly apprehended and nobly met it. "He returned back from him, and took a yoke of oxen, and slew them, and boiled their flesh with the instruments of the oxen [the wood of his ploughing implements], and gave unto the people, and they did eat: then he arose, and went after Elijah, and ministered unto him" (I Kings 19:19-21). We know not if even his father and mother had time to be called to this hasty feast. But this much is plain, that, though in affluent circumstances, he gave up his lower calling, with all its prospects, for the higher and at that time perilous, office to which he was called. What now is the bearing of these two cases? Did Elisha do wrong in bidding them farewell with whom he was associated in his early calling? Or, if not, would this disciple have done wrong if he had done the same thing, and in the same spirit, with Elisha? Clearly not. Elisha's doing it proved that he could *with safety* do it; and our Lord's warning is not against bidding them farewell which were at home at his house, but against the probable *fatal consequences* of that step; lest the embraces of earthly relationship should prove too strong for him, and he should never return to follow Christ. Accordingly, we have called this the Irresolute or Wavering Disciple.

62. No man . . .—As ploughing requires an eye intent on the furrow to be made, and is marred the instant one turns about, so will they come short of salvation who prosecute the work of God with a distracted attention, a divided heart. Though the reference seems chiefly to ministers, the application is general. The expression "looking back" has a manifest reference to "Lot's wife" (Gen. 19:26; and see on ch. 17:32). It is not *actual return* to the world, but a *reluctance to break with it*.

ADAM CLARKE

man. A Hebrew phrase, expressive of humiliation and debasement; and, on that account, applied emphatically to himself by the meek and lowly Jesus. Besides, it seems here to be used to point out the incarnation of the Son of God, according to the predictions of the prophets, Ps. viii. 5; Dan. vii. 13. And as our Lord was now showing forth His eternal divinity in the miracles He wrought, He seems studious to prove to them the certainty of His incarnation, because on this depended the atonement for sin. Indeed our Lord seems more intent on giving the proofs of His *humanity* than of His *divinity*, the latter being necessarily manifested by the miracles which He was continually working.

Another of his disciples. This does not mean any of the twelve, but one of those who were constant hearers of our Lord's preaching, the name of *disciple* being common to all those who professed to believe in Him, John vi. 66. *Bury my father*. Probably his father was old, and apparently near death; but it was a maxim among the Jews that, if a man had any duty to perform to the dead, he was, for that time, free from the observance of any other precept or duty.

Let the dead bury their dead. It was usual for the Jews to consider a man as *dead* who had departed from the precepts of the law; and, on this ground, every transgressor was reputed a dead man. Our Lord's saying, being in common use, had nothing difficult in it to a Jew. Natural death is the separation of the body and soul; spiritual death, the separation of God and the soul. Men who live in sin are dead to God. Leave the *spiritually* dead to bury their *natural* dead.

61. *Another also said*. This circumstance is not mentioned by any of the other Evangelists; and Matthew alone mentions the former case, vv. 57-58. *Let me first go bid them farewell, which are at home*. "Permit me to set in order my affairs at home." Those who understand the Greek text will see at once that it will bear this translation well, and that this is the most natural. This person seems to have had in view the case of Elisha, who made a similar request to the Prophet Elijah, 1 Kings xix. 19-20, which request was granted by the prophet. But our Lord, seeing that this person had too much attachment to the earth, and that his return to worldly employments, though for a short time, was likely to become the means of stifling the good desires which he now felt, refused to grant him that permission.

62. *Put his hand to the plow*. Can any person properly discharge the work of the ministry who is engaged in secular employments? A farmer and a minister of the gospel are incompatible characters. As a person who holds the plow cannot keep on a straight furrow if he look behind him, so he who is employed in the work of the ministry cannot do the work of an evangelist if he turn his desires to worldly profits. Such a person is not *fit*, "properly dis-

MATTHEW HENRY

is in order to sowing. Those are not fit to be employed in sowing who know not how to break up the fallow ground, but, when they have *laid their hand to the plough*, upon every occasion look back and think of quitting it. Looking back inclines to *drawing back*, and *drawing back* is to *perdition*. Those are not fit for heaven, who, having set their faces heavenward, face about. But he, and he only, that *endures to the end, shall be saved*.

CHAPTER 10

Verses 1–16

We have here the sending forth of seventy disciples, two and two. This is not taken notice of by the other evangelists: but the instructions here given them are much the same with those given to the twelve.

I. Their number: they were seventy. As in the choice of twelve apostles Christ has an eye to the twelve patriarchs, the twelve tribes, and the twelve princes of those tribes, so here he seems to have an eye to the *seventy* elders of Israel.

1. We are glad to find that Christ had so many followers fit to be sent forth; his labour was not altogether in vain, though he met with much opposition. These *seventy*, though they did not attend him so closely and constantly as the *twelve* did, were nevertheless the constant hearers of his doctrine, and witnesses of his miracles, and believed in him. These seventy are those of whom Peter speaks as "*the men who companied with us all the time that the Lord Jesus went in and out among us*," and were part of the one hundred and twenty there spoken of, Acts i. 15, 21. Many of those that were the companions of the apostles, whom we read of in the Acts and the Epistles, we may suppose, were of these seventy disciples.

2. We are glad to find there was work for so many ministers, hearers for so many preachers: thus the grain of mustard-seed began to *grow*, and the savour of the leaven to diffuse itself in the meal.

II. Their work and business: He sent them *two and two*, that they might strengthen and encourage one another. He sent them, not to all the cities of Israel, as he did the *twelve*, but only *to every city and place whither he himself would come* (*v.* 1), as his harbingers. Two things they were ordered to do, the same that Christ did wherever he came: 1. They must *heal the sick* (*v.* 9), heal them *in the name of Jesus*, which would make people long to see this Jesus, and ready to entertain him whose name was so powerful. 2. They must publish the approach of the kingdom of God: *The kingdom of God is come nigh to you*. It is good to be made sensible of our advantages and opportunities, that we may lay hold of them. When the *kingdom of God comes nigh us*, it concerns us to go forth to meet it.

III. The instructions he gives them.

1. They must set out with prayer (*v.* 2). They must be duly affected with the necessities of the souls of men. They must *look about*, and see how *great the harvest was*. There was corn ready to shed and be lost for want of hands to gather it in. They must likewise be concerned that the *labourers were so few*. It is common for tradesmen not to care how few there are of their own trade; but Christ would have the labourers in his vineyard reckon it a matter of complaint when the *labourers are few*. They must earnestly desire to receive their mission from God, that *he* would send them forth as *labourers into his harvest*, and that he would send others forth; for, if God send them forth, they may hope he will go along with them and give them success.

2. They must set out with an expectation of trouble and persecution: "*Behold, I send you forth as lambs among wolves;* but *go your ways*. Your enemies will be as *wolves*. But you must be as *lambs*, peaceable and patient, though made an easy prey of." It would have been very hard thus to be sent forth as *sheep among wolves*, if he had not endued them with his spirit and courage.

3. They must not encumber themselves, as if they were going a long voyage, but depend upon God and their friends to provide: "Carry neither a *purse* for money, nor a *scrip* or knapsack for clothes or victuals, nor new *shoes* (as before to the twelve, *ch.* ix. 3); and *salute no man by the way*." (1) They must go as men *in haste*, must not hinder or retard themselves with needless ceremonies or compliments. (2) They must go as *men of business*, business that relates to another world, and therefore must not entangle themselves with conversation about secular affairs. (3) They must go as *serious* men.

4. They must show, not only *their goodwill*, but *God's goodwill*, to all to whom they came, *v.* 5, 6. (1) The charge given them was, Whatsoever *house* they *entered into*, they must say, *Peace be to this house*.

JAMIESON, FAUSSET, BROWN

CHAPTER 10

Vss. 1-24. MISSION OF THE SEVENTY DISCIPLES, AND THEIR RETURN. As our Lord's end approaches, the preparations for the establishment of the coming Kingdom are quickened and extended. **1. the Lord**—a becoming title here, as this appointment was an act truly *lordly* [BENGEL]. **other seventy also**—rather, "others (also in number), 70"; probably with allusion to the seventy elders of Israel on whom the Spirit descended in the wilderness (Num. 11:24, 25). The mission, unlike that of the Twelve, was evidently quite *temporary*. All the instructions are in keeping with a brief and hasty *pioneering* mission, intended to supply what of general preparation for coming events the Lord's own visit afterwards to the same "cities and places" (vs. 1) would not, from want of time, now suffice to accomplish; whereas the instructions to the Twelve, besides embracing all those to the Seventy, contemplate *world-wide* and *permanent* effects. Accordingly, after their return from this single missionary tour, we never again read of the Seventy.

2. the harvest . . . —(See on Matt. 9:37, 38). **The harvest truly is plenteous**—His eye doubtless rested immediately on the Jewish field, but this he saw widening into the vast field of "the world" (ch. 13:38), teeming with souls having to be gathered to Him. **but the labourers**—men divinely qualified and called to gather them in. **Pray ye therefore the Lord of the harvest**—the great Lord and Proprietor of all. Cf. John 15:1, "I am the true vine, and My Father is the husbandman." **that he will send forth labourers into his harvest**—The word properly means "thrust forth"; but this emphatic sense disappears in some places, as in vs. 25, and John 10:4—"When He *putteth forth* His own sheep." (See on ch. 4:1.)

3-12. (See on Matt. 10: 7-16). **Behold, I send you forth**—The "I" here is emphatic, holding up Himself as the Fountain of the Gospel ministry, as He is also the Great Burden of it. **as sheep**—defenseless—**in the midst of wolves**—ready to make a prey of you (John 10:12). To be left exposed, as sheep to wolves, would have been startling enough; but that the sheep should be *sent* among the wolves would sound strange indeed. No wonder this announcement begins with the exclamation, "Behold."

And when ye come into an house—or "the house," but it means not the worthy house, but the house ye first enter, to try if it be worthy. **salute it**—show it the usual civilities. **And if the house be worthy**—showing this by giving you a welcome—**let your peace come upon it**—This is best explained by the injunction to the Seventy, "And into whatsoever house ye enter, first say, Peace be to this house" (Luke 10:5). This was

ADAM CLARKE

posed," has not his mind properly directed towards the heavenly inheritance, and is not *fit* to show the way to others. In both these verses there is a plain reference to the call of Elisha.

CHAPTER 10

1. *The Lord appointed other seventy*. Rather, "seventy others," not *other seventy*, as our translation has it, which seems to intimate that he had appointed seventy before this time, though probably the word *other* has a reference to the twelve chosen first. He not only chose twelve disciples to be constantly with Him, but He chose seventy others to go before Him. Our blessed Lord formed everything in His Church on the model of the Jewish church; and why? Because it was the pattern shown by God himself, the divine form, which pointed out the heavenly substance which now began to be established in its place. As He before had chosen twelve apostles, in reference to the twelve patriarchs, who were the chiefs of the twelve tribes, He now "publicly appointed" (for so the word means) *seventy* others, as Moses did the seventy elders whom he associated with himself to assist him in the government of the people; see Exod. xviii. 19; xxiv. 1-9. These Christ sent by *two and two*: (1) to teach them the necessity of concord among the ministers of righteousness; (2) that in the mouths of two witnesses everything might be established; and (3) that they might comfort and support each other in their difficult labor. See on Mark vi. 7. Several MSS. and versions have *seventy-two*. Sometimes the Jews chose six out of each tribe; this was the number of the great Sanhedrin.

2. *That he would send forth*. There seems to be an allusion here to the case of reapers who, though the harvest was perfectly ripe, yet were in no hurry to cut it down. News of this is brought to *the Lord of the harvest*, the farmer, and he is entreated to exert his authority, and hurry them out; and this he does because the harvest is spoiling for want of being reaped and gathered in. See the notes on Matt. ix. 37-38.

4. *Carry neither purse, nor scrip*. See on Matt. x. 9, etc., and Mark vi. 8, etc.

Nor scrip for your journey. To carry provisions. It was a leathern pouch hung about their necks, in which they put their victuals. This was, properly, the shepherd's bag.

If the house be worthy. If that family be proper for a preacher to lodge in, and the master be ready to embrace the message of salvation. *Your peace*. The blessings you have prayed for

MATTHEW HENRY

Here, [1] They are supposed to enter into *private houses*; for, being not admitted into the synagogues, they were forced to preach where they could have liberty. And, as their public preaching was driven into houses, so thither they carried it. Christ's church was at first very much *a church in the house.* [2] They are instructed to say, "*Peace be to this house. Salute no man by the way* in compliment, but to those into whose house ye enter, say, *Peace be to you,* with seriousness and in reality." Christ's ministers go into all the world, to say, in Christ's name, *Peace be to you.* We are to *propose* peace to all, to *preach peace by Jesus Christ, peace on earth,* and to invite the children of men to come and take the benefit of it. We are to *pray* for peace to all.

(2) The success was to be different, according to the different dispositions of those whom they preached to and prayed for. According as the inhabitants were sons of peace or not, so their peace should or should not *rest upon the house.* "You will meet with some that are the *sons of peace,* that are ready to admit the word of the gospel in the light and love of it. As to those, *your peace* shall find them out and *rest upon them*; your prayers for them shall be heard, the promises of the gospel shall be *confirmed* to them. You will meet with others that are no ways disposed to hear or heed your message, whole houses that have not one *son of peace* in them." Now it is certain that our peace shall *not come* upon *them.* But it shall *return to us again*; that is, we shall have the comfort of having done our duty to God and discharged our trust. Our peace shall return to us again, not only to be enjoyed by ourselves, but to be communicated to others, them that are *sons of peace.*

5. They must *receive* the kindnesses of those that should *entertain* them and *bid them welcome, v.* 7, 8. "Those that receive the gospel will receive you that preach it, and give you entertainment." (1) "Be not *shy*; do not suspect your welcome, nor be afraid of being troublesome, but *eat and drink* heartily *such things as they give.* You will deserve it, for *the labourer is worthy of his hire,* and it is not an act of charity, but of justice, in those who are *taught in the word to communicate to those that teach them.*" (2) "Be not *nice* and *curious* in your diet: *Eat and drink such things as they give* (*v.* 7), *such things as are set before you, v.* 8. Be thankful for plain food, and do not find fault, though it be not dressed according to art." It ill becomes Christ's disciples to be *desirous of dainties.* Probably, Christ here refers to the traditions of the elders about their meat, but Christ would not have them to regard those things, but eat what was given them, *asking no question for conscience' sake.*

6. They must *denounce* the judgments of God against those who should *reject* them and their *message*: "If you *enter into a city,* and they *do not receive you,* leave them, *v.* 10. If they will not *give you welcome* into their houses, do you *give them warning* in their streets." He orders them to (*ch.* ix. 5) do as he had ordered the apostles to do: "Say to them: *Even the dust of your city, which cleaveth on us, we do wipe off against you, v.* 11. From them do not receive any kindnesses at all, be not beholden to them." It shall be a witness for Christ's messengers that they had been there according to their Master's order; *tender* and *refusal* were a discharge of their trust. "But tell them plainly, and bid them *be sure* of it, *The kingdom of God is come nigh to you.* Here is a fair offer made you; if you have not the benefit of it, it is your own fault. Now that the *kingdom of God is come nigh to you,* if you will not come up to it, and come into it, your sin will be inexcusable." The fairer offers we have of grace and life by Christ, the more we shall have to answer for another day, if we slight these offers: *It shall be more tolerable for Sodom than for that city, v.* 12. The Sodomites indeed rejected the warning given them by Lot; but rejecting the gospel is a more heinous crime.

Upon this occasion, the evangelist repeats,

(1) The particular doom of those cities wherein most of Christ's mighty works were done, which we had, Matt. xi. 20, &c. [1] They enjoyed greater privileges. Christ's *mighty works were done in them.* They were hereby *exalted to heaven.* They were brought as near heaven as external means could bring them. [2] God's design in favouring them thus was to bring them to *repentance* and *reformation* of life, *to sit in sackcloth and ashes.* [3] Their frustrating this design, and their receiving the grace of God therein in vain. It is implied that they *repented not*; they did not bring forth fruits agreeable to the advantages they enjoyed. [4] There was reason to think, morally speaking, that, if Christ had gone to Tyre and Sidon, Gentile cities, they would have repented *long ago,* so speedy would their repentance

JAMIESON, FAUSSET, BROWN

the ancient salutation of the East, and it prevails to this day. But from the lips of Christ and His messengers, it means something far higher, both in the gift and the giving of it, than in the current salutation. (See on John 14:27.) **but if it be not worthy, let your peace return to you**—If your peace finds a shut, instead of an open, door in the heart of any household, take it back to yourselves, who know how to value it; and it will taste the sweeter to you for having been offered, even though rejected.

son of peace—inwardly prepared to embrace your message of peace. See note on "worthy," (Matt. 10:13).

the workman is worthy of his meat—his "food" or "maintenance"; a principle which, being universally recognized in secular affairs, is here authoritatively applied to the services of the Lord's workmen, and by Paul repeatedly and touchingly employed in his appeals to the churches (Rom. 15:27; I Cor. 9:11; Gal. 6:6), and once as "scripture" (I Tim. 5:18).

12-15. (See on Matt. 11:20-24).

for Sodom—Tyre and Sidon were ruined by commercial prosperity; Sodom sank through its vile pollutions: but the doom of otherwise correct persons who, amidst a blaze of light, reject the Saviour, shall be *less endurable* than that of any of these.

ADAM CLARKE

shall come upon the family; God will prosper them in their bodies, souls, and substance. *Let your peace.* The blessings prayed for, return to you. "It shall turn back upon yourselves." They shall get nothing, and you shall have an increase.

6. *The son of peace.* In the Jewish style, a man who has any good or bad quality is called the *son* of it. Thus, wise men are called "the children of wisdom," Matt. xi. 19; Luke vii. 35. So, likewise, what a man is doomed to, he is called *the son* of, as in Eph. ii. 3, wicked men are styled the "children of wrath"; so Judas is called "the son of perdition," John xvii. 12; and a man who deserves to die is called, 2 Sam. xii. 5, a "son of death." *Son of peace* in the text not only means a peaceable, quiet man, but one also of good report for his uprightness and benevolence.

7. *The labourer is worthy.* See on Matt. x. 8. *Go not from house to house.* See on Matt. x. 11. *The workman is worthy of his meat.* "Of his maintenance." It is a maintenance, and that only, which a minister of God is to expect, and that he has a divine right to; but not to make a fortune, or lay up wealth. Besides, it is the *workman,* he that labors in the Word and doctrine, that is to get even this.

Into whatsoever city or town ye shall enter. In the commencement of Christianity, Christ and His preachers were all itinerant. *Enquire who in it is worthy.* That is, of a good character; for a preacher of the gospel should be careful of his reputation, and lodge only with those who are of a regular life. *There abide till ye go thence.* "Go not from house to house," Luke x. 7. Acting contrary to this precept has often brought a great disgrace on the gospel of God. Stay in your own lodging as much as possible, that you may have time for prayer and study. Seldom frequent the tables of the rich and great; if you do, it will unavoidably prove a snare to you.

9. *The kingdom of God is come nigh unto you.* "Is just upon you." This was the general text on which they were to preach all their sermons. See it explained, Matt. iii. 2.

11. *Even the very dust of your city.* See on Matt. x. 14-15.

13. *Woe unto thee, Chorazin!* See on Matt. xi. 21-24.

MATTHEW HENRY

have been, and that in *sackcloth and ashes*, so deep would it have been. [5] The doom of those who thus receive the grace of God in vain will be very fearful. They that were *thus exalted*, not making use of their elevation, will be *thrust down to hell.* [6] In the day of judgment Tyre and Sidon will fare better, and it will be more tolerable for them than for these cities.

(2) The general rule which Christ would go by, as to those to whom he sent his ministers: He will reckon himself treated according as they treated his ministers, *v.* 16. "*He that heareth you, heareth me.* He that *despiseth you* doth in effect *despise me*, nay, he *despiseth him that sent me.*" And they who *despise* the faithful ministers of Christ, and turn their backs upon their ministry, will be reckoned with as despisers of God and Christ.

Verses 17–24

I. What account they gave him of the success of their expedition: *They returned again with joy* (*v.* 17); not complaining of the fatigue of their journeys, but rejoicing in their success, especially in casting out unclean spirits: *Lord, even the devils are subject unto us through thy name.* They give Christ the glory of this: It is *through thy name*. All our victories over Satan are obtained by power derived from Jesus Christ. We must *in his name* enter the lists with our spiritual enemies. If the work be done *in* his name, the honour is due *to* his name. They speak of it with an air of exultation: *Even the devils* are *subject to us.* If devils are *subject to us*, what can stand before us?

II. How he received this account.

1. He confirmed what they said, as agreeing with his own observation (*v.* 18): I *saw Satan fall as lightning from heaven.* Satan and his kingdom fell before the preaching of the gospel. He falls *as lightning falls from heaven*, so suddenly, so irrecoverably. Satan *falls from heaven* when he falls from the throne in men's hearts. And Christ foresaw that the preaching of the gospel would wherever it went pull down Satan's kingdom. *Now is the prince of this world cast out.*

2. He repeated, ratified, and enlarged their commission: *Behold I give you power to tread on serpents, v.* 19. They had employed their power vigorously against Satan, and now Christ entrusts them with greater power. (1) An *offensive* power, power to *tread on serpents and scorpions*, devils and malignant spirits, the old serpent. As the devils have now been *subject to you*, so they shall still be. (2) *A defensive* power: "*Nothing shall by any means hurt you;* not *serpents* nor *scorpions.* If wicked men be as *serpents* to you, and you *dwell* among those *scorpions*, you may despise their rage, and *tread* upon it. They may *hiss*, but they cannot *hurt.*"

3. He directed them to turn their joy into the right *channel* (*v.* 20): "*Notwithstanding in this rejoice not, that the spirits are subject unto you.* Do not rejoice in this *only*, or in this *chiefly*, but *rather rejoice because your names are written in heaven*, because you are the children of God through faith." Christ could tell them that their *names were written in heaven*, for it is the *Lamb's book of life* that they are written in. Power to become the children of God is to be valued more than a power to work miracles; for we read of those who did *in Christ's name cast out devils*, and yet will be disowned by Christ in the great day. But they whose *names are written in heaven* shall never perish; they are *Christ's sheep*, to whom he will *give eternal life.* Holy love is *a more excellent way* than speaking with tongues.

4. He offered up a solemn thanksgiving to his Father, *v.* 21, 22. This we had before (Matt. xi. 25–27), only here it is prefixed that *in that hour Jesus rejoiced.* In *that hour* in which he saw Satan fall, *in that hour he rejoiced.* Christ's joy was a solid substantial joy, an inward joy: *he rejoiced in spirit.* Before he applied himself to *thank his Father*, he stirred up himself to *rejoice*; for, as *thankful praise* is the genuine language of *holy joy*, so *holy joy* is the root and spring of *thankful praise.* Two things he gives thanks for:

(1) For what was *revealed* by the *Father* through the *Son*: *I thank thee, O Father, Lord of heaven and earth, v.* 21. Now that which he gives thanks for is, [1] That the counsels of God concerning man's reconciliation to himself were *revealed* to some of the children of men, who might be fit also to *teach others*; *he* has *revealed* that which had been *kept secret* from the beginning of the world. [2] That they were revealed to *babes*, to those who were but *children in understanding*, till God by his Spirit elevated their faculties. We have reason to thank God, not so much for the honour he has hereby put upon babes, as for the honour he has hereby done himself in perfecting strength *out of weakness.* [3] That, at the

JAMIESON, FAUSSET, BROWN

16. He that . . .—(See on Matt. 10:40).

17. returned—evidently not long away. **Lord . . .**—"Thou hast exceeded Thy promise, for '*even the devils . . .*'." The possession of such power, not being expressly in their commission, as in that to the Twelve (ch. 9:1), filled them with more astonishment and joy than all else. **through thy name**—taking no credit to themselves, but feeling lifted into a region of unimagined superiority to the powers of evil simply through their connection with Christ.

18. I beheld—As much of the force of this glorious statement depends on the nice shade of sense indicated by the *imperfect tense* in the original, it should be brought out in the translation: "I was beholding Satan as lightning falling from heaven"; i.e., "I followed you on your mission, and watched its triumphs; while you were wondering at the subjection to you of devils in My name, a grander spectacle *was opening* to My view; sudden as the darting of lightning from heaven to earth, lo! Satan was beheld falling from heaven!" How remarkable is this, that by that law of association which connects a part with the whole, those feeble triumphs of the Seventy seem to have not only brought vividly before the Redeemer the whole ultimate result of His mission, but compressed it into a moment and quickened it into the rapidity of lightning! *N. B.*—The word rendered "*devils,*" is always used for those spiritual agents employed in *demoniacal possessions*—never for the ordinary agency of Satan in rational men. When therefore the Seventy say, "the *devils* [demons] are subject to us," and Jesus replies, "Mine eye was beholding *Satan falling,*" it is plain that He meant to raise their minds not only from the *particular* to the *general*, but from a very *temporary* form of satanic operation to *the entire kingdom of evil.* (See John 12:31; and cf. Isa. 14:12). **19. Behold, I give you . . .**—not for any renewal of their mission, though probably many of them afterwards became ministers of Christ; but simply as disciples. **serpents and scorpions**—the latter more venomous than the former: literally, in the first instance (Mark 16:17, 18; Acts 28:5); but the next words, "*and over all the power of the enemy, and nothing shall by any means hurt you,*" show that the glorious power of faith to "overcome the world" and "quench all the fiery darts of the wicked one," by the communication and maintenance of which to His people He makes them *innocuous*, is what is meant (I John 5:4; Eph. 6:16). **20. rejoice not, . . .**—i.e., not so much. So far from forbidding it, He takes occasion from it to tell them what had been passing in His own mind. But as power over demons was after all intoxicating, He gives them a higher joy to *balance* it, the joy of having their names in Heaven's register (Phil. 4:3). **21, 22. Jesus . . . said . . . .**—The very same sublime words were uttered by our Lord on a former similar occasion (Matt. 11:25-27, on which see *Note*); but (1) There we are merely told that He "answered and said" thus; here, He "*rejoiced in spirit* and said . . ." (2) There it was merely "at that time" (or season) that He spoke thus, meaning with a general reference to the rejection of His gospel by the self-sufficient; here, "*In that hour* Jesus said," with express reference probably to the humble class from which He had to draw the Seventy, and the similar class that had chiefly welcomed their message. "Rejoice" is too weak a word. It is "exulted in spirit"—evidently giving visible expression to His unusual emotions; while, at the same time, the words "in spirit" are meant to convey to the reader the *depth* of them. This is one of those rare

ADAM CLARKE

15. *To hell.* To hades. See this explained, Matt. xi. 23.
Shalt be brought down to hell. Perhaps not meaning here the place of torment, but rather a state of desolation. The original word is *Hades*—the invisible receptacle or mansion of the dead, answering to *sheol*, in Hebrew; and implying, often, (1) the grave; (2) the state of separate souls, or unseen world of spirits, whether of torment, Luke xvi. 23, or in general, Rev. i. 18; vi. 8; xx. 13-14. The word *hell*, used in the common translation, conveys now an improper meaning of the original word, because *hell* is used only to signify the place of the damned.

18. *I beheld Satan.* Or "Satan himself"—"The very Satan, the supreme adversary"—falling *as lightning*, with the utmost suddenness, as a flash of lightning falls from the clouds, and at the same time in the most observable manner. The fall was both very sudden and very apparent.

19. *To tread on serpents.* It is possible that by *serpents and scorpions* our Lord means the scribes and Pharisees, whom He calls "serpents" and a "brood of vipers," Matt. xxiii. 33, because through the subtility and venom of the old *serpent*, the devil, they opposed Him and His doctrine. And by trampling on these, it is likely that He means they should get a complete victory over such; as it was an ancient custom to trample on the kings and generals who had been taken in battle, to signify the complete conquest which had been gained over them. See Josh. x. 24. See also Rom. xvi. 20.

20. *Because your names are written in heaven.* This form of speech is taken from the ancient custom of writing the names of all the citizens in a public register, that the several families might be known, and the inheritances properly preserved. This custom is still observed even in these kingdoms, though not particularly noticed. Every child that is born in the land is ordered to be *registered*, with the names of its parents, and the time when born, baptized, or registered; and this register is generally kept in the parish church, or in some public place of safety. Such a register as this is called in Phil. iv. 3; Rev. iii. 5, "the book of life," i.e., the book or register where the persons were enrolled as they came into life.

21. *Rejoiced in spirit.* Was truly and heartily joyous, felt an inward triumph. But *the Holy Spirit* is the reading here of numerous MSS. and versions. These might be considered sufficient authority to admit the word into the text.

I thank thee. Bishop Pearce justly observes the thanks are meant to be given to God for revealing them to babes, not for hiding them from the others. *Thou hast hid.* That is, Thou hast not revealed them to the scribes and Pharisees, who idolized their own wisdom; but Thou *hast revealed them* to the simple and humble of heart.

MATTHEW HENRY

same time when he revealed them unto babes, he *hid them from the wise and prudent*, the Gentile philosophers, the Jewish rabbin. He *did not reveal* the things of the gospel to them, nor employ them in preaching up his kingdom. Paul indeed was bred a scholar among the wise and prudent; but he became a *babe* when he became an apostle, and made neither show nor use of any other knowledge than that of *Christ and him crucified*, 1 Cor. ii. 2, 4. [4] That God herein acted by way of sovereignty: *Even so, Father, for so it seemed good in thy sight.* If God gives his grace and the knowledge of his son to some that are less likely, and does not give it to others whom we should think better able to deliver it with advantage, this must satisfy. He chooses to entrust the dispensing of his gospel in the hands of those who with a *divine energy* will give it the *setting on*, rather than in theirs who with *human art* will give it the *setting off*.

(2) For what was *secret* between the *Father* and *the Son, v.* 22. [1] The vast *confidence* that the Father *puts* in the Son: *All things are delivered to me of my Father.* In him all fulness must *dwell*, and from him it must be *derived*: he is the great *trustee* that manages all the concerns of God's kingdom. [2] The good understanding that there is between the Father and the Son: *No man knows who the Son is but the Father*, nor *who the Father is but the Son, and he to whom the Son* by the Spirit *will reveal him.*

5. He told his disciples how well it was for them that they had these things revealed to them, *v.* 23, 24. He *turned to his disciples*, designing to make them sensible how much it was for their happiness, that they knew the mysteries of the kingdom and were employed to lead others into the knowledge of them. (1) What a step it is *towards* something better. Though the bare knowledge of these things is not saving, yet it puts us in the way of salvation: *Blessed are the eyes which see the things which we see.* (2) What a step it is *above* those that went before them: "*Many prophets and righteous men*" (so it is in Matt. xiii. 17), "*many prophets and kings*" (so it is here), "have *desired* to see and hear those things which you are daily and intimately conversant with, and *have not seen* and *heard* them." The honour and happiness of the New Testament saints far exceed those even of the *prophets* and *kings* of the Old Testament. The general ideas which the Old Testament saints had of the graces and glories of the Messiah's kingdom, made them wish a thousand times that they might see the substance of those things of which they had faint shadows.

Verses 25-37

We have here Christ's discourse with a lawyer about some points of conscience, which we are all concerned to be rightly informed in, and are so here, from Christ.

I. We are concerned to know what that good is which we should do in *this* life, in order to our attaining *eternal life.* A question to this purport was proposed to our Saviour by a *certain lawyer*, only with a design to *try* him, *v.* 25. The lawyer *stood up*, and *asked him, Master, what shall I do to inherit eternal life?* If Christ had anything peculiar to prescribe, by this question he would get it out of him; if not, he would expose his doctrine as needless; or, perhaps, he had no malicious design against Christ, only he was willing to have a little talk with him, just as people go to church to hear what the minister will say. This was a good question: *What shall I do to inherit eternal life?* But it lost all its goodness when it was proposed with an ill design. It is not enough to speak of the things of God, and to enquire about them, but we must do it with a suitable concern.

1. How Christ turned him over to the divine law. Though he knew the thoughts and intents of his heart, he did not answer him according to the folly of that, but according to the wisdom and goodness of the question he asked. He answered him with a question: *What is written in the law? How readest thou? v.* 26. Christ will catechize him, and make him know himself. The studies of his profession would inform him; let him practise according to his knowledge, and he should not come short of *eternal life.* It will be of great use to us, in our way to heaven, to consider *what is written in the law*, and *what we read* there. We must have recourse to our bibles, to the law, as it is now in the hand of Christ, and walk in the way that is shown us there. Having it *written*, it is our duty to read it, to read it with understanding so that, when there is occasion, we may be able to tell *what is written in the law*, and *how we read.*

2. What a good account he gave of the law, of the principal commandments of the law. He did not, like a Pharisee, refer himself to the tradition of the

JAMIESON, FAUSSET, BROWN

cases in which the veil is lifted from off the Redeemer's inner man, that, angel-like, we may "look into it" for a moment (I Pet. 1:12). Let us gaze on it with reverential wonder, and as we perceive what it was that produced that mysterious ecstasy, we shall find rising in our hearts a still rapture—"Oh, the depths!"

23, 24.—(See on Matt. 13:16, 17).

25-37. QUESTION OF A LAWYER, AND PARABLE OF THE GOOD SAMARITAN.

25. tempted him—"tested him"; in no hostile spirit, yet with no tender anxiety for light on that question of questions, but just to see what insight this great Galilean teacher had.

26. What is written in the law—apposite question to a doctor of the *law*, and putting him in turn to the test [BENGEL].

ADAM CLARKE

CHARLES H. SPURGEON:

The Savior's joy was that through the Father's grace men were being enlightened. The seventy disciples had been from city to city, working miracles and preaching the gospel, and their Master was glad when they returned with tidings of success: "In that hour Jesus rejoiced in spirit." It pleases Jesus when the gospel has free course, and God is glorified thereby. Then, in measure, He sees of the travail of His soul, and is filled with satisfaction. Shall we not find our joy where He finds His? Shall we not enter into the joy of the Lord? Whenever we hear good news of a village evangelized, of a township moved by the glad tidings, of a country long shut up from the gospel at length opened to the world, let us feel our highest and deepest joy. Rather let us rejoice in this than in business prosperity or personal advantage. What if we can find no joy in our own circumstances, what if even spiritual affairs within our soul are full of difficulty; let us joy and rejoice that God the Father is revealing the light of His gospel among the sons of men. Be this our highest wish, "Thy kingdom come," and in that coming kingdom let us find our utmost happiness. Be sure that the joy which warmed the heart of Christ can do us no hurt: it must be a pure, sacred, and ennobling joy, and therefore let us indulge in it very largely. Christ's joy lay in the Father's sending forth His light and His truth, making men to see things which prophets and kings had desired to behold, but had not been favored to see. Jesus rejoiced in this, that the blessings of grace were being revealed by the Father.

—*The Treasury of the New Testament*

But blessed are your eyes. You improve the light which God has given you, and you receive an increase of heavenly wisdom by every miracle and by every sermon.

Many prophets and righteous men. These lived by and died in the faith of the promised Messiah; the fullness of the time was not then come for His manifestation in the flesh.

A lawyer. "A teacher of the law." What is called *lawyer* in the common translation conveys a wrong idea to most readers. These teachers of the law were the same as the scribes.

ALEXANDER MACLAREN:

The story is not, properly speaking, a parable, or imaginary narrative of something in the physical world intended to be translated into something in the spiritual region, but it is an illustration (by an imaginary narrative) of the actual virtue in question. Every detail is beautifully adapted to bring out the lesson that the obligation of neighborly affection has nothing to do with nearness of race or religion, but is as wide as humanity. The wounded man was probably a Jew, but it is significant that his nationality is not mentioned. He is "a certain man," that is all. The Samaritan did not ask where he was born before he helped him. So Christ teaches us that sorrow and need and sympathy and help are of no nationality.—*Expositions of Holy Scripture*

MATTHEW HENRY

siders, but fastened upon the two first and great commandments of the law, which included all the rest, *v.* 27. We must *love God with all our hearts,* must look upon him as the best of beings, in himself most amiable, and infinitely perfect and excellent. Our love to him must be sincere, hearty, and fervent; it must be a superlative love, a love that is as strong as death, but an intelligent love. It must be an *entire* love; he must have our *whole* souls, and must be served with *all that is within us.* We must love our neighbours as *ourselves,* which we shall easily do, if we, as we ought to do, love God *better than ourselves.* We must do all the good we can in the world and no hurt, and must fix it as a rule to ourselves to do to others as we would they should do to us; and this is to love our neighbour *as ourselves.*

3. Christ's approbation of what he said, *v.* 28. What he said that was good Christ commended: *Thou hast answered right.* Christ himself fastened upon these as the two great commandments of the law (Matt. xxii. 37). So far is right; but the hardest part of this work yet remains: "*This do, and thou shalt live;* thou shalt *inherit eternal life.*"

4. His care to avoid the conviction which was now ready to fasten upon him. When Christ said, *This do, and thou shalt live,* he began to be aware that Christ intended to draw from him an acknowledgment that he *had not done this.* He was *willing to justify himself,* and therefore cared not for carrying on that discourse. Many ask good questions with a design rather to *justify themselves* than to *inform themselves,* rather proudly to show what is good in them than humbly to see what is bad in them.

II. We are concerned to know who is our neighbour. This is another of this lawyer's queries. As to loving God, he was willing to say no more of it; but, as to his *neighbour,* he was sure that there he had come up to the rule, for he had always been very kind and respectful to all about him. Now observe,

1. What was the corrupt notion of the Jewish teachers in this matter. "Where he saith, *Thou shalt love thy neighbour, he excepts all Gentiles,* for they are not *our neighbours,* but those only that are of our own nation and religion." If they saw a Gentile in *danger of death,* they thought themselves under no obligation to help to *save his life.*

2. How Christ corrected this inhuman notion, and showed, by a parable, that whomsoever we *have need* to receive kindness *from,* and *find ready* to show us the kindness *we need,* we cannot but look upon as *our neighbour.*

(1) The parable itself, which represents to us a poor Jew in distressed circumstances, succoured and relieved by a good Samaritan. Let us see here,

[1] How he was *abused* by his *enemies.* The honest man was travelling peaceably upon his lawful business in the road, and it was a great road that led from Jerusalem to Jericho, *v.* 30. Probably it happened lately, just as it is here related. This poor man *fell among thieves.* They were very *barbarous;* they not only took his money, but stripped him of his clothes, and they *wounded him,* and left him *half dead,* ready to die of his wounds. What reason have we to thank God for our preservation from perils by robbers!

[2] How he was *slighted* by those who should have been his friends, one a priest and the other a Levite, men of professed sanctity, whose offices obliged them to tenderness and compassion, who ought to have taught others their duty in such a case as this. Many of the courses of the priests had their residence in Jericho, and thence came up to Jerusalem, and so back again, which occasioned abundance of *passing* and *repassing* of priests that way, and Levites their attendants. They came *this way,* and saw the poor wounded man. The Levite not only saw him, but *came and looked on him, v.* 32. But they *passed by on the other side;* when they saw his case, they got as far off him as ever they could.

[3] How he was *succoured* and *relieved* by a *stranger,* a *certain Samaritan,* of that nation which of all others the Jews most despised and detested and would have no dealings with. This man had some humanity in him, *v.* 33. The priest had his heart hardened against one of *his own people,* but the Samaritan had his opened towards one of *another* people. *When he saw him he had compassion on him.* Though he was a Jew, he was a man, and a man in *misery,* and the Samaritan has learned to honour all men; and therefore pities him, as he himself would desire and expect to be pitied in the like case. The *compassion* of this Samaritan was not an idle compassion; but, when he *drew out his soul,* he *reached forth his hand* also to this poor *needy* creature. See how friendly this good Samaritan was. He *went to* the poor man, whom the priest and Levite kept at a distance from. He did the surgeon's part, for want of a better. He *bound up his wounds,* making use of his own linen,

JAMIESON, FAUSSET, BROWN

27. Thou shalt . . .—the answer Christ Himself gave to another lawyer. (See on Mark 12:29-33).

28. he said . . .—"Right; THIS do, and life is thine"—laying such emphasis on "this" as to indicate, without expressing it, *where the real difficulty to a sinner lay,* and thus nonplussing the questioner himself.

29. willing—"wishing," to get himself out of the difficulty, by throwing on Jesus the definition of "neighbor," which the Jews interpreted very narrowly and technically, as excluding Samaritans and Gentiles [ALFORD].

30. A certain man—a Jew. **from Jerusalem to Jericho**—a distance of nineteen miles northeast, a deep and very fertile hollow—"the *Temple* of Judea" [TRENCH]. **thieves**—"robbers." The road, being rocky and desolate, was a notorious haunt of robbers, then and for ages after, and even to this day.

31, 32. came down a . . . priest . . . and a Levite—Jericho, the second city of Judea, was a city of the priests and Levites, and thousands of them lived there. The two here mentioned are supposed, apparently, to be returning from *temple duties,* but they "had not learnt what that meaneth, 'I will have mercy and not sacrifice' [TRENCH]. **saw him**—It was not *inadvertently* that he acted. **came and looked**—a further aggravation. **passed by**—although the law expressly required the opposite treatment even of the *beast* not only of their *brethren,* but of their *enemy* (Deut. 22:4; Exod. 23.4, 5. Cf. Isa. 58:7). **33. Samaritan**—one excommunicated by the Jews, a byword among them, synonymous with heretic and devil (John 8:48; See on ch. 17:18). **had compassion**—His best is mentioned first; for "He who gives outward things gives something *external to himself,* but he who imparts compassion and tears gives him something *from his very self"* [GREGORY the Great, in TRENCH]. No doubt the priest and Levite had their excuses—'Tisn't safe to be lingering here; besides, he's past recovery; and then, mayn't suspicion rest upon ourselves? So might the Samaritan have reasoned, *but did not* [TRENCH]. Nor did he say, He's a Jew, who would have had no dealings with me (John 4:9), and why should I with him?

ADAM CLARKE

27. *Thou shalt love the Lord.* See this important subject explained at large on Matt. xxii. 37-40. *Thy neighbour as thyself.* See the nature of *self-love* explained on Matt. xix. 19.

Thou shalt love thy neighbour as thyself. Self-love, as it is generally called, has been grievously declaimed against, even by religious people, as a most pernicious and dreadful evil. But they have not understood the subject on which they spoke. They have denominated that intense propensity which unregenerate men feel to gratify their carnal appetites and vicious passions self-love, whereas it might be more properly termed self-hatred or self-murder. If I am to love my neighbor as myself, and this "love worketh no ill to his neighbour," then self-love, in the sense in which our Lord uses it, is something excellent.

29. *Willing to justify himself.* Wishing to make it appear that he was a righteous man, and that consequently he was in the straight road to the kingdom of God, said, *Who is my neighbour?* supposing our Lord would have at once answered, "Every Jew is to be considered as such, and the Jews only." Now as he imagined he had never been deficient in his conduct to any person of his own nation, he thought he had amply fulfilled the law. This is the sense in which the Jews understood the word *neighbour,* as may be seen from Lev. xxix. 15-18. But our Lord shows here that the acts of kindness which a man is bound to perform to his neighbor when in distress, he should perform to any person, of whatever nation, religion, or kindred, whom he finds in necessity. As the word signifies one who is "near," this very circumstance makes any person our neighbor whom we know; and, if in distress, an object of our most compassionate regard.

30. *And Jesus answering.* Rather, "Then Jesus took him up." This I believe to be the meaning of the word; he threw out a challenge, and our Lord "took him up" on his own ground. *A certain man went down from Jerusalem.* This was the most public road in all Judea, as it was the grand thoroughfare between these two cities for the courses of priests, 12,000 of whom are said to have resided at Jericho. *Fell among thieves.* At this time the whole land of Judea was much infested with hordes of banditti, and it is not unlikely that many robberies might have been committed on that very road to which our Lord refers.

31. *And by chance.* Properly means the "coincidence of time and circumstance." At the time in which the poor Jew was half dead, through the wounds which he had received, a priest came where he was.

31-32. *Priest* and *Levite* are mentioned here, partly because they were the most frequent travellers on this road, and partly to show that these were the persons who, from the nature of their office, were most obliged to perform works of mercy, and from whom a person in distress had a right to expect immediate succor and comfort; and their inhuman conduct here was a flat breach of the law, Deut. xxii. 1-4.

33. *Samaritan* is mentioned merely to show that he was a person from whom a Jew had no right to expect any help or relief, because of the enmity which subsisted between the two nations.

MATTHEW HENRY

it is likely, for that purpose; and poured *in oil and wine*; wine to wash the wound, and oil to mollify it, and close it up. He did all he could as one whose heart bled with them. He *set him on his own beast*, and went on foot himself, and *brought him to an inn.* We suppose this Samaritan went upon business; but he understood that both his own business and God's sacrifice too must give place to such an act of mercy as this. He *took care of him* in the inn, got him to bed, had food for him that was proper, and due attendance, and, it may be, prayed with him. As if he had been his own child, when he left him next morning, he left money with the landlord, and passed his word for what he should spend more. *Twopence* of their money would go a great way; however, here it was an earnest of satisfaction to the full of all demands. All this was kind and generous, and as much as one could have expected from a friend or a brother; and yet here it is done by a stranger and foreigner.

Now this parable is applicable to another purpose than that for which it was intended; and does excellently set forth the kindness and love of God our Saviour towards sinful miserable man. We were like this poor distressed traveller. The law of Moses *passes by on the other side*, as having neither pity nor power to help us; but then comes the blessed Jesus, that good Samaritan; he has compassion on us. He takes care of us. This magnifies the riches of his love, and obliges us all to say, "How much are we indebted, and what shall we render?"

(2) The application of the parable. [1] The truth contained in it is extorted from the lawyer's own mouth. Saith Christ, "*Which of these three was neighbour to him that fell among thieves* (*v.* 36). Which of these did the neighbour's part?" To this the lawyer would not answer, "Doubtless, the Samaritan was"; but, "*He that showed mercy on him;* doubtless, he was a good neighbour to him." [2] The duty inferred from it is pressed home upon the lawyer's own conscience: *Go, and do thou likewise*. If a Samaritan does well that helps a distressed Jew, certainly a Jew does not well if he refuses in like manner to help a distressed Samaritan. "And therefore *go thou* and do as the Samaritan did, whenever occasion offers: show mercy to those that need thy help, and do it freely, and with concern and compassion, though they be not of thy own nation." This lawyer thought to have puzzled Christ himself; but Christ sends him to school to a Samaritan, to learn his duty: "Go, and do like him." It is the duty of everyone of us to succour, help, and relieve all that are in distress and necessity, and of lawyers particularly.

Verses 38–42

I. The entertainment which Martha gave to Christ and his disciples at her house, *v.* 38.

1. Christ's coming to the village where Martha lived: *As they went* he *entered into a certain village*. This village was *Bethany*, nigh to Jerusalem. Christ honoured the country-villages with his presence and favour, and not the great and populous cities only; for, as he *chose privacy*, so he *countenanced poverty*.

2. His reception at Martha's house: *A certain woman, named Martha, received him into her house*, and made him welcome. There were some who were Christ's particular friends, whom he loved more than his other friends, and them he visited most frequently. He *loved* this family (John xi. 5), and often invited himself to them. It is called Martha's house, for, probably, she was a widow, and was the housekeeper. Though at this time it was grown dangerous to entertain him, especially so near Jerusalem, yet she cared not what hazard she ran for his name's sake. Though there were many that rejected him, and would not entertain him, yet there was one that would bid him welcome.

II. The attendance which Mary, the sister of Martha, gave upon the word of Christ, *v.* 20. 1. She *heard his word*. It seems, our Lord Jesus, as soon as he came into Martha's house, addressed himself to his great work of preaching the gospel. A good sermon is never the worse for being preached in a house. Since Christ is forward to speak, we should be *swift to hear*. She *sat* to hear, which denotes a close attention. Her mind was composed, and she resolved not to catch a word now and then, but to receive all that Christ delivered. If we sit with him at his feet now, we shall sit with him on his throne shortly.

III. The care of Martha about her domestic affairs: But Martha *was cumbered about much serving* (*v.* 40), and that was the reason why she was not where Mary was. Housekeepers know what care and bustle there must be when a great entertainment is to be made. Observe here,

1. Something *commendable*, which must not be

JAMIESON, FAUSSET, BROWN

oil and wine—the remedies used in such cases all over the East (Isa. 1:6), and elsewhere; the *wine* to cleanse the wounds, the *oil* to assuage their smartings. **on his own beast**—himself going on foot.

35. two pence—equal to two day's wages of a laborer, and enough for several days' support. **36. Which . . . was neighbour?**—a most dexterous way of putting the question: (1) Turning the question from, "Whom am I to love as my neighbour?" to "Who is the man that shows that love?" (2) Compelling the lawyer to give a reply very different from what he would like—not only condemning his own nation, but those of them who should be the most exemplary. (3) Making him commend one of a deeply hated race. And he does it, but it is almost extorted. For he does not answer, "The Samaritan"—that would have sounded heterodox, heretical —but"He that showed mercy on him." It comes to the same thing, no doubt, but the circumlocution is significant. **37. Go . . .**—O exquisite, matchless teaching! What new fountains of charity has not this opened up in the human spirit—rivers in the wilderness, streams in the desert! What noble Christian institutions have not such words founded, all undreamed of till that wondrous One came to bless this heartless world of ours with His incomparable love—first in words, and then in deeds which have translated His words into flesh and blood, and poured the life of them through that humanity which He made His own! Was this parable, now, designed to magnify the law of love, and to show who fulfils it and who not? And who did this as never man did it, as our Brother Man, "our Neighbor?" The priests and Levites had not strengthened the diseased, nor bound up the broken (Ezek. 34:4), while He bound up the brokenhearted (Isa. 61:1), and poured into all wounded spirits the balm of sweetest consolation. All the Fathers saw through the thin veil of this noblest of stories, *the* Story of love, and never wearied of tracing the analogy (though sometimes fancifully enough) [TRENCH]. "He hungered," exclaims GREGORY of Nazianzen (in the fourth century), "but He fed thousands; He was weary, but He is the Rest of the weary; He is saluted 'Samaritan' and 'Demoniac,' but He *saves him that went down from Jerusalem and fell among thieves*," etc.

38-42. MARTHA AND MARY. **38. certain village**—Bethany (John 11:1), which Luke so speaks of, having no farther occasion to notice it. **received him . . . her house**—The house belonged to her, and she appears throughout to be the older sister.

39. which also—"who for her part," in contrast with Martha. **sat**—"seated herself." From the custom of sitting *beneath* an instructor, the phrase "sitting at one's feet" came to mean being a disciple of any one (Acts 22:3). **heard**—rather, "kept listening" to His word.

40. cumbered—"distracted." **came to him**—"presented herself before Him," as from another apartment, in which her sister had "*left* her to serve (or make preparation) *alone*."

ADAM CLARKE

34. *Pouring in oil and wine*. These, beaten together, appear to have been used formerly as a common medicine for fresh wounds. Bind up a fresh cut immediately in a soft rag or lint moistened with pure olive oil, and the parts will heal by what is called the first intention, and more speedily than by any other means.

35. *Two pence*. Two denarii.

36. *Which . . . was neighbour?* Which fulfilled the duty which one neighbor owes to another?

37. *He that shewed mercy*. Or "so much mercy." His prejudice would not permit him to name the Samaritan, yet his conscience obliged him to acknowledge that he was the only righteous person of the three. *Go, and do thou likewise*. Be even to your enemy in distress as kind, humane, and merciful as this Samaritan was.

38. *Received him*. "Kindly received." She received Him in a friendly manner, under her roof, and entertained Him hospitably. So the word is used in the best Greek writers. Martha is supposed by some to have been a widow, with whom her brother, Lazarus, and sister, Mary, lodged.

39. *Sat at Jesus' feet*. This was the posture of the Jewish scholars while listening to the instructions of the rabbins. It is in this sense that Paul says he was "brought up at the feet of Gamaliel," Acts xxii. 3.

40. *Martha was cumbered*. "Perplexed." She was harassed with different cares and employments at the same time, one drawing one way, and another, another—a proper description of a worldly mind. But in Martha's favor it may be justly said that all her anxiety was to provide

MATTHEW HENRY

overlooked. Here was a commendable *respect to our Lord Jesus.* It was not for ostentation, but purely to testify her goodwill to him, that she made this entertainment. Here was a commendable *care of her household affairs.* It is the duty of those who have the charge of families to *look well to the ways of their household.* The affectation of state and the love of ease make many families neglected.

2. Here was something *culpable.* She was for *much serving.* Her heart was upon it, to have a very sumptuous and splendid entertainment. She was in care, *concerning much attendance.* It does not become the disciples of Christ to affect *much serving;* what need is there of *much serving,* when much less will serve? She was *cumbered* about it; she was just *distracted* with it. Note, Whatever cares the providence of God casts upon us we must not be *cumbered* with them. *Care* is good and duty; but *cumber* is sin and folly. She was *then cumbered about much serving* when she should have been with her sister, sitting at Christ's feet to hear his word.

IV. The *complaint* which Martha made to Christ against her sister Mary (*v.* 40): "*Lord, dost thou not care that my sister has left me to serve alone?* Bid her come and help me."

1. This complaint of Martha's may be considered as a *discovery* of her *worldliness;* it was the language of her inordinate care and cumber. The inordinacy of worldly cares and pursuits is often the occasion of disturbance in families and of strife and contention among relations. Martha, being angry at her sister, appealed to Christ, and would have him say that she *did well to be angry. Lord, dost thou not care that my sister has left me to serve alone?* When Martha was caring, she must have Mary, and Christ and all, to *care* too, or else she is not pleased. Those are not always in the right that are most forward to appeal to God; we must therefore take heed, lest at any time we expect that Christ should espouse our unjust and groundless quarrels. The cares which he casts upon us we may cheerfully cast upon him, but not those which we foolishly draw upon ourselves.

2. It may be considered as a discouragement of Mary's piety and devotion. Her sister should have *commended* her for it, but, instead of this, she *condemns* her as wanting in her duty. It is no strange thing for those that are zealous in religion to meet, not only with opposition from enemies, but with blame and censure from their friends.

V. The reproof which Christ gave to Martha for her inordinate care, *v.* 41. *Martha, Martha, thou art careful and troubled about many things,* whereas but *one thing is needful.*

1. He reproved her, though he was at this time her guest. *As many as Christ loves he rebukes and chastens.* Even those that are dear to Christ, if anything be amiss in them, shall be sure to hear of it.

2. When he reproved her, he called her by her name, *Martha.* He repeated her name, *Martha, Martha;* he speaks as one in earnest, and deeply concerned for her welfare. Those that are *entangled* in the cares of this life are not easily *disentangled.*

3. That which he reproved her for was her being *careful and troubled about many things.* Christ reproves her, both for the *intenseness* of her care ("Thou art *careful and troubled, divided* and *disturbed* by thy care"), and for the *extensiveness of it,* "about *many things.* Poor Martha, thou hast many things to fret at, and this puts thee out of humour, whereas less ado would serve." Inordinate care or trouble about many things in this world is a common fault among Christ's disciples. If they fret for no just cause, it is just with him to order them something to fret at.

4. That which aggravated the sin and folly of her care was that *but one thing is needful. The one thing needful* is certainly meant of that which Mary made her choice—*sitting at* Christ's feet, to hear his word. She was troubled about *many things,* when she should have applied herself to one; godliness *unites* the heart, which the world had *divided.* The *many things* she was troubled about were *needless,* while the *one thing* she neglected was *needful.* Martha's care and work were good in their proper season and place; but now she had something else to do, which was unspeakably more needful. She expected Christ to have blamed Mary for not doing as she did, but he blamed her for not doing as Mary did. The day will come when Martha will wish she had set where Mary did.

VI. Christ's approbation and commendation of Mary for her serious piety: *Mary hath chosen the good part.*

1. She had justly given the preference to that which best deserved it; for *one thing is needful,* this one thing that she has done. Serious godliness is a *needful* thing, it is the *one thing needful.* Nothing but this will go with us into another world.

2. She had herein wisely done well for herself.

JAMIESON, FAUSSET, BROWN

carest thou not . . . my sister . . .—"Lord, here am I with everything to do, and this sister of mine will not lay a hand to anything; thus I miss something from Thy lips, and Thou from our hands." **bid her . . .**—She presumes not to stop Christ's teaching by calling her sister away, and thus leaving Him without His one auditor, nor did she hope perhaps to succeed if she had tried.

41. Martha, Martha—emphatically redoubling upon the name. **careful and cumbered**—the one word expressing the inward *worrying anxiety* that her preparations should be worthy of her Lord; the other, the outward *bustle* of those preparations. **many things**—"much service" (vs. 40); too elaborate preparation, which so engrossed her attention that she missed her Lord's teaching.

42. one thing . . .—The idea of "Short work and little of it suffices for Me" is not so much the *lower sense* of these weighty words, as *supposed* in them, as the basis of something far loftier than any precept on economy. Underneath that idea is couched another, as to the littleness both of elaborate preparation for the present life and *of that life itself,* compared with another.

chosen the good part—not in the general sense of Moses' choice (Heb. 11:25), and Joshua's (Josh. 24:15), and David's (Ps. 119:30); i.e., of good in opposition to *bad;* but, of two good ways of serving and pleasing the Lord, choosing *the better.* Wherein, then, was Mary's better than Martha's? Hear what follows.

ADAM CLARKE

suitable and timely entertainment for our Lord and His disciples. And we should not, on the merest supposition, attribute earthly-mindedness to a woman whose character stands unimpeachable in the gospel; and who, by entertaining Christ and His disciples, and providing liberally for them, gave the highest proof that she was influenced by liberality and benevolence, and not by parsimony or covetousness.

Dost thou not care? Dost Thou not think it wrong that my sister thus leaves me to provide and prepare this supper, *alone?*

41. *Thou art careful and troubled.* "You are distracted, your mind is divided," in consequence of which "you are disturbed," your spirit is thrown into a tumult. *About many things.* Getting a variety of things ready for this entertainment, much more than are necessary on such an occasion.

42. *One thing is needful.* This is the end of the sentence, according to Bengel. "Now Mary hath chosen . . ." begins a new one. One single dish, the simplest and plainest possible, is such as best suits Me and My disciples, whose meat and drink it is to do the will of our Heavenly Father. *Mary hath chosen that good part.* That is, of hearing My word, of which she shall not be deprived, it being at present of infinitely greater importance to attend to My teaching than to attend to any domestic concerns. While you are busily employed in providing that portion of perishing food for perishing bodies, Mary has chosen that spiritual *portion* which endures forever, and which *shall not be taken away from her.* Therefore I cannot command her to leave her present employment, and go and help you bring forward a variety of matters which are by no means necessary at this time. The words *one thing is needful,* on which we lay so much stress, are wanting in some of the most ancient MSS., and are omitted by some of the fathers, who quote all the rest of the passage—a plain proof that the meaning which we take out of them was not thought of in very ancient times; and in other MSS., versions, and fathers there is an unusual variety of readings where even the thing, or something like it, is retained. Some have it thus: "Martha, Martha, thou laborest much, and yet a little is sufficient, yea, one thing only." Others: "And only one thing is

G. CAMPBELL MORGAN:

Of Martha, Luke tells us she "was cumbered about much serving"; a far better word for us today, with our modern method of speech, is the word distracted. She was distracted by much serving. What a great soul this Martha was. Jesus was the guest, and the one thing of supreme importance in the heart of Martha was that He should have adequate welcome. I can see her. I have met her in this life, haven't you? Those hurrying feet, those swiftly moving fingers; love suddenly suggesting something else to make the welcome more perfect. Love always multiplies itself. She went to do something, and on her way, love suggested two other things, and she moved a little more quickly; and while she was going to do these, four were suggested; and then she hurried after the four, and by the time she has begun those, the four are eight things crowding in; and by the time eight are begun, there are sixteen, and so she became distracted! God bless her; a great soul. But she was trying to express love in service, and it reacted. It was a sad reaction. She got so distracted that the next thing we see her doing—think of this woman whose one concern was to make Jesus welcome—we see her rushing in and complaining of His carelessness as well as her sister's. She said, "Dost thou not care?"—*The Gospel According to Luke*

MATTHEW HENRY

Christ *justified Mary* against her sister's clamours. Sooner or later, Mary's choice will be justified, and all those who make that choice, and abide by it. But this was not all; he *applauded* her for her wisdom: *She hath chosen the good part;* for she chose to be with Christ, and took a better way of *honouring* Christ and of *pleasing* him, by receiving his word into her heart, than Martha did by providing for his entertainment in her house. (1) A *part with Christ* is a *good part*; it is a part for the soul and eternity. (2) It is a part that shall *never be taken away from those that have it. Nothing shall separate us from the love of Christ,* and our part in that love. Men and devils *cannot* take it away from us, and God and Christ *will not.* (3) It is the wisdom and duty of everyone of us to choose this *good part.* Mary was at her choice whether she would partake with Martha in her care, and get the reputation of a fine *housekeeper*, or sit at the feet of Christ and approve herself a *zealous disciple*; and, by her choice in this particular, Christ judges of her general choice.

JAMIESON, FAUSSET, BROWN

not be taken away—Martha's choice would be taken from her, for *her services would die with her*; Mary's *never,* being spiritual and eternal. Both were true-hearted disciples, but the one was absorbed in the higher, the other in the lower of two ways of honoring their common Lord. Yet neither despised, or would willingly neglect, the other's occupation. The one represents the *contemplative,* the other the *active* style of the Christian character. A Church full of Marys would perhaps be as great an evil as a Church full of Marthas. Both are needed, each to be the complement of the other.

ADAM CLARKE

required." Others: "Thou art anxious and embarrassed about many things, when that which is needful is very small." Others: "But here there need only a few things." Others: "But a few things, or one only, is necessary." Now these are the readings of almost all the ancient versions; and we plainly perceive by them that what we term the *one thing needful* is not understood by one of them as referring to the salvation of the soul, but to the provision then to be made. In short, I wonder how the present most exceptionable mode of interpretation ever obtained, as having no countenance in the text, ancient MSS. or versions, and as being false in itself. For even Christ himself could not say that sitting at His feet and hearing His word was the one thing needful. Repentance, faith, prayer, obedience, and a thousand other things are necessary to our salvation, besides merely hearing the doctrines of Christ, even with the humblest heart.

MATTHEW HENRY — CHAPTER 11

Verses 1–13

Prayer is one of the great laws of natural religion. One great design therefore of Christianity is to *assist us in prayer*, to enforce the duty upon us, to instruct us in it, and encourage us to expect advantage by it.

I. We find Christ himself *praying in a certain place.* This evangelist has taken particular notice of Christ's *praying often*, more than any other of the evangelists: when he was baptized (*ch.* iii. 21), he was *praying*; he *withdrew into the wilderness, and prayed* (*ch.* v. 16); he *went out into a mountain to pray, and continued all night in prayer* (*ch.* vi. 12): he was *alone praying* (*ch.* ix. 18); soon after, he *went up into a mountain to pray*, and *as he prayed he was transfigured* (*ch.* ix. 28, 29); and here he was *praying in a certain place.*

II. His disciples applied themselves to him for direction in prayer. When he was praying, they asked, *Lord, teach us to pray.* They came to him with this request, *when he ceased*; for they would not disturb him when he was at prayer. *One of his disciples* said, *Lord, teach us.* Though Christ is *apt to teach*, yet he will for this be enquired of.

1. Their request is, "*Lord, teach us to pray.*" It becomes the disciples of Christ to apply themselves to him for instruction in prayer. *Lord, teach us to pray*, is itself a good prayer, and a very needful one, for it is a hard thing to *pray well*; and it is Jesus Christ only that can *teach us*, by his word and Spirit, *how to pray.* "Give me a mouth and wisdom in prayer, that I may speak as I ought; *teach me what I shall say.*"

2. Their plea is, "*As John also taught his disciples.* He took care to instruct his disciples in this necessary duty, and we would be taught as they were." Whereas the Jews' prayers were generally adorations, and praises of God, and doxologies, John taught his disciples such prayers as were more filled up with petitions and requests. "Now, Lord, teach us this, to be added to those benedictions of the name of God which we have been accustomed to from our childhood." Christ did there teach them a prayer consisting wholly of petitions, and even omitting the doxology which had been affixed; and the *Amen.*

III. Christ gave them direction, much the same as he had given them before in his sermon upon the mount, Matt. vi. 9, &c. They would find all their requests couched in these few words, and would be able, in words of their own, to expatiate and enlarge upon them.

1. There are some differences between the Lord's prayer in Matthew and in Luke. There is a difference in the fourth petition. In Matthew we pray, "Give us daily bread *this day*": here, "Give it us *day by day.* Give us *each day* the bread which our bodies require, as they call for it." Let us have bread *today* for *today*, and to*morrow* for to*morrow*; for thus we may be kept in a *continual dependence* upon God, as children upon their parents, and may find ourselves under *fresh* obligations to do the work of every day in the day, according as the *duty of the day requires*, because we have from God the supplies of every day in the day, according as the *necessity of the day requires.* Here is likewise some difference in the fifth petition. In Matthew it is, *Forgive us our debts*, as we forgive: here it is, *Forgive us our sins. For we forgive.* This is a very necessary qualification for forgiveness, and, if God have wrought it in us, we may plead that work of his grace for the enforcing of our petitions for the pardon of our sins: "Lord, forgive us, for thou hast thyself inclined us to forgive others." There is another addition here; we plead not only in general, We forgive *our debtors*, but in particular, "We profess *to forgive everyone that is*

JAMIESON, FAUSSET, BROWN — CHAPTER 11

Vss. 1-13. THE DISCIPLES TAUGHT TO PRAY. **1. one . . .**—struck with either the matter or the manner of our Lord's prayers.

as John . . .—From this reference to John, it is possible that disciple had not heard the Sermon on the Mount. Nothing of John's *inner* teaching (to his own disciples) has been preserved to us, but we may be sure he never taught his disciples to say, "Our Father." **2-4.** (See on Matt. 6:9-13).

3. day by day . . .—an extension of the petition in Matthew for "*this day's*" supply, to every successive day's necessities. The closing doxology, wanting here, is wanting also in all the best and most ancient copies of Matthew's Gospel. Perhaps our Lord purposely left that part *open:* and as the grand Jewish doxologies were ever resounding, and passed immediately and naturally, in all their hallowed familiarity into the Christian Church, probably this prayer was never used in the Christian assemblies but in its present form, as we find it in Matthew, while in Luke it has been allowed to stand as originally uttered.

ADAM CLARKE — CHAPTER 11

1-5. *Teach us to pray.* See the nature of prayer, with an ample explanation of the different parts of the Lord's Prayer, treated of in Matt. vi. 5-15. The prayer related here by Luke is not precisely the same as that mentioned by Matthew; and indeed it is not likely that it was given at the same time. There are many variations in the MSS. in this prayer, but they seem to have proceeded principally from the desire of rendering this similar to that in Matthew. Attempts of this nature have given birth to multitudes of the various readings in the MSS. of the New Testament. It should be remarked also that there is no vestige of the doxology found in Matthew in any copy of Luke's Gospel.

Give us this day our daily bread. The word *epiousion* has greatly perplexed critics and commentators. I find upwards of thirty different explanations of it. It is found in no Greek writer before the Evangelists. The interpretation of Theophylact, one of the best of the Greek fathers, has ever appeared to me to be the most correct, "Bread, sufficient for our substance and support," i.e., that quantity of food which is necessary to support our health and strength, by being changed into the substance of our bodies.

And forgive us our debts. Sin is represented here under the notion of a debt, and as our sins are many, they are here called *debts.* God made man that he might live to His glory, and gave him a law to walk by; and if, when he does anything that tends not to glorify God, he contracts a debt with divine justice, how much more is he debtor when he breaks the law by actual transgression! *Forgive us.* Man has nothing to pay; if his debts are not forgiven, they must stand charged against him forever, as he is absolutely insolvent. Forgiveness, therefore, must come from the free mercy of God in Christ. *As we forgive our debtors.* It was a maxim among the ancient Jews that no man should lie down in his bed without forgiving those who had offended him. That man condemns himself to suffer eternal punishment who makes use of this prayer with revenge and hatred in his heart.

MATTHEW HENRY

indebted to us." Here also the doxology in the close is wholly omitted, and the *Amen.* He left a vacuum here, to be filled up by a doxology more peculiar to the Christian institutes, ascribing glory to *Father, Son and Holy Ghost.*

2. Yet it is, for substance, the same; and we shall therefore here only gather up some general lessons from it.

(1) That in prayer we ought to come to God as children to *a Father*, a common Father to us and *all mankind.*

(2) That at the same time, and in the same petitions, which we address to God for *ourselves*, we should take in with us *all the children of men.* A rooted principle of *catholic charity* should go along with us throughout this prayer, which is so worded as to be accommodated to that noble principle.

(3) That in order to the confirming of the habit of heavenly-mindedness in us, we should, with an eye of faith look *heavenward*, and view the God we pray to as our Father *in heaven.*

(4) That in prayer we must *seek first the kingdom of God and the righteousness thereof*, by ascribing honour to his name, his *holy* name, and power to his government. O that both the one and the other may be more manifested.

(5) That the *principles* and *practices* of the *unseen* world (which therefor by *faith* only we are *apprized of*), are the *great original—the ἀρχέτυπον*, to which we should desire that the principles and practices of this *lower* world may be more conformable. Those words, *As in heaven, so on earth*, refer to all the first three petitions.

(6) That those who faithfully and sincerely mind the kingdom of God may humbly hope that *all other things shall be added to them*, and they may in faith pray for them. If our first chief desire and care be that God's name may be sanctified, his kingdom come, and his will be done, we may then come boldly to the throne of grace for our *daily bread.*

(7) That in our prayers for temporal blessings we must *moderate* our desires, and confine them to a *competency.* The expression here used of *day by day* is the very same with our *daily bread.*

(8) That sins are debts which we are daily contracting, and which therefore we should every day pray for the forgiveness of. Every day adds to the score of our guilt, and it is a miracle of mercy that we have so much encouragement given us to come every day to the throne of grace, to pray for the pardon of our sins of daily infirmity. God *multiplies to pardon* beyond seventy times seven.

(9) That we have no reason to expect that God would forgive our sins against him, if we do not *sincerely* forgive those that have at any time affronted us or been injurious to us.

(10) That temptations to sin should be as much dreaded and deprecated by us as ruin by sin. We must be as earnest with God that we may not be led into it as that we may not be led by that to sin, and by sin to ruin.

(11) That God is to be depended upon for our deliverance *from all evil*; and we should pray, not only that we may not be left to ourselves to run into evil, but that we may not be left to Satan to bring evil upon us.

IV. He stirs up and encourages importunity, fervency, and constancy, in prayer, by showing,

1. That importunity will go far in our dealings with men, *v.* 5–8. Suppose a man, upon a sudden emergency, goes to borrow a loaf or two of bread of a neighbour, at an unseasonable time of night, not for himself, but for his friend that came unexpectedly to him. His neighbour will be loth to accommodate him, for he has wakened him with his knocking, and put him out of humour, and he has a great deal to say in his excuse. But his neighbour will have no nay, therefore he continues *knocking* still, and tells him he will do so till he has what he comes for; so that he must give it to him, to be rid of him: *He will rise and give him as many as he needs, because of his importunity.* We prevail with men by importunity because they are *displeased* with it, but with God because he is *pleased* with it. Now this similitude may be of use to us to *direct* us in prayer. (1) We must come to God with *boldness* and *confidence* for what we need, as a man does to the house of his neighbour or friend, who, he knows, loves him, and is inclined to be kind to him. (2) We must come for *bread*, for that which is *needful.* (3) We must come to him by prayer *for others* as well as *for ourselves.* This man did not come for bread for himself, but for his friend. We cannot come to God upon a more pleasing errand than when we come to him for grace to enable us to do good. (4) We may come with the more boldness to God in a strait, if it be a strait that we have not brought ourselves into by

JAMIESON, FAUSSET, BROWN

Invocation: **Our Father which art in heaven.** In the former clause we express His nearness to us; in the latter, His distance from us. (See Eccles. 5:2; Isa. 66:1). Holy, loving familiarity suggests the one; awful reverence the other. In calling Him "Father" we express a relationship we have all known and felt surrounding us even from our infancy; but in calling Him our Father "who art in heaven," we contrast Him with the fathers we all have here below, and so raise our souls to that "heaven" where He dwells, and that Majesty and Glory which are there as in their proper home. These first words of the Lord's Prayer—this invocation with which it opens—what a brightness and warmth does it throw over the whole prayer, and into what a serene region does it introduce the praying believer, the child of God, as he thus approaches Him! It is true that the paternal relationship of God to His people is by no means strange to the Old Testament. (See Deut. 32:6; Ps. 103:13; Isa. 63:16; Jer. 3:4, 19; Mal. 1:6; 2:10.) But these are only glimpses—the "back parts" (Exod. 33:23), if we may so say, in comparison with the "open face" of our Father revealed in Jesus. (See on II Cor. 3:18). Nor is it too much to say, that the view which our Lord gives, throughout this His very first lengthened discourse, of "our Father in heaven," beggars all that was ever taught, even in God's own Word, or conceived before by His saints, on this subject.

The great majority of the best critics (taking the word to be compounded of *ousia*, "*substance*," or "being") understand by it the "staff of *life*," the bread of *subsistence*, and so the sense will be, "Give us this day the bread which this day's necessities require." In this case, the rendering of our authorized version (after the *Vulgate*, LUTHER and some of the best modern critics)—"our daily bread"—is, in sense, accurate enough. (See Prov. 30:8.) Among commentators, there was early shown an inclination to understand this as a prayer for the heavenly bread, or spiritual nourishment; and in this they have been followed by many superior expositors, even down to our own times. But as this is quite unnatural, so it deprives the Christian of one of the sweetest of his privileges—to cast his bodily wants in this short prayer, by one simple petition, upon his heavenly Father. No doubt the spiritual mind will, from "the meat that perisheth," naturally rise in thought to "that meat which endureth to everlasting life." But let it be enough that the petition about bodily wants irresistibly *suggests* a higher petition; and let us not rob ourselves—out of a morbid spirituality—of our one petition in this prayer for that bodily provision which the immediate sequel of this discourse shows that our heavenly Father has so much at heart. In limiting our petitions, however, to provision *for the day*, what a spirit of childlike dependence does the Lord both demand and beget!

5-8. at midnight . . . for a friend is come—The heat in warm countries makes evening preferable to day for travelling; but "midnight" is everywhere a most *unseasonable* hour of call, and for that very reason it is here selected. **Trouble me not**—the *trouble* making him insensible both to the urgency of the case and the claims of friendship. **I cannot**—without exertion which he would not make.

8. importunity—The word is a strong one—"shamelessness"; persisting in the face of all that seemed reasonable, and refusing to take a denial. **as many . . .**—His reluctance once overcome, all the claims of friendship and necessity are felt to the full. The sense is obvious: If the churlish and self-indulgent—deaf both to friendship and necessity—can after a positive refusal, be won over, by sheer persistency, to do all that is needed, *how much more* may the same determined perseverance in prayer be expected to prevail with Him whose very nature is "*rich* unto all that call upon Him" (Rom. 10:12).

ADAM CLARKE

Which art in heaven. The phrase, *Our Father which art in heaven* was very common among the ancient Jews, and was used by them precisely in the same sense as it is used here by our Lord. This phrase in the Scriptures seems used to express: (1) His omnipresence. "The . . . heaven of heavens cannot contain thee," 1 Kings viii. 27. (2) His majesty and dominion over His creatures. "Art not thou God in heaven? and rulest not thou over all the kingdoms of the heathen?" 2 Chron. xx. 6 (3) His power and might. "Art not thou God in heaven? . . . and in thine hand is there not power and might, so that none is able to withstand thee?" 2 Chron. xx. 6 (4) His omniscience. "The Lord's throne is in heaven: his eyes behold, his eyelids try, the children of men," Ps. xi. 4. (5) His infinite purity and holiness. Thou art "the high and lofty One that inhabiteth eternity, whose name is Holy," Isa. lvii. 15. *Hallowed. Hagiazo* from a negative, and *ge, the earth*, a thing *separated from the earth*, or from earthly purposes and employments. As the word *sanctified* or *hallowed*, in Scripture, is frequently used for the consecration of a thing or person to a holy use or office, as the Levites, firstborn, Tabernacle, Temple, and their utensils, which were all set apart from every earthly, common, or profane use, and employed wholly in the service of God, so the Divine Majesty may be said to be sanctified by us, in analogy to those things, viz., when we separate Him from, and in our conceptions and desires exalt Him above, earth and all things. *Thy name.* That is, God himself, with all the attributes of His divine nature—His power, wisdom, justice, mercy. We hallow God's name: (1) with our *lips*, when all our conversation is holy, and we speak of those things which are meet to minister grace to the hearers; (2) in our *thoughts*, when we suppress every rising evil, and have our tempers regulated by His grace and Spirit; (3) in our *lives*, when we begin, continue, and end our works to His glory; (4) in our *families*, when we endeavor to bring up our *children* in the discipline and admonition of the Lord; (5) in a particular *calling* or *business*, when we separate the falsity, deception, and lying, commonly practiced, from it, buying and selling as in the sight of the holy and just God.

4. *Deliver us from evil.* **Literally, "Deliver us from the wicked one."**

6. *In his journey is come.* **Or perhaps more literally, "A friend of mine is come to me out of his way," which renders the case more urgent—a friend of mine, benighted, belated, and who has lost his way, is come unto me.**

MATTHEW HENRY

our own folly and carelessness, but Providence has led us into it. This man would not have wanted bread if his friend had not come in *unexpectedly*. The care which Providence casts upon us, we may with cheerfulness cast back upon Providence. If importunity could prevail thus with *a man* who was angry at it, much more with a God who is infinitely more kind, and is not angry at our importunity, but accepts it. If he do not answer our prayers presently, yet he will in due time, if we continue to pray.

2. That God has promised to give us what we ask of him. We have not only the goodness of nature to take comfort from, but the word which he has spoken (*v.* 9, 10): "*Ask, and it shall be given you.*" *I say unto you.* We have it from Christ's own mouth. We must not only *ask*, but we must *seek*, must second our prayers with our endeavours; and, in *asking* and *seeking*, we must continue *pressing*, still knocking at the same door, and we shall at length prevail. *Every one that asketh receiveth*, even the meanest saint that asks in faith. When we ask of God those things which Christ has here directed us to ask, that his name may be sanctified, that his kingdom may come, and his will be done, in these requests we must be importunate.

V. He gives us both instruction and encouragement in prayer from the consideration of our relation to God as a Father.

1. An *appeal* to the *bowels* of *earthly fathers*: "Let any of you that *is a father* tell me, if his son *ask bread, will he give him a stone*? *If he ask a fish will he for a fish give him a serpent?* Or, *if he shall ask an egg* for his supper (an egg and to bed), *will he offer him a scorpion*? You know you could not be so unnatural to your own children," *v.* 11, 12.

2. An *application* of this to the *blessings* of our *heavenly Father* (*v.* 13): *If ye then, being evil, give good gifts to your children, much more shall God give you the Spirit.* He shall give *good things*; so it is in Matthew. Observe,

(1) The direction he gives us what to *pray for.* We must ask for the *Holy Spirit*, not only as necessary in order to our *praying well*, but as inclusive of all the good things we are to pray for.

(2) The *encouragement* he gives us to hope that we shall speed in this prayer: *Your heavenly Father will give.* It is *in his power* to give the Spirit; he has all good things to bestow, wrapped up in that one; but that is not all, it is *in his promise.* If our earthly parents, though *evil*, be yet so kind, if they, though *weak*, be yet so *knowing*, that they not only give, but give with discretion, give what is best, much more will our *heavenly Father* give us his *Holy Spirit*.

Verses 14–26

The substance of these verses we had in Matt. xii. 22, &c. Christ is here giving a general proof of his divine mission, by a particular proof of his power over Satan. Here too he gives an earnest of the success of that undertaking. He is here casting out *a devil* that made the poor possessed man *dumb*: in Matthew we are told that he was *blind* and *dumb*. When the devil was forced out by the word of Christ, the *dumb* spoke immediately, and the lips were opened to show forth his praise.

I. Some were *affected* with this miracle. The people *wondered*; they admired the power of God.

II. Others were *offended* at it, and suggested that it was by virtue of a league with Beelzebub, the prince of the devils, that he did this, *v.* 15. Some, to *corroborate* this suggestion and *confront* the evidence of Christ's miraculous power, challenged him to *give them a sign from heaven* (*v.* 16), to confirm his doctrine. As if a *sign from heaven* could not have been given them as well by a compact and collusion with *the prince of the power of the air*, as the *casting out of a devil.* Obstinate infidelity will never be at a loss for something to say in its own excuse, though ever so frivolous and absurd. Christ here returns a full and direct answer in which he shows,

1. That it can by no means be imagined that such a subtle prince as Satan is should ever agree to measures that had such a direct tendency to his own overthrow, *v.* 17, 18. Jesus *knew their thoughts*, even when they industriously thought to conceal them, and he said, "You yourselves cannot but see the groundlessness of this charge; for it is an allowed maxim that no interest can stand that is divided against itself; not the more *public* interest of a *kingdom*, nor the *private* interest of a house or family; if either the one or the other be *divided against itself*, it cannot stand. Now, if Satan should thus be *divided against himself*, he would hasten his own overthrow."

2. That it was a very partial ill-natured thing for them to impute that in him to a compact with Satan which

JAMIESON, FAUSSET, BROWN

9-13. (See on Matt. 7:7-11.) **Ask, and it shall be given you; seek, and ye shall find; knock, and it shall be opened unto you**—Though there seems evidently a climax here, expressive of more and more importunity, yet each of these terms used presents what we desire of God in a different light. We *ask* for what we *wish;* we *seek* for what we *miss;* we *knock* for that from which we feel ourselves *shut out.* Answering to this threefold representation is the triple assurance of success to our believing efforts. "But ah!" might some humble disciple say, "I cannot persuade myself that *I* have any interest with God." To meet this, our Lord repeats the triple assurance He had just given, but in such a form as to silence every such complaint. **For every one that asketh receiveth; and he that seeketh findeth; and to him that knocketh it shall be opened**—Of course, it is presumed that he asks aright—i.e., in faith—and with an honest purpose to make use of what he receives. "If any of you lack wisdom, let him ask of God. But let him ask in faith, nothing wavering [undecided whether to be altogether on the Lord's side]. For he that wavereth is like a wave of the sea driven with the wind and tossed. For *let not that man think that he shall receive any thing of the Lord*" (Jas 1:5-7).

13. **the Holy Spirit**—in Matthew (7:11), "good gifts"; the former, the Gift of gifts descending on the Church through Christ, and comprehending the latter.

14-36. Blind and Dumb Demoniac Healed—Charge of Being in League with Hell, and Reply—Demand of a Sign, and Reply. (See on Matt. 12:22-45). **14. dumb**—blind also (Matthew 12:22).

But when the Pharisees heard it—Mark (3:22) says, "the scribes which came down from Jerusalem"; so that this had been a hostile party of the ecclesiastics, who had come all the way from Jerusalem to collect materials for a charge against Him. (See on vs. 14.) **they said, This fellow**—an expression of contempt—**doth not cast out devils, but by Beelzebub**—rather, Beelzebul (see on ch. 10:25)—**the prince of the devils**—Two things are here implied—first, that the bitterest enemies of our Lord were unable to deny the reality of His miracles; and next, that they believed in an *organized internal kingdom of evil,* under one chief. This belief would be of small consequence, had not our Lord set His seal to it; but this He immediately does. Stung by the unsophisticated testimony of "all the people," they had no way of holding out against His claims but the desperate shift of ascribing His miracles to Satan. **And Jesus knew their thoughts**—"called them" (Mark 3:23). **and said unto them, Every kingdom divided against itself is brought to desolation; and every city or house**—household—**divided against itself shall not stand: And if Satan cast out Satan, he is divided against himself; how shall then his kingdom stand?**—The argument here is irresistible. "No organized society can stand—whether kingdom, city, or household—when turned against itself; such intestine war is suicidal: But the works I do are destructive of Satan's kingdom: That I should be in league with Satan, therefore, is incredible and absurd."

ADAM CLARKE

9. *And* [or, therefore] *I say unto you, Ask,* Be importunate with God, not so much to prevail on Him to save you, as to get yourselves brought into a proper disposition to receive that mercy which He is ever disposed to give. He who is not importunate for the salvation of his soul does not feel the need of being saved; and were God to communicate His mercy to such they could not be expected to be grateful for it, as favors are prized and esteemed only in proportion to the sense men have of their necessity and importance.

13. *The Holy Spirit.* Or, as several MSS. have it, *the good spirit.* See on Matt. vii. 11.

14. *Casting out a devil.* See on Matt. xii. 22.

One possessed with a devil, blind, and dumb. A person from whom the indwelling demon took away both sight and hearing. Satan makes himself master of the heart, the eyes, and the tongue of the sinner. His heart he fills with the love of sin; his eyes he blinds that he may not see his guilt, and the perdition which awaits him; and his tongue he hinders from prayer and supplication, though he gives it increasing liberty in blasphemies, lies, slanders, etc. None but Jesus can redeem from this threefold captivity.

MATTHEW HENRY

yet they applauded and admired in others that were of their own nation (*v.* 19): "*By whom do your sons cast them out?* Some of your own *kindred*, some of your own *followers*, have undertaken, in the name of the God of Israel, to cast out devils, and they were never charged with such a hellish combination." It is gross hypocrisy to *condemn* that in those who *reprove* us which yet we *allow* in those that *flatter* us.

3. That, in opposing the conviction of this miracle, they were enemies to themselves, for they thrust from them the kingdom of God (*v.* 20): "*If I with the finger of God cast out devils, no doubt the kingdom of God is come upon you*, and if you receive it not, it is at your peril." In Matthew it is *by the Spirit of God*, here *by the finger of God*. He needed not make bare his *everlasting arm*; that roaring lion, when *he* pleases, is crushed, like a moth, with a touch of *a finger*.

4. That his casting out devils was really the destroying of them and their power, *v.* 21, 22. When Christ cast out devils he was *stronger than they*, and could do it *by force*, and did it so as to ruin Satan's power. Now this is applicable to Christ's victories over Satan both in the world and in the hearts of particular persons. And so we may observe here,

(1) The miserable condition of an unconverted sinner. In his heart, which was fitted to be a habitation of God, the devil has his palace; and all the powers and faculties of the soul are *his goods*. The heart is a *palace*, a noble dwelling; but the unsanctified heart is the *devil's palace*. The devil, as a *strong man armed, keeps* this palace. All the prejudices with which he hardens men's hearts against truth and holiness are the *strongholds* which he erects for the *keeping of his palace*. There is a kind of *peace* in the palace of an unconverted soul, while the devil, as a *strong man armed*, keeps it. The sinner has a good opinion of himself, is very secure and merry; he flatters himself in his own eyes, and cries peace to himself. Before Christ appeared, all was quiet, because all *went one way*; but the preaching of the gospel disturbed the peace of the devil's palace.

(2) The wonderful change that is made in conversion. *Satan* is a *strong man armed;* but our Lord Jesus is *stronger than he*, see the manner of this victory: *He comes upon him* by surprise, when his *goods are in peace* and *overcomes* him. See the evidences of this victory. *First*, He *takes from him all his armour wherein he trusted*. Christ disarms him. When the power of sin and corruption in the soul is broken then Satan's *armour* is *taken away*. *Secondly*, He *divides the spoils*; he *takes possession* of them for himself. All the endowments of mind and body are now converted to Christ's service. Yet this is not all; he *makes a distribution* of them among his followers, and gives to all believers the benefit of that victory. Hence Christ infers that, since the whole drift of his doctrine and miracles was to break the power of the devil, it was the duty of all to join with him, to receive his gospel and come heartily into the interests of it; for otherwise they would justly be reckoned as siding with the enemy (*v.* 23): *He that is not with me is against me*.

5. That there was a vast difference between the devil's *going out* by compact and his being *cast out* by compulsion. Those out of whom Christ *cast him* he never entered into again, for so was Christ's charge (Mark ix. 25); whereas, if he had *gone out*, whenever he saw fit he would have made a re-entry, *v.* 24–26. Christ, as he gives a *total*, so he gives a *final*, defeat to the enemy. Here we have,

(1) The condition of a *formal hypocrite*, his *bright side* and his *dark side*. His heart still remains the *devil's house*, and yet [1] The *unclean spirit is gone out*. He was not *driven out*, but he *went out*, withdrew for a time, so that the man seemed not to be under the power of Satan as formerly. [2] The *house is swept* from common pollutions by a partial reformation. The house is *swept*, but it is not *washed*; the house must be *washed*, or it is *none of his*. Sweeping takes off only the loose dirt, while the sin that *besets* the sinner, is untouched. It is swept from the filth that lies open to the eye of the world, but it is not searched and ransacked for secret filthiness. It is *swept*, but the *leprosy is in the wall*. [3] The house is *garnished* with common gifts and graces. It is not *furnished* with any true grace, but *garnished* with the pictures of all graces. It is all paint and varnish, not real, not lasting. The house is *garnished*, but the property is not altered; it was never surrendered to Christ.

(2) Here is the condition of a *final apostate*, into whom the devil returns after he had *gone out*: *Then goes he, and takes seven other spirits more wicked than himself* (*v.* 26). These *enter in* without any difficulty or opposition; they are welcomed, and they *dwell there*; and the *last state of that man is worse than the first*. Hypocrisy is the high road to apostasy. Where

JAMIESON, FAUSSET, BROWN

And if I by Beelzebub cast out devils, by whom do your children—"your sons," meaning here the "disciples" or pupils of the Pharisees, who were so termed after the familiar language of the Old Testament in speaking of the sons of the prophets (I Kings 20:35; II Kings 2:3, etc.). Our Lord here seems to admit that such works were wrought by them; in which case the Pharisees stood self-condemned, as expressed in Luke (11:19), "Therefore shall they be your judges."

20. the finger of God—"the Spirit of God" (Matt. 12:28); the former figuratively denoting the *power* of God, the latter the *living Personal Agent* in every exercise of it.

21, 22. strong man—meaning *Satan*. **armed**—pointing to all the subtle and varied methods by which he wields his dark power over men. **keepeth**—"guardeth." **his palace**—*man* whether viewed more largely or in individual souls—how significant of what men are to Satan! **in peace**—undisturbed, secure in his possession. **22. a stronger than he**—*Christ:* Glorious title, in relation to Satan! **come upon him and overcome him**—sublimely expressing the Redeemer's approach, as the Seed of the woman, to bruise the Serpent's head. **taketh from him all his armour**—"his panoply," "his complete armor." Vain would be the victory, were not the *means of regaining* his lost power wrested from him. It is this that completes the triumph and ensures the final overthrow of his kingdom. The parable that immediately follows (vss. 24-26) is just the *reverse of this*. (See on Matt. 12:43-35.) In the one case, Satan is *dislodged by Christ,* and so finds, in all future assaults, the house *preoccupied;* in the other, he merely goes out and comes in again, finding the house "EMPTY" (Matt. 12:44) of any rival, and all ready to welcome him back. This explains the important saying that comes in *between the two parables* (vs. 23). *Neutrality in religion there is none.* The absence of positive attachment to Christ involves hostility to Him. **23. gathereth . . . scattereth**—referring probably to gleaners. The meaning seems to be, Whatever in religion is disconnected from Christ comes to nothing.

CHARLES H. SPURGEON:

Is there a conflict going on in you? Remember faith gets the victory. Look to Jesus—look to Jesus, and the battle is won. Cast your poor spirit upon Jesus. Now burn that broom: it is of no use to go on sweeping, you want washing—washing with blood! Come, now, spare that money of yours with which you are going to buy garnishings—they are all rubbish; buy no more. I counsel thee buy of Him gold tried in the fire. Come to His precious blood, and be really made clean. Your church-goings, your chapel-goings, your prayers, your almsgivings, your fastings, your feelings, your good works, are all nothing—so much dross and dung—if you try to sweep and garnish your house with them. Cast them all away; fly from your good works as you would from your bad ones. No more expect to be saved by anything that you can feel that is good than you would expect to be saved by anything that you feel that is bad. Only Jesus can do helpless sinners good.

—*The Treasury of the New Testament*

ADAM CLARKE

19. *Beelzebub.* See on Matt. x. 25.

By whom do your children cast them out? Children, or sons, of the prophets means the disciples of the prophets; and children or sons of the Pharisees, disciples of the Pharisees. From Acts xix. 13-14, it is evident there were *exorcists* among the Jews, and from our Lord's saying here, it is also evident that the disciples of the Pharisees did cast out demons, or at least those who educated them wished to have it believed that they had such a power. Our Lord's argument here is extremely conclusive: If the man who casts our demons proves himself thereby to be in league with and influenced by Satan, then your disciples, and you who taught them, are all of you in league with the devil.

20. *Finger of God.* See on Exod. viii. 19.

This is the finger of God. That is, The power and skill of God are here evident. Probably before this the magicians supposed Moses and Aaron to be conjurers, like themselves; but now they are convinced that no man could do these miracles which these holy men did, unless God were with him. God permits evil spirits to manifest themselves in a certain way that men may see that there is a spiritual world and be on their guard against seduction. He at the same time shows that all these agents are under His control, that men may have confidence in His goodness and power.

Else how can one enter into a strong man's house? Men, through sin, are become the very house and dwelling place of Satan, having of their own accord surrendered themselves to this unjust possessor; for whoever gives up his soul to sin gives it up to the devil. It is Jesus, and Jesus alone, who can deliver from the power of this bondage. When Satan is cast out, Jesus purifies and dwells in the heart.

He that is not with me is against me. There is no medium between loving the Lord and being His enemy—between belonging to Christ or to Satan. If we be on the side of the devil, we must expect to go to the devil's hell; if we be on the side of Christ, we may expect to go to His heaven.

Scattereth abroad. This seems to have been a proverbial form of speech, and may be a metaphor taken from shepherds. He who does not help the true shepherd to gather his flock into the fold is, most likely, one who wishes to scatter them, that he may have the opportunity of stealing and destroying them.

Into my house. The soul of that person from whom he had been expelled by the power of Christ, and out of which he was to have been kept by continual prayer, faith, and watchfulness. *He findeth it empty.* "Unoccupied," empty of the former inhabitant, and ready to receive a new one, denoting a soul that has lost the life and power of godliness and the testimony of the Holy Spirit. *Swept, and garnished.* Idle, or unemployed, it may refer here to the person as well as to his state. His affections and desires are no longer busied with the things of God, but gad about, like an idle person, among the vanities of a perishing world. *Swept,* from love, meekness, and all the fruits of the Spirit; and *garnished,* "adorned, decorated," with the vain, showy trifles of folly and fashion.

Seven other spirits more wicked. Seven was a favorite number with the Jews, implying frequently, with them, something "perfect, completed, filled up," for such is the proper import of the Hebrew word *sheva* or *shevang,* nearly allied in sound to our *seven. The last state of that man is worse than the first.* His soul, before influenced by the Spirit of God, dilated and ex-

MATTHEW HENRY

secret haunts of sin are kept up conscience is debauched, and the *close* hypocrite commonly proves an *open* apostate. The last state of such is *worse than the first*, in respect both of sin and punishment. Apostates are usually the worst of men; their consciences are seared, and their sins of all others the most aggravated. In the other world they will *receive the greater damnation.*

Verses 27, 28

We had not this passage in the other evangelists.

1. The applause which an affectionate, honest, well-meaning woman gave to our Lord Jesus, upon hearing his excellent discourses. This good woman admired them: *As he spoke these things* (*v.* 27), a *certain woman of the company* was so pleased that she could not forbear crying out, "*Blessed is the womb that bore thee.* Happy the woman that has thee for her son. I should have thought myself very happy to have been the mother of one that *speaks as never man spoke*, that has so much of the grace of heaven in him, and is so great a blessing to this earth." To all that believe the word of Christ the person of Christ is precious.

2. The occasion which Christ took from this to pronounce *them* more happy who are his faithful and obedient followers than she was who bore and nursed him. *Yea, rather, blessed are they that hear the word of God, and keep it*, *v.* 28. This is intended partly as a *check* to her, for doting so much upon his bodily presence, partly as an *encouragement* to her to hope that she might be as happy as his own mother, if she would *hear the word of God and keep it.* Those only are truly blessed that hear it and *keep* it.

Verses 29-36

I. What is the *sign* we may *expect* from God for the *confirmation* of our *faith.* The great and most convincing proof of Christ's being sent of God was the resurrection of Christ from the dead.

1. A reproof to the people for demanding other signs than what had already been given them in great plenty: *The people were gathered thickly together* (*v.* 29), a vast crowd of them. Christ knew what brought such a multitude together; they came *seeking a sign*, they came to gaze, to have something to talk of when they went home.

2. A promise that yet there should be *one sign* more given them, even the *sign of Jonas the prophet*, which in Matthew is explained as meaning the *resurrection of Christ.* But, if this do not work upon them, let them look for nothing but utter ruin: *The Son of man shall be a sign to this generation* (*v.* 30), a sign speaking to them, though a sign spoken against by them.

3. A warning to them to improve this sign. The *queen of Sheba* would *rise up in judgment against them*, and condemn *their unbelief*, *v.* 31. She was a stranger to the commonwealth of Israel, and yet she came from the uttermost parts of the earth to *hear his wisdom*, not only to satisfy her curiosity, but to inform her mind; and, behold, a *greater than Solomon is here.* Yet these wretched Jews will give no manner of regard to what Christ says to them, though he be in the midst of them. The Ninevites would rise up in judgment against them (*v.* 32): They *repented at the preaching of Jonas*; but here is preaching which far exceeds that of Jonas, and yet none are startled by it, to turn *from their evil way*, as the Ninevites did.

II. What is the *sign* that God *expects* from us for the *evidencing* of our faith, and that is the serious practice of that religion which we profess to believe.

1. They had *the light.* For God, having *lighted the candle* of the gospel, did not put it in a *secret place*, or *under a bushel*; Christ did not preach in corners. It is a great privilege that the light of the gospel is put on a *candlestick*, so that all that come in may *see it*, and may *see by it.*

2. Having the *light*, their concern was to have the *sight.* Be the *object* ever so *clear*, if the *organ* be not *right*, we are never the better: *The light of the body is the eye* (*v.* 34). So the light of the soul is its power of discerning between good and evil, truth and falsehood. Now, according as this is, so the light of divine revelation is to us, and our benefit by it. (1) If this eye of the soul be *single*, if it see *clear*, if it aim at *truth* only, and seek it for its own sake, the *whole body*, that is, the whole soul, is *full of light.* If our understanding admits the gospel in its full light, it fills the soul, and it has enough to *fill* it. And if the soul be thus *filled, having no part dark*, then *the whole soul shall be full of light. It was darkness* itself, but is now light in the Lord, *as when the bright shining of a candle doth give thee light*, *v.* 36. The gospel will come into those souls whose doors and

JAMIESON, FAUSSET, BROWN

27, 28. as he spake these things, a . . . woman of the company—of the multitude, the crowd. A charming little incident and profoundly instructive. With true womanly feeling, she envies the mother of such a wonderful Teacher. Well, and higher and better than she had said as much before her (ch. 1:28. 42); and our Lord is far from condemning it. He only holds up—as "*blessed rather*"—the hearers and keepers of God's word; in other words, *the humblest real saint of God.* (See on Matt. 12:49, 50). How utterly alien is this sentiment from the teaching of the Church of Rome, which would excommunicate any one of its members who dared to talk in the spirit of this glorious saying!

29-32. (See on Matt. 12:39-42.) **An evil and adulterous generation**—This latter expression is best explained by Jeremiah 3:20, "Surely as a wife treacherously departeth from her husband, so have ye dealt treacherously with Me, O house of Israel, saith the Lord." For this was the relationship in which He stood to the covenant people—"I am married unto you" (Jer. 3:14). **seeketh after a sign**—In the eye of Jesus this class were but the spokesmen of their generation, the exponents of the reigning spirit of unbelief. **and there shall no sign be given to it, but the sign of the prophet Jonas.**

The men of Nineveh shall rise in judgment with this generation, . . .—The Ninevites, though heathens, repented at a man's preaching; while they, God's covenant people, repented not at the preaching of the Son of God—whose supreme dignity is rather implied here than expressed. **The queen of the south shall rise up in the judgment with this generation . . .**—The queen of Sheba (a tract in Arabia, near the shores of the Red Sea) came from a remote country, "south" of Judea, to hear the wisdom of a mere man, though a gifted one, and was transported with wonder at what she saw and heard (I Kings 10:1-9). They, when a Greater than Solomon had come *to them*, despised and rejected, slighted and slandered Him.

33-36. (See on Matt. 5:14-16; 6:22, 23.) But vs. 36 here is peculiarly vivid, expressing what pure, beautiful, broad perceptions *the clarity of the inward eye* imparts. **The light** [the lamp] **of the body is the eye: if therefore thine eye be single**—simple, clear. As applied to the outward eye, this means general soundness; particularly, not looking two ways. Here, as also in classical Greek, it is used figuratively to denote the simplicity of the mind's eye, singleness of purpose, looking right at its object, as opposed to having two ends in view. (See Prov. 4:25-27.) **thy whole body shall be full of light**—illuminated. As with the bodily vision, the man who looks with a good, sound eye, walks in light, seeing every object clear; so a simple and persistent purpose to serve and please God in everything will make the whole character consistent and bright. **But if thine eye be evil**—distempered, or, as we should say, If we have got a *bad* eye—**thy whole body shall be full of darkness**—darkened. As a vitiated eye, or an eye that looks not straight and full at its object, sees nothing as it is, so a mind and heart divided between heaven and earth is all dark. **If therefore the light**

ADAM CLARKE

panded under its heavenly influences, becomes more capable of refinement in iniquity, as its powers are more capacious than formerly. Evil habits are formed and strengthened by relapses; and relapses are multiplied, and become more incurable, through new habits.

27. *A certain woman . . . lifted up her voice, and said.* It was very natural for a *woman*, who was probably a mother, to exclaim thus. She thought that the happiness of the woman who was mother to such a Son was great indeed; but our blessed Lord shows her that even the holy Virgin could not be benefited by her merely being the mother of His human nature, and that only they were happy who carried Christ in their hearts. True happiness is found in *hearing* the glad tidings of salvation by Christ Jesus, and *keeping* them in a holy heart, and *practicing* them in an unblamable life.

29. *This is an evil generation.* Or, "This is a wicked race of men." See on Matt. xii. 38-42.

An evil and adulterous generation. Or "race of people." Our Lord terms the Jews an adulterous race. Under the old covenant, the Jewish nation was represented as in a marriage contract with the Lord of hosts, as believers in the new covenant are represented as the spouse of Christ. All unfaithfulness and disobedience was considered as a breach of this marriage contract; hence the persons who were thus guilty are denominated adulterers and adulteresses.

The queen of the south. In 1 Kings x. 1, this queen is said to be of Saba, which was a city and province of Arabia Felix, to the south, or southeast, of Judea. *Uttermost parts of the earth.* A form of speech which merely signifies "a great distance."

33. *No man, when he hath lighted.* See on Matt. v. 15. Our Lord intimates that if He worked a miracle among such an obstinate people, who were determined to disbelieve every evidence of His messiahship, He should act as a man who lighted a candle and then covered it with a bushel, which must prevent the accomplishment of the end for which it was lighted.

34. *The light of the body is the eye.* Or, "The eye is the lamp of the body." See on Matt. vi. 22.

36. *The whole shall be full of light.* Or "altogether enlightened"; i.e., when the eye is perfect, it enlightens the whole body. Every object within the reach of the eye is as completely seen as if there was an eye in every

MATTHEW HENRY

windows are thrown open to receive it. (2) If the eye of the soul be *evil*, it is no wonder that the *whole body*, the whole soul, should be *full of darkness*, *v.* 34. The inference hence therefore is, *Take heed that the light which is in thee be not darkness*, *v.* 35. Be sincere in your enquiries after truth, and ready to receive the light, and love, and power of it; and not as the men of *this generation* to whom Christ preached, who never sincerely *desired* to know God's will, nor *designed* to do it, and therefore no wonder that they *walked on in darkness*.

Verses 37–54

Christ here says many of those things to a Pharisee and his guests, in a *private* conversation at table, which he afterwards said in a *public* discourse in the temple (Matt. 23); for what he said in public and private was *of a piece*.

I. Christ's going to dine with a Pharisee that very civilly invited him to his house (*v.* 37): *As he spoke a certain Pharisee* interrupted him with a request to him to come and *dine with him*. We know not the mind of this Pharisee; but, whatever it was, Christ knew it: if he meant ill, he shall know Christ does not fear him; if well, he shall know Christ is willing to do him good: so *he went in, and sat down to meat*. Christ's disciples must learn of him to be *conversable*, and not *morose*. Though we have need to be *cautious* what company we keep, yet we need not be *rigid*.

II. The offence which the Pharisee took at Christ for not *washing before dinner*, *v.* 38. He wondered that a man of his sanctity should sit down to meat, and not first *wash his hands*; the Pharisee himself and all his guests, no doubt, *washing*. The ceremonial law consisted in *divers washings*, but this was none of them, and therefore Christ would not practise it, though he knew that offence would be taken at his omitting it.

III. The sharp reproof which Christ gave to the Pharisees.

1. He reproves them for placing religion so much in those instances of it which are only external, and fall under the eye of man, while those were not only *postponed*, but quite *expunged*, which respect the soul, and fall under the eye of God, *v.* 39, 40. (1) The absurdity they were guilty of: "*You Pharisees make clean the outside* only, you wash your hands with water, but do not *wash your hearts from wickedness*." Those can never be reckoned *cleanly* servants that wash only the *outside of the cup* or *the platter*, and take no care to make clean the *inside*. The frame or temper of the mind in every religious service is as the *inside* of the cup and platter; the impurity of this *infects* the services. To live under the dominion of spiritual wickedness, is as great an affront to God as it would be for a servant to give the cup into his master's hand, clean wiped from all the dust on the outside, but *within* full of cobwebs and spiders. *Ravening* and *wickedness* are the dangerous damning sins of many who have made the *outside of the cup* clean from the more gross, and scandalous, and inexcusable sins of whoredom and drunkenness. (2) A particular instance of the absurdity of it, "*Ye fools, did not he that made that which is without make that which is within also?* (*v.* 40). Did not that God who in the law of Moses appointed divers ceremonial washings, appoint also that you should cleanse and purify your hearts? He who made laws for that which is *without*, did not he even in those laws further intend something within. Did not God, who made us these bodies, make us *these souls* also? Now, if he made both, he justly expects we should take care of both; and therefore not only wash the *body*, but wash the spirit, which he is the Father of, and get the leprosy in the heart cleansed?"

To this he subjoins a rule for making our creature-comforts clean to us (*v.* 41): "Instead of *washing your hands* before you go to meat, *give alms of such things as you have*, let the poor have their share out of them, and then *all things are clean to you*, and you may use them comfortably." Here is a plain allusion to the law of Moses, by which it was provided that certain portions of the increase of their land should be given *to the Levite, the stranger, the fatherless, and the widow*; and, when that was done, what was reserved for their own use was *clean to them*. Deut. xvi. 12–15. *Then* we can with comfort enjoy the gifts of God's bounty ourselves when we *send portions to them for whom nothing is prepared*. What we have is not our own, unless God have his dues out of it; and it is by *liberality to the poor* that we clear up to ourselves our *liberty* to make use of our creature-comforts.

2. He reproves them for laying stress upon trifles, and neglecting the weighty matters of the law, *v.* 42. Those laws which related only to the *means of religion*

JAMIESON, FAUSSET, BROWN

that is in thee be darkness, how great is that darkness!—As the conscience is the regulative faculty, and a man's inward purpose, scope, aim in life, determines his character—if these be not simple and heavenward, but distorted and double, what must all the other faculties and principles of our nature be which take their direction and character from these, and what must the whole man and the whole life be but a mass of darkness? In Luke (11:36) the converse of this statement very strikingly expresses what pure, beautiful, broad perceptions the *clarity of the inward eye* imparts: "If thy whole body therefore be full of light, having no part dark, the whole shall be full of light, as when the bright shining of a candle doth give thee light." But now for the application of this.

37-54. Denunciation of the Pharisees. **38. marvelled . . .**—(See on Mark 7:2-4).

39-41. cup and platter—remarkable example of our Lord's way of drawing the most striking illustrations of great truths from the most familiar objects and incidents of life. **ravening**—rapacity.

40. that which is without . . .—i.e., He to whom belongs the outer life, and right to demand its subjection to Himself—is the inner man less His?

41. give alms . . . and . . . all . . . clean—a principle of immense value. As the greed of these hypocrites was one of the most prominent features of their character (ch. 16:14; Matt. 23:14), our Lord bids them exemplify the opposite character, and then their *outside*, ruled by this, would be beautiful in the eye of God, and their meals would be eaten with clean hands, though never so fouled with the business of this worky world. (See Eccles. 9:7.)

ADAM CLARKE

part. So the eye is to every part of the body what the lamp is to every part of the house. When the light of Christ dwells fully in the heart, it extends its influence to every thought, word, and action, and directs its possessor how he is to act in all places and circumstances.

37. *To dine*. The word signifies the *first* eating of the day. The Jews made but two meals in the day; their *ariston* may be called their "breakfast" or their "dinner," because it was both, and was but a slight meal. Their chief meal was their supper, after the heat of the day was over; and the same was the principal meal among the Greeks and Romans.

38. *First washed*. See on Mark vii. 2-4.

Except they wash their hands. The hand to the wrist—"Unless they wash the hand up to the wrist, *eat not*." This sort of washing was, and still continues to be, an act of religion in the Eastern countries. It is particularly commanded in the Koran, Surat, v, v. 7, "O believers, when ye wish to pray, wash your faces, and your hands up to the elbows—and your feet up to the ankles," which custom it is likely Mohammed borrowed from the Jews. The Jewish doctrine is this: "If a man neglect the washing, he shall be eradicated from this world."

Except they wash. Or "dip." But instead of the word in the text, the famous Codex Vaticanus (B), eight others, and Euthymius have *sprinkle*. However the Jews sometimes washed their hands previously to their eating; at other times they simply dipped or plunged them into the water. *Of cups*. Any kind of earthen vessels. *Pots*. "Of measures," a measure for liquids, formed from the Latin *sextarius*, equal to a pint and a half English. *Of brasen vessels*. These, if polluted, were only to be washed or passed through the fire, whereas the earthen vessels were to be broken. *And of tables*. "Beds, couches." This is wanting in some MSS.

40. *Did not he that made that which is without?* God has made you such, both as to your bodies and souls, as He intended should show forth His praise. But can you think that the purpose of God can be accomplished by you while you attend only to external legal purifications, your hearts being full of rapine and wickedness?

41. *Give alms of such things as ye have*. Meaning either what was within the dishes spoken of before, or what was within their houses or power, or what they had "at hand." Far from spoiling the poor by wicked exactions, rather *give* them *alms* of everything you possess; and when a part of everything you *have* is sincerely consecrated to God for the use of the poor, then all that remains will be *clean* unto you. You will have the blessing of God in your basket and store, and everything will be sanctified to you. These verses are very difficult, and are variously translated and interpreted by critics and divines. I have given what I believe to be our Lord's meaning, in the preceding paraphrase.

MATTHEW HENRY

they were very exact in the observance of: *Ye pay tithe of mint and rue*, pay it in kind and to the full. By this they would gain a reputation with the people as strict observers of the law. Now Christ does not condemn them for being so exact in paying tithes (*these things ought ye to have done*), but for thinking that this would atone for the neglect of their greater duties. Those laws which relate to the *essentials of religion* they made nothing of: *You pass over judgment and the love of God*, you make no conscience of giving men their *dues* and God your *hearts*.

3. He reproves them for their pride and vanity (*v.* 43): "*Ye love the uppermost seats in the synagogues*, and *you love greetings in the markets*." It is not sitting uppermost, or being greeted, that is reproved, but *loving it*.

4. He reproves them for their hypocrisy (*v.* 44): "*You are as graves* overgrown with grass, which therefore *appear not*, and *the men that walk over them are not aware of them*, and so they contract the ceremonial pollution which by the law arose from the *touch of a grave*." These Pharisees were *within* full of *abominations*, as a grave of putrefaction; and yet they concealed it so artfully that it did not appear, so that they who conversed with them, and followed their doctrine, were infected with their corruptions and ill morals, and yet suspected no danger by them. The contagion *insinuated* itself, and was *insensibly* caught, and those that caught it thought themselves never the worse.

IV. The testimony which he bore also against the lawyers or scribes, who made it their business to *expound* the law, as the Pharisees did to *observe* the law.

1. There was one of that profession who resented what he said against the Pharisees (*v.* 45): "*Master, thus saying thou reproachest us also.*" It is the folly of those who are wedded to their sins, and resolved not to part with them, to make an *ill use* of the faithful and friendly admonitions given them, which come from love, and to have their passions provoked by them as if they were intended for *reproaches*. This lawyer espoused the Pharisee's cause, and so made himself partaker of his sins.

2. Our Lord Jesus thereupon took them to task (*v.* 46): *Woe unto you also, ye lawyers;* and again (*v.* 52): *Woe unto you, lawyers.* They blessed themselves in the reputation they had among the people, but Christ denounced *woes* against them, for he sees not as man sees. Those who quarrel with the reproofs of others, and suspect them to be reproaches to them, do but get *woes of their own* by so doing.

(1) The lawyers are reproved for making the services of religion more *burdensome* to others, but more *easy* to themselves, than God had made them (*v.* 46): "*You lade men with burdens grievous to be borne, but you yourselves touch them not with one of your fingers*"; that is, [1] "You will not *burden* yourselves with them, nor be yourselves bound by those restraints with which you hamper others." [2] "You will not *lighten* them, *you will not touch them*, that is, either to repeal them or to dispense with them when you find them to be burdensome and grievous to the people." They would come in with *both hands* to dispense with a command of God, but not with a *finger* to mitigate the rigour of any of the traditions of the elders.

(2) They are reproved for pretending a veneration for the memory of the prophets whom their fathers killed, when yet they hated and persecuted those in their own day who were sent to them on the same errand, *v.* 47–49. [1] These hypocrites *built the sepulchres of the prophets*; that is, they erected monuments over their graves, in honour of them. They were not so superstitious as to enshrine their relics, or to think their devotions the more acceptable to God for being offered at the *tombs of the martyrs*; but, as if they owned themselves the *children of the prophets*, they *repaired* and *beautified* the monuments sacred to their *pious memory*. [2] Notwithstanding this, they had an inveterate *enmity* to those in their *own day* that came to them in the *spirit* and *power* of those prophets. For the *Wisdom of God said* that they would *slay* and *persecute* the prophets and apostles that would be sent them. The *Wisdom of God* would thus make trial of them by sending them prophets, to reprove them for their sins and warn them of the judgments of God. "*I will send them prophets* under the style and title of apostles, and these they shall not only contradict and oppose, but *slay* and *persecute*, and put to death." [3] Therefore God will justly put another construction upon their *building* the *tombs* of the prophets, and it shall be interpreted their *allowing the deeds of their fathers* (*v.* 45); the *building* of *their sepulchres* shall have this sense put upon it, that they resolved to keep them in their graves whom their fathers had

JAMIESON, FAUSSET, BROWN

42. mint . . . rue . . .—founding on Leviticus 27:30, which they interpreted rigidly. Our Lord purposely names the most trifling products of the earth, as examples of what they punctiliously exacted the tenth of. **judgment and the love of God**—in Matthew 23:25, "judgment, mercy, and *faith*." The reference is to Micah 6:6-8, whose third element of all acceptable religion, "walking humbly with God," comprehends both "love" and "faith." (See on Mark 12:29, 32, 33.) The same tendency to merge greater duties in less besets us still, *but it is the characteristic of hypocrites.* **these ought ye . . .**—There is no need for one set of duties to jostle out another; but of the *greater*, our Lord says, "Ye *ought to have done*" them; of the *lesser*, only "ye ought *not to leave them undone.*" **43. uppermost seats**—See on ch. 14:7-11. **greetings**—(See on Matt. 23:7-10). **44. appear not . . .**—As one might unconsciously walk over a grave concealed from view, and thus contract ceremonial defilement, so the plausible exterior of the Pharisees kept people from perceiving the pollution they contracted from coming in contact with such corrupt characters. (See Ps. 5:9; Rom. 3:13; a different illustration from Matt. 23:27.)

46. burdens grievous . . .—referring not so much to the irksomeness of the legal rites (though they were irksome, Acts 15:10), as to the heartless rigor with which they were enforced, and by men of shameless inconsistency.

47, 48. ye build . . .—Out of pretended respect and honor, they repaired and beautified the sepulchres of the prophets, and with whining hypocrisy said, "If we had been in the days of our fathers, we should not have been partakers with them in the blood of the prophets," while all the time they "were witnesses to themselves that they were the children of them that killed the prophets" (Matt. 23:29, 30); convicting themselves daily of as exact a resemblance in spirit and character to the very classes over whose deeds they pretended to mourn, as child to parent. **49-51. said the wisdom . . . .**—a remarkable variation of the words in Matthew 23:34, "Behold *I* SEND." As there seems plainly an allusion to ancient warnings of what God would do with so incorrigible a people, so here Christ, stepping majestically into the place of God, so to speak, says, "Now I am going to carry all that out." *Could this be other than the Lord of Israel in the flesh*?

ADAM CLARKE

42. *Ye tithe mint and rue.* See on Matt. xxiii. 23.

43. *Ye love the uppermost seats.* Every one of them affected to be a ruler in the synagogues.

44. *Ye are as graves which appear not.* In Matt. xxiii. 27 our Lord tells them that they exactly resembled whitewashed tombs; they had no fairness but on the outside. But here He says they are like hidden tombs, graves which were not distinguished by any outward decorations and were not elevated above the ground, so that those who walked over them did not consider what corruption was within. So they, under the veil of hypocrisy, covered their iniquities, so that those who had any intercourse or connection with them did not perceive what accomplished knaves they had to do with.

45. *Thou reproachest us.* He alone who searches the heart could unmask these hypocrites; and He did it so effectually that their own consciences acknowledged the guilt, and reechoed their own reproach.

46. *Ye lade men with burdens.* By insisting on the observance of the traditions of the elders, to which it appears, by the way, they paid no great attention themselves. See on Matt. xxiii. 4.

47. *Ye build the sepulchres.* That is, you rebuild and beautify them.

48. *Truly ye bear witness.* You acknowledge that those of old who killed the prophets were your *fathers*, and you are about to show, by your conduct towards Me and My apostles, that you are as capable of murdering a prophet now as they were of old.

49. *The wisdom of God.* These seem to be Luke's words, and to mean that Jesus, *the wisdom of God* (as He is called, 1 Cor. i. 24), added the words which follow here, on that occasion, and this interpretation of the words is agreeable to that of Matthew, who makes Jesus speak in His own person: "Wherefore, behold, I send unto you prophets," Matt. xxiii. 34.

MATTHEW HENRY

…rried thither. [4] They must expect no other …n to be reckoned with, as the *fillers up* of the …asure of persecution, *v.* 50, 51. It shall all be …uired *of this generation* whose sin in persecuting …rist's apostles would exceed any of the sins of …t kind that their fathers were guilty of. Their …struction by the Romans was so terrible that it …ght well be reckoned the completing of God's …ngeance upon that persecuting nation.

(3) They are reproved for opposing the gospel of …rist, *v.* 52. They had not, according to the duty … their place, faithfully expounded to the people …ose scriptures of the Old Testament which pointed … the Messiah. Instead of that, they had perverted …ose texts by their corrupt glosses upon them, and …s is called *taking away the key of knowledge*; …stead of *using* that key for the people, and helping …em to use it aright, they *hid it* from them; this is …lled, in Matthew, *shutting up the kingdom of heaven …ainst men*, Matt. xxiii. 13. They themselves did …ot embrace the gospel of Christ, though by their …quaintance with the Old Testament they could …ot but know that the *time was fulfilled*, and the …*ngdom of God was at hand*, and yet would not …emselves *enter into it*. Them that without any …uidance or assistance of theirs were *entering in* they …d all they could to *hinder* and discourage, by …reatening to *cast them out of the synagogue*. It is …ad for people to be averse to revelation, but much …orse to be adverse to it.

Lastly, In the close of the chapter we are told how …pitefully and maliciously the scribes and *Pharisees* …ontrived to draw him into a snare, *v.* 53, 54. They …ould not bear those cutting reproofs which they …ust own to be just, as if, because his reproofs were …warm, they hoped to stir him up to some intemperate …eat and passion, so as to put him off his guard, …hey *began to urge him vehemently*, and to *provoke …im to speak of many things, laying wait* for something which might serve the design they had of making him either *odious* to the people, or *obnoxious* to the government, or both. Faithful reprovers of sin must expect to have many enemies. That we may bear trials of this kind with patience, and get through them with prudence, let us *consider him who endured such contradiction of sinners against himself.*

JAMIESON, FAUSSET, BROWN

50. all . . . required of this generation—As it was only in the last generation of them that "the iniquity of the Amorites was full" (Gen. 15:16), and then the abominations of ages were at once completely and awfully avenged, so the iniquity of Israel was allowed to accumulate from age to age till in that generation it came to the full, and the whole collected vengeance of Heaven broke at once over its devoted head. In the first French Revolution the same awful principle was exemplified, and *Christendom has not done with it yet.* **prophets**—in the New Testament sense (Matt. 23:34; see I Cor. 12:28). **51. blood of Zacharias**—Probably the allusion is not to any recent murder, but to II Chronicles 24:20-22, as the *last recorded* and most suitable case for illustration. And as Zacharias' last words were, "The Lord *require it,*" so they are warned that "of that generation it should be *required.*" **52. key of knowledge**—not the key to open knowledge, but knowledge, the only key to open heaven. In Matthew 23:13, they are accused of *shutting heaven;* here of *taking away the key*, which was worse. A right knowledge of God's Word is eternal life (John 17:3); but this they took away from the people, substituting for it their wretched traditions.

53, 54. Exceedingly vivid and affecting. They were stung to the quick—and can we wonder?—yet had not materials for the charge they were preparing against Him. **provoke him . . .**—"to harass Him with questions."

ADAM CLARKE

50. *That the blood.* That the particle may be translated "so that," pointing out the event only, nor the design or intention, Bishop Pearce has well shown in his note on this place, where he refers to a like use of the word in chap. ix. 45; xiv. 20; John x. 17; Rom. v. 20; xi. 11; 1 Cor. i. 15, 31.

51. *From the blood of Abel.* See this subject explained at large on Matt. xxiii. 35. *Required.* May be translated either by the word "visited" or "revenged," and the latter word evidently conveys the meaning of our Lord. They are here represented as having this blood among them; and it is intimated that God will come by and by to *require* it, and to inquire how it was shed, and to punish those who shed it.

52. *Ye have taken away the key of knowledge.* By your traditions you have taken away the true method of interpreting the prophecies; you have given a wrong meaning to those scriptures which speak of the kingdom of the Messiah, and the people are thereby hindered from entering into it.

53. *Began to urge him vehemently.* They "began to be furious." They found themselves completely unmasked in the presence of a vast concourse of people. They therefore questioned Him on a variety of points, and hoped by the multitude and impertinence of their questions to puzzle or irritate Him, so as to induce Him to "speak rashly" (for this is the import of the word), that they might find some subject of accusation against Him.

MATTHEW HENRY

CHAPTER 12

Verses 1–12

I. A vast auditory that was got together to hear Christ preach. The *scribes* and *Pharisees* sought *to accuse him*, but the people still *admired* him, attended on him, and did him honour. *In the meantime* (*v.* 1), while he was in the Pharisee's house, the people got together for an afternoon sermon, a sermon after *dinner*, after dinner with a Pharisee; and he would not disappoint them. Though in the morning sermon, when they were *gathered thickly together* (*ch.* xi. 29), he had severely reproved them, yet they renewed their attendance on him; so much better could the people bear *their* reproofs than the Pharisees *theirs.* The more the Pharisees strove to drive the people from Christ, the more flocking there was to him. Here was an *innumerable multitude of people gathered together, so that they trode one upon another.* It is a good sight to see people thus forward to hear the word. When the net is cast where there is such a multitude of fish, it may be hoped that some will be enclosed.

II. The instructions which he gave his followers.

1. He began with a caution against *hypocrisy.* This he said *to his disciples first of all.* These were his more peculiar charge, and therefore he particularly *warned them* as his *beloved sons;* they made more profession of religion than others, and hypocrisy in *that* was the sin they were most in danger of. Hypocrisy would be worse in them than in others. Christ's disciples were, for aught we know, the *best men* then in the world, yet they needed to be cautioned against hypocrisy. Christ said this to the disciples, *in the hearing* of this great multitude, to add the greater weight to the caution, and to let the world know that he would not countenance hypocrisy, no, not in *his own disciples.*

(1) The description of that sin which he warns them against: *It is the leaven of the Pharisees.* It is *leaven*; it is *spreading* as leaven, *insinuating* itself into the whole man, and all that he does; it is *swelling* and *souring* as leaven, for it puffs men up with pride, embitters them with malice, and makes their service unacceptable to God. It is the leaven of the Pharisees: "It is the sin they are most of them found in. Take heed of imitating them; do not dissemble in Christianity as they do in Judaism."

(2) A good reason against it: "*For there is nothing*

JAMIESON, FAUSSET, BROWN

CHAPTER 12

VSS. 1-12. WARNING AGAINST HYPOCRISY. **1-3. meantime**—in close connection, probably, with the foregoing scene. Our Lord had been *speaking out* more plainly than ever before, as matters were coming to a head between Him and His enemies, and this seems to have suggested to His own mind the warning here. He had just Himself illustriously exemplified His own precepts.

his disciples first of all—afterwards to "the multitudes" (vs. 54).

ADAM CLARKE

CHAPTER 12

1. *An innumerable multitude of people.* "Myriads of people." A myriad is 10,000, and myriads must, at the very lowest, mean 20,000. But the word is often used to signify a crowd or multitude which cannot be readily numbered. There was doubtless a vast crowd assembled on this occasion, and many of them were deeply instructed by the very important discourse which our Lord delivered.

Leaven of the Pharisees. See Matt. xvi. 1-12. *Which is hypocrisy.* These words are supposed by some to be an addition to the text, because it does not appear that it is their *hypocrisy* to which Christ alludes, but their false doctrines. They had, however, a large proportion of both.

MATTHEW HENRY

covered that shall not be revealed, v. 2, 3. Sooner or later, truth will come out. If you *speak in darkness* that which is inconsistent with your public professions, *it shall be heard in the light*; some way or other it shall be discovered, and your folly and falsehood will be *made manifest.*" If men's religion prevail not to conquer and cure the wickedness of their hearts, it shall not always serve for a cloak. The day is coming when hypocrites will be stripped of their fig-leaves.

2. To this he added a charge to them to be faithful to the trust reposed in them, and not to betray it, through cowardice or base fear. "Whether men will *hear*, or whether they will *forbear*, tell them the *truth*, the *whole* truth, and *nothing but* the truth; what has been spoken to you *privately*, that do you preach *publicly*, whoever is offended." It was likely to be a *suffering* cause, though never a *sinking* one; let them therefore arm themselves with courage; and divers arguments are furnished here to steel them with a holy resolution in their work.

(1) "The power of your enemies is a limited power (*v.* 4): *I say unto you, my friends*" (Christ's disciples are his friends, he calls them *friends*, and gives them this *friendly* advice), "*be not afraid.*" Those whom Christ owns for *his friends* need not be afraid of any enemies. "*Be not afraid*, no, not of them that *kill the body; after that there is no more that they can do.*" Those can do Christ's disciples no real harm who can but *kill the body*, for they only send that to its rest, and the soul to its joy, the sooner.

(2) God is to be feared more than the most powerful men: "*I will forewarn you whom you shall fear* (*v.* 5). By *owning Christ* you may incur the wrath of men, but by *denying* Christ, and disowning him, you will incur the wrath of God, which has power to send *you to hell.* Therefore *I say unto you, Fear him.*" "It is true," said that blessed martyr, Bishop Hooper, "life is sweet, and death bitter; but eternal life is more sweet, and eternal death more bitter."

(3) The lives of good Christians and good ministers are the particular care of divine Providence, *v.* 6, 7. Providence takes cognizance of the *meanest creatures*, even of *the sparrows.* "Though they are of such small account that *five* of them are sold for *two farthings*, yet not one of them is *forgotten of God.* Now, *you are of more value than many sparrows*, and therefore you may be sure you *are not forgotten.*" Providence takes cognizance of the *meanest interest* of the disciples of Christ: "*Even the very hairs of your head are all numbered* (*v.* 7); much more are your sighs and tears numbered, and the drops of your blood, which you shed for Christ's name's sake."

(4) "You will be owned or disowned by Christ, according as you now own or disown him," *v.* 8, 9. To engage us to *confess Christ before men*, how dear soever it may cost us, we are assured that they who *confess Christ* now shall be owned by him in the great day *before the angels of God.* Jesus Christ will *confess*, not only that he suffered for them, but that they suffered *for him*, and what greater honour can be done them? To deter us from *denying* Christ we are here assured that those who *deny Christ*, whatever they may save by it, though it were life itself, and whatever they may *gain* by it, will be vast losers at last, for they shall be *denied before the angels of God*; Christ will not know them, will not own them.

(5) The errand they were shortly to be sent out upon was of the highest and last importance, *v.* 10. Let them be bold in preaching the gospel, for a sorer and heavier doom would attend those that rejected them (after the Spirit was poured upon them, which was to be the *last* method of conviction) than those that now rejected Christ himself. "*Whosoever shall speak a word against the Son of man*, it is capable of some excuse: *Father, forgive them, for they know not what they do.* But unto him that *blasphemes the Holy Ghost*, the privilege of the *forgiveness of sins* shall be denied; he shall have no benefit by Christ and his gospel." There were hopes of those who, though not convinced by them at first, yet admired them, but those who *blasphemed* them were given over.

(6) Whatever trials they should be called out to, they should be sufficiently furnished for them, and honourably brought through them, *v.* 11, 12. The faithful martyr for Christ has not only *sufferings* to *undergo*, but a *testimony* to *bear*, a *good confession* to *witness*, and is concerned to do that *well*, so that the cause of Christ may not suffer, though he suffer for it; and, if this be his care, let him cast it upon God: "When they *bring you into the synagogues*, or before *magistrates and powers*, to be examined about your doctrine, *take no thought what ye shall answer*," [1] "That you may *save yourselves.* If it be the will of God that you should come off, and your time is not yet come, he will bring it about effectually." [2] "That you may *serve your Master*; aim at this, but do not perplex yourselves about it, for *the Holy*

JAMIESON, FAUSSET, BROWN

covered—from the view. **2. hid**—from knowledge. "Tis no use concealing anything, for all will one day come out. Give free and fearless utterance then to all the truth." (Cf. I Cor. 4:3, 5).

4, 5. I say . . .—You will say, That may cost us our life. Be it so; but, "My friends,' there their power ends." He calls them "my friends" here, not in any loose sense, but, as we think, from the feeling He then had that in this "killing of the bodv" *He and they* were going to be affectingly one with each other. **Fear Him . . .—Fear Him**—how striking the repetition here! *Only the one fear would effectually expel the other.* **after he hath killed . . .**—Learn here —(1) To play false with one's convictions to save one's life, may fail of its end after all, for God can inflict a violent death in some other and equally formidable way. (2) There is a *hell*, it seems, for the body as well as the soul; consequently, sufferings adapted to the one as well as the other. (3) *Fear of hell* is a divinely authorized and needed motive of action even to Christ's "friends." (4) As Christ's meekness and gentleness were not compromised by such harsh notes as these, so those servants of Christ lack their Master's spirit who soften down all such language to please ears 'polite.' (See on Mark 9:43-48.) **6, 7. five . . . for two farthings**—In Matthew 10:29 it is two for one farthing"; so if one took two farthings' worth, he got one in addition—of such small value were they. **than many sparrows**—not "than millions of sparrows"; the charm and power of our Lord's teaching is very much in this simplicity.

8, 9. confess . . . deny . . .—The point lies in doing it "before men," because one has to do it "despising the *shame.*" But when done, the Lord holds Himself bound to repay it *in kind* by confessing such "before the angels of God." For the rest, see on ch. 9:26.

10. Son of man . . . Holy Ghost—(See on Matt. 12:31, 32).

What, then, is this sin against the Holy Ghost—the unpardonable sin? One thing is clear: Its unpardonableness cannot arise from anything in the nature of sin itself; for that would be a naked contradiction to the emphatic declaration of vs. 31, that all manner of sin is pardonable. And what is this but the fundamental truth of the Gospel? (See Acts 13:38, 39; Rom. 3:22, 24; I John 1:7, etc.). Then, again when it is said (vs. 32), that to speak against or blaspheme the Son of man is pardonable, but the blasphemy against the Holy Ghost is not pardonable, it is not to be conceived that this arises from any greater sanctity in the one blessed Person than the other. These remarks so narrow the question that the true sense of our Lord's words seem to disclose themselves at once. It is a contrast between slandering "the Son of man" *in His veiled condition and unfinished work*—which might be done "ignorantly, in unbelief" (I Tim. 1:13), and slandering the same blessed Person after the blaze of glory which *the Holy Ghost* was soon to throw around His claims, and in the full knowledge of all

ADAM CLARKE

2. *There is nothing covered.* See the no on Matt. v. 15; x. 26-27; Mark iv. 22.

For there is nothing covered. God se everything; this is consolation to the uprig and dismay to the wicked. And He will bri into judgment every work, and every sec thing, whether good or bad, Eccles. xii. 14.

5. *Fear him.* Even the friends of God ar commanded to fear God, as a Being who ha authority to send both body and soul into hel Therefore it is proper even for the most hol persons to maintain a fear of God, as the Pun isher of all unrighteousness.

6. *Are not five sparrows sold for two farthings?* See this explained on Matt. x. 29, from which place we learn that two sparrows were sold for one farthing, and here that *five* were sold for *two farthings.*

7. *Fear not therefore.* Want of faith in the providence and goodness of God is the source of all human inquietudes and fears. He has undertaken to save and defend those to the uttermost who trust in Him.

8. *Shall confess.* See on Matt. x. 32-33.

Whosoever therefore shall confess me before men. That is, whosoever shall acknowledge Me to be the Messiah, and have his heart and life regulated by My spirit and doctrine. It is not merely sufficient to have the heart right before God; there must be a firm, manly, and public profession of Christ before men.

Whosoever shall deny me. Whosoever prefers his worldly interest to his duty to God sets a greater value on earthly than on heavenly things, and prefers the friendship of men to the approbation of God. Let it be remembered that to be renounced by Christ is to have Him for neither Mediator nor Saviour. To appear before the tribunal of God without having Christ for our Advocate, and, on the contrary, to have Him there as our Judge, and a Witness against us—how can a man think of this and not die with horror!

10. *Him that blasphemeth.* See the sin *against the Holy Ghost* explained, Matt. xii. 32.

11. *Unto magistrates, and powers.* See Matt. x. 17-20. *Take ye no thought.* See Matt. vi. 25; x. 19.

MATTHEW HENRY

Ghost, as a Spirit of wisdom, *shall teach you what you ought to say*, and how to say it, so that it may be for the honour of God and his cause."

Verses 13–21

I. The application that was made to Christ by one of his hearers, desiring him to interpose *between him and his brother* in a matter that concerned the estate of the family (*v.* 13): "*Master, speak to my brother that he divide the inheritance with me.*" Some think that his brother *did him wrong*, and that he appealed to Christ to *right him*. Such brethren there are in the world, who have no sense at all either of *natural equity* or *natural affection*. They who are so wronged have a God to go to, who will *execute* judgment and justice for *those that are oppressed*. Others think that he had a mind to *do his brother wrong*, and would have Christ to *assist him*; that, whereas the law gave the elder brother a double portion of the estate, he would have Christ to *alter that law*, and oblige his brother to *divide the inheritance* equally *with him*. It was not a lawful desire of getting his own, but a *sinful* desire of getting more than his own.

II. Christ's refusal to interpose this in matter (*v.* 14): *Man, who made me a judge or divider over you?* Christ will not assume either a *legislative* power, or a *judicial* power. He corrects the man's mistake. If he had come to him to desire him to assist his pursuit of the heavenly inheritance, Christ would have given him his best help; but as to this matter he has nothing to do. Whatever he did, he could tell by what authority he did it, and who gave him that authority. Now this shows us what is the nature and constitution of Christ's kingdom. It is a spiritual kingdom, and not of this world. 1. It does not interfere with civil powers. Christianity leaves the matter as it found it, as to civil power. 2. It does not intermeddle with civil rights; it obliges all to do justly, according to the settled rules of equity. 3. It does not *encourage* our *expectations* of worldly advantages by our religion. 4. It does not *encourage* our *contests* with our brethren, and our being rigorous and high in our demands.

III. The necessary caution which Christ took occasion from this to give to his hearers.

1. The caution itself (*v.* 15): *Take heed and beware of covetousness;* ὁρᾶτε—"*Observe yourselves*, keep a *jealous eye* upon your own hearts, lest covetous principles steal into them; and φυλάσσεσθε—*preserve yourselves*, keep a *strict hand* upon your own hearts, lest covetous principles rule and give law in them."

2. An argument to enforce this caution: *For a man's life consisteth not in the abundance of the things which he possesseth;* that is, "our happiness and comfort do not depend upon our having a great deal of the wealth of this world." The life of the *soul*, undoubtedly, does not depend upon it. The things of the world will not suit the nature of a soul, nor supply its needs, nor satisfy its desires. Even the life of the body and the happiness of that do not consist in an *abundance* of these things; for many live very contentedly and easily, who have but a little of the wealth of it (a dinner of herbs with holy love is better than a *feast of fat things*); and, on the other hand, many live very miserably who have a great deal of the things of this world.

3. The illustration of this by a parable, which is intended for the enforcing of that necessary caution to us all, to *take heed of covetousness*. The parable gives us the life and death of a *rich man*, and leaves us to judge whether he was a *happy* man.

(1) Here is an account of his worldly wealth and abundance (*v.* 16): *The ground of a certain rich man brought forth plentifully.* His wealth lay much in the fruits of the earth. He had a great deal of ground, and his ground was *fruitful*; much would have *more*, and he *had more*.

(2) Here are the workings of his heart. We are here told what *he thought within himself*, *v.* 17. The God of heaven knows and observes whatever we think within ourselves, and we are accountable to him for it. Let us here observe,

[1] What his *cares* and *concerns* were. When he saw an extraordinary crop upon his ground, instead of *thanking God* for it, or rejoicing in the opportunity it would give him of doing the more good, he afflicts himself with this thought, *What shall I do, because I have no room where to bestow my fruits?* He speaks as one *at a loss*, and full of perplexity. *What shall I do now?* The poorest beggar in the country, that did not know where to get a meal's meat, could not have said a more anxious word. Even the *abundance* of the rich will not suffer them to *sleep*, for thinking what they shall do with what they have. The rich man seems to speak it with a sigh, *What shall I do?*

JAMIESON, FAUSSET, BROWN

that. This would be to slander Him with eyes open, or to do it "presumptuously."

13-53. COVETOUSNESS—WATCHFULNESS—SUPERIORITY TO EARTHLY TIES. **13. Master . . .**—i.e., "Great Preacher of righteousness, help; there is need of Thee in this rapacious world; here am I the victim of injustice, and that from my own brother, who withholds from me my rightful share of the inheritance that has fallen to us." In this most inopportune intrusion upon the solemnities of our Lord's teaching, there is a mixture of the absurd and the irreverent, the one, however, occasioning the other. The man had not the least idea that his case was not of as urgent a nature, and as worthy the attention of our Lord, as anything else He could deal with.

14. Man, . . .—*Contrast this style of address with* "my friends," (vs. 4). **who . . .**—a question literally repudiating the office which Moses assumed (Exod. 2:14). *The influence of religious teachers in the external relations of life has ever been immense, when only the* INDIRECT *effect of their teaching; but whenever they intermeddle* DIRECTLY *with secular and political matters, the spell of that influence is broken.*

15. unto them—the multitude around Him (vs. 1). **of covetousness**—The best copies have "all," i.e., "every kind of covetousness"; because as this was one of the more plausible forms of it, so He would strike at once at the *root* of the evil. **a man's life . . .**—a singularly weighty maxim, and not less so because its meaning and its truth are equally evident.

ALEXANDER MACLAREN:

Covetousness is folly because it grasps at worldly good under the false belief that thereby it will secure the true good of life; but when it has made its pile, it finds that it is no nearer peace of heart, rest, nobleness, or joy than before, and has probably lost much of both in the process of making it. The mad race after wealth, which is the sin of this luxurious, greedy, commercial age, is the consequence of a lie—that life does consist in the abundance of possessions. It consists in knowing "thee the only true God, and Jesus Christ, whom thou hast sent." Is there any saying of Jesus Christ's more revolutionary or less believed by His professed followers than this?

The story of the rich fool is not a parable in the narrower meaning of that word—that is, a description of some event or thing in the natural sphere, transferred by analogy to the spiritual—but an imaginary narrative exemplifying in a concrete instance the characteristics of the class of covetous men. The first point noted is that accumulated wealth breeds anxiety rather than satisfaction. The man is embarrassed by his abundance. The trouble of knowing how to keep it is as great as the labor of acquiring it, and the enjoyment of it is still in the future. Many a rich man is more worried about his securities than he was in making his money. There are so many "bags with holes" that he is at his wits' end for investments, and the first thing he looks at in his morning's paper is the stock report, the sight of which often spoils his breakfast. *(Continued on next page)*

ADAM CLARKE

13. *Speak to my brother, that he divide.* Among the Jews, the children had the inheritance of their fathers divided among them; the eldest had a double portion, but all the rest had equal parts. It is likely the person complained of in the text was the elder brother, and he wished to keep the whole to himself—a case which is far from being uncommon.

14. *A judge.* Without some judgment given in the case, no division could be made; therefore Jesus added the word *judge*. A minister of Christ ought not to concern himself with secular affairs any further than charity and the order of discipline require it. Better to leave all these things to the civil magistrate, unless where a lawsuit may be prevented, and the matter decided to the satisfaction or acquiescence of both parties.

15. *Beware of covetousness.* Or rather, "Beware of all inordinate desires." I add "all," on the authority of many MSS., versions, and several of the primitive fathers. Inordinate desires—from *pleion*, "more," and *echein*, "to have"; the desire to have *more* and *more*, let a person possess whatever he may—such a disposition of mind is never satisfied; for as soon as one object is gained, the heart goes out after another. *Consisteth not in the abundance.* That is, "dependeth not on the abundance." It is not superfluities that support man's life, but necessaries. What is necessary, God gives liberally; what is superfluous, He has not promised. Nor can a man's life be preserved by the abundance of his possessions; to prove this Jesus spoke the following parable.

16. *The ground of a certain rich man.* He had generally what is called good luck in his farm and this was a remarkably plentiful year.

17. *He thought within himself.* Began to be puzzled in consequence of the increase of his goods. Riches, though ever so well acquired, produce nothing but vexation and embarrassment.

MATTHEW HENRY

And if you ask, Why, what is the matter? Truly he has *abundance* of wealth, and wants a place to *put it in*, that is all.

[2] What his *projects* and *purposes* were (*v.* 18): "*This will I do, I will pull down my barns*, and I will *build greater, and there will I bestow all my fruits and my goods*, and then I shall be at ease." It was folly for him to call the fruits of the ground *his* fruits and *his* goods. What we have is but *lent* us for our use, the property is still in God; we are but stewards of our *Lord's goods*. It was folly for him to *hoard up* what he had, and then to think it *well bestowed*. There will I bestow it *all*; as if none must be bestowed upon the poor, and *the stranger*, the *fatherless and the widow*, but all in the great barn. It was folly for him to let his *mind* rise with his *condition*; to talk of bigger barns, as if the next year must needs be as fruitful as this, and much more abundant, whereas the barn might be as much too big the next year as it was too little this. It was folly for him to think to ease his care by building new barns, for the building of them would but increase his care; those know this who know anything of the spirit of building. It was folly for him to contrive and resolve all this *absolutely* and *without reserve*. This *I will* do. *I will*; without so much as that necessary proviso, *If the Lord will, I shall live*, James iv. 13–15. Peremptory projects are foolish projects; for our times are in God's hand, and not in our own, and we do not so much as *know what shall be on the morrow*.

[3] What his *pleasing hopes* and *expectations* were. "Then *I will say to my soul, Soul, thou hast much goods laid up for many years*; now *take thine ease, eat, drink, and be merry*," *v.* 19. Here also appears his folly. It was folly for him to put off his comfort in his abundance till he had compassed his projects concerning it. When he has built bigger barns, then he will *take his ease*; and might he not as well have *done that now*? It was folly for him to be confident that his goods were *laid up for many years*, whereas in an hour's time they might be burnt to the ground and all that was laid up in them, perhaps by lightning. A few years may make a great change; *moth and rust may corrupt, or thieves break through and steal*. It was folly for him to count upon certain *ease*, whereas there are many things that may make people uneasy in the midst of their greatest abundance. One dead fly may spoil a whole pot of precious ointment; and one thorn a whole bed of down. Pain and sickness of body, disagreeableness of relations, and especially a guilty conscience, may rob a man of his ease, who has ever so much of the wealth of this world. It was folly for him to think of making no other use of his plenty than to *eat* and *drink*, and to *be merry*; to indulge the flesh, and gratify the sensual appetite, without any thought of doing good to others: as if we *lived* to eat, and did not *eat* to *live*. It was the greatest folly of all to say all this to his *soul*. If he had said, *Body, take thine ease*, for *thou hast goods laid up for many years*, there had been sense in it; but the soul was no way interested in a barn full of corn or a bag full of gold. If he had had the *soul of a swine*, he might have *blessed it* with the satisfaction of *eating* and *drinking*. It is the great absurdity which the children of this world are guilty of that they portion their souls in the wealth of the world and the pleasures of sense.

(3) Here is God's sentence upon all this. He said to himself, *Take thine ease*. If God had said so too, the man had been happy. *But God said* quite otherwise; God said he did ill for himself: *Thou fool, this night thy soul shall be required of thee, v.* 20. *God said to him*, that is, decreed this concerning him. This was said when he was *in the fulness of his sufficiency*, when his eyes were held waking upon his bed with his cares and contrivances about enlarging his barns. When he was forecasting this, and then lulled himself asleep again with a pleasing dream of many years' enjoyment, *then* God said this to him. Now observe what God said,

The character he gave him: *Thou fool*, thou *Nabal*, alluding to the story of Nabal, that *fool* (Nabal is his name, and folly is with him). Carnal worldlings are fools, and the day is coming when God will call them by their own name, *Thou fool*, and they will call themselves so.

The sentence he passed upon him, a sentence of death: *This night thy soul shall be required of thee*; and then *whose shall those things be which thou hast provided*? He thought he had goods that should be his for many years, but he must part from them *this night*; he thought he should enjoy them himself, but he must leave them to he knows not who.

First, It is a *force*, an *arrest*; it is the *requiring of the soul*; what hast thou to do with a soul, who canst use it no better? Thy soul shall be *required*. A good man cheerfully resigns his soul at death, and gives it

JAMIESON, FAUSSET, BROWN

The next point is the selfish and arrogant sense of possession, as betrayed by the repetition of "my"—my fruits, my barns, my corn, and my goods. He has no thought of God, nor of his own stewardship. He recognizes no claim on his wealth. If he had looked a little beyond himself, he would have seen many places where he could have bestowed his fruits. Were there no poor at his gates? He had better have poured some riches into the laps of these than have built a new barn. Corn laid up would breed weevils; dispersed, it would bring blessings.

Again, this type of covetous men is a fool because he reckons on "many years." The goods may last, but will he? He can make sure that they will suffice for a long time, but he cannot make sure of the long time. Again, he blunders tragically in his estimate of the power of worldly goods to satisfy. "Eat, drink," might be said to his body, but to say it to his soul, and to fancy that these pleasures of sense would put it at ease, is the fatal error which gnaws like a worm at the root of every worldly life. The word here rendered "take thine ease" is cognate with Christ's in His great promise, "Ye shall find rest unto your souls." Not in abundance of worldly goods, but in union with Him, is that rest to be found which the covetous man vainly promises himself in filled barns and luxurious idleness.

There is a grim contrast between what the rich man said and what God said. The man's words were empty breath; God's are powers, and what He says is a deed. The divine decree comes crashing into the abortive human plans like a thunder-clap into a wood full of singing birds, and they are all stricken silent. So little does life consist in possessions that all the abundance cannot keep the breath in a man for one moment. His life is "required of him," not only in the sense that he has to give it up, but also inasmuch as he has to answer for it. In that requirement the selfishly used wealth will be "a swift witness against" him, and instead of ministering to life or ease, will "eat his flesh as fire." Molten gold dropping on flesh burns badly. Wealth, trusted in and selfishly clutched, without recognition of God the giver or of others' claims to share it, will burn still worse.
—*Expositions of Holy Scripture*

19. a certain rich man . . .—Why is this man called a "fool?" (1) Because he deemed a life of secure and abundant earthly enjoyment the summit of human felicity. (2) Because, possessing the means of this, through prosperity in his calling, he flattered himself that he had a long lease of such enjoyment, and nothing to do but give himself up to it. Nothing else is laid to his charge.

20, 21. this night . . .—This sudden cutting short of his career is designed to express not only the folly of building securely upon the future, but of throwing one's whole soul into what may at any moment be gone. "Thy *soul* shall be required of thee" is put in opposition to his own treatment of it, "I will say to my *soul, Soul*, . . ." **whose shall those things be . . .**—Cf. Psalm 39:6, "He heapeth up riches and *knoweth not who shall gather them*."

ADAM CLARKE

18. *I will pull down*. The rich are full of designs concerning this life, but in general take no thought about eternity till the time that their goods and their lives are both taken away.

19. *Soul, thou hast much goods*. Great possessions are generally accompanied with pride, idleness, and luxury; and these are the greatest enemies to salvation.

20. *Thou fool*. To imagine that a man's comfort and peace can depend upon temporal things, or to suppose that these can satisfy the wishes of an immortal spirit!

***This night*. What a dreadful awakening of a soul, long asleep in sin! He is now hurried into the presence of his Maker; none of his worldly goods can accompany him, and he has not a particle of heavenly treasure!**

MATTHEW HENRY

up; but a worldly man has it *torn* from him with violence. *They shall require thy soul.* God shall require it; he shall require an account of it. "Man, woman, what hast thou done with thy soul. Give an account of that stewardship."

Secondly, It is a *surprise*, an *unexpected* force. It is in *the night*. The time of death is day-time to a good man; it is his morning. But it is night to a worldling, a dark night. It is *this night*, this *present* night, without delay. This *pleasant* night, when thou art promising thyself many years to come, now thou must die. In the midst of all, here is an end of all.

Thirdly, It is the leaving of all *those things* behind *which they have provided*. All that which they have placed their happiness in, and built their hope upon, they must leave behind.

Fourthly, It is leaving them to they *know not who*: "Then *whose shall those things be*? Not *thine* to be sure, and thou knowest not what *they* will prove for whom thou didst design them, thy children and relations, whether they will be *wise* or *fools* (Eccles. ii. 18, 19), whether such as will bless thy memory or curse it, be a credit to thy family or a blemish, do good or hurt with what thou leavest them." If many a man could have foreseen to whom his house would have come after his death, he would rather have burned it than beautified it.

Fifthly, It is a demonstration of his folly. *At his end he shall be a fool*, for then it will appear that he took pains to lay up treasure in a world he was hastening from, but took no care to lay it up in the world he was hastening to.

Lastly, Here is the application of this parable (*v.* 21): *So is he that layeth up treasure for himself, and is not rich towards God.* This is the way and this is the end of such a man.

1. The description of a worldly man: He *lays up treasure for himself*, for *himself* in opposition to God, for that *self* that is to be *denied*. It is his error that he counts his *flesh himself*, as if the *body* were the *man*. It is his error that he makes it his business to *lay up for the flesh*, which he calls laying up *for himself*. It is his error that he counts those things his *treasure* which are thus *laid up* for the world, and the body, and the life that now is. The greatest error of all is that he is in no care to be *rich towards God*, rich in the *things of God*. Many who have abundance of this world are wholly destitute of that which will enrich their souls, which will make them rich towards God, rich for eternity.

2. The folly and misery of a worldly man: *So is he*. Our Lord Jesus Christ has here told us what his end will be. It is the unspeakable folly of the most of men to mind that which is merely for the body and for time, more than that which is for the soul and eternity.

Verses 22–40

"*Therefore*, because there are so many that are ruined by covetousness, *I say unto you*, my disciples, take heed of it." *Thou, O man of God, flee these things*, as well as thou, O man of the world, 1 Tim. vi. 11.

I. He charges them not to afflict themselves with disquieting perplexing cares about the necessary supports of life: *Take no thought for your life, v.* 22. In the foregoing parable he had given us warning against that branch of covetousness of which rich people are most in danger. He here warns them against another branch of covetousness, which they are most in temptation to that have but a little of this world, and that was, an *anxious solicitude* about the necessary supports of life: "*Take no thought for your life what ye shall eat* or *what ye shall put on*." This is the caution he had largely insisted upon, Matt. vi. 25, &c.; and the arguments here used are much the same.

1. God, who has done the greater for us, may be depended upon to do the less. He has given us *life* and a *body*, and therefore we may cheerfully leave it to him to provide *meat* for the support of that life, and *raiment* for the defence of that body.

2. God, who provides for the inferior creatures, may be depended upon to provide. "Trust God for *meat*, for he *feeds the ravens* (*v.* 24); they *neither sow nor reap*, and yet they are *fed*. Now consider *how much better ye are than the fowls*, than the ravens. Trust God for clothing, for he clothes the lilies (*v.* 27, 28); they *toil not*, they *spin not*, and yet, as the flower grows up, it appears wonderfully *beautified*. Now, if God has so clothed the flowers, *shall he not much more clothe* you?" Then let them not be *of little faith*. Our inordinate cares are owing to the weakness of our faith; for a powerful practical belief of the all-sufficiency of God would be mighty, through God, to the pulling down of the strongholds of these disquieting perplexing imaginations.

F. B. MEYER:

The doom of the money lover. Our Lord did not come into our world as an earthly judge, adjusting differences between man and man. He lays down great principles, obedience to which will bring heaven into human lives. One of the greatest of these is enunciated in verse 15. Covetousness is as much a temptation of the poor man who is wronged as of his rich oppressor; and love for money will inevitably, in poor and rich, becloud the vision and disturb the inner peace. The worth of a man cannot be computed by the amount that stands to his credit. Not what you have, but what you are—that is your value in the eyes of God. Some men live to get; see to it that you live to be.

It is absurd to suppose that the soul can take its ease just because its barns are bursting with goods. Goods are not good! The soul cannot live on corn! Merriment cannot come to a heart that is smitten by remorse and shadowed by the remonstrances of an evil conscience! Besides, we cannot take with us our possessions when we cross the river. We can only take our character—our things pass into other hands.—*Bible Commentary*

JAMIESON, FAUSSET, BROWN

21. So is he . . .—Such is a picture of his folly here, and of its awful issue. **is not rich . . .**—lives to amass and enjoy riches which terminate on *self*, but as to the riches of God's favor, which is life (Ps. 30:5), of "precious" faith (II Peter 1:1; Jas. 2:5), of good works (I Tim. 6:18), of wisdom which is better than rubies (Prov. 8:11)—lives and dies *a beggar*!

22-31.—(See on Matthew 6:25-33.)

Therefore I say unto you, Take no thought—"Be not solicitous." The English word "thought," when our version was made, expressed this idea of "solicitude," "anxious concern"—as may be seen in any old English classic; and in the same sense it is used in I Samuel 9:5, etc. But this sense of the word has now nearly gone out, and so the mere English reader is apt to be perplexed. *Thought* or forethought, for temporal things—in the sense of reflection, consideration—is required alike by Scripture and common sense. It is that anxious solicitude, that oppressive care, which springs from unbelieving doubts and misgivings, which alone is here condemned. (See Phil. 4:6). **for your life, what ye shall eat, or what ye shall drink; nor yet for your body, what ye shall put on**—In Luke (12:29) our Lord adds, "neither be ye unsettled"—not "of doubtful mind," as in our version. When "careful (or 'full of care') about nothing," but committing all in prayer and supplication with thanksgiving unto God, the apostle assures us that "the peace of God, which passeth all understanding, shall keep our hearts and minds in Christ Jesus" (Phil. 4:6, 7); i.e., shall guard both our feelings and our thoughts from undue agitation, and keep them in a holy calm. But when we commit our whole temporal condition to the wit of our own minds, we get into that "unsettled" state against which our Lord exhorts His disciples. **Is not the life more than meat [food] and the body than raiment?**—If God, then, gives and keeps up the greater—the life, the body—will He withhold the less, food to sustain life and raiment to clothe the body?

ADAM CLARKE

21. *So is he.* That is, "thus will it be." This is not an individual case; all who make this life their portion, and who are destitute of the peace and salvation of God, shall, sooner or later, be surprised in the same way. *Layeth up treasure for himself.* This is the essential characteristic of a covetous man. He desires riches; he gets them; he lays them up, not for the necessary uses to which they might be devoted, but *for himself*—to please himself, and to gratify his avaricious soul. Such a person is commonly called a "miser," i.e., literally, a wretched, "miserable" man.

22. *Take no thought.* Be not anxiously careful. See on Matt. vi. 25.

Therefore. "On this account," namely, that you may not serve mammon, but have unshaken confidence in God, *I say unto you. Take no thought.* Be not anxiously careful. Prudent care is never forbidden by our Lord, but only that anxious, distracting solicitude which, by dividing the mind and drawing it different ways, renders it utterly incapable of attending to any solemn or important concern. In this and the following verses our Lord lays down several reasons why men should not disquiet themselves about the wants of life or concerning the future. The *first* is the experience of greater benefits already received. *Is not the life more than meat, and the body than raiment?* Can He who gave us our bodies, and breathed into them the breath of life, before we could ask them from Him, refuse us that which is necessary to preserve both, and when we ask it in humble confidence?

Behold the fowls of the air. The *second* reason why we should not be anxiously concerned about the future is the example of the smaller animals, which the providence of God feeds without their own labor, though He be not their father.

MATTHEW HENRY

3. Our cares are fruitless, vain, and insignificant. They will not gain us our wishes, and therefore ought not to hinder our repose (*v.* 25): "*Which of you by taking thought can add to his stature one cubit?* Now if ye be *not able to do that which is least*, if it be not in your power to alter your statures, why should you perplex yourselves about other things, which are as much out of your power?" As in our *stature*, so in our *state*, it is our wisdom to take *it as it is*, and make the best of it; for fretting and vexing, carping and caring will not mend it.

4. An inordinate anxious pursuit of the things of this world, even necessary things, very ill becomes the disciples of Christ (*v.* 29, 30): "*Seek not ye what ye shall eat, or what ye shall drink;* do not you afflict yourselves with perplexing cares." Let not the disciples of Christ thus *seek* their food, but ask it of God day by day; let them not be *of doubtful mind;* blown hither and thither with every wind. Be even and steady, and have your hearts fixed; *live not in careful suspense;* let not your minds be continually perplexed between hope and fear, ever upon the rack. Let not the children of God make themselves uneasy; for,

(1) This is to make themselves like the children of this world: "*All these things do the nations of the world seek after*, *v.* 30. They that take care for this world only, and not for the other, look no further than what they shall *eat* and *drink*. But it ill becomes you to do so. When inordinate cares prevail over us, we should think, "What am I, a Christian or a heathen? If a Christian, shall I rank myself with Gentiles, and join with them in their pursuits?"

(2) It is needless for them to disquiet themselves with care about the necessary supports of life: "*Your Father knows that you have need of these things*, and will supply your needs *according to his riches in glory*; for he is *your Father*, and therefore will take care that you *want no good thing*."

(3) They have better things to mind and pursue (*v.* 31): "*But rather seek ye the kingdom of God*, and mind this, you, my disciples, who are to *preach the kingdom of God*. Let all that have souls to save *seek the kingdom of God*, in which only they can be *safe*. Then *all these things shall be added to you.* Mind the affairs of your souls with diligence and care, and then trust God with all your other affairs."

(4) They have better things to expect and hope for: *Fear not, little flock*, *v.* 32. When we frighten ourselves with an apprehension of evil to come, we put ourselves upon the stretch of care how to avoid it, when after all perhaps it is but the creature of our own imagination. Therefore *fear not, little flock*, for *it is your Father's good pleasure to give you the kingdom*. This comfortable word we had not in Matthew. [1] Christ's flock in this world is a *little flock*. The church is a vineyard, a garden, a small spot, compared with the wilderness of this world. [2] Though it be a little flock, quite *over-numbered* by its enemies, yet it is the will of Christ that they should not *be afraid*: "*Fear not, little flock*, but see yourselves safe under the protection and conduct of the great and good Shepherd." [3] God has *a kingdom* in store for all that belong to Christ's *little flock*, a crown of glory (1 Pet. v. 4). [4] The kingdom is given according to the *good pleasure* of the Father: *It is your Father's good pleasure;* it is given not of debt, but of grace. [5] The believing hopes and prospects of *the kingdom* should silence and suppress the fears of Christ's little flock in this world. "Fear no trouble; for, though it should come, it shall not come between you and the kingdom." (That is not an evil worth trembling at the thought of which cannot separate us from the love of God.)

II. He charged them to make sure work for their souls, by laying up their treasure in heaven, *v.* 33, 34.

1. "*Sell that ye have*, and *give alms*," that is, "rather than want wherewith to relieve those that are truly *necessitous*, sell what you have that is *superfluous*, and give it *to the poor*. *Sell what you have*, if you find it a hindrance from, or incumbrance in, the service of Christ. Do not sell to *hoard up* the money, or because you can make more of it by usury, but *sell and give alms*; what is given in alms, in a right manner, is put out to the *best* interest, upon the *best* security."

2. "*Set your hearts upon the other world. Provide yourselves bags that wax not old.*" Grace will *go with us* into another world, for it is *woven in* the soul; and our good works will *follow us*. These will be *treasures in heaven*, that will enrich us to eternity. (1) It is treasure that will not be *exhausted*; we may spend upon it to eternity; there is no danger of seeing the bottom of it. (2) It is treasure that we are in no danger of being robbed of; what is laid up in heaven is out of the reach of enemies. (3) It is treasure that will not *spoil* with *keeping*, any more than it will *waste* with *spending*; the *moth* does not *corrupt* it. We have

JAMIESON, FAUSSET, BROWN

25, 26. which of you . . .—Corroding solicitude will not bring you the least of the things ye fret about, though it may double the evil of wanting them. And if not the least, why vex yourselves about things of more consequence?

29. of doubtful . . .—unsettled mind. put off your balance.

for your heavenly Father knoweth that ye have need of all these things—How precious this word! Food and raiment are pronounced *needful* to God's children; and He who could say, "No man knoweth the Father but the Son, and he to whomsoever the Son will reveal Him" (ch. 11:27), says with an authority which none but Himself could claim, "Your heavenly Father *knoweth* that ye have need of all these things." Will not that suffice you, O ye needy ones of the household of faith? **But seek ye first the kingdom of God, and his righteousness; and all these things shall be added unto you**—This is the great summing up. Strictly speaking, it has to do only with the subject of the present section—the right state of the heart with reference to heavenly and earthly things; but being couched in the form of a brief general directory, it is so comprehensive in its grasp as to embrace the whole subject of this discourse. And, as if to make this the more evident, the two keynotes of this great sermon seem purposely struck in it—"the KINGDOM" and "the RIGHTEOUSNESS" of the kingdom—as the grand objects, in the supreme pursuit of which all things needful for the present life will be added to us. The precise sense of every word in this golden verse should be carefully weighed.

32. little flock . . .—How sublime and touching a contrast between this tender and pitying appellation, "Little flock" (in the original a double diminutive, which in German can be expressed, but not in English)—and the "good pleasure" of the Father to give them the Kingdom; the one recalling the insignificance and helplessness of that then literal handful of disciples, the other holding up to their view the eternal love that encircled them, the everlasting arms that were underneath them, and the high inheritance awaiting them!—"the kingdom"; grand word; then why not "bread" (vs. 31 [BENGEL]. Well might He say, "Fear not!"

33, 34. Sell . . .—This is but a more vivid expression of Matthew 6:19-21 (see *Note* there).

ADAM CLARKE

25. *To his stature one cubit?* See on Matt. vi. 27.

Which of you by taking thought can add one cubit unto his stature? The *third* reason against these carking cares is the unprofitableness of human solicitude, unless God vouchsafe to bless it. What can our uneasiness do but render us still more unworthy of the divine care?

28. *Into the oven.* See the note on Matt. vi. 30.

29. *Neither be ye of doubtful mind.* Or "in anxious suspense."

30. *The nations of the world seek after.* Or "earnestly seek"; to seek one thing after another, to be continually and eagerly coveting. This is the employment of the nations of this world, utterly regardless of God and eternity! It is the essence of heathenism to live only for this life; and it is the property of Christianity to lead men to live here in reference to another and better world.

32. *Fear not, little flock.* Or "very little flock." This is what some term a double diminutive, and, literally translated, is "little, little flock." Though this refers solely to the apostles and first believers, of whom it was literally true, yet we may say that the number of genuine believers has been, and is still, small in comparison of heathens and false Christians. *It is your Father's good pleasure.* "It hath pleased," though this tense joined with an infinitive has often the force of the present. Our Lord intimates, God has already given you that Kingdom which consists in righteousness, peace, and joy in the Holy Ghost, and has undertaken to protect and save you to the uttermost. Therefore, fear not; the smallness of your number cannot hurt you, for Omnipotence itself has undertaken your cause.

33. *Sell that ye have.* Dispose of your goods. Be not like the foolish man already mentioned, who laid up the produce of his fields, without permitting the poor to partake of God's bounty. Turn the fruits of your fields (which are beyond what you need for your own support) into money, and give it in alms; and the treasure thus *laid out* shall be as *laid up* for yourselves and families in heaven.

34. *Where your treasure is.* Men fix their hearts on their treasures, and often resort to the place where they have deposited them, to see that all is safe and secure. Let God be the Treasure of your soul, and let your heart go frequently to the place where His honor dwelleth.

MATTHEW HENRY

laid up our treasure in heaven if our *hearts* be *there* while we are *here* (*v.* 34). But, if your hearts be set upon the earth and the things of it, it is to be feared that you have your treasure and portion in it, and are undone when you leave it.

III. He charges them to get ready, and to keep in a readiness for Christ's coming, *v.* 35, &c.

1. Christ is our *Master*, and we are his *servants*, not only *working* servants, but *waiting* servants. We must be as men that *wait for their Lord*, that sit up late while he stays out late, to be ready to receive him.

2. Christ our Master, though now *gone from us*, will *return again*. Christ's servants are now in a state of expectation, *looking for their Master's glorious appearing*. He *will come* to take cognizance of his servants, and they shall either stay with him or be turned out of doors, according as they are found in that day.

3. The time of our Master's return is uncertain; it will be *far* in the night, when he has long *deferred* his coming; in the *second watch*, just before midnight, or in the *third watch*, next after midnight, *v.* 38. *The Son of man cometh at an hour that ye think not* (*v.* 40). This bespeaks the prevailing security of the greatest part of men, who are *unthinking*, so that, whenever he comes, it is *in an hour that they think not*.

4. That which he expects and requires from his servants is that they be *ready to open to him immediately* (*v.* 36), that is, that they be found *as* his servants, with their *loins girded about*, having their long garments tucked up (which otherwise would hang about them, and hinder them), and *their lights burning*, with which to light their master into the house.

5. Those servants will be happy who shall be found ready when their Lord shall come (*v.* 37): *Blessed are those servants* who, after having waited long, are then found awake and aware of his first approach, of his first knock; and again (*v.* 38): *Blessed are those servants*. He *will make them sit down to meat, and will serve them*. For the bridegroom to wait upon his bride at table is not uncommon, but to wait upon his servants is not *the manner of men*; yet Jesus Christ did once, to show his condescension, *gird himself*, and *serve them*, when he *washed their feet* (John xiii. 4, 5).

6. We are *therefore* kept at uncertainty concerning the precise time of his coming that we may be always ready: *The good man of the house, if he had known what hour the thief would have come*, though he were ever so careless a man, *would* yet *have watched*, *v.* 39. But we do not know at what hour the alarm will be given us, and therefore are concerned never to be off our guard. Or this may intimate the miserable case of those who are careless and unbelieving in this great matter. We have notice of the day of the Lord's coming, *as a thief in the night*, and yet do not thus *watch*. If men will take such care of their houses, O let us be thus wise for our souls: *Be ye therefore ready also*, as ready as the good man of the house would be *if he knew what hour the thief would come*.

Verses 41-53

I. Peter's question, which he put to Christ upon occasion of the foregoing parable (*v.* 41): *"Lord, speakest thou this parable to us, or also to all*—to all the hearers?" Peter was now, as often, spokesman for the disciples. We have reason to bless God that there are some such forward men; let those that are such take heed of being proud. Now Peter desires Christ to explain himself. Lord, said Peter, was it intended for *us*, or for *all*? To this Christ gives a direct answer (Mark xiii. 37): *What I say unto you, I say unto all.* Yet here he seems to show that the apostles were primarily concerned in it. *Speakest thou this to us?* Doth this word belong to me? Speak it to *my heart*.

II. Christ's reply to this question, directed to Peter and the rest of the disciples. This that follows is peculiarly adapted to ministers, who are the *stewards* in Christ's house.

1. What was their *duty* as *stewards*, and what the *trust* committed to them. They are made *rulers of God's household*, under Christ, whose own the house is; ministers derive an authority from Christ. Their business is to give God's children and servants *their portion of meat*, that which is proper for them; convictions and comfort to those to whom they respectively belong; to give it to them *in due season*; a word *in season* to him *that is weary*. Herein they must approve themselves *faithful* and *wise*; *faithful* to their Master, and faithful to their fellow-servants; and *wise*. Ministers must be both *skilful* and *faithful*.

2. What would be their happiness if they approved themselves faithful and wise (*v.* 43): *Blessed is that*

JAMIESON, FAUSSET, BROWN

38. second . . . third watch—To find them ready to receive Him at any hour of day or night, when one might least of all expect Him, is peculiarly blessed. A servant may be truly faithful, even though taken so far unawares that he has not everything in *such* order and readiness for his master's return as he thinks is due to him, and both could and would have had if he had had notice of the time of his coming, and so may not be willing to open to him *"immediately,"* but fly to preparation, and let his master knock again ere he admit him, and even then *not with full joy*. A too common case this with Christians. But if the servant have himself and all under his charge in such a state that at any hour when his master knocks, he can open to him "immediately," and hail his "return"—that is the most enviable, "blessed" servant of all. **35-40. loins . . . girded**—to fasten up the long outer garment, always done before travel and work (II Kings 4:29; Acts 12:8). The meaning is, Be in readiness. **lights . . .** (See on Matt. 25:1).

return from the wedding not come to it, as in the parable of the virgins. Both have their spiritual significance; but *preparedness for Christ's coming* is the prominent idea. **37. gird himself . . .**—"a promise the most august of all: Thus will the Bridegroom entertain his friends [nay, servants] on the solemn Nuptial Day" [BENGEL].

41-48. unto us or even to all?—us the Twelve, or all this vast audience?

42. Who then . . .—answering the question indirectly by another question, from which they were left to gather what it would be:—To you certainly in the first instance, representing the "stewards" of the "household" I am about to collect, but generally to all "servants" in My house. **faithful and wise**—*Fidelity* is the first requisite in a servant, *wisdom* (discretion and judgment in the exercise of his functions), the next.

ADAM CLARKE

38. *If he shall come in the second watch.* See the note on Matt. xiv. 25.

35. *Let your loins.* Be active, diligent, determined, ready; let all hindrances be removed out of the way, and let the candle of the Lord be always found burning brightly in your hand.

37. *He shall gird himself.* Alluding to the long garments which were worn in the Eastern countries; and which, in travelling and serving, were tucked up in their belts. That those among the Romans who waited on the company at table were *girded*, and had their clothes tucked up, appears from what Horace says, "He runs about like a girded waiter."

A. T. ROBERTSON:

41. "Peter said" (*Eipen de ho Petros*). This whole paragraph from verse 22 to verse 40 had been addressed directly to the disciples. Hence it is not surprising to find Peter putting in a question. This incident confirms also the impression that Luke is giving actual historical data in the environment of these discourses. He is certain that the Twelve are meant, but he desires to know if others are included, for he had spoken to the multitude in verses 13 to 21. Recall Mark 13:37. This interruption is somewhat like that on the Mount of Transfiguration (Luke 9:33) and is characteristic of Peter. Was it the magnificent promise in verse 37 that stirred Peter's impulsiveness? It is certainly more than a literary device of Luke. Peter's question draws out a parabolic reply by Jesus (42-48).
—*Word Pictures in the New Testament*

42. *Faithful and wise steward.* Those appear to have been stewards among the Jews whose business it was to provide all the members of a family, not only with food, but with raiment.

MATTHEW HENRY

servant, (1) That is *doing*, and is not idle. (2) That is *so* doing, doing as he should be, by public preaching and personal application. (3) That is *found* so doing when his Lord comes. Now his happiness is illustrated by the preferment of a steward that has approved himself within a lower and narrower degree of service; he shall be preferred to a larger and higher (*v.* 44): *He will make him ruler over all that he has.* Ministers that obtain mercy of the Lord to be faithful shall obtain further mercy to be abundantly rewarded for their faithfulness in the day of the Lord.

3. What a dreadful reckoning there would be if they were treacherous and unfaithful, *v.* 45, 46. We had all this before in Matthew, and therefore shall here only observe, (1) *He saith in his heart, My Lord delays his coming.* Christ's patience is very often misinterpreted as *delay*, to the *dis*couragement of his people, and the *en*couragement of his enemies. (2) The persecutors of God's people are commonly abandoned to security and sensuality; *they beat their fellow-servants*, and then *eat and drink with the drunken*, altogether unconcerned either at their own sin or their brethren's sufferings. (3) Death and judgment will be very terrible to all wicked people, but especially to wicked ministers. It will be a surprise to them: *At an hour when they are not aware.*

4. What an aggravation it would be of their sin and punishment that they knew their duty, and did not do it (*v.* 47, 48): *That servant that knew his lord's will, and did it not, shall be beaten with many stripes*; and *he that knew not shall be beaten with few stripes*, his punishment shall be mitigated. Here seems to be an allusion to the law, which made a distinction between sins committed through ignorance, and presumptuous sins (Num. xv. 29, 30). (1) Ignorance of our duty is an extenuation of sin. He *that knew not his lord's will*, and *did things worthy of stripes*, he shall *be beaten*, because he might have known his duty better, but *with few stripes*; his ignorance excuses in part, but not wholly. Thus *through ignorance* the Jews put Christ to death, and Christ pleaded that ignorance in their excuse: *They know not what they do.* (2) The knowledge of our duty is an aggravation of our sin: *That servant that knew his lord's will* shall be *beaten with many stripes.* God will justly inflict more upon him because it argues a great degree of wilfulness and contempt to sin against knowledge. Here is a good reason for this added: *To whomsoever much is given, of him shall be much required.* Those that have greater capacities of mind than others, more knowledge and learning, more acquaintance and converse with the scriptures, to them *much is given*, and their account will be accordingly.

III. A further discourse concerning his own sufferings, and concerning the sufferings of his followers. In general (*v.* 49): *I am come to send fire on the earth.* By this some understand the preaching of the gospel, and the pouring out of the Spirit, holy fire; and it was *already kindled.* But, by what follows, it seems rather to be understood of the fire of *persecution.* Christ is not the Author of it, as it is the sin of the incendiaries, the *persecutors*; but he *permits* it as a *refining* fire for the *trial* of the *persecuted.*

1. He must himself suffer many things; he must pass through this fire that was already kindled (*v.* 50): *I have a baptism to be baptized with.* Afflictions are compared both to *fire* and *water*, Ps. lxvi. 12. Christ's sufferings were both. He calls them a *baptism* (Matt. xx. 22); for he was watered or sprinkled with them, and dipped into them, as Israel was baptized *in the sea*, 1 Cor. x. 2. Christ's *foresight* of his sufferings: *I am to be baptized with a baptism.* He calls his sufferings by a name that *mitigates* them; it is a baptism, not a deluge; I must be *dipped* in them, not *drowned* in them; and by a name that *sanctifies* them, for baptism is a sacred rite. Christ's *forwardness* to his sufferings: *How am I straitened till it be accomplished!* He longed for the time when he should suffer and die, having an eye to the glorious issue of his sufferings. Christ's sufferings were the *travail of his soul*, which he cheerfully underwent. So much was his heart set upon the redemption and salvation of man.

2. He tells those about him that they also must bear with hardships and difficulties (*v.* 51): "*Suppose ye that I came to give peace on earth?*" It is intimated that they went upon this supposition, that the gospel would meet with a *universal* welcome, that people would *unanimously* embrace it, that Christ would at least give them *peace.* "But," saith Christ, "you will be mistaken, the event will declare the contrary, and therefore do not flatter yourselves into a fool's paradise. You will find:

(1) "That the effect of the preaching of the gospel will be *division.*" Not but that the design of the gospel and its proper tendency are to unite the children of men to one another, to knit them together in holy

JAMIESON, FAUSSET, BROWN

steward—house-steward, whose it was to distribute to the servants their allotted portion of food. **shall make**—will deem fit to be made. **44. make him ruler over all he hath**—will advance him to the highest post, referring to the world to come. (See Matt. 25:21, 23.)

45. begin to beat ...—In the confidence that his Lord's return will not be speedy, he throws off the role of servant and plays the master, maltreating those faithful servants who refuse to join him, seizing on and revelling in the fulness of his master's board; intending, when he has got his fill, to resume the mask of fidelity ere his master appear. **46. cut him in sunder**—a punishment not unknown in the East; cf. Hebrews 11:37, "sawn asunder" (I Sam. 15:33; Dan. 2:5). **the unbelievers**—the unfaithful, those unworthy of trust (Matt. 24:51), "the hypocrites," falsely calling themselves "servants." **48. knew not**—i.e., knew but *partially;* for *some* knowledge is presupposed both in the name "servant" of Christ, and his being liable to punishment at all. **many ... few stripes**—degrees of future punishment proportioned to the knowledge sinned against. Even heathens are not without knowledge enough for future judgment; but the reference here is not to such. It is a solemn truth, and though *general,* like all other revelations of the future world, discloses a tangible and momentous principle in its awards.

49-53. to send—cast. **fire**—"the higher spiritual element of life which Jesus came to introduce into this earth (cf. Matt. 3:11), with reference to its mighty effects in quickening all that is akin to it and *destroying all that is opposed.* To cause this element of life to take up its abode on earth, and wholly to pervade human hearts with its warmth, was the lofty destiny of the Redeemer" [OLSHAUSEN: so CALVIN, STIER, ALFORD, etc.]. **what will I ...**—an obscure expression, uttered under deep and half-smothered emotion. In its general import all are agreed; but the nearest to the precise meaning seems to be, "And what should I have to desire if it were once already kindled?" [BENGEL and BLOOMFIELD]. **50. But ... a baptism ....**—clearly, His own bloody baptism, first to take place. **how ... straitened**—not, "how do I long for its accomplishment," as many understand it, thus making it but a repetition of the former verse; but "what a pressure of spirit is upon Me." **till it be accomplished**—till it be over. Before a promiscuous audience, such obscure language was fit on a theme like this; but oh, what surges of mysterious emotion in the view of what was now so near at hand does it reveal!

51. peace ....? Nay—the reverse of peace, *in the first instance.* (See on Matt. 10:34-36.) The connection of all this with the foregoing warnings about hypocrisy, covetousness, and watchfulness, is deeply solemn: "My conflict hasten apace; Mine over, yours begins; and then, let the servants tread in their Master's steps, uttering their testimony entire and fearless, neither loving nor dreading the world, anticipating awful wrenches of the dearest ties in life, but looking forward, as I do, to the completion of their testimony, when, reaching the haven after the tempest, they shall enter into the joy of their Lord."

ADAM CLARKE

W. E. VINE:

OIKONOMOS primarily denoted the manager of a household or estate (*oikos*, a house, *nemo*, to arrange), a steward (such were usually slaves or freedmen), Luke 12:42; 16:1, 3, 8; 1 Cor. 4:2; Gal. 4:2; R.V. (A.V., "governors"); in Rom. 16:23, the "treasurer" (R.V.) of a city; it is used metaphorically, in the wider sense, of a steward in general (a) of preachers of the gospel and teachers of the Word of God (1 Cor. 4:1); (b) of elders or bishops in churches (Tit. 1:7); (c) of believers generally (1 Pet. 4:10).—*Vine's Expository Dictionary*

46. *With the unbelievers.* Or, rather, "the unfaithful." Persons who had the light and knowledge of God's Word, but made an improper use of the privileges they received.

47. *Shall be beaten with many stripes.* Criminals among the Jews could not be beaten with more than forty stripes; and as this was the sum of the severity to which a whipping could extend, it may be all that our Lord here means. But, in some cases, a man was adjudged to receive fourscore stripes! How could this be, when the law had decreed only forty? Answer: By doubling the crime. He received forty for each crime; if he were guilty of two offenses, he might receive fourscore.

48. *Shall be beaten with few.* For petty offenses the Jews in many cases inflicted so few as four, five, and six stripes.

From this and the preceding verse we find that it is a crime to be ignorant of God's will, because to everyone God has given less or more of the means of instruction.

49. *I am come to send fire.* See this subject largely explained on Matt. x. 34, etc. From the connection in which these words stand, both in this place and in Matthew, it appears as if our Lord intended by the word *fire,* not only the consuming influence of the Roman sword, but also the influence of His own Spirit in the destruction of sin. In both these senses this *fire* was *already kindled.* As yet, however, it appeared but as a spark, but was soon to break out into an all-consuming flame.

50. *But I have a baptism.* The fire, though already kindled, cannot burn up till after the Jews have put Me to death. Then the Roman sword shall come, and the Spirit of judgment, burning, and purification shall be poured out.

51. *To give peace.* See Matt. x. 34.

Think not that I am come to send peace. The meaning of this difficult passage will be plain when we consider the import of the Jews word *peace,* and the expectation of the Jews. The word *shalom* was used among the Hebrews to express all possible blessings, temporal and spiritual, but especially the former. The import of our Lord's teaching here is this: Do not imagine, as the Jews in general vainly do, that I am come to *send forth,* by forcing out the Roman power, that temporal prosperity which

MATTHEW HENRY

love, and, if all would receive it, this would be the effect of it; but there being multitudes that not only will not receive it, but oppose it, it proves, though not the *cause*, yet the *occasion* of *division.* While *the strong man armed kept his palace*, in the Gentile world, *his goods were at peace.* The sects of philosophers agreed well enough, so did the worshippers of different deities; but when the gospel was preached, and many were turned from the power of Satan to God, then there was a disturbance. Some *distinguished* themselves by embracing the gospel, and others were angry that they did so. Yea, and among them that received the gospel there would be *division*; and Christ permits it for holy ends, that Christians may learn and practise mutual forbearance.

(2) "That this *division* will reach into private families" (*v.* 53): *The father shall be divided against the son, and the son against the father*, when the one turns Christian and the other does not; for the one that does turn Christian will be zealous by arguments and endearments to turn the other too. The one that continues in unbelief will be provoked, and will hate and persecute the one that by his faith and obedience witnesses against, and condemns, his unbelief and disobedience. Even *mothers* and *daughters* fall out about religion; and those that believe not are ready to deliver up those that believe, though otherwise very near and dear to them. We find in the *Acts* that, wherever the gospel came, *persecution* was *stirred up*; it was *everywhere spoken against*, and there was *no small stir about that way.* Therefore let not the disciples of Christ promise themselves *peace upon earth.*

Verses 54–59

Having given his disciples *their* lesson in the foregoing verses, here Christ turns to *the people*, and gives them *theirs*, *v.* 54. In general, he would have them be as wise in the affairs of their souls as they are in their outward affairs.

I. Let them learn to *discern the way of God towards them*, that they may *prepare* accordingly. They were *weather-wise*, could foresee when there would be *rain* and when there would be *hot weather* (*v.* 54, 55). Even in regard to changes of the weather God gives warning to us what is coming, and art has improved the notices of nature in weather-glasses. From what *has been* we conjecture what *will be*. See the benefit of experience; by *taking notice* we may come to *give notice*. Whoso is wise will *observe* and *learn*.

1. The particulars of the presages: "*When you see a cloud arising out of the west*, perhaps it is at first *no bigger than a man's hand* (1 Kings xviii. 44), but you say, There is a shower in the womb of it, and it proves so. When you *observe* the *south wind blow*, you say, *There will be heat*, and it usually *comes to pass*"; yet nature has not tied itself to such a track but that *sometimes* we are mistaken in our prognostics.

2. The inferences from them (*v.* 56): "*Ye hypocrites*, who pretend to be wise, but really are not so, *how is it that you do not discern this time?* Why are you not aware that you have now an opportunity which you *will not have long*, and which you *may never have again*?" *Now is the accepted time*, now or never. It is the folly and misery of man that he *knows not his time*. This was the ruin of the men of that generation, that they *knew not the day of their visitation, ch.* xix. 44. He adds, "*Yea, and why even of yourselves, judge ye not what is right?*" *v.* 57. If men would allow themselves the liberty of *judging what is right*, they would soon find that all Christ's precepts concerning all things are right, and that there is nothing more equitable in itself, than to submit to them and be ruled by them.

II. Let them hasten to *make their peace with God* in time, before it be too late, *v.* 58, 59. This we had upon another occasion, Matt. v. 25, 26. 1. We reckon it our wisdom in our temporal affairs to *compound* with those with whom we cannot *contend*. "*When thou goest with thine adversary to the magistrate*, and thou art in danger of being cast, thou knowest it is the most prudent course to make the matter up between yourselves; *as thou art in the way, give diligence to be delivered from him.*" Wise men will not let their quarrels go to an extremity, but accommodate them in time. 2. Let us do thus in the affairs of our souls. We have by sin made God our *adversary*, and he has both *right* and *might* on his side. Christ, to whom all judgment is committed, is the magistrate before whom we are hastening to appear: if we stand a trial before him, the cause will certainly go against us, the *Judge* will *deliver* us to the *officer*, and we shall be *cast into the prison* of hell, *till the last mite be paid*, which will not be to all eternity. Christ's sufferings were short, yet the *value* of them made them fully satisfactory. Now, in con-

JAMIESON, FAUSSET, BROWN

And a man's foes shall be they of his own household—This saying, which is quoted, as is the whole verse, from Micah 7:6, is but an extension of the Psalmist's complaint (Ps. 41:9; 55: 12-14), which had its most affecting illustration in the treason of Judas against our Lord Himself (John 13:18; Matt. 26:48-50). Hence would arise the necessity of a choice between Christ and the nearest relations, which would put them to the severest test.

54-59. NOT DISCERNING THE SIGNS OF THE TIME. **54. to the people**—"the multitude," a word of special warning to the thoughtless crowd, before dismissing them. (See on Matt. 16:2, 3).

56. how . . . not discern . . .—unable to perceive what a critical period that was for the Jewish Church. **57. why even of yourselves . . .**—They might say, To do this requires more knowledge of Scripture and providence than we possess; but He sends them to their own conscience, as enough to show them who He was, and win them to immediate discipleship.

58. When thou goest . . .—(See on Matt. 5:25, 26). The *urgency of the case with them, and the necessity, for their own safety, of immediate decision,* was the object of these striking words.

ADAM CLARKE

they long for. I am not come for this purpose, but to send forth the Roman sword, to cut off a disobedient and rebellious nation, the cup of whose iniquity is already full, and whose crimes cry aloud for speedy vengeance.

I am come to set a man at variance. The spirit of Christ can have no union with the spirit of the world. Even a father, while unconverted, will oppose a godly child. Thus the spirit that is in those who sin against God is opposed to that spirit which is in the followers of the Most High.

52. *Five in one house divided.* See on Matt. x. 35-36.

A man's foes shall be they of his own household. Our Lord refers here to their own traditions. So *Sota*, fol. 49. "A little before the coming of the Messiah, the son shall insult the father, the daughter rebel against her mother, the daughter-in-law against her mother-in-law; and each man shall have his own household for his enemies."

54. *A cloud rise.* See on Matt. xvi. 2-3.

56. *This time?* Can you not discover from the writings of the prophets and from the events which now take place that this is the time of the Messiah, and that I am the very Person foretold by them?

57. *And why . . judge ye?* Even without the express declarations of the prophets, you might, from what you see and hear yourselves, discern that God has now visited His people in such a manner as He never did before.

58. *When thou goest with thine adversary.* This and the next verse are a part of our Lord's Sermon on the Mount. See them explained, Matt. v. 25-26. *Give diligence.* "Give labor," do everything in your power to get free before a suit commences. *The officer.* Properly signifies such an officer as was appointed to levy the fines imposed by the law for a violation of any of its precepts.

59. *Till thou hast paid the very last mite.* And when can this be, if we understand the text spiritually? Can weeping, wailing, and gnashing

MATTHEW HENRY

sideration of this, let us give diligence to be delivered *out of* the hands of God as an adversary, into his hands as a Father, and this *as we are in the way*, which has the chief stress laid upon it here. While we are alive, we are *in the way*; and *now* is our *time*, by repentance and faith, to get the quarrel made up, while it may be done, before it be too late. Let us take hold on the arm of the Lord stretched out in this gracious offer, that we may make peace.

ADAM CLARKE

of teeth pay to divine justice the debt a sinner has contracted? This is impossible. Let him who readeth understand.

MATTHEW HENRY

CHAPTER 13

Verses 1–5

We have here, I. Tidings brought to Christ of the death of some Galileans lately, whose blood *Pilate had mingled with their sacrifices*, *v.* 1.

1. What this tragical story was. It is briefly related here, and is not met with in any of the historians of those times. The Galileans being Herod's subjects, it is probable that this outrage committed upon them by Pilate occasioned the quarrel that was between Herod and Pilate, which we read of in *ch.* xxiii. 12. We are not told what number they were, perhaps *but a few*; but the circumstance remarked is that he *mingled their blood with their sacrifices*. Though perhaps they had reason to fear Pilate's malice, yet they would not keep away from Jerusalem, whither the law obliged them to go up with their sacrifices. Neither the holiness of the place nor of the work would be a protection to them from the fury of an unjust judge, *who neither feared God nor regarded man*. The altar, which used to be a sanctuary and place of shelter, is now become a snare and a trap, a place of danger and slaughter.

2. Why it was related *at this season* to our Lord Jesus. Perhaps merely as a matter of news, which they supposed he had not heard before, and as a thing which they lamented and believed he would do so too. Perhaps it was intended as a confirmation of what Christ had said in the close of the foregoing chapter, concerning the necessity of making our peace with God in time, "Master, here is a fresh instance of some that were very suddenly *delivered to the officer*, that were taken away by death when they little expected it; and therefore we have all need to be ready." It will be of good use to us both to explain the word of God and to enforce it upon ourselves by observing the providences of God. Perhaps they would stir him up, being himself of Galilee, and a prophet, to find out a way to revenge the death of these Galileans upon Herod. Perhaps this was told Christ to *deter* him from going up to Jerusalem, to worship (*v.* 22), lest Pilate should serve him as he had served those Galileans. Now, lest Pilate, when his hand was in, should proceed further, they think it advisable that Christ should for the present keep out of the way. Christ's answer intimates that they told him this with a spiteful *innuendo*, that without doubt they were secretly bad men, else God would not have permitted Pilate thus barbarously to cut them off. It was very invidious; rather than they would allow them to be martyrs they would, without any colour of proof, suppose them to be malefactors. This fate of theirs was capable not only of a favourable, but an honourable construction.

II. Christ's reply to this report.

1. He seconded it with another story, which, like it, gave an instance of people's being taken away by sudden death. It is not long since *the tower of Siloam fell*, and there were eighteen persons killed and buried in the ruins of it. It was a sad story; yet such melancholy accidents we often hear of. Towers, that were built for safety, often prove men's destruction.

2. He cautioned his hearers not to make an ill use of these and similar events, nor take occasion thence to censure *great sufferers*, as if they were *therefore* to be accounted *great sinners*: *Suppose ye that these Galileans were sinners above all the Galileans, because they suffered such things? I tell you nay*, *v.* 2, 3. Perhaps they that told him the story of the Galileans were Jews, and were glad of anything that furnished them with matter of reflection upon the Galileans, and therefore Christ retorted upon them the story of the *men of Jerusalem*, that came to an untimely end. "Now suppose ye that *those eighteen* who met with their death from the tower of Siloam, while perhaps they were expecting their cure from the pool of Siloam, were *debtors* to divine justice *above all men that dwelt at Jerusalem*? *I tell you nay*." We cannot judge of men's *sins* by their *sufferings* in this world; for many are thrown into the furnace as gold to be purified, not as dross and chaff to be consumed. We must therefore not be harsh in our censures of those that are afflicted more than their neighbours, lest we add sorrow to the sorrowful. If we

JAMIESON, FAUSSET, BROWN

CHAPTER 13

Vss. 1-9. The Lesson, "Repent or Perish," Suggested by Two Recent Incidents, and Illustrated by the Parable of the Barren Fig Tree. **1-3. Galileans**—possibly the followers of Judas of Galilee, who, some twenty years before this, taught that Jews should not pay tribute to the Romans, and of whom we learn, from Acts 5:37, that he drew after him a multitude of followers, who on his being slain were all dispersed. About this time that party would be at its height, and if Pilate caused this detachment of them to be waylaid and put to death as they were offering their sacrifices at one of the festivals, that would be "mingling their blood with their sacrifices" [Grotius, Webster and Wilkinson, but doubted by De Wette, Meyer, Alford, etc.]. News of this being brought to our Lord, to draw out His views of such, and whether it was not a judgment of Heaven, He simply points them to the practical view of the matter: "These men are not signal examples of divine vengeance, as ye suppose; but every impenitent sinner—*ye yourselves*, except ye repent—shall be like monuments of the judgment of Heaven, and in a more awful sense."

ADAM CLARKE

CHAPTER 13

1. *At that season*. At what time this happened is not easy to determine, but it appears that it was now a piece of news which was told to Christ and His disciples for the first time. *Whose blood Pilate had mingled*. This piece of history is not recorded (as far as I can find) by Josephus; however, he states that the Galileans were the most seditious people in the land. They belonged properly to Herod's jurisdiction; but, as they kept the great feasts at Jerusalem, they probably, by their tumultuous behavior at some one of them, gave Pilate, who was a mortal enemy to Herod, a pretext to fall upon and slay many of them and thus, perhaps, sacrifice the people to the resentment he had against the prince.

CHARLES H. SPURGEON:

To all those who hastily look on every calamity as a judgment, I would speak in the earnest hope of setting them right. Let me begin, then, by saying: My dear brethren, do not you see that what you say is not true? and that is the best of reasons why you should not say it. Does not your own experience and observation teach you that one event happens both to the righteous and to the wicked? It is true, the wicked man sometimes falls dead in the street; but has not the minister fallen dead in the pulpit? It is true that a pleasure boat, in which men were seeking their own pleasure on Sunday, has suddenly gone down; but is it not equally true that a ship which contained none but godly men, who were bound upon an excursion to preach the gospel, has gone down too? The visible providence of God has no respect of persons; and a storm may gather round the "John Williams" missionary ship quite as well as around a vessel filled with riotous sinners.

Why do you not perceive that the providence of God has been, in fact, in its outward dealings, rather harder upon the good than upon the bad? For, did not Paul say, as he looked upon the miseries of the righteous in his day, "If in this life only we have hope in Christ, we are of all men most miserable"? The path of righteousness has often conducted men to the rack, to the prison, to the gibbet, to the stake; while the road of sin has often led a man to empire, to dominion, and to high esteem among his fellows. It is not true that in this world God does punish men for sin, and reward them for their good deeds. For, did not David say, "I have seen the wicked in great power, and spreading himself like a green bay tree"? And did not this perplex the Psalmist for a little season, until he went into the sanctuary of God, and he understood their end? Although your faith assures you that the ultimate result of providence will work out only good to the people of God, yet your life, though it be but a brief part of the divine drama of history, must have taught you that providence does not outwardly discriminate between the righteous and the wicked—that the righteous perish suddenly as well as the wicked—that the plague knows no difference between the sinner and the saint—and that the sword of war is alike pitiless to the sons of God and the sons of Belial.

—*The Treasury of the New Testament*

JAMIESON, FAUSSET, BROWN

4, 5. tower in Siloam—probably one of the towers of the city wall, near the pool of Siloam. Of its fall nothing is known.

ALBERT BARNES:

From this account of the Galileans we may learn: (1) That men are very prone to infer, when any great calamity happens to others, that they are peculiarly guilty. See the Book of Job, and the reasoning of his three "friends." (2) That that conclusion, in the way in which it is usually drawn, is erroneous. If we see a man bloated, and haggard, and poor, who is in the habit of intoxication, we may infer properly that he is guilty, and that God hates his sin and punishes it. So we may infer of the effects of licentiousness. But we should not thus infer when a man's house is burned down, or when his children die, or when he is visited with a loss of health; nor should we infer it of the nations that

ADAM CLARKE

4. *The tower in Siloam*. This tower was probably built over one of the porticoes near the pool, which is mentioned in John ix. 7. See also Neh. iii. 15. "Debtors," a Jewish phrase for *sinners*. Persons professing to be under the law are bound by the law to be obedient to all its precepts; those who obey not are reckoned "debtors" to the law, or rather to that divine justice from which the law came.

MATTHEW HENRY

will be judging, we have enough to do to judge ourselves. And we might as justly conclude that the *oppressors on whose side are power* and success, are the greatest saints, as that the *oppressed* are the *greatest sinners*. Let us, in our censures of others, do as we would be done by; for as we do we shall be done by: *Judge not, that ye be not judged*, Matt. vii. 1.

3. On these stories he founded a call to repentance, adding to each of them this awakening word, *Except ye repent, ye shall all likewise perish, v.* 3-5. (1) This intimates that we all deserve to *perish* as much as *they did*. It must moderate our censures, not only that we are *sinners*, but that we are as great sinners as they, have as much sin to repent of as they had to suffer for. (2) That therefore we are all concerned to *repent*, to be sorry for what we have done amiss, and to do so no more. The judgments of God upon others are loud calls to us to *repent*. (3) That repentance is the way to escape perishing, and it is a sure way. (4) That, if we repent not, we shall certainly perish, as others have done before us. Except we repent, we shall perish eternally, as they perished out of this world. The same Jesus that calls us to *repent because the kingdom of heaven is at hand*, bids us *repent* because otherwise we shall perish; so that he has set before us life and death, good and evil, and put us to our choice.

Verses 6-9

This parable is intended to enforce that word of warning immediately going before, "*Except ye repent, ye shall all likewise perish.*"

I. This parable primarily refers to the nation and people of the Jews. God chose them for his own, made them a people near to him, expected answerable returns of duty and obedience from them, which he would have accounted *fruit*; but they disappointed his expectations; they were a reproach instead of being a credit to their profession. Upon this, he justly determined to abandon them; but, upon Christ's intercession, he graciously gave them further time and further mercy; tried them, as it were, another year, by sending his apostles among them, to call them to repentance, and in Christ's name to offer them pardon. Some of them were wrought upon to *repent*, and bring forth fruit, and with them all was well; but the body of the nation continued impenitent and unfruitful, and ruin without remedy came upon them.

II. Yet it has a further reference, and is designed for the awakening of all that enjoy the means of grace to see to it that the temper of their minds and the tenor of their lives be answerable to their opportunities, for that is the *fruit* required.

1. The advantages which this fig-tree had. It was *planted in a vineyard*, in better soil, and where it had more care taken of it than other fig-trees had, that commonly grew by the *way-side*, Matt. xxi. 19. This fig-tree belonged to a *certain man*. The church of God is *his vineyard*. We are *fig-trees planted* in this vineyard. It is a distinguishing favour.

2. The owner's expectation from it: *He came, and sought fruit thereon*. He did not *send*, but came himself. Christ came into this world, *came to his own*, seeking fruit. The God of heaven requires and expects *fruit* from those that have a place in his vineyard. *Leaves* will not serve, crying, *Lord, Lord*; *blossoms* will not serve, beginning well and promising fair; there must be *fruit*. Our thoughts, words, and actions must be according to the gospel, light and love.

3. The disappointment of his expectation: *He found none*, not one fig. It is sad to think how many enjoy the privileges of the gospel, and yet do nothing at all to the honour of God.

(1) He here complains of it to the dresser of the vineyard: I come, *seeking fruit*, but am disappointed—*I find none*.

(2) He aggravates it, with two considerations: [1] That he had waited long, and yet was disappointed. As he was not *high* in his expectations, he only expected fruit, not *much* fruit, so he was not *hasty, he came three years*, year after year. In general, it teaches us that the patience of God is stretched out to longsuffering with many that enjoy the gospel, and do not bring forth the fruits of it. How many times three years has God come to many of us, *seeking fruit*, but has *found none*. [2] That this fig-tree did not only not bring forth fruit, but did hurt; it *cumbered the ground*; it took up the room of a fruitful tree, and was injurious to all about it. Those who do not *do good* commonly *do hurt* by the influence of their bad example. And the mischief is the greater, and the ground the more cumbered, if it be a high, large, spreading tree, and if it be an old tree of long standing.

4. The doom passed upon it: *Cut it down*. No other

JAMIESON, FAUSSET, BROWN

are afflicted with famine, or the plague, or with the ravages of war; nor should we infer it when a man is killed by lightning, or when he perishes by the blowing up of a steamboat. Those who thus perish may be far more virtuous than many that live. (3) This is not a world of retribution. Good and evil are mingled; the good and the bad suffer, and all are exposed here to calamity. (4) There is another world—a future state—a world where the good will be happy and the wicked punished. There all that is irregular on earth will be regulated; all that appears unequal will be made equal; all that is chaotic will be reduced to order. (5) When men are disposed to speak about the great guilt of others, and the calamities that come upon them, they should inquire about themselves. What is their character? what is their condition? It may be that they are in quite as much danger of perishing as those are whom they regard as so wicked. (6) We must repent or we shall perish. No matter what befalls others, we are sinners; we are to die; we shall be lost unless we repent. Let us, then, think of ourselves rather than of others; and when we hear of any signal calamity happening to others, let us remember that there is calamity in another world as well as here; and that while our fellow sinners are exposed to trials here, we may be exposed to more awful woes there. Woe there is eternal; here, a calamity like that produced by a falling tower is soon over.—*Popular Commentary*

6-9. fig tree—Israel, as the visible witness of God in the world, but generally all within the pale of the visible Church of God; a familiar figure (cf. Isa. 5:1-7; John 15:1-8, etc.).

vineyard—a spot selected for its fertility, separated from the surrounding fields, and cultivated with special care, with a view solely to *fruit*.

came and sought fruit—a heart turned to God; the fruits of righteousness; cf. Matthew 21:33, 34, and Isaiah 5:2, "He *looked* that it should bring forth fruit"; He has a *right* to it, and will *require* it.

7. three years—a long enough trial for a fig tree, and so denoting probably just a *sufficient* period of culture for spiritual fruit. The supposed allusion to the duration of our Lord's ministry is precarious.

ADAM CLARKE

5. ***Ye shall all likewise perish.*** **"In a like way, in the same manner." This prediction of our Lord was literally fulfilled. When the city was taken by the Romans, multitudes of the priests, who were going on with their sacrifices, were slain, and their blood mingled with the blood of their victims; and multitudes were buried under the ruins of the walls, houses, and Temple. See Josephus, *War*, b. vi, cc. iv—vi.**

6. ***A certain man.*** **Many meanings are given to this parable, and divines may abound in them. The sense which our Lord designed to convey by it appears to be the following: (1)** ***A person,*** **God Almighty. (2)** ***Had a fig tree,*** **the Jewish church.**

(3) ***Planted in his vineyard***—**established in the land of Judea.**

(4) ***He came seeking fruit***—**He required that the Jewish people should walk in righteousness, in proportion to the spiritual culture He bestowed on them.**

7. ***Behold these three years.*** **From this circumstance in the parable it may be reasonably concluded that Jesus had been, at the time of saying this, exercising His ministry for three years past; and from what is said in v. 8 of letting it alone this year also, it may be concluded likewise that this parable was spoken about a** ***year*** **before Christ's crucifixion.**

(6) ***Cut it down***—**let the Roman sword be unsheathed against it.**

MATTHEW HENRY

can be expected concerning barren trees than that they should be *cut down.* And with good reason, for *why cumbers it the ground?* What reason is there why it should have a place in the vineyard to no purpose?

5. The dresser's intercession for it. Christ is the great Intercessor. Ministers are intercessors; those we *preach to* we should *pray for*.

(1) What it is he prays for, and that is a reprieve: *Lord, let it alone this year also.* He doth not pray, "Lord, let it never be cut down," but, "Lord, not now." It is desirable to have a barren tree reprieved. Some have not yet *grace to repent*, yet it is a mercy to them to have *space to repent*. We owe it to Christ, the great Intercessor, that *barren* trees are not cut down immediately. We are encouraged to pray to God for the merciful reprieve of barren fig-trees: "Lord, *let them alone*; bear with them a little longer, and wait to be gracious." Thus must we stand in the gap, to turn away wrath. Reprieves of mercy are but for a time: *Let it alone this year also.* When God has borne long, we may hope he will bear yet a little longer, but we cannot expect he should bear always. *Reprieves* may be obtained by the prayers of others for us, but not *pardons*; there must be our own faith, and repentance, and prayers.

(2) How he promises to improve this reprieve: *Till I shall dig about it, and dung it.* In general, our prayers must always be seconded with our endeavours. Thus in all our prayers we must request God's grace, with a humble resolution to do our duty, else we mock God, and show that we do not rightly value the mercies we pray for. The dresser of the vineyard engages to do *his* part, and therein teaches ministers to do *theirs*. He will *dig about* the tree and will *dung* it. Unfruitful Christians must be *awakened* by the terrors of the law, which *break up the fallow ground*, and then encouraged by the promises of the gospel, which are warming and fattening, as manure to the tree. Both methods must be tried; the one prepares for the other, and all little enough.

(3) Upon what foot he leaves the matter: "Let us try what we can do with it one year more, *and, if it bear fruit, well*," *v.* 9. The word *well* is not in the original, but the expression is abrupt: *If it bear fruit!* —supply it how you please, so as to express how wonderfully well-pleased both the owner and dresser will be. Unfruitful professors of religion, if after long unfruitfulness they will repent, and amend, and bring forth fruit, shall find *all is well.* God will be *pleased*, ministers' hands will be strengthened. Nay, there will be joy in heaven for it; the ground will be no longer cumbered, but bettered, the vineyard beautified, and the good trees in it made better. As for the tree itself, it is *well* for it; it shall *receive blessing from God* (Heb. vi. 7); it shall be *purged*, and *shall bring forth more fruit.*

But he adds, *If not, then after that thou shalt cut it down.* Though God bear long, he will not bear always. Barren trees will certainly be *cut down* at last, and *cast into the fire.* The longer God has *waited* the greater will their destruction be: to be cut down *after that* will be sad indeed. Cutting down, though it is work that shall be done, is work that God does not take pleasure in. Those that now intercede for barren trees, if they persist in their unfruitfulness will be even content to see them cut down. Their best friends will acquiesce in the righteous judgment of God.

Verses 10–17

I. The miraculous cure of a woman that had been long under a spirit of infirmity. Our Lord Jesus spent his *sabbaths* in the *synagogues, v.* 10. We should make conscience of doing so, and not think we can spend the sabbath as well at home in reading a good book. And, when he was in the synagogues on the sabbath day, *he was teaching there.* He was in his element when he was teaching. Now to confirm the doctrine he preached, he wrought a miracle, a miracle of mercy.

1. The object of charity was a woman in the synagogue that had *a spirit of infirmity eighteen years, v.* 11. She had an infirmity which was such that she was *bowed together*, and could *in no wise lift up herself*; she could not stand erect. Though she was under this infirmity, yet she went to the *synagogue on the sabbath day.* Even bodily infirmities, unless they be very grievous indeed, should not keep us from public worship on sabbath days; for God can help us, beyond our expectation.

2. The offer of this cure to one that sought it not bespeaks the preventing mercy and grace of Christ: *When Jesus saw her, he called her to him, v.* 12. *Before she called he answered.* She came to him to be *taught*, and to get good to her soul, and then Christ gave this relief to her bodily infirmity. Those whose

JAMIESON, FAUSSET, BROWN

cut it down—indignant language. **cumbereth**—not only doing no good, but wasting ground.

8. He answering . . .—Christ, as Intercessor, loath to see it cut down so long as there was any hope (see vs. 34).

dig . . .—loosen the earth about it and enrich it with manure; pointing to changes of method in the divine treatment of the impenitent, in order to freshen spiritual culture.

9. if fruit, well—Genuine repentance, however late, avails to save (Ch. 23:42, 43).

after that . . .—The final perdition of such as, after the utmost limits of reasonable forbearance, are found fruitless, will be pre-eminently and confessedly just (Prov. 1:24-31; Ezek. 24:13).

10-17. Woman of Eighteen Year's Infirmity Healed on the Sabbath.

11. spirit of infirmity—Cf. vs. 17, "whom *Satan* hath bound." From this it is probable, though not certain, that her protracted infirmity was the effect of some milder form of *possession;* yet she was "a daughter of Abraham," in the same gracious sense, no doubt, as Zaccheus, after his conversion, was "a son of Abraham" (ch. 19:9).

12, 13. said . . . Woman . . . and laid—both at once.

ADAM CLARKE

Why cumbereth it the ground? Or in other words, "Why should the ground be also useless?" The tree itself brings forth no fruit; let it be cut down that a more profitable one may be planted in its place.

(5) *The vinedresser*—the Lord Jesus, for God hath committed all judgment to the Son, John v. 22.

(7) *Let it alone*—Christ is represented as Intercessor for sinners, for whose sake the day of their probation is often lengthened; during which time He is constantly employed in doing everything that has a tendency to promote their salvation.

CHARLES H. SPURGEON:

The comparison of a man to a tree, and of human works to fruit, is exceedingly common in Scripture, because it is most suggestive, natural, and appropriate. As fruit is the production of the tree's life, and the end for which the tree exists, so obedience to the divine will, and holiness unto the Lord, should be the product of man's life, and for it he was at first created. When men plant trees in a vineyard, they very naturally expect to find fruit thereon; and if at the age and season of fruitbearing they find no produce, their natural and justifiable expectation is disappointed. Even thus, speaking after the manner of men, it is natural that the great Maker of all should look for the good fruit of obedience and love from the men who are the objects of His providential care, and be grieved when he meets with no return. Man is very much more God's property than a tree can ever be the property of the man who plants a vineyard; and as God has spent so much more skill and wisdom in the creation of a man than a husbandman can have spent in the mere planting of trees, it becomes the more natural that God should look for fruit from His creature, man; and the more reasonable that His most righteous requirements should not be refused. Trees that bring not forth fruit must be cut down; and sinners who bring not forth repentance, faith, and holiness must die. It is only a matter of time as to whether or not the vineyard shall be cleared of the incumbrance of its barren trees; it is but a matter of time as to when the world shall be delivered from the burdensome presence of barren souls. It stands to reason that barren trees which soon become the haunts of all sorts of mischief-doing creatures should be a nuisance to the vineyard; neither can sinners be permitted forever to become the dwelling places of evil spirits, and the dens of iniquity: a thorough riddance must be made of impenitent sinners as well as of rotten trees. There is a time for felling fruitless trees, and there is an appointed season for hewing down and casting into the fire the useless sinner.

—The Treasury of the New Testament

G. CAMPBELL MORGAN:

Let us first look at the woman at the center of the picture. Eighteen years, says Luke, she had been "bowed together." That is a medical term, and it is not found anywhere else in the New Testament. The Greek word might be translated quite accurately as "bent double." We are told, moreover, that she "could in no wise lift herself up." "Lift herself up" is again a medical term. It occurs in one other place in the New Testament, in John eight, where it speaks of Jesus in the temple and the woman taken in the act of sin. There John says, "He lifted himself up." She was quite unable to look up. If you had met her, she could not have looked at you; bent double, her eyes were always on the

MATTHEW HENRY

first and chief care is for their souls do best befriend the true interests of their bodies likewise.

3. The cure effectually and immediately wrought bespeaks his almighty power. He *laid his hands on her*, and said, "*Woman, thou art loosed from thine infirmity.*" Though *she could in no wise lift up herself*, Christ could lift her up, and enable her to lift up herself. She that had been *crooked* was *immediately made straight*. This cure represents the work of Christ's grace upon the souls of people, in the *conversion* of sinners. Unsanctified hearts are under this *spirit of infirmity*; they are distorted. They can in no wise *lift up themselves* to God and heaven; the bent of the soul is the quite contrary way. Such crooked souls seek not to Christ; but he calls them to him, speaks a healing word to them, by which he *looses them from their infirmity*, makes the soul *straight*. The grace of God can make that straight which the sin of man has made crooked. In the *consolation* of good people. Many of the children of God are long under a *spirit of infirmity*, a spirit of bondage. Christ, by his Spirit of adoption, looses them from this infirmity in due time.

4. The present effect of this cure upon the *soul* of the patient as well as upon her *body*. She *glorified God*. When crooked souls are made straight, they will show it by their glorifying God.

II. The offence that was taken at this by the *ruler of the synagogue*. He *had indignation* at it, because it was *on the sabbath day*, *v.* 14. What light can shine so clear, so strong, that a spirit of bigotry will not serve to shut men's eyes against it? He said *to the people*, reflecting upon Christ in what he said, *There are six days in which men ought to work, in them therefore come and be healed, and not on the sabbath day*. See here how light he made of the miracles Christ wrought, as if they were *things of course*: "You may *come* and be healed any day of the week." Christ's cures were become, in his eyes, cheap and common things. This was evidently *the work of God*; and, when God tied us out from working that day, did he tie himself out? The same word in Hebrew signifies both *godly* and *merciful* (*chesed*), to intimate that works of *mercy* and *charity* are in a manner works of *piety* and therefore very proper on sabbath days.

III. Christ's justification of himself in what he had done (*v.* 15): *The Lord then answered him, Thou hypocrite*. We *must* judge charitably, and *can* judge only according to the outward appearance. Christ knew that he had a real enmity to him and to his gospel, that he did but cloak this with a pretended zeal for the sabbath day. Christ could have told him this, but he vouchsafes to reason the case with him.

1. He *appeals* to the common practice among the Jews, which was never disallowed, that of *watering* their cattle on the sabbath day. Those cattle that are kept up in the stable are constantly *loosed from the stall on the sabbath day, and led away to watering*. It would be a barbarous thing not to do it. Letting the cattle *rest* on the sabbath day, would be worse than working them, if they must be made to fast on that day.

2. He applies this to the present case (*v.* 16): "Must the *ox* and the *ass* have compassion shown them on the sabbath day, and shall not this woman be *loosed* from a much *greater* grievance? She is *a daughter of Abraham*; she is *your sister*, and shall she be denied a favour that you grant to an ox or an ass? She is *a daughter of Abraham*, and therefore is entitled to the Messiah's blessings. She is one whom Satan *has bound*. Therefore it was not only an act of charity to the poor woman, but of piety to God, to break the power of the devil. She has been in this deplorable condition *lo, these eighteen years*, and therefore, now that there is an opportunity of delivering her, it ought not to be deferred *a day* longer. Any of you would have thought eighteen years' affliction full long enough."

IV. The different effect that this had upon those that heard him.

1. What a confusion this was to the malice of his persecutors: *When he had said these things, all his adversaries were ashamed* (*v.* 17). It was not a shame that worked repentance, but rather indignation.

2. What a confirmation this was to the faith of his friends: *All the people* rejoiced *for all the glorious things that were done by him*. The shame of his foes was the joy of his followers. The things Christ did were *glorious things*, and we ought to rejoice in them.

Verses 18–22

I. The gospel's progress foretold in two parables, which we had before, Matt. xiii. 31–33. Christ undertakes here to show *what the kingdom of God is like* (*v.* 18): "*Whereunto shall I liken the kingdom of God? v.* 20. It will be quite another thing from what you

JAMIESON, FAUSSET, BROWN

14. with indignation—not so much at the sabbath violation as at the glorification of Christ. (Cf. Matt. 21:15) [Trench]. **said to the people**—"Not daring directly to find fault with the Lord, he seeks circuitously to reach Him through the people, who were more under his influence, and whom he feared less" [Trench].

15. the Lord—(See on ch. 10:1). **hypocrite!**—How "the faithful and true Witness" tears off the masks which men wear! **his ox . . .**—(see on Matt. 12:9-13; and ch. 6:9).

16. ought not . . .—How gloriously the Lord vindicates the superior claims of this woman, in consideration of the sadness and long duration of her suffering, and of her dignity notwithstanding, as an heir of the promise!

ADAM CLARKE

ground, and she "could in no wise lift herself up."

Luke tells us in a very significant phrase that she "had a spirit of infirmity," and therefore was bent double, and therefore could not raise herself.

The interpretation of that phrase, "a spirit of infirmity," is found in verse sixteen. Jesus said of her, "Ought not this woman, being a daughter of Abraham, whom Satan had bound." The spirit of infirmity was an evil spirit. This woman was held in the grip of a physical malady, described by this physician-evangelist and writer, as bent double, with no ability to straighten herself at all; and Jesus says, "Satan had bound her."

Here, then, was a case in which an evil spirit had produced a physical malady that lasted eighteen years. There is no suggestion in this story that there was anything of immorality in this woman's life. She was the victim of a demon activity, under what circumstances we do not know, producing a physical disability and holding the woman in it for eighteen long years. There is no hint of this mastery having produced an immoral effect in her life. As a matter of fact, here she was in the synagogue. She had found her way to the place of worship, and when Jesus presently called her a daughter of Abraham, He did not merely mean she was a Jewess; that was patent. He was using the term in its full spiritual significance as revealing her faith in God. Here, then, was a case of physical suffering that was directly produced by the power of Satan. I am not attempting to explain this. There may be many other such cases in the world. There are things we have not fathomed yet in life concerning the mystery of suffering and the power of evil. We take the facts as revealed, and proceed to consider the action of Jesus.

Then He spoke to her. He called her "Woman." There are other occasions when He used the term, and on His lips it was ever a word of infinite and beautiful tenderness. Then He touched her, as He said, "Woman, thou art loosed from thine infirmity," and in a moment she was straight. A characteristic of the healing work of Jesus was that it was immediate, it was complete. There was no wondering whether the person was healed when He healed. There was no hysterical delay. People may fling their crutches away, and have to pick them up again. They never picked them up again when He healed. The woman was healed, she was completely healed, "immediately she was made straight."

Now let us listen to the ruler of the synagogue. He was angry. In the words of Scripture, "he was moved with indignation." The ruler of the synagogue, devoted to the worship of God, angry! Why? There was a woman who had entered the synagogue, a cripple, a derelict, a sufferer, now standing erect and glorifying God.

As I look at the ruler, I see that a man who has lost his sense of the worth of humanity has lost his sense of the truth about God. He did not know God. One the contrary, Jesus, knowing God, knew the value of humanity. A man who has lost his vision of God, and does not know God, has always lost his sense of the value of human life. But a man who knows God, knows the value of every human life, and knows that the tithing of mint and anise and rue and cummin are trivialities by comparison with the necessity for righteousness and truth and justice and mercy.—*The Gospel According to Luke*

MATTHEW HENRY

expect. You expect it will appear *great*, and will arrive at its perfection all of a sudden; but you are mistaken, *it is like a grain of mustard-seed*, a little thing, makes but a little figure, and promises but little; yet, when sown it *waxes a great tree, v.* 19." Many perhaps were prejudiced against the gospel, because its beginning was so small. Christ would remove this prejudice, by assuring them that though *its beginning was small its latter end should greatly increase*; so that many should come upon the wing, to lodge in the branches of it. "You expect it will make its way by *external* means, but it shall work *like leaven*, silently and insensibly, and without any force or violence," *v.* 21. A little leaven leaveneth the whole lump; so the doctrine of Christ will strangely *diffuse* its relish into the world of mankind. But you must *give it time*, and you will find it does wonders. By degrees *the whole will be leavened*.

II. Christ's progress towards Jerusalem recorded: *He went through the cities and villages, teaching and journeying, v.* 22. Here we find Christ journeying towards Jerusalem, to the feast of dedication, which was *in the winter*, when travelling was uncomfortable.

Verses 23-30

I. A question put to our Lord Jesus. Who it was that put it we are not told, whether a friend or a foe. The question was, *Are there few that are saved? v.* 23. Perhaps it was a *captious* question. If he should say that many would be saved, they would reproach him as too loose; if few, they would reproach him as precise and strait-laced. In nothing do men more betray their ignorance than in judging of the salvation of others. Perhaps it was a *curious* question, a nice speculation. Many are more inquisitive respecting who shall be saved, and who not, than respecting what they shall do to be saved. Perhaps it was an *admiring* question. He had taken notice how strict the law of Christ was, and how bad the world was, and, comparing these together, cries out, "How few are there that will be saved!" We have reason to wonder that of the many to whom the word of salvation is sent there are so few to whom it is indeed a saving word. Perhaps it was an *enquiring* question: "*If there be few that be saved*, what then? What influence should this have upon me?"

II. Christ's answer to this question. Our Saviour did not give a direct answer to this enquiry, for he came to *guide* men's *consciences*, not to *gratify* their *curiosity*. Not, "What shall become of such and such?" But, "What shall I do, and what will become of me?"

1. A quickening exhortation and direction: *Strive to enter in at the strait gate*. This is directed not to him only that asked the question, but to all: *Strive ye*. All that will be saved must *enter in at the strait gate*, and must submit to a strict discipline. Those that would enter in at the strait gate must *strive to enter*. It is a hard matter to get to heaven, and a point that will not be gained without a great deal of care and pains. "*Be in an agony;* strive as those that run for a prize; excite and exert ourselves to the utmost."

2. Divers awakening considerations.

(1) Think how many take *some pains* for salvation and yet perish because they do not take *enough*. *Many will seek to enter in, and shall not be able;* they *seek*, but they do not *strive*. The reason why many come short of grace and glory is because they rest in a *lazy seeking*. They have a *good mind to happiness*, and a *good opinion of holiness*, and take some *good steps* towards both. But their convictions are weak; their desires are cold, and their endeavours feeble, and there is no strength or steadiness in their resolutions; and thus they *come short*.

(2) Think of the *distinguishing* day that is coming and the *decisions* of that day: The *Master of the house* will *rise up, and shut to the door, v.* 25. Now he seems as if he left things at large; but the day is coming when he will *rise up, and shut to the door*. What door? A door of *distinction*. Now, within the temple of the church there are *carnal* professors who worship in the *outer-court*, and *spiritual* professors who worship *within the veil*; between these the door is now open. But, when the *Master of the house is risen up*, the door will be shut between them, that those who are in the *outer-court* may be kept out. As to those *that are filthy*, shut the door upon them, that those who are within may be kept within, that those who are *holy may be holy still*. The door is shut to *separate* between the *precious* and the *vile*. A door of *denial* and exclusion. The door of *mercy* and *grace* has long *stood open* to them, but they would *not come in by it*; they hoped to get to heaven by their own merits, and therefore when the Master of the house is risen up he will justly *shut that door*.

(3) Think how many who were very *confident* that they should be *saved* will be rejected in the day of

JAMIESON, FAUSSET, BROWN

18-30. Miscellaneous Teachings. **18-21. mustard seed ... leaven**—See on Mark 4:30-32). The parable of "the Leaven" sets forth, perhaps, rather the *inward* growth of the kingdom, while "the Mustard Seed" seems to point chiefly to the *outward*. It being a woman's work to knead, it seems a refinement to say that "the woman" here represents *the Church*, as the instrument of depositing the leaven. Nor does it yield much satisfaction to understand the "three measures of meal" of that threefold division of our nature into "spirit, soul, and body," (alluded to in I Thess. 5:23) or of the threefold partition of the world among the three sons of Noah (Gen. 10:32), as some do. It yields more real satisfaction to see in this brief parable just the *all-penetrating* and *assimilating* quality of the Gospel, by virtue of which it will yet mould all institutions and tribes of men, and exhibit over the whole earth one "Kingdom of our Lord and of His Christ." (See on Rev. 11:15.)

23. Lord ...—one of those curious questions by talking of which some flatter themselves they are *religious*.

said unto them—the multitude; taking no notice of the man or his question, save as furnishing the occasion of a solemn warning not to trifle with so momentous a matter as "salvation." **24. Strive**—The word signifies to "contend" as for the mastery, to "struggle," expressive of the *difficulty* of being saved, as if one would have to *force his way in*. **strait gate**—another figure of the same. (See *Note* on Matt. 7:13, 14).

for many ... will seek—*desire*, i.e., with a mere wish or slothful endeavor. **and shall not be able**—because it must be made a *life-and-death struggle*.

25. master of the house is risen up and hath shut to the door—awfully sublime and vivid picture! At present he is represented as in a *sitting* posture, as if calmly looking on to see who will "strive," while entrance is practicable, and who will merely "seek" to enter in. But this is to have an end, by the great Master of the house Himself rising and shutting the door, after which there will be *no admittance*.

ADAM CLARKE

18-19. *The kingdom . . . is like a grain of mustard seed*. See on Matt. xiii. 31.

21. *Like leaven*. See this explained, Matt. xiii. 33.

22. *Journeying toward Jerusalem*. Luke represents all that is said, from chap. ix. 51, as having been done and spoken while Christ was on His last journey to Jerusalem.

Enter ye in at the strait gate. The words in the original are very emphatic: Enter in (to the kingdom of Heaven) through this strait gate, i.e., of doing to everyone as you would he should do unto you; for this alone seems to be the *strait gate* which our Lord alludes to. *For wide is the gate*. And very "broad"; a spacious, roomy place that leadeth forward into that *destruction*, meaning eternal misery.

Because strait is the gate. Instead of *because*, I should prefer "how," which reading is supported by a great majority of the best MSS., versions, and fathers. How strait is that gate! This mode of expression more forcibly points out the difficulty of the way to the Kingdom. *Few there be that find it*. The strait gate signifies literally what we call a wicket, i.e., a little door in a large gate. *Gate*, among the Jews, signifies, metaphorically, the entrance, introduction, or means of acquiring anything. So they talk of the gate of repentance, the gate of prayers and the gate of tears. When God, say they, shut the gate of paradise against Adam, He opened to him the gate of repentance.

24. *Many . . . will seek*. They *seek*—wish and desire; but they do not *strive*. Therefore, because they will not "agonize"—will not be in earnest—they shall not get in.

25. *And hath shut to the door*. See the notes on Matt. vii. 22-23 and xxv. 10-41.

MATTHEW HENRY

trial, and you will say that there are *few* that *shall be saved* and that we are all concerned to *strive.* Consider,

[1] How far their hope carried them, even to *heaven's gate.* There they *stand and knock,* knock as those that belong to the house, *saying,* "*Lord, Lord, open to us,* for we think we have a right to enter." Many are ruined by an ill-grounded hope of heaven, which they never distrusted or called in question. They call Christ, *Lord;* they are desirous now to enter in by that door which they had formerly made light of.

[2] What *grounds* they had for this *confidence.* Let us see what their plea is, *v.* 26. They had been *Christ's guests* and had shared in his favours: *We have eaten and drunk in thy presence,* at thy table. They had been *Christ's hearers:* "*Thou hast taught in our streets.* Wouldest thou teach us, and not save us?"

[3] How their confidence will fail them. Christ will say to them, *I know you not whence you are, v.* 25. And again (*v.* 27), *I tell you, I know you not, depart from me. First,* He *disowns* them: "*I know you not;* you do not belong to my family." *The Lord knows them that are his,* but them that are not he does not know, he has nothing to do with them. *Secondly,* He *discards* them: *Depart from me.* "Depart from my door, here is nothing for you." *Thirdly,* He gives them such a character as is the reason of this doom: *You are workers of iniquity.* This is their ruin, that, under a pretence of piety, they did the devil's drudgery in Christ's livery.

[4] How terrible their punishment will be (*v.* 28): *There shall be weeping and gnashing of teeth,* the utmost degree of grief and indignation: *You shall see the patriarchs and prophets in the kingdom of God, and yourselves thrust out.* The *Old Testament saints* are in the kingdom of God; they *saw his day* at a distance and it reflected comfort upon them. *New Testament sinners* will be *thrust out* of the kingdom of God. They shall be *thrust out* with shame, as having no part or lot in the matter. The sight of the saint's glory will be a great aggravation of sinner's misery.

(4) Think who are they that shall be saved, notwithstanding: *They shall come from the east and the west; and the last shall be first, v.* 29, 30. By what Christ said, it appears that but *few shall be saved* of those who we think most likely. Yet do not say then that the gospel is preached in vain. There shall come many from all parts of the Gentile world that shall be admitted. When we come to heaven, we shall meet a great many there whom we little thought to have met there, and miss a great many thence whom we verily expected to have found there. Those who *sit down in the kingdom of God* are such as had taken pains to get thither, for they came from far—*from the east and from the west, from the north and from the south.* This shows that they who would enter into that kingdom must *strive.* Many who stood fair for heaven came short, and others who seemed cast behind will win and wear this prize, and therefore it concerns us to *strive to enter.* Shall I, who started first, and stood nearest, miss of heaven, when others, less likely, enter into it? If it be got by striving, why should not I strive?

Verses 31–35

I. A suggestion to Christ of his danger from Herod, now that he was in Galilee, within Herod's jurisdiction (*v.* 31): *Certain of the Pharisees came* to Christ, and said, *Get thee* out of this country, and *depart hence,* for otherwise *Herod will kill thee.* Some think that these Pharisees had no ground at all for this, but that they framed this lie, to drive him out of Galilee, and to drive him into Judea,where they knew there were those that really sought his life. But, Christ's answer being directed to Herod himself, it should seem that the Pharisees had ground for what they said, and that Herod was enraged against Christ, and designed him a mischief. Herod was willing to get rid of Christ. He hoped to *frighten him away* by sending him this threatening message.

II. His defiance of Herod's rage: *Go you, and tell that fox* so, *v.* 32. In calling him a *fox,* he gives him his true character; for he was subtle as a fox, noted for his craft, and treachery, and baseness. And, though it is a black and ugly character, yet it did not ill become Christ to give it to him. For Christ was a prophet, and prophets always had a liberty of speech in reproving princes and great men. Therefore it became him to call this proud king by his own name: "Go, and tell *that* fox that *I do not fear him.* I know that I must die, and must die shortly; I expect it, *the third day,*" that is, "very shortly; my hour is at hand. If Herod should kill me, he will not surprise me. Tell him I do not fear him; when I die, *I shall be perfected;* I shall have completed my

JAMIESON, FAUSSET, BROWN

Lord, Lord—emphatic reduplication, expressive of the earnestness *now* felt, but too late. (See on Matt. 7:21, 22).

26, 27. See on the similar passage (Matt. 7:22, 23). **eaten and drunk . . .**—We have sat with Thee at the same table. **taught in our streets**—Do we not remember listening in our own streets to Thy teaching? Surely *we* are not to be denied admittance? **But he shall say . . .**—*No nearness of external communion with Christ will avail at the great day, in place of that "holiness without which no man shall see the Lord."* Observe the *style* which Christ intimates that He will then assume, that of absolute Disposer of men's eternal destinies, and contrast it with His "despised and rejected" condition at that time.

ALEXANDER MACLAREN:

Boldly and searchingly personal as the preceding words had been, the final turn of Christ's answer must have had a still sharper and more distasteful edge. He had struck a blow at Jewish trust in outward connection with Messiah as ensuring participation in His kingdom. He now says that the Gentiles shall fill the vacant places. Many Jews will be unable to enter, for all their seeking, but still there will be many saved; for troops of hated Gentiles shall come from every corner of the earth, and the sight of them sitting beside the fathers of the nation, while Israel after the flesh is shut out, will move the excluded to weeping—the token of sorrow, which yet has in it no softening nor entrance-securing effect, because it passes into "gnashing of teeth," the sign of anger. Such sorrow worketh death.

—*Expositions of Holy Scripture*

31-35. MESSAGE TO HEROD. **31. and depart hence**—and "go forward," *push on.* He was on His way out of Perea, east of Jordan, and in Herod's dominions, "journeying towards Jerusalem" (vs. 22). Haunted by guilty fears, probably, Herod wanted to get rid of Him (see on Mark 6:14), and seems, from our Lord's answer, to have sent these Pharisees, under pretense of a friendly hint, to persuade Him that the sooner He got beyond Herod's jurisdiction the better it would be for His own safety. Our Lord saw through both of them, and sends the cunning ruler a message couched in dignified and befitting irony.

32. that fox—that crafty, cruel enemy of God's innocent servants.

ADAM CLARKE

Not every one. The sense of this verse seems to be this: No person, by merely acknowledging My authority, believing in the divinity of My nature, professing faith in the perfection of My righteousness, and the infinite merit of My atonement, *shall enter into the kingdom of heaven*—shall have any part with God in glory; but *he that doeth the will of my Father*—he who gets the bad tree rooted up, the good tree planted, and continues to bring forth fruit to the glory and praise of God.

Many will say to me in that day. "In that very day," viz., the day of judgment—*Have we not prophesied,* taught, publicly preached, *in thy name;* acknowledging Thee to be the only Saviour, and proclaiming Thee as such to others; *cast out demons,* impure spirits, who had taken possession of the bodies of men; *done many wonderful works,* miracles, being assisted by supernatural agency to invert even the course of nature, and thus prove the truth of the doctrine we preached?

28. *Abraham, and Isaac.* See on Matt. viii. 11, where the figures and allusions made use of here are particularly explained.

29. *They shall come.* That is, the Gentiles, in every part of the world, shall receive the gospel of the grace of God, when the Jews shall have rejected it.

30. *There are last which shall be first.* See on Matt. xix. 30.

31. *Depart hence.* It is probable that the place from which Christ was desired to depart was Galilee or Perea, for beyond this Herod had no jurisdiction. *Herod will kill thee.* Lactantius says that this Herod was the person who chiefly instigated the Jewish rulers to put our Lord to death—fearing lest himself should be expelled from the kingdom if Christ should be permitted to set up His.

32. *Tell that fox.* Herod was a very vicious prince, and lived in public incest with his sister-in-law, Mark vi. 17. A fox among the Jews appears to have been the emblem of a wicked ruler who united cunning with cruelty, and was always plotting how he might aggrandize himself by spoiling the people.

MATTHEW HENRY

business"; *I shall be consecrated.* When Christ died, he is said to have *sanctified himself*; he consecrated himself to his priestly office with his own blood. "I know that neither he nor any one else can kill me *till I have done my work. I will cast out devils, and do cures, today and tomorrow,* in spite of him and all his threats. It is not in his power to hinder me. I must *go about* preaching and healing, *today, and tomorrow, and the day following.*" It is good for us to look upon the time we have before us as but a little, that we may thereby be quickened to *do the work of the day in its day.* And it is a comfort to us, in reference to the power and malice of our enemies, that they can have no power to take us off as long as God has any work for us to do. "I know that Herod can do me no harm, not only because *my time* is not yet come, but because the place appointed for my death is Jerusalem, which is not within his jurisdiction: *It cannot be that a prophet perish out of Jerusalem.*" Now none undertook to try prophets, but the great sanhedrim, which always sat at Jerusalem; and therefore, if a *prophet* be *put to death,* it must be at Jerusalem.

III. His lamentation for Jerusalem, and his denunciation of wrath against that city, *v.* 34, 35. This we had in Matt. xxiii. 37-39. 1. The wickedness of persons and places that more eminently than others profess relation to God is in a particular manner provoking and grieving to the Lord Jesus. How pathetically does he speak of the sin and ruin of that holy city! *O Jerusalem! O Jerusalem!* 2. Those that enjoy great plenty of the means of grace, if they are not profited by them, are often prejudiced against them. If men's corruptions are not conquered, they are provoked. 3. Jesus Christ has shown himself willing to receive and entertain poor souls that come to him: *How often would I have gathered thy children together,* as a hen gathereth her brood under her wings, with such care and tenderness! 4. *I would,* I often would, and *ye would not.* Christ's willingness aggravates sinners' unwillingness. 5. The house that Christ leaves is *left desolate.* The temple is desolate if Christ has deserted it. He leaves it *to them*; let them take it to themselves, and make their best of it, Christ will trouble it no more. 6. Christ justly withdraws from those that drive him from them. They would not be *gathered* by him, and therefore, saith he, "*You shall not see me* any more." 7. The judgment of the great day will effectually convince unbelievers that would not now be convinced: "Then you will say, *Blessed is he that cometh*"—"you *will not see me* to be the Messiah till then when it is too late."

CHAPTER 14

Verses 1-6

I. *The Son of man came eating and drinking,* conversing familiarly with all sorts of people. Here he *went into the house of one of the chief Pharisees to eat bread on the sabbath day, v.* 1. See how favourable God is to us, that he allows us time, even on his own day, for bodily refreshments; and how careful we should be not to abuse that liberty. Christ went only to *eat bread,* to take such refreshment as was necessary on the sabbath day. Our sabbath meals must, with a particular care, be guarded against all manner of excess.

II. He *went about doing good.* Here was *a certain man before him who had the dropsy, v.* 2. Christ *prevented him* with the blessings of his goodness, and *before he called* he answered him. It is a happy thing to be where Christ is. This man had the *dropsy,* it is probable, in a high degree.

III. He *endured the contradiction of sinners against himself: They watched him, v.* 1. The Pharisee that invited him, it should seem, did it with a design to pick some quarrel with him. When Christ asked them *whether* they thought it *lawful to heal on the sabbath day* they would say neither *yea* nor *nay,* for their design was to *inform against him,* not to be *informed by him.* They would not say *it was lawful to heal,* they could not for shame say it was *not lawful.* Good men have often been persecuted for doing that which even their persecutors could not but own to be lawful and good. Many a *good work* Christ did, for which they *cast stones* at him and his name.

IV. Christ would not be hindered from *doing good* by the *opposition* and *contradiction* of sinners. He *took him, and healed him, and let him go, v.* 4. He *took him,* that is, he *laid hands* on him, to cure him; *he embraced him,* took him in his arms, big and unwieldly as he was (for so dropsical people generally are), and reduced him to shape. Christ cured even *that* disease, perfectly cured it, in a moment. He then let him go, lest the Pharisees should fall upon him for *being healed,* for what absurdities would not

JAMIESON, FAUSSET, BROWN

Behold, I cast out devils and I do cures—i.e., "Plot on and ply thy wiles; I also have My plans; My works of mercy are nearing completion, but some yet remain; I have work for to-day and to-morrow too, and the third day; by that time I shall be where his jurisdiction reaches not; the guilt of My blood shall not lie at his door; that dark deed is reserved for others." He does not say, I preach the Gospel—that would have made little impression upon Herod—in the light of the *merciful* character of Christ's *actions* the *malice* of Herod's snares is laid bare [BENGEL]. **to-day, to-morrow, the third day**—remarkable language expressive of *successive steps* of His work yet remaining, the calm *deliberateness* with which He meant to go through with them, one after another, to the last, unmoved by Herod's threat, yet the *rapid march* with which they were now hastening to completion. (Cf. John 22:18.) **I shall be perfected**—I finish my course, I attain completion. **33. it cannot be that a prophet . . .**—"*It would never do* that . . ."—awful severity of satire this upon "the bloody city!" "He seeks to kill me, does he? Ah! I must be out of Herod's jurisdiction for that. Go tell him I neither fly from him nor fear him, but Jerusalem is the prophets' slaughter-house." **34, 35. O Jerusalem . . .**—(See on Matt. 23:37, 39).

How ineffably grand and melting is this apostrophe! It is the very heart of God pouring itself forth through human flesh and speech. It is this incarnation of the innermost life and love of Deity, pleading with men, bleeding for them, and ascending only to open His arms to them and win them back by the power of this story of matchless love, that has conquered the world, that will yet "draw all men unto Him," and beautify and ennoble Humanity itself! "Jerusalem" here does not mean the mere city or its inhabitants; nor is it to be viewed merely as the metropolis of the *nation,* but as the *center of their religious life*—"the city of their solemnities, whither the tribes went up, to give thanks unto the name of the Lord"; and at this moment it was full of them. It is the whole family of God, then, which is here apostrophized by a name dear to every Jew, recalling to him all that was distinctive and precious in his religion.

CHAPTER 14

Vss. 1-24. HEALING OF A DROPSICAL MAN, AND MANIFOLD TEACHINGS AT A SABBATH FEAST.

2. man before him—not one of the company, since this was apparently *before* the guests sat down, and probably the man came in hope of a cure, though not expressly soliciting it [DE WETTE]. **3-6.** (See on Matt. 12:11, 12.)

Is it lawful to heal on the sabbath days? that they might accuse him—Matthew and Luke say they "watched Him whether He would heal on the sabbath day." They were now come to the length of dogging His steps, to collect materials for a charge of impiety against Him. It is probable that it was to their *thoughts* rather than their words that Jesus addressed Himself in what follows.

Then saith he to the man, Stretch forth thine hand. And he stretched it forth—the power to obey going forth with the word of command. **and it was restored whole, like as the other**—The poor man, having faith in this wonderful Healer—which no doubt the whole scene would singularly help to strengthen—disregarded the proud and venomous Pharisees, and thus gloriously put them to shame.

ADAM CLARKE

To day and to morrow. I am to work miracles for two days more, and on the third day I shall be put to death. But it is probable that this phrase only means that He had but a short time to live, without specifying its duration. *Perfected.* Or "finished." I shall then have accomplished the purpose for which I came into the world, leaving nothing undone which the counsel of God designed Me to complete. Hence, in reference to our Lord, the word implies His dying, as the plan of human redemption was not finished till He bowed His head and gave up the ghost on the Cross; see John xix. 30, where the same word is used. It is used also in reference to Christ's *death,* Heb. ii. 10; v. 9; see also Acts xx. 24 and Heb. xii. 23.

33. *I must walk.* I must continue to work miracles and teach for a short time yet, and then I shall die in Jerusalem. Therefore I cannot depart, according to the advice given Me (v. 31), nor can a hair of My head fall to the ground till My work be all done. *Perish out of Jerusalem.* A man who professes to be a *prophet* can be tried on that ground only by the grand Sanhedrin, which always resides at Jerusalem; and as the Jews are about to put Me to death, under the pretense of My being a false prophet, therefore My sentence must come from this city and My death take place in it.

35. *Your house.* The Temple—called here *your house,* not "My house"—I acknowledge it no longer; I have abandoned it, and will dwell in it no more forever. So He said, 2 Chron. xxxvi. 17, when He delivered the Temple into the hands of the Chaldeans—*the house of their sanctuary.* A similar form of speech is found, Exod. xxxii. 7, where the Lord said to Moses, "Thy people," to intimate that He acknowledged them no longer for His followers. But some think that our Lord means, not the Temple, but the whole commonwealth of the Jews.

CHAPTER 14

1. *Chief Pharisees.* Or "one of the rulers of the Pharisees." A man who was of the sect of the Pharisees, and one of the rulers of the people. *To eat bread on the sabbath day.* But why is it that there should be an invitation or dinner given on the Sabbath day? Answer: The Jews purchased and prepared the best viands they could procure for the Sabbath day, in order to do it honor. As the Sabbath is intended for the benefit of both the body and soul of man, it should not be a day of austerity or fasting, especially among the laboring poor. The most wholesome and nutritive food should be then procured if possible, that both body and soul may feel the influence of this divine appointment, and give God the glory of His grace. On this blessed day let every man eat his bread with gladness and singleness of heart, praising God. *They watched him.* Or "were maliciously watching." The conduct of this Pharisee was most execrable. Professing friendship and affection, he invited our blessed Lord to his table, merely that he might have a more favorable opportunity of watching His conduct, that he might accuse Him and take away His life. In eating and drinking people feel generally less restraint than at other times and are apt to converse more freely. The man who can take such an advantage over one of his own guests must have a baseness of soul of which we would have thought that devils alone were capable.

2. *The dropsy.* "Dropsical." Probably the insidious Pharisee had brought this dropsical man to the place, not doubting that our Lord's eye would affect His heart, and that He would instantly cure him; and then he could most plausibly accuse Him for a breach of the Sabbath. If this were the case, and it is likely, how deep must have been the perfidy and malice of

MATTHEW HENRY

such men as they were be guilty of?

V. Our Lord Jesus *did nothing but what he could justify*, *v.* 5, 6. He still answered their thoughts, and made them *hold their peace* for *shame* who before held their peace for *subtlety*, by an appeal to their own practice. *Which of you shall have an ass or an ox fallen into a pit, and will not pull him out on the sabbath day*, and that straightway, not deferring it till the sabbath be over, lest it perish? It is not so much out of *compassion to the poor creature* that they do it as a concern for their own interest. It is *their own ox*, and *their own ass*, that is worth money, that they will dispense with the law of the sabbath for the *saving of*. Many can easily dispense with that, for their own interest, which they cannot dispense with for God's glory and the good of their brethren. This question *silenced* them: *They could not answer him again to these things*, *v.* 6. Christ will be justified when he speaks.

Verses 7–14

Our Lord Jesus here sets us an example of profitable edifying discourse at our tables, when we are in company with our friends. When he was in company with strangers, nay, with enemies that *watched him*, he took occasion to reprove what he saw amiss in them, and to instruct them. We must not only not allow any corrupt communication at our tables, but we must go beyond common harmless talk, and should take occasion from God's goodness to us at our tables to speak well of him, and learn to *spiritualise* common things. Our Lord Jesus was among persons of quality, yet, as one that had not respect of persons,

I. He takes occasion to reprove *the guests* for striving to *sit uppermost*.

1. He observed how these lawyers and Pharisees affected the *highest seats*, *v.* 7. He had charged that sort of men with this in general, *ch.* xi. 43. Here he brings home the charge to particular persons. He *marked* how they *chose out the chief rooms*; every man, as he came in, got as near the best seat as he could. Even in the common actions of life, Christ's eye is upon us, and he *marks* what we do.

2. He observed how those who were thus aspiring often exposed themselves, and came off *with a slur*; whereas those who were modest, and seated themselves in the lowest seats, often *gained respect* by it. Those who assume the highest seats, may perhaps be *degraded*, and forced to *come down* to give place to one *more honourable*, *v.* 8, 9. It ought to check our high thoughts of ourselves to think how many there are that are *more honourable* than we, not only in respect of worldly dignities, but of personal merits and accomplishments. The master of the feast will marshal his guests, and will not see the *more honourable* kept out of the seat that is his due, and therefore will make bold to take him lower that usurped it: *Give this man place*. Pride will have *shame*, and will at last have a *fall*. Those who content themselves with the lowest seats, are likely to be preferred (*v.* 10): "Go, and *seat thyself in the lowest room*, as taking it for granted that thy friend has guests to come that are of better rank and quality than thou art; but perhaps it may not prove so, and then it will be said to thee, *Friend, go up higher*." The way to *rise high* is to *begin low*: "*Thou shalt have honour and respect before those that sit with thee*. They will see thee to be an *honourable man*. Honour appears the brighter for shining *out of obscurity*. They will likewise see thee to be a *humble man*, which is the greatest honour of all." A parable out of one of the rabbin is somewhat like this. "Three men," said he, "were bidden to a feast; one sat highest, For, said he, I am a prince; the other next, For, said he, I am a wise man; the other lowest, For, said he, I am a humble man. The king seated the humble man highest, and put the prince lowest."

3. He applied this generally, and would have us all learn not to *mind high things*. Pride and ambition are disgraceful before men: for *whosoever exalteth himself shall be abased*; but humility and self-denial are really honourable: *he that humbleth himself shall be exalted*, *v.* 11.

II. He takes occasion to reprove the master of the feast for inviting so many *rich people*, when he should rather have *invited the poor*. Our Saviour here teaches us that the using of what we have in works of charity is better than using it in magnificent housekeeping.

1. "Covet not to *treat the rich*; invite not *thy friends, and brethren, and neighbours, that are rich*," *v.* 12. This does not *prohibit* the entertaining of such, for the cultivating of friendship among relations and neighbours. "Do not make a common custom of it. One feast for the rich will make a great many meals

JAMIESON, FAUSSET, BROWN

Resistless appeal! "A righteous man regardeth the life of his beast" (Prov. 12:10), and would instinctively rescue it from death or suffering on the sabbath day; how much more his nobler fellow man! But the reasoning, as given in the other two Gospels, is singularly striking: "But He knew their thoughts, and said to the man which had the withered hand, Rise up, and stand forth in the midst. And he arose and stood forth. Then said Jesus unto them, I will ask you one thing: Is it lawful on the sabbath days to do good, or to do evil? to save life, or to destroy it?" (Luke 6:8, 9), or as in Mark (3:4), "to kill?" He thus shuts them up to this startling alternative: "Not to do good, when it is in the power of our hand to do it, is to do evil; not to save life, when we can, is to kill"—and must the letter of the sabbath rest be kept at this expense? This unexpected thrust shut their mouths. By this great ethical principle our Lord, we see, held Himself bound, as man. But here we must turn to Mark, whose graphic details make the second Gospel so exceedingly precious. "When He had looked round about on them with anger, being grieved for the hardness of their hearts, He saith unto the man" (Mark 3:5). This is one of the very few passages in the Gospel history which reveal our Lord's *feelings*. How holy this anger was appears from the "grief" which mingled with it at "the hardness of their hearts."

7-11. a parable—showing that His design was not so much to inculcate mere politeness or good manners, as *underneath* this to teach something *deeper* (vs. 11). **chief rooms**—principal seats, in the middle part of the couch on which they reclined at meals, esteemed the most honorable.

8. wedding—and seating thyself at the wedding *feast*. Our Lord avoids the appearance of personality by this delicate allusion to a different kind of entertainment than this of his host [BENGEL]. **9. the lowest**—not a *lower* merely [BENGEL]. **with shame**—"To be lowest is only ignominious to him who affects the highest" [BENGEL]. **10. Friend**—said to the *modest* guest only, not the proud one (vs. 9) [BENGEL]. **worship**—honor. The whole of this is but a reproduction of Proverbs 25:6, 7. But it was reserved for the matchless Teacher to *utter articulately*, and *apply to the regulation of the minutest features of social life*, such *great laws of the Kingdom of God* as that of vs. 11.

"whosoever . . ."—couching them in a chaste simplicity and proverbial terseness of style which makes them "apples of gold in a setting of silver." (See on ch. 18:14.)

12-14. call not thy friends—Jesus certainly did not mean us to dispense with the duties of ordinary fellowship, but, remitting these to their proper place, inculcates what is better [BENGEL].

ADAM CLARKE

the Pharisee!

4. *They held their peace*. They could not answer the question but in the affirmative; and as they were determined to accuse Him if He did heal the man, they could not give an answer but such as would condemn themselves, and therefore they were silent.

7. *They chose out the chief rooms*. When custom and law have regulated and settled places in public assemblies, a man who is obliged to attend may take the place which belongs to him, without injury to himself or to others. When nothing of this nature is settled, the law of humility and the love of order are the only judges of what is proper. To take the highest place when it is not our due is public vanity; obstinately to refuse it when offered is another instance of the same vice, though private and concealed. Humility takes as much care to avoid the ostentation of an affected refusal as the open seeking of a superior place. In this parable our Lord only repeats advices which the rabbins had given to their pupils, but were too proud to conform to themselves. Rabbi Akiba said, "Go two or three seats lower than the place that belongs to thee, and sit there till they say unto thee, 'Go up higher'; but do not take the uppermost seat, lest they say unto thee, 'Come down': for it is better that they should say unto thee, 'Go up, go up'; than that they should say, 'Come down, come down.'"

11. *For whosoever exalteth himself*. This is the unchangeable conduct of God. He is ever abasing the proud, and giving grace, honor, and glory to the humble.

12. *Call not thy friends*. Our Lord certainly does not mean that a man should not entertain, at particular times, his friends. But what He inculcates here is charity to the poor; and what He condemns is those entertainments which are given to the rich either to flatter them or to procure a similar return.

MATTHEW HENRY

for the poor. Be not *proud of it*." Many *make feasts* only to *make a show*, and thus rob their families, to please their fancies. "Aim not at being paid again in your own coin." This is that which our Saviour blames in making such entertainments: "You commonly do it in hopes that you will be invited by them, and so *a recompense will be made you*."

2. "Be forward to *relieve the poor* (*v.* 13, 14): *When thou makest a feast* invite *the poor and maimed*, such as have nothing to live upon, nor are able to work for their living. These are objects of charity; they want necessaries; furnish them, and they will recompense thee with their prayers. They will go away, and thank God for thee. Say not that thou art a *loser*, because *they cannot recompense thee*, for *thou shalt be recompensed at the resurrection of the just*." Works of charity perhaps may not be rewarded *in this world*, for the things of this world are not the *best things*, but they shall *in no wise lose their reward*. It will be found that the longest voyages make the richest returns.

Verses 15–24

I. The occasion of the discourse was given by one of the guests, who said to him, *Blessed is he that shall eat bread in the kingdom of God* (*v.* 15).

1. But with what design does this man bring it in here? (1) Perhaps this man, fearing he should put the company out of humour, started this, to *divert* the discourse to something else. Or, (2) Admiring the good rules which Christ had now given, but despairing to see them lived up to, he longs for *the kingdom of God*, and pronounces them *blessed* who shall have a place in that kingdom. Or, (3) Christ having mentioned *the resurrection of the just*, he here confirms what he said, "Yea, Lord, they that shall be recompensed in the resurrection of the just, shall *eat bread in the kingdom*." Or, (4) Observing Christ to be silent, he was willing to draw him in again to further discourse; and he knew nothing more likely to engage him than to mention the *kingdom of God*. Even those that are not of ability to carry on good discourse themselves ought to put in a word now and then, to help it forward.

2. Now what this man said was a plain and acknowledged truth, and it was quoted very *appositely* now that they were *sitting at meat*. This thought will be very seasonable when we are partaking of bodily refreshments: *Blessed are they that shall eat bread in the kingdom of God*. (1) In the kingdom of grace. Christ promised his disciples that they should *eat and drink with him in his kingdom*. (2) In the kingdom of glory. Blessed are they that shall sit down at that table, whence they shall rise no more.

II. The parable which our Lord Jesus put forth upon this occasion, *v.* 16, &c. "But who are they that shall enjoy that privilege? You Jews will generally reject it, and the Gentiles will be the greatest sharers in it." Now in the parable we may observe,

1. The free grace and mercy of God, shining in the gospel of Christ; it appears,

(1) In the rich provision he has made for poor souls (*v.* 16): *A certain man made a great supper*. It is called a *supper*, because in those countries supper time was the chief feasting time.

(2) In the gracious invitation given us to come and partake of this provision. A general invitation given: He *bade many*. Christ invited the whole nation and people of the Jews to partake of the benefits of his gospel. Christ in the gospel, as he keeps a *good* house, keeps an *open* house. A particular memorandum given; the servant was sent round to put them in mind of it: *Come, for all things are now ready*. This is the call now given to us: "*All things are now ready*, now is the *accepted time*; and therefore *come now*; do not delay; accept the invitation; believe yourselves welcome."

2. The cold entertainment which the grace of the gospel meets with. The invited guests declined coming. *They all with one consent began to make excuse*, *v.* 18. They all found out some pretence or other to shift off their attendance. This bespeaks the general neglect of the Jewish nation to close with Christ. It also intimates the backwardness there is in most people to close with the gospel call. They cannot for shame avow their refusal, but they desire to be *excused*. They were *unanimous* in it; *with one voice*. Here were *two* that were *purchasers*. One had *bought a piece of ground* which was represented to him to be a good bargain, and he must needs *go and see* whether it was so or no; and therefore *I pray thee have me excused*. But what a frivolous excuse was this! He might have deferred going to see his piece of ground till the next day, and have found it in the same place and plight it was now in. Another had purchased *stock* for his land. "*I have bought five yoke of oxen* for the plough, and I must just now go

JAMIESON, FAUSSET, BROWN

lest . . . a recompense be given thee—a fear the world is not afflicted with [BENGEL]. The meaning, however, is that no *exercise of principle* is involved in it, as selfishness itself will suffice to prompt to it (Matt. 5:46, 47). **13. call the poor**—"Such God Himself calls" (vs. 21) [BENGEL]. **14. blessed**—acting from disinterested, god-like compassion for the wretched.

15-24. when one . . . heard . . . he said, Blessed . . .—As our Lord's words seemed to hold forth the future "recompense" under the idea of a great Feast, the thought passes through this man's mind, how blessed they would be who should be honored to sit down to it. Our Lord's reply is in substance this: "The great Feast is prepared already; the invitations are issued, *but declined;* the feast, notwithstanding, shall not want abundance of guests; but not one of its present contemners—who shall yet come to sue for admission—shall be allowed to taste of it." This shows what was lacking in the seemingly pious exclamation of this man. It was Balaam's, "Let me *die the death* of the righteous, and let my *last end* be like his" (Num. 23:10), without any anxiety about *living his life;* fondly wishing that all were right with him *at last,* while all heedless of the precious *present.*

16. a great supper—(Cf. Isa. 25:6). **bade many**—*historically,* the Jews (see on Matt. 22:3); generally, those within the pale of professed discipleship. **17. supper-time . . . all now ready**—pointing undoubtedly to the now ripening preparations for the great Gospel call. (See on Matt. 22:4.)

18. all began to make excuse—(Cf. Matthew 22:5). Three excuses, given as specimens of the rest, answer to "the *care of this world*" (vs. 18), "the *deceitfulness of riches*" (vs. 19), and "the *pleasures of this life*" (vs. 20), which "choke the word" (Matt. 13:22 and ch. 8:14). Each differs from the other, and each has its own plausibility, but *all come to the same result:* "We have other things to attend to, more pressing just now." Nobody is represented as saying, I *will not* come; nay, all the answers imply that *but for* certain things they *would* come, and when these are out of the way they *will* come. So it certainly is in the case intended, for the last words clearly imply that the *refusers* will one day become *petitioners.*

ADAM CLARKE

14. *For they cannot recompense thee.* Because you have done it for God's sake only, and they cannot make you a recompense, therefore God will consider himself your Debtor, and will recompense you in the resurrection of the righteous.

16-24. *A certain man made a great supper.* See a similar parable to this, though not spoken on the same occasion, explained, Matt. xxii. 1-14.

The kingdom of heaven. It appears from Luke xiv. 15 that it was at an entertainment that this parable was originally spoken. It was a constant practice of our Lord to take the subjects of His discourses from the persons present, or from the circumstances of times, persons, and places. See chap. xvi. 6; John iv. 7-10; vi. 26-27; vii. 37. A preacher that can do so can never be at a loss for text or sermon. *A marriage for his son.* "A marriage feast." Or a feast of inauguration, when his son was put in possession of the government, and thus he and his new subjects became married together. See 1 Kings i. 5-9, 19, 25, where such a feast is mentioned. From this parable it appears plain that: (1) the king means the great God; (2) his son, the Lord Jesus; (3) the marriage, His incarnation, or espousing human nature, by taking it into union with himself; (4) the marriage feast, the economy of the gospel, during which men are invited to partake of the blessings purchased by, and consequent on, the incarnation and death of our blessed Lord; (5) by those who had been bidden, or "invited," v. 3, are meant the Jews in general, who had this union of Christ with human nature, and His sacrifice for sin, pointed out by various rites, ceremonies, and sacrifices under the law, and who by all the prophets had been constantly invited to believe in and receive the promised Messiah; (6) by the servants, we are to understand the first preachers of the gospel, proclaiming salvation to the Jews—John the Baptist and the seventy disciples, Luke x. 1 may be here particularly intended; (7) by the other servants, v. 4, the apostles seem to be meant, who, though they were to preach the gospel to the whole world, yet were to begin at Jerusalem, Luke xxiv. 47, with the first offers of mercy; (8) by their making light of it, v. 5, is pointed out their neglect of this salvation, and their preferring secular enjoyments to the kingdom of Christ; (9) by injuriously using some and slaying others of his servants, v. 6, is pointed out the persecution raised against the apostles by the Jews, in which some of them were martyred; (10) by sending forth his troops, v. 7, is meant the commission given to the Romans against Judea; and by the burning of their city, the total destruction of Jerusalem by Titus, the son of Vespasian, which happened about forty years after.

MATTHEW HENRY

and *prove them*, and therefore excuse me for this time." The former intimates that inordinate *complacency* in the world, this the inordinate *care* and *concern* about the world, which keep people from Christ and his grace. It is very criminal, when we are called to any duty, to make excuses for our neglect of it: it is a sign that there are convictions that it is duty, but no inclination to it. These things here were, [1] *Little things.* It had better become them to have said, "I am invited *to eat bread in the kingdom of God*, and therefore must be excused from going to see the *ground* or the *oxen*." [2] *Lawful things. Things lawful in themselves*, when the heart is too much set upon them, *prove fatal* hindrances in religion. Here was one that was *newly married* (*v.* 30): *I have married a wife, and therefore*, in short, *I cannot come.* He pretends that he *cannot*, when the truth is he *will not*. Thus many pretend *inability* for the duties of religion when really they have an *aversion* to them. Our affection to our relations often proves a hindrance to us in our duty to God. He might have gone and taken his wife along with him; they would both have been welcome.

3. The account which was brought to the master of the feast of the affront put upon him by his friends, who now showed how little they valued him (*v.* 21): *That servant came, and showed his lord these things*, told him with surprise that he was likely to sup alone. He made the matter neither better nor worse, but related it just as it was. Ministers must give account of the success of their ministry. They must do it now at the throne of grace. If they see of *the travail of their soul*, they must go to God with their *thanks*; if they *labour in vain*, they must go to God with their *complaints*. The apostle urges this as a reason why people should give ear to the word of God sent them by his ministers; for *they watch for your souls, as those that must give account*, Heb. xiii. 17.

4. The master's just resentment of this affront: *He was angry*, *v.* 21. The ingratitude of those that slight gospel offers, and the contempt they put upon the God of heaven thereby, are a very great provocation to him, and justly so. Abused mercy turns into the greatest wrath. *None of the men that were bidden shall taste of my supper.* Grace despised is grace forfeited, like Esau's birthright. They that will not have Christ when they *may* shall not have him when they *would*.

5. The care that was taken to furnish the table with guests, as well as meat. "Go" (saith he to the servants), "*go first into the streets and lanes of the city* that you may invite those that will be glad to come, bring in *hither the poor and the maimed, the halt and the blind*; pick up the common beggars." They soon gather an abundance of such guests: *Lord, it is done as thou hast commanded.* Many of the Jews are brought in, not of the scribes and Pharisees, but publicans and sinners; these are *the poor and the maimed.* But *yet there is room* for more guests. "Go, then, *secondly, into the highways and hedges.* Go out into the country, and pick up the vagrants, or those that are returning now in the evening from their work in the field, and *compel them to come in*, not by force of arms, but by force of arguments. Be earnest with them; for in this case it will be necessary to convince them that the invitation is *sincere*. They will hardly believe that they shall be welcome, and therefore do not leave them till you have prevailed with them." This refers to the *calling of the Gentiles*, and with them the church was filled. (1) The provision made for precious souls in the gospel of Christ shall appear not to have been made *in vain*; for, if some *reject it*, yet others will thankfully *accept* the offer of it. (2) Those that are very poor and low in the world shall be as welcome to Christ as the rich and great. Christ here plainly refers to what he had said just before, to invite to our tables *the poor amd maimed, the lame and blind*, *v.* 13. His condescensions and compassions towards them should engage ours. (3) Many times the gospel has the *greatest success* among those that are *least likely* to have the benefit of it. The publicans and harlots went into the kingdom of God before the scribes and Pharisees; *so the last shall be first, and the first last.* Let us not be *confident* concerning those that are most forward, nor despair of those that are least promising. (4) Christ's ministers must be both very expeditious and very importunate in inviting to the gospel feast: "*Go out quickly* (*v.* 21); lose no time, because *all things are now ready*." (5) Though many have been brought in to partake of the benefits of the gospel, yet still *there is room for more.* There is in him enough for all, and enough for each; and the gospel excludes none that do not exclude themselves. (6) Christ's house, though it be *large*, shall at last be *filled*.

JAMIESON, FAUSSET, BROWN

A. B. SIMPSON:

First, the friends of the host, who here represent the ordinary hearers of the Gospel; perhaps we may say the worldly and nominal adherents of Christianity. They rejected the invitation. They did it very politely, as proud and worldly sinners still do. The first class declined on account of pressing business engagements, perhaps connected with first starting in life and beginning to acquire earthly possessions. This man has bought his piece of ground. He is just commencing to accumulate wealth, and is too busy to go to the feast. The second has bought five yoke of oxen. This represents an advanced stage of worldly success and occupation; he is now getting to be a very busy man. He is stocking his farm by the half score at a time and rapidly growing rich. And so he for the present puts off the kind invitation. The third has married a wife, and is still more peremptory in his refusal. He cannot come; and evidently he regards the religion of Jesus as incompatible with the thorough enjoyment of the pleasures of the world. Everything in its place. The bridal party, the honeymoon, the dance and revel are inconsistent in his view with the table of the Lord; and he allows the endearments, attachments, and pleasures of life to outweigh the claims of Christ, and the value of his soul.

The three forms of worldly obstruction which here stand in the way of the Gospel are worldly business, worldly wealth and worldly pleasure. With some, it is the eager desire to grow rich. With some, it is the increasing preoccupation of constant drive and absorbing business. With others, it is the love of pleasure and the influence of friends. From these various causes the great proportion of the invited guests still stay away from Christ. Indeed, the parable represents every one of them as refusing. It looks as though the whole body of nominal professors was ultimately going to reject the Gospel.—*Christ in the Bible*

21. came and told . . .—saying as in Isaiah 53:1. "It is the part of ministers to report to the Lord in their prayers the compliance or refusal of their hearers" [BENGEL].

angry—in one sense a *gracious* word, showing how sincere he was in issuing his invitations (Ezek. 33:11). But it is the *slight* put upon him, the sense of which is intended to be marked by this word.

streets and lanes—*historically*, those within the same pale of "the city" of God as the former class, but the despised and outcasts of the nation, the "publicans and sinners" [TRENCH]; generally, all similar classes, usually overlooked in the first provision for supplying the means of grace to a community, half heathen in the midst of revealed light, and in every sense miserable. **22. yet there is room**—implying that these classes *had* embraced the invitation (Matt. 21:32; Mark 12:37; last clause; John 7:48, 49); and beautifully expressing the longing that should fill the hearts of ministers to see their Master's table filled. **23. highways and hedges**—outside the city altogether; *historically*, the heathen, sunk in the lowest depths of spiritual wretchedness, as being beyond the pale of all that is revealed and saving, "without Christ, strangers from the covenant of promise, having no hope, and without God in the world" (Eph. 2:12); generally, all such still. Thus, this parable *prophetically* contemplates the extension of the kingdom of God to the whole world; and *spiritually*, directs the Gospel invitations to be carried to the lowest strata, and be brought in contact with the outermost circles, of human society. **compel them to come in**—not as if they would make the "excuses" of the first class, but because it would be hard to get them over two difficulties: (1) "We are not fit company for such a feast." (2) "We have no proper dress, and are ill in order for such a presence." How fitly does this represent the difficulties and fears of the *sincere*! How is this met? "Take no excuse—make them come as they are—bring them along with you." What a directory for ministers of Christ! **that my house may be filled**—"Grace no more than nature will endure a vacuum" [BENGEL]. **24. I say unto you, That none**—Our Lord here appears to throw off the veil of the parable, and proclaim the Supper *His own*, intimating that when transferred and transformed into its final glorious form, and the refusers themselves would give all for another opportunity, *He* will not allow one of them to taste it. (*N.B.*—This parable must not be confounded with that of Prov. 1:24-33; *The Marriage Supper*, Matt. 22:2-14.)

ADAM CLARKE

Go ye therefore into the highways. "Cross- or by-paths"; the places where two or more roads met in one, leading into the city, where people were coming together from various quarters of the country. Luke adds "hedges," to point out the people to whom the apostles were sent, as either miserable vagabonds or the most indigent poor, who were wandering about the country, or sitting by the sides of the ways and hedges, imploring relief. This verse points out the final rejection of the Jews and the calling of the Gentiles. It was a custom among the Jews, when a rich man made a feast, to go out and invite in all destitute travellers. *As many as ye shall find, bid to the marriage.* God sends His salvation to every soul, that all may believe and be saved.

23. *Compel them to come in.* "Prevail" on them by the most earnest entreaties. The word is used by Matthew, chap. xiv. 22, and by Mark, chap. vi. 45; in both places when Christ is said to "constrain" His disciples to get into the vessel, nothing but His commanding or persuading them to do it can be reasonably understood.

MATTHEW HENRY

Verses 25–35

He is in these verses directing his discourse to the multitudes that crowded after him, and his exhortation to them is to understand the terms of discipleship.

I. How zealous people were in their attendance on Christ (*v.* 25): *There went great multitudes with him*, many for love and more for company. Here was a *mixed multitude*.

II. How *considerate* he would have them to be in their *zeal*. Those that undertake to follow Christ must count upon the worst, and prepare accordingly.

1. He tells them what the worst is that they must count upon. He takes it for granted that they had a mind to be *his disciples*. They expected that he should say, "If any man come to me, and be my disciple, he shall have wealth and honour in abundance." But he tells them quite the contrary.

(1) They must be willing to *quit* that which was *very dear*, rather than quit their interest in Christ, *v.* 26. A man cannot be Christ's disciple but he must *hate father, and mother, and his own life*. He is not *sincere*, he will not be *constant* and persevering, unless he love Christ better than anything in this world. Mention is not made here of *houses* and *lands*; philosophy will teach a man to look upon these with contempt; but Christianity carries it higher. Every good man loves *his relations*; and yet, if he be a disciple of Christ, he must comparatively *hate them*. Not that their persons must be in any degree hated, but our comfort and satisfaction in them must be lost and swallowed up in our love to Christ. When our duty to our parents comes in competition with our evident duty to Christ, we must give Christ the preference. If we must either *deny Christ* or be *banished* from our families and relations (as many of the primitive Christians were), we must rather lose their society than his favour. Every man loves *his own life*, no man ever yet *hated it*; and we cannot be Christ's disciples if we do not love him better than our own lives. The experience of the pleasures of the *spiritual life*, and the believing hopes and prospects of *eternal life* will make this *hard saying* easy. When tribulation and persecution arise because of the word, then chiefly the trial is. Yet even in *days of* peace this matter is sometimes brought to the trial. Those that are ashamed to confess him, for fear of disobliging a relation or friend, or losing a customer, give cause to suspect that they love him better than Christ.

(2) That they must be willing to *bear* that which was very *heavy* (*v.* 27): *Whosoever doth not bear his cross*, and so *come after me*, he *cannot be my disciple*. Though the disciples of Christ are not *all crucified*, yet they all *bear their cross*. They must be content to be put into an ill name, for no name is more ignominious than *Furcifer—the bearer of the gibbet*. He must bear his cross, and *come after Christ*; that is, he must bear it in the way of his duty, whenever it lies in that way. He must bear it when Christ calls him to it, and live in hope of a recompense with him.

2. He bids them count upon it, and then consider of it. It is better never to begin than not to proceed; and therefore before we begin we must consider what it is to proceed. This is to act rationally, and as becomes men. The cause of Christ will bear a scrutiny. Satan shows the best, but hides the worst. This considering of the case is necessary to perseverance. Our Saviour here illustrates the necessity of it by two similitudes. We are like a man that undertakes to *build a tower*, and therefore must consider the *expense of it* (*v.* 28–30): *Which of you, intending to build a tower sitteth not down first, and counteth the cost?* Let him compare the charge with his purse, lest he make himself to be laughed at, by *beginning to build* what he is *not able to finish*. All that take upon them a profession of religion undertake to *build a tower*. Begin low, and lay the foundation deep, lay it on the rock, and make sure work, and then aim as high as heaven. Those that intend to build this tower must *sit down and count the cost*. Let them consider that it *will cost them* a life of self-denial and watchfulness. It *may*, perhaps, *cost them* their reputation among men, and all that is dear to them in this world, even life itself. And if it should cost us all this, what is it in comparison with what it cost Christ? Many that begin to *build this tower* do not *go on with it*, nor persevere in it, and it is their folly. It is true, we have none of us in ourselves *sufficient to finish* this tower, but Christ hath said, *My grace is sufficient for thee*. Nothing is more *shameful* than for those that have begun well in religion to break off.

(2) When we undertake to be Christ's disciples we are like a man that *goes to war*, and therefore must consider the *hazard* of it, *v.* 31, 32. A king that declares war against a neighbouring prince considers whether he has strength wherewith to make his part

JAMIESON, FAUSSET, BROWN

25-35. ADDRESS TO GREAT MULTITUDES TRAVELLING WITH HIM.

25. great multitudes with him—on His final journey to Jerusalem. The "great multitudes" were doubtless people going to the passover, who moved along in clusters (ch. 2:44), and who on this occasion falling in with our Lord had formed themselves into one mass about Him. **26, 27. If any man . . .**—(See on Matt. 10:34-36, and Mark 8:34, 35).

He that loveth father or mother more than me, is not worthy of me; and he that loveth son or daughter more than me, is not worthy of me—(Cf. Deut. 33:9). As the preference of the one would, in the case supposed, necessitate the abandonment of the other, our Lord here, with a sublime, yet awful self-respect, asserts His own claims to supreme affection.

And he that taketh not his cross, and followeth after me, is not worthy of me—a saying which our Lord once and again emphatically reiterates (ch. 16:24; Luke 9:23; 14:27). We have become so accustomed to this expression—"taking up one's cross"—in the sense of "being prepared for trials in general for Christ's sake," that we are apt to lose sight of its primary and proper sense here—"a preparedness to go forth even to crucifixion," as when our Lord had to bear His own cross on His way to Calvary—a saying the more remarkable as our Lord had not as yet given a hint that He would die this death, nor was crucifixion a Jewish mode of capital punishment.

28-33. which of you . . .—Common sense teaches men not to *begin* any costly work without first seeing that they have wherewithal to *finish*. And he who does otherwise exposes himself to general ridicule. Nor will any wise potentate enter on a war with any hostile power without first seeing to it that, despite formidable odds (two to one), he be able to stand his ground; and if he has no hope of this, he will feel that nothing remains for him but to make the best terms he can. *"Even so,"* says our Lord, "in the warfare you will each have to wage as My disciples, despise not your enemy's strength, for the odds are all against you; and you had better see to it that, despite every disadvantage, you still have wherewithal to hold out and win the day, or else not begin at all, and make the best you can in such awful circumstances." In this simple sense of the parable (STIER, ALFORD, etc., go wide of the mark here in making the enemy to be *God*, because of the "conditions of peace," vs. 32), two things are taught: (1) Better not begin (Rev. 3:15), than begin and not finish. (2) Though the contest for salvation be on our part an awfully unequal one, *the human will*, in the exercise of that "faith which overcometh the world" (I John 5:4), and nerved by power from above, which "out of *weakness*

ADAM CLARKE

26. *And hate not*. Matthew, chap. x. 37, expresses the true meaning of this word, when he says, "He that loveth father or mother more than me." In chap. vi. 24 he uses the word *hate* in the same sense. When we read, Rom. ix. 13, "Jacob have I loved, but Esau have I hated," the meaning is simply, I have loved Jacob, the Israelites, more than Esau, the Edomites. That this is no arbitrary interpretation of the word *hate*, but one agreeable to the Hebrew idiom, appears from what is said on Gen. xxix. 30-31, where Leah's being *hated* is explained by Rachel's being loved more than Leah.

A. T. ROBERTSON:

26. "Hateth not" (*ou misei*). An old and very strong verb *miseo*, to hate, detest. The Orientals use strong language where cooler spirits would speak of preference or indifference. But even so Jesus does not here mean that one must hate his father or mother of necessity or as such, for Matt. 15:4 proves the opposite. It is only where the element of choice comes in (Matt. 6:24) as it sometimes does when father or mother opposes Christ. Then one must not hesitate. The language here is more sharply put than in Matt. 10:37. The *ou* here coalesces with the verb *misei* in this conditional clause of the first class determined as fulfilled. It is the language of exaggerated contrast, it is true, but it must not be watered down till the point is gone. In mentioning "and wife," Jesus has really made a comment on the excuse given in verse 20 (I married a wife and so I am not able to come). "And his own life also" (*eti te kai ten psuchen heautou*). Note *te kai*, both—and. "The *te* (BL) binds all the particulars into one bundle of *renuncianda*" (Bruce). Note this same triple group of conjunctions (*eti te kai*) in Acts 21:28, "And moreover also," "even going as far as his own life." Martyrdom should be an ever-present possibility to the Christian, not to be courted, but not to be shunned.

—Word Pictures in the New Testament

28. *To build a tower*. Probably this means no more than a dwelling house, on the top of which, according to the Asiatic manner, battlements were built, both to take the fresh air on, and to serve for refuge from and defense against an enemy. It was also used for prayer and meditation. This parable represents the absurdity of those who undertook to be disciples of Christ without considering what difficulties they were to meet with, and what strength they had to enable them to go through with the undertaking. He that will be a true disciple of Jesus Christ shall require no less than the mighty power of God to support him, as both hell and earth will unite to destroy him.

MATTHEW HENRY

good, and, if not, he will lay aside his thoughts of war. *Is not* the Christian *life a warfare?* We must fight every step we go, so restless are our spiritual enemies in their opposition. We ought to consider whether we can *endure the hardness* which a good soldier of Jesus Christ must expect and count upon, before we enlist ourselves under Christ's banner. Of the two it is better to make the best terms we can with the world than pretend to renounce it and afterwards *return to it*. That *young man* that could not find in his heart to part with his possessions for Christ did better to go away from Christ *sorrowing* than to have stayed with him *dissembling*.

This parable is another way applicable, and may be taken as designed to teach us to begin *speedily* to be religious, rather than to begin *cautiously*; and may mean the same with Matt. v. 25, *Agree with thine adversary quickly*. Those that persist in sin make war against God. The proudest and most daring sinner is no equal match for God. In consideration of this, it is our interest to make peace with him. We need not send to *desire conditions of peace*; they are offered to us, and are unexceptionable. Let us acquaint ourselves with them, and be at peace; do this in time, *while the other is yet a great way off*.

But the application of this parable here (*v.* 33) is to the consideration that ought to be exercised when we take upon us a profession of religion. Enter upon a profession of religion, as those that know that *except you forsake all you have you cannot be Christ's disciples*.

3. He warns them against apostasy, for that would make them utterly useless, *v.* 34, 35. Good Christians are *the salt of the earth*, and good ministers especially (Matt. v. 13); *salt is good* and of great use. Degenerate Christians, who, rather than part with what they have in the world, will throw up their profession, are like *salt that has lost its savour*, that is the most useless worthless thing in the world; it has no manner of virtue or good property in it. It can never be recovered: *Wherewith shall it be seasoned?* You cannot salt it. This intimates that it is extremely difficult, and next to impossible, to recover an apostate, Heb. vi. 4–6. It is of no use. It is *not fit*, as dung is, *for the land*, to manure that, nor will it be the better if it be laid in the dunghill to rot. A professor of religion whose mind and manners are depraved is the most *insipid* animal that can be. It is abandoned: *Men cast it out*, they will have no more to do with it. Such scandalous professors ought to be cast out of the church, because there is danger that others will be infected by them. Our Saviour concludes this with a call to all to take notice of it, and to take warning: *He that hath ears to hear, let him hear.*

JAMIESON, FAUSSET, BROWN

makes it *strong*" (Heb. 11:34; I Pet. 1:5), becomes heroical and will come off "more than conqueror." But without *absolute surrender of self* the contest is hopeless (vs. 33).

ALEXANDER MACLAREN:

There are two kinds of "forsaking all that we have." One is the forsaking by which we become disciples; and the other, by which we continue true disciples. The conviction that they had not sufficient to finish is the very conviction that Christ wished to root in the minds of the crowds. He exhibits the difficulties in order that they may feel they cannot cope with them. What then? That they may "forsake" all their own power to cope with them.

That is the first kind of "forsaking all that we have." That makes a disciple. The recognition of my own utter impotence to do the things which yet I see must be done is the underside of trust in Him. And that trust in Him brings the power that makes it possible for us to do the things which we cannot of ourselves do, and the consciousness of the impotence to do which is the first step toward doing them. It is the self-sufficient man who is sure to be bankrupt before he has finished his building; but he who has no confidence in himself, and recognizes the fact that he cannot build, will go to Jesus Christ and say, "Lord, I am poor and needy. Come Thou thyself and be my strength." Such a forsaking of all that we have in the recognition of our own poverty and powerlessness brings into the field an Ally for our reinforcement that has more than the twenty thousand that are coming against us, and will make us strong.—*Expositions of Holy Scripture*

34. 35. salt . . .—(See on Matt. 5:13-16; and Mark 9:50).

but if the salt have lost his savour—"become unsavory" or "insipid"; losing its saline or salting property. The meaning is: If that Christianity on which the health of the world depends, does in any age, region, or individual, exist only in *name*, or if it contain not those *saving elements* for want of which the world languishes, **wherewith shall it be salted?**—How shall the salting qualities be restored it? (Cf. Mark 9:50.) Whether salt ever does lose its saline property—about which there is a difference of opinion—is a question of no moment here. The point of the case lies in the supposition—that *if it should lose it,* the consequence would be as here described. So with Christians. The question is not: Can, or do, the saints ever totally lose that grace which makes them a blessing to their fellow men? But, What is to be the issue of that Christianity which is found wanting in those elements which can alone stay the corruption and season the tastelessness of an all-pervading carnality?

ADAM CLARKE

33. *Whosoever he be of you.* This seems to be addressed particularly to those who were then, and who were to be, preachers of His gospel, and who were to travel over all countries publishing salvation to a lost world.

MATTHEW HENRY

CHAPTER 15

Verses 1–10

Here is, I. The diligent attendance of the publicans and sinners upon Christ's ministry. *Great multitudes* of Jews *went with him* (*ch.* xiv. 25), with such an assurance of admission into the kingdom of God that he found it requisite to say that to them which would shake their vain hopes. Here multitudes of *publicans* and *sinners* drew near to him, with a humble modest fear of being *rejected* by him, and to them he found it requisite to give encouragement. The *publicans* were perhaps some of them *bad men*, but they were all industriously put into an *ill name*, because of the prejudices of the Jewish nation against their office. They are sometimes ranked with *harlots* (Matt. xxi. 32); here and elsewhere with *sinners.* They drew near to him, not, as some did, for curiosity to *see him*, nor as others did, to solicit for cures, but to hear his excellent doctrine. In all our approaches to Christ we must have this in our eye, to *hear him*; to hear the instructions he gives us, and his answers to our prayers.

II. The offence which the *scribes* and *Pharisees* took at this. They *murmured, This man receiveth sinners, and eateth with them, v.* 2. 1. They were angry that *publicans* and *heathens* had the means of grace allowed them, and were encouraged to hope for pardon upon repentance. 2. They thought it inconsistent with the dignity of his character, to make himself familiar with such sort of people, and to *eat with them.* They could not, for shame, condemn him for *preaching to them*, and therefore they reproached him for *eating with them,* which was more expressly contrary to the tradition of the elders.

III. Christ's justifying himself in it, by showing that the worse these people were, the more glory would redound to God, and the more joy there would be in heaven, if by his preaching they were brought to repentance. It would be a more pleasing sight in

JAMIESON, FAUSSET, BROWN

CHAPTER 15

VSS. 1-32. PUBLICANS AND SINNERS WELCOMED BY CHRIST—THREE PARABLES TO EXPLAIN THIS. **1. drew near . . . all the publicans and sinners . . .**—drawn around Him by the extraordinary adaptation of His teaching to their case, who, till He appeared—at least His forerunner—might well say, "No man careth for my soul."

2. murmured, saying . . .—took it ill, were scandalized at Him, and insinuated (on the principle that a man is known by the company he keeps) that He must have some secret sympathy with their *character.* But oh, what a truth of unspeakable preciousness do their lips, as on other occasions, unconsciously utter! Now follow three parables representing the sinner: (1) *in his stupidity;* (2) as *all-unconscious of his lost condition;* (3) *knowingly and willingly estranged from God* [BENGEL]. The first two set forth the *seeking* love of God; the last, His *receiving* love [TRENCH].

ADAM CLARKE

CHAPTER 15

1. *Publicans and sinners.* "Taxgatherers and heathens"; persons who believed neither in Christ nor in Moses. See the note on chap. vii. 36. Concerning the "taxgatherers," see the note on Matt. v. 46.

The publicans. That is, "taxgatherers." A farmer or collector of the taxes or public revenues. This class of men were detestable among the Romans, the Greeks, and the Jews for their intolerable rapacity and avarice. They were abhorred in an especial manner by the Jews, to whom the Roman government was odious. These, assisting in collecting the Roman tribute, were considered as betrayers of the liberties of their country, and abettors of those who enslaved it.

2. *Receiveth sinners.* He "receives them cordially, affectionately," takes them to His bosom, for so the word implies.

MATTHEW HENRY

heaven to see publicans and sinners live an orderly sort of life than to see *scribes* and *Pharisees* go on in living such a life. This he here illustrates by two parables.

1. The parable of the *lost sheep*. Something like it we had in Matt. xviii. 12. There it was designed to show the care God takes for the preservation of saints; here it is designed to show the pleasure God takes in the conversion of sinners. We have here,

(1) The case of a sinner that goes on in sinful ways. He is like a *lost sheep*, a sheep *gone astray*; he is *lost* to God; *lost* to the flock; *lost* to himself: he knows not where he is, wanders endlessly, is continually exposed to the beasts of prey, subject to frights and terrors, taken from under the shepherd's care, and wanting the green pastures; and he cannot of himself find the way back to the fold.

(2) The care the God of heaven takes of poor wandering sinners. There is a particular care to be taken of this lost sheep; and though he has a hundred sheep, yet he will not *lose* that *one*, but he goes after it, and shows abundance of care in *finding it out*. He follows it, looking about for it, until he *finds* it. God follows backsliding sinners until at length they are wrought upon to think of returning. Though he finds it *weary* and not able to bear being driven home, yet he does not leave it to perish, but *lays it on his shoulders*, and, with a great deal of tenderness and labour, brings it to the fold. God sends his Son to *seek and save that which was lost, ch.* xix. 10. Christ is said to *gather the lambs in his arms*, and carry *them in his bosom*, denoting his pity and tenderness. Here he is said to bear them *upon his shoulders*; those can never perish whom he carries upon his shoulders.

(3) The pleasure that God takes in repenting returning sinners. He *lays it on his shoulders rejoicing*, and the joy is the greater because he began to be out of hope of finding it; and he *calls his friends and neighbours, saying, Rejoice with me*. Observe, he calls it *his sheep*, though a *stray*, a wandering sheep. Therefore he looks after it himself: *I have found it;* he did not send a servant, but his own Son, the great and good Shepherd, who will find what he seeks, and will be found of those that seek him not.

2. The parable of the *lost piece of silver*. (1) The *loser* is here supposed to be *a woman*. She has *ten pieces of silver*, and out of them loses only one. Notwithstanding the sinfulness and misery of the world of mankind there are nine to one, nay, in the foregoing parable there are ninety-nine to one, that retain their integrity, in whom God *is* praised, and never *was* dishonoured. (2) That which is lost is a piece of silver. The soul is *silver*, of intrinsic worth and value; not base metal, as iron or lead, but *silver*. It is *silver coin*. It is stamped with God's *image and superscription*. This silver was lost *in the dirt*; a soul plunged in the world is like a piece of money in the dirt; anyone would say, It is a thousand pities that it should *lie there*. (3) Here is a great deal of care and pains taken in quest of it. The woman *lights a candle, sweeps the house*, and *seeks diligently till she finds it*. This represents the various means and methods God makes use of to bring lost souls home to himself: he has *lighted the candle* of the gospel, not to show himself the way to us, but to show us the way to him; his heart is upon it, to bring lost souls to himself. (4) Here is a great deal of joy for the finding of it: *Rejoice with me, for I have found the piece which I had lost, v.* 9. Those that rejoice desire that others should rejoice with them. The pleasing surprise of finding it put her, for the present, into a kind of transport—*I have found, I have found*, is the language of joy.

3. The explication of these two parables is to the same purport (*v.* 7, 10): *There is joy in heaven, joy in the presence of the angels of God, over one sinner that repenteth*, more than *over* a great number of *just persons, who need no repentance.*

(1) The *repentance* and *conversion of sinners* on earth are *matter of joy* and rejoicing *in heaven*. It is possible that the greatest sinners may be brought to repentance. While there is life there is hope, and the worst are not to be despaired of. God will *delight* to show them mercy. There is always *joy in heaven*. God *rejoiceth in all his works*, but particularly in the works of his grace. He rejoiceth to do good to penitent sinners. He rejoiceth not only in the conversion of nations, but even over *one sinner that repenteth*, though but *one*. The good angels will be glad that mercy is shown them. The redemption of mankind was matter of joy in the presence of the angels; for they sung, *Glory to God in the highest, ch.* ii. 14.

(2) There is more joy over *one sinner that repenteth* than there is *over ninety-nine just persons, who need no repentance*. More joy for the conversion of the sinners of the Gentiles, and of those publicans that

JAMIESON, FAUSSET, BROWN

3-7. I. THE LOST SHEEP—occurring again (Matt. 18:12-14); but there to show how precious one of His sheep is to the Good Shepherd; here, to show that the shepherd, though the sheep stray never so widely, will seek it out, and when he hath found, will rejoice over it. **4. leave the ninety and nine**—bend all His attention and care, as it were, to the one object of recovering the lost sheep; not saying. " 'Tis but one; let it go; enough remain." **go after . . . until . . .**—pointing to all the diversified means which God sets in operation for recovering sinners.

6. Rejoice with me . . .—The principle here is, that one feels *exuberant joy* to be almost too much for himself to bear alone, and is positively relieved by having others to *share it with him*. (See on vs. 10.)

8-10. II. THE LOST COIN. **sweep the house**—"not done without *dust* on man's part" [BENGEL].

7. ninety-nine just . . . needing no repentance—not *angels*, whose place in these parables is very different from this; but those represented by the *prodigal's wellbehaved brother*, who have "served their Father" many years and not at any time transgressed His commandment (in the outrageous sense of the prodigal). (See on vss. 29, 31.) In other words, *such as have grown up from childhood* in the fear of God and as the sheep of His pasture. Our Lord does not *say* "the Pharisees and scribes" were such; but as there *was* undoubtedly such a class, while "the publicans and sinners" were confessedly the strayed sheep and the prodigal children, He leaves them to fill up the place of the other class, *if they could.*

10. Likewise—on the same principle. **joy . . .**—Note carefully the language here—not "joy *on the part,*" but "joy *in the presence* of the angels of God." True to the

ADAM CLARKE

4. *What man of you?* Our Lord spoke this and the following parable to justify His conduct in receiving and conversing with sinners. *An hundred sheep.* Parables similar to this are frequent among the Jewish writers. The whole flock of mankind, both Jews and Gentiles, belongs unto this divine Shepherd; and it is but reasonable to expect that the gracious Proprietor will look after those who have gone astray, and bring them back to the flock. The lost sheep is an emblem of a heedless, thoughtless sinner, one who follows the corrupt dictates of his own heart without ever reflecting upon his conduct or considering what will be the issue of his unholy course of life. No creature strays more easily than a sheep; none is more heedless; and none so incapable of finding its way back to the flock, when once gone astray. It will bleat for the flock, and still run on in an opposite direction to the place where the flock is; this I have often noticed. No creature is more defenseless than a sheep, and more exposed to be devoured by dogs and wild beasts. Even the fowls of the air seek its destruction. I have known ravens often attempt to destroy lambs by picking out their eyes, in which, when they have succeeded, as the creature does not see whither it is going, it soon falls an easy prey to its destroyer.

8. *Ten pieces of silver.* "Ten drachmas." I think it always best to retain the names of these ancient coins, and to state their value in English money. Every reader will naturally wish to know by what names such and such coins were called in the countries in which they were current. The Grecian *drachma* was worth about the same as the Roman *denarius.* The *drachma* that was lost is also a very expressive emblem of a sinner who is estranged from God, and enslaved to habits of iniquity. The longer a piece of money is lost, the less probability is there of its being again found. So the sinner sinks deeper and deeper into the impurities of sin and gets the image and superscription of his Maker defaced from his heart.

7. *Just persons, which need no repentance.* Who do not require "such a change of mind and purpose" as these do—who are not so profligate, and cannot repent of sins they have never committed. Distinctions of this kind frequently occur in the Jewish writings. There are many persons who have been brought up in a sober and regular course of life, attending the ordinances of God and being true and just in all their dealings; these most materially differ from the heathens mentioned in v. 1, because they believe in God, and attend the means of grace. They differ also essentially from the taxgatherers mentioned in the same place, because they wrong no man and are upright in their dealings. Therefore they cannot repent of the sins of a heathen, which they have not practiced; nor of the rapine of a taxgatherer, of which they have never been guilty. As, therefore, these *just persons* are put in opposition to the taxgatherers and heathens, we may at once see the scope and design of our Lord's words. These needed no

MATTHEW HENRY

now heard Christ preach, than for all the praises and devotions, and all the *God I thank thee*, of the Pharisees, and the other self-justifying Jews, who thought that they *needed no repentance*. Christ tells them that God was more praised *in*, and pleased *with*, the penitent broken heart of one of those despised, envied sinners, than all the long prayers which the scribes and Pharisees made, who could not see anything amiss in themselves; more joy for the conversion of one such great sinner than for the regular conversion of one that had always conducted himself decently and well, and comparatively *needs no repentance*. Not but that it is best not to go astray; but the grace of God is more manifested in the *reducing* of great sinners than in the *conducting* of those that never went astray. And many times those that have been great sinners before their conversion prove more eminently and zealously good after. They to whom much is forgiven will love much. We are moved with a more sensible joy for the recovery of what we had lost than for the continuance of what we had always enjoyed, for health *out of* sickness than for health *without* sickness. A constant course of religion may in itself be more valuable, and yet a sudden return from an evil course and way of sin may yield a more surprising pleasure.

Verses 11–32

We have here the parable of the prodigal son, the scope of which is the same with those before. But the circumstances of the parable do much more largely and fully set forth the riches of gospel grace, and it has been, and will be while the world stands, of unspeakable use to poor sinners.

I. The parable represents God as a *common Father* to all mankind. He is *our Father*, for he has the *educating* and *portioning* of us. Our Saviour hereby intimates to those proud Pharisees that these publicans and sinners, whom they thus despised, were their brethren, and therefore they ought to be glad of any kindness shown them.

II. It represents the children of men as of *different* characters. He had *two sons*, one of them a solid grave youth, *reserved* and *austere*, sober himself, but not at all *good-humoured* to those about him; such a one would adhere to his education, and not be easily drawn from it; but the other *volatile* and *mercurial*, and impatient of restraint, roving, and willing to try his fortune, and, if he fall into ill hands, likely to be a rake. Now this latter represents the publicans and sinners, and the Gentiles. The former represents the Jews in general, and particularly the Pharisees. The *younger son* is the prodigal.

1. His *riot* and *ramble* when he was a prodigal, and the extravagances and miseries he fell into.

(1) What his request to his father was (*v.* 12): *He said to his father, "Father, give me"*—he might have put a little more in his mouth, and have said, *Pray give me*, or, *Sir, if you please, give me*, but he makes an imperious demand—"*give me the portion of goods that falleth to me;* that which falls to me as *my due*." It is bad, and the beginning of worse, when men look upon God's gifts as debts. "*Give it me all* at present in possession, and I will never expect anything in *reversion*, anything *hereafter*." The great folly of sinners is being content to have *their portion in hand*, now in this lifetime to *receive their good things*. They look only at the things that are seen, and covet only a present gratification, but have no care for a future felicity. And why did he desire to have his portion in his own hands? [1] He was *weary* of his *father's government*, and was fond of liberty falsely so called. See the folly of many young men, who never think themselves their own masters till they have broken all God's bands in sunder, and, instead of them, bound themselves with the cords of their own lust. Here is the original of the apostasy of sinners from God; they will not be tied up to the rules of *God's government*; they will themselves *be as gods*, knowing no other *good and evil* than what themselves please. [2] He was willing to get *from under his father's eye*. A shyness of God, and a willingness to disbelieve his omniscience, are at the bottom of the wickedness of the wicked. [3] He was distrustful of his *father's management*. He would have his *portion of goods* himself, for he thought that his father would limit him in his present expenses, and that he did not like. [4] He was *proud of himself*, and had a *great conceit of his own sufficiency*. He thought that if he had put his portion in his own hands he could manage it better than his father did, and make a better figure with it. There are more young people ruined by *pride* than by any one lust whatsoever.

(2) How kind his father was to him: *He divided unto them his living*. He computed what he had to dispose of between his sons, and gave the younger son *his share*, and offered the elder his; but, it should

JAMIESON, FAUSSET, BROWN

idea of the parables. The Great Shepherd. The Great Owner Himself, is He *whose the joy properly is over His own recovered property;* but so vast and exuberant is it (Zech. 8:17), that as if He could not keep it to Himself, He "calleth His friends and neighbors together"—His whole celestial family—saying, "Rejoice WITH ME, for I have found *My* sheep-My-piece," etc. In this sublime sense it is "joy," *before "or in the presence* of the angels"; they only "catch the flying joy," sharing it *with Him*! The application of this to the reception of those publicans and sinners that stood around our Lord is grand in the extreme: "Ye turn from these lost ones with disdain, and because I do not the same, ye murmur at it: but a very different feeling is cherished in heaven. There, the recovery of even one such outcast is watched with interest and hailed with joy; nor are they left to come home of themselves or perish; for lo! even now the great Shepherd is going after His lost sheep, and the Owner is making diligent search for the lost property; and He is finding it, too, and bringing it back with joy, and all heaven is full of it." (Let the reader mark what sublime claims Himself our Lord covertly puts in here—as if in Him they beheld, all unknown to themselves, nothing less than heaven in the habiliments of earth, the Great Shepherd above, clothed in a garment of flesh, come "to seek and to save that which was lost")! **11-32. III. THE PRODIGAL SON.**

12. the younger—as the more thoughtless. **said . . .**—weary of restraint, panting for independence, unable longer to abide the check of a father's eye. *This is man* impatient of divine control, desiring to be independent of God, seeking to be his own master; that "sin of sins, in which all subsequent sins are included as in their germ, for they are but the unfolding of this one" [TRENCH].

he divided . . .—Thus "God, when His service no longer appears a perfect freedom, and man promises himself something far better elsewhere, allows him to make the trial; and he shall discover, if need be

ADAM CLARKE

repentance in comparison of the others, as not being guilty of their crimes. And as these belonged, by outward profession at least, to the flock of God, and were sincere and upright according to their light, they are considered as being in no danger of being *lost;* and as they fear God, and work righteousness according to their light, He will take care to make those further discoveries to them of the purity of His nature, the holiness of His law, and the necessity of the atonement, which He sees to be necessary. On this ground, the owner is represented as feeling more joy in consequence of finding *one sheep* that was *lost,* there having been almost no hope of its recovery, than he feels at seeing ninety and nine still safe under his care.

12. *Give me the portion of goods.* It may seem strange that such a demand should be made, and that the parent should have acceded to it, when he knew that it was to minister to his debauches that his profligate son made the demand here specified. But the matter will appear plain when it is considered that it has been an immemorial custom in the East for sons to demand and receive their portion of the inheritance during their father's lifetime; and the parent, however aware of the dissipated inclinations of the child, could not legally refuse to comply with the application.

ALBERT BARNES:

1. "And he said." Jesus, to illustrate still further the sentiment which he had uttered, and to show that it was proper to rejoice over repenting sinners, proceeds to show it by a most beautiful and instructive parable. We shall see its beauty and propriety by remembering that the design of it was simply to justify his conduct in receiving sinners, and to show that to rejoice over their return was proper. This he shows by the feelings of a father rejoicing over the return of an ungrateful and dissipated son.—*Popular Commentary*

ALEXANDER MACLAREN:

The desire to be independent is good, but when it can only be attained by being dependent on him whose authority is irksome, it takes another color. This foolish boy wished to be able to use his father's property as his own, but he had to get the father's consent first. It is a poor beginning of independence when it has to be set up in business by a gift.

That is the essential absurdity in our attempts to do without God and to shake off His control. We can only get power to seem to do it by misusing His gifts. When we say, "Who is Lord over us?" the tongues which say it were given us by Him. The next step soon followed. "Not many days after," of course, for the sense of ownership could not be kept up while near the father. A man who wishes to enjoy worldly good without reference to God is obliged, in self-defense, to hustle God out of his thoughts as soon and as completely as possible.

(Continued on next page)

MATTHEW HENRY

seem, he desired his father to keep it in his own hands still, and we may see what he got by it (*v.* 31): *All that I have is thine.* He gave the younger son what he asked. He had as much as he expected, and perhaps more. [1] Thus he might *now see his father's kindness,* how willing he was to please him and make him easy. [2] Thus he would in a little time be made to see *his own folly,* and that he was not such a wise manager for himself.

(3) How he managed himself when he had got his portion in his own hands. He set himself to spend it as fast as he could, and, in a little time he made himself a beggar: *not many days after, v.* 13. That which the younger son determined was to *be gone* presently, and, in order to that, he *gathered all together.*

Now the condition of the prodigal in this ramble of his represents to us a *sinful state,* into which man has fallen.

[1] A sinful state is a state of *departure* and *distance* from God. It is the *sinfulness* of sin that it is an apostasy from God. He *took his journey* from his father's house. Sinners are fled from God. They get as far off him as they can. The world is the *far country* in which they take up their residence. It is the misery of sinners that they are afar off from God, and are going further and further from him. What is hell itself, but being *afar off* from God?

[2] A sinful state is a *spending* state: There he *wasted his substance with riotous living* (*v.* 13), devoured it *with harlots* (*v.* 30), and in a little time *he had spent all, v.* 14. He bought fine clothes, associated with those that helped him to make an end of what he had in a little time. But this is to be applied spiritually. Wilful sinners *waste* their patrimony; for they misemploy their thoughts and all the powers of their souls, do not only bury, but embezzle; the talents they are entrusted to trade with, and the gifts of Providence, which were intended to enable them to serve God and to do good with, are made the food and fuel of their lusts. The soul that is made a drudge, either to the world or to the flesh, *wastes its substance,* and *lives riotously.*

[3] A sinful state is a *wanting* state: *When he had spent all there arose a mighty famine in that land,* and he *began to be in want, v.* 14. Wilful waste brings woeful want. Riotous living in time, perhaps in a little time, brings men to a *morsel of bread,* especially when *bad times* hasten on the consequences of *bad husbandry.* This represents the misery of *sinners,* who have thrown away *their own mercies.* These they *gave away* for the pleasure of sense, and the wealth of the world, and then are ready to perish for want of them. Sinners want necessaries for their souls; they have neither food nor raiment for them, nor any provision for hereafter. A sinful state is like a land where *famine reigns.* Sinners are *wretchedly* and *miserably poor,* and, what aggravates it, they brought themselves into that condition.

[4] A sinful state is *a vile servile state.* When this young man's riot had brought him to want his want brought him to servitude. *He went, and joined himself to a citizen of that country, v.* 15. The same wicked life that before was represented by *riotous living* is here represented by *servile living.* How did this young gentleman debase and disparage himself, when he hired himself into such a service and under such a master as this! He *sent him into the fields,* not to feed sheep but to *feed swine.* The business of the devil's servants is to *make provision for the flesh, to fulfil the lusts thereof,* and that is no better than feeding greedy, dirty, noisy swine; and how can rational immortal souls more disgrace themselves?

[5] A sinful state is a state of *perpetual dissatisfaction. He would fain have filled his belly with the husks which the swine did eat, v.* 16. A fine pass my young master had brought himself to, to be fellow-commoner with the swine! That which sinners, when they *depart from God,* promise themselves *satisfaction in,* will certainly disappoint them; they are *labouring for that which satisfieth not,* Isa. lv. 2. Husks are food for swine, but not for men. The wealth of the world and the entertainments of sense will serve for bodies; but what are these to *precious souls*? They neither suit their nature, nor satisfy their desires, nor supply their needs.

[6] A sinful state is a state which *cannot expect relief from any creature.* This prodigal, when he would not earn his bread by *working,* took to *begging;* but *no man gave unto him.* Those who depart from God cannot be helped by any creature. In vain do we cry to the world and the flesh; they have that which will *poison* a soul, but have nothing to give it which will *feed* and *nourish* it.

[7] A sinful state is a *state of death*: *This my son was dead, v.* 23, 32. A sinner is not only dead in law, as he is under a sentence of death, but dead in tres-

JAMIESON, FAUSSET, BROWN

by saddest proof, that to depart from Him is not to throw off the yoke, but to exchange a light yoke for a heavy one, and one gracious Master for a thousand imperious tyrants and lords" [TRENCH].

13. not many days—intoxicated with his new-found resources, and eager for the luxury of using them at will.

a far country—beyond all danger of interference from home.

wasted . . .—So long as it lasted, the inward monitor (Isa. 55:2) would be silenced (Isa. 9:10; 57:10; Amos 4:6-10). **riotous living**—(vs. 30), "with harlots." Ah! but this reaches farther than the sensualist; for "in the deep symbolical language of Scripture fornication is the standing image of idolatry; they are in fact ever spoken of as one and the same sin, considered now in its fleshly, now in its spiritual aspect" (Jer. 3; Ezek. 16 and 17), [TRENCH].

14. when he had spent all . . . a mighty famine—a mysterious providence holding back the famine till he was in circumstances to feel it in all its rigor. Thus, like Jonah, whom the storm did not overtake till on the mighty deep at the mercy of the waves, does the sinner feel as if "the stars in their courses were fighting against" him (Judg. 5:20). **in want**—the first stage of his bitter experience, and preparation for a change.

15. joined himself . . .—his pride not yet humbled, unable to brook the shame of a return. **to feed swine**—glad to keep life anyhow, behold the son sank into a swineherd—among the Jews, on account of the prohibition of swine's flesh, emphatically vile!" "He who begins by using the world as a servant, to minister to his pleasure, ends by reversing the relationship" [TRENCH].

16. would fain have filled—rather, "was fain to fill," ate greedily of the only food he could get. **the husks**—"the hulls of a leguminous plant which in the East is the food of cattle and swine, and often the nourishment of the poorest in times of distress" [STIER]. **no man gave . . . him**—not this food, for that he had, but *anything better* (Jer. 30:14). This was his lowest depth—*perishing unpitied, alone in the world,* and *ready to disappear from it unmissed*! But this is just the blessed turning-point; midnight before dawn of day (II Chron. 12:8; 33:11-13; Jer. 2:19).

ADAM CLARKE

The "far country" is easily reached; and it is far, though a step can land us in it. A narrow bay may compel a long journey round its head before those on its opposite shores can meet. Sin takes us far away from God, and the root of all sin is that desire of living to one's self which began the prodigal's evil course.

The third step in his downward career, wasting his substance in riotous living, comes naturally after the two others; for all self-centered life is in deepest truth waste, and the special forms of gross dissipation to which youth is tempted are only too apt to follow the first sense of being their own masters, and removed from the safeguards of their earthly father's home. Many a lad in our great cities goes through the very stages of the parable, and, when a mother's eye is no longer on him, plunges into filthy debauchery. But living which does not outrage the proprieties may be riotous all the same; for all conduct which ignores God and asserts self as supreme is flagrantly against the very nature of man, and is reckless waste.

—*Expositions of Holy Scripture*

13. *Riotous living.* In a course of life that led him to *spend all.*

15. *To feed swine.* The basest and vilest of all employments and, to a Jew, peculiarly degrading. Shame, contempt, and distress are wedded to sin, and can never be divorced. No character could be meaner in the sight of a Jew than that of a swineherd. Herodotus informs us that in Egypt they were not permitted to mingle with civil society, nor to appear in the worship of the gods, nor would the very dregs of the people have any matrimonial connections with them.

16. *With the husks.* Bochart, I think, has proved that *keratia* does not mean *husks.* He shows also that the original word means the fruit of the *charub* tree, which grows plentifully in Syria. This kind of pulse was made use of to feed *swine.*

MATTHEW HENRY

passes and sins, destitute of spiritual life; no union with Christ, no living to God, and therefore *dead*. The prodigal in the *far country* was *dead* to his father and his family, and it is his own doing.

[8] A sinful state is a *lost state*: *This my son was lost*—lost to everything that was good—lost to his father's house. Souls that are separated from God are *lost* souls; lost as a *traveller* that is out of his way, and, if infinite mercy prevent not, will soon be lost irrecoverably.

[9] A sinful state is a state of *madness* and *frenzy*. This is intimated in that expression (*v*. 17), *when he came to himself*, which intimates that he had been *beside himself*. Surely he was so when he left his father's house, and much more so when he joined himself to the citizen of that country. Sinners, like those that are *mad*, destroy themselves with *foolish lusts*, and yet at the same time deceive themselves with foolish *hopes*.

2. We have here his *return* from this *ramble*. Now observe here,

(1) What was the *occasion* of his return and repentance. It was his *affliction*; when he was in *want*, then he *came to himself*. Afflictions, when they are sanctified by divine grace, prove happy means of turning sinners from the error of their ways. When we find the insufficiency of creatures to make us happy, and have tried all other ways of relief for our poor souls in vain, then it is time to think of returning to God. When we see what miserable comforters, what physicians of no value, all but Christ are; no *man gives unto us* what we need, then surely we shall apply ourselves to Jesus Christ.

(2) What was the *preparative* for it; it was *consideration*. He said within himself when he recovered his right mind, *How many hired servants of my father's have bread enough!* Consideration is the first step towards conversion. He considered how bad his condition was: *I perish with hunger*. Not only, "I am *hungry*," but, "*I perish with hunger*." Sinners will not come to the service of Christ till they are brought to see themselves just ready to perish in the service of sin. And though we be thus driven to Christ he will not think himself dishonoured by our being forced to him, but rather honoured by his being applied to in a desperate case.

He considered how much better it might be made if he would but return: *How many hired servants of my father's have bread enough, and to spare*, such a good house does he keep! In our *Father's house* there is bread for all his family. There is *enough* and to *spare*, enough for all, enough for each, enough and *to spare* for *charity*. There are *crumbs* that fall from his table, which many would be glad of, and thankful for. Even the *hired servants* in God's family are well provided for. The consideration of this should encourage sinners, that have gone astray from God, to think of returning to him.

(3) What was the *purpose* of it. His consideration issues, at length, in this conclusion: *I will arise, and go to my father*. Good purposes are good things, but still good performances are all in all. He determined what to do: *I will arise and go to my father*. Though he be in a *far country*, a great way off from his father's house, yet, far as it is, he will return; every step of backsliding from God must be a step back again in return to him. Observe with what resolution he speaks: "*I will arise, and go to my father;* I am resolved I will, whatever the issue be." He determined what to say. True repentance is a *rising*, and *coming* to God. But what words shall we take with us? In all our addresses to God, it is good to deliberate with ourselves beforehand what we shall say, that we may *order our cause before him*. Let us observe what he purposed to say.

First, He would confess his fault and folly: *I have sinned*. Forasmuch as we have all sinned, it behoves us to own that we have sinned. The confession of sin is required and insisted upon, as a necessary condition of peace and pardon. If we plead *not guilty*, we put ourselves upon a trial. If *guilty*, with a contrite, penitent, and obedient heart, we refer ourselves to the covenant of grace, which offers forgiveness to those that *confess their sins*.

Secondly, He would be so far from extenuating the matter that he would *lay a load* upon himself for it: I have sinned *against Heaven*, and *before thee*. Let those that are *undutiful* to their *earthly parents* think of this; they sin *against Heaven, and before God*. Offences against them are offences against God. Sin is committed in contempt of God's authority over us: *We have sinned against Heaven*. The malignity of sin aims high; it is *against Heaven*. Yet it is *impotent* malice, for we cannot hurt the heavens. Nay, it is foolish malice; what is shot *against the heavens* will return upon the head of him that shoots it. It is committed in contempt of God's eye upon us:

JAMIESON, FAUSSET, BROWN

17. came to himself—Before, he had been "beside himself" (Eccles. 9:3), in what sense will presently appear.

how many hired . . .—What a testimony to the *nature* of the home he had left! But did he not know all this ere he departed and every day of his voluntary exile? He did, and he did not. His heart being wholly estranged from home and steeped in selfish gratification, his father's house never came within the range of his vision, or but as another name for bondage and gloom. Now empty, desolate, withered, perishing, *home*, with all its peace, plenty, freedom, dignity, starts into view, fills all his visions as a warm and living reality, and breaks his heart.

18. I will arise and go to my FATHER—The change has come at last, and what a change!—couched in terms of such exquisite simplicity and power as if expressly framed for all heart-broken penitents. **Father . . .**—Mark the term. Though "no more *worthy* to be called his son," the prodigal sinner is taught to claim the *defiled*, but *still existing* relationship, asking not to be made a servant, but *remaining a son* to be made "*as* a servant," willing to take the lowest place and do the meanest work. Ah! and is it come to this? Once it was, "Any place rather than home." Now, "Oh, that home! Could I but dare to hope that the door of it would not be closed against me, how gladly would I take any place and do any work, happy only to be there at all." Well, *that is conversion*—nothing absolutely new, yet all new; old familiar things seen in a new light and for the first time as realities of overwhelming magnitude and power. *How this is brought about the parable says not*. (We have that abundantly elsewhere, Phil. 2:13, etc.). Its one object is to paint the *welcome home* of the greatest sinners, when (no matter for the present *how*) they "arise and go *to their* Father."

ADAM CLARKE

17. *When he came to himself*. A state of sin is represented in the sacred writings as a course of folly and madness, and repentance is represented as a restoration to sound sense. *I perish with hunger!* "Here" is added by some MSS. and most of the versions.

18. *Against heaven*. That is, "against God." The Jews often make use of this periphrasis in order to avoid mentioning the name of God, which they have ever treated with the utmost reverence. But some contend that it should be translated "even unto heaven"; a Hebraism for, I have sinned exceedingly, beyond all description.

CHARLES H. SPURGEON:

When a sinner comes to himself, he soon comes to his God. This poor prodigal, soon after he came to himself, said, "I will arise, and go to my father." What led him back to his father? Very briefly let me answer that question.

First, *his memory aroused him*. He recollected his father's house, he remembered the past, his own riotous living. Do not try to forget all that has happened; the terrible recollections of a misspent past may be the means of leading you to a new life. Set memory to work.

Next, *his misery bestirred him*. Every pang of hunger that he felt, the sight of his rags, the degradation of associating with swine—all those things drove him back to his father. Oh, sirs, let your very needs, your cravings, your misery, drive you to your God!

Then, *his fears whipped him back*. He said, "I perish with hunger." He had not perished yet, but he was afraid that he soon would do so; he feared that he really would die, for he felt so faint. Oh, sirs, see what will become of you if you do die in your sins! What awaits you but an endless future of limitless misery? Sin will follow you into eternity, and will increase upon you there, and as you shall go on to sin, so shall you go on to sorrow ever-increasing. A deeper degradation and a more tremendous penalty will accompany your sin in the world to come; therefore, let your fears drive you home, as they drove home the poor prodigal.

Meanwhile, *his hope drew him*. This gentle cord was as powerful as the heavy whip: "In my father's house there is bread enough and to spare; I need not perish with hunger, I may yet be filled." Oh, think of what you may yet be! Poor sinner, think of what God can do and is ready to do for you, to do for you even tonight! How happy He can make you! How peaceful and how blessed! So let your hope draw you to him.

Then, *his resolve moved him*. He said, "I will arise, and go to my father." All else drove him or drew him, and now he is resolved to return home. He rose up from the earth on which he had been sitting amidst his filthiness, and he said, "I will." Then the man became a man; he had come to himself, the manhood had come back to him, and he said, "I will, I will."

—The Treasury of the New Testament

MATTHEW HENRY

"I have sinned *against Heaven*, and yet *before thee*."

Thirdly, He would acknowledge himself to have forfeited all the privileges of the family: *I am no more worthy to be called thy son*, *v.* 19. He does not deny the relation (for that was all he had to trust to), but he owns that his father might justly deny the relation. He had, at his own demand, the portion of goods that belonged to him, and had reason to expect no more. It becomes sinners to acknowledge themselves unworthy to receive any favour from God.

Fourthly, He would nevertheless sue for admission into the family, though it were into the meanest post there: "*Make me as one of thy hired servants;* that is good enough, and too good for me." If it be imposed on him as a mortification to sit with the servants, he will not only submit to it, but count it a preferment in comparison with his present state. "*Make me as a hired servant*, that I may show I love my father's house as much as ever I slighted it."

Fifthly, In all this he would have an eye to his father as a father: "*I will arise, and go to my father, and will say unto him, Father*. Eyeing God as a Father, and our Father, will be of great use in our repentance and return to him. It will make our sorrow for sin genuine, our resolutions against it strong, and encourage us to hope for pardon. God delights to be called *Father* both by penitents and petitioners.

(4) What was the performance of this purpose: *He arose, and came to his father*. His good resolve he put in execution without delay; he struck while the iron was hot. Have we said that we will arise and go? Let us immediately arise and come. He did not come halfway, and then pretend that he was tired and could get no further, but, weak and weary as he was, he made a thorough business of it.

3. We have here his reception and entertainment with his father: *He came to his father;* but was he welcome? Yes, heartily welcome. And, by the way, it is an example to parents whose children have been foolish and disobedient, if they repent, not to be harsh and severe with them, but to be governed by the wisdom that is from above, which is *gentle and easy to be entreated*. But it is chiefly designed to set forth the grace and mercy of God to poor sinners that repent and return to him, and his readiness to forgive them. Now here observe,

(1) The great love and affection wherewith the father received the son: *When he was yet a great way off his father saw him*, *v.* 20. He expressed his kindness before the son expressed his repentance. Even *before we call he answers*; for he knows what is in our hearts. How lively are the images presented here! [1] Here were *eyes of mercy*, and those eyes quick-sighted: *When he was yet a great way off his father saw him*, as if from the top of some high tower he had been looking that way which his son was gone, with such a thought as this, "O that I could see yonder wretched son of mine coming home!" This intimates God's desire of the conversion of sinners, and his readiness to meet them that are coming towards him. He is aware of the first inclination towards him. [2] Here were *bowels of mercy*, yearning at the sight of his son: *He had compassion*. Misery is the object of pity, even the misery of a sinner; though he has brought it upon himself, yet God compassionates. [3] Here were *feet of mercy*, and those feet quick-paced: *He ran*. The prodigal son came slowly, under a burden of shame and fear; but the tender father ran to meet him with his encouragements. [4] Here were *arms of mercy*, and those arms stretched out to embrace him: *He fell on his neck*. Though guilty and deserving to be beaten, though dirty and newly come from feeding swine, yet he thus takes him in his arms, and lays him in his bosom. Thus dear are true penitents to God, thus welcome to the Lord Jesus. [5] Here were *lips of mercy*. *He kissed him*. This kiss not only *assured* him of his *welcome*, but *sealed his pardon*; his former follies shall be all forgiven, nor is one word said by way of upbraiding.

(2) The penitent submission which the poor prodigal made to his father (*v.* 21): He *said unto him, Father, I have sinned*. As it commends the good father's kindness that he showed it before the prodigal expressed his repentance, so it commends the prodigal's repentance that he expressed it after his father had shown him so much kindness. When he had received the kiss which sealed his pardon, yet he said, *Father, I have sinned*. Even those that have received the pardon of their sins must have in their hearts a sincere contrition for it. The more we see of God's readiness to *forgive us*, the more difficult it should be to us to *forgive ourselves*.

(3) The splendid provision which this kind father made for the returning prodigal. One word we find in his purpose to say (*v.* 19) which we do not find that he did say (*v.* 21), and that was, *Make me as*

JAMIESON, FAUSSET, BROWN

20. a great way off—Oh yes, when but the face is turned *homeward*, though as yet far, far away, our Father recognizes His own child in us, and bounds to meet us—not saying, Let him come to Me and sue for pardon first, but Himself taking the first step.

fell on his neck and kissed him—What! In all his filth? Yes. In all his rags? Yes. In all his haggard, shattered wretchedness? Yes. "Our Father who art in heaven," is this Thy portraiture? It is even so (Jer. 31:20). And because it is so, I wonder not that such incomparable teaching hath made the world new.

21. Father, I have sinned . . .—"This confession is uttered *after the kiss of reconciliation*" (Ezek. 16:63) [TRENCH].

ADAM CLARKE

20. *And kissed him.* Or "kissed him again and again." The father thus showed his great tenderness towards him, and his great affection for him.

ALEXANDER MACLAREN:

There is no sign that his conscience smote him or that his heart woke in love to his father. His stomach, and it only, urged him to go home. He did, indeed, feel that he had been wrong and had forfeited the right to be called a son; but he did not care much for losing that name or even for losing the love to which it had the right if only he could get as much to eat as one of the hired servants, whose relation to the master was less close, and, in patriarchal times, less happy, than that of slaves born in the house.

One good thing about the lad was that he did not let the grass grow under his feet, but, as soon as he had made the resolution, began to carry it into effect. The bane of many a resolve to go back to God is that it is delayed by procrastination. The ragged prodigal has not much to leave which need hold him, but many such a one says, "I will arise and go to my father tomorrow," and lets all the tomorrows become yesterdays and is sitting among the swine still.

Low as the prodigal's motive for return was, the fact of his return was enough. So is it in regard to our attitude to the gospel. Men may be drawn to give heed to its invitations from the instinct of self-preservation, or from their sense of hungry need and the belief that in it they will find the food they crave for, while there may be little consciousness of longing for more from the Father than the satisfaction of felt wants. The longing for a place in the Father's heart will spring up later, but the beginning of most men's taking refuge in God as revealed in Christ is the gnawing of a hungry heart. The call to all is, "Ho, everyone that thirsteth, come ye to the waters, and he that hath no money; come ye, buy, and eat."—*Expositions of Holy Scripture*

MATTHEW HENRY

one of thy hired servants. We cannot think that he forgot it, much less that he changed his mind, but his father interrupted him, prevented his saying it: "Hold, son, thou art heartily welcome, and, though not *worthy to be called a son*, shalt be treated as a *dear son.*" He who is thus entertained at first needs not ask to be made *as a hired servant*, It is strange that here is not one word of rebuke: "You could never find the way home till beaten hither with your own rod." No, here is nothing like this; which intimates that, when God forgives the sins of true penitents, he forgets them, he remembers them no more. But this is not all; here is rich and royal provision made for him, far beyond what he did or could expect. He would have thought it sufficient if his father had but taken notice of him, and bid him go to the kitchen, and get his dinner with his servants; but God does for those who cast themselves upon his mercy, abundantly above what they are able to ask or think. The prodigal came home between hope and fear, fear of being rejected and hope of being received; but his father was not only better to him than his fears, but better to him than his hopes.

[1] He came home *in rags*, and his father not only *clothed* him, but *adorned* him. He *said to the servants, Bring forth the best robe, and put it on him.* The worst old clothes in the house might have served; but the father calls not for a *coat*, but for a *robe*, the *best robe*. "*That robe, that principal robe*, you know which I mean. Bring hither that robe, and put it on him; he will be ashamed to wear it, and think that it ill becomes him who comes home in such a dirty pickle, but *put it on him*, and *put a ring on his hand*, a signet-ring, with the arms of the family, in token of his being owned as a branch of the family." He came home barefoot, his feet perhaps sore with travel, and therefore, "Put *shoes on his feet.*" Thus does the grace of God provide for true penitents. *First*, The *righteousness of Christ* is the robe with which they are clothed; they *put on the Lord Jesus Christ*. A *new nature* is this *best robe*; true penitents are clothed with this. *Secondly*, The *earnest* of the Spirit is the *ring on the hand*. "*Put a ring on his hand*, to be before him a constant memorial of his father's kindness, that he may never forget it." *Thirdly*, The *preparation of the gospel of peace* is as *shoes for our feet* (Eph. vi. 15). It intimates that they shall go on cheerfully, and with resolution, in the way of religion, as a man does when he has shoes on his feet, above what he does when he is barefoot.

[2] He came home *hungry*, and his father not only *fed him*, but *feasted him* (*v.* 23): "*Bring hither the fatted calf* and *kill it*, that my son may be satisfied with the best we have." The fatted calf can never be better bestowed. It was a great change with the prodigal, who just before *would fain have filled his belly with husks*. How sweet will the supplies of the new covenant be, to those who have been *labouring in vain* for satisfaction in the creature! Now he found his own words made good, *In my father's house there is bread enough and to spare*.

(4) The great joy and rejoicing occasioned by his return. The bringing of the fatted calf was designed to be not only a *feast* for him, but a *festival* for the family: "*Let us all eat, and be merry*, for it is a good day; for *this my son was dead*; we thought that he was dead, but behold *he lives*; he *was lost*, we gave him up for lost, but he *is found*." The conversion of a soul from sin to God is the raising of that soul from death to life, and the finding of that which seemed to be lost: it is a great, and wonderful, and happy change. It is such a change as that upon the face of the earth when the spring returns. The conversion of sinners is greatly pleasing to the God of heaven, and all that belong to his family ought to rejoice in it; those in heaven *do*, and those on earth *should*. It was *the father* that began the joy, and set all the rest on rejoicing. The family complied with the master: *They began to be merry*. God's children and servants ought to be affected with things as he is.

4. We have here the *repining and envying of the elder brother*, which is described by way of reproof to the scribes and Pharisees. He represents it so as not to aggravate the matter, but as allowing them still the privileges of elder brethren. Christ, when he reproved them for their faults, yet accosted them mildly, to smooth them into a good temper towards the poor publicans. But by the *elder brother* here we may understand those who are really good, and never went astray, who *comparatively* need no repentance; and to such these words in the close, *Son, thou art ever with me*, are applicable without any difficulty, but not to the scribes and Pharisees. Now concerning the elder brother, observe,

(1) How *foolish* and *fretful* he was upon occasion of his brother's reception, and how he was disgusted at it. It seems he was abroad *in the field* when his

JAMIESON, FAUSSET, BROWN

A. B. SIMPSON:

There was much that was wrong in the spirit and repentance of the prodigal. There was much of pride still lingering in his heart, and he was really determined to buy his way back to his father's favor; or, at least, to earn some place as a servant at his board. It was a self-righteous idea, which always clings to the fallen heart. I will do something to deserve God's mercy. "I will say to my father, Father, I have sinned and am no more worthy to be called thy son." This is all right; but, "make me one of thy hired servants" is the very self-righteousness which Christ and His apostles declared shut the Pharisees out of the kingdom of heaven. It is the sinner still comforting himself with the thought that he is going to do better, and somehow make up for his past misdeeds by trying to serve God. Happily, when he got back, his father choked all this out of him before he was able to utter it. He let him say, "I have sinned and am no more worthy to be called thy son," and then he stopped short all the rest of his studied speech by his overflowing welcome and his fatherly reconciliation. Therefore, although our penitence may be imperfect, and our faith be weak and faltering, let us come the best we can. This is the beautiful teaching of this parable, and it comes out with still more force in the next division.—*Christ in the Bible*

22. But the Father said . . .—The son has not said all he purposed, not so much, because the father's demonstrations had rekindled the filial, and swallowed up all servile feeling [TRENCH] (see on the word "Father," vs. 18), but because the father's heart is made to appear too full to listen, at that moment, to more in this strain. **the best robe**—Cf. Zech. 3:4, 5, "Take away the filthy garments from him; behold I have clothed thee with change of raiment; and they clothed him with garments" (Isa. 61:10; Rev. 3:18). **a ring**—(Cf. Gen. 41:42; Jas. 2:2). **shoes**—Slaves went barefoot. Thus, we have here a threefold symbol of *freedom* and *honor*, restored, as the fruit of *perfect reconciliation.*

23. the fatted calf—kept for festive occasions.

24. my son—now *twice* his son. **dead . . . lost**—to *me;* to *himself*—to my service, my satisfaction; to his own dignity, peace, profit. **alive again . . . found**—to all these. **merry**—(See on vs. 10).

25. in the field—engaged in his father's business: cf. vs. 29, "These many years do I *serve* thee."

ADAM CLARKE

22. *Bring forth the best robe.* "Bring out that chief garment," the garment which was laid by, to be used only on birthdays or festival times. *Put a ring on his hand.* Giving a ring was in ancient times a mark of honor and dignity. See Gen. xli. 42; 1 Kings xxi. 8; Esther viii. 2; Dan. vi. 17; Jas. ii. 2. *Shoes on his feet.* Formerly those who were captivated had their shoes taken off, Isa. xx. 1; and when they were restored to liberty their shoes were restored. See 2 Chron. xxviii. 15.

23. *The fatted calf, and kill it.* "Sacrifice it." In ancient times the animals provided for public feasts were first sacrificed to God. The blood of the beast being poured out before God, by way of atonement for sin, the flesh was considered as consecrated, and the guests were considered as feeding on divine food.

24. *Was dead.* Lost to all good—given up to all evil. In this figurative sense the word is used by the best Greek writers.

25. *His elder son.* Meaning probably persons of a regular moral life, who needed no repentance in comparison of the prodigal already described. *In the field.* Attending the concerns of the farm.

MATTHEW HENRY

brother came, and by the time he had returned home the *mirth* was *begun*: *When he drew nigh to the house he heard music and dancing, v.* 25. He enquired *what these things meant* (*v.* 26), and was informed that his brother was come, and his father had made him a feast for his *welcome home*, and great joy there was because he had received him *safe and sound, v.* 27. It is but one word in the original, he had *received* him *ὑγιαίνοντα—in health*, well both in body and mind. He received him not only well in body, but a penitent, returned to his *right mind*, cured of his vices, else he had not been received *safe* and *sound*. Now this offended him to the highest degree: *He was angry, and would not go in* (*v.* 28), because he would intimate to his father that he should have kept out his younger brother. This shows what is a common fault,

[1] In men's families. Those who have always been a comfort to their parents think they should have the monopoly of their parents' favours, and are apt to be *too sharp* upon those who have transgressed.

[2] In God's family. Those who are comparatively *innocents* seldom know how to be compassionate towards those who are manifestly *penitents*. The language of such we have here, in what the *elder brother* said (*v.* 29, 30). *First*, He *boasted of himself* and *his own virtue* and *obedience*. *Lo, these many years do I serve thee, neither transgressed I at any time thy commandment*. It is too common for those that are better than their neighbours to boast of it. I am apt to think that this elder brother said more than was true, that he had never *transgressed his father's commands*, for then I believe he would not have been so obstinate as now he was to *his father's entreaties*. Those that have long served God, and been kept from gross sins, have a great deal to be humbly thankful for, but nothing proudly to boast of. *Secondly*, He *complained of his father*: *Thou never gavest me a kid, that I might make merry with my friends*. He was out of humour now, else he would not have made this complaint; for, no question, if he had asked such a thing at any time, he might have had it at the first word. The *killing of the fatted calf* put him upon making this peevish reflection. When men are *in a passion* they are apt to reflect in a way they would not if they were in their right mind. He had many a time been merry with him and the family; but his father had never given him so much as a kid, which was but a small token of love compared with the *fatted calf*. Those that think *highly* of themselves and their services are apt to think *hardly* of their master and meanly of his favours. We ought to own ourselves utterly unworthy of those mercies which God has thought fit to give us, and therefore we must not *complain*. He would have had a kid, to *make merry with his friends* abroad, whereas the *fatted calf* was given to his brother, not to *make merry with his friends* abroad, but *with the family* at home: the mirth of God's children should be with their father and his family, and not with *any other friends*. *Thirdly*, He was very *ill-humoured* towards his younger brother. Some good people are apt to be overtaken in this fault, to look with disdain upon those who have not preserved their reputation so clean as they have done, though they have given very good evidence of their repentance and reformation. This is not the Spirit of Christ, but of the Pharisees. Let us observe the instances of it. 1. He *would not go in*; one house shall not hold him and his own brother, no, not his *father's house*. Though we are to shun the society of those sinners by whom we are in danger of being infected, yet we must not be shy of the company of penitent sinners, by whom we may get good. He saw that his father had *taken him in*, and yet he would not *go in* to him. We think too well of ourselves, if we cannot find in our hearts to *receive* those whom God *hath received*, and who are taken into friendship and fellowship with him. 2. He would not call him *brother*; but *this thy son*, which sounds arrogant, and not without reflection upon his father. Let us give our relations the titles that belong to them. Let the rich call the poor *brethren*, and let the innocents call the penitents so. 3. He *aggravated his brother's faults*, and made the worst of them: He *is thy son, who hath devoured thy living with harlots*. He had spent his own portion foolishly enough (whether *upon harlots* or no we are not told before, perhaps that was only the language of the elder brother's jealousy and ill will), but that he had devoured *all his father's living* was false; the father had still a good estate. Now this shows how apt we are to *make the worst* of everything, and to set it out in the blackest colours, which is not doing as we would be done by, nor as our heavenly Father does by us. 4. He *grudged* him the *kindness* that his father *showed him*: *Thou hast killed for him the fatted calf*. It is a wrong thing to *envy* penitents

JAMIESON, FAUSSET, BROWN

29. these many years . . . neither transgressed I at any time . . .—The words are not to be pressed too far. He is merely contrasting *his constancy of love and service* with the conduct of his brother; just as Job, resenting the charge of *hypocrisy* by his friends, speaks as if nothing could be laid to his charge (Job 23:10-12), and David too (Ps. 18:20-24). *The father attests the truth of all he says.* **never . . . a kid**—I say not a *calf*, but not even a kid. **that I might make merry with my friends**—Here lay his misapprehension. It was no entertainment for the gratification of the prodigal: it was a *father's* expression of the joy *he* felt at his recovery.

thy son . . . thy living—How unworthy a reflection on the common father of both, for the one not only to disown the other, but fling him over upon his father, as if he should say, Take him, and have joy of him!

ADAM CLARKE

He heard music. Symphonias, a number of sounds mingled together, as in a concert. *Dancing*. But Le Clerc denies that the word means *dancing* at all, as it properly means a "choir of singers." The "symphony" mentioned before may mean the musical instruments which accompanied the choirs of singers.

28. *He was angry*. This refers to the indignation of the scribes and Pharisees, mentioned in vv. 1-2. In every point of view, the anger of the old son was improper and unreasonable. He had already received his part of the inheritance (see v. 12), and his profligate brother had received no more than what was his just dividend. Besides, what the father had acquired since that division he had a right to dispose of as he pleased, even to give it all to one son; nor did the ancient customs of the Asiatic countries permit the other children to claim any share in such property thus disposed of.

29. *Never gavest me a kid*. It is evident from v. 12 that the father gave him his portion when his profligate brother claimed his, for he divided his whole substance between them. And though he had not claimed it, so as to separate from, and live independently of, his father, yet he might have done so whenever he chose; and therefore his complaining was both undutiful and unjust.

30. *This thy son*. "This son of thine"—words expressive of supreme contempt. *This son*—he would not condescend to call him by his name, or to acknowledge him for his brother; and at the same time bitterly reproaches his amiable father for his affectionate tenderness, and readiness to receive his once undutiful, but now penitent, child!

G. CAMPBELL MORGAN:

There is another son. What are we to do with this elder son? It is rather interesting how men have struggled to explain this. I have heard it said that this is the difference between the Jew and the Gentile. That is very absurd, because we cannot say of the Jew what the father said of this son. The difference is not between Jew and Gentile. The difference is between two sons, one self-righteous and the other a sinner.

But that is not all. Look at this elder son. What do we find? He was devoted to his father's law, and he was devoted to his father's service; but he was entirely out of sympathy with his father's heart; and therefore unable to set the true value upon his brother. The Pharisees and scribes were the men Jesus was looking at when He talked about the elder son. He was taking them at their own valuation, devoted to the law and service of God. To them He said, in effect, "You cannot understand God, you cannot understand the heart of God; if you did, you could not look with contempt upon these men outside, with whom I am mixing." The elder son was out of sympathy with the heart of his father. How many sons of God are like that, even in the Church today!

—The Gospel According to Luke

MATTHEW HENRY

the grace of God. As we must not envy those that *are* the worst of sinners the gifts of common providence, so we must not envy those that *have been* the worst of sinners the gifts of covenant love upon their repentance; we must not envy them any extraordinary gift which God bestows upon them. Paul, before his conversion, had been a prodigal, yet when after his conversion he had greater measures of grace given him than the other apostles, they who were the elder brethren did not envy him his visions and revelations, nor his more extensive usefulness, but *glorified God in him*, which ought to be an example to us, as the reverse of this elder brother.

(2) Let us now see how *favourable* and *friendly* his father was in *his carriage towards him* when he was thus sour and ill-humoured. This is as surprising as the former. Methinks the mercy and grace of our God in Christ shine almost as brightly in his tender and gentle bearing with *peevish saints*, as before in his reception of prodigal sinners upon their repentance. The disciples of Christ themselves had many infirmities, and were men subject to like passions as others, yet Christ bore with them.

[1] When he would not come in, his *father came out, and entreated him*, accosted him mildly, gave him good words, and desired him to come in. He might justly have said, "If he will not come in, let him stay out. Is not the house my own? and may I not do what I please in it? Is not the fatted calf my own? and may I not do what I please with it?" No, as he went to meet the younger son, so now he goes to court the elder. This is designed to represent to us the goodness of God; how strangely gentle and winning he has been towards those that were strangely froward and provoking. It is to teach all superiors to be mild and gentle with their inferiors, even when they are in a fault and passionately justify themselves in it. Even in that case let fathers *not provoke their children to more wrath*, and let *masters forbear threatening*, and both show all *meekness*.

[2] His father assured him that the kind entertainment he gave his younger brother was neither any reflection upon him nor should be any prejudice to him (*v.* 31): "*Son, thou art ever with me;* the reception of him is no rejection of thee, nor what is laid out on him any sensible diminution of what I design for thee; *all that I have is thine*, by an indefeasible title." If he had not *given him a kid to make merry with his friends*, he had allowed him to eat bread at his table continually; and it is better to be *happy with our Father* in heaven than *merry* with any *friend* we have in this world. *First*, It is the unspeakable happiness of all the children of God, that they are, and shall be, ever with him. All that he has is theirs; for, *if children, then heirs*, Rom. viii. 17. *Secondly, Therefore* we ought not to envy others God's grace to them because we shall have never the less for their sharing in it. If we be true believers, all that God is, all that he has, is *ours*; and, if others come to be true believers, all that he is, and all that he has, is theirs too, and yet we have not the less, as they that walk in the light and warmth of the sun have all the benefit they can have by it, and yet not the less for others having as much.

[3] His father gave him a good reason, *It was meet that we should make merry and be glad, v.* 32. He might have insisted upon his own authority: "It was *my will* that the family should make merry and be glad." But it does not become even those that have authority to be vouching and appealing to it upon every occasion, which does but make it cheap and common; it is better to give a convincing reason, as the father does here: *It was meet that we should make merry* for the return of a prodigal son, more than for the perseverance of a dutiful son; for, though the latter is a greater blessing to a family, yet the former is a more sensible pleasure. Any family would be much more transported with joy at the raising of a dead child to life, than for the continued life and health of many children. We do not find that the elder brother made any reply to what his father said, which intimates that he was well reconciled to his prodigal brother; and his father put him in mind that he was his brother: *This thy brother*. A good man, though he have not such a command of himself at all times as to *keep his temper*, yet will, with the grace of God, *recover his temper.*

JAMIESON, FAUSSET, BROWN

ALBERT BARNES:

30. "This thy son." This son of "thine." This is an expression of great contempt. He did not call him his brother, but his father's son, to show at once his contempt for his younger brother and for his father for having received him as he did. Never was there a more striking instance of petty malice, or more unjustifiable disregard of a father's conduct and will.

"Thy living." Thy property. This is still designed to irritate the father and set him against his younger son. It was true that the younger son had been guilty and foolish and ungrateful; but he was penitent, and that was of more consequence to the father than all his property; and in the joy that he was penitent and was safe, he forgot his ingratitude and folly. So should the elder son have done.

31. "All I have is thine." The property was divided. What remained was in reality the elder son's. He was heir to it all, and had a right, if he chose, to use it. He had therefore no right to complain.

This instructive and beautiful parable was designed to vindicate the conduct of Jesus—to show that it was right to receive sinners, and that the conduct of the Pharisees was unreasonable. The elder son represents the Pharisees; the younger, the returning sinner, whether Jew or Gentile; and the father, God, who is willing to receive them. The parable had the designed effect. It silenced the adversaries of Jesus and vindicated his own conduct. There is not, perhaps, anywhere to be found a more beautiful and touching narrative than this. Every circumstance is tender and happily chosen; every word has a meaning; every image is beautiful; and the narrative closes just where it is fitted to make the deepest impression.—*Popular Commentary*

came his father out, and entreated him—"Like as a father pitieth his children, so the Lord pitieth them that fear Him" (Ps. 103:13). As it is the elder brother who now errs, so it is *the same paternal compassion* which had fallen on the neck of the younger that comes forth and pleads with the elder.

31. Son . . .—The father resents not the insult—how could he, after the largeness of heart which had kissed the returning prodigal? He calmly expostulates with him, "Son, listen to reason. What need for special, exuberant joy over thee? Didst thou say, 'Lo, these many years do I serve thee?' In that saidst thou truly; but *just for that reason* do I not set the whole household a-rejoicing over thee. For thee is reserved *what is higher still*—a tranquil lifelong satisfaction in thee, as a true-hearted faithful son in thy father's house, nor of the inheritance reserved for thee is aught alienated by this festive and fitting joy over the once foolish but now wise and newly recovered one."

32. It was meet—Was it possible he should simply take his long vacant place in the family without one special sign of wonder and delight at the change? Would that have been *nature?* But *this* being the meaning of the festivity, it would for that very reason be *temporary*. In time, the dutifulness of even the younger son would become the *law* and not the *exception;* he too at length might venture to say, "Lo, these many years do I serve thee"; and of him the father would say, "Son, thou art ever with me." In that case, therefore, it would *not* be "meet that they should make merry and be glad." The lessons are obvious, but how beautiful! (1) The deeper sunk and the longer estranged any sinner is, the more exuberant is the joy which his recovery occasions. (2) Such joy is *not* the portion of those whose whole lives have been spent in the service of their Father in heaven. (3) Instead of grudging the want of this, they should deem it the highest testimony to their lifelong fidelity, that something better is reserved for them—the deep, abiding complacency of their Father in heaven.

ADAM CLARKE

31. *All that I have is thine.* See on v. 28.

32. *This thy brother.* Or "this brother of thine." To awaken this ill-natured, angry, inhumane man to a proper sense of his duty, to both his parent and his brother, this amiable father returns him his own unkind words, but in a widely different spirit. This son of mine to whom I show mercy is *your brother,* to whom you should show tenderness and affection, especially as he is no longer the person he was. He was dead in sin—he is quickened by the power of God; he was *lost* to you, to me, to himself, and to our God, but now he is *found.* This, as well as the two preceding parables, was designed to vindicate the conduct of our blessed Lord in receiving taxgatherers and heathens. And as the Jews, to whom it was addressed, could not but approve of the conduct of this benevolent father, and reprobate that of his elder son, so they could not but justify the conduct of Christ towards those outcasts of men, and at least in the silence of their hearts pass sentence of condemnation upon themselves.

MATTHEW HENRY

CHAPTER 16

We mistake if we imagine that the design of Christ's doctrine and holy religion was either to amuse us with notions of divine mysteries or to entertain us with notions of divine mercies. No, the divine revelation of both these in the gospel is intended to engage and quicken us to the practice of Christian duties, to the duty of beneficence and doing good to those who stand in need of anything that either we have or can do for them. We are but *stewards of the manifold grace of God.* It is our wisdom to think how we may make what we have in the world turn to a good account. If we would act wisely, we must be as diligent and industrious to employ our riches in the acts of piety and charity, in order to promote our future and eternal welfare, as worldly men are in laying them out to the greatest temporal profit.

I. The parable itself, in which all the children of men are represented as *stewards* of what they have in this world. Whatever we have, the property of it is God's; we have only the use of it.

1. Here is the *dishonesty* of this *steward.* He *wasted his lord's goods,* and for this he was *accused to his lord, v.* 1. We are all *liable* to the same charge. We have not made a due improvement of what God has entrusted us with in this world. That we may not be for this *judged of our Lord,* it concerns us to *judge ourselves.*

2. His *discharge* out of his place. His lord *called for him,* and said, "*How is it that I hear this of thee?*" He speaks as one sorry to find himself disappointed in him: it troubles him to hear it; but the steward cannot deny it, and therefore there is no remedy, he must make up his accounts, and be gone in a little time, *v.* 2. Now this is designed to teach us, (1) That we must all of us shortly be discharged from *our stewardship* in this world. Death will come, and *dismiss* us from our stewardship, others will come in our places. (2) That our discharge from our stewardship at death is *just,* and what we have deserved, for we have wasted our Lord's goods. (3) That when our stewardship is taken from us we must *give an account* of it to our Lord.

3. His *after-wisdom.* Now he began to consider, *What shall I do? v.* 3. He would have done well to have considered this before, but it is better to *consider* late than never. He must live; which way shall he have a livelihood? (1) He knows that he has not such a degree of industry in him as to get his living by work: "*I cannot dig.*" But why can he not dig? The truth is, he is *lazy.* His *cannot* is a *will not*; it is not a natural but a moral disability that he labours under. He *cannot dig,* for he was never used to it. (2) He knows that he has not such a degree of *humility* as to get his bread by begging: *To beg I am ashamed.* This was the language of his pride, as the former of his slothfulness. This steward had more reason to be ashamed of cheating his master than of begging his bread. (3) He therefore determines to make friends of his lord's debtors: "*I am resolved what to do* (*v.* 4). I am acquainted with my lord's tenants, have done them many a good turn, and now I will do them one more, which will so oblige them that they will bid me welcome to their houses. Till I can better dispose of myself, I will quarter upon them, and go from one good house to another." Accordingly, he sent for one, who owed his lord *a hundred measures of oil*: *Take thy bill,* said he, and *sit down quickly, and write fifty* (*v.* 6); so he reduced his debt to the one half. "*Sit down quickly,* and do it, lest we be taken treating, and suspected." He took another, who owed his lord *a hundred measures of wheat,* and bade him write *fourscore* (*v.* 7). See here what uncertain things our worldly possessions are; they are most so to those who have most of them, who devolve upon others all the care concerning them, and so put it into their power to *cheat them.* See also what treachery is to be found even among those in whom trust is reposed. Though this steward is turned out for dealing dishonestly, yet still he does so. So rare is it for men to mend of a fault, though they smart for it.

4. The approbation of this: *The lord commended the unjust steward, because he had done wisely, v.* 8. It may be meant of *his lord,* the lord of that servant, who yet was pleased with his ingenuity and policy for himself; but, taking it so, the latter part of the verse must be the words of *our Lord,* and therefore I think the whole is meant of him. He does not commend him because he had done *falsely* to his master, but because he had done *wisely* for himself. Yet perhaps herein he did well for his master too, and but justly with the tenants. He knew what *hard bargains* he had *set them,* so that they could not *pay their rent.* He now, at going off, did as he ought to do both in justice and charity. He had been *all for his lord,* but now he begins to consider the tenants, that he might

JAMIESON, FAUSSET, BROWN

CHAPTER 16

Vss. 1-31. Parables of the Unjust Steward and of the Rich Man and Lazarus, or, the Right Use of Money.

1. steward—manager of his estate. **accused**—informed upon. **had wasted**—rather, "was wasting."

3. cannot dig . . . to beg, ashamed—therefore, when dismissed, shall be in utter want.

4. may receive me . . .—Observe his one object—*when cast out of one home to secure another.* This is the key to the parable, on which there have been many differing views. **5-7. fifty . . . fourscore**—deducting a half from the debt of the one, and a fifth from that of the other.

8. the lord—evidently the steward's lord, so called in vss. 3, 5. **commended . . .**—not for his "injustice," but "because he had done *wisely,*" or prudently; with commendable *foresight* and *skilful adaptation of means to end.*

ADAM CLARKE

CHAPTER 16

1. *A steward.* One who superintends domestic concerns, and ministers to the support of the family, having the products of the field and business put into his hands for this very purpose. *Wasted his goods.* Had been profuse and profligate, and had embezzled his master's substance.

2. *Give an account of thy.* Produce your books of receipts and disbursements, that I may see whether the accusation against you is true or false. The original may be translated, "Give up the business of the stewardship."

3. *I cannot dig.* He could not submit to become a common day laborer, which was both a severe and base employment. *To beg I am ashamed.* And as these were the only honest ways left him to procure a morsel of bread, and he would not submit to either, he found he must continue the system of knavery, in order to provide for his idleness and luxury, or else starve.

4. *They may receive me.* That is, the debtors and tenants, who paid their debts and rents, not in money, but in kind; such as wheat, oil, and other produce of their lands.

6. *An hundred measures of oil.* "A hundred baths." The *bath* was the largest measure of capacity among the Hebrews, except the *homer,* of which it was the tenth part: see Ezek. xlv. 11, 14. It is equal to the *ephah,* i.e., to seven gallons and a half of our measure. *Take thy bill.* "Your account." The writing in which the debt was specified, together with the obligation to pay so much, at such and such times. This appears to have been in the handwriting of the debtor, and probably signed by the steward, and this precluded imposition on each part. To prevent all appearance of forgery in this case, he is desired to write it over again, and to cancel the old engagement.

7. *An hundred measures of wheat.* "A hundred cors." *Koros,* from the Hebrew *cor,* was the largest measure of capacity among the Hebrews, whether for solids or liquids. As the *bath* was equal to the *ephah,* so the *cor* was equal to the *homer.* It contained about seventy-five gallons and five pints English.

8. *The lord commended.* Viz., the master of this unjust steward. He spoke highly of the address and cunning of his iniquitous servant. He had, on his own principles, made a very prudent provision for his support; but his master no more approved of his conduct in this than he did in his wasting his substance before. From the ambiguous and improper manner in which this is expressed in the common English translation, it has been supposed that our blessed

F. B. MEYER:

The right use of money. We are all stewards, but how much we waste! Well might our Master deprive us of our position and trust! The unjust steward used his opportunity of ingratiating himself with the tenants at the landowner's cost. He thus secured for himself a welcome to their homes, but his deceit came to light and he was dismissed. Our Master did not commend his fraud, but pointed out that the children of this world are singularly alive to their future and prepare for its contingencies. If they make a wrong use of money to provide for the future, how much more should Christians make a right use of it, so that when they die they may be welcomed to the eternal home by those whom they have benefited!—*Bible Commentary*

MATTHEW HENRY

have *their favour* when he had lost *his lord's.* Now this forecast of his, for a comfortable subsistence in this world, shames our improvidence for another world: *The children of this world are wiser for their generation*, better consult their worldly interest and advantage, than the *children of light*, in *their generation*, that is, in the concerns of their souls and eternity. (1) The wisdom of worldly people in the concerns of this world is to be *imitated* by us in the concerns of our souls: it is their principle to improve their opportunities, to do that first which is most needful. O that we were thus wise in our spiritual affairs! (2) The children of light are commonly *outdone* by the children of this world. Not that the children of this world are *truly wise*; it is only *in their generation.* But in that they are *wiser than the children of light in theirs.* We live as if we were to be *here always* and as if there were not *another life after this.* Though as *children of the light* we cannot but see *another world* before us, yet we do not prepare for it, do not send our best effects and best affections thither, as we should.

II. The application of this parable, and the inferences drawn from it (*v.* 9): "*I say unto you*, you my disciples" (for to them this parable is directed, *v.* 1), "though you have but little in this world, consider how you may do good with that little." Observe,

1. What it is that our Lord Jesus here exhorts us to: "*Make to yourselves friends of the mammon of unrighteousness.*" It is the wisdom of the men of this world so to manage their money as that they may have the benefit of it hereafter, and not for this present only. Now we should learn of them to make use of our money so as that we may be the better for it hereafter in another world, as they do in hopes to be the better for it hereafter in this world. And in our case, though whatever we have *are our Lord's goods*, yet, as long as we dispose of them among *our Lord's tenants* and for their advantage, it is so far from being reckoned a wrong to our Lord, that it is a duty to him as well as policy for ourselves. (1) The things of this world are the *mammon of unrighteousness*, or the false *mammon.* Riches are perishing things, and will disappoint those that raise their expectations from them. (2) Though this *mammon of unrighteousness* is not to be *trusted to* for a happiness, yet it may and must be *made use of* in subserviency to our pursuit of that which is our happiness. Though we cannot find true satisfaction in it, yet we may *make to ourselves friends* with it. (3) At death we must all *fail*, *ὅταν ἐκλίπητε—when ye suffer an eclipse.* Death eclipses us. A tradesman is said to *fail* when he becomes a *bankrupt.* We must all thus fail shortly; death shuts up the shop, seals up the hand. (4) It ought to be our great concern to make it sure to ourselves, that *when* we *fail* at death we may be *received into everlasting habitations* in heaven. Christ is gone before, to prepare a place for those that are his, and is there ready to *receive them.* See 1 Tim. vi. 17–19, which explains this here.

2. With what arguments he presses this exhortation. (1) If we do not make a right use of the *gifts of God's providence*, how can we expect from him the *gifts of his spiritual grace*? Our unfaithfulness in the use of them may be justly reckoned a *forfeiture* of that grace which is necessary to bring us to glory, *v.* 10–14. The riches of this world are the *less*; grace and glory are the *greater.* Now if we be unfaithful in the less, it may justly be feared that we should be so in the gifts of God's grace, and therefore they will be denied us: *He that is faithful in that which is least is faithful also in much*, He that serves God, and does good, with his money, will serve God, and do good, with the more noble and valuable talents of wisdom and grace, but he that buries the *one talent* of this world's wealth will never improve the *five talents* of spiritual riches. The riches of this world are the *unrighteous mammon*, which is hastening from us apace, and, if we would make any advantage of it, we must bestir ourselves quickly; if we do not, how can we expect to be entrusted with spiritual riches, which are the only *true riches*? *v.* 11. Let us be convinced of this, that those are *truly* rich, and *very* rich, who are rich in *faith*, and rich *towards God*, rich in Christ, the *kingdom of God and the righteousness thereof.* If other things be added to us, by using them well we may take the faster hold of the *true riches*, and may be qualified to receive yet *more grace* from God. To a man that is *faithful in the unrighteous mammon*, he gives the *true riches.* The riches of this world are *another man's.* They are not *our own*; for they are God's. They are *another man's*; we have them from others; we use them for others; and we must shortly leave them to others. But spiritual and eternal riches are *our own inseparably*; they are a good part that will never be taken away from us. If we make Christ our own, and the promises our own, and heaven our own, we have that which we

JAMIESON, FAUSSET, BROWN

children of this world—so ch. 20:34; cf. Psalm 17:14 ("their portion in this life"); Philippians 3:19 ("mind earthly things"); Psalm 4:6, 7. **in**—or "for"—**their generation**—i.e., for the purposes of the "world" they are "of." The greater wisdom (or shrewdness) of the one, in *adaptation of means to ends,* and in energetic, determined prosecution of them, is none of it for *God* and *eternity*—a region they were never in, an atmosphere they never breathed, an undiscovered world, an unborn existence to them—but all for the purposes of their own grovelling and fleeting generation. **children of light**—(so John 12:36; Eph. 5:8; I Thess. 5:5). Yet this is only "as night-birds see better in the dark than those of the day—owls than eagles" [CAJETAN and TRENCH]. But we may learn lessons from them, as our Lord now shows, and "be wise as *serpents.*"

9. Make . . . friends of—Turn to your advantage; i.e., as the steward did, "by showing mercy to the poor" (Dan. 4:27; cf. 12:33; 14:13, 14).

mammon of unrighteousness—treacherous, precarious. (See on Matt. 6:24.) **ye fail**—in respect of life. **they may receive you**—not generally, "ye may be received" (as ch. 6:38, "shall *men* give"), but "those ye have relieved may rise up as witnesses for you" at the great day. Then, like the steward, when turned out of one home shall ye secure another; but better than he, a heavenly for an earthly, an everlasting for a temporary habitation. Money is not here made the key to heaven, more than "the deeds done in the body" in general, according to which, as a test of character—but not by the merit of which—men are to be judged (II Cor. 5:10, and see Matt. 25:34-40).

10. He . . .—a maxim of great pregnancy and value; rising from the *prudence* which the steward had to the *fidelity* which he had not, the "*harmlessness* of the dove, to which the serpent" with all his "*wisdom*" is a total stranger. Fidelity depends not on the *amount entrusted,* but on the *sense of responsibility.* He that feels this in little will feel it in much, and conversely. **11, 12. unrighteous mammon**—To the whole of this He applies the disparaging term "what is least," in contrast with "the true riches."

12. another man's . . . your own—an important turn to the subject. Here all we have is *on trust* as stewards, who have an account to render. Hereafter, what the faithful have will be *their own property,* being no longer on probation, but in secure, undisturbed, rightful, everlasting possession and enjoyment of all that is graciously bestowed on us. Thus money is neither to be *idolized* nor *despised;* we must sit loose to it and use it for God's glory.

ADAM CLARKE

Lord commended the conduct of this wicked man; but the word there translated *lord* simply means the "master" of the unjust steward. *The children of this world.* Such as mind worldly things only, without regarding God or their souls. A phrase by which the Jews always designate the Gentiles. *Children of light.* Such as are illuminated by the Spirit of God, and regard worldly things only as far as they may subserve the great purposes of their salvation, and become the instruments of good to others. But ordinarily the former evidence more carefulness and prudence in providing for the support and comfort of this life than the latter do in providing for another world.

9. *The mammon of unrighteousness.* Literally, "the mammon of injustice." Riches promise much, and perform nothing; they excite hope and confidence, and deceive both. In making a man depend on them for happiness, they rob him of the salvation of God and of eternal glory. For these reasons they are represented as unjust and deceitful. *When ye fail.* That is, when ye "die." The Septuagint use the word in this very sense, Jer. xlii. 17, 22. So does Josephus, *War*, chap. iv. 1, 9. *They may receive you.* The expression seems to be a mere Hebraism: *they may receive you*, for "ye shall be received"; i.e., God shall admit you, if you make a faithful use of His gifts and graces. He who does not make a faithful use of what he has received from his Maker has no reason to hope for eternal felicity.

10. *He that is faithful in that which is least.* He who has the genuine principles of fidelity in him will make a point of conscience of carefully attending to even the smallest things; and it is by habituating himself to act uprightly in little things that he acquires the gracious habit of acting with propriety, fidelity, honor, and conscience in matters of the greatest concern. On the contrary, he who does not act uprightly in small matters will seldom feel himself bound to pay much attention to the dictates of honor and conscience, in cases of high importance. Can we reasonably expect that a man who is continually falling by little things has power to resist temptations to great evils?

12. *That which is another man's.* Or rather "another's." That is, worldly riches, called another's: (1) Because they belong to God, and He has not designed that they should be any man's portion; (2) Because they are continually changing their possessors, being in the way of commerce, and in providence going from one to another. *That which is your own.* Grace and glory, which God has particularly designed for you.

MATTHEW HENRY

may truly call *our own.* But how can we expect God should *enrich us* with these if we do not serve him with our worldly possessions, of which we are but stewards?

(2) We have no other way to prove ourselves the servants of God than by giving up ourselves so entirely to his service as to make all our worldly gain serviceable to us in his service (*v.* 13): *No servant can serve two masters.* If a man will *love* the world, and *hold to that,* it cannot be but he will *hate God* and *despise* him. But, on the other hand, if a man will *love God,* and *adhere* to him, he will comparatively *hate* the world, and the things of the world shall be made to help him in serving God and working out his salvation. The matter is here laid plainly before us: *Ye cannot serve God and mammon.* So divided are their interests that their services can never be *compounded.*

3. We are here told what entertainment this doctrine of Christ met with among the Pharisees.

(1) They wickedly *ridiculed* him, *v.* 14. *The Pharisees, who were covetous, heard all these things,* and could not contradict him, but *they derided him.* Let us consider this as their *sin,* and the fruit of their *covetousness,* which was their reigning sin. Many that make a great profession of religion and abound in the exercise of devotion, are yet ruined by the love of the world. These covetous Pharisees could not bear to have that *touched,* which was their *Delilah,* their darling lust; for this they derided him, *they snuffled up their noses at him,* or blew their noses on him. It is an expression of the utmost scorn and disdain imaginable. They laughed at him for going so contrary to the opinion and way of the world. It is common for those to *make a jest* of the word of God who are resolved that they will not be ruled by it. Our Lord Jesus endured not only the *contradiction* of sinners, but their *contempt.* He that spoke as never man spoke was bantered and ridiculed, that his faithful ministers, whose preaching is unjustly *derided,* may not be disheartened at it. It is no disgrace to a man to be laughed at, but to deserve to be laughed at.

(2) He justly reproved them for *deceiving* themselves with the shows and colours of piety, *v.* 15. **Here is,**

[1] Their *specious outside. First,* They *justified themselves before men;* they denied whatever ill was laid to their charge. They claimed to be looked upon as men of singular sanctity and devotion: "*You are they that* make it your business to court the opinion of men, and will justify yourselves before the world; you are *notorious* for this." *Secondly,* They were *highly esteemed among men.* Men did not only *acquit* them, but *applauded* them, not only as *good men,* but as the *best of men.*

[2] Their *odious inside,* which was under the eye of God: "He *knows your heart,* and it is in his sight an *abomination.*" It is folly to *justify ourselves before men,* and to think this enough to bear us out, that men *know no ill* of us; for God, who knows our hearts, knows that ill of us which no one else can know. This ought to check our value for ourselves, that *God knows our hearts,* for we have reason to abase and distrust ourselves. It is folly to judge of persons and things by the opinion of men concerning them, and to go down with the stream of vulgar estimate; for that which is *highly esteemed among men* is perhaps *an abomination in the sight of God,* who sees things as they are. There are those whom men despise and condemn who yet are accepted and approved of God, 2 Cor. x. 18.

(3) He turned from them to the publicans and sinners, as more likely to be wrought upon by his gospel than those covetous conceited Pharisees (*v.* 16): "The *law and the prophets were* indeed *until John;* but since John Baptist appeared *the kingdom of God is preached. Every man presses* into the gospel kingdom, Gentiles as well as Jews. It is not as the Jewish economy was, when *salvation was of the Jews;* but it is made a particular personal concern, and therefore *every man* that is convinced he has a soul to save, thrusts to get in, lest he should come short." Some give this sense of it; they derided Christ for speaking in contempt of riches, for, thought they, were there not many promises of riches and other temporal good things in the *law and the prophets*? "It is true," saith Christ, "so it was, but now that the kingdom of God is begun to be preached, blessed are the poor, and the mourners, and the persecuted. Now that the *gospel is preached* the eyes of the people are opened, they *press* with a holy violence into the kingdom of God." Those that would go to heaven must take pains, must strive against the stream, must press against the crowd that are going the contrary way.

(4) Yet still he protests against any design to in-

JAMIESON, FAUSSET, BROWN

13. can serve—be *entirely at the command* of; and this is true even where the services are not opposed. **hate . . . love**—showing that the two *here intended* are in uncompromising hostility to each other: an awfully searching principle!

14-18. covetous . . . derided him—sneered at Him; their master-sin being too plainly struck at for them to relish. But it was easier to *run down* than to *refute*

15. justify yourselves—make a show of righteousness. **highly esteemed among men**—generally carried away by plausible appearances. (See I Sam. 16:7; and ch. 14:11.)

16. The law . . .—(See on Matt. 11:13). **every man presseth . . .**—Publicans and sinners, all indiscriminately, are eagerly pressing into it; and ye, interested adherents of the mere forms of an economy which is passing away, "discerning not the signs of this time," will allow the tide to go past you and be found a stranded monument of blindness and obstinacy.

ADAM CLARKE

13. *No servant can serve two masters.* The heart will be either wholly taken up with God or wholly engrossed with the world.

14. *They derided him.* Or rather, "They treated Him with the utmost contempt." So we may translate the original words, which literally signify, "They turned up their noses at Him."

15. *Ye . . . justify yourselves.* "You declare yourselves to be just."

16. *The law and the prophets were until John.* The law and the prophets continued to be the sole teachers till John came, who first began to proclaim the glad tidings of the kingdom of God. And now, he who wishes to be made a partaker of the blessings of that Kingdom must "rush speedily" into it, as there will be but a short time before an utter destruction shall fall upon this ungodly race. They who wish to be saved must imitate those who take a city by storm—rush into it, without delay, as the Romans are about to do into Jerusalem.

A. T. ROBERTSON:

14. "Who were lovers of money" (*philarguroi huparchontes*). Literally, being lovers of money. *Philarguroi* is an old word, but in the N.T. only here and 2 Tim. 3:2. It is from *philos* and *arguros.* "Heard" (*ekouon*). Imperfect active, were listening all the while Jesus was talking to the disciples (vv. 1-13). "And they scoffed at him" (*kai exemukterizon*). Imperfect active again of *ekmukterizo.* LXX where late writers use simple verb. In the N.T. only here and Luke 23:35. It means to turn out or up the nose at one, to sneer, to scoff. The Romans had a phrase, *naso adunco suspendere,* to hang on the hooked nose (the subject of ridicule). These money-loving Pharisees were quick to see that the words of Jesus about the wise use of money applied to them. They had stood without comment the three parables aimed directly at them (the lost sheep, the lost coin, the lost son). But now they do not remain quiet while they hear the fourth parable spoken to the disciples. No words were apparently spoken, but their eyes, noses, faces were eloquent with a fine disdain.
—*Word Pictures in the New Testament*

MATTHEW HENRY

validate the law (*v.* 17): *It is easier for heaven and earth to pass than for one tittle of the law to fail.* The moral law is confirmed and ratified; the duties enjoined by it are duties still; the sins forbidden by it are sins still. The ceremonial law is perfected in the gospel, and its shades are filled up with the gospel colours; not *one tittle* of that *fails*, for it is found printed off in the gospel. There were some things which were connived at by the law, for the preventing of greater mischiefs, the permission of which the gospel has indeed taken away, but without any detriment or disparagement to the law, as in the case of divorce (*v.* 18), which we had before, Matt. v. 32; xix. 9. His gospel is intended to strike at the bitter root of men's corrupt appetites and passions, to kill them, and pluck them up; and therefore they must not be so far *indulged* as that permission *did* indulge them, for the more they are indulged the more impetuous and headstrong they grow.

Verses 19–31

As the parable of the prodigal son set before us the grace of the gospel, so this sets before us the *wrath to come*, and is designed for our awakening. The tendency of the gospel of Christ is both to reconcile us to poverty and affliction and to arm us against temptations to worldliness and sensuality. Now this parable goes very far in prosecuting those two great intentions. This parable is not like Christ's other parables, in which spiritual things are represented by similitudes borrowed from worldly things, as those of the sower and the seed. But here the *spiritual things themselves* are represented in a narrative or description of the different state of good and bad in this world and the other. It is *matter of fact* that is true every day, that poor godly people die away out of their miseries, and go to heavenly bliss and joy; and that rich epicures, who live in luxury, and are unmerciful to the poor, die, and go into a state of insupportable torment. Is this a parable? What similitude is there in this? Our Saviour came to bring us acquainted with another world, and here he does it. In this description (for so I shall choose to call it) we may observe,

I. The different condition of a *wicked rich man*, and a *godly poor man*, in this world. The Jews of old were ready to make prosperity one of the marks of a good man so that they could hardly have any favourable thoughts of a *poor man*. This mistake Christ, upon all occasions, set himself to correct, and here very fully, where we have,

1. A wicked man, and one that will be for ever miserable, in the height of prosperity (*v.* 19): *There was a certain rich man.* From the Latin we commonly call him *Dives—a rich man*; but he has no name given him, as the poor man has. Now we are told concerning this rich man,

(1) That he was *clothed in purple and fine linen*, and that was his *adorning*. He had *fine linen* for *pleasure*, and clean, no doubt, every day; night-linen, and day-linen. He had *purple* for *state*. He never appeared abroad but in great magnificence.

(2) He *fared sumptuously every day*. His table was furnished with all the varieties and dainties that nature and art could supply; his side-table richly adorned with plate; his servants, who waited at table, in rich liveries; and the guests at his table, no doubt, such as he thought *graced* it. Well, and what harm was there in all this? It is no sin to be rich, no sin to wear purple and fine linen, nor to keep a plentiful table, if a man's estate will afford it. Nor are we told that he got his estate by fraud, oppression, or extortion, no, nor that he was drunk, or made others drunk. [1] Christ would hereby show that a man may have a great deal of the wealth, and yet lie and perish for ever under God's wrath and curse. We cannot infer from men's living great either that God loves them *in* giving them so much, or that they love God *for* giving them so much. [2] That plenty and pleasure are very *dangerous*. This man might have been happy if he had not had great possessions and enjoyments. [3] That the indulgence of the body, and the ease and pleasure of that, are the ruin of many a soul. It is true, eating good meat and wearing good clothes are lawful; but they often become the food and fuel of pride and luxury, and so turn into sin to us. [4] That feasting ourselves and our friends, and, at the same time, forgetting the distresses of the poor and afflicted, are very provoking to God and damning to the soul.

2. Here is a godly man in the depth of adversity and distress (*v.* 20): *There was a certain beggar, named Lazarus.* This poor man was reduced to the last extremity, as miserable as you can suppose a man to be in this world.

JAMIESON, FAUSSET, BROWN

17. it is easier . . .—(See on Matt. 5:17, 18).

18. putteth away his wife . . .—(See on Matt. 19:3-9). Far from intending to weaken the force of the law, in these allusions to a new economy, our Lord, in this unexpected way, sends home its high requirements with a pungency which the Pharisees would not fail to feel.

19. purple and fine linen . . .—(Cf. Esther 8:15; Rev. 18:12); wanting nothing which taste and appetite craved and money could procure.

ADAM CLARKE

18. *Putteth away* (or divorceth) *his wife.* See on Matt. v. 31-32; xix. 9-10; Mark x. 12, where the question concerning divorce is considered at large.

19. *There was a certain rich man.* This account of the rich man and Lazarus is either a parable or a real history. If it be a parable, it is what may be; if it be a history, it is that which has been. Either a man may live as is here described, and go to perdition when he dies; or some have lived in this way, and are now suffering the torments of an eternal fire. The account is equally instructive in whichsoever of these lights it is viewed. *There was a certain rich man.* Here is the *first* degree of his reprobation—he got all he could, and kept all to himself. He *was clothed in purple and fine linen.* Purple was a very precious and costly stuff; but our Lord does not say that in the use of it he exceeded the bounds of his income, nor of his rank in life. Yet our Lord lays this down as a *second* cause of his perdition. He *fared sumptuously every day.* Now let it be observed that the law of Moses, under which this man lived, forbade nothing on this point but excess in eating and drinking. Besides, this rich man is not accused of having eaten food which was prohibited by the law, or of having neglected the abstinences and fasts prescribed by it. It is true, he is said to have feasted *sumptuously every day;* but our Lord does not intimate that this was carried to excess, or that it ministered to debauch. What are his crimes? (1) He was *rich.* (2) He was *finely clothed.* And (3) he *feasted well.* No other evil is spoken of him. In comparison of thousands he was not only blameless, but he was a virtuous man.

20. *There was a certain beggar named Lazarus.* His name is mentioned because his character was good and his end glorious, and because it is the purpose of God that the righteous shall be had in everlasting remembrance. *Lazarus,*

A. B. SIMPSON:

This remarkable and most solemn picture carries us forward from the present to the eternal world and reveals the judgments and recompenses which await each individual at the close of the present life.

First, we have the picture of two lives in vivid contrast. The one is a man who has everything that this world can afford without God. He is not necessarily a wicked man in the common sense of that word; he is simply a worldly man without God. His portion is purely earthly; but it is complete as such a portion can be. He is rich and lives in luxury, and every indulgence. His taste and vanity are gratified by the most elegant and costly apparel. His sensual appetites are ministered to by every form of physical gratification. He dwells in a splendid mansion and no doubt is surrounded by a retinue of servants and a circle of admiring friends; and perhaps, has all that affection can add to the more refined enjoyments of life; but that is all.

The other is a man that has nothing that the world values. He is a poor, diseased beggar, without the means even of obtaining his necessary food, except through the charity of this very rich man; and without a friend to minister to his sufferings, except the dogs that licked his sores. It is the uttermost contrast of earthly conditions. But as the one compensation, he has God and the hope of heaven. This is not intended to glorify poverty, or to depreciate wealth; but simply to show how little the world is worth without God, and how much God is worth without the world.—*Christ in the Bible*

MATTHEW HENRY

(1) His body was *full of sores*, like Job. To be sick and weak in body is a great affliction; but sores are more *painful* to the patient, and more *loathsome* to those about him.

(2) He was forced to beg his bread. He was so sore and lame that he could not go himself, but was carried by some compassionate hand or other, and *laid at the rich man's gate*. Those that are not able to help the poor with their *purses* should help them with their *pains*; those that cannot lend them *a penny* should lend them *a hand*. Lazarus, in his distress, had nothing of his own to subsist on.

[1] His expectations from the rich man's table: *He desired to be fed with the crumbs, v.* 21. He did not look for a mess from off his table, though he ought to have had one, but would be thankful for the crumbs from under the table, nay, the leavings of his dogs. Now this is taken notice of to show, *First*, What was the distress, and what the disposition, of the poor man. He was *poor*, but he was *poor in spirit*, contentedly poor. He did not lie at the rich man's gate complaining, and bawling, but silently and modestly desiring to be *fed with the crumbs*. Here is a child of wrath and an heir of hell sitting in the house, faring sumptuously; and a child of love and an heir of heaven lying at the gate, perishing for hunger. And is men's spiritual state to be judged of then by their outward condition? *Secondly*, What was the temper of the rich man towards him. We are not told that he abused him, but it is intimated that he slighted him. Here was a *real* object of charity, and a very *moving* one, which spoke for itself; it was presented to him at *his own gate*. A *little* thing would be a *great* kindness to him, and yet he took no cognizance of his case, but let him lie there. It is not enough not to oppress and trample upon the poor; we shall be found unfaithful stewards of our Lord's goods if we do not succour and relieve them. The reason given for the most fearful doom is, *I was hungry, and you gave me no meat*. I wonder how those rich people who have read the gospel of Christ, and say that they believe it, can be so unconcerned as they often are in the necessities and miseries of the poor and afflicted.

[2] The usage he had from the dogs: *The dogs came and licked his sores*. The rich man kept a kennel of hounds, it may be, or other dogs, and these were fed to the full, when poor Lazarus could not get enough to keep him alive. Those will have a great deal to answer for hereafter that feed their dogs, but neglect the poor. Those offend God, nay, and they put a contempt upon human nature, that pamper their dogs and horses, and let the families of their poor neighbours starve. Now those dogs *came and licked the* sores of poor Lazarus, which may be taken, *First*, As an aggravation of his misery. His sores were *bloody*, which tempted the dogs to come and lick them. The dogs were like their master, and thought they fared sumptuously when they regaled themselves with human gore. Or, it may be taken, *Secondly*, as some relief to him in his misery; the master was *hard-hearted* towards him, *but* the dogs *came and licked his sores*, which mollified and eased them. The dogs were more kind to him that their master was.

II. The *different condition* of this *godly poor man*, and this *wicked rich man, at* and *after death*.

1. They both died (*v.* 22): The *beggar died*; the *rich man also died*. Death is the common lot of rich and poor, godly and ungodly; there they meet together. Saints die, that they may bring their sorrows to an end, and may enter upon their joys. Sinners die, that they may go to give up their account. It concerns both rich and poor to prepare for death, for it waits for them both.

2. The beggar *died first*. God often takes godly people out of the world, when he leaves the wicked to flourish still. Since he could find no other shelter or resting-place, he was *hid in the grave*.

3. The rich man *died and was buried*. Nothing is said of the interment of the poor man. They dug a hole anywhere, and tumbled his body in. But the rich man had a pompous funeral; probably he had a funeral oration in praise of him, and his generous way of living, and the good table he kept, which those would commend that had been feasted at it. How foreign is the ceremony of a funeral to the happiness of the man!

4. The beggar died and was *carried by angels into Abraham's bosom*. How much did the honour done to his soul, by this convoy of it to its rest, exceed the honour done to the rich man, by the carrying of his body with so much magnificence to its grave! (1) His soul *existed* in a state of separation from the body. It did not *die*, or *fall asleep*, with the body. (2) His soul *removed* to another world, it returned to

JAMIESON, FAUSSET, BROWN

20, 21. laid—having to be carried and put down. **full of sores**—open, running, "not closed, nor bound up, nor mollified with ointment" (Isa. 1:6).

21. desiring to be fed with—but was not [GROTIUS, BENGEL, MEYER, TRENCH, etc.]. The words may mean indeed "was fain to feed on," or "gladly fed on," as in ch. 15:16 [ALFORD, WEBSTER and WILKINSON, etc.]. But the context rather favors the former.

licked . . .—a touching act of brute pity, in the absence of human relief. It is a case of heartless indifference, amidst luxuries of every kind, to one of God's poorest and most afflicted ones, presented daily before the eye.

22. died—His burial was too unimportant to mention; while "the rich man died and *was buried*"—his carcass carried in pomp to its earthly restingplace.

ADAM CLARKE

a contraction of the word *Eliezar*, which signifies the "help or assistance of God"—a name properly given to a man who was both poor and afflicted, and had no help but that which came from heaven.

G. CAMPBELL MORGAN:

"And desiring to be fed with the crumbs that fell from the rich man's table." Don't put in there, "and no man gave unto him." That is from the parable of the prodigal son. I have heard those words positively added in that connection. He may have received the crumbs. We are not told he did not. We have simply a picture of abject poverty, of a pauper on life's highway, without question through certain social conditions, because the sequel proves that he was a godly man.

And Jesus added: "Yea, even the dogs came and licked his sores." There was more kindness in the dogs than in the heart of the man who lived in the house, in purple and fine-twined linen. Even if we suppose that Lazarus did gain the scraps from the rich man's table, the rich man would not know about it. There was no generosity in letting him have the crumbs. We do not prove our care for any poor, wretched beggar by the wayside when we give away the things we have already flung away, rummage sales notwithstanding!

That is our Lord's contrast. Now, the Pharisees would have spurned the beggar and glorified the success of the wealthy man.

But the story of the two men is not ended. Our Lord went on with it. Something happened.

"It came to pass, that the beggar died. And the rich man also died." They both died. The man with all his wealth could not bribe the grim rider upon the pale horse. He died. The beggar could not postpone the event. He died! They shared the common lot. They are both dead. That company of Pharisees, if there had been any sorrow, might have said of the beggar, "Poor wretch! what a blessing a man like that should have gone!" But of the other they would have said: "It is very sad this man has gone. We wonder what he was worth!" Indeed, they might have said: "What a successful man! Let us write his story for the encouragement of youth."

They both died! Is that all? No, said Jesus, that is not all. Death comes to all, but it does not end all. It does not end all for the rich man. It does not end all for the beggar. It does not end all for any man.

—*The Gospel According to Luke*

The rich man also died, and was buried. There is no mention of this latter circumstance in the case of Lazarus. He was buried, no doubt—necessity required this; but he had the burial of a pauper, while the pomp and pride of the other followed him to the tomb.

MATTHEW HENRY

God who gave it, to its native country. The spirit of a man goes upward. (3) Angels took care of it; it was *carried by angels.* They are ministering spirits to the heirs of salvation, not only while they live, but when they die. The soul of man, if not chained to this earth and clogged by it as unsanctified souls are, has in itself an elastic virtue, by which it *springs upward* as soon as it gets clear of the body; but Christ will not trust those that are his to that, and therefore will send special messengers to fetch them to himself. Saints shall be brought home, not only safely, but honourably. What were the bearers at the rich man's funeral, though, probably, those of the first rank, compared with Lazarus's bearers? (4) It was carried *into Abraham's bosom.* Abraham was the *father of the faithful*; and whither should the souls of the faithful be gathered but to him. He was carried *to his bosom,* that is, to feast with him. The *saints in heaven* sit *down with Abraham, and Isaac, and Jacob.* Abraham was a great and rich man, yet in heaven he does not disdain to lay poor Lazarus in his bosom. Rich saints and poor meet in heaven. *He* is laid in the bosom of Abraham, whom the rich glutton scorned to *set with the dogs of his flock.*

5. The next news you hear of the *rich man* is that *in hell he lifted up his eyes, being in torment, v.* 23.

(1) His state is very miserable. *He is in hell,* in *hades,* in the state of separate souls, and there he is in *the utmost misery* and *anguish* possible. As the souls of the faithful, immediately *after they are delivered from the burden of the flesh, are in joy and felicity,* so wicked and unsanctified souls, immediately after they are fetched from the pleasures of the flesh by death, are in misery and torment endless, useless, and remediless. This *rich man* had entirely devoted himself to the pleasures of the *world of sense,* and therefore was wholly unfit for the pleasures of the *world of spirits*; to such a carnal mind as his they would indeed be no pleasure, and therefore he is of course excluded from them.

(2) The misery of his state is aggravated by his knowledge of the happiness of Lazarus: He *lifts up his eyes,* and *sees Abraham afar off,* and *Lazarus in his bosom.* He now began to consider what was become of Lazarus. He does not find him where he himself is, nay, he plainly sees him afar off in the bosom of Abraham. [1] He saw *Abraham afar off.* To see Abraham we should think a pleasing sight; but to see him afar off was a tormenting sight. [2] He saw *Lazarus in his bosom.* The sight of him brought to his mind his own cruel and barbarous conduct towards him; and the sight of him in that happiness made his own misery the more grievous.

III. An account of what passed between the rich man and Abraham in the separate state.

1. The request which the rich man made to Abraham for some mitigation of his present misery, *v.* 24. Seeing Abraham afar off, *he cried to him.* He that used to *command* aloud now *begs* aloud. The songs of his riot and revels are all turned into lamentations. Observe here,

(1) The title he gives to Abraham: *Father Abraham.* There are many in hell that can call Abraham *father.* Perhaps this rich man, in his carnal mirth, had ridiculed Abraham and the story of Abraham, as the scoffers of the latter days do; but now he gives him a title of respect, *Father Abraham.* The day is coming when wicked men will be glad to scrape acquaintance with the righteous, and to claim kindred to them, though now they slight them.

(2) The representation he makes to him of his present deplorable condition: *I am tormented in this flame.* It is the torment of his soul that he complains of, and therefore it is such a fire as will operate upon souls; and such a fire the *wrath of God* is, fastening upon a guilty conscience; such a fire horror of mind is, and the reproaches of a self-accusing self-condemning heart.

(3) His request to Abraham, in consideration of this misery: *Have mercy on me.* The day is coming when those that make light of divine mercy will beg hard for it. He that had no mercy on Lazarus, yet expects Lazarus should have mercy on him; "for," thinks he, "Lazarus is better natured than ever I was." The particular favour he begs is, *Send Lazarus, that he may dip the tip of his finger in water, and cool my tongue.* [1] Here he complains of the torment of his *tongue* particularly. The *tongue* is one of the organs of speech, and by the torment of that he is put in mind of all the wicked words that he had spoken against God and man, all his *hard speeches,* and *filthy speeches*; by his words *he is condemned,* and therefore in his tongue he is tormented. The tongue is also one of the organs of *tasting,* and therefore the torments of that will remind him of his inordinate relish of the delights of sense. [2] He desires a *drop of water to cool his tongue.* He asks

JAMIESON, FAUSSET, BROWN

in to Abraham's bosom—as if seen reclining next to Him at the heavenly feast (Matt. 8:11).

23. in hell—not the final place of the lost (for which another word is used), but as we say "the unseen world." But as the object here is certainly to depict the *whole torment* of the one and the *perfect bliss* of the other, it comes in this case to much the same.

seeth Abraham—not God, to whom therefore he cannot cry [BENGEL].

24. Father Abraham—a well-founded, but unavailing, claim of natural descent (ch. 3:8; John 8:37).

mercy on me—who never showed any (Jas. 2:3). **send Lazarus**—the pining victim of his merciless neglect. **that he may**—take me hence? No; that he dares not to ask. **dip . . . tongue**—i.e., the *least* conceivable and the *most momentary* abatement of his torment; that is all. But even this he is told is (1) *unreasonable.*

ADAM CLARKE

22. *Abraham's bosom,* an allusion to the custom at Jewish feasts, when three persons reclining on their left elbows on a couch, the person whose head came near the breast of the other was said to lie in his bosom. So it is said of the beloved disciple, John xiii. 25. *Abraham's bosom* was a phrase used among the Jews to signify the paradise of God.

23. *And seeth Abraham afar off, and Lazarus in his bosom.* He sees Lazarus clothed with glory and immortality—this is the first circumstance in his punishment. What a contrast! What a desire does he feel to resemble him, and what rage and despair because he is not like him!

ALBERT BARNES:

24. "Father Abraham." The Jews considered it a signal honor that Abraham was their father—that is, that they were descendants from him. Though this man was now in misery, yet he seems not to have abandoned the idea of his relation to the father of the faithful. The Jews supposed that departed spirits might know and converse with each other. See Lightfoot on this place. Our Savior speaks in conformity with that prevailing opinion; and as it was not easy to convey ideas about the spiritual world without some such representation, he therefore speaks in the language which was usual in his time. We are not, however, to suppose that this was literally true, but only that it was designed to represent more clearly the sufferings of the rich man in hell.

—*Popular Commentary*

MATTHEW HENRY

as small a thing as could be asked, *a drop of water* to cool his tongue for one moment. [3] He desires that Lazarus might bring it. He *names* him, because he *knows* him, and thinks Lazarus will not be unwilling to do him this good office for old acquaintance' sake. There is a day coming when those that now hate and despise the people of God would gladly receive kindness from them.

2. The reply which Abraham gave to this request. In general, he did not grant it. See how justly this rich man is paid in his own coin. He that denied a crumb is denied a drop. Now it is said to us, *Ask, and it shall be given you;* but, if we let slip this accepted time, we may ask, and it shall not be given us.

(1) He calls him *son*, a kind and civil title. He had been a son, but a rebellious one, and now an abandoned disinherited one.

(2) He puts him in mind of what had been both his own condition and the condition of Lazarus, in their *life-time: Son, remember;* this is a cutting word. Now sinners are called upon to *remember*, but they do not, they will not. "*Son, remember* thy Creator, thy Redeemer, remember thy latter end"; but they can forget that for which they have their memories. "*Son, remember* the many warnings that were given thee, remember the fair offers made thee of eternal life and glory, which thou wouldest not accept!" But that which he is here put in mind of is, [1] That *thou in thy life-time receivedst thy good things.* He does not tell him that he had *abused* them, but that he had *received* them: "Remember what a bountiful benefactor God has been to thee; thou canst not therefore say he owes thee anything, no, not a *drop of water*. What he gave thee *thou receivedst*, and that was all. Thou hast been the grave of God's blessings, in which they were buried, not the field of them, in which they were sown. Thou receivedst *thy good things*. They were the things which thou didst choose for *thy good things*, which were in thine eye the *best things*. Thou wast for the *good things of thy life-time*, and hadst no thought of better things in another life. The day of thy *good things* is past and gone." [2] "What *evil things Lazarus received.* Think what a large share of miseries he had *in his life-time.* Thou hadst *as much good* as could be thought to fall to the lot of so *bad a man*, and he *as much evil* as could be thought to fall to the lot of *so good a man.* He *received* his evil things; he *received* them as physic appointed for the cure of his spiritual distempers, and the cure was effected." As wicked people have *good things* in this life only, godly people have evil things only *in this life.* Now Abraham awakens his conscience to remind him how he had behaved towards Lazarus; he cannot forget that then he would not help Lazarus, and how then could he expect that Lazarus should now help him?

(3) He puts him in mind of Lazarus's present bliss, and his own misery: *Now he is comforted, and thou art tormented.* Heaven is *comfort*, and hell is *torment*: heaven is *joy*, hell is *weeping, and wailing*. Heaven will be heaven indeed to those that go thither through many and great calamities in this world. When they are fallen asleep in Christ, you may truly say, "Now *they are comforted*; now *all their tears are wiped away*." In heaven there is everlasting consolation. And, on the other hand, hell will be hell indeed to those that go thither from the midst of the enjoyment of all the delights and pleasures of sense.

(4) He assures him that it was to no purpose to think of having any relief by the ministry of Lazarus; for (*v.* 26), *Besides all this, between us and you there is a great gulf fixed, a great chasm.* The kindest saint in heaven cannot make a visit to the congregation of the dead and damned, to comfort or relieve any there who once were their friends. "*They that would pass hence to you cannot.*" The most daring sinner in hell cannot force his way out of that prison. *They cannot pass to us that would come thence.* In this world, blessed be God, there is no gulf fixed between a state of nature and grace, but we may pass from the one to the other, from sin to God. It might have been prevented *in time*, but it cannot now be remedied *to eternity*. A stone is rolled to the door of the pit, which cannot be rolled back.

3. The further request he had to make to his father Abraham. having an opportunity of speaking to Abraham, he will improve it for his relations whom he has left behind.

(1) He begs that Lazarus might be *sent to his father's house. I pray thee therefore, father, v.* 27. Again he calls upon Abraham. Surely thou wilt be so compassionate as not to deny this. Send him back *to my father's house*; he knows well enough where it is, has been there many a time. He knows I have *five brethren* there; they will *know him*, and will regard what he saith. Let him *testify to them*; let him tell

JAMIESON, FAUSSET, BROWN

ALEXANDER MACLAREN:

"Son, remember!" It is the voice, the first voice, the perpetual voice, which meets every man when he steps across the threshold of earth into the presence chamber of eternity. All the future is so built upon and interwoven with the past that for the saved and for the lost alike this word might almost be taken as the motto of their whole situation, as the explanation of their whole condition. Memory in another world is indispensable to the gladness of the glad, and strikes the deepest note in the sadness of the lost. There can be no need to dwell at any length on the simple introductory thought, that there must be memory in a future state. Unless there were remembrance, there could be no sense of individuality. A man cannot have any conviction that he is himself, but by constant, though often unconscious, operation of this subtle act of remembrance. There can be no sense of personal identity except in proportion as there is clearness of recollection. Then again, if that future state be a state of retribution, there must be memory. Otherwise, there might be joy, and there might be sorrow; but the why and the wherefore of either would be entirely struck out of a man's consciousness, and the one could not be felt as reward nor the other as punishment. If, then, we are to rise from the grave the same men that we are laid in it, and if the future life has this for its characteristic, that it is a state either of recompense and reward or of retribution and suffering, then, for both, the clearness and constant action of memory are certainly needed. But it is not to the simple fact of its existence that I desire to direct your attention now. I wish, rather, to suggest to you one or two modifications under which it must apparently work in another world. When men remember *there*, they will remember very differently from the way in which they remember *here*. These changes constitute, on the one hand, an instrument of torture; and, on the other, a foundation of all our gladness.

—Expositions of Holy Scripture

25, 26. Son—stinging acknowledgment of the claimed relationship. **thou . . . Lazarus . . .**—As it is a great law of God's kingdom, that *the nature of our present desires shall rule that of our future bliss*, so by that law, he whose "good things," craved and enjoyed, were all bounded by time, could look for none after his connection with time had come to an end (ch. 6:24). But by this law, he whose "evil things," all crowded into the present life, drove him to seek, and find, consolation in a life beyond the grave, is by death released from all evil and ushered into unmixed and uninterrupted good (ch. 6:21). (2) It is *impossible*.

26. besides all this—independently of this consideration. **a great gulf fixed**—*By an irrevocable decree* there has been placed a vast impassable abyss between the two states, and the occupants of each.

27-31. Then he said—now abandoning all hope for himself—**send him to my father's house . . .**—no waking up of good in the heart of the lost, but bitter reproach against God and the old economy, as not warning him sufficiently [TRENCH]. The answer of Abraham is, They *are* sufficiently warned.

ADAM CLARKE

25. *Son, remember that thou in thy lifetime receivedst thy good things.* The remembrance of the good things possessed in life, and now to be enjoyed no more forever, together with the remembrance of grace offered or abused, will form a circumstance in the perdition of the ungodly.

26. *Beside all this, between us and you there is a great gulf.* The eternal purpose of God, formed on the principles of eternal reason, separates the persons and the places of abode of the righteous and the wicked, so that there can be no intercourse: *They which would pass from hence to you cannot; neither can they pass to us, that would come from thence.* The iniquitous conduct of relatives and friends, who have been perverted by the bad example of those who are lost, is a source of present punishment to them; and if they come also to the same place of torment, must be, to those who were the instruments of bringing them thither, an eternal source of anguish. "Send Lazarus to my father's family, for I have five brothers, that he may earnestly testify to them, that they come not to this place of torment." These brothers had probably been influenced by his example to content themselves with an earthly portion, and to neglect their immortal souls. Those who have been instruments of bringing others into hell shall suffer the deeper perdition on that account.

MATTHEW HENRY

them what condition I am in. Let him warn them not to tread in my steps *lest they also come into this place of torment*, *v.* 28. He does not say, "Give me leave to go to them, that I may testify to them"; his going would frighten them out of their *wits*; but, "Send Lazarus, whose address will be less terrible, and yet his testimony sufficient to frighten them out of their *sins*." Now he desired the preventing of their ruin, in tenderness to *them*, for whom he could not but retain a *natural affection*.

(2) Abraham denies him this favour too. There is no request granted in hell. Abraham leaves them to the testimony of Moses and the prophets. Here is their privilege: *They have Moses and the prophets;* and their duty: "*Let them hear them*, and mix faith with them, and that will be sufficient to keep them from this place of torment."

(3) He urges his request yet further (*v.* 30): "*Nay, father Abraham*, they have Moses and the prophets, yet it may be hoped, *if one went to them from the dead, they would repent*, that would be a more sensible conviction to them. They are used to Moses and the prophets; but this would be a *new thing*, and more startling; surely this would bring them to *repent*." Foolish men are apt to think any method of conviction better than that which God has chosen and appointed.

(4) Abraham insists upon the denial of it (*v.* 31): "*If they hear not Moses and the prophets, neither will they be persuaded though one rose from the dead.*" The same strength of corruption that breaks through the convictions of the written word would certainly triumph over those by a witness *from the dead*. The scripture is now the ordinary way of God's making known his mind to us, and it is sufficient.

JAMIESON, FAUSSET, BROWN

30. Nay—giving the lie to Abraham. **if . . .**—a principle of awful magnitude and importance. The greatest miracle will have no effect on those who are determined not to believe. A *real* Lazarus soon "rose from the dead," but the sight of him by crowds of people, inclined thereby to Christ, only crowned the unbelief and hastened the murderous plots of the Pharisees against the Lord of glory; nor has His own resurrection, far more overpowering, yet won over that "crooked and perverse nation."

ADAM CLARKE

29. *They have Moses and the prophets.* This plainly supposes they were all Jewish believers; they had these writings in their hands, but they did not permit them to influence their lives.

30. *If one went to them from the dead.* Many are desirous to see an inhabitant of the other world, and converse with him, in order to know what passes there. Make way! Here is a damned soul, which Jesus Christ has evoked from the hell of fire! Hear him! Hear him tell of his torments! Hear him utter his regrets!

31. *If they hear not Moses.* This answer of Abraham contains two remarkable propositions: (1) That the Sacred Writings contain such proofs of a divine origin that, though all the dead were to arise to convince an unbeliever of the truths therein declared, the conviction could not be greater nor the proof more evident of the divinity and truth of these sacred records than that which themselves afford; (2) That to escape eternal perdition and get at last into eternal glory, a man is to receive the testimonies of God and to walk according to their dictates.

MATTHEW HENRY

CHAPTER 17

Verses 1–10

Note, I. That the *giving of offences* is a *great sin*, *v.*1, 2. We can expect no other than that offences will come. *It is* almost *impossible but that offences will come*, and therefore we are concerned to provide accordingly; but *woe to him through whom they come*, his doom will be heavy (*v.* 2). They perish under a load of guilt more *ponderous* than that of *millstones*. This includes a woe, 1. To persecutors who offer any injury to the least of Christ's *little ones*. 2. To seducers, who corrupt the truths of Christ, and so *trouble the minds of the disciples*. 3. To those who live scandalously, and thereby weaken the hands and sadden the hearts of God's people.

II. That the *forgiving of offences* is a *great duty* (*v.* 3): *Take heed to yourselves*. This may refer either to what goes before, or to what follows: *Take heed that you offend not one of these little ones*. Or, "When *your brother trespasses against you, take heed to yourselves at such a time*, lest you be put into a passion."

1. If you are permitted to *rebuke him*, you are advised to do so. Smother not the resentment, but give it vent. *Tell him his faults;* and, it may be, you will perceive that you mistook him, that it was not a *trespass against you*, but an *oversight*, and then you will beg his pardon for misunderstanding him.

2. You are commanded, upon his repentance, to forgive him: *If he repent, forgive him;* forget the injury, never think of it again. Though he do not repent, you must not therefore bear malice to him, nor meditate revenge.

3. You are to repeat this every time he repeats his trespass, *v.* 4. If he could be supposed to be either so negligent as to *trespass against thee seven times in a day*, and as often profess himself sorry for his fault, continue to *forgive him*. Christians should be of a forgiving spirit, willing to make the best of everybody, and they should contrive as much to show that they have forgiven an injury as others to show that they resent it.

III. That we have all need to get our *faith* strengthened, because, as that grace grows, all other graces grow. 1. The address which the disciples made to Christ, for the strengthening of their faith, *v.* 5. *The apostles* themselves yet acknowledged the weakness and deficiency of their faith, and saw their need of Christ's grace for the improvement of it; they *said unto the Lord*, "*Increase our faith.*" The increase of our faith is what we should earnestly desire. They put up this prayer to Christ upon occasion of his pressing upon them the duty of forgiving injuries: "*Lord, increase our faith*, or we shall never be able to practise such a difficult duty as this." Faith in God's pardoning mercy will enable us to get over the greatest difficulties that lie in the way of our forgiving our brother. 2. The assurance Christ gave them of the wonderful efficacy of true faith (*v.* 6): "*If ye have faith*

JAMIESON, FAUSSET, BROWN

CHAPTER 17

Vss. 1-10. OFFENSES—FAITH—HUMILITY. **1, 2.** (See on Matt. 18:6, 7.)

For whosoever shall offend one of these little ones that believe in me—or, shall cause them to stumble; referring probably to the effect which such unsavory disputes as they had held would have upon the inquiring and hopeful who came in contact with them, leading to the belief that after all they were no better than others. **it is better for him that a millstone were hanged about his neck**—The word here is simply "millstone," without expressing of which kind. But in Matthew 18:6 it is the "ass-turned" kind, far heavier than the small hand-mill turned by female slaves, as in Luke 17:35. It is of course the same which is meant here. **and he were cast into the sea**—meaning, that if by such a death that stumbling were prevented, and so its eternal consequences averted, it would be a happy thing for them. Here follows a striking verse in Matthew 18:7, "Woe unto the world because of offences!" (There will be stumblings and falls and loss of souls enough from the world's treatment of disciples, without any addition from you: dreadful will be its doom in consequence; see that ye share not in it.) "For it must needs be that offences come; but woe to that man by whom the offence cometh!" (The struggle between light and darkness will inevitably cause stumblings, but not less guilty is he who wilfully makes any to stumble.)

3, 4. (See on Matt. 18:15-17, 21, 22.) **seven times**—not a *lower* measure of the forgiving spirit than the "seventy times seven" enjoined on Peter, which was occasioned by his asking if he was to *stop* at seven times. "No," is the virtual answer, "though it come to seventy times that number, if only he ask forgiveness in sincerity."

5. Lord—(See on ch. 10:1). **increase our faith**—moved by the difficulty of avoiding and forgiving "offenses." This is the only instance in which *a spiritual operation upon their souls* was solicited of Christ by the Twelve; but a kindred and higher prayer had been offered before, by one with far fewer opportunities. (See on Mark 9:24.)

ADAM CLARKE

CHAPTER 17

1. *It is impossible but that offences will come.* Such is the corrupt state of the human heart that, notwithstanding all the influences of grace and the promises of glory, men will continue to sin against God; and His justice must continue to punish.

2. *A millstone.* To have a millstone hanged about the neck was a common proverb.

3-4. *If thy brother trespass.* See the notes on Matt. xviii. 21-22.

5. *Increase our faith.* This work of pardoning every offense of every man, and that continually, seemed so difficult, even to the disciples themselves, that they saw, without an extraordinary degree of faith, they should never be able to keep this command.

MATTHEW HENRY

as a grain of mustard-seed, so small as mustard-seed, or so sharp as mustard-seed, so pungent, so exciting to all other graces, nothing would be too hard for you, that was fit to be done for the glory of God, yea, though it were the *transplanting of a tree* from the earth *to the sea.*" As with God *nothing is impossible,* so are all *things possible to him that can believe.*

IV. That, whatever we do in the service of Christ, we must be very humble. Even the apostles themselves, who did so much more for Christ than others, must not think that they had thereby made him their debtor. 1. We are all *God's servants.* Our whole strength and our whole time are to be employed for him. 2. As God's servants, it becomes us to fill up our time with duty, we ought to make the end of one service the beginning of another. The servant that has been *ploughing,* or *feeding cattle, in the field,* when he *comes home* at night has work to do still; he must *wait at table, v.* 7, 8. When we have been *working for God,* still we must be *waiting on God.* 3. Our principal care here must be to do the duty of our relation, and leave it to our Master to give us the comfort of it. No servant expects that his master should say to him, *Go and sit down to meat*; it is time enough to do that when we have *done our day's work.* Let us be in care to finish our work, and then the reward will come in due time. 4. It is fit that Christ should be served before us: *Make ready wherewith I may sup, and afterwards thou shalt eat and drink.* 5. Christ's servants, when they are to wait upon him, must *gird themselves,* must free themselves from everything that is entangling and encumbering. We must then *gird ourselves,* to attend him. This is expected from servants, and Christ might require it from us, but he does not insist upon it. He was *among his disciples as one that served,* and came not *to be ministered unto, but to minister*; witness his washing his disciples' feet. 6. Christ's servants do not so much as merit his thanks for any service they do him: *"Does he thank that servant?"* No good works of ours can merit anything at the hand of God. 7. Whatever we do for Christ, it is no more than is our duty to do. Though we should *do all things that are commanded us,* and alas! in many things we come short of this, it is but what we are bound to by that first and great commandment of *loving God* with *all our heart and soul.* 8. The best servants of Christ must humbly acknowledge that they are *unprofitable servants.* God cannot be a *gainer* by our services, and therefore cannot be made a *debtor* by them. It becomes us therefore to call ourselves *unprofitable servants,* but to call his service a profitable service.

Verses 11-19

We have here an account of the cure of ten lepers, which we had not in any other of the evangelists. The leprosy was a disease which the Jews supposed to be, more than other diseases, a mark of God's displeasure; and therefore Christ, who came to take away sin, took particular care to cleanse the lepers that fell in his way. Christ was now in his way to Jerusalem, about the mid-way. He was now in the frontier-country, the marches that lay between Samaria and Galilee.

I. The address of these lepers to Christ. They were ten in a company; for, though they were shut out from society with others, yet those that were infected were at liberty to converse with one another. 1. They *met* Christ *as he entered into a certain village.* They did not stay till he had refreshed himself, but met him as he *entered* the town, weary as he was; and yet he did not put them off. 2. They *stood afar off.* A sense of our spiritual leprosy should make us very humble in all our approaches to Christ. Who are we, that we should draw near to him that is infinitely pure? 3. Their request was unanimous, and very importunate (*v.* 13): *They lifted up their voices* and cried, *Jesus, Master, have mercy on us.* Those that expect help from Christ must take him for their Master. If he be *Master,* he will be *Jesus, a Saviour.* They ask not in particular to be cured of their leprosy, but, *Have mercy on us;* and it is enough to refer ourselves to the compassions of Christ, for they *fail not.*

II. Christ sent them to *the priest,* to be *inspected* by him. He did not tell them positively that they should be *cured,* but bade them *go show themselves to the priests, v.* 14. This was a trial of their obedience. Those that expect Christ's favours must take them in his way and method. They all *went to the priest.* As the ceremonial law was yet in force, Christ took care that it should be observed.

III. *As they went, they were cleansed. Then,* we may expect God to meet us with mercy when we are found in the way of duty. If we do what we can, God will not be wanting to do that for us which we cannot. Though the means will not heal thee of

JAMIESON, FAUSSET, BROWN

sycamine—mulberry. (See on Mark 11:22-24.)

7-10. say unto him by and by—The "by and by" (or rather "directly") should be joined not to the *saying* but the *going:* "Go directly." The connection here is: "But when your faith *has* been so increased as both to avoid and forgive offenses, and do things impossible to all but faith, be not puffed up as though you had laid the Lord under any obligations to you."

9. I trow not—or, as we say, when much more is meant, "I should think not."

10. unprofitable—a word which, though usually denoting the *opposite* of profit, is here used simply in its *negative* sense. "We have not, as his servants, profited or benefited God at all." (Cf. Job 22:2, 3; Rom. 11:35.)

11-19. TEN LEPERS CLEANSED. **11-13. through the midst of Samaria and Galilee**—probably on the *confines* of both.

12. stood afar off—(Cf. Lev. 13: 45, 46). **13. they lifted up**—their common misery drawing these poor outcasts together (II Kings 7:3), nay, making them forget the fierce national antipathy of Jew and Samaritan [TRENCH] **Jesus . . .**—(Cf. Matt. 20:30-33). How quick a teacher is felt misery, even though as here the teaching may be soon forgotten!

14. show yourselves—as cleansed persons. (See on Matt. 8:4.) Thus too would the Samaritan be taught that "salvation is of the Jews" (John 4:22). **as they went, were cleansed**—In how many different ways were our Lord's cures wrought, and this different from all the rest.

ADAM CLARKE

6. *As a grain of mustard seed.* A faith that increases and thrives as that is described to do. *This sycamine.* The words seem to intimate that they were standing by such a tree. The *sycamine* is probably the same as the "sycomore." Jerome, who was well-acquainted with these countries, translates the word "mulberry tree." *Be thou plucked up by the root.* See the note on Matt. xxi. 21, where it is shown that this mode of speech refers to the accomplishment of things very difficult, but not impossible.

7-9. *Which of you, having a servant?* It is never supposed that the master waits on the servant—the servant is bound to wait on his master, and to do everything for him to the uttermost of his power. Nor does the former expect thanks for it, for he is bound by his agreement to act thus because of the stipulated reward, which is considered as being equal in value to all the service that he can perform.

10. *We are unprofitable servants.* This text has often been produced to prove that no man can live without committing sin against God. But let it be observed the text says *unprofitable servants,* not sinful servants.

12. *Which stood afar off.* They kept at a distance, because forbidden by law and custom to come near to those who were sound, for fear of infecting them. See Lev. xiii. 46; Num. v. 2; 2 Kings xv. 5.

13. *They lifted up their voices.* They cried with one accord—they were all equally necessitous, and there was but one voice among them all, though ten were engaged in crying at the same time. As they were companions in suffering, they were also companions in prayer.

14. *Shew yourselves unto the priests.* According to the direction, Lev. xiii. 2, etc.; xiv. 2 etc. Our Lord intended that their cure should be received by faith. They depended on His goodness and power; and though they had no promise, yet they went at His command to do that which those only were required by the law to do who were already healed. *And . . . as they went,* in this spirit of implicit faith, *they were cleansed.* God highly honors this kind of faith

MATTHEW HENRY

themselves, God will heal thee in the diligent use of those means.

IV. One of them, and but one, *returned, to give thanks, v.* 15. When he *saw that he was healed* he *turned back* towards him who was the Author of his cure, whom he wished to have the glory of it. He appears to have been very hearty and affectionate in his thanksgivings: *With a loud voice he glorified God, v.* 13. Those that have received mercy from God should publish it to others. But he also made a particular address of thanks to Christ (*v.* 16): *He fell down at his feet*, and *gave him thanks.* We ought to give thanks for the favours Christ bestows upon us, and particularly for recoveries from sickness. It becomes us also to be very humble in our thanksgivings, as well as in our prayers.

V. Christ took notice of this one that had thus distinguished himself; for, it seems, he was a Samaritan whereas the rest were Jews, *v.* 16. The Samaritans had not the pure knowledge and worship of God among them that the Jews had, and yet it was one of them that *glorified God*, when the Jews forgot.

1. The particular notice Christ took of him, and the ingratitude of those that were sharers with him in the mercy—that he who was a *stranger* was the only one that *returned to give glory to God, v.* 17, 18. (1) How *rich* Christ is in *doing good: Were there not ten cleansed?* Here was a cure by *wholesale*, a whole *hospital* healed with *one* word's speaking. We shall have never the less grace for others sharing it. (2) How *poor* we are in our returns: "*Where are the nine?*" Ingratitude is a very common sin. Of the many that receive mercy from God, there are but few, very few, that *return to give thanks.* (3) How those often prove most grateful from whom it was least expected. A Samaritan gives thanks, and a Jew does not. This serves here to aggravate the ingratitude of those Jews of whom Christ speaks.

2. The great encouragement Christ gave him, *v.* 19. The rest had their *cure*, and had it not *revoked*, but he had his cure confirmed particularly; *Thy faith hath made thee whole.* The rest were *made whole* by the power of Christ, in compassion to their distress; but he was made whole *by his faith*, by which Christ saw him distinguished from the rest.

I. Here is the demand of the Pharisees concerning it, which occasioned this discourse. They asked *when the kingdom of God should come.* They understood, perhaps, that Christ had taught his disciples to pray for the coming of it, and they had long preached that it was *at hand.* "Now," say the Pharisees, "when will that glorious view open?"

II. Christ's reply to this demand, directed to the Pharisees first, and afterwards to his own disciples (*v.* 22); what he said to both, he saith to us.

1. That the kingdom of the Messiah was to be a *spiritual kingdom.* They asked *when* it would come. "You know not what you ask," saith Christ; "it may come, and you not be aware of it." For it has not an *external show*, as other kingdoms have, the advancements and revolutions of which fill the newspapers. "No," saith Christ, "it will have a silent entrance; it *cometh not with observation.*" They desired to have their curiosity satisfied concerning the *time* of it. Christ will have their mistakes rectified concerning the nature of it. When Messiah the Prince comes to set up his kingdom, they shall not say, *Lo here*, or *Lo there*, as when a prince goes in progress to visit his territories. Christ will not come with all this talk; it will not be set up in this or that particular place. Those who confine Christianity and the church to this place or that party, cry, *Lo here*, or *Lo there*; so do they who make prosperity and external pomp a mark of the true church. "It has a *spiritual* influence: *The kingdom of God is within you.*" It is not of this world. Its glory does not strike men's fancies, but affects their spirits, and its power is over their souls and consciences. The *kingdom of God* will not change men's outward condition, but their hearts and lives. Then it *comes* when it makes those humble, and serious, and heavenly, that were proud, and vain; and therefore look for the kingdom of God in the revolutions of the heart. The kingdom of God is *among you*; so some read it. "You enquire when it will come, and are not aware that it is already begun to be set up *in the midst of you.* It is *in your* nation, though not in your hearts." It is the folly of many curious enquirers concerning the times to come that they look for that *before them* which is already *among them.*

2. That the setting up of this kingdom was a work that would meet with a great deal of *opposition* and *interruption, v.* 22. The *disciples* thought they should carry all before them, but Christ tells them it would be otherwise: "*The days will come when you shall desire to see one of the days of the Son of man*, and *shall not see it.* At first, indeed, you will have won-

JAMIESON, FAUSSET, BROWN

G. CAMPBELL MORGAN:

"Were not the ten cleansed? but where are the nine?" What a revelation of the fact that Christ values gratitude and misses it when it is not expressed. We had another illustration of it in chapter seven. When He went to the house of Simon, He missed the common courtesy of the Eastern home. "You gave me no water for my feet, you gave me no kiss, my head with oil you did not anoint"; you neglected the common courtesies. Are we not all in danger of being among the nine, rather than being represented by the one, forgetting and failing in our praising? We have almost lost the art of pure praise.—*The Gospel According to Luke*

17, 18. Were there not ten cleansed—rather, were not *the ten* cleansed? i.e., the whole of them—an example (by the way) of Christ's omniscience [BENGEL]. **18. this stranger**—"this alien" (literally, "of another race"). The language is that of wonder and admiration, as is expressly said of another exhibition of Gentile faith (Matt. 8:10).

19. Arise—for he had "fallen down on his face at His feet" (vs. 16) and there lain prostrate. **faith made thee whole**—not as the others, merely in body, but in that higher spiritual sense with which His constant language has so familiarized us.

20-37. COMING OF THE KINGDOM OF GOD AND OF THE SON OF MAN. **20-25. when . . .**—To meet the erroneous views not only of the Pharisees, but of the disciples themselves, our Lord addresses both, announcing the coming of the kingdom under different aspects. "It cometh not with observation"—with watching or lying in wait, as for something outwardly imposing and at once revealing itself.

21. Lo here! . . . lo there!—shut up within *this* or *that* sharply defined and visible geographical or ecclesiastical limit. **within you**—is of an internal and *spiritual* character (as contrasted with their *outside* views of it). But it has its *external* side too.

22. The days—rather "Days." **will come**—as in ch. 19: 43, when, amidst calamities, etc., you will anxiously look for a deliverer, and deceivers will put themselves forward in this character. **one of the days of the Son of man**—Himself again among them but for one day; as we say when all seems to be

ADAM CLARKE

and makes it the instrument in His hand of working many miracles. He who will not believe till he receives what he calls a reason for it is never likely to get his soul saved. The highest, the most sovereign reason that can be given for believing is that God has commanded it.

15. *One of them, when he saw that he was healed.* It seems that he did not wait to go first to the priest, but turned immediately back, and gave public praise to the kind hand from which he had received his cure.

16. *He was a Samaritan.* One who professed a very corrupt religion, and from whom much less was to be expected than from the other nine, who probably were Jews.

18. *This stranger.* Often God receives more praise and affectionate obedience from those who had long lived without His knowledge and fear than from those who were bred up among His people and who profess to be called by His name. The simple reason is, Those who have much forgiven will love much, chap. vii. 47.

19. *Thy faith hath made thee whole.* Your faith has been the means of receiving that influence by which you have been cleansed.

20. *Cometh not with observation.* "With scrupulous observation."

21. *Lo here! or, lo there!* Perhaps those Pharisees thought that the Messiah was kept secret, in some private place, known only to some of their rulers; and that by and by He should be proclaimed in a similar way to that in which Joash was by Jehoiada the priest. See the account, 2 Chron. xxiii. 1-11.

22. *When ye shall desire to see one of the days.* As it was our Lord's constant custom to support and comfort the minds of His disciples, we cannot suppose that He intimates here that they shall be left destitute of those blessings necessary for their support in a day of trial.

MATTHEW HENRY

derful success" (so they had, when *thousands* were added to the church *in a day*); "but do not think it will be always so; people will grow cool to it." This looks forward to his disciples in after-ages; they must expect much disappointment. Ministers and churches will sometimes be under *outward restraints*. Then they will wish to see such days of opportunity as they have formerly enjoyed. God teaches us to know the worth of such mercies by the want of them. Sometimes they will be under *inward restraints*. Then they shall wish to see such *victorious triumphant* days as they have sometimes seen. We must not think that Christ's church and cause are lost because not always alike visible and prevailing.

3. That Christ and his kingdom are not to be looked for in this or that particular place, but his appearance will be general in all places at once (*v.* 23, 24): "*They will say to you, See here, or, See there. Go not after them, nor follow them.* The kingdom of God was not designed to be the glory of one people only, but to *give light to the Gentiles*; for *as the lightning that lightens out of one part under heaven, and shines* all on a sudden irresistibly *to the other part under heaven, so shall also the Son of man be in his day.* The gospel that is to set up Christ's kingdom in the world shall *fly like lightning* through the nations. The kingdom of the Messiah is not to be a *local* thing, but is to be dispersed far and wide over the face of the whole earth." The design of the setting up of Christ's kingdom was not to make one *nation great*, but to make *all nations good*—some, at least, of all nations.

4. That the Messiah must *suffer* before he must *reign* (*v.* 25): "*First must he suffer many things* and *be rejected of this generation;* and, if he be thus treated, his disciples must expect no other than to *suffer* and be *rejected* too for his sake. We must go by the cross to the crown. The *Son of man must suffer many things.* Pain, and shame, and death, are those *many things.* He must be *rejected by this generation* of unbelieving Jews, before he be embraced by another generation of believing Gentiles."

5. That the setting up of the kingdom of the Messiah would introduce the destruction of the Jewish nation. Observe,

(1) How it had been with sinners formerly. Think how it was with the men of Sodom, who were *wicked, and sinners before the Lord exceedingly*. Now observe, [1] That they had *fair warning given them.* Noah was a *preacher of righteousness* to the old world; so was Lot to the Sodomites. [2] That they did not regard the warning given them. They were very secure. They were all very merry, and yet very busy too. When they should have been, as the men of Nineveh, *fasting and praying, repenting* and *reforming*, they were going on securely, *eating flesh*, and *drinking wine*. [3] That they continued in their security and sensuality, till the threatened judgment came. [4] That God took care for the preservation of those that were his. Noah entered *into the ark*, and there he was safe; Lot went out of Sodom, and so went out of harm's way. [5] That they were surprised with the ruin which they would not fear. The *flood came*, and destroyed all the sinners of the old world; *fire and brimstone* came, and *destroyed* all the sinners of Sodom. But that which is especially intended here is to show what a dreadful surprise destruction will be to those who are secure and sensual.

(2) How it will be with sinners still (*v.* 30): *Thus shall it be in the day when the Son of man is revealed.* They have warning given by Christ now, and will have it repeated to them by the apostles after him; but it will be all *in vain*. One would have thought that this discourse of our Saviour's, which was public, should have awakened them; but it did not.

6. That it ought to be the care of his disciples and followers to distinguish themselves from the unbelieving Jews in that day, and, leaving them, to flee at the signal given, according to the direction that should be given. This flight of theirs from Jerusalem must be *expeditious*, and must not be retarded by any concern about their worldly affairs (*v.* 31): "*He that shall be on the house-top, let him not come down, to take his stuff away.*" It will be better to leave his stuff behind him than to stay to look after it, and *perish with them that believe not*. It will be their concern to do as Lot and his family were charged to do: *Escape for thy life. Save yourselves from this untoward generation.* When they have made their escape, they must not think of returning (*v.* 32): "*Remember Lot's wife* and do not *look back*, as she did; be not loth to leave a place marked for destruction." Let them not *look back*, lest they should be tempted to *go back*; nay, lest that be construed a *going back in heart*, or an evidence that the heart was left behind. There would be no other way of saving their lives

JAMIESON, FAUSSET, BROWN

going wrong and the one person who could keep them right is removed [NEANDER in STIER, etc.]. "This is said to guard against the mistake of supposing that His visible presence would accompany the manifestation and establishment of His kingdom" [WEBSTER and WILKINSON].

23. they shall say, See here . . . go not . . .—a warning to all so-called expositors of prophecy and their followers, who cry, Lo there and see here, every time that war breaks out or revolutions occur. **24. as lightning . . . so . . . the Son of man**—i.e., it will be as manifest. The Lord speaks here of His coming and manifestation in a prophetically indefinite manner, and in these preparatory words *blends into one the distinctive epochs* [STIER]. When the whole polity of the Jews, civil and ecclesiastical alike, was broken up at once, and its continuance rendered impossible by the destruction of Jerusalem, it became as manifest to all as the lightning of heaven that the kingdom of God had ceased to exist in its old, and had entered on a new and perfectly different form. So it may be again, ere its final and greatest change at the personal coming of Christ, and of which the words in their highest sense are alone true. **But first . . . suffer . . .**—This shows that the more immediate reference of the previous verse is to an event *soon* to follow the death of Christ. It was designed to withdraw the attention of "His disciples" from the *glare* in which His foregoing words had invested the approaching establishment of His kingdom.

26-30. eat . . . married . . . planted . . .—all the ordinary occupations and enjoyments of life. Though the antediluvian world and the cities of the plain were awfully wicked, it is not their *wickedness*, but their *worldliness*, their unbelief and indifference to the future, their *unpreparedness*, that is here held up as a warning. *N.B.*—These recorded events of Old Testament history—denied or explained away nowadays by not a few—are referred to here as *facts*.

31-33. to take it away . . . Remember . . .—a warning against that *lingering reluctance to part with present treasures* which induces some to remain in a burning house, in hopes of saving this and that precious article till consumed and buried in its ruins. The cases here supposed, though different, are similar. **Lot's wife**—her *"look back,"* for that is all that is said of her, and her recorded *doom*. Her heart was in Sodom still, and the "look" just said, "And must I bid it adieu?" **Whosoever . . .**—(See on ch. 9:23-27).

ADAM CLARKE

When He says, *Ye shall desire to see one of the days of the Son of man*, He either means, you of this nation, you Jews, and addresses His disciples as if they should bear witness to the truth of the declaration, intimating that heavy calamities were about to fall upon them, and that they should desire in vain to have those opportunities of returning to God which now they rejected; or He means that such should the distressed state of this people be that the disciples would through pity and tenderness desire the removal of those punishments from them which could not be removed because the cup of their iniquity was full. But the former is more likely to be the sense of the place.

24. *As the lightning, that lighteneth.* See this particularly explained, Matt. xxiv. 27-28.

25. *But first must he suffer many things.* As the cup of the iniquity of this people shall not be full till they have finally rejected and crucified the Lord of life and glory, so this desolation cannot take place till after My death.

26. *As it was in the days of Noe.* See on Matt. xxiv. 38.

27. *They did eat, they drank.* They spent their whole lives in reference to this world, and made no sort of provision for their immortal souls. So it was when the Romans came to destroy Judea; there was a universal carelessness, and no one seemed to regard the warnings given by the Son of God.

31. *He which shall be upon the house top.* See this explained on Matt. xxiv. 17.

32. *Remember Lot's wife.* Relinquish everything, rather than lose your souls. She "looked back," Gen. xix. 26; probably she turned back also to carry some of her goods away—for so much the preceding verse seems to intimate—and became a monument of the divine displeasure, and of her own folly and sin.

33. *Whosoever shall seek to save his life.* These or similar words were spoken on another occasion. See on Matt. x. 39; xvi. 25-26.

MATTHEW HENRY

(*v.* 33): "*Whosoever shall seek to save his life*, he shall *lose it*; but whosoever is willing to venture his life, he shall *preserve* his life, for he shall make sure of *eternal life*."

7. That all good Christians should certainly escape, but many of them very *narrowly*, *v.* 34–36. When God's judgments are laying all waste, he will take an effectual course to preserve those that are his: *two in a bed, one taken and the other left*. Sooner or later it shall be made to appear that the Lord knows them that are his and them that are not.

8. That this distinguishing, dividing, discriminating work shall be done in all places, as far as the kingdom of God shall extend, *v.* 37. *Where, Lord?* They had enquired concerning the time, and he would not gratify their curiosity, they therefore tried him with another question: "*Where, Lord?*" The answer is proverbial: *Wheresoever the body is, thither will the eagles be gathered together*. (1) Wherever the wicked are, they shall *be found out* by the judgments of God; as wherever a dead carcase is, the birds make a prey of it. The judgments of God shall fasten upon them, as the eagles do upon the prey. (2) Wherever the godly are, who are marked for preservation, they *shall be found* happy in the enjoyment of Christ. Wherever Christ is, believers will flock to him, and meet in him, as eagles about the prey, by the instinct of the new nature. *Wherever the body is*, wherever the gospel is preached, thither will pious souls resort, there they will find Christ. Wherever Christ records his name he will meet his people, and bless them.

CHAPTER 18

Verses 1–8

This parable has its key hanging at the door. Christ spoke it to teach us that *men ought always to pray and not to faint*, *v.* 1. It supposes that all God's people are *praying* people; all God's children send to him *statedly*, and upon *every emergency*. It is our privilege and honour that we *may* pray. It is our duty; we *ought to pray*. It is to be our constant work; we ought *always* to pray. We must pray, and never grow weary of praying, till it comes to be swallowed up in everlasting praise. But that which seems particularly designed here is to teach us constancy and perseverance in our requests for some spiritual mercies that we are in pursuit of, relating either to ourselves or to the church of God. When we are praying for strength against our spiritual enemies, our lusts and corruptions, we must continue instant in prayer, must pray and *not faint*, for we shall not *seek God's face in vain*.

I. Christ shows, by a parable, the *power of importunity* among men. He gives you an instance of an honest cause that succeeded before an unjust judge, not by the equity or compassionableness of it, but purely by *dint of importunity*. 1. The bad character of the judge that was in a certain city. He *neither feared God nor regarded man*; he took no care to do his duty either to God or man; he was a perfect stranger both to godliness and honour. It is not strange if those that have cast off the fear of their Creator be altogether regardless of their fellow-creatures; where no *fear of God* is no good is to be expected. Such a prevalency of irreligion and inhumanity is bad in any, but very bad in a *judge*. Instead of doing good with his power he will be in danger of doing hurt. 2. The distressed case of a poor widow. She had manifestly right on her side; but, it should seem, she tied not herself to the formalities of the law, but made personal application to the judge from day to day, still crying, *Avenge me of mine adversary*, that is, *Do me justice against mine adversary*. Magistrates are particularly charged, not only not to do *violence to the widow* (Jer. xxii. 3), but to *judge the fatherless*, and *plead for the widow* (Isa. i. 17). 3. The difficulty and discouragement she met with in her cause: *He would not for awhile*. According to his usual practice, he took no notice of her cause; for she had no bribe to give him, so that he did not at all incline to redress her grievances. 4. The gaining of her point by continually *dunning* this unjust *judge* (*v.* 5): "*Because this widow troubleth me* I will hear her cause, and do her justice, lest by her clamour to me she weary me; for she is resolved that she will give me no rest till it is done, and therefore I will do it, to save myself further trouble; as good at first as at last." Thus she got justice done her by continual craving.

II. He applies this for the encouragement of God's praying people.

1. He assures them that God will at length be gracious to them (*v.* 6): *Hear what the unjust judge saith, and shall not God avenge his own elect?* Observe, (1) What it is that they desire and expect: that God

JAMIESON, FAUSSET, BROWN

34. two in one bed—the prepared and unprepared mingled in closest intercourse together in the ordinary walks and fellowships of life, when the moment of severance arrives. Awful truth! realized before the destruction of Jerusalem, when the Christians found themselves forced by their Lord's directions (ch. 21:21) at once and for ever away from their old associates; but most of all when the second coming of Christ shall burst upon a heedless world. **37. Where**—shall this occur? **Wheresoever . . .**—"As birds of prey scent out the carrion, so wherever is found a mass of incurable moral and spiritual corruption, there will be seen alighting the ministers of divine judgment," a proverbial saying terrifically verfied at the destruction of Jerusalem, and many times since, though its most tremendous illustration will be at the world's final day.

CHAPTER 18

Vss. 1-8. PARABLE OF THE IMPORTUNATE WIDOW. **1-5. always**—Cf. vs. 7, "night and day." **faint**—lose heart, or slacken.

2. feared not . . . neither regarded—defying the vengeance of God and despising the opinion of men.

widow—weak, desolate, defenseless (I Tim. 5:5, which is taken from this). **3. came**—kept coming. See vs. 5, "her continual coming." **Avenge me**—i.e., rid me of the oppression of. **5. continual coming**—coming for ever.

6-8. the Lord—a name expressive of the *authoritative* style in which He interprets His own parable.

ADAM CLARKE

34 and 36. On the subject of these verses see Matt. xxiv. 40-41. The thirty-sixth verse is, without doubt, an interpolation. It was probably borrowed from Matt. xxiv. 40. The whole verse is wanting in most MSS. and versions and in many of the fathers.

37. *Where, Lord?* In what place shall all these dreadful evils fall? The answer our Lord gives in a figure, the application of which they are to make themselves. Where the "dead carcass" is, there will be the "birds of prey"—where the sin is, there will the punishment be. *Thither will the eagles* (or vultures) *be gathered together*.

CHAPTER 18

1. *Men ought always to pray.* Therefore the plain meaning and moral of the parable are evident; viz., that as afflictions and desolations were coming on the land, and they should have need of much patience and continual fortitude, and the constant influence and protection of the Almighty, therefore they should be instant in prayer. It states, further, that men should never cease praying for that the necessity of which God has given them to feel till they receive a full answer to their prayers. No other meaning need be searched for in this parable; Luke, who perfectly knew his Master's meaning, has explained it as above.

2. *A judge, which feared not God, neither regarded man.* It is no wonder that our Lord calls this person an "unrighteous judge," v. 6. Because this person *feared not God*, he paid no attention to the calls of justice; and because he respected not *man*, he was unmoved at the complaint of the widow.

3. *Avenge me of mine adversary.* The original had better be translated, "Do me justice against, or vindicate me from, my adversary." If the woman had come to get revenge, as our common translation intimates, I think our blessed Lord would never have permitted her to have the honor of a place in the sacred records. She desired to have justice, and that only; and by her importunity she got that which the unrighteous judge had no inclination to give, but merely for his own ease.

4. *He said within himself.* How many actions which appear good have neither the love of God nor that of our neighbor, but only self-love of the basest kind, for their principle and motive!

5. *She weary me.* "Stun me." A metaphor taken from boxers, who bruise each other, and by beating each other about the face "blacken the eyes." See 1 Cor. ix. 27.

6. *Hear what the unjust judge saith.* Our blessed Lord intimates that we should reason thus with ourselves: "If a person of such an infamous character as this judge was could yield to the pressing and continual solicitations of a poor widow, for whom he felt nothing but contempt, how much more ready must God be, who is infinitely good and merciful, and who loves His creatures in the tenderest manner, to give

MATTHEW HENRY

would *avenge his own elect.* There are a people in the world that are God's people, his *own elect.* And this he has an eye to in all he does for them. God's own elect meet with a great deal of trouble and opposition in this world; there are *many adversaries.* That which is wanted and waited for is God's preserving and protecting them.

(2) What it is that is required of God's people: they must *cry day and night to him.* This he has made their duty, and to this he has promised mercy. We ought to be particular in praying against our spiritual enemies, like this importunate widow. Lord, mortify *this* corruption. Lord, arm me against *this* temptation. We ought to concern ourselves for the persecuted and oppressed churches, and to pray that God would do them justice. We must *cry* with earnestness; we must cry *day and night*; we must *wrestle with God.* God's praying people are told to *give him no rest,* Isa. lxii. 6, 7.

(3) What discouragements they may perhaps meet with in their prayers. He may *bear long with them.* He *exercises patience towards* the adversaries of his people, and he *exercises the patience of his people.*

(4) What assurance they have that mercy will come at last, though it be delayed. If this widow prevail by being importunate, much more shall God's elect prevail. [1] This widow was a *stranger,* but God's praying people are his own elect, whom he knows, and loves. [2] She was but *one,* but the praying people of God are *many.* Saints on earth besiege the throne of grace with their united prayers. [3] She came to a *judge* that bade her *keep her distance*; we come to a *Father* that bids us *come boldly* to him. [4] She came to an *unjust judge*; we come to a *righteous Father.* [5] She came to this judge purely upon her own account; but God is himself engaged in the cause which we are soliciting. [6] She had no friend to speak for her, but we have an *Advocate with the Father,* his own Son, who *ever lives to make intercession* for us. [7] She had no encouragement given her to ask; but we have a promise that it shall be given to us. [8] She could have access to the judge only at some certain times; but we may cry to God *day and night,* at all hours. [9] Her importunity was provoking to the judge, but our importunity is pleasing to God, and therefore we may hope, shall avail much, if it be an effectual fervent prayer.

2. He intimates to them that, notwithstanding this, they will begin to be weary of waiting for him (*v.* 8): "*Nevertheless, when the Son of man cometh, shall he find faith on the earth?*" Now, when he comes, will he find faith on the earth? The question implies a strong negation: No, he will not; he himself foresees it.

(1) It supposes that *faith* is the great thing that Jesus Christ *looks for.* He does not ask, Is there innocency? but, *Is there faith?*

(2) It supposes that if there were faith, though ever so little, he would *find it out.*

(3) It is foretold that, when Christ comes he will find but *little faith.* [1] In general, he will find but *few good people.* Many that have the form and fashion of godliness, but few that have faith, that are sincere and honest. [2] In particular, he will find few that have *faith* concerning his coming. It intimates that Christ may, and will, delay his coming so long as that, *First,* Wicked people will begin to *defy it,* and his delay will harden them in their wickedness. *Secondly,* Even his own people will begin to *despair* of it. But this is our comfort, that, when the time appointed comes, it will appear that the unbelief of man has not made the promise of God of no effect.

Verses 9–14

The scope of this parable likewise is prefixed to it. He designed it for the conviction of some who *trusted in themselves that they were righteous, and despised others.* 1. They were such as had a great conceit of themselves; they thought themselves as holy as they needed to be, and holier than all their neighbours. 2. They had a confidence in themselves before God. They *trusted in themselves as being righteous*; they thought they had made God their debtor. 3. They despised others. This is called a *parable,* though the e be nothing of similitude in it. It is matter of fact every day.

I. Here are both these addressing themselves to the duty of prayer at the same place and time (*v.* 10): *Two men went up into the temple to pray.* It was not the hour of public prayer, but they went thither to offer up their personal devotions. The *Pharisee* and the *publican* both went to *the temple to pray.* Among the worshippers of God there is a mixture of good and bad. The Pharisee, proud as he was, could not think himself above prayer; nor could the publican, humble as he was, think himself shut out from the benefit of it. The Pharisee went *to the temple* to

JAMIESON, FAUSSET, BROWN

7. shall not God—not unjust, but the infinitely righteous Judge. **avenge**—redeem from oppression. **his own elect**—not like this widow, the object of indifference and contempt, but dear to Him as the apple of the eye (Zech. 2:8). **cry day and night**—whose every cry enters into the ears of the Lord of Sabaoth (Jas. 5:4), and how much more their incessant and persevering cries! **bear long with them**—rather, "in their case," or "on their account" (as Jas. 5:7, "for it"), [GROTIUS, DE WETTE, etc.]. **8. speedily**—as if pained at the long delay, impatient for the destined moment to interpose. (Cf. Prov. 29:1.)

Nevertheless . . .—i.e., Yet ere the Son of man comes to redress the wrongs of His Church, so low will the hope of relief sink, through the length of the delay, that one will be fain to ask, Will He find any faith of a coming avenger left on the earth? From this we learn: (1) That the *primary* and *historical* reference of this parable is to the Church in its *widowed,* desolate, oppressed, defenseless condition during the present absence of her Lord in the heavens; (2) That in these circumstances importunate, persevering prayer for deliverance is the Church's fitting exercise; (3) That notwithstanding every encouragement to this, so long will the answer be delayed, while the need of relief continues the same, and all hope of deliverance will have nearly died out, and "faith" of Christ's coming scarcely to be found. But the application of the parable to *prayer in general* is so obvious as to have nearly hidden its more direct reference, and so precious that one cannot allow it to disappear in any public and historical interpretation.

9-14. PARABLE OF THE PHARISEE AND THE PUBLICAN.

ADAM CLARKE

His utmost salvation to all them who diligently seek it!"

7. *And shall not God avenge his own elect?* And will not God, the righteous Judge, "do justice for His chosen?" As God has graciously promised to give salvation to every soul that comes unto Him through His Son, and has put His Spirit in their hearts, inducing them to cry unto Him incessantly for it, the goodness of His nature and the promise of His grace bind Him to hear the prayers they offer unto Him, and to grant them all that salvation which He has led them by His promise and Spirit to request. *Which cry day and night unto him.* This is a genuine characteristic of the true elect or disciples of Christ. They feel they have neither light, power, nor goodness but as they receive them from Him; and, as He is the Desire of their souls, they incessantly seek that they may be upheld and saved by Him. *Though he bear long with them.* Rather, "and He is compassionate towards them," and consequently not at all like to the unrighteous judge.

8. *He will avenge them speedily.* Or, "He will do them justice speedily"—"instantly, in a trice." (1) Because He has promised it; and (2) Because He is inclined to do it.

When the Son of man cometh. To require the produce of the seed of the Kingdom sown among this people. *Shall he find faith on the earth?* Or rather, "Shall He find fidelity in this land?" Shall He find that the soil has brought forth a harvest proportioned to the culture bestowed on it?

9. *Despised.* "Disdained, made nothing of others, treated them with sovereign contempt." Our Lord grants that the Pharisees made clean the outside; but, alas! what pride, vainglory, and contempt for others, were lodged within!

10. *Publican.* See an account of these on Matt. v. 46. Both these persons *went up into the temple to pray,* i.e., to worship God. They were probably both Jews, and felt themselves led by different motives to attend at the Temple, at the hour of prayer: the one to return thanks for the mercies he had received; the other to implore that grace which alone could redeem him from his sins.

CHARLES H. SPURGEON:

When Jesus comes He will look for precious faith. He has more regard for faith than for all else that earth can yield Him. Our returning Lord will care nothing for the treasures of the rich or the honors of the great. He will not look for the abilities we have manifested, nor the influence we have acquired; but He will look for our faith. It is His glory that He is "believed on in the world," and to that He will have respect. This is the jewel for which He is searching. This heavenly merchantman counts faith to be the pearl of great price—faith is precious to Jesus as well as to us. The last day will be occupied with a great scrutiny, and that scrutiny will be made upon the essential point—where is there faith, and where is there no faith? He that believeth is saved; he that believeth not is condemned. A search warrant will be issued for our houses and our hearts, and the inquiry will be: Where is your faith? Did you honor Christ by trusting His Word and His blood, or did you not? Did you glorify God by believing His revelation and depending upon His promise, or did you not? The fact that our Lord, at His coming, will seek for faith should cause us to think very highly of faith.

—The Treasury of the New Testament

MATTHEW HENRY

pray because it was a *public* place, and therefore he should have many eyes upon him. The character Christ gave of the Pharisees, that *all their works they did to be seen of men*, gives us occasion for this suspicion. There are many whom we see *every day* at the temple, whom, it is to be feared, we shall not see in the great day at Christ's right hand. The Pharisee came to the temple upon a *compliment*, the publican upon business; the Pharisee to make his appearance, the publican to make his request. God sees with what disposition and design we come to wait upon him.

II. Here is the Pharisee's address to God (for a prayer I cannot call it): He *stood* and *prayed thus with himself* (*v.* 11, 12); *standing by himself, he prayed thus*, so some read it; he was wholly intent upon himself, had nothing in his eye but *self*, not God's glory. That which he is here supposed to say is that which shows,

1. That he *trusted to himself that he was righteous*. A great many good things he said of himself, which we will suppose to be true. He was not an *extortioner*. He was not *unjust* in any of his dealings; he did no man any wrong; he was *no adulterer*. Yet this was not all: he *fasted twice in the week*. Thus he glorified God with his body: yet that was not all; he *gave tithes of all that he possessed*, and so glorified God with his worldly estate. Yet he was not accepted; and why was he not? (1) His giving God thanks for this seems to be a mere formality. He does not say, *By the grace of God I am what I am*, as Paul did, but turns it off with a slight, *God, I thank thee*. (2) He makes his boast of this as if all his business to the temple was to tell God Almighty how very good he was. (3) He *trusted* to it as a righteousness. (4) Here is not one word of prayer in all he saith. He went *up to the temple to pray*, but forgot his errand. He thought he had need of nothing, no, not of the favour and grace of God, which, it would seem, he did not think worth asking.

2. That he *despised others*. (1) He thought meanly of all mankind but himself: *I thank thee that I am not as other men are*. We may have reason to thank God that we are not as *some men* are, but to speak as if *we* only were good, is to judge by wholesale. (2) He thought meanly in a particular manner of this publican. He knew that he was a publican, and therefore very uncharitably concluded that he was an *extortioner, unjust*, and all that is naught. Suppose it had been so, what business had he to take notice of it? Could not he *say his prayers* without reproaching his neighbours? And was he as much pleased with the publican's badness as with his own goodness?

III. Here is the publican's address to God, which was the reverse of the Pharisee's, as full of *humility* and *humiliation* as his was of *pride* and *ostentation*; as full of *repentance* for sin, and *desire* towards God, as his was of *confidence* in *himself*.

1. He expressed his repentance and humility in *what he did*. (1) He *stood afar off*. The publican *kept at a distance* under a sense of unworthiness to draw near to God. Hereby he owned that God might justly *behold him afar off*, and that it was a great favour that God was pleased to admit him *thus nigh*. (2) He *would not lift up so much as his eyes to heaven*. He did *lift up his heart* to God in the heavens, in *holy desires*, but, through prevailing shame and humiliation, he did not lift up his eyes in *holy confidence* and *courage*. The dejection of his looks is an indication of the dejection of his mind at the thought of sin. (3) He *smote upon his breast*. The sinner's heart first smites him in a penitent rebuke. Sinner, what hast thou done? And then he smites his heart with penitent remorse: *O wretched man that I am!*

2. He expressed it *in what he said*. His prayer was *short*. Sighs and groans swallowed up his words; but what he said was to the purpose: *God, be merciful to me a sinner*. And blessed be God that we have this prayer upon record as an answered prayer. (1) He owns himself *a sinner* by nature, by practice, guilty before God. The Pharisee denies himself to be a *sinner*. But the publican gives himself no other character than that of a *sinner*. (2) He has no dependence but upon the *mercy of God*. The Pharisee had insisted upon the *merit* of his fastings and tithes; but the poor publican disclaims all thought of merit, and flies to mercy as his city of refuge. "Justice condemns me; nothing will save me but mercy, mercy." (3) He earnestly prays for the benefit of that mercy: "*O God, be merciful*, be *propitious, to me*." He comes as a beggar for an alms, when he is ready to perish for hunger. Probably he repeated this prayer with renewed affections, but still this was the burden of the song: *God, be merciful to me a sinner*.

IV. Here is the publican's *acceptance with God*. There were those who would cry up the Pharisee, and who would look with contempt upon this

JAMIESON, FAUSSET, BROWN

11, 12. stood—as the Jews in prayer (Mark 11:25). **God . . .**—To have been kept from gross iniquities was undoubtedly a just cause of thankfulness to God; but instead of the devoutly humble, admiring frame which this should inspire, the Pharisee arrogantly severs himself from the rest of mankind, as quite above them, and, with a contemptuous look at the poor publican, thanks God that he has not to stand afar off like him, to hang down his head like a bulrush and beat his breast like him. But these are only his *moral* excellencies. His *religious* merits complete his grounds for congratulation. Not confining himself to the one divinely prescribed annual fast (Lev. 16:29), he was not behind the most rigid, who fasted on the second and fifth days of every week [LIGHTFOOT], and gave the tenth not only of what the law laid under tithing, but of "all his gains." Thus, besides doing *all his duty*, he did *works of supererogation;* while sins to confess and spiritual wants to be supplied he seems to have felt none. What a picture of the Pharisaic character and religion!

13. standing afar off—as unworthy to draw near; but that was the way *to get* near (Ps. 34:18; Isa. 57:15). **would not lift up**—blushing and ashamed to do so (Ezra 9:6).

smote . . .—kept smiting; for anguish (ch. 23:48), and self-reproach (Jer. 31:19).

be merciful—"be propitiated," a very unusual word in such a sense, only once else used in the New Testament, in the sense of "making reconciliation" by sacrifice (Heb. 2:17). There *may* therefore, be some allusion to this here, though not likely. **a sinner**—literally, "*the* sinner"; i.e., "If ever there was one, I am he."

ADAM CLARKE

11. *Stood and prayed thus with himself.* Or "stood by himself and prayed," as some would translate the words. *God, I thank thee.* In Matt. v. 20, our Lord says, "Unless your righteousness abounds more than that of the scribes and Pharisees, you shall not enter into the kingdom of God." Now the righteousness of the scribes and Pharisees is described here by a Pharisee himself. We find it was twofold: (1) It consisted in doing no harm to others, (2) In attending all the ordinances of God, then established in the Jewish economy; and in these things they were not like *other men*, the bulk of the inhabitants of the land paying little or no attention to them. That the Pharisees were in their origin a pure and holy people can admit of little doubt, but that they had awfully degenerated before our Lord's time is sufficiently evident. They had lost the spirit of their institution, and retained nothing else than its external regulations. This Pharisee did no harm to others—I am not rapacious, nor unjust, nor an adulterer.

12. He observed the ordinances of religion—*I fast twice in the week.* The Jewish days of fasting, in each week, were the second and fifth, what we call Monday and Thursday. These were instituted in remembrance of Moses' going up to the mount to give the law, which they suppose to have been on the fifth day; and of his descent, after he had received the two tables, which they suppose was on the second day of the week. *I give tithes of all that I possess.* Or "of all I acquire."

13. *The publican, standing afar off.* Not because he was a heathen and dared not approach the holy place (for it is likely he was a Jew), but because he was a true penitent, and felt himself utterly unworthy to appear before God. *Would not lift up . . . his eyes.* Holding down the head, with the eyes fixed upon the earth, was (1) a sign of deep distress, (2) of a consciousness and confession of guilt, and (3) it was the very posture that the Jewish rabbins required in those who prayed to God. So the Pharisee appears to have forgotten one of his own precepts. *But smote upon his breast.* Smiting the breast was a token of excessive grief, commonly practiced in all nations. It seems to intimate a desire in the penitent to punish that heart through the evil propensities of which the sin deplored had been committed.

God be merciful to me. "Be propitious toward me through sacrifice"—or, Let an atonement be made for me. I am a sinner, and cannot be saved but in this way. The Greek word often signifies to make expiation for sin. We see then, at once, the reason why our blessed Lord said that the taxgatherer "went down to his house

MATTHEW HENRY

sneaking whining publican. But our Lord Jesus assures us that this poor, penitent, broken-hearted publican *went to his house justified, rather than the other.* The Pharisee thought that if one of them must be justified, and not the other, certainly it must be he rather than the publican. "No," saith Christ, "*I tell you* it is the publican rather than the Pharisee." The proud Pharisee goes away rejected of God; he is *not justified.* He is not accepted as righteous in God's sight, because he is so righteous in his own sight; but the publican obtains the remission of his sins, and he whom the Pharisee would not set *with the dogs of his flock* God sets with the *children of his family.* Proud men, who *exalt themselves,* are *rivals with God,* and therefore *they shall* certainly be *abased.* Humble men, who *abase themselves,* are *subject to God,* and they shall be *exalted.* See how the punishment answers the sin: *He that exalteth himself shall be abased.* See how the recompense answers the duty: *He that humbles himself shall be exalted.* See also the power of God's grace in bringing good out of evil; the publican had been a great sinner, and out of the greatness of his sin was brought the greatness of his repentance. It was good that the Pharisee was no extortioner, nor unjust; but the devil made him proud of this, to his ruin.

Verses 15–17

1. Those who are themselves blessed in Christ should desire to have their children also blessed in him. They brought to him *infants,* very young, not able to go, sucking children, as some think. None are too little, too young, to bring to Christ. 2. One gracious touch of Christ's will make our children happy. They *brought infants to him, that he might touch them.* 3. It is no strange thing for those who make their application to Jesus Christ, for themselves or for their children, to meet with discouragement: *When the disciples saw it* they *rebuked them.* 4. Many whom the disciples rebuke the Master invites: *Jesus called them unto him.* 5. It is the mind of Christ that *little children* should be brought to him: "*Suffer little children to come to me, and forbid them not;* let nothing be done to hinder them, for they shall be as welcome as any." 6. The children of those who belong to the kingdom of God do likewise belong to that kingdom, as the children of freemen are freemen. 7. Those grown people are most welcome to him who have in them most of the disposition of children (*v.* 17): *Whosoever shall not receive the kingdom of God as a little child,* that is, receive the benefits of it with humility and thankfulness, gladly owning himself indebted to free grace for them; unless a man be brought to this self-denying frame he shall *in no wise enter* into that kingdom.

Verses 18–30

I. Christ's discourse with a ruler, that had a good mind to be directed by him in the way to heaven.

1. Luke takes notice of it that he was a *ruler.* Few of the rulers had any esteem for Christ, but here was one that had.

2. The great thing we are everyone of us concerned to enquire after is, *what we shall do to inherit eternal life.*

3. Those who would inherit eternal life must apply themselves to Jesus Christ as their *Master,* their *teaching* Master, and their *ruling* Master. There is no learning the way to heaven but in the school of Christ.

4. Those who come to Christ as their Master must believe him to have not only a *divine mission,* but a *divine goodness.* "*Why callest thou me good?* Thou knowest *there is none good but one, that is, God.*"

JAMIESON, FAUSSET, BROWN

14. rather than the other—The meaning is, "and not the other"; for the Pharisee was not seeking justification, and felt no need of it. This great law of the Kingdom of God is, in the teaching of Christ, inscribed, as in letters of gold, over its entrance gate. And in how many different forms is it repeated (Ps. 138:6; 147:6; ch. 1:53). To be *self-emptied,* or, "poor in spirit," is the fundamental and indispensable preparation for the reception of the "grace which bringeth salvation": wherever this exists, the "mourning" for it which precedes "comfort" and the earnest "hungerings and thirstings after righteousness" which are rewarded by the "fulness" of it, will, as we see here, be surely found. Such, therefore, and such only, are the justified ones (Job 33:27, 28; Ps. 34:18; Isa. 57:15).

15-17. LITTLE CHILDREN BROUGHT TO CHRIST. **infants**—showing that some, at least, of those called in Matthew (19:13) and Mark (10:13) simply "little" or "young children," were literally "*babes.*" **touch them**—or, as more fully in Matthew, "put His hands on them and *pray,*" or invoke a "blessing" on them (Mark 10:16), according to venerable custom (Gen. 48:14, 15). **rebuked them**—Repeatedly the disciples thus interposed to save annoyance and interruption to their Master; but, as the result showed, *always against the mind of Christ* (Matt. 15:23; ch. 18:39, 40). Here, it is plain from our Lord's reply, that they thought the intrusion a useless one, as *infants* were not capable of receiving anything from Him. His ministrations were for *grown people.* **16. But Jesus**—*much displeased,"* says Mark (10:14); and invaluable addition. **said**—"SUFFER THE LITTLE CHILDREN TO COME UNTO ME"—"AND FORBID THEM NOT," is the important addition of Matthew (19:14) and Mark (10:14). What words are these from the lips of Christ! The price of them is above rubies. But the *reason* assigned, "FOR OF SUCH IS THE KINGDOM OF GOD," or "of heaven," as in Matthew 19:14, completes the previous information here conveyed; especially as interpreted by what immediately follows: "AND HE TOOK THEM UP IN HIS ARMS, PUT HIS HANDS UPON THEM, AND BLESSED THEM" (Mark 10:16). It is surely not to be conceived that all our Lord meant was to inform us, that seeing *grown people* must become childlike in order to be capable of the Kingdom of God, therefore they should not hinder *infants* from coming to Him, and therefore He took up and blessed *the infants themselves.* Was it not just the grave mistake of the disciples that infants should not be brought to Christ, because only grown people could profit by Him, which "much displeased" our Lord? And though He took the irresistible opportunity of lowering their pride of reason, by informing them that, in order to enter the Kingdom, "*instead of the children first becoming like them, they must themselves become like the children*" [RICHTER in STIER], this was but by the way; and, returning to the *children themselves,* He took them up in His gracious arms, put His hands upon them and blessed them, for no conceivable reason but to show that *they were thereby made capable,* AS INFANTS, *of the Kingdom of God.* And if so, then "*Can any man forbid water that these should not be baptized which have received the Holy Ghost as well as we?"* (Acts 10:47). But such application of the baptismal water can have no warrant here, save where the infants have been *previously brought to Christ Himself* for His benediction, and only as the *sign and seal* of that benediction.

18-30. THE RICH YOUNG RULER, AND DISCOURSE THEREON. This case presents some remarkable points. (1) The man was of irreproachable moral character; and this amidst all the temptations of *youth,* for he was a "young man" (Matt. 19:22), and *wealth,* for "he was very rich" (vs. 23; Mark 10:22). (2) But restless notwithstanding, his heart craves eternal life. (3) Unlike the "rulers," to whose class he belonged (vs. 18), he so far believed in Jesus as to be persuaded He could authoritatively direct him on this vital point. (4) So earnest is he that he comes "running" and even "kneeling before Him," and that when He was gone forth *into the war* (Mark 10:17)—the high-road, by this time crowded with travellers to the passover; undeterred by the virulent opposition of the class he belonged to as a "ruler" and by the shame he might be expected to feel at broaching such a question in the hearing of a crowd and on the open road. **19. Why . . .**—Did our Lord mean then to teach that God only ought to be called "good"? Impossible, for that had been to contradict all Scripture teaching, and His own, too (Ps. 112:5; Matt. 25:21; Titus 1:8). Unless therefore we are to ascribe captiousness to our Lord, He could have had but one object — *to raise the*

ADAM CLARKE

justified rather than the other"; he sought for mercy through an atonement for sin, which was the only way in which God had from the beginning purposed to save sinners. As the Pharisee depended on his doing no harm and observing the ordinances of religion for his acceptance with God, according to the economy of grace and justice, he must be rejected. For as all had sinned and come short of the glory of God, and no man could make an atonement for his sins, so he who did not take refuge in that which God's mercy had provided must be excluded from the kingdom of Heaven.

14. *Went down to his house justified.* His sin blotted out, and himself accepted. *Rather than the other.* That is, the other was not accepted, because he exalted himself—he made use of the mercies which he acknowledged he owed to God, to make claims on the divine approbation, and to monopolize the salvation of the Most High!

15-17. *They brought unto him also infants.* On these verses the reader is requested to consult the notes on Matt. xix. 13-14 and on Mark x. 16.

Then were there brought unto him little children. These are termed by Luke, chap. xviii. 15, "infants," very young children; and it was on this account, probably, that the disciples rebuked the parents, thinking them too young to receive good. *That he should put his hands.* It was a common custom among the Jews to lay their hands on the heads of those whom they blessed or for whom they prayed. This seems to have been done by way of dedication or consecration to God—the person being considered as the sacred property of God ever after.

Of such is the kingdom of heaven. Or, "The kingdom of heaven is composed of such." A great part of God's kingdom is composed of such literally, and those only who resemble little children shall be received into it; see on chap. xviii. 3. Christ loves little children because He loves simplicity and innocence; He has sanctified their very age by passing through it himself—the holy Jesus was once a little child.

18-23. *A certain ruler.* See the case of this person largely explained on Matt. xix. 16-22 and Mark x. 21-22.

One came. Much instruction may be had from seriously attending to the conduct, spirit, and question of this person. (1) He came running, Mark x. 17, and he was deeply convinced of the importance of his business, and seriously determined to seek so as to find. (2) He kneeled, or caught Him by the knees, thus evidencing his humility, and addressing himself only to mercy. (3) He came in the spirit of a disciple, or scholar, desiring to be taught a matter of the utmost importance to him—Good teacher. (4) He came in the spirit of obedience; he had worked hard to no purpose, and he is still willing to work, provided he can have a prospect of succeeding—*What good thing shall I do?* (5) His question was the most interesting and important that any soul can ask of God—How shall I be saved?

Why callest thou me good? Or, "Why do you question Me concerning that good thing?" The whole passage therefore may be read thus:

MATTHEW HENRY

5. Our Master, Christ himself, has not altered the way to heaven from what it was before his coming, but has only made it more plain, and easy, and comfortable. *Thou knowest the commandments.* Wouldest thou inherit eternal life? Govern thyself by the commandments.

6. The duties of the second table must be conscientiously observed. Nor is it enough to keep ourselves free from the gross violations of these commandments, but we must *know these commandments* in their extent and spiritual nature.

7. Men think themselves *innocent* because they are *ignorant*; so this ruler did. He said, *All these have I kept from my youth up*, v. 21. He boasts that he began *early* in a course of virtue, that he had continued in it to this day, and that he had not in any instance transgressed. Had he been acquainted with the nature of the divine law, and with the workings of his own heart,—had he been but Christ's disciple awhile, he would have said quite the contrary: "*All these have* I broken from my youth up."

8. The great things are how we stand affected to Christ and to our brethren, to this world and to the other. If he have a true *affection to Christ*, he will *come and follow him* whatever it cost him. None shall inherit eternal life who are not willing to follow the Lamb whithersoever he goes. If he have a true *affection to his brethren*, he will *distribute to the poor*. If he think meanly of *this world* he will not stick at *selling what he has* for the relief of God's poor. If he think highly of the other world, he will desire no more than to have *treasure in heaven*.

9. There are many that have a great deal in them that is very commendable, and yet they perish *for lack of some one thing*; so this *ruler* here; he broke with Christ upon this, which would part between him and his estate.

10. Many that are loth to leave Christ, yet do leave him. Their corruptions carry the day at last. If one must be quitted, it shall be their God, not their worldly gain.

II. Christ's discourse with his disciples upon this occasion, in which we may observe, 1. Riches are a great hindrance to many in the way to heaven. He *saw that he was very sorrowful*, and was sorry for him; but thence he infers, *How hardly shall they that have riches enter into the kingdom of God! v.* 24. Having a great estate, it had a great influence upon him, and he chose rather to take his leave of Christ than to lay himself under an obligation to dispose of his estate in charitable uses. Christ asserts the difficulty of the salvation of rich people very emphatically: *It is easier for a camel to go through a needle's eye than for a rich man to enter into the kingdom of God, v.* 25. 2. It is really very hard for any to get to heaven. If we must *sell all*, or break with Christ, *who then can be saved*? *v.* 26. They do not find fault with what Christ required as hard and unreasonable. But they know how closely the hearts of most men cleave to this world, and are ready to despair of their being ever brought to this. 3. There are such difficulties in the way of our salvation as could never be got over but by that grace of God which is almighty. The *things which are impossible with men*, these things are *possible with God*. His grace can work upon the soul, so as to alter the bent and bias of it, and give it a contrary ply. 4. There is an aptness in us to speak too much of what we have left and lost for Christ. This appears in Peter: *Lo we have left all, and followed thee, v.* 28. When it came in his way, he could not forbear magnifying his own and his brethren's affection to Christ, in *quitting* all to follow him. 5. Whatever we have left for Christ, it shall without fail be abundantly made up to us in this world and that to come (*v.* 29, 30): *No man has left* the comfort of his estate or relations *for the kingdom of God's sake, who shall not receive manifold more in this present time*, in the pleasures of communion with God and of a good conscience, advantages which will abundantly countervail all their losses. In the world to come they *shall receive life everlasting*, which is the thing that the ruler seemed to have his eye and heart upon.

JAMIESON, FAUSSET, BROWN

youth's ideas of Himself, as not to be classed merely with other "good masters," and declining to receive this title *apart from* the "One" who is essentially and only "good." This indeed is but distantly hinted; but unless this is seen in *the background* of our Lord's words, nothing worthy of Him can be made out of them. (Hence, *Socinianism*, instead of having any support here, is only baffled by it.) **20. Thou knowest . . .**—Matthew is more complete here: "but if thou wilt enter into life, keep the commandments. He saith unto him, Which?"—as if he had said, Point me out one of them which I have not kept?—"Jesus said, Thou shalt . . ." (Matt. 19: 17, 18). Our Lord purposely confines Himself to the *second* table, which He would consider easy to keep, enumerating them all—for in Mark (10:19), "Defraud not" stands for the *tenth* (else the eighth is twice repeated). In Matthew the *sum* of this second table of the law is added, "Thou shalt love thy neighbor as thyself," as if to see if he would venture to say he had kept *that*. **21. All these . . .**—"what lack I yet?" adds Matthew. Ah! this gives us a glimpse of his heart. Doubtless he was perfectly sincere; but something within whispered to him that *his* keeping of the commandments was *too easy* a way of getting to heaven. He felt something beyond this to be necessary; after keeping all the commandments he was at a loss to know what that could be; and he came to Jesus just upon that point. "Then," says Mark (10:21), "Jesus beholding him loved him," or "looked lovingly upon him." His sincerity, frankness, and nearness to the kingdom of God, in themselves most winning qualities, won our Lord's regard even though he turned his back upon Him—a lesson to those who can see nothing lovable save in the regenerate. **22. lackest . . . one thing**—Ah! but that a fundamental, fatal lack. **sell . . .**—As riches were his idol, our Lord, who knew if from the first, lays His great authoritative grasp at once upon it, saying, "Now give Me up that, and all is right." No general direction about the disposal of riches, then, is here given, save that we are to sit loose to them and lay them at the feet of Him who gave them. He who does this with all he has, whether rich or poor, is a true heir of the kingdom of heaven. **23-25. was very sorrowful**—Matthew more fully, "*went away* sorrowful"; Mark still more, "was sad" or "sullen" at that saying, and "went away grieved." Sorry he was, very sorry, to part with Christ; but to part with his riches would have cost him a pang more. When Riches or Heaven, on Christ's terms, were the alternative, the result showed to which side the balance inclined. Thus was he shown to lack the one all-comprehensive requirement of the law—the *absolute subjection of the heart to God*, and this want vitiated all his other obediences. **24. when Jesus saw**—Mark says, He "looked round about"—as if first following the departing youth with His eye—"and saith unto His disciples." **how hardly . . .**—with what difficulty. In Mark an explanation is added, "How hard is it for them that *trust* in riches . . ."—i.e., with what difficulty is this idolatrous trust conquered, without which they cannot enter; and this is introduced by the word "children"—sweet diminutive of affection and pity (John 21:5). **easier for a camel . . .**—a proverbial expression denoting literally a thing impossible, but figuratively, very difficult. **26, 27. For . . .**—"At that rate none can be saved": "Well, it does pass *human* power, but not *divine*. **28-30. Lo . . .**—in the simplicity of his heart (as is evident from the reply), conscious that the required surrender had been made, and generously taking in his brethren with him—"*we*"; not in the spirit of the young ruler. "All these have I kept," **left all**—"The workmen's little is as much his 'all' as the prince's much [BENGEL]. In Matthew (19:27) he adds, "What shall we have therefore?" How shall it fare with us? **29. There is no man . . .**—graciously acknowledging at once the completeness and the acceptableness of the surrender as a thing already made. **house . . .**—The specification is still more minute in Matthew and Mark, to take in *every* form of self-sacrifice. **for the kingdom of God's sake**—in Mark, "for MY sake and the Gospel's." See on ch. 6:22. **30. manifold more in this present time**—in Matthew (19:29) "an hundredfold," to which Mark (10:30) gives this most interesting addition, "Now in this present time, houses, and brethren, and sisters, and mothers, and children, and lands, with persecutions." We have here the blessed promise of a *reconstruction of all human relationships and affections on a Christian basis and in a Christian state, after being sacrificed, in their natural form, on the altar of love to Christ.* This He calls "manifold more"—"an hundredfold more"—than what they sacrificed.

ADAM CLARKE

"O Teacher! what good thing shall I do that I may have eternal life? And He said unto him, Why do you question Me concerning that good thing? There is One that is good." *Keep the commandments.* From this we may learn that God's great design in giving His law to the Jews was to lead them to the expectation and enjoyment of eternal life. But as all the law referred to Christ, and He became "the end of the law for righteousness" (justification) to all that believe, so He is to be received, in order to have the end accomplished which the law proposed.

All these things have I kept. I have made these precepts the rule of my life. There is a difference worthy of notice between this and our Lord's word. He says, v. 17, *keep*, earnestly, diligently, as with watch and ward, probably referring not only to the letter but to the spirit. The young man modestly says, All these have I "observed"; I have paid attention to, and endeavored to regulate my conduct by them. I have "kept them in custody." *What lack I yet?* He felt a troubled conscience, and a mind unassured of the approbation of God; and he clearly perceived that something was wanting to make him truly happy.

If thou wilt be perfect. "Be complete," have the business "finished," and all hindrances to your salvation removed, *go and sell that thou hast*—go and dispose of your possessions, to which it is evident his heart was too much attached, *and give to the poor*—for your goods will be a continual snare to you if you keep them; *and thou shalt have treasure in heaven*—the loss, if it can be called such, shall be made amply up to you in that eternal life about which you inquired; *and come and follow me*—be My disciple, and I will appoint you to preach the kingdom of God to others.

Went away sorrowful. Men undergo great agony of mind while they are in suspense between the love of the world and the love of their souls. *He had great possessions.* And what were these in comparison of peace of conscience and mental rest?

24. *How hardly shall they that have riches.* See the notes on this discourse of our Lord, on Matt. xix. 24-30 and Mark x. 30.

A rich man shall hardly enter. That is, into the spirit and privileges of the gospel in this world, and through them into the Kingdom of glory.

A camel. It was a mode of expression common among the Jews, and signified a thing impossible. Hence this proverb: "No man sees a palm tree of gold, nor an elephant passing through the eye of a needle."

28. *We have left all.* Our trades, our houses, and families. The reader is desired to consult the notes on Matt. iv. 20; xix. 27, etc.

29. *That hath left house, or parents.* See on Matt. xix. 28-29 and Mark x. 29-30.

MATTHEW HENRY

Verses 31-34

I. The notice Christ gave to his disciples of his sufferings and death approaching, and of the glorious issue of them. Two things are here which we had not in the other evangelists:—1. The *sufferings* of Christ are here spoken of as the *fulfilling of the scriptures. All things that are written by the prophets concerning the Son of man shall be accomplished.* This proves that the scriptures are the *word of God*, for they had their exact and full accomplishment; and that Jesus Christ was *sent of God*, for they had their accomplishment *in him*. This makes the *offence of the cross to cease*, and puts an honour upon it. *Thus it was written, and thus it behoved Christ to suffer.* 2. The ignominy and disgrace done to Christ in his sufferings are here most insisted upon. The other evangelists had said that he should be *mocked*; but here it is added, *He shall be spitefully treated*, shall have all possible reproach put upon him. But here, as always, when Christ spoke of his sufferings and death, he foretold his resurrection as that which took off both the terror and reproach of his sufferings: *The third day he shall rise again.*

II. The confusion that the disciples were hereby put into. This was so contrary to the notions they had had of the Messiah and his kingdom that *they understood none of these things*, *v.* 34. Their prejudices were so strong that they *would not* understand them literally, and they *could not* understand them otherwise, so that they did not understand them at all. This saying was *hidden from them*, they could not receive it. They were so intent upon those prophecies that spoke of his glory that they overlooked those that spoke of his *sufferings*. *Therefore* it is that people run into mistakes, because they *read their Bibles by the halves*, and are as partial in the prophets as they are *in the law*. Thus now we are too apt, in reading, the prophecies that are yet to be fulfilled, to have our expectations raised of the glorious state of the church in the latter days. But we overlook its wilderness sackcloth state, and are willing to fancy that is over.

Verses 35-43

Christ came not only to bring *light* to a *dark* world, and so to set before us the *objects* we are to have in view, but also to give *sight* to blind *souls*, to enable them to view those objects. We have now an account of one to whom he *gave sight* near Jericho. Mark gives us an account of one, and names him, whom he cured *as he went out of Jericho*, Mark x. 46. Matthew speaks of two whom he cured *as they departed* from Jericho, Matt. xx. 30. Luke says it was *when he was near* to Jericho.

I. This poor blind man *sat by the wayside, begging*, *v.* 35. It seems, he was not only *blind*, but *poor*; the fitter emblem of the world of mankind which Christ came to heal and save. He sat begging, for he was blind, and could not work for his living. Such objects of charity *by the wayside* ought not to be overlooked by us. Christ here cast a favourable eye upon a *common beggar*.

II. Hearing the noise of a multitude passing by, he asked *what it meant*, *v.* 36. This we had not before. It teaches us that it is good to be *inquisitive*, and that those who are so some time or other find the benefit of it. Those who want their *sight* should make so much the better use of their *hearing*, and, when they cannot see with their own eyes, should, by *asking questions*, make use of other people's eyes. So this blind man did, and by that means came to understand that Jesus of Nazareth *passed by*, *v.* 37.

III. His prayer has in it a great deal both of faith and fervency: *Jesus, thou Son of David, have mercy on me*, *v.* 38. He believes he is able to help and succour him, and earnestly begs his favour: "*Have mercy on me.*" *Have mercy on us;* for Christ's mercy includes all.

IV. Those who are in good earnest for Christ's favours and blessings will not be put by from the pursuit of them, though they meet with opposition and rebuke. They who went along chid him as troublesome to the Master, noisy and impertinent, and bade him *hold his peace*. The check given him was but as a dam to a full stream, which makes it swell so much the more: he *cried the louder, Thou Son of David, have mercy on me.*

V. Christ encourages poor beggars and invites them to come to him: *He commanded him to be brought to him.* Christ has more tenderness and compassion for distressed supplicants than any of his followers have. Those who had checked him must now lend him their hands to lead him to Christ.

VI. Though Christ knows all our wants, he will know them from us (*v.* 41): *What wilt thou that I shall do unto thee?* This man poured out his soul before Christ, when he said, *Lord, that I may receive my sight.*

JAMIESON, FAUSSET, BROWN

Our Lord was Himself the first to exemplify this *new adjustment of His own relationships.* (See on Matt. 12:49, 50; and on II Cor. 6:14-18.) But this "with persecutions"; for how could such a transfer take place without the most cruel wrenches to flesh and blood? but the persecution would haply follow them into their new and higher circle, breaking that up too! But best of all, "in the world to come life everlasting." And

When the shore is won at last
Who will count the billows past?
KEBLE

These promises are for *every one* who forsakes his all for Christ. But in Matthew (19:28) this is prefaced by a special promise to *the Twelve*: "Verily I say unto you, That ye which have followed Me in the Regeneration, when the Son of man shall sit in the throne of His glory, ye also shall sit on twelve thrones judging the twelve tribes of Israel." Ye who have now adhered to Me shall, in the new kingdom, rule, or give law to, the great Christian world, here set forth in Jewish dress as the twelve tribes, presided over by the twelve apostles on so many judicial thrones. In this sense certainly the promise has been illustriously fulfilled [CALVIN, GROTIUS, LIGHTFOOT, etc.]. But if the promise refers to the yet future glory (as may be thought from ch. 22:28-30, and as most take it), it points to the highest personal distinction of the first founders of the Christian Church.

31-34. FULLER ANNOUNCEMENT OF HIS APPROACHING DEATH AND RESURRECTION. (See on Mark 10:32-34). **31. all written by the prophets concerning the Son of man . . . be accomplished**—showing how Christ Himself read, and would have us to read, the Old Testament, in which some otherwise evangelical interpreters find no prophecies, or *virtually* none, of the sufferings of the Son of man. **34. understood none . . .**—The Evangelist seems unable to say strongly enough how entirely hidden from them at that time was the *sense* of these exceeding plain statements: no doubt to add weight to their subsequent testimony, which from this very circumstance was prodigious, and with all the simple-hearted irresistible.

35-43. BLIND MAN HEALED. In Matthew 20: 29-34, they are *two*, as in the case of the Demoniac of Gadara. In Matthew and Mark (10:46-52) the occurrence is connected with Christ's *departure from* Jericho; in Luke with His *approach to it.* Many ways of accounting for these slight divergences of detail have been proposed. Perhaps, *if we knew all the facts*, we should see no difficulty; but that we have been left so far in the dark shows that the thing is of no moment any way. One thing is plain, there could have been no collusion among the authors of these Gospels, else they would have taken care to remove these "spots on the sun."

38. son of David . . .—(See on Matthew 12:23).

39. rebuked . . .—(See on vs. 15). **so much the more**—that *importunity* so commended in the Syrophœnician woman, and so often enjoined (ch. 11:5-13; 18:1-8). **40. commanded . . .**—Mark has this interesting addition: "And they call the blind man, saying unto him, Be of good comfort, rise, He calleth thee"—just as one earnestly desiring an interview with some exalted person, but told by one official after another that it is vain to wait, as he will not succeed (they know it), yet persists in waiting for some answer to his suit, and at length the door opens, and a servant appears, saying, "You will be admitted—he has called you." *And are there no other suitors to Jesus who sometimes fare*

ADAM CLARKE

31. *Behold, we go up to Jerusalem.* See the notes on this discourse, Matt. xx. 17-19 and Mark x. 32.

33. *And the third day he shall rise again.* See Hos. vi. 2; and let the reader observe that the passage should be read thus: "In the third day He will raise Him up, and we shall live before Him"; His resurrection shall be the pledge, token, and cause of ours.

34. *They understood none of these things.* Notwithstanding all the information which Christ had given them concerning this awful subject, they could not as yet fully comprehend how the Messiah should suffer; or how their Master, whose power they knew was unlimited, should permit the Jews and Gentiles to torment and slay Him as He here intimates they would.

35. *A certain blind man.* Bartimaeus. See this transaction explained at large on Matt. xx. 29-34 and Mark x. 46, etc.

Two blind men. Mark x. 46 and Luke xviii. 35 mention only one blind man, Bartimaeus. Probably he was mentioned by the other Evangelists as being a person well-known before and after his cure. *Sitting by the way side.* In the likeliest place to receive alms, because of the multitudes going and coming between Jerusalem and Jericho.

Cried out. Though God had deprived them, for wise reasons, of their eyes, He left them the use of their speech. It is never so ill with us but it might be much worse; let us therefore be submissive and thankful.

MATTHEW HENRY	JAMIESON, FAUSSET, BROWN	ADAM CLARKE

MATTHEW HENRY

VII. The prayer of faith shall not be in vain (*v.* 42); Christ said, *Receive thy sight, thy faith hath saved thee.* True faith will produce fervency in prayer, and both together will fetch in abundance of the fruits of Christ's favour.

VIII. The *grace of Christ* ought to be thankfully acknowledged, *v.* 43. 1. The poor beggar himself, that had his sight restored, *followed Christ, glorifying God.* Those whom he healed *pleased him* best when they *praised God*, as those shall *please God* best who *praise Christ* and do him honour. 2. The *people that saw it* could not forbear *giving praise to God.* We must give praise to God for his mercies to others as well as for mercies to ourselves.

JAMIESON, FAUSSET, BROWN

thus? "And he, casting away his garment"—how lively is this touch, evidently of an eye-witness, expressive of his earnestness and joy—"came to Jesus" (Mark 10:49, 50). **41-43. What wilt thou . . .** —to try them; to deepen their present consciousness of need; and to draw out their faith in Him. **Lord** "*Rabboni*" (Mark 10:51); an emphatic and confiding exclamation. (See on John 9.)

ADAM CLARKE

That our eyes may be opened. He who feels his own sore, and the plague of his heart, has no great need of a prompter in prayer. A hungry man can easily ask bread; he has no need to go to a book to get expressions to state his wants in. His hunger tells him he wants food, and he tells this to the person from whom he expects relief.

MATTHEW HENRY

CHAPTER 19

Verses 1-10

Many, no doubt, were converted to the faith of Christ of whom no account is kept in the gospels; but the conversion of some, whose case had something in it extraordinary, is recorded, as this of Zaccheus. Christ passed through Jericho, *v.* 1. This city was built under a curse, yet Christ honoured it with his presence, for the gospel *takes away the curse.*

I. Who, and what, this Zaccheus was. His name bespeaks him a Jew. 1. His calling, and the post he was in: *He was the chief among the publicans.* Here was one that was *chief* of the publicans, that enquired after him. God has his remnant among all sorts. Christ came to save even the *chief of sinners*, and therefore even the *chief of publicans.* 2. His circumstances in the world were very considerable: *He was rich.* Christ had lately shown how *hard* it is for *rich people to enter into the kingdom of God*, yet presently produces an instance of one rich man that had been lost, and was found, and that not as the prodigal by being reduced to want.

II. How he came in Christ's way. 1. He had a great *curiosity to see Jesus, v.* 3. It is natural to us to come in sight, if we can, of those whose fame has filled our ears; at least, we shall be able to say hereafter that we have seen such and such *great men.* We should now *seek to see Jesus* with an eye of faith, to see *who he is*; *We would see Jesus.* 2. He could not get his curiosity gratified in this matter because he was *little*, and the crowd was *great.* Christ did not study to *show himself.* As *one of us*, he was *lost in a crowd.* Many that are little of stature have large souls, and are lively in spirit. 3. Because he would not disappoint his curiosity he *forgot his gravity*, and *ran before*, like a boy, and *climbed up into a sycamore-tree, to see him.* Those that sincerely desire a sight of Christ will use the proper means for gaining a sight of him. Those that find themselves *little* must take all the advantages they can get to *raise themselves* to a sight of Christ. Let not dwarfs despair, with good help, by aiming high to reach high.

III. The notice Christ took of him, the call he gave him to a further acquaintance (*v.* 5), and the efficacy of that call, *v.* 6. 1. Christ *invited himself* to Zaccheus's house. Christ *looked* up into the tree, and *saw* Zaccheus. He came to look upon Christ, but little thought of being taken notice of by Christ. See how Christ *prevented* him with the blessings of his goodness, and *outdid* his expectations; and see how he *encouraged* very weak beginnings. He that had a mind to know Christ shall be *known of him*; he that only courted to see him shall be admitted to converse with him. And sometimes those that come to hear the word of Christ, as Zaccheus did, only for curiosity, have their consciences awakened, and their hearts changed. Christ called him *by name, Zaccheus.* He bade him *make haste, and come down.* Zaccheus must not hesitate, but hasten. He must *come down*, for Christ intends this day to *bait at his house*, and *stay* an hour or two with him. 2. Zaccheus was *overjoyed* to have such an honour put upon his house (*v.* 6): *He made haste, and came down, and received him joyfully;* and his receiving him *into his house* was an indication and token of his receiving him *into his heart.* How often has Christ said to us, *Open to me*, when we have made excuses! Zaccheus's forwardness to receive Christ will shame us.

IV. The offence which the people took. Those narrow-souled censorious Jews *murmured*, saying that he was *gone to be a guest with a man that is a sinner*; and were not they themselves sinful men? Was it not Christ's errand to seek and save *men* that are *sinners*? Now this was very unjust to blame Christ for going to *his house*: 1. Though he was a *publican*, and many of the publicans were *bad men*, it did not therefore follow that they were *all so.* We must take heed of condemning men in the lump, for at God's bar every man will be judged as he is. 2. Though he *had been a sinner*, it did not therefore follow that

JAMIESON, FAUSSET, BROWN

CHAPTER 19

Vss. 1-10. ZACCHEUS THE PUBLICAN. The name is Jewish.

2-4. chief among the publicans—farming a considerable district, with others under him. **rich**—Illgotten riches some of it certainly was. (See on vs. 8).

3. who he was—what sort of person. *Curiosity* then was his only motive, though his determination not to be baulked was overruled for more than he sought.

4. sycamore—the Egyptian fig, with leaves like the mulberry.

5, 6. looked up . . .—in the full knowledge of who was in the tree, and preparatory to addressing him.

Zaccheus . . . whom he had never seen in the flesh, nor probably heard of. "He calleth His own sheep *by name* and leadeth them out" (John 10:3). **make haste, and come down**—to which he literally responded—"he made haste and came down." **for to-day . . .** —Our Lord *invites Himself*, and in *royal* style, which waits not for invitations, but as the honor is done to the subject, not the sovereign, announces the purpose of royalty to partake of the subject's hospitalities. Manifestly our Lord speaks as knowing how the privilege would be appreciated. **to-day . . . abide**—(Cf. John 1:39), probably over night. **6. joyfully**—Whence this so sudden "joy" in the cold bosom of an avaricious publican? The internal revolution was as perfect as instantaneous. "He spake and it was done." "Then shall the lame man leap as an hart, and the tongue of the dumb sing" (Isa. 35:6). **7. to be guest**—or *lodge:* something more than "eating with" such (ch. 15:2). **a sinner**—that *was* one but a minute ago, but now is

ADAM CLARKE

CHAPTER 19

1. *Entered and passed through.* "Was passing through." Our Lord had not as yet passed *through Jericho*—He was only "passing" through it; for the house of Zacchaeus, in which He was to lodge, v. 5, was in it.

2. *Zacchaeus.* It is not unlikely that this person was a Jew by birth; see v. 9. But because he had engaged in a business so infamous, in the eyes of the Jews, he was considered as a mere heathen, v. 7. *Chief among the publicans.* Either a farmer-general of the taxes, who had subordinate collectors under him, or else the most respectable and honorable man among that class at Jericho. *He was rich.* And therefore the more unlikely to pay attention to an impoverished Messiah, preaching a doctrine of universal mortification and self-denial.

3. *And he sought to see Jesus who he was.* So the mere principle of curiosity in him led to his conversion and salvation, and to that of his whole family, v. 9.

4. *He ran before.* The shortness of his stature was amply compensated by his agility and invention. Had he been as tall as the generality of the crowd, he might have been equally unnoticed with the rest. His getting into the tree made him conspicuous; had he not been so low of stature he would not have done so. Even the imperfections of our persons may become subservient to the grace of God in our eternal salvation. As the Passover was at hand, the road was probably crowded with people going to Jerusalem, but the fame of the cure of the blind man was probably the cause of the concourse at this time.

6. *Received him joyfully.* He had now seen who He was, and he wished to hear what He was; and therefore he rejoiced in the honor that God had now conferred upon him. How often does Christ make the proposal of lodging, not only in our house, but in our heart, without its being accepted!

7. *To be guest with a man that is a sinner.* Meaning either that he was a heathen or, though by birth a Jew, yet as bad as a heathen, because of his unholy and oppressive office.

MATTHEW HENRY

he was now as bad as he had been. God allows room for repentance, and so must we. 3. Though he was *now a sinner*, they ought not to blame Christ for going to him. Whither should the physician go but to the sick?

V. The proofs which Zaccheus gave publicly that he was now a *penitent*, *v.* 8. By his *good works* he will evidence the *sincerity* of his *faith* and *repentance*. He *stood*, which denotes his saying it deliberately and with solemnity, in the nature of a vow to God. He addressed himself to Christ in it, not to the people, but to the Lord. He makes it appear that there is a change *in his heart* (and that is repentance), for there is a change in his way.

1. Zaccheus had a good estate. He resolves that for the future he will be all towards God, and do good to others with it: *Behold, Lord, the half of my goods I give to the poor*. "I *do* give it now," saith Zaccheus; "though hitherto I have been uncharitable to the poor, now I will relieve them, and give so much the more for having neglected the duty so long, even the *half of my goods*." Zaccheus would give one moiety to the poor, which would oblige him to retrench all his extravagant expenses. This he mentions here as a fruit of his repentance.

2. Zaccheus was conscious to himself that he had not gotten all he had honestly and fairly. He promises to make restitution: "If *I have taken anything from any man by false accusation*, exacting more than was appointed, I promise to restore him *four-fold*." (1) He seems plainly to own that he had *done wrong*. True penitents will own themselves not only in general guilty before God, but will particularly reflect upon that which, by reason of their business and employment in the world, has most easily beset them. (2) He admits that he had done wrong *by false accusation*. They had the ear of the government, which gave them an opportunity of gratifying their revenge if they bore a man an ill will. (3) He promises to restore *four-fold*. He does not say, "If I be sued, and compelled to it, I will make restitution" (some are *honest* when they cannot help it); but he will do it *voluntarily*. Those who are convinced of having done wrong cannot evidence the sincerity of their repentance but by *making restitution*. He does not think that his giving half his estate to the poor will atone for the wrong he has done. It is no charity, but hypocrisy, to give that which is *none of our own*; and we are not to reckon that our own which we have not come honestly by.

VI. Christ's *approbation* and *acceptance* of Zaccheus's conversion, *v.* 9, 10.

1. Zaccheus is declared to be now a *happy man*. *This day is salvation come to this house*. Now that he is *converted* he is in effect *saved*. Christ is come *to his house*, and, where Christ comes, he brings salvation along with him. Yet this is not all. Salvation this day *comes to his house*. (1) When Zaccheus becomes a convert, he will be, more than he had been, a *blessing to his house*. He will bring the means of grace and salvation to his house. He that is charitable to the poor does a kindness to his own house, and brings a blessing upon it. (2) When Zaccheus is brought to Christ himself his *family* also become related to Christ, and so *salvation comes to his house*, for that he is *a son of Abraham*, that *blessing* of Abraham which comes upon the publicans, *upon the Gentiles*, through faith, that God will be a God *to them and to their children*. Zaccheus is by birth a son of Abraham, but, being a publican, he was deemed a heathen. Being a true penitent, he is become as good a son of Abraham as if he had never been a publican.

2. What Christ had done was consonant to the great design and intention of his coming into the world, *v.* 10. With the same argument he had before justified his conversing with publicans, Matt. ix. 13. There he pleaded that he came to *call sinners to repentance*; now that he came to *seek and save that which was lost*. (1) The *deplorable case* of the *sons of men*: they were *lost*. The whole world of mankind, by the fall, is become a *lost world*: as a traveller is lost when he has missed his way in a wilderness, as a sick man is lost when his disease is incurable. (2) The *gracious design* of the *Son of God*: he came to *seek and save*, to seek in order to saving. He came from heaven to earth (a long journey), to *seek* that which was *lost* (which had *wandered and gone astray*), and to bring it back (Matt. xviii. 11, 12), and to *save* that which was lost, which was perishing. Christ undertook the cause when it was given up for *lost*. Christ *came* into this lost world to seek and save it. His design was to *save*. In prosecution of that design, he *sought*, took all probable means to effect that salvation. He seeks those that sought him not, and asked not for him, as Zaccheus here.

JAMIESON, FAUSSET, BROWN

not. This mighty change, however, was all unknown to them. But they shall know it presently. "Sinner" would refer both to his office, vile in the eyes of a Jew, and to his character, which it is evident was not good. **8-10. stood**—before all.

said unto the Lord, Behold, Lord—Mark how frequently Luke uses this title, and always where lordly *authority, dignity,* or *power* is intended.

if I have—i.e., "so far as I have," for evidently the "if" is so used (as in Philippians 4:8). **taken by false accusation**—defrauded, overcharged (ch. 3:12, 13). **fourfold**—The Roman law required this; the Jewish law, but the principal and a fifth more (Num. 5:7). There was no *demand* made for either; but, as if to revenge himself on his hitherto reigning sin (see on John 20:28), and to testify the change he had experienced, besides surrendering the half of his *fair* gains to the poor, he voluntarily determines to give up all that was ill-gotten, quadrupled. He gratefully addressed this to the "Lord," to whom he owed the wonderful change.

9. Jesus said unto him—but also before all. **This day . . .**—memorable saying! Salvation already come, but not a day old. **to this house**—so expressed probably to meet the taunt, "He is gone to be guest . . ." The house is no longer polluted; it is now fit to receive Me. But *salvation to a house* is an exceedingly precious idea, expressing the new air that would henceforth breathe in it, and the new impulses from its head which would reach its members (Ps. 118:15; Acts 16:15, 16, 31). **son of Abraham**—He was that by birth, but here it means a partaker of his *faith*, being mentioned as the sufficient explanation of *salvation* having come to him.

10. lost—and such "lost" ones as this Zaccheus. (See on ch. 15:32). What encouragement is there in this narrative to hope for unexpected conversions!

ADAM CLARKE

8. *If I have taken any thing . . . by false accusation. Esychophantesa*, from *sychon*, "a fig," and *phaino*, "I show or declare"; for among the primitive Athenians, when the use of that fruit was first found out, or in the time of a dearth when all sorts of provisions were exceedingly scarce, it was enacted that no figs should be exported from Attica; and this law (not being actually repealed when a plentiful harvest had rendered it useless by taking away the reason of it) gave occasion to ill-natured and malicious fellows to accuse all persons they found breaking the letter of it; and from them all busy informers have ever since been branded with the name of "sycophants." *I restore him fourfold*. This restitution the Roman laws obliged the taxgatherers to make, when it was proved they had abused their power by oppressing the people. See the observations at the end of Genesis xlii and Num. v. 7.

ALEXANDER MACLAREN:

The one transforming agency is the love of Christ received into the heart. I do not suppose that Zacchaeus knew as much about Jesus Christ even after the conversation as we do; nor did he see His love in that supreme death on the cross as we do. But the love of the Lord made a deep dint in his heart and revolutionized his whole nature. The thing that will alter the whole current and set of a man's affections, that will upset his estimate of the relative value of material and spiritual, and that will turn him inside out and upside down, and make a new man of him, is the revelation of the supreme love that in Jesus Christ has come into the world, with an individualizing regard to each of us, and has died on the cross for the salvation of us all. Nothing else will do it. People had frowned on Zacchaeus and it made him bitter. They had execrated and persecuted him; and his only response was setting his teeth more firmly and turning the screw a little tighter when he had the chance. You can drive a man into devilry by contempt. If you want to melt him into goodness, try love. The one transforming power is faith in the love of Jesus Christ.

Further, the one test of a true reception of Him is the abandonment of past evil and restitution for it as far as possible. People say that our Gospel is unreal and sentimental, and a number of other ugly adjectives. Well! If it ever is so, it is the fault of the speakers and not of the Gospel. For its demands from every man that accepts it are intensely practical, and nothing short of a complete turning of his back upon his old self, shown in the conclusive forsaking of former evil, however profitable or pleasant, and reparation for harm done to men, satisfies them.—*Expositions of Holy Scripture*

MATTHEW HENRY

Verses 11–27

Our Lord Jesus is now upon his way to Jerusalem, to his last passover.

I. How the expectations of his friends were *raised* upon this occasion: *They thought that the kingdom of God would immediately appear, v.* 11. The Pharisees expected it about this time (*ch.* xvii. 20), and, it seems, so did Christ's own disciples. The disciples thought that their Master would introduce it, but with temporal pomp and power. Jerusalem, they concluded, must be the seat of his kingdom, and therefore, now that he is going directly thither, they doubt not but in a little time to see him upon the throne there. Even good men are subject to mistakes concerning the kingdom of Christ.

II. How their expectations were *checked*, and the mistakes *rectified*; and this he does in three things:—

1. They expected that he should appear in his glory now *presently*, but he tells them that he must not be publicly installed in his kingdom for a great while yet. He is like *a certain nobleman*, he *goes into a far country, to receive for himself a kingdom.* He must receive the kingdom, and then *return.* Christ returned when the Spirit was poured out, when Jerusalem was destroyed. But his chief return here meant is that at the great day, of which we are yet in expectation.

2. They expected that his apostles and immediate attendants should be advanced to dignity and honour, that they should all be made princes and peers, privy-counsellors and judges, and have all the pomp and preferments of the court and of the town. But Christ here tells them that, instead of this, he designed them to be *men of business*; they must expect no other preferment in this world than that of the trading end of the town; he would set them up with a stock under their hands, that they might employ it themselves, in serving him and the interest of his kingdom among men. That is the true honour of a Christian and a minister which will enable us to look upon all temporal honours with a holy contempt. The apostles had dreamed of *sitting on his right hand and on his left in his kingdom*, and were pleasing themselves with this dream; but Christ tells them that which would fill them with serious thoughts, instead of those *aspiring* ones.

(1) They have a *great work* to do now. Their Master leaves them, and, at parting, he gives each of them a *pound.* This signifies the same thing with the talents in the parable that is parallel to this (Matt. xxv). But perhaps it is in the parable thus represented to make them the more humble; their honour in this world is only that of *traders*, and that not of first-rate merchants. He gave these pounds to his servants, with this charge: *Occupy till I come.* Or, as it might much better be translated, *Trade till I come—Be busy.* So the word properly signifies. "Now," saith he, "mind your business, and make a business of it; set about it in good earnest, and stick to it." All Christians have *business* to do for Christ in this world, and ministers especially; the former were not *baptized*, nor the latter *ordained*, to be *idle.* Those that are called to business for Christ he furnishes with gifts necessary for their business; and, on the other hand, from those to whom he gives power he expects service. He delivers the *pounds* with this charge, Go work, go trade. We must continue to mind our business *till our Master comes.*

(2) They have a *great account* to make shortly. These servants are *called to him that he might know what every man had gained by trading.* They that trade diligently and faithfully in the service of Christ shall be *gainers.* Many a labouring tradesman has been a loser; but those that trade for Christ shall be *gainers.* The conversion of souls is the *winning* of them; every true convert is clear gain to Jesus Christ. Ministers are but factors for him, and to him they must give account what fish they have enclosed in the gospel-net, that is, what they have *gained by trading.*

First, The *good account* which was given by *some* of the servants, and the master's approbation of them. Two such are instanced, *v.* 16, 19. 1. They had both made considerable improvements, but not both *alike*; one had gained *ten pounds* by his trading, and another *five.* All that are alike *faithful* are not alike *successful.* And perhaps, though they were both faithful, one of them took more pains, and applied himself more closely to his business, than the other, and sped accordingly. 2. They both acknowledged their obligations to their Master: Lord, it is not *my* industry, but *thy* pound, that has gained *ten pounds.* God must have all the glory of all our gains. 3. They were both commended for their fidelity and industry: *Well done, thou good servant, v.* 17. And to the other he *said likewise, v.* 19. If he says *Well done*, the matter is not great who says otherwise. 4. They were

JAMIESON, FAUSSET, BROWN

11-27. Parable of the Pounds. A different parable from that of the Talents (Matt. 25:14-30). For, (1) This parable was spoken "when He was *nigh* to Jerusalem" (vs. 11); that one, some days after entering it, and from the Mount of Olives. (2) This parable was spoken to the promiscuous crowd; that, to the Twelve alone. Accordingly, (3) Besides the "servants" in this parable, who profess subjection to Him, there is a class of "citizens" who refuse to own Him, and who are treated differently, whereas in the parable of the talents, spoken to the *former* class alone, this latter class is omitted. (4) In the Talents, each servant receives a different number of them (5, 2, 1); in the Pounds all receive the same one pound, which is but about the 60th part of a talent; also, in the talents, each shows the same fidelity by doubling what he received (the 5 are made 10, the 2, 4); in the Pounds, each receiving the same, render a *different* return (one making his pound 10, another 5). Plainly, therefore, the intended lesson is different; the one illustrating *equal fidelity with different degrees of advantage;* the other, *different degrees of improvement of the same opportunities*; yet with all this difference, the parables are remarkably similar. **12. a far country**—said to put down the notion that He was just on His way to set up His kingdom, and to inaugurate it by His personal presence. **to receive . . . a kingdom**—be invested with royalty; as when Herod went to Rome and was there made king; a striking expression of what our Lord went away for and received, "sitting down at the right hand of the Majesty on high." **to return**—at His second coming.

13. Occupy—"negotiate," "do business," with the resources entrusted. **14. his citizens**—His proper subjects; meaning the Jews, who expressly repudiating our Lord's claims said, "We have no king but Caesar" (John 19:15). In Christendom, these correspond to infidel rejecters of Christianity, as distinguished from professed Christians.

15-26. (See on Matt. 25:19-29).

After a long time the lord of those servants cometh and reckoneth with them—That any one—within the lifetime of the apostles at least—with such words before them, should think that Jesus had given any reason to expect His Second Appearing within that period, would seem strange, did we not know the tendency of enthusiastic, ill-regulated love of His appearing ever to take this turn.

—How beautifully does this illustrate what the beloved disciple says of "boldness in the day of judgment," and his desire that "when He shall appear we may have confidence, and not be ashamed before Him at His coming!" (I John 4:17; 2:28). **His lord said unto him, Well done**—a single word, not of bare satisfaction, but of warm and delighted commendation. And from what Lips!–

ADAM CLARKE

11. *Immediately appear.* Perhaps the generality of His followers thought that on His arrival at Jerusalem He would proclaim himself king.

12. *A certain nobleman.* In the following parable there are two distinct morals intended: (1) the behavior of the *citizens* to the nobleman, and (2) the behavior of his own *servants* to him. (1) By the behavior of the *citizens*, and their punishment (verses 14, 27), we are taught that the Jews, who were the people of Christ, would reject Him, and try to prevent His reigning over them in His spiritual kingdom, and would for that crime be severely punished by the destruction of their state. And this moral is all that answers to the introductory words, v. 11, "They thought that the kingdom of God should immediately appear." (2) The other moral extends itself through the whole of the parable, viz., that the disciples of Christ, who are His *servants*, and who made a good improvement of the favors granted them by the gospel, should be rewarded in proportion to the improvement made under the means of grace. The meaning of the different parts of this parable appears to be as follows. *A certain nobleman*—The Lord Jesus, who was shortly to be crucified by the Jews. *Went into a far country.* Ascended to the right hand of the Divine Majesty. *To receive . . . a kingdom.* To take possession of the mediatorial Kingdom, the right to which, as Messiah, He had acquired by His sufferings; see Phil. ii. 8-9; Heb. i. 3, 8-9. In these words there is an allusion to the custom of those days, when they who had kingdoms or governments given unto them went to Rome to receive that dignity from the emperors. In proof of this, see Josephus, *Ant.*, 1. xiv, c. xiv, where we find Herod went to Rome to receive the sanction and authority of the Roman emperor. And, from lib. xvii, c. 3, we learn that his successors acted in the same way. *And to return.* To judge and punish the rebellious Jews.

13. *Ten servants.* All those who professed to receive His doctrine. *Ten* was a kind of sacred number among the Hebrews, as well as *seven. Ten pounds.* Ten *minas.* It appears from Ezek. xlv. 12 to have been equal to sixty shekels in money.

14. *His citizens.* Or "countrymen"—the Jewish people, who professed to be subjects of the kingdom of God. *Hated him.* Despised Him for the meanness of His birth, His crucifixion to the world, and for the holiness of His doctrine. Neither mortification nor holiness suits the dispositions of the carnal mind. *Sent a message after him.* As, in v. 12, there is an allusion to a person's going to Rome, when elected to be ruler of a province or kingdom, to receive that dignity from the hand of the emperor, so it is here intimated that, after the person went to receive this dignity, some of the discontented citizens took the opportunity to send an embassy to the emperor to prevent him from establishing the object of their hatred in the government. *We will not have this man.* The Jews rejected Jesus Christ, would not submit to His government, and a short time after this preferred even a murderer to Him.

15. *When he was returned.* When He came to punish the disobedient Jews, and when He shall come to judge the world. See the parable of the *talents*, Matt. xxv. 14, etc.

16. *Lord, thy pound hath gained ten.* The principal difference between this parable and that of the talents above referred to is that the *mina* given to each seems to point out the gift of the gospel, which is the same to all who hear it; but the talents distributed in different proportions according to each man's ability seem to intimate that God has given different capacities and advantages to men, by which this one gift of the gospel may be differently improved.

MATTHEW HENRY

preferred in proportion to the improvement they had made: "*Because thou hast been faithful in a very little, have thou authority over ten cities.*" Those are in a fair way to rise who are content to begin low. Two things are hereby promised the apostles: (1) That when they have taken pains to *plant* many churches they shall have great respect paid them, and have a great interest in the love and esteem of good Christians. (2) That, when they have served their generation, according to the will of Christ, in the other world they shall reign as kings with Christ. The happiness of heaven will be a much greater advancement to a good minister or Christian than it would be to a poor tradesman to be made governor of ten cities. He that had gained but *five pounds* had dominion over *five cities*. There are *degrees of glory* in heaven; every vessel will be alike *full*, but not alike *large*. And the degrees of glory there will be according to the degrees of usefulness here.

Secondly, The *bad account* that was given by *one* of them, and the sentence passed upon him, *v.* 20, &c. 1. He owned that he had not *traded* with the pound with which he had been entrusted (*v.* 20): "*Lord, behold, here is thy pound;* it is true, I have not made it *more*, but withal I have not made it *less*; I have kept it safely *laid up in a napkin*." This represents the carelessness of those who have gifts, but never lay out themselves to do good with them. It is all one to them whether the interests of Christ's kingdom sink or swim, go backward or forward; for their parts, they will take no care about it. Those are the servants that lay up their pound *in a napkin* who think it enough to say that they have done no hurt in the world, but *did no good*. 2. He justified himself with a plea that made the matter worse and not better (*v.* 21): *I feared thee, because thou art an austere man. Austere* is the Greek word itself: a *sharp* man: *Thou takest up that which thou laidst not down.* He thought that it was *reaping where he did not sow*; whereas really it was reaping where he *had sown*. He had no reason to *fear* his master's austerity. This was a mere sham, a frivolous groundless excuse for his idleness. 3. His excuse is turned upon him: *Out of thine own mouth will I judge thee, thou wicked servant*, *v.* 22. He will be *condemned* by his crime, but *self-condemned* by his plea. If thou hadst had any regard to my interest, thou mightest have put my money *into the bank*, that I might have had, not only *my own*, but my own *with usury*. If he durst not *trade* for fear of *losing* the principal, yet that would be no excuse for his not setting it out to interest, where it would be sure. Whatever may be the pretences of slothful professors, the true reason of it is a reigning indifference to the interests of Christ and his kingdom. They care not whether religion gets ground or loses ground, so long as they can but live at ease. 4. His pound is taken from him, *v.* 34. It is fit that those should *lose* their gifts who will not *use* them. *Take from him the pound.* 5. It is given to him that had the *ten pounds*. When this was objected against because he had so much already (*Lord, he has ten pounds, v.* 25), it is answered (*v.* 26), *Unto everyone that hath shall be given.* It is the rule of justice, (1) That those should be most encouraged who have been most industrious. To him that hath gotten shall more be given, that he may be in a capacity to get more. (2) That those who have their gifts, as if they had them not, should be deprived of them. To those who endeavour to increase the grace they have, God will impart more; those who neglect it, and suffer it to decline, can expect no other than that God should do so too.

3. Another thing they expected was, that, when the kingdom of God should appear, the body of the Jewish nation would immediately fall in with it. Christ tells them that, after his departure, the generality of them would persist in their obstinacy and rebellion. This is shown here,

(1) In the message which his citizens sent after him, *v.* 14. When he was gone to be invested in his kingdom, then they continued their enmity to him, and said, *We will not have this man to reign over us.* This was fulfilled in the prevailing infidelity of the Jews after the ascension of Christ. They would not submit their necks to his yoke. It speaks the language of all unbelievers; they could be content that Christ should *save them*, but they will not have him to *reign over them.*

(2) In the sentence passed upon them at his return: *Those mine enemies bring hither*, *v.* 27. When his faithful subjects are preferred and rewarded, then he will take vengeance on his enemies. When the *kingdom of God appeared* then vengeance was taken on those irreconcilable enemies to Christ and his government; they were *brought forth and slain before him.* But this is applicable to all others who *persist* in their infidelity. Utter ruin will certainly be the portion

JAMIESON, FAUSSET, BROWN

ten . . . five cities—different degrees of future gracious reward, proportioned to the measure of present fidelity.

This depicts the conduct of all those who shut up their gifts from the active service of Christ, without actually prostituting them to unworthy uses. Fitly, therefore, may it, at least, comprehend those, to whom TRENCH refers, who, in the early Church, pleaded that they had enough to do with their own souls, and were afraid of losing them in trying to save others; and so, instead of being the salt of the earth, thought rather of keeping their own saltness by withdrawing sometimes into caves and wildernesses, from all those active ministries of love by which they might have served their brethren.

Then he which had received the one talent came and said, Lord, I knew thee that thou art an hard man—harsh. The word in Luke (19:21) is "austere."—**reaping where thou hast not sown, and gathering where thou hast not strawed**—The sense is obvious: "I knew thou wast one whom it was impossible to serve, one whom nothing would please: exacting what was impracticable, and dissatisfied with what was attainable." Thus do men secretly think of God as a hard Master, and virtually throw on Him the blame of their fruitlessness. **25. And I was afraid**—of making matters worse by meddling with it at all.

Thou wicked and slothful servant—"Wicked" or "bad" means "falsehearted," as opposed to the others, who are emphatically styled "*good* servants." The addition of "slothful" is to mark the precise nature of his wickedness: it consisted, it seems, not in his doing anything *against*, but simply *nothing for* his master.

For whosoever hath—i.e., keeps; as a thing which he values. **to him shall be given, and he shall have more abundance**—He will be rewarded by an increase of what he so much prizes. **but whosoever hath not**—who lets this go or lie unused, as a thing on which he sets no value. **from him shall be taken away even that he hath**—or as it is in Luke (8:18), "what he seemeth to have," or, thinketh he hath. This is a principle of immense importance, and, like other weighty sayings, appears to have been uttered by our Lord on more than one occasion, and in different connections. (See on ch. 25:9.) As a great ethical principle, we see it in operation everywhere, under the general law of *habit;* in virtue of which moral principles become stronger by exercise, while by disuse, or the exercise of their contraries, they wax weaker, and at length expire. The same principle reigns in the intellectual world, and even in the animal—if not in the vegetable also—as the facts of physiology sufficiently prove. Here, however, it is viewed as a divine ordination, as a judicial retribution in continual operation under the divine administration.

ADAM CLARKE

17. *Over ten cities.* This is to be understood as referring to the new kingdom which the nobleman had just received. His former trustiest and most faithful servants he now represents as being made governors under him over a number of cities, according to the capacity he found in each, which capacity was known by by the improvement of the minas.

20. *Lord, behold, here is thy pound.* See Matt. xxv. 18.

(1) See the *ingratitude* of this servant. His master gave him a talent, capable of being improved to his own present and eternal advantage; but he slights the mercy of his lord. (2) See his *idleness.* Rather than exert himself to improve what he has received, he goes and hides it. (3) See his gross *error*. He digs to hide it—puts himself to more trouble to render the mercy of God to him of none effect than he would have had in combating and conquering the world, the devil, and the flesh. (4) See his *injustice*. He takes his master's money, and neither improves nor designs to improve it, even while he is living on and consuming that bounty which would have been sufficient for a faithful servant. (5) Hear the *absurdity* of his *reasoning*. *Lord, I knew thee that thou art an hard* (or avaricious) *man, reaping where thou hast not sown*, v. 24. The wicked excuse of this faithless servant confuted itself and condemned him.

23. *With usury.* "With its produce," i.e., what the loan of the money is fairly worth, after paying the person sufficiently for using it.

26. *And from him that hath not.* See this particularly explained, Matt. xiii. 12.

Whosoever hath, to him shall be given. This is an allusion to a common custom in all countries. He who possesses much or is rich, to such a person presents are ordinarily given. *Whosoever hath not, from him shall be taken away even that he hath.* That is, the poor man; he that has little may be easily made a prey of, and so lose his little.

27. *Those mine enemies . . . bring hither.* The Jews, whom I shall shortly slay by the sword of the Romans.

MATTHEW HENRY

of all Christ's enemies. *Bring them hither*, to have their frivolous pleas overruled, and to receive sentence according to their merits. Those that *will not have Christ to reign over them* shall be reputed and dealt with as his enemies. Those will be accounted so that will not submit to Christ's yoke, but will be their own masters. Whoever will not be *ruled* by the grace of Christ will inevitably be ruined by the wrath of Christ.

Verses 28–40

We have here the same account of Christ's riding in some sort of triumph (such as it was) into Jerusalem which we had before in Matthew and Mark.

I. Jesus Christ was forward and willing to suffer and die for us. He went forward *to Jerusalem* knowing very well the *things* that should *befall him there*, and yet *he went before, ascending up to Jerusalem*, *v.* 28. He was the foremost of the company. Was he so forward to suffer and die for us, and shall we draw back from any service we are capable of doing for him?

II. It was no ways inconsistent either with Christ's humility or with this present state of humiliation to make a *public entry* into Jerusalem a little before he died. The ignominy of his death might appear the greater.

III. Christ is entitled to a dominion over all the creatures. Christ sent to fetch an *ass* and her *colt* from their *owner's* and *master's crib*, when he had occasion for their service.

IV. Christ has all men's hearts both under his eye and in his hand. He could influence those to whom the ass and the colt belonged to consent to their taking them away, as soon as they were told that the Lord had occasion for them.

V. Those that go on Christ's errands are sure to speed (*v.* 32). It is a comfort to Christ's messengers that they shall bring what they are sent for, if indeed the Lord has occasion for it.

VI. The disciples of Christ, who fetch that for him from others which he has occasion for, should not think that enough, but, whatever they have themselves wherewith he may be served, they should be ready to serve him with it. Those disciples not only fetched the ass's colt for him, but *cast their* own *garments upon the colt*.

VII. Christ's triumphs are the matter of his disciples' praises. When Christ came nigh to Jerusalem, God put it of a sudden into the hearts of the *whole multitude of the disciples*, not of the twelve only, *to rejoice and praise God* (*v.* 37), and the *spreading of their clothes in the way* (*v.* 36) was a common expression of joy. Observe, What was the matter or occasion of their joy and praise. They praised God *for all the mighty works they had seen*, especially the *raising of Lazarus*, which is particularly mentioned, John xii. 17, 18. See how they expressed their joy and praise (*v.* 38): *Blessed be the king that cometh in the name of the Lord.* Christ is *the king*; he *comes in the name of the Lord. Blessed be he.* Let us *praise him*, let God *prosper him. Peace in heaven.* Let the God of heaven send peace and success to his undertaking, and then there will be *glory in the highest.* Compare this song of the saints on earth with that of the angels, *ch.* ii. 14. They both agree to give glory to God in the highest. The angels say, *On earth peace.* The saints say, *Peace in heaven.* Such is the communion we have with the holy angels that, as *they* rejoice in the *peace on earth*, so *we* rejoice in the *peace in heaven.*

VIII. Christ's triumphs, and his disciples' joyful praises of them, are the vexation of proud Pharisees. There were some Pharisees among *the multitude* who were enraged at them. They thought that he would not admit such acclamations as these, and therefore expected that he should *rebuke his disciples*, *v.* 39. As he despises the contempt of the proud, so he accepts the praises of the humble.

IX. Whether men praise Christ or no he will, and shall, and must be praised (*v.* 40): *If these should hold their peace the stones would immediately cry out*, rather than that Christ should not be praised. Pharisees would silence the praises of Christ, but they cannot gain their point; for as God can *out of stones raise up children unto Abraham*, so he can out of the mouths of those children perfect praise.

Verses 41–48

The great Ambassador from heaven is here making his public entry into Jerusalem, not to be *respected* there, but to be *rejected.* See here two instances of his love to that place and his concern for it.

I. The *tears he shed* for the *approaching ruin* of the *city* (*v.* 41): *When he was come near, he beheld*

JAMIESON, FAUSSET, BROWN

27. bring hither . . .—(Cf. I Sam. 15:32, 33). Referring to the awful destruction of Jerusalem, but pointing to the final destruction of all that are found in open rebellion against Christ.

28-44. Christ's Triumphant Entry into Jerusalem, and Tears over It. (See on Matt. 21:1-11). **29-38.**

Bethphage—"house of figs," a village which with Bethany lay along the further side of Mount Olivet, east of Jerusalem. **30. whereon . . .** (See on John 19:41). **31. the Lord hath need . . .**—He both knew all and had the key of the human heart. (See on vs. 5.)

Perhaps the owner was a disciple. **35. set Jesus on**—He allowing this, as befitting the *state* He was for the first and only time assuming.

37. whole multitude . . .—The language here is very grand, intended to express a burst of admiration far wider and deeper than ever had been witnessed before.

38. Blessed be the King . . .—Mark more fully, "Hosanna," i.e., "*Save now,*" the words of Psalm 118:25, which were understood to refer to Messiah; and so they add, "to the Son of David, blessed is He that cometh in the name of the Lord (Ps. 118:26), Hosanna in the highest." This was the very loftiest style in which He could be saluted as the promised Deliverer. **peace . . .**—(See on ch. 2:13, 14).

40. the stones . . .—Hitherto the Lord had discouraged all demonstrations in His favor; latterly He had *begun* an opposite course; on this one occasion He seems to yield His whole soul to the wide and deep acclaim with a mysterious satisfaction, regarding it as *so necessary* a part of the regal dignity in which as Messiah He for this last time entered the city, that if not offered by the vast multitude, it would have been *wrung out of the stones* rather than be withheld (Hab. 2:11).

ADAM CLARKE

28. *He went before.* Perhaps it means that He walked at the head of His disciples, and that He and His disciples kept on the road before other companies who were then also on their way to Jerusalem, in order to be present at the feast.

29-38. See this Triumphal Entry into Jerusalem explained at large on Matt. xxi. 1-11 and Mark xi. 1-10.

Bethphage. A place on the west declivity of Mount Olivet, from which it is thought the whole declivity and part of the valley took their name. It is supposed to have derived its name from the fig trees which grew there.

And put on them their clothes. Thus acknowledging Him to be their King, for this was a custom observed by the people when they found that God had appointed a man to the kingdom.

Hosanna to the son of David. When persons applied to the king for help, or for a redress of grievances, they used the word *hosanna.* "Save now!" or "Save, we beseech thee!" *Son of David.* A well-known epithet of the Messiah. *He that cometh in the name.* He who comes in the name and authority of the Most High. *Hosanna in the highest.* Either meaning, Let the heavenly hosts join with us in magnifying this august Being!—or, let the utmost degrees of hosanna, of salvation, and deliverance, be communicated to Thy people! Probably there is an allusion here to the custom of the Jews in the Feast of Tabernacles. During the first seven days of that feast they went once round the altar, each day, with palm and other branches in their hands, singing hosanna. But on the eighth day of that feast they walked seven times round the altar, singing the hosanna; and this was termed the "great hosanna"; i.e., "Assist with the greatest succor."

40. *If these should hold their peace, the stones would immediately cry out.* Of such importance is My present conduct to you and to others, being expressly predicted by one of your own prophets, Zech. ix. 9, as pointing out the triumph of humility over pride, and of meekness over rage and malice, as signifying the salvation which I bring to the lost souls of men, that, if this multitude were silent, God would give even to the stones a voice, that the advent of the Messiah might be duly celebrated.

MATTHEW HENRY

the city, and wept over it. Probably, it was when he was coming down the descent of the hill from the *mount of Olives,* where he had a full view of the city, and his eye affected his heart, and his heart his eye again. See here,

1. What a tender spirit Christ was of; we never read that he laughed, but we often find him in tears.

2. That Jesus Christ *wept* when all about him were *rejoicing,* to show how little he was elevated with the applause and acclamation of the people.

3. That he *wept over Jerusalem.* There are cities to be wept over, and none to be more lamented than Jerusalem. But why did Christ weep at the sight of Jerusalem? He himself gives us the reason of his tears.

(1) Jerusalem has not improved the day of her opportunities. He wept, and said, *If thou hadst known, even thou at least in this thy day, the things that belong to thy peace*—but thou *dost not know the day of thy visitation, v.* 44. The manner of speaking is abrupt: *If thou hadst known! O that thou hadst,* so some take it. Or, *If thou hadst known, well;* like that of the *fig-tree, ch.* xiii. 9. How happy had it been for thee! What he says lays all the blame of Jerusalem's impending ruin upon herself. [1] There are things which *belong to our peace,* which we are all concerned to *know* and *understand.* The things that belong to our peace are those things that relate to our present and future welfare; these we must know with application. [2] There is a *time of visitation* when those things which *belong to our peace* may be *known by us.* When we enjoy the means of grace in great plenty, and have the word of God powerfully preached to us—then is the *time of visitation.* [3] With those that have long neglected the time of their visitation, if at last their eyes be opened, and they bethink themselves, all will be well yet. Those shall not be refused that come into the vineyard *at the eleventh hour.* [4] It is the amazing folly of multitudes that enjoy the means of grace, that they do not improve the day of their opportunities. The *things of their peace* are revealed to them, but are not minded or regarded by them; they *hide their eyes* from them. They are not aware of the *accepted time* and the *day of salvation,* and so let it slip and perish through mere carelessness. None are so *blind* as those that will not *see.* [5] The sin and folly of those that persist in a contempt of gospel grace are a great grief to the Lord Jesus, and should be so to us. He looks with weeping eyes upon lost souls, that continue impenitent. He had rather that they would *turn and live* than *go on and die,* for he is not willing that any should perish.

(2) Jerusalem cannot escape the day of her desolation. The *things of her peace* are now in a manner hidden from her eyes. Not but that after this the gospel was preached to them by the apostles, and multitudes were convinced and converted. But as to the body of the nation, and the leading part of it, they were sealed up under unbelief. They were justly given up to *judicial* blindness and hardness. Neglecting the great salvation often brings temporal judgments upon a people; it did so upon Jerusalem. [1] The Romans besieged the city, *cast a trench about it, compassed it round,* and *kept their* inhabitants in *on every side.* [2] They *laid it even with the ground.* Titus commanded his soldiers to *dig up the city,* and the whole compass of it was levelled, except three towers. Not only the city, but the citizens were laid even with the ground (*thy children within thee*), by the cruel slaughters that were made of them: and there was scarcely one stone *left upon another.* This was because they *knew not the day of their visitation.*

II. The *zeal he showed* for the *present purification of the temple.*

1. Christ cleared it of those who profaned it. He went straight to the temple, and *began to cast out the buyers and sellers, v.* 45. Its purity was more its glory than its wealth was. Christ gave a reason for his dislodging the temple-merchants, *v.* 46. The temple is a *house of prayer,* set apart for communion with God: the *buyers* and *sellers* made it a *den of thieves* by the fraudulent bargains they made there. It would be a distraction to those who came there to pray.

2. He put it to the best use that ever it was put to, for he *taught daily in the temple, v.* 47. Now, when Christ preached in the temple, observe here, (1) How spiteful the church-rulers were against him (*v.* 47): *The chief priests and scribes, and the chief of the people, sought to destroy him.* (2) How respectful the common people were to him. They were *very attentive to hear him.* The people paid him great respect, attended on his preaching with diligence. Some read it, *All the people, as they heard him, took his part;* and so his enemies *could not find what they might* do against him.

JAMIESON, FAUSSET, BROWN

41-44. when beheld . . . wept,—Cf. Lamentations 3:51, "Mine eye affecteth mine heart"; the heart again affecting the eye. Under this sympathetic law of the relation of mind and body, Jesus, in His beautiful, tender humanity, was constituted even as we. What a contrast to the immediately preceding profound joy! He yielded Himself alike freely to both. (See on Matt. 23:37.

42. at least in this . . .—even at this moving moment. (See on ch. 13:9). **thy peace**—thinking perhaps of the name of the city (Heb. 7:2) [WEBSTER and WILKINSON]. How much is included in this word!

now . . . hid—It was His among His *last* open efforts to "gather them," but their eyes were judicially closed.

43. a trench—a rampart; first of wood, and when this was burnt, a built wall, four miles in circuit, built in three days—so determined were they. This "cut off all hope of escape," and consigned the city to unparalleled horrors. (See JOSEPHUS, *Jewish Wars,* vss. 6: 2; 12:3, 4.) All here predicted was with dreadful literality fulfilled.

45-48. SECOND CLEANSING OF THE TEMPLE, AND SUBSEQUENT TEACHING. **45, 46.** As the first cleansing was on His *first* visit to Jerusalem (John 2:13-22), so this second cleansing was on His last. **den of thieves**—banded together for plunder, reckless of principle. The mild term "house of merchandise,' used on the former occasion, was now unsuitable.

47. sought—continued seeking, i.e., daily, as He taught. **48. were very attentive to hear him**—hung upon His words.

ADAM CLARKE

41. *And wept over it.* See Matt. xxiii. 37.

42. *The things which belong unto thy peace!* It is very likely that our Lord here alludes to the meaning of the word Jerusalem, *yereh,* "he shall see," and *shalom,* "peace or prosperity."

Now, because the inhabitants of it had not "seen" this "peace" and salvation, because they had refused to open their eyes, and behold this glorious light of heaven which shone among them, therefore He said, *Now they are hid from thine eyes,* still alluding to the import of the name.

43. *Cast a trench about thee.* This was literally fulfilled when this city was besieged by Titus. Josephus gives a very particular account of the building of this wall, which he says was effected in three days, though it was not less than thirty-nine furlongs in circumference; and that, when this wall and trench were completed, the Jews were so enclosed on every side that no person could escape out of the city, and no provision could be brought in, so that they were reduced to the most terrible distress by the famine which ensued. The whole account is well worth the reader's attention. See Josephus, *War,* book v, chap. xii, secs. 1-3.

44. *The time of thy visitation.* That is, the time of God's gracious offers of mercy to you. This took in all the time which elapsed from the preaching of John the Baptist to the coming of the Roman armies, which included a period of above forty years.

45. *Went into the temple.* See all this transaction explained, Matt. xxi. 12-16.

47. *And he taught daily in the temple.* This He did for five or six days before His crucifixion. Some suppose that it was on Monday in the Passion Week that He thus entered into Jerusalem and purified the Temple; and on Thursday He was seized late at night. During these four days He taught in the Temple, and lodged each night at Bethany.

48. *Were very attentive to hear him.* Or, "They heard Him with the utmost attention";

MATTHEW HENRY

Till his hour was come his interest in the common people protected him; but, when his hour was come, the chief priests' influence upon the common people delivered him up.

CHAPTER 20

Verses 1–8

Nothing is added here to what we had in the other evangelists; but only in the first verse, where we are told,

I. That he was now *teaching the people in the temple*, and *preaching the gospel*. Christ was a preacher of his own gospel. He not only *purchased* the salvation for us, but *published* it to us. This likewise puts an honour upon the preachers of the gospel. It puts an honour upon the *popular preachers* of the gospel; Christ condescended to the capacities of the *people* in preaching the gospel, and *taught them*.

II. That his enemies are here said to *come upon him*. The word is used only here, and it intimates, 1. That they thought to surprise him with this question; they *came upon him* suddenly.

2. That they thought to frighten him with this question. From this story itself we may learn, (1) That it is not to be thought strange, if even that which is evident be disputed and called in question by those that shut their eyes against the light. Christ's miracles plainly showed *by what authority he did these things*. (2) Those that question Christ's authority will have their folly made manifest unto all men. Christ answered these priests and scribes with a question concerning the baptism of John: *Was it from heaven or of men?* They all knew it was *from heaven*. And this question gravelled them, and ran them aground, and served to shame them before the people. (3) It is not strange if those that are governed by reputation and secular interest imprison the plainest truths, as these priests and scribes did who would not own that John's baptism was *from heaven*, and had no other reason why they did not say it was *of men* but because they *feared the people*. What good can be expected from men of such a spirit? (4) Those that bury the knowledge they have are justly denied further knowledge, *v.* 7, 8.

Verses 9–19

Christ spoke this parable against those who were resolved not to own his authority.

I. The parable has nothing added here to what we had before in Matthew and Mark. The scope of it is to show that the Jewish nation had provoked God to abandon them to ruin. It teaches us, 1. That those who enjoy the privileges of the visible church are as tenants and farmers that have a vineyard to look after, and rent to pay for it. God, by setting up revealed religion, hath planted a vineyard, which he lets out, *v.* 9. And they have *vineyard work* to do, needful and constant work, but pleasant and profitable. They have also *vineyard-fruits* to present to the Lord of the vineyard. There are rents to be paid and services to be done. 2. That the work of God's ministers is to call upon those who enjoy the privileges of the church to *bring forth fruit* accordingly. They are God's rent-gatherers, *v.* 10. 3. That it has often been the lot of God's faithful servants to be wretchedly abused by his own tenants. They that are resolved not to do their duty to God cannot bear to be called upon to do it. 4. That God sent his Son into the world to *gather the fruits of the vineyard*. The prophets spoke as *servants*, but Christ *as a Son*; to send him, one would have thought, should have won upon them. 5. That those who reject Christ's ministers would reject Christ himself. They said, *This is the heir, come let us kill him.* When they slew the servants, there were other servants sent. "But, if we can but be the death of the son, there is never another son to be sent; we may have a quiet possession of the vineyard for ourselves." Therefore they took the bold step, they *cast him out of the vineyard, and killed him.* 6. That the putting of Christ to death filled up the measure of the Jewish iniquity. No other could be expected than that God should *destroy those wicked husbandmen.* Those that live in the neglect of their duty to God know not what degrees of sin and destruction they are running themselves into.

II. To the application of the parable is added here, which we had not before, their deprecation of the doom included in it (*v.* 16): *When they heard it, they said, God forbid—Let not this be done*, so it should be read. And see what a cheat they put upon themselves, to think to avoid it by a cold *God forbid*, when they do nothing towards the preventing of it. Now observe what Christ said. 1. He *beheld them.* This is taken notice of only by this evangelist, *v.* 17. He *looked upon* them with pity and compassion. He

JAMIESON, FAUSSET, BROWN

CHAPTER 20

Vss. 1-19. The Authority of Jesus questioned, and His Reply—Parable of the Wicked Husbandmen. (See on Matthew 21:23.) **2. these things**—particularly the clearing of the temple.

4. baptism of John—his whole ministry and mission, of which baptism was the seal. **5. Why then believed ye him not?**—i.e., in his testimony to Jesus, the sum of his whole witness. **7. could not tell**—crooked, cringing hypocrites! No wonder Jesus gave you no answer (Matt. 7:6). But what dignity and composure does our Lord display as He turns their question upon themselves!

9-13. vineyard—(See on ch. 13:6). In Matthew 21:33 additional points are given, taken literally from Isaiah 5:2, to fix down the application and sustain it by Old Testament authority. **husbandmen**—the ordinary spiritual guides of the people, under whose care and culture the fruits of righteousness might be yielded. **went . . .**—leaving it to the laws of the spiritual husbandry during the whole length of the Jewish economy. (See on Mark 4:26.) **10. beat . . .**—(Matt. 21:35); i.e., the prophets, extraordinary messengers raised up from time to time. (See on Matt. 23:37.) **13. my beloved son**—Mark (12:6) still more affectingly, "Having yet therefore one son, his well-beloved"; our Lord thus severing Himself from all merely *human* messengers, and claiming *Sonship* in its loftiest sense. (Cf. Heb. 3:3-6.) **it may be**—"surely"; implying the almost unimaginable guilt of *not* doing so. **14. reasoned among themselves . . .**—(Cf. Genesis 37:18-20; John 11:47-53). **the heir**—sublime expression of the great truth, that God's inheritance was destined for, and in due time to come into the possession of, His Son *in our nature* (Heb. 1:2). **inheritance . . . ours**—and so from mere *servants* we may become *lords;* the deep aim of the depraved heart, and literally *"the root of all evil."* **15. cast him out of the vineyard**—(Cf. Hebrews 13:11-13; I Kings 21:13; John 19:17). **16. He shall come . . .**—This answer was given by the Pharisees themselves (Matt. 21:41), thus pronouncing their own righteous doom. Matthew alone (21:43) gives the naked application, that "the kingdom of God should be taken from them, and given to a nation bringing forth the fruits thereof"—the great evangelical community of the faithful, chiefly Gentiles. **God forbid**—His whole meaning now bursting upon them. **17-19. written**—(in Ps. 118:22, 23. See on ch. 19:38). The Kingdom of God is here a Temple, in the erection of which *a certain stone,* rejected as unsuitable by

ADAM CLARKE

literally, "They hung upon Him, hearing." The same form of speech is used often by both Greek and Latin writers of the best repute.

CHAPTER 20

1. *One of those days.* Supposed to have been one of the four last days of His life, mentioned in chap. xix. 47, probably Tuesday before the Passover.

2. *By what authority.* See the note on Matt. xxi. 23-27.

By what authority doest thou these things? The things which the chief priests allude to were His receiving the acclamations of the people as the promised Messiah, His casting the traders out of the Temple, and His teaching the people publicly in it.

The baptism of John. Had John a divine commission or not for his baptism and preaching? Our Lord here takes the wise in their own cunning. He knew the estimation John was in among the people, and He plainly saw that if they gave any answer at all they must convict themselves; and so they saw, when they came to examine the question.

We cannot tell, said they; which, in the words of truth, should have been, "We will not tell," for we will not have this man for the Messiah; because, if we acknowledge John as His forerunner, we must, of necessity, receive Jesus as the Christ.

9. *A certain man planted a vineyard.* **See this parable largely explained, Matt. xxi. 33-46. See also on Mark xii. 4-9.**

He sent his servants. Prophets, which, from time to time, He sent to the Jewish nation to call both priests and people back to the purity of His holy religion. *Receive the fruits of it.* Alluding to the ancient custom of paying the rent of a farm in kind; that is, by a part of the produce of the farm.

Beat one. "Took his skin off, flayed him," probably alluding to some who had been excessively scourged.

Other servants. There is not a moment in which God does not shower down His gifts upon men, and require the fruit of them. *More than the first.* Or more honorable.

Last of all he sent . . . his son. This requires no comment. Our Lord plainly means himself. *They will reverence.* They will reflect upon their conduct and blush for shame because of it, when they see my son.

Said among themselves. Alluding to the conspiracies which were then forming against the life of our blessed Lord, in the councils of the Jewish elders and chief priests. See chap. xxvii. 1.

Cast him out of the vineyard. Utterly rejected the counsel of God against themselves, and would neither acknowledge the authority of Christ nor submit to His teaching.

16. *God forbid.* Or, "Let it not be." Our phrase, *God forbid,* answers pretty well to the meaning of the Greek, but it is no translation.

MATTHEW HENRY

beheld them, to see if they would blush at their own folly. 2. He referred them to the scripture: "*What is this then that is written? The stone which the builders rejected is become the head of the corner.*" The Lord Jesus will be exalted to the Father's right hand. Even those that stumble at him *shall be broken*—it will be their ruin; but as to those that not only reject him, but hate and persecute him, he will fall upon them and crush them to pieces—will *grind them to powder*.

Lastly, We are told how the chief priests and scribes were exasperated by this parable (*v.* 19): *They perceived that he had spoken this parable against them.* They fall into a rage at him and *sought to lay hands on him.* And it was only because they *feared the people*, that they did not now fly in his face, and take him by the throat. They were just ready to make his words good: *This is the heir, come let us kill him.* Christ tells them that instead of *kissing the Son* of God they would *kill him.* They do, in effect, say this: "And so we will; have at him now." And, though they deprecate the punishment of the sin, in the next breath they are projecting the commission of it.

Verses 20-26

We have here Christ's evading a snare which his enemies laid for him, by proposing a question to him about tribute.

I. The mischief designed him. The plot was to *deliver him unto the power and authority of the governor, v.* 20. They could not themselves put him to death by course of law, nor otherwise than by a *popular tumult.* They hoped to gain their point, if they could but incense the governor against him. Thus Christ's word must be fulfilled that he should be *delivered into the hands of the Gentiles.*

II. The persons they employed. They were *spies, who should feign themselves just men.* It is no new thing for *bad men* to feign themselves *just men.* A spy must go in disguise. These spies must take on them to have a value for Christ's judgment, and therefore must desire his advice in a case of conscience.

III. The question they proposed. Their preface is very courtly: *Master, we know that thou sayest and teachest rightly, v.* 21. Thus they thought to flatter him into an incautious freedom and openness with them. They were much mistaken who thought thus to impose upon the humble Jesus. He *accepts not the person of any*, but it is as true that he knows the hearts of all, and knew theirs, though they *spoke fair.* It was certain that he *taught the way of God truly*; but he knew that they were unworthy to be taught by him, who came to *take hold of his words*, not to be *taken hold of* by them. Their case is very nice: "Is it lawful *for us*" (this is added here in Luke), "*to give tribute to Caesar*?" Their pride and covetousness made them loth to pay taxes, and then they would have it a question whether it was lawful or no. Now if Christ should say that *it was lawful* the people would take it ill. But if he should say that *it was not lawful* as they expected he would, then they should have something to accuse him of to the governor.

IV. His evading the snare which they laid for him: *He perceived their craftiness, v.* 23. He did not give them a direct answer, but reproved them for offering to impose upon him—*Why tempt ye me? Show me a penny;* he asked them whose money it was, whose stamp it bore, who coined it. They owned, "It is Caesar's money." "Why then," saith Christ, "you should first have asked whether it was lawful to *pay* and *receive* Caesar's money among yourselves, and to admit that to be the instrument of your commerce. You must therefore *render to Caesar the things that are Caesar's.* But in sacred things God only is your King. You must *render to God the things that are God's.*"

V. The confusion they were hereby put into, *v.* 26. The snare is broken: *They could not take hold of his words before the people.* They *marvelled at his answer*, it was so discreet and unexceptionable. Their mouths are stopped; they *held their peace.* They durst ask him nothing else, lest he should shame and expose them.

Verses 27-38

I. In every age there have been men of corrupt minds, that have endeavoured to subvert the fundamental principles of revealed religion. The Sadducees deny that *there is any resurrection*, any *future state*, no world of spirits, no state of recompense and retribution for what was done in the body. Take away this, and all religion falls to the ground.

II. It is common for those that design to undermine any truth of God to perplex it. So these Sadducees did when they would weaken people's faith in the doctrine of the resurrection. The case perhaps

JAMIESON, FAUSSET, BROWN

the spiritual builders, is, by the great Lord of the House, made the keystone of the whole. On that Stone the builders were now "falling" and being "broken" (Isa. 8:15), "sustaining great spiritual hurt; but soon that Stone should fall upon *them* and grind them to powder" (Dan. 2:34, 35; Zech. 12:3)—in their *corporate* capacity in the tremendous destruction of Jerusalem, but *personally*, as unbelievers, in a more awful sense still. **19. the same hour**—hardly able to restrain their rage.

20-40. ENTANGLING QUESTIONS ABOUT TRIBUTE AND THE RESURRECTION—THE REPLIES. **20-26. sent forth**—after consulting (Matt. 22:15) on the best plan.

spies—"of the Pharisees and Herodians" (Mark 12:13). See on Mark 3:6. **21. we know ...**—hoping by flattery to throw Him off His guard

22. tribute—(See on Matt. 17:24).

25. things which be Cæsar's—Putting it in this general form, it was impossible for sedition itself to dispute it, and yet it dissolved the snare. **and unto God**—How much there is in this profound but to them startling addition to the maxim, and how incomparable is the whole for fulness, brevity, clearness, weight!

27-34. no resurrection—"nor angel nor spirit" (Acts 23:8); the *materialists* of the day.

ADAM CLARKE

The stone. R. Solom. Jarchi, on Micah v, says this *stone* means the Messiah. This seems to have been originally spoken of David, who was at first rejected by the Jewish rulers, but was afterwards chosen by the Lord to be the great ruler of His people, Israel. The quotation is taken from Ps. cxviii. 22. *The builders.* The chief priests and elders of the people, with the doctors of the law. *Rejected.* An expression borrowed from masons, who, finding a stone, which being tried in a particular place, and appearing improper for it, is thrown aside, and another taken; however, at last, it may happen that the very stone which had been before rejected may be found the most suitable as the headstone of the corner.

18. *Grind him to powder.* See on Matt. xxi. 44.

20. *They watched him.* "Insidiously watching."

See on chap. xiv. 1. *Spies.* One who crouches in some secret place to spy, listen, catch, or hurt. Hesychius explains the word by "those who lie in wait," or in "ambush," to surprise and slay. Josephus uses the word to signify a person bribed for a particular purpose. No doubt the persons mentioned in the text were men of the basest principles and were hired by the malicious Pharisees to do what they attempted in vain to perform.

22. *Is it lawful for us to give tribute unto Caesar?* See this insidious but important question considered at large on Matt. xxii. 16-22.

Whose is this image and superscription? He knew well enough whose they were, but He showed the excellency of His wisdom in making them answer to their own confusion. They came to ensnare our Lord in His discourse, and now they are ensnared in their own. He who digs a pit for his neighbor ordinarily falls into it himself.

They say unto him, Caesar's. The *image* was the head of the emperor; the *superscription*, his titles. Tiberius was emperor at this time. *Render therefore unto Caesar.* The conclusion is drawn from their own premises. You acknowledge this to be Caesar's coin; this coin is current in your land; the currency of this coin shows the country to be under the Roman government; and your acknowledgment that it is Caesar's proves you have submitted. Do not, therefore, be unjust; but render to Caesar the things which you acknowledge to be his; at the same time, be not impious, but render unto God the things which belong to God. The image of princes stamped on their coin denotes that temporal things belong all to their government. The image of God stamped on the soul denotes that all its faculties and powers belong to the Most High, and should be employed in His service.

When they had heard these words, they marvelled. And well they might—"Never man spake like this man." By this decision Caesar is satisfied—he gets his own to the uttermost farthing. God is glorified—His honor is in every respect secured. And the people are edified—one of the most difficult questions that could possibly come before them is answered in such a way as to relieve their consciences and direct their conduct.

MATTHEW HENRY

was matter of fact of a woman that had *seven husbands*. Now in the resurrection *whose wife shall she be*?

III. There is a great deal of difference between the state of the children of men on earth and that of the children of God in heaven.

1. The children of men in this world *marry, and are given in marriage*. Much of our business in this world is to raise and build up families, and to provide for them. Much of our pleasure in this world is in our relations, our wives and children; nature inclines to it. Marriage is instituted for the comfort of human life.

2. The world to come is quite another thing; it is called *that world*, by way of emphasis and eminency. (1) Who shall be the inhabitants of *that world*: They that shall be *accounted worthy to obtain it*. They have not a *legal* worthiness, but an *evangelical* worthiness. It is a worthiness imputed by which we are glorified, as well as a righteousness imputed by which we are justified. They are by grace made and *counted worthy to obtain that world*; it intimates some *difficulty* in reaching after it, and danger of coming short. We must *so run* as that we may obtain. They shall obtain the *resurrection from the dead*, that is, the blessed resurrection.

(2) What shall be the happy state of the inhabitants of that world we cannot express or conceive, 1. Cor. ii. 9. See what Christ here says of it. [1] They *neither marry nor are given in marriage*. Those that have entered into the joy of their Lord are entirely taken up with that. Into that *new Jerusalem* there enters nothing that defiles. [2] They cannot *die any more*; and this comes in as a reason why they do not *marry*. Where there are no burials, there is no need of weddings. This crowns the comfort of that world that there is no more death there. Here death reigns, but thence it is for ever excluded. [3] They are *equal unto the angels*. In the other evangelists it was said, They are *as the angels*, but here they are said to be *equal to the angels—angels' peers*; they have a glory and bliss no way inferior to that of the holy angels. Saints, when they come to heaven, shall be *naturalised*. They have in all respects equal privileges with them that were free-born, the angels that are the natives and aborigines of that country. [4] They *are the children of God*, and so they are as the angels. We have the nature and disposition of sons, but that will not be *perfected* till we come to heaven. [5] They are the *children of the resurrection*, that is, they are made capable of the employments and enjoyments of the future state. They are the *children of God*, being the *children of the resurrection*.

IV. It is an undoubted truth that there is another life after this (*v*. 37, 38): *Moses showed this, as it was shown to Moses at the bush*, when he *calleth the Lord*, the *God of Abraham, and the God of Isaac, and the God of Jacob. Abraham, Isaac, and Jacob*, were then *dead* as to our world; they had departed out of it many years before; how then could God say, not *I was*, but *I am* the *God of Abraham*? We must therefore conclude that they were then in being in another world; for *God is not the God of the dead, but of the living*. Luke here adds, *For all live unto him*, that is, all who, like them, are true believers; though they are dead, yet they *do live*. But there is more in it yet; when God called himself *the God* of these patriarchs, he meant that he was their felicity and portion, their *exceeding great reward*, Gen. xv. 1. Therefore there must be another life after this, in which he will do that for them that will amount to a *discharge in full* of that promise.

Verses 39–47

The scribes were *students* in the law, and *expositors* of it to the people, men in reputation for wisdom and honour, but the generality of them were enemies to Christ and his gospel.

I. We have them here commending the reply which Christ made to the Sadducees: *Certain of the scribes said, Master, thou hast well said*, *v*. 39. Even the scribes commended his performance, and owned that he said well. Many that call themselves Christians come short even of this spirit.

II. We have them here struck with an awe of Christ, and of his wisdom and authority (*v*. 40): *They durst not ask him any questions at all*. His own disciples, being willing to receive his doctrine, durst *ask him any question*; but the Sadducees durst ask him none.

III. We have them here *puzzled* and run aground with a question concerning the Messiah, *v*. 41. It was plain by many scriptures that Christ was to be the *Son of David*; even the blind man knew this (*ch*. xviii. 39); and yet it was plain that David called the Messiah *his Lord* (*v*. 42, 44): *The Lord said to my Lord*, Ps. cx. 1. Now if he be *his Son*, why doth he call him *his Lord*? If he be *his Lord*, why do *we* call him *his Son*? They could not reconcile this

JAMIESON, FAUSSET, BROWN

34. said unto them—In Matthew 22:29, the reply begins with this important statement:—"Ye do err, not knowing the Scriptures," regarding the future state, "nor the power of God," before which a thousand such difficulties vanish (also Mark 12:24).

36. neither . . . die any more—Marriage is ordained to perpetuate the human family; but as there will be no breaches by death in the future state, this ordinance will cease. **equal**—or "like." **unto the angels**—i.e., in the *immortality* of their nature.

children of God—not in respect of *character* but *nature;* "being the children of the resurrection" to an undecaying existence (Rom. 8:21, 23). And thus the children of their Father's immortality (I Tim. 6:16).

37, 38. even Moses—whom they had just quoted to entangle Him. **not . . . of the dead, . . . for all . . .**—To God, no human being is dead, or ever will be; but all sustain an abiding conscious relation to Him. But the "all" here meant "those who shall be accounted worthy to obtain that world." These *sustain a gracious covenant relation to God, which cannot be dissolved*. In this sense our Lord affirms that for Moses to call the Lord the "God" of His patriarchal servants if at that moment they had no existence, would be unworthy of Him. He "would be *ashamed* to be called their God, if He had not prepared for them a city" (Heb. 11:16). How precious are these glimpses of the *resurrection state!*

39. scribes . . . well said—enjoying His victory over the Sadducees. **they durst not**—neither party, both for the time utterly foiled.

41-47. Christ Baffles the Pharisees by a Question about David and Messiah, and Denounces the Scribes. **41. said . . .**—"What think ye of Christ [the promised and expected Messiah]? Whose son is He [to be]? They say unto Him, The son of David. He saith unto them, How then doth David in spirit [by the Holy Ghost, Mark 12:36] call Him Lord?" (Matt. 22:42, 43). The dif-

ADAM CLARKE

29. *There were therefore seven brethren.* See on Matt. xxii. 23-33.

34. *The children of this world.* Men and women in their present state of mortality and probation, procreation being necessary to restore the waste made by death, and to keep up the population of the earth.

36. *Equal unto the angels.* Who neither marry nor die.

38. *All live unto him.* There is a remarkable passage in Josephus' account of the Maccabees, chap. xvi, which proves that the best informed Jews believed that the souls of righteous men were in the presence of God in a state of happiness. "They who lose their lives for the sake of God, live unto God, as do Abraham, Isaac, and Jacob, and the rest of the patriarchs." So the resurrection of the dead, and the immortality and immateriality of the soul, were not strange or unknown doctrines among the Jews.

40. *They durst not ask.* Or "did not venture" to ask any other question, for fear of being again confounded, as they had already been.

41. *How say they?* See the note on Matt. xxii. 42-46.

43. *Thy footstool.* Literally, "the footstool of Thy feet." They shall not only be so far humbled that the feet may be set on them; but they shall be actually subjected, and put completely under that Christ whom they now despise and are about to crucify.

MATTHEW HENRY

seeming contradiction; thanks be to God, we can; that Christ, *as God*, was David's Lord, but Christ, *as man*, was David's Son.

IV. We have them here described in their black characters, *v.* 45–47. Christ bids his disciples *beware of the scribes*, that is,

1. "Take heed of being drawn *into sin* by them; beware of such a spirit as they are governed by."

2. "Take heed of being *brought into trouble* by them," in the same sense that he had said (Matt. x. 17), "*Beware of men, for they will deliver you up to the councils;* beware of the scribes, for they will do so. Beware of them, they are *proud* and *haughty*. They *desire to* walk about the streets in *long robes*, as those that are above business, and as those that take state, and take place." They loved in their hearts to have people make their obeisance to them *in the markets*. They *loved the highest seats in the synagogues* and *the chief rooms at feasts*, and looked upon themselves with great conceit and upon all about them with great contempt. "They are *covetous and oppressive*, and make their religion a cloak and cover for crime. They *devour widows' houses. For a show they make long prayers*."

Christ reads them their doom in a few words: *These shall receive a more abundant judgment*, a double damnation. *Dissembled piety is double iniquity.*

JAMIESON, FAUSSET, BROWN

ficulty can only be solved by the *higher* and *lower*—the *divine* and *human* natures of our Lord (Matt. 1:23). Mark the testimony here given to the *inspiration* of the Old Testament (cf. ch. 24:44). **46, 47. Beware . . .**—(See on Matt. 23:5; and on ch. 14:7).

devour . . .—taking advantage of their helpless condition and confiding character, to obtain possession of their property, while by their "long prayers" they made them believe they were raised far above "filthy lucre." So much "the greater damnation" awaits them. What a lifelike description of the Romish clergy, the true successors of "the scribes!"

ADAM CLARKE

46. *Beware of the scribes.* Take heed that you are not seduced by those who should show you the way of salvation. See on Matt. xxiii. 4-14.

The scribes and the Pharisees sit in Moses' seat. They "sat" there formerly by divine appointment; they *sit* there now by divine permission. What our Lord says here refers to their expounding the Scriptures, for it was the custom of the Jewish doctors to *sit* while they expounded the law and prophets, chap. v. 1; Luke iv. 20-22, and to stand up when they read them. By the *seat* of Moses we are to understand authority to teach the law. Moses was the great teacher of the Jewish people, and the scribes are here represented as his successors.

MATTHEW HENRY

CHAPTER 21

Verses 1–4

This short passage of story we had before in Mark. It is thus recorded twice, to teach us, 1. That *charity* to the poor is a *main matter* in religion. Our Lord Jesus took all occasions to commend it and recommend it. 2. That Jesus Christ has his eye upon us, to observe what we give to the poor. Christ, though intent upon his preaching, looked up, to see what *gifts were cast into the treasury, v.* 1. He observes whether we give largely and liberally, in proportion to what we have, or whether we be sneaking and paltry in it. He observes whether we give charitably and with a willing mind, or grudgingly and with reluctance. And this should encourage us to be abundant in it. He sees in secret, and will reward openly. 3. That Christ observes and accepts the charity of the poor in a particular manner. Those that have nothing *to give* may yet *do* a great deal in charity by ministering to the poor, and helping them. But here was one that was herself poor and yet *gave* what little she had to the treasury. It was but *two mites*, which make a farthing; but Christ magnified it as a piece of charity exceeding all the rest: *She has cast in more than they all.* Christ does not blame her for indiscretion; but commended her liberality, which proceeded from a belief of and dependence upon God's providence to take care of her. 4. That, whatever may be called *the offerings of God*, we ought to have a respect for, and to our power, yea, and beyond our power, to contribute cheerfully to.

Verses 5–19

See here, I. With what admiration some spoke of the external pomp and magnificence of the temple. They took notice of it to him *how it was adorned with goodly stones and gifts, v.* 5. They thought their Master should be as much affected with those things as they were. When we *speak of the temple*, it should be of the presence of God in it.

II. Christ spoke of their being all made desolate very shortly (*v.* 6): "*As for those things which you behold, the days will come in which there shall not be left one stone upon another*. This building shall yet be utterly ruined."

III. With what curiosity those about him enquire concerning the time when this great desolation should be: *Master, when shall these things be? v.* 7. It is natural to us to covet to know future things, when we are more concerned to ask what is our duty in the prospect of these things, and how we may prepare for them. They enquire *what sign there shall be when these things shall come to pass*. They ask not for a *present* sign, to confirm the prediction itself, but what the future signs will be of the approaching accomplishment of the prediction.

IV. With what clearness and fulness Christ answers their enquiries.

1. They must expect to hear of false Christs and false prophets appearing (*v.* 8): *Many shall come in my name*, usurping the title and character of the Messiah. They shall say, *I am he*. To encourage people to follow them, they added, "*The time draws near* when the kingdom shall be restored to Israel." When they asked solicitously and eagerly, *Master, when shall these things be?* the first word Christ said

JAMIESON, FAUSSET, BROWN

CHAPTER 21

Vss. 1-4. The Widow's Two Mites. **looked up**—He had "sat down over against the treasury" (Mark 12:41), probably to rest, for He had continued long standing as he taught in the temple-court (Mark 11:27), and "looking up He saw"—as in Zaccheus' case, not quite casually. **the rich . . .**—"the people," says Mark 12:41 "cast money into the treasury, and many rich cast in much"; i.e., into chests deposited in one of the courts of the temple to receive the offerings of the people towards its maintenance (II Kings 12:9; John 8:20). **2. two mites**—"which make a farthing" (Mark 12:42), the smallest Jewish coin. "She might have kept one" [Bengel]. **3. And he said**—"to His disciples," whom He "called to Him" (Mark 12:43), to teach from it a great future lesson. **more than . . . all**—in proportion to her means, which is God's standard (II Cor. 8:12). **4. of their abundance**—their *superfluity;* what they had to spare," or beyond what they needed. **of her penury**—or "want" (Mark 12:44)—her *deficiency*, of what was *less* than her own wants required, "all the living she had." Mark still more emphatically, "all that she had—her whole subsistence." Note: (1) *As temple offerings are needed still for the service of Christ at home and abroad, so "looking down" now, as then "up," Me "sees" who "cast in," and how much.* (2) *Christ's standard of commendable offering is not our superfluity, but our deficiency*—not what will never be missed, but what costs us some real sacrifice, and just in proportion to the relative amount of that sacrifice. (See II Cor. 8:1-3.)

5-38. Christ's Prophecy of the Destruction of Jerusalem, and warnings to Prepare for His Second Coming, Suggested by It—His Days and Nights during His Last Week. **5-7.** (See on Matt. 24:1-3.)

8. the time—of the Kingdom, in its full glory.

ADAM CLARKE

CHAPTER 21

1. *The rich men casting their gifts into the treasury.* See all this, vv. 1-4, explained on Mark xii. 41-44.

2. *A certain poor widow.* A widow "miserably poor," and her being miserably poor heightened the merit of the action. *Two mites.* Which Mark says, chap. xii. 42, make a "farthing," or *quadrans*, the fourth part of an *as*, or "penny," as we term it. In Plutarch's time we find the smallest piece of brass coin in use among the Romans was the *quadrans*, but it appears that a smaller piece of money was in circulation among the Jews in our Lord's time, called here, and in Mark, chap. xii. 42, a *lepton*, i.e., "small, diminished." In ancient times our penny used to be marked with a deep indented cross, dividing the piece into four equal parts, which, when broken in two, made the halfpenny, and, when broken into four, made the "fourthing," what we have corrupted into *farthing*. Probably the Roman *quadrans* was divided in this way for the convenience of the poor.

5. *Goodly stones.* Or "costly stones." It has been thought by some that this relates not so much to the stones of which the Temple was built as to the precious stones with which it was decorated. For an account of the stones of the Temple, see on Mark xiii. 1. *And gifts.* Or "consecrated things," "consecrated to sacred uses."

6. *One stone upon another.* This was literally fulfilled. See Matt. xxiv. 2.

8. *Many shall come in my name.* Usurping My name; calling themselves the Messiah. See Matt. xxiv. 5. Concerning this prediction of the destruction of Jerusalem and its literal accomplishment, see the notes on Matt. xxiv. 1-42.

MATTHEW HENRY

was, *Take heed that you be not deceived.* Those that are most *inquisitive* in the things of God (though it is very good to be so) are in most danger of being imposed upon. *"Go you not after them."* If we are sure that Jesus is the Christ, and his doctrine is the *gospel of God*, we must be deaf to all intimations of another Christ and another gospel.

2. They must expect to hear of great commotions in the nations. There shall be *bloody wars* (*v.* 10): *Nation shall rise against nation.* There shall be *earthquakes, in divers places.* There shall be *famines* and *pestilences.* God has various ways of punishing a provoking people. Though spiritual judgments are more commonly inflicted in gospel times, yet God makes use of temporal judgments also. There shall be *fearful sights* and *great signs from heaven.* *"Be not terrified.* Others will be frightened at them, but be not you frightened, *v.* 2. As to the *fearful sights*, let them not be fearful to you. You fall into the hands of God. Trust therefore in him, and *be not afraid.* It is your interest to *make the best of that which is*, for all your fears cannot alter it: *these things must first come to pass.* There is *worse behind. The end is not by and by*, not *suddenly.* Be not *terrified*, for, if you begin so quickly to be discouraged, how will you bear up under what is yet before you?"

3. They must expect to be themselves for *signs* and *wonders* in Israel. *"Before all these, they shall lay their hands on you.* This must be considered not only as the *suffering* of the *persecuted*, but as the *sin* of the *persecutors.*" The ruin of a people is always introduced by their sin.

(1) Christ tells them what hard things they should suffer for his name's sake. They should *sit down and count the cost.* The Christians, having themselves been originally Jews, might expect fair quarter with them; but Christ bids them not expect it: *They shall deliver you up to the synagogues* to be scourged there. They shall *deliver you into prisons, that* you may be *brought before kings and rulers for my name's sake.* "Your own relations will betray you (*v.* 16), *your parents, brethren, and kinsfolks, and friends.* You will be called to *resist unto blood. Some of you shall they cause to be put to death. You shall be hated of all men for my name's sake.*" This is worse than death itself. They were hated of *all men*, that is, of all bad men, who could not bear the light of the gospel (because it discovered their evil deeds). The wicked world, which hated to be reformed, hated Christ, the great Redeemer, and all that were his, for his sake.

(2) He encourages them to bear up under their trials, and to go on in their work. God will bring glory both to himself and them out of their sufferings: *"It shall turn to you for a testimony, v.* 13. Your being set up thus for a mark, and publicly *persecuted*, will make you the more taken notice of. Your being brought *before kings and rulers* will give you an opportunity of preaching the gospel to them. Your suffering such severe things, and being so hated by the worst of men, will be a testimony that you are good. Your courage, and cheerfulness, and constancy under your sufferings will be a testimony for you, that you believe what you preach, that you are supported by a divine power. God will stand by you, and own you, and assist you, and you shall be well furnished with instructions, *v.* 14, 15. *Settle it in your hearts, not to meditate before what you shall answer;* do not *depend* upon your own wit and ingenuity, and do not *distrust* or *despair* of the immediate and extraordinary aids of the divine grace. I promise you the special assistance of divine grace: *I will give you a mouth and wisdom."* A *mouth* and *wisdom* together completely fit a man both for services and sufferings; *wisdom* to know what to say, and a *mouth* wherewith to say it. Those that plead Christ's cause may depend upon him to give them *a mouth and wisdom* to enable them to answer for themselves. They are enabled to say that both for him and themselves which *all their adversaries are not able to gainsay or resist*, Acts iv, v and vi. "You shall suffer no real damage by all the hardships they shall put upon you (*v.* 18): *There shall not a hair of your head perish.*" Shall some of them lose their heads, and yet not lose a hair? Take it figuratively in the same sense that Christ saith, *He that loseth his life for my sake shall find it.* To this end he had said (Matt. x. 30), *The hairs of your head are all numbered.* We do not reckon that *lost* or *perishing* which is laid out for good purposes. If we drop the body itself for Christ's name's sake, it does not perish, but is well bestowed. "It shall be abundantly recompensed." Though we may be losers for Christ, we shall not, we cannot, be losers by him in the end. "It is therefore your duty and interest to maintain a holy sincerity and serenity of mind, which will keep you always easy (*v.* 19): *In your patience*

JAMIESON, FAUSSET, BROWN

go . . . not . . . after them—"I come not so very soon" (II Thess. 2:1, 2) [Stier].

10. Nation . . .—Matthew and Mark add, "All these are the beginning of sorrows," or travailpangs, to which heavy calamities are compared (Jer. 4:31, etc.).

9-11. not terrified—(See vs. 19; Isa. 8:11-14).

end not by and by—or immediately, not yet (Matt. 24:6; Mark 13:7): i.e., "Worse must come before all is over."

12. brought before . . .—The book of Acts verifies all this.

13. for a testimony—an opportunity of bearing testimony.

18. not a hair . . . perish—He had just said (vs. 16) they should be *put to death;* showing that this precious promise is far above immunity from mere bodily harm, and furnishing a key to the right interpretation of Psalm 91, and such like. Matthew adds the following: "And because iniquity shall abound, the love of many," the many or the most—the generality of professed disciples—"shall wax cold." But he that endureth to the end shall be saved. Sad illustrations of the effect of abounding iniquity in cooling the love of faithful disciples we have in the *Epistle of James*, written about this period referred to, and too frequently ever since (Heb. 10:38, 39;

ADAM CLARKE

9. *Commotions.* Seditions and civil dissensions, with which no people were more agitated than the Jews.

11. *Fearful sights.* What these were the reader will find in detail on Matt. xxiv. 7.

12. *Synagogues.* Or "assemblies." See these all explained on Mark xiii. 9.

13. *It shall turn to you for a testimony.* That is, it shall turn out on your part for a testimony to them (your persecutors) that you are thoroughly persuaded of the truth of what you teach and that you are no impostors.

14. *Settle it therefore.* See on Matt. x. 19.

15. *I will give you a mouth and wisdom.* A mouth must appear plain to every person to be used here for a "ready utterance" or "eloquence" in speaking. They shall have an abundance of wisdom to know what to say, and they shall have an irresistible eloquence to say what they ought.

18. *But there shall not an hair of your head perish.* A proverbial expression for, You shall not suffer any essential injury. Every genuine Christian shall escape when this desolation comes upon the Jewish state.

MATTHEW HENRY

possess ye your souls." It is our duty and interest at all times, especially in perilous times, to secure the possession of our own souls, that they be not distempered now, nor our possession of them disturbed and interrupted. "*Possess your souls*, be your own men. Keep under the tumults of passion, that neither grief nor fear may tyrannise over you." It is by patience, Christian patience, that we keep possession of our own souls. "Set patience upon the guard, and keep out all those impressions which would ruffle you and put you out of temper."

Verses 20–28

He here comes to show them what all those things would issue in at last, namely, the destruction of Jerusalem, which would be a little day of judgment, a type and figure of Christ's second coming.

I. He tells them that they should see Jerusalem besieged, *compassed with armies* (*v.* 20), and, when they saw this, they might conclude that *its desolation was nigh.*

II. He warns them, upon this signal given, to shift for their own safety (*v.* 21): "*Then let them that are in Judæa flee to the mountains; let them that are in the midst of it depart out*, and let not them that are in the countries and villages about enter into the city. Do you abandon a city and country which you see God has abandoned and given up to ruin."

III. He foretells the terrible havoc that should be made of the Jewish nation (*v.* 22): *Those are the days of vengeance* so often spoken of by the Old Testament prophets. All their predictions must now be fulfilled. *All things that are written must be fulfilled* at length. Reprieves are not pardons. The greatness of that destruction is set forth. It is *wrath upon this people*, the wrath of God. Of particular terror it would be to women with child, and poor mothers that are nurses. There should be general confusion all the nation over.

IV. He describes the issue of the struggles between the Jews and the Romans. Multitudes of them *shall fall by the edge of the sword.* The siege of Jerusalem was, in effect, a military execution. The rest shall be *led away captive*; not into *one* nation, but *into all nations.* Jerusalem itself was *trodden down of the Gentiles.* The Romans laid it quite waste.

V. He describes the great frights that people should generally be in. Many frightful *sights* shall be *in the sun, moon, and stars*, and here in this lower world, the *sea and the waves roaring.* The effect of this shall be universal confusion and consternation *upon the earth, distress of nations with perplexity, v.* 25. *Men's hearts shall fail them for fear* (*v.* 26), dying away for fear, still trembling for fear of worse, and *looking after those things which are coming upon the world.* The *powers of heaven shall be shaken*, and then the pillars of the earth cannot but tremble. As that day was all terror and destruction to the unbelieving Jews, so the great day will be to all unbelievers.

VI. He makes this to be a kind of *appearing of the Son of man: Then shall they see the Son of man coming in a cloud, with power and great glory, v.* 27. The destruction of Jerusalem was in a particular manner an act of Christ's judgment, so that it might justly be looked upon as *a coming of the Son of man, in power and great glory*, but *in the clouds.* Now this was, 1. An *evidence* of the first coming of the Messiah. Those that would not have him to *reign over them* shall have him to *triumph over them.* 2. It was an *earnest* of his second coming.

VII. He encourages all the faithful disciples (*v.* 28) "*When these things begin to come to pass, then* do you look *up*, look heavenward, in faith, hope, and prayer, and *lift up your heads for your redemption draws nigh.*" When Christ came he came to redeem the Christians that were persecuted and oppressed. When he comes to judge the world at the last day, he will *redeem* all that are his, from all their grievances. When they see that day approaching, they can *lift up their heads with joy*, knowing that *their redemption draws nigh.*

VIII. Here is one word of prediction that looks further than the destruction of the Jewish nation, which is not easily understood; we have it in *v.* 24: *Jerusalem shall be trodden down of the Gentiles, till the times of the Gentiles be fulfilled.* 1. Some understand it of what is past. The Gentiles shall keep possession of it, and it shall be purely Gentile, till a great part of the Gentile world shall have become Christian. 2. Others understand it of what is yet to come. Jerusalem shall be possessed by the Gentiles, till the time come when the kingdoms of this world shall become Christ's kingdoms, and then all the Jews shall be converted.

JAMIESON, FAUSSET, BROWN

Rev. 2:10). "And this gospel of the kingdom shall be preached in all the world for a witness, and then shall the end come" (Matt. 24:14). God never sends judgment without previous warning; and there can be no doubt that the Jews, already dispersed over most known countries, had nearly all heard the Gospel "as a witness," before the end of the Jewish state. The same principle was repeated and will repeat itself to *the* end. **20, 21. by armies**—encamped armies, i.e., besieged: "the abomination of desolation" (meaning the Roman ensigns, as the symbols of an idolatrous, pagan, unclean power) "spoken of by Daniel the prophet" (Dan. 9:27) "standing where it ought not" (Mark 13:14). "Whoso readeth [that prophecy] let him understand" (Matt. 24:15). **Then . . . flee . . .**—EUSEBIUS says the Christians fled to *Pella*, at the north extremity of Perea, being "prophetically directed"; perhaps by some prophetic intimation still more explicit than this, which still would be their *chart.* **23. woe unto**—"alas for." **with child . . .**—from the greater suffering it would involve; as also "flight in winter, and on the sabbath," which they were to "pray" against (Matt. 24:20), the one as more trying to the body, the other to the soul. "For then shall be tribulation such as was not since the beginning of the world, nor ever shall be"—language not unusual in the Old Testament for tremendous calamities, though of this it may perhaps be literally said, "And except those days should be shortened, there should no flesh be saved, but for the elect's sake those days shall be shortened" (Matt. 24:21, 22). But for this merciful "shortening," brought about by a remarkable concurrence of causes, the whole nation would have perished, in which there yet remained a remnant to be afterwards gathered out. Here in Matthew and Mark are some particulars about "false Christs," who should, "*if possible*"—a precious clause—"deceive the very elect." (Cf. II Thess. 2:9-11; Rev. 13:13.) **24. Jerusalem . . . trodden down . . . until . . .**—Implying (1) that one day Jerusalem shall cease to be "trodden down by the *Gentiles*" (Rev. 11:2), as then by pagan so now by Mohammedan unbelievers; (2) that this shall be at the "completion" of "the times of the Gentiles," which from Romans 11:25 (taken from this) we conclude to mean till the Gentiles have had their *full time* of that place in the Church which the Jews in *their time* had before them—after which, the Jews being again "graffed into their own olive tree," one Church of Jew and Gentile together shall fill the earth (Rom. 11). What a vista this opens up! **25-28. signs . . .**—Though the grandeur of this language carries the mind over the head of all periods but that of Christ's second coming, nearly every expression will be found used of the Lord's coming in terrible national judgments, as of Babylon, etc.; and from vss. 28, 32, it seems undeniable that its *immediate* reference was to the destruction of Jerusalem, though its *ultimate* reference beyond doubt is to Christ's final coming.

28. redemption—from the oppression of ecclesiastical despotism and legal bondage by the total subversion of the Jewish state and the firm establishment of the evangelical kingdom (vs. 31). But the words are of far wider and more precious import. Matthew (24:30) says, "And then shall appear *the sign* of the Son of man in heaven," evidently something distinct from Himself, mentioned immediately after. What this was intended to mean, interpreters are not agreed. But as before Christ came to destroy Jerusalem, some appalling portents were seen in the air, so before His personal appearing it is likely that something *analogous* will be witnessed, though of what nature it is vain to conjecture.

ADAM CLARKE

19. *In your patience.* Rather, "your perseverance," your faithful continuance in My word and doctrine. *Possess ye your souls.* You will preserve your souls. You shall escape the Roman sword, and not one of you shall perish in the destruction of Jerusalem. Instead of "possess, or preserve ye," I read "ye shall preserve." This reading is supported by many of the MSS., versions, and fathers.

22. *These be the days of vengeance.* See on Matt. xxiv. 21.

24. *They shall fall by the edge of the sword.* Those who perished in the siege are reckoned to be not less than eleven hundred thousand. See Matt. xxiv. 22. *And shall be led away captive.* To the number of ninety-seven thousand. See Josephus, *War*, b. vi, c. ix, s. 2-3, and on Matt. xxiv. 31. *Trodden down of the Gentiles.* Judea was so completely subjugated that the very land itself was sold by Vespasian; the Gentiles possessing it, while the Jews were either nearly all killed or led away into captivity. *Of the Gentiles be fulfilled.* Till the different nations of the earth, to whom God shall have given the dominion over this land, have accomplished all that which the Lord hath appointed them to do; and till the time of their conversion to God take place.

25. *The sea and the waves roaring.* Figuratively pointing out the immense Roman armies by which Judea was to be overrun and destroyed.

26. *Men's hearts failing them for fear.* Or "men fainting away through fear, being ready to die." *Coming on the earth.* Or "coming upon this land."

ALEXANDER MACLAREN:

A gleam of hope shoots through the stormy prospect, for the treading down of Jerusalem by the Gentiles has a term set to it. It is to continue "till the times of the Gentiles are fulfilled." That expression is important, for it clearly implies that these "times" are of considerable duration, and it thus places a period of undefined extent between the fall of Jerusalem and the subsequent prophecy. The word used for "times" generally carries with it the notion of opportunity, and here seems to indicate that the breakup of the Jewish national existence would usher in a period in which the "Gentiles" would have the kingdom of God offered to them. The history of the world since the city fell is the best comment on this saying.

—*Expositions of Holy Scripture*

MATTHEW HENRY

Verses 29–38

I. Christ appoints his disciples to observe the signs of the times, which they might judge by, as they could judge of the approach of summer by the budding forth of the trees, *v.* 29–31. As in the kingdom of nature there is a chain of causes, so in the kingdom of providence there is a consequence of one event upon another. When we see the ruin of persecuting powers hastening on, we may thence infer that *the kingdom of God is nigh at hand.*

II. He charges them to look upon those things as *sure* and very *near.* The destruction of the Jewish nation, 1. Was *near* (*v.* 32): *This generation shall not pass away till all be fulfilled.* There were some now alive that should see it. 2. It was *sure*; the decree was gone forth (*v.* 33): "*Heaven and earth shall pass away* sooner than any word of mine: but *my words shall not.*"

III. He cautions them against security and sensuality (*v.* 34, 35): *Take heed to yourselves.* This is the word of command given to all Christ's disciples. We cannot be *safe* if we be *secure.* It concerns us at *all* times, but especially at *some* times, to be very cautious. 1. What our *danger* is: that *the day* of death and judgment should *come upon us unawares,* when we do not *expect* it, and are not *prepared* for it, lest it *come upon us as a snare.* 2. What our *duty* is: we must *take heed lest our hearts be overcharged.* Two things we must watch against, lest our hearts be overcharged with them: (1) The indulging of the appetites of the body: *Take heed lest you be overcharged with surfeiting and drunkenness,* the immoderate use of meat and drink. They stupefy the conscience, and cause the mind to be *unaffected* with those things that are most *affecting.* (2) The inordinate pursuit of the good things of this world. The heart is overcharged with the *cares of this life.* This is the snare of the men of business, that *will be rich.*

IV. He counsels them to prepare and get ready for this great day, *v.* 36. Here see, 1. What should be *our aim*: that we may be *accounted worthy to escape all these things.* Yet we must aim not only to *escape that,* but to *stand before the Son of man*; not only to stand *acquitted* before him as our Judge, but to *stand before him,* to attend on him as our Master, and serve him day and night, always to *behold his face.* The saints are here said to be *accounted worthy,* as before, *ch.* xx. 35. God, by the goodwill of his grace towards them, *accounts them worthy* of it. A great part of our worthiness lies in an acknowledgment of our own unworthiness. 2. What should be our *actings* in these aims: *Watch therefore, and pray always.* Watching and praying must go together. Those that would make sure of the joys to come, must *watch* and *pray.* (1) To keep a guard upon themselves. "Watch against sin, watch to every duty. Be awake, and keep awake." (2) To keep up their communion with God: "*Pray always.*" Those shall be accounted worthy to live a life of praise in the other world that live a life of prayer in this world.

V. In the last two verses we have an account how Christ disposed of himself during those three or four days between his riding in triumph into Jerusalem and the night in which he was betrayed. 1. He was *all day teaching in the temple.* He was an indefatigable preacher; he preached in the face of opposition, and in the midst of those that he knew sought occasion against him. 2. At night he went out to lodge at a friend's house, in the mount of Olives. 3. Early in the morning he was in the temple again, and the people were forward to hear one that they saw forward to preach (*v.* 38): *They all came early in the morning to hear him.* Sometimes the taste and relish which serious, honest, plain people have of good preaching are more to be valued and judged by than the opinion of the witty and learned.

JAMIESON, FAUSSET, BROWN

32. This generation—not "this nation," as some interpret it, which, though admissible in itself, seems very unnatural here. It is rather as in ch. 9:27.

34-37. surfeiting, and drunkenness—All animal excesses, quenching spirituality. **cares of this life**—(See on Mark 4:7, 19).

36. Watch . . . pray . . .—the two great duties which in prospect of trial are constantly enjoined. These warnings, suggested by the need of preparedness for the tremendous calamities approaching, and the total wreck of the existing state of things, are the *general improvement* of the whole discourse, carrying the mind forward to Judgment and Vengeance of another kind and on a grander and more awful scale—not ecclesiastical or political but personal, not temporal but eternal—when all safety and blessedness will be found to lie in being able to "STAND BEFORE THE SON OF MAN" in the glory of His personal appearing.

37, 38. in the daytime—of this His last week. **abode in the mount**—i.e., at Bethany (Matt. 21:17).

ADAM CLARKE

29. *He spake to them a parable.* Illustrated all these predicted facts by the simile of a fig tree. See this explained on Matt. xxiv. 32.

31. *The kingdom of God is nigh at hand.* After the destruction of the Jewish state, the doctrine of Christ crucified shall be preached everywhere, and everywhere prevail.

32. *This generation.* This race of men; but see on Matt. xxiv. 34 and Mark xiii. 30.

34. *Take heed to yourselves.* See our Lord's parable relative to this matter explained, Mark xiii. 34.

Be overcharged. Literally, "be made heavy," as is generally the case with those who have eaten or drunk too much.

35. *The face of the whole earth.* Or "of this whole land." The land of Judea, on which these heavy judgments were to fall.

36. *Watch ye therefore, and pray always.* Perhaps we should connect "continually" with *watch,* as it appears to be the most natural order. Indeed the word "continually" belongs equally to both *watch* and *pray;* and no man is safe, at any time, who does not attend to this advice as literally as possible. *That shall come to pass.* That is, the tribulations which are on their way to overwhelm and destroy the Jewish people. These are sufficiently stated in the preceding verses. *To stand before the Son of man.* To be *acquitted* and to be *condemned* are expressed, in Rom. xiv. 4, by "standing" and "falling." Those who were faithful to the grace they had received were not only not destroyed in the destruction of Jerusalem, but became heralds of the grace and mercy of God to the nations. Thus they were counted worthy *to stand before the Son of man*—to minister salvation in His name.

37. *And in the day time.* Or "every day." This probably relates to the last four days of His life already mentioned. *Abode in the mount.* He taught all day in the Temple, and withdrew every evening and lodged in Bethany, a town at the foot or on the declivity of the Mount of Olives.

MATTHEW HENRY

CHAPTER 22

Verses 1–6

Christ is here delivered up, *when the feast of unleavened bread drew nigh, v.* 1. Here we have,

I. His sworn enemies contriving it (*v.* 2), *the chief priests,* and the scribes, *seeking how they might kill him.* Could they have had their will, it had been soon done, but they *feared the people.*

II. A treacherous disciple joining in with them, Judas surnamed *Iscariot.* He is here said to be *of the number of the twelve.* One would wonder that one of *that number,* who could not but *know Christ,* should be so base as to betray him. How he who knew Christ so well yet came to betray him we are here told: *Satan entered into Judas, v.* 3. It was the devil's work. Whoever betrays Christ, or his truths or ways, it is Satan that puts them upon it. Judas knew how desirous the chief priests were to get Christ into their

JAMIESON, FAUSSET, BROWN

CHAPTER 22

VSS. 1-6. CONSPIRACY OF THE JEWISH AUTHORITIES TO PUT JESUS TO DEATH—COMPACT WITH JUDAS. **1, 2.** (See on Matt. 26:1-5.) **3. Then entered Satan . . .**—but not yet in the full sense. The awful stages of it were these: (1) *Covetousness* being his master-passion, the Lord let it reveal itself and gather strength by entrusting him with "the bag" (John 12:6), as treasurer to Himself and the Twelve. (2) In the discharge of that most sacred trust he became "a thief," appropriating its contents from time to time to his own use. Satan, seeing this door into his heart standing wide open, determines to enter by it, but cautiously (II Cor. 2:11); first merely "*putting it into his heart* to betray Him" (John 13:2), suggesting the thought to him that by this means he might enrich himself. (3) This

ADAM CLARKE

CHAPTER 22

1. *The feast of unleavened bread.* See this largely explained, Exod. xxiii. 14; xxiii. 2-40; and on Matt. xxvi. 2.

2. *They feared the people.* The great mass of the people seem to have been convinced that Christ was at least a prophet sent from God, and it is likely they kept steady in their attachment to Him. The multitude, who are represented as clamoring for His blood at the Crucifixion, appear to have been a mere mob, formed out of the creatures of the chief priests and Pharisees.

3. *Then entered Satan into Judas.* The devil filled the heart of Judas with avarice, and that infamous passion led him to commit the crime here specified. This at once accounts for the

MATTHEW HENRY

hands. He therefore went himself, and made the motion to them, *v.* 4. When you see Judas communing with the *chief priests*, be sure some mischief is hatching.

III. The issue of the treaty between them. 1. Judas must *betray Christ to them*, and this they would be *glad of*. 2. They must give him a sum of money for doing it, and this he would be glad of (*v.* 5): *They covenanted to give him money.* Judas sought *opportunity to betray him.* He gained the advantage he sought, and fixed the time and place where it might be done, *in the absence of the multitude*, and *without tumult.*

Verses 7–20

I. The preparation that was made for Christ's eating the passover with his disciples, upon the very *day of unleavened bread, when the passover must be killed* according to the law, *v.* 7. He sent Peter and John to *prepare the passover.* He directed those whom he employed whither they should go (*v.* 9, 10): *they must follow a man bearing a pitcher of water*, and he must be their guide to the house. He directed them thus, to teach them to depend upon the conduct of Providence, and to follow that, *step by step.* Being come to the house, they must desire the master of the house to show them a room (*v.* 11), and he will readily do it, *v.* 12. The disciples found their guide, and the house, and the room, just as he had said to them (*v.* 13). They got everything in readiness for *the passover*, *v.* 11.

II. The solemnizing of the passover. When *the hour was come he sat down*, and *the twelve apostles with him*, Judas not excepted. Though Judas has already been guilty of an *overt act* of treason, yet, it not being publicly known, Christ admits him to sit down with the rest at the passover. Now observe.

1. How Christ *bids this passover welcome* (*v.* 15): "*With desire I have desired* to *eat this passover with you before I suffer.*" He knew it was to be the prologue to his sufferings, and *therefore* he desired it, because it was in order to his Father's glory and man's redemption. Shall we be *backward* to any service for him who was so *forward* in the work of our salvation? See the love he had to his disciples; he desired to eat it *with them*, that he and they might have a little time together for private conversation. He was now about to leave them, but was very desirous to *eat this passover with hem before he suffered*, as if the comfort of that would carry him the more cheerfully through his sufferings.

2. How Christ in it *takes his leave of all passovers* (*v.* 16): "*I will not any more eat thereof until it be fulfilled in the kingdom of God.*" (1) It was fulfilled when *Christ our Passover was sacrificed for us.* (2) It was fulfilled in the *Lord's supper*, an ordinance of the gospel kingdom, in which the passover had its accomplishment. They ate of it, and Christ might be said to eat with them, because of the spiritual communion they had with him in that ordinance. (3) The complete accomplishment of that commemoration of liberty will be in the kingdom of glory. What he had said of his eating of the paschal lamb, he repeats concerning his drinking of the *passover wine*, the cup of *blessing*, or of thanksgiving. This cup *he took*, according to the custom, and *gave thanks* and then said, *Take this, and divide it among yourselves*, *v.* 17. This is not said afterwards of the sacramental cup, which, being the *New Testament in his blood*, he might give into everyone's hand, to teach them to make a particular application of it to their own souls; but, as for the paschal cup, it is enough to say, "*Take* it, and *divide it among yourselves*, *v.* 18. *I will not drink of the fruit of the vine any more, till the kingdom of God shall come.*" Christ dying next day was its fulfilment.

III. The institution of the Lord's supper, *v.* 19, 20. The *passover* and the *deliverance* out of Egypt were *typical* and *prophetic signs* of a Christ to come, who should by dying deliver us from sin and death, and the tyranny of Satan. Therefore the Lord's supper is instituted to be a commemorative sign or memorial of a Christ already come, that *has* by dying delivered us.

1. The *breaking of Christ's body* as a *sacrifice for us* is here commemorated by the *breaking of bread*: *This is my body which is given for you.* This bread that was given for us is given *to us* to be food for our souls, this bread that was *broken* and *given for us*, to satisfy for the guilt of our sins, is *broken* and *given to us*, to satisfy the desire of our souls. And this we do in *remembrance* of what he did for us, when he died for us, and for a *memorial* of what we *do*, in making ourselves *partakers of him*, and joining ourselves to him in an everlasting covenant.

JAMIESON, FAUSSET, BROWN

thought was probably converted into a settled purpose by what took place in Simon's house at Bethany. (See on Matt. 26:6, and John 12:4-8.) (4) Starting back, perhaps, or mercifully held back, for some time, the determination to carry it into immediate effect was not consummated till, sitting at the paschal supper, *"Satan entered into him"* (see on John 13:27), and conscience, effectually stifled, only rose again to be his tormentor. What lessons in all this for every one (Eph. 4:27; Jas. 4:7; I Pet. 5:8, 9)! **5. money**—"thirty pieces of silver" (Matt. 26:15); thirty shekels, the fine payable for man-or maidservant accidentally killed (Exod. 21:32), and equal to $25 in our money—"a *goodly price* that I was priced at of them" (Zech. 11:13). (See on John 19:16.) **6. in the absence, . . .**—(See on Matt. 26:5).

7-38. LAST PASSOVER—INSTITUTION OF THE SUPPER—DISCOURSE AT THE TABLE. **7. the day of unleavened bread**—strictly the 15th Nisan (part of our March and April) *after* the paschal lamb was killed; but here, the 14th (Thursday). Into the difficult questions raised on this we cannot here enter. **10-13. when ye are entered the city**—He Himself probably stayed at Bethany during the day. **there shall a man . . .**—(See on ch. 19:29-32).

14-18. the hour—about 6 P.M. Between three and this hour the lamb was killed (Exod. 12:6, *Margin*).

15. With desire . . . desired—"earnestly have I longed" (as Gen. 31:30, "sore longedst"). Why? It was to be His *last* "before He suffered"—and so became *"Christ our Passover sacrificed for us"* (I Cor. 5:7), when it was *"fulfilled* in the Kingdom of God," the typical ordinance thenceforth disappearing.

17. took the cup—the first of several partaken of in this service. **divide it among . . .**—i.e., It is to be *your* last as well as Mine, "until the Kingdom of God come," or as it is beautifully given in Matthew 26:29, "until that day when I shall drink it new with you in my Father's kingdom." It was *the point of transition between two economies and their two great festivals*, the one about to close for ever, the other immediately to open and run its majestic career until from earth it be transferred to heaven.

ADAM CLARKE

whole of this most unprincipled and unnatural transaction.

4. *And captains.* Among the priests who were in waiting at the Temple, some were appointed for a guard to the Temple, and over these were "commanding officers."

5. *They . . . covenanted to give him money.* Matthew says thirty pieces, or staters, of silver, the common price of the meanest slave.

6. *And he promised.* That is, to do it—or he accepted the proposal.

7. *The passover.* That on which they feasted, viz., the sacrificed paschal lamb.

8-13. *He sent Peter and John.* See the subject of these verses largely explained on Matt. xxvi. 17-19 and Mark xiv. 13, 15.

14. *And when the hour was come.* That is, the evening. See Matt. xxvi. 20 and Mark xiv. 17.

15. *With desire I have desired.* A Hebraism for "I have desired most earnestly." Our Lord's meaning seems to be that, having purposed to redeem a lost world by His blood, He ardently longed for the time in which He was to offer himself up. Such love did the holy Jesus bear to the human race. This eucharistic Passover was celebrated once, by way of anticipation, before the bloody sacrifice of the Victim of salvation, and before the deliverance it was appointed to commemorate, as the figurative Passover had been likewise once celebrated before the going out of Egypt and the deliverance of God's chosen people.

16. *Until it be fulfilled in the kingdom of God.* That is, until that of which the Passover is a type is fulfilled in My death, through which the kingdom of God, or of Heaven (see Matt. iii. 2), shall be established among men.

17. *He took the cup.* This was not the sacramental cup, for that was taken after supper, v. 20, but was the cup which was ordinarily taken before supper. *Divide it among yourselves.* Pass the cup from one to another; thus the cup which Christ gave to the first person on His right hand continued to be handed from one to another till it came to the last person on His left.

18. *I will not drink of the fruit of the vine.* That is, before the time of another Passover the Holy Ghost shall descend, the gospel of the Kingdom be established, and the sacramental supper shall take place of the paschal lamb; for in a few hours His crucifixion was to take place.

19. *Took bread.* See the nature and design of the Lord's Supper explained in the notes on Matt. xxvi. 26-29. *This do in remembrance of me.* That the Jews in eating the Passover did it to represent the sufferings of the Messiah is evident from the tract *Pesachim,* fol. 119.

MATTHEW HENRY

2. The *shedding* of *Christ's blood*, by which the atonement was made, as represented by the wine in the cup. It *commemorates* the purchase of the covenant by the blood of Christ, and *confirms* the promises of the covenant. In all our commemorations of the shedding of Christ's blood, we must have an eye to it as shed for us; *who loved me, and gave himself for me.*

Verses 21–38

We have here Christ's discourse with his disciples after supper, much of which is new here; and in St. John's gospel we shall find other additions.

I. He discoursed with them concerning him that should betray him. 1. He signifies to them that the traitor was now among them, and one of them, *v.* 21. By placing this after the institution of the Lord's supper, though in Matthew and Mark it is placed before it, it seems plain that Judas did receive the Lord's supper, did *eat of that bread* and *drink of that cup*; for, after the solemnity was over, Christ said, *Behold, the hand of him that betrayeth me is with me on the table.* 2. He foretells that the treason would take effect (*v.* 22): *Truly the Son of man goes as it was determined*; for he is delivered up by the counsel and foreknowledge of God. Christ was not driven to his sufferings, but cheerfully *went to them.* 3. He threatens the traitor: *Woe to that man by whom he is betrayed.* Though God has *determined* that Christ shall be betrayed, and he himself has cheerfully submitted to it, yet Judas's sin or punishment is not at all the less. 4. He frightens the rest of the disciples into a suspicion of themselves, by saying that it was one of them (*v.* 23): *They began to enquire among themselves who it was that should do this thing.*

II. Concerning the strife that was among them for precedency or supremacy.

1. See what the dispute was: *Which of them should be accounted the greatest.* How inconsistent is this with that in the verse before! There they were enquiring which would be the traitor, and here which should be the prince. What a self-contradiction is the deceitful heart of man!

2. See what Christ said to this dispute. He was not sharp upon them but mildly showed them the sin and folly of it.

(1) This was to make themselves like the *kings of the Gentiles, v.* 25. They *exercise lordship* over their subjects. The *exercising of lordship* better becomes the *kings of the Gentiles* than the ministers of Christ. *They that exercise authority*, they are called *Benefactors*, they call themselves so, and so their flatterers call them. However they may really serve themselves, they would be thought to *serve their country.* One of the Ptolemies was surnamed *The Benefactor.* Now our Saviour, by taking notice of this, intimates, [1] That to *do good* is much more honourable than to *look great.* By their own confession, a benefactor to his country is much more valued than a ruler of his country. [2] That to *do good* is the surest way to be great. He would have his disciples believe, that their greatest honour would be to do all the good they could in the world. If they have that which is confessedly the *greater* honour, of being benefactors, let them despise the less, of being rulers.

(2) It was to make themselves unlike Christ himself: "*You shall not be so,*" *v.* 26, 27. "It was never intended that you should *rule* any otherwise than by the power of truth and grace, but that you should *serve.*" Here is the rule Christ gave to his disciples: He that is *greater among you,* that is *senior*, let him be as the *younger.* Their age and honour, instead of warranting them to take their ease, bind them to double work. And he *that is chief,* let him be *as he that* serves. Here is the example which he himself gave to this rule: *Whether is greater, he that sitteth at meat or he that serveth?* He was ready to do any office of kindness and service for them; witness his *washing* their feet.

(3) They ought not to strive for worldly honour and grandeur, because he had better honours in reserve for them, a *kingdom, a feast,* a *throne,* wherein they should all share alike, *v.* 28–30.

[1] Christ's commendation of his disciples for their faithfulness to him. It is spoken with an air of encomium and applause: "*You are they who have continued with me in my temptations,* you are they who have stood by me and stuck to me." His disciples continued with him, and were afflicted in all his afflictions. It was but little help that they could give him; nevertheless, he took it kindly that they *continued with him,* and he here owns their kindness. Christ's disciples had been very defective in their duty. We find them guilty of many mistakes and weaknesses: yet their Master passes all by and forgets it. *You are they who have continued with me.* Thus does he praise at parting, to show how willing

JAMIESON, FAUSSET, BROWN

21, 22. (See on John 13:21, etc.)

He will therefore speak it out in terms not to be misunderstood. But how much it cost Him to do this, appears from the "trouble" that came over His "spirit"—visible emotion, no doubt—before He got it uttered. What wounded susceptibility does this disclose, and what exquisite delicacy in His social intercourse with the Twelve, to whom He cannot, without an effort, break the subject!

24-30.

there was—or "had been," referring probably to some symptoms of the former strife which had reappeared, perhaps on seeing the whole paschal arrangements committed to two of the Twelve. (See on Mark 10:42-45.)

25. benefactors—a title which the vanity of princes eagerly coveted.

26.

But ye . . . not—Of how little avail has this condemnation of "lordship" and vain titles been against the vanity of Christian ecclesiastics?

28.

continued . . .—affecting evidence of Christ's tender susceptibility to human sympathy and support! (See on John 6:66, 67; 16:32.)

ADAM CLARKE

20. *This cup is the new testament in my blood.* Perhaps it might be better to paraphrase the passage thus: "This cup which is poured out for you signifies the blood of the new covenant, which is shortly to be ratified in (or by) the shedding of My blood." Or, "This cup is the new covenant, poured out for you with My blood"; that is, the paschal sacrifice and My sacrifice happen together.

22. *The Son of man goeth.* That is, He is about to die. "Going, going away, and departing" are used, by the best Greek and Latin writers, for "death" and "dying."

23. *They began to inquire among themselves.* See the notes on Matt. xxvi. 23-24.

25. *Are called benefactors.* The very Greek word used by the Evangelist was the surname of some of the Ptolemies of Egypt: *Ptolemy Euergetes,* i.e., "the Benefactor." It was a custom among the ancient Romans to distribute part of the lands which they had conquered on the frontiers of the empire to their soldiers. Those who enjoyed such lands were called *beneficiarii,* beneficed persons; and the lands themselves were termed *beneficia,* benefices, as being held on the *beneficence* of the sovereign. And it is no wonder that such sovereigns, however tyrannical or oppressive they might have been in other respects, were termed *benefactors* by those who were thus dependent on their bounty.

26. *Let him be as the younger.* Dr Lightfoot justly conjectures that Peter was the eldest of all the disciples; and he supposes that the strife was kindled between him and the sons of Zebedee, James and John. These three disciples were those whom Christ had distinguished by peculiar marks of His favor; and therefore it is natural to conclude that the strife lay between these three, the two brothers and Peter. Shall we or Peter be at the head? Neither, says our Lord. *Let him,* Peter, *who is chief* (the eldest) *among you, be as* John, *the younger.*

MATTHEW HENRY

he is to make the best of those whose hearts he knows to be upright with him.

[2] The recompence he designed them for their fidelity: *I appoint unto you a kingdom.* Understand it, *First,* Of what should be done for them in this world. God gave his Son a *kingdom among men,* the gospel church. This *kingdom* he *appointed* to his apostles and their successors in the ministry of the gospel. This is the honour reserved for you. Or, *Secondly,* Of what should be done for them in the other world. God will give them *the kingdom.* They shall *eat and drink at Christ's table in his kingdom,* of which he had spoken, *v.* 16, 18. They shall partake of those joys and pleasures which were the recompence of his services and sufferings. The *highest dignities*: "You shall *sit down with me on my throne,*" Rev. iii. 21.

III. Concerning Peter's denying him.

1. The general notice Christ gives to Peter of the devil's design upon him and the rest of the apostles (*v.* 31): *The Lord said, Simon, Simon, Satan hath desired to have you, that he may sift you as wheat.* Peter, who used to be the *mouth* of the rest in speaking to Christ, is here made the *ear* of the rest; and what is designed for warning to them all (*all you shall be offended, because of me*) is directed to Peter, being in a particular manner struck at by the tempter: *Satan has desired to have you.* "Give me leave to try them," saith Satan, "and Peter particularly." He desired to have them, *that he might sift them,* that he might show them to be chaff, and not wheat. Satan could not sift them unless God gave him leave: He *desired to have them,* "*He has challenged you* to prove you a company of hypocrites, and Peter especially, the forwardest of you."

2. The particular encouragement he gave to Peter: "*I have prayed for thee:* thou wilt be most violently assaulted, *but I have prayed for thee, that thy faith fail not.*" Though there may be many failings in the faith of true believers, yet there shall not be a total and final failure of their faith. It is owing to the mediation and intercession of Jesus Christ that the faith of his disciples, though sometimes sadly shaken, yet is not sunk. They are *kept by the power of God* and the prayer of Christ.

3. The charge he gives to Peter to help others: "*When thou art converted, strengthen thy brethren;* when thou hast found thy faith kept from failing, labour to confirm the faith of others; when thou hast found mercy with God thyself, encourage others to hope that they also shall find mercy." Those that have fallen into sin must be *converted from it.* Those that through grace are converted from sin must do what they can to strengthen their brethren that stand, and to prevent *their falling*; see Ps. li. 11-13.

4. Peter's declared resolution to cleave to Christ, whatever it cost him (*v.* 33): *Lord, I am ready to go with thee, both into prison and to death.* This was a great word, and yet I believe no more than he meant at this time, and thought he should *make good* too. All the true disciples of Christ sincerely desire and design to *follow him, withersoever he goes.*

5. Christ's express prediction of his denying him thrice (*v.* 34): "*I tell thee, Peter, the cock shall not crow this day before thou even deny that thou knowest me.*" Christ knows us better than we know ourselves. It is well for us that Christ knows where we are weak better than we do, and therefore where to come in with grace sufficient.

IV. Concerning the condition of all the disciples.

1. He appeals to them concerning what had been, *v.* 35. He had owned that they had been faithful servants to him, *v.* 28. *When I sent you without purse, lacked you anything?* He owns that he had sent them out in a very poor and bare condition. If God thus send us out into the world, let us remember that better than us have thus begun low. Notwithstanding this, they had *lacked nothing*; and they readily acknowledged it: "*Nothing, Lord.*" It is good for us often to review the providences of God, and to observe how we have got through the straits and difficulties we have met with. Christ is a good Master, and his service a good service; for though his servants may sometimes be brought low, yet he will help them. We must reckon ourselves well done by if we have had the necessary supports of life, though we have lived from hand to mouth. They had wanted nothing.

2. He gives them notice of a very great change of their circumstances now approaching. He that was their Master was now entering upon his sufferings, which he had often foretold (*v.* 37): "Now *that which is written must be fulfilled in me. He was numbered among the transgressors.* This is *yet to be accomplished,* and then *the things concerning me* will have an end; then I shall say, *It is finished.*" It may be the comfort of suffering Christians, as it was of a suffer-

JAMIESON, FAUSSET, BROWN

29. I appoint . . .—Who is this that dispenses kingdoms, nay, the Kingdom of kingdoms, within an hour or two of His apprehension, and less than a day of His shameful death? These sublime contrasts, however, perpetually meet and entrance us in this matchless history. **30. eat and drink . . .**—(See on vs. 16, and on ch. 18:28, etc.).

31-34. Simon, Simon—(See on ch. 10:41). **desired to have**—rather, "hath obtained you," properly "asked and obtained"; alluding to Job (1:6-12; 2:1-6), whom he solicited and obtained that he might sift him as wheat, insinuating as "the accuser of the brethren" (Rev. 12:10), that he would find chaff enough in his religion, if indeed there was any wheat at all. **to have you**—not Peter only, but them *all.*

32. But I have prayed—have been doing it already. **for thee**—as most in danger. (See on vss. 61, 62.) **fail not**—i.e., entirely; for partially it did fail.

converted—brought back afresh as a penitent disciple. **strengthen . . .**—i.e., make use of thy bitter experience for the fortifying of thy tempted brethren.

33. I am ready . . .—honest-hearted, warmly-attached disciple, thinking thy present feelings immovable as a rock, thou shalt find them in the hour of temptation unstable as water: "I have been praying for thee," therefore thy faith shall not perish; but thinking this superfluous, thou shalt find that "he that trusteth in his own heart is a fool" (Prov. 28:26). **34. cock . . . crow**—"twice" (Mark 14:30).

35-38. But now—that you are going forth not as before on a temporary mission, provided for without purse or scrip, but into scenes of continued and severe trial, your *methods* must be different; for purse and scrip will now be needed for support, and the usual means of defense.

37. the things concerning me—decreed and written.

ADAM CLARKE

29. *I appoint unto you a kingdom, as my Father hath appointed unto me.* Our Lord is probably to be understood as promising that they should get a Kingdom, a state of blessedness, as He should get it—they must go through much tribulation in order to enter into the kingdom of God.

31. *Simon, Simon.* When a name is thus repeated in the sacred writings, it appears to be always intended as an expression of love, manifested by a warning voice. As if He had said, While you and the others are contending for supremacy, Satan is endeavoring to destroy you all; but I have prayed for you, as being in most danger. *Satan hath desired to have you.* That is, all the apostles but particularly the three contenders; the plural pronoun sufficiently proves that these words were not addressed to Peter alone. Satan had already got one, Judas; he had nearly got another, Peter; and he wished to have all. But we see by this that the devil cannot even tempt a man unless he receive permission. He desires to do all evil; he is permitted only to do some.

32. *I have prayed for thee.* From the natural forwardness and impetuosity of your own spirit, you will be brought into the most imminent danger; "but I have supplicated for you, that your faith may not utterly fail"—"fall utterly or entirely off." Peter's faith did *fail,* but not utterly; he did *fall,* but he did not fall off, apostatize, or forsake his Master and His cause finally, as Judas did. Everybody sees, from Peter's denial of his Lord, that his faith did fail, and his great courage too; and yet they read, in the common translation, that Christ prayed that it might *not fail.* Can they then conceive that our Lord's prayer was heard? The translation which I have given above removes this embarrassment and apparent contradiction. *When thou art converted.* Restored to a sense of your folly and sin, and to Me and My cause—establish these *thy brethren.* All the disciples forsook Jesus and fled, merely through fear of losing their lives; Peter, who continued for a while near Him, denied his Master with oaths, and repeated this thrice. Our Lord seems to intimate that, after this fall, Peter would become more cautious and circumspect than ever; and that he should become uncommonly strong in the faith, which was the case; and that, notwithstanding the baseness of his past conduct, he should be a proper instrument for strengthening the feebleminded, and supporting the weak. His two Epistles to the persecuted Christians show how well he was qualified for this important work.

34. *The cock shall not crow this day.* Matt. xxvi. 34 and Mark xiv. 30 say "this night"; both expressions are right, because the Jewish day, of twenty-four hours, began with the evening, and ended at the evening of the following day. On Peter's denial, see the notes on Matt. xxvi. 31-35.

35. *When I sent you without purse.* See the notes on Matt. x. 9-10.

MATTHEW HENRY

ing Christ, that their sufferings were foretold. They *will have an end*, and will end well, everlastingly well. They must now in some degree suffer *with* their Master; and, when he is gone, they must expect to suffer *like* him. They must not now expect that their friends would be so kind and generous to them as they had been; and therefore, *He that has a purse, let him take it.* They must now expect that their enemies would be more fierce upon them than they had been, and they would need magazines as well as stores: *He that has no sword* will find a great want of it, and will be ready to wish that he had sold his garment and bought one. But the *sword of the Spirit* is the sword which the disciples of Christ must furnish themselves with. *Christ having suffered for us*, we must *arm ourselves* with the same mind, with a holy resignation to the will of God, and then we are better prepared than if we had sold a coat to buy a sword. The disciples hereupon enquire what strength they had, and find they had among them *two swords* (*v.* 38), of which one was Peter's. But he intimates how little he would have them depend upon this when he saith, *It is enough.* Two swords are sufficient for those who need more, having God himself to be *the shield of their help and the sword of their excellency.*

Verses 39–46

We have here the awful story of Christ's *agony in the garden.* In it Christ entered the lists with the powers of darkness, and yet conquered them.

I. What we have in this passage which we had before is, 1. That when Christ went out, *his disciples* (eleven of them, for Judas had given them the slip) *followed him.* Having continued with him hitherto in his temptations, they would not leave him now. 2. That he went to the place *where he was wont* to be private, which intimates that Christ was often alone, to teach us to be so. 3. That he exhorted his disciples to *pray* that, though the approaching trial could not be avoided, yet they might not in it *enter into temptation* to sin. 4. That he withdrew from them, and prayed himself. He withdrew about a *stone's cast*, and there he *kneeled down* (so it is here); but the other evangelists say that afterwards he *fell on his face*, and there *prayed* that, if it were the will of God, this cup of suffering might be *removed from him.* 5. That he, knowing it to be his Father's will that he should suffer and die, withdrew that petition, resigned himself to his heavenly Father's will: "*Nevertheless not my will be done*, not the will of my human nature, but the will of God, let that be done." 6. That his disciples were *asleep* when he was at prayer, and when they should have been themselves praying, *v.* 45. When he *rose from prayer*, he *found them sleeping.* See what a favourable construction is here put upon it, which we had not in the other evangelists—they were *sleeping for sorrow.* This teaches us to make the best of our brethren's infirmities, and, if there be one cause better than another, charitably impute them to that. 7. That when he awoke them, then he exhorted them to pray (*v.* 46): "*Why sleep ye? Rise and pray.*" When we find ourselves entering into temptation, it concerns us to *rise and pray*, Lord, help me in this *time of need.*

II. There are three things in this passage which we had not in the other evangelists:

1. That when Christ was in his agony, *there appeared* to him *an angel from heaven, strengthening him, v.* 43. When he was not delivered from his sufferings, yet he was *strengthened* and supported under them, and that was *equivalent.* If God proportion the shoulders to the burden, we shall have no reason to complain, whatever he is pleased to lay upon us. The angels ministered to the Lord Jesus in his sufferings. He could have had legions of them to rescue him; but he made use of his ministration only to *strengthen him.*

2. That, *being in an agony, he prayed more earnestly, v.* 44. As his sorrow and trouble grew upon him, he grew more importunate in prayer. Prayer, though never out of season, is in a special manner seasonable when we are in an agony; and the stronger our agonies are the more lively and frequent our prayers should be.

3. That, in this agony, *his sweat was as it were great drops of blood falling down to the ground.* There is some dispute among the critics whether this *sweat* is only *compared to* drops of *blood*, or whether *real* blood mingled with it, so that it was in colour like blood, and might truly be called a *bloody sweat*; the matter is not great. Every pore was as it were a bleeding wound, and his blood stained all his raiment. This showed the *travail of his soul.*

Verses 47–53

I. The marking of him by Judas. Here a numerous party appears, and Judas at the head of them, for

JAMIESON, FAUSSET, BROWN

have an end—are rapidly drawing to a close. **38. two swords . . . enough**—they thinking He referred to present defense, while His answer showed He meant something else.

39-46. AGONY IN THE GARDEN. **39. as . . . wont**—(See John 18:2). **40. the place**—the Garden of Gethsemane, on the west or city side of the mount. Comparing all the accounts of this mysterious scene, the facts appear to be these: (1) He bade nine of the Twelve remain "here" while He went and prayed "yonder." (2) He "took the other three, Peter, James, and John, and began to be sore amazed [appalled], sorrowful, and very heavy [oppressed], and said, My soul is exceeding sorrowful even unto death"—'I feel as if nature would sink under this load, as if life were ebbing out, and death coming before its time'—"tarry ye here, and watch with Me"; not, 'Witness for Me,' but, 'Bear Me company.' It did Him good, it seems, to have them beside Him. (3) But soon even they were too much for Him: He must be alone. "He was withdrawn from them about a stone's-cast"—though near enough for them to be competent witnesses—and kneeled down, uttering that most affecting prayer (Mark 14:36), that if possible "the cup," of His approaching *death*, "might pass from Him, but if not, His Father's will be done": implying that *in itself* it was so purely revolting that only its being the Father's will would induce Him to taste it, but that *in that view* of it He was perfectly prepared to drink it. It is no struggle between a reluctant and a compliant will, but between two views of one event—an *abstract* and a *relative* view of it, in the one of which it was *revolting*, in the other *welcome.* By signifying how it felt in the *one* view, He shows His beautiful oneness with ourselves in nature and feeling; by expressing how He regarded it in the other light, He reveals His absolute obediential subjection to His Father. (4) On this, having a momentary relief, for it came upon Him, we imagine, by surges, He returns to the three, and finding them sleeping, He addresses them affectingly, particularly *Peter*, as in Mark 14:37, 38. He then (5) goes back, not now to kneel, but fell on His face on the ground, saying the same words, but with this turn, "If this cup *may not pass* . . ." (Matt. 26:42)—i.e., 'Yes, I understand this mysterious silence (Ps. 22:1-6); it may not pass; I am to drink it, and I will'—"Thy will be done!" (6) Again, for a moment relieved, He returns and finds them "sleeping for sorrow," warns them as before, but puts a loving construction upon it, separating between the "willing spirit" and the "weak flesh." (7) Once more, returning to His solitary spot, the surges rise higher, beat more tempestuously, and seem ready to overwhelm Him. To fortify Him for this, "there appeared an angel unto Him from heaven strengthening Him"—not to minister light or comfort (He was to have none of that, and they were not needed nor fitted to convey it), but purely to sustain and brace up sinking nature for a yet hotter and fiercer struggle. And now, He is "in an agony, and prays more earnestly"—even Christ's prayer, it seems, admitted of and now demanded such increase—"and His sweat was as it were great drops [literally clots] of blood falling down to the ground." What was this? *Not His proper sacrificial offering,* though essential to it. It was just the internal struggle, apparently hushing itself before, but now swelling up again, convulsing His whole inner man, and this so affecting His animal nature that the sweat oozed out from every pore in thick drops of blood, falling to the ground. It was just *shuddering nature* and *indomitable will* struggling together. But again the cry, If it must be, *Thy will be done,* issues from His lips, and all is over. "The bitterness of death is past." He has anticipated and rehearsed His final conflict, and won the victory—now on the theater of an *invincible will,* as then on the arena of the Cross. 'I *will* suffer,' is the grand result of Gethsemane: "It is finished" is the shout that bursts from the Cross. The Will without the Deed had been all in vain; but His work was consummated when He carried the now manifested Will into the palpable Deed, "*by the which* WILL *we are sanctified* THROUGH THE OFFERING OF THE BODY OF JESUS CHRIST ONCE FOR ALL" (Heb. 10:10). (8) At the close of the whole scene, finding them still sleeping (worn out with continued sorrow and racking anxiety), He bids them, with an irony of deep emotion, "sleep on now and take their rest, the hour is come, the Son of man is betrayed into the hands of sinners, rise, let us be going, the traitor is at hand." And while He spoke, Judas approached with his armed band. Thus they proved "miserable comforters," broken

ADAM CLARKE

36. *He that hath no sword.* The word stands rather oddly in the passage. The verse, translated in the order in which it stands, is as follows: "And he who hath none, let him sell his garment and buy—a sword." [Some] think that it was a proverbial expression, intimating a time of great difficulty and danger, and that now the disciples had need to look to themselves, for His murderers were at hand. The reader will observe that these words were spoken to the disciples just before He went to the Garden of Gethsemane, and that the danger was now so very near that there could be no time for any of them to go and sell his garment in order to purchase a sword to defend himself and his Master from the attack of the Jewish mob. Judea was at this time, as we have already noticed, much infested by robbers; while our Lord was with His disciples, they were perfectly safe, being shielded by His miraculous power. Shortly they must go into every part of the land and would need weapons to defend themselves.

37. *Must yet be accomplished.* Probably meaning that, though this prophecy did refer to some particular matter in the time of the prophet, yet it "farther" related to Christ, and could not have its complete accomplishment but in His crucifixion as a criminal. *For the things concerning me have an end.* As if He had said: My work is now almost done; yours is only beginning. I am now about to be crucified and numbered with the transgressors. Think what will be done to you, and what ought to be done by you; and then think if this be a time for you to be contending with each other.

38. *Lord, behold, here are two swords. And he said unto them, It is enough.* These words cannot be well understood as being an answer to the supposed command of Christ for everyone who had no sword to go and sell his garment and buy one, for in this case they were not *enough,* or "sufficient," as nine of the disciples must be without any instrument of defense. But they may be understood as pointing out the readiness and determination of Peter, and perhaps some others, to defend our Lord: "Thou shalt not be treated as a transgressor; here are two swords, and we will fight for Thee." In v. 33, Peter had said he was ready to go with Christ either to prison or death which showed his strong resolution to stand by and defend his Master, even at the expense of his life. But, alas, he depended too much on himself! *It is enough.* The meaning probably is, There is enough said on the subject; as immediately after this He entered into His agony. I must here confess that the matter about the *swords* appears to me very obscure. I am afraid I do not understand it, and I know of none who does. Schoettgen and Lightfoot have said much on the subject; others have endeavored to get rid of the difficulty by translating a "knife," which was necessary on long journeys for providing forage and fuel, as they were to depend wholly on their own industry, under God, for all the necessaries of life while going through the nations of the earth, preaching the gospel to Jews and Gentiles. I cannot say which sense the reader should prefer.

40. *When he was at the place.* Viz., Gethsemane. On this agony of our Lord see the notes on Matt. xxvi. 36-46.

43. *There appeared an angel . . . from heaven.* It was as necessary that the fullest evidence should be given, not only of our Lord's divinity, but also of His humanity. His miracles sufficiently attested the former; His hunger, weariness, and agony in the garden, as well as His death and burial, were proofs of the latter. As man, He needs the assistance of an angel to support His body, worn down by fatigue and suffering. See at the end of v. 44.

44. *Prayed more earnestly.* With greater emphasis and earnestness than usual, with strong crying and tears, Heb. v. 7; the reason given for which is that He was *in an agony. Drops of blood.* Some have thought that the meaning of the words is that the sweat was so profuse that every drop was as large as a drop of blood, not that the sweat was blood itself, but this does not appear likely. There have been cases in which persons in a debilitated state of body, through horror of soul, have had their sweat

MATTHEW HENRY

he was *guide to them that took Jesus*; they knew not where to *find him*, but he brought them to the place: when they were there, they knew not which was he, but Judas told them that whomsoever he should kiss, that same was he; so he *drew near to him to kiss him*. Luke takes notice of the question Christ asked him, which we have not in the other evangelists: *Judas, betrayest thou the Son of man with a kiss? v.* 48. Must one of his own disciples betray him? Must he be betrayed with a kiss? Was ever a love-token so desecrated and abused?

II. The effort which his disciples made for his protection (*v.* 49): *When they saw what would follow*, they said, "*Lord, shall we smite with the sword?* Thou didst allow us to *have* two swords, shall we now make use of them?" But they were in too much *haste* and too much *heat* to stay for an answer. Peter, aiming at the head of one of the servants of the *high priest*, missed his blow, and *cut off his right ear*. The other evangelists tell us what was the check Christ gave to Peter for it. Luke here tells us, 1. How Christ excused the blow: *Suffer ye thus far, v.* 51. He said this to his enemies who came to take him, to pacify them, that they might not be provoked by it to fall upon the disciples. He *speaks them fair*, and, as it were, *begs their pardon* for an assault made upon them by one of his followers, to teach us to give good words even to our enemies. 2. How he cured the wound: *He touched his ear, and healed him;* fastened his ear on again. Christ hereby gave them a proof, (1) Of his power. He that could *heal* could *destroy* if he pleased. (2) Of his mercy and goodness. Christ here gave an illustrious example to his own rule of *doing good to them that hate us*, as afterwards he did of *praying for them that despitefully use us*. Those who render good for evil do as Christ did.

III. Christ's expostulation with the officers to show what an absurd thing it was for them to make all this rout and noise, *v.* 52, 53. Luke tells us that it was said to the *chief priests and captains of the temple*, so that they were all ecclesiastics, retainers to the temple, who were employed in this odious piece of service.

1. How Christ *reasons* with them concerning their proceedings. What occasion was there for them to come out in the dead of the night, and *with swords and staves?* They knew that he was one that would not *resist*. Why then *are ye come out as against a thief*? They knew he was one that would not *abscond*, for he was daily with them in the temple, in the midst of them.

2. How he reconciles himself to their proceedings; and this we had not before: "*But this is your hour, and the power of darkness.* How hard soever it may seem that I should be thus exposed, I submit, for so it is determined. Now the *power of darkness*, Satan, *the ruler of the darkness of this world*, is permitted to do his worst. Let him do his worst." It is *the power of darkness* that *rides master*, and darkness must give way to light, and the power of darkness be made to truckle to the prince of light.

Verses 54–62

We have here the melancholy story of Peter's denying his Master. Notice is not taken here, as was in the other evangelists of Christ's being now upon his examination before the high priest, only of his being brought into *the high priest's house, v.* 54. But the manner of expression is observable. They *took him, and led him, and brought him*, which methinks intimates that they were in confusion. Struck with inward terror upon what they had seen and heard, they took him the furthest way about, such a hurry were they in in their own bosoms.

I. Peter's falling. It began in *sneaking*. He *followed Christ*; this was well. But he followed *afar off*. He thought to trim the matter, to *follow Christ*, and so to satisfy his conscience, but to follow *afar off*, and so to save his reputation, and sleep in a whole skin. It proceeded in associating himself with the high priest's servants. The *servants kindled a fire in the midst of the hall* and *sat down together*. *Peter sat down among them*, as if he had been one of them. His fall itself was disclaiming all acquaintance with Christ, because he was now in distress and danger. He was charged by a sorry simple maid with being retainer to this *Jesus*. She *looked wistfully* upon him as he *sat by the fire; and this man was with him*, saith she. And Peter, as he had not the courage to *own* the charge, so he had not the wit and presence of mind to *turn it off*, and therefore flatly and plainly denies it: *Woman, I know him not*. His fall was repeated a second time (*v.* 58): *After a little while another saw him*, and said, "*Even thou art one of them.*" *Not I*, saith Peter; *Man, I am not*. And a *third* time, *about the space of an hour after another* confidently affirms, *strenuously* asserts it. "*Of a truth this fellow*

JAMIESON, FAUSSET, BROWN

reeds; and thus in His whole work He was *alone*, and "of the people there was none with Him."

47-54. Betrayal and Apprehension of Jesus—Flight of His Disciples.

Then Simon Peter, having a sword, drew it, and smote the high priest's servant, and cut off his right ear. The servant's name was Malchus—None of the other Evangelists mention the name either of the ardent disciple or of his victim. John being "known to the high priest" (vs. 15), the mention of the servant's name by *him* is quite natural, and an interesting mark of truth in a small matter. As to the *right* ear, specified both here and in Luke, the man was "likely foremost of those who advanced to seize Jesus, and presented himself in the attitude of a combatant; hence his right side would be exposed to attack. The blow of Peter was evidently aimed vertically at his head" [Wester and Wilkinson]. **Then said Jesus**—"Suffer ye thus far" (Luke 22:51). **Put up thy sword into the sheath: the cup which my Father hath given me, shall I not drink it?**—This expresses *both the feelings* which struggled in the Lord's breast during the Agony in the garden—*aversion to the cup* viewed *in itself*, but, *in the light of the Father's will*, perfect *preparedness to drink it*. (See on Luke 22:39-46.) Matthew adds to the address to Peter the following:—"For all they that take the sword shall perish by the sword" (Matt. 26:52)—i.e., 'Those who take the sword must run all the risks of human warfare; but Mine is a warfare whose weapons, as they are not carnal, are attended with no such hazards, but carry certain victory.' "Thinkest thou that I cannot now"—even after things have proceeded so far—"pray to My Father, and He shall presently give Me"—rather, 'place at My disposal'—"more than twelve legions of angels"; with allusion, possibly, to the one angel who had, in His agony, "appeared to Him from heaven strengthening Him" (Luke 22:43); and in the precise number, alluding to the *twelve* who needed the help, Himself and His eleven disciples. (The full complement of a legion of Roman soldiers was six thousand.) "But how then shall the scripture be fulfilled that thus it must be?" (Matt. 26:53, 54.) He could not suffer, according to the Scripture, if He allowed Himself to be delivered from the predicted death. "And He touched his ear and healed him" (Luke 22:51); for "the Son of man came not to destroy men's lives, but to save them" (Luke 9. 56), and, even while they were destroying His, to save theirs.

Then the band . . . took Jesus—but not till He had made them feel that "no man took His life from Him, but that He laid it down of Himself." **And led him away**—"In that hour," says Matthew (26:55, 56), and probably now, on the way to judgment. when the crowds were pressing upon Him, "said Jesus to the multitudes, Are ye come out as against a thief, with swords and staves, for to take Me"—expressive of the indignity which He felt to be thus done to Him—"I sat daily with you in the temple, and ye laid no hold on Me. But this" (adds Luke 22:53) "is your hour and the power of darkness." Matthew continues—"But all this was done that the scriptures of the prophets might be fulfilled. Then all the disciples forsook Him and fled" (Matt. 26:56)—thus fulfilling His prediction (Mark 14:27; ch. 16:32).

55-62. Jesus before Caiaphas—Fall of Peter. The particulars of these two sections require a combination of all the narratives, for which see on John 18:1-27.

ADAM CLARKE

tinged with blood. Dr. Mead from Galen observes, "Cases sometimes happen in which, through mental pressure, the pores may be so dilated that the blood may issue from them; so that there may be a bloody sweat."

48. *Betrayest thou the Son of man with a kiss?* Do you attempt to kiss Me as a friend, while you are delivering Me up into the hands of My enemies? We need not wonder at all this, as Satan himself had entered into the heart of this traitor; see v. 3. Consequently we can expect nothing from him but what is fell, deceitful, and cruel.

51. *Suffer ye thus far.* Or, "Suffer Me to go thus far." As they had now a firm hold of Christ, Matt. xxvi. 50, He wished them to permit Him to go as far as Malchus, whose ear was cut off, that He might heal it. However, the words may be understood as an address to His disciples: "Let them proceed"; make no resistance; for in this way only are the Scriptures to be fulfilled.

53. *I was daily with you in the temple.* Alluding to the four preceding days, during the whole of which He taught in the Temple, see chap. xxi. 37 and Matt. xxi. 17. *This is your hour, and the power of darkness.* That is, the time in which you are permitted to unrein your malice, which you could not do before, because God did not permit you; and so perfectly are you under His control that neither you nor the prince of darkness can proceed a hair's breadth against Me but through this permission. What a comfortable thought is it to the followers of Christ that neither men nor demons can act against them but by the permission of their Heavenly Father, and that He will not suffer any of those who trust in Him to be tried above what they are able to bear, and will make the trial issue in their greater salvation and in His glory!

56. *A certain maid beheld him.* Or "attentively beholding him." And this she did by the help of the light of the fire at which Peter sat.

57. *And he denied him.* See the notes on Matt. xxvi. 58, 69, etc.

MATTHEW HENRY

also was with him, let him deny it if he can, for you may all perceive *he is a Galilean."* Peter now not only denies that he is a disciple of Christ, but that he knows anything of him (*v.* 60): *"Man, I know not what thou sayest."*

II. *Peter's getting up again.* See how happily he recovered himself.

1. The *cock crew,* and this startled him and put him upon thinking. Small accidents may involve great consequences.

2. *The Lord turned and looked upon him.* This circumstance we had not in the other evangelists, but it is a very remarkable one. Though Christ had now his back upon Peter, and was upon his trial, yet he knew all that Peter said. Christ takes more notice of what we say and do than we think he does. When Peter disowned Christ, yet Christ did not disown him. It is well for us that Christ does not deal with us as we deal with him. Christ *looked upon Peter,* for he knew that, though he had denied him with his lips, yet his eye would still be towards him. He only gave him *a look,* which none but Peter would understand the meaning of. (1) It was a *convincing* look. Peter said that he did not *know Christ.* Christ *turned, and looked upon him,* as if should say, "Dost thou not know me, Peter?" (2) It was a *chiding* look. (3) It was an *expostulating* upbraiding look: "What Peter, art thou he that disownest me now? Thou that wast the most forward to confess me to be the Son of God, and didst solemnly promise thou wouldest never disown me?" (4) It was a *compassionate* look; he looked upon him with tenderness. **"Poor Peter! How art thou fallen and undone if I do not help thee!"** (5) It was a *directing* look. Christ *guided him with his eye* to *retire,* and bethink himself a little. (6) It was a *significant* look: it signified the conveying of grace to Peter's heart. The crowing of the cock would not have brought him to repentance without this look. Power went along with this look to change the heart of Peter.

3. *Peter remembered the words of the Lord.*

4. Then *Peter went out, and wept bitterly.* One look from Christ melted him into tears of godly sorrow for sin.

Verses 63–71

I. How our Lord Jesus was *abused* by the servants of the high priest. They that *held Jesus mocked him,* and *smote him* (*v.* 63). They made sport with him: this sorrowful night to him shall be a merry night to them. They *hood-winked* him and then, they *struck him on the face,* and continued to do so till he named the person that smote him (*v.* 64), intending hereby an affront to his prophetical office. *Many other things blasphemously spoke they against him, v.* 65.

II. How he was accused and condemned by the great sanhedrim, consisting of the *elders of the people, the chief priests, and the scribes,* who were all up betimes, and got together *as soon as it was day,* to prosecute this matter. They would not have been up so early for any good work.

1. They ask him, *Art thou the Christ?* They could not prove it upon him that he had ever said so *in so many words,* and therefore urged him to own it to them, *v.* 67. If they had asked him this question with a willingness to admit that he was the Christ, it had been *well;* but they asked it with a resolution not to believe him, but a design to ensnare him.

2. He justly complained of their unfair and unjust usage of him, *v.* 67, 68. "But," saith he, *"If I tell you that I am the Christ, you will not believe.* Why should the cause be brought on before you who have already prejudged it? *If I ask you* what you have to object against the proofs I produce, *you will not answer me. You will neither answer me nor let me go;* if I be *not* the Christ, you ought to *answer* the arguments with which I prove that I am; if I be, you ought to *let me go;* but you will do neither."

3. He referred them to his second coming, for the full proof of his being the Christ (*v.* 69): *"Hereafter shall the Son of man sit on the right hand of the power of God,* and then you will not need to ask whether he be the Christ or no."

4. Hence they inferred that he set up himself as the Son of God, and asked him *whether he were so* or *no* (*v.* 70): *Art thou then the Son of God?* He called himself the *Son of man,* referring to Daniel's vision of the *Son of man,* Dan. vii. 13, 14. But they understood so much as to know that if he was *that Son* of man, he was also *the Son of God.*

5. He owns himself to be the Son of God: *Ye say that I am;* that is, "I am, as ye say."

6. Upon this they ground his condemnation (*v.* 71): *What need we any further witness?* It was true, they needed not any further witness to prove that he said he was *the Son of God,* they had it from *his own mouth.*

JAMIESON, FAUSSET, BROWN

immediately—"while he yet spake" (Luke 22:60). **the cock crew**—As Mark is the only Evangelist who tells us that our Lord predicted that the cock should crow *twice* (ch. 14:30), so he only mentions that it *did* crow twice (vs. 72). The other Evangelists, who tell us merely that our Lord predicted that "before the cock should *crow* he would deny Him thrice" (Matt. 26:34; Luke 22:34; John 13:38), mention only *one actual* crowing, which was Mark's last. This is something affecting in this Evangelist—who, according to the earliest tradition (confirmed by internal evidence), derived his materials so largely from Peter as to have been styled his *"interpreter,"* being the *only one* who gives both the sad prediction and its still sadder fulfilment *in full.* It seems to show that Peter himself not only retained through all his after-life the most vivid recollection of the circumstances of his fall, but that he was willing that others should know them too. The immediately *subsequent* acts are given in full only in Luke (22:61, 62): "And the Lord turned and looked upon Peter," from the hall of judgment to the court, in the way already explained. But who can tell what lightning flashes of wounded love and piercing reproach shot from that "look" through the eye of Peter into his heart! "And Peter remembered the word of the Lord, how He had said unto him, Before the cock crow, thou shalt deny Me thrice. And Peter went out and wept bitterly." How different from the sequel of Judas' act! Doubtless the hearts of the two men towards the Saviour were perfectly different from the first; and the treason of Judas was but the consummation of the wretched man's resistance of the blaze of light in the midst of which he had lived for three years, while Peter's denial was but a momentary obscuration of the heavenly light and love to his Master which ruled his life. But the immediate cause of the revulsion, which made Peter "weep bitterly," was, beyond all doubt, this heart-piercing "look" which his Lord gave him. And remembering the Saviour's own words at the table, "Simon, Simon, Satan hath desired to have you that he may sift you as wheat, *but I have prayed* [rather, 'I prayed'] *for thee that thy faith fail not"* (see on Luke 22:31, 32), may we not say that *this prayer fetched down all that there was in that "look"* to pierce and break the heart of Peter, to keep it from despair, to work in it "repentance unto salvation not to be repented of," and at length, under other healing touches, to "restore his soul?" (See on Mark 16:7.)

63-71. Jesus Condemned to Die and Shamefully Entreated. (See on Mark 14:53-63; John 18:19, etc.; and on vss. 55-62.)

Art thou the Christ, the Son of the Blessed?—Why our Lord should have answered this question, when He was silent as to the former, we might not have quite seen, but for Matthew, who says (26:63) that the high priest *put Him upon solemn oath,* saying, "I adjure Thee by the living God, that Thou tell us whether Thou be the Christ, the Son of God." Such an adjuration was understood to render an answer legally necessary (Lev. 5:1). **And Jesus said, I am**—or, as in Matthew 26:64, "Thou hast said [it]." In Luke, however (22:70), the answer, "Ye say that I am," should be rendered—as De Wette, Meyer, Ellicott, and the best critics agree that the preposition requires—"Ye say [it], for I am [so]." Some words, however, were spoken by our Lord before giving His answer to this solemn question. These are recorded by Luke alone (22:67, 68): "Art Thou the Christ [they asked]? tell us. And He said unto them, If I tell you, ye will not believe: and if I also ask [interrogate] "you, ye will not answer Me, nor let Me go." This seems to have been uttered before giving His direct answer, as a calm remonstrance and dignified protest against the prejudgment of His case and the unfairness of their mode of procedure. But now let us hear the rest of the answer, in which the conscious majesty of Jesus breaks forth from behind the dark cloud which overhung Him as He stood before the Council. **and**—in that character—**ye shall see the Son of man sitting on the right hand of power, and coming in the clouds of heaven**—In Matthew (26:64) a slightly different but interesting turn is given to it by one word: "Thou hast said [it]: nevertheless"—We prefer this sense of the word to "besides," which some recent critics decide for—"I say unto you, Hereafter shall ye see the Son of man sit on the right hand of power, and coming in the clouds of heaven." The word rendered "hereafter" means, not "at some future time" (as today "hereafter commonly does), but what the English word originally

ADAM CLARKE

Peter remembered the word of Jesus. Luke says, chap. xxii. 61, "The Lord turned, and looked upon Peter." *And wept bitterly.* Felt bitter anguish of soul, which evidenced itself by the tears of contrition which flowed plentifully from his eyes. "Let him that standeth take heed lest he fall." Where the mighty have been slain, what shall support the feeble? Only the grace of the almighty God. This transaction is recorded by the inspired penmen: (1) That all may watch unto prayer, and shun the occasions of sin. (2) That if a man be unhappily overtaken in a fault, he may not despair, but cast himself immediately with a contrite heart on the infinite tenderness and compassion of God.

62. *And Peter went out.* The word Peter is omitted by many good MSS., and some of the ancient versions.

63. *Mocked him, and smote him.* This and the following verses are placed by Matthew and Mark before the relation of Peter's denial. For their explanation, see on Matt. xxvi. 67-68.

68. *And if I also ask you.* Concerning the Christ, in case you cannot give Me such an answer as may prove I am not the Christ, you will not let Me go; for I know you are determined to put Me to death.

69. *Hereafter.* "From this very time." The kingdom of God is now going to be set up. See the note on Matt. xvi. 27-28.

70. *Art thou then the Son of God?* They all insisted on an answer to this question, and the high priest particularly put it to Him, Matt. xxvi. 63.

71. *We ourselves have heard.* We have heard Him profess himself the Son of God; He is therefore guilty of blasphemy, and, as an impious pretender to a divine mission, we must proceed against and condemn Him to death. See the note on Matt. xxvi. 66. Thus they proceeded as far as they could; He must now be brought before Pilate, as the Jews had no power to put Him to death. His trial before Pilate is related in the subsequent chapter.

On our Lord's agony in the garden, related in the forty-third and forty-fourth verses, much has been written, but to little purpose. The cause of this agony seems not to have been well understood, and there have been many wild conjectures concerning it. Some think it was occasioned by "the Divine wrath pressing in upon him; for, as he was bearing the sin of the world, God looked on and treated him as if he were a sinner." There is something very shocking in this supposition; and yet it is truly astonishing how general it is. The ministry of the angel, in this case, is a sufficient refutation of this opinion; for what sort of strength could an angel give Christ against God's indignation? Indeed the ministry of the angel, who must have been sent from God, and sent in love too, is a full proof that God's wrath was not poured out on our blessed Redeemer at this time. What renders this circumstance more difficult is that there is no mention of it in any of the other Evangelists; and it is worthy of remark that, among many of the ancients, the authenticity of these two verses, the forty-third and forty-fourth, has been doubted, and in consequence they are omitted in several MSS. and in some versions and fathers. The Codex Alexandrinus and the Codex Vaticanus omit both verses; in some other very ancient MSS. they stand with an *asterisk* before them, as a mark of dubiousness. They are, however, extant in such a vast number of MSS., versions, and fathers as to leave no doubt with most critics of their authenticity. After all that has been said or perhaps can be said on this subject there will remain mysteries which only the bright light of the eternal world can sufficiently illustrate. That Christ was now suffering, "the just for the unjust, that he might bring us to God," and that He was bearing in His body the punishment due to their sins, I have no doubt; and that the agony of His mind in these vicarious sufferings caused the effusion of the bloody sweat from His body may be easily credited without supposing Him to be at all under the displeasure of His Heavenly Father. For as God can see nothing but as it is, He

MATTHEW HENRY

They cannot think it possible that he should be the Messiah, if he appear not, as they expect, in worldly pomp and grandeur.

CHAPTER 23

Verses 1–12

Our Lord Jesus was condemned as a blasphemer in the spiritual court. When they had *condemned* him, they knew they could not *put him to death*, and therefore took another course.

I. They accused him before Pilate. The *whole multitude of them arose, led him unto Pilate*, and they demanded justice against him, not as a blasphemer (that was no crime that he took cognizance of), but as one disaffected to the Roman government, which they in their hearts did not look upon as any crime at all.

1. Here is the indictment drawn up against him (*v.* 2). They misrepresented him, (1) As making the people *rebel against Caesar*. It was true, and Pilate knew it, that there was a general uneasiness in the people under the Roman yoke. They would have Pilate believe that this Jesus was active to foment that general discontent: *We have found him perverting the nation.* Christ had particularly taught that they *ought to give tribute to Caesar*, and yet he is here falsely accused as *forbidding to give tribute to Caesar*. Innocency is no fence against calumny. (2) As making himself a *rival with Caesar*, though the very reason why they rejected him was because he did not offer to do anything against Caesar; yet this is what they charged him with, that he said, *he himself is Christ a king*.

2. His pleading to the indictment: *Pilate asked him, Art thou the king of the Jews? v.* 3. To which he answered, *Thou sayest it;* that is, "It is as thou sayest." Christ's kingdom is wholly spiritual, and will not interfere with Caesar's jurisdiction. All that knew him knew that he never pretended to be the *king of the Jews*, in opposition to Caesar as supreme.

3. Pilate's declaration of his innocency (*v.* 4): He *said to the chief priests, and the people, "I find no fault in this man."*

4. The continued fury and outrage of the prosecutors, *v.* 5. Instead of being moderated by Pilate's declaration of his innocency they were the more exasperated, more exceedingly *fierce*. We do not find that they have any particular fact to produce, but they resolve to carry it with noise and confidence: *He stirs up the people, teaching throughout all Judæa, beginning from Galilee to this place.* He did *stir up the people*, but it was to everything that was virtuous and praiseworthy. He did *teach*, but they could not charge him with teaching any doctrine that tended to disturb the public peace.

II. They accused him before Herod. 1. Pilate removed him and his cause to Herod's court. The accusers mentioned Galilee. "Why," said Pilate, "is he of that country? Is he a Galilean?" *v.* 6. "Yes," said they. "Let us send him to Herod then," said Pilate, "since he belongs to Herod's jurisdiction." Pilate was already sick of the cause, and desirous to rid his hands of it. 2. Herod was very willing to have the examining of him (*v.* 8): *When he saw Jesus he was exceedingly glad.* He had *heard many things of him* in Galilee, and he *longed to see him*, but purely out of curiosity; and it was only to gratify this that he *hoped to have seen some miracle done by him.* In order to this, he *questioned with him in many things.* But Jesus *answered him nothing*; nor would he gratify him so much as with the performance of one miracle. The poorest beggar, that asked a miracle for the relief of his necessity, was *never denied*; but this proud prince, is denied. He might have seen Christ and his wondrous works many a time in Galilee, and *would not*. Now he would see them, and *shall not*; because he knew not the day of his visitation. Miracles must not be made cheap, nor Omnipotence be at the beck of the greatest potentate. 3. His prosecutors appeared against him before Herod. *They stood, and vehemently accused him* (*v.* 10), *impudently* and *boldly*, so the word signifies. 4. Herod was very *abusive* to him: He, with *his men of war, set him at nought.* They *made nothing* of him; so the word is. They laughed at him as one that had lost his power, and was become weak as other men. Herod was more *abusive* to Christ than Pilate was. Herod arrayed Christ in a *gorgeous robe*, as a mock-king; and so he taught Pilate's soldiers afterwards to do him the same indignity. 5. Herod sent him back to Pilate, and it proved an occasion of the making of them friends. Herod would not condemn him as a malefactor, and therefore *sent him again to Pilate* (*v.* 11), and so returned Pilate's civility and respect; and this mutual obligation brought them to a better understanding

JAMIESON, FAUSSET, BROWN

signified "after here," "after now," or "from this time." Accordingly, in Luke 22:69, the words used mean "from now."

CHAPTER 23

Vss. 1-5. JESUS BEFORE PILATE. (See on Mark 15:1-5; and John 18:28-19:22.)

–I find in him no fault–no crime. This so exasperated "the chief priests and elders" that, afraid of losing their prey, they poured forth a volley of charges against Him, as appears from Luke 23:4, 5: on Pilate's affirming His innocence, "they were *the more fierce*, saying, He stirreth up the people, teaching throughout all Jewry, beginning from Galilee to this place." They see no hope of getting Pilate's sanction to His death unless they can fasten upon Him a charge of conspiracy against the government; and as *Galilee* was noted for its turbulence (Luke 13:1; Acts 5:37), and our Lord's ministry lay chiefly there, they artfully introduce it to give color to their charge. "And the chief priests accused Him of *many things*, but He answered nothing (Mark 15.3). Then said Pilate unto Him, Hearest Thou not how many things they witness against Thee? And He answered him to never a word, insomuch that the governor marvelled greatly" (Matt. 27:13, 14). See on Mark 15:3-5. In his perplexity, Pilate, hearing of Galilee, bethinks himself of the expedient of sending Him to Herod, in the hope of thereby further shaking off responsibility in the case. See on Mark 15:6, and on Luke 23:6-12. The return of the prisoner only deepened the perplexity of Pilate, who, "calling together the chief priests, rulers, and people," tells them plainly that not one of their charges against "this man" had been made good, while even Herod, to whose jurisdiction he more naturally belonged, had done nothing to Him: He "will therefore chastise and release him" (Luke 23:13-16).

6-12. JESUS BEFORE HEROD. (See on Mark 15:6). **7. sent him to Herod**–hoping thus to escape the dilemma of an unjust condemnation or an unpopular release. **at Jerusalem . . . at that time**–to keep the passover.

8. some miracle–Fine sport thou expectedst, as the Philistines with Samson (Judg. 16:25), O coarse, crafty, cruel tyrant! But thou hast been baulked before (see on ch. 13:31-33), and shalt be again. **9. answered . . . nothing**–(See Matt. 7:6).

10. stood and vehemently accused him–no doubt both of *treason* before the *king*, and of *blasphemy*, for the king was a *Jew*. **11. his men of war**–his bodyguard. **set him at naught . . .**–stung with disappointment at His refusal to amuse him with miracles or answer any of his questions. **gorgeous robe**–bright robe. If this mean (as sometimes) of shining white, this being the royal color among the Jews, it may have been in derision of His claim to be "King of the Jews." But if so, "He in reality honored Him, as did Pilate with His true title blazoned on the cross" [BENGEL]. **sent him again to Pilate**–instead of releasing him as he ought, having established nothing against Him (vss. 14, 15). "Thus he implicated himself with Pilate

ADAM CLARKE

could not see Him as a sinner who was purity itself. In every act Jesus was that beloved Son in whom the Father was ever well pleased.

CHAPTER 23

1. *The whole multitude.* It seems most probable that the chief priests, elders, scribes, and captains of the Temple, together with their servants, dependents, and other persons hired for the purpose, made up the multitude mentioned here. The common people were generally favorers of Christ; and for this reason the Jewish rulers caused Him to be apprehended in the night and in the absence of the people, chap. xxii. 6, and it was now but just the break of day, xxii. 66.

2. *Perverting the nation.* The Greek word signifies "stirring up to disaffection and rebellion." Many MSS. and versions add "our" *nation.* They intimated that He not only preached corrupt doctrine, but that He endeavored to make them disaffected towards the Roman government, for which they now pretended to feel a strong affection! *Forbidding to give tribute to Caesar.* These were the falsest slanders that could be invented. The whole of our Lord's conduct disproved them. And His decision in the case of the question about the lawfulness of paying tribute to Caesar, Matt. xxii. 21, was so fully known that we find Pilate paid not the least attention to such evidently malicious and unfounded accusations. Neither Christ nor any of His followers, from that day until now, ever forbade the paying tribute to Caesar; that is, constitutional taxes to a lawful prince.

7. *Herod's jurisdiction.* The city of Nazareth, in which Christ had continued till He was thirty years of age, and that of Capernaum, in which He principally resided the last years of His life, were both in lower Galilee, of which Herod Antipas was tetrarch. Pilate was probably glad of this opportunity to pay a little respect to Herod, whom it is likely he had irritated, and with whom he now wished to be friends. See v. 12.

10. *The chief priests . . . vehemently accused him.* Corrupt priests and teachers are generally the most implacable enemies of Christ and His truth. Evil passions betray those who are slaves to them. An affected moderation would have rendered these accusers less suspected, their accusations more probable, and the envy less visible than this vehemence. But envy seldom or never consults prudence, and God permits this to be so for the honor of truth and innocence.

11. *A gorgeous robe.* It probably means a "white robe," for it was the custom of the Jewish nobility to wear such. Hence in Rev. iii. 4 it is said of the saints, "They shall walk with me in white [garments]: for they are worthy." In such a robe Herod, by way of mockery, caused our Lord to be clothed; but the nobility among the Romans wearing purple for the most part, Pilate's soldiers, who were Romans, put on Jesus a "purple robe," Mark xv. 17; John xix. 2—both of them following the custom of their own country, when, by way of mocking our Lord as a King, they clothed Him in robes of state.

MATTHEW HENRY

one of another, *v.* 12. They had been *at enmity between themselves.* Observe how those that quarrelled with one another yet could unite against Christ. Christ is the great peacemaker; both Pilate and Herod owned his innocency, and their agreeing in this cured their disagreeing in other things.

Verses 13–25

We have here the blessed Jesus run down by the mob, and hurried to the cross in the storm of a popular noise and tumult.

I. Pilate solemnly protests that he believes he has done nothing worthy of death or of bonds. And, if he did believe so, he ought immediately to have *discharged* him. But, being himself a bad man, he had no kindness for Christ, and was afraid of displeasing the people; and therefore, for want of integrity, he *called together the chief priests, and rulers, and people,* and will hear what they have to say (*v.* 14): "*You have brought,*" said he, "*this man to me,* and *I have examined him before you,* and have heard all you have to allege against him, and I can make nothing of it: *I find no fault in him.*"

II. He appeals to Herod concerning him (*v.* 15): "*I sent you to him,* and he has *sent him back;* in his opinion, his crimes are not capital. He has laughed at him as a weak man, but has not stigmatized him as a dangerous man." He thought Bedlam a fitter place for him than Tyburn.

III. He proposes to release him, if they will but consent to it. He ought to have done it without asking leave of them. But the fear of man brings many into this snare, that, they will do an unjust thing rather than pull an old house about their ears. To please the people, 1. He will release him under the notion of a malefactor, because *of necessity he must release one* (*v.* 17). 2. He will *chastise* him, and release him. If *no fault* is to be *found in him,* why should he be chastised?

IV. The people choose rather to have Barabbas released. He was imprisoned for a *sedition made in the city,* and for *murder,* yet this was the criminal that was preferred before Christ: *Away with this man, and release unto us Barabbas, v.* 18, 19.

V. When Pilate urged the second time that Christ should be released, they cried out, *Crucify him, crucify him, v.* 20, 21. Nothing less will serve but he must be crucified: *Crucify him, crucify him.*

VI. When Pilate the third time reasoned with them they were the more peremptory and outrageous (*v.* 22): "*Why? What evil hath he done?* Name his crime. *I have found no cause of death, I will chastise him and let him go.*" But they were *instant with loud voices,* not requesting, but *requiring, that he might be crucified;* as if they had as much right to demand the crucifying of one that was innocent as the release of one that was guilty.

VII. Pilate's yielding, at length. The voice of the people and of the *chief priests prevailed.* He *gave sentence that it should be as they required, v.* 24. This is repeated, in *v.* 25, with the aggravating circumstance of the release of Barabbas: *He released unto them him that for sedition and murder was cast into prison,* because *him they had desired;* but he *delivered Jesus to their will,* and he could not deal more barbarously with him than to deliver him to *their will.*

Verses 26–31

It is strange with what expedition they went through his trial. He was brought before the chief priests at break of day (*ch.* xxii. 66), after that to Pilate, then to Herod, then to Pilate again; and there seems to have been a long struggle between Pilate and the people about him. He was scourged, and crowned with thorns, and contumeliously used, and all this was done in four or five hours' time, or six at most, for he was crucified between nine o'clock and twelve. Never anyone was so *chased out of the world* as Christ was. Now as they led him away to death we find,

I. One that was a *bearer,* that carried his cross, *Simon* by name, *a Cyrenian.* They laid Christ's cross upon him, that he might *bear it after Jesus* (*v.* 26), lest Jesus should faint under it. It was pity, but a *cruel pity,* that gave him this ease.

II. Many that were *mourners.* The common people, were moved with compassion towards him, because they had reason to think he suffered unjustly. This drew a great crowd after him, as is usual at executions. *A great company of people followed him,* especially of women (*v.* 27); they *also bewailed and lamented him.* Though there were many that reproached and reviled him, yet there were some that valued him, and pitied him. Many bewail Christ that do not believe in him, and lament him that do not love him above all. He found time and heart to take cognizance of their tears. Christ *died lamented.* He *turned to them,* and bade them *not weep for him, but for themselves,*

JAMIESON, FAUSSET, BROWN

in all the guilt of His condemnation, and with him accordingly he is classed" (Acts 4:27) [BENGEL]. **at enmity**—perhaps about some point of disputed jurisdiction, which this exchange of the Prisoner might tend to heal.

13-38. JESUS AGAIN BEFORE PILATE—DELIVERED UP—LED AWAY TO BE CRUCIFIED. (See on Mark 15:6-15; and John 19:2-17.)

Luke 23:13-16: **And Pilate, when he had called together the chief priests and the rulers and the people, said unto them, Ye have brought this man unto me, as one that perverteth the people: and, behold, I, having examined him before you**—from the first three Gospels we should conclude that the whole examination hitherto had been in their presence, while John represents it as private; but in all likelihood the reference here is to what is related in verses 3-5, though too briefly to enable us to see the precise form which the examination took throughout—**have found no fault in this man touching those things whereof ye accuse him: No, nor yet Herod: for I sent you to him; and, lo, nothing worthy of death is done unto him**—or rather, "by him," as the phrase sometimes means classically, and here must be held to mean. **I will therefore chastise him, and let him go.** "When, therefore, I have corrected, I will dismiss Him." Though the kind of correction which he proposed to inflict was not specified by Pilate on this occasion, there can be no doubt that scourging was what he meant, and the event soon proved it. It seems strange to our ideas of justice that a Roman governor should propose to punish, however lightly, a prisoner whose innocence he had just proclaimed. But it was of the nature of a well-meant, yet indefensible offer, in hope of saving the prisoner's life.

Matt. 27:15-23: "Now at that feast the governor was wont to release unto the people a prisoner, whom they would. And they had then a notable [or notorious] prisoner called Barabbas"—"which," says Mark (15:7), "lay bound with them that had made insurrection with him" or "with his fellow insurgents, who had committed murder in the insurrection." But in Luke (23:19) the murder is expressly ascribed to this Barabbas, who is also called "a robber." He was evidently the ringleader of this lawless gang; and there we learn that the "sedition" here referred to was "made in the city." "And the multitude," says Mark, "crying aloud, began to desire him to do as he had ever done unto them." This is peculiar to Mark, and enables us vividly to realize the rising of the popular excitement before which Pilate—reluctantly though it was—gave way. But this clamor for the exercise of his usual clemency at the feast suggested another expedient for saving his conscience—the selection of Jesus as the prisoner of his choice for this release; not doubting that between Jesus and such a villain as this Barabbas they would for very shame be forced to prefer the former. But he little knew his men, if he thought that. "Therefore," continues Matthew, "when they were gathered together, Pilate saith unto them, Whom will ye that I release unto you? Barabbas, or Jesus which is called Christ? For he knew that for envy they had delivered him"—that is, out of jealousy at the popularity of Jesus, and fear of losing their own. This would seem to show that Pilate was not ignorant of the leading facts of this case.

Cyrenian—of Cyrene, in Libya, on the north coast of Africa, where were many Jews who had a synagogue at Jerusalem (Acts 6:9, and see 2:10). He was "the father of Alexander and Rufus" (Mark 15:21), probably better known afterwards than himself, as disciples. (See Rom. 16:13.) **out of the country**—and casually drawn into that part of the crowd. **laid the cross**—"Him they compel to bear His cross," (Matt. 27:32)—sweet compulsion, if it issued in him or his sons *voluntarily* "taking up *their* cross!" It would appear that our Lord had first to bear His own cross (John 19:17), but being from exhaustion unable to proceed, it was laid on another to bear it "after Him."

ADAM CLARKE

12. *Pilate and Herod were made friends.* I do not find any account of the cause of the enmity which subsisted between Herod and Pilate given by ancient authors, and the conjectures of the moderns on the subject should be considered as mere guesses. It is generally supposed that this enmity arose from what is related in chap. xiii of the Galileans whose blood Pilate had mingled with that of their sacrifices. These were Herod's subjects, and Pilate seems to have fallen on them at the time they were offering sacrifices to God at the Temple.

15. *No, nor yet Herod: for I sent you to him.* That is, to see whether he could find that Christ had ever attempted to raise any disaffection or sedition among the Galileans, among whom He had spent the principal part of His life; and yet Herod has not been able to find out any evil in His conduct. Your own accusations I have fully weighed, and find them frivolous to the last degree. Instead of *for I sent you to him,* many MSS., with some versions, read, "For he hath sent Him to us." As if he had said, "Herod had sent Him back to us, which is a sure proof that he had found no blame in Him." *Nothing worthy of death is done unto him.* Or rather, "Nothing worthy of death is committed by Him," not *done unto him.*

17. *For of necessity he must release one.* That is, he was under the necessity of releasing one at this feast. The custom, however it originated, had now been so completely established that Pilate was obliged to attend to it.

18. *Away with this man.* That is, "Put Him to death"—literally, "Take this One away," i.e., to punishment, to death.

22. *I have found no cause of death in him.* "I find no crime worthy of death in Him." There is nothing proved against Him that can at all justify me in putting Him to death. So here our blessed Lord was in the most formal manner justified by His judge. Now as this decision was publicly known, and perhaps registered, it is evident that Christ died as an innocent Person, and not as a malefactor. On the fullest conviction of His innocence, His judge pronounced Him guiltless, after having patiently heard everything that the inventive malice of these wicked men could allege against Him; and when he wished to dismiss Him, a violent mob took and murdered Him.

26. *Simon, a Cyrenian.* See on Matt. xxvii. 32.

27. *Bewailed and lamented him.* "Beat their breasts."

MATTHEW HENRY

v. 28.

1. He gives them a general direction concerning their lamentations: *Daughters of Jerusalem, weep not for me.* They must not weep for him only, but rather let them *weep for themselves and for their children.* When with an eye of faith we behold Christ crucified we ought to weep, not for him, but for ourselves. The death of Christ was a thing peculiar; it was his victory and triumph over his enemies; it was our deliverance, and the purchase of eternal life for us. And therefore let us weep, not for him, but for our own sins, and the sins of our children, that were the cause of his death.

2. He gives them a particular reason why they should *weep for themselves and for their children*: "*For behold* sad times are coming upon your city." He had lately wept over Jerusalem himself, and now he bids them weep over it. Christ's tears should set us weeping. Now the destruction of Jerusalem is here foretold by two proverbial sayings, which both bespeak it very terrible, that what people commonly dread they would then desire, to be *written childless* and to be *buried alive.* (1) They would wish to be *written childless.* They will envy those that have none, and say, *Blessed are the barren, and the wombs that never bare.* (2) They would wish to be *buried alive*: *They shall begin to say to the mountains, Fall on us, and to the hills, Cover us, v.* 30. They shall wish to be hid in the darkest caves, that they may be out of the noise of these calamities. They will be willing to be sheltered upon any terms, though with the hazard of being crushed to pieces.

3. He shows how natural it was for them to infer this desolation from his sufferings. *If they do these things in a green tree, what shall be done in the dry? v.* 31. Christ was a *green tree,* fruitful and flourishing; now, if such things were done to him, we may thence infer what would have been done to the whole race of mankind if he had not *interposed,* and what shall be done to those that continue dry trees, notwithstanding all that is done to make them fruitful. The consideration of the bitter sufferings of our Lord Jesus should engage us to stand in awe of the justice of God. The best saints, compared with Christ, are *dry trees*; if he suffer, why may not they expect to suffer?

Verses 32-43

I. Divers passages which we had before in Matthew and Mark concerning Christ's sufferings. 1. That there were *two others, malefactors, led with him* to the place of execution. 2. That he was crucified at a place called *Calvary—the place of a skull.* He was *crucified.* This was a painful and shameful death above any other. 3. That he was crucified *in the midst between two thieves.* Thus he was not only treated as a transgressor, but *numbered with them.* 4. That the soldiers who were employed in the execution seized his garments as their fee, and divided them among themselves *by lot*: *They parted his raiment and cast lots.* 5. That he was reviled and reproached: *The people stood beholding,* and *the rulers* stood among the rabble, *and derided him,* and they said, *He saved others, let him save himself.* They challenged him to save himself from the cross, when he was saving others by the cross: *If he be the Christ, the chosen of God,* let him save himself. They *mocked him* (*v.* 36, 37); they made sport with him, and made a jest of his sufferings. And they said, *If thou be the king of the Jews, save thyself.* 6. That the superscription over his head, setting forth his crime, was, *This is the King of the Jews, v.* 38. He is put to death for pretending to be the king of the Jews; but God intended it to be a declaration of what he really was: he is *the king of the Jews,* and his cross is the way to his crown. This was written in those that were called the three learned languages, *Greek, and Latin, and Hebrew.* It was written in these three languages that it might be known and read of all men. In these three languages is Jesus Christ *proclaimed king.*

II. Here are two passages which we had not before, and they are very remarkable ones.

1. Christ's prayer for his enemies (*v.* 34): *Father, forgive them.* Seven remarkable words Christ spoke after he was nailed to the cross, and before he died, and this is the first. As soon as ever he was fastened to the cross, or while they were nailing him, he prayed this prayer, in which observe,

(1) The petition: *Father, forgive them.* The sin they were now guilty of might justly have been made unpardonable. No, these are particularly *prayed for.* Now he made intercession for transgressors. Now the sayings of Christ upon the cross as well as his sufferings had a further intention than they seemed to have. This was explicatory of the intent and meaning of his death: "*Father, forgive them,* not only these, but all that shall repent, and believe the gospel." The great thing which Christ died to pur-

JAMIESON, FAUSSET, BROWN

27-31. women—not the precious Galilean women (vs. 49), but part of the crowd. **28. not for me . . .**—noble spirit of compassion, rising above His own dread endurances, in tender commiseration of sufferings yet in the distance and far lighter, but *without His supports and consolations!*

30. mountains . . . hills . . .—(Hos. 10:8), flying hither and thither as they did in despair for shelter, during the siege; a very slight premonition of cries of another and more awful kind (Isa. 2:10, 19, 21; Rev. 6:16, 17).

31. green tree—that naturally resists the fire. **the dry**—that attracts the fire, being its proper fuel. The proverb here plainly means: "If such sufferings alight upon the innnocent One, the very Lamb of God, what must be in store for those who are provoking the flames?"

32-38, 44-46. CRUCIFIXION AND DEATH OF THE LORD JESUS. (See on John 19:17-30.)

they crucified him, and two others with him—"malefactors" (Luke 23:33), "thieves" (rather "robbers," Matt. 27:38; Mark 15:27). **on either side one and Jesus in the midst**—a hellish expedient, to hold Him up as the worst of the three. But in this, as in many other of their doings, "the scripture was fulfilled, which saith (Isa. 53:12), *And he was numbered with the transgressors*"—(Mark 15:28)—though the prediction reaches deeper.

Pilate wrote a title, and put it on the cross . . . Jesus of Nazareth, the King of the Jews . . . and it was written in Hebrew—or Syro-Chaldaic, the language of the country—**and Greek**—the current language—**and Latin**—the official language. These were the chief languages of the earth, and this secured that all spectators should be able to read it. Stung by this, the Jewish ecclesiastics entreat that it may be so altered as to express, not His real dignity, but His false claim to it. But Pilate thought he had yielded quite enough to them; and having intended expressly to spite and insult them by this title, for having got him to act against his own sense of justice, he peremptorily refused them. And thus, amidst the conflicting passions of men, was proclaimed, in the chief tongues of mankind, from the Cross itself and in circumstances which threw upon it a lurid yet grand light, the truth which drew the Magi to His manger, and will yet be owned by all the world!

"Then said Jesus"—['probably while being nailed to the CROSS'] [OLSHAUSEN], "FATHER, FORGIVE THEM, FOR THEY KNOW NOT WHAT THEY DO" (Luke 23:34)—and again the Scripture was fulfilled which said, "And He made intercession for the transgressors" (Isa. 53:17); though this also reaches deeper. (See Acts 3:17; 13:27; and cf. I Tim. 1:13). Often have we

ADAM CLARKE

28. *Weep not for me.* Many pious persons have been greatly distressed in their minds because they could not weep on reading or hearing of the sufferings of Christ. For the relief of all such let it be forever known that no human spirit can possibly take any part in the passion of the Messiah. His sufferings were such as only God manifested in the flesh could bear; and as they were all of an expiatory nature, no man can taste of or share in them.

30. *Mountains, fall on us.* As this refers to the destruction of Jerusalem, and as the same expressions are used in Rev. vi. 16, Dr. Lightfoot conjectures that the whole of that chapter may relate to the same event.

31. *If they do these things in a green tree.* This seems to be a proverbial expression, the sense of which is: If they spare not a tree which, by the beauty of its foliage, abundance and excellence of its fruits, deserves to be preserved, then the tree which is dry and withered will surely be cut down. If an innocent Man be put to death in the very face of justice, in opposition to all its dictates and decisions, by a people who profess to be governed and directed by divine laws, what desolation, injustice, and oppression may not be expected when anarchy and confusion sit in the place where judgment and justice formerly presided? Our Lord alludes prophetically to those tribulations which fell upon the Jewish people about forty years after.

32. *Two other, malefactors.* Should certainly be translated "two others, malefactors," as in the Bibles published by the King's printer, Edinburgh. As it now stands in the text, it seems to intimate that our blessed Lord was also a *malefactor.*

33. *The place which is called Calvary.* See on Matt. xxvii. 33. *They crucified him.* See the nature of this punishment explained, Matt. xxvii. 35.

33. *A place called Golgotha.* From the Hebrew *golgoleth,* "a skull," probably so called from the many skulls of those who had suffered crucificion and other capital punishments scattered up and down in the place. It is the same as Calvary, *Calvaria,* i.e., *calvi capitis area,* the place of bare skulls. Some think the place was thus called because it was in the form of a human skull. It is likely that it was the place of public execution.

In the prayer, *Father, forgive them,* that word of prophecy was fulfilled, "He made intercession for the transgressors," Isa. liii. 12.

MATTHEW HENRY

chase and procure for us is the forgiveness of sin. His blood speaks this: *Father, forgive them.* Though they were his persecutors and murderers, he prayed, Father, forgive *them.*

(2) The plea: *For they know not what they do;* for, *if they had known,* they would not have crucified him. The crucifiers of Christ *know not what they do.* There is a kind of ignorance that does in part excuse sin: ignorance through want of the means of knowledge or of a capacity to receive instruction. The crucifiers of Christ were kept in ignorance by their rulers, and had prejudices against him instilled into them, so that in what they did against Christ and his doctrine they thought they did God service. Such are to be pitied and prayed for. We must in prayer call God *Father.* The great thing we must beg of God, both for ourselves and others, is the forgiveness of sins. We must pray for *our enemies,* and those that hate and persecute us; and we must be earnest with God in prayer for the forgiveness of their sins, their sins against us. This is Christ's example to his own rule (Matt. v. 44, 45, *Love your enemies*). If Christ loved and prayed for such enemies, what enemies can we have that we are not obliged to *love* and *pray for*?

2. The conversion of the thief upon the cross. Christ was crucified between two thieves, and in them were represented the different effects which the cross of Christ would have upon the children of men. Now the cross of Christ is to some a *savour of life unto life,* to others of *death unto death.*

(1) Here was one of these malefactors that was *hardened to the last.* Near to the cross of Christ, he *railed on him,* as others did (*v.* 39): he said, *If thou be the Christ save thyself and us.* Though he was now in pain and agony, yet this did not humble his proud spirit, nor teach him to give good language, no, not to his fellow-sufferer. He challenges Christ to *save both himself and them.* There are some that have the impudence to rail at Christ, and yet the confidence to expect to be saved by him.

(2) Here was the other of them that was *softened at the last.* This malefactor was snatched as a brand out of the burning, and made a monument of divine mercy and grace. This gives no encouragement to any to put off their repentance, for, though it is certain that true repentance is never too late, it is as certain that late repentance is seldom true. He never had any offer of Christ, nor day or grace, before now: he was designed to be made a singular instance of the power of Christ's grace. Christ, having conquered Satan in the destruction of Judas and the preservation of Peter, erects this further trophy of his victory over him. We shall see the case to be extraordinary if we observe,

[1] The extraordinary operations of God's grace upon him, which appeared in what he said.

First, See what he said to the other malefactor, *v.* 40, 41. 1. He reproved him for railing at Christ, as destitute of the *fear of God*: *Dost not thou fear God?* This implies that it was the fear of God which restrained him from following the multitude to do this evil. "If thou hadst any humanity in thee, thou wouldest not insult over one that is thy fellow-sufferer; *thou art in the same condition;* thou art a *dying man* too." 2. He owns that he deserves what was done to him: *We indeed justly. We received the due reward of our deeds.* True penitents acknowledge the justice of God in all the punishments of their sin. God has *done right,* but *we have done wickedly.* 3. He believes Christ to have suffered *wrongfully.* This penitent thief is convinced, by his conduct in his sufferings, that *he has done nothing amiss.* The chief priests would have him crucified *between* the malefactors, as *one of them*; but this thief has more sense than they.

Secondly, See what he said to our Lord Jesus: *Lord, remember me when thou comest into thy kingdom, v.* 42. This is the prayer of a *dying sinner* to a *dying Saviour.* It was the honour of Christ to be *thus prayed to.* It was the happiness of the thief *thus to pray*; perhaps he never prayed before, and yet now was heard, and saved at the last gasp. Observe his *faith* in this prayer. In his confession of sin (*v.* 41) he discovered *repentance towards God.* In this petition he discovered *faith towards our Lord Jesus Christ.* He owns him to be *Lord,* and to have a *kingdom,* and that he was going to that kingdom, and that those should be happy whom he favoured; and to *believe* and *confess* all this was a *great thing* at this time of day. He believed *another life* after this, and desired to be happy in *that* life, not as the other thief, to be *saved from the cross,* but to be well provided for when the cross had done its worst. Observe his humility in this prayer. All he begs is, *Lord, remember me,* referring himself to Christ in what way to remember him. Christ remembered this thief. There is an air of importunity and fervency in this prayer.

JAMIESON, FAUSSET, BROWN

occasion to observe how our Lord is the first to fulfil His own precepts—thus furnishing the right interpretation and the perfect Model of them. (See on Matt. 5:44.) How quickly was it seen in "His martyr Stephen," that though He had left the earth in Person, His Spirit remained behind, and Himself could, in some of His brightest lineaments, be reproduced in His disciples! (Acts 7:60.) And what does the world in every age owe to these few words, spoken *where* and *as* they were spoken!

39-43. THE TWO THIEVES. **39. railed on him**—catching up the universal derision, but with a turn of his own. Jesus, "reviled, reviles not again"; but another voice from the cross shall nobly wipe out this dishonor and turn it to the unspeakable glory of the dying Redeemer.

40. Dost not thou—"thou" is emphatic: 'Let others jeer, but dost *thou?*' **fear God**—Hast thou no fear of meeting Him so soon as thy righteous Judge? Thou art within an hour or two of eternity, and dost thou spend it in reckless disregard of coming judgment? **in the same condemnation**—He has been condemned to die, but is it better with thee? Doth even a common lot kindle no sympathy in thy breast? **41. we . . . justly . . .**—He owns the worst of his crimes and deserts, and would fain shame his fellow into the same. **nothing amiss**—lit., "out of place"; hence "unnatural"; a striking term here. Our Lord was not charged with *ordinary crime,* but only with laying claim to office and honors which amounted to blasphemy. The charge of treason had not even a show of truth, as Pilate told His enemies. In this defense then there seems more than meets the eye. 'He made Himself the promised Messiah, the Son of God; but in this He "did nothing amiss"; He ate with publicans and sinners, and bade all the weary and heavy laden come and rest under His wing; but in this He "did nothing amiss": He claimed to be Lord of the Kingdom of God, to shut it at will, but also to open it at pleasure even to such as we are; but in this He "did nothing amiss!"' Does His next speech imply *less* than this? Observe: (1) His frank confession and genuine selfcondemnation. (2) His astonishment and horror at the very different state of his fellow's mind. (3) His anxiety to bring him to a better mind while yet there was hope. (4) His noble testimony, not only to the innocence of Jesus, but to all that this implied of the rightfulness of His claims. **42. said to Jesus . . .**—Observe here (1) The "kingdom" referred to was one *beyond the grave;* for it is inconceivable that he should have expected Him to come down from the cross to erect any *temporal* kingdom. (2) This he calls Christ's own

F. B. MEYER:

The signs of renewal, wrought in the heart of the penitent thief, showed the sure work of the Holy Spirit. These were: the fear of God, the sense of justice in his suffering, the confession of evil deeds, the recognition of our Lord's sinlessness and dignity, and the anticipation of his coming kingdom. We may begin a day under the dull skies of earth and close it where there is no need of sun or moon (Phil. 1:23; 2 Cor. 5:6). The rent veil (Heb. 10:20). Dying saints have often passed home with our Lord's last words on their lips (Ps. 31:5; Acts 7:59).

—Bible Commentary

ADAM CLARKE

34. *They know not what they do.* If ignorance does not excuse a crime, it at least diminishes the atrocity of it. However, these persons well knew that they were crucifying an innocent man; but they did not know that by this act of theirs they were bringing down on themselves and on their country the heaviest judgments of God.

35. *Derided him.* "Treated Him with the utmost contempt," in the most infamous manner. See the meaning of this word explained, chap. xvi. 14.

36. *Offering him vinegar.* See on Matt. xxvii. 34. Vinegar or small sour wine was a common drink of the Roman soldiers; and it is supposed that wherever they were on duty they had a vessel of this liquor standing by. It appears that at least two cups were given to our Lord: one before He was nailed to the Cross, viz., of wine mingled with myrrh; and another of vinegar, while He hung on the Cross. Some think there were three cups: one of wine mixed with myrrh; the second, of vinegar mingled with gall; and the third, of simple vinegar. Allow these three cups, and the different expressions in all the Evangelists will be included.

38. *A superscription.* See Matt. xxvii. 37. *In letters of Greek, and Latin, and Hebrew.* The inscription was written in all these languages, which were the most common, that all might see the reason why He was put to death. The inscription was written in Greek, on account of the Hellenistic Jews, who were then at Jerusalem because of the Passover; it was written in Latin, that being the language of the government under which He was crucified; and it was written in Hebrew, that being the language of the place in which this deed of darkness was committed. But, by the good providence of God, the inscription itself exculpated Him and proved the Jews to be rebels against, and murderers of, their King. See the note on Matt. xxvii. 37. It is not to be wondered at that they wished Pilate to alter this inscription, John xix. 21, as it was a record of their infamy.

39. *One of the malefactors which were hanged.* It is likely that the two robbers were not nailed to their crosses, but only tied to them by cords, and thus they are represented in ancient paintings. If not nailed, they could not have suffered much, and therefore they were found still alive when the soldiers came to give the *coup de grace,* which put a speedy end to their lives, John xix. 31-33.

40. *Dost not thou fear God?* The sufferings of this person had been sanctified to him, so that his heart was open to receive help from the hand of the Lord. He is a genuine penitent, and gives the fullest proof he can give of it, viz., the acknowledgment of the justice of his sentence. He had sinned, and he acknowledges his sin; his heart believes unto righteousness, and with his tongue he makes confession unto salvation. While he condemns himself, he bears testimony that Jesus was innocent. Bishop Pearce supposes that these were not robbers in the common sense of the word, but Jews who took up arms on the principle that the Romans were not to be submitted to and that their levies of tribute money were oppressive, and therefore they made no scruple to rob all the Romans they met with. These Jews Josephus calls "robbers," the same term used by the Evangelists. This opinion gains some strength from the penitent thief's confession: *We receive the due reward of our deeds*—we rose up against the government, and committed depredations in the country; *but this man hath done nothing amiss*—"out of place, disorderly," nothing calculated to raise sedition or insurrection.

42. *Lord, remember me.* It is worthy of remark that this man appears to have been the first who believed in the intercession of Christ.

MATTHEW HENRY

He does, as it were, breathe out his soul in it: "*Lord, remember me;* I desire no more; into thy hands I commit my case." To be remembered by Christ, now that he is in his kingdom, is what we should earnestly desire and pray for, and it will be enough to secure our welfare living and dying.

[2] The extraordinary grants of Christ's favour to him: *Jesus said unto him*: "*Verily I say unto thee*, I say *Amen* to this prayer: nay, thou shalt have more than thou didst ask, *This day thou shalt be with me in paradise*," *v.* 43.

First, To whom this was spoken: to the penitent thief. Though Christ himself was now in the greatest struggle and agony, yet he had a word of comfort to speak to a poor penitent. Even great sinners, if they be true penitents, shall, through Christ, obtain not only the pardon of their sins, but a place in the paradise of God.

Secondly, By whom this was spoken. This was another mediatorial word which Christ spoke to explain the true intent and meaning of his sufferings; as he died to purchase the *forgiveness of sins* for us (*v.* 34), so also to purchase *eternal life* for us. By this word we are given to understand that Jesus Christ died to *open the kingdom of heaven to all penitent obedient believers*. 1. Christ here lets us know that he was going to paradise himself. He went by the cross to the crown, and we must not think of going any other way. 2. He lets all penitent believers know that when they die they shall go to be with him there. See here how the happiness of heaven is set forth to us. (1) It is *paradise*, a garden of pleasure, the *paradise of God* (Rev. ii. 7). (2) It is being *with Christ* there. That is the happiness of heaven. (3) It is immediate upon death: *This day shalt thou be with me*, tonight, before tomorrow.

Verses 44–49

I. Christ's dying *magnified* by the *prodigies* that attended it. 1. The *darkening of the sun at noon-day*. It was now about the *sixth hour*, that is, twelve o'clock at noon; and there was a *darkness over all the earth until the ninth hour*. 2. The *rending of the veil of the temple*. The former prodigy was in the *heavens*, this in the *temple*; for both these are the houses of God. By this rending of the veil was signified the taking away of the ceremonial law, and of all other difficulties and discouragements in our approaches to God, so that now we may *come boldly to the throne of grace*.

II. Christ's dying *explained* (*v.* 46) by the words with which he breathed out his soul. Jesus *had cried* with a loud voice when he said, *Why hast thou forsaken me?* So we are told in Matthew and Mark, and, it should seem, it was with a *loud voice* that he said this too. He said, *Father, into thy hands I commend my spirit*. He borrowed these words from his father David (Ps. xxxi. 5). Christ died with scripture in his mouth. In this address to God he calls him *Father*. When he complained of being forsaken, he cried, *Eli, Eli, My God, my God*; but, to show that that dreadful agony of his soul was now over, he here calls God *Father*. Christ made use of these words in a sense peculiar to himself as Mediator. He was now to *make his soul an offering for our sin* (Isa. liii. 10), to *give his life a ransom for many* (Matt. xx. 28). Now by these words he *offered up the sacrifice*, did, as it were, lay his hand upon the head of it, and surrender it. "I *deposit* it, I pay it down into thy hands. Father, accept of my life and soul instead of the lives and souls of the sinners I die for." *The goodwill of the offerer* was requisite to the acceptance of the offering. He commends his spirit into his Father's hand, to be *received* into paradise, and *returned* the third day. Christ has fitted those words of David to the purpose of dying saints, and hath, as it were, sanctified them for their use. We must show that we are freely willing to die, that we firmly believe in another life after this, by saying, *Father, into thy hands I commend my spirit*.

III. Christ's dying improved by the impressions it made upon those that attended him.

1. The centurion that had command of the guard was much affected with what he saw, *v.* 47. He was a Roman, a Gentile, and yet he *glorified God*. And he bore a testimony to the patient sufferer: "*Certainly this was a righteous man.*" His testimony in Matthew and Mark goes further: *Truly this was the Son of God*.

2. The disinterested spectators could not but be concerned. This is taken notice of only here, *v.* 48. *All the people that came together to that sight, beholding the things which were done*, could not but go away very serious. *They smote their breasts, and returned*. They laid the thing very much to heart for the present. Probably these very people were of those that had cried, *Crucify him, crucify him*, and,

JAMIESON, FAUSSET, BROWN

(Thy) kingdom. (3) As such, he sees in Christ the absolute right to dispose of that kingdom to whom He pleased. (4) He does not presume to *ask* a place in that kingdom, though that is what he means, but with a humility quite affecting, just says, "Lord, *remember me* when . . . ." Yet was there mighty faith in that word. If Christ will but "think upon him" (Neh. 5:19), at that august moment when He "cometh into His kingdom," it will do. 'Only assure me that then Thou wilt not forget such a wretch as I, that once hung by Thy side, and I am content.' Now contrast with this bright act of faith the darkness even of the apostles' minds, who could hardly be got to believe that their Master would die at all, who now were almost despairing of Him, and who when dead had almost buried their hopes in His grave. Consider, too, the man's previous *disadvantages* and *bad life*. And then mark how his faith comes out—not in protestations, 'Lord, I cannot doubt, I am firmly persuaded that Thou art Lord of a kingdom, that death cannot disannul Thy title nor impede the assumption of it in due time,' etc.—but as having no shadow of doubt, and rising above it as a question altogether, he just says, "Lord, remember me *when* Thou comest . . ." Was ever faith like this exhibited upon earth? It looks as if the brightest crown had been reserved for the Saviour's head at His darkest moment! **43. Jesus said . . .**—The dying Redeemer speaks as if He Himself viewed it in this light. It was a "song in the night." It ministered cheer to His spirit in the midnight gloom that now enwrapt it. **Verily I say unto thee**—'Since thou speakest as to the king, with kingly authority speak I to thee.' **to-day**—"Thou art prepared for a long delay before I come into My kingdom, but not a day's delay shall there be for thee; thou shalt not be parted from Me even for a moment, but together we shall go, and with Me, ere this day expire, shalt thou be in Paradise" (future bliss, II Cor. 12:4; Rev. 2:7). Learn (1) How "One is taken and another left"; (2) How easily divine teaching can raise the rudest and worst above the best instructed and most devoted servants of Christ; (3) How *presumption* and *despair* on a death hour are equally discountenanced here, the one in the impenitent thief, the other in his penitent fellow.

"And when Jesus had cried with a loud voice" (Luke 23:46). This "*loud voice,*" noticed by three of the Evangelists, does not imply, as some able interpreters contend, that our Lord's strength was so far from being exhausted that He needed not to die then, and surrendered up His life sooner than Nature required, merely because it was the appointed time. It was indeed the appointed time, but time that He should be "crucified *through weakness*" (I Cor. 13:4), and Nature was now reaching its utmost exhaustion. But just as even His own dying saints, particularly the martyrs of Jesus, have sometimes had such gleams of coming glory immediately before breathing their last, as to impart to them a strength to utter their feelings which has amazed the bystanders, so this *mighty voice* of the expiring Redeemer was nothing else but the exultant spirit of the Dying Victor, receiving the fruit of His travail just about to be embraced, and nerving the organs of utterance to an ecstatic expression of its sublime feelings (not so much in the *immediately* following words of tranquil surrender, in Luke, as in the *final* shout, recorded only by John): "FATHER, INTO THY HANDS I COMMEND MY SPIRIT!" (Luke 23:46). Yes, the darkness is past, and the true light now shineth. His soul has emerged from its mysterious horrors; "*My God*" is heard no more, but in unclouded light He yields sublime into His *Father's* hands the infinitely precious spirit—using here also the words of those matchless Psalms (31:5) which were ever on His lips.

47-56. SIGNS AND CIRCUMSTANCES FOLLOWING HIS DEATH—HIS BURIAL. (See on Matt. 27:51-56, 62-66; John 19:31-42.) **Now when the centurion**—the military superintendent of the execution. **and they that were with him watching Jesus, saw the earthquake**—or felt it and witnessed its effects. **and those things that were done**—reflecting upon the entire transaction. **they feared greatly**—convinced of the presence of a Divine Hand. **saying, Truly this was the Son of God**—There cannot be a reasonable doubt that this expression was used in the Jewish sense, and that it points to the claim which Jesus made to be the Son of God, and on which His condemnation expressly turned. The meaning, then, clearly is that He must have been what He professed to be; in other words,

ADAM CLARKE

43. *In paradise*. The Garden of Eden, mentioned in Gen. ii. 8, is also called, from the Septuagint, the "garden of Paradise." The word *Eden* signifies "pleasure" and "delight." Several places were thus called; see Gen. iv. 16; 2 Kings xix. 12; Isa. xxxvii. 12; Ezek. xxvii. 23; and Amos i. 5—and such places probably had this name from their "fertility, pleasant situation." In this light the Septuagint have viewed Gen. ii. 8, as they render the passage thus: "God planted a paradise in Eden." Hence the word has been transplanted into the New Testament, and is used to signify a place of exquisite pleasure and delight.

Paradise was in the beginning the habitation of man in his state of innocence, in which he enjoyed that presence of his Maker which constituted his supreme happiness. Our Lord's words intimate that this penitent should be immediately taken to the abode of the spirits of the just, where he should enjoy the presence and approbation of the Most High.

44. *Darkness over all the earth*. See the note on Matt. xxvii. 45. The darkness began at the sixth hour, about our twelve o'clock at noon, and lasted till the ninth hour, which answered to our three o'clock in the afternoon.

45. *The veil . . . was rent*. See Matt. xxvii. 51.

The veil of the temple was rent. That is, the veil which separated the holy place, where the priests ministered, from the holy of holies, into which the high priest only entered, and that once a year, to make a general expiation for the sins of the people. This rending of the veil was emblematical, and pointed out that the separation between Jews and Gentiles was now abolished, and that the privilege of the high priest was now communicated to all mankind. All might henceforth have access to the throne of grace, through the one great Atonement and Mediator, the Lord Jesus. See this beautifully illustrated in Heb. x. 19-22.

46. *Into thy hands I commend my spirit*. Or, "I will commit My spirit"—"I deposit My soul in Thy hands." Another proof of the immateriality of the soul, and of its separate existence when the body is dead.

48. *And all the people*. All were deeply affected except the priests, and those whom they had employed to serve their base purposes. The darkness, earthquake, etc., had brought terror and consternation into every heart.

MATTHEW HENRY

when he was nailed to the cross, reviled and blasphemed him; but now they had not only their mouths stopped, but their consciences startled. Yet, it should seem, the impression soon wore off: *They smote their breasts, and returned.* They did not show any further token of respect to Christ, but went home; and we have reason to fear that in a little time they quite forgot it. Thus many that see Christ evidently set forth crucified among them in the word and sacraments are a little affected for the present, but it does not continue. They see Christ's face and admire him; but they *go away, and straightway forget what manner of man he is,* and what reason they have to love him.

3. His own friends and followers were obliged to keep their distance, and yet got as near as they could and durst, to see what was done (*v.* 49): *All his acquaintance stood afar off;* this was part of his sufferings. And *the women that followed him from Galilee were beholding these things.* Now was Christ *set for a sign that should be spoken against,* as *Simeon foretold,* that the thoughts of many hearts might be revealed *ch.* ii. 34, 35.

Verses 50–56

We have here an account of Christ's burial.

I. Who buried him. His acquaintance *stood afar off*; but God raised up a *man named Joseph, v.* 50. His character is that he was *a good man and a just,* a man of unspotted reputation for virtue and piety, not only *just* to all, but good to all that needed him; he was a person of quality, a counsellor, a member of the sanhedrim, one of the elders of the Jewish church. Though he was of that body of men who had put Christ to death, yet he *had not consented to their counsel and deed* (*v.* 51). Nay, he not only *dissented* openly from those that were enemies to Christ, but he *consented* secretly with those that were his friends: *He himself waited for the kingdom of God.* There are many who, though they do not make any show in their outward profession, yet will be more ready to do him a piece of real service, than others who make a greater figure and noise.

II. What he did towards the burying of him. 1. He *went to Pilate* and *begged the body of Jesus.* 2. He *took it down, it should seem,* with his own hands, and *wrapped it in linen.* It was the manner of the Jews to *roll* the bodies of the dead, as we do little children in their *swaddling-clothes,* so that the piece of fine linen, which he bought whole, he cut into many pieces for this purpose.

III. Where he was buried. *In a sepulchre that was hewn in stone.* But it was *a sepulchre in which never man before was laid.*

IV. When he was buried. *On the day of the preparation, when the sabbath drew on, v.* 54. This is given as a reason why they made such haste with the funeral, because the *sabbath drew* on. Weeping must not hinder sowing. Though they were in tears for the death of Christ, yet they must apply themselves to the sanctifying of the sabbath.

V. Who attended the funeral; not any of the disciples, but only *the women that came with him from Galilee* (*v.* 55), who, as they stayed by him while he hung on the cross, so they *followed* him, and *beheld the sepulchre,* and *how his body was laid in it.* They were led to this, not by their curiosity, but by their affection to the Lord Jesus.

VI. What preparation was made for the embalming of his body after he was buried (*v.* 56): *They returned, and prepared spices and ointments,* which was more an evidence of their love than of their faith; for had they *remembered* and *believed* that he should *rise again the third day,* they would have spared their *cost* and *pains* herein. But, busy as they were in this preparation, they *rested on the sabbath day.*

JAMIESON, FAUSSET, BROWN

that He was no impostor. There was no medium between those two. See, on the similar testimony of the penitent thief—"This man hath done nothing amiss"—on Luke 23:41

And many women were there beholding afar off, which followed Jesus—The sense here would be better brought out by the use of the pluperfect, "which had followed Jesus." **from Galilee, ministering unto him**—As these dear women had ministered to Him during His glorious missionary tours *in* Galilee (see on Luke 8:1-3), so from this statement it should seem that they accompanied him and ministered to His wants *from* Galilee on His final journey to Jerusalem.

Joseph of Arimathea—"a rich man" (Matt. 27:57), thus fulfilling Isaiah 53:9; "an honorable counsellor," a member of the Sanhedrim, and of good condition, "which also waited for the kingdom of God" (Mark 15:43), a devout expectant of Messiah's kingdom; "a good man and a just, the same had not consented to the counsel and deed of them" (Luke 23:50, 51—he had gone the length, perhaps, of dissenting and protesting in open council against the condemnation of our Lord); "who also himself was Jesus' disciple" (Matt. 27:57). **being a disciple of Jesus, but secretly, for fear of the Jews**—"He went in boldly unto Pilate" (Mark 15:43)—lit., "having taken courage went in," or "had the boldness to go in." Mark alone, as his manner is, notices the *boldness* which this required. The act would without doubt identify him *for the first time* with the disciples of Christ. Marvellous it certainly is, that one who while Jesus was yet alive merely refrained from condemning Him, not having the courage to espouse His cause by one positive act, should, now that He was dead, and His cause apparently dead with Him, summon up courage to go in personally to the Roman governor and ask permission to take down and inter the body. But if this be the first instance, it is not the last, that *a seemingly dead Christ has wakened a sympathy which a living one had failed to evoke. The heroism of faith is usually kindled by desperate circumstances, and is not seldom displayed by those who before were the most timid, and scarce known as disciples at all.*

Now the next day, that followed the day of the preparation—i.e., after six o'clock of our *Saturday* evening. The crucifixion took place on the *Friday* and all was not over till shortly before sunset, when the Jewish sabbath commenced; and "that sabbath day was an high day" (John 19:31), being the first day of the feast of unleavened bread. That day being over at six on Saturday evening, they hastened to take their measures.

ADAM CLARKE

50-51. *Joseph . . . of Arimathaea.* See the notes on Matt. xxvii. 57-60 and those especially on Mark xv. 43.

When the even. This must have been about three o'clock or a little after; for our Lord having expired about three o'clock, v. 46, and the Jewish Passover beginning about four, it was necessary that Joseph, who would not fail to eat the Passover at the usual time, should have obtained and buried the body of Christ some time before four o'clock. But such was the general consternation, occasioned by the prodigies that took place on this most awful occasion, that we may safely conjecture that nothing was done in order, and perhaps the Passover itself was not eaten at the usual hour, if at all, that day. *A rich man.* He was a counsellor of the great Sanhedrin, Luke xxiii. 50; and, from the accounts given of him by the Evangelists, we learn that he was a man of the greatest respectability. He now acted a more honorable part than all the disciples of our Lord. He was of Arimathaea, or Rama, in the tribe of Benjamin, Matt. ii. 17, but lived ordinarily in Jerusalem as being a member of the great council.

54. *And the sabbath drew on.* Or, "The Sabbath was lighting up," i.e., with the candles which the Jews light just before six in the evening, when the Sabbath commences. The same word is used for the dawning of the day, Matt. xxviii. 1.

55. *The women also, which came.* These were Mary of Magdala, Joanna, and Mary the mother of James, chap. xxiv. 10. To these three, Mark, in chap. xvi. 1, adds, Salome; but some think that this was only a surname of one of these Marys.

56. *Prepared spices and ointments.* This was in order to embalm Him, which sufficiently proves that they had no hope of His resurrection the third day. *And rested the sabbath day.* For though the Jewish canons allowed all works necessary for the dead to be done, even on the Sabbath, such as washing and anointing, provided they moved not a limb of the dead person, yet, as the Jews had put Christ to death under the pretense of His being a malefactor, it would not have been either prudent or safe to appear too forward in the present business; and therefore they rested on the Sabbath.

MATTHEW HENRY

CHAPTER 24

Verses 1–12

The *infallible proofs* of his resurrection are *things revealed which belong to us and to our children.* Some of them we have here in these verses.

I. We have here the affection and respect which the good women that had followed Christ showed to him, after he was dead and buried, *v.* 1. As soon as ever they could, after the sabbath was over, they *came to the sepulchre,* to embalm his body, to anoint the head and face, and perhaps the wounded hands and feet, and to scatter sweet spices upon and about the body as it is usual with us to strew flowers about the dead bodies and graves of our friends. The zeal of these good women for Christ did continue. The spices they had prepared the evening before the sabbath, they brought to the sepulchre on the morning after the sabbath, early, very early. What is

JAMIESON, FAUSSET, BROWN

CHAPTER 24

Vss. 1-12. Angelic Announcement to the Women that Christ Is Risen—Peter's Visit to the Empty Sepulchre. (See on Mark 16:1-8; and Matt. 28:1-5.)

ADAM CLARKE

CHAPTER 24

1. *Bringing the spices.* To embalm the body of our Lord; but Nicodemus and Joseph of Arimathaea had done this before the body was laid in the tomb. See John xix. 39-40. But there was a second embalming found necessary. The first must have been hastily and imperfectly performed; the spices now brought by the women were intended to complete the preceding operation. *And certain others with them.* This clause is wanting in some MSS. and versions. Dionysius Alexandrinus and Eusebius also omit it. The omission is approved by Mill, Bengel, Wetstein, Griesbach, and others.

MATTHEW HENRY

prepared for Christ, let it be used for him. Notice is taken of the names of these women, *Mary Magdalene*, and *Joanna*, and *Mary* the Mother of James. Notice is also taken of certain others with them, *v.* 1, and again, *v.* 10. These, who had not joined in preparing the spices, would yet go along with them to the sepulchre; as if the number of Christ's friends increased when he was dead.

II. The surprise they were in, when they found the stone rolled away and the grave empty (*v.* 2, 3); they were *much perplexed* at that (*v.* 4), that *the stone was rolled away from the sepulchre*, and that they *found not the body of the Lord Jesus.* Good Christians often perplex themselves about that with which they should comfort and encourage themselves.

III. The plain account which they had of Christ's resurrection from two angels, who appeared to them *in shining garments.* The women, when they saw the angels, *were afraid*, they *bowed down their faces to the earth*, to look for their dear Master in the grave. They would rather find him in his *grave-clothes* than angels themselves in their *shining-garments*. They upbraid the women with the absurdity of the search they were making: *Why seek ye the living among the dead? v.* 5. Witness is hereby given to Christ that he is *living*, and it is the comfort of all the saints, *I know that my Redeemer liveth*; for because he lives we shall live also. But a reproof is given to those that look for him *among the dead.* They assure them that he is risen from the dead (*v.* 6): "*He is not here, but is risen*; he has quitted his grave." They refer them to his own words: *Remember what he spoke to you, when he was yet in Galilee.* If they had duly believed and observed the prediction of it, they would easily have believed the thing itself when it came to pass. The angels repeat to them what Christ had often said in their hearing, *The Son of man must be delivered into the hands of sinful men.* He told them that he *must be crucified.* Would not this bring to their mind that which always followed, *The third day he shall rise again?* These angels from heaven bring not any *new gospel*, but put them in mind of the sayings of Christ, and teach them how to improve and apply them.

IV. Their satisfaction in this account, *v.* 8. They *remembered his words*, when they were thus put in mind of them, and thence concluded that if he was risen it was no more than they had reason to expect. A seasonable remembrance of the words of Christ will help us to a right understanding of his providence.

V. The report they brought of this to the apostles: *They returned from the sepulchre, and told all these things to the eleven, and to all the rest* of Christ's disciples, *v.* 9. In a little time, that morning, they all had notice of it. But we are told (*v.* 11) how the report was received: *Their words seemed to them as idle tales, and they believed them not.* They thought it was only the fancy of the women, and imputed it to the power of imagination; for they also had forgotten Christ's words. One cannot but be amazed at the stupidity of these disciples,—who had themselves so often professed that they believed Christ to be the Son of God, had been so often told that he must die and rise again, and then enter into his glory, had seen him more than once raise the dead,—that they should be so backward to believe.

VI. The enquiry which Peter made hereupon, *v.* 12. It was Mary Magdalene that brought the report to him, as appears, John xx. 1, 2, where this story of his running to the sepulchre is more particularly related. 1. Peter hastened to the sepulchre upon the report. Perhaps, he had not been so ready to go thither now if the women had not told him that *the watch was fled.* Many that are *swift-footed* enough when there is no danger are but *cow-hearted* when there is. 2. He looked into the sepulchre, and took notice how orderly the linen clothes in which Christ was wrapped were taken off, and folded up, and laid by themselves, but the body gone. He was very particular in making his observations, as if he would rather credit his own eyes than the testimony of the angels. 3. He went away *wondering in himself; at that which was come to pass.* He is only amazed with the thing, and knows not what to make of it. There is many a thing puzzling and perplexing to us which would be both plain and profitable if we did but rightly understand the words of Christ.

Verses 13–35

This appearance of Christ to the *two disciples* going to Emmaus was mentioned, and but just mentioned, before (Mark xvi. 12); here it is largely related. It happened the same day that Christ rose, the first day of the new world that rose with him. One of these two disciples was *Cleopas*; who the other was is not certain. It was one of those that were associated with the eleven, mentioned *v.* 9.

I. The *walk* and *talk* of these two disciples: *They*

JAMIESON, FAUSSET, BROWN

10. Joanna—(See on ch. 8:1-3).

G. CAMPBELL MORGAN:

We see the women engaged in a great ministry of love, but a ministry all filled with sorrow and hopelessness. Very beautiful it is to see them coming, bringing their spices. They brought them to show their love for a dead Master. They thought of Him as dead. They loved Him with a great love. Love is stronger than death. Their love for Him had not ceased. Their faith in Him had not failed. But the things they had hoped for had not been realized. He was mastered, beaten, put to death, but still they loved Him, and they came to find a dead body and honor it.

—*The Gospel According to Luke*

5. Why . . .—Astonishing question! not "the *risen,*" but "*the Living One*" (cf. Rev. 1: 18); and the surprise expressed in it implies an *incongruity* in His being there at all, as if, though He might *submit* to it, "it was impossible He should be *holden* of it" (Acts 2:24). **6. in Galilee**—to which these women themselves belonged (ch. 23: 55).

7. saying . . .—How remarkable it is to hear angels quoting a whole sentence of Christ's to the disciples, mentioning where it was uttered, and wondering it was not fresh in their memory, as doubtless it was in theirs! (I Tim. 3:16, "seen of angels," and I Pet. 1:12.)

12. Peter . . .—(See on John 20:1-10).

13-35. CHRIST APPEARS TO THE TWO GOING TO EMMAUS. **13. two of them**—One was *Cleopas* (vs. 18); who the other was is mere conjecture.

ADAM CLARKE

10. *And Joanna.* She was the wife of Chuza, Herod's steward. See chap. viii. 3.

2. *They found the stone rolled away.* An angel from God had done this before they reached the tomb, Matt. xxviii. 2. On this case we cannot help remarking that when persons have strong confidence in God obstacles do not hinder them from undertaking whatever they have reason to believe He requires; and the removal of them they leave to Him.

3. *And found not the body of the Lord.* His holy soul was in paradise, chap. xxiii. 43; and the Evangelist mentions the body particularly, to show that this only was subject to death.

5. *Why seek ye the living among the dead?* This was a common form of speech among the Jews and seems to be applied to those who were foolishly, impertinently, or absurdly employed. As places of burial were unclean, it was not reasonable to suppose that the living should frequent them; or that if any was missing, he was likely to be found in such places.

7. *Sinful men.* Or "heathens," i.e., the Romans by whom only He could be put to death, for the Jews themselves acknowledged that this power was now vested in the hands of the Roman governor alone. See John xix. 15.

8. *They remembered his words.* Even the simple recollection of the words of Christ becomes often a source of comfort and support to those who are distressed or tempted, for His words are the words of eternal life.

12. *Then arose Peter.* John went with him, and got to the tomb before him. See John xx. 2-3. *The linen clothes laid by themselves.* Or "the linen clothes only." This was the fine linen which Joseph of Arimathaea bought, and wrapped the body in, Mark xv. 46. Small as this circumstance may at first view appear, it is, nevertheless, no mean proof of the resurrection of our Lord. Had the body been stolen away, all that was wrapped about it would have been taken away with it, as the delay which must have been occasioned by stripping it might have led to the detection of the theft; nor would the disciples have run such a risk if they had stolen Him, when stripping the body could have answered no end. This circumstance is related still more particularly by John, chap. xx. 5-7. Peter "saw the linen clothes lying . . . and the napkin, that was about his head, not lying with the linen clothes, but wrapped together in a place by itself."

13. *Behold, two of them.* This long and interesting account is not mentioned by Matthew nor John, and is only glanced at by Mark, chap. xvi. 12-13. One of these disciples was Cleopas, v. 18, and the other is supposed by many learned men, both ancient and modern, to have been Luke himself. See the sketch of his life prefixed to these notes.

MATTHEW HENRY

went to a village called Emmaus, which is reckoned to be about two hours' walk from Jerusalem, *v.* 13. The accounts brought them that morning of their Master's resurrection seemed to them *as idle tales*. But as they travelled they *talked together of all those things which had happened*, *v.* 14. They *talked over these things*, reasoning with themselves concerning the probabilities of Christ's resurrection.

II. The good company they met with upon the road, when Jesus himself came, and joined himself to them (*v.* 15): *They communed together, and reasoned. Jesus himself drew near*, as a stranger who, seeing them travel the same way that he *went*, told them that he should be *glad of their company*. Where but two together are well employed in work of that kind Christ will come to them, and make a third. Two thus twisted in faith and love become a *threefold cord, not easily broken*. They in their communings and reasonings together were searching for Christ, and now Christ comes to them. They who seek Christ shall find him. But, though they had Christ with them, they were not at first aware of it (*v.* 16): *Their eyes were held, that they should not know him*. No matter *how* it was, but *so* it was they did not *know him*, Christ so ordering it that they might the more freely discourse with him and he with them.

III. The conference that was between Christ and them, when he knew them, and they knew not him. Now Christ and his disciples, as is usual when friends meet incognito, or in a disguise, are here crossing questions.

1. Christ's first question to them is concerning *their* present *sadness*: *What manner of communications are these that you have one with another as you walk, and are sad? v.* 17.

(1) They were *sad*. They had lost their dear Master, and were, in their own apprehensions, quite disappointed in their expectations from him. They had given up the cause, and knew not what course to take to retrieve it. Though he was risen from the dead, yet either they did not know it or did not believe it, and so they were still in sorrow. Christ's disciples are often sad and sorrowful even when they have reason to rejoice. They had *communications one with another* concerning Christ. It becomes Christians to talk of Christ, not only of God and his providence, but of Christ and his grace and love. Good company and good converse are an excellent antidote against prevailing melancholy. Giving *vent* to the grief may perhaps give *ease* to the grieved. Joint mourners should be mutual comforters; comforts sometimes come best from such.

(2) Christ came up to them, and enquired into the matter of their talk: *What manner of communications are these?* Though Christ had now entered into his state of exaltation, yet he continued tender of his disciples. Our Lord Jesus takes notice of the sorrow and sadness of his disciples, and is afflicted in their afflictions. Christ has thereby taught us to be *conversable*. It does not become Christians to be morose and shy, but to take pleasure in good society. We are hereby taught to be *compassionate*. When we see our friends in sorrow and sadness, we should, like Christ here, take cognizance of their grief.

2. In answer to this, they put a question to him concerning *his strangeness*. *Art thou only a stranger in Jerusalem, and hast not known the things that are come to pass there in these days?* Cleopas gave him a civil answer. We ought to be civil to those who are civil to us. It was a dangerous time now with Christ's disciples; yet he was not jealous of this stranger, that he had any design upon them, to inform against them. He is full of Christ himself and of his death and sufferings, and wonders that everybody else is not so too: "What! art thou such a stranger in Jerusalem as not to know what has been done to our Master there?" He is very willing to inform this stranger concerning Christ. He would not have anyone that had the face of a man to be ignorant of Christ. And it is observable that these disciples, who were so forward to instruct the stranger, were instructed by him; for to him that has, and uses what he has, shall be given. It appears, by what Cleopas says, that the death of Christ made a great noise in Jerusalem, so that it could not be imagined that any man should be such a stranger in the city as not to know of it.

3. Christ, by way of reply, asked concerning *their knowledge* (*v.* 19): *He said unto them, What things?* thus making himself yet more a stranger. Jesus Christ made light of his own sufferings, in comparison with the joy set before him. See with what unconcernedness he looks back upon his sufferings. He had reason to know what things; for to him they were bitter things, and heavy things, and yet he asks, *What things?* They must tell him *what things* they know, and then he will tell them what was the meaning

JAMIESON, FAUSSET, BROWN

Emmaus—about seven and a half miles from Jerusalem. They probably lived there and were going home after the Passover.

14-16. communed and reasoned—exchanged views and feelings, weighing afresh all the facts, as detailed in vss. 18-24. **drew near**—coming up behind them as from Jerusalem.

eyes holden—Partly He was "in another form" (Mark 16:12), and partly there seems to have been an operation on their own vision; though certainly, as they did not believe that He was alive, His company as a fellow traveller was the last thing they would expect.

17-24. communication . . .—The words imply the earnest discussion that had appeared in their manner.

18. knowest not . . .—If he knew not the events of the last few days in Jerusalem, he must be a mere sojourner; if he did, how could he suppose they would be talking of anything else? How artless all this!

ADAM CLARKE

Threescore furlongs. Some MSS. say 160 furlongs, but this is a mistake, for Josephus assigns the same distance to this village from Jerusalem as the Evangelist does. "Ammaus is sixty stadia distant from Jerusalem," about 7 English miles and three-quarters. A *stadium* was about 243 yards.

15. *And reasoned.* Concerning the probability or improbability of Christ being the Messiah, or of His resurrection from the dead. It was a laudable custom of the Jews, and very common also, to converse about the law in all their journeyings; and now they had especial reason to discourse together, of both the law and the prophets, from the transactions which had recently taken place.

16. *Their eyes were holden.* It does not appear that there was anything supernatural here, for the reason why these persons (who were not apostles, see v. 33) did not recollect our Lord is given by Mark, chap. xvi. 12, who says that Christ appeared to them in another form.

CHARLES H. SPURGEON:

Christian people, commune together, but let your communications always be like these which are recorded in this chapter. Speak of Him, talk of Him, what you know of Him, of your sorrows about Him, even of your neglects of Him, of your ill treatment of Him, your sins against Him. Talk of these things one to the other, for so long as they are about Him it will be good even to confess your faults one to another. It will lead you to pray one for another and to join your prayers together, so that there will be greater strength in the petitions; for if two of you are agreed, you know what power that sweet agreement has with heaven. "They that feared the Lord spake often one to another." A blessed practice, an ancient practice, an edifying practice, a God-honoring practice, one which so pleased God that He turned eavesdropper—came under the window to listen to what they said, and took His notebook and recorded it, "a book of remembrance was written"; and He has published it and given His blessing to "those that fear the Lord and that think upon his name."

—The Treasury of the New Testament

18. *Cleopas.* The same as Alphaeus, father of the Apostle James, Mark iii. 18, and husband of the sister of the Virgin, John xix. 25. *Art thou only a stranger?* As if he had said, What has been done in Jerusalem within these few days has been so public, so awful, and so universally known that, if you had been but a lodger in the city for a single night, I cannot conceive how you could miss hearing of these things. Indeed, you appear to be the *only* person unacquainted with them.

MATTHEW HENRY

of these things, and lead them into the mystery of them.

4. They, hereupon, gave him a particular account concerning Christ. Observe the story they tell, *v.* 19, &c.

(1) Here is a summary of Christ's *life* and *character*. The *things* they are full of are concerning *Jesus of Nazareth*, who *was a prophet*, a teacher come from God. He confirmed it by many glorious miracles, miracles of mercy, so that he was *mighty in deed and word before God and all the people*. He had great acceptance with God, and a great reputation in the country. Many are *great before all the people*, who are not so *before God*, but Christ was mighty *before God and all the people*. Those were strangers in Jerusalem that did not know this.

(2) Here is a modest narrative of his sufferings and death, *v.* 20. "The *chief priests and our rulers delivered him to be condemned to death*, and *they have crucified him*." It is strange that they did not lay a greater load upon those that had been guilty of crucifying Christ.

(3) Here is an intimation of their disappointment in him, as the reason of their sadness: "*We trusted that it had been he who should have redeemed Israel*," *v.* 21; great things expected from him, by them that *looked for redemption*, and in it for the consolation of Israel. Now, if *hope deferred makes the heart sick*, hope disappointed, especially such a hope, kills the heart. *We trusted* (say they) *that it had been he that should have redeemed Israel*. And is it not he that doth redeem Israel? Nay, is he not by his death paying the price of their redemption? So that now, since that most difficult part of his undertaking was got over, they had more reason than ever to *trust* that *this was he that should deliver Israel*.

(4) Here is an account of their present amazement. "*This is the third day* since he was crucified and died, and that was the day when it was expected, if ever, that he should rise again and show himself as publicly in honour as he had been shown three days before in disgrace, but all is silent." They own that there was a report among them that he was risen, but they seem to speak of it very slightly (*v.* 22, 23): "*Certain women also of our company made us astonished*, who were *early at the sepulchre*, and found the body gone, and they said that they had *seen a vision of angels, who said that he was alive;* but we are ready to think it was only their fancy. Women are easily imposed upon." They acknowledge that some of the apostles had visited the sepulchre, and found it empty, *v.* 24. "But *him they saw not*, and therefore we have reason to fear that he *is not risen*, for, if he be, surely he would have *shown himself* to them: so that we have no great reason to think that he is risen. Our hopes were all nailed to his cross, and buried in his grave."

(5) Our Lord Jesus, though not known by face to them, makes himself known to them by his word.

[1] He reproves them for the weakness of their faith in the scriptures of the Old Testament: *O fools, and slow of heart to believe*, *v.* 25. Christ called them *fools*, not as it signifies *wicked men*, but as it signifies *weak men*. That which is condemned in them as their *foolishness* is, *First*, Their *slowness to believe*. Christ tells us that those are *fools* who are *slow of heart to believe*, and are kept from it by prejudices never impartially examined. *Secondly*, Their slowness to believe *the writings of the prophets*. Were we but more *conversant* with the scripture, and the divine counsels as far as they are made known in the scripture, we should not be subject to such perplexities as we often *entangle* ourselves in.

[2] He shows them that the sufferings of Christ were really the appointed way to his glory, and he could not go to it any other way (*v.* 26): "*Ought not the Christ* to *have suffered these things, and to enter into his glory?*" The cross of Christ was that to which they could not reconcile themselves; now here he shows them two things which take off the offence of the cross: *First*, That the Messiah *ought to suffer* these things; and therefore his sufferings were not only no objection against his being the Messiah, but really a proof of it. He could not have been a *Saviour*, if he had not been a *sufferer*. *Secondly*, That, when he had suffered these things, he should *enter into his glory*, which he did at his resurrection. It is called *his* glory, and it was the glory he had before the world was. He *ought* to suffer first, and then to enter into his glory. We are directed to expect the crown of *thorns* and then that of *glory*.

[3] He expounded to them the scriptures of the Old Testament, and showed them how they were fulfilled in Jesus of Nazareth (*v.* 27): *Beginning at Moses* he went in order through *all the prophets*, and *expounded to them the things concerning himself*, showing that the sufferings he had now gone through were the accomplishment of them. There are things dispersed

JAMIESON, FAUSSET, BROWN

19. Concerning Jesus . . .—As if feeling it a relief to have some-one to unburden his thoughts and feelings to, this disciple goes over the main facts in his own desponding style, and this was just what our Lord wished.

21. we trusted . . .—They expected the promised Deliverance at His hand, but in the current sense of it, not by His death. **besides all this**—not only did His death seem to give the fatal blow to their hopes, but He had been two days dead already, and this was the third. It is true, they add, some of our women gave us a surprise, telling us of a vision of angels they had at the empty grave this morning that said He was alive, and some of ourselves who went thither confirmed their statement; but then Himself they saw not. A doleful tale truly, told out of the deepest despondency.

fools—senseless, without understanding.

26. Ought not Christ—"the Christ," "the Messiah." **to suffer . . . and enter**—i.e., through the gate of suffering (and suffering "*these things*," or *such a death*) to enter into His glory. 'Ye believe in the glory; but these very sufferings are the predicted gate of entrance into it.'

27. Moses and all the prophets . . .—Here our Lord both teaches us the reverence due to Old Testament Scripture, and the great burden of it—"Himself."

ADAM CLARKE

19. *Which was a prophet*. "A man prophet," a genuine prophet; but this has been considered as a Hebraism: "for, in Exod. ii. 14, a *man prince* is simply a *prince;* and in 1 Sam. xxxi. 3, *men archers* mean no more than *archers*." But my own opinion is that this word is often used to deepen the signification; so in the above quotations: *Who made thee a man prince* (i.e., a mighty sovereign) *and a judge over us?* Exod. ii. 14. And, *The battle went sore against Saul*, and the *men archers* (i.e., the stout, or well-aiming archers) *hit him*, 1 Sam. xxxi. 3. So *aner prophetes* here signifies, He was a "genuine prophet," nothing like those false ones by whom the people have been so often deceived; and He has proved the divinity of His mission by His heavenly teaching and astonishing miracles. *Mighty in deed and word*. Irresistibly eloquent. "Powerful in deed," working incontrovertible miracles.

21-24. Cleopas paints the real state of his own mind in these verses. In his relation there is scarcely anything well connected. Important points are referred to, and not explained, though he considered the person to whom he spoke as entirely unacquainted with these transactions. His own hopes and fears he cannot help mixing with the narration, and throwing over the whole that confusion that dwells in his own heart. The narration is not at all in Luke's style; but as it is probable he was the other disciple who was present, and had heard the words of Cleopas, he gave them in that simple, natural, artless manner in which they were spoken. Had the account been forged, those simple, natural touches would not have appeared. *To day is the third day*. Our Lord had often said that He would rise again the third day; and though Alphaeus had little hope of this resurrection, yet he could not help recollecting the words he had heard, especially as they seemed to be confirmed by the relation of the women, vv. 22-24.

25. *O fools, and slow of heart to believe*. "Inconsiderate" men, justly termed such because they had not properly attended to the description given of the Messiah by the prophets, nor to His teaching and miracles, as proofs that He alone was the Person they described. *Slow of heart*. "Backward," not easy to be persuaded of the truth, always giving way to doubtfulness and distrust. This very imperfection in them is a strong evidence of the truth of the doctrine which they afterwards believed, and proclaimed to the world. Had they not had the fullest assurance of these things, they never would have credited them; and it is no small honor to the new-covenant Scriptures that such persons were chosen, first to believe them; secondly, to proclaim them in the world; and, thirdly, to die on the evidence of those truths, the blessed influence of which they felt in their own hearts and fully exemplified in their lives.

26. *Ought not Christ to have suffered?* "Was it not necessary that the Christ should suffer?" This was the way in which sin must be expiated and without this no soul could have been saved. The suffering Messiah is He alone by whom Israel and the world can be saved.

27. *Beginning at Moses*. What a sermon this must have been, where all the prophecies relative to the incarnation, birth, teaching, miracles, sufferings, death, and resurrection of the blessed Jesus were all adduced, illustrated, and applied

MATTHEW HENRY

throughout *all the scriptures* concerning Christ. You cannot go far in any part of scripture but you meet with something that has reference to Christ, some prophecy, some promise, some prayer, some type or other. A golden thread of gospel grace runs through the whole web of the Old Testament. The things concerning Christ need to be *expounded.* They were delivered darkly, according to that dispensation: but now that the veil is taken away the New Testament expounds the Old. Jesus Christ is himself the best expositor of scripture, particularly the scriptures concerning himself. In *studying* the scriptures, it is good to be *methodical,* for the Old Testament light shone *gradually* to the *perfect day,* and it is good to observe how *at sundry times,* and in *divers manners,* God spoke to the fathers *concerning* his Son, by whom he has now *spoken* to us. Some begin their bible at the wrong end, who study the Revelation first.

IV. Here is the discovery which Christ at length made of himself to them. One would have given a great deal for a copy of the sermon Christ preached to them by the way, of that exposition of the bible which he gave them. The disciples are so charmed with it, that they think they are come too soon to their journey's end; but so it is: *They drew nigh to the village whither they went* (*v.* 28). And now,

1. They courted his stay with them: *He made as though he would have gone further;* he did not *say* that he would but he seemed to them to be going further. He would have gone further if they had not courted his stay. Those that would have Christ dwell with them must invite him, and be importunate with him. If he seem to *draw off* from us, it is but to draw out our importunity; as here, *they constrained him;* with a kind and friendly violence, saying, *Abide with us.* Those that have experienced the pleasure and profit of communion with Christ cannot but covet more of his company, and beg of him, not only to *walk with them* all day, but to *abide with them* at night. Christ yielded to their importunity: He *went in, to tarry with them.* He has promised that *if any man open the door,* to bid him welcome, he will *come in to him,* Rev. iii. 20.

2. He manifested himself to them, *v.* 30, 31. We may suppose that he continued his discourse with them, which he began upon the road. While supper was getting ready (which perhaps was soon done, the provision was so small and mean), it is probable that he entertained them. But still they little thought that it was Jesus himself that was all this while talking with them, till at length he was pleased to throw off his disguise. They began to suspect it was he, when, as they *sat down to meat*: *He took bread, and blessed it,* and *brake it, and gave to them.* This was not a *miraculous* meal like that of the five loaves, nor a *sacramental* meal like that of the eucharist, but a *common* meal; yet Christ here did the same as he did in those, to teach us to keep up our communion with God through Christ in common providences as well as in special ordinances. Wherever we *sit down to eat,* let us set Christ at the upper end of the table, take our meat as *blessed to us* by him, and *eat and drink* to his glory, and receive contentedly and thankfully what he is pleased to *carve* out to us, be the fare ever so coarse and mean. *Their eyes were opened,* and then they saw who it was, and *knew him* well enough. The mists were scattered, the veil was taken off, and then they made no question but it was their Master. He might put on the shape of another, but no other could put on his; and therefore it must be he. See how Christ by his Spirit and grace makes himself known. The work is completed by the opening of the eyes of their mind. If he that gives the revelation do not give the understanding, we are in the dark still.

3. He immediately disappeared: *He vanished out of their sight.* He *became not visible by them.* As soon as he had given his disciples one glimpse of him he was gone. Such short and transient views have we of Christ in this world; we see him, but in a little while lose the sight of him again.

V. Here is the reflection which these disciples made upon this conference, and the report which they made of it to their brethren at Jerusalem.

1. The reflection they each of them made upon the influence which Christ's discourse had upon them (*v.* 32): *They said one to another, Did not our hearts burn within us?* Thus do they not so much compare *notes* as compare *hearts,* in the review of the sermon Christ had preached to them. They found the preaching powerful, even when they knew not the preacher. It made things very plain and clear to them; and, which was more, brought a *divine heat* with a *divine light* into their souls. Now this they take notice of, for the confirming of their belief, that it was indeed, as at last they saw, *Jesus himself* that had been talking with them all along. See here, (1) What *preaching*

JAMIESON, FAUSSET, BROWN

G. CAMPBELL MORGAN:

I never read this without having the feeling that I would have given anything to travel that road, and hear what He had to say. One could almost imaginatively follow some of the things as one thinks of the Old Testament. They listened to this Stranger as He took their own sacred writings and interpreted to them their deepest meaning. They listened to Him as He revealed to them the profoundest depths in the suggestive ritual of the Mosaic economy, as He breathed in their ears the secret of the love which lay at the heart of the ancient law. They listened to Him as He traced the messianic note in the music of all the prophets.

—The Gospel According to Luke

28-31. made as though . . .—(Cf. Mark 6:48; Gen. 18:3, 5; 32:24-26). **29. constrained . . .**—But for this, the whole design of the interview had been lost; but *it was not to be lost,* for He who only wished to be constrained had kindled a longing in the hearts of His travelling companions which was not to be so easily put off. And does not this still repeat itself in the interviews of the Saviour with His loving, longing disciples? Else why do they say,

> Abide with me from morn to eve,
> For without Thee I cannot live;
> Abide with me when night is nigh,
> For without Thee I cannot die.
> KEBLE

30-31. he took . . . and blessed . . and their eyes were opened—The stranger first startles them by taking the place of master at their own table, but on proceeding to that act which reproduced the whole scene of the last Supper, a rush of associations and recollections disclosed their guest, and He stood confessed before their astonished gaze—THEIR RISEN LORD! They were going to gaze on Him, perhaps embrace Him, but that moment He is gone! It was enough.

32-34. They now tell each to the other how their hearts burned—were fired—within them at His talk and His expositions of Scripture. 'Ah! this accounts for it: We could not understand the glow of self-evidencing light, love, glory that ravished our hearts; but now we do.' They cannot rest—how could they?—they must go straight back and tell the news. They find the eleven, but ere they have time to tell their tale, their ears are saluted with the thrilling news, "The Lord is risen indeed, and hath appeared to *Simon.*" Most touch-

ADAM CLARKE

to himself, by an appeal to the well-known facts which had taken place during His life! We are almost irresistibly impelled to exclaim, What a pity this discourse has not been preserved! No wonder their hearts burned within them while hearing such a sermon from such a Preacher! The law and the prophets had all borne testimony, either directly or indirectly, to Christ; and we may naturally suppose that these prophecies and references were those which our Lord at this time explained and applied to himself. See v. 32.

28. *He made as though he would have gone further.* That is, "He was going on, as though He intended to go farther"; and so He doubtless would had they not earnestly pressed Him to lodge with them. His preaching had made a deep impression upon their hearts, v. 32, and now they feel it their greatest privilege to entertain the Preacher.

29. *For it is toward evening.* And consequently both inconvenient and unsafe to proceed to another village. *And he went in.* And so He will to you, you penitent soul! Therefore take courage, and be not faithless but believing.

30. *He took bread.* This was the office of the master and father of a family, and this was our Lord's usual custom among His disciples. Those whom Christ lodges with He feeds, and feeds too with bread that He has blessed, and this feeding not only strengthens but also enlightens the soul.

31. *Their eyes were opened.* But we are not to imagine that He administered the holy Eucharist at this time; there is not the most distant evidence of this. It was a mere family meal, and ended before it was well begun. *They knew him.* His acting as father of the family, in taking, blessing, and distributing the bread among them, caused them to recollect those lips which they had often heard speak, and those hands by which they had often been fed. Perhaps He also threw off the disguise which He had before assumed, and now appeared in His own person. *He vanished out of their sight.* Probably, during their surprise, He took the opportunity of withdrawing from the place, leaving them to reflect and meditate on what they had heard and seen.

32. *Did not our heart burn within us?* His word was in our heart as a burning fire, Jer. xx. 9. Our hearts waxed hot within us, and while we were musing the fire burned, Ps. xxxix. 3. In some such way as this the words of the disciples may be understood.

MATTHEW HENRY

is likely to *do good*—such as Christ's was, *plain preaching—he talked with us by the way;* and scriptural preaching—*he opened to us the scriptures.* Ministers should show people their religion in their bibles, they must show that they make that the fountain of their knowledge and the foundation of their faith. (2) What *hearing* is likely to *do good*—that which makes the *heart burn*; when we are much affected with the things of God, especially with the love of Christ in dying for us, and have our hearts thereby drawn out in love to him, and drawn up in holy desires and devotions, then our hearts *burn within us.*

2. The report they brought of this to their brethren at Jerusalem (*v.* 33): *They rose up the same hour*, so transported with joy at the discovery Christ had made of himself to them that they could not stay to make an end of their supper, but returned with all speed to Jerusalem, though it was towards evening. Now that they had seen Christ they could not rest till they had brought the good news to the disciples, both for the confirmation of their trembling faith and for the comfort of their sorrowful spirits. It is the duty of those to whom Christ has manifested himself to let others know what he has done for their souls. These disciples were *full* of this matter themselves, and must go to their brethren, to give vent to their joys. (1) How they found them relating another proof of the resurrection of Christ. They found the eleven, and those that were their usual companions, *gathered together* late in the night, and they found them *saying* among themselves, and when these two came in, they repeated to them with joy and triumph, *The Lord is risen indeed, and hath appeared to Simon*, *v.* 34. That Peter had a sight of him before the rest of the disciples had appears 1 Cor. xv. 5, where it is said, *He was seen of Cephas, then of the twelve.* The angel having ordered the women to tell Peter of it particularly (Mark xvi. 7), for his comfort, it is highly probable that our Lord Jesus did himself the same day appear to Peter, though we have no particular narrative of it. This he had related to his brethren; but, observe, Peter does not here proclaim it, and boast of it, himself, but the other disciples speak of it with exultation, *The Lord is risen indeed.* He has appeared not only to the women, but to Simon. (2) How they seconded their evidence with an account of what they had seen (*v.* 35): *They told what things were done in the way.* The words that were spoken by Christ to them in the way are here called the *things* that were *done in the way*; for the words that Christ speaks are not an empty sound, wondrous things are *done* by them, done *by the way*, by the by as it were, where it is not expected. They told also how he was at length *known to them in the breaking of bread.*

Verses 36–49

Five times Christ was seen the same day that he rose: by Mary Magdalene alone in the garden (John xx. 14), by the women as they were going to tell the disciples (Matt. xxviii. 9), by Peter alone, by the two disciples going to Emmaus, and now at night by the eleven.

I. The great *surprise* which his appearing gave them. He came in among them very *seasonably*, as they were comparing notes concerning the proofs of his resurrection: *As they thus spoke, Jesus himself stood in the midst of them*, and *put it out of question.* 1. The *comfort* Christ spoke to them: *Peace be unto you.* This intimates in general that it was a kind visit which Christ now paid them, a visit of love and friendship. They did not *credit* those who had seen him; therefore he *comes himself.* He had promised that after his resurrection he *would see them in Galilee*; but so desirous was he to see them that he anticipated the appointment and *sees them at Jerusalem.* Christ is often *better than his word*, but never *worse.* Now his first word to them was, *Peace be to you.* Thus Christ would at the first word intimate to them that he did not come to quarrel with Peter for *denying* him and the rest for *running away* from him; no, he *came peaceably*, to signify to them that he had forgiven them. 2. The *fright* which they put themselves into upon it (*v.* 37): They were *terrified*, supposing that *they had seen a spirit*, because he was in the midst of them ere they were aware. The word used (Matt. xiv. 26), when they said *It is a spirit*, is a *spectre*, an *apparition*; but the word here used properly signifies a *spirit*; they supposed it to be a spirit not clothed with a real body.

II. The great *satisfaction* which his discourse gave them, wherein we have,

1. The reproof he gave them for their causeless fears: *Why are you troubled, and why do thoughts arise in your hearts? v.* 38. Observe here, (1) That when at any time we are *troubled, thoughts* are apt to *rise in our hearts* that do us hurt. Sometimes the

JAMIESON, FAUSSET, BROWN

ing and precious intelligence this. The only one of the Eleven to whom He appeared *alone* was he, it seems, who had so shamefully denied Him. What passed at that interview we shall never know here. Probably it was too sacred for disclosure. (See on Mark 16:7.) The two from Emmaus now relate what had happened to them, and while thus comparing notes of their Lord's appearances, lo! Christ Himself stands in the midst of them. What encouragement to doubting, dark, true-hearted disciples!

ALEXANDER MACLAREN:

The other appearances of the risen Lord to individuals on the day of Resurrection are narrated with much particularity and a considerable length. John gives us the lovely account of our Lord's conversation with Mary Magdalene; Luke gives us in full detail the story of the interview with the two travelers on the road to Emmaus. Here is another appearance, known to "the eleven, and them that were with them," on the Resurrection evening, and enumerated by Paul in his list of the appearances of the Lord, the account of which was the common gospel of himself and all the others, and yet deep silence is preserved in regard to it. No word escaped Peter's lips as to what passed in the conversation between the denier and his Lord. That is very significant.

The other appearances of the risen Lord to individuals on the day of Resurrection suggest their own reasons. He appeared first to Mary Magdalene because she loved much. The love that made a timid woman brave, and the sorrow that filled her heart, to the exclusion of everything else, drew Jesus to her. The two on the road to Emmaus were puzzled, honest, painful seekers after truth. It was worth Christ's while to spend hours of that day of Resurrection in clearing, questioning, and confirming sincere minds.

Does not this other appearance explain itself? The brief spasm of cowardice and denial had changed into penitence when the Lord looked, and the bitter tears that fell were not only because of the denial, but because of the wound of that sharp arrow, the poisoned barb of which we are happy if we have not felt the thought—"He will never know how ashamed and miserable I am; and His last look was reproach, and I shall never see His face anymore." To respond to and to satisfy love, to clear and to steady thought, to soothe the agony of a penitent, were worthy works for the risen Lord. I venture to think that such a record of the use of such a day bears historical truth on its very face, because it is so absolutely unlike what myth-making or hallucination or the excited imagination of enthusiasts would have produced if these had been the sources of the story of the Resurrection.

—*Expositions of Holy Scripture*

36-53. Jesus Appears to the Assembled Disciples—His Ascension. **36. Jesus . . . stood**—(See on John 20:19).

37, 38. a spirit—the ghost of their dead Lord, but not Himself in the body (Acts 12:15; Matt. 14:26).

thoughts—rather, reasonings; i.e., whether He were risen or no, and whether this was His very self.

ADAM CLARKE

F. B. MEYER:

How swiftly the seven and a half miles must have sped in such company; and what new light illumined the pages of the Old Testament! All the Bible is full of him, but we need to be shown its meaning. It is only through suffering that we shall come to the glory. But why should not life be one sweet walk of fellowship with One whom we cannot see, but whose presence fills our hearts with burning love until suddenly the veil shall part in twain (1 Pet. 1:8).

—*Bible Commentary*

34. *Saying, The Lord is risen indeed.* The meaning here is that these two disciples found the apostles, and those who were with them, unanimously testifying that Christ had risen from the dead. It is not the two disciples to whom we are to refer the word *saying*, but to the body of the disciples.

35. *And they.* The two disciples who were just come from Emmaus "related what had happened to them on the way," going to Emmaus, "and how He had been known unto them in the breaking of bread," while supping together at the above village.

36. *And as they thus spake.* While the two disciples who were going to Emmaus were conversing about Christ, He joined himself to their company. Now while they and the apostles are confirming each other in their belief of His resurrection, Jesus comes in, to remove every doubt, and to give them the fullest evidence of it. And it is ever true that wherever two or three are gathered together in His name He is in the midst of them. *Peace be unto you.* The usual salutation among the Jews. "May you prosper in body and soul, and enjoy every heavenly and earthly good!"

MATTHEW HENRY

trouble is the effect of the *thoughts* that *arise in our hearts.* Sometimes the thoughts arising in the heart are the effect of the trouble, without are fightings and then within are fears. (2) That many of the troublesome thoughts with which our minds are disquieted arise from our mistakes concerning Christ. They here thought that they had *seen a Spirit*, when they saw Christ. When Christ is by his Spirit convincing and humbling us, when he is by his providence trying and converting us, we *mistake him*, as if he designed our hurt, and this troubles us. (3) That all the troublesome thoughts which rise in our hearts at any time are known to the Lord Jesus. He chid his disciples for such *thoughts*, to teach us to chide ourselves for them.

2. The proof he gave them of his resurrection, both for the *silencing* of their *fears* and for the *strengthening* of their *faith.* Two proofs he gives them:

(1) He shows them his body, particularly *his hands and his feet.* "*Behold my hands and my feet;* you see I have *hands* and *feet*, and therefore have a *true* body; and you see the marks of the nails in my hands and feet, and therefore it is *my own* body, the *same* that you saw crucified, and not a *borrowed* one." He lays down this prinicple—that a *spirit has not flesh and bones.* Now hence he infers, "*It is I myself*, whom you have been so intimately acquainted with, and have had such familiar conversation with; it is *I myself*, whom you have reason to rejoice in, and not to be afraid of." [1] He appeals to their *sight*, *shows* them *his hands* and *his feet*, which were pierced with the nails. Christ retained the marks of them in his glorified body, that they might be proofs that it was he himself; and he was willing that they should be *seen.* He afterwards showed them to Thomas, for he is not ashamed of his sufferings for us; little reason then have we to be ashamed of them, or of ours for him. [2] He appeals to their *touch*: *Handle me, and see.* He would not let Mary Magdalene touch him at that time, John xx. 17. But the disciples here are entrusted to do it, that they who were to preach his resurrection, and to suffer for doing so, might be themselves abundantly satisfied concerning it. He bade them *handle him*, that they might be convinced that he was not a *spirit.* There were many heretics in the primitive times who said that Christ had never any substantial body, was neither really born nor truly suffered. Blessed be God, these heresies have long since been *buried*; and we know and are sure that Jesus Christ was no *spirit* or *apparition*, but had a true and real body, even after his resurrection.

(2) He *eats* with them, to show that he had a real and true body. Peter lays a great stress upon this (Acts x. 41): We *did eat and drink with him after he rose from the dead.*

[1] When they *saw his hands and his feet, They believed not for joy, and wondered, v.* 41. It was their infirmity that they *believed not*, that *yet* they believed not. This very much corroborates the truth of Christ's resurrection that the disciples were so slow to believe it. Instead of stealing away his body, and saying, *He is risen*, when he is not, as the chief priests suggested they would do, they are ready to say again and again, *He is not risen*, when he is. When afterwards they did believe it, and venture their all upon it, it was not but upon the fullest demonstration of the thing that could be. But, though it was their infirmity, yet it was an excusable one; for it was not from any contempt of the evidence offered them that they believed not. They *believed not for joy*; they thought it too good news to be true. They *wondered*; they thought it not only *too good*, but *too great*, to be true.

[2] For their further conviction and encouragement, he *called for some meat.* He here did actually *eat* with *them* and *the rest*, to show that his body was really and truly *returned to life.* They gave him *a piece of a broiled fish, and of a honey-comb, v.* 42. This was mean fare; yet, if it be the fare of the disciples, their Master will fare as they do, because in the kingdom of our Father they shall fare as he does.

3. The *insight* he gave them into the word of God. He refers them to the *word* which they had *heard* from him when he was with them (*v.* 44): *These are the words which I said unto you while I was yet with you.* We should better *understand* what Christ *does*, if we did but better *remember* what he hath *said.* He refers them to the *word* they had read in the Old Testament: *All things must be fulfilled which were written.* Whatever they found written concerning the Messiah in the Old Testament must be fulfilled in him, what was written concerning his sufferings as well as what was written concerning his kingdom. *All things* must be fulfilled, even the *hardest*, even the *heaviest.* The several parts of the Old Testament are here mentioned, as containing each of them things

JAMIESON, FAUSSET, BROWN

CHARLES H. SPURGEON:

He has not lost His habit of chiding unbelief and encouraging faith; for as soon as He has risen, and speaks with His disciples, He asks them, "Why are ye troubled? and why do thoughts arise in your hearts?" He loves you to believe in Him, and be at rest. Find if you can, beloved, one occasion in which Jesus inculcated doubt, or bade men dwell in uncertainty. The apostles of unbelief are everywhere today, and they imagine that they are doing God service by spreading what they call "honest doubt." This is death to all joy! Poison to all peace! The Savior did not so. He would have them take extraordinary measures to get rid of their doubt. "Handle me," He says." It was going a long way to say that, but He would sooner be handled than His people should doubt! Ordinarily it might not be meet for them to touch Him. Had He not said to the women, "Touch me not"? But what may not be allowable ordinarily becomes proper when necessity demands it. The removal of their doubt as to our Lord's resurrection needed that they should handle Him, and therefore He bids them do so. Oh, beloved, you that are troubled and vexed with thoughts, and therefore get no comfort out of your religion because of your mistrust, your Lord would have you come very near to Him, and put His gospel to any test which will satisfy you. He cannot bear you to doubt. He appeals tenderly, saying "O thou of little faith, wherefore didst thou doubt?" He would at this moment still encourage you to taste and see that the Lord is good.—*The Treasury of the New Testament*

39-43. Behold . . .—lovingly offering them both *ocular* and *tangible* demonstration of the reality of His resurrection. **a spirit hath not**—an important statement regarding "spirits." **flesh and bones**—He says not "flesh and *blood*"; for the blood is the life of the animal and corruptible body (Gen. 9:4), which "cannot inherit the kingdom of God" (I Cor. 15:50; but "flesh and bones," implying the *identity*, but *with diversity of laws*, of the resurrection-body. (See on John 20:24-28.)

believed not for joy . . .—They did believe, else they had not rejoiced [BENGEL]. But it seemed *too good* to be true (Ps. 126:1, 2).

42. honeycomb—common frugal fare, anciently. **43. eat before them**—i.e., let them see Him doing it: not for His own necessity, but their conviction.

44-49. These are the words . . .—i.e., "Now you will understand what seemed so dark to you when I told you about the Son of man being put to death and rising again (ch. 18:31-34). **while . . . yet with you**—a striking expression, implying that He was now, as the dead and risen Saviour, virtually dissevered from this scene of mortality, and from all ordinary intercourse with His mortal disciples.

ADAM CLARKE

37-39. *And supposed that they had seen a spirit.* But if there be no such thing as a disembodied spirit, would not our Lord have shown them their error? Instead of this, He confirms them in their opinion, by saying, *A spirit hath not flesh and bones, as ye see me have;* therefore He says, *Handle me, and see me.* They probably imagined that it was the soul only of our blessed Lord which they saw; but they were soon fully convinced of the identity of His person and the reality of His resurrection; for (1) they saw His body, (2) they heard Him speak, (3) they handled Him, (4) they saw Him eat a piece of broiled fish and honeycomb, which they gave Him. In these things it was impossible for them to have been deceived.

41. *They yet believed not for joy.* They were so overcome with the joy of His resurrection that they did not, for some time, properly receive the evidence that was before them—as we phrase it, they thought the news too good to be true.

ALEXANDER MACLAREN:

Note Luke's explanation of the persistent incredulity, as being "for joy." It is like his notice that the three in Gethsemane "slept for sorrow." Great emotion sometimes produces effects opposite to what might have been expected. Who can wonder that the mighty fact which turned the black smoke of despair into bright flame should have seemed too good to be true? The little notice brings the disciples near to our experience and sympathy. Christ's loving forbearance and condescending affording of more than sufficient evidence show how little changed He was by death and resurrection. He is as little changed by sitting at the right hand of God. Still He is patient with our slow hearts. Still He meets our hesitating faith with lavish assurances. Still he lets us touch Him, if not with the hand of sense, with the truer contact of spirit; and we may have as firm personal experience of the reality of His life and presence as had that wondering company in the upper room.

—*Expositions of Holy Scripture*

MATTHEW HENRY

concerning Christ: *The law of Moses*, the *prophets*, the *Psalms*. See in what various ways of writing God did of old reveal his will. By an immediate present work upon their minds he gave them to apprehend the true intent and meaning of the Old Testament prophecies of Christ: *Then opened he their understanding, that they might understand the scriptures*, *v*. 45. In his discourse with the two disciples he took the veil from off the text, by *opening* the scriptures; here he took the veil from off the heart, *by opening the mind*. Jesus Christ by his Spirit operates on the minds of men. He has access to our Spirits and can immediately influence them. Even good men need to have their *understandings opened*; for though they are not *darkness*, yet in many things they are *in the dark*. Christ's way of working faith in the soul is by *opening the understanding*. Thus he comes into the soul by the *door*. The design of opening the understanding is *that we may understand the scriptures*; not that we may be *wise above what is written*, but that we may be *wiser in what is written*. Christ's scholars never learn *above their bibles* in this world; but they need to be learning still more and more *out of their bibles*.

4. The instructions he gave them as *apostles*: "*You are* to be *witnesses of these things* (*v*. 48), to carry the notice of them to all the world. You are fully assured of these things yourselves, you are eye and ear-witnesses of them; go, and assure the world of them."

(1) *What they must preach*. They must preach the gospel. They must take their bibles along with them, and must show people how it was written of old concerning the Messiah, and the glories and graces of his kingdom, and then must tell them how all this was fulfilled in the Lord Jesus. The great *gospel truth* concerning the *death* and *resurrection* of Jesus Christ must be *published* to the children of men (*v*. 46): *Thus it was written*, and therefore, *thus it behoved Christ to suffer*. "Go, and tell the world that Christ *suffered*, as it was written of him. Go, preach *Christ crucified*; be not ashamed of his cross, not ashamed of a suffering Jesus. Tell them that it *behoved him to suffer*, that it was necessary to the taking away of the sin of the world. That he rose from the dead on *the third day*. In this also the *scriptures* were *fulfilled*. Go, and tell them, then, that he that *was dead is alive*, and *lives for evermore*, and *has the keys of death and the grave*." The great *gospel duty* of *repentance* must be *pressed* upon the children of men. *Repentance for sin* must be preached in *Christ's name*, and by his authority, *v*. 47. "Go, and tell all people that they must turn to the service of God in Christ. Their hearts and lives must be changed." The great *gospel privilege* of the *remission of sins* must be *proposed* to all, and assured to all that *repent*, and *believe the gospel*. "Go, tell a guilty world that *there is hope* concerning them."

(2) *To whom they must preach*. They must preach this *among all nations*. They must disperse themselves and carry this light along with them wherever they go. The prophets had preached *repentance* and *remission* to the *Jews*, but the apostles must preach them to *all the world*. None are *exempted* from the obligations the gospel lays upon men to *repent*, nor are any *excluded* from those inestimable benefits. They must *begin at Jerusalem*. There the gospel day must dawn. And why must they begin there? *First*, Because *thus it was written*, and therefore it *behoved them* to take this method. *The word of the* Lord must *go forth from Jerusalem*, Isa. ii. 3. *Secondly*, Because there the matters of fact on which the gospel was founded were transacted; and therefore there they were first attested. So strong, so bright, is the first shining forth of the glory of the risen Redeemer that it dares face those daring enemies of his and sets them at defiance. *Thirdly*, Because he would give us a further example of forgiving enemies. The first offer of gospel grace is made to Jerusalem, and thousands there are in a little time brought to partake of that grace.

(3) What *assistance they should have in preaching*. *Behold, I send the promise of my Father upon you*, and *you shall be endued with power from on high*, *v*. 49. He here assures them that in a little time the Spirit should be poured out upon them in greater measures than ever, and they should thereby be furnished with all those gifts and graces which were necessary to their discharge of this great trust. Those who *receive the Holy Ghost* are thereby *endued with a power from on high*. Christ's apostles could never have planted his gospel, and set up his kingdom in the world, as they did, if they had not been endued with such a power. *This power from on high* was the *promise of the Father*. And, if it be the *promise of the Father*, we may be sure that the promise is *inviolable* and the thing promised *invaluable*. Christ's ambassadors must stay till they have their powers.

JAMIESON, FAUSSET, BROWN

law . . . prophets . . . psalms—the three Jewish divisions of the Old Testament Scriptures. **45. Then opened he . . .**—a statement of unspeakable value; expressing, on the one hand, Christ's *immediate access to the human spirit* and *absolute power over it*, to the adjustment of its vision, and permanent rectification for spiritual discernment (than which it is impossible to conceive a stronger evidence of His proper divinity); and, on the other hand, making it certain that the *manner of interpreting the Old Testament which the apostles afterwards employed* (see the Acts and Epistles), *has the direct sanction of Christ Himself*.

48. witnesses—(Cf. Acts 1:8, 22).

46. behoved Christ—(See on vs. 26.)

47. beginning at Jerusalem—(1) As the metropolis and heart of the then existing kingdom of God:—"to the Jew first" (Rom. 1:16; Acts 13:46; Isa. 2:3, see on Matt. 10:6). (2) As the great reservoir and laboratory of all the sin and crime of the nation, thus proclaiming for all time that there is mercy in Christ for the chief of sinners. (See on Matt. 23: 37.)

49. I send—the present tense, to intimate its nearness. **promise of my Father**—i.e., what My Father hath promised; the Holy Ghost, of which Christ is the authoritative Dispenser (John 14:7; Rev. 3:1, 5:6). **endued**—invested, or clothed with; implying, as the parallels show (Rom. 13:14; I Cor. 15:53; Gal. 3: 27; Col. 3:9, 10), their being *so penetrated and acted upon by conscious supernatural "power"* (in the full sense of that word) *as to stamp with divine authority the whole exercise of their apostolic office*, including, of course, their *pen* as well as their *mouth*.

ADAM CLARKE

44. *The law . . . the prophets, and . . . the psalms*. The common Jewish division of the writings of the old covenant is the following, and indeed seems to be the same to which our Lord alludes: (1) The law, *thorah*, including Genesis, Exodus, Leviticus, Numbers, and Deuteronomy. (2) The prophets, *nabiaim*, or "teachers," including Joshua, Judges, the two Books of Samuel, and the two Books of Kings; these were termed the "former prophets." Isaiah, Jeremiah, Ezekiel, Hosea, Joel, Amos, Obadiah, Jonah, Micah, Nahum, Habakkuk, Zephaniah, Haggai, Zechariah, and Malachi—these were termed the "latter prophets." (3) The hagiographa (*holy writings*), *kethuvim*, which comprehended the Psalms, Proverbs, Job, Canticles, Ruth, Lamentations, Ecclesiastes, Esther, Daniel, Ezra, Nehemiah, and the two Books of Chronicles. The Jews made anciently only twenty-two books of the whole, to bring them to the number of the letters in the Hebrew alphabet; and this they did by joining Ruth to Judges, making the two Books of Samuel only one, and so of Kings and Chronicles, joining the Lamentations to Jeremiah, and making the twelve minor prophets only one book.

45. *Then opened he their understanding*. "He fully opened." They had a measure of light before, so that they discerned the Scriptures to be the true *Word* of God, and to speak of the Messiah; but they had not light sufficient to enable them to apply these Scriptures to their Lord and Master. But now, by the influence of Christ, they see not only the prophecies which pointed out the Messiah, but also the Messiah who was pointed out by these prophecies. The Book of God may be received in general as a divine Revelation, but the proper meaning, reference, and application of the Scriptures can be discerned only by the light of Christ. Even the very plain Word of God is a dead letter to those who are not enlightened by the grace of Christ. And why? Because this Word speaks of spiritual and heavenly things, and the carnal mind of man cannot discern them. They who receive not this inward teaching continue dark and dead while they live.

47. *Remission of sins*. The "taking away"—removal of *sins*, in general—everything that relates to the destruction of the power, the pardoning of the guilt, and the purification of the heart from the very nature of sin. *Should be preached in his name*. See the office of a proclaimer, herald, or preacher explained in the note on Matt. iii. 1. *In his name*. On His authority, and in virtue of the atonement made by Him. For on what other ground could the inhabitants of the earth expect *remission of sins? Among all nations*. Because God wills the salvation of all, and Jesus Christ by His grace has tasted death for every man, Heb. ii. 9. *Beginning at Jerusalem*. Making the first overtures of mercy to My murderers! If, then, the sinners of Jerusalem might repent, believe, and be saved, none on this side of hell need despair.

48. *Ye are witnesses of these things*. He gave them a full commission to proclaim these glad tidings of peace and salvation to a lost world. The disciples were *witnesses* not only that Christ had suffered and risen again from the dead, but also that He opens the understanding by the inspiration of His Spirit, that He gives repentance, that He pardons sin and purifies from all unrighteousness, and that He is not willing that any should perish, but that all should come unto the knowledge of the truth and be saved.

49. *The promise of my Father*. That is, the *Holy Ghost*, promised, John xv. 26. See Acts i. 4; ii. 33.

The promise of the Father. The Holy Spirit, which indeed was the grand promise of the New Testament, as Jesus Christ was of the Old. How properly do we still pray, and how necessary is the prayer, "Cleanse the thoughts of our hearts by the inspiration of thy Holy Spirit, that we may perfectly love thee, and worthily magnify thy name, through Jesus Christ our Lord! Amen."—Communion Service. *Ye have heard of me*. In His particular conversations with His disciples, such as those related in John xiv. 16-26; xv. 26; xvi. 7-15.

MATTHEW HENRY

Though, one would think, never was such haste as now for the preaching of the gospel, yet the preachers must tarry till they be endued with power from on high.

Verses 50–53

His ascension into heaven, of which we have a very brief narrative in these verses.

I. How solemnly Christ took leave of his disciples. He had business to do in both worlds, and accordingly came from heaven to earth in his incarnation, to despatch his business here, and, having finished this, he returned to heaven, to reside there. 1. Whence he ascended: from *Bethany*, near Jerusalem, adjoining to the *mount of Olives*. There was the *garden* in which his sufferings began, there he was in his agony; and Bethany signifies *the house of sorrow*. Those that would go to heaven must ascend thither from the house of sufferings and sorrow. And here it was that awhile ago he began his triumphant entry into Jerusalem, *ch.* xix. 29. 2. Who were the witnesses of his ascension: *He led out his disciples* to see him. The disciples did not see him rise out of the grave, because his resurrection was capable of being proved by their seeing him alive afterwards; but they saw him *ascend* into heaven, because they could not otherwise have an *ocular* demonstration of his ascension. 3. What was the farewell he gave them: *He lifted up his hands, and blessed them.* He did not go away in displeasure, but in love; he left a blessing behind him. He blessed them to show that, having loved his own which were in the world, he loved them unto the end. 4. How he left them: *While he was blessing them, he was parted from them;* to intimate that his being parted from them did not put an end to his blessing them. He *began* to bless them on earth, but he went to heaven to *go on* with it. 5. How his ascension is described. (1) He was *parted from them.* Those that love us, and pray for us, and instruct us, must be *parted from us.* Those that knew him after the flesh must now henceforth know him so no more. (2) He was *carried up into heaven.* There needed no chariot of fire, nor horses of fire; he knew the way.

II. How cheerfully his disciples continued their attendance on him. They paid their homage to him at his going away: *They worshipped him, v.* 52. He *blessed them*, in token of gratitude for which they *worshipped him.* The cloud that received him out of their sight did not put them or their services out of his sight. They *returned to Jerusalem with great joy.* Thither they went, and there they stayed *with great joy.* This was a wonderful change. When Christ told them that he must leave them sorrow filled their hearts; yet now that they see him go they are *filled with joy.* They abounded in acts of devotion while they were in expectation of the promise of the Father, *v.* 53. They attended the temple-service at the hours of prayer. *They were continually in the temple*, as their Master was when he was at Jerusalem. Temple-sacrifices, they knew, were superseded by Christ's sacrifice, but the temple-songs they joined in. Nothing better prepares the mind for the receiving of the Holy Ghost than holy joy and praise. Fears are silenced, sorrows sweetened and allayed, and hopes kept up. *Amen.* Let him be continually praised and blessed.

JAMIESON, FAUSSET, BROWN

50-53. to Bethany—not to the village itself, but on the *descent* to it from Mount Olivet.

51. while he blessed . . . parted . . .—Sweet intimation! Incarnate Love, Crucified Love, Risen Love, now on the wing for heaven, waiting only those odorous gales which were to waft Him to the skies, goes away in benedictions, that in the character of Glorified, Enthroned Love, He might continue His benedictions, but in yet higher form, until He come again! And oh, if angels were so transported at His birth into this scene of tears and death, what must have been their ecstasy as they welcomed and attended Him "far above all heavens" into the presence-chamber, and conducted Him to the right hand of the Majesty on High! Thou hast an everlasting right, O my Saviour, to that august place. The brightness of the Father's glory, enshrined in our nature, hath won it well; for He poured out His soul unto death, and led captivity captive, receiving gifts for men, yea for the rebellious, that the Lord God might dwell among them. Thou art the King of glory, O Christ. Lift up your heads, O ye gates, be lifted up, ye everlasting doors, that the King of glory may come in! Even so wilt Thou change these vile bodies of ours, that they may be like unto Thine own glorious body; and then with gladness and rejoicing shall they be brought, they shall enter into the King's palace! **52. worshipped him**—certainly in the strictest sense of adoration. **returned to Jerusalem**—as instructed to do: but not till after gazing, as if entranced, up into the blue vault in which He had disappeared, they were gently checked by two shining ones, who assured them He would come again to them in the like manner as He had gone into heaven. (See on Acts 1:10, 11.) This made them return, not with disappointment at His removal, but "with great joy." **53. were continually in the temple**—i.e., every day at the regular hours of prayer till the day of Pentecost.

ADAM CLARKE

CHARLES H. SPURGEON:

Our Lord Jesus, having spoiled the grave, and so proved His power over things that are under the earth, tarried for forty days among men, and so claimed His power over the earth itself, and then ascended through the air to show that the dominion of the prince of the power of the air was broken, and, finally, entered into the heaven of heavens to claim sovereignty there, that so, from the lowest depths up to the extremest heights, He might take possession of His vast domains. I like to think of Him as traversing His dominions from end to end, like a conqueror looking over the provinces which have been subdued by His might.

—*The Treasury of the New Testament*

51. *Carried up into heaven.* Into that heaven from which He had descended, **John i. 18; iii. 13.** This was forty days after His resurrection, **Acts i. 3**, during which time He had given the most convincing proofs of that resurrection, not only to the apostles, but to many others, to upwards of five hundred at one time, **1 Cor. xv. 6.** As in His life they had seen the way to the Kingdom, and in His death the price of the Kingdom, so in His ascension they had the fullest proof to the immortality of the soul, the resurrection of the human body, and of His continual intercession at the right hand of God. There are some remarkable circumstances relative to this ascension mentioned in **Acts i. 4-12.**

53. *Were continually in the temple.* Especially till the Day of Pentecost came, when they received the promise mentioned, **v. 49.** *Praising and blessing God.* Magnifying His mercy and speaking good of His name. Thus the days of their mourning were ended, and they began that life upon earth in which they still live in the kingdom of God.

I cannot close these observations with a more profitable word than what is contained in that truly apostolic and sublime prayer for the second *Sunday in Advent;* and may he who reads it weigh every word in the spirit of faith and devotion! "Blessed God! who hast caused all holy scriptures to be written for our learning; grant that we may in such wise *hear* them, *read, mark, learn,* and *inwardly digest* them, that, by patience and comfort of thy holy word, we may embrace and ever hold fast the blessed hope of everlasting life, which thou hast given us in our Saviour Jesus Christ!"

Now "unto him that loved us, and washed us from our sins in his own blood, and hath made us kings and priests unto God and his Father; to him be glory and dominion for ever and ever. Amen."

THE GOSPEL ACCORDING TO JOHN

I. From everlasting (1:1-18)
A. The Word essentially (1:1-14)
1. The two relations (1:1, 14)
2. The two creations (1:2-13)
B. The witnesses (1:15-17)
1. The old: John—prophet (1:15)
2. The new: John—apostle (1:16, 17)
C. The Word evangelically (1:18)

II. God manifest (1:19-19:42)
A. In the world (1:19-12:50)
1. Prologue (1:19-51)
2. The manifestation (2:1-11:46)
3. Epilogue (11:47-12:50)
B. To His own (13:1-17:26)
1. Love (13:1-14:15)
2. Light (14:16-31)
3. Life (15:1-16:33)
4. The prayer of the Word (17:1-26)
C. By the cross (18:1-19:42)
1. Love: deserted and faithful (18:1-19:16)
2. Light: eclipsed and dawning (19:17-30)
3. Life: laid down and given (19:31-42)

III. To everlasting (20:1-21:25)
A. Abiding life (20:1-18)
1. The empty tomb (20:1-10)
2. The living Lord (20:11-18)
B. Abiding light (20:19-31)
1. The disciples (20:19-23)
2. Thomas (20:24-29)
3. Unrecorded signs (20:30, 31)
C. Abiding love (21:1-25)
1. Breakfast (21:1-14)
2. Love triumphant (21:15-23)
3. Unrecorded deeds (21:24, 25)

It is not important when and where this gospel was written; we are sure that it was given to John, the brother of James, one of the twelve apostles, distinguished by the honorable character of "that disciple whom Jesus loved." The ancients tell us that John lived longest of all the twelve apostles, and was the only one who died a natural death. Some of them say that he wrote this gospel at Ephesus in opposition to the heresy of the Ebionites, who held that our Lord was a mere man. It is clear that he wrote last of the four evangelists, and, comparing his gospel with theirs, we may observe (1) that he relates what they had omitted; he brings up the rear, gleans up what they had passed by; (2) that he gives us more of the *mystery* of that of which the other evangelists gave us only the *history*. Some of the ancients observe that the other evangelists wrote more of the *bodily* things of Christ; but John writes of the *spiritual* things of the gospel, the life and soul of it.

MATTHEW HENRY

CHAPTER 1

Verses 1–5

Let us enquire what there is in those strong lines. The evangelist here lays down the great truth he is to prove, that Jesus Christ is God, one with the Father.

I. Of whom he speaks—*The Word—ὁ λόγος*. This is an idiom peculiar to John's writings. Even the vulgar Jews were taught that the *Word of God* was the same with God. The evangelist, in the close of his discourse (*v.* 18), plainly tells us why he calls Christ *the Word—because he is the only begotten Son, who is in the bosom of the Father, and has declared him. Word* is two-fold: *Word conceived,* and *word uttered.* 1. There is the *word conceived,* that is, *thought*, which is the first and only immediate product and conception of the soul. And thus the second person in the Trinity is fitly called *the Word*; for he is the *first-begotten of the Father.* There is nothing we are more sure of then *that we think*, yet nothing we are more in the dark about then *how we think.* Surely then the generations and births of the eternal mind may well be allowed to be great mysteries of godliness, the bottom of which we cannot fathom, while yet we adore the depth. 2. There is the *word uttered,* and this is *speech*, the chief and most natural indication of the mind. And thus Christ is *the Word,* for *by him* God has in *these last days spoken to us.* He has made known God's mind to us, as a man's word or speech makes known his thoughts. John Baptist was *the voice*, but Christ *the Word.*

II. What he saith of him.

1. His existence in the beginning: *In the beginning was the Word.* This bespeaks his existence, not only before his incarnation, but before all time. The world was *from* the beginning, but the Word was *in* the beginning. The Word had a being before the world had a beginning. He that *was* in the beginning *never* began, and therefore was *ever.*

2. His co-existence with the Father: *The Word was with God, and the Word was God.* It is repeated in *v.* 2: *the same* was *in the beginning with God*, that is, he was so from eternity. In the beginning the world was *from God*, but the Word was *with God*, as ever with him. The Word was with God, (1) In respect of *essence* and *substance*; for the *Word was God.* (2) In respect of *complacency* and *felicity*. There was a glory and happiness which Christ had *with God*

JAMIESON, FAUSSET, BROWN

CHAPTER 1

Vss. 1-14. THE WORD MADE FLESH. **1. In the beginning**—of all time and created existence, for this Word gave it being (vss. 3, 10); therefore, "before the world was" (ch. 17:5, 24); or, from all eternity.

was the Word—He *who is to God what man's word is to himself, the manifestation or expression of himself to those without him.* (See on vs. 18.) On the *origin* of this most lofty and now for ever consecrated title of Christ, this is not the place to speak. It occurs only in the writings of this seraphic apostle. **was with God**—having a conscious personal existence *distinct from God* (as one is from the person he is "with"), but *inseparable from Him* and *associated with Him* (vs. 18; ch. 17:5; I John 1:2), where "THE FATHER" is used in the same sense as "GOD" here. **was God**—in substance and essence GOD; or was possessed of essential or proper divinity. Thus, each of these brief but pregnant statements is the complement of the other, correcting any misapprehensions which the

ADAM CLARKE

CHAPTER 1

1. *In the beginning.* That is, before anything was formed—ere God began the great work of creation. This is the meaning of the word in Gen. i. 1, to which the Evangelist evidently alludes. This phrase fully proves, in the mouth of an inspired writer, that Jesus Christ was no part of the creation, as He existed when no part of that existed; and that consequently He is no creature, as all created nature was formed by Him; for "without him was not any thing made that was made," v. 3. Now as what was before creation must be eternal, and as what gave being to all things could not have borrowed or derived its being from anything, therefore Jesus, who was before all things and who made all things, must necessarily be the eternal God.

Was the Word. Or "existed the Logos." This term "Logos" should be left untranslated, for the very same reason the names *Jesus* and *Christ* are left untranslated. And as it would be highly improper to say, "the Deliverer, the Anointed," instead of "Jesus Christ," so I deem it improper to say, "the Word," instead of *the Logos.* But as every appellative of the Saviour of the world was descriptive of some excellence in His person, nature, or work, so the epithet *Logos,* which signifies "a word spoken, speech, eloquence, doctrine, reason, or the faculty of reasoning," is very properly applied to Him who is the "true Light, which lighteth every man that cometh into the world," v. 9; who is the Fountain of all wisdom; who giveth being, life,

MATTHEW HENRY

before the world was (*ch.* xvii. 5). (3) In respect of *counsel* and *design.* So that this grand affair of man's reconciliation to God was concerted between the Father and Son from eternity.

3. His agency in making the world, *v.* 3. This is here, (1) Expressly asserted: *All things were made by him.* He was *with God, active* in the divine operations in the beginning of time. Not as the workman cuts by his axe, but as the body sees by the eye. (2) The contrary is denied: *Without him was not anything made that was made,* from the highest angel to the meanest worm. God the Father did nothing without him in that work. This proves that *he is God.* This proves the excellency of the Christian religion, that the author and founder of it is the same that was the author and founder of the world. This shows how well qualified he was for the work of our redemption and salvation. He is appointed the author of our bliss who was the author of our being.

4. The original of life and light that is in him: *In him was life, v.* 4. This further proves that he is God. (1) He has *life in himself;* not only the *true God,* but the *living God.* (2) All living creatures have their life in him; all the *life* too that is in the creation is derived from him. He is that Word by which man lives more than by bread, Matt. iv. 4. (3) Reasonable creatures have their *light* from him; that *life* which is *the light of men* comes from him. Life in man is something greater and nobler than it is in other creatures; it is *rational,* and not merely *animal.* The *spirit of a man is the candle of the Lord,* and it was the eternal Word that lighted this candle. The light of reason, as well as the life of sense, is derived from him. From whom may we better expect the light of divine revelation than from him who gave us the light of human reason?

5. The manifestation of him to the children of men. Whence is it that he has been so little taken notice of and regarded? To this he answers (*v.* 5), *The light shines, but the darkness comprehends it not.*

(1) The discovery of the eternal Word to the lapsed world, even before he was manifested in the flesh: *The light shineth in darkness.* [1] The eternal Word, *as God,* shines in *the darkness* of *natural conscience.* Something of the power of the divine Word all mankind have an innate sense of. [2] The eternal Word shone in the darkness of the Old Testament prophecies and promises. He that had commanded the light of this world to shine out of darkness was himself long a light *shining in darkness.*

(2) The disability of the degenerate world to receive this discovery: *The darkness comprehended it not.* The darkness of error and sin overpowered and quite eclipsed this light. The Jews who had the light of the Old Testament, yet comprehended not Christ in it. It was therefore requisite that Christ should come, both to rectify the errors of the Gentile world and to improve the truths of the Jewish church.

Verses 5–14

The evangelist designs to bring in John Baptist bearing an honourable testimony to Jesus Christ. Now in these verses, before he does this,

I. He gives us some account of the witness he is about to produce. His name was *John,* which signifies *gracious.*

1. We are here told concerning him, in general, that he was a *man sent of God.* He was a *man,* a mere man. God is pleased to speak to us by men like ourselves. He was *sent from God,* he was God's *messenger.* God gave him both his mission and his message. John wrought no miracle, but the strictness and purity of his life and doctrine, were plain indications that he was *sent of God.*

2. We are here told what his office and business were (*v.* 7): *The same came for a witness, for a testimony.* The legal institutions had been long a testimony for God, in the Jewish church. But now divine revelation is to be turned into another channel. There was a profound silence concerning him, till John Baptist came for a witness to him. (1) The matter of his testimony: *He came to bear witness to the light.* Light is a thing which witnesses for itself. Christ's light needs not man's testimony, but the world's darkness does. John was like the night watchman that goes round the town, proclaiming the approach of the morning light to those that have closed their eyes. He was sent of God to proclaim that dispensation at hand which would bring life and immortality to light. (2) The design of his testimony: *That all men through him might believe;* not in him, but in Christ. He taught men to look through him, and pass through him, to Christ. If they would but receive this witness of man, they would soon find that the witness of God was greater. It was designed

JAMIESON, FAUSSET, BROWN

others might occasion. Was the Word *eternal?* It was *not* the eternity of *"the Father,"* but of a conscious personal existence *distinct from Him and associated with Him.* Was the Word thus "with God?" It was not the distinctness and the fellowship of *another being,* as if there were *more Gods than one,* but of One who was *Himself God*—in such sense that the *absolute unity* of the God head, the great principle of all religion, is only transferred from the region of shadowy abstraction to the region of essential life and love. But why all this definition? Not to give us any *abstract information* about certain mysterious distinctions in the Godhead, but solely to let the reader know *who it was that* in the fulness of time *"was made flesh."* After each verse, then, the reader must say, "It was He who is thus, and thus, and thus described, who was made flesh." **2. The same . . .**—See what property of the Word the stress is laid upon—His *eternal distinctness,* in unity, from God—the Father (John 1:2). **3. All things . . .**—all things *absolutely* (as is evident from vs. 10; I Cor. 8:6; Col. 1:16, 17; but put beyond question by what follows). "Without Him was *not one thing* made [brought into being] that was made." This is a denial of the *eternity* and *non-creation* of matter, which was held by the whole thinking world *outside of Judaism and Christianity:* or rather, its proper *creation* was never so much as dreamt of save by the children of *revealed religion.* **4. In Him was life**—*essentially* and *originally,* as the previous verses show to be the meaning. Thus He is *the Living Word,* or, as He is called in I John 1:1,2, "the Word of Life." **the life . . . the light of men**—All that in men which is *true light*—knowledge, integrity, intelligent, willing subjection to God, love to Him and to their fellow creatures, wisdom, purity, holy joy, rational happiness—all this "light of men" has its fountain in the essential original "life" of "the Word" (I John 1:5-7; Ps. 36:9). **5. shineth in darkness . . .**—in this dark, fallen world, or in mankind "sitting in darkness and the shadow of death," *with no ability to find the way either of truth or of holiness.* In this thick darkness, and consequent intellectual and moral obliquity, "the light of the Word" shineth—*by all the rays whether of natural or revealed teaching which men* (apart from the Incarnation of the Word) *are favored with.* **the darkness comprehended it not**—*did not take it in,* a brief summary of the effect of all the strivings of this *un*incarnate Word throughout this wide world from the beginning, and a hint of the necessity of His putting on *flesh,* if any recovery of men was to be effected (I Cor. 1:21).

6-9. The Evangelist here *approaches* his grand thesis, so paving his way for the full statement of it in vs. 14, that we may be able to bear the bright light of it, and take in its length and breadth and depth and height.

ADAM CLARKE

light, knowledge, and reason to all men; who is the grand Source of revelation, who has declared God unto mankind; who spake by the prophets, "for the testimony of Jesus is the spirit of prophecy," Rev. xix. 10; who has illustrated life and immortality by His gospel, 2 Tim. i. 10; and who has fully made manifest the deep mysteries which lay hidden in the bosom of the invisible God from all eternity, John i. 18. The apostle does not borrow this mode of speech from the writings of Plato, as some have imagined; he took it from the scriptures of the Old Testament, and from the subsequent style of the ancient Jews. *And the Word was God.* Or "God was the Logos"; therefore no subordinate being, no second to the Most High, but the supreme, eternal Jehovah.

3. *All things were made by him.* That is, by this Logos. In Gen. i. 1, God is said to have created all things; in this verse, Christ is said to have created all things. The same unerring Spirit spoke in Moses and in the Evangelists; therefore Christ and the Father are One.

4. *In him was life.* This expression is not to be understood of natural life, but of that life eternal which He revealed to the world, 2 Tim. i. 10; to which He taught the way, chap. xiv. 6; which He promised to believers, chap. x. 28; which He purchased for them, chap. vi. 51, 53-54; which He is appointed to give them, chap. xvii. 2; and to which He will raise them up, v. 29, because He hath the life in himself, v. 26.

5. *And the light shineth in darkness.* By *darkness* here may be understood: (1) the heathen world, Eph. v. 8; (2) the Jewish people; (3) the fallen spirit of man. *Comprehended it not.* "Prevented it not—hindered it not."

6. *Whose name was John.* This was John the Baptist; see his name and the nature of his office explained, Mark i. 4 and Matt. iii. 1-3.

7. *That all men through him might believe.* He testified that Jesus was the *true Light*—the true Teacher of the way to the Kingdom of glory, and the Lamb or Sacrifice of God, which was to bear away the sin of the world, v. 29, and

MATTHEW HENRY

that all men through him might believe, excluding none that did not exclude themselves.

3. We are here cautioned not to mistake him for the light who only came to bear witness to it (*v.* 8): *He was not that light.* He was a star, like that which guided the wise men to Christ, a morning star; but he was not the Sun. The evangelist here, when he speaks very honourably of him, yet shows that he must give place to Christ. He was great as the prophet of the Highest, but not the Highest himself. We must take heed of over-valuing ministers, as well as of under-valuing them; they are not our lords, but ministers by whom we believe. Those who usurp the honour of Christ forfeit the honour of being the servants of Christ; yet John was very serviceable as a witness to the light, though he was not that light. Those may be of great use to us who yet shine with a borrowed light.

II. Before he goes on with John's testimony, he returns to give us a further account of this Jesus, to show the graces of his incarnation.

1. Christ was the *true Light* (*v.* 9). Christ is the great light that deserves to be called so. Other lights are but figuratively and equivocally called so: Christ is the true light. But how does Christ enlighten every man that comes into the world? (1) By his creating power he enlightens every man with the light of reason; all the beauty it puts upon us, are from Christ. (2) By the publication of his gospel to all nations he does in effect enlighten every man. John Baptist was a light but he lightened only Jerusalem and Judæa, like a candle that enlightens one room; but Christ is the true light, for he is a light to enlighten the Gentiles. Divine revelation is not now to be confined, as it had been, to one people, but to be diffused to all people, Matt. v. 15. Whatever light any man has, he is indebted to Christ for it, whether it be natural or supernatural.

2. Christ *was in the world*, *v.* 10. This speaks of his being in the world when he took our nature upon him, and dwelt among us. *I am come into the world.* He left a world of bliss and glory, and was here in this melancholy miserable world. He was in the world, but not of it. The greatest honour that ever was put upon this world was that the Son of God was once *in the world.* It should reconcile us to our present abode in *this* world that once Christ was *here.* What reason Christ had to expect the most affectionate and respectful welcome possible in this world; for *the world was made by him. Therefore* he came to save a lost world because it was a world of his own making. The world was *made by him*, and therefore ought to do him homage. What cold entertainment he met with, notwithstanding: *The world knew him not.* The *ox knows his owner*, but the more brutish world did not. They did not own him, did not bid him welcome, because they did not *know him.* When he shall come as a Judge the world shall *know* him.

3. He *came to his own* (*v.* 11); not only to the world, which was *his own*, but to the people of Israel, that were peculiarly *his own.* To them he was *first sent.* He came to his own, to seek and save them, because they were *his own.* The generality *rejected* him: *His own received him not.* He had reason to expect that those who were his own should have bidden him welcome. He came among them himself, introduced with signs and wonders, and himself the greatest; and therefore it is not said of them, as it was of the world (*v.* 10), that they *knew him not*; but *his own*, though they could not but know him, yet *received him not.* Many who in profession are *Christ's own*, yet do not *receive him*, because they will not part with their sins, nor have him to *reign over them.* Yet there was a remnant who *owned* him, and were faithful to him. There were those that *received* him (*v.* 12): *But as many as received him.* There were many of *them* that were wrought upon to submit to Christ, and many more that *were not of that fold.* The true Christian's *description* and *property*; and that is, that he *receives Christ*, and *believes on his name.* Believing in Christ's name is *receiving* him as a gift from God. We must receive his doctrine as true and good; and we must receive the image of his grace, and impressions of his love, as the governing principle of our affections and actions. The true Christians' dignity and privilege are twofold:

First, The *privilege of adoption*: *To them gave he power to become the sons of God.* Hitherto, the adoption pertained to the Jews only; but now, by faith in Christ, Gentiles are the *children of God.* To them gave he a *right*; *this power have all the saints.* It is the unspeakable privilege of all good Christians, that they are become the *children of God.* If they be the *children of God*, they *become* so, are *made* so. *Behold what manner of love is this*, 1 John iii. 1. God calls them *his children*, they call him *Father.* The privilege of adoption is entirely owing to *Jesus*

JAMIESON, FAUSSET, BROWN

8. not that Light—(See on ch. 5:35). What a testimony to John to have to explain that "he was *not* that Light!" Yet was he but a foil to set it off, his night-taper dwindling before the Dayspring from on high (ch. 3:30).

lighteth every man . . .—rather, "which, coming into the world, enlighteneth every man"; or, is "the Light of the world" (ch. 9:5). "Coming into the world" is a superfluous and quite unusual description of "every man"; but it is of all descriptions of Christ amongst the most familiar, especially in the writings of this Evangelist (ch. 12:46; 16:28; 18:37; I John 4:9; I Tim. 1:15, etc.).

10-13. He was in the world . . .—The language here is nearly as wonderful as the thought. Observe its compact simplicity, its sonorousness—"the world" resounding in each of its three members—and the enigmatic form in which it is couched, startling the reader and setting his ingenuity a-working to solve the stupendous enigma of *Christ ignored in His own world.* "The world," in the first two clauses, plainly means the *created* world, *into* which *He* came, says vs. 9; "*in* it He was," says this verse. By His Incarnation, He became *an inhabitant of it,* and bound up with it. Yet it "was made by Him" (vss. 3, 4, 5). Here, then, it is merely alluded to, in contrast partly with His being *in* it, but still more with the reception He met with from it. "The world that knew Him not" (I John 3:1) is of course the intelligent world of mankind. (See on vss. 11, 12.) Taking the first two clauses as one statement, we try to apprehend it by thinking of the infant Christ conceived in the womb and born in the arms of His own creature, and of the Man Christ Jesus breathing His own air, treading His own ground, supported by substances to which He Himself gave being, and the Creator of the very men whom He came to save. But the most vivid commentary on this entire verse will be got by tracing (in His matchless history) Him of whom it speaks walking amidst all the elements of nature, the diseases of men and death itself, the secrets of the human heart, and "the rulers of the darkness of this world" in all their number, subtlety, and malignity, not only with absolute ease, as their conscious Lord, but, as we might say, with full consciousness on their part of the presence of their Maker, whose will to one and all of them was law. And this is He of whom it is added, "the world knew Him not!" **11. his own**—"His own" (property or possession), for the word is in the *neuter* gender. It means His own land, city, temple, Messianic rights and possessions. **and his own**—"His own" (people); for now the word is *masculine.* It means the Jews, as the "peculiar people." Both *they* and their *land,* with all that this included, were "HIS OWN," not so much as part of "the world which was made by Him," but as "THE HEIR" of the inheritance (Luke 20:14; see also on Matt. 22:1). **received him not**—*nationally*, as God's chosen witnesses. **12. But as many**—*individuals,* of the "disobedient and gainsaying people." **gave he power**—The word signifies both *authority* and *ability,* and both are certainly meant here. **to become**—Mark these words: Jesus is the Son of God; He is never said to have become such. **the sons**—or more simply, "sons of God," in *name* and in *nature.* **believe on his name**—*a phrase never used in Scripture of any mere creature,* to express the credit given to human testimony, even of prophets or apostles, inasmuch it carries with it the idea of *trust* proper only towards GOD. In this

ADAM CLARKE

invited men to believe in Him for the remission of their sins, that they might receive the baptism of the Holy Ghost, vv. 32-34.

9. *Which lighteth every man.* As Christ is the Spring and Fountain of all wisdom, so all the wisdom that is in man comes from Him. The human intellect is a ray from His brightness; and reason itself springs from this Logos, the eternal Reason. Some of the most eminent rabbins understand Isa. lx. 1, "Arise, shine; for thy light is come," of the Messiah, who was to illuminate Israel. *That cometh into the world.* Or "coming into the world." This heavenly light shines into the soul of every man, to convince of sin, righteousness, and judgment; and it is through this light, which no man brings into the world with him, but which Christ mercifully gives to him on his coming into it, that what is termed conscience among men is produced. No man could discern good from evil were it not for this light thus supernaturally and graciously restored.

10. *He was in the world.* From its very commencement—He governed the universe—regulated His Church—spake by His prophets—and often, as the Angel or Messenger of Jehovah, appeared to them and to the patriarchs. *The world knew him not.* "Did not acknowledge Him"; for the Jewish rulers *knew* well enough that He was "a teacher come from God," but they did not choose to acknowledge Him as such.

11. *He came unto his own.* "To those of His own family, city, country"; "and His own people"—His own citizens, brethren, subjects. *Received him not.* Would not acknowledge Him as the Messiah, nor believe in Him for salvation.

12. *Gave he power.* "Privilege, honor, dignity, or right." He who is made a child of God enjoys the greatest "privilege" which the Divine Being can confer on this side of eternity. Those who accept Jesus Christ as He is offered to them in the gospel have, through His blood, a "right" to this sonship; for by that sacrifice this blessing was purchased, and the fullest promises of God confirm it to all who believe. And those

MATTHEW HENRY

Christ; he *gave* this power to them that believe on his name. The Son of God became a Son of man, that the sons and daughters of men might become the sons and daughters of God Almighty.

Secondly, The *privilege of regeneration* (*v*. 13): *Which were born*. All the children of God are born again; all that are adopted are regenerated. Now here we have an account of the original of this new birth. 1. Negatively. (1) It is *not of blood, not of the will of the flesh*, nor of *corruptible seed*. We do not become the children of God as we become the children of our natural parents. Grace does not run in the blood, as corruption does. (2) It is not *produced* by the natural power of our own will. As it is not of *blood*, nor of *the will of the flesh*, so neither is it of the *will of man*. It is the grace of God that makes us willing to be *his*. But, 2. Positively: it is of *God*. This new birth is owing to the word of God as the means and to the Spirit of God as the great and sole author. True believers are *born of God*, 1 John iii. 9; v. 1.

4. The *word was made flesh*, *v*. 14. This expresses Christ's incarnation more clearly than what went before. Now that the fulness of time was come he was sent forth after another manner, *made of a woman*.

(1) The *human nature of Christ* with which he was veiled. *The word was made flesh. Forasmuch as the children* who were to become the sons of God, *were partakers of flesh and blood, he also himself likewise took part of the same*, Heb. ii. 14. John here saith, *He was God*, but *He was made flesh*. Compare *v*. 1 with this. He subjected himself to the miseries and calamities of the human nature. *Flesh* bespeaks *man tainted with sin*, and Christ appeared *in the likeness of sinful flesh* (Rom. viii. 3), and was made *sin for us*, 2 Cor. v. 21, and *condemned sin in the flesh*, Rom. viii. 3. The *Word of the Lord*, who was made flesh, *endures for ever*; when made flesh, he ceased not to be the Word of God. He *dwelt among us*. Having taken upon him the nature of man, he put himself into the place and condition of other men. Having taken a *body* of the same mould with ours, in it he came, and resided in the same world with us. He *dwelt among us*, us worms of the earth, us that were *corrupt* and *depraved*, and revolted from God. When we look upon the upper world, how mean and contemptible does this flesh, this body, appear, which we carry about with us, and this world in which our lot is cast. But that the eternal Word was *made flesh*, and dwelt in this world as we do should make us willing to abide in the flesh while God has any work for us to do. He dwelt *among* the Jews. Though the Jews were unkind to him, yet he continued to dwell among them. He *dwelt* among us. He was in the world, not as a wayfaring man that tarries but for a night, but he *dwelt* among us. The original word is observable, he dwelt *as in a tabernacle*, which intimates, that he dwelt here in very *mean* circumstances, as shepherds that dwell in tents. That his stay among us was not to be perpetual. He dwelt here as *in a tent*, not as at *home*. That as of old God dwelt in the tabernacle of Moses, so now he dwells in the human nature of Christ. And we are to make all our addresses to God through Christ.

(2) The *beams of his divine glory* that *darted* through this *veil of flesh*: *We beheld his glory, the glory as of the only begotten of the Father, full of grace and truth*. The sun is still the fountain of light, though eclipsed or clouded; so Christ was still the brightness of his Father's glory. There were those that saw through the veil.

[1] Who were the witnesses of this glory: *we*, his disciples and followers, we among whom he *dwelt*. Other men discover their weaknesses to those that are most familiar with them, but it was not so with Christ; those that were most intimate with him saw most of his glory. They saw the glory of his divinity, while others saw only the veil of his human nature.

[2] What evidence they had of it: *We saw it*. They had not their evidence by report, at secondhand, but were themselves eyewitnesses, *We saw it*. The word signifies a fixed abiding sight. This apostle himself explains this: *What we declare unto you* of the Word of life is what we have *seen with our eyes*, and what *we have looked upon*, 1 John i. 1.

[3] What the glory was: *The glory as of the only begotten of the Father*. The glory of the *Word made flesh* was such a glory as became the only *begotten Son of God*, and could not be the glory of any other. Jesus Christ is the only begotten of the Father. Believers are the children of God by the special favour of adoption and the special grace of regeneration. They are in a sense *of a like nature*, and have the image of his perfections; but Christ is *of the same nature*. He was evidently declared to be the only begotten of the Father, by that which was seen of his glory when he dwelt among us. His divine glory

JAMIESON, FAUSSET, BROWN

sense of *supreme faith*, as due to Him who "gives those that *believe in Himself* power to become sons of God," it is manifestly used here. **13. Which were born**—a sonship therefore not of mere title and privilege, but of *nature*, the soul being made conscious of the vital capacities, perceptions, and emotions of *a child of God*, before unknown. **not of blood . . .**—not of superior human descent, not of human generation at all, not of man in any manner of way. By this elaborate threefold denial of the *human* source of this sonship, immense force is given to what follows—"*but of God*." Right royal gift, and He who confers must be absolutely divine. For who would not worship Him who can bring him into the family, and evoke within him the very life, of the sons of God? **14. And the Word . . .**—*To raise the reader to the altitude of this climax were the thirteen foregoing verses written.* **was made flesh**—BECAME MAN, in man's present frail, mortal condition, denoted by the word "flesh" (Isa. 40:6; I Pet. 1:24). It is directed probably against the *Docetæ*, who held that Christ was not really but only *apparently* man; against whom this gentle spirit is vehement in his Epistles (I John 4:3; II John 7:10, 11), [LUCKE, etc.]. Nor could He be too much so, for with the verity of the Incarnation all substantial Christianity vanishes. But now, married to our nature, henceforth He is as *personally conscious of all that is strictly human as of all that is properly divine;* and our nature is in His Person redeemed and quickened, ennobled and transfigured. **and dwelt**—tabernacled or pitched his tent; a word peculiar to John, who uses it four times, all in the sense of *a permanent stay* (Rev. 7:15; 12:12; 13:6; 21:3). For ever wedded to our "*flesh*," He has entered this tabernacle to "go no more out." The allusion is to that tabernacle where dwelt the *Shekinah* (see on Matt. 23:38, 39), or manifested "GLORY OF THE LORD," and with reference to God's *permanent dwelling among His people* (Lev. 26:11; Ps. 68:18; 132:13, 14; Ezek. 37:27). This is put almost beyond doubt by what immediately follows, **"And we beheld His glory"** [LUCKE, MEYER, DE WETTE, which last critic, rising higher than usual, says that thus were perfected all former partial manifestations of God in *an essentially Personal and historically Human* manifestation].

and we beheld his glory—not by the eye of *sense*, which saw in Him only "the carpenter." His glory was "spiritually discerned" (I Cor. 2:7-15; II Cor. 3:18; 4:4, 6; 5:16)—the glory of surpassing grace, love, tenderness, wisdom, purity, spirituality; majesty and meekness, richness and poverty, power and weakness, meeting together in unique contrast; ever attracting and at times ravishing the "babes" that followed and forsook all for Him.

the glory as of the only begotten of the Father—(See on Luke 1:35); not *like*, but "such as (belongs to)," such as *became* or was *befitting* the only begotten of the Father [CHRYSOSTOM in LUCKE, CALVIN, etc.], according to a wellknown use of the word "as."

ADAM CLARKE

who are engrafted in the heavenly family have the highest "honor" and "dignity" to which it is possible for a human soul to arrive.

13. *Which were born, not of blood*. Who were regenerated, "not of bloods"—the union of father and mother, or of a distinguished or illustrious ancestry, for the Hebrew language makes use of the *plural* to point out the dignity or excellence of a thing; and probably by this the Evangelist intended to show his countrymen that having Abraham and Sarah for their parents would not entitle them to the blessings of the new covenant, as no man could lay claim to them but in consequence of being born of God. Therefore neither *the will of the flesh* (anything that the corrupt heart of man could purpose or determine in its own behalf) nor *the will of man* (anything that another may be disposed to do in our behalf) can avail here. This new birth must come through the *will of God*—through His own unlimited power and boundless mercy, prescribing salvation by Christ Jesus alone.

14. *And the Word was made flesh*. That very Person who was in the beginning—who was with God—and who was God, v. 1, in the fullness of time became flesh—became incarnated by the power of the Holy Ghost, in the womb of the Virgin. Allowing this apostle to have written by divine inspiration, is not this verse, taken in connection with v. 1, an absolute and incontestable proof of the proper and eternal Godhead of Christ Jesus? *And dwelt among us*. "And tabernacled among us," the human nature which He took of the Virgin being as the shrine, house, or temple in which His immaculate deity condescended to dwell. The word is probably an allusion to the divine Shekinah in the Jewish Temple; and as God has represented the whole gospel dispensation by the types and ceremonies of the old covenant, so the Shekinah in the Tabernacle and Temple pointed out this manifestation of God in the flesh. The word is thus used by the Jewish writers; it signifies with them a manifestation of the divine Shekinah.

We beheld his glory. This refers to the Transfiguration, at which John was present, in company with Peter and James.

The glory as of the only begotten. That is, such a glory as "became," or was "proper to," the Son of God; for thus the particle *hos* should be here understood. There is also here an allusion to the manifestations of God above the ark in the Tabernacle (see Exod. xxv. 22; Num. vii. 89); and this connects itself with the first clause, "He tabernacled," or "fixed His tent among us." While God dwelt in the Tabernacle, among the Jews, the priests saw His glory; and while Jesus dwelt among men His glory was manifested in His

MATTHEW HENRY

appeared in the holiness and heavenliness of his doctrine; in his miracles; it appeared in the purity, goodness, and beneficence, of his whole conversation. God's goodness is his glory, and he went about doing good. Perhaps the evangelist had a particular regard to the glory of his *transfiguration*, of which he was an eyewitness.

[4] What advantage those he dwelt among had from this. In the old tabernacle wherein God dwelt was the *law*, in *this* was grace; in that were *types*, in this was *truth*. He was *full of grace and truth*, the two great things that fallen man stands in need of. He was full *of grace*, and therefore qualified to intercede for us; and full *of truth*, and therefore fit to instruct us. He had a fulness of knowledge and a fulness of compassion.

Verses 15–18

I. The evangelist begins again to give us John Baptist's testimony concerning Christ, *v.* 15.

1. *How he expressed* his testimony: He *cried*, according to the prediction that he should be *the voice of one crying*. The Old Testament prophets cried aloud, to show people their *sins*; this New Testament prophet cried aloud, to show people their *Saviour*. It was an open *public* testimony, proclaimed, that all manner of persons might take notice of it. He was free and hearty in bearing this testimony. He *cried* as one that was both *well assured* of the truth to which he witnesses and *well affected* to it.

2. What his *testimony* was. He appeals to what he had said at the beginning of his ministry, when he had directed them to expect one that should *come after him*, whose forerunner he was. Now what he had then said he applies to this Jesus whom he had lately baptized: *This was he of whom I spoke*. In *this* he went beyond all the Old Testament prophets that he particularly specified the person.

(1) He had given the preference to this Jesus: *He that comes after me* is preferred before me as the prince or peer that *comes after* is preferred before the harbinger or gentleman-usher that makes way for him. Jesus Christ, who was to be called the *Son of the highest* (Luke i. 32), was preferred before John Baptist, who was to be called only the *prophet of the Highest*, Luke i. 76. John was a great man, yet he was forward to give the preference to him to whom it belonged. All the ministers of Christ must prefer him and his interest before themselves and their own interests. He comes *after me*, and yet is *preferred before me*. God dispenses his gifts according to his good pleasure, and many times crosses hands, as Jacob did. Paul far outstripped those that were in Christ before him.

(2) He gives here a good reason for it: *For he was before me*. In respect of *seniority*: he was *before me*, for he was before Abraham, *ch.* viii. 58. I am but of yesterday, he from eternity. In respect of supremacy: he is my Master, I am his minister and messenger."

II. He returns again to speak of Jesus Christ, and cannot go on with John Baptist's testimony till *v.* 19. The 16th verse has a manifest connection with *v.* 14, where the incarnate Word was said to be *full of grace and truth*. He has a fountain of fulness overflowing: *We all have received*. *All we* believers; as many as received him (*v.* 16), received from him. All true believers receive from Christ's fulness; the best and greatest saints cannot live without him, the meanest and weakest may live by him. This excludes proud boasting, that we have nothing but *we have received it*; and silences perplexing fears, that we want nothing but *we may receive it*.

1. We have received *grace for grace*. Our receivings by Christ are all summed up in this one word, *grace*; so great a gift, so rich, so invaluable; we have received *no less* than grace. It is repeated, *grace for grace*.

(1) The blessing received. It is *grace*; the goodwill of God towards us, and the good work of God in us. God's goodwill works the good work, and then the good work qualifies us for further tokens of his good will. As the cistern receives water from the fulness of the fountain, the branches sap from the fulness of the root, and the air light from the fulness of the sun, so we receive grace from the fulness of Christ.

(2) The manner of its reception: *Grace for grace*. The phrase is singular, and interpreters put different senses upon it, each of which will be of use to illustrate the unsearchable riches of the grace of Christ. *Grace for grace* bespeaks, [1] The *freeness* of this grace. It is grace for grace' sake. We receive grace, not for *our sakes*. It is grace *to us* for the sake of Jesus Christ. [2] The *fulness* of this grace. *Grace for grace* is abundance of grace, grace upon grace. It is a blessing poured out, that there shall not be room to receive it: one grace a pledge of more

JAMIESON, FAUSSET, BROWN

full of grace and truth—So it should read. "He dwelt among us full of grace and truth"; or, in Old Testament phrase, "Mercy and truth," denoting the whole fruit of God's purposes of love towards sinners of mankind, which until now existed only in *promise*, and the *fulfilment* at length of that promise in Christ; in one great word, "*the* SURE MERCIES *of David*" (Isa. 55:3; Acts 13:34; cf. II Sam. 23:5). In His Person all that Grace and Truth which had been floating so long in shadowy forms, and darting into the souls of the poor and needy its broken beams, took everlasting possession of human flesh and filled it full. By this Incarnation of Grace and Truth, the teaching of thousands of years was at once transcended and beggared, and the family of God sprang into Manhood.

15. A SAYING OF THE BAPTIST CONFIRMATORY OF THIS. **after me**—in *official manifestation*. **before me**—*in rank and dignity*.

for he was before me—in *existence;* "His goings forth being from of old, from everlasting" (Mic. 5:2). (Anything lower than this His words cannot mean); i.e., "My Successor is my Superior, for He was my Predecessor." This enigmatic play upon the different senses of the words "before" and "after" was doubtless employed by the Baptist to arrest attention, and rivet the thought; and the Evangelist introduces it just to clinch his own statements.

16-18. SAME SUBJECT CONTINUED. **of his fulness**—of "grace and truth," resuming the thread of vs. 14.

grace for grace—i.e., grace upon grace (so all the best interpreters), in successive communications and larger measures, as each was able to take it in. Observe, the word "truth" is here dropped. "Grace" being the chosen New Testament word for the whole fulness of the new covenant, all that dwells in Christ for men.

ADAM CLARKE

gracious words and miraculous acts. *The only begotten of the Father*. That is, the only Person born of a woman whose human nature never came by the ordinary way of generation, it being a mere creation in the womb of the Virgin by the energy of the Holy Ghost. *Full of grace and truth*. Full of favor, kindness, and mercy to men; teaching the way to the kingdom of God, with all the simplicity, plainness, dignity, and energy of *truth*.

15. *Of him*. The glorious Personage before mentioned. John the Baptist, whose history was well-known to the persons to whom this Gospel came in the beginning, *bare witness . . . and [he] cried*—being deeply convinced of the importance and truth of the subject, he delivered his testimony with the utmost zeal and earnestness, saying, *This was he of whom I spake, He that cometh after me*—for I am no other than the voice of the crier in the wilderness, Isa. xl. 3, the forerunner of the Messiah. *Was before me*. Speaking by the prophets, and warning your fathers to repent and return to God, as I now warn you;

for he was before me—He was from eternity, and from Him I have derived both my being and my ministry.

16. *And of his fulness*. Of the plenitude of His grace and mercy, by which He made an atonement for sin, and of the plenitude of His wisdom and truth, by which the mysteries of heaven have been revealed and the science of eternal truth taught, *have all we received*. All we apostles have received *grace* or mercy to pardon our sins, and *truth* to enable us so to write and speak concerning these things, that those who attend to our testimony shall be unerringly directed in the way of salvation, and with us continue to receive "grace upon grace," one blessing after another, till they are filled with all the fullness of God. It is only necessary to add that John seems here to refer to the gospel as succeeding the law. The law was certainly a dispensation of both *grace* and *truth*, for it pointed out the gracious design of God to save men by Christ Jesus. But the gospel, which had now taken place, introduced that plenitude of *grace* and *truth* to the whole world, which the law had only shadowed forth to the Jewish people, and which they imagined should have been restrained to themselves alone. In the most gracious economy of God, one dispensation of mercy and truth is designed to make way for, and to be followed by, another and a greater. Thus the law succeeded the patriarchal dispensation, and the gospel the law; more and more of the plenitude of the grace of the gospel becomes daily manifest to the genuine followers of Christ; and to those who are faithful unto

MATTHEW HENRY

grace. [3] The *serviceableness* of this grace. *Grace for grace* is grace for the promoting and advancing of grace. Gracious vouchsafements for gracious performances; grace is a talent to be traded with. [4] The *substitution* of New Testament grace *in the room and stead* of Old Testament grace. And this sense is confirmed by what follows (*v.* 17); for the Old Testament had grace in type, the New Testament has grace in truth. This is grace instead of grace. [5] It bespeaks the *augmentation* and *continuance of grace. Grace for grace* is one grace to improve, confirm, and perfect another grace. [6] *Grace for grace* is grace in us answering to grace in him, as the impression upon the wax answers the seal line for line. The grace we receive from Christ *changes us into the same image.*

2. We have received *grace and truth, v.* 17. He had said (*v.* 14) that Christ was *full of grace and truth;* now here he says that by him *grace and truth* came to us. From Christ we *receive grace;* this is a string he delights to harp upon, he cannot go off from it. Two things he further observes in this verse concerning this grace: (1) Its *preference* above the law of Moses: *The law was given by Moses,* and it was a glorious discovery; but the gospel of Christ is a much clearer discovery. That which was given by Moses was purely terrifying and threatening, but that which is given by Jesus Christ has all the beneficial uses of the law, but not the terror, for it is *grace.* The endearments of love are the genius of the gospel, not the affrightments of law and the curse. (2) Its *connection* with truth: *grace and truth.* In the gospel we have the discovery of the greatest *truths* to be embraced by the understanding, as well as of the richest *grace* to be embraced by the will and affections. It is *grace and truth* with reference to the *law* that was *given by Moses.* For it is, [1] The performance of all the Old Testament promises. [2] It is the substance of all the Old Testament types and shadows. He is the *true* paschal lamb, the *true* scape-goat, the true *manna.* They had grace in the picture; we have grace in the person. *Grace and truth came, was made;* the same word that was used (*v.* 3) concerning Christ's *making all things.* By him this *grace and truth* do *consist.*

3. Another thing we receive from Christ is a clear revelation of God to us (*v.* 18): He hath *declared* God to us, whom *no man hath seen at any time.*

(1) The insufficiency of all other discoveries: *No man hath seen God at any time.* This intimates, [1] That the nature of God being *spiritual,* he is invisible to bodily eyes. We have therefore need to *live by faith,* by which we *see him that is invisible,* Heb. xi. 27. [2] That the revelation which God made of himself in the Old Testament was very short and imperfect, in comparison with that which he has made by Christ: *No man hath seen God at any time.* But *this* recommends Christ's holy religion to us that it was founded by one that had seen God, and knew more of his mind that anyone else ever did.

(2) The all-sufficiency of the gospel discovery proved from its author: *The only-begotten Son, who is in the bosom of the Father, he has declared him.* Observe here, How *fit* he was to make this discovery. He is *the only-begotten Son;* and who so likely to know the Father as the Son? or in whom is the Father better known than in the Son? Matt. xi. 27. He is *in the bosom of the Father.* 1. In the bosom of his *special love,* dear to him, in *whom he was well pleased.* 2. In the bosom of his *secret counsels.* None so fit as he to make known God, for none knew his mind as he did.

(3) How *free* he was in making this discovery: *He hath declared.* Not only that which was hid *of God,* but that which was hid *in* God. It signifies a plain, clear, and full discovery. He that runs may now read the will of God and the way of salvation. This is the *grace,* this the *truth,* that came by Jesus Christ.

Verses 19–28

We have here the testimony of John, which he delivered to the messengers who were sent from Jerusalem to examine him.

I. Who they were that sent to him, and who they were that were sent. They that sent to him were *the Jews at Jerusalem.* One would think that they should have understood the times so well as to know that the Messiah was at hand, and therefore have known him that was his forerunner, but, instead of this, they sent messengers to *cross questions* with him. Secular learning, honour, and power, seldom dispose men's minds to the reception of divine light. They that were sent were, (1) *Priests and Levites.* John Baptist was himself a priest of the seed of Aaron, and therefore it was not fit that he should be examined by any but priests. (2) They were *of the Pharisees* that thought they needed no repentance.

II. On what errand they were sent; it was to enquire

JAMIESON, FAUSSET, BROWN

17. For . . .—The Law elicits the consciousness of sin and the need of redemption; it only typifies the reality. The Gospel, on the contrary, actually communicates reality and power from above (cf. Rom. 6:14). Hence Paul terms the Old Testament "shadow," while he calls the New Testament "substance" (Col. 2:17), [OLSHAUSEN].

18. No man—"No one," in the widest sense. **hath seen God**—by immediate gaze, or direct intuition.

in the bosom of the Father—A remarkable expression, used only here, presupposing *the Son's conscious existence distinct from the Father,* and expressing *His immediate and most endeared access to, and absolute acquaintance with, Him.* **he**—emphatic; *q.d.,* "He and He only hath declared Him," because He only *can.*

19-36. THE BAPTIST'S TESTIMONY TO CHRIST. **19. record**—testimony. **the Jews**—i.e., the heads of the nation, the members of the Sanhedrim. *In this peculiar sense our Evangelist seems always to use the term.*

ADAM CLARKE

death, a heaven full of eternal glory will soon succeed to the grace of the gospel.

17. *The law was given by Moses.* Moses received the law from God, and through him it was given to the Jews, Acts vii. 38. *But grace and truth.* Which he had already mentioned, and which were to be the subject of the book which he was now writing, *came* to all mankind "through Jesus Christ," who is the Mediator of the new covenant, as Moses was of the old, Heb. viii. 6; ix. 15; Gal. iii. 19. *Jesus Christ.* "Jesus the Christ, the Messiah," or anointed Prophet, Priest, and King, sent from heaven.

18. *No man hath seen God at any time.* Moses and others heard His voice, and saw the cloud and the fire, which were the symbols of His presence; but such a manifestation of God as had now taken place, in the person of Jesus Christ, had never before been exhibited to the world. It is likely that the word *seen,* here, is put for "known," as in chap. iii. 32; 1 John iii. 2, 6; and 3 John, v. 11; and this sense the latter clause of the verse seems to require—*No man,* how highly soever favored, "hath fully known God, at any time," in any nation or age.

The only begotten Son, which is in the bosom of the Father, who was intimately acquainted with all the counsels of the Most High, *he hath declared him,* hath announced the divine oracles unto men; for in this sense the word is used by the best Greek writers. "Lying in the bosom" is spoken of in reference to the Asiatic custom of reclining while at meals. The person who was next the other was said to "lie in his bosom"; and he who had this place in reference to the master of the feast was supposed to share his peculiar regards, and to be in a state of the utmost favor and intimacy with him.

19. *And this is the record of John.* He persisted in this assertion, testifying to the Jews that this Jesus was *the Christ.*

concerning John and *his baptism.* They did not send for John; they thought it was good to keep him at a distance. They enquire concerning him, 1. To satisfy their curiosity. The doctrine of repentance was to them strange doctrine. 2. It was to show their authority. 3. It was with a design to *suppress* him and silence him.

III. What was the answer he gave them, and his account, both concerning himself and concerning his baptism.

1. Concerning himself. They asked him, *Thou, who art thou?* John's appearing in the world was surprising. His spirit, his converse, his doctrine, had something in them which commanded and gained respect; but he did not give out himself to be *some great one.* He was more industrious to *do good* than to *appear great.* He answers their interrogatory,

Negatively. He was not that great one whom some took him to be. God's faithful witnesses stand more upon their guard *against undue respect* than against *unjust contempt.* John disowns himself to be *the Christ* (*v.* 20): *He said, I am not the Christ.* Observe how emphatically this is here expressed concerning John: He *confessed, and denied not, but confessed;* it denotes his vehemence and constancy in making this protestation. *I am not the Christ, not I;* another is at hand, who is he, but I am not, His disowning himself to be the Christ is called his *confessing* and not *denying* Christ. He disowns himself to be Elias, *v.* 21. The Jews expected the person of Elias to return from heaven. Hearing of John's character, doctrine, and baptism, and observing that he appeared as one dropped from heaven, it is no wonder that they were ready to take him for this Elijah; but he disowned this honour too. He was indeed prophesied of under the name of Elijah (Mal. iv. 5), and he came in the *spirit and power of Elias* (Luke i. 17), and was the Elias that was to come (Matt. xi. 14); but he was not the person of Elias. He was the Elias that God had promised, not the Elias that they foolishly dreamed of. Elias did come, and *they knew him not* (Matt. xvii. 12); because they had promised themselves such an Elias as God never promised them. He disowns himself to be that *prophet. First,* He was not *that* prophet which Moses said *the Lord* would *raise up to them of their brethren. Secondly,* He was not such a prophet as they expected and wished for, who would interpose in public affairs, and rescue them from under the Roman yoke. *Thirdly,* He was not one of the old prophets raised from the dead.

The committee sent to examine him pressed for a positive answer (*v.* 22), urging the authority of *those that sent them*: "*Tell us, What art thou?* that we may *give an answer* to those that sent us." John was looked upon as a man of sincerity, and therefore they believed he would be fair and above-board, and give a plain answer to a plain question: *What sayest thou of thyself?* And he did so, *I am the voice of one crying in the wilderness.* He gives his answer in the words of scripture, to show that the scripture was fulfilled in him. He gives his answer in very humble, modest, self-denying expressions. He chooses to apply that scripture to himself which bespeaks him little: *I am the voice, mere voice.* He gives such an account of himself as might awaken them to hearken to him; for he *was the voice* (see Isa. xl. 3), a voice to alarm, an articulate voice to instruct. Ministers are but the *voice,* by which God is pleased to communicate his mind. *First,* He was a *human* voice. The people were prepared to receive the law by the voice of thunders; but they were prepared for the gospel by the voice of a man like ourselves, *a still small voice. Secondly,* He was the voice of *one crying,* which denotes, 1. His *earnestness* and *importunity*; he *cried aloud, and did not spare.* Ministers must preach as those that are in earnest. Those words are not likely to *thaw* the hearers' hearts that *freeze* between the speaker's lips. 2. His *open publication* of the doctrine he preached. *Thirdly,* It was in the *wilderness* that this voice was crying; in a place of silence and solitude, out of the noise of the world and the hurry of its business. *Fourthly,* That which he cried was, *Make straight the way of the Lord.* He came to *rectify* the mistakes of people concerning the ways of God. The scribes and Pharisees had made them crooked. Now John Baptist calls people to return to the original rule.

2. Here is his testimony concerning *his baptism.* (1) The enquiry which the committee made about it: *Why baptizest thou, if thou be not the Christ, nor Elias, nor that prophet? v.* 25. They readily apprehended baptism to be fitly and properly used as a sacred rite or ceremony, to signify the cleansing of them from the pollutions of their former state. That sign was made use of in the Christian church. Christ did not affect novelty, nor should his ministers.

A. T. ROBERTSON:

"When the Jews sent unto him" (*hote apesteilan pros auton hoi Ioudaioi*). John, writing in Ephesus near the close of the first century long after the destruction of Jerusalem, constantly uses the phrase "the Jews" as descriptive of the people as distinct from the Gentile world and from the followers of Christ (at first Jews also). Often he uses it of the Jewish leaders and rulers in particular who soon took a hostile attitude toward both John and Jesus. Here it is the Jews from Jerusalem who sent (*apesteilan,* first aorist active indicative of *apostello*). "Priests and Levites" (*hiereis kai Leueitas*). Sadducees these were. In verse 24 the author explains that it was the Pharisees who sent the Sadducees. The Synoptics throw a flood of light on this circumstance, for in Matt. 3:7 we are told that the Baptist called the Pharisees and Sadducees "offspring of vipers" (Luke 3:7). Popular interest in John grew till people were wondering "in their hearts concerning John whether haply he were the Christ" (Luke 3:15). So the Sanhedrin finally sent a committee to John to get his own view of himself, but the Pharisees saw to it that Sadducees were sent. "Who art thou?" (*su tis ei*). Direct question preserved and note proleptic position of *su,* "Thou, who art thou?" The committee from the Sanhedrin put the question sharply up to John to define his claims concerning the Messiah.

—*Word Pictures in the New Testament*

20. confessed . . .—i.e., While many were ready to hail him as the Christ, he neither gave the slightest ground for such views, nor the least entertainment to them. **21. Elias**—in His own proper person. **that prophet**—announced in Deuteronomy 18:15, etc., about whom they seem not to have been agreed whether he were the same with the Messiah or no.

G. CAMPBELL MORGAN:

These men were intelligent; they were sent by the Pharisees, trained in the lore of their own religion. They began by suggesting, "Art thou the Christ?" The reply was clear, "I am not the Christ." Then they went back to Malachi, and they said, "Malachi said that before the Christ comes Elijah would come again. Are you Elijah?" He said, "I am not." Then they went back further. They went to Moses and said, "Art thou the prophet?" The interpretation of that question is found in Deuteronomy 18:15. Moses had said that God should one day raise up a prophet like unto him. These men were employing their own Scriptures. Art thou the Messiah? Art thou Elijah? Well then, art thou the prophet? Every time the answer was a denial. Then they said, "Who art thou? that we may give an answer to them that sent us." We cannot go back with negatives. Tell us, "Who art thou? What sayest thou of thyself?"

His reply was very suggestive. It implies that they had knowledge of their own Scriptures; they had the messianic hope; they were familiar with Malachi; and they knew the prediction of Moses. So he took them to the great central prophecy of Isaiah: "I am the voice of one crying in the wilderness, Make straight the way of the Lord, as said Isaiah the prophet."

Then these men did what men often do when they are surprised. They raised a ritualistic technicality. They said, "Why then baptizest thou, if thou art not the Christ, neither Elijah, neither the prophet?" In reply he interpreted his mission. "I baptize in water." That is all. They knew what his baptism in water had meant. They knew what had preceded it in his preaching, and what baptism in water at his hands had signified. He had called them to repent and be baptized unto the remission of sins; repentance, the confession of guilt, and baptism, a sign of the need for remission.

—*The Gospel According to John*

25. Why baptizest thou, if not . . .—Thinking he disclaimed any special connection with Messiah's kingdom, they demand his right to gather disciples by baptism.

20. *He confessed, and denied not; but confessed.* A common mode of Jewish phraseology. John renounces himself, that Jesus may be All in All.

21. *Art thou Elias?* The scribes themselves had taught that Elijah was to come before the Messiah. See Matt. xvii. 10; and this belief of theirs they supported by a literal construction of Mal. iv. 5. *Art thou that prophet?* The prophet spoken of by Moses, Deut. xviii. 15, 18. This text they had also misunderstood, for the prophet or teacher promised by Moses was no other than the Messiah himself. See Acts iii. 22. But the Jews had a tradition that Jeremiah was to return to life, and restore the pot of manna, the ark of the covenant, etc., which he had hidden that the Babylonians might not get them. Besides this, they had a general expectation that all the prophets should come to life in the days of the Messiah. *I am not.* I am not the prophet which you expect, nor Elijah—though he was the Elijah that was to come; for in the spirit and power of that eminent prophet he came, proclaiming the necessity of reformation in Israel. See Matt. xi. 14; xvii. 10-13.

22. *That we may give an answer to them that sent us.* These Pharisees were probably a deputation from the grand Sanhedrin, the members of which, hearing of the success of the Baptist's preaching, were puzzled to know what to make of him, and seriously desired to hear from himself what he professed to be.

23. *I am the voice of one crying.* See the notes on Matt. iii. 3; Mark i. 4-5.

25. *Why baptizest thou then?* Baptism was a very common ceremony among the Jews, who never received a proselyte into the full enjoyment of a Jew's privileges till he was both baptized and circumcised. But such baptisms were never performed except by an ordinance of the Sanhedrin, or in the presence of three

MATTHEW HENRY

They expected it would be used in the days of the Messiah. It is taken for granted that Christ, and Elias, and *that prophet*, would baptize, when they came to *purify a polluted world*. Divine grace has provided for the cleansing of this new world *from its filth*. They would therefore know by what authority John baptized. His denying himself to be Elias, or *that prophet*, subjected him to this further question, *Why baptizest thou?*

(2) The account he gave of it, *v.* 26, 27. He owned himself to be only the minister of the outward sign: "*I baptize with water*, and that is all. I cannot confer the spiritual grace signified by it." He directed them to one who was greater than himself, and would do that for them which he could not do. John gave the same account to this committee that he had given to the people (*v.* 15): *This was he of whom I spoke*. He tells them of Christ's *presence among them* now at this time: *There stands one among you, whom you know not*. Christ stood among the common people, and was as one of them. Much true worth lies hid in this world; obscurity is often the lot of real excellency. God himself is often nearer to us than we are aware of. The kingdom of God was abroad and already *among them*, Luke xvii. 21. He tells them of Christ's *preference above himself*: He comes *after me*, and yet is *preferred before me*, "Whose *shoe-latchet I am not worthy to loose*." If so great a man as John accounted himself unworthy of the honour of being near Christ, how unworthy then should we account ourselves! Now, one would think, these chief priests and Pharisees, should presently have asked who, and where, this excellent person was. No, they came to molest John, not to receive any instructions from him. They might have known Christ, and would not. Notice is taken of the place where all this was done: *In Bethabara beyond Jordan*, *v.* 28. Bethabara signifies the *house of passage*; there was opened the way into the gospel state by Jesus Christ. He made this confession in the same place where he was *baptizing*, that all those who attended his baptism might be witnesses of it.

Verses 29-36

We have in these verses an account of John's testimony concerning Jesus Christ, which he witnessed to his own disciples that followed him. As soon as ever Christ was *baptized* he was immediately hurried into the wilderness, to be *tempted*; and there he was forty days. During his absence John had continued to bear testimony to him, but now at last he *sees Jesus coming to him*. Now here are *two testimonies* borne by John to Christ, but those two *agree in one*.

I. Here is his testimony to Christ, and here four things are witnessed by him concerning Christ.

1. That he is *the Lamb of God which taketh away the sin of the world*, *v.* 29. Let us learn here,

(1) That Jesus Christ is the *Lamb of God*, which bespeaks him the great sacrifice, by which atonement is made for sin, and man reconciled to God. Of all the legal sacrifices he chooses to allude to the *lambs* that were offered with a special reference to the *daily sacrifice*, which was offered every morning and evening continually, and that was always a *lamb*; to the *paschal lamb*, the blood of which secured the Israelites from the stroke of the destroying angel. Christ is *our passover*. Christ, who was to make atonement for sin, is called the *Lamb of God*.

(2) That Jesus Christ, as the *Lamb of God, takes away the sin of the world*. John Baptist had called people to repent of their sins, in order to the remission of them. Now here he shows how and by whom that remission was to be expected. This ground of hope we have—Jesus Christ is *the Lamb of God*. [1] He *takes away sin*. He came to take away the guilt of sin by the merit of his death. To take away the power of sin by the Spirit of his grace. *He is taking away* the sin of the world, which denotes it a continued act. He is always *taking away* sin. [2] He takes away the *sin of the world*; purchases pardon for all of what country, nation, or language, soever they be. The Lamb of God was offered to be a propitiation for the *sin of the whole world*; see 1 John ii. 2. If Christ takes away the sin of the world, then why not my sin? [3] He does this by *taking it upon himself*. He is the Lamb of God, that *bears the sin of the world*; so the margin reads it. He bears it *from us*; he *bore the sin of many*, as the scape-goat had the sins of Israel put upon his head, Lev. xvi. 21. God has found out a way of abolishing the sin, and yet sparing the sinner, by making his Son *sin for us*.

(3) That it is our duty to *behold* the Lamb of God thus taking away the *sin of the world*. See him taking away sin, and let that increase our hatred of sin. Let it increase our love to Christ.

2. That this was he of whom he had spoken before (*v.* 30, 31): *This is he of whom I said, After me cometh*

JAMIESON, FAUSSET, BROWN

26. there standeth—This must have been spoken after the baptism of Christ, and possibly just after His temptation (see on vs. 29).

28. Bethabara—Rather, Bethany (according to nearly all the best and most ancient MSS.); not the Bethany of Lazarus, but another of the same name, and distinguished from it as lying "beyond Jordan," on the east.

29. seeth Jesus—fresh, probably, from the scene of the temptation. **coming unto him**—as to congenial company (Acts 4:23), and to receive from him His first greeting. **and saith**—catching a sublime inspiration at the sight of Him approaching. **the Lamb of God**—the one God-ordained, God-gifted sacrificial offering.

that taketh away—*taketh up* and *taketh away*. The word signifies both, as does the corresponding Hebrew word. Applied to sin, it means to *be chargeable with the guilt of it* (Exod. 28:38; Lev. 5:1; Ezek. 18:20), and to *bear it away* (as often). In the Levitical victims both ideas met, as they do in Christ, the people's guilt being viewed as *transferred* to them, *avenged* in their death, and so *borne away* by them (Lev. 4:15; 16:15, 21, 22; and cf. Isa. 53:6-12; II Cor. 5:21). **the sin**—The *singular* number being used to mark the *collective burden* and *all-embracing efficacy*. **of the world**—not of Israel only, for whom the typical victims were exclusively offered. Wherever there shall live a sinner throughout the wide world, sinking under that burden too heavy for him to bear, he shall find in this "Lamb of God," a shoulder equal to the weight. The right note was struck at the first—balm, doubtless, to Christ's own spirit; nor was ever after, or ever will be, a more glorious utterance.

ADAM CLARKE

magistrates. Besides, they never baptized any Jew or Jewess, nor even those who were the children of their proselytes; for, as all these were considered as born in the covenant, they had no need of baptism, which was used only as an introductory rite. Now, as John had in this respect altered the common custom so very essentially, admitting to his baptism the Jews in general, the Sanhedrin took it for granted that no man had authority to make such changes, unless especially commissioned from on high; and that only *the prophet*, or *Elijah*, or the *Messiah* himself could have authority to act as John did.

26. *I baptize with water*. See on Mark i. 8. I use the common form, though I direct the baptized to a different end, viz., that they shall repent of their sins and believe in the Messiah. *There standeth one among you*. That is, the Person whose forerunner I am is now dwelling in the land of Judea and will shortly make His appearance among you. Christ was not present when John spoke thus, as may be seen from v. 29.

27. *Is preferred before me*. "Who was before me." This clause is wanting in a few of the MSS. and versions, and in some of the primitive fathers.

28. *These things were done in Bethabara*. It is very probable that the word *Bethany* should be inserted here instead of *Bethabara*. This reading, in the judgment of the best critics, is the genuine one. It is supported by many authorities, including some of the most eminent of the primitive fathers, before the time of Origen, who is supposed to have first changed the reading. *Bethabara* signifies literally "the house of passage," and is thought to be the place where the Israelites passed the river Jordan under Joshua. There was a place called *Bethany*, about two miles from Jerusalem, at the foot of the Mount of Olives. But there was another of the same name, beyond Jordan, in the tribe of Reuben. It was probably of this that the Evangelist speaks; and Origen, not knowing of this second Bethany, altered the reading to *Bethabara*.

29. *The next day*. The day after that on which the Jews had been with John, v. 19. *Behold the Lamb of God*. This was said in allusion to what was spoken in Isa. liii. 7. Jesus was the true Lamb or Sacrifice required and appointed by God, of which those offered daily in the Tabernacle and Temple, Exod. xxix. 38-39, and especially the paschal lamb, were only the types and representatives. See Exod. xii. 4-5; 1 Cor. v. 7. The continual morning and evening sacrifice of a lamb, under the Jewish law, was intended to point out the continual efficacy of the blood of atonement; for even at the throne of God, Jesus Christ is ever represented as a Lamb newly slain, Rev. v. 6. But John, pointing to Christ, calls Him emphatically *the Lamb of God*. All the lambs which had been hitherto offered had been furnished by men; this was provided by God, as the only sufficient and available Sacrifice for the sin of the world.

MATTHEW HENRY

a man. This honour John had above all the prophets, that, whereas they spoke of him as one that should come, he saw him already come. Such a difference there is between present *faith* and future *vision.* He refers to what he had himself said of him before: *This is he of whom I said.* Though Christ appeared not in any external pomp or grandeur, yet John is not ashamed to own, *This is he whom I* meant, who is *preferred before me.* And it was necessary that John should thus show them the person, otherwise they could not have believed that one who made so mean a figure should be he of whom John had spoken such great things. He protests against any confederacy or combination with this Jesus: *And I knew him not.* There was no acquaintance at all between them; John had no personal knowledge of Jesus till he saw him come to his baptism. They who are taught believe and confess one whom they have not seen, and blessed are they who *yet have believed.* The great intention of John's ministry and baptism was to introduce Jesus Christ. That he should be *made manifest to Israel, therefore am I come baptizing with water.* Though John did not know Jesus by face, yet he knew that he should be made manifest. We may know the certainty of that which yet we do not fully know the nature and intention of. The general assurance John had that Christ *should be made manifest* served to carry him with diligence and resolution through his work: *Therefore am I come.* God reveals himself to his people by degrees. At first, John knew no more concerning Christ but that he should be made manifest; and now he is favoured with a sight of him.

3. That this was he *upon whom the Spirit descended from heaven like a dove.* For the confirming of his testimony concerning Christ, he here vouches the extraordinary appearance at his baptism, in which God himself bore witness to him. We are here told (*v.* 32–34),

(1) That John Baptist saw it: He *bore record*; attested it, with all the seriousness and solemnity of *witness-bearing.* He made affidavit of it: *I saw the Spirit descending* from heaven. John could not see the *Spirit,* but he saw the dove which was a sign and representation of the Spirit. God's children are made manifest by their *graces*; their glories are reserved for their future state. He descended *like a dove*—an emblem of meekness, and wildness, and gentleness. The dove brought the olive-branch of peace, Gen. viii. 11. The Spirit that descended upon Christ *abode upon him.* The *Spirit did not* move him at times, but *at all times.*

(2) That he was *told to expect it.* It was an *instituted* sign given him before, by which he might certainly know it (*v.* 33): *I knew him not. He that sent me to baptize* gave me this sign, *Upon whom thou shalt see the Spirit descending, the same is he.* See here what sure grounds John went upon. He did not run *without sending*: God *sent him to baptize.* He had a warrant from heaven for what he did. When a minister's call is clear, his comfort is sure, though his success is not always so. He did not run *without speeding*; for, when he was sent to *baptize with water,* he was directed to one that should *baptize with the Holy Ghost.* It is a great comfort to Christ's ministers, that he whose ministers they are can put life, and soul, and power into their ministrations; can speak to the heart what they speak to the ear, and *breathe* upon the dry bones to which they *prophesy.* God had before given him a sign: "On whom thou shalt see the Spirit descend, *that same is he.*" This not only prevented any mistakes, but gave him boldness in his testimony. When he had such assurance as this given him, he could speak with assurance.

4. That he is *the Son of God.* This is the conclusion of John's testimony, that in which all the particulars centre (*v.* 34): *I saw, and bore record, that this is the Son of God.* The truth asserted is, *that this is the Son of God.* This was the peculiar Christian creed, that Jesus is the Son of God (Matt. xvi. 16), and here is the first framing of it. John's testimony to it: "*I saw, and bore record.*" What he *saw* he was forward to *bear record* of. What he *bore record* of was what he *saw.* Christ's witnesses were eyewitnesses.

II. Here is John's testimony to Christ, the next day after, *v.* 35, 36. *John stood looking upon Jesus as he walked.* It should seem, John was in close conversation with *two* of his disciples. He saw Jesus *walking.* He was *looking upon Jesus*; he looked steadfastly, and fixed his eyes upon him. Those that would lead others to Christ must be diligent and frequent in the *contemplation* of him themselves. 2. He repeated the same testimony which he had given to Christ the day before. Christ's sacrifice for the taking away of the sin of the world ought especially to be insisted upon by all good ministers: Christ, the Lamb of God, *Christ and him crucified.* 3. He intended this especially

JAMIESON, FAUSSET, BROWN

31-34. knew him not—Living mostly apart, the one at Nazareth, the other in the Judean desert—to prevent all appearance of collusion, John only knew that at a definite time after his own call, his Master would show Himself. As He drew near for baptism one day, the last of all the crowd, the spirit of the Baptist heaving under a divine presentiment that the moment had at length arrived, and an air of unwonted serenity and dignity, not without traits, probably, of the family features, appearing in this Stranger, the Spirit said to him as to Samuel of his youthful type, "Arise, anoint Him, for this is He!" (I Sam. 16:12). But *the* sign which he was told to expect was the visible descent of the Spirit upon Him as He emerged out of the baptismal water. *Then,* catching up the voice from heaven, "he saw and bare record that this is the Son of God."

A. B. SIMPSON:

This was the visible descent of the Holy Spirit upon Jesus, in the form of a dove, and was designed to be an open and manifest testimony to His messiahship and divinity that no one could gainsay. It was also, as we learn from the other evangelists, accompanied by the voice of God, proclaiming, "This is my beloved Son, in whom I am well pleased." To John himself this sign had already been promised as the special token of the Messiah. The voice of God had whispered to him, "Upon whom thou shalt see the Spirit descending and remaining on him, the same is he which baptizeth with the Holy Ghost." This is ever still the highest testimony that God can give to any of His servants. The same Holy Spirit is the witness of Christianity by His unceasing manifestations of grace and power in the ministry of God's servants and the lives of His children. The form in which the Holy Spirit came to Christ, as a dove, suggests the idea of gentleness, peace and love as the special attributes of His life and ministry.

—*Christ in the Bible*

35. John stood—"was standing," at his accustomed place. **36. looking**—having fixed his eyes, with significant gaze, on Jesus. **as he walked**—but not now *to him.* To have done this once (see on vs. 29) was humility enough [BENGEL]. **Behold . . .**—The repetition of that wonderful proclamation, in identical terms and without another word, could only have been meant as a gentle hint to go after Him—as they did.

ADAM CLARKE

31. *And I knew him not.* John did not know our Lord personally, and perhaps had never seen Him, at the time he spoke the words in v. 15. Nor is it any wonder that the Baptist should have been unacquainted with Christ, as he had spent thirty years in the hill country of Hebron, and our Lord remained in a state of great privacy in the obscure city of Nazareth, in the extreme borders of Galilee. *But that he should be made manifest to Israel.* One design of My publicly baptizing Jesus was that He, coming to my baptism, should be shown to be what He is, by some extraordinary sign from heaven.

32. *I saw the Spirit descending.* See the notes on Matt. iii. 16-17.

33. *He that sent me . . . said unto me.* From this we may clearly perceive that John had a most intimate acquaintance with the Divine Being; and received not only his call and mission at first, but every subsequent direction, by immediate, unequivocal inspiration.

35. *The next day.* After that mentioned in v. 29. *Two of his disciples.* One of them was Andrew, v. 40, and it is very likely that John himself was the other; in everything in which he might receive honor he studiously endeavors to conceal his own name.

36. *And looking upon Jesus.* "Attentively beholding"—to view with steadfastness and attention. He who desires to discover the glories and excellencies of this Lamb of God must thus look on Him. At first sight He appears only as a man among men, and as dying in testimony to the truth, as many others have died. But on a

MATTHEW HENRY

for his two disciples that stood with him; he was willing to turn them over to Christ. He did not reckon that he lost those disciples who went over from him to Christ, any more than the schoolmaster reckons that scholar lost whom he sends to the university. John gathered disciples, not for himself, but for Christ. Humble, generous souls will give others their due praise without fear of diminishing themselves by it.

Verses 37–42

We have here the turning over of two disciples from John to Jesus, and one of them fetching in a third, and these are the first-fruits of Christ's disciples.

I. Andrew and another with him were the two that John Baptist had directed to Christ, *v.* 37. Who the other was we are not told.

1. Here is their readiness to go over to Christ. They heard him speak of Christ as the *Lamb of God, that takes away the sin of the world*, and this made them *follow him*.

2. The kind notice Christ took of them, *v.* 38. He was soon aware of them, and *turned*, and *saw them following*. Christ takes early cognizance of the first motions of a soul towards him. He did not stay till they begged leave to speak with him, but spoke first. When there is communion between a soul and Christ, it is he that *begins the discourse*. He saith unto them, "*What seek ye?*" It is a kind invitation of them into his acquaintance: "Come, what have you to say to me?" Those whose business it is to instruct people in the affairs of their souls should be humble, and mild, and easy of access. The question Christ put to them is what we should all put to ourselves when we begin to follow Christ: "*What seek ye?* What do we design and desire? Do we seek a teacher, ruler, and reconciler? In following Christ, do we seek the favour of God and eternal life?"

3. Their modest enquiry concerning the place of his abode: *Rabbi, where dwellest thou?* In calling him *Rabbi*, they intimated that their design in coming to him was to be *taught by him*; *rabbi* signifies a *master*, a teaching master. These came to Christ to be his scholars, so must all those that apply themselves to him. In asking *where he dwelt*, they intimate a desire to be better acquainted with him. They would attend him at some seasonable time, when he should appoint. Civility and good manners well become those who follow Christ. They hoped to have more from him than they could have now by the way. They resolved to make a business, not a by-business of conversing with Christ. Those that have had some communion with Christ cannot but desire a *further communion* with him; a *fixed communion* with him; where they may sit down at his feet. It is not enough to take a turn with Christ now and then, but we must *lodge with him*.

4. The courteous invitation Christ gave them to his lodgings: *He saith unto them, Come and see.* He invites them to come to his lodgings: the nearer we approach to Christ, the more we see of his beauty. Deceivers maintain their interest in their followers by keeping them at a distance, but that which Christ desired to recommend him to the esteem and affections of his followers was that they would *come and see*. He invites them to come *immediately* and without delay. There is never a better time. It is best taking people when they are in a good mind; strike while the iron is hot. It is wisdom to embrace the present opportunities: *Now is the accepted time*.

5. Their cheerful and (no doubt) thankful acceptance of his invitation: *They came and saw where he dwelt*, and *abode with him that day*. They readily went along with him. Gracious souls cheerfully accept Christ's gracious invitations. It is good being where Christ is, wherever it be. They *abode with him that day* ("Master, it is good to be here"); and he bade them welcome. It was about the tenth hour.

II. Andrew brought his brother Peter to Christ. Andrew had the honour first to be acquainted with Christ, and to be the instrument of bringing Peter to him.

1. The *information* which Andrew gave to Peter.

(1) *He first finds his own brother Simon;* his finding implies his seeking him. *He first findeth Simon* who came only to attend on John, but has his expectations out-done; he meets with Jesus.

(2) He told him whom they had found: *We have found the Messias.* He speaks *humbly*; not, "I have found," but "*We* have," rejoicing that he had shared with others in it. He speaks *exultingly*: *We have found.* He proclaims it, for he knows that he shall have never the less in Christ for others sharing. He speaks *intelligently*: *We have found the Messias*, which was more than had yet been said. He speaks more clearly concerning Christ than ever *his teacher* had done.

(3) He *brought him to Jesus*, brought him to the

JAMIESON, FAUSSET, BROWN

37-51. First Gathering of Disciples—John, Andrew, Simon, Philip, Nathanael.

38. What seek ye—gentle, winning question, remarkable as the Redeemer's *first public utterance.* (See on Matt. 12:18-20.) **where dwellest thou**—i.e., "That is a question we cannot answer in a moment; but had we Thy company for a calm hour in private, gladly should we open our burden."

39. Come and see—His *second utterance,* more winning still.

tenth hour—not 10 A.M. (as some), according to *Roman,* but 4 P.M., according to *Jewish* reckoning, which John follows. The hour is mentioned to show why they stayed out the day with him—because little of it remained. **40. One . . . was Andrew**—The other was doubtless our Evangelist himself. His great sensitiveness is touchingly shown in his representation of this first contact with the Lord; the circumstances are present to him in the minutest details; he still remembers the very hour. But "he reports no particulars of those discourses of the Lord by which he was bound to Him for the whole of His life; he allows everything personal to retire" [Olshausen]. **Peter's brother**—and the elder of the two. **41. have found the Messias**—The previous preparation of their simple hearts under the Baptist's ministry, made quick work of this blessed conviction, while others hesitated till doubt settled into obduracy. *So it is still.* **42. brought him to Jesus**—Happy brothers that thus do to each other!

ADAM CLARKE

more attentive consideration He appears to be no less than God manifest in the flesh, and by His death making an atonement for the sin of the world. *Behold the Lamb of God!* By this the Baptist designed to direct the attention of his own disciples to Jesus, not only as the great Sacrifice for the sin of the world, but also as the complete Teacher of heavenly truth.

38. *What seek ye?* These disciples might have felt some embarrassment in addressing our blessed Lord, after hearing the character which the Baptist gave of Him; to remove or prevent this, He graciously accosts them, and gives them an opportunity of explaining themselves to Him. Such questions, we may conceive, the blessed Jesus still puts to those who in simplicity of heart desire an acquaintance with Him. A question of this nature we may profitably ask ourselves: *What seek ye?* In this place? In the company you frequent? In the conversation in which you engage? In the affairs with which you are occupied? In the works which you perform? *Rabbi.* "Teacher." Behold the modesty of these disciples—we wish to be scholars; we are ignorant—we desire to be taught; we believe Thou art a Teacher come from God. *Where dwellest thou?* That we may come and receive Thy instructions.

39. *Come and see.* If those who know not the salvation of God would *come* at the command of Christ, they should soon *see* that with Him is the fountain of life, and in His light they should see light. *The tenth hour.* Generally supposed to be about what we call four o'clock in the afternoon. According to chap. xi. 9, the Jews reckoned twelve hours in the day; and of course each hour of the day, thus reckoned, must have been something longer or shorter, according to the different times of the year in that climate. The sixth hour with them answered to our twelve o'clock, as appears from what Josephus says in his life, chap. liv. "That on the Sabbath day it was the rule for the Jews to go to dinner at the sixth hour." Dr. Macknight, however, is of opinion that the Evangelist is to be understood as speaking of the Roman hour, which was ten o'clock in the morning; and, as the Evangelist remarks, *They . . . abode with him that day,* it implies that there was a considerable portion of time spent with our Lord. But had it been the Jewish tenth hour, it would have been useless to remark their abiding with Him that day, as there were only two hours of it still remaining.

41. *Findeth his own brother Simon.* Every man who has been brought to an acquaintance with God should endeavor to bring at least another with him; and his first attention should be fixed upon those of his own household.

MATTHEW HENRY	JAMIESON, FAUSSET, BROWN	ADAM CLARKE

fountain-head. Now this was an instance of true love to his brother. We ought with a particular concern and application to seek the spiritual welfare of those that are related to us; for their relation to us adds both to the *obligation* and to the *opportunity* of doing good to their souls. It was an effect of his day's conversation with Christ. Hereby it appeared that Andrew had *been with Jesus* that he was so full of him. He knew there was enough in Christ for all; and, having tasted that he is gracious, he could not rest till those he loved had tasted it too. True grace hates monopolies, and loves not to eat its morsels alone.

2. The *entertainment* which Jesus Christ gave to Peter, *v.* 42.

(1) Christ called him by his name: *When Jesus beheld him, he said, Thou art Simon, the son of Jona.* Some observe the signification of these names: *Simon—obedient, Jona—a dove.* An obedient dove-like spirit qualifies us to be the disciples of Christ.

(2) He gave him a new name: *Cephas.* His giving him a name intimates *Christ's favour* to him. By this Christ adopted him into his family as one of his own. The name which he gave him bespeaks his *fidelity* to Christ: *Thou shalt be called Cephas* (that is Hebrew for *a stone:*), *which is by interpretation Peter.* Peter's natural temper was stiff, and hardy, and resolute, which I take to be the principal reason why Christ called him *Cephas—a stone.* When Christ afterwards prayed for him, that his faith might not fail, that so he might be firm to Christ himself, then he *made him* what he here called him, *Cephas—a stone.* Those that come to Christ must come with a fixed resolution to be firm and constant to him, *like a stone,* and it is by his grace that they are so.

Verses 43–51

We have here the call of Philip and Nathanael.

I. Philip was called immediately by Christ himself, not as Andrew, who was directed to Christ by John or Peter, who was invited by his brother. God has various methods of bringing his chosen ones home to himself. *Jesus findeth Philip.* Christ sought us, and found us, before we made any enquiries after him. The name *Philip* is of Greek origin, and much used among the Gentiles, yet Christ changed not his name. He was called the *day following.* When work is to be done for God, we must not *lose a day.* Jesus *would go forth into Galilee.* Christ will find out all those that are given to him. Philip was brought to be a disciple by the power of Christ going along with that word, *Follow me.* We are told that Philip was of Bethsaida, and Andrew and Peter were so too, *v.* 44. Bethsaida was a wicked place (Matt. xi. 21), yet even *there* was a remnant, according to the election of grace.

II. Nathanael was invited to Christ by Philip.

1. What passed between Philip and Nathanael.

(1) The joyful news that Philip brought to Nathanael, *v.* 45. Philip, though newly come to an acquaintance with Christ himself, yet steps aside to seek Nathanael. O, saith Philip, *we have found him of whom Moses and the prophets did write.* What a transport of joy Philip was in, upon this new acquaintance with Christ: "We have found him whom we have so long wished and waited for; at last, *he is come, he is come,* and *we* have found him!" What an advantage it was to him that he was so well acquainted with the scriptures of the Old Testament, which prepared his mind for the reception of evangelical light. It was his weakness to say, *We have found him,* for Christ found them before they found Christ. He did not yet *apprehend,* as Paul did, how he was *apprehended of Christ Jesus.*

(2) The objection which Nathanael made against this, *Can any good thing come out of Nazareth? v.* 46. [1] His *caution* was commendable; our rule is, *Prove all things.* [2] His objection arose from ignorance. If he meant that the Messiah, that great good thing, could not come out of Nazareth, so far he was right, but then he was ignorant of the matter of *fact,* that this Jesus was born at Bethlehem; so that the blunder Philip made, in calling him *Jesus of Nazareth,* occasioned this objection.

(3) The short reply which Philip gave to this objection: *Come and see.* We may *know* enough to *satisfy* ourselves, and yet not be able to *say* enough to *silence* a subtle adversary. It was his *wisdom* and zeal that, when he could not answer the objection himself, he would have him go to one that could: *Come and see.* Not, *Go and see,* but, "*Come,* and I will go along with thee." Many people are kept from the ways of religion by the unreasonable prejudices they have conceived against religion, upon the account of some foreign circumstances which do not at all touch the merits of the case.

2. What passed between Nathanael and our Lord Jesus. He came and *saw,* not in vain.

beheld him—fixed his eyes on him, with significant gaze (as vs. 36). **Cephas . . . stone**—(See on Matt. 16:18).

43. would go . . . into Galilee—for from His baptism He had sojourned in *Judea* (showing that the calling at the Sea of Galilee (Matt. 4:18) was a *subsequent* one; see on Luke 5:1). **Follow me**—the first express call given, the former three having come to Him spontaneously. **44. the city of Andrew and Peter**—of their *birth* probably, for they seem to have *lived* at Capernaum (Mark 1:29).

45. Nathanael—(See on Matt. 10:3). **Moses**—(See ch. 5:46). **son of Joseph**—the current way of speaking. (See Luke 3:23.)

46. any good out of Nazareth—remembering Bethlehem, perhaps, as Messiah's predicted birthplace, and Nazareth having no *express* prophetic place at all, besides being in no repute. The question sprang from mere dread of mistake in a matter so vital.

Come and see—Noble remedy against preconceived opinions [BENGEL]. Philip, though he could not perhaps solve his difficulty, could show him how to get rid of it. (See on ch. 6:68.)

42. *Cephas, which is by interpretation, A stone.* The reason why this name was given to Simon, who was ever afterwards called Peter, may be seen in the notes on Matt. xvi. 18-19.

43. *Philip.* This apostle was a native of Bethsaida in Galilee. He must not be confounded with Philip the deacon, spoken of in Acts vi. 5.

45. *Nathanael.* This apostle is supposed to be the same with *Bartholomew,* which is very likely, for these reasons: (1) That the Evangelists who mention Bartholomew say nothing of Nathanael; and that John, who speaks of Nathanael, says nothing of Bartholomew. (2) No notice is taken anywhere of Bartholomew's vocation, unless his and that of Nathanael mentioned here be the same. (3) The name of Bartholomew is not a proper name; it signifies the "son of Ptolomy"; and Nathanael might have been his own name. (4) John seems to rank Nathanael with the apostles when he says that Peter and Thomas, the two sons of Zebedee, Nathanael, and two other disciples, being gone a fishing, Jesus showed himself to them, John xxi. 2-4. *Moses in the law.* See Gen. iii. 15; xxii. 18; xlix. 10; Deut. xviii. 18. *And the prophets.* See Isa. iv. 2; vii. 14; ix. 5; xl. 10; liii. 1, etc.; Jer. xxiii. 5; xxxiii. 14-15; Ezek. xxiv. 23; xxxvii. 24; Dan. ix. 24; Mic. v. 2; Zech. vi. 12; ix. 9; xii. 10.

46. *Can there any good thing come out of Nazareth?* Bishop Pearce supposes that the *ti anathon* of the Evangelist has some particular force in it: for, in Jer. xxxiii. 14, God says, "I will perform *that good thing* which I have promised"; and this, in v. 15, is explained to mean his causing "the Branch of righteousness [i.e., the Messiah] to grow up unto David," from whom Jesus was descended. In this view, Nathanael's question seems to imply that not Nazareth, but Bethlehem, was to be the birthplace of the Messiah, according to what the chief priests and scribes had determined, Matt. ii. 4-6. If this conjecture be not thought solid, we may suppose that Nazareth, at this time, was become so abandoned that no good could be expected from any of those who dwelt in it,

MATTHEW HENRY

(1) *Jesus saw him* coming. He said of him to those about him, *Behold an Israelite indeed.* He *commended* him; not to flatter him, but perhaps because he knew him to be a *modest* man. Nathanael had objected against Christ; but Christ hereby showed that he excused it, because he knew his heart was upright. He commended him for his *integrity. Behold an Israelite indeed. All are not Israel that are of Israel;* here, however, was *an Israelite indeed.* A sincere follower of the good example of Israel. He was a genuine son of *honest Jacob.* A sincere professor of the faith of Israel: he was really as good as he seemed, and his practice was *of a piece* with his profession. He is the Jew that is one *inwardly*, so is he *the Christian.* He is one in whom is *no guile*: *no guile* towards men; a man that one may trust; *no guile* towards God, sincere in his repentance for sin. He does not say without *guilt*, but without *guile.* An Israelite indeed, a miracle of divine grace.

(2) Nathanael is much surprised at this.

[1] Here is Nathanael's modesty: "*Whence knowest thou me*, me that am unworthy of thy cognizance?" This was an evidence of his sincerity, that he did not catch at the praise he met with. Doth Christ know us? Let us covet to know him.

[2] Here is Christ's further *manifestation* of himself to him: *Before Philip called thee, I saw thee. First*, He gives him to understand that he *knew him*, and so manifests his divinity. *Secondly*, That before Philip called him he saw him under the fig-tree. Christ has knowledge of us before we have any knowledge of him. His eye was upon him when he was *under the fig-tree*; this was a private token which nobody understood but Nathanael: "When thou wast retired *under the fig-tree* I had then my eye upon thee, and saw that which was very acceptable." It is most probable that Nathanael under the fig-tree was employed in meditation, and prayer, and communion with God. *Sitting under the* fig-tree denotes quietness and composedness of spirit, which much befriend communion with God.

(3) Nathanael hereby obtained a full assurance of faith in Jesus Christ (*v.* 49): *Rabbi, thou art the Son of God, thou art the king of Israel;* that is, in short, thou art the true Messiah. Observe here, how *firmly* he believed *with the heart.* Now he asks no more, *Can any good thing come out of Nazareth?* How *freely* he confessed *with the mouth.* He confesses Christ's prophetical office, in calling him *Rabbi.* He confesses his divine nature and mission, in calling him the Son of God. He confesses, "*Thou art the king of Israel.*" If he be the Son of God, he is king of the Israel of God.

(4) Christ hereupon raises the hopes and expectations of Nathanael to something further and greater than all this, *v.* 50, 51.

[1] He here signifies his acceptance, and (it should seem) his admiration, of the ready faith of Nathanael: *Because I said, I saw thee under the fig-tree, believest thou?* It was a sign that Nathanael's heart was prepared beforehand, else the work had not been done so suddenly.

[2] He promises him much greater helps for the confirmation and increase of his faith.

First, In general: "*Thou shalt see greater things than these*"; the miracles of Christ, and his resurrection. Those who truly believe the gospel will find its evidences grow upon them. Whatever discoveries Christ is pleased to make of himself here in this world, he hath still greater things than these to make known to them.

Secondly, In particular: "Not thou only, but you, all you my disciples, you *shall see heaven opened.*" *Verily, verily I say unto you*, which commands both a *fixed attention* to what is said as very weighty, and a *full assent* to it as undoubtedly true. None used this word at the beginning of a sentence but Christ, though the Jews often used it at the close of a prayer. It is a solemn asseveration. Now see what it is that Christ assures them of: *Hereafter*, or *ere long*, ye shall see heaven opened. *The Son of man* is a title frequently applied to him in the gospel, but always by himself. Nathanael had called him the *Son of God* and *king of Israel*: he calls himself *Son of man* to express his *humility*, and to teach his *humanity.* They are great things which he here foretells: *You shall see heaven opened*, and *the angels of God ascending and descending upon the Son of man.* It was fulfilled in the many ministrations of the angels to our Lord Jesus, especially that at his ascension, when heaven was opened to receive him, and the angels *ascended* and *descended*, and this in the sight of the disciples. Christ's ascension was the great proof of his mission, and much confirmed the faith of his disciples. We may understand it of Christ's *miracles.* Christ is now beginning a dispensation of miracles. Immediately after this, Christ began to work miracles, *ch.* ii. 11.

JAMIESON, FAUSSET, BROWN

47. an Israelite indeed . . . no guile—not only no hypocrite, but with a guileless simplicity not always found even in God's own people, ready to follow wherever truth might lead him, saying, Samuel-like, "Speak, Lord, for Thy servant heareth."

48. Whence knowest thou me—conscious that his very heart had been read, and at this critical moment more than ever before. **Before Philip called thee**—showing He knew all that passed between Philip and him at a distance. **when . . . under the fig tree . . .**—where retirement for meditation and prayer was not uncommon [LIGHTFOOT]. Thither, probably—hearing that his master's Master had at length appeared, and heaving with mingled eagerness to behold Him and dread of deception—he had retired to pour out his guileless heart for light and guidance, ending with such a prayer as this, "Show me a token for good!" (See on Luke 2:8.) Now he has it, 'Thou guileless one, that fig tree scene, with all its heaving anxieties, deep pleadings and tremulous hopes—I saw it all.' The first words of Jesus had astonished, but this quite overpowered and won him.

49. Son of God . . . King of Israel—the one denoting His person, the other His office. How much loftier this than anything Philip had said to him! But just as the earth's vital powers, the longer they are frostbound, take the greater spring when at length set free, so souls, like Nathanael and Thomas (see on ch. 20:28), the outgoings of whose faith are hindered for a time, take the start of their more easy-going brethren when loosed and let go.

51. Because I said . . .—"So quickly convinced, and on this evidence only?"—an expression of admiration.

Hereafter . . .—The key to this great saying is Jacob's vision (Gen. 28:12-22), to which the allusion plainly is. To show the patriarch that though alone and friendless on earth his interests were busying all heaven, he was made to see "heaven opened and the angels of God ascending and descending upon a" mystic "*ladder* reaching from heaven to earth." 'By and by,' says Jesus here, 'ye shall see this communication between heaven and earth thrown wide open, and *the Son of man the real Ladder of this intercourse.*'

ADAM CLARKE

and that its wickedness had passed into a proverb: Can anything good be found in Nazareth? *Come and see.* He who candidly examines the evidences of the religion of Christ will infallibly become a believer. No history ever published among men has so many external and internal proofs of authenticity as does this.

47. *Behold an Israelite indeed.* A worthy descendant of the patriarch Jacob, who not only professes to believe in Israel's God, but who worships Him in sincerity and truth, according to his light. *In whom is no guile!* To find a man, living in the midst of so much corruption, walking in uprightness before his Maker, was a subject worthy the attention of God himself. Behold this man! and, while you see and admire, imitate his conduct.

48. *Whence knowest thou me?* He was not yet acquainted with the divinity of Christ, could not conceive that He could search his heart, and therefore asks how He could acquire this knowledge of him, or who had given him that character. *Under the fig tree.* Probably engaged in prayer with God for the speedy appearing of the salvation of Israel; and the shade of this fig tree was perhaps the ordinary place of retreat for this upright man. It is not "a fig tree," but *the fig tree,* one particularly distinguished from the others.

49. *Rabbi.* That is, "Teacher!" and so this word should be translated. *Thou art the Son of God.* The promised Messiah. *Thou art the King of Israel.* The real Descendant of David, who was to sit on that spiritual throne of which the throne of David was the type.

50. *Because I said unto thee, I saw thee.* As you have credited My divine mission on this simple proof, that I saw you when and where no human eye, placed where Mine was, could see you, your faith shall not rest merely upon this, *for you shall see greater things than these*—more numerous and express proofs of My eternal power and Godhead.

51. *Verily, verily.* Amen, amen. The doubling of this word probably came from this circumstance: that it was written both in Hebrew and in Greek, signifying, "It is true." *Heaven open.* This seems to be a figurative expression. (1) Christ may be understood by this saying to mean that a clear and abundant revelation of God's will should now be made unto men; that heaven itself should, as it were, be laid *open,* and all the mysteries which had been shut up and hidden in it from eternity, relative to the salvation and glorification of man, should be now fully revealed. (2) That by the *angels of God ascending and descending* is to be understood that a perpetual intercourse should now be opened between heaven and earth through the medium of Christ, who was God manifested in the flesh. Our blessed Lord is represented in His mediatorial capacity as the Ambassador of God to men; and *the angels ascending and descending upon the Son of man* is a metaphor taken from the custom of dispatching couriers or messengers from the prince to his ambassador in a foreign court, and from the ambassador back to the prince. This metaphor will receive considerable light when compared with 2 Cor. v. 19-20: "God was in Christ, reconciling the world unto himself . . . we are ambassadors for Christ, as though God did beseech you by us: we pray you in Christ's stead, be ye reconciled to God."

MATTHEW HENRY

CHAPTER 2

We have here the story of Christ's miraculous conversion of water into wine at a marriage in Cana of Galilee. He could have wrought miracles before, but, miracles being designed for the sacred and solemn seals of his doctrine, he began not to work any till he began to preach.

I. The occasion of this miracle. Maimonides observes it to be to the honour of Moses that all the signs he did in the wilderness he did *upon necessity*; we needed food, he brought us manna, and so did Christ.

1. The time: the *third day* after he came into Galilee. The evangelist keeps a journal of occurrences. Our Master filled up his time better than his servants do, and never lay down at night complaining that he had *lost a day*.

2. The place: it was at Cana in Galilee. Christ began to work miracles in an obscure corner of the country. His doctrine and miracles would not be so much opposed by the plain and honest Galileans as they would be at Jerusalem.

3. The occasion itself was a *marriage*. The *mother of Jesus* is said to be *there*. The honour which Christ hereby put upon the ordinance of marriage, that he graced the solemnity of it, not only with his presence, but with his first miracle. There was a *marriage*, a *marriage-feast*, to grace the solemnity. Marriages were usually celebrated with festivals.

4. Christ and his mother and disciples were principal guests at this entertainment. *The mother of Jesus was there;* no mention being made of Joseph, we conclude him dead before this. Jesus was *called*, and he came, and feasted with them. Christ was to come in a way different from that of John Baptist, who came *neither eating nor drinking*. *There was a marriage, and Jesus was called*. It is very desirable, when there is a *marriage*, to have Jesus Christ *present* at it; to have the marriage owned and blessed by him: the *marriage* is then *honourable* indeed. They that would have Christ with them at their marriage must invite him by prayer; that is the messenger that must be sent to heaven for him; and he will come. And he will turn the water into wine. The disciples also were invited. They had thrown themselves upon his care, and they soon found that, though he had no wealth, he had good friends. Those that *follow* Christ shall *feast* with him, they shall *fare* as he *fares*. Love to Christ is testified by a love to those that are his.

II. The miracle itself.

1. They *wanted wine*, *v.* 3. There was *want* at a *feast*; though much was provided, yet all was spent. While we are in this world we sometimes find ourselves *in straits*, even then when we think ourselves in the *fulness of our sufficiency*. If always *spending*, perhaps all is spent ere we are aware. There was want at a *marriage feast*. It should seem, Christ and his disciples were the occasion of this want, but they who straiten themselves for Christ shall not lose by him.

2. The *mother of Jesus* solicited him to assist her friends. We are told (*v.* 3–5) what passed between Christ and his mother.

(1) She acquaints him with the difficulty they were in (*v.* 3): *She saith unto him, They have no wine*. Some think that she did not expect from him any miraculous supply (he having as yet wrought no miracle). But, most probably, she looked for a miracle. The bridegroom might have sent out for more wine, but she was for going to the fountain-head. We ought to be concerned for the wants and straits of our friends. In our own and our friends' straits it is our wisdom and duty to apply ourselves to Christ by prayer. In our addresses to Christ, we must not prescribe to him, but humbly spread our case before him.

(2) He gave her a reprimand for it. Here is,

[1] The rebuke itself: *Woman, what have I to do with thee?* As many as Christ loves, he rebukes and chastens. He calls her *woman*, not *mother*. When we begin to be assuming, we should be reminded what we are, *men* and *women*, frail, foolish, and corrupt. Now this was intended to be, *First*, A check to his mother for interposing in a matter which was the act of his Godhead, which had no dependence on her, and which she was not the mother of. The greatest advancements must not make us forget ourselves and our place, nor the familiarity to which the covenant of grace admits us breed contempt, irreverence, or any kind of degree of presumption. *Secondly*, It was an instruction to others of his relations that they must never expect him to have any regard to his kindred according to the flesh, in his working miracles, who in this matter were no more to him than other people. In the things of God we must not *know faces*.

JAMIESON, FAUSSET, BROWN

CHAPTER 2

VSS. 1-12. FIRST MIRACLE, WATER MADE WINE—BRIEF VISIT TO CAPERNAUM.

1. third day—He would take two days to reach Galilee, and this was the third.

mother there—it being probably some relative's marriage. *John never names her* [BENGEL].

3. no wine—evidently expecting some display of His glory, and hinting that now was His time.

4, 5. Woman—no term of disrespect in the language of that day (ch. 19:26). **what . . . to do with thee**—i.e., 'In my Father's business I have to do with Him only.' 'Twas a gentle rebuke for *officious interference*, entering a region from which all creatures were excluded (cf. Acts 4:19, 20).

ADAM CLARKE

CHAPTER 2

1. *Cana of Galilee*. This was a small city in the tribe of Asher, Josh. xix. 28, and by saying this was Cana of *Galilee*, the Evangelist distinguishes it from another Cana which was in the tribe of Ephraim, in the Samaritan country. See Josh. xvi. 8; xvii. 9. Some suppose that the *third day* mentioned here refers to the third day of the marriage feast, such feasts lasting among the Jews seven days. See Judg. xiv. 12, 17-18.

3. *They have no wine*. Though the blessed Virgin is supposed never to have seen her Son work a miracle before this time, yet she seems to have expected Him to do something extraordinary on this occasion, as from her acquaintance with Him she must have formed some adequate idea of His power and goodness.

4. *Woman, what have I to do with thee?* "O woman, what is this to you and Me?" This is an abrupt denial, as if He had said: "We are not employed to provide the necessaries for this feast; this matter belongs to others, who should have made a proper and sufficient provision for the persons they had invited." The words seem to convey a reproof to the Virgin for meddling with that which did not particularly concern her. But here indeed there appears to be no blame. It is very likely the bride or bridegroom's family were relatives of the blessed Virgin; and she would naturally suppose that our Lord would feel interested for the honor and comfort of the family, and knowing that He possessed extraordinary power, made this application to Him to come forward to their assistance. Our Lord's answer to His mother, if properly translated, is far from being disrespect-

ALEXANDER MACLAREN:

The first point, which John makes all but as emphatic as the miracle itself, is the new relation between Mary and Jesus, the lesson she had to learn, and her sweet triumphant trust. Now that she sees her Son surrounded by His disciples, the secret hope which she had nourished silently for so long bursts into flame, and she turns to Him with beautiful faith in His power to help, even in the small present need. What an example of her first word to Him sets us all! Like the two sad sisters at Bethany, she is sure that to tell Him of trouble is enough, for that His own heart will impel Him to share, and perchance to relieve it. Let us tell Jesus our wants and leave Him to deal with them as He knows how.—*Expositions of Holy Scripture*

MATTHEW HENRY

[2] The reason of this rebuke: *Mine hour is not yet come.* For everything Christ did, and that was done to him, he had *his hour*, the *fixed* time and the *fittest* time. "Mine hour for *working miracles* is not yet come." Yet afterwards he wrought this, before the hour, because he foresaw it would confirm the faith of his infant disciples (*v.* 11): so that this was an earnest of the many miracles he would work when his *hour was come.* His mother moved him to help them *when the wine began to fail* (so it may be read, *v.* 3), but his hour was not yet come till it was quite spent. This teaches us that man's extremity is God's opportunity. Then *his hour is come* when we are reduced to the utmost strait, and know not what to do. The delays of mercy are not to be construed the denials of prayer.

(3) Notwithstanding this, she encouraged herself with expectations, that he would help, for she bade the servants *observe his orders, v.* 5. She took the reproof very submissively, and did not reply to it. It is best not to deserve reproof from Christ, but next best to be meek and quiet under it, and to count it a kindness. She kept her hope in Christ's mercy. When we come to God in Christ for any mercy, two things discourage us: Sense of *our own follies* and infirmities and fear of *our Lord's frowns and rebukes.* Afflictions are continued, deliverances delayed, and God seems angry at our prayers. This was the case of the mother of our Lord here, and yet she encourages herself with hope that he will at length give an answer of peace, to teach us to wrestle with God even when he seems in his providence to walk contrary to us. She directed the servants to have an eye *to him*, and not to make their applications to her. She directed them punctually to observe his orders: "*Whatsoever he saith unto you, do it.*" Those that expect Christ's *favours* must with an implicit obedience observe his *orders.* The way of duty is the way to mercy; and Christ's methods must not be objected against.

(4) Christ did at length miraculously supply them; for he is often better than his word, but never worse.

[1] The miracle itself was *turning water into wine*; the substance of water acquiring a new form, and having all the accidents and qualities of wine. By this Christ showed himself to be the God of nature, who maketh the earth to bring forth wine. The beginning of Christ's miracles was turning water into wine; the blessing of the gospel turns water into wine. Christ hereby showed that his errand into the world was to heighten and improve creature-comforts to all believers, and make them comforts indeed.

[2] The circumstances of it magnified it and freed it from all suspicion of cheat.

First, It was done in water-pots (*v.* 6): *There were set there six water-pots of stone.* 1. For what use these water-pots were intended: for the legal purifications enjoined by the law of God, and many more by the tradition of the elders. They used much water in their washing, for which reason here were six large water-pots provided. It was a saying among them—*He who uses much water in washing will gain much wealth in this world.* 2. To what use Christ put them; to be the receptacles of the miraculous wine. Thus Christ came to bring in the grace of the gospel, which is as *wine*, instead of the shadows of the law, which were as water. These were *water-pots,* that had never been used to have wine in them; and of *stone*, which is not apt to retain the scent of former liquors, if ever they had had wine in them. They contained *two or three firkins apiece*; the quantity is uncertain, but very considerable. Christ gives like himself, gives abundantly, according to his riches in glory.

Secondly, The water-pots were filled *up to the brim* by the servants at Christ's word, *v.* 7.

Thirdly, The miracle was wrought suddenly, and in such a manner as greatly magnified it.

a. As soon as they had filled the water-pots, he said, *Draw out now* (*v.* 8), and it was done. Without any ceremony, in the eye of the spectators. He sits still in his place, says not a word, but *wills* the thing, and so works it. Christ does great things and marvellous *without noise*, works manifest changes in a hidden way, without any hesitation or uncertainty in his own breast. With the greatest assurance imaginable, though it was his *first miracle*, he recommends it to the master of the feast *first.* As he knew what he *would* do, so he knew what he *could* do. All was good, very good, even in the beginning.

b. Our Lord Jesus directed the servants, (*a*) *To draw it out;* to be drank. Christ's works are all *for use.* Has he turned thy water into wine, given thee knowledge and grace? It is to *profit withal*; and therefore *draw out now.* Those that would know Christ must make trial of him. (*b*) To present it to

JAMIESON, FAUSSET, BROWN

mine hour...—hinting that He *would* do something, but at His own time; and so she understood it (vs. 5).

CHARLES H. SPURGEON:

Now, concerning this miracle, it may well be remarked how simple and unostentatious it was. One might have expected that when the great Lord of all came here in human form, He would commence His miraculous career by summoning the scribes and Pharisees at least, if not the kings and princes of the earth, to see the marks of His calling and the guarantees and warrants of His commission; gathering them all together to work some miracle before them, as Moses and Aaron did before Pharaoh, that they might be convinced of His messiahship. He does nothing of the kind. He goes to a simple wedding among poor people, and there in the simplest and most natural way He displays His glory. When the water is to be turned into wine, when He selects that as the first miracle, He does not call for the master of the feast even, or for the bridegroom himself, or for any of the guests, and begin to say, "You clearly perceive that your wine is all gone. Now, I am about to show you a great marvel, to turn water into wine." No, He does it quietly with the servants. He tells them to fill the waterpots: He uses the baths. He does not ask for any new vessels, but uses what were there, making no fuss or parade. He uses water, too, of which they had abundance, and works the miracle, if I may so speak, in the most commonplace and natural style; and that is just the style of Jesus Christ. Now, if it had been a Romish miracle, it would have been done in a very mysterious, theatrical, sensational way, with no end of paraphernalia; but, being a genuine miracle, it is done just as nearly after the course of nature as the supernatural can go. Jesus does not have the waterpots emptied and then fill them with wine, but He goes as far with nature as nature will go, and uses water to make the wine from; therein following the processes of His providence which are at work every day. When the water drops from heaven and flows into the earth to the roots of the vine, and so swells out the clusters with ruddy juice, it is through water that wine is produced. There is only a difference as to time whether the wine is created in the cluster, or in the waterpots. Our Lord does not call for any strangers to do it, but the ordinary servants shall bring ordinary water; and while they are drawing out the water, or what appears to them to be water, the servants shall perceive that the water has been turned into wine.

—The Treasury of the New Testament

6. firkins—about seven and a half gallons in Jewish, or nine in Attic measure; each of these huge water jars, therefore, holding some twenty or more gallons, for washings at such feasts (Mark 7:4).

7,
8. Fill... draw... bear...—directing all, but Himself touching nothing, to prevent all appearance of collusion.

ADAM CLARKE

ful. He addresses the Virgin as He did the Syrophoenician woman, Matt. xv. 28; as He did the Samaritan woman, John iv. 21; as He addressed His disconsolate mother when He hung upon the Cross, chap. xix. 26; as He did His most affectionate friend Mary Magdalene, chap. xx. 15, and as the angels had addressed her before, v. 13; and as Paul does the believing Christian woman, 1 Cor. vii. 16—in all which places the same term which occurs in this verse is used, and where certainly no kind of disrespect is intended. *Mine hour is not yet come.* Or my "time," for in this sense the word is often taken. My time for working a miracle is not yet fully come. What I do, I do when necessary, and not before. Nature is unsteady, full of haste, and ever blundering in consequence. It is the folly and sin of men that they are ever finding fault with the divine providence. According to them, God never does anything in due time—He is too early or too late; whereas it is utterly impossible for the divine wisdom to forestall itself or for the divine goodness to delay what is necessary.

5. *His mother saith.* The Virgin seems to have understood our Lord as hinted above. It was not yet time to grant them a supply, because the want had not as yet been generally felt. But, silently receiving the respectful caution, she saw that miracle should be wrought when it best suited the purposes of the divine wisdom.

6. *After the manner of the purifying of the Jews.* Or "for the purpose of the purifying of the Jews." The preposition which I have translated "for the purpose" often denotes in the best Greek writers the final cause of a thing. These six vessels were set in a convenient place, for the purpose of the Jews washing their hands before they sat down to meat, and probably for other purposes of purification. See this custom referred to in Matt. xv. 2.

Containing two or three firkins apiece. "Measures" or *metretes.* [Some] make each *metretes* to contain ten gallons and two pints.

MATTHEW HENRY

the governor of the feast. Though he was not treated as the Master of the feast, he kindly approved himself a friend to the feast, and, if not its founder, yet its best benefactor. This *governor* was the monitor of the feast, whose office it was to see that each had enough, and none did exceed, and that there were no indecencies or disorders. Feasts have need of governors, because too many, when they are at feasts, have not the government of themselves. Some think that this *governor* was priest or Levite that craved a blessing and gave thanks, and Christ would have the cup brought to him, that he might bless it, and bless God for it; for the extraordinary tokens of Christ's presence and power were not to supersede, or jostle out, the ordinary rules and methods of piety and devotion.

Fourthly, The wine which was thus miraculously provided was of the best and richest kind, which was acknowledged by the governor of the feast, *v.* 9, 10. 1. It was certain that this was *wine.* The governor knew this when he drank it, though he knew not *whence it was;* the servants knew whence it was, but had not yet tasted it. 2. That it was the best wine. Christ's works commend themselves even to those that know not their author. The products of miracles were always the best in their kind. This the governor of the feast takes notice of to the bridegroom, with an air of pleasantness, as *uncommon.* The common method was otherwise. Good wine is brought out to the best advantage at the beginning of a feast, but *when they have well drank,* good wine is but thrown away upon them, worse will serve then. See the vanity of all the pleasures of sense; they soon surfeit, but never satisfy; the longer they are enjoyed, the less pleasant they grow. *Thou hast kept the good wine until now;* not knowing to whom they were indebted for this good wine, he returns the thanks of the table to the bridegroom. Christ, in providing thus plentifully for the guests, though he hereby allows a sober cheerful use of wine, especially in times of rejoicing (Neh. viii. 10), yet he does not invalidate his own caution, which is, that our hearts be not *at any time,* no not at a marriage feast, *overcharged with surfeiting and drunkenness,* Luke xxi. 34. Temperance *per force* is a thankless virtue; but if divine providence gives us abundance of the delights of sense, and divine grace enables us to use them moderately, this is self-denial that is praiseworthy. Two considerations, drawn from this story, may be sufficient at any time to fortify us against temptations to intemperance: *First,* That our meat and drink are the *gifts of God's bounty* to us. It is therefore ungrateful and impious to abuse them. *Secondly,* That, wherever we are, Christ has his eye upon us. He has given us a specimen of the method he takes in dealing with those that deal with him, which is, to reserve the *best* for the *last,* and therefore they must *deal upon trust.* The pleasures of sin give their colour in the cup, but *at the last bite;* but the pleasures of religion will be *pleasures for evermore.*

III. In the conclusion of this story (*v.* 11) we are told, 1. That this was *the beginning of miracles* which Jesus did. He himself was the greatest miracle of all; but this was the first that was wrought *by* him. He had power, but there was a *time of the hiding of his power.* 2. That herein he *manifested his glory;* hereby he proved himself to be the Son of God. 3. That *his disciples believed on him.* Those whom he had called (*ch.* i), now saw this, shared in it, and had their faith strengthened by it. Even the faith that is true is at first but weak. The strongest men were once babes, so were the strongest Christians.

Verses 12–22

I. The short visit Christ made to Capernaum, *v.* 12. It is called *his own city* (Matt. ix. 1), because he made it his headquarters in Galilee, and what little rest he had was there. It was a place of concourse, and *therefore* Christ chose it, that the fame of his doctrine and miracles might thence spread the further.

1. The company that attended him thither: *his mother, his brethren, and his disciples.* Wherever Christ went, (1) He *would not* go alone, but would take those with him who had put themselves under his guidance. (2) He *could not* go alone, but they would follow him, because they liked the sweetness either of his doctrine or of his wine, *ch.* vi. 26. His mother, yet followed him; not to intercede with him, but to learn of him. His *brethren,* who were at the marriage, and *his disciples,* attended him wherever he went. It should seem, people were more affected with Christ's miracles at first than they were afterwards, when custom made them seem less strange.

2. His continuance there, which was at this time *not many days.* Christ was still upon the remove, would not confine his usefulness to *one* place, because *many* needed him. He did not stay long at Capernaum

JAMIESON, FAUSSET, BROWN

9, 10. well drunk—"drunk abundantly" (as Song of Sol. 5:1), speaking of the general practice. **the good . . . till now**—thus testifying, while ignorant of the source of supply, not only that it was real wine, but better than any at the feast.

11. manifested forth his glory—Nothing in the least like this is said of the miracles of prophet or apostle, nor could without manifest blasphemy be said of any mere creature. Observe, (1) At a marriage Christ made His first public appearance in any company, and at a marriage He wrought His first miracle—the noblest sanction that could be given to that God-given institution. (2) As the miracle did not make *bad good,* but *good better,* so Christianity only redeems, sanctifies, and ennobles the beneficent but abused institution of marriage; and Christ's whole work only turns the water of earth into the wine of heaven. Thus "this beginning of miracles" exhibited the character and "manifested forth the glory" of His entire Mission. (3) As Christ countenanced our seasons of *festivity,* so also that greater *fulness* which befits such; so far was He from encouraging that *asceticism* which has since been so often put for all religion. (4) The character and authority ascribed by Romanists to the Virgin is directly in the teeth of this and other scriptures.

12. Capernaum—on the Sea of Galilee. (See on Matt. 9:1.)

his mother and his brethren—(See on Luke 2:51, and Matt. 13:54-56).

ADAM CLARKE

8. *Governor of the feast.* The original word signifies one who is "chief or head over three couches, or tables." In the Asiatic countries, they take their meals reclining on small, low couches. And when many people are present, so that they cannot all eat together, three of these low tables or couches are put together in form of a crescent, and one of the guests is appointed to take charge of the persons who sit at these tables. Hence the appellation of *architriclinus,* the "chief over three couches or tables," which in process of time became applied to the *governor* or "steward" of a feast, let the guests be many or few; and such person, having conducted the business well, had a festive crown put on his head by the guests at the conclusion of the feast. *And they bare it.* A question has been asked, "Did our Lord turn all the water into wine which the six measures contained?" To which I answer: There is no proof that He did; and I take it for granted that He did not. It may be asked, "How could a part be turned into wine, and not the whole?" To which I answer: The water, in all likelihood, was changed into wine *as it was drawn out,* and not otherwise. "But did not our Lord by this miracle minister to vice, by producing an excess of inebriating liquor?" No; for the following reasons: (1) The company was a select and holy company, where no excess could be permitted. And (2) our Lord does not appear to have furnished any extra quantity, but only what was necessary. "But it is intimated in the text that the guests were nearly intoxicated before this miraculous addition to their wine took place; for the Evangelist says, 'when they have become intoxicated.'" I answer: (1) It is not intimated, even in the most indirect manner, that *these* guests were at all intoxicated. (2) The words are not spoken of the persons at *that* wedding at all; the governor of the feast only states that such was the common custom at feasts of this nature, without intimating that any such custom prevailed there. (3) The original word bears a widely different meaning from that which the objection forces upon it. The verbs signify not only "to inebriate" but "to take wine, to drink wine, to drink enough"; and in this sense the verb is evidently used in the Septuagint, Gen. xliii. 34; Cant. v. 1; Hag. i. 6.

10. *The good wine until now.* That which our Lord now made being perfectly pure and highly nutritive.

11. *This beginning of miracles.* It was probably the first He ever wrought; at any rate, it was the first He wrought after His baptism and the first He wrought publicly. *His glory.* His supreme divinity, chap. i. 14. *His disciples believed on him.* Were more abundantly confirmed in their faith that He was either the promised Messiah or a most extraordinary prophet, in the fullest intercourse with the ever blessed God.

MATTHEW HENRY

because the passover was at hand, and he must attend it at Jerusalem.

II. The passover he kept at Jerusalem; it is the *first* after his baptism. Christ, being *made under the law*, observed the passover at Jerusalem. He went up to Jerusalem when *the passover was at hand*, that he might be there *with the first*. Christ kept the passover at Jerusalem yearly, ever since he was twelve years old, but now that he has entered upon his public ministry we may expect something more from him than before; and two things he did there:

1. He *purged the temple, v.* 14–17.

(1) The first place we find him in at Jerusalem was the *temple*, and, it should seem, he did not make any public appearance till he came thither.

(2) The first work we find him at in the temple was the *purging* of it. He first *purged out* what was amiss and then taught them to do well. He expects that all who come to him should reform their hearts and lives. And this he has taught us by purging the temple. See here, What were the corruptions that were to be purged out. He found a market in one of the courts of the temple, that which was called the *court of the Gentiles*. They sold *oxen, and sheep, and doves*, for sacrifice; not for common use, but for the convenience of those who came out of the country, and could not bring their sacrifices *in kind* along with them. This *market* was admitted into the temple by the chief priests, for filthy lucre. Great corruptions in the church owe their rise to the love of money. They *changed money*, for the convenience of those that were to pay a half-shekel for the service of the tabernacle, and no doubt they got by it. See what course our Lord took to purge out those corruptions. He did not complain to the chief priests, for he knew they countenanced those corruptions. But he himself,

First, Drove out the sheep and oxen, and those that *sold them*. He never used *force* to drive any *into* the temple, but only to drive those out that profaned it. He made a scourge of *small cords*, which probably they had led their sheep and oxen with. Sinners prepare the scourges with which they themselves will be driven out from the temple of the Lord.

Secondly, He *poured out the changers' money*. In *pouring out* the money, he showed his contempt of it. In *overthrowing* the tables, he showed his displeasure against those that make religion a matter of worldly gain. Money-changers in the temple are the scandal of it.

Thirdly, He said to them that sold doves (sacrifices for the poor), *Take these things hence*. The sparrows and swallows were welcome, that were left to God's providence (Ps. lxxxiv. 3), but not the doves, that were appropriated to man's profit. God's temple must not be made a pigeon-house.

Fourthly, He gave them a good reason for what he did: *Make not my Father's house a house of merchandise*.

a. Here is a reason why they should not profane the temple, because it was the *house of God*. Merchandise is a good thing in the exchange, but not in the temple. It was *sacrilege*; it was robbing God. It was to debase that which was solemn and awful, and to make it mean. It was to make the business of religion subservient to a secular interest. Those make God's house a house of merchandise whose minds are filled with cares about the worldly business when they are attending on religious exercises, as those who perform divine offices for filthy lucre.

b. Here is a reason why he was concerned to purge it, because it *was his Father's house*. Therefore he had authority to purge it, as a Son *over his own house*. Therefore he had a zeal for the purging of it: "It is *my Father's house*, and therefore I cannot bear to see it profaned, and *him* dishonoured." Christ's purging the temple thus may justly be reckoned among his *wonderful works*. Considering, (*a*) That he did it without the *assistance* of any of his *friends*. (*b*) That he did it without the *resistance* of any of his *enemies*. The corruption was too plain to be justified; sinners' own consciences are reformers' best friends; yet that was not all, there was a divine power put forth herein, a power over the spirits of men.

Fifthly, Here is the remark which his disciples made upon it (*v.* 17): *They remembered that it was written, The zeal of thine house hath eaten me up*. One scripture came to their thoughts, which taught them to reconcile this action both with the meekness of the *Lamb of God* and with the majesty of the *King of Israel*; for David, speaking of the Messiah, takes notice of his *zeal for God's house*, as so great that it even *ate him up*. 1. The disciples came to understand the meaning of what Christ did, by remembering the scriptures: *They remembered* now *that it was written*. The word of God and the works of God do mutually explain and illustrate each other. See of what great use it is to

JAMIESON, FAUSSET, BROWN

13-25. CHRIST'S FIRST PASSOVER—FIRST CLEANSING OF THE TEMPLE. **14-17. in the temple**—not the temple itself, as vs. 19-21, but the *temple-court*.

sold oxen . . .—for the convenience of those who had to offer them in sacrifice. **changers of money**—of Roman into Jewish money, in which the temple dues (see on Matt. 17:24) had to be paid. **15. small cords**—likely some of the rushes spread for bedding, and when twisted used to tie up the cattle there collected. "Not by this slender whip but by divine majesty was the ejection accomplished, the whip being but a sign of the scourge of divine anger" [GROTIUS]. **poured out . . . overthrew . . .**—thus expressing the mingled indignation and authority of the impulse.

16. my Father's house—How close the resemblance of these remarkable words to Luke 2:49; the same *consciousness of intrinsic relation to the temple*—as the seat of His Father's most august worship, and so the symbol of all that is due to Him on earth—dictating both speeches. Only, when but a youth, *with no authority,* He was simply "a SON IN His own house"; now He was "a SON OVER His own house" (Hebrews 3:6), the proper Representative, and in flesh "the Heir," of his Father's rights. **house of merchandise**—There was nothing wrong in the merchandise; but to bring it, for their own and others' convenience, into that most sacred place, was a high-handed profanation which the eye of Jesus could not endure.

ADAM CLARKE

13. *And the Jews' passover was at hand.* This was the reason why He stayed but a few days at Capernaum, v. 12, as He wished to be present at the celebration of this feast at Jerusalem. This was the *first* passover after Christ's baptism. The *second* is mentioned in Luke vi. 1; the *third*, in John vi. 4; and the *fourth*, which was that at which He was crucified, in chap. xi. 55. From which it appears: (1) that our blessed Lord continued His public ministry about three years and a half, according to the prophecy of Daniel, chap. ix. 27; and (2) that, having been baptized about the beginning of His thirtieth year, He was crucified precisely in the middle of His thirty-third.

14. *Found in the temple those that sold oxen.* This is a *similar* fact to that mentioned in Matt. xxi. 12; Mark xi. 15; Luke xix. 45. If it be the *same* fact, then John anticipates three years of time in relating it here, as that cleansing of the Temple mentioned by the other Evangelists took place in the last week of our Lord's life. Mr. Mann, Dr. Priestley, and Bishop Pearce contend that our Lord cleansed the Temple only *once*, and that was at the last Passover. Calvin, Dr. Lardner, Bishop Hurd, and Bishop Newcome contend that He purged the Temple *twice;* and that this mentioned by John was the *first* cleansing, which none of the other Evangelists have mentioned. The vindication of God's house from profanation was the *first* and the *last* care of our Lord, and it is probable He began and finished His public ministry by this significant act. It certainly appears that John directly asserts an early cleansing of the Temple by the series of His history, as the other three Evangelists assert a later cleansing of it. And though the act mentioned here seems to be nearly the same with that mentioned by the other Evangelists, yet there are some differences. John alone mentions the "scourge of rushes" and the casting out of the "sheep and oxen." Besides, there is a considerable difference in our Lord's manner of doing it. In the cleansing mentioned by the three Evangelists, He assumes a vast deal of authority and speaks more pointedly concerning himself than He appears to do in this cleansing mentioned by John. The reason which has been given is, In the first cleansing He was just entering upon His public ministry, and therefore avoided (as much as was consistent with the accomplishment of His work) the giving any offence to the Jewish rulers; but in the last cleansing He was just concluding His ministry, being about to offer up His life for the salvation of the world, in consequence of which He speaks fully and without reserve.

17. *The zeal of thine house.* See Ps. lix. 10. Zeal to promote Thy glory, and to keep Thy worship pure.

MATTHEW HENRY

the disciples of Christ to be *ready* and *mighty* in the scriptures, and to have their memories well stored with scripture truths. 2. The scripture they remembered was very apposite: *The zeal of thine house hath eaten me up.* All the graces that were to be found among the Old Testament saints were eminently in Christ, and particularly this of zeal for the house of God. Zeal for the house of God forbids us to consult our own credit, ease, and safety, when they come in competition with Christ's service, and sometimes carries on our souls in our duty so far and so fast that our bodies cannot keep pace with them.

2. Christ gave a sign to those who demanded it to prove his authority for so doing.

(1) Their demand of a sign: *Then answered the Jews,* that is the multitude of the people, with their leaders. When they could object nothing against the thing itself, they questioned his authority to do it: "*What sign showest thou unto us.*" What had he to do to undertake it, who was in no office there? But was not the thing itself sign enough?

(2) Christ's answer to this demand, *v.* 19. A sign in something *to come,* the truth of which must appear by the event. The sign that he gives them is his own *death* and *resurrection.* He refers them to that which would be. He foretells his death and resurrection, not in plain terms, but in figurative expressions: *Destroy this temple, and in three days I will raise it up.* Thus he spoke in parables to those who were willingly ignorant, that *they might not perceive,* Matt. xiii. 13, 14. Those that will not see shall not see. Nay, this figurative speech used here proved such a *stumbling-block* to them that it was produced in evidence against him at his trial, Matt. xxvi. 60, 61. He foretells his death by the Jews' malice, in these words, *Destroy you this temple.* Christ, even at the beginning of his ministry, had a clear foresight of all his sufferings at the end of it, and yet went on cheerfully in it. He foretells his resurrection by his own power: In *three days I will raise it up.* There were others that *were raised,* but Christ raised himself. He chose to express this by *destroying* and *re-edifying* the temple. *First,* Because he was now to justify himself in purging the temple, which they had profaned: "You that defile one temple will destroy another; and I will prove my authority to *purge* what you have *defiled* by *raising* what you will *destroy.*"

(3) "*Forty and six years was this temple in building,* v. 20. Temple work was always slow work and canst thou make such quick work of it?" They show *some knowledge*; they could tell how long the temple was in building. They show *more ignorance, First,* Of the *meaning of Christ's words. Secondly,* Of *the almighty power of Christ,* as if he could do no more than another man.

(4) A vindication of Christ's answer from their cavil. *He spoke of the temple of his body, v.* 21. Some think that when he said, Destroy *this* temple, he pointed to his own body; however, it is certain that he *spoke of the temple of his body.* Like the temple it was built by immediate divine direction. Like the temple, it was a *holy house*; it is called *that holy thing.* It was, like the temple, the habitation, of God's glory; there the eternal Word dwelt. He is *Emmanuel —God with us.* Worshippers looked *towards* that house. So we must worship God with an eye to Christ.

(5) A reflection which the disciples made upon this, long after (*v.* 22): *When he was risen from the dead his disciples remembered that he had said this.* The memories of Christ's disciples should be like the treasure of the good householder, furnished with things both *new* and *old,* Matt. xiii. 52. *They remembered* that saying *when he was risen from the dead.* They laid up the saying in their hearts, and afterwards it became both intelligible and useful. The juniors in years and profession should treasure up those truths of which at present they do not well understand either the meaning or the use, for they will be serviceable to them hereafter. This saying of Christ revived in the memories of his disciples *when he was risen from the dead*; and why then? Because *then* the Spirit was poured out to bring things to their remembrance which Christ had said to them. That very day that Christ rose from the dead he *opened their understandings,* Luke xxiv. 45. Because then this saying of Christ was fulfilled. When the temple of his body had been *destroyed* and was *raised again,* and that upon the *third day,* then they remembered this. See what use they made of it: *They believed the scripture, and the word that Jesus had said.* They were slow of heart to believe (Luke xxiv. 25), but they were *sure.* The *scripture* and the *words of Christ* are here put together, because they mutually illustrate and strengthen each other.

Verses 23–25

I. Our Lord Jesus, when he was at Jerusalem at

JAMIESON, FAUSSET, BROWN

17. eaten me up—a glorious feature in the predicted character of the suffering Messiah (Ps. 69:9), and rising high even in some not worthy to loose the latchet of His shoes. (Exod. 32:19 etc.).

18-22. What sign . . .—Though the *act* and the *words* of Christ, taken together, were sign enough, they were unconvinced: yet they were *awed,* and though at His very next appearance at Jerusalem they "sought to kill Him" for speaking of "His Father" just as He did now (ch. 5:18), they, at this early stage, only ask a sign. **19. Destroy this temple . . .**—(See on Mark 14:58, 59).

20. Forty-six years—From the eighteenth year of Herod till then was just forty-six years [JOSEPHUS, *Antiquities,* xv. 11. 1].

21. temple of his body—in which was enshrined the glory of the eternal Word. (See on ch. 1:14.) By its resurrection the true Temple of God upon earth was reared up, of which the stone one was but a shadow; so that the allusion is not *quite* exclusively to Himself, but takes in that Temple of which He is the foundation, and all believers are the "lively stones." (I Pet. 2:4, 5.)

22. believed the scripture—on this subject; i.e., what was meant, which was hid from them till then. Mark (1) *The act by which Christ signalized His first public appearance in the Temple.* Taking "His fan in His hand, He purges His floor," not thoroughly indeed, but enough to *foreshadow His last act* towards that faithless people—*to sweep them out of God's house.* (2) The sign of His authority to do this is the announcement, at this first outset of His ministry, of that coming death by their hands, and resurrection by His own, which were to pave the way for their judicial ejection.

ADAM CLARKE

18. *What sign shewest thou?* When Moses came to deliver Israel he gave signs, or miracles, that he acted under a divine commission. What miracle dost Thou work to show us that Thou art vested with similar authority?

19. *Destroy this temple.* "This very temple," perhaps pointing to His body at the same time.

20. *Forty and six years was this temple in building.* The Temple of which the Jews spoke was begun to be rebuilt by Herod the Great in the eighteenth year of his reign (see Josephus). But though he finished the main work in nine years and a half, yet some additional buildings or repairs were constantly carried on for many years afterwards. Herod began the work sixteen years before the birth of our Lord; the transactions which are here related took place in the thirtieth year of our Lord, which make the term exactly forty-six years. Josephus has told us that the whole of the buildings belonging to the Temple were not finished till Nero's reign, when Albinus, the governor of Judea, was succeeded by Gessius Florus, which was eighty years after the eighteenth year of Herod's reign.

21. *Of the temple of his body.* Rather, "the temple, His body." His body had no particular temple; but it was the temple of His divinity—the place in which, as in the ancient Temple, His Godhead dwelt. See how the Jews perverted these words, Matt. xxvi. 60, and the notes there.

22. *Remembered that he had said this unto them. Unto them* is wanting in many MSS. and versions.

They believed the scripture. The scripture which the Evangelist immediately refers to may have been Ps. xvi. 10. Compare this with Acts ii. 31-32 and with chap. xiii. 35-37. See also Ps. ii. 7, and compare it with Heb. i. 5, and chap. v. 5, and with Acts xiii. 33. They understood these scriptures in a sense in which they never before understood them.

MATTHEW HENRY

the passover, did preach and work miracles. The time was holy time, *the feast-day*, and Christ took that opportunity of preaching, when the concourse of people was great.

II. Hereby many were brought to *believe in his name*, to acknowledge him a *teacher come from God*, as Nicodemus did (*ch.* iii. 2).

III. Yet *Jesus did not commit himself unto them* (*v.* 24): Christ did not see cause to repose any confidence in these new converts at Jerusalem, either, 1. Because they were *false*, at least some of them. He had more disciples that he could trust among the Galileans than among the dwellers at Jerusalem. Or, 2. Because they were *weak*. (1) They were *timorous*, and wanted zeal and courage. In times of difficulty and danger, cowards are not fit to be trusted. Or, (2) They were *tumultuous*, and wanted discretion and management.

IV. The reason why he did not *commit himself* to them was because he *knew* them (*v.* 25), knew the wickedness of some and the weakness of others. The evangelist takes this occasion to assert Christ's omniscience. He *knew all men*, not only their names and faces, as it is possible for us to know many, but their nature, dispositions, affections, designs, as we do not know *any man*, scarcely *ourselves*. He knows them that are truly his, knows their integrity and knows their infirmity too. He *needed not that any should testify of man*. His knowledge was not by information from others, but by his own infallible intuition. He *knew what was in man*. We know what is done *by men*; Christ knows what is *in them*. How fit is Christ to be the *Saviour of men*, very fit to be the physician, who has such a perfect knowledge of the patient's state and case, temper and distemper; knows what is in him! How fit also to be the *Judge of all*! The Lord comes to his temple, and none come to him but a parcel of weak simple people, that he can neither have *credit* from nor put *confidence* in.

CHAPTER 3

Verses 1–21

We found, in the close of the foregoing chapter, that few were brought to Christ at Jerusalem; yet here was *one*, a considerable one.

I. Who this Nicodemus was. Not many mighty and noble are called; yet some are, and here was one. *Not many of the rulers, or of the Pharisees*. This was a *man of the Pharisees*, bred to learning, a scholar. Let it not be said that all Christ's followers are *unlearned and ignorant men*. He was a *ruler of the Jews*, and a member of the great sanhedrim, a man of authority in Jerusalem. Bad as things were, there were some rulers *well inclined*. Nicodemus continued in his place, and did what he *could*, when he could not do what he *would*.

II. His solemn address to our Lord Jesus Christ, *v.* 2.

1. When he came: *He came to Jesus by night*, did not think it enough to hear his public discourses. He resolved to talk with him by himself, where he might be free with him. He made this address *by night*, which may be considered, (1) As an act of *prudence* and *discretion*. Christ was engaged all day in *public* work, and he would not interrupt him then, but observed *Christ's hour*, and waited on him when he was *at leisure*. Christ had many enemies, and therefore Nicodemus came to him *incognito*, lest being known to the chief priests they should be the more enraged against Christ. (2) As an act of *zeal*. He would rather take time from the diversions of the *evening*, or the rest of the *night*, than not converse with Christ. When others were sleeping, he was getting knowledge. He knew not how soon Christ might leave the town, nor what might happen betwixt that and another feast, and therefore would lose no time. In the night his converse with Christ would be more free, and less liable to disturbance. (3) As an act of *fear* and *cowardice*. He was afraid, or ashamed, to be *seen* with Christ, and therefore came *in the night*. Though he came by night, Christ bade him welcome, accepted his integrity, and pardoned his infirmity, and hereby taught his ministers to encourage good beginnings, though weak. Though now he came *by night*, yet afterwards he owned Christ *publicly*, *ch.* vii. 50; xix. 39. The grace which is at first but a grain of mustard-seed may grow to be a great tree.

2. What he said. He comes immediately to the business; he calls Christ *Rabbi*, which signifies a *great man*. There are hopes of those who have a respect for Christ, and think and speak honourably of him. He tells Christ how far *he had attained*: We *know that thou art a teacher*. (1) His *assertion*

JAMIESON, FAUSSET, BROWN

23-25. in the feast day—the foregoing things occurring probably before the feast began. **many believed**—superficially, struck merely by "the miracles He did." Of these we have no record.

24. did not commit—"entrust," or let Himself down familiarly to them, as to His genuine disciples.

25. knew what was in man—It is impossible for language more clearly to assert of Christ what in Jeremiah 17:9, 10, and elsewhere, is denied of all mere creatures.

CHAPTER 3

Vss. 1-21. Night Interview of Nicodemus with Jesus. 1, 2. Nicodemus—In this member of the Sanhedrim sincerity and timidity are seen struggling together. One of those superficial "believers" mentioned in ch. 2:23, 24, yet inwardly craving further satisfaction, he comes to Jesus in quest of it, but comes "by night" (see ch. 19:38, 39; 12:42); he avows his conviction that He was "come from God"—*an expression never applied to a merely human messenger*, and probably meaning more here—but only as "a *teacher*," and in His miracles he sees a proof merely that "God is with Him." Thus, while unable to repress his convictions, he is afraid of committing himself too far.

ALEXANDER MACLAREN:

"He came to Jesus by night," half-ashamed and wholly afraid of speaking out the conviction that was working in him. He was a man in position. He could not compromise himself in the eyes of his co-Sanhedrists. "It would be a grave thing for a man like me to be found in converse with this new rabbi and apparent prophet. I must go cautiously, and have regard to my reputation and my standing in the world; and shall steal to Him by night." There is something wrong with any convictions about Jesus Christ which let themselves be huddled up in secret. The true apprehension of Him is like a fire in a man's bones that makes him "weary of forbearing" when he locks his lips, and forces him to speak. If Christians can be speechless, there is something dreadfully wrong with their Christianity. If they do not regard Jesus Christ in such an aspect as to oblige them to stand out in the world and say, "Whatever anybody says or thinks about it, I am Christ's man," then be sure that they do not yet know Him as they ought to.

Nicodemus said, "Rabbi, we know." He is giving Jesus Christ a certificate, duly signed and sealed by rabbinical authority. He evidently thinks it is no small matter that he and some of his fellows should have been disposed to look with favor upon this new teacher. And so he comes, if not patronizing the young man, at all

ADAM CLARKE

23. *Many believed in his name*. They believed Him to be the promised Messiah, but did not believe in Him to the salvation of their souls; for we find from the following verse that their hearts were not at all changed, because our blessed Lord could not trust himself to them.

CHAPTER 3

1. *Nicodemus, a ruler of the Jews*. One of the members of the grand Sanhedrin, for such were ordinarily styled *rulers* among the Jews.

2. *Came to Jesus by night*. He had matters of the utmost importance on which he wished to consult Christ; and he chose the *night* season, perhaps less through the fear of man than through a desire to have Jesus alone, as he found Him all the day encompassed with the multitude, so that it was impossible for him to get an opportunity to speak fully on those weighty affairs concerning which he intended to consult Him.

Rabbi. "My Master" or "Teacher," a title of respect given to the Jewish doctors, something like our "Doctor of Divinity," i.e., teacher of divine things. But as there may be many found among us who, though they bear the title, are no teachers, so it was among the

MATTHEW HENRY

concerning Christ: *Thou art a teacher come from God;* supported with divine inspiration and divine authority. He came first to be a *teacher*; for he would rule by the power of truth, not of the sword. (2) His *assurance* of it: *We know, not only I,* but *others*; so he took it for granted, the thing being so plain and self-evident. (3) The ground of this assurance: *No man can do those miracles that thou doest, except God be with him.* Here was Nicodemus, a judicious, sensible, inquisitive man, one that had all the *reason* and *opportunity* imaginable to examine them, so fully satisfied that they were real miracles that he was wrought upon by them to go contrary to the stream of those of his own rank. We are directed what inference to draw from Christ's miracles: Therefore we are to receive him as a *teacher come from God.*

III. The discourse between Christ and Nicodemus hereupon, see *v.* 11, 12. Four things our Saviour here discourses of:

1. Concerning the *necessity and nature of regeneration* or the *new birth, v.* 3–8. Now we must consider this,

(1) As *pertinently answered* to Nicodemus's address. Jesus *answered, v.* 3. It was not enough for him to admire Christ's miracles, and acknowledge his mission, but he must be *born again.* It is plain that he expected the *kingdom of heaven* now shortly to appear. He is betimes aware of the dawning of that day. But Christ tells him that he can have no benefit by that *change of the state,* unless there be a *change of the spirit,* equivalent to a new birth. When Nicodemus owned Christ a *teacher come from God,* he plainly intimated a desire to know what this revelation was, and Christ declares it.

(2) As *positively* and *vehemently* asserted by our Lord Jesus: *Verily, verily, I say unto thee, except a man be born again he cannot see the kingdom of God.* Observe,

[1] What it is that is required: to be *born again.* We must *live a new life.* Birth is the beginning of life; to be *born again* is to begin anew. We must not think to patch up the old building, but begin from the foundation. We must *have a new nature,* new principles, new affections, new aims. We must be born *ἄνωθεν*, which signifies both *again,* and *from above.* We must be born *anew.* Our souls must be *fashioned* and *enlivened* anew. We must be born *from above.* This new birth has its rise *from heaven,* it is to be born to a *divine* and *heavenly* life.

[2] The indispensable necessity of this: "Except *a man be born again, he cannot see the kingdom of God.*" Except we be *born from above,* we cannot *see* this. We cannot *understand* the *nature* of it. We cannot *receive the comfort* of it. Regeneration is absolutely necessary to our happiness here and hereafter. It will appear, in the nature of the thing, that we must be *born again,* because it is impossible that we should be *happy* if we be not *holy.*

This great truth of the necessity of regeneration being thus solemnly laid down,

a. It is objected against by Nicodemus (*v.* 4): *How can a man be born when he is old? Can he enter the second time into his mother's womb, and be born?* Herein appears, (*a*) His weakness in knowledge; what Christ spoke spiritually he seems to have understood after a corporal and carnal manner, as if there was such a connection between the soul and the body that there could be no fashioning the *heart anew* but by forming the *bones anew.* It is a great surprise to him to hear of being *born again.* Could he be better bred and born than bred and born an Israelite. They that are proud of their *first birth* are hardly brought to a *new birth.* (*b*) His willingness to be taught. He does not turn his back upon Christ because of his hard saying, but ingenuously acknowledges his ignorance. "Lord, make me to understand this, for it is a riddle to me; I am such a fool as to know no other way for a man to be born than of his mother." When we meet with that in the things of God which is *dark,* and *hard to be understood,* we must continue our attendance upon the means of knowledge.

b. It is opened and further explained by our Lord Jesus, *v.* 5–8. From the objection he takes occasion to repeat and confirm what he had said (*v.* 5): "*Verily, verily I say unto thee,* the very same that I said before." Though Nicodemus understood not the mystery of regeneration, yet Christ asserts the necessity of it as positively as before. It is folly to think of evading the obligation of evangelical precepts, by pleading that they are unintelligible. To expound and clear what he had said he further shows,

(*a*) The *author* of this blessed change, and who it is that works it. To be born again is to be *born of the Spirit, v.* 5–8. The change is not wrought by any wisdom or power of our own, but by the power and influence of the blessed Spirit of grace.

JAMIESON, FAUSSET, BROWN

events extremely conscious of his own condescension in recognizing Him with his "We know."

Had he the right to speak for any of his colleagues? If so, then at that very early stage of our Lord's ministry there was a conviction beginning to work in that body of ecclesiastics which casts a very lurid light on their subsequent proceedings. It was a good long while after, when Jesus Christ's attitude toward them had been a little more clearly made out than it was at the beginning, that they said officially, "As for this fellow, we know not whence he is." They "knew" when He did not seem to be trenching on their prerogatives, or driving His Ithuriel-spear through their traditional professions of orthodoxy and punctilious casuistries. But when He trod on their toes, when He ripped up their pretensions, when He began to show His antagonism to their formalism and traditionalism, *then* they did not know where He came from.—*Expositions of Holy Scripture*

3. Except . . .—This blunt and curt reply was plainly meant to shake the whole edifice of the man's religion, in order to lay a deeper and more enduring foundation. Nicodemus probably thought he had gone a long way, and expected, perhaps, to be complimented on his candor. Instead of this, he is virtually told that he has raised a question which he is not in a capacity to solve, and that before approaching it, *his spiritual vision required to be rectified by an entire revolution on his inner man.* Had the man been less sincere, this would certainly have repelled him; but with persons in his mixed state of mind—to which Jesus was no stranger (ch. 2:25)—such methods speed better than more honeyed words and gradual approaches. **a man**—not *a Jew* merely; the necessity is a universal one. **born again**—or, as it were, *begin life anew* in relation to God; his manner of thinking, feeling, and acting, with reference to spiritual things, undergoing *a fundamental and permanent revolution.* **cannot see**—can have no part in (just as one is said to "see life," "see death," etc.). **the kingdom of God**—whether in its beginnings here (Luke 16:16), or its consummation hereafter (Matt. 25:34; Eph. 5:5).

4. How . . .—The figure of the new birth, if it had been meant only of *Gentile proselytes* to the Jewish religion, would have been intelligible enough to Nicodemus, being quite in keeping with the language of that day; but that *Jews themselves* should need a new birth was to him incomprehensible.

5. of water and of the Spirit—A twofold explanation of the "new birth," so startling to Nicodemus. To a Jewish ecclesiastic, so familiar with the symbolical application of water, in every variety

ADAM CLARKE

Jews; and perhaps it was in reference to this that Nicodemus uses the word *didaskalos* immediately after, by which, in chap. i. 39, John translates the word rabbi. *Rabbi,* teacher, is often no more than a title of respect; *didaskalos* signifies a person who not only has the name of teacher but who actually does teach. *We know that thou art a teacher come from God. We,* all the members of the grand Sanhedrin, and all the rulers of the people, who have paid proper attention to Thy doctrine and miracles. We are all convinced of this, though we are not all candid enough to own it. It is possible, however, that *we know* signifies no more than "it is known, it is generally acknowledged and allowed," *that thou art a teacher come from God. No man can do these miracles.* It is on the evidence of Thy miracles that I ground my opinion of Thee. No man can do what Thou dost unless the omnipotence of God be with him.

3. *Jesus answered.* Not in the language of compliment; He saw the state of Nicodemus' soul, and He immediately addressed himself to him on a subject the most interesting and important. But what connection is there between our Lord's reply and the address of Nicodemus? Probably our Lord saw that the object of his visit was to inquire about the Messiah's kingdom; and in reference to this He immediately says, *Except a man be born again.* The repetition of *amen,* or *verily, verily,* among the Jewish writers, was considered of equal import with the most solemn oath. *Be born again.* Or "from above"; different to that new birth which the Jews supposed every baptized proselyte enjoyed; for they held that the Gentile who became a proselyte was like a newborn child. This birth was of water from below; the birth for which Christ contends is "from above"—by the agency of the Holy Spirit. Every man must have two births: one from heaven, the other from earth—one of his body, the other of his soul. Without the first he cannot see nor enjoy this world; without the last he cannot see nor enjoy the kingdom of God. As there is an absolute necessity that a child should be born into the world, that he may see its light, contemplate its glories, and enjoy its good, so there is an absolute necessity that the soul should be brought out of its state of darkness and sin, through the light and power of the grace of Christ, that it may be able to *see,* or to "discern," the glories and excellencies of the kingdom of Christ here, and be prepared for the enjoyment of the Kingdom of glory hereafter. The Jews had some general notion of the new birth; but, like many among Christians, they put the acts of proselytism, baptism, etc., in the place of the Holy Spirit and His influence. They acknowledged that a man must be born again; but they made that new birth to consist in profession, confession, and external washing. The new birth which is here spoken of comprehends not only what is termed justification or pardon but also sanctification or holiness. Sin must be pardoned and the impurity of the heart washed away before any soul can possibly enter into the kingdom of God. As this new birth implies the renewing of the whole soul in righteousness and true holiness, it is not a matter that may be dispensed with. Heaven is a place of holiness, and nothing but what is like itself can ever enter into it.

4. *How can a man be born when he is old?* It is probable that Nicodemus was pretty far advanced in age at this time; and from his answer we may plainly perceive that, like the rest of the Jews, and like multitudes of Christians, he rested in the letter, without paying proper attention to the spirit. The shadow, without the thing signified, had hitherto satisfied him. Our Lord knew him to be in this state, and this was the cause of His pointed address to him.

5. *Of water and of the Spirit.* To the baptism of water a man was admitted when he became a proselyte to the Jewish religion; and, in this baptism, he promised in the most solemn man-

MATTHEW HENRY

(*b*) The *nature* of this change, and what that is which is wrought; it is *spirit*, *v.* 6. Those that are regenerated are made *spiritual*. The dictates and interests of the rational and immortal soul have retrieved the dominion they ought to have over the flesh.

(*c*) The *necessity* of this change. Christ here shows that it is necessary in the *nature of the thing*: *That which is born of the flesh is flesh*, *v.* 6. 1. We are here told *what we are*: We are *flesh*. The soul is still a spiritual substance, but so wedded to the flesh, so captivated by the will of the flesh, that it is justly called *flesh*. And what communion can there be between God, who is a *spirit*, and a soul in this condition? 2. How we *came to be so*; by being *born of the flesh*. It is a corruption that is bred *in the bone* with us. The corrupt nature, which is *flesh*, takes rise from our *first birth*; and therefore the new nature, which is *spirit*, must take rise from a second birth. Nicodemus spoke of entering again into his mother's womb, and being born; but, if he could do so, to what purpose? If he were born of his mother a hundred times, that would not mend the matter, for still that *which is born of the flesh is flesh*. Corruption and sin are woven into our nature; we are *shapen in iniquity*. It is not enough to put on a new coat or a new face, but we must put on the *new man*. Christ makes it further necessary, by his own word: *Marvel not that I said unto thee, You must be born again*, *v.* 7. Christ hath said it. He who is the great Physician of souls, knows their case, and what is necessary to their cure,—he hath said, *You must be born again*. We are not to *marvel* at it; for when we consider the holiness of the God with whom we have to do, the depravity of our nature, we shall not think it strange that so much stress is laid upon this as the one thing needful, that *we must be born again*.

(*d*) This change is illustrated by two comparisons. *First*, The regenerating work of the Spirit is compared to *water*, *v.* 5. To be born again is to be *born of water* and of the Spirit. That which is primarily intended here is to show that the Spirit, in sanctifying a soul, (1) *Cleanses* and purifies it as water, takes away its filth. (2) Cools and refreshes it, as water does the hunted hart and the weary traveller. It is probable that Christ had an eye to the ordinance of baptism, which John had used and he himself had begun to use, "You must be born again of the Spirit," which regeneration by the Spirit should be signified by washing with water, as the visible sign of that spiritual grace. *Secondly*, It is compared to *wind*: *The wind bloweth where it listeth, so is every one that is born of the Spirit*, *v.* 8. The same word signifies both the wind and the Spirit. The Spirit, in regeneration, works *arbitrarily*, and as a free agent. The Spirit dispenses his influences where, and when, on whom, and in what measure and degrees, he pleases. He works *powerfully*, and with evident effects: *Thou hearest the sound thereof;* though its causes are hidden, its effects are manifest. He works *mysteriously*, and in secret hidden ways. *Thou canst not tell whence it comes, nor whither it goes.* How it gathers and how it spends its strength is a riddle to us; so the manner and methods of the Spirit's working are a mystery.

2. The *certainty and sublimity of gospel truths.*

(1) The objection which Nicodemus still made (*v.* 9): *How can these things be?* Christ's explication of the doctrine of the necessity of regeneration, it should seem, made it never the clearer to him. The corruption of nature which makes it *necessary*, and the way of the Spirit which makes it *practicable*, are as much mysteries to him as the thing itself. Thus many will neither believe the truths of Christianity nor submit to the laws of it further than *they please*. Christ shall be their teacher, provided they may choose their lesson. Nicodemus owns himself ignorant of Christ's meaning, after all: "*How can these things be?* They are things I do not understand, my capacity will not reach them." Because this doctrine was *unintelligible* to him he questions the truth of it. Many think that that cannot be *proved* which they cannot *believe*.

(2) The reproof which Christ gave him for his dullness and ignorance: "*Art thou a master in Israel*, and yet not only unacquainted with the doctrine of regeneration, but incapable of understanding it?" This word is a reproof, [1] To those who undertake to teach others and yet are ignorant and unskilful in the world of righteousness themselves. [2] To those that spend their time in notions and ceremonies in religion, niceties and criticisms in the scripture, and neglect that which is practical. Two words in the reproof are very emphatic: *First*, The place where his lot was cast: in *Israel*, where divine revelation was. He might have learned this out of the Old Testament. *Secondly*, The things he was thus ignorant in: *these*

JAMIESON, FAUSSET, BROWN

of way and form of expression, this language was fitted to show that the thing intended was no other than a *thorough spiritual purification by the operation of the Holy Ghost*. Indeed, element of *water* and operation of *the Spirit* are brought together in a glorious evangelical prediction of Ezekiel (36:25-27), which Nicodemus might have been reminded of had such spiritualities not been almost lost in the reigning formalism. Already had the symbol of water been embodied in an initiatory ordinance, in the baptism of the Jewish expectants of Messiah by the Baptist, not to speak of the baptism of Gentile proselytes before that; and in the Christian Church it was soon to become the great visible door of entrance into "the kingdom of God," *the reality being the sole work of the Holy Ghost* [Titus 3:5]. **6-8. That which is born . . .**—A great universal proposition; "That which is begotten carries within itself the nature of that which begat it" [OLSHAUSEN]. **flesh**—Not the mere material body, but all that comes into the world by birth, *the entire man;* yet not humanity simply, but in its corrupted, depraved condition, *in complete subjection to the law of the fall* (Rom. 8:1-9). So that though a man "*could* enter a second time into his mother's womb and be born," he would be no nearer this "new birth" than before (Job 14:4; Ps. 51:5). **is spirit**—*partakes of and possesses His spiritual nature.* **7. Marvel not . . .**—If a spiritual nature only can see and enter the kingdom of God; if all we bring into the world with us be the reverse of spiritual; and if this spirituality be solely of the Holy Ghost, no wonder a new birth is indispensable. **Ye must**—"*Ye,* says Jesus, not *we*" [BENGEL]. After those universal propositions, about what "*a man*" must be, to "enter the kingdom of God,"—this is remarkable, showing that our Lord meant to hold Himself forth as "*separate from sinners*."

8. The wind . . .—*Breath* and *spirit* (one word both in Hebrew and Greek) are constantly brought together in Scripture as analogous (Job 27:3; 33:4; Ezek. 37:9-14). **canst not tell . . .**—The laws which govern the motion of the *winds* are even yet but partially discovered; but the risings, fallings, and change in direction many times in a day, of those *gentle breezes* here referred to, will probably ever be a mystery to us: So of the operation of the Holy Ghost in the new birth.

9, 10. How . . .—Though the subject still confounds him, the necessity and possibility of the new birth is no longer the point with him, but the nature of it and how it is brought about [LUTHARDT]. "From this moment Nicodemus *says nothing more*, but has sunk unto a disciple who has found his true teacher. *Therefore* the Saviour now graciously advances in His communications of truth, and once more solemnly brings to the mind of this teacher in Israel, now become a learner, his own not guiltless *ignorance*, that He may then proceed to utter, out of the fulness of His divine knowledge, such farther testimonies both of earthly and heavenly things as his docile scholar may to his own profit receive" [STIER]. **master**—"teacher." The question clearly implies that *the doctrine of regeneration is so far disclosed in the Old Testament that Nicodemus was culpable in being ignorant of it.* Nor is it merely as something that should be experienced *under the* Gospel that the Old Testament holds it forth—as many distinguished critics allege, denying that there was any such thing as regeneration before Christ. For our Lord's proposition is universal, that no fallen man is or can be spiritual without a regenerating operation of the Holy Ghost, and the necessity of a *spiritual obedience* under whatever name, in opposition to mere mechanical services, is proclaimed throughout all the Old Testament.

ADAM CLARKE

ner to renounce idolatry, to take the God of Israel for his God, and to have his life conformed to the precepts of the divine law. But the water which was used on the occasion was only an emblem of the Holy Spirit. The soul was considered as in a state of defilement because of past sin. Now, as by that water the body was washed, cleansed, and refreshed, so, by the influences of the Holy Spirit, the soul was to be purified from its defilement and strengthened to walk in the way of truth and holiness. When John came baptizing with water, he gave the Jews the plainest intimations that this would not suffice; that it was only typical of that baptism of the Holy Ghost, under the similitude of fire, which they must all receive from Jesus Christ. See Matt. iii. 11. Therefore our Lord asserts that a man must be *born of water and of the Spirit,* i.e., of the Holy Ghost, which, represented under the similitude of *water*, cleanses, refreshes, and purifies the soul. Though baptism by water into the Christian faith was necessary to every Jew and Gentile that entered into the kingdom of the Messiah, it is not necessary that by water and the Spirit (in this place) we should understand two different things. It is probably only an elliptical form of speech for the Holy Spirit under the similitude of water; as, in Matt. iii. 3, "the Holy Ghost and fire" do not mean two things, but one, viz., the Holy Ghost under the similitude of fire—pervading every part, refining and purifying the whole.

6. *That which is born of the flesh is flesh.* This is the answer to the objection made by Nicodemus in v. 4. "Can a man enter the second time into his mother's womb, and be born?"

8. *The wind bloweth.* Though the manner in which this new birth is effected by the Divine Spirit be incomprehensible to us, yet we must not on this ground suppose it to be impossible. The wind blows in a variety of directions—we hear its sound, perceive its operation in the motion of the trees, etc., and feel it on ourselves—but we cannot discern the air itself; we only know that it exists by the effects which it produces. *So is every one that is born of the Spirit;* the effects are as discernible and as sensible as those of the wind, but itself we cannot see. But he who is born of God knows that he is thus born. "The Spirit itself," the grand Agent in this new birth, "beareth witness with our spirit," that he is born of God, Rom. viii. 16; for "he that believeth . . . hath the witness in himself," 1 John iv. 13 and v. 10; Gal. iv. 6. And so does this Spirit work in and by him that others, though they see not the principle, can easily discern the change produced; for "whatsoever is born of God overcometh the world," 1 John v. 4.

9. *How can these things be?* Our Lord had very plainly told him how these things could be, and illustrated the new birth by one of the most proper similes that could be chosen; but so intent was this great man on making everything submit to the testimony of his senses that he appears unwilling to believe anything unless he can comprehend it. This is the case with many—they profess to believe because they comprehend, but they are impostors who speak thus. There is not a man in the universe that can fully comprehend one operation, either of God or of His instrument nature; and yet they must believe, and do believe, though they never did nor ever can fully comprehend, or account for, the objects of their faith.

10. *Art thou a master of Israel?* Have you taken upon you to guide the blind into the way of truth, and yet know not that truth yourself? Do you command proselytes to be baptized with water as an emblem of a new birth, and are you unacquainted with the cause, necessity, na-

MATTHEW HENRY

things, these *necessary* things, these *great* things, these *divine* things.

(3) Christ's discourse, hereupon, of the certainty and sublimity of gospel truths (*v.* 11–13). Observe here,

[1] That the truths Christ taught were very *certain* and what we may venture upon (*v.* 11): *We speak that we do know.* The truths of Christ are of undoubted certainty. We have all the reason in the world to be assured that the sayings of Christ are *faithful sayings*, and such as we may venture our souls upon. Whatever Christ spoke, he spoke *of his own knowledge.* The things are thus sure, thus clear; and yet *you receive not our witness.*

[2] The truths Christ taught, though communicated in language and expressions borrowed from common and earthly things, yet were most sublime and heavenly; this is intimated, *v.* 12: "*I have told them earthly things*, that is, have told them the great things of God in similitudes taken from earthly things, to make them the more easy and intelligible, as that of the *new birth* and the *wind*, and lisped to you in your own language, and cannot make you to understand my doctrine. If such *familiar expressions* be stumbling-blocks, what would *abstract ideas* be, and spiritual things painted *proper?*" The things of the gospel are *heavenly* things, out of the road of the enquiries of human reason, and much more out of the reach of its discoveries. He considers our *frame*, that we are *of* the earth, and our *place*, that we are *on* the earth, and therefore speaks to us earthly things, and makes things sensible the vehicle of things spiritual, to make them the more easy and familiar to us. Earthly things are despised because they are *vulgar*, and heavenly things because they are *abstruse*; and so, whatever method is taken, still some fault or other is found with it.

[3] Our Lord Jesus, and he alone, was fit to reveal to us a doctrine thus certain, thus sublime: *No man hath ascended up into heaven but he*, *v.* 13. None but Christ was able to reveal to us the will of God for our salvation. Nicodemus addressed Christ as a prophet; but he must know that he is greater than all the Old Testament prophets, for none of them *had ascended into heaven.* No man hath attained to the certain knowledge of God and heavenly things as Christ has. It is not for us to send to heaven for instructions; we must wait to receive what instructions Heaven will send to us. Jesus Christ is able to reveal the will of God to us; for it is *he that came down from heaven* and *is in heaven.* He had said (*v.* 12), *How shall ye believe, if I tell you of heavenly things?* He gives them an instance of those *heavenly things* when he tells them of one that *came down from heaven*, and yet is the *Son of man.* If the regeneration of the *soul of man* is such a mystery, what then is the incarnation of the *Son of God*? We have here an intimation of Christ's two distinct natures in one person. He gives them a proof of his ability to speak to them *heavenly things* by telling them, (1) That *he came down from heaven.* The intercourse settled between God and man began *above.* We love him, and send to him, because he first loved us, and sent to us. Now this intimates, [1] Christ's divine nature. [2] His intimate acquaintance with the divine counsels. [3] The *manifestation of God.* The New Testament shows us God *coming down* from heaven, to teach and save us. Herein he commended his love. (2) That *he is the Son of man*, by which the Jews always understand to be meant the Messiah. (3) That he *is in heaven.* Now at this time, when he is talking with Nicodemus on earth, yet, as God, he is *in heaven.*

3. Christ here discourses of the *great design of his own coming into the world, and the happiness of those that believe in him*, *v.* 14–18. Here we have the very marrow and quintessence of the whole gospel, that Jesus Christ came to seek and to save the children of men from death, and recover them to life. This saving here is opposed to condemning, *v.* 16–18.

(1) Jesus Christ came to save us by *healing* us, as the children of Israel that were stung with fiery serpents were cured and *lived* by looking up to the brazen serpent.

First, The *deadly* and *destructive* nature of *sin*, which is implied here. The guilt of sin is like the *pain* of the biting of a fiery serpent; the power of corruption is like the *venom* diffused thereby. The curses of the law are as fiery serpents, so are all the tokens of divine wrath.

Secondly, The powerful remedy provided against this fatal malady. The case of poor sinners is deplorable; but is it desperate? Thanks be to God, it is not. The *Son of man is lifted up*, as the *serpent of brass* was by Moses. It was a *serpent of brass* that cured them. It was made in the shape of a *fiery serpent*, and yet had no poison, no sting, fitly representing Christ; as harmless as a serpent of brass. It was

JAMIESON, FAUSSET, BROWN

11-13. We speak that we know, and . . . have seen—i.e., by *absolute* knowledge and *immediate* vision of God, which "the only-begotten Son in the bosom of the Father" claims as exclusively His own (ch. 1:18). The "we" and "our" are here used, though Himself only is intended, in emphatic contrast, probably, with the opening words of Nicodemus, "Rabbi, *we know* . . . ." **ye receive not . . .**—referring to the *class* to which Nicodemus belonged, but from which he was beginning to be separated in spirit. **12. earthly things**—such as *regeneration,* the gate of entrance to the kingdom of God *on earth,* and which Nicodemus should have understood better, as a truth even of that more *earthly* economy to which he belonged. **heavenly things**—the things of the new and more heavenly evangelical economy, only to be fully understood after the effusion of the Spirit from heaven through the exalted Saviour.

13. no man hath ascended . . .—There is something paradoxical in this language—'No one has gone up but He that came down, even He who is at once both up and down.' Doubtless it was intended to startle and constrain His auditor to think that there must be mysterious elements in His Person. The old Socinians, to subvert the doctrine of the pre-existence of Christ, seized upon this passage as teaching that the man Jesus was secretly caught up to heaven to receive His instructions, and then "came down from heaven" to deliver them. But the sense manifestly is this: 'The perfect knowledge of God is not obtained by any man's going up from earth to heaven to receive it—no man hath so ascended—but He whose *proper habitation,* in His essential and eternal nature, is heaven, hath, by taking human flesh, descended as the "Son of man" to disclose the Father, whom He knows by immediate gaze alike in the flesh as before He assumed it, being essentially and unchangeably "in the bosom of the Father" ' (ch. 1:18).

14-16. And as Moses . . .—Here now we have the "heavenly things," as before the "earthly," but under a veil, for the reason mentioned in vs. 12. The crucifixion of Messiah is twice after this veiled under the same lively term—"*uplifting,*" ch. 8:28; 12:32, 33. Here it is still further veiled—though to us who know what it means, rendered vastly more instructive—by reference to the brazen serpent. The venom of the fiery serpents, shooting through the veins of the rebellious Israelites, was spreading death through the camp—lively emblem of the perishing condition of men by reason of sin. In both cases the remedy was divinely provided. In both the way of cure strikingly resembled that of the disease. Stung by serpents, by a serpent they are healed. By "fiery serpents" bitten—serpents, probably, with skin spotted fiery-red (KURTZ)—the instrument of cure is a serpent of brass or copper, having at a distance *the same appearance.* So in redemption, as by man came death, by Man also comes life—Man, too, "*in the likeness of sinful flesh,*" differing in nothing *outward and apparent* from those who, pervaded by the poison of the serpent, were ready to perish. But as the uplifted serpent had none of the venom of which the serpent-bitten people were dying, so while the whole human family were perishing of the deadly wound inflicted on it by the old serpent, "the Second Man," who arose over humanity with healing in His wings, was without spot or wrinkle, or any such thing. In both cases the remedy is *conspicuously displayed;* in the one case on a pole, in the other on the cross, to "draw all men unto Him"

ADAM CLARKE

ture, and effects of that new birth? "But I am taught to believe that this baptism is regeneration." Then you are taught to believe a falsity. Whereby are such persons made the children of grace? Not by the water, but by the "death unto sin," and the "new birth unto righteousness"; i.e., through the agency of the Holy Ghost sin is destroyed and the soul filled with holiness.

11. *We speak that we do know.* I and My disciples do not profess to teach a religion which we do not understand nor exemplify in our conduct. A strong but delicate reproof to Nicodemus, who, though a master of Israel, did not understand the very rudiments of the doctrine of salvation.

12. *If I have told you earthly things.* If after I have illustrated this new birth by a most expressive metaphor taken from earthly things, and after all you believe not, how can you believe should I tell you of *heavenly things,* in such language as angels use, where earthly images and illustrations can have no place? Or if you, a teacher in Israel, do not understand the nature of such an earthly thing, or custom of the kingdom established over the Jewish nation, as being born of baptism, practiced every day in the initiation of proselytes, how will you understand such heavenly things as the initiation of My disciples by the baptism of the Holy Ghost and fire from heaven, if I should proceed further on the subject?

13. *No man hath ascended.* This seems a figurative expression for "No man hath known the mysteries of the kingdom of God," as in Deut. xxx. 12; Ps. lxxiii. 17; Prov. xxx. 4; Rom. xi. 34. And the expression is founded upon this generally received maxim: That to be perfectly acquainted with the concerns of a place, it is necessary for a person to be on the spot. But our Lord probably spoke to correct a false notion among the Jews, viz., that Moses had ascended to heaven in order to get the law. It is not Moses who is to be heard now, but Jesus; Moses did not ascend to heaven, but the Son of Man is come down from heaven to reveal the divine will. *That came down.* The incarnation of Christ is represented under the notion of His *coming down* from heaven to dwell upon earth.

14. *As Moses lifted up.* He shows the reason why He descended from heaven, that He might be lifted up, i.e., crucified, for the salvation of mankind, and be, by the appointment of God, as certain a Remedy for sinful souls as the brazen serpent elevated on a pole, Num. xxi. 9, was for the bodies of the Israelites which had been bitten by the fiery serpents in the wilderness.

MATTHEW HENRY

lifted up upon a pole, and so *must* the Son of man be lifted up. Christ is lifted up, [1] In his *crucifixion.* He was lifted up upon the cross. His death is called his being *lifted up, ch.* xii. 32, 33. [2] In his *exaltation.* He was lifted up to the Father's right hand. He was lifted up to the cross, to be further lifted up to the crown. [3] In the *publishing* and *preaching* of his everlasting gospel. Being thus lifted up, it was appointed for the cure. He that sent the plague provided the remedy. It was God himself that *found the ransom.* He whom we have offended is *our peace.*

Thirdly, The way of *applying* this remedy, and that is by *believing*. Everyone that *looked up to it* did well, Num. xxi. 9. He hath said, *Look, and be saved* (Isa. xlv. 22), look and live.

Fourthly, The great encouragements given us by faith to look up to him. *a.* It was for this end that he was *lifted up*, that his followers might be saved. *b.* The offer that is made of salvation by him is general, *whosoever believes* without exception. *c.* The salvation offered is complete. They *shall not perish.* They shall *have eternal life.*

(2) Jesus Christ came to save us by *pardoning us, v.* 16, 17. Here is *gospel* indeed, good *news*, the best that ever came from heaven to earth.

First, Here is God's *love*, in *giving his Son for the world* (*v.* 16). [1]. The great *gospel mystery* revealed: *God so loved the world that he gave his only-begotten Son. a.* Jesus Christ is the *only-begotten Son of God.* Now know we that he loves us, when he has given his *only-begotten Son for us. b.* In order to the redemption and salvation of man, it pleased God to *give his only-begotten Son.* He *gave him*, that is, he gave him up to suffer and die for us. His enemies could not have *taken him* if his Father had not *given* him. *c.* Herein God has commended his *love to the world*; God so *loved the world*, so really, so richly. Behold, and wonder, that the *great God* should love such a *worthless* world; that the *holy God* should love such a *wicked* world. The Jews vainly conceited that the Messiah should be sent only in love to *their nation*; but Christ tells them that he came in love to the *whole world*, Gentiles as well as Jews. Through him there is a *general offer* of life and salvation made to all. So *far God loved the world* that he sent his Son with this fair proposal, that *whosoever believes in him shall not perish. Salvation* has been *of the Jews*, but now Christ is *known as salvation to the ends of the earth.* [2]. Here is the great *gospel duty*, and that is to *believe in Jesus Christ.* [3]. Here is the great gospel benefit: *That whosoever believes in Christ shall not perish.* God has taken away their sin, they shall not die; a pardon is purchased. They are entitled to the joys of heaven: they shall *have everlasting life.*

Secondly, Here is God's design in sending his Son into the world: it was *that the world through him might be saved.* He came into the world with salvation in *his eye*, with salvation *in his hand* (*v.* 17): *God sent his Son into the world*; sent him as his agent or ambassador, as resident. We are concerned to enquire on what errand he comes: *Is it peace?* And this scripture returns the answer, *Peaceably.* He did not come to *condemn the world.* We had reason enough to expect that he should, for it is a guilty world; it is *convicted.* Justly may such a world as this be *condemned.* He came with full powers indeed to *execute judgment* (*ch.* v. 22, 27), but did not begin with a judgment of condemnation, but put us upon a new trial before a *throne of grace.* He came *that the world through him might be saved.* God was in Christ *reconciling the world to himself*, and so *saving* it. This is good news to a convinced conscience, healing to broken bones and bleeding wounds, that Christ, our judge, came not to *condemn*, but to *save.*

(3) From all this is inferred the happiness of true believers: *He that believeth on him is not condemned, v.* 18. This denotes more than a reprieve; he *is not condemned*, that is, he is acquitted; and if he be not condemned he is discharged. *Who is he that condemns? It is Christ that died.* The cross perhaps lies heavy upon him, but he is saved from the curse: condemned *by the world*, it may be, but not *condemned with the world*, Rom. viii. 1.

4. The *deplorable condition of those that persist in unbelief and wilful ignorance, v.* 18–21.

(1) Read here the doom of those that will not *believe in Christ*: they *are condemned already.* [1] How great the *sin* of unbelievers is. They *believe not in the name of the only-begotten Son of God*, who is infinitely *true*, and deserves to be believed, *infinitely good*, and deserves to be embraced. God sent one to save us that was *dearest* to himself; and shall not he be *dearest to us*? [2] How great the *misery* of unbelievers is: they are *condemned already.* A *certain* condemnation. A *present* condemnation. They are condemned already, for their own hearts condemn them.

JAMIESON, FAUSSET, BROWN

(ch. 12:32). In both cases it is by *directing the eye to the uplifted Remedy* that the cure is effected; in the one case the bodily eye, in the other the gaze of the soul by "believing in Him," as in that glorious ancient proclamation—"*Look* unto me and be ye saved, all the ends of the earth . . ." (Isa. 45:22). Both methods are stumbling to human reason. What, to any thinking Israelite, could seem more unlikely than that a deadly poison should be dried up in his body by simply looking on a reptile of brass? Such a stumbling block to the Jews and to the Greeks foolishness was faith in the crucified Nazarene as a way of deliverance from eternal perdition. Yet was the warrant in both cases to expect a cure equally rational and well grounded. As the serpent was *God's ordinance* for the cure of every bitten Israelite, so is Christ for the salvation of every perishing sinner—the one however a purely *arbitrary* ordinance, the other divinely *adapted* to man's complicated maladies. In both cases the efficacy is the same. As one simple look at the serpent, however distant and however weak, brought an instantaneous cure, even so, real faith in the Lord Jesus, however tremulous, however distant—be it but *real* faith—brings certain and instant healing to the perishing soul. In a word, the consequences of disobedience are the same in both. Doubtless many bitten Israelites, galling as their case was, would *reason* rather than *obey*, would *speculate* on the absurdity of expecting the bite of a living serpent to be cured by looking at a piece of dead metal in the shape of one—speculate thus *till they died.* Alas! is not salvation by a crucified Redeemer subjected to like treatment? Has the offense of the cross" yet ceased? (Cf. II Kings 5:12). **16. For God so loved . . .**—What proclamation of the Gospel has been so oft on the lips of missionaries and preachers in every age since it was first uttered? What has sent such thrilling sensations through millions of mankind? What has been honored to bring such multitudes to the feet of Christ? What to kindle in the cold and selfish breasts of mortals the fires of selfsacrificing love to mankind, as these words of transparent simplicity, yet overpowering majesty? The picture embraces several distinct compartments: "THE WORLD"—in its widest sense—*ready "to perish"*; the immense "LOVE OF GOD" *to that perishing world*, measurable only, and conceivable only, by the gift which it drew forth from Him; THE GIFT itself—"He *so* loved the world that He *gave His* only begotten Son," or, in the language of Paul, "*spared not* His own Son" (Rom. 8:32), or in that addressed to Abraham when ready to offer Isaac on the altar, "*withheld not* His Son, His only Son, whom He loved" (Gen. 22:16); the FRUIT of this stupendous gift—not only *deliverance from* impending "*perdition*," but *the bestowal of everlasting life*; and the MODE in which all takes effect—by "*believing*" on the Son. How would Nicodemus' narrow Judaism become invisible in the blaze of this Sun of righteousness seen rising on "the world" with healing in His wings! **17-21. not to condemn . . .**—A statement of vast importance. Though "condemnation" is to many the *issue* of Christ's mission (vs. 19), it is not the *object* of His mission, which is purely a *saving* one.

18. is not condemned—Having, immediately on his believing, "passed from death unto life" (ch. 5:24).

condemned already—Rejecting the one way of deliverance from that "condemnation" which God gave His Son to *remove*, and so wilfully *remaining* condemned.

ADAM CLARKE

CHARLES H. SPURGEON:

The only thing we have to do with Christ Jesus crucified is to lift Him up and preach Him. There is many a man who could speak only in a ploughman's dialect, who will wear a bright and starry crown in heaven, because he lifted Christ up, and sinners saw and lived. And there is many a learned doctor, who spoke with the brogue of the Egyptian, and, with the dark and mysterious language, he talked he knew not what, who, after having ended his course, shall enter heaven without a solitary star in his crown, never having lifted up Christ, nor won crowns for his Master. Let each of us who are called to the solemn work of the ministry remember that we are not called to lift up doctrine, or church governments, or particular denominations; our business is to lift up Christ Jesus and to preach Him fully. There may be times when church government is to be discussed, and peculiar doctrines are to be vindicated. God forbid that we should silence any part of the truth; but the main work of the ministry —its everyday work—is just exhibiting Christ and crying out to sinners, "Believe, believe, believe on Him who is the Lamb of God that taketh away the sins of the world."

—*The Treasury of the New Testament*

16. *For God so loved the world.* Such a love as that which induced God to give His only begotten Son to die for the world could not be described; Jesus Christ does not attempt it. He has put an eternity of meaning in the particle *so* and left a subject for everlasting contemplation, wonder, and praise, to angels and to men. The same Evangelist uses a similar mode of expression, 1 Epist. iii. 1: "Behold, what manner of love the Father hath bestowed upon us."

17. *For God sent not.* It was the opinion of the Jews that the Gentiles, whom they often term "the world," and "nations of the world," were to be destroyed in the days of the Messiah. Christ corrects this false opinion and teaches here a contrary doctrine. God, by giving His Son and publishing His design in giving Him, shows that He purposes the salvation, not the destruction, of the world—the Gentile people. Nevertheless, those who will not receive the salvation He had provided for them, whether Jews or Gentiles, must necessarily perish; for this plain reason, there is but one remedy, and they refuse to apply it.

18. *He that believeth.* As stated before on v. 16. *Is not condemned.* For past sin, that being forgiven on his believing in Christ. *But he that believeth not.* When the gospel is preached to him, and the way of salvation made plain.

Is condemned already. Continues under the condemnation which divine justice has passed upon all sinners; and has this superadded, *He hath not believed in the name of the only begotten Son of God,* and therefore is guilty of the grossest insult to the divine majesty in neglecting, slighting, and despising the salvation which the infinite mercy of God had provided for him.

MATTHEW HENRY

A condemnation *grounded upon their former guilt. He is condemned already, because he has not believed.* Unbelief is a sin against the *remedy.*

(2) Read also the doom of those that would not so much as *know him, v.* 19. And *this is the condemnation, that light is come into the world, and they loved darkness rather.* The gospel is light, and, when the gospel came, *light came into the world.* Light is *self-evidencing,* so is the gospel; it proves its own divine origin. Light is *discovering,* and *truly the light is sweet.* A dark place indeed the world would be without it. It is the unspeakable folly of the most of men that they loved darkness rather than *this* light. Sinners that were wedded to their lusts loved their ignorance and mistakes rather than the truths of Christ. Wretched man is in love with his sickness, in love with his slavery, and will not be made *free,* will not be *made whole.* The true reason why men love darkness rather than light is *because their deeds are evil.* Their case is sad, and, because they are resolved that they will not *mend* it, they are resolved that they will not *see it.* Wilful ignorance is so far from excusing sin that it will be found to aggravate the condemnation: *This is the condemnation,* that they shut their eyes against the light, and will not so much as admit a parley with Christ and his gospel. We must account in the judgment not only for the knowledge we *sinned against,* but for the knowledge we *sinned away.* It is a common observation that *everyone that doeth evil hateth the light, v.* 20. Evil-doers seek concealment, out of a sense of shame and fear of punishment. *They come not to this light,* but keep as far off it as they can, *lest their deeds should be reproved.* The light of the gospel is sent into the *world* to *reprove the evil deeds* of sinners; to *show* people *their transgressions,* to show that to be sin which was not thought to be so, *that sin by the* new *commandment* might appear *exceeding sinful.* The gospel has its convictions, to make way for its consolations. It is for this reason that evil-doers *hate the light* of the gospel. There were those who *had done evil* and were sorry for it, who bade this light welcome, as the *publicans and harlots.* But he that *does evil,* and resolves to go on in it, *hateth the light.* Christ is hated because sin is loved. They who do not *come to the light* thereby evidence a secret *hatred* of the light. On the other hand, upright hearts bid this light welcome (*v.* 21): *He that doeth truth cometh to the light.* As it *convinces* and *terrifies* evil-doers, so it *confirms* and *comforts* those that walk in their integrity. The character of a *good man.* He is one that *doeth truth.* Though sometimes he comes short of *doing good,* the good he would do, yet he *doeth truth,* he aims honestly; he has his infirmities, but holds fast his integrity. He is one that *cometh to the light.* He that *doeth truth* is willing to know the *truth* by himself, and to *have his deeds made manifest.* He is solicitous to *know* what the will of God is, and resolves to *do it,* though ever so contrary to his own will and interest. Here is the character of a *good work*: it is *wrought in God.* Our works are *then* good, when the will of God is the rule of them and the glory of God the end of them; when they are done in his strength and for his sake. Nicodemus, though he was puzzled at first, yet afterwards became a faithful disciple of Christ.

Verses 22-36

I. Christ's removal into the land of Judæa (*v.* 22). Our Lord Jesus, after he entered upon his public work, travelled much, and removed often. Many a weary step he took to do good to souls. The *Sun of righteousness* took a large circuit to diffuse his light and heat, Ps. xix. 6. He was not wont to stay long at Jerusalem. *After these things,* after he had had this discourse with Nicodemus, he came into the land of Judæa; not so much for *greater privacy* as for *greater usefulness.* His preaching and miracles, perhaps, made *most noise* at Jerusalem, the fountain-head of news, but did *least good* there. When he came into the land of Judæa his *disciples came with him.* There he *tarried with them.* Those that are ready to *go with Christ* shall find him as ready to *stay with them.* There *he baptized.* John began to baptize in the land of Judæa (Matt. iii. 1), therefore Christ began there. He himself *baptized* not, with his own hand, but his disciples by his orders and directions, as appears, *ch.* iv. 2. Holy ordinances are Christ's, though administered by weak men.

II. John's continuance in his work, as long as his opportunities lasted, *v.* 23, 24. Here we are told,

1. That *John was baptizing.* Christ's baptism, was, for substance, the same with John's, and therefore they did not at all clash or interfere with one another. (1) Christ began the work of preaching and baptizing before *John laid it down,* so the wheels might be kept going. It is a comfort to useful men, when they are

JAMIESON, FAUSSET, BROWN

19. this is the condemnation . . .—emphatically so, *revealing* the condemnation already existing, and *sealing up* under it those who will not be delivered from it. **light is come into the world**—in the Person of Him to whom Nicodemus was listening. **loved darkness . . .**—This can only be known by the deliberate rejection of Christ, but that *does* fearfully reveal it.

20. reproved—by detection.

21. doeth truth—whose only object in life is to be and do what will bear the light. Therefore he loves and "comes to the light," that all he is and does, being thus thoroughly tested, may be seen to have nothing in it but what is divinely wrought and divinely approved. This is the "Israelite, indeed, in whom is no guile."

22-36. Jesus in the Neighborhood of the Baptist—His Noble Testimony to His Master. **22-24. land of Judea**—the rural parts of that province, the foregoing conversation being held in the capital.

ADAM CLARKE

19. *This is the condemnation.* That is, this is the reason why some shall finally perish, not that they came into the world with a perverted and corrupt nature, which is true; nor that they lived many years in the practice of sin, which is also true; but because they refused to receive the salvation which God sent to them. *Light is come.* That is, Jesus, the Sun of righteousness, the Fountain of light and life, diffusing His benign influences everywhere, and favoring men with a clear and full revelation of the divine will. *Men loved darkness.* Have preferred sin to holiness, Belial to Christ, and hell to heaven. *Chashac,* "darkness," is frequently used by the Jewish writers for the angel of death and for the devil. *Because their deeds were evil.* An allusion to robbers and cutthroats, who practice their abominations in the night season for fear of being detected.

20. *For every one that doeth evil hateth the light.* He who doth vile or abominable things, alluding to the subject mentioned in the preceding verse.

Lest his deeds should be reproved. Or "discovered." To "manifest" or "discover" is one sense of the original word in the best Greek writers, and is evidently its meaning in this place.

21. *Wrought in God.* In His presence, and through His assistance. This is the end of our Lord's discourse to Nicodemus; and though we are not informed here of any good effects produced by it, yet we learn from other scriptures that it had produced the most blessed effects in his mind, and that from this time he became a disciple of Christ. He publicly defended our Lord in the Sanhedrin, of which he was probably a member, chap. vii. 50; and, with Joseph of Arimathaea, gave Him an honorable funeral, chap. xix. 39, when all His bosom friends had deserted Him.

22. *Came . . . into the land of Judaea.* Jerusalem itself, where Christ held the preceding discourse with Nicodemus, was in Judea; but the Evangelist means that our Lord quitted the city and its suburbs and went into the country parts. The same distinction between Jerusalem and Judea is made in Acts i. 8; x. 39; and in 1 Macc. iii. 34; 2 Macc. i. 1, 10.

MATTHEW HENRY

going off the stage, to see those rising up who are likely to fill up their place. (2) John continued the work of preaching and baptizing though Christ had *taken it up*. There was still work for John to do, for Christ was not yet *generally known*, nor were the minds of people *thoroughly prepared* for him by repentance. *He goes on* with his work, till Providence lays him aside. The greater gifts of some do not *render* the labours of others, that come short of them, *needless* and *useless*; there is work enough for all hands. They are sullen that will sit down and do nothing when they see themselves outshone.

2. That he baptized in Ænon near Salim, places we find nowhere else mentioned. Wherever it was, it seems that John removed from *place to place*. Ministers must follow their opportunities. He chose a place where there was much water, that is, many *streams* of water; so that wherever he met with any that were willing to submit to his baptism water was at hand to baptize.

3. That thither people *came to him* and *were baptized*. Some refer this both to John and to Jesus: some came to John, some to Jesus, and, as their baptism was one, so were their hearts.

4. It is noted (*v.* 24) that *John was not yet cast into prison*. John never desisted from his work as long as he had his liberty.

III. A contest between *John's disciples and the Jews about purifying*, *v.* 25. 1. Who were the disputants: *some of John's disciples, and the Jews* who had not submitted to his baptism of repentance. Penitents and impenitents divide this sinful world. 2. What was the matter in dispute: *about purifying*, about *religious washing*. We may suppose that John's disciples cried up his baptism, his purifying, and gave the preference to that as perfecting and superseding all the purifications of the Jews, and they were in the right. No doubt the Jews with as much assurance applauded the *purifyings* that were in use among them. It is very likely that the Jews in this dispute, when they could not *deny* the excellent nature and design of John's baptism, raised an objection against it from Christ's baptism, which gave occasion for the complaint that follows here (*v.* 26). Thus objections are made against the gospel from the advancement and improvement of gospel light, as if childhood and manhood were contrary to each other, and the superstructure were against the foundation.

IV. A complaint which John's disciples made to their master concerning Christ and his baptizing, *v.* 26. They come to their master, and tell him, "*Rabbi, he that was with thee*; he *baptizeth, and all men come to him*." They suggest that Christ's setting up a baptism of his own was a piece of presumption, as if John, having first set up this rite of baptizing, must have, as it were, a patent for the invention: "*He that was with thee beyond Jordan, behold, the same, baptizes*." They suggest that it was a piece of ingratitude to John. He *to whom thou barest witness* baptizes; as if Jesus owed all his reputation to the honourable character John gave of him. But Christ needed not John's testimony, *ch.* v. 36. He reflected more honour upon John than he received from him. John was *just* to Christ, in bearing witness to him; and Christ's answering his testimony did rather enrich than impoverish John's ministry. They conclude that it would be a total eclipse to John's baptism: "*All men come to him*." Aiming at the monopoly of honour and respect has been in all ages the bane of the church, and the shame of its members and ministers. We mistake if we think that the excelling gifts and graces, and labours and usefulness, of one, are a diminution and disparagement to another that has obtained mercy to be faithful. We must leave it to God to choose, employ, and honour his own instruments as he pleaseth.

V. Here is John's answer, *v.* 27, &c. It was no *disturbance* to him, but what he wished for. He therefore checked the complaint, and took this occasion to confirm the testimonies he had formerly borne to Christ as superior to him.

1. John here *abases himself in comparison with Christ*, *v.* 27–30.

(1) *John acquiesces* in the divine disposal (*v.* 27): *A man can receive nothing except it be given him from heaven*. Different employments are according to the direction of divine Providence, different endowments according to the distribution of the divine grace. We should not *envy* those that have a larger share of gifts than we have, or move in a larger sphere of usefulness. John reminds his disciples that Jesus would not have thus excelled him *except he had received it from heaven*, and, if God gave him *the Spirit without measure* (*v.* 34), shall they grudge at it? We should not be *discontented*, though we be inferior to, others in gifts and usefulness, and be eclipsed by their excellencies. John was ready to

JAMIESON, FAUSSET, BROWN

23. Ænon . . . Salim—on the west of Jordan. (Cf. vs. 26 with ch. 1:28.)

baptized—in the sense explained in ch. 4:2.

24. John not yet cast into prison—Hence it is plain that our Lord's ministry did not *commence* with the imprisonment of John, though, but for this, we should have drawn that inference from Matthew 4:12 and Mark's (1:14) express statement. **25, 26. between some of**—rather, "on the part of." **and the Jews**—rather (according to the best MSS.), "and a Jew," **about purifying**—i.e,, baptizing, the symbolical meaning of washing with water being put (as in ch. 2:6) for the act itself. As John and Jesus were the only teachers who baptized Jews, discussions might easily arise between the Baptist's disciples and such Jews as declined to submit to that rite.

26. Rabbi . . .—'Master, this man tells us that He to whom thou barest such generous witness beyond Jordan is requiting thy generosity by drawing all the people away to Himself. At this rate, thou shalt soon have no disciples at all.' The reply to this is one of the noblest and most affecting utterances that ever came from the lips of man.

A man can receive . . .—can assume nothing, i.e., lawfully and with any success; i.e., Every man has his work and sphere appointed him from above. Even Christ Himself came under this law (Heb. 5:4).

ADAM CLARKE

23. *In Aenon*. This place was eight miles southward from Scythopolis, between Salim and Jordan. *There was much water*. And this was equally necessary where such multitudes were baptized, whether the ceremony was performed by dipping or sprinkling. But as the Jewish custom required the persons to stand in the water, and, having been instructed, and entered into a covenant to renounce all idolatry, and take the God of Israel for their God, then plunge themselves under the water, it is probable that the rite was thus performed at Aenon.

And baptized. It is not clear that Christ did baptize any with water, but His disciples did—chap. iv. 2; and what they did, by His authority and command, is attributed to himself. It is a common custom, in all countries and in all languages, to attribute the operations of those who are under the government and direction of another to him by whom they are directed and governed.

25. *John's disciples and the Jews*. Instead of *Jews*, some versions and fathers read, "a Jew." The *person* here spoken of was probably one who had been baptized by the disciples of our Lord, and the subject of debate seems to have been whether the baptism of John or that of Christ was the most efficacious towards *purifying*.

26. *And they came unto John*. That he might decide the question.

27. *A man can receive nothing*. Or, "A man can receive nothing from heaven, unless it be given him." I have received, not only my commission, but the power also by which I have executed it, from above. As I took it up at God's command, so I am ready to lay it down when He pleases. I have told you from the beginning that I was only the forerunner of the Messiah; and was sent, not to form a separate party, but to point out to men that Lamb of God which takes away the sin of the world, v. 28.

MATTHEW HENRY | JAMIESON, FAUSSET, BROWN | ADAM CLARKE

own that it was God that gave him the interest he had in the love and esteem of the people; and, if now his interest decline, God's will be done! When he has fulfilled his ministry, he can contentedly see it go out of date.

(2) John appeals to the testimony he had formerly given concerning Christ (*v.* 28). I said, again and again, *I am not the Christ, but I am sent before him.* Neither the frowns of the chief priests, nor the flatteries of his own disciples, could make him change his note. Now this serves here, [1] As a *conviction* to his disciples of the unreasonableness of their complaint. "Now," saith John, "do you not remember what the testimony was that I did bear? Did I not say, *I am not the Christ*? Did I not say, *I am sent before him*? Why then does it seem strange to you that I should stand by and give way to him?" [2] As a *comfort* to himself that he had never *given* his disciples *any occasions* thus to set him up in competition with Christ; but, on the contrary, had particularly *cautioned* them against this mistake. John had not only not encouraged them to hope that he was the Messiah, but had plainly told them the contrary. It is a common excuse for those who have undue honour paid them—*If the people will be deceived, let them;* but that is an ill maxim for those to go by whose business it is to *undeceive* people.

(3) John professes the great satisfaction he had in the advancement of Christ, he *rejoiced* in it. This he expresses (*v.* 29) by an elegant similitude. He compares our Saviour to the *bridegroom*: "*He that hath the bride is the bridegroom.* Do *all men come to him*? It is his right." As far as particular souls are devoted to him in faith and love, so far the bridegroom has the bride. He compares himself to the *friend of the bridegroom*, assists him in prosecuting the match, speaks a good word for him, rejoices most of all when he *has the bride. The friend of the bridegroom stands, and hears him; rejoices with joy because of the bridegroom's voice.* Faithful ministers are friends of the bridegroom, to recommend him to the children of men; to bring letters and messages from him, for he courts by proxy. The friends of the bridegroom must *stand, and hear the bridegroom's voice*; must receive instructions from him, and attend his orders. The espousing of souls to Jesus Christ, in faith and love, is the fulfilling of the joy of every good minister. Surely they have *no greater joy*.

(4) He owns it highly fit and necessary that the reputation and interest of Christ should be advanced, and his own diminished (*v.* 30): *He must increase, but I must decrease.* John speaks of Christ's increase and his own decrease as highly *just* and *agreeable*, and affording him entire satisfaction. He was *well pleased* to see the kingdom of Christ getting ground: "*He must increase.*" The kingdom of Christ is, and will be, a growing kingdom, like the light of the morning, like the grain of mustard-seed. He was not at all *displeased* that the effect of this was the diminishing of his own interest: *I must decrease.* The shining forth of the glory of Christ eclipses the lustre of all other glory. As the light of the morning increases, that of the morning star decreases. We must cheerfully be content to be *anything*, to be *nothing*, so that Christ may be *all*.

2. John Baptist here *advances* Christ, and instructs his disciples concerning him.

(1) Concerning the *dignity of Christ's person* (*v.* 31): *He that cometh from above is above all.* He supposes his divine origin, that he *came from above*, from *heaven.* None but he that came from heaven was fit to show us the will of heaven, or the way to heaven. Hence he infers his sovereign authority: he is *above all*, above all things and all persons. When we come to speak of the honours of the Lord Jesus, we can say but this, *He is above all.* This he further illustrates by the meanness of those who stood in competition with him: *He that is of the earth, is earthly*, has his converse with earthly things, and his concern is for them. The prophets and apostles were of the same mould with other men; they were but *earthen vessels*, though they had a rich treasure lodged in them.

(2) Concerning the *excellency and certainty of his doctrine.* He, for his part, *spoke of the earth*, and so do all those that are *of the earth.* The prophets were men; *of themselves* they could not speak but *of the earth.* The preaching of the prophets and of John was but low and flat compared with Christ's preaching; as heaven is high above the earth, so were his thoughts above theirs. But he that cometh from heaven is above all the prophets that ever lived on earth. The doctrine of Christ is here recommended to us,

First, As infallibly *sure* and *certain*, and to be entertained accordingly (*v.* 32): *What he hath seen and heard, that he testifieth.* 1. Christ's divine knowledge; he testified nothing but *what he had seen and heard.* What he discovered of the divine nature was what he

F. B. MEYER:

John shows the greatness of humility. It is expressly stated in 4:2 that Jesus baptized through his disciples. This controversy arose with a Jew who was comparing the respective baptisms of John and the Lord. Perhaps he stirred John's followers with jealousy as he contrasted the crowds that gathered round the new teacher with the waning popularity of the old. But the Baptist had no sense of being aggrieved. His answer is one of the noblest ever made by human lips: "My work has been definitely assigned to me. It has been enough for me to fulfill it. The rapture of the Bridegroom and his success in wooing hearts is not for me. It is enough to behold his joy. He must increase, and I must decrease, but I sorrow not. Indeed, my joy is filled to the brim because of his success."

What a blessing it would be if we could enshrine in our hearts this immortal maxim: "A man can receive nothing except it be given him from heaven!" What we have is God's gift; let us hold it reverently. What another person has is God's gift to him; we have no right to find fault with his dealings with another of his servants. Our orbits are distinct; all we have to do is shine our brightest where he has placed us, confident that he knows best.—*Bible Commentary*

27-30. A man . . .—'I do my heaven-prescribed work, and that is enough for me. Would you have me mount into my Master's place? Said I not unto you, I am not the Christ? The Bride is not mine, why should the people stay with me? Mine it is to point the burdened to the Lamb of God that taketh away the sin of the world, to tell them there is Balm in Gilead, and a Physician there. And shall I grudge to see them, in obedience to the call, flying as a cloud, and as doves to their windows? Whose is the Bride but the Bridegroom's? Enough for me to be the Bridegroom's *friend*, sent by Him to negotiate the match, privileged to bring together the Saviour and those He is come to seek and to save, and rejoicing with joy unspeakable if I may but "stand and hear the Bridegroom's voice," witnessing the blessed espousals. Say ye, then, they go from me to Him? Ye bring me glad tidings of great joy. He must increase, but I must decrease; this, my joy, therefore is fulfilled.'

31-34. He that . . .—Here is the reason why He must increase while all human teachers must decrease. The Master "cometh from above"—descending from *His proper element*, the region of those "heavenly things" which He came to reveal, and so, although mingling with men and things on the earth, is not "of the earth," either in Person or Word. The servants, on the contrary, springing of earth, are of the earth, and their testimony, even though divine in authority, partakes necessarily of their own earthiness. (So strongly did the Baptist feel this contrast that the last clause just repeats the first.) It is impossible for a sharper line of distinction to be drawn between Christ and all human teachers, even when divinely commissioned and speaking by the power of the Holy Ghost. And who does not perceive it? The words of prophets and apostles are undeniable and most precious truth; but in the words of Christ we hear a voice as from the excellent Glory, the Eternal Word making Himself heard in our own flesh. **32. what he hath seen and heard**—(See on vs. 11 and ch. 1:18).

29. *He that hath the bride.* The congregation of believers. *Is the bridegroom.* The Lord Jesus, the Head of the Church. *The friend of the bridegroom.* The person whom the Greeks called the *paranymph.* There were two at each wedding: one waited on the bride, the other on the bridegroom. Their business was to serve them, to inspect the concerns of the bridechamber, and afterwards to reconcile differences between husband and wife, when any took place. John considers himself as standing in this relation to the Lord Jesus, while espousing human nature and converting souls to himself; this is the meaning of "standeth by," i.e., ready to serve.

30. *He must increase.* His present success is but the beginning of a most glorious and universal spread of righteousness, peace, truth, and goodwill among men. *I must decrease.* My baptism and teaching, as pointing out the coming Messiah, must *cease;* because the Messiah is now come, and has entered publicly on the work of His glorious ministry.

31. *Is above all.* This blessed Bridegroom, who has descended from heaven, v. 13, is above all, superior to Moses, the prophets, and me. *He that is of the earth.* John himself, who was born in the common way of man. *Speaketh of the earth.* Cannot speak of heavenly things as Christ can do, and only represents divine matters by these earthly ordinances, for the spirit and meaning of which you must all go to the Messiah himself.

MATTHEW HENRY	JAMIESON, FAUSSET, BROWN	ADAM CLARKE

had *seen*; what he revealed of the mind of God was what he had *heard* immediately from him. The prophets testified what was made known to them in dreams and visions, but not what they had seen and heard. The gospel of Christ is not a doubtful opinion, like an hypothesis or new notion in philosophy, but it is a revelation of the mind of God, which is of *eternal truth* in itself. 2. His divine grace and goodness. Christ's preaching is here called his *testifying*, to denote, (1) The *convincing evidence* of it; it was not *reported* as news by hearsay, but it was *testified* as evidence given in court. (2) The affectionate earnestness of the delivery of it.

From the *certainty* of Christ's doctrine, John takes occasion, to lament the infidelity of the most of men. They receive it not, they will not hear it, or give credit to it. This he speaks of not only as a matter of *wonder* but as a matter of *grief*; John's disciples grieved that *all men came to Christ* (*v.* 26); they thought his followers too many. But John grieves that *no man came to him*; he thought them too few. The unbelief of sinners is the grief of saints. He takes occasion to commend the faith of the chosen remnant (*v.* 33): *He that hath received his testimony* hath *set to his seal that God is true.* God is true, though we do not *set our seal to it*; his truth needs not our faith to support it, but by faith we do ourselves the honour and justice to subscribe to his truth. God's promises are all *yea* and *amen*; by faith we put our *amen* to them. By believing in Christ we set to our seal that God is true to all the promises which he has made *concerning Christ*. That he is true to all the promises he has made *in Christ*. Being satisfied that he is *true*, we are willing to deal with him *upon trust*.

Secondly, It is recommended to us as a *divine* doctrine (*v.* 34): *For he whom God hath sent speaketh the word of God, for God giveth not the Spirit by measure unto him.* 1. He spoke the *words of God*. Both substance and language were divine. He proved himself *sent of God* (*ch.* iii. 2), and therefore his words are to be received as the words of God. 2. He spoke as no other prophet did; for *God giveth not the Spirit by measure to him.* The Old Testament prophets had the Spirit, and in different degrees. But, whereas God gave them the Spirit by *measure*, he gave him to Christ *without measure*. The Spirit was not in Christ as in a vessel, but as in a fountain, as in a bottomless ocean.

(3) Concerning *the power and authority he is invested with.* He is the *beloved Son of the Father* (*v.* 35): *The Father loveth the Son.* The prophets were faithful as servants, but Christ as a Son. He continued his love to him even in his estate of humiliation, loved him never the less for his poverty, and sufferings. He is *Lord of all*. The Father *hath given all things into his hand.* Love is generous. Having given *him the Spirit without measure*, he gave him *all things*. All *power*; so it is explained, Matt. xxviii. 18. He has *power over all flesh*, the *heathen* given *him for his inheritance*. Both the golden sceptre and the iron rod are given into his hand. All *grace* is given into his hand as the channel of conveyance. We are unworthy that the Father should give those things *into our hands*. The things he intended for us he gives *into his hands*, who is worthy. They are given *into his hands*, by him to be given into ours. The riches of the new covenant are deposited in so sure, so kind, so good a hand, the hand of him that purchased them for us.

He is the object of that faith which is made the great condition of eternal happiness: *He that believeth on the Son, hath life, v.* 36. It is the *conclusion of the whole matter*. As God offers and conveys good things to us by the *testimony* of Jesus Christ, so we receive and partake of those favours by *believing* the testimony. This way of *receiving* fitly answers that way of *giving*. We have here the sum of that gospel which is to be preached to every creature. Here is,

First, The blessed state of all true Christians: *He that believes on the Son hath everlasting life.* Not only *believes him*, that what he saith is true, but believes *on him*, and confides in him. The benefit of true Christianity is no less than *everlasting life*. True believers, even now, *have* everlasting life; not only they shall have it hereafter, but they have it now. They have the Son of God, and in him *they have life*. Grace is glory begun.

Secondly, The wretched and miserable condition of unbelievers: *He that believeth not the Son* is undone. The word includes both *incredulity* and *disobedience*. They *cannot be happy* in this world, nor that to come: *He shall not see life*, that life which Christ came to bestow. They *cannot but be miserable*: *The wrath of God abides upon* an unbeliever.

no man receiveth . . .—John's disciples had said, "*All* come to Him" (vs. 26). The Baptist here virtually says, Would it were so, but alas! they are next to "*none*" [BENGEL]. They were far readier to receive himself, and obliged him to say, I am not the Christ, and he seems pained at this. **33. hath set to His seal . . .**—gives glory to God whose words Christ speaks, not as prophets and apostles by a partial communication of the Spirit to them.

34. for God giveth not the Spirit by measure—Here, again, the sharpest conceivable line of distinction is drawn between Christ and all human-inspired teachers: 'They have the Spirit in a *limited* degree; but God giveth not [to Him] the Spirit *by measure*.' It means the entire fulness of divine life and divine power. The present tense "*giveth*," very aptly points out the permanent communication of the Spirit by the Father to the Son, so that a constant flow and reflow of living power is to be understood (Cf. ch. 1:15) [OLSHAUSEN].

35, 36. The Father loveth . . .—See on Matthew 11:27, where we have the "*delivering over* of all things into the hands of the Son," while here we have the deep spring of that august act in the Father's ineffable "*love of the Son.*"

36. hath everlasting life—already has it. (See on vs. 18 and ch. 5:24). **shall not see life**—The contrast here is striking: The one has already a life that will endure for ever—the other not only has it not now, but shall never have it—never see it. **abideth on him**—It was on Him before, and not being *removed* in the only possible way, by "believing on the Son," it necessarily *remaineth* on him! *N.B.*—How flatly does this contradict the teaching of many in our day, that there neither was, nor is, anything *in God* against sinners which needed to be removed by Christ, but only *in men* against God!

32. *And no man receiveth his testimony.* Or, "And this his testimony no man taketh up." That is, the testimony which John had borne to the Jews that Jesus was the promised Messiah. *No man taketh up.* No person is found to tread in my steps and to publish to the Jews that this is the Christ, the Saviour of the world.

33. *Hath set to his seal.* That is, hath hereby confirmed the truth of the testimony which he has borne. As a testator sets his seal to an instrument in order to confirm it, and such instrument is considered as fully confirmed by having the testator's seal affixed to it, so I, by taking up this testimony of Christ and proclaiming it to the Jews, have fully confirmed it, as I know it to be a truth; which knowledge I have from the immediate inspiration of the Holy Spirit.

34. *For God giveth not the Spirit by measure.* He is the most perfect of all teachers, as having received the Holy Spirit as none before Him ever did. Without measure—not for a particular time, people, purpose, etc., but for the whole compass of time, and in reference to all eternity. It is worthy of remark that this was fully done after the outpouring of the Spirit on the Day of Pentecost, Acts ii. 1, as may be clearly seen in all the apostolic Epistles. The Jews observe that the Holy Spirit was given only in certain measures to the prophets; some writing only one book, others two.

35. *All things into his hand.* See on Matt. xi. 27. A principal design of John is to show that Christ was infinitely above every teacher, prophet, and divine messenger that had ever yet appeared. The prophets had various gifts: some had visions, other dreams; some had the gift of *teaching*, others of comforting, etc. But none possessed all these gifts; Christ alone possessed their plenitude, and is all things in all.

36. *Hath everlasting life.* He has already the seed of this life in his soul, having been made a partaker of the grace and spirit of Him in whom he has believed. *He that believeth not.* Or "obeyeth not." *Shall not see life.* Shall never enjoy it, there being no way to the kingdom of God but through Christ Jesus, Acts iv. 12. And none can expect to enter into this Kingdom but those who obey Him; for to such only He is the Author of eternal salvation, Heb. v. 9. *But the wrath of God abideth on him.* The "displeasure" of God. I should prefer "displeasure" to *wrath*, because the common acceptation of the latter (*fury, rage*) is not properly applicable here. Perhaps the original word is used in the same sense here as in Rom. ii. 5; iii. 5; xiii. 4-5; Eph. v. 6; 1 Thess. i. 10; v. 9, where it evidently means "punishment," which is the effect of irritated justice. Taken in this sense, we may consider the phrase as a Hebraism: "punishment of God," i.e., the most heavy and awful of all punishments—such as sin deserves, and such as it becomes divine justice to inflict. And this *abideth on him*—endures as long as his unbelief and disobedience remain!

MATTHEW HENRY

CHAPTER 4

Now he left Judæa four months before harvest (*v.* 35).

I. He *made disciples.* His ministry was successful, notwithstanding the opposition it met with. It is Christ's prerogative to *make disciples,* to form and fashion them to his will. *The Christian is made such, not born such.*

II. He *baptized* those whom he *made disciples;* not himself, but by the ministry of his disciples, *v.* 2. Because he would put a difference between his baptism and that of John, who baptized all himself, He would put honour upon his disciples, and so train them up to further services. He would teach us that what is done by his ministers, according to his direction, he owns as done by himself.

III. He made and baptized *more disciples than John.* Christ's converse was more winning than John's.

IV. The Pharisees were informed of this. When the Pharisees thought they had got rid of John, Jesus appears. That which grieved them was that Christ made so many disciples. The success of the gospel exasperates its enemies.

V. Our Lord Jesus knew very well what informations were given in against him. None can dig so deep as to *hide their counsels from the Lord.*

VI. Hereupon our Lord Jesus *left Judæa* and *departed again* to go to Galilee. He *left Judæa,* because he was likely to be persecuted there even to the death. Christ quitted the country, and went where what he did would be less provoking than just under their eye. His hour was not yet come. He had not finished his testimony, and therefore would not surrender or expose himself. The disciples he had gathered in Judæa were not able to bear hardships, and therefore he would not expose them. Hereby he gave an example to his own rule: *When they persecute you in one city, flee to another.* We are not called to suffer, while we may avoid it without sin; and therefore we may change our place. He departed into Galilee, because he had work to do there, and many friends and fewer enemies.

Verses 4–26

We have here an account of the good Christ did in Samaria. The Samaritans, both in *blood* and *religion,* were *mongrel Jews.* They worshipped the God of Israel only, to whom they erected a temple on mount Gerizim. The Samaritans would not admit Christ, when they saw he was going to Jerusalem (Luke ix. 53); the Jews thought they could not give him a worse name than to say, *He is a Samaritan.*

I. Christ's coming into Samaria. He charges his disciples not to *enter into any city of the Samaritans* (Matt. x. 5), nor did he here preach publicly, or work any miracle, his eye being to *the lost sheep of the house of Israel.* What kindness he here did them was only a *crumb* of the children's bread that casually *fell from the master's table.*

1. His *road* from Judæa to Galilee lay through the *country* of Samaria (*v.* 4): *He must needs go through Samaria.* There was no other way, unless he would have fetched a compass on the other side *Jordan,* a great way about. We should not go into places of temptation but when we *needs must;* and then we should not reside in them, but *hasten through* them. It was happy for Samaria that it lay *in Christ's way.* 2. His baiting place happened to be at a *city of Samaria.* The place is described. It was called *Sychar;* probably the same with *Sichem,* or *Shechem.* Shechem yielded the first proselyte that ever came into the church of Israel (Gen. xxxiv. 24), and now it is the first place where the gospel is preached out of the commonwealth of Israel. Abimelech was made king here; it was Jeroboam's royal seat; but the evangelist takes notice of Jacob's interest there, which was more its honour than its crowned heads. Here lay Jacob's ground, the *parcel of ground which Jacob* gave to his son Joseph. Here was Jacob's well. *Being wearied with his journey, he sat thus on the well.* We have here our Lord Jesus labouring under the common fatigue of travellers. He was *wearied with his journey. Because* it was the sixth hour, the time of the heat of the day, therefore he was weary. He was a *true man,* and subject to the common infirmities of the human nature. He was a *poor man,* else he might have travelled on horseback or in a chariot. When we are carried easily, let us think on the weariness of our Master. It should seem that he was not of a robust constitution; it should seem, his disciples were not tired, for they went into the town without any difficulty. Bodies of the finest mould are most sensible of fatigue, and can worst bear it. We have him here betaking himself to the common relief of travellers: *Being wearied, he sat thus on the well.* He sat *thus,* in an *uneasy posture.*

II. His discourse with a Samaritan woman. This

JAMIESON, FAUSSET, BROWN

CHAPTER 4

Vss. 1-42. CHRIST AND THE WOMAN OF SAMARIA—THE SAMARITANS OF SYCHAR.

2. **Jesus baptized not**—John being a servant baptized with his own hand; Christ as the Master, "baptizing with the Holy Ghost," administered the outward symbol only through His disciples.

1-4. the Lord knew—not by report, but in the sense of ch. 2:25, for which reason He is here styled "the Lord."

3. left Judea—to avoid persecution, which at that early stage would have marred His work. **departed into Galilee**—by which time John had been cast into prison (Mark 1:14).

4. must needs go through Samaria—for a geographical reason, no doubt, as it lay straight in his way, but certainly not without a higher design. **5. cometh . . . to**—i.e., as far as: for He remained at some distance from it. **Sychar**—the "Shechem" of the Old Testament, about thirty-four miles from Jerusalem, afterwards called "Neapolis," and now "Nablous."

6-8. wearied . . . sat thus—i.e., "as you might fancy a weary man would"; an instance of the graphic style of St. John [WEBSTER and WILKINSON]. In fact, this is perhaps the most *human* of all the scenes of our Lord's earthly history. We seem to be beside Him, overhearing all that is here recorded, nor could any painting of the scene on canvas, however perfect, do other than lower the conception which this exquisite narrative conveys to the devout and intelligent reader. But with all that is *human,* how much also of the *divine* have we here, both blended in one glorious manifestation of the majesty, grace, pity, patience with which "the Lord" imparts light and life to this unlikeliest of strangers, standing midway between Jews and heathens. **the sixth hour**—*noonday,* reckoning from 6 A.M. From Song of Solomon 1: 7 we know, as from other sources, that the very flocks "rested at noon." But Jesus, whose maxim

ADAM CLARKE

CHAPTER 4

1. *Jesus made and baptized.* These seem to be quoted as the very words which were brought to the Pharisees; and, from our Lord's conduct after this information, we may take it for granted that they were so irritated that they were determined to seek an occasion to take away His life; in consequence of which, leaving Judea, He withdrew into Galilee.

2. *Jesus himself baptized not.* See chap. iii. 22.

G. CAMPBELL MORGAN:

The Lord knew that the account of His success was reaching the Pharisees. Quite evidently remarkable success was attending that ministry of Jesus, which was collateral with that of John. That success was evidenced by the fear expressed by John's disciples when they said, "All men go after him." The account of this success was now reaching the Pharisees. On that account, He left Judea. The implication is quite self-evident, that this knowledge was precipitating conflict between himself and the Pharisees. Already we have seen how in connection with His second sign—His first in the Temple, when He cleansed it—that He came into conflict with them. Now news came to these men that the One whose action in the Temple had raised their objection was marvelously successful in His ministry, even more so than John. The Lord knew that this would mean conflict; and on that account He left Judea.

—*The Gospel According to John*

4. *And he must needs go through Samaria.* Or, "It was necessary for Him to pass through Samaria." From Jerusalem to Galilee through Samaria, according to Josephus, was three days' journey.

5. *A city . . . called Sychar.* This city was anciently called Shechem. It seems to have been situated at the foot of Mount Gerizim, in the province of Samaria, on which the temple of the Samaritans was built. After the ruin of Samaria by Salmanezer, Sychar, or Shechem, became the capital of the Samaritans; and it continued so, according to Josephus, *Ant.* l. xi, c. 8, in the time of Alexander the Great. It was about ten miles from Shiloh, forty from Jerusalem, and fifty-two from Jericho. It probably got the name of Sychar, which signifies "drunken," from the drunkenness of his inhabitants. With this crime the Prophet Isaiah (ch. xxviii. 1, 3, 7-8) solemnly charges the Ephraimites, within whose limits the city stood. This place is remarkable in the Scriptures: (1) As being that where Abram first stopped on his coming from Haran to Canaan; (2) Where God first appeared to that patriarch, and promised to give the land to his seed; (3) The place where Abram first built an altar to the Lord, and called upon His name, Gen. xii. 7. *That Jacob gave to his son Joseph.* Jacob had bought this field from the children of Hamor, the father of Shechem, for a hundred pieces of silver, or lambs, Gen. xxxiii. 19; and in it he built an altar, which he dedicated to *El Elohey Yishrael,* the strong God, the covenant God of Israel, v. 19. This, Jacob left as a private or overplus inheritance to Joseph and his children. See Gen. xlviii. 21-22 and Josh. xxiv. 32.

6. *The sixth hour.* About twelve o'clock; see the notes on chap. i. 30. The *time* is noted here: (1) To account for Christ's *fatigue*—He had already travelled several hours. (2) To

MATTHEW HENRY

discourse is reducible to four heads:

1. They discourse *concerning the water, v.* 7-15.

(1) Notice is taken of the *circumstances* that gave occasion to this discourse. There comes a *woman* of Samaria to *draw water.* She had no servant to be a *drawer of water;* she would do it herself. See here, How the divine Providence brings about glorious purposes by events which seem to us fortuitous and accidental. His disciples were *gone away into the city to buy meat.* Christ did not go into the city to eat, but sent his disciples to fetch his meat thither; not because he scrupled eating in a Samaritan city, but, [1] Because he had a good work to do at that well. [2] Because it was more private and retired, more cheap and homely, to have his dinner brought him thither, than to go into the town for it. Christ could eat his dinner as well upon a *draw well* as in the best inn in the town. He often preached to multitudes yet here he condescends to teach a single person, a woman, a poor woman, a stranger, a Samaritan, to teach his ministers to do likewise, as those that know what a glorious achievement it is to help to save, though but *one soul,* from death.

(2) Let us observe the *particulars* of this discourse. Jesus begins with a modest request for a draught of water: *Give me to drink.* He that *for our sakes became poor* here becomes a beggar. Christ asked for it because he would draw on further discourse with her. Christ is still begging in his poor members, and a *cup of cold water,* given to them in his name, shall not lose its reward. The woman quarrels with him because he did not carry on the humour of his own nation (*v.* 9): *How is it?* Observe, *First,* What a mortal feud there was between the Jews and the Samaritans: *The Jews have no dealings with the Samaritans.* Quarrels about religion are usually the most implacable of all quarrels. They plainly show that however their religion may be *true* they are not *truly religious. Secondly,* How ready the woman was to upbraid Christ with the haughtiness and ill nature of the Jewish nation: *How is it that thou, being a Jew, askest drink of me?* Moderate men of all sides are *men wondered at.* Two things this woman wonders at: That he should *ask* this kindness; for it was the pride of the Jews that they would endure any hardship rather than be beholden to a Samaritan. We must, like our Master, put on *goodness* and *kindness,* though it should be ever so much the genius of our country, or the humour of our party, to be morose and ill-natured. This woman expected that Christ should be as other Jews were. No rule but has some exceptions. She wonders that he should *expect to receive* this kindness from her that was a Samaritan. Christ takes this occasion to instruct her in divine things: *If thou knewest the gift of God, thou wouldst have asked, v.* 10. He waives her objection of the feud between the Jews and Samaritans. Some differences are best *healed* by avoiding all occasions of *entering into dispute* about them. Christ will convert this woman, showing her her need of a Saviour. He fills her with an apprehension that she had now an opportunity of gaining that which would be of unspeakable advantage to her. Christ tells her expressly that she had now a season of grace.

[1] He hints to her what she *should know,* but was ignorant of: *If thou knewest the gift of God, who it is that saith, Give me to drink.* She saw him to be a Jew, a poor weary traveller; but he would have her know something more concerning him. Jesus Christ is the *gift of God,* the richest token of God's love to us. It is an unspeakable privilege to have this gift of God proposed and offered to us. It is he that saith, *Give me to drink;* this gift comes begging to thee.

[2] He hopes concerning her, what she would have done if she had known him: *Thou wouldst have asked.* Those that would have any benefit by Christ must ask for it. Those that have a right knowledge of Christ will seek to him. Christ knows what they that want the means of knowledge would have done if they had had them.

[3] He assures her what he would have done for her if she had applied to him: "He *would have given thee living water.*" By this living water is meant the *Spirit,* who is not like the water in the bottom of the well, but like *living* or *running* water. The Spirit of grace is as *living water.* Jesus Christ *can* and *will* give the Holy Spirit to them that ask him. The woman cavils at the gracious intimation which Christ gave her (*v.* 11, 12): *Thou hast nothing to draw with;* and besides, *Art thou greater than our father Jacob?* What he spoke figuratively, she took literally; Nicodemus did so too. She does not think him capable of furnishing her with any water: *Thou hast nothing to draw with,* and *the well is deep.* But there are those who will not believe his promise, unless the means of the performance of it be *visible;* as if he could not

JAMIESON, FAUSSET, BROWN

was, "I must work the works of Him that sent Me while it is day" (ch. 9:4), seems to have denied Himself that repose, at least on this occasion, probably that He might reach this well when He knew the woman would be there. Once there, however, He accepts . . . the grateful ease of a seat on the patriarchal stone. But what music is that which I hear from His lips, "Come unto Me, all ye that labor and are heavy laden, and I will give you rest" (Matt. 11:28).

7. Give me to drink—for the heat of a noonday sun had parched His lips. But "in the last, that great day of the feast," Jesus stood and cried, saying, "If any man thirst let him come unto Me and *drink*" (ch. 7:37).

9-12. How is it that thou—not altogether refusing, yet wondering at so unusual a request from a Jew, as His dress and dialect would at once discover Him to be, to a Samaritan. **For . . .**—It is this national antipathy that gives point to the parable of the good Samaritan (Luke 10:30-37), and the thankfulness of the Samaritan leper (Luke 17:16, 18).

10. If thou knewest . . .—i.e., 'In Me thou seest only a petitioner to thee but if thou knewest who that Petitioner is, and the Gift that God is giving to men, thou wouldst have changed places with Him, gladly suing of Him living water—nor shouldst thou have sued in vain" (gently reflecting on her for not immediately meeting His request).

ADAM CLARKE

account for His *thirst*—the sun had at this time waxed hot. (3) To account for the disciples going to *buy food,* v. 8, because this was the ordinary time of *dinner* among the Jews. See the note referred to above. Dr. Macknight thinks the *sixth hour* to be the Roman six o'clock in the afternoon.

7. *There cometh a woman of Samaria to draw water.* That this was the employment of the females, we see in different parts of the Sacred Writings. See Gen. xxiv. 11, etc.; Exod. ii. 16. The Jews say that those who wished to get wives went to the wells where young women were accustomed to come and draw water; and it is supposed that women of ill fame frequented such places also.

9. *That thou, being a Jew.* Probably the inhabitants of Judea distinguished themselves from those of Samaria by some peculiar mode of dress, and by this the Samaritan woman might have known Christ. But it is likely that our Lord spoke the Galilean dialect, by which we find, from Mark xiv. 70, a Jew of that district might easily be known. *The Jews have no dealings with the Samaritans.* Perhaps better, "Jews have no communion with Samaritans." These words appear to be added by the Evangelist himself, in explanation of the woman's question. The original word has been variously translated and understood. It has been understood to mean the Jews will be "under no kind of obligation" to the Samaritans—will borrow nothing from them—will not drink out of the same cup or well with them—will not sit down to meals with them, nor eat out of the same vessel—will have no religious connection, no commercial dealings with them. The word "communion," I think, fully expresses the sense of the original; and, being as extensive in its meaning as our word *dealings,* is capable of as general an interpretation. The deadly hatred that subsisted between these two nations is known to all. The Jews cursed them, and believed them to be accursed. Their most merciful wish to the Samaritans was that they might have no part in the resurrection; or, in other words, that they might be annihilated.

10. *If thou knewest the gift of God.* "Free gift." A *gift* is anything that is given for which no equivalent has been or is to be returned; a "free gift" is that which has been given without asking or entreaty. Such a gift of kindness was Jesus Christ to the world, chap. iii. 16; and through Him comes the gift of the Spirit, which those who believe on His name were to receive. *Living water.* By this expression, which was common to the inhabitants both of the East and of the West, is always meant "spring water," in opposition to dead, stagnant water contained in ponds, pools, tanks, or cisterns; and what our Lord means by it is evidently the Holy Spirit, as may be seen from chap. vii. 38-39. As water quenches the thirst, refreshes and invigorates the body, purifies things defiled, and renders the earth fruitful, so it is an apt emblem of the gift of the Holy Ghost, which so satisfies the souls that receive it that they thirst no more for earthly good; it purifies also from all spiritual defilement, on which account it is emphatically styled the *Holy* Spirit; and it makes those who receive it fruitful in every good word and work.

11. *Thou hast nothing to draw with.* "Thou hast no bucket." Good water is not plentiful in the East; and travellers are often obliged to carry leathern bottles or buckets with them, and a line also, to let them down into the deep wells, in order to draw up water. If the well was in our Lord's time, as it was found by

MATTHEW HENRY

draw water without our buckets. She asks scornfully, "*Whence hast thou this living water?* I see not whence thou canst have it." The fountain of life is hid with Christ. Christ has enough for us, though we see not whence he has it. She does not think it possible that he should furnish her with any better water, *Art thou greater than our father Jacob, who gave us the well?*

[4] We will suppose the tradition true, that Jacob *himself, and his children, and cattle, did drink of this well.* And we may observe from it, the power and providence of God, in the continuance of the fountains of water from generation to generation.

[5] Yet, allowing that to be true, she was out in several things. In calling Jacob *father.* What authority had the Samaritans to reckon themselves of the seed of Jacob? She is out in claiming this well as Jacob's gift. But thus we are apt to call the *messengers* of God's gifts the *donors* of them, and to look so much at the hands they *pass through* as to forget the hand they *come from.* She was out in speaking of Christ as not worthy to be compared with our father Jacob. An over-fond veneration for antiquity makes God's graces, in the good people of our own day, to be slighted. Christ makes it out that the *living water* he had to give was far better than that of Jacob's well, *v.* 13, 14. Christ did not cast her off, but encouraged her. He shows her that the water of Jacob's well yielded but a *transient* satisfaction: "*Whoso drinketh of this water shall thirst again.* It is no better than other water; it will quench the present thirst, but the thirst will return." This intimates, *a.* The *infirmities* of our bodies in this present state; they are ever *craving.* Life is a fire, a *lamp,* which will soon go out, without continual supplies of fuel and oil. *b.* The *imperfections* of all our comforts in this world; they are not lasting. Yesterday's meat and drink will not do to-day's work. But the living waters he would give should yield a lasting satisfaction and bliss, *v.* 14. Whoever partakes of the Spirit of grace,

(*a*) He shall *never thirst.* A *desiring* thirst he has, nothing more *than* God, still more and more *of* God; but not a *despairing* thirst.

(*b*) He shall never thirst, because this water that Christ gives *shall be in him a well of water. He* can never be reduced to extremity that has in himself a *fountain* of supply and satisfaction, *ever ready,* for it shall be *in him.* He needs not sneak to the world for comfort. Believers have in them a *well of water,* overflowing, ever flowing. It is *springing up,* ever in motion. If good truths *stagnate* in our souls, like standing water, they do not answer the end of our receiving them. It is springing up *unto everlasting* life, which intimates the *aims* of gracious actings. Spiritual life springs up towards its own perfection in eternal life. It will continue springing up till it come to perfection, eternal life at last. And now is not this water better than that of Jacob's well? The woman begs of him to give her some of this water (*v.* 15): *Give me this water, that I thirst not.* Some think that she speaks *tauntingly,* and ridicules what Christ had said as mere stuff. "A rare invention; it will save me a great deal of *pain* if I *thirst not,* and a great deal of *pains* if I never *come hither to draw.*" Others think that it was a *well-meant* but weak and ignorant desire. *Whatever it be,* let me have it. *Ease,* or saving of labour, is a valuable good to poor labouring people. Even those that are weak and ignorant may yet have some faint and fluctuating desires towards Christ and his gifts.

2. The next subject of discourse with this woman is *concerning her husband, v.* 16–18. It was not to let fall the discourse of the water of life that Christ started this, but it was with a gracious design. Waiving the discourse about the living water, he sets himself to awaken her conscience, and then she would more easily apprehend the remedy by grace. And this is the method of dealing with souls; they must first be made *weary* and *heavy-laden* under the burden of sin, and then brought to Christ for rest. This is the course of spiritual physic.

(1) How discreetly and decently Christ introduces this discourse (*v.* 16): *Go, call thy husband, and come hither.* The order Christ gave her had a *very good colour:* "*Call thy husband,* that he may teach thee, and help thee to understand these things. *Call thy husband,* that he may learn with thee: that then you may be *heirs together of the grace of life.*" As it had a good colour, so it had a *good design;* for hence he would take occasion to call her sin to remembrance. There is need of art and prudence in giving reproofs.

(2) How industriously the woman seeks to evade the conviction, and yet insensibly convicts herself. She said, *I have no husband.*

(3) How closely our Lord Jesus brings home the

JAMIESON, FAUSSET, BROWN

12. Art thou greater . . .—already perceiving in this Stranger a claim to some mysterious greatness. **our father Jacob**—for when it went well with the Jews, they claimed kindred with them, as being descended from Joseph; but when misfortunes befell the Jews, they disowned all connection with them [JOSEPHUS, 9. 14, 3].

14. thirst again . . . never thirst . . .—The contrast here is fundamental and all comprehensive. "This water" plainly means 'this natural water and *all satisfactions of a like earthly and perishable nature.*' Coming to us *from without,* and reaching only the *superficial* parts of our nature, they are soon spent, and need to be anew supplied as much as if we had never experienced them before, while the deeper wants of our being are not reached by them at all; whereas the "water" that Christ gives—*spiritual life*—is struck out of the very depths of our being, making the soul not a *cistern,* for holding water *poured into it from without,* but a *fountain* (the word had been better so rendered, to distinguish it from the word rendered "well" in vs. 11), springing, gushing, bubbling up and flowing forth *within* us, ever fresh, ever living. *The indwelling of the Holy Ghost as the Spirit of Christ* is the secret of this life with all its enduring energies and satisfactions, as is expressly said (ch. 7:37-39). "Never thirsting," then, means simply that such souls have the supplies *at home.* **into everlasting life**—carrying the thoughts up from the eternal freshness and vitality of these waters to the great ocean in which they have their confluence. "Thither may I arrive!" [BENGEL].

15-18. give me this water . . .—This is not obtuseness—that is giving way—it expresses a wondering desire after she scarce knew what from this mysterious Stranger.

16. call thy husband—now proceeding to arouse her slumbering conscience by laying bare the guilty life she was leading, and by the minute details which that life furnished, not only bringing her sin vividly up before her, but preparing her to receive in His true character that wonderful Stranger to whom her whole life, in its minutest particulars, evidently lay open.

ADAM CLARKE

Mr. Maundrell, thirty-five yards deep, it would require a considerable line to reach it; and with such it is not likely that even the disciples of our Lord were provided. The woman might well say, *The well is deep,* and *thou hast nothing to draw with . . . whence then hast thou that living water?*

12. *Our father Jacob.* The *ancient* Samaritans were undoubtedly the descendants of Jacob, for they were the ten tribes that revolted in the reign of Rehoboam. But those in our Lord's time were not genuine Israelites, but a corrupted race, sprung from a mixture of different nations sent thither by Salmanezer, king of the Assyrians. See 2 Kings xvii.

14. *Springing up into everlasting life.* On this account he can never thirst; for how can he lack water who has in himself a living, eternal spring?

15. *Give me this water.* She did not as yet comprehend our Lord's meaning; but her curiosity was much excited, and this was the design of our Lord, that He might have her mind properly prepared to receive the great truths which He was about to announce.

16. *Call thy husband.* Our Lord appears to have spoken these words for two purposes: (1) To make the woman consider her own state; (2) To show her that He knew her heart and the secret actions of her life, and was therefore well qualified to teach her heavenly truths.

MATTHEW HENRY

conviction to her conscience. It is probable that he said more than is here recorded, for she thought that he told her all that ever she did (*v.* 29). A *surprising narrative* of her *past* conversation: *Thou hast had five husbands.* A severe reproof of her present state of life: *He whom thou now hast is not thy husband.* So that, in short, *she lived in adultery.* Yet observe how mildly Christ tells her of it; *He with whom thou livest is not thy husband:* and then leaves it to her own conscience to say the rest. Yet in this he puts a better construction than it would well bear upon what she said: *Thou hast well said I have no husband;* and again, *In that saidst thou truly.* What she intended as a *denial of the fact* he favourably interpreted as a *confession of the fault.* Those who would win souls should *make the best* of them, whereby they may hope to *work* upon their *good-nature*; for, if they *make the worst* of them, they certainly *exasperate* their *ill-nature.*

3. The next subject of discourse with this woman is concerning *the place of worship, v.* 19–24.

(1) A case of conscience concerning the place of worship, *v.* 19, 20.

[1] The inducement she had to put this case: *Sir, I perceive that thou art a prophet.* She does not deny the truth of what he had charged her with, nor is she put into a passion by it, as many are when they are touched in a sore place, but (which is a rare thing) can bear to be told of a fault. She goes further: *First,* She speaks respectfully to him, calls him *Sir.* This was the effect of Christ's meekness in reproving her; he gave her no ill language, and then she gave him none. *Secondly,* She acknowledges him to be a *prophet. Thirdly,* She desires some further instruction from him.

[2] The case itself that she propounded concerning the *place of religious worship in public.* She knew she must worship God, and desired to do it aright; and therefore, meeting with a prophet, begs his direction. It was agreed between the Jews and the Samaritans that God is to be worshipped (even those who were such fools as to worship *false* gods were not such brutes as to worship none). But the matter in variance was *where* they should worship God. Observe how she states the case:

As for the Samaritans: *Our fathers worshipped in this mountain*; there the Samaritan temple was built by Sanballat. Whatever the temple was the place was holy; it was mount *Gerizim,* the mount on which the blessings were pronounced. It might plead prescription: *Our fathers* worshipped here. She thinks they have antiquity, tradition, and succession, on their side. As to the Jews: *You say* that *in Jerusalem is the place where men ought to worship.* The Samaritans governed themselves by the five books of Moses. Now, though they found frequent mention there of the place God would choose, yet they did not find it named there; and therefore thought themselves at liberty to set up another place.

(2) Christ's answer to this case of conscience, *v.* 21, &c. He puts *a slight* upon the question concerning the place of worship (*v.* 21): "*Woman, believe me;* that which thou hast been taught to lay so much weight on shall be set aside as a thing *indifferent.*" *The hour comes when you shall neither in this mountain nor yet at Jerusalem worship the Father.* A period shall be put to all niceness and all differences about the place of worship. It shall be a thing perfectly indifferent whether in either of these places or any other men worship God, for they shall not be tied to any place; neither *here* nor *there,* but *both,* and *anywhere,* and *everywhere.* He *lays a stress* upon other things. When he made so light of the place of worship he did not intend to lessen our concern about the thing itself. As to the present state of the controversy, he *determines* against the Samaritan worship, *v.* 22. The Samaritans were certainly *in the wrong,* because they were out in the object of their worship. *But you worship you know not what.* Ignorance is so far from being the *mother* of devotion that it is the *murderer* of it. That the Jews were certainly *in the right.* "*We know what we worship.* We go upon sure grounds in our worship." Those who by the scriptures have obtained some knowledge of God may worship him *comfortably* to themselves, and *acceptably* to him, for they *know what they worship.* Worship may be *true* where yet it is not *pure* and *entire.* Our Lord Jesus was pleased to reckon himself among the *worshippers* of God: *We worship.* Let not the greatest of men think the worship of God below them, when the Son of God himself did not. *Salvation is of the Jews;* and therefore they know what they worship, and what grounds they go upon in their worship. The author of eternal salvation comes of the Jews, and is sent first to *bless* them. The means of eternal salvation are afforded to them. The *word of salvation* was *of the Jews.* Having shown

JAMIESON, FAUSSET, BROWN

19, 20. Sir I perceive . . .—Seeing herself all revealed, does she now break down and ask what hopes there might be for one so guilty? Nay, her convictions have not reached that point yet. She ingeniously shifts the subject from a personal to a public question. It is not, "Alas, what a wicked life am I leading!" but "Lo, what a wonderful prophet I got into conversation with! He will be able to settle that interminable dispute between us and the Jews. Sir, you must know all about such matters—our fathers hold to this mountain here," pointing to *Gerizim* in Samaria, "as the divinely consecrated place of worship, but ye Jews say that *Jerusalem* is the proper place—which of us is right?" How slowly does the human heart submit to *thorough* humiliation! (Compare the *prodigal;* see on Luke 15:15). Doubtless our Lord saw through the fetch; but does He say, "That question is not the point just now, but have you been living in the way described, yea or nay? Till this is disposed of I cannot be drawn into theological controversies." The Prince of preachers takes another method: He humors the poor woman, letting her take her own way, allowing her to lead while He follows—but thus only the more effectually gaining His object. He answers her question, pours light into her mind on the *spirituality* of all true worship, as of its glorious Object, and so brings her insensibly to the point at which He could disclose to her wondering mind whom she was all the while speaking to. **21-24. Woman . . .** Here are three weighty pieces of information: (1) The point raised will very soon cease to be of any moment, for a total change of dispensation is about to come over the Church. (2) The Samaritans are wrong, not only as to the *place,* but the whole *grounds* and *nature* of their worship, while in all these respects the truth lies with the Jews. (3) As God is a *Spirit,* so He both *invites* and *demands* a *spiritual worship,* and already all is in preparation for a *spiritual economy,* more in harmony with the true nature of acceptable service than the ceremonial worship by consecrated *persons, place,* and *times,* which God for a time has seen meet to keep up till fulness of the time should come. **neither in this mountain nor yet at Jerusalem**—i.e., *exclusively* (Mal. 1:11; I Tim. 2:8). **worship the Father**—She had talked simply of "worship"; our Lord brings up before her the great OBJECT of all acceptable worship—"THE FATHER."

22. Ye worship ye know not what—without any *revealed authority,* and so very much in the dark. In this sense, the Jews *knew what they were about.* But the most glorious thing here is the reason assigned, *"For salvation is of the Jews,"* intimating to her that *Salvation* was not a thing left to be reached by any one who might vaguely desire it of a God of mercy, but something that had been *revealed, prepared, deposited with a particular people,* and must be sought *in connection with, and as issuing from them;* and that people "the Jews."

ADAM CLARKE

18. *Thou hast had five husbands.* It is not clear that this woman was a prostitute. She might have been legally married to those five, and might have been divorced through some misbehavior of her own, not amounting to adultery; for the adulteress was to be put to death, by both the Jewish and the Samaritan law, not divorced. Or she might have been cast off through some caprice of her husband; for, in the time of our Lord, divorces were very common among the Jews, so that a man put away his wife for any fault. See the note on Matt. v. 31. *He whom thou now hast is not thy husband.* Bishop Pearce would translate this clause in the following manner: "There is no husband whom thou now hast"—or, less literally, "Thou hast no husband now." Probably the meaning is, Thou art contracted to another, but not yet brought home; therefore he is not yet thy husband.

19. *I perceive that thou art a prophet.* And therefore thought Him well qualified to decide the grand question in dispute between the Jews and the Samaritans; but she did not perceive Him to be the Messiah.

20. *Worshipped in this mountain.* Probably pointing to Mount Gerizim, at the foot of which Sychar was situated. The patriarchs had worshipped here—Jacob built an altar on this mountain, and worshipped the true God; see Gen. xxii. 2; xxxiii. 20. Thus she could say, *Our fathers worshipped in this mountain.* On this mountain Sanballat had built them a temple, about 332 years before our Lord's incarnation. See Joseph., *Antiq.* xi, c. viii, s. 4, and 2 Macc. vi. 2.

21. *The hour cometh.* The time was now at hand in which the spiritual worship of God was about to be established in the earth, and all the Jewish rites and ceremonies entirely abolished. *Worship the Father.* This epithet shows the mild, benignant, and tender nature of the gospel dispensation. Men are called to worship their Heavenly Father, and to consider themselves as His children. In reference to this, our Lord's prayer begins, *Our Father which art in heaven.* See v. 23.

22. *Ye worship ye know not what.* The Samaritans believed in the same God with the Jews; but, as they rejected all the prophetical writings, they had but an imperfect knowledge of the Deity. Besides, as they incorporated the worship of idols with His worship, they might be justly said to worship Him whom they did not properly know. See the account of their motley worship, 2 Kings xvii. 26-34. But after Sanballat had built the temple on Mount Gerizim, the idolatrous worship of the Cutheans and Sepharvites, etc., was entirely laid aside, the same religious service being performed in the Samaritan temple which was performed in that at Jerusalem. *We know what we worship.* We Jews acknowledge all the attributes of His nature, and offer to Him only the sacrifices prescribed in the law. *Salvation is of the Jews.* "Salvation is from the Jews." *Salvation* seems here to mean the Saviour, the Messiah, as it does

MATTHEW HENRY

that the place is *indifferent*, he comes to show what is *necessary* and *essential*—that we worship God *in spirit and in truth*, *v.* 23, 24. The stress is upon the state of *mind* in which we worship him. It concerns us to be right, not only in the *object* of our worship, but in the *manner* of it; and it is this which Christ here instructs us in.

[1] The revolution which should introduce this change: *The hour cometh, and now is.* The *perfect day is coming*, and now it *dawns*.

[2]. The blessed change itself. *True worshippers shall worship the Father in spirit and in truth.* As creatures, we worship the Father of *all*: as Christians, we worship *the Father of our Lord Jesus*. Now the change shall be in the *nature* of the worship. Christians shall worship God, not in the ceremonial observances of the Mosaic institution, but in *spiritual* ordinances; in the *temper* and *disposition* of the worshippers. All *should*, and they will, worship God *in spirit and in truth*. It is spoken of (*v.* 23) as their character, and (*v.* 24) as their duty. It is required of all that worship God that they worship him *in spirit and in truth*. We must worship God *in spirit*, Phil. iii. 3. We must depend upon *God's Spirit* for strength and assistance. We must worship him with fixedness of thought and a flame of affection, with *all that is within us*. *In truth*, that is, in *sincerity*. We must mind the power more than the form. God must be thus worshipped, because they only are accounted the *true* worshippers. The gospel erects a spiritual way of worship, so that the professors of the gospel do not live up to gospel light and laws, if they do not worship God *in spirit and in truth*. For the *Father seeketh such worshippers of him*. Such worshippers are very rare. The gate of spiritual worshipping is strait. Such worship is necessary, and what the God of heaven insists upon. God is greatly well pleased with and graciously accepts such worship and such worshippers. His *seeking* such worshippers implies his *making* them such. Christ came to *declare God* to us (*ch.* i. 18), and this he has declared concerning him; he declared it to this poor Samaritan woman, for the meanest are concerned to know God. *God is a spirit*. It is easier to say what God is not than what he is. The spirituality of the divine nature is a very good reason for the spirituality of divine worship. If we do not worship God, who is *a spirit, in the spirit*, we miss the *end* of worship.

4. The last subject of discourse with this woman is concerning the Messiah, *v.* 25, 26.

(1) The faith of the woman, by which she expected the Messiah: *I know that Messias cometh—and he will tell us all things*. She had nothing to object against what Christ had said; his discourse was what might become the Messiah; but *from him* she would receive it, and in the meantime she thinks it best to suspend her belief. Thus many have no heart to the price *in their hand*, because they think they have a better *in their eye*. Whom she expects: *I know that Messias cometh*. The Jews and Samaritans agreed in the expectation of the Messiah and his kingdom. Those who knew least knew this, that Messias was to come. *Messias, who is called Christ*. The evangelist, though he retains the Hebrew word *Messias*, takes care to render it by a Greek word of the same signification, *who is called Christ—Anointed*. What she expects from him: "*He will tell us all things*. He will tell us the mind of God fully and clearly, and keep back nothing." Now this implies an acknowledgment, *First*, Of the imperfection of the discovery they now had of the divine will, and the rule they had of the divine worship. *Secondly*, Of the sufficiency of the Messiah to make this change: "*He will tell us all things* which we want to know, and about which we wrangle in the dark."

(2) The favour of our Lord Jesus in making himself known to her: *I that speak to thee am he*, *v.* 26. Christ did never make himself known so expressly to any as he did here to this poor Samaritan, and to the blind man (*ch.* ix. 37). Christ would thus put an honour upon such as were poor and despised. This woman had never had any opportunity of seeing Christ's miracles, which were then the ordinary method of conviction. God can make the light of grace shine *into the heart* even where he doth not make the light of the gospel shine *in the face*. This woman was better prepared to receive such a discovery than others were. Christ will manifest himself to those who with an honest humble heart desire to be acquainted with him: *I that speak to thee am he*. See here, How near Jesus Christ was to her, when she knew not who he was, Gen. xxviii. 16. Many are lamenting Christ's absence, and longing for his presence, when at the same time he is speaking to them. Christ makes himself known to us by *speaking* to us: *I that speak unto thee, I am he.*

JAMIESON, FAUSSET, BROWN

23. hour cometh, and now is—evidently meaning her to understand that this new economy was in some sense being set up while He was talking to her, a sense which would in a few minutes so far appear, when He told her plainly He was *the Christ*.

25, 26. I know Messias cometh . . . when He is come . . .—If we take our Lord's immediate disclosure of Himself, in answer to this, as the proper key to its meaning to *His ear*, we can hardly doubt that the woman was already *all but prepared for even this startling announcement*, which indeed she seems (from vs. 29) to have already begun to suspect by His revealing her to herself. Thus quickly, under so matchless a Teacher, was she brought up from her sunken condition to a frame of mind and heart capable of the noblest revelations. **tell us all things**—an expectation founded probably on Deuteronomy 18:15.

26. I that speak . . am he—He scarce ever said anything like this to His own people, the Jews. He had magnified them to the woman, and yet to themselves He is to the last far more reserved than to her—*proving* rather than plainly *telling* them He was the Christ. But what would not have been *safe* among them was safe enough with her, whose *simplicity* at this stage of the conversation appears from the sequel to have become perfect. What now will the woman say? We listen, the scene has changed, a new party arrives, the disciples have been to Sychar, at some distance, to buy bread, and on their return are astonished at the company their Lord has been holding in their absence.

ADAM CLARKE

in Luke ii. 30; Acts iv. 12; and so the woman appears to have understood it, v. 25. The Messiah was to spring from the Jews—from them, the preaching of the gospel and the knowledge of the truth were to go to all the nations of the world. It was to the Jews that the promises were made; and it was in their prophetic Scriptures, which the Samaritans rejected, that Jesus Christ was proclaimed and described. See Isa. xi. 3.

23. *The true worshippers shall worship the Father in spirit.* The worship of the Samaritans was a defective worship—they did not receive the prophetical writings. That of the Jews was a carnal worship, dealing only in the letter, and referring to the spirit and design, which were at a distance, by types and ceremonies.

24. *God is a Spirit.* This is one of the first, the greatest, the most sublime, and necessary truths in the compass of nature! There is a God, the Cause of all things—the Fountain of all perfection—without parts or dimensions, for He is eternal—filling the heavens and the earth—pervading, governing, and upholding all things, for He is an infinite Spirit! A man worships God in *spirit* when, under the influence of the Holy Ghost, he brings all his affections, appetites, and desires to the throne of God; and he worships Him in *truth* when every purpose and passion of his heart, and when every act of his religious worship, is guided and regulated by the word of God.

25. *I know that Messias cometh.* Though they did not receive the prophetic writings, yet the tradition of the advent of the Messiah, which was common among the Jews, and founded on promises contained even in the books of Moses, was generally received among the Samaritans also. *Which is called Christ.* This appears to be the Evangelist's explanation of the Hebrew word, according to his custom; chap. i. 38, 41-42; ix. 7, etc. For we cannot suppose that the woman understood Greek, so as to translate the Hebrew word to our Lord; or that she should suppose that a person who was a Jew, v. 9, and a prohpet, v. 19, could stand in need of this interpretation. *He will tell us all things.* Relative to the nature of God, the nature of His worship, and the proper place to adore Him in.

26. *Jesus saith unto her, I . . . am he.* Our Lord never spoke in such direct terms concerning himself to His own countrymen; nor even to His own disciples, till a little before His death. The reason given by Bishop Pearce is the following: The woman being alone when Jesus said it and being a Samaritan, He had no reason to apprehend that the Samaritans, if they knew His claim, would disturb His ministry before the time of His suffering came—which seems to have been the reason why He concealed it so long from His own countrymen.

MATTHEW HENRY

Verses 27–42

I. The *interruption given to this discourse* by the disciples' coming. Just when the discourse was brought to a head, *then came the disciples.* They wondered at Christ's converse with this woman, marvelled that he talked thus earnestly with a woman, a strange woman alone, especially with a Samaritan woman. They wondered he should condescend to talk with such a poor contemptible woman, forgetting what despicable men they themselves were when Christ first called them. Yet they acquiesced in it; they knew it was for some good reason, and therefore none of them asked, *What seekest thou?* or, *Why talkest thou with her?* All is well which Jesus Christ saith and doeth. Whatever they *thought*, they said *nothing.*

II. The notice which the woman gave to her neighbours, *v.* 28, 29. Observe here,

1. How she *forgot her errand to the well, v.* 28. She *went her way.* She withdrew, in civility to Christ, that he might have leisure to *eat his dinner.* She delighted in his discourse, but would not be *rude.* She supposed that Jesus would go forward in his journey, and therefore hastened to tell her neighbours. See how she improved time. When opportunities of *getting good* cease we should seek opportunities of *doing good.* Notice is taken of her *leaving her water-pot* or *pail.* She left it in kindness to Christ, that he might have water to drink with his dinner. She left it that she might make the more haste into the city. She left her water-pot, as one *careless of it,* being wholly taken up with better things.

2. How she *minded her errand to the town.* She *went into the city,* and said to *the men,* to every man she met in the streets: *Come, see a man who told me all things that ever I did. Is not this the Christ?* Observe,

(1) How *solicitous* she was to *have her friends and neighbours* acquainted with Christ. When she had found that treasure, she *called together her friends and neighbours* (as Luke xv. 9), not only to *rejoice with her,* but to share with her. Has he done us the honour to make himself known to us? Let us do him the honour to make him known to others; nor can we do ourselves a greater honour. This woman becomes an apostle. I have most *opportunity,* and therefore lie under the greatest *obligations,* to do good to those that live near me.

(2) How fair and ingenuous she was in the notice she gave them concerning this stranger. She *tells them* plainly what induced her to admire him: *He has told me all things that ever I did.* No more is recorded than what he told her of her husbands. He told her that which none knew but God and her own conscience. Two things affected her: *First, the extent of his knowledge.* We ourselves cannot tell *all things that ever we did. Secondly, The power of his word.* This made a great impression upon her, that he told her her *secret sins.* "*Come see a man* that has told me of my sins." She fastens upon that part of Christ's discourse which one would think she would have been most shy of repeating. That *knowledge of Christ* into which we are led by the conviction of sin and humiliation is most likely to be *sound* and *saving.* She *invites them to come and see* him. Not barely, "Come and look upon him" (she does not invite them to him as a *show*), but "Come and converse with him; come and *hear his wisdom,* as I have done." She would not undertake to manage the arguments which had convinced her, in such a manner as to convince others; all that see the evidence of truth themselves are not able to make others see it. Jesus was now at the town's end. "Now come see him." Shall we not go over the threshold to see him whose day prophets and kings desired to see? She resolves to *appeal to themselves, Is this not the Christ?* She does not peremptorily say, "He is the Messiah." She will not impose her faith upon them, but only propose it to them. By such fair but forcible appeals as these men's judgments and consciences are sometimes taken hold of ere they are aware.

(3) What success she had in this invitation: *They went out of the city, and came to him, v.* 30. They *came unto him*; did not send for him into the city to them, they *went out to him.* Those that would know Christ must meet him where he records his name.

III. Christ's discourse with his disciples while the woman was absent, *v.* 31–38. See how industrious our Lord Jesus was to *redeem time,* to husband every minute of it. It were well if we could *thus* gather up the fragments of time. Two things are observable in this discourse:

1. How Christ *expresses the delight* which he himself had in his work. Now with this work we here find him wholly taken up. For,

(1) *He neglected his meat and drink for his work.* When he sat down upon the well, he was *weary,* and

JAMIESON, FAUSSET, BROWN

27. marvelled that he talked with the woman—It never probably occurred to them to marvel that He talked with *themselves;* yet in His eye, as the sequel shows, He was quite as nobly employed. How poor, if not false, are many of our most plausible estimates! **no man said . . . What? . . . Why?**—awed by the spectacle, and thinking there must be something under it. **28-30. left her water-pot**—How exquisitely natural! The presence of strangers made her feel that it was time for her to withdraw, and He who knew what was in her heart, and what she was going to the city to do, let her go without exchanging a word with her in the hearing of others. Their interview was too sacred, and the effect on the woman too overpowering (not to speak of His own deep emotion) to allow of its being continued. But this one artless touch—that she "left her water-pot"—speaks volumes. The living water was already beginning to spring up within her; she found that man doth not live by bread nor by water only, and that there was a water of wondrous virtue that raised people above meat and drink, and the vessels that held them, and all human things. In short, she was transported, forgot everything but One, and her heart running over with the tale she had to tell, she hastens home and pours it out.

CHARLES H. SPURGEON:

Notice that the woman *leaves her waterpot.* The Spirit of God thought well to record this circumstance, and therefore I think there must be a measure of teaching in it. She left her waterpot, first, for speed. Perhaps you thought it was an ordinary English waterpot such as you water the garden with: possibly you so picture it, rose and all. Nothing of the sort. It was a big jar, or large pitcher of earthenware, she had to carry on her head or her shoulder, quite a load for her, and so she left it that she might run the more quickly. She was a wise woman to leave her waterpot when she wanted to move rapidly. Others think she did so because she was so taken up with her errand that she forgot her pitcher. It is blessed forgetfulness which comes of absorption in a holy design. When the King's business requireth haste, it is wise to leave behind everything that would hinder.

—*The Treasury of the New Testament*

29. is not this the Christ—The *form* of the question (in the *Greek*) is a distant, modest way of only half *insinuating* what it seemed hardly fitting for her to *affirm;* nor does she refer to what He said of Himself, but solely to His disclosure to her of the particulars of her own life.

30. they went out . . .—How different from the Jews! and richly was their openness to conviction rewarded. **31-38. meantime**—i.e., while the woman was away.

ADAM CLARKE

27. *Came his disciples.* From the town, whither they went to buy food, v. 8. *Marvelled that he talked with the woman.* Because it was contrary to the custom of the Eastern countries; and there are many canons, among the rabbins, against it. To the present time, if a man meet even his own wife in the street, he does not speak to her; and this is done to keep up the appearance of a chastity and temperance of which the Eastern world knows nothing. *Yet no man said.* They were awed by His majesty, and knew that He must have sufficient reasons to induce Him to act a part to which He was not at all accustomed.

28. *Left her waterpot.* She was so penetrated with the great truths which Jesus had announced that she forgot her errand to the well, and returned to the city without the water for which she came out!

29. *All things that ever I did.* The Jews believed that one essential characteristic of the Messiah would be that He should be able to tell the secrets of all hearts. This they believed was predicted, Isa. xi. 2-3.

30. *They went out of the city.* Such effect had the simple testimony of the woman on their minds. *And came unto him.* Or "were coming to Him"; for they did not reach Him immediately, all that discourse between Him and His disciples mentioned in vv. 31-39 inclusive having taken place before the people of Sychar got to the well.

MATTHEW HENRY

needed refreshment; but this opportunity of saving souls made him forget his weariness and hunger. And he minded *his food* so little that his disciples were forced to invite him to it: *They prayed him, Master, eat.* It was an instance of their *love to him* that they invited him; but it was a greater instance of his *love to souls* that he needed invitation. He minded it so little that they suspected he had had meat brought him in their absence (*v.* 33): *Has any man brought him aught to eat?* He had so little appetite for his dinner that they were ready to think he had dined already.

(2) He *made his work his meat and drink.* The work he *had done* in instructing the woman, the work he *had to do* among the Samaritans, this was *meat and drink* to him. Never did a hungry man, or an epicure, expect a plentiful feast with so much desire, nor feed upon its dainties with so much delight, as our Lord Jesus expected and improved an opportunity of doing good to souls. It was such *meat* as the disciples *knew not of.* This may be said of good Christians too, that they have meat to eat which others know not of, joy with which a stranger does not intermeddle. Now this word made them ask, *Has any man brought him aught to eat?* The reason why his work was his meat and drink was because it was his Father's work, his Father's will: *My meat is to do the will of him that sent me, v.* 34. The salvation of sinners is the *will of God,* and the instruction of them in order thereunto is *his work.* He made this work his business and delight. When his body needed food, his mind was so taken up with this that he forgot both hunger and thirst, both meat and drink. He was *earnest* and in care to go *through* it, and to *finish his work.* He resolved never to quit it, nor lay it down, till he could say, *It is finished.* Many have zeal to carry them *out* at first, but not zeal to carry them *on* to the last.

2. See here how Christ excites his disciples to diligence in *their* work; they were workers *with him,* and therefore should be workers *like him.* The work they had to do was to *preach the gospel.* Now this work he here compares to *harvest work, v.* 35–38. Harvest time is *busy* time; all hands must be then at work. Harvest time is *opportunity,* a short and limited time, and harvest work is work that must be done *then* or not at all. Now he here suggests three things to them to quicken them to diligence:

(1) That it was *necessary work,* and the *occasion* for it very urgent and pressing (*v.* 35): *You say, It is four months to harvest;* but I say, *The fields are already white.* [A saying concerning the *corn-harvest;* there *are yet four months, and then comes harvest.* "You say, for the encouragement of the sower at seed-time, that it will be but four months to the harvest."] God has not only promised us a harvest every year, but has appointed the *weeks of harvest;* so that we know *when to expect it.* Christ's saying concerning the *gospel harvest: Look, the fields are already white unto the harvest.* Here in *this* place there was harvest work for *him* to do. They would have him to *eat, v.* 31. "Eat!" saith he, "I have other work to do, that is more needful; *look* what crowds of Samaritans are coming that are ready to receive the gospel." People's forwardness to hear the word is a great excitement to ministers' diligence and liveliness in preaching it. There are multitudes as ready to receive the gospel as a field of corn that is fully ripe is ready to be reaped. The fields were now made *white to the harvest.* It is a great encouragement to us to engage in any work for God, if we understand by the signs of the times that this is the proper season for that work. John Baptist had *made ready a people prepared for the Lord.* Since he began to preach the kingdom of God *every man pressed into it,* Luke xvi. 16. This, therefore, was a time to *thrust in their sickle.* It was *necessary* to work now. If the corn that is *ripe* be not reaped, it will *shed* and be lost. If souls that are under convictions be not helped now, their hopeful beginnings will come to nothing.

(2) That it was *profitable* and *advantageous* work, which they themselves would be gainers by (*v.* 36): "*He that reapeth receiveth wages.*" Christ's reapers never have cause to say they served a hard Master. His work is *its own wages.* Christ's reapers have *fruit: He gathereth fruit unto life eternal;* that is, he shall both save himself and those that hear him. This is the comfort of faithful ministers, that their work has a tendency to the eternal salvation of precious souls: They have *joy: That he that sows and they that reap may rejoice together.* The minister who is the happy instrument of beginning a good work is *he that sows;* he that is employed to carry it on and perfect it is *he that reaps:* and both shall rejoice together. The reapers share in the *joy of harvest.*

(3) That it was *easy work,* and work that was half done to their hands by those that were gone before

JAMIESON, FAUSSET, BROWN

Master, eat–*Fatigue* and *thirst* we saw He felt; here is revealed another of our common infirmities to which the Lord was subject–*hunger.*

32. meat ye know not of–What spirituality of mind! 'I *have* been eating all the while, and such food as ye dream not of.' What can that be? they ask each other; have any supplies been brought Him in our absence? He knows what they are saying though He hears it not. **34. My meat is . . .**–'A Servant here to fulfil a prescribed work, to *do* and to *finish,* that is "meat" to Me; and of this, while you were away, I have had My fill.' And of what does He speak thus? Of the condescension, pity, patience, wisdom He had been laying out upon *one soul*–a very humble woman, and in some respects repulsive too! But He had gained her, and through her was going to gain more, and lay perhaps the foundations of a great work in the country of Samaria; and this filled His whole soul and raised Him above the sense of natural hunger (Matt. 4:4).

35. yet four months, and then harvest–i.e., 'In current speech, ye say thus at this season; but lift up your eyes and look upon those fields in the light of *another* husbandry, for lo! *in that sense,* they are even now white to harvest, ready for the sickle.' The simple beauty of this language is only surpassed by the glow of holy emotion in the Redeemer's own soul which it expresses. It refers to the *ripeness* of these Sycharites for accession to Him, and the joy of this great Lord of the reapers over the anticipated ingathering. Oh, could we but *so,* "lift up our eyes and look" upon many fields abroad and at home, which to dull sense appear unpromising, as *He* beheld those of Samaria, what movements, as yet scarce in embryo, and accessions to Christ, as yet seemingly far distant, might we not discern as quite near at hand, and thus, amidst difficulties and discouragements too much for nature to sustain, be cheered–*as our Lord Himself was* in circumstances far more overwhelming–with "songs in the night!"

36. he that reapeth . . .–As our Lord could not mean that the reaper only, and not the sower, received "wages," in the sense of *personal reward* for his work, the "wages" here can be no other than the joy of having such a harvest to gather in–the joy of "gathering fruit unto life eternal." **rejoice together**–The blessed issue of the whole ingathering is the interest alike of the sower as of the reaper; it is no more the fruit of the last operation than of the first; and just as there can be no reaping without previous sowing, so have those servants of Christ, to whom is assigned the pleasant task of merely reaping the spiritual harvest, no work to do, and no joy to taste, that has not been prepared to their hand by the toilsome and often thankless work of their predecessors in the field. *The joy,* therefore, *of the great harvest*

ADAM CLARKE

31. *Master, eat.* They knew that He was greatly spent both with hunger and fatigue.

32. *I have meat to eat that ye know not of.* Our blessed Lord seizes every opportunity to raise the minds of His apostles to heavenly things through the medium of earthly matters.

33. *Hath any man brought Him ought to eat?* Has He got food in any preternatural way? They could not help remembering the miraculous interventions of divine providence in feeding Elijah by the ravens, at the brook Cherith, 1 Kings xvii. 4-6, and by the ministry of an angel, chap. xix. 5-8, and our Lord's preternatural repast in the wilderness, after His victory over Satan, Matt. iv. 11.

34. *My meat is to do the will of him that sent me.* In these words our blessed Lord teaches a lesson of zeal and earnestness to His apostles, and to all their successors in the Christian ministry. Let the salvation of souls lie nearer your heart then life itself. Let eating and drinking, labor and rest, reading, thinking, study, prayer, and all things be directed to the accomplishment of this great work.

35. *There are yet four months, and then cometh harvest?* In Palestine the harvest did not begin till after the Passover, which was fixed on the fourteenth of the month Nisan, which answers to our March, and sometimes extends into April. The barley harvest was the first, after that the wheat; and both were finished by Pentecost. For in the Feast of Pentecost the firstfruits of all the harvest were carried to the Temple and waved before the Lord. See Lev. xxiii. 11. *Lift up your eyes, and look on the fields,* over which it is likely the Samaritans were then coming in troops, guided by the woman who had already received the light of the gospel of peace. *The fields . . . are white already to harvest.* Multitudes of Samaritans are coming to believe on Me, and to be saved unto eternal life. Probably they had a kind of *white* raiment.

36. *And he that reapeth receiveth wages.* Or, "And already the reaper receiveth wages." By making the word "already" the beginning of this verse, on the authority of some excellent MSS. and versions, a more consistent sense is obtained than from the common arrangement, where "already" terminates the preceding verse.

MATTHEW HENRY

them: *One soweth, and another reapeth*, *v.* 37, 38. Moses, and the prophets, and John Baptist, had *paved* the way to the gospel. *I sent you to reap that whereupon you bestowed* no *labour*. This intimates *two things* concerning the Old Testament ministry: It was very much *short* of the New Testament ministry. Moses and the *prophets* sowed, but they could not be said to *reap*. Their writings have done much more good since they left us than ever their preaching did. It was very *serviceable* to the New Testament ministry, and made way for it. Had it not been for the seed sown by the prophets, this Samaritan woman could not have said, *We know that Messias cometh*. This also intimates *two things* concerning the ministry of the *apostles of Christ*. It was a *fruitful* ministry: they were reapers that gathered in a great harvest. It was much *facilitated* by the writings of the prophets. The prophets *sowed in tears*, crying out, *We have laboured in vain;* the apostles *reaped in joy*, saying, *Thanks be to God, who always causeth us to triumph*. From the labours of ministers that are dead and gone much good fruit may be reaped by the people that *survive* them and the ministers that *succeed* them. See what reason we have to bless God for those that are *gone before us*. We are *entered into their labours*.

IV. The *good effect* which this visit Christ made to the Samaritans had upon them, *v.* 39–42. See what impressions were made on them,

1. By the *woman's testimony* concerning *Christ*; and the testimony no more than this, *He told me all that ever I did*. And *two things* they were brought to:

(1) To *credit* Christ's *word* (*v.* 39): *Many of the Samaritans of that city believed on him for the saying of the woman*. Who they were that believed: *Many of the Samaritans*, who were not of the house of Israel. Their faith was an *earnest* of the *faith* of the Gentiles. Upon what inducement they believed: *For the saying of the woman*. See here, *First*, How God is sometimes pleased to use very weak and unlikely instruments for the beginning and carrying on of a good work. *Secondly*, How great a matter a little fire kindles. Our Saviour, by instructing one poor woman, spread instruction to a whole town. Let not ministers be either *careless* in their preaching, or *discouraged* in it, because their hearers are *few* and *mean*; for, by doing good to *them*, good may be conveyed to *more*. See how good it is to speak *experimentally* of Christ. Those are most likely to do good that can tell what God has done *for their souls*.

(2) To *court his stay* among them (*v.* 40): When they were come to him *they besought him that he would tarry with them*. Upon the woman's report, they believed him to be a prophet, and *came to him*; and, when they *saw* him, they respected him as a prophet. They begged he would tarry with them that they might *testify their respect* to him; that they might receive instruction from him. Many would have flocked to one that would tell them *their fortune*, but these flocked to one that would tell them *their faults*. The Jews drove him from them: while the Samaritans invited him to them. The *proof* of the gospel's success is not always according to the *probability*, nor what is *experienced* according to what is *expected*. Christ granted their request. He *abode there*. When he had an opportunity of doing good, he *abode there*. We are told what impressions were made upon them by Christ's own word (*v.* 41, 42), what he *said* and *did* there is not related. He said and did that which convinced them that he was the Christ; and the labours of a minister are best told by the good fruit of them. *Now their eyes saw him;* and the effect was, [1] That their number grew (*v.* 41): *Many more believed*. [2] That their faith grew. Those who had been wrought upon by the report of the woman now saw cause to say, *Now we believe, not because of thy saying*, *v.* 42. Here are three things in which their *faith grew*: *a.* In the matter of it. Upon the testimony of the woman, they believed him to be *a prophet*; but now that they have conversed with him they believe that he is *the Christ*, the *Anointed One*, and that, being the *Christ*, he is the *Saviour of the world*. They believed him to be the Saviour not only of the Jews, but *of the world*, which they hoped would take them in, though Samaritans. *b.* In the *certainty* of it; their faith now grew up to a full assurance: *We know* that this is indeed the *Christ*. *c.* In the *ground* of it: *Now we believe, not because of thy saying, for we have heard him ourselves*. They had before *believed for her saying*: "*Now we believe* because we have *heard him ourselves*. We are abundantly satisfied and assured that *this is the Christ*." In this instance we may see how *faith comes by hearing*. Faith comes *to the birth* by hearing the *report of men*. The instructions of parents and preachers *recommend* the doctrine of Christ *to our acquaintance*. Faith *comes*

JAMIESON, FAUSSET, BROWN

festivity will be the common joy of all who have taken any part in the work from the first operation to the last. (See Deut. 16:11, 14; Ps. 126:6; Isa. 9:3.) What encouragement is here for those "fishers of men" who "have toiled all the night" of their official life, and, to human appearance, "have taken nothing!" **38. I sent you . . .**—The *I* is emphatic—I, the Lord of the whole harvest: "sent you," points to their *past* appointment to the apostleship, though it has reference only to their *future* discharge of it, for they had nothing to do with the present ingathering of the Sycharites. **ye bestowed no labour**—meaning that much of their future success would arise from the *preparation already made* for them. (See on vs. 42.) **others laboured**—Referring to the Old Testament laborers, the Baptist, and *by implication* Himself, though He studiously keeps this in the background, *that the line of distinction between Himself and all His servants might not be lost sight of*. "Christ represents Himself as the Husbandman [rather the Lord of the laborers], who has the direction both of the sowing and of the harvest, who commissions *all* the agents—those of the Old Testament as well as of the New—and therefore does not stand on a level with either the sowers or the reapers" [OLSHAUSEN].

39-42. many . . . believed . . .—The truth of vs. 35 begins to appear. These Samaritans were the foundation of the Church afterwards built up there. No miracle appears to have been wrought there [but unparalleled supernatural knowledge displayed]: "*we have heard Him ourselves*" sufficed to raise their faith to a point never attained by the Jews, and hardly as yet by the disciples—that He was "the Saviour of *the world*" [ALFORD]. "This incident is further remarkable as a rare instance of the Lord's ministry producing *an awakening on a large scale*" [OLSHAUSEN].

40. abode two days—Two precious days, surely, to the Redeemer Himself! Unsought, He had come to His own, yet His own received Him not: now those who were not His own had come to Him, been won by Him, and invited Him to their town that others might share with them in the benefit of His wonderful ministry. Here, then, would He solace His already wounded spirit and have in this outfield village triumph of His grace, a sublime foretaste of the inbringing of the whole Gentile world into the Church.

ADAM CLARKE

37. *Herein is that saying true, One soweth, and another reapeth*. Or, "One is the sower, and another is the reaper." In what respects you, of this business, this proverb is true—*One is the sower;* for I have sent you to reap, to preach My gospel and gain converts, where you have not labored—have not sown the first seeds of eternal life. Others have labored—the patriarchs and prophets—and you are entered into the fruits of their labors.

39. *Many of the Samaritans . . . believed on him for the saying of the woman*. This woman was the first apostle of Christ in Samaria! She went and told her fellow citizens that the Messiah was come, and gave for proof that He had told her the most secret things she had ever done; see on v. 29. This word, which is twice repeated, in v. 29 and here, strongly intimates that a more particular conversation had taken place between our Lord and the Samaritan woman than what is here related.

40. *He abode there two days*. We are not told that He wrought any miracles among them. This does not appear to have been necessary; they were a simplehearted, teachable people, and they credited Him on the evidence of His own eternal truth. Why are not miracles wrought now? Miracles were only for the establishment of the doctrines of Christianity where they were first preached. We profess to believe these doctrines; therefore, to us, miracles would be useless. Where the doctrine is credited, no miracle is necessary; the Samaritans believed, and no miracle was wrought among them, for the simple reason that it was not necessary.

42. *We have heard him ourselves*. On seeing and hearing our Lord, the faith of those who had already believed on the woman's testimony was abundantly confirmed; and, besides those, many others believed who had not heard the woman speak. *This is indeed the Christ*. The promised Messiah. *The Saviour of the world*. Not of the Jews only, but of the Samaritans, and of the whole Gentile world.

MATTHEW HENRY

to its growth, by hearing the testimony of Christ himself; and this goes further, and recommends his doctrine *to our acceptance*. We were induced to look into the scriptures *by the saying* of those who told us that in them they had found eternal life; now we believe, *not for their saying*, but because we have searched them ourselves: and our faith *stands not in the wisdom of men, but in the power of God*.

Thus was the seed of the gospel sown in Samaria.

Verses 43–54

I. Christ's *coming* into Galilee, *v.* 43. *After two days* he left them because *he must preach to other cities*, Luke iv. 43. *He went into Galilee*.

1. Whither Christ went; into Galilee, but not to Nazareth, which was strictly *his own* country. He went among the villages, but declined going to Nazareth, for a reason here given, which *Jesus himself testified*: That a *prophet has no honour in his own country*. The honour due to the Lord's prophets has very often been denied them. This *due* honour is most frequently denied them *in their own country*. Christ's near kinsmen spoke most slightly of him, *ch.* vii. 5. Men's pride and envy make them scorn to be instructed by those who once were their school-fellows and play-fellows. It is just with God to deny his gospel to those that despise the ministers of it. They that mock the messengers forfeit the benefit of the message.

2. What entertainment he met with among the Galileans in the country (*v.* 45): They *received him*. Christ and his gospel are not sent in vain; if they have not honour with *some*, they shall have with *others*. Now the reason given why these Galileans were so ready to receive Christ is because they had seen *the miracles he did at Jerusalem*, *v.* 45. They went up to Jerusalem at the feast, the feast of the passover. They *went up to the feast*, and there they became acquainted with Christ. They that are diligent and constant in attending on public ordinances some time or other meet with more spiritual benefit than they expect. At Jerusalem they *saw* Christ's miracles. The miracles were wrought for the benefit of those at Jerusalem; yet the Galileans got more advantage by them than they did for whom they were chiefly designed. Thus the word preached to a *mixed multitude* may perhaps edify *occasional* hearers more than the constant auditory.

3. What city he went to. He chose to go to Cana of Galilee, *where he had made the water wine* (*v.* 46). The evangelist mentions this miracle here to teach us to keep in remembrance what we *have seen of the* works of Christ.

II. His *curing* the *nobleman's son*. This story is not recorded by any other of the evangelists.

1. Who the *petitioner* was, and who the *patient*: the petitioner was a *nobleman*; the patient was his son: *There was a certain nobleman*. The father a nobleman and yet the son sick; for dignities and titles of honour will be no security from the assaults of sickness and death. It was fifteen miles from Capernaum to Cana, where Christ now was; yet this affliction in his family sent him so far to Christ.

2. How the petitioner made *his application* to the physician. He *went to him* himself, and *besought him to come and heal his son*, *v.* 47. See here, His *tender affection* to his son, that when he was sick he would spare no pains to get help for him. His *great respect* to our Lord Jesus, that he would come himself to wait upon him, and that he *besought him*, when, as a man in authority, he might have ordered his attendance. The greatest men, when they come to God, must become beggars. As to the errand he came upon, we may observe a mixture in *his faith*. There was *sincerity* in it; he did believe that Christ could heal his son. Yet there was *infirmity* in his faith; he thought he could not heal him at a distance, and therefore he besought him that he would *come down* and heal him. We are encouraged to *pray*, but we are not allowed to prescribe: Lord, heal me; but, whether with a word or a touch, *thy will be done*.

3. The gentle rebuke he met with in this address (*v.* 48): *Jesus said to him*, *"Except you see signs and wonders, you will not believe."* Though he was a *nobleman*, and now in *grief* about his son, yet Christ gives him a reproof. Christ first shows him his sin and weakness, to prepare him for mercy, and then grants his request. Those whom Christ intends to honour with his *favours* he first *humbles* with his *frowns*. Whereas they had heard by credible and incontestable report of the miracles he had wrought in other places, they could not believe except they saw them with their own eyes. They must be *honoured*, and they must be *humoured*, or they will not be *convinced*. Whereas they had seen divers miracles which sufficiently proved Christ to be a teacher come from God, they would go no further in believing than

JAMIESON, FAUSSET, BROWN

43-54. SECOND GALILEAN MIRACLE—HEALING OF THE COURTIER'S SON. **43, 44. after two days**—lit., the two days of His stay at Sychar. **For Jesus testified . . .**—This verse had occasioned much discussion. For it seems strange, if "His own country" here means *Nazareth*, which was in Galilee, that it should be said He came to Galilee *because* in one of its towns He expected no good reception. But all will be simple and natural if we fill up the statement thus: 'He went into the region of Galilee, but not, as might have been expected, to that part of it called "His own country," Nazareth (see Mark 6:4; Luke 4:24), *for* He acted on the maxim which He oft repeated, that a prophet . . .

45. received—welcomed Him. **having seen . . . at the feast**—proud, perhaps, of their Countryman's wonderful works at Jerusalem, and possibly won by this circumstance to regard His claims as at least worthy of respectful investigation. Even this our Lord did not despise, for saving conversion often begins in less than this (so Zaccheus, Luke 19:3-10). **for they also went**—i.e., it was their practice to go up to the feast.

46, 47. nobleman—courtier, king's servant, or one connected with a royal household; such as Chuza (Luke 8:3), or Manaen (Acts 13:1). **heard that Jesus was come out of Judea**—"where he had doubtless seen or heard what things Jesus had done at Jerusalem" (vs. 45), [BENGEL].

come down—for Capernaum was down on the northwest shore of the Sea of Galilee.

48-54. Except ye see signs . . .—He *did* believe, both as his coming and his urgent entreaty show; but how imperfectly we shall see; and our Lord would deepen his faith by such a blunt and seemingly rough answer as He made to Nicodemus.

ADAM CLARKE

44. *Jesus himself testified.* He bore testimony to the general truth of the following proverb. See on Matt. xiii. 57.

45. *The Galilaeans received him.* They received Him as the promised Messiah because of the miracles which they had seen Him perform at Jerusalem, at the Passover. See chap. ii. 23.

46. *Where he made the water wine.* See the notes on chap. ii. 1, etc. Cana was on the road from Nazareth to Capernaum and the Sea of Tiberias. *A certain nobleman.* An officer of the king's court, for this is the meaning of the original word. This officer belonged to Herod Antipas, who was then tetrarch of Galilee. This officer, whoever he was, appears to have had his ordinary abode at Capernaum; and hearing that Christ was at Cana, he came expressly from Capernaum thither to entreat Him to heal his child.

48. *Except ye see signs and wonders.* Our Lord did not tell this man that he had no faith, but that he had not enough. If he had had none, he would not have come from Capernaum to Cana to beg Him to heal his son. If he had had enough, he would have been contented with recommending his son to our Lord, without entreating Him to go to Capernaum to heal him, which intimates that he did not believe our Lord could do it at a distance. But the words are not addressed to the nobleman alone, but to all the Galilean Jews in general; for our Lord uses the plural number, which He never does when addressing an individual. These people differed widely from the people of Sychar; they

MATTHEW HENRY

they were *driven* by signs and wonders. The *spiritual* power of the word did not *affect them*, did not *attract* them, but only the *sensible* power of miracles.

4. His continued importunity in his address (*v.* 49): *Sir, come down ere my child die.* He took the reproof patiently; he spoke to Christ respectfully. And, as he did not take the reproof for an affront, so he did not take it for a denial, but still prosecuted his request, and continued to wrestle till he prevailed. He is so wholly taken up with concern about his child that he can mind nothing else. He still discovered the weakness of his faith in the power of Christ. He must have Christ to come down, thinking that else he could do the child no kindness. He believes that Christ could heal a *sick* child, but not that he could raise a *dead* child, "O *come down, ere my child die*," as if then it would be too late. He forgot that Elijah and Elisha had raised dead children; and is Christ's power inferior to theirs? Observe what haste he is in: *Come down, ere my child die;* as if there were danger of Christ's slipping his time.

5. The answer of peace which Christ gave (*v.* 50): *Go thy way, thy son liveth.* Christ here gives us an instance of his *power*, that he not only could heal, but could heal with so much ease. Here is nothing *said*, nothing *done*, nothing *ordered* to be done, and yet the cure wrought. This nobleman would have Christ *come down and heal his son*; Christ will heal his son, and not *come down.* And thus the cure is the sooner wrought, the nobleman's mistake rectified, and his faith confirmed; so that the thing was better done in Christ's way. When he denies what we ask, he gives what is much more to our advantage. He observed the nobleman to be *in pain* about his son, and therefore Christ dropped the reproof, and gave him assurance of the recovery of his child; for he knows how a father *pities his children.*

6. The nobleman's belief of the word of Christ: He *believed*, and *went away*. He is satisfied with the method Christ took. Now he *sees no sign or wonder*, and yet *believes* the wonder done. Christ said, *Thy son liveth*, and the man *believed* him. Christ said, *Go thy way;* and, as an evidence of the sincerity of his faith, he *went his way.*

7. The further confirmation of his faith, by comparing notes with his servants at his return. His servants met him with the agreeable news of the child's recovery, *v.* 51. Christ said, *Thy son liveth*; and now the servants say the same. Good news will meet those that hope in God's word. He enquired what hour the child began to recover (*v.* 52). He was desirous to have his faith confirmed. The diligent comparison of the works of Christ with his word will be of great use to us for the confirming of our faith. This was the course the nobleman took: *He enquired of the servants the hour when he began to amend;* and they told him, *Yesterday at the seventh hour* the *fever left him*; not only he began to amend, but he was perfectly well on a sudden; so *the father knew that it was at the same hour* when Jesus said to him, *Thy son liveth.* Two things would help to confirm his faith: *First*, That the child's recovery was *sudden* and not *gradual.* They name the precise time to an hour: *Yesterday*, not *about*, but *at* the seventh hour, *the fever left him.* The word of Christ did not work like physic, which must have time to operate, and produce the effect, and perhaps *cures by expectation* only; no, with Christ it was *he spoke and it was done;* not, He spoke and it was *set a-doing. Secondly*, That it was just at the same time that Christ spoke to him: *at that very hour.* The synchronisms and coincidents of events add very much to the beauty and harmony of Providence. In men's works, distance of place is the delay of time and the retarding of business; but it is not so in the works of Christ.

8. The *happy effect and issue of this.* The bringing of the cure to the family brought salvation to it. The nobleman *himself believed.* He had before *believed* the word of Christ; but now he *believed in Christ.* Christ has many ways of gaining the heart, and by the grant of a *temporal* mercy may make way for *better* things. His *whole house* believed likewise. Because of the *interest* they all had in the miracle, which preserved the *blossom* and *hopes* of the family; this affected them all, and endeared Christ to them. This was a *nobleman*, and probably he had a *great household*; but, when he comes into Christ's school, he brings them all along with him. What a blessed change was here in this house, occasioned by the sickness of the child! This should reconcile us to afflictions; we know not what good may follow from them.

9. Here is the evangelist's remark upon this cure (*v.* 54); *This is the second miracle*, referring to *ch.* ii. 11. In Judæa he had wrought many miracles. They had the first offer; but, being driven thence, he wrought miracles in Galilee. Somewhere or other Christ will

JAMIESON, FAUSSET, BROWN

49. come down ere my child die—'While we talk, the case is at its crisis, and if Thou come not instantly, all is over. This was faith, but partial, and our Lord would perfect it. The man cannot believe the cure could be wrought without the Physician coming to the patient—the thought of such a thing evidently never occurred to him. But Jesus will in a moment bring him up to this.

50. Go thy way; thy son liveth—Both effects instantaneously followed:—"The man believed the word," and the cure, shooting quicker than lightning from Cana to Capernaum, was felt by the dying youth. In token of faith, the father takes his leave of Christ—in the circumstances this evidenced full faith. The servants hasten to convey the joyful tidings to the anxious parents, whose faith now only wants one confirmation.

"When began he to amend?" "Yesterday, at the seventh hour, the fever left him"—the very hour in which was uttered that great word, "Thy son liveth!" So "himself believed and his whole house." He *had* believed before this, first very imperfectly; then with assured confidence of Christ's word; but now with a faith crowned by "sight." And the wave rolled from the head to the members of his household. "To-day is salvation come to this *house*" (Luke 19:9); and no mean house this!

second miracle Jesus did—i.e., in Cana; done "after He came out of Judea," as the former before.

ADAM CLARKE

had neither a love of the truth nor simplicity of heart, and would not believe anything from heaven unless forced on their minds by the most striking miracles. They were favored with the ministry of John Baptist; but, as that was not accompanied with miracles, it was not generally credited. They required the miracles of Christ in order that they might credit the advent of the Messiah.

49. *Sir, come down.* He did not think our Lord could cure him without being present, and seems here to feel himself hurt because our Lord did not come at his first entreaty. It is difficult for a proud man, or a man in office, to humble himself or to treat even God Almighty with proper respect.

50. *Go thy way; they son liveth.* Had our Lord gone with him, as he wished, his unbelief could not have been fully removed, as he would have still thought that our Lord's power could not reach from Cana to Capernaum. In order to destroy his unbelief at once, and bring him into the fullness of the faith of His supreme power, He cures him, being apparently absent, by that energy through which He fills both the heavens and the earth. Here it may be observed that our blessed Lord did what this man requested Him to do, but not in the way in which he wished it to be done. God will save all to the uttermost who call upon Him, but not in the way in which they may desire. Eternal life is the free gift of God, and He has a right to give it as He pleases; and He always gives His gifts in that way in which His glory is best promoted, and our eternal interest secured. *The man believed the word.* And yet it appears that he had suspended his faith upon a certain condition: "If I find on my return that my son is healed, I will believe that Jesus is the Messiah."

52. *Then enquired he of them the hour.* The servants, overjoyed to find their master's son so suddenly restored, set off to meet him, that they might impart to him tidings which they knew would be so very agreeable; and he, intent on having his faith settled, began immediately to inquire what time it was when the fever left him, to see whether his cure was the effect of some natural cause or whether it was done by the power of Christ. *Yesterday at the seventh hour.* At the time we would call one o'clock.

53. *So the father knew.* He had the fullest proof that his son's cure was supernatural, and that it was wrought by the Lord Jesus. *Himself believed, and his whole house.* He and his whole family became true converts to the doctrine of the manifested Messiah. The whole family, impressed with the great kindness of God in sending health to the child, were the more easily led to believe in the Lord Jesus. The sickness of the child became the means of salvation to all the household. They no doubt thought at first that God was dealing hardly with them, when threatening to remove the child; but now they see that in very faithfulness God had afflicted them. Let us learn never to murmur against God, or think that He does not act kindly towards us.

54. *This is again the second miracle.* The first miracle which Christ performed was in this same city of Cana, just after His baptism; and this second took place after His arrival

MATTHEW HENRY

find a welcome. People may, if they please, shut the sun out of *their own houses*, but they cannot shut it *out of the world*. This is noted to be the *second miracle*, to remind us of the first. *Fresh* mercies should revive the remembrance of former mercies, as former mercies should encourage our hopes of further mercies. Probably, the patient being a person of quality, when this nobleman applied himself to Christ, multitudes followed. What abundance of good may great men do, if they be good men!

CHAPTER 5

Verses 1–16

This miraculous cure is not recorded by any other of the evangelists, who confine themselves mostly to the miracles wrought in Galilee, but John relates those wrought at Jerusalem.

I. *The time when* this cure was wrought: it was at a *feast of the Jews*, that is, the passover, for that was the most celebrated feast. Christ, though residing in Galilee, yet *went up to Jerusalem* at the feast, *v.* 1. It was an *opportunity of good*; there were great numbers gathered together there at that time; it was a general rendezvous, from all parts of the country, besides proselytes from other nations. It was to be hoped that they were in a *good frame*, for they came together to *worship God*. Now a mind *inclined to devotion lies very open* to the further discoveries of divine light and love.

II. The *place where* this cure was wrought: at the *pool of Bethesda*, which had a miraculous healing virtue in it, *v.* 2–4.

1. Where it was situated: *At Jerusalem, by the sheep-market*. Some think it was near the temple, and, if so, it yielded a melancholy but profitable spectacle to those that went up to the temple to pray.

2. How it was called: It was a *pool which is called in Hebrew, Bethesda—the house of mercy*; for therein appeared much of the *mercy of God* to the sick and diseased. In a world of so much misery as this is, it is well that there are some *Bethesdas*.

3. How it was fitted up: It had *five porches* in which the sick lay. Thus the charity of men concurred with the mercy of God for the relief of the distressed. Nature has provided *remedies*, but men must provide *hospitals*.

4. How it was frequented with sick and cripples (*v.* 3): *In these lay a great multitude of impotent folks*. How many are the afflictions of the afflicted in this world! It may do us good to visit the hospitals sometimes, that we may take occasion, from the calamities of others, to thank God for our comforts. The evangelist specifies three sorts of diseased people that lay here, *blind, halt*, and *withered*. These are mentioned because, being least able to help themselves into the water, they lay longest waiting in the *porches*. O that men were as wise for their souls, and as solicitous to get their spiritual diseases healed!

5. What virtue it had for the cure of these impotent folks (*v.* 4): *An angel went down*, and *troubled the water;* and *whoso first stepped in was made whole*. The virtue this pool had was supernatural.

(1) The *preparation* of the medicine by an angel, who *went down into the pool*, and *stirred the water*. See what mean offices the holy angels condescend to. If we would do the will of God as the angels do it, we must think nothing below us but sin. The *troubling of the water* was the signal given of the descent of the angel. The waters of the sanctuary are then *healing* when they are put in *motion*. Ministers must *stir up the gift* that is in them. When they are cold and dull in their ministrations, the waters *settle* and are not apt to *heal*. The angel descended, to *stir the water at a certain season*.

(2) The *operation* of the medicine: *Whoever first stepped in was made whole*. What disease soever it was, this water cured it. The power of miracles *succeeds* where the power of nature *succumbs*. He that first stepped in had the benefit, not those that lingered and came in afterwards. This teaches us to observe and improve our opportunities, that we slip not a season which may never return.

Now this is all the account we have of this *standing* miracle. It was a *token* of God's goodwill to that people, and an indication that, though they had been long without prophets and miracles, yet God had not *cast them off*. It was a type of the Messiah that arises *with healing under his wings*.

III. The patient on whom this cure was wrought (*v.* 5): one that *had been infirm thirty-eight years*. His *disease* was *grievous*: He had an *infirmity*; he had lost the use of his limbs. It is sad to have the

JAMIESON, FAUSSET, BROWN

CHAPTER 5

Vss. 1-47. THE IMPOTENT MAN HEALED—DISCOURSE OCCASIONED BY THE PERSECUTION ARISING THEREUPON. **1. a feast of the Jews**—*What feast*? No question has more divided the Harmonists of the Gospels, and the duration of our Lord's ministry may be said to hinge on it. For if, as the majority have thought (until of late years) it was a *Passover*, His ministry lasted three and a half years; if not, probably a year less. Those who are dissatisfied with the Passover-view all differ among themselves what other feast it was, and some of the most acute think there are no grounds for deciding. In our judgment the evidence is in favor of its being a *Passover*, but the reasons cannot be stated here.

2, 3. sheep [market]—The supplement should be (as in *Margin*) 'sheep [gate]', mentioned in Nehemiah 3:1, 32. **Bethesda**—i.e., 'house (place) of mercy,' from the cures wrought there. **five porches**—for shelter to the patients. **3. impotent**—infirm.

4. an angel . . .—This miracle differed in two points from all other miracles recorded in Scripture: (1) It was not one, but a succession of miracles periodically wrought: (2) As it was only wrought "when the waters were troubled," so only upon one patient at a time, and that the patient "who first stepped in after the troubling of the waters." But this only the more undeniably fixed its miraculous character. We have heard of many waters having a medicinal virtue; but what water was ever known to cure *instantaneously* a single disease? And who ever heard of any water curing all, even the most diverse diseases—"blind, halt, withered"—alike? Above all, who ever heard of such a thing being done "only at a certain season," and most singularly of all, doing it only to the first person who stepped in after the moving of the waters? Any of these peculiarities—much more all taken together—must have proclaimed the supernatural character of the cures wrought. (If the text here be genuine, there can be no doubt of the miracle, as there were multitudes living when this Gospel was published who, from their own knowledge of Jerusalem, could have exposed the falsehood of the Evangelist, if no such cure had been known there. The want of vs. 4 and part of vs. 3 in some good MSS., and the use of some unusual words in the passage, are more easily accounted for than the evidence in their favor if they were not originally in the text. Indeed vs. 7 is unintelligible without vs. 4. The *internal* evidence brought against it is merely the *unlikelihood* of such a miracle—a principle which will carry us a great deal farther if we allow it to weigh against positive evidence). **5-9. thirty-eight years**—but not all that time at the pool. This was probably the most pitiable of all the cases, and *therefore* selected.

ADAM CLARKE

here from Jerusalem, whence, we have seen, He was driven by the persecution raised against Him by the scribes and Pharisees. By construing the word *again*, with *he came*, that confusion which is evident in the common version is entirely removed.

CHAPTER 5

1. *A feast*. This is generally supposed, by the best critics, to have been the Feast of the Passover, which was the most eminent feast among the Jews. In several excellent MSS. the article is added, *the feast*, the grand, the principal festival. Petavius supposes that the feast of *Purim* is here meant; and one MS. reads the feast of *Tabernacles*. Several of the primitive fathers believe *Pentecost* to be intended; and they are followed by many of the moderns, because, in chap. vii. 2, mention is made of the feast of *Tabernacles*, which followed *Pentecost*, and was about the latter end of our September. Lightfoot has observed that the other Evangelists speak very sparingly of our Lord's acts in Judea. They mention nothing of the Passovers, from our Lord's baptism till His death, excepting the very last; but John points at them all. The *first* he speaks of in chap. ii. 13; the *third*, in chap. vi. 4; the *fourth*, in chap. xii. 1; and the *second*, in this place. For although he does not call it the Passover, but a *feast* in general, yet the circumstances agree best with this feast; and our Lord's words, chap. iv. 35, seem to cast light on this subject.

2. *There is*. This is thought by some to be a proof that John wrote his Gospel before the destruction of Jerusalem, and that the pool and its porticoes were still remaining. Though there can be little doubt that Jerusalem was destroyed many years before John wrote, yet this does not necessarily imply that the pool and its porticoes must have been destroyed too. It, or something in its place, is shown to travellers to the present day. But instead of *is*, both the Syriac, all the Arabic, Persic, Armenian, and Nonnus read "was," which is to me some proof that it did not exist when these versions were made, and that the pool which is shown now is not the original. *By the sheep market*. Rather, "gate"; see Neh. iii. 1, 32; xii. 39. This was in all probability the gate through which the sheep were brought which were offered in sacrifice in the Temple. *Bethesda*. This word is variously written in the MSS. and versions, but this reading is the genuine one. Bethesda, or according to the Hebrew *Bethchasdah*, signifies literally "the house of mercy." It got this name probably from the cures which God mercifully performed there. It is likely the porticoes were built for the more convenient reception of the poor and distressed, who came hither to be healed.

3. *Waiting for the moving of the water*. This clause, with the whole of the fourth verse, is wanting in some MSS. and versions; but I think there is no sufficient evidence against their authenticity.

4. *Certain season*. This probably refers to the time of the feast, during which only this miraculous virtue lasted. It is not likely that the angel appeared to the people—his descent might be only known by the ebullition caused in the waters. Was not the whole a type of Christ? See Zech. xiii. 1. He is the true *Bethesda*, or "house of mercy," the "fountain opened to the house of David and to the inhabitants of Jerusalem for sin and for uncleanness," unto which all the diseased may come, and find health and life eternal.

5. *Had an infirmity thirty and eight years*. The length of the time he had been afflicted makes the miracle of his cure the greater. There could have been no collusion in this case. As his affliction had lasted thirty-eight years, it must have been known to multitudes; therefore he could not be a person prepared for the occasion. All Christ's miracles have been wrought in such a way and on such per-

MATTHEW HENRY

body so disabled that instead of being the soul's instrument, it is become, even in the affairs of this life, its burden. What reason have we to thank God for bodily strength, to use it for him. The *duration* of it was *tedious*: *Thirty-eight years*. He was lame longer than most live. Shall we complain of one wearisome night, or one fit of illness, who perhaps for many years have scarcely known what it has been to be a day sick, when many others, better than we, have scarcely known what it has been to be a day well?

IV. The cure and the circumstances of it briefly related, *v.* 6–9.

1. *Jesus saw him lie.* Observe, When Christ came up to Jerusalem he visited not the palaces, but the hospitals, an *indication* of his great design in coming into the world, which was to seek and save the sick and wounded. There was a great multitude of poor cripples here at Bethesda, but Christ fastened his eye upon this one. Christ delights to help the helpless. He had often been disappointed of a cure; therefore Christ took him for his patient: it is his honour to side with the weakest.

2. He knew and considered *how long he had lain* in this condition.

3. He asked him, *Wilt thou be made whole?* A strange question to be asked one that had been so long ill. Some indeed would not be made whole, because their sores serve them to beg by. Christ put it to him, to *express* his own pity and concern for him. Christ is tenderly inquisitive concerning the desires of those that are in affliction, to teach them to value the mercy, and to excite in them desires after it. In spiritual cases, people are not willing to be cured of their sins. If people were willing to be *made whole*, the work were half done, for Christ is willing to heal, if we be but willing to be healed.

4. The poor impotent man takes this opportunity to set forth the misery of his case: *Sir, I have no man to put me into the pool*, *v.* 7. He complains for want of friends to help him in: "*I have no man*, no friend to do me that kindness." One would think that some of those who had been themselves healed should have lent him a hand. To the sick and impotent it is as true a piece of charity to work for them as to relieve them. He bewails his infelicity, that very often when *he* was coming *another stepped in before him*. But a step between him and a cure, and yet he continues impotent. There is no getting over the old maxim, *Every one for himself*. Having been so often disappointed, he begins to despair, and now is Christ's time to come to his relief. And observe further, to his praise, that, though he had waited so long in vain, yet still he continued lying by the pool-side, hoping that sometime or other help would come.

5. Our Lord Jesus hereupon cures him with a word.

(1) The word he said: *Rise, take up thy bed*, *v.* 8. He is bidden to *rise and walk*; a strange command to be given to an *impotent* man, that had been long disabled. He must *rise and walk*, that is, attempt to do it, and in the *essay* he should receive strength to do it. If he had not attempted to help himself, he had not been cured, yet it does not therefore follow that, when he did rise and walk, it was by his own strength; no, it was by the power of Christ. He is bidden to *take up his bed*. *First*, To make it to appear that it was a *perfect cure*, and purely miraculous; for he did not recover strength by degrees, but from the extremity of weakness and impotency he suddenly stepped into the highest degree of bodily strength. He, who this minute was not able to turn himself in his bed, the next minute was able to carry his bed. *Secondly*, It was to *proclaim* the cure. Being the sabbath day, whoever carried a burden through the streets made himself very remarkable, and everyone would enquire what was the meaning of it. Christ would thus witness against the tradition of the elders. The case may be such that it may become a work of *necessity*, or *mercy*, to carry a bed on the sabbath day; but here it was more, it was a work of *piety*. He would hereby try the faith and obedience of his patient. Those that have been *healed by Christ's word* should be *ruled by his word*.

(2) The efficacy of this word (*v.* 9). *Immediately he was made whole*. What a joyful surprise was this to the poor cripple, to find himself all of a sudden so easy, so strong, so able to help himself! What a new world was he in, in an instant! He *took up his bed and walked*, and did not care who blamed him or threatened him for it.

V. What became of the poor man after he was cured.

1. What passed between him and the Jews who saw him carry his bed on the sabbath day. The Jews quarrelled with the man, telling him that *it was not lawful*, *v.* 10. Thus far was commendable, that,

JAMIESON, FAUSSET, BROWN

6. saw him lie and knew . . .—As He doubtless visited the spot just to perform this cure, so He knows where to find His patient, and the whole previous history of his case (ch. 2:25).

Wilt thou be made whole?—Could anyone doubt that a sick man would like to be made whole, or that the patients came thither, and this man had returned again and again, just in hope of a cure? But our Lord asked the question. (1) To fasten attention upon Himself; (2) By making him detail his case to deepen in him the feeling of entire helplessness; (3) By so singular a question to beget in his desponding heart the hope of a cure. (Cf. Mark 10: 51.) **Sir, I have no man . . .**—Instead of *saying* he wished to be cured, he just tells with piteous simplicity how fruitless had been all his efforts to obtain it, and how *helpless* and all but *hopeless* he was. Yet not quite. For here he is at the pool, waiting on. It seemed of no use; nay, only tantalizing—"While I am coming, another steppeth down before me"—the fruit was snatched from his lips. Yet he will not go away. He may get nothing by staying, he may drop into his grave ere he get into the pool; but by going from the appointed, divine way of healing, he can get nothing. Wait therefore he will, wait he does, and when Christ comes to heal him, lo! he is waiting his turn. *What an attitude for a sinner* at Mercy's gate! The man's hopes seemed low enough ere Christ came to him. He might have said, just before "Jesus passed by that way," 'This is no use; I'll never get in; let me die at home.' Then all had been lost. But he *held on*, and his perseverance was rewarded with a glorious cure. Probably some rays of hope darted into his heart as he told his tale before those Eyes whose glance measured his whole case. But the word of command consummates his preparation to receive the cure, and instantaneously works it. **8. Rise, take up thy bed . . .**—"Immediately" he did so. "He *spake* and it was *done*." The slinging of his portable couch over his shoulders was designed to show the perfection of the cure.

9. the same day was the sabbath—Beyond all doubt this was intentional, as in so many other healings, in order that when opposition arose on this account men might be compelled to listen to His claims and His teaching. **10-16. The Jews**—i.e., *those in authority*. (See on ch. 1:19.) **it is not lawful to carry thy bed**—a glorious testimony to the cure, as *instantaneous* and *complete*, from the lips of the most prejudiced! (And what a contrast does it, as all our Lord's miracles, present to the bungling miracles of the Church of Rome!) **In** *ordinary* circumstances, the

ADAM CLARKE

sons and occasions as abolutely to preclude all possibility of the suspicion of imposture.

6. *Wilt thou be made whole?* Christ, by asking this question, designed to excite in this person faith, hope, and a greater desire of being healed. He wished him to reflect on his miserable state, that he might be the better prepared to receive a cure, and to value it when it came.

ALEXANDER MACLAREN:

This poor man, sick and impotent for thirty-eight years—many of which he had spent, as it would appear, day by day, wearily dragging his paralyzed limbs to the fountain with daily diminishing hope—attracts the regard of Christ when He enters, and He puts to him the strange question, "Wilt thou be made whole?" Surely there was no need to ask that; but no doubt the many disappointments and the long years of waiting and of suffering had stamped apathy upon the sufferer's face, and Christ saw that the first thing that was needed, in order that His healing power might have a point of contact in the man's nature, was to kindle some little flicker of hope in him once more.

And so, no doubt, with a smile on His face, which converted the question into an offer, He says: "Wilt thou be made whole?" meaning thereby to say, "I will heal thee if thou wilt." And there comes the weary answer, as if the man had said: "Will I be made whole? What have I been lying here all these years for? I have nobody to put me into the pool."

—*Expositions of Holy Scripture*

8. *Rise, take up thy bed, and walk.* Jesus speaks here as God. He speaks in no name but His own, and with an authority which belongs to God alone. And what is the consequence? The man became whole immediately; and this sudden restoration to health and strength was an incontestable proof of the omnipotence of Christ. It has been remarked that our Lord, after having performed a miracle, was accustomed to connect some circumstance with it which attested its truth. After the miracle of the five loaves, He ordered the fragments to be collected, which were more in quantity than the loaves themselves, though several thousands had been fed. When He changed the water into wine, He ordered some to be taken first to the steward of the feast, that he might taste and bear testimony to its genuineness and excellency. When He cured the lepers, He commanded them to show themselves to the priests, whose business it was to judge of the cure. So here, He judged it necessary, after having cured this infirm man, to order him not only to *arise*, but to *take up his bed*, and *walk*, which sufficiently attested the miracle which He had wrought.

MATTHEW HENRY

while they knew not by *what authority* he did it, they were jealous for the honour of the sabbath. The man justified himself in what he did by a warrant that would bear him out, *v.* 11. "I do not do it in contempt of the law and the sabbath. He that could work such a miracle as to *make me whole* no doubt might give me such a command as to carry *my bed.* He that was so kind as to make me whole would not be so unkind as to bid me do what is sinful." The Jews enquired further who it was that gave him this warrant (*v.* 12): *What man is that?* How industriously they *overlooked* that which might be a ground of their *faith in Christ.* They resolve to look upon Christ as a *mere man*: *What man is that?* They were resolved that they would never own him to be the *Son of God.* They resolve to look upon him as a bad *man.* He who bade this man carry his bed was certainly a delinquent. The poor man was unable to give them any account of him: *He wist not who he was, v.* 13. Christ was *unknown* to him when he healed him. Christ does many a good turn for those that know him not. He enlightens, strengthens, quickens, comforts us, and we *wist not who he is.* For the present he *kept himself unknown*; for as soon as he had wrought the cure he *conveyed himself away, a multitude being in that place.* This is mentioned to show, either, *First, How* Christ conveyed himself away—by retiring into the crowd, so as not to be distinguished from a common person. Or, *Secondly, Why* he conveyed himself away, because there was *a multitude* there, and he industriously avoided both the *applause* of those who would admire the miracle and *cry that up,* and the censure of those who would censure him as a sabbath-breaker, and *run him down.* Christ left the miracle to commend itself, and the man on whom it was wrought to justify it.

2. What passed at their next interview, *v.* 14.

(1) Where Christ found him: *in the temple.* Christ *went to the temple.* The man that was cured *went to the temple.* There Christ found him. Thither he straightway went because he had, *by his infirmity,* been so long *detained* thence. Perhaps he had not been there for thirty-eight years. His first visit shall be to the temple. Because he had *by his recovery* a good errand thither; he went up to the temple to return thanks to God for his recovery. Because he had, by *carrying his bed,* seemed to put a contempt on the sabbath, he would thus show that he had an honour for it. Works of necessity and mercy are allowed; but when they are over we must *go to the temple.*

(2) What he said to him. He now applies himself to the healing of his soul. He gives him a *memento* of his cure: *Behold thou art made whole.* Christ calls his attention to it. Let the impressions of it abide, and never be lost. He gives him a caution against sin, *Being made whole, sin no more.* This implies that his disease was the punishment of sin. While those chronical diseases lasted, they prevented the outward acts of many sins, and therefore watchfulness was the more necessary when the disability was removed. When the trouble which only dammed up the current is over, the waters will return to their old course. It is common for people, when they are sick, to *promise much,* when newly recovered to *perform something,* but after awhile to *forget all.* He gives him warning of his danger: *Lest a worse thing come to thee.* Christ knew that he was one of those that must be *frightened* from sin. There is something *worse* that will come to him if he relapse into sin after God has *given him such a deliverance.*

VI. The notice which the poor simple man gave to the Jews concerning Christ, *v.* 15. He told them it was Jesus that had *made him whole.* The rage and enmity of the Jews against him: *Therefore did the* rulers of the Jews *persecute Jesus.* See, (1) How absurd and unreasonable their enmity to Christ was. *Therefore,* because he had made a poor sick man well, they persecuted him, because he did good in Israel. (2) How bloody and cruel it was: *They sought to slay him.* (3) How it was varnished over with a colour of zeal for the honour of the sabbath; for this was the pretended crime, *Because he had done these things on the sabbath day.* Thus hypocrites often cover their real enmity against the *power* of godliness with a pretended zeal for the *form of it.*

Verses 17–30

We have here Christ's discourse upon occasion of his being accused as a sabbath-breaker.

I. The doctrine laid down, by which he justified what he did on the sabbath day (*v.* 17): *He answered them, My father worketh hitherto, and I work.* Waving all other pleas, he insists upon that which was *equivalent to the whole,* and abides by it, which he had mentioned, Matt. xii. 8. *The Son of man is Lord even of the sabbath day.* 1. He pleads that he was the *Son of God,* plainly intimated in his calling *God his*

JAMIESON, FAUSSET, BROWN

rulers had the law on their side (Neh. 13:15; Jer. 17:21). But when the man referred them to "Him that had made him whole" as his authority, the argument was resistless. Yet they ingeniously parried the thrust, asking him, not who had "made him whole"—that would have condemned themselves and defeated their purpose—but who had bidden him "take up his bed and walk," in other words, who had dared to order a breach of the sabbath? Tis time we were looking after Him—thus hoping to shake the man's faith in his Healer.

13. he that was healed wist not . . .—That some one, with unparelleled generosity, tenderness and power, had done it, the man knew well enough: but as he had never heard of Him before, so he disappeared too quickly for any inquiries. **conveyed himself away**—slipped out of the crowd that had gathered, to avoid both hasty popularity and precipitate hatred (Matt. 12:14-19).

14. findeth him in the temple—saying, perhaps, "I will go into Thy house with burnt offerings, I will pay my vows which my lips have uttered and my mouth hath spoken when I was in trouble" (Ps. 66:13, 14). Jesus, there Himself for His own ends, "findeth him there"—*not all accidentally,* be assured.

sin no more . . .—a glimpse this of the reckless life he had probably led *before* his thirty-eight years' infirmity had come upon him, and which not improbably had brought on, in the just judgment of God, his chronic complaint. Fearful illustration this of "the severity of God," but glorious manifestation of our Lord's insight into "what was in man."

15. The man departed and told . . .—little thinking how unwelcome his grateful and eager testimony would be. "The darkness received not the light which was pouring its rays upon it" (John 1:5, 11), [OLSHAUSEN]. **16. because he had done these things on the sabbath day**—What to these hypocritical religionists was the doing of the most glorious and beneficent miracles, compared with the atrocity of doing them on the sabbath day! Having given them this handle, on purpose to raise the first public controversy with them, and thus open a fitting opportunity of laying His claims before them, He rises at once to the whole height of them, in a statement which for grandeur and terseness exceeds almost anything that ever afterwards fell from Him, at least to His enemies. **17, 18. My Father worketh hitherto and I work**—The "*I*" is emphatic; 'The creative and conservative activity of My Father has known no sabbath-cessation from the beginning until now, *and that is the law of My working.*'

ADAM CLARKE

11. *He that made me whole.* The poor man reasoned conclusively: He who could work such a miracle must be at least the best of men. Now a good man will neither do evil himself nor command others to do it. But he who cured me ordered me to carry my bed; therefore there can be no evil in it.

13. *Jesus had conveyed himself away.* Or "had withdrawn himself." And this He might easily do, as there was a crowd in the place. Some think the words indicate that Jesus withdrew on seeing a multitude in the place, i.e., raising a tumult, because of the man's carrying his bed. He had not yet finished His work and would not expose himself to the envy and malice of the Jewish rulers.

14. *Jesus findeth him in the temple.* The man being conscious that it was through the mercy of God that he was restored (though he did not as yet know distinctly who Christ was) went to the Temple to return thanks to God for his cure. Whether this was on the same day or some other does not distinctly appear; it was probably the same day, after he had carried home his couch.

Sin no more, lest a worse thing come unto thee. Our Lord, intending to disclose to this man who He was, gave him two proofs of the perfection of His knowledge. (1) He showed him that He knew the secret of the past—*sin no more,* thereby intimating that his former sins were the cause of his long affliction. (2) He showed him that He knew the future—*lest a worse thing come unto thee;* if your iniquity be repeated, your punishment will be increased.

15. *The man departed, and told the Jews.* He did not say it was Jesus who had ordered him to carry his bed, but it was Jesus who had cured him; and he left them to draw the inference, viz., that this Jesus must have the miraculous power of God.

17. *My Father worketh hitherto, and I work.* Or, "As My Father worketh until now." God created the world in six days; on the seventh He rested from all creating acts and set it apart to be an everlasting memorial of His

MATTHEW HENRY

Father. 2. That he was a worker together with God. *My Father worketh hitherto.* But I also *work with him.* As God created all things by Christ, so he supports and governs all by him. He that does all is Lord of all, and therefore *Lord of the sabbath.*

II. The offence that was taken at his doctrine (*v.* 18): *The Jews sought the more to kill him.* His defence was made his offence. They sought to kill him,

1. Because he had broken the sabbath.

2. He had said also *that God was his Father.* Now they pretend a jealousy for *God's honour,* and charge Christ with it as a heinous crime that he made himself equal with God. This was justly inferred from what he said, that he was the *Son of God,* and that God was *his Father.* He had said that he worked with his Father, and hereby he made himself equal with God. Yet it was unjustly imputed to him as an offence that he equalled himself with God, for he was and is God. Therefore Christ, in answer to this charge, makes out his claim and proves that he is equal with God in power and glory.

III. Christ's discourse upon this occasion. In these verses he explains, and afterwards confirms, his commission, as Mediator. And, as the honours he is hereby *entitled to* are such as it is not fit for any creature to receive, so the work he is hereby entrusted with is such as it is not possible for any creature to go through with, and therefore he is God.

1. *In general.* He is one with the Father in all he does as Mediator. It is ushered in with a solemn preface (*v.* 19): *Verily, verily, I say unto you.* This intimates that the things declared are, (1) Very awful and great. (2) Very sure. (3) That they are matters purely of divine revelation, which we could not otherwise have come to the knowledge of. Two things he saith in general concerning the Son's oneness with the Father in working:

[1] That the Son *conforms to the Father* (*v.* 19): *The Son can do nothing of himself but what he sees the Father do; for these things does the Son.* The Lord Jesus, as Mediator, is *Obedient to his Father's will.* Christ was so entirely devoted to his Father's will that it was impossible for him in anything to act separately. He is *observant of his Father's counsel;* he can, he will, do nothing *but what he sees the Father do.* No man can *find out the work of God,* but the only-begotten Son, sees what he does, is intimately acquainted with his purposes, and has the plan of them ever before him. What the Father did in his counsels, the Son had ever in his view, and still he had his eye upon it. Yet he is *equal* with the Father in *working;* for *what things soever* the Father does *these also does the Son likewise;* he did the *same* things, not *such* things, but the *same things;* and he did them in the *same manner,* with the same authority, the same energy and efficacy.

[2] That the Father *communicates* to the Son, *v.* 20.

First, The inducement to it: *The Father loveth the Son.* Christ was now hated of men, but he comforted himself with this, that his Father loved him.

Secondly, The instances of it. He shows it, 1. In what he *does* communicate to him: *He shows him all things that himself doth.* He shows him all things *which he does,* that is, which the *Son* does; all that the Son does is by direction from the Father; he *shows* him. 2. In what he *will* communicate; he will *show him greater works than these.* Works of greater *power* than the *curing of the impotent man;* for he should raise the dead, and should himself rise from the dead. Many are brought to marvel at Christ's works, whereby he has the honour of them, who are not brought to believe, by which they would have the benefit of them.

2. *In particular.* He proves his equality with the Father, by specifying some of those works which he does that are the peculiar works of God. This is enlarged upon, *v.* 21–30.

(1) Observe what is here said concerning the Mediator's power to *raise the dead* and *give life.* [1] His *authority* to do it (*v.* 21): *As the Father raiseth up the dead,* so *the Son quickeneth whom he will.* It is God's prerogative to raise the dead, and give life. A *resurrection from the dead* never lay in the common road of nature, nor ever fell within the thought of those that studied only the compass of nature's power. It is purely the work of a divine power, and the knowledge of it purely by divine revelation. The Mediator is invested with this prerogative: *He quickens whom he will.* He does not enliven things by natural necessity, as the sun does, whose beams revive of course; but he acts as a free agent. As he has the power, so he has the wisdom and sovereignty, of a God; has the *key of the grave and of death.*

[2] His *ability* to do it, because *he has life in himself, as the Father has, v.* 26. It is certain that the Father *has life in himself.* He is a sovereign giver of

JAMIESON, FAUSSET, BROWN

God was his Father—lit., "His own [or peculiar] Father," (as in Rom. 8:32). The addition is their own, but a very proper one. **making himself equal with God**—rightly gathering this to be His meaning, not from the mere words "My Father," but from His claim of right to act as His Father did in the like high sphere, and by the same law of ceaseless activity in that sphere. And as, instead of instantly disclaiming any such meaning—as He must have done if it was false—He positively sets His seal to it in the following verses, merely explaining how consistent such claim was with the prerogatives of His Father, it is beyond all doubt that we have here an assumption of *peculiar personal Sonship,* or participation in the Father's essential nature.

19, 20. **the Son can do nothing of himself**—i.e., *apart from* and *in rivalry of* the Father, as they supposed. The meaning is, 'The Son can have no separate *interest* or *action* from the Father.' **for what things . . .** 'On the contrary, whatever the Father doeth that same doeth the Son,' likewise—'in the like manner.' What claim to absolute equality with the Father could exceed this: not only to do *the same things,* but to do them *as the Father does them?*

Father loveth . . . and showeth him all . . .—As love has no concealments, so it results from the perfect fellowship and mutual endearment of the Father and the Son (see on ch. 1:1, 18), whose interests are one, even as their nature, that the Father communicates to the Son all His counsels, and what has been thus shown to the Son is by Him executed in His mediatorial character. "With the Father, *doing* is *willing;* it is only the Son who *acts in Time*" [ALFORD]. Three things here are clear: (1) The *personal distinctions* in the Godhead. (2) Unity of *action* among the Persons results from unity of *nature.* (3) Their oneness of interest is no unconscious or involuntary thing, but a thing of glorious *consciousness, will,* and *love,* of which the Persons themselves are the proper Objects. **show him greater things . . .**—referring to what He goes on to mention (vss. 21-31), comprised in two great words, LIFE and JUDGMENT, which STIER beautifully calls God's *Regalia.* Yet these, Christ says, the Father and He do in common. **21-23. raiseth the dead and quickeneth them**—one act in two stages. This is His absolute prerogative as God. **so the Son quickeneth**—i.e., raiseth up and quickeneth. **whom he will**—not only *doing the same divine act,* but doing it *as the result of His own will,* even as the Father does it. This statement is of immense importance in relation to the miracles of Christ, distinguishing them from similar miracles of prophets and apostles, who as *human instruments* were employed to perform super-natural actions, while Christ did all as the Father's *commissioned Servant* indeed, but *in the exercise of His own absolute right of action.*

ADAM CLARKE

work. But though He rested from creating, He never ceased from preserving and governing that which He had formed. In this respect He can keep no sabbaths; for nothing can continue to exist or answer the end proposed by the divine wisdom and goodness without the continual energy of God. So *I work*—I am constantly employed in the same way, governing and supporting all things, comforting the wretched, and saving the lost; and to Me, in this respect, there is no Sabbath.

18. *Making himself equal with God.* This the Jews understood from the preceding verse, nor did they take a wrong meaning out of our Lord's words; for He plainly stated that, whatever was the Father's work, His was the same, thus showing that He and the Father were *one.* They had now found out two pretenses to take away His life. One was that He had broken the Sabbath—"dissolved," as they pretended, the obligation of keeping it holy. The other was that He was guilty of blasphemy, in *making himself equal with God.* For both of these crimes a man, according to the law, must suffer death. See Num. xv. 32; Lev. xxiv. 11, 14, 16.

19. *The Son can do nothing of himself.* Because of His inseparable union with the Father; nor can the Father do anything of *himself,* because of His infinite unity with the Son. *What things soever he doeth, these also doeth the Son.* The conclusion from our Lord's argument is: If I have broken the Sabbath, so has God also, for I can do nothing but what I see Him doing.

20. *Greater works than these.* Two of these He immediately mentions: *raising the dead,* v. 21; and *judging the world,* v. 22. *That ye may marvel.* Or "so as to make you wonder." Our Lord sometimes speaks of himself as God, and sometimes as the Ambassador of God. As He had a human and a divine nature, this distinction was essentially necessary.

21. *As the Father raiseth up the dead.* This He did in the case of the widow's son at Sarepta, I Kings xvii. 22, by the ministry of the Prophet Elijah. And again, in the case of the Shunammite's son, 2 Kings iv. 32-35, by the ministry of the Prophet Elisha. *The Son quickeneth whom he will.* He raiseth from death to life whomsoever He pleases. So He did, for He raised the ruler's daughter, Mark v. 35-42; the widow's son at Nain, Luke vii. 11-15; and Lazarus, at Bethany, John xi. 14-44. *Whom he will.* Here our Lord points out His sovereign power and independence; He gives life according to His own will—not being obliged to supplicate for the power by which it was done, as the prophets did, His own will being absolute and sufficient in every case.

MATTHEW HENRY

life; he has the disposal of life in himself; and of all good (for so *life* sometimes signifies). He is to his creatures the fountain of life, and all good. It is as certain that he has *given to the Son to have life in himself.* The Son, as Redeemer, is the original of all spiritual life and good; is that to the church which the Father is to the world. The kingdom of grace, and all the life in that kingdom, are as fully and absolutely in the hand of the Redeemer as the kingdom of providence is in the hand of the Creator.

[3] His *acting* according to this authority and ability. There are two resurrections performed by his powerful word, both which are here spoken of:

A resurrection that *now is* (*v.* 29), a resurrection from the depth of sin to the life of righteousness. *The hour is coming, and now is.* It is a resurrection begun already. This is plainly distinguished from that in *v.* 28, which speaks of the resurrection at the end of time. Some think this was fulfilled in those whom he miraculously raised to life. I rather understand it of the power of the doctrine of Christ, for the recovering and quickening of those that were *dead in trespasses and sins*, Eph. ii. 1. The *hour* was *coming* when dead souls should be made alive by the *preaching* of the gospel: nay, it *then was*, while Christ was upon earth. It is to be applied to all the wonderful success of the gospel, among both Jews and Gentiles; an hour which still *is*, and is still *coming*. Sinners are spiritually *dead*, miserable, but neither sensible of their misery nor able to help themselves out of it. The conversion of a soul to God is its resurrection from death to life; then it begins to live when it begins to *live to God*. It is by the *voice of the Son of God* that souls are raised to spiritual life. *The dead shall hear* the *voice of the Son of God*.

The voice of Christ must be heard by us, that we may live by it. A resurrection yet *to come*; this is spoken of, *v.* 28, 29. When this resurrection shall be: *The hour is coming*. It is *not yet* come, it is not the hour spoken of at *v.* 25, that is coming, and *now is*. It *will certainly* come, it is coming on, nearer every day. How far off it is we know not. Who shall be raised: *All that are in the graves*. Christ here tells us that *all* must appear before the Judge, and therefore *all* must be raised. The grave is the prison of dead bodies, where they are *detained*. Yet, in prospect of their resurrection, we may call it their *bed*, where they sleep to be *awaked* again. How they shall be raised. (*a*) The efficient of this resurrection: *They shall hear his voice*. A divine power shall go along with the voice, to put life into them, and enable them to obey it. (*b*) The effect of it: *They shall come forth* out of their graves. They shall *appear* before Christ's tribunal. To what they shall be raised; to a different state of happiness or misery, according to their different character.

(*a*) *They that have done good shall come forth to the resurrection of life;* they shall live again, to live for ever. It will be well in the great day with those only that have *done good*. They shall be *admitted* into the presence of God, and that is life, it is better than life.

(*b*) *They that have done evil to the resurrection of damnation;* they shall live again, to be for ever dying.

(2) Observe what is here said concerning the Mediator's *authority to execute judgment*, *v.* 22–24, 27. As he has an almighty power, so he has a sovereign jurisdiction. Christ's commission or delegation to the office of a judge, which is twice spoken of here (*v.* 22): *He hath committed all judgment to the Son;* and again (*v.* 27): *He hath given him authority*.

First, The *Father judges no man*; he is pleased to govern by Jesus Christ. He does not *rule* us by the *mere* right of *creation*. Having made us, he *may* do what he *pleases* with us, as the potter with the clay; yet he does not take advantage of this. The Mediator having undertaken to make a *vicarious* satisfaction, the matter is referred to him.

Secondly, *He has committed all judgment to the Son.* It is God in Christ that reconciles the world, and to him he has given power to confer eternal life. The book of life is the Lamb's book; by his award we must stand or fall. He is constituted sole manager of the judgment of the great day. The final and universal judgment is committed to the Son of Man.

Thirdly, He has *given him authority to execute judgment also*, *v.* 27. He that *executes judgment* upon them is the same that would have *wrought salvation* for them. Whence he has that authority: the Father *gave it to him*. Now all this redounds very much to the honour of Christ, and very much to the comfort of all believers, who may with the greatest assurance venture their all in such hands. He has all judgment committed to him for two reasons:

First, Because he is the *Son of man*; which denotes these three things: 1. His humiliation and gracious

JAMIESON, FAUSSET, BROWN

26. given to the Son . . .—Does this refer to the essential life of the Son before all time (ch. 1:4) [as most of the Fathers, and OLSHAUSEN, STIER, ALFORD, etc., among the moderns], or to the purpose of God that this essential life should reside in the Person of the Incarnate Son, and be manifested thus to the world? [CALVIN, LUCKE, LUTHARDT, etc.] The question is as difficult as the subject is high. But as all that Christ says of His *essential* relation to the Father is intended to explain and exalt His *mediatorial* functions, so the one seems in our Lord's own mind and language mainly the starting-point of the other. **28. Marvel not at this**—this committal of all judgment **to *the Son of man.*** **for the hour is coming**—He adds not in this case (as in vs. 25), "and now is," because this was not to be till the close of the whole dispensation of mercy.

25-29. The hour cometh—in its whole fulness, at Pentecost. **and now is**—in its beginnings. **the dead**—the *spiritually* dead, as is clear from vs. 28. Here He rises from the calmer phrase "hearing *his word*" (vs. 24), to the grander expression, "hearing *the voice of the Son of God,*" to signify that as it finds men in a *dead* condition, so it carries with it a *resurrection-power*. **shall live**—in the sense of vs. 24.

29. resurrection of life—i.e., to life everlasting (Matt. 25:46). **of damnation**—It would have been harsh to say 'the resurrection of death,' though that is meant, for sinners rise *from death to death* [BENGEL]. The resurrection of both classes is an exercise of *sovereign authority;* but in the one case it is an act of *grace*, in the other of *justice.* (Cf. Dan. 12:2, from which the language is taken.) How awfully grand are these unfoldings of His dignity and authority from the mouth of Christ Himself! And they are all in the *third person;* in what follows He resumes the *first person.*

22. For the Father judgeth no man . . .—rather, "For neither doth the Father judge any man," implying that the same "thing was meant in the former verse of the quickening of the dead"—both acts being done, not by the Father *and* the Son, as though twice done, but by the Father *through* the Son as His voluntary Agent. **all judgment**—judgment in its most comprehensive sense, or as we should say, all *administration.*

27. because he is the Son of man—This seems to confirm the last re-

ADAM CLARKE

A. T. ROBERTSON:

26. "In himself" (*en heautoi*). The living God possesses life wholly in himself, and so he has bestowed this power of life to the Son as already stated in the Prologue of the Logos (1:3). For "gave" (*edoken*, timeless aorist active indicative), see also 3:35; 17:2, 24. The particles "as" (*hosper*) and "so" (*houtos*) mark here the fact, not the degree (Westcott).

—*Word Pictures in the New Testament*

25. *The dead shall hear the voice.* Three kinds of death are mentioned in the Scriptures: *natural, spiritual,* and *eternal.* The *first* consists in the separation of the body and soul; the *second*, in the separation of God and the soul; the *third*, in the separation of body and soul from God in the other world. Answerable to these three kinds of death, there is a threefold life: *natural* life, which consists in the union of the soul and body; *spiritual* life, which consists in the union of God and the soul, by faith and love; *eternal* life, which consists in the communion of the body and soul with God, by holiness, in the realms of bliss.

22. *The Father judgeth no man.* This confirms what He had said before, vv. 17, 19, that the Father acts not without the Son, nor the Son without the Father; their acts are common, their power equal.

27. *Because he is the Son of man.* Because He is the Messiah; for in this sense the phrase *Son of man* is often to be understood.

MATTHEW HENRY

condescension. To this low estate he stooped. Because he condescended to be the *Son of Man*, his Father made him *Lord of all*, Phil. ii. 8, 9. 2. His affinity and alliance to us. Being the *Son of man*, he is of the same nature with those whom he is *set over*. 3. His being the Messiah promised. He is the Messiah, and therefore is invested with all this power. Christ usually called himself the *Son of man*, which was the more humble title, and bespeaks him a prince and Saviour, not to the Jewish nation only, but to the whole race of mankind.

Secondly, That all men should honour the Son, v. 23. The honouring of Jesus Christ is here spoken of as God's great design, and as man's great duty. We must *honour the Son*, must *confess that he is Lord*, and worship him; must honour him who was dishonoured for us. *Even as they honour the Father*. This *supposes* it to be our duty to *honour the Father*, and *directs* us *to honour the Son*. To enforce this law, it is added, *He that honours not the Son honours not the Father* who has sent him. Some pretend a reverence for the Creator, and speak *honourably* of him, who make light of the Redeemer, and speak *contemptibly* of him. Indignities done to the Lord Jesus reflect upon God himself. The Father counts himself struck as through him. The reason of this is because it is the *Father who hath sent him*. Affronts to an ambassador are justly resented by the prince that sends him. Here is the rule by which the Son goes in executing this commission (*v.* 24): *He that heareth and believeth* hath *everlasting life*. Here we have the substance of the whole gospel.

First, The *character* of a Christian: *He that heareth my word, and believeth on him that sent me*. To be a Christian indeed is to *hear the word of Christ*. It is not enough to be within hearing of it, we must hear and obey, it must abide by the gospel of Christ as the fixed rule of our faith and practice. To *believe on him that sent him*; for Christ's design is to *bring us to God*. Christ is our *way*; God is our rest.

Secondly, The *charter* of a Christian. A charter of pardon: *He shall not come into condemnation*. The grace of the gospel is a full discharge from the curse of the law. A charter of privileges: He is *passed out of death to life. Hear and live, believe and live*, is what we may venture our souls upon. Here is the righteousness of his proceedings (*v.* 30). *My judgment is just*. His judgments are certainly just, for they are directed by the Father's *wisdom*: *I can of my ownself* do nothing, but *as I hear I judge*, as he had said before (*v.* 19). The Son *can do nothing but what he sees the Father do*; so here, nothing but what he hears the Father *say*: *As I hear*, 1. From the secret eternal counsels of the Father, *so I judge*. Would we know what we may depend upon in our dealing with God? *Hear the word* of Christ. What Christ has adjudged is an exact copy or counterpart of what the Father has decreed. 2. From the published records of the Old Testament. Christ, in all the execution of his undertaking, had an eye to the scripture. *As it was written in the volume of the book*. By the Father's *will*: *My judgment is just, because I seek not my own will*, but *his who sent me*. Not as if the will of Christ were contrary to the will of the Father. Christ has, as man, the natural and innocent affections of the human nature, *sense of pain* and *pleasure*, an inclination to life, an aversion to death: yet he *pleased not himself*, but acquiesced entirely in the will of his Father. What he did as Mediator was not the result of any *peculiar* or *particular* purpose and design of his own, but he was therein guided by his Father's will.

Verses 31–47

I. He *sets aside* his own testimony of himself (*v.* 31): "*If I bear witness of myself*, though it is infallibly true (*ch.* viii. 14), you will not admit it."

II. He produces other witnesses that bear testimony to him that he was sent of God.

1. The Father himself bore testimony to him (*v.* 32): *There is another that beareth witness*. I take this to be meant of God the Father. The seal which the Father put to his commission: He *beareth witness of me*, not only has done so by a voice from heaven, but still does so by the tokens of his presence with me. The satisfaction Christ had in this testimony: "*I know that the witness which he witnesseth of me is true*."

2. John Baptist witnessed to Christ, *v.* 33, &c. John came to *bear witness of the light* (*ch.* i. 7).

(1) Now the testimony of John was a *solemn* and public testimony: You sent an embassy of priests and Levites to John, which gave him an opportunity of publishing what he had to say. It was a *true* testimony: *He bore witness to the truth*. Christ does not say, *He bore witness to me*, but, like an honest man. *He bore witness to the truth*.

(2) Two things are added concerning John's

JAMIESON, FAUSSET, BROWN

mark, that what Christ had properly in view was the indwelling of the Son's essential life in *humanity* as the great *theater* and *medium* of divine display, in both the great departments of His work—*lifegiving and judgment*. The appointment *of a Judge in our own nature* is one of the most beautiful arrangements of divine wisdom in redemption.

23. honour the Son as . . . the Father—As he who believes that Christ in the foregoing verses has given a true account of His relation to the Father must of necessity hold Him entitled to the same *honor* as the Father, so He here adds that it was the Father's express intention in making over all judgment to the Son, that men *should* thus honor Him. **honoureth not the Father . . .**—does not do it in fact, whatever he may imagine, and will be held as not doing it by the Father Himself, who will accept no homage which is not accorded to His own Son.

24. believeth on him that sent me—i.e., believeth in Him as having sent Me. I have spoken of the Son's right not only to heal the sick but to raise from the dead, and quicken whom He will: And now I say unto you, *That life-giving operation has already passed upon all who receive My words as the Sent of the Father* on the great errand of mercy. **hath everlasting life**—immediately on his believing (cf. ch. 3:18; I John 5:12, 13). **is passed**—'hath passed over' "from death unto life." What a transition! (Cf. I John 3:14).

30-32. of mine own self do nothing—i.e., apart from the Father, or in any interest than My own. (See on vs. 19.) **as I hear**—i.e., "My judgments are all *anticipated* in the bosom of My Father, to which I have immediate access, and by Me only *responded to* and *reflected*. They cannot therefore err, as I live for one end only, to carry into effect the will of Him that sent Me."

31. If I . . . witness of myself—standing alone, and setting up any separate interest.

32. There is another—i.e., *the Father*, as is plain from the connection. How brightly the distinction of the Persons shines out here! **and I know that the witness . . .**—"This is the Son's testimony to the Father's truth (see ch. 7:28; 8:26, 55). It testifies to the full consciousness on the part of the Son, even in the days of His humiliation, of the righteousness of the Father" [ALFORD]. And thus He cheered His spirit under the cloud of human opposition which was already gathering over His head.

ADAM CLARKE

23. *That all men should honour the Son*. If then the Son is to be honored, even as the Father is honored, then the Son must be God, as receiving that worship which belongs to God alone. To worship any creature is idolatry. Christ is to be honored even as the Father is honored; therefore Christ is not a creature, and, if not a creature, consequently the Creator. *He that honoureth not the Son*. God will not receive that man's adoration who refuses to honor Jesus, *even as* He honors Him. The Jews expected the Messiah as a great and powerful prince; but they never thought of a person coming in that character enrobed with all the attributes of Godhead. To lead them off from this error our Lord spoke the words recorded in these verses.

24. *He that heareth my word*—My doctrine—*and believeth on him that sent me*—he who credits My divine mission, that I am come to give light and life to the world by My doctrine and death—*hath everlasting life*—the seed of this life is sown in his heart the moment he believes—*and shall not come into condemnation*, "into judgment"—that which will speedily come on this unbelieving race, and that which shall overwhelm the wicked in the great day. *But is passed from death unto life*. Has "changed his country, or place of abode." Death is the country where every Christless soul lives. The man who knows not God lives a dying life or a living death; but he who believes in the Son of God passes over from the empire of death to the empire of life.

30. *I can of mine own self do nothing*. Because of My intimate union with God. See on v. 19. *I seek not mine own will*. I do not, I cannot attempt to do anything without God. This, that is, the Son of Man, the human nature which is the temple of My divinity, chap. i. 14, is perfectly subject to the deity that dwells in it. In this respect our blessed Lord is the perfect Pattern of all His followers. In everything their wills should submit to the will of their Heavenly Father.

31. *If I bear witness*. If I had no proof to bring of My being the Messiah, and equal to God, common sense would direct you to reject My testimony; but the mighty power of God, by which I work My miracles, sufficiently attests that My pretensions are well-founded.

32. *There is another*. God the Father, who by His Spirit in your prophets described My person, office, and miracles. You read these Scriptures, and you cannot help seeing that they testify of Me. No person ever did answer the description there given but myself, and I answer to that description in the fullest sense of the word.

33. *Ye sent unto John*. I am not without human testimony of the most respectable kind. *Ye sent unto John, and he bare witness*.

MATTHEW HENRY

testimony:

[1] That it was a testimony *more than he needed to vouch* (*v.* 34): *I receive not testimony from man.* Christ needs no testimonials or certificates, but what his own worth and excellency bring with him; why then did Christ here urge the testimony of John? Why, *these things I say, that you may be saved.* This he aimed at in all this discourse, to save not his own life, but the souls of others. Christ desires and designs the salvation even of his enemies and persecutors.

[2] That it was a testimony *to the man,* because John Baptist was one whom *they* had a respect for (*v.* 35). *First,* The character of John Baptist: *He was a burning and a shining light.* He was *a light,* not *light* (so Christ was *the* light), but *a luminary,* a derived subordinate light. He was a *burning* light, which denotes *sincerity*; painted fire may be made to shine, but that which burns is true fire. It denotes also his *activity,* zeal, and fervency. Fire is always working on itself or something else, so is a good minister. He was a *shining* light, which denotes either his *exemplary conversation,* in which our light should shine (Matt. v. 16), or an *eminent* diffusive influence. *Secondly,* The affections of the people to him: *You were willing for a season to rejoice in his light.* 1. It was a *transport* that they were *in,* upon the appearing of John: "*You delighted to rejoice in his light;* you were very proud that you had such a man among you. You were willing to *dance,* and make a noise about this light, as boys about a bonfire." 2. It was but *transient,* and soon over: "You were fond of him for *a season,* as little children are fond of a new thing, but soon grew weary of him, and said that *he had a devil,* and now you have him in prison." It is common for forward and noisy professors to cool and fall off. These here rejoiced in John's light, but never walked in it. Christ mentions their respect to John, to *condemn* them for their present opposition to himself. If they had continued their veneration for John they would have embraced Christ.

3. Christ's own works witnessed to him (*v.* 36): *I have a testimony greater than that of John;* for *if we believe the witness of men,* the *witness of God is greater,* 1 John v. 9. We must be glad of all the supports that offer themselves for the confirmation of our faith, though they may not amount to a demonstration; we have occasion for them all. Now this greater testimony was that of the *works* which *his Father had given him to finish.* In general the whole course of his life and ministry. All that work of which he said when he died, *It is finished*; all he said and did was *holy* and *heavenly,* and a divine purity, power and grace shone in it, proving abundantly that he was *sent of God.* In particular, the miracles he wrought for the proof of his divine mission witnessed of him. Now it is here said, (1) That these works were *given him by the Father,* that is, he was both *appointed* and *empowered* to work them. (2) They were given to him to *finish*; and his finishing them proves a divine power. (3) These works did *bear witness of him,* did prove that he was sent of God. That the Father had sent him as *a Father,* not as a master sends his servant on an errand, but as a father sends his son to take possession for himself.

4. He produces, more fully than before, his Father's testimony concerning him (*v.* 37): *The Father that sent me hath borne witness of me.* God was pleased to bear witness of his Son himself by a voice from heaven at his baptism (Matt. iii. 17): *This is my beloved Son.* Those whom God *sends* he will *bear witness* of; where he gives a commission, he will not fail to seal it. Where God demands belief, he will not fail to give sufficient *evidence,* as he has done concerning Christ. If God himself thus bore witness of Christ, how came it to pass that he was not universally received by the Jewish nation and their rulers? To this Christ here answers that it was for two reasons: (1) Because they were not acquainted with such extraordinary revelations of God and his will: *You have neither heard his voice at any time, nor seen his shape,* or *appearance.* They showed themselves to be as ignorant of God as we are of a man we never either saw or heard. Ignorance of God is the true reason of men's rejecting the record he has given concerning his Son. (2) Because they were not affected with the ordinary ways by which God had revealed himself to them: *You have not his word abiding in you, v.* 38. *First,* The word of God was not in them; it was *among them,* but not *in them,* in their hearts: not ruling in their souls, but only shining in their eyes and sounding in their ears. What did it avail them that they had the oracles of God *committed* to them (Rom. iii. 2), when they had not these oracles *commanding* in them? If they had, they would readily have embraced Christ. *Secondly,* It did not *abide.* Many have the word of God coming into them, and making some impressions for awhile, but it does not

JAMIESON, FAUSSET, BROWN

33-35. Ye sent unto John—(See ch. 1:19, etc.). **receive not testimony . . . from man**—i.e., depend not on human testimony. **but . . . that ye might be saved**—'I refer to him merely to aid your salvation.'

35. He was a burning and a shining light—lit., "*the* burning and shining lamp" (or torch):—i.e., 'the great light of his day.' Christ is never called by the humble word here applied to John—a *light-bearer*—studiously used to distinguish him from his Master, but ever *the Light* in the most absolute sense. (See on ch. 1:6.)

willing for a season—i.e., till they saw that it pointed whither they were not prepared to go. **to rejoice in his light**—There is a play of irony here, referring to the hollow delight with which his testimony tickled them.

36-38. I have greater witness—rather, The witness which I have is greater. **the works . . . bear witness of me**—not simply as *miracles* nor even as a miracle of *mercy,* but these miracles, *as He did them,* with a *will* and a *power,* a *majesty* and a *grace* manifestly *His own.*

37. the Father himself . . . hath borne witness of me—not referring, probably, to the voice of His baptism, but (as seems from what follows) to the testimony of the Old Testament Scripture [CALVIN, LUCKE, MEYER, LUTHARDT, etc.].

neither heard his voice . . .—never recognized Him in this character. (The words are "designedly mysterious, like many others which our Lord uttered" [STIER]. **38. not his word abiding in you**—passing now from the *Witness* to the *testimony* borne by Him in "the lively oracles": both were alike strangers to their breasts, as was evidenced by their rejecting Him to whom all that witness was borne.

ADAM CLARKE

34. *But I receive not testimony from man* (only). I have no need of John's testimony; the works that I do bear sufficient testimony to Me, v. 36. *But these things I say.* You believed John to be a prophet. A prophet cannot lie; he bore testimony that I am the Lamb of God, that beareth away the sin of the world, chap. i. 29. Therefore, that you may be saved by believing in Me as such, I have appealed to John's testimony.

35. *He was a burning and a shining light.* "He was a burning and a shining lamp." The expression of "lamp" our Lord took from the ordinary custom of the Jews, who termed their eminent doctors "the lamps of Israel." *Burning* may refer to the zeal with which John executed his message; and *shining* may refer to the clearness of the testimony which he bore concerning Christ. He who wishes to save souls must both *burn* and *shine;* the clear light of the knowledge of the sacred records must fill his understanding, and the holy flame of loving zeal must occupy his heart. Zeal without knowledge is continually blundering, and knowledge without zeal makes no converts to Christ. *For a season.* The time between his beginning to preach and his being cast into prison. *To rejoice.* "To jump for joy," as we would express it. They were exceedingly rejoiced to hear that the Messiah was come, because they expected Him to deliver them out of the hands of the Romans. But when a spiritual deliverance, of infinitely greater moment, was preached to them, they rejected both it and the light which made it manifest.

36. *But I have greater witness.* However decisive the judgment of such a man as John may be, nevertheless I am not obliged to depend on his testimony alone; for I have a greater one, that of Him whom you acknowledge to be your God. And how do I prove that this God bears testimony to Me? By My *works*: these miracles, which attest My mission and prove by themselves that nothing less than unlimited power and boundless love could ever produce them.

37. *The Father himself . . . hath borne witness.* That is, by His prophets. *Ye have neither heard his voice.* I make these words, with Bishop Pearce, a parenthesis. The sense is—"Not that My Father ever appeared visibly or spake audibly to any of you; but He did it by the mouths of His prophets." Lately, however, He had added to their testimony His own voice from heaven on the day of Christ's baptism. See Matt. iii. 17.

38. *Ye have not his word abiding in you.* Though you believe the Scriptures to be of God, yet you do not let them take hold of your hearts—His word is in your mouth, but not in your mind.

MATTHEW HENRY

abide with them; it is not constantly in them, as a man at home, but only now and then, as a *wayfaring man.* But how did it appear that they *had not the word of God abiding in them?* It appeared by this, *Whom he hath sent, him ye believe not.* The indwelling of the word, and Spirit, and grace of God in us, is best tried by its effects, particularly by our *receiving what he sends,* especially Christ whom he hath sent.

5. The next witness he calls is the Old Testament, and to it he appeals (*v.* 39, &c.): *Search the scriptures.*

(1) This may be read, either, [1] "*You search the scriptures,* and you do well to do so." Christ owns that they did indeed search the scriptures, but it was in search of their *own glory.* It is possible for men to be very studious in the letter of the scripture, and yet to be strangers to the power and influence of it. Or, [2] As we read it: *Search the scriptures.* It was spoken to *them* in the nature of an *appeal.* When appeals are made to the scriptures they must be searched. Search the whole book of scripture *throughout,* compare one passage with another, and explain one by another. We must likewise search particular passages *to the bottom,* and see not what they *seem* to say, but what they say *indeed.* It is spoken to *us* in the nature of an *advice.* All those who would *find Christ* must *search the scriptures,* which denotes, 1. *Diligence* in seeking, close application of mind. 2. *Desire* and *design* of finding. We must often ask, "What am I now searching for?" We must search as those that *sink* for gold or silver, or that *dive* for pearl.

(2) Now there are two things which we are here directed to have in our eye, in our searching the scripture: *heaven* our end, and *Christ* our way. [1] *For in them you think you have eternal life.* The scripture assures us of an eternal state set before us, and offers to us an eternal life in that state. But to the Jews Christ saith only, *You think* you have *eternal life* in the scriptures. They looked for it by the bare reading and studying of the scripture. It was a common but corrupt saying among them, *He that has the words of the law has eternal life.* [2] We must *search the scriptures for Christ,* as the new and living *way* that leads to this *end.* These are *they that testify of me.* The scriptures, even those of the Old Testament, *testify* of Christ, and by them God *bears witness* to him. The Jews knew very well that the Old Testament testified of the Messiah, and were critical in their remarks upon the passages that looked that way; and yet were careless, and wretchedly overseen, in the application of them. *Therefore* we must *search the scriptures,* because they testify of Christ; for this is *life eternal, to know him.* Christ is the treasure hid in the field of the scriptures, the water in those wells.

(3) To this testimony he annexes a reproof in four instances.

[1] Their *neglect of him* and his doctrine: "*You will not come to me, that you might have life,*" *v.* 40. Their estrangement from Christ was the fault not so much of their *understandings* as of their *wills.* Christ offered life, and it was not accepted. There is *life* to be had with Jesus Christ for poor souls. Life is the perfection of our being, and inclusive of all happiness; and Christ is our life. Those that would have this life must *come* to Jesus Christ for it, we may have it for the coming for. The only reason why sinners die is because they *will not come* to Christ; it is not because they *cannot,* but because they *will* not. They will not be cured, for they will not observe the methods of cure. Those words (*v.* 41), *I receive not honour from men,* come in in a parenthesis, to obviate an objection against him, as if he sought his own glory in obliging all to come to *him.* He did not *covet* nor *court* the applause of men. He *had not* the applause of men. Instead of *receiving honour* from men, he received a great deal of *dishonour* and disgrace from men. He *needed* not the applause of men; it was no addition to his glory.

[2] Their *want of the love of God* (*v.* 42): "*I know you that you have not the love of God in you.*" The reason why people *slight Christ* is because they do not *love God.* He charged them (*v.* 37) with *ignorance* of God, and here with want of love to him; *therefore* men have not the love of God because they desire not the knowledge of him. The crime charged upon them: *You have not the love of God in you.* They pretended a great love to God, and thought they proved it by their zeal for the law, and yet they were really without the love of God. There are many who make a great profession of religion who yet show they want the love of God by their neglect of Christ. They hate his holiness and undervalue his goodness. It is the love of God *in* us, that love seated *in the heart,* that God will *accept;* the love *shed abroad* there. The proof of this charge, is given by the personal knowledge of Christ. *I know you.* Christ sees through all our disguises, and can say to each of us, *I know thee.*

JAMIESON, FAUSSET, BROWN

39-42. Search the scriptures . . .—'In the Scriptures ye find your charter of eternal life; go search them then, and you will find that I am the Great Burden of their testimony; yet ye will not come to Me for that life eternal which you profess to find there, and of which they tell you I am the appointed Dispenser.' (Cf. Acts 17:11, 12.) How touching and gracious are these last words! Observe here (1) The honor which Christ gives to the Scriptures, as a record which all *have a right* and *are bound* to search—the reverse of which the Church of Rome teaches; (2) The opposite extreme is, resting in the mere *Book* without *the living Christ,* to direct the soul to whom is its main use and chiefest glory.

41. I receive not honour from men—contrasting His own end with theirs, which was to obtain *human applause.*

42. not the love of God in you—which would inspire you with a single desire to know His mind and will, and yield yourselves to it, in spite of prejudice and regardless of consequences.

ALBERT BARNES:

39. "Search the scriptures." The word translated search here means to search diligently or anxiously. It is applied to miners, who search for precious metals—who look anxiously for the bed of the ore with an intensity or anxiety proportionate to their sense of the value of the metal. It is applied by Homer to a lioness robbed of her whelps, and who searches the plain to trace out the footsteps of the man who has robbed her. It is also applied by him to dogs tracing their game by searching them out by the scent of the foot. It means a diligent, faithful, anxious investigation. The word may be either in the indicative or imperative mood. In our translation it is in the imperative, as if Jesus *commanded* them to search the Scriptures. Cyril, Erasmus, Beza, Bengel, Kuinoel, Tholuck, De Wette, and others, give it as in the indicative; Chrysostom, Augustine, Luther, Calvin, Wetstein, Stier, Alford, and others, regard it as in the imperative, or as a command. It is impossible to determine which is the true interpretation. Either of them makes good sense, and it is proper to use the passage in either signification. There is abundant evidence that the Jews did search the books of the Old Testament. It is equally clear that all men ought to do it.
—*Popular Commentary*

ADAM CLARKE

39. *Search the scriptures.* This should be translated, not in the imperative, but in the indicative mood—thus, "You search the Scriptures diligently." That these words are commonly read in the imperative mood is sufficiently known; but this reading can never accord well with the following verse, nor can the force and energy of the words be perceived by this version. The rabbins strongly recommend the study of the Scriptures. The *Talmud, Tract. Shabbath,* fol. 30, brings in God thus addressing David: "I am better pleased with one day in which thou sittest and studiest the law, than I shall be with a thousand sacrifices which thy son Solomon shall offer upon my altar." The word which might be translated, "You search diligently," is very expressive. Homer, *Il.* xviii. l. 321, applies it to a *lion* deprived of his whelps, who "scours the plains, and *traces* the *footsteps* of the man." And in *Odyss.* xix. l. 436, to *dogs tracing* their game by the *scent* of the *foot.* In the Septuagint the verb answers to the Hebrew *chapash,* "to search by uncovering"; to *chakar,* "to search minutely, to explore"; to *chashaph,* "to strip, make bare"; and to *mashash,* "to feel, search by feeling." It is, says Chrysostom, "a metaphor taken from those who dig deep, and search for metals in the bowels of the earth. They look for the bed where the metal lies, and break every clod, and sift and examine the whole, in order to discover the ore."

40. *And ye will not come to me.* Though you thus search the Scriptures, in hopes of finding the Messiah and eternal life in them, yet *ye will not come to me,* believe in Me, and be My disciples, though so clearly pointed out by them, that you may have that eternal life, which can come only through Me.

41. *I receive not honour from men.* I do not stand in need of you or your testimony. I act through neither self-interest nor vanity. Your salvation can add nothing to Me, nor can your destruction injure Me. I speak only through My love for your souls, that you may be saved.

42. *But I know you, that ye have not.* Do not say that you oppose Me through zeal for God's honor and love for His name, because I make myself equal to Him; no, this is not the case. I know the dispositions of your souls; and I know you have neither *love* for His name nor zeal for His glory. You read the Scriptures, but you do not enter into their meaning.

MATTHEW HENRY

Christ knows men better than *their neighbours know them.* Christ knows men better than *they know themselves.* We may deceive ourselves, but we cannot deceive him.

[3] Another charge is their readiness to entertain false christs and false prophets (*v.* 43): *I am come in my Father's name, and you receive me not. If another shall come in his own name, him you will receive.* They would not receive Christ, who came in his Father's name. They hearken to everyone that will set up in his own name. They forsake their own mercies, which is bad enough; and it is for *lying vanities*, which is worse. Those are false prophets who come in their own name. It is just with God to suffer those to be deceived with false prophets who receive not the truth. They that shut their eyes against the true light are given up to wander endlessly after *false lights*, and to be led aside after every *ignis fatuus.* They loathe the manna, and at the same time *feed upon ashes.*

[4] They are charged with pride and vain-glory, and unbelief, and the effect of them, *v.* 44. They *therefore* slighted and undervalued Christ because they *admired* and *overvalued themselves.*

First, their ambition of worldly honour. Christ despised it, *v.* 41. They set their hearts upon it: *You receive honour one of another.* "You desire to receive it, and aim at this in all you do. You give honour to others, and applaud them, only that they may return it, and may applaud you. What respect is shown to you you *receive* yourselves, and do not transmit to God."

Secondly, Their neglect of spiritual honour, called here *the honour that comes from God only. This honour have all the saints.* All that believe in Christ, through him receive the honour that comes from God. This honour that comes from God we must *seek*; we must account it *our reward*, as the Pharisees accounted the praise of men.

Thirdly, The influence this had upon their infidelity. *How can you believe* who are thus affected? The ambition and affectation of worldly honour are a great hindrance to faith in Christ. How can they believe, the summit of whose ambition is to *make a fair show in the flesh*?

6. The last witness here called is Moses, *v.* 45, &c. Christ here shows them,

(1) That Moses was a witness against the unbelieving Jews: *There is one that accuses you, even Moses.* This may be understood either, [1] As showing the difference between the law and the gospel. Moses, that is, the law, *accuses you*, for by the law is the knowledge of sin; it *condemns* you. But it is not the design of Christ's gospel to *accuse* us: *Think not that I will accuse you.* He came to be an advocate, not an accuser; to reconcile God and man. Or, [2] As showing the manifest unreasonableness of their infidelity: "Think not that I will appeal from your bar to God's and challenge you to answer there for what you do against me, as injured innocency usually does." Instead of *accusing* his crucifiers to his Father, he prayed, *Father, forgive them.* Nor let them mistake concerning Moses, as if he would stand by them in rejecting Christ; no, *There is one that accuses you, even Moses in whom you trust.* The Jews *trusted* in Moses, and thought their having his laws and ordinances would save them. Those that confide in their privileges will find that those very privileges will be witnesses against them.

(2) That Moses was a witness for Christ and to his doctrine (*v.* 46, 47): *He wrote of me.* The ceremonies of the law of Moses were *figures of him that was to come.* Christ here shows that Moses was so far from writing against Christ that he wrote *for him*, and *of him.* Christ here charges it on the Jews that they *did not believe Moses.* He had said (*v.* 45) that they *trusted* in Moses, they trusted to his name, but they did not receive his doctrine in its true sense and meaning. He proves this charge from their disbelief of him: *Had you believed Moses, you would have believed me.* Many say that they believe, whose actions give their words the lie. Those who rightly believe one part of scripture will receive every part. From their disbelief of Moses he infers that it was not strange that they rejected him: *If you believe not his writings, how shall you believe my words?* "If you do not believe sacred *writings*, those oracles which are in black and white, which is the most certain way of conveyance, *how shall you believe my words*, words being usually less regarded? If you believe not what Moses spoke and wrote of me, how shall you believe me and my mission?" If we admit not the premises, how shall we admit the conclusion. If therefore we believe not the divine inspiration of those writings, how shall we receive the doctrine of Christ?

Thus ends Christ's plea for himself. Their *mouths* were *stopped* for the present.

JAMIESON, FAUSSET, BROWN

42-47. if another shall come . . .—How strikingly has this been verified in the history of the Jews! "From the time of the true Christ to our time, sixty-four false Christs have been reckoned by whom they have been deceived" [BENGEL].

How can ye believe . . .—(See on vss. 40, 41). The "*will not*" of vs. 40, and "*cannot*" here are just different features of the same awful state of the human heart.

45. Do not think I will accuse you—'My errand hither is not to collect evidence to condemn you at God's bar.'

one that judgeth you, Moses . . .—'Alas! that will be too well done by another, and him the object of all your religious boastings—Moses,' here put for "*the Law*," the basis of the Old Testament Scriptures. **46. he wrote of me**—"an important testimony to the subject of the whole Pentateuch—'of Me' " [ALFORD].

47. If ye believe not . . .—(See on Luke 16:31). **his writings . . . my words**—a remarkable contrast, not *absolutely* exalting Old Testament Scripture above His own words, but pointing to the office of those venerable documents to *prepare* Christ's way, to the necessity universally felt for *documentary* testimony in revealed religion, and perhaps (as STIER adds) to the relation which the comparative "*letter*" of the Old Testament holds to the more flowing "words" of "spirit and life" which characterize the New Testament.

ADAM CLARKE

43. *I am come in my Father's name.* With all His influence and authority. Among the rabbins it was essential to a teacher's credit that he should be able to support his doctrine by the authority of some eminent persons who had gone before. *If another shall come in his own name.* Having no divine influence and no other authority than his own, *him ye will receive.* For an account of these false Christs, see the notes on Matt. xxiv. 5.

44. *How can ye believe, which receive honour?* The grand obstacle to the salvation of the scribes and Pharisees was their pride, vanity, and self-love. They lived on each other's praise. If they had acknowledged Christ as the only Teacher, they must have given up the good opinion of the multitude; and they chose rather to lose their souls than to forfeit their reputation among men! *From God only.* Or "from the only God."

45. *Do not think that I will accuse you.* You have accused Me with a breach of the Sabbath, which accusation I have demonstrated to be false. I could, in return, accuse you, and substantiate the accusation, with the breach of the whole law; but this I need not do, for *Moses, in whom ye trust,* accuses you. You read his law, acknowledge you should obey it, and yet break it both in the letter and in the spirit.

46. *He wrote of me.* For instance, in reciting the prophecy of Jacob, Gen. xlix. 10: "The sceptre shall not depart from Judah, nor a lawgiver from between his feet, until Shiloh come; and unto him shall the gathering of the people be." And in Deut. xviii. 18: "I will raise them up a Prophet from among their brethren, like unto thee, and will put my words in his mouth." Compare this with Acts iii. 22 and vii. 37.

47. *But if ye believe not his writings.* If you lay them not to heart—if you draw not those conclusions from them which their very letter, as well as their spirit, authorizes you to draw—*how shall ye believe my words,* against which you have taken up the most ungrounded prejudice?

ALBERT BARNES:

44. "Which receive honor one of another." Who are studious of praise, and live for pride, ambition, and vain glory. This desire, Jesus says, was the great reason why they would not believe on him. They were unwilling to renounce their worldly honors and become the followers of one so humble and unostentatious as he was. They expected a Messiah of pomp and splendor, and would not submit to one so despised and of so lowly a rank. Had the Messiah come, as they expected, with pomp and power, it would have been an honor, in their view, to follow him; as it was, they despised and rejected him. The great reason why the multitudes do not believe is their attachment to human honors, or their pride, and vanity, and ambition. These are so strong that while they continue they cannot and will not believe. They might, however, renounce these things, and then, the obstacles being removed, they would believe. Learn: (1) A man cannot believe the gospel while he is wholly under the influence of ambition. The two are not compatible. The religion of the gospel is humility, and a man who has not that cannot be a Christian. (2) Great numbers are deterred from being Christians by pride and ambition. Probably there is no single thing that prevents so many young men from becoming Christians as this passion. The proud and ambitious heart refuses to bow to the humiliating terms of the gospel. (3) Though while a man is under this governing principle he cannot believe the gospel, yet this proves nothing about his ability to lay that aside, and to yield to truth.
—*Popular Commentary*

MATTHEW HENRY

CHAPTER 6

We have here an account of Christ's feeding five thousand men with five loaves and two fishes. It is the only passage of the actions of *Christ's life* that is recorded by all the four evangelists. John relates this, because of the reference the following discourse has to it.

I. The *place* and *time* where and when this miracle was wrought.

1. The country that Christ was in (*v.* 1): *He went over the sea of Galilee.* Christ did not go directly over but made a *coasting* voyage to another place on the same side.

2. The company that he was attended with: *A great multitude followed him, because they saw his miracles, v.* 2. Our Lord Jesus, while he went about *doing good,* lived continually in *a crowd.* Good and useful men must not complain of a *hurry* of business, when they are serving God. It will be time enough to *enjoy ourselves* when we come to that world where we shall *enjoy God.* Christ's miracles drew many *after him* that were not effectually drawn *to him.*

3. Christ's posting himself advantageously to entertain them (*v.* 3): *He went up into a mountain,* and there he *sat with his disciples,* Christ was now driven to be a *field preacher*; but his word was never the worse for that to those who followed him still, not only when he *went out* to a desert place, but when he *went up* to a mountain, though *up-hill* be *against heart.* Whoever would might come, and find him there. He sat *with his disciples.*

4. The time when it was. *After those things.* We are told (*v.* 4) that it was *when the passover was nigh.* It was a custom with the Jews religiously to observe the approach of the passover *thirty days* before. Perhaps, the approach of the passover, when everyone knew Christ would go up to Jerusalem, and be absent for some time, made the multitude attend the more diligently on him. The prospect of losing our opportunities should quicken us to improve them with double diligence.

II. The miracle itself.

1. The notice Christ took of the crowd that attended him (*v.* 5): He *lifted up his eyes,* and *saw a great company come to him.* Christ showed himself pleased with their attendance, and concerned for their welfare, to teach us to *condescend to those of low estate,* and not to *set* those *with the dogs of our flock* whom Christ hath set with the lambs of his.

2. The enquiry he made concerning the way of providing for them. He directed himself to Philip, who had been his disciple from the first, and had seen all his miracles, and particularly that of his turning water into wine. Those that have been witnesses of Christ's works, and have shared in the benefit of them, are inexcusable if they say, *Can he furnish a table in the wilderness?* Philip was of Bethsaida, in the neighbourhood of which town Christ now was, and therefore he was most likely to help them to provision at the best hand. Now Christ asked, *Whence shall we buy bread, that these* may eat? He takes it for granted that they must all *eat with him.* One would think that when he had taught and healed them he had done his part; yet he is solicitous to entertain them. Those that will accept Christ's spiritual gifts, instead of *paying* for them, shall be *paid* for their acceptance of them. His enquiry is, *Whence shall we buy bread?* He will buy to give, and we must *labour* that we may give, Eph. iv. 28.

3. The design of this enquiry; it was only to try the faith of Philip, *for he himself knew what he would do, v.* 6. When we know not, he *himself knows what he will do.* When Christ is pleased to *puzzle* his people, it is only with a design to *prove* them.

4. Philip's answer to this question: "*Two hundred pennyworth of bread is not sufficient, v.* 7. Neither will the country afford so much bread, nor can we afford to lay out so much money." Philip would go as near hand as he could, would have *everyone to take a little.* Christ might now have said to him, as he did afterwards, Have I *been so long with you, and yet hast thou not known me, Philip?* We are apt thus to distrust God's power when visible and ordinary means fails, that is, to trust him no further than we can see him.

5. The information which Christ received concerning the provision they had. It was Andrew who acquainted Christ with what they had at hand; and in this we may see,

(1) The *strength* of his *love* to those for whom he saw his Master concerned, in that he was willing to bring out all they had, though he knew not but they might want themselves, and anyone would have said, *Charity begins at home.* He did not go about to conceal it. It was *five barley loaves,* and two small fishes. The provision was *coarse* and *ordinary*; they were *barley loaves.* Christ and his disciples were glad of

JAMIESON, FAUSSET, BROWN

CHAPTER 6

Vss. 1-13. FIVE THOUSAND MIRACULOUSLY FED. (See on Mark 6:31-44.)

3. a mountain—somewhere in that hilly range which skirts the east side of the lake.

4. passover . . . was nigh—but for the reason mentioned (ch. 7:1), Jesus kept away from it, remaining in Galilee.

F. B. MEYER:

The multitude satisfied with food. In this chapter we have a further illustration of John's method in selecting for his purpose the miracles which became the texts of our Lord's discourses. These multitudes had evidently gathered on their way to Jerusalem to celebrate the Passover. The imminence of that great festival, when the worshipers not only sacrificed but partook of the slain lamb, gave point to much that our Lord said after this memorable feeding of the multitude.

Christ often tests us to see what we shall say and do in the presence of overwhelming difficulty, but he always knows the way out. We at once begin to calculate our paltry resources and to confess their inadequacy. We come back to explain that when we have done our utmost, we can provide very little. Then he steps in, determined that everyone shall be "filled," with an ample supply left over. He makes his guests sit down in comfort on the grass, because there is plenty of time, as well as an abundance of food, for a happy and comfortable meal. We must bring him what we have, however slender; must enter into his great plan and arrange the people for the banquet; must distribute the food and gather up the broken pieces. The world is to be fed by the cooperation of Christ and his Church.

—*Bible Commentary*

ADAM CLARKE

CHAPTER 6

1. *After these things.* This is a sort of indefinite expression, from which we can gather nothing relative to the time in which these things happened. *Jesus went over the sea of Galilee.* Or, as some translate the words, "by the side of the sea of Galilee." From Luke, chap. ix. 10, we learn that this was a desert place in the vicinity of Bethsaida. The sea of *Galilee, Gennesaret,* and *Tiberias* are the same in the New Testament with the sea of *Cinnereth* in the Old. *Tiberias* was a city in Galilee, situated on the western side of the lake.

2. *They saw his miracles which he did.* John does not mention these miracles but Matthew details them, from chap. xii. 2 to chap. xiv. 13. John seems more intent on supplying the deficiencies of the other Evangelists than in writing a connected history himself.

3. *Went up into a mountain.* This mountain must have been in the desert of Bethsaida, in the territories of Philip, tetrarch of Galilee. Our Lord withdrew to this place for a little rest; for He and His disciples had been so thronged with the multitudes, continually coming and going, that they had not time to take necessary food. See Mark vi. 31.

4. *And the passover . . . was nigh.* This happened about ten or twelve days before the third Passover which Christ celebrated after His baptism. For a particular account of our Lord's four Passovers see the note on chap. ii. 13. For thirty days before the Passover there were great preparations made by the Jews, but especially in the last nineteen days, in order to celebrate the feast with due solemnity.

5. *Saw a great company.* See this miracle explained at large on Matt. xiv. 13, etc.; Mark vi. 31, etc.; Luke ix. 10, etc. In speaking of the Passovers and various other matters it does not appear that John follows any strict chronological order. *Saith unto Philip.* This, with what follows to the end of the seventh verse, is not mentioned by any of the other Evangelists. *Philip* was probably the provider for the disciples, as Judas was the treasurer. *Whence shall we buy bread?* Instead of *shall we buy,* I should read "may we buy," which is the reading of many MSS. As Philip was of Bethsaida, chap. i. 44; xii. 21, he must have been much better acquainted with the country in which they then were than any other of the disciples.

6. *This he said to prove him.* To try his faith, and to see whether he and the other apostles had paid proper attention to the miracles which they had already seen Him work; and to draw their attention more particularly to that which He was now about to perform. This is an observation of the Evangelist himself, who often interweaves his own judgment with the facts he relates, which Matthew rarely ever does.

8. *Andrew, Simon Peter's brother, saith.* The other Evangelists attribute this answer to the apostles in general. See the passages referred to above.

9. *There is a lad here.* A "little boy," or "servant," probably one who carried the apostles' provisions, or who came on purpose to sell his bread and fish. *Five barley loaves. Barley* bore scarcely one-third of the value of wheat in the East; see Rev. vi. 6. That it was a very mean fare appears from Ezek. xiii. 19, where the false prophetesses are said to pollute the name

MATTHEW HENRY

barley-bread. It does not follow hence that we should tie ourselves to such coarse fare, and place religion in it (when God brings that which is finer to our hands, let us receive it, and be thankful). Barley-bread is what Christ *had*, and better than we *deserve*. It was but *short* and *scanty*; there were but *five loaves*, and those so small that one little lad carried them all. There were but two fishes, and those *small* ones. The provision of *bread* was *little*, but that of *fish* was *less* in proportion to it, so that many a bit of dry bread they must eat before they could make a meal. Well, Andrew was willing that the people should have this, as far as it would go. A distrustful fear of wanting ourselves should not hinder us from needful charity to others.

(2) See here the *weakness* of his *faith* in that word, "*But what are they among so many?*" Philip and he had not that actual consideration of the power of Christ which they should have had.

6. The directions Christ gave the disciples to seat the guests (*v.* 10): "*Make the men sit down.*" This was like *sending providence to market*, and going to buy without money. (1) The furniture of the dining-room: *there was much grass in that place.* Here was this plenty of grass where Christ was preaching; the gospel brings other blessings along with it. This plenty of grass made the place the more commodious for those that must sit on the ground, and served them for cushions, and, considering what Christ says of the grass of the field (Matt. vi. 29, 30), these excelled those of Ahasuerus: nature's pomp is the most glorious. (2) The number of the guests: *About five thousand:* a great entertainment, representing that of the gospel, which is a *feast for all nations* (Isa. xxv. 6), a feast for all *comers*.

7. The distribution of the provision, *v.* 11. It was done with thanksgiving: *He gave thanks.* We ought to give thanks to God for our food, for it is a mercy to have it. Though our provision be coarse and scanty, though we have neither plenty nor dainty, yet we must give thanks to God for what we have. It was distributed from the hands of Christ by the hands of his disciples, *v.* 11. All our comforts come to us *originally* from the hand of Christ; whoever *brings* them, it is he that *sends* them. It was done to universal satisfaction. They did not everyone take a little, but all had *as much as they would.* How agreeable this miraculous food may be supposed to have been, above common food. Those whom Christ feeds with the bread of life he does not stint. There were but *two small fishes*, and yet they had *of them* too *as much as they would.* Those who call feeding upon fish *fasting*, reproach the entertainment Christ here made, which was a *full feast.*

8. The care that was taken of the broken meat. The orders Christ gave concerning it (*v.* 12): *When they were filled* Christ *said to the disciples, Gather up the fragments.* We must always take care that we make no waste of any of God's good creatures; for the grant we have of them is with this proviso, *wilful waste only excepted.* It is just with God to bring us to the want of that which we make waste of. When we are filled we must remember that others want, and we may want. Those that would have wherewith to be *charitable* must be *provident.* Christ did not order the broken meat to be gathered up till all were filled; we must not begin to hoard and lay up till all is laid out that ought to be. The observance of these orders (*v.* 13): *They filled twelve baskets with the fragments*, which was an evidence not only of the *truth* of the miracle, that they were fed, but of the *greatness* of it; they were not only filled, but there was all this over and above. See how large the divine bounty is; bread enough, and to spare, in our Father's house. The fragments filled twelve baskets, one for each disciple; they were thus repaid with interest for their willingness to part with what they had for public service.

III. Here is the influence which this miracle had upon the people (*v.* 14): *They said, This is of a truth that prophet.* Even the vulgar Jews with great assurance expected the Messiah to come into the world, and to be a *great prophet.* The Pharisees despised them as *not knowing the law*; but, it should seem, they knew more of him that is the *end of the law* than the Pharisees did. The miracles which Christ wrought did clearly demonstrate that he was the *Messiah* promised, a teacher come from God, the great prophet. There were many who were convinced he was that prophet that should come into the world who yet did not cordially receive his doctrine. It is possible for men to acknowledge that Christ is that prophet, and yet to turn a deaf ear to him.

Verses 15–21

I. Christ's retirement from the multitude.

1. What induced him to retire; because he per-

JAMIESON, FAUSSET, BROWN

ALEXANDER MACLAREN:

Christ's preparation for making our poor resources adequate for anything is to drive home into our hearts the consciousness of their insufficiency. We need, first of all, to be brought to this: "All that I have is this wretched little stock; and what is that measured against the work that I have to do and the claims upon me?" Only when we are brought to that can His great power pour itself into us and fill us with rejoicing and overcoming strength. The old mystics used to say, and they said truly: "You must be emptied of yourself before you can be filled by God." And the first thing for any man to learn, in preparation for receiving a mightier power than his own into his opening heart, is to know that all his own strength is utter and absolute weakness. "What are they among so many?" When we have once gone right down into the depths of felt impotence, and when our work has risen before us, as if it were far too great for our poor strengths which are weaknesses, then we are brought, and only then, into the position in which we may begin to hope that power equal to our desire will be poured into our souls.

And so the last of the preparations that I will touch upon is that majestic preparation for blessing by obedience. "And Jesus said, Make the men sit down." And there they sat themselves, as Mark puts it in his picturesque way, like so many garden plots—the rectangular oblongs in a garden in which pot herbs are grown—on the green grass, below the blue sky, by the side of the quiet lake. Cannot you fancy how some of them seated themselves with a scoff, and some with a quiet smile of incredulity; and some half sheepishly and reluctantly; and some in mute expectancy; and some in foolish wonder; and yet all of them with a partial obedience? And says John in the true translation: "So the men sat down, therefore Jesus took the loaves." Sit you down where He bids you, and your mouths will not be long empty. Do the things He tells you, and you will get the food that you need. Our business is to obey and to wait, and His business is, when we are seated, to open His hand and let the mercy drop. So much for the preparations for this great miracle.—*Expositions of Holy Scripture*

14-21. JESUS WALKS ON THE SEA. (See also on Mark 6:45-56.) **14, 15. that prophet**—(See on ch. 1:21).

ADAM CLARKE

of God "for handfuls of barley," i.e., for the meanest reward. And Plutarch, in *Apoph.*, p. 174, speaking concerning the flight of Artaxerxes Mnemon, says he was reduced to such distress as to be obliged to eat barley bread. *Two small fishes.* The word signifies "whatever is eaten with bread," to perfect the meal, or to help the digestion.

10. *There was much grass in the place.* Perhaps newly mown grass, or hay, is meant (so the Vulgate *foenum*), and this circumstance marks out more particularly that the Passover was at hand. In Palestine the grass is ready for mowing in March, and this miracle seems to have been wrought only a few days before the commencement of that festival.

11. *Jesus took the loaves.* See the notes on Matt. xiv. 19-21. As there were 5 loaves and 5,000 people, so there was one loaf to every thousand men, independently of the women and children.

12. *Gather up the fragments.* Among the Jews the *peah*, or residue after a meal, was the property of the servitors.

14. *This is of a truth that prophet.* Spoken of in Deut. xviii. 15, viz., the Messiah. How near were these people at this time to the kingdom of Heaven!

MATTHEW HENRY

ceived that those who acknowledged him to be that prophet would come, and *take him by force, to make him a king, v.* 15. Now here we have an instance,

(1) Of the irregular zeal of some of Christ's followers; nothing would serve but they would make him *a king*. This was *an act of zeal* for the honour of Christ. They were concerned to see so great a benefactor to the world so little esteemed in it; and therefore they would make him a king. Those whom Christ has feasted with the royal dainties of heaven should, in return for his favour, make him *their* king, and set him upon the throne in their souls. It was an *irregular* zeal. It was grounded upon a mistake concerning the nature of Christ's kingdom, as if it were to be *of this world*, and he must appear with outward pomp. Such a king as this they would make him, which was as great a disparagement to his glory as it would be to lacker gold or paint a ruby. Right notions of Christ's kingdom would keep us to right methods for advancing it. It was excited by the love of the flesh; they would make *him* their king who could feed them so plentifully without their toil, and save them from the curse of *eating their bread in the sweat of their face*. It was intended to carry on a *secular* design; they hoped this might be a fair opportunity of shaking off the Roman yoke. Thus is religion often prostituted to a secular interest, and Christ is served only to *serve a turn. Jesus is usually sought after for something else, not for his own sake.* It was contrary to the mind of our Lord Jesus himself; for they would take him *by force*, whether he would or no.

(2) Of the humility of the Lord Jesus, that he *departed*; so far was he from countenancing the design that he effectually quashed it. Herein he has left a testimony against ambition and affectation of worldly honour. Let us not then covet to be the *idols of the crowd*, nor be *desirous of vain-glory*. It is a testimony also against faction and sedition, treason and rebellion, and whatever tends to disturb the peace of kings and provinces. *Whither* he retired: *He departed again into a mountain, into the* mountain, the mountain where he had preached (*v.* 3), and then returned to it alone, to be private. Christ chose sometimes to be alone for the more free converse with God, and our own souls are *never less alone, than when alone.*

II. The disciples' distress at sea.

1. Here is their *going down to the sea* in a ship (*v.* 16, 17): *When even was come*, and they had done their day's work, it was time to look homeward, and therefore they went aboard, and set sail for Capernaum.

2. Here is the *stormy wind* arising. They had lately been feasted at Christ's table; but after the sunshine of comfort expect a storm. *It was now dark.* Sometimes the people of God are in trouble, and cannot see their way out; in the dark concerning the cause of their trouble, concerning the design and tendency of it, and what the issue will be. Jesus *was not come to them.* The absence of Christ is the great aggravation of the troubles of Christians. The *sea rose by reason of a great wind.* It was calm and fair when they put to sea, but it arose when they were *at sea*. In times of tranquillity we must prepare for trouble, for it may arise when we little think of it. Clouds and darkness sometimes surround the children of the light, and of the day.

3. Here is Christ's seasonable approach to them, *v.* 19. *They had rowed about twenty-five or thirty furlongs.* And, when they were got off a good way at sea, they *see Jesus walking on the sea.* The power Christ has over the laws and customs of nature. Christ walked *upon* the water as upon dry land. The concern Christ has for his disciples in distress: *He drew nigh to the ship.* He will not leave them comfortless when they seem to be *tossed with tempests* and *not comforted.* The relief Christ gives to his disciples in their fears. They *were afraid*, more afraid of an apparition (for so they supposed him to be) than of the winds and waves. When they thought a demon haunted them, they were more terrified than they had been while they saw nothing in it but what was natural. Our real distresses are often much increased by our imaginary ones. We are often not only *worse frightened than hurt*, but *then* most *frightened* when we are ready to be *helped.* How affectionately did Christ silence their fears with that compassionate word (*v.* 20), *It is I, be not afraid!* Nothing more powerful to comfort saints than this, "*I am Jesus whom thou lovest:* be not afraid of me, nor of the storm." When trouble is nigh Christ is nigh.

4. Here is their speedy arrival at the port they were bound for, *v.* 17. They *welcomed* Christ into the ship; they *willingly received him.* Christ's absenting himself for a time is but so much the more to *endear himself*, at his return, to his disciples. Christ

JAMIESON, FAUSSET, BROWN

A. B. SIMPSON:

This is one of Christ's most impressive miracles, showing His absolute command over all the laws and forces of nature; and the scale upon which it was wrought was so magnificent that it left the profoundest impression on the multitudes who witnessed it. So much so, indeed, that in the enthusiasm of the moment they impetuously determined to compel Him to become the leader of a great popular movement, and allow them to make Him their actual king. Of course, this was but a superficial, and even a selfish movement. He knew their hearts better than they themselves did, and a few days afterward declared to them, "Ye seek not me because ye saw the miracles, but because ye did eat of the loaves and were filled." The Greek word in this last sentence denotes the grossest, the most animal satisfaction. They wanted a king that could gratify their earthly desires, and give them immunity from laboring and suffering, but had no appreciation of Christ's higher character and teaching. At the same time, their testimony, on this occasion, was sincere and spontaneous, as far as they knew themselves, and bears witness to the power of Christ and the influence of His mighty works.

—*Christ in the Bible*

15. departed . . . to a mountain himself alone—(1) to *rest*, which He came to this "desert place" on purpose to do before the miracle of the loaves, but could not for the multitude that followed Him (see on Mark 6:31); and (2) *"to pray"* (Matt. 14:23; Mark 6:46). But from His mountain-top He kept watching the ship (see on vs. 18), and doubtless prayed both for them, and with a view to the new manifestation which He was to give them of His glory. **16, 17. when even was come**—(See on Mark 6:35). **entered into a ship**—*"constrained"* to do so by their Master (Matt. 14:22; Mark 6:45), in order to put an end to the misdirected excitement in His favor (vs. 15), into which the disciples themselves may have been somewhat drawn. The word "constrained" implies reluctance on their part, perhaps from unwillingness to part with their Master and embark at night, leaving Him alone on the mountain. **went**—rather, "were proceeding." **toward Capernaum**—Mark says (6:45), "unto Bethsaida," meaning "Bethsaida of Galilee" (ch. 12:21), on the west side of the lake. The place they left was of the same name (see on Mark 6:31). **Jesus was not come to them**—They probably lingered in hopes of His still joining them, and so let the darkness come on. **18, 19. sea arose . . .**—and they were "now in the midst of it" (Matt. 14:24). Mark adds the graphic and touching particular, "He saw them toiling in rowing" (6:48), putting forth all their strength to buffet the waves and bear on against a head wind, but to little effect. He *saw* this from His mountain-top, and through the darkness of the night, for His heart was all with them; yet would He not go to their relief till His own time came. **19. they see Jesus**—"about the fourth watch of the night" (Matt. 14:25; Mark 6:48), or between three and six in the morning. **walking on the sea**—What Job (9:8) celebrates as the distinguishing prerogative of GOD, "WHO ALONE spreadeth out the heavens, and TREADETH UPON THE WAVES OF THE SEA"—what AGUR challenges as GOD's unapproachable prerogative, to "GATHER THE WIND IN HIS FISTS, and BIND THE WATERS IN A GARMENT" (Prov. 30:4)—lo! this is here done *in flesh*, by "THE SON OF MAN." **drawing nigh to the ship**—yet as though He *"would have passed by them,"* Mark 6: 48 (cf. Luke 24:28; Gen. 18:3:5; 32:24-26). *they were afraid*—"cried out for fear" (Matt. 14:26), "supposing it had been a spirit" (Mark 6:49). He would appear to them at first like a dark moving speck upon the waters; then as a human figure, but—in the dark tempestuous sky, and not dreaming that it could be their Lord—they take it for a spirit. (How often thus we miscall our chiefest mercies—not only thinking them distant when they are near, but thinking the best the worst!) **20. It is I; be not afraid**—Matthew and Mark give before these exhilarating words, that to them well-known one, "Be of good cheer!" **21. willingly received him into the ship**—their first fears being now converted

ADAM CLARKE

15. *Take him by force, to make him a king.* The Jews had often suffered by famine in those times in which their enemies were permitted to prevail over them; but, finding that Jesus had such power as to multiply a few loaves to feed thousands, they took it for granted that while He was at their head no evil could possibly happen to them and therefore were determined immediately to proclaim Him king and rid themselves at once of Herod and the Romans. Our Lord perceiving this, either by some words which they had dropped or by His penetration of their hearts, retired before the project had been fully formed or could be put into execution. It was not till a considerable time afterwards that even the disciples fully understood that His kingdom was not of this world. *Into a mountain.* That on which He was with His disciples previously to His working this miracle; see v. 3. Matthew, chap. xiv. 22-23, and Mark, vi. 45-46, say that before this Jesus constrained His disciples to embark in the vessel and go along the seacoast towards Capernaum, or Bethsaida—see here v. 17, and the note on Mark vi. 45; and that after they were gone He dismissed the multitudes, having no doubt given them such advices as the nature of the case required, after which He went into the mountain to pray.

17. *Toward Capernaum.* Mark says, chap. vi. 45, that our Lord commanded them to go along to Bethsaida; and in the course of the history we find they got neither to Bethsaida nor Capernaum, but landed in the country of Gennesaret, Matt. xiv. 34. Our Lord seems to have desired them to go to either Bethsaida or Capernaum, which were only a very few miles distant, and on the same side of the sea. The reason why they could reach neither was the storm which the Evangelists say rose at the time, and the wind being contrary.

19. *Had rowed.* Their vessel was a small one only, something of the boat kind. As to sails, if they had any they could not now venture to carry them because of the storm. *Five and twenty or thirty furlongs.* Between three and four miles.

MATTHEW HENRY

brought them safely to the shore: *Immediately the ship was at the land whither they went.* The ship of the church may be much shattered and distressed, yet it shall come safe to the harbour at last. The disciples had rowed hard, but could not make their point till they had got Christ in the ship, and then the work was *done suddenly.* If we have received Christ Jesus the Lord, though the night be dark and the wind high, yet we may comfort ourselves with this, that we shall be at shore shortly, and are nearer to it than we think we are.

Verses 22–27

I. The careful enquiry which the people made after Christ, *v.* 23, 24. They saw Christ retire to the mountain. They way-laid his return, and *the day following,*

1. They were *much at a loss* for him. He was gone, and they knew not what was become of him. They saw there was *no boat there* but that in which the disciples went off. They observed also that *Jesus did not go with his disciples,* but that they went off alone.

2. They were very *industrious in seeking* him. They searched the places thereabouts, and when *they saw that Jesus was not there, nor his disciples,* they resolved to search elsewhere. Those whom Christ has feasted with the bread of life should have their souls carried out in earnest desires towards him. Much would have more, in communion with Christ. They resolved to go to Capernaum in quest of him. Thither his disciples were gone; and they knew he would not be long absent from *them.* Providence favoured them with an opportunity of going thither, for there *came other boats from Tiberias,* nigh to the place where they did *eat bread.* Those that in sincerity seek Christ are commonly owned and assisted by Providence in those pursuits. The evangelist adds, *After that the Lord had given thanks,* v. 11. So much were the disciples affected with their Master's giving thanks that they could never forget the impressions made upon them by it. This was the grace and beauty of that meal, and made it remarkable; their hearts burned within them.

3. *They also took shipping, and came to Capernaum, seeking for Jesus.* Their convictions being strong, and their desires warm, they followed him. Good motions are often crushed, and come to nothing, for want of being *prosecuted* in *time.* They came to Capernaum, and, for aught that appears, had a *calm* and *pleasant* passage, while his sincere disciples had a *rough* and *stormy* one. It is not strange if it fare worst with the best men in this evil world. They *came, seeking Jesus.*

II. The success of this enquiry: *They found him on the other side of the sea, v.* 25. It is worth while to cross a sea to seek Christ, if we may but find him at last. These people appeared afterwards to be unsound, and not actuated by any good principle, and yet were thus zealous. If men have *no more* to show for their love to Christ than their running after sermons and prayers, and their pangs of affection to good preaching, they have reason to suspect themselves no better than this *eager crowd.* But though these people were no better principled, and Christ knew it, yet he was willing to be found of them.

III. The question they put to him: *Rabbi, when camest thou hither?* It should seem by *v.* 59 that they found him *in the synagogue.* There they found him, and all they had to say to him was, *Rabbi, when camest thou hither?* Their enquiry refers not only to the *time,* but to the *manner,* of his conveying himself thither; not only *When,* but "*How* camest thou hither?" They were curious in asking concerning Christ's motions, but not solicitous to observe their own.

IV. The answer Christ gave them, such an answer as their case required.

1. He discovers the *corrupt principle* they *acted from* in following him (*v.* 26): "*Verily, verily, I say unto you. You seek me;* that is well, but it is not from a good principle." Christ knows not only *what* we do, but *why* we do it. *Not because you saw the miracles.* It was for their own bellies' sake: *Because you did eat of the loaves, and were filled;* not because he taught them, but because he fed them. He had given them a *full* meal's meat: *They did eat, and were filled;* and some of them perhaps were so poor that they had not known of a long time before now what it was to have enough, to eat and leave. A *cheap* meal's meat, that cost them nothing. Many follow Christ for *loaves,* and not for *love.* These people *complimented* Christ with Rabbi, yet he told them thus faithfully of their hypocrisy; his ministers must hence learn not to flatter those that flatter them, but to give faithful reproofs where there is cause for them.

2. He directs them to better principles (*v.* 27): *Labour for that meat which endures to everlasting life.* His design is,

JAMIESON, FAUSSET, BROWN

into wonder and delight. **and immediately the ship was at the land**—This additional miracle, for as such it is manifestly related, is recorded here alone. Yet all that is meant seems to be that as the storm was suddenly calmed, so the little bark—propelled by the secret power of the Lord of Nature now sailing in it—glided through the now unruffled waters, and while they were wrapt in wonder at what had happened, not heeding their rapid motion, *was found* at port, to their still further surprise.

22-71. Jesus, Followed by the Multitudes to Capernaum, Discourses to Them in the Synagogue of the Bread of Life—Effect of this on Two Classes of the Disciples. **22-24.** These verses are a little involved, from the Evangelist's desire to mention every circumstance, however minute, that might call up the scene as vividly to the reader as it stood before his own view. **The day following**—the miracle of the loaves, and the stormy night; the day on which they landed at Capernaum. **the people which stood on the other side of the sea**—not the whole multitude that had been fed, but only such of them as remained over night about the shore, i.e., on the *east* side of the lake; for we are supposed to have come, with Jesus and His disciples in the ship, to the *west* side, to Capernaum. **saw that there was none other boat there . . .**—The meaning is, the people had observed that there had been only one boat on the east side where they were; namely, the one in which the disciples had crossed at night to the other, the west side, and they had also observed that Jesus had not gone on board that boat, but His disciples had put off without Him: "Howbeit," adds the Evangelist, in a lively parenthesis, "there came other boats from Tiberias" (which lay near the southwest coast of the lake), whose passengers were part of the multitude that had followed Jesus to the east side, and been miraculously fed; these boats were fastened somewhere (says the Evangelist) "nigh unto the place where they did eat bread, after that the Lord had given thanks"—thus he refers to the glorious "miracle of the loaves"—and now they were put in requisition to convey the people back again to the west side. For when "the people saw that Jesus was not there, neither His disciples, they also took shipping [in these boats] and came to Capernaum, seeking for Jesus." **25. when they had found him on the other side**—at Capernaum—**they said . . .**—astonished at His *being* there, and wondering *how* He could have accomplished it, whether by land or water, and *when* He came; for being quite unaware of His having walked upon the sea and landed with the disciples in the ship, they could not see how, unless He had travelled all night round the head of the lake alone, He could have reached Capernaum, and even then, how He could have arrived before themselves.

26. Ye seek me . . .—Jesus does not put them through their difficulty, says nothing of His treading on the waves of the sea, nor even notices their question, but takes advantage of the favorable moment for pointing out to them how forward, flippant, and superficial were their views, and how low their desires. "Ye seek Me not because ye saw the miracles"—lit., 'the *signs,*' i.e., supernatural tokens of a higher presence, and a divine commission, "but because ye did eat of the loaves and were filled." From this He proceeds at once to that *other Bread,* just as, with the woman of Samaria, to that *other Water* (ch. 4). We should have supposed all that follows to have been delivered by the wayside, or wherever they happened first to meet. But from vs. 59 we gather that they had probably met about the door of the synagogue—"for that was the day in which they assembled in their synagogues" [Lightfoot]—and that on being asked, at the close of the service, if He had any word of exhortation to the people, He had taken the two breads, the *perishing* and the *living* bread, for the subject of His profound and extraordinary discourse.

ADAM CLARKE

21. *Immediately the ship was at the land.* How far they were from the place at which they landed when our Lord came to them, we know not. But the Evangelist seems to speak of their sudden arrival there as extraordinary and miraculous.

23. *There came other boats.* After Jesus and His disciples had departed. *From Tiberias.* Herod Antipas built this city near the lake of Gennesaret, in the best parts of Galilee, and called it *Tiberias,* in honor of Tiberius, the Roman emperor; see Jos., *Ant.,* book xviii, chap. 2, sec. 3.

24. *They also took shipping.* That is, as many of them as could get accommodated with boats took them, and thus got to Capernaum. But many others doubtless went thither on foot, as it is not at all likely that five or six thousand persons could get boats enough to carry them.

25. *On the other side of the sea.* That is, on the seacoast, to the northward of it, where Capernaum lies in the land of Gennesaret. It was in one of the synagogues of Capernaum that He delivered the following discourse; see v. 59.

26. *Ye seek me, not because ye saw.* Though the miracle of the loaves was one of the most astonishing that ever was wrought upon earth; and though this people had, by the testimony of all their senses, the most convincing proof of its reality; yet we find many of them paid little attention to it, and regarded the omnipotent hand of God in it no further than it went to satisfy the demands of their appetite! Most men are willing to receive temporal good from the hands of God; and there are few, very few, who are willing to receive spiritual blessings.

MATTHEW HENRY

(1) To moderate our worldly pursuits: *Labour not for the meat that perishes.* We must not make the things of this world our chief care and concern. The things of the world are *meat that perishes.* Worldly wealth, honour, and pleasure, are *meat*; they *feed the fancy* (and many times this is all) and *fill the belly.* These are things which men *hunger* after as *meat.* Those that have the largest share of them are not sure to have them while they live, but are sure to leave them and lose them when they die. It is therefore folly for us inordinately to labour after them. We must not make these perishing things our *chief good.*

(2) To quicken and excite our gracious pursuits: "*Labour for that meat* which belongs to the soul." It is *unspeakably desirable*: It is meat which *endures to everlasting life*; it is a happiness which will last as long as we must, which not only itself endures eternally, but will nourish us up to everlasting life. It is *undoubtedly attainable.* It is that *which the Son of man shall give. First,* Who gives this meat: the *Son of man,* who has power to give eternal life, with all the means of it. We are told to *labour for it,* as if it were to be got by our own industry, and sold upon that valuable consideration. But, when we have laboured ever so much for it, we have not merited it as our *hire,* but the Son of man *gives it.* And what more free than gift? *Secondly,* What authority he has to give it; for *him has God the Father sealed.* He has *sealed him,* that is, has given him full authority to deal between God and man, as God's *ambassador* to man and man's *intercessor* with God, and has proved his commission by miracles.

Verses 28–59

He gave them leave to ask him questions, and did not resent the interruption as an affront. Those that would be apt to teach must be swift to hear, and study to answer.

I. They enquire what work they must do, and he answers them, *v.* 28, 29. Their *enquiry* was *pertinent* enough (*v.* 28): *What shall we do, that we may work the works of God?* A humble serious question, showing them to be, at least for the present, in a good mind, and willing to know and do their duty. They were convinced that those who would obtain this everlasting meat, (1) Must aim to do something great. Those who *look high* in their expectations, must *aim high* in those endeavours, and study to *do the works of God,* distinguished from the works of worldly men in their worldly pursuits. It is not enough to speak the words of God, but we must do the works of God. (2) Must be willing to do anything: *What shall we do?* Lord, I am ready to do whatever thou shalt appoint. Christ's answer was plain enough (*v.* 29): *This is the work of God that ye believe.* The work of faith is the work of God. They enquire after the *works* of God (in the plural number), being careful about *many things*; but Christ directs them to the one thing needful; that *you believe.* Without faith you cannot please God. That faith is the work of God which closes with Christ; to *rest* upon him, and *resign ourselves* to him.

II. Christ having told them that the *Son of man* would *give them this meat,* they enquire concerning him.

1. Their enquiry is after *a sign* (*v.* 30): *What sign showest thou?* Thus far they were right, that, since he required them to give him *credit,* he should produce his *credentials.* But *herein* they missed it,

(1) That they overlooked the many miracles which they had seen wrought by him. Is this a time of day to ask, "What sign showest thou?" especially at Capernaum, where he had done so *many mighty works.* Were not these very persons but the other day miraculously fed by him? None so blind as they that will not see.

(2) That they preferred the miraculous feeding of Israel in the wilderness before all the miracles Christ wrought (*v.* 31): *Our fathers did eat manna in the desert.* They quote a scripture for it: *He gave them bread from heaven.* What a good use might be made of this story to which they here refer! Yet see how these people perverted it, and made an ill use of it. Christ reproved them for their fondness of the miraculous bread, and bade them not set their hearts upon *meat which perisheth.* Under colour of *magnifying* the miracles of Moses, they tacitly *undervalue* this miracle of Christ. Christ fed them but once, and then reproved those who followed him in hope to be still fed. Moses fed his followers forty years, and miracles were not their rarities, but their daily bread: Christ fed them with bread out of *the earth,* barley-bread, and fishes out of *the sea*; but Moses fed Israel with bread *from heaven,* angel's food. Thus big did these Jews talk of the *manna* which *their fathers did eat*; but their fathers had slighted it, and called it *light*

JAMIESON, FAUSSET, BROWN

27. which the Son of man—taking that title of Himself which denoted His incarnate life. **shall give unto you**—in the sense of vs. 51. **him hath God the Father sealed**—marked out and authenticated for that transcendent office, to impart to the world the bread of an everlasting life, and this in the character of "the Son of *man*."

28-31. What shall we do . . . the works of God—such works as God will approve. Different answers may be given to such a question, according to the *spirit* which prompts the inquiry. (See Hos. 6:6-8; Luke 3:12-14.) Here our Lord, knowing whom He had to deal with, shapes His reply accordingly.

29. This is the work of God . . .—That lies at the threshold of all acceptable obedience, being not only the prerequisite to it, but the proper spring of it—in that sense, the work of works, emphatically "*the* work of God."

What sign showest thou . . .—But how could they ask "a sign," when many of them scarce a day before had witnessed such a "sign" as had never till then been vouchsafed to men; when after witnessing it, they could hardly be restrained from making Him a king; when they followed Him from the one side of the lake to the other; and when, in the opening words of this very discourse, He had chided them for seeking Him, "not because they *saw the signs,*" but for the loaves? The truth seems to be that they were confounded by the *novel claims* which our Lord had just advanced. In proposing to make Him a king, it was for far other purposes than dispensing to the world the bread of an everlasting life; and when He seemed to raise His claims even higher still, by representing it as the grand "work of God," that they should believe *on Himself* as His Sent One, they saw very clearly that He was making a demand upon them beyond anything they were prepared to accord to Him, and beyond all that man had ever before made. Hence their question, "What dost Thou *work?*" **31. Our fathers did eat manna . . .**—insinuating the inferiority of Christ's miracle of the loaves to those of Moses: 'When Moses claimed the confidence of the fathers, "he gave them bread from heaven to eat"—not for a few thousands, but for millions, and not once only, but daily throughout their wilderness journey.'

ADAM CLARKE

27. *Labour not for the meat.* That is, for that "only," but "also for the bread." *Him hath God the Father sealed.* By this expression our Lord points out the commission which, as the Messiah, He received from the Father, to be Prophet and Priest to an ignorant, sinful world. As a person who wishes to communicate his mind to another who is at a distance writes a letter, seals it with his own seal, and sends it directed to the person for whom it was written, so Christ, who lay in the bosom of the Father, came to interpret the divine will to man, bearing the image, superscription, and seal of God in the immaculate holiness of His nature, the unsullied truth of His doctrine, and in the astonishing evidence of His miracles. But He came also as a Priest, to make an atonement for sin; and the bread which nourishes unto eternal life, He tells us, v. 51, is His body, which He gives for the life of the world; and to this sacrifice of himself the words *him hath God the Father sealed* seem especially to relate. It certainly was a custom, among nations contiguous to Judea, to set a seal upon the victim which was deemed proper for sacrifice.

28. *That we might work the works of God.* That is, divine works, or such as God can approve.

29. *This is the work of God, that ye believe.* There is nothing you can be employed in more acceptable to God than in yielding to the evidence set before you, and acknowledging Me as your Messiah and the Saviour of a lost world.

30. *What sign?* "What miracle?" So the word is evidently used in John ii. 11, 23, and in many other places. *That we may see, and believe thee.* That, having *seen* the miracle, we may *believe* Thee to be the promised Messiah. They had already seen the miracle of the five loaves, and did not believe; and it was impossible for them to see anything more descriptive of unlimited power and goodness.

31. *Our fathers did eat manna in the desert.* Their argument seems to run thus: Thou hast, we grant, fed 5,000 men with 5 loaves and 2 small fishes, but what is this in comparison of what Moses did in the desert, who for forty years fed more than a million of persons with bread from heaven? Do something like this, and then we will believe in Thee, as we have believed in Moses.

MATTHEW HENRY

bread, Num. xxi. 5. Thus apt are we to slight and overlook the appearances of God's power and grace in our own times, while we pretend to admire the wonders of which *our fathers told us*.

2. Here is Christ's reply to this enquiry. It was true that their fathers did eat *manna* in the desert. But, it was not Moses that gave it to them, he was but the instrument, and therefore they must look beyond him to God. Moses gave them not either *that* bread or *that* water. He *informs* them concerning the *true* manna: *But my Father giveth you the true bread from heaven;* the *bread from heaven* is *now given*, not to *your fathers*, but *to you*, for whom the *better things were reserved*: he is *now giving* you that *bread from heaven*, which is *truly* so called.

III. Christ, having replied to their enquiries, takes further occasion to discourse of *himself* under the similitude of *bread*, and of *believing* under the similitude of *eating and drinking*; to which, together with his putting both together in the *eating* of *his flesh* and *drinking* of his *blood*, and with the remarks made upon it by the hearers, the rest of this conference may be reduced.

1. Christ having spoken of *himself* as the great *gift of God*, and the *true bread* (*v.* 32), largely *explains* and *confirms* this. He here shows that he is the *true bread*; this he repeats again and again, *v.* 33, 35, 48–51. Observe, (1) That Christ is *bread*, is that to the soul which bread is to the body; *it is the staff of life*. Our bodies could better live without food than our souls without Christ. (2) That he is the *bread of God* (*v.* 33), divine bread; the bread of God's family, his *children's bread*. (3) That he is the *bread of life* (*v.* 35, and again, *v.* 48), *that* bread of life. Christ is the bread of life, for he is the fruit of the *tree of life*. He is the *living bread* (so he explains himself, *v.* 51): *I am the living bread*. Bread is itself a dead thing, but Christ is himself *living bread*, and nourishes by his own power. Christ is ever living, everlasting bread. The doctrine of Christ crucified is now as strengthening and comforting to a believer as ever it was. *He gives life unto the world* (*v.* 33). The *manna* did only preserve and support life. Christ *gives* life to those that were dead in sin. The manna was ordained only for the life of the Israelites, but Christ is given for the *life of the world*. (4) That he is the *bread which came down from heaven*; this is often repeated here, *v.* 33, 50, 51, 58. This denotes, the divinity of Christ's person; the divine original of all that good which flows to us through him. (5) That he is *that bread* of which the *manna* was a type and figure (*v.* 58), the true bread, *v.* 32. There was *manna* enough for them all; so in Christ a fulness of grace for all believers; he that *gathers much* of this *manna* will have none to spare when he comes to use it, and he that gathers little, when his grace comes to be perfected in glory, shall find that *he has no lack*. He here shows what his undertaking was, giving us an account of his business among men, *v.* 38–40. He came from heaven upon his Father's business (*v.* 38), not to *do his own will, but the will of him that sent him*. He *came from heaven*; we may well ask with wonder, "What moved him to such an expedition?" Here he tells us that he came to do, not *his own will*, but the will of his Father. "I am come to *do the will of him that sent me*." He came into the world as God's great agent and the world's great physician. The scope of his whole life was to glorify God and do good to men. He acquaints us, in particular, with that will of the Father which he came to do.

First, The *private instructions* given to Christ to save all the chosen remnant; and this is the *covenant of redemption* between the Father and the Son (*v.* 38): *This is the Father's will, who hath sent me;* that *of all whom he hath given me I should lose none*. There is a certain number of the children of men *given* by the Father to Jesus Christ, to be his care, and so to be to him for a name and a praise. Those whom God chose to be the objects of his special love he lodged as a trust in the hands of Christ. Jesus Christ has undertaken that he will *lose none* of those that were thus *given him* of the Father. Christ's undertaking for those that are given him extends to the resurrection of their bodies. *I will raise it up again at the last day*. Christ's undertaking will never be accomplished till the resurrection. The spring and original of all this is the *sovereign will of God*.

Secondly, The *public instructions* which were to be given to the children of men, upon what terms, they might obtain salvation by Christ; and this is the *covenant of grace* between God and man. Who the particular persons were that were given to Christ is a *secret*. Though their names are concealed, their characters are published. An offer is made that by it those that were given to Christ might be brought to him (*v.* 40): "*This is the will of him that sent me,*

JAMIESON, FAUSSET, BROWN

32, 33. Moses gave you not . . .—'It was not Moses that gave you the manna, and even it was but from the lower heavens; "but *My Father* giveth you *the true bread*," and that *"from heaven."* '

33. the bread of God is he . . .—This verse is perhaps best left in its own transparent grandeur—holding up the Bread Itself as *divine, spiritual,* and *eternal;* its ordained Fountain and essential Substance, *"Him who came down from heaven to give it"* (that Eternal Life which was with the Father and was manifested unto us, I John 1:2); and its designed objects, *"the world."*

35. I am the bread of life—Henceforth the discourse is all *in the first person,* "I," "Me," which occur in one form or other, as STIER reckons, thirty-five times.

51. I am . . .—Understand, it is of MYSELF I now speak as the Bread from heaven; of ME if a man eat he shall live for ever; and "THE BREAD WHICH I WILL GIVE IS MY FLESH, WHICH I WILL GIVE FOR THE LIFE OF THE WORLD." Here, for the first time in this high discourse, our Lord explicitly introduces His sacrificial *death*—for only rationalists can doubt this—not only as that which constitutes Him the Bread of life to men, but as THAT very element IN HIM WHICH POSSESSES THE LIFE-GIVING VIRTUE.—"From this time we hear no more (in this discourse) of 'Bread'; this figure is dropped, and the reality takes its place" [STIER]. The words "I will *give*" may be compared with the words of institution at the Supper, "This is My body which is *given* for you" (Luke 22:19), or in Paul's report of it, "*broken* for you" (I Cor. 11:24).

These, then, being the two members of the general opening statement, what follows is meant to take in both, "For I came down from heaven not to do Mine own will"—to play an independent part—"but [in respect to both the foregoing things, the *divine* and the *human* side of salvation] the will of Him that sent Me." What this twofold will of Him that sent Him is, we are next sublimely told (vss. 39, 40): "And this"—in the *first* place—"is the will of Him that sent Me, that of all [everything] which He hath given Me (taking up the identical words of vs. 37), I should lose nothing, but should raise it up at the last day." The meaning is not, of course, that He is charged to keep the objects entrusted to Him *as He received them,* so as they should merely suffer nothing in His hands. For as they were just "perishing" *sinners* of Adam's family, to let "nothing" of such "be lost," but "raise them up at the last day," must involve, *first,* giving His flesh for them" (vs. 51), that they "might not perish, but have everlasting life"; and *then,* after "keeping them from falling," raising their sleeping dust in incorruption and glory, and presenting them, body and soul, perfect and entire, wanting nothing, to Him who gave them to Him, saying, "Behold I and the children which God hath given Me." So much for the *first* will of Him that sent Him, the *divine* side of man's salvation, whose every stage and movement is inscrutable to us, but infallibly certain. "And this"—in the *second* place—"is the will of Him that sent Me, that

ADAM CLARKE

32. *Moses gave you not that bread from heaven.* Our Lord refutes the argument of the Jews by proving: (1) That it was not Moses, but God, who gave the manna; (2) That this bread was not the *true* bread, but was merely a type of it; (3) That God had given them now a Bread infinitely more excellent; (4) That himself is that heavenly nourishment of which He spake, and who was typified by the manna in the desert.

35. *I am the bread of life.* That is, the Bread which gives *life,* and preserves from death. *He that cometh to me.* The person who receives My doctrine and believes in Me as the great atoning Sacrifice shall be perfectly satisfied and never more feel misery of mind. All the guilt of his sins shall be blotted out, and his soul shall be purified unto God; and, being enabled to love Him with all his heart, he shall rest, fully, supremely, and finally happy, in his God.

50. *This is the bread.* I am come for this very purpose, that men may believe in Me and have eternal life.

38. *Not to do mine own will.* I am come, not to act according to human motives, passions, or prejudices; but according to infinite wisdom, goodness, and mercy. Jewish passions and prejudices would reject publicans and sinners as those alluded to, and shut the gate of heaven against the Gentiles; but God's mercy receives them, and I am come to manifest that mercy to men.

39. *I should lose nothing.* It is the will of God that every soul who believes should continue in the faith, and have a resurrection unto life eternal. But He wills this continuance in salvation without purposing to force the persons so to continue. God may will a thing to be without willing that it *shall be.* Judas was given to Christ by the Father, chap. xvii. 12. The Father willed that this Judas should continue in the faith, and have a resurrection unto life eternal; but Judas sinned and perished. Now it is evident that God willed that Judas *might be* saved, without willing that he *must* be saved infallibly and unconditionally. When a man is a worker together with the grace of God, he is saved; when he receives that grace of God in vain, he is lost—not through a lack of will or mercy in God, but through lack of his cooperation with divine grace. God saves no man as a stock or a stone, but as a reasonable being and free agent. "That which thou hast heard, thou mayest hold fast, and persevere in, if thou wilt," says Augustine. *Raise it up again at the last day.* The Jews believed that the wicked should have no resurrection; and that the principle that led to the resurrection of the body, in the righteous, was the indwelling Spirit of God.

40. *This is the will of him that sent me.*

MATTHEW HENRY

that *every one* that *sees the Son, and believes on him*, may have *everlasting life*, and *I will raise him up*." Is it not reviving to hear this? *Eternal life* may be had, if it be not our own fault. The crown of glory is set before us as the prize of our high calling, which we may run for and obtain. Every one may have it. This everlasting life is sure to all those who believe in Christ. He that *sees the Son*, and *believes on him*, shall be saved. I rather understand *seeing* here to mean the same thing with *believing*. Everyone that *sees the Son*, that is, *believes on him*, sees him with an eye of faith. It is not a *blind* faith that Christ requires, that we should be willing to have our *eyes put out*, and then follow him, but that we should *see him*, and see what ground we go upon in our faith. Those who believe in Jesus Christ, shall be raised up by his power at the last day. He had it in charge as his Father's will (*v.* 39), and here he solemnly makes it his own undertaking: *I will raise him up*.

2. Now Christ discoursing thus concerning himself, as the *bread of life* that came down from heaven, let us see what remarks his hearers made upon it.

(1) When they heard of such a thing as the *bread of God*, which *gives life*, they heartily prayed for it (*v.* 34): *Lord, evermore give us this bread*. I take this request to be made, though ignorantly, yet honestly, and to be well meant. General and confused notions of divine things produce some kind of desires towards them. Those who have an indistinct knowledge of the things of God, who see men as trees walking, make, as I may call them, *inarticulate* prayers for spiritual blessings. They think the favour of God a *good thing*, and heaven a *fine place*, while they have no value nor desire at all for that holiness which is necessary.

(2) But, when they understood that by this *bread of life* Jesus meant *himself*, then they *despised* it. *They murmured at him*. This comes in immediately after that solemn declaration which Christ had made of God's will and his own undertaking concerning man's salvation (*v.* 39, 40), which certainly were some of the most weighty and gracious words that ever proceeded out of the mouth of our Lord Jesus. One would think that when they heard that God had thus *visited* them, they should have *bowed their heads and worshipped*; but on the contrary, they *murmured*, quarrelled with what Christ said. Many that will not professedly contradict the doctrine of Christ yet say in their hearts that they *do not like it*. That which offended them was Christ's asserting his origin to be *from heaven*, *v.* 41, 42. How is it that he saith, *I came down from heaven?* That which they thought justified them herein was that they knew his extraction on earth: *Is not this Jesus the son of Joseph, whose father and mother we know?* They took it amiss that he should say that he came down from heaven, when he was *one of them*.

3. Christ, having spoken of faith as the great *work of God* (*v.* 29), discourses largely concerning this work.

(1) He shows what it is to *believe in Christ*. He that *comes to* me is the same with him that *believes in me* (*v.* 35), and again (*v.* 37): *He that comes unto me*; so *v.* 44, 45. Repentance towards God is *coming to him* as our chief good and highest end; and so faith towards our Lord Jesus Christ is coming to him as our prince and Saviour, and our way to the Father. When he was here on earth it was more than barely coming where he was; so it is now more than coming to his word and ordinances. It is to *feed upon Christ* (*v.* 51): *If any man eat of this bread*. The former denotes applying ourselves to Christ; this denotes applying Christ to ourselves.

(2) He shows what is to be got by believing in Christ. What shall we be the better if we *feed upon him*? *Want* and *death* are the chief things we dread. They shall never want, *never hunger, never thirst*, *v.* 35. Desires they have, earnest desires, but these so abundantly satisfied, that they cannot be called hunger and thirst, which are uneasy and painful. They shall *never die*, not die eternally. He that believes on Christ *has everlasting life* (*v.* 47). Union with Christ and communion with God in Christ are *everlasting life* begun. Whereas they that did *eat manna* died, Christ is such bread as a man may eat of and never die, *v.* 49, 50. [1] The insufficiency of the typical manna: *Your fathers did eat manna in the wilderness, and are dead*. Those that did eat manna, angel's food, died, like other men. Many of them died for their unbelief and murmurings. Their eating manna was no security to *them* from the *wrath of God*, as believing in Christ is to *us*. The rest of them died in a course of nature, and their carcases fell in that wilderness where they did *eat manna*. Let them not then boast so much of *manna*. [2] The all-sufficiency of the true *manna*: *This is the bread that cometh down from heaven, that a man may eat thereof and not*

JAMIESON, FAUSSET, BROWN

every one which seeth the Son and believeth [seeing the Son believeth] on Him, may have everlasting life, and I will raise him up at the last day." This is the *human* side of the same thing as in the foregoing verse, and answering to "*Him that cometh unto Me I will in no wise cast out*"; i.e., I have it expressly in charge that everyone that *so* "beholdeth" [so vieweth] the Son as to believe on Him shall have everlasting life; and, that *none* of Him be lost, "I will raise him up at the last day." (See on vs. 54.)

34. Lord, evermore give us this bread—speaking now with a certain reverence (as at vs. 25), the perpetuity of the manna floating perhaps in their minds, and much like the Samaritan woman, when her eyes were but half opened, "Sir, give Me this water . . ." (ch. 4:15).

41-46. Jews murmured—muttered, not in our Lord's hearing, but He knew it (vs. 43; ch. 2:25). **he said, I am the bread . . .**—Missing the sense and glory of this, and having no relish for such sublimities, they harp upon the "Bread from heaven." 'What *can* this mean? Do we not know all about Him—where, when, and of whom He was born? And yet He says He came down from heaven!'

he that cometh to me—to obtain what the soul craves, and as the only all-sufficient and ordained source of supply. **hunger . . . thirst**—shall have conscious and abiding satisfaction.

47-51. He that believeth . . .—(See on ch. 3:36; 5: 24). **48. I am the bread of life . . .**—'As he that believeth in Me hath everlasting life, so I am Myself the everlasting *Sustenance* of that life.' (Repeated from vs. 35.) **49. Your fathers**—of whom ye spake (vs. 31); not "*ours*," by which He would hint that *He* had a higher descent, of which they dreamt not [BENGEL]. **did eat manna . . . and are dead**—recurring to their own point about the manna, as one of the noblest of the *ordained* preparatory illustrations of His own office: 'Your fathers, ye say, ate manna in the wilderness; and ye say well, for so they did, *but they are dead*—even they whose carcasses fell in the wilderness did eat of that bread; the Bread whereof I speak cometh down from heaven, which the manna never did, that men, eating of it, may *live for ever*.'

ADAM CLARKE

Lest they should take a wrong meaning out of His words, as many have done since, He tells them that, far from any person being excluded from His mercy, it was the will of God that everyone who saw Him might believe and be saved. The power without which they could not believe He freely gave them, but the use of that power was their own. God gives the grace of repentance and faith to every man, but He neither repents nor believes for any man. Each must repent for his own sins, and believe in the Lord Jesus, through the grace given, or perish.

34. *Lord, evermore give us this bread*. Either meaning, "Let the miracle of the manna be renewed, and continue among us forever"; or, "Let that Bread of which Thou hast spoken become our constant nourishment." The Jews expected that when the Messiah should come He would give them all manner of delicacies, and, among the rest, manna, wine, and spicy oil.

41. *The Jews then murmured*. Because the whole of His discourse went to prove that He was infinitely greater than Moses, and that He alone could give present peace and eternal glory to men.

49. *Your fathers did eat manna . . . and are dead*. That bread neither preserved their bodies alive nor entitled them to life eternal; but those who receive My salvation shall not only be raised again in the last day, but shall inherit eternal life. It was an opinion of the Jews themselves that their fathers who perished in the wilderness should never have a resurrection. Our Lord takes them on their own ground: You acknowledge that your fathers who fell in the wilderness shall never have a resurrection, and yet they ate of the manna. Therefore that manna is not the bread that preserves to everlasting life, according even to your own concession.

A. B. SIMPSON:

The opposition of the Jews was on account of His high pretensions in contrast with what they knew of His obscure human origin. "Is not this Jesus, son of Joseph, whose father and mother we know? How is it that he saith, I came down from heaven?" Jesus answers them that no one can understand His divine character without divine teaching. "No man can come to me except my Father draw him." And this, He adds, lest they should excuse themselves by saying that the Father had not drawn them: "Every man therefore that hath heard of the Father and hath learned, cometh unto me." That is to say, the Father is teaching and willing to teach all who will learn; but they are not willing to be thus definitely taught and drawn. Then He adds two new thoughts to His former teaching, respecting the life He brings to men. First, the life it brings is not like the nourishment imparted by the manna, mere mortal life, but it is everlasting life. "Your fathers did eat manna and are dead; he that believeth on me hath everlasting life." The other thought is, that this life must come through His death: "The bread which I will give is my flesh, which I will give for the life of the world."
—Christ in the Bible

MATTHEW HENRY

die. Not die, that is, not perish, not come short of the heavenly Canaan. *If any man eat of this bread, he shall live for ever, v.* 51. This is the meaning of this *never dying*: though he go down to *death*, he shall pass through it to that world where there shall be *no more death.* To *live for ever* is not to *be* for ever, but to be *happy* for ever.

(3) He shows what encouragements we have to believe in Christ. Christ here speaks of some who *had seen him and yet believed not, v.* 36. Faith is not always the effect of sight; the soldiers were eye-witnesses of his resurrection, and yet, instead of *believing* in him, they *belied* him. Two things, to encourage our faith: That the Son will bid all those welcome that come to him (*v.* 37): *Him that cometh to me I will in no wise cast out.* How welcome should this word be to our souls which bids us welcome to Christ! The duty required is a pure gospel duty: to *come to Christ*, that we may come to God by him. His beauty and love must *draw* us to him; sense of need and fear of danger must *drive* us to him; anything to bring us to Christ. The promise is a pure gospel promise: *I will in no wise cast out.* There are two negatives: *I will not, no, I will not.* Much favour is expressed here. We have reason to fear that he should *cast us out.* We may justly expect that he should frown upon us, and shut his doors against us; but he obviates these fears with this assurance, he *will not* do it; will not reject us though we are sinful. More favour is implied than is expressed; when it is said that he will not cast them out the meaning is, He will receive them, and give them all that which they come to him for. That the Father will, without fail, bring all those to him in due time that were given him.

First, He here *assures* us *that* this shall be done: *All that the Father giveth me shall come to me, v.* 37. Christ had complained (*v.* 36) of those who, though they had *seen* him, yet would not believe on him; and then he adds this for *their* conviction and awakening. How can we think that God gave us to Christ if we give ourselves to the world and the flesh? For *his own* comfort and encouragement he adds: *All that the Father gives him shall come to him.* Here we have, (*a*) The election described: *All that the father giveth me*, and all that belongs to them; all their services, all their interests. As all that he has is *theirs*, so all that they have is *his*. God was now about to *give him the heathen for his inheritance* (Ps. ii. 8). And though the Jews, who *saw* him, *believed not* on him, yet these (saith he) shall *come to me*; the other sheep, which are not of this fold, shall be *brought, ch.* x. 15, 16. (*b*) The effect of it secured: *They shall come to me.* This is not in the nature of a *promise*, but a *prediction.* None of them shall be forgotten; not a grain of God's corn shall be lost. They are by nature *alienated* from Christ, and averse to him, and yet *they shall come.* Not, They shall be *driven* to me, but, They shall come freely, shall be made *willing*.

Secondly, How shall those who are given to Christ be brought to him? Two things are to be done in order to it:

a. Their *understandings* shall be *enlightened*; this is promised, *v.* 45, 46. It is written in the prophets, *And they shall be all taught of God; they shall all know me.* In order to our *believing in Jesus Christ*, it is necessary that we be *taught of God.* That there be a *divine revelation made to us.* There are some things which *even nature teaches*, but to bring us to Christ there is need of a higher light. That there be a *divine work wrought in us.* God, in giving us reason, teaches us more than the *beasts of the earth*; but in giving us faith he teaches more than the *natural man.* All that are *genuine*, are *taught of God*; he hath undertaken their education. It follows then, by way of inference from this, that *every man* that has *heard and learned of the Father comes to Christ, v.* 45. Except God by his grace enlighten our minds and not only *tell* us, that we may *hear*, but teach us, that we may *learn* the truth as it is in Jesus, we shall never be brought to believe in Christ. Those who do not *come to Christ* have never *heard* nor *learned* of the Father; for, if they had, doubtless they would have come to Christ. In vain do men pretend to be *taught of God* if they believe not in Christ. But lest any should dream of a visible appearance of God the Father, he adds (*v.* 46): *Not that any man hath seen the Father.* God, in enlightening men's eyes and teaching them, works in a spiritual way. The Father of spirits hath access to, and influence upon, men's spirits, undiscerned. Those that have not seen his face have felt his power. Those that *learn of the Father* must learn of Christ, who alone hath seen him.

b. Their *wills* shall be *bowed.* In the depraved soul of fallen man there is a rebellion of the will against the right dictates of the understanding. It is there-

JAMIESON, FAUSSET, BROWN

36. But . . . ye have seen me, and believe not—seen Him not in His mere bodily presence, but in all the majesty of His life, His teaching, His works. "AND HIM THAT COMETH TO ME I WILL IN NO WISE CAST OUT." As the former was the *divine*, this is just the *human* side of the same thing. True, the "coming" ones of the second clause are just the "given" ones of the first. But had our Lord merely said, "*When those* that have been given Me of My Father shall come to Me, I will receive them"—besides being very flat, the impression conveyed would have been quite different, sounding as if there were *no other laws in operation*, in the movement of sinners to Christ, but such as are wholly *divine* and *inscrutable* to us; whereas, though He does speak of it as a sublime certainty which men's *refusals* cannot frustrate, He speaks of that certainty as taking effect only by men's *voluntary advances* to Him and acceptance of Him—"Him that cometh to Me," "whosoever will," throwing the door wide open. Only it is not the simply *willing*, but the actually *coming*, whom He will not cast out; for the word here employed usually denotes *arrival*, as distinguished from the ordinary word, which rather expresses the *act of coming* (see ch. 8:42, *Greek*), [WEBSTER and WILKINSON]. "In no wise" is an emphatic negative, to meet the fears of the timid (as in Rev. 21:27, to meet the presumption of the hardened). **37-40. All that . . .**—This comprehensive and very grand passage is expressed with a peculiar artistic precision. The opening general statement (vs. 37) consists of two members: (1) "ALL THAT THE FATHER GIVETH ME SHALL COME TO ME"—i.e., 'Though ye, as I told you, have no faith in Me, My errand into the world shall in no wise be defeated; for all that the Father giveth Me shall infallibly come to Me.' Observe, what is *given* Him by the Father is expressed in the *singular* number and *neuter* gender—lit., 'everything'; while those who *come to* Him are put in the *masculine* gender and *singular* number—'every one.' The *whole mass*, so to speak, is gifted by the Father to the Son as a *unity*, which the Son evolves, one by one, in the execution of His trust. So ch. 17:2, "that He should give eternal life to *all that which* Thou hast given Him" [BENGEL]. This "*shall*" expresses the glorious *certainty* of it, the Father being pledged to see to it that the gift be no empty mockery.

45. written in the prophets—in Isaiah 54:13; Jeremiah 31:33, 34; other similar passages may also have been in view. Our Lord thus falls back upon Scripture authority for this seemingly hard saying. **all taught of God**—not by *external* revelation merely, but by *internal illumination*, corresponding to the "drawing" of vs. 44.

Every man therefore . . .—i.e., who hath been thus efficaciously taught of Him. **cometh unto me**—*with absolute certainty*, yet in the sense above given of "drawing"; i.e., 'As none can come to Me but as divinely drawn, so none thus drawn shall fail to come.' **Not that any man hath seen . . .**—Lest they should confound that "hearing and learning of the Father," to which believers are admitted by divine *teaching*, with His own immediate access to Him, He here throws in a parenthetical explanation; stating, as explicitly as words could do it, how totally different the two cases were, and that only He who is **"from God" hath this naked,** immediate access to the Father. (See ch. 1:18).

ADAM CLARKE

I will in no wise cast out. The words are exceedingly emphatic—"I will by no means thrust out of doors." Our blessed Lord alludes to the case of a person in deep distress and poverty who comes to a nobleman's house, in order to get relief. The person appears; and the owner, far from treating the poor man with asperity, welcomes, receives him kindly, and supplies his wants. So does Jesus. Never did He reject the suit of a penitent, however grievous his crimes might have been.

37. *All that the Father giveth me.* The neuter gender, *pan*, is probably used here for the masculine, *pas. Shall come to me.* All that are drawn by the Father, v. 44, i.e., all those who are influenced by His Spirit, and yield to those influences. "For as many as are led [not driven or dragged] by the Spirit of God, they are the sons [children] of God," Rom. viii. 14. God sent His prophets to proclaim His salvation to this people; and He accompanied their preaching with the influence of His Spirit. Those who yielded were saved; those who did not yield to these drawings were lost.

45. *It is written in the prophets.* Isa. liv. 13; Jer. xxxi. 34. *They shall be all taught of God.* This explains the preceding verse. God teaches a man to know himself, that, finding his need of salvation, he may flee to lay hold on the hope which his Heavenly Father has set before him in the gospel. God draws men by His *love*, and by showing them what His love has done for them. *Fear* repels, but *love* attracts. He who is ever preaching the terrors of the law, and representing God as a vindictive judge, will never bring sinners to Him. They are afraid of this terrible God; but they love Him who "so loved the world, that he gave his only begotten Son, that whosoever believeth in him should not perish, but have everlasting life."

46. *Not that any man hath seen the Father.* He does not teach men by appearing personally before them, or by any other outward voice than that of His Word and messengers; but He teaches by His Spirit. *He which is of God.* That is, Christ alone. Neither Moses nor any of the prophets had ever seen God. Jesus, who lay in the bosom of the Father, saw and revealed Him, chap. i. 18.

MATTHEW HENRY

fore requisite that there be a work of grace wrought upon the will, which is here called *drawing* (*v.* 44): *No man can come to me except the Father, who hath sent me, draw him.* The Jews murmured at the doctrine of Christ. Christ said (*v.* 43), "*Murmur not among yourselves;* lay not the fault of your dislike of my doctrine one upon another. Your antipathies to the truths of God are so strong that nothing less than a divine power can conquer them. *No man can come to me except the Father, who hath sent me, draw him,*" *v.* 44. (*a*) The nature of the work: It is *drawing*, which denotes not a *force* put upon the will, but a *change* wrought in the will. A new bias is given to the soul, by which it inclines to God. He that *formed the spirit of man* knows how to new-mould the soul. (*b*) The necessity of it: *No man*, in this weak and helpless state, can come to Christ without it. (*c*) The author of it: The *Father who hath sent me.* The Father would not send him on a fruitless errand. So, having sent Christ to save souls, he sends souls to him to be saved by him. (*d*) The crown and perfection of this work: And *I will raise him up at the last day.* This is four times mentioned in this discourse. If he undertakes this, surely he *can* do anything. Let our expectations be carried out towards a happiness reserved for the *last day*.

4. Christ comes more particularly to show *what of himself* is this bread, *v.* 51–58, where he still prosecutes the metaphor of food. *The bread that I will give is my flesh* (*v.* 51), *the flesh of the Son of man and his blood, v.* 53. *His flesh is meat indeed, and his blood is drink indeed, v.* 53. We must *eat the flesh of the Son of man and drink his blood* (*v.* 53); and again (*v.* 54), *Whoso eateth my flesh and drinketh my blood;* and the same words (*v.* 56, 57), he that *eateth me.*

(1) Let us see how this discourse of Christ was liable to mistake and misconstruction. It was misconstrued by the carnal *Jews* (*v.* 52): *They strove among themselves: How can this man give us his flesh to eat?* Christ spoke (*v.* 51) of giving his flesh *for us*, to suffer and die; but they understood it of his giving it *to us*, to be eaten. It is misunderstood by many who hence infer that, if they take the sacrament when they die, they shall certainly go to heaven.

(2) Let us see how this discourse of Christ is to be understood.

[1] What is meant by the *flesh and blood of Christ.* It is called (*v.* 53), *The flesh of the Son of man, and his blood.* It is said to be *given for the life of the world*, that is, *First, Instead* of the *life of the world*, which was *forfeited* by sin, Christ gives his own flesh as a ransom. *Secondly*, In *order to* the *life of the world*, to purchase a *general* offer of eternal life to all the world. So that the *flesh and blood* of the Son of man denote Christ and *him crucified*, and the redemption wrought out by him. The promises of the covenant, and eternal life; these are called *the flesh and blood* of Christ, 1. Because they are purchased by the breaking of his body, and the shedding of his blood. 2. Because they are meat and drink to our souls. He had before compared himself to *bread*, which is necessary food; here to *flesh*, which is delicious. It is *meat indeed*, and *drink indeed*; in opposition to the shows and shadows with which the world shams off those that feed upon it.

[2] What is meant by *eating this flesh* and *drinking* this *blood*. It is certain that it means neither more nor less than believing in Christ. *Believing in Christ* includes these four things, which *eating and drinking* do: *First*, It implies an *appetite* to Christ. This spiritual eating and drinking begins with *hungering* and *thirsting* (Matt. v. 6): "Give me Christ or else I die." *Secondly*, An *application* of Christ to ourselves. Meat *looked upon* will not nourish us, but meat *fed upon*. We must so accept of Christ as to appropriate him to ourselves. *Thirdly*, A *delight* in Christ and his salvation. The doctrine of Christ crucified must be *meat and drink* to us, most pleasant and delightful. *Fourthly*, A *derivation of nourishment* from him and a dependence upon him for the support and comfort of our spiritual life, and the strength, growth, and vigour of the new man. It is to live upon him as we do upon our meat. When afterwards he would institute some outward sensible signs, by which to represent our *communicating* of the benefits of his death, he chose those of *eating* and *drinking*, and made them *sacramental* actions.

(3) Having thus explained the general meaning of this part of Christ's discourse, the particulars are reducible to two heads:

[1] The *necessity* of our *feeding upon Christ* (*v.* 53): *Except you eat the flesh of the Son of man, and drink his blood, you have no life in you. First*, It is a certain sign that you *have no* spiritual *life* in you if you have no *desire* towards Christ, nor *delight* in him. If the soul does not *hunger* and *thirst*, certainly it does not

JAMIESON, FAUSSET, BROWN

43. Murmur not . . . 44. No man—i.e., Be not either startled or stumbled at these sayings; for it needs divine teaching to understand them, divine drawing to submit to them. **can come to me**—in the sense of vs. 35. **except the Father which hath sent me**—i.e., the Father *as the Sender of Me* and *to carry out the design of My mission.* **draw him**—by an *internal* and *efficacious* operation; though by all the means of rational conviction, and in a way altogether consonant to their moral nature (Song of Sol. 1:4; Jer. 31:3; Hos. 11:3, 4). **raise him up . . .**—See on vs. 54.

52. Jews strove among themselves—arguing the point together. **How can . . .**—i.e., Give us His flesh to eat? Absurd. **53-58. Except ye eat the flesh . . . and drink the blood . . . no life . . .**—The harshest word He had yet uttered in their ears. They asked how it was *possible* to eat His flesh. He answers, with great solemnity, "It is *indispensable.*" Yet even here a thoughtful hearer might find something to temper the harshness. He says they must not only "eat His *flesh*" but "drink His *blood*," which could not but suggest the idea of His *death*—implied in the separation of one's flesh from his blood. And as He had already hinted that it was to be something very different from a *natural* death, saying, "My flesh I will give for the life of the world" (vs. 51), it must have been pretty plain to candid hearers that He meant something above the gross idea which the bare terms expressed. And farther, when He added that they "had no *life* in them unless they thus ate and drank," it was impossible they should think He meant that the *temporal* life they were then living was dependent on their eating and drinking, in this gross sense, His flesh and blood. Yet the whole statement was certainly confounding, and beyond doubt was meant to be so. Our Lord had told them that in spite of all they had "seen" in Him, they "did not believe" (vs. 36). For *their* conviction therefore he does not here lay Himself out; but having the ear not only of them but of the more *candid and thoughtful* in the crowded synagogue, and the miracle of the loaves having led up to the most exalted of all views of His Person and Office, He takes advantage of their very difficulties and objections to announce, for all time, those most profound truths which are here expressed, regardless of the disgust of the unteachable, and the prejudices even of the most sincere, which His language would seem only designed to deepen. The *truth* really conveyed here is no other than that expressed in vs. 51, though in more emphatic terms —that He Himself, in the virtue of His sacrificial death, is the spiritual and eternal life of men; and that unless men voluntarily appropriate to themselves this death, in its sacrificial virtue, so as to become the very life and nourishment of their inner man, they have no spiritual and eternal life at all. Not as if His death were the *only* thing of value, but it is what gives all else in Christ's Incarnate Person, Life, and Office, their whole value *to us sinners.* **54. Whoso eateth . . . hath . . .**—The former verse said that *unless* they partook of Him they had no life; this adds, that *whoever* does so "hath eternal life." **And I will raise him up at the last day**—For the *fourth* time this is repeated (see vss. 39, 40, 44)—showing most clearly that the "eternal life" which such a man "*hath*" cannot be the same with the *future* resurrection-life from which it is carefully distinguished each time, but a

ADAM CLARKE

44. *Except the Father . . . draw him.* But how is a man drawn? Augustine answers from the poet, "A man is attracted by that which he delights in." Show green herbage to a sheep; he is drawn by it. Show nuts to a child, and he is drawn by them. They run wherever the person runs who shows these things. They run after him, but they are not forced to follow; they run through the desire they feel to get the things they delight in. So God draws man. He shows him his wants—He shows the Saviour whom He has provided for him. The man feels himself a lost sinner; and, through the desire which he finds to escape hell and get to heaven, he comes unto Christ, that he may be justified by His blood. Unless God thus draw, no man will ever come to Christ; because none could, without this drawing, ever feel the need of a Saviour. Drawing, or alluring, not dragging, is here to be understood. The best Greek writers use the verb in the same sense of "alluring, inciting."

51. *Is my flesh, which I will give.* Our Lord explains His meaning more fully in these words than He had done before. Having spoken so much of the bread which feeds and nourishes the soul and preserves from death, the attention of His hearers was fixed upon His words, which to them appeared inexplicable; and they desired to know what their meaning was. He then told them that the bread meant His *flesh* (His life), which He was about to give up to save the life of the world. Here our Lord plainly declares that His death was to be a vicarious sacrifice and atonement for the sin of the world; and that as no human life could be preserved unless there was *bread* (proper nourishment) received, so no soul could be saved but by the merit of His death.

52. *How can this man give us his flesh to eat?* Our Lord removes this difficulty, and answers the question in v. 63.

53. *Except ye eat the flesh of the Son of man.* Unless you be made partakers of the blessings about to be purchased by My blood, passion, and violent death, you cannot be saved. Bishop Pearce justly observes that the ideas of eating and drinking are here borrowed to express "partaking of" and "sharing in." Thus spiritual happiness on earth, and even in heaven, is expressed by eating and drinking; instances of which may be seen in Matt. viii. 11; xxvi. 29; Luke xiv. 15; xxii. 30; and Rev. ii. 17. Those who were made partakers of the Holy Spirit are said by Paul, 1 Cor. xii. 13, to be "made to drink into [or of] one Spirit." This, indeed, was a very common mode of expression among the Jews.

54. *Hath eternal life.* This can never be understood of the sacrament of the Lord's Supper: (1) Because this was not instituted till a year after, at the last Passover; (2) It cannot be said that those who do not receive that sacrament must perish everlastingly; (3) Nor can it be

MATTHEW HENRY

live. Secondly, It is certain that you *can have* no spiritual life, unless you derive it from Christ by faith; separated from him you can do nothing. Our bodies may as well live without meat as our souls without Christ.

[2] The *benefit* and *advantage* of it, in two things: *First*, We shall be *one with Christ* (*v.* 56): *He that eats my flesh, and drinks my blood*, he *dwelleth in me, and I in him*. By faith we have a close and intimate union with Christ; he is *in us*, and we *in him*. Such is the union between Christ and believers that he shares in their griefs, and they share in his graces and joys; he *sups* with them upon their bitter herbs, and *they with him* upon his *rich dainties*.

Secondly, We shall *live*, shall live eternally, *by him*. We shall *live by him* (*v.* 57): *As the living Father hath sent me, and I live by the Father, so he that eateth me, even he shall live by me*. True believers receive this divine life by virtue of their union with Christ. *He that eateth me*, or feeds on me, *even he shall live by me*: those that live *upon* Christ shall live *by* him. Because he lives, we shall live also. We shall live *eternally* by him (*v.* 54): *Whoso eateth my flesh, and drinketh my blood*, he *hath eternal life*. He shall live *for ever*, *v.* 58.

Lastly, The historian concludes with an account *where* Christ had this discourse with the Jews (*v.* 59): *In the synagogue as he taught*. This was that in his discourse which was new. Christ pleaded this upon his trial (*ch.* xviii. 20): *I ever taught in the synagogue*.

Verses 60–71

We have here an account of the effects of Christ's discourse.

I. To some it was a *savour of death unto death*; not only to the Jews, but even to many of *his disciples*.

1. Their murmurings at the doctrine they heard (*v.* 60); not a few, but many of them, were offended at it. See what they say to it (*v.* 60): *This is a hard saying, who can hear it?* They do not like it themselves. Now, when they found it a hard saying, if they had humbly begged of Christ to have *declared unto them this parable*, he would have opened it, and their understandings too. They think it impossible that anyone else should like it: "*Who can hear it?* Surely none can." Thus the scoffers at religion are ready to undertake that all the intelligent part of mankind concur with them. Thanks be to God, thousands have *heard* these sayings of Christ, and have found them not only easy, but pleasant.

2. Christ's animadversions upon their murmurings.

(1) He well enough knew their murmurings, *v.* 61. Christ *knew* them; he saw them, he heard them. He knew it *in himself*, not by any information given him, but by his own divine omniscience. Thoughts are words to Christ; we should therefore take heed not only what we say and do, but what we think.

(2) He well enough knew how to answer them: "*Doth this offend you?*" We may justly wonder that so much offence should be taken at the doctrine of Christ for so little cause. Christ speaks of it here with wonder: "*Doth this offend you?*" He gives them a hint of his ascension into heaven, as that which would give an irresistible evidence of the truth of his doctrine (*v.* 62): *What and if you shall see the Son of man ascend up where he was before?* If this be so hard a saying that you cannot hear it, how will you digest it when I tell you of my returning *to* heaven, whence I came down? Those who stumble at smaller difficulties should consider how they will get over greater. "You think I take too much upon me when I say, *I came down from heaven*, for it was with this that you quarrelled (*v.* 42); but will you think so when you see me return to heaven?" Christ did often refer himself thus to *subsequent* proofs. He gives them a general key to this and all such parabolical discourses, teaching them that they are to be understood spiritually: *It is the spirit that quickeneth, the flesh profiteth nothing*, *v.* 63. The bare participation of ordinances, unless the Spirit of God work with them, and quicken the soul by them, *profits nothing*; the word and ordinances, if the Spirit works with them, are as food to a living man, if not, they are as food to a dead man. The doctrine of eating Christ's flesh and drinking his blood, if it be understood literally, *profits nothing*. The spiritual sense of meaning of it quickens the soul, makes it *alive* and *lively*: *The words that I speak unto you, they are spirit, and they are life*. To believe that Christ died for me, to derive from that doctrine strength and comfort, this is the *spirit and life* of that saying, and, construing it thus, it is an excellent saying. The reason why men *dislike* Christ's sayings is because they *mistake* them. The literal sense of a parable does us no good, we are never the wiser for it. *The flesh profits nothing;* but *the Spirit quickeneth*. They found fault with Christ's sayings, whereas the fault was in themselves; it is

JAMIESON, FAUSSET, BROWN

life communicated *here below* immediately on believing (ch. 3:36; 5:24, 25); and giving to *the resurrection of the body* as that which consummates the redemption *of the entire man*, a prominence which in the current theology, it is to be feared, it has seldom had. (See Rom. 8:23; I Cor. 15, throughout.) **56. He that eateth . . . dwelleth in me and I in him**—As our food becomes incorporated with ourselves, so Christ and those who eat His flesh and drink His blood become spiritually *one life*, though *personally* distinct. **57. As the living Father hath sent me**—to communicate His own life. **and I live by the Father**—lit., "because of the Father"; My life and His being one, but Mine that of a *Son*, whose it is to be "*of* the Father." (See ch. 1:18; 5:26.) **he that eateth me, . . . shall live by me**—lit., 'because of Me.' So that though *one spiritual life* with Him, "the Head of every man is Christ, as the head of Christ is God" (I Cor. 11:3; 3:23). **58. This is that bread . . .**—a sort of summing up of the whole discourse, on which let this one further remark suffice—that as our Lord, instead of softening down His figurative sublimities, or even putting them in naked phraseology, leaves the great truths of His Person and Office, and our participation of Him and it, enshrined for all time in those glorious forms of speech, so when we attempt to strip the truth of these figures, figures though they be, it goes away from us, like water when the vessel is broken, and our wisdom lies in raising our own spirit, and attuning our own ear, to our Lord's chosen modes of expression. (It should be added that although this discourse has nothing to do with the Sacrament of the Supper, the Sacrament has everything to do with it, as *the visible embodiment* of these figures, and, to the believing partaker, a *real*, yea, and the most lively and affecting participation of His flesh and blood, and nourishment thereby of the spiritual and eternal life, here below.) **59. These things said he in the synagogue**—which seems to imply that what follows took place after the congregation had broken up. **60-65. Many . . . of his disciples**—His pretty constant followers, though an outer circle of them. **hard saying**—not merely harsh, but insufferable, as the word often means in the Old Testament. **who can hear**—submit to listen to it.

61. Doth this offend . . . What and if . . .—i.e., 'If ye are stumbled at what I *have* said, how will ye bear what I *now* say?' Not that His ascension itself would stumble them more than His death, but that after recoiling from the *mention* of the one, they would not be in a state of mind to take in the other.

the flesh profiteth nothing—Much of His discourse was *about* "flesh"; but flesh as such, mere flesh, could profit nothing, much less impart that *life* which the Holy Spirit alone communicates to the soul.

the words that I speak . . . are spirit and . . . life—The whole burden of the discourse is "*spirit*," not mere flesh, and "*life*" in its highest, not its lowest sense, and the words I have employed are to be interpreted solely in that sense.

ADAM CLARKE

supposed that all those who do receive it are necessarily and eternally saved. On the contrary, Paul intimates that many who received it at Corinth perished because they received it unworthily, not discerning the Lord's body, not distinguishing between it and a common meal, and not properly considering that Sacrifice for sin of which the sacrament of the Lord's Supper was a type; see 1 Cor. xi. 30.

55. *My flesh is meat indeed, and my blood is drink indeed.* Or rather, "My flesh is the true meat." In both clauses of this verse, instead of the *adverb* I read the *adjective*, agreeing with *brosis*. This reading is supported by many MSS. Our Lord terms His flesh the "true meat," and His blood the "true drink," because those who received His grace merited by His death would be really nourished and supported thereby unto eternal life.

56. *Dwelleth in me, and I in him.* Of all connections and unions, none is so intimate and complete as that which is effected by the digestion of aliments, because they are changed into the *very substance* of him who eats them; and this our Lord makes the model of that union which subsists between himself and genuine believers. He lives in them, and they in Him; for they are made partakers of the divine nature, 2 Pet. i. 4.

57. *So he that eateth me, even he shall live by me.* From which we learn that the union between Christ and His followers shall be similar to that which subsists between God and Christ.

59. *In the synagogue . . . in Capernaum.* From v. 26 to this verse the Evangelist gives us the discourse which our Lord preached in the synagogue, in which He was repeatedly interrupted by the Jews; but this gave Him the fuller opportunity to proclaim the whole truth relative to His passion and death, to edify the disciples, and confute these gainsayers.

60. *Many therefore of his disciples.* So it appears that He had many more than the twelve who constantly accompanied Him. *This is an hard saying; who can hear it?* Who can digest such doctrine as this? It is intolerable; it is impracticable.

62. *If ye shall see the Son of man ascend.* You need not be stumbled at what I say concerning eating My flesh and drinking My blood, for you shall soon have the fullest proof that this is *figuratively* spoken, for I shall ascend with the same body with which I shall arise from the dead; therefore My flesh and blood, far from being eaten by men, shall not even be found among them.

63. *It is the spirit that quickeneth.* It is the spiritual sense only of My words that is to be attended to, and through which life is to be attained, 2 Cor. iii. 6. Such only as eat and drink what I have mentioned, in a spiritual sense, are to expect eternal life. *The words that I speak.* Instead of *I speak*, I read, "I have spoken," on the authority of many MSS. This is an important reading, and plainly shows that our Lord's words here do not refer to any new point of doctrine which He was then inculcating, but to what He had spoken concerning His being the living Bread, and concerning the eating of His flesh and drinking of His blood, in the preceding verses. *Are spirit, and they are life.* As My words are to be spiritually understood, so the life they promise is of a spiritual nature.

MATTHEW HENRY

only to *sensual* minds that spiritual things are *senseless* and *sapless*, spiritual minds *relish* them, see 1 Cor. ii. 14, 15. He gives them an intimation of his *knowledge of them*, and that he had expected no better from them, though they called themselves his disciples, *v.* 64, 65.

First, They did not *believe his report*. Among those who are *nominal Christians*, there are many who are *real infidels*. The unbelief of hypocrites is naked and open before the eyes of Christ. He *knew from the beginning* who they were that *believed*, and who of the twelve should betray him; who were sincere, as Nathanael (*ch.* i. 47), and who were not. It is Christ's prerogative to *know the heart*; he knows who they are that *believe not*, but dissemble in their profession. If we pretend to judge men's hearts, we step into Christ's throne. We are often deceived in men, and see cause to change our sentiments of them.

Secondly, The reason why they did not believe his report was because the *arm of the Lord* was not *revealed* to them (*v.* 65): *Therefore said I unto you that no man can come to me, except it be given unto him of my Father;* referring to *v.* 44. There he had said that none could *come to him, except the Father draw him*; here he saith, *except it be given him of my Father*, which shows that God *draws* souls by giving them grace and strength, and a heart to come.

3. We have here their final apostasy from Christ hereupon: *From that time many of his disciples went back, and walked no more with him*, *v.* 66: the *backsliding* of these *disciples*. They had entered themselves in Christ's school, but they *went back*, did not only play truant for once, but took leave of him. Here were *many* that *went back*. It is often so; when some backslide many backslide with them; the disease is infectious. The occasion of this backsliding: *From that time*, from the time that Christ preached this comfortable doctrine, that he is the *bread of life*, and that those who by faith feed *upon him* shall live *by him*. The corrupt and wicked heart of man often makes that an occasion of offence which is indeed matter of the greatest comfort. That which is the undoubted word and truth of Christ must be faithfully delivered, whoever may be offended at it. Men's humours must be captivated to God's word, and not God's word accommodated to men's. The degree of their apostasy: *They walked no more with him*, returned no more to him and attended no more upon his ministry.

II. This discourse was to others a *savour of life unto life*. *Many went back*, but, thanks be to God, all did not.

1. The affectionate question which Christ put to the twelve (*v.* 67): *Will you also go away?* He saith nothing to those who went back. It was no great *loss* of those whom he never *had*; lightly come, lightly go; but he takes this occasion to speak to the twelve, to confirm them: *Will you also go away?* (1) "It is *at your choice* whether you will or no; if you will forsake me, now is the time, when so many do." Christ will detain none with him against their wills; his soldiers are volunteers, not pressed men. The twelve had now had time enough to try how they liked Christ and his doctrine. He here allows them a power of revocation, and leaves them at their liberty. (2) "It is *at your peril* if you do go away." They have not been so intimate with me as you have been, nor received so many favours from me; they are gone, but will *you* also go? The nearer we have been to Christ and the longer we have been with him, the more mercies we have received from him the greater will be our sin if we desert him. (3) "I have reason *to think you will not. I hope better things of you,* for *you are they that have continued with me*," Luke xxii. 28. Christ and believers know one another too well to part upon every displeasure.

2. The believing reply which Peter, in the name of the rest, made to this question, *v.* 68, 69. Peter was upon all occasions the *mouth of the rest*, not so much because he had more of his Master's ear than they, but because he had more tongue of his own; and what he said was sometimes approved and sometimes reprimanded (Matt. xvi. 17, 23)—the common lot of those who are swift to speak. Here is a good resolution to adhere to Christ: "*Lord, to whom shall we go?* No, Lord, we like our choice too well to change." Those who leave Christ would do well to consider to whom they will go. "*Whither shall we go?* Shall we make our court to the world? It will certainly *deceive* us. Shall we return to sin? It will certainly *destroy* us. Shall we leave the *fountain of living waters* for *broken cisterns*?" The disciples resolve to continue their pursuit of life and happiness, and will adhere to Christ as their guide. "If ever we find the way to happiness, it must be in following thee." Let those who find fault with this religion find a better before they quit it. Here is a good reason

JAMIESON, FAUSSET, BROWN

64. But there are some . . .—i.e., "But it matters little to some of you in what sense I speak, for ye believe not." This was said, adds the Evangelist, not merely of the outer but of the inner circle of His disciples; for He knew the traitor, though it was not yet time to expose him.

65. **Therefore said I . . .**—i.e., "That was why I spoke to you of the necessity of divine teaching which some of you are strangers to." **except it were given him**—plainly showing that by the Father's "drawing" (vs. 44) was meant an *internal* and *efficacious* operation, for in recalling the statement here He says, it must be "*given* to a man to come" to Christ. **66-71. From that time . . .**—or, in consequence of this. Those last words of our Lord seemed to have given them the finishing stroke—they could not stand it any longer.

walked no more—Many a journey, it may be, they had taken with Him, but now they gave Him up finally!

67. **the twelve**—the first time they are thus mentioned in this Gospel. **Will ye also go away?**—Affecting appeal! Evidently Christ *felt* the desertion of Him even by those miserable men who could not abide His statements; and seeing a disturbance even of the *wheat* by the violence of the wind which blew away the *chaff* (not yet visibly showing itself, but open to His eyes of fire), He would *nip it in the bud* by this home question.

68. Then Simon Peter—whose forwardness in this case was noble, and to the wounded spirit of His Lord doubtless very grateful. **Lord, to whom . . .**—i.e., 'We cannot deny that *we* have been staggered as well as they, and seeing so many go away who, as we thought, might have been retained by teaching a little less hard to take in, our own endurance has been severely tried, nor have we been able to stop short of the question, Shall *we* follow the rest, and give it up? But when it came to this, our light returned, and our hearts were reassured. For as soon as we thought of going away, there arose upon us that awful question, "To WHOM shall we go?" To the lifeless formalism and wretched traditions of the elders? to the gods many and lords many of the

ADAM CLARKE

64. *But there are some of you that believe not.* This is addressed to Judas, and to those disciples who left Him, v. 66. *And who should betray him.* Or "who would deliver Him up."

65. *Therefore said I unto you.* V. 44; see the note there. *Except it were given unto him.* None can come at first unless he be drawn by the Father; and none can continue unless he continue under those sacred influences which God gives only to those who do not receive His first graces in vain. Augustine himself grants that it was the sole fault of these disciples that they did not believe and were saved. "If I be asked why these could not believe, I immediately answer, because they would not."

66. *Many of his disciples went back.* They no longer associated with Him nor professed to acknowledge Him as the Messiah. None of these were of the twelve.

67. *Will ye also go away?* Or, "Do ye also desire?" These words are very emphatic. Will you abandon Me?—you, whom I have distinguished with innumerable marks of My affection—you, whom I have chosen out of the world to be My companions—you, to whom I have revealed the secrets of the eternal world—you, who have been witnesses of all My miracles—you, whom I intend to seat with Me on My throne in glory; will you go away?

68. *Simon Peter answered.* With his usual zeal and readiness, speaking in behalf of the whole, *To whom shall we go?* Where shall we find a more gracious master—a more powerful redeemer—a more suitable saviour? *Thou* [*alone*] *hast the words of eternal life.*

MATTHEW HENRY

for this resolution. It was not the inconsiderate resolve of a blind affection, but the result of mature deliberation. The disciples were resolved never to go away from Christ because of the *advantage* they promised themselves by him: *Thou hast the words of eternal life.* The word of his doctrine showed the way to *eternal life*, and directed us what to do, that we might inherit it. His *having the words of eternal life* is the same with his having *power to give eternal life.* He had in the foregoing discourse assured *eternal life* to his followers; these disciples fastened upon this plain saying, and therefore resolved to stick to him, when the others overlooked this, and fastened upon the *hard sayings*, and therefore forsook him. Though we cannot account for every mystery, every obscurity, in Christ's doctrine, yet we know that it is the word of eternal life, and therefore must live and die by it. Because of the assurance they had concerning him (*v.* 69): *We believe, and are sure, that thou art that Christ.* The *doctrine* they believed: that this Jesus was the Messiah promised to the fathers, and that he was not a mere man, but the Son of the living God. The *degree* of their faith: it rose up to a full assurance: *We are sure.* When we have so strong a faith in the gospel of Christ as boldly to venture our souls *upon it*, then, and not till then, we shall be willing to venture everything else for it.

3. The melancholy remark which our Lord Jesus made upon this reply of Peter's (*v.* 70, 71): *Have not I chosen you twelve, and one of you is a devil?* And the evangelist tells us whom he meant: *he spoke of Judas Iscariot.* Peter had undertaken for them all that they would be faithful to their Master. Now Christ does not condemn his charity (it is always good to hope the best), but he tacitly corrects his confidence. We must not be too sure concerning any. God knows those that are his; we do not. Hypocrites and betrayers of Christ are no better than devils. Judas, into whose *heart* Satan entered, and filled it, is called a *devil.* Many that are *seeming* saints are *real* devils. It is *strange*, and to be wondered at; *Christ* speaks of it with wonder: *Have not I?* It is *sad*, and to be lamented. The disguises of hypocrites however they may deceive men cannot deceive Christ. Christ's *divine sight*, far better than any *double sight*, can see spirits. There are those who are chosen by Christ to special services who yet prove false to him: *I have chosen you* and yet one of *you* is a devil. In the most *select* societies on this side heaven it is no new thing to meet with those that are corrupt. Of the twelve that were chosen to an intimate conversation with an *incarnate Deity*, one was an *incarnate devil.* The historian lays an emphasis upon this, that Judas was *one of the twelve* that were so dignified and distinguished. Let us not reject the twelve because *one of them is a devil.* There is a society within the veil into which no unclean thing shall enter.

JAMIESON, FAUSSET, BROWN

heathen around us? or to blank unbelief? Nay, Lord, we are shut up. *They* have none of that "ETERNAL LIFE" to offer us whereof Thou hast been discoursing, in words rich and ravishing as well as in words staggering to human wisdom. That life we cannot want; that life we have learnt to crave as a necessity of the deeper nature which Thou hast awakened: "*the words* of that eternal life" (the authority to *reveal* it and the power to confer it). Thou hast: Therefore will we stay with Thee—"we *must.*"

69. And we believe . . .—(See on Matt. 16:16). Peter seems to have added this not merely—probably not so much—as an assurance *to his Lord* of his heart's belief in Him, as for the purpose of fortifying *himself* and his faithful brethren against that *recoil* from his Lord's harsh statements which he was probably struggling against with difficulty at that moment. N.B.—There are seasons when one's faith is tried to the utmost, particularly by speculative difficulties; the spiritual eye then swims, and all truth seems ready to depart from us. At such seasons, a clear perception that to abandon the faith of Christ is *to face black desolation, ruin and death;* and on recoiling from this, to be able to fall back, not merely on *first principles and immovable foundations,* but on *personal experience of a Living Lord in whom all truth is wrapt up and made flesh for our very benefit*—this is a relief unspeakable. Under that blessed Wing taking shelter, until we are again fit to grapple with the questions that have staggered us, we at length either find our way through them, or attain to a calm satisfaction in the discovery that they lie beyond the limits of present apprehension. **70. Have not I chosen . . . and one of you is a devil:**—'Well said, Simon-Barjonas, but that "we" embraces not so wide a circle as in the simplicity of thine heart thou thinkest; for though I have chosen you but twelve, one even of these is a "devil" ' (the temple, the tool of that wicked one).

ADAM CLARKE

69. *We believe.* On the authority of Thy word; *and are sure*—"have known," by the evidence of Thy miracles, *that thou art that Christ,* the promised Messiah. Instead of *Christ, the Son of the living God,* some excellent MSS. read "the holy one of God."

70. *Have not I chosen you twelve?* Have I not, in an especial manner, called you to believe in My name, and chosen you to be My disciples, and the propagators of My doctrine? *Nevertheless, one of you is a devil,* or "accuser," enlisted on the side of Satan, who was a murderer from the beginning.

71. *He spake of Judas . . . for he it was that should betray him.* "He who was about to deliver Him up." By referring to this matter so often, did not our blessed Lord intend to warn Judas? Was not the evil fully exposed to his view? And who dare say that it was impossible for him to avoid what he had so often been warned against?

CHAPTER 7

Verses 1–13

I. The reason given why Christ spent more of his time in Galilee than in Judæa (*v.* 1): *because the Jews*, the people in Judæa and Jerusalem, sought to *kill him*, for curing the impotent man on the sabbath day, *ch.* v. 16. It is not said, He *durst not*, but, He *would not*, walk in Jewry; it was not through fear and cowardice that he declined it, but in *prudence*, because his hour was not yet come. Christ will withdraw from those that drive him from them. In times of imminent peril it is not only *allowable*, but *advisable*, to *withdraw*, and to choose the service of those places which are least perilous, Matt. x. 23. If the providence of God casts persons of *merit* into places of obscurity and little note, it must not be thought strange; it was the lot of our Master himself. He did not sit still in Galilee, but *walked*; he went about doing good. When we cannot do *what* and *where* we *would*, we must do *what* and *where* we *can*.

II. The approach of the *feast of tabernacles* (*v.* 2), one of the three solemnities which called for the personal attendance of all the males at Jerusalem. This feast was still religiously observed. Divine institutions are never antiquated, nor go out of date, by length of time: nor must wilderness mercies ever be forgotten.

III. Christ's discourse with his *brethren.* They interposed to advise him in his conduct.

1. Their ambition and vain-glory in urging him to make a more public appearance than he did: "*Depart hence,*" said they, "*and go into Judæa*" (*v.* 3).

(1) They give two reasons for this advice: That it would be an encouragement to those in and about Jerusalem. They would have had the disciples *there* particularly countenanced, and thought the time

CHAPTER 7

Vss. 1-53. CHRIST AT THE FEAST OF TABERNACLES. **1, 2. After these things**—i.e., *all that is recorded after ch.* 5:18. **walked in Galilee**—continuing His labors there, instead of going to Judea, as might have been expected. **sought to kill him . . .**—referring back to ch. 5:18. *Hence it appears that our Lord did not attend the Passover mentioned in* ch. 6:4—being the *third* since His ministry began, if the feast mentioned in ch. 5:1 was a Passover.

2. feast of tabernacles . . . at hand—This was the last of the three annual festivals, celebrated on the 15th of the 7th month (September). (See Lev. 23:33, etc.; Deut. 16:13, etc.; Neh. 8:14-18).

3-5. His brethren said—(See on Matt. 13:54-56). **Depart . . . into Judea . . .**—In vs. 5 this speech is as-

CHAPTER 7

1. *After these things.* John passes from the preceding discourse of our Lord, which He delivered a little before the Passover, chap. vi. 4, to the Feast of Tabernacles, which happened six months after, and thus omits many things mentioned by the other Evangelists which our blessed Lord said and did during that time. He had already gone over Galilee four or five times; and He continued there, because He found that the hatred of the Jews was such that they would kill Him if they could meet with Him in Judea; and His time to suffer was not yet come. *For he would not walk in Jewry.* He found greater scope for the exercise of His important ministry in Galilee than in Judea, as the chief priests were continually plotting His death.

2. *Feast of tabernacles.* This feast was celebrated on the fifteenth day of the month *Tisri,* answering to the last half of our September and the first half of October. This month was the seventh of the ecclesiastical, and first of the civil, year. The feast took its name from the tents which were erected about the Temple, in public places, in courts, on the flat roofs of their houses, and in gardens; in which the Jews dwelt for eight days, in commemoration of the forty years during which their fathers dwelt in the wilderness. It was one of the three solemn annual feasts in which all the males were obliged, by the law, to appear at Jerusalem. This feast was celebrated in the following manner. All the people cut down branches of palm trees,

MATTHEW HENRY

he spent among his Galilean disciples wasted and thrown away, and his miracles turning to no account unless those at Jerusalem saw them. That it would be for the advancement of his name, *There is no man that does anything in secret* if he himself *seeks to be known* openly. They took it for granted that Christ sought to make himself known: "*If thou do these things*, venture abroad, and *show thyself to the world*. It is high time to think of being *great*."

(2) The evangelist notes it is an evidence of their infidelity: *For neither did his brethren believe in him* (*v.* 5). They that hear his word and keep it are the kindred he values. There were those who were akin to Christ according to the flesh who did believe in him, and yet others did not believe in him.

(3) What was there amiss in the advice which they gave him? It was a sign that they *did not believe him* able to guide them, when they did not think him sufficient to guide himself. They discovered a great carelessness about his safety, when they would have him go to Judæa, where they knew the Jews sought to kill him. Perhaps they were weary of his company in Galilee, and this was, in effect, a desire that he would *depart out of their coasts*. They tacitly reproach him as *mean-spirited*, that he durst not trust himself upon the stage of public action, which, if he had any courage and *greatness of soul*, he would do, and not sneak thus and skulk in a corner. They seem to question the truth of the miracles he wrought, in saying, "*If thou do these things*, if they will bear the test of a public scrutiny in the courts above, produce them there." They think Christ altogether such a one as themselves, and as desirous as they to *make a fair show in the flesh*. Self was at the bottom of all; if he would make himself as great as he might, they, being his kinsmen, should share in his honour. Many go to public ordinances, only to *show themselves*, and all their care is to make a *good appearance*.

2. The prudence and humility of our Lord Jesus, *v.* 6–8. Though there were so many base insinuations in it, he answered them mildly. We should learn of our Master to reply with meekness, and where it is easy to find much amiss, to seem not to see it, and wink at the affront.

(1) He shows the difference between himself and them, in two things: [1] His *time* was *set*, so was not *theirs*: *My time is not yet come, but your time is always ready*. Those who live useless lives have *their time always ready*; they can go and come when they please. But those whose *time* is filled up with *duty* will often find themselves *straitened*, and they have *not yet time* for that which others can do *at any time*. The confinement of business is a thousand times better than the liberty of idleness. We, who are ignorant and short-sighted, are apt to prescribe to him. The present time is *our* time, but he is fittest to judge, and, it may be, *his time is not yet come*. Therefore wait with patience for *his time*. [2] His *life* was *sought*, so was not *theirs*, *v.* 7. They, in *showing themselves* to the world, did not expose themselves: "*The world cannot hate you*, for you are *of the world*." Unholy souls, whom the holy God *cannot love*, the world that lies in wickedness *cannot hate*; but Christ, in showing himself to the world, laid himself open to the greatest danger; for *me it hateth*. Christ was not only *slighted*, but *hated*. But why did the world hate Christ? "Because" (saith he), "*I testify of it, that the works of it are evil*." The works of an evil world are *evil works*; as the tree is, so are the fruits. It is a great uneasiness and provocation to the world to be convicted of the evil of its works. Whatever is *pretended*, the *real* cause of the world's enmity to the gospel is the testimony it bears against sin and sinners. It is better to incur the world's hatred, by testifying against its wickedness, than gain its good-will by going down the stream with it.

(2) He dismisses them, with a design to stay behind for some time in Galilee (*v.* 8): *Go you up to this feast, I go not up yet*. He allows their going to the feast. He denies them his company. Those who go to ordinances for ostentation, or to serve some secular purpose, go without Christ, and will speed accordingly. If the presence of Christ go not with us, to what purpose should we go up? When we are going to, or coming from, solemn ordinances, it becomes us to be careful what company we *have* and *choose*, lest the coal of good affections be quenched by corrupt communications. *I go not up yet to this feast;* he does not say, I will not go up at all, but not yet. The reason he gives is, *My time is not yet fully come*.

3. Christ's continuance in Galilee till his *full time* was come, *v.* 9. He, saying these things to them, *abode still in Galilee*. He would not depart from his own purpose. It becomes the followers of Christ thus to be *steady*, and not to *use lightness*.

4. His going up to the feast when his time was come. (1) *When* he went: *When his brethren were*

JAMIESON, FAUSSET, BROWN

cribed to their *unbelief*. But as they were in the "upper room" among the one hundred and twenty disciples who waited for the descent of the Spirit after the Lord's ascension (Acts 1:14), they seem to have had their prejudices removed, perhaps after His resurrection. Indeed here their language is more that of strong prejudice and suspicion (*such as near relatives, even the best, too frequently show in such cases*), than from unbelief. There was also, probably, a tincture of *vanity* in it. 'Thou hast many disciples in Judea; here in Galilee they are fast dropping off; it is not like one who advances the claims Thou dost to linger so long here, away from the city of our solemnities, where surely "the kingdom of our father David" is to be set up: "seeking," as Thou dost, "to be known openly," those miracles of Thine ought not to be confined to this distant corner, but submitted at headquarters to the inspection of "the world."' (See Ps. 69:8, "I am become a stranger to *my brethren*, an alien unto *my mother's children*!")

6-10. My time is not yet come—i.e., for showing Himself to the world. **your time is always ready**—i.e., 'It matters little when we go up, for ye have no great plans in life, and nothing hangs upon your movements. With Me it is otherwise; on every movement of Mine there hangs what ye know not. The world has no quarrel with you, for ye bear no testimony against it, and so draw down upon yourselves none of its wrath; but I am here to lift up My voice against its hypocrisy, and denounce its abominations; therefore it cannot endure Me, and one false step might precipitate its fury on its Victim's head before the time. Away, therefore, to the feast as soon as it suits you; I follow at the fitting moment, but "My time is not yet full come."'

ADAM CLARKE

willows, and myrtles (and tied them together with gold and silver cords, or with ribbons), which they carried with them all day, took them into their synagogues and kept them by them while at prayers. On the other days of the feast they carried them with them into the Temple and walked round the altar with them in their hands, singing, "Hosanna!" i.e., "Save, we beseech Thee!" —the trumpets sounding on all sides. To this feast John seems to refer, Rev. vii. 9-10, where he represents the saints standing before the throne, with palm branches in their hands, singing, "Salvation to God." On the seventh day of the feast, they went seven times round the altar, and this was called the "great Hosanna." But the ceremony at which the Jews testified most joy was that of pouring out the water, which was done on the eighth day of the feast. A priest drew some water out of the Pool of Siloam, in a golden vessel, and brought it into the Temple; and at the time of the morning sacrifice, while the members of the sacrifice were on the altar, he went up and poured this water mingled with wine upon it, the people all the while singing, with transports of joy, Isaiah xii, especially v. 6: "With joy shall ye draw water out of the wells of salvation." To this part of the ceremony our Lord appears to allude in v. 37 of this chapter.

3. *His brethren . . . said*. It is generally supposed that these were the children of the sisters of his mother, Mary; but some of the ancients have stated that Joseph had several children by a former wife. No solid proof can be alleged against this, nor can we pretend to say that these were not the children of Joseph and Mary. Our blessed Lord, it is true, was her Firstborn, while she was yet a virgin; but no man can prove that He was her last.

4. *No man that doeth any thing in secret*. They took it for granted that Christ was influenced by the same spirit which themselves felt, and that therefore He should use every opportunity of exhibiting himself to the public, that He might get into repute; and they hoped that a part of His honor would be reflected back upon themselves, as being His near relations.

5. *Neither did his brethren believe in him*. They did not receive Him as the promised Messiah; but, having seen so many of His miracles, they could not but consider Him as an eminent prophet. They supposed that if He were the Messiah He would wish to manifest himself as such to the world; and because He did not do so they did not believe that He was the Salvation of Israel.

6. *My time is not yet come*. It is probable our Lord meant no more than this, that He had some business to transact before He could go to Jerusalem; but His brethren, having nothing to hinder them, might set off immediately. Others think He spoke of His passion: My time of suffering is not yet come. as you are still in friendship with the world, you need not be under any apprehension of danger; you may go when you please. The first sense I think is the best.

7. *The world cannot hate you*. The Jews will not persecute you, because you are in their sentiments and interests. *But me it hateth*. Because I condemn its injustice, its pride, its ambition, and its maxims by My life and doctrine. It is very likely that the term *world* means here the Jewish people only.

8. *I go not up yet unto this feast*. Porphyry accuses our blessed Lord of falsehood, because He said here, I will not go to this feast, and yet afterwards He went; and some interpreters have made more ado than was necessary in order to reconcile this seeming contradiction. To me the whole seems very simple and plain. Our Lord did not say, "I will not go to this feast"; but merely, I go not yet or am not "going," i.e., at present; because, as He said in v. 6 and repeats here, His time was not yet come—He had other business to transact before He could go.

MATTHEW HENRY

gone up. He went up *after them*. His carnal brethren went up *first*, and then he went. It is not, Who comes *first*? that will be the question, but, Who come *fittest*? If we bring our hearts *with us*, it is no matter who gets *before us*. (2) *How* he went, *as if he were hiding himself: not openly, but as it were in secret*. Provided the work of God be done effectually, it is best done when done with *least noise*. We may do the work of God *privately*, and yet not do it *deceitfully*.

5. The great expectation that there was of him among the Jews at Jerusalem, *v.* 11–14. They could not but think of him (*v.* 11): *The Jews sought him at the feast, and said, Where is he?* They hoped the feast would bring him to Jerusalem, and then they should see him. If an opportunity of acquaintance with Christ come to their door, they can like it well enough. They *sought him at the feast*. Those who would *see* Christ at a feast must *seek* him there. Perhaps it was his enemies that were thus waiting an opportunity to seize him. They said, *Where is he?—where is that fellow?* Thus scornfully and contemptibly do they speak of him. When they should have welcomed the feast as an opportunity of serving God, they were glad of it as an opportunity of persecuting Christ. The people differed much in their sentiments concerning him (*v.* 12): *There was much murmuring*, or *muttering*, rather *among the people concerning him*. The enmity of the rulers against Christ caused him to be so much the more talked of. This ground the gospel of Christ has got by the opposition made to it. By being *everywhere spoken against*, it has come to be everywhere *spoken of*, and by this means has been spread the further. This murmuring was not *against* Christ, but *concerning* him; some murmured at the rulers, because they did not countenance and encourage him: others murmured at them, because they did not silence and restrain him. Christ and his religion have been, and will be, the subject of much controversy, and debate, Luke xii. 51, 52. But the noise and rencounter of liberty and business are preferable, surely, to the silence and agreement of a prison. Some said, *He is a good man*. This was a truth, but it was far short of being the *whole truth*. He was the *Son of God*. Many who have no *ill* thoughts of Christ have yet *low* thoughts of him, they do not *say enough*. Even those who would not believe him to be the Messiah could not but own he was a *good man*. Others said, *Nay, but he deceiveth the people*; if this had been true, he had been a very bad man. It must be taken for granted that there was some undiscovered cheat at the bottom, because it was the interest of the chief priests to oppose him and run him down. They were frightened by their superiors from speaking much of him (*v.* 13): *No man spoke openly of him, for fear of the Jews*. Either, they durst not openly speak *well* of him. Or they durst not speak *at all* of him openly. Because nothing could justly be said *against* him, they would not suffer anything to be said *of* him.

Verses 14–36

I. Christ's public preaching in the temple (*v.* 14): He *went up into the temple, and taught*. His sermon is not recorded. But that which is observable here is that it was *about the midst of the feast*. Why did he not go to the temple *sooner*, to preach? Because the people would have more leisure to hear him when they had spent some days in their booths. Because he would choose to appear when both his friends and his enemies had done looking for him. But why did he appear thus publicly now? Surely it was to *shame* his persecutors. By showing that he did not fear them; by taking their work out of their hands. Their office was to teach the people in the temple. But they taught for doctrines the commandments of men, and therefore he goes up to the temple and teaches the people.

II. His discourse with the Jews hereupon.

1. Concerning *his doctrine*.

(1) How the Jews *admired* it (*v.* 15): *They marvelled*, saying, *How knoweth this man letters, having never learned?* Our Lord Jesus was not educated in the schools of the prophets, or at the feet of the rabbin. Having received the Spirit *without measure*, he needed not to receive any knowledge *from man, or by man*. Christ *had letters*, though he had never *learned* them. It is necessary that Christ's ministers should have *learning*, and since they cannot expect to have it by inspiration, they must take pains to get it in an ordinary way. Christ's having learning, though he had not been taught it, made him truly great and wonderful. Some, it is likely, took notice of it to his honour. Others, probably, mentioned it in disparagement and contempt of him: Whatever he *seems* to have, he cannot really have any true learning, for he was never at the university, nor took his degree. Some perhaps suggested that he had got his learning

JAMIESON, FAUSSET, BROWN

10. then went he . . . not openly—not "in the (caravan) company" [MEYER]. See on Luke 2:44.) **as it were in secret**—rather, in a manner secretly; perhaps by some other route, and in a way not to attract notice.

11-13. Jews—the rulers—**sought him**—for no good end. Where is He?—He had not been at Jerusalem for probably *a year and a half*.

12. much murmuring—buzzing. **among the people**—the multitudes; the natural expression of a Jewish writer, indicating without design the crowded state of Jerusalem at this festival [WEBSTER and WILKINSON].

a good man . . . Nay . . . deceiveth . . .—the two opposite views of His claims, that they were *honest*, and that they were an *imposture*. **none spake openly of him**—i.e., in His favor, "for fear of the [*ruling*] Jews."

14, 15. about the midst of the feast—the fourth or fifth day of the eight, during which it lasted. **went up into the temple and taught**—The word denotes *formal* and *continuous teaching*, as *distinguished* from mere casual sayings. This was probably *the first time* that He did so thus openly in Jerusalem. He had kept back till the feast was half through, to let the stir about Him subside, and entering the city unexpectedly, had begun His "teaching" at the temple, and created a certain awe, before the wrath of the rulers had time to break it.

15. How knoweth . . . letters—learning (Acts 26:24). **having never learned**—at any rabbinical school, as Paul under Gamaliel. These rulers knew well enough that He had not *studied* under any human teacher—an important admission against ancient and modern attempts to trace our Lord's wisdom to human sources [MEYER]. Probably His teaching on this occasion was *expository*, manifesting that unrivalled faculty and depth which in the Sermon on the Mount had excited the astonishment of all.

ADAM CLARKE

11. *Then the Jews sought him*. By Jews here are to be understood the scribes, Pharisees, and rulers of the people, and not the inhabitants of the province of Judea.

12. *Some said, He is a good man*. The multitude were divided in their opinions concerning Him. Those who knew Him best said. *He is a good man*. Those who spoke according to the character given Him by the priests said, *Nay; but he deceiveth the people*.

15. *How knoweth this man letters, having never learned?* The Jewish learning consisted in the knowledge of their own Scriptures and the traditions of their elders. As these branches of learning were taught at the Jewish schools, and our Lord had never attended there, they were astonished to find Him excelling in that sort of learning of which they themselves professed to be the sole teachers.

MATTHEW HENRY

by magic arts. Since they know not how he could be a scholar, they will think him a conjuror.

(2) What he *asserted* concerning it; three things:

[1] That his *doctrine* is *divine* (*v.* 16): *My doctrine is not mine, but his that sent me.* They were offended because he undertook to *teach* though he had never learned, in answer to which he tells them that his doctrine was such as was not to be *learned.* It was a *divine revelation.* "*My doctrine is not mine,* but *his that sent me*; it does not centre in myself, nor lead ultimately to myself, but to him that sent me."

[2] That the most competent judges are those that with a sincere and upright heart desire and endeavour to do the will of God (*v.* 17): *If any man be willing to do the will of God he shall know of the doctrine whether it be of God or whether I speak of myself. First,* What the question is, concerning the doctrine of Christ, *whether it be of God* or no. Christ himself was willing to have his doctrine enquired into, much more should his ministers. *Secondly,* Who are likely to succeed in this search: those that *do the will of God,* at least are desirous to do it. Who they are that *will do the will of God.* Such as are resolved by the grace of God, when they find out what the will of God is, to conform to it. Whence it is that such a one shall know of the truth of Christ's doctrine. Christ has promised to *give knowledge* to such; he hath said, *He shall know.* Those who improve the light they have shall be secured by divine grace. He that is inclined to submit to the rules of the divine law is disposed to admit the rays of divine light.

[3] That hereby it appeared that Christ, as a teacher, did not speak *of himself, v.* 18. See here the character of a deceiver: he *seeketh his own glory,* which is a sign that he *speaks of himself.* Here is the description of the *cheat*: they *speak of themselves,* and have no commission nor instructions from God; no warrant but their own will, no inspiration but their own imagination. They consult purely *their own glory*; self-seekers are self-speakers. Those who speak *from God* will speak *for God,* and for his glory. See the contrary character Christ gives of himself and his doctrine: *He that seeks his glory that sent him, he is true.* He was *sent of God.* Those teachers, and those only, who are sent of God, are to be received and entertained by us. He *sought the glory of God.* It was both the tendency of his doctrine and the tenor of his whole conversation to *glorify God.* This was a proof that he was *true.* False teachers are most *unrighteous*; they are unjust to God whose name they abuse, and unjust to the souls of men whom they impose upon. But Christ made it appear that he was *true,* that he was really what he said he was.

2. They discourse concerning the *crime* that was laid to his charge for curing the impotent man, and bidding him carry his bed on the sabbath day. He argues against them by way of *recrimination, v.* 19. How could they for shame censure him for a breach of the law of Moses, when they themselves were such notorious breakers of it? *Did not Moses give you the law?* But it was their wickedness that *none of them kept the law.* Their neglect of the law was universal: *None of you keepeth* it. They boasted of the law, and pretended a zeal for it, and yet none of them kept it; like those who say that they are for the church, and yet never go to church. It was an aggravation of their wickedness, in persecuting Christ; "*None of you keepeth the law,* why then go ye about to kill me for not keeping it?" Those are commonly most censorious of others who are most faulty themselves. Those that support themselves and their interest by persecution and violence, whatever they pretend, are not keepers of the law of God.

Here the *people* rudely interrupted him (*v.* 20): *Thou hast a devil; who goes about to kill thee?* This intimates the *good opinion* they had of their rulers, who, they think, would never attempt so atrocious a thing as to kill him. The *ill opinion* they had of our Lord Jesus: "*Thou hast a devil,* thou art possessed with a lying spirit, and art a *bad man* for saying so"; so some: or rather, "Thou art melancholy, and art a *weak man*; thou frightenest thyself with causeless fears." Not only open frenzies, but silent melancholies were then commonly imputed to the power of Satan. "Thou art crazed, hast a distempered brain." Let us not think it strange if the best of men are put under the worst of characters. Those who would be like Christ must put up with affronts, must not *regard* them, much less *resent* them, and least of all *revenge* them. He argues by way of appeal and vindication.

(1) He appeals to *their own sentiments* of this miracle: "*I have done one work, and you all marvel, v.* 21. You cannot choose but marvel at it as truly great."

(2) He appeals to their own practice in other instances: "*I have done one work* on the sabbath, and you all marvel, you make a mighty strange thing of

JAMIESON, FAUSSET, BROWN

16-18. doctrine . . . not mine . . .—i.e., from Myself unauthorized; I am here by commission.

17. If any man will do his will . . .—'is willing,' or 'wishes to do.' **whether . . . of God or . . . of myself**—from above or from beneath; is divine or an imposture of Mine. A principle of immense importance, showing, on the one hand, that *singleness of desire to please God is the grand inlet to light on all questions vitally affecting one's eternal interests,* and on the other, that *the want of his,* whether perceived or not, *is the chief cause of infidelity amidst the light of revealed religion.* **18. seeketh his own glory . . .**—(See on ch. 5:41-44).

19, 20. Did not Moses . . .—i.e., In opposing Me ye pretend zeal for Moses, but to the spirit and end of that law which he gave ye are total strangers, and in "going about to kill Me" ye are its greatest enemies.

20. The people answered, Thou hast a devil: who goeth about to kill thee?—This was said by *the multitude,* who as yet had no bad feeling to Jesus, and were not in the secret of the plot hatching, as our Lord knew, against Him.

21-24. I have done one work . . .—Taking no notice of the popular appeal, as there were those there who knew well enough what He meant, He recalls His cure of the impotent man, and the murderous rage it had kindled (ch. 5:9, 16, 18). It may seem strange

ADAM CLARKE

16. *My doctrine is not mine.* Our blessed Lord, in the character of Messiah, might as well say, *My doctrine is not mine,* as an ambassador might say, I speak not my own words, but his who sent me.

17. *If any man will do his will.* I will give you a sure rule by which you may judge of My doctrine: If you really wish to do the will of God, begin the practice of it; and take My doctrine and apply it to all that you know God requires of man.

18. *He that speaketh of himself.* I will give you another rule whereby you shall know whether I am from God or not: If I speak so as to procure My own glory, to gratify vanity, or to secure and promote My secular interests, then reject Me as a deceiver and as a false prophet. *And no unrighteousness is in him.* Or, "There is no falsehood in him."

19. *Did not Moses give you the law?* The scribes and Pharisees announced our Lord to the multitude as a deceiver; and they grounded their calumny on this, that He was not an exact observer of the law, for He had healed a man on the Sabbath day, chap. v. 9-10, and consequently must be a false prophet. Now they insinuated that the interests of religion required Him to be put to death (1) as a violator of the law and (2) as a false prophet and deceiver of the people. To destroy this evil reasoning our Lord speaks in this wise; If I deserve death for curing a man on the Sabbath and desiring him to carry home his bed, which you consider a violation of the law, you are more culpable than I am, for you circumcise a child on the Sabbath, which requires much more bustle and is of so much less use than what I have done to the infirm man.

21. *I have done one work.* That of curing the impotent man, already referred to. See chap. v. 9. *And ye all marvel.* Or, "You all marvel because of this."

MATTHEW HENRY

it, that a religious man should dare do such a thing. If it be lawful for you, nay, and your duty, to circumcise a child on the sabbath day, much more was it lawful and good for me to heal a diseased man on that day."

First, The rise and origin of circumcision: *Moses gave you circumcision.* Circumcision is said to *be given*, and (*v.* 23) they are said to *receive it.* The ordinances of God, and particularly those which are seals of the covenant, are *gifts given to men*, and are to be received as such. Moses did not give it them, but God; nay, it was not of Moses first, but *of the fathers, v.* 22. It was ordained long before, for it was a seal of the righteousness of faith, and was part of that blessing of Abraham which was to come upon the Gentiles.

Secondly, The respect paid to the law of circumcision above that of the sabbath. If a child was born one sabbath day it was without fail circumcised the next.

Thirdly, The inference Christ draws hence in justification of himself (*v.* 23): *A man-child on the sabbath day receives circumcision, that the law of circumcision might not be broken.* "Now, if this be allowed by yourselves, how unreasonable are you, who are *angry with me because I have made a man every whit whole on the sabbath day*!" It was a spiteful anger, anger with gall in it. It is very absurd and unreasonable for us to condemn others for that in which we justify ourselves. Observe the comparison Christ here makes between their *circumcising a child* and his *healing a man* on the sabbath day. Circumcision was but a ceremonial institution. What Christ did was a good work by the law of nature. Circumcision *made sore*; but what Christ did made whole. Whereas, when they had circumcised a child, their care was only to heal up that part which was circumcised, which might be done and yet the child remain under other illnesses, Christ had made this man *every whit whole. I have made the whole man healthful* and sound. The *whole body* was *healed.* Nay, Christ not only healed his body, but his soul too, by that admonition, *Go, and sin no more*, and so indeed made the *whole man* sound.

He concludes this argument with that rule (*v.* 24): *Judge not according to the appearance, but judge righteous judgment.* This may be applied, either, *First*, In particular, to this work. Be not partial in your judgment; judge not *with respect of persons.* Or, *Secondly*, In general, to Christ's person and preaching, which they were offended at. Those things that are false commonly appear best when they are judged of *according to the outward appearance*, they appear most plausible *prima facie—at the first glance.* It was this that gained the Pharisees such an interest and reputation, that they *appeared right* unto men (Matt. xxiii. 27, 28), and men judged of them by that appearance. "But," saith Christ, "be not too confident that all are real saints who are seeming ones." Those who undertook to judge whether he was the Son of God or no by his *outward appearance* were not likely to *judge righteous judgment.* If a divine power accompanied him, and God bore him witness, and the scriptures were fulfilled in him, they ought to receive him, and to judge by faith, and not by the sight of the eye. We must not judge concerncerning any by their *outward appearance*, not by their titles, the figure they make in the world, and their fluttering show, but by their intrinsic worth, and the gifts and graces of God's Spirit in them.

3. Christ discourses with them here concerning *himself*, whence he came, and whither he was going, *v.* 25–36.

(1) *Whence he came, v.* 25–31.

[1] The objection concerning this stated by some of the inhabitants of Jerusalem, who seem to have been of all others most prejudiced against him, *v.* 25. Our Lord Jesus has often met with the least welcome from those that one would expect the best from. But it was not without some just cause that it came into a proverb. *The nearer the church the further from God.*

First, Reflecting on the rulers, because they let him alone: *Is not this he whom they seek to kill?* "Why do they not do it then? Lo, *he speaketh boldly*, and *they say nothing to him*; do *the rulers know indeed that this is the very Christ?" v.* 26. Here they slyly and maliciously insinuate two things, to exasperate the rulers against Christ. *a.* That by conniving at his preaching they *brought their authority into contempt.* "If our rulers will suffer themselves to be thus trampled upon, they may thank themselves if none stand in awe of them." The worst of persecutions have often been carried on under colour of the necessary support of authority and government. *b.* That hereby they brought *their judgment* into *suspicion*: *Do they know that this is the Christ?* It is spoken

JAMIESON, FAUSSET, BROWN

that He should refer to an event a year and a half old, as if but newly done. But their present attempt "to kill Him" brought up the past scene vividly, not only to Him, but without doubt to them, too, if indeed they had ever forgotten it; and by this fearless reference to it, exposing their hypocrisy and dark designs, He gave His position great moral strength. **22. Moses . . . gave you circumcision . . .**—Though servile work was forbidden on the sabbath, the circumcision of males on that day (which certainly was a servile work) was counted no infringement of the Law. How much less ought fault to be found with One who had made a man "every whit whole"—or rather, 'a man's entire body whole'—on the sabbath-day? What a testimony to the reality of the miracle, none daring to meet the bold appeal.

24. Judge not . . .—i.e., Rise above the *letter* into the *spirit* of the law.

25-27. some of them of Jerusalem—the citizens, who, knowing the long-formed purpose of the rulers to put Jesus to death, wondered that they were now letting Him teach openly. **26. Do the rulers know . . .**—Have they got some new light in favor of His claims?

ADAM CLARKE

22. *But of the fathers.* That is, it came "from the patriarchs." Circumcision was not, properly speaking, one of the laws of the Mosaic institution, it having been given at first to Abraham, and continued among his posterity till the giving of the law, Gen. xvii. 9-10, etc. *Ye . . . circumcise a man.* That is, a male child, for every male child was circumcised when eight days old; and if the eighth day after its birth happened to be a Sabbath, it was nevertheless circumcised, that the law might not be broken which had enjoined the circumcision to take place at that time, Lev. xii. 3.

23. *Every whit whole.* Some think that the original words should be translated "the whole man"; and that the meaning is that the blessed Saviour made him whole in both body and soul. This makes the miracle the greater, and shows still more forcibly the necessity of doing it without delay.

24. *Judge not according to the appearance.* Attend to the law, not merely in the letter, but in its spirit and design. Learn that the law which commands men to rest on the Sabbath day is subordinate to the law of mercy and love, which requires them to be ever active to promote God's glory in the comfort and salvation of their fellow creatures. And endeavor to judge of the merit or demerit of an action, not from the first impression it may make upon your prejudices, but from its tendency, and the motives of the person, as far as it is possible for you to acquaint yourselves with them, still believing the best where you have no certain proof to the contrary.

26. *That this is the very Christ.* In most of the common printed editions *alethos* is found, *the very Christ;* but the word is wanting in many MSS. and several editions. Calmet observes that the multitude which heard our Lord at this time was composed of three different classes of persons: (1) The rulers, priests, and Pharisees, declared enemies of Christ; (2) The inhabitants of Jerusalem, who knew the sentiments of their rulers concerning Him; (3) The strangers, who from different quarters had come up to Jerusa-

MATTHEW HENRY

ironically. "How came they to change their mind?" When religion and the profession of Christ's name are *out of fashion*, and consequently *out of repute*, many are strongly tempted to persecute and oppose them, only that they may not be thought to favour them and incline to them. It was strange that the rulers, thus irritated, did not seize Christ; but his hour was not yet come; and God can tie men's hands to admiration, though he should not turn their hearts.

Secondly, By their exception against his being the Christ, in which appeared more malice than matter, *v.* 27. "We have this argument against it, that *we know this man, whence he is; but when Christ comes no man knows whence he is*." They *despised him* because they knew *whence he was*. Familiarity breeds contempt, and we are apt to disdain the *use* of those whom we know the *rise of*. Christ's own received him not, because he was *their own*, for which very reason they should the rather have loved him.

[2] Christ's answer to this objection, *v.* 28, 29. He spoke freely and boldly, he *cried in the temple, as he taught*; to express his earnestness, being *grieved for the hardness of their hearts*. There may be a vehemency in contending for the truth where yet there is no intemperate heat nor passion. We may instruct gainsayers with warmth, and yet with *meekness*. Whoever has ears to hear, let him hear this. His answer to their cavil is, *a*. By way of *concession*, "*You both know me, and you know whence I am. You know me*, you think you know me; but you are mistaken; you take me to be the carpenter's son, and born at Nazareth, but it is not so." *b*. By way of *negation*, denying that that which they did see in him, and know of him, was all that was to be known. He will tell them what they knew not, *from whom* he came. (*a*) That he did not *come of himself*. (*b*) That he was sent of his Father; this is twice mentioned. (*c*) That he was *from his Father* as the beams from the sun. (*d*) *That the Father who sent him is true;* he had promised to give the Messiah. He that made the promise is *true*, and has performed it. He *is true*, and will fulfil the promise in the calling of the Gentiles. (*e*) That these unbelieving Jews did *not know the Father*: *He that sent me, whom you know not*. There is much ignorance of God even with many that have a *form of knowledge*; and the true reason why people reject Christ is because they do not *know God*. (*f*) Our Lord Jesus was intimately acquainted with the Father that *sent him*: *but I know him*. He was not at all *in doubt* concerning his mission from him, nor at all *in the dark* concerning the work he had to do.

[3] The provocation which this gave to his enemies, *v.* 30. *They sought therefore to take him*. But nobody touched him, *because his hour was not yet come*. God has wicked men in a chain. The malice of persecutors is *impotent* even when it is most *impetuous*, and, when Satan *fills their hearts*, yet God *ties their hands*. God's servants are sometimes wonderfully protected by indiscernible unaccountable means. Christ had *his hour* set. So have all his people and all his ministers. Nor can all the powers of hell and earth prevail against them, until they have *finished their testimony*.

[4] The good effect which Christ's discourse had upon some of his hearers (*v.* 31): *Many of the people believed on him*. Even where the gospel meets with opposition there may yet be a great deal of good done. *Who* they were that believed; not a few, but many, more than one would have expected when the stream ran so strongly the other way. But these *many* were *of the people*. We must not measure the prosperity of the gospel by its success among the great ones; nor must ministers say that they labour in vain, though none but the *poor* receive the gospel. What *induced* them to believe: the *miracles which he did*. How *weak* their faith was: they do not positively assert, as the Samaritans did, *This is indeed the Christ*, but they only argue, *When Christ comes will he do more miracles than these?* "Therefore why may not this be he?" They *believe* it, but have not courage to own it. Even weak faith may be true faith, and so *accepted*, by the Lord Jesus.

(2) *Whither he was going*, *v.* 32-36.

[1] The design of the Pharisees and chief priests against him, *v.* 32. The provocation given them was that they had information brought them by their spies, that *the people murmured such things concerning him*, that there were many who had a respect and value for him. Though the people did but whisper these things, yet the Pharisees were enraged at it. The Pharisees were sensible that if Christ did thus *increase* they must *decrease*. The project they laid hereupon was to seize Jesus, and take him into custody: *They sent officers to take him*. The most effectual way to disperse the flock is to *smite the shepherd*. The Pharisees *as such*, had no power, and

JAMIESON, FAUSSET, BROWN

27. Howbeit we know this man . . .—This seems to refer to some current opinion that Messiah's origin would be mysterious (not *altogether* wrong), from which they concluded that Jesus could not be He, since they knew all about His family at Nazareth.

28, 29. cried Jesus—in a louder tone, and more solemn, witnessing style than usual.

Ye both . . .—i.e., 'Yes, ye know both Myself and My local parentage, "and (*yet*) I am not come of Myself."

he that sent me is true . . .—Probably the meaning is, 'He that sent Me is the only *real* Sender of any one.'

30-32. sought to take . . . none laid hands—their *impotence* being equal to their *malignity*.

31. When Christ cometh, will he . . .—i.e., If this be not the Christ, what can the Christ do, when He does come, which has not been anticipated and eclipsed by this man? This was evidently the language of friendly persons, overborne by their spiteful superiors, but unable to keep quite silent. **32. heard that the people murmured**—that mutterings to this effect were going about, and thought it high time to stop Him if He was not to be allowed to carry away the people.

ADAM CLARKE

lem to the feast, and who heard Christ attentively, being ignorant of the designs of the rulers against Him. Our Lord addresses himself in this discourse principally to His enemies. The strange Jews were those who were astonished when Christ said, v. 20, that they sought to kill Him. And the Jews of Jerusalem were those who, knowing the disposition of the rulers, and seeing Christ speak openly, no man attempting to seize Him, addressed each other in the foregoing words, *Do the rulers know indeed that this is the Christ?* imagining that the chief priests had at last been convinced that Jesus was the Messiah.

27. *No man knoweth whence he is*. The generality of the people knew very well that the Messiah was to be born in Bethlehem, in the city, and of the family, of David; see v. 42. But from Isaiah liii. 8, "Who shall declare his generation?" they probably thought that there should be something so peculiarly mysterious in His birth, or in the manner of His appearing, that no person could fully understand.

28. *Ye both know me, and ye know whence I am*. Perhaps they should be read interrogatively: "Do you both know Me, and know whence I am?" Our Lord takes them up on their own profession and argues from it. Since you have got so much information concerning Me, add this to it, to make it complete; viz., that *I am not come of myself*, am no self-created or self-authorized prophet. I came from God; the testimony of John the Baptist, the descent of the Holy Ghost, the voice from heaven, the purity and excellence of My doctrine, and the multitude of My miracles sufficiently attest this. Now God is *true*, who has borne testimony to Me. But you know Him not; therefore it is that this testimony is disregarded.

31. *Will he do more miracles?* It was the belief of the Jews, and they founded it upon Isa. xxxv. 5, that, when the Messiah came, He would do all kinds of miracles. And in order that they might have the fullest proof of the divine mission of Christ, it had pleased God to cause miracles to cease for between four and five hundred years, and that John the Baptist himself had not wrought any. His miracles, therefore, were a full proof of His divine mission.

32. *The people murmured such things*. The people began to be convinced that He was the Messiah; and this being generally whispered about, the Pharisees thought it high time to put Him to death, lest the people should believe on Him. Therefore they *sent officers to take him*.

MATTHEW HENRY

therefore they got the *chief priests* to join with them. As *the world by wisdom knew not God*, so the Jewish church by their wisdom knew not Christ.

[2] The discourse of our Lord Jesus hereupon (*v.* 33, 34): *Yet a little while I am with you, and then I go to him that sent me; you shall seek me, and shall not find me; and where I am, thither you cannot come.* These words, like the pillar of cloud and fire, have a *bright* side and a *dark* side.

First, They have a *bright side* towards our Lord Jesus himself. Three things Christ here comforted himself with: That he had but *a little time* to continue here in this troublesome world. His warfare will shortly be accomplished. Whomsoever we are *with* in this world, friends or foes, it is but a *little while* that we shall be with them. We must be *awhile* with those that are pricking briars and grieving thorns; but thanks be to God, it is but a little while, and we shall be out of their reach. That he should *go to him that sent him.* When I have done my work with you, then, and not till then, I go to him *that sent me.* Let those who suffer for Christ comfort themselves with this, that they have a God to go to, and are going to him, to be for ever with him. That none of their persecutions could follow him to heaven: *You shall seek me, and shall not find me.* It adds to the happiness of glorified saints that they are out of the reach of the devil and all his wicked instruments.

Secondly, These words have a *black and dark side* towards those that hated and persecuted Christ. They now longed to be rid of him. According to their choice so shall their doom be. He will not trouble them long, yet a little while and he will *depart* from them. They that are weary of Christ need no more to make them miserable than to have *their wish.* They would certainly repent their choice when it was too late. They should in vain seek the presence of the Messiah: "*You shall seek me, and shall not find me.*" Those who now seek Christ shall find him, but the day is coming when those who now refuse him *shall seek him, and shall not find him.* They should in vain expect a place in heaven: *Where I am*, and where all believers shall be with me, *thither ye cannot come.* They are disabled by their own iniquity and infidelity: *You cannot come*, because you *will not.* Indeed heaven would be no heaven to them.

[3] Their descant upon this discourse (*v.* 35, 36): *They said among themselves; Whither will he go? First*, Their wilful ignorance and blindness. He had expressly said whither he would go—to him that sent him, to his Father in heaven, and yet they ask, *Whither will he go?* and, *What manner of saying is this? Secondly*, Their daring contempt of Christ's threatenings. Instead of trembling at that terrible word, *You shall seek me, and not find me*, they banter it and make a jest of it. *Thirdly*, Their inveterate malice and rage against Christ. All they dreaded in his *departure* was that he would be out of the reach of their power: "*Whither will he go, that we shall not find him?*" *Fourthly*, Their proud disdain of the Gentiles, whom they here call the *dispersed of the Gentiles.* Will he make his court to them? "Will he go and *teach the Gentiles*? Will he carry his doctrine to them?" So common is it for those who have lost the power of religion to be very jealous for the monopoly of the name. They now made a *jest* of his going *to teach the Gentiles*; but not long after he did it *in good earnest* by his apostles and ministers.

Verses 37-44

I. Christ's discourse, with the explication of it, *v.* 37-39. It is probable that these are only short hints of what he enlarged upon, but they have in them the substance of the whole gospel; here is a *gospel invitation* to *come to Christ*, and a *gospel promise* of comfort and happiness in him.

1. *When* he gave this invitation: *On the last day* of the feast of tabernacles, *that great day.* Much people were gathered together, and, if the invitation were given to *many*, it might be hoped that *some* would accept of it. The people were now returning to their homes, and he would give them this to carry away with them as his parting word. When a great congregation is about to scatter, it is affecting to think that in all probability they will never come all together again in this world, and therefore, if we can say or do anything to help them to heaven, that must be the time. It is good to be lively at the close of an ordinance. Christ made this offer *on the last day of the feast.* He will try them once more, and, if they will yet hear his voice, they shall live. It would be half a year before there would be another feast, and in that time they would many of them be in their graves. *Behold now is the accepted time.*

2. *How* he gave this invitation: *Jesus stood and cried*, which denotes his great earnestness and importunity. Love to souls will make preachers lively. His desire

JAMIESON, FAUSSET, BROWN

33, 34. Yet a little while . . .—i.e., 'Your desire to be rid of Me will be for you all too soon fulfilled. Yet a little while and we part company—for ever; for I go whither ye cannot come: nor, even when ye at length seek Him whom ye now despise, shall ye be able to find Him'—referring not to any penitential, but to purely selfish cries in their time of desperation.

35, 36. Whither will he go . . .—They cannot comprehend Him, but seem awed by the solemn grandeur of His warning. He takes no notice, however, of their questions.

37-39. the last day, that great day of the feast—the eigthth (Lev. 23:39). It was a sabbath, the last feast day of the year, and distinguished by very remarkable ceremonies. "The generally joyous character of this feast broke out on this day into loud jubilation, particularly at the solemn moment when the priest, as was done on every day of this festival, brought forth, in golden vessels, water from the stream of Siloah, which flowed under the temple-mountain, and solemnly poured it upon the altar. Then the words of Isaiah 12:3 were sung, "*With joy shall ye draw water out of the wells of Salvation,*" and thus the symbolical reference of this act, intimated in vs. 39, was expressed" [OLSHAUSEN]. So ecstatic was the joy with which this ceremony was performed—accompanied with sound of trumpets—that it used to be said, "Whoever had not witnessed it had never seen rejoicing at all" [LIGHTFOOT]. On this high occasion, then, He who had already drawn all eyes upon Him by His supernatural power and

ADAM CLARKE

33. *Yet a little while am I with you.* As He knew that the Pharisees had designed to take and put Him to death, and that in about six months from this time, as some conjecture, He should be crucified, He took the present opportunity of giving this information to the common people, who were best disposed towards Him, that they might lay their hearts to His teaching and profit by it while they had the privilege of enjoying it. The word *autois*, "to them," in the beginning of this verse, is wanting in many MSS. Our Lord did not speak these words to the officers who came to apprehend Him, as *autois* here implies, but to the common people, merely to show that He was not ignorant of the designs of the Pharisees, though they had not yet been able to put them into practice.

34. *Ye shall seek me, and shall not find me.* When the Roman armies come against you, you will vainly seek for a deliverer. But you shall be cut off in your sins, because you did not believe in Me. And *where I am*—in the Kingdom of glory—*ye cannot come*, for nothing that is unholy shall enter into the New Jerusalem.

35. *The dispersed among the Gentiles.* Or "Greeks." By the *dispersed* are meant here the Jews who were scattered through various parts of that empire which Alexander the Great had founded in Greece, Syria, Egypt, and Asia Minor, where the Greek language was used and where the Jewish Scriptures in the Greek version of the Septuagint were read.

37. *In the last day, that great day of the feast.* This was the eighth day, and was called the *great day* because of certain traditional observances, and not on account of any excellence which it derived from the original institution. On the seven days they professed to offer sacrifices for the seventy nations of the earth, but on the eighth day they offered sacrifices for Israel; therefore the eighth day was more highly esteemed than any of the others. See the account of the Feast of Tabernacles, in the note on v. 2. It was probably when they went to draw water from the Pool of Siloam, and while they were pouring it out at the foot of the altar, that our Lord spoke these words.

MATTHEW HENRY

was that all might take notice, and take hold of this invitation. He *stood*, and *cried*, that he might the better be heard. The heathen oracles were delivered privately by them that *peeped and muttered*; but the oracles of the gospel were proclaimed by one that *stood, and cried*.

3. The invitation itself is very general: *If any man* thirst, whoever he be, he is invited to Christ. It is also very *gracious*: "*If any man thirst, let him come to me and drink*. If any man desires to be truly and eternally happy, let him apply himself to me."

(1) The persons invited are such as *thirst*, which may be understood, either, [1] Of the *indigence* of their cases; either as to their *outward* condition (let his poverty and afflictions draw him to Christ for that peace which the world can neither give nor take away), or as to their *inward* state: "If any man want spiritual blessings, he may be supplied by me." Or, [2] Of the *inclination* of their souls and their desires towards a spiritual happiness. If any man hunger and thirst after righteousness.

(2) The invitation itself: *Let him come to me*. Let him *go to Christ* as the fountain of living waters.

(3) The satisfaction promised: Let him come *and drink*, he shall have that which will not only *refresh*, but *replenish*.

4. A gracious promise annexed to this gracious call (*v*. 38): *He that believeth on me, out of his belly shall flow*: (1) See here what it is to come to Christ: It is *to believe on him, as the scripture hath said*. We must not frame a Christ according to our fancy, but believe in a Christ according to the scripture. (2) See how thirsty souls, that come to Christ, shall be made *to drink*. Israel drank of the *rock that followed them*, but believers drink of a rock *in them, Christ in them*. Provision is made not only for their *present* satisfaction, but for their *continual perpetual* comfort. *Living water*, *running* water, which the Hebrew language calls *living*, because still in motion. The graces and comforts of the Spirit are compared to *living* (meaning *running*) *water*: *Rivers* of living water. The comfort flows in both *plentifully* and *constantly* as a river; strong as a stream to bear down the oppositions of doubts and fears. These flow out of his heart or soul. There *gracious principles* are planted; and out of the heart, in which the Spirit dwells, flow the *issues of life*. Where there are *springs* of grace and comfort in the soul they will *send forth streams*. Grace and comfort will *evidence themselves*. A holy heart will be seen in a holy life; the tree is known by its fruits, and the fountain by its streams. They will *communicate themselves* for the benefit of others; a good man is a common good.

Those words, *as the scripture hath said*, seem to refer to some promise in the Old Testament to this purport, and there are many. It was a custom of the Jews which they received by tradition, *the last day of the feast* of tabernacles to have a solemnity, which they called *the pouring out of water*. They fetched a golden vessel of water from the pool of Siloam, brought it into the temple with sound of trumpet and other ceremonies, and, upon the ascent to the altar, poured it out before the Lord with all possible expressions of joy. It is thought that our Saviour might here allude to this custom. Believers shall have the comfort, not of a vessel of water fetched from a pool, but of a river flowing from themselves.

5. Here is the evangelist's exposition of this promise (*v*. 39): *This spoke he of the Spirit*, of the gifts, graces, and comforts of the Spirit. It is promised to *all that believe* on Christ that they shall *receive the Holy Ghost*. Some received his miraculous gifts; all receive his sanctifying graces. The Spirit dwelling and working in believers is as a *fountain of living* running *water*, out of which plentiful streams flow, cooling and cleansing as water, mollifying and moistening as water, making them fruitful, and others joyful. This plentiful effusion of the Spirit was yet the matter of a promise; for *the Holy Ghost was not yet given, because Jesus was not yet glorified*. It was certain that he should be glorified, but he was as yet in a state of humiliation and contempt. And, if Christ must wait for his glory, let not us think it much to wait for ours. *The Holy Ghost was not yet given*. If we compare the clear knowledge and strong grace of the disciples of Christ themselves, after the day of Pentecost, with their darkness and weakness before, we shall understand in what sense *the Holy Ghost was not yet given*; the earnests and first-fruits of the Spirit were given, but the full harvest was not yet come. The *Holy Ghost* was *not yet given* in such rivers of living water as should issue forth to water the whole earth, even the Gentile world. The reason why *the Holy Ghost was not given* was because *Jesus was not yet glorified*. The death of Christ is sometimes called his glorification; for in his cross he conquered and triumphed. The gift of the Holy Ghost was pur-

JAMIESON, FAUSSET, BROWN

unrivalled teaching—"JESUS stood," probably in some elevated position, "and cried," as if making proclamation in the audience of all the people, "IF ANY MAN THIRST, LET HIM COME UNTO ME AND DRINK!" What an offer! The deepest cravings of the human spirit are here, as in the Old Testament, expressed by the figure of *"thirst,"* and the eternal satisfaction of them by *"drinking."* To the woman of Samaria He had said almost the same thing, and in the same terms (John 4:13, 14). But what to her was simply affirmed to her as a *fact*, is here turned into a world-wide *proclamation;* and whereas there, the *gift* by Him of the living water is the most prominent idea—in contrast with her hesitation to give Him the perishable water of Jacob's well—here, the prominence is given to *Himself* as the Well-spring of all satisfaction. He had in Galilee invited all the WEARY AND HEAVYLADEN of the human family to come under His wing and they should find REST (Matt. 11:28), which is just the same deep want, and the same profound relief of it, under another and equally grateful figure. He had in the synagogue of Capernaum (ch. 6) announced Himself, in every variety of form, as "the BREAD of Life," and as both able and authorized to appease the "HUNGER," and quench the "THIRST," of all that apply to Him. There is, and there can be, nothing beyond that here. But what was on all those occasions uttered in private, or addressed to a provincial audience, is here sounded forth in the streets of the great religious metropolis, and in language of surpassing majesty, simplicity, and grace. *It is just Jehovah's ancient proclamation now sounding forth through human flesh,* "HO, EVERY ONE THAT THIRSTETH, COME YE TO THE WATERS, AND HE THAT HATH NO MONEY . . . !" (Isa. 55:1). In this light we have but two alternatives; either to say with Caiaphas of Him that uttered such words, "*He is guilty of death*," or falling down before Him to exclaim with Thomas, "MY LORD AND MY GOD!"

38. as the scripture hath said—These words belong to what follows, "Out of his belly, as the scripture hath said, shall flow . . ." referring not to any particular passage, but to such as Isaiah 58:11; Joel 3:18; Zechariah 14:8; Ezekiel 47:1-12; in most of which the idea is that of waters issuing from beneath the temple, to which our Lord compares Himself and those who believe in Him. **out of his belly**—i.e., his inner man, his soul, as in Proverbs 20:27. **rivers of living water**—(See on ch. 4:13, 14). It refers primarily to the *copiousness*, but indirectly also to the *diffusiveness*, of this living water to the good of others.

39. This spake he of the Spirit—who, by His direct personal agency, opens up this spring of living waters in the human spirit (ch. 3:6), and by His indwelling in the renewed soul ensures their *unfailing flow*. **they that believe . . .**—As the Holy Ghost is, in the rendemption of man, entirely *at the service of Christ*, as His Agent, so it is *only in believing connection with Christ* that any one "receives" the Spirit. **for the Holy Ghost was not yet [given]**—Beyond all doubt the word "given," or some similar word, is the right supplement. In ch. 16:7 the Holy Ghost is represented not only as the *gift of Christ*, but a gift the communication of which was *dependent upon His own departure to the Father*. Now as Christ was *not yet gone*, so the Holy Ghost *was not yet given*. **Jesus not yet glorified**—The word *"glorified"* is here used advisedly, to teach the reader not only that the *departure* of Christ to the Father was *indispensable* to the giving of the Spirit, but that this illustrious Gift, direct from the hands of the ascended Saviour, was God's intimation to the world that He whom it had cast out, crucified, and slain, was "His Elect, in whom His soul delighted," and that it was through the smiting of that Rock that the waters of the Spirit—for which the Church was waiting, and with pomp at the feast of tabernacles proclaiming its expectation—had gushed forth upon a thirsty world.

ADAM CLARKE

F. B. MEYER:

There is a deep inner lesson for us all in these words. We sometimes wonder why we have not received the Spirit and why our lives are not channels through which He pours in mighty rivers to make desert hearts and lives blossom and sing. How gladly would we part with all beside if we might be conscious that not tiny streamlets, not one river of holy influence merely, but that rivers were issuing from us as the waters from the temple threshold!

Is not the reason to be sought in our neglect to glorify Christ? We have never yet abandoned ourselves to Him, content to live the branch-life, with no other aim than to realize the one purpose of his most blessed life, the glorifying of the Father. We have never seriously made it our life-purpose to glorify the Lord Jesus. There has been no triumphal entry into our hearts, no enthronization, no challenge to the gates of our soul that they should lift themselves up to admit the King of Glory.

—Great Verses Through the Bible

38. *He that believeth on me, as the scripture hath said.* He who receives Me as the Messiah, according to what the Scripture has said concerning Me—My person, birth, conduct, preaching, and miracles being compared with what is written there, as ascertaining the true Messiah. *Out of his belly*—"from his heart and soul"; for in his soul shall this Spirit dwell. *Living water*. As a true spring is ever supplied with water from the great deep with which it has communication, so shall the soul of the genuine believer be supplied with light, life, love, and liberty, and all the other graces of the indwelling Spirit from the indwelling Christ. The Jews frequently compare the gifts and influences of the Holy Spirit to water in general. The Scriptures abound in this metaphor. See Ps. xxxvi. 8-9; Isa. xliv. 3-4; Joel ii. 23.

39. *Was not yet given.* "Given" is added by many MSS. and several of the primitive fathers. The word seems necessary to the completion of the sense.

MATTHEW HENRY

chased by the blood of Christ: the Holy Ghost was not given. There was not so much need of the Spirit, while Christ himself was here upon earth, as there was when he was gone. Though the Holy Ghost was not yet given, yet he was *promised.* Though the gifts of Christ's grace are *long deferred,* while we are waiting for the good promise, we have the promise to live upon.

II. The consequents of this discourse. In general, it occasioned differences: *There was a division among the people because of him, v.* 43. There were diversities of opinions, and those managed with heat and contention; various sentiments, and those such as set them at *variance.* Think we that Christ came to send peace. No, the effect of the preaching of his gospel would be *division,* for, while some are *gathered to it* others will be *gathered against it.* This is no more the fault of the gospel than it is the fault of a wholesome medicine that it stirs up the *peccant* humours in the body, in order to the discharge of them.

1. Some were *taken with him*: *Many of the people, when they heard this saying,* could not but think highly of him. Some of them said, *Of a truth this is the prophet,* the harbinger and forerunner of the Messiah. Others went further, and said, *This is the Christ* (*v.* 41), the Messiah himself. We do not find that these people became his disciples and followers; a good opinion of Christ is far short of a lively faith in Christ; many give Christ a good word that give him no more.

2. Others were *prejudiced against him.* No sooner was this great truth started, that *Jesus is the Christ,* than immediately it was contradicted and argued against. That his rise and origin were (as they took it for granted) out of Galilee, was thought enough to answer all the arguments for his being the Christ. For, *shall Christ come out of Galilee?* Has not *the scripture said that Christ comes of the seed of David*? See here, (1) A laudable knowledge of the scripture. This even the common people knew by the traditional expositions which their scribes gave them. Many that espouse some corrupt notions, seem to be very ready in the scriptures, when indeed they know little more than those scriptures which they have been taught to *pervert.* (2) A culpable ignorance of our Lord Jesus. They speak of it as certain and past dispute that *Jesus was of Galilee,* whereas by enquiring they might have known that he was the Son of David, and a native of Bethlehem.

3. Others were *enraged against him,* and they *would have taken him, v.* 44. Though what he said was most sweet and gracious, yet they were exasperated against him for it. They *would have taken him*; but no man *laid hands on him,* because his hour was not come. As the malice of Christ's enemies is always *unreasonable,* so sometimes the suspension of it is *unaccountable.*

Verses 45–53

The chief priests and Pharisees are here contriving how to suppress Christ; though this was the *great day of the feast,* they attended not the religious services of the day. They sat in the council-chamber, expecting Christ to be brought a prisoner to them, as they had issued out warrants for apprehending him, *v.* 32.

I. What passed between them and their own officers, who returned without him.

1. The reproof they gave the officers for not executing the warrant they gave them: *Why have you not brought him?* It vexed them that those who were their own creatures should thus disappoint them.

2. The reason which the officers gave: *Never man spoke like this man, v.* 46. This was a very great truth, that *never any man spoke with* that wisdom, and power, and grace, that convincing clearness, and that charming sweetness, wherewith Christ spoke. The very officers that were sent to take him were taken with him, and acknowledged this. They could not but prefer him before all those that sat in Moses's seat. Thus Christ was preserved by the power God has upon the consciences even of bad men. They said this to their lords and masters, who could not endure to hear anything that tended to the honour of Christ and yet could not avoid hearing this. Their own officers, who could not be suspected to be biassed in favour of Christ, are witnesses against them.

3. The Pharisees endeavour to secure their officers to their interest, and to beget in them prejudices against Christ. They suggest two things: (1) That if they embrace the gospel of Christ they will *deceive themselves* (*v.* 47): *Are you also deceived?* Christianity has, from its first rise, been represented to the world as a great cheat upon it, and they that embraced it as men *deceived,* then when they began to be *undeceived,* observe what a *compliment* the Pharisees paid to these officers: "*Are you also deceived?* What! men of your sense?" They endeavour to prejudice them against

JAMIESON, FAUSSET, BROWN

40-43. Many . . . when they heard this . . . said, Of a truth . . .—The only wonder is they did not all say it. "But their minds were blinded." **Others, This is the Christ**—(See on ch. 1:21). **Shall Christ come out of Galilee . . . scripture said . . . of the seed of David and out of . . . Bethlehem . . .**—We accept this spontaneous testimony to our David-descended, Bethlehemborn Saviour. Had those who gave it made the inquiry which the case demanded, they would have found that Jesus "came out of Galilee" and "out of Bethlehem" both, alike in fulfilment of prophecy as in point of fact. (Matt. 2:23; 4:13-16.)

44-49. would have taken him, but . . .—(See on vs. 30). **45. Then came the officers**—"sent to take him" (vs. 32). **Why . . . not brought him?**—already thirsting for their Victim, and thinking it an easy matter to seize and bring Him. **46. Never man spake like this man**—Noble testimony of unsophisticated men! Doubtless they were strangers to the profound intent of Christ's teaching, but there was that in it which by its mysterious grandeur and transparent purity and grace, held them spellbound. No doubt it was of God that they should so feel, that their arm might be paralyzed, as Christ's hour was not yet come; but even in human teaching there has sometimes been felt such a divine power, that men who came to kill them (e.g., ROWLAND HISS) have confessed to all that they were unmanned.

47. ye also deceived—In their own servants this seemed intolerable.

ADAM CLARKE

43. *There was a division.* A "schism"; they were divided in sentiment and separated into parties.

40. *Of a truth this is the Prophet.* The great prophet or "teacher" spoken of by Moses, Deut. xviii. 15, which they improperly distinguished from the Messiah, v. 41.

41. *Shall Christ come out of Galilee?* As the prophets had declared that the Messiah was to come from the tribe of Judah and from the family of David, and should be born in the city of Bethlehem, these Jews, imagining that Christ had been born in Galilee, concluded that He could not be the Messiah.

42. *Where David was?* That is, where he was born, 1 Sam. xvi. 1, 4, and where he was before he became king in Israel.

44. *Would have taken him.* Or "they wished to seize Him." And this they would have done, and destroyed Him too at that time, had they been unanimous; but their being divided in opinion, v. 43, was the cause, under God, why His life was at that time preserved. How true are the words of the prophet: "The wrath of man shall praise thee: the remainder of wrath shalt thou restrain," Ps. lxxvi. 10!

45. *Then came the officers.* They had followed Him for several days, seeking for a proper opportunity to seize on Him, when they might fix some charge of sedition upon Him; but the more they listened, the more they were convinced of His innocence, purity, and consummate wisdom.

46. *Never man spake like this man.* Though these officers had gone on the errand of their masters, they had not entered into their spirit. They were sent to apprehend a seditious man and a false prophet. They came where Jesus taught; they found Him to be a different Person to the description they received from their masters, and therefore did not attempt to touch or molest Him. No doubt they expected when they told their employers the truth that they would have commended them and acknowledged their own mistake, but these simple people were not in the secret of their masters' malice.

MATTHEW HENRY

Christ by persuading them to think well of themselves. (2) That they will *disparage themselves*. Most men, even in their religion, are willing to be governed by the example of those of the *first rank*; these officers therefore, are desired to consider,

(1) That, if they become disciples of Christ, they go contrary to those who were persons of quality and reputation: "*Have any of the rulers, or of the Pharisees, believed on him?*" Some of the rulers did embrace Christ and more believed in him, but wanted courage to confess him (*ch.* xii. 42); but, when the interest of Christ runs low in the world, it is common for its adversaries to represent it as lower than really it is. The cause of Christ has seldom had rulers and Pharisees on its side. *Self-denial* and the *cross* are hard lessons to *rulers* and *Pharisees*. This has confirmed many in their prejudices against Christ, that the rulers and Pharisees have been no friends. If *rulers* and *Pharisees* do not believe in Christ, they that do believe in him will be the most singular, unfashionable, ungenteel people in the world. Thus are people foolishly willing to be damned for fashion-sake.

(2) That they will link themselves with the despicable vulgar sort of people (*v.* 43): *But this people, who know not the law, are cursed. First,* How scornfully and disdainfully they speak of them: *This people.* As the wisdom of God has often chosen base things, and things which are despised, so the folly of men has commonly debased and despised those whom God has chosen. *Secondly,* How unjustly they reproach them: *They know not the law.* Perhaps many of those whom they thus despised *knew the law,* and the prophets too, better than they did. Many a plain, honest, unlearned disciple of Christ attains to a more clear, sound, and useful knowledge of the word of God, than some great scholars with all their wit and learning. Whose fault was it but theirs, who should have *taught them better? Thirdly,* How magisterially they pronounce sentence upon them: they are *cursed.* We are unable to *try,* and therefore unfit to *condemn,* and our rule is, *Bless, and curse not.* They use this odious word, they are *cursed,* to express their own indignation, and to frighten their officers from having anything to do with them.

II. What passed between them and Nicodemus, *v.* 50, &c.

1. The just and rational objection which Nicodemus made against their proceedings.

(1) Who it was that appeared against them; it was Nicodemus, *he that came to Jesus by night, being one of them, v.* 50. Though he had been with Jesus, and taken him for his teacher, yet he retained his place in the council, and his vote among them. Some impute this to his *weakness* and cowardice. It seems rather to have been his *wisdom* not immediately to throw up his place, because there he might have opportunity of serving Christ, and stemming the tide of the Jewish rage. God has his remnant among all sorts, and many times finds, or puts, or makes, some good in the worst places and societies. Though at first he came to Jesus *by night,* for fear of being known; yet, when there was occasion, he boldly appeared in defence of Christ, and opposed the whole council. Thus many believers who at first were timorous have at length, by divine grace, grown courageous. Let none justify the disguising of their faith by the example of Nicodemus, unless, like him, they be ready openly to appear in the cause of Christ, though they stand alone in it; for so Nicodemus did here, and *ch.* xix. 39.

(2) What he alleged against their proceedings (*v.* 51): *Doth our law judge any man before it hear him* and *know what he doeth?* He prudently argues from the principles of their own law, and an incontestable rule of justice, that no man is to be condemned *unheard.* Whereas they had reproached the people, as *ignorant of the law,* he here tacitly retorts the charge upon themselves. The law is here said to *judge,* and *hear,* and *know.* It is highly fit that none should come under the *sentence* of the law, till they have first undergone the *scrutiny* of it. Judges have two ears, to remind them to hear both sides. Persons are to be judged, not by what is *said* of them, but by what they *do.* Facts, and not faces, must be known in judgment; and the *scale* of justice must be used before the *sword* of justice.

2. What was said to this objection. Here is no direct reply given to it. What was lacking in *reason* they made up in railing and reproach. Whoever are *against reason* give cause to suspect that *reason* is *against them.* See how they taunt him: *Art thou also of Galilee?* (*v.* 52).

(1) How *false* the grounds of their arguing were. They suppose that Christ was of Galilee, and this was false. They suppose that because most of his disciples were Galileans they were all such. They

JAMIESON, FAUSSET, BROWN

48. any of the rulers or . . . Pharisees believed—"Many of them" did, including Nicodemus and Joseph, but not one of these had openly "confessed Him" (ch. 12:42), and this appeal must have stung such of them as heard it to the quick.

49. But this people—lit., "multitude," meaning the *ignorant rabble.* It is a pity that these important distinctions, so marked in the orginal of this Gospel, should not be also in our version.) **knoweth not the law**—i.e., by school learning, which only subverted it by human traditions.

are cursed—a cursed set (a kind of swearing at them, out of mingled rage and scorn).

50-53. Nicodemus—reappearing to us after nearly three years' absence from the history, as a member of the council, probably then sitting.

51. Doth our law . . .—a very proper, but all too tame rejoinder, and evidently more from pressure of conscience than any design to pronounce *positively* in the case. "The feebleness of his defense of Jesus has a strong contrast in the fierceness of the rejoinders of the Pharisees" [WEBSTER and WILKINSON].

52. thou of Galilee—in this taunt expressing their scorn of the party. Even a word of caution, or the gentlest proposal to inquire before condemning, was with them equivalent to an espousal of the hated One. **Search . . . out of Galilee . . . no prophet**—Strange! For had not *Jonah* (of

ADAM CLARKE

48. *Have any of the rulers . . . believed on him?* Very few. But is this a proof that He is not of God? No, truly. If He were of the world, the world would love its own. The religion of Christ has been in general rejected by the rulers of this world.

49. *This people.* "This rabble." The common people were treated by the Pharisees with the most sovereign contempt. They were termed *am ha-arets,* "people of the earth," and were not thought worthy to have a resurrection to eternal life.

50. *Nicodemus . . . being one of them.* That is, a Pharisee, and a ruler of the Jews; see on chap. iii. 1.

51. *Doth our law judge any man?* "The man," i.e., who is accused. Perhaps Nicodemus did not refer so much to anything in the law of Moses as to what was commonly practiced among them. Josephus says, *Ant.*, b. xiv, c. 9, s. 3, "That the law has forbidden any man to be put to death, though wicked, unless he be first condemned to die by the Sanhedrin." It was probably to this law that Nicodemus here alludes. See laws relative to this point in Deut. xvii. 8, etc.; xix. 15.

52. *Art thou also of Galilee?* They knew very well that he was not, but they spoke this by way of reproach. As if they had said, You are no better than He is, as you take His part. *Search, and look.* Examine the Scriptures, search the public registers, and you will see that out of Galilee there arises no prophet. This conclusion, says Calmet, was false, because Jonah was of Gath-hepher, in Galilee; see 2 Kings xiv. 25, compared with Josh. xix. 13. The Prophet Nahum was also a Galilean, for he was of the tribe of Simeon.

53. *And every man went.* The authority and influence of Nicodemus, in this case, was so great that the Sanhedrin broke up without being able

MATTHEW HENRY

suppose that out of Galilee no prophet had *risen*, yet this was false too.

(2) How *absurd* their arguings were upon these grounds. Is any man of worth and virtue ever the worse for the poverty and obscurity of his country? Supposing no prophet had risen out of Galilee, yet it is not impossible that any should arise thence.

3. The hasty adjournment of the court hereupon. They broke up the assembly in confusion, and with precipitation, and *every man went to his own house*. All the policy of the close cabal was broken to pieces with one plain honest word. They were not willing to hear Nicodemus, because they could not answer him.

JAMIESON, FAUSSET, BROWN

Gathhepher) and even Elijah (of Thisbe) arisen out of Galilee? And there it may be more, of whom we have no record. But rage is blind, and deep prejudice distorts all facts. Yet it looks as if they were afraid of losing Nicodemus, when they take the trouble to reason the point at all. It was just *because* he had "searched," as they advised him, that he went the length even that he did. **53. every man went unto his own home**—*finding their plot could not at that time be carried into effect.* Is your rage thus impotent, ye chief priests?

ADAM CLARKE

to conclude anything. As the feast was now ended, they were not obliged to continue any longer in or about Jerusalem, and therefore all returned to their respective dwellings. This verse and the first eleven verses of the following chapter are wanting in several MSS. Some of those which retain the paragraph mark it with obelisks, as a proof of spuriousness. Those which do retain it have it with such a variety of reading as is nowhere else found in the sacred writings. Professor Griesbach leaves the whole paragraph in the text with notes of doubtfulness. Most of the modern critics consider it as resting on no solid authority.

MATTHEW HENRY — CHAPTER 8

Verses 1–11

I. His retirement in the evening out of the town (*v.* 1): *He went unto the mount of olives.* He went out of Jerusalem, perhaps because he had no friend there that had either kindness or courage enough to give him a night's lodging; while his persecutors had *houses* of their own to go to (*ch.* vii. 53). In the daytime, when he had work to do in the temple, he willingly exposed himself. But in the night, he withdrew into the country, and sheltered himself there.

II. His return in the morning to the temple, and to his work there, *v.* 2.

1. What a diligent preacher Christ was: *Early in the morning he came again, and taught.* Three things were taken notice of here concerning Christ's preaching. (1) The time: *Early in the morning.* When a day's work is to be done for God and souls it is good to take the day before us. (2) The place: *In the temple;* not so much because it was a *consecrated* place as because it was not a *place of concourse.* (3) His posture: *He sat down,* and taught, as one having authority.

2. How diligently his preaching was attended upon: *All the people came unto him.* Though the rulers were displeased at those that came to hear him, yet they would come; and *he taught them,* though they were angry at *him* too.

III. His dealing with those that brought to him the *woman taken in adultery, tempting* him.

1. The case proposed to him by the scribes and Pharisees, who herein contrived to pick a quarrel with him, *v.* 3–6.

(1) They set the prisoner to the bar (*v.* 3): they brought him *a woman taken in adultery.* Those that were *taken in adultery* were by the Jewish law to be put to death. The scribes and Pharisees bring her to Christ, and set her in the midst of the assembly, as if they would leave her wholly to the judgment of Christ.

(2) They prefer an indictment against her: *Master, this woman was taken in adultery, v.* 4. Here they call him *Master* whom but the day before they had called a *deceiver.* The crime for which the prisoner stands indicted is no less than adultery. The Pharisees seemed to have a great zeal against the sin, when it appeared afterwards that they themselves were not free from it. It is common for those that are indulgent to their own sin to be severe against the sins of others. The proof of the crime, an incontestable proof; she was *taken in the act.* Sometimes it proves a mercy to sinners to have their sin brought to light. Better our sin should *shame* us than *damn* us.

(3) They produce the statute in this case upon which she was indicted, *v.* 5. Moses in the law commanded *that such should be stoned.* Adultery is an exceedingly sinful sin. It is the violation of a divine institution in innocency, by the indulgence of one of the basest lusts of man in his degeneracy.

(4) They pray his judgment in the case: "*But what sayest thou,* who pretendest to be a teacher come from God to repeal old laws and enact new ones?" If they had asked this question in sincerity, it had been very commendable. But *this they said tempting him, that they might have to accuse him, v.* 6. If he should confirm the sentence of the law, they would censure him as inconsistent with himself (he having received publicans and harlots) and with the character of the Messiah, who should be meek, and have salvation. If he should acquit her they would represent him, *First,* As an enemy to the law of Moses. *Secondly,* As a friend to sinners and, consequently a favourer of sin; than which no reflection could be more invidious upon one that professed the strictness, purity, and business of a prophet.

2. The method he took to resolve this case, and so to break this snare.

(1) He seemed to slight it, and turned a deaf ear to it: He *stooped down, and wrote on the ground.*

JAMIESON, FAUSSET, BROWN — CHAPTER 8

Vss. 1-11. The Woman Taken in Adultery. **1, 2. Jesus went unto the Mount of Olives**—This should have formed the last verse of the foregoing chapter. "The return of the people to the inert quiet and security of their *dwellings* (ch. 7:53), at the close of the feast, is designedly contrasted with our Lord's *homeless* way, so to speak, of spending the short night, who is early in the morning on the scene again. One cannot well see why what is recorded in Luke 21:37, 38 may not even thus early have taken place; it might have been the Lord's ordinary custom from the beginning to leave the brilliant misery of the city every night, that so He might compose His sorrowful and interceding heart, and collect His energies for new labors of love; preferring for His resting-place Bethany, and the *Mount of Olives,* the scene thus consecrated by many preparatory prayers for His final humiliation and exaltation" [Stier].

3-6. scribes and Pharisees—foiled in their yesterday's attempt, and hoping to succeed better in this. **4. woman . . . in adultery . . .**

5. Moses . . . commanded . . . should be stoned—simply put to death (Deut. 22:22), but in aggravated cases, at least in later times, this was probably by stoning (Ezek. 16:40). **but what sayest thou**—hoping, whatever He might answer, to put Him in the wrong:—if He said, Stone her, that would seem a stepping out of His province; if He forbade it, that would hold Him up as a relaxer of the public morals. But these cunning hypocrites were overmatched.

6. stooped down—It will be observed He was *sitting* when they came to Him.

ADAM CLARKE — CHAPTER 8

G. CAMPBELL MORGAN:

When on the previous day He had made His great call, "If any man thirst," He had *stood,* which marked a distinct difference in His attitude for the moment. He stood as a herald. Now He went back and resumed the attitude of the teacher: He sat down. When He stood and uttered that call, He was not teaching, but making a proclamation. Now, going back, He again assumed the position of the teacher. The crowds gathered round Him. As they listened to Him, there was a stir, a movement in the crowd, and there came into the midst certain scribes and Pharisees, bringing a woman. It is impossible to read the story without realizing the brutal indelicacy of their action. Whatever this woman had done, and however guilty she was, legally they had no right to drag her into the public gaze. The Sanhedrin had its sittings in the very next part of the Temple to where Jesus was teaching. Probably they intended to take her there presently; but they had no right to drag her into publicity.

—The Gospel According to John

3. *A woman taken in adultery.* It is allowed that adultery was exceedingly common at this time, so common that they had ceased to put the law in force against it. The waters of jealousy were no longer drunk, the culprits, or those suspected of this crime, being so very numerous; and the men who were guilty themselves dared not try their suspected wives, as it was believed the waters would have no evil effect upon the wife if the husband himself had been criminal. See the whole of the process on the waters of jealousy in the notes on Num. v. 14.

5. *That such should be stoned.* It is not strictly true that Moses ordered adultery in general to be punished by stoning. The law simply says that the adulterer and the adulteress shall be "put to death," Lev. xx. 10; Deut. xxii. 22. The rabbins say they were strangled. This they affirm was the ordinary mode of punishment where the species of death was not marked in the law. If the person guilty of an act of this kind had been betrothed, but not married, she was to be stoned, Deut. xxii. 23. But if she was the daughter of a priest, she was to be burned alive, Lev. xxi. 9. It appears from Ezek. xvi. 38, 40 that adulteresses in the time of that prophet were stoned and pierced with a sword.

6. *That they might have to accuse him.* Had our Lord condemned the woman to death, they might have accused Him to Pilate, as arrogating to himself the power of life and death, which the Romans had taken away from the Jews. Besides, the Roman laws did not condemn an adulteress to be put to death. On the other hand, if He had said she should not be put to death, they might have represented Him to the people as One who decided contrary to the law and favored the crime of which the woman was accused. *With his finger wrote.* Several MSS.

MATTHEW HENRY

It is impossible to tell, and therefore needless to ask, what he wrote; but this is the only mention made in the gospels of Christ's writing. Christ by this teaches us to be slow to speak when difficult cases are proposed to us, not quickly to shoot our bolt. Think twice before we speak once. But, when Christ seemed as though he heard them not, he made it appear that he not only heard their words, but knew their thoughts.

(2) He turned the conviction of the prisoner upon the prosecutors, *v.* 7.

[1] They *continued asking him*, and his seeming not to take notice of them made them the more vehement; for now they thought sure enough that they had run him aground. Therefore they pushed on their appeal to him with vigour; whereas they should have construed his disregard of them as a check to their design, and an intimation to them to desist.

[2] At last he put them all to shame and silence with one word: *He lifted up himself* and *said unto them, He that is without sin among you, let him first cast a stone at her.* He neither reflected upon the law nor excused the prisoner's guilt, nor did he on the other hand encourage the prosecution or countenance their heat. When we cannot make our point by steering a direct course, it is good to fetch a compass. They came with design to accuse him, but they were forced to accuse themselves. He here refers to that rule which the law of Moses prescribed in the execution of criminals, that the *hand of the witnesses must be first upon them* (Deut. xvii. 7), as in the stoning of Stephen, Acts vii. 58. Christ puts it to them whether, according to their own law, they would dare to be the executioners. Durst they take away that life with their hands which they were now taking away with their tongues? He builds upon an uncontested maxim in morality. They are not better than self-condemned who judge others, and yet themselves do the same thing: "If there be any of you who is *without sin*, let him cast the first stone at her." Whenever we find fault with others, we ought to reflect upon ourselves, and to be more severe against sin in ourselves than in others. We ought to be favourable, though not to the sins, yet to the persons, of those that offend, considering ourselves and our own corrupt nature. Let this restrain us from *throwing stones* at our brethren. Those that are any way obliged to animadvert upon the faults of others are concerned to look well to themselves, and keep themselves pure. If you are without sin, stand to the charge, and let the adulteress be executed; but, if not, though she be guilty, while you that present her are equally so, according to your own rule she shall be free. He aimed to bring, not only the prisoner to repentance, by showing her his mercy, but the prosecutors too, by showing them their sins. They sought to ensnare him; he sought to convince and convert them.

[3] Having given them this startling word, he left them to consider of it, *and again stooped down*, and *wrote on the ground*, *v.* 8. The matter was lodged in their own breasts, let them make the best of it there. Some Greek copies here read, He *wrote on the ground, the sins of everyone of them.* But he does not write men's sins *in the sand*; no, they are written as with a *pen of iron* (Jer. xvii. 1), never to be forgotten till they are forgiven.

[4] The scribes and Pharisees were so strangely thunderstruck with the words of Christ that they let fall their persecution of Christ, whom they durst no further tempt, and their prosecution of the woman, whom they durst no longer accuse (*v.* 9): *They went out one by one.* Perhaps his writing on the ground frightened them, as the handwriting on the wall frightened Belshazzar. Happy they who have no reason to be afraid of Christ's writing! What he said frightened them by sending them to their own consciences; he had *shown them to themselves*, and they were afraid his next word would show them to the world. They went out *one by one*, that they might go out *softly*; they went away by *stealth*, as *people being ashamed*. The order of their departure is taken notice of, *beginning at the eldest*. If the eldest quit the field, and retreat ingloriously, no marvel if the younger follow them. 1. The *force* of the word of Christ for the conviction of sinners: *They who heard it were convicted by their own consciences.* Conscience is God's deputy in the soul, and one word from him will set it on work, Heb. iv. 12. Even scribes and Pharisees are by the power of Christ's word made to retire with shame. 2. The *folly* of sinners under these convictions. It is folly for those that are under convictions to make it their principal care to *avoid shame*. Our care should be more to save our souls than to save our credit. The scribes and Pharisees had the wound *opened*, and now they should have been desirous to have it *searched*, and then it might have

JAMIESON, FAUSSET, BROWN

with his finger wrote on the ground—The words of our translators in italics ("as though He heard them not") have hardly improved the sense, for it is scarcely probable He could wish that to be thought. Rather He wished to show them His aversion to enter on the subject. But as this did not suit them, they "continue asking Him," pressing for an answer. At last, raising Himself He said.

7. He that is without sin—not meaning sinless altogether; nor yet, guiltless of a literal breach of the Seventh Commandment; but probably, he whose conscience acquits him of *any such* sin. **cast a stone**—"*the* stone," meaning the first one (Deut. 17:7).

8. again he stooped down and wrote—The design of this second stooping and writing on the ground was evidently to give her accusers an opportunity to slink away unobserved *by Him*, and so avoid an exposure to His eye which they could ill have stood. Accordingly it is added.

ADAM CLARKE

add *their sins who accused her, and the sins of all men.* There are many idle conjectures concerning what our Lord wrote on the ground. We never find that Christ wrote anything before or after this, and what He wrote at this time we know not.

7. *He that is without sin.* Meaning the same kind of sin, adultery, fornication. *Let him first cast a stone at her.* Or "upon her." The Jewish method of stoning, according to the rabbins, was as follows: The culprit, half naked, the hands tied behind the back, was placed on a scaffold, ten or twelve feet high. The witnesses, who stood with her, pushed her off with great force. If she was killed by the fall, there was nothing further done; but if she was not, one of the witnesses took up a very large stone, and dashed it upon her breast, which generally was the *coup de grace*, or finishing stroke.

A. B. SIMPSON:

Here was a case of flagrant sin for which no excuse was offered, and all the hostile use His enemies would make of any necessities of the situation, especially the leniency on His part toward her, seemed to demand that He should act with righteous severity, at least according to the strict letter of the law. By a stroke of infinite wisdom He silences her accusers in a moment, and sends them from the room, more confounded than she, under the conviction of their own consciences; and then, by an act of sovereign grace, He forgives her sin without condoning or excusing it in the least degree, and dismisses her with the tender, solemn charge, "Neither do I condemn thee, go and sin no more."

One beautiful act of His delicate grace shines preeminent in all this incident. It was the refusal to look in the face of this poor woman while her accusers were present. Stooping down, He busied himself writing on the ground, and seeming to pay no attention to their bitter charges. This is the beautiful attitude which He still occupies in regard to His people's sins and the devil's charges against them. He listens as though He heard them not. "Who shall lay anything to the charge of God's elect?" But although He forgives, He forgives with a purity as beautiful as His grace is blessed, and speaks to her heart the solemn charge, which the truly forgiven never can forget, "Go and sin no more."

—Christ in the Bible

9. *Being convicted by their own conscience.* So it is likely they were all guilty of similar crimes. *Their own* is not in the original, and is needless; *being convicted by conscience* is expressive enough. *Beginning at the eldest, even unto the last.* "From the most honorable to those of the least repute." In this sense the words are undoubtedly to be understood.

MATTHEW HENRY

been *healed*. It is folly for those that are under convictions to *get away from Jesus Christ*, for he is the only one that can heal the wounds of conscience. To whom will they go?

[5] When the *self-conceited* prosecutors quitted the field, the *self-condemned* prisoner stood her ground: *Jesus was left alone and the woman standing in the midst*, where they set her, *v.* 3. She did not seek to make her escape. Her prosecutors had appealed unto Jesus, and to him she would go. Those whose cause is brought before our Lord Jesus will never have occasion to remove it into any other court. Our cause is lodged in the gospel court; we are *left with Jesus alone*, it is with him only that we have now to deal. Let his gospel *rule us*, and it will infallibly *save us*.

[6] Here is the conclusion of the trial: *Jesus lifted up himself, and he saw none but the woman, v.* 10, 11. The woman, it is likely, stood trembling at the bar, as one doubtful of the issue. Christ was *without sin*, and might cast the first stone; but though none more severe than he against sin, none more compassionate than he to sinners, for he is infinitely gracious and merciful, and this poor malefactor finds him so. The prosecutors are called: *Where are those thine accusers? Hath no man condemned thee?* He asked, that he might shame them, who declined his judgment, and encourage her who resolved to abide by it. They do not appear when the question is asked: *Hath no man condemned thee?* She said, *No man, Lord.* She speaks respectfully to Christ, calls him *Lord*, but is silent concerning her prosecutors. She does not triumph in their retreat nor insult over them as witnesses against themselves, not against her. But she answered the question which concerned herself. *Has no man condemned thee?* True penitents find it enough to give an account of themselves to God, and will not undertake to give account of other people. The prisoner is therefore discharged: *Neither do I condemn thee; go, and sin no more.* 1. Her discharge from the temporal punishment: "If they do not condemn thee to be *stoned to death*, neither *do I.*" Christ would not condemn this woman, (*a*) Because it was *none of his business*; would not intermeddle in secular affairs. (*b*) Because she was prosecuted by those that were more guilty than she and could not for shame insist upon their demand of justice against her. When Christ dismissed her, it was with this caution, *Go, and sin no more.* The fairer the escape was, the fairer the warning was to go and sin no more. Those who help to save the life of a criminal should, as Christ here, help to save the soul with this caution. 2. Her discharge from the eternal punishment. For Christ to say, *I do not condemn thee* is, in effect, to say, *I do forgive thee*; and the *Son of man had power on earth to forgive sins.* He knew the tenderness and sincere repentance of the prisoner, and therefore said that which would comfort her. Those are truly happy whom Christ *doth not condemn.* Christ will not condemn those who, though they have sinned, will *go and sin no more.* Christ's favour to us in the remission of the sins that are past should be a prevailing argument with us to *go and sin no more.*

Verses 12-20

The rest of the chapter is taken up with debates between Christ and contradicting sinners. There were other Pharisees (*v.* 13) to confront Christ, who had brass enough in their foreheads to keep them in countenance.

I. A great doctrine laid down, with the application of it.

1. The doctrine is, *That Christ is the light of the world* (*v.* 12): *Then spoke Jesus again unto them.* They had turned a deaf ear to what he said, and yet he *spoke again to them*, saying, *I am the light of the world.* He was expected to be a *light to enlighten the Gentiles* (Luke ii. 32), and so the *light of the world.* The visible light of the world is the sun. One sun enlightens the whole world, so does one Christ, and there needs no more. What a dungeon would the world be without the sun. So would it be without Christ by whom *light came into the world.* 2. The inference from this doctrine is, *He that followeth me shall not walk in darkness*, but *shall have the light of life.* It is our duty to *follow him.* Christ is the *true light.* It is not enough to *look at* this light, and to *gaze* upon it, but we must follow it, believe in it, and walk in it, for it is a light to *our feet*, not *our eyes* only. It is the happiness of those who follow Christ that they *shall not walk in darkness.* They shall have the *light of life*, the light of spiritual life in this world and of everlasting life in the other world. Follow Christ, and we shall follow him to heaven.

II. The objection which the Pharisees made against this doctrine: *Thou bearest record of thyself; thy record is not true, v.* 13. The objection was very

JAMIESON, FAUSSET, BROWN

9. they . . . convicted . . . went out one by one . . . Jesus was left alone—i.e., without one of her accusers remaining; for it is added—**the woman in the midst**—i.e., of the remaining audience. While the trap failed to catch Him for whom it was laid, it caught those who laid it. Stunned by the unexpected home-thrust, they immediately made off—which makes the impudence of those impure hypocrites in dragging such a case before the public eye the more disgusting.

10. Woman . . .—What inimitable tenderness and grace! Conscious of her own guilt, and till now in the hands of men who had talked of stoning her, wondering at the *skill* with which her accusers had been dispersed, and the *grace* of the few words addressed to herself, she would be disposed to listen, with a reverence and teachableness before unknown, to our Lord's admonition. "And Jesus said unto her, Neither do I condemn thee, go and sin no more." He pronounces no pardon upon the woman (such as, "Thy sins are forgiven thee" —"Go in peace"), much less does He say that she had done nothing condemnable; He simply leaves the matter where it was. He meddles not with the magistrate's office, nor acts the *Judge* in any sense (ch. 12:47). But in saying, "Go and sin no more," which had been before said to one who undoubtedly believed (ch. 5:14), more is probably implied than expressed. If brought suddenly to conviction of sin, admiration of her Deliverer, and a willingness to be admonished and guided by Him, this call to begin a new life may have carried with it what would ensure and naturally bring about a permanent change. (This whole narrative is wanting in some of the earliest and most valuable MSS., and those which have it vary to some extent. The internal evidence in its favor is almost overpowering. It is easy to account for its *omission*, though genuine; but if not so, it is next to impossible to account for its *insertion*).

12-59. FURTHER DISCOURSES OF JESUS—ATTEMPT TO STONE HIM. **12. I am the light of the world**—As the former references to *water* (chs. 4 and 7) and to *bread* (ch. 6) were occasioned by outward occurrences, so this one to *light*. In "the treasury" where it was spoken (see on vs. 20) stood two colossal golden lamp-stands, on which hung a multitude of lamps, lighted after the evening sacrifice (probably every evening during the feast of tabernacles), diffusing their brilliancy, it is said, over all the city. Around these the people danced with great rejoicing. Now, as amidst the festivities of the *water* from Siloam Jesus cried, saying, "If any man thirst, let him come unto me and drink," so now amidst the blaze and the joyousness of this illumination, He proclaims, "I AM THE LIGHT OF THE WORLD"—plainly in the most *absolute* sense. For though He gives His disciples the same title, they are only "light *in the Lord*" (Eph. 5:8); and though He calls the Baptist "the burning and shining light" (or "*lamp*" of his day, ch. 5:35), yet "he was *not that Light*, but was sent to bear witness of that Light: that was THE TRUE LIGHT which, coming into the world, *lighteth every man*" (ch. 1:8, 9). Under this magnificent title Messiah was promised of old (Isa. 42:6; Mal. 4:2, etc.). **he that followeth me**—as one does a light going before him, and as the Israelites did the pillar of bright cloud in the wilderness. **but shall have the light of life**—the light, as of a new world, a newly awakened spiritual and eternal life. **13-19. bearest record of thyself; thy record is not true**—How does He meet this

ADAM CLARKE

The woman standing in the midst. But if they all went out, how could she be in the midst? It is not said that all the people whom our Lord had been instructing went out, but only her accusers; see v. 2. The rest undoubtedly continued with their Teacher.

11. *Neither do I condemn thee.* After weighing what has been adduced in favor of its authenticity and seriously considering its state in the MSS., I must confess the evidence in its favor does not appear to me to be striking. Yet I by no means would have it expunged from the text. It may however be necessary to observe that a very perfect connection subsists between v. 52 of chap. vii and v. 12 of this chapter—all the intermediate verses having been omitted by MSS. of the first antiquity and authority. In some MSS. it is found at the end of this Gospel; in others a vacant place is left in this chapter; and in others it is placed after the twenty-first chapter of Luke.

12. *Then spake Jesus again unto them.* Allowing the story about the woman taken in adultery to be authentic and to stand here in its proper place, we may consider that our Lord, having begun to teach the people in the Temple, was interrupted by the introduction of this woman by the scribes and Pharisees; and now, having dismissed them and the woman also, He resumes His discourse. *I am the light of the world.* The Fountain whence all intellectual light and spiritual understanding proceed; without Me all is darkness, misery, and death. The Divine Being was by the rabbins denominated *The light of the world.* So in *Bamidbar Rabbi:* "The Israelites said to God, O Lord of the universe, thou commandest us to light lamps to thee, yet thou art the light of the world: and with thee the light dwelleth." Our Lord, therefore, assumes here a well-known character of the Supreme Being, and with this we find the Jews were greatly offended. *Shall not walk in darkness.* He shall be saved from ignorance, infidelity, and sin. He *shall have the light of life*—such a light as brings and supports life. The sun, the fountain of light, is also the fountain of life; by its vivifying influences, all things live—neither animal nor vegetative life could exist were it not for its influence. Jesus, the Sun of Righteousness, Mal. iv. 2, is the Fountain of all spiritual and eternal life. His light brings life with it, and they who walk in

MATTHEW HENRY

unjust, for they made that his crime which in the case of one who introduced a divine revelation was necessary and unavoidable. Did not Moses and all the prophets bear witness of themselves when they avouched themselves to be God's messengers? Futhermore they overlooked the testimony of all the other witnesses. Had he only borne record of himself, his testimony had indeed been *suspicious*, and the belief of it might have been *suspended*.

III. Christ's reply to this objection, *v.* 14. He is the light of the world, and it is the property of light to be self-evidencing. First principles prove themselves. He urges three things to prove that his testimony, though of himself, was true and cogent.

1. That he was conscious to himself of his own authority. He did not speak as one at uncertainty. *I know whence I came, and whither I go.* He knew that he came *from the Father*, and was going *to him*, came *from glory*, and was going *to glory*.

2. That they are very incompetent judges of him. Because they were *ignorant*: *You cannot tell whence I came, and whither I go.* He had told them of his coming from heaven and returning to heaven, but it was *foolishness to them*, they *received it not*. They took upon them to judge of that which they did not understand. Because they were *partial* (*v.* 15): *You judge after the flesh.* The judgment cannot be right when the rule is wrong. The Jews judged of Christ and his gospel by outward appearances, and thought it impossible he should be the light of the world; as if the sun under a cloud were no sun. Because they were *unjust* and *unfair* towards him, intimated in this "*I judge no man;* I neither make nor meddle with your political affairs." He thus *judged no man*. It was very unreasonable for them to *judge him after the flesh*.

3. That his testimony of himself was sufficiently supported and corroborated by the testimony of his Father *with him and for him* (*v.* 16): *And yet, if I judge, my judgment is true.* Consider him then,

(1) As a judge: "*If I judge, my judgment is true. If I should judge*, my judgment must be true, and then you would be condemned." Now that which makes his judgment unexceptionable is his Father's concurrence with him: *I am not alone, but I and the Father.* He did not act *separately*, but in his own name and his Father's. His Father's commission was to him: "It is the Father that *sent me*." No doubt his *judgment* was *true* and valid.

(2) Look upon him as *a witness*. As such his testimony was true and unexceptionable; this he shows, *v.* 17, 18. He quotes a maxim of the Jewish law, *v.* 17: That *the testimony of two men is true*. If nothing appear to the contrary it is taken for granted to be *true*. He applies this to the case in hand (*v.* 18): *I am one that bear witness of myself, and the Father that sent me bears witness of me.* Behold two witnesses! Now if the testimony of two distinct persons, that are *men*, and therefore may deceive or be deceived, is conclusive, much more ought the testimony of the Son of God concerning himself, backed with the testimony of his Father concerning him, to command assent. In conclusion, we are told how their tongues were let loose, and their hands tied.

First, How their tongues were let loose, *v.* 19. They set themselves to *cross question* with him.

a. How they evaded the *conviction*. *Then said they unto him, Where is thy Father?* They might easily have understood that when he spoke of his *Father* he meant no other than God himself; yet they pretend to understand him of a common person. They bid him *call his witness*, and challenge him, if he can, to produce him: *Where is thy Father?* Thus, as Christ said of them (*v.* 15), they *judge after the flesh*. Thus they turned it off with a taunt.

b. How he evaded the *cavil* with a further *conviction*; he charged them with wilful ignorance: "*You neither know me nor my Father.* It is to no purpose to discourse to you about divine things, who talk of them as blind men do of colours." He charges them with ignorance of God: "*You know not my Father.*" Their eyes were darkened that they could not see the light of his glory shining *in the face of Jesus Christ*. The *little children* of the Christian church *know the Father*, but these rulers of the Jews did not, because they would not so know him. He shows them the true cause of their ignorance of God: *If you had known me, you would have known my Father also.* The reason why men are ignorant of God is because they are unacquainted with Jesus Christ. In knowing him we should know the Father. If we *knew Christ* better, we should *know the Father* better.

Secondly, See how their hands were tied, though their tongues were thus let loose. *These words spoke Jesus in the treasury.* Now the priests might easily, with the assistance of the janizaries that were at their beck, either have seized him and exposed him to the rage of the mob, or, at least, have *silenced* him. Yet

JAMIESON, FAUSSET, BROWN

specious cavil? Not by disputing the wholesome human maxim that "self-praise is no praise," but by affirming that He was *an exception to the rule*, or rather, that *it had no application to Him*.

14. for I know whence I came, and whither I go . . .—(See on ch. 7:28, 29). **15. Ye judge after the flesh**—with no spiritual apprehension. **I judge no man.**

16. And yet if I judge, my judgment is true . . .—Ye not only *form* your carnal and warped judgments of Me, but are bent on carrying them into effect; I, though I form and utter My judgment of you, am not here to carry this into execution—that is reserved to a future day; yet the judgment I now pronounce and the witness I now bear is not Mine only as ye suppose, but His also that sent Me. (See on ch. 5:31, 32.) And these are the two witnesses to any fact which your law requires.

20. These words spake Jesus in the treasury—a division, so called, of the fore-court of the temple, part of the court of the women [JOSEPHUS, *Antiquities*, xix. 6. 2, etc.), which may confirm the genuineness of vss. 2-11, as the place where the woman was brought.

ADAM CLARKE

His light live in His life. Some suppose our Lord alludes to the custom of lighting lamps or torches on the first day of the Feast of Tabernacles. But as these words seem to have been spoken the day after that last and great day of the feast, mentioned in chap. vii. 37, they may rather be considered as referring to the following custom. It has already been observed that the Jews added a ninth day to this feast, which day they termed "the feast of joy for the law"; and on that day they were accustomed to take all the sacred books out of the chest where they had been deposited, and put a lighted candle in their place, in allusion to Prov. vi. 23: "For the commandment is a lamp [or candle]; and the law is light"; or to Ps. cxix. 105: "Thy word is a lamp unto my feet, and a light unto my path." If this custom existed in the time of our Lord, it is most likely that it is to it He here alludes, as it must have happened about the same time in which these words were spoken. As the Messiah was frequently spoken of by the prophets under the emblem of light (see Isa. lx. 1; xlix. 6; ix. 2), the Pharisees must at once perceive that He intended to recommend himself to the people as the Messiah, when He said, *I am the light of the world.*

13. *Thou bearest record.* As if they had said, Dost Thou imagine that we shall believe Thee, in a matter so important, on Thy bare assertion? Had these people attended to the teaching and miracles of Christ, they would have seen that His pretensions to the Messiahship were supported by the most irrefragable testimony.

14. *I know whence I came.* I came from God, and am going to God, and can neither do nor say anything but what leads to and glorifies Him.

15. *Ye judge after the flesh.* Because I appear in the form of man, judging from this appearance, you think I am but a mere man—pay attention to My teaching and miracles, and you shall then see that nothing less than infinite wisdom and unlimited power could teach and do what I have taught and performed.

19. *Ye neither know me.* You know neither the Messiah nor the God that sent Him. *If ye had known me.* If you had received My teaching, you would have got such an acquaintance with the nature and attributes of God as you never could have had and never can have any other way. That is a true saying, "No man hath seen God at any time; the only begotten Son, which is in the bosom of the Father, he hath declared him." The nature and perfections of God never can be properly known but in the light of the gospel of Jesus Christ.

20. *The treasury.* Lightfoot observes, from the rabbins, that the treasury was in what was called the "court of the women"—that there were thirteen chests in it; in the thirteenth only the women were permitted to put their offerings. Probably the other twelve were placed there in reference to the twelve tribes, each perhaps inscribed with the name of one of Jacob's twelve

ALBERT BARNES:

18. "I am one that bear witness of myself." In human courts a man is not allowed to bear witness of himself, because he has a personal interest in the case, and the court could have no proof of the impartiality of the evidence; but in the case of Jesus it was otherwise. When one has no party ends to serve; when he is willing to deny himself; when he makes great sacrifices; and when, by his life, he gives every evidence of sincerity, his own testimony may be admitted in evidence of his motives and designs. This was the case with Jesus and his apostles. And though in a legal or criminal case such testimony would not be admitted, yet, in an argument on moral subjects, about the will and purpose of him who sent him, it would not be right to reject the testimony of one who gave so many proofs that he came from God.

"The Father—beareth witness of me." By the voice from heaven at his baptism (Matt. 3:17), and by the miracles which Jesus wrought, as well as by the prophecies of the Old Testament. We may here remark that there is a distinction between the Father and the Son. They are both represented as bearing testimony; yet, they are not divided. They are not different beings. They bear testimony to the same thing, and are one in counsel, in plan, in essence, and in glory.—*Popular Commentary*

MATTHEW HENRY

even *in the temple,* where they had him in their reach, *no man laid hands on him,* for *his hour was not yet come.* 1. The restraint laid upon his persecutors by an invisible power. God can set bounds to the wrath of men, as he does to the waves of the sea. 2. The reason of this restraint: *His hour was not yet come.* The frequent mention of this, intimates how much the time of our departure out of the world depends upon the fixed counsel and decree of God. It *will* come, it is coming; not yet come, but it is at hand. *My times are in thy hands;* and better there than in our own.

Verses 21–30

Christ here gives fair warning to the careless unbelieving Jews to consider what would be the consequence of their infidelity.

I. The wrath threatened (*v.* 21): *Jesus said again unto them.* He continued to teach, in kindness to those few who received his doctrine, which is an example to ministers to go on with their work, notwithstanding opposition, because a remnant shall be saved. Here Christ changes his voice; he had *piped to them* in the offers of his grace, and they *had not danced;* now he mourns to them in the denunciations of his wrath, to try if they would lament. He said *I go my way, and you shall seek me, and shall die in your sins. Whither I go you cannot come.* Every word is terrible, and bespeaks spiritual judgments, which are the sorest of all judgments. Four things are here threatened against the Jews.

1. Christ's departure from them: *I go my way.* But woe to those from whom Christ departs. He *bade often farewell,* as one *loth to depart,* and willing to be invited.

2. Their enmity to the true Messiah, and their infatuated enquiries after another Messiah when he was gone away. *You shall seek me,* which intimates either, (1) Their *enmity* to the *true Christ*: "You shall seek to ruin my interest, by persecuting my doctrine and followers." Or, (2) Their *enquiries* after *false Christs*: "You shall continue your expectations of the Messiah, of a Christ to come, when he is already come."

3. Their final impenitency: *You shall die in your sins.* Here it is meant especially of the sin of unbelief. Those that live in unbelief are for ever undone if they die in unbelief. Many that have long lived in sin are, through grace, saved by a timely repentance from *dying in sin.*

4. Their eternal separation from Christ. *Whither I go you cannot come.* When Christ left the world he went to paradise. Thither he took the penitent thief with him, that did not die in his sins; but the impenitent not only *shall not* come to him, but they *cannot*; for heaven would not be heaven to those that die unsanctified and unmeet for it.

II. The jest they made of this threatening. They turned it into ridicule (*v.* 22): *Will he kill himself?* What slight thoughts they had of Christ's threatenings; they could make themselves and one another merry with them. What ill thoughts they had of Christ's meaning, as if he had an inhuman design upon his own life. They had put a much more favourable construction upon this word of his (*ch.* vii. 34, 35): *Will he go to the dispersed among the Gentiles?* But see how indulged malice grows more and more malicious.

III. The confirmation of what he had said.

1. He had said, *Whither I go you cannot come* (*v.* 23): *You are from beneath, I am from above; you are of this world, I am not of this world.* You are *of those things which are beneath.* You are *in with these things,* how can you come where I go, when your spirit and disposition are so directly contrary to mine? The *spirit of the Lord Jesus* was—not of *this world,* but from *above.* None shall be with him but those who are *born from above* and have their *conversation in heaven.* How contrary to this *their* spirit was: "*You are from beneath.*" What communion could Christ have with them?

2. He had said, *You shall die in your sins,* and here he stands to it. He gives this further reason for it, *If you believe not that I am he, you shall die in your sins, v.* 34. (1) What we are required to believe: *that I am he;* he that should come, he that you expect the Messias to be. I do not only call myself so, but I *am he.* True faith does not *amuse* the soul with an empty sound of words, but *affects* it. (2) How necessary it is that we believe this. If we have not this faith, *we shall die in our sins.* We cannot be saved from the power of sin while we live, and therefore shall certainly continue in it to the last. None but the *Spirit* of Christ's grace will be an agent powerful enough to turn us from sin to God. If Christ do not cure us, our case is desperate, and we shall *die in our*

JAMIESON, FAUSSET, BROWN

no man laid hands on him . . .—(See on ch. 7:30). In the dialogue that follows, the conflict waxes sharper on both sides, till rising to its climax, they take up stones to stone him.

21-25. Then said Jesus again unto them, I go my way . . .—(See on ch. 7:34).

22. Then said the Jews, Will he kill himself?—seeing something more in His words than before (ch. 7:35), but their question more malignant and scornful.

23. Ye are from beneath; I am from above—contrasting Himself, not as in ch. 3:31, simply with *earthborn messengers of God,* but *with men sprung from and breathing an opposite element* from His, which rendered it impossible that He and they should have any present fellowship, or dwell eternally together. (See again on ch. 7:34: also vs. 44.)

24. if ye believe not that I am he, ye shall die in your sins—They knew well enough what He meant (Mark 13:6, *Gr.;* cf. Matt. 24:5). But He would not, by speaking it out, give them the materials for a charge for which they were watching. At the same time, one is irresistibly reminded by such language, so far transcending what is becoming in *men,* of those ancient declarations of the God of Israel, "I AM HE" (Deut. 32:39; Isa. 43:10, 13; 46:4; 48:12). See on ch. 6:20.

ADAM CLARKE

sons. *His hour was not yet come.* The time was not arrived in which He had determined to give himself up into the hands of His crucifiers.

21. *Then said Jesus again unto them.* He had said the same things to them the day before. See chap. vii. 34. *Ye shall seek me.* When your calamities come upon you, you shall in vain seek for the help of the Messiah, whom you now reject and whom you shall shortly crucify.

22. *Will he kill himself?* They now understood that He spoke concerning His death; but before, chap. vii. 35, they thought He spoke of going to some of the Grecian provinces to preach to the dispersed Jews.

23. *Ye are from beneath.* You are capable of murder, and of self-murder too, because you have nothing of God in you. They verified this character in murdering the Lord Jesus; and many of them afterwards, to escape famine, put an end to their own lives.

A. T. ROBERTSON:

21. "Again" (*palin*). Probably *palin* (again) in verse 12 refers to a day after the feast is over since the last day is mentioned in 7:37. So then here again we probably move on to another day still beyond that in verse 12. "And ye shall seek me" (*kai zetesete me*). As in 7:34, "the search of despair" (Bernard), seeking for the Messiah when it is too late, the tragedy of Judaism today (1:11). "And ye shall die in your sin" (*kai en tei hamartiai humon apothaneisthe*). Future middle indicative of *apothnesko* which is the emphatic word here (Ezek. 3:18; 18:18; Prov. 24:9). Note singular *hamartiai* (sin) here, but plural *hamartiais* (sins) when the phrase is repeated in verse 24 (sin in its essence, sin in its acts). "Ye cannot come" (*humeis ou dunasthe elthein*). Precise language of 7:34 to the Jews and to the apostles in 13:33.

22. "Will he kill himself?" (*meti apoktenei heauton*). Negative answer formally expected, but there is a manifest sneer in the query. "The mockery in these words is alike subtle and bitter" (Vincent). It was a different group of Jews in 7:31 who cynically suggested that he was going to work among the Greeks in the Dispersion. Here they infer that Jesus refers to the next world. They suggest the depths of Gehenna for him as the abode of suicides (Josephus, *War* III. viii. 5). Of course the rabbis could not join Jesus there! Edersheim argues against this view.
— Word Pictures in the New Testament

MATTHEW HENRY

sins. Without faith we cannot be saved from the punishment of sin when we die. This implies the great gospel promise: *If we believe that Christ is he,* and receive him accordingly, *we shall not die in our sins.* Believers die in Christ, in his love, in his arms.

IV. Here is a further discourse concerning *himself, v.* 25–29.

1. The question which the Jews put to him (*v.* 25): *Who art thou?* He had said, You must believe that *I am he.* His not saying expressly who he was, they turned to his reproach, as if he knew not what to say of himself: "*Who art thou?*"

2. His answer to this question, wherein he directs them three ways for information:

(1) He refers them to *what he had said* all along: "Do you ask who I am? *Even the same that I said unto you from the beginning.*" I am *the same that I said to you from the beginning* of time in the scriptures of the Old Testament; *from the beginning* of my public ministry. The account he had already given of himself he resolved to *abide by.* To this he refers them for an answer to their question.

(2) He refers them to his Father's judgment (*v.* 26): "*I have many things to say, and to judge of you. I speak to the world* (to which I am sent as an ambassador) *those things which I have heard of him.*"

[1] He suppresses his accusation of them. He had *many things* to charge them with, but for the present he had said enough.

[2] He enters his appeal against them to his Father: *He that sent me.* Here two things comfort him: *First,* That he had been *true to his Father,* and to the trust reposed in him: *I speak to the world* (for his gospel was to be preached to every creature) *those things which I have heard of him. Secondly,* That his Father would be *true to him.* Though he should not *accuse* them to his Father, yet the Father, who sent him, would undoubtedly reckon. Christ would not accuse them; "for," saith he, "he that sent me is true, and will pass judgment on them." Upon this part of our Saviour's discourse the evangelist has a melancholy remark (*v.* 27): *They understood not that he spoke to them of the Father.* Though Christ spoke so plainly of God as his Father in heaven, yet they did not understand whom he meant. Day and night are alike to the blind.

(3) He refers them to *their own convictions* hereafter, *v.* 28, 29. Now observe here,

[1] *What* they should ere long be *convinced of*: "*You shall know that I am he.* You shall be made to know it in your own consciences, the convictions of which, though you may *stifle,* yet you cannot *baffle.*" Two things they should be convinced of, *First,* That he did nothing *of himself,* of himself without the Father. Of false prophets it is said that they prophesied *out of their own hearts,* and followed *their own spirits. Secondly,* That as *his Father taught him* so he *spoke these things,* that he was not *self-taught,* but *taught of God.*

[2] *When* they should be convinced of this: *When you have lifted up the Son of man,* lifted him up upon the cross, as the brazen serpent upon the pole (*ch.* iii. 14). Or the expression denotes that his death was his exaltation. They *lifted him up* to the cross, but then he lifted up himself to his Father. Observe with what tenderness and mildness Christ here speaks to those who he certainly knew would put him to death. Christ speaks of his death as that which would be a powerful conviction of the infidelity of the Jews. *When you have lifted up the Son of man, then shall you know* this. Careless and unthinking people are often taught the worth of mercies by the want of them. The guilt of their sin would so awaken their consciences that they would be put upon serious enquiries after a Saviour, and then would know that Jesus was he who alone could save them. And so it proved, when, being told that with wicked hands they had *crucified and slain* the Son of God, they cried out, *What shall we do?* (Acts ii. 36). There would be such signs and wonders attending his death as would give a stronger proof of his being the Messiah than any that had been yet given. By the death of Christ the pouring out of the Spirit was purchased, who would convince the world that *Jesus is he.* The judgments which the Jews brought upon themselves, by putting Christ to death, were a sensible conviction to the most hardened among them that *Jesus was he.*

[3] What supported our Lord Jesus in the mean time (*v.* 29): *He that sent me is with me, for the Father hath not left me alone,* for *I do always those things that please him.* The assurance which Christ had of his Father's *presence* with him: *He that sent me is with me.* This greatly *emboldens* our faith in Christ and our reliance upon his word. The King of kings accompanied his own ambassador, and *never left him alone,* either solitary or weak; it also *aggravated* the wickedness of those that opposed him. The

JAMIESON, FAUSSET, BROWN

25. Who art thou?—hoping thus to extort an explicit answer; but they are disappointed.

26, 27. I have many things to say and to judge of you; but he that sent me is true . . .—i.e., I could, and at the fitting time, will say and judge many things of you (referring perhaps to the work of the Spirit which is for *judgment* as well as *salvation, ch.* 16:8), but what I do say is just the message My Father hath given Me to deliver.

28-30. When ye have lifted up the Son of man—The plainest intimation He had yet given *in public* of *the manner* and the *authors* of His death. **then shall ye know that I am he . . .**—i.e., *find out,* or have sufficient evidence, how true was all He said, though they would be far from owning it.

29. the Father hath not left me alone; for I do always those things that please him . . .—i.e., To you, who gnash upon Me with your teeth, and frown down all open appearance for Me, I seem to stand uncountenanced and alone; but I have a sympathy and support transcending all human applause; I came hither to do My Father's will, and in the doing of it have not ceased to please Him; therefore is He ever by Me with His approving smile, His cheering words, His supporting arm.

ADAM CLARKE

25. *Who art thou?* This marks the indignation of the Pharisees—as if they had said: Who art Thou that takest upon Thee to deal out threatenings in this manner against us? *Jesus saith unto them, Even the same that I said unto you from the beginning.* Rather, "Just what I have already told you," i.e., that "I am the light of the world"—the Christ—the Saviour of mankind.

26. *I have many things to say and to judge of you.* Or "to speak and to condemn."

28. *When ye have lifted up.* When you have crucified Me, and thus filled up the measure of your iniquities, you shall know that I am the Christ by the signs that shall follow; and you shall know that what I spoke is true by the judgments that shall follow. To be lifted up is a common mode of expression among the Jewish writers for "to die" or "to be killed."

29. *The Father hath not left me alone.* Though you shall have power to put Me to death, yet this shall not be because He has abandoned Me. No—He is ever with Me, because I do that which pleases Him; and it is His pleasure that I should lay down My life for the salvation of the world.

G. CAMPBELL MORGAN:

"When you have lifted up the Son of man you will know." In these words we catch the accents of the everlasting mercy. He had spoken to them in anger. He had had to tell them the truth. They were from beneath; and all their attitude was mastered by hell. But He was in the world under the mastery of high heaven. One day, He told them, the revelation would come to them. When they had lifted up the Son of man, they would understand. "I do always the things that please my Father"; and within those are the things to which I refer, the lifting up of the Son of man. So in the midst of all the bitterness of opposition, and the sternness of rebuke, there was the vibrant tenderness of the everlasting mercy.—*The Gospel According to John*

ground of this assurance: *For I do always those things that please him.* His whole undertaking is called the *pleasure of the Lord* (Isa. liii. 10). His management of that affair was in nothing *displeasing* to his Father. Our Lord Jesus never offended his Father in anything, he *fulfilled all righteousness.* God's servants may *then* expect God's presence with them when they *choose* and do *those things that please him.*

V. Here is the good effect which this discourse of Christ's had upon some of his hearers (*v.* 30): *As he spoke these words many believed on him.* There is a remnant who *believe to the saving of the soul.* If Israel, the whole body of the people, *be not gathered,* yet there are those of them in whom Christ will be *glorious.* When Christ told them that if they *believed not* they should *die in their sins,* they thought it was time to look about them. Sometimes there is a *wide door opened,* and an *effectual* one, even where there are *many adversaries.* The gospel sometimes gains great victories where it meets with great opposition. Let this encourage God's ministers to preach the gospel, though it be with *much contention,* for they shall not *labour in vain.* Many may be *secretly* brought home to God by those endeavours which are openly contradicted.

Verses 31–37

I. A comfortable doctrine laid down concerning the *spiritual liberty* of Christ's disciples. Christ, knowing that his doctrine began to work upon some of his hearers addressed himself to those *weak* believers.

1. How graciously the Lord Jesus looks to those that *tremble at his word,* and are ready to receive it; and will not pass by those who set themselves in his way, without speaking to them.

2. How carefully he cherishes the beginnings of grace. In what he said to them, we have two things, which he saith to all that should at any time believe: (1) The character of a true disciple of Christ: *If you continue in my word, then are you my disciples indeed.* He lays down this for a settled rule, that he would own none for his disciples but those that *continued in his word.* It highly concerns those that are not *strong in faith* to see to it that they be *sound in the faith.* Let those who have thoughts of covenanting with Christ have no thoughts of reserving a power of revocation. Children are sent to school, and bound apprentices, only for a *few years;* but those only are Christ's who are willing to be bound to him *for the term of life.* Those only that *continue in Christ's word* shall be accepted as his *disciples indeed.* It is *to dwell* in Christ's word, as a man does at home, which is his centre, and rest, and refuge.

(2) The privilege of a true disciple of Christ. Here are two precious promises, *v.* 32. "*You shall know the truth.*" Even those who are true believers may be, and are, much in the dark concerning many things which they should know. God's children are but children, and understand and speak as children. Did we not need to be taught, we should not need to be disciples. It is a very great privilege to *know the truth.* Christ's scholars are sure to be well taught. *The truth shall make you free;* that is, *First,* The truth which Christ teaches tends to make men free, Isa. lxi. 1. It makes us *free from* our spiritual enemies, free *in* the service of God, free *to* the privileges of sons. *Secondly,* The knowing, entertaining, and believing, of this truth does actually *make us free,* free from prejudices, mistakes, and false notions, free from the dominion of lust and passion; and restores the soul to the government of itself. The mind, by admitting the truth of Christ is vastly enlarged, and has scope and compass given it and never acts with so true a liberty as when it acts under a divine command, 2 Cor. iii. 17.

II. The offence which the carnal Jews took at this doctrine. They cavilled at it, *v.* 33. With a great deal of pride and envy they answered him, "*We Jews are Abraham's seed,* and therefore are *free-born; we were never in bondage to any man; how sayest thou then, You shall be made free?*"

1. What it was that they were grieved at; it was an *innuendo* in those words, *You shall be made free,* as if the Jewish nation were in some sort of bondage. 2. What it was that they alleged against it. (1) "We are Abraham's seed." It is common for a sinking decaying family to boast of the glory and dignity of its ancestors, and to borrow honour from that name to which they repay disgrace; so the Jews here did. It is the common fault and folly of those that have pious parentage and education to trust to their privilege, and boast of it, as if it would atone for the want of real holiness. Saving benefits are not conveyed by *entail* to us and our issue, nor can a title to heaven be made by *descent.* They are not all Israel that are of Israel. (2) *We were never in bondage*

30. As he spake these words, many believed on him—Instead of wondering at this, the wonder would be if words of such unearthly, surpassing grandeur *could* be uttered without captivating *some* that heard them. And just as "all that sat in the council" to try Stephen "*saw his face*"—though expecting nothing but death—"*as it had been the face of an angel*" (Acts 6:15), so may we suppose that, full of the sweet supporting sense of His Father's presence, amidst the rage and scorn of the rulers, a divine benignity beamed from His countenance, irradiated the words that fell from Him, and won over the candid "many" of His audience.

31-33. Then said Jesus to those Jews who believed, If ye continue in my word, then are ye my disciples indeed . . .—The impression produced by the last words of our Lord may have become visible by some decisive movement, and here He takes advantage of it to press on them "*continuance*" in the faith, since then only were they His real disciples (cf. ch. 15:3-8), and then should they *experimentally* "know the truth," and "by the truth be made (*spiritually*) free."

33. They answered him, We be Abraham's seed, and were never in bondage to any man . . .—Who said this? Not surely the very class just spoken of as won over by His divine words, and exhorted to continue in them. Most interpreters seem to think so; but it is hard to ascribe such a petulant speech to the newly gained disciples, even in the lowest sense, much less persons *so* gained as they were. It came, probably, from persons mixed up with them in the same part of the crowd, but of a very different spirit. The *pride* of the Jewish nation, even now after centuries of humiliation, is the most striking feature of their character. 'Talk of freedom to *us*? Pray when or to whom were we ever in bondage?' This bluster sounds almost ludicrous from such a nation. Had they forgotten their long and bitter bondage in Egypt? their dreary captivity in Babylon? their present bondage to the Roman yoke, and their restless eagerness to throw it off? But probably they

30. *As he spake these words, many believed on him.* The same sun that hardens the clay softens the wax. This discourse, which proved the savor of death unto death to the obstinate Pharisees, became the savor of life unto life to many of the simplehearted people.

31. *If ye continue in my word.* Or "in this doctrine of Mine." It is not enough to receive God's truth—we must retain and walk in it. And it is only when we receive the truth, love it, keep it, and walk in it, that we are the genuine disciples of Christ.

32. *Ye shall know the truth.* Shall have a constant experimental knowledge of its power and efficacy. *And the truth shall make you free.* It was a maxim of the Jews "that no man was free, but he who exercised himself in the meditation of the law." No man is truly free but he in whose heart the power of sin is destroyed, and who has received the Spirit of adoption, through which he cries, "Abba! Father!" See Rom. viii. 15. The bondage of sin is the most grievous bondage, and freedom from its guilt and influence is the greatest liberty.

33. *They answered.* That is, the other Jews who had not believed—the carping, cavilling Pharisees already mentioned; for the words cannot be spoken of the simple people who had already believed.

MATTHEW HENRY

to any man. How false this allegation was. I wonder how they could have the assurance to say a thing in the face of a congregation which was so notoriously *untrue.* Were they not at this time tributaries to the Romans, and, though not in a *personal,* yet in a *national* bondage to them, and groaning to be made free? How foolish the application was. Christ had spoken of a liberty wherewith the *truth* would make them free, which must be meant of a *spiritual* liberty, for truth as it is the enriching, so it is the *enfranchising* of the mind, and the *enlarging* of that from the captivity of error and prejudice; and yet they plead against the offer of *spiritual* liberty that they were never in *corporal* thraldom. Carnal hearts are sensible of no other grievances than those that molest the body and injure their secular affairs. Discourse to them of the bondage of sin, a captivity to Satan, and a liberty by Christ—and *you bring certain strange things to their ears.*

III. Our Saviour's vindication of his doctrine, *v.* 34–37, where he does these four things:

1. He shows that it was possible that they might be in a state of bondage (*v.* 34): *Whosoever commits sin* is the servant of sin. Christ further explains what he had said for their edification. (1) The preface is very solemn: *Verily, verily, I say unto you.* The style of the prophets was, *Thus saith the Lord,* for they were *faithful* as *servants;* but Christ, being a Son, speaks in his own name: *I say unto you.* He pawns his veracity upon it.

(2) The truth is of universal concern: *Whosoever commits sin is the servant of sin,* and sadly needs to be made free. See who it is on whom this brand is fastened—on him that *commits sin.* There is not a *just man* upon earth, that *lives, and sins not;* yet every one that sins is not a servant of sin, for then God would have no servants; but he that *makes sin,* that *makes choice* of sin, who walks after the flesh, and *makes a trade* of sin. See what the brand is which Christ fastens upon those that thus *commit sin.* He stigmatizes them, gives them a mark of servitude. They are *servants of sin.* He does the work of sin, supports its interest, and accepts its wages, Rom. vi. 16.

2. He shows them that their having a place in the house of God would not entitle them to the inheritance of sons: for (*v.* 35) *the servant abideth not in the house for ever, but the son* of the family abideth ever. (1) This points primarily at the rejection of the Jewish church and nation. Israel had been *God's son,* his *first-born.* Christ tells them that having made themselves servants they should not *abide in the house for ever.* "Think not to be made free from sin by the rites and ceremonies of the law of Moses, for Moses was but a servant. But, if the Son make you free, it is well," *v.* 36. (2) It looks further, to the rejection of all that are the *servants of sin.* True believers only are accounted free, and shall abide for ever in the house.

3. He shows them the way of deliverance. The case of those that are the servants of sin is sad, but thanks be to God it is not helpless, it is not hopeless. He who is *the Son* has a power both of manumission and of adoption (*v.* 36): *If the Son shall make you free, you shall be free indeed.*

(1) Jesus Christ in the gospel offers us *our freedom.* [1] To *discharge prisoners;* this he does in *justification,* by making satisfaction for *our guilt,* and for *our debts.* Christ, as our surety, compounds with the creditor, answers the demands of injured justice with more than an *equivalent.* [2] He has a power to rescue *bond-slaves,* and this he does in *sanctification;* by the powerful operations of his Spirit, he breaks the power of corruption in the soul, rallies the scattered forces of reason and virtue, and so the soul is made free. [3] He has a power to *naturalize strangers and foreigners,* and this he does in *adoption.* This is a further act of grace. There is a charter of privileges as well as pardon.

(2) Those whom Christ makes free are *free indeed.* It is not the word used (*v.* 31) for disciples *indeed,* but *really.* The truth and certainty of the promise, the liberty which the Jews boasted of was an *imaginary* liberty; but the liberty which Christ gives is a certain thing, it is real. The servants of sin promise themselves liberty and fancy themselves free, but they cheat themselves. None are *free indeed* but those whom Christ *makes free.* The singular excellency of the freedom promised; it is a freedom that deserves the name. It is a *glorious* liberty. It is *substance,* while the things of the world are shadows.

4. He applies this in answer to their boasts of relation to Abraham (*v.* 37): *"I know that you are Abraham's seed, but now you seek to kill me, because my word hath no place in you."*

(1) The dignity of their extraction admitted: *"I know that you are Abraham's seed."* They boasted of

JAMIESON, FAUSSET, BROWN

saw that our Lord pointed to something else—freedom, perhaps, from the leaders of sects or parties—and were not willing to allow their subjection even to these. Our Lord, therefore, though He knew what slaves they were in this sense, drives the ploughshare somewhat deeper than this, to a bondage they little dreamt of.

34, 35. Whosoever committeth sin—i.e., *liveth in the commission* of it—(Cf. I John 3:8; Matt. 7:23). **is the servant of sin**—i.e., the *bond-servant,* or *slave* of it; for the question is not about free service, but who are in *bondage.* (Cf. II Pet. 2:19; Rev. 6:16.) The great truth here expressed was not unknown to heathen moralists; but it was applied only to *vice,* for they were total strangers to what in revealed religion is called *sin.* The thought of *slaves* and *freemen* in the house suggests to our Lord a wider idea.

35. And the servant abideth not in the house for ever, but the Son abideth ever—i.e., 'And if your connection with the family of God be that of BOND-SERVANTS, ye have no *natural tie* to the house; your tie is essentially *uncertain and precarious.* But the SON'S relationship to the FATHER is a *natural and essential* one; it is an indefeasible tie; His abode in it is *perpetual* and *of right:* That is My relationship, My tie: If, then, ye would have your connection with God's family made *real, rightful, permanent,* ye must by the Son be *manumitted* and *adopted* as sons and daughters of the Lord Almighty.' In this sublime statement there is no doubt a *subordinate* allusion to Genesis 21:10, *"Cast out* this *bondwoman and her son,* for *the son of this bondwoman shall not be heir with my son,* with Isaac." (Cf. Gal. 4:22-30.)

37-41. ye seek to kill me—He had said this to their face before: He now repeats it, and they do not deny it; yet are they held back, as by some marvellous spell—it was the awe which His combined dignity, courage, and benignity struck into them.

ADAM CLARKE

Were never in bondage to any man. This assertion was not only false, but it was ridiculous in the extreme, seeing their whole history, sacred and profane, is full of recitals of their servitude in Egypt, in Chaldea, under the Persians, under the Macedonians, and under the Romans.

34. *Whosoever committeth sin is the servant of sin.* Or "is the slave of sin." This was the slavery of which Christ spoke, and deliverance from it was the liberty which He promised.

35. *And the servant abideth not in the house.* Or, rather, "Now the slave abideth not in the family." As if Jesus had said: And now that I am speaking of a *slave,* I will add one thing more, viz., a slave has no right to any part of the inheritance in the family to which he belongs; but the *son,* the legitimate son, has a right.

CHARLES H. SPURGEON:

When Christ sets free no chains can bind again. Let the Master say to me, "Captive, I have delivered thee," and it is done. Come on, come on, ye fiends of the pit! Mightier is he who is for us than all they who be against us. Come on, come on, temptations of the world, but if the Lord be on our side, whom shall we fear? If He be our defense, who shall be our destruction? Come on, come on, ye foul corruptions, come on, ye machinations and temptations of my own deceitful heart, but He who hath begun the good work in me will carry it on and perfect it to the end. Gather ye, gather ye, gather ye, all your hosts together, ye who are the foes of God and the enemies of man, and come at once with concentrated fury and with hellish might against my spirit, but if God acquitteth, who is he that condemneth? Who shall separate us from the love of God which is in Christ Jesus our Lord? Yon black stream of health shall never wash out the mark of Christian liberty. That skeleton monarch bears no yoke which he can put upon a believer's neck. We will shout victory when we are breast-deep amidst the last billows and grapple with the king upon the pale horse: we will throw the rider and win the victory in the last struggle, according as it is written, "Thanks be unto God which giveth us the victory through our Lord Jesus Christ." Sparta and Greece refused to wear the yoke of Persia and broke the proud king's pomp; but we are free in a nobler sense. We refuse the yoke of Satan and will overcome his power as Christ overcame it in the days gone by.—*The Treasury of the New Testament*

MATTHEW HENRY

their descent from *Abraham*, as that which *aggrandized* their names; whereas really it did but *aggravate* their crimes.

(2) The inconsistency of their practice with this dignity: *But you seek to kill me.* They had attempted it several times, and were now designing it, which quickly appeared (*v.* 58), when they *took up stones to cast at him.*

(3) The reason of this inconsistency. It is because *my word hath no place in you.* Some of the critics read it, *My word does not penetrate into you;* it descended as the rain, but it came upon them as the rain upon the rock, which it runs off, and did not soak into their hearts, as the rain upon the ploughed ground. Our translation is very significant: *It has no place in you.* The words of Christ ought to have a place in us, the innermost and uppermost place,—a *dwelling* place, as a man at home, and not as a stranger or sojourner,—a *working* place; it must have room to operate, to work sin out of us, and to work grace in us; it must have a *ruling* place, its place must be *upon the throne.* There are many that make a profession of religion in whom *the word of* Christ has no place; they will not *allow* it a place, for they do not like it. Other things possess the place it should have in us. Where the word of God has no place no good is to be expected, for room is left there for all wickedness.

Verses 38–47

Here Christ and the Jews are still at issue.

I. He here traces the difference between his sentiments and theirs to a different rise and origin (*v.* 38): *I speak that which I have seen with my Father,* and *you do what you have seen with your father.*

1. Christ's *doctrine* was from *heaven. I speak that which I have seen.* The discoveries Christ has made to us of God and another world are not grounded upon guess and hearsay. It is what I have seen *with my Father.* The doctrine of Christ is not a plausible hypothesis, supported by probable arguments. It was not only what he had *heard from* his Father, but what he had *seen with him.* It was Christ's prerogative to have *seen* what he *spoke,* and to *speak* what he had *seen.*

2. Their *doings* were from hell: "*You do that which you have seen with your father.*" As a child that is trained up with his father learns his father's words and fashions, and grows like him by imitation as well as by a natural image, so these Jews made themselves as like the devil as if they had industriously set him before them for their pattern.

II. He answers their vain-glorious boasts of relation to Abraham and to God as their fathers.

1. They pleaded relation to Abraham, and he replies to this plea. *They said, Abraham is our father, v.* 39. In this they intended, (1) To do honour to themselves, and to make themselves look great. (2) They designed to cast an odium upon Christ as if he reflected upon the patriarch Abraham, in speaking of their father as one they had learned evil from. Now Christ overthrows this plea by a plain and cogent argument: "Abraham's children will do the works of Abraham, but you do not do Abraham's works, therefore you are not Abraham's children." The proposition is plain: *If you were Abraham's children* then you would *do the works of Abraham.* Those only are reckoned the seed of Abraham, who *tread in the steps of* his faith and obedience. Those who would approve themselves Abraham's seed must not only be of Abraham's faith, but do Abraham's works (James ii. 21, 22). The assumption is evident likewise: *But you do not do* the works of Abraham, for *you seek to kill me, a man that has told you the truth, which I have heard of God; this did not Abraham, v.* 40. He shows them what their work was which they were now about; they *sought to kill him.* They were so *unnatural* as to seek the life of *a man* who had done them no harm, nor given them any provocation. They were so *ungrateful* as to seek the life of one who had *told them the truth.* They were so *ungodly* as to seek the life of one who told them the truth *which he had heard from God.* He shows them that this did not become the children of Abraham; for *this did not Abraham.* "He did nothing like this." He was famous for his humanity, and for his piety. Abraham believed God; they were obstinate in unbelief. "He would not have done thus if he had lived now, or I had lived then." The conclusion follows of course (*v.* 41): "You are not Abraham's children, but father yourselves upon another family (*v.* 41); there is *a father whose deeds you do.*" He does not *yet* say plainly that he means the devil. He tried whether they would suffer their own consciences to infer from what he said that they were the devil's children.

2. So far were they from owning their unworthiness of relation to Abraham that they pleaded re-

JAMIESON, FAUSSET, BROWN

because my word hath no place in you—When did ever *human prophet* so speak of His words? They tell us of "the word of the Lord" coming to them. But here is One who holds up "His word" as that which ought to find entrance and abiding room for itself in the souls of all who hear it.

38. my Father . . . your father—(See on vs. 23).

39. If ye were Abraham's children, ye would do the works of Abraham—He had just said He "knew they were Abraham's children," i.e., according to the *flesh;* but the children of his *faith and holiness* they were not, but the reverse.

40. this did not Abraham—In so doing ye act in direct opposition to him.

ADAM CLARKE

37. *My word hath no place in you.* Or, "This doctrine of Mine has no place in you." You hear the truths of God but you do not heed them; the word of life has no influence over you. And how can it when you seek to kill Me because I proclaim this truth to you? From what is here said it is manifest, says Dr. Lightfoot, that the whole tendency of our Saviour's discourse is to show the Jews that they are the seed of that serpent which was to bruise the heel of the Messiah. Else what could that mean, v. 44: "Ye are of your father the devil"; i.e., "Ye are the seed of the serpent"?

38. *I speak that which I have seen.* I speak nothing but that unchangeable, eternal truth which I have received from the bosom of God.

Ye do that which ye have seen. Instead of *ye have seen* I think we should read "ye have heard," on the authority of some MSS. Jesus saw the Father, for He was the Word that was with God from eternity. The Jews did not see; they only felt and heard their father the devil.

39. *If ye were Abraham's children.* Griesbach reads *ye are* instead of *ye were,* on the authority of some MSS. *Ye would do the works of Abraham.* As the son has the nature of his father in him, and naturally imitates him, so if you were the children of Abraham you would imitate him in his faith, obedience, and uprightness. But this you do not, for you seek to kill Me merely because I tell you the truth. Abraham never did anything like this; therefore you have no spiritual relationship to him.

41. *Ye do the deeds of your father.* You have certainly another father than Abraham—one who has instilled his own malignant nature into you; and as you seek to murder Me for telling you the truth, you must be the offspring of him who was a murderer from the beginning, and stood not in the truth, v. 44.

MATTHEW HENRY

lation to God himself as their Father: "We are *not born of fornication, we have one Father, even God.*"

(1) Some understand this literally. They were Hebrews of the Hebrews; and, being born in *lawful* wedlock, they might call God *Father.*

(2) Others take it figuratively. They begin to be aware now that Christ spoke of a *spiritual* father, of the father of their religion. They deny themselves to be a generation of idolaters: "We are *not born of fornication,* are not the children of idolatrous parents." If they meant no more than that they themselves were not idolaters, what then? A man may be free from idolatry, and yet perish in another iniquity. They boast themselves to be true worshippers of the true God. We have not many fathers, as the heathens had. *The Lord our God is one Lord and one Father,* and therefore it is well with us. Now our Saviour gives a full answer to this fallacious plea (*v.* 42, 43), and proves, by two arguments, that they had no right to call God Father.

First, They did not love Christ: *if God were your Father, you would love me.* He had disproved their relation to Abraham by their going about to kill him (*v.* 40), but here he disproves their relation to God by their not loving and owning him. All that have God for their Father have a true love to Jesus Christ. God has taken various methods to prove us, and this was one: he sent his Son into the world, concluding that all that called him Father would bid *him* welcome. By this our adoption will be proved or disproved—Did we love Christ, or no? If they were God's children they would *love him.* He was the *Son of God.* Now this could not but recommend him to the affections of all that were *born of God.* He was *sent of God.* Observe the emphasis he lays upon this: *I came from God; neither came I of myself, but he sent me.* He came to *gather together in one the children of God* (*ch.* xi. 52). And would not all God's children embrace with both arms a messenger sent from their Father on *such* errands?

Secondly, They did not understand him. They did not understand the language and dialect of the family: *You do not understand my speech* (*v.* 43). Those that had made the word of the Creator familiar to them needed no other key to the dialect of the Redeemer. And the reason why they did not understand Christ's speech made the matter much worse: *Even because you cannot hear my word,* that is, "You cannot persuade yourselves to hear it without prejudice, as it should be heard." The meaning of this *cannot* is an obstinate *will not.* They do not like it nor love it, and therefore they will not understand it. *You cannot hear my words,* for you have *stopped your ears.*

III. He comes next to tell them plainly whose children they were: *You are of your father the devil, v.* 44. If they were not God's children, they were the devil's.

This is a high charge, and sounds very harsh and horrid, and therefore our Saviour fully proves it,

1. By a general argument: *The lusts of your father you will do.* (1) "You *do* the devil's lusts, the lusts which he would have you to fulfil, and are *led captive by him at his will.*" The peculiar lusts of the devil are *spiritual wickedness;* pride and envy, and wrath and malice; enmity to that which is good, and enticing others to that which is evil; these are lusts which the devil fulfils. (2) You *will do* the devil's lusts. The more there is of the *will* in these lusts, the more there is of the devil in them. "The lusts of your father you *delight to do,*" they are rolled under the tongue as a sweet morsel.

2. By two particular instances, wherein they manifestly resembled the devil—*murder* and *lying.*

(1) He was *a murderer from the beginning.* He was a *hater of man,* and so in disposition a murderer of him. He was man's tempter to *that* sin which brought death into the world. The great tempter is the great destroyer. The Jews called the devil *the angel of death.* If the devil had not been very strong in Cain, he could not have done such an unnatural thing as to kill his own brother. Now herein these Jews were followers of him, and were murderers, like him; murderers of souls, sworn enemies of Christ, and now ready to be his betrayers and murderers. *Now you seek to kill me.*

(2) He was *a liar.* He is a *deserter* from the truth; he *abode not in the truth.* The truth which Christ was now preaching, and which the Jews opposed; herein they did *like their father the devil.* He is *destitute* of the truth: *There is no truth in him.* There is no truth, nothing you can confide in, in him, nor in anything he says or does. He is a friend and patron of lying: *When he speaketh a lie he speaketh of his own.* Three things are here said of the devil with reference to the sin of lying: *First,* That he is *a liar;* his oracles were lying oracles, his prophets lying prophets. All his temptations are carried on by lies, calling

JAMIESON, FAUSSET, BROWN

41. We be not born of fornication . . . we have one Father, God—meaning, as is generally allowed, that they were not an illegitimate race in point of *religion,* pretending only to be God's people, but were decended from His own chosen Abraham.

42, 43.

If God were your Father, ye would love me—'If ye had anything of His moral image, as children have their father's likeness, ye would love Me, for I am immediately of Him and directly from Him. But "My speech" (meaning His peculiar style of expressing Himself on these subjects) is unintelligible to you because ye cannot take in the truth which it conveys.

44. Ye are of your father the devil—"This is one of the most decisive testimonies to the *objective* (outward) *personality* of the devil. It is quite impossible to suppose an accommodation to Jewish views, or a metaphorical form of speech, in so solemn an assertion as this" [ALFORD]. **the lusts of your father**—his impure, malignant, ungodly propensities, inclinations, desires. **ye will do**—are willing to do; not of any *blind necessity of nature,* but of *pure natural inclination.*

He was a murderer from the beginning—The reference is not to *Cain* [as LOCKE, DE WETTE, ALFORD, etc.], but to *Adam* [GROTIUS, CALVIN, MEYER, LUTHARDT, etc.]. The death of the human race, in its widest sense, is ascribed to the murderous seducer of our race. **and abode not in the truth**—As, strictly speaking, the word means "abideth," it has been denied that the *fall* of Satan from a former holy state is here expressed [LOCKE, etc.], and some superior interpreters think it only *implied* [OLSHAUSEN, etc.]. But though the *form* of the thought is present—not past—this is to express the important idea, that his whole character and activity are just *a continual aberration from his own original truth or rectitude;* and thus his fall is not only the *implied basis* of the thought, but *part of the statement itself,* properly interpreted and brought out. **no truth in him**—void of all that holy, transparent rectitude which, as His creature, he originally possessed. **When he speaketh a lie, he speaketh of his own**—perhaps his own resources, treasures (Matt. 12:35) [ALFORD].

ADAM CLARKE

We be not born of fornication. We are not a mixed, spurious breed—our tribes and families have been kept distinct—we are descended from Abraham by his legal wife, Sarah. *We have one Father, even God.* In the spiritual sense of father and son we are not a spurious, that is, an *idolatrous* race; because we acknowledge none as our spiritual father, and worship none as such, but the true God.

42. *If God were your Father, ye would love me.* I came from God, and it would be absurd to suppose that you would persecute Me if you were under the influence of God. The children of the same father should not murder each other.

43. *Why do ye not understand my speech?* "This My mode of speaking"—when illustrating spiritual by natural things. *Because ye cannot hear my word.* That is, you cannot bear My doctrine. It comes too close to you; it searches your hearts, detects your hypocrisy, and exposes your iniquitous intentions and designs. And as you are determined not to leave your sins, so you are purposed not to hear My doctrine.

44. *Ye are of your father the devil.* You are the seed of the old serpent. See on v. 37. *The lusts of your father.* Like father, like son. What Satan desires, you desire, because you are filled with his nature.

He was a murderer from the beginning. It was through him that Adam transgressed, in consequence of which death entered into the world, and slew him and all his posterity. *Abode not in the truth.* "He stood not in the truth"—was once in a state of glorious felicity, but fell from it; and, being deprived of all good himself, he could not endure that others should enjoy any. *He speaketh of his own.* "He speaketh of his own offspring," or, "from his own disposition," for he is the father and fountain of all error and falsity; and all who are deceived by him, and partake of his disposition, falsity, and cruelty are his offspring. *For he is a liar, and the father of it*—literally, "his father also."

MATTHEW HENRY

evil good and good evil. Secondly, That when he *speaks a lie* he *speaks of his own.* It is the proper *idiom* of his language. *Thirdly,* That he is the *father of it.* He is the author and founder of all lies. He is the father of *every liar.* God made men with a disposition to truth. It is congruous to reason and natural light, that we should speak truth; but the devil, the author of sin, is the father of liars, who begat them, who trained them up in the *way of lying,* whom they resemble and obey.

IV. Christ, having thus proved all murderers and all liars to be the devil's children, comes in the following verses to assist them in the application of it to themselves. Two things he charges upon them:

1. That they would not *believe the word of truth* (*v.* 45).

(1) Two ways it may be taken: [1] "Though I tell you the truth, yet you will not believe me." They would not believe that he told them the truth. The greatest truths with some gained not the least credit; for they *rebelled against the light.* Or, [2] *Because I tell you the truth* (so we read it) therefore *you believe me not.* They would not receive him, nor entertain him as a prophet, because he showed them their faces in a glass that would not flatter them. Miserable is the case of those to whom the light of divine truth is become a torment.

(2) Now, to show them the unreasonableness of their infidelity, he condescends to put the matter to this fair issue, *v.* 46. If *he* were in an error, why did they not convince him? But (saith Christ) *which of you convinceth me of sin?* Their accusations were malicious groundless calumnies, and *utterly false.* The very judge that condemned him owned he *found no fault in him.* The only way not to be convicted of sin is not to sin. If *they* were in an error, why were they not convinced by him? *"If I say the truth, why do you not believe me?* If you cannot convince me of error, you must own that I *say the truth,* and why do you not then *give me credit?"* It will be found that the reason why we believe not in Jesus Christ is because we are not willing to part with our sins, and deny ourselves, and serve God faithfully.

2. Another thing charged upon them is that they would not hear the words of God (*v.* 47).

(1) A doctrine laid down: *He that is of God heareth God's words.* He is *willing* and *ready* to hear them, is sincerely desirous to know what the mind of God is, and cheerfully embraces whatever he knows to be so. He *apprehends* and *discerns* them, he so hears them as to perceive the *voice of God* in them, as they of the family know the master's tread, and the master's knock, as the sheep know the voice of their shepherd from that of a stranger.

(2) The application of this doctrine: *You therefore hear them not, because you are not of God.* Your being thus deaf and dead to the words of God is a plain evidence that you are *not of God.* Or, their not being of God was the reason why they did not profitably *hear the words of God,* which Christ spoke. If the word of the kingdom do not bring forth fruit, the blame is to be laid upon the soil, not upon the seed.

Verses 46–50

I. Hitherto they had cavilled at his doctrine, but, having shown themselves uneasy when he complained (*v.* 43, 47) that they would not hear him, now at length they fall to downright railing, *v.* 48. The scribes and Pharisees scornfully turned off the conviction with this: *Say we not well that thou art a Samaritan, and hast a devil?*

1. The blasphemous character commonly given of our Lord Jesus among the wicked Jews. (1) That he was a Samaritan. Thus they exposed him to the ill will of the people, with whom you could not put a man into a worse name than to call him *a Samaritan.* They had often enough called him *a Galilean—a mean man*; they will have him a *Samaritan —a bad man.* Great endeavours have in all ages been used to make good people odious by putting them under black characters, and it is easy to run that down with a crowd and a cry which is once put into an ill name. (2) That *he had a devil*; that he was *in league with the devil.* That he was possessed with a devil, that he was a melancholy man, whose brain was *clouded,* or a mad man, whose brain was *heated,* and that which he said was no more to be believed than the extravagant rambles of a distracted man.

2. How they undertook to justify this character: *Say we not well that thou art so?* Their hearts were more hardened and their prejudices confirmed. They value themselves on their enmity to Christ, as if they had never spoken *better* than when they spoke the worst they could of Jesus Christ. It is bad to say and do ill, but it is worse to *stand to it.*

II. The meekness and mercifulness of Heaven shining in Christ's reply, *v.* 49, 50.

JAMIESON, FAUSSET, BROWN

(The word is *plural.*) It means that he has no temptation to it *from without;* it is purely *self-begotten,* springing from a nature which is nothing but obliquity. **the father of it**—i.e., of lying: all the falsehood in the world owes its existence to him. What a verse is this! It holds up the devil (1) as the murderer of the human race; but as this is meant here in the more profound sense of *spiritual* death, it holds him up, (2) as the spiritual parent of this fallen human family, communicating to his offspring his own evil passions and universal obliquity, and stimulating these into active exercise. But as there is "a stronger than he," who comes upon him and overcomes him (Luke 11:21, 22), it is only such as "love the darkness," who are addressed as children of the devil (Matt. 13:38; I John 3:8-10). **45-47. And because I tell you the truth, ye believe me not**—not *although,* but just *because* He did so, for the reason given in the former verse. Had He been *less* true they would have hailed Him more readily.

46. Which of you convinceth me of sin—"Convicteth," bringeth home a charge of sin. Glorious dilemma! 'Convict Me of sin, and reject Me: If not, why stand ye out against My claims?' Of course, they could only be supposed to impeach His *life;* but in One who had already passed through unparalleled complications, and had continually to deal with friends and foes of every sort and degree, such a challenge thrown wide among His bitterest enemies, can amount to nothing short of a claim to *absolute sinlessness.*

48-51. Say we not well that thou art a Samaritan, and hast a devil?—What intense and virulent scorn! (See Heb. 12:3.) The "say we not well" refers to ch. 7:20. "A Samaritan" means more than "no Israelite at all"; it means one who *pretended, but had no manner of claim* to the title—retorting perhaps, this denial of their *true* descent from Abraham.

ADAM CLARKE

46. *Which of you convinceth me of sin?* Do you pretend to reject the truths which I announce, because My life does not correspond to the doctrines I have taught? But can any of you prove Me guilty of any fault? But it is probable that *sin* is put here in opposition to *truth* in the same verse, and then it should be rendered "falsehood." The very best Greek writers use the word in the same sense.

48. *Thou art a Samaritan.* This is the only time in which the Jews gave our Lord this title of reproach, and they probably grounded it on His having preached among them and lodged in their villages. See the account in chap. iv; but *Samaritan,* among them, meant a person unworthy of any credit. *Hast a devil.* Art possessed by an evil spirit and art, in consequence, deranged.

ALBERT BARNES:

46. "Which of you convinceth me?" To *convince,* with us, means to satisfy a man's own mind of the truth of anything; but this is not its meaning here. It rather means to *convict.* Which of you can prove that I am guilty of sin? "Of sin." The word sin here evidently means error, falsehood, or impostor. It stands opposed to truth. The argument of the Savior is this: A doctrine might be rejected if it could be proved that he that delivered it was an impostor; but as you cannot prove this of me, you are bound to receive my words.

47. "He that is of God." He that loves, fears, and honors God. "Heareth God's words." Listens to, or attends to the doctrines or commandments of God, as a child who loves his parent will regard and obey his commandments. This is an evidence of true piety. A willingness to receive all that God teaches us, and to obey all his commandments, is an undoubted proof that we are his friends (John 14:21; 1 John 2:4; 3:24). As the Jews did not show a readiness to obey the commands of God, it proved that they were not of him, and to this was owing their rejection of the Lord Jesus.

—*Popular Commentary*

MATTHEW HENRY

1. He denies their charge against him: *I have not a devil.* The imputation is unjust; "I am neither actuated by a devil, nor in compact with one."

2. He asserts the sincerity of his own intentions: But *I honour my Father.* It also proves that he *had not a devil*; for, if he had, he would not honour God.

3. He complains of the wrong they did him by their calumnies: *You do dishonour me.* By this it appears that, as man, he had a tender sense of the disgrace and indignity done him. Christ honoured his Father so as never man did, and yet was himself dishonoured so as never man was; for, though God has promised that those who honour him he will honour, he never promised that men should honour them.

4. He clears himself from the imputation of vain glory, *v.* 50. His *contempt* of worldly honour: *I seek not mine own glory.* He did not aim at this nor covet preferment in the world. "*You do dishonour me,* but cannot disturb me, for I *seek not my own glory.*" Those who are dead to men's praise can safely bear their contempt. His *comfort* under worldly dishonour: *There is one that seeketh and judgeth.* In two things Christ made it appear that he *sought not his own glory.* (1) He did not *court* men's respect. In reference to this he saith, "*There is one that seeketh.*" God will seek *their* honour that do not seek *their own*; for before honour is humility. (2) He did not *revenge* men's affronts, and in reference to this he saith, "*There is one that judgeth,* that will vindicate my honour." If we be humble appellants and patient expectants, we shall find, to our comfort, *there is one that judgeth.*

Verses 51–59

I. The doctrine of the immortality of believers laid down, *v.* 51. It is ushered in with the usual solemn preface, *Verily, verily, I say unto you, If a man keep my sayings, he shall never see death.* 1. The *character* of a believer: he is one that *keeps the sayings* of the Lord Jesus—*my word.* This we must not only *receive,* but *keep*; not only *have,* but *hold.* We must keep it in mind and memory, keep it in love and affection, keep in it as our way, keep to it as our rule. 2. The *privilege* of a believer: *He shall by no means see death for ever;* so it is in the original. Not as if the bodies of believers were secured from the stroke of death. How then is this promise made good that they *shall not see death*? The property of death is so altered to them that they do not see it as death, they do not see the terror of death. Their sight does not *terminate* in death, they look so clearly, so comfortably, through death, and beyond death, that they overlook death, and *see it not.* They shall not see death *for ever.* The day will come when *death shall be swallowed up in victory.* They are perfectly delivered from *eternal death.* They shall have their everlasting lot where there will be *no more death,* where they *cannot die any more.*

II. The Jews cavil at this doctrine. They lay hold of this occasion to reproach him that makes them so kind an offer: *Now we know that thou hast a devil. Abraham is dead.*

1. Their *railing*: "*Now we know that thou hast a devil.*" If he had not abundantly proved himself a *teacher come from God,* his promises of immortality to his credulous followers might justly have been ridiculed, and charity itself would have imputed them to a crazed fancy; but his doctrine was evidently divine, his miracles confirmed it, and the Jews' religion taught them to expect such a prophet, and to believe in him.

2. Their *reasoning.* They look upon him as guilty of an insufferable piece of arrogance, in making himself greater than *Abraham and the prophets*: *Abraham is dead,* and *the prophets,* they are dead too. It is true that Abraham and the prophets were great men, great in the favour of God, and great in the esteem of all good men. It is true that they *kept God's sayings.* It is true that they *died*; they never pretended to *have,* much less to *give,* immortality. It was their honour that they *died in faith,* but die they must. Why should a good man be afraid to die when Abraham is dead, and the prophets are dead? They have *tracked* the way through that darksome valley, which should reconcile us to death and help to take off the terror of it. Now they think Christ talks madly when he saith, *If a man keep my sayings, he shall never taste death.* Now their arguing goes upon two mistakes: [1] They understood Christ of an immortality in this world. God is still the *God of Abraham* and the *God of the holy prophets.* God is not the God of the dead, but of the living; therefore Abraham and the prophets are still alive, and, as Christ meant it, they had not *seen* nor *tasted* death. [2] They thought none could be greater than Abraham and the prophets, whereas they could not but know that the Messiah would be greater than Abraham or any of the prophets. Instead of inferring from Christ's making himself greater than Abraham that he had a *devil,*

JAMIESON, FAUSSET, BROWN

49. Jesus answered, I have not a devil—What calm dignity is here! Verily, "when reviled, He reviled not again" (I Pet. 2:23). Cf. Paul (Acts 26:25), "I am not mad . . ." He adds not, "Nor am I a Samaritan," that He might not even seem to partake of their contempt for a race that had already welcomed Him as the Christ, and began to be blessed by Him. **I honour my Father, and ye do dishonour me**—the language of *wounded feeling.* But the *interior* of His soul at such moments is only to be seen in such prophetic utterances as these, "For thy sake I have borne reproach; shame hath covered my face; I am become a *stranger* unto my brethren, an *alien* unto my mother's children. For the zeal of thine house hath eaten me up, and *the reproaches of them that* reproached thee are fallen upon me" (Ps. 69: 7-9.) **50. I seek not mine own glory: there is one that seeketh**—i.e., evidently, *'that seeketh My glory'*; *requiring* "all men to honor the Son even as they honor the Father"; judicially *treating* him "who honoreth not the Son as honoring not the Father that hath sent Him" (ch. 5:23; and cf. Matt. 17:5); but giving to Him (ch. 6:37) such as will yet cast their crowns before His throne, in whom He "shall see of the travail of his soul, and be satisfied" (Isa. 53:11).

51. If a man keep my saying, he shall never see death—Partly thus vindicating His lofty claims as Lord of the kingdom of life everlasting, and, at the same time, holding out even to His revilers the scepter of grace. The word *"keep"* is in harmony with vs. 31, "If ye *continue* in My word," expressing the permanency, as a living and paramount principle, of that faith to which He referred: *"never see death,"* though virtually uttered before (ch. 5:24; 6:40, 47, 51), is the strongest and most naked statement of a very glorious truth yet given. (In ch. 11:26 it is repeated in nearly identical terms.)

52, 53. Then said the Jews unto him, Now we know that thou hast a devil . . .—'Thou art now self-convicted; only a demoniac could speak so; the most illustrious of our fathers are dead, and Thou promisest exemption from death to anyone who will keep *Thy saying*! pray, who art Thou?'

ADAM CLARKE

49. *I have not a devil.* The first part of the charge was too futile; if taken literally, it was both absurd and impossible. They did not believe it themselves, and therefore our Lord does not stop a moment to refute it; but He answers to the second with the utmost meekness and conclusiveness: I honor God. This is what no demon can do nor any man who is under such influence.

50. *I seek not mine own glory.* Another proof that I am not influenced by any spirit but that which proceeds from God. But there is *one that seeketh*—i.e., My glory—*and judgeth*—will punish you for your determined obstinacy and iniquity.

51. *Shall never see death.* He shall never come under the power of the death of the soul, but shall live eternally with Me in glory.

CHARLES H. SPURGEON:

The false charge was the occasion of our Lord's uttering a great truth. On they rush, furious in their rage, but He flashes in their faces the light of truth. To put down error, lift up truth. Thus their deadly saying was met by a living saying: "Verily, verily, I say unto you, If a man keep my saying, he shall never see death." Nothing so baffles the adversaries of the faith as to utter with unshaken confidence the truth of God. The truth which Jesus stated was full of promise; and if they willfully rejected His promise, it became worse to them than a threatening. Christ's rejected promises curdle into woes. If these men, when He said to them, "If a man keep my saying, he shall never see death," yet went on reviling Him, then their consciences, when afterward awakened, would say to them, "He that believeth not shall not see life; but the wrath of God abideth on him." If the believer shall never see death, then the unbeliever shall never see life. Thus the gospel itself becomes "a savor of death unto death" to those who refuse it; and the very word which proclaims eternal life threatens eternal death to the willfully unbelieving.

—The Treasury of the New Testament

MATTHEW HENRY

they should have inferred that he was the Christ; but their eyes were blinded. They scornfully asked, *Whom makest thou thyself?*

III. Christ's reply; still he vouchsafes to reason with them. This was the *day of his patience.*

1. In his answer he insists not upon his own testimony concerning himself, but waives it as not sufficient nor conclusive (*v.* 54): *If I honour myself, my honour is nothing.* Honour of our own creating is a mere chimera, has nothing in it, and therefore is called *vain-glory.* Self-admirers are self-*deceivers.*

2. He refers himself to *his* Father, God; and to *their* father, Abraham.

(1) To his Father, *God*: *It is my Father that honoureth me.* He *derived* from his Father all the honour he now claimed. He *depended* upon his Father for all the honour he further *looked for.* Christ and all that are his depend upon God for their honour; and he that is sure of honour where he is known cares not though he be slighted where he is in disguise.

First, He here takes occasion to show the reason of *their* incredulity, and this was their *unacquaintedness* with God; You *say of him that he is your God, yet you have not known him.* The profession they made of relation to God: "*You say that he is your God.*" Many pretend to have an interest in God, and say that he is *theirs,* who yet have no just cause to say so. What will it avail us to say, He is *our God,* if we be not in sincerity *his people.* Their ignorance of him: *Yet you have not known him. You know him not at* all. Or, *You know him not aright;* and this is as bad as not knowing him at all, or worse. Men may be able to dispute subtly concerning God, and *not know him.* It is only the name of God which they have learned to talk of. They knew not God; and therefore perceived not the image of God, nor the voice of God in Christ. The reason why men receive not the *gospel of Christ* is because they have not the *knowledge of God.*

Secondly, He gives them the reason of *his* assurance that his Father would *honour* him and *own him*: *But I know him;* and again, *I know him*; which bespeaks his *confidence* in him. He *professes* his knowledge of his Father, with the greatest certainty: *If I should say I know him not, I should be a liar like unto you.* He would not deny his relation to God, to humour the Jews. If he should, he would be found a false witness against God and himself. He *proves* his knowledge of his Father: *I know him and keep his sayings,* or *his word.* He kept *his Father's* word, and *his own word* with the Father. Christ requires of us (*v.* 51) that we *keep his sayings*; and he has set before us a copy of obedience: he *kept his Father's sayings*; well might he who *learned obedience* teach it. Christ by this evinced that he knew the Father.

(2) Christ refers them to *their* father, and that was Abraham.

[1] Christ asserts Abraham's prospect of him, and respect to him: *Your father Abraham rejoiced to see my day, and he saw it, and was glad, v.* 56. Two things he here speaks of as instances of that patriarch's respect to the promised Messiah:

First, The ambition he had to *see his day*: *He rejoiced—he leaped at it.* The word must here signify a transport of *desire* rather than of *joy,* for otherwise the latter part of the verse would be a tautology; he *saw it, and was glad.* The notices he had received of the Messiah to come had raised in him an expectation of something *great,* which he earnestly longed to know more of. Those who rightly know anything of Christ cannot but be earnestly desirous to know more of him. Those who discern the dawning of the light of the Sun of righteousness cannot but wish to see his rising. Abraham desired to see Christ's day, though it was at a great distance; but this degenerate seed of his discerned not his day, nor bade it welcome when it came.

Secondly, The satisfaction he had in what he did see of it: *He saw it, and was glad.*

a. How God gratified the pious desire of Abraham; he longed to see Christ's day, and he *saw it.* He saw something of it, more *afterwards* than he did at first. To him that desires and prays for more of the knowledge of Christ, God will give more. But how did Abraham see Christ's day? Some understand it of the sight he had of it in the other world. The longings of gracious souls after Jesus Christ will be fully satisfied when they come to heaven, and not till then. It is more commonly understood of some sight he had of *Christ's day* in this world. They that *received not the promises,* yet *saw them afar off.* There is room to conjecture that Abraham had some vision of Christ and his day, which is not recorded in his story.

b. How *Abraham* entertained these discoveries of Christ's day: *He saw, and was glad.* He was glad of what he *saw* of God's favour to himself, and glad of what he *foresaw* of the mercy God had in store

JAMIESON, FAUSSET, BROWN

54-56. If I honour myself, my honour is nothing . . .—(See on ch. 5:31, etc.).

I shall be a liar like unto you—now rising to the summit of holy, naked severity, thereby to draw this long dialogue to a head.

56. Abraham rejoiced to see my day . . .—exulted, or exceedingly rejoiced that he should see, he exulted to see it, i.e., by *anticipation.* Nay, **he saw it and was glad**—he *actually* beheld it, to his joy. If this mean no more than that he had a prophetic foresight of the gospel-day—the second clause just repeating the first—how could the Jews understand our Lord to mean that He "had seen Abraham"? And if it mean that Abraham was *then beholding,* in his disembodied spirit, the incarnate Messiah [STIER, ALFORD, etc.], the words seem very unsuitable to express it. It expresses something *past*—"he *saw* My day, and *was* glad," i.e., surely *while he lived.* He seems to refer to the familiar intercourse which Abraham had with *God,* who is once and again in the history called *"the Angel of the Lord,"* and whom Christ here identifies with Himself. On those occasions, Abraham "saw ME" [OLSHAUSEN, though he thinks the reference is to some unrecorded scene]. If this be the meaning, all that follows is quite natural.

ADAM CLARKE

54. *Your God.* Many MSS. and most of the versions read *our* instead of *your.* The variation is of very little consequence. They called God their God, while enemies to Him in both their spirit and conduct.

56. *Abraham rejoiced to see my day.* Or "he earnestly desired to see My day"; his soul "leaped" forward in earnest hope and strong expectation that he might see the incarnation of Jesus Christ. *And he saw it.* Not only in the first promise, Gen. iii. 15, for the other patriarchs saw this as well as he; and not only in that promise which was made particularly to himself, Gen. xii. 7; xxii. 18 (compared with Gal. iii. 16), that the Messiah should spring from his family. But he saw this day especially when Jehovah appeared to him in a human form, Gen. xviii. 2, 17, which many suppose to have been a manifestation of the Lord Jesus.

MATTHEW HENRY

for the world. A believing sight of Christ and his day will put gladness into the heart. No joy like the joy of faith; we are never acquainted with true pleasure till we are acquainted with Christ.

[2] The Jews cavil at this, and reproach him for it (*v.* 57): *Thou art not yet fifty years old, and hast thou seen Abraham?* They suppose it a very absurd thing for him to pretend to have seen Abraham, who was *dead* so many ages before he was born. Now this gave them occasion to *despise his youth*, as if he were *but of yesterday, and knew* nothing: *Thou art not yet fifty years old.*

[3] Our Saviour gives an effectual answer to this cavil, by a solemn assertion of his own seniority even to Abraham himself (*v.* 58): "*Verily, verily, I say unto you;* I say it to your faces, take it how you will: *Before Abraham was, I am. Before Abraham was made or born, I am.*" The change of the word is observable, and bespeaks Abraham a creature, and himself the Creator. *Before Abraham he was,* as God. *I am,* is the name of God. He does not say, *I was,* but *I am,* for he is the first and the last. He was the appointed Messiah, long before Abraham.

[4] This great word ended the dispute *abruptly*: they could bear to hear no more from him, and he needed to say no more to them. Their inveterate prejudice against the holy spiritual doctrine and law of Christ, baffled all the methods of conviction. They were *enraged* at Christ for what he said: *They took up stones to cast at him, v.* 59. Perhaps they looked upon him as a blasphemer, and such were indeed to be stoned, but they must be first legally tried and convicted. Farewell justice and order if every man pretend to execute a law at his pleasure. Who would think that ever there should be such wickedness as this in men? Thus everyone has a stone to throw at his holy religion. He made his *escape* out of their hands. Jesus *hid himself.* Not that Christ was afraid or ashamed to stand by what he had said, but his *hour was not yet come*, and he would countenance the flight of his ministers and people in times of persecution. He *departed*, he *went out of the temple*, going *through the midst of them*, undiscovered, and *so passed by*. This was not a cowardly inglorious flight, nor such as argued either guilt or fear. It was an instance of his power over his enemies, and that they could do no more against him than he gave them leave to do. They now thought they had made sure of him and yet he *passed through the midst* of them, and thus he left them to fume. It was an instance of his prudent provision for his own safety. Thus he gave an example to his own rule, *When they persecute you in one city flee to another.* It was a righteous deserting of those who stoned him from among them. Christ will not long stay with those who bid him be gone. Christ now *went through* the midst of the Jews, and none of them courted his stay, nor stirred up himself to take hold of him, but were even content to let him go. God never forsakes any till they have first provoked him to withdraw, and will have none of him. When Christ left them it is said that he passed by silently and unobserved; so that they were not aware of him. Christ's departures from a church, or a particular soul, are often *secret*. As *the kingdom of God comes not,* so it *goes not, with observation.* Thus it was with these forsaken Jews, God left them, and they never missed him.

JAMIESON, FAUSSET, BROWN

57-59. Then said the Jews unto him, Thou art not yet fifty years old—"No inference can be drawn from this as to the age of our Lord at the time as man. Fifty years was with the Jews the completion of manhood" [ALFORD]. **and hast thou seen Abraham?**—He had said Abraham saw *Him,* as being his peculiar privilege. They give the opposite turn to it—"Hast Thou seen *Abraham?*" as an honor too great for Him to pretend to. **58. Before Abraham was, I am**—The words rendered "was" and "am" are quite different. The one clause means, 'Abraham was *brought into being'*; the other, *'I exist.'* The statement therefore is not that *Christ came into existence before Abraham did* (as Arians affirm is the meaning), but that He never *came* into being at all, but *existed* before Abraham had a being; in other words, existed before *creation*, or *eternally* (as ch. 1:1).

In that sense the Jews plainly understood Him, since "then took they up stones to cast at Him," *just as they had before done when they saw that He made Himself equal with God* (ch. 5:18). **hid himself**—(See on Luke 4:30).

ADAM CLARKE

ALBERT BARNES:

57. "Fifty years old." Jesus is supposed to have been at this time about thirty-three. It is remarkable that when he was so young they should have mentioned the number fifty, but they probably designed to prevent the possibility of a reply. Had they said forty they might have apprehended a reply, or could not be so certain that they were correct. "Hast thou seen Abraham?" It is remarkable, also, that they perverted his words. His affirmation was not that *he* had seen Abraham, but that *Abraham* had seen his day. The design of Jesus was to show that he was greater than Abraham (v. 53). To do this, he says that Abraham, great as he was, earnestly desired to see his time, thus acknowledging his inferiority to the Messiah. The Jews perverted this, and affirmed that it was impossible that he and Abraham should have seen each other.—*Popular Commentary*

59. *Then took they up stones.* It appears that the Jews understood Him as asserting His Godhead; and, supposing Him to be a blasphemer, they proceeded to stone Him, according to the law, Lev. xxiv. 16. *But Jesus hid himself.* In all probability He rendered himself invisible—though some will have it that He conveyed himself away from those Jews who were His enemies, by mixing himself with the many who believed on Him (vv. 30-31) and who, we may suppose, favored His escape. *Going through the midst of them, and so passed by.* These words are wanting in the Codex Bezae, and in several editions and versions. Erasmus, Grotius, Beza, Pearce, and Griesbach think them not genuine.

A. T. ROBERTSON:

59. "They took up stones therefore" (*eran oun lithous*). First aorist active indicative of *airo,* inferential use of *oun.* The time for argument had past. "To cast at him" (*hina balosin ep auton*). Final clause with *hina* and the second aorist active subjunctive of *ballo.* Vivid picture of a mob ready to kill Jesus, already beginning to do so. "Hid himself" (*ekrube*). Second aorist passive indicative of *krupto.* He was hidden. No Docetic vanishing, but quietly and boldly Jesus went out of the temple. His hour had not yet come. Once again three months later the Pharisees will try to kill him, but he will pass out of their hands (10:39).—*Word Pictures in the New Testament*

MATTHEW HENRY — CHAPTER 9

Verses 1–7

I. The notice which our Lord Jesus took of the piteous case of this poor blind man (*v.* 1): *As Jesus passed by he saw a man which was blind from his birth.* Though the Jews had so basely abused him, yet he did not miss any opportunity of doing good among them. The cure of this blind man was a kindness to *the public*, enabling him to work for his living who before was a charge and burden to the neighbourhood. It is noble, and generous, and Christ-like, to be willing to *serve the public*. Though he was in his flight from a threatening danger, and escaping for his life, yet he willingly halted and stayed awhile to show mercy to this poor man. We make more haste than good speed when we out-run opportunities of doing good. Christ took this poor blind man in his way, and cured him *as he passed by*. Thus should we take occasions of doing good, even as we *pass by*, wherever we are. The condition of this poor man was very sad. He was *blind*, and had been so *from his birth.* He that is *blind* has no *enjoyment* of the light, but he that is *born blind* has no *idea* of it. Methinks such a one would give a great deal to have his curiosity satisfied with but one day's sight of light and colours,

JAMIESON, FAUSSET, BROWN — CHAPTER 9

VSS. 1-41. THE OPENING OF THE EYES OF ONE BORN BLIND, AND WHAT FOLLOWED ON IT. **1-5. as Jesus passed by, he saw a man which was blind from birth**—and who "sat begging" (vs. 8).

ADAM CLARKE — CHAPTER 9

1. *And as Jesus passed by.* This chapter is a continuation of the preceding, and therefore the word *Jesus* is not in the Greek text; it begins simply thus—"And passing along." Having left the Temple, where the Jews were going to stone Him (chap. viii. 59), it is probable our Lord went, according to His custom, to the Mount of Olives. The next day, which was the Sabbath, v. 14, He met a man who had been born blind, sitting in some public place, and asking alms from those who passed by, v. 8.

MATTHEW HENRY

shapes and figures, though he were never to see them more. Let us bless God that it was not our case. The eye is one of the most curious parts of the body, its structure exceedingly nice and fine. What a mercy is it that there was no miscarriage in the making of ours! Christ cured many that were blind by disease or accident, but here he cured one that was *born blind*; that he might give an instance of his power to help in the most desperate cases. That he might give a *specimen* of the work of his grace, upon the souls of sinners, which gives sight to those that were by nature blind. The compassions of our Lord Jesus towards him were very tender. He *saw him*; and looked upon him with concern. Others saw him, but not as he did. Christ is often found of those that seek him not, nor see him.

II. The discourse between Christ and his disciples concerning this man.

1. The question which the disciples put to their Master, *v.* 2. When Christ looked upon him, they had an eye to him too; Christ's compassion should kindle ours. But they did not move Christ to heal him. Instead of this, they started a very odd question concerning him: *Rabbi, who sinned, this man or his parents, that he was born blind?* Now this question of theirs was,

(1) *Uncharitably censorious.* They take it for granted that this extraordinary calamity was the punishment of some uncommon wickedness. The greatest sufferers are not *therefore* to be looked upon as the greatest sinners. The grace of repentance calls our own afflictions *punishments*, but the grace of charity calls the afflictions of others *trials*.

(2) It was *unnecessarily curious.* They ask, *Who were the criminals, this man or his parents?* And what was this to them? Or what good would it do them to know it? We are apt to be more inquisitive concerning other people's sins than concerning our own. To judge ourselves is our duty, but to judge our brother is our sin. They enquire, [1] Whether this man was punished thus for some sin of his own, either committed or foreseen before his birth. The Pharisees seem to have had the same opinion of his case when they said, *Thou wast altogether born in sin* (*v.* 34). Or, [2] Whether he was punished for the wickedness of his parents, which God sometimes *visits upon the children.* It is a good reason why parents should take heed of sin, lest their children smart for it when they are gone. Being at a loss what construction to put upon this providence, they desire to be informed. The equity of God's dispensations is always certain, but not always to be accounted for, for his *judgments are a great deep.*

2. Christ's answer to this question.

(1) He gives the reason of this poor man's blindness: "*Neither has this man sinned nor his parents*, but he was born blind, that now at last *the works of God should be made manifest in him,*" *v.* 3. Here Christ told them two things concerning such uncommon calamities: That they are not always inflicted as punishments of sin. Many are made much more *miserable* than others in this life who are not at all more *sinful.* It was not any uncommon guilt that God had an eye to in inflicting this upon him. Misfortunes are sometimes intended purely *for the glory of God*, and the *manifesting of his works.* If God be glorified, either by us or in us, we were not made *in vain.* This man was *born blind, that the works of God might be manifest in him. First,* That the *attributes of God* might be made manifest in him, especially that his extraordinary power and goodness might be manifested in curing him. The difficulties of providence, otherwise unaccountable, may be resolved into this—God intends in them to *show* himself. Those who regard him not in the ordinary course of things are sometimes alarmed by things extraordinary. *Secondly,* That the counsels of God might be manifested in him. He was *born blind* that our Lord Jesus might prove himself sent of God to be the true light to the world. It was now a great while since this man was born blind, and yet it never appeared till now *why* he was so. The sentences in the book of providence are sometimes *long*, and you must read a great way before you can apprehend the sense of them.

(2) He gives the reason of his own forwardness and readiness to help and heal him, *v.* 4, 5. *I must work the works of him that sent me while it is day; the night cometh, when no man can work.* It was the sabbath day, on which works of necessity might be done, and he proves this to be a work of necessity.

[1] It was his Father's will: *I must work the works of him that sent me.* Whom God sends he employs, for he sends none to be idle. He was a worker together with God. He was pleased to lay himself under the strongest obligations to do the business he was sent about: I *must work.* Christ laid out himself with

JAMIESON, FAUSSET, BROWN

ALEXANDER MACLAREN:

"As Jesus passed by," says the story, "he saw a man which was blind from his birth." He fixes His eye upon him. No cry from the blind man's lips draws Him. He sits there unconscious of the kind eyes that were fastened upon him. The disciples stand at Christ's side and have no share in His feelings. They ask Him to do nothing. To them the blind man is—what? A theological problem. No trace of pity touches their hearts. They do not even seem to have reckoned upon or expected Christ's miraculous intervention. And that is a very remarkable feature in the Gospels. At all events, they evidently do not expect it here; but all that the sight of this lifelong sufferer does in them is to raise a question, "Who did sin; he or his parents?" Perhaps they do not quite see to the bottom of the alternative that they are suggesting; and we need not trouble ourselves to ask whether there was a full-blown notion of the preexistence of the man's soul in their minds as they ask the question. Perhaps they remembered the impotent man to whom our Lord said, "Go and sin no more lest a worse thing come unto thee." And they may have thought that they had His sanction to the doctrine—as old as Job's friends—that wherever there was great suffering there must first have been great sin.

—*Expositions of Holy Scripture*

2. who did sin, this man or his parents, that he was born blind—not in a former state of existence, in which, as respects the wicked, the Jews did not believe; but, perhaps, expressing loosely that sin *somewhere* had surely been the cause of this calamity.

3. Neither . . . this man . . .—The cause was neither in himself nor his parents, but, in order to the manifestation of "the works of God," in his cure.

4. I must work the works of him that sent me . . .—a most interesting statement from the mouth of Christ; intimating, (1) that He had a precise work to do upon earth, with every particular of it arranged and laid out to Him; (2) that all He did upon earth was just "the works of God"—particularly "going about *doing good,*" though not exclusively by miracles; (3) that each work had its precise *time* and *place* in His programme of instructions, so to speak; hence, (4) that as His period for work had definite termina-

ADAM CLARKE

2. *Who did sin, this man, or his parents?* The doctrine of the transmigration of souls appears to have been an article in the creed of the Pharisees, and it was pretty general among both the Greeks and the Asiatics. The Pythagoreans believed the souls of men were sent into other bodies for the punishment of some sin which they had committed in a preexistent state. This seems to have been the foundation of the disciples' question to our Lord.

3. *Neither hath this man sinned, nor his parents.* That is, the blindness of this person is not occasioned by any sin of his own, nor of his parents; but has happened in the ordinary course of divine providence, and shall now become the instrument of salvation to his soul, edification to others, and glory to God. Many of the Jews thought that marks on the body were proofs of sin in the soul.

4. *While it is day.* Though I plainly perceive that the cure of this man will draw down upon Me the malice of the Jewish rulers, yet I must accomplish the work for which I came into the world while it is day—while the term of this life of Mine shall last. It was about six months after this that our Lord was crucified. It is very likely that the day was now declining and night coming on, and He took occasion from this circumstance to introduce the elegant metaphor immediately following. By this we are taught

MATTHEW HENRY

the utmost vigour and industry in his work. He *worked the works* he had to do. It is not enough to look at our work, and talk over it, but we must work it.

[2] Now was his opportunity. I must work *while it is day*, while the light lasts which is given to work by. Christ himself had *his day*. All the work he had to do *in his own person* here on earth was to be done *before his death*; the time of his living in this world is *the day* here spoken of. The time of our life is our day. Day-time is the proper season for work; during the day of life we must be busy, not waste day-time, nor play by *daylight*; it will be time enough to rest when our day is done.

[3] The period of his opportunity was at hand, and therefore he would be busy: *The night comes when no man can work*. It will come certainly, may come suddenly, is coming nearer and nearer. We cannot compute how nigh our sun is, it may go down at noon: nor can we promise ourselves a twilight between the day of life and the night of death. When the night comes we *cannot work*. When night comes, *call the labourers*; we must then *show our work*, and receive according to the things done. It is too late to *bid* when the inch of candle is *dropped*.

[4] His business in the world was to enlighten it (*v.* 5): *As long as I am in the world, I am the light of the world*. He had said this before, *ch.* viii. 12. Christ would cure this blind man, the representative of a blind world, because he came to be *the light of the world*, not only to give *light*, but to give *sight*. Now this gives us a great *encouragement* to come to him. Which way should we turn our eyes, but to the light? We partake of the sun's light, and so we may of Christ's grace, without money and without price. A good *example* of usefulness in the world. What Christ saith of himself, he saith of his disciples: *You are lights in the world*, and, if so, *Let your light shine*. What were candles made for but to burn?

III. The manner of the cure of the blind man, *v.* 6, 7. The circumstances of the miracle are singular, and no doubt significant. *When he had thus spoken* he addressed himself to the opening of the blind man's eyes. He did not defer it till the sabbath was past, when it would give less offence. What good we have opportunity of doing we should do quickly; he that will never do a good work till there is nothing to be objected against it will leave many a good work for ever undone.

1. The preparation of the eye-salve. Christ *spat on the ground, and made clay of the spittle*. He made clay of his own spittle, because there was no water near; and he would teach us to be willing to take up with that which is *next hand*, if it will but serve the turn. Why should we *go about* for that which may as well be had and done a *nearer way*?

2. The application of it to the place: *He anointed the eyes of the blind man with the clay*. Like a tender physician; he did it himself with his own hand, though the patient was a beggar. Daubing clay on the eyes would *close them* up, but never *open them*. The power of God often works by contraries. The design of the gospel is to *open men's eyes*. Now the eye-salve that does the work is of Christ's preparing. We must come to Christ for *the eye-salve*. He only is *able*, and he only is *appointed*, to make it up. The means used in this work are very weak, and unlikely, and are made effectual only by the power of Christ. And the method Christ takes is first to make men feel themselves blind, and then to give them sight.

3. The directions given to the patient, *v.* 7. His physician said to him, *Go, wash in the pool of Siloam*. Christ would hereby try his obedience, and whether he would with an implicit faith obey the orders of one he was so much a stranger to. He would likewise try how he stood affected to the tradition of the elders, which taught that it was not lawful to wash the eyes on the sabbath day. He would hereby represent the method of spiritual healing, in which, though the effect is owing purely to his power and grace, there is duty to be done by us. Go, search the scriptures, attend upon the ministry, converse with the wise; this is like washing in the pool of Siloam. Promised graces must be expected in the way of instituted ordinances. Concerning the pool of Siloam observe that it was supplied with water from Mount Zion, living waters, which were *healing*. The evangelist takes notice of the signification of the name, its being interpreted *sent*. Christ is often called the *sent of God*, so that when Christ sent him to the pool of Siloam he did in effect send him to himself. *Go, wash in the fountain opened*, a fountain of life, not a *pool*.

4. The patient's obedience to these directions: *He went his way therefore*, and *he washed his eyes*. In confidence of Christ's power, as well as in obedience to his command, he went, and washed.

5. The cure effected: *He came seeing*. So when the

JAMIESON, FAUSSET, BROWN

tion, so by letting any one service pass by its allotted time, the whole would be disarranged, marred, and driven beyond its destined period for completion; (5) that He acted ever under the impulse of these considerations, as man—"the night cometh when no man [or no one] can work." What lessons are here for others, and what encouragement from such Example!

5. As long as I am in the world, I am the light of the world—not as if He would cease, after that, to be so; but that He must make full proof of His fidelity while His earthly career lasted by displaying His glory. "As before the raising of Lazarus (ch. 11:25), He announces Himself as *the Resurrection and the Life*, so now He sets Himself forth as the source of the archetypal spiritual light, of which the natural, now about to be conferred, is only a derivation and symbol" [ALFORD].

6, 7. he spat on the ground, and made clay . . . and he anointed the eyes of the blind man . . . —These operations were not so incongruous in their nature as might appear, though it were absurd to imagine that they contributed in the least degree to the effect which followed. (See on Mark 6:13; and 7:33, 34).

7. Go, wash in Siloam which is . . ., Sent . . .—(See II Kings 5:10, 14). As the prescribed action was purely symbolical in its design, so in connection with it the Evangelist notices the symbolical name of the pool as in this case bearing testimony to him who was *sent* to do what it only *symbolized*. (See Isa. 8:6, where this same pool is used figuratively to denote "the streams that make glad the city of God," and which, humble though they be, betoken *a present God of Israel*.)

ADAM CLARKE

that no opportunity for doing good should be omitted—*day* representing the opportunity: *night*, the loss of that opportunity.

5. *I am the light of the world*. Like the sun, it is My business to dispense light and heat everywhere, and to neglect no opportunity that may offer to enlighten and save the bodies and souls of men. See chap. viii. 12.

6. *Anointed the eyes of the blind man*. It would be difficult to find out the reason which induced our Lord to act thus. It is certain this procedure can never be supposed to have been any likely medical means to restore sight to a man who was born blind; this action, therefore, had no tendency to assist the miracle. The Jews believed that there was some virtue in spittle to cure the diseases of the eye, but then they always accompanied this with some charm. Perhaps the best lesson we can learn from this is that God will do His own work in His own way; and, to hide pride from man, will often accomplish the most beneficial ends by means not only simple or despicable in themselves, but by such also as appear entirely contrary, in their nature and operation, to the end proposed to be effected by them.

7. *By interpretation, Sent*. From the Hebrew *shalach*, "he sent"; either because it was looked upon as a gift sent from God, for the use of the city, or because its waters were directed or sent by canals or pipes, into different quarters, for the same purpose.

MATTHEW HENRY

pangs and struggles of the new birth are over, the bands of sin fly off with them, and a glorious light and liberty succeed. Such is the power of Christ. What cannot *he* do who could do *this*, and do it *thus*? This man let Christ do what *he* pleased, and did what he appointed him to do, and so was cured. Those that would be healed by Christ must be ruled by him. He *came back* from the pool wondering and wondered at; he came *seeing*. This represents the benefit gracious souls find in attending on instituted ordinances, according to Christ's appointment; they have gone trembling, and come away triumphing; have gone *blind*, and come away *seeing*, come away singing.

Verses 8–12

Such a wonderful event as the giving of sight to a man born blind could not but be the talk of the town. Here we are told what the neighbours said of it, for the confirmation of the matter of fact. That which at first was not believed without *scrutiny* may afterwards be admitted without *scruple*.

I. Whether this was the same man that had before been blind, *v.* 8.

1. The neighbours could not but be amazed when they saw that he had his eyesight, and they said, *Is not this he that sat and begged?* When he could not labour, his parents not being able to maintain him, he *begged*. Those who cannot otherwise subsist must not be *ashamed to beg*; let no man be ashamed of anything but sin. There are some common beggars that are objects of charity, that should be distinguished; and we must not let the bees starve for the sake of the drones or wasps that are among them. The truth of the miracle was the better attested, and there were more to witness against those infidel Jews who would not believe *that he had been blind* than if he had been maintained in his father's house. Note, Christ's condescension. When it was for the advantage of his miracles that they should be wrought on those that were remarkable, he pitched upon those that were made so by their poverty and misery, not by their dignity.

2. Some said, *This is he*, the very same man; and these are witnesses to the truth of the miracle, for they had long known him stone-blind. Others said, *He is not he, but is like him*, and so, by their confession, if it be he, it is a great miracle that is wrought upon him. Think, [1] Of the wisdom and power of Providence in ordering such a universal variety of the faces of men and women, so that no two are so alike but that they may be distinguished, which is necessary to society, and commerce, and the administration of justice. [2] Of the wonderful change which the converting grace of God makes upon some who before were very wicked and vile, but are thereby so universally and visibly altered that one would not take them to be the same person.

3. This controversy was soon decided by the man himself: *He said, I am he*, "I am he that was blind, but now see, and am a monument of the mercy and grace of God." Those who are savingly enlightened by the grace of God should be ready to own what they were before.

II. How he came to have his eyes opened, *v.* 10–12. They will now turn aside, and *see this great sight*, and enquire further concerning it. Two things these neighbours enquire after:

1. The manner of the cure: *How were thine eyes opened?* It is good to observe the way and method of God's works, and they will appear the more wonderful. In answer to this enquiry the poor man gives them a plain and full account of the matter: *A man that is called Jesus made clay—and I received sight*, *v.* 11. Those who have experienced God's power and goodness, in temporal or spiritual things, should be ready upon all occasions to communicate their experiences. It is a debt we owe to our benefactor, and to our brethren. God's favours are lost *upon* us, when they are lost *with us*, and go no further.

2. The author of it (*v.* 12): *Where is he?* Some perhaps asked this question out of curiosity. "Where is he, that we may see him?" Others, perhaps, asked out of ill-will. "Where is he, that we may *seize* him?" The unthinking crowd will have ill thoughts of those that are put into an ill name. Some, we hope, asked this question out of *goodwill*. "Where is he, that we may be acquainted with him?" In answer to this, he could say nothing: *I know not*. As soon as Christ had sent him to the pool of Siloam, it should seem, he withdrew immediately. The man had never seen Jesus, for by the time that he had gained his sight he had lost his Physician. None of all the new and surprising objects that presented themselves could be so grateful to him as one sight of Christ, but as yet he knew no more of him than that he was called *Jesus—a Saviour*. Thus in the work of grace

JAMIESON, FAUSSET, BROWN

F. B. MEYER:

Jesus opens blind eyes. At the close of the previous chapter our Lord bore the contradiction of sinners against himself. The Jews had caught up the stones gathered to repair the temple, in order to inflict the doom of the blasphemer; but Jesus passed through them unscathed and began to descend the great steps.To human gaze there was need for Jesus to hasten from his foes (8:59); in *his* thought there was greater need to heal this blind beggar. In the most leisurely manner, therefore, he made clay and wrought this miracle of sight. His heart was at rest in God. No great thing is wrought by those who live in perpetual ferment. Through the quiet heart God works his own works, and there will be time enough to get them all done before "the night cometh, when no man can work."

Our Lord perceived that beneath the unpromising exterior of this man were elements of nobility, which he set himself to elicit. The clay which the man found suddenly applied to his eyes awakened wonder, hope, expectation, and faith. It was a ladder by which he climbed from the pit of despair to the mount of joy. The walk to Siloam was a further venture of faith; but there were other steps to be taken before he attained to the full stature of his discipleship. Some were forced on him by opposition; to others he was led by Christ himself.—*Bible Commentary*

8-15. **The neighbours therefore . . . said, Is not this he that sat and begged**—Here are a number of details to identify the newly seeing with the long-known blind beggar.

CHARLES H. SPURGEON:

In this man's healing, and in the salvation of every chosen soul, we shall see *The Great Healer Conspicuous*. If anyone among us shall ever be saved, the Savior will be made great thereby. If we are pardoned, we shall not be honored by the forgiveness, but the royal hand which signed and sealed the pardon shall be greatly extolled. If our eyes are opened, we shall not be made famous for sight, but He that opened our eyes will be made illustrious by the cure. It was thus in this case, and rightly so.

To begin with, in this man's mind, as soon as ever he received sight, "a man that was named Jesus" *came to the forefront*. Jesus was to him the most important person in existence. All that he knew of Him at first was that He was a man named Jesus; and under that character Jesus filled the whole horizon of his vision. He was more to him than those learned Pharisees, or than all his neighbors put together. Jesus was exceeding great, for He had opened his eyes. By and by, fixing his mind upon that figure, he saw more in it and declared, "He is a prophet." He boldly said this when he was running great risks by doing so. To their faces he told the carping Pharisees, "He is a prophet." A little further on he came to this, that he believed Him to be the Son of God, and worshiped Him. Now, my dear friend, if you are saved by Jesus, your star must set, but the star of Jesus must rise and increase in brilliance till it becomes no more a star, but a sun, making your day and flooding your whole soul with light. If we are saved, Christ Jesus must and will have the glory of it. None on earth or in heaven can rival Jesus in the esteem of souls brought from darkness to light: He is everybody to them. Do you dislike this? Do you want a share of the spoils, a fragment of the glory? Go your way and be blind, for your condition can never be altered while you refuse to honor the Savior. He that openeth a man's eyes deserves his grateful praises evermore.—*The Treasury of the New Testament*

ADAM CLARKE

8. *That he was blind.* Instead of this, "when he begged," or "was a beggar," is the reading of many MSS. This is in all probability the true reading.

9. *Some said, This is he.* This miracle was not wrought in private—nor before a few persons—nor was it lightly credited. Those who knew him before were divided in their opinion concerning him—not whether the man who sat there begging was blind before, for this was known to all; nor whether the person now before them saw clearly, for this was now notorious; but whether this was the person who was born blind, and who used to sit begging in a particular place. *Others said, He is like him.* This was very natural, for certainly the restoration of his sight must have given him a very different appearance to what he had before.

11. *A man that is called Jesus.* The whole of this relation is simple and artless in the highest degree. The blind man had never seen Jesus, but he had heard of His name—he felt that He had put something on his eyes, which he afterwards found to be clay—but how this was made he could not tell, because he could not see Jesus when He did it. Therefore he does not say, "He made clay of spittle"—but simply, "He made clay, and spread it upon my eyes."

12. *Where is he?* They had designed to seize and deliver Him up to the Sanhedrin, as a violator of the law, because He had done this on the Sabbath day.

MATTHEW HENRY

wrought upon the soul we see the change, but see not the hand that makes it.

Verses 13–34

One would have expected that such a miracle as Christ wrought upon the blind man would have silenced and shamed all opposition, but it had the contrary effect; instead of being embraced as a prophet for it, he is prosecuted as a criminal.

I. *They brought to the Pharisees him that aforetime was blind, v.* 13. Some think that those who brought this man to the Pharisees did it with a *good design,* to show them that this Jesus was not what they represented him, but one that gave considerable proofs of a divine mission. It should seem, rather, that they did it with an *ill design.*

II. That which is good was never maligned but under the imputation of something evil. And the crime objected here (*v.* 14) was that *it was the sabbath day when Jesus made the clay, and opened his eyes.* The traditions of the Jews had made that to be a violation of the law of the sabbath which was far from being so. But it may be asked, "Why would Christ not only work miracles on the sabbath day, but work them in such a manner as he knew would give offence to the Jews? Could he not have cured this blind man without making clay?" He would not seem to yield to the usurped power of the scribes and Pharisees. Christ was made under the law of God, but not under their law. He did it that he might, both by word and action, expound the law of the fourth commandment. Works of necessity and mercy are allowed, and the sabbath-rest to be kept, not so much for its own sake as in order to the sabbath-work.

III. The trial and examination of this matter by the Pharisees, *v.* 15. So much passion, prejudice, and ill-humour, and so little reason, appear here, that the discourse is nothing but crossing questions. Their enmity to Christ had divested them of all manner of humanity, and divinity too. Let us see how they teased this man.

1. They interrogated him concerning the cure itself. They *did not believe* that he was *born blind.* This was not a prudent caution, but a prejudiced infidelity. However, it was a good way that they took for the clearing of this: *They called the parents of the man who had received his sight.* This they did in hopes to disprove the miracle. God so ordered and overruled this counsel of theirs that it turned to the more effectual proof of the miracle, and left them under a necessity of being either convinced or confounded. Now in this part of the examination we have the questions that were put to them (*v.* 19): They *asked them,* "*Is this your son? Do you say he was born blind? How then doth he now see?* That is impossible, and therefore you had better unsay it." Those who cannot bear the light of truth do all they can to *eclipse* it, and hinder the discovery of it. Their answers to these interrogatories. They fully attest that which they could safely say in this matter (*v.* 20): *We know that this is our son,* and we know that he was *born blind.* It had cost them many a sad thought, and many a careful troublesome hour, about him. Those who are ashamed of their children because of their bodily infirmities, may take a reproof from *these* parents, who freely owned, This is *our son,* though he was *born blind.* They cautiously decline giving any evidence concerning his cure. They were not themselves eye-witnesses of it, and could say nothing to it *of their own knowledge.* Observe how warily they express themselves (*v.* 21): "*By what means he now seeth we know not,* or *who has opened his eyes we know not.*" Now these parents of the blind man were bound in gratitude to have borne their testimony to the honour of the Lord Jesus, who had done their son so great a kindness; but they had not courage to do it, and then thought it might serve to atone for their not appearing in favour of him that they said nothing to his prejudice. They refer themselves and the court to him: *He is of age, ask him, he shall speak for himself.* This man, though he was *born blind,* seems to have been of quick understanding above many. Thus God often by a kind providence makes up in the mind what is wanting in the body. His parents' turning them over to him was only to save themselves from trouble. See the reason why they were so cautious (*v.* 22, 23): *Because they feared the Jews.* Because they would shift trouble off from themselves. Near is my friend, and near is my child, and perhaps near is my religion, but *nearer is myself.* Note,

(1) The *late law* which the sanhedrim had made. If any man within their jurisdiction did *confess* that Jesus *was Christ, he should be put out of the synagogue.* [1] The crime designed to be punished, and that was embracing Jesus of Nazareth as the promised Messiah,

JAMIESON, FAUSSET, BROWN

13. They brought to the Pharisees—sitting probably in council, and chiefly of that sect (ch. 7:47, 48).

18-23. the Jews did not believe . . . he had been born blind . . . till they called the parents of him that had received his sight—Foiled by the testimony of the young man himself, they hope to throw doubt on the fact by close questioning his parents, who, perceiving the snare laid for them, ingeniously escape it by testifying simply to the identity of their son, and his birth-blindness, leaving it to himself, as a competent witness, to speak as to the cure. They prevaricated, however, in saying they "knew not who had opened his eyes," for "they feared the Jews," who had come to an understanding (probably after what is recorded (ch. 7:50, etc.) but by this time well known), that whoever owned Him as the Christ would be put out of the synagogue—i.e., not simply *excluded,* but *excommunicated.*

ADAM CLARKE

13. *They brought to the Pharisees.* These had the chief rule, and determined all controversies among the people; in every case of religion, their judgment was final. The people, now fully convinced that the man had been cured, brought him to the Pharisees, that they might determine how this was done and whether it had been done legally.

14. *It was the sabbath.* Some of the ancient rabbins taught, and they have been followed by some moderns not much better skilled in physic than themselves, that the saliva is a cure for several disorders of the eyes; but the former held this to be contrary to the law if applied on the Sabbath.

18. *But the Jews did not believe.* All the subterfuge they could use was simply to sin against their conscience, by asserting that the man had not been blind. But out of this subterfuge they were soon driven by the testimony of the parents, who, if tried further on this subject, might have produced as witness, not only the whole neighborhood, but nearly the whole city; for it appears the man got his bread by publicly begging, v. 8.

21. *He is of age.* Literally, "he has stature," i.e., he is a full-grown man; and in this sense the phrase is used by the best Greek writers. Mature age was fixed among the Jews at thirty years.

22. *Put out of the synagogue.* That is, "excommunicated"—separated from all religious connection with those who worshipped God. This was the lesser kind of excommunication among the Jews and was against the followers of Christ till after the Resurrection.

MATTHEW HENRY

and confessing of him. They themselves did expect a Messiah, but they could by no means bear to think that this Jesus should be he. *First,* Because his precepts were all so contrary to their traditional *laws.* The spiritual worship he prescribed overthrew their formalities. Humility and mortification, repentance and self-denial, were lessons new to them and sounded harsh and strange in their ears. *Secondly,* Because his promises and appearances were so contrary to their traditional hopes. Now to hear of a Messiah whose outward circumstances were all mean and poor, and at the same time bade his followers expect the cross, and count upon persecution; this was such a disappointment to all their hopes, that they could never be reconciled to it. Right or wrong, it must be *crushed.*

[2] The penalty to be inflicted for this crime. If any should own himself a disciple of Jesus, he should therefore be *put out of the synagogue,* as one that had rendered himself unworthy of the honours, and incapable of the privileges, of their church. Nor was this merely an ecclesiastical censure. It was, in effect, an *outlawry.* Christ's holy religion, from its first rise, has been opposed by penal laws made against the professors of it. The church's artillery, when the command of it has fallen into ill hands, has often been turned against itself. It is no new thing to see those cast out of the synagogue that were the greatest ornaments and blessings of it. They had already agreed it. Thus early were they aware of his growing interest, and already agreed to do their utmost to suppress it.

(2) The influence which this law had upon the parents of the blind man. They declined saying anything of Christ, *because they feared the Jews.* Christ had incurred the frowns of the government to do their son a kindness, but they would not incur them to do him any honour. Let us now go on with the examination of the man himself.

(3) They enquired of *him* concerning the *manner of the cure, v.* 15, 16.

[1] The same question which his neighbours had put to him *now again the Pharisees asked him, how he had received his sight.* This they enquired not with any sincere desire to find out the truth, but with a desire to find an occasion against Christ.

[2] The same answer, in effect, which he had before given to his neighbours, he here repeats to the Pharisees: *He put clay upon mine eyes, and I washed, and do see.* In the former account he said, *I washed, and received sight;* but lest they should think it was only a glimpse, he now says, "*I do see;* it is a complete and lasting cure."

[3] The remarks made upon this story were very different, and occasioned a debate in the court, *v.* 16.

First, Some took this occasion to censure and condemn Christ. Some of the Pharisees said, *This man is not of God, because he keepeth not the sabbath day.* The doctrine upon which this censure is grounded is very true—that those *are not of God* who do not *keep the sabbath day.* Those that are of God will *keep the commandments of God;* and this is his commandment, that we sanctify the sabbath. The application of it to our Saviour is very unjust, for he did religiously observe the sabbath day, never did otherwise than *well* on the sabbath day. He did not keep the sabbath according to the tradition of the elders, but he kept it according to the command of God. Much unrighteousness and uncharitable judging is occasioned by men's making the rules of religion more strict than God has made them, and adding their own fancies to God's appointments. Everything that we take for a rule of practice must not presently be made a rule of judgment.

Secondly, Others spoke in his favour, and very pertinently urged, *How can a man that is a sinner do such miracles?* There were some that were witnesses for Christ, even in the midst of his enemies. The matter of fact was plain, that this was a true miracle. Such things as these could never be done by a *man that is a sinner.* Such a one may indeed show some *signs and lying wonders,* but not such signs and true wonders as Christ wrought. Thus there was a *division among them.* Thus God defeats the counsels of his enemies by dividing them.

2. Their enquiry concerning the *author* of it.

(1) What the man said of him. They ask him (*v.* 17), "*What sayest thou of him, seeing that he has opened thine eyes?*" If he should speak *slightly* of Christ, in answer to this, as he might be tempted to do, to please them, they would have triumphed in it. Nothing confirms Christ's enemies in their enmity to him so much as the slights put upon him by those that have passed for his friends. But if he should speak honourably of Christ, they would prosecute him. They would make him an example. Or perhaps

JAMIESON, FAUSSET, BROWN

16, 17. This man is not of God . . . —(See on ch. 5:9, 16).

ADAM CLARKE

16. *This man is not of God.* He can neither be the Messiah nor a prophet, for He has broken the Sabbath. The Jews always argued falsely on this principle. The law relative to the observation of the Sabbath never forbade any work but what was of the servile and unnecessary kind. Works of necessity and mercy never could be forbidden on that day by Him whose name is Mercy, and whose nature is love; for the Sabbath was made for man, and not man for the Sabbath. Were it otherwise, the Sabbath would be rather a curse than a blessing.

How can a man that is a sinner? They knew very well that, though magicians and impostors might do things apparently miraculous, yet nothing really good could be performed by them. *And there was a division among them. Schisma,* "a schism," a decided difference of opinion, which caused a separation of the assembly.

ALBERT BARNES:

"If any man did confess that he was Christ." Did acknowledge that he was "the Messiah." They had prejudged the case, and were determined to put down all free inquiry, and not to be convinced by any means. "Put out of the synagogue." This took place in the temple, or near the temple. It does not refer, therefore, to any immediate and violent putting forth from the place where they were. It refers to excommunication from the synagogue. Among the Jews there were two grades of excommunication; the one for lighter offenses, of which they mentioned twenty-four causes; the other for greater offenses. The first excluded a man for thirty days from the privilege of entering a synagogue, and from coming nearer to his wife or friends than four cubits. The other was a solemn exclusion forever from the worship of the synagogue, attended with awful maledictions and curses, and an exclusion from all intercourse with the people. This was called "the curse," and so thoroughly excluded the person from all communion whatever with his countrymen, that they were not allowed to sell to him anything, even the necessaries of life (Buxtorf). It is probable that this latter punishment was what they intended to inflict if anyone should confess that Jesus was the Messiah; and it was the fear of this terrible punishment that deterred his parents from expressing their opinion.
—*Popular Commentary*

MATTHEW HENRY

Christ's friends proposed to have the man's own sentiments concerning his physician, since he appeared to be a sensible man. Those whose eyes Christ has opened know best what to say of him. What think we of Christ? To this question the poor man makes a short, plain, and direct answer: *He is a prophet.* It should seem, this man had not any thoughts that Christ was the Messiah, the great prophet. This blind man thought well of Christ according to the light he had, though he did not think well enough of him. This poor blind beggar had a clearer judgment of the things pertaining to the kingdom of God than the *masters in Israel.*

(2) What they said of him, in reply to the man's testimony. Finding that indeed a *notable miracle was wrought*, and they *could not deny it*, they do all they can to shake the good opinion the man had of him that opened his eyes, and to convince him that Christ was a bad man (*v.* 24): *Give God the praise, we know that this man is a sinner.* Two ways this is understood: By way of *advice*, to take heed of ascribing the praise of his cure to a sinful man, but to give it all to God. When God makes use of men that are sinners as instruments of good to us, we must *give God the glory*, and yet there is gratitude owing to the instruments. It was a good word, *Give God the praise*, but here it was ill used. By way of *adjuration*; "We know that this man is *a sinner*; this we are sure of, therefore *give God praise.* In God's name, man, tell the truth." See how basely they speak of the Lord Jesus: *We know that this man is a sinner*, is a man of sin. Their insolence and pride. They know very well that he is a sinner, and nobody can convince them of the contrary. He had challenged them to their faces (*ch.* viii. 46) to *convince him of sin*, and they had nothing to say; but now behind his back they speak of him as a malefactor. Thus false accusers make up in confidence what is wanting in proof. The injury and indignity hereby done to the Lord Jesus. When he became man, he took upon him the form not only of a *servant*, but of a *sinner.* Being *made sin for us*, he despised even this shame.

3. The debate that arose between the Pharisees and this poor man concerning Christ. They say, *He is a sinner;* he says, *He is a prophet.* It is an encouragement to those who are called out to witness for Christ to find with what prudence and courage this man managed his defence, according to the promise, *It shall be given you in that same hour what you shall speak.* Now in the parley we may observe three steps:

(1) He sticks to the certain matter of fact the evidence of which they endeavour to shake. He adheres to that which to himself, at least, was past dispute (*v.* 25): "*Whether he be a sinner or no I know not,*" or, as it might better be rendered, "*If he be a sinner, I know it not,* for this *one thing I know, that whereas I was blind, now I see,* and therefore he is a *prophet;* I am both able and bound to speak well of him." He tacitly reproves their great assurance of the ill character they gave of the blessed Jesus: "I, who know him as well as you do, cannot give him any such character." He boldly relies upon his own experience of the power and goodness of the holy Jesus, and resolves to abide by it. There is no disputing against experience. As Christ's mercies are most valued by those that have felt the want of them, so the most powerful and durable affections to Christ are those that arise from an experimental knowledge of him. Thus in the work of grace in the soul, though we cannot tell when and how, the blessed change was wrought, yet we may take the comfort of it if we can say, through grace, "*Whereas I was blind, now I see.*" A needless repetition of their enquiries into it (*v.* 26): *What did he to thee? How opened he thine eyes?* They asked these questions, because they wanted something to say, and would rather speak *impertinently* than seem to be silenced; because they hoped, by putting the man upon repeating his evidence, to catch him tripping in it.

(2) He upbraids them with their invincible prejudices, and they revile him as a disciple of Jesus, *v.* 27–29.

[1] Their wilful and unreasonable opposition to the evidence of this miracle, *v.* 27. He would not gratify them with a repetition of the story: *I have told you already, and you did not hear, wherefore would you hear it again, will you also be his disciples?* Some think that he spoke *seriously*, and really expecting that they would be convinced. But it rather seems to be spoken *ironically*: "*Will you be his disciples?* No, I know you abhor the thoughts of it." Those that wilfully shut their eyes against the light, as these Pharisees here did, *First,* Make themselves contemptible and base. *Secondly,* They forfeit all the benefit of further instruction. They that have been told once, and *would not hear*, why should they be told it again? *Thirdly,* They hereby *receive the grace*

JAMIESON, FAUSSET, BROWN

Others said . . .—such as Nicodemus and Joseph. **the blind man . . . said, He is a prophet**—rightly viewing the miracle as but a "sign" of His prophetic commission.

24-34. Give God the praise; we know that this man is a sinner—not wishing him to own, even to the praise of God, that a miracle had been wrought upon him, but to show more regard to the honor of God than ascribe any such act to one who was a sinner.

25. He answered and said, Whether a sinner or no . . .—Not that the man meant to insinuate any doubt in his own mind on the point of His being "a sinner," but as his *opinion* on such a point would be of no consequence to others, he would speak only to what he *knew* as *fact* in his *own case.*

26. Then said they . . . again, What did he to thee . . .—hoping by repeated questions to ensnare him, but the youth is more than a match for them.

27. I have told you already . . . will ye also be his disciples?—In a vein of keen irony he treats their questions as those of anxious inquirers, almost ready for discipleship! Stung by this, they retort upon *him* as the disciple (and here they plainly were not wrong); for themselves, they fall back upon Moses; about *him* there could be no doubt; but who knew about this upstart?

ADAM CLARKE

17. *He is a prophet.* They had intended to lay snares for the poor man, that, getting him to acknowledge Christ for the Messiah, they might put him out of the synagogue, v. 22, or put him to death, that such a witness to the divine power of Christ might not appear against them. But, as the mercy of God had given him his sight, so the wisdom of God taught him how to escape the snares laid for his ruin. If they allow that Jesus was a prophet, then, even in their sense, He might break the law of the Sabbath, and be guiltless. Or if they did not allow Him to be a prophet, they must account for the miracle some other way than by the power of God; as from Satan or his agents no good can proceed—to do this it was impossible. So the wisdom of God taught the poor man to give them such an answer as put them into a complete dilemma, from which they could not possibly extricate themselves.

24. *Give God the praise.* Having called the man a second time, they proceeded to deal with him in the most solemn manner; and therefore they put him to his oath; for the words above were the form of an oath, proposed by the chief magistrate to those who were to give evidence to any particular fact, or to attest anything, as produced by or belonging to the Lord. But while they solemnly put him to his oath, they endeavored to put their own words in his mouth, viz., he *is a sinner*—a pretender to the prophetic character, and a transgressor of the law of God; assert this, or you will not please us.

25. *Whereas I was blind, now I see.* He pays no attention to their cavils, nor to their perversion of justice; but in the simplicity of his heart speaks to the fact of the reality of which he was ready to give them the most substantial evidence.

27. *I have told you already.* So he did, v. 15. And did you not hear? You certainly did. Why then do you wish to *hear it again?* Is it because you wish to become His disciples? The poor man continued steady in his testimony; and by putting this question to them, he knew he should soon put an end to the debate.

MATTHEW HENRY

of God in vain. This is implied in that, "*Will you be his disciples?*" Those who will not see cause to embrace Christ, and join with his followers, yet, one would think, should see cause enough not to hate and persecute him and them.

[2] For this they scorn and revile him, *v.* 28. When they could not resist the wisdom and spirit by which he spoke, they broke out into a passion. The method commonly taken by unreasonable man is to make out with railing what is wanting in truth and reason.

First, They taunted this man for his affection to Christ; they said, *Thou art his disciple.* They *reviled him.* The Vulgate reads it, *they cursed him*; and what was their curse? It was this, *Be thou his disciple.* "May such a curse" (saith St. Austin here) "ever be on us and on our children!" They had no reason to call this man a *disciple of* Christ. He had spoken favourably of a kindness Christ had done him, and this they could not bear.

Secondly, They gloried in their relation to Moses as their Master: "*We are Moses's disciples.*" These Pharisees had before boasted of their good parentage: *We are Abraham's seed;* here they boast of their good education, *We are Moses's disciples;* as if these would save them. There was a perfect harmony between Christ and Moses; they might be disciples of Moses and become the disciples of Christ too; and yet they here put them in opposition. If we rightly understand the matter, we shall see God's grace and man's duty meet together and kiss and befriend each other.

Thirdly, They gave some sort of reason for their adhering to Moses against Christ (*v.* 29): *We know that God spoke unto Moses; as for this fellow, we know not whence he is.* But did they not know that they must expect another prophet, and a further revelation of the mind of God? yet, when our Lord Jesus did appear, they not only forfeited, but forsook, their own mercies. In this argument of theirs observe, *a.* How impertinently they allege that which none of his followers ever denied: *We know that God spoke unto Moses*, and, thanks be to God, we know it too. Moses was a prophet, it is true, and might not Jesus be a prophet also? *b.* How absurdly they urge their ignorance of Christ as a reason to justify their contempt of him: *As for this fellow.* Thus scornfully do they speak of the blessed Jesus, as if they did not think it worth while to charge their memories with a name so inconsiderable. *As for this fellow*, this sorry fellow, *we know not whence he is.* It was not long ago that the Jews had made the contrary to this an objection against Christ (*ch.* vii. 27): *We know this man whence he is, but when Christ comes no man knows whence he is.* Thus they could with the greatest assurance either affirm or deny the same thing, according as they saw it would serve their turn. See the absurdity of infidelity. Men will not know the doctrine of Christ because they are resolved they will not believe it, and then pretend they do not believe it because they do not know it.

4. He reasons with them, and they excommunicate him.

(1) The poor man, finding that he had reason on his side, grows more bold. He wonders at their obstinate infidelity (*v.* 30). He bravely answered, "*Why, herein is a marvellous thing*, that *you know not whence he is*, and yet he has opened mine eyes." Two things he wonders at: [1] That they should be strangers to a man so *famous.* He that could open the eyes of the blind must certainly be a considerable man, and worth taking notice of. That they should talk as if they thought it below them to take cognizance of such a man as this, this is a strange thing indeed. There are many who pass for learned and knowing men, who have no concern, no, not so much as a curiosity, to acquaint themselves with that which the *angels desire to look into.* [2] That they should question the divine mission of one that had undoubtedly wrought a divine miracle. "Now this is strange," saith the poor man, "that the miracle wrought upon me has not convinced you, that you should thus shut your eyes against the light." Had Christ opened the eyes of the Pharisees, they would not have doubted his being a prophet. He argues strongly against them, *v.* 31-33. The man here proves not only that he was *not a sinner* (*v.* 31), but that he was *of God*, *v.* 33.

a. He argues here, (*a*) With great knowledge. Though he could not read a letter of the book, he was well acquainted with the scripture; he had wanted the sense of seeing, yet had well improved that of hearing, by which faith cometh. (*b*) With great zeal for the honour of Christ. (*c*) With great boldness, and courage. Those that are ambitious of the favours of God must not be afraid of the frowns of men.

b. His argument may be reduced into form, somewhat like that of David, Ps. lxvi. 18-20. *If I regard iniquity in my heart, God will not hear me. But verily*

JAMIESON, FAUSSET, BROWN

30. The man answered, Herein is a marvellous thing, that ye know not from whence he is, and yet he hath opened mine eyes—He had no need to say another word; but waxing bolder in defense of his Benefactor, and his views brightening by the very courage which it demanded, he puts it to them how they could pretend inability to tell whether one who opened the eyes of a man born blind was "of God" or "a sinner"—from above or from beneath—and proceeds to argue the case with remarkable power. So irresistible was his argument that their rage burst forth in a speech of intense Pharisaism, 'Thou wast altogether born in sins, and dost thou teach us?—*thou,* a base-born, uneducated, impudent youth, teach *us,* the trained, constituted, recognized guides of the people in the things of God! Out upon thee!

A. B. SIMPSON:

The testimony of this man is full of manly courage and keen discernment. He faces the whole synagogue and stands fearlessly for his Deliverer, amazed that anybody could doubt that One to whom God could give such power was a true teacher and divine messenger. Like many still who are not afraid to witness for all that God has done for them, his persecution ended in his being expelled from the synagogue. But like every similar trial, it brought him a greater blessing, for then the Master met him and led him into a deeper revelation of His own character and love; and prostrate at Jesus' feet his spiritual vision was now open and he recognized and worshiped the Son of God as his own Savior and Lord. It teaches us that as we are true to Christ and to the light and blessing He gives us, He will lead us on and more freely meet us in every trial and suffering with the higher revelation of himself.

—*Christ in the Bible*

ADAM CLARKE

28. *Then they reviled him.* They spoke "cutting, piercing" words. Solomon talks of some who spoke "like the piercings of a sword," Prov. xiii. 18. And the Psalmist speaks of words that are like "drawn swords," Ps. lv. 21, words which show that the person who speaks them has his heart full of murderous intentions; and that, if he had the same power with a sword as he has with his tongue, he would destroy him whom he thus reproaches.

29. *We know not from whence he is.* As if they had said: We have the fullest assurance that the commission of Moses was divine, but we have no proof that this Man has such a commission: and should we leave Moses, and attach ourselves to this Stranger? No.

30. *Why herein is a marvellous thing.* As if he had said, "This is wonderful indeed!" Is it possible that such persons as you are, whose business it is to distinguish good from evil, and who pretend to know a true from a false prophet, cannot decide in a case so plain? Has not the Man opened my eyes? Is not the miracle known to all the town; and could anyone do it who was not endued with the power of God?

MATTHEW HENRY

God hath heard me; blessed be God.

(*a*) He lays it down for an undoubted truth that none but good men are the favourites of heaven (*v.* 31): *Now we know that God heareth not sinners* but *if any man be a worshipper of God, and does his will, him he heareth.* The assertions, rightly understood, are true. Be it spoken to the terror of the wicked, *God heareth not sinners.* This bespeaks no discouragement to repenting returning sinners, but to those that go on still in their trespasses. God will not *hear* them. Be it spoken to the comfort of the righteous, *If any man be a worshipper of God, and does his will, him he heareth.* The complete character of a good man: he is one that *worships God,* and *does his will.* The unspeakable comfort of such a man: him *God hears;* hears his prayers, and answers them.

(*b*) He magnifies the miracles which Christ had wrought, to strengthen the argument the more (*v.* 32): *Since the world began was it not heard that any man opened the eyes of one that was born blind.* It was a true miracle, and above the power of nature; it was never heard that any man, by the use of natural means, had cured one that was *born blind.* It was an extraordinary miracle, and beyond the precedents of former miracles. Moses wrought miraculous plagues, but Christ wrought miraculous cures.

(*c*) He therefore concludes, *If this man were not of God, he could do nothing.* What Christ did on earth sufficiently demonstrated what he was in heaven. We may each of us know by this whether we are of God or no: *What do we?* What do we more than others?

(2) The Pharisees fell foul upon him, and broke off the discourse, *v.* 34. What they *said.* Having nothing to reply to his argument, they reflected upon his person: *Thou wast altogether born in sin, and dost thou teach it?* [1] How they despised him: "*Thou wast not only born in sin,* as every man is, but altogether so, and bearing about with thee in thy body as well as in thy soul the marks of that corruption; thou waste one whom nature *stigmatized.*" It was most unjust to take notice of it now that the cure had not only rolled away the reproach of his blindness, but had *signalised* him as a favourite of Heaven. [2] How they *disdain* to learn of him: *Dost thou teach us?* A mighty emphasis must be laid here upon *thou* and *us.* "What! wilt *thou,* a silly sorry fellow, ignorant and illiterate, wilt thou pretend to teach *us,* that sit in Moses's chair. Proud men scorn to be taught, especially by their inferiors, whereas we should never think ourselves too old, nor too wise, nor too good, to learn. Those that have much wealth would have more; and why not those that have much knowledge? What they did: They *cast him out.* Some understand it only of a rude and scornful dismission of him from their council-board. But it seems rather to be a judicial act; they excommunicated him.

Verses 35–38

I. The tender care which our Lord Jesus took of this poor man (*v.* 35): *When Jesus heard that they had cast him out,* then he *found him,* which implies his seeking him and looking after him, that he might encourage and comfort him, 1. Because he had spoken so very well, so bravely, so boldly, in defence of the Lord Jesus. Jesus Christ will be sure to stand by his witnesses, and own those that own him and his truth and ways. It shall redound not only to our credit hereafter, but our comfort now. 2. Because the Pharisees had cast him out. Here was one poor man suffering for Christ, and he took care that as his afflictions abounded his consolations should *much more abound.* Happy are they who have a friend from whom men cannot debar them. Jesus Christ will graciously find and receive those who for his sake are unjustly rejected and cast out by men.

II. The comfortable converse Christ had with him. Christ gives him further instruction; for he that is faithful in a little shall be entrusted with more, Matt. xiii. 12.

1. Our Lord Jesus examines his faith: "*Dost thou believe on the Son of God?*" The Messiah is here called the *Son of God.* Christ, that he might give us an idea of his kingdom, as purely spiritual and divine, calls himself the *Son of God.*

2. The poor man solicitously enquires concerning the Messiah he was to believe in, professing his readiness to embrace him (*v.* 36): *Who is he, Lord, that I may believe on him?* Some think he did know that Jesus, who cured him, was the Son of God, but did not know which was Jesus, and therefore, supposing this person that talked with him to be a follower of Jesus, desired him to do him the favour to direct him to his master. Others think he did know that this person who talked with him was Jesus, whom he believed a great and good man and a prophet, but did not yet know that he was the Son of God. "Thou

JAMIESON, FAUSSET, BROWN

31. they cast him out—judicially, no doubt, as well in fact. The allusion to his being "born in sins" seems a tacit admission of his being blind from birth—the very thing they had been so unwilling to own. But rage and enmity to truth are seldom consistent in their outbreaks. The friends of this excommunicated youth, crowding around him with their sympathy, would probably express surprise that One who could work such a cure should be unable to protect his patient from the persecution it had raised against him, or should possess the power without using it. Nor would it be strange if such thoughts should arise in the youth's own mind. But if they did, it is certain, from what follows, that they made no lodgment there, conscious as he was that "wheras he was blind, now he saw," and satisfied that if his Benefactor "were not of God, He could do nothing" (vs. 33). There was a word for him too, which, if whispered in his ear from the oracles of God, would seem expressly designed to describe his case, and prepare him for the coming interview with his gracious Friend. "Hear the word of the Lord, ye that tremble at His word. *Your brethren that hated you, that cast you out for My name's sake, said, Let the Lord be glorified;* BUT HE SHALL APPEAR TO YOUR JOY, *and they shall be ashamed*" (Isa. 66:5). But how was *He* engaged to whom such noble testimony had been given, and for whom such persecution had been borne? Uttering, perhaps, in secret, "with strong crying and tears," the words of the prophetic psalm, "Let not them that wait on Thee, O Lord God of hosts, be ashamed for my sake; let none that seek Thee be confounded for my sake, O God of Israel; because for Thy sake I have borne reproach . . . and the reproaches of them that reproached Thee are fallen upon me" (Ps. 69:6, 7, 9). **35-38. Jesus heard**—i.e., by intelligence brought Him. **that they had cast him out; and when he had found him**—by accident? Not very likely. Sympathy in that breast could not long keep aloof from its object.

he said unto him, Dost thou believe on the Son of God?—A question stretching purposely beyond his present attainments, in order the more quickly to lead him—in his present teachable frame—into the highest truth. **36. He answered and said, Who is he, Lord, that I may believe on him?**—"His reply is affirmative, and believing by anticipation, promising faith as soon as Jesus shall say who He is" [STIER].

ADAM CLARKE

31. *God heareth not sinners.* I believe the word signifies "heathens," or persons not proselyted to the Jewish religion; and therefore it is put in opposition to "a worshipper of [the true] God." But in what sense may it be said, following our common version, that *God heareth not sinners?* When they regard iniquity in their heart—when they wish to be saved, and yet abide in their sins—when they will not separate themselves from the workers and works of iniquity.

32. *Since the world began.* "From the age"—probably meaning from the commencement of time. Neither Moses nor the prophets have ever opened the eyes of a man who was born blind. If this Person then were not the best of beings, would God grant Him a privilege which He has hitherto denied to His choicest favorites? *Opened the eyes of one that was born blind.* That there are cases in which a person who was born blind may be restored to sight by surgical means we know, but no such means were used by Christ. And it is worthy of remark that from the foundation of the world no person *born blind* has been restored to sight, even by surgical operation, till about the year of our Lord 1728, when the celebrated Dr. Cheselden, by couching the eyes of a young man, fourteen years of age, who had been born blind, restored him to perfect soundness. This was the effect of well-directed surgery; that performed by Christ was a miracle.

33. *If this man were not of God.* A very just conclusion: God is the Fountain of all good. All good must proceed from Him, and no good can be done but through Him. If this Person were not commissioned by the good God, He could not perform such beneficent miracles as these.

34. *Thou wast altogether born in sins.* You have not only been a vile wretch in some other preexistent state, but your parents also have been grossly iniquitous; therefore you and they are punished by this blindness. *And they cast him out.* They immediately "excommunicated" him, as the margin properly reads—drove him from their assembly with disdain, and forbade his further appearing in the worship of God. Thus a simple man, guided by the Spirit of truth, and continuing steady in his testimony, utterly confounded the most eminent Jewish doctors.

35. *Dost thou believe on the Son of God?* This was the same with, "Dost thou believe on the Messiah?" for these two characters were inseparable.

36. *Who is he, Lord?* It is very likely that the blind man did not know that it was Jesus the Christ who now spoke to him, for it is evident he had never seen Him before this time; and he might now see Him without knowing that He was the Person by whom he was cured, till our Lord made that discovery of himself mentioned in the following verse.

MATTHEW HENRY

who hast given me bodily sight, tell me, O tell me, who and where this Son of God is." The question was rational and just: *Who is he, Lord, that I may believe on him?*

3. Our Lord Jesus graciously reveals himself to him as that Son of God: *Thou hast both seen him, and it is he that talketh with thee, v.* 37. We do not find that Christ did thus expressly, and in so many words, reveal himself to any other as to this man here and to the woman of *Samaria*. He left others to find out by arguments who he was. Christ here describes himself to this man by two things: (1) *Thou hast seen him.* Now he was made sensible, more than ever, what an unspeakable mercy it was to be cured of his blindness, that he might see the Son of God. The greatest comfort of bodily eyesight is its serviceableness to our faith and the interests of our souls. Can we say that by faith we have seen Christ, seen him in his beauty and glory? Let us give him the praise, who opened our eyes. (2) *It is he that talketh with thee.* Great princes are willing to be *seen* by those whom yet they will not vouchsafe to *talk with*. But Christ talks with those whose desires are towards him, and manifests himself to them, as he did to the two disciples, when he talked their hearts warm, Luke xxiv. 32. This poor man was solicitously enquiring after the Saviour, when at the same time he saw him, and was talking with him. Jesus Christ is often nearer the souls that seek him than they themselves are aware of.

4. The poor man readily entertains this surprising revelation and said, *Lord, I believe, and he worshipped him.* He professed his faith in Christ: *Lord, I believe thee to be the Son of God.* He would not dispute anything that *he* said who had shown such mercy to him, and wrought such a miracle for him. Believing with the heart, he thus confesses with the mouth; and now the bruised reed was become a cedar. He paid his homage to him: *He worshipped him.* In worshipping Jesus he owned him to be God. Those who believe in him will see all the reason in the world to worship him. We never read any more of this man.

Verses 39–41

I. The account Christ gives of his design in coming into the world (*v.* 39): *For judgment I am* come. What Christ spoke, he spoke not as a preacher in the pulpit, but as a king upon the throne, and a judge upon the bench.

1. His business in the world was *great*. He came *for judgment*. To preach a doctrine and a law which would try men, and effectually discover and distinguish them. To put a difference between men, by revealing the thoughts of many hearts, and laying open men's true characters.

2. This great truth he explains by a metaphor borrowed from the miracle which he had lately wrought. That *those who see not might see, and that those who see might be made blind.* (1) This is applicable to nations and people. The Gentiles see a great light, while blindness is *happened unto Israel*, and their eyes are darkened. (2) To particular persons. Christ came into the world, [1] Intentionally and designedly to give sight to those that were spiritually blind; by his word to reveal the object, and by his Spirit to heal the organ, that many precious souls might be turned *from darkness to light*. [2] Eventually, and in the issue, *that those who see might be made blind*; that those who have a high conceit of their own wisdom, and set up that in contradiction to divine revelation, might be sealed up in ignorance. The preaching of the cross was foolishness to those who by wisdom *knew not God*.

II. The Pharisees' cavil at this. They said, *Are we blind also?* When Christ said that *those who saw* should by his coming be made blind, they apprehended that he meant them, who were the *seers* of the people, and valued themselves on their *insight* and *foresight*. "We know that the common people are blind; but *are we blind also*?" Frequently those that need reproof most, and deserve it best, though they have wit enough to discern a *tacit* one, have not grace enough to bear a *just* one. These Pharisees took this reproof for a reproach.

III. Christ's answer to this cavil, which, if it did not convince them, yet silenced them: *If you were blind you should have no sin; but now you say, We see, therefore your sin remaineth.* They gloried that they were not blind, but would *see with their own eyes*, having abilities, as they thought, sufficient for their own guidance. This very thing which they gloried in, Christ here tells them, was their shame and ruin.

1. *If you were blind, you would have no sin.* If you were blind you would have had comparatively *no sin*. The times of ignorance God *winked at*. It will be more tolerable with those that perish for lack of vision than with those that *rebel against the light*. "If you had been sensible of your own blindness you

JAMIESON, FAUSSET, BROWN

37. Jesus said unto him, Thou hast both seen him—the new sense of sight having at that moment its highest exercise, in gazing upon "the Light of the world."

38. he said, Lord, I believe: and he worshipped him—a *faith* and a *worship*, beyond doubt, meant to express far more than he would think proper to any human "prophet" (vs. 17)—the unstudied, resistless expression, probably of SUPREME faith and adoration, though without the full understanding of what that implied.

39-41. Jesus said—perhaps at the same time, but after a crowd, including some of the skeptical and scornful rulers, had, on seeing Jesus talking with the healed youth, hastened to the spot. **that they which see not might see . . .**—rising to that *sight* of which the natural vision communicated to the youth was but the symbol. (See on vs. 5, and cf. Luke 4:18.) **that they which see might be made blind**—judicially incapable of apprehending and receiving the truth, to which they have wilfully shut their eyes.

40. Are we blind also?—We, the constituted, recognized guides of the people in spiritual things? pride and rage prompting the question.

41. If ye were blind—wanted light to discern My claims, and only waited to receive it—**ye should have no sin**—none of the guilt of shutting out the light.

ADAM CLARKE

G. CAMPBELL MORGAN:

Observe the ascending scale in this man's consciousness of Jesus. "A man called Jesus"; "He is a prophet"; "If this man were not from God, he could do nothing"; "Lord, I believe. And he worshipped him."

Thus the scene ends with Jesus receiving the worship of a man. An excommunicated man, a man put out of the synagogue, is received into relationship with God in the act of his submission and his worship.

—*The Gospel According to John*

38. *And he said, Lord, I believe.* That is, I believe Thou art the Messiah; and, to give the fullest proof of the sincerity of his faith, he fell down before and adored Him. Never having seen Jesus before, but simply knowing that a person of that name had opened his eyes, he had only considered Him as a holy man and a prophet. But now that he sees and hears Him, he is convinced of His divinity, and glorifies Him as his Saviour. The word *kyrie* has two meanings; it signifies "Lord," or Sovereign Ruler, and "Sir," a title of civil respect. In the latter sense it seems evidently used in the thirty-sixth verse, because the poor man did not then know that Jesus was the Messiah; in the former sense it is used in this verse—now the healed man knew the quality of his Benefactor.

39. *For judgment I am come.* I am come to manifest and execute the just judgment of God: (1) By giving sight to the blind and light to the Gentiles, who sit in darkness, (2) By removing the true light from those who, pretending to make a proper use of it, only abuse the mercy of God. In a word, salvation shall be taken away from the Jews, because they reject it; and the kingdom of God shall be given to the Gentiles.

40. *Are we blind also?* These Pharisees understood Christ as speaking of blindness in a spiritual sense, and wished to know if He considered them in that state.

41. *If ye were blind.* If you had not had sufficient opportunities to have acquainted yourselves with My divine nature, by the unparalleled miracles which I have wrought before you and the holy doctrine which I have preached, then your rejecting Me could not be

MATTHEW HENRY

would soon have accepted Christ as your guide, and then you would *have had no sin.*" Those that are convinced of their disease are in a fair way to be cured, for there is not a greater hindrance to the salvation of souls than self-sufficiency.

2. "*But now you say, We see;* now that you have knowledge, and are instructed out of the law, and now that you think you see your way better than anybody can show it you, *therefore your sin remains.*" And as those are most blind who *will not see*, so their blindness is most dangerous who fancy they do see. Hearest thou the Pharisees say, *We see? There is more hope of a fool*, of a publican and a harlot, than of such.

CHAPTER 10

Verses 1–18

The Pharisees supported themselves in their opposition to Christ with this principle, that they were the *pastors of the church*, and that Jesus was an intruder and an imposter, and therefore the people were bound in duty to stick to *them*, against *him*. In opposition to this, Christ here describes who were the false shepherds, and who the true, leaving them to infer what they were.

I. Here is the parable or similitude proposed (*v.* 1-5). *Verily, verily, I say unto you,—Amen, amen.* This vehement asseveration intimates the certainty and weight of what he said.

1. In the parable we have, (1) A thief and a robber, that comes to do mischief to the flock, and damage to the owner, *v.* 1. *He enters not by the door*, as having no lawful cause of entry, but *climbs up some other way.* How industrious are wicked people to do mischief! This should shame us out of our slothfulness and cowardice in the service of God. (2) The character that distinguishes the rightful owner. *He enters in by the door* (*v.* 2), and he comes to do them some good office or other. Sheep need man's care, and, in return for it, are serviceable to man, they clothe and feed those by whom they are coted and fed. (3) The ready entrance that the shepherd finds: *To him the porter openeth*, *v.* 3. (4) The care he takes. The *sheep hear his voice*, and, which is more, he *calls his own sheep by name*, so exact is the notice he takes of them, and he leads them out from the fold to the green pastures (*v.* 4, 5). He does not drive them, but (such was the custom in those times) he goes before them, and they, being used to it, *follow him*, and are safe. (5) The strange attendance of the sheep upon the shepherd: *They know his voice*, and *a stranger will they not follow*, but will flee from him, not *knowing his voice.*

2. Good men are fitly compared to sheep. Men, as creatures depending on their Creator, are called the *sheep of his pasture.* The church of God in the world is a *sheepfold*, into which the *children of God* that were scattered abroad are *gathered together* (*ch.* xi. 52). This sheepfold lies much exposed to thieves and robbers; *wolves* in sheep's clothing, Matt. vii. 15. The great Shepherd of the sheep takes wonderful care of the flock and of all that belong to it. God is the great Shepherd, Ps. xxiii. 1. The under-shepherds, who are entrusted to feed the flock of God, ought to be careful and faithful in the discharge of that trust. Ministers must serve them in their spiritual interests, must *feed their souls* with the word of God. They must know the members of their flocks by name, and watch over them; must lead them into the pastures of public ordinances, be their mouth to God and God's to them. Those who are truly the sheep of Christ will be very observant of their Shepherd, and very cautious and shy of strangers. *They follow their Shepherd*, for they *know his voice*, having both a discerning ear, and an obedient heart. *They flee from a stranger*, and dread following him, because they know not his voice.

II. The Jews' ignorance of the drift and meaning of this discourse (*v.* 6): *Jesus spoke this parable to them, but they understood not what the things were which he spoke unto them.* The Pharisees had a great conceit of their own knowledge, and yet they had not sense enough to *understand the things that Jesus spoke of*; they were above their capacity. Frequently the greatest pretenders to knowledge are most ignorant in the things of God.

III. Christ's explication of this parable. Christ, in the parable, had distinguished the shepherd from the robber by this, that he *enters in by the door.* He makes himself to be both *the door* by which the shepherd enters and the shepherd that enters in by the door.

1. Christ is *the door.* He saith it to the Jews, who would be thought God's only sheep, and to the Pharisees, who would be thought their only shepherds:

JAMIESON, FAUSSET, BROWN

ye say, We see; therefore your sin remaineth—Your claim to possess light, while rejecting Me, is that which seals you up in the guilt of unbelief.

CHAPTER 10

Vss. 1-21. THE GOOD SHEPHERD. This discourse seems plainly to be a continuation of the closing verses of ch. 9. The figure was familiar to the Jewish ear (from Jer. 23; Ezek. 34; Zech. 11, etc.). "This simple creature [the sheep] has this special note among all animals, that it quickly hears the voice of the shepherd, follows no one else, depends entirely on him, and seeks help from him alone—cannot help itself, but is shut up to another's aid" [LUTHER in STIER]. **1, 2. He that entereth not by the door**—the legitimate way (without saying what that was, as yet). **into the sheepfold**—the sacred enclosure of God's true people. **climbeth up some other way**—not referring to the assumption of ecclesiastical office without an external call, for those Jewish rulers, specially aimed at, had this (Matt. 23:2), but to the want of a true spiritual commission, the seal of heaven going along with the outward authority; it is the assumption of the spiritual guidance of the people *without this* that is meant. **2. he that entereth in by the door is the shepherd of the sheep**—a true, divinely recognized shepherd. **3. To him the porter openeth**—i.e., *right of free access* is given, by order of Him to whom the sheep belong; for it is better not to give the allusion a more specific interpretation [CALVIN, MEYER, LUTHARDT]. **and the sheep hear his voice**—This and all that follows, though it admits of important *application* to every faithful shepherd of God's flock, is in its direct and highest sense true only of "the great Shepherd of the sheep," who in the first five verses seems plainly, under the simple character of a true shepherd, to be drawing His own portrait [LAMPE, STIER, etc.].

7-14. I am the door of the sheep—i.e., *the way in* to the fold, with all blessed privileges, both for shepherds and sheep (cf. ch. 14:6; Eph. 2: 18).

ADAM CLARKE

imputed to you as sin. But because you say, *We see*—we are perfectly capable of judging between a true and false prophet, and can from the Scriptures point out the Messiah by His works—on this account you are guilty. And your sin is of no common nature; it *remaineth;* i.e., it shall not be expiated. As you have rejected the Lord from being your Deliverer, so the Lord has rejected you from being His people. When the Scripture speaks of sin "remaining," it is always put in opposition to pardon; for pardon is termed the "taking away of sin," chap. i. 29; Ps. xxxii. 5.

CHAPTER 10

1. *Verily, verily.* Our Lord introduces this discourse in a most solemn manner, *Verily, verily*—Amen, amen!—"It is true, it is true!"—a Hebraism for, This is a most important and interesting truth, a truth of the utmost concern to mankind. *He that entereth not by the door.* Christ assures us, v. 7, that he is *the door;* whoever, therefore, enters not by Jesus Christ into the pastoral office is no other than *a thief and a robber* in the sheepfold. And he enters not by Jesus Christ who enters with a prospect of any other interest besides that of Christ and His people. Ambition, avarice, love of ease, a desire to enjoy the conveniences of life, to be distinguished from the crowd, to promote the interests of one's family, and even the whole design of providing against want—these are all ways by which thieves and robbers enter into the Church. Acting through motives of self-interest and with the desire of providing for himself and his family are innocent, yea, laudable, in a secular business; but to enter into the ministerial office through motives of this kind is highly criminal before God.

2. *He that entereth in by the door.* Observe here the marks, qualities, and duties of a good pastor. The *first* mark is that he has a lawful entrance into the ministry by the internal call of Christ, namely, by an impulse proceeding from His Spirit, upon considerations which respect only His glory, and upon motives which aim at nothing but the good of His Church, the salvation of souls, the doing the will of God, and the sacrificing himself entirely to His service, and to that of the meanest of His flock.

3. *To him the porter openeth.* In the porter opening the door to the true shepherd we may discover the *second* mark of a true minister—his labor is crowned with success. The Holy Spirit opens his way into the hearts of his hearers and he becomes the instrument of their salvation. See Col. iv. 3; 2 Cor. ii. 12; 1 Cor. xvi. 9; Rev. iii. 8. *The sheep hear his voice.* A *third* mark of a good shepherd is that he speaks so as to instruct the people—*the sheep hear his voice.* A man who preaches in such a language as the people cannot comprehend may do for a stage-player or a mountebank, but not for a minister of Christ. *He calleth his own sheep by name.* A *fourth* mark of a good pastor is that he is well acquainted with his flock; he knows them by name—he takes care to acquaint himself with the spiritual states of all those that are entrusted to him. *And leadeth them out.* A *fifth* mark of a good shepherd is, he *leads* the flock, does not lord it over God's heritage, nor attempt by any rigorous discipline not founded on the gospel of Christ to drive men into the way of life; nor drive them out of it, which many do, by a severity which is a disgrace to the mild gospel of the God of peace and love. He leads them out of themselves to Christ, *out* of the follies, diversions, and amusements of the world, into the path of Christian holiness.

4. *He goeth before them.* A *sixth* mark of a true pastor is, he gives them a good example; he not only preaches, but he lives, the truth of the gospel. He enters into the depths of the salvation of God. The minister who is in this state of salvation *the sheep*, genuine Christians, will *follow . . . for they know his voice.* It was the custom in the Eastern countries for the shepherd to go at the head of his sheep, and they followed him from pasture to pasture.

5. *And a stranger will they not follow.* That

MATTHEW HENRY

I am the door of the sheepfold.

(1) In general, he is as a *door shut*, to keep out thieves and robbers, and such as are not fit to be admitted. He is as a *door open* for passage and communication. By Christ, as the door, we have our first admission into the flock of God. By him God comes to his church, visits it, and communicates himself to it. By him, as the door, the sheep are at last admitted into the heavenly kingdom.

(2) More particularly,

[1] Christ is the door of *the shepherds*, so that none who come not in by him are to be accounted pastors, but *thieves and robbers* (though they pretended to be *shepherds*); but the *sheep did not hear them*. The character given of them: they are *thieves and robbers* (*v.* 8); all that *went before him*, that assumed a precedency and superiority above him. They condemned our Saviour as a thief and a robber, because he did not come in by them as the door, but he shows that they ought to have been admitted by him. The care taken to preserve the sheep from them: *But the sheep did not hear them*. Those that were spiritual and heavenly could by no means approve of the traditions of the elders, nor relish their formalities.

[2] Christ is the door of *the sheep* (*v.* 9): *By me if any man enter into the sheepfold*, he *shall be saved;* he *shall go in and out*. *First*, Plain directions how to come into the fold: we must come in *by Jesus Christ* as the door. By faith in him we come into covenant and communion with God. *Secondly*, Precious promises to those who observe this direction. They *shall be saved hereafter*; this is the privilege of *their home*. They shall be *for ever happy*. In the meantime they shall *go in and out and find pasture*; this is the privilege of *their way*. True believers are *at home* in Christ; when they go out, they are not *shut out* as strangers, but have liberty to come in again; when they come in, they are not *shut in* as trespassers, but have liberty to go out. They go out to the field in the morning, they come into the fold at night; and they *find pasture* in both: grass in the field, fodder in the fold.

2. Christ is the *shepherd*, *v.* 11, &c. God has constituted his Son Jesus to be our *shepherd*; and here again and again he owns the relation. He expects all that attendance and observance which the shepherds in those countries had from their flocks.

(1) Christ is *a shepherd*, and not as the thief. The mischievous design of the thief (*v.* 10): *The thief cometh not* but to *steal, and to kill, and to destroy*. Those whom they *steal*, whose hearts and affections they steal from Christ and his pastures, they *kill and destroy* spiritually. Deceivers of souls are murderers of souls. The gracious design of the shepherd; he is come,

First, To *give life to the sheep*. Christ saith, *I am come among men*, [1] That *they might have life*. He came to put life into the flock, the church in general, which had seemed rather like a valley full of dry bones than like a pasture covered over with flocks. He came to *give life* to particular believers. Life is inclusive of all good. [2] That they might have it *more abundantly*, that they might have a life *more abundant* than could have been expected or than we are *able to ask or think*. But it may be construed *that they might have abundance*. Christ came to give life and *something more*, something *better*, life with advantage. Life in abundance is *eternal life*, life and *much more*.

Secondly, To *give his life for the sheep*, and this that he might give life *to them* (*v.* 11): *The good shepherd giveth his life for the sheep*. It is the property of every good shepherd to hazard and expose his life for the sheep. It was the prerogative of the great Shepherd to give his life to purchase his flock.

(2) Christ is *a good shepherd*, and not as a hireling. There were many that were not thieves, yet were very careless in the discharge of their duty, and through their neglect the flock was greatly damaged. Christ here *calls himself the good shepherd* (*v.* 11), and again (*v.* 14). Jesus Christ is the best of shepherds, none so skilful, so faithful, so tender, as he. He *proves himself* so, in opposition to all hirelings, *v.* 12–14. The carelessness of the unfaithful shepherd described (*v.* 12, 13); he that is a hireling, *whose own the sheep are not, sees the wolf coming*, and *leaves the sheep*, for in truth he *careth not for them*. Evil shepherds, magistrates and ministers, are here described both by their bad principles and their bad practices. Their *bad principles*, the root of their bad practices. What makes those that have the charge of souls in trying times to betray their trust, and in quiet times not to mind it? It is because they are *hirelings*, and *care not for the sheep*. The wealth of the world is the chief of their good; it is because they are *hirelings*. They undertook the shepherds' office, as a trade to live

JAMIESON, FAUSSET, BROWN

8. All that ever came before me—the false prophets; not as claiming the prerogatives of Messiah, but as perverters of the people from the way of life, all pointing to Him [OLSHAUSEN]. **the sheep did not hear them**—the instinct of their divinely taught hearts preserving them from seducers, and attaching them to the heaven-sent prophets, of whom it is said that "the Spirit of Christ was in them" (I Peter 1:11).

9. by me if any man enter in—whether shepherd or sheep. **shall be saved**—the great object of the pastoral office, as of all the divine arrangements towards mankind. **and shall go in and out and find pasture**—*in*, as to a place of *safety* and *repose; out*, as to "green pastures and still waters" (Ps. 23:2) for nourishment and refreshing, and all this only transferred to another clime, and enjoyed in another manner, at the close of this earthly scene (Rev. 7:17).

10. I am come that they might have life, and . . . more abundantly—not merely to *preserve* but *impart* LIFE, and communicate it in rich and unfailing exuberance. What a claim! Yet it is only an echo of all His teaching; and He who uttered these and like words must be either a blasphemer, all worthy of the death He died, or "God with us"—there can be no middle course. **11. I am the good shepherd**—emphatically, and, in the sense intended, exclusively so (Isa. 40:11; Ezek. 34:23; 37:24; Zech. 13:7). **the good shepherd giveth his life for the sheep**—Though this may be said of literal shepherds, who, even for their brute flock, have, like David, encountered "the lion and the bear" at the risk of their own lives, and still more of faithful pastors who, like the early bishops of Rome, have been the foremost to brave the fury of their enemies against the flock committed to their care; yet here, beyond doubt, it points to the struggle which was to issue in the willing surrender of the Redeemer's own life, to save His sheep from destruction. **12. an hireling . . . whose own the sheep are not**—who has no *property* in them. By this He points to His own peculiar relation to the sheep, the same as His Father's, the great Proprietor and Lord of the flock, who styles Him "My Shepherd, *the Man that is My Fellow*" (Zech. 13:7), and though faithful undershepherds are so in their Master's interest, that they feel a measure of His own concern for their charge, the language is strictly applicable only to "the Son over His own house" (Heb. 3:6). **seeth the wolf coming**—not *the devil* distinctively, as some take it [STIER, ALFORD, etc.], but generally whoever comes upon the flock with hostile intent, in whatever form: though the wicked one, no doubt, is *at the bottom* of such movements [LUTHARDT].

ADAM CLARKE

is, a man who, pretending to be a shepherd of the flock of God, is a *stranger* to that salvation which he professes to preach.

7. *I am the door of the sheep*. It is through Me only that a man can have a lawful entrance into the ministry; and it is through Me alone that mankind can be saved.

8. *All that ever came before me*. Or, as some translate, "all that came instead of Me," i.e., all that came as the Christ, or Messiah, such as Theudas, and Judas the Gaulonite, who are mentioned, Acts v. 36-37; and who were indeed no other than thieves, plundering the country wherever they came; and murderers, not only slaying the simple people who resisted them, but leading the multitudes of their followers to the slaughter. But our Lord probably refers to the scribes and Pharisees, who pretended to show the way of salvation to the people—who in fact stole into the fold, and clothed themselves with the fleece, and devoured the sheep. The thief and the robber should be properly distinguished; one takes by cunning and stealth, the other openly and by violence.

9. *I am the door: by me if any man enter*. Those who come for salvation to God, through Christ, shall obtain it. *He shall be saved*—he shall have his sins blotted out, his soul purified, and himself preserved unto eternal life. *Go in and out*. This phrase, in the style of the Hebrews, points out all the actions of a man's life and the liberty he has of acting or not acting. A good shepherd conducts his flock to the fields where good pasturage is to be found, watches over them while there, and brings them back again and secures them in the fold.

10. *But for to steal, and to kill, and to destroy*. Those who enter into the priesthood that they may enjoy the revenues of the Church are the basest and vilest of thieves and murderers. Their ungodly conduct is a snare to the simple, and the occasion of much scandal to the cause of Christ. Their doctrine is deadly; they are not commissioned by Christ, and therefore they cannot profit the people. Their character is well pointed out by the Prophet Ezekiel, chap. xxxiv. 2, etc.: "Woe be to the shepherds of Israel that do feed themselves! . . . Ye eat the fat, and ye clothe you with the wool, ye kill them that are fed: but ye feed not the flock." *That they might have life*. My doctrine tends to life, because it is the true doctrine—that of the false and bad shepherds tends to death, because it neither comes from nor can lead to that God who is the Fountain of life.

11. *I am the good shepherd*. Whose character is the very reverse of that which has already been described. In vv. 7 and 9, our Lord had called himself "the door of the sheep," as being the sole Way to glory, and Entrance into eternal life. Here He changes the thought, and calls himself the *shepherd*, because of what He was to do for them that believe in Him, in order to prepare them for eternal glory. *Giveth his life for the sheep*. That is, gives up His soul as a sacrifice to save them from eternal death.

MATTHEW HENRY

and grow rich by. It is the love of money, and of their own bellies, that carries them on in it. Those are *hirelings* that love the wages more than the work. The work of their place is the least of their care. They *value not the sheep*, are unconcerned in the souls of others. They *seek their own things*. What can be expected but that they will flee when *the wolf comes*. He *careth not for the sheep*, for he is one *whose own the sheep are not*. Their *bad practices*, the effect of these bad principles, *v.* 12. How basely the hireling deserts his post; when he sees *the wolf coming* he *leaves the sheep and flees*. Those who mind their safety more than their duty are an easy prey to Satan's temptations. How fatal the consequences are! *The wolf catches them*, and *scatters the sheep*, and woeful havoc is made of the flock. See here the grace and tenderness of the good Shepherd. The Lord Jesus is, and will be, as he ever has been, *the good Shepherd*. Here are two great instances of the shepherd's goodness.

[1] His *acquainting* himself with his flock.

a. He is acquainted with all that *are now of his flock* (*v.* 14, 15), as the good Shepherd (*v.* 3, 4): *I know my sheep and am known of mine*. They know one another very well, and knowledge notes affection. Christ *knows his sheep*. He knows who are his sheep, and who are not; he knows the sheep under their many infirmities, and the goats under their most plausible disguises. He *knows* them, that is, he approves and accepts of them. He is *known of them*. They observe him with an eye of faith. It is not so much our knowing him as our being known of him that is our happiness. Upon this occasion Christ mentions (*v.* 15) the mutual acquaintance between his Father and himself: *As the Father knoweth me, even so know I the Father*. *First*, As the *ground* of that intimate acquaintance and relation which subsist between Christ and believers. The Lord Jesus *knows whom he hath chosen*, and is sure of them (*ch.* xiii. 18), and they also *know whom they have trusted*, and are sure of him (2 Tim. i. 12), and the ground of both is the perfect knowledge which the Father and the Son had of one another's mind. *Secondly*, As an apt similitude, illustrating the intimacy that is between Christ and believers. It may be connected with the foregoing words, thus: *I know my sheep, and am known of mine, even as the Father knows me, and I know the Father*. As the Father knew the Son, and loved him, so Christ knows his sheep, and has a watchful tender eye upon them. As the Son knew the Father, loved and obeyed him, so believers know Christ.

b. He is acquainted with those that are *hereafter to be of this flock* (*v.* 16): *Other sheep I have, which are not of this fold; them also I must bring*.

(*a*) The eye that Christ had to the poor Gentiles. He had sometimes intimated his special concern for *the lost sheep of the house of Israel*, but, saith he, *I have other sheep*. Those who in process of time should believe in Christ, from among the Gentiles, are here called *sheep*. Christ has a right to many a soul of which he has not yet the possession. Christ speaks of those *other sheep* to take off the contempt that was put upon him, as having but a *little flock*, and therefore, if a *good* shepherd, yet a *poor* shepherd: "But," saith he, "I have more sheep than you see."

(*b*) The purposes and resolves of his grace concerning them: "*Them also I must bring.*" But why *must* he bring them? What was the necessity? The *necessity of their case* required it. Like sheep, they will never come back, of themselves. The *necessity of his own engagements* required it; he must bring them, or he would not be faithful to his trust.

(*c*) The happy effect and consequence of this. "They shall hear my voice. It shall be heard *by them*; I will speak, and give to them to hear." Faith comes by hearing. *There shall be one fold and one shepherd*. As there is one shepherd, so there shall be one fold. Both Jews and Gentiles shall be incorporated in one church. Being united to Christ, they shall unite in him; two sticks shall become one in the hand of the Lord.

[2] Christ's *offering up himself for his sheep v.* 15, 17, 18.

a. He declares his purpose of *dying for his flock* (*v.* 15): *I lay down my life for the sheep*. He laid down his life not only for the good of the sheep, but *in their stead*. Thousands of sheep had been offered in sacrifice for their shepherds, as sin-offerings, but here, by a surprising reverse, the shepherd is sacrificed for the sheep. Though the smiting of the shepherd be for the present the *scattering* of the flock, it is in order to the gathering of them in.

b. He takes off the offence of the cross by four considerations:

(*a*) That his *laying down his life for the sheep* entitled him to the honours and powers of his exalted state (*v.* 17): "*Therefore doth my Father love me,*

JAMIESON, FAUSSET, BROWN

ALEXANDER MACLAREN:

"I know my sheep." That is a knowledge like the knowledge of the shepherd, a bond of close intimacy. But He does not know them by reason of looking at them and thinking about them. It is something far more blessed than that. He knows me because He loves me; He knows me because He has sympathy with me, and I know Him, if I know Him at all, by my love, my sympathy, and my communion. A loveless heart does not know the Shepherd, and unless the Sherpherd's heart was all love, He would not know His sheep. The Shepherd's love is an individualized love. He knows His flock as a flock because He knows the units of it, and we can rest ourselves upon the personal knowledge, which is personal love and sympathy, of Jesus Christ.—*Expositions of Holy Scripture*

14. I am the good shepherd, and know my sheep—in the peculiar sense of II Timothy 2:19. **am known of mine**—the soul's response to the voice that has inwardly and efficaciously called it; for of this mutual loving acquaintance ours is the *effect* of His. "The Redeemer's knowledge of us is the *active* element, penetrating us with His power and life; that of believers is the *passive* principle, the reception of His life and light. In this reception, however, an assimilation of the soul to the sublime Object of its knowledge and love takes place; and thus an activity, though a derived one, is unfolded, which shows itself in obedience to His commands" [OLSHAUSEN]. From this mutual knowledge Jesus rises to another and loftier reciprocity of knowledge. **15-18. As the Father knoweth me, even so know I the Father**—What claim to absolute equality with the Father could exceed this? (See on Matt. 11:27.)

16. other sheep I have . . . not of this fold: them also I must bring—He means the perishing Gentiles, *already His "sheep"* in the love of His heart and the purpose of His grace to "*bring them*" in due time.

they shall hear my voice—*This is not the language of mere foresight that they would believe, but the expression of a purpose to draw them to Himself by an inward and efficacious call, which would infallibly issue in their spontaneous accession to Him.* **and there shall be one fold**—rather "one flock" (for the word for "fold," as in the foregoing verses, is quite different).

and I lay down my life for the sheep—How sublime this, immediately following the lofty claim of the preceding clause! 'Tis the riches and the poverty of "the Word made flesh"—one glorious Person reaching at once up to the Throne and down even to the dust of death, "that we might live through Him." A candid interpretation of the words, "*for the sheep*," ought to go far to establish the special relation of the vicarious death of Christ to the Church.

ADAM CLARKE

14. *I . . . know my sheep*. I know "them that are Mine."

16. *Other sheep I have*. The Gentiles and Samaritans. As if our Lord had said, Do not imagine that I shall lay down My life for the Jews, exclusively of all other people. No, I shall die also for the Gentiles; and, though they *are not of this fold* now, those among them that believe shall be united with the believing Jews, and made one fold under one Shepherd, Eph. ii. 13-17.

MATTHEW HENRY

because I lay down my life." He was *therefore* beloved of the Father because he undertook to *die for the sheep*. Did he think God's love recompence sufficient for all his services and sufferings, and shall we think it too little for ours, and court the smiles of the world to make it up?

(*b*) That his laying down his life was in order to his resuming it: *I lay down my life, that I may receive it again.* God loved him too well to leave him in the grave. He yielded to death, as if he were smitten before it, that he might the more gloriously conquer death, and triumph over the grave.

(*c*) That he was perfectly voluntary in his sufferings and death (*v.* 18). "I freely *lay it down of myself*, for I *have power to lay it down, and to take it again.*" See here the power of Christ, as the Lord of life. He had power to *keep his life* against all the world. Though Christ's life seemed to be taken by storm, yet really it was surrendered, otherwise it had been impregnable. *No man taketh my life from me.* He had power to *lay down his life.* [*a*] He had ability to do it. He could, when he pleased, slip the knot of union between soul and body. Having voluntarily *taken up* a body, he could voluntarily lay it down again. [*b*] He had authority to do it. We are not at liberty to do it; but Christ had a sovereign authority to dispose of his own life as he pleased. He had power to *take it again*; we have not. Our life, once laid down, is *as water spilt upon the ground*; but Christ, when he laid down his life, still had it within reach, and could resume it. See here the grace of Christ; he *laid it down of himself* for our redemption. He offered himself to be the Saviour.

(*d*) That he did all this by the express order and appointment of his Father: *This commandment have I received of my Father.*

Verses 19–21

The people's different sentiments concerning Christ. There was a division, a *schism*, among them. Such a ferment as this they had been in before (*ch.* vii. 43; ix. 16); and where there has once been a division a little thing will make a division again. Rents are sooner made than made up or mended. But it is better that men should be *divided* about the doctrine of Christ than *united* in the service of sin.

I. Some upon this occasion spoke ill of Christ and of his sayings. They said, *He has a devil, and is mad, why do you hear him?* They reproach him as a demoniac. He is a distracted man, no more to be heard than the rambles of a man in bedlam. They ridicule his hearers: "*Why hear you him?*" Men would not thus be laughed out of their necessary food, and yet suffer themselves to be laughed out of what is more necessary.

II. Others stood up in defence of him, and, though the stream ran strong, dared to swim against it. They could not bear to hear him thus abused. If they could say no more of him, this they would maintain, that he was a man in his wits, that he had not a devil, that he was neither senseless nor graceless. Two things they plead: 1. The excellency of his doctrine: "*These are not the words of him that hath a devil.* These are not the words of one that is either violently possessed with a devil or voluntarily in league with the devil." So much of holiness there is in the words of Christ that we may conclude they are *not the words of one that has a devil*, and therefore are the words of one that was sent of God. 2. The power of his miracles: *Can a devil open the eyes of the blind?* Neither mad men nor bad men can work miracles. The devil will sooner put out men's eyes than open them. Therefore Jesus *had not a devil.*

Verses 22–38

It is hard to say which is more strange, the gracious words that came out of his mouth or the spiteful ones that came out of theirs.

I. *It was at the feast of dedication, and it was winter*, a feast that was annually observed by consent, in remembrance of the dedication of a new altar and the purging of the temple, by Judas Maccabæus. The return of their liberty was to them as life from the dead, and, in remembrance of it, they kept an annual feast about the beginning of *December*, and seven days after. The celebrating of it was not confined to Jerusalem, but every one observed it in his own place, not as a *holy time*, but as a *good time.*

II. The place where it was (*v.* 23): *Jesus walked in the temple in Solomon's porch. He walked*, ready to give audience to any that should apply to him, and to offer them his services. Those that have anything to say to Christ may find him in the temple and walk with him there.

III. The conference itself.

1. A weighty question put to him by the Jews, *v.* 24. They *came round about him*, to tease him; he was

JAMIESON, FAUSSET, BROWN

17. Therefore doth my Father love me, because I lay down my life . . .—As the highest act of the Son's love to the Father was the laying down of His life for the sheep at His "commandment," so the Father's love to Him as His *incarnate* Son reaches its consummation, and finds its highest justification, in that sublimest and most affecting of all acts. **that I might take it again**—His resurrection-life being indispensable to the accomplishment of the fruit of His death. **18. No man taketh it from me, but I lay it down myself: I have power to lay it down, and I have power to take it again**—It is impossible for language more plainly and emphatically to express the *absolute voluntariness* of Christ's death, such a voluntariness as it would be manifest presumption in any mere *creature* to affirm of his own death. It is beyond all doubt the language of One who was conscious that *His life was His own* (which no creature's is), and therefore His to surrender or retain *at will.* Here lay the glory of His sacrifice, that it was *purely* voluntary. The claim of "power to take it again" is no less important, as showing that His resurrection, though ascribed to the Father, in the sense we shall presently see, was nevertheless *His own assertion of His own right to life* as soon as the purposes of His voluntary death were accomplished. **This commandment**—to "lay down His-life, that He might take it again." **have I received of my Father**—So that Christ died at once by "command" of His Father, and by such a voluntary obedience to that command as has made Him (so to speak) infinitely dear to the Father. The *necessity* of Christ's death, in the light of these profound sayings, must be manifest to all but the superficial student.

19-21. There was a division . . . again among the Jews for these sayings—the light and the darkness revealing themselves with increasing clearness in the separation of the teachable from the obstinately prejudiced. The one saw in Him only "a devil and a madman"; the other revolted at the thought that *such words* could come from one possessed, and sight be given to the blind by a demoniac; showing clearly that a deeper impression had been made upon them than their words expressed.

22-42. DISCOURSE AT THE FEAST OF DEDICATION—FROM THE FURY OF HIS ENEMIES JESUS ESCAPES BEYOND JORDAN, WHERE MANY BELIEVE ON HIM. **22, 23. it was . . . the feast of the dedication**—celebrated rather more than *two months* after the feast of tabernacles, during which intermediate period our Lord seems to have remained in the neighborhood of Jerusalem. It was instituted by Judas Maccabeus, to commemorate the purification of the temple from the profanations to which it had been subjected by Antiochus Epiphanes 165 B.C., and kept for eight days, from the 25th Chisleu (December), the day on which Judas began the first joyous celebration of it (I Maccabees 4:52, 56, 59; and JOSEPHUS, *Antiquities*, xii. 7. 7). **it was winter**—implying some *inclemency*. Therefore **Jesus walked . . . in Solomon's porch**—for shelter. This portico was on the east side of the temple, and Josephus says it was part of the original structure of Solomon [*Antiquities*, xx. 9. 7]. **24. Then came the Jews**—*the rulers*. (See on ch. 1:19.)

ADAM CLARKE

17. *Therefore doth my Father love me.* As I shall be shortly crucified by you, do not imagine that I am abandoned by My Heavenly Father and therefore fall thus into your hands. The Father loveth Me particularly on this account, because I am going to *lay down my life* for the life of the world. Again, do not suppose that I shall be put to death by your rulers because I have not strength to resist them. *I lay down my life* voluntarily and cheerfully. No one can *take* it away from Me; see v. 18. And I shall give you the fullest proof of My supreme power by raising, in three days, that very crucified, wounded body from the grave.

18. *I have power.* Or "authority."

19. *There was a division.* "A schism." They were divided in their opinions; one part received the light, and the other resisted it. *Again.* There was a dissension of this kind before among the same people; see chap. ix. 16.

20. *He hath a devil, and is mad.* So, then, a demoniac and a madman were not exactly the same in the apprehension of the Jews; no more than the effect is the same with the cause which produces it. Some will have it that, when the Jews told our Lord that He had a demon, they meant no more than that He was deranged; but here these matters are evidently distinguished. They believed Him to be possessed by a demon, who deranged his faculties, and that He must have been a wicked man, and a deceiver, thus to be put under the power of such a spirit.

21. *These are not the words of him that hath a devil.* If He were deranged by an unclean spirit, His words would bear a similitude to the spirit that produced them; but these are words of deep sense, soberness, and piety. Besides, could a demoniac open the eyes of blind men? This is not the work of a demon. Now we have seen that this Man has restored a man who was born blind. Therefore it is demonstrably evident that He is neither a madman nor a demoniac.

22. *The feast of the dedication.* This was a feast instituted by Judas Maccabaeus in commemoration of his purifying the Temple after it had been defiled by Antiochus Epiphanes. This feast began on the twenty-fifth of the month, *Cisleu* (which answers to the eighteenth of our December), and continued for eight days. When Antiochus had heard that the Jews had made great rejoicings on account of a report that had been spread of his death, he hastened out of Egypt to Jerusalem, took the city by storm, and slew of the inhabitants in three days 40,000 persons; and 40,000 more he sold for slaves to the neighboring nations. Not contented with this, he sacrificed a great sow on the altar of burnt offerings; and, broth being made by his command of some of the flesh, he sprinkled it all over the Temple, that he might defile it to the uttermost. After this, the whole of the Temple service seems to have been suspended for three years; see 1 Macc. iv. 36, etc. Judas Maccabaeus restored the Temple service and cleansed it from pollution. *It was winter.* Or, "It was stormy or rainy weather." And this is the reason, probably, why our Lord is represented as walking in "Solomon's porch," or portico, v. 23. Though it certainly was in *winter* when this feast was held, yet it does not appear that the word above refers so much to the time of the year as to the state of the weather.

23. *Solomon's porch.* By what we find in Jo-

MATTHEW HENRY

waiting for an opportunity to do them a kindness. Ill-will for good-will is no rare and uncommon return. They came about him pretending an impartial and importunate enquiry after truth, but intending a general assault upon our Lord Jesus: *How long dost thou make us to doubt? If thou be the Christ tell us.* They quarrel with him, as if he had unfairly held them in suspense hitherto. "*How long dost thou keep us in suspense?* How long are we kept debating whether thou be the Christ or no?" It was the effect of their infidelity, and powerful prejudices. The struggle was between their convictions, which told them he was Christ, and their corruptions, which said, No, because he was not such a Christ as they expected. They laid the blame of their doubting upon Christ himself, as if he *made them to* doubt by inconsistency with himself. Christ would make us to believe; we make ourselves to *doubt*. They challenge him to give a direct and categorical answer: "*If thou be the Christ, tell us plainly, in so many words,* either that thou art the Christ, or, as John Baptist, that thou art not," *ch.* i. 20. Now this pressing query of theirs was *seemingly good*; but it was *really bad*, and put with an ill design. Everyone knew the Messiah was to be a king, and therefore whoever pretended to be the Messiah would be prosecuted as a traitor, which was the thing they would have been at.

2. Christ's answer to this question.

(1) He justifies himself, referring them, [1] To what he had said: *I have told you.* He had told them that he was the Son of God, the Son of man. And is not this the Christ then? *You believed not.* They pretended that they only doubted, but Christ tells them that they did not believe. It is not for us to teach God how he should teach us, but to be thankful for divine revelation as we have it. [2] He refers them to his works, to the example of his life, and especially to his miracles. No man could do those miracles except God were with him, and God would not be with him to attest a forgery.

(2) He condemns them for their obstinate unbelief: "*You believed not.*" But the reason he gives is very surprising: "*You believed not, because you are not of my sheep.* You are not disposed to be my followers, you will not herd yourselves with my sheep, will not come and see, come and hear my voice." Rooted antipathies to the gospel of Christ are the bonds of iniquity and infidelity.

(3) He takes this occasion to describe both the gracious disposition and the happy state of those that are his sheep.

[1] To convince them that they were not his sheep, he tells them what were the characters of his sheep. They *hear his voice* (*v.* 27), for they know it to be his (*v.* 4), and he has undertaken that they shall hear it, *v.* 16. They discern it. They delight in it. They do according to it. Christ will not account those his sheep that are deaf to his calls, deaf to his charms. They *follow him.* The word of command has always been, *Follow me.* We must *tread in his steps—follow the Lamb whithersoever he goes.* In vain do we *hear his voice* if we do not *follow him.*

[2] To convince them that it was their great unhappiness and misery not to be of Christ's sheep, he here describes the blessed state and case of those that are. Our Lord Jesus *takes cognizance* of his sheep: They *hear my voice*, and *I know them.* He distinguishes them from others (2 Tim. ii. 19), has a particular regard to every individual (Ps. xxxiv. 6). He has provided a happiness for them: *I give unto them eternal life, v.* 28. Man has a living soul; therefore the happiness provided is life. Man has an immortal soul: therefore the happiness provided is eternal life. *Life eternal* is the felicity and chief good of a *soul immortal. I give it* to them; it is given by the free grace of Jesus Christ. Not *I will* give it, but *I do* give it; it is a present gift. He gives the assurance of it, heaven in the seed, in the bud, in the embryo. He has undertaken for their security and preservation to this happiness. *They shall by no means perish for ever;* so the words are. As there is an eternal life, so there is an eternal destruction. They shall not *come into condemnation.* Shepherds that have large flocks often lose some of the sheep and suffer them to perish; but Christ has engaged that none of his sheep shall perish, not one. They cannot be kept from their *everlasting happiness.* His own power is engaged for them: *Neither shall any man pluck them out of my hand.* The Shepherd is so careful of their welfare that he has them not only within his fold, but *in his hand*, and taken under his special protection. Yet their enemies are so daring that they attempt to pluck them out of his hand; but they cannot, they shall not do it. Those are safe who are in the hands of the Lord Jesus. His Father's power is likewise engaged for their preservation, *v.* 29. *a.* The power of the Father: *My Father is greater than all;* greater

JAMIESON, FAUSSET, BROWN

How long dost thou make us to doubt—"hold us in suspense" (*marg.*). **If thou be the Christ, tell us plainly**—But when the plainest *evidence* of it was resisted, what weight could a mere *assertion* of it have?

25, 26. Jesus answered them, I told you—i.e., in substance, what I am (e.g. ch. 7:37, 38; 8: 12, 35, 36, 58).

26. ye believe not, because ye are not of my sheep, as I said—referring to the whole strain of the Parable of the Sheep, (vs. 1, etc.).

27-30. My sheep hear my voice . . .—(See on vs. 8). **I give unto them eternal life**—not "will give them"; for it is a present gift. (See on ch. 3: 36; 5:24.) It is a very grand utterance, couched in the language of majestic authority.

29. My Father, which gave them me—(See on ch. 6:37-39). **is greater than all**—with whom no adverse power can contend. It is a general expression of an admitted truth, and what follows shows for what purpose it was uttered, "and none is able to pluck them out of My Father's hand." The impossibility of true believers being lost, in the midst of all the temptations which they may encounter, does not consist in their fidelity and decision, but is founded upon the *power of God.* Here the doctrine of predestination is presented in its sublime and sacred aspect; there is a predestination of the holy, which is taught from one end of the Scriptures to the other; not, indeed, of such a nature that an "irresistible grace" *compels* the opposing will of man (of course not), but so that that will of man which receives and loves the commands of God is *produced* only by God's grace [OLSHAUSEN—a testimony all the more valuable, being given in spite of *Lutheran* prejudice].

ADAM CLARKE

sephus, a portico built by Solomon, on the east side of the outer court of the Temple, was left standing by Herod when he rebuilt the Temple. This portico was 400 cubits long and was left standing, probably, because of its grandeur and beauty. But when Agrippa came to Jerusalem, a few years before the destruction of the city by the Romans, and about eighty years after Herod had begun his building (till which time what Herod had begun was not completed), the Jews solicited Agrippa to repair this portico at his own expense, using for argument not only that the building was growing ruinous but that otherwise 18,000 workmen, who had all of them, until then, been employed in carrying on the works of the Temple, would be all at once deprived of a livelihood.

24. *How long dost thou make us to doubt?* Or, "How long dost Thou kill us with suspense?" The Jews asked this question through extreme perfidiousness. They wished to get Him to declare himself king of the Jews, that they might accuse him to the Roman governor; and by it they insolently insinuated that all the proofs He had hitherto given them of His divine mission were good for nothing.

25. *I told you.* That is, I told you before what I tell you now again, that "the works which I do bear testimony to Me."

27. *My sheep hear my voice;* but you will not hear. My sheep *follow me;* but you will neither follow nor acknowledge Me. Any person who reads without prejudice may easily see that our Lord does not at all insinuate that these persons could not believe because God had made it impossible to them, but simply because they did not hear and follow Christ, which the whole of our blessed Lord's discourse proves that they might have done. The sheep of Christ are not those who are included in any eternal decree, to the exclusion of others from eternal mercy; but they are those who hear, believe in, follow, and obey the Saviour of the world.

28. *They shall never perish.* Why? Because they hear My voice, and follow Me; therefore I know, I approve of and love them, and *give unto them eternal life.* They who continue to hear Christ's voice, and to follow Him, shall never perish. They give themselves up to God—believe so on Jesus that He lives in their hearts. God hath given unto them "eternal life, and this life is in his Son. He that hath the Son hath life," 1 John v. 11-12. Now it is evident that only those who have Christ living in and governing their souls, so that they possess the mind that was in Him, are His sheep—are those that shall never perish, because they have this eternal life abiding in them. Therefore to talk of a man's being one of the elect—one that shall never perish—one who shall have eternal life—who shall never be plucked out of the hand of God, while he lives in sin, has no Christ in his heart, has either never received or fallen away from the grace of God, is as contrary to common sense as it is to the nature and testimonies of the Most High. Final perseverance implies final faithfulness—he that endures to the end shall be saved—he that is faithful unto death shall have a crown of life. And will any man attempt to say that he who does not endure to the end and is unfaithful shall ever enter into life?

MATTHEW HENRY

than all the other *friends* of the church, all the other shepherds, magistrates or ministers. Those shepherds slumber and sleep, but he keeps his flock day and night. He is greater than all the enemies of the church. He is *greater than all* the combined force of hell and earth. The devil and his angels have had many a push, many a pluck for the mastery, but have never yet prevailed. *b.* The interest of the Father in the sheep: "It is my Father *that gave them to me*," and therefore God will still look after them. All the divine power is engaged for the accomplishment of all the divine counsels. *c.* The safety of the saints inferred from these two. *None* (neither man nor devil) is *able to pluck them out of the Father's hand.* Christ had himself experienced the power of his Father *upholding* and *strengthening* him, and therefore puts all his followers into his hand too. He that secured the glory of the Redeemer will secure the glory of the redeemed. Further to corroborate the security, he asserts: "*I and my Father are one.*" The Jews understood him as hereby making himself God (*v.* 33), and he did not deny it. None could pluck them out *of his hand* because they could not pluck them out *of the Father's hand.*

IV. The rage of the Jews. *The Jews took up stones again, v.* 31. It is not the word that is used before (*ch.* viii. 59), but *they carried stones*—great stones, such as they used in stoning malefactors. The absurdity of this insult will appear if we consider that they had *imperiously*, not to say *impudently*, challenged him to tell them plainly whether he was the Christ or no; and yet now they condemned him as a malefactor. If the preachers of the truth propose it *modestly*, they are branded as cowards; if *boldly*, as insolent. When they had before made a similar attempt it was in vain; he *escaped through the midst of them* (*ch.* viii. 59); yet they repeat their baffled attempt. Daring sinners will throw stones at heaven, though they return upon their own heads.

V. Christ's tender expostulation with them (*v.* 32): *Jesus answered* what they *did*, for we do not find that they *said anything*. He mildly replied, *Many good works have I shown you from my Father: for which of those works do you stone me?* Words so very tender that one would think they should have melted a heart of stone. In dealing with his enemies he still argued from his works (men evidence what they *are* by what they *do*), his *good works*; the expression signifies both *great works* and *good works.*

1. The divine power of his works convicted them of the most obstinate infidelity. They were works *from his Father*. These works he *showed* them; he did them openly before the people. He did not show his works by candle-light, as those that are concerned only for *show*, but he showed them at noon-day before the world, *ch.* xviii. 20. His works were an incontestable *demonstration* of the validity of his commission.

2. The divine grace of his works convicted them of the most base ingratitude. The works he did among them were not only works of wonder to amaze them, but works of love and kindness to do them good, and so make them good. "*Now, for which of these do you stone me?* If therefore you will pick a quarrel with me, it must be for some good work; tell me for which." When he asks, *For which of these do you stone me?* as he intimates the abundant satisfaction he had in his own innocency, so he puts his persecutors upon considering what was the true reason of their enmity, and asking: *Why persecute we him?*

VI. Their vindication of the attempt they made upon Christ, *v.* 33.

1. They would not be thought such enemies to their country as to persecute him for a good work: *For a good work we stone thee not.* For indeed they would scarcely allow any of his works to be so. But, if he had done any good works, they would not own that they stoned him *for them.* Thus, though most absurd, they could not be brought to own their absurdities.

2. They would be thought such friends to God as to prosecute him for blasphemy: *Because that thou, being a man, makest thyself God.*

(1) A pretended zeal for the law. They seem mightily concerned for the honour of the divine majesty. A blasphemer was to be *stoned*, Lev. xxiv. 16. The vilest practices are often varnished with plausible pretences. As nothing is more *courageous* than a well-informed conscience, so nothing is more *outrageous* than a mistaken one.

(2) A real enmity to the gospel by representing Christ as a blasphemer. It is no new thing for the worst of characters to be put upon the best of men, by those that resolve to give them the worst of treatment. The crime laid to his charge is *blasphemy.*

JAMIESON, FAUSSET, BROWN

30. I and my Father are one—Our language admits not of the precision of the original in this great saying. "*Are*" is in the *masculine* gender—"we (two persons) are"; while "*one*" is *neuter*—"*one thing.*" Perhaps "*one interest*" expresses, as nearly as may be, the purport of the saying. There seemed to be some contradiction between His saying they had been given by His Father into *His own* hands, out of which they could not be plucked, and then saying that none could pluck them out of *His Father's* hands, as if they had not been given *out of* them. '*Neither have they,*' says He; 'though He has given them to Me, they are as much in His own almighty hands as ever—they *cannot be,* and when given to Me they *are not,* given away from Himself; for HE AND I HAVE ALL IN COMMON.' Thus it will be seen, that, though *oneness of essence* is not the precise thing here affirmed, that truth is *the basis of what is affirmed,* without which it would not be true. And Augustine was right in saying the "*We are*" condemns the *Sabellians* (who denied the *distinction of Persons* in the Godhead), while the "*one*" (as explained) condemns the *Arians* (who denied the unity of their essence). **31. Then the Jews took up stones again to stone Him**—and for precisely the same thing as before (ch. 8:58, 59).

32. Many good works have I showed you—i.e., works of pure benevolence (as in Acts 10:38, "Who went about doing good . . ."; see Mark 7:37).

from my Father not so much by His power, but as directly *commissioned by Him to do them.* This He says to meet the imputation of unwarrantable assumption of the divine prerogatives [LUTHARDT].

for which of those works do ye stone me?—"are ye stoning (i.e., going to stone) me?"

33. for a blasphemy—whose legal punishment was stoning (Lev. 24:11-16). **thou, being a man**—i.e., a man only. **makest thyself God**—Twice before they understood Him to advance the same claim, and both times they prepared themselves to avenge what they took to be the insulted honor of God, as here, in the way directed by their law (ch. 5:18; 8:59).

ADAM CLARKE

30. *I and my Father are one.* If Jesus Christ were not God, could He have said these words without being guilty of blasphemy? It is worthy of remark that Christ does not say, *I and my Father,* which *my* our translation very improperly supplies, and which in this place would have conveyed a widely different meaning; for then it would imply that the human nature of Christ, of which alone, I conceive, God is ever said to be the Father in Scripture, was equal to the Most High. But He says, speaking then as God over all, "I and the Father"—the Creator of all things, the Judge of all men, the Father of the spirits of all flesh—*are one,* one in nature, one in all the attributes of Godhead, and one in all the operations of those attributes; and so it is evident the Jews understood Him.

31. *The Jews took up stones.* To stone Him as a blasphemer, Lev. xxiv. 14-16, because He said He was one with God. The Evangelist adds the word *again,* because they had attempted to do this before; see chap. viii. 59. But it seems they were prevented from doing this now by the following discourse.

32. *Many good works have I shewed you.* I have healed your sick, delivered those of you who were possessed from the power of demons; I have fed multitudes of your poor, and I have taught you in all places, at all times, without expense, with patience; and is this My reward? To "show good works or good things" is a Hebraism which signifies to do them really, to give good things liberally.

33. *But for blasphemy.* I have elsewhere shown that the original word, when applied to men, signifies "to speak injuriously" of their persons, character, connections, etc.; but when applied to God it signifies "to speak impiously," i.e., contrary to His nature, perfections, the wisdom of His providence, or goodness of His works. *Thou, being a man.* That is, only a man—*makest thyself God.* When Christ said before, v. 30, "I and the Father are one," had the Jews understood Him as only saying He

MATTHEW HENRY

The proof of the crime: *Thou, being a man, makest thyself God.* As it is God's glory that *he is God,* so it is his glory that *besides him there is no other.* Thus far they were in the right, that what Christ said of himself amounted to this—that he was God, for he had said that he was *one with the Father* and that he would *give eternal life;* and Christ does not deny it. They were much mistaken when they looked upon him as a *mere man,* and that the Godhead he claimed was of his own making.

VII. Christ's reply to their accusation and his making good those claims which they imputed to him as blasphemous (*v.* 34, &c.), by two arguments:

1. By an argument taken from *God's word.* It is written (Ps. lxxxii. 6), *I have said, You are gods.* If they were gods, much more am I.

(1) How he explains the text (*v.* 35): *He called them gods to whom the word of God came, and the scripture cannot be broken.* We are sure that the scripture *cannot be broken* or found fault with. Every word of God is *right.*

(2) How he applies it. *Say you of him whom the Father hath sanctified, Thou blasphemest?* [1] The honour done him by the *Father:* He *sanctified him,* and *sent him into the world.* Our Lord Jesus was himself the *Word,* and had the *Spirit without measure.* He was sent *into the world* as Lord of all. The Father's sanctifying and sending him is here vouched as a sufficient warrant for his calling himself the *Son of God.* [2] The dishonour done him by the Jews, that he was a *blasphemer,* because he called himself the *Son of God:* "*Say you of him* so and so? Dare you say so? Have you brow and brass enough to tell the God of truth that he lies? What! say you of the Son of God that *he is a blasphemer?*" If devils, whom he came to condemn, had said so of him, it had not been so strange; but that *men,* whom he came to teach and save, should say so of him, *be astonished, O heavens! at this.*

2. By an argument taken from *his own works.* He here makes out his own claims, and proves that he and the Father are one (*v.* 37, 38): *If I do not the works of my Father, believe me not.*

(1) *From what* he argues—from his works. As he proved himself sent of God by the *divinity* of his works, so we must prove ourselves allied to Christ by the *Christianity* of ours. [1] The argument is very cogent; for the works he did were the *works of his Father,* which the Father only could do, and which could not be done in the ordinary course of nature. The miracles which the apostles wrought in his name corroborated this argument, and continued the evidence of it when he was gone. [2] It is proposed as fairly as can be desired, and put to a short issue. *If I do not the works of my Father, believe me not.* He does not demand an assent to his divine mission further than he gave proof of it. Christ is no hard master, who expects to reap in assents where he has not sown in arguments. "But if I do *the works of my Father, though you believe not me,* yet *believe the works;* believe your own eyes, your own reason." The invisible things of the Redeemer were seen by his miracles, and by all his works both of power and mercy; so that those who were not convinced by these works were *without excuse.*

(2) *For what* he argues—*that you may know and believe* that *the Father is in me and I in him;* which is the same with what he had said (*v.* 30): *I and my Father are one.* This we must *know;* not know and *explain,* but know and *believe* it; acknowledging and adoring the depth, when we cannot find the bottom.

Verses 39–42

We have here the issue of the conference with the Jews. Here we are told,

I. How they attacked him by force. Therefore *they sought again to take him, v.* 39. Because he persevered in the same testimony concerning himself, they persisted in their malice against him. They express the same resentment, and justify their attempt to stone him by another attempt to take him.

II. How he avoided them by flight. He *escaped out of their hands,* not by the interposal of any friend that helped him, but by his own wisdom he *got clear* of them. And he who knew how to *deliver himself* no doubt knows how to *deliver the godly out of temptation,* and to make *a way for them to escape.*

III. How he disposed of himself in his retirement: He *went away again beyond Jordan, v.* 40.

1. What *shelter* he found there. He went into a private part of the country, and *there he abode;* there he found some rest and quietness, when in Jerusalem he could find none. Christ and his gospel have often found better entertainment among the plain country-people than among *the wise, the mighty, the noble,* 1 Cor. i. 26, 27.

JAMIESON, FAUSSET, BROWN

34-36. Is it not written in your law—in Psalm 82:6, respecting judges or magistrates. **Ye are gods**—being the *official representatives* and *commissioned agents* of God. **If he called them gods unto whom the word of God came . . . Say ye of him whom the Father hath sanctified and sent into the world, Thou blasphemest**—The whole force of this reasoning, which has been but in part seized by the commentators, lies in what is said of the two parties compared. The *comparison* of Himself with mere men, divinely commissioned, is intended to show [as NEANDER well expresses it] that the idea of a communication of the Divine Majesty to human nature was by no means foreign to the revelations of the Old Testament; but there is also a *contrast* between Himself and all merely human representatives of God—the one "*sanctified by the Father and sent into the world*"; the other, "*to whom the word of God* [merely] *came,*" which is expressly designed to prevent His being massed up with them as only one of many human officials of God. *It is never said of Christ* that "the word of the Lord came to Him"; whereas this is the well-known formula by which the divine commission, even to the highest of *mere men,* is expressed, as John the Baptist (Luke 3:2). The reason is that given by the Baptist himself (see on ch. 3:31). The contrast is between those "to whom the word of God came"—men of the earth, earthy, who were merely privileged to get a divine *message* to utter (if prophets), or a divine *office* to discharge (if judges)—and "Him whom (not being of the earth at all) *the Father sanctified* (or set apart), and *sent into the world,*" an expression *never used of any merely human messenger of God,* and *used only of Himself.* **because, I said, I am the Son of God**—It is worthy of special notice that our Lord *had not said,* in so many words, that He was the Son of God, on this occasion. But He had said what beyond doubt amounted to it—namely, that He gave His sheep eternal life, and none could pluck them out of His hand; that He had got them from His Father, in whose hands, though given to Him, they still remained, and out of whose hand none could pluck them; and that they were *the indefeasible property of both,* inasmuch as "He and His Father were one." Our Lord considers all this as just saying of Himself, "I am the Son of God"—*one nature* with Him, yet mysteriously *of Him.* The parenthesis (vs. 35), "and the Scripture cannot be broken," referring to the terms used of magistrates in the 82d Psalm, has an important bearing on the *authority* of the living oracles. "The Scripture, as the expressed will of the unchangeable God, is itself unchangeable and indissoluble" [OLSHAUSEN]. (Cf. Matt. 5:17.) **37-39. though ye believe not me, believe the works**—There was in Christ's words, independently of any miracles, a self-evidencing truth, majesty and grace, which those who had any spiritual susceptibility were unable to resist (ch. 7:46; 8:30). But, for those who wanted this, "the works" were a mighty help. When these failed, the case was desperate indeed. **that ye may know and believe that the Father is in me, and I in him**—thus reiterating His claim to essential *oneness with the Father,* which He had only *seemed* to soften down, that He might calm their rage and get their ear again for a moment. **39. Therefore they sought again to take him**—true to their original understanding of His words, for they saw perfectly well that He *meant* to "make Himself God" throughout all this dialogue. **he escaped out of their hand**—(See on Luke 4:30; ch. 8:59). **40-42. went away again beyond Jordan . . . the place where John at first baptized**—(See on ch. 1:28).

ADAM CLARKE

had a unity of sentiments with the Father, they would not have attempted to treat Him for this as a blasphemer; because in this sense Abraham, Isaac, Moses, David, and all the prophets were one with God. But what irritated them so much was that they understood Him as speaking of a unity of nature. Therefore they say here, *Thou makest thyself God;* which word they understood, not in a figurative, metaphorical, or improper sense, but in the most literal meaning of the term.

34. *Is it not written in your law?* The words which our Lord quotes are taken from Ps. lxxxii. 6, which shows that under the word *law* our Lord comprised the Jewish sacred writings in general. *Ye are gods.* That is, "judges," who are called *elohim.* That judges are here meant appears from Ps. lxxxii. 2, etc., and also from what follows here.

35. *And the scripture cannot be broken.* "Dissolved," rendered of none effect; i.e., it cannot be gainsaid or set aside. Every man must believe this, because it is the declaration of God. If those were termed *gods* who were only earthly magistrates, fallible mortals—and that they are termed gods is evident from that Scripture which cannot be gainsaid—what greater reason then have I to say, *I am the Son of God,* and one with God, when, as Messiah, I have been "consecrated," sent into the world, to instruct and save men; and when, as God, I have wrought miracles which could be performed by no power less than that of omnipotence?

37. *If I do not the works.* I desire you to believe only on the evidence of My works; if I do not do such works as God only can perform, then believe Me not.

38. *Believe the works.* Though you do not now credit what I have said to you, yet consider My works, and then you will see that these works prove that "I am in the Father, and the Father in me"; and, consequently, that I and the Father are one.

39. *They sought again to take him.* They could not reply to His arguments but by stones. The evidence of the truth could not be resisted, and they endeavored to destroy the Person who spoke it. *But he escaped.* In such a way as we know not, for the Evangelist has not specified the manner of it.

MATTHEW HENRY

2. What *success* he found there. He chose to go thither, where John at first baptized (*ch.* i. 28), because there could not but remain some impressions of John's ministry and baptism thereabouts, which would dispose them to receive Christ. The event in some measure answered expectation; for we are told,

(1) That they flocked after him (*v.* 41): *Many resorted to him*. The return of the means of grace to a place, commonly occasions a great stirring of affections.

(2) That they reasoned in his favour as much as those at Jerusalem sought objections against him. They said, *John did no miracle, but all things that John spoke of this man were true*. Two things they considered: That Christ far exceeded John Baptist's power, for *John did no miracle*, but Jesus does many; whence it is easy to infer that Jesus is greater than John. How great then is this Jesus! Christ is best known and acknowledged by such a comparison with others as sets him superlatively above others. That Christ exactly answered John Baptist's testimony. All things that *John said of this man were true*. Great things John had said of him, which raised their expectations. They acknowledged him as great as John had said he would be. When we get acquainted with Christ, and come to know him experimentally, we find that the reality exceeds the report, 1 Kings x. 6, 7. John Baptist was now dead and gone, and yet his hearers profited by what they had heard formerly. They were confirmed in their belief that *John was a prophet*, who foretold such things. They were prepared to believe that *Jesus was the Christ*. The success and efficacy of the words preached are not confined to the life of the preacher, nor do they expire with his breath.

(3) That many believed on him there. They gave up themselves to him as his disciples, *v.* 42. They were *many*. It was where John had had great success; *there* many believed on the Lord Jesus. Where the preaching of the doctrine of repentance has had success, there the preaching of the doctrine of reconciliation is most likely to be prosperous. Where John had been acceptable, Jesus will not be unacceptable.

JAMIESON, FAUSSET, BROWN

41. many resorted to him—on whom the ministry of the Baptist had left permanent impressions. **John did no miracle, but all things John spake of this man were true**—what they now heard and saw in Jesus only confirming in their minds the divinity of His forerunner's mission, though unaccompanied by any of His Master's miracles. And thus, "many believed on Him there."

ADAM CLARKE

40. *Where John at first baptized*. That is, at Bethabara; see chap. i. 28. Afterwards, John baptized at Aenon, chap. iii. 23.

42. *Many believed on him there*. The people believed on Him: (1) because of the testimony of John the Baptist, whom they knew to be a good and a wise man, and a prophet of the Lord; and (2) because of the miracles which they saw Jesus work. These fully proved that all that John had said of Him was true.

MATTHEW HENRY — CHAPTER 11

Verses 1–16

I. A particular account of the parties principally concerned in this story, *v.* 1, 2. They lived at *Bethany*, a village not far from Jerusalem, where Christ usually lodged when he came up to the feasts. It is here called the *town of Mary and Martha*. Here was a brother named *Lazarus*. Here were two sisters, *Martha* and *Mary*, who seem to have been the housekeepers. Here was a decent, happy, well-ordered family, and a family that Christ was very much conversant with. One of the sisters is particularly described to be *that Mary which anointed the Lord with ointment*, *v.* 2. It refers to that anointing of Christ which this evangelist relates (*ch.* xii. 3). This was she *whose brother Lazarus was sick*; and the sickness of those we love is our affliction. The more friends we have the more frequently we are thus afflicted by sympathy. The multiplying of our comforts is but the multiplying of our cares and crosses.

II. The tidings that were sent to our Lord Jesus of the sickness of Lazarus, *v.* 3. *His sisters* knew where Jesus was, and they sent a special messenger to him, in which they manifest, 1. The affection and concern they had for their brother. They showed their love to him now that he was sick, for a *brother is born for adversity*, and so is a sister too. 2. The regard they had to the Lord Jesus, whom they were willing to make acquainted with all their concerns. The message they sent was very short, barely relating the case with the tender insinuation of a powerful plea, *Lord, behold, he whom thou lovest is sick*. They do not say, Lord, behold, he *who loveth thee*, but *he whom thou lovest*. Our love to him is not worth speaking of, but his to us can never be enough spoken of. It is no new thing for those whom Christ loves to be sick: all things come alike to all. It is a great comfort to us, when we are sick, to have those about us that will pray for us. We have reason to love and pray for those whom we have reason to think Christ loves and cares for.

III. An account how Christ entertained the tidings brought him.

1. He prognosticated the event and issue of the sickness. Two things he prognosticates:

(1) *This sickness is not unto death*. It was mortal, proved *fatal*, and no doubt but Lazarus was truly dead for four days. It came not, as in a common case, to be a summons to the grave. That was not the

JAMIESON, FAUSSET, BROWN — CHAPTER 11

Vss. 1-46. LAZARUS RAISED FROM THE DEAD—THE CONSEQUENCES OF THIS. **1. of Bethany**—at the east side of Mount Olivet. **the town of Mary and her sister Martha**—thus distinguishing it from the other Bethany, "beyond Jordan." (See on ch. 1: 28; 10:40.) **2. It was that Mary who anointed the Lord with ointment . . .**—This, though not recorded by our Evangelist till ch. 12:3, was so well known in the teaching of all the churches, according to our Lord's prediction (Matt. 26:13), that it is here alluded to by anticipation, as the most natural way of identifying her; and she is first named, though the younger, as the more distinguished of the two. She "anointed THE LORD," says the Evangelist—led doubtless to the use of this term here, as he was about to exhibit Him illustriously as the *Lord of Life*.

3-5. his sisters sent unto him, saying, Lord, he whom thou lovest is sick—a most womanly appeal, yet how reverential, to the known affection of her Lord for the patient. (See vss. 5, 11.) "Those whom Christ loves are no more exempt than others from their share of earthly trouble and anguish: rather are they bound over to it more surely" [TRENCH].

4. When Jesus heard that, he said, This sickness is not unto death—to *result* in death—**but**

ADAM CLARKE — CHAPTER 11

1. *Lazarus, of Bethany*. John, who seldom relates anything but what the other Evangelists have omitted, does not tell us what gave rise to that familiar acquaintance and friendship that subsisted between our Lord and this family. It is surprising that the other Evangelists have omitted so remarkable an account as this, in which some of the finest traits in our Lord's character are exhibited. The conjecture of Grotius has a good deal of weight. He thinks that the other three Evangelists wrote their histories during the life of Lazarus, and that they did not mention him for fear of exciting the malice of the Jews against him. And indeed we find, from chap. xii. 10, that they sought to put Lazarus to death also, that our Lord might not have one monument of His power and goodness remaining in the land. Probably both Lazarus and his sisters were dead before John wrote. *Bethany* was situated at the foot of the Mount of Olives, about two miles from Jerusalem.

2. *It was that Mary which anointed*. There is much disagreement between learned men relative to the two anointings of our Lord, and the persons who performed these acts. The various conjectures concerning these points the reader will find in the notes on Matt. xxvi. 7, etc. Some think that the anointing of which the Evangelist speaks is that mentioned in chap. xii. 1, etc., and which happened about six days before the Passover. John, therefore, is supposed to *anticipate* the account, because it served more particularly to designate the person of whom he was speaking.

3. *He whom thou lovest is sick*. Nothing could be more simple, nor more modest, than this prayer. They do not say, Come and heal him; or, Command the disease to depart even where Thou art, and it will obey Thee. They content themselves with simply stating the case and using an indirect but a most forcible argument to induce our Lord to show forth His power and goodness.

MATTHEW HENRY

final effect of this sickness. He *died*, and yet it might be said he did not *die*. Death is an everlasting farewell to this world; and in this sense it was *not unto death*. The sickness of good people, how threatening soever, is *not unto death*. The body's death to this world is the soul's birth into another world.

(2) *But it is for the glory of God*. The afflictions of the saints are designed for the glory of God. The sweetest mercies are those which are occasioned by trouble. Let this reconcile us to the darkest dispensations of Providence, they are all for the glory of God; and, if God be glorified, we ought to be satisfied. It was *that the Son of God might be glorified thereby*, as it gave him occasion to work that glorious miracle, the *raising of him from the dead*. Let this comfort those whom Christ loves under all their grievances that the design of them all is that *the Son of God may be glorified thereby*.

2. He deferred visiting his patient, *v.* 5, 6. They had pleaded, *Lord, it is he whom thou lovest*, and the plea is allowed (*v.* 5): *Jesus loved Martha, and her sister, and Lazarus*. Now one would think it should follow, *When he heard therefore that he was sick* he made all the haste that he could to him. But he took the contrary way to show his love. Instead of coming post to him, he abode *two days still in the same place where he was*. (1) He *loved them* and therefore he deferred coming to them, that he might try them, that their trial might at last *be found to praise and honour*. (2) He *loved them*, that is, he designed to do something great and extraordinary for them. Therefore he delayed coming to them, that Lazarus might be *dead* and *buried* before he came. Deferring his relief so long, he had an opportunity of doing more for him than for *any*. God hath gracious intentions even in seeming delays. Christ's friends at Bethany were not out of his thoughts, though he made no haste to them.

IV. The discourse he had with his disciples, *v.* 7-16. Two things he discourses about—his own *danger* and Lazarus's *death*.

1. His own danger in going into Judæa, *v.* 7-10.

(1) He saith (*v.* 7): "*Let us go into Judæa again.*" Now this may be considered, [1] As a purpose of his kindness to his friends at Bethany. When he knew they were brought to the last extremity, "Now," saith he, "let us go to Judæa." Christ will arise in favour of his people when *the time to favour them, yea, the set time, is come*; and the worst time is commonly the set time. In the depths of affliction, let this therefore keep us out of the depths of despair, that man's extremity is God's opportunity. [2] As a trial of the courage of the disciples, whether they would venture to follow him thither. To go to Judæa, which was so lately made *too hot* for them, was a saying that *proved them. Let us go*. Christ never brings his people into any peril but he accompanies them in it.

(2) Their objection against this journey (*v.* 8): *Master, the Jews of late sought to stone thee, and goest thou thither again?* They remind him of the danger he had been in there not long since. Christ's disciples are apt to make a greater matter of sufferings than their Master does. The rememberance of the fright was fresh in their minds. They marvel that he will *go thither again*. "Wilt thou favour those with thy presence that have expelled thee out of their coasts? *Goest thou thither again*, where thou hast been so ill used?" Had Christ been inclined to shift off suffering, he did not want friends to persuade him to it. They discover at the same time a distrust of his power, as if he could not secure both himself and them now in Judæa as well as he had done formerly; a secret fear of suffering themselves, for they count upon this if he suffer.

(3) Christ's answer to this objection (*v.* 9, 10): *Are there not twelve hours in the day?* Divine Providence has given us daylight to work by. Man's life is a *day*; this day is divided into divers ages, states, and opportunities, as into hours; the consideration of this should make us not only *very busy*, as to the *work* of life, but also *very easy* as to the perils of life; our day shall be lengthened out till our work be done. He shows the comfort and satisfaction which a man has while he keeps in the way of his duty: *If any man walk in the day, he stumbles not*. He does not *hesitate* in his own mind, but, *walking uprightly*, *walks surely*. As he that walks in the day stumbles not, but goes on steadily and cheerfully in his way, *because he sees the light of this world*, and by it sees his way before him; so a good man, relies upon the word of God as his rule, and regards the glory of God as his end, *because he sees* those two great lights. He is furnished with a faithful guide in all his doubts, and a powerful guard in all his dangers. Christ, wherever he went, walked *in the day*, and so shall we, if we follow his steps. He shows the pain and peril

JAMIESON, FAUSSET, BROWN

for the glory of God, that the Son of God may be glorified thereby—i.e., by this glory of God. (See *Gr.*) Remarkable language this, which from creature lips would have been intolerable. It means that the glory of GOD manifested in the resurrection of dead Lazarus would be shown to be the glory, *personally* and immediately, of THE SON.

5. Jesus loved Martha and her sister and Lazarus—what a picture!—one that in every age has attracted the admiration of the whole Christian Church. No wonder that those miserable skeptics who have carped at the ethical system of the Gospel, as not embracing private friendships in the list of its virtues, have been referred to the Saviour's peculiar regard for this family as a triumphant refutation, if such were needed. **6. When he heard he was sick, he abode two days still . . . where he was**—at least twenty-five miles off. Beyond all doubt this was just to let things come to their worst, in order to display His glory. But how trying, meantime, to the faith of his friends, and how unlike the way in which love to a dying friend usually shows itself, on which it is plain that Mary reckoned. But the ways of *divine* are not as the ways of *human* love. Often they are the reverse. When His people are sick, in body or spirit; when their case is waxing more and more desperate every day; when all hope of recovery is about to expire—just then and therefore it is that *"He abides two days still in the same place where He is."* Can they still hope against hope? Often they do not; but "this is their infirmity." For it is His chosen style of acting. We have been well taught it, and should not *now* have the lesson to learn. From the days of Moses was it given sublimely forth as the character of His grandest interpositions, that "the Lord will judge His people and repent Himself for His servants"—*when He seeth that their power is gone* (Deut. 32:36). **7-10. Let us go into Judea again**—He was now in Perea, "beyond Jordan."

8. His disciples say unto him, Master, the Jews of late sought . . .—lit., 'were (just) now seeking' "to stone thee" (ch. 10:31). **goest thou thither again?**—*to certain death*, as vs. 16 shows they thought.

9. Jesus answered, Are there not twelve hours in the day?—(See on ch. 9:4). Our Lord's day had now reached its eleventh hour, and having till now "walked in the day," He would not *mistime* the remaining and more critical part of His work, which would be as fatal, He says, as omitting it altogether; for "if *a man* (so He speaks, putting Himself under the same great law of duty as all other men—if a man) walk in the night, he stumbleth, because there is no light in him."

ADAM CLARKE

4. *This sickness is not unto death*. Not to final privation of life at this time; but a temporary death shall be now permitted, that the glory of God may appear in the miracle of his resurrection. It is very likely that this verse contains the message which Christ sent back by the person whom the afflicted sisters had sent to Him.

5. *Now Jesus loved Martha, and her sister, and Lazarus*. Therefore His staying two days longer in Bethabara was not through lack of affection for this distressed family, but merely that He might have a more favorable opportunity of proving to them how much He loved them. Christ never denies a less favor but in order to confer a greater. God's delays in answering prayers offered to Him by persons in distress are often proofs of His purpose to confer some great kindness; and they are also proofs that His wisdom finds it necessary to permit an increase of the affliction, that His goodness may be more conspicuous in its removal.

8. *The Jews of late sought to stone thee*. It was but a few weeks before that they were going to stone Him in the Temple, on the day of the Feast of the Dedication, chap. x. 31.

9. *Are there not twelve hours in the day?* Our Lord alludes to the case of a traveller who has to walk the whole day. The *day* points out the time of life—the *night*, that of death. He has already used the same mode of speech in chap. ix. 4: "I must work the works of him that sent me, while it is day: the night cometh, when no man can work." Here He refers to what the apostles had just said—"The Jews were but just now going to stone Thee." *Are there not*, said He, *twelve hours in the day?* I have not travelled these twelve hours yet—My last hour is not yet come; and the Jews, with all their malice and hatred, shall not be able to bring it a moment sooner than God has purposed. *If any man walk in the day, he stumbleth not*. A traveller should use the day to walk in, and not the night. During the day he has the sun, the light of this world; he sees his way, and does not stumble. But if he walk in the night, he stumbleth, because there is no light

MATTHEW HENRY

a man is in who walks not according to this rule (*v.* 10): *If a man walk in the night, he stumbles.* If a man walk in the way of his heart, and according to the course of this world—he falls into temptations and snares. He stumbles, *because there is no light in him,* for light in us is that to our moral actions which light about us is to our natural actions.

2. The death of Lazarus *v.* 11-16.

(1) The notice Christ gave his disciples of the death of Lazarus, *v.* 11. He then gives them plain intelligence of the death of Lazarus: *Our friend Lazarus sleepeth.* See here how Christ calls a believer and a believer's death. He calls a believer his friend: *Our friend Lazarus.* Those whom Christ is pleased to own as his friends all his disciples should take for *theirs.* Christ speaks of Lazarus as their common friend: *Our friend.* Death itself does not break the bond of friendship between Christ and a believer. Lazarus is dead, and yet he is still *our friend.* He calls the death of a believer a *sleep*: *he sleepeth.* It is good to call death by such names and titles as will help to make it more *familiar* and less *formidable* to us. Why should not the believing hope of that resurrection to eternal life make it as easy to us to put off the body and die as it is to put off our clothes and go to sleep? A good Christian, when he dies, does but sleep: he rests from the labours of the day past, and is refreshing himself for the next morning. To the godly it is a bed, and all its bands as the soft and downy fetters of an easy quiet sleep. It is but putting off our clothes to be mended and trimmed up for the marriage day. Particular intimations of his favourable intentions concerning Lazarus: *but I go, that I may awake him out of sleep.* Christ had no sooner said, *Our friend sleeps,* but presently he adds, *I go, that I may awake him.* When Christ tells his people at any time how bad the case is he lets them know in the same breath how easily, how quickly, he can mend it. Christ's telling his disciples that this was his business to Judæa might help to take off their fear of going with him thither; and, besides, it was to do a kindness to a family to which they were all obliged.

(2) Their mistake, and the blunder they made about it (*v.* 12, 13): They said, *Lord, if he sleep, he shall do well.* This intimates, [1] *Some concern they* had for their friend Lazarus; they hoped he would recover. Now that they heard he slept they concluded the worst was past. Sleep is often nature's physic. This is true of the sleep of death; if a good Christian so *sleep,* he shall do well. [2] A *greater concern* for themselves. It was now needless for Christ to go to him, and expose himself and them. Thus we are willing to hope that the good work which we are called to do will do itself if there be peril in the doing of it.

(3) This mistake of theirs rectified (*v.* 13): *Jesus spoke of his death.* How dull of understanding Christ's disciples as yet were. Frequently death is called a sleep in the Old Testament. They should have understood Christ when he spoke scripture language. What Christ undertakes to do, we may be sure, is something great and uncommon, and a work *worthy of himself.* How carefully the evangelist corrects this error: *Jesus spoke of his death.*

(4) The plain and express declaration which Jesus made to them of the death of Lazarus, and his resolution to go to Bethany, *v.* 14, 15. He gives them notice of the death of Lazarus; what he had before said darkly he now says plainly: *Lazarus is dead, v.* 14. He gives them the reason why he had delayed so long: *I am glad for your sakes that I was not there.* Now that he went and raised him from the dead, as there were many brought to *believe on him* who before did not (*v.* 45), so there was much done towards the perfecting of what was lacking in the faith of those that did, which Christ aimed at: *To the intent that you may believe.* He resolves now to go to Bethany, and take his disciples along with him: *Let us go unto him.* Death cannot separate us from the love of Christ, nor put us out of the reach of his calls. Perhaps those who said, If he sleep there is *no need* to go, were ready to say, If he be dead it is to *no purpose* to go.

(5) Thomas exciting his fellow-disciples cheerfully to attend their Master's motions (*v.* 16): *Thomas, who is called Didymus.* Thomas in Hebrew and Didymus in Greek signify a *twin.* Probably Thomas was a *twin.* He said *to his fellow-disciples* very courageously, *Let us also go that we may die with him; with him,* that is,

[1] With Lazarus, who was now dead; so some take it. Perhaps Thomas had a particular intimacy with him. "If we *survive,* we know not how to *live without him.*" Thus we are sometimes ready to think our lives bound up in the lives of some that were dear to us: but God will teach us to live, and to live com-

JAMIESON, FAUSSET, BROWN

11-16. Our friend Lazarus sleepeth; but I go that I may wake him out of sleep—Illustrious title! "*Our friend* Lazarus." To *Abraham only* is it accorded in the Old Testament, and not till *after his death,* (II Chron. 20:7; Isa. 41:8, to which our attention is called in the New Testament (Jas. 2:23). When Jesus came in the flesh, His forerunner applied this name, in a certain sense, to himself (ch. 3:29); and into the same fellowship the Lord's chosen disciples are declared to have come (ch. 15: 13-15). "The phrase here employed, 'our friend Lazarus, means more than 'he whom *Thou* lovest' in vs. 3, for it implies that Christ's affection was *reciprocated* by Lazarus" [LAMPE]. Our Lord had been told only that Lazarus was "sick." But the change which his two days' delay had produced is here tenderly alluded to. Doubtless, His spirit was all the while with His dying, and now dead "friend." The symbol of "sleep" for *death* is common to all languages, and familiar to us in the Old Testament. In the New Testament, however, a higher meaning is put into it, in relation to believers in Jesus (see on I Thess. 4:14), a sense hinted at, and clearly, in Psalm 17:15 [LUTHARDT]; and the "awaking out of sleep" acquires a corresponding sense far transcending bare resuscitation.

12. if he sleep, he shall do well—lit., "be preserved"; i.e., recover. 'Why then go to Judea?'

14. Then said Jesus unto them plainly, Lazarus is dead—'Sleep [says BENGEL, beautifully] is the death of the saints, in the language of heaven; but this language the disciples here understood not; incomparable is the generosity of the divine manner of discoursing, but such is the slowness of men's apprehension that Scripture often has to descend to the more miserable style of human discourse; cf. Matthew 16:11.' **15. I am glad for your sakes I was not there**—This certainly implies that if He had been present, Lazarus would not have died; not because He could not have resisted the importunities of the sisters, but because, in presence of the personal Life, death could not have reached His friend [LUTHARDT]. "It is beautifully congruous to the divine decorum that in presence of the Prince of Life no one is ever said to have died" [BENGEL]. **that ye may believe**—This is added to explain His "gladness"' at not having been present. His friend's death, as such, could not have been to Him "joyous"; the sequel shows it was "grievous"; but *for them* it was safe. Phil. 3:1). **16. Thomas, ... called Didymus**—or "the twin." **Let us also go, that we may die with him**—lovely spirit, though tinged with some sadness, such as reappears at ch. 14:5, showing the tendency of this disciple to take the *dark* view of things. On a memorable occasion this tendency opened the door to downright, though but momentary, unbelief (ch. 20:25). Here, however, though alleged by many interpreters there is nothing of the sort. He perceives clearly how this journey to Judea will end, as respects his Master, and not only sees in it peril to themselves, as they

ADAM CLARKE

"in it," v. 10; i.e., there is no sun above the horizon. The words *en auto,* v. 10, refer not to the man, but to the world, the sun, its light, not being above the horizon.

11. *Lazarus sleepeth.* It was very common among the Jews to express death by sleep; and the expressions "falling asleep," "sleeping with their fathers" were in great use among them. The Hebrews probably used this form of speech to signify their belief in the immortality of the soul and the resurrection of the body. It is certain that our Lord received no intimation of Lazarus' death from any person, and that He knew it through that power by which He knows all things.

12. *If he sleep, he shall do well.* That is, "if he sleep only." Though the word sleep frequently meant death (see Acts vii. 60; 1 Cor. xi. 30; xv. 18, 20), yet, as it was an ambiguous term, the disciples appear here to have mistaken its meaning. *If he sleep, he shall do well,* or "recover," became a proverbial form of speech among the Jews. In most diseases sleep is a very favorable prognostic.

15. *I am glad for your sakes that I was not there.* "I tell you plainly, Lazarus is dead; and I am glad I was not there—if I had been, I should have been prevailed on to heal him almost as soon as he fell sick, and I should not have had so striking an occasion to manifest the glory of God to you, and to establish you in the faith."

16. *Thomas, which is called Didymus. Thomas,* or Thaom, was his Hebrew name, and signifies a "twin." *Didymus* is a literal translation of the Hebrew word into Greek. *Let us also go, that we may die with him.* That is, "Seeing we cannot dissuade our Lord from going, and His death is likely to be the inevitable consequence, let us give Him the fullest proof we can of our love, by going and suffering death with Him." Some think Thomas spoke these words peevishly, and that they should be translated thus, "Must we also go, and expose

MATTHEW HENRY

fortably, upon himself, when those are gone without whom we thought we could not live. "If we die, we hope to be *happy with him*." Such a firm belief he has of a happiness on the other side death that he is willing they should all go and *die with him*. The more of our friends are translated hence, the fewer cords we have to bind us to this earth, and the more to draw our hearts heavenwards.

[2] "Let us go and die *with our Master*," and so I rather think it is meant. "If he will go into danger, let us also go, according to the command we received, *Follow me*." Thomas knew so much of the malice of the Jews against Christ that it was no foreign supposition that he was now going to die. Thomas manifests a gracious readiness to die with Christ himself, flowing from strong affections to him. A zealous desire to help his fellow-disciples into the same frame: "*Let us go* and *die with him;* who would desire to survive such a Master?" Thus, in difficult times, Christians should animate one another.

Verses 17–32

The matter being determined, that Christ will go to Judæa, and his disciples with him, they address themselves to their journey.

At length, he comes near to Bethany, which is said to be about *fifteen furlongs* from Jerusalem, *v.* 18. Notice is taken of this, that this miracle was in effect wrought *in Jerusalem*.

I. What posture he found his friends there in. When we part from our friends we know not what changes may affect us or them before we meet again.

1. He found his friend Lazarus *in the grave*, *v.* 17. Lazarus had been *four days buried*. Promised salvations, though they always come surely, yet often come slowly.

2. He found his friends that survived *in grief. Many of the Jews came to Martha and Mary to comfort them.* Ordinarily, where death is there are *mourners*. Here was Martha's house, a house where the fear of God was, and on which his blessing rested, yet made a *house of mourning*. Grace will keep sorrow from the heart (*ch.* xiv. 1), not from the house. Where there are mourners there ought to be comforters. It is a duty we owe to those that are in sorrow to mourn with them, and to comfort them. They comforted them *concerning their brother*, that is, by speaking to them of him, not only of the good name he left behind, but of the happy state he was gone to. We have reason to be comforted concerning those who are gone before us to a happiness where they have no need of us. This visit which the Jews made to Martha and Mary is an evidence that they were persons of distinction. There was also a providence in it, that so many Jews should come together, just at this time, that they might be unexceptionable witnesses of the miracle.

II. What passed between him and his surviving friends. His departures endear his returns, and his absence teaches us how to value his presence.

1. The interview between Christ and Martha.

(1) We are told that she *went and met him, v.* 20. It should seem that Martha was earnestly expecting Christ's arrival, and enquiring for it. However it was, she heard of his coming before he arrived. Martha, when the good news was brought that Jesus was coming, threw all aside, and *went and met him.* When Martha went to meet Jesus, Mary *sat still in the house*. Some think she did *not* hear the tidings, while Martha, who was busied in the household-affairs, had early notice of it. Others think she *did* hear that Christ was come, but was so overwhelmed with sorrow that she did not care to stir. Comparing this story with that in Luke x. 38, &c., we may observe the different tempers of these two sisters. Martha's natural temper was active and busy; she loved to be here and there, and at the end of everything; and this had been a snare to her when by it she was not only careful and cumbered about many things, but hindered from the exercises of devotion: but now in a day of affliction this active temper did her a kindness, kept the grief from her heart, and made her forward to meet Christ, and so she received comfort from him the sooner. On the other hand, Mary's natural temper was contemplative and reserved. This had been formerly an advantage to her, when it was placed at her Christ's feet, to hear his word, and enabled her there to attend upon him without those distractions with which Martha was cumbered; but now in the day of affliction that same temper proved a snare to her, made her less able to grapple with her grief, and disposed her to melancholy. See here how much it will be our wisdom carefully to watch against the temptations, and improve the advantages, of our natural temper.

(2) Here is fully related the discourse between

JAMIESON, FAUSSET, BROWN

all did, but feels as if he could not and cared not to survive his Master's sacrifice to the fury of His enemies. It was that kind of affection which, living only in the light of its Object, cannot contemplate, or has no heart for life, without it.

18. Bethany was nigh Jerusalem, about fifteen furlongs—rather less than two miles; mentioned to explain the visits of sympathy noticed in the following words, which the proximity of the two places facilitated.

17-19. **when Jesus came, he found that he had lain in the grave four days**—If he died on the day the tidings came of his illness—and was, according to the Jewish custom, buried the same day (see JAHN'S *Archæology*, and vs. 39; Acts 5:5, 6, 10)—and if Jesus, after two days' farther stay in Perea, set out on the day following for Bethany, some ten hours' journey, that would make out the four days; the first and last being incomplete [MEYER]. **19. many of the Jews came to Martha and Mary to comfort them**—Thus were provided, in a most natural way, so many witnesses of the glorious miracle that was to follow, as to put the fact beyond possible question.

20-22. **Martha, as soon as she heard that Jesus was coming, went and met him**—true to the *energy* and *activity* of her character, as seen in Luke 10:38-42. (See *Notes* there.) **but Mary sat . . . in the house**—equally true to her *placid* character. These undesigned touches not only charmingly illustrate the minute *historic fidelity* of both narratives, but their *inner harmony*.

ADAM CLARKE

ourselves to destruction with Him?" But I think the first sense is to be preferred. When a matter is spoken which concerns the moral character of a person and which may be understood in a good and a bad sense, that sense which is most favorable to the person should certainly be adopted.

18. *Fifteen furlongs.* About two miles, for the Jewish miles contained about seven furlongs and a half.

17. *He had lain in the grave four days already.* Our Lord probably left Bethabara the day, or the day after, Lazarus died. He came to Bethany three days after; and it appears that Lazarus had been buried about four days and consequently that he had been put in the grave the day or day after he died. Though it was the Jewish custom to embalm their dead, yet we find, from v. 39, that he had not been embalmed; and God wisely ordered this, that the miracle might appear the more striking.

19. *Many of the Jews came.* Bethany being so nigh to Jerusalem, many of the relatives and friends of the family came, according to the Jewish custom, to mourn with the afflicted sisters. Mourning, among the Jews, lasted about thirty days. The first three days were termed days of weeping; then followed seven of lamentation. During the three days the mourner did no servile work; and if anyone saluted him, he did not return the salutation. During the seven days he did no servile work, except in private—lay with his bed on the floor—did not put on his sandals—did not wash nor anoint himself—had his head covered. All the thirty days he continued unshaven, wore no white or new clothes, and did not sew up the rents which he had made in his garments.

20. *Martha . . . went and met him.* Some suppose she was the eldest of the two sisters—she seems to have had the management of the house. See Luke x. 40. *Mary sat still in the house.* It is likely that by this circumstance the Evangelist intended to convey the idea of her sorrow and distress, because anciently afflicted persons were accustomed to put themselves in this posture, as expressive of their distress, their grief having rendered them as it were immovable.

G. CAMPBELL MORGAN:

Martha hurried from the house to meet Him. In doing so she violated the conventionalities of the East. Mary observed them. She sat in the house, remaining in the seclusion of the home. Martha, honest, angry, as I cannot help believing, hurried to meet Him, and when she met Him, she said, "Lord, if thou hadst been here, my brother had not died." Of course it is very difficult to interpret dogmatically, but when Mary came she said exactly the same thing. But surely there was a tremendous difference between the intention of Martha and the intention of Mary. I have no doubt whatever that Martha's intention was that of honest, sincere, protesting disappointment. As though she had said, "Why did you not hurry? If thou hadst been here, my brother had not died." But she still believed in Him. She still had confidence in Him, and that in a very wonderful way, as witness her words: "And even now I know that, whatsoever thou shalt ask of God, God will give thee." She had tremendous confidence in Him, and yet, as a matter of fact, she did not quite mean that. She thought she did. She was perfectly honest, but she did not expect her brother back.
—The Gospel According to John

MATTHEW HENRY

Christ and Martha.

[1] Martha's address to Christ, *v.* 21, 22.

First, She complains of Christ's long absence and delay. *Lord, if thou hadst been here, my brother had not died.* Here is, 1. Some evidence of faith. She believed Christ's *power,* that he could have prevented his death. She believed his *pity,* that if he had but seen Lazarus in his extreme illness, he would have had compassion. 2. Here are sad instances of unbelief. Her faith was true, but weak as a bruised reed, for she limits the power of Christ, in saying, *If thou hadst been here;* whereas she ought to have known that Christ could cure at a distance. She reflects likewise upon the wisdom and kindness of Christ, that he did not hasten to them when they sent for him, and now might as well have stayed away.

Secondly, Yet she corrects and comforts herself. At least, she blames herself for blaming her Master, and for suggesting that he comes too late: *for I know that even now, whatsoever thou wilt ask of God, God will give it to thee.* 1. How *willing* her hope was. She humbly recommends the case to the wise and compassionate consideration of the Lord Jesus. When we know not what in particular to ask or expect, let us in general refer ourselves to God. 2. How *weak* her faith was. She should have said, "Lord, thou canst do whatsoever thou wilt"; but she only says, "Thou canst obtain whatsoever thou prayest for." His power is always predominant, his intercession always prevalent.

[2] The comfortable word which Christ gave to Martha (*v.* 23): *Jesus saith unto her, Thy brother shall rise again.* Martha, in her complaint, looked back. We are apt, in such cases, to add to our own trouble, by fancying what *might have been.* Christ directs Martha, and us in her, to look forward, and to think what *shall be. Thy brother shall rise again.* This was true of Lazarus in a sense peculiar to him: he was now presently to be raised. It is applicable to all the saints. Think you hear Christ saying, "Thy parent, thy child, thy yoke-fellow, shall rise again."

[3] The faith which Martha mixed with this word, and the unbelief mixed with this faith, *v.* 24. She accounts it a *faithful saying* that *he shall rise again at the last day.* Yet she seems to think this saying not so well worthy of all acceptation as really it was. *I know that he shall rise again at the last day;* and is not this enough? She seems to think it is not. Thus, by our discontent under present crosses, we greatly undervalue our future hopes.

[4] The further instruction and encouragement which Jesus Christ gave her. He said to her, *I am the resurrection and the life, v.* 25, 26. Two things Christ possesses her with the belief of.

First, The power of Christ, his sovereign power: *I am the resurrection and the life.* Martha believed that at his prayer God would give any thing, but he would have her know that by his word he could work anything. It is an unspeakable comfort to all good Christians that Jesus Christ is the resurrection and the life, and will be so to them. *Resurrection* is a return to life; Christ is the author of that return, and of that life to which it is a return.

Secondly, The promises of the new covenant. To whom these promises are made—to those that believe in Jesus Christ. The condition of the latter promise is thus expressed: *Whosoever liveth and believeth in me,* which may be understood, either, of *natural* life: *Whosoever lives in this world,* whether he be Jew or Gentile, if he believes in Christ, he shall live by him. Or, of *spiritual* life. He that *lives* and *believes* is he that by faith is born again to a heavenly and divine life. What the promises are (*v.* 25): *Though he die, yet shall he live,* nay, *he shall never die, v.* 26.

a. For the *body;* here is the promise of a *blessed resurrection.* Though the body be dead because of sin yet it *shall live again.* The body shall be raised a glorious body.

b. For the *soul;* here is the promise of a *blessed immortality.* He that *liveth and believeth* shall *never die.* That spiritual life shall never be extinguished, but perfected in eternal life. The *mortality* of the body shall at length be *swallowed up of life;* but the life of the soul shall be immediately at death swallowed up of immortality. Christ asks her, "*Believest thou this?* Canst thou take my word for it?" Martha was doting upon her brother's being raised to life in this world; before Christ gave her hopes of this, he directed her thoughts to another life, another world. The crosses and comforts of this present time would not make such an impression upon us as they do if we did but believe the things of eternity as we ought.

[5] Martha's unfeigned assent yielded to what Christ said, *v.* 27. We have here Martha's creed, the good confession she witnessed. And it is the *conclusion of the whole matter.*

First, Here is the *guide of her faith,* and that is the

JAMIESON, FAUSSET, BROWN

21. Then said Martha . . . Lord, if thou hadst been here, my brother had not died—As Mary afterwards said the same thing (vs. 32), it is plain they had made this very natural remark to each other, perhaps many times during these four sad days, and not without having their confidence in His love at times overclouded. Such trials of faith, however, are not peculiar to them.

22. But I know that even now . . .—Energetic characters are usually sanguine, the rainbow of hope peering through the drenching cloud. **whatsoever thou wilt ask of God, God will give it thee**—i.e., 'even to the restoration of my dead brother to life,' for that plainly is her meaning, as the sequel shows.

23-27. Jesus saith unto her, Thy brother shall rise again—purposely expressing Himself in general terms, to draw her out.

24. Martha said, . . . I know that he shall rise again . . . at the last day—'But are we never to see him in life till then?'

25. Jesus said, I am the resurrection and the life—*'The whole power to restore, impart, and maintain* life, resides in Me.' (See on ch. 1:4; 5:21.) What higher claim to supreme divinity than this grand saying can be conceived?

he that believeth in me, though . . . dead . . . shall he live—i.e., The believer's death shall be swallowed up in life, and his life shall never sink into death. As death comes by sin, it is His to dissolve it; and as life flows through His righteousness, it is His to communicate and eternally maintain it (Rom. 5:21). The temporary separation of soul and body is here regarded as not even interrupting, much less impairing, the new and everlasting life imparted by Jesus to His believing people.

Believest thou this?—Canst thou take this in?

ADAM CLARKE

21. *If thou hadst been here, my brother had not died.* Mary said the same words to him a little after, v. 32, which proves that these sisters had not a complete knowledge of the omnipotence of Christ. They thought He could cure at hand, but not at a distance; or they thought that it was because He did not know of their brother's indisposition that He permitted him to die.

22. *I know, that even now.* She durst not ask so great a favor in direct terms; she only intimated modestly that she knew He could do it.

23. *Thy brother shall rise again.* That is, directly; for it was by raising him immediately from the dead that He intended to comfort her.

24. *I know that he shall rise again in the resurrection.* The doctrine of the resurrection of the dead was then commonly received; and though it was our Lord who fully exemplified it by His own resurrection, yet the opinion was common, not only among God's people, but among all those who believed in the God of Israel. The Jewish writings after the Captivity are full of this doctrine. See 2 Macc. vii. 9, 14, 23, 36; xii. 43; xiv. 46; Wisd. v. 1, 7, 17; vi. 6-7.

25. *I am the resurrection, and the life.* You say that your brother shall rise again in the resurrection at the last day; but by whom shall he arise if not by Me, who am the Author of the resurrection and the Source of life? And is it not as easy for Me to raise him now as to raise him then?

Though he were dead. Every man who has believed or shall believe in Me, though his believing shall not prevent him from dying a natural death, yet his body shall be reanimated, and he shall live with Me in an eternal glory. And everyone who is now dead, dead to God, dead in trespasses and sins, if he believe in Me, trust on Me as his sole Saviour, he shall *live,* shall be quickened by My Spirit, and live a life of faith, working by love.

26. *Shall never die.* Or "shall not die forever." Though he die a temporal death, he shall not continue under its power forever, but shall have a resurrection to life eternal.

Believest thou this? God has determined to work in the behalf of men only in proportion to their faith in Him. It was necessary, therefore, that these persons should be well instructed concerning His nature, that they might find no obstacles to their faith.

MATTHEW HENRY

word of Christ. She takes it entire as Christ had said it: *Yea, Lord.* Faith is an echo to divine revelation, returns the same words.

Secondly, The *ground of her faith,* and that is the authority of Christ. She has recourse to the foundation, for the support of the superstructure. "*I have believed* that thou art Christ, and therefore *I do believe* this." What she believed and confessed concerning Jesus. That he was the Christ; that he was the *Son of God;* that it was *he who should come.* That blessing of blessings she embraced as *present.* What she inferred hence. If she admits this, that Jesus is the Christ, there is no difficulty in believing that he is the resurrection and the life. He is the fountain of light and truth, and we may take all his sayings for faithful and divine. He is the fountain of life and blessedness, and we may therefore depend upon his ability.

2. The interview between Christ and Mary.

(1) The notice which Martha gave her of Christ's coming (*v.* 28): *When she had so said, she went her way,* and *called Mary her sister.* Time was when Martha would have drawn Mary from Christ, to come and help her in *much serving* (Luke x. 40). Here she is industrious to draw her to Christ. She called her *secretly.* She called her by order from Christ: *The Master is come, and calleth for thee.* She triumphs in his arrival: *The Master is come.* He whom we have long wished and waited for, *he is come, he is come;* this was the best cordial in the present distress. She invites her sister to go and meet him: "*He calls for thee.*" When Christ our Master comes, he *calls for us.* He calls for thee in particular, for thee *by name.* If he calls thee, he will cure thee, he will comfort thee.

(2) The haste with which Mary made to Christ (*v.* 29): *As soon as she heard* that the *Master was come,* she *arose quickly,* and came to him. She little thought how near he was to her, for he is often nearer to them that mourn in Zion than they are aware of. The least intimation of Christ's gracious approaches is enough to a lively faith, which stands ready to take the hint, and answer the first call. She did not consult her neighbours, the Jews that were *with her, comforting her;* she left them all, to come to him.

(3) We are told (*v.* 30) where she found the Master; *in that place where Martha met him.* Christ's love to his work. He stayed near the place where the grave was, that he might be ready to go to it. Mary's love to Christ; still she *loved much.* Though Christ had seemed unkind in his delays, yet she could take nothing amiss from him.

(4) The misconstruction which the Jews made of her going away so hastily (*v.* 31): They said, *She goes to the grave, to weep there.* Martha bore up better under this affliction than Mary did, who was a woman of tender and sorrowful spirit; such was her natural temper. These comforters therefore concluded when she went out, it was to go *to the grave and weep there.* [1] What often is the folly and fault of mourners; they contrive how to aggravate their own grief, and to make bad worse. We are apt to fasten upon those things that aggravate the affliction, when it is our duty to reconcile ourselves to the will of God in it. [2] What is the wisdom and duty of comforters; and that is, to prevent as much as may be, the revival of the sorrow, and to divert it. Those Jews that followed Mary were thereby led to Christ, and became the witnesses of one of his most glorious miracles. It is good cleaving to Christ's friends in their sorrows, for thereby we may come to know him better.

(5) Mary's address to our Lord Jesus (*v.* 32): She came and *fell down at his feet* and said with many tears (as appears *v.* 33), *Lord, if thou hadst been here, my brother had not died,* as Martha said before. *She fell down at his feet,* which was more than Martha did, who had a greater command of her passions. This Mary had sat *at Christ's feet to hear his word* (Luke x. 39), and here we find her there on another errand. Those that in a day of peace place themselves at Christ's feet, to receive instructions from him, may with comfort and confidence in a day of trouble cast themselves at his feet with hope to find favour with him. Mary hereby made profession of the Christian faith as truly as Martha did, and in effect said, *I believe that thou art the Christ.* This she did in presence of *the Jews* that attended her, who, though friends to her and her family, yet were bitter enemies to Christ. Let them resent it as they pleased, she falls at his feet. Her address is very pathetic: *Lord, if thou hadst been here, my brother had not died.* Christ's delay was designed for the best, and proved so; yet both the sisters very indecently *cast the same in his teeth,* and in effect charge him with the death of their brother. Mary added no more, as Martha did. She said less than Martha, but wept more; and tears of devout affection have a voice, in the ears of Christ;

JAMIESON, FAUSSET, BROWN

27. Yea, . . . I believe that thou art the Christ, the Son of God . . .—i.e., And having *such* faith in Thee, I can believe all which that comprehends. While she had a glimmering perception that Resurrection, in every sense of the word, belonged to the Messianic office and Sonship of Jesus, she means, by this way of expressing herself, to cover much that she felt her ignorance of—as no doubt belonging to Him.

28-32. The Master is come and calleth for thee—The narrative does not give us this interesting detail, but Martha's words do.

29. As soon as she heard that, she arose quickly—affection for her Lord, assurance of His sympathy, and His hope of interposition, putting a spring into her distressed spirit.

31. The Jews . . . followed her . . . to the grave—Thus *casually* were provided witnesses of the glorious miracle that followed, *not prejudiced,* certainly, *in favor* of Him who wrought it. **to weep there**—according to Jewish practice, for some days after burial.

fell at his feet—more impassioned than her sister, though her words were fewer. (See on vs. 21.)

ADAM CLARKE

27. *Yea, Lord: I believe.* "I have believed." Either meaning that she had believed this for some time past or that, since He began to teach her, her faith had been considerably increased. Martha here acknowledges Christ for the Messiah promised to their fathers; but her faith goes no further; and, having received some hope of her brother's present resurrection, she waited for no further instruction, but ran to call her sister.

28. *The Master is come.* This was the appellation which He had to the family; and from these words it appears that Christ had inquired for Mary, desiring to have her present, that He might strengthen her faith, previously to His raising her brother.

30. *Jesus was not yet come into the town.* As the Jewish burying places were without their cities and villages, it appears that the place where our Saviour was, when Martha met Him, was not far from the place where Lazarus was buried.

31. *She goeth unto the grave to weep there.* It appears that it was the custom for the nearest relatives of the deceased to go at times during the three days of weeping, accompanied by their friends and neighbors, to mourn near the graves of the deceased. They supposed that for three days the spirit hovered about the place where the body was laid, to see whether it might be again permitted to enter; but when it saw the face change, it knew that all hope was now past. It was on this ground that the seven days of lamentation succeeded the three days of weeping, because all hope was now taken away.

MATTHEW HENRY

no rhetoric like this.

Verses 33–44

I. Christ's tender *sympathy* with his afflicted friends, which appeared three ways:—

1. By the inward groans and troubles of his spirit (*v.* 33): *Jesus saw Mary weeping* and the *Jews that came with her weeping; he groaned in the spirit, and was troubled.* The griefs of the sons of men represented in the tears of Mary and her friends. What an emblem was here of this world, this vale of tears! Religion teaches us likewise to *weep with them that weep*, as these Jews wept with Mary. Those that truly love their friends will share with them in their joys and griefs; for what is friendship but a communication of affections? The grace of the Son of God and his compassion towards those that are in misery. *In all their afflictions he is afflicted*, Isa. lxiii. 9. When Christ saw them all in tears, He *groaned in the spirit.* This was an expression of his feeling sense of the calamitous state of human life, and the power of death. Having now to make a vigorous attack upon death and the grave, he thus stirred up himself to the encounter. It was an expression of his kind sympathy with his friends that were in sorrow. Christ not only seemed concerned, but he *groaned in the spirit;* he was inwardly and sincerely affected with the case. Christ's was a deep and a hearty sigh. He was *troubled.* He *troubled himself;* so the phrase is, very significantly. He was never troubled, but when he *troubled himself*, as he saw cause. He often *composed* himself to trouble, but was never discomposed or disordered by it.

2. His concern for them appeared by his *kind enquiry*, (*v.* 34): Where *have you laid him?* He would thus divert the grief of his mourning friends, by raising their expectations of something great.

3. It appeared by *his tears*. Those about him desired him to *come and see.*

(1) As he was going to the grave, *Jesus wept*, *v.* 35. A very short verse, but it affords many useful instructions. Jesus Christ was really and truly man, susceptible of the impressions of joy, and grief. Christ gave this proof of his humanity, in both senses of the word; that, as a man, he could weep, and, as a merciful man, he *would weep*, before he gave this proof of his divinity. He was *a man of sorrows*, and *acquainted with grief*, as was foretold, Isa. liii. 3. We never read that he laughed, but more than once we have him in tears. Tears of compassion well become Christians, and make them most to resemble Christ.

(2) Different constructions were put upon Christ's weeping. Some made a kind and candid interpretation of it (*v.* 36): *Then said the Jews, Behold how he loved him!* They seem to wonder that he should have so strong an affection for one to whom he was not related. It becomes us, according to this example of Christ, to show our love to our friends, both living and dying. Though our tears profit not the dead, they embalm their memory. When he only dropped a tear over Lazarus, they said, *See how he loved him!* Much more reason have we to say so, for whom he hath laid down his life: *See how he loved us!* Others make a peevish unfair reflection upon it (*v.* 37): *Could not this man, who opened the eyes of the blind*, have prevented the death of Lazarus? If he could have prevented it he would, and therefore because he *did not* they incline to think that he *could not*. Therefore it might justly be questioned whether he did indeed *open the eyes of the blind*. His not working this miracle they thought enough to invalidate the former. Christ soon convinced these *whisperers*, by raising Lazarus from the dead, which was the greater work, that he could have prevented his death.

II. Christ's approach to the grave.

1. Christ repeats his groans (*v.* 38): *Again groaning in himself, he comes to the grave;* he groaned, (1) Being displeased at the unbelief of those who spoke doubtingly of his power, and blamed him for not preventing the death of Lazarus. He never groaned so much for his own pains and sufferings as for the sins and follies of men. (2) Being affected with the fresh lamentations which, it is likely, the mourning sisters made, when they came near the grave, his tender spirit was sensibly touched with their wailings. Ministers, when they are sent by the preaching of the gospel to raise dead souls, should be much affected with the deplorable condition of those they preach to and pray for, and groan in themselves to think of it.

2. The grave wherein Lazarus lay is here described: *It was a cave, and a stone lay upon it;* and such was the sepulchre in which Christ was buried. They reckoned the solemnity of the funeral ended when the stone was rolled to the grave, or, as here, *laid upon it*.

3. Orders are given to remove the stone (*v.* 39): *Take away the stone.* He would have this stone removed, that all the standers-by might see the body

JAMIESON, FAUSSET, BROWN

33-38. When Jesus . . . saw her weeping, and the Jews . . . weeping . . . , he groaned in the spirit—the tears of Mary and her friends acting sympathetically upon Jesus, and **drawing forth His emotions.** What a vivid and beautiful outcoming of His *real* humanity! The word here rendered "groaned" does not mean "sighed" or "grieved," but rather "powerfully checked his emotion"—made a visible effort to restrain those tears which were ready to gush from His eyes. **and was troubled**—rather, "troubled himself" (*Margin*); referring probably to this visible difficulty of repressing His emotions.

34. Where have ye laid him? . . . Lord, come and see—Perhaps it was to retain composure enough to ask this question, and on receiving the answer to proceed with them to the spot, that He checked Himself. **35. Jesus wept**—This beautifully conveys the sublime brevity of the two original words; else "*shed tears*" might have better conveyed the difference between the word here used and that twice employed in vs. 33, and there properly rendered "weeping," denoting the loud wail for the dead, while that of Jesus consisted of *silent tears.* Is it for nothing that the Evangelist, some *sixty years* after it occurred, holds up to all ages with such touching brevity the sublime spectacle of *the Son of God in tears?* What a seal of His perfect oneness with us in the most redeeming feature of our stricken humanity! But was there nothing in those tears beyond sorrow for human suffering and death? Could these *effects* move Him without suggesting the *cause?* Who can doubt that in His ear every feature of the scene proclaimed that stern law of the Kingdom, "*The wages of sin is death,*" and that this element in His visible emotion underlay all the rest? **36. Then said the Jews, Behold how he loved him!**—We thank you, O ye visitors from Jerusalem, for this spontaneous testimony to the *human* tenderness of the Son of God. **37. And**—rather "But"—**some . . . said, Could not this man, which opened the eyes of the blind, have caused that this man should not have died?**—The former exclamation came from the better-feeling portion of the spectators; this betokens a measure of suspicion. It hardly goes the length of attesting the miracle on the blind man; but 'if (as everybody says) He did that, why could He not also have kept Lazarus alive?' As to the restoration of the dead man to life, they never so much as thought of it. But *this disposition to dictate to divine power, and almost to peril our confidence in it upon its doing our bidding, is not confined to men of no faith.* **38. Jesus again groaning in himself**—i.e., as at vs. 33, checked or repressed His rising feelings, in the former instance, of sorrow, here of righteous indignation at their unreasonable unbelief; (cf. Mark 3:5) [WEBSTER and WILKINSON]. But here, too, struggling emotion was deeper, now that His eye was about to rest on the spot where lay, in the still horrors of death, His *friend.*

a cave—the cavity, natural or artificial, of a rock. This, with the number of condoling visitors from Jerusalem, and the costly ointment with which Mary afterwards anointed Jesus at Bethany, all go to show that the family was in good circumstances. **39-44. Jesus said, Take ye away the stone**—spoken to the attendants of Martha and Mary; for it was a work of

ADAM CLARKE

33. ***He groaned in the spirit.*** **Here the blessed Jesus shows himself to be truly man; and a Man, too, who, notwithstanding His amazing dignity and excellence, did not feel it beneath Him to sympathize with the distressed, and weep with those who wept. After this example of our Lord, shall we say that it is weakness, folly, and sin to weep for the loss of relatives?**

35. ***Jesus wept.*** **The least verse in the Bible, yet inferior to none.**

37. ***Could not this man, which opened the eyes?*** **Through the maliciousness of their hearts these Jews considered the tears of Jesus as a proof of His weakness.**

38. ***It was a cave.*** **It is likely that several of the Jewish burying places were made in the sides of rocks.**

39. ***Take ye away the stone.*** **He desired to convince all those who were at the place, and**

MATTHEW HENRY

lie dead in the sepulchre, and that way might be made for its coming out, and it might appear to be a true body, and not a *ghost* or *spectre*. It is a good step towards the raising of a soul to spiritual life when prejudices are removed and got over and way made for the word to the heart.

4. An objection made by Martha against the opening of the grave: *Lord, by this time he stinketh, for he has been dead four days*. Probably Martha perceived the body to smell, as they were removing the stone, and therefore cried out thus.

(1) It is easy to observe hence the nature of human bodies: four days are but a little while, yet what a great change will this time make with the body of man. Christ rose the third day because he was not to *see corruption*.

(2) Some think she said it in a due tenderness to the dead body. She did not care that it should be thus publicly shown and made a spectacle of. Others think she said it out of a concern for Christ. If there were any thing noisome she would not have her Master near it; but he was none of those tender and delicate ones that cannot bear an ill smell; if he had, he would not have visited the world of mankind, which sin had made a perfect dunghill. It should seem, by Christ's answer, that it was the language of her unbelief and distrust: "Lord, it is too late now. It is impossible that this putrid carcase should *live*." She gives up his case as helpless and hopeless. This distrustful word of hers served to make the miracle both the more evident and the more illustrious. Her suggesting that it *could not be done* puts the more honour upon him that *did it*.

5. The gentle reproof Christ gave to Martha (*v.* 40): *Said I not unto thee that if thou wouldest believe thou shouldest see the glory of God?* Our Lord Jesus has given us all the assurances imaginable that a sincere faith shall at length be crowned with a blessed vision. If we will take Christ's word, and rely on his power and faithfulness, we shall see the glory of God, and be happy in the sight. We have need to be often reminded of these *sure mercies* with which our Lord Jesus hath encouraged us. We are apt to forget what Christ has spoken, and need him to put us in mind of it by his Spirit: "*Said I not unto thee* so and so? And dost thou think that he will ever unsay it?"

6. The opening of the grave, notwithstanding Martha's objection (*v.* 41): *Then they took away the stone*. If we will see the glory of God, we must let Christ take his own way. *They took away the stone*, and this was all they could do; Christ only could *give life*.

III. The miracle itself wrought.

1. He applies himself to his *living Father in heaven*. The gesture he used was very significant: *He lifted up his eyes*. What is prayer, but the ascent of the soul to God, and the directing of its affections and motions heavenward? He *lifted up* his eyes, looking beyond the grave where Lazarus lay, and overlooking all the difficulties that arose thence. His address to God was with great assurance: *Father, I thank thee that thou hast heard me*. He has here taught us, by his own example, *First*, In prayer to call God Father. *Secondly*, In our *prayers* to *praise him*, and thankfully to acknowledge former favours. But our Saviour's thanksgiving here was intended to express the unshaken assurance he had of the effecting of this miracle. He speaks of this as his own act (*v.* 11): *I go, that I may awake him;* yet he speaks of it as what he had obtained by prayer, for his Father *heard him*. Christ speaks of this miracle as an answer to prayer. He was pleased thus to *honour prayer*, making it the key wherewith even he unlocked the treasures of divine power and grace. Christ, being assured that his prayer was answered, professes:

(1) His thankful acceptance of this answer: *I thank thee that thou hast heard me*. He triumphs before the victory. We may by faith in the promise have a prospect of mercy before it be actually given in, and give God thanks for it. Mercies in answer to prayer ought in a special manner to be acknowledged with thankfulness. Besides the grant of the mercy itself, we are to value it as a great favour to have our poor prayers taken notice of. As God *answers* us with mercy, even *before we call*, so we should answer him with praise even before he grants.

(2) His cheerful assurance of a ready answer at any time (*v.* 42): *And I know that thou hearest me always*. "*I gave thanks*" (saith he) "for being heard in this, because I am sure to be heard in every thing." The Father *heard him always*, which may encourage us to depend upon his intercession, and put all our petitions into his hand, for we are sure that him the Father *hears always*. The confidence he had: *I knew it*. We cannot have such a particular assurance as he had; but this we know, that *whatsoever we ask according to his will he heareth us*, 1 John v. 14, 15. But why

JAMIESON, FAUSSET, BROWN

no little labor [GROTIUS]. According to the Talmudists, it was forbidden to open a grave after the stone was placed upon it. Besides other dangers, they were apprehensive of legal impurity by contact with the dead. Hence they avoided coming nearer a grave than four cubits [MAIMONIDES in LAMPE]. But He who touched the leper, and the bier of the widow of Nain's son, rises here also above these Judaic memorials of evils, every one of which He had come to roll away. *Observe here what our Lord did Himself, and what He made others do*. As Elijah himself repaired the altar on Carmel, arranged the wood, cut the victim, and placed the pieces on the fuel, but made the bystanders fill the surrounding trench with water, that no suspicion might arise of fire having been secretly applied to the pile (I Kings 18:30-35); so our Lord would let the most skeptical see that, without laying a hand on the stone that covered His friend, He could recall him to life. But what could be done by human hand He orders to be done, reserving only to Himself what transcended the ability of all creatures. **Martha, the sister of . . . the dead**—and as such the proper guardian of the precious remains; the relationship being *here* mentioned to account for her venturing gently to remonstrate against their exposure, in a state of decomposition, to eyes that had loved him so tenderly in life. **Lord, by this time he stinketh, for he hath been dead four days**—(See on vs. 17). It is wrong to suppose from this [as LAMPE and others do] that, like the bystanders, she had not thought of his restoration to life. But the glimmerings of hope which she cherished from the first (vs. 22), and which had been brightened by what Jesus said to her (vss. 23-27), had suffered a momentary eclipse on the proposal to expose the now sightless corpse. *To such fluctuations all real faith is subject in dark hours.* (See, for example, the case of Job.) **40. Jesus saith unto her, Said I not unto thee, that if thou wouldest believe, thou shouldest see the glory of God?**—He had not said those very words, but this was the scope of all that He had uttered to her about His life-giving power (vss. 23, 25, 26); a gentle yet emphatic and most instructive rebuke: 'Why doth the restoration of life, even to a decomposing corpse, seem hopeless in the presence of the Resurrection and the Life? Hast thou yet to learn that "if thou canst believe, all things are possible to him that believeth?"' (Mark 9:23).

41. Jesus lifted up his eyes—an expression marking His calm solemnity. (Cf. ch. 17:1.)

Father, I thank thee that thou hast heard me—rather, "heardest Me," referring to a specific prayer offered by Him, probably on intelligence of the case reaching Him (vss. 3,4); for His living and loving oneness with the Father was maintained and manifested in the flesh, not merely by the spontaneous and uninterrupted outgoing of Each to Each in spirit, but by specific actings of faith and exercises of prayer about each successive case as it emerged. He prayed [says LUTHARDT well] not for what He wanted, but for the manifestation of what He had; and having the bright consciousness of the answer in the felt liberty to ask it, and the assurance that it was at hand, He gives thanks for this with a grand simplicity before performing the act. **42. And**—rather "Yet"—**I knew that thou hearest me always, but because of the people that stand by I said it, that they might believe that thou hast sent me**—Instead of praying now, He simply gives thanks for answer to prayer offered ere He left Perea, and adds that His doing even this, in the audience of the people, was not from any doubt of the prevalency of His prayers in any case, but to show the people that *He did nothing without His Father, but all by direct communication with Him.*

ADAM CLARKE

especially those who took away the stone, that Lazarus was not only dead, but that putrescency had already taken place, that it might not afterwards be said that Lazarus had only fallen into a lethargy, but that the greatness of the miracle might be fully evinced.

He stinketh. The body is in a state of putrefaction. The Greek word signifies simply "to smell," whether the scent be good or bad; but the circumstances of the case sufficiently show that the latter is its meaning here. *For he hath been dead four days*. "This is the fourth day," i.e., since his interment. Christ himself was buried on the same day on which He was crucified, see chap. xix. 42, and it is likely that Lazarus was buried also on the same day on which he died.

40. *If thou wouldest believe*. So it appears that it is faith alone that interests the miraculous and saving power of God in behalf of men.

41. *Where the dead was laid*. These words are wanting in some MSS. *Father, I thank thee*. As it was a common opinion that great miracles might be wrought by the power and in the name of the devil, Jesus lifted up His eyes to heaven, and invoked the supreme God before these unbelieving Jews, that they might see that it was by His power, and by His only, that this miracle was done.

MATTHEW HENRY

should Christ give this public intimation of his obtaining this miracle by prayer? It is *because of the people who stand by, that they may believe that thou hast sent me;* for *prayer may preach.* It was to obviate the objections of his enemies. It was blasphemously suggested by the Pharisees that he wrought his miracles by compact with the devil; now, to evidence the contrary, he openly made his address to God, using *prayers*, and not *charms*, with elevated eyes and voice professing his dependence on Heaven. It was to corroborate the faith of those that were well inclined to him: *That they may believe that thou hast sent me.* Christ proves his mission by raising to life one that was dead.

2. He now applies himself to his *dead friend.* He *cried with a loud voice, Lazarus come forth.*

(1) He could have raised Lazarus by a silent exertion of his power and will, but he did it by a call, a loud call.

[1] To be significant of the power then put forth for the raising of Lazarus. The soul of Lazarus, which was to be called back, was at a distance, not hovering about the grave, as the Jews fancied, but removed to Hades. It is natural to speak loud when we call to those at a distance. The body of Lazarus, which was to be called up, was *asleep*, and we usually speak loud when we would awake any out of sleep.

[2] To be typical of other works of wonder which the power of Christ was to effect. This loud call was a figure, *First*, Of the gospel call, by which dead souls were to be brought out of the grave of sin. *Secondly*, Of the sound of the archangel's trumpet at the last day, with which they that sleep in the dust shall be awakened when Christ shall *descend with a shout.*

(2) This *loud call* was but *short*, yet *mighty through God.* He calls him by name, Lazarus, as we call those by their names whom we would wake out of a fast sleep. He calls him *out of the grave.* He does not say unto him, *Live;* but he saith to him, *Move*, for when by the grace of Christ we live spiritually we must stir up ourselves to *move;* the grave of sin and this world is no place for those whom Christ has quickened, and therefore they must *come forth.* The event was according to the intention: *He that was dead came forth, v.* 44. Power went along with the word of Christ to reunite the soul and body of Lazarus, and then he came forth. The miracle is described, not by its invisible springs, to satisfy our curiosity, but by its visible effects, to confirm our faith. If any ask whether Lazarus, after he was raised, could give an account or description of his soul's removal out of the body or return to it, or what he saw in the other world, I suppose both these changes were so unaccountable to himself that it was not lawful nor possible to express it. Let us not covet to be wise above what is written, and this is all that is written concerning the resurrection of that Lazarus, that *he that was dead came forth.*

(3) This miracle was wrought, [1] *Speedily.* Nothing intervenes between the command, *Come forth*, and the effect, *He came forth.* [2] *Perfectly.* He was so thoroughly revived that he got up out of his grave as strongly as ever he got up out of his bed, and returned not only to life, but health. He was not raised to serve a present turn, but to live as other men. He came out of his grave, though he was fettered with his grave-clothes, with which he was *bound hand and foot*, and *his face bound about with a napkin* (for so the manner of the Jews was to bury); and he came forth in the same dress wherein he was buried, that it might appear that it was he himself and not another. The standers-by, in unbinding him, would *handle him, and see him, that it was he himself*, and so be witnesses of the miracle. How little we carry away with us, when we leave the world—only a winding-sheet and a coffin; there is no change of raiment in the grave, nothing but a single suit of grave-clothes. Lazarus being *come forth*, hampered and embarrassed with his grave-clothes, we may well imagine that those about the grave were exceedingly surprised and frightened at it. Christ, to make the thing familiar, sets them to work: "*Loose him*, slacken his grave-clothes, that they may serve for day-clothes till he comes to his house."

Verses 45–57

We have here an account of the consequences of this glorious miracle.

I. Some were invited by it, and induced to believe. Many of the Jews, when they *saw the things that Jesus did, believed on him.* They had often heard of his miracles, and yet evaded the conviction of them, by calling in question the matter of fact; but now that they had themselves seen this done their unbelief was conquered. These were some of those Jews that came to Mary, to comfort her. When we are doing good offices to others we put ourselves in the way of

JAMIESON, FAUSSET, BROWN

43, 44.

and when he had thus spoken, he cried with a loud voice—On one other occasion only did He this—on the *cross.* His last utterance was a "loud cry" (Matt. 27:50). "He shall not cry," said the prophet, nor, in His ministry, did He. What a sublime contrast is this "loud cry" to the magical "whisperings" and "mutterings" of which we read in Isaiah 8:19; 29:4 [as GROTIUS remarks]! It is second only to the grandeur of that voice which shall raise all the dead (ch. 5:28, 29; I Thess. 4:16).

44. Jesus saith unto them, Loose him and let him go—Jesus will no more do this Himself than roll away the stone. The one was the necessary *preparation* for resurrection, the other the necessary *sequel* to it. THE LIFE-GIVING ACT ALONE HE RESERVES TO HIMSELF. So *in the quickening of the dead to spiritual life, human instrumentality is employed first to prepare the way, and then to turn it to account.*

ADAM CLARKE

43. *He cried with a loud voice.* In chap. v. 25, our Lord had said that the time was coming in which the dead should hear the voice of the Son of God and live. He now fulfills that prediction and cries aloud, that the people may take notice, and see that even death is subject to the sovereign command of Christ.

44. *Bound hand and foot with graveclothes.* "Swathed about with rollers." These were long slips of linen a few inches in breadth with which the body and limbs of the dead were swathed, and especially those who were embalmed, that the aromatics might be kept in contact with the flesh. But as it is evident that Lazarus had not been embalmed, it is probable that his limbs were not swathed together, as is the constant case with those who are embalmed, but separately, so that he could come out of the tomb at the command of Christ, though he could not walk freely till the rollers were taken away. *Loose him, and let him go.* He would have the disciples and those who were at hand take part in this business, that the fullest conviction might rest on every person's mind concerning the reality of what was wrought. He whom the grace of Christ converts and restores to life comes forth at His call from the dark, dismal grave of sin, in which his soul has long been buried. He walks, according to the command of Christ, in newness of life; and gives, by the holiness of his conduct, the fullest proof to all his acquaintance that he is alive from the dead.

45. *Many of the Jews . . . believed on him.* They saw that the miracle was incontestable, and they were determined to resist the truth no longer. Their friendly visit to these distressed sisters became the means of their conversion.

G. CAMPBELL MORGAN:

Someone asks, "Why did Jesus have to cry with a loud voice?" That is a child's question, and therefore it is the sort of question that admits to the kingdom of heaven and truth. It does look as though He had to cry in a loud voice to make Lazarus hear. But we know that is not so. Profundity is in the simplicities. He raised His voice that the crowd might hear. He had prayed to his Father that the multitude may believe, and now that all may hear what He does, He raised His voice. With a loud voice He spoke. Moreover, the habit of that time, and indeed of today in the case of all sorts of sorcerers and wizards communicating with the dead, was and is that of muttering incantations that nobody but themselves understand. I am not sure that this was not also the reason of the loud voice. "He cried with a loud voice, Lazarus, come forth."

But far more important than that, He spoke as to somebody who could hear Him. Martha would not have thought of calling Lazarus. Mary in her wailing might have called upon her brother, "O Lazarus, Lazarus!" But she would never have dreamed that he could hear her. Jesus spoke as to one who could hear. He knew that Lazarus was not dead. He told Martha that he was asleep, he was not dead. When He went into the house of Jairus, He said, "Talitha cumi," that exquisitely beautiful little phrase so badly rendered "Damsel arise," which should be, "Little lamb arise." He expected her to hear Him. She did! That was His attitude now. His was the voice which needed no raising for that purpose; but that carried over the borderline, and could be heard on the other side.

—The Gospel According to John

MATTHEW HENRY

receiving favours from God.

II. Others were irritated by it, and hardened in their unbelief.

1. The *informers* were so (*v.* 46): *Some of them went to the Pharisees and told them what things Jesus had done,* with a spiteful design to excite those who needed no spur the more vigorously to prosecute him. A most *obstinate infidelity,* refusing to yield to the most powerful means of conviction. A most *inveterate enmity.* If they would not be satisfied that he was to be believed in as the Christ, yet one would think they should have been mollified, and persuaded not to persecute him.

2. The judges, *the blind leaders,* of the people were no less exasperated by the report made to them.

(1) A special council is called and held (*v.* 47): *Then gathered the chief priests and Pharisees a council.* This council was called, not only for joint advice, but for mutual irritation; that so they might exasperate and inflame one another with enmity and rage against Christ.

(2) The case is proposed, and shown to be weighty and of great consequence.

[1] The matter to be debated was what course they should take with this Jesus; they said, *What do we? For this man doeth many miracles.* They own the truth of Christ's miracles, and that he had wrought many of them; they are therefore witnesses against themselves, for they acknowledge his credentials and yet deny his commission. They consider what is to be done, and chide themselves that they have not done something sooner effectually to crush him. They do not take it at all into their consideration whether they shall not receive him and own him as the Messiah; but they take it for granted that he is an enemy, and as such is to be run down: "*What do we?* Shall we be always talking, and bring nothing to pass?"

[2] That which made this matter weighty was the peril they apprehended their church and nation to be in from the Romans (*v.* 48): "If we do not silence him, *all men will believe on him*; and, this being the setting up of a new king, the Romans *will come* and *take away our place and nation.*" See what an opinion they have of their own *power.* They speak as if they thought Christ's progress depended upon their connivance; as if it were in their power to conquer him who had conquered death.

a. They take on them to prophecy that if he have liberty to go on, *all men will believe on him.* Thus do they now make his interest formidable, though, to serve another turn, these same men strove to make it contemptible, *ch.* vii. 48, *Have any of the rulers believed on him?* This was the thing they were afraid of, that men would *believe on him.*

b. They foretell that if the generality of the nation be *drawn after him,* the rage of the Romans will be *drawn upon them.* They *will come and take away our place.* Here appeared a cowardice. Had they kept their integrity, they needed not to have feared the Romans; but they speak like a dispirited people. When men lose their piety they lose their courage. It was false that there was any danger of the Romans' being irritated against their nation by the progress of Christ's gospel. He taught men to give tribute to Cæsar, and not to *resist evil.* The Roman governor, at his trial, could *find no fault in him.* Pretended fears are often the colour of malicious designs. The enemies of Christ and his gospel have often coloured their enmity with a seeming care for the *public good* and the *common safety,* and have branded his prophets and ministers as men that *turn the world upside down.* Carnal policy commonly sets up *reasons of state,* in opposition to *rules of justice.* That calamity which we seek to escape by sin we take the most effectual course to bring upon our own heads.

(3) Caiaphas makes a malicious but mystical speech in the council.

[1] The *malice* of it appears evident at first view, *v.* 49, 50. He, being the high priest, took upon him to decide the matter. "*You know nothing at all.* It is soon determined, if you consider that received maxim, *That it is expedient for us that one man should die for the people.*"

First, The counsellor was Caiaphas, who was *high priest that same year.*

Secondly, the drift of the advice was, in short, this, That some way or other must be found out to put Jesus to death. Caiaphas does not say, Let him be silenced, but *die he must.*

Thirdly, This is plausibly insinuated. He suggests his own sagacity. How scornfully does he say, "*You know nothing,* who are but common priests. Thus it is common for those in authority to impose their corrupt dictates by virtue of that; and, because they *should be* the wisest and best, to expect that everybody should believe they *are so.* He takes it for granted that the case is plain and past dispute. Reason and

JAMIESON, FAUSSET, BROWN

45, 46. many . . . which . . . had seen . . . believed . . . . But some . . . went . . . to the Pharisees and told them what Jesus had done—the two classes which continually reappear in the Gospel history; nor is there ever any great work of God which does not produce both. "It is remarkable that on each of the three occasions on which our Lord raised the dead, a large number of persons was assembled. In two instances, the resurrection of the widow's son and of Lazarus, these were all witnesses of the miracle; in the third (of Jairus' daughter) they were necessarily cognizant of it. Yet this important circumstance is in each case only incidentally noticed by the historians, not put forward or appealed to as a proof of their veracity. In regard to this miracle, we observe a greater degree of preparation, both in the provident arrangement of events, and in our Lord's actions and words than in any other. The preceding miracle (cure of the man born blind) is distinguished from all others by the open and formal investigation of its facts. And both these miracles, the most public and best attested of all, are related by John, who wrote long after the other Evangelists" [WEBSTER and WILKINSON]. **47-54. What do we? for this man doeth many miracles.**—'While we trifle, "this man," by His "many miracles," will carry all before Him; the popular enthusiasm will bring on a revolution, which will precipitate the Romans upon us, and our all will go down in one common ruin.' What a testimony to the reality of our Lord's miracles, and their resistless effect, from His bitterest enemies!

ALEXANDER MACLAREN:

The resurrection of Lazarus had raised a wave of popular excitement. Any stir among the people was dangerous, especially at the Passover time, which was nigh at hand, when Jerusalem would be filled with crowds of men, ready to take fire from any spark that might fall among them. So a hasty meeting of the principal ecclesiastical council of the Jews was summoned in order to discuss the situation and concert measures for repressing the nascent enthusiasm. One might have expected to find there some disposition to inquire honestly into the claims of a teacher who had such a witness to His claims as a man alive that had been dead. But nothing of the sort appears in their ignoble calculations. Like all weak men, they feel that "something must be done," and are perfectly unable to say what. They admit Christ's miracles: "This man doeth many miracles," but they are not a bit the nearer to recognizing His mission, being therein disobedient to their law and untrue to their office. They fear that any disturbance will bring Rome's heavy hand down on them, and lead to the loss of what national life they still possess. But even that fear is not patriotism nor religion. It is pure self-interest. "They will take away *our* place"—the Temple, probably—"and our nation." The holy things were, in their eyes, their special property. And so, at this supreme moment, big with the fate of themselves and of their nation, their whole anxiety is about personal interests.

—*Expositions of Holy Scripture*

ADAM CLARKE

47. *Then gathered the chief priests and the Pharisees a council.* The Pharisees, as such, had no power to assemble councils; and therefore only those are meant who were scribes or elders of the people, in conjunction with Annas and his son-in-law, Caiaphas, who were the high priests here mentioned. See chap. xviii. 13, 24.

What do we? This last miracle was so clear, plain, and incontestable that they were driven now to their wits' end. Their own spies had come and borne testimony of it.

48. *All men will believe on him.* If we permit Him to work but a few more miracles like these last two (the cure of the blind man and the resurrection of Lazarus), He will be universally acknowledged for the Messiah; the people will proclaim Him king; and the Romans, who can suffer no government here but their own, will be so irritated that they will send their armies against us and destroy our Temple and utterly dissolve our civil and ecclesiastical existence. *Both our place and nation.* Literally, "this place," but that the Temple only is understood is clear from Acts vi. 13-14; 2 Macc. i. 14; ii. 18; iii. 18; v. 16-17; x. 7; where it is uniformly called "the place," or "the holy place," because they considered it the most glorious and excellent place in the world. When men act in opposition to God's counsel, the very evils which they expect thereby to avoid will come upon them. They said, If we do not put Jesus to death, the Romans will destroy both our Temple and nation. Now it was because they put Him to death that the Romans burned and razed their Temple to the ground and put a final period to their political existence. See Matt. xxii. 7 and the notes on chap. xxiv.

49. *Caiaphas being the high priest that same year.* By the law of Moses, Exod. xl. 15, the office of high priest was for life, and the son of Aaron's race always succeeded his father. But at this time the high priesthood was almost annual. The Romans and Herod put down and raised up whom they pleased, and when they pleased, without attending to any other rule than merely that the person put in this office should be of the sacerdotal race. According to Josephus, *Ant.* xviii, c. 3, the proper name of this person was Joseph, and Caiaphas was his surname. He possessed the high priesthood for eight or nine years and was deposed by Vitellius, governor of Judea. *Ye know nothing.* Of the perilous state in which you stand.

MATTHEW HENRY

justice are often run down with a high hand. *Truth is fallen in the streets*, and, when it is down, down with it; and *equity cannot enter*, and, when it is out, out with it. He insists upon a maxim in politics, That the welfare of communities is to be preferred before that of particular persons. *It is expedient for us* that *one man die for the people.* Caiaphas craftily insinuates that the greatest and best man ought to think his life well spent, nay well lost, to save his country from ruin. The case ought to have been put thus: Was it expedient for them to bring upon themselves and upon their nation the guilt of blood, for the securing of their civil interests? Carnal policy, while it thinks to *save all* by sin, *ruins all* at last.

[2] The *mystery* that was in this counsel of Caiaphas does not appear at first view, but the evangelist leads us into it (*v.* 51, 52): *This spoke he not of himself.* In these words he prophesied, though he himself was not aware of it, *that Jesus should die for that nation.* Here is a precious comment upon a pernicious text. Charity teaches us to put the most favourable construction upon men's words and actions that they will bear; but piety teaches us to make a good improvement of them. If wicked men *are God's hand* to humble and reform us, why may they not be God's mouth to instruct and convince us? As the hearts of all men are in God's hand, so are their tongues.

(4) The evangelist explains and enlarges upon Caiaphas's words.

[1] He explains what he said. He did not *speak it of himself.* As it was an artifice to stir up the council against Christ, he spoke it of himself, but as it was an *oracle*, declaring it the purpose and design of God, he did not speak it of himself.

First, He *prophesied*, and those that prophesied did not, in their prophecying, *speak of themselves*. But is Caiaphas also among the prophets? He is so, *this once*. God can and often does make wicked men instruments to serve his own purposes, even contrary to their own intentions. Words of prophecy in the mouth are no infallible evidence of a principle of grace in the heart. *Lord, Lord, have we not prophesied in thy name?* will be rejected as a frivolous plea.

Secondly, He prophesied, *being high priest that year;* not that his being high priest did at all dispose or qualify him to be a prophet. Being high priest, God was pleased to put this significant word into his mouth rather than into the mouth of any other, that it might be the more observed or the non-observance of it the more aggravated.

Thirdly, The matter of his prophecy was *that Jesus should die for that nation.* He meant by *that nation* those in it that obstinately adhered to Judaism, but God meant those in it that would receive the doctrine of Christ, and become followers of him. It is a great thing that is here prophesied: That Jesus should *die*, die for others, not only *for their good*, but *in their stead*. If the whole nation of the Jews had unanimously believed in Christ, and received his gospel, they had been not only saved eternally, but saved as a nation from their grievances.

[2] The evangelist enlarges upon this word of Caiaphas (*v.* 52), *not for that nation only*, but *that also he should gather together in one the children of God that were scattered abroad.*

First, The persons Christ died for: *Not for the nation* of the Jews *only*. He must die for *the children of God that were scattered abroad.* Some understand it of the children of God that were then *in being*, scattered abroad in the Gentile world, *devout men* of every nation that *feared God* and worshipped him. Christ died to incorporate these in one great society. Others take in with these all that belong to the election of grace, who are called the children of God. There are those that *fear him throughout all generations*; to all these he had an eye in the atonement he made. As he prayed, so he died, for *all that should believe on him.*

Secondly, The purpose and intention of his death: he died to *gather in* those who wandered, and to *gather together in one* those who were scattered. Christ's dying is, 1. The great *attractive of our hearts;* for this end he is lifted up, to draw men to him. His love in dying for us is the great lodestone of our love. 2. The great *centre of our unity.* He gathers them together *in one.* All the saints in all places and ages meet in Christ.

(5) The result of this debate (*v.* 53): *From that day they took counsel together, to put him to death.* They now understood one another's minds, and so each was fixed in his own, that Jesus must die. What before they had thought of *severally* now they *jointly* concurred in, and so strengthened the hands one of another in this wickedness. Evil men confirm and encourage themselves and one another in evil practices, by comparing notes; then the wickedness which before seemed impracticable appears not only possible, but easy to be effected. What before they wished done,

JAMIESON, FAUSSET, BROWN

TODAY'S DICTIONARY OF THE BIBLE:

Caiaphas, the Jewish high priest (A.D. 27-36) at the beginning of our Lord's public ministry, in the reign of Tiberius (Luke 3:1), and also at the time of his condemnation and crucifixion (Matt. 26:3, 57; John 11:49; 18:13, 14). He held this office during the whole of Pilate's administration. His wife was the daughter of Annas, who had formerly been high priest, and was probably the vicar or deputy (Heb. *sagan*) of Caiaphas. He was of the sect of the Sadducees (Acts 5:17) and was a member of the council when he gave his opinion that Jesus should be put to death "for the people, and that the whole nation perish not" (John 11:50). In these words he unconsciously uttered a prophecy. "Like Saul, he was a prophet in spite of himself." Caiaphas had no power to inflict the punishment of death, and therefore Jesus was sent to Pilate, the Roman governor, that he might duly pronounce the sentence against him (Matt. 27:2; John 18:28). At a later period his hostility to the gospel is still apparent (Acts 4:6).

Caiaphas . . . prophesied that Jesus should die for that nation.—He meant nothing more than that the way to prevent the apprehended ruin of the nation was to make a sacrifice of the Disturber of their peace. But in giving utterance to this suggestion of political expediency, he was so guided as to give forth a divine prediction of deep significance; and God so ordered it that it should come from the lips of the high priest for that memorable year, the recognized head of God's visible people, whose ancient office, symbolized by the Urim and Thummim, was to decide in the last resort, all vital questions as the oracle of the divine will.

and not for that nation only . . .—These are the Evangelist's words, not Caiaphas'.

53. they took council together to put him to death—Caiaphas but expressed what the party was secretly wishing, but afraid to propose.

ADAM CLARKE

50. *Nor consider.* Instead of ye do not *consider*, which properly conveys the idea of "conferring" or "talking together," *neither do ye reason* or *consider rightly* is the reading of several MSS. and some of the primitive fathers. *That one man should die for the people.* In saying these remarkable words Caiaphas had no other intention than merely to state that it was better to put Jesus to death than to expose the whole nation to ruin on His account. His maxim was, It is better to sacrifice one man than a whole nation.

51. *This spake he not of himself.* Wicked and worthless as he was, God so guided his tongue that, contrary to his intention, he pronounced a prophecy of the death of Jesus Christ. I have already remarked that the doctrine of a vicarious atonement had gained, long before this time, universal credit in the world. Words similar to these of Caiaphas are, by the prince of all the Roman poets, put in the mouth of Neptune, when promising Venus that the fleet of Aeneas should be preserved, and his whole crew should be saved, one only excepted, whose death he speaks of in these remarkable words: "One life shall fall, that many may be saved." This victim the poet informs us was Palinurus, the pilot of Aeneas' own ship, who was precipitated into the deep by a divine influence.

52. *And not for that nation only.* These, and the preceding words in v. 51, are John's explication of what was prophetic in the words of Caiaphas; as if John had said, He is indeed to die for the sins of the Jewish nation, but not for theirs alone, but for the sins of the whole world. See His own words afterwards, 1 John ii. 1-2. *Gather together in one.* That He should "collect into one body"; form one Church out of the Jewish and Gentile believers. *Children of God that were scattered abroad.* Probably John meant only the Jews who were dispersed among all nations since the conquest of Judea by the Romans (these are called "the dispersed," chap. vii. 35, and Jas. i. 1); and it is because he refers to these only that he terms them here *the children of God*, which was an ancient character of the Jewish people; see Deut. xxxii. 5; Isa. xliii. 6; xlv. 11; Jer. xxxii. 1. Taking his words in this sense, then his meaning is this: that Christ was to die, not only for the then inhabitants of Judea, but for all the Jewish race wheresoever scattered; and that the consequence would be that they should be all collected from their various dispersions and made one body. This comports with the predictions of Paul, Rom. xi. 1-32.

53. *They took counsel together.* They were of one accord in the business, and had fully made up their minds on the subject; they waited only for a proper opportunity to put Him to death.

MATTHEW HENRY

but *wanted a colour for*, now they are furnished with a plausible pretence to justify themselves in.

(6) Christ hereupon absconded, *v.* 54. *He walked no more openly among the Jews.* He withdrew into an obscure part of the country, so obscure that the name of the town he retired to is scarcely met with anywhere else. He went to a country *near the wilderness.* He entered into a city called Ephraim. Thither his disciples went with him; neither would they leave him in solitude, nor would he leave them in danger. But why would Christ abscond now? It was not because he either feared the power of his enemies or distrusted his own power. He retired to put a mark of his displeasure upon Jerusalem and the people of the Jews. They rejected him and his gospel; justly therefore did he remove himself and his gospel from them. It was a sad presage of that thick darkness which was shortly to come upon Jerusalem, because she knew not the day of her visitation. It was to render the cruelty of his enemies the more inexcusable. He would try whether their anger would be turned away by his retirement into privacy. His hour was *not yet come*, and therefore he declined danger. His retirement, for awhile, was to make his return into Jerusalem the more remarkable and illustrious. This swelled the acclamations of joy with which his well-wishers welcomed him when he rode triumphantly into the city.

(7) The strict enquiry made for him during his recess, *v.* 55–57.

[1] The occasion of it was the approach of the passover, at which they expected his presence, according to custom (*v.* 55): *The Jews' passover was nigh at hand*, a festival which shone bright in their calendar. Now the passover being at hand, *many went out of* all parts of *the country to Jerusalem, to purify themselves.* This was either: A *necessary purification* of those who had contracted any ceremonial pollution. Or: A *voluntary purification*, by fasting and prayer, and other religious exercises, which many spent some time in before the passover.

[2] The enquiry was very solicitous: *They said, What think you, that he will not come to the feast? v.* 56. Some think this was said by those who wished well to him, and expected his coming. Those who came early out of the country, that they might purify themselves, were very desirous to meet with Christ, and perhaps came up the sooner with that expectation. They enquired what news of Christ? It should rather seem that they were his enemies who made this enquiry after him. When they should have been assisting those that came to purify themselves, according to the duty of their place, they were plotting against Christ. Their asking, *What think you? Will he not come up to the feast?* implies, *a.* An invidious reflection upon Christ, as if he would omit his attendance on the feast of the Lord for fear of exposing himself. It is sad to see holy ordinances prostituted to such unholy purposes. *b.* A fearful apprehension that they had of missing their game: "*Will he not come up to the feast?* If he do not, our measures are broken."

[3] The orders for the apprehending of him were very strict, *v.* 57. The great sanhedrim issued out a proclamation, strictly charging and requiring that if any person *knew where he was* they should show it, that he might be taken. See, *First*, How intent they were upon this prosecution. *Secondly*, How willing they were to involve others in the guilt with them. It is an aggravation of the sins of wicked rulers that they commonly make those that are under them instruments of their unrighteousness.

CHAPTER 12

Verses 1–11

I. The *kind visit* our Lord Jesus paid to his friends at Bethany, *v.* 1. He came up out of the country, *six days before the passover*, and took up at Bethany. He lodged here with his friend Lazarus, whom he had lately *raised from the dead.* His coming to Bethany now may be considered.

1. As a preface to the passover he intended to celebrate, to which reference is made in assigning the date of his coming: *Six days before the passover.*

2. As a voluntary exposing of himself to the fury of his enemies; now that his hour was at hand he came within their reach. Our Lord Jesus was voluntary in his sufferings; his life was not *forced* from him, but *resigned.* As the strength of his persecutors could not overpower him, so their subtlety could not surprise him. As there is a time when we are allowed to shift for our own preservation, so there is a time when we are called to hazard our lives in the cause of God.

3. As an instance of his kindness to his friends at Bethany, whom he loved. This was a farewell visit.

JAMIESON, FAUSSET, BROWN

Jesus . . . walked no more openly among the Jews—How could He, unless He had wished to die before His time? **near to the wilderness**—of Judea. **a city called Ephraim**—between Jerusalem and Jericho.

55-57. passover . . . at hand . . . many went . . . up . . . before the passover, to purify themselves—from any legal uncleanness which would have disqualified them from keeping the feast. This is mentioned to introduce the graphic statement which follows.

56. sought they for Jesus, and spake among themselves, as they stood in the temple—giving forth the various conjectures and speculations about the probability of His coming to the feast. **that he will not come**—The form of this question implies the opinion that He *would* come.

57. chief priests and the Pharisees had given a commandment that if any knew where he were, he should show it, that they might take him—This is mentioned to account for the conjectures whether He would come, in spite of this determination to seize Him.

CHAPTER 12

Vss. 1-11. The Anointing at Bethany. (See on Matt. 26:6-13.) **1-8. six days before the passover**—i.e., on the sixth day before it; probably after sunset on *Friday* evening, or the commencement of the Jewish *sabbath* preceding the passover.

ADAM CLARKE

54. *Walked no more openly.* He did not go as before through the cities and villages, teaching, preaching, and healing the sick. *A city called Ephraim.* Variously written in the MSS., Ephraim, Ephrem, Ephram, and Ephratha. This was a little village situated in the neighborhood of Bethel; for the scripture (2 Chron. xiii. 19) and Josephus join them both together. Eusebius and Jerome say it was about twenty miles north of Jerusalem.

55. *The Jews' passover was nigh at hand.* It is not necessary to suppose that this verse has any particular connection with the preceding. Most chronologists agree that our Lord spent at least two months in Ephraim. This was the last Passover which our Lord attended, and it was at this one that He suffered death for the salvation of a lost world. As the Passover was nigh, many of the inhabitants of Ephraim and its neighborhood went up to Jerusalem, some time (perhaps seven or eight days, for so much time was required to purify those who had touched the dead) before the feast, that they might purify themselves, and not eat the Passover otherwise than prescribed in the law. Many of the country people, in the time of Hezekiah, committed a trespass by not attending to this; see 2 Chron. xxx. 18-19. Those mentioned in the text wished to avoid this inconvenience.

56. *Then sought they for Jesus.* Probably those of Ephraim, in whose company Christ is supposed to have departed for the feast, but, having stayed behind, perhaps at Jericho, or its vicinity, the others had not missed Him till they came to the Temple, and then inquired among each other whether He would not attend the feast. Or the persons mentioned in the text might have been the agents of the high priest, and hearing that Christ had been at Ephraim, came and inquired among the people that came from that quarter whether Jesus would not attend the festival, knowing that He was punctual in His attendance on all the Jewish solemnities.

57. *Had given a commandment.* Had given order; "positive order," or "injunction," and perhaps with a grievous penalty, that no one should keep the place of His residence a secret. This was their hour, and the power of darkness; and now they were fully determined to take away His life. The order here spoken of was given in consequence of the determination of the council, mentioned in vv. 48-53.

CHAPTER 12

1. *Six days before the passover.* Reckoning the day of the Passover to be the last of the six.

MATTHEW HENRY

Bethany is here described to be the town *where Lazarus was, whom he raised from the dead.* The miracle wrought here put a new honour upon the place, and made it remarkable. Where he has sown plentifully, he observes whether it comes up again.

II. The *kind entertainment* which his friends there gave him: They *made him a supper* (*v.* 2). It is queried whether this was the same with that which is recorded, Matt. xxvi. 6, &c., in the house of Simon. Most commentators think it was. Let us see the account of this entertainment. They *made him a supper;* for with them, ordinarily, supper was the best meal. This they did in token of their respect and gratitude, for a feast is made for *friendship*; and that they might have an opportunity of free and pleasant conversation with him, for a feast is made for *fellowship*. Martha *served.* She did not think it below her to *serve*, when Christ sat at meat; nor should we think it a dishonour to stoop to any service whereby Christ may be honoured. Christ had formerly reproved Martha for being *troubled with much serving*. But she did not therefore leave off serving, as some, who, when they are reproved for one extreme, peevishly run into another; no, still she *served.* Better be a *waiter* at Christ's table than a *guest* at the table of a prince. Lazarus was *one of those that sat at meat*. It proved the truth of his resurrection, as it did of Christ's, that there were those who did *eat and drink with him*, Acts x. 41. He *sat at meat*, as a momument of the miracle Christ had wrought. Those whom Christ has *raised up* to a spiritual life are made to *sit together with him*.

III. The particular respect which Mary showed him, *v.* 3. She had a *pound of ointment of spikenard, very costly*, and with this she *anointed the feet of Jesus*, and she *wiped them with her hair*, and *the house was filled with the odour of the ointment*. Doubtless she intended this as a token of her love to Christ. By this her love to Christ appears to have been a *generous* love. If she had anything more valuable than another, that must be brought out for the honour of Christ. Those who love Christ truly love him so much better than this world as to be willing to lay out the best they have for him. A *condescending* love; she not only bestowed her ointment upon Christ, but with her own hands poured it upon him. Nay, she did not, as usual, anoint his *head* with it, but his *feet*. True love, as it does not spare charges, so it does not spare pains, in honouring Christ. A *believing* love; there was faith working by this love, faith in Jesus as the Messiah, the Christ, the Anointed. *God's Anointed* should be *our Anointed*. Let us pour on him the ointment of our best affections. The *filling of the house* with the pleasant *odour of the ointment*. Those who entertain Christ in their hearts and houses bring a sweet odour into them.

IV. Judas's dislike of Mary's token of her respect to Christ, *v.* 4, 5.

1. The person that carped at it was Judas, *one of his disciples*; not one of their nature, but only one of their number. Judas was an apostle, a preacher of the gospel, and yet one that discouraged this instance of pious affection. It is sad to see the life of religion discountenanced by such as are bound by their office to assist and encourage it. But this was he that should *betray Christ*.

2. The pretence with which he covered his dislike (*v.* 5): "*Why was not this ointment* sold for three hundred pence, and *given to the poor?*" Here is worldly wisdom passing a censure upon pious zeal. Those who value themselves upon their *secular policy*, and undervalue others for their *serious piety*, have more in them of the spirit of Judas than they would be thought to have. Here is charity to the poor secretly made a cloak for covetousness. Many excuse themselves from *laying out* in charity under pretence of *laying up* for charity. Judas asked, *Why was it not given to the poor?* We must not conclude that those do no acceptable piece of service who do not do it in our way. Proud men think all ill-advised who do not advise with them.

3. The detection and discovery of Judas's hypocrisy herein, *v.* 6. *This he said, not that he cared for the poor, but because he was a thief, and had the bag.* It did not come from a principle of charity: *Not that he cared for the poor.* What were the poor to him any further than he might serve his own ends? Thus some warmly contend for the *power* of the church, as others for its *purity*, when perhaps it is all one to them whether its *true interest* sink or swim, but under the pretence of this they are advancing themselves. It did come from a principle of covetousness. The truth of the matter was, he would rather have had it in money, to be put in the common stock, and then he knew what to do with it.

(1) Judas was treasurer of Christ's household. See what *estate* Jesus and his disciples had to live upon. Only a *bag*, wherein they kept just enough for their

JAMIESON, FAUSSET, BROWN

2. **Martha served**—This, with what is afterwards said of Mary's way of honoring her Lord, is so true to the character in which those two women appear in Luke 10:38-42, as to constitute one of the strongest and most delightful confirmations of the truth of both narratives. (See also on ch. 11:20.) **Lazarus . . . sat at the table**—"*Between the raised Lazarus and the healed leper* [Simon, Mark 14:3], *the Lord probably sits as between two trophies of His glory*" [STIER].

3. **spikenard**—or pure *nard*, a celebrated aromatic (Song of Sol. 1:12). **anointed the feet of Jesus**—and "poured it on His head" (Matt. 26:7; Mark 14:3). The only use of this was to refresh and exhilarate—a grateful compliment in the East, amidst the closeness of a heated atmosphere, with many guests at a feast. Such was the form in which Mary's love to Christ, at so much cost to herself, poured itself out.

4. **Judas . . . who should betray him**—For the reason why this is here mentioned, see on Matthew 26:6. **5. three hundred pence**—about $50.

6. **had the bag**—the purse. **bare what was put therein**—not, bare it off by theft, though that he did; but simply, had charge of its contents, was treasurer to Jesus and the Twelve. How worthy of notice is this arrangement, by which an avaricious and dishonest person was not only taken into the number of the Twelve, but entrusted with the custody of their little property! The purposes which this served are obvious enough; but it is further noticeable, that the remotest hint was never given to the eleven of His true character, nor did the disciples most favored with the intimacy of Jesus ever suspect him, till a few minutes before he voluntarily separated himself from their company—for ever!

ADAM CLARKE

F. B. MEYER:

Love's fragrant gift. Martha's service reminds us of Luke 10:41. The earlier Gospels (Matt. 26; Mark 14) do not mention Mary's name, probably because the whole family might have suffered for their intimate identification with Jesus (see v. 10). But when this Gospel was written, the beloved trio had been gathered home to God.

There was no value in the spikenard except to refresh and comfort, but this was sufficient to warrant Mary's act. We must not always be considering the utilitarian side of service. There are hours of holy ecstasy when we are lifted out of ourselves in the expression of our love to Jesus, in ways that to cold and calculating onlookers seem mere extravagance. In her absorption in him whom she loved, Mary has incited myriads to similar acts. But her love stirred up the evil in the heart of Judas, as summer's lovely sunshine extracts poison from stagnant ponds. Our Advocate will screen us from our dread accuser. He interpreted Mary's motive. She knew that her Lord would be crucified, and as she thought that there would be no opportunity for love to perform the last offices, she beforehand anointed him for the burial.

—*Bible Commentary*

5. *Three hundred pence.* Or denarii.

6. *Not that he cared for the poor.* There should be a particular emphasis laid on the word *he*, as the Evangelist studies to show the most determined detestation to his conduct. *And bare what was put therein.* Or rather, as some eminent critics contend, "and stole what was put in it." This seems the proper meaning of *ebastazen;* and in this sense it is used, chap. xx. 15: "If thou hast stolen Him away." In the same sense the word is used by Josephus, *Ant.*, b. xii, c. 5, s. 4, where, speaking of the pillage of the Temple by Antiochus, he says, "He carried off, or stole, also the vessels of the Lord." If stealing were not intended by the Evangelist, the word itself must be con-

MATTHEW HENRY

subsistence, giving the overplus, if any were, to the poor. This bag was supplied by the contributions of good people, and the Master and his disciples had all *in common*; for our sakes he *became poor*. See who was the *steward* of the little they had; it was Judas, he was purse-bearer. He was the least and lowest of all the disciples; it was not Peter nor John that was made steward. Secular employments, as they are a digression, so they are a degradation to a minister of the gospel. He was desirous of the place. He loved in his heart to be fingering money, and therefore had the moneybag committed to him. The bag he chose, and the bag he had. Strong inclinations to sin within are often justly punished with strong temptations to sin without. We have little reason to be fond of the bag, or proud of it, for at the best we are but stewards of it.

(2) Being trusted with the bag, he was *a thief*. The reigning love of money is *heart-theft* as much as anger and revenge are *heart-murder*. Those to whom the management and disposal of public money is committed have need to be governed by steady principles of justice and honesty, that no blot cleave to their hands. Judas, who had betrayed his trust, soon after betrayed his Master.

V. Christ's justification of what Mary did (*v.* 7, 8): *Let her alone*. Hereby he intimated his acceptance of her kindness. As it was a token of her goodwill, he signified himself well-pleased with it. Christ would not have those censured nor discouraged who sincerely design to please him, though in their honest endeavours there be not all the discretion that may be. Christ puts a favourable construction upon what she did, which those that condemned it were not aware of: *Against the day of my burying she has kept this*. "The day of my burying is now at hand, and she has anointed a body that is already *as good as dead*." Providence does often so open a door of opportunity to good Christians, that the expressions of their pious zeal prove to be more *seasonable*, and more *beautiful*, than any foresight of their own could make them. He gives a sufficient answer to Judas's objection, *v.* 8. It is so ordered in the kingdom of Providence that *the poor we have always with us*. It is so ordered in the kingdom of grace that the church should not always have the bodily presence of Jesus Christ: "*Me you have not always*." Opportunities are to be improved, and those opportunities first and most vigorously which are likely to be of the shortest continuance. That good duty which may be done *at any time* ought to give way to that which cannot be done but *just now*.

VI. The public notice which was taken of our Lord Jesus here at this supper in Bethany (*v.* 9): *Much people of the Jews knew that he was there*, and *they came* flocking thither. They came to see Jesus, whose name was very much magnified by the late miracle he had wrought in raising Lazarus. They came, not to hear him, but to gratify their curiosity with a sight of him. It being known where Christ was, multitudes came to him. They came to see Lazarus and Christ together, which was a very inviting sight. Some came for the confirmation of their faith in Christ. Others came only for the gratifying of their curiosity, that they might say they had seen a man who had been dead and buried, and yet lived again; so that Lazarus served for a *show*.

VII. The indignation of the chief priests at the growing interest of our Lord Jesus (*v.* 10, 11): They *consulted how they might put Lazarus also to death*, because that *by reason of him many of the Jews went away, and believed on Jesus*. Here observe,

1. How vain and unsuccessful their attempts against Christ had hitherto been. They had done all they could to alienate the people from him, and yet many of the Jews were so overcome by the convincing evidence of Christ's miracles that they *went away* from the party of the priests, *and believed* on *Jesus*; and it was by reason of Lazarus; his resurrection put life into their faith. What was impossible to him that could raise the dead?

2. How absurd and unreasonable that Lazarus must be put to death. It was a sign that they *neither feared God nor regarded man*. If they had feared God, they would not have done such an act of defiance to him. God will have Lazarus to live by a miracle, and they will have him to die by malice. Lazarus is singled out to be the object of their special hatred, because God has distinguished him by the tokens of his peculiar love. One would think that they should rather have consulted how they might have joined in friendship with Lazarus and his family, and by their mediation have reconciled themselves to this Jesus whom they had persecuted. If they had regarded man, they would not have done such an act of injustice to Lazarus, an innocent man, to whose charge they could not pretend to lay any crime.

JAMIESON, FAUSSET, BROWN

7. said Jesus, Let her alone, against the day of my burying hath she done this—not that she thought of His burial, much less reserved any of her nard to anoint her dead Lord. But as the time was so near at hand when that office would have to be performed, *and she was not to have that privilege even after the spices were brought for the purpose* (Mark 16:1), He lovingly *regards it as done now*. **8. the poor always... with you**—referring to Deuteronomy 15:11. **but me... not always**—a gentle hint of His approaching departure. He adds (Mark 14:8), "*She hath done what she could*," a noble testimony, embodying a principle of immense importance. "Verily, I say unto you, Wheresoever this Gospel shall be preached in the whole world, there shall also this, that this woman hath done, be told for a memorial of her" (Matt. 26:13; Mark 14:9). "In the act of love done to Him she had erected to herself an eternal monument, as lasting as the Gospel, the eternal word of God. From generation to generation this remarkable prophecy of the Lord has been fulfilled; and even we, in explaining this saying of the Redeemer, of necessity contribute to its accomplishment" [OLSHAUSEN]. "Who but Himself had the power to ensure to any work of man, even if resounding in his own time through the whole earth, an imperishable remembrance in the stream of history? Behold once more here, the majesty of His royal judicial supremacy in the government of the world, in this, Verily I say unto you" [STIER]. Beautiful are the lessons here: (1) *Love to Christ transfigures the humblest services*. All, indeed, who have themselves a heart value its least outgoings beyond the most costly mechanical performances; but how does it endear the Saviour to us to find Him endorsing the principle as His own standard in judging of character and deeds!

What though in poor and humble guise
Thou here didst sojourn, cottage-born,
Yet from Thy glory in the skies
Our earthly gold Thou didst not scorn.
For Love delights to bring her best,
And where Love is, that offering evermore is blest.
Love on the Saviour's dying head
Her spikenard drops unblam'd may pour,
May mount His cross, and wrap Him dead
In spices from the golden shore.

KEBLE

(2) Works of *utility* should never be set in opposition to the promptings of self-sacrificing *love*, and the sincerity of those who do so is to be suspected. Under the mask of concern for the poor at home, how many excuse themselves from all care of the perishing heathen abroad. (3) Amidst conflicting duties, that which our "hand (*presently*) findeth to do" is to be preferred, and even a less duty *only to be done now* to a greater *that can be done at any time*. (4) "If there be first a willing mind, it is accepted according to that a man hath, and not according to that he hath not" (II Cor. 8:12).—"She hath done what she could." (5) As Jesus beheld in spirit the universal diffusion of His Gospel, while His lowest depth of humiliation was only approaching, so He regards *the facts of His earthly history* as constituting *the substance of this Gospel*, and the relation of them as just the "preaching of this Gospel." Not that preachers are to confine themselves to a bare narration of these facts, but that they are to make their whole preaching turn upon them as its grand center, and derive from them its proper vitality; all that goes before this in the Bible being but the *preparation* for them, and all that follows but the *sequel*. **9-11.** Crowds of the Jerusalem Jews hastened to Bethany, not so much to see Jesus, whom they knew to be there, as to see dead Lazarus alive; and this, issuing in their accession to Christ, led to a plot against the life of Lazarus also, as the only means of arresting the triumphs of Jesus (see vs. 19)—to such a pitch had these chief priests come of diabolical determination to shut out the light from themselves, and quench it from the earth!

ADAM CLARKE

sidered as superfluous; for when we are told that he had the *bag*, we need not be informed that he had what was *in* it. But the apostle says *he was a thief*, and because he was a thief and had the common purse in his power, therefore he stole as much as he conveniently could without subjecting himself to detection. And as he saw that the death of Christ was at hand, he wished to secure a provision for himself before he left the company of the apostles. The *bag* meant originally the little box, or sheath, in which the tongues or reeds used for pipes were carried. The Greek word is used in Hebrew letters by the Talmudists to signify a "purse, scrip, chest, coffer." As our Lord and His disciples lived on charity, a bag or scrip was provided to carry those pious donations by which they were supported. And Judas was steward and treasurer to this holy company.

7. *Let her alone: against the day of my burying hath she kept this*. Several MSS. and versions read thus: "Let her alone, that she may keep it to the day of my embalming." This reading, which has the approbation of Mill, Bengel, Griesbach, Pearce, and others, intimates that only a part of the ointment was then used, and that the rest was kept till the time that the women came to embalm the body of Jesus, Luke xxiv. 1.

9. *Much people of the Jews*. John, who was a Galilean, often gives the title of *Jews* to those who were inhabitants of Jerusalem.

10. *Consulted that they might put Lazarus also to death*. As long as he lived they saw an incontestable proof of the divine power of Christ; therefore they wished to put Him to death, because many of the Jews, who came to see him through curiosity, became converts to Christ through his testimony.

MATTHEW HENRY

Verses 12-19

I. The respect that was paid to our Lord Jesus by the common people, *v.* 12, 13.

1. Who they were that paid him this respect: *much people—a great crowd* of those that came up to the feast; not the inhabitants of Jerusalem, but the country people. The nearer the temple of the Lord, the further from the Lord of the temple. They were such as *came up to the feast.* Perhaps they had been Christ's hearers in the country, and great admirers of him there, and therefore were forward to testify their respect to him at Jerusalem. Perhaps they were those more *devout Jews* that came up to the feast some time before, to purify themselves, that were more inclined to religion than their neighbours, and these were they that were so forward to honour Christ. They were not the rulers, nor the great men, that went out to meet Christ, but the commonalty. But Christ is honoured more by the multitude than by the magnificence of his followers; for he values men by their souls, not their names and titles of honour.

2. On what occasion they did it: *They heard that Jesus was coming to Jerusalem.* They had enquired for him (*ch.* xi. 55, 56): *Will he not come up to the feast?* Now when they heard he was coming, they bestirred themselves, to give him an agreeable reception.

3. In what way they expressed their respect. Such as they had they gave him; and even this despicable crowd was a faint resemblance of that glorious company which John saw *before the throne, and before the Lamb,* Rev. vii. 9, 10. Though these were not before the throne, they were before the Lamb. There it is said of that celestial choir,

(1) That they had palms in their hands, and so had these *branches of palm-trees.* The palm-tree has ever been an emblem of victory and triumph. Christ was now by his death to conquer principalities and powers. Though he was but girding on the harness, yet he could boast as though he had put it off.

(2) That they *cried with a loud voice, saying, Salvation to our God* (Rev. vii. 10); so did these here, they shouted before him, *Hosanna, blessed is the king of Israel, that comes in the name of the Lord;* and *hosanna* signifies *salvation.* [1] They acknowledge our Lord Jesus to be the king of Israel, that comes *in the name of the Lord.* They own him to be a king, which bespeaks both his dignity and honour, which we must adore; and his dominion and power, to which we must submit. A rightful king, coming in *the name of the Lord.* The promised and long-expected king, Messiah the prince, for he is *king of Israel.* [2] They heartily wish well to his kingdom, which is the meaning of hosanna. In crying hosanna they prayed for three things: That his kingdom might come in the light and knowledge of it, and in the power and efficacy of it. That it might conquer. That it might continue. Hosanna is, *Let the king live for ever.* [3] They bid him welcome in Jerusalem: "*Welcome is he that cometh; come in thou blessed of the Lord.*" Thus we must every one of us bid Christ welcome into our hearts. Faith saith, *Blessed is he that cometh.*

II. The posture Christ puts himself into for receiving the respect that was paid him (*v.* 14): *When he had found a young ass,* he *sat thereon.* It was but a poor sort of figure he made, he alone upon an ass, and a crowd of people about him shouting *Hosanna.* This was much more of state than he used to take; he used to travel on foot, but now was mounted. Yet it was much less of state than the great ones of the world usually take. His kingdom was not of this world, and therefore came not with outward pomp.

III. The fulfilling of the scripture in this: *As it is written, Fear not, daughter of Sion, v.* 15.

1. It was foretold that Zion's king should come, should come *thus, sitting on an ass's colt.* Though he comes but slowly (an ass is slow-paced), yet he comes surely, and with such expressions of condescension as greatly encourage his loyal subjects. Humble supplicants may reach to speak with him.

2. The daughter of Zion is therefore called upon to *behold her king. Fear not.* In the prophecy, Zion is told to rejoice greatly, and to shout, but here it is rendered, *Fear not.* Unbelieving fears are enemies to spiritual joys; if they be cured, if they be conquered, joy will come of course. If the case be so that we cannot reach to the exultations of joy, yet we should labour to get from under the oppressions of fear. *Rejoice greatly;* at least, *fear not.*

IV. The remark respecting the disciples (*v.* 16): *They understood not at first,* but when *Jesus was glorified* they remembered that *these things were written of him,* and that they and others had *done these things to him.*

1. See here the imperfection of the disciples; *they understood not these things at first.* They did not consider that they were performing the ceremony of

JAMIESON, FAUSSET, BROWN

12-19. CHRIST'S TRIUMPHAL ENTRY INTO JERUSALEM. (See on Matt. 21:1-9; and Luke 19:29-36. **12. On the next day**—the Lord's day, or Sunday (see on vs. 1); the tenth day of the Jewish month Nisan, on which the paschal lamb was set apart to be "kept up until the 14th day of the same month, when the whole assembly of the congregation of Israel were to kill it in the evening" (Exod. 12:3, 6). Even so, from the day of this solemn entry into Jerusalem, "Christ our Passover" was virtually set apart to be "sacrificed for us" (I Cor. 5:7).

ADAM CLARKE

13. *Took branches.* See on Matt. xxi. 1, etc., and Mark xi. 1-6, where this transaction is largely explained.

ALEXANDER MACLAREN:

The difference between John's account of the entry into Jerusalem and those of the Synoptic Gospels is very characteristic. His is much briefer, but it brings the essentials out clearly, and is particular in showing its place as a link in the chain that drew on the final catastrophe, and in noting its effect on various classes.

"The next day" (v. 12) was probably the Sunday before the crucifixion. To understand the events of that day, we must try to realize how rapidly, and, as the rulers thought, dangerously, excitement was rising among the crowds who had come up for the Passover, and who had heard of the raising of Lazarus. The Passover was always a time when national feeling was ready to blaze up, and any spark might light the fire. It looked as if Lazarus were going to be the match this time, and so, on the Saturday, the rulers had made up their minds to have him put out of the way in order to stop the current that was setting in, of acceptance of Jesus as the Messiah.

They had already made up their minds to dispose of Jesus, and now, with cynical contempt for justice, they determined to "put Lazarus also to death." So there were to be two men who were to "die for the people." Keeping all this wave of popular feeling in view, it might have been expected that Jesus would, as hitherto, have escaped into privacy, or discouraged the offered homage of a crowd whose messianic ideal was so different from His.

John is mainly concerned in bringing out two points in his version of the incident. First, he tells us what we should not have gathered from the other Evangelists, that the triumphal procession began in Jerusalem, not in Bethany. It was the direct result of the ebullition of enthusiasm occasioned by the raising of Lazarus. The course of events seems to have been that "the common people of the Jews" came streaming out to Bethany on the Sunday to gape and gaze at the risen man and Him who had raised him, that they and some of those who had been present at the raising went back to the city and carried thither the intelligence that Jesus was coming in from Bethany next day, and that then the procession to meet Him was organized.

The meaning of the popular demonstration was plain—from the palm branches, signs of victory and rejoicing, and from the chant, which is in part taken from Psalm 118. The messianic application of that quote is made unmistakable by the addition, "even the King of Israel." In the Psalm, "he that cometh in the name of Jehovah," means the worshiper drawing near to the Temple, but the added words divert the expression to Jesus, hail Him as the King, and invoke Him as "Savior." Little did that shouting crowd understand what sort of a Savior He was. Deliverance from Rome was what they where thinking of.—*Expositions of Holy Scripture*

MATTHEW HENRY

the inauguration of Zion's king. The scripture is often fulfilled by the agency of those who have not themselves an eye to the scripture in what they do. That which afterwards is clear was at first dark and doubtful. It well becomes the disciples of Christ to reflect upon the follies and weaknesses of their first beginning, that they may have compassion on the ignorant. *When I was a child, I spoke as a child.*

2. See here the improvement of the disciples in their adult state.

(1) When they understood it: *When Jesus was glorified.* Till then they did not rightly apprehend the nature of his kingdom. Till then the Spirit was not poured out, who was to lead them into all truth.

(2) How they understood it; they compared the prophecy with the event. *Then remembered they that these things were written of him.* The remembrance of what is written will enable us to understand what is done, and the observation of what is done will help us to understand what is written.

V. The reason which induced the people to pay this respect to our Lord Jesus. It was because of the illustrious miracle he had lately wrought in raising Lazarus.

1. See here what account and what assurance they had of this miracle; no doubt, the city rang of it. Those who considered it as a proof of Christ's mission, and a ground of their faith in him, traced the report to those who were eye-witnesses of it, that they might *know the certainty* of it. *The people therefore that* stood by *when he called Lazarus* out of his grave, *bore record, v.* 17. They unanimously averred the thing to be true, beyond dispute or contradiction. The truth of Christ's miracles was evidenced by incontestable proofs.

2. What influence it had upon them (*v.* 18): *For this cause the people met him.* Some, out of curiosity, were desirous to see one that had done such a wonderful work. Others, out of conscience, studied to do him honour, as the one sent of God.

VI. The indignation of the Pharisees at all this. They own that they had got no ground against him; that they *prevailed nothing.* Those who oppose Christ, will be made to perceive that they prevail nothing. God will accomplish his own purposes in spite of them, and the little efforts of their impotent malice. *You prevail nothing, you profit nothing.* There is nothing got by opposing Christ. They own that he had got ground: *The world is gone after him.* Yet here, like Caiaphas, ere they were aware, they prophesied that *the world would go after him.* 1. Thus they *express* their own vexation; their envy makes them fret. Considering how great these Pharisees were, one would think they needed not grudge Christ so inconsiderable a piece of honour as was now done him; but proud men would monopolize honour, and have none share with them. 2. Thus they excite themselves, and one another, to a more vigorous carrying on of the war against Christ. Thus the enemies of religion are made more resolute and active by being baffled; and shall its friends be disheartened with every disappointment, who know its cause is righteous and will at last be victorious?

Verses 20–26

Honour is here paid to Christ by certain Greeks that enquired for him.

I. We are told who they were that paid this honour to our Lord Jesus: *Certain Greeks among* the people who *came up to worship at the feast, v.* 20. Some think they were *Jews of the dispersion,* that were scattered among the Gentiles, and were called *Greeks.* Others think they were Gentiles, those whom they called *proselytes of the gate,* such as the eunuch and Cornelius. There were devout worshippers of the true God even among those that were strangers to the commonwealth of Israel. Though these Greeks, if uncircumcised, were not admitted to eat the passover, yet they came to *worship at the feast.* We must thankfully use the privileges we have, though there may be others from which we are shut out.

II. What was the honour they paid him: they desired to be acquainted with him, *v.* 21. Having a desire to see Christ, they were industrious in the use of proper means. They did not rest in bare wishes, but resolved to try what could be done. They made their application to Philip, one of his disciples. Some think that they had acquaintance with him formerly. It is good to know those who know the Lord. I think that they applied to him only because they saw him a close follower of Christ. Those that would see Jesus by faith now that he is in heaven must apply to his ministers, whom he has appointed for this purpose, to guide poor souls in their enquiries after him. The bringing of these Greeks to the knowledge of Christ by the means of Philip signified the agency of the apostles,

JAMIESON, FAUSSET, BROWN

when Jesus was glorified, then remembered they that these things were written of him . . .—The Spirit, descending on them from the glorified Saviour at Pentecost, opened their eyes suddenly to the true sense of the Old Testament, brought vividly to their recollection this and other Messianic predictions, and to their unspeakable astonishment showed them that they, and all the actors in these scenes, had been unconsciously fulfilling those predictions.

A. T. ROBERTSON:

19. "The Pharisees therefore said among themselves" (*hoi oun Pharisaioi eipan pros heautous*). Graphic picture of the predicament of the Pharisees standing off and watching the enthusiastic crowds sweep by. As people usually do, they blame each other for the defeat of their plots against Jesus and for his final victory, as it seemed. "Behold how ye prevail nothing" (*theoreite hoti ouk opheleite ouden*). It was a pathetic confession of failure because the rest of the plotters had bungled the whole thing. "Ye help nothing at all" by your plots and plans. "Lo, the world is gone after him" (*ide ho kosmos opiso autou apelthen*). Exclamatory use of *ide* and timeless aorist active indicative of *aperchomai.* The "world" is a bunch of fools, they feel, but see for yourselves. And the Sanhedrin had advertised to "find" Jesus! They can find him now!

—*Word Pictures in the New Testament*

20-36. **Some Greeks Desire to See Jesus—The Discourse and Scene Thereupon. 20-22. Greeks**—Not Grecian Jews, but Greek proselytes to the Jewish faith, who were wont to attend the annual festivals, particularly this primary one, the Passover.

The same came therefore to Philip . . . of Bethsaida—possibly as being from the same quarter. **saying, Sir, we would see Jesus**—certainly in a far better sense than Zaccheus (Luke 19:3). Perhaps He was then in that part of the temple court to which Gentile proselytes had no access. "These men from the *west* represent, at the end of Christ's life, what the wise men from the *east* represented at its beginning; but those come to the cross of the King, even as these to His manger" [Stier].

ADAM CLARKE

16. *Then remembered they.* After the ascension of Christ, the disciples saw the meaning of many prophecies which referred to Christ, and applied them to Him, which they had not fully comprehended before. Indeed it is only in the light of the new covenant that the old is to be fully understood.

17. *When he called.* It appears that these people who had seen Him raise Lazarus from the dead were publishing abroad the miracle, which increased the popularity of Christ and the envy of the Pharisees.

19. *Ye prevail nothing.* By either your threatenings or excommunications. *The world is gone after him.* The whole mass of the people are becoming His disciples. This is a very common form of expression among the Jews, and simply answers to the French, *tout le monde,* and to the English, "everybody"—the bulk of the people.

20. *Certain Greeks.* There are three opinions concerning these: (1) That they were proselytes of the gate or covenant, who came up to worship the true God at this feast; (2) That they were real Jews, who lived in Grecian provinces, and spoke the Greek language; (3) That they were mere Gentiles, who never knew the true God; and, hearing of the fame of the Temple or the miracles of our Lord, came to offer sacrifices to Jehovah and to worship Him according to the manner of the people of that land. Of these opinions the reader may choose, but the first seems best founded.

MATTHEW HENRY

and the use made of their ministry in the conversion of the Gentiles. Their address to Philip was in short this: *Sir, we would see Jesus.* They gave him a title of respect, because he was in relation to Christ. Their business is, they would *see Jesus*; not only see his face, that they might be able to say, when they came home, they had seen one that was so much talked of; but they would have some free conversation with him, and be taught by him. Now that they were come to worship at the feast, they would see Jesus. In our attendance upon holy ordinances, and particularly the gospel passover, the great desire of our souls should be to see Jesus. We miss of our end in coming if we do not see Jesus. The report which Philip made of this to his Master, *v.* 22. He tells Andrew. They agree that it must be made; but then he would have Andrew go along with him. Christ's ministers should be helpful to one another and concur in helping souls to Christ. It should seem that Andrew and Philip brought this message to Christ when he was teaching in public, for we read (*v.* 29) of the *people that stood by.*

III. Christ's acceptance of this honour. He foretells both the honour which he himself should have in being followed (*v.* 23, 24) and the honour which those should have that followed him, *v.* 25, 26.

1. He foresees that plentiful harvest, in the conversion of the Gentiles, of which this was as it were the first-fruits, *v.* 23. *The hour is come when the Son of man shall be glorified.* The end designed hereby, and that is the glorifying of the Redeemer: "And is it so? Do the Gentiles begin to enquire after me? Then the hour is come for the *glorifying of the Son of man.*" This was no surprise to Christ, but a paradox to those about him. The calling of the Gentiles greatly redounded to the glory of the Son of man. The multiplying of the redeemed was the magnifying of the Redeemer. There was a time, a set time, for the glorifying of the Son of man, and he speaks of the approach of it with exultation and triumph: *The hour is come.* The strange way in which this end was to be attained, and that was by the death of Christ, intimated in that similitude (*v.* 24): "*Verily, verily, I say unto you, except a corn of wheat fall into the ground* and *die,* it *abideth alone,* and you never see any more of it; but *if it die* it *bringeth forth much fruit.*" The necessity of Christ's humiliation intimated. He would never have been the living quickening head and root of the church if he had not descended from heaven to this accursed earth and ascended from earth to the accursed tree, and so accomplished our redemption. He must *pour out his soul unto death.* The advantage of Christ's humiliation illustrated. He *fell to the ground* in his incarnation; but this was not all: *he died.* He lay in the grave like seed under the clods; but as the seed comes up again green, and fresh, and flourishing, and with a great increase, so one dying Christ gathered to himself thousands of living Christians. The salvation of souls hitherto, and henceforward to the end of time, is all owing to the dying of this *corn of wheat.*

2. He promises an abundant recompence to those who should cordially embrace him, and should make it appear that they do so by their faithfulness.

(1) In suffering for him (*v.* 25): *He that loves his life shall lose it;* but he that hates *his life in this world,* shall *keep it unto life eternal.* The great design of his religion is to wean us from this world, by setting before us another world.

[1] See here the fatal consequences of an inordinate love of life; many a man hugs himself to death, and loses his life by overloving it. He that so loves his animal life shall thereby shorten his days, shall lose the life he is so fond of, and another infinitely better. He that is so much in love with the life of the body, as to deny Christ, he shall lose it, that is, lose a real happiness in the other world, while he thinks to secure an imaginary one in this. He that gives his soul, his God, his heaven, for it, buys life too dear.

[2] See also the blessed recompence of a holy contempt of life. He that so hates the life of the body as to venture it for the preserving of the life of his soul shall find both in eternal life. It is required of the disciples of Christ that they hate *their life in this world.* Our life in this world includes all the enjoyments of our present state. We must hate, that is, despise them as vain and insufficient to make us happy, and cheerfully part with them whenever they come in competition with the service of Christ. See here much of the *power of godliness*—that it conquers the strongest natural affections; and much of the *mystery of godliness*—that it is the greatest wisdom, and yet makes men hate their own lives. Those who, in love to Christ, hate their own lives in this world, shall be abundantly recompenced in the resurrection of the just. *He that hateth his life shall keep it.*

(2) In serving him (*v.* 26): *If any man* profess *to serve*

JAMIESON, FAUSSET, BROWN

Philip . . . telleth Andrew—As follow townsmen of Bethsaida (ch. 1:44), these two seem to have drawn to each other. **Andrew and Philip tell Jesus**—The minuteness of these details, while they add to the graphic force of the narrative, serves to prepare us for something important to come out of this introduction.

23-26. Jesus answered them, The hour is come that the Son of man should be glorified—i.e., They would see Jesus, would they? Yet a little moment, and they shall see Him so as now they dream not of. The middle wall of partition that keeps them out from the commonwealth of Israel is on the eve of breaking down, "and I, if I be lifted up from the earth, shall draw all men unto Me"; I see them "flying as a cloud, and as doves to their cotes"—a glorious event that will be for the Son of man, by which this is to be brought about. It is His *death* He thus sublimely and delicately alluded to. Lost in the scenes of triumph which this desire of the Greeks to see Him called up before His view, He gives no direct answer to their petition for an interview, but sees the cross which was to bring them gilded with glory. **24. Except a corn of wheat fall into the ground and die, it abideth alone; but if it die, it bringeth forth much fruit**—The *necessity* of His death is here brightly expressed, and its proper operation and fruit—*life springing forth out of death*—imaged forth by a beautiful and deeply significant law of the vegetable kingdom. For a double reason, no doubt, this was uttered—to explain what he had said of His death, as the hour of His own glorification, and to sustain His own Spirit under the agitation which was mysteriously coming over it in the view of that death.

He that loveth his life shall lose it; and he that hateth his life in this world shall keep it unto life eternal—(See on Luke 9:24). Did our Lord mean to exclude Himself from the operation of the great principle here expressed—*selfrenunciation the law of self-preservation;* and its converse, *self-preservation the law of self-destruction?* On the contrary, as He became Man to exemplify this fundamental law of the Kingdom of God in its most sublime form, so the very utterance of it on this occasion served to sustain His own Spirit in the double prospect to which He had just alluded.

ADAM CLARKE

22. *Andrew and Philip tell Jesus.* How pleasing to God is this union when the ministers of His gospel agree and unite together to bring souls to Christ!

23. *The hour is come, that the Son of man.* The time is just at hand in which the gospel shall be preached to all nations, the middle wall of partition broken down, and Jews and Gentiles united in one fold. But this could not be till after His death and resurrection, as the succeeding verse teaches.

24. *Except a corn of wheat fall into the ground and die.* Our Lord compares himself to a grain of wheat; His death, to a grain sown and decomposed in the ground; His resurrection, to the blade which springs up from the dead grain, which grain, thus dying, brings forth an abundance of fruit. I must die to be glorified; and, unless I am glorified, I cannot establish a glorious Church of Jews and Gentiles upon earth.

25. *He that loveth his life.* See on Matt. x. 39; Luke xiv. 26. I am about to give up My life for the salvation of men; but I shall speedily receive it back with everlasting honor, by My resurrection from the dead. In this I should be imitated by My disciples, who should, when called to it, lay down their lives for the truth; and if they do, they shall receive them again with everlasting honor.

MATTHEW HENRY

me, let him *follow me*; and *where I am*, there *let my servant be*; so some read it, as part of the duty. We read it as part of the promise, *there shall he be* in happiness with me. And, lest this should seem a small matter, he adds, *If any man serve me, him will my Father honour*. The Greeks desired to see Jesus (*v.* 21), but Christ lets them know that it was not enough to see him, they must *serve him*. In taking servants it is usual to fix both the work and the wages; Christ does both here.

[1] Here is the work which Christ expects from his servants. Let them attend their Master's movements: *If any man serve me, let him follow me*. Christians must follow Christ, *do the things that he says, walk as he also walked*. We must go whither he leads us, and in the way he leads us. Let them attend their Master's repose: *Where I am, there let my servant be*, to wait upon me. Christ is where his church is; and *there let his servants be*, to present themselves before him, and receive instructions from him.

[2] Here are the wages which Christ promises to his servants.

First, They shall be happy with him: *Where I am, there shall also my servant be*. Doubtless, he means being with him in paradise. Christ speaks of heaven's happiness as if he were already in it: Where *I am*; because he was sure of it, and near to it. And the same joy and glory which he thought recompence enough for all his services and sufferings are proposed to his servants as the recompence of theirs. Those that follow him in the way shall be with him in the end.

Secondly, They shall be honoured by his Father; he will make them amends for all their pains and loss, by conferring an honour upon them, far beyond what such worthless worms of the earth could expect to receive. The reward is honour, true lasting honour, the highest honour; it is the honour that comes from God. Those that wait on Christ God will put honour upon. Those that serve Christ must humble themselves, and are commonly vilified by the world, in recompence of both which they shall be exalted in due time.

What became of those Greeks we are not told, but are willing to hope that those who thus asked the way to heaven, with their faces thitherward, found it, and walked in it.

Verses 27–36

Honour is here done to Christ by his Father in a voice from heaven, which gave occasion to a further conference with the people.

I. Christ's address to his Father, upon occasion of the trouble which seized his spirit at this time: *Now is my soul troubled*, *v.* 27. A strange word to come from Christ's mouth, and at this time surprising, for it comes in the midst of divers pleasing prospects, in which, one would think, he should have said, Now is my soul *pleased*. Trouble of soul sometimes follows after great enlargements of spirit.

1. Christ's dread of his approaching sufferings: *Now is my soul troubled*. Now were the first throes of the travail of his soul. The sin of our soul was the trouble of Christ's soul. The trouble of his soul was designed to ease the trouble of our souls. Christ was *now* troubled, but it would not be so always, it would not be so long. The same is the comfort of Christians in their troubles; they are but *for a moment*, and will be turned into joy.

2. The strait he seems to be in hereupon: *And what shall I say?* Christ speaks like one at a loss, as if what he should choose he wot not. There was a struggle between the work he had taken upon him, which required sufferings, and the nature he had taken upon him, which dreaded them; between these two he here pauses with, *What shall I say?*

3. His prayer to God in this strait: *Father, save me from this hour, out of this hour*, praying, not so much that it might not come as that he might be brought through it. This was the language of innocent nature, and its feelings poured forth in prayer. Christ was voluntary in his sufferings, and yet prayed to be saved from them. Prayer against a trouble may very well consist with patience under it and submission to the will of God in it. The time of his suffering was, (1) A set time. (2) A short time. An hour is soon over, so were Christ's sufferings; he could see through them to the *joy set before him*.

4. His acquiescence in his Father's will, notwithstanding. *But for this cause came I to this hour.* Innocent nature got the first word, but divine wisdom and love got the last. Those who would proceed regularly must go upon second thoughts. With the second thought he checked himself: *For this cause came I to this hour;* he does not silence himself with this, that he could not avoid it, but satisfies himself with this, that he would not avoid it. This should reconcile us to the darkest hours of our lives.

JAMIESON, FAUSSET, BROWN

26. If any man serve me, let him follow me; and where I am, there shall also my servant be: If any man serve me, him will my Father honour—*Jesus here claims the same absolute subjection to Himself, as the law of men's exaltation to honor, as He yielded to the Father.*

ADAM CLARKE

26. *If any man serve me.* To such a person a twofold promise is given: (1) He shall be with Christ, in eternal fellowship with Him; and (2) He shall be honored by the Lord; he shall have an abundant recompense in glory.

ALEXANDER MACLAREN:

What does He mean by this commandment, "Follow me"? Of course I need not remind you that it brings all duty down to the imitation of Jesus Christ. That is a commonplace I do not need to dwell upon, nor to follow out into the many regions into which it would lead us, and where we might find fruitful subjects of contemplation; because I desire, in a sentence or two, to insist upon the special form of following which is here enjoined. It is a very grand thing to talk about the imitation of Christ, and even in its most superficial acceptation it is a good guide for all men. But no man has penetrated to the depths of that stringent and all-comprehensive commandment who has not recognized that there is one special thing in which Christ is to be our Pattern, and that is in regard to the very thing in which we think that He is most unique and inimitable. It is His Cross, and not His life; it is His death, and not His virtues, which He is here thinking about, and laying it upon all of us as the encyclopedia and sum of all morality that we should be conformed to it.

Christ's death is the pattern which is here set before us. Of course we cannot imitate that in its effects, except in a very secondary and figurative fashion. But the spirit that underlay it, as the supreme Example of self-sacrifice, is commended to us all as the royal law for our lives, and unless we are conformed thereto we have no right to call ourselves Christ's disciples. To die for the sake of higher life, to give up our own will utterly in obedience to God, and in the unselfish desire to help and bless others, that is the Alpha and the Omega of discipleship. It always has been so and always will be so. And so, dear brethren, let us lay it to our own hearts, and make very stringent inquiry into our own conduct, whether we have ever come within sight of what makes a true disciple—that we should be "conformable unto his death."—*Expositions of Holy Scripture*

JAMIESON, FAUSSET, BROWN

27, 28. Now is my soul troubled—He means at the prospect of His death, just alluded to. Strange view of the Cross this, immediately after representing it as the hour of His glory! (vs. 23.) But the two views naturally meet, and blend into one. It was the Greeks, one might say, that troubled Him. Ah! they shall see Jesus, but *to Him* it shall be a costly sight.

and what shall I say?—He is in a strait betwixt two. The death of the cross was, and could not but be, appalling to His spirit. But to shrink from absolute subjection to the Father, was worse still. In asking Himself, "What shall I say?" He seems as if thinking aloud, feeling His way between two dread alternatives, looking both of them sternly in the face, measuring, weighing them, in order that the choice actually made might be seen, *and even by himself the more vividly felt,* to be a profound, deliberate, spontaneous election. **Father, save me from this hour**—To take this as a question—"Shall I say, Father, save me . . ."—as some eminent editors and interpreters do, is unnatural and jejune. It is a real petition, like that in Gethsemane, "Let this cup pass from Me"; only whereas *there* He prefaces the prayer with an "If it be possible," *here* He follows it up with what is tantamount to that—"Nevertheless for this cause came I unto this hour." The sentiment conveyed, then, by the prayer, in both cases, is twofold: (1) that only one thing could reconcile Him to the death of the cross—its being His Father's will He should endure it—and (2) that in this view of it He yielded Himself freely to it. *What He recoils from is not subjection to His Father's will: but to show how tremendous a self-sacrifice that obedience involved,* He first asks the Father to save Him from it, and then signifies how

ADAM CLARKE

27. *Now is my soul troubled.* Our blessed Lord took upon Him our weaknesses, that He might sanctify them to us. As a man He was *troubled* at the prospect of a violent death. Nature abhors death. God has implanted that abhorrence in nature, that it might become a principle of self-preservation; and it is to this that we owe all that prudence and caution by which we avoid danger. When we see Jesus working miracles which demonstrate His omnipotence, we should be led to conclude that He was not man were it not for such passages as these. The reader must ever remember that it was essentially necessary that He should be man, for without being such He could not have died for the sin of the world.

And what shall I say? Father, save me from this hour. Which may be paraphrased thus: "And why should I say, Father, save Me from this hour, when for this cause I am come to this hour?" The common version makes our blessed Lord contradict himself here, by not attending to the proper punctuation of the passage, and by translating the particle *ti* as *what,* instead of *why* or *how.*

MATTHEW HENRY

5. His regard to his Father's honour herein. *Father, glorify thy name*, to the same purport with *Father, thy will be done*; for God's will is for his own glory. This expresses more than barely a submission to the will of God; it is a consecration of his sufferings to the glory of God. It was a mediatorial word, and was spoken by him as our surety, who had undertaken to satisfy divine justice for our sin. Our Lord Jesus interposed, undertook to satisfy God's injured honour, and he did it by his humiliation. Now here he makes a tender of this satisfaction as an equivalent: "*Father, glorify thy name*; let the debt be levied upon me." Thus he restored that which he took not away.

II. The Father's answer to this address. 1. How this answer was given. By a voice from heaven. 2. What the answer was. It was an express return to that petition, *Father, glorify thy name: I have glorified it* already, and *I will glorify it yet again*. (1) The name of God had been glorified in the life of Christ, in his doctrine and miracles, and all the examples he gave of holiness and goodness. (2) It should be further glorified in the death and sufferings of Christ. His wisdom and power, his justice and holiness, his truth and goodness, were greatly glorified. God accepted the satisfaction, and declared himself well pleased. What God has done for the glorifying of his own name is an encouragement to us to expect what he will yet further do.

III. The opinion of the standers-by concerning this voice, *v.* 29. Some of them said that *it thundered*; others said that certainly *an angel spoke to him*. Now this shows, 1. That it was a real thing. 2. That they were loth to admit so plain a proof of Christ's divine mission. They would rather say that it was this, or that, or any thing, than that God spoke to him in answer to his prayer.

IV. The account which our Saviour himself gives of this voice.

1. Why it was sent (*v.* 30): "It came *not because of me, but for your sakes*, that all you who heard it may *believe that the Father hath sent me*." What is said from heaven concerning our Lord Jesus, is said for our sakes, that we may be brought to rest upon him. "That you my disciples, who are to follow me in sufferings, may therein be comforted with the same comforts that carry me on."

2. What was the meaning of it. Two things God intended when he said that he would *glorify his own name*:—

(1) That by the death of Christ Satan should be conquered (*v.* 31): *Now is the judgment*. He speaks with a divine exultation and triumph. "Now the year of my redeemed is come: *now, now*, that great work is to be done which has been so long thought of in the divine counsels." The matter of the triumph is, [1] That *now is the judgment of the world;* take it as a medical term: "Now is the *crisis* of this world." The sick and diseased world is now upon the turning point; this is the critical day upon which the trembling scale will turn for life or death, to all mankind. Or, rather, it is a law term, "Now, judgment is entered." The death of Christ was the *judgment of this world. First*, It is a judgment of discovery and distinction. Now is the trial of this world, for men shall have their character according as the cross of Christ is to them. By this men are judged, what they think of the death of Christ. *Secondly*, It is a judgment of favour and absolution. Christ upon the cross interposed between a righteous God and a guilty world. It was as it were the judgment of this world, for an everlasting righteousness was thereby brought in, not for Jews only, but the whole world. *Thirdly*, It is a judgment of condemnation given against the powers of darkness; see *ch.* xvi. 11. Satan's dominion is declared to be a usurpation. The judgment of this world is, that it belongs to Christ, and not to Satan. That *now is the prince of this world cast out*. It is the devil that is here called the *prince of this world*, because he rules over the men of the world by the things of the world. He is said to be *cast out*, to be *now* cast out. Christ reconciling the world to God by the merit of his death, broke the power of death, and cast out Satan as a destroyer; Christ, reducing the world to God by the doctrine of his cross, broke the power of sin, and cast out Satan as a deceiver. With what assurance Christ here speaks of the victory over Satan; it is as good as done, and even when he yields to death he triumphs over it.

(2) That by the death of Christ souls should be converted, and this would be the casting out of Satan (*v.* 32): *If I be lifted up from the earth, I will draw all men unto me*. Here observe two things:—

[1] The great design of our Lord Jesus, which was to *draw all men to him*, not the Jews only, but the Gentiles also. Observe here how Christ himself is all in all in the conversion of a soul. It is Christ that draws. He does not drive by force, but draws as the loadstone; the soul is *made willing*. It is to Christ

JAMIESON, FAUSSET, BROWN

perfectly He knows that He is there for the very purpose of enduring it. Only by letting these mysterious words speak their full meaning do they become intelligible and consistent. As for those **who see** ***no bitter elements in the death of Christ***— nothing beyond mere dying—what can they make of such a scene? and when they place it over against the feelings with which thousands of His adoring followers have welcomed death for His sake, how can they hold Him up to the admiration of men?

28. Father, glorify thy name—by a present testimony. **I have both glorified it**—referring specially to the voice from heaven at His *baptism*, and again at His *transfiguration*. **and will glorify it again**—i.e., in the yet future scenes of His still deeper necessity; although this promise was a present and sublime testimony, which would irradiate the clouded spirit of the Son of man.

29-33. The people therefore that stood by, said, It thundered; others, An angel spake to him—some hearing only a sound, others an articulate, but to them unintelligible voice.

30. Jesus . . . said, This voice came not because of me, but for your sakes—i.e., probably, to correct the unfavorable impressions which His momentary agitation and mysterious prayer for deliverance may have produced on the bystanders.

31. Now is the judgment of this world—the world that "crucified the Lord of glory" (I Cor. 2:8), considered as a vast and complicated kingdom of Satan, breathing his spirit, doing his work, and involved in his doom, which Christ's death by its hands irrevocably sealed.

now shall the prince of this world be cast out— How differently is that fast-approaching "hour" regarded in the kingdoms of darkness and of light! "The hour of relief; from the dread Troubler of our peace—how near it is! Yet a little moment, and the day is ours!" So it was calculated and felt in the one region. "Now shall the prince of this world be cast out," is a somewhat different view of the same event. We know who was right. Though yet under a veil, He sees the triumphs of the Cross in unclouded and transporting light.

32. And I, if I be lifted up from the earth, will draw all men unto me—The "I" here is emphatic—I, taking the place of the world's ejected prince. "If lifted up," means not only *after that I have been lifted up*, but, *through the virtue of that uplifting*. And truly, the death of the Cross, in all its significance, revealed in the light, and borne in upon the heart, by the power of the Holy Ghost, possesses an at-

ADAM CLARKE

28. *Father, glorify thy name*. By the *name* of God is to be understood himself, in all His attributes: His wisdom, truth, mercy, justice, holiness, which were all more abundantly glorified by Christ's death and resurrection (i.e., shown forth in their own excellence) than they had ever been before. Christ teaches here a lesson of submission to the divine will.

29. *The people . . . said that it thundered: others said, An angel spake to him*. Bishop Pearce says, Probably there was thunder as well as a voice, as in Exod. xix. 16-17, and some persons, who were at a small distance, might hear the thunder without hearing the voice, while others heard the voice too; and these last said, "An angel hath spoken to Him."

30. *This voice came not because of me, but for your sakes*. Probably meaning those Greeks who had been brought to Him by Philip and Andrew. The Jews had frequent opportunities of seeing His miracles and of being convinced that He was the Messiah; but these Greeks, who were to be a firstfruits of the Gentiles, had never any such opportunity. For their sakes, therefore, to confirm them in the faith, this miraculous voice appears to have come from heaven.

31. *Now is the judgment of this world*. The judgment spoken of in this place is applied by some to the punishment which was about to fall on the Jewish people for rejecting Christ.

And the ruler or *prince of this world* is understood to be Satan, who had blinded the eyes of the Jews and hardened their hearts, that they might not believe on the Son of God. But his kingdom, not only among the Jews, but in all the world, was about to be destroyed by the abolition of idolatry and the vocation of the Gentiles.

32. *I . . . will draw all men unto me*. After I shall have died and risen again, by the preaching of My Word and the influence of My Spirit I shall attract and illuminate both Jews and Gentiles. It was one of the peculiar characteristics of the Messiah that unto Him should the "gathering of the people be," Gen. xlix. 10. And probably our Lord refers to the prophecy, Isa

MATTHEW HENRY

that we are drawn. He that was shy and distrustful of him is brought to love him and trust in him—drawn up to his terms, into his arms.

[2] The strange method he took to accomplish his design by *being lifted up from the earth. This he spoke signifying by what death he should die*, the death of the cross. He that was crucified was first nailed to the cross, and then lifted up upon it. The word here used signifies an honourable advancement: *If I be exalted;* he reckoned his sufferings his honour. Now Christ's drawing all men to him followed his being *lifted up from the earth.* It followed after it in time. The great increase of the church was after the death of Christ. It followed upon it as a blessed consequence of it. The cross of Christ, though to some a *stumbling-stone*, is to others a *loadstone.* Some make it an allusion to the lifting up of the brazen serpent in the wilderness, which drew all those to it who were stung with fiery serpents. O what flocking was there to it! So there was to Christ, when salvation through him was preached to all nations; see *ch.* iii. 14, 15. Perhaps it has some reference to the posture in which Christ was crucified, with his arms stretched out, to invite all to him, and embrace all that come.

V. The people's exception against what he said, *v.* 34. Though they had heard the voice from heaven, they object, and pick quarrels with him. Christ had called himself the *Son of man* (*v.* 23), which they knew to be one of the titles of the Messiah. He had also said that the *Son of man must be lifted up*, which they understood of his dying.

1. They alleged those scriptures of the Old Testament which speak of the perpetuity of the Messiah, from all which they inferred that the Messiah should not die. Their perverseness in opposing this to what Jesus had said will appear if we consider: That, when they vouched the scripture to prove that the Messiah *abideth for ever*, they took no notice of those texts which speak of the Messiah's death and sufferings. Had they never heard out of the law that he should *pour out his soul unto death* (Isa. liii. 12), and particularly that his *hands and feet* should be pierced? Why then do they make so strange of the *lifting up of the Son of man?* That, when they opposed what Christ said concerning the sufferings of the Son of man, they took no notice of what he had said concerning his glory and exaltation. In the doctrine of Christ there are paradoxes, which to men of corrupt minds are stones of stumbling.

2. They asked hereupon, *Who is this Son of man?* "Thou sayest, *The Son of man must die*; we have proved the Messiah must not, and where is then thy Messiahship?" They would rather have no Christ than a suffering one.

VI. What Christ said to this exception. They might, if they pleased, answer it themselves: man dies, and yet is immortal, and abideth for ever, so the *Son of man.* He gives them a serious caution to take heed of trifling away the day of their opportunities (*v.* 35, 36): "*Yet a little while is the light with you;* therefore *walk while you have the light.*"

1. In general, we may observe here: The concern Christ has for the souls of men, and his desire of their welfare. With what tenderness does he here admonish those to look well to themselves who were contriving all against him! The method he takes with these objectors, *with meekness instructing those that opposed themselves*, 2 Tim. ii. 25.

2. Particularly we have here,

(1) The advantage they enjoyed in having Christ and his gospel among them, with the shortness and uncertainty of their enjoyment of it: *Yet a little while is the light with you.* Christ is this light. His dying upon the cross was as consistent with his *abiding for ever* as the setting of the sun every night is with his perpetuity. The Jews at this time had the *light with them*; they had Christ's bodily presence. It was to be but a little while with them; Christ would shortly leave them. It is good for us all to consider what a little while we are to have the light with us. Time is short, and perhaps opportunity not so long.

(2) The warning given them to make the best of this privilege while they enjoyed it: *Walk while you have the light;* as travellers who make the best of their way forward, that they may not be benighted in their journey. It is our business to walk, to press forward towards heaven. The best time of walking is while we have the light. The day is the proper season for work, as the night is for rest. We are highly concerned thus to improve our opportunities, for fear lest our day be finished before we have finished our day's work and our day's journey: "*Lest darkness come upon you.*"

(3) The sad condition of those who have sinned away the gospel. *They walk in darkness*, and know neither *where* they go, nor *whither* they go. Set aside the instructions of the Christian doctrine, and we

JAMIESON, FAUSSET, BROWN

traction over the wide world—to civilized and savage, learned and illiterate, alike—which breaks down all opposition, assimilates all to itself, and forms out of the most heterogeneous and discordant materials a kingdom of surpassing glory, whose uniting principle is adoring subjection "to Him that loved them." "Will draw all men 'UNTO ME,'" says He. What lips could venture to utter such a word but His, which "dropt as an honeycomb," whose manner of speaking was evermore in the same spirit of conscious equality with the Father? **33. This he said, signifying what death he should die**—i.e., "by being lifted up from the earth" on "the accursed tree" (ch. 3:14; 8:28).

34. We have heard out of the law—the scriptures of the Old Testament (referring to such places as Ps. 89:28, 29; 110:4; Dan. 2:44; 7:13, 14).

that Christ—the Christ "endureth for ever." **and how sayest thou, The Son of Man must be lifted up . . .**—How can that consist with this "uplifting?" They saw very well both that He was holding Himself up as *the Christ* and *a Christ to die a violent death;* and as that ran counter to all their ideas of the Messianic prophecies, they were glad to get this seeming advantage to justify their unyielding attitude.

35, 36. Yet a little while is the light with you. Walk while ye have the light, . . .—Instead of answering their question, He warns them, with mingled majesty and tenderness, against trifling with their last brief opportunity, and entreats them to let in the Light while they have it in the midst of them, that they themselves might be "light in the Lord." In this case, all the clouds which hung around His Person and Mission would speedily be dispelled, while if they continued to hate the light, bootless were all His answers to their merely speculative or captious questions. (See on Luke 13:23.)

ADAM CLARKE

xi. 10, which peculiarly belonged to the Gentiles: "There shall be a root of Jesse, which shall stand for an ensign of the people; to it shall the Gentiles seek: and his rest shall be glorious." There is an allusion here to the ensigns or colors of commanders of regiments, elevated on high places on long poles, that the people might see where the pavilion of their general was and so flock to his standard.

34. *We have heard out of the law.* That is, out of the sacred writings. The words here are quoted from Ps. cx. 4; but the Jews called every part of the sacred writings by the name *The Law*, in opposition to the words or sayings of the scribes. *That Christ abideth for ever.* There was no part of the law nor of the Scripture that said the Messiah should not die; but there are several passages that say as expressly as they can that Christ must die, and die for the sin of the world, too. See especially Isa. liii. 1, etc.; Dan. ix. 24, 27. But as there were several passages that spoke of the perpetuity of His reign, as Isa. ix. 7; Ezek. xxxvii. 25; Dan. vii. 14, they probably confounded the one with the other, and thus drew the conclusion, The Messiah cannot die; for the Scripture hath said, His throne, kingdom, and reign shall be eternal. The prophets, as well as the Evangelists and apostles, speak sometimes of the *divine*, sometimes of the *human* nature of Christ. When they speak of the former, they show forth its glory, excellence, omnipotence, omniscience, and eternity; when they speak of the latter, they show forth its humiliations, afflictions, sufferings, and death. And those who do not make the proper distinction between the two natures of Christ, the human and the divine, will ever make blunders as well as the Jews.

35. *Yet a little while is the light with you.* In answer to their objection, our Lord compares himself to a light which was about to disappear for a short time and afterwards to shine forth with more abundant luster; but not to their comfort, if they continued to reject its present beamings. He exhorts them to follow this light while it is among them. The Christ shall abide forever, it is true; but He will not always be visible. When He shall depart from you, you shall be left in the thickest darkness, in impenitence and hardness of heart. Then shall you wish to see one of the days of the Son of Man, and shall not see it, Luke xvii. 22. Then shall ye seek Me, but shall not find Me, John

MATTHEW HENRY

know little of the difference between good and evil. He is going to destruction, and knows not his danger, for he is either sleeping or dancing at the pit's brink.

(4) The great duty and interest of every one of us inferred from all this (*v.* 36): *While you have light, believe in the light.* This is an admonition to them not to out-stand their market, but to accept the offer when it was made to them: the same Christ saith to all who enjoy the gospel. It is the duty of every one of us *to believe in the gospel light*, to subscribe to the truths it discovers, for it is a light to our eyes, and to follow its guidance, for it is a light to our feet. We are concerned to do this while we have the light. Those that have God for their Father are children of light, for God is light.

VII. Christ's retiring from them, hereupon: *These things spoke Jesus and departed, and did hide himself from them.* 1. For their conviction and awakening. If they will not regard what he hath said, he will have nothing more to say to them. Christ justly removes the means of grace from those that quarrel with him. 2. For his own preservation. He hid himself from their rage and fury. What he said irritated and exasperated them, and they were made worse by that which should have made them better.

Verses 37–41

We have here the honour done to our Lord Jesus by the Old Testament prophets, who foretold and lamented the infidelity of the many that believed not on him. Two things are here said concerning this untractable people, and both were forefold by the evangelical prophet Isaiah, that they *did not* believe, and that they *could not* believe.

I. They did not believe (*v.* 37): *Though he had done so many miracles before them.*

1. The abundance of the means of conviction. He *did miracles, so many miracles;* both so many and so great. Two things concerning them he here insists upon:—The number of them; they were *many*, and every new miracle confirmed the reality of all that went before. Being all *miracles of mercy*, the more there were the more good was done. The notoriety of them. He wrought these miracles *before them*, not in a corner, but before many witnesses.

2. The inefficacy of these means: *Yet they believed not on him.* These *saw*, and yet *believed not*.

3. The fulfilling of the scripture in this (*v.* 38): *That the saying of Esaias might be fulfilled.* The more improbable any event is, the more does a divine foresight appear in the prediction of it. One could not have imagined that the kingdom of the Messiah, supported with such pregnant proofs, should have met with so much opposition among the Jews, and therefore their unbelief is called a *marvellous work, and a wonder*, Isa. xxix. 14. Christ himself *marvelled at it*, but it was what Isaiah foretold (Isa. liii. 1). The gospel is here called *their report*: *Who has believed* our *hearing*, which we have heard from God, and which you have heard from us. Many hear it, but few heed it and embrace it: *Who hath believed it?* Here and there one, but none to speak of. It is spoken of as a thing to be greatly lamented that so few believe the report of the gospel. The reason why men believe not the report of the gospel is because *the arm of the Lord* is not *revealed* to them. They saw Christ's miracles, but did not see the *arm of the Lord revealed in them.*

II. They could not believe, *because Esaias said, He hath blinded their eyes.* This is a hard saying, who can explain it? God damns none by mere sovereignty; yet it is said, *They could not believe.*

1. They *could not* believe, that is, they *would not*; they were obstinately resolved in their infidelity. This is a *moral* impotency, like that of one that is accustomed to do evil, Jer. xiii. 23.

2. They could not because Esaias had said, *He hath blinded their eyes.* It is certain that God is not the author of sin, and yet,

(1) There is a righteous hand of God sometimes to be acknowledged in the blindness of those who persist in impenitency and unbelief, by which they are justly punished for their former resistance of the divine light. If God withhold abused grace, and give men over to indulged lusts, then he *blinds their eyes*, and *hardens their hearts*, and these are spiritual judgments. Observe the method of conversion implied here. Sinners are brought to *see with their eyes*, to discern the reality of divine things. *To understand with their heart*, not only to assent and approve, but to consent and accept. To be *converted*, and effectually turned from sin to Christ. Then God will *heal* them; will *pardon* their sins, and mortify their corruptions, which are as lurking diseases.

(2) Judicial blindness and hardness are in the word of God threatened against those who wilfully persist in wickedness. Known unto God are all his works, and all ours too. Christ knew before who would

JAMIESON, FAUSSET, BROWN

36. These things spake Jesus, and departed, and did hide himself from them—He who spake as never man spake, and immediately after words fraught with unspeakable dignity and love, had to "hide Himself" from His auditors! What then must *they* have been? He retired, probably to Bethany. (The parallels are: Matt. 21:17; Luke 21:37.)

37-41. It is the manner of this Evangelist alone to record his own reflections on the scenes he describes; but here, having arrived at what was virtually the close of our Lord's public ministry, he casts an affecting glance over the fruitlessness of His whole ministry on the bulk of the now doomed people. **37. though he had done so many miracles**—The word used suggests their *nature* as well as *number*.

38. That the saying of Esaias . . . might be fulfilled. This unbelief did not at all set aside the purposes of God, but, on the contrary, fulfilled them.

39-40. Therefore they could not believe, because Esaias said again, He hath blinded their eyes, that they should not see . . . That this expresses *a positive divine act*, by which those who wilfully close their eyes and harden their hearts against the truth are judicially *shut up* in their unbelief and impenitence, is admitted by all candid critics [as OLSHAUSEN], though many of them think it necessary to contend that this is in no way inconsistent with the liberty of the human will, which of course it is not.

ADAM CLARKE

vii. 34. For the kingdom of God shall be taken from you, and given to the Gentiles, Matt. xxi. 43. If you do not believe in Me now, you shall then wish you had done it, when wishing shall be forever fruitless. Instead of *with you*, "among you" is the reading of some MSS.

36. *Children of light.* Let the light, the truth of Christ, so dwell in and work by you that you may be all light in the Lord; that as truly as a child is the produce of his own parent and partakes of his nature, so you may be children of the light, having nothing in you but truth and righteousness. *Did hide himself from them.* Either by rendering himself invisible or by suddenly mingling with the crowd, so that they could not perceive Him. See chap. viii. 59. Probably it means no more than that He withdrew from them and went to Bethany, as was His custom, a little before His crucifixion; and concealed himself there during the night, and taught publicly every day in the Temple. It was in the night season that they endeavored to seize upon Him, in the absence of the multitude.

37. *Yet they believed not on him.* Though the miracles were wrought for this very purpose, that they might believe in Christ, and escape the coming wrath, and every evidence was given that Jesus was the Messiah, yet they did not believe; but they were blinded by their passions, and obstinately hardened their hearts against the truth.

38. *That the saying of Esaias.* Or, "Thus the word of Isaiah was fulfilled." *Our report.* The testimony of the prophets concerning the person, office, sufferings, death, and sacrifice of the Messiah. See Isa. liii. 1, etc. *The arm of the Lord.* The power, strength, and miracles of Christ.

39. *Therefore they could not believe.* Why? Because they did not believe the report of the prophets concerning Christ; therefore they credited not the miracles which He wrought as a proof that He was the Person foretold by the prophets, and promised to their fathers. The prophecy of Isaiah was neither the cause nor the motive of their unbelief; it was a simple prediction, which imposed no necessity on them to resist the offers of mercy. Thus then saith Augustine: "If I be asked why they could not believe? I immediately answer, Because they would not. And God, having foreseen their bad will, foretold it by the prophet."

40. *And I should heal them.* This verse is taken from Isa. vi. 9, and perhaps refers more to the judgments that should fall upon them as a nation, which God was determined should not be averted, than it does to their eternal state. To suppose that the text meant that God was unwilling that they should turn unto Him, lest He should be obliged to save them, is an insupportable blasphemy.

MATTHEW HENRY

betray him.

(3) What God has foretold will certainly come to pass, and so it might be said that *therefore* they *could not believe*. Such is the knowledge of God that he cannot be deceived in what he foresees, and such his truth that he cannot deceive in what he foretells. Yet be it observed that the prophecy did not name particular persons. It pointed at the body of the Jewish nation; yet still reserving a remnant, which reserve was sufficient to keep a door of hope open to particular persons; for each one might say, Why may not I be of that remnant?

Lastly, The evangelist, having quoted the prophecy, shows (*v.* 41) that its principal reference was to the days of the Messiah: *These things said Esaias when he saw his glory, and spoke of him.* We read in the prophecy that this was said to Esaias, Isa. vi. 8, 9. But here we are told that it was said *by him* to the purpose. For nothing was said by him as a prophet which was not first said to him; nor was anything said to him which was not afterwards said by him to those to whom he was sent. The vision which the prophet there had of the *glory of God* is here said to be his *seeing the glory* of Jesus Christ; He *saw his glory*. It is said that the prophet there *spoke of him*. It might be objected against his doctrine, If it was from heaven, why did not the Jews believe it? It was not for want of evidence, but because their *ears were heavy*. It was spoken of Christ, that he should be glorified in the ruin of an unbelieving multitude, as well as in the salvation of a distinguished remnant.

Verses 42–43

Some honour was done to Christ by these rulers: for they *believed on him*; but they did not do him honour enough, for they had not courage to own their faith in him. Many professed more kindness for Christ than really they had; these had more kindness for him than they were willing to profess.

I. See the power of the word in the convictions that many of them were under. They *believed on him* as Nicodemus, received him as a teacher come from God. Many cannot but approve of that in their hearts which yet outwardly they are shy of. It may be, there are more good people than we think there are. Some are really better than they seem to be. Their faults are known, but their repentance is not; a man's goodness may be concealed by a *culpable* yet pardonable weakness, which he himself truly repents of. Nor have all who are good the same faculty of appearing to be so.

II. See the power of the world in the smothering of these convictions. They believed in Christ, but because of the Pharisees they durst not confess him. Wherein they failed and were defective: They did not *confess* Christ. There is cause to question the sincerity of that faith which is either afraid or ashamed to show itself. What they feared: being *put out of the synagogue*, which they thought would be a disgrace and damage to them. What was at the bottom of this fear: *They loved the praise of men*, chose it as a more valuable good than the *praise of God*. They set these two in the scale one against the other. 1. They set the praise of men in one scale, and considered how good it was to give praise to men and receive praise from men. They would not confess Christ, lest they should thereby derogate from the reputation of the Pharisees, and forfeit their own. Besides, the followers of Christ were put into an *ill name*, and were looked upon with contempt, which those who had been used to honour could not bear. Each one thought that if he should declare himself in favour of Christ he should stand alone, whereas, if anyone had had resolution to *break the ice*, he would have had more *seconds* than he thought of. 2. They put the praise of God in the other scale. They were sensible that by confessing Christ they should both give praise to God, and have praise from God; but, 3. They gave the preference to the praise of men, and this turned the scale. Many come short of the glory of God by having a regard to the applause of men. Love of the praise of men, as a by-end in that which is good, will make a man a hypocrite when religion is in fashion. Love of the praise of men, as a base principle in that which is evil, will make a man an apostate when religion is in disgrace.

Verses 44–50

We have here the honour Christ not assumed, but asserted, to himself, in the account he gave of his mission. As this evangelist records it, it was his last public discourse; all that follows was private with his disciples. He *cried and said.* The raising of his voice and crying intimate, 1. His boldness in speaking. Though they had not courage openly to profess faith in his doctrine, he had courage openly to publish it; if they were ashamed of it, he was not. 2. His earnestness in speaking. He cried as one that was importu-

JAMIESON, FAUSSET, BROWN

41. These things said Esaias, when he saw his glory, and spake of him—a key of immense importance to the opening of Isaiah's vision (Isa. 6), and all similar Old Testament representations. "THE SON is the King Jehovah who rules in the Old Testament and appears to the elect, as in the New Testament. THE SPIRIT, the invisible Minister of the Son, is the Director of the Church and the Revealer in the sanctuary of the heart" [OLSHAUSEN].

42, 43. among the chief rulers also—rather, even of the rulers; such as Nicodemus and Joseph. **because of the Pharisees**—i.e., the *leaders* of the sects; for they were of it themselves. **put out of the synagogue**—See on ch. 9:22, 34.

43. they loved the praise of men more than the praise of God—"a severe remark, considering that several at least of these persons afterwards boldly confessed Christ. It indicates the displeasure with which God regarded their conduct at this time, and with which He continues to regard similar conduct" [WEBSTER and WILKINSON].

44-50. Jesus cried—in a loud tone, and with peculiar solemnity. (Cf. ch. 7:37.)

ADAM CLARKE

41. *When he saw his glory.* Isa. vi. 1, etc. "I saw also the Lord [Jehovah] sitting upon a throne, high and lifted up, and his train filled the temple. Above it stood the seraphims . . . And one cried unto another, and said, Holy, holy, holy, is the Lord of hosts: the whole earth is full of his glory."

42. *Among the chief rulers also many believed on him.* We know the names of only two of them, Nicodemus and Joseph of Arimathaea.

But . . . they did not confess him. Or "it." They were as yet weak in the faith, and could not bear the reproach of the cross of Christ. Besides, the principal rulers had determined to excommunicate every person who acknowledged Christ for the Messiah; see chap. ix. 22.

43. *They loved the praise of men.* The "glory" or honor that cometh from men.

44. *Jesus cried and said.* This is our Lord's concluding discourse to this wicked people. Probably this and the following verses should be understood as a part of the discourse which was left off at the thirty-sixth verse. *Jesus cried*—He spoke these words aloud, and showed His earnest desire for their salvation.

MATTHEW HENRY

nate, and in good earnest in what he said. 3. It denotes his desire that all might take notice of it. This being the last time of the publication of his gospel by himself in person, he makes proclamation. Now what is this closing summary of all Christ's discourses? It is much like that of Moses (Deut. xxx. 15): *See, I have set before you life and death.* So Christ here takes leave of the temple, with a solemn declaration of three things:—

I. The privileges and dignities of those that believe.

1. By believing in Christ we are brought into an *honourable acquaintance with God* (*v.* 44, 45): *He that believes on me, believes on him that sent me.* He does not believe in a mere man, but he believes in one that is the Son of God. His faith does not terminate in Christ, but through him it is carried out to the Father, to whom we come by Christ as our way. This is illustrated, *v.* 45. He that *sees me sees him that sent me;* in getting an acquaintance with Christ, we come to the knowledge of God. God makes himself known in the face of Christ (2 Cor. iv. 6). All that have a believing sight of Christ are led by him to the knowledge of God. God is pleased to deal with fallen man by proxy.

2. We are hereby brought into a comfortable enjoyment of ourselves (*v.* 46): *I am come a light into the world, that whoever believes in me should not abide in darkness.* (1) The character of Christ: *I am come a light into the world,* to be a light to it. (2) The comfort of Christians: They *do not abide in darkness.* They do not continue in that dark condition in which they were by nature; they are *light in the Lord.* Light is sown for them. They are delivered from that darkness which *abideth for ever.*

II. The peril and danger of those that believe not, (*v.* 47, 48): "*If any man hear my words, and believe not, I judge him not; though I judge him not, there is one that judgeth him.*"

1. Who they are whose unbelief is here condemned: those who *hear Christ's words* and yet *believe them not.* Those shall not be condemned for their infidelity that never had, nor could have, the gospel; every man shall be judged according to the dispensation of light he was under.

2. What is their unbelief: not receiving Christ's word; it is interpreted (*v.* 48) a *rejecting* of Christ. Where the banner of the gospel is displayed, no neutrality is admitted.

3. The wonderful patience and forbearance of our Lord Jesus: *I judge him not.* He had work of another nature to do first, and that was to *save the world.* To offer salvation to all the world, and thus far to save them that it is their own fault if they be not saved.

4. The certain and unavoidable judgment of unbelievers at the great day, the day of the revelation of the righteous judgment of God. There is *one that judgeth them.* Nothing is more dreadful than abused patience, and grace trampled on. Their final judgment is reserved to the *last day.* The word of Christ will judge them then: *The words that I have spoken, the same shall judge* the unbeliever *in the last day.* Christ's words will judge unbelievers. As the evidence of their crime, they will convict them. As the rule of their doom, they will condemn them.

III. A solemn declaration of the authority Christ had to demand our faith, *v.* 49, 50.

1. The commission which our Lord Jesus received from the Father (*v.* 49): *I have not spoken of myself; but the Father gave me a commandment what I should say.* This is the same with what he said *ch.* vii. 16. *My doctrine is, Not mine,* for *I have not spoken of myself.* It was his that sent him. God the Father gave him his commission. His instructions are called a *commandment.* Our Lord Jesus learned obedience himself, before he taught it to us, though he was a Son. *The Lord God commanded* the first Adam, and he by his disobedience ruined us; he commanded the second Adam, and he by his obedience saved us.

2. The scope of this commission: *I know that his commandment is life everlasting, v.* 50. The commission given to Christ had a reference to the everlasting state of the children of men, and was in order to their everlasting life and happiness in that state. The command given him was life everlasting. This Christ says he knew: "I know it is so." Those who disobey Christ despise everlasting life, and renounce it.

3. Christ's exact observance of the commission and instructions given him: *Whatsoever I speak,* it is *as the Father said unto me.* As the faithful witness delivers souls, so did he, and spoke the truth, the whole truth, and nothing but the truth. This is a great encouragement to faith; the sayings of Christ, rightly understood, are what we may venture our souls upon. It is a great example of obedience. Christ said as he was bidden. This is the honour he values himself upon, that what the Father had said to him that he spoke. By an unfeigned belief of every word of Christ,

JAMIESON, FAUSSET, BROWN

and said, He that believeth . . .—This seems to be a supplementary record of some weighty proclamations, for which there had been found no natural place before, and introduced here as a sort of *summary and winding up* of His whole testimony.

G. CAMPBELL MORGAN:

"I am come a light into the world, that whosoever believeth on me may not abide in the darkness. And if any man hear my sayings, and keep them not, I judge him not; for I came not to judge the world, but to save the world. He that rejecteth me and receiveth not my sayings, hath one that judgeth him; the word that I spake, the same shall judge him in the last day." We must not disassociate this from what He had already said. Nevertheless this is personal: I am come a light into the world. I have brought into the world that which it had lost, the light of life that comes when God is there, and is recognized. That is the light. I am come a light into the world; and if any man hear My sayings, *rhemata,* not the word, but the sayings, the individual sayings; and keep them not, I do not judge; I did not come to judge. I came to save. But that man is judged. And how is he judged? By the very words that having heard, he refuses to obey. They are the words that judge him in the last day.

The last movement was a return to the first. He goes back to emphasize His relationship with God. "I spake not from myself; but the Father which sent me, he hath given me a commandment, what I should say, and what I should speak. And I know that his commandment is life eternal; the things therefore which I speak, even as the Father hath said unto me, so I speak."

What self-emptying all through. And yet what daring. He had been speaking. Men had heard His sayings. They were not His. They are the sayings of God. They are the words of God. Who else ever made that claim. For nineteen hundred years the sacramental host has grown and multiplied of those who have found it to be true that in the words of Jesus, they have heard the voice of God.

Thus the account of the public ministry of Jesus ends. Fourteen signs have been grouped, eight in the realm of works, six in the realm of words; and as John distinctly says, "many other signs." We have no complete list either of His words or His works; but we have illustrations of them in this grouping of John. So many signs, yet they believed not. If we take this Gospel of John, and also Matthew, Mark, and Luke, and end there, with their account of the saying and doing of Jesus in beneficence and in revelation, then we are face to face with failure. Yet we know the story is not that of failure. The Christian Church, using the word in its fine, universal sense, all down the ages proves that it has not been failure. And why not? Because He did not end there. His teaching, wondrous teaching; His beneficent doing in the realm of miraculous exercise of power, wondrous and amazing—left the mass unbelieving. They were all unbelieving in a measure. You get little glimpses of it after the resurrection. In Matthew, in the last chapter when they went up to meet Him in Galilee, it is said that some disbelieved. Ultimate saving faith broke in waves of possibility and power only after the death and the resurrection and the ascension, when the Holy Spirit was poured out upon men.

—*The Gospel According to John*

ADAM CLARKE

Believeth not on me (only), *but on him that sent me.* Here He asserts again His indivisible unity with the Father. He who believes on the Son believes on the Father; he who hath seen the Son hath seen the Father; he who honors the Son honors the Father. Though it was for asserting this (His oneness with God) that they were going to crucify Him, yet He retracts nothing of what He had spoken, but strongly reasserts it in the very jaws of death!

46. *I am come a light into the world.* Probably referring to what His forerunner had said, chap. i. 5. Before the coming of this Saviour, this Sun of Righteousness, into the world, all was darkness. At His rising the darkness is dispersed; but it profits only those whose eyes are open to receive the rays of this Sun of Righteousness.

47. *And believe not.* "And keep them not," is the reading of some MSS. A man must *hear* the words of Christ in order to *believe* them; and he must *believe* in order to keep them; and he must keep them in order to his salvation. *I judge him not.* I need not to do it; the words of Moses and the prophets judge and condemn him.

48. *The word that I have spoken, the same shall judge him.* You shall be judged according to My doctrine. The maxims which you have heard from My mouth shall be those on which you shall be tried in the great day; and you shall be condemned or acquitted according as you have believed or obeyed them, or according as you have despised and violated them. See this proved, Matt. xxv. 35, etc.

49. *Gave me a commandment.* Or "commission." Christ, as the Messiah, received His "commission" from God: what He should command—everything that related to the foundation and establishment of the Christian institution; and what He should speak—all His private conversations with His disciples or others, He, as man, commanded and spoke through the constant inspiration of the Holy Spirit.

50. *I know that his commandment is life everlasting.* These words of our Lord are similar to that saying in John's First Epistle, chap. v. 11-12. "This is the record, that God hath given to us eternal life, and this life is in his Son. He that hath the Son hath life." God's *commandment* or "commission" is, Preach salvation to a lost world, and give thyself a Ransom for all; and whoever believes on Thee shall not perish, but have everlasting life. The public work of our Lord was now done; and the remnant of His time, previously to His crucifixion, He spent in teaching His disciples—instructing them in the nature of His kingdom, His intercession, and the mission of the Holy Spirit; and in that heavenly life which all true believers live with the Father, through faith in the Son, by the operation of the Holy Ghost.

MATTHEW HENRY

and an entire subjection of soul to it, we must give him the glory due to his name.

CHAPTER 13

Verses 1–17

It has generally been taken for granted by commentators that Christ's washing his disciples' feet, and the discourse that followed it, were the same night in which he was betrayed, and at the same sitting wherein he ate the passover and instituted the Lord's supper. This evangelist, making it his business to gather up those passages which the others had omitted, industriously omits those which the others had recorded, which occasions some difficulty in putting them together. It is here said (*v.* 1) to be *before the feast of the passover*.

In these verses we have the story of Christ's washing his disciples' feet. But why would Christ do this? A wise man will not do a thing that looks odd and unusual, but for very good causes and considerations. The transaction was very solemn, and four reasons are here intimated why Christ did this: 1. That he might testify his love to his disciples, *v.* 1, 2. 2. That he might give an instance of his own voluntary humility, *v.* 3–5. 3. That he might signify to them spiritual washing, which is referred to in his discourse with Peter, *v.* 6–11. 4. That he might set them an example, *v.* 12–17.

I. Christ washed his disciples' feet that he might give a proof of that great love wherewith he loved them, *v.* 1, 2.

1. Our Lord Jesus, *having loved his own that were in the world, loved them to the end*, *v.* 1.

(1) This is true of the disciples that were his immediate followers, in particular the twelve. These were his own in the world, his bosom-friends. These he loved, he called them into fellowship with himself, was always tender of them. He allowed them to be very free with him, and bore with their infirmities. He loved them to the end; he never took away his loving kindness. Though there were some persons of quality that espoused his cause, he did not lay aside his old friends, but still stuck to his poor fishermen. Though he reproved them often, he never ceased to love them and take care of them.

(2) It is true of all believers. Our Lord Jesus has a people in the world that are his own. *His own;* where *his own* were spoken of that *received him not*, as a man's cattle are his own, which yet he may, when he pleases, dispose of. But here it is, *his own persons*, as a man's wife and children are his own. Christ has a cordial love for his own that are in the world. He was now going to his own in heaven; but he seems most concerned for his own on earth, because they most needed his care: the sickly child is most indulged. Those whom Christ loves *he loves to the end*. Nothing can separate a believer *from the love of Christ*; he loves his own *unto perfection*.

2. Christ manifested his love to them by washing their feet. Thus he would show that as his love to them was constant so it was condescending, would put honour upon them as great and surprising as for a lord to serve his servants. The disciples had just now betrayed the weakness of their love to him, in grudging the ointment that was poured upon his head (Matt. xxvi. 8), yet he presently gives this proof of his love to them. Our infirmities are foils to Christ's kindnesses, and set them off.

3. He chose this time to do it, for two reasons:

(1) Because now *he knew that his hour was come when he should depart out of this world to the Father*. The change that was to pass over our Lord Jesus; he must *depart*. As Christ himself, so all believers, when they depart out of the world, *go to the Father*. It is a departure *out of the world*, and it is a going *to the Father* and the fruition of him as ours. The time of this change: *His hour was come*. It is sometimes called his enemies' hour (Luke xxii. 53), the hour of their triumph; sometimes his hour, the hour of his triumph. His foresight of it: He *knew that his hour was come;* he knew from the beginning that it would come, but now he knew that it *was come*.

(2) Because the *devil had now put it into the heart of Judas to betray him*, *v.* 2. These words in a parenthesis may be considered, [1] As tracing Judas's treason to its origin. What way of access the devil has to men's hearts we cannot tell. But there are some sins in their own nature so exceedingly sinful, that it is plain Satan lays the egg of them in a heart disposed to be the nest to hatch them in. [2] As intimating a reason why Christ now washed his disciples' feet. Judas being now resolved to betray him, the time of his departure could not be far off. The more malicious we perceive our enemies to be against us,

JAMIESON, FAUSSET, BROWN

CHAPTER 13

VSS. 1-20. AT THE LAST SUPPER JESUS WASHES THE DISCIPLES' FEET—THE DISCOURSE ARISING THEREUPON. **1. when Jesus knew that his hour was come that he should depart out of this world unto the Father**—On these beautiful euphemisms, see on Luke 9:31, 51.

having loved his own which were in the world, he loved them unto the end—The meaning is, that on the very edge of His last sufferings, when it might have been supposed that He would be absorbed in His own awful prospects, He was so far from forgetting "His own," who were to be left struggling "in the world" after He had "departed out of it to the Father" (ch. 17:11), that in His care for them He seemed scarce to think of Himself save in connection with them: "Herein is love," not only "enduring to the end," but most affectingly manifested when, judging by a human standard, least to be expected.

2. supper being ended—rather, being prepared, being served, or, going on; for that it was not "ended" is plain from vs. 26.

the devil having now—or, "already"—**put into the heart of Judas . . . to betray him**—referring to the agreement he had *already* made with the chief priests (Luke 22:3-6).

ADAM CLARKE

CHAPTER 13

1. *Now before the feast of the passover, when Jesus knew*. Or, as some translate, "Now Jesus having known, before the feast of the passover, that his hour was come." The supper mentioned in v. 2 is supposed to have been that on the Thursday evening, when the Feast of the Passover began; and though, in our common translation, this passage seems to place the supper *before* that feast, yet, according to the amended translation, what is here said is consistent with what we read in the other Evangelists.

Having loved his own. His disciples. *Which were in the world*. Who were to continue longer in its troubles and difficulties. *He loved them unto the end*. Continued His fervent affection towards them to His latest breath, and gave them that convincing proof of it which is mentioned in v. 5. That the disciples alone are meant here every man must see.

2. *And supper being ended*. Rather, "while supper was preparing." To support this new translation of the words, it may be remarked that, from vv. 26 and 30, it appears that the supper was not then *ended*. Nay, it is probable that it was not then begun; because the washing of feet (v. 5) was usually practiced by the Jews before they entered upon their meals, as may be gathered from Luke vii. 44, and from the reason of the custom. I think that John wrote, not *genomenou*, but *ginomenou*, as in some MSS., which latter reading is approved by several eminent critics, and should be translated as above. By the *supper* I suppose to be meant, not only the eating of it, but the preparing and dressing of it, and doing all things necessary previously to the eating of it. The devil had, before this time of the supper, put it into Judas' heart to betray his Master. See Matt. xxvi. 14, etc.; Mark xiv. 10-11; and Luke xxii. 3, etc. Calmet observes that John, designing only to supply what was omitted by the other Evangelists, passes over all the transactions of the Tuesday, Wednesday, and Thursday before the Passion, and at once goes from Monday evening to Thursday evening. It is remarkable that John says nothing about the institution of the Holy Sacrament, which Matthew (xxvi. 26, etc.), Mark (xiv. 22, etc.), and Luke (xxii. 19, etc.) describe so particularly. No other reason can be assigned for this than that he found it completely done by the others, and that he designed only to supply their defects. *The devil having now put into the heart*. Judas formed his plot six days before this, on occasion of what happened at the house of Simon the leper.

MATTHEW HENRY

the more industrious we should be to prepare for the worst that may come. Judas being now got into the snare, and the devil aiming at Peter and the rest of them (Luke xxii. 31), Christ would fortify his own against him. If the wolf has seized one of the flock, it is time for the shepherd to look well to the rest. Antidotes must be stirring, when the infection is begun. Judas, who was now plotting to betray him, was *one of the twelve.* Now Christ would hereby show that he did not design to cast them all off for the faults of one. Though one had a devil, and was a traitor, yet they should fare never the worse for that. Christ had still a kindness for his disciples though there was a Judas among them and he knew it.

II. Christ washed his disciples' feet that he might let all the world know how low he could stoop in love to his own. This is intimated, *v.* 3–5. *Jesus knowing* that *the Father had given all things into his hand, rises from supper,* and, to the great surprise of the company, *washed his disciples' feet.*

1. Here is the rightful advancement of the Lord Jesus. *The Father had given all things into his hands;* had given him a power over all. See Matt. xi. 27. He is *heir of all things.* He *came from God.* This implies that he was in the beginning with God. He came from God as the Son of God, and the sent of God. He *went to God.* That which comes from God shall go to God; those that are born from heaven are bound for heaven. He *knew* all this; was not like a prince in the cradle, that knows nothing of the honour he is born to. He had a full view of all the honours of his exalted state, and yet stooped thus low. But how does this come in here? It may come in as that which supported him under his sufferings. Judas was now betraying him, and he knew it, yet, knowing also *that he came from God and went to God,* he did not draw back. It seems to come in as a foil to his condescension. That is given as an inducement to Christ to stoop which should rather have been a reason for his taking state; for God's thoughts are not as ours.

2. Here is the voluntary abasement of our Lord Jesus. A well-grounded assurance of heaven and happiness, instead of puffing a man up with pride, will make and keep him very humble. Now that which Christ humbled himself to was to *wash his disciples' feet.* The action itself was mean and servile, and that which servants of the lowest rank were employed in. If he had washed their hands or faces, it had been great condescension; but for Christ to stoop to such a piece of drudgery as this may well excite our admiration. He did this for his own disciples, who in themselves were of a low and despicable condition, not curious about their bodies; their feet, it is likely, were seldom washed, and therefore very dirty. They were his servants, and such as should have washed his feet. Many of great spirits otherwise will do a mean thing to curry favour with their superiors; they rise by stooping, and climb by cringing; but for Christ to do this to *his disciples* could be no act of policy, but pure humility. He *rose from supper* to do it. Though we translate it (*v.* 2) *supper being ended,* it might be better read, *there being a supper made,* for he sat down again (*v.* 12), and we find him dipping a sop (*v.* 26), so that he did it in the midst of his meal, and thereby taught us, (1) Not to reckon it a disturbance to be called from our meal to do God or our brother any real service. Christ would not leave his preaching to oblige his nearest relations (Mark iii. 33), but would leave his supper to show his love to his disciples. (2) Not to be over nice about our meat. It would have turned many a squeamish stomach to wash dirty feet at supper-time; but Christ did it, not that we might learn to be rude and slovenly (cleanliness and godliness will do well together), not to indulge, but mortify, the delicacy of the appetite, giving good manners their due place, and no more. He put himself into the garb of a servant, to do it: he *laid aside* his *garments.* We must address ourselves to duty as those that in earnest buckle to business. He did it with all the humble ceremony that could be. He *girded himself with the towel;* he *poured water into the basin,* and then *washed their feet* and *wiped them.* Nothing appears to the contrary but that he washed the feet of Judas, for he was present, *v.* 26. Jesus here washed the feet of a sinner, the worst of sinners, who was at this time contriving to betray him.

III. Christ washed his disciples' feet that he might signify to them the cleansing of the soul from the pollutions of sin. This is plainly intimated in his discourse with Peter upon it, *v.* 6–11.

1. The surprise Peter was in (*v.* 6): *Then cometh he to Simon Peter,* and bids him put out his feet to be washed. It is most probable that when he *went about* this service (which is all that is meant by his *beginning* to wash, *v.* 5)he took Peter first, and that the rest would not have suffered it, if they had not first heard it explained in what passed between Christ and Peter.

JAMIESON, FAUSSET, BROWN

ALBERT BARNES:

"The devil." The leader or prince of evil spirits. "Having now put it into the heart." Literally, having "cast it" into the heart. Eph. 6:16: "The fiery darts of the wicked" (see Acts 5:3; Luke 12:3). The meaning of this passage is that Satan inclined the mind of Judas to do this, or he tempted him to betray his Master. We know not precisely how this was done, but we know that it was by means of his avarice. Satan could tempt no one unless there was some inclination of the mind, some natural or depraved propensity that he could make use of. He presents objects in alluring forms fitted to that propensity, and under the influence of a strong or a corrupt inclination the soul yields to sin. In the case of Judas it was the love of money; and it was necessary to present to him only the possibility of obtaining money, and it found him ready for any crime.—*Popular Commentary*

3. Jesus knowing that the Father had given all things into his hands . . .—This verse is very sublime, and as a preface to what follows, were we not familiar with it, would fill us with inexpressible surprise. An unclouded perception of His relation to the Father, the commission He held from Him, and His approaching return to Him, possessed His soul.

G. CAMPBELL MORGAN:

He knew that it was the hour when "he should depart out of this world unto the Father." Not a word is said here and now about the way of His going, but only the fact that His going would bring Him to the Father. When the Greeks came, He said, "The hour is come that the Son of man should be glorified." So here the reference was not to the method of His going, but to the fact, and to the issue of it. "Knowing that his hour was come that he should depart out of this world unto the Father." It is of supreme importance that we should understand the Scripture's teaching about the mind of Jesus as He approached His cross. Too often the death of Jesus is spoken of as a martyrdom, the heroic surrender to the inevitable in circumstances. There is no scintilla of truth in that view of the cross. The New Testament accounts all reveal Him as moving with the mien and attitude of One carrying out a divine program: His soul troubled, but always seeing through the gloom to the glory. "Knowing that his hour was come that he should depart out of this world unto the Father."

But again, "Jesus knowing that the Father had given all things into his hands." That statement is significantly placed: "The devil having already put into the heart of Judas Iscariot, Simon's son, to betray him, Jesus knowing that the Father had given all things into his hands." Judas had willed, and the devil had willed; but Jesus knew that He was already by the Father's appointment in supreme authority. Presently He will say to this self-same group, "All authority hath been given unto me in heaven and on earth." He knew it now.—*The Gospel According to John*

4, 5. He riseth from supper, and laid aside his—outer—**garments**—which would have impeded the operation of washing. **and took a towel and girded himself**—assuming a servant's dress. **5. began to wash**—proceeded to wash. *Beyond all doubt the feet of Judas were washed,* as of all the rest.

ADAM CLARKE

3. *Knowing that the Father had given.* Our Lord, seeing himself almost at the end of His race, and being about to leave His apostles, thought it necessary to leave them a lesson of humility exemplified by himself, to deliver them from the bad influence of those false ideas which they formed concerning the nature of His kingdom.

4. *He riseth from supper.* Not from eating, as Bishop Pearce has well observed, but from His place at table; probably the dishes were not as yet laid down, though the guests were seated. According to the custom of the Jews and other Asiatics, this washing must have taken place before the supper. *Laid aside his garments.* That is, His gown or upper coat, with the girdle wherewith it was girded close to his tunic or undercoat; and, instead of this girdle, He tied a *towel* about Him: (1) that He might appear in the character of a servant; and (2) that He might have it in readiness to dry their feet after He had washed them.

5. *Poureth water into a bason.* This was the office of the meanest slaves. When David sent to Abigail, to inform her that he had chosen her for wife, she arose and said: "Behold, let thine handmaid be a servant to wash the feet of the servants of my lord," 1 Sam. xxv. 41. Some of the ancients have supposed that our Lord began with washing the feet of Judas, to inspire him with sentiments of compunction and remorse, to melt him down with kindness, and to show all His disciples how they should act towards their enemies.

MATTHEW HENRY

Peter was startled at the proposal: *Lord* (saith he) *dost thou wash my feet?* What *thou*, our Lord and Master, whom we know and believe to be the Son of God, do this for *me*, a worthless worm of the earth, *a sinful man, O Lord?* Shall those hands wash my feet which with a touch have cleansed lepers, given sight to the blind, and raised the dead? Very willingly would Peter have taken the basin and towel, and washed his Master's feet, and been proud of the honour. For *my Master* to wash my feet is such a paradox as I cannot understand.

2. The immediate satisfaction Christ gave. This was at least sufficient to silence his objections (*v.* 7): *What I do, thou knowest not now, but thou shalt know hereafter.* Here are two reasons why Peter must submit:

(1) Because he was at present in the dark concerning it, and ought not to oppose what he did not understand. Christ would teach Peter an *implicit obedience*: "*What I do thou knowest not now*, and therefore art no competent judge of it."

(2) Because there was something considerable in it, of which he should hereafter know the meaning: "*Thou shalt know hereafter.* Our Lord Jesus does many things the meaning of which even his own disciples do not for the present know, but they *shall know afterwards.* Subsequent providences explain preceding ones; and we see afterwards the kind tendency of events that seemed most cross; and the way which we thought was *about* proved the *right way.* We must let Christ take his own way, and we shall find in the issue it was the best way.

3. Peter's peremptory refusal to let Christ wash his feet (*v.* 8): *Thou shalt by no means wash my feet; no, never.* It is the language of a fixed resolution. Here was a show of humility and modesty. Peter herein seemed to have, and no doubt he really had, a great respect for his Master. Under this show of humility there was a real contradiction to the will of the Lord Jesus. It is not humility, but infidelity, to put away the offers of the gospel, as if too rich to be made to us or too good news to be true.

4. Christ's insisting upon his offer: *If I wash thee not, thou hast no part with me.* A severe caution against disobedience: "*If I wash thee not*, if thou continue refractory, thou shalt not be owned as one of my disciples." If Peter will dispute the commands he ought to obey, he does in effect renounce his allegiance. A declaration of the necessity of spiritual washing: "*If I wash not* thy soul from the pollution of sin, *thou hast no part with me.*" All those, and those only, that are spiritually washed by Christ, have a part in Christ. It is that *good part* the having of which is the *one thing needful.* It is necessary to our having a part in Christ that he wash us.

5. Peter's more than submission, his earnest request, to be washed by Christ, *v.* 9: *Lord, wash not my feet only, but also my hands and my head.* How soon is Peter's mind changed! Let us therefore not be peremptory in any resolve, because we may soon see cause to retract it, but cautious in taking up a purpose we will be tenacious of.

(1) How ready Peter is to recede from what he had said: "Lord, what a fool was I to speak such a hasty word!" Now that the washing of him appeared to be an act of Christ's grace he admits it; but disliked it when it seemed only an act of humiliation. Good men, when they see their error, will not be loth to recant it.

(2) How importunate he is for the purifying grace of the Lord Jesus, and the universal influence of it, even upon his hands and head. An exclusion from having a part in him, is the most formidable evil in the eyes of all that are enlightened. And for fear of this we should be earnest with God in prayer, that he will wash us. "*Lord, wash not my feet only* from the gross pollutions that cleave to them, *but also my hands and my head* from the spots which they have contracted, and the undiscerned filth which proceeds by perspiration from the body itself."

6. Christ's further explication of this sign.

(1) With reference to his disciples that were faithful to him (*v.* 10): *He that is washed* all over in the bath, *needeth not save to wash his feet*, his hands and head having been washed, and he having only dirtied his feet in walking home. Peter had gone from one extreme to the other. At first he would not let Christ wash his feet; and now he overlooks what Christ had done for him in his baptism, and what was signified thereby. See here what is the privilege and comfort of such as are in a justified state; they are washed by Christ, and are *clean every whit.* The heart may be swept and garnished, and yet still remain the devil's palace; but, if it be washed, it belongs to Christ, and he will not lose it. See what ought to be the daily care of those who through grace are in a justified state, and that is to wash their feet; to cleanse themselves from the guilt they contract daily through infirmity and inadver-

JAMIESON, FAUSSET, BROWN

6-11. Peter saith . . . Lord, dost thou wash my feet?—Our language cannot bring out the intensely vivid contrast between the *"Thou"* and the *"my,"* which, by bringing them together, the original expresses, for it is not good English to say, "Lord, *Thou my* feet dost wash?" But *every word* of this question is emphatic. Thus far, and in the question itself, there was nothing but the most profound and beautiful astonishment at a condescension to him quite incomprehensible. Accordingly, though there can be no doubt that already Peter's heart rebelled against it as a thing not to be tolerated, Jesus ministers no rebuke as yet, but only bids him wait a little, and he should understand it all. **7. Jesus answered and said . . ., What I do thou knowest not now**—i.e., Such condescension *does* need explanation; it *is* fitted to astonish.

but thou shalt know hereafter—afterwards, meaning *presently;* though viewed as a general maxim, applicable to all dark sayings in God's Word, and dark doings in God's providence, these words are full of consolation.

8. Peter saith unto him, Thou shalt never wash . . .—more emphatically, 'Never shalt Thou wash my feet': i.e., 'That is an incongruity to which I can never submit.' How like the man! **If I wash thee not, thou hast no part with me**—What Peter could not submit to was, that the Master should serve His servant. But *the whole saving work of Christ was one continued series of such services, ending with and consummated by the most self-sacrificing and transcendent of all services:* THE SON OF MAN CAME *not to be ministered unto, but* TO MINISTER, AND TO GIVE HIS LIFE A RANSOM FOR MANY. (See on Mark 10:45.) If Peter then could not submit to let his Master go down so low as to wash his feet, *how should he suffer himself to be served by Him at all?* This is couched under the one pregnant word "wash," which though applicable to the *lower* operation which Peter resisted, is the familiar scriptural symbol of that *higher* cleansing, which Peter little thought he was at the same time virtually putting from him. *It is not humility to refuse what the Lord deigns to do for us, or to deny what He has done,* but it is self-willed presumption—*not rare, however, in those inner circles of lofty religious profession and traditional spirituality, which are found wherever Christian truth has enjoyed long and undisturbed possession.* The truest humility is to receive reverentially, and thankfully to own, the gifts of grace. **9. Lord, not my feet only, but also my hands and my head**—i.e., 'To be severed from Thee, Lord, is death to me: **If that be the meaning of my speech, I tread upon it; and if to be washed of Thee have such significance, then not my feet only, but hands, head, and all, be washed!'** This artless expression of clinging, life-and-death attachment to Jesus, and felt dependence upon Him for his whole spiritual wellbeing, compared with the similar saying in ch. 6:68, 69 (on which see *Notes*), furnishes such evidence of *historic verity* such as no thoroughly honest mind can resist.

10. He that is washed—in this *thorough* sense, to express which the word is carefully changed to one meaning to wash *as in a bath.* **needeth not**—to be *so* washed any more. **save to wash his feet**—needeth to do no more than wash his feet (and here the former word is resumed, meaning to wash *the hands or feet*). **but is clean every whit**—as a whole. This sentence is singularly instructive. Of the *two cleansings,* the one points to that which takes place at the *commencement* of the Christian life, embracing *complete absolution from sin as a guilty state,* and *entire deliverance from it as a polluted life* (Rev. 1:5; I Cor. 6:11)—or, in the language of theology, *Justification* and *Regeneration.* This cleansing is effected *once for all,* and is never repeated. The other cleansing, described as that of

ADAM CLARKE

6. *Lord, dost thou wash my feet?* Every word here is exceedingly emphatic. Peter had often seen the great humility of his Lord, but never saw His condescension so particularly marked as in this instance.

7. *What I do thou knowest not now.* As if our Lord had said, Permit Me to do it now, and I will shortly explain to you the nature of this action, and My motives for doing it. *Thou shalt know hereafter.* After this business is finished. And so we find He explained the whole to them as soon as He had finished the washing; see vv. 12-17.

CHARLES H. SPURGEON:

Let us come at once to the teaching of the Savior, and let it be surrounded with an unusual interest, because it is His *dying* teaching. Let us see Him as He girds himself with the towel, remembering that He was soon to be girt with the bands of death; let us see Him, I say, with a more profound interest, because He is just upon the verge of these terrible depths where all the waves and billows of Jehovah's justice dashed over Him. His sermon beginning, "Let not your heart be troubled," is His swan song; these are the last drops of His life that He is now spending; at the supper table you have the wine, which He keeps until now. As we see Him washing His disciples' feet, we shall discover choice love worthy of the last solemn hour of departure.

—*The Treasury of the New Testament*

10. *He that is washed.* That is, he who has been in the bath, as probably all the apostles had lately been, in order to prepare themselves the better for the paschal solemnity; for on that occasion it was the custom of the Jews to bathe twice. *Needeth not save to wash his feet.* To cleanse them from any dirt or dust that might have adhered to them, in consequence of walking from the bath to the place of supper. The washing, therefore, of the *feet* of such persons was all that was necessary, previously to their sitting down to table.

MATTHEW HENRY

tence, by the renewed exercise of repentance. We must also wash our feet by constant watchfulness against everything that is defiling. The provision made for our cleansing should not make us presumptuous, but the more cautious. From yesterday's pardon we should fetch an argument against this day's temptation.

(2) With reflection upon Judas: *And you are clean, but not all, v.* 10, 11. He washed them himself, and then said, *You are clean;* but he excepts Judas: *not all.* Many have the sign that have not the thing signified. Christ sees it necessary to let his disciples know that they are not all clean; that we may all be jealous over ourselves (*Is it I? Lord, is it I* that am among the clean, yet not clean?)

IV. Christ washed his disciples' feet to set before us an example. This explication he gave of what he had done, when he had done it, *v.* 12–17.

1. With what solemnity he gave an account of the meaning of what he had done (*v.* 12): *After he had washed their feet,* he said, *Know you what I have done?*

(1) He adjourned the explication until he had finished the transaction: To try their submission and implicit obedience, that they might learn to acquiesce in his will when they could not give a reason for it. Because it was proper to finish the riddle before he unriddled it.

(2) Before he explained it, he asked them if they could construe it: *Know you what I have done to you?* He puts this question to them, not only to make them sensible of their ignorance, but to raise their desires and expectations of instruction.

2. Upon what he grounds that which he had to say (*v.* 13): "*You call me Master and Lord,* and *you say well,* for *so I am.*" He that is our Redeemer and Saviour is, in order to that, our Lord and Master. He is our Master—our teacher and instructor. He is our Lord—our ruler and owner. It becomes the disciples of Christ to call him Master and Lord, not in compliment, but in reality; not by constraint, but with delight. Our calling Christ Master and Lord is an obligation upon us to receive and observe the instructions he gives us. We are bound in honour and honesty to be observant of him.

3. The lesson which he hereby taught: *You also ought to wash one another's feet, v.* 14.

(1) Some have understood this literally, that Christians should, in a solemn religious manner, *wash one another's feet,* in token of their condescending love to one another. St. Ambrose took it so, and practised it in the church of Milan. St. Austin saith that those Christians who did not do it with their hands, yet (he hoped) did it with their hearts in humility; but he saith, It is much better to do it with the hands also. What Christ has done Christians should not disdain to do.

(2) But doubtless it is to be understood figuratively. Three things our Master hereby designed to teach us: [1] A humble condescension. We must learn of our Master to be *lowly in heart* (Matt. xi. 29). Christ had often taught his disciples humility, and they had forgotten the lesson; but now he teaches them in such a way as surely they could never forget. [2] A condescension to be serviceable. To wash one another's feet is to stoop to the meanest offices of love, for the real good and benefit one of another. We must not grudge to take care and pains, and to spend time, for the good of those to whom we are not under any particular obligations, even of our inferiors. The duty is *mutual;* we must both accept help from our brethren and afford help to our brethren. [3] A serviceableness to the sanctification one of another: *You ought to wash one another's feet,* from the pollutions of sin. We cannot satisfy for one another's sins, but we may help to purify one another from sin. We must in the first place wash ourselves; this charity must begin at home, but it must not end there; we must sorrow for the failings and follies of our brethren, must wash our brethren's polluted feet in tears.

4. Here is the enforcing of this command from the example of what Christ had now done: *If I your Lord and Master have* done it to you, you ought to do it *to one another.* I am *your Master,* and therefore you ought to *learn of me* (*v.* 15); for in this, *I have given you an example,* that *you should do* to others, *as I have done* to you. What a good teacher Christ is. He teaches by example as well as doctrine, and for this end came into this world, that he might set us a copy; and it is a copy without one false stroke. What good scholars we must be. We must *do as he hath done;* he gave us a copy, that we should write after it. Christ's example herein is to be followed by ministers in particular, in whom the graces of humility and holy love should especially appear. When Christ sent his apostles abroad, it was with this charge: *become all things to all men,* 1 Cor. ix. 22. What I have done to your dirty feet that do you to the polluted souls of

JAMIESON, FAUSSET, BROWN

"the feet," is *such as one walking from a bath quite cleansed still needs, in consequence of his contact with the earth.* (Cf. Exod. 30:18, 19.) It is the *daily* cleansing which we are taught to seek, when in the spirit of adoption we say, "Our Father which art in heaven—*forgive us our debts*"; and, when burdened with the sense of manifold shortcomings —as what tender spirit of a Christian is not?—is it not a relief to be permitted thus to wash our feet after a day's contact with the earth? This is not to call in question the completeness of our past justification. Our Lord, while graciously insisting on washing Peter's feet, refuses to extend the cleansing farther, that the symbolical instruction intended to be conveyed might not be marred. **and ye are clean**—in the first and *whole* sense. **but not all**—important, as showing that Judas, instead of being as true-hearted a disciple as the rest at first, and merely *falling away* afterwards—as many represent it—*never experienced that cleansing at all which made the others what they were.* **12-15. Know ye what I have done?**—i.e., its intent. The question, however, was put merely to summon their attention to His own answer.

13. Ye call me Master—Teacher—**and Lord**—*learning* of Him in the one capacity, *obeying* Him in the other. **and ye say well, for so I am**—The conscious dignity with which this claim is made is remarkable, following immediately on His laying aside the towel of service. Yet what is this whole history but a succession of such astonishing contrast from first to last?

14. If I then—the Lord—**have washed your feet**—the servants'—**ye**—but fellow servants—**ought to wash one another's feet**—not in the narrow sense of a literal washing, profanely caricatured by popes and emperors, but by the very humblest *real* services one to another.

ADAM CLARKE

Ye are clean, but not all. Eleven of you are upright and sincere; the twelfth is a traitor. So it appears He had washed the feet of all the twelve; but as no external ablutions can purify a hypocrite or a traitor, therefore Judas still remained unclean.

12. *Know ye what I have done?* Our Lord had told Peter, in the presence of the rest, v. 7, that he should afterwards know what was the intent and meaning of this washing; and now He begins to fulfill His promise. Therefore I think it more likely that He gives a *command,* here, than asks a *question,* as He knew himself that they did not comprehend His design. On this account *ginoskete* might be translated in the imperative mood, "Consider what I have done."

13. *Ye call me Master and Lord.* Similar to *Rabbi,* and *Mar,* titles very common among the Jewish doctors. This double title was not given except to the most accredited teachers.

14. *Ye also ought to wash one another's feet.* That is, you should be ready, after My example, to condescend to all the weakness of your brethren, to be willing to do the meanest offices for them, and to prefer the least of them in honor to yourselves.

A. B. SIMPSON:

The first lesson taught by this picture is that of Christ's humility. Like Him, we cannot truly stoop until we have learned our high calling and know that we are indeed the sons of God. Then we shall not fear the most menial service or think that the lowliest place can degrade our true dignity, but shall prove that we are the chief by becoming the servant of all. The next lesson is love, that, instead of exposing the stains of one another, seeks to wash them away. But the deepest spiritual teaching of these words is the unfolding of Christ's own constant cleansing as our ever living Advocate and High Priest. Still He is girded with the towel, and still He stoops to cleanse the saints of defilement from our feet day by day.—*Christ in the Bible*

MATTHEW HENRY

sinners; *wash them.* Christians likewise are here taught to condescend to each other in love, unasked, unpaid; we must not be mercenary in the services of love. I am *your Master*, and you are my disciples (*v.* 16), *the servant is not greater than his Lord, neither he that is sent greater than he that sent him.* Christ had urged this (Matt. x. 24, 25) as a reason why they should not think it strange if they suffered as he did; here he urges it as a reason why they should not think it much to humble themselves as he did. What he did not think a disparagement to him, they must not think a disparagement to them. Christ reminds them of their place as his servants; they were not better men than their Master. We need to be put in mind of this, that we are not *greater than our Lord.* Christ, by humbling himself, has dignified humility. We commonly say to those who disdain to do such or such a thing, As good as you have done it; and true indeed it is, if our Master has done it. When we see our Master serving, we cannot see but how ill it becomes us to be domineering.

5. Our Saviour closes this part of his discourse: *If you know these things, happy are you if you do them.* Most people think, Happy are those that rise and rule. Washing one another's feet will never get estates and preferments; but Christ saith, notwithstanding this, Happy are those that stoop and obey. Since they had such excellent precepts given them, recommended by such an excellent pattern, it will be necessary to the completing of their happiness that they practise accordingly. This is applicable to the commands of Christ in general. Though it is a great advantage to know our duty, yet we shall come short of happiness if we do not do our duty. Knowing is in order to doing, James iv. 17. It is knowing and doing that will demonstrate us of *Christ's kingdom*, and wise builders. It is to be applied especially to this command of humility. Nothing is better known than this, that we should be humble. Few will own themselves to be proud, for it is as inexcusable a sin, and as hateful, as any other; and yet how little is to be seen of true humility. Most know these things so well as to expect that others should do accordingly to them, but not so well as to do so themselves.

Verses 18–30

We have here the discovery of Judas's plot to betray his Master. Christ knew it from the beginning; but now first he discovered it to his disciples.

I. Christ gives them a general intimation of it (*v.* 18): *I speak not of you all*, for *I know whom I have chosen*, but the scripture will be fulfilled (Ps. xli. 9), *He that eateth bread with me hath lifted up his heel against me.*

1. He intimates to them that they were not all right. He had said (*v.* 10), *You are clean, but not all.* So here, *I speak not of you all.* What is said of the excellencies of Christ's disciples cannot be said of all that are called so. There is a mixture of bad with good in the best societies, a Judas among the apostles.

2. He himself knew who were right, and who were not: *I know whom I have chosen.* Those that are chosen, Christ himself had the choosing of them. Those that are chosen are known to Christ, for he never forgets any whom he has once had in his thoughts of love, 2 Tim. ii. 19.

3. In the treachery of him that proved false to him the scripture was fulfilled. Christ took one into his family whom he foresaw to be a traitor, *that the scripture might be fulfilled.* This our Saviour applies to Judas. Judas, as an apostle, was admitted to the highest privilege: he did *eat bread with Christ.* He was favoured by him, one of those with whom he was intimately conversant. He saith, He did *eat bread with me*; such as he had, his disciples had their share of, Judas among the rest. Wherever he went, Judas was welcome with him, sat at table with his Master, and in all respects fared as he fared. He ate miraculous bread with him, when the loaves were multiplied, ate the passover with him. All that eat bread with Christ are not his disciples indeed. Judas was guilty of the basest treachery; he *lifted up the heel* against Christ. He forsook him, *v.* 30. He despised him. He became an enemy to him. It is no new thing for those that were Christ's seeming friends to prove his real enemies.

II. He gives them a reason why he told them beforehand of the treachery of Judas (*v.* 19): "*Now I tell you before it come, that when it is come to pass you may* be confirmed in your *belief that I am he.*" By his clear and certain foresight of things to come, of which he gave incontestable proof, he proved himself to be the true God. By this application of the types and prophecies of the Old Testament to himself, he proved himself to be the true Messiah.

III. He gives a word of encouragement to his apostles, and all his ministers whom he employs in

JAMIESON, FAUSSET, BROWN

16, 17. The servant is not greater than his lord . . .—an oft-repeated saying (Matt. 10: 24, etc.).

If ye know these things, happy are ye if ye do them—a hint that even among real Christians the *doing* of such things would come lamentably short of the *knowing*.

18, 19. I speak not of you all—the "happy *are* ye," of vs. 17, being on no supposition applicable to Judas.

I know whom I have chosen—in the *higher* sense. **But that the scripture may be fulfilled**—i.e., one has been added to your number, by no accident or mistake, who is none of Mine, but just that he might fulfil his predicted destiny. **He that eateth bread with me**—"did eat of *my bread*" (Ps. 41:9), as one of My family; admitted to the nearest familiarity of discipleship and of social life. **hath lifted up his heel against me**—turned upon Me, adding *insult* to injury. (Cf. Heb. 10:29.) In the Psalm the immediate reference is to Ahithophel's treachery against David (II Sam. 17), one of those scenes in which the parallel of his story with that of His great Antitype is exceedingly striking. "The eating bread derives a fearful meaning from the participation in the sacramental supper, a meaning which must be applied for ever to all unworthy communicants, as well as to all betrayers of Christ who eat the bread of His Church" [STIER, with whom, and others, we agree in thinking that Judas partook of the Lord's Supper.] **19. I tell you before . . . that when it comes to pass, ye may believe**—and it came to pass when they deeply needed such confirmation.

ADAM CLARKE

16. *The servant is not greater than his lord.* Christ has ennobled the acts of humility by practicing them himself. The true glory of a Christian consists in being, in his measure, as humble as his Lord. *Neither he that is sent.* "Nor an apostle." As I think these words were intended for the suppression of all worldly ambition and lordly conduct in the apostles and their successors in the ministry, therefore I think the original word *apostolos* should be translated "apostle," rather than *he that is sent*, because the former rendering ascertains and determines the meaning better.

17. *If ye know these things, happy.* True happiness consists in the knowledge of God, and in obedience to Him. A man is not happy because he knows much; but because he receives much of the divine nature and is, in all his conduct, conformed to the divine will.

18. *I speak not of you all.* This is a continuation of that discourse which was left off at the tenth verse. The preceding verses may be read in a parenthesis.

I know whom I have chosen. I am not deceived in My choice; I perfectly foresaw everything that has happened, or can happen. I have chosen Judas, not as a wicked man, nor that he should become such; but I plainly foresaw that he would abuse My bounty, give way to iniquity, deliver Me into the hands of My enemies, and bring ruin upon himself. *That the scripture may be fulfilled.* Or, "Thus the scripture is fulfilled." Christ applies to Judas what David had said of his rebellious son Absalom, Ps. xli. 9, who was one of the most express emblems of this traitor. *He that eateth bread with me.* That is, he who was in habits of the utmost intimacy with Me. *Hath lifted up his heel.* An illusion to a restive, ill-natured horse, that sometimes kicks even the person who feeds and takes care of him.

19. *That . . . ye may believe.* These frequent predictions of His death, so circumstantial in themselves, had the most direct tendency to confirm the disciples, not only in the belief of His being the Messiah, but also in that of His omniscience.

MATTHEW HENRY

his service (*v.* 20): *He that receiveth whomsoever I send receiveth me.* Christ had told his disciples that they must humble and abase themselves. "Now," saith he, "though there may be those that will despise you for your condescension, yet there will be those that will do you honour, and shall be honoured for so doing." Those who know themselves dignified by Christ's commission may be content to be vilified in the world's opinion. As Christ will think never the worse of them for Judas's crime, so he will own them, and will raise up such as shall receive them. Those that had received Judas when he was a preacher were never the worse, though he afterwards proved a traitor; for he was one whom Christ sent. Those who appear to be sent of Christ we must receive, till the contrary appear. Though some, by entertaining strangers, have entertained robbers unawares, thereby some have entertained angels. The abuses put upon our charity, will neither justify our uncharitableness, nor lose us the reward of our charity. We are here encouraged to receive ministers as *sent of Christ*: "*He that receiveth whomsoever I send*, though weak and poor, yet if he deliver my message, he that entertains him shall be owned as a friend of mine." It is *receiving Christ Jesus the Lord* himself. We are here encouraged to receive Christ as sent of God: *He that* thus *receiveth me*, receiveth the Father also. *He that receiveth me* as his prince and Saviour receiveth *him that sent me* as his portion and felicity.

IV. Christ more particularly notifies to them the plot (*v.* 21): *When Jesus had thus said*, he was *troubled in spirit*, and *he testified*, he solemnly declared it: "*One of you shall betray me.*" This did not determine Judas to the sin by any fatal necessity; for, though the event did follow according to the prediction, yet not from the prediction. Christ is not the author of sin. As to this heinous sin of Judas, 1. Christ foresaw it. He *knows what is in men* better than they do themselves, and therefore sees what will be done by them. 2. He foretold it, not only for the sake of the rest of the disciples, but for the sake of Judas himself, that he might take warning. Traitors proceed not in their plots when they find they are discovered; surely Judas, when he finds that his Master knows his design, will retreat in time. 3. He spoke of it with a manifest concern; he was *troubled in spirit* when he mentioned it. The falls of the disciples of Christ are a great trouble of spirit to their Master; the sins of Christians are the grief of Christ. "What! *One of you betray me?*" This went to his heart, as the undutifulness of children grieves those who have *nourished and brought them up.*

V. The disciples quickly take the alarm; and therefore *looked one upon another*, with a manifest concern, *doubting of whom he spoke.* It struck such a horror upon them that they knew not well which way to look, nor what to say. They saw their Master troubled, and therefore they were troubled. That which grieves Christ is, and should be, a grief to all that are his. Hereby they endeavoured to *discover* the traitor. Christ thus perplexed his disciples for a time, that he might *humble them, and prove them*, might excite in them a jealousy of themselves. It is good for us sometimes to be put to a gaze, to be put to a pause.

VI. The disciples were solicitous to get their Master to explain himself.

1. Of all the disciples John was most fit to ask, because he was the favourite, and sat next his Master (*v.* 23): *There was leaning on Jesus's bosom one of the disciples whom Jesus loved.* It appears that this was John, by comparing *ch.* xxi. 20, 24. The particular kindness which Jesus had for him; he was *the disciple whom Jesus loved.* He loved them all (*v.* 1), but John was particularly dear to him. His name signifies *gracious.* Among the disciples of Christ some are dearer to him than others. His place at this time: He was *leaning on Jesus's bosom.* It seems to be an extraordinary expression of endearment. Those who lay themselves at Christ's feet, he will lay in his bosom. Yet he conceals his name. He puts this instead of his name, to show that he was pleased with it; it is his title of honour, that he was *the disciple whom Jesus loved.*

2. Of all the disciples Peter was most forward to know, *v.* 24. Peter, sitting at some distance, beckoned to John to ask. Peter was generally the leading man. Where men's natural tempers lead them to be thus bold in answering and asking, if kept under the laws of humility and wisdom, they make men very serviceable. God gives his gifts variously; but it must be noted that it was not Peter, but John, that was the beloved disciple. The reason why Peter did not himself ask was because John had a much fairer opportunity to whisper the question into the ear of Christ, and to receive a like private answer. It is good to improve our interest in those that are near to Christ. Do we know any that we have reason to think lie in

JAMIESON, FAUSSET, BROWN

20. He that receiveth whomsoever I send, receiveth me . . .—(See on Matt. 10:40). The connection here seems to be that despite the dishonor done to Him by Judas, and similar treatment awaiting themselves, they were to be cheered by the assurance that their office, even as His own, was divine.

21-30. THE TRAITOR INDICATED—HE LEAVES THE SUPPER ROOM. **21. When Jesus had thus said, he was troubled in spirit, and testified, and said, Verily, verily, I say unto you, One of you shall betray me**—The announcement of vs. 18 seems not to have been plain enough to be quite apprehended, save by the traitor himself. He will therefore speak it out in terms not to be misunderstood. But how much it cost Him to do this, appears from the "trouble" that came over His "spirit"—visible emotion, no doubt—before He got it uttered. What wounded susceptibility does this disclose, and what exquisite delicacy in His social intercourse with the Twelve, to whom He cannot, without an effort, break the subject! **22. the disciples looked one on another, doubting of whom he spake**—Further intensely interesting particulars are given in the other Gospels: (1) "They were exceeding sorrowful" (Matt. 26:22). (2) "They began to inquire among themselves which of them it was that should do this thing" (Luke 22:23). (3) "They began to say unto Him one by one, Is it I, and another, Is it I?" (Mark 14:19). Generous, simple hearts! They abhorred the thought, but, instead of putting it on others, each was only anxious to purge *himself*, and know if *he* could be the wretch. Their putting it at once to Jesus Himself, as knowing doubtless who was to do it, was the best, as it certainly was the most spontaneous and artless evidence of their innocence. (4) Jesus, apparently while this questioning was going on, added, "The Son of man goeth as it is written of Him, but woe unto that man by whom the Son of man is betrayed! It had been good for that man if he had not been born" (Matt. 26:24). (5) "Judas," *last of all*, "answered and said, *Lord, is it I?*" evidently feeling that when all were saying this, if he held his peace, that of itself would draw suspicion upon him. To prevent this the question is wrung out of him, but perhaps, amidst the stir and excitement at the table, in a half-suppressed tone as we are inclined to think the answer also was—"Thou hast said" (Matt. 26:25), or possibly by little more than a sign; for from vs. 28 it is evident that till the moment when he went out, he was not openly discovered. **23-26. there was leaning on Jesus' bosom one of his disciples, whom Jesus loved**—Thus modestly does our Evangelist denote himself, as reclining next to Jesus at the table.

Peter . . . beckoned to him to ask who it should be of whom he spake—reclining probably at the corresponding place on the other side of Jesus.

ADAM CLARKE

20. *He that receiveth whomsoever I send.* See similar words, Matt. x. 40. Our Lord spoke this to comfort His disciples. He showed them that, although they should be rejected by many, they would be received by several; and that whoever received them should reap the utmost benefit by it.

21. *Was troubled in spirit.* See the note on chap. xi. 33. *And testified.* Spoke with great earnestness. *Shall betray me.* "Will deliver Me up." Judas had already betrayed our blessed Lord, and he was now on the point of delivering Him up into the hands of the chief priests. By all these warnings, did not our Lord intend that Judas should be benefited—that he should repent of his iniquity, and turn and find mercy?

22. *Looked one on another, doubting of whom he spake.* See the notes on Matt. xxvi. 20-25. Everyone but Judas, conscious of his own innocence, looked about upon all the rest, wondering who in that company could be such a traitor. Even Judas himself is not suspected. **Is not this a proof that his general conduct had been such as to subject him to no suspicion?**

23. *Now there was leaning on Jesus' bosom.* The Jews of those days at their suppers reclined, supported by their left arms, on couches placed round the table, as the Greeks and Romans did. On each couch there were two or three persons; and the head of one of them came near to the bosom of him who reclined above him on the same couch. The person here mentioned was John, the writer of this history, who, being more tenderly loved by Christ than the rest, had always that place at table which was nearest to his Lord.

MATTHEW HENRY

Christ's bosom? Let us beg of them to speak a good word for us.

3. The question was asked accordingly (*v.* 25): *He then, lying at the breast of Jesus, saith unto him, Lord, who is it?* Now here John shows: A regard to his fellow-disciple. Those who lie in Christ's bosom may often learn from those who lie at his feet and be reminded of that which they did not of themselves think of. A reverence of his Master. Though he whispered this in Christ's ear, yet he called him Lord; the familiarity he was admitted to did not at all lessen his respect for his Master. The more intimate communion gracious souls have with Christ, the more sensible they are of his worthiness and their own unworthiness.

4. Christ gave a speedy answer to this question, but whispered it in John's ear; for it appears (*v.* 29) that the rest were still ignorant of the matter. *He it is to whom I shall give a sop, when I have dipped it.* And *when he had dipped the sop, he gave it to Judas.* Christ notified the traitor by a sign. He could have told John by name who he was. The false brethren we are to stand upon our guard against are not made known to us by words, but by signs; they are to be known to us by *their fruits.* That sign was a sop. Christ sometimes gives sops to traitors; worldly riches, honours, and pleasures are sops (if I may so speak), which Providence sometimes gives into the hands of wicked men. We must not be outrageous against those whom we know to be very malicious against us. Christ carved to Judas as kindly as to any at the table, though he knew he was then plotting his death.

VII. Judas himself, instead of being convinced hereby of his wickedness, was the more confirmed in it.

1. The devil hereupon took possession of him (*v.* 27): *After the sop, Satan entered into him.* Satan entered into him to possess him with a prevailing prejudice against Christ, and a contempt of him, to excite in him a covetous desire of the wages of unrighteousness and a resolution to stick at nothing for the obtaining of them. Was not Satan in him before? How then is it said that now *Satan entered into him?* Judas was all along a devil (*ch.* vi. 70), but now Satan gained a more full possession of him. Though the devil is in every wicked man that does his works, yet sometimes he enters more manifestly and more powerfully than at other times. How came Satan to enter into him *after the sop?* Perhaps he was aware that it was the discovery of him, and it made him desperate in his resolutions. Many are made worse by the gifts of Christ's bounty, and are confirmed in their impenitency by that which should have led them to repentance.

2. Christ hereupon dismissed him: *Then said Jesus unto him, What thou doest, do quickly.* Abandoning him to the conduct and power of Satan. Christ knew that Satan had entered into him, and had peaceable possession; and now he gives him up as hopeless. The various methods Christ had used for his conviction were ineffectual. When the evil spirit is willingly admitted, the good Spirit justly withdraws. Challenging him to do his worst: "I do not fear thee, I am ready for thee."

3. Those that were at table understood not what he meant (*v.* 28, 29): *No man at table knew for what intent* he spoke this to him. They did not suspect that Christ said it to Judas as a traitor, because it did not enter into their heads that Judas was such a one, or would prove so. Christ's disciples were so well taught to love one another that they could not easily learn to suspect one another. They therefore took it for granted that he said it to him as treasurer of the household, giving him orders for the laying out of some money. In works of piety: *Buy those things that we have need of against the feast.* Or in works of charity: *That he should give something to the poor.* Our Lord Jesus, though he lived upon alms himself (Luke viii. 3), yet gave alms to the poor, a little out of a little. Though he might very well be excused, not only because he was poor himself, but because he did so much good in other ways, curing so many *gratis*; yet, to set us an example, he gave for the relief of the poor. The time of a religious feast was thought a proper time for works of charity. When he celebrated the passover he ordered something for the poor. When we experience God's bounty to us, this should make us bountiful to the poor.

4. Judas hereupon sets himself vigorously to pursue his design against him: He *went away.*

(1) His speedy departure: *He went out presently.* For fear of being more plainly discovered to the company. He went out as one weary of Christ's company and the society of his apostles. Christ needed not to expel him, he expelled himself. *He went out* to prosecute his design. Now that Satan had got into him he hurried him on.

JAMIESON, FAUSSET, BROWN

25. He then lying—rather leaning over on Jesus' bosom—**saith**—*in a whisper,* "Lord, who is it?"

26. Jesus answered—*also inaudibly,* the answer being communicated to Peter perhaps from behind—**He . . . to whom I shall give a sop when I have dipped it**—a piece of the bread soaked in the wine or the sauce of the dish; one of the ancient ways of testifying peculiar regard; cf. vs. 18, *"he that eateth bread with Me."* **And when he had dipped . . . he gave it to Judas . . .**—Thus the sign of Judas' treachery was an affecting expression, and the last, of the Saviour's wounded love!

27-30. after the sop Satan entered into him—Very solemn are these brief hints of the successive steps by which Judas reached the climax of his guilt. "The devil had already put it into his heart to betray his Lord." Yet who can tell what struggles he went through ere he brought himself to carry that suggestion into effect? Even after this, however, his compunctions were not at an end. With the thirty pieces of silver already in his possession, he seems still to have quailed—and can we wonder? When Jesus stooped to wash his feet, it may be the last struggle was reaching its crisis. But that word of the Psalm, about "one that ate of his bread who would lift up his heel against Him," probably all but turned the dread scale, and the still more explicit announcement, that one of those sitting with Him at the table should betray Him, would beget the thought, "I am detected; it is now too late to draw back." At that moment the sop is given; offer of friendship is once more made—and how affectingly! But already "Satan has *entered into him,"* and though the Saviour's act might seem enough to recall him even yet, hell is now in his bosom, and he says within himself, "The die is cast; now let me go through with it; fear, begone!" (See on Matt. 12:43-45.) **Then said Jesus unto him, That thou doest, do quickly**—i.e., Why linger here? Thy presence is a restraint, and thy work stands still; thou hast the wages of iniquity, go work for it! **28-29. no man . . . knew for what intent he spake this unto him . . . some thought . . . Jesus . . . said . . . , But what we need . . . or, . . . give . . . to the poor**—a very important statement, as showing how carefully Jesus had kept the secret, and Judas his hypocrisy, to the last.

30. He then, having received the sop, went immediately out—severing himself *for ever* from that holy society with which he never had any spiritual sympathy.

ADAM CLARKE

25. *He then lying on Jesus' breast.* Laying his head against the breast of Christ, in a loving, respectful manner. As the expressions in the text are different here from those in the preceding verse, it shows that John altered his position at table, in order to ask the question which Peter suggested, which he probably did by whispering to our Lord. For from v. 28 we may learn that the other disciples had not heard what John said; and it is likely that the following words—"It is he to whom I shall give the morsel when I have dipped it," were whispered back by Christ to John.

26. *And when he had dipped the sop.* Dr. Lightfoot observes that it was no unusual thing to dip a sop and give it to any person; and it is probable that the rest of the disciples considered it as given to Judas that he might hurry to do some work on which He wished to employ him, and not wait to finish his supper in a regular manner.

27. *Satan entered into him.* He had entered into him before, and now he enters again, to strengthen him in his purpose of delivering up his Master. But the morsel was not the cause of this entering in; the giving of it only marks the time in which the devil confirmed Judas in his traitorous purpose. Some have thought that this morsel was the sacrament of the Lord's Supper, but this is an utter mistake.

That thou doest, do quickly. As if He had said: "You are past all counsel; you have filled up the measure of your iniquity, and have wholly abandoned yourself to Satan. What you are determined to do, and I to permit, do directly; delay not. I am ready."

29. *Give something to the poor.* It is well-known that our Lord and His disciples lived on public charity, and yet they gave alms out of what they had thus received. From this we learn that even those who live on charity themselves are expected to divide a little with those who are in deeper distress and want.

MATTHEW HENRY

(2) The time of his departure: *It was night.* [1] Though it was night, he made no difficulty of the coldness and darkness of the night. This should shame us out of our slothfulness and cowardice in the service of Christ, that the devil's servants are so earnest and venturous in his service. [2] Because it was night, and this gave him advantage of privacy and concealment. Those whose deeds are evil love darkness rather than light.

Verses 31–35

This and what follows, to the end of *ch.* xiv., was Christ's table-talk with his disciples. When supper was done, Judas went out. Christ begins this discourse. Those especially that by their place, reputation, and gifts, *command the company,* to whom *men give ear,* ought to use the opportunity of doing them good.

I. Concerning the great mystery of his own death and sufferings, about which they were as yet so much in the dark, much less did they understand the meaning of it. Christ did not begin this discourse until Judas was gone out. The presence of wicked people is often a hindrance to good discourse. When Judas *was gone out,* Christ said, *Now is the Son of man glorified.* Christ is glorified by the purifying of Christian societies: corruptions in his church are a reproach to him. Now Judas was gone to set the wheels a-going, in order to his being put to death: *Now is the Son of man glorified,* meaning, *Now he is crucified.*

1. Here is something which Christ instructs them in, concerning his sufferings, that was very *comforting.*

(1) That he should himself be glorified in them. Now the Son of man is to be exposed to the greatest ignominy, and dishonoured both by the cowardice of his friends and the insolence of his enemies; yet *now he is glorified.* Now he is to obtain a glorious victory over Satan and all the powers of darkness. Now he is to work out a glorious deliverance for his people, by his death to reconcile them to God, and bring in an everlasting righteousness and happiness for them. Now he is to give a glorious example of self-denial and patience under the cross, and love to the souls of men, such as will make him to be for ever admired. Christ had been glorified in many miracles he had wrought, and yet he speaks of his being glorified *now* in his sufferings, as if that were more than all his other glories.

(2) That God the Father should be glorified in them. The sufferings of Christ were: The satisfaction of God's justice, and so God was glorified in them. They were the manifestation of his holiness and mercy. God is love, and herein he hath commended his love.

(3) That he should himself be greatly glorified after them, in consideration of God's being greatly glorified by them, *v.* 32. [1] He is sure that God will glorify him. Hell and earth set themselves to vilify Christ, but God resolved to glorify him. He glorified him in his sufferings by the amazing signs and wonders which attended them, and extorted even from his crucifiers an acknowledgment that he was the Son of God. [2] That he will glorify him *in himself.* In Christ himself. He will glorify him in his own person. This supposes his speedy resurrection. [3] That he will glorify him straightway. He looked upon the joy and glory set before him, not only as great, but as near. Good services done to earthly princes often remain long unrewarded; but Christ had his preferments presently. [4] All this in consideration of God's being glorified in and by his sufferings: *Seeing God is glorified in him,* God shall in like manner glorify him in himself. Those who mind the business of glorifying God no doubt shall have the happiness of being glorified with him.

2. Here is something which was *awakening,* for as yet they were slow of heart to understand it (*v.* 33). Two serious words:

(1) That his stay in this world they would find to be very short. *Little children.* This compellation does not bespeak so much their weakness as his tenderness. Know this, then, that *yet a little while I am with you.* Let them improve the advantage they now had. We must make the best of the helps we have for our souls while we have them. Let them not dote upon his bodily presence. They must think of living without it; not be always little children, but go alone, without their nurses.

(2) That their following him to the other world they would find to be very difficult. What he had said to the Jews (*ch.* vii. 34) he saith to his disciples. Christ tells them here, [1] That when he was gone they would feel the want of him: *You shall seek me.* We are often taught the worth of mercies by the want of them. The presence of the Comforter was not such a *sensible* satisfaction as his bodily presence would have been. But observe, Christ said to the Jews, You shall seek me and *not find me;* but to the disciples he only saith, *You shall seek me.* They should find that which was tantamount, and should not seek in vain. [2] That

JAMIESON, FAUSSET, BROWN

and it was night—but far blacker night in the soul of Judas than in the sky over his head.

31-38. DISCOURSE AFTER THE TRAITOR'S DEPARTURE—PETER'S SELF-CONFIDENCE—HIS FALL PREDICTED. **31. when he was gone out, Jesus said, Now is the Son of man glorified**—These remarkable words plainly imply that up to this moment our Lord had spoken *under a painful restraint,* the presence of a traitor within the little circle of His holiest fellowship on earth preventing the free and full outpouring of His heart; as is evident, indeed, from those oft-recurring clauses, "Ye are not all clean," "I speak not of you all," etc. "Now" the restraint is removed, and the embankment which kept in the mighty volume of living waters having broken down, they burst forth in a torrent which only ceases on His leaving the supper room and entering on the next stage of His great work—the scene in the Garden. But with what words is the silence first broken on the departure of Judas? By no reflections on the traitor, and, what is still more wonderful, by no reference to the dread character of His own approaching sufferings. He does not even name them, save by announcing, as with a burst of triumph, that the hour of His *glory* has arrived! And what is very remarkable, in five brief clauses He repeats this word "glorify" *five times,* as if to His view a coruscation of glories played at that moment about the Cross. (See on ch. 12:23.) **God is glorified in him**—the glory of Each reaching its zenith in the Death of the Cross!

32. If God be glorified in him, God shall also—in return and reward of this highest of all services ever rendered to Him, or capable of being rendered—

glorify him in himself, and . . . straightway glorify him—referring now to the Resurrection and Exaltation of Christ *after* this service was over, including all the honor and glory then put upon Him, and that will for ever encircle Him as Head of the new creation.

33-35. Little children—From the height of His own glory He now descends, with sweet pity, to His "little children," *all now His own.* This term of endearment, nowhere else used in the Gospels, and once only employed by Paul (Gal. 4:19), is appropriated by the beloved disciple himself, who no fewer than seven times employs it in his first Epistle.

Ye shall seek me—feel the want of Me. **as I said to the Jews**—ch. 7:34; 8:21. But oh in what a different sense!

ADAM CLARKE

31. *Now is the Son of man glorified.* "Hath been glorified." Now it fully appears that I am the Person appointed to redeem a lost world by My blood. I have already been glorified by this appointment, and am about to be further glorified by My death, resurrection, and ascension.

ALEXANDER MACLAREN:

"Now is the Son of man glorified." There blend, in that last act of our Lord's—for His death was His act—in strange fashion, the two contradictory ideas of glory and shame; like some sky, all full of dark thunderclouds, and yet between them the brightest blue and the blazing sunshine. In the cross, Death crowns Him the Prince of Life, and His cross is His throne. All His life long He was the Light of the World, but the very noontide hour of His glory was that hour when the shadow of eclipse lay over all the land, and He hung on the cross dying in the dark. At His "eventide it was light." "He endured the cross, despising the shame"; and lo! the shame flashed up into the very brightness of glory, and the ignominy and the suffering became the jewels of His crown. "Now is the Son of man glorified."

—*Expositions of Holy Scripture*

32. *And shall straightway glorify him.* Or "glorify Him immediately"; as He did, not only in the miracles wrought at His death, but also in that remarkable case mentioned, chap. xviii. 6, when the whole crowd that came to seize Him were driven back with a word of His mouth, and fell to the ground.

33. *Little children.* Or, rather, "beloved children"—a word frequently used by this apostle in his Epistles. It is an expression which implies great tenderness and affection, and such as a fond mother uses to her most beloved babes. Now that Judas was gone out, He could use this epithet without any restriction of meaning. *Yet a little while.* The end of My life is at hand; Judas is gone to consummate his treason; I have but a few hours to be with you, and by and by you shall be scattered.

Ye shall seek me. For a few days you shall feel great distress because of My absence. *Whither I go, ye cannot come.* Your time is not up.

MATTHEW HENRY

whither he went they *could not come*. Christ tells them that they could not follow him only to quicken them to so much the more diligence and care. They could not follow him to his cross, for they had not courage and resolution. Nor could they follow him to his crown.

II. He discourses with them concerning the great duty of brotherly love (*v.* 34, 35): *You shall love one another.* Now that they must expect such treatment as their Master had, it concerned them by brotherly love to strengthen one another's hands. Three arguments for mutual love are here urged:

1. The command of their Master (*v.* 34): *A new commandment I give unto you.* He not only commends it, not only counsels but commands it, and makes it one of the fundamental laws of his kingdom. It is *a new commandment.* It is a renewed commandment. It is like an old book in a new edition corrected and enlarged. This commandment has been so corrupted that when Christ revised it, it might well be called a *new commandment.* The law of brotherly love was forgotten as obsolete and out of date; so that as it came from Christ new, it was new to the people. It is an everlasting command; so strangely new as to be always so. It shall be new to eternity, when faith and hope are antiquated. As Christ gives it, it is *new.* Before it was, *Thou shalt love thy neighbour;* now it is, You shall love *one another*; it is pressed in a more winning way when it is thus pressed as mutual duty owing to one another.

2. The example of their Saviour is another argument for brotherly love: *As I have loved you.* It is this that makes it a *new commandment.* Understand this of all the instances of Christ's love to his disciples. Thus he *had* loved them, and thus they *must* love one another, and love *to the end.* It may be understood of the special instance of love which he was now about to give, in laying down his life for them. *Greater love hath no man than this, ch.* xv. 13. We must love one another in some respects after the *same manner*; we must set this before us as our copy. It must be love *to the souls* one of another. We must also love one another from *this motive*, and upon this consideration —because Christ has loved us.

3. The reputation of their profession (*v.* 35): *By this shall all men know that you are my disciples, if you have love one to another.* We must have love, not only show love, but have it in the root and habit of it; have it *ready.* Brotherly love is the badge of Christ's disciples. This is the livery of his family; this he would have them *noted for*, as that wherein they excelled all others —their loving one another. This was what their Master was famous for; and therefore, if you see any people more affectionate one to another than what is common, say, "Certainly these are the followers of Christ, they have been with Jesus." The heart of Christ was very much upon it. In this they must be *singular*; whereas the way of the world is to be *everyone for himself*, they should be hearty for one another. He does not say, *By this shall men know* that you are my disciples—if you *work miracles*, for a worker of miracles is but a cipher without charity (1 Cor. xiii. 1, 2). It is the true honour of Christ's disciples to excel in brotherly love. Christians were known by their affection to one another. Their adversaries took notice of it, and said, *See how these Christians love one another.* If the followers of Christ do not love one another, they give just cause to suspect their own sincerity. When our brethren stand in need of help from us, when they are any ways rivals with or provoking to us, and so we have an occasion to forgive, in such cases as this it will be known whether we have this badge of Christ's disciples.

Verses 36-38

In these verses we have,

I. Peter's curiosity.

1. Peter's question was bold and blunt (*v.* 36): *Lord, whither goest thou?* referring to what Christ had said (*v.* 33), *Whither I go, you cannot come.* It is a common fault among us to be more desirous to have our curiosity gratified than our consciences directed. It is easy to observe it in the converse of Christians, how soon a discourse of that which is plain and edifying is dropped, and no more said to it; which in a matter of doubtful disputation runs into an endless strife of words.

2. Christ's answer. He did not gratify him, but said what he had said before (*v.* 36): Let this suffice, *thou canst not follow me now, but thou shalt follow me hereafter.* We may understand it of his following him to the cross. When Christ was seized, he provided for the safety of his disciples. *Let these go their way*, because they could not *follow him now.* Christ considers the frame of his disciples. The day shall be as the strength is. Peter, though designed for martyrdom, cannot follow Christ now, but he *shall follow* him here-

JAMIESON, FAUSSET, BROWN

34. a new commandment I give unto you, That ye love one another; as I have loved you, that ye also love one another—This was the *new* feature of it. Christ's love to His people in giving His life a ransom for them was altogether new, and consequently as a Model and Standard for theirs to one another. It is not, however, something transcending the great moral law, which is "the *old* commandment" (I John 2:7, and see on Mark 12:28-33), but that law *in a new and peculiar form.* Hence it is said to be both *new* and *old* (I John 2:7, 8).

35. By this shall all men know that ye are my disciples—the disciples of Him who laid down His life for those He loved. **if ye have love one to another**—for My sake, and as one in Me; for to *such* love men outside the circle of believers know right well they are entire strangers. Alas, how little of it there is even within this circle!

36-38. Peter said—seeing plainly in these directions how to behave themselves, that He was indeed going from them. **Lord, whither goest thou?**—having hardly a glimmer of the real truth.

Jesus answered, . . . thou canst not follow me now, but thou shalt follow me afterwards—How different from what He said to the Jews: "Whither I go *ye cannot come*" (ch. 8:21).

ADAM CLARKE

34. *A new commandment I give unto you.* In what sense are we to understand that this was a *new* commandment? "Thou shalt love thy neighbour as thyself," was a positive precept of the law, Lev. xix. 18, and it is the very same that Christ repeats here; how then was it *new?*

Our Lord answers this question, Even *as I have loved you.* Now Christ more than fulfilled the Mosaic precept; He not only loved His neighbor as himself, but He loved him more than himself, for He laid down His life for men. In this He calls upon the disciples to imitate Him, to be ready on all occasions to lay down their lives for each other.

35. *By this shall all men know.* From this time forward, this mutual and disinterested love shall become the essential and distinctive mark of all My disciples. When they love one another with pure hearts, fervently, even unto death, then shall it fully appear that they are disciples of that Person who laid down His life for His sheep, and who became, by dying, a Ransom for all. The disciples of different teachers were known by their habits, or some particular creed or rite, or point of austerity, which they had adopted; but the disciples of Christ were known by this love which they bore to each other. The primitive Christians were particularly known by this among the Gentiles. Tertullian, in his *Apology,* gives us their very words: "See, said they, how they love one another, and are ready to lay down their lives for each other."

36. *Thou canst not follow me now.* You have not faith strong enough to die for Me, nor is your work yet done; but hereafter you shall suffer for My sake, and die in defense of My truth. See chap. xxi. 18.

MATTHEW HENRY

after; he shall be crucified at last, like his Master. Let him not think that because he escapes suffering now he shall never suffer. We may be reserved for greater trials than we have yet known. We may understand it of his following him to the crown: "No," saith Christ, "*thou canst not follow me now. Thou shalt follow me afterwards*, after thou hast fought the good fight." There is a wilderness between the Red Sea and Canaan.

II. Peter's confidence.

1. Peter makes a daring protestation of his constancy. "*Lord, why cannot I follow thee now? I will lay down my life for thy sake.*" Having heard his Master so often speak of his own sufferings, surely he could not understand him any otherwise than of his going away by death; and he resolves as Thomas did that he will *go and die with him*; and better die with him than live without him. What an affectionate love Peter had to our Lord Jesus: "*I will lay down my life for thy sake.*" Peter spoke as he thought, and though he was inconsiderate he was not insincere. How ill he took it to have it questioned: "*Lord, why cannot I follow thee now?* Dost thou suspect my fidelity to thee?" It is with regret that true love hears its own sincerity arraigned. We are apt to think that we can do anything, and take it amiss to be told that this and the other we cannot do, whereas without Christ we can do nothing.

2. Christ gives him a surprising prediction of his inconstancy, *v.* 38. He upbraids Peter with his confidence: ***Wilt thou lay down thy life for my sake?*** **Christ** hereby puts Peter upon second thoughts, that he might insert into it that necessary proviso, "Lord, *thy grace enabling me*, I will lay down my life for thy sake." "Wilt thou undertake to die for me? What! thou that trembledst to walk upon the water to me? It was an easy thing to leave thy boats and nets to follow me, but not so easy to lay down thy life." It is good for us to shame ourselves out of our presumptuous confidence in ourselves. What a fool am I to talk so big. He plainly foretells his cowardice in the critical hour. Christ solemnly asserts it with, *Verily, verily, I say unto thee, the cock shall not crow till thou hast denied me thrice: the cock shall not crow*, shall not have crowed his crowing out, till thou hast again and again denied me. The crowing of the cock was to be the occasion of his repentance. Christ not only foresaw that Judas would betray him, but he foresaw that Peter would deny him though he did not design it, but the contrary. He knows not only the wickedness of sinners but the weakness of saints. Christ told Peter that he would deny him. That he would do this not once only by a hasty slip of the tongue, but would repeat it a second and a third time. We may well imagine what a mortification it was to Peter's confidence of his own courage to be told this. The most secure are commonly the least safe; and those most shamefully betray their own weakness that most confidently presume upon their own strength, 1 Cor. x. 12.

JAMIESON, FAUSSET, BROWN

37. why not . . . now? I will lay down my life for thy sake—He seems now to see that it was *death* Christ referred to as what would sever Him from them, but is not staggered at following Him thither.

Jesus answered, **38. Wilt thou lay down thy life for my sake?**—In this repetition of Peter's words there is deep though affectionate irony, and this Peter himself would feel for many a day after his recovery, as he retraced the painful particulars. **Verily . . . The cock . . .**—See on Luke 22:31-34.

ADAM CLARKE

37. *Why cannot I follow thee now?* Peter probably thought that our Lord intended to go on some long journey, which would necessarily subject Him to many inconveniences and fatigue; and he felt quite disposed to follow Him in this supposed journey, at all hazards. He saw no reason, because he did not see our Lord's meaning, why he could not follow Him *now. I will lay down my life for thy sake.* Poor Peter! You were sincere, but you did not know your own strength. You were at this time willing to die, but when the time came were not able. Christ must first die for Peter, before Peter can die for Him. Let no man think he can do anything good without the immediate assistance of God. Peter's denial should be an eternal warning to all self-confident persons; though there be sincerity and goodwill at the bottom, yet in the trial these cannot perform that office which belongs to the power of God. We should *will*, and then look to God for *power* to execute; without Him we can do nothing.

F. B. MEYER:

Heaven delayed. "Thou canst not follow me now." The emphasis is not on the cannot. It is as though the Master said, "The hindrance is not in some arbitrary edict of divine power, but in the infinite knowledge and wisdom that cannot err." Peter was not fit to go. There were lessons of the utmost importance waiting for him to acquire in the near future. He must learn to know himself, and Christ, and the grace of the Holy Spirit. When he proudly vaunted that he would lay down his life for Jesus, he gave incontestable evidence that he did not know himself; and there was every reason to think that he was similarly deceived when he supposed that he was fit to quit earth's discipline, and enter on heaven's blessed enjoyment. He must exchange his own strivings and resolvings for the gracious indwelling of the Spirit of Pentecost; he must learn the glorious energy of the indwelling Savior; he must be girded by another and carried whither he would not; and only then would the time of his putting off of the tabernacle of the body arrive.—*Great Verses Through the Bible*

MATTHEW HENRY

CHAPTER 14

Verses 1–3

I. A general caution which Christ gives to his disciples against *trouble of heart* (*v.* 1): *Let not your heart be troubled.*

1. How Christ took notice of it. Perhaps it was apparent in their looks; at least it was intelligible to the Lord Jesus, who is acquainted with all our secret undiscovered sorrows, with the wound that bleeds inwardly. He takes cognizance of all the trouble which his people are at any time in danger of being overwhelmed with. Many things concurred to trouble the disciples now.

(1) Christ had just told them of the unkindness he should receive from some of them, and this troubled them all. Christ comforts them; though a godly jealousy over ourselves is of great use to keep us humble and watchful, yet it must not prevail to the disquieting of our spirits and the damping of our holy joy.

(2) He had just told them of his own departure from them, that he should not only go away, but go away in a cloud of sufferings. When we now look upon Christ pierced, we cannot but *mourn and be in bitterness*, though we see the glorious issue and fruit of it; much more grievous must be the sight to them, who could then look no further. If Christ depart from them, [1] They will think themselves shamefully disappointed; for they looked that this had been he that should have delivered Israel. [2] They will think themselves sadly deserted and exposed. Now, in reference to all these, *Let not your hearts be troubled.* Here are three words, upon any of which the emphasis may significantly be laid. Upon the word *troubled.*

JAMIESON, FAUSSET, BROWN

CHAPTER 14

VSS. 1-31. DISCOURSE AT THE TABLE, AFTER SUPPER. We now come to that portion of the evangelical history which we may with propriety call its *Holy of Holies*. Our Evangelist, like a consecrated priest, alone opens up to us the view into this sanctuary. It is the record of the last moments spent by the Lord in the midst of His disciples before His passion, when words full of heavenly thought flowed from His sacred lips. All that His heart, glowing with love, had still to say to His friends, was compressed into this short season. At first (from ch. 13:31) the intercourse took the form of conversation; sitting at table, they talked familiarly together. But when (14:31) the repast was finished, the language of Christ assumed a loftier strain; the disciples, assembled around their Master, listened to the words of life, and seldom spoke a word (only ch. 16:17, 29). At length, in the Redeemer's sublime intercessory prayer, His full soul was poured forth in express petitions to His heavenly Father on behalf of those who were His own. It is a peculiarity of these last chapters, that they treat almost exclusively of the most profound relations—as that of the Son to the Father, and of both to the Spirit, that of Christ to the Church, of the Church to the world, and so forth. Moreover, a considerable portion of these sublime communications surpassed the point of view to which the disciples had at that time attained; hence the Redeemer frequently repeats the same sentiments in order to impress them more deeply upon their minds, and, because of what they still did not un-

ADAM CLARKE

CHAPTER 14

1. *Let not your heart be troubled.* After having answered Peter's question, He addresses himself again to His disciples, and tells them not to be afflicted at His leaving them, nor to lose courage because of what He said concerning Peter's denying Him; that if they reposed their confidence in God, He would protect them; and that, howsoever they might see Him treated, they should believe in Him more firmly, as His sufferings, death, and resurrection should be to them the most positive proof of His being the Messiah, the Saviour of the world.

MATTHEW HENRY

Be not *like the troubled sea when* it cannot rest. He does not say, "Let not your hearts be sensible of the griefs, or sad because of them," but, "Be not ruffled and discomposed." Upon the word *heart*: "*Let not your heart be troubled.*" Keep possession of your own souls when you can keep possession of nothing else. The heart is the main fort; whatever you do, keep trouble from this. Upon the word *your*: "You that are my disciples and followers, be not you so, for you know better." Herein Christ's disciples should *do more than others*, should keep their minds quiet, when everything else is unquiet.

2. The remedy he prescribes; in general, *believe.* (1) Some read it in both parts imperatively, "*Believe in God*, and his perfections and providence, *believe also in me*, and my mediation." (2) We read the former as an acknowledgment that they did believe in God. "But, if you would effectually provide against a stormy day, *believe also in me.*" By believing in Christ as the Mediator between God and man, our belief in God becomes comfortable. Those that rightly believe in God will believe in Jesus Christ, and believing in God through Jesus Christ is an excellent means of keeping trouble from the heart. The joy of faith is the best remedy against the griefs of sense.

II. Here is a particular direction to act faith upon the promise of eternal life, *v.* 2, 3. But what must they trust God and Christ for? Trust them for a happiness to come, for a happiness to last as long as the immortal soul and the eternal world shall last. The saints have encouraged themselves with this in their greatest extremities. *That heaven would make amends for all.* Let us see how this is suggested here.

1. Believe and consider that really there is such a happiness: *In my Father's house there are many mansions; if it were not so, I would have told you, v.* 2.

(1) See under what notion the happiness of heaven is here represented: as *mansions.* Heaven is a house, not a tent or tabernacle. It is a Father's house: *my Father's house*; and his Father is our Father. All true believers shall be welcome to that happiness as to their home. There are *mansions* there. Distinct dwellings, an apartment for each. Our individuality shall not be lost there. Durable dwellings. The house itself is lasting; our estate in it is not for a term of years, but a perpetuity. Here we are as in an inn; in heaven we shall gain a settlement. There are *many* mansions, for there are many sons to be brought to glory.

(2) See what assurance we have of the reality of the happiness itself: "*If it were not so, I would have told you.*" The assurance is built: Upon the veracity of his word. Upon the sincerity of his affection to them. As he is true, and would not impose upon them himself, so he is kind, and would not suffer them to be imposed upon. He loves us too well, and means us too well, to disappoint the expectations of his own raising.

2. Believe and consider that the design of Christ's going away was to prepare a place in heaven for his disciples. He went to prepare a place for us; to take possession for us, as our advocate or attorney, and so to secure our title as indefeasible; to make provision. The happiness of heaven yet must be further fitted up for man. It consisting much in the presence of Christ there, it was therefore necessary that he should *go before.* Heaven would be an *unready* place for a Christian if Christ were not there.

3. Believe and consider that *therefore* he would certainly come again (*v.* 3): "*If I go and prepare a place for you, I will come again, and receive you to myself, that where I am there you may be also.*" Now these are comfortable words indeed. (1) That Jesus Christ will come again; intimating the certainty of it. We say, We are coming, when we are busy in preparing for our coming, and so he is. (2) That he will come again to receive all his faithful followers to himself. The coming of Christ is in order to our gathering *together unto him.* (3) That where he is there they shall be also. This intimates that the quintessence of heaven's happiness is being with Christ *there. That where I am;* where I am to be shortly, where I am to be eternally; there you shall be shortly, there you shall be eternally: not only spectators of his glory, but sharers in it. (4) That this may be inferred from his *going to prepare a place* for us, for his preparations shall not be in vain. He will not build and furnish lodgings, and let them stand empty. If he has prepared the place for us, he will prepare us for it, and in due time put us in possession of it.

Verses 4–11

Christ, having set the happiness of heaven before them as the end, here shows them himself as the way to it. *You know*, 1. "You may know; it is none of the *secret things* which belong not to you, but one of the *things revealed.*" 2. "You do know; you know that which is the home and which is the way, though per-

JAMIESON, FAUSSET, BROWN

derstand, points them to the Holy Spirit, who would remind them of all His sayings, and lead them into all truth (14:26)" [OLSHAUSEN]. **1. Let not your heart be troubled . . .**—What myriads of souls have not these opening words cheered, in deepest gloom, since first they were uttered!

ye believe in God— absolutely. **believe also in me**—i.e., Have the *same trust* in Me. What less, and what else, can these words mean? And if so, what a demand to make by one sitting familiarly with them at the supper table! Cf. the saying in ch. 5:17, for which the Jews took up stones to stone Him, as "making himself equal with God" (vs. 18). But it is no *transfer of our trust from its proper Object;* it is but *the concentration of our trust in the Unseen and Impalpable One upon His Own Incarnate Son,* by which that trust, instead of the distant, unsteady, and too often cold and scarce real thing it otherwise is, acquires a conscious reality, warmth, and power, which makes all things new. *This is Christianity in brief.*

2. In my Father's house are many mansions—and so room for all, and a place for each.

if not, I would have told you—i.e., I would tell you so at once; I would not deceive you.

I go to prepare a place for you—to obtain for you a right to be there, and to possess your "place." **3. I will come again and receive you unto myself**—*strictly*, at His Personal appearing; but in a secondary and comforting sense, to each individually. Mark again the claim made:—to come again to receive His people *to Himself*, that where *He is* there they may be also. *He thinks it ought to be enough to be assured that they shall be where He is and in His keeping.*

ADAM CLARKE

Ye believe in God, believe also in me. It is best to read both the verbs in the imperative mood—Place your confidence in God, and in Me as the Mediator between God and man, vv. 12-14; expect the utmost support from God, but expect it all through Me. The disciples began to lose all hope of a secular kingdom, and were discouraged in consequence. Christ promises them a spiritual and heavenly inheritance, and thus lifts up their drooping hearts.

2. *In my Father's house.* The Kingdom of glory. *Many mansions.* Though I have said before that where I am going you cannot come now, yet do not think that we shall be forever separated. I am going to that state of glory where there is not only a place of supreme eminence for myself, but also places for all My disciples—various degrees of glory suited to the various capacities and attainments of My followers. Our Lord alludes here to the Temple, which was called the "house of God," in the precincts of which there were a great number of chambers, 1 Kings vi. 5; Ezra viii. 29; Jer. xxxv. 2, 4; xxxvi. 10. *If it were not so, I would have told you.* If your places were not prepared in the kingdom of God, I would not have permitted you to have indulged a vain hope concerning future blessedness.

3. *And if I go.* And when I shall have gone and prepared a place for you—opened the Kingdom of an eternal glory for your reception, and for the reception of all that shall die in the faith—*I will come again*, after My resurrection, and give you the fullest assurances of this state of blessedness; and confirm you in the faith, by My grace and the effusion of My Spirit.

4. *And whither I go ye know.* I have told you this so often and so plainly that you must certainly have comprehended what I have said.

MATTHEW HENRY

haps not as the home and as the way. You have been told it, and cannot but know."

I. Thomas enquired concerning the way (*v.* 5).

He said, "*Lord, we know not whither thou goest, and how can we know the way?*" Christ's testimony concerning their knowledge made them more sensible of their ignorance, and more inquisitive after further light. Thomas here shows more modesty than Peter. Peter was the more solicitous to know *whither Christ went*. Thomas here seems more solicitous to know *the way*. His confession of his ignorance was commendable enough. If good men be in the dark, and know it but in part, yet they are willing to own their defects. The cause of his ignorance was culpable. They knew not whither Christ went, because they dreamed of a temporal kingdom. Their fancy ran upon his going to some remarkable city or other, there to be anointed king. Where these castles in the air were to be built, east, west, north, or south, they could not tell, and therefore knew not the way. Had Thomas understood, that Christ was going to the invisible world, he would not have said, *Lord, we do not know the way.*

II. Now to this complaint of their ignorance Christ gives a full answer, *v.* 6, 7. Thomas had enquired both whither he went and what was the way, and Christ answers both these enquiries. They knew him, and he was the way; they knew the Father, and he was the end; and therefore, *whither I go you know, and the way you know*. Believe in God as the end, and in me as the way (*v.* 1).

(1) He speaks of himself as the way, *v.* 6. *I am the way; no man comes to the Father but by me.*

[1] The nature of his mediation: He is *the way, the truth, and the life*. Let us consider these first distinctly. Christ is *the way*. In him God and man meet, and are brought together. We could not get to the tree of life in the way of innocency; but Christ is another way to it. The disciples followed him, and Christ tells them that while they continued following him, they would never be out of their way. He is *the truth*; as truth is opposed to falsehood and error. When we enquire for truth, we need learn no more than *the truth as it is in Jesus*; as truth is opposed to fallacy and deceit; as true as truth itself. He is *the life*; for we are *alive unto God* only in and *through Jesus Christ*. Let us consider these jointly. Christ is *the way, the truth, and the life*. He is the beginning, the middle, and the end. He is *the true and living way*; there are *truth and life* in the way, as well as at the end of it. He is *the true way to life*. Other ways may seem right, but the end of them is *the way of death*.

[2] The necessity of his mediation: *No man cometh to the Father but by me.* Fallen man cannot come to him as a Father, otherwise than by Christ as Mediator.

(2) He speaks of his Father as the end (*v.* 7): "*If you had known me, you would have known my Father also; and henceforth you know him and have seen him.*" A tacit rebuke to them for their dullness and carelessness in not acquainting themselves with Jesus Christ: *If you had known me——*. They knew him, and yet did not know him so well as they might and should have known him. Christ had said to the Jews (*ch.* viii. 19): *If you had known me, you would have known my Father also;* and here the same to his disciples; for it is hard to say which is the more strange, the wilful ignorance of those that are enemies to the light, or the defects and mistakes of *the children of light*. He was well satisfied concerning their sincerity, notwithstanding the weakness of their understanding: "*And henceforth you know him, and have seen him,*" for in the face of Christ we see the glory of God. Many of the disciples of Christ have more knowledge and more grace than they think they have. Those that know God do not all at once know that they know him.

III. Philip enquired concerning the Father (*v.* 8), and Christ answered him, *v.* 9–11.

1. Philip's request for some extraordinary discovery of the Father. From an earnest desire of further light, he cries out, *Show us the Father*. "That is what we want, that is what we would have: *Show us the Father and it sufficeth us.*" This supposes an earnest desire of acquaintance with God as a Father. The petition is, "*Show us the Father.*" The plea is, *It sufficeth us*. Grant us but one sight of the Father, and we have enough. In the knowledge of God as our Father the soul is satisfied; a sight of the Father is a heaven upon earth. "Let us see the Father with our bodily eyes, as we see thee, *and it sufficeth us.*" It manifests not only the weakness of his faith, but his ignorance of the gospel way of manifesting *the Father*. Christ's institutions have provided better for the confirmation of our faith than our own inventions would.

2. Christ's reply, *v.* 9–11.

(1) He refers him to what he had seen, *v.* 9. "*Have I been so long time with you, and yet hast thou not known me, Philip?* Now, *he that hath seen me hath seen*

JAMIESON, FAUSSET, BROWN

4-7. whither I go ye know . . . Thomas saith, Lord, we know not whither thou goest . . ., Jesus saith, I am the way . . .—By saying this, He meant rather to draw out their inquiries and reply to them. Christ is "THE WAY" to the Father—"no man cometh unto the Father but by Me"; He is "THE TRUTH" of all we find in the Father when we get to Him, "For in Him dwelleth all the fulness of the Godhead bodily" (Col. 2:9), and He is all "THE LIFE" that shall ever flow to us and bless us from the Godhead thus approached and thus manifested in Him—"this is the true God and eternal life" (I John 5:20).

7. from henceforth—now, or from this time, understand.

8-12. The substance of this passage is that the Son is the ordained and perfect manifestation of the Father, that His own word for this ought to His disciples to be enough; that if any doubts remained His works ought to remove them (see on ch. 10:37, 38); but yet that these works of His were designed merely to aid weak faith, and would be repeated, nay exceeded, by His disciples, in virtue of the power He would confer on them after His departure. His miracles the apostles wrought, though wholly in His name and by His power, and the "greater" works—not in degree but in kind—were the conversion of thousands in a day, by His Spirit accompanying them.

ADAM CLARKE

5. *Lord, we know not.* Thomas, perhaps, thought that our Lord only spoke of His going some distance from the place where He then was.

6. *I am the way* that leads to the Father; *the truth* that teaches the knowledge of God, and directs in the way; *the life* that animates all those who seek and serve Him, and which is to be enjoyed eternally at the end of the way.

7. *If ye had known me, ye should have known my Father.* Because I and the Father are one, chap. x. 30. Or, If you had properly examined the intention and design of the law, you would have been convinced that it referred to Me; and that all that I have done and instituted was according to the design and intention of the Father, as expressed in that law.

8. *Shew us the Father.* As if he had said, We have seen and adored Thee, and our happiness will be complete if Thou show us the Father. The demand of Philip was similar to that made by Moses, Exod. xxxiii. 18. He wished to see the glory of God. In Peter, James, or John, this would have been inexcusable; but Philip had not seen the Transfiguration on the mount.

MATTHEW HENRY

the Father; and how sayest thou then, Show us the Father?" He reproves him for two things: [1] For not improving his acquaintance with Christ to a clear and distinct knowledge of him: "*Hast thou not known me, Philip?*" Philip, the first day he came to him, declared that he knew him to be the Messiah (*ch.* i. 45), and yet to this day did *not know the Father* in him. Many know Christ, who yet do not know what they might know of him, nor see what they should see in him. *I have been so long time with thee.* Christ expects that our proficiency should be in some measure according to our standing, that we should not be always babes. [2] For his infirmity in the prayer made, *Show us the Father.* Herein appears much of the weakness of Christ's disciples that they *know not what to pray for as they ought* (Rom. viii. 26), but often *ask amiss* (Jas. iv. 3). He instructs him, and gives him a maxim which justifies what he had said (*v.* 7): *You know the Father, and have seen him;* and answered what Philip had asked, *Show us the Father. He that hath seen me hath seen the Father.* All that saw *Christ in the flesh* might *have seen the Father* in him. All that saw Christ by faith did *see the Father* in him, though they were not suddenly aware that they did so. The holiness of God shone in the spotless purity of Christ's life, and his grace in all the acts of grace he did.

(2) He refers him to what he had reason to believe (*v.* 10, 11): "*Believest thou not that I am in the Father, and the Father in me,* and therefore that in *seeing me* thou hast *seen the Father?*" What it is which we are to believe: *That I am in the Father, and the Father in me;* that is, as he had said (*ch.* x. 30), *I and my Father are one.* In knowing Christ we know the Father; and in seeing him we see the Father. What inducements we have to believe this. We must believe it: For his word's sake: *The words that I speak to you, I speak not of myself. He spoke not of himself* only, but the mind of God according to the eternal counsels. For his works' sake: *The Father that dwelleth in me, he doeth them;* and therefore *believe me for their sake.* The Father is said to *dwell* in him. The Father so dwells in Christ that in him he may *be found*, as a man where he dwells. *Seek ye the Lord, seek* him in Christ, and *he will be found*, for in him he dwells. *He doeth the works.* Many works of power, and works of mercy, Christ did, and the Father did them in him. We are bound to believe this, *for the very works' sake.* Christ's miracles are proofs of his divine mission, not only for the conviction of infidels, but for the confirmation of the faith of his own disciples.

Verses 12–14

The disciples, as they were full of grief to think of parting with their Master, so they were full of care what would become of themselves when he was gone. If he leave them, they will be *as sheep having no shepherd.* Christ here assures them that they should be clothed with powers sufficient to bear them out.

I. Great power on earth (*v.* 12): *He that believeth on me, the works that I do shall he do also.* This magnifies his power more than anything, that he not only wrought miracles himself, but gave power to others to do so too.

1. Two things he assures them of:

(1) That they should be enabled to do such works as he had done. Did Christ *heal the sick, cleanse the leper, raise the dead?* So should they. Did he convince and convert sinners, and draw multitudes to him? So should they. Though he should depart, the work should not cease, nor fall to the ground; and it is still in the doing.

(2) That they should do *greater works than these.* In the kingdom of nature they should work greater miracles. No miracle is little, but some to our apprehension seem greater than others. Christ wrought miracles for two or three years in one country, but his followers wrought miracles in his name for many ages in divers countries. In the kingdom of grace, they should obtain greater victories by the gospel than had been obtained while Christ was upon earth. The truth is, the captivating of so great a part of the world to Christ, was the miracle of all.

2. The reason Christ gives for this is, *Because I go unto my Father.* "*Because I go*, it will be requisite that you should have such a power. *Because I go to the Father*, I shall be in a capacity to furnish you with such a power."

II. Great *power in heaven:* "*Whatsoever you shall ask, that will I do*" (*v.* 13, 14).

1. In what way they were to derive power from him, when he was gone to the Father—by prayer. When dear friends are to be removed to a distance from each other, they provide for the settling of a correspondence; thus, when Christ was going to his Father, he tells his disciples how they might write to him upon every occasion, and send their epistles by a safe

JAMIESON, FAUSSET, BROWN

ALEXANDER MACLAREN:

The vehement burst with which Philip interrupts the calm flow of our Lord's discourse is not the product of mere frivolity or curiosity. One hears the ring of earnestness in it, and the yearnings of many years find voice. Philip had felt out of his depth, no doubt, in the profound teachings which our Lord had been giving, but His last words about seeing God set a familiar chord vibrating. As an Old Testament believer he knew that Moses had once led the elders of Israel up to the mount where "they saw the God of Israel," and that to many others had been granted sensible manifestations of the divine presence. As a disciple he longed for some similar sign to confirm his faith. As a man he was conscious of the deep need which all of us have, whether we are conscious of it or not, for something more real and tangible than an unseeable and unknowable God. The peculiarities of Philip's temperament strengthened the desire. The first appearance that he makes in the Gospels is characteristically like this his last. To all Nathanael's objections he had only the reply, "Come and see." And here he says: "Oh! if we could *see* the Father it would be enough." He was one of the men to whom seeing is believing, and so he speaks.

His petition is childlike in its simplicity, beautiful in its trust, noble and true in its estimate of what men need. He longs to see God. He believes that Christ can show God; he is sure that the sight of God will satisfy the heart. These are errors, or truths, according to what is meant by "seeing." Philip meant a palpable manifestation, and so far he was wrong. Give the word its highest and its truest meaning, and Philip's error becomes grand truth. Our Lord gently, lovingly, and with only a hint of rebuke, answers the request and seeks to disengage the error from the truth.

There is a word of sadness and tenderness, of suppressed pain and of grieved affection, in the first words of our Lord's reply. "Have I been so long time with you, and yet hast thou not known me, Philip?" He seldom names His disciples. When He does, there is a deep cadence of affection in the designation. This man was one of the first disciples, the little original band called by Christ himself, and thus had been with Him all the time of His ministry, and the Master wonders with a gentle wonder that, before eyes that loved Him as much as Philip's did, His continual self-revelation had been made to so little purpose. In the answer, in its first portion, there lies the reiteration of the thoughts that the sight of Christ is the sight of God—"He that hath seen me hath seen the Father"—and that not to know Christ as thus showing God is not to know Him at all—"Thou hast not known me, Philip." Further, there is the thought that the sight of God in Christ is sufficient, "How sayest thou, Shew us the Father?"

—*Expositions of Holy Scripture*

13, 14. whatsoever ye . . . ask in my name—as Mediator—**that will I do**—as Head and Lord of the kingdom of God. This comprehensive promise is emphatically repeated in vs. 14.

ADAM CLARKE

9. *He that hath seen me hath seen the Father.* Could any *creature* say these words? Do they not evidently imply that Christ declared himself to His disciples to be the everlasting God?

10. *I am in the Father, and the Father in me.* We are essentially one, and those who have seen Me have seen Him who sent me. *He doeth the works.* We are not only one in nature, but one also in operation. The works which I have done bear witness of the infinite perfection of My nature. Such miracles as I have wrought could be performed only by unlimited power.

12. *And greater works than these.* The miracles which I have wrought could not have been wrought but by the omnipotence of God, but that omnipotence can work *greater.* And those who believe on My name shall, through My almighty power, be enabled to work *greater* miracles than those which I have ordinarily wrought. Perhaps the *greater works* refer to the immense multitudes that were brought to God by the ministry of the apostles. *Because I go unto my Father.* Where I shall be an Intercessor for you, that—

13. *Whatsoever ye shall ask in my name.* To enable you to perform these miracles, and to convert souls, may be granted you. Besides, by going unto the Father, I shall receive the Holy Spirit, and send down His abundant influences into the hearts of those who believe.

MATTHEW HENRY

and ready way of conveyance. "Let me hear from you by prayer, and you shall hear from me by the Spirit." And it is still open to us. Humility prescribed: *You shall ask*. They could demand nothing of him as a debt, but must be humble supplicants, beg or starve, beg or perish. Liberty allowed: "Ask anything, anything that is good and proper for you; anything, provided you know what you ask." Occasions vary, but they shall be welcome to the throne of grace upon every occasion.

2. In what name they were to present their petitions: *Ask in my name*. They were to plead his merit and intercession, and to depend upon it. If we ask *in our own name*, we cannot expect to speed, for, being strangers, we have *no name* in heaven; being sinners, we have an *ill name* there; but Christ's is a good name, well known in heaven.

3. What success they should have in their prayers: "What you ask, *that will I do*," *v.* 13. And again (*v.* 14), "*I will do it*. You may be sure I will: not only it shall be done, but *I will do it*." By faith in his name we may have what we will for the asking.

4. For what reason their prayers should speed so well: *That the Father may be glorified in the Son. Hallowed be thy name* is an answered prayer, and is put first, because, if the heart be sincere in this, it does in a manner *consecrate* all the other petitions. This Christ will aim at in granting, and for the sake of this will do what they ask. The wisdom, power, and goodness of God were magnified in the Redeemer when his apostles and ministers were enabled to do such great things, both in the proofs of their doctrine and in the successes of it.

Verses 15–17

Christ here promises to send the Spirit, whose office it should be to be their Comforter, to *impress* these things upon them.

I. He premises to this a memento of duty (*v.* 15): *If you love me, keep my commandments*. We must not expect comfort but in the way of duty. When they were in care what would become of them now, he bids them *keep his commandments*. In difficult times our care concerning the events of the day should be swallowed up in a care concerning the duty of the day. When they were showing their love to Christ by their grieving to think of his departure, and the sorrow which filled their hearts, he bids them, if they would show their love to him, do it, not by these weak and feminine passions, but by a universal obedience to his commands; this is better than sacrifice, better than tears. When Christ has given them precious promises he lays down this as a limitation of the promises, "Provided you keep my commandments, from a principle of love to me."

II. He promises this great and unspeakable blessing to them, *v.* 16, 17.

1. It is promised that they shall have *another comforter*. This is the great New Testament promise; a promise adapted to the present distress of the disciples, who were in sorrow, and needed a comforter.

(1) The blessing promised. The word is used only here in these discourses of Christ's, and 1 John ii. 1, where he translates it an *advocate*. You shall have another *advocate*. The office of the Spirit was to be Christ's advocate with them and others, to plead his cause, and take care of his concerns, on earth. When Christ was with them he spoke for them; but now that he is leaving them, the Spirit of the Father shall speak in them, Matt. x. 19, 20. And the cause cannot miscarry that is pleaded by such an advocate. You shall have another *master* or *teacher*, another *exhorter*. While they had Christ with them he excited and exhorted them to their duty; but now he leaves one with them that shall do this as effectually. Another *comforter*. Christ comforted his disciples when he was with them, and now that he was leaving them in their greatest need he promises them *another*.

(2) The giver of this blessing: *The Father* shall give him. The same that gave the Son to be our Saviour will give his Spirit to be our comforter.

(3) How this blessing is procured—by the intercession of the Lord Jesus: *I will pray the Father*. When Christ saith, *I will pray the Father*, it does not suppose that the Father is unwilling, but only that the gift of the Spirit is a fruit of Christ's mediation.

(4) The continuance of this blessing: *That he may abide with you for ever*. "*With you, as long as you live*. You shall never know the want of a comforter." There are everlasting consolations provided for us. They must disperse, and therefore a comforter that would be with them all, in all places alike, was alone fit to be with them for ever: "With your successors, when you are gone, to the end of time."

2. This comforter is the *Spirit of truth, whom you know*, *v.* 16, 17.

(1) The comforter promised is *the Spirit*, one who

JAMIESON, FAUSSET, BROWN

CHARLES H. SPURGEON:

Observe how our Savior puts this *if* concerning love, in such a way as to teach us that *love must be prior to obedience*. The text is not, "Keep My commandments, and then love Me." No, we do not expect pure streams till the fountain is cleansed. Nor does He say, "Keep My commandments, and love Me at the same time," as two separate things, although that might in a measure correspond with truth. But love is put first, because it is first in importance and first in experience. "If ye love me"—we must begin with love: then "keep my commandments." Obedience must have love for its mother, nurse, and food. The essence of obedience lies in the hearty love which prompts the deed rather than in the deed itself. I can conceive it possible that a man might, in his outward life, keep Christ's commandments, and yet might never keep them at all so as to be accepted before God. If he became obedient by compulsion, but would have disobeyed if he dared, then his heart was not right before God, and his actions were of little worth. The commandments are to be kept out of love to Him who gave them. In obedience, to love is to live: if we love Christ we live Christ. Love to the person of our Lord is the very salt of our sacrifices. To put it most practically, I often say to myself, "Today I have performed all the duties of my office; but have I been careful to abide in my Lord's love? I have not failed as to doing all that was possible to me; I have gone from early morning till late at night, packing as much work as possible into every hour, and trying to do it with all my heart. But have I, after all, done this as unto the Lord and for His sake?" I tremble lest I should serve God merely because I happen to be a minister and am called to preach His word; or because the natural routine of the day carries me through it. I am concerned that I may be impelled by no force but the love of Jesus. This fear often humbles me in the dust, and prevents all glorying in what I have done.

—The Treasury of the New Testament

he shall give you another Comforter—a word used only by John; in his *Gospel* with reference to the Holy Spirit, in his *First Epistle* (2:1), with reference to Christ Himself. Its proper sense is an "advocate," "patron," "helper." In this sense it is plainly meant of Christ (I John 2:1), and in this sense it comprehends all the *comfort* as well as *aid* of the Spirit's work. The Spirit is here promised as One who would *supply Christ's own place* in His absence.

15-17. If ye love me, keep my commandments. And I will pray the Father . . .—This connection seems designed to teach that the proper temple for the indwelling Spirit of Jesus is a heart filled with that love to Him which lives actively for Him, and so this was the fitting preparation for the promised gift.

that he may abide with you for ever—never go away, as Jesus was going to do in the body.

ADAM CLARKE

15. *If ye love me, keep my commandments.* Do not be afflicted at the thought of My being separated from you; the most solid proof you can give of your attachment to and affection for Me is to keep My commandments. This I shall receive as a greater proof of your affection than your tears.

Another Comforter. The word *paracletos* signifies not only a *comforter*, but also an "advocate," a "defender" of a cause, a "counsellor, patron, mediator." Christ is thus termed, 1 John ii. 1, where the common translation renders the word "advocate." Christ is thus called because He is represented as transacting the concerns of our souls with God; and for this cause, He tells us, He goes unto the Father, v. 12. The Holy Spirit is thus called because He transacts the cause of God and Christ with us, explains to us the nature and importance of the great atonement, shows the necessity of it, counsels us to receive it, instructs us how to lay hold on it, vindicates our claim to it, and makes intercessions in us with unutterable groanings. As Christ acted with His disciples while He sojourned with them, so the Holy Ghost acts with those who believe in His name.

16. *I will pray the Father.* After having made an atonement for the sin of the world, I will become the Mediator between God and man; and through My mediation and intercession shall all the blessings of grace and glory be acquired.

For ever. As the death and atonement of Christ will be necessary to man till the conclusion of the world, so the office of the Holy Spirit must be continued among men till the end of time. Therefore says Christ, "He shall continue with you forever," teaching, comforting, advising, defending, and interceding for you and for all My followers to the end of time.

17. *The Spirit of truth.* The Spirit, or Holy Ghost, whose essential office is to manifest,

MATTHEW HENRY

should do his work in a spiritual way and manner.

(2) He is the *Spirit of truth.* He will be true to you, and to his undertaking for you. He will *teach you the truth.* The Spirit of truth shall not only *lead you into all truth*, but others by your ministry. Christ is the truth, and he is the Spirit of Christ.

(3) He is one *whom the world cannot receive*; but *you know him. Therefore he abideth with you.* The disciples of Christ are here distinguished from the world; they are the children and heirs of another world, not of this. It is the misery of those that are invincibly devoted to the world that they *cannot receive* the Spirit of truth. Where the spirit of the world has the ascendant, the Spirit of God is excluded. Therefore men *cannot receive the Spirit of truth* because they *see him not, neither know him.* The comforts of the Spirit are *foolishness to them*, as much as ever the cross of Christ was. Speak to the children of this world of the operations of the Spirit, and you are as a barbarian to them. The best knowledge of the Spirit of truth is that which is got by experience: *You know him, for he dwelleth with you.* Christ had dwelt with them, and by their acquaintance with him they could not but know *the Spirit of truth.* The experiences of the saints are the explications of the promises. He *dwelleth with you, and shall be in you*, for the blessed Spirit doth not use to shift his lodging. Those that know him know how to invite him and bid him welcome; and therefore he shall be in them, as the light in the air, as the sap in the tree, and their union with him inseparable. The gift of the Holy Ghost is a peculiar gift, bestowed upon the disciples of Christ in a distinguishing way—upon them, and not the world. No comforts are comparable to those which make no show, make no noise.

Verses 18–24

When friends are parting, it is a common request they make to each other, "Pray let us hear from you as often as you can": this Christ engaged to his disciples, that out of sight they should not be out of mind.

I. He promises that he would continue his care of them (*v.* 18): "*I will not leave you orphans*, or *fatherless; I will come to you.*" His departure from them was neither total nor final. Not total. "Though I leave you without my bodily presence, yet I do not leave you without comfort." The case of true believers, though sometimes it may be sorrowful, is never comfortless, because they are never orphans: for God is their Father. Not final: *I will come to you.* "I will come speedily to you at my resurrection." He had often said, *The third day I will rise again.* "I will be coming daily to you in my Spirit"; in the tokens of his love, and visits of his grace, he is still coming. The consideration of Christ's coming to us saves us from being comfortless in his removals from us.

II. He promises that they should continue their acquaintance with him (*v.* 19, 20): *Yet a little while, and the world sees me no more.* The malignant world thought they had seen enough of him, and *cried, Away with him, crucify him;* and so shall their doom be; they shall see him no more. But his disciples have communion with him in his absence.

1. *You see me.* They saw him with their bodily eyes after his resurrection. And *then were the disciples glad when they saw the Lord.* They saw him with an eye of faith after his ascension; saw that in him which the world saw not.

2. *Because I live, you shall live also.* That which grieved them was, that their Master was dying, and they counted upon nothing else but to die with him. No, saith Christ, *I live.* Not only, I shall live, as he saith of them, but, I do live. We are not comfortless, while *we know that our Redeemer lives.* Therefore *you shall live also.* The life of Christians is bound up in the life of Christ; as sure and as long as he lives, those that by faith are united to him shall live also. This life is hid with Christ; if the head and root live, the members and branches live also.

3. You shall have the assurance of this (*v.* 20): *At that day you shall know* that *I am in my Father, and you in me, and I in you.* These glorious mysteries will be fully known in heaven. Now it appears not *what we shall be*, but then it will appear what we were. They were more fully known after the pouring out of the Spirit upon the apostles; at that day divine light should shine, and their eyes should see more clearly, like the blind man's at the second touch of Christ's hand, who at first only *saw men as trees walking.* They are known by all that receive the Spirit of truth. They know that *Christ is in the Father*, is one with the Father, by their experience of what he has wrought for them and in them. That Christ is in them. That they are in Christ, for the relation is mutual. Christ in them and they in Christ, which

JAMIESON, FAUSSET, BROWN

17. whom the world cannot receive . . .—(See I Cor. 2:14). **he dwelleth with you, and shall be in you**—Though the proper fulness of both these was yet future, our Lord, by using both the present and the future, seems plainly to say that they *already* had the germ of this great blessing.

18-20. I will not leave you comfortless—in a bereaved and desolate condition; or (as *Margin*) "orphans." **I will come to you**—"I come" or "am coming" to you; i.e., plainly *by the Spirit*, since it was to make His departure to be *no bereavement.*

19. world seeth—beholdeth—**me no more, but ye see**—behold—**me**—His bodily presence, being all the sight of Him which "the world" ever had, or was capable of, it "beheld Him no more" after His departure to the Father; but by the coming of the Spirit, the presence of Christ was not only *continued* to His spiritually enlightened disciples, but rendered *far more efficacious and blissful* than His bodily presence had been *before* the Spirit's coming. **because I live**—not '*shall* live,' only when raised from the dead; for it is His unextinguishable, divine life of which He speaks, in view of which His *death and resurrection* were but as shadows passing over the sun's glorious disk. (Cf. Luke 24:5; Rev. 1:18, "the Living One"). And this grand saying Jesus uttered *with death immediately in view.* What a brightness does this throw over the next clause, "ye shall live also!" "Knowest thou not," said LUTHER to the King of Terrors, "that thou didst devour the Lord Christ, but wert obliged to give Him back, and wert devoured of Him? So thou must leave me undevoured because I abide in Him, and live and suffer for His name's sake. Men may hunt me out of the world—that I care not for—but I shall not on that account abide in death. I shall live with my Lord Christ, since I know and believe that *He liveth!*" [quoted in STIER]. **20. At that day**—of the Spirit's coming. **ye shall know that I am in my Father, ye in me, I in you**—(See on ch. 17:22, 23).

ADAM CLARKE

vindicate, and apply the *truth. The world cannot receive.* By the *world*, John means those who are influenced only by the desire of the flesh, the desire of the eye, and the pride of life, 1 John ii. 16. Now these cannot receive the Spirit of truth, because they see *him not*, have no spiritual discernment, attend to nothing but the dictates of their corrupt passions and affections, and will admit of no influence but what can be an object of their senses. *But ye know him.* You have already received a measure of the truth, and you believe in this Spirit. Probably our Lord refers to the knowledge which they should afterwards attain; in this sense the passage has been understood by the *Vulgate*—"Ye shall know him." *For he dwelleth with you.* Or, "He shall dwell with you"; and this, it is very evident, is the meaning of the Evangelist, who not unfrequently uses the present for the future tense.

18. *I will not leave you comfortless.* Literally, "orphans." The disciples of a particular teacher among the Hebrews called him "father"; his scholars were called his *children*, and, on his death, were considered as orphans. Christ calls His disciples "children, beloved children," chap. xiii. 33; and now that He is about to be removed from them by death, He assures them that they shall not be left fatherless, or without a teacher; for in a little time He should come again (rise from the dead), and after His ascension they should be made partakers of that Spirit which would be their Comforter, Advocate, Teacher, and Guide forever.

19. *Because I live.* As surely as I shall rise from the dead, so shall you. My resurrection shall be the proof and pledge of yours. And *because I live* a life of intercession for you at the right hand of God, you shall live a life of grace and peace here, and a life of glory hereafter.

20. *That I am in my Father.* After My resurrection, you shall be more fully convinced of this important truth, that I and the Father are one; for I will live in you by the energy of My Spirit, and you shall live in Me by faith, love, and obedience.

MATTHEW HENRY

speaks an intimate and inseparable union. Union with Christ is the life of believers. The knowledge of this union is their unspeakable joy and satisfaction.

III. He promises that he would love them, and manifest himself to them, *v.* 21–24.

1. Who they are whom Christ will accept as lovers of him; those that *have his commandments, and keep them.* The kind things he here said to his disciples were intended not for those only that were *now* his *followers*, but for all that should *believe in him through their word.* The duty of those who claim the dignity of being disciples. Having Christ's commandments, we must keep them. Having them in our heads, we must keep them in our hearts and lives. The dignity of those that do the duty of disciples. Not those that have the greatest wit and know how to talk for him, or the greatest estate to lay out for him, but those that *keep his commandments.* The surest evidence of our love to Christ is obedience to the laws of Christ.

2. What returns he will make to them for their love. (1) They shall have the Father's love: *He that loveth me shall be loved of my Father.* We could not love God if he did not first give us his grace to love him. He loves them, and lets them know that he loves them. God so loves the Son as to love all those that love him. (2) They shall have Christ's love: *And I will love him.* God will love him as a Father, and I will love him as a brother, an elder brother. In the nature of God, nothing shines more brightly than this, that *God is love.* And in the undertaking of Christ nothing appears more glorious than this, that *he loved us.* Christ was now leaving his disciples, but promises to continue his love to them. He bears them on his heart, and ever lives interceding for them. (3) They shall have the comfort of that love: *I will manifest myself to him.* Being promised to all that *love him and keep his commandments*, it must be construed so as to extend to them.

3. What occurred upon Christ's making this promise.

(1) One of the disciples expresses his wonder and surprise at it, *v.* 22. [1] Who it was that said this—*Judas, not Iscariot.* Two of Christ's disciples were of that name: one of them was the traitor, the other was the brother of James (Luke vi. 16). There was a very good man, and a very bad man, called by the same name; for names commend us not to God, nor do they make men worse. Judas the apostle was never the worse, nor Judas the apostate ever the better, for being namesakes. The evangelist carefully distinguishes between them. Take heed of mistaking; let us not confound the precious and the vile. [2] What he said—*Lord how is it? First,* The weakness of his understanding. He expected the temporal kingdom of the Messiah, that it should appear in external pomp and power. "*What is the matter* now, that thou wilt not show thyself openly as is expected." *Secondly,* The strength of his affections. *Lord, how is it?* He is amazed at the condescensions of divine grace. What is there in us to deserve so great a favour? It is justly *marvellous in our eyes*; for it is unaccountable, and must be resolved into free and sovereign grace.

(2) Christ explains and confirms what he had said, *v.* 23, 24.

[1] He further explains the condition of the promise, which was loving him, and keeping his commandments. Love is the root, obedience is the fruit. Where a sincere love to Christ is in the heart, there will be obedience: "*If a man love me* indeed, he will *keep my words.*" Where love is, duty follows of course, is easy and natural, and flows from a principle of gratitude. Where there is no true love to Christ there will be no care to obey him: *He that loveth me not keepeth not my sayings*, *v.* 24. Certainly those do not love him that believe not his truths, and obey not his laws, to whom Christ's sayings are but as idle tales, which he heeds not, or hard sayings, which he likes not. Why should Christ be familiar with those that will be strange to him?

[2] He further explains the promise (*v.* 23): *If a man thus love me, I will manifest myself to him. My Father will love him;* this he had said before (*v.* 21), and here repeats it for the confirming of our faith. Jude wondered that Christ should *manifest himself to them. We will come unto him, and make our abode with him.* Not only, *I will,* but *We will, I and the Father.* Wherever Christ is formed the image of God is stamped. Not only, "*I will show myself to him* at a distance," but, "*We will come to him,* to be near him, to be with him." Not only, "I will give him a transient view of me, or make him a short and running visit," but, *We will take up our abode with him.* God will not only love obedient believers, but he will rest in love to them. He will be with them as at his home.

[3] He gives a good reason both to bind us to observe the condition and encourage us to depend

JAMIESON, FAUSSET, BROWN

ALEXANDER MACLAREN:

In like manner, our Lord says, the practical obedience to His commandments is the sure sign and test of love. I need not dwell upon that. There are two motives for keeping commandments—one because they are commandments, and one because we love Him that commands. The one is slavery, the other is liberty. The one is like the Arctic regions, cold and barren; the other is like tropical lands, full of warmth and sunshine, glorious and glad fertility.

The form of the sentence suggests how easy it is for people to delude themselves about their love to Jesus Christ. That emphatic "he" and the putting first of the character before its root is pointed out are directed against false pretensions to love. The love that Christ stamps with His hallmark, and passes as genuine, is no mere emotion, however passionate, however sweet; no mere sentiment, however pure, however deep. The tiniest little rivulet that drives a mill is better than a Niagara that rushes and foams and tumbles idly. And there is much so-called love to Jesus Christ that goes masquerading up and down the world, from which the paint is stripped by the sharp application of the words of my text. Character and conduct are the true demonstrations of Christian love, and it is only love so attested that He accepts.—*Expositions of Holy Scripture*

21. He that hath my commandments and keepeth them . . .—(See on vss. 15, 16). **my Father and I will love him**—Mark the sharp line of distinction here, not only between the Divine Persons but the actings of love in Each respectively, towards true disciples.

22. Judas saith . . . , not Iscariot—Beautiful parenthesis this! The traitor being no longer present, we needed not to be told that this question came not from *him*. But it is as if the Evangelist had said, "A very different Judas from the traitor, and a very different question from any that he would have put. Indeed [as one in STIER says], we never read of Iscariot that he entered in any way into his Master's words, or ever put a question even of rash curiosity (though it may be he did, but that nothing from *him* was deemed fit for immortality in the Gospels but his name and treason). **"how . . . manifest thyself to us, and not to the world**—a most natural and proper question, founded on vs. 19, though interpreters speak against it as *Jewish*.

23. we will come and make our abode with him—Astonishing statement! In the Father's "coming" He "refers to the revelation of Him *as a Father* to the soul, which does not take place till the Spirit comes into the heart, teaching it to cry, *Abba,* Father" [OLSHAUSEN]. The "abode" means a permanent, eternal stay! (Cf. Lev. 26:11, 12: Ezek. 37:26, 27; II Cor. 6:16; and *contrast* Jer. 14: 8).

ADAM CLARKE

21. *He it is that loveth me.* See on v. 15. *And will manifest myself to him.* All My faithful disciples shall see Me after My resurrection; and I will manifest My power and goodness to all those who believe in and obey Me, even to the end of the world.

22. *Judas.* The same as Thaddeus and Lebbeus, the brother of James, and author of what is called the Epistle of Jude. *How is it?* Or, "How can it be?"—"What is to happen?"—On what account is it? Judas, who was probably thinking that the kingdom of Christ should extend over all the earth, wonders how this can be, and yet Christ manifest himself only to His disciples and not to the world, v. 19. To this our Lord, in a more express manner than He had done before, answers:

23. *If a man.* Not only My present disciples, but all those who shall believe on Me through their word, or that of their successors. *Love me.* Receive me as his Saviour, and get the love of God shed abroad in his heart by the Holy Ghost. *He will keep my words.* Observe all My sayings, and have his affections and conduct regulated by My Spirit and doctrine. *My Father will love him.* Call him His child; support, defend, and preserve him as such.

And we will come unto him. God the Father, through His Son, will continue to pour out His choicest blessings upon his head and upon his heart. *And make our abode with him.* Will make his heart our temple, where God, the Father, Son, and Spirit, shall rest, receive homage, and dwell to eternity.

MATTHEW HENRY

upon the promise. *The word which you hear is not mine, but his that sent me, v.* 24. To this purport he had often spoken (*ch.* vii. 16). The stress of duty is laid upon the precept of Christ as our rule. The stress of our comfort is laid upon the promise of Christ. It concerns us to enquire whether the security be sufficient for us to venture our all upon; and this satisfies us that it is, that the promise is not Christ's bare word, but the Father's which sent him.

Verses 25–27

Two things Christ here comforts his disciples with:

I. That they should be under the tuition of his Spirit, *v.* 25, 26. Christ would have them reflect upon the instructions he had given them: *These things have I spoken unto you being yet present with you.* What he had said he did not retract. What he had spoken he had spoken, and would abide by it. Christ would find out a way of speaking to them after his departure from them, *v.* 26.

(1) On whose account he should be sent: "The Father will send him *in my name*; that is, for *my sake*." He came in his Father's name: the Spirit comes in his name to carry on his undertaking.

(2) On what errand he should be sent: *He shall teach you all things.* He shall teach them all things necessary for them either to learn themselves, or to teach others; for those that would teach the things of God must first themselves be taught of God. *He shall bring all things to your remembrance whatsoever I have said unto you.* Many a good lesson Christ had taught them, which they had forgotten. The Spirit shall not teach them a new gospel, but bring to their minds that which they had been taught, by leading them into the understanding of it. To all the saints the Spirit of grace is given to be a remembrancer.

II. That they should be under the influence of his peace (*v.* 27): *Peace I leave with you.* When Christ was about to leave the world he *made his will.* His soul he committed to his Father; his body he bequeathed to Joseph, to be decently interred; his clothes fell to the soldiers; his mother he left to the care of John: but what should he leave to his poor disciples, that had left all for him? Silver and gold he had none; but he left them that which was infinitely better, *his peace.* "*I leave you,* but I leave *my peace* with you." He did not part in anger, but in love; for this was his farewell, *Peace I leave with you.*

1. The legacy that is here bequeathed: *Peace, my peace.* Peace is put for all good. Peace is put for reconciliation and love; the peace bequeathed is peace with God. Peace *in our own bosoms* seems to be especially meant. It is the peace on which the angels congratulated men at his birth, Luke ii. 14.

2. To whom this legacy is bequeathed: "To you, my disciples and followers." This legacy was left to them and their successors, to them and all true Christians in all ages.

3. In what manner it is left: *Not as the world giveth, give I unto you.* "I do not compliment you with *Peace be unto you*; no, it is not a mere formality, but a real blessing. The gifts I give to you are not such as this world gives." The world's gifts concern only the body and time; Christ's gifts enrich the soul for eternity. The peace which Christ gives is infinitely more valuable than that which the world gives. As is the difference between a killing lethargy and a reviving refreshing sleep, such is the difference between Christ's peace and the world's.

4. What use they should make of it: *Let not your heart be troubled, neither let it be afraid.* This comes in here as the conclusion of the whole matter; he had said (*v.* 1), *Let not your heart be troubled,* and here he repeats it as that for which he had now given sufficient reason.

Verses 28–31

Christ here gives his disciples another reason why their hearts should not be troubled for his going away; and that is, because his heart was not. He comforted himself,

I. That, though he went away, he should *come again*: "*You have heard how I have said, I go away, and come again.*" Christ encouraged himself with *this,* in his sufferings and death, that he should *come again,* and the same should comfort us in our departure at death; we go away to come again; the leave we take of our friends at that parting is only a good night, not a final farewell.

II. That he *went to his Father*: "*If you loved me, you would rejoice* because, though I leave you, *I go unto the Father*; for *my Father is greater than I.*" It is matter of joy. His departure had a bright side as well as a dark side. The reason of this is, because *the Father is greater than he.* His state with his Father would be much more excellent and glorious

JAMIESON, FAUSSET, BROWN

25, 26. he shall teach you all things, and bring all to . . . remembrance, whatsoever I have said unto you–(See on vss. 16, 17). As the Son came in *the Father's* name, so the Father shall send the Spirit "*in My name,*" says Jesus, i.e., with like divine *power* and *authority* to reproduce in their souls what Christ taught them, "bringing to living consciousness what lay like slumbering germs in their minds" [OLSHAUSEN]. *On this rests the credibility and ultimate divine authority of* THE GOSPEL HISTORY. The whole of what is here said of THE SPIRIT is decisive of His divine *personality.* "He who can regard all the *personal* expressions, applied to the Spirit in these three chapters ("teaching," "reminding," "testifying," "coming," "convincing," "guiding," "speaking," "hearing," "prophesying," "taking") as being no other than a long drawnout figure, deserves not to be recognized even as an interpreter of intelligible words, much less an expositor of Holy Scripture" [STIER]. **27. Peace I leave with you, my peace I give unto you**–If the two preceding verses sounded like a note of preparation for drawing the discourse to a close, this would sound like a farewell. But oh, how different from ordinary adieus! It *is* a parting word, but of richest import, the customary "peace" of a parting friend sublimed and transfigured. As "the Prince of Peace" (Isa. 9:6) He brought it into flesh, carried it about in His Own Person ("My peace") died to make it ours, left it as the heritage of His disciples upon earth, implants and maintains it by His Spirit in their hearts. Many a legacy is "left" that is never "given" to the legatee, many a gift destined that never reaches its proper object. But Christ is the Executor of His own Testament; the peace He "*leaves*" He "*gives*"; Thus all is secure. **not as the world giveth**–in contrast with the world, He gives *sincerely, substantially, eternally.*

28. If ye loved me, ye would rejoice, because I said, I go unto the Father, for my Father is greater than I–These words, which Arians and Socinians perpetually quote as triumphant evidence against the proper Divinity of Christ, really yield no intelligible sense on their principles. Were a holy *man* on his deathbed, beholding his friends in

ADAM CLARKE

24. *He that loveth me not.* Hence we learn that the man who is not obedient to the testimonies of Christ does not love Him.

26. *He shall teach you all things.* If in the things which I have already spoken to you there appear to you any obscurity, the Holy Spirit, the Advocate, Counsellor, and Instructor, will take away all your doubts, free you from all embarrassment, and give you a perfect understanding in all things; and this Spirit ye shall shortly receive. *And bring all things to your remembrance.* Here Christ promises them that inspiration of the Holy Spirit which enabled them not only to give a true history of His life and death, but also gave them the most perfect recollection of all the words which He had spoken to them, so that they have been able to transmit to posterity the identical words which Jesus uttered in His sermons, and in His different discourses with them, the Jews, and others.

27. *Peace I leave with you.* The Jewish form of salutation and benediction. A wish of peace among them is thus to be understood. "May you prosper in body and soul, and enjoy every earthly and heavenly good!" *My peace I give unto you.* Such tranquillity of soul, such uninterrupted happiness of mind, such everlasting friendship with God as I enjoy, may ye all enjoy! And such blessedness I bequeath unto you; it is My last, My best, My dying legacy. *Not as the world giveth.* Not as the Jews, in empty wishes; not as the people of the world, in empty compliments. Their salutations and benedictions are generally matters of custom and polite ceremony, given without desire or design; but I mean what I say. What I wish you, that I will give you. To His followers Jesus gives peace, procures it, preserves it, and establishes it. He is the Author, Prince, Promoter, and Keeper of peace. *Neither let it be afraid.* Let not your heart "shrink back" through fear of any approaching evil. This is the proper meaning of the word. In a few hours you will be most powerfully assaulted, but stand firm. The evil will fall only upon Me; and this evil will result in your comfort and salvation, and in the redemption of a lost world.

28. *I go away.* To the Father by My death. *And come again unto you.* By My resurrection. *Ye would rejoice.* Because, as the Messiah, I am going to receive a Kingdom, and power, and glory, forever. Therefore as My friends you should rejoice in My elevation, though for a while it may put you to the pain of being separated from Me. Besides, I am going that I may send you the Holy Spirit, who shall fill you with the fullness of God. On your own account, therefore, you should have rejoiced and not mourned. *My Father is greater than I.*

MATTHEW HENRY

than his present state. Christ raises the thoughts and expectations of his disciples to something greater than that in which now they thought all their happiness bound up. The kingdom of the Father will be greater than the mediatorial kingdom. The disciples of Christ should show that they love him by their rejoicing in the glories of his exaltation. Many that love Christ, let their love run out in a wrong channel; they think if they love him they must be continually in pain because of him; whereas those that love him should *rejoice in Christ Jesus.*

III. That his going away would be a means of confirming the faith of his disciples (*v.* 29): *I have told you before it come to pass, that, when it is come to pass, you might believe.* See this reason, *ch.* xiii. 19; xvi. 4. Christ told his disciples of his death because it would afterwards redound to the confirmation of their faith. He who foretold these things had a divine prescience. The things foretold were according to the divine purpose. Let them therefore not be troubled at that which would be for the confirmation of their faith.

IV. That he was sure of a victory over Satan (*v.* 30): "*Henceforth I will not talk much with you.*" He had a great deal of good talk with them after this (*ch.* xv. and xvi.), but, in comparison with what he had said, it was not much. One reason why he would not talk much with them was because he had now other work to apply himself to: *The prince of this world comes.* He called the devil the *prince of this world, ch.* xii. 31. Christ tells them that the *prince of this world* was his enemy. But *he has nothing in me.* 1. The prospect Christ had of an approaching conflict, not only with men, but with the powers of darkness. The devil had set upon him with his temptations (Matt. iv), had offered him the *kingdoms of this world. Then the devil departed from him for a season.* "But now," says Christ, "I see him rallying again." The foresight of a temptation gives us great advantage in our resistance of it; for, being forewarned, we should be forearmed. 2. The assurance he had of good success in the conflict: *He hath nothing in me.* There was no guilt in Christ. Christ having done no evil, Satan, though he prevailed to crucify him, could not prevail to terrify him; though he hurried him to death, yet not to despair. When Satan comes to disquiet us, he has something in us to perplex us with, for we have all sinned; but, when he would disturb Christ, he found no occasion against him. There was no corruption in Christ. Such was the spotless purity of his nature that he was above the possibility of sinning.

V. That his departure was in obedience to his Father. *That the world may know that I love the Father, v.* 31.

1. Confirming what he had often said, that his undertaking, as Mediator, was a demonstration to the world, of his compliance with the Father. As it was an evidence of his love to man that he died for his salvation, so it was of his love to God that he died for his glory. It demonstrates also his obedience to his Father: "*As the Father gave me commandment, even so I do.*" The best evidence of our love to the Father is our doing as he hath given us commandment. The command of God is sufficient to bear us out in that which is most disputed by others, and therefore should be sufficient to bear us up in that which is most difficult to ourselves.

2. Concluding what he had now said; *that the world may know that I love the Father.* You shall see how cheerfully I can meet the appointed cross: "*Arise, let us go hence.*" When we talk of troubles at a distance, it is easy to say, *Lord, I will follow thee whithersoever thou goest.* When an unavoidable cross lies in the way of duty, then to say, "*Arise, let us go* to meet it," instead of going out of our way to miss it, this lets *the world know that we love the Father.* In these words he gives his disciples an encouragement to follow him. He does not say, *I must go;* but, *Let us go.* He calls them out to no hardships but what he himself goes before them in as their leader. He gives them an example, teaching them at all times to sit loose to all things here below, and often to think and speak of leaving them. When we sit down under Christ's shadow with delight, and say, *It is good to be here;* yet we must think of rising and going hence; going down from the mount.

JAMIESON, FAUSSET, BROWN

tears at the prospect of losing him, to say, "Ye ought rather to joy than weep for me, and would if ye really loved me," "the speech would be quite natural. But if they should ask him, *why* joy at his departure was more suitable than sorrow, would they not start back with astonishment, if not horror, were he to reply, "*Because my Father is greater than I?*" Does not this strange speech from Christ's lips, then, *presuppose such teaching* on His part as would make it extremely difficult for them to think He could gain anything by departing to the Father, and make it necessary for Him to say expressly that there was a sense in which He *could* do so? Thus, this startling explanation seems plainly intended to correct such misapprehensions as might arise from the emphatic and reiterated teaching of *His proper equality with the Father*—as if so Exalted a Person were incapable of any accession by transition from this dismal scene to a cloudless heaven and the very bosom of the Father—and by assuring them that this was *not* the case, to make them forget their own sorrow in His approaching joy. **30, 31. Hereafter I will not talk much with you**—'I have a little more to say, but My work hastens apace, and the approach of the adversary will cut it short.'

for the prince of this world—See on ch. 12:31. **cometh**—with hostile intent, for a last grand attack, having failed in His first formidable assault (Luke 4) from which he "departed [only] *for a season*" (vs. 13). **and hath nothing in me**—*nothing of His own—nothing to fasten on.* Glorious saying! The *truth* of it is, that which makes the Person and Work of Christ the life of the world (Heb. 9:14; I John 3:5; II Cor. 5:21.

31. But that the world may know that I love the Father . . .—The sense must be completed thus: 'But to the Prince of the world, though he has nothing in Me, I shall yield Myself up even unto death, that the world may know that I love and obey the Father, whose commandment it is that I give My life a ransom for many.' **Arise, let us go hence**—Did they then, at this stage of the discourse, leave the supper room, as some able interpreters conclude? If so, we think our Evangelist would have mentioned it: see ch. 18:1, which seems clearly to intimate that they then only left the upper room. But what do the words mean if not this? We think it was the dictate of that saying of earlier date, "I have a baptism to be baptized with, and *how am I straitened till it be accomplished!*"—a spontaneous and irrepressible expression of the deep eagerness of His spirit to get into the conflict, and that if, as is likely, it was responded to somewhat too literally by the guests who hung on His lips, in the way of a movement to depart, a wave of His hand, would be enough to show that He had yet more to say ere they broke up; and that disciple, whose pen was dipped in a love to his Master which made *their* movements of small consequence save when essential to the illustration of *His* words, would record this little outburst of the Lamb hastening to the slaughter, in the very midst of His lofty discourse; while the effect of it, if any, upon His hearers, as of no consequence, would naturally enough be passed over.

ADAM CLARKE

In v. 24, Christ tells His disciples that the Father had sent Him; i.e., in His quality of Messiah, He was sent by the Father to instruct and to save mankind. Now, as the sender is greater than the sent, chap. xiii. 16, so in this sense is the Father greater than the Son; and in this sense was the passage understood by Origen, Jerome, Novatian, and Vigilius, who read the text thus: "The Father, who sent me, is greater than I."

29. *I have told you before it come to pass.* Lest My death should be a stumbling block to you, I have spoken of it beforehand, and showed you the necessity of it, that when it happens you may believe that, as I could predict it so clearly and so circumstantially, so all the good which I have promised shall be the result may be confidently expected by you; and that your sorrow, if not entirely removed, may at least be much mitigated.

30. *The prince of this world. Of this* is omitted by many MSS. I rather think the omission of the pronoun makes the sense more general; for had He said *this world,* the words might have been restrained to the Jewish state or to the Roman government. But who is the person called here the *prince of the world?* Mr. Wakefield thinks that Christ speaks here of himself, as He does in chap. xii. 31, and translates this verse and the following thus: "For the ruler of this world is coming; and I have nothing now to do, but to convince the world that I love the Father, and do as he commanded me." Others think that our Lord refers to the Roman government, the ruler of the world, who, by its deputy, Pilate, was going to judge Him, but who should "find nothing" (which is the reading found in some excellent MSS. and versions, and is followed by almost all the primitive fathers) as a just cause of death in Him; and this indeed Pilate witnessed in the most solemn manner. See chap. xviii. 38; xix. 4, 12; see also Luke xxiii. 4, etc., and Matt. xxvii. 24. But the most general opinion is that Satan is meant, who is called the "prince of the power of the air," Eph. ii. 2; and who is supposed to be the same that is called "the god of this world," 2 Cor. iv. 4; and who at his last and most desperate trial, the agony in the garden, should be convinced that there was nothing of his nature in Christ, nothing that would coincide with his solicitations, and that he should find himself completely foiled in all his attacks, and plainly foresee the impending ruin of his kingdom. It is very difficult to ascertain the real meaning here; of the different opinions proposed above, the reader must take that which he deems the most likely.

31. *Arise, let us go hence.* Calmet supposes that Christ, having rendered thanks to God, and sung the usual hymn, Matt. xxvi. 30; Mark xiv. 26, rose from the table, left the city, and went towards the Garden of Olives, or Garden of Gethsemane, on the road to which a part of the following discourse was delivered. It was now about midnight, and the moon was almost full, it being the fourteenth day of her age, about the time in which the Jewish Passover was to be slain.

MATTHEW HENRY

CHAPTER 15

Here Christ discourses concerning the fruit, *the fruits of the Spirit*, under the similitude of a vine.

I. The doctrine of this similitude.

1. Jesus Christ is *the vine, the true vine*. He is pleased to speak of himself under low and humble comparisons. He is *the vine*, planted in the vineyard, and not a spontaneous product; planted in the earth, for he is *the Word made flesh*. The vine is a spreading plant, and Christ will be known as *salvation to the ends of the earth*. The fruit of the vine honours God and cheers man, so does the fruit of Christ's mediation. He is *the true vine*, as truth is opposed to pretence and counterfeit. Unfruitful trees are said to *lie*, but Christ is a vine that will not deceive.

2. Believers are branches of this vine, which supposes that Christ is the root of the vine. The root bears the tree (Rom. xi. 18), diffuses sap to it, and is all in all to its flourishing and fruitfulness; and in Christ are all supports and supplies. The branches of the vine are many, yet, meeting in the root, are all but one vine; thus all good Christians, though in place and opinion distant from each other, yet meet in Christ, the centre of their unity.

3. *The Father is the husbandman, the land-worker*. Though *the earth is the Lord's*, it yields him no fruit unless he work it. God has not only a propriety in, but a care of, the vine and all the branches. Never was any husbandman so wise, so watchful, about his vineyard, as God is about his church, which therefore must needs prosper.

II. The duty taught us by this similitude.

1. We must be fruitful. From a vine we look for grapes, and from a Christian we look for Christianity; this is the *fruit*, a Christian temper and disposition, a Christian life and conversation. We must honour God, and do good, and this is bearing fruit. The disciples here must be fruitful, as Christians, in all *the fruits of righteousness*, and as apostles, in diffusing the savour of the knowledge of Christ.

(1) The doom of the unfruitful (*v.* 2): They are *taken away*. It is here intimated that there are many who pass for *branches* in Christ who yet do *not bear fruit*. Being only tied to him by the thread of an outward profession, though they seem to be branches, they will soon be seen to be dry ones. Unfruitful professors are unfaithful professors; professors, and no more. It is here threatened that they shall be *taken away*.

(2) The promise made to the fruitful: *He purgeth them, that they may bring forth more fruit*. Further fruitfulness is the blessed reward of forward fruitfulness. Even fruitful branches, in order to their further fruitfulness, have need of purging or pruning. The best have that in them which is peccant; some notions, passions, or humours, that want to be purged away. These shall be taken off by degrees in the proper season. The purging of fruitful branches is the care and work of the great husbandman.

(3) The benefits which believers have. *Now you are clean, v.* 3. Their society was clean, now that Judas was expelled. Till they were got clear of him *they were not all clean*. They were each of them clean, that is, sanctified, by the truth of Christ (*ch.* xvii. 17). Apply it to all believers. The word of Christ is spoken to them; there is a cleansing virtue in that word. It cleanses as fire cleanses the gold from its dross, and as physic cleanses the body from its disease.

(4) The glory that will redound to God by our fruitfulness, *v.* 8. If we *bear much fruit*, herein our Father will be glorified. The fruitfulness of all Christians is to the glory of God. By the eminent good works of Christians many are brought to *glorify our Father who is in heaven*. So shall we be Christ's disciples indeed. So shall we both evidence our discipleship and adorn it, and be to our Master *for a name and a praise*. And the more fruit we bring forth, the more we abound in that which is good, the more he is glorified.

2. In order to our fruitfulness, we must abide in Christ.

(1) The duty enjoined (*v.* 4): *Abide in me, and I in you*. Those that are come to Christ must abide in him: "*Abide in me, and I in you. Abide in me*, and then fear not but I will *abide in you*"; for the communion between Christ and believers never fails on his side. The knot of the branch abides in the vine, and the sap of the vine abides in the branch, and so there is a constant communication between them.

(2) The necessity of our abiding in Christ, in order to our fruitfulness (*v.* 4, 5): "*You cannot bring forth fruit, except you abide in me*; but, if you do, you *bring forth much fruit; for without me you can do nothing*." So necessary is it to our happiness that we be fruitful, that the best argument to engage us to abide in Christ is, that otherwise we cannot be fruitful.

JAMIESON, FAUSSET, BROWN

CHAPTER 15

VSS. 1-27. DISCOURSE AT THE SUPPER TABLE CONTINUED. **1-8.** *The spiritual oneness of Christ and His people, and His relation to them as the Source of all their spiritual life and fruitfulness*, are here beautifully set forth by a figure familiar to Jewish ears (Isa. 5:1, etc.). **I am the true vine**—of whom the vine of *nature* is but a shadow.

my Father is the husbandman—the great Proprietor of the vineyard, the Lord of the spiritual kingdom. (It is surely unnecessary to point out the claim to *supreme divinity* involved in this.)

2. Every branch in me that beareth not fruit . . . every branch that beareth fruit—As in a fruit tree, some branches may be *fruitful*, others quite *barren*, according as there is a *vital connection* between the branch and the stock, or *no vital connection;* so the disciples of Christ may be spiritually fruitful or the reverse, according as they are *vitally* and *spiritually connected* with Christ, or but *externally* and *mechanically attached* to Him. The fruitless He "taketh away" (see on vs. 6); the fruitful He "purgeth" (cleanseth, pruneth)—*stripping it*, as the husbandman does, *of what is rank* (Mark 4:19), "that it may bring forth more fruit"; a process often painful, but no less needful and beneficial than in the natural husbandry.

3. Now—rather, 'Already.' **ye are clean through**—by reason of—**the word I have spoken to you**—already in a purified, fruitful condition, in consequence of the long action upon them of that searching "word" which was "as a refiner's fire" (Mal. 3:2, 3).

8. glorified that ye bear much fruit—not only from His delight in it for its own sake, but as from 'the juices of the Living Vine.' **so shall ye be my disciples**—*evidence* your discipleship.

4. Abide in me, and I in you; as the branch cannot bear fruit of itself, except it abide in the vine . . .—As all spiritual fruitfulness had been ascribed to the mutual *inhabitation*, and living, active *interpenetration* (so to speak) of Christ and His disciples, so here the keeping up of this vital connection is made essential to continued fruitfulness. **5. without me**—apart, or vitally disconnected from Me. **ye can do nothing**—spiritually, acceptably.

ADAM CLARKE

CHAPTER 15

F. B. MEYER:

The condition of fruitfulness. The vine is not able to do its work in the world without its branches; they stretch far from the root, to bear its strength and sweetness to those who stand outside the wall (Gen. 49:22). We need the Lord Jesus, but he also needs us. Without us he cannot bless men as he would. What a sublime thought is here—that Jesus needs something which I can yield him! Service to God and man is possible only through abiding union in him. Let us yield ourselves to be pruned by the Word that we may not need the pruning of awful sorrows. It is said that three out of five of the vineberries are cut off that the remainder may attain their full size. How many of our own promptings have to be excised in order that our best fruit may be yielded!—*Bible Commentary*

2. *Every branch in me.* I stand in the same relation to My followers, and they to Me, as the vine to the branches, and the branches to the vine. *He taketh away.* As the vinedresser will remove every unfruitful branch from the vine, so will My Father remove every unfruitful member from My mystical body—such as Judas, the unbelieving Jews, the apostatizing disciples, and all false and merely nominal Christians, who are attached to the vine by faith in the word and divine mission of Christ, while they live not in His life and Spirit and bring forth no fruit to the glory of God. *He purgeth it.* "He pruneth." The branch which bears not fruit, the husbandman "taketh it away." But the branch that beareth fruit, "He taketh away from it"; i.e., He prunes away excrescences, and removes everything that might hinder its increasing fruitfulness. The verb "I take away" signifies ordinarily to "cleanse, purge, purify," but is certainly to be taken in the sense of "pruning," or "cutting off," in this text.

3. *Now ye are clean.* "Ye are pruned." As our Lord has not changed the metaphor, it would be wrong to change the expression. *Through the word.* "Through that word"—that doctrine of holiness which I have incessantly preached unto you, and which you have received. Perhaps our Lord more immediately refers here to the words which He had spoken concerning Judas, chap. xiii. 21-30, in consequence of which Judas went out and finished his bargain with the chief priests. He being gone off, the body of the apostles was purified; and thus he might say, *Now ye are clean through the word which I have spoken unto you.*

8. *Herein is my Father glorified.* Or "honored." It is the honor of the husbandman to have good, strong, vigorous vines, plentifully laden with fruit. So it is the honor of God to have strong, vigorous, holy children, entirely freed from sin, and perfectly filled with His love.

4. *Abide in me.* Hold fast faith and a good conscience; and let no trials turn you aside from the truth. *And I will abide in you*—you shall receive every help and influence from Me that your souls can require in order to preserve and save them to eternal life.

5. *Without me ye can do nothing.* "Separated from Me, ye can do nothing at all." God can do without man, but man cannot do without God. Following the metaphor of our Lord, it would be just as possible to do any good without Him as for a branch to live, thrive, and bring forth fruit while cut off from that tree from which it not only derives its juices but its very existence also.

MATTHEW HENRY

Abiding in Christ is necessary in order to our doing much good. He that is constant in the exercise of faith in Christ and love to him, *bringeth forth much fruit.* A life of faith in the Son of God is incomparably the most excellent life a man can live in this world. It is necessary to our doing any good. It is the root and spring of all good: "*Without me you can do nothing:* not only no great thing, but nothing." *Without Christ we can do nothing* aright, nothing that will be fruit pleasing to God or profitable to ourselves. We depend upon Christ, not only as the vine upon the wall, for support; but, as the branch on the root, for sap.

(3) The fatal consequences of forsaking Christ (*v.* 6): *If any man abide not in me, he is cast forth as a branch.* This is a description of the fearful state of hypocrites that are *not in Christ.* They are cast forth as dry and withered branches, which are plucked off because they cumber the tree. It is just that those who reject him should be rejected by him. Those that abide not in Christ shall be abandoned by him. They are withered, as a branch broken off from the tree. Those that abide not in Christ in a little time wither and come to nothing. Those that bear no fruit after a while will bear no leaves. *Men gather them.* Satan's agents and emissaries pick them up, and make an easy prey of them. *They are burned;* this follows, of course, but it is here added very emphatically, and makes the threatening very terrible.

(4) The blessed privilege which those have that *abide in Christ* (*v.* 7): *If my words abide in you, you shall ask what you will and it shall be done.* How our union with Christ is maintained: *If you abide in me;* he had said before, *and I in you;* here he explains himself, *and my words abide in you.* It is in the word that we receive and embrace him; and so where the *word of Christ dwells richly* there Christ dwells. If the word be in us as at home, then we abide in Christ, and he in us. How our communion with Christ is maintained: *You shall ask what you will, and it shall be done to you.* And what can we desire more than to have what we will for the asking? Those that abide in Christ as their heart's delight shall have, through Christ, their heart's desire. If we abide in Christ, and his word in us, we shall not ask anything but what is proper to be done for us. The promises abiding in us lie ready to be turned into prayers; and the prayers so regulated cannot but speed.

Verses 9–17

Christ, who is love itself, is here discoursing concerning love, a fourfold love.

I. Concerning the Father's love to him. 1. The Father did love him (*v.* 9): *As the Father hath loved me.* He was the Son of his love. And yet God so *loved the world* as to deliver him up for us all. Those whom God loves as a Father may despise the hatred of all the world. 2. He abode in his Father's love, *v.* 10. Because he continued to love his Father, he went cheerfully through his sufferings, and therefore his Father continued to love him. 3. Therefore he abode in his Father's love because he kept his Father's law: *I have kept my Father's commandments,* and so *abide in his love.* Christ satisfied for us by obeying the law of redemption, and so he abode in his love, and restored us to it.

II. Concerning his own love to his disciples. Though he leaves them, he loves them.

1. The pattern of this love: *As the Father has loved me, so have I loved you.* As the Father loved him, who was most worthy, he loved them, who were most unworthy. The Father loved him as his Son, and he loves them as his children. The Father was well pleased with him, that he might be well pleased with us in him; and loved him, that in him, as beloved, he might *make us accepted.*

2. The proofs and products of this love.

(1) Christ loved his disciples, for he laid down his life for them (*v.* 13): *Greater love hath no man than this,* to *lay down his life for his friend.* And this is the love wherewith *Christ hath loved us.* See the extent of the love of the children of men to one another. The highest proof of it is laying down one's life for a friend, to save his life. It is love in the highest degree, which is *strong as death.* See the excellency of the love of Christ. He has not only equalled, but exceeded, the most illustrious lovers. Others have thus laid down their lives for their friends, but Christ laid down his for us *when we were enemies,* Rom. v. 8, 10. *Those hearts must be harder than iron or stone which are not softened by such incomparable sweetness of divine love.*—Calvin.

(2) Christ loved his disciples, for he took them into a covenant of friendship with himself, *v.* 14, 15. The followers of Christ are the friends of Christ. Those that do the duty of his servants are admitted

JAMIESON, FAUSSET, BROWN

6. If a man abide not in me, he is cast forth as a branch . . . withered . . . cast into the fire . . . burned—The one proper use of the vine is to *bear fruit;* failing this, it is good for one other thing—*fuel.* (See Ezek. 15:1-5.) How awfully striking the figure, in this view of it!

7. If ye abide in me, and my words . . . in you—Mark the change from the inhabitation of *Himself* to that of His *words,* paving the way for the subsequent exhortations (vss. 9, 10). **ask what ye will, and it shall be done unto you**—because this indwelling of His words in them would secure the harmony of their askings with the divine will.

Greater love hath no man than this, that a man lay down his life for his friends—The emphasis lies not on "friends," but on "*laying down his life*" for them; i.e., 'One can show no greater regard for those dear to him than to give his life for them, and this is the love ye shall find in Me.'

14. Ye are my friends, if ye do whatsoever I command you—hold yourselves in absolute subjection to Me.

ADAM CLARKE

6. *If a man abide not in me.* Our Lord in the plainest manner intimates that a person may as truly be united to Him as the branch is to the tree that produces it, and yet be afterwards cut off and cast into the fire, because he has not brought forth fruit to the glory of his God. No man can cut off a branch from a tree to which that branch was never united; it is absurd, and contrary to the letter and spirit of the metaphor, to talk of being "seemingly" in Christ—because this means nothing. If there was only a seeming union, there could be only a seeming excision. So the matter is just where it began; nothing is done on either side, and nothing said to any purpose. *He is cast forth.* Observe that person who abides not in Christ, in a believing, loving, obedient spirit, (1) Is *cut off* from Jesus, having no longer any right or title to Him or to His salvation. (2) He is *withered*—deprived of all the influences of God's grace and Spirit. (3) He is *gathered*—becomes (through the judgment of God) again united with backsliders like himself and other workers of iniquity. And, being abandoned to his own heart and Satan, he (4) is *cast into the fire*—separated from God's people, from God himself, and from the glory of His power. And (5) he is *burned*—is eternally tormented with the devil and his angels, and with all those who have lived and died in their iniquity.

7. *If ye abide in me.* Observe, (1) That in order to have influence with God, we must be united to Christ—*if ye abide in me.* (2) That in order to be preserved in this union, we must have our lives regulated by the doctrine of Christ—*and my words abide in you.* (3) That to profit by this union and doctrine, we must pray—*ye shall ask.* (4) That every heavenly blessing shall be given to those who continue in this union with a loving, obedient, praying spirit—*ye shall ask what ye will.*

13. *That a man lay down his life for his friends.* No man can carry his love for his friend farther than this; for when he gives up his life, he gives up all that he has. This proof of My love for you I shall give in a few hours, and the doctrine which I recommend to you I am just going to exemplify myself.

ALEXANDER MACLAREN:

What shall we say about these mysterious and profound first words of this verse? They carry us into the very depths of divinity, and suggest for us that wonderful analogy between the relation of the Father to the Son, and that of the Son to His disciples, which appears over and over again in the solemnities of these last hours and words of Jesus. Christ here claims to be, in a unique and solitary fashion, the object of the Father's love, and He claims to be able to love like God. "As the Father hath loved me, so have I loved you"; as deeply, as purely, as fully, as eternally, and with all the unnameable perfectnesses which must belong to the divine affection, does Christ declare that He loves us.

I know not whether the majesty and uniqueness of His nature stand out more clearly in the one or in the other of these assertions. As beloved of God, and as loving like God, He equally claims for himself a place which none other can fill, and declares that the love which falls on us from His pierced and bleeding heart is really the love of God.

In this mysterious, awful, tender, perfect affection, He exhorts us to abide. That comes yet closer to our hearts than the other phrase of which it is the modification, and in some sense the explanation. The command to abide in Him suggests much that is blessed, but to have all that mysterious abiding in Him resolved into abiding in His love is infinitely tenderer, and draws us still closer to himself.—*Expositions of Holy Scripture*

MATTHEW HENRY

and advanced to the dignity of his friends. This honour have all Christ's servants. Christ takes believers to be his friends. Though they often show themselves unfriendly, he is a friend that loves at all times. He will not *call them servants.* He will *call them his friends*; he will not only love them, but will let them know it. Though Christ called *them his friends*, they called themselves *his servants*: Peter, *a servant of Christ* (1 Pet. i. 1), and so James, *ch.* i. 1. The more honour Christ puts upon us, the more honour we should study to do him; the higher in his eyes, the lower in our own.

(3) Christ loved his disciples, for he was very free in communicating his mind to them (*v.* 15). "*All things that I have heard of my Father I have declared unto you.*" Jesus Christ has faithfully handed to us what he received of the Father, Matt. xi. 27. The great things relating to man's redemption Christ declared to his disciples, that they might declare them to others.

(4) Christ loved his disciples, for he chose and ordained them (*v.* 16): *I have chosen you, and ordained you.* His love to them appeared,

[1] In their election to their apostleship: *I have chosen you twelve.* It did not begin on their side: *You have not chosen me*, but I first *chose you.* It is fit that Christ should have the choosing of his own ministers; still he does it. Though ministers make that holy calling their own choice, Christ's choice is prior to theirs and directs and determines it.

[2] In their ordination: *I have ordained you;* "*I have put you* into commission." It was a mighty confidence he reposed in them. The treasure of the gospel was committed to them that it might be propagated; *that you may go* from place to place all the world over, and *bring forth fruit.* They were ordained, not to sit still, but to go about. They were ordained, not to beat the air, but to be instrumental for the bringing of nations into obedience to Christ. Those whom Christ ordains shall not labour in vain. The church of Christ was not to be a short-lived thing. It did not *come up in a night*, nor should it *perish in a night.* As one generation of ministers and Christians has passed away, still another has come. Thus *their fruit remains* to this day, and shall do while the earth remains.

[3] His love to them appeared in the interest they had at the throne of grace: *Whatsoever you shall ask of my Father, in my name, he will give it you.* Probably this refers in the first place to the power of working miracles, which was to be drawn out by prayer. "Whatever help from heaven you have occasion for at any time, it is but ask and have." We have a God to go to who is a Father. We come in a good name. Whatever errand we come upon to the throne of grace, we may with a humble boldness mention Christ's name in it. An answer of peace is promised us. What you come for shall be given you.

III. Concerning the disciples' love to Christ. Three things he exhorts them to:

1. To continue in his love, *v.* 9. "Continue in your love to me, and in mine to you." All that love Christ should continue in their love to him. *Continue in my love.* Keep up your love to me, and then all the troubles you meet with will be easy. Let not the troubles you meet with for Christ's sake quench your love to Christ, but rather quicken it.

2. To let his joy remain in them, and fill them, *v.* 11.

(1) That his joy might remain in them. That *my joy in you may remain.* If they bring forth much fruit, and continue in his love, he will continue to rejoice in them as he had done. Fruitful and faithful disciples are the joy of the Lord Jesus. That *my joy*, that is, your joy in me, *may remain.* It is the will of Christ that his disciples should constantly and continually rejoice in him, Phil. iv. 4. The joy of those who abide in Christ's love is a continual feast.

(2) *That your joy might be full;* not only that you might be full of joy, but that your joy in me and in my love may rise higher and higher, till it come to perfection. Those and those only that have Christ's joy remaining in them have their joy full; worldly joys soon surfeit but never satisfy. The design of Christ in his word is to *fill the joy* of his people.

3. To evidence their love to him by keeping his commandments: *If you keep my commandments, you shall abide in my love, v.* 10. The promise: *You shall abide in my love* as in a dwelling place, at home in Christ's love; as in a resting-place, at ease in Christ's love; as in a stronghold, safe in it. "*You shall abide in my love*, you shall have grace and strength to persevere in loving me." The condition of the promise: *If you keep my commandments.* The disciples were to keep Christ's commandments, not only by a constant conformity to them themselves, but by a faithful delivery of them to others; they

JAMIESON, FAUSSET, BROWN

15. **Henceforth I call you not servants**—i.e., *in the sense explained* in the next words; for servants He still calls them (vs. 20), and they delight to call themselves so, in the sense of being "under law to Christ" (I Cor. 9:20). **the servant knoweth not what his lord doeth**—knows nothing of his master's *plans* and *reasons,* but simply receives and executes his orders. **but . . . friends, for all things that I have heard of my Father I have made known unto you**—admitted you to free, unrestrained fellowship, keeping back nothing from you which I have received to communicate. (Cf. Gen. 18:17; Ps. 25: 14; Isa. 50:4.)

16. Ye have not chosen me, but I . . . you—a wholesale memento after the lofty things He had just said about their mutual indwelling, and the unreservedness of the friendship they had been admitted to.

ordained—appointed—**you, that ye should go and bring forth fruit**—i.e., give yourselves to it. **and that your fruit should remain**—showing itself to be an imperishable and ever growing principle. (Cf. Prov. 4:18; II John 8.)

that whatsoever ye shall ask . . .—(See on vs. 7).

9-11. continue ye in my love—not, 'Continue to love Me,' but, 'Continue in the possession and enjoyment of My love to you'; as is evident from the next words.

10. If ye keep my commandments, ye shall abide in my love—the obedient spirit of true discipleship cherishing and attracting the continuance and increase of Christ's love; and this, He adds, was the secret even of His own abiding in His Father's love!

ADAM CLARKE

15. *Henceforth I call you not servants.* Which He at least indirectly had done, chap. xiii. 16; Matt. x. 24-25; Luke xvii. 10. *I have called you friends.* I have admitted you into a state of the most intimate fellowship with myself, and have made known unto you whatsoever I have heard from the Father which, in your present circumstances, it was necessary for you to be instructed in.

16. *Ye have not chosen me.* You have not elected Me as your Teacher; I have called you to be My disciples, witnesses and depositories of the truth. It was customary among the Jews for every person to choose his own teacher.

And ordained you. Rather, "I have appointed you." The word is *etheka*, "I have put or placed you," i.e., in the vine.

11. *That my joy may remain in you.* That the joy which I now feel, on account of your steady, affectionate attachment to Me, may be lasting, I give you both warnings and directions, that you may abide in the faith. *That your joy might be full.* Or "complete"—"filled up"; a metaphor taken from a vessel into which water or any other thing is poured till it is full to the brim.

10. *If ye keep my commandments.* Hence we learn that it is impossible to retain a sense of God's pardoning love without continuing in the obedience of faith.

MATTHEW HENRY

were to keep them as trustees.

To induce them to keep his commandments, he urges his own example: *As I have kept my Father's commandments, and abide in his love.* The necessity of it to their interest in him (*v.* 14): "*You are my friends if you do whatsoever I command you.*" Those only will be accounted Christ's faithful friends that approve themselves his obedient servants. It is universal obedience to Christ that is the only acceptable obedience.

IV. Concerning the *disciples' love one to another.* We must keep his commandments, and this is his commandment, that we *love one another, v.* 12, and again, *v.* 17. No one duty of religion is more frequently inculcated, nor more pathetically urged upon us, by our Lord Jesus, than that of mutual love. It is here recommended by Christ's pattern (*v.* 12): *as I have loved you.* We should love one another, as, and because, Christ has loved us. *Go you and do likewise.* It is required by his precept. Observe how differently it is expressed in these two verses, and both very emphatic. 1. *This is my commandment* (*v.* 12), as if this were the most necessary of all the commandments. Christ, foreseeing the addictedness of the Christian church to uncharitableness, has laid most stress upon this precept. 2. *These things I command you, v.* 17. He speaks as if he were about to give them many things in charge, and yet names this only, *that you love one another.*

Verses 18–25

Here Christ discourses concerning *hatred,* which is the character and genius of the devil's kingdom, as love is of the kingdom of Christ.

I. Who they are in whom this hatred is found—the world, the children of this world, as distinguished from the children of God. The calling of these *the world* intimates, 1. Their number; there were a world of people that opposed Christ and Christianity. I fear, if we should put it to the vote between Christ and Satan, Satan would out-poll us quite. 2. Their confederacy. Jews and Gentiles, that could agree in nothing else, agreed to persecute Christ's ministers. 3. Their spirit and disposition; they are *men of the world.* The people of God are taught to hate the sins of sinners, yet not their persons, but to love and do good to all men. A malicious, spiteful, envious spirit, is not the spirit of Christ, but of the world.

II. Who they are against whom this hatred is levelled—against the disciples of Christ, against Christ himself, and against the Father.

1. The world hates the disciples of Christ: *The world hateth you* (*v.* 19).

(1) Observe how this comes in here. Christ had expressed the great kindness he had for them as friends; but there was given them a *thorn in the flesh,* reproaches and persecutions for Christ's sake. He had appointed them their work, but tells them what hardships they should meet with in it. He had charged them to *love one another,* and need enough they had to love one another, for the world would hate them. Those that are in the midst of enemies are concerned to hold together.

(2) Observe what is here included. The world's enmity against the followers of Christ: it *hateth them.* Whom Christ blesseth the world curseth. The favourites and heirs of heaven have never been the darlings of this world. The fruits of that enmity, *v.* 20. They will persecute you. It is the common lot of those who will live godly in Christ Jesus to *suffer persecution.* He sent them forth as sheep in the midst of wolves. Another fruit of their enmity is implied, that they would reject their doctrine. When Christ says, *If they have kept my sayings, they will keep yours,* he means, They will keep yours, and regard yours, no more than they have regarded and kept mine. The causes of that enmity. The world will hate them,

First, Because they do not belong to it (*v.* 19): "*If you were of the world,* of its spirit, *the world would love you* as its own." We are not to wonder if those that are devoted to the world are caressed by it as its friends. Nor are we to wonder if those that are delivered from the world are maligned by it as its enemies. The reason why Christ's disciples are not of the world is because Christ hath chosen them out of it. This is the reason why the world hates them. The glory which they are designed for sets them above the world, and so makes them the objects of its envy. The grace which they are endued with sets them against the world. They witness against it, and are not conformed to it. This would support them under all the calamities which the world's hatred would bring upon them, that they were hated because they were the chosen ones of the Lord Jesus. This was no just cause for the world's hatred of them.

JAMIESON, FAUSSET, BROWN

12-16. That ye love one another . . .—(See on ch. 13:34, 35).

17-21. The substance of these important verses has occurred more than once before. (See on Matt. 10: 34-36; Luke 12:49-53 etc.).

F. B. MEYER:

Suffering for Jesus' sake. We have been appointed for the one purpose of bearing imperishable fruit, but our holy service to the world will never be appreciated. The world has its own god and religion. It hates without cause. The more Christlike we are, the closer we shall be identified with his sufferings. There is no limit to the hatred and persecution which the world will vent on those who have ceased to belong to it because of their identification with the Crucified. But through the pitiless storm, we must be glad; there must be no slackening of our love, which will as certainly conquer hate as tomorrow's sun the darkness (vv. 26, 27). In each Christian century there has been this double witness of the Spirit in the Church. The voice of the Church has testified to the living Christ, not arguing but attesting; and to each word of testimony the Holy Spirit had borne assenting witness. Christian apologetics are of less importance than the witness of obscure but Spirit-led lives.—*Bible Commentary*

ADAM CLARKE

12. *That ye love one another.* See on chap. xiii. 34. So deeply was this commandment engraven on the heart of this Evangelist that Jerome says that in his extreme old age, when he used to be carried to the public assemblies of the believers, his constant saying was, "Little children, love one another." His disciples, wearied at last with the constant repetition of the same words, asked him why he constantly said the same thing. "Because [said he] it is the commandment of the Lord, and the observation of it alone is sufficient."

18. *If the world hate you.* As the followers of Christ were to be exposed to the hatred of the world, it was no small consolation to them to know that that hatred would be only in proportion to their faith and holiness; and that, consequently, instead of being troubled at the prospect of persecution, they should rejoice because that should always be a proof to them that they were in the very path in which Jesus himself had trod.

20. *If they have kept my saying.* Or "doctrine." Whosoever acknowledges Me for the Christ will acknowledge you for My ministers. Some translate the passage thus: "If they have watched My sayings," i.e., with an intent to accuse Me for something which I have said, "they will watch yours also"; therefore be on your guard. *Paraterein* has this sense, as we have had occasion to observe before; and perhaps *terein* has the same sense here, as it is much more agreeable to the context.

19. *Ye are not of the world . . . therefore.* On this very account, because you do not join in fellowship with those who know not God, therefore they hate you.

MATTHEW HENRY

If men hate us for that for which they should love and value us, we have reason to pity them. This was just cause for their own joy. Those hug themselves whom the world hates, but whom Christ loves.

Secondly, Another cause. will be because you do belong to Christ (*v.* 21): *For my name's sake.* Whatever is pretended, this is the ground of the quarrel, they hate Christ's disciples because they *bear his name*, and *bear up his name* in the world. It is the character of Christ's disciples that they stand up for his name. It has commonly been the lot of those that appear for Christ's name to suffer for so doing, to suffer *all these things. If you be reproached for the name of Christ, happy are you* (1 Pet. iv. 14). *If we suffer with Christ*, and for Christ, *we shall reign with him.*

Thirdly. It is the world's ignorance that is the true cause of its enmity to the disciples of Christ (*v.* 21): *Because they know not him that sent me.* They know not God. They know not God as him that sent our Lord Jesus. We do not rightly know God if we do not know him in Christ.

2. The world hates Christ himself. And this is spoken of here for two ends:

(1) To mitigate the trouble of his followers, arising from the world's hatred (*v.* 18): *You know that it hated me before you.* We read it as signifying priority of time. But it may be read as expressing his superiority over them: "*You know* that it hated me, *your first*, your chief and captain." If Christ was hated, can we expect that any virtue or merit of ours should screen us from malice. If our Master, the founder of our religion, met with so much opposition in the planting of it, his servants and followers can look for no other in propagating and professing it. For this he refers them (*v.* 20) to his own word: *Remember the word that I said unto you.* A plain truth: *The servant is not greater than his Lord.* The servant is inferior to his lord. The plainest truths are sometimes the strongest arguments for the hardest duties. A proper inference drawn from it: "*If they have persecuted me they will also persecute you;* you may expect it, for," [1] "You will do the same that I have done to provoke them; you will reprove them for their sins, and give them strict rules of holy living, which they will not bear." [2] "You cannot do more than I have done to oblige them. Let none wonder if they suffer ill for doing well. *If they have kept my sayings, they will keep yours also;* as there have been a few that have been wrought upon by my preaching, so there will be by yours a few."

(2) To aggravate the wickedness of this unbelieving world, and to discover its exceeding sinfulness. The world is generally in an ill name in scripture, and nothing can put it into a worse name than this, that it hated Jesus Christ. Two things he insists upon to aggravate the wickedness of those that hated him:

[1] That there was the greatest reason imaginable why they should love him.

First, His words were such as merited their love (*v.* 22): "*If I had not spoken unto them they had not had sin.* But now they have no pretence, no excuse for their sin." The advantage which those have that enjoy the gospel; Christ in it comes and speaks to them; he spoke in person to the men of that generation, and is still speaking to us. Every word of his carries with it a condescending tenderness, able, one would think, to charm the deafest adder. The excuse which those have that enjoy not the gospel: "*If I had not spoken to them they had not had sin.*" Not this kind of sin. They had not been chargeable with a contempt of Christ. As *sin is not imputed where there is no law*, so unbelief is not imputed where there is no gospel. Not such a degree of sin. If they had not had the gospel among them, their other sins had not been so bad. The aggravated guilt which those lie under to whom Christ has *come and spoken in vain. They have no cloak for their sin;* they are altogether inexcusable. The word of Christ strips sin of its cloak, that it may appear sin.

Secondly, His works were such as merited their love (*v.* 24): "*If I had not done among them* such works as *no other man ever did, they had not had sin;* their unbelief and enmity had been excusable." But he produced satisfactory proofs of his divine mission, *works which no other man did.* His miracles, his mercies, works of wonder and works of grace, prove him sent of God, and sent on a kind errand. Christ's works were such as *no man ever did.* No common person that had not a commission from heaven, and God with him, could work miracles, *ch.* iii. 2. They were all good works, works of mercy. One that was so universally useful should have been universally beloved, and yet even he is hated. The works of Christ enhance the guilt of sinners' enmity to him. If they had only heard his words, and not seen his

JAMIESON, FAUSSET, BROWN

22-25. (See on ch. 9: 39-41.) **If I had not come and spoken unto them, they had not had sin**—*comparatively* none; all other sins being light compared with the rejection of the Son of God. **now they have no cloak for their sin**—rather, 'pretext.'

24. If I had not done . . . the works which none other . . . did—(See on ch. 12:37).

ADAM CLARKE

21. *Because they know not him that sent me.* This is the foundation of all religious persecution; those who are guilty of it, whether in church or state, know nothing about God.

22. *But now they have no cloke for their sin.* They are without "excuse." See the margin, and see the note on chap. ix. 41. Christ had done such works as demonstrated Him to be the Messiah—yet they rejected Him; here lay their sin. And this sin, and the punishment to which it exposed them, still remain; for they still continue to reject the Lord that bought them.

ALEXANDER MACLAREN:

These words strike a discord in the midst of the sweet music to which we have been listening. The keynote of all that has preceded has been love—the love of Christ's friends to one another, and of all to Him, as an answer to His love to all. That love, which is one, whether it rise to Him or is diffused on the level of earth, is the result of that unity of life between the Vine and the branches, of which our Lord has been speaking such great and wonderful things. But that unity of life between Christians and Christ has another consequence than the spread of love. Just because it binds them to Him in a sacred community, it separates them from those who do not share in His life, and hence the "hate" of our context is the shadow of "love"; and there result two communities—to use the much abused words that designate them—the Church and "the World"; and the antagonism between these is deep, fundamental, and perpetual.

Unquestionably, our Lord is here speaking with special reference to the Apostles, who, in a very tragic sense, were "sent forth as sheep in the midst of wolves." If we may trust tradition, every one of that little company, Speaker as well as hearers, died a martyr's death, with the exception of John himself, who was preserved from it by a miracle. But, be that as it may, our Lord is here laying down a universal statement of the permanent condition of things; and there is no more reason for restricting the force of these words to the original hearers of them than there is for restricting the force of any of the rest of this wonderful discourse. "The world" will be in antagonism to the Church until the world ceases to be a world, because it obeys the King; and then, and not till then, will it cease to be hostile to His subjects.—*Expositions of Holy Scripture*

MATTHEW HENRY

works, unbelief might have pleaded want of proof. They saw Christ to be studious to do them a kindness; yet they hated him. And we see in his word that great love wherewith he loved us, and yet are not wrought upon by it.

[2] That there was no reason at all why they should hate him (*v.* 25): "*This comes to pass that the word might be fulfilled which is written in their law, They hated me without a cause.*" Those that hate Christ hate him without any just cause; enmity to Christ is unreasonable enmity. Christ was the greatest blessing imaginable to his country, and yet was hated. He testified indeed that *their works were evil*, with a design to make them good, but to hate him for this cause was to hate him without cause. Herein the scripture was fulfilled. Those that hated Christ did not design therein to fulfil the scripture; but God, in permitting it, confirms our faith in Christ as the Messiah that even this was foretold concerning him, and, being foretold, was accomplished in him. And we must not think it strange or hard if it have a further accomplishment in us.

3. In Christ the world hates God himself; this is twice said here (*v.* 23): *He that hateth me hates my Father also.* And again, *v.* 24, They have *seen and hated both me and my Father.* There are those that hate God. Those who cannot bring themselves to deny that there is a God, and yet wish there were none, they see and hate him. Hatred of Christ will be adjudged hatred of God. What entertainment the Son has, that the Father has. Let an unbelieving world know that their enmity to the gospel of Christ will be looked upon as an enmity to the blessed God himself; and let all that suffer for righteousness' sake take comfort from this; if God himself be hated in them, they need not be either ashamed of their cause or afraid of the issue.

Verses 26–27

Christ having spoken of the great opposition which his gospel was likely to meet with here intimates what effectual provision was made for supporting it, both by the principal testimony of the Spirit (*v.* 26), and the subordinate testimony of the apostles (*v.* 27).

I. It is here promised that the blessed Spirit shall maintain the cause of Christ in the world. "*When the Comforter is come, who proceedeth from the Father,* and *whom I will send, he shall testify of me.*" We have more in this verse concerning the Holy Ghost than in any one verse besides in the Bible.

1. Here is an account of him. In his essence He is *the Spirit of truth, who proceedeth from the Father.* He is spoken of as a distinct person; as a divine person, that *proceedeth from the Father.* The spirit or breath of man, called the *breath of life*, proceeds from the man, and by it invigorated he sometimes exerts his strength to *blow out* what he would extinguish, and *blow up* what he would excite. Thus the blessed Spirit is the emanation of divine light, and the energy of divine power.

2. In his mission. He will come in a more plentiful effusion of his gifts, graces, and powers, than had ever yet been. *I will send him to you from the Father.* He had said (*ch.* xiv. 16), *I will pray the Father, and he shall send you the Comforter.* Here he says, *I will send him.* The Spirit was sent, (1) By Christ as Mediator, now *ascended on high* to *give gifts unto men.* (2) From the Father: "Not only from heaven, my Father's house, but according to my Father's will and appointment." (3) To the apostles to instruct them in their preaching.

3. In his office and operations, which are two: One implied in the title given to him; he is the *Comforter*, or *Advocate.* An advocate for Christ, to maintain his cause against the world's infidelity, a comforter to the saints against the world's hatred. Another expressed: *He shall testify of me.* He is not only an advocate, but a witness for Jesus Christ. The power of the ministry is derived from the Spirit, for he qualifies ministers; and the power of Christianity too, for he sanctifies Christians, and in both testifies of Christ.

II. It is here promised that the apostles also should have the honour of being Christ's witnesses (*v.* 27): *And you also shall bear witness* of me.

1. The apostles were appointed to be witnesses for Christ in the world. When he had said, *The Spirit shall testify*, he adds, *And you also shall bear witness.* The Spirit's working is not to supersede, but to engage and encourage ours. Though the Spirit testify, ministers also must bear their testimony. The work cut out for them; they were to attest the truth, the whole truth, and nothing but the truth, concerning Christ. Though Christ's disciples fled upon his trial before the high priest and Pilate, yet after the Spirit was poured out upon them they appeared courageous in vindication of the cause of Christ. The truth of

JAMIESON, FAUSSET, BROWN

25. that the word might be fulfilled . . . , They hated me without a cause—quoted from the Messianic Psalm 69:4, applied also in the same sense in ch. 2:17; Acts 1:20; Romans 11:9, 10; 15:3.

26, 27.—(See on ch. 14:16, 17).

27. ye also shall bear witness—rather, "are witnesses"; with reference indeed to their *future* witness-bearing, but putting the emphasis upon their *present* ample opportunities for acquiring their qualifications for that great office, inasmuch as they had been "with Him from the beginning." (See on Luke 1:2.)

ADAM CLARKE

25. *Written in their law.* See on chap. x. 34. These words are taken from Ps. lxix. 4. This psalm is applied to Christ, chap. ii. 17; xix. 28; to the vengeance of God against Judea, Acts i. 20. The psalm seems entirely prophetic of Christ.

26. *But when the Comforter is come.* See on chap. xiv. 16.

26-27. *He shall testify . . . and ye also shall bear witness.* He shall bear His testimony in your souls, and you shall bear this testimony to the world. Our Lord appears to reason thus: In every respect the unbelief of the Jews is inexcusable. They believe not My doctrine, notwithstanding its purity and holiness. They believe not in the Father who sent Me, notwithstanding I have confirmed My mission by the most astonishing miracles. One thing only remains now to be done, i.e., to send them the Holy Spirit, to convince them of sin, righteousness, and judgment; and this He shall do, not only by His influence upon their hearts, but also by your words. And when they shall have resisted this Spirit, then the cup of their iniquity shall be filled, and wrath shall come upon them to the uttermost.

ALBERT BARNES:

25. "In their law" (Ps. 35:19). All the Old Testament was sometimes called "the law." The meaning here is that the same thing happened to him which did to the psalmist. The same words which David used respecting his enemies would express, also, the conduct of the Jews and their treatment of the Messiah. In both cases it was without cause. Jesus had broken no law, he had done no injury to his country or to any individual. It is still true that sinners hate him in the same way. He injures no one, but, amid all their hatred, he seeks their welfare; and, while they reject him in a manner for which they can give no reason in the day of judgment, he still follows them with mercies and entreats them to return to him. Who has ever had any reason to hate the Lord Jesus? What injury has he ever done to any one of the human race? What evil has he ever said or thought of any one of them? What cause or reason had the Jews for putting him to death? What reason has the sinner for hating him now? What reason for neglecting him? No one can give a reason for it that will satisfy his own conscience, none that has the least show of plausibility. Yet no being on earth has ever been more hated, despised, or neglected, and in every instance it has been "without a cause."
—*Popular Commentary*

ALEXANDER MACLAREN:

The Comforter whom Christ sends is no mere drier of men's tears and gentle Consoler of human sorrows, but He is a mightier Spirit than that, and the word by which He is described in our text, which means "one who is summoned to the side of another," conveys the idea of a helper who is brought to the man to be helped, in order to render whatever aid and succour that man's weakness and circumstances may require. The verses before our text suggest what sort of aid and succour the disciples will need. They are to be as sheep in the midst of wolves. Their defenseless purity will need a Protector, a strong Shepherd. They stand alone among enemies. There must be someone beside them to fight for them, to shield and to encourage them, to be their Safety and their Peace. And that Paraclete, who is called to our side, comes for the special help which these special circumstances require, and is a strong Spirit who will be our Champion and our Ally, whatever antagonism may storm against us, and however strong and well armed may be the assaulting legions of the world's hate.

Then, still further, the other designation here of this strong Succourer and Friend is "the Spirit of truth," by which is designated, not so much His characteristic attribute, as rather the weapon which He wields, or the material with which He works. The "truth" is His instrument; that is to say, the Spirit of God sent by Jesus Christ is the Strengthener, the Encourager, the Comforter, the Fighter for us and with us, because He wields that great body of truth, the perfect revelation of God, and man, and duty, and salvation, which is embodied in the incarnation and work of Jesus Christ our Lord. The truth is His weapon, and it is by it that He makes us strong.—*Expositions of Holy Scripture*

MATTHEW HENRY

the Christian religion was to be proved very much by the evidence of matter of fact, especially Christ's resurrection, of which the apostles were in a particular manner chosen witnesses (Acts x. 41). Christ's ministers are his witnesses. The honour put upon them hereby—that they should be *workers together with God*. "The *Spirit shall testify of me*, and you also *shall bear witness*." This might encourage them against the hatred and contempt of the world, that Christ had honoured them.

2. They were qualified to be so: *You have been with me from the beginning*. They not only heard his public sermons, but had constant private converse with him. Others saw the wonderful and merciful works that he did in their own town and country only, those that went about with him were witnesses of them all. Those are best able to bear witness for Christ that have themselves been with him, by faith, hope, and love. Ministers must first learn Christ, and then preach him. Those speak best of the things of God that speak experimentally. It is particularly a great advantage to have been acquainted with Christ *from the beginning*. To have been with him from the beginning of our days. An early acquaintance and constant converse with the gospel of Christ will make a man like a good householder.

JAMIESON, FAUSSET, BROWN

ADAM CLARKE

A. B. SIMPSON:

The mission of the Comforter with respect to the disciples. Already, in the preceding discourse, He has been revealed as their indwelling Teacher and Monitor. Here He is represented still more fully in this respect, as the patient and gentle Guide, who will supplement the present instructions of the Master by such fuller unfoldings of the truth as they may be able to bear from time to time, and, especially, the truths respecting the future and the second coming of the Lord—the whole prophetic horizon, which was to be opened to their view a little later. "He will guide you unto all truth, and show you things to come" (v. 13). He was also to be to them the spirit of testimony. "He shall testify of me, and ye shall also bear witness, because ye have been with me from the beginning." —*Christ in the Bible*

CHAPTER 16

Verses 1–6

Christ dealt faithfully with his disciples when he sent them forth. He told them the worst, that they might sit down and count the cost.

I. He gives them a reason why he alarmed them thus: *These things have I spoken unto you, that you should not be offended, v.* 1. The disciples of Christ are apt to be offended at the cross; and the offence of the cross is a dangerous temptation, even to good men, to turn back from the ways of God. Our Lord Jesus, by giving us notice of trouble, designed to take off the terror of it, that it might not be a surprise to us. We can easily welcome a guest we expect, and *being forewarned are forearmed*.

II. He foretells particularly what they should suffer (*v.* 2): "Those that have power to do it shall *put you out of their synagogues; they shall kill you*." *Behold two swords* drawn against the followers of the Lord Jesus.

1. The sword of ecclesiastical censure. They shall *cast you out of their synagogues*. At first, they scourged them in their synagogues as contemners of the law (Matt. x. 17), and at length cast them out as incorrigible. "They shall cast you out of the congregation of Israel, put you into the condition of an outlaw," *to be knocked on the head, like another wolf*. Many a good truth has been branded with an anathema.

2. The sword of civil power. When you are expelled as heretics, they will *kill you, and think they do God service*. You will find them really cruel: They will *kill you*. The twelve apostles (we are told) were all put to death, except John. You will find them *seemingly conscientious*; they will think they do God service. It is possible for those that are real enemies to God's service to pretend a mighty zeal for it. The devil's work has many a time been done in God's livery. It is common to patronise an enmity to religion with a colour of duty to God. God's people have suffered the greatest hardships from conscientious persecutors. This does not at all lessen the sin of the persecutors, but it does enhance the sufferings of the persecuted, to die under the character of being enemies to God.

III. He gives them the true reason of the world's enmity and rage against them (*v.* 3): "*These things will they do unto you, because they have not known the Father, nor me*." Many that pretend to know God are wretchedly ignorant of him. Those that are ignorant of Christ cannot have any right knowledge of God. Those are very ignorant indeed of God and Christ that think it an acceptable piece of service to persecute good people.

IV. He tells them why he gave them notice of this now, and why not sooner. Why he told them of it now (*v.* 4), not to discourage them, but that, "when *the time shall come* you may *remember that I told you*." When suffering times come it will be of use to us to remember what Christ has told us of sufferings. The trouble may be the less grievous, for we were told of it before. So that it ought not to be a surprise to us. Why he did not tell them of it sooner: *I spoke not this to you from the beginning* because *I was with you*. While he was with them, he bore the shock of the world's malice, and stood in the front of the battle. But we do find that from the beginning

CHAPTER 16

VSS. 1-33. DISCOURSE AT THE SUPPER TABLE CONCLUDED. **1-5. These things have I spoken unto you, that ye should not be offended**—both the *warnings* and the *encouragements* just given.

2. They shall put you out of the synagogue—(ch. 9:22; 12:42). **the time cometh, that whosoever killeth you will think that he doeth God service**—The words mean *religious service*—'that he is offering a service to God.' (So Saul of Tarsus, Gal. 1:13, 14; Phil. 3:6.)

4. these things I said not . . . at—from—**the beginning**—He *had* said it pretty early (Luke 6: 22), but not quite as in vs. 2. **because I was with you.**

CHAPTER 16

1. *These things have I spoken.* Particularly what is mentioned in the two last chapters. *Be offended.* "That ye should not be stumbled." May not fall away from the faith, nor receive any injury to your souls, as that man does to his body who stumbles or falls over a stone or block in the way which he has not discovered.

2. *They shall put you out of the synagogues.* They will "excommunicate" you. In these excommunications they were spoiled of all their substance; see Ezra x. 8 and Heb. x. 34, and deprived of their character, their influence, and every necessary of life. *That whosoever killeth you.* This Paul found; for more than forty Jews bound themselves under a curse that they would neither eat nor drink till they had killed him, Acts xxiii. 12-13; and agreeably to this, it is said, in that Tract of the Talmud which is entitled *Bammidbar,* R. xxi. ad. Num. xxv. 13: "He who sheds the blood of the ungodly, is equal to him who brings an offering to God."

3. *Because they have not known the Father.* Ignorance of the benevolence of God, and of the philanthropy of Christ, is the grand fountain whence all religious persecution and intolerance proceed.

4. *At the beginning.* I would not trouble you by speaking of these things pointedly at first, when I chose you to be My disciples, but have referred them to the present time, lest you should be discouraged, and now declare them only because it is absolutely necessary that you should be put upon your guard.

MATTHEW HENRY

he bade them prepare for sufferings.

V. He expresses a very affectionate concern for the present sadness of his disciples (*v.* 5, 6): "*Now I go my way to him that sent me;* and *none of you asketh me, Whither goest thou?* But, instead of enquiring after that which would comfort you, you pore upon that which looks melancholy."

1. He had told them that he was about to leave them: *Now I go my way.* He was not driven away by force, but voluntarily departed. He went *to him that sent him,* to give an account of his negotiation.

2. He had told them what hard things they must suffer when he was gone. They would be tempted to think they had made a sorry bargain of it. Their Master sympathizes with them, yet blames them, (1) They were careless of the means of comfort: *None of you asks me, Whither goest thou?* Peter had started this question (*ch.* xiii. 36), and Thomas had seconded it (*ch.* xiv. 5), but they did not pursue it. See what a compassionate teacher Christ is. Many a teacher will not endure that the learner should ask the same question twice; if he cannot take a thing quickly, let him go without it; but our Lord Jesus knows how to deal with babes, that must be taught with *precept upon precept.* Enquiry into the design and tendency of the darkest dispensations of Providence would help to reconcile us to them. It will silence us to ask, Whence come they? but will abundantly satisfy us to ask, Whither go they? for we know they *work for good,* Rom. viii. 28.

(2) They were too intent upon the occasions of their grief: *Sorrow has filled their hearts.* By looking at that only which made against them, and overlooking that which made for them, they were so full of sorrow that there was no room left for joy. It is the common fault and folly of melancholy Christians to dwell only upon the dark side of the cloud. That which filled the disciples' hearts with sorrow was too great an affection to this present life. They were big with hopes of their Master's external kingdom and glory. Nothing is a greater prejudice to our joy in God than *the love of the world*; and *the sorrow of the world,* the consequence of it.

Verses 7–15

Three things we have here concerning *the Comforter's coming*:

I. Christ's departure was absolutely necessary to the Comforter's coming, *v.* 7. Christ saw cause to assert it with a more than ordinary solemnity: *I tell you the truth.*

1. *It is expedient,* not only for me, but *for you* also, *that I go away.* Our Lord Jesus is always for that which is most expedient for us, and gives us the physic we are loth to take, because he knows it is good for us.

2. *It was therefore expedient* because it was in order to the sending of the Spirit.

(1) Christ's going was in order to the Comforter's coming. *If I go not away, the Comforter will not come.* He that gives freely may recall one gift before he bestows another, while we would fondly hold all. The sending of the Spirit was to be the fruit of Christ's purchase, and that purchase was to be made by his death. It was to be an answer to his intercession within the veil. See *ch.* xiv. 16. Thus must this gift be both paid for, and prayed for, by our Lord Jesus. The disciples must be weaned from his bodily presence before they were duly prepared to receive the spiritual aids and comforts of a new dispensation. *If I depart I will send him to you.* Though he *departs, he sends the Comforter*; nay, he departs on purpose to send him.

(2) The presence of Christ's Spirit in his church is so much more desirable than his bodily presence, that it was really expedient for us that he should go away. His corporal presence could be but in one place at one time, but his Spirit is wherever *two or three are gathered in his name.* Christ's bodily presence draws men's eyes, his Spirit draws their hearts.

II. The coming of *the Spirit* was absolutely necessary to the carrying on of Christ's interests on earth (*v.* 8): *And when he is come he will reprove,* or, *he will convince the world,* concerning *sin, righteousness, and judgment.*

1. See here on what errand he is sent. To *reprove.* The Spirit, by the word and conscience, is a reprover. To *convince.* It is a law-term, and speaks the office of the judge in summing up the evidence. He shall *convince,* that is, "He shall put to silence the adversaries of Christ and his cause." Convincing work is the Spirit's work; man may open the cause, but it is the Spirit only that can open the heart. The Spirit is called the *Comforter* (*v.* 7), and here it is said, *He shall convince.* One could think this were cold comfort, but it is the method the Spirit takes, first to convince, and then to comfort; first to lay open the wound, and then to apply healing medicines.

JAMIESON, FAUSSET, BROWN

5. But now I go my way to him that sent me—While He was with them, the world's hatred was directed chiefly against Himself; but His departure would bring it down upon them as His representatives. **and none of you asketh me, Whither goest thou?**—They *had* done so in a sort (ch. 13:36; 14:5); but He wished more intelligent and eager inquiry on the subject.

6, 7. But because I have said these things . . . , sorrow hath filled your heart—Sorrow had too much paralyzed them, and He would rouse their energies.

7. It is expedient for you that I go away—

My Saviour, can it ever be
That I should gain by losing thee?
KEBLE

Yes. **for if I go not away, the Comforter will not come unto you, but if I depart, I will send him unto you**—(See on ch. 7:39; 14:16).

8. And when he is come, he will . . .—This is one of the passages most pregnant with thought in the profound discourses of Christ; with a few great strokes depicting all and every part of the ministry of the Holy Ghost in the world—His operation with reference to individuals as well as the mass, on believers and unbelievers alike [OLSHAUSEN]. **he will reprove**—This is too weak a word to express what is meant. *Reproof* is indeed implied in the term employed, and doubtless the word begins with it. But *convict* or *convince* is the thing intended; and as the one expresses the work of the Spirit on the *unbelieving* portion of mankind, and the other on the *believing,* it is better not to restrict it to either.

ADAM CLARKE

5. *None of you asketh me, Whither goest thou?* In chap. xiii. 36, Peter had asked, "Lord, whither goest thou?"—and Thomas much the same in chap. xiv. 5, both of whom had received an answer. But now, at the time when Jesus was speaking this, none of them asked this question, because their hearts were filled with sorrow, v. 6.

7. *It is expedient for you that I go away.* In other places He had shown them the absolute necessity of His death for the salvation of men; see Matt. xx. 19; xxvi. 2; Mark ix. 31; x. 33; Luke ix. 44; xviii. 32. This He does not repeat here, but shows them that, by the order of God, the Holy Spirit cannot come to them, nor to the world, unless He first die; and consequently men cannot be saved but in this way.

8. *He will reprove.* He will demonstrate these matters so clearly as to leave no doubt on the minds of those who are simple of heart, and so fully as to confound and shut the mouths of those who are gainsayers.

MATTHEW HENRY

2. See who they are whom he is to reprove and convince: *The world.* He shall give the world the most powerful means of conviction, the gospel, fully proved. He shall sufficiently provide for the silencing of the objections and prejudices of the world against the gospel. He shall savingly convince many in the world, some in every age, in every place. Even this malignant world the Spirit shall work upon; and the conviction of sinners is the comfort of faithful ministers.

3. See what the Spirit shall convince the world of.

(1) *Of sin* (*v.* 9), *because they believe not on me.* The Spirit is sent to convince sinners of sin, not barely to tell them of it; in conviction there is more than this; it is to prove it upon them, and force them to own it. The Spirit convinces of the fact of sin, of the fault of sin, of the folly of sin, of the filth of sin, and, lastly, of the fruit of sin, that the end thereof is death. The Spirit, in conviction, fastens especially upon the sin of unbelief, their not believing in Christ, *First,* As the great reigning sin. There was, and is, a world of people, that believe not in Jesus Christ, and they are not sensible that it is their sin. Those transgress who, when *God speaketh to us by his Son, refuse him that speaketh. Secondly,* As the great ruining sin. Every sin is so in its own nature. It is a sin against the remedy. *Thirdly,* As that which is at the bottom of all sin. The Spirit shall convince the world that the true reason why sin reigns among them is because they are not by faith united to Christ.

(2) *Of righteousness, because I go to my Father, and you see me no more, v.* 10. We may understand this, [1] Of Christ's personal righteousness. He shall convince the world that Jesus of Nazareth was Christ the righteous, as the centurion owned (Luke xxiii. 47), *Certainly this was a righteous man.* Now by what medium or argument will the Spirit convince men of the sincerity of the Lord Jesus? Their *seeing him no more* will contribute something towards the removal of their prejudices. His *going to the Father* would be a full conviction of it. The coming of the Spirit, according to the promise, was a proof of Christ's exaltation to God's *right hand* (Acts ii. 33), and this was a demonstration of his righteousness. [2] Of Christ's righteousness communicated to us for our justification and salvation. The Spirit shall convince men of this righteousness. Having shown them their need of a righteousness, lest this should drive them to despair he will show them where it is to be had. It was hard to convince those of this righteousness that *went about to establish their own,* but the Spirit will do it. Christ's ascension is the great argument proper to convince men of this righteousness: *I go to the Father, and you shall see me no more.* Now that we are sure he is *at the right hand of God* we are sure of being justified through him.

(3) *Of judgment, because the prince of this world is judged, v.* 11. The devil, *the prince of this world,* was judged, was discovered to be a great deceiver and destroyer. He was cast out of the souls of people by the grace of God working with the gospel of Christ. The Spirit convinces the world of judgment. By *the judgment of the prince of this world,* it appears that Christ is stronger than Satan. He shall show that Christ's errand into the world was to set things to right in it. All will be well when his power is broken who made all the mischief. If Satan be thus subdued by Christ, we may be sure no other power can stand before him.

III. The coming of the Spirit would be of unspeakable advantage to the disciples themselves. The Spirit has work to do, not only on the enemies of Christ, but upon his servants and agents, and therefore it was *expedient for them that he should go away.*

1. The tender sense he had of their present weakness (*v.* 12): *I have yet many things to say unto you, but you cannot bear them now.* See what a teacher Christ is. None like him for copiousness. Treasures of wisdom and knowledge are hid in him. None like him for compassion; he would have told them more of *the things pertaining to the kingdom of God,* but they could not bear it, it would have confounded and stumbled them, rather than have given them any satisfaction.

2. He assures them of sufficient assistances. "*But when he, the Spirit of truth, is come,* all will be well." He shall undertake to guide the apostles, and glorify Christ.

(1) To guide the apostles. That they do not miss their way: *He will guide you.* The Spirit is given us to be our guide, to go along with us. That they do not come short of their end: *He will guide them into all truth,* as the skilful pilot guides the ship into the port it is bound for. To be led *into a truth* is more than barely to know it; it is to be intimately and experimentally acquainted with it. It denotes a gradual discovery of truth shining more and more.

JAMIESON, FAUSSET, BROWN

9. Of sin, because they believe not on me—As all sin has its root in unbelief, so the most aggravated form of unbelief is the rejection of Christ. The Spirit, however, in fastening this truth upon the conscience, does not *extinguish,* but, on the contrary, does *consummate and intensify, the sense of all other sins.*

10. Of righteousness, because I go to my Father, and ye see me no more—Beyond doubt, it is *Christ's personal righteousness* which the Spirit was to bring home to the sinner's heart. The evidence of this was to lie in the great *historical fact,* that He had "gone to His Father and was no more visible to men":—for if His claim to be the Son of God, the Saviour of the world, had been a lie, how should the Father, who is "a jealous God," have raised such a blasphemer from the dead and exalted him to His right hand? But if He was the "Faithful and True Witness," the Father's "Righteous Servant," "His Elect, in whom His soul delighted," then was His departure to the Father, and consequent disappearance from the view of men, but the fitting consummation, the august reward, of all that He did here below, the seal of His mission, the glorification of the testimony which He bore on earth, by the reception of its Bearer to the Father's bosom. This triumphant vindication of Christ's *rectitude* is to us divine evidence, bright as heaven, that He is indeed the Saviour of the world, God's Righteous Servant to justify many, because He bare their iniquities (Isa. 53:11). Thus the Spirit, in this clause, is seen convincing men that there is in Christ perfect relief under the sense of *sin* of which He had before convinced them; and so far from mourning over His absence from us, as an irreparable loss, we learn to glory in it, as the evidence of His perfect acceptance on our behalf, exclaiming with one who understood this point, "Who shall lay anything to the charge of God's elect? It is God that justifieth: Who is he that condemneth? It is Christ that died; *yea, rather, that is risen again, who is even at the right hand of God . . .*" (Rom. 8:33, 34). **11. Of judgment, because the prince of this world is judged**—By supposing that the *final judgment* is here meant, the point of this clause is, even by good interpreters, quite missed. The statement, "The prince of this world is *judged,*" means, beyond all reasonable doubt, the same as that in ch. 12:31, "Now shall the prince of this world be *cast out*"; and both mean that his dominion over men, or his power to enslave and so to ruin them, is destroyed. The death of Christ "judged" or judicially overthrew him, and he was thereupon "cast out" or expelled from his usurped dominion (Heb. 2:14; I John 3:8; Col. 2:15). Thus, then, the Spirit shall bring home to men's conscience: (1) the sense of *sin,* consummated in the rejection of Him who came to "take away the sin of the world"; (2) the sense of perfect relief in the *righteousness* of the Father's Servant, now fetched from the earth that spurned Him to that bosom where from everlasting He had dwelt; and (3) the sense of emancipation from the fetters of Satan, whose *judgment* brings to men liberty to be holy, and transformation out of servants of the devil into sons and daughters of the Lord Almighty. To one class of men, however, all this will carry *conviction* only; they "will not come to Christ"—revealed though He be to them as the life-giving One—that they may have life. Such, abiding voluntarily under the dominion of the prince of this world, are *judged in his judgment,* the visible consummation of which will be at the great day. To another class, however, this blessed teaching will have another issue—translating them out of the kingdom of darkness into the kingdom of God's dear Son. **12-15. when he, the Spirit of truth, is come . . . he shall not speak of himself**—i.e., *from* Himself, but, like Christ Himself, "what He hears," what is given Him to communicate.

ADAM CLARKE

The world. The Jewish nation first, and afterwards the Gentile world; for His influences shall not be confined to one people, place, or time.

9. *Of sin.* Of the sin of the Jews in not receiving Me as the Messiah, though My mission was accredited by the very miracles which the prophets foretold; see Isa. xxxv. 3-6. This was literally fulfilled on the Day of Pentecost, when the Spirit was given; for multitudes of Jews were then convinced of this sin, and converted to God. See Acts ii. 37.

10. *Of righteousness.* Of My innocence and holiness, because I go away to My Father, of which My resurrection from the dead and My ascension to heaven shall be complete proofs.

11. *Of judgment.* Of the false judgment of the Jews in condemning the Lord Jesus, who, as some think, is intended here by the ruler *of this world.* Others think that Satan is meant, whose usurped power over the world was now to be greatly restrained, and by and by totally destroyed; see chap. xii. 31; Col. ii. 15; Rev. xi. 15; xii. 10-11. Perhaps our Lord's meaning is that, as a most astonishing judgment or punishment was now about to fall upon the Jews in consequence of their obstinate infidelity, the Holy Ghost by the ministry of the apostles should demonstrate that this judgment, severe as it might seem, was amply merited by this worst of all people. One general exposition may be given of these three verses. The Holy Spirit will convince the world of *sin* committed, and guilt and condemnation thereby incurred; of *righteousness*—of the necessity of being pardoned, and made righteous through the blood of the Lamb, who, after being offered up for sin, went to the Father, ever to appear in His presence as our intercessor; and of *judgment*—of the great day thereof, when none shall be able to stand but those whose sins are pardoned and whose souls are made righteous. In all that our Lord says here, there seems to be an allusion to the office of an advocate in a cause, in a court of justice; who, by producing witnesses and pleading upon the proof, convicts the opposite party of sin, demonstrates the righteousness of his client, and shows the necessity of passing judgment upon the accuser.

13. *He will guide you.* He will consider your feeble infant state; and, as a father leads his child by the hand, so will the Holy Spirit lead and guide you.

MATTHEW HENRY | JAMIESON, FAUSSET, BROWN | ADAM CLARKE

But how into *all truth*? Into the whole truth relating to their embassy; whatever was needful or useful for them to know; what truths they were to teach others the Spirit would teach them. Into nothing but the truth. All that *he shall guide you into* shall be *truth*. [1] "The Spirit shall teach nothing but the truth, *for he shall not speak of himself, but whatsoever he shall hear, that*, and that only, *shall he speak*." The testimony of the Spirit, in the word and by the apostles, is what we may rely upon. We may venture our souls upon the Spirit's word. The testimony of the Spirit always concurs with the word of Christ, *for he does not speak of himself*. Men's word and spirit often disagree, but the eternal Word and the eternal Spirit never do. [2] "He shall teach you all truth, for *he will show you things to come*." The Spirit was in the apostles a Spirit of prophecy. This was a great satisfaction to their own minds, and of use to them in their conduct. We should not grudge that the Spirit does not now *show us things to come* in this world, let it suffice that the Spirit in the word hath *shown us things to come* in the other world, which are our chief concern.

(2) The Spirit undertook to glorify Christ, *v.* 14, 15. Even the sending of the Spirit was the glorifying of Christ. It was the honour of the Redeemer that the Spirit was both sent in his name and sent on his errand, to carry on and perfect his undertaking. All the gifts and graces of the Spirit, all the preaching and all the writing of the apostles, the tongues, and miracles, were to glorify Christ. The Spirit glorified Christ by leading his followers into *the truth as it is in Jesus*. *First*, The Spirit should communicate the things of Christ to them: *He shall receive of mine, and shall show it unto you*. All that the Spirit shows us, all that he gives us for our strength and quickening, did all belong to Christ, and was had from him. The Spirit came not to erect a new kingdom, but to advance and establish the same kingdom that Christ had erected. *Secondly*, Herein the things of God should be communicated to us. *All things that the Father hath are mine*. All that *grace and truth* which God designed to show to us he lodged in the hands of the Lord Jesus. Spiritual blessings in heavenly things are given by the Father to the Son for us, and the Son entrusts the Spirit to convey them to us.

Verses 16–22

I. Observe the intimation he gave them of the comfort he designed them, *v.* 16.

1. That they should now shortly lose the sight of him: *A little while, and you shall not see me;* and therefore, if they had any good question to ask him, they must ask quickly. It is good to consider how near to a period our seasons of grace are, that we may be quickened to improve them. They lost the sight of Christ at his death. The most that death does to our Christian friends is to take them out of our sight, only out of sight, and then not out of mind. At his ascension, when he withdrew from them, *out of their sight*; *a cloud received* him, and *they saw him no more*.

2. That yet they should speedily recover the sight of him: *Again a little while, and you shall see me*. His farewell was not a final farewell. (1) At his resurrection, soon after his death, when *he showed himself alive*, by many infallible proofs. (2) By the pouring out of the Spirit, soon after his ascension. The Spirit's coming was Christ's visit to his disciples, not a transient but a permanent one. (3) At his second coming.

3. He assigns the reason: "*Because I go to the Father*." This refers rather to his going away at death, and return at his resurrection, than his going away at his ascension, and his return at the end of time; for it was his death that was their grief, not his ascension. Thus we may say of our ministers and Christian friends, *Yet a little while, and we shall not see them*. It is certain that we must part shortly, and yet not part for ever. It is but a good night to those whom we hope to see with *joy in the morning*.

II. The perplexity of the disciples. They were at a loss what to make of it (*v.* 17, 18): *Some of them said among themselves, What is this that he saith to us?* Though Christ had often spoken to this purport before, yet still they were in the dark. 1. The disciples' weakness, in that they could not understand so plain a saying. Having told them so often in plain terms that he should *be killed, and the third day rise again;* yet, say they, *We cannot tell what he saith. Sorrow had filled their heart*, and made them unapt to receive the impressions of comfort. Mistakes cause griefs, and then griefs confirm mistakes. The notion of Christ's secular kingdom was so deeply rooted in them. When we think the scripture must be made to agree with the false ideas we have imbibed, no wonder that we complain of its

he will show you things to come—referring specially to those revelations which, in the Epistles partially, but most fully in the Apocalypse, open up a vista into the Future of the Kingdom of God, whose horizon is the everlasting hills. **14. He shall glorify me; for he shall receive of mine and show it unto you**—Thus the whole design of the Spirit's office is to glorify Christ—not in His own Person, for this was done by the Father when He exalted Him to His own right hand—but in the view and estimation of men. For this purpose He was to *"receive of Christ"—all the truth relating to Christ—"and show it unto them,"* or make them to discern it in its own light. The *subjective* nature of the Spirit's teaching—the discovery to the souls of men of what is Christ *outwardly*—is here very clearly expressed; and, at the same time, the vanity of looking for revelations of the Spirit which shall do anything beyond throwing light in the soul upon what Christ Himself is, and taught, and did upon earth. **15. All things that the Father hath are mine**—a plainer expression than this of *absolute community* with the Father in all things cannot be conceived, though the "all things" here have reference to the things of the Kingdom of Grace, which the Spirit was to receive that He might show it to us. We have here a wonderful glimpse into the *inner relations of the Godhead*.

16-22. A little while, and ye shall not see me; and again a little while, and ye shall see me, because I go to the Father—The joy of the world at their not seeing Him seems to show that His removal from them by *death* was what He meant; and in that case, their joy at again seeing Him points to their transport at His reappearance amongst them on His *Resurrection,* when they could no longer doubt His identity. At the same time the sorrow of the widowed Church in the absence of her Lord in the heavens, and her transport at His personal return, are certainly here expressed.

CHARLES H. SPURGEON:

Ah, brothers! the Holy Ghost never comes to glorify *us*, or to glorify a denomination, or, I think, even to glorify a systematic arrangement of doctrines. He comes to glorify Christ. If we want to be in accord with Him, we must preach in order to glorify Christ. May we never have this thought, "I will put that bit in; it will tell well. The friends will feel that oratory is not quite extinct, that Demosthenes lives again in this village." No, no. I should say, brother, though it is a very delightful piece, strike that out ruthlessly; because if you have had a thought of that kind, you had better not put yourself in the way of temptation by using it. "Yes, that is a magnificent sentence! I do not know where I met with it, or whether it is my own, I am afraid that most of our friends will not understand it; but then it will give them an impression that they have a deep thinker in their pulpit." Well then, it may be very admirable, and, further, it might be a very right thing to give them that precious piece; but if you have that thought about it, strike it out. Strike it out ruthlessly. Say, "No, no, no! If it is not distinctly my aim to glorify Christ, I am not in accord with the aim of the Holy Ghost, and I cannot expect His help. We shall not be pulling the same way, and therefore, I will have nothing of which I cannot say that I am saying it simply, sincerely, and only that I may glorify Christ."
—*The Treasury of the New Testament*

15. *All things that the Father hath are mine.* If Christ had not been equal to God, could He have said this without blasphemy? *And shew it unto you.* As Christ is represented as the Ambassador of the Father, so the Holy Spirit is represented as the Ambassador of the Son, coming vested with His authority, as the Interpreter and Executor of His will.

16. *A little while.* He had but a few hours to live. *And ye shall not see me.* I shall be hidden from your view in the grave.

Again, a little while. In three days after My death. *Ye shall see me.* I will rise again, and show myself to you. Or, As I am going by My ascension to the Father, in a short time, you shall see Me personally no more; but in a little while I shall pour out My Spirit upon you, and others through your ministry; and you shall see Me virtually in the great and wonderful work which shall then take place in the hearts and lives of men.

18. *What is this that he saith?* They knew from what He had said that He was to die, but knew not what He meant by their seeing Him again in a little time.

MATTHEW HENRY

difficulty; but, when our reasonings are captivated to revelation, the matter becomes easy. It should seem, that which puzzled them was the *little while*. They could not conceive how he should leave them quickly. Thus it is hard for us to represent to ourselves that change as near which yet we know will come certainly, and may come suddenly. 2. Their willingness to be instructed. When they were at a loss about the meaning of Christ's words, they conferred together upon it. By mutual converse about divine things we both borrow the light of others and improve our own. We must revolve what we cannot explain, and wait *till God shall reveal even this unto us*.

III. The further explication of what Christ had said.

1. See here *why* Christ explained it (*v.* 19); because he *knew they were desirous to ask him*. The knots we cannot untie we must bring to him. Christ *knew they were desirous to ask him*, but were bashful and ashamed to ask. Christ instructed those who he *knew were desirous to ask him*, though they did not ask. Who they are that Christ will teach. The humble, that confess their ignorance. The diligent, that use the means they have: "*Do you enquire?* You shall be taught."

2. See here *how* he explained it. He explains it by their sorrowing and rejoicing, because we commonly measure things according as they affect us (*v.* 20): *You shall weep and lament, but the world shall rejoice and you shall be sorrowful, but your sorrow will be turned into joy*. Believers have joy or sorrow according as they have or have not a sight of Christ.

(1) What Christ says here, and *v.* 21, 22, of their sorrow and joy, is primarily to be understood of the present state of the disciples. Their grief foretold: *You shall weep and lament, and you shall be sorrowful*. They wept for him because they loved him; the pain of our friend is a pain to ourselves. They wept for themselves, and their own loss. Christ has given notice to his disciples beforehand to expect sorrow, that they may treasure up comforts accordingly. The world's rejoicing: *But the world shall rejoice*. That which is the grief of saints is the joy of sinners. Those that are *strangers to Christ* will continue in their carnal mirth. Those that are *enemies to Christ* will rejoice because they hope they have conquered him. Let it be no surprise to us if we see others triumphing, when we are *trembling for the ark*. The return of joy. *But your sorrow shall be turned into joy*. The sorrow of the true Christian, *is but for a moment. The disciples were glad when they saw the Lord*. His resurrection was *life from the dead* to them, and their sorrow for Christ's sufferings was turned into joy. They were *sorrowful, and yet always rejoicing* (2 Cor. vi. 10), had sorrowful lives and yet joyful hearts.

(2) It is applicable to all the faithful followers of the Lamb.

[1] Their condition and disposition are both mournful. Those that are acquainted with Christ must, as he was, be *acquainted with grief*. They mourn with sufferers that mourn, and mourn for sinners that mourn not for themselves.

[2] The world, at the same time, goes away with all the mirth. Mirth and pleasures are surely none of the best things, for then the worst men would not have so large a share of them, and the favourites of heaven be such strangers to them.

[3] Spiritual mourning will shortly be turned into eternal rejoicing. Their sorrow will not only be followed with joy, but turned into it. It is the will of Christ that his people should be a comforted people.

First, Here is the parable itself (*v.* 21): *A woman, when she is in travail, hath sorrow because her hour is come, but as soon as she is delivered of the child she remembers no more the anguish, for joy that a man is born into the world*. The fruit of the curse according to the sentence (Gen. iii. 16), *In sorrow shalt thou bring forth*. See what this world is; all its roses are surrounded with thorns. This comes of sin. The fruit of the blessing, in *the joy there is for a child born into the world*. The fruit of a blessing is matter of joy; the birth of a living child is the parents' joy. Though children are certain cares, uncertain comforts, and often prove the greatest crosses, yet it is natural to us to rejoice at their birth. Now this is very proper to set forth, (*a*) The sorrows of Christ's disciples in this world; they are sure and sharp, but not to last long, and in order to a joyful product. (*b*) Their joys after these sorrows, which will *wipe away all tears*. When they reap the fruit of all their services and sorrows, the toil and anguish of this world will be no more remembered.

Secondly, The application of the similitude (*v.* 22): "*You now have sorrow, but I will see you again*."

a. Here again he tells them of their *sorrow*: "*You now therefore have sorrow; therefore*, because I am leaving you." Christ's withdrawings are just cause

JAMIESON, FAUSSET, BROWN

ALEXANDER MACLAREN:

"Jesus knew that they were desirous to ask him." He knows all our difficulties and perplexities. Perhaps it is His supernatural knowledge that is indicated in the words before us, or perhaps it is merely that He saw them whispering among themselves and so inferred their wish. Be that as it may, we may take the comfort that we have to do with a Teacher who accurately understands how much we understand and where we grope, and will shape His teaching according to our necessities.

He had not a word of rebuke for the slowness of their apprehension. He might well have said to them, "O fools and slow of heart to believe!" But that word was not addressed to them then, though two of them deserved it and got it, after events had thrown light on His teaching. He never rebukes us for either our stupidity or for our carelessness, but "has long patience" with us.

He does give them a kind of rebuke. "Do ye inquire *among yourselves*?" That is a hopeful source to go to for knowledge. Why did they not ask Him, instead of whispering and muttering behind Him, as if two people equally ignorant could help each other to knowledge? Inquiry "among yourselves" is folly; to ask Him is wisdom.—*Expositions of Holy Scripture*

G. CAMPBELL MORGAN:

"A little while" was the little while of darkness into which they then were passing. "Verily, verily, I say unto you, that ye shall weep and lament." He was looking at the cross, their weeping and lamenting, while the world would be rejoicing. "The world will think when they have put Me on the cross they have gotten rid of Me, and so will it seem to you. You will be weeping and sorrowful; and the world will be glad."

Then the high, wondrous, beauteous declaration: "Ye shall be sorrowful, but your sorrow shall be turned into joy." Not after your sorrow you will obtain joy. No, the very sorrow, the very thing causing your sorrow will be transmuted into joy. The joy will come out of the sorrow. "Your sorrow shall be turned into joy."

In that connection He employed that fine, tender, exquisite illustration of a woman in travail, to interpret the sorrow in the hour to which they were going, and in the hour to which He was going. In effect He said, "Your sorrows will be birthpangs, leading to life. A little while that you will not see Me, the little while of your darkness, and pain, and tears; but that is going to be turned into your joy." He was telling them beforehand. I do not think they understood Him at the time, but I am sure they came to understand Him by and by.—*The Gospel According to John*

ADAM CLARKE

20. *Ye shall weep and lament*. To see Me crucified and laid in the grave. *But the world shall rejoice*. The chief priests, scribes, Pharisees, and persecuting Jews in general will triumph, hoping that their bad cause is crowned with success. *But your sorrow shall be turned into joy*. When you see Me risen from the dead. It is very evident that our Lord uses the word *world* in several parts of this discourse of His to signify the unbelieving and rebellious Jews.

21. *For joy that a man is born*. *Anthropos* is put here for a "human creature," whether male or female, as *homo* among the Romans denoted either man or woman.

MATTHEW HENRY

of grief to his disciples. When the sun sets, the sunflower will hang the head.

b. He, more largely than before, assures them of a return of joy. Three things recommend the joy: The cause of it: "*I will see you again.*" Christ will graciously return to those that wait for him. Men, when they are exalted, will scarcely look upon their inferiors; but the exalted Jesus will visit his disciples. Christ's returns are returns of joy to all his disciples. The cordiality of it: *Your heart shall rejoice.* Joy in the heart is solid, and not flashy; it is secret, it is sweet, it is sure, and not easily broken in upon. The continuance of it: *Your joy no man taketh from you.* They would if they could; but they shall not prevail. Some understand it of the eternal joy of those that are glorified. Our joys on earth we are liable to be robbed of by a thousand accidents, but heavenly joys are everlasting. I rather understand it of the spiritual joys of those that are sanctified. They could not rob them of their joy, because they could not *separate them from the love of Christ*, could not rob them of their God, nor of their *treasure in heaven.*

Verses 23–27

An answer to their askings is here promised. Now there are two ways of asking: asking by way of enquiry, which is the asking of the ignorant; and asking by way of request, which is the asking of the indigent. Christ here speaks of both.

I. By way of enquiry, they should not need to ask (*v.* 23): "*In that day you shall ask me nothing.* You shall not need to enquire." In the story *of the apostles' Acts* we seldom find them asking questions, for they were constantly under a divine guidance. Asking questions supposes us at a loss, or at least at a stand, and the best of us have need to ask questions.

Now for this he gives a reason (*v.* 25): "*These things have I spoken unto you in proverbs, but the time cometh when I shall show you plainly of the Father*, so that you shall not need to ask questions."

1. The great thing Christ would lead them into was the knowledge of God: "*I will show you the Father.*" When Christ would express the greatest favour intended for his disciples, he tells them that he would *show them plainly of the Father*; for what is the happiness of heaven, but immediately and everlastingly to see God?

2. Of this he had hitherto spoken to them in proverbs. Christ had expounded his parables privately to the disciples. (1) Considering their dullness, and unaptness to receive what he said to them, he might be said to speak in proverbs; what he said to them was as a book sealed. (2) Comparing the discoveries he had made to them with what he would make to them, all hitherto had been but proverbs. (3) Confining it to what he had said of *the Father*, what he had said was very dark, compared with what was shortly to be revealed.

3. He would speak to them *plainly* of the Father. When the Spirit was poured out, the apostles attained to a much greater knowledge of divine things than they had before. But this promise will have its full accomplishment in heaven, where we shall see the Father as he is. While we are here, we have many questions to ask, but in that day we shall see all things clearly, and *ask no more questions.*

II. He promises that by way of request they should ask nothing in vain. It is taken for granted that all Christ's disciples give themselves to prayer. Their instruction, direction, strength, and success, must be fetched in by prayer.

1. Here is an express promise of a grant, *v.* 23. The preface to this promise leaves no room to question it: "*Verily, verily, I say unto you.*" The golden sceptre is here held out to us, with this word, *What is thy petition, and it shall be granted?* For he says, *Whatsoever you shall ask the Father in my name, he will give it to you.* What would we more? The promise is as express as we can desire. (1) We are here taught how to seek; we must *ask the Father in Christ's name.* Asking of the Father includes a sense of spiritual wants and a desire of spiritual blessings, with a conviction that they are to be had from God only. Asking in Christ's name includes an acknowledgment of our own unworthiness, and an entire dependence upon Christ. (2) We are here told how we shall speed: *He will give it to you.* What more can we wish for? Christ had promised them great illumination by the Spirit, but they must pray for it. They must continue praying. Perfect fruition is reserved for the land of our rest; asking and receiving are the comfort of the land of our pilgrimage.

2. Here is an invitation for them to petition. Great men permit addresses, but Christ calls upon us to petition, *v.* 24.

JAMIESON, FAUSSET, BROWN

ALBERT BARNES:

"Your joy no man taketh from you." You shall be so firmly persuaded that I have risen and that I am the Messiah that neither the threats nor persecutions of men shall ever be able to shake your faith and produce doubt or unbelief, and thus take away your joy. This prediction was remarkably fulfilled. It is evident that after his ascension not one of the apostles ever doubted for a moment that he had risen from the dead. No persecution or trial was able to shake their faith; and thus, amid all their afflictions, they had an unshaken source of joy. *—Popular Commentary*

23-28. In that day—of the dispensation of the Spirit (as in ch. 14:20). **ye shall ask**—inquire of—**me nothing**—by reason of the fulness of the Spirit's teaching (ch. 14:26; 16:13; and cf. I John 2: 27).

25. in proverbs—in obscure language, opposed to "showing plainly"—i.e., by the Spirit's teaching.

ADAM CLARKE

22. *Your joy no man taketh from you.* Or "shall take away." Some excellent MSS. and versions read the verb in the future tense. Our Lord's meaning appears to have been this: that His resurrection should be so *completely demonstrated* to them that they should never have a doubt concerning it; and consequently that their joy should be great and permanent, knowing that the atonement was made, the victory gained, and the kingdom of Heaven opened to all believers.

23. *Ye shall ask me nothing.* Ye shall then be led, by that Spirit which guides into all truth, to consider Me in the character of Mediator in the kingdom of God, and to address your prayers to the Father in *my name*—in the name of Jesus, the Saviour, because I have died to redeem you —in the name of Christ, the Anointed, because I have ascended to send down the gift of the Holy Ghost.

25. *In proverbs.* That is, words which, besides their plain, literal meaning, have another, viz., a spiritual or figurative one. I have represented heavenly things to you through the medium of earthly. *The time cometh.* Viz., the interval from His resurrection to His ascension, which consisted of forty days, during which He instructed His disciples in the most sublime mysteries and truths of His kingdom, Acts. i. 3.

A. B. SIMPSON:

The first word translated "ask" (v. 23) does not mean to pray, but to inquire about matters with respect to which they are in perplexity. He means that in the coming day, the light will be so plain and clear that they will not need to inquire, as they do now, "What is this that he saith? We cannot tell what he saith"; but they shall plainly understand His will and teachings, and His Father's love.

And, as to prayer, they shall have a higher place of access and confidence, for they shall ask in His name, even as He asks, which they have not yet been able to do, because His redemption work was not complete, and His heavenly priesthood, in their behalf, had not begun. But henceforth He shall be at the Father's side in their interests, and their petitions shall be received at the heavenly throne even as His own; nor will He need to plead for them as for strangers, or aliens, for the Father himself loves them, even as He loves His Son, and His intercession is not so much to propitiate an angry Father and constrain from His reluctant hands the answer to His people's prayers, as that He is to be the channel through whom the answer will come, and the Mediator who receives our petition as they ascend to heaven, in their imperfection and ignorance, purifying them with His holy intercession, and then presenting them with the added incense of His own merits as His very own prayers. *—Christ in the Bible*

MATTHEW HENRY

(1) He looks back upon their practice hitherto: *Hitherto have you asked nothing in my name.* This refers either, [1] To the matter of their prayers: "You have asked nothing comparatively, nothing to what you might have asked." See what a generous benefactor our Lord Jesus is; he gives liberally, and is so far from upbraiding us with the frequency and largeness of his gifts that he rather upbraids us with the seldomness and straitness of our requests. Or, [2] To the name in which they prayed. They prayed many a prayer, but never so expressly in the name of Christ as now he was directing them to do; for he had not as yet offered up that great sacrifice in the virtue of which our prayers were to be accepted, the incense whereof was to perfume all our devotions.

(2) He looks forward to their practice for the future: *Ask, and you shall receive, that your joy may be full.* He directs them to ask for all that which they needed and he had promised. He assures them that they shall *receive.* What we ask from a principle of grace God will graciously give, that hereby *their joy shall be full.* This denotes, *First,* The blessed effect of the *prayer of faith*; it helps to fill up the *joy of faith.* When we are told to *rejoice evermore,* it follows immediately, *Pray without ceasing.* See how high we are to aim in prayer—not only at peace, but joy. Or, *Secondly,* The blessed effects of the *answer of peace*: "Ask, and you shall receive that which will *fill your joy.*"

3. Here are the grounds upon which they might hope to speed (*v.* 26, 27), which are summed up in short by the apostle (1 John ii. 1): "*We have an advocate with the Father.*"

(1) We have an advocate: "*I say not unto you that I will pray the Father for you.*" He speaks as if they needed not any further favours, when he had prevailed for the gift of the Holy Ghost to *make intercession within them*; as if they had no further need of him to pray for them now; but we shall find that he does more for us than he says he will.

(2) We have to do with a Father: *For the Father himself loveth you.* The disciples of Christ are the beloved of God himself. Observe what an emphasis is laid upon this: "*The Father himself loveth you.*" The Father himself, whose favour you have forfeited, and with whom you need an advocate, he himself now loves you. Why the Father loved the disciples of Christ: *Because you have loved me, and have believed that I came out from God,* that is, because you are my disciples indeed. The character of Christ's disciples; they love him, because they *believe he came out from God.* Faith in Christ works by love to him. If we believe him to be our Saviour, we cannot but love him as the most kind to us. Observe with what respect Christ is pleased to speak of his disciples' love to him; he speaks of it as that which recommended them to his Father's favour. What advantage Christ's faithful disciples have, the Father loves them, and that because they love Christ. What encouragement this gave them in prayer. They need not fear speeding when they came to one that loved them. This cautions us against hard thoughts of God. When we are taught in prayer to plead Christ's merit and intercession, it is not as if all the kindness were in Christ only. We owe Christ's merit to God's mercy in giving him for us. Let it cherish and confirm in us good thoughts of God. Believers, that love Christ, ought to know that God loves them.

Verses 28–33

Two things Christ here comforts his disciples with:

I. With an assurance that, though he was leaving the world, he was returning to his Father, *v.* 28–32.

1. A plain declaration of Christ's mission from the Father, and his return to him (*v.* 28): *I came forth from the Father, and am come into the world. Again, I leave the world and go to the Father.* This is the conclusion of the whole matter.

(1) These two great truths are here, [1] Contracted. Brief summaries of Christian doctrine are of great use to young beginners. The principles of the oracles of God brought into a little compass in creeds and catechisms have, like the beams of the sun contracted in a burning glass, conveyed divine light and heat with a wonderful power. [2] Compared. There is an admirable harmony in divine truths; they both corroborate and illustrate one another; Christ's coming and his going do so. Christ had commended his disciples for believing that he came forth from God (*v.* 27), and thence infers the necessity of his returning to God again. The due improvement of what we know and own would help us into the understanding of that which seems difficult and doubtful.

(2) If we ask concerning the Redeemer *whence he came,* and *whither he went,* we are told, [1] That he *came from the Father,* and he came into this world,

JAMIESON, FAUSSET, BROWN

24. Hitherto have ye asked nothing in my name—for "prayer *in the name of* Christ, and prayer to Christ, presuppose His *glorification*" [OLSHAUSEN]. **ask**—when I am gone, "in My name."

26. I say not . . ., I will pray the Father for you—as if He were not of *Himself* disposed to aid you: Christ does pray the Father for His people, but not for the purpose of inclining an *unwilling* ear.

27. For the Father himself loveth you, because ye have loved me—This love of theirs is that which is called forth by God's eternal love in the gift of His Son *mirrored* in the hearts of those who believe, and resting on His dear Son.

28. I came forth from the Father . . .—i.e., 'And ye are right, for I have indeed so come forth,and shall soon return whence I came.' This echo of the truth, alluded to in the preceding verse, seems like *thinking aloud,* as if it were grateful to His own spirit on such a subject and at such an hour.

ADAM CLARKE

24. *Hitherto have ye asked nothing in my name.* You have not as yet considered Me the great Mediator between God and man; but this is one of the truths which shall be more fully revealed to you by the Holy Spirit.

Ask. In My name; and *ye shall receive*—all the salvation you thus request; the consequence of which shall be *that your joy* shall *be full*—you shall be thoroughly happy in being made completely holy.

26. *I say not unto you, that I will pray the Father for you.* I need not tell you that I will continue as your Intercessor; I have already given you so many proofs of My love that you cannot possibly doubt this. Besides, the Father himself needs no entreaty to do you good, for He loves you, and is graciously disposed to save you to the uttermost, because "you have loved Me and believed in Me as coming from God," for the salvation of the world.

28. *I came forth from the Father.* With whom I existed from eternity in glory. *Am come into the world.* By my incarnation. *I leave the world.* By My death. *And go to the Father.* By My ascension. These four words contain the whole economy of the gospel of man's salvation, and a consummate abridgment of the Christian faith. This gave the disciples a key to the whole of our Lord's discourse; and especially to that part, v. 16, that had so exceedingly embarrassed them, as appears by vv. 17-18.

MATTHEW HENRY

this world of mankind. Here his business lay, and hither he came to attend it. He left his home for this strange country; his palace for this cottage. [2] That, when he had done his work on earth, he left the world, and went back to his Father. That still he is spiritually present with his church, and will be to the end.

2. The disciples' satisfaction in this declaration (*v.* 29, 30): *Lo, now speakest thou plainly.* It should seem, this one word of Christ did them more good than all the rest. Two things they improved in.

(1) In knowledge: *Lo, now speakest thou plainly.* Divine truths are most likely to do good when they are spoken plainly. When Christ is pleased to speak plainly to our souls we have reason to rejoice in it.

(2) In faith: *Now are we sure.*

[1] What was the matter of their faith: *We believe that thou camest forth from God.* He had said (*v.* 27) that they did believe this; "Lord" (say they) "we do believe it."

[2] What was the motive of their faith—his omniscience. This proved him a teacher come from God, and more than a prophet, that he knew all things. Those know Christ best that know him by experience, that can say of his power, It works in me; of his love, He loved me. This confirmed the faith of the disciples here. *And needest not that any man should ask thee.* Christ's aptness to teach. He prevents us with his instructions and needs not to be importuned. His ability to teach. The best of teachers can only answer what is spoken, but Christ can answer what is thought.

3. The gentle rebuke Christ gave the disciples, *v.* 31, 32. Observing how they triumphed in their attainments, he said, "*Do you now believe?* Alas! you know not your own weakness; you will very shortly *be scattered every man to his own,*" &c.

(1) A question, designed to put them upon consideration: *Do you now believe?* "If now, why not sooner?" Those who are at last persuaded to believe have reason to be ashamed that they stood it out so long. "If now, why not ever? When an hour of temptation comes, where will your faith be then?"

(2) A prediction of their fall. In a little time they would all desert him, which was fulfilled that very night. They were scattered from one another; they shifted everyone for his own safety. Scattered from him: *You shall leave me alone.* They should have been witnesses for him upon his trial, but they were ashamed of his chain, and afraid of sharing with him in his sufferings, and left him alone. Many a good cause, when it is distressed by its enemies, is deserted by its friends. Those that are tried, do not always prove trusty. If we at any time find our friends unkind to us, let us remember that Christ's were so to him. When they left him alone, they were scattered *every man to his own.* Everyone went his own way, where he fancied he should be most safe. Christ knew before that his disciples would thus desert him in the critical moment, and yet he was still tender of them. We are ready to say of some, "If we could have foreseen their ingratitude, we would not have been so prodigal of our favours to them"; Christ did foresee theirs, and yet was kind to them. He told them of it: "*Do you now believe?* Be not high-minded, but fear." Even when we are taking the comfort of our graces, it is good to be reminded of our danger from our corruptions. When our faith is strong, our love flaming, and our evidences are clear, yet we cannot infer thence that *tomorrow shall be as this day.* Even when we have most reason to think we stand, yet we have reason enough to take heed lest we fall. He spoke of it as a thing very near. *The hour was* already *come* when they would be as shy of him as ever they had been fond of him.

(3) An assurance of his own comfort notwithstanding: *Yet I am not alone. The Father is with me.* We may consider this as a privilege peculiar to the Lord Jesus. The divine nature did not desert the human nature, but supported it. Even when he complained of his Father's forsaking him, yet he called him *My God,* and was so well assured of his favourable presence with him as to commit his Spirit into his hand. This he had comforted himself with all along (*ch.* viii. 29), *He that sent me is with me, the Father hath not left me alone.* As a privilege common to all believers. When they are alone, they are *not alone,* but *the Father is with them.* When solitude is their choice—Nathaniel under the fig-tree, Peter upon the house-top, meditating and praying—the Father is with them. Those that converse with God in solitude are never less alone than when alone. A good God and a good heart are good company at any time. When solitude is their affliction, they are not so much alone as they are thought to be, *the Father is with them.* While we have God's favourable

JAMIESON, FAUSSET, BROWN

29, 30. His disciples said, . . . now speakest thou plainly, and speakest no proverb—hardly more so than before; the time for perfect plainness was yet to come; but having caught a glimpse of His meaning (it was nothing more), they eagerly express their satisfaction, as if glad to make anything of His words. How touchingly does this show both the simplicity of their hearts and the infantile character of their faith!

31-33. Jesus answered . . ., Do ye now believe?—i.e., 'It is well ye do, for it is soon to be tested, and in a way ye little expect.'

the hour cometh, yea, is now come, that ye shall be scattered, every man to his own, and shall leave me alone; and yet I am not alone—A deep and awful sense of *wrong* experienced is certainly expressed here, but how lovingly! That He was not to be utterly deserted, that there was One who would not forsake Him, was to Him matter of ineffable support and consolation; but that He should be without all *human* countenance and cheer, who as Man was exquisitely sensitive to the law of sympathy, would fill themselves with as much *shame,* when they afterwards recurred to it, as the Redeemer's heart in His hour of need with pungent *sorrow.* "I looked for some to take pity, but there was none; and for comforters, but I found none" (Ps. 69:20).

because the Father is with me—how near, and with what sustaining power, who can express?

ADAM CLARKE

29. *Lo, now speakest thou plainly.* The disciples received more light now on the nature of Christ's person and office than they had ever done before.

30. *Now are we sure that thou knowest all things.* Is not the following the meaning of the disciples? We believe that Thou art not only the Messiah who came out from God, but that Thou art that God who searchest the heart and triest the reins, and needest not to be asked in order to make Thee acquainted with the necessities of Thy creatures; for Thou perfectly knowest their wants, and art infinitely disposed to relieve them.

31. *Do ye now believe?* And will you continue to believe? You are now fully convinced; and will you in the hour of trial retain your conviction, and prove faithful and steady?

32. *The hour cometh.* You shall shortly have need of all the faith you profess. You now believe Me to be the Omniscient; but you will find difficulty to maintain this faith when you see Me seized, condemned, and crucified as a malefactor. Yes, your faith will be then so shaken that you shall run away, each striving to save himself at his "own home," or among his "kindred."

ALEXANDER MACLAREN:

We have here the calm consciousness of unbroken communion. Jesus Christ's sense of union with the Father was deep, close, constant, in manner and measure altogether transcending any experience of ours. But still He sets before us a pattern of what we should aim at in these great words. They show the path of comfort for every lonely heart. "I am not alone, for the Father is with Me." If earth be dark, let us look to heaven. If the world with its millions seems to have no friend in it for us, let us turn to Him who never leaves us. If dear ones are torn from our grasp, let us grasp God. Solitude is bitter; but, like other bitters, it is a tonic. It is not all loss if the trees which with their leafy beauty shut out the sky from us are felled, and so we see the blue.

—*Expositions of Holy Scripture*

MATTHEW HENRY

presence with us, we are happy, though all the world forsake us.

II. He comforts them with a promise of peace in him, by virtue of his victory over the world, whatever troubles they might meet with in it (*v.* 33): "*These things have I spoken, that in me you might have peace;* for *in the world you shall have tribulation. I have overcome the world.*"

1. The end Christ aimed at: *That in him they might have peace.* His departure from them was really for the best. It is the will of Christ that his disciples should have peace within, whatever their troubles may be without. Peace in Christ is the only true peace. Through him we have peace with God, and so in him we have peace in our own minds. The word of Christ aims at this, *that in him we may have peace.*

2. The entertainment they were likely to meet with in the world. It has been the lot of Christ's disciples to have more or less tribulation in this world. Men persecute them because they are so good, and God corrects them because they are no better. So between both *they shall have tribulation.*

3. The encouragement Christ gives them: "*But be of good cheer*, have a good heart on it, all shall be well." In the midst of the tribulations of this world it is the duty and interest of Christ's disciples to be of good cheer; as sorrowful indeed, in compliance with the temper of the climate, and yet always rejoicing, always cheerful, even *in tribulation*, Rom. v. 3.

4. The ground of that encouragement: *I have overcome the world.* Christ's victory is a Christian triumph. When he sends his disciples to preach the gospel to all the world, "Be *of good cheer*," says he, "*I have overcome the world.*" He overcame the evil things of the world by submitting to them; he endured the cross, despising it and the shame of it; and he overcame the good things of it by being wholly dead to them. Never was there such a conqueror of the world as Christ was, and we ought to be encouraged by it. Christ has overcome the world before us; so that we may look upon it as a conquered enemy. He has conquered it for us, as the captain of our salvation. By his cross the world is *crucified to us*, which bespeaks it completely conquered. Christ having overcome the world, believers have nothing to do but to pursue their victory, and this we do by faith. *We are more than conquerors through him that loved us.*

CHAPTER 17

Verses 1–5

I. The circumstances of this prayer, *v.* 1. None of his prayers are recorded so fully as this.

1. The time when he prayed this prayer; when he had *spoken these words*, had given the foregoing farewell to his disciples. (1) It was a prayer after sermon; when he had spoken from God to them, he turned to speak to God for them. Those we preach to we must pray for. The word preached should be prayed over, for God *gives the increase.* (2) It was a prayer after sacrament. He closed the solemnity with this prayer, that God would preserve the good impressions of the ordinance upon them. (3) It was a family prayer. Christ's disciples were his family, and, to set a good example before masters of families, he blessed his household, prayed for them and with them. (4) It was a parting prayer. When we and our friends are parting, it is good to part with prayer, Acts xx. 36. (5) It was a prayer that was a preface to his sacrifice, which he was now about to offer on earth. Christ prayed then as a priest now offering sacrifice, in the virtue of which all prayers were to be made. (6) It was a prayer that was a specimen of his intercession, which he ever lives to make for us within the veil.

2. The outward expression of fervent desire which he used in this prayer: He *lifted up his eyes to heaven.* He was pleased thus to sanctify this gesture to those that use it, and justify it against those that ridicule it. *Sursum corda* was anciently used as a call to prayer, *Up with your hearts*, up to heaven.

II. The first part of the prayer itself, in which Christ prays for himself.

1. He prays to God as a Father: He *lifted up his eyes, and said, Father.* If God be our Father, we have liberty of access to him, and great expectations from him. Christ calls him here *holy Father* (*v.* 11), and *righteous Father*, *v.* 25. For it will be of great use to us in prayer to call God as we hope to find him.

2. He prayed for himself first. Though Christ, as God, was prayed to, Christ, as man, prayed. What he had purchased he must ask for; and shall

JAMIESON, FAUSSET, BROWN

33. These things I have spoken unto you—not the immediately preceding words, but this whole discourse, of which these were the very last words, and which He thus winds up. **that in me ye might have peace**—in the sublime sense before explained. (See on ch. 14:27.)

In the world ye shall have tribulation—specially arising from its deadly opposition to those who "are not of the world, but chosen out of the world." So that the "peace" promised was far from an unruffled one.

I have overcome the world—not only *before* you, but *for* you, that ye may be able to do the same (I John 5:4, 5).

CHAPTER 17

Vss. 1-26. The Intercessory Prayer. (See on ch. 14:1.) Had this prayer *not* been recorded, what reverential reader would not have exclaimed, Oh, to have been within hearing of such a prayer as that must have been, which wound up the whole of His past ministry and formed the point of transition to the dark scenes which immediately followed! But here it is, and with such signature of the Lips that uttered it that we seem rather to hear it from Himself than read it from the pen of His faithful reporter.

1-3. These words spake Jesus, and lifted up his eyes—"John very seldom depicts the gestures or looks of our Lord, as here. But this was an occasion of which the impression was indelible, and the upward look could not be passed over" [Alford].

ADAM CLARKE

33. *That in me ye might have peace.* I give you this warning as another proof that I know all things, and to the end that you may look to Me alone for peace and happiness. The peace of God is ever to be understood as including all possible blessedness—light, strength, comfort, support, a sense of the divine favor, unction of the Holy Spirit, purification of heart, and all these to be enjoyed *in Christ.*

In the world ye shall have tribulation. Or, as most of the very best MSS. read, "ye have"—the tribulation is at hand; you are just about to be plunged into it. *But be of good cheer.* Do not despond on account of what I have said. The world shall not be able to overcome you, how severely soever it may try you.

I have overcome the world. I am just now going by My death to put it and its god to the rout. My apparent weakness shall be My victory; My ignominy shall be My glory; and the victory which the world, the devil, and My adversaries in general shall appear to gain over Me shall be their own lasting defeat and My eternal triumph.

CHAPTER 17

1. *These words spake Jesus.* That is, what is related in the preceding chapters.

I. Our Lord's Prayer for Himself, vv. 1-5

Father. Here our Lord addresses the whole divine nature, as He is now performing His last acts in His state of humiliation.

MATTHEW HENRY

we expect to have what we never merited, but have a thousand times forfeited, unless we pray for it? It gives great encouragement to praying people. Time was when he that is advocate for us had a cause of his own to solicit, and this he was to solicit in the same method that is prescribed to us, *by prayers and supplications* (Heb. v. 7). Christ began with prayer for himself, and afterwards prayed for his disciples; this charity must begin at home, though it must not end there. Christ was much shorter in his prayer for himself than in his prayer for his disciples. Our prayers for the church must not be crowded into a corner of our prayers. Now here are two petitions which Christ puts up for himself, and these two are one. This one petition, *Glorify thou me*, is twice put up, because it has a double reference. To the prosecution of his undertaking further: *Glorify me, that I may glorify thee*, *v.* 1–3. And to the performance of his undertaking hitherto: "*Glorify me, for I have glorified thee*. I have done my part, and now, Lord, do thine," *v.* 4, 5.

(1) Christ here prays to be *glorified*, in order to his *glorifying God* (*v.* 1): *Glorify thy Son that thy Son may glorify thee*.

[1] What he prays for—that he might be glorified in this world. The Father glorified the *Son* upon earth; even in his sufferings, by the signs and wonders which attended them. Then the Father not only justified, but glorified the Son; even by his sufferings; when he was crucified, he was magnified, he was glorified. It was in his cross that he conquered Satan and death; his thorns were a crown. Much more after his sufferings. The Father glorified the Son when he *raised him from the dead*.

[2] What he pleads to enforce this request.

First, He pleads relation: *Glorify thy Son*. Those that have received the adoption of sons may in faith pray for the inheritance of sons; if sanctified, then glorified.

Secondly, He pleads the time: *The hour is come*. He had often said his hour was not yet come; but now it was come, and he knew it. He calls it *this hour* (*ch.* xii. 27), and here *the hour*. The hour of the Redeemer's death, which was also the hour of the Redeemer's birth, was the most signal and remarkable hour, and, without doubt, the most critical, that ever was since the clock of time was first set going. 1. "*The hour is come* in the midst of which I need to to be owned." The decisive battle between heaven and hell is now to be fought. "*Now glorify thy Son*, now give him victory, now let thy Son be so upheld as not to fail nor be discouraged." He *glorified his Son* when he made the cross his triumphant chariot. 2. *The hour is come* when I am *to be glorified*. Good Christians in a trying hour, particularly a dying hour, may thus plead: "*Now the hour is come*, stand by me, now or never: now *the earthly tabernacle is to be dissolved, the hour is come that I should be glorified*," 2 Cor. v. 1.

Thirdly, He pleads the Father's own interest and concern herein: *That thy Son may also glorify thee*; that he might glorify the Father two ways: By *the death of the cross. Father, glorify thy name*, expressed the great intention of his sufferings. "Father, own me in my sufferings, that I may honour thee by them." By the doctrine of the cross now shortly to be published to the world. If God had not glorified Christ crucified, *by raising him from the dead*, his whole undertaking had been crushed; therefore *glorify me, that I may glorify thee*. Now hereby he hath taught us what to eye and aim at in our prayers—that is, the honour of God. "Do this and the other for thy servant, that thy servant may glorify thee. Give me health, that I may glorify thee with my body; success, that I may glorify thee with my estate," &c. *Hallowed be thy name* must be our first petition, which must fix our end in all other petitions, 1 Pet. iv. 11. He hath taught us what to expect and hope for. If we sincerely set ourselves to glorify our Father, he will give us the grace he knows sufficient, and the opportunity he sees convenient. But, if we secretly honour ourselves more than him, instead of honouring ourselves, we shall shame ourselves.

Fourthly, He pleads his commission (*v.* 2, 3); he desires to glorify his Father, in conformity to the commission given him. Now see here the power of the Mediator.

a. The origin of his power: *Thou hast given him power;* he has it from God, *to whom all power belongs*. The church's king is no usurper, as the prince of this world is; Christ's right to rule is incontestable.

b. The extent of his power: He has *power over all flesh*. Over all mankind. Being now mediating between God and man, he here *pleads his power over all flesh*. They were men whom he was to subdue and save; out of that race he had a remnant given him, and therefore all that rank of beings was *put under his feet*. Over mankind considered as corrupt and

JAMIESON, FAUSSET, BROWN

ALBERT BARNES:

1. "These words." The words addressed to them in the preceding chapters. They were proceeding to the garden of Gethsemane. It adds much to the interest of this prayer that it was offered in the stillness of the night, in the open air, and in the peculiarly tender circumstances in which Jesus and his apostles were. It is the longest prayer recorded in the New Testament. It was offered on the most tender and solemn occasion that has ever occurred in our world, and it is perhaps the most sublime composition to be found anywhere. Jesus was about to die. Having expressed his love to his disciples, and made known to them his last desires, he now commends them to the protection and blessing of the God of grace. This prayer is moreover a specimen of the manner of his intercession, and evinces the interest which he felt in behalf of all who should become his followers in all ages of the world.—*Popular Commentary*

glorify thy Son—Put honor upon Thy Son, by countenancing, sustaining, and carrying Him through that "hour."

Father, the hour is come—See on ch. 13:31,

G. CAMPBELL MORGAN:

Mark the arresting words with which He began: "Father, the hour is come." All through John we have found references to that hour. It began away back when talking to His mother at Cana He said, "Mine hour is not yet come." Now He said, "Father, the hour is come." To this hour He had been looking forward from the beginning; for it, He had been preparing in all His teaching and all His doing; it was this hour which had constituted the underlying passion, urge of His life. "Father, the hour is come." In the presence of that consciousness, He expressed two desires for himself. The first is contained in the early verses, "Glorify thy Son, that the Son may glorify thee; even as thou gavest him authority over all flesh, that whatsoever thou hast given him, to them he should give eternal life. And this is life eternal, that they should know thee the only true God, and him whom thou didst send, even Jesus Christ. I glorified thee on the earth, having accomplished the work which thou hast given me to do."

What is the desire? "Glorify thy Son, that the Son may glorify thee." He did not say, "Glorify Me that I may glorify Thee." Of course that is what is meant, but the very method of statement is significant. It was not personal, but relative. He was thinking of himself in His intimate relationship with His Father, "Thy Son . . . the Son." Whereas the prayer is personal, as we have said, the first expressed desire maintains His sense of relationship, and all which that meant at that hour. "The hour is come; glorify thy Son, that the Son may glorify thee." He was expressing His desire that the Son might be glorified. What for? That the Son may glorify the Father. The deepest passion of His heart was the glory of God. The deepest passion of the heart of Jesus was not the saving of men, but the glory of God; and then the saving of men, because that is for the glory of God.

—*The Gospel According to John*

2. given—gavest—**him power over all flesh**—(See on Matt. 11:27; 28:18-20).

ADAM CLARKE

Glorify thy Son. Cause Him to be acknowledged as the promised Messiah by the Jewish people, and as the universal Saviour by the Gentile world; and let such proofs of His Godhead be given as shall serve to convince and instruct mankind. *That thy Son also may glorify thee.* That by dying He may magnify Thy law and make it honorable, respected among men—show the strictness of Thy justice, and the immaculate purity of Thy nature.

2. *As thou hast given him power.* As the Messiah, Jesus Christ, received from the Father *universal dominion. All flesh*, i.e., all the "human race," was given unto Him, that by one sacrifice of himself He might reconcile them all to God, having by His grace tasted death for every man, Heb. ii. 9.

MATTHEW HENRY

fallen. If man had not in this sense been flesh, he had not needed a Redeemer. Over this sinful race the Lord Jesus has all power; and *all judgment is committed to him.* Whom he does not rule, he over-rules.

c. The grand intention and design of this power: *That he should give eternal life to as many as thou hast given him.* Here is the Father making over the elect to the Redeemer, and giving them to him as the crown and recompence of his undertaking. Here is the Son undertaking to secure the happiness of those that were given him, that he would *give eternal life to them.* He has lives and crowns to give, eternal lives that never die, immortal crowns that never fade. Now consider how great the Lord Jesus is, and how gracious he is. He sanctifies them in this world, gives them the spiritual life which is eternal life in the bud and embryo. Grace in the soul is heaven in that soul. He will glorify them in the other world; their happiness shall be completed in the vision and fruition of God. We are *called to his kingdom and glory,* and *begotten to the inheritance.* What is last in execution was first in intention, and *that is eternal life.* Christ's dominion over the children of men is in order to the salvation of the children of God. The administration of the kingdoms of providence and grace are put into the same hand, that all things may be made to concur for good to the called.

d. Here is a further explication of this grand design (*v.* 3): "*This is life eternal, to know thee the only true God.*" Here is,

(*a*) The great end which the Christian religion sets before us, and that is, eternal life. This he was to reveal to all, and secure to all that were given him. By the gospel *life and immortality are brought to light,* are brought to hand.

(*b*) The sure way of attaining this blessed end, which is, by the right knowledge of God and Jesus Christ: "*This is life eternal, to know thee,* which may be taken two ways: [*a*] *Life eternal* lies in the knowledge of God and Jesus Christ. Those that are brought into union with Christ, and live a life of communion with God in Christ, will say. "If this be heaven, heaven is sweet." [*b*] The knowledge of God and Christ leads to life eternal. The Christian religion shows us the way to heaven, *First,* By directing us to God, for Christ died to *bring us to God.* He is the true God, the only true God; the service of him is the only true religion. *Secondly,* By directing us to Jesus Christ: *Jesus Christ whom thou hast sent.* If man had continued innocent, the knowledge of the only true God would have been life eternal to him; but now that he is fallen there must be something more. We are therefore concerned to know Christ as our Redeemer. It is life eternal to believe in Christ; and this he has undertaken to give. Those that are acquainted with God and Christ are already in the suburbs of life eternal.

(2) Christ here prays to be glorified in consideration of his having glorified the Father hitherto, *v.* 4, 5. The meaning of the former petition was, Glorify me in this world; the meaning of the latter is, Glorify me in the other world.

[1] With what comfort Christ reflects on the life he had lived on earth: *I have glorified thee, and finished my work.* He pleases himself in reviewing the service he had done his Father. This is here recorded for the honour of Christ, that his life upon earth did in all respects fully answer the end of his coming into the world. 1. Our Lord Jesus had work given him to do. His Father gave him his work, both appointed him to it and assisted him in it. 2. *The work that was given him to do* he finished. It was as good as done, he was giving it its finishing stroke. 3. Herein he glorified his Father. It is the glory of God that *his work is perfect,* and the same is the glory of the Redeemer; what he is the author of he will be the finisher of. It is recorded for example to all, *that we may follow his example.* We must make it our business to do the work God has appointed us to do. We must aim at the glory of God in all. We must persevere herein to the end of our days; we must not sit down till we have finished our work. It is recorded for encouragement to all those that rest upon him. If he has *finished the work that was given him to do,* then he is a complete Saviour, and did not do his work by the halves.

[2] See with what confidence he expects *the joy set before him* (*v.* 5): *Now, O Father, glorify thou me.* *First,* See here what he prayed for: *Glorify thou me,* as before, *v.* 1. What his Father had promised him yet he must pray for; promises are not designed to supersede prayers, but to be the guide of our desires and the ground of our hopes. 1. It is a glory with God; not only, *Glorify my name on earth,* but, *Glorify me with thine own self.* The prayers of the lower world draw out grace and peace *from God our Father and our Lord Jesus Christ* in conjunction; and thus the Father has glorified him with himself.

JAMIESON, FAUSSET, BROWN

give eternal life to as many as . . .—lit., "to all that which thou hast given him." (See on ch. 6:37-40.)

3.
this is—that—**life eternal, that they might**—may—**know . . .**—This life eternal, then, is not mere conscious and unending existence, but a life of acquaintance with God in Christ (Job 22:21). **thee, the only true God**—the sole personal living God; in glorious contrast equally with heathen *polytheism,* philosophic *naturalism,* and mystic *pantheism.* **and Jesus Christ whom thou hast sent**—This is the only place where our Lord gives Himself this compound name, afterwards so current in apostolic preaching and writing. Here the terms are used in their strict signification—"JESUS," because He "*saves* His people from their sins"; "CHRIST," as *anointed* with the measureless fulness of the Holy Ghost for the exercise of His saving offices (see on Matt. 1:16); "WHOM THOU HAST SENT," in the plenitude of Divine Authority and Power, to save. "The very juxtaposition here of *Jesus Christ* with *the Father* is a proof, by implication, of our Lord's Godhead. The knowledge of *God and a creature* could not be eternal life, and such an association of the one with the other would be inconceivable" [ALFORD].

4.
5. I have glorified thee on the earth—rather, "I glorified" (for the thing is conceived as now *past*). **I have finished**—(I finished)—**the work which thou gavest me to do**—It is very important to preserve in the translation the *past* tense, used in the original, otherwise it might be thought that the work already "*finished*" was only what He had done *before uttering that prayer;* whereas it will be observed that our Lord speaks throughout as already beyond this present scene (vs. 12, etc.), and so must be supposed to include in His "finished work" the "decease which He was to accomplish at Jerusalem."

5. And now—in return. **glorify thou me**—The "*I Thee*" and "*Thou Me*" are so placed in the original, each beside its fellow, as to show that A PERFECT RECIPROCITY OF SERVICES of the Son to the Father first, and then of the Father to the Son in return, is what our Lord means here to express.

ADAM CLARKE

That he should give eternal life. As all were delivered into His power, and He poured out His blood to redeem all, then the design of God is that all should have eternal life, because all are given for this purpose to Christ.

3. *This is life eternal.* It is called *eternal life* to show that it reaches beyond the limits of time, and that it necessarily implies: (1) the immortality of the soul; (2) the resurrection of the body; and (3) that it is never to end, hence called "a life ever living." *The only true God.* The way to attain this eternal life is to acknowledge, worship, and obey, the one only true God, and to accept as Teacher, Sacrifice, and Saviour, the Lord Jesus, the one and only true Messiah.

4. *I have glorified thee.* Our Lord, considering himself as already sacrificed for the sin of the world, speaks of having completed the work which God had given Him to do; and He looks forward to that time when, through the preaching of His gospel, His sacrifice should be acknowledged, and the true God should be known and worshipped by the whole world.

MATTHEW HENRY

2. It is *the glory he had with God before the world was.* (1) Jesus Christ, as God, had a being *before the world was.* Our religion acquaints us with one that *was before all things, and by whom all things consist.* (2) His glory with the Father is from everlasting. Christ undertook the work of redemption, not because he needed glory, for he had a glory *with the Father before the world,* but because we needed glory. (3) Jesus Christ in his state of humiliation divested himself of this glory. He was *God manifested in the flesh,* not in his glory. (4) In his exalted state he resumed this glory. He does not pray to be glorified with the princes and great men of the earth: no; he that knew both worlds, chose it in the glory of the other world, as far exceeding all the glory of this. *Let the same mind be in us. Father, glorify thou me with thine own self.*

Secondly, See here what he pleaded: *I have glorified thee;* and now, *glorify thou me.* There was an equity in it, and an admirable becomingness, *that, if God was glorified in him, he should glorify him in himself.* If the Father was a gainer in his glory by the Son's humiliation, it was fit the Son should be no loser by it, at long run, in his glory. It was according to the covenant between them. It was *for the joy set before him* that *he endured the cross.* He still expects the completing of his exaltation, because he perfected his undertaking. By the glorifying of Christ we are satisfied that God was satisfied, and therein a real demonstration was given that his Father was well pleased in him as his beloved Son. Thus we must be taught that those, and only those who glorify God on earth shall be glorified with the Father, when they must be no more in this world.

Verses 6–10

Christ, having prayed for himself, comes next to pray for those that are his.

I. Whom he did not pray for (*v.* 9): *I pray not for the world.* It is not meant of the world of mankind in general (he prays for that here, *v.* 21, *That the world may believe that thou hast sent me*). Take the world for a heap of unwinnowed corn in the floor, and God loves it, Christ prays for it, and dies for it, *for a blessing is in it.* Then take the world for the remaining heap of rejected, worthless chaff. For these Christ does not pray; not but that there are some things which he intercedes with God for on their behalf, as the dresser for the reprieve of the barren tree; but he does not pray for them in this prayer. He does not say, I pray against the world, but, *I pray not for them,* I pass them by, and leave them to themselves. We that know not who are chosen, and who are passed by, must *pray for all men,* 1 Tim. ii. 1, 4. While there is life, there is hope, and room for prayer.

II. Whom he did pray for; the children of men. He prays *for those that were given him,* who receive and believe the words of Christ, *v.* 6, 8. He prays *for all that should believe on him* (*v.* 20). Not only the petitions that follow, but those also which went before, must be construed to extend to all believers, in every place and every age.

III. What are the general pleas with which he introduces his petitions for them. They are five:

1. The charge he had received concerning them: *Thine they were, and thou gavest them me* (*v.* 6), and again (*v.* 9), *Those whom thou hast given me.* This is meant primarily of the disciples that then were. They were given in order to their being the publishers of his gospel and the planters of his church. When they left all to follow him, this was the secret spring of that strange resolution: they were given to him, else they had not given themselves to him. The apostleship and ministry, which are Christ's gift to the church, were first the Father's gift to Jesus Christ. Christ received this gift for men, that he might give it to men. It lays a mighty obligation upon the ministers of the gospel to devote themselves entirely to Christ's service, as being *given to him,* but it is designed to extend to all the elect, for they are elsewhere said to be given to Christ (*ch.* vi. 37, 39).

(1) The Father had authority to give them: *Thine they were,* his own in three ways: *First,* They were creatures, and their lives and beings were derived from him. *Secondly,* They were criminals, and their lives and beings were forfeited to him. It was a remnant of fallen mankind that was given to Christ to be redeemed, that might have been made sacrifices to justice when they were pitched upon to be the *monuments of mercy. Thirdly,* They were chosen; they were set apart for God. This he insists upon again (*v.* 7): *All things whatsoever thou hast given me are of thee;* they *are all of thee,* and therefore, Father, I bring them all to thee, that they may be all for thee.

(2) He did accordingly give them to the Son: *Thou gavest them to me,* as sheep to the shepherd,

JAMIESON, FAUSSET, BROWN

with the glory which I had with thee before the world was—when "in the beginning the Word was *with God*" (ch. 1:1), "the only-begotten Son *in the bosom of the Father*" (ch. 1:18). With this pre-existent glory, which He veiled on earth, He asks to be reinvested, the design of the veiling being accomplished—not, however, simply as before, but *now in our nature.*

6-8. From praying for Himself He now comes to pray for His disciples. **not for the world**—for they had been given Him *"out of* the world" (vs. 6), and had been already transformed into the very *opposite* of it. The things sought for them, indeed, are applicable only to such.

to the men thou gavest me out of the world (See on ch. 6:37-40).

ADAM CLARKE

5. *Before the world was.* That is, from eternity, before there was any creation—so the phrase, and others similar to it, are taken in the sacred writings; see v. 24; Ps. xc. 2; Eph. i. 4. See chap. i. 1.

II. Our Lord's Prayer for His Disciples, vv. 6-19

9. *I pray not for the world.* I am not yet come to that part of My intercession; see v. 20. I am now wholly employed for My disciples, that they may be properly qualified to preach My salvation to the ends of the earth. Jesus here imitates the high priest, the second part of whose prayer, on the day of expiation, was for the *priests,* the *sons of Aaron.* These words may also be understood as applying to the rebellious Jews. God's wrath was about to descend upon them, and Christ prays that His own followers might be kept from the evil, v. 15. But He does not thus pray for the *world,* the rebellious Jews, because the cup of their iniquity was full, and their judgment slumbered not.

The men which thou gavest me. That is, the apostles, who, having received this knowledge from Christ, were by their preaching and writings to spread it through the whole world. *Out of the world.* From among the Jewish people; for in this sense is the word *kosmos* to be understood in various parts of our Lord's last discourses. *Thine they were.* Objects of Thy choice; *and thou gavest them me* from among this very unbelieving people, that they might be My disciples and the heralds of My salvation.

ALBERT BARNES:

"Before the world was." There could not be a more distinct and clear declaration of the preexistence of Christ than this. It means before the creation of the world; before there was any world. Of course, the speaker here must have existed then, and this is equivalent to saying that he existed from eternity (see John 1:1, 2; 6:62; 3:13; 16:28). The glory which he had then was that which was proper to the Son of God, represented by the expression "being in the bosom of the Father" (John 1:18), denoting intimacy, friendship, united felicity. The Son of God, by becoming incarnate, is represented as "humbling himself" (Greek, he "emptied himself"), Phil. 2:8. He laid aside for a time the external aspect of honor, and consented to become despised, and to assume the form of a servant. He now prays that God would raise him up to the dignity and honor which he had before his incarnation. This is the state to which he is now exalted, with the additional honor of having made atonement for sin, and having opened the way to save a race of rebels from eternal death. The lowest condition on earth is frequently connected with the highest honors of heaven. Man looks on the outward appearance. God looks to him that is humble and of a contrite spirit.—*Popular Commentary*

MATTHEW HENRY

to be kept; as patients to the physician, to be cured; children to a tutor, to be educated. They were delivered to Christ, that the election of grace might not be frustrated, *that not one*, no not *of the little ones, might perish*, that the undertaking of Christ might not be fruitless. He should *see of the travail of his soul and be satisfied* (Isa. liii. 10, 11).

2. The care he had taken of them to teach them (*v.* 6): *I have manifested thy name to them. I have given to them the words which thou gavest to me*, *v.* 8. Observe here, The great design of Christ's doctrine, which was to manifest God's name, to declare him that he might be better loved and worshipped. His faithful discharge of this undertaking: *I have* done it. His fidelity appears in the truth of his doctrine. It agreed exactly with the instructions he received from his Father. Ministers, in wording their message, must have an eye to *the words which the Holy Ghost teaches*. In the tendency of his doctrine, which was to manifest God's name, He did not seek himself, but aimed to magnify his Father. It is Christ's prerogative to manifest God's name to the souls of the children of men. He only has acquaintance with the Father, and so is able to open the truth; and he only has access to the spirits of men, and so is able to open the understanding. Ministers may *publish the name of the Lord*, but Christ only can manifest that name. Ministers may speak the words of God to us, but Christ can give us his words, can put them in us. Sooner or later, Christ will manifest God's name to all that were given him.

3. The good effect of the care he had taken of them (*v.* 6): *They have kept thy word* (*v.* 7), *they have known that all things are of thee* (*v.* 8); *they have received thy words, and have known surely that I came out from thee, and have believed that thou didst send me.*

(1) What success the doctrine of Christ had among those *that were given to him.* "They have received the words which I gave them, as the ground receives the seed, and the earth drinks in the rain." The word was to them an *ingrafted word. "They have kept thy word;* they have conformed to it." Christ's commandment is then only kept when it is obeyed. It was requisite that these should *keep what was committed to them*, for it was to be transmitted by them to every place for every age. "They have understood the word, They have been aware *that all things whatsoever thou hast given me are of thee.*" All Christ's offices and powers, all the gifts of the Spirit, all his graces and comforts, were all from God, designed by his grace, for his own glory in man's salvation. We may therefore venture our souls upon Christ's mediation. If the righteousness be of God's appointing, we shall be justified; if the grace be of his dispensing, we shall be sanctified. They have set their seal to it: *They have known surely that I came out from God*, *v.* 8. What it is to believe; it is to *know surely*, to know *that it is so of a truth.* We may know surely that which we neither do nor can know fully. *We walk by faith*, which knows surely, *not yet by sight*, which knows clearly. What it is we are to believe: *that Jesus Christ came out from God*, and that God did send him. Therefore all the doctrines of Christ are to be received as divine truths, and all his promises depended upon as divine securities.

(2) How Jesus Christ here speaks of this: As pleased with it himself. Their constant adherence to him, their gradual improvements, and their great attainments at last, were his joy. Christ is a Master that delights in the proficiency of his scholars. He accepts the sincerity of their faith, and graciously passes by the infirmity of it. As pleading it with his Father. He is praying for *those that were given to him*; and he pleads that they had given themselves to him. Those that keep Christ's word, and believe on him, let Christ alone to commend them, and, which is more, to recommend them to his Father.

4. He pleads the Father's own interest in them (*v.* 9): *I pray for them, for they are thine. All mine are thine, and thine are mine.*

(1) The plea particularly urged for his disciples: *They are thine.* The consigning of the elect to Christ was so far from making them less the Father's that it was in order to making them the more so. Christ has *redeemed us*, not to himself only, but *to God.* This is a good plea in prayer, Christ here pleads it, *They are thine;* we may plead it for ourselves, *I am thine, save me*; and for others: "*They are thy people. They are thine.* Wilt thou not secure them, that they may not be run down by the devil and the world? *They are thine*, own them as thine."

(2) The foundation on which this plea is grounded: *All mine are thine, and thine are mine.* This bespeaks the Father and Son to be one in essence and one in interest. What the Father has as Creator is delivered over to the Son. *All things are delivered to him* (Matt. xi. 27); nothing is excepted but *he that did put all*

JAMIESON, FAUSSET, BROWN

I have manifested—I manifested—**thy name**—His whole character towards mankind.

8. they . . . have known surely that I came out from thee—(See on ch. 16:30, 31).

ADAM CLARKE

6. *I have manifested thy name.* I have brought it into light, and caused it to shine in itself, and to illuminate others. A little of the divine nature was known by the works of creation; a little more was known by the Mosaic revelation. But the full manifestation of God, His nature, and His attributes came only through the revelation of Christ.

And they have kept thy word. Though their countrymen have rejected it; and they have received Me as Thy well-beloved Son in whom Thou delightest.

8. *I have given unto them the words.* I have delivered Thy doctrine to them, so that they have had a pure teaching immediately from heaven. *And have known surely.* Are fully convinced and acknowledge that I am the promised Messiah, and that they are to look for none other, and that My mission and doctrine are all divine.

ALEXANDER MACLAREN:

In verse 9 Jesus assumes the great office of Intercessor. "I pray for them" is not so much prayer as His solemn presentation of himself before the Father as the High Priest of His people. It marks an epoch in His work. The task of bringing God to man is substantially complete. That of bringing men by supplication to God is now to begin. It is the revelation of the permanent office of the departed Lord. Moses on the Mount holds up the rod, and Israel prevails (Ex. 17:9). The limitation of this prayer to the disciples applies only to the special occasion, and has no bearing on the sweep of His redeeming purpose or the desires of His all-pitying heart. The reasons for His intercession follow in verses 9-11a. The disciples are the Father's, and continue so even when "given" to Christ, in accordance with the community of possession, which oneness of nature and perfectness of love establish between the Father and the Son. God cannot but care for those who are His. The Son cannot but pray for those who are His. Their having recognized Him for what He was binds Him to pray for them. He is glorified in His disciples, and if we show forth His character, He will be our Advocate.
—Expositions of Holy Scripture

9-14. I pray for them—not as individuals merely, but as representatives of all such in every succeeding age (see on vs. 20).

10. all mine are thine, and thine are mine—lit., "All My things are Thine and Thy things are Mine." (On this use of the *neuter* gender, see on ch. 6:37-40.) Absolute COMMUNITY OF PROPERTY between the Father and the Son is here expressed as nakedly as words can do it. (See on vs. 5.)

MATTHEW HENRY

things under him. What the Son has as Redeemer is designed for the Father. All the benefits of redemption purchased by the Son are intended for the Father's praise: *All mine are thine.* The Son owns none for his that are not devoted to the service of the Father. In a limited sense, every true believer may say, *All thine are mine.* In an unlimited sense every true believer does say, Lord, *all mine are thine*; all laid at his feet, to be serviceable to him. "Lord, take care of what I have, for it is *all thine*."

5. He pleads his own concern in them: *I am glorified in them.* (1) *I have been glorified in them.* What little honour Christ had in this world was among his disciples, and therefore *I pray for them.* (2) "*I am to be glorified in them*; they are to bear up my name. *I am glorified in them*, therefore, I concern myself for them. Therefore I commit them to the Father, who has engaged to glorify the Son, and, upon this account, will have a gracious eye to those in whom he is glorified."

Verses 11–16

After the general pleas follow the particular petitions he puts up for them. They all relate to spiritual blessings in heavenly things. The prosperity of the soul is the best prosperity. They are such blessings as were suited to their present state and case. Christ's intercession is always pertinent. Our *advocate with the father* is acquainted with all the particulars of our wants. He is large and full in the petitions, to teach us fervency and importunity in prayer, wrestling as Jacob, *I will not let thee go, except thou bless me.*

Now the first thing Christ prays for is their preservation. Keeping supposes danger, and their danger arose *from the world; the evil* of this he begs they might be kept from.

I. The request itself: *Keep them from the world.* There were two ways of their being delivered from the world:

1. By taking them out of it; and he does not pray that they might be so delivered: *I pray not that thou shouldest take them out of the world.*

(1) "I pray not that they may be speedily removed by death." If the world will be vexatious to them, the readiest way to secure them would be to hasten them out of it. Send chariots and horses of fire for them, to fetch them to heaven. Christ would not pray so for his disciples. Because he came to conquer those intemperate passions which make men impatient of life, it is his will that we should take up our cross, and not outrun it. Because he had work for them to do in the world, the world could ill spare them. In pity therefore to this dark world, Christ would not have these lights removed out of it, especially for the sake of those in the world that were to *believe in him through their word.* They must each in his own order die a martyr, but not till they have finished their testimony. The taking of good people out of the world is a thing by no means to be desired. Though Christ loves his disciples, he does not presently send for them to heaven, but leaves them for some time in this world, that they may be ripened for heaven. Many good people are spared to live, because they can ill be spared to die.

(2) "I pray not that they may be exempted from the troubles of this world, and taken out of the toil and terror of it." *Not that, being freed from all trouble, they may bask in luxurious ease, but that by the help of God they may be preserved in a scene of danger;* so Calvin. Not that they may be kept from all conflict with the world, but that they may not be overcome by it. It is more the honour of a Christian soldier by faith to *overcome the world* than by a monastical vow to retreat from it; and more for the honour of Christ to serve him in a city than to serve him in a cell.

2. By keeping them from the corruption that is in the world, *v.* 11, 15. Here are three branches of this petition:

(1) *Holy Father, keep those whom thou hast given me.* Christ was now leaving them. He does here commit them to the custody of his Father. It is the unspeakable comfort of all believers that Christ himself has committed them to the care of God. Those cannot but be safe whom the almighty God keeps, and he cannot but keep those whom the Son of his love commits to him. He here puts them under the divine protection. To this prayer is owing the wonderful preservation of the gospel ministry and gospel church in the world unto this day. He puts them under the divine tuition. We need God's power not only to put us into a state of grace, but to keep us in it. The titles he gives to him he prays to, and them he prays for, enforce the petition. He speaks to God as a *holy Father.* If he be a holy God and hate sin, he will make those holy that are his, and

JAMIESON, FAUSSET, BROWN

15-19. I pray not that thou shouldest take them out of the world—for that, though it would secure their own safety, would leave the world unblessed by their testimony.

Holy Father—an expression He nowhere else uses. *"Father"* is His wonted appellation, but *"Holy"* is here prefixed, because His appeal was to that perfection of the Father's nature, to "keep" or preserve them from being tainted by the unholy atmosphere of "the world" they were still in.

ADAM CLARKE

10. *I am glorified in them.* Christ speaks of the things which were not, but which should be, as though they were. He anticipates the glorifying of His name by the successful preaching of the apostles.

15. *That thou shouldest take them out of the world.* They must not yet leave the land of Judea; they had not as yet borne their testimony here, concerning Christ crucified and risen again from the dead.

JOHN WESLEY:

10. "All things that are mine are thine, and that are thine are mine." These are very lofty and strong expressions, too grand for any mere creature to use; as implying that all things whatsoever, inclusive of the divine nature, perfections, and operations, are the common property of the Father and the Son. This is the original ground of that peculiar property which both have in the persons who were given to Christ as Mediator; according to what is said of his being glorified by them; namely, believing in him, and so acknowledging his glory.
—*Expositions of Holy Scripture*

ALEXANDER MACLAREN:

In the petition itself (v. 11b), observe the invocation "Holy Father!" with special reference to the prayer for preservation from the corruption of the world. God's holiness is the pledge that He will make us holy, since He is "Father" as well. Observe the substance of the request, that the disciples should be kept, as in a fortress, within the enclosing circle of the name which God has given to Jesus. The name is the manifestation of the divine nature. It was given to Jesus, inasmuch as He, "the Word," had from the beginning the office of revealing God; and that which was spoken of the Angel of the Covenant is true in highest reality of Jesus: "My name is in Him." "The name of the Lord is a strong tower: the righteous runneth into it and is safe."—*Expositions of Holy Scripture*

MATTHEW HENRY

keep them from sin, which they also hate and dread as the greatest evil. If he be a Father, he will take care of his own children; who else should? He speaks of them as those whom the Father had *given him*. What we receive as our Father's gifts, we may comfortably remit to our Father's care.

(2) *Keep* them *through thine own name:* keep them for thy name's sake. Those may with comfort plead it that are indeed more concerned for the honour of God's name than for any interest of their own. Keep them in thy name. "Keep them in the knowledge and fear of thy name; keep them in the profession and service of thy name, whatever it cost them." Keep them by or through thy name. "Keep them by thine own power, in thine own hand. Let thy name be their strong tower."

(3) *Keep them from the evil*, or out of the evil. He had taught them to pray daily, *Deliver us from evil*, and this would encourage them to pray. "Keep them from the evil one. Keep them from Satan as a tempter, that their faith may not fail. Keep them from him as a destroyer. Keep them from the evil thing, that is, sin. Keep them, that they do no evil. Keep them from the evil of the world, and of their tribulation in it, so that it may have no sting in it." Not that they might be kept from affliction, but kept through it.

II. The reasons with which he enforces these requests, which are five:

1. He pleads that hitherto he had kept them (*v.* 12): "*While I was with them in the world, I have kept them in thy name*, they are all safe, and none of them missing, *but the son of perdition*; he is lost, that the scripture might be fulfilled."

(1) Christ's faithful discharge of his undertaking: *While he was with them, he kept them*, and his care concerning them was not in vain. Many that followed him awhile took offence at something or other, and went off; but he kept the twelve that they should not go away. *While he was with them*, he kept them in a visible manner. When he was gone from them, they must be kept in a more spiritual manner. Comforts and supports are sometimes given and sometimes withheld; but, when they are withdrawn, yet they are not left comfortless. What Christ here says is true of all the saints while they are here in this world; Christ keeps them *in God's name*. They are weak, and cannot keep themselves. They are, in God's account, valuable and worth the keeping; his treasure, his jewels. Their salvation is designed, for to this it is that they are kept, 1 Pet. i. 5. The righteous are preserved for the day of bliss. They are the charge of the Lord Jesus; he keeps them, and exposed himself like the good shepherd for the preservation of the sheep.

(2) The comfortable account he gives of his undertaking: *None of them is lost*. Jesus Christ will certainly keep all that were given to him; they may think themselves lost, and may be nearly lost (in imminent peril); but it is the Father's will that he should *lose none*, and none he will lose.

(3) A brand put upon Judas, as none of those whom he had undertaken to keep. He was among those that were given to Christ, but not of them. But the apostasy and ruin of Judas were no reproach at all to his Master, or his family. He was *the son of perdition*, and therefore not one of those that were given to Christ to be kept. It is an awful consideration that one of the apostles proved a son of perdition. No man's place or name in the church will secure him from ruin, if his heart be not right with God. The scripture was fulfilled; the sin of Judas was foreseen and foretold, and the event would certainly follow after the prediction as a consequent, though it cannot be said necessarily to follow from it as an effect.

2. He pleads that he was now under a necessity of leaving them (*v.* 11): "Keep them now. Keep them, *that they may be one* with us *as we are* with each other."

(1) With what pleasure he speaks of his own departure. He expresses himself concerning it with an air of triumph and exultation, with reference both to the world he left and the world he removed to. "*Now I am no more in the world.* Now farewell to this provoking troublesome world. Now the welcome hour is at hand when I shall be *no more in it*." It should be a pleasure to those that have their home in the other world to think of being *no more in this world*. What is there here that should court our stay? *Now I come to thee.* To get clear of the world is but the one half of the comfort of a dying Christ, of a dying Christian; the far better half is to think of going to the Father. Those who love God cannot but be pleased to think of coming to him, though it be through the valley of the shadow of death. It is to be *present with the Lord*, like children fetched

JAMIESON, FAUSSET, BROWN

keep through thine own name—rather, 'in thy name'; in the exercise of that gracious and holy character for which He was known.

but . . . keep them from the evil—all evil in and of the world.

12. I kept—guarded—**them in thy name**—acting as Thy Representative on earth.

none of them is lost, but the son of perdition—It is not implied here that the son of perdition was one of those whom the Father had given to the Son, but rather the contrary (ch. 13:18) [Webster and Wilkinson]. It is just as in Luke 4:26, 27, where we are not to suppose that the woman of *Sarepta* (in Sidon) was one of the widows of *Israel*, nor Naaman the *Syrian* one of the lepers in *Israel*, though the language—the same as here—might *seem* to express it. **son of perdition**—doomed to it (II Thess. 2:3; Mark 14:21).

that they may be one—See on vs. 21.

11. I am no more in the world—(see on vs. 4) **but these are in the world**—i.e., Though My struggles are at an end, theirs are not; though I have gotten beyond the scene of strife, I cannot sever Myself in spirit from them, left behind and only just entering on their great conflict.

ADAM CLARKE

Keep through thine own name those whom thou hast given me. Instead of *those whom thou hast given me*, many MSS. read *ho*, which refers to *thy name*, immediately preceding. The whole passage should be read thus: "Holy Father, keep them through Thy own name which Thou hast given me, that they may be one." By the *name*, here, it is evident that the doctrine or knowledge of the true God is intended; as if our Lord had said, Keep them in that doctrine which Thou hast given Me, that they may be one. This reading is supported by the most ample evidence and indisputable authority.

12. *I kept them in thy name.* In Thy doctrine and truth.

But the son of perdition. So we find that Judas, whom all account to have been lost, and whose case at best is extremely dubious, was first given by God to Christ. But why was he lost? Because, says Augustine, he would not be *saved;* and he further adds, After the commission of his crime, he might have returned to God and have found mercy. *Perdition* or "destruction" is personified; and Judas is represented as being her *son*, i.e., one of the worst of men. *That the scripture might be fulfilled.* Or, "Thus the scripture is fulfilled"; see Ps. xli. 9; cix. 8, compared with Acts i. 20.

That they may be one. That they and all that believe through their word (the doctrine which I have given them) may be one body, united by one Spirit to Me, their living Head. The union which Christ recommends here and prays for is so complete and glorious as to be fitly represented by that union which subsists between the Father and the Son.

11. *I am no more in the world.* I am just going to leave the world, and therefore they shall stand in need of peculiar assistance and support. They have need of all the influence of My intercession, that they may be preserved in Thy truth.

MATTHEW HENRY

home from school to their father's house.

(2) With what a tender concern he speaks of those whom he left behind: "*But these are in the world. Holy Father, keep them;* they will want my presence, let them have thine. They have now more need than ever to be kept, and will be lost if thou do not keep them." When our Lord Jesus was going to the Father, he carried with him a tender concern for *his own that are in the world.* When he is out of their sight they are not out of his, much less out of his mind. When Christ would express the utmost need his disciples had of divine preservation, he only says, *They are in the world;* this bespeaks danger enough to those who are bound for heaven.

3. He pleads what a satisfaction it would be to them to know themselves safe, and what a satisfaction it would be to him to see them easy: *I speak this, that they may have my joy fulfilled in themselves, v.* 13.

(1) Christ earnestly desired the fulness of the joy of his disciples, for it is his will that they should rejoice evermore. When they thought their joy in him was brought to an end, then was it advanced nearer to perfection than ever it had been, and they were fuller of it. We are here taught to found our joy in Christ. Christ is a Christian's joy, his chief joy. Joy in the world is withering with it; joy in Christ is everlasting, like him. To build up our joy with diligence. No part of the Christian life is pressed upon us more earnestly, Phil. iii. 1; iv. 4. To aim at the perfection of this joy.

(2) In order hereunto, he did thus solemnly commit them to his Father's care and keeping: *These things I speak in the world.* Saying this in the world would be a greater satisfaction and encouragement to them, and would enable them to *rejoice in tribulation.* Christ has not only treasured up comforts for his people, but has given out comforts to them. He here condescended to publish his last will and testament, and (which many a testator is shy of) lets them know what legacies he had left them, and how well they were secured. Christ's intercession for us is enough to fulfil our joy in him; nothing more effectual to silence all our fears and mistrusts than this, that he always appears in the presence of God for us. See Heb. vii. 25.

4. He pleads the ill usage they were likely to meet with in the world, for his sake (*v.* 14): "*I have given them thy word, and they have received it,* and therefore *the world hath hated them,* because they are *not of the world,* any more than I." The world's enmity to Christ's followers. While Christ was with them it hates them, much more would it do so when by their more extensive preaching of the gospel they would *turn the world upside down.* "Father, stand their friend," says Christ. "Let them have thy love, for the world's hatred is entailed upon them." It is God's honour to take part with the weaker side, and to help the helpless. The reasons of this enmity, which strengthen the plea. One reason is because they had received the word of God by the hand of Christ, when the greatest part of the world rejected it. Those that receive Christ's goodwill and good word must expect the world's ill will and ill word. Gospel ministers have been in a particular manner hated by the world, because they call men out of the world, and separate them from it, and so condemn the world. "*Father, keep them,* they are sufferers for thee." Those that keep the word of Christ's patience are entitled to special protection in the hour of temptation. That cause which makes a martyr may well make a joyful sufferer. Another reason is more express; the world hates them, because they *are not of the world.* Those to whom the word of Christ comes in power are not of the world, and therefore the world bears them a grudge.

5. He pleads their conformity to himself in a holy non-conformity to the world (*v.* 16): "Father, keep them, *they are not of the world, even as I am not of the world.*" Those may in faith commit themselves to God's custody, who are *as Christ was in this world.* God will love those that are like Christ. (1) Jesus Christ was not of this world; he never had been of it. This intimates, *First,* His state; he was none of the world's favourites nor darlings; worldly possessions he had none, not even *where to lay his head*; nor worldly power. *Secondly,* His Spirit; he was perfectly dead to the world, the prince of this world had nothing in him. (2) Therefore true Christians are not of this world. It is their lot to be despised by the world; they are not in favour with the world any more than their Master before them was. It is their privilege to be delivered from the world. It is their duty and character to be dead to the world. Christ's disciples were weak, and had many infirmities; yet this he could say for them, They were not of the world and therefore he recommends them to the care of Heaven.

JAMIESON, FAUSSET, BROWN

13. I speak in the world, that they might have my joy fulfilled in themselves—i.e., Such a strain befits rather the upper sanctuary than the scene of conflict; but I speak so *"in the world,"* that My joy, the joy I experience in knowing that such intercessions are to be made for them by their absent Lord, may be tasted by those who now hear them, and by all who shall hereafter read the record of them,'

16. They are not of the world, even as I am not of the world—(See on ch. 15:18, 19). This is reiterated here, to pave the way for the prayer which follows.

ALEXANDER MACLAREN:

Going away so soon, He yearned to leave them sharers of His own emotions in the prospect of His departure to the Father, and therefore He had admitted them (and us) to hear this sacred outpouring of His desires. If we laid to heart the blessed revelations of this disclosure of Christ's heart, and followed Him with faithful gaze as He ascends to the Father, and realized our share in that triumph, our empty vessels would be filled by some of that same joy which was His. Earthly joy can never be full; Christian joy should never be anything less than full. —*Expositions of Holy Scripture*

ADAM CLARKE

13. *My joy fulfilled in themselves.* See on chap. xv. 11.

14. *I have given them thy word.* Or "Thy doctrine." *And the world hath hated them.* The Jewish rulers have hated them.

F. B. MEYER:

In the world, but not of the world. What is "the world"? The inspired definition is given in 1 John 2:16. Enumerating her three offsprings, the apostle goes on the say, "All that is in the world . . . is not of the Father," that is, does not originate or proceed from him. We might reverse the proposition and say, "All that does not emanate from the Father, and which is inconsistent with perfect love and purity and truth, is of the world."

The spirit of the world permeates society. All its plans, aims, and activities belong to the present passing show. "Under the sun" is the suggestion of Ecclesiastes. The world has always been in collision with Christ, because his teaching reverses everything that the world prizes. In its beatitudes, its methods of pleasure and acquisition, its view and use of power, and its attitude toward God, the difference is wide as the poles. But its hatred is welcome to the followers of Christ, as proving that they are on the Master's track, and in his fellowship they are abundantly compensated.—*Bible Commentary*

MATTHEW HENRY

Verses 17-19

The next thing he prayed for them was that they might be sanctified; not only kept from evil, but made good.

I. Here is the petition (*v.* 17): *Sanctify them through thy truth; thy word is truth.* He desires they may be sanctified,

1. As Christians, 1 Thess. v. 23.

(1) The grace desired—sanctification. He prays, *Father, sanctify them.* "Confirm the work of sanctification in them, rivet their good resolutions. Carry on that good work in them; let the *light shine more and more.* Complete it, sanctify them throughout and to the end." He cannot for shame own them as his, either here or hereafter, or present them to his Father, if they be not sanctified. Those that through grace are sanctified have need to be sanctified more and more. Not to go forward is to go backward; *he that is holy must be holy still,* more holy still. It is God that sanctifies as well as God that justifies.

(2) The means of conferring this grace—*through thy truth, thy word is truth.* Divine revelation, as it now stands in the written word, is not only pure truth without mixture, but entire truth without deficiency. This word of truth should be the outward and ordinary means of our sanctification. It is the seed of the new birth, and the food of the new life.

2. As ministers. "*Sanctify them,* let their call to the apostleship be ratified in heaven. Qualify them for the office, with Christian graces and ministerial gifts. Separate them to the office. I have called them, they have consented; Father, say *Amen* to it. Own them in the office; let thy hand go along with them. Sanctify them to thy truth, to be the preachers of thy truth to the world." Jesus Christ intercedes for his ministers with a particular concern, and recommends to his Father's grace those stars he carries in his right hand. The great thing to be asked of God for gospel ministers is that they may be sanctified, entirely devoted to God, and experimentally acquainted with the influence of that word upon their own hearts which they preach to others.

II. We have here two pleas to enforce the petition,

1. The mission they had from him (*v.* 18): "*As thou hast sent me into the world,* so now *have I sent them into the world.*"

(1) Christ speaks with great assurance of his own mission: *Thou hast sent me into the world.* He was sent of God to say what he said, and do what he did, and be what he is to those that believe on him.

(2) He speaks of the commission he had given his disciples: "*So have I sent them* on the same errand"; to preach the same doctrine that he preached. He gave them their commission (*ch.* xx. 21) with a reference to his own, and it magnifies their office that it comes from Christ, and that there is some affinity between the commission given to the ministers of reconciliation and that given to the Mediator. Only they are sent as servants, he as a Son. Christ was concerned so much for them, because he had himself put them into a difficult office, which required great abilities for the due discharge of it. Whom Christ sends he will stand by. What he calls us out to he will fit us out for, and bear us out in. He committed them to his Father, because he was concerned in their cause, their mission being in prosecution of his. The Father *sanctified him* when *he sent him into the world, ch.* x. 36. Now, they being sent as he was, let them also be sanctified.

2. The merit he had for them is another thing here pleaded (*v.* 19): *For their sakes I sanctify myself.* (1) Christ's designation of himself to the work and office of Mediator: *I sanctified myself.* He entirely devoted himself to the undertaking, and all the parts of it, especially that which he was now going about—the *offering up of himself without spot unto God, by the eternal Spirit.* This he pleads with his Father, for his intercession is made in the virtue of his satisfaction. (2) Christ's design of kindness to his disciples herein; it is *for their sakes,* that *they may be sanctified,* that they may be saints and ministers, duly qualified and accepted of God. The office of the ministry is the purchase of Christ's blood, and one of the blessed fruits of his satisfaction. The real holiness of all good Christians is the fruit of Christ's death. He *gave himself for his church,* to *sanctify it.* And he that designed the end designed also the means, that they might be sanctified *by the truth.* The word of truth receives its sanctifying virtue and power from the death of Christ. And this Christ has prayed for, for all that are his; for *this is his will, even their sanctification,* which encourages them to pray for it.

Verses 20-23

Next to their purity he prays for their unity.

I. Who are included in this prayer (*v.* 20): "*Not these only,* but *for those also who shall believe on me*

JAMIESON, FAUSSET, BROWN

17. Sanctify them—As the former prayer, "*Keep* them," was *negative,* asking *protection* for them from the poisonous element which surrounded and pressed upon their renewed nature, so this prayer, "*Sanctify* them," is positive, asking the *advancement and completion* of their begun sanctification. **through—in—thy truth**—God's revealed truth, as the medium or element of sanctification; a statement this of immense importance. **thy word is truth**—(Cf. ch. 15:3; Col. 1:5; Eph. 1:13).

18. As thou hast sent—sentest—**me into the world, even so have I also sent**—sent I also—**them into the world**—As their mission was to carry into effect the purposes of their Master's mission, so our Lord speaks of the *authority* in both cases as *co-ordinate.*

And for their sakes I sanctify—consecrate—**myself, that they also might**—may—**be sanctified**—consecrated. The only difference between the application of the same term to Christ and the disciples is, as applied to Christ, that it means *only* to "consecrate"; whereas, in application to the disciples, it means to consecrate with the *additional idea* of previous sanctification, since nothing but what is holy can be presented as an offering. The whole self-sacrificing work of the disciples appears here as a mere *result* of the offering of Christ [OLSHAUSEN]. **through 'in—the truth**—Though the article is wanting in the original here, we are not to translate, as in the margin, "*truly* sanctified"; for the reference seems plainly to be "the truth" mentioned in vs. 17. (See there.)

ADAM CLARKE

17. *Sanctify them. Hagiason,* from *a,* negative, and *ge,* "the earth." This word has two meanings: (1) It signifies to "consecrate," to "separate" from earth and common use, and to "devote" or "dedicate" to God and His service. (2) It signifies to "make holy" or "pure." The prayer of Christ may be understood in both these senses. He prayed (1) that they might be fully consecrated to the work of the ministry, and separated from all worldly concerns; (2) that they might be holy, and patterns of all holiness to those to whom they announced the salvation of God. *Through thy truth.* It is not only according to the truth of God that ministers are to be set apart to the sacred work; but it is from that truth, and according to it, that they must preach to others. That doctrine which is not drawn from the truth of God can never save souls.

18. *As thou hast sent me . . . so have I also sent them.* The apostles had the same commission which Christ had, considered as man—they were endued with the same Spirit, so that they could not err, and their word was accompanied with the same success.

19. *I sanctify myself.* I "consecrate" and "devote" myself to death—that I may thereby purchase eternal salvation for them. There seems to be here an allusion to the entering of the high priest into the holy of holies, when, having offered the sacrifice, he sprinkled the blood before the ark of the covenant. So Jesus entered into the holiest of all by His own blood, in order to obtain everlasting redemption for men; see Heb. ix. 11-13. The word *hagiazo,* to "consecrate" or "sanctify," is used in the sense of devoting to death, in Jer. xii. 3, both in the Hebrew and in the Septuagint; the Hebrew signifies also to "sacrifice."

MATTHEW HENRY

through their word. I pray *for them all.*" Those, and those only, are interested in the mediation of Christ, that believe in him. They that lived then, *saw and believed,* but they in after ages *have not seen,* and yet *have believed.* It is *through the word* that souls are brought to believe on Christ. He does not here pray at a venture. Christ knew very well whom he prayed for. Jesus Christ intercedes not only for great and eminent believers, but for the meanest and weakest. The Good Shepherd has an eye even to *the poor of the flock.* Jesus Christ in his mediation had an actual regard to those that were yet unborn, the *other sheep* which he *must yet bring.*

II. What is intended in this prayer (*v.* 21): *That they all may be one.* The same was said before (*v.* 11), *that they may be one as we are,* and again, *v.* 22. The heart of Christ was much upon this. Let them be not only of *one heart,* but of *one mouth,* speaking the same thing. The oneness prayed for in *v.* 21 respects all believers. It is the prayer of Christ for all that are his—*that they all may be one,* one in us (*v.* 21), one *as we are one* (*v.* 22), made *perfect in one, v.* 23.

1. That they might all be *incorporated in one body.* "Father, look upon them all as one. Though they live in distant places, and in several ages, yet let them be united in me their common head." As Christ died, so he prayed, to *gather them all in one.*

2. That they might all be animated by one Spirit. This is plainly implied in this—*that they may be one in us.* Let them all be stamped with the same image and superscription, and influenced by the same power.

3. That they might all be *knit together* in the bond of love and charity, all of one heart. *That they all may be one.* In judgment and sentiment; not in every little thing—this is neither possible nor needful, but in the great things of God, and in them, by the virtue of this prayer. In disposition and inclination. They have all a new heart, and it is *one heart.* In their designs and aims. In their desires and prayers; though they differ in words and the manner of expressions, yet they pray for the same things in effect. In love and affection. That which Christ here prays for is that *communion of saints* which we profess to believe. But this prayer of Christ will not have its complete answer till all the saints come to heaven, for then, and not till then, they shall be *perfect in one.*

III. What is intimated by way of plea to enforce this petition.

1. The oneness that is between the Father and the Son, which is mentioned again and again, *v.* 11, 21–23. It is taken for granted that the Father and Son are one, one in mutual endearments. The *Father loveth the Son,* and the Son always pleased the Father. They are one in design. The intimacy of this oneness is expressed in these words, *thou in me, and I in thee.* This is insisted on in Christ's prayer for his disciples' oneness, (1) As the pattern of that oneness. Believers are one in some measure as God and Christ are one; they are united by a divine nature, by the power of divine grace, in pursuance of the divine counsels. It is a holy union, for holy ends; not a body politic for any secular purpose. It is a complete union. (2) As the centre of that oneness; that they may be *one in us.* There is *one God* and *one Mediator.* That is a conspiracy, not a union, which doth not centre in God as the end, and Christ as the way. All who are truly united to God and Christ, who *are one,* will soon be *united one to another.* (3) As a plea for that oneness. The Creator and Redeemer are one in interest and design; but to what purpose are they so, if all believers be not one body with Christ, and do not jointly receive grace for grace from him, as he has received it for them? Those words, *I in them, and thou in me,* show what that union is which is so necessary, not only to the beauty, but to the very being, of his church. Union with Christ: *I in them.* Union with God through him: *Thou in me,* so as by me to be in them. Union with each other, resulting from these: *that they* hereby *may be made perfect in one.* We are complete in him.

2. The design of Christ in all his communications of light and grace to them (*v.* 22): "*The glory which thou gavest me, I have* accordingly *given them, that they may be one, as we are one;* so that those gifts will be in vain, if they be not one." Now these gifts are either, (1) Those that were conferred upon the apostles. The glory of being God's ambassadors to the world, and erecting the throne of God's kingdom among men—this glory was given to Christ, and some of the honour he put upon them when he sent them to *disciple all nations.* Or, (2) Those that are given in common to all believers. The glory of being in covenant with the Father was the glory which the Father gave to the Redeemer, and he has confirmed it to the redeemed. This honour he says he *hath given them.* He gave it to them, that they *might*

JAMIESON, FAUSSET, BROWN

20-23. Neither pray I for these alone—This very important explanation, uttered in condescension to the hearers and readers of this prayer in all time, is meant not merely of what follows, but of the whole prayer. **them also which shall believe**—The majority of the best MSS. read "which believe," all future time being viewed as *present,* while the present is viewed as past and gone.

21. that they all may be one, as thou, Father, art in me, and I in thee, that they may be one in us—*The indwelling Spirit of the Father and the Son* is the one perfect bond of union, knitting up into a living unity, first all believers amongst themselves; next, this unity into one still higher, with the Father and the Son. (Observe, that Christ *never mixes Himself up with His disciples as He associates Himself with the Father,* but says I in THEM and THEY in US.) **that the world may believe that thou hast sent**—sentest—**me**—So the grand impression upon the world at large, that the mission of Christ is divine, is to be made by *the unity of His disciples.* Of course, then, it must be something that shall be *visible* or perceptible to the world. What is it, then? Not certainly a merely formal, mechanical unity of ecclesiastical machinery. For as that may, and to a large extent does, exist in both the Western and Eastern churches, with little of the Spirit of Christ, yea much, much with which the Spirit of Christ cannot dwell so instead of convincing the world *beyond its own pale* of the divinity of the Gospel, it generates infidelity to a large extent within its own bosom. But the Spirit of Christ, illuminating, transforming, and reigning in the hearts of the genuine disciples of Christ, drawing them to each other as members of one family, and prompting them to loving co-operation for the good of the world—this is what, when sufficiently glowing and extended, shall force conviction upon the world that Christianity is divine. Doubtless, the more that differences among Christians disappear—the more they can agree even in minor matters—the impression upon the world may be expected to be greater. But it is not *dependent* upon this; for living and loving oneness in Christ is sometimes more touchingly seen even amidst and in spite of minor differences, than where no such differences exist to try the strength of their deeper unity. Yet till this living brotherhood in Christ shall show itself strong enough to destroy the sectarianism, selfishness, carnality, and apathy that eat out the heart of Christianity in all the visible sections of it, in vain shall we expect the world to be overawed by it. It is when "the Spirit shall be poured upon us from on high," as a Spirit of truth and love, and upon all parts of the Christian territory alike, melting down differences and heart-burnings, kindling astonishment and shame at past unfruitfulness, drawing forth longings of catholic affection, and yearnings over a world lying in wickedness, embodying themselves in palpable forms and active measures—it is then that we may expect the effect here announced to be produced, and then it will be irresistible. *Should not Christians ponder these things? Should not the same mind be in them which was also in Christ Jesus about this matter? Should not His prayer be theirs?*

22. And the glory which thou gavest—hast given—**me I have given them, that they may be one, even as we are one**—The last clause shows the meaning of the first. It is not the *future* glory of the heavenly state, but the secret of that *present* unity just before spoken of; *the glory,* therefore, *of the indwelling Spirit of Christ;* the glory of an accepted state, of a holy character, of every grace. **23. I in them, and thou in me, that they may be made perfect in one**—(See on vs. 21).

ADAM CLARKE

III. OUR LORD'S PRAYER FOR HIS CHURCH, and for all who would believe on His name, through the preaching of the apostles and their successors

20. *Neither pray I for these alone.* This prayer extends itself through all ages, and takes in every soul that believes in the Lord Jesus. And what is it that Christ asks in behalf of His followers? The greatest of blessings: unity, peace, love, and eternal glory.

21. *That they all may be one.* This prayer was literally answered to the first believers, who were all of one heart and of one soul, Acts iv. 32. And why is it that believers are not in the same spirit now? Because they neither attend to the example nor to the truth of Christ.

CHARLES H. SPURGEON:

We hear much moaning over our divisions. There may be some that are to be deplored among ecclesiastical confederacies, but in the spiritual Church of the living God, I really am at a loss to discover the divisions which are so loudly proclaimed. It strikes me that the tokens of union are much more prominent than the tokens of division. But what are they? First there is a union *in judgment* upon all vital matters. I converse with a spiritual man, and no matter what he calls himself, when we talk of sin, pardon, Jesus, the Holy Spirit, and such like themes, we are agreed. We speak of our blessed Lord. My friend says that Jesus is fair and lovely; so say I. He says that he has nothing else to trust to but the precious blood; nor have I anything beside. I tell him that I find myself a poor, weak creature; he laments the same. I live in his house a little while. We pray together at the family altar. You could not tell which it was that prayed. Calvinist or Arminian, we pray so exactly alike, and when we open the hymn book, very likely if he happens to be a Wesleyan he chooses to sing, "Jesus, Lover of My Soul." I will sing it, and then next morning he will sing with me, "Rock of Ages, Cleft for Me." If the Spirit of God be in us, we are all agreed upon great points. Let me say that among true saints the points of union even in matters of judgment are ninety-nine, and the points of difference are only as one. In *experimental points,* as face answers to face, so does the heart of man to man. Only get upon experimental topics concerning soul dealings with God, leave the letter and get to the spirit, crack the shells and eat the kernel of spiritual truth, and you will find that the points of agreement between genuine Christians are something marvelous. But this union is to be seen most plainly in union of *heart.* I am told that Christians do not love each other. I am very sorry if that be true, but I rather doubt it, for I suspect that those who do not love each other are not Christians. Where the Spirit of God is there must be love, and if I have once known and recognized any man to be my brother in Christ Jesus, the love of Christ constrains me no more to think of him as a stranger or foreigner, but a fellow citizen with the saints.

—*The Treasury of the New Testament*

22. *And the glory which thou gavest me I have given them.* As Christ, according to His human nature, is termed the Son of God, He may be understood as saying: "I have communicated to all those who believe, or shall believe, in Me the glorious privilege of becoming sons of God; that, being all adopted children of the same Father, they may abide in peace, love, and unity."

MATTHEW HENRY

be one, to entitle them to the privilege of unity. The gift of the Spirit, that great glory which the Father gave to the Son, by him to be given to all believers, makes them one, to engage them to the duty of unity. That in consideration of what they have in one God and one Christ, and of what they hope for in one heaven, they may be of one mind and one mouth. Worldly glory sets men at variance; for if some be advanced others are eclipsed. The more Christians are taken up with the glory Christ has given them, the less desirous they will be of vain-glory, and, consequently, the less disposed to quarrel.

3. He pleads the happy influence their oneness would have upon others. This is twice urged (*v.* 21): *That the world may believe that thou hast sent me.* And again (*v.* 23): *That the world may know it.* Believers must know what they believe, and why and wherefore they believe it. Those who believe *at a venture,* venture too far. Now Christ here shows,

(1) His goodwill to the world of mankind in general. Herein he is of his Father's mind, that he would have all men to be saved. Therefore it is his will that no stone be left unturned, for the conviction and conversion of the world. We must in our places do our utmost to further men's salvation.

(2) The good fruit of the church's oneness; it will be an evidence of the truth of Christianity, and a means of bringing many to embrace it. In general, it will recommend Christianity to the world. The embodying of Christians in one society will greatly promote Christianity. When the world shall see so many of those that were its children changed from what they themselves sometimes were, they will be ready to say, *We will go with you, for we see that God is with you.* The uniting of Christians in love and charity is the beauty of their profession, and invites others to join with them. When Christianity, instead of causing quarrels about itself, makes all other strifes to cease,—when it disposes men to be kind and loving, studious to preserve and promote peace, this will recommend it to all that have anything either of natural religion or natural affection in them. In particular, it will beget in men good thoughts of Christ: They will know and believe that *thou hast sent me.* By this it will appear that Christ was sent of God, in that his religion prevails to join so many of different capacities, tempers, and interests in other things, in one body by faith, with one heart by love. Of Christians: They will *know that thou hast loved them as thou hast loved me.* 1. The privilege of believers: *the Father* himself loveth them with a love resembling his love to his Son, for they are loved in him with an everlasting love. 2. The evidence, that of their being one: it will appear that God loves us, if we *love one another with a pure heart.* See how much good it would do to the world to know better how dear to God all good Christians are. Those that have so much of God's love would have more of ours.

Verses 24–26

I. A petition for the glorifying of all those that were given to Christ (*v.* 24): *Father, I will that they may be with me.*

1. The connection of this request with those foregoing. He had prayed that God would sanctify them; and now he prays that he would crown all his gifts with their glorification. In this method we must pray, first for grace, and then for glory; for in this method God gives.

2. The manner of the request: *Father, I will.* Here, as before, he addresses himself to God as a Father, and therein we must do likewise; but when he says, *I will,* he speaks a language such as does not become ordinary petitioners. This intimates the authority of his intercession in general; his word was with power in heaven, as well as on earth. It intimates his particular authority in this matter; he had a power to *give eternal life* (*v.* 2), and, pursuant to that power, he says, *Father, I will.*

3. The request itself—that all the elect might come to be with him in heaven at last.

(1) Under what notion we are to hope for heaven? Wherein does that happiness consist? Three things make heaven: It is to be where Christ is: *Where I am,* am to be shortly, am to be eternally. In this world we are but *on our passage;* there we truly are where we are to be for ever. It is to be with him where he is. The happiness of the place will consist in his presence. The very heaven of heaven is to be with Christ. It is to *behold his glory, which the Father* has given him. The glory of the Redeemer is the brightness of heaven. The Lamb is the light of the new Jerusalem, Rev. xxi. 23. God shows his glory there, as he does his grace here, through Christ. The felicity of the redeemed consists very much in the beholding of this glory. They will see into those springs of love from

JAMIESON, FAUSSET, BROWN

24-26. Father, I will—The majesty of this style of speaking is quite transparent. No petty criticism will be allowed to fritter it away in any but superficial or perverted readers.

be with me where I am—(See on ch. 14:3). **that they may behold my glory which thou hast given me**—(See on vs. 5.) Christ regards it as glory enough for us to be admitted to see and gaze for ever upon *His* glory! This is 'the beatific vision'; but it shall be no mere vision, for "we shall be like Him, because we shall see Him as He is" (I John 3:2).

ADAM CLARKE

That the world may believe. We have already seen that the word *cosmos, world,* is used in several parts of this last discourse of our Lord to signify the "Jewish people" only.

23. *That the world may know.* That the Jewish people first, and secondly the Gentiles, may acknowledge Me as the true Messiah, and be saved unto life eternal.

24. *That they may behold my glory.* That they may enjoy eternal felicity with Me in Thy kingdom. So the word is used, chap. iii. 3; Matt. v. 8.

ALBERT BARNES:

23. "May be made perfect in one." That their union may be complete. That there may be no jars, discords, or contentions. A machine is perfect or complete when it has all its parts and is in good order—when there is no portion of it wanting. So the union of Christians, for which the Savior prayed, would be complete or perfect if there were no controversies, no envyings, no contentions, and no heartburnings and jealousies. It is worthy of remark here how entirely *the union of his people* occupied the mind of Jesus as he drew near to death. He saw the danger of strifes and contentions in the church. He knew the imperfections of even the best of men. He saw how prone they would be to passion and ambition; how ready to mistake love of sect or party for zeal for pure religion; how selfish and worldly men in the church might divide his followers, and produce unholy feeling and contention; and he saw, also, how much this would do to dishonor religion. Hence he took occasion, when he was about to die, to impress the importance of union on his disciples.

By solemn admonition, and by most tender and affecting appeals to God in supplication, he showed *his* sense of the value of this union. He used the most sublime and impressive illustration; he adverted to the eternal union between the Father and himself; he reminded them of his love, and of the effect that their union would have on the world, to fix it more deeply in their hearts. The effect has shown the infinite wisdom of the Savior. The contentions and strifes of Christians have shown his knowledge in foreseeing it. The effect of all this on religion has shown that he understood the value of union. Christians have contended long enough. It is time that they should hear the parting admonitions of their Redeemer, and go unitedly against their common foe. The world still lies in wickedness; and the friends of Jesus, bound by the cords of eternal love, should advance together against the common enemy, and spread the triumphs of the gospel around the globe. All that is needful now, under the blessing of God, to convince the world that God sent the Lord Jesus is that very union among all Christians for which he prayed; and when that union of feeling, and purpose, and action shall take place, the task of sending the gospel to all nations will be soon accomplished, and the morning of the millennial glory will dawn upon the world.—*Popular Commentary*

MATTHEW HENRY

which flow all the streams of grace. They shall *be changed into the same image, from glory to glory.*

(2) Upon what ground we are to hope for heaven; because he hath said, *Father, I will.* Our sanctification is our evidence, but it is the will of Christ that is our title. Christ speaks here as if he did not count his own happiness complete unless he had his elect to share with him in it.

4. The argument to back this request: *for thou lovedst me before the foundation of the world.* This is a reason, (1) Why he expected this glory himself. Thou wilt *give it to me, for thou lovedst me. The Father loves the Son,* is infinitely well pleased in his undertaking, and *therefore has given all things into his hands.* He is said to love him as Mediator *before the foundation of the world.* Or, (2) Why he expected that those who *were given to him* should be with him to share in his glory: *"Thou lovedst me,* and them in me, and canst deny me nothing I ask for them."

II. The conclusion of the prayer.

1. The respect he had to his Father, *v.* 25.

(1) The title he gives to God: *O righteous Father.* When he prayed that they might be sanctified, he called him *holy Father*; when he prays that they may be glorified, he calls him *righteous Father.*

(2) The character he gives of the world: *The world has not known thee.* Ignorance of God overspreads the world of mankind; this is the darkness they sit in. These disciples needed the aids of special grace, both because of the necessity of their work, and also because of the difficulty of their work—therefore keep them. They were qualified for further peculiar favours, for they had that knowledge of God which the world had not.

(3) The plea he insists upon for himself: *But I have known thee.* Christ knew the Father as no one else ever did, and therefore, in this prayer, came to him with confidence, as we do to one we know. When he had said, *The world has not known thee,* one would expect it should follow, *but they have known thee;* no, their knowledge was not to be boasted of, *but I have known thee.* There is nothing in us to recommend us to God's favour, but all our interest in him, and intercourse with him, result from Christ's interest and intercourse. We are unworthy, but he is worthy.

(4) The plea he insists upon for his disciples: *And they have known that thou hast sent me.* Hereby they are distinguished from the unbelieving world. To know and believe in Jesus Christ, in the midst of a world that persists in ignorance and infidelity, shall certainly be crowned with distinguishing glory. Singular faith qualifies for singular favours. Hereby they partake of the benefit of his acquaintance with the Father: *"I have known thee,* and these *have known that thou hast sent me."* Knowing Christ as sent of God, they have, in him, known the Father. "Father, look after them for my sake."

2. The respect he had to his disciples (*v.* 26): "I have led them into the knowledge of thee, *that the love wherewith thou hast loved me may be in them, and I in them.*"

(1) What Christ had done for them: *I have declared unto them thy name.* This he had done for those that were his immediate followers. This he has done for all that believe on him. We are indebted to Christ for all the knowledge we have of the Father's name. Those whom Christ recommends to the favour of God he first leads into an acquaintance with God.

(2) What he intended to do yet further for them: *I will declare it.* To the disciples he designed to give further instructions after his resurrection (Acts i. 3), by the pouring out of the Spirit after his ascension; and to all believers, into whose hearts he hath shined, he shines more and more.

(3) What he aimed at in all this; to secure and advance their real happiness in two things:

[1] Communion with God: "Therefore I have given them the knowledge of thy name, *that thy love, wherewith thou hast loved me, may be in them.* Let the *Spirit of love,* with which thou hast filled me, *be in them.*" Christ declares his Father's name to believers, that with that divine light darted into their minds a divine love may be shed abroad in their hearts, that they may partake of a divine nature. When God's love to us comes to be in us, it is like the virtue which the loadstone gives the needle, inclining it to move towards the pole; it draws out the soul towards God. Let them not only be interested in the love of God, let them have the comfort of that interest; that they may not only know God, but *know that they know him.* It is *the love of God* thus *shed abroad in the heart* that fills it with joy, Rom. v. 3, 5. We may not only be satisfied with his loving kindness, but be satisfied of it. This we must press after; if we have it, we must thank Christ for it; if we want it, we may thank ourselves.

[2] Union with Christ in order hereunto: *And I in*

JAMIESON, FAUSSET, BROWN

A. T. ROBERTSON:

24. "I will" (*thelo*). Perfect identity of his will with that of the Father in "this moment of spiritual exaltation" (Bernard), though in Gethsemane Jesus distinguishes between his human will and that of the Father (Mark 14:36). "Where I am" (*hopou eimi ego*). That is heaven, to be with Jesus (12:26; 13:36; 14:3; Rom. 8:17; 2 Tim. 2:11). "That they may behold" (*hina theorosin*). Another purpose clause with *hina* and the present active subjunctive of *theoreo,* "that they may keep on beholding," the endless joy of seeing Jesus "as he is" (1 John 3:2) in heaven. "Before the foundation of the world" (*pro kataboles kosmou*). This same phrase in Eph. 1:4 and 1 Pet. 1:20 and six other times we have *katabole kosmou* (Matt. 25:34; Luke 11:50; Heb. 4:3; 9:26; Rev. 13:8; 17:8). Here we find the same preincarnate consciousness of Christ seen in 17:5.

—Word Pictures in the New Testament

O righteous Father, the world hath not known thee—knew thee not. **but I have known**—knew—**thee,**

and these have known—knew—**that thou hast sent**—sentest—**me**—As before He said *"Holy* Father," when desiring the display of that perfection on His disciples (vs. 11), so here He styles Him *"Righteous* Father," because He is appealing to His righteousness or justice, to make a distinction between those two diametrically opposite classes—*"the world,"* on the one hand, which would not "know the Father, though brought so nigh to it in the Son of His love, and, on the other, *Himself,* who recognized and owned Him, *and even His disciples,* who owned His mission from the Father.

26. And I have declared—I made known or communicated—**thy name**—in His past ministry. **and will declare it**—in yet larger measure, by the gift of the Holy Ghost at Pentecost and through all succeeding ages.

that the love wherewith thou hast loved—lovedst—**me may be in them, and I in them**—This eternal love of the Father, resting first on Christ, is by His Spirit imparted to and takes up its permanent abode in all that believe in Him; and "He abiding in them and they in Him" (ch. 15:5), they are *"one Spirit."* "With this lofty thought the Redeemer closes His prayer for His disciples, and in them for His Church through all ages. He has compressed into the last moments given Him for conversation with His own the most sublime and glorious sentiments ever uttered by mortal lips. But hardly has the sound of the last word died away, when He passes with the disciples over the brook Kedron to Gethsemane—and the bitter conflict draws on. The seed of the new world must be sown in Death, that thence Life may spring up" [OLSHAUSEN].

ADAM CLARKE

25. *The world hath not known thee.* Has not acknowledged Me. See on chap. i. 11-12.

And these have known. Here our Lord, returning to the disciples, speaks: (1) of their having received Him as the Messiah; (2) of His making the Father known unto them; (3) of His purpose to continue to influence them by the Spirit of truth. that they might be perfectly united to God by an indwelling Saviour forever.

26. *I have declared unto them thy name.* I have taught them the true doctrine. *And will declare it.* This He did: (1) by the conversations He had with His disciples after His resurrection, during the space of forty days; (2) by the Holy Spirit, who was poured out upon them on the Day of Pentecost.

MATTHEW HENRY

them. There is no getting into the love of God but through Christ, nor can we keep ourselves in that love but by abiding in Christ. It is *Christ in us* that is *the* only *hope of glory* that will *not make us ashamed,* Col. i. 27. All our communion with God, the reception of his love to us with our return of love to him again, passes through the hands of the Lord Jesus. Christ had said but a little before, *I in them* (*v.* 23), and here it is repeated, and the prayer closed with it, to show how much the heart of Christ was set upon it. "*I in them;* let me have this, and I desire no more." Let us therefore make sure our union with Christ, and then take the comfort of his intercession. *This* prayer had an end, but *that* he ever lives to make.

CHAPTER 18

Verses 1–12

The hour was now come that *the captain of our salvation,* who was to be *made perfect by sufferings,* should engage the enemy. *Let us turn aside now, and see this great sight.*

I. Our Lord Jesus, like a bold champion, takes the field first (*v.* 1, 2): *When he had spoken these words,* he would lose no time, but *went forth with his disciples,* and *he went over the brook Cedron where was a garden.*

1. Our Lord Jesus entered upon his sufferings *when he had spoken these words.* Christ had said all he had to say as a prophet, and now he addresses himself to the discharge of his office as a priest, to *make his soul an offering for sin;* and, when he had gone through this, he entered upon his kingly office. Having by his sermon prepared his disciples for this hour of trial, and by his prayer prepared himself for it, he then courageously went out to meet it. When he had put on his armour, he entered the lists, and not till then. Christ will not engage those that are in any conflict, but he will first do that for them which is necessary to prepare them for it. We may, with an unshaken resolution, venture through the greatest hardships in the way of duty.

2. *He went forth with his disciples.* He would do as he was wont to do, and not alter his method, either to meet the cross or to miss it, when his hour was come. It was his custom when he was at Jerusalem to retire at night *to the mount of Olives.* This being his custom, he would not be put out of his method by the foresight of his sufferings. He was as unwilling that there should be *an uproar among the people* as his enemies were. If he had been seized in the city, and a tumult raised thereby, mischief might have been done, and a great deal of blood shed, and therefore he withdrew. When we find ourselves involved in trouble, we should be afraid of involving others with us. It is no disgrace to the followers of Christ to fall tamely. Those who aim at honour from men value themselves upon a resolution to sell their lives as dearly as they can; but those who know that their blood is precious to Christ need not stand upon such terms. He would set us an example of retirement from the world. We must lay aside, and leave behind, the crowds, and cares, and comforts, of cities, even holy cities, if we would cheerfully take up our cross.

3. He went *over the brook Cedron.* He must go over this to go to *the mount of Olives,* but the notice taken of it intimates that there was something in it significant. *The brook Cedron, the black brook,* so called either from the darkness of the valley it ran through or the colour of the water, tainted with the dirt of the city. The godly kings of Judah had burnt and destroyed the idols they found at *the brook Cedron.* Into that brook the abominable things were cast. Christ began his passion by the same brook.

4. He entered into a garden. This circumstance is taken notice of only by this evangelist, that Christ's sufferings began in a garden. In the garden of Eden sin began; there the Redeemer was promised. Christ was buried also in a garden. Let us, when we walk in our gardens, take occasion thence to meditate on Christ's sufferings in a garden, to which we owe all the pleasure we have in our gardens. When we are in the midst of our possessions and enjoyments, we must keep up an expectation of troubles, for our gardens of delight are in a vale of tears.

5. He had his disciples with him. They must be witnesses of his sufferings, and his patience under them, that they might with the more assurance and affection preach them to the world, and be themselves prepared to suffer. He would take them into the danger to show them their weakness. Christ sometimes brings his people into difficulties that he may magnify himself in their deliverance.

6. Judas the traitor *knew the place.* A solitary garden is a proper place for meditation and prayer,

JAMIESON, FAUSSET, BROWN

CHAPTER 18

VSS. 1-13. BETRAYAL AND APPREHENSION OF JESUS.

1-3. over the brook Kedron—a deep, dark ravine, to the northeast of Jerusalem, through which flowed this small storm-brook or winter-torrent, and which in summer is dried up.

where was a garden—at the foot of the Mount of Olives, "called Gethsemane; i.e., olive press (Matt. 26:30, 36).

2. Judas . . . knew the place, for Jesus ofttimes—see ch. 8:1; Luke 21:37—**resorted thither with his disciples**—The baseness of this abuse of knowledge in Judas, derived from admission to the closest privacies of his Master, is most touchingly conveyed here, though nothing beyond bare narrative is expressed. Jesus, however, knowing that in this spot Judas would expect to find Him, instead of avoiding it, hies Him thither, as a Lamb to the slaughter. "No man taketh My life from Me, but I lay it down of Myself" (ch. 10:18). Besides, the scene which was to fill up the little breathing-time, the

ADAM CLARKE

Our Lord's sermon, which He concluded by the prayer recorded in this chapter, begins at v. 13 of chap. xiii and is one of the most excellent that can be conceived. His Sermon on the Mount shows men what they should *do,* so as to please God; this sermon shows them *how* they are to do the things prescribed in the other. In the former the reader sees a strict morality which he fears he shall never be able to perform. In this he sees all things are possible to him who believes; for that very God who made him shall dwell in his heart, and enable him to do all that He pleases to employ him in.

CHAPTER 18

1. *Over the brook Cedron.* Having finished the prayer related in the preceding chapter, our Lord went straight to the Garden of Gethsemane, Matt. xxvi. 36, which was in the Mount of Olives, eastward of Jerusalem. This mount was separated from the city by a very narrow valley, through the midst of which the brook Cedron ran. Cedron is a very small rivulet, about six or seven feet broad, nor is it constantly supplied with water, being dry all the year except during the rains. It is mentioned in the Old Testament: 2 Sam. xv. 23; 1 Kings xv. 13; 2 Kings xxiii. 4. And it appears the Evangelist mentions it here only to call to remembrance what happened to David when he was driven from Jerusalem by his son Absalom, and he and his followers obliged to pass the brook Cedron on foot; see 2 Sam. xv. 23. All this was a very expressive figure of what happened now to this Second David by the treachery of one of His own disciples. *A garden.* Gethsemane; see on Matt. xxvi. 36. John mentions nothing of the agony in the garden; probably because he found it so amply related by all the other Evangelists. As that account should come in here, the reader is desired to consult the notes on Matt. xxvi. 36-47. See also Mark xiv. 30-36 and Luke xxii. 40-44.

2. *Judas . . . knew the place.* As many had come from different quarters to celebrate the Passover at Jerusalem, it could not be an easy matter to find lodging in the city. Jesus therefore chose to pass the night in the garden with His disciples, which, from this verse and from Luke xxii. 39, we find was His frequent custom, though He often lodged in Bethany. But as He had supped in the city this evening, Judas took it for granted that He had not gone to Bethany, and therefore was to be met with in the garden; and having given this informa-

TODAY'S DICTIONARY OF THE BIBLE:

Kidron = Kedron = Cedron—turbid—the winter torrent which flows through the Valley of Jehoshaphat, on the eastern side of Jerusalem, between the city and the Mount of Olives. This valley is known in Scripture only by the name "the brook Kidron." David crossed this brook barefoot and weeping, when fleeing from Absalom (2 Sam. 15:23, 30), and it was frequently crossed by our Lord in his journeyings back and forth (John 18:1). Here Asa burned the obscene idols of his mother (1 Kings 15:13), and here Athaliah was executed (2 Kings 11:16). It afterward became the receptacle for all manner of impurities (2 Chron. 29:16; 30:14); and in the time of Josiah this valley was the common cemetery of the city (2 Kings 23:6; comp. Jer. 26:23).

Through this mountain ravine no water runs, except after heavy rains in the mountains round about Jerusalem. Its length from its head to en-Rogel is 2¾ miles. Its precipitous, rocky banks are filled with ancient tombs, especially the left bank opposite the temple area. The greatest desire of the Jews is to be buried there, from the idea that the Kidron is the "valley of Jehoshaphat" mentioned in Joel 3:2.

Below en-Rogel the Kidron has no historical or sacred interest. It runs in a winding course through the wilderness of Judea to the northwestern shore of the Dead Sea. Its whole length, in a straight line, is only some 20 miles, but in this space its descent is about 3,912 feet.

Recent excavations have brought to light the fact that the old bed of the Kidron is about 40 feet lower than its present bed, and about 70 feet nearer the sanctuary wall.

MATTHEW HENRY

that we may pray over the impressions made and the vows renewed, and clench the nail. Mention is made of Judas's knowing the place, (1) To aggravate the sin of Judas, that he would betray his Master, and that he would make use of his familiarity with Christ, as giving him an opportunity of betraying him; a generous mind would have scorned to do so base a thing. (2) To magnify the love of Christ, that, though he knew where the traitor would seek him, thither he went to be found of him. Thus he showed himself willing to suffer and die for us. It was late in the night (we may suppose eight or nine o'clock) when Christ went out to the garden. When others were going to bed, he was going to prayer, going to suffer.

II. *The captain of our salvation* having taken the field, the enemy attacks him (*v.* 3): Judas with his men comes thither. This evangelist passes over Christ's agony, because the other three had fully related it.

1. The persons employed in this action—*a band of men and officers from the chief priests, with Judas.* (1) Here is a multitude engaged against Christ—*a band of men.* Christ's friends were few, his enemies many. (2) Here is a mixed multitude; the band of men were Gentiles, Roman soldiers, the *officers of the chief priests.* The officers of their courts were Jews; these had an enmity to each other, but were united against Christ. (3) It is a commissioned multitude who have received orders *from the chief priests,* and it is likely that they had a warrant to take him up, *for they feared the people.* See what enemies Christ and his gospel have had, and are likely to have, numerous and potent; ecclesiastical and civil powers combined against them. (4) All under the direction of Judas. He *received* this *band of men.* He thought himself wonderfully preferred from coming in the rear of the contemptible twelve to be placed at the head of these formidable hundreds.

2. The preparation they had made for an attack: They came *with lanterns, and torches, and weapons.* If Christ should abscond, though they had moonlight, they would have occasion for their lights. It was folly to light a candle to seek the Sun by. If he should resist, they would have occasion for their arms. *The weapons of his warfare were spiritual,* and at these *weapons* he had often beaten them, therefore they have now recourse to other *weapons, swords and staves.*

III. Our Lord Jesus gloriously repulsed the first onset of the enemy, *v.* 4-6.

1. How he received them.

(1) He met them with a very soft and mild question (*v.* 4): *Knowing all things that should come upon him,* undisturbed and undaunted, he *went forth* to meet them, and softly asked, "*Whom seek you?*" See here, Christ's foresight of his sufferings: he *knew all those things that should come upon him.* We should not covet to know what shall come upon us; it would but anticipate our pain; *sufficient unto the day is the evil thereof:* yet it will do us good to expect sufferings in general. "It is but the cost we sat down and counted upon." Christ's forwardness to his sufferings. When the people would have forced him to a crown, he withdrew, and hid himself (*ch.* vi. 15); but, when they came to force him to a cross, he offered himself; for he came to this world to suffer and went to the other world to reign. This will not warrant us needlessly to expose ourselves to trouble, but we are called to suffering when we have no way to avoid it but by sin.

(2) He met them with a very calm and mild answer when they told him whom they were in quest of, *v.* 5. They said, *Jesus of Nazareth;* and he said, *I am he.* It is highly probable that at least the officers of the temple had often seen him. Judas knew him well enough, and yet none of them could pretend to say, *Thou art the man* we seek. In their enquiries for him they called him *Jesus of Nazareth.* It was a name of reproach given him, to darken the evidence of his being the Messiah. By this it appears that they knew him not, whence he was. He fairly answers them: *I am he.* Though they called him Jesus of Nazareth, he answered to the name, for he despised the reproach; he might have said, *I am not he,* for he was *Jesus of Bethlehem.* He has hereby taught us to own him, whatever it cost us; not to be *ashamed of him or his words.* Particular notice is taken *that Judas stood with them.* He that used to stand with those that followed Christ now stood with those that fought against him. This is mentioned: To show the impudence of Judas. One would wonder where he got the confidence with which he now faced his Master, and *was not ashamed.* To show that Judas was particularly aimed at in the power which went along with that word, *I am he,* to foil the aggressors.

2. See how he terrified them, and obliged them to

JAMIESON, FAUSSET, BROWN

awful interval, between the Supper and the Apprehension—like the "silence in heaven for about the space of half an hour" between the breaking of the Apocalyptic Seals and the peal of the Trumpets of war (Rev. 8:1)—the AGONY—would have been too terrible for the upper room; nor would He cloud the delightful associations of the *last Passover* and the *first Supper* by pouring out the anguish of His soul there. The garden, however, with its amplitude, its shady olives, its endeared associations, would be congenial to His heart. Here He had room enough to retire—first, from eight of them, and then from the more favored three; and here, when that mysterious scene was over, the stillness would only be broken by the tread of the traitor. **3. Judas then**—"He that was called Judas, one of the Twelve," says Luke, in language which brands him with peculiar infamy, as *in* the sacred circle while in no sense *of* it. **a band of men**—"the *detachment* of the Roman cohort on duty at the festival for the purpose of maintaining order" [WEBSTER and WILKINSON]. **officers from the chief priests and Pharisees**—captains of the temple and armed Levites. **lanterns and torches**—It was full moon, but in case He should have secreted Himself somewhere in the dark ravine, they bring the means of exploring its hiding-places—little knowing whom they had to do with. "Now he that betrayed Him had given them a sign, saying, Whomsoever I shall kiss, that same is He, hold Him fast" (Matt. 26:48). The cold-bloodedness of this speech was only exceeded by the deed itself. "And Judas went before them [Luke 22:47], and forthwith he came to Jesus, and said, Hail, Master, and kissed Him" (Matt. 26:49; cf. Exod. 4:27; 18:7; Luke 7:45). The impudence of this atrocious deed shows how thoroughly he had by this time mastered all his scruples. If the dialogue between our Lord and His captors was *before* this, as some interpreters think it was, the kiss of Judas was purely gratuitous, and probably to make good his right to the money; our Lord having presented Himself unexpectedly before them, and rendered it unnecessary for any one to point Him out. But a comparison of the narratives seems to show that our Lord's "coming forth" to the band was *subsequent* to the interview of Judas. "And Jesus said unto him, Friend"—not the endearing term "friend" (in ch. 15:15), but "companion," a word used on occasions of remonstrance or rebuke (as in Matt. 20:13; 22:12)—"Wherefore art thou come?" (Matt. 26:50). "Betrayest thou the Son of man with a kiss"—imprinting upon the foulest act the mark of tenderest affection? What *wounded feeling* does this express! Of this Jesus showed Himself on various occasions keenly susceptible—as all generous and beautiful natures do. **4-9. Jesus . . . , knowing all things that should come**—were coming—**upon him, went forth**—from the shade of the trees, probably, into open view, indicating His sublime preparedness to meet His captors. **Whom seek ye?**—partly to prevent a rush of the soldiery upon the disciples [BENGEL]; and see Mark 14:51, 52, as showing a tendency to this: but still more as part of that courage and majesty which so overawed them. He would not wait to be *taken.*

5. They answered . . . , Jesus of Nazareth—just the sort of blunt, straightforward reply one expects from military men, simply acting on their instructions. **I am He**—(See on ch. 6:20).

Judas . . . stood with them—No more is recorded here of *his* part of the scene, but we have found the gap painfully supplied by all the other Evangelists.

ADAM CLARKE

tion to the priests, they gave him some soldiers and others that he might be the better enabled to seize and bring Him away.

3. *A band.* "The band" or "troop." Some think that the *spira* was the same as the Roman *cohort,* and was the tenth part of a legion, which consisted sometimes of 4,200 and sometimes of 5,000 foot. But Raphelius, on Matt. xxvii. 27, has clearly proved, from Polybius, that the *spira* was no more than a tenth of the fourth part of a legion. And as the number of the legions was uncertain, and their divisions not at all equal, no person can tell how many the band or *spira* contained. This band was probably those Roman soldiers given by the governor for the defense of the Temple, and the *officers* were those who belonged to the Sanhedrin. *With lanterns and torches.* With these they had intended to search the corners and caverns, provided Christ had hidden himself; for they could not have needed them for any other purpose, it being now the fourteenth day of the moon's age, in the month Nisan, and consequently it appeared full and bright. The *weapons* mentioned here were probably no other than clubs, staves, and instruments of that kind, as we may gather from Matt. xxvi. 55; Mark xiv. 48; Luke xxii. 52. The swords mentioned by the other Evangelists were probably those of the Roman soldiers; the clubs and staves belonged to the chief priest's officers.

4. *Jesus therefore, knowing all things.* He had gone through all His preaching, working of miracles, and passion, and had nothing to do now but to offer up himself on the Cross; He therefore went forth to meet them, to deliver himself up to death.

5. *Jesus of Nazareth.* They did not say this till after Judas kissed Christ, which was the sign which he had agreed with the soldiers to give them that they might know whom they were to seize; see Matt. xxvi. 48.

MATTHEW HENRY

retire (*v.* 6): *They went backward, and fell to the ground.* This word, *I am he*, had revived his disciples, and raised them up, but the same word strikes his enemies down. Hereby he showed plainly,

(1) What he could have done with them. When he struck them down, he could have struck them dead. But he would not do so. He would only show that his life was not forced from him, but *he laid it down of himself*, as he had said. He would give an instance of his patience and forbearance and his compassionate love to his very enemies. In striking them down, and no more, he gave them both a call to repent and space to repent.

(2) What he will do at last with all his implacable enemies, *that will not repent to give him glory; they shall flee, they shall fall before him.*

IV. Having given his enemies a repulse, he gives his friends a protection, *v.* 7-9.

1. He continued to expose himself to their rage, *v.* 7. When they were down, one would have thought Christ should have made his escape; when they were up again, one would have thought they should have let fall their pursuit. They are as eager as ever to seize him. They cannot imagine what ailed them, but will impute it to anything rather than Christ's power. There are hearts so very hard in sin that nothing will work upon them to reduce and reclaim them. He is as willing as ever to be seized. When they were fallen before him, he asked them the same question, *Whom seek you?* And they gave him the same answer, *Jesus of Nazareth.* In their repeating the same answer, they showed an obstinacy in their wicked way; they still call him *Jesus of Nazareth*, with as much disdain as ever, and Judas is as unrelenting as any of them.

2. He contrived to secure his disciples from their rage. When he shows his courage with reference to himself, *I have told you that I am he*, he shows his care for his disciples, *Let these go their way.* This aggravated the sin of the disciples in forsaking him, and particularly Peter's in denying him. When Christ said, *Let these go their way*, he intended,

(1) To manifest his affectionate concern for his disciples. When he exposed himself, he excused them, because they were not as yet fit to suffer. It would have been as much as their souls, and the lives of their souls, were worth, to bring them into sufferings now. And, besides, they had other work to do; they must go their way, for they are to go into all the world, to preach the gospel. Christ gives us a great encouragement to follow him. He considers our frame, will wisely time the cross, and proportion it to our strength. He gives us a good example of love to our brethren. We must not consult our own ease and safety only, but others' as well as our own, and in some cases more than our own.

(2) To give a specimen of his undertaking as Mediator. When he offered himself to suffer and die, it was that we might escape.

3. He confirmed the word which he had spoken a little before (*ch.* xvii. 12), *Of those whom thou gavest me, I have lost none.* Though Christ's keeping them was meant especially of the preservation of their souls from sin, yet it is here applied to the preservation of their natural lives. Christ will preserve the natural life for the service to which it is designed. It shall be held in life as long as any use is to be made of it. This preservation of the disciples was a spiritual preservation. They were now so weak in faith and resolution that in all probability, if they had been called out to suffer at this time, some of them, at least the weaker of them, would have been lost; and therefore, that he might *lose none*, he would not expose them.

V. He rebukes the rashness of one of them, and represses the violence of his followers, *v.* 10, 11.

1. Peter's rashness. He had a sword. They had two swords among them all (Luke xxii. 38), and Peter, being entrusted with one, drew it; and *he smote one of the high priest's servants*, and *cut off his right ear. The servant's name*, for the greater certainty of the narrative, is recorded; it *was Malchus.*

(1) We must here acknowledge Peter's goodwill; he had an honest zeal for his Master, though now misguided. He had lately promised to venture his life for him, and would now make his words good.

(2) Yet we must acknowledge Peter's ill conduct; and, though his good intention did excuse, yet it would not justify him. [1] He had no warrant from his Master for what he did. Christ's soldiers must wait the word of command, and not outrun it. [2] He resisted the powers that were, which Christ had never countenanced, but forbidden (Matt. v. 39). [3] He opposed his Master's sufferings. Thus, while he seemed to fight for Christ, he fought against him. [4] He broke the capitulation his Master had lately

JAMIESON, FAUSSET, BROWN

6. As soon then as he said unto them, I am He, they went backward—recoiled. **and fell to the ground**—struck down by a power such as that which smote Saul of Tarsus and his companions to the earth (Acts 26:14). It was the glorious effulgence of the majesty of Christ which overpowered them. "This, occurring before His surrender, would show His *power* over His enemies, and so the *freedom* with which He gave Himself up" [MEYER].

7. Then asked he them again, Whom seek ye?—Giving them a door of escape from the guilt of a deed which *now* they were able in some measure to understand. **Jesus of Nazareth**—The stunning effect of His first answer wearing off, they think only of the necessity of executing their orders.

8. I have told you that I am He: if therefore ye seek me, let these go their way—Wonderful self-possession, and consideration for others, in such circumstances!

9. That the saying might be fulfilled which he spake, Of them which thou gavest me have I lost none—The reference is to such sayings as ch. 6:39; 17:12; showing how conscious the Evangelist was, that in reporting his Lord's former sayings, he was giving them not in *substance* merely, but in *form* also. Observe, also, how the preservation of the disciples on this occasion is viewed as part that *deeper preservation* undoubtedly intended in the saying quoted.

10, 11. Then Simon Peter, having a sword, drew it, and smote the high priest's servant, and cut off his right ear. The servant's name was Malchus—None of the other Evangelists mention the name either of the ardent disciple or of his victim. John being "known to the high priest" (vs. 15), the mention of the servant's name by *him* is quite natural, and an interesting mark of truth in a small matter. As to the *right* ear, specified both here and in Luke, the man was "likely foremost of those who advanced to seize Jesus, and presented himself in the attitude of a combatant; hence his right side would be exposed to attack. The blow of Peter was evidently aimed vertically at his head" [WESTER and WILKINSON].

ADAM CLARKE

6. *They went backward, and fell to the ground.* None of the other Evangelists mentions this very important circumstance. Our Lord chose to give them this proof of His infinite power that they might know that their power could not prevail against Him if He chose to exert His might, seeing that the very breath of His mouth confounded, drove back, and struck them down to the earth. Thus by the blast of God they might have perished, and by the breath of His nostrils they might have been consumed, Job. iv. 9.

8. *Let these go their way.* These words are rather words of authority than words of entreaty. I voluntarily give myself up to you, but you must not molest one of these My disciples.

10. *Having a sword.* See the note on Luke xxii. 36. *Cut off his right ear.* He probably designed to have cut his skull in two, but God turned it aside, and only permitted the ear to be taken off; and this He would not have suffered, but only that He might have the opportunity of giving them a most striking proof of His divinity in working an astonishing miracle on the occasion. See the notes on Matt. xxvi. 51-56. The other three Evangelists mention this transaction; but neither gives the name of Peter nor of Malchus, probably because both persons were alive when they wrote; but it is likely both had been long dead before John published his history.

MATTHEW HENRY

made with the enemy. When he said, *Let these go their way*, he in effect passed his word for their good behaviour; this Peter heard, and yet would not be bound by it. [5] He foolishly exposed himself and his fellow disciples to the fury of this enraged multitude. Many have been guilty of self-destruction, in their zeal for self-preservation. [6] Peter played the coward so soon after this (denying his Master) that we have reason to think his courage failed him; whereas the true Christian hero will appear in the cause of Christ, not only when it is prevailing, but when it seems to be declining; will be on the right side, though it be not the rising side.

(3) We must acknowledge God's overruling providence in giving Christ an opportunity to manifest his power and goodness in healing the hurt, Luke xxii. 51.

2. The rebuke his Master gave him (*v.* 11): *Put up thy sword into the sheath*. It is a gentle reproof, because it was his zeal that carried him beyond the bounds of discretion. Many think their being in grief and distress will excuse them if they be hot and hasty with those about them; but Christ has here set us an example of meekness in sufferings.

3. The reason for this rebuke: *The cup which my Father has given me, shall I not drink it?* Christ gives us, (1) A full proof of his own submission to his Father's will. Of all that was amiss in what Peter did, he seems to resent nothing so much as that he would have hindered his sufferings now that his *hour was come*. He was willing to drink of this cup, though it was a bitter cup. He drank it, that he might put into our hands the cup of salvation. He is willing to drink it, because *his Father put it into his hand*. (2) A fair pattern to us of submission to God's will. We must *pledge* Christ in the cup that he drank of (Matt. xx. 23). It is but a *cup*; a small matter comparatively. It is a cup that is given us; sufferings are gifts. It is given us by a Father, who has a Father's affection, and means us no hurt.

VI. He calmly surrendered, and yielded himself a prisoner, not because he could not have made his escape, but because he would not.

1. How they seized him: *They took Jesus*. Only some few of them could lay hands on him, but it is charged upon them all, for they were all aiding and abetting. In treason there are no accessories; all are principals. They had so often been frustrated in their attempts to seize him that now we may suppose they flew upon him with so much the more violence.

2. How they secured him: *They bound him*. This particular of his sufferings is taken notice of only by this evangelist, that, as soon as ever he was taken, he was bound, pinioned, handcuffed.

(1) This shows the spite of his persecutors. They bound him, that they might torment him, and put him in pain; that they might disgrace him, and put him to shame; that they might prevent his escape. They bound him as one already condemned, for they were resolved to prosecute him to the death. Christ had bound the consciences of his persecutors with the power of his word, which galled them; and, to be revenged on him, they laid these bonds on him.

(2) Christ's being bound was very significant. Before they bound him, he had bound himself to the work and office of a Mediator. He was already bound to the horns of the altar with the cords of his own love to man, and duty to his Father. Guilt is a bond on the soul, by which we are bound over to the judgment of God; corruption is a bond on the soul, by which we are bound under the power of Satan. Christ, to free us from those bonds, himself submitted to be bound for us. To his bonds we owe our liberty. Thus the Son maketh us free. Christ was bound, that he might bind us to duty and obedience. His bonds for us are bonds upon us, by which we are for ever obliged to love him and serve him. Christ's bonds for us were designed to make our bonds for him easy to us, to sanctify and sweeten them; these enabled Paul and Silas to sing in the stocks.

Verses 13–27

We have here an account of Christ's arraignment before the high priest, and some circumstances that occurred therein which were omitted by the other evangelists. Peter's denying him, of which the other evangelists had given the entire story by itself, is interwoven with the other passages. The crime laid to his charge having relation to religion, the judges of the spiritual court took it to fall directly under their cognizance. Both Jews and Gentiles seized him, and so both Jews and Gentiles tried and condemned him, for he died for the sins of both.

I. Having seized him, they *led him away to Annas first*, *v.* 13. 1. They *led him away*, led him in triumph, as a trophy of their victory. They hurried him away

JAMIESON, FAUSSET, BROWN

11. Then said Jesus—"Suffer ye thus far" (Luke 22:51). **Put up thy sword into the sheath: the cup which my Father hath given me, shall I not drink it?**—This expresses *both the feelings* which struggled in the Lord's breast during the Agony in the garden—*aversion to the cup* viewed *in itself*, but, *in the light of the Father's will*, perfect *preparedness to drink it*. (See on Luke 22:39-46.) Matthew adds to the address to Peter the following:—"For all they that take the sword shall perish by the sword" (Matt. 26:52)—i.e., 'Those who take the sword must run all the risks of human warfare; but Mine is a warfare whose weapons, as they are not carnal, are attended with no such hazards, but carry certain victory.' "Thinkest thou that I cannot now"—even after things have proceeded so far—"pray to My Father, and He shall presently give Me"—rather, 'place at My disposal'—"more than twelve legions of angels"; with allusion, possibly, to the one angel who had, in His agony, "appeared to Him from heaven strengthening Him" (Luke 22:43); and in the precise number, alluding to the *twelve* who needed the help, Himself and His eleven disciples. (The full complement of a legion of Roman soldiers was six thousand.) "But how then shall the scripture be fulfilled that thus it must be?" (Matt. 26:53, 54.) He could not suffer, according to the Scripture, if He allowed Himself to be delivered from the predicted death. "And He touched his ear and healed him" (Luke 22:51); for "the Son of man came not to destroy men's lives, but to save them" (Luke 9. 56), and, even while they were destroying His, to save theirs. **12. Then the band . . . took Jesus**—but not till He had made them feel that "no man took His life from Him, but that He laid it down of Himself."

13. And led him away—"In that hour," says Matthew (26:55, 56), and probably now, on the way to judgment. when the crowds were press-

ADAM CLARKE

11. *The cup which my Father hath given me.* The cup sometimes signifies the lot of life, whether prosperous or adverse: here it signifies the final sufferings of Christ.

12. *The captain.* The *chiliarch*, or "chief over one thousand men." He was probably the prefect, or captain, of the Temple guard.

G. CAMPBELL MORGAN:

"Then they bound him." I never read it without laughing. Yes they bound Him, and see how many it took to do it: the band, and the council, and the chief captain (he is specially named), and all the police. They rushed at Him, and they bound Him. *They* bound *Him*? They thought they bound Him. What did bind Him? Love for me! Love for you! That was what bound Him; not the hempen cords of those foolish men, but the eternal cords of the Divine Love.

Still they bound Him, and they took Him to Annas. John only gives an account of the arraignment of Jesus before Annas, which was quite a preliminary matter. He tells us in the twenty-fourth verse that Annas bound Him again, and sent Him to Caiaphas. John omits entirely the account of our Lord's examination before Caiaphas and the Sanhedrin, recorded by Matthew and Mark. At verse twenty-eight we read, "They led Jesus therefore from Caiaphas into the palace." Thus omitting the appearing before Caiaphas, and the Sanhedrin, John gives the story of the preliminary arraignment of Jesus.—*The Gospel According to John*

MATTHEW HENRY

with violence, as if he had been the worst and vilest of malefactors. We had been led away of our own impetuous lusts, and led captive by Satan at his will, and, that we might be rescued, Christ was led away, led captive by Satan's agents and instruments. 2. They led him away to their masters that sent them. It was now about midnight, and one would think they should have put him in ward till it was a proper time to call a court; but he is hurried away immediately, not to the justices of peace, to be committed, but to the judges to be condemned; so extremely violent was the prosecution. 3. They led him to Annas first. Probably his house lay in the way. To gratify him therefore with the assurance of their success, they produce their prisoner before him. Christ, the great sacrifice, was presented to him, and sent away bound, as approved and ready for the altar. This Annas was father-in-law to Caiaphas the high priest. Acquaintance and alliance with wicked people are a great confirmation to many in their wicked ways.

II. Annas being as willing as any of them to have the prosecution pushed on, sent him bound to Caiaphas.

1. The power of Caiaphas intimated (*v.* 13). He was *high priest that same year.* The high priest's commission was during life; but there were now such frequent changes that it was become almost an annual office. While they were undermining one another, God was overturning them all. Caiaphas was high priest that same year when Messiah was to be cut off. When a bad thing was to be done by a high priest, Providence so ordered it that a bad man should be in the chair to do it. It was the ruin of Caiaphas that he was high priest that year, and so became a ringleader in the putting of Christ to death. Many a man's advancement has lost him his reputation, and he had not been dishonoured if he had not been preferred.

2. The malice of Caiaphas, which is intimated (*v.* 14) by the repeating of what he had said some time before, that *it was expedient that one man should die for the people.* This was that Caiaphas that governed himself and the church by rules of policy, in defiance of the rules of equity. His case was adjudged before it was heard, and they were already resolved what to do with him; *he must die;* so that his trial was a jest. It is a testimony to the innocence of our Lord Jesus, from the mouth of one of his worst enemies, who owned that he fell a sacrifice to the public good, and that it was not just he should die, but *expedient* only.

3. The concurrence of Annas in the prosecution of Christ. He made himself a partaker in guilt, (1) With the captain and officers, by continuing him bound when he should have loosed him. It was more excusable in the rude soldiers to bind him than in Annas, who should have known better, to continue him bound. (2) With the chief priest and council. This Annas was not present with them, yet thus he became a *partaker of their evil deeds.*

III. In the house of Caiaphas, Simon Peter began to deny his Master, *v.* 15-18.

1. It was with much ado that Peter got into the hall where the court was sitting, an account of which we have, *v.* 15, 16.

(1) Peter's kindness to Christ, which (though it proved no kindness) appeared in two things: [1] That he *followed Jesus* when he was *led away;* though at first he fled with the rest, yet afterwards he took heart a little, and followed at some distance, calling to mind the promises he had made to adhere to him, whatever it should cost him. Those that truly love and value Christ will follow him all weathers and all ways. [2] When he could not get in where Jesus was in the midst of his enemies, he *stood at the door without,* willing to be as near him as he could, and waiting for an opportunity to get nearer. As it proved, he did but run himself into a snare. Christ, who knew him better than he knew himself, had expressly told him (*ch.* xiii. 36), *Whither I go thou canst not follow me now,* and had told him again and again that he would deny him; and he had lately had experience of his own weakness in forsaking him. (2) The other disciple's kindness to Peter, which yet, as it proved, was no kindness either. St. John several times in this gospel speaking of himself as another disciple, many interpreters have been led by this to fancy that this other disciple here was John. But I see no reason to think that this other disciple was John, or one of the twelve; other sheep Christ had, which were not of the fold. As there are many who seem disciples and are not so, so there are many who are disciples and seem not so. There are good people hid in courts, even in Nero's, as well as hid in crowds. This other disciple showed a respect to Peter, in introducing him, not only to gratify

JAMIESON, FAUSSET, BROWN

ing upon Him, "said Jesus to the multitudes, Are ye come out as against a thief, with swords and staves, for to take Me"—expressive of the indignity which He felt to be thus done to Him—"I sat daily with you in the temple, and ye laid no hold on Me. But this" (adds Luke 22:53) "is your hour and the power of darkness." Matthew continues—"But all this was done that the scriptures of the prophets might be fulfilled. Then all the disciples forsook Him and fled" (Matt. 26:56)—thus fulfilling His prediction (Mark 14:27; ch. 16:32).

13-27. JESUS BEFORE ANNAS AND CAIAPHAS—FALL OF PETER. **13, 14. And led him away to Annas first**—(See on Luke 3:2, and on Matt. 26:57).

Jesus Is Brought Privately before Annas, the Father-in-Law of Caiaphas (John 18:13, 14). 13. "And they led Him away to Annas first; for he was father-in-law to Caiaphas, which was the high priest that same year." This successful Annas, as ELLICOT remarks, was appointed high priest by Quirinus, A.D. 12, and after holding the office for several years, was deposed by Valerius Gratius, Pilate's predecessor in the procuratorship of Judea [JOSEPHUS, *Antiquities,* xviii. 2. 1, etc.]. He appears, however, to have possessed vast influence, having obtained the high priesthood, not only for his son Eleazar, and his son-in-law Caiaphas, but subsequently for four other sons, under the last of whom James, the brother of our Lord, was put to death (*ibid* xx. 9. 1). It is thus highly probable that, besides having the title of "high priest" merely as one who had filled the office, he to a great degree retained the powers he had formerly exercised, and came to be regarded practically as a kind of rightful high priest. 14. "Now Caiaphas was he which gave counsel to the Jews, that it was expedient that one man should die for the people." See on John 11:50. What passed between Annas and our Lord during this interval the beloved disciple reserves till he has related the beginning of Peter's fall. To this, then, as recorded by our own Evangelist, let us meanwhile listen.

15-18. Simon Peter followed Jesus—Natural though this was, and safe enough, had he only "watched and prayed that he enter not into temptation," as his Master bade him (Matt. 26:41), it was, in his case, a fatal step.

and . . . another disciple—Rather, the other disciple"—our Evangelist himself, no doubt. **known unto the high priest**—(See on vs. 10). **went in with Jesus into the palace of the high priest. 16. But Peter stood at the door without**—by preconcerted arrangement with his friend till he should get access for him. **Then went out that other . . . and spake to her that kept the door, and brought in Peter**—The *naturalness* of these small details is not unworthy of notice. This other disciple first made good his own entrance on the score of acquaintance with the high priest; this secured, he goes forth again, now as a privi-

ADAM CLARKE

13. *To Annas.* This man must have had great authority in his nation: (1) Because he had been a long time high priest; (2) Because he had no less than five sons who successively enjoyed the dignity of the high priesthood; and (3) Because his son-in-law Caiaphas was at this time in possession of that office. It is likely that Annas was chief of the Sanhedrin and that it was to him in that office that Christ was first brought. *That same year.* The office was now no longer during life as formerly. See the note on chap. xi. 49. What is related in the twenty-fourth verse, "Now Annas had sent him bound unto Caiaphas," comes properly in after the thirteenth verse. See the margin.

14. *Caiaphas was he, which gave counsel.* Therefore he was an improper person to sit in judgment on Christ, whom He had prejudged and precondemned; see on chap. xi. 50-52. But Christ must not be treated according to the rules of justice; if He had, He could not have been put to death.

15. *And . . . another disciple.* There are many conjectures who this disciple was. Jerome, Chrysostom, Theophylact, Nonnus, Lyra, Erasmus, Piscator, and others say it was John. It is true John frequently mentions himself in the third person; but then he has always "whom Jesus loved," as in chap. xiii. 23; xix. 26; xxi. 7, 20, except in chap. xix. 35, where he has plainly pointed out himself as writer of this Gospel. But in the place before us he has mentioned no circumstance by which that disciple may be known to be John. To this may be added that John being not only a Galilean, but a fisherman

MATTHEW HENRY

affection, but to give him an opportunity of being serviceable to his Master upon his trial. But this kindness proved no kindness, nay a great diskindness; by letting him into the high priest's hall, he let him into temptation, and the consequence was bad.

2. Peter, having got in, was immediately assaulted with the temptation, *v.* 17.

(1) How slight the attack was. It was but a silly maid, of so small account that she was set to keep the door, that challenged him, and she only asked him carelessly, *Art not thou one of this man's disciples?* Peter would have had some reason to take the alarm if Malchus had set upon him, and had said, "This is he that cut off my ear, and I will have his head for it."

(2) How speedy the surrender was. Without taking time to recollect himself, he suddenly answered, *I am not.* All his care being for his own safety, he thought he could not secure this but by a peremptory denial.

(3) Yet he goes further into the temptation: *And the servants and officers stood there, and Peter with them, v.* 18.

[1] See how the servants made much of themselves; the night being cold, they made a fire in the hall. They cared not what became of Christ; all their care was to sit and warm themselves.

[2] See how Peter herded himself with them. *He sat and warmed himself.* It was a fault bad enough that he did not attend his Master, and appear for him at the upper end of the hall. He might have been a witness for him, at least, he might have been a witness to him. He might have learned by his Master's example how to carry himself when it should come to his turn to suffer thus; yet neither his conscience nor his curiosity could bring him into the court. It was much worse that he joined himself with those that were his Master's enemies: *He stood with them, and warmed himself.* A little thing will draw those into bad company that will be drawn to it by the love of a good fire. If Peter's zeal for his Master had not frozen, but had continued in the heat it seemed to be of but a few hours before, he had not had occasion to warm himself now. Peter was much to be blamed, 1. Because he associated with these wicked men. Doubtless they were diverting themselves with this night's expedition, scoffing at Christ; and what sort of entertainment would this give to Peter? If Peter had not so much courage as to appear publicly for his Master, yet he might have had so much devotion as to retire into a corner, and weep in secret for his Master's sufferings, and his own sin in forsaking him. 2. Because he desired to be thought *one of them.* Is this Peter? It is ill warming ourselves with those with whom we are in danger of burning ourselves.

IV. Peter, Christ's friend, having begun to deny him, the high priest, his enemy, begins to accuse him, *v.* 19-21. It should seem, the first attempt was to prove him a teacher of false doctrine, which this evangelist relates; and, when they failed in the proof of this, then they charged him with blasphemy, which is related by the other evangelists.

1. The articles or heads upon which Christ was examined (*v.* 19): concerning *his disciples and his doctrine.*

(1) The irregularity of the process; it was against all law and equity. Now that he is their prisoner they have nothing to *lay to his charge.* Against all reason and justice, he is put on to be his own accuser.

(2) The intention. The *high priest then* examined him upon those interrogatories which would touch his life. [1] Concerning his disciples, that he might charge him with sedition. Some think his question concerning his disciples was, "What is now become of them all? Why do they not appear?" upbraiding him with their cowardice in deserting him, and thus adding to the affliction of it. [2] Concerning his doctrine, that they might charge him with heresy. This was a matter properly cognizable in that court, therefore a prophet could not perish but at Jerusalem, where that court sat. They said nothing to him concerning his miracles, by which he had done so much good, because of these they were sure they could take no hold.

2. The appeal Christ made, in answer to these interrogatories. As to his disciples, he said nothing, because it was an impertinent question. His having disciples was no more than what was practised and allowed by their own doctors. If Caiaphas designed to ensnare them, it was in kindness to them that Christ said nothing of them, for he had said, *Let these go their way.* If he meant to upbraid him with their cowardice, no wonder that he said nothing. He would say nothing to condemn them, and could say nothing to justify them. As to his doctrine, he said nothing in particular, but in general referred himself to those that heard him, *v.* 20, 21.

[1] He tacitly charges his judges with illegal pro-

JAMIESON, FAUSSET, BROWN

leged person, to make interest for Peter's admission. But thus our poor disciple is in the coils of the serpent.

17. Then saith the damsel that kept the door—"one of the maids of the high priest," says Mark (14:66). "When she saw Peter warming himself, she looked upon him and said" (Mark 14:67). Luke is more graphic (22:56)—She "beheld him as he sat by the fire (lit., 'the light'), and earnestly looked on him (fixed her gaze upon him), and said." "His demeanor and timidity, which must have vividly showed themselves, as it so generally happens, leading to the recognition of him" [OLSHAUSEN]. **Art thou not also one of this man's disciples?**—i.e., thou as well as "that other disciple," whom she knew to be one, but did not challenge, perceiving that he was a privileged person. **He saith, I am not**—"He denied before them all, saying, I know not what thou sayest" (Matt. 26:70)—a common form of point-blank denial; "I know [supply 'Him'] not, neither understand I what thou sayest" (Mark 14:68); "Woman, I know Him not" (Luke 22:57). This was THE FIRST DENIAL. "And he went out into the porch [thinking, perhaps, to steal away], *and the cock crew,*" (Mark 14:68).

18. And the servants and officers—the menials and some of the "band" that "took Jesus." **stood there, who had made**—'having made'—**a fire of coals, for it was cold, and they warmed themselves**—"John alone notices the material (charcoal) of which the fire was made, and the reason for a fire—the coldness of the night" [WEBSTER and WILKINSON]. "Peter went in and sat with the servants to see the end (Matt. 26:58), and warmed himself at the fire" (Mark 14:54). These two statements are extremely interesting. His wishing to "see the end," or issue of these proceedings, was what led him into the palace, for he evidently feared the worst. But once in, the serpent coil is drawn closer; it is a cold night, and why should not he take advantage of the fire as well as others? Besides, in the talk of the crowd about the all-engrossing topic, he may pick up something which he would like to hear. "And as Peter was beneath in the palace" (Mark 14:66). Matthew (26:69) says, "sat *without* in the palace." According to Oriental architecture, and especially in large buildings, as here, the street door—or heavy folding gate through which single persons entered by a wicket kept by a porter—opened by a passage or "porch" (Mark 14:68) into a quadrangular *court,* here called the "palace" or *hall,* which was *open above,* and is frequently *paved* with flagstones. In the center of this court the "fire" would be kindled (in a brazier). At the upper end of it, probably, was the chamber in which the trial was held, *open to the court* and *not far from the fire* (Luke 22:61), but on a higher level; for Mark says the court was "*beneath*" it. The ascent was, perhaps, by a short flight of steps. This explanation will make the intensely interesting details more intelligible.

19-21. The high priest . . . asked Jesus of his disciples, and of his doctrine—probably to entrap Him into some statements which might be used against Him at the trial. From our Lord's answer it would seem that "His disciples" were understood to be some secret party.

ADAM CLARKE

by trade, it is not likely that he should have been known to the high priest, as it is here said of that disciple who followed Jesus with Peter. The conjecture of Grotius is the most likely, viz., that it was the person at whose house Jesus had supped. Augustine, *Tract* 113, speaks like a man of sound sense: We should not decide hastily, says he, on a subject concerning which the Scripture is silent.

18. *Servants and officers.* These belonged to the chief priests; the Roman soldiers had probably been dismissed after having conducted Christ to Annas.

F. B. MEYER:

Fear undermines loyalty. Apparently a preliminary and private examination was held while the Sanhedrin was being hastily summoned. The other disciple was evidently John. It was a mistake for Peter to throw himself into such a vortex of trial. His foolhardiness and curiosity led him thither. While the Master was before one bar, Peter stood at another, but how egregiously he failed! In spite of his brave talk, he was swept off his feet—as we shall be unless we have learned to avail ourselves of that power which is made perfect only in weakness. Peter's fall was due to his self-confidence and lack of prayer. Those who are weak should beware of exposing themselves in places and company where they are liable to fail. Do not warm yourself at the world's fires.

Three lessons emerge from Peter's failure: (1) Let us not sleep through the precious moments which heaven affords before each hour of trial, but use them for putting on the whole armor of God that we may be able to stand in the evil day. (2) Let us not vaunt our own strength. We need more than resolution to sustain us in the hour of conflict. (3) Let us not cast ourselves down from the mountainside unless absolutely sure that God bids us to do so. He will not otherwise give his angels charge to keep us.—*Bible Commentary*

19. *Asked Jesus of his disciples, and of hi doctrine.* He probably asked Him by what au thority, or in virtue of what right, He collecte disciples, formed a different sect, preached a nev doctrine, and set himself up for a public Re former? As religion was interested in thes things, the high priest was considered as bein the proper judge. But all this, with what fol lows, was transacted by night, and this wa contrary to established laws. For the *Talmu* states that "criminal processes can neither com mence nor terminate, but during the course o the day. If the person be acquitted, the sentenc

MATTHEW HENRY

ceedings. He appeals to the settled rules of their own court, whether they dealt fairly by him. *Why ask you me?* Which implies two absurdities in judgment: *First,* "*Why ask you me now* concerning my doctrine, when you have already condemned it?" They had made an order of court for excommunicating all that owned him (*ch.* ix. 22), and now they come to ask what his doctrine is! *Secondly,* "*Why ask you me?* Must I accuse myself?"

[2] He insists upon his fair and open dealing with them in the publication of his doctrine. Christ clears himself very fully. *First,* As to the manner of his preaching. He spoke openly *with freedom and plainness of speech.* Christ explained himself fully, with, *Verily, verily, I say unto you. Secondly,* As to the persons he preached to: *He spoke to the world,* to all that had *ears to hear,* and were willing to hear him, high or low, learned or unlearned, Jew or Gentile, friend or foe. *Thirdly,* As to the places he preached in. When he was in the country, he preached ordinarily in the synagogues; when he came up to Jerusalem, he preached the same doctrine in the temple. Though he often preached in private houses, and on mountains, and by the seaside, yet what he preached in private was the very same with what he delivered publicly. The doctrine of Christ needs not be ashamed to appear in the most numerous assembly, for it carries its own strength and beauty along with it. *Fourthly,* As to the doctrine itself. *In secret have I said nothing.* He sought no corners, for he feared no colours, nor said anything that he needed to be ashamed of; what he did speak in private to his disciples he ordered them to proclaim on the house-tops, Matt. x. 27.

[3] He appeals to those that had heard him, and desires that they might be examined: "*Ask those that heard me what I said unto them.*" He means not his friends and followers, who might be presumed to speak in his favour, but, Ask any impartial hearer. The doctrine of Christ may safely appeal to all that know it. Those who will judge impartially cannot but witness to it.

V. While the judges were examining him, the servants that stood by were abusing him, *v.* 22, 23.

1. It was a base affront which one of the officers gave him; this insolent fellow *struck him with the palm of his hand,* saying, *Answerest thou the high priest so?*

(1) He *struck him—he gave him a blow.* It was unjust to strike one that neither said nor did amiss; it was cowardly to strike one that had his hands tied; and barbarous to strike a prisoner at the bar. Here was a breach of the peace in the face of the court, and yet the judges countenanced it.

(2) He checked him in a haughty imperious manner: *Answerest thou the high priest so?* As if the blessed Jesus were not good enough to speak to his master, but, like a rude and ignorant prisoner, must be controlled by the jailer, and taught how to behave. It was done to please the high priest, and to curry favour with him; for what he said implied a jealousy for the dignity of the high priest. Wicked rulers will not want wicked servants, who will *help forward the affliction* of those whom their masters persecute.

2. Christ bore this affront with wonderful meekness and patience (*v.* 23): "*If I have spoken evil, bear witness of the evil.* But if well, *why smitest thou me?*" Christ did not here *turn the other cheek,* by which it appears that that rule, Matt. v. 39, is not to be understood literally. Comparing Christ's precept with his pattern, we learn that in such cases we must not be our own avengers, nor judges in our own cause. Our resentment of injuries done us must always be rational, and never passionate; such Christ's here was.

VI. While the servants were thus abusing him, Peter was proceeding to deny him, *v.* 25-27.

1. He repeated the sin the second time, *v.* 25. While he was warming himself with the servants, they asked him, *Art not thou one of his disciples?* He, perhaps, fearing he should be seized, if he should own it, flatly denied it, and said, *I am not.*

(1) It was his great folly to thrust himself into the temptation, by continuing in the company. He stayed to warm himself; but those that warm themselves with evil doers grow cold towards good people and good things, and those that are fond of the devil's fire-side are in danger of the devil's fire.

(2) It was his great unhappiness that he was again assaulted by the temptation. [1] The subtlety of the tempter in running down one whom he saw falling; not a maid now, but all the servants. Yielding to one temptation invites another, and perhaps a stronger. Satan redoubles his attacks when we give ground. [2] The danger of bad company. We commonly study to approve ourselves to those with whom we choose to associate. As we choose our people we choose our praise; we are therefore concerned to make the first choice well.

JAMIESON, FAUSSET, BROWN

20. I spake—have spoken—**openly to the world**—See ch. 7:4. **I ever taught in the synagogues and in the temple, whither the Jews always resort**—courting publicity, though with sublime noiselessness. **in secret have I said**—spake I—**nothing**—i.e., nothing of any different nature; all His private communications with the Twelve being but explanations and developments of His public teaching. (Cf. Isa. 45:19; 48:16). **21. Why askest thou me? ask them which heard me . . . they know what I . . . said**—This seems to imply that He saw the attempt to draw Him into selfcrimination, and resented it by falling back upon the right of every accused party to have some charge laid against Him by competent witnesses.

22. struck Jesus with the palm . . . Answerest Thou the high priest so—(See Isa. 50:6; and cf. Acts 23:2).

23. If I have spoken . . .—'if I spoke' evil, in reply to the high priest. **if well**—He does not say "If *not*" *evil,* as if His reply were merely unobjectionable: "*well*" seems to challenge more than this as due to His remonstrance [BENGEL]. This shows that Matthew 5:39 is not to be taken to the letter. **24-27. Now Annas had sent him bound unto Caiaphas**—Our translators so render the words, understanding that the foregoing interview took place before *Caiaphas;* Annas, declining to meddle with the case, having sent Him to Caiaphas *at once.* But the words here literally are, "Annas sent Him [not '*had* sent Him] to Caiaphas"—and the "now" being of doubtful authority. Thus read, the verse affords no evidence that He was sent to Caiaphas *before* the interview just recorded, but implies rather the contrary. We take this interview, then, with some of the ablest interpreters, to be a preliminary and non-official one with *Annas,* at an hour of the night when Caiaphas' Council could not convene; and one that ought not to be confounded with that solemn one recorded by the other Evangelists, when all were assembled and witnesses called. But *the building in which both met with Jesus appears to have been the same, the room only being different, and the court, of course, in that case, one.* **25. And Simon Peter was standing and warming himself. They said therefore . . . , Art thou not also one of his disciples?**—In Matthew 26:71 the *second* charge was made by "another maid, when he was gone out into the porch," who "saw him, and said unto them that were there, This [fellow] was also with Jesus of

ADAM CLARKE

may be pronounced during that day; but, if he be condemned, the sentence cannot be pronounced till the next day. But no kind of judgment is to be executed, either on the eve of the Sabbath, or the eve of any festival." Nevertheless, to the lasting infamy of this people, Christ was judicially interrogated and condemned during the night; and on the night, too, of the Passover, or, according to others, on the eve of that feast. Thus all the forms of justice were insulted and outraged in the case of our Lord. In this "his humiliation his judgment was taken away," Acts viii. 33.

20. *I spake openly to the world.* To every person in the land indiscriminately—to the people at large. This is another proof that John uses the term *world* to mean the Jewish people only, for it is certain our Lord did not preach to the Gentiles. The answer of our Lord, mentioned in this and the following verse, is such as became a Person conscious of His own innocence and confident in the righteousness of His cause. I have taught in the Temple, in the synagogues, in all the principal cities, towns, and villages, and through all the country. I have had no secret school. You and your emissaries have watched Me everywhere. No doctrine has ever proceeded from My lips but what was agreeable to the righteousness of the law and the purity of God. Ask those who have attended our public ministrations and hear whether they can prove that I or My disciples have preached any false doctrines, have ever troubled society, or disturbed the state. Attend to the ordinary course of justice, call witnesses, let them make their depositions, and then proceed to judge according to the evidence brought before you.

22. *One of the officers . . . struck Jesus.* This was an outrage to all justice. For a prisoner, before he is condemned, is ever considered to be under the especial protection of justice; nor has anyone a right to touch him but according to the direction of the law. But it has been observed before that if justice had been done to Christ He could have neither suffered nor died.

24. *Now Annas had sent him.* It has been observed before that the proper place of this verse is immediately after the thirteenth; and if it be allowed to stand here it should be read in a parenthesis and considered as a recapitulation of what had been done before.

MATTHEW HENRY

(3) It was his great weakness to yield to the temptation, and to say, *I am not one* of his disciples, as one ashamed of that which was his honour. When Christ was admired and treated with respect, Peter prided himself, in this, that he was a disciple of Christ. Thus many who seem fond of the reputation of religion when it is in fashion are ashamed of the reproach of it.

2. He repeated the sin the third time, *v.* 26, 27. Here he was attacked by one of the servants, who was kinsman to Malchus, who gave him the lie with great assurance: "*Did not I see thee in the garden with him?*" Peter then denied again.

(1) Before his relation to Christ was only suspected, here it is proved upon him by one that saw him with Jesus. Those who by sin think to help themselves out of trouble do but entangle and embarrass themselves the more. Dare to be brave, for truth will out. Notice is taken of this servant's being akin to Malchus, because this circumstance would make it the more a terror to Peter. We should not make any man in particular our enemy if we can help it. He that may need a friend should not make a foe. Though here was sufficient evidence against Peter to have prosecuted him, yet he escapes, has no harm done him. We are often drawn into sin by groundless causeless fears, which a small degree of wisdom and resolution would make nothing of.

(2) His yielding to it was no less base than the former: *He denied again.* The nature of sin in general: *the heart is hardened by the deceitfulness of it,* Heb. iii. 13. *The beginning of sin is as the letting forth of water,* when once the fence is broken men easily go from bad to worse. Of the sin of lying in particular; it is a fruitful sin; one lie needs another to support it, and that another.

(3) *Immediately the cock crew;* and this is all that is here said of his repentance, it being recorded by the other evangelists. The crowing of the cock to others was an accidental thing, and had no significancy, but to Peter it was the voice of God.

Verses 28–40

We have here an account of Christ's arraignment before Pilate, the Roman governor, in the praetor's house, or *hall of judgment*; thither they hurried him, to get him condemned in the Roman court, and executed by the Roman power. They took this course, 1. That he might be put to death the more legally and regularly; not stoned in a popular tumult, as Stephen, but put to death with the present formalities of justice. 2. That he might be put to death the more safely. If they could engage the Roman government in the matter, there would be little danger of an uproar. 3. That he might be put to death with more reproach to himself. *The death of the cross,* being of all deaths the most ignominious, they were desirous by it to put an indelible mark of infamy upon him. This therefore they harped upon, *Crucify him.* 4. That he might be put to death with less reproach to them. It was an invidious thing to put one to death that had done so much good, and therefore they were willing to throw the odium upon the Roman government. Thus many are more afraid of the scandal of a bad action than of the sin of it. (1) Their industry in the prosecution: *It was early,* when most people were in their beds. Now that they had him in their hands, they would lose no time till they had him upon the cross. (2) Their superstition and vile hypocrisy: *The chief priests and elders went not into the judgment-hall lest they should be defiled,* but kept out of doors, *that they might eat the passover,* and therefore would not go into the court, for fear of touching a Gentile, and thereby contracting, not a legal, but only a traditional pollution. This they scrupled, but made no scruple of breaking through all the laws of equity to persecute Christ to the death.

I. Pilate's conference with the prosecutors. They were called first, and stated what they had to say against the prisoner, *v.* 29–32.

1. The judge calls for the indictment. Because they would not come into the hall, *he went out to them.* Here are three things commendable in him: (1) His diligent and close application to business. Men in public trusts must not love their ease. (2) His condescending to the humour of the people. He might have said, "If they be so nice as not to come in to me, let them go home as they came"; but Pilate insists not upon it, and goes out to them. (3) His adherence to the rule of justice, in demanding the accusation: "*What accusation bring you against this man?* What is the crime you charge him with, and what proof have you of it?"

2. The prosecutors demand judgment against him upon a general surmise that he was a criminal (*v.* 30): *If he were not a malefactor we would not have de-*

JAMIESON, FAUSSET, BROWN

Nazareth." So also Mark 14:69. But in Luke 22:58 it is said, "After a little while" (from the time of the first denial), "another [*man*] saw him, and said, Thou art also of them." Possibly it was thrown at him by more than one; but these circumstantial variations only confirm the truth of the narrative. **He denied it, and said, I am not**—in Matthew 26:72, "He denied *with an oath,* I do not know the man." This was THE SECOND DENIAL. **26. One of the servants of the high priest, being his kinsman, whose ear Peter cut off, saith, Did not I see thee in the garden with him**—No doubt his relationship to Malchus drew attention to the man who smote him, and this enabled him to identify Peter. "Sad reprisals!" [BENGEL]. The other Evangelists make his detection to turn upon his *dialect.* "After a while ['about the space of one hour after,' Luke 22:59] came unto him they that stood by and said to Peter, Surely thou also art one of them, for thy speech betrayeth thee" (Matt. 26: 73). "Thou art a Galilean, and thy speech agreeth thereto" (Mark 14:70; and so Luke 22:59). The Galilean dialect had a more *Syrian* cast than that of Judea. *If Peter had held his peace,* this peculiarity had not been observed; but hoping, probably, to put them off the scent by joining in the *fireside talk,* he only thus revealed himself. **27. Peter then denied again**—But, if the challenge of Malchus' kinsman was made simultaneously with this on account of his Galilean dialect, it was no simple denial; for Matthew 26:74 says, "Then began he to *curse and to swear,* saying, I know not the man." So Mark 14:71. This was THE THIRD DENIAL. **and immediately**—"while he yet spake" (Luke 22:60): **the cock crew**—As Mark is the only Evangelist who tells us that our Lord predicted that the cock should crow *twice* (ch. 14:30), so he only mentions that it *did* crow twice (vs. 72). The other Evangelists, who tell us merely that our Lord predicted that "before the cock should *crow* he would deny Him thrice" (Matt. 26:34; Luke 22:34; John 13:38), mention only *one actual* crowing, which was Mark's last. This is something affecting in this Evangelist —who, according to the earliest tradition (confirmed by internal evidence), derived his materials so largely from Peter as to have been styled his "*interpreter,*" being the *only one* who gives both the sad prediction and its still sadder fulfilment *in full.* It seems to show that Peter himself not only retained through all his after-life the most vivid recollection of the circumstances of his fall, but that he was willing that others should know them too. The immediately *subsequent* acts are given in full only in Luke (22:61, 62): "And the Lord turned and looked upon Peter," from the hall of judgment to the court, in the way already explained. But who can tell what lightning flashes of wounded love and piercing reproach shot from that "look" through the eye of Peter into his heart! "And Peter remembered the word of the Lord, how He had said unto him, Before the cock crow, thou shalt deny Me thrice. And Peter went out and wept bitterly." **28. Then led they Jesus from Caiaphas to the hall of judgment**—but not till "in the morning the chief priests held a consultation with the elders and scribes and the whole council against Him to put Him to death, and bound Him" (Matt. 27:1; and see on Mark 15:1). The word here rendered "hall of judgment" is from the Latin, and denotes 'the palace of the governor of a Roman province.' **they themselves went not into the judgment hall lest they should be defiled**—by contact with ceremonially unclean Gentiles. **but that they might eat the passover**—If this refer to the principal part of the festival, the eating of the lamb, the question is, how our Lord and His disciples came to eat it the night before; and, as it was an *evening* meal, how ceremonial defilement contracted in the *morning* would unfit them for partaking of it, as after 6 o'clock it was reckoned a new day. These are questions which have occasioned immense research and learned treatises. But as the usages of the Jews appear to have somewhat varied at different times, and our present knowledge of them is not sufficient to clear up all difficulties, they are among the not very important questions which probably will never be entirely solved.

29-32. Pilate went out to them, and said, What accusation bring ye against this man?—State your charge. **30. If he were not a malefactor, we would not**

ADAM CLARKE

27. *And immediately the cock crew.* Peter denied our Lord three times. His first denial took place when he was without, or beneath, in the hall of Caiaphas' house. He was not in the higher part where Christ stood before the high priest, but without that division of the hall and in the lower part with the servants and officers, at the fire kindled in the midst of the hall, vv. 16, 18; and the girl who kept the door had entered into the hall, where she charged Peter. His second denial was a short time after the first, Luke xxii. 58. Having once denied his Master, he naturally retired from the place where his accuser was to the vestibule of the hall, Matt. xxvi. 71, and it was the time of the first cock-crowing, or soon after midnight. After his remaining here a short time, perhaps an hour, another girl saw him and said to them who were standing by in the vestibule that he was one of them. Peter, to avoid this charge, withdrew into the hall and warmed himself. The girl, and those to whom she had spoken, followed him, the communication between the two places being immediate. Here a man enforced the charge of the girl, according to Luke; and others urged it, according to John; and Peter denied Jesus vehemently. His third denial was in the hall within sight of Jesus, though at such a distance from Him that Jesus could not know what passed but in a supernatural way. And about an hour after his second denial those who stood by founded a third charge against him, on his being a Galilean, which Luke says, chap. xxii. 59, one in particular strongly affirmed; and which, according to John, v. 26, was supported by one of Malchus' relations. This occasioned a more vehement denial than before, and immediately the cock crew the second time. The first denial may have been between our twelve and one, and the second between our two and three. The time of Peter's denials happened during the space of the third Roman watch, or that division of the night between twelve and three, which is called "cock-crowing," Mark xiii. 35.

28. *The hall of judgment.* To the praetorium. This was the house where Pilate lodged; hence called in our margin *Pilate's house.* The praetorium is so called from being the dwelling place of the *praetor,* or chief of the province. It was also the place where he held his court and tried causes. John has omitted all that passed in the house of Caiaphas—the accusations brought against Christ, the false witnesses, the insults which He received in the house of the high priest, and the assembling of the grand council, or Sanhedrin. These he found amply detailed by the other three Evangelists, and for this reason it appears that he omitted them. John's is properly a supplementary Gospel. *Lest they should be defiled.* The Jews considered even the touch of a Gentile as a legal defilement, and therefore would not venture into the praetorium for fear of contracting some impurity, which would have obliged them to separate themselves from all religious ordinances till the evening, Lev. xv. 10-11, 19-20. *That they might eat the passover.* Some maintain that *to pascha* here does not mean the paschal lamb but the other sacrifices which were offered during the paschal solemnity—for this had been eaten the evening before; and that our Lord was crucified the day after the Passover. Others have maintained that the paschal lamb is here meant, that this was the proper day for sacrificing it, that it was on the very hour in which it was offered that Christ expired on the Cross, and that therefore our Lord did not eat the paschal lamb this year, or that He ate it some hours before the common time. That Jesus ate a Passover this last year of His life is sufficiently evident from Matt. xxvi. 17-19; Mark xiv. 12-18; Luke xxii. 8-15; and that He ate this Passover some hours before the ordinary time and was himself slain at that hour in which the paschal lamb was ordered by the law to be sacrificed is highly probable, if not absolutely certain.

29. *Pilate then went out.* This was an act of condescension; but, as the Romans had confirmed to the Jews the free use of all their rites and ceremonies, the governor could not do less then comply with them in this matter. He went out to them, that they might not b-

MATTHEW HENRY

livered him to thee. This bespeaks them, (1) Very rude and uncivil to Pilate. He put the most reasonable question to them that could be; but, if it had been the most absurd, they could not have answered him with more disdain. (2) Very spiteful and malicious towards our Lord Jesus. They will presume him guilty who could prove himself innocent. They say, "He is an evil-doer." He an evil-doer who *went about doing good!* It is no new thing for the best of benefactors to be branded and run down as the worst of malefactors. (3) Very proud and conceited of themselves, and their own judgment and justice.

3. The judge remands him to their own court (*v.* 31): "*Take you him, and judge him according to your* own *law.*" Some think Pilate herein complimented them, acknowledging the remains of their power, and allowing them to exert it. Saith Pilate, "Go as far as your law will allow you, and, if you go further, it shall be connived at." This he said, willing to do the Jews a pleasure, but unwilling to do them the service they required. (2) Others think he upbraided them with their present state of weakness and subjection. Saith Pilate, "You have found him guilty by your own law, condemn him, if you dare, by your own law." Some think Pilate here reflects upon the law of Moses, as if it allowed them what the Roman law would by no means allow—the judging of a man unheard.

4. They disown any authority as judges: "*It is not lawful for us to put any man to death.*" Some think they had lost their power to give judgment in matters of life and death only by their own carelessness. Others think their power was taken from them by the Romans. Their acknowledgment of this they designed for a compliment to Pilate, and to atone for their rudeness (*v.* 30). However, there was a providence in it, *That the saying of Jesus might be fulfilled, which he spoke, signifying what death he should die, v.* 32. Even those who designed the defeating of Christ's sayings were made serviceable to the fulfilling of them by an overruling hand of God. Those sayings of Christ in particular were fulfilled which he had spoken concerning his own death. Two sayings of Christ concerning his death were fulfilled, by the Jews declining to *judge him according to their law. First,* He had said that he should be *delivered to the Gentiles,* and that *they should put him to death* (Matt. xx. 19; Mark x. 33; Luke xviii. 32, 33). *Secondly,* He had said that he should be crucified (Matt. xx. 19; xxvi. 2), *lifted up, ch.* iii. 14; xii. 32. Now if they had *judged him by their law,* he had been stoned. It was therefore necessary that Christ should be put to death by the Romans. As the Roman power had brought him to be born at Bethlehem, so now to die upon a cross, and both according to the scriptures.

II. Here is Pilate's conference with the prisoner, *v.* 33, &c.

1. The prisoner set to the bar. Pilate, after he had conferred with the chief priests at his door, entered into the hall, and called for Jesus to be brought in. Pilate entered into judgment with him, that God might not enter into judgment with us.

2. His examination. The other evangelists tell us that his accusers had laid it to his charge that *he perverted the nation, forbidding to give tribute to Caesar.*

(1) Here is a question put to him, with a design to find out something upon which to ground an accusation: "*Art thou the king of the Jews?*" Some think Pilate asked this with an air of scorn and contempt: "What! *art thou a king? Art thou the king of the Jews,* by whom thou art thus hated and persecuted?" Since it could not be proved he ever said it, he would constrain him to say it now, that he might proceed upon his own confession.

(2) Christ answers this question with another as an intimation to Pilate to consider upon what grounds he went (*v.* 34): "*Sayest thou this thing of thyself or did others tell it thee of me?* It is plain that thou hast no reason to *say this of thyself.*" Pilate was bound by his office to take care of the interests of the Roman government, but he could not say that this was in any danger, or suffered any damage, from anything our Lord Jesus had ever said or done. [2] "If others *tell it of me* thou oughtest to consider whether those who represent me as an *enemy to Caesar* are not really such themselves." If Pilate had been as inquisitive as he ought to have been in this matter, he would have found that the true reason why the chief priests were outrageous against Jesus was because he did not set up a temporal kingdom in opposition to the Roman power. Not answering this expectation of theirs, they charged that upon him of which they were themselves most notoriously guilty—disaffection to and design against the present government.

JAMIESON, FAUSSET, BROWN

have delivered him up unto thee—They were conscious they *had no case* of which Pilate could take cognizance, and therefore insinuate that they had already found Him worthy of death by their own law; but not having the power, under the Roman government, to carry their sentence into execution, they had come merely for his sanction.

32. That the saying . . . might be fulfilled which he spake, signifying what death he should die—i.e., by *crucifixion* (ch. 12:32, 33; Matt. 20:19); which being a Roman mode of execution, could only be carried into effect by order of the governor. (The Jewish mode in such cases as this was by *stoning.*)

33-38. Pilate . . . called Jesus, and said . . . , Art thou the King of the Jews?—In Luke 23:2 they charge our Lord before Pilate with "perverting the nation, and forbidding to give tribute to Cæsar, saying that He Himself is Christ a king." Perhaps this was what occasioned Pilate's question.

34. Jesus answered . . . , Sayest thou this of thyself, or did others tell it thee of me?—an important question for our Lord's case, to bring out whether the word "*King*" were meant in a *political* sense, with which Pilate had a right to deal, or whether he were merely *put up* to it by His accusers, who had no claims to charge Him but such as were of a purely *religious* nature, with which Pilate had nothing to do.

ADAM CLARKE

obliged to come into the hall and thus run the risk of being defiled.

30. *If he were not a malefactor.* So they did not wish to make Pilate the judge, but the executor of the sentence which they had already illegally passed.

31. *It is not lawful for us to put any man to death.* They might have judged Jesus according to their law, as Pilate bade them do, but they could only excommunicate or scourge Him. They might have voted Him worthy of death, but they could not put Him to death, if anything of a secular nature were charged against Him. The power of life and death was in all probability taken from the Jews when Archelaus, king of Judea, was banished to Vienna, and Judea was made a Roman province; and this happened more than fifty years before the destruction of Jerusalem. But the Romans suffered Herod, mentioned in Acts xii, to exercise the power of life and death during his reign. After all, I think it probable that, though the power of life and death was taken away from the Jews as far as it concerned affairs of state, yet it was continued to them in matters which were wholly of an ecclesiastical nature; and that they only applied thus to Pilate to persuade him that they were proceeding against Christ as an enemy of the state, and not as a transgressor of their own peculiar laws and customs. Hence, though they assert that He should die according to their law, because He made himself the Son of God, chap. xix. 7, yet they lay peculiar stress on His being an enemy to the Roman government; and when they found Pilate disposed to let Him go, they asserted that if he did he was not Caesar's friend, v. 12. It was this that intimidated Pilate and induced him to give Him up, that they might crucify Him.

32. *That the saying of Jesus might be fulfilled.* Or, "Thus the word was fulfilled." God permitted the Jews to lose the power of life and death, in the sense before stated, that according to the Roman laws, which punished sedition with the cross, Christ might be crucified, according to His own prediction, chap. xii. 32 and iii. 14.

33. *Art thou the King of the Jews?* Luke says expressly, xxiii. 2, that when the Jews brought Him to Pilate they began to accuse Him as a rebel, who said He was King of the Jews, and forbade the people to pay tribute to Caesar. It was in consequence of this accusation that Pilate asked the question mentioned in the text.

34. *Sayest thou this thing of thyself?* That is, Is it because My enemies thus accuse Me or because you have any suspicion of Me that you ask this question?

MATTHEW HENRY

(3) Pilate resents Christ's answer, and takes it very ill, *v.* 35. This is a direct answer to Christ's question, *v.* 34. Christ had asked him whether he spoke of himself. "No," says he; "*am I a Jew?*" Observe with what disdain Pilate asks, *Am I a Jew?* A man of sense and honour reckoned it a scandal to be counted a Jew. Christ had asked him whether others told him. "Yes," says he, "and those *thine own people*, and *the priests*; and therefore I have nothing to do but to proceed upon their information." Christ had declined answering that question, *Art thou the king of the Jews?* And therefore Pilate puts another question: "*What hast thou done?* Surely there cannot be all this smoke without some fire, what is it?"

(4) Christ, in his next reply, gives a more full answer to Pilate's former question, *Art thou a king?* explaining in what sense he was a king, *v.* 36.

[1] An account of the nature and constitution of Christ's kingdom: It *is not of this world.* Christ is a king, and has a kingdom, but *not of this world.* Its rise is not from this world. Its nature is not worldly; it is a kingdom within men, set up in their hearts and consciences. Its guards and supports are not worldly; its weapons are spiritual. Its tendency and design are not worldly. Its subjects, though they are in the world, yet *are not of the world.* They are neither the world's pupils nor its darlings, neither governed by its wisdom nor enriched with its wealth.

[2] An evidence of the spiritual nature of Christ's kingdom produced. *If my kingdom were of this world, then would my servants fight, that I should not be delivered to the Jews.* His followers did not offer to fight; there was no uproar, no attempt to rescue him. He did not order them to fight; nay, he forbade them, knowing that what would have been the destruction of any worldly kingdom would be the advancement and establishment of his. *Now* you may see *my kingdom is not from hence*; in the world, but not of it.

(5) In answer to Pilate's further query, he replies yet more directly, *v.* 37. Pilate's plain question: "*Art thou a king then?* Thou speakest of a kingdom thou hast; art thou then, in any sense, a king? Explain thyself." The good confession which our Lord Jesus witnessed before Pontius Pilate: *Thou sayest that I am a king*, that is, It is as thou sayest, I am a king. He grants himself to be a king, though not in the sense that Pilate meant. Though Christ *took upon him the form of a servant*, yet even then he justly claimed the honour and authority of a king. He explains himself, and shows how he is a king, as *he came to bear witness of the truth*; he rules in the minds of men by the power of truth. *He came to be a witness*, a witness for the God that made the world, and against sin that ruins the world, and by this *word of his testimony* he sets up and keeps up, his kingdom. Christ's errand into the world, and his business in the world, were *to bear witness to the truth.* To reveal it, to discover to the world that which otherwise could not have been known concerning God and his *goodwill to men, ch.* xvii. 26. To confirm it. By his miracles *he bore witness to the truth* of religion, *that all men through him might believe.* Now by doing this he is a king, and sets up a kingdom. The spirit and genius, of Christ's kingdom, is truth, divine truth. When he said, *I am the truth*, he said, in effect, I am a king. He conquers by the convincing evidence of truth; he rules by the commanding power of truth. He came *a light into the world*, and rules as the sun by day. The subjects of this kingdom are those that are *of the truth.* All that are in love with truth will hear the voice of Christ, for greater, better, surer, sweeter truths can nowhere be found than are found in Christ, by whom *grace and truth came.*

(6) Pilate, hereupon, puts a good question to him, but does not stay for an answer, *v.* 38. He said, *What is truth?* and *immediately went out again.* It is certain that this was a good question. Truth is that *pearl of great price* which the human understanding is in quest of; for it cannot rest but in that which is, or at least is apprehended to be, truth. But many put this question that have not patience enough to persevere in their search after truth, or not humility and sincerity enough to receive it when they have found it. It is uncertain with what design Pilate asked this question. Perhaps he spoke it as a learner, as one that began to think well of Christ. Some think he spoke it as a judge, enquiring further into the cause: "Tell me what the truth of it is, the true state of this matter." Others think he spoke it as a scoffer: "Thou talkest of truth; canst thou tell what truth is, or give me a definition of it?" Like men of no religion, who take a pleasure in bantering all religions, he ridicules both sides; and therefore Christ made him no reply. But, though Christ would not tell Pilate what is truth, he has told his disciples, and by them

JAMIESON, FAUSSET, BROWN

35. Pilate answered, Am I a Jew? Thine own nation and the chief priests delivered thee to me: What hast thou done?—i.e., Jewish questions I neither understand nor meddle with; but Thou art here on a charge which, though it *seems* only Jewish, *may* yet involve treasonable matter: As *they* state it, I cannot decide the point; tell me, then, what procedure of Thine has brought Thee into this position.' In modern phrase, Pilate's object in this question was merely to determine the *relevancy* of the charge. **36. Jesus answered, My kingdom is not of this world**—He does not say 'not *over*,' but 'not of this world'—i.e., in its *origin* and *nature;* therefore 'no such kingdom as need give thee or thy master the least alarm.' **if my kingdom were of this world, then would my servants fight, that I should not be delivered to the Jews**—"A very convincing argument; for if His servants did not fight to prevent their King from being delivered up to His enemies, much less would they use force for the establishment of His kingdom" [WEBSTER and WILKINSON]. **but now**—but the fact is. **is my kingdom not from hence**—Our Lord only says whence His kingdom is *not*—first simply affirming it, next giving proof of it, then reaffirming it. This was all that Pilate had to do with. The *positive* nature of His kingdom He would not obtrude upon one who was as little able to comprehend it, as entitled officially to information about it. (It is worthy of notice that the "MY," which occurs *four* times in this one verse—*thrice* of His *kingdom,* and *once* of His *servants*—is put in the emphatic form.) **37. Art thou a king then?**—There was no sarcasm or disdain in this question [as THOLUCK, ALFORD, and others, allege], else our Lord's answer would have been different. Putting emphasis upon "*thou,*" his question betrays a mixture of *surprise* and *uneasiness,* partly at the possibility of there being, after all, something dangerous under the claim, and partly from a certain awe which our Lord's demeanor probably struck into him. **Thou sayest that I am a king**—It is even so. **To this end was I** ('have I been') **born, and for this cause came I**—am I come—**into the world, that I may bear witness to the truth**—His *birth* expresses His manhood; His *coming into the world,* His existence before assuming humanity: The truth, then, here affirmed, though Pilate would catch little of it, was that *His Incarnation was expressly in order to the assumption of Royalty in our nature.* Yet, instead of saying, He came to be a King, which is His meaning, He says He came to *testify to the truth.* Why this? Because, in such circumstances it required a noble courage not to flinch from His royal claims; and our Lord, *conscious that He was putting forth that courage,* gives a turn to His confession expressive of it. It is to this that Paul alludes, in those remarkable words to Timothy: "I charge thee before God, who quickeneth all things, and before Christ Jesus, who, *in the presence* of Pontius Pilate, witnessed *the good confession*" (I Tim. 6:13). This one act of our Lord's life, His courageous witness-bearing before the governor, was selected as an encouraging example of the *fidelity* which Timothy ought to display. As the Lord [says OLSHAUSEN beautifully] owned Himself *the Son of God* before the most exalted theocratic council, so He confessed His *regal dignity* in presence of the representative of the highest political authority on earth. **Every one that is of the truth heareth my voice**—Our Lord here not only affirms that His word had in it a self-evidencing, self-recommending power, but gently insinuated the *true secret of the growth and grandeur of His kingdom*—as A KINGDOM OF TRUTH, in its highest sense, into which all souls who have learned to live and count all things but loss for the truth are, by a most heavenly attraction, drawn as into their proper element; THE KING of whom Jesus is, fetching them in and ruling them by His captivating power over their hearts. **38. Pilate saith unto him, What is truth?**—i.e., 'Thou stirrest the question of questions, which the thoughtful of every age have asked, but never man yet answered.' **And when he had said this**—as if, by putting such a question, he was getting into interminable and unseasonable inquiries, when this business demanded rather prompt action—**he went out again unto the Jews**—thus missing a noble opportunity for himself, and giving utterance to that consciousness of the want of all intellectual and moral certainty, which was the feeling of every thoughtful mind at that time. "The only certainty," says the elder PLINY, "is that nothing is certain, nor more miserable than man, nor more proud. The fearful laxity of morals at that time must doubtless be traced in a great degree to this skepticism. The revelation of the eternal

ADAM CLARKE

35. *Am I a Jew?* That is, I am not a Jew, and cannot judge whether Thou art what is called the Christ, the King of the Jews. It is Thine own countrymen, and their spiritual rulers, who delivered Thee up to me with the above accusation. *What hast thou done?* If Thou dost not profess thyself King over this people, and an enemy to Caesar, what is it that Thou hast done for which they desire Thy condemnation?

36. *My kingdom is not of this world.* It is purely spiritual and divine. If it had been of a secular nature, then My servants would have contended—they would have opposed force with force, as the kingdoms of this world do in their wars; but as *my kingdom is not of this world,* therefore no resistance has been made.

37. *Thou sayest.* A common form of expression for "Yes, it is so." I was born into the world that I might set up and maintain a spiritual government, but this government is established in and by truth. All that love truth hear My voice and attend to the spiritual doctrines I preach. It is by *truth* alone that I influence the minds and govern the manners of My subjects.

38. *What is truth?* Among the sages of that time there were many opinions concerning *truth,* and some had even supposed that it was a thing utterly out of the reach of men. Pilate perhaps might have asked the question in a mocking way; and his not staying to get an answer indicated that he either despaired of getting a satisfactory one or that he was indifferent about it.

MATTHEW HENRY

has told us, *ch.* xiv. 6.

III. The result of both these conferences with the prosecutors and the prisoner (*v.* 38–40).

1. The judge appeared his friend.

(1) He publicly declared him innocent, *v.* 38. *I find in him no fault at all.* Nothing criminal appears against him. This solemn declaration of Christ's innocency was, [1] For the justification and honour of the Lord Jesus. Though he was treated as the worst of malefactors he had never merited such treatment. [2] For explaining the design and intention of his death, that he did not die for any sin of his own, and therefore he died as a sacrifice for our sins, and that, *one man should die for the people, ch.* xi. 50. [3] For aggravating the sin of the Jews that prosecuted him with so much violence. Our Lord Jesus, though brought in not guilty, is still run down as a malefactor, and his blood thirsted for.

(2) He proposed an expedient for his discharge (*v.* 39): *You have a custom, that I should release to you a prisoner at the passover;* shall it be this king of the Jews. It was an appeal to the people, as appears, Matt. xxvii. 15. Probably he had heard how this Jesus had been attended but the other day with the hosannas of the common people, and therefore he made no doubt but they would demand the release of Jesus. He allows their custom, in honour of the passover, which was a memorial of their release. He offers to release Jesus to them, according to the custom. If he *found no fault in him,* he was bound in conscience to discharge him. But he was willing to trim the matter, and please all sides, being governed more by worldly wisdom than by the rules of equity.

2. The people appeared his enemies (*v.* 40): *They cried all again, Not this man, but Barabbas.* Observe how fierce and outrageous they were. Pilate proposed the thing to them calmly, but they resolved in it a heat, and gave in their resolution with clamour and noise. There is cause to suspect a deficiency of reason and justice on that side which calls in the assistance of popular tumult. How foolish and absurd they were, as is intimated in the short account here given of the other candidate: *Now Barabbas was a robber,* and therefore, [1] A breaker of the law of God; and yet he shall be spared. [2] An enemy to the public safety and personal property. The clamour of the town is wont to be against robbers, yet here it is for one. Thus those do who prefer their sins before Christ. Sin is a robber, and yet foolishly chosen rather than Christ, who would truly enrich us.

JAMIESON, FAUSSET, BROWN

truth alone was able to breathe new life into ruined human nature, and that in the apprehension of complete redemption" [OLSHAUSEN]. **and saith unto them**—in the hearing of our Lord, who had been brought forth—**I find in him no fault**—no crime. This so exasperated "the chief priests and elders" that, afraid of losing their prey, they poured forth a volley of charges against Him, as appears from Luke 23:4, 5: on Pilate's affirming His innocence, "they were *the more fierce,* saying, He stirreth up the people, teaching throughout all Jewry, beginning from Galilee to this place." They see no hope of getting Pilate's sanction to His death unless they can fasten upon Him a charge of conspiracy against the government; and as *Galilee* was noted for its turbulence (Luke 13:1; Acts 5:37), and our Lord's ministry lay chiefly there, they artfully introduce it to give color to their charge. "And the chief priests accused Him of *many things,* but He answered nothing (Mark 15.3). Then said Pilate unto Him, Hearest Thou not how many things they witness against Thee? And He answered him to never a word, insomuch that the governor marvelled greatly" (Matt. 27:13, 14). See on Mark 15:3-5. In his perplexity, Pilate, hearing of Galilee, bethinks himself of the expedient of sending Him to Herod, in the hope of thereby further shaking off responsibility in the case. See on Mark 15:6, and on Luke 23:6-12. The return of the prisoner only deepened the perplexity of Pilate, who, "calling together the chief priests, rulers, and people," tells them plainly that not one of their charges against "this man" had been made good, while even Herod, to whose jurisdiction he more naturally belonged, had done nothing to Him: He "will therefore chastise and release him" (Luke 23:13-16). **39. But ye have a custom that I should release one unto you at the passover . . .**—See on Mark 15:7-11. "On the typical import of the choice of Christ to suffer, by which Barabbas was set free, see Leviticus 16, particularly vss. 5-10, where the subject is the *sin offering* on the great day of atonement" [KRAFFT in LUTHARDT].

ADAM CLARKE

I find in him no fault. Having asked the above question, and being convinced of our Lord's innocence, he went out to the Jews to testify his conviction, and to deliver Him, if possible, out of their hands.

39. *But ye have a custom.* Nothing relative to the origin or reason of this custom is known. Commentators have swum in an ocean of conjecture on this point.

40. *Barabbas was a robber.* See Matt. xxvii. 16.

MATTHEW HENRY

CHAPTER 19

Verses 1–15

Here is a further account of the unfair trial which they gave to our Lord Jesus. The prosecutors carried it on with great confusion among the people, and the judge with great confusion in his own breast.

I. The judge abuses the prisoner, though he declares him innocent, and hopes therewith to pacify the prosecutors.

1. He ordered him to be whipped as a criminal, *v.* 1. *Pilate,* being disappointed in his project of releasing him upon the people's choice, *took Jesus, and scourged him.* Matthew and Mark mention his scourging after his condemnation, but here it appears to have been before. Luke speaks of Pilate's offering to *chastise him, and let him go,* which must be before sentence. This scourging of him was designed only to pacify the Jews. The Roman scourgings were ordinarily very severe, not limited, as among the Jews, to *forty stripes;* yet this pain and shame Christ submitted to for our sakes. (1) *That the scripture might be fulfilled,* which spoke of *the chastisement of our peace* being *upon him* (Isa. liii 5). He himself likewise had foretold it, Matt. xx. 19; Mark x. 34; Luke xviii. 33. (2) *That by his stripes we might be healed.* The physician scourged, and so the patient healed. (3) That stripes, for his sake, might be sanctified and made easy to his followers. Christ's stripes take out the sting of theirs.

2. He turned him over to his soldiers, to be ridiculed and made sport with as a fool (*v.* 2, 3): *The soldiers put a crown of thorns upon his head; they put on him a purple robe;* and they complimented him with, *Hail, king of the Jews,* and then *smote him with their hands.*

(1) See here the baseness and injustice of Pilate. Pilate did this: To oblige his soldiers' merry humour, and perhaps his own too. *Herod,* as well as *his men of war,* had just before done the same, Luke xxiii. 11. It was as good as a stage-play to them, now that it was a festival time. To oblige the Jews' malicious humour.

JAMIESON, FAUSSET, BROWN

CHAPTER 19

Vss. 1-16. JESUS BEFORE PILATE—SCOURGED—TREATED WITH OTHER SEVERITIES AND INSULTS—DELIVERED UP, AND LED AWAY TO BE CRUCIFIED. **1-3. Pilate took Jesus and scourged him**—in hope of appeasing them. (See on Mark 15:15.) "And the soldiers led Him away into the palace, and they call the whole band" (Mark 15:16)—the body of the military cohort stationed there—to take part in the mock coronation now to be enacted.

2. the soldiers platted a crown of thorns, and put it on his head—in mockery of a regal *crown.*

ADAM CLARKE

CHAPTER 19

1. *Pilate therefore took Jesus, and scourged him.* That is, caused Him to be scourged. As our Lord was scourged by order of Pilate, it is probable He was scourged in the Roman manner, which was much more severe than that of the Jews. The latter never gave more than thirty-nine blows; for the law had absolutely forbidden a man to be abused, or his flesh cut in this chastisement, Deut. xxv. 3. Though it was customary to scourge the person who was to be crucified, yet it appears that Pilate had another end in view by scourging our Lord. He hoped that this would satisfy the Jews, and that he might then dismiss Jesus. This appears from Luke xxiii. 16.

2. *Platted a crown of thorns.* See on Matt. xxvii. 29.

MATTHEW HENRY

(2) See here the rudeness and insolence of the soldiers. Thus hath Christ's holy religion been basely misrepresented, dressed up by bad men at their pleasure, and so exposed to contempt and ridicule. They clothe him with a mock-robe. And as Christ is here represented as a king in conceit only, so is his religion as a concern in conceit only, and God and the soul, sin and duty, heaven and hell, are with many all chimeras. They crown him with thorns, as if to submit to the control of God and conscience were to thrust one's head into a thicket of thorns; but this is an unjust imputation; *thorns and snares are in the way of the froward*, but roses and laurels in religion's ways.

(3) See here the wonderful condescension of our Lord Jesus. Great and generous minds can bear anything better than ignominy, yet this the great and holy Jesus submitted to for us. See and admire, the invincible patience of a sufferer, the invincible love and kindness of a Saviour. Herein he commended his love, that he would not only die for us, but die as a fool dies. He *endureth the pain*; not the pangs of death only, but, as if these were too little, he submitted to those previous pains. Shall we complain of a thorn in the flesh, and of being buffeted by affliction. Christ humbled himself to bear those thorns in the head, and those buffetings, to save and teach us. He *despised the shame*, the shame of a fool's coat, and the mock-respect paid him, with, *Hail, king of the Jews.* He that bore these sham honours was recompensed with real honours, and so shall we, if we patiently suffer shame for him.

II. Pilate presents him to the prosecutors in hope that they would now be satisfied, *v.* 4, 5. Here he proposes two things to their consideration:

1. That he had not found anything in him which made him obnoxious to the Roman government (*v.* 4): *I find no fault in him.* If he found no fault in him, why did he bring him out to his prosecutors, and not immediately release him, as he ought to have done? Thinking to trim the matter, to please the people by scourging Christ, and save his conscience by not crucifying him, behold he does both. It is common for those who think to keep themselves from greater sins by venturing upon less sins to run into both.

2. That he had done that to him which would make him the less dangerous to them and to their government, *v.* 5. He brought him out to them, wearing the crown of thorns, his head and face all bloody, and said, *Behold the man*, treating him as a slave, and exposing him to contempt, after which he supposed the people would never look upon him with any respect. Little did Pilate think with what veneration even these sufferings of Christ would in after ages be commemorated by the best and greatest of men. Our Lord Jesus shows himself dressed up in all the marks of ignominy. He came forth, willing to be made a spectacle. Did he go forth thus bearing our reproach? Let us go forth to him *bearing his reproach.* Pilate saith unto them, with a design to appease them, *Behold the man*; not so much to move their pity, Behold a man worthy your compassion, as to silence their jealousies, Behold a man not worthy your suspicion. The word however is very affecting: *Behold the man.* It is good for everyone of us to behold the man Christ Jesus in his sufferings. "Behold him, and mourn because of him. Behold him, and love him; be still *looking unto Jesus.*"

III. The prosecutors were but the more exasperated, *v.* 6, 7.

1. Their clamour and outrage. *The chief priests cried out*, and their officers joined with them in crying, *Crucify him, crucify him.* The common people perhaps would have acquiesced in Pilate's declaration of his innocency. Their malice against Christ was unreasonable and most absurd, in that they offer not to make good their charge against him; but, though he be innocent, he must be crucified. It was insatiable and very cruel. Neither the extremity of his scourging, nor his patience under it, could mollify them in the least. It was violent and exceedingly resolute; they will have it their own way. Were they so violent in running down our Lord Jesus, and in crying, *Crucify him, crucify him?* and shall not we be vigorous and zealous in crying, *Crown him, Crown him?* Shall not our love to him quicken our endeavours for him and his kingdom?

2. The check Pilate gave to their fury: "*Take you him and crucify him.*" He knew they could not, they durst not, crucify him; but it is as if he should say, "You shall not make me a drudge to your malice." A good resolve, if he would but have stuck to it. He found no fault in him, and therefore should not have continued to parley with the prosecutors. Those that would be safe from sin should be deaf to temptation. Nay, he should have secured the prisoner from

JAMIESON, FAUSSET, BROWN

and they put on him a purple robe—in mockery of the *imperial purple;* first "stripping him" (Matt. 27:28) of His own outer garment. The robe may have been the "gorgeous" one in which Herod arrayed and sent Him back to Pilate (Luke 23:11). "And they put a reed into His right hand" (Matt. 27:29)—in mockery of the regal *scepter.* "And they bowed the knee before Him" (Matt. 27:29).

3. And said, Hail, King of the Jews!—doing Him derisive homage, in the form used on approaching the emperors. "And they spit upon Him, and took the reed and smote Him on the head" (Matt. 27:30). The best comment on these affecting details is to *cover the face.* **4, 5. Pilate . . . went forth again, and saith . . . , Behold, I bring**—am bringing, i.e., going to bring—**him forth to you, that ye may know I find no fault in him**—and, by scourging Him and allowing the soldiers to make sport of Him, have gone as far to meet your exasperation as can be expected from a judge.

5. Then Jesus came forth, wearing the crown of thorns, and the purple robe. And Pilate saith unto them, Behold the man!—There is no reason to think that *contempt* dictated this speech. There was clearly a struggle in the breast of this wretched man. Not only was he reluctant to surrender to mere clamor an innocent man, but a feeling of anxiety about His mysterious claims, as is plain from what follows, was beginning to rack his breast, and the object of his exclamation seems to have been to *move their pity.* But, be *his* meaning what it may, those three words have been eagerly appropriated by all Christendom, and enshrined for ever in its heart as a sublime expression of its calm, rapt admiration of its suffering Lord.

6, 7. When the chief priests . . . saw him, they cried out—their fiendish rage kindling afresh at the sight of Him—**Crucify him, crucify him**—(See on Mark 15:14).

Pilate saith unto them, Take ye him, and crucify him; for I find no fault in him—as if this would relieve *him* of the responsibility of the deed, who, by surrendering Him, incurred it all!

ADAM CLARKE

ALEXANDER MACLAREN:

The cruel scourging, which, in Roman hands, was a much more severe punishment than the Jewish "beating with rods," and often ended in death, was inflicted on the silent, unresisting Christ, not because His judge thought that it was deserved, but to please accusers whose charge he knew to be absurd. The underlings naturally followed their betters' example, and after they had executed Pilate's orders to scourge, they covered the bleeding wounds with some robe, perhaps ragged, but of the royal color, and crushed the twisted wreath of thornbranch down on the brows to make fresh wounds there. The jest of crowning such a poor, helpless creature as Jesus seemed to them was exactly on the level of such rude natures, and would be the more exquisite to them because it was double-barrelled, and insulted the nation as well as the "King." They came in a string, as the tense of the original word suggests, and offered their mock reverence. But that sport became tame after a little, and mockery passed into violence, as it always does in such natures. These rough legionaries were cruel and brutal, and they were unconscious witnesses to His kingship as founded on suffering; but they were innocent as compared with the polished gentleman on the judgment seat who prostituted justice, and the learned Pharisees outside who were howling for blood.

In verses 4-8 the scene changes again to without the palace and shows us Pilate trying another expedient, equally in vain. The hesitating governor has no chance with the resolute, rooted hate of the rulers. Jesus silently and unresistingly follows Pilate from the hall, still wearing the mockery of royal pomp. Pilate had calculated that the sight of Him in such guise, and bleeding from the lash, might turn hate into contempt, and perhaps give a touch of pity. "Behold the man!" as he meant it, was as if he had said, "Is this poor, bruised, spiritless sufferer worth hate or fear? Does He look like a king or a dangerous enemy?" Pilate for once drops the scoff of calling Him their King, and seeks to conciliate and move to pity. The profound meanings which later ages have delighted to find in his words, however warrantable, are no part of their design as spoken, and we gain a better lesson from the scene by keeping close to the thoughts of the actors. What a contrast between the vacillation of the governor, on the one hand, afraid to do right and reluctant to do wrong, and the dogged malignity of the rulers and their tools on the other, and the calm, meek endurance of the silent Christ, knowing all their thoughts, pitying all, and fixed in loving resolve, even firmer than the rulers' hate, to bear the utmost that He might save a world!

Some pity may have stirred in the crowd, but the priests and their immediate dependants silenced it by their yell of fresh hate at the sight of the prisoner. Note how John gives the very impression of the fierce, brief roar, like that of wild beasts for their prey, by his "Crucify, crucify!" without addition of the person. Pilate lost patience at last, and angrily and half seriously gives permission to them to take the law into their own hands. He really means, "I will not be your tool, and if my conviction of this Man's innocence is to be of no account, *you* must punish Him; for *I* will not." How far he meant to abdicate authority, and how far he was launching sarcasms, it is difficult to say. Throughout he is sarcastic, and thereby indicates his weakness, indemnifying himself for being thwarted by sneers which sit so ill on authority.

—*Expositions of Holy Scripture*

MATTHEW HENRY

their insults. But Pilate had not courage enough to act according to his conscience.

3. The further colour which the prosecutors gave to their demand (*v.* 7): *We have a law, and by our law he ought to die, because he made himself the Son of God.* They *made their boast of the law.* They had indeed an excellent law, but in vain did they boast of their law, when they abused it to such bad purposes. They discover a restless and inveterate malice against our Lord Jesus. They urged this, that he pretended himself a God. Thus they turn every stone to take him off. They pervert the law, and make that the instrument of their malice. It was true that blasphemers were to be put to death. Whoever falsely pretended to be the Son of God was guilty of blasphemy. It was false that Christ pretended to be the Son of God, for he really was so. That which was his honour, and might have been their happiness, they impute to him as a crime, for which he ought to die; yet he ought not to be crucified, for this was no death inflicted by their law.

IV. The judge brings the prisoner again to his trial, upon this new suggestion.

1. The concern Pilate was in, when he heard this alleged (*v.* 8): When he heard that his prisoner pretended not to royalty only, but to deity, he was *the more afraid.* There was the more danger of offending the people if he should acquit him. Though he might hope to pacify their rage against a pretended king, he could never reconcile them to a pretended God. There was the more danger of offending his own conscience if he should condemn him. "Is he one" (thinks Pilate) "that makes himself *the Son of God?* and what if it should prove that he is so? What will become of me then?"

2. His further examination of our Lord Jesus thereupon, *v.* 9. He resumed the debate, went into the judgment-hall, and asked Christ, *Whence art thou?*

(1) The place he chose for this examination: He *went into the judgment-hall* for privacy, that he might be out of the noise and clamour of the crowd. Those that would find out the truth as it is in Jesus must get out of the noise of prejudice, and retire as it were into the judgment-hall, to converse with Christ alone.

(2) The question he put to him: *Whence art thou?* Art thou from men or from heaven? From beneath or from above?

(3) The silence of our Lord Jesus; but *Jesus gave him no answer.* This was not a sullen silence, in contempt of the court, nor was it because he knew not what to say. It was a patient silence. This silence loudly bespoke his submission to his Father's will in his present sufferings. He was silent, because he would say nothing to hinder his sufferings. It was a prudent silence. When the chief priests asked him, *Art thou the Son of the Blessed?* he answered, *I am;* but when Pilate asked him he knew he did not understand his own question, having no notion of the Messiah, and of his being the *Son of God,* and therefore to what purpose should he reply to him whose head was filled with the pagan theology?

(4) The haughty check which Pilate gave him for his silence (*v.* 10): *"Speakest thou not unto me? Knowest thou not that I have power to crucify thee, and have power to release thee?"* Observe here how Pilate magnifies himself, and boasts of his own authority. Men in power are apt to be puffed up with their power, and the more absolute and arbitrary it is the more it gratifies and humours their pride. How he tramples upon our blessed Saviour: *Speakest thou not unto me?* He reflects upon him as if he were undutiful and disrespectful to those in authority or as if he were ungrateful to one that had been tender of him, as if he were unwise for himself. If Christ had indeed sought to save his life, now had been his time to have spoken.

(5) Christ's pertinent answer to this check, *v.* 11. [1] He boldly rebukes his arrogance: "*Thou couldest have no power at all against me, except it were given thee from above.*" Though Christ did not think fit to answer him when he was impertinent, yet he did think fit to answer him when he was imperious. When Pilate used his power, Christ silently submitted to it; but, when he grew proud of it, he made him know himself: "All the power thou hast is given thee from above." His power in general, as a magistrate, was a limited power, and he could do no more than God would suffer him to do. Let the proud oppressors know that there is *a higher than they.* And let this silence the murmurings of the oppressed, let it comfort them that their persecutors can do no more than God will let them. Pilate never fancied himself to look so great as now, when he sat in judgment upon such a prisoner as this, who was looked upon by many as the *Son of God* and king of Israel. But Christ lets him know that he was herein but an instrument in

JAMIESON, FAUSSET, BROWN

7. The Jews answered him, We have a law, and by our law he ought to die, because he made himself the Son of God—Their criminal charges having come to nothing, they give up that point, and as Pilate was throwing the whole responsibility upon them, they retreat into their own Jewish law, by which, as claiming equality with God (see on ch. 5:18 and 8:59), He ought to die; insinuating that it was Pilate's duty, even as civil governor, to protect their law from such insult.

8-11. When Pilate . . . heard this saying, he was the more afraid—the name "SON OF GOD," the lofty sense evidently attached to it by His Jewish accusers, the dialogue he had already held with Him, and the dream of his wife (Matt. 27:19), all working together in the breast of the wretched man.

9. and went again into the judgment hall, and saith to Jesus, Whence art thou?—beyond all doubt a question relating not to His *mission* but to His personal *origin.*

Jesus gave him no answer—He had said enough; the time for answering such a question was past; the weak and wavering governor is already on the point of giving way.

10. Then saith Pilate unto him, Speakest thou not to me?—The "me" is the emphatic word in the question. He falls back upon the *pride of office,* which doubtless tended to blunt the workings of his conscience. **knowest thou not that I have power to crucify thee, and have power to release thee?**—said to work upon Him at once by *fear* and by *hope.*

11. Thou couldest—rather 'shouldst'—**have no power at all against me**—neither to crucify nor to release, nor to do anything whatever against Me [BENGEL]. **except it were**—'unless it had been'—**given thee from above**—i.e., 'Thou thinkest too much of thy power, Pilate: against Me that power is none, save what is meted out to thee by special divine appointment, for a special end.'

ADAM CLARKE

7. *We have a law.* In Lev. xxiv. 14-16 we find that blasphemers of God were to be put to death; and the chief priests having charged Jesus with blasphemy, they therefore voted that He deserved to die. They might refer also to the law against false prophets, Deut. xviii. 20. *The Son of God.* It is certain that the Jews understood this in a very peculiar sense. When Christ called himself *the Son of God,* they understood it to imply positive equality to the Supreme Being; and, if they were wrong, our Lord never attempted to correct them.

8. *He was the more afraid.* While Jesus was accused only as a disturber of the peace of the nation, which accusation Pilate knew to be false, he knew he could deliver Him, because the judgment in that case belonged to himself. But when the Jews brought a charge against Him of the most capital nature, from their own laws, he then saw that he had everything to fear if he did not deliver Jesus to their will. The Sanhedrin must not be offended—the populace must not be irritated. From the former a complaint might be sent against him to Caesar; the latter might revolt, or proceed to some acts of violence, the end of which could not be foreseen. Pilate was certainly to be pitied. He saw what was right and he wished to do it, but he had not sufficient firmness of mind. Some suppose that Pilate's fear arose from hearing that Jesus had said He was *the Son of God;* because Pilate, who was a polytheist, believed that it was possible for the offspring of the gods to visit mortals; and he was afraid to condemn Jesus, for fear of offending some of the supreme deities. Perhaps the question in the succeeding verse refers to this.

9. *Whence art thou?* This certainly does not mean, From what country art Thou? for Pilate knew this well enough; but it appears he made this inquiry to know who were the parents of Christ; what were His pretensions, and whether He really were a demigod, such as the heathens believed in. To this question we find our Lord gave no answer. He had already told him that His kingdom was not of this world; and that He came to erect a spiritual Kingdom, not a temporal one, chap. xviii. 36-37. This answer He deemed sufficient; and He did not choose to satisfy a criminal curiosity, nor to enter into any debate concerning the absurdity of the heathen worship.

MATTHEW HENRY

God's hand.

[2] He mildly excuses his sin, in comparison with the sin of the ringleaders: "*Therefore he that delivered me unto thee* lies under greater guilt." It is plainly intimated that what Pilate did was sin, a great sin, and that the forces which the Jews put upon him would not justify him. The guilt of others will not acquit us, nor will it avail in the great day to say that others were worse than we. Yet theirs that delivered him to Pilate was the greater sin. By this it appears that all sins are not equal, but some more heinous than others. *He that delivered Christ to Pilate* was either, 1. The people of the Jews, who cried out, *Crucify him, crucify him*. They had seen Christ's miracles, which Pilate had not, and therefore it was much worse in them to appear against him than in Pilate. 2. Or Caiaphas in particular, who first advised his death, *ch.* xi. 49, 50. The sin of Caiaphas was abundantly greater than the sin of Pilate. Caiaphas prosecuted Christ from pure enmity and of malice prepense. Pilate condemned him purely for fear of the people, and it was a hasty resolution which he had not time to cool upon. 3. Some think Christ means Judas. The sin of Judas was, upon many accounts, greater than the sin of Pilate. The sin of Judas was a leading sin, and let in all that followed. He was a *guide to them that took Jesus*.

V. Pilate struggles with the Jews to deliver Jesus out of their hands, but in vain.

1. Pilate seems more zealous than before to get Jesus discharged (*v.* 12): *Thenceforth*, though Christ found fault with him, he still continued to find no fault in Christ, but *sought to release him*. If Pilate's policy had not prevailed above his justice, he would not have been long seeking to release him, but would have done it.

2. The Jews were more violent to get Jesus crucified. Still they carry on their design with noise and clamour as before. They laboured to get him cried down by a multitude, and it is no hard matter to pack a mob. A few madmen may out-shout many wise men, and then fancy themselves to speak the sense (when it is but the nonsense) of a nation, but it is not so easy a thing to change the sense of the people as it is to misrepresent it. In this outcry they sought: To blacken the prisoner as an enemy to Caesar. They will have it that he *speaks against Caesar*. It has always been the artifice of the enemies of religion to represent it as hurtful to kings and provinces, when it would be highly beneficial to both. To frighten the judge, as no friend to Caesar: "If thou *let this man go thou art not Caesar's friend*." They intimate a threatening that they would inform against him, and here they touched him in a sensible and very tender part. A pretended zeal for that which is good often serves to cover a real malice against that which is better.

3. Pilate slightly endeavoured to banter them out of their fury, and yet, in doing this, yielded to the rapid stream, *v.* 13-15. After he had seemed now as if he would have made a vigorous resistance upon this attack (*v.* 12), he basely surrendered.

(1) What it was that shocked Pilate (*v.* 13): "*When he heard that saying*, that he could not be sure of Caesar's favour, if he did not put Jesus to death, then he thought it was time to look about him." Those that bind up their happiness in the favour of men make themselves an easy prey to the temptations of Satan.

(2) What preparation was made for a definitive sentence upon this matter: *Pilate brought Jesus forth*, and then *sat down in the judgment-seat*. Christ was condemned with all the ceremony that could be. Notice is here taken of the place and time. The place where Christ was condemned: in a *place called the Pavement, but in Hebrew, Gabbatha*, probably the place where he used to sit to try causes or criminals. The time, *v.* 14. It was the preparation of the passover, and *about the sixth hour*. 1. The day: It was the preparation of the passover, that is, for the passover-sabbath. It was when they should have been purging out the old leaven, to get ready for the passover; but the better the day the worse the deed. 2. The hour: *It was about the sixth hour*. Some ancient Greek and Latin manuscripts read it about the third hour, which agrees with Mark xv. 25. And it appears by Matt. xxvii. 45 that he was upon the cross before the sixth hour. From the third to the sixth hour (which was, as we call it, church-time) on that day, they were employed in this wickedness; so that for this day, though they were priests, they dropped the temple-service.

(3) The rencounter Pilate had with the Jews, endeavouring in vain to stem the tide of their rage. He saith unto the Jews: "*Behold your king*, that is, him whom you accuse as a pretender to the crown. Is this a man likely to be dangerous to the government?" Pilate, though he was far from meaning so, seems as if he were the voice of God to them. Christ,

JAMIESON, FAUSSET, BROWN

therefore he that delivered me unto thee—Caiaphas, too wit—but he only as representing the Jewish authorities as a body. **hath the greater sin**—as having better opportunities and more knowledge of such matters.

And from thenceforth—particularly this speech, which seems to have filled him with awe, and redoubled his anxiety. **Pilate sought to release him**—i.e., to gain their *consent* to it, for he could have done it at once on his authority.

but the Jews cried—seeing their advantage, and not slow to profit by it. **If thou let this man go, thou art not Cæsar's friend . . .**—"This was equivalent to a threat of *impeachment*, which we know was much dreaded by such officers as the procurators, especially of the character of Pilate or Felix. It also consummates the treachery and disgrace of the Jewish rulers, who were willing, for the purpose of destroying Jesus, to affect a zeal for the supremacy of a foreign prince" (See vs. 15.) [WEBSTER and WILKINSON].

When Pilate . . . heard that, . . . he brougt Jesus forth, and sat down in—['upon']—**the judgment seat**—that he might pronounce sentence against the Prisoner, on this charge, the more solemnly—**in a place called the Pavement**—a tesselated pavement, much used by the Romans—**in the Hebrew, Gabbatha**—from its being *raised*. **14. It was the preparation**—i.e., the day before the Jewish sabbath. **and about the sixth hour**—The true reading here is probably, "the *third* hour"—or 9 A.M.—which agrees best with the whole series of events, as well as with the other Evangelists.

he saith to the Jews, Behold your King!—Having now made up his mind to yield to them, he takes a sort of quiet revenge on them by this irony, which he knew would sting them. This only reawakens their cry to despatch Him.

ADAM CLARKE

11. *Hath the greater sin.* It is a sin in you to condemn Me, while you are convinced in your conscience that I am innocent; but the Jews who delivered Me to you, and Judas, who delivered Me to the Jews, have the greater crime to answer for.

12. *Pilate sought to release him.* Pilate made five several attempts to release our Lord, as we may learn from Luke xxiii. 4, 15, 20, 22; John xix. 4, 12-13.

Thou art not Caesar's friend. You do not act like a person who has the interest of the emperor at heart. This insinuation determined Pilate to make no longer resistance; he was afraid of being accused, and he knew Tiberius was one of the most jealous and distrustful princes in the world. During his reign accusations of conspiracies were much in fashion; they were founded on the silliest pretenses and punished with excessive rigor.

13. *The Pavement.* Literally, "a stone pavement." Probably it was that place in the open court where the chair of justice was set, for the prefects of provinces always held their courts of justice in the open air, and which was paved with stones of various colors, like that of Ahasuerus, Esther i. 6, of red, blue white, and black marble; what we still term Mosaic work, or something in imitation of it *Gabbatha.* That is, "an elevated place"; from *gabah*, "high, raised up." It is very likely that the judgment seat was considerably elevated in the court, and that the governor went up to it by steps; and perhaps these very steps were what was called *the Pavement.* The place was probably called *Lithostroton*, or *the Pavement* the seat of judgment, *Gabbatha*, the "raised or elevated" place.

14. *It was the preparation of the passover* That is, the time in which they were just preparing to kill the paschal lamb. Critics differ widely concerning the time of our Lord's crucifixion, and this verse is variously understood Some think it signifies merely the preparation of the Sabbath, and that it is called *the preparation of the passover* because the preparation of the Sabbath happened that year on the eve of the Passover. Others think that the preparation of the Sabbath is distinctly spoken of in v. 31, and was different from what is here mentioned. Contending nations may be more easily reconciled than contending critics. *Behold your King!* This was probably intended as an irony; and by thus turning their pretended serious apprehensions into ridicule, he hoped still to release Him.

MATTHEW HENRY

now crowned with thorns, is, as a king at his coronation, offered to the people: "*Behold your king.*" They cried out with the greatest indignation, *Away with him, away with him.* "*Take him,* he is none of ours; we disown him; *away with him* out of our sight." Had not Christ been thus rejected of men, we had been for ever rejected of God. It shows how we ought to treat our sins. We are often in scripture said to crucify sin, in conformity to Christ's death. With a pious indignation we should run down sin in us, as they with an impious indignation ran him down who was made sin for us. Pilate, willing to have Jesus released, asks them, *Shall I crucify your king?* To stop their mouths, by showing them how absurd it was for them to reject one who offered himself to them to be their king. Though he saw no cause to fear him, they might see cause to hope for something from him. To stop the mouth of his own conscience. "If this Jesus be a king" (thinks Pilate), "he is only king of the Jews. If they refuse him, and will have their king crucified, what is that to me?" The chief priests cried out, *We have no king but Caesar*. This they knew would please Pilate, and so they hoped to carry their point, though at the same time they hated Caesar and his government. What a righteous thing it was with God to bring upon them that ruin by the Romans which followed not long after. They adhere to Caesar, and to Caesar they shall go. God soon gave them enough of their Caesars. Henceforward they were rebels to the Caesars, and the Caesars tyrants to them, and their disaffection ended in the overthrow of their place and nation. It is just with God to make that a scourge and plague to us which we prefer before Christ.

Verses 16–18

We have here sentence of death passed upon our Lord Jesus, and execution done soon after. A mighty struggle Pilate had had within him; but at length his convictions yielded, and his corruptions prevailed, the fear of man having a greater power over him than the fear of God.

I. *Pilate gave judgment* against Christ and signed the warrant for his execution, *v.* 16. Pilate sinned against his conscience; he had again and again pronounced him innocent, and yet at last condemned him as guilty. He was a man of a haughty and implacable spirit. Fearing therefore that he should be complained of, he was willing to gratify the Jews. Now this makes the matter much worse. For a man that was so wilful in other things, and of so fierce a resolution, to be overcome in a thing of this nature, shows him to be a bad man indeed, that could better bear the wronging of his conscience than the crossing of his humour. He endeavoured to transfer the guilt upon the Jews. He *delivered him* to the prosecutors, the chief priests and elders; so excusing the wrong to his own conscience with this, that it was but a permissive condemnation, and that he did not put Christ to death, but only connived at those that did it.

II. Judgment was no sooner given than the prosecutors, having gained their point, resolved to lose no time lest Pilate should change his mind. And also lest there should be *an uproar among the people*. It were well if we would be thus expeditious in that which is good, and not stay for more difficulties.

1. They immediately hurried away the prisoner. The chief priests greedily flew upon the prey which they had been long waiting for. Or *they*, that is, the soldiers, took him and led him away. Both the priests and the soldiers joined in leading him away. By the law of Moses the prosecutors were to be the executioners. And the priests here were proud of the office. He was led forth for us, that we might escape.

2. To add to his misery, they obliged him to carry his cross (*v.* 17), according to the custom among the Romans. Their crosses did not stand up constantly. Everyone that was crucified had a cross of his own. Christ's carrying his cross may be considered as a part of his sufferings; he endured the cross literally. The blessed body of the Lord Jesus was tender; it had now lately been harassed and tired out; his shoulders were sore with the stripes they had given him; every jog of the cross would renew his smart, and be apt to strike the thorns he was crowned with into his head; yet all this he patiently underwent. He was made a curse for us, and therefore on him was the cross. Our Master hereby taught all his disciples to take up their cross, and follow him. Whatever cross he calls us out to bear at any time, we must remember that he bore the cross first. He bore that end of the cross that had the curse upon it; this was the heavy end; and hence all that are his are enabled to call their afflictions for him *light*.

3. They brought him to the place of execution: He *went forth*, not dragged against his will, but voluntary in his sufferings. He went forth out of the

JAMIESON, FAUSSET, BROWN

15. crucify your King? . . . We have no king but Cæsar—"Some of those who thus cried died miserably in rebellion against Cæsar forty years afterwards. But it suited their present purpose" [ALFORD].

16. Then delivered he him therefore unto them to be crucified . . .—(See on Mark 15:15).

17-30. CRUCIFIXION AND DEATH OF THE LORD JESUS. **17. And he bearing his cross**—(See on Luke 23:26). **went forth**—Cf. Hebrews 13:11-13, "without the camp"; "without the gate." On arriving at the place, "they gave Him vinegar to drink mingled with gall [wine mingled with myrrh, Mark 15:23], and when He had tasted thereof, He would not drink" (Matt. 27:34). This potion was stupefying, and given to criminals just before execution, to deaden the sense of pain.

Fill high the bowl, and spice it well, and pour
The dews oblivious: for the Cross is sharp,
The Cross is sharp, and He
Is tenderer than a lamb.
[KEBLE]

But *our Lord would die with every faculty clear, and in full sensibility to all His sufferings.*

Thou wilt feel all, that Thou may'st pity all;
And rather would'st Thou wrestle with strong pain
Than overcloud Thy soul,
So clear in agony,
Or lose one glimpse of Heaven before the time,
O most entire and perfect Sacrifice,
Renewed in every pulse.
[KEBLE]

ADAM CLARKE

15. *Away with him.* Probably this means, "Kill Him."

G. CAMPBELL MORGAN:

"Upon this Pilate sought to release him. The Jews cried out, saying, If thou release this man, thou art not Ceasar's friend; every one that maketh himself a king speaketh against Caesar." In that sentence the Jewish nation expressed, through its rulers, their final subjugation by Gentile power, and their rejection of their birthright inheritance. They bowed the neck to Caesar in order to murder Jesus. "When Pilate therefore heard these words, he brought Jesus out, and sat down in the judgment seat at a place called The Pavement, but in Hebrew, Gabbatha. Now it was the preparation of the Passover; it was about the sixth hour." He made one more effort to release Jesus as he said, "Behold, your King! They therefore cried out, Away with him, away with him, crucify him." And again he said, now perhaps in defeat and disappointed mockery, "Shall I crucify your King?" Then the final word of the priests, "We have no king but Caesar." "Then therefore he delivered him unto them to be crucified."

—*The Gospel According to John*

16. *Then delivered he him.* This was not till after he had washed his hands, Matt. xxvii. 24, to show by that symbolical action that he was innocent of the death of Christ. John omits this circumstance, together with the insults which Christ received from the soldiers. See Matt. xxvii. 26, etc.; Mark xv. 16, etc.

17. *Bearing his cross.* He bore it all alone first. When He could no longer carry the whole through weakness, occasioned by the ill usage He had received, Simon, a Cyrenian, helped Him to carry it; see the note on Matt. xxvii. 32. *Golgotha.* See on Matt. xxvii. 33.

MATTHEW HENRY

city, for he was *crucified without the gate*, Heb. xiii. 12. And, to put the greater infamy upon his sufferings, he was brought to the common place of execution, a place called *Golgotha, the place of a skull.* There Christ suffered, because he was *made sin for us.*

4. There they crucified him, and the other malefactors with him (*v.* 18): *There they crucified him.* (1) What death Christ died; the death of the cross, a bloody, painful, shameful death, a cursed death. He was lifted up as the brazen serpent. His hands were stretched out to invite and embrace us. (2) In what company he died: *Two others with him.* This exposed him much to the people's contempt and hatred, who are apt to judge of persons by the lump, and are not curious in distinguishing, and would conclude him not only a malefactor because he was yoked with malefactors, but the worst of the three because put in the midst. But thus the scripture was fulfilled, *He was numbered among the transgressors.* He died among the criminals, and mingled his blood with theirs who were sacrificed to public justice.

And now let us pause awhile, and with an eye of faith look upon Jesus. Was ever sorrow like unto his sorrow? See him bleeding, see him struggling, see him dying, see him and love him, love him and live to him, and study what we shall render.

Verses 19–30

Here are some remarkable circumstances of Christ's dying more fully related than before.

I. The title set up over his head.

1. The inscription itself which Pilate wrote, and ordered to be fixed to the top of the cross, declaring the cause for which he was crucified, *v.* 19. It was this, *Jesus of Nazareth, the King of the Jews.* Pilate intended this for his reproach, that he, being *Jesus of Nazareth*, should pretend to be king of the Jews, and set up in competition with Caesar. But God overruled this matter: That it might be a further testimony to the innocence of our Lord Jesus; for here was an accusation which, as it was worded, contained no crime. That it might show forth his dignity and honour. This is Jesus a Saviour, dying for the good of his people, as Caiaphas had foretold.

2. The notice taken of this inscription (*v.* 20): *Many of the Jews read it*, not only those of Jerusalem, but those from other countries, that came up to worship at the feast. Multitudes read it, and it occasioned a great variety of reflections and speculations. Christ himself was set for a sign, a title. The title was so much read: Because the place where Jesus was crucified, though without the gate, was yet *nigh the city.* It is an advantage to have the means of knowing Christ brought to our doors. Because it was written in Hebrew, and Greek, and Latin; they all understood one or other of these languages. Everyone would be curious to enquire what it was which was so industriously published in the three most-known languages. In each of these Christ is proclaimed king. It was intimated thereby that Jesus Christ should be a Saviour to all nations, and not to the Jews only; and also that every nation should hear *in their own tongue the wonderful works* of the Redeemer. It teaches us that the knowledge of Christ ought to be diffused throughout every nation in their own tongue, that people may converse as freely with the scriptures as they do with their neighbours.

3. The offence which the prosecutors took at it, *v.* 21. They would not have it written, *the king of the Jews*; but that he said *I am the king of the Jews.* Here they show themselves: Very spiteful and malicious against Christ. To justify themselves they thought themselves concerned to represent him as a usurper of honours and powers that he was not entitled to. Foolishly jealous of the honour of their nation. They scorned to have it said that this was their king. Very impertinent and troublesome to Pilate. They could not but be sensible that they had forced him, against his mind, to condemn Christ. Though they had charged him with pretending to be the king of the Jews, yet they had not proved it

4. The judge's resolution to adhere to it: "*What I have written I have written.*"

1. Hereby an affront was put upon the chief priests. By this inscription he insinuates: That, notwithstanding their pretences, they were not sincere in their affections to Caesar and his government. That such a king as this, so mean and despicable, was good enough to be the king of the Jews. That they had been very unjust in prosecuting this Jesus, when there was no fault to be found in him.

2. Hereby honour was done to the Lord Jesus. Pilate stuck to it with resolution, that he was the king of the Jews. When the Jews reject Christ Pilate, a Gentile, sticks to it that he is a king, which was an earnest of what came to pass soon after, when the Gentiles submitted to the kingdom of the Messiah.

JAMIESON, FAUSSET, BROWN

18. they crucified him, and two others with him—"malefactors" (Luke 23:33), "thieves" (rather "robbers," Matt. 27:38; Mark 15:27). **on either side one and Jesus in the midst**—a hellish expedient, to hold Him up as the worst of the three. But in this, as in many other of their doings, "the scripture was fulfilled, which saith (Isa. 53:12), *And he was numbered with the transgressors*"—(Mark 15:28)—though the prediction reaches deeper. "Then said Jesus"—['probably while being nailed to the CROSS'] [OLSHAUSEN], "FATHER, FORGIVE THEM, FOR THEY KNOW NOT WHAT THEY DO" (Luke 23:34)—and again the Scripture was fulfilled which said, "And He made intercession for the transgressors" (Isa. 53:12), though this also reaches deeper. (See Acts 3:17; 13:27; and cf. I Tim. 1:13). Often have we occasion to observe how our Lord is the first to fulfil His own precepts—thus furnishing the right interpretation and the perfect Model of them. (See on Matt. 5:44.) How quickly was it seen in "His martyr Stephen," that though He had left the earth in Person, His Spirit remained behind, and Himself could, in some of His brightest lineaments, be reproduced in His disciples! (Acts 7:60.) And what does the world in every age owe to these few words, spoken *where* and *as* they were spoken!

19-22. Pilate wrote a title, and put it on the cross . . . Jesus of Nazareth, the King of the Jews . . . **and it was written in Hebrew**—or Syro-Chaldaic, the language of the country—**and Greek**—the current language—**and Latin**—the official language. These were the chief languages of the earth, and this secured that all spectators should be able to read it. Stung by this, the Jewish ecclesiastics entreat that it may be so altered as to express, not His real dignity, but His false claim to it. But Pilate thought he had yielded quite enough to them; and having intended expressly to spite and insult them by this title, for having got him to act against his own sense of justice, he peremptorily refused them. And thus, amidst the conflicting passions of men, was proclaimed, in the chief tongues of mankind, from the Cross itself and in circumstances which threw upon it a lurid yet grand light, the truth which drew the Magi to His manger, and will yet be owned by all the world!

ADAM CLARKE

18. *Two other.* Matthew and Mark in the parallel places calls them robbers or murderers; they probably belonged to the gang of Barabbas.

19. *Pilate wrote a title.* See on Matt. xxvii. 37.

20. *Hebrew, and Greek, and Latin.* See on Luke xxiii. 38.

22. *What I have written I have written.* That is, I will not alter what I have written. The Roman laws forbad the sentence to be altered when once pronounced; and as this inscription was considered as the sentence pronounced against our Lord, therefore it could not be changed. But this form of speech is common in the Jewish writings, and means simply, What is done shall continue. Pilate seems to speak prophetically. This is the King of the Jews; they shall have no other Messiah forever.

MATTHEW HENRY

II. The dividing of his garments among the executioners, *v.* 23, 24. Four soldiers were employed, who, *when they had crucified Jesus*, had nailed him to the cross, and lifted it up, and him upon it, and nothing more was to be done than to wait his expiring, went to make a dividend of his clothes. And so they *made four parts*, as nearly of the same value as they could, *to every soldier a part*; but *his coat, without seam, woven from the top throughout*, they *cast lots for it*. 1. The shame they put upon our Lord Jesus. The shame of nakedness came in with sin. He therefore who was made sin for us bore that shame. 2. The wages with which these soldiers paid themselves for crucifying Christ. They were willing to do it for his old clothes. Nothing is to be done so bad, but there will be found men bad enough to do it for a trifle. 3. The sport they made about his seamless coat. We read not of anything about him valuable or remarkable but this. Tradition says, his mother wove it for him, and adds this further, that it was made for him when he was a child. But this is a groundless fancy. The soldiers thought it a pity to rend it for then it would unravel; they would *therefore cast lots for it*. While Christ was in his dying agonies, they were merrily dividing his spoils. The preserving of Christ's seamless coat is commonly alluded to to show the care all Christians ought to take that they rend not the church of Christ with strifes and divisions. 4. The fulfilling of the scripture in this. David, in spirit, foretold this very circumstance of Christ's sufferings, in that passage, Ps. xxii. 18. *These things herefore the soldiers did.*

III. The care that he took of his poor mother.

1. His mother attends him to his death (*v.* 25): *There stood by the cross his mother*, and some of his elations and friends with her. At first, they stood ear, as it is said here; but afterwards, it is probable, he soldiers forced them to stand afar off, as it is aid in Matthew and Mark. See here the tender ffection of these pious women. When all his disiples, except John, had forsaken him, they continued heir attendance on him. They were not deterred by he fury of the enemy nor the horror of the sight; hey could not rescue him nor relieve him, yet they ttended him. We may easily suppose what an ffliction it was to these poor women to see him thus bused, especially to the blessed virgin. Now was ulfilled Simeon's word, *A sword shall pierce through hy own soul*, Luke ii. 35. His torments were her ortures, and her heart bled with his wounds. We nay justly admire the power of divine grace in suporting these women, especially the virgin Mary. We do not find his mother wringing her hands or naking an outcry; but *standing by the cross*, and her iends with her. Surely she and they were strengthned by a divine power to this degree of patience. We know not what we can bear till we are tried, and hen we know who has said, *My grace is sufficient or thee.*

2. He tenderly provides for his mother. It is robable that Joseph was long since dead, and that er son Jesus had supported her, and now that he was ying what would become of her? He saw her anding by, and he saw John standing not far off, nd so he settled a new relation between his beloved other and his beloved disciple: "*Woman, behold y son*," and to him, "*Behold thy mother*." And so *om that hour that disciple took her to his own home.* (1) The care Christ took of his dear mother. He as not so much taken up with a sense of his sufferings as to forget his friends. He had no other way provide for his mother than by his interest in a end, which he does here. He calls her *woman*, not other, because mother would have been a cutting ord to her that was already wounded to the heart ith grief. He directs her to look upon John as her n. An instance of divine goodness. Sometimes, hen God removes one comfort from us, he raises another for us, perhaps where we looked not r it. Let none therefore reckon all gone with one stern dried up, for from the same fountain another ay be filled. An instance of filial duty. Christ has re taught children to provide for the comfort of eir aged parents. Children at their death, according their ability, should provide for their parents, they survive them, and need their kindness. (2) The confidence he reposed in the beloved sciple. It is to him he says, *Behold thy mother.* is was an honour put upon John, and a testimony th to his prudence and to his fidelity. It is a great nour to be employed for Christ, and to be entrusted th any of his interest in the world. It would be a re and some charge to John; but he cheerfully cepted it, *and took her to his own home.* Those that ly love Christ, and are beloved of him, will be d of an opportunity to do any service to him or .

JAMIESON, FAUSSET, BROWN

23, 24. Then the soldiers, when they had crucified Jesus, took his garments, and made four parts; to every soldier—the four who nailed Him to the cross, and whose perquisite they were. **a part, and also his coat**—the Roman *tunic*, or close-fitting vest. **without seam, woven from the top throughout**—"perhaps denoting considerable skill and labor as necessary to produce such a garment, the work probably of one or more of the women who ministered in such things unto Him, Luke 8:3" [WEBSTER and WILKINSON]. **24. Let us not rend it, but cast lots . . ., whose it shall be, that the scripture might be fulfilled which saith, They parted my raiment among them; and for my vesture they did cast lots . . .** (Psalm 22:18). That a prediction so exceedingly specific—distinguishing one piece of dress from others, and announcing that while *those* should be parted amongst several, *that* should be given by lot to one person—that such a prediction should not only be fulfilled to the letter, but by a party of heathen military, without interference from either the friends of the enemies of the Crucified One, is surely worthy to be ranked among the wonders of this all-wonderful scene.

25-27. Now there stood by the cross of Jesus his mother, and his mother's sister, Mary, wife of Cleophas—This should be read, as in *margin*, "*Clopas*," the same as "Alpheus" (Matt. 10:3). The "Cleopas" of Luke 24:18 was a different person. **26. When Jesus . . . saw his mother, and the disciple whom he loved, standing by, he saith to his mother,** WOMAN, BEHOLD THY SON! **27. Then saith he to the disciple,** BEHOLD THY MOTHER! —What forgetfulness of self, what filial love, and to the "mother" and "son" what parting words! **from that hour . . . took her to his own home**—or, home with him; for his father Zebedee and his mother Salome were both alive, and the latter here present (Mark 15:40). See on Matthew 13:55. Now occurred the supernatural *darkness*, recorded by all the other Evangelists, but not here. "Now from the sixth hour (12, noon) there was darkness over all the land unto the ninth hour" (Matt. 27: 45). No ordinary eclipse of the sun could have occurred at this time, it being then *full moon*, and this obscuration lasted about *twelve times* the length of any ordinary eclipse. (Cf. Exod. 10:21, 23). Beyond doubt, the divine intention of the portent was to invest this darkest of all tragedies with a gloom expressive of its real character. "And about the ninth hour Jesus cried, ELI, ELI, LAMA SABACHTHANI . . . *My God, My God, why hast Thou forsaken Me*?" (Matt. 27:46). As the darkness commenced at the sixth hour, the second of the Jewish hours of prayer, so it continued till the ninth hour, *the hour of the evening sacrifice*, increasing probably in depth, and *reaching its deepest gloom at the moment of this mysterious cry*, when the flame of the one great "Evening Sacrifice" was burning fiercest. The words were made to His hand. They are the opening words of a Psalm (the 22d) full of the last "sufferings of Christ and the following glories" (I Pet. 1:11). "FATHER," was the cry in the first prayer which He uttered on the cross, for matters had not then come to the worst. "Father" was the cry of His last prayer, for matters had then passed their worst. But at this crisis of His sufferings, "Father" does not issue from His lips, for the light of a Father's countenance was then mysteriously eclipsed. He falls back, however, on a title expressive of His *official* relation, which, though lower and more distant in itself, yet when grasped in pure and naked faith was mighty in its claims, and rich in psalmodic associations. And what deep earnestness is conveyed by the redoubling of this title! But as for the cry itself, it will never be fully comprehended. An absolute desertion is not indeed to be thought of; but a total eclipse of the *felt* sense of God's presence it certainly expresses. It expresses *surprise*, as under the experience of something not only *never before known*, but *inexplicable* on the footing which had till then subsisted between Him and God. *It is a question which the lost cannot utter.* They are forsaken, *but they know why.* Jesus is forsaken, but *does not know and demands to know why.* It is thus *the cry of conscious innocence*, but of innocence unavailing to draw down, at that moment, the least token of approval from the unseen Judge—innocence whose only recognition at that moment lay in the thick surrounding gloom which but reflected the horror of great darkness that invested His own spirit. *There was indeed a cause for it*, and He knew it too—the "why" must not be pressed so far as to exclude this. *He must taste this bitterest of the wages of sin "who did no sin."*

ADAM CLARKE

23. *To every soldier a part.* So it appears there were four soldiers employed in nailing Him to and rearing up the Cross. Our Lord was now in the grand office of High Priest, and was about to offer the expiatory Victim for the sin of the world. And it is worthy of remark that the very dress He was in was similar to that of the Jewish high priest. The following is the description given of his dress by Josephus: "Now this coat (*chiton*) was not composed of two pieces, nor was it sewed together upon the shoulders and sides, but it was one long vestment, so woven as to have an opening for the neck; not an oblique one, but parted all along the back and breast: it was also parted where the hands were to come out."

24. *That the scripture might be fulfilled.* The words are taken from Ps. xxii. 18, where it appears they were spoken prophetically of this treatment which Jesus received, upwards of a thousand years before it took place! But it should be remarked that this form of speech, which frequently occurs, often means no more than that the thing so fell out that such a portion of Scripture may be exactly applied to it.

25. *Mary the wife of Cleophas.* She is said, in Matt. xxvii. 56 and Mark xv. 40, to have been the mother of James the Less and of Joses; and this James, her son, is said, in Matt. x. 3, to have been the son of Alphaeus; hence it seems that Alphaeus and Cleophas were the same person. To which may be added that Hegesippus is quoted by Eusebius as saying that Cleophas was the brother of Joseph, the husband of the Virgin. In many cases it is very difficult to distinguish the different Marys mentioned by the Evangelists.

26. *The disciple . . . whom he loved.* John, the writer of this Gospel. *Woman, behold thy son!* This is a remarkable expression, and has been much misunderstood. It conveys no idea of disrespect, nor of unconcern, as has been commonly supposed. "Man" and "woman" were titles of as much respect among the Hebrews as "sir" and "madam" are among us. But why did not Jesus call her "Mother"? Probably because He wished to spare her feelings; He would not mention a name the very sound of which must have wrung her heart with additional sorrow. On this account He said, *Behold thy son!* This was the language of pure natural affection. It is probable that it was because the keeping of the blessed Virgin was entrusted to him that he was the only disciple of our Lord who died a natural death, God having preserved him for the sake of the person whom He gave him in charge. It is very likely that Joseph was dead previously to this, and that this was the reason why the desolate Virgin is committed to the care of the beloved disciple.

MATTHEW HENRY

IV. The fulfilling of the scripture, in the giving of him vinegar to drink, *v.* 28, 29.

1. How much respect Christ showed to the scripture (*v.* 28): *Knowing that all things were accomplished, that the scripture might be fulfilled, he saith, I thirst.*

(1) It was not at all strange that he was thirsty. Well might he thirst after all the toil and hurry which he had undergone, and being now in the agonies of death, ready to expire purely by the loss of blood and extremity of pain.

(2) But the reason of his complaining of it is somewhat surprising; it is the only word he spoke that looked like complaint of his outward sufferings. He cried, *I thirst.* He would thus express *the travail of his soul.* He thirsted after the accomplishment of the work of our redemption. He would thus take care to see the scripture fulfilled. Hitherto, all had been accomplished, and he knew it. The scripture had foretold his thirst, and therefore he himself related it, because it could not otherwise be known, saying, *I thirst.* The scripture had foretold that in his thirst he should have vinegar given him to drink, Ps. lxix. 21.

2. See how little respect his persecutors showed to him (*v.* 29): *There was set a vessel full of vinegar,* probably according to the custom at all executions of this nature; with this *they filled a sponge, and they put it upon hyssop,* a hyssop-stalk, and with this heaved it to his mouth. A drop of water would have cooled his tongue better than a draught of vinegar. When heaven denied him a beam of light earth denied him a drop of water, and put vinegar in the room of it.

V. The dying word wherewith he breathed out his soul (*v.* 30): *When he had received the vinegar he said, It is finished;* and, with that, *bowed his head, and gave up the ghost.*

1. What he said, and we may suppose him to say it with triumph and exultation—*It is finished.* (1) *It is finished,* that is, the malice and enmity of his persecutors had now done their worst. (2) *It is finished,* that is, the counsel and commandment of his Father concerning his sufferings were now fulfilled. He had said, when he entered upon his sufferings, *Father, thy will be done;* and now he saith with pleasure, *It is done.* (3) *It is finished,* that is, all the types and prophecies of the Old Testament, which pointed at the sufferings of the Messiah, were accomplished and answered. (4) *It is finished,* that is, the ceremonial law is abolished. The substance is now come, and all the shadows are done away. (5) *It is finished,* that is, sin is finished, and an end made of transgression. *The Lamb of God was sacrificed to take away the sin of the world,* and it is done. (6) *It is finished,* that is, his sufferings were now finished. The storm is over, the worst is past, and he is just entering upon *the joy set before him.* Let all that *suffer for Christ,* and with Christ, comfort themselves with this, *that yet a little while* and they also shall say, *It is finished.* (7) *It is finished,* that is, his life was now finished, he was just ready to breathe his last. This we must all come to shortly. (8) *It is finished,* that is, the work of man's redemption and salvation is now completed, a fatal blow given to the power of Satan, a fountain of grace opened that shall ever flow. *He that has begun a good work will perform it;* the mystery of God shall be finished.

2. What he did: *He bowed his head, and gave up the ghost. He gave up the ghost.* His life was not forcibly extorted from him, but freely resigned. He had said, *Father, into thy hands I commit my spirit,* and, accordingly, he did give up his spirit, paid down the price of pardon and life at his Father's hands. *He bowed his head.* Those that were crucified, in dying stretched up their heads to gasp for breath, and did not drop their heads till they had breathed their last; but Christ *bowed his head* first, composing himself, as it were, to fall asleep.

Verses 31–37

This passage concerning the piercing of Christ's side after his death is recorded only by this evangelist.

I. Observe the superstition of the Jews, which occasioned it (*v.* 31): *Because it was the preparation for the sabbath, and that sabbath day was a high day,* they would *not have the dead bodies to remain on the crosses on the sabbath-day,* but *besought Pilate that their legs might be broken,* and that then they might be buried out of sight. 1. The esteem they would be thought to have for the approaching sabbath. Every sabbath day is a holy day, and a good day, but this was a high day, *a great day.* Sacrament-days, supper-days, communion-days are high days, and there ought to be more than ordinary preparation for them. 2. The reproach which they reckoned it would be to that day if the dead bodies should be left hanging on the crosses. Dead bodies were not to be left at any time. Many strangers from all parts

JAMIESON, FAUSSET, BROWN

28-30. After this, Jesus knowing that all things were now accomplished—i.e., the moment for the fulfilment of the last of them; for there was one other small particular, and the time was come for that too, in consequence of the burning thirst which the fevered state of His frame occasioned (Ps. 22:15). **that the scripture**—Ps. 69:21—**might be fulfilled, saith, I thirst.**

Now there was set a vessel full of vinegar—see on the offer of the soldiers vinegar, above—**and they**—"one of them," (Matt. 27:48). **29. filled a sponge with vinegar, and put it upon**—a stalk of—**hyssop, and put it to his mouth**—Though a stalk of this plant does not exceed eigtheen inches in length, it would suffice, as the feet of crucified persons were not raised high. "The rest said, Let be"—[i.e., as would seem, 'Stop that officious service'] "let us see whether Elias will come to save Him" (Matt. 27:49). This was the last cruelty He was to suffer, but it was one of the most unfeeling. "And when Jesus had cried with a loud voice" (Luke 23:46). This "*loud voice,*" noticed by three of the Evangelists, does not imply, as some able interpreters contend, that our Lord's strength was so far from being exhausted that He needed not to die then, and surrendered up His life sooner than Nature required, merely because it was the appointed time. It was indeed the appointed time, but time that He should be "crucified *through weakness*" (I Cor. 13:4), and Nature was now reaching its utmost exhaustion. But just as even His own dying saints, particularly the martyrs of Jesus, have sometimes had such gleams of coming glory immediately before breathing their last, as to impart to them a strength to utter their feelings which has amazed the bystanders, so this *mighty voice* of the expiring Redeemer was nothing else but the exultant spirit of the Dying Victor, receiving the fruit of His travail just about to be embraced, and nerving the organs of utterance to an ecstatic expression of its sublime feelings (not so much in the *immediately* following words of tranquil surrender, in Luke, as in the *final* shout, recorded only by John): "FATHER, INTO THY HANDS I COMMEND MY SPIRIT!" (Luke 23:46). Yes, the darkness is past, and the true light now shineth. His soul has emerged from its mysterious horrors; "*My God*" is heard no more, but in unclouded light He yields sublime into His *Father's* hands the infinitely precious spirit—using here also the words of those matchless Psalms (31:5) which were ever on His lips. "As the Father receives the spirit of Jesus, so Jesus receives those of the faithful" (Acts 7:59) [BENGEL]. And now comes the expiring mighty shout—**30. It is finished! and he bowed his head and gave up the ghost.** What is finished? The Law is fulfilled as never before, nor since, in His "obedience unto death, even the death of the cross"; Messianic prophecy is accomplished; Redemption is completed; "He hath finished the transgression, and made reconciliation for iniquity, and brought in everlasting righteousness, and sealed up the vision and prophecy, and anointed a holy of holies"; He has inaugurated the kingdom of God and given birth to a new world.

31-42. BURIAL OF CHRIST. **31-37. the preparation**—sabbath eve. **that the bodies should not remain**—over night, against the Mosaic law (Deut. 21:22, 23). **on the sabbath day, for that sabbath day was an high**—or 'great'—**day**—the first day of unleavened bread, and, as concurring with an ordinary sabbath, the most solemn season of the ecclesiastical year. Hence their peculiar jealousy lest the law should be infringed.

ADAM CLARKE

28. *I thirst.* The scripture that referred to His drinking the vinegar is Ps. lxix. 21. The fatigue which He had undergone, the grief He had felt, the heat of the day, and the loss of blood were the natural causes of this thirst.

29. *A vessel full of vinegar.* This was probably that tart small wine which we are assured was the common drink of the Roman soldiers. Our word *vinegar* comes from the French *vin aigre, sour* or "tart wine." This vinegar must not be confounded with the "vinegar and gall" mentioned in Matt. xxvii. 34 and Mark xv. 23. That, being a stupefying potion, intended to alleviate His pain, He refused to drink; but of this He took a little, and then expired, v. 30. *And put it upon hyssop.* Or, according to others, "putting hyssop about it."

30. *It is finished.* As if He had said: "I hav executed the great designs of the Almighty—have satisfied the demands of His justice—I hav accomplished all that was written in the proph ets, and suffered the utmost malice of M enemies; and now the way to the holy of holie is made manifest through My blood." An awfu yet a glorious finish!

31. *It was the preparation.* Every Sabbat had a preparation which began at the nint hour (that is, three o'clock) the preceding eve ning. Josephus, *Ant.*, b. xvi, c. 6, s. 2, recite an edict of the Emperor Augustus in favor c the Jews, which orders "that no one shall b obliged to give bail or surety on the Sabbat day, nor on the preparation before it, after th ninth hour." The time fixed here was un doubtedly in conformity to the Jewish custon as they began their preparation at three o'cloc on the Friday evening. *That the bodies shoul not remain.* For the law, Deut. xxi. 22-2 ordered that the bodies of criminals should n hang all night; and they did not wish to hav the Sabbath profaned by either taking the down on that day or letting them hang disturb the joy of that holy time. *For th sabbath day was an high day.* (1) Because was the Sabbath. (2) Because it was the da on which all the people presented themselv in the Temple according to the command, Exo xxiii. 17. (3) Because that was the day c which the sheaf of the firstfruits was offere according to the command, Lev. xxiii. 10-1 So that upon this day there happened to three solemnities in one. It might be prope called a high day because the Passover fell that Sabbath.

MATTHEW HENRY

being then at Jerusalem, it would have been an offence to them; nor could they well bear the sight of Christ's crucified body. 3. Their petition to Pilate, that their bodies, now as good as dead, might be despatched by the breaking of their legs, which would carry them off in the most exquisite pain. The pretended sanctity of hypocrites is abominable. They made no conscience of bringing an innocent and excellent person to the cross, and yet scrupled letting a dead body hang upon the cross.

II. The despatching of the *two thieves that were crucified with him, v.* 32. Pilate gave orders as they desired; *and the soldiers came and broke the legs of the two thieves.* One of these thieves was a penitent, and had received from Christ an assurance that he should shortly be with him in paradise, and yet died in the same pain and misery that the other thief did. The extremity of dying agonies is no obstruction to the living comforts that wait for holy souls on the other side death.

III. The trial that was made whether Christ was dead or no.

1. They supposed him to be dead, and therefore *did not break his legs, v.* 33. Jesus died in less time than persons crucified ordinarily did. It was to show that he laid down his life of himself. He yielded to death, yet he was not conquered. His enemies were satisfied he was really dead.

2. Because they would be sure he was dead they would put it past dispute. *One of the soldiers with a spear pierced his side and forthwith came thereout blood and water, v.* 34.

(1) The soldier hereby designed to decide the question whether he was dead or no, and by this honourable wound in his side to supersede the ignominious method of despatch they took with the other two. Tradition says that this soldier's name was *Longinus.*

(2) But God had a further design herein. To give an evidence of the truth of his death, in order to the proof of his resurrection. He was certainly dead, for this spear broke up the very fountains of life. To give an illustration of the design of his death. There was much of mystery in it, and its being so solemnly attested (*v.* 35) intimates there was something miraculous in it. It was very significant; this same apostle refers to it as a very considerable thing, 1 John v. 6, 8. The opening of his side was significant. When we would protest our sincerity, we wish there were a window in our hearts, that the thoughts and intents of them might be visible to all. Through this window, opened in Christ's side, you may look into his heart, and see love flaming there, love strong as death. *The blood and water* that flowed out of it were significant. They signified the two great benefits which all believers partake of through Christ—blood for atonement, water for purification. Guilt contracted must be expiated by blood; stains contracted must be done away by *the water of purification.* These two must always go together. Christ has joined them together, and we must not think to put them asunder. They both flowed from the pierced side of our Redeemer. They signified the two great ordinances of baptism and the Lord's supper. It is not the water in the font that will be to us *the washing of regeneration,* but the water out of the side of Christ; not the blood of the grape that will refresh the soul, but the blood out of the side of Christ.

IV. The attestation of the truth of this by an eyewitness (*v.* 35), the evangelist himself.

1. What a competent witness he was of the matters of fact. What he bore record of he saw; he was an eye-witness of it. What he saw he faithfully bore record of; he told not only the truth, but the whole truth. *His record is* undoubtedly *true,* for he wrote from the dictates of the Spirit of truth. He had himself a full assurance of the truth of what he wrote: *He knows that he saith true.* He *therefore* witnessed these things, *that we might believe*; to draw men to believe the gospel in order to their eternal welfare.

2. What care he showed in this particular instance. Let this silence the fears of weak Christians, and encourage their hopes. There came both water and blood out of Christ's pierced side, both to justify and sanctify them; and if you ask, How can we be sure of this? you may be sure, for *he that saw it bore record.*

V. The accomplishment of the scripture in all this (*v.* 36): *That the scripture might be fulfilled.*

1. The scripture was fulfilled in the preserving of his legs from being broken; therein that word was fulfilled, *A bone of him shall not be broken.* There was a promise of this made indeed to all *the righteous,* but principally pointing at *Jesus Christ the righteous* (Ps. xxxiv. 20). There was a type of this in the paschal lamb (Num. ix. 12): *You shall not break*

JAMIESON, FAUSSET, BROWN

besought Pilate that their legs might be broken—to hasten their death, which was done in such cases with clubs.

33. But when they came to Jesus, and saw that he was dead already—there being in *His* case elements of suffering, unknown to the malefactors, which might naturally hasten His death, lingering though it always was in such cases, not to speak of His *previous* sufferings. **they brake not his legs**—a fact of vast importance, as showing that the *reality* of His death was visible to those whose business it was to see to it. The *other* divine purpose served by it will appear presently. **34. But one of the soldiers**—to make assurance of the fact doubly sure—**with a spear pierced his side**—making a wound deep and wide, as indeed is plain from ch. 20:27, 29. Had life still remained, it must have fled now—

and forthwith came thereout blood and water—"It is now well known that the effect of long-continued and intense agony is frequently to produce a secretion of a colorless lymph within the pericardium (the membrane enveloping the heart), amounting in many cases to a very considerable quantity" [WEBSTER and WILKINSON].

35. And he that saw it bare record—hath borne witness—**and his witness is true, and he knoweth that he saith true, that ye might believe**—This solemn way of referring to his own testimony in this matter has no reference to what he says in his Epistle about Christ's "coming by water and blood" (see on I John 5:6), but is intended to call attention both to the fulfilment of Scripture in these particulars, and to the undeniable evidence he was thus furnishing of the *reality* of Christ's death, and consequently of His resurrection; perhaps also to meet the growing tendency, in the Asiatic churches, to deny the reality of our Lord's body, or that "Jesus Christ is come in the flesh" (I John 4:1-3). **36. that the scripture should be fulfilled, A bone of him shall not be broken**—The reference is to the paschal lamb, as to which this ordinance was stringent (Exod. 12:46; Num. 9:12. Cf. I Cor. 5:7). But though we are to see here the fulfilment of a very definite typical ordinance, we shall, on searching deeper, see in it *a remarkable divine interposition to protect the sacred body of Christ from the last indignity after He had finished the work given Him to do.* Every imaginable indignity had been permitted *before that,* up to the moment of His death. But no sooner is that over than an Unseen hand is found to have provided against the clubs of the rude soldiers coming in contact with that temple of the Godhead. Very different from such violence was that *spear-thrust,* for which not only doubting Thomas would thank the soldier, but intelligent believers in every age, to whom the certainty of their Lord's death and resurrection is the life of their whole Christianity.

ADAM CLARKE

Their legs might be broken. Lactantius says that it was a common custom to break the legs or other bones of criminals upon the cross; and this appears to have been a kind of *coup de grace,* the sooner to put them out of pain.

34. *With a spear pierced his side.* The soldier who pierced our Lord's side has been called by the Roman Catholic writers *Longinus,* which seems to be a corruption of *lonche,* a *spear* or "dart." They moreover tell us that this man was converted—that it was he who said, "Truly this was the Son of God"—that he travelled into Cappadocia, and there preached the gospel of Christ, and received the crown of martyrdom. But this deserves the same credit as the other legends of the Popish church.

Blood and water. It may be naturally supposed that the spear went through the pericardium and pierced the heart; that the water proceeded from the former, and the blood from the latter. Ambrose, Augustine, and Chrysostom make the *blood* an emblem of the Eucharist, and the *water* an emblem of baptism. Others represent them as the emblem of the old and new covenants. Protestants have thought them the emblems of justification, which is through the *blood* of the Lamb, and sanctification, which is through the *washing* of regeneration; and it is in reference to the first notion that they mingle the wine with water in the sacrament of the Lord's Supper. The issuing of the blood and water appears to be only a natural effect of the above cause, and probably nothing mystical or spiritual was intended by it. However it affords the fullest proof that Jesus *died* for our sins.

35. *He that saw it.* Most probably John himself, who must have been pretty near the Cross to have been able to distinguish between the blood and the water as they issued from the side of our blessed Lord. *And he knoweth.* This appears to be an appeal to the Lord Jesus for the truth of the testimony which he had now delivered. But why such a solemn appeal unless there was something miraculous in this matter? It might appear to him necessary: (1) because the other Evangelists had not noticed it; (2) because it contained the most decisive proof of the *death* of Christ, as a wound such as this was could not have been inflicted (though other causes had been wanting) without occasioning the death of the person, and on His *dying* for men depended the salvation of the world; and (3) because two important prophecies were fulfilled by this very circumstance, both of which designated more particularly the person of the Messiah. "A bone of him shall not be broken," Exod. xii. 46; Num. ix. 12; Ps. xxxiv. 20. "They shall look upon me whom they have pierced," Zech. xii. 10; Ps. xxii. 16.

MATTHEW HENRY

any bone of it. He is *the Lamb of God* (*ch.* i. 29), and, as the true passover, his bones were kept unbroken. There was a significancy in it; the strength of the body is in the bones. The Hebrew word for the bones signifies the strength. Though *he be crucified in weakness* his strength to save is not at all broken. Sin breaks our bones but it did not break Christ's bones; he stood firm under the burden, mighty to save.

2. *The scripture was fulfilled* in *the piercing of his side* (*v.* 27): *They shall look on me whom they had pierced;* so it is written, Zech. xii. 10. It is here implied that the Messiah shall be pierced; and here it had a more full accomplishment than in *the piercing of his hands and feet.* It is promised that *when the Spirit is poured out they shall look on him and mourn.* This was in part fulfilled when many of those that were his betrayers and murderers *were pricked to the heart*, and brought to believe in him. We have all been guilty of piercing the Lord Jesus, and are all concerned with suitable affections to look on him.

Verses 38–42

We have here an account of the burial of the blessed body of our Lord Jesus. Come and see a burial that conquered the grave, and buried it, a burial that beautified the grave and softened it for all believers.

I. The body begged, *v.* 38. This was done by *Joseph of Arimathea,* of whom no mention is made in all the New Testament story, but only in the narrative which each of the evangelists gives us of Christ's burial. 1. The character of this Joseph. He was a disciple of Christ *in secret*, a better friend to Christ than he would willingly be known to be. It was his honour that he was a disciple of Christ; and some such there are, that are themselves great men, and unavoidably linked with bad men. But it was his weakness that he was so secretly. Christ may have many that are his disciples sincerely, though secretly; better secretly than not at all, especially, if like Joseph, here, they grow stronger and stronger. Some who in less trials have been timorous, yet in greater have been very courageous; so Joseph here. To Pilate the governor he *went boldly*, and yet *feared the Jews.* The impotent malice of those that can but censure, and revile, is sometimes more formidable even to wise and good men than one would think. 2. The part he bore in this affair. He, having access to Pilate, desired leave of him to dispose of the body. His disciples were gone; if nobody appeared, the Jews or soldiers would bury him with the thieves. When God has work to do he can find out such as are proper to do it, and embolden them for it. Observe it as an instance of the humiliation of Christ, that his dead body lay at the mercy of a heathen judge, and must be begged before it could be buried.

II. The embalming prepared, *v.* 39. This was done by Nicodemus, another person of quality, and in a public post. He brought a *mixture of myrrh and aloes.* 1. The character of Nicodemus, which is much the same with that of Joseph; he was a secret friend to Christ. He at first *came to Jesus by night*, but now owned him publicly, as before, *ch.* vii. 50, 51. That grace which at first is like a bruised reed may afterwards become like a strong cedar. It is a wonder that Joseph and Nicodemus, men of such interest, did not appear sooner, and solicit Pilate not to condemn Christ. Begging his life would have been a nobler piece of service than begging his body. 2. The kindness of Nicodemus. Joseph served Christ with his interest, Nicodemus with his purse. Probably, they agreed it between them, because they were straightened in time. But why did they made this ado about Christ's dead body? Some think we may see in it the weakness of their faith. What need of such furniture of the grave for one that, like a way-faring man, did but turn aside into it, to *tarry for a night or two*? However, we may plainly see in it the strength of their love. Hereby they showed the value they had for his person and doctrine, and that it was not lessened by the reproach of the cross. They showed not only the charitable respect of committing his body to the earth, but the honourable respect shown to great men. This they might do, and yet believe and look for his resurrection. Since God designed honour for this body, they would put honour upon it.

III. The body got ready, *v.* 40. They *took it*, and, having washed it from blood and dust, *wound it in linen clothes*, with the spices, as *the manner of the Jews is to bury.* Here was care taken of Christ's body: It was *wound in linen clothes.* Among clothing that belongs to us, Christ put on even the grave-clothes, to make them easy to us, and to enable us to call them our wedding-clothes. Dead bodies

JAMIESON, FAUSSET, BROWN

37. And again another scripture saith, They shall look on him whom they pierced—The quotation is from Zechariah 12:10; not taken as usual from the Septuagint (the current Greek version), which here is all wrong, but direct from the Hebrew. And there is a remarkable nicety in the choice of the words employed both by the prophet and the Evangelist for "piercing." The word in Zechariah means to *thrust through* with spear, javelin, sword, or any such weapon. In that sense it is used in all the ten places, besides this, where it is found. How suitable this was to express the action of the Roman soldier, is manifest; and our Evangelist uses the exactly corresponding word, which the Septuagint certainly does not. Very *different is the other word* for "*pierce*" in Psalm 22:16, "*They pierced my hands and my feet.*" The word there used is one signifying to *bore* as with an awl or hammer. How striking are these small niceties! **38-40. Joseph of Arimathea**—"a rich man" (Matt. 27:57), thus fulfilling Isaiah 53:9; "an honorable counsellor," a member of the Sanhedrim, and of good condition, "which also waited for the kingdom of God" (Mark 15:43), a devout expectant of Messiah's kingdom; "a good man and a just, the same had not consented to the counsel and deed of them" (Luke 23:50, 51—he had gone the length, perhaps, of dissenting and protesting in open council against the condemnation of our Lord); "who also himself was Jesus' disciple" (Matt. 27:57). **being a disciple of Jesus, but secretly, for fear of the Jews**—"He went in boldly unto Pilate" (Mark 15:43)—lit., "having taken courage went in," or "had the boldness to go in." Mark alone, as his manner is, notices the *boldness* which this required. The act would without doubt identify him *for the first time* with the disciples of Christ. Marvellous it certainly is, that one who while Jesus was yet alive merely refrained from condemning Him, not having the courage to espouse His cause by one positive act, should, now that He was dead, and His cause apparently dead with Him, summon up courage to go in personally to the Roman governor and ask permission to take down and inter the body. But if this be the first instance, it is not the last, that *a seemingly dead Christ has wakened a sympathy which a living one had failed to evoke. The heroism of faith is usually kindled by desperate circumstances, and is not seldom displayed by those who before were the most timid, and scarce known as disciples at all.* "And Pilate marvelled if he were"—rather "wondered that he was" "already dead." "And calling the centurion, he asked him whether He had been any while dead"—Pilate could hardly credit what Joseph had told him, that He had been dead "some time," and, before giving up the body to His friends, would learn how the fact stood from the centurion, whose business it was to oversee the execution. "And when he knew it of the centurion," that it was as Joseph had said, "he gave"—rather 'made a gift of'—"the body to Joseph"; struck, possibly, with the rank of the petitioner and the dignified boldness of the petition, in contrast with the spirit of the other party and the low rank to which he had been led to believe all the followers of Christ belonged. Nor would he be unwilling to show that he was not going to carry this black affair any farther. But, whatever were Pilate's motives, two most blessed objects were thus secured: (1) *The reality of our Lord's death was attested* by the party of all others most competent to decide on it, and certainly free from all bias—the officer in attendance—in full reliance on whose testimony Pilate surrendered the body: (2) The dead Redeemer, thus delivered out of the hands of His enemies, and committed by the supreme political authority to the care of His friends, was thereby protected from all further indignities; a thing most befitting indeed, now that His work was done, but impossible, so far as we can see, if His enemies had been at liberty to do with Him as they pleased. How wonderful are even the minutest features of this matchless History! **39. also Nicodemus, which at the first came to Jesus by night**—"This remark corresponds to the secrecy of Joseph's discipleship, just noticed, and calls attention to the similarity of their previous character and conduct, and the remarkable change which had now taken place" [WEBSTER and WILKINSON]. **brought . . . myrrh and aloes, about an hundred pounds weight**—an immense quantity, betokening the greatness of their love, but part of it probably intended as a layer for the spot on which the body was to lie. (See II Chron. 16:14) [MEYER]. **40. Then took they the**

ADAM CLARKE

38. *Joseph of Arimathaea.* See on Matt. xxvii. 57-60; and particularly Mark xv. 42-43.

39. *Nicodemus.* See on chap. iii. 1. *Myrrh and aloes.* Which drugs were used to preserve bodies from putrefaction.

TODAY'S DICTIONARY OF THE BIBLE:

Joseph, a native of Arimathea, probably the Ramah of the Old Testament (1 Sam. 1:19), a man of wealth, and a member of the Sanhedrin (Matt. 27:57; Luke 23:50, 51), an "honorable counselor, who waited for the kingdom of God." As soon as he heard the tidings of Christ's death, he "went in boldly [*lit.* having summoned courage, he went] unto Pilate, and craved the body of Jesus." Pilate, having ascertained from the centurion that the death had really taken place, granted Joseph's request, who immediately, having purchased fine linen (Mark 15:46), proceeded to Golgotha to take the body down from the cross. There, assisted by Nicodemus, he took down the body and wrapped it in the fine linen, sprinkling it with the myrrh and aloes which Nicodemus had brought (John 19:39), and then conveyed the body to the new tomb hewn by Joseph himself out of a rock in his garden nearby. There they laid it, in the presence of Mary Magdalene, Mary the mother of Joses, and other women, and rolled a great stone to the entrance, and departed (Luke 23:53, 55). This was done in haste, "for the Sabbath was drawing on" (comp. Isa. 53:9).

MATTHEW HENRY

and graves are noisome and offensive. No ointment or perfume can rejoice the heart so as the grave of our Redeemer does, where there is faith to perceive the fragrant odours of it. In conformity to this example, we ought to have regard to the dead bodies of Christians; not to enshrine and adore their relics, but carefully to deposit them, the dust in the dust, as those who believe that the dead bodies of the saints are still united to Christ. The resurrection of the saints will be in virtue of Christ's resurrection, and therefore in burying them we should have an eye to Christ's burial.

IV. The grave pitched upon, in a garden which belonged to Joseph of Arimathea, very near the place where he was crucified. There was a sepulchre not yet used.

1. Christ was buried without the city, for thus the manner of the Jews was to bury. There was then a peculiar reason for it, because the touching of a grave contracted a ceremonial pollution: but now that the resurrection of Christ has altered the property of the grave, we need not keep at such a distance from it. Those that would not superstitiously, but by faith, visit the holy sepulchre, must go forth out of the noise of this world.

2. Christ was buried in a garden. Joseph had his sepulchre in his garden that it might be a memento: To himself while living. The garden is a proper place for meditation, and a sepulchre there may furnish us with a proper subject for meditation. To his heirs and successors when he was gone. It is good to acquaint ourselves with the *place of our fathers' sepulchres*; and perhaps we might make our own less formidable if we made theirs more familiar. In a sepulchre in a garden Christ's body was laid. In the garden of Eden death and the grave first received their power, and now in a garden they are conquered.

3. He was buried in a new sepulchre. This was so ordered, (1) For the honour of Christ. He that was born from a virgin-womb must rise from a virgin-tomb. (2) For the confirming of the truth of his resurrection, that it might not be suggested that it was not he, but some other that rose. He that has *made all things new* has new-made the grave for us.

V. The funeral solemnized (*v.* 42): *There laid they Jesus.* There they laid him because it was the preparation day.

1. The deference which the Jews paid to the sabbath, and to the day of preparation. This day had been ill kept by the chief priests, who called themselves the church, but was well kept by the disciples of Christ, who were branded as dangerous to the church; and it is often so. They would not put off the funeral till the sabbath day, because the sabbath is to be a day of holy rest and joy. They would not drive it too late on the day of preparation for the sabbath.

2. The convenience they took of an adjoining sepulchre; the sepulchre they made use of was *nigh at hand.* It was so ordered that he should be laid in a sepulchre nigh at hand: Because he was to lie there but awhile, as in an inn, and therefore he took the first that offered itself. Because this was a new sepulchre. Those that prepared it little thought who should handsel it. We are hereby taught not to be over-curious in the place of our burial. Where the tree falls, why should it not lie? For Christ was buried in the sepulchre that was next at hand.

Thus without pomp or solemnity is the body of Jesus laid in the cold and silent grave. Here lies death itself slain, and the grave conquered. *Thanks be to God, who giveth us the victory.*

JAMIESON, FAUSSET, BROWN

body of Jesus, and wound it in linen clothes with the spices, as the manner of the Jews is to bury—the mixed and pulverized myrrh and aloes shaken into the folds, and the entire body, thus swathed, wrapt in an outer covering of "clean linen cloth" (Matt. 27:59). Had the Lord's own friends had the least reason to think that the spark of life was still in Him, would *they* have done this? But even if one could conceive them mistaken, could anyone have lain thus enveloped for the period during which He was in the grave, and life still remained? Impossible. When, therefore, He walked forth from the tomb, we can say with the most absolute certainty, "Now is Christ *risen from the dead,* and become the first fruits of them that slept" (I Cor. 15:20). No wonder that the learned and the barbarians alike were prepared to die for the name of the Lord Jesus; for such evidence was to the unsophisticated resistless. (No mention is made of *anointing* in this operation. No doubt it was a hurried proceeding, for fear of interruption, and because it was close on the sabbath, the women seem to have set this as their proper task "as soon as the sabbath should be past" (Mark 16:1). But as the Lord graciously held it as undesignedly anticipated by Mary at Bethany (Mark 14:8), so this was probably all the anointing, in the strict sense of it, which He received. **41, 42. Now in the place where he was crucified there was a garden, and in the garden a new sepulchre**—The choice of this tomb was, on *their* part, dictated by the double circumstance that it was so near at hand, and by its belonging to a friend of the Lord; and as there was need of haste, even they would be struck with the providence which thus supplied it. "There laid they Jesus therefore, because of the Jew's preparation-day, for the sepulchre was nigh at hand." But there was one recommendation of it which probably would not strike them; but God had it in view. Not its being "hewn out of a rock" (Mark 15:46), accessible only at the entrance, which doubtless would impress them with its security and suitableness. But it was "a *new* sepulchre" (vs. 41), "*wherein never man before was laid*" (Luke 23:53): and Matthew (27:60) says that Joseph laid Him "in *his own new tomb,* which he had hewn out in the rock"—doubtless for his own use, though the Lord had higher use for it. Thus as He rode into Jerusalem on an ass "*whereon never man before had sat,*" so now He shall lie in a tomb *wherein never man before had lain,* that from these specimens it may be seen that in all things He was "SEPARATE FROM SINNERS."

ADAM CLARKE

G. CAMPBELL MORGAN:

Always in those rock-hewn tombs, there was a porch; into that they carried the dead body. There they brought the body of Jesus, and there we see these two men wrapping it round, with a hundred pounds of spices intermixed with the wrappings. John is careful to say they buried Him "as the custom of the Jews is to bury." That is to say not after the Egyptian manner, or the manner of other nations, which meant embalming, and the mutilation of the body. The Jews never mutilated a dead body, but wrapped it in spices in the cloths, and last of all a final winding sheet. The wrapping of those dead bodies was a work of singular complexity.—*The Gospel According to John*

41. *There was a garden.* It was an ancient custom for particular families to have burying places in their gardens. See 2 Kings xxi. 18, 26. *New sepulchre.* See on Matt. xxvii. 60.

42. *Because of the Jews' preparation.* From this it may be conjectured that they had designed to put Him in a more magnificent tomb, or that they intended to make one expressly for himself after the Passover, or that they had designed to put Him somewhere else, but could not do it for want of time; and that they put Him here because the tomb *was nigh.* It appears plainly, from embalming, that none of these persons had any hope of the resurrection of Christ. They considered Him as a great and eminent prophet, and treated Him as such.

MATTHEW HENRY — CHAPTER 20

Verses 1–10

There was no one thing of which the apostles were more concerned to produce substantial proof than the resurrection of their Master, 1. Because it was that which he himself appealed to as the last and most cogent proof of his being the Messiah. And therefore enemies were most solicitous to stifle the notice of this. 2. Because it was upon this the performance of his undertaking for our redemption and salvation did depend. 3. Because he never showed himself alive after his resurrection to all the people, Acts x. 40, 41. But the demonstrations of his resurrection should be reserved as a favour for his particular friends, and by them be published to the world, that those might be blessed who have not seen, and yet have believed.

In these verses we have the first step towards the proof of Christ's resurrection, which is, that the sepulchre was found empty.

I. Mary Magdalene, coming to the sepulchre, finds the *stone taken away.* This evangelist does not men-

JAMIESON, FAUSSET, BROWN — CHAPTER 20

VSS. 1-18. MARY'S VISIT TO THE SEPULCHRE, AND RETURN TO IT WITH PETER AND JOHN—HER RISEN LORD APPEARS TO HER.

1, 2. The first day . . . cometh Mary Magdalene early . . .—(See on Mark 16:1-4; and Matt. 28:1, 2).

ADAM CLARKE — CHAPTER 20

1. *The first day of the week.* On what we call Sunday morning, the morning after the Jewish Sabbath. As Christ had been buried in haste, these holy women had bought aromatics, Mark xvi. 1; Luke xxiv. 1, to embalm Him afresh, and in a more complete manner than it could have been done by Joseph and Nicodemus.

John mentions only Mary of Magdala, because he appears to wish to give a more detailed history of her conduct than of any of the rest.

MATTHEW HENRY

tion the other women that went with Mary Magdalene, but her only. Much was forgiven her, therefore she loved much. She had shown her affection to him while he lived, attended his doctrine, ministered to him of her substance, Luke viii. 2, 3. The continued instances of her respect to him at and after his death prove the sincerity of her love. Love to Christ, if it be cordial, will be constant. Her love to Christ was *strong as death,* the death of the cross, for it stood by that.

1. She *came to the sepulchre,* to wash the dead body with her tears, for she *went to the grave, to weep there,* and to *anoint it with the ointment* she had prepared. It must be an extraordinary affection to the person which will endear his grave to us. It is especially frightful to the weak and timorous sex. Love to Christ will take off the terror of death and the grave. If we cannot come to Christ but through that darksome valley, even in that, if we love him, we shall *fear no evil.*

2. She came as soon as she could. Upon the *first day of the week,* as soon as ever the sabbath was gone. This was the first Christian sabbath, and she begins it accordingly with enquiries after Christ. She came *early, while it was yet dark.* Those who would seek Christ so as to find him must seek him early. Seek him solicitously; be up early for fear of missing him. Seek him industriously. Seek him betimes. That day is in a fair way to be well ended that is thus begun. Those that diligently enquire after Christ *while it is yet dark* shall have such light given them concerning him as shall shine *more and more.*

3. She found the stone taken away, which she had seen *rolled to the door of the sepulchre.* Now this was, (1) A surprise to her. Christ crucified is the fountain of life. His grave is one of the wells of salvation; if we come to it in faith, we shall find the stone rolled away and free access to the comforts of it. Surprising comforts are the frequent encouragements of early seekers. (2) The beginning of a glorious discovery; the Lord was risen, though she did not at first apprehend it so. Those that are most constant in their adherence to Christ have commonly the first and sweetest notices of the divine grace. Mary Magdalene, who followed Christ to the last in his humiliation, met him with the first in his exaltation.

II. Finding the stone taken away, she hastens back to Peter and John: "*They have taken the Lord out of the sepulchre, and we know not where they have laid him.*" She found the stone gone, looked into the grave, and saw it empty. Now one would expect that the first thought that offered itself would have been, Surely the Lord is risen; for whenever he had told them that he should be crucified, he still subjoined in the same breath that *the third day he should rise again.* Could she now see the grave empty, and yet have no thought of the resurrection enter into her mind? When we come to reflect upon our own conduct in a *cloudy and dark day,* we shall stand amazed at our dulness and forgetfulness, that we could miss of such thoughts as afterwards appear obvious. She suggested, *They have taken away the Lord.* Whatever was her suspicion, it seems it was a great vexation and disturbance to her that the body was gone; whereas, if she had understood it rightly, nothing could be more happy. Weak believers often make that the matter of their complaint which is really just ground of hope, and matter of joy. She did not stand poring upon the grief herself, but acquaints her friends with it. The communication of sorrows is one good improvement of the communion of saints. Peter, though he had denied his Master, had not deserted his Master's friends; by this appears the sincerity of his repentance. And the disciples' keeping up their intimacy with him as formerly, teaches us to restore those that have been faulty. If God has received them upon their repentance, why should not we?

III. Peter and John go with all speed to the sepulchre, *v.* 3, 4. Some think that the other disciples were with Peter and John when the news came; for they *told these things to the eleven,* Luke xxiv. 9. Yet none of them went to the sepulchre but Peter and John, who were often distinguished from the rest by special favours. It is well when those that are more honoured than others with the privileges of disciples are more active than others in the duty of disciples, more willing to take pains and run hazards. See here what use we should make of the experience of others. When Mary told them what she had seen, they would go and see with their own eyes. Do others tell us of the comfort and benefit of ordinances? Let us be engaged thereby to make trial of them. See how ready we should be to share with our friends in their cares and fears. Peter and John hastened to the sepulchre. See what haste we should make in a good work. Peter and John consulted neither their

JAMIESON, FAUSSET, BROWN

she runneth and cometh to Simon Peter, and to the other disciple whom Jesus loved, and saith unto them, They have taken away the Lord out of the sepulchre—Dear disciple! thy dead Lord is to thee "the Lord" still.

ADAM CLARKE

But the other Evangelists speak of three persons who went together to the tomb, viz., Mary of Magdala, Mary the mother of James, and Salome, Matt. xxviii. 1; Mark xvi. 1.

2. *Then she runneth.* This was after the women had seen the angels, who said He was risen from the dead, Luke xxiv. 4. She told not only Peter and John but the other apostles also, Matt. xxviii. 8; but only the two disciples above mentioned went to the tomb to see whether what she had said was true. *They have taken away the Lord.* She mentions nothing of what the angels had said, in her hurry and confusion; she speaks things only by halves; and probably the vision of angels might have appeared to her only as an illusion of her own fancy, and not to be any further regarded.

A. B. SIMPSON:

Mary at the sepulchre, or the new revelation of the risen Lord (John 20:1-18). This woman was singularly honored by the love of her risen Lord, as the first witness of His resurrection. She had been saved from more than perhaps any of His disciples. His strong arm of love had rescued her from the sevenfold possession of demoniacal power. There is no reason to suppose that her womanhood had been degraded by the sin which has been associated with her name, but something more terrific, and on her part involuntary and irresistible, had bound perhaps all the powers of her body and soul. Set free by His almighty love, her heart was now bound to Him by cords of everlasting love. No sadder or truer heart lingered at the cross through the dark hours of His dying agony, and no more fearless or devoted feet hastened on the Easter morning to anoint His body in Joseph's sepulchre. Finding the stone rolled away and the door open, she hastens to tell His brethren, Peter and John. When they have come and gone, she lingers still in the garden, believing that the body has been removed by the gardener's hands, perhaps, because of its being inconvenient to keep it longer. It is then that Jesus appears to her, disguised at first in a form that she mistakes for the gardener; but the disguise only brings out more beautifully her tender love. Her willing hands are ready to bear away the precious body, but His living voice dispels the illusion, and her hands clasp with rapture the feet of her Lord.—*Christ in the Bible*

ALEXANDER MACLAREN:

Peter and John at the tomb, the dawning of faith, and the continuance of bewildered wonder. In the account, we may observe, first, the characteristic conduct of each of the two. Peter is first to set out, and John follows, both men doing according to their kind. The younger runs faster than his companion. He looked into the tomb, and saw the wrappings lying; but the reverent awe which holds back finer natures kept him from venturing in. Peter is not said to have looked before entering. He loved with all his heart, but his love was impetuous and practical, and he went straight in, and felt no reason why he should pause. His boldness encouraged his friend, as the example of strong natures does.—*Expositions of Holy Scripture*

MATTHEW HENRY

ease nor their gravity, but ran to the sepulchre. See what a good thing it is to have good company in a good work. See what a laudable emulation it is among disciples to strive which shall excel in that which is good. It was no breach of ill manners for John to outrun Peter. We must do our best, and neither envy those that can do better, nor despise those that do as they can, though they come behind. He that got foremost in this race was *the disciple whom Jesus loved.* Sense of Christ's love to us, kindling love in us to him again, will make us to excel in virtue. He that was cast behind was Peter, who had denied his Master, and was in sorrow and shame for it. When conscience is offended we lose ground.

IV. Peter and John, having come to the sepulchre, prosecute the enquiry.

1. John went no further than Mary Magdalene had done. He had the curiosity to look into the sepulchre, and saw it was empty. He *stooped down,* and *looked in.* Those that would find the knowledge of Christ must stoop down, and look in. Yet he had not courage to go into the sepulchre. The warmest affections are not always accompanied with the boldest resolutions.

2. Peter went in first and made a more exact discovery than John had done, *v.* 6, 7. While John was with much caution looking in, he came, and with great courage *went into the sepulchre.* The boldness of Peter, and how God dispenses his gifts variously. John could out-run Peter, but Peter could out-dare John. Some disciples are quick, and they are useful to quicken those that are slow; others are bold, and they are useful to embolden those that are timorous. Those who in good earnest seek after Christ must not frighten themselves with bugbears and foolish fancies. Good Christians need not be afraid of the grave, since Christ has lain in it. Let us therefore not indulge, but conquer, the fear we are apt to conceive upon the sight of a dead body, or being alone among the graves. We must be willing to go through the grave to Christ; that way he went to his glory, and so must we. If we cannot see God's face and live, better die than never see it. The posture in which he found things in the sepulchre. Christ had left his grave-clothes behind him there. He laid them aside because he arose to die no more. Lazarus came out with his grave-clothes on, for he was to use them again. When we arise from the death of sin to the life of righteousness, we must leave our grave-clothes behind us, must put off all our corruptions. Christ left those in the grave, as it were, for our use; if the grave be a bed to the saints, thus he hath sheeted that bed, and made it ready for them. The grave-clothes were found in very good order, which serves for an evidence that his body was not stolen away while men slept. Peter's boldness encouraged John; now he took heart and ventured in (*v.* 8), and *he saw and believed.* He began to believe that Jesus was risen to life again.

(1) John followed Peter in venturing. He durst not have gone into the sepulchre if Peter had not gone in first. It is good to be emboldened in a good work by the boldness of others. The dread of difficulty and danger will be taken off by observing the resolution and courage of others. Perhaps John's quickness had made Peter run faster, and now Peter's boldness makes John venture further. John not only associated with Peter, but thought it no disparagement to follow him.

(2) John got the start of Peter in believing. Peter saw and wondered (Luke xxiv. 12), but John saw and believed. A mind disposed to contemplation may perhaps sooner receive the evidence of divine truth than a mind disposed to action. But what was the reason that they were so slow of heart to believe? The evangelist tells us (*v.* 9), as yet they *knew not the scripture* that he must *rise again from the dead. First,* How unapt the disciples themselves were, at first, to believe the resurrection of Christ, which confirms the testimony they afterwards gave with so much assurance concerning it; for, by their backwardness to believe it, it appears that they were not credulous concerning it, nor of those simple ones that believe every word. It was to them as a strange thing, and one of the furthest things from their thoughts. Peter and John were so shy of believing it at first that nothing less than the most convincing proof could bring them to testify it afterwards with so much assurance. Hereby it appears that they were not only honest men, who would not deceive others, but cautious men, who would not themselves be imposed upon. *Secondly,* The reason of their slowness to believe; because as yet they *knew not the scripture.* This seems to be the evangelist's acknowledgment of his own fault among the rest.

3. Peter and John pursued their enquiry no further, hovering between faith and unbelief (*v.* 10): *The*

JAMIESON, FAUSSET, BROWN

3-10. Peter therefore went forth, and that other disciple, and came first to the sepulchre.—These particulars have a singular air of artless truth about them. Mary, in her grief, runs to the two apostles who were soon to be so closely associated in proclaiming the Saviour's resurrection, and they, followed by Mary, hasten to see with their own eyes. The younger disciple outruns the older; love haply supplying swifter wings. He stoops, he gazes in, but enters not the open sepulchre, held back probably by a reverential fear. The bolder Peter, coming up, goes in at once, and is rewarded with bright evidence of what had happened.

6-7. seeth the linen clothes lie—lying—**And the napkin, that was about his head, not lying with the linen clothes**—not loosely, as if hastily thrown down, and indicative of a hurried and disorderly removal—**but wrapped**—folded—**together in a place by itself**—showing with what grand tranquillity "the Living One" had walked forth from "the dead" (Luke 24:5). "Doubtless the two attendant angels (vs. 12) did this service for the Rising One, the one disposing of the linen clothes, the other of the napkin" [BENGEL]. **8. Then went in . . . that other disciple which came first to the sepulchre**—The repetition of this, in connection with his not having gone in till after Peter, seems to show that at the moment of penning these words the advantage which each of these loving disciples had of the other was present to his mind. **and he saw and believed**—Probably he means, though he does not say, that he believed in his Lord's resurrection more immediately and certainly than Peter.

9. For as yet they knew—i.e., understood—**not the scripture that he must rise again from the dead.**—In other words, they believed in His resurrection at first, not because they were prepared by Scripture to expect it; but *facts* carried resistless conviction of it in the first instance to their minds, and furnished a key to the Scripture predictions of it.

ADAM CLARKE

4. *Outrun Peter.* Not because he had a greater desire to see into the truth of these things, but because he was younger and lighter of foot.

6. *Seeth the linen clothes lie.* To "look steadily" at anything, so as to discover what it is and to be satisfied with viewing it.

7. *Wrapped together in a place by itself.* The providence of God ordered these very little matters, so that they became the fullest proofs against the lie of the chief priests that the body had been stolden away by the disciples. If the body had been stolen away, those who took it would not have stopped to strip the clothes from it and to wrap them up and lay them by in separate places.

8. *That other disciple.* John. *Saw.* That the body was not there. *And believed.* That it had been taken away, as Mary had said; but he did not believe that He was risen from the dead. See what follows.

9. *They knew not the scripture.* Viz., Ps. xvi. 9-10: "Thou wilt not leave my soul in hell"—For Thou wilt not abandon My life to the grave, nor "suffer thine Holy One to see corruption." It was certainly a reproach to the disciples that they had not understood this prophecy, when our Lord had often given them the most direct information concerning it. However, this ingenuous confession of John in a matter so dishonorable to himself is a full proof of his sincerity and of the truth of his narration.

G. CAMPBELL MORGAN:

In these few verses John shows that these disciples, Mary, John, and Peter, used their eyes, but he uses different words to describe how they did so. It is said that Mary "seeth" the stone rolled away. It is said when John arrived, that "he seeth the linen cloths lying." It is said Peter "beholdeth the linen cloths lying, and the napkin" in separation. Then it is said that John "saw."

Mary "seeth," and the Greek verb is *blepo,* which means just to see, quite the ordinary word. When John came, and stooping, looked in, he also saw in that way, the linen cloths lying. When Peter came, he beheld. The word for Peter's use of his eyes is *theoreo.* This word suggests far more than mere seeing. It means that he looked critically and carefully. We are not told of any effect produced upon him. I am sure an effect was produced. Then John, encouraged, went in. Now we have an entirely different word. It is the word *eido.* This word, while describing the use of the eyes, always conveys the ideal of apprehension and understanding of the thing seen. When John went in, he saw, that is, he understood, and therefore believed. Intelligent apprehension produced absolute conviction.—*The Gospel According to John*

MATTHEW HENRY

disciples went away to their own home. For fear of being taken up upon suspicion of a design to steal away the body, or of being charged with it now that it was gone. In difficult dangerous times it is hard even for good men to go on in their work with the resolution that becomes them. Because they were at a loss, and knew not what to do next, nor what to make of what they had seen; which is an instance of their weakness as yet. It is probable that the rest of the disciples were together; to them they return, to make report of what they had discovered. It is observable that before Peter and John came to the sepulchre an angel had appeared there, rolled away the stone, frightened the guard, and comforted the women; as soon as they were gone from the sepulchre, Mary Magdalene here sees two angels in the sepulchre (*v.* 12), and yet Peter and John come to the sepulchre, and go into it, and see none. Angels appear and disappear at pleasure, according to the orders and instructions given them. They may be, and are really, where they are not visibly. This favour was shown to those who were early and constant in their enquiries after Christ, and was the reward of those that came first and stayed last, but denied to those that made a transient visit.

Verses 11–18

I. The constancy and fervency of Mary Magdalene's affection to the Lord Jesus, *v.* 11.

1. She stayed at the sepulchre, when Peter and John were gone, because there her Master had lain. This good woman, though she has lost him, will abide by his grave for his sake, and continue in his love even when she wants the comfort of it.

2. She stayed there weeping, and these tears loudly bespoke her affection to her Master. Those that have lost Christ have cause to weep. Those that seek Christ must weep, not for him, but for themselves.

3. *As she wept, she looked into the sepulchre.* When we are in search of something that we have lost we look again and again in the place where we last left it, and expected to have found it. Weeping must not hinder seeking. Though she wept, she *stooped down and looked in.*

II. The vision she had of two angels in the sepulchre, *v.* 12.

1. The description of the persons she saw. They were *two angels in white, sitting* one *at the head,* and the other at the *feet,* of the grave. Their nature. They were angels, messengers from heaven, sent on purpose: To honour the Son. Now that the Son of God was again to be brought into the world, the angels have a charge to attend him, as they did at his birth. To comfort the saints, and, by giving them notice that the Lord was risen, to prepare them for the sight of him. Their number: *two,* not a *multitude of the heavenly host,* to sing praise, only two, to bear witness. Their array: They were *in white,* denoting their purity and holiness. Glorified saints, when they come to be as the angels, shall *walk with Christ in white.* Their posture and place: They sat in Christ's grave. These angels went into the grave, to teach us not to be afraid of it. Matters are so ordered that the grave is not much out of our way to heaven. These angelic guards, keeping possession of the sepulchre, when they had frightened away the guards, represents Christ's victory over the powers of darkness. Their sitting to face one another, one at his bed's head, the other at his bed's feet, may also remind us of the two cherubim, placed one at either end of the mercy-seat, looking one at another. Christ crucified was the great propitiary, at the head and feet of which were these two cherubim, not with flaming swords, to keep us from, but welcome messengers, to direct us to, the way of life.

2. Their compassionate enquiry into the cause of Mary Magdalene's grief (*v.* 13): *Woman, why weepest thou?* A rebuke to her weeping: "*Why weepest thou,* when thou hast cause to rejoice?" Many of the floods of our tears would *dry away* before such a search as this into the fountain of them. It was designed to show how much angels are concerned at the griefs of the saints. Christians should thus sympathize with one another. It was only to make an occasion of informing her of that which would turn her mourning into rejoicing.

3. The melancholy account of her present distress: *Because they have taken away* the blessed body I came to embalm, *and I know not where they have laid it.* (1) The weakness of her faith. We often perplex ourselves needlessly with imaginary difficulties, which faith would discover to us as real advantages. (2) The strength of her love. Mary Magdalene is not diverted from her enquiries by the surprise of the vision, nor satisfied with the honour of it; but still she harps upon the same string: *They have taken away my Lord.* A sight of angels and their smiles

JAMIESON, FAUSSET, BROWN

11-15. But Mary stood without at the sepulchre weeping . . .—Brief was the stay of those two men. But Mary, arriving perhaps by another direction after they left, lingers at the spot, weeping for her missing Lord. As she gazes through her tears on the open tomb, she also ventures to stoop down and look into it, when lo! "two angels in white" (as from the world of light, and see on Matt. 28:3) appear to her in a "sitting" posture, "as having finished some business, and awaiting some one to impart tidings to" [BENGEL].

12. one at the head, and the other at the feet where the body of Jesus had lain—not merely proclaiming silently the *entire* charge they had had of the body of Christ [quoted in LUTHARDT], but rather, possibly, calling mute attention to the narrow space within which the Lord of glory had contracted Himself; as if they would say, Come, see within what limits, marked off by the interval here between us two, *the Lord* lay! But she is in tears, and these suit not the scene of so glorious an Exit. They are going to point out to her the incongruity.

13. Woman, why weepest thou?—You would think the vision too much for a lone woman. But absorbed in the one Object of her affection and pursuit, she speaks out her grief without fear.

Because . . .—i.e., Can I choose but weep, when "they have taken away . . ." repeating her very words to Peter and John. On this she turned herself and saw Jesus Himself standing beside her, but took Him for the gardener. Clad therefore in some such style He must have been. But if any ask, as too curious interpreters do, whence He got those habiliments, we answer [with OLSHAUSEN and LUTHARDT] where the two angels got theirs. Nor did the voice of

ADAM CLARKE

10. *Unto their own home.* Either to their own houses, if they still had any, or to those of their friends, or to those where they had a hired lodging, and where they met together for religious purposes.

11. *But Mary stood without.* She remained some time after Peter and John had returned to their own homes.

12. *Seeth two angels.* She knew these to be angels by their white and glistering robes. Matthew and Mark mention but one angel—probably that one only that spoke, v. 13. *One at the head, and the other at the feet.* So were the cherubim placed at each end of the mercy seat, Exod. xxv. 18-19.

13. *They have taken away my Lord.* It was conjectured, on chap. xix. 42, that the body of our Lord was put here only for the time being, that, after the Sabbath, they might carry it to a more proper place. Mary seems to refer to this: *They have taken away my Lord, and I know not where they have laid him.* This removal she probably attributed to some of our Lord's disciples or to some of His friends.

MATTHEW HENRY

will not suffice without a sight of Christ and God's smiles in him. Nay, the sight of angels is but an opportunity of pursuing her enquiries after Christ. The angels asked her, *Why weepest thou?* I have cause enough to weep, says she, for *they have taken away my Lord*. None know, but those who have experienced it, the sorrow of a deserted soul, that has had comfortable evidences of the love of God in Christ, but has now lost them, and walks in darkness.

III. Christ's appearing to her while she was talking with the angels. Christ himself steps in. Mary would fain know where her Lord is, and behold he is at her right hand. Those that will be content with nothing short of a sight of Christ shall be put off with nothing less. Christ, in manifesting himself to those that seek him, often outdoes their expectations. Mary longs to see the dead body of Christ, and behold she sees him alive. Thus he does for his praying people more than they are able to ask or think.

(1) He did at first conceal himself from her.

[1] He stood as a common person, and she looked upon him accordingly, *v.* 14. She *turned herself back* from talking with the angels, and *sees Jesus himself* standing, and yet she *knew not that it was Jesus. The Lord is nigh unto them that are of a broken heart* (Ps. xxxiv. 18), nearer than they are aware. Those that seek Christ, though they do not see him, may yet be sure he is not far from them. Those that diligently seek the Lord will turn every way in their enquiry after him. *Mary turned herself back*, in hopes of some discoveries. It was her earnest desire in seeking that made her turn every way. Christ is often near his people, and they are not aware of him. She *knew not that it was Jesus*.

[2] He asked her a common question, and she answered him accordingly, *v.* 15.

First, The question he asked her was what anyone would have asked her: "*Woman, why weepest thou? Whom seekest thou?*" It should seem, this was the first word Christ spoke after his resurrection: "*Why weepest thou?*" Christ takes cognizance: Of his people's griefs, and enquires, *Why weep you?* Of his people's cares, and enquires, *Whom seek you, and what would you have?* When he knows they are seeking him, yet he will know it from them.

Secondly, The reply she made him is natural enough. *Supposing him to be the gardener, Sir, if thou hast carried him hence*, pray *tell me where thou hast laid him, and I will take him away*. 1. The error of her understanding. She supposed our Lord Jesus to be the gardener. Troubled spirits, in a cloudy and dark day, are apt to misrepresent Christ to themselves. 2. The truth of her affection. See how her heart was set upon finding Christ. She puts the question to everyone she meets. When she speaks of Christ, she does not name him; but, *If thou have borne him hence*, taking it for granted that this gardener was full of thoughts concerning this Jesus as well as she. Another evidence of the strength of her affection was that, wherever he was laid, she would undertake to remove him. Such a body was much more than she could pretend to carry; but true love thinks it can do no more than it can, and makes nothing of difficulties. Christ needs not to stay where he is thought a burden.

(2) How Christ at length made himself known to her, and gave her infallible assurances of his resurrection.

[1] How Christ discovered himself to this good woman (*v.* 16): *Jesus saith unto her, Mary*. It was said with that air of kindness with which he was wont to speak to her. Now he changed his voice, and spoke like himself, not like the gardener. Christ's *sheep know his voice, ch.* x. 4. This one word, *Mary*, was like that to the disciples in the storm, *It is I*.

[2] How readily she received this discovery. She turned herself and said, *Rabboni, My Master*. The title of respect she gives him: *My Master*. *Rabbon* was with them a more honourable title than *Rabbi*; and therefore Mary chooses that, and adds a note of appropriation, *My great Master*. Notwithstanding the freedom of communion which Christ is pleased to admit us to, he is our *Master*. With what liveliness of affection she gives this title to Christ. *She turned* from the angels to look unto Jesus. We must take off our regards from all creatures, even the brightest and best, to fix them upon Christ. When *she thought it had been the gardener*, she looked another way while speaking to him; but now that she knew the voice of Christ *she turned herself*.

[3] The further instructions that Christ gave her (*v.* 17): "*Touch me not*, but go and carry the news to the disciples."

First, He diverts her from the expectation of familiar society and conversation with him at this time: *Touch me not, for I am not yet ascended*. Mary was

JAMIESON, FAUSSET, BROWN

His first words disclose Him to Mary—"Woman, why weepest thou? whom seekest thou?" He will *try* her ere he *tell* her. She answers not the stranger's question, but comes straight to her point with him.

ALEXANDER MACLAREN:

The presence of angels was a trifle to Mary, who had only one thought—the absence of her Lord. Surely that touch in her unmoved answer, as if speaking to men, is beyond the reach of art. She says "*My* Lord" now, and "*I* know not," but otherwise repeats her former words, unmoved by any hope caught from John. Her clinging love needed more than an empty grave and folded clothes and waiting angels to stay its tears, and she turned indifferently and wearily away from the interruption of the question to plunge again into her sorrow. Chrysostom suggests that she "turned herself," because she saw in the angels' looks that they saw Christ suddenly appearing behind her; but the preceding explanation seems better. Her not knowing Jesus might be accounted for by her absorbing grief. One who looked at white-robed angels, and saw nothing extraordinary, would give but a careless glance at the approaching figure, and might well fail to recognize Him.—*Expositions of Holy Scripture*

15. Sir, if thou have borne him hence—borne *whom?* She says not. She can think only of *One*, and thinks others must understand her. It reminds one of the question of the Spouse, "Saw ye him whom my soul loveth?" (Song of Sol. 3:3.) **tell me where thou hast laid him, and I will take him away**—Wilt thou, dear fragile woman? But it is the language of sublime affection, that thinks itself fit for anything if once in possession of its Object. It is enough. Like Joseph, He can no longer restrain Himself (Gen. 45:1).

16, 17. Jesus saith unto her, Mary—It is not now the distant, though respectful, "Woman." It is the oft-repeated name, uttered, no doubt, with all the wonted manner, and bringing a rush of unutterable and overpowering associations with it.

She turned herself, and saith to him, Rabboni!—But that single word of transported recognition was not enough for woman's full heart. Not knowing the change which had passed upon Him, she hastens to express by her action what words failed to clothe; but she is checked.

ADAM CLARKE

14. *She turned herself back*. Or "she was turned back," i.e., to go again with the other women to Jerusalem, who had already departed; but she had not as yet gone so far as to be out of the garden. *Knew not that it was Jesus*. John has here omitted what the angels said to the women about Christ's being risen, probably because it was so particularly related by the other Evangelists: Matt. xxviii. 5-7; Mark xvi. 6-7; Luke xxiv. 5-7. Mary was so absorbed in grief that she paid but little attention to the person of our Lord, and therefore did not at first discern it to be He; nor could she imagine such an appearance possible, as she had no conception of His resurrection from the dead. She was therefore in every way unprepared to recognize the person of our Lord.

15. *Supposing him to be the gardener*. The inspector or overseer of the garden, the person who had the charge of the workmen, and the care of the produce of the garden, and who rendered account to the owner. *And I will take him away*. How true is the proverb, "Love feels no load"! Jesus was in the prime of life when He was crucified, and had a hundred pounds' weight of spices added to His body; and yet Mary thinks of nothing less than carrying Him away with her if she can but find where He is laid!

16. *Mary*. This word was no doubt spoken with uncommon emphasis; and the usual sound of Christ's voice accompanied it, so as immediately to prove that it must be Jesus. What transports of joy must have filled this woman's heart! Let it be remarked that Mary Magdalene sought Jesus more fervently and continued more affectionately attached to Him than any of the rest; therefore to her first Jesus is pleased to show himself, and she is made the first herald of the gospel of a risen Saviour.

MATTHEW HENRY

ready to express her joy by affectionate embraces of him, which Christ here forbids at this time. *Touch me not* for I am to ascend to heaven. He bade the disciples touch him, for the confirmation of their faith. She must believe him, and adore him, but must not expect to be familiar with him as formerly. He forbids her to dote upon his bodily presence, and leads her to the spiritual communion which she should have with him after he was ascended to his Father. Though *I am not yet ascended, go to my brethren, and tell them, I am to ascend.* As before his death, so now after his resurrection, he still harps upon this. They must look higher than his bodily presence, and look further than the present state of things. "*Touch me not*, stay not now to make any further enquiries, or give any further expressions of joy, for *I am not yet ascended.* The best service thou canst do now is to carry the tidings to the disciples; lose no time therefore, but go away with all speed." Mary must not stay to talk with her Master, but must carry his message; for it is a day of good tidings.

Secondly, He directs her what message to carry to his disciples: *But go to my brethren, and tell them that I ascend.* To whom this message is sent: *Go to my brethren* with it. He was now entering upon his glory, yet he owns his disciples as his brethren. He had called them friends, but never brethren till now. Though Christ be high, yet he is not haughty. Notwithstanding his elevation, he disdains not to own his poor relations. He had never seen them together since *they all forsook him and fled.* He forgives, he forgets, and does not upbraid. By whom it is sent: by *Mary Magdalene, out of whom had been cast seven devils.* This was her reward for her constancy in adhering to Christ; she becomes an apostle to the apostles. What the message itself is: *I ascend to my Father.*

a. Our joint-relation to God, resulting from our union with Christ, is an unspeakable comfort. He says, He is *my Father, and your Father*; *my God, and your God.* It is the great dignity of believers that *the Father of our Lord Jesus Christ* is, in him, *their Father.* He is ours by a gracious adoption; yet even this warrants us to call him, as Christ did, *Abba, Father.* It is the great condescension of Christ that he is pleased to own the believer's God for his God: *My God, your God;* the God of the Redeemer, to support him, that he might be the God of the redeemed, to save them.

b. Christ's ascension into heaven is likewise an unspeakable comfort: "Tell them I must shortly ascend." *(a)* A word of caution to these disciples, not to expect the continuance of his bodily presence on earth. "I am risen, not to stay with them, but to go on their errand to heaven." Thus those who are raised to a spiritual life must reckon that they rise to ascend. Let them not think that this earth is to be their home and rest; no, being born from heaven, they are bound for heaven. I ascend, therefore must I seek things above. *(b)* A word of comfort to them, and to all *that shall believe in him through their word*; he was then ascending, he is now *ascended to his Father, and our Father.* He says it with triumph, that those who love him may rejoice. He ascended as our forerunner, *to prepare a place for us*, and to be ready to receive us.

Some make these words, *I ascend to my God and your God*, to include a promise of our resurrection. *Because I live, you shall live also.*

IV. Here is Mary Magdalene's faithful report to the disciples (*v.* 18): *She came and told the disciples that she had seen the Lord.* Peter and John had left her seeking him carefully with tears, and would not stay to seek him with her. Now she found it was a living body and a glorified one; so that she found what she sought, and, what was infinitely better, she had joy in her sight of the Master herself. When God comforts us, it is with this design, that we may comfort others. And as she told them what she had seen, so also what she had heard; *that he had spoken these things unto her* as a message to be delivered to them.

Verses 19–25

The infallible proof of Christ's resurrection was his *showing himself alive*, Acts i. 3. In these verses, we have an account of his first appearance to the college of the disciples, on the day on which he rose. He had sent them the tidings of his resurrection, but to confirm their faith in him, he came himself, that they might not have it by hearsay only, but might themselves be eye-witnesses of his being alive.

I. When and where this appearance was, *v.* 19. It was *the same day, being the first day of the week.*

There are three secondary ordinances (as I may call them) instituted by our Lord Jesus, to continue in his church; these are, the Lord's day, solemn

JAMIESON, FAUSSET, BROWN

17. Jesus saith unto her, Touch me not, for I am not yet ascended to my Father—Old familiarities must now give place to new and more awful yet sweeter approaches; but for these the time has not come yet. This seems the spirit, at least, of these mysterious words, on which much difference of opinion has obtained, and not much that is satisfactory said.

but go to my brethren—(Cf. Matt. 28:10; Heb. 2:11, 17). That He had still our Humanity, and therefore "*is not ashamed to call us brethren*," is indeed grandly evidenced by these words. But it is worthy of most reverential notice, that *we nowhere read of anyone who presumed to call Him Brother.* "My brethren: Blessed Jesus, who are these? Were they not Thy followers? yea, Thy forsakers? How dost Thou raise these titles with Thyself! At first they were Thy *servants;* then *disciples;* a little before Thy death, they were Thy *friends;* now, after Thy resurrection, they were Thy *brethren.* But oh, mercy without measure! how wilt Thou, how canst Thou call *them* brethren whom, in Thy last parting, Thou foundest fugitives? Did they not run from Thee? Did not one of them rather leave his inmost coat behind him than not be quit of Thee? And yet Thou sayest, 'Go, tell My brethren! It is not in the power of the sins of our infirmity to unbrother us'" [BISHOP HALL]. **I ascend unto my Father and your Father, and to my God and your God**—words of incomparable glory! Jesus had called God habitually His *Father,* and on one occasion, in His darkest moment, His *God.* But both are here united, expressing that full-orbed relationship which embraces in its vast sweep at once Himself and His redeemed. Yet, note well, He says not, *Our* Father and *our* God. All the deepest of the Church fathers were wont to call attention to this, as expressly designed to distinguish between what God is to Him and to us—*His Father essentially, ours not so: our God essentially, His not so: His God only in connection with us: our God only in connection with Him.*

18. Mary Magdalene came and told the disciples that she had seen the Lord, and that he had spoken these things unto her—*To a woman was this honor given to be the first that saw the risen Redeemer,* and *that woman was not His mother.* (See on Mark 16:9.)

19-23. JESUS APPEARS TO THE ASSEMBLED DISCIPLES.

ADAM CLARKE

17. *Touch me not.* "Cling not to Me." *Aptomai* has this sense in Job xxxi. 7, where the Septuagint use it for the Hebrew *dabak,* which signifies to "cleave, cling, stick, or be glued to." From Matt. xxviii. 9, it appears that some of the women "held him by the feet, and worshipped him." This probably Mary did; and our Lord seems to have spoken to her to this effect: "Spend no longer time with Me now. I am not going immediately to heaven—you will have several opportunities of seeing Me again. But go and tell My disciples that I am, by and by, to ascend to My Father and God, who is your Father and God also. Therefore, let them take courage."

ALBERT BARNES:

17. *"Touch me not."* This passage has given rise to a variety of interpretations. Jesus required Thomas to touch him (v. 27), and it has been difficult to ascertain why he forbade this now to Mary. The reason why he directed Thomas to do this was that he doubted whether he had been restored to life. Mary did not doubt that. The reason why he forbade her to touch him now is to be sought in the circumstances of the case. Mary, filled with joy and gratitude, was about to prostrate herself at his feet, disposed to *remain* with him, and offer him there her homage as her risen Lord. This is probably included in the word "touch" in this place; and the language of Jesus may mean this: "Do not approach me *now* for this purpose. Do not *delay* here. Other opportunities will yet be afforded to see me. I have not yet ascended—that is, I am not *about* to ascend *immediately*, but shall remain yet on earth to afford opportunity to my disciples to enjoy my presence." From Matt. 23:9, it appears that the women, when they met Jesus, "held him by the feet and worshipped him." This species of adoration it was probably the intention of Mary to offer, and this, *at that time*, Jesus forbade, and directed her to go at once and give his disciples notice that he had risen. "My brethren" (see 15:15). "My Father and your Father." Nothing was better fitted to afford them consolation than this assurance that *his* God was *theirs*, and that, though he had been slain, they were still indissolubly united in attachment to the same Father and God.

—*Popular Commentary*

18. *Told the disciples . . . that he had spoken these things.* Mark says, chap. xvi. 11, that the afflicted apostles could not believe what she had said. They seem to have considered it as an effect of her troubled imagination.

MATTHEW HENRY | JAMIESON, FAUSSET, BROWN | ADAM CLARKE

assemblies, and a standing ministry. The mind of Christ concerning each of these is plainly intimated to us in these verses: of the first two, here, in the circumstances of this appearance, the other *v.* 21.

1. Here is a Christian sabbath observed by the disciples, and owned by our Lord Jesus. The visit Christ made to his disciples was on *the first day of the week*. And the first day of the week is (I think) the only day of the week, or month, or year, that is ever mentioned by number in all the New Testament; and this is several times spoken of as a day religiously observed. Thus, in effect, he blessed and sanctified that day.

2. Here is a Christian assembly solemnized by the disciples, and also owned by the Lord Jesus. Probably the disciples met here for some religious exercise, to pray together. They met to know one another's minds, strengthen one another's hands, and concert proper measures to be taken in the present critical juncture. This meeting was private, because they durst not appear publicly. They met in a house, but they kept the door shut, that they might not be seen together, and that none might come among them but such as they knew; for they feared the Jews. Those *sheep of the flock were scattered* in the storm; but sheep are sociable, and will come together again. It is no new thing for the assemblies of Christ's disciples to be driven into corners, and forced into the wilderness. God's people have been often obliged to *enter into their chambers, and shut their doors*, as here, *for fear of the Jews*.

II. What was said and done in this visit Christ made to his disciples. When they were assembled, Jesus came among them. *Where two or three are gathered together in his name, he will be in the midst of them.* He came, though *the doors were shut*. It is a comfort to Christ's disciples, when their solemn assemblies are reduced to privacy, that no doors can shut out Christ's presence from them. We have five things in this appearance of Christ:

1. His kind and familiar salutation of his disciples: *He said, Peace be unto you*. The phrase was common, but the sense was now peculiar. *Peace be unto you* is as much as, All good be to you, all peace always by all means. Christ had left them his peace for their legacy, *ch.* xiv. 27. He here makes prompt payment of the legacy: *Peace be unto you*. Peace with God, peace in your own consciences, peace with one another; all this peace be with you; not peace with the world, but peace in Christ. His sudden appearing in *the midst of them*, could not but put them into some disorder and consternation, the noise of which waves he stills with this word, *Peace be unto you*.

2. His clear and undeniable manifestation of himself to them, *v.* 20. And here observe: The method he took to convince them of the truth of his resurrection. None could desire a further proof than the scars or marks of the wounds in the body. The marks of the wounds remained in the body of the Lord Jesus even after his resurrection, that they might be demonstrations of the truth of it. Conquerors glory in the marks of their wounds. Christ's wounds were to speak on earth that it was he himself, and therefore he arose with them; they were to speak in heaven, in the intercession he must ever live to make, and therefore he ascended with them. These marks he showed to his disciples, for their conviction. They had not only the satisfaction of seeing him look with the same countenance, and hearing him speak with the same voice, but they had the further evidence of these peculiar marks: he opened his hands to them, that they might see the marks of the wounds on them; he opened his breast, to show them the wound there. The exalted Redeemer will ever show himself open-handed and open-hearted to all his faithful friends and followers. The impression it made upon them. They were convinced that they saw the Lord; so was their faith confirmed. Thus many true believers, who, while they were weak, feared their comforts were but imaginary, afterwards find them, through grace, real and substantial. *Then they were glad.* The evangelist seems to write it with somewhat of transport and triumph. *Then! then! were the disciples glad, when they saw the Lord.* How would it revive the heart of these disciples to hear that Jesus is again alive! It is life from the dead to them. Now that word of Christ was fulfilled (*ch.* xvi. 22), *I will see you again, and your heart shall rejoice.* This wiped away all tears from their eyes.

3. The commission he gave them to be his agents in the planting of his church, *v.* 21.

(1) The preface to their commission, which was the solemn repetition of the salutation before: *Peace be unto you.* The former salutation was to still the tumult of their fear, that they might calmly attend to the proofs of his resurrection; this was to reduce

G. CAMPBELL MORGAN:

But they were gathered together. What brought them back? They had been scattered every one to his own. They had fled when the thunderstorm burst upon His head. But now they were together again. The only thing that brought them together again was the stories that they had heard in the early morning that He was alive, that He was risen from the dead. They had not understood the fact of His resurrection. John tells us that in this very chapter at an earlier point. But there were those who said they had seen Him. Through the intervening hours, as recorded by other of the evangelists, others had seen Him. They were afraid. The doors were shut. And yet inside they were surely talking of their Lord, and of these strange things. I think I am warranted in saying that by the story of the two walking to Emmaus. They were walking disconsolately away from Jerusalem when our Lord joined them. He asked them what they were talking about, and why they looked so sad. They said, "Are you only a lodger in Jerusalem, are you only tarrying for a night? Don't you know the things that are happening?" And He said to them, "What things?" Then they told Him, "Jesus of Nazareth . . . a Prophet mighty in deed and word. . . . We hoped that it was he which should redeem Israel." I am always convinced that the two going to Emmaus were men, because they said, "Certain women of our company" say that they have seen Him, as though it were possibly a delusion. They were all talking about Him. Thus they were gathered, with the conflicting emotions of wonder, of hope, of fear.
—*The Gospel According to John*

19-23. the same day at evening, the first day of the week, the doors being shut where the disciples were assembled for fear of the Jews, came Jesus—plainly not by the ordinary way of entrance.

and saith unto them Peace be unto you—not the mere *wish* that even His own exalted peace might be theirs (ch. 14:27), but conveying it into their hearts, even as He "opened their understandings to understand the scriptures" (Luke 24:45).

when he had so said, he showed them his hands and his side—not only as *ocular* and *tangible* evidence of the *reality* of His resurrection (see on Luke 24:37-43), but as through "the *power* of that resurrection" dispensing all His peace to men. **Then were the disciples glad when they saw the Lord.**

19. *The doors were shut . . . for fear of the Jews.* We do not find that the Jews designed to molest the disciples; but, as they had proceeded so far as to put Christ to death, the faith of the disciples not being very strong, they were led to think that they should be the next victims if found. Some think, therefore, that they had the doors not only *shut* but barricaded. Nevertheless Jesus came in, **the doors being** shut, i.e., while they continued shut. **But how?** By His almighty power; and further we know not. Yet it is quite possible that no miraculous influence is here intended. The doors might be shut for fear of the Jews; and Jesus might open them, and enter in the ordinary way. Where there is no need for a miracle, a miracle is never wrought. The Evangelist has omitted the appearing of our Lord to the other women who came from the tomb, Matt. xxviii. 9, and that to the two disciples who were going to Emmaus, Luke xxiv. 13, etc., which all happened in the course of this same day. *Peace be unto you.* His usual salutation and benediction. May every blessing of heaven and earth which you need be granted unto you!

20. *He shewed unto them his hands and his side.* So it appears that His body bore the marks of the nails and the spear; and these marks were preserved that the disciples might be the more fully convinced of the reality of His resurrection.

F. B. MEYER:

The risen Christ brings peace. Evidently our Lord was clothed in the spiritual body of which the apostle speaks, not subject to the laws governing physical life. Twice he uttered the salutation, "Peace be unto you." The first time he accompanied his words with the indication of his wounds: "He shewed unto them his hands and his side." This was the peace of forgiveness, falling on conscience-stricken hearts as the dew distills on parched herbage. "Look at the wounds of Jesus!" cried Staupitz to Luther, and there is, indeed, no other sign which can give rest to the penitent. This is the peace of the evening hour, when we come back from the soil and fret of the world and need to have our feet washed and our heart quieted.

The second time the message of peace was accompanied by an injunction to go forth into the world, as he was sent from the Father, on the great errand of world evangelization. Then he breathed on them and said, "Receive ye the Holy Ghost," which shortly after was to descend as a rushing, mighty wind. There is no way of remitting sin but by preaching the gospel of reconciliation, with the Holy Spirit accompanying our message. This is the peace of the morning, when we go forth to our post of duty or danger.—*Bible Commentary*

21. Then said Jesus—prepared now to listen to Him in a new character. **Peace be unto you.**

MATTHEW HENRY

the transport of their joy, that they might sedately hear what he had further to say to them. To encourage them to accept of the commission he was giving them. In the issue, it would be peace to them. Christ was now sending the disciples to publish peace to the world, and he here not only confers it upon them but commits it to them as a trust to be by them transmitted.

(2) The commission itself: *As my Father hath sent me, even so send I you.* It is easy to understand how Christ sent them; he appointed them to go on with his work upon earth. He sent them authorized with a divine warrant, armed with a divine power. Hence they were called *apostles*—men *sent*. But how Christ sent them as the Father sent him is not so easily understood; certainly their commissions and powers were infinitely inferior to his. [1] Their work was of the same kind with his, and they were to go on where he left off. As he was sent to bear witness to the truth, so were they; not to be mediators of the reconciliation, but only preachers and publishers of it. As the Father sent him *to the lost sheep of the house of Israel*, so he sent them into all the world. [2] He had a power to send them equal to that which the Father had to send him. By the same authority that the Father sent me do I send you. Had he an incontestable authority, and an irresistible ability, for his work? so had they for theirs. *As the Father hath sent me:* by virtue of the authority given him as a Mediator, he gave authority to them, to act for him, and in his name, so that those who received them, or rejected them, received or rejected him, and him that sent him, *ch.* xiii. 20.

4. The qualifying of them (*v.* 22): *He breathed on them, and said, Receive ye the Holy Ghost.*

(1) The sign he used: *He breathed on them;* not only to show them, by this breath of life, that he himself was really alive, but to signify to them the spiritual life and power which they should receive from him. As *the breath of the Almighty* gave life to man and began the old world, so the breath of the mighty Saviour gave life to his ministers, and began a new world. The Spirit is the breath of Christ, *proceeding from the Son. The breath of God* is put for the power of his wrath, but the breath of Christ signifies the power of his grace; the breathing of threatenings is changed into the breathings of love by the mediation of Christ. The Spirit is the gift of Christ. The apostles communicated the Holy Ghost by the laying on of hands, for they could only carry it as messengers; but Christ conferred the Holy Ghost by breathing, for he is the author of the gift.

(2) The solemn grant he made: "*Receive ye the Holy Ghost.*" *First*, Christ hereby gives them assurance of the Spirit's aid in their future work: "*I send you*, and you shall have the Spirit to go along with you." Whom Christ employs he will clothe with his Spirit, and furnish with all needful powers. *Secondly*, He hereby gives them experience of the Spirit's influences in their present case. He had shown them his hands and his side, to convince them of the truth of his resurrection. "Therefore *receive ye the Holy Ghost*, to work faith in you." They were now in danger of the Jews: "Therefore receive ye the Holy Ghost, to work courage in you." What Christ said to them he says to all true believers, *Receive ye the Holy Ghost*.

5. One particular branch of the power given them particularized (*v.* 23): "*Whosesoever sins you remit*, they are remitted to them; *and whosesoever sins you retain, they are retained.*" How this follows upon their receiving the Holy Ghost; for, if they had not had an extraordinary spirit of discerning, they had not been fit to be entrusted with such an authority. Yet it must be understood as a general charter to the church and her ministers, encouraging the faithful stewards of the mysteries of God to stand to the gospel they were sent to preach, for that God himself will stand to it. Christ, being risen for our justification, sends his gospel heralds to proclaim the act of indemnity now passed. Those whom the gospel acquits shall be acquitted, and those whom the gospel condemns shall be condemned, which puts immense honour upon the ministry, and should put immense courage into ministers. Two ways, and both as having authority: (1) By sound doctrine. They are commissioned to tell the world that salvation is to be had upon gospel terms, and no other. (2) By a strict discipline, applying the general rule of the gospel to particular persons.

III. The incredulity of Thomas, which introduced Christ's second appearance.

1. Here is Thomas's absence, *v.* 24. He is said to be *one of the twelve*, though now eleven. They were but eleven, and one of them was missing: Christ's disciples will never be all together till the general assembly at the great day. By his absence he missed

JAMIESON, FAUSSET, BROWN

As my Father hath sent me, so send I you—(See on ch. 17:18).

22. he breathed on them—a symbolical conveyance to them of the Spirit.

and saith, Receive ye the Holy Ghost—an earnest and first fruits of the more copious Pentecostal effusion.

Whose soever sins ye remit, they are remitted unto them . . .—In any *literal* and *authoritative* sense *this power was never exercised by one of the apostles*, and plainly *was never understood by themselves as possessed by them or conveyed to them.* (See on Matthew 16:19.) The power to intrude upon the relation between men and God cannot have been given by Christ to His ministers in any but a *ministerial* or *declarative* sense—as the authorized interpreters of His word, while in the *actings* of His ministers, the real nature of the power committed to them is seen in the exercise of *church discipline*.

24-29. Jesus Again Appears to the Assembled Disciples. **24, 25. But Thomas** (see on ch. 14: 16) **. . . was not with them when Jesus came**—why, we know not, though we are loath to think [with Stier, Alford and Luthardt] it was *intentional*,

ADAM CLARKE

21. *Even so send I you.* As I was sent to proclaim the truth of the Most High, and to convert sinners to God, I send you for the very same purpose, clothed with the very same authority, and influenced by the very same Spirit.

22. *He breathed on them.* Intimating, by this, that they were to be made new men, in order to be properly qualified for the work to which He had called them. For in this breathing He evidently alluded to the first creation of man, when God breathed into him the breath of lives, and he became a living soul, the breath or Spirit of God (*ruach Elohim*) being the grand principle and cause of his spiritual and divine life.

Receive ye the Holy Ghost. From this act of our Lord, the influences of the Holy Spirit on the souls of men have been termed His "inspiration"; from *in*, "into," and *spiro*, "I breathe." Every word of Christ which is received in the heart by faith comes accompanied by this divine breathing; and without this there is neither light nor life.

23. *Whose soever sins ye remit.* See the note on Matt. xvi. 19 and xviii. 18. It is certain God alone can forgive sins; and it would be not only blasphemous but grossly absurd to say that any creature could remit the guilt of a transgression which had been committed against the Creator. The apostles received from the Lord the doctrine of reconciliation and the doctrine of condemnation. They who believed on the Son of God, in consequence of their preaching, had their sins remitted; and they who would not believe were declared to lie under condemnation.

24. *Thomas . . . called Didymus.* See this name explained, chap. xi. 16. *Was not with them.* And by absenting himself from the company of the disciples he lost this precious opportunity of seeing and hearing Christ, and

MATTHEW HENRY

the satisfaction of seeing his Master risen, and of sharing with the disciples in their joy upon that occasion.

2. The account which the other disciples gave him, *v.* 25. They *said unto him, We have seen the Lord.* It seems, though Thomas was then from them, he was not long from them; absentees for a time must not be condemned as apostates for ever: Thomas is not Judas. With what exultation they speak it. "*We have seen the Lord*, and we wish thou hadst been here, to see him too." The disciples of Christ should endeavour to *build up one another in their most holy faith*, both by repeating what they have heard to those that were absent, and also by communicating what they have experienced. Those that by faith have seen the Lord, and tasted that he is gracious, should tell others what God has done for their souls; only let boasting be excluded.

3. The objections Thomas raised against the evidence. "*Except I shall* not only *see in his hands the print of the nails*, but put my finger into it, *and thrust my hand* into the wound *in his side, I will not believe*." Some conjecture him to have been a man of a rough, morose temper, apt to speak peevishly; for all good people are not alike happy in their temper. There was certainly much amiss in his conduct. He had either not heeded, or not duly regarded, what Christ had so often said, that he would *rise again the third day*. He did not pay a just deference to the testimony of his fellow-disciples. They all ten of them concurred in the testimony with great assurance; and yet he could not persuade himself to say that *their record was true*. It was not, however, their veracity that he questioned, but their prudence; he feared they were too credulous. He tempted Christ when he would be convinced by his own method, or not at all. Thomas ties up his faith to this evidence. Either he will be humoured, and have his fancy gratified, or he will not believe. The open avowal of this in the presence of the disciples was an offence and discouragement to them. As one coward makes many, so does one unbeliever, one sceptic. His proclaiming his infidelity, and that so peremptorily, might be of ill consequence to the rest.

Verses 26–31

We have here an account of another appearance of Christ, when Thomas was now with them.

I. When it was: *After eight days*, which must therefore be, as that was, *the first day of the week*.

1. He deferred his next appearance for some time, to show his disciples that he was as one that belonged to another world, and visited this only now and then, when there was occasion. In the beginning of his ministry he had been forty days unseen, tempted by the evil Spirit. In the beginning of his glory he was forty days, for the most part unseen, attended by good spirits.

2. He deferred it so long as seven days. That he might put a rebuke upon Thomas for his incredulity. He cannot have such another opportunity for several days. He that slips one tide must stay a good while for another. A very melancholy week Thomas had of it, while the other disciples were full of joy. That he might try the faith and patience of the rest. They had gained a great point when they were satisfied that they had seen the Lord. He would try whether they could keep the ground they had got. He would gradually wean them from his bodily presence, which they had depended too much upon. That he might put an honour upon the first day of the week, and give a plain intimation of his will, that it should be observed in his church as the Christian sabbath. The religious observance of that day has been thence transmitted down to us through every age of the church.

II. Where, and how, Christ made them this visit. It was at Jerusalem, for the doors were shut now, as before, for fear of the Jews. Thomas was with them; though he had withdrawn himself once, yet not a second time. When we have lost one opportunity, we should give the more earnest heed to lay hold on the next. It is a good sign if such a loss whet our desires, and a bad sign if it cool them. The disciples admitted him among them. They did not receive him to doubtful disputation, but bade him welcome to come and see. Christ did not appear to Thomas till he found him in society with the rest of his disciples. He would have all the disciples witnesses of the rebuke he gave to Thomas, and yet withal of the tender care he had of him. Christ *came* in among them, and *stood in the midst*. See the condescension of our Lord Jesus. For the benefit of his church, he lingered on earth, and visited the little private meetings of his poor disciples, and is in the midst of them. He saluted them all as he had done before; he said, *Peace be unto you.* This was no vain repetition, but

JAMIESON, FAUSSET, BROWN

from sullen despondency. The fact merely is here stated, as a loving apology for his slowness of belief. **25. We have seen the Lord**—This way of speaking of Jesus (as vs. 20 and 21:7), so suited to His resurrection-state, was soon to become the prevailing style.

Except I see in his hands the print of the nails, and put my finger into the print of the nails, and thrust my hand into his side, I will not believe—The very form of this speech betokens the strength of the unbelief. "It is not, *If I shall see I shall believe*, but, *Unless I shall see I will not believe;* nor does he expect to see, although the others tell him they had" [BENGEL]. How Christ Himself viewed this state of mind, we know from Mark 16: 14, "He upbraided them with their unbelief and hardness of heart because they believed not them which had seen Him after He was risen." But whence sprang this pertinacity of resistance in *such* minds? Not certainly from reluctance to believe, but as in Nathanael (see on ch. 1:46) from mere dread of mistake in so vital a matter.

26-29. And after eight days—i.e., on the eighth, or first day of the preceding week. They probably met every day during the preceding week, but their Lord designedly reserved His second appearance among them till the recurrence of His resurrection day, that He might thus inaugurate the delightful sanctities of THE LORD'S DAY (Rev. 1:10).

disciples were within, and Thomas with them . . . Jesus . . . stood in the midst, and said, Peace be unto you.

ADAM CLARKE

of receiving (at this time) the inestimable blessing of the Holy Ghost. Where two or three are assembled in the name of Christ, He is in the midst of them. Christ had said this before; Thomas should have remembered it, and not have forsaken the company of the disciples. What is the consequence? His unbelief becomes (1) Utterly *unreasonable*. Ten of his brethren witnessed that they had seen Christ, v. 15; but he rejected their testimony. (2) His unbelief became *obstinate*. He was determined not to believe on any evidence that it might please God to give him; he would believe according to his own prejudices, or not at all. (3) His unbelief became *presumptuous*. A view of the person of Christ will not suffice; he will not believe that it is He unless he can put his finger into the holes made by the nails in his Lord's hand, and thrust his hand into the wound made by the spear in His side. Thomas had lost much good, and gained much evil, and yet was insensible of his state. Behold the consequences of forsaking the assemblies of God's people! Jesus comes to the meeting—a disciple is found out of his place, who might have been there; and he is not only not blessed, but his heart becomes hardened and darkened through the deceitfulness of sin. It was through God's mere mercy that Thomas ever had another opportunity of being convinced of his error.

26. *After eight days*. It seems likely that this was precisely on that day on which Christ had appeared to them before, and from this we may learn that this was the weekly meeting of the apostles; and though Thomas was not found at the former meeting, he was determined not to be absent from this. According to His custom, Jesus came again; for He cannot forget His promise—two or three are assembled in His name, and He was engaged to be among them.

CHARLES H. SPURGEON:

On the second occasion Thomas is present, and he is the only one out of the eleven who is vexed with doubts. He cannot think it possible that the Lord Jesus, who was nailed to the cross, and whose side was pierced, could have really risen from the dead. Observe joyfully the Lord's patience with him. All the others had been doubtful too, and the Lord had gently upbraided them for their unbelief and the hardness of their hearts; but Thomas is not convinced by the tenfold testimony of his brethren, who each one well deserved his implicit confidence. After the plain way in which the Lord had told His disciples that He should be crucified and would rise again from the dead, they ought to have expected the resurrection; and inasmuch as they did not they were to be blamed: what shall we say of him who in addition to all this had heard the witness of his ten comrades who had actually seen the Lord? Yet there he is, the one doubter, the one sturdy questioner who has laid down most stringent requirements as to the only way in which he will be brought to believe. Will not his Lord be provoked by his obstinacy? See how patient Jesus is!

—*The Treasury of the New Testament*

MATTHEW HENRY

significant of the abundant peace which Christ gives, and of the continuance of his blessings.

III. What passed between Christ and Thomas at this meeting; and that only is recorded.

1. Christ's gracious condescension to Thomas, *v.* 27. He singled him out from the rest: "*Reach hither, thy finger*, and *behold my hands*, the *print of the nails; reach hither thy hand*, and *thrust it into my side.*" (1) An implicit rebuke of Thomas's incredulity, in the plain reference to what Thomas had said, answering it word for word. There is not an unbelieving word on our tongues, no, nor thought in our minds, but it is known to the Lord Jesus. (2) An express condescension to his weakness. He suffers his wisdom to be prescribed to. Christ is pleased here to accommodate himself even to Thomas's fancy in a needless thing, rather than leave him in his unbelief. He suffers his wounds to be raked into, allows Thomas even to thrust his hand into his side, if then at last he would believe. Thus, for the confirmation of our faith, he has instituted an ordinance on purpose to keep his death in remembrance. And in that ordinance wherein we *show the Lord's death* we are called, as it were, to put our finger *into the print of the nails. Reach hither thy hand* to him, who reacheth forth his helping, inviting, giving hand to thee.

It is an affecting word with which Christ closes up what he had to say to Thomas: *Be not faithless but believing*. This warning is given to us all: *Be not faithless;* for, if we are faithless, we are Christless and graceless, hopeless and joyless.

2. Thomas's believing consent to Jesus Christ. He is now ashamed of his incredulity, and cries out, *My Lord and my God*, *v.* 28. We are not told whether he did put his finger into the print of the nails. Christ says (*v.* 29), *Thou hast seen, and believed;* seeing sufficed. And now faith comes off a conqueror.

(1) Thomas is now fully satisfied of the truth of Christ's resurrection. His slowness and backwardness to believe may help to strengthen our faith.

(2) He therefore believed him to be Lord and God, and we are to believe him so. [1] We must believe his deity—that he is God; not a man made God, but God made man. [2] His mediation—that he is Lord, the one Lord, to settle the great concerns that lie between God and man, and to establish the correspondence that was necessary to our happiness.

(3) He consented to him as his Lord and his God. We must accept of Christ to be that to us which the Father hath appointed him. This is the vital act of faith, He is mine.

(4) He made an open profession of this. He says it to Christ, *Thou art* my Lord and my God; or, speaking to his brethren, *This is* my Lord and my God. Do we accept of Christ as our *Lord God*? We must go to him, and tell him so, tell others so, as those that triumph in our relation to Christ. Thomas speaks with an ardency of affection as one that took hold of Christ with all his might, *My Lord* and *my God*.

3. The judgment of Christ upon the whole (*v.* 29): "*Thomas, because thou hast seen me, thou hast believed*; but *blessed are those that have not seen, and yet have believed.*" Christ owns Thomas a believer. Sound and sincere believers, though they be slow and weak, shall be graciously accepted of the Lord Jesus. No sooner did Thomas consent to Christ than Christ gives him the comfort of it, and lets him know that he believes. He upbraids him with his former incredulity. He had been so backward to believe, and came so slowly to his own comforts. Those that in sincerity have closed with Christ see a great deal of reason to lament that they did not do it sooner. It was not without much ado that he was brought to believe at last. If no evidence must be admitted but that of our own senses, and we must believe nothing but what we ourselves are eyewitnesses of, how must the world be converted to the faith of Christ? He is therefore justly blamed for laying so much stress upon this.

He commends the faith of those who believe upon easier terms. Thomas, as a believer, was truly blessed; but rather *blessed are those that have not seen* Christ's miracles, and especially his resurrection; blessed are those that see not these, and yet believe in Christ. This may look forward upon those who should afterwards believe, the Gentiles, who had never seen Christ in the flesh. This faith is more praiseworthy than theirs who saw and believed. It evidences a better temper of mind in those that do believe. He that believes upon that sight has his resistance conquered by a sort of violence; but he that believes without it is more noble. It is a greater instance of the power of divine grace. Flesh and blood contribute more to their faith that see and believe, than to theirs who see not and yet believe.

IV. The remark which the evangelist makes like an historian drawing towards a conclusion, *v.* 30, 31.

JAMIESON, FAUSSET, BROWN

27. Then saith he to Thomas, Reach hither . . . behold . . . put it into my side, and be not faithless, but believing—"There is something rhythmical in these words, and they are purposely couched in the words of Thomas himself, to put him to shame" [LUTHARDT]. But with what condescension and gentleness is this done!

28. Thomas answered and said unto him, My Lord and my God—That Thomas did *not* do what Jesus invited him to do, and what he had made the condition of his believing, seems plain from vs. 29 ("Because thou hast *seen* Me, thou hast believed"). He is overpowered, and the glory of Christ now breaks upon him in a flood. His exclamation surpasses all that had been yet uttered, nor can it be surpassed by anything that ever will be uttered in earth or heaven. On the striking parallel in Nathanael, see on ch. 1:49. The Socinian invasion of the supreme divinity of Christ here manifestly taught—as if it were a mere call upon God in a fit of astonishment—is beneath notice, save for the profanity it charges upon this disciple, and the straits to which it shows themselves reduced.

29. because thou hast seen me, thou hast believed—words of measured commendation, but of indirect and doubtless painfully-felt rebuke: i.e., 'Thou hast indeed believed; it is well: it is only on the evidence of thy senses, and after peremptorily refusing all evidence short of that.'

blessed they that have not seen, and yet have believed—"Wonderful indeed and rich in blessing for us who have not seen Him, is this closing word of the Gospel" [ALFORD].

ADAM CLARKE

27. *Then saith he to Thomas.* Through His infinite compassion He addressed him in a particular manner, condescending in this case to accommodate himself to the prejudices of an obstinate, though sincere, disciple. *Reach hither thy finger.* And it is very probable that Thomas did so, for his unbelief was too deeply rooted to be easily cured.

28. *Thomas answered.* Those who deny the Godhead of Christ would have us to believe that these words are an exclamation of Thomas, made through surprise, and that they were addressed to the Father and not to Christ. However, a man must do violence to every rule of construction who can apply the address here to any but Christ. The text is plain: Jesus comes in—sees Thomas, and addresses him, desiring him to come to Him and put his finger into the print of the nails. Thomas, perfectly satisfied of the reality of our Lord's resurrection, *said unto him, My Lord and my God.* Thomas was the first who gave the title of *God* to Jesus; and by this glorious confession made some amends for his former obstinate incredulity.

29. *Thomas.* This word is omitted by almost every MS., version, and ancient commentator of importance.

Blessed are they. You have seen and therefore you have believed, and now you are blessed; you are now happy—fully convinced of My resurrection. Yet no less blessed shall all those be who believe in My resurrection without the evidence you have had.

MATTHEW HENRY

1. He assures us that many other things occurred, which are *not written in the book*; *many signs.* There were other signs, many others, for the confirmation of our faith. Those that recorded the resurrection of Christ were not put to fish for evidence, to take up such short and scanty proofs as they could find, and make up the rest with conjecture. No, they had evidence enough and to spare. The disciples, in whose presence these other signs were done, were to be preachers of Christ's resurrection to others, and therefore it was requisite they should have proofs of it *in abundance.* We need not ask why they were not all written, or why not more than these, or others than these. Had this history been a mere human composition, it had been swelled with a multitude of depositions and affidavits, to prove the contested truth of Christ's resurrection; but, being a divine history, the penmen write with a noble security, sufficient to convince those that were willing to be taught and to condemn those that were obstinate in their unbelief; and, if this satisfy not, more would not. Men produce all they have to say, that they may gain credit; but God does not, for he can give faith. Had this history been written for the entertainment of the curious, it would have been more copious, but it was written to bring men to believe, and enough is said to answer that intention.

2. He instructs us in the design of recording what we do find here (*v.* 31): "*That you might believe* upon these evidences; that you might believe that Jesus is the Christ, the Son of God."

(1) The design of those that wrote the gospel. The evangelists wrote without any view of temporal benefit to themselves or others, but to bring men to Christ and heaven, and to persuade men to believe.

(2) The duty of those that read and hear the gospel. It is their duty to believe, to embrace, the doctrine of Christ. [1] What the great gospel truth is which we are to believe—that *Jesus is that Christ,* that *Son of God.* He is the Christ, *anointed* of God to be a prince and a Saviour. He is the Son of God, endued with the power of God and entitled to the glory of God. [2] What the great gospel blessedness is which we are to hope for—*That believing we shall have life through his name.* This is: To direct our faith. Life through Christ's name is what we must propose to ourselves as the fulness of our joy. To encourage our faith. Upon the prospect of some great advantage, men will venture far; and greater advantage there cannot be than that which is offered by the *words of this life.* It includes both spiritual life and eternal life. Both are through Christ's name and both indefeasibly sure to all true believers.

JAMIESON, FAUSSET, BROWN

30, 31. FIRST CLOSE OF THIS GOSPEL. The connection of these verses with the last words of vs. 29 is beautiful: i.e., And indeed, as the Lord pronounced them blessed who not having seen Him have yet believed, so for that one end have the whole contents of this Gospel been recorded, that all who read it may believe on Him, and believing, have life in that blessed name. **30. many other signs**—miracles.

31. But these are written—as sufficient specimens. **the Christ, the Son of God**—the one His *official,* the other His *personal,* title. **believing . . . may have life**—(See on ch. 6:51-54).

ADAM CLARKE

30. *Many other signs truly did Jesus.* That is, besides the two mentioned here, vv. 19 and 26, viz., Christ's entering into the house in a miraculous manner twice, notwithstanding the doors were fast shut; see on v. 19. The other miracles which our Lord did, and which are not related here, were such as were necessary to the disciples only, and therefore not revealed to mankind at large.

31. *That ye might believe.* What is here recorded is to give a full proof of the divinity of Christ; that He is the promised Messiah; that He really suffered and rose again from the dead; and that through Him every believer might have eternal life.

CHAPTER 21

/erses 1–14

We have here an account of Christ's appearance to is disciples at the sea of Tiberias. 1. Let us compare his appearance with those that *went before.* In those Christ showed himself to his disciples when they vere met upon a Lord's day, and when they were all ogether; but in this he showed himself to some of hem upon a week-day, when they were fishing. Christ has many ways of making himself known to his eople; sometimes by his Spirit he visits them when hey are employed in common business. 2. Let us ompare it with that which followed at the mountain n Galilee, where Christ had appointed them to neet him, Matt. xxviii. 16. Now this appearance vas while they were waiting for that, that they might ot be weary of waiting.

I. Who they were to whom Christ now showed imself (*v.* 2): not to all the twelve, but to seven of hem only. Nathanael is mentioned as one of them, vhom we have not met with since *ch.* i. But some hink he was the same with Bartholomew. It is good or the disciples of Christ to be much together; in ommon conversation, and about common business. Christ chose to manifest himself to them when they ere together, that they might be joint witnesses of e same matter of fact. Thomas was one of them, nd is named next to Peter, as if he now kept closer to e meetings of the apostles than ever.

II. How they were employed, *v.* 3.

1. Their agreement to go a-fishing. For my part, ays Peter, *I will go a-fishing*; *We will go with thee* en, say they. Though commonly two of a trade annot agree, yet they could. They did it, (1) To edeem time, and not be idle. The hour for entering pon action was not come. Now, in the meantime, ather than do nothing, they would go a-fishing; not or recreation, but for business. It is an instance kewise of their industry, and bespeaks them good usbands of their time. While they were waiting,

CHAPTER 21

VSS. 1-23. SUPPLEMENTARY PARTICULARS. (That this chapter was added by another hand has been asserted, against clear evidence to the contrary, by some late critics, chiefly because the Evangelist had *concluded* his part of the work with ch. 20:30, 31. But neither in the Epistles of the New Testament, nor in other good authors, is it unusual to insert supplementary matter, and so have more than one conclusion). **1, 2. Jesus showed**—manifested—**himself again . . . and on this wise he manifested himself**—This way of speaking shows that after His resurrection He appeared to them but *occasionally, unexpectedly,* and in a way quite *unearthly,* though yet *really* and *corporeally.* **2. Nathanael**—(See on Matt. 10:3).

3-6. Peter saith unto them, I go a fishing—(See on Luke 5:11).

CHAPTER 21

1. *Jesus shewed himself again.* After that our Lord had appeared several times to the women, and to the apostles at Jerusalem, and at the tomb, He bade them go into Galilee, giving them the promise of meeting them there, Matt. xxviii. 7; Mark xvi. 7. This promise we find He fulfilled in the way John relates here. This was the seventh appearance of our Lord after the Resurrection. Matthew, chap. xxviii. 16, has but just mentioned it; of it the rest of the Evangelists say nothing, and this is the reason why John gives it so particularly.

3. *Peter saith . . . I go a fishing.* Previously to the crucifixion of our Lord, the temporal necessities of himself and His disciples appear to have been supplied by the charity of individuals, Luke viii. 3. As it is probable that the scandal of the Cross had now shut up this source of support, the disciples, not fully knowing how they were to be employed, purposed to return to their former occupation of fishing in order to gain a livelihood; and therefore

MATTHEW HENRY

they would not be idling. Those who would give an account of their time with joy should contrive to fill up the vacancies of it. (2) That they might help to maintain themselves and not be burdensome to any.

2. Their disappointment in their fishing. That night they caught nothing. The hand of the diligent often returns empty. Even good men may come short of desired success in their honest undertakings. Providence so ordered it that all that night they should catch nothing, that the miraculous draught of fishes in the morning might be the more acceptable. In those disappointments which to us are very grievous God has often designs that are very gracious.

III. After what manner Christ made himself known to them. It is said (*v.* 1), *He showed himself.* Four things are observable in the appearance of Christ to them:

1. He showed himself to them seasonably (*v.* 4): *When the morning was now come,* Jesus *stood on the shore.* Christ's time of making himself known to his people is when they are most at a loss. When they think they have lost themselves, he will let them know that they have not lost him. Christ appeared to them, not *walking upon the water,* but *standing upon the shore,* because now they were to make towards him. It is a comfort to us, when our passage is rough and stormy, that our Master is at shore, and we are hastening to him.

2. He showed himself to them gradually. The disciples *knew not,* all at once, *that it was Jesus.* Christ is often nearer to us than we think he is.

3. He showed himself to them by an instance of his pity, *v.* 5. He called to them, *Children,* "*Lads have you any meat?*" (1) The compellation is very familiar; he speaks unto them with the care and tenderness of a father: *Children.* They were not children in age, but they were his children, the children which God had given him. (2) The question is very kind: *Have you any meat? The Lord is for the body,* 1 Cor. vi. 13. Christ takes cognizance of the temporal wants of his people, and has promised them not only grace sufficient, but food convenient. Christ looks into the cottages of the poor, and asks, *Children, have you any meat?* Christ takes care of them, takes care for them. Christ has herein set us an example of compassionate concern for our brethren. There are many poor householders disabled for labour, or disappointed in it, that are reduced to straits, whom the rich should enquire after thus, *Have you any meat?* For the most necessitous are commonly the least clamorous. The disciples gave a short answer. They said, *No.* Christ put the question to them, not because he did not know their wants, but because he would know them *from them.* Those that would have supplies from Christ must own themselves empty and needy.

4. He showed himself to them by an instance of his power (*v.* 6): he ordered them to *cast the net on the right side of the ship.* And then they, who were going home empty-handed, were enriched with a great draught of fishes. (1) The orders Christ gave them, and the promise annexed to those orders: *Cast the net* there in such a place, and *you shall find.* Divine providence extends itself to things most minute, and they are happy that know how to take hints thence in the conduct of their affairs. (2) Their obedience of these orders, and the good success of it. As yet *they knew not that it was Jesus*; however, they were willing to be advised by anybody. In being thus observant of strangers, they were obedient to their Master unawares. And it sped wonderfully well; now they had a draught that paid them for all their pains. There is nothing lost by observing Christ's orders. Now the draught of fishes may be considered, [1] As a miracle in itself. Christ manifests himself to his people by doing that for them which none else can do. [2] As a mercy to them. When their ingenuity and industry failed them, the power of Christ came in opportunely for their relief. [3] As the memorial of a former mercy, with which Christ had formerly recompensed Peter for the loan of his boat, Luke v. 4, &c. Both that and this affected him much, as meeting him in his own element, in his own employment. Latter favours are designed to bring to mind former favours, that eaten bread may not be forgotten. [4] As a mystery, and very significant of that work to which Christ was now sending them forth. When, soon after this, three thousand were converted in one day, then the net was *cast on the right side of the ship.* It is an encouragement to Christ's ministers to continue their diligence in their work. One happy draught, at length, may be sufficient to repay many years of toil at the gospel net.

IV. How the disciples received this discovery, *v.* 7, 8.

1. John was the most intelligent and quick-sighted

JAMIESON, FAUSSET, BROWN

that night . . . caught nothing—as at the first miraculous draught (see on Luke 5:5); no doubt so ordered that the miracle might strike them the more by contrast. The same principle is seen in operation throughout much of Christ's ministry, and is indeed a great law of God's spiritual procedure with His people.

4. Jesus stood—(Cf. ch. 20:19, 26). **but the disciples knew not it was Jesus**—Perhaps there had been some considerable interval since the last manifestation, and having agreed to betake themselves to their secular employment, they would be unprepared to expect Him.

5. Children—This term would not necessarily identify Him, being not unusual from any superior; but when they did recognize Him, they would feel it sweetly like Himself. **have ye any meat?**—provisions, supplies, meaning *fish.*

They answered . . ., No—This was in His wonted style, making them *tell* their case, and so the better prepare them for what was coming.

6. he said unto them, Cast the net on the right side of the ship—no doubt, by this very specific direction, intending to reveal to them His knowledge of the deep and power over it.

ADAM CLARKE

the seven, mentioned in v. 2, embarked on the Sea of Tiberias, otherwise called the Sea of Galilee.

That night they caught nothing. God had so ordered it that they might be the more struck with the miracle which He afterwards wrought.

4. *Knew not that it was Jesus.* Probably because it was either not light enough, or He was at too great a distance, or He had assumed another form, as in Mark xvi. 12.

5. *Children.* A term of familiarity and affectionate kindness; it literally signifies "little children" or "beloved children." *Any meat.* Anything that is eaten with bread, or suchlike solid substances, to make the deglutition the more easy. Here it evidently means any kind of fish; and our Lord seems to have appeared at first in the character of a person who wished to purchase a part of what they had caught.

A. B. SIMPSON:

The command of Christ to cast the net on the other side and the immediate results in the miraculous draught of fishes reveal the Master. John is the first to recognize Him, because his spirit was the least clouded by unbelief, and Peter is the first to plunge for the shore. The other disciples followed in a little fishing boat, dragging the loaded net and landing it, with Peter's help, with its enormous store of great fishes, every one of which is safely landed and the net unbroken. All this is so different from the former miracle, where the net broke and the ship began to sink, and Peter in guilty awe begged the Master to depart from him because he felt unworthy of His presence, that it must itself have suggested to their minds the higher lessons it has taught the church of service for Christ and the church.

The chief of these lessons is the higher service upon which they were now to enter into fellowship with their risen Lord, and of which Peter, who had just dragged the net to land, was to be the first illustrious example, through his harvest of souls on the day of Pentecost. They were to learn the vanity and unselfishness of all their wisdom and strength in the Master's work, and the necessity of His presence and guidance as they cast the Gospel net into the sea of sinful men. Only as He stood upon the shore were they able to cast it upon the right side, and only as they spake and acted in fellowship with Him would they be able to bring to land the souls they sought to save. But henceforth that presence and power was to be their resource.—*Christ in the Bible*

MATTHEW HENRY

disciple. He whom Jesus loved was the first that said, *It is the Lord.* His secret is with his favourites. When John was himself aware that it was the Lord, he communicated his knowledge to those with him. Those that know Christ themselves should endeavour to bring others acquainted with him; we need not engross him, there is enough in him for us all. John tells Peter particularly, knowing he would be glad to see him above any of them.

2. Peter was the most zealous and warmhearted disciple; for as soon as he heard it was the Lord the ship could not hold him, but into the sea he throws himself that he might come first to Christ. He showed his respect to Christ by *girding his fisher's coat* about him, that he might appear before his Master in the best clothes he had, and he girt it to him that he might make the best of his way through the water to Christ. He showed the strength of his affection to Christ by casting himself into the sea; and either wading or swimming to shore, to come to him. *He cast himself into the sea* with precipitation; sink or swim, he would show his goodwill and aim to be with Jesus. Peter had had much forgiven, and made it appear he loved much by his willingness to run hazards, to come to him. Those that have been with Jesus will be willing to swim through a stormy sea to come to him.

3. The rest of the disciples were careful and honest hearted. They hastened in the boat to the shore, and made the best of their way (*v.* 8). (1) How variously God dispenses his gifts. Some excel, as Peter and John; are very eminent in gifts and graces; others are but ordinary disciples, that mind their duty, and are faithful to him, and yet both the one and the other, the eminent and the obscure, shall sit down together with Christ in glory; nay, and perhaps *the last shall be first.* Some, like John, are eminently contemplative, have great gifts of knowledge, and serve the church with them; others, like Peter, are eminently active and courageous, and are thus very serviceable to their generation. Some are useful as the church's eyes, others as the church's hands, and all for the good of the body. (2) What a great deal of difference there may be between some good people and others in the way of their honouring Christ, and yet both *accepted of him.* Peter ought not to be censured for casting himself into the sea, but commended for his zeal and the strength of his affection; and so must those be who, in love to Christ, quit the world, with Mary, to *sit at his feet.* But others serve Christ more in the affairs of the world. They continue in that ship, drag the net, and bring the fish to shore, as the other disciples here; and such ought not to be censured as worldly, for they, in their place, are as truly serving Christ as the other, even in serving tables. Christ was well placed with both, and so must we be.

V. What entertainment the Lord Jesus gave them.

1. He had provision ready for them. When they came to land, wet and cold, weary and hungry, they found a good fire there to warm them and dry them, and fish and bread. We need not be curious in enquiring whence this fire, and fish, and bread. Here was nothing stately or delicate. We should be content with mean things, for Christ was. We may be comforted in this instance of Christ's care of his disciples. He kindly provided for those fishermen, when they came weary from their work. It is encouraging to Christ's ministers that they may depend upon him who employs them to provide for them. Let them content themselves with what they have here; they have better things in reserve.

2. He called for some of that which they had caught, *v.* 10, 11.

(1) The command Christ gave them to bring their draught of fish to shore: "Bring of the fish hither, which you have now caught." He would have them eat the labour of their hands. What is got by God's blessing on our own industry and honest labour hath a peculiar sweetness in it. Christ would hereby teach us to use what we have. He would have them taste the gifts of his miraculous bounty. The benefits Christ bestows upon us are not to be buried and laid up, but to be used and laid out. He would give a specimen of the spiritual entertainment he has for all believers—that *he sups with them, and they with him.* Ministers, who are fishers of men, must bring all they catch to their Master.

(2) Their obedience to this command, *v.* 11. It was said (*v.* 6), *They were not able to draw the net to shore, for the multitude of fishes.* Thus the fishers of men, when they have enclosed souls in the gospel net, cannot bring them to shore, and complete the good work begun, without the continued influence of the divine grace. Who it was that was most active in landing the fishes: it was Peter, who, as in the former instance (*v.* 7), had shown a more

JAMIESON, FAUSSET, BROWN

7-11. that disciple whom Jesus loved, said, It is the Lord—again having the advantage of his brother in quickness of recognition (see on ch. 20:8), to be followed by an alacrity in Peter *all his own.*

he was naked—his vest only on, worn next the body. **cast himself into the sea**—the shallow part, not more than a hundred yards from the water's edge (vs. 8), not meaning therefore to swim, but to get sooner to Jesus than in the full boat which they could hardly draw to shore.

8. the other disciples came in a little ship—by ship.

9. they saw—'see'—**a fire of coals, and fish laid thereon, and bread**—By comparing this with I Kings 19:6, and similar passages, the unseen agency by which Jesus made this provision will appear evident.

10. Jesus saith unto them, Bring of the fish ye have now caught—Observe the double supply thus provided—His and theirs. The meaning of this will perhaps appear presently.

ADAM CLARKE

7. *His fisher's coat.* Or "his upper coat." *He was naked.* He was only in his "vest." *Naked* is often used to signify the absence of this upper garment only. In 1 Sam. xix. 24, when Saul had put off his upper garments, he is said to have been "naked"; and David, when girded only with a linen ephod, is said to have been "uncovered," in 2 Sam. vi. 14, 20. *Cast himself into the sea.* It is likely that they were in very shallow water; and, as they were only 200 cubits from the land, it is possible that Peter only stepped into the water that he might assist them to draw the boat to land, which was now heavily laden.

8. *Dragging the net.* It is probable that this was that species of fishing in which the net was stretched from the shore out into the sea. The persons who were in the boat, and who shot the net, fetched a compass, and bringing in a hawser, which was attached to the other end of the net, those who were on shore helped them to drag it in. As the net was sunk with weights to the bottom, and the top floated on the water by corks, or pieces of light wood, all the fish that happened to come within the compass of the net were of course dragged to shore. The sovereign power of Christ had in this case miraculously collected the fish to that part where He ordered the disciples to cast the net.

9. *They saw a fire.* This appears to have been a new miracle. It could not have been a fire which the disciples had there, for it is remarked as something new. Besides, they had caught no fish, v. 5, and here was a small fish upon the coals, and a loaf of bread provided to eat with it. The whole appears to have been miraculously prepared by Christ.

6. *For the multitude of fishes.* This was intended as an emblem of the immense number of souls which should be converted to God by their ministry, according to the promise of Christ, Matt. iv. 19.

MATTHEW HENRY

zealous affection to his Master's person than any of them, so in this he showed a more ready obedience to his Master's command; but all that are faithful are not alike forward. The number of the fishes that were caught. They were in all a *hundred and fifty and three*, and all *great fishes*. A further instance of Christ's care of them: *For all there were so many* and *great fishes* too, *yet was not the net broken;* so that they lost none of their fish, nor damaged their net. The net of the gospel has enclosed multitudes, three thousand in one day, and yet is not broken; it is still as mighty as ever to bring souls to God.

3. He invited them to dinner. Observing that *they were afraid to ask him, Who art thou?* because they *knew it was their Lord*, he called to them very familiarly, *Come and dine*.

(1) See here how free Christ was with his disciples; he treated them as friends. *Come, and dine* with me. The call Christ gives his disciples into communion with him in grace here. Christ is a friend; come, dine with him, he will bid you welcome. The call he will give them into the fruition of him in glory hereafter. Christ has wherewithal to dine all his friends and followers; there is room and provision enough for them all.

(2) See how reverent the disciples were before Christ. They were somewhat shy of using the freedom he invited them to. *None of them durst ask him, Who art thou?* Either, because they would not be so bold with him. They had very good reason to think it was he, and could be no other. Or, because they would not so far betray their own folly. They must be stupid indeed if they questioned whether it was he or no. We should be ashamed of our distrusts. Groundless doubts must be stifled, and not started.

4. He carved for them, as the master of the feast, *v.* 13. *He comes, and takes bread himself*, and *gives them, and fish likewise*. The entertainment here was but ordinary; it was only a fish-dinner, plain and homely. Hunger is the best sauce. Christ *showed himself alive by eating*, not showed himself a prince by feasting. Christ himself began. He would show that he had a true body, which was capable of eating. The apostles produced this as one proof of his resurrection, that *they had eaten and drank with him*, Acts x. 41. He gave the meat about to all his guests. He not only provided it for them, but he himself divided it among them, and put it into their hands. Thus to him we owe the application, as well as the purchase, of the benefits of redemption.

The evangelist leave them at dinner, and makes this remark (*v.* 14): *This is now the third time that Jesus showed himself alive to his disciples*. Though he had appeared to Mary, to the women, to the two disciples, and to Cephas, yet he had but twice before this appeared to any company of them together. This is taken notice of, (1) For confirming the truth of his resurrection; the vision was doubled, was trebled, for the thing was certain. (2) As an instance of Christ's continued kindness to his disciples; once, and again, and a third time, he visited them. It is good to keep account of Christ's gracious visits. *This is now the third;* have we made a due improvement of *the first and second*? *This is the third*, perhaps it may be the last.

Verses 15–19

We have here Christ's discourse with Peter after dinner.

I. He examines his love to him, and gives him a charge concerning his flock, *v.* 15–17.

1. When Christ entered into this discourse with Peter.—It was after they had dined. Christ foresaw that what he had to say to Peter would give him some uneasiness. Peter was conscious to himself that he had incurred his Master's displeasure, and could expect no other than to be upbraided with his ingratitude. Twice, if not thrice, he had seen his Master since his resurrection, and he said not a word to him of it. We may suppose Peter full of doubts upon what terms he stood with his Master; sometimes hoping the best, yet not without some fears. But now, at length, his Master put him out of his pain. *When they had dined* together, in token of reconciliation, then discoursed he with him about it as with a friend. Peter had reproached himself for it, and therefore Christ did not reproach him for it. Being satisfied in his sincerity, the offence was not only forgiven, but forgotten; and Christ let him know that he was as dear to him as ever. Herein he has given us an encouraging instance of his tenderness towards penitents.

2. What was the discourse itself. Here was the same question three times asked, the same answer three times returned, and the same reply three times

JAMIESON, FAUSSET, BROWN

11. Peter went up—into the boat; went aboard. **and drew the net to land full of great fishes, an hundred and fifty and three; and for all there were so many, yet was not the net broken**—The manifest reference here to the former miraculous draught (Luke 5:1-11) furnishes the key to this scene. There the draught was *symbolical* of the success of their future ministry: While "Peter and all that were with him were astonished at the draught of the fishes which they had taken, Jesus said unto him, Fear not, from henceforth thou shalt catch men." Nay, when first called, in the act of "casting their net into the sea, for they were fishers," the same *symbolic* reference was made to their secular occupation: "Follow Me, and I will make you fishers of men" (Matt. 4:18, 19). Here, then, if but the same symbolic reference be kept in view, the design of the whole scene will, we think, be clear. The *multitude* and the *size* of the fishes *they* caught symbolically foreshadowed the vast success of their now fast approaching ministry, and this only as a beginning of successive draughts, through the agency of a Christian ministry, till, "as the waters cover the sea, the earth should be full of the knowledge of the Lord." And whereas, at the first miraculous draught, the net "was breaking" through the weight of what it contained—expressive of *the difficulty with which, after they had "caught men," they would be able to retain, or keep them from escaping back into the world*—while here, "for all they were so many, yet was not the net broken," are we not reminded of such sayings as these (chap. 10:28): "I give unto My sheep eternal life, and they shall never perish, neither shall any pluck them out of My hand" [LUTHARDT]? But it is not through the agency of a Christian ministry that all true disciples are gathered. Jesus Himself, by unseen methods, gathers some, who afterwards are recognized by the constituted fishers of men, and mingle with the fruit of their labors. And are not these symbolized by that portion of our Galilean repast which the fishers found, in some unseen way, made ready to their hand? **12-14. none . . . durst ask him, Who art thou, knowing it was the Lord**—implying that they *would* have liked Him just to say, "It is I"; but having such convincing *evidence* they were afraid of being "upbraided for their unbelief and hardness of heart" if they ventured to put the question. **13. Jesus . . . taketh** [the] **bread, and giveth them, and** [the] **fish likewise**—See on Luke 24:30.

14. This is the third time that Jesus showed himself—was manifested—**to his disciples**—His *assembled* disciples; for if we reckon His appearances to individual disciples, they were more.

when they had dined, Jesus saith—Silence appears to have reigned during the meal; unbroken on *His* part, that by their mute observation of Him they might have their assurance of His identity the more confirmed; and on *theirs,* from reverential shrinking to speak till He did.

ADAM CLARKE

12. *Come and dine.* Though this is the literal translation of the word, yet it must be observed that it was not dinner time, being as yet early in the morning, v. 4; but Kypke has largely shown that the original word is used by Homer, Xenophon, and Plutarch to signify "breakfast," or any early meal, as well as what we term "dinner." It might perhaps appear singular; otherwise it would be as agreeable to the use of the Greek word to have translated it, "Come and breakfast."

Durst ask him. Ever since the confession of Thomas, a proper awe of the deity of Christ had possessed their minds.

13. *And giveth them.* Eating likewise with them, as Luke expressly says, chap. xxiv. 43.

14. *This is now the third time.* That is, this was the third time He appeared unto the apostles when all or most of them were together. He appeared to ten of them, chap. xx. 19; again to eleven of them, v. 26; and at this time to seven of them, v. 2 of this chapter. But when the other Evangelists are collated we shall find that this was the seventh time in which He had manifested himself after He arose from the dead. (1) He appeared to Mary of Magdala, Mark xvi. 9; John xx. 15-16. (2) To the holy women who came from the tomb, Matt. xxviii. 9. (3) To the two disciples who went to Emmaus, Luke xxiv. 13, etc. (4) To Peter alone, Luke xxiv. 34. (5) To the ten, in the absence of Thomas, chap. xx. 19. (6) Eight days after to the eleven, Thomas being present, v. 26. (7) To the seven, mentioned in v. 2 of this chapter, which was between the eighth and fortieth day after His resurrection. Besides these *seven* appearances, He showed himself (8) to the disciples on a certain mountain in Galilee, Matt. xxviii. 16. If the appearance mentioned by Paul, 1 Cor. xv. 6, to upwards of 500 brethren at once—if this be not the same with His appearance on a mountain in Galilee, it must be considered the ninth. According to the same apostle, He was seen of James, 1 Cor. xv. 7, which may have been the tenth appearance. And after this to all the apostles when, at Bethany, He ascended to heaven in their presence. See Mark xvi. 19-20; Luke xxiv. 50-53; Acts i. 3-12; 1 Cor. xv. 7. This appears to have been the eleventh time in which He distinctly manifested himself after His resurrection. But there might have been many other manifestations which the Evangelists have not thought proper to enumerate, as not being connected with anything of singular weight or importance.

MATTHEW HENRY

given. The same thing was repeated by our Saviour, the more to affect Peter. It is repeated by the evangelist, the more to affect us, and all that read it.

(1) Three times Christ asks Peter whether he loves him or no. The first time the question is, *Simon, son of Jonas, lovest thou me more than these?* Now he calls him: *Simon, son of Jonas.* He speaks to him by name, the more to affect him, as Luke xxii. 31. *Simon, Simon.* He does not call him *Cephas,* nor *Peter,* the name he had given him, but his original name, *Simon.* Yet he gives him no hard language, but as he had called him when he pronounced him blessed, *Simon Bar-jona,* Matt. xvi. 17. How he catechises him: *Lovest thou me more than these?*

First, Lovest thou me? If we would try whether we are Christ's disciples indeed, this must be the enquiry, Do we love him? 1. His fall had given occasion to doubt of his love: "Peter, I have cause to suspect thy love; for if thou hadst loved me thou wouldst not have been ashamed and afraid to own me in my sufferings." We must not reckon it an affront to have our sincerity questioned, when we ourselves have done that which makes it questionable. The question is affecting: "Dost thou love me? Give but proof of this, and the affront shall be passed by, and no more said of it." Peter had professed himself a penitent, witness his tears; he was now upon his probation as a penitent; but the question is not, "Simon, how much hast thou wept?" but, "Dost thou love me?" It is this that will make the other expressions of repentance acceptable. *Much is forgiven her,* not because *she wept much,* but because *she loved much.* 2. His function would give occasion for the exercise of his *love.* Before Christ would commit his *sheep* to his care, he asked him, *Lovest thou me?* Christ has such a tender regard to his flock that he will not trust it with any but those that love him. Those that do not truly love Christ will never truly love the souls of men; nor will that minister love his work that does not love his Master. Nothing but the love of Christ will constrain ministers to go cheerfully through the difficulties and discouragements they meet with in their work. But this love will make their work easy, and them in good earnest in it.

Secondly, Lovest thou me more than these? 1. "*Lovest thou me more than thou lovest these?*" Dost thou love me more than thou dost James or John, or Andrew? Those do not love Christ aright that do not love him better than the best friend they have in the world. 2. "*Lovest thou me more than these love me,*" more than any of the rest of the disciples love me? And then the question is intended to upbraid him with his vain-glorious boast, *Though all men should deny thee, yet will not I.* Or, to intimate to him that he had now more reason to love him than any of them had, for more had been forgiven to him than to any of them. It is no breach of the peace to strive which shall love Christ best.

Thirdly, The second and third time that Christ put this question, 1. He left out the comparison *more than these,* because Peter modestly left it out, not willing to compare himself with his brethren, much less to prefer himself before them. Though we cannot say, *We* love Christ more than others do, yet we shall be accepted if we can say, We love him indeed. 2. In the last he altered the word. In the first two enquiries, the original word is: *Dost thou retain a kindness for me?* In answer to which Peter uses another word, more emphatic, *I love thee dearly.* In putting the question the last time, Christ uses that word.

(2) Three times Peter returns the same answer to Christ: *Yea, Lord, thou knowest that I love thee.* [1] Peter does not pretend to love Christ more than the rest of the disciples did. Though we must aim to be better than others, yet we must, *in lowliness of mind, esteem others better than ourselves;* for we know more evil of ourselves than we do of any of our brethren. [2] Yet he professes again and again that he loves Christ: *Yea, Lord,* surely *I love thee.* He had a grateful sense of his kindness, his desire was towards him, and his delight in him, as one he should be unspeakably happy in. This amounts to a profession of repentance for his sin, for it grieves us to have affronted one we love; and to a promise of adherence to him for the future: *Lord, I love thee,* and *will never leave thee.* Christ *prayed that his faith might not fail* (Luke xxii. 32), and, because his faith did not fail, his love did not; for faith will work by love. Christ puts his trial upon this issue: *Dost thou love me?* And Peter joins issue upon it: *Lord, I love thee.* [3] He appeals to Christ himself for the proof of it: *Thou knowest that I love thee;* and *the third time* yet more emphatically: *Thou knowest all things, thou knowest that I love thee.* He calls Christ himself to witness. Peter was sure that Christ knew all things, and particularly that he knew the heart.

JAMIESON, FAUSSET, BROWN

15. Simon, son of Jonas, lovest thou me more than these?—referring lovingly to those sad words of Peter, shortly before denying his Lord, "Though *all men* shall be offended because of Thee, *yet will I never* be offended" (Matt. 26:33), and intending by this allusion to bring the whole scene vividly before his mind and put him to shame.

16. He saith to him . . . the second time . . . lovest thou me . . .—In this repetition of the question, though the wound was meant to be reopened, the words "*more than these*" are not repeated; for Christ is a *tender* as well as *skilful* Physician, and Peter's silence on that point was confession enough of his sin and folly. On Peter's repeating his protestation in the same words, our Lord rises higher in the manifestation of His restoring grace.

17. He saith unto him the third time, Simon, son of Jonas, lovest thou me?

Yea, Lord; thou knowest that I love thee—He adds not, "more than these," but prefixes a touching appeal to the Saviour's own omniscience for the truth of his protestation, which makes it a totally different kind of speech from his former.

ADAM CLARKE

15. *Simon . . . lovest thou me?* Peter had thrice denied his Lord, and now Christ gives him an opportunity in some measure to repair his fault by a triple confession. *More than these?* This was a kind of reproach to Peter. He had professed a more affectionate attachment to Christ than the rest; he had been more forward in making professions of friendship and love than any of the others; and no one (Judas excepted) had treated his Lord so basely. As he had before intimated that his attachment to his Master was *more* than that of the rest, our Lord now puts the question to him, "Dost thou love Me more than these?"

G. CAMPBELL MORGAN:

The qualifications for the doing of the work are then revealed. He said, "Simon, are you devoted to Me?" The word our Lord used is far more than emotional. It describes complete devotion. Simon dared not climb to the height of the word used by his Lord. He honestly replied that he loved Him, using the purely emotional word. He asked him again, "Are you devoted to Me?" and again he dared not climb. He said, "I love You." Then with infinite grace, the Lord came down to Simon's word, "Do you love Me?" Simon did not like that. He did not like Jesus coming down to the lower word. But still he used it, "Lord, Thou knowest all things, Thou knowest that I love Thee."

The qualifications, then, for feeding lambs and shepherding sheep is that of love of the Lord. But do not let us forget that the love He seeks is the love of absolute devotion.

—*The Gospel According to John*

To which Peter made the most modest reply—*Thou knowest that I love thee,* but no longer dwells on the strength of his love, nor compares himself with even the meanest of his brethren. He had before cast the very unkind reflection on his brethren, "Though all . . . be offended because of thee, yet will I never be offended," Matt. xxvi. 33. But he had now learned, by dreadful experience, that he who trusts his own heart is a fool; and that a man's sufficiency for good is of the Lord alone. The words *more than these,* Bishop Pearce thinks refer to the provisions they were eating, or to their secular employments. But it appears to me that our Lord refers to the profession made by Peter, which I have quoted above. It is remarkable that in these three questions our Lord uses the verb *agapao,* which signifies to "love affectionately, ardently, supremely, perfectly"; and that Peter always replies using the verb *phileo,* which signifies to "love," to "like," to "regard," to "feel friendship" for another. As if our Lord had said, "Peter, do you love Me ardently and supremely?" To which he answers, "Lord, I feel an affection for Thee—I do esteem Thee—but dare, at present, say no more."

MATTHEW HENRY

Peter was satisfied of this, that Christ, who knew all things, knew the sincerity of his love to him. It is a terror to a hypocrite to think that Christ knows all things. But it is a comfort to a sincere Christian. Christ knows us better than we know ourselves. Though we know not our own uprightness, he knows it. [4] *He was grieved* when Christ asked him the *third time, Lovest thou me? v.* 17. It put him in mind of his threefold denial of Christ. Every remembrance of past sins, even pardoned sins, renews the sorrow of a true penitent. It put him in fear lest his Master foresaw some further miscarriage of his. "Surely," thinks Peter, "my Master would not thus put me upon the rack if he did not see some cause for it. What would become of me if I should be again tempted?"

(3) Three times Christ committed the care of his flock to Peter: *Feed my lambs; feed my sheep; feed my sheep.* Those whom Christ committed to Peter's care were his lambs and his sheep. In this flock some are lambs, others are sheep. The Shepherd here takes care of both, and of the lambs first, for upon all occasions he showed a particular tenderness for them. The charge he gives him concerning them is to feed them. The word used in *v.* 15, 17, strictly signifies to *give them food*; but the word used in *v.* 16 signifies more largely to do all the offices of a shepherd to them. It is the duty of all Christ's ministers to feed his lambs and sheep. *Feed them,* that is, teach them. *Feed them,* that is, "Lead them to the green pastures, ministering all the ordinances to them. Feed them by personal application to their respective state and case; not only lay meat before them, but feed those with it that are wilful and will not, or weak and cannot feed themselves." But why did he give this charge particularly to Peter? The particular application to Peter here was designed to restore him to his apostleship, now that he repented. This commission given to Peter was an evidence that Christ was reconciled to him, else he would never have reposed such a confidence in him. Christ, when he forgave Peter, trusted him with the most valuable treasure he had on earth. It was designed to quicken him to a diligent discharge of his office as an apostle. Peter was always forward to speak and act, and, lest he should be tempted to take upon him the directing of the shepherds, he is charged to feed the sheep. If he will be doing, let him do this, and pretend no further. What Christ said to him he said to all his disciples; he charged them all, not only to be fishers of men by the conversion of sinners, but feeders of the flock, by the edification of saints.

II. Having confirmed to him the honour of an apostle, he now tells him of further preferment designed him—the honour of a martyr.

1. How his martyrdom is foretold (*v.* 18): *Thou shalt stretch forth thy hands* and *another shall gird thee* (as a prisoner that is pinioned) *and carry thee whither thou wouldest not.*

(1) He prefaces the notice he gives to Peter of his sufferings with a solemn asseveration, *Verily, verily, I say unto thee.* It was not spoken of as a thing probable, but as a thing certain, *I say it to thee.* As Christ foresaw all his own sufferings, so he foresaw the sufferings of all his followers. Having charged him to feed his sheep, he bids him not to expect ease and honour in it, but trouble and persecution.

(2) He foretells particularly that he should die by the hands of an executioner. The tradition of the ancients informs us that Peter was crucified at Rome under Nero. The pomp and solemnity of an execution add much to the terror of death. Death, in these horried shapes, has often been the lot of Christ's faithful ones. It was a violent death that he should be carried to, such a death as even innocent nature could not think of without dread. He that puts on the Christian does not put off the man. Christ himself prayed against the bitter cup. A natural aversion to pain and death is well reconcilable with a holy submission to the will of God in both.

(3) He compares this with his former liberty. "Time was when *thou girdedst thyself and walkedst whither thou wouldest.*" Where trouble comes we are apt to fret the more at the grievances of restraint, sickness, and poverty, because we have known the sweets of liberty, health, and plenty. But we may turn it the other way: "How many years of prosperity have I enjoyed more than I deserved and improved? And, having received good, shall I not receive evil also?" What a change may possibly be made with us, as to our condition in this world! What a change is presently made with those that leave all to follow Christ! They must no longer walk whither they will, but whither he will.

(4) Christ tells Peter he should suffer thus in his old age. His enemies would hasten him out of the

JAMIESON, FAUSSET, BROWN

Peter was grieved because he said the third time . . . —This was the Physician's deepest incision into the wound, while yet smarting under the two former probings. Not till now would Peter discern the object of this succession of thrusts. The *third* time reveals it all, bringing up such a rush of dreadful recollections before his view, of his "*thrice* denying that he knew Him," that he feels it to the quick. It was fitting that he should; it was meant that he should. But this accomplished, the painful dialogue concludes with a delightful "Feed My sheep"; as if He should say, 'Now, Simon, the last speck of the cloud which overhung thee since that night of nights is dispelled: Henceforth thou art to Me and to My work as if no such scene had ever happened'

Feed—keep—**my sheep**—It has been observed that the word here is studiously changed, from one signifying simply to *feed,* to one signifying to *tend* as a shepherd, denoting the *abiding* exercise of that vocation, and in its highest functions.

He saith unto him, Feed my lambs—It is surely wrong to view this term as a mere diminutive of affection, and as meaning the same thing as "the sheep" [WEBSTER and WILKINSON]. It is much more according to usage to understand by the "lambs" *young and tender* disciples, whether in age or Christian standing (Isa. 40:11; I John 2:12, 13), and by the "sheep" the more *mature.* Shall we say (with many) that Peter was here reinstated in office? Not exactly, since he was not actually excluded from it. But after such conduct as his, the deep wound which the honor of Christ had received, the stain brought on his office, the damage done to his high standing among his brethren, and even his own comfort, in prospect of the great work before him, required some such renewal of his call and re-establishment of his position as this.

when . . . old thou shalt stretch forth thine hands—to be bound for execution, though not necessarily meaning *on a cross.* There is no reason, however, to doubt the very early tradition that Peter's death was by crucifixion.

18, 19. When thou wast young—embracing the whole period of life to the verge of old age. **thou girdedst thyself, and walkedst whither thou wouldest**—wast thine own master.

ADAM CLARKE

There is another remarkable change of terms in this place. In vv. 15 and 17 our Lord uses the verb *bosko,* "to feed"; and in v. 16 He uses the word *poimaino,* which signifies to "tend a flock"—not only to "feed," but to "take care of, guide, govern, defend"—by which He seems to intimate that it is not sufficient merely to offer the Bread of Life to the congregation of the Lord, but he must take care that the sheep be properly collected, attended to, regulated, guided. Every spiritual shepherd of Christ has a flock, composed of lambs—"young converts"—and sheep—"experienced Christians"—to feed, guide, regulate, and govern. To be properly qualified for this, his wisdom and holiness should always exceed those of his flock.

18. *Thou shalt stretch forth thy hands.* Wetstein observes that it was a custom at Rome to put the necks of those who were to be crucified into a yoke, and to stretch out their hands and fasten them to the end of it; and having thus led them through the city they were carried out to be crucified. Thus then Peter was girded, chained, and carried whither he would not—not that he was unwilling to die for Christ, but he was a man—he did not love death, but he loved his life less than he loved his God.

MATTHEW HENRY

world violently when he was about to retire out of it peaceably. God would shelter him from the rage of his enemies till he should come to be old, that he might be made the fitter for sufferings, and the church might the longer enjoy his services.

2. The explication of this prediction (*v.* 19), *This spake he* to Peter, *signifying by what death he should glorify God.* It is not only *appointed to all once to die*, but it is appointed to each what death he shall die. There is one way into the world, but many ways out, and God has determined which way we should go. It is the great concern of every good man, whatever death he dies, to glorify God in it. When we die patiently, die cheerfully, and die usefully, we glorify God in dying. The death of the martyrs was in a special manner for the glorifying of God. The blood of the martyrs has been the seed of the church. Those who thereby at such an expense honour him he will honour.

3. The word of command he gives him hereupon: *When he had spoken thus, he saith unto him, Follow me.* This word, *Follow me*, was a further confirmation of his restoration to his Master's favour, for *Follow me* was the first call. It was an explication of the prediction of his sufferings. *Follow me:* "Expect to be treated as I have been, *for the disciple is not greater than his Lord.*" It was to encourage him in faithfulness and diligence in his work as an apostle. He had told him to *feed his sheep*, and let him set his Master before him as an example. Herein they did follow him, and it was their present honour; who would be ashamed to follow such a leader? Hereafter they should follow him, and that would be their future happiness. Those that faithfully follow Christ in grace shall certainly follow him to glory.

Verses 20–25

I. The conference Christ had with Peter concerning John.

1. The eye Peter cast upon him (*v.* 20): Peter followed him, and *turning about he sees the disciple whom Jesus loved following* likewise. (1) How John is described. He does not name himself, but gives such a description of himself as sufficiently informs us whom he meant. *He was the disciple whom Jesus loved.* It is probable that mention is here made of John's having *leaned on Jesus's breast* and his enquiring concerning the traitor, which he did at the instigation of Peter (*ch.* xiii. 24), as a reason why Peter made the following enquiry concerning him. Then John was in the favourite's place, and he improved the opportunity to oblige Peter. And now that Peter was in the favourite's place, called to take a walk with Christ, he thought himself bound in gratitude to put such a question for John as he thought would oblige him, we all being desirous to know things to come. As we have interest at the throne of grace, we should improve it for the benefit of one another. This is the *communion of saints.* (2) What he did: He also followed Jesus; where he was there also would this servant of his be. What Christ said to Peter he took as said to himself; for that word of command, *Follow me*, was given to all the disciples. (3) The notice Peter took of it: *He, turning about, seeth him.* [1] A culpable diversion from following his Master. The best men find it hard to *attend upon the Lord without distraction.* A needless and unseasonable regard to our brethren often diverts us from communion with God. Or, [2] A laudable concern for his fellow-disciples. He was not so elevated with the honour his Master did him as to deny a kind look to one that followed.

2. The enquiry Peter made concerning him (*v.* 21): "*Lord, and what shall this man do?* What shall be his work, and his lot?" Now this may be taken as the language, (1) Of concern for John, and kindness to him. Here comes thy beloved disciple, hast thou nothing to say to him? Wilt thou not tell how he must be employed, and how he must be honoured? (2) Or of uneasiness at what Christ had said to him concerning his sufferings: "Lord, must I alone be *carried whither I would not?* Must this man have no share of the cross?" (3) Or of curiosity, and a fond desire of knowing things to come. It seems, by Christ's answer, there was something amiss in the question. He seems more concerned for another than for himself. So apt are we to be busy in other men's matters, but negligent in the concerns of our own souls—quick-sighted abroad, but dim-sighted at home. He seems more concerned about events than about duty. We need not ask, "What shall be the lot of those that shall come after us?" Scripture-predictions must be eyed for the directing of our consciences, not the satisfiying or our curiosity.

3. Christ's reply to this enquiry (*v.* 22), "*If I will that he tarry till I come, what is that to thee. Follow*

JAMIESON, FAUSSET, BROWN

19. This spake he, signifying by what death he should glorify God—not, therefore, a mere prediction of the manner of his *death,* but of the *honor* to be conferred upon him by dying for his Master. And, indeed, beyond doubt, this prediction was intended to follow up his triple restoration:—'Yes, Simon, thou shalt not only feed My lambs, and feed My sheep, but after a long career of such service, shalt be counted worthy to die for the name of the Lord Jesus.'

And when he had spoken this, he saith unto him, Follow me—By thus connecting the utterance of this prediction with the invitation to follow Him, the Evangelist would indicate the deeper sense in which the call was understood, not merely to go along with Him at that moment, but to come after Him, "*taking up his cross.*"

20, 21. Peter, turning about—showing that he followed immediately as directed. **seeth the disciple whom Jesus loved following; which also leaned on Jesus' breast at supper, and said, Lord, which is he that betrayeth thee?**—The Evangelist makes these allusions to the peculiar familiarity to which he had been admitted on the most memorable of all occasions, perhaps lovingly to account for Peter's somewhat forward question about him to Jesus; which is the rather probable, as it was at Peter's suggestion that he put the question about the traitor which he here recalls (ch. 13:24, 25).

21. Peter . . . saith to Jesus, Lord, and what shall this man do?—What of this man? or, How shall it fare with him?

ADAM CLARKE

19. *Should glorify God.* Ancient writers state that, about thirty-four years after this, Peter was crucified; and that he deemed it so glorious a thing to die for Christ that he begged to be crucified with his head downwards, not considering himself worthy to die in the same posture in which his Lord did.

Follow me. Whether our Lord meant by these words that Peter was to walk with Him a little way for a private interview, or whether He meant that he was to imitate His example, or be conformed to Him in the manner of His death, is very uncertain.

CHARLES H. SPURGEON:

The name before us is *a name in which John felt himself most at home.* No other title would so well describe him. His own name, "John," means the "gift of God," and he was a precious gift from God the Father to His suffering Son, and a great comfort to the Savior during the years of His abode among men. Jesus doubtless counted him to be His Jonathan, His John, His God gift, and He treasured him as such; but John does not so much think of his being of any service to his Lord as of that which his Lord had been to him. He calls himself "that disciple whom Jesus loved" because he recognized the delightful obligation which springs out of great love, and wished ever to be under its royal influence. He looked on Jesus' love as the source and root of everything about himself which was gracious and commendable. If he had any courage, if he had any faithfulness, if he had any depth of knowledge, it was because Jesus had loved these things into him. All the sweet flowers which bloomed in the garden of his heart were planted there by the hand of Christ's love, so when he called himself "that disciple whom Jesus loved," he felt that he had gone to the root and bottom of the matter, and explained the main reason of his being what he was.

This endearing name was very precious to him, because it evoked the sunniest memories of all his life. Those short years in which he had been with Jesus must have been looked upon by him in his old age with great transport, as the crown and glory of his earthly existence. I do not wonder that he saw Christ again in Patmos, after having seen Him once in Palestine as he did see Him; for such sights are very apt to repeat themselves. Such sights, I say; for John's view of his Lord was no ordinary one. There is at times an echo to sights as well as to sounds; and he who saw the Lord with John's eagle eye, with his deep-seated inner eye, was the likeliest man in all the world to see Him over again in vision as he did see Him amidst the rocks of the Aegean Sea. All the memories of the best part of his life were awakened by the name which he bore, and by its power he oft renewed that intimate communion with the living Christ which had lived on during the horrors of the crucifixion, and lasted to the end of his days. That charming name set all the bells of his soul a-ringing: does it not sound right musically?—"The disciple whom Jesus loved."

—*The Treasury of the New Testament*

MATTHEW HENRY

thou me."

(1) There seems to be here an intimation of Christ's purpose concerning John. That he should not die a violent death, like Peter, but should tarry till Christ himself came by a natural death to fetch him to himself. The most credible of the ancient historians tell us that John was the only one of all the twelve that did not actually die a martyr. He at length died in his bed in a good old age. Though the crown of martyrdom is bright and glorious, yet the beloved disciple comes short of it.

(2) Others think that it is only a rebuke to Peter's curiosity. "Suppose I should design that John should never die, what does that concern thee? I have told thee how thou must die; it is enough for thee to know that, *Follow thou me.*" It is the will of Christ that his disciples should mind their own present duty, and not be curious about future events concerning either themselves or others. There are many things we are apt to be solicitous about that are nothing to us. Other people's characters are nothing to us; it is out of our line to judge them. Other people's affairs are nothing to us to intermeddle in. What do you think will become of such and such? is a common question, which may easily be answered with another: *What is that to me?* To his own Master he stands or falls. Secret things belong not to us. The great thing that is all in all to us is duty, and not event; for duty is ours, events are God's. Now all our duty is summed up in this one of following Christ. And, if we will closely attend to the duty of following Christ, we shall find neither heart nor time to meddle with that which does not belong to us.

4. The mistake which arose from this saying of Christ, that *that disciple should not die.*

(1) The easy rise of a mistake in the church by misconstruing the sayings of Christ. Because John must not die a martyr, they conclude he must not die at all. They were inclined to expect it because they could not choose but desire it. We are apt to dote too much on men and means, instruments and external helps; whereas God will change his workmen, and yet carry on his work. There is no need of immortal ministers to be the guides of the church, while it is under the conduct of an eternal Spirit. Perhaps they were confirmed in their expectations when they now found that John survived all the rest of the apostles. However, it took rise from a saying of Christ's, misunderstood, and then made a saying of the church. Hence learn the uncertainly of human tradition, and the folly of building our faith upon it. Here was a tradition, an apostolical tradition, a saying that *went abroad among the brethren.* It was early; it was common; it was public; and yet it was false. Let the scripture be its own interpreter and explain itself. The aptness of men to misinterpret the sayings of Christ. The scriptures themselves have been wrested by the unlearned and unstable.

(2) The easy rectifying of such mistakes by adhering to the word of Christ. So the evangelist here corrects that saying among the brethren, by repeating the very words of Christ. He said, *If I will that he tarry till I come, what is that to thee?* He said so, and no more. Let the words of Christ speak for themselves. The best end of men's controversies would be to keep to the express words of scripture. Scripture language is the safest and most proper vehicle of scripture truth. As the scripture itself is the best weapon wherewith to wound all dangerous errors, so the scripture itself is the best weapon-salve to heal the wounds that are made by different modes of expression concerning the same truths. Those that cannot agree in the same logic and metaphysics, may yet agree in the same scripture terms, and then may agree to love one another.

II. We have here the conclusion of this gospel, *v.* 24, 25.

1. This gospel concludes with an account of the penman of it (*v.* 24): *This is the disciple which testifies of these things* to the present age, and wrote these things for the benefit of posterity. Those who wrote the history of Christ were not ashamed to put their names to it. John here does in effect subscribe his name. The record of Christ's life and death was drawn up by men of known integrity, who were ready to *seal it with their blood.* Those who wrote the history of Christ wrote upon their own knowledge. The penman of this history was a disciple, one that had leaned on Christ's breast, that had himself heard his sermons, had seen his miracles, and the proofs of his resurrection. This is he who testifies what he was well assured of. Those who wrote the history of Christ, as they testified what they had seen, so they wrote what they had first testified. It was published by word of mouth, with the greatest assurance, before it was committed to writing. What they wrote they wrote as an affidavit, which they would abide by.

JAMIESON, FAUSSET, BROWN

22, 23. Jesus saith to him, If I will that he tarry till I come, what is that to thee? follow thou me—From the fact that John alone of the Twelve survived the destruction of Jerusalem, and so witnessed the commencement of that series of events which belongs to "the last days," many good interpreters think that this is a virtual prediction of fact, and not a mere supposition. But this is very doubtful, and it seems more natural to consider our Lord as intending to give *no positive indication* of John's fate at all, but to signify that this was a matter which belonged to the Master of both, who would disclose or conceal it as He thought proper, and that Peter's part was to mind his own affairs. Accordingly, in "follow thou Me," the word "*thou*" is emphatic. Observe the absolute disposal of human life which Christ claims: "*If I will* that he tarry till I come . . . ."

23. Then went this saying abroad among the brethren, that that disciple should not die—into which they the more easily fell from the prevalent expectation that Christ's second coming was then near at hand. **yet Jesus said not unto him, He shall not die**—The Evangelist is jealous for His Master's honor, which his death might be thought to compromise if such a misunderstanding should not be corrected.

24, 25. FINAL CLOSE OF THIS GOSPEL. **24. This is the disciple which testifieth of these things, and wrote these things**—thus identifying the author of this book with all that it says of this disciple.

ADAM CLARKE

ALEXANDER MACLAREN:

We have in that majestic "If I will!" the revelation of the risen Christ as the Lord of life and death.

In His charge to Peter, Christ had asserted His right absolutely to control His servant's conduct and fix his place in the world, and His power to foresee and forecast his destiny and his end. But in these words He goes a step further. "I *will* that he tarry"; to communicate life and to sustain life is a divine prerogative; to act by the bare utterance of His will upon physical nature is a divine prerogative. Jesus Christ here claims that His will goes out with sovereign power among the perplexities of human history and into the depths of that mystery of life; and that He, the Son of Man, "quickens whom he will," and has power "to kill and to make alive." The words would be absurd, if not something worse, upon any but divine lips, that opened with conscious authority, and whose Utterer knew that His hand was laid upon the innermost springs of being.

So, in this entirely incidental fashion, you have one of the strongest and plainest instances of the quiet, unostentatious and habitual manner in which Jesus Christ claimed for himself properly divine prerogatives.

Remember that He who thus spoke was standing before these seven men there, in the morning light, on the beach, fresh from the grave. His resurrection had proved Him to be the Lord of death. He had bound it to His chariot wheels as a Conqueror. He had risen and He stood there before them with no more mark of the corruption of the grave upon Him than there are traces of the foul water in which a seabird may have floated, on its white wing that flashes in the sunshine as it soars. And surely as these men looked to Christ, "declared to be the Son of God with power, by his resurrection from the dead," they may have begun, however "foolish and slow of heart" they were "to believe," to understand that "to this end Christ both died and rose and revived, that he might be the Lord both of the dead and of the living," both of death and of life.

—*Expositions of Holy Scripture*

22. *If I will that he tarry till I come.* Augustine, Bede, and others understood the passage thus: If I will that he remain till I come and take him away by a natural death, what is that to you? Follow Me to your crucifixion. On this it may be observed that all antiquity agrees that John, if he did die, was the only disciple who was taken away by a natural death. Others imagine that our Lord was only now taking Peter aside to speak something to him in private, and that Peter, seeing John following, wished to know whether he should come along with them; and that our Lord's answer stated that John should remain in that place till Christ and Peter returned to him—and to this meaning of the passage many eminent critics incline. I rather lean to this opinion.

24. *This is the disciple.* It is, I think, very likely that these two verses were added by some of the believers at that time, as a testimony to the truth of the preceding narration; and I allow, with Bishop Pearce and others, that it is possible that John may mean himself when he says *we know*; yet I think that it is very unlikely.

MATTHEW HENRY

It was graciously appointed that the history of Christ should be put into writing, that it might spread to every place, and last through every age.

2. It concludes with an attestation of the truth of what had been here related: *We know that his testimony is true.* The testimony of one who is an eye-witness, is of unspotted reputation, and puts it into writing for the greater certainty, is an unexceptionable evidence. *We know,* that is, All the world knows, that the testimony of such a one is valid. The truth of the gospel comes confirmed by all the evidence we can rationally desire or expect. Then let the doctrine recommend itself, and let the miracles prove it to be of God. It expresses the satisfaction of the churches *at that time* concerning the truth of what is here related. Not as if an inspired writing needed any attestation from men, but hereby they recommended it to the notice of the churches. Or, it expresses the evangelist's own assurance of the truth of what he wrote. The evangelists themselves were entirely satisfied of the truth of what they have testified and transmitted to us. They ventured both this life and the other upon it; threw away this life, and depended upon another.

3. It concludes with an *et cetera,* with a reference to *many other things* said and done by our Lord Jesus, *v.* 25. If they should be written at large, even the world itself could not contain the books that might be written. If it be asked why the gospels are not larger, it may be answered,

(1) It was not because they had exhausted their subject, and had nothing more to write that was worth writing. Everything that Christ said and did was worth our notice. His miracles were many, very many, of many kinds, and the same often repeated. The repetition of the miracles before a great variety of witnesses, helped very much to prove them true miracles. Every new miracle rendered the report of the former the more credible; and the multitude of them renders the whole report incontestable. When we speak of Christ, we have a copious subject before us; the reality exceeds the report, and, after all, *the one half is not told us.* St. Paul quotes one of Christ's sayings, which is not recorded by any of the evangelists (Acts xx. 35), and doubtless there were many more.

(2) But it was for these three reasons: Because it was not needful to write more. What is written is a sufficient revelation of the doctrine of Christ and the proof of it. If we do not believe and improve what is written, neither should we if there had been much more. It was not possible to write all. It would be such a large and overgrown history as never was; such as would jostle out all other writings, and leave us no room for them. It would have been an endless thing. It was not advisable to write much; for *the world,* in a moral sense, *could not contain the books that should be written. The world could not contain.* It is the word that is used, *ch.* viii. 37, "My word *has no place* in you." They would have been so many that they would have found no room. All people's time would have been spent in reading, and other duties would thereby have been crowded out. Much is overlooked of what is written, much forgotten, and much made the matter of doubtful disputation; this would have been the case much more if there had been such a world of books. Especially since it was requisite that what was written should be meditated upon and expounded, which God wisely thought fit to leave room for. Let us be thankful for the books that are written, and not prize them the less for their plainness and brevity, and long to be above, where our capacities shall be so elevated and enlarged that there will be no danger of their being over-loaded.

The evangelist, concluding with *Amen,* thereby sets to his seal, and let us set to ours, an *Amen* of faith, that it is true, all true; and an *Amen* of satisfaction in what is written, as able to make us wise to salvation. *Amen;* so be it.

JAMIESON, FAUSSET, BROWN

we know that his testimony is true—(Cf. ch. 19:35).

25. And there are many other things which Jesus did—(Cf. ch. 20:30, 31).

if . . . written every one, I suppose—an expression used to show that what follows is not to be pressed too far. **even the world itself would not hold the books . . .**—not a *mere* hyperbolical expression, unlike the sublime simplicity of this writer, but intended to let his reader know that, even now that he had done, he felt his materials so far from being exhausted, that he was still running over, and could multiply "Gospels" to almost any extent within the strict limits of what "Jesus did." But in the *limitation* of these matchless histories, in point of number, there is as much of that divine wisdom which has presided over and pervades the living oracles, as in their *variety* and *fulness.*

ADAM CLARKE

ALBERT BARNES:

25. "Many other things." Many miracles (20:30). Many discourses delivered. "I suppose." This is evidently the figure of speech called a hyperbole. It is a mode of speech where the words express more or less than is literally true. It is common among all writers; and as the sacred writers, in recording a revelation to men, used human language, it was proper that they should express themselves as men ordinarily do if they wished to be understood. This figure of speech is commonly the effect of surprise, or having the mind full of some object, and not having words to express the ideas: at the same time, the words convey no falsehood. The statement is to be taken as it would be understood among the persons to whom it is addressed; and as no one supposes that the author means to be understood literally, so there is no deception in the case, and consequently no impeachment of his veracity or inspiration. Thus, when Longinus said of a man that "he was the owner of a piece of ground not larger than a Lacedaemonian letter," no one understood him literally. He meant, evidently, a very small piece of land, and no one would be deceived. So Virgil says of a man, "he was so tall as to reach the stars," and means only that he was very tall. So when John says that the world could not contain the books that would be written if all the deeds and sayings of Jesus were recorded, he clearly intends nothing more than that a great many books would be required, or that it would be extremely difficult to record them all; intimating that his life was active, that his discourses were numerous, and that he had not pretended to give them all, but only such as would go to establish the main point for which he wrote—that he was the Messiah (20:30, 31).—*Popular Commentary*

25. *Could not contain.* Origen's signification of the word is to "admit of" or "receive favorably." As if he had said, The miracles of Christ are so many, and so astonishing, that if the whole were to be detailed the world would not receive the account with proper faith; but enough is recorded that men may believe that Jesus is the Son of God, and that in believing they may have life through His name, chap. xx. 31. We have already seen that this apostle often uses the term world to designate the Jewish people only; and if it have this sense here, which is possible, it will at once vindicate the above exposition. As if he had said, Were I to detail all the signs and miracles which Jesus did among His disciples, and in the private families where He sojourned, the Jewish people themselves would not receive nor credit these accounts; but enough is written to prove that this Christ was the promised Messiah.

THE ACTS OF THE APOSTLES

I. The Church formed (1:1-2:4)
A. The key note—the continuity of Christ (1:1)
1. King—proceeding to empire (Matthew)
2. Servant—serving and suffering (Mark)
3. Man—realizing and revealing (Luke)
4. God—manifest (John)
B. The last glimpse of the old conditions (1:2-26)
1. Christ alone (1:2-11)
2. Disciples alone (1:12-26)
C. The creation of the new (2:1-4)
1. The units
2. The unity

II. The church witnessing (2:5-28:31)
A. In Jerusalem (2:5-7:60)
1. The first impression (2:5-13)
2. The first message (2:14-47)
3. The first opposition (3:1-4:31)
4. The first communism (4:32-37)
5. The first discipline (5:1-16)
6. The first persecution (5:17-42)
7. The first organization (6:1-7)
8. The first martyr (6:8-7:60)
B. In Judea and Samaria (8:1-25)
1. The scattered witnesses (8:1-4)
2. Samaria (8:5-25)
C. To the uttermost part of the earth (8:26-28:31)
1. Toward Africa (8:26-40)
2. Toward Asia (9:1-16:5)
a. Saul—the instrument found (9:1-31)
b. Peter (9:32-11:18)
c. Barnabas and Saul (11:19-30)
d. Herod (12:1-24)
e. Paul—the instrument commissioned (12:25-13:4)
f. Paul—the instrument used (13:5-14:28)
g. The council at Jerusalem (15:1-35)
h. Separation between Barnabas and Paul (15:36-16:5)
3. Toward Europe (16:6-18:18)
4. In Asia (18:19-26:32)
a. Ephesus (18:19-21)
b. Visitation (18:22-23)
c. Ephesus (18:24-19:41)
d. Three months in Europe (20:1-6)
e. Troas (20:7-12)
f. Journey to Jerusalem (20:13-21:16)
g. Jerusalem (21:17-23:30)
h. Caesarea (23:31-26:32)
5. In Europe (27:1-28:31)
a. The long journey (27:1-28:15)
b. Rome (28:16-31)

We have with an abundant satisfaction seen the foundation of our holy religion laid in the history of our blessed Savior. Upon this rock the Christian church is built. How it began to be built is recorded in the Acts.

The history of this book may be considered—

I. *As looking back to the preceding gospels.* The promises made in the gospels, we find made good in the Acts, particularly the great promises of the descent of the Holy Ghost. The powers lodged in them, we here find exerted in miracles wrought on the bodies of people—miracles of mercy, miracles of judgment, and much greater miracles wrought on the minds of people. The proofs of Christ's resurrection with which the gospels closed are here abundantly corroborated according to the word of Christ, that his resurrection should be the most convincing proof of his divine mission. Christ had told his disciples that they should be his witnesses, and this book brings them in witnessing for him. That dayspring from on high the first appearing of which we there discerned, we here find shining more and more. *The kingdom of heaven,* which was then *at hand,* is here set up. Christ's predictions of the virulent persecutions which the preachers of the gospel should be afflicted with we here find abundantly fulfilled, and also the assurances he gave them of extraordinary supports and comforts under their sufferings. This latter part of the history of the New Testament exactly answers to the word of Christ in the former part of it: and thus they mutually confirm and illustrate each other.

II. *As looking forward to the following epistles.* This book introduces them and is a key to them. We are members of the Christian church, that "tabernacle of God among men." Now this book gives us an account of the framing and rearing of that tabernacle. The four gospels showed us how the foundation of that house was laid; this shows us how the superstructure began to be raised among the Jews, the Samaritans, and the Gentiles.

Two things more are to be observed concerning this book: (1) The penman of it. It was written by Luke, who wrote the third of the four gospels, which bears his name. This Luke was very much a companion of Paul in his services and sufferings. "Only Luke is with me" (2 Tim. 4:11). We may know by his style in the latter part of this book when and where he was with him, for then he writes, We did so and so (16:10; 20:6). (2) The title of it: *The Acts of the Apostles.* (a) It is the history of the apostles; yet there is in it the history of Stephen, Barnabas, and some other apostolic men. It is the history of Peter and Paul only that is here recorded; Peter the apostle of the circumcision, and Paul the apostle of the Gentiles (Gal. 2:7). (b) It is called their *acts,* or *doings.* The apostles were active men; and though the wonders they did were by the word, yet they are fitly called *their acts*; they spoke *and it was done.*

MATTHEW HENRY

CHAPTER 1

Verses 1–5

I. Theophilus is put in mind, and we in him, of St. Luke's gospel, which it will be of use for us to cast an eye upon.

1. His patron, to whom he dedicates this book, is Theophilus, *v.* 1. The directing some of the books of the scripture so is an intimation to each of us to receive them as if directed to us in particular, to us by name.

2. His gospel is here called *the former treatise which he had made.* He made the former treatise, and now is divinely inspired to make this, for Christ's scholars must *go on towards perfection,* and not think that their former labours will excuse them from further labours. St. Luke, because he had laid the foundation in a former treatise, will build upon it in this. Let not new sermons and new books make us forget old ones, but put us in mind of them, and help us to improve them.

3. The contents of his gospel were *that, all that, which Jesus began both to do and teach.* (1) Christ both did and taught. Those are the best ministers

JAMIESON, FAUSSET, BROWN

CHAPTER 1

Vss. 1-11. INTRODUCTION—LAST DAYS OF OUR LORD UPON EARTH—HIS ASCENSION. **1, 2. former treatise**—Luke's Gospel. **Theophilus**—(See on Luke 1:3).

began to do and teach—a very important statement, dividing the work of Christ into two great branches: the one embracing His work *on earth,* the other His subsequent work *from heaven;*

ADAM CLARKE

CHAPTER 1

1. *The former treatise.* The Gospel according to Luke, which is here most evidently intended. *O Theophilus.* See the note on Luke i. 3. *To do and teach.* These two words comprise His miracles and sermons.

MATTHEW HENRY

that both do and teach, whose lives are a constant sermon. (2) *He began both to do and teach;* he laid the foundation. His apostles were to carry on and continue what he began. Christ set them in, and then left them to go on, but sent his Spirit to empower them. It is a comfort to those who are endeavouring to carry on the work of the gospel that Christ himself began it. (3) The four evangelists, and Luke particularly, have handed down to us *all that Jesus began both to do and to teach*; not all the particulars; but all the heads, that by them we may judge of the rest.

4. The period of the evangelical story is fixed *to the day in which he was taken up*, *v.* 2. Then it was that he left this world, and his bodily presence was no more in it.

II. The truth of Christ's resurrection is maintained and evidenced, *v.* 3. The great evidence of his resurrection was that *he showed himself alive to his apostles*; and *he was seen of them.* 1. The proofs were infallible, both that he was *alive* (he walked and talked with them, he ate and drank with them) and that *it was he himself, and not another*; for he showed them again and again the marks of *the wounds in his hands, and feet, and side.* 2. They were many, and often repeated: *He was seen by them forty days*, not constantly residing with them, but frequently appearing to them.

III. A general hint given of the instructions he furnished his disciples with. He instructed them concerning the work they were to do: *He gave commandments to the apostles whom he had chosen.* Those whom he elected into the apostleship expected he should give them preferments, instead of which *he gave them commandments. He gave them commandments through the Holy Ghost.* In giving them the Holy Ghost, he gave them his commandments; for the Comforter will be a commander. He instructed them concerning the doctrine they were to preach: *He spoke to them of the things pertaining to the kingdom of God.* He had given them a general idea of that kingdom, but here he instructed them more in the nature of it, as a kingdom of grace in this world and of glory in the other, to prepare them to receive the Holy Ghost, and to go through that which they were designed for. It was one of the proofs of Christ's resurrection; the disciples, to whom *he showed himself alive*, knew that it was he, not only by what he showed them, but by what he said to them. None but he could speak thus clearly, thus fully, *of the things pertaining to the kingdom of God.*

IV. A particular assurance given them that they should now shortly receive the Holy Ghost (*v.* 4, 5).

1. The command he gives them to wait. This was to raise their expectations. They must wait till the time appointed, which is now *not many days hence.* Those that by faith hope promised mercies will come must with patience wait till they do come. They must wait in the place appointed, *in Jerusalem.* There Christ was put to shame, there he will have his honour done him, and this favour is done to Jerusalem to teach us to forgive our enemies and persecutors. The apostles were now to put on a public character. Jerusalem was the fittest candlestick for those lights to be set up in.

2. The assurance he gives them that they shall not wait in vain.

(1) The blessing designed them shall come: *You shall be baptized with the Holy Ghost.* They had already been breathed upon with the Holy Ghost (John xx. 22), and they had found the benefit of it; but now they shall have larger measures of his gifts, graces, and comforts. "You shall be cleansed and purified by the Holy Ghost," as the priests were baptized and washed with water, when they were consecrated to the sacred function: "They had the sign; you shall have the thing signified. You shall thereby be more effectually than ever engaged to our Master. You shall be tied so fast to Christ that you shall never forsake him again."

(2) Now this gift of the Holy Ghost he speaks of, [1] As *the promise of the Father, which they had heard of him*, and might therefore depend upon. *First*, The Spirit was given by promise. The Spirit of God is not given as the spirit of men is given us, but by the word of God. That the gift may be the more valuable. That it may be the more sure. That it may be of grace, and may be received by faith. As Christ, so the Spirit, is received by faith. *Secondly*, It was *the promise of the Father,*—of Christ's Father; our Father. He will give the Spirit as *the Father of mercies*; it is *the promise of the Father. Thirdly*, This promise of the Father they had heard from Christ many a time. He assured them, again and again, that *the Comforter* should come. This confirms the promise of God that we have heard it from Jesus Christ.

[2] As the prediction of John Baptist (*v.* 5): "You

JAMIESON, FAUSSET, BROWN

the one in His own Person, the other by His Spirit; the one the "beginning," the other the continuance of the same work; the one complete when He sat down at the right hand of the Majesty on high, the other to continue till His second appearing; the one recorded in "The Gospels," the *beginnings* only of the other related in this book of "The Acts." "Hence the grand history of what Jesus did and taught does not conclude with His departure to the Father; but Luke now begins it in a higher strain; for all the subsequent labors of the apostles are just an exhibition of *the ministry of the glorified Redeemer Himself,* because they were acting under His authority, and He was the principle that operated in them all" [OLSHAUSEN].

3-5. showed himself alive—As the author is about to tell us that *"the resurrection of the Lord Jesus"* was the great burden of apostolic preaching, so the subject is here fitly introduced by an allusion to the primary evidence on which that great fact rests, the repeated and undeniable manifestations of Himself in the body to the assembled disciples, who, instead of being predisposed to believe it, had to be overpowered by the resistless evidence of their own senses, and were slow of yielding even to this (Mark 16:14). **after his passion**—or, suffering. This primary sense of the word "passion" has fallen into disuse; but it is nobly consecrated in the phraseology of the Church to express the Redeemer's final endurances. **seen of them forty days**—This important specification of time occurs here only.

after he, through the Holy Ghost, had given commandments...—referring to the charge recorded in Matthew 28:18-20; Mark 16:15-18; Luke 24:44-49. It is worthy of notice that nowhere else are such communications of the risen Redeemer said to have been given "through the Holy Ghost." In general, this might have been said of all He uttered and all He did in His official character; for it was for this very end that God "gave not the Spirit by measure unto Him" (John 3:34). But after His resurrection, as if to signify the new relation in which He now stood to the Church, He signalized His first meeting with the assembled disciples by *breathing* on them (immediately after dispensing to them His *peace*) and saying, *"Receive ye the Holy Ghost,"* thus anticipating the donation of the Spirit from His hands (see on John 20:21, 22); and on the same principle His parting charges are here said to have been given "through the Holy Ghost," as if to mark that He was now all redolent with the Spirit; that what had been husbanded, during His suffering work, for His own necessary uses, had now been set free, was already overflowing from Himself to His disciples, and needed but His ascension and glorification to flow all forth. (See on John 7:39.)

speaking of—rather 'speaking'—**the things pertaining to the kingdom of God**—till now only in germ, but soon to take visible form; the earliest and the latest burden of His teaching on earth. **4. should not depart from Jerusalem**—because the Spirit was to glorify the existing economy, by descending on the disciples at its metropolitan seat, and at the next of its great festivals after the ascension of the Church's Head; in order that "out of Zion might go forth the law, and the word of the Lord from Jerusalem" (Isa. 2: 3; and cf. Luke 24:49). **5. ye shall be baptized with the Holy Ghost not many days hence**—*ten* days hence, as appears from Leviticus 23:15, 16; but it was expressed thus indefinitely to exercise their faith.

ADAM CLARKE

3. ***To whom . . . he shewed himself alive . . . by many infallible proofs.*** By many proofs of such a nature, and connected with such circumstances, as to render them indubitable; for this is the import of the Greek word.

4. ***And, being assembled together.*** Instead of "being assembled together," several good MSS. and versions read "living or eating together," which refers the conversation reported here to some particular time when He sat at meat with His disciples.

Pertaining to the kingdom of God. Whatever concerned the doctrine, discipline, and establishment of the Christian Church.

5. ***Ye shall be baptized with the Holy Ghost not many days hence.*** John baptized with water, which was a sign of penitence, in reference to the remission of sin; but Christ baptizes with the Holy Ghost, for the destruction of sin, the illumination of the mind, and the consolation of the heart.

The promise of the Father. The Holy Spirit, which indeed was the grand promise of the New Testament, as Jesus Christ was of the Old. How properly do we still pray, and how necessary is the prayer, "Cleanse the thoughts of our hearts by the inspiration of thy Holy Spirit, that we may perfectly love thee, and worthily magnify thy name, through Jesus Christ our Lord! Amen."—Communion Service. ***Ye have heard of me.*** In His particular conversations with His disciples, such as those related in John xiv. 16-26; xv. 26; xvi. 7-15.

MATTHEW HENRY

have not only heard it from me, but you had it from John; he said (Matt. iii. 11), *I indeed baptize you with water, but he that comes after me shall baptize you with the Holy Ghost.*" It is a great honour that Christ now does to John. Thus *he confirmeth the word of his servants, his messengers.* But Christ can do more than any of his ministers. It is an honour to them to be employed in dispensing the means of grace, but it is his prerogative to give *the Spirit of grace.*

(3) Now this gift of the Holy Ghost thus promised is that which we find the apostles received in the next chapter, for in that this promise had its full accomplishment. Other scriptures speak of *the gift of the Holy Ghost* to ordinary believers; this speaks of that particular power which the first preachers of the gospel were endued with. By virtue of this promise we receive the New Testament as of divine inspiration.

Verses 6–11

They came together to be *the witnesses* of his ascension.

I. The question they asked him at this interview. *Lord, wilt thou at this time restore again the kingdom to Israel?* Two ways this may be taken:

1. "Surely thou wilt not at all restore it to the present rulers of Israel. What! Shall those that hate and persecute thee and us be trusted with power?" Or rather,

2. "Surely thou wilt now restore it to the Jewish nation, as far as it will submit to thee." Now two things were amiss in this question:

(1) Their expectation of the thing itself. They thought Christ would *restore the kingdom to Israel,* whereas Christ came to set up his own kingdom, and that a kingdom of heaven, not to *restore the kingdom to Israel,* an earthly kingdom. See here, [1] How apt even good men are to place the happiness of the church too much in external pomp and power. We are told to expect the cross in this world, and to wait for the kingdom in the other world. [2] How apt we are to retain what we have imbibed, and how hard it is to get over the prejudices of education. The disciples were long before they could be brought to have any idea of his kingdom as spiritual. [3] How naturally we are biased in favour of our own people. The kingdoms of this world were to become his whether Israel should sink or swim. [4] How apt we are to misunderstand scripture and to expound scripture by our schemes, whereas we ought to form our schemes by the scriptures.

(2) Their enquiry concerning the time of it: "*Lord, wilt thou* do it *at this time?*" They were inquisitive into that which their Master had never encouraged them to enquire into. They were impatient for the setting up of that kingdom in which they promised themselves so great a share. Christ had told them that they should *sit on thrones* (Luke xxii. 30), and now nothing will serve them but they must be in the throne immediately.

II. The check which Christ gave to this question, *v. 7: It is not for you to know the times and seasons.* That mistake would soon be rectified by the pouring out of the Spirit, after which they never had any more thoughts of the temporal kingdom. There is a sense of the expectation which is true, the setting up of the gospel kingdom in the world. But he checks their enquiry after the time.

1. The knowledge of this is not allowed to them: *It is not for you to know.* (1) Christ is now parting from them, and yet he gives them this rebuke; a caution to his church to take heed of splitting upon the rock which was fatal to our first parents—an inordinate desire of forbidden knowledge. (2) Christ had given his disciples a great deal of knowledge above others. He here lets them understand that there were some things which it was not for them to know. We shall see how little reason we have to be proud of our knowledge when we consider how many things we are ignorant of. (3) Christ had given his disciples instructions sufficient for the discharge of their duty, and in this knowledge he will have them to be satisfied. (4) Christ had himself told his disciples *the things pertaining to the kingdom of God,* and had promised that the Spirit should *show them things to come.* He had likewise given them *signs of the times.* But they must not expect nor desire to know either all the particulars of future events or the exact times of them. As to the times and seasons of the year, we know, in general, there will be summer and winter counterchanged, but we know not particularly which day will be fair or which foul, either in summer or in winter. What this or that particular *day will bring forth* we cannot tell, but must accommodate ourselves to it, whatever it is, and make the best of it.

2. The knowledge of it is reserved to God; it is

JAMIESON, FAUSSET, BROWN

A. B. SIMPSON:

He was to be a Person as real as Christ himself. It is not something that we receive from God in this deeper life, but somebody who comes to make himself known to us, to make himself real to us, and to be in us the source of all our strength and happiness.

He was to come as the Spirit of power. Man is the weakest of beings, weaker than the elements around him, weaker even than the brutes over whom he was sent to exercise dominion. But the Holy Ghost comes to give him power, to make his life effectual, and when the Holy Spirit comes into our life He does something. He accomplishes something. He is more than a sentiment, a feeling, a fancy. He is an infinite force that makes our life powerful, and enables us to accomplish all for which we are called as the disciples of Christ. It is power over sin, power over self, power over the world, power over sickness, power over Satan, power to be, to do, to suffer, and to overcome.
—*Christ in the Bible*

6-8. wilt thou at this time restore the kingdom to Israel?—Doubtless their carnal views of Messiah's kingdom had by this time been modified, though how far it is impossible to say. But, as they plainly looked for *some* restoration of the kingdom to Israel, so they are neither rebuked nor contradicted on this point.

ALEXANDER MACLAREN:

The promise of this great gift, the nature of which they but dimly knew, set the Apostles' expectations on tiptoe, and they seem to have thought that their reception of it was in some way the herald of the establishment of the messianic kingdom. So it was, but in a very different fashion from their dream. They had not learned so much from the forty days' instructions concerning the kingdom as to be free from their old Jewish notions, which color their question, "Wilt thou at this time restore again the kingdom to Israel?" They believed that Jesus could establish His kingdom when He would. They were right, and also wrong—right, for He is King; wrong, for its establishment is not to be effected by a single act of power, but by the slow process of preaching the gospel.

Our Lord does not deal with their misconceptions which could only be cured by time and events; but He lays down great principles, which we need as much as the Eleven did. The "times and seasons," the long stretches of days, and the critical epoch-making moments, are known to God only; our business is not to speculate curiously about these, but to do the plain duty which is incumbent on the Church at all times. The perpetual office of Christ's people to be His witnesses, their equipment for that function (the power of the Holy Spirit), and the sphere of their work (namely, in ever-widening circles, Jerusalem, Samaria, and the whole world) are laid down, not for the first hearers only, but for all ages and for each individual, in these last words of the Lord as He stood on Olivet, ready to depart.—*Expositions of Holy Scripture*

7. It is not for you to know the times . . .—implying not only that this was *not* the time, but that the question was irrelevant to their present business and future work.

ADAM CLARKE

6. *At this time restore again the kingdom.* That the disciples, in common with the Jews, expected the Messiah's kingdom to be at least in part secular, I have often had occasion to note. In this opinion they continued less or more till the Day of Pentecost, when the mighty outpouring of the Holy Spirit taught them the spiritual nature of the kingdom of Christ. The Kingdom had now for a considerable time been taken away from Israel; the Romans, not the Israelites, had the government. The object of the disciples' question seems to have been this: to gain information, from their all-knowing Master, whether the time was now fully come in which the Romans should be thrust out and Israel made, as formerly, an independent kingdom.

7. *The times or the seasons. Times* here may signify any large portion of a period, era, or century; and *seasons,* the particular part, season or opportunity in that period in which it might be proper to do any particular work.

MATTHEW HENRY

what *the Father hath put in his own power.* None besides can reveal the times and seasons to come. He has not thought fit to let you know the times and seasons. He hath not said that he will not give you to know something more than you do of the times and seasons, but he has put it in his own power to do it or not, as he thinks fit.

III. He appoints them their work, and with authority assures them of success in it. "Know this (*v.* 8) that you shall receive a spiritual *power*, by the *descent of the Holy Ghost upon you, you shall be witnesses unto me*; and your testimony shall be received here in Jerusalem, in the country about, and all the world over," *v.* 8. If Christ make us serviceable to his honour in our own day and generation, let this be enough for us. Christ here tells them,

1. That their work should be honourable and glorious: *You shall be witnesses unto me.* They shall proclaim him king. They must openly and solemnly preach his gospel to the world. They shall confirm their testimony, not as witnesses do, with an oath, but with the divine seal of miracles and supernatural gifts: *You shall be martyrs to me;* for they attested the truth of the gospel with their sufferings, even unto death.

2. That their power for this work should be sufficient. They had not strength of their own for it, nor wisdom nor courage enough. "*But you shall receive the power of the Holy Ghost coming upon you.* You shall have power to preach the gospel, and to confirm it both by miracles and by sufferings." Those whom he employs in his service he will qualify for it.

3. That their influence should be great and very extensive: "*You shall be witnesses: In Jerusalem;* there you must begin. Your light shall thence shine throughout all Judæa. Thence you shall proceed *to Samaria.* Your usefulness shall reach *to the uttermost part of the earth.*"

IV. Having left these instructions with them, he leaves them (*v.* 9): *When he had spoken these things he blessed them* (so we were told, Luke xxiv. 50); and *while they beheld him, he was taken up, and a cloud received him out of their sight.* He began his ascension in the sight of his disciples, even *while they beheld.* They saw him go up towards heaven, and had actually their eye upon him with so much care and earnestness of mind that they could not be deceived. He *vanished out of their sight, in a cloud.* It was a bright cloud that overshadowed him in his transfiguration, and most probably this was so, Matt. xvii. 5. By the clouds there is a sort of communication kept up between the upper and lower world; in them the vapours are sent up from the earth, and the dews sent down from heaven. Fitly therefore does he ascend in a cloud who is *the Mediator between God and man*, by whom God's mercies come down upon us and our prayers come up to him. This was the last that was seen of him.

V. The disciples, when he had gone out of their sight, yet still continued *looking up steadfastly to heaven* (*v.* 10). 1. Perhaps they hoped that Christ would come back to them again, so much did they still dote upon his bodily presence, though he had told them that *it was expedient for them that he should go away.* 2. Perhaps they expected to see some change in the visible heavens now upon Christ's ascension. Christ had told them that hereafter they should *see heaven opened* (John i. 51), and why should not they expect it now?

VI. Two angels appeared to them. To show how much Christ had at heart the concerns of his church on earth, he sent back to his disciples two of those that came to meet him, who appear as *two men in white apparel.* Now we are told what the angels said to them, 1. To check their curiosity: *You men of Galilee, why stand you gazing up into heaven?* What would you see? You have seen all that you were called together to see, and why do you look any further? *Why stand you gazing?* Christ's disciples should never stand at a gaze, because they have a sure rule to go by. 2. To confirm their faith concerning Christ's second coming. Their Master had often told them of this: "*This same Jesus, who is taken up from you into heaven will come in like manner thence, as you have seen him go thither.*" (1) "*This same Jesus,* who came once in disgrace to be judged, will come again in glory to judge." (2) "He *shall come in like manner.* He is gone away in a *cloud.* You have now lost the sight of him in the clouds; and *whither he is gone you cannot follow him now,* but shall then." When we stand gazing and trifling, the consideration of our Master's second coming should quicken and awaken us; and, when we stand gazing and trembling, the consideration of it should comfort and encourage us.

JAMIESON, FAUSSET, BROWN

8. receive power—See Luke 24:49. **and ye shall be witnesses unto me . . . in Jerusalem . . . in all Judea . . . and unto the uttermost part of the earth**—*This order of apostolic preaching and success supplies the proper key to the plan of the Acts,* which relates first the progress of the Gospel "in Jerusalem, and all Judea and Samaria" (ch. 1 to ch. 9), and then "unto the uttermost part of the earth" (ch. 10 to ch. 28).

9-11. while they beheld, he was taken up—See on Luke 24:50-53. Lest it should be thought He had disappeared when they were looking in some other direction, and so was only *concluded* to have gone up to heaven, it is here expressly said that "*while they were looking* He was taken up, and a cloud received Him *out of their sight.*" So Elijah, "If thou *see me* when I am taken from thee" (II Kings 2:10); "And Elisha *saw* it" (vs. 12). (See on Luke 9:32.)

10. while they looked steadfastly toward heaven—following Him with their eager eyes, in rapt amazement. Not, however, as a mere fact is this recorded, but as a part of that resistless evidence of their senses on which their whole subsequent testimony was to be borne.

two men in white apparel—angels in human form, as in Luke 24:4. **11. Ye men of Galilee, why stand ye gazing up into heaven . . .**—'as if your now glorified Head were gone from you never to return: He is coming again; not another, but "this same Jesus"; and "as ye have seen Him go, in the like manner shall He come"—as *personally,* as *visibly,* as *gloriously;* and let the joyful expectation of this coming swallow up the sorrow of that departure.'

ADAM CLARKE

8. *But ye shall receive power.* Translating different terms of the original by the same English word is a source of misapprehension and error. We must not understand *dynamis,* which we translate *power* in this verse, as we do *exousia,* translated by the same word in the preceding verse. In the latter, God's infinite "authority" over all times and seasons, and His uncompellable liberty of acting or not acting in any given case, are particularly pointed out. In the other, the "energy" communicated by Him to His disciples through which they were enabled to work miracles is particularly intended; and *dynamis,* in general, signifies such power. The disciples were to be made instruments in the establishment of the kingdom of Christ, but this must be by the *energy* of the Holy Ghost sent down from heaven. *Ye shall be witnesses.* Though the word *earth* is often used to denote Judea alone, yet here it is probable it is to be taken in its largest extent. All the inhabitants of the globe might at that period be considered divisible into three classes: (1) The Jews, who adhered to the law of Moses and the prophetic writings, worshipping the true God only and keeping up the Temple service as prescribed in their law; (2) The Samaritans, a mongrel people who worshipped the God of Israel in connection with other gods, 2 Kings xvii. 5, etc., and who had no kind of religious connection with the Jews; and (3) the Gentiles, the heathens through all other parts of the world, who were addicted to idolatry alone and had no knowledge of the true God. By the terms in the text we may see the extent to which this commission of instruction and salvation was designed to reach: to the Jews, to the Samaritans, and to *the uttermost part of the earth,* i.e., to the Gentile nations. Thus, to the *whole human race* the gospel of the Kingdom was to be proclaimed.

9. *He was taken up.* He was speaking face-to-face with them, and *while they beheld, he was taken up.* He began to ascend to heaven, and they continued to look after Him till *a cloud received him out of their sight*—till He had ascended above the region of the clouds, by the density of which all further distinct vision was prevented.

10. *Looked stedfastly.* Keeping their eyes intensely fixed on their ascending Lord, continuing to look even after He had ascended above the region of the inferior clouds.

Two men stood by them. Doubtless angels in human shape. *In white apparel.* As emblematical of their purity, happiness, and glory.

MATTHEW HENRY

Verses 12–14

I. When Christ ascended—*from the mount of Olives* (*v.* 12). There he began his sufferings, and therefore there he rolled away the reproach of them by his glorious ascension. Thus would he enter upon his kingdom in the sight of Jerusalem. This mount is here said to be near Jerusalem, *a sabbath day's journey* from it; no further than devout people used to walk out on a sabbath evening, after the public worship was over, for meditation. Some reckon it a thousand paces; some seven furlongs. Thus far it is a rule to us, not to journey on the sabbath any more than in order to the sabbath work; and as far as is necessary to this we are not only allowed, but enjoined.

II. Whither the disciples returned: They came to Jerusalem, according to their Master's appointment. It should seem that though immediately after Christ's resurrection they were watched, yet after it was known that they were gone into Galilee no notice was taken of their return to Jerusalem. God can find out hiding-places for his people in the midst of their enemies. At Jerusalem they *went up into an upper room, and there abode.* There they assembled every day, in expectation of the descent of the Spirit. *They were continually in the temple* (Luke xxiv. 53), but that was *in the courts of the temple, at the hours of prayer,* where they could not be hindered from attending; but, it should seem, this upper room was in a private house.

III. Who the disciples were, that kept together. The eleven apostles are here named (*v.* 13), so is Mary the mother of our Lord (*v.* 14), and it is the last time that ever any mention is made of her. There were others, the brethren of our Lord, and, to make up *the hundred and twenty* spoken of (*v.* 15), we may suppose that all or most of the *seventy disciples* were with them.

IV. How they spent their time: *They all continued with one accord in prayer and supplication. They prayed, and made supplication.* All God's people are praying people. It was now a time of trouble and danger, and, *Is any afflicted? Let him pray.* They had new work before them, and, before they entered upon it, *they were instant in prayer to God.* Before they were first sent forth Christ spent time in prayer for them, and now they spent time in prayer for themselves. Those are in the best frame to receive spiritual blessings that are in a praying frame. God will be enquired of for promised mercies, and the nearer the performance seems to be the more earnest we should be in prayer for it. *They continued in prayer.* It is said (Luke xxiv. 53), *They were praising and blessing God;* here, *They continued in prayer and supplication.* Praise for the promise is a decent way of begging for the performance, and praise for former mercy of begging further mercy. They did this *with one accord.* Those who so keep *the unity of the Spirit in the bond of peace* are best prepared to receive the *comforts of the Holy Ghost.*

Verses 15–26

The sin of Judas made a vacancy in the college of the apostles. If they were but eleven, it would occasion everyone to enquire what had become of the twelfth; therefore care was taken, to fill up the vacancy.

I. The persons concerned in this affair. The house consisted of *about a hundred and twenty.* This was *the number of the names,* that is, the persons. Here was the beginning of the Christian church: this hundred and twenty was the grain of mustard-seed that grew into a tree, the leaven that leavened the whole lump. The speaker was Peter, who had been, and still was, the most forward man. Peter, being designed to be the apostle of the circumcision, while the sacred story stays among the Jews, he is still brought in, as afterwards, when it comes to speak of the Gentiles, it keeps to the story of Paul.

II. The proposal which Peter made for the choice of another apostle. He *stood up in the midst of the disciples, v.* 15.

1. The account he gives of the vacancy made by the death of Judas, in which he is very particular, and takes notice of the fulfilling of the scriptures in it.

(1) The power to which Judas had been advanced (*v.* 17): *He was numbered with us, and had obtained part of this ministry.* What will it avail us to be added to the number of Christians, if we partake not of the spirit and nature of Christians?

(2) The sin of Judas. He was *guide to those that took Jesus.* He had the impudence to appear openly at the head of the party that seized him. He went before them to the place, and gave the word of command: *That same is he, hold him fast.* Ringleaders in sin are the worst of sinners.

(3) The ruin of Judas by this sin. Perceiving the

JAMIESON, FAUSSET, BROWN

12-26. RETURN OF THE ELEVEN TO JERUSALEM—PROCEEDINGS IN THE UPPER ROOM TILL PENTECOST. **12-14. a sabbath day's journey**—about 2000 cubits. **went up into an upper room**—perhaps the same "large upper room" where with their Lord they had celebrated the last Passover and the first Supper (Luke 22:12). **where abode**—not lodged, but had for their place of rendezvous. **Peter . . .**—See on Matthew 10:2-4. **14. continued with one accord**—knit by a bond stronger than death. **in prayer and supplication**—for the promised baptism, the need of which in their orphan state would be increasingly felt. **and Mary the mother of Jesus**—distinguished from the other "women," but "so as to exclude the idea of her having any pre-eminence over the disciples. We find her with the rest in prayer to her glorified Son" [WEBSTER and WILKINSON]. *This is the last mention of her in the New Testament.* The fable of the *Assumption of the Virgin* has no foundation even in tradition [ALFORD]. **with his brethren**—See on John 7:3-5.

15-26. in those days—of expectant prayer, and probably towards the close of them, when the nature of their future work began more clearly to dawn upon them, and the Holy Ghost, already "breathed" on the Eleven (John 20:22), was stirring in Peter, who was to be the leading spirit of the infant community (Matt. 16:19). **the number . . . about an hundred and twenty**—Many, therefore, of the "500 brethren" who saw their risen Lord "at once" (I Cor. 15:6), must have remained in Galilee.

ADAM CLARKE

13. *They went up into an upper room.* This was either a room in the Temple or in the house of one of the disciples, where this holy company was accustomed to meet. In Luke xxiv. 53, it is said that, after their return from Mount Olivet, "they were continually in the temple, praising and blessing God." It is probable, therefore, that the *upper room* mentioned in this verse is that apartment of the Temple mentioned above. But still it is not certain that this place should be so understood, as we have the fullest proofs that the *upper rooms* in private houses were used for the purpose of reading the law and conferring together on religious matters. Add to this that the room here mentioned seems to have been the place where all the apostles lodged, and therefore most probably a private house.

14. *These . . . continued . . . in prayer and supplication.* Waiting for the promise of the Father, according to the direction of our Lord, Luke xxiv. 49. The words *and supplication* are omitted by some MSS. *With the women.* Probably those who had been witnesses of His resurrection, with the immediate relatives of the apostles. Peter we know was married, Matt. viii. 14, and so might others of the disciples; and therefore the wives of the apostles, as well as of other pious men, may be here intended.

15. *In the midst of the disciples.* But instead of this, *brethren* is the reading of some MSS. This seems the best reading because of what immediately follows; for it was not among the *disciples* merely that He stood, but among the whole company, which amounted to 120. It is remarkable that this was the number which the Jews required to form a council in any city; and it is likely that in reference to this the disciples had gathered together, with themselves, the number of 120, chosen out of the many who already had been converted by the ministry of our Lord, the 12 disciples, and the 70 whom He had sent forth to preach, Luke x. 1, etc. Thus they formed a complete council in presence of which the important business of electing a person in the place of Judas was to be transacted.

17. *Obtained part of this ministry.* "He obtained the lot of this ministry"—not that he or any of the twelve apostles were chosen to this ministry by lot; but as "lot" signifies the portion a man has in life, what comes to him in the course of the divine providence, or as an especial gift of God's goodness, it is used here, as in many other parts of the sacred writings, to signify office or station.

MATTHEW HENRY

chief priests to seek the life of Christ and his disciples, he thought to save his by going over to them, and not only so, but to get an estate under them. [1] He lost his money shamefully enough (*v.* 18): *He purchased a field* with the *thirty pieces of silver,* which were the *reward of his iniquity.* He thought to have purchased a field for himself, but it proved the purchase of a field to bury strangers in; and what was he or any of his the better for this?

[2] He lost his life more shamefully. We were told (Matt. xxvii. 5) that he *went away* in despair; here it is added, he *fell headlong.* He *burst asunder in the midst,* so that *all his bowels tumbled out.* Bowelling is part of the punishment of traitors.

(4) The public notice that was taken of this: *It was known to all the dwellers in Jerusalem.* It was, as it were, put into the newspapers, and was all the talk of the town, as a remarkable judgment of God upon him that betrayed his Master, *v.* 19. It was in everybody's mouth, and nobody disputed the truth of the fact. *It was known,* that is, it was known to be true. Here is one proof of the notoriety of the thing mentioned, that the field was called *Aceldama —the field of blood,* because it was bought with the *price of blood.*

(5) The fulfilling of the scriptures in this, *that it must needs be fulfilled, v.* 16. Let none be surprised nor stumble at it, for David had not only foretold his sin, but had also foretold his punishment: *Let his habitation be desolate.* The substitution of another in his room. His *bishopric,* or *his office shall another take.* We are not to think the worse of any office that God has instituted either for the wickedness of any that are in that office or for the ignominious punishment of that wickedness; nor will God suffer any purpose of his to be frustrated, or any work of his to be undone, for the miscarriages of those that are entrusted therewith. Judas is hanged, but his bishopric is not lost. Christ's cause shall never be lost for want of witnesses.

2. The motion he makes for the choice of another apostle, *v.* 21, 22. (1) How the person must be qualified that must fill up the vacancy. It must be one of *these men that have companied with us all the time that the Lord Jesus went in and out among us, beginning from the baptism of John, unto that same day that he was taken up from us.* Those that have been diligent in the discharge of their duty in a lower station, are fittest to be preferred to a higher; those that have been faithful in a little shall be entrusted with more. None shall be an apostle but one that has companied with the apostles, and that continually. (2) To what work he is called. He must be *a witness with us of his resurrection.* By this it appears that others of the disciples were with the eleven when Christ appeared to them. The great thing which the apostles were to attest to the world was Christ's resurrection. See what the apostles were ordained to, not to a secular dignity and dominion, but to preach Christ, and the power of his resurrection.

JAMIESON, FAUSSET, BROWN

TODAY'S DICTIONARY OF THE BIBLE:

Judas, son of Simon (John 6:71; 13:2, 26), surnamed Iscariot—i.e., a man of Kerioth (Josh. 15:25). His name is uniformly the last in the list of the apostles, as given in the synoptic (i.e., the first three) Gospels. The evil of his nature probably gradually unfolded itself till "Satan entered into him" (John 13:27), and he betrayed our Lord (18:3, 5). Afterward he owned his sin with "an exceeding bitter cry," and cast the money he had received as the wages of his iniquity down on the floor of the sanctuary, and "departed and went and hanged himself" (Matt. 27:5). He perished in his guilt, and went "to his own place" (Acts 1:25). The statement in Acts 1:18 that he "falling headlong, burst asunder in the midst, and all his bowels gushed out" is in no way contrary to that in Matt. 27:5. The suicide first hanged himself, perhaps over the valley of Hinnom, "and the rope giving way, or the branch to which he hung breaking, he fell down headlong on his face, and was crushed and mangled on the rocky pavement below."

Why such a man was chosen to be an apostle we do not know, but it is written that "Jesus knew from the beginning who should betray him" (John 6:64). Nor can any answer be satisfactorily given to the question as to the motives that led Judas to betray his Master. Of the motives that have been assigned we need not care to fix on any one as that which simply led him on. Crime is, for the most part, the result of a hundred motives rushing with bewildering fury through the mind of the criminal.

18. **falling headlong . . .**—This information supplements, but by no means contradicts, what is said in Matthew 27:5.

20. **his bishopric**—or 'charge.' The words are a combination of Psalms 69:25 and 109:8; in which the apostle discerns a greater than David, and a worse than Ahithophel and his fellow conspirators against David.

21. **all the time the Lord Jesus went in and out among us**—in the close intimacies of a three years' public life.

22. **Beginning from the baptism of John**—by whom our Lord was not only Himself baptized, but first officially announced and introduced to his own disciples. **unto that same day when he was taken up from us, must one be ordained to be a witness with us of his resurrection**—How clearly is the primary office of the apostles here expressed: (1) to testify, from personal observation, to the one great fact of "the resurrection of the Lord Jesus"; (2) to show how this glorified His whole previous life, of which they were constant observers, and established His divine claims.

ADAM CLARKE

18. *Purchased a field with the reward of iniquity.* Probably Judas did not purchase the field himself, but the money for which he sold his Lord was thus applied; see Matt. xxvii. 6-8. It is possible, however, that he might have designed to purchase a field or piece of ground with this reward of his iniquity, and might have been in treaty for it, though he did not close the bargain, as his bringing the money to the treasury proves. The priests, knowing his intentions, might have completed the purchase, and, as Judas was now dead, applied the field thus bought for the burial of strangers, i.e., Jews from foreign parts, or others who, visiting Jerusalem, had died there. Though this case is possible, yet the passage will bear a very consistent interpretation without the assistance of this conjecture; for in ordinary conversation we often attribute to a man what is the consequence of his own actions, though such consequence was never designed nor wished for by himself. Thus we say of a man embarking in a hazardous enterprise, "He is gone to seek his death"; of one whose conduct has been ruinous to his reputation, "He has disgraced himself"; of another who has suffered much in consequence of his crimes, "He has purchased repentance at a high price." All these, though undesigned, were consequences of certain acts, as the buying of the field was the consequence of Judas' treason. *And falling headlong, he burst asunder. It* is very likely that the eighteenth and nineteenth verses are not the words of Peter, but of the historian Luke, and should be read in a parenthesis; then the seventeenth and twentieth verses will make a connected sense.

19. *It was known unto all the dwellers at Jerusalem.* The repentance of Judas, his dying testimony in behalf of our Lord's innocence, and his tragic death were publicly known, as was also the transaction about the purchase of the field; and hence arose the name by which it was publicly known. *That field is called in their proper tongue, Aceldama.* This *proper tongue* was not the Hebrew; that had long ceased to be the proper tongue in Palestine. It was a sort of Chaldaio-Syriac which was commonly spoken.

16. *The Holy Ghost by the mouth of David.* This is a strong attestation to the divine inspiration of the Book of Psalms. They were dictated by the Holy Spirit and spoken by the mouth of David.

20. *For it is written in the book of Psalms.* The places usually referred to are Ps. lxix. 25: "Let their habitation be desolate; and let none dwell in their tents"; and Ps. cix. 8: "Let his days be few; and let another take his office," *pekudato,* "his overseership, his charge of visitation or superintendence"—translated by the Septuagint, *ten episcopen,* and Vulgate, *episcopatum;* and we, following both, *bishopric,* but not with sufficient propriety. For surely the office or charge of Judas was widely different from what we call *bishopric,* the diocese, estate, and emoluments of a bishop. *Episcopos,* which was corrupted by our Saxon ancestors into *biscop,* and by us into "bishop," signifies literally an "overseer or superintendent."

21. *Which have companied with us.* They judged it necessary to fill up this blank in the apostolate by a person who had been an eyewitness of the acts of our Lord. *Went in and out.* A phrase which includes all the actions of life.

22. *Beginning from the baptism of John.* From the time that Christ was baptized by John in Jordan, for it was at that time that His public ministry properly began. *Must one be ordained.* This translation misleads every reader who cannot examine the original text. There is no term for *ordained* in the Greek; "to be" is the only word in the verse to which this interpretation can be applied. The New Testament printed at London, by Robert Barker, the king's printer, in 1615, renders this and the preceding verse more faithfully and more clearly than our common version: "Wherefore of these men who have companied with us, all the time that the Lord Jesus was conversant among us, beginning from the baptism of John unto the day he was taken up from us, must one of them be made a witness with us of his resurrection." The word *ordained* would naturally lead most readers to suppose that some ecclesiastical rite was used

MATTHEW HENRY

III. The nomination of the person that was to succeed Judas.

1. Two, who were known to have been Christ's constant attendants, were set up as candidates for the place (*v.* 23): *They appointed two.* The two they nominated were *Joseph* and *Matthias*, of neither of whom do we read elsewhere. These two were both of them so well qualified for the office, that they could not tell which of them was the fitter, but all agreed it must be one of these two.

2. They applied to God by prayer for direction, *which of these two? v.* 24, 25. (1) They appeal to God as the searcher of hearts: "*Thou, Lord, who knowest the hearts of all men.*" When an apostle was to be chosen he must be chosen by his heart and the temper and disposition of that. It is comfortable to us, in our prayers for the welfare of the church and its ministers, that the God to whom we pray *knows the hearts of all men*, can make them fit for his purpose by giving them another spirit. (2) They desire to know which of these God had chosen: *Lord*, show us this. It is fit that God should choose his own servants. (3) They are ready to receive him as a brother whom God hath chosen, to *take part of this ministry and apostleship from which Judas by transgression fell*, that he might go *to his own place*, the place of a traitor, the fittest place for him. Those that betray Christ, as they fall from the dignity of relation to him, so they fall into all misery. Our Saviour had said that Judas's own place should be such that *it had been better for him that he had never been born* (Matt. xxvi. 24).

(4) The doubt was determined by lot (*v.* 26), which is an appeal to God, and lawful to be used for determining matters not otherwise determinable, provided it be done in a solemn religious manner, and with prayer, the prayer of faith. Thus the number of the apostles was made up.

JAMIESON, FAUSSET, BROWN

23. they appointed—'put up' in nomination; meaning not the Eleven but the whole company, of whom Peter was the spokesman. **two**—The choice would lie between a very few.

24. prayed and said, Thou, Lord . . .—"The word 'Lord,' placed absolutely, denotes in the New Testament almost universally THE SON; and the words, 'Show whom Thou hast chosen,' are decisive. The apostles are just Christ's messengers: It is He that sends them, and of Him they bear witness. Here, therefore, we have the first example of a prayer offered to the exalted Redeemer; furnishing indirectly the strongest proof of His divinity" [OLSHAUSEN]. **which knowest the hearts of all men**—See John 2:24, 25; 21:15-17; Revelation 2:23. **25. that he might go to his own place**—A euphemistic or softened expression of the awful future of the traitor, implying not only destined habitation but congenial element.

26. was numbered—'voted in' by general suffrage. **with the eleven apostles**—completing the broken Twelve.

ADAM CLARKE

on the occasion, such as imposition of hands, although nothing of the kind appears to have been employed.

23. *They appointed two.* These two were probably of the number of the seventy disciples, and in this respect well fitted to fill up the place. It is likely that the disciples themselves were divided in opinion which of these two was the most proper person, and therefore laid the matter before God, that He might decide it by the lot. No more than two candidates were presented, probably because the attention of the brethren had been drawn to those two alone, as having been most intimately acquainted with our Lord, or in being better qualified for the work than any of the rest.

24. *Thou, Lord, which knowest the hearts.* "Searcher of hearts" seems to be used here as an attribute of God; He knows the hearts, the most secret purposes, intentions, and dispositions of all men. And because He is the Knower of hearts, He knew which of these men He had qualified the best, by natural and gracious dispositions and powers, for the important work to which one of them was now to be appointed.

25. *That he may take part of this ministry.* Instead of "the lot," which we translate *part*, "the place" is the reading of some MSS. and from them the verse may be read thus, "That he may take the place of this ministry and apostleship (from which Judas fell), and go to his own place." Some of the best critics assert that the words belong to Matthias—*his own place* being the office to which he was about to be elected. Should any object that this could not be called *his own place* because he was not yet appointed to it, but hell might be properly called Judas' own place because by treason and covetousness he was fully prepared for that place of torment, it may be answered that the *own* or proper *place* of a man is that for which he is eligible from being qualified for it, though he may not yet possess such a place.

26. *They gave forth their lots.* In what manner this or any other question was decided by lot, we cannot precisely say. The most simple form was to put two stones, pieces of board, metal, or slips of parchment, with the names of the persons inscribed on them, into an urn; and after prayer, sacrifice, etc., to put in the hand and draw out one of the lots, and then the case was decided. *He was numbered with the eleven apostles.* The word comes from "together with," "according to," and a "pebble or small stone," used for lots, and as a means of enumeration among the Greeks, Romans, and Egyptians; hence the words "calculate, calculation," from *calculus*, a small stone or pebble. From this use of the word, though it signifies in general to sum up, associate, we may conjecture that the calculus or pebble was used on this occasion.

CHAPTER 2

Verses 1–4

We have here an account of the descent of the Holy Ghost.

I. When, and where, this was done.

1. It was *when the day of pentecost was fully come.* (1) The Holy Ghost came down at the time of a solemn feast, because there was then a great concourse of people to Jerusalem from all parts, which would make the fame of it to be spread the sooner and further. Thus now, as before at the passover, the Jewish feasts served to toll the bell for gospel services. (2) This feast of pentecost was kept in remembrance of the giving of the law upon Mount Sinai. Fitly, therefore, is the Holy Ghost given at that feast, in fire and in tongues, for the promulgation of the evangelical law, not as that to one nation, but to every creature. (3) This feast of pentecost happened on the *first day of the week*, which was a confirmation of it to be the Christian sabbath, to be a standing memorial in his church of those two great blessings—the resurrection of Christ, and the pouring out of the Spirit. Every Lord's day in the year, I think, there should be a full and particular notice taken in our prayers and praises of these.

CHAPTER 2

VSS. 1-13. DESCENT OF THE SPIRIT—THE DISCIPLES SPEAK WITH TONGUES—AMAZEMENT OF THE MULTITUDE. **1-4. when the day of Pentecost was fully come**—The fiftieth from the morrow after the first Passover sabbath (Lev. 23:15, 16).

CHAPTER 2

1. *When the day of Pentecost was fully come.* The Feast of Pentecost was celebrated fifty days after the Passover, and has its name from *penteconta*, "fifty." It commenced on the fiftieth day, reckoned from the first day of unleavened bread, i.e., on the morrow after the paschal lamb was offered. The law relative to this feast is found in Lev. xxiii. 15-16, in these words: "And ye shall count unto you from the morrow after the sabbath, from the day that ye brought the sheaf of the wave offering; seven sabbaths shall be complete: even unto the morrow after the seventh sabbath shall ye number fifty days." This feast was instituted in commemoration of the giving the law on Mount Sinai, and is therefore sometimes called by the Jews "the joy of the law," and frequently the Feast of Weeks. There is a correspondence between the giving of the law, which is celebrated by this Feast of Pentecost, together with the crucifixion of our Lord, which took place at the Passover and this descent of the Holy Spirit, which happened at this Pentecost. At the Passover the Israelites were delivered from Egyptian bondage; this was a type of the thraldom in which the human race were to Satan and sin. At the Passover, Jesus Christ, who was typified by the paschal lamb, was sacrificed for the sin

MATTHEW HENRY

2. It was when *they were all with one accord in one place.* What place it was we are not told particularly. But it was at Jerusalem, because this had been the place which God chose, and the prophecy was that thence the word of the Lord should go forth. Here God had promised to meet them and bless them; here therefore he meets them with this blessing of blessings. He did this honour to Jerusalem, to teach us not to fall out with places, for God has his remnant in all places; he had this in Jerusalem. Here the disciples were in one place. And here they were *with one accord.* They had prayed more together of late than usual (*ch.* i. 14), and this made them love one another better. By his grace he thus prepared them for the gift of the Holy Ghost; for that blessed dove comes not where there is noise and clamour, but moves upon the face of the still waters, not the rugged ones. Would we have the Spirit *poured out upon us from on high*? Let us all be of one accord; let us agree to love one another.

II. How, and in what manner, the Holy Ghost came upon them. We often read in the Old Testament of God's coming down in a cloud. And Christ went up to heaven in a cloud. But the Holy Ghost did not descend in a cloud; for he was to dispel and scatter the clouds that overspread men's minds.

1. Here is an audible summons given them to awaken their expectations, *v.* 2. It came *suddenly*, but was at the height immediately. It came sooner than they expected, and startled even those that were now together waiting. It was *a sound from heaven.* It was the sound of a wind, for the way of the Spirit is like that of the wind (John iii. 8), *thou hearest the sound thereof, but canst not tell whence it comes nor whither it goes.* It was a *rushing mighty wind*; it was strong and violent, and came with great force, as if it would bear down all before it. This was to signify the powerful influences and operations of the Spirit of God. *It filled* not only the room, but *all the house where they were sitting.* This wind filling the house would strike an awe upon the disciples, and help to put them into a very serious frame, for the receiving of the Holy Ghost. Thus the convictions of the Spirit make way for his comforts; and the rough blasts of that blessed wind prepare the soul for its soft and gentle gales.

2. Here is a visible sign of the gift. They saw *cloven tongues, like as of fire* (*v.* 3), and *it sat*, rested upon each of them. There is a meteor which naturalists call *ignis lambens—a gentle flame*, not a devouring fire; such was this.

(1) There was an outward sensible sign, for the confirming of the faith of the disciples themselves.

(2) The sign given was fire, that John Baptist's saying concerning Christ might be fulfilled, *He shall baptize you with the Holy Ghost and with fire.* They were now celebrating the memorial of the giving of the law upon mount Sinai; and as that was given in fire, so is the gospel. The Spirit, like fire, melts the heart, burns up the dross, and kindles pious and devout affections in the soul. This is that fire which Christ came to send upon the earth.

(3) This fire appeared in cloven tongues. The operations of the Spirit were many; that of speaking with divers tongues was one, and to that this sign had a reference. They were tongues. By him Christ would speak to the world, and he gave the Spirit to the disciples to endue them with a power to publish and proclaim to the world what they knew. These tongues were cloven. The tongues were divided, and yet they still continued all of one accord; for there may be a sincere unity of affections where yet there is a diversity of expression.

(4) This fire sat upon them to denote the constant residence of the Holy Ghost with them. The disciples of Christ had the gifts of the Spirit always with them, though the sign, we may suppose, soon disappeared.

III. What was the immediate effect of this? 1. *They were all filled with the Holy Ghost.* They were filled with the graces of the Spirit, and were more than ever under his sanctifying influences. They were more filled with the comforts of the Spirit, rejoiced more than ever in the love of Christ and the hope of heaven. They were also filled with the gifts of the Holy Ghost. They were endued with miraculous powers for the furtherance of the gospel. It seems evident that not only the twelve apostles, but all the hundred and twenty disciples were *filled with the Holy Ghost* alike at this time. The *all* here must refer to the *all* that were together, *v.* 1. 2. *They began to speak with other tongues*, besides their native language. They spoke not matters of common conversation, but the word of God, and the praises of his name, *as the Spirit gave them utterance.* We may suppose that they understood not only themselves but one another too. They spoke not from any previous thought or meditation, but *as the*

JAMIESON, FAUSSET, BROWN

with one accord—the solemnity of the day, perhaps, unconsciously raising their expectations.

2. And suddenly there came a sound from heaven, as of a rushing mighty wind . . .—"The whole description is so picturesque and striking that it could only come from an eyewitness" [OLSHAUSEN]. The suddenness, strength, and diffusiveness of the sound strike with deepest awe the whole company, and thus complete their preparation for the heavenly gift. Wind was a familiar emblem of the Spirit (Ezek. 37:9; John 3:8; 20:22). But this was not a rush of actual wind. It was only a sound *"as of"* it.

3. cloven tongues, like as of fire . . .—'disparted tonques,' i.e., tongue-shaped, flamelike appearances, rising from a common center or root, and resting upon each of that large company:—beautiful visible symbol of the burning energy of the Spirit now descending in all His plenitude upon the Church, and about to pour itself through every tongue, and over every tribe of men under heaven!

ADAM CLARKE

of the world, and by this sacrifice redemption from sin and Satan is now procured and proclaimed. On Pentecost, God gave His law on Mount Sinai, accompanied with thunderings and lightnings. On Pentecost, God sent down His Holy Spirit, like a rushing mighty wind; and tongues of fire sat upon each disciple, in order that, by His influence, that new law of light and life might be promulgated and established. *They were all with one accord in one place.* It is probable that the *all* here mentioned means the 120 spoken of in chap. i. 15, who were all together at the election of Matthias. *In one place.* Where this place was we cannot tell. It was probably in the Temple, as seems to be intimated in v. 46, where it is said they were "daily with one accord in the temple"; and as this was the third hour of the day, v. 15, which was the Jewish hour of morning prayer, it is most probable that the Temple was the place in which they were assembled.

2. *A sound from heaven.* Probably thunder is meant, which is the harbinger of the Divine Presence. *Rushing mighty wind.* There is a good deal of similarity between this account and that of the appearance of God to Elijah, 1 Kings xix. 11-12, where the strong wind, the earthquake, and the fire were harbingers of the Almighty's presence, and prepared the heart of Elijah to hear the small still voice. So this *sound* and the *mighty rushing wind* prepared the apostles to receive the influences and gifts of the Holy Spirit. In both cases the *sound, strong wind,* and *fire,* although *natural* agents, were *supernaturally* employed.

3. *Cloven tongues like as of fire.* The *tongues* were the emblem of the languages they were to speak. The *cloven tongues* pointed out the diversity of those languages; and the *fire* seemed to intimate that the whole would be a spiritual gift, and be the means of bringing light and life to the souls who should hear them preach the everlasting gospel in those languages. *Sat upon each of them.* That unusual appearances of fire were considered emblems of the presence and influence of God both the Scriptures and the Jewish writings amply prove. Thus God manifested himself to Moses when He appointed him to deliver Israel, Exod. iii. 2-3; and thus He manifested himself when He delivered the law on Mount Sinai, Exod. xix. 16-20. *It sat upon each.* That is, one of those tongues, like flames, sat upon the head of each disciple; and the continuance of the appearance, which is indicated by the word *sat,* shows that there could be no illusion in the case. I still think that in all this case the agent was natural, but supernaturally employed.

MATTHEW HENRY

Spirit gave them utterance; he furnished them with the matter as well as the language. Now this was, (1) A very great miracle; it was a miracle upon the mind, for in the mind words are framed. They had not only never learned these languages, for aught that appears, they had never so much as heard these languages spoken. They were neither scholars nor travellers. Peter indeed was forward enough to speak in his own tongue, but the rest of them were no spokesmen. He that made man's mouth new-made theirs. (2) A very proper, needful, and serviceable miracle. The language the disciples spoke was Syriac, a dialect of the Hebrew. They were commissioned to *preach the gospel to every creature, to disciple all nations*. But here is an insuperable difficulty at the threshold. And therefore, to prove that Christ could give authority to preach to the nations, he gives ability to preach to them in their own language. This may well be reckoned, all things considered, a greater work than the miraculous cures Christ wrought. It was the first effect of the *pouring out of the Spirit* upon them.

Verses 5–13

We have here an account of the public notice that was taken of this extraordinary gift.

I. The great concourse of people that there was now at Jerusalem. *There were dwelling at Jerusalem* Jews that were *devout men, out of every nation under heaven*, denoting that there were some from most of the then known parts of the world. Jerusalem at that time was a rendezvous of religious people. 1. We may here see what were some of those countries whence those strangers came (*v.* 9–11), some from the eastern countries, as the *Parthians, Medes, Elamites, and dwellers in Mesopotamia*; thence we come in order to Judæa. Next come the inhabitants of Cappadocia, Pontus, and that country which was particularly called *Asia*. Next come the dwellers in *Phrygia and Pamphylia*, which lay westward, also the *strangers of Rome*; there were some also that dwelt in the southern parts of *Egypt, in the parts of Libya about Cyrene*; there were also some from the island of Crete, and some from the deserts of Arabia; but they were all either Jews originally, or *proselytes* to the Jewish religion. The Jewish writers about this time speak of the Jews as *dwelling everywhere through the whole earth*; and that *there is not a people upon earth among whom some Jews do not inhabit*. 2. We may enquire what brought all those Jews and proselytes together to Jerusalem at this time? for they are said to dwell there. There was at this time a general expectation of the appearing of the Messiah. This brought those who were most zealous and devout to Jerusalem, to sojourn there.

II. The amazement with which these strangers were seized when they heard the disciples speak in their own tongues.

1. They observe that the speakers are all Galileans, that know no other than their mother tongue (*v.* 7). God chose the weak and foolish things of the world to confound the wise and mighty.

2. They acknowledge that they spoke intelligibly and readily their own language; *We hear every man in our own tongue wherein we were born* (*v.* 8). *We do hear them speak in our tongues the wonderful works of God*, *v.* 11. It was not only a surprise, but a pleasing surprise, to them to hear the language of their own country spoken. (1) The things they heard the apostles discourse of were the *wonderful works of God, the great things of God*. It is probable that the apostles spoke of Christ, and redemption by him, and the grace of the gospel; and these are indeed the *great things of God*. (2) They heard them both praise God for these great things and instruct the people concerning these things, *in their own tongue*. Now

JAMIESON, FAUSSET, BROWN

4. they . . . began to speak with . . . tongues . . .—real, living languages, as is plain from what follows. The thing uttered, probably the same by all, was "the wonderful works of God," perhaps in the inspired words of the Old Testament evangelical hymns; though it is next to certain that the speakers themselves understood nothing of what they uttered (see on I Cor. 14).

5-11. there were dwelling at Jerusalem Jews, devout men out of every nation—not, it would seem, permanently settled there (see vs. 9), though the language seems to imply more than a temporary visit to keep this one feast. **9. Parthians . . .**—Beginning with the farthest east, the Parthians, the enumeration proceeds farther and farther westward till it comes to Judea; next come the western countries, from Cappadocia to Pamphylia; then the southern, from Egypt to Cyrene; finally, apart from all geographical consideration, Cretes and Arabians are placed together. This enumeration is evidently designed to convey an impression of universality [BAUMGARTEN].

G. CAMPBELL MORGAN:

All the references in Acts, Corinthians, and Ephesians show that the exercise of tongues consisted of ecstatic utterance. These people were not preaching, they were praising; they were not indulging in set discourse, they were pouring out the rapture that filled their souls. In the filling of the Spirit there had come to them a new vision of their Lord, and a new consciousness of His life throbbing through their lives. They realized that all the hopes and aspirations of the past were being fulfilled. They knew that the river of God had come by the way of the altar, and that they were in the full flood tide of its healing and life-giving waters. They were praising God for His mighty works.

Did they know they were speaking in other tongues? One cannot be at all sure that they did. Were they familiar with the tongues in which they were speaking? Probably not. They praised with a new inspiration; they poured out their songs, and lo, Parthians, Medes, and Elamites, sojourners from Rome, people from Mesopotamia, men of all dialects, listened; and they heard the songs in their own language, with perfect accuracy and distinctness. The Resurrection was the first note in their singing, as it came to be the first note in apostolic preaching. One could almost wish that one could have listened to that first chanting of the Church, in which the singers set forth the mighty works of God.

We may now consider the impressions made upon Jerusalem. "They were all amazed, and were perplexed, saying one to another, What meaneth this? But others mocking said, They are filled with new wine." In that one statement we have a record of the first impression made by the Church in Jerusalem. It was a threefold impression. First, amazement; second, perplexity; third, criticism.

ADAM CLARKE

4. *To speak with other tongues.* At the building of Babel the language of the people was confounded, and in consequence of this they became scattered over the face of the earth. At this foundation of the Christian Church, the gift of various languages was given to the apostles that the scattered nations might be gathered, and united under one Shepherd and Superintendent of all souls. *As the Spirit gave them utterance.* The word seems to imply such utterance as proceeded from immediate inspiration and included oracular communications.

5. *Devout men, out of every nation.* Either by these we are simply to understand Jews who were born in different countries and had now come up to Jerusalem to be present at the Passover, and for purposes of traffic, or proselytes to Judaism who had come up for the same purpose; for I cannot suppose that the term *devout men* can be applied to any other.

9. *Parthians.* Parthia anciently included the northern part of modern Persia; it was situated between the Caspian Sea and Persian Gulf, rather to the eastward of both. *Medes.* Media was a country lying in the vicinity of the Caspian Sea, having Parthia on the east, Assyria on the south, and Mesopotamia on the west. *Elamites.* Probably inhabitants of that country now called Persia; both the *Medes* and *Elamites* were a neighboring people, dwelling beyond the Tigris. *Mesopotamia.* Situated between the Tigris and Euphrates rivers. *Judaea.* This word has exceedingly puzzled commentators and critics, and most suspect that it is not the true reading. *Cappadocia* was an ancient kingdom of Asia, comprehending all that country that lies between Mount Taurus and the Euxine Sea. *Pontus* was anciently a very powerful kingdom of Asia, originally a part of Cappadocia. *Asia.* Meaning probably Asia Minor.

10. *Phrygia.* A country in Asia Minor, southward of Pontus. *Pamphylia.* The ancient name of the country between Lycia and Cilicia, near the Mediterranean Sea. *Egypt.* A very extensive country of Africa. *Libya.* In a general way, among the Greeks, signified Africa; but the northern part, in the vicinity of Cyrene, is here meant. *Cyrene.* A country in Africa on the coast of the Mediterranean Sea, southward of the most western point of the Island of Crete. *Strangers of Rome.* Persons dwelling at Rome and speaking the Latin language, partly consisting of regularly descended *Jews* and *proselytes* to the Jewish religion.

11. *Cretes.* Natives of Crete, a large and noted island in the eastern part of the Mediterranean Sea. *Arabians.* Natives of Arabia, a well-known country of Asia, having the Red Sea on the west, the Persian Gulf on the east, Judea on the north, and the Indian Ocean on the south. *The wonderful works of God.* Such as the incarnation of Christ; His various miracles, preaching, death, resurrection, and ascension, and the design of God to save the world through Him. From this one circumstance we may learn that all the people enumerated above were either *Jews* or *proselytes;* and that there were probably none that could be, strictly speaking, called heathens among them.

6. *When this was noised abroad.* If we suppose that there was a considerable peal of thunder, which produced the mighty rushing *wind* already noticed in v. 2, then the whole city must have been alarmed; and as various circumstances might direct their attention to the Temple, having flocked thither they were further astonished and confounded to hear the disciples of Christ addressing the mixed multitude in the languages of the different countries from which these people had come. *Every man heard them speak in his own language.* We may naturally suppose that, as soon as any person presented himself to one of these disciples, he the disciple, was immediately enabled to address him in his own language, however various this had been from the Jewish or Galilean dialects.

7. *Are not all these . . . Galilaeans?* Persons who know no other dialect, save that of their own country. Persons wholly uneducated, and consequently naturally ignorant of those languages which they now speak so fluently.

8. *How hear we every man in our own tongue?* Some have supposed from this that th

MATTHEW HENRY

though, perhaps they were got to be so much masters of the Jewish language that they could have understood the meaning of the disciples if they had spoken that language, yet this was more strange, and helped to convince their judgment, that this doctrine was of God. It was more kind, and helped to engage their affections. And this is to us a plain intimation of the mind and will of God, that the scriptures should be read, and public worship performed, in the vulgar languages of the nations.

3. They wonder at it (*v.* 12): *They were all amazed;* they were in doubt what the meaning of it was. They asked themselves and one another—*What is the tendency of this?* They will *turn aside, and see this great sight.*

III. The scorn which some made of it, probably the scribes and Pharisees, and chief priests; they said, *These men are full of new wine,* they have drunk too much this festival-time, *v.* 13. These, being native Jews, knew not, as the others did, that what was spoken was really the languages of other nations, and therefore took it to be gibberish and nonsense, such as drunkards sometimes talk. And, if they called the Master of the house a wine-bibber, no marvel if they so called those of his household.

Verses 14–36

We have here the first-fruits of the Spirit, in the sermon which Peter preached immediately, directed to the Jews, even to those that mocked; for he begins with the notice of that (*v.* 15), and addresses his discourse (*v.* 14) *to the men of Judæa and the inhabitants of Jerusalem.* It was not by Peter's preaching only, but that of all, *that three thousand souls were* that day converted, but Peter's sermon only is recorded. He that had sneakingly denied Christ now as courageously confesses him.

I. His introduction: *Peter stood up* (*v.* 14) *with the eleven.* Those that were of greatest authority stood up to speak to the scoffing Jews. Thus among Christ's ministers, some of greater gifts are called out to instruct those that oppose themselves, to take hold of sword and spear. *Peter lifted up his voice,* as one that was both well assured of what he said, and was neither afraid nor ashamed to own it. He applied himself to *the men of Judæa,* "and you especially *that dwell at Jerusalem, be this known unto you, and hearken to my words.*"

II. His answer to their blasphemous calumny (*v.* 15): "*These men are not drunken, as you suppose.* These disciples of Christ, that now *speak with other tongues,* speak good sense, and know what they say. You cannot think they are drunk, for *it is but the third hour of the day,*" nine of the clock in the morning; and before this time, on the sabbaths and solemn feasts, the Jews did not eat nor drink.

III. His account of the miraculous effusion of the Spirit. Two things he resolves it into: that it was the fulfilling of the scripture, and the fruit of Christ's resurrection and ascension.

1. That it was the accomplishment of the prophecies of the Old Testament. He specifies one, that of *the prophet Joel, ch.* ii. 28. It is observable that though Peter *was filled with the Holy Ghost,* yet he did not set aside the scriptures, nor think himself above them. Christ's scholars never learn above their Bible.

(1) The text itself that Peter quotes, *v.* 17–21. It refers to *the last days,* the times of the gospel, which are called *the last days* because the dispensation of God's kingdom among men, which the gospel sets up, is the last dispensation of divine grace. "It was prophesied of and promised, and therefore you ought to expect it, and not to be surprised at it; to desire it, and bid it welcome." The apostle quotes the whole paragraph, for it is good to take scripture entire; how it was foretold,

[1] That there should be a more plentiful and extensive effusion of the Spirit of grace from on high than had ever yet been. Now *the Spirit shall be poured out,* not only upon the Jews, but *upon all flesh,* Gentiles as well as Jews. The Jewish doctors taught that the Spirit came only upon wise and rich men, and such as were of the seed of Israel; but God will not tie himself to their rules.

[2] That the Spirit should be in them a Spirit of prophecy. This power shall be given without distinction of sex—not only *your sons,* but *your daughters shall prophesy;* without distinction of age—both *your young men and your old men shall see visions, and dream dreams,* the *servants and handmaids* shall receive of *the Spirit, and shall prophesy* (*v.* 18); men and women, whom God calls his servants and his handmaids. The mention of *the daughters* (*v.* 17) and *the handmaidens* (*v.* 18) would make one think that *the women* (*ch.* i. 14) received the extraordinary gifts of the Holy Ghost, as well as the men.

[3] That one great thing which they should prophesy

JAMIESON, FAUSSET, BROWN

What was this amazement? It was mental arrest; not yet illumination. They did not know the meaning of what they heard and saw; but they wondered. Out of wonder worship is born. Where wonder ceases worship ceases. Wonder is not worship, but it is the first movement toward worship. For the moment, Jerusalem was compelled to turn from other interests to attend to this matter. It was only a beginning, but it was a beginning. For a brief hour or two at least, men left the schools, and the disputations, and the quarrelings, forgot their differences, and united in common amazement in the presence of something in their midst for which they could not account. The amazement was mental arrest, a compulsion laid upon the men of a city to turn from all other matters in wonder.

As they observed, and as they listened, they were not only amazed; they were perplexed. If amazement is mental arrest, perplexity is mental defeat; not yet illumination. The amazement meant that they did not know. The perplexity meant that they knew they did not know. There is no moment more hopeful to an intellectual soul than that in which it comes to the point of known ignorance. That is the opportunity for discovery.—*The Acts of the Apostles*

14-36. PETER, FOR THE FIRST TIME, PUBLICLY PREACHES CHRIST. **14-21. Peter, standing up with the eleven**—in advance, perhaps, of the rest.

these are not drunken—meaning, not the Eleven, but the body of the disciples. **but the third hour**—9 A.M. (see Eccles. 10:16; Isa. 5:11; I Thess. 5:17).

17. in the last days—meaning, the days of the Messiah (Isa. 2:2); as closing all preparatory arrangements, and constituting the final dispensation of God's kingdom on earth.

pour out of my Spirit—in contrast with the mere drops of all preceding time. **upon all flesh**—hitherto confined to the seed of Abraham.

sons . . . daughters . . . young men . . . old men . . . servants . . . handmaidens—without distinction of sex, age, or rank. **see visions . . . dream dreams**—This is a mere accommodation to the ways in which the Spirit operated under the ancient economy, when the prediction was delivered; for in the New Testament, visions and dreams are rather the exception than the rule.

ADAM CLARKE

miracle was not so much wrought on the disciples as on their hearers; imagining that, although the disciples spoke their own tongue, yet every man so understood what was spoken as if it had been spoken in the language in which he was born. Though this is by no means so likely as the opinion which states that the disciples themselves spoke all these different languages, yet the miracle is the same howsoever it be taken.

13. *These men are full of new wine.* Rather "sweet wine"; cannot mean the *mustum,* or *new wine,* as there could be none in Judea so early as Pentecost.

14. *Peter, standing up with the eleven.* They probably spoke by turns, not all together; but Peter began the discourse. *All ye that dwell at Jerusalem.* Would be better translated by the word "sojourn," because they were not inhabitants of Judea, but the strangers mentioned in vv. 9-11, who had come up to the feast.

15. *But the third hour of the day.* That is, about nine o'clock in the morning, previously to which the Jews scarcely ever ate or drank, for that hour was the hour of prayer. This custom appears to have been so common that even the most intemperate among the Jews were not known to transgress it.

17. *In the last days.* The time of the Messiah; and so the phrase was understood among the Jews.

Your sons and your daughters shall prophesy. The word *prophesy* is not to be understood here as implying the knowledge and discovery of future events, but signifies to teach and proclaim the great truths of God, especially those which concerned redemption by Jesus Christ. *Your young men shall see visions.* These were two of the various ways in which God revealed himself under the Old Testament. Sometimes He revealed himself by a symbol, which was a sufficient proof of the Divine Presence; fire was the most ordinary, as it was the most expressive, symbol. Thus He appeared to Moses on Mount Horeb, and afterwards at Sinai; to Abraham, Genesis xv; to Elijah, 1 Kings xix. 11-12. At other times He revealed himself by angelic ministry; this was frequent, especially in the days of the patriarchs, of which we find many instances in the Book of Genesis. By *dreams* He discovered His will in numerous instances. See the remarkable case of Joseph, Gen. xxxvii. 5, 9; of Jacob, Gen. xxviii. 1 ff.; xlvi. 2 ff.; of Pharaoh, Gen. xli. 1-7; of Nebuchadnezzar, Dan. iv. 10-17.

18. *On my servants and on my handmaidens.*

MATTHEW HENRY

of should be the judgment that was coming upon the Jewish nation. Those that would not submit to the power of God's grace should fall and lie under the pourings out of the vials of his wrath. Those shall break that will not bend. *First,* The destruction of Jerusalem, which was about forty years after Christ's death, is here called *that great and notable day of the Lord.* The desolation itself was such as was never brought upon any place or nation, either before or since. It was *the day of the Lord,* for it was the day of his vengeance upon that people for crucifying Christ. It was a little day of judgment; it was a *notable day.* The destruction of the Jews was the deliverance of the Christians. *Secondly,* The terrible presages of that destruction are here foretold: *There shall be wonders in heaven above, the sun turned into darkness and the moon into blood; and signs* too *in the earth beneath, blood and fire.* Josephus, in his preface to his history of the wars of the Jews, speaks of the signs and prodigies that preceded them, terrible thunders, lightnings, and earthquakes; there was a fiery comet that hung over the city for a year, and a flaming sword was seen pointing down upon it. *The fire and vapour of smoke* literally came to pass in the burning of their cities, and towns, and synagogues, and temple at last. *Thirdly,* The signal preservation of the Lord's people is here promised (*v.* 21): *Whosoever shall call upon the name of the Lord Jesus shall be saved.* In the destruction by the Romans not one Christian perished. The saved remnant are a praying people: *they call on the name of the Lord.* It is *the name of the Lord* which *they call upon* that is *their strong tower.*

(2) The application of this prophecy to the present event (*v.* 16): *This is that which was spoken by the prophet Joel.* This is that effusion of the Spirit upon all flesh which should come, and we are to look for no other. This Spirit of grace, the Advocate, or Comforter, that was given now, according to the promise, will, according to the same promise, continue with the church on earth to the end.

2. That it was the gift of Christ. From this *gift of the Holy Ghost,* he takes occasion to preach unto them Jesus (*v.* 22): "*You men of Israel, hear these words.*"

(1) An abstract of the history of the life of Christ, *v.* 22. He calls him *Jesus of Nazareth.* He was *a man approved of God among you,* censured and condemned by men, but approved of God: *a man marked out by God.* "You yourselves are witnesses how he became famous by *miracles, wonders, and signs, which God did by him; for no man could do such works unless God were with him.*" See what a stress Peter lays upon Christ's miracles. The matter of fact was not to be denied: "They were done *in the midst of you, as you yourselves also know.* You have been eyewitnesses of his miracles." The inference from them cannot be disputed; certainly God approved him, *declared him to be the Son of God* and *the Saviour of the world.*

(2) An account of his death and sufferings. This was the greatest miracle of all, that a man approved of God should thus seem to be abandoned of him; and a man thus approved among the people, should be thus abandoned by them too. But both these mysteries are here explained (*v.* 23). As God's act; and in him it was an act of wonderful grace and wisdom. He *delivered him to death.* And yet there was nothing in this that signified the disapproving of him; for it was done by *the determinate counsel and foreknowledge of God.* This reconciled him to the cross: *Father, thy will be done;* and *Father, glorify thy name.* As the people's act; and in them it was an act of prodigious sin and folly. It was their voluntary act and deed, from a principle morally evil, and therefore "they were *wicked hands with which you have crucified and slain* him." It is probable that some of those were here present who had cried, *Crucify him, crucify him.* He charges it particularly on them the more effectually to bring them to faith and repentance.

(3) An attestation of his resurrection (*v.* 24): *Whom God raised up;* the same that delivered him *to death* delivers him *from death.*

[1] He describes his resurrection: God *loosed the pains of death, because it was impossible that he should be holden of it.* From *these pains and sorrows of soul the Father loosed him,* when at his death he said, *It is finished.* Most refer this to the resurrection of Christ's body. Christ was imprisoned for our debt, was thrown into the bands of death; but it was not possible he should be detained there, for he had life in himself and had conquered the prince of death.

[2] He attests the truth of his resurrection (*v.* 32): *God hath raised him up, whereof we all are witnesses.* They *received power,* by the *descent of the Holy Ghost upon them,* on purpose that they might be skilful,

JAMIESON, FAUSSET, BROWN

19. I will show wonders . . .—referring to the signs which were to precede the destruction of Jerusalem (see on Luke 21: 25-28).

21. whosoever shall call on the name of the Lord shall be saved—This points to the permanent establishment of the economy of salvation, which followed on the breaking up of the Jewish state.

22-28. a man approved of God—rather, 'authenticated,' 'proved,' or 'demonstrated to be from God.' **by miracles . . . which God did by him**—This is not a low view of our Lord's miracles, as has been alleged, nor inconsistent with John 2: 11, but is in strict accordance with His progress from humiliation to glory, and with His own words in John 5:19. This view of Christ is here dwelt on to exhibit to the Jews the whole course of Jesus of Nazareth as the ordinance and doing of *the God of Israel* [ALFORD].

23. determinate counsel and foreknowledge—God's fixed plan and perfect foresight of all the steps involved in it. **ye have taken, and by wicked hands have crucified and slain**—How strikingly is the criminality of Christ's murderers here presented in harmony with the eternal purpose to surrender Him into their hands!

24. was not possible he should be holden of it—Glorious saying! It was indeed impossible that "the Living One" should remain "among the dead" (Luke 24:5); but here, the impossibility seems to refer to the prophetic assurance that He should not see corruption.

ADAM CLARKE

This properly means persons of the lowest condition, such as male and female slaves. As the Jews asserted that the spirit of prophecy never rested upon a poor man, these words are quoted to show that, under the gospel dispensation, neither bond nor free, male nor female, is excluded from sharing in the gifts and graces of the Divine Spirit.

19. *I will shew wonders.* It is likely that both the prophet and the apostle refer to the calamities that fell upon the Jews at the destruction of Jerusalem, and the fearful signs and portents that preceded those calamities. *Blood, and fire, and vapour of smoke.* Skirmishes and assassinations over the land, and wasting the country with fire and sword.

20. *The sun shall be turned into darkness, and the moon into blood.* These are figurative representations of *eclipses,* intended most probably to point but the fall of the *civil* and *ecclesiastical* state in Judea.

21. *Whosoever shall call on the name of the Lord shall be saved.* The predicted ruin is now impending, and only such as receive the gospel of the Son of God shall be saved. And that none but the *Christians* did escape, when God poured out these judgments, is well-known; and that all the Christians did escape, not one of them perishing in these devastations, stands attested by the most respectable authority. See the note on Matt. xxiv. 13.

16. *Spoken by the prophet Joel.* The prophecy which he delivered so long ago is just now fulfilled; and this is another proof that Jesus, whom you have crucified, is the Messiah.

22. *A man approved of God.* "Celebrated, famous." The sense of the verse seems to be this: "Jesus of Nazareth, a Man sent of God, and celebrated among you by miracles, wonders, and signs," and all these done in such profusion as had never been done by the best of your most accredited prophets. And these signs were such as demonstrated His Divine mission.

23. *By the determinate counsel;* that counsel of God which "defined the time, place, and circumstance," according to His foreknowledge. *By wicked hands have crucified and slain.* I think this refers to the Romans, and not to the Jews, the former being the agents to execute the evil purposes of the latter. It is well-known that the punishment of the cross was not a Jewish, but a Roman, punishment. Hence we may infer that by *the hands of the wicked,* the Romans are meant, being called *anomoi,* "without law," because they had no revelation from God.

24. *Whom God hath raised up.* For as God alone gave Him up to death, so God alone raised Him up from death. *Having loosed the pains of death.* "Removed the pains or sufferings of death." Instead of *death,* several MSS. have "hell," or the "place of separate spirits"; and perhaps it was on no better authority than this various reading, supported but by slender evidence, that "He descended into hell" became an article in what is called the Apostles' Creed. And on this article many a popish legend has been builded, to the discredit of sober sense and true religion.

MATTHEW HENRY

faithful, and courageous witnesses.

[3] He showed it to be the fulfilling of the scripture, *it was impossible that he should be holden* by *death* and *the grave; for David speaks* of his being raised.

First, The text quoted at large (*v.* 25-28). 1. The constant regard that our Lord Jesus had to his Father: *I foresaw the Lord before me continually.* He set before him his Father's glory as his end in all—*for he saw* that his sufferings would redound abundantly to the honour of God. 2. The assurance he had of his Father's presence and power: *"He is on my right hand, that I should not be moved."* If God be at our right hand we shall not be moved. 3. The cheerfulness with which our Lord Jesus went on in his work. *"I shall not be moved,* therefore *doth my heart rejoice, and my tongue is glad."* It was a constant pleasure to our Lord Jesus to look *to the end of his work*, it does his heart good to think how the issue would answer the design. 4. The happy issue of his death and sufferings. *My flesh shall rest; it shall rest in hope, that thou wilt not leave my soul in hell;* what follows is the matter of his hope. (1) The soul shall not continue in a state of separation from the body: *"Thou wilt not leave my soul in hell"* (in *hades*, in *the invisible state*, so *hades* properly signifies). (2) The body shall lie but a little while in the grave: *Thou wilt not suffer thy Holy One to see corruption.* He must die, but he must *not see corruption.* (3) His death and sufferings should be an inlet to a blessed immortality: *"Thou hast made known to me the ways of life*, and by me made them known to the world, and laid them open." (4) That all his sorrows and sufferings should end in perfect felicity: *Thou shalt make me full of joy with thy countenance.* The reward set before him was *joy*, a *fulness of joy*, and that in God's *countenance.* That is *the joy of our Lord*, into which all his shall enter, and in which they shall be for ever happy.

Secondly, The comment upon this text. He addresses himself to them with a title of respect, *Men and brethren, v.* 29. "Give me leave *freely to speak to you concerning the patriarch David.* David cannot be understood here as speaking of himself, but of the Christ to come." He could not say *that of himself*, for *he died, and was buried, and his sepulchre remained in Jerusalem till now.* He could never say of himself that **he** *should not see corruption*; for it was plain he did see corruption. Therefore certainly he spoke *it as a prophet*, with an eye to the Messiah. David knew that the Messiah should descend from his loins (*v.* 30), *that God had sworn to him, that of the fruit of his loins, according to the flesh, he would raise up Christ to sit on his throne.* When our Lord Jesus was born, it was promised *that the Lord God would give him the throne of his Father David*, Luke i. 32. *According to the spirit*, and by his divine nature, he was *to be David's Lord*, not his son. When he says that *his soul should not be left in its separate state, nor his flesh see corruption*, without doubt he must be understood to speak of the resurrection of Christ, *v.* 31. And as *Christ died*, so *he rose again, according to the scriptures;* and *that he did so we are witnesses.* Here is a glance at his ascension too. As David did not rise from the dead, so neither did he *ascend into the heavens*, *v.* 34. And further, in another psalm, he plainly shows that he spoke of another person, and such another as was his Lord (Ps. cx. 1): *"The Lord said unto my Lord, Sit thou at my right hand until I make thy foes thy footstool," v.* 35.

(4) The application of this discourse.

[1] This explains the meaning of the present wonderful effusion of the Spirit. Some of the people had asked (*v.* 12), *What meaneth this?* I will tell you the meaning of it, says Peter. *This Jesus being exalted by the right hand of God*, and *having received of the Father the promise of the Holy Ghost, hath shed forth this which you now see and hear. The gift of the Holy Ghost* was a performance of divine promises already made; this is the promise that includes all the rest. It was a pledge of all divine favours further intended; what you now see and hear is but an earnest of greater things.

[2] This proves that Christ Jesus is the true Messiah and Saviour of the world; this he closes his sermon with (*v.* 36): *Therefore let all the house of Israel know assuredly that God has made that same Jesus whom you have crucified both Lord and Christ.* They were charged to *tell no man that he was Jesus the Christ* till after his resurrection (Matt. xvii. 9); but now it must be *proclaimed.* It is not proposed as probable, but deposed as certain: *Let them know it assuredly. First,* That God has glorified him *whom they have crucified.* God had glorified him, and the indignities they had done him served as a foil to his lustre. *Secondly,* That he has glorified him to such a degree as to make him *both Lord and Christ.* This is the great truth of the gospel *that that same Jesus that was crucified at Jerusalem is Lord and Christ.*

JAMIESON, FAUSSET, BROWN

27. wilt not leave my soul in hell—in its disembodied state (see on Luke 16:23). **neither ... suffer thine Holy One to see corruption**—in the grave.

28. Thou hast made known to me the ways of life—i.e., resurrection-life. **thou shalt make me full of joy with thy countenance**—i.e., in glory; as is plain from the whole connection and the actual words of the 16th Psalm.

29-36. David ... is ... dead and buried ...—Peter, full of the Holy Ghost, sees in this 16th Psalm, one Holy Man, whose life of high devotedness and lofty spirituality is crowned with the assurance, that though He taste of death, He shall rise again without seeing corruption, and be admitted to the bliss of God's immediate presence. Now as this was palpably untrue of David, it could be meant only of One other, even of Him whom David was taught to expect as the final Occupant of the throne of Israel. (Those, therefore, and they are many, who take David himself to be the subject of this Psalm, and the words quoted to refer to Christ only *in a more eminent* sense, nullify the whole argument of the apostle.) The Psalm is then affirmed to have had its only proper fulfilment in JESUS, of whose resurrection and ascension they were witnesses, while the glorious effusion of the Spirit by the hand of the ascended One, setting an infallible seal upon all, was even then witnessed by the thousands who stood listening to Him. A further illustration of Messiah's ascension and session at God's right hand is drawn from Psalm 110:1, in which David cannot be thought to speak of himself, seeing he is still in his grave.

36. Therefore—i.e., to sum up all. **let all the house of Israel**—for in this first discourse the appeal is formally made to the whole house of Israel, as the then existing Kingdom of God. **know assuredly**—by indisputable facts, fulfilled predictions, and the seal of the Holy Ghost set upon all. **that God hath made**—for Peter's object was to show them that, instead of interfering with the arrangements of the God of Israel, these events were His own high movements. **this same Jesus, whom ye have crucified**—"The sting is at the close" [BENGEL]. To prove to them merely that Jesus was the Messiah might have left them all unchanged in heart. But to convince them that He whom they had crucified had been by the right hand of God exalted, and constituted the "LORD" whom David in spirit adored, to whom every knee shall bow, and the CHRIST of God, was to bring them to "look on Him whom they had pierced and mourn for Him."

ADAM CLARKE

25. *For David speaketh concerning him.* The quotation here is made from Psalm xvi, which contains a most remarkable prophecy concerning Christ, every word of which applies to Him, and to Him exclusively.

26. *And my tongue was glad.* In the Hebrew it is, "And my glory was glad"; but the Evangelist follows the Septuagint. And what is to be understood by "glory" here? Why, the "soul," certainly, and not the *tongue.*

27. *Thou wilt not leave my soul in hell.* "In hades," that is, the state of separate spirits, or the state of the dead. *To see corruption.* "Dust thou art, and unto dust thou shalt return," was a sentence pronounced on man after the Fall; therefore this sentence could be executed on none but those who were fallen. But Jesus, being conceived without sin, neither partook of human corruption nor was involved in the condemnation of fallen human nature; consequently it was impossible for His body to *see corruption;* and it could not have undergone the temporary death, to which it was not naturally liable, had it not been for the purpose of making an atonement.

28. *Thou hast made known to me the ways of life.* That is, the way from the region of death, or state of the dead and separate spirits; so that I shall resume the same body, and live the same kind of life, as I had before I gave up My life for the sin of the world.

29. *Let me freely speak . . . of the patriarch David.* Dr. Lightfoot: "That this passage, *Thou shalt not leave my soul in hell*, is not to be applied to David himself appears in that I may confidently aver concerning him, that he was *dead* and *buried*, and never rose again; but his soul was left in the state of the dead, and he saw corruption, for his sepulchre is with us to this day."

30. *According to the flesh, he would raise up Christ.* This whole clause is wanting in some MSS.

31. *That his soul was not left in hell.* The words *his soul* are omitted by some MSS.

32. *Whereof we all are witnesses.* That is, the whole 120 saw Him after He rose from the dead, and were all ready, in the face of persecution and death, to attest this great truth.

34. *David is not ascended.* Consequently he has not sent forth this extraordinary gift; but it comes from his Lord, of whom he said, *The Lord said unto my Lord.*

35. *Until I make thy foes thy footstool.* It was usual with conquerors to put their feet on the necks of vanquished leaders, as emblematical of the state of subjection to which they were reduced, and the total extinction of their power.

36. *Both Lord and Christ.* Not only the Messiah, but the supreme Governor of all things and all persons, Jews and Gentiles, angels and men. In the preceding discourse, Peter assumes a fact which none would attempt to deny, viz., that Jesus had been lately crucified by them. He then proves (1) His resurrection, (2) His ascension, (3) His exaltation to the right hand of God, (4) the effusion of the Holy Spirit, which was the fruit of His glorification, and which had not only been promised by himself but foretold by their own prophets; in consequence of which it was indisputably proved (5) that this same Jesus whom they had crucified was the promised Messiah; and if so, (6) the Governor of the universe, from whose power and justice they had everything to dread, as they refused to receive His proffered mercy and kindness.

MATTHEW HENRY

Verses 37–41

We have seen the wonderful effect of the pouring out of the Spirit, in its influence upon the preachers of the gospel. We are now to see another blessed fruit of the pouring out of the Spirit in its influence upon the hearers of the gospel. From the first delivery of that divine message, it appeared that there was a divine power going along with it. We have here the first-fruits of that vast harvest of souls which by it were gathered in to Jesus Christ. Let us see the method of it.

I. They were put upon a serious enquiry, *v.* 37. *When they heard they were pricked to the heart,* and, under a deep concern applied themselves to the preachers with this question, *What shall we do?* It was very strange that such impressions should be made upon such hard hearts all of a sudden. Peter had charged them with having a hand, a *wicked hand,* in his death, which was likely to have exasperated them against him; yet, when they heard this plain scriptural sermon, they were much affected with it.

1. It put them in pain: *They were pricked in their hearts.* Peter awakened their consciences, touched them to the quick. Sinners, when their eyes are opened, cannot but be *pricked to the heart* for sin.

2. It put them upon enquiry.

(1) To whom they thus addressed themselves: *To Peter and to the rest of the apostles.* By them they had been convinced, and therefore by them they expect to be counselled and comforted. They call them *men* and *brethren,* as Peter had called them (*v.* 29): it is a style of friendship and love. Ministers are spiritual physicians, and it is good for people to be free and familiar with those ministers, as men and their brethren, who deal for their souls as for their own.

(2) What the address is: *What shall we do?* [1] They speak as men at a stand, that did not know what to do: "*Is that Jesus* whom we have crucified both *Lord and Christ?* Then what will become of us who crucified him?" No way of being happy but by seeing ourselves miserable. When we find ourselves in danger of being lost for ever, there is hope of our being made for ever. [2] They speak as men at a point, that were resolved to do anything they should be directed to immediately. Those that are convinced of sin would gladly know the way to peace and pardon.

II. Peter and the other apostles direct them in short what they must do, *v.* 38, 39. Sinners convinced must be encouraged; though their case is sad it is not desperate, there is hope for them.

1. He here shows them the course they must take. *Repent;* this is a plank after shipwreck. This was the same duty that John the Baptist and Christ had preached, and it is still insisted on: "*Repent, repent;* change your mind, change your way." *Be baptized every one of you in the name of Jesus Christ;* that is, "firmly believe the doctrine of Christ, and make an open solemn profession of this, and renounce your infidelity." They must be baptized *in the name of Jesus Christ.* Believe in the name of Jesus, that he is the Christ, the Messias promised to the fathers. They must be baptized *in his name* for the *remission of sins.* This is pressed upon each particular person: *Every one of you.* "Even those of you that have been the greatest sinners, if they repent and believe, are welcome to be baptized. There is grace enough in Christ for everyone of you, be you ever so many, and grace suited to the case of everyone."

2. He gives them encouragement to take this course: (1) "It shall be for *the remission of sins.*" Repent of your sin, and it shall not be your ruin; be baptized into the faith of Christ, and in truth you shall be justified. Aim at this, and depend upon Christ for it, and this you shall have. (2) "You shall *receive the gift of the Holy Ghost* as well as we." All that receive the remission of sins *receive the gift of the Holy Ghost.* (3) "Your children shall still have an interest in the covenant, for the promise of the remission of sins, and the gift of the Holy Ghost, is *to you and to your children,*" *v.* 39. Now it is proper for an Israelite to ask, "What must be done with my children? Must they be thrown out, or taken in with me?" "Taken in" (says Peter) "by all means; for the promise is as much to you and to your children now as ever it was." (4) "Though the promise is still extended to your children, yet it is not confined to you and them, but the benefit of it is *designed* for *all that are afar off.*" To this general the following limitation must refer, *even as many of them,* as many particular persons in each nation, *as the Lord our God shall call.* God can make his call to reach those that are ever so far off.

III. These directions are followed with a needful caution (*v.* 40): *With many other words did he testify.* He had said much in a little (*v.* 38, 39), yet he had more to say. When we have heard those words which have done our souls good, we cannot but wish to hear

JAMIESON, FAUSSET, BROWN

37-40. pricked in their hearts—the begun fulfilment of Zechariah 12:10, whose full accomplishment is reserved for the day when "all Israel shall be saved" (see on Rom. 11).

what shall we do?—This is that beautiful spirit of genuine compunction and childlike docility, which, discovering its whole past career to have been one frightful mistake, seeks only to be set right for the future, be the change involved and the sacrifices required what they may. So Saul of Tarsus (ch. 9:6).

38. Repent—The word denotes *change of mind,* and here includes the reception of the Gospel as the proper issue of that revolution of mind which they were then undergoing. **baptized . . . for the remission of sins**—as the visible seal of that remission. **39. For the promise**—of the Holy Ghost, through the risen Saviour, as the grand blessing of the new covenant. **all afar off**—the **Gentiles** (as in Eph. 2:17, but "to the Jew first."

40. with many other words did he testify and exhort—Thus we have here but a summary of Peter's discourse; though from the next words it would seem that only the more practical parts, the home

ADAM CLARKE

CHARLES H. SPURGEON:

Peter's discourse was not distinguished by any special rhetorical display: he used not the words of man's wisdom or eloquence. It was not an oration, but it was a heart-moving argument, entreaty, and exhortation. He gave his hearers a simple, well-reasoned, scriptural discourse, sustained by the facts of experience; and every passage of it pointed to the Lord Jesus. It was in these respects a model of what a sermon ought to be as to its contents. His plea was personally addressed to the people who stood before him, and it had a practical and pressing relation to them and to their conduct. It was aimed, not at the head, but at the heart. Every word of it was directed to the conscience and the affections. It was plain, practical, personal, and persuasive; and in this it was a model of what a sermon ought to be as to its aim and style.

Yet Peter could not have spoken otherwise under the impression of the divine Spirit: his speech was as the oracles of God, a true product of a divine inspiration. Under the circumstances, any other kind of address would have been sadly out of place. A flashy, dazzling oration would have been a piece of horrible irreverance to the Holy Ghost; and Peter would have been guilty of the blood of souls if he had attempted it. In sober earnestness he kept to the plain facts of the case, setting them in the light of God's Word; and then with all his might he pressed home the truth upon those for whose salvation he was laboring. May it ever be the preacher's one desire to win men to repentance toward God and faith in our Lord Jesus Christ. May no minister wish to be admired, but may he long that his Lord and Master may be sought after! May none bewilder their people with the clouds of theoretic philosophy, but refresh them with the rain of revealed truth! Oh, that we could so preach that our hearers should be at once pricked in their hearts, and so be led at once to believe in our Lord Jesus, and immediately to come forward and confess their faith in His name!

—*The Treasury of the New Testament*

38. *Peter said unto them, Repent.* Humble yourselves before God, and deeply deplore the sins you have committed; pray earnestly for mercy, and deprecate the displeasure of incensed justice. For a definition of repentance, see on Matt. iii. 2. *And be baptized every one of you.* Take on you the public profession of the religion of Christ, by being baptized in His name, and thus acknowledge yourselves to be His disciples and servants. *For the remission of sins.* "In reference to the remission or removal of sins," baptism pointing out the purifying influences of the Holy Spirit. *Ye shall receive the gift of the Holy Ghost.* Receive the baptism, in reference to the removal of sins, and you shall receive the Holy Ghost, by whose agency alone the efficacy of the blood of the covenant is applied, and by whose refining power the heart is purified.

39. *For the promise is unto you.* Jews of the land of Judea. Not only the fulfillment of the *promise* which he had lately recited from the prophecy of Joel was made to them, but in this promise was also included the purification from sin, with every gift and grace of the Holy Spirit. *To all that are afar off.* To the Jews wherever dispersed, and to all the Gentile nations. *Even as many as the Lord our God shall call,* i.e., all to whom, in the course of His providence and grace, He shall send the preaching of Christ crucified.

MATTHEW HENRY

more. Among other things he said, *Save yourselves from this untoward generation.* "Give diligence to save yourselves from their ruin. *Repent, and be baptized;* and then you shall not be sharers in destruction with those with whom you have been sharers in sin. In order to this continue not with them in their sin. *Save yourselves* from this *untoward generation.* Partake not with them in their sins, that you share not with them in their plagues." To separate ourselves from wicked people is the only way to save ourselves from them. If we consider whither they are hastening, we shall see it is better to have the trouble of swimming against their stream than the danger of being carried down their stream. Those that repent of their sins, and give up themselves to Jesus Christ, must evidence their sincerity by breaking off all intimate society with wicked people.

IV. Here is the happy success and issue of this, *v.* 41. The Spirit wrought with the word, and wrought wonders by it. These same persons that had many of them been eye-witnesses of the death of Christ, were yet wrought upon by the preaching of the word. They received the word; and *then* only the word does us good, when we do receive it, and bid it welcome. They gladly received it. Herod *heard* the word gladly, but these gladly *received* it. They were baptized and enrolled themselves among the disciples of Christ by that sacred rite and ceremony which he had instituted. Those that receive the Christian covenant ought to receive the Christian baptism. Hereby there were added to the disciples to the number of about *three thousand souls that same day.* All those that had received the Holy Ghost had their tongues at work to preach, and their hands at work to baptize; for it was time to be busy, when such a harvest was to be gathered in. The conversion of these three thousand with these words was a *greater work* than the feeding of four or five thousand with a few loaves. These were *added to them.* When we take God for our God, we must take his people to be our people.

Verses 42-47

In these verses we have the history of the *truly primitive church,* its state of infancy indeed, but, like that, the state of its greatest *innocence.*

I. They kept close to holy ordinances. Christianity will dispose the soul to communion with God in all those ways wherein he has appointed us to meet him and promised to meet us.

1. They were diligent and constant in their attendance upon the *preaching of the word.* They *continued in the apostles' doctrine.* Those who have given up their names to Christ must make conscience of hearing his word.

2. They kept up the *communion of saints.* They continued *in fellowship* (*v.* 42), and *continued daily with one accord in the temple, v.* 46. They were much together. Wherever you saw one disciple, you would see more, like *birds of a feather.* See how these Christians love one another. They had fellowship with one another in religious worship. They met *in the temple:* there was their rendezvous; for joint-fellowship with God is the best fellowship we can have with one another. They were daily in the temple. Worshipping God is to be our daily work. They were *with one accord;* not only no discord nor strife, but a great deal of holy love among them.

3. They frequently joined in the ordinance of the Lord's supper. They continued *in the breaking of bread.* They broke bread *from house to house;* they administered that ordinance in private houses; and they went from one to another of these little synagogues or domestic chapels, and there celebrated the eucharist with those that usually met there to worship God.

4. They continued *in prayers. After* the Spirit was poured out, as well as before, they continued instant in prayer; for prayer will never be superseded till it comes to be swallowed up in everlasting praise.

5. They abounded in thanksgiving; were continually *praising God, v.* 47. This should have a part in every prayer, and not be crowded into a corner.

II. They were loving one to another and their joining together in holy ordinances very much endeared them to one another.

1. They had frequent meetings for Christian converse (*v.* 44): *All that believed were together.* They associated together, and so both expressed and increased their mutual love.

2. They had *all things common.* There was such a readiness to help one another that it might be said, They had *all things common,* according to the law of friendship.

JAMIESON, FAUSSET, BROWN

appeals, are omitted. **Save yourselves from this untoward generation**—as if Peter already foresaw the hopeless impenitence of the nation at large, and would have his hearers hasten in for themselves and secure their own salvation.

41-47. BEAUTIFUL BEGINNINGS OF THE CHRISTIAN CHURCH. **41-47. they that gladly received his word were baptized**—"It is difficult to say how 3000 could be baptized in one day, according to the old practice of a complete submersion; and the more as in Jerusalem there was no water at hand except Kidron and a few pools. The difficulty can only be removed by supposing that they already employed sprinkling, or baptized in houses in large vessels. Formal submersion in rivers, or larger quantities of water, probably took place only where the locality conveniently allowed it" [OLSHAUSEN]. **the same day there were added to them about 3000 souls**—fitting inauguration of the new kingdom, as an economy of the Spirit!

42. continued steadfastly in—'attended constantly upon.' **the apostles' doctrine**—'teaching'; giving themselves up to the instructions which, in their raw state, would be indispensable to the consolidation of the immense multitude suddenly admitted to visible discipleship. **fellowship**—in its largest sense.

46. daily . . . in the temple—observing the hours of Jewish worship-

breaking of bread—not certainly in the Lord's Supper alone, but rather in frugal repasts taken together, with which the Lord's Supper was probably conjoined until abuses and persecution led to the discontinuance of the common meal. **prayers**—probably, stated seasons of it.

47. Praising God—"Go thy way, eat thy bread with joy, and drink thy wine with a merry heart, *for God now accepteth thy works*" (Eccles. 9:7, see also on ch. 8:39).

44. all that believed were together, and had all things common—(See on ch. 4:34-37).

ADAM CLARKE

40. *Save yourselves from this untoward generation.* Separate yourselves from them. "Be saved." The power is present with you; make a proper use of it, and you shall be delivered from their obstinate unbelief, and the punishment that awaits it in the destruction of them and their city by the Romans.

41. *They that gladly received his word.* The word which signifies "joyfully, readily, willingly" implies that they approved of the doctrine delivered, that they were glad to hear of this way of salvation, and that they began immediately to act according to its dictates. The word is however omitted by some MSS. *Were baptized.* That is, in the name of Jesus, v. 38, for this was the criterion of a Jew's conversion. This baptism was a very powerful means to prevent their apostasy; they had, by receiving baptism in the name of Jesus, renounced Judaism and all the political advantages connected with it. Dr. Lightfoot has well remarked that the Gentiles who received the Christian doctrine were baptized in the "name of the Father, and the Son, and the Holy Ghost"; whereas the Jewish converts, for the reasons already given, were baptized in the "name of the Lord Jesus." *Were added . . . three thousand souls.* They went over from one party to another. The Greek writers make use of this verb to signify that act by which cities, towns, or provinces changed their masters, and put themselves under another government. So these 3,000 persons left the scribes and Pharisees, and put themselves under the teaching of the apostles, professing the Christian doctrine, and acknowledging that Christ was come, and that He who was lately crucified by the Jews was the promised and only Messiah; and in this faith they were baptized. These 3,000 were not converted under one discourse, nor in one place, nor by one person. All the apostles preached, some in one language, and some in another; and not in one house—for where was there one at that time that could hold such a multitude of people? For, out of the multitudes that heard, 3,000 were converted. The truth seems to be this: All the apostles preached in different parts of the city during the course of that day; and "in that day" 3,000 converts were the fruits of the conjoint exertions of these holy men.

42. *They continued stedfastly in the apostles' doctrine.* They received it, retained it, and acted on its principles. *And fellowship. Koinonia,* "community," meaning association for religious and spiritual purposes.

46. *They, continuing daily with one accord in the temple.* They were present at all the times of public worship, and joined together in prayers and praises to God; for it is not to be supposed that they continued to offer any of the sacrifices prescribed by the law.

And in breaking of bread. Whether this means the holy Eucharist or their common meals, it is difficult to say. *Breaking of bread* was that act which preceded a feast or meal, and which was performed by the master of the house when he pronounced the blessing—what we would call "grace" before meat.

44. *And all that believed.* "The believers," i.e., those who conscientiously credited the doctrine concerning the incarnation, crucifixion, resurrection, and ascension of Jesus Christ, and had, in consequence, received redemption in His blood. *Were together.* "These words signify either, in one time, chap. iii. 1; or in one place, chap. ii. 1; or in one thing. The last of these three senses seems to be the most proper here; for it is not probable that the believers, who were then 3,000 in number, v. 41, besides the 120 spoken of in chap. i. 15, were used all to meet at one time, or in one place, in Jerusalem." *And had all things common.* Perhaps this has not been understood. At all the public religious feasts in Jerusalem there was a sort of community of goods. No man at such times hired houses or beds in Jerusalem; all were lent *gratis* by the owners. Also, provisions of water were made for them at the public expense.

MATTHEW HENRY

3. They were very cheerful; they did *eat their meat with gladness and singleness of heart.* They brought the comforts of *God's table* along with them to *their own.* It made them very pleasant, and enlarged their hearts with holy joy. None have such cause to be cheerful as good Christians have; it is a pity but that they should always have hearts to be so. It made them very liberal to their poor brethren. They did *eat their meat with singleness of heart—with liberality of heart;* so some: they did not eat their morsels alone, but bade the poor welcome to their table. It becomes Christians to be open-hearted and open-handed.

4. They raised a fund for charity (*v.* 45): They *sold their possessions and goods,* and *parted* the money to their brethren, *as every man had need.* This was to destroy not property, but selfishness. Herein, probably, they had an eye to the command which Christ gave to the rich man, as a test of his sincerity, *Sell that thou hast, and give to the poor.* Not that this was intended for an example to be a constant binding rule. But here the case was extraordinary. They were under no obligation of a divine command to do this, as appears by what Peter said to Ananias (*ch.* v. 4): *Was it not in thine own power?* But it was a very commendable instance of their love to their brethren, their compassion to the poor, and their great zeal for the encouraging of Christianity, and the nursing of it in its infancy. Our rule is, to give according as God has blessed us.

III. God owned them, and gave them signal tokens of his presence with them (*v.* 43): *Many wonders and signs were done by the apostles.*

But the Lord's giving them power to work miracles was not all he did for them; he *added to the church daily.* The word in their mouths *did wonders,* and God blessed their endeavours.

IV. The people were influenced by it. They *feared them* (*v.* 43): *Fear came upon every soul.* They had abundance of spiritual gifts that were truly honourable, which possessed men with an inward reverence for them. The *souls* of people were strangely influenced by their awful preaching and living. They *favoured them.* Though we have reason to think there were those that despised them, yet far the greater part of the common people had a kindness for them—they *had favour with all the people.* Here we find them *in favour with them all,* by which it appears that their prosecuting Christ was a sort of force put upon them by the artifices of the priests; now they returned to their wits, to their right mind. Undissembled piety and charity will command respect; and cheerfulness in serving God will recommend religion to those that are without. They *fell over* to them. Some or other were daily coming in, and they were such as *should be saved.*

CHAPTER 3

Verses 1-11

We were told in general (*ch.* ii. 43) that *many signs and wonders were done by the apostles.* Here we have one given us for an instance.

I. The persons by whose ministry this miracle was wrought were Peter and John.

Peter and John had each of them a brother among the twelve, yet now they seem to be knit together more closely than either of them to his brother, for the bond of friendship is sometimes stronger than that of relation. Peter and John seem to have had a peculiar intimacy after Christ's resurrection more than before. It was good evidence of Peter's acceptance with God, upon his repentance, that Christ's favourite was made his bosom friend.

II. The time and place are here set down. It was in *the temple,* whither *Peter and John went up together.* There were the shoals of fish among which the net of the gospel was to be cast. It is good to go up to the temple, to attend on public ordinances; and it is comfortable to go up together to the temple. The best society is society in worshipping God. It was *at the hour of prayer.* There must be a house of prayer and an hour of prayer. It is of use for private Christians so far to have their hours of prayer as may serve, though not to bind, yet to remind, conscience.

III. The patient on whom this miraculous cure was wrought, *v.* 2. He was a poor lame beggar at the temple gate. 1. He was a cripple, not by accident, but born so. He was *lame from his mother's womb.* Such piteous cases show us what we all are by nature spiritually: *without strength,* lame from our birth, unable to work or walk in God's service. 2. He was a beggar. Being unable to work for his living, he must live upon alms; such are God's poor. He was *laid daily at one of the gates of the temple* to *ask alms of those that entered into the temple.* Those that need,

JAMIESON, FAUSSET, BROWN

—and breaking bread from house to house—Rather, 'at home' (*margin*), i.e., in *private,* as contrasted with their *temple*-worship, but in some stated place or places of meeting. **eat their meat with gladness**—'exultation'—**and singleness of heart.**

43. fear came upon every soul—A deep awe rested upon the whole community.

having favour with all the people—commending themselves by their lovely demeanor to the admiration of all who observed them. **And the Lord**—i.e., JESUS, as the glorified Head and Ruler of the Church. **added**—kept adding; i.e., to the visible community of believers, though the words "to the Church" are wanting in the most ancient MSS. **such as should be saved**—Rather, 'the saved,' or 'those who were being saved.' "The young Church had but few peculiarities in its outward form, or even in its doctrine: the single discriminating principle of its few members was that they all recognized the crucified Jesus of Nazareth as the Messiah. This confession would have been a thing of no importance, if it had only presented itself as a naked declaration, and would never in such a case have been able to form a community that would spread itself over the whole Roman empire. It acquired its value only through the power of the Holy Ghost, passing from the apostles as they preached to the hearers; for He brought the confession from the very hearts of men (I Cor. 12:3), and like a burning flame made their souls glow with love. By the power of this Spirit, therefore, we behold the first Christians not only in a state of active fellowship, but also internally changed: the narrow views of the natural man are broken through; they have their possessions in common, and they regard themselves as one family" [OLSHAUSEN].

CHAPTER 3

VSS. 1-26. PETER HEALS A LAME MAN AT THE TEMPLE GATE—HIS ADDRESS TO THE WONDERING MULTITUDE. **1-11. Peter and John**—already associated by their Master, first with James (Mark 1:29; 5:37; 9:2), then by themselves (Luke 22:8; and see John 13:23, 24). Now we find them constantly together, but John (yet young) only as a silent actor. **went up**—were going up, were on their way.

2. a certain man lame from his mother's womb—and now "above 40 years old" (ch. 4:22)—**was carried**—was wont to be carried.

ADAM CLARKE

Therefore a sort of community of goods was no strange thing at Jerusalem at such times as these. It appears, however, that this community of goods was carried further; for we are informed, v. 45, that they *sold their possessions and goods, and parted them to all men, as every man had need.* But this probably means that, as in consequence of this remarkable outpouring of the Spirit of God and their conversion they were detained longer at Jerusalem than they had originally intended, they formed a kind of community for the time being, that none might suffer want on the present occasion; as no doubt the unbelieving Jews, who were mockers, v. 13, would treat these new converts with the most marked disapprobation.

Breaking bread from house to house. This may signify that select companies, who were contiguous to each other, frequently ate together at their respective lodgings on their return from public worship. But *kat'oikon,* which we translate *from house to house,* is repeatedly used by the Greek writers for "at home" (see margin); for though they had all things in common, each person lived at his own table. *Breaking bread* is used to express the act of taking their meals. The bread of the Jews was thin, hard, and dry, and was never cut with the knife as ours is, but was simply broken by the hand. *With gladness and singleness of heart.* A true picture of genuine Christian fellowship. They ate their bread; they had no severe fasts. The Holy Spirit had done in their souls, by His refining influence, what others vainly expect from bodily austerities. It may also be said that, if they had no severe fasts, they had no splendid feasts; all was moderation, and all was contentment. They were full of *gladness,* spiritual joy and happiness; and *singleness of heart,* every man worthy of the confidence of his neighbor.

47. *And the Lord added to the church daily such as should be saved.* Though many approved of the life and manners of these primitive Christians, yet they did not become members of this holy Church, God permitting none to be *added* to it but those who were "saved" from their sins and prejudices. Our translation *such as should be saved* is improper and insupportable. The original means simply and solely those who were then saved; those who were redeemed from their sins, and baptized into the faith of Jesus Christ.

CHAPTER 3

1. Peter and John went up together. The words which we translate *together,* and which are the first words in this chapter in the Greek text, are added by several MSS. and versions to the last verse of the preceding chapter. But they do not make as good a sense there as they do here; and should be translated, not *together,* which really makes no sense here, but "at that time"; intimating that this transaction occurred about the same time as those which are mentioned at the close of the former chapter. *At the hour of prayer.* This, as is immediately added, was the *ninth* hour, which answers, in a general way, to our three o'clock in the afternoon. It appears that there were *three* hours of the day destined by the Jews to public prayer; perhaps they are referred to by David, Ps. lv. 17: "Evening, and morning, and at noon, will I pray, and cry aloud." There are three distinct times marked in the Book of the Acts. The third hour, chap. ii. 15, answering, as we have already seen, to nearly our nine o'clock in the morning; the sixth hour, chap. x. 9, answering to about twelve with us; and the ninth hour, mentioned in this verse, and answering to our three in the afternoon. I should be glad to know that every Christian in the universe observed the same rule. It is the most natural division of the day; and he who conscientiously observes these three stated times of prayer will infallibly grow in grace and in the knowledge of Jesus Christ our Lord.

2. *A . . . man lame from his mother's womb.* The case of this man must have been well-known: (1) from the long standing of his in-

MATTHEW HENRY

and cannot work, must not be ashamed to beg. Our prayers and our alms should go together. Objects of charity should be in a particular manner welcome to us when we go up to the temple to pray; it is a pity that common beggars at church doors should any of them be of such a character as to discourage charity; but they ought not always to be overlooked: some there are surely that merit regard, and better feed ten drones, yea, and some wasps, than let one bee starve. The gate of the temple at which he was laid is here named: it was called *Beautiful*. It was no diminution to the beauty of this gate that a poor man lay there begging. 3. He begged of Peter and John (*v.* 3), begged an alms; this was the utmost he expected from them. He *asked an alms*, and had a cure.

IV. We have here the method of the cure.

1. His expectations were raised. Peter, instead of turning his eyes from him, *fastened his eyes upon him*, *v.* 4. John did so too, they said, *Look on us*. This gave him cause to expect that he should *receive something from them*, and therefore he *gave heed to them*, *v.* 5. We must come to God with hearts fixed and expectations raised. We must look up to heaven and expect to receive.

2. His expectation of an alms was disappointed. *Peter said*, "*Silver and gold have I none.*" It is not often that Christ's friends and favourites have abundance of the wealth of this world. Peter and John had abundance of money laid at their feet, but this was appropriated to the maintenance of the poor of the church. Public trusts ought to be strictly and faithfully observed. Many who are well inclined to works of charity are yet not in a capacity of doing anything considerable, while others, who have wherewithal to do much, have not a heart to do anything.

3. His expectations were quite outdone. Peter had no money to give him. He had that which was better, such a power from heaven, as to be able to cure his disease. Those who are poor in the world may yet be rich, very rich, in spiritual gifts. He gave him that which was better—the cure of his disease. This would enable him to work for his living, so that he would not need to beg any more; nay, he would *have to give to those that needed*. When Peter had no silver and gold to give, yet (says he) *such as I have I give thee*. Those who have not silver and gold have their limbs and senses, and with these may be serviceable to the blind, and lame, and sick, and if they be not, neither would they give to them if they had silver and gold. How the cure was wrought. Peter bids a lame man *rise up and walk*, which would have been a banter upon him if he had not premised *in the name of Jesus Christ of Nazareth*. He bids the cripple *rise up and walk*. If he attempt to rise and walk, and depend upon a divine power to enable him to do it, he shall be enabled; and by rising and walking he must evidence that that power has wrought upon him; and then let him take the comfort, and let God have the praise. Peter lent his hand, and helped him (*v.* 7): *He took him by the right hand and lifted him up*. When God by his word commands us to rise, and walk in the way of his commandments, he will give his Spirit to take us by the hand, and lift us up. If we set ourselves to do what we can, God has promised his grace to enable us to do what we cannot. *His feet and ankle-bones received strength*; he does his part, and Peter does his, and yet it is Christ that does all: it is he that puts strength into him.

V. Here is the impression which this cure made upon the patient himself. He leaped up, in obedience to the command, *Arise*. He started up, as one refreshed with sleep, that questioned not his own strength. The incomes of strength were sudden, and he was no less sudden in showing them. He stood, and walked. He trod strongly, and moved steadily; and this was to manifest the cure. Those who have had experience of the working of divine grace upon them should evidence what they have experienced. Has God put strength into us? Let us stand up resolutely for him, and walk cheerfully with him. He *held Peter and John*, *v.* 11. We need not ask why he held them. I believe he scarcely knew himself: but it was in a transport of joy that he embraced them. Thus he testified his affection to them; he held them, and would not let them go. Those whom God hath healed love those whom he made instruments of their healing, and see the need of their further help. He *entered with them into the temple*. His strong affection to them held them; but it could not hold them so fast as to keep them out of the temple. He is resolved to go with them, and the rather because they are going into the temple. Like the impotent man whom Christ cured, he was presently found in the temple, John v. 14. He was there *walking, and leaping, and praising God*. The strength God has given us, both in mind and body, should be made use of to his praise. This

JAMIESON, FAUSSET, BROWN

4. Peter fastening his eyes on him with John, said, Look on us. 5. And he gave heed—that, through the eye, faith might be aided in its birth.

6. Silver and gold have I none, but such as I have give I thee.—What a lofty superiority breathes in these words!

In the name of Jesus Christ of Nazareth rise up and walk.—These words, uttered with supernatural power, doubtless begat in this poor man the faith that sent healing virtue through his diseased members.

7. And he took . . . and lifted him up—precisely what his Lord had done to his own mother-in-law (Mark 1:31). **his feet**—'soles'—**and ankle bones . . .**—the technical language of a physician (Col. 4:14).

11. the lame man . . . held . . .—This is human nature.

8. leaping up, stood . . . walked . . . entered the temple walking, leaping, and praising God—Every word here is emphatic, expressing the perfection of the cure, as vs. 7 its immediateness.

ADAM CLARKE

firmity; (2) from his being daily exposed in a place so public. It appears that he had no power to walk, and was what we term a "cripple," for he was carried to the gate of the Temple, and laid there in order to excite compassion. These circumstances are all marked by Luke, the more fully to show the greatness and incontestable nature of the miracle. *The gate . . . which is called Beautiful*. There are different opinions concerning this gate. Josephus observes (Bell, *Jud.*, l. v, c. 5, s. 3) that the Temple had nine gates, which were on every side covered with gold and silver; but there was one gate which was without the holy house, and was of Corinthian brass, and greatly excelled those which were only covered with gold and silver. The magnitudes of the other gates were equal one to another; but that of the Corinthian gate, which opened on the east, over against the gate of the holy house itself, was much larger. "For its height was fifty cubits, and its doors were forty cubits, and it was adorned after a most costly manner, as having much richer and thicker plates of silver and gold upon them than upon the other." This last was probably the gate which is here called *Beautiful;* because it was on the outside of the Temple, to which there was an easy access, and because it was evidently the most costly, according to the account in Josephus.

4. *Look on us*. He wished to excite and engage his attention that he might see what was done to produce his miraculous cure, and, it is likely, took this occasion to direct his faith to Jesus Christ. Peter and John probably felt themselves suddenly drawn by the Holy Spirit to pronounce the healing name in behalf of this poor man.

5. *Expecting to receive something of them*. Because it was a constant custom for all who entered the Temple to carry money with them to give to the treasury, or to the poor, or to both. It was on this ground that the friends of the lame man laid him at the gate of the Temple, as this was the most likely place to receive alms.

6. *Silver and gold have I none*. Though it was customary for all those who entered the Temple to carry some money with them, for the purposes mentioned above, yet so poor were the apostles that they had nothing to give, either to the sacred treasury or to the distressed. The popish writers are very dexterous at forming analogies between Peter and the pope, but it is worthy of note that they have not attempted any here. Thomas Aquinas, surnamed the angelical doctor, who was highly esteemed by Pope Innocent IV, going one day into the pope's chamber, where they were reckoning large sums of money, the pope, addressing himself to Aquinas, said: "You see that the Church is no longer in an age in which she can say, *Silver and gold have I none?*" "It is true, holy father," replied the angelical doctor, "nor can she now say to the lame man, *Rise up and walk!*" . .

7. *Immediately his feet and ancle bones received strength*. The suddenness of the cure was the proof of the miracle; his walking and leaping were the evidences of it.

11. *Held Peter and John*. He felt the strongest affection for them, as the instruments by which the divine influence was conveyed to his diseased body. *In the porch that is called Solomon's*. On this portico see Bishop Pearce's note, inserted in this work, John x. 23.

8. *Walking, and leaping, and praising God*. These actions are very naturally described. *He walked* in obedience to the command of the apostle to rise up and walk; *he leaped*, to try the strength of his limbs, and to be convinced

MATTHEW HENRY

man, as soon as he could leap, leaped for joy in God, and praised him. All true converts walk and praise God; but perhaps young converts leap more in his praises.

VI. How the people that were eye-witnesses of this miracle were influenced by it. 1. They were entirely satisfied in the truth of the miracle. *They knew it was he that sat begging at the beautiful gate of the temple, v.* 10. He had sat there so long that they all knew him. They now saw him *walking and praising God* (*v.* 9). He was now as loud in praising God as he had before been in begging relief. Mercies are then perfected, when they are sanctified. 2. They were astonished at it: They were *filled with wonder and amazement* (*v.* 10); *greatly wondering, v.* 11. There seems to have been this effect of the pouring out of the Spirit, that the people were much more affected with the miracles the apostles wrought than they had been with those that had been wrought by Christ himself. 3. They gathered about Peter and John: *All the people ran together unto them in Solomon's porch.* Here the people met, to see this great sight.

Verses 12-26

We have here the sermon which Peter preached. *When Peter saw it.* When he saw the people got together in a crowd, he took that opportunity to preach Christ to them. When he saw the people affected with the miracle, he sowed the gospel seed in the ground which was thus prepared to receive it. When he saw the people ready to adore him and John, he diverted their respect from them, that it might be directed to Christ only.

I. He humbly disclaims the honour of the miracle. He addresses himself to them as *men of Israel*, men to whom pertained, not only the law and the promises, but the gospel and the performances. Two things he asks them: 1. Why they were so surprised at the miracle itself: *Why marvel you at this?* It was indeed marvellous, but it was no more than what Christ had done many a time. It was but a little before that Christ had *raised Lazarus from the dead*; and why should this then seem so strange? Stupid people think that strange now which might have been familiar to them if it had not been their own fault. Christ had lately risen from the dead himself; why did they not marvel at this? 2. Why they gave so much of the praise of it to them, who were only the instruments of it: *Why look you so earnestly on us?* It was certain that they *had made this man to walk*, by which it appeared that the apostles not only were sent of God, but were sent to be blessings to the world. Yet they did not do it by any *power or holiness of their own.* The power they did it by was wholly derived from Christ. The power which Christ gave them to do it they had not deserved: it was not by their own holiness. Peter was a sinful man. Yet he wrought miracles in Christ's name. It was the people's fault that they attributed it to their power and holiness. The instruments of God's favour to us, must not be idolized. It was the praise of Peter and John that they would not take the honour of this miracle to themselves, but carefully transmitted it to Christ. Useful men must see to it that they be very humble.

II. He preaches Christ to them.

1. He preaches Christ, as the true Messiah promised to the fathers (*v.* 13). He is Jesus the Son of God. He is *his Son Jesus*; to him dear as a Son; to us, *Jesus*, a Saviour. God hath glorified him, in raising him up. He hath glorified him as *the God of our fathers, the God of Abraham, of Isaac, and of Jacob.* God sent him into the world, pursuant to the promises made to those patriarchs. The gospel they preached was the revelation of the mind and will of the God of Abraham.

2. He charges them flatly and plainly with the murder of this Jesus: "*You delivered him up*, and you of the common people were influenced to clamour against him, as if he had been a public grievance." *You denied him*, and you disowned him, could not look upon him as the Messiah, because he came not in external pomp and power; *you denied him in the presence of Pilate.* "You were worse than Pilate, for he would have released him, if you had let him follow his own judgment. *You denied the holy One and the Just.*" The holiness and justice of the Lord Jesus, which are something more than his innocency, were a great aggravation of the sin of those that put him to death. "*You desired a murderer to be released*, and Christ crucified." *You killed the prince of life.* "You preserved *a murderer*, a destroyer of life; and destroyed the Saviour, *the author of life. You killed the prince of life*, and so not only forsook, but rebelled against your own mercies."

3. He attests his resurrection as before, *ch.* ii. 32. "You thought *the prince of life* might be deprived of his life. *But of his resurrection we are all*

JAMIESON, FAUSSET, BROWN

9. all the people saw him . . .—as they assembled at the hour of public prayer, in the temple courts; so that the miracle had the utmost publicity. **10. they knew that it was he which sat for alms . . .**—(Cf. John 9:8).

all the people ran together unto them in the porch . . .—How vividly do these graphic details bring the whole scene before us! Thus was Peter again furnished with a vast audience, whose wonder at the spectacle of the healed beggar clinging to his benefactors prepared them to listen with reverence to his words.

12-16. why marvel at this?—For miracles are marvels only in relation to the limited powers of man.

as though by our own power or holiness we had made this man to walk.—Neither the might nor the merit of the cure are due to us, mere agents of Him whom we preach.

13. The God of Abraham . . .—See on ch. 2:22, 36. **hath glorified his Son Jesus**—rather, 'his Servant Jesus,' as the same word is rendered in Matthew 12:18, but in that high sense in which Isaiah applies it always to Messiah (Isa. 42:1; 49:6; 52:13; 53:11). When 'Son' is intended a different word is used.

whom ye delivered up . . .—With what heroic courage does Peter here charge his auditors with the heaviest of all conceivable crimes, and with what terrific strength of language are these charges clothed!

15. killed the Prince of life—Glorious paradox, but how piercing to the conscience of the auditors.

ADAM CLARKE

of the reality of the cure; *he praised God*, as a testimony of the gratitude he felt for the cure he had received. Now was fulfilled, in the most literal manner, the words of the Prophet Isaiah, chap. xxxv. 6: "Then shall the lame man leap as an hart."

9. *And all the people saw him.* The miracle was wrought in the most public manner, and in the most public place, and in a place where the best judgment could be formed of it. For, as it was a divine operation, the priests were the most proper persons to judge of it; and under their notice it was now wrought.

ALBERT BARNES:

"Why marvel ye at this?" The particular thing which he intended to reprove here was not that they wondered, for that was proper; but that they looked on himself and John as if they had been the authors of this healing. They ought to have understood it. The Jews were sufficiently acquainted with miracles to interpret them and to know whence they proceeded; and they ought not, therefore, to ascribe them to *man*, but to inquire *why* they had been wrought *by God.* "Why look ye?" Why do ye fix the eyes with amazement on us, as though we could do this? Why not look at once to God? "By our own power." By any art of healing or by any medicine we had done this. "Or holiness." Piety. As if God had bestowed this on us on account of our personal and eminent piety. It may be remarked that here was ample opportunity for them to establish a reputation of their own. The people were disposed to pay them honor; they might at once have laid claim to vast authority over them; but they refused all such personal honor and ascribed all to the Lord Jesus. Whatever success may attend the ministers of the gospel, or however much the world may be disposed to do them honor, they should disclaim all power in themselves, and ascribe it to the Lord Jesus Christ. It is not by the talents or personal holiness of ministers, valuable as these are, that men are saved; it is only by the power of God, designed to honor his Son (see 2 Cor. 3:5, 6).
—*Popular Commentary*

12. *As though by our own power.* "Miraculous energy." *Or holiness.* Meaning "religious attachment to the worship of God." Do not think that we have wrought this miracle by any power of our own; or that any supereminent piety in us should have induced God thus to honor us, by enabling us to work it.

13. *The God of Abraham.* This was wisely introduced, to show them that He whom they called their God had acknowledged Jesus Christ for His Son, and wrought this miracle in His name; and by thus honoring Jesus, whom they slew, He had charged home the guilt of that murder upon them. *Denied him in the presence of Pilate.* You have renounced Him as your King, and denounced Him to death as a malefactor, when Pilate, convinced of His perfect innocense, was *determined,* "judged" it proper and just, to let Him go. Pilate wished to act according to justice; you acted contrary to justice and equity in all their forms.

14. *Ye denied the Holy One.* A manifest reference to Ps. xvi. 10: "Thou wilt not . . . suffer thine Holy One to see corruption." *And desired a murderer.* Barabbas. The case must have been fresh in their own remembrance. Like cleaves to like, and begets its like; they were murderers themselves, and so Christ calls them, Matt. xxii. 7, and they preferred a murderer to the holy and righteous One of God.

15. *And killed the Prince of life.* "The author of this life," not only implying that all life proceeds from Jesus Christ as its Source, but that the life-giving influence of that religion which they were now proclaiming came all through Him. *Archegos* signifies a "prime leader or author, a captain." In Heb. ii. 10, Christ is

MATTHEW HENRY

witnesses."

4. He ascribes the cure of this impotent man to the power of Christ (*v.* 16): *His name, through faith in his name, has made this man strong.* He repeats it again, *The faith which is by him hath given him this soundness.* (1) He appeals to themselves concerning the truth of the miracle; the man on whom it was wrought is one *whom you see, and know.* The miracle was wrought publicly, *in the presence of you all,* in the gate of the temple. The cure is complete; it is a *perfect soundness*; you see the man walks and leaps. (2) He acquaints them with the power by which it was wrought. It is done by the name of Christ. That name which Christ has above every name; his authority, his command has done it; as writs run in the king's name, though it is an inferior officer that executes them. The power of Christ is fetched in *through faith in his name,* and it is for his sake, that he may have the glory of it. Those that wrought this miracle by faith derived power from Christ to work it, and therefore returned all the glory to him. Peter both confirmed the great gospel truth they were to preach to the world—that Jesus Christ is the fountain of all power and grace, and the great healer and Saviour—and recommended the great gospel duty of faith in him as the only way of receiving benefit by him. Thus does Peter preach unto them Jesus, and him crucified.

III. He encourages them to hope that they might find mercy; he does all he can to convince them, yet is careful not to drive them to despair. 1. He mollifies their crime by a candid imputation of it to their ignorance. He saw it needful to mitigate the rigour of the charge by calling them *brethren*; and well might he call them so, for he had been himself a brother with them in this iniquity: he had *denied the Holy One and the Just,* and sworn that he did not know him. *I know that through ignorance you did it, as did also your rulers, v.* 17. This was the language of Peter's charity, and teaches us to make the best of those whom we desire to make better. He has the example of his Master's praying for his crucifiers, and pleading in their behalf that they knew not what they did. Perhaps some of the rulers, and of the people did it through malice; but the generality went down the stream, and did it through ignorance. 2. He mollifies the effects of their crime, it was *according to the scriptures* (*v.* 18). So he himself saith: *Thus it is written, and thus it behoved Christ to suffer.* "You fulfilled the scripture, and did not know it; *God,* by your hands, *hath fulfilled what he showed by the mouth of all his prophets, that Christ should suffer*; this was his design but you had views of your own, and were altogether ignorant of this design. God was fulfilling the scripture when you were gratifying your own passions." This is no extenuation at all of their sin in hating and persecuting Christ *to the death,* yet it was an encouragment to them to repent, and hope for mercy. The death and sufferings of Christ were for *the remission of sins,* and the ground of that display of mercy for which he now encouraged them to hope.

IV. He exhorts them all to turn Christians.

1. He tells them what they must believe. They must believe that Jesus Christ is the promised seed, *v.* 25. *Jesus,* who was of *the seed of Abraham, according to the flesh,* and *in him all the families of the earth are blessed,* and not the families of Israel only. They must believe that Jesus Christ is a prophet, *that prophet like unto Moses* whom God had promised to *raise up to them from among their brethren, v.* 22. Christ is a prophet, for by him God speaks unto us. He is a *prophet like unto Moses.* He was a deliverer of his people out of bondage, like Moses. Moses was *faithful as a servant,* Christ *as a Son.* Moses was a pattern of meekness and patience, so is Christ. *There was no prophet like unto Moses,* but a greater than Moses is here where Christ is. He is a prophet of God's raising up. He was raised up unto Israel in the first place. They had the first offer of divine grace made to them; and therefore he was *raised up from among them.* If he come to his own, one would think, they should receive him. The Old Testament church was blessed with many prophets from *Samuel, and those that follow after, v.* 24; but, these servants being abused, last of all God sent them his Son. They must believe *that times of refreshing will come from the presence of the Lord* (*v.* 19), and that they will be *the times of the restitution of all things, v.* 21. The absence of the Lord occasions many of the securities of sinners and the distrusts of saints; but his presence is hastening on, which will for ever silence both. The presence of the Lord will introduce, (1) *The restitution of all things* (*v.* 21); the renovation of the whole creation; that *end of all things which God hath spoken of by the mouth of all his holy prophets since the world began.* This is more clearly

JAMIESON, FAUSSET, BROWN

16. his name, through faith in his name, hath made this man strong . . .—With what skill does the apostle use the miracle both to glorify his ascended Lord and bring the guilt of His blood more resistlessly home to his audience!

17-21. And now, brethren.—Our preacher, like his Master, "will not break the bruised reed." His heaviest charges are prompted by love, which now hastens to assuage the wounds it was necessary to inflict. **I wot**—'know.' **through ignorance ye did it**—(See *marginal reference*).

18. that Christ—The best MSS. read, 'that His Christ'—**should suffer**—The doctrine of a SUFFERING MESSIAH was totally at variance with the current views of the Jewish Church, and hard to digest even by the Twelve, up to the day of their Lord's resurrection. Our preacher himself revolted at it, and protested against it, when first nakedly announced, for which he received a terrible rebuke. Here he affirms it to be the fundamental truth of ancient prophecy realized unwittingly by the Jews themselves, yet by a glorious divine ordination. How great a change had the Pentecostal illumination wrought upon his views!

22-26. a prophet . . . like unto me—particularly *in intimacy of communication with God* (Num. 12:6-8), *and as the mediatorial Head of a new order of things* (Heb. 3:2-6). Peter takes it for granted that, in the light of all he had just said, it would be seen at once that One only had any claim to be that Prophet.

24. foretold of these days—of Messiah; all pointing to "the time of reformation" (Heb. 9:10), though with more or less distinctness.

21. until the times—embracing the whole period between the ascension and the second advent of Christ. **restitution of all things**—comprehending, probably, the rectification of all the disorders of the fall.

ADAM CLARKE

called the "captain of . . . salvation." He teaches the doctrine of life and salvation, leads the way in which men should walk, and has purchased the eternal life and glory which are to be enjoyed at the end of the way. So the Jews preferred a son of death, a destroyer of life, to the Author and Procurer of life and immortality!

16. *And his name.* Jesus, the Saviour; *through faith in his name,* as the Saviour, and Author of life, and all its concomitant blessings, such as health.

17. *I wot.* "I know." Wot is from Anglo-Saxon; and hence "wit," science or understanding. *Through ignorance ye did it.* This is a very tender excuse for them; and one which seems to be necessary in order to show them that their state was not utterly desperate. For if all that they did to Christ had been through absolute malice (they well knowing who He was), if any sin could be supposed to be unpardonable, it must have been theirs. Peter, foreseeing that they might be tempted thus to think, and consequently to despair of salvation, tells them that their offense was extenuated by their ignorance of the Person they had tormented and crucified.

18. *But those things . . . he hath so fulfilled.* Your ignorance and malice have been overruled by the sovereign wisdom and power of God, and have become the instruments of fulfilling the divine purpose, that Christ must suffer in order to make an atonement for the sin of the world. *All his prophets* had declared this; some of them in express terms, others indirectly and by symbols.

22. *Moses truly said unto the fathers.* From this appeal to Moses it is evident that Peter wished them to understand that Jesus Christ was come, not as an ordinary prophet, to exhort to repentance and amendment, but as a Legislator, who was to give them a new law, and whose commands and precepts they were to obey, on pain of endless destruction.

The times of restitution of all things. The word *apokatastasis* from *apo,* which signifies "from," and *kathistanein,* to "establish or settle" anything, viz., in a good state; and, when *apo* is added to it, then this preposition implies that this good state in which it is settled was preceded by a bad one, from which the change is made to a good one. So in chap. i. 6, when the disciples said to Christ, "Wilt thou at this time

MATTHEW HENRY

and plainly revealed in the New Testament than it had been before. (2) With this will come *the times of refreshing* (v. 19), like a cool shade to those *that have borne the burden and heat of the day.* All Christians look for *a rest that remains for the people of God*, after the travails and toils of their present state. The refreshing that then *comes from the presence of the Lord* will continue eternally in the presence of the Lord.

2. He tells them what they must do. They must *repent*; they must begin anew. Peter, who had himself denied Christ, repented, and he would have them to do so too. They must *be converted*, must face about; they must *return to the Lord their God*. It is not enough to repent of sin, but we must be converted from it, and not return to it again. They must hear Christ, the great prophet: "*Him shall you hear in all things whatsoever he shall say unto you.* Hear him with a divine faith, as prophets should be heard. *Hear him in all things;* let his laws govern all your actions. Whatever he saith to you, bid it welcome." It is at our peril if we turn a deaf ear to his call (v. 23): *Every soul that will not hear that prophet shall be destroyed from among the people.* Those that will not be advised by the Saviour can expect no other than to fall into the hands of the destroyer.

3. He tells them what they might expect.

(1) That they should have the pardon of their sins (v. 19): *Repent, and be converted, that your sins may be blotted out.* The remission of sin is the blotting of it out. When God forgives sin he remembers it no more against the sinner; it is forgotten, as that which is blotted out. We cannot expect our sins should be pardoned unless we repent of them, and turn from them to God. If no repentance, no remission. Hopes of the pardon of sin upon repentance should be a powerful inducement to us to repent. This was the first and great argument, *Repent, for the kingdom of heaven is at hand.* The most comfortable fruit of the forgiveness of our sins will be *when the times of refreshing shall come.* During these times of toil and conflict (doubts and fears within, troubles and dangers without) we cannot have that full satisfaction of our pardon, and in it, that we shall have when the refreshing times come, which shall wipe away all tears.

(2) That they should have the comfort of Christ's coming (v. 20, 21): "*He shall send Jesus Christ, that before was preached unto you.* If you *repent and be converted*, you shall find no want of him; some way or other he shall be seen of you." We must not expect Christ's personal presence with us in this world; for the heavens, which received him out of the sight of the disciples, must retain him till the end of time. We must live by that faith in him which is *the evidence of things not seen.* Yet it is promised that he shall be sent to all that repent and are converted (v. 20): "*He shall send Jesus Christ, who was preached to you.* You shall have his spiritual presence. He that is sent into the world shall be sent to you; you shall have the comfort of his being sent. The sending of Christ to judge the world, at the end of time, will be a blessing to you." It seems to refer to this, for till then *the heavens must receive him*, v. 21.

4. He tells them what ground they had to expect these things, if they were converted to Christ.

(1) As Israelites they were, above any other, God's favourite nation. *You are the children of the prophets and of the covenant.* A double privilege. [1] They were *the children of the prophets.* You are of that people from among whom prophets were raised up, and to whom prophets were sent. Those of the latter ages of the church, when prophecy had ceased, might yet be fitly called *the children of the prophets*, because they heard *the voices of the prophets, which were read in their synagogues every sabbath day, ch.* xiii. 27. Now this should quicken them to embrace Christ. Those that are blessed with prophets and prophecy (as all are that have the scriptures) are concerned not to receive the grace of God therein in vain. [2] They were *the children*, that is, the heirs, *of the covenant which God made with our Fathers.* "The promise of the Messiah was made to you, and therefore you may hope it shall be made good to you." If all the kindreds of the earth were to be blessed in Christ, much more that kindred, *his kinsmen according to the flesh.*

(2) As Israelites, they had the first offer of the grace of the New Testament. To them the Redeemer was first sent, which was an encouragement to them to hope that if they did repent, and were converted, he should be yet further sent for their comfort (v. 20): *He shall send Jesus Christ*, for to you first he hath sent him, v. 26. *Unto you first, God, having raised up his Son Jesus from the dead, sent him to bless you*, especially that great blessing of *turning every one of you from his iniquities.* [1] We are here told whence

JAMIESON, FAUSSET, BROWN

19. when the times of refreshing shall come—rather, 'in order that the times of refreshing may come'; that long period of repose, prosperity and joy, which all the prophets hold forth to the distracted Church and this miserable world, as eventually to come, and which is here, as in all the prophets, made to turn upon the national conversion of Israel.

him shall ye hear in all things . . .—This part of the prediction is emphatically added, in order to shut up the audience to the obedience of faith, on pain of being finally "cut off" from the congregation of the righteous (Ps. 1:1).

20. he shall send Jesus Christ—The true reading is, 'He shall send your predestinated [or foreordained] Messiah, Jesus.'

25. Ye are the children . . . of the covenant—and so the natural heirs of its promises. **in thy seed . . .**—(See on Gal. 3:8, etc.).

26. God, having raised up—not from the dead, but having provided, prepared, and given. **his Son Jesus**—'His Servant Jesus' (see on vs. 13). **sent him to bless you**—lit., 'sent Him blessing you,' as if laden with blessing.

ADAM CLARKE

restore again the kingdom to Israel?" they meant, as the Greek word implies, Wilt Thou take the kingdom from the Romans, and give it back to the Jews? Now as the word is here connected with *which God hath spoken by the mouth of all his holy prophets*, it must mean the accomplishment of all the prophecies and promises contained in the Old Testament relative to the kingdom of Christ upon earth, the whole reign of grace, from the ascension of our Lord till His coming again, for of all these things have the holy prophets spoken; and as the grace of the gospel was intended to destroy the reign of sin, its energetic influence is represented as restoring all things, destroying the bad state, and establishing the good—taking the kingdom out of the hands of sin and Satan, and putting it into those of righteousness and truth. This is done in every believing soul; all things are restored to their primitive order. Therefore the words are to be applied to this, and no other meaning. *All his holy prophets. All* is omitted by some MSS. *Since the world began. Ap'aionos;* as *aion* signifies complete and everduring existence or eternity, it is sometimes applied, by way of accommodation, to denote the whole course of any one period, such as the Mosaic dispensation. See the note on Gen. xxi. 33. It may therefore here refer to that state of things from the giving of the law; and as Moses is mentioned in the next verse, and none before him, it is probable that the phrase should be so understood here. But if we apply it to the commencement of time, the sense is still good.

19. *Repent ye therefore.* Now that you are convinced that this was the Messiah, let your minds be changed and your hearts become contrite for the sins you have committed. *And be converted.* Turn to God through this Christ, deeply deploring your transgressions and believing on His name; *that your sins may be blotted out*, which are not only recorded against you, but for which you are condemned by the justice of God; and the punishment due to them must be executed upon you, unless prevented by your repentance, and turning to Him whom you have pierced. The blotting *out of* sins may refer to the ceremony of the waters of jealousy, where the curse that was written in the book was to be *blotted out* with the bitter water. See the note on Num. v. 23. *When the times of refreshing shall come.* "That the times of refreshing may come." *Anapsyxis* signifies a "breathing time, or respite," and may be here applied to the space that elapsed from this time till the destruction of Jerusalem by the Romans. This was a time of respite, which God gave them to repent of their sins, and be converted to himself. Taking the word in the sense of refreshment in general, it may mean the whole reign of the Kingdom of grace, and the blessings which God gives here below to all genuine believers, peace, love, joy, and communion with himself. See on v. 21.

20. *Which before was preached unto you.* Instead of *before . . . preached*, some MSS. have, who was "before designed, or appointed"; and this is without doubt the true reading. Christ crucified was the Person whom God had from the beginning "appointed" or "designed" for the Jewish people.

21. *Whom the heaven must receive.* He has already appeared upon earth, and accomplished the end of His appearing; He has ascended unto heaven to administer the concerns of His kingdom, and there He shall continue till He comes again to judge the quick and the dead.

25. *Ye are the children of the prophets.* As you are the children or disciples of the prophets, you are bound to believe their predictions, and obey their precepts; and not only so, but you are entitled to their promises. Your duty and your interest go hand in hand; and there is not a blessing contained in the covenant which was made with your fathers but belongs to you. Now as this covenant respected the blessings of the gospel, you must believe in Jesus Christ, in order to be put in possession of all those blessings.

26. *Unto you first God, having raised up.* As you are the children of the prophets and of the covenant, the first offers of salvation belong to you, and God thus makes them to you. God designs to *bless you;*

MATTHEW HENRY

Christ had his mission: *God raised up his Son Jesus, and sent him.* God raised him up when he constituted him a prophet. He sent him to bear witness of the truth, sent him to seek and save lost souls. Some refer *the raising of him up to the resurrection.* Though having raised him up, he seemed presently to take him from us, yet he did really send him afresh to us in his gospel and Spirit. [2] To whom he was sent: "*Unto you first,* you that are *the children of the prophets, and of the covenant.*" The personal ministry of Christ, as that of the prophets, was confined to the Jews; *to the lost sheep of the house of Israel,* and he forbade the disciples he then sent forth to go any further. After his resurrection, he was to be preached indeed to all nations, but they must *begin at Jerusalem,* Luke xxiv. 47. And, when they went to other nations, they first preached to the Jews they found therein. So far were they from being excluded for their putting Christ to death, that, when he is risen, he is first sent to them. [3] On what errand he was sent: "*He is sent to you first, to bless you;* not to condemn you, as you deserve, but to justify you." Christ's errand into the world was to bless us, and, when he left the world, he left a blessing behind him, for he was *parted from the disciples as he blessed them,* Luke xxiv. 51. It is by Christ that God sends blessings to us, and through him only we can expect to receive them. The great blessing was the turning of us away from our iniquities, that we may be qualified to receive all other blessings. Sin is that to which naturally we cleave; the design of divine grace is to turn us from it, nay, to turn us against it, that we may not only forsake it, but hate it. "Therefore, do your part: *repent, and be converted,* because Christ is ready to do his, *in turning you from your iniquities,* and so blessing you."

JAMIESON, FAUSSET, BROWN

in turning away every one of you from his iniquities—i.e., 'Hitherto we have all been looking too much for a Messiah who should shed outward blessings upon the nation generally, and through it upon the world. But we have learned other things, and now announce to you that the great blessing with which Messiah has come laden is the turning away of every one of you from his iniquities.' With what divine skill does the apostle, founding on resistless facts, here drive home to the conscience of his auditors their guilt in crucifying the Lord of Glory; then soothe their awakened minds by assurances of forgiveness on turning to the Lord, and a glorious future as soon as this shall come to pass, to terminate with the Personal Return of Christ from the heavens whither He has ascended; ending all with warnings, from their own Scriptures, to submit to Him if they would not perish, and calls to receive from Him the blessings of salvation.

ADAM CLARKE

but it is by *turning away every one of you from his iniquities.* The salvation promised in the covenant is a salvation from sin, not from the Romans; and no man can have his sin blotted out who does not turn away from it.

MATTHEW HENRY

CHAPTER 4

Verses 1–4

We have here the powers of darkness appearing against them to put a stop to them. Let Christ's servants be ever so resolute, Satan's agents will be spiteful; and therefore, let Satan's agents be ever so spiteful, Christ's servants ought to be resolute.

I. The apostles, Peter and John, went on in their work, and did not labour in vain.

1. The preachers faithfully deliver the doctrine of Christ: *They spoke unto the people, v.* 1. *They taught the people;* taught those that as yet did not believe, for their conviction and conversion; and taught those that did believe, for their comfort and establishment. *They preached through Jesus the resurrection from the dead.* The doctrine of the resurrection of the dead was verified in Jesus. They preached the resurrection of Christ as their warrant for what they did. It is secured by him to all believers. This *they preached through Jesus Christ,* attainable through him, and through him only. They meddled not with matters of state, but kept to their business, and preached to the people heaven as their end and Christ as their way.

2. The hearers cheerfully receive it (*v.* 4): *Many of those who heard the word believed, to the number of about five thousand.* Though the preachers were persecuted, the word prevailed; for sometimes the church's suffering days have been her growing days: the days of her infancy were so.

II. The chief priests and their party did what they could to crush them; their hands were tied awhile, but their hearts were not in the least changed. 1. Who they were that appeared against the apostles. They were *the priests.* With them was joined *the captain of the temple,* who, it is supposed, was a Roman officer. Still here were both Jews and Gentiles confederate against Christ. *The Sadducees* also, who denied *the being of spirits* and *the future state,* were zealous against them. 2. How they stood affected to the apostles' preaching: *They were grieved that they taught the people, v.* 2. It grieved them, both that the gospel doctrine was preached, and that the people were so ready to hear it. It vexed them to see that his gospel got ground, instead of losing it. Miserable is their case to whom the glory of Christ's kingdom is a grief. It grieved them that the apostles *preached through Jesus the resurrection from the dead.* The Sadducees were grieved that the resurrection from the dead was preached; for they opposed that doctrine. The chief priests were grieved that they preached the resurrection of the dead through Jesus; they would rather give up that important article than have it preached and proved to be through Jesus. 3. How far they proceeded against the apostles (*v.* 3): *They laid hands on them,* and *put them in hold* until the next day. See how God trains up his servants for sufferings

JAMIESON, FAUSSET, BROWN

CHAPTER 4

Vss. 1-13. PETER AND JOHN BEFORE THE SANHEDRIM. **4. the number of the men**—or males, exclusive of women; though the word sometimes includes both. **about five thousand**—and this in Jerusalem, where the means of detecting the imposture or crushing the fanaticism, if such it had been, were within everyone's reach, and where there was every inducement to sift it to the bottom.

1-12. the captain—of the Levitical guard—**of the temple**—annoyed at the disturbance created around it. **and the Sadducees**—who "say that there is no resurrection" (ch. 23:8), irritated at the apostles "preaching through [rather, 'in'] Jesus the resurrection from the dead"; for the resurrection of Christ, if a fact, effectually overthrew the Sadducean doctrine.

ADAM CLARKE

CHAPTER 4

4. *The number . . . was about five thousand.* That is, as I understand the passage, the 120 which were converted before Pentecost, the 3,000 converted at Pentecost, and 1,880 converted since the conversion of the 3,000, making in the whole 5,000, or *about* that number.

1. *The priests.* These persons had evidenced the most implacable enmity against Christ from the beginning. *The Sadducees.* Whose whole system was now in danger by the preaching of the resurrection of Christ; for they believed not in the immortality of the soul nor in any future world.

2. *Being grieved.* They were "thoroughly fatigued" with the continuance of this preaching; their minds suffered more labor, through vexation at the success of the apostles, than the bodies of the apostles did in their fatiguing exercise of preaching during the whole day.

A. T. ROBERTSON:

"The captain of the temple" (*ho strategos tou hierou*). Twenty-four bands of Levites guarded the temple, one guard at a time. They watched the gates. The commander of each band was called captain (*strategos*). Josephus names this captain of the temple police next to the high priest (*War.* VI. 5, 3). "The Sadducees" (*hoi Saddoukaioi*). Most of the priests were Sadducees now and all the chief priests since John Hyrcanus I deserted the Pharisees (Josephus, *Ant.* XVII. 10, 6; XVIII. 1, 4; XX. 9, 1). The Sadducees were slow to line up with the Pharisees against Jesus, but they now take the lead against Peter and John. "Came upon them" (*epestesan autois*). Second aorist active indicative (intransitive). Burst upon them suddenly or stood by them in a hostile attitude here (Luke 20:1; 24:4; Acts 6:12; 17:5; 22:20; 23:11).—*Word Pictures in the New Testament*

MATTHEW HENRY

by degrees; now they resist unto bonds only, but afterwards to blood.

Verses 5–14

We have here the trial of Peter and John before the judges of the ecclesiastical court.

I. Here is the court set. An extraordinary court, it should seem, was called on purpose upon this occasion. 1. The time when the court sat (*v.* 5)—*on the morrow.* They adjourned it to the morrow, and no longer; for they were impatient to get them silenced. 2. The place where—in Jerusalem (*v.* 6), where there were so many that looked for redemption before it came, yet there were more that would not look upon it when it did come. 3. The judges of the court. (1) Their general character: they were *rulers, elders,* and *scribes, v.* 5. The scribes were men of learning. The rulers and elders were men in power. The gospel of Christ had both the learning and power of the world against it. (2) The names of some of them, who were most considerable. Here were Annas and Caiaphas, ringleaders in this persecution; Annas the president of the sanhedrim, and Caiaphas the high priest (though Annas is here called so). However they were both equally malignant against Christ and his gospel. There were others likewise that were *of the kindred of the high priest,* who having dependence on him, would be sure to say as he said. Great relations, and not good, have been a snare to many.

II. The prisoners are arraigned, *v.* 7. They are brought to the bar; they *set them in the midst,* for the sanhedrim sat in a circle. The question they asked them was, "*By what power, or by what name, have you done this?* Who commissioned you to preach such a doctrine as this, and empowered you to work such a miracle as this?" They knew very well that they preached Jesus (*v.* 2), yet they asked them, to tease them, and try if they could get anything out of them that looked criminal.

III. The plea they put in, not so much to clear and secure themselves as to advance the name and honour of their Master.

1. By whom this plea was drawn up: it was dictated by the Holy Ghost. The apostles set themselves to preach Christ and then Christ made good to them his promise, that the Holy Ghost should *give them in that same hour what they should speak.* Christ's faithful advocates shall never want instructions, Mark xiii. 11.

2. To whom it was given in: Peter addresses himself to the judges of the court, as the *rulers of the people, and elders of* Israel; for the wickedness of those in power does not divest them of their power, but the consideration of the power they are entrusted with should prevail to divest them of their wickedness.

3. What the plea is.

(1) What they did was in the name of Jesus Christ, which was a direct answer to the question the court asked them (*v.* 9, 10): "*If we this day be examined* for *a good deed done to the impotent man, by what means,* or by whom, *he is made whole,* we have an answer ready. *Be it known to you all,* and not to you only, but *to all the people of Israel that by the name of Jesus Christ, whom you crucified,* and *whom God hath raised from the dead, even by him doth this man stand here before you whole,* a monument of the power of the Lord Jesus." He justifies what he and his colleague had done in curing the lame man. It was a *good deed.* "Now, if we be reckoned with for this good deed, we have no reason to be ashamed. Let those be ashamed who bring us into trouble for it." It is no new thing for good men to suffer ill for doing well. He transfers all the praise and glory of this good deed to Jesus Christ. "It is by him, and not by any power of ours, that this man is cured. Let the Lord alone be exalted, no matter what becomes of us." He charges it upon the judges themselves, that they had been the murderers of this Jesus: "It is he *whom you crucified.*" He endeavours to convince them of sin, of that sin which was most likely to startle conscience—their putting Christ to death. Peter will miss no occasion to tell them of it. He attests the resurrection of Christ as the strongest testimony for him, and against his persecutors: "God *raised him from the dead*; they took away his life, but God gave it to him again." He preaches this to all the bystanders: "*Be it known to you all,* to *all the people of Israel,* that wonders are wrought in the name of Jesus, not by repeating it as a charm, but believing in it as a divine revelation of grace and goodwill to men.

(2) The name of this Jesus is that name alone by which we can be saved. It is not an indifferent thing, but of absolute necessity, that people believe in this name, and call upon it. We are obliged to it in duty to God, and in compliance with his designs (*v.* 11): "*This is the stone which was set at nought of*

JAMIESON, FAUSSET, BROWN

5. their rulers . . .—This was a regular meeting of the Sanhedrim (see on Matt. 2:4).

6. Annas . . . and Caiaphas—(See on Luke 3:2). **John and Alexander**—of whom nothing is known.

7. By what power or . . . name have ye done this—thus admitting the reality of the miracle, which afterwards they confess themselves unable to deny (vs. 16).

8. Then, filled with the Holy Ghost, said—(See Mark 13:11; Luke 21:15).

10. Be it known unto you . . . and to all the people of Israel—as if emitting a formal judicial testimony to the entire nation through its rulers now convened. **by the name of Jesus . . .**—(See on ch. 3:13, etc). **even by him doth this man stand before you whole**—for from vs. 14 it appears that the healed man was at that moment before their eyes.

ADAM CLARKE

5. *Their rulers, and elders, and scribes.* Those with the high priest, Annas, formed the Sanhedrin, or grand council of the Jews.

6. *Annas.* Though this man, was not now actually in the office of high priest, yet he had possessed it for eleven years, bore the title all his life, and had the honor of seeing five of his sons fill that eminent place after him—an honor that never happened to any other person from the commencement of the Mosaic institution. *And Caiaphas.* He was son-in-law to Annas, John xviii. 13; was now high priest, and the same who, a short time before, condemned Christ to be crucified. *And John.* Dr. Lightfoot conjectures, with great probability, that this was Jochanan ben Zaccai, who was very famous at that time in the Jewish nation. *And Alexander.* This was probably Alexander Lysimachus, one of the richest Jews of his time, who made great presents to the Temple and was highly esteemed by King Agrippa. *Of the kindred of the high priest.* Or rather, "of the race of the high priests," i.e., of the family out of which the high priests were chosen. It may, however, comprehend those who belonged to the families of Annas and Caiaphas, and all who were connected with the sacerdotal family. Luke distinctly mentions all these to show how formidable the enemies were against whom the infant Church of Christ had to contend.

7. *By what power, or by what name, have ye done this?* It seems that this council were convinced that the lame man was miraculously healed, but it is very likely that they believed the whole to be the effect of magic; and as all intercourse with familiar spirits, and all spells, charms, etc., were unlawful, they probably hoped that on examination this business would come out, and that then these disturbers of their peace would be put to death. Hence they inquired *by what power,* by what supernatural energy; or *in what name,* by what mode of incantation; and who is the spirit you invoke, in order to do these things?

8. *Then Peter, filled with the Holy Ghost.* Who guided him into all truth, and raised him far above the fear of man, placing him in a widely different state of mind to that in which he was found when, in the hall of Caiaphas, he denied his Master through fear of a servant girl. But now was fulfilled the promise of Christ, Matt. x. 18-20: "And ye shall be brought before governors and kings for my sake . . . but . . . take no thought how or what ye shall speak . . . For it is not ye that speak, but the Spirit of your Father which speaketh in you."

10. *By the name of Jesus Christ of Nazareth.* This was a very bold declaration in the presence of such an assembly, but he felt he stood on good ground. The cure of the lame man the day before was notorious. His long infirmity was well-known; his person could be easily identified; and he was now standing before them whole and sound. They themselves therefore could judge whether the miracle was true or false. But the reality of it was not questioned, nor was there any difficulty about the instruments that were employed; the only question was, *How* have you done this? and in *whose name?* Peter immediately answers, We have done it in the name of Jesus of Nazareth, whom *ye crucified,* and whom God hath *raised from the dead.*

MATTHEW HENRY

you builders, you that are *the rulers of the people, and the elders of Israel*, that should be the builders of the church. Here was a stone offered you, to be put in the chief place of the building; but you rejected it, threw it by as good for nothing. But this stone is *now become the head of the corner*." Probably St. Peter here chose to make use of this quotation because Christ had himself made use of it not long before this, Matt. xxi. 42. Scripture is a tried weapon in our spiritual conflicts: let us therefore stick to it. We are obliged to it for our own interest. We cannot be saved but by Jesus Christ (*v.* 12): *Neither is there salvation in any other*. As there is no other name by which diseased bodies can be cured, so there is no other by which sinful souls can be saved. Our salvation is our chief concern. Our salvation is not in ourselves; we can destroy ourselves, but we cannot save ourselves. This is the honour of Christ's name, that it is the only name whereby we must be saved. This name is *given*. God has appointed it. It is given *under heaven*. He has all power both in the upper and in the lower world. It is given *among men*, who need salvation. We may be saved by his name, and we cannot be saved by any other. How far those may find favour with God who have not the knowledge of Christ, yet live up to the light they have, it is not our business to determine. Whatever saving favour such may receive it is upon the account of Christ, and for his sake only; so that still *there is no salvation in any other*.

IV. The stand that the court was put to, *v.* 13, 14.

1. They could not deny the cure of the lame man to be both a good deed and a miracle. They had *nothing to say against it* (*v.* 14).

2. They could not face down Peter and John. This was a miracle not inferior to the cure of the lame man. They see *the boldness of Peter and John*, *v.* 13. They appeared not only undaunted by the rulers, but daring and daunting to them. The courage of Christ's faithful confessors has often been the confusion of their cruel persecutors. (1) What increased their wonder: *They perceived that they were unlearned and ignorant men*. They enquired and found that they were born in Galilee, that they were bred fishermen, and had no learned education. And yet speak to them of the Messiah and his kingdom, and they speak so pertinently and so fluently, and are so ready in the scriptures that the most learned judge upon the bench is not able to answer them. They were *ignorant men*—men that had not any public character or employment, which made them wonder to see what freedom they took. (2) What made their wonder in a great measure to cease: they *took knowledge of them that they had been with Jesus*. When they understood that *they had been with Jesus* they knew what to impute their boldness to. Those that *have been with Jesus* should conduct themselves, in everything, so that those who converse with them may *take knowledge of them that they have been with Jesus*. One may know that they have been in the mount by the shining of their faces.

Verses 15–22

We have here the issue of the trial. They came off now with flying colours.

I. Here is the consultation of the court and their proceeding thereupon.

1. The prisoners were ordered to withdraw (*v.* 15): They *commanded them to go aside out of the council*, willing enough to get clear of them (they spoke so home to their consciences). The designs of Christ's enemies are carried on in close cabals, as if they would hide their counsels from the Lord.

2. A debate arose upon this matter: *They conferred among themselves*. The question proposed was, *What shall we do to these men? v.* 16. If they would have yielded to the convincing commanding power of truth, it had been easy to say what they should do to these men. But, when men will not be persuaded to do what they should do, it is no marvel that they are ever and anon at a loss what to do.

3. They came at last to a resolution, in two things: (1) That it was not safe to punish the apostles. Now they could not find how they might punish Peter and John, *because of the people*. They knew it would be an unrighteous thing to punish them, and therefore should have been restrained from it by the fear of God; but they considered it only as a dangerous thing, and therefore were held in from it only by the fear of *the people*. [1] The people were convinced of the truth of the miracle; it was a *notable miracle—a known miracle*. This was a known instance of the power of Christ, and a proof of his doctrine. That it was wrought for the confirmation of the doctrine they preached, was *manifest to all that dwelt in Jerusalem*: it was an opinion universally received.

JAMIESON, FAUSSET, BROWN

11. This is the stone which was set at naught of you builders . . .—This application of Psalm 118:22, already made by our Lord Himself before some of the same "builders" (Matt. 21:42), is here repeated with peculiar propriety after the deed of rejection had been consummated, and the rejected One had, by His exaltation to the right hand of the Majesty on high, become "the head of the corner." **12. Neither is there salvation in any other; for there is none other name under heaven given among men whereby we must be saved**—How sublimely does the apostle, in these closing words, shut up these rulers of Israel to Jesus for salvation, and in what universal and emphatic terms does he hold up his Lord as the one Hope of men!

13-17. perceived that they were unlearned and ignorant men—i.e., uninstructed in the learning of the Jewish schools, and of the common sort; men in private life, untrained to teaching. **took knowledge of them that they had been with Jesus**—recognized them as having been in His company; remembering possibly, that they had seen them with Him [MEYER, BLOOMFIELD, ALFORD]; but, more probably, perceiving in their whole bearing what identified them with Jesus: i.e., 'We thought we had got rid of Him; but lo! He reappears in these men, and all that troubled us in the Nazarene Himself has yet to be put down in these His disciples.' What a testimony to these primitive witnesses! Would that the same could be said of their successors!

16. a notable miracle . . . done by them is manifest to all . . . in Jerusalem; and we cannot deny it—And why should ye wish to deny it, O ye rulers, but that ye hate the light, and will not come to the light lest your deeds should be reproved?

ADAM CLARKE

11. *This is the stone which was set at nought of you builders*. By your rejection and crucifixion of Jesus Christ you have fulfilled one of your own prophecies, Ps. cxviii. 22; and as one part of this prophecy is now so literally fulfilled, you may rest assured, so shall the other; and this rejected *stone* shall speedily become *the head* stone *of the corner*.

12. *For there is none other name*. Not only no other person, but no *name* except that divinely appointed one, Matt. i. 21, by which salvation from sin can be expected—*none* given *under heaven*—no other means ever devised by God himself for the salvation of a lost world.

14. *They could say nothing against it*. They could not gainsay the apostolic doctrine, for that was supported by the miraculous fact before them. If the doctrine be false, the man cannot have been miraculously healed; if the man be miraculously healed, then the doctrine must be true that it is by the name of Jesus of Nazareth that he has been healed.

13. *The boldness of Peter and John*. The "freedom and fluency" with which they spoke; for they spoke now from the immediate influence of the Holy Ghost, and their word was with power. *That they were unlearned and ignorant men*. *Agrammatoi*, persons without literature, not brought up in nor given to literary pursuits—*and ignorant, idiotai*, persons in private life, brought up in its occupations alone. It does not mean ignorance in the common acceptation of the term, and our translation is very improper. In no sense of the word could any of the apostles be called *ignorant men*; for though their spiritual knowledge came all from heaven, yet in all other matters they seem to have been men of good, sound, strong common sense. *They took knowledge of them* may imply that they got information that they had been disciples of Christ, and probably they might have seen them in our Lord's company. *That they had been with Jesus*. Had they not had His teaching, the present company would soon have confounded them; but they spoke with so much power and authority that the whole Sanhedrin was confounded.

16. *A notable miracle hath been done*. A miracle has been wrought, and this miracle is "known," and acknowledged to be such. All Jerusalem knew that he was lame—lame from his birth, and that he had long begged at the Beautiful Gate of the Temple; and now all

G. CAMPBELL MORGAN:

What impression did they make upon the council? The impression they made was "that they had been with Jesus." Men filled with the Spirit always make that impression. That is the impression which the filling of the Spirit creates. If a man shall tell me he has received specific gifts at some specific hour which he describes, and the impression he makes upon me is antagonistic to the mind of Jesus, I know that he is not filled with the Spirit. The word "ignorant" used to describe these men is a little unfortunate; "plebeian" would better convey the idea. They were unlearned and plebeian men, that is, men of the common class. But they had boldness of speech, and boldness does not merely mean braveness, but clarity, clearness of statement.

On another occasion when Jesus was talking in the metropolitan center of the learning of His time, they said: "How knoweth this man letters, having never learned?" This puzzle was repeated in the case of Peter and John. Notice the mistake they made. This was the result of their own philosophy. They spoke of the men as having been with Jesus, in a past tense. What was the truth? Chirst was in the men, and speaking through the men; and the similarity which they detected was not that lingering from contact with a lost teacher, but that created by the presence of the living Christ.

Then followed the conference. The prisoners were excluded; and we see the measure of the intelligence of the Sanhedrin. First we note their discovery of the relation of Peter and John to Jesus, and the certainty of the miracle, and their decision not to attempt to deny it. We see also the measure of their ignorance in their decision to threaten these men. Imagine any court threatening a man who is filled with the Holy Spirit. But, of course, there was no Holy Spirit according to their philosophy, and therefore that was the proper thing to do. If one man be threatened by a Tribunal, composed of the forces of culture, there is little hope of him; but if that man be filled with the Holy Spirit, he will challenge the whole company, and the victory will be with him.

—*The Acts of the Apostles*

MATTHEW HENRY

They themselves, with all the craftiness and all the effrontery they had, *could not deny it* to be a true miracle; everybody would have hooted at them if they had. They could easily deny it to their own consciences, but not to the world. [2] All men *glorified God for that which was done*. Even those that were not persuaded by it to believe in Christ could not but give praise to God for it.

(2) That it was nevertheless necessary to silence them for the future, *v.* 17, 18. All their care is that the doctrine of Christ *spread no further among the people*; as if that healing institution were a plague begun, the contagion of which must be stopped. To prevent the further spreading of this doctrine, [1] They charge the apostles never to preach it any more, that *no man speak at all nor teach in the name of Jesus*, *v.* 18. "Not only that you do not preach this doctrine publicly, but that you *speak henceforth to no man*, not to any particular person privately, *in this name*," *v.* 17. There is not a greater service done to the devil's kingdom than the silencing of faithful ministers, and putting those under a bushel that are the lights of the world. [2] They threaten them if they do: it is at their peril. Christ had not only charged them to preach the gospel to every creature, but had promised to bear them out in it. Those who know how to put a just value upon Christ's promises know how to put a just contempt upon the world's threatenings.

II. Here is the courageous resolution of the prisoners to go on in their work, and their declaration of this resolution, *v.* 19, 20. Peter and John jointly put in the answer: "*Whether it be right in the sight of God to hearken unto you more than unto God, judge you; for we cannot forbear speaking the things which we have seen and heard.*" The prudence of the serpent would have directed them to be silent. But the boldness of the lion directed them thus to set their persecutors at defiance. They justify themselves in it with two things: 1. The command of God: "You charge us not to preach the gospel; he has charged us to preach it; now whom must we obey, God or you?" Nothing can be more absurd than to hearken unto weak and fallible men more than unto a God that is infinitely wise and holy. The case is so plain and self-evident, that we will venture to leave it to yourselves to judge of it. Can you think it *right in the sight of God* to break a divine command in obedience to a human injunction? 2. The convictions of their consciences. They *could not but speak those things which they had seen and heard.* (1) They felt the influence of it upon themselves, what a blessed change it had wrought upon them. Those speak the doctrine of Christ best that have felt the power of it. (2) They knew the importance of it to others. They look with concern upon perishing souls, and know that they cannot escape eternal ruin but by Jesus Christ, and therefore will be faithful to them in giving them warning. They are things *which we have seen and heard*, and therefore are fully assured of ourselves: and things which we only have seen and heard, and therefore, if we do not publish them, who will? Who can?

III. Here is the discharge of the prisoners (*v.* 21): *They further threatened them*, and then *let them go*. 1. Because they durst not contradict the people, who *glorified God for that which was done*. As rulers by the ordinance of God are made a terror and restraint to wicked people, so people are sometimes by the providence of God made a terror and restraint to wicked rulers. 2. Because they could not contradict the miracle: *For* (*v.* 22) *the man was above forty years old on whom this miracle of healing was shown*. The miracle was so much the greater, he having been lame *from his mother's womb, ch.* iii. 2. If those that have been long accustomed to evil, are cured of their spiritual impotency to good, the power of divine grace is therein so much the more magnified. The truth of it was so much the better attested; for *the man being above forty years old*, he was able when he was asked, to *speak for himself*.

Verses 23–31

We hear no more at present of the chief priests, but are to attend those *two witnesses*.

I. Their return to their brethren (*v.* 23): *Being let go, they went to their own company.* As soon as ever they were at liberty, they went to their old friends. 1. Though God had highly honoured them, in calling them out to be his witnesses, yet they were not puffed up with the honour done them, but *went to their own company*. No advancement in gifts or usefulness should make us think ourselves above either the duties or the privileges of the communion of saints. 2. Though their enemies had severely threatened them, yet they *went to their own company*. Christ's followers do best in company, provided it be in their own com-

JAMIESON, FAUSSET, BROWN

17. But that it spread no further . . . let us straitly—strictly—**threaten . . . that they speak henceforth to no man in this name**—Impotent device! Little knew they the fire that was burning in the bones of those heroic disciples.

18-22. Whether it be right . . . to hearken to you more than . . . God, judge ye. 20. For we cannot but speak the things which we have seen and heard—There is here a wonderful union of sober, respectful appeal to the better reason of their judges, and calm, deep determination to abide the consequences of a constrained testimony, which betokens a power above their own resting upon them, according to promise.

21. finding nothing how they might punish them, because of the people—not at a loss for a pretext, but at a loss how to do it so as not to rouse the opposition of the people.

23-37. Peter and John, Dismissed from the Sanhedrin, Report the Proceedings to the Assembled Disciples—They Engage in Prayer—The Astonishing Answer and Results. **23-30. being let go, they went to their own company**—Observe the two opposite classes, representing the two interests which were about to come into deadly conflict.

ADAM CLARKE

Jerusalem knew that he was healed, and there was no means by which such a self-evident fact could be disproved.

17. *But that it spread no further.* Not the news of the miraculous healing of the lame man, but the doctrine and influence which these men preached and exerted. More than a thousand people had already professed faith in Christ in consequence of this miracle (see v. 4); and if this teaching should be permitted to go on, probably accompanied with similar miracles, they had reason to believe that all Jerusalem (themselves excepted, who had steeled their hearts against all good) should be converted to the religion of Him whom they had lately crucified. *Let us straitly threaten them.* "Let us threaten them with threatening," a Hebraism, and a proof that Luke has translated the words of the council into Greek, just as they were spoken. *That they speak . . . to no man in this name.* Nothing so ominous to them as the name of Christ crucified, because they themselves had been His crucifiers. On this account they could not bear to hear salvation preached to mankind through Him of whom they had been the betrayers and murderers, and who was soon likely to have no enemies but themselves.

21. *When they had further threatened them.* When they had added to their former threatenings, repeating the former menaces and adding new penalties. *Because of the people.* The people saw the miracle, confessed the finger of God, believed on the Lord Jesus, and thus became converts to the Christian faith; and the converts were now so numerous that the Sanhedrin was afraid to proceed to any extremities, lest an insurrection should be the consequence.

22. *The man was above forty years old.* The disease was of long standing, and consequently the more inveterate; but all difficulties, small or great, yield equally to the sovereign power of God.

23. *They went to their own company.* This was properly the first persecution that had been raised up against the Church since the resurrection of Christ; and as the rest of the disciples must have known that Peter and John had been cast into prison, and that they were to be examined before the Sanhedrin, and knowing the evil disposition of the rulers toward their brethren, they doubtless made joint supplication to God for their safety. In this employment it is likely Peter and John found them on their return from the council, and repeated to them all their treatment, with the threats of the chief priests and elders.

MATTHEW HENRY

pany.

II. The account they gave them of what had passed: They *reported all that the chief priests and elders had said to them.* They related it to them, 1. That they might know what to expect both from men and from God. From men they might expect everything that was terrifying, but from God everything that was encouraging. 2. That they might have it recorded for the confirmation of our faith touching the resurrection of Christ. These apostles told the chief priests to their faces that God had *raised up Jesus from the dead.* They had not the confidence to deny it, but, in the silliest and most sneaking manner imaginable, bade the apostles not to tell anybody of it. 3. That they might now join with them in prayers and praises.

III. Their address to God upon this occasion: *When they heard they lifted up their voice to God with one accord, v.* 24. One in the name of the rest *lifted up his voice to God* and the rest joined with him, *with one mind* (so the word signifies); their hearts went along with him, and so, though but one spoke, they all prayed.

1. Their adoration of God as the Creator of the world (*v.* 24). They *said,* "*O Lord. thou art God our Master and sovereign Ruler*" (so the word signifies), "thou art the God *who hast made heaven and earth, and the sea.*" The heathen worship gods which they have made, we are worshipping the God that made us and all the world. And it is very proper to begin our prayers, as well as our creed, with the acknowledgment of this, that God is the *Father almighty, Maker of heaven and earth, and of all things visible and invisible.* The Christian religion was intended to confirm and improve, not to eclipse nor jostle out, the truths and dictates of natural religion. It is a great encouragement to God's servants that they serve the God that made all things, and is able to strengthen them under all their difficulties.

2. Their reconciling themselves to the present dispensations of Providence, by reflecting upon the Old Testament, *v.* 25, 26. *Thus he spoke by the mouth of his servant David.* Let it not therefore be a surprise to them, for the *scripture must be fulfilled.* It was foretold, Ps. ii. 1, 2. (1) That the heathen would rage at Christ and his kingdom. (2) That the people would imagine all the things that could be against it. (3) That the kings of the earth, particularly, would stand up in opposition to the kingdom of Christ. (4) That the rulers would gather together against God and Christ. Where the power is in many rulers, councils, and senates, they *gather together against the Lord and against his Christ.* What is done against Christ, God takes as done against himself. Christianity was opposed and fought against by them, and yet it made its way.

3. Their representation of the present accomplishment of those predictions. What was foretold we see fulfilled, *v.* 27, 28. It is *of a truth* that Herod and Pilate, the two Roman governors with the *people of Israel,* were *gathered together against thy holy child Jesus whom thou hast anointed.* (1) The wise and holy designs God had concerning Christ. He is here called the *child Jesus.* The word signifies both a son and a servant. He was the Son of God; and yet in the work of redemption he acted as his Father's servant. It was he whom God anointed, and thence he was called the Lord's Christ, *v.* 26. God that anointed Christ determined what should be done to him. He was anointed to be a Saviour, and therefore it was determined he should be a sacrifice to make atonement for sin. He must die. God wisely determined before by what hands it should be done. He must therefore be *delivered into the hands of sinners. God's hand and his counsel determined it.* His hand and his counsel always agree: for *whatsoever the Lord pleased that did he.* (2) The wicked and unholy instruments that were employed in the executing of this design. Herod and Pilate, Gentiles and Jews, who had been at variance with each other, united against Christ. Sin is not the less evil for God's bringing good out of it, but he is by this the more glorified.

4. Their petition with reference to the case at this time.

(1) That God would take cognizance of the malice of their enemies: *Now, Lord, behold their threatenings, v.* 29. And *now, Lord*; there is an emphasis upon the *now.* Then is God's time to appear for his people, when the power of their enemies is most daring and threatening. They do not dictate to God what he shall do, but refer themselves to him. To thee we appeal, *behold their threatenings,* and either tie their hands or turn their hearts. It is a comfort to us that if we be unjustly threatened we may make ourselves easy to spreading the case before the Lord, and leaving it with him.

(2) That God, by his grace, would keep up their

JAMIESON, FAUSSET, BROWN

F. B. MEYER:

Help from on high. Like draws like; Judas went to his own place, and the apostles to their own company. The best answer to threats is prayer. The apostles' one petition just then was for boldness. They scorned to ask for their own safety; it was enough if Jesus was glorified.

What a note of jubilant triumph was in that glorious prayer, offered by this threatened little band! They realized that they were under the special protection of God, who had made the world, had spoken by the prophets, and was the Father of Jesus. They thought that more miracles of healing would promote their cause; but though they did not realize it at the time, their unity, love, hope, willingness to share their goods, coupled with their intrepid bearing, were their most potent arguments. Notice that in their consciousness, it was God's hand that was being stretched out to heal, though their hands were the immediate channel of its beneficent operations. They had been filled before, but they were filled again. It is our privilege to claim repeated infillings to make good our leakage and evaporation.—*Bible Commentary*

24. they lifted up their voice—the assembled disciples, on hearing Peter's report. **with one accord**—the breasts of all present echoing every word of this sublime prayer. **Lord**—See on Luke 2:29. Applied to God, the term expresses absolute authority. **God which hast made heaven and earth**—against whom, therefore, all creatures are powerless.

25. by the mouth of . . . David—to whom the Jews ascribed the 2d Psalm, though anonymous; and internal evidence confirms it. David's spirit sees with astonishment "the heathen, the people, the kings and princes of the earth," in deadly combination against the sway of Jehovah and *His Anointed* (his Messiah, or Christ), and asks "why" it is. This fierce confederacy our praying disciples see in full operation, in the "gathering together of Herod and Pilate, the Gentiles (the Roman authority), and the people of Israel, against God's holy Child ('Servant') Jesus." (See on ch. 3:13). The best ancient copies read, after "were gathered together," *'in this city,'* which probably answers to "upon my holy hill of Zion," in the Psalm.

thy hand and thy counsel determined . . . to be done—i.e., "Thy counsel" determined to be done by "Thy hand."

29. now, Lord, behold their threatenings—Recognizing in the threatenings of the Sanhedrim a declaration of war by the combined powers of the world against their infant cause, they seek not enthusiastically to hide from themselves its critical position, but calmly ask the Lord of heaven and earth to "look upon their threatenings."

ADAM CLARKE

24. *Lord, thou art God.* "Thou, God, art the sovereign Lord." Thy rule is universal, and Thy power unlimited.

26. *Against the Lord, and against his Christ* should be translated "against His Anointed," because it particularly agrees with "whom thou hast anointed," in the succeeding verse.

27. There is a parenthesis in this verse that is not sufficiently noticed. It should be read in connection with v. 28, thus: "For of a truth against thy holy child Jesus, whom thou hast anointed (for to do whatsoever thy hand and thy counsel determined before to be done), both Herod, and Pontius Pilate, with the Gentiles, and the people of Israel, were gathered together." It is evident that what God's *hand and . . . counsel determined before to be done* was not that which Herod, Pontius Pilate, the Gentiles (Romans) and the people of Israel had done and were doing; for then their rage and vain counsel would be such as God himself had determined should take place, which is both impious and absurd. But these gathered together to hinder what God had before determined that His Christ or Anointed should perform; and thus the passage is undoubtedly to be understood. *Were gathered together.* "In this very city" is added by some MSS. This makes the words much more emphatic; in this Thy own city, these different and in all other cases dissentient powers are leagued together against Thine Anointed, and are determined to prevent the accomplishment of Thy purpose.

29. *And now, Lord, behold their threatenings.* It is not against us, but against Thee, that they conspire; it is not to prevent the success of our preaching, but to bring to nought Thy counsel. The whole of their enmity is against Thee. Now, Lord, look upon it; consider this. *And grant unto thy servants.* While we are endeavoring to fulfill Thy counsels, and can do nothing without Thee, sustain our courage, that we may proclaim Thy truth with boldness and irresistible power.

MATTHEW HENRY

spirits: *Grant unto thy servants that with all boldness they may speak thy word.* Their prayer is not, "*Lord, behold their threatenings,* and frighten them," but, "*Behold their threatenings,* and animate us." They do not pray, "Lord, give us a fair opportunity to retire from our work, now that it is become dangerous"; but, "Lord, give us grace to go on in our work, and not to be afraid." Those that are sent on God's errands ought to deliver their message with boldness, not doubting of what they say, nor of being borne out in saying it. God is to be sought unto for an ability to speak his word with boldness. The threatenings of our enemies should rather stir us up to so much the more courage. Are they daring that fight against Christ? For shame, let not us be sneaking that are for him.

(3) That God would still give them power to work miracles for the confirmation of the doctrine they preached: *Lord, grant us boldness, by stretching forth thy hand to heal.* Nothing emboldens faithful ministers more in their work than the tokens of God's presence with them. They pray: *That signs and wonders might be done by the name of the holy child Jesus,* which would be convincing to the people, and confounding to the enemies. It is the honour of Christ that they aim at that the wonders might be done by the name of Jesus.

IV. The gracious answer God gave. God gave them a sign of the acceptance of their prayers (*v.* 31): *When they had prayed, the place was shaken where they were assembled together.* This shaking of the place was designed to awaken and raise their expectations, and to give them a sensible token that God was with them of a truth. This was to show them what reason they had to fear God more, and then they would fear man less. The place was shaken, that their faith might be established and unshaken. God gave them greater degrees of his Spirit. Their prayer, without doubt, was accepted, for it was answered: *They were all filled with the Holy Ghost,* by which they were not only encouraged, but enabled to speak the word of God with boldness. The Holy Ghost taught them not only *what* to speak, but *how* to speak. They were *filled with the Holy Ghost* at the bar (*v.* 8), and now *filled with the Holy Ghost* in the pulpit. We have here an instance of the performance of that promise, *that God will give the Holy Spirit to those that ask him* (Luke xi. 13), for it was in answer to prayer that *they were filled with the Holy Ghost*: we have also an example of the improvement of that gift; have it and use it, use it and have more of it. *They spoke the word with all boldness.* Talents must be traded with, not buried.

Verses 32–37

I. The disciples loved one another dearly. *The multitude of those that believed were of one heart, and of one soul* (*v.* 32). 1. There were multitudes that believed; even in Jerusalem *there were three thousand* converted on one day, and *five thousand* on another, and, besides these, *there were added to the church daily.* The increase of the church is the glory of it. 2. They *were all of one heart, and of one soul.* Though there were many, very many, of different ages, tempers, and conditions, in the world, they were unanimous in the faith of Christ, and, being all *joined to the Lord, they were joined to one another in holy love.* This was the blessed fruit of Christ's dying precept to his disciples, to *love one another,* and his dying prayer for them, *that they all might be one. They were all of one heart, and one soul.* Thus it was then, and we may not despair of seeing it so again.

II. The ministers went on in their work with great vigour and success (*v.* 33). *With great power gave the apostles witness of the resurrection of the Lord Jesus.* The resurrection of Christ, rightly understood, will let us into the great mysteries of religion. By the great power wherewith the apostles attested the resurrection may be meant the great vigour, spirit, and courage, with which they published this doctrine; they did it not softly and diffidently, but with liveliness and resolution. Or it may mean the miracles which they wrought to confirm their doctrine. God himself, in them, *bearing witness* too.

III. The beauty of the Lord our God shone upon them: *Great grace was upon them all, grace* that had something *great* in it (magnificent and very extraordinary) *was upon them all.* Christ poured out abundance of *grace upon them.* There were evident fruits of this grace in all they said and did. Some think it includes the favour they were in with the people. Everyone saw a beauty and excellency in them, and respected them.

IV. They were very liberal to the poor.

1. They insisted not upon property, which even children seem to have a sense of and a jealousy for,

JAMIESON, FAUSSET, BROWN

that with all boldness they may speak thy word—Rising above self, they ask only fearless courage to testify for their Master, and divine attestation to their testimony by miracles of healing, etc., in His name.

31-37. place was shaken—glorious token of the commotion which the Gospel was to make (ch. 17:6; cf. 16:26), and the overthrow of all opposing powers in which this was to issue.

they were all filled with the Holy Ghost, and spake . . .—The Spirit rested upon the entire community, first, in the very way they had asked, so that they "spake the word with boldness" (vss. 29, 31); next, in melting down all selfishness, and absorbing even the feeling of individuality in an intense and glowing realization of Christian unity. The community of goods was but an outward expression of this, and natural in such circumstances.

33. with great power—effect on men's minds. **great grace was upon them all**—The grace of God copiously rested on the whole community.

ADAM CLARKE

30. *By stretching forth thine hand to heal.* Show that it is Thy truth which we proclaim, and confirm it with miracles, and show how highly Thou hast magnified Thy Son, Jesus, whom they have despised and crucified, by causing signs and wonders to be wrought in His name. *Thy holy child Jesus* should be translated "Thy holy Servant," as in v. 25, "thy servant David," not "Thy child David." The word is the same in both places.

31. *The place was shaken.* This earthquake was an evidence of the presence of God, and a most direct answer to their prayer, as far as that prayer concerned themselves. The earthquake proclaimed the stretched-out arm of God, and showed them that resistance against His counsels and determinations must come to nought.

***And they were all filled with the Holy Ghost.* And in consequence of this, *they spake the word of God with boldness*—a pointed answer to a second part of their request, v. 29. Though these disciples had received the Holy Spirit on the Day of Pentecost, yet they were capable of larger communications; and what they had then received did not preclude the necessity of frequent supplies on emergent occasions. Neither apostle nor private Christian can subsist in the divine life without frequent influences from on high.**

32. *The multitude of them that believed.* The whole 5,000, mentioned in v. 4, and probably many others who had been converted by the ministry of the other apostles since that time. *Were of one heart and of one soul.* Were in a state of the most perfect friendship and affection. *They had all things common.* See the notes on chap. ii. 44. See below, v. 34.

33. *With great power gave the apostles witness.* This power they received from the Holy Spirit, who enabled them, "with striking miracles," to give proof of *the resurrection of the Lord Jesus;* for this is the point that was particularly to be proved. That He was slain and buried, all knew; that He rose again from the dead, many knew; but it was necessary to give such proofs as should convince and confound all. *Great grace was upon them all.* They all received much of the favor or grace of God, and they had much favor with all who feared God. In both these ways this clause may be understood.

MATTHEW HENRY

and which worldly people triumph in. *No man said that aught of the things which he possessed was his own, v.* 32. They did not take away property, but they were indifferent to it. They did not call it their own, because they had, in affection, forsaken all for Christ. We can call nothing our own but sin. *No man said that what he had was his own;* for he was *ready to distribute, willing to communicate.* Those that had estates were not solicitous to lay up, but very willing to lay out, and would straiten themselves to help their brethren. *Meum—mine,* and *tuum—thine,* are the great makebates. Men's holding their own, and grasping at more than their own, are the rise of wars and fightings.

2. They abounded in charity, *they had all things common;* for (*v.* 34) *there was not any among them that lacked.* As there were many poor that received the gospel, so there were some rich that were able to maintain them, and the grace of God made them willing. The gospel hath laid *all things common,* not so that the poor are allowed to rob the rich, but so that the rich are appointed to relieve the poor.

3. They did many of them sell their estates: *As many as had possession of lands or houses sold them, v.* 34. We are here told what they did with the money that was so raised: They *laid it at the apostles' feet*—they left it to them to be disposed of as they thought fit. *Distribution was made unto every man according as he had need.* Great care ought to be taken in the distribution of public charity. That it be given to such as have need. Those who have real need, above all, those that are reduced to want for well doing ought to be taken care of, and provided for. That it be given *to every man according as he has need,* without partiality or respect of persons.

Here is one particular person mentioned: *Barnabas,* afterwards Paul's colleague. [1] The account here given concerning him, *v.* 36. His name was *Joses;* he was of *the tribe of Levi.* He was born in Cyprus, a great way off from Jerusalem. Notice is taken of the apostles' changing his name after he associated with them. He was respected by the apostles, who, in token of their value for him, gave him a name, *Barnabas. A son of consolation* (so we read it)—a cheerful Christian, and this enlarged his heart in charity to the poor; eminent for comforting the Lord's people; he had an admirable facility that way. There were two among the apostles that were called *Boanerges—sons of thunder* (Mark iii. 17); but here was a *son of consolation* with them. Each had his several gift. Let the one search the wound, and then let the other heal it and bind it up. [2] Here is an account of his great generosity. This is particularly taken notice of, because of the eminency of his services afterwards in the church of God. Or perhaps this is mentioned because it was a leading card, and an example to others: *He having land, he sold it, brought the money, and laid it at the apostles' feet.* And he lost nothing upon the balance of the account, when he himself was, in effect, numbered among the apostles, by that word of the Holy Ghost, *Separate me Barnabas and Saul for the work whereunto I have called them, ch.* xiii. 2. Thus, for the respect he showed to the apostles as apostles, he had an apostle's reward.

CHAPTER 5

Verses 1–11

The chapter begins with a melancholy *but.* As every man, so every church, in its best state has its *but.* The disciples seemed to be all exceedingly good; *but* there were hypocrites among them. There is a mixture of bad with good in the best societies of this side heaven; tares will grow among the wheat until the harvest. They came up to that perfection which Christ recommended to the rich young man—they *sold what they had, and gave to the poor; but* even that proved a cloak and cover of hypocrisy. The signs and wonders which the apostles wrought were hitherto miracles of mercy; *but* now comes in a miracle of judgment that God may be both loved and feared.

I. The sin of Ananias and Sapphira his wife. 1. They were ambitious of being thought eminent disciples when really they were not true disciples. They *sold a possession, and brought the money to the apostles' feet,* that they might not seem to be behind the very chief of believers. It is possible that hypocrites may deny themselves in one thing, but then it is to serve themselves in another. Ananias and Sapphira would take upon them a profession of Christianity, *and make a fair show in the flesh* with it, when they knew they could not go through with the Christian profession. It is often of fatal consequence for people to go a greater length in profession than their

JAMIESON, FAUSSET, BROWN

35. laid . . . at the apostles' feet—sitting, it may be, above the rest. But the expression may be merely derived from that practice, and here meant figuratively.

36. Joses . . .—This is specified merely as an eminent example of that spirit of generous sacrifice which pervaded all. **son of consolation**—no doubt so surnamed from the character of his ministry. **a Levite**—who, though as a tribe having no inheritance, might and did acquire property as individuals (Deut. 18:8). **Cyprus**—a well-known island in the Mediterranean.

CHAPTER 5

Vss. 1-11. ANANIAS AND SAPPHIRA. "The first trace of a shade upon the bright form of the young Church. Probably among the new Christians a kind of holy rivalry had sprung up, every one eager to place his means at the disposal of the apostles" [OLSHAUSEN]. Thus might the newborn zeal of some outrun their abiding principle, while others might be tempted to seek credit for a liberality which was not in their character.

ADAM CLARKE

34. ***Neither was there any among them that lacked.*** **It was customary with the Jews to call the poor together to eat of the sacrifices; but as the priests were incensed against Christ and Christianity, consequently the Christian poor could have no advantage of this kind. Therefore by making a common stock for the present necessity the poor were supplied; so there was none among them that lacked. This provision therefore of the community of goods, which could be but temporary, was made both suitably and seasonably.**

36. ***The son of consolation.*** **As *paraclesis* signifies "exhortation," as well as *consolation,* and is indeed distinguished from the latter, 1 Cor. xiv. 3, the original name was probably *Bar naba,* or *Bar nebia,* which signifies the "son of prophecy or exhortation." This is certainly one sense which prophecy has in the New Testament; and in this way Barnabas distinguished himself among the apostles. See chap. xi. 23. Barnabas "exhorted them all, that with purpose of heart they would cleave unto the Lord."** ***A Levite, and of the country of Cyprus.*** **Cyprus is an island in the Mediterranean Sea, off Cilicia, and not very distant from the Jewish coast. The Jews were very numerous in that island. Though he was a Levite, he might have had land of his own by private purchase. The Levites, as a tribe, had no land in Israel; but the individuals certainly might make purchases anywhere.**

It is worthy of remark that the two apostles of the Gentiles, though of Jewish extraction, were both born in Gentile countries; Paul in Cilicia, Barnabas in Cyprus. This gave them many advantages: served to remove prejudices from the heathens; and gave them no doubt much facility in the Greek tongue, without which they could have done but little in Asia Minor, nor in most parts of the Roman Empire where they travelled. How admirably does God determine even the place of our birth and the bounds of our habitation! The man whom He calls to His work He will take care to endue with every necessary qualification. And is it too much to say that God never did call a man to preach the gospel whom He did not qualify in such a manner that both the workman and the work should appear to be of God? Some have said that "ignorance is the mother of devotion." Devotion and religion are both scandalized by the saying. Every genuine minister of Christ has an enlightened heart; and to this it is his duty to add a well-cultivated mind. A blockhead never did, and never can, make a minister.

CHAPTER 5

1. ***But a certain man named Ananias.*** **The import of his name, *chananiyah,* the "grace or mercy of the Lord," agrees very ill with his conduct.**

MATTHEW HENRY	JAMIESON, FAUSSET, BROWN	ADAM CLARKE

inward principle will admit of. 2. They were covetous of the wealth of the world, and distrustful of God and his providence: *They sold their land*, and in a pang of zeal, designed to dedicate the whole of the purchase-money to pious uses; but, when the money was received, their heart failed them, and *they kept back part of the price* (*v.* 2), because they loved the money. They could not take God's word that they should be provided for, but thought they would play a wiser part than the rest had done, and lay up for a rainy day. As if there were not an all-sufficiency in God to make up the whole to them. If they had been thorough-paced worldlings, they would not have sold their possession; and, if they had been thorough-paced Christians, they would not have detained part of the price. 3. They thought to deceive the apostles, and make them believe they brought the whole purchase-money. They came and *laid the money at the apostles' feet*, as if it were their all.

II. The indictment of Ananias, which proved both his condemnation and execution for this sin. When he brought the money Peter took him to task about it. He charges him peremptorily with the crime, showing it to him in its own colour, *v.* 3, 4. The Spirit of God in Peter not only discovered the fact but likewise discerned the principle of reigning infidelity in the heart of Ananias, which was at the bottom of it. Had it been a sin of infirmity, through the surprise of a temptation, Peter would have bidden him go home, and repent of his folly. He here showed him,

1. The origin of his sin: *Satan filled his heart;* he not only suggested it to him, and put it into his head, but hurried him on with resolution to do it.

2. The sin itself: *He lied to the Holy Ghost;* a sin of such a heinous nature that he could not have been guilty of it if Satan had not filled his heart. We read it, *to lie unto the Holy Ghost*, which reading is countenanced by *v.* 4, *Thou hast not lied unto men, but unto God.* Ananias told a lie; he told Peter that he had sold a possession and this was the purchase-money. He did as the rest did who brought the whole price, and would be thought to do so, and expected the praise those had that did so. Many are brought to gross lying by reigning pride, and affectation of the applause of men, particularly in works of charity to the poor. Those that boast of good works they never did, or promise good works they never do, or make the good works they do more or better than really they are, come under the guilt of Ananias's lie. He told this lie *to the Holy Ghost*. It was not so much to the apostles as to the Holy Ghost in them that the money was brought, and that was said which was said, *v.* 4, *Thou hast not lied unto men but thou hast lied unto God.*

3. The aggravations of the sin (*v.* 4): *While it remained, was it not thine own? And, after it was sold, was it not in thine own power?* (1) "Thou wast under no temptation *to keep back part of the price*; before it was sold it was thy own, and when it was sold it was in thy own power to dispose of the money at thy pleasure." Or, (2) "Thou wast under no necessity of selling thy land at all, nor bringing any of the money to the apostles' feet. Thou mightest have kept the money, if thou hadst pleased, and the land too." It is better not to vow than to vow and not to pay, so better had it been for him not to have pretended to do the good work than thus to do it by the halves. "*When it was sold, it was in thine own power;* but it was not so when it was vowed." Thus, in giving our hearts to God, we are not admitted to divide them. Satan, like the mother whose own the child was not, would take up with a half; but God will have all or none.

4. All this guilt is charged upon him: *Why hast thou conceived this thing in thine heart?* He is said to have conceived it in his own heart, which shows that we cannot extenuate our sins by laying the fault of them upon the devil; he tempts, but he cannot force. The close of the charge is very high, but very just: *Thou hast not lied unto men, but unto God.* If we think to put a cheat upon God, we shall prove in the end to have put a fatal cheat upon our own souls.

III. The death and burial of Ananias, *v.* 5, 6.

1. He died upon the spot: *Ananias, hearing these words, was speechless:* he had nothing to say for himself; but this was not all. He *fell down, and gave up the ghost.* See the power of the word of God in the mouth of the apostles. As there are those whom the gospel justifies, so there are those whom it condemns. This punishment of Ananias may seem severe, but we are sure it was just. It was a great affront which Ananias put upon the Holy Ghost, as if he could be imposed upon. It was designed to deter others from the like presumptions. The doing of this by the ministry of Peter, who himself with a lie denied his Master, intimates that it

2. kept back part of the price, his wife also being privy to it—The coolness with which they planned the deception aggravated the guilt of this couple. **brought a certain part**—pretending it to be the whole proceeds of the sale.

3-6. why hath Satan filled—'why . . . fill—'why hast thou suffered him to fill'—**thine heart . . .** —so criminally entertaining his suggestion? Cf. vs. 4, "why hast thou conceived this thing in thine heart?" And see John 13:2, 27. **to lie to the Holy Ghost**—to men under His supernatural illumination.

4. While it remained, was it not thine own? and after it was sold, was it not in thine own power?—from which we see how purely voluntary were all these sacrifices for the support of the infant community.

not lied to men but God—to men so entirely the instruments of the directing Spirit that the lie was rather told to Him: language clearly implying both the distinct *personality* and the proper *divinity* of the Holy Ghost. **5 Ananias . . . gave up the ghost . . . great fear came on all that heard these things**—on those without the Christian circle; who, instead of disparaging the followers of the Lord Jesus, as they might otherwise have done on the discovery of such hypocrisy, were awed at the manifest presence of Divinity among them, and the mysterious power of throwing off such corrupt matter which rested upon the young Church.

2. *Kept back part of the price.* Ananias and Sapphira evidently were persons who professed faith in Christ with the rest of the disciples. While all were making sacrifices for the present necessity, they came forward among the rest, pretending to bring all the money they had received for a possession (of what kind we know not) which they had sold. A *part* of this price, however, they kept back, not being willing to trust entirely to the bounty of Providence, as the others did.

3. *Why hath Satan filled thine heart?* The verb which we translate *to fill,* Kypke has showed by many examples to signify to "instigate, excite, impel," and it was a common belief, as well among the heathens as among the Jews and Christians, that when a man did evil he was excited to it by the influence and malice of an evil spirit. *To lie to the Holy Ghost.* "To deceive the Holy Spirit." Every lie is told with the intention to deceive; and they wished to deceive the apostles, and, in effect, that Holy Spirit under whose influence they professed to act. Lying against the Holy Ghost is in the next verse said to be lying against God; therefore the Holy Ghost is *God. To keep back part of the price.* The verb is used by the Greek writers to signify "purloining part of the public money." The word is used here with great propriety, as the money for which the estate was sold was public property, as it was for this purpose alone that the sale was made.

5. *Fell down, and gave up the ghost.* "Falling down, he expired, breathed his last." "Gave up the ghost" is a very improper translation here.

MATTHEW HENRY

was not the resentment of a wrong done to himself; for then he would have forgiven this affront, and endeavoured to bring this offender to repentance; but it was the act of the Spirit of God in Peter: to him the indignity was done, and by him the punishment was inflicted.

2. He was buried immediately, for this was the manner of the Jews (*v.* 6): *The young men wound up* the dead body in grave-clothes, *carried it out* and *buried it.*

IV. The reckoning with Sapphira, the wife of Ananias. *She came in about three hours after,* for *she knew not what had been done.*

1. She was found guilty of sharing with her husband in his sin, by a question that Peter asked her (*v.* 8): *Tell me whether you sold the land for so much?* Saith she, "We had no more, but that was every farthing we received." Ananias and his wife agreed to tell the same story; they thought they might safely stand in the lie, and should gain credit to it. It is sad to see those relations who should quicken one another to that which is good harden one another in that which is evil.

2. Sentence was passed upon her, that she should partake in her husband's doom, *v.* 9.

(1) Her sin is opened: *How is it that you have agreed together to tempt the Spirit of the Lord?* Before he passes sentence he shows her the evil of her sin. They tempted the Spirit of the Lord. They saw that the apostles had the gift of tongues; but had they the gift of discerning spirits? Those that presume upon security and impunity in sin tempt the Spirit of God. They agreed together to do it. It is hard to say which is worse between yoke-fellows and other relations—a discord in good or concord in evil.

(2) Her doom is read: *Behold, the feet of those who have buried thy husband are at the door, and* they *shall carry thee out.*

3. The sentence executed itself. *Then she fell down straightway at his feet.* Some sinners God makes quick work with, while others he bears long with; for which difference, doubtless, there are good reasons; but he is not accountable to us for them. And many instances there are of sudden deaths which are not to be looked upon as the punishment of some gross sin, like this. We must not think that all who die suddenly are sinners above others; perhaps it is in favour to them, that they have a quick passage: however, it is forewarning to all to be always ready. But here it is plain that it was in judgment. Some put the question concerning the eternal state of Ananias and Sapphira, and incline to think that the destruction of the flesh was that *the spirit might be saved in the day of the Lord Jesus.* But secret things belong not to us. It is said, *She fell down at Peter's feet.* The *young men* coming in *found her dead. They carried her out and buried her by her husband.* Some ask whether the apostles kept the money which they did bring. What they brought was not polluted to those to whom they brought it; but what they kept back was polluted to those that kept it back.

V. The impression that this made upon the people. Notice is taken of this in the midst of the story (*v.* 5): *Great fear came upon all that heard these things.* And again (*v.* 11), *Great fear came upon all the church, and upon as many as heard these things.* Those that had joined themselves to the church were thereby struck with an awe of God and of his judgments. It was not a damp or check to their holy joy, but it taught them to be serious in it, and to rejoice with trembling.

Verses 12–16

I. Here is a general account of the miracles which the apostles wrought (*v.* 12): *By the hands of the apostles were many signs and wonders wrought among the people.* God had come out of his place to punish, but now returns to his place, to his mercy-seat again. The miracles they wrought proved their divine mission. They were signs and wonders, such wonders as were confessedly signs of a divine presence and power.

II. We are here told what were the effects of these miracles.

1. The church was hereby kept together: *They were all with one accord in Solomon's porch.* They met in the temple, Solomon's porch. Those who permitted buyers and sellers could not for shame prohibit such preachers and healers there. They all met in public worship. They were there with one accord. The separation of hypocrites should make the sincere cleave so much the closer to each other.

2. It gained the apostles very great respect. *Of the rest* of their company *durst no man join himself to them,* as their equal or an associate with them. All *the people magnified them.* Though the chief priests did all they could to make them contemptible, this did not hinder the people from magnifying them.

JAMIESON, FAUSSET, BROWN

the young men—some of the younger and more active members of the church, not as office-bearers, nor coming forward now for the first time, but who probably had already volunteered their services in making subordinate arrangements. In every thriving Christian community such volunteers may be expected, and will be found eminently useful. **7-11. Tell me whether ye sold the land for so much**—naming the sum.

9. How is it that ye have agreed together—See on vs. 2. **to tempt the Spirit** *try* whether they could escape detection by that omniscient Spirit of whose supernatural presence with the apostles they had had such full evidence.

feet of them that buried thy husband are at the door—How awfully graphic!

10. buried her by her husband—The later Jews buried before sunset of the day of death.

11. great fear on all the church . . .—This effect on the Christian community itself was the chief design of so startling a judgment; which had its counterpart, as the sin itself had, in *Achan* (Josh. 7), while the *time*—at the commencement of a new career—was similar.

12-26. The Progress of the New Cause Leads to the Arrest of the Apostles—They Are Miraculously Delivered from Prison, Resume Their Teaching, But Allow Themselves to Be Conducted before the Sanhedrim. **12. Solomon's Porch**—See on John 10:23.

13-16. of the rest durst no man join himself . . .—Of the unconverted none ventured, after what had taken place, to profess discipleship; but yet their number continually increased.

ADAM CLARKE

6. *The young men arose.* Some of the stout young men belonging to the disciples then present, who were the fittest to undertake a work of this kind, which required considerable bodily exertion. *Buried him.* This was on the same day in which he died. It was a clear case that he was dead, and dead by a judgment of God that would not be revoked.

G. CAMPBELL MORGAN:

This was the true nature of the new conditions. The discerning Spirit was at work, and the atmosphere was such that it was impossible for a man with a lie in his heart to come in without the lie being known and detected. The thing that astonishes and fills us with awe is not the death of Ananias and Sapphira. It is rather that of the purity of the Church that compelled that death; compelled it, not by law and control, but by the atmosphere of the Spirit in which the Church was purified, and in which the Church was wholly and absolutely at the disposal of the Spirit. There was once a flaming sword that guarded the way to the tree of life. How flaming, in the power of holiness, was this atmosphere into which if a man passed with the profession of generosity on his lips and a lie in his heart, he was immediately arrested and smitten. I look back upon the great scene, and it is not the death of a man that fills me with awe, but that of the Church's condition. That little company of believing souls, a growing company all the time, but still comparatively a small company, was the Body of Christ, His instrument for the revealing of His will, and the carrying out of His will. It was dominated by the Spirit, and so was mastered by His love, walked in His light, and was energized by His life. There came into that assembly a man with a lie upon his lips; and in a moment one spokesman of the fellowship addressed him with a faithfulness that could only be the outcome of the Spirit's indwelling, inspiration, and interpretation. Peter had no mixed motive in his heart, he had no desire to retain the patronage of Ananias because he was a wealthy man; but being a man wholly at the disposal of the Spirit for the doing of the work of Christ, his word was that of terrific directness.

—The Acts of the Apostles

10. *Yielded up the ghost.* It was not by Peter's words, nor through Peter's prayers, nor through shame, nor through remorse, that this guilty pair died, but by an immediate judgment of God. It was right in this infant state of the Church to show God's displeasure against deceit, fraud, and hypocrisy. Had this guilty pair been permitted to live after they had done this evil, this long-suffering would have been infallibly abused by others; and instead of leading them who had sinned to repentance might have led them to hardness of heart by causing them to presume on the mercy of God. That hypocrisy may be afraid to show her face, God makes these two an example of His justice.

11. *Great fear came upon all the church.* This judgment answered the end for which it was inflicted; a deeply religious fear occupied every mind, and hypocrisy and deception were banished from this holy assembly.

12. *Solomon's porch.* See the note on John x. 23.

13. *And of the rest durst no man join himself to them.* Who were these called *the rest?* Calmet observes that the Jewish nation was then divided into many different sects, who entertained widely different opinions on various articles. The apostles adopted none of these jarring sentiments, and none of the different sects dared to join themselves to them; neither Pharisees, Sadducees, nor Herodians, as such, were found in this simple, holy Church.

MATTHEW HENRY

The apostles were far from magnifying themselves, and yet the people magnified them; for those that humble themselves shall be exalted, and those honoured that honour God only.

3. The church increased in number (*v.* 14): *Believers were the more added to the Lord*, even *multitudes both of men and women.* They were so far from being deterred by the example that was made of Ananias and Sapphira that they were rather invited by it into a society that kept such a strict discipline. Many have been brought to the Lord, and yet there is room for others to be added to him, added to the number of those that are united to him. Notice is taken of the conversion of *women* as well as *men.* As among those that followed Christ while he was upon earth, so among those that believed on him after he went to heaven, great notice was taken of the good women.

4. The apostles had abundance of patients, and gained abundance of reputation by the cure of them all, *v.* 15, 16. So many *signs and wonders were wrought by the apostles* that all manner of people put in for the benefit of them, both in city and country, and had it. In the city: They *brought forth their sick into the streets.* And they *laid them on beds and couches that at least the shadow of Peter, passing by, might overshadow some of them*, though it could not reach them all; and it had the desired effect, as the woman's touch of the hem of Christ's garment had; and in this that word of Christ was fulfilled, *Greater works than these shall you do.* And, if such miracles were wrought by Peter's shadow, we have reason to think they were so by the other apostles, as by the handkerchiefs from Paul's body (*ch.* xix. 12). In the country towns: Multitudes came to Jerusalem from *the cities round about, bringing sick folks* and *those that were vexed with unclean spirits*, and they were *healed every one*; distempered bodies and distempered minds were set to rights. Thus opportunity was given to the apostles, both to convince people's judgments of the heavenly origin of the doctrine they preached, and also to engage people's affections both to them and it.

Verses 17–25

Never did any good work go on with any hope of success, but it met with opposition. It would have been strange if the apostles had gone on thus teaching and healing and had had no check. In these verses we have the malice of hell and the grace of heaven struggling about them, the one to drive them off from this good work, the other to animate them in it.

I. The priests were enraged at them, and shut them up in prison, *v.* 17, 18. 1. Who their enemies and persecutors were. The high priest was the ringleader, Annas or Caiaphas. Those that were most forward to join with the high priest herein were the *sect of the Sadducees*, who had a particular enmity to the gospel of Christ, because it confirmed the resurrection of the dead, and the future state, which they denied. 2. How they were affected towards them, ill affected, and exasperated to the last degree. They *rose up* in a passion, being *filled with indignation* at the apostles for preaching the doctrine of Christ, and curing the sick,—at the people for hearing them, and bringing the sick to them to be cured. 3. How they proceeded against them (*v.* 18): *They laid their hands on them*, and *put them in the common prison*, among the worst of malefactors. (1) To put a restraint upon them. While they had them in prison they kept them from going on in their work, and this they reckoned a good point gained. (2) To put a terror upon them, and so to drive them off from their work. The last time they had them before them, they only threatened them (*ch.* iv. 21); but, now they imprisoned them, to make them afraid of them. (3) To put a disgrace upon them, and therefore they chose to clap them up in the common prison.

II. God sent his angel to release them out of prison. The powers of darkness fight against them, but the Father of lights fights for them. The Lord will never desert his witnesses, his advocates, but will certainly stand by them.

1. The apostles are discharged from their imprisonment (*v.* 19): *The angel of the Lord by night opened the prison doors*, and, in spite of the keepers that *stood without before the doors, brought forth* the prisoners (see *v.* 23). There is no prison so dark, so strong, but God can both visit his people in it, and fetch them out of it.

2. They are charged to go on with their work. The angel bade them, *Go, stand, and speak in the temple to the people all the words of this life*, *v.* 20. When they were miraculously set at liberty it was that they might go on with their work with so much the more boldness. Recoveries from sickness, releases out of trouble, are granted us, not that we may enjoy the comforts of our life, but that God may be honoured with the services of our life. Where

JAMIESON, FAUSSET, BROWN

15. into the streets—'in every street.' **on beds and couches**—The words denote the softer couches of the rich and the meaner cribs of the poor [BENGEL]. **shadow of Peter . . . might overshadow some of them**—Cf. ch. 19:12; Luke 8: 46. So Elisha. Now the predicted greatness of Peter (Matt. 16:18), as the directing spirit of the early Church, was at its height.

17-23. sect of the Sadducees—See on ch. 4:2 for the reason why this is specified.

19. by night—the same night.

20. all the words of this life—beautiful expression for that Life in the Risen One which was the burden of their preaching!

ADAM CLARKE

15. *That . . . the shadow of Peter passing by.* I cannot see all the miraculous influence here that others profess to see. The people who had seen the miracles wrought by the apostles pressed with their sick to share the healing benefit. As there must have been many diseased people, it is not likely that the apostles, who generally addressed such persons, prayed, and used imposition of hands, could reach all those that were brought to them as fast as the solicitude of their friends could wish. As therefore they could not get Peter or the other apostles personally to all their sick, they thought if they placed them on that side of the way where the shadow was projected (the sun probably now declining, and consequently the shadow lengthening) they should be healed by the *shadow* of the man passing over them, in whose person such miraculous powers were lodged. But it does not appear that the persons who thus thought and acted were of the number of those converts already made to the faith of Christ, nor does it appear that any person was healed in this way.

16. *Sick folks, and them which were vexed with unclean spirits.* Here it is evident that *sick people* are distinguished from those who were *vexed with unclean spirits;* and therefore they were not one and the same thing. The same distinction is made in Matt. iv. 24; x. 1; Mark i. 32, 34; xvi. 17-18; and Luke iv. 40-41 and vii. 21.

17. *The high priest . . . and . . . the sect of the Sadducees.* "The heresy of the Sadducees." In this place, as well as in several others, the word *hairesis*, "heresy," has no evil meaning in itself. It signifies a "sect" or "party," whether good or bad, distinguished from any other sect. *Hairesis, heresy,* comes from *haireo*, "I choose," and was anciently applied to the different "sects" of the heathen philosophers, the members of each sect having chosen their own in preference to all the others. *Were filled with indignation.* With "zeal." *Zelos* signifies a vehement affection or disposition of the mind, which, according to its object, is either good or bad, laudable or blamable. Its meaning in this place is easily discerned, and not improperly translated *indignation* in our version.

19. *But the angel of the Lord . . . opened the prison doors.* This was done: (1) To increase the confidence of the apostles, by showing them that they were under the continual care of God; and (2) To show the Jewish rulers that they were fighting against God while persecuting His followers and attempting to prevent them from preaching the gospel.

20. *All the words of this life.* This is another periphrasis for "gospel." Go to *the temple*—the most public place, and *speak . . . to the people*—who come there to worship according to the law, *the words of this life*—the whole doctrine of salvation from sin and death; and show that the law is fulfilled in the sacrifice of Jesus, and that by His resurrection He has brought life and immortality to light.

MATTHEW HENRY

they must preach: *Speak in the temple.* One would think it had been prudent to go on with it in a more private place. No; "Speak in the temple, for this is the place of concourse, this is your Father's house." It is not for the preachers of Christ's gospel to retire into corners, as long as they can have any opportunity of preaching in the great congregation. To whom they must preach: "*Speak to the people,* who are willing and desirous to be taught, and whose souls are as precious to Christ as the souls of the greatest." How they must preach: *Go, stand, and speak,* which intimates, not only that they must speak publicly, but that they must speak boldly and resolutely. What they must speak: *All the words of this life.* "Go, and preach the same to the world, that others may be comforted with the same comforts with which you yourselves are comforted of God. Of this life emphatically; this heavenly, divine life, in comparison with which the present earthly life does not deserve the name." The gospel is concerning matters of life and death, and ministers must preach it and people hear it accordingly. They must speak *all the words of this life,* and not conceal any. Christ's witnesses are sworn to speak the whole truth.

III. They went on with their work (*v.* 21): *When they heard this* they *returned to Solomon's porch, v.* 12. It was a great satisfaction to them to have these fresh orders. Now that the angel ordered them to go preach in the temple, their way was plain, and they ventured without any difficulty, entered into the temple, and feared not the face of man. If we may but be satisfied concerning our duty, our business is to keep close to this, and then we may cheerfully trust God with our safety. They set themselves immediately to execute them. They *entered into the temple early in the morning,* and taught them the gospel of the kingdom: and did not at all fear what man could do unto them. The whole treasure of the gospel is lodged in their hands; if they be silent now the springs are shut up, and the whole work falls to the ground and is made to cease. When God gives opportunity of doing good, though we be under the restraint and terror of human powers, we should venture far rather than let go such an opportunity.

IV. The high priest and his party went on with their prosecution, *v.* 21. They *called the council together,* a great and extraordinary council, for they summoned *all the senate of the children of Israel.*

1. How they were prepared to crush the gospel of Christ and the preachers of it, for they raised the whole posse. The last time they had the apostles in custody they convened them only before a committee of those that were of the kindred of the high priest, but now they called together *all the eldership.* Thus God ordered it, that the confusion of the enemies, and the apostles' testimony against them, might be more public, and that those might hear the gospel who would not hear it otherwise than from the bar.

2. How they were disappointed, and had their faces filled with shame. An officer is despatched immediately to fetch the prisoners to the bar. (1) The officers come and tell them that they are not to be found in the prison, *v.* 22, 23. They were gone, and the report which the officers make is, "*The prison-door truly found we shut with all safety, the keepers standing without before the doors,* but when we went in *we found no man* therein." Which way the angel fetched them we are not told; however it was, they were gone. The Lord knows, though we do not, how to deliver the godly out of temptation, and how to loose those that are in bonds for his name's sake, and he will do it, as here, when he has occasion for them (*v.* 24): *When the high priest, and the captain of the temple,* and the *chief priests, heard these things,* they were all at a plunge, and looked one upon another, *doubting what this thing should be.* They were at their wits' end, having never been so disappointed in all their lives of anything they were so sure of. Those often distress and embarrass themselves that think to distress and embarrass the cause of Christ. (2) Their doubt is, in part, determined; and yet their vexation is increased by another messenger, who brings them word that their prisoners are preaching in the temple (*v.* 25): "*Behold, the men whom you put in prison are now standing in the temple,* under your nose and in defiance of you, *teaching the people.*" Now this confounded them more than anything. Common malefactors may have art enough to break prison; but those are uncommon ones that have courage enough to avow it when they have so done.

Verses 26–42

We are not told what it was that the apostles preached to the people; but what passed between them and the council we have here an account of; for in their sufferings there appeared more of a divine power and energy than even in their preaching.

CHARLES H. SPURGEON:

It is clear from the text that they were to take a conspicuous place and speak boldly: "Go, stand in the temple." Go where the Sanhedrin holds its sittings, where the high priest and his Sadducean comrades are on the watch. Let not the danger hinder you. Go where all can see you; stand up and stand out. Wherever the people are, there let your voices be heard. Be there perseveringly, taking your stand, and keeping it till removed by force. The object was to make the gospel known; therefore, let them go to headquarters, let them stand in the chief place of concourse, let them be in the resort of the devout, let them challenge the observation of pilgrims from every corner of the land. Brethren, it is not ours to hide in holes and in corners; our gospel is like the sun, whose line has gone out through all the earth. Let us not speak timidly, for we have not received the spirit of fear, neither will we hide our candle under a bushel. We are to publish the tidings of that life from the dead which has brought life for the dead.

"Speak unto the people." "Unto the people"—that does not mean the poor to the exclusion of the rich, nor the many to the exclusion of the few. The expression is most comprehensive, and embraces both the masses and the classes. If the men of the council would hear them, let them speak to them. They did so, alas! with small result. This is a truly gospel word of command; for the gospel is glad tidings to all people, and it is to be preached to every creature under heaven. A restricted audience is an unevangelic idea. Go and speak unto the people, then—to all sorts of people, to everybody. Let not a soul escape if you can help it, for your mission is to all mankind. Oh, gospel fishermen, spread the great seine net, which will encompass a great multitude of fishes, and with diligence draw it to shore.—*The Treasury of the New Testament*

JAMIESON, FAUSSET, BROWN

21. entered into the temple . . .—How self-possessed! the indwelling Spirit raising them above fear.

called . . . all the senate . . .—an unusually general convention, though hastily summoned.

23. the prison . . . shut . . . keepers . . . before the doors, but . . . no man within—the reverse of the miracle in ch. 16:26; a similar contrast to that of the nets at the miraculous draughts of fishes (Luke 5:6; and John 21:11). **24-26. they doubted**—'were in perplexity.'

ADAM CLARKE

21. *Called the council together.* The "Sanhedrin."

23. *The prison truly found we shut.* All the doors were properly bolted and the keepers at their post; *but when we had opened,* for it appears they were alone in possession of the keys. How much this must have increased their astonishment when they found that the doors were not broken open, the guards properly posted, and everything as they left it!

24. *They doubted of them whereunto this would grow.* They did not know what to think of the apostles, whether they had saved themselves by magic or whether they were delivered by a real miracle; and they were at a loss to tell what the issue of these things would be.

MATTHEW HENRY

I. The seizing of the apostles a second time. They brought them without violence. One would think they had reason to do so, in reverence to the temple, and for fear of the apostles, lest they should strike them, as they did Ananias. But all that restrained their violence was their fear of the people, who had such a veneration for the apostles that they would have stoned the officers if they had offered them any abuse. 2. Yet they brought them to those who were resolved to take violent courses with them (*v.* 27): They *brought them, to set them before the council.* Thus the powers that should have been a terror to evil works and workers became so to the good.

II. Their examination. The high priest told them what it was they had to lay to their charge, *v.* 28. 1. They had disobeyed the commands of authority (*v.* 28): "*Did not we* strictly *charge and command you that you should not teach in this name?* But you have disobeyed our commands." *Did not we command you?* Yes, they did; but did not Peter at the same time tell them that God's authority was superior to theirs, and his commands must take place of theirs? And they had forgotten this. 2. They had spread false doctrine among the people. "*You have filled Jerusalem with your doctrine,* and thereby have disturbed the public peace." 3. They had a malicious design against the government, as having made itself justly odious both to God and man: "*You intend to bring this man's blood,* the guilt of it before God, the shame of it before men, *upon us.*" See here how those who with a great deal of presumption will do an evil thing yet cannot bear to hear of it afterwards. When they were in the heat of the persecution they could cry daringly enough, "*His blood be upon us and upon our children.*" But now they take it as a great affront to have his blood laid at their door.

III. Their answer to the charge exhibited against them: *Peter and the other apostles* all spoke to the same purport; they spoke as one and the same Spirit gave them utterance.

1. They justified themselves in their disobedience (*v.* 29): *We ought to obey God rather than men.* God had commanded them to teach in the name of Christ, and therefore they ought to do it, though the chief priests forbade them. Those rulers have a great deal to answer for, who punish men for disobedience to them in that which is their duty to God.

2. They justified themselves in doing what they could to fill Jerusalem with the doctrine of Christ, and if they thereby bring his blood upon them they may thank themselves.

(1) The chief priests are told to their faces the indignities they did to this Jesus: "*You slew him and hanged him on a tree.*" People's being unwilling to hear of their faults is no good reason why they should not be faithfully told of them. It is a common excuse made for not reproving sin that the times will not bear it. But those whose office it is to reprove must not be awed by this; the times must bear it, and shall bear it.

(2) They are told also what honours God put upon this Jesus, and then let them judge who was in the right, the persecutors of his doctrine or the preachers of it. He calls God the *God of our fathers.* The God of *Abraham, Isaac,* and *Jacob,* is the *God and Father of our Lord Jesus Christ*; see what honour he did him. [1] He *raised him up.* "You put him to death, but God has restored him to life, so that God and you are manifestly contesting about this Jesus; and which must we side with?" [2] He *exalted him with his right hand.* "You loaded him with disgrace, but God has crowned him with honour; and ought we not to honour him whom God honours? God has *given him a name above every name.*" [3] "He has appointed him to be *a prince and a saviour.*" There is no having Christ to be our Saviour, unless we be willing to take him for our prince. We cannot expect to be redeemed and healed by him, unless we give up ourselves to be ruled by him. Faith takes an entire Christ, that came, not to save us in our sins, but to save us from our sins. [4] He is appointed to *give repentance to Israel and remission of sins.* Therefore they must preach in his name to the people of Israel, for his favours were designed primarily and principally for them. Why should the rulers and elders of Israel oppose one who came with no less a blessing to Israel than repentance and pardon? But repentance and remission of sins are blessings they neither value nor see their need of. Repentance and remission go together; wherever repentance is wrought remission is without fail granted. On the other hand, no remission without repentance. It is Jesus Christ that gives both repentance and remission. Are we appointed to repent? Christ is appointed to give repentance. The new heart is his work, and the broken spirit a sacrifice of his providing; and, when he has given repentance, if he should not give re-

JAMIESON, FAUSSET, BROWN

26. without violence, for they feared...—hardened ecclesiastics, all unawed by the miraculous tokens of God's presence with the apostles, and the fear of the mob only before their eyes!

27-42. SECOND APPEARANCE AND TESTIMONY BEFORE THE SANHEDRIM—ITS RAGE CALMED BY GAMALIEL—BEING DISMISSED, THEY DEPART REJOICING, AND CONTINUE THEIR PREACHING. **27, 28. ye have filled Jerusalem with your doctrine**—noble testimony to the success of their preaching, and (for the reason mentioned on ch. 4:4) to the truth of their testimony, from reluctant lips! **intend to bring this man's blood upon us**—They avoid naming Him whom Peter gloried in holding up [BENGEL]. In speaking thus, they seem to betray a disagreeable recollection of their own recent imprecation, "His blood be upon us..." (Matt. 27:25), and of the traitor's words as he threw down the money, "I have sinned in that I have betrayed innocent blood" (Matt. 27:4). **29, 30. Then Peter...**—See on ch. 2:22, and on ch. 3:13, etc.

G. CAMPBELL MORGAN:

Peter's brave answer is the type of answer that thousands of trembling women and meek men have given. His tone is severer now than on his former appearance. Now he has no courteous recognition of the court's authority. Now he brushes aside all Annas's attempts to impose on him the sanctity of its decrees, and flatly denies that the Council has any more right to command than any other "men." They claimed to be depositaries of God's judgments. This revolutionary fisherman sees nothing in them but "men," whose commands point one way, while God's point the other. The angel bade them "speak"; the Council had bid them be dumb. To state the opposition was to determine their duty. Formerly Peter had said "judge ye," which command it is right to obey. Now, he wraps his refusal in no folds of courtesy, but thrusts the naked "We must obey God" in the Council's face. That was a great moment in the history of the world and the Church. How much lay in it, as in a seed—Luther's "Here I stand, I can do none other. God help me! Amen"; Plymouth Rock, and many a glorious and blood-stained page in the records of martyrdom.

—*The Acts of the Apostles*

31. Prince and a Saviour—the first word expressing that *Royalty* which all Israel looked for in Messiah, the second the *Saving* character of it which they had utterly lost sight of. Each of these features in our Lord's work enters into the other, and both make one glorious whole (cf. ch. 3:15; Heb. 2:10). **to give**—dispensing as a "Prince." **repentance and remission of sins**—as a "Saviour"; "repentance" embracing all that change which issues in the faith which secures "forgiveness" (cf. ch. 2:38; 20:21). How gloriously is Christ here exhibited; not, as in other places, as the *Medium*, but as the *Dispenser* of all spiritual blessings!

ADAM CLARKE

26. *Brought them without violence.* On receiving the information mentioned above, proper officers were sent to seize and bring them before the council. The officers, on reaching the Temple, found the multitude gladly receiving the doctrine of the apostles and so intent on hearing all the words of this life that they were afraid to show any hostility to the apostles, lest the people should stone them. We may therefore conclude that the officers entreated them to accompany them to the council; and that they felt it their duty to obey every ordinance of man for the Lord's sake and so cheerfully went with them, trusting in the Lord their God.

28. *Did not we straitly command you?* "With commanding did we not command you?"; a Hebraism—another proof of the accuracy and fidelity of Luke, who seems always to give every man's speech as he delivered it—not the substance, but the very words. See chap. iv. 17. *Not teach in this name.* That is, of Jesus as the Christ or Messiah. *Intend to bring this man's blood upon us.* You speak in such a way of Him to the people as to persuade them that we have crucified an innocent Man.

29. *We ought to obey God rather than men.* The same answer they gave before, chap. iv. 19, founded on the same reason, which still stood good. We have received our commission from *God;* we dare not lay it down at the desire or command of *men.*

30. *The God of our fathers raised up Jesus.* It was well to introduce this, that the council might at once see that they preached no strange God; and that He who so highly honored the patriarchs, Moses, and the prophets had yet more highly honored Jesus Christ in raising Him from the dead and seating Him at His right hand, and proclaiming Him as the only Giver of salvation and the repentance which leads to it. *Whom ye slew.* They charge them again with the murder of Christ, as they had done before, chap. iv. 10-12.

31. *Him hath God exalted with his right hand.* By a supereminent display of His "almighty power," for so the *right hand* of God often means. *A Prince.* The Leader or Director in the way. See the notes on chap. iii. 15 and 19. *And a Saviour.* "A Deliverer or Preserver." The word *soter* comes from *sozo,* to "save, deliver, preserve, escape from death or danger, bring into a state of security or safety." *Jesus* and *Saviour* are nearly of the same import. He alone delivers from sin, death, and hell; by Him alone we escape from the snares and dangers to which we are exposed: and it is by and in Him, and in connection with Him, that we are preserved blameless and harmless. He alone can save the soul from sin and preserve it in that state of salvation. *Forgiveness of sins.* The "taking away of sins." This is not to be restrained to the mere act of justification; it implies the removal of sin, whether its power, guilt, or impurity be considered. Through Jesus we have the destruction of the power, the pardon of the guilt, and the cleansing from the pollution, of sin. The two words in italics in this text, *to be,* are impertinently introduced; it reads much better without them.

MATTHEW HENRY

mission he would *forsake the work of his own hands*. [5] All this is well attested, *First*, by the apostles themselves. "*We are his witnesses*, and if we should be silent, as you would have us, we should betray a trust." When a cause is trying, witnesses ought not to be silenced, for the issue of the cause depends on their testimony. *Secondly*, By the Spirit of God. *The Holy Ghost is witness*, a witness from heaven. For this end the Holy Ghost is given us, whose operations we cannot stifle. The giving of the Holy Ghost to obedient believers, not only to bring them to the obedience of faith, but to make them eminently useful therein, is a very strong proof of the truth of Christianity. *Lastly*, The giving of the Holy Ghost to those that obey Christ is a plain evidence that it is the will of God that Christ should be obeyed; "judge then whether we ought to obey you in opposition to him."

IV. The impression which the apostles' defence of themselves made upon the court. Surely such fair reasoning could not but clear the prisoners, and convert the judges. They raged against it, and were filled, 1. With indignation: They were *cut to the heart*, angry to see their own sin set in order before them; stark mad to find that the gospel of Christ had so much to say for itself. When a sermon was preached to the people to this purport, they were *pricked to the heart*, in remorse and godly sorrow, *ch.* ii. 37. These here were *cut to the heart* with rage and indignation. 2. With malice against the apostles themselves. Since they see they cannot stop their mouths any other way than by stopping their breath, they *take counsel to slay them*. While the apostles went on in the service of Christ, with a holy security and serenity of mind, their persecutors went on in their opposition to Christ, with a constant perplexity and perturbation of mind, and vexation to themselves.

V. The grave advice which Gamaliel gave upon this occasion. This Gamaliel is here said to be a *Pharisee* by his profession and sect, and by office a *doctor of the law*. Paul was brought up at his feet (*ch.* xxii. 3). He is here said to be *in reputation among all the people*. He was a moderate man, and not apt to go in with furious measures. Men of temper and charity are justly had in reputation, for checking the incendiaries that otherwise would set the world on fire.

1. The necessary caution he gives to the council: *He commanded to put the apostles forth a little while. You men of Israel*, saith he, *take heed to yourselves*, consider what you do, or *intend to do, as touching these men*, *v.* 25. He calls them *men of Israel*, to enforce this caution: "You are men, that should be governed by reason; you are men of Israel, that should be governed by revelation. *Take heed to yourselves*." The persecutors of God's people had best look to themselves, lest they fall into the pit which they dig.

2. The cases he cites. Two instances he gives of factious seditious men, whose attempts came to nothing of themselves; whence he infers that if these men were indeed such as they represented them their cause would sink with its own weight.

(1) There was one *Theudas, boasting himself to be somebody*. He observes here (*v.* 26) concerning him, how far he prevailed: "*A number of men, about four hundred* in all, joined themselves to him." How soon his pretensions were all dashed: "When *he was slain, all, as many as obeyed him, were scattered*. Now compare that case with this. You have slain Jesus, the ringleader of this faction. Now if he was an impostor and pretender, his death will be the death of his cause."

(2) The case was the same with *Judas of Galilee*, *v.* 37. [1] The attempt he made. It is said to be *after this*, which some read, *besides this*. It is not easy to determine particularly when these events happened. It is probable that they were cases which lately happened, and were fresh in memory. This *Judas drew away much people after him*. [2] Here is the defeat of his attempt, *he also perished, and all, even as many as obeyed him*, were dispersed.

3. His opinion upon the whole matter.

(1) That they should not persecute the apostles (*v.* 38): *Now I say unto you*, "*Refrain from these men; let not our hand be upon them*." It is uncertain whether he spoke this out of policy. The apostles did not attempt anything by outward force. Why should any outward force be used against them? Or, whether it was only the language of a mild quiet spirit. Or, whether God put this word into his mouth beyond his own intention. We are sure there was an overruling Providence in it, that the servants of Christ might not only come off, but come off honourably.

(2) That they should refer this matter to Providence: "Wait the issue. *If it be of men, it will come to nought* of itself; *if of God, it will stand*, in spite of all your powers and policies." That which is apparently wicked and immoral must be suppressed, but that

JAMIESON, FAUSSET, BROWN

32, 33. we are his witnesses . . . and the Holy Ghost—They as competent human witnesses to facts, and the Holy Ghost as attesting them by undeniable miracles.

33. cut to the heart and took—'were taking'—**counsel to slay them**—How different this feeling and the effect of it from that "pricking of the heart" which drew from the first converts on the day of Pentecost the cry, "Men and brethren, what shall we do?" (ch. 2:37). The words used in the two places are strikingly different.

34. Then stood up . . . Gamaliel—in all probability one of that name celebrated in the Jewish writings for his wisdom, the son of Simeon (possibly the same who took the infant Saviour in his arms, Luke 2:25-35), and grandson of Hillel, another celebrated rabbi. He died eighteen years before the destruction of Jerusalem [LIGHTFOOT].

35-39. Theudas—not the same with a deceiver of that name whom Josephus mentions as heading an insurrection some twelve years after this [*Antiquities*, 20. 5. 1], but some other of whom he makes no mention. Such insurrections were frequent.

37. Judas of Galilee—See on Luke 2:2, and 13:1-3 [JOSEPHUS, *Antiquities*, 13. 1. 1].

ADAM CLARKE

32. *We are his witnesses*. The word *his* is omitted by several MSS. It does not seem to be necessary. *Of these things*. "Of these transactions"; i.e., of Christ's life and miracles, and of your murderous proceedings against Him. *To them that obey him*. We obey God, not you; and therefore God gives us this Spirit, which is in us a Fountain of light, life, love, and power.

33. *They were cut to the heart*. Literally, "they were sawn through." They were stung to the heart, not with compunction nor remorse, but with spite, malice, and revenge. For, having the murder of Christ thus brought home to their consciences, in the first feelings of their malice and revenge they thought of destroying the persons who had witnessed their nefarious conduct.

34. *A Pharisee, named Gamaliel, a doctor of the law*. "This," says Dr. Lightfoot, "was Rabban Gamaliel the first; commonly, by way of distinction, called Rabban Gamaliel the elder. He was president of the council after the death of his own father, Rabban Simeon, who was the son of Hillel. He was Paul's master, and the thirty-fifth receiver of the traditions, and on this account might not be improperly termed *a doctor of the law*, because he was one that kept and handed down the Cabala received from Mount Sinai. He died eighteen years before the destruction of Jerusalem, his son *Simeon* succeeding him in the chair, who perished in the ruins of the city." Though probably no favorer of Christianity, yet for a Pharisee he seems to have possessed a more liberal mind than most of his brethren; the following advice was at once humane, sensible, candid, and enlightened.

35. *What ye intend to do*. "What you are about to do." They had already intended to destroy them; and they were now about to do it.

36. *Rose up Theudas*. Josephus, *Ant.*, l. xx, c. 4, s. 1, mentions one named *Theudas* who was the author of an insurrection, about whom there has been much controversy whether he were the person spoken of here by Gamaliel. Every circumstance, as related by Josephus, agrees well enough with what is referred to here except the chronology; for the Theudas mentioned by Josephus made his insurrection when Fadus was governor of Judea, which was at least ten years after the time in which the apostles were brought before this council. Much labor has been thrown away in unsuccessful attempts to reconcile the historian and the Evangelist, when it is very probable they speak of different transactions. Dr. Lightfoot thinks that "Josephus has made a slip in his chronology." I confess the matter does not appear to me of so much consequence. *Boasting himself to be somebody*. "Saying that he was a great personage," i.e., according to the supposition of Bishop Pearce, setting himself up to be king of the Jews.

37. *Judas of Galilee*. Josephus mentions the insurrection made by Judas of Galilee, *Ant.*, l. xviii, c. 1, and says it was when Cyrenius was governor of Syria. Pearce supposes that there were two "taxations" or "enrollments"; and that the one mentioned here took place ten years after that mentioned in Luke ii.

38. *Refrain from these men*. Do not molest them; leave them to God. For if this counsel and work be of man it will come to nought, like the rebellion of Theudas, and that of Judas of Galilee.

MATTHEW HENRY

which has a show of good, and it is doubtful whether it be of God or men, it is best to let it alone, and let it take its fate. Christ rules by the power of truth, not of the sword. [1] "If this *counsel, and this work, be of men, it will come to nothing.* If it be the counsel and work of foolish crack-brained men, they will run themselves out of breath. They will make themselves ridiculous. If it be the counsel and work of politic and designing men, let them alone awhile, and their knavery will be manifest to all men. Providence will never countenance it. *It will come to nothing* in a little time; there is no occasion to kill that which, if you give it a little time, will die of itself. The unnecessary use of power is an abuse of it." [2] "If it should prove *that this counsel and this work is of God*, then what do you think of persecuting them, of this attempt of yours (*v.* 33) *to slay them?* You must conclude it to be a fruitless attempt against them: *If it be of God, you cannot overthrow it.*" It may be the comfort of all who are sincerely on God's side, that whatsoever is of God cannot be overthrown totally and finally, though it may be very vigorously opposed; it may be run upon, but cannot be run down. "A dangerous attempt to yourselves. Pray let it alone, *lest haply you be found even to fight against God.*" Those that hate and abuse God's faithful people, that restrain and silence his faithful ministers, fight against God. Well, this was the advice of Gamaliel: we wish it were duly considered by those that persecute for conscience' sake.

VI. The determination of the council upon the whole matter, *v.* 40. Thus far they agreed with Gamaliel that they let fall the design of putting the apostles to death. Yet they could not forbear giving some vent to their rage. *They beat them*, scourged them as malefactors, and notice is taken (*v.* 41) of the ignominy of it. Thus they thought to make them ashamed of preaching, and the people ashamed of hearing them. *They commanded them that they should not speak* any more *in the name of Jesus.*

VII. The wonderful courage and constancy of the apostles. *They departed from the council*, and we do not find one word they said by way of reflection upon the court, *but committed their cause to him* to whom Gamaliel had referred it.

1. They bore their sufferings with an invincible cheerfulness (*v.* 41): When *they went out*, instead of being ashamed of Christ, *they rejoiced that they were counted worthy to suffer shame for his name.* They were men that had never done anything to make themselves vile, and therefore could not but have a sense of the shame they suffered, which was more grievous to them than the smart, as it usually is to ingenuous minds; but they considered that it was for the name of Christ that they were thus abused, and their sufferings should be made to contribute to the further advancement of his name. They reckoned it an honour *that they were counted worthy to suffer shame, that they were honoured to be dishonoured for Christ.* Reproach for Christ is true preferment. They rejoiced in it, remembering what their Master had said to them at their first setting out (Matt. v. 11, 12): *When men shall revile you, and persecute you, rejoice and be exceedingly glad.* They rejoiced *that they suffered shame.* If we suffer ill for doing well, provided we suffer it well, we ought to rejoice in that grace which enables us so to do.

2. They went on in their work with indefatigable diligence (*v.* 42): They were commanded *not to preach*, and *yet they ceased not to teach and preach.* When they preached—*daily*; every day, as duly as the day came. Where they preached—both publicly *in the temple*, and privately *in every house.* Though in the temple they were under the eye of their enemies, yet they did not confine themselves to their own houses, but ventured into the post of danger; and though they had the liberty of the temple, yet they made no difficulty of preaching in houses, in every house, even the poorest cottage. What was the subject matter of their preaching: *They preached Jesus Christ.* They did *not preach themselves, but Christ.* This was the preaching that gave most offence to the priests, but they would not alter their subject to please them. It ought to be the constant business of gospel ministers to preach Christ; *Christ, and him crucified; Christ, and him glorified.*

JAMIESON, FAUSSET, BROWN

38. if . . . of men, it will come to naught—This neutral policy was true wisdom, in the then temper of the council. But individual neutrality is hostility to Christ, as He Himself teaches (Luke 11:23).

40-42. beaten them—for disobeying their orders (cf. Luke 23:16).

departed . . . rejoicing that they were counted worthy to suffer shame for his name—'thought worthy by God to be dishonored by man' (Matt. 5:12; I Pet. 4:14, 16) [WEBSTER and WILKINSON]. *This was their first taste of persecution, and it felt sweet for His sake whose disciples they were.*

42. in every house—in private. (See on ch. 2:46.) **ceased not to preach Jesus Christ**—i.e., Jesus (to be the) Christ.

ALBERT BARNES:

"This counsel or this work be of men." This plan or purpose. If the apostles had originated it for the purposes of imposture. "It will come to nought." Gamaliel *inferred* that from the two instances which he specified. They had been suppresed without the interference of the Sanhedrin; and he inferred that this would also die away if it was a human device. It will be remembered that this is the mere advice of Gamaliel, who was not inspired, and that this opinion should not be adduced to guide us, except as it was an instance of great shrewdness and prudence. It is doubtless right to oppose error in the proper way and with the proper temper, not with arms, or vituperation, or with the civil power, but with argument and kind entreaty.

But the sentiment of Gamaliel is full of wisdom in regard to error. For, (1) The very way to exalt error into notice, and to confirm men in it, is to oppose it in a harsh, authoritative, and unkind manner. (2) Error, if left alone, will often die away itself. The interest of men in it will often cease as soon as it ceases to be opposed; and, having nothing to fan the flame, it will expire. It is not so with truth. (3) In this respect the remark may be applied to the Christian religion. It has stood too long, and in too many circumstances of prosperity and adversity, to be of men. It has been subjected to all trials from its pretended friends and real foes; and it still lives as vigorous and flourishing as ever. Kingdoms have changed; empires have risen and fallen since Gamaliel spoke this; systems of opinion and belief have had their day, and expired; but the preservation of the Christian religion, unchanged through so many revolutions, and in so many fiery trials, shows that it is not of men, but of God. The argument for the divine origin of the Christian religion from its perpetuity is one that can be applied to no other system that has been, or that now exists.—*Popular Commentary*

ADAM CLARKE

40. *To him they agreed.* That is, not to stay the apostles nor to attempt any further to imprison them. But their malevolence could not be thus easily satisfied, and therefore they beat them—probably gave each of them thirty-nine stripes; and having commanded them not to speak in the name of Jesus, they let them go.

41. *Rejoicing that they were counted worthy.* The whole verse may be read thus: "But they departed rejoicing from the presence of the Sanhedrin, because they were deemed worthy to be dishonored on account of the name." The word *his* is omitted by some MSS. The name probably by this time distinguished both the Author of salvation and the sacred system of doctrine which the apostles preached.

42. *Daily in the temple.* That is, at the hours of morning and evening prayer; for they felt it their duty to worship God in public, and to help others to make a profitable use of the practice. Every man that professes Christianity should in this respect also copy their conduct; nor can any man be considered to have any religion who does not attend on the public worship of his Maker. *They ceased not to teach and preach Jesus.* Far from desisting, they became more zealous, yea, incessant, in their work. They took advantage of the public assemblies in the Temple, as well as of all private opportunities, to *teach* all the truths of their holy religion; and to *preach*, proclaim Jesus as the only Messiah, that He who was crucified rose from the dead and was exalted a Prince and a Saviour at the right hand of God.

MATTHEW HENRY

CHAPTER 6

Verses 1–7

I. An unhappy disagreement among some of the church members was prudently taken up in time (*v.* 1): *When the number of the disciples was multiplied there arose a murmuring.*

1. It does our hearts good to find *that the number of the disciples is multiplied*, as, no doubt, it vexed *the priests and Sadducees* to see it. The opposition that the preaching of the gospel met with contributed to the success of it. The preachers were beaten, threatened, and abused, and yet the people received their doctrine, invited thereto by their wonderful patience and cheerfulness under their trials.

2. Yet it casts a damp upon us to find that the multiplying of the disciples proves an occasion of discord. Now that they were multiplied they began to murmur. *There arose a murmuring*, not an open falling out, but a secret heart-burning.

(1) The complainants were *the Grecians against the Hebrews*—the Jews that were scattered in Greece, and other parts, many of whom being at Jerusalem at the feast embraced the faith of Christ. These complained against the Hebrews, the native Jews. Some of each of these became Christians, and their joint-embracing of the faith of Christ did not prevail to extinguish the little jealousies they had one of another before their conversion. But all are alike welcome to Christ, and should be, for his sake, dear to one another.

(2) The complaint of these Grecians was *that their widows were neglected in the daily administration.* The first contention in the Christian church was about a money-matter. A great deal of money was gathered for the relief of the poor, but, as often happens in such cases, it was impossible to please everybody in the laying of it out. *The apostles* no doubt designed to do it with the utmost impartiality, and yet here they are complained to, and tacitly complained of, *that the Grecian widows were neglected.* Perhaps this complaint was groundless and unjust. Those who, upon any account, lie under disadvantages (as the Grecian Jews did, in comparison with those that were Hebrews of the Hebrews) are apt to be jealous that they are slighted when really they are not so; and it is the common fault of poor people that they are querulous and clamorous, and apt to find fault that more is not given them. There are envy and covetousness to be found among the poor as well as among the rich. We will suppose there might be some occasion for their complaint. As those that have the administration of public justice ought in a particular manner to protect widows from injury, so those that have the administration of public charity ought in a particular manner to provide for widows what is necessary. In the best-ordered church in the world there will be something amiss, some grievances, or at least some complaints; those are the best that have the least and the fewest.

II. The happy accommodating of this matter. The apostles had hitherto the directing of the matter. Some persons must be chosen to manage this matter who have more leisure to attend to it than the apostles had.

1. How the method was proposed by the apostles: They *called the multitude of the disciples unto them.* The twelve themselves would not determine anything without them. Those might be best able to advise who were more conversant in the affairs of this life than the apostles were.

(1) The apostles could by no means admit so great a diversion from their great work (*v.* 2): *It is not reasonable that we should leave the word of God and serve tables.* This was foreign to the business which the apostles were called to. They were *to preach the word of God.* They thought that was work enough for a whole man. If they serve tables, they must, in some measure, *leave the word of God.* They will no more be drawn from their preaching by the money laid at their feet than they will be driven from it by the stripes laid on their backs. Preaching the gospel is the best work that a minister can be employed in. He must not entangle himself in the affairs of this life, no, not in the outward business of the house of God.

(2) They therefore desire *that seven men* might be chosen whose business it should be *to serve tables*, *v.* 2. The business must be minded, must be better minded than it had been, and than the apostles could mind it; and therefore proper persons must be chosen, that everything might be done decently and in order, and no person nor thing neglected. The persons must be duly qualified. The people are to choose, and the apostles to ordain. *Look out seven men.* These must be *of honest report*, men free from

JAMIESON, FAUSSET, BROWN

CHAPTER 6

Vss. 1-7. First Election of Deacons. **1. the Grecians**—the Greek-speaking Jews, mostly born in the provinces. **the Hebrews**—those Jews born in Palestine who used their native tongue, and were wont to look down on the "Grecians" as an inferior class.

were neglected—'overlooked' by those whom the apostles employed, and who were probably of the Hebrew class, as being the most numerous. The complaint was in all likelihood well founded, though we cannot suspect the distributors of intentional partiality. "It was really just an emulation of love, each party wishing to have their own poor taken care of in the best manner" [Olshausen]. **the daily ministration**—the daily distribution of alms or of food, probably the latter.

2-4. the multitude—the general body of the disciples. **It is not reason**—The word expresses dislike; i.e. 'We cannot submit.' **to leave the word of God**—to have our time and attention withdrawn from preaching; which, it thus appears, they regarded as their primary duty. **to serve tables**—oversee the distribution of provisions.

3. look ye out among you—i.e., ye, "the multitude," from among yourselves. **seven men of honest report**—good reputation (ch. 10:22; I Tim. 3: 7).

ADAM CLARKE

CHAPTER 6

1. *A murmuring of the Grecians against the Hebrews.* Those who are here termed Grecians, or Hellenists, were Jews who sojourned now at Jerusalem but lived in countries where the Greek language was spoken, and probably in general knew no other. They are distinguished here from those called *Hebrews*, by which we are to understand native Jews, who spoke what was then termed the Hebrew language, a sort of Chaldaio-Syriac. The foreign or Hellenistic Jews began to be jealous that their widows were neglected in the daily ministration, that they either had not the proportion or were not duly served, the Palestine Jews being partial to those of their own country. This shows that the community of goods could never have been designed to become general. Indeed, it was no ordinance of God; and, in any state of society, must in general be impracticable.

2. *It is not reason.* "It is not pleasing, proper, or fitting," *that we should leave the word of God*, that we should give up ourselves or confide to others the doctrine of salvation which God has commanded us to preach unto the people. *And serve tables.* Become providers of daily bread for your widows and poor. Others can do this, to whom our important office is not intrusted.

3. *Wherefore . . . look ye out among you seven men.* Choose persons in whom you can all confide, who will distribute the provisions impartially and in due time; and let these persons be the objects of the choice of both the Hebrews and the Hellenists, that all cause of murmuring and discontent may be done away. Probably the *seven* men were to take each his day of service, and then there would be a superintendent for these widows for each day of the week. *Of honest report.* Persons to whose character there is authentic "testimony," well-known and accredited.

ALBERT BARNES:

"Of the Grecians." There has been much diversity of opinion in regard to these persons, whether they were Jews who had lived among the Gentiles, and who spoke the Greek language, or whether they were proselytes from the Gentiles. The former is probably the correct opinion. The word here used is not that which is commonly employed to designate the inhabitants of Greece, but it properly denotes those who imitate the customs and habits of the Greeks, who use the Greek language, etc. In the time when the gospel was first preached, there were two classes of Jews: those who remained in Palestine, who used the Hebrew language, and who were appropriately called *Hebrews*; and those who were scattered among the Gentiles, who spoke the Greek language, and who used in their synagogues the Greek translation of the Old Testament, the Septuagint, who were called *Hellenists*, or, as it is in our translation, *Grecians.* These were doubtless the persons mentioned here—not those who were proselyted from Gentiles, but those of Jewish origin who were not natives of Judea, who had come up to Jerusalem to attend the great festivals.

Dissensions would very likely arise between these two classes of persons. The Jews of Palestine would pride themselves much on the fact that they dwelt in the land of the patriarchs and the land of promise; that they used the language which their fathers spoke, and in which the oracles of God were given; and that they were constantly near the temple, and regularly engaged in its solemnities. On the other hand, the Jews from other parts of the world would be suspicious, jealous, and envious of their brethren, and would be likely to charge them with partiality, or of taking advantage in their association with them. These occasions of strife would not be destroyed by their conversion to Christianity, and one of them is furnished on this occasion.—*Popular Commentary*

MATTHEW HENRY

scandal, that were looked upon by their neighbours as men of integrity, that might be trusted, well spoken of for everything that is virtuous. They must be *full of the Holy Ghost*. They must not only be honest men, but they must be men of ability and men of courage, hereby appearing to be *full of the Holy Ghost*. They must be *full of wisdom*. It was not enough that they were honest, good men, but they must be discreet, judicious men, that could not be imposed upon: *full of the Holy Ghost, and wisdom*, that is, of the Holy Ghost as a Spirit of wisdom. Those must be full of wisdom who are entrusted with public money, that it may be disposed of, not only with fidelity, but with frugality. The people must nominate the persons: "*Look you out among yourselves seven men.*" They might be presumed to know better, or at least were fitter to enquire, what character men had, than the apostles. The apostles will ordain them to the service, will give them their charge, and give them their authority. *Whom we may appoint over this business*, to take care of it, and to see that there be neither waste nor want.

(3) The apostles engage to addict themselves wholly to their work as ministers, if they can but get fairly quit of this troublesome office (*v.* 4): *We will give ourselves continually to prayer, and to the ministry of the word.* See here, [1] What are the two great gospel ordinances—*the word, and prayer*. By these two the kingdom of Christ must be advanced, and additions made to it. [2] What is the great business of gospel ministers—to give themselves continually to prayer, and to the ministry of the word. They must be God's mouth to the people in the ministry of the word, and the people's mouth to God in prayer. In order to the conviction and conversion of sinners, and the edification and consolation of saints, we must not only offer up our prayers for them, but we must minister the word to them. Nor must we only minister the word to them, but we must pray for them. God's grace can do all without our preaching, but our preaching can do nothing without God's grace. Those ministers, without doubt, are the successors of the apostles, who give themselves continually to prayer, and to the ministry of the word.

2. How this proposal was agreed to by the disciples. It was not imposed, but proposed. *The saying pleased the whole multitude, v.* 5.

(1) They pitched upon the persons. The majority of votes fell upon the persons here named; and the rest both of the candidates and the electors acquiesced. The overseers of the poor were chosen by the suffrage of the people, in which yet a regard is to be had to the providence of God. We have a list of the persons chosen. We may conjecture, concerning these seven, [1] That they were such as had sold their estates, and brought the money into the common stock; those were fittest to be entrusted with the distribution of it who had been most generous in the contribution to it. [2] That these seven were all of the Grecian or Hellenist Jews, for they have all Greek names, and this would be most likely *to silence the murmurings of the Grecians*. *Nicolas*, it is plain, was one of them, for he was *a proselyte of Antioch*. The first named is *Stephen, a man full of faith and of the Holy Ghost, full of fidelity, full of courage* (so some), for he was *full of the Holy Ghost*, of his gifts and graces. He was an extraordinary man, and excelled in everything that was good: his name signifies *a crown*. *Philip* is put next, afterwards ordained to the office of an evangelist, a companion and assistant to the apostles, for so he is expressly called, *ch.* xxi. 8. And his preaching and baptizing (which we read of *ch.* viii. 12) were certainly not as a deacon, but as an evangelist. The last named is *Nicolas*, who, some say, afterwards degenerated (as the Judas among these seven) and was the founder of *the sect of the Nicolaitans* which we read of (Rev. ii. 6, 15), and which Christ there says, once and again, was a thing he hated. But some of the ancients clear him from this charge, and tell us that, though that vile impure sect denominated themselves from him, yet it was unjustly, and because he only insisted much upon it *that those that had wives should be as though they had none*, thence they wickedly inferred *that those that had wives should have them in common*, which therefore Tertullian, when he speaks of the community of goods, particularly excepts: *Omnia indiscreta apud nos, prœter uxores—All things are common among us, except our wives*—Apol. cap. 39.

(2) The apostles appointed them to this work of serving tables for the present, *v.* 6. They prayed with them, and for them. All that are employed in the service of the church ought to be committed to the conduct of the divine grace by the prayers of the church. *They laid their hands on them.* Having by prayer implored a blessing upon them, they did by the laying on of hands assure them that the blessing was conferred in answer to the prayer; and this was

JAMIESON, FAUSSET, BROWN

full of the Holy Ghost—not full of miraculous gifts, which would have been no qualification for the duties required, but *spiritually gifted* (although on two of them miraculous power did rest). **and wisdom**—discretion, aptitude for practical business. **whom we may appoint**—for while the *election* was vested in the Christian people, the *appointment* lay with the apostles, as spiritual rulers.

4. we will give ourselves to prayer—public prayer, as along with preaching their great work.

5. Stephen . . .—As this and the following names are all Greek, it is likely they were all of the "Grecian" class, which would effectually restore mutual confidence.

when they had prayed, they laid their hands on them—the one proclaiming that all official gifts flowed from the Church's glorified Head, the other symbolizing the communication of these to the chosen office-bearers through the recognized channels.

ADAM CLARKE

Full of the Holy Ghost. Saved into the spirit of the gospel dispensation, and made partakers of that Holy Ghost by which the soul is sanctified, and endued with those graces which constitute the mind that was in Christ. *And wisdom.* Prudence, discretion, and economy; for mere piety and uprightness could not be sufficient where so many must be pleased, and where frugality, impartiality, and liberality, must ever walk hand in hand. *Whom we may appoint.* Instead of *we may appoint*, "we shall appoint" is the reading of several MSS. It makes, however, very little difference in the sense.

4. *We will give ourselves continually to prayer.* "We will steadfastly and invariably attend," we will carefully keep our hearts to this work. The word is very emphatic.

5. *Stephen, a man full of faith and of the Holy Ghost.* A person every way properly fitted for his work, and thus qualified to be the first martyr of the Christian Church. *Nicolas a proselyte of Antioch.* A heathen Greek, who had not only believed in the God of Israel but had also received circumcision, and consequently was a "proselyte of the covenant." As this is the only proselyte mentioned here, we may presume that all the rest were native Jews.

6. *And when they had prayed.* The apostles prayed for these persons, that they might in every respect be qualified for their office and be made successful in it. And when they had done this they *laid their hands* upon them, and by this rite appointed them to their office.

G. CAMPBELL MORGAN:

The first thing in this organism was the setting free of the apostles for their own work, setting them free from high work which nevertheless hindered them from doing their own. It was high and holy work, this work of caring for the distress existing among the members of the Church. It is always high and holy work, every part of the business of the Church—the swinging open of the door, the reception of the man who comes across the threshold, and placing him in relation to service and work. It is great in every detail, but the doing of it hinders the men who are called to the preaching of the Word. The apostles said: "It is not fit that we should forsake the word of God"—not to do a low thing, a mean thing, a vulgar thing; but to do a high and holy thing, if the high and holy thing prevents our fulfillment of that which is our specific work. The first organization was designed to set the preacher of the Word free from everything except prayer and the preaching of the Word. "We will continue steadfastly in prayer and in the ministry of the word."

Notice the process, the method, under the apostolic guidance. They instructed the people as to how they should act, and ratified their choice, but the appointment of the seven was a Church appointment. The whole multitude of disciples were gathered together; and they—the whole multitude, not the apostles—chose these men. The details of election are not given. This is in keeping with the utter absence of ecclesiastical detail which characterizes the apostolic records. The perpetual presence of the Holy Spirit was to be the safeguard of method and of choice. That which is final and necessary is the presence of the Spirit, His safeguarding of the organization, His selection of the proper men for the proper work, His making known the will of the Lord for the whole company of disciples, under the direction of the apostolic teaching and apostolic authority. These are things that are very simple, and yet they are of supreme importance.—*The Acts of the Apostles*

MATTHEW HENRY

giving them authority to execute that office.

III. The advancement of the church hereupon. When things were thus put into good order in the church then religion got ground, *v.* 7. *The word of God increased.* Now that the apostles resolved to stick more closely than ever to their preaching, it spread the gospel further. Ministers disentangling themselves from secular employments, and addicting themselves entirely to their work, will contribute very much, as a means, to the success of the gospel. Christians became numerous: *The number of the disciples multiplied in Jerusalem greatly.* When Christ was upon earth, his ministry had least success in Jerusalem; yet now that city affords most converts. God has his remnant even in the worst of places. *A great company of the priests were obedient to the faith. Then* is the word and grace of God greatly magnified when those are wrought upon by it that were least likely. It should seem, they came *in a body*; many of them agreed together, for the keeping up of one another's credit, and the strengthening of one another's hands, to join at once in giving up their names to Christ: *a great crowd of priests* were by the grace of God helped over their prejudices, and *were obedient to the faith.* They embraced the doctrine of the gospel; their understandings were captivated to the power of the truths of Christ. They evinced the sincerity of their believing the gospel of Christ by a cheerful compliance with all the rules and precepts of the gospel.

Verses 8–15

Stephen, no doubt, was diligent and faithful in the discharge of his office. Being called to that office, he did not think it below him to do the duty of it. And, being faithful in a little, he was entrusted with more. We find him here called out to very honourable services, and owned in them.

I. He proved the truth of the gospel, by working miracles in Christ's name, *v.* 8. He was *full of faith and power.* Those that are full of faith are full of power, because by faith the power of God is engaged for us. By faith we are emptied of self, and so are filled with Christ. Being so *he did great wonders and miracles among the people,* openly, and in the sight of all; for Christ's miracles feared not the strictest scrutiny.

II. He pleaded the cause of Christianity against those that opposed it (*v.* 9, 10); he served the interests of religion as a disputant, in the high places of the field, while others were serving them as vinedressers and husbandmen.

1. We are here told who were his opponents, *v.* 9. They were Jews, but Hellenist Jews. It was with difficulty that they retained the practice of it in the country where they lived, and not without great expense and toil that they kept up their attendance at Jerusalem, and this made them more active sticklers for Judaism than those were whose profession of their religion was cheap and easy. They were *of the synagogue which is called the synagogue of the Libertines*; the Romans called those *Liberti,* or *Libertini,* who, slaves by birth, were manumitted, or made freemen. Some think that these Libertines were such of the Jews as had obtained the Roman freedom, as Paul had (*ch.* 27, 28). There were others that belonged to the synagogue of the Cyrenians and Alexandrians, and others who were of Cilicia and Asia. The Jews that were born in other countries, and had concerns in them, had frequent occasion to reside in Jerusalem. Each nation had its synagogue, as in London there are French, and Dutch, and Danish churches. Now those that were in these synagogues, being confident of the goodness of their cause, and their own sufficiency to manage it, would undertake to run down Christianity by force of argument. It was a fair and rational way of dealing with it, and what religion is always ready to admit. But why did they dispute with Stephen? And why not with the apostles themselves? Some think because they despised the apostles as *unlearned and ignorant men*; but Stephen was bred a scholar, and they thought it their honour to meddle with their match. Others think it was because they stood in awe of the apostles. Perhaps, they having given a public challenge, Stephen was chosen by the disciples to be their champion. Stephen, who was only a deacon in the church, and a very sharp young man, of bright parts, was appointed to this service. It is probable that they disputed with Stephen because he was zealous to argue with them and convince them, and this was the service to which God had called them.

2. We are here told how he carried the point in this dispute (*v.* 10): *They were not able to resist the wisdom and the Spirit by which he spoke.* They could neither support their own arguments nor answer his. Though they were not convinced, yet they were confounded.

JAMIESON, FAUSSET, BROWN

7. word of God increased . . . disciples multiplied in Jerusalem greatly—prosperity crowning the beautiful spirit which reigned in this mother community. **a great company of the priests were obedient . . .**—This was the crowning triumph of the Gospel, whose *peaceful* prosperity was now at its greatest height. After Stephen's teaching and trial made it clear that sacerdotal interests could not stand with the Gospel, such priestly accessions became rare indeed. Note (1) how easily misunderstandings may arise among the most loving and devoted followers of the Lord Jesus: but (2) How quickly and effectually such misunderstandings may be healed, where honest intentions, love, and wisdom reign: (3) What a beautiful model for imitation is furnished by the class here complained of, who, though themselves the majority, chose the new office-bearers from amongst the complaining minority! (4) How superior to the lust of power do the apostles here show themselves to be, in not only divesting themselves of the immediate superintendence of temporal affairs in the Christian community, but giving the choice of those who were to be entrusted with it to the disciples at large! (5) How little of formal organization did the apostles give to the Church at first, and when an emergency arose which demanded something more, how entirely was the remedy suggested by the reason of the thing! (6) Though the new office-bearers are not expressly called *Deacons* here, it is universally admitted that this was the first institution of that order in the Church; the success of the expedient securing its permanency, and the qualifications for "the office of a Deacon" being laid down in one of the apostolical Epistles immediately after those of "a Bishop" (I Tim. 3:8-13).

8-15. STEPHEN ARRAIGNED BEFORE THE SANHEDRIM. **8. And Stephen . . .**—The foregoing narrative seems to be only an introduction to what follows. **full of faith**—rather, 'of grace,' as the best MSS. read.

9, 10. synagogue of the Libertines—Jewish freedmen; manumitted Roman captives, or the children of such, expelled from Rome (as appears from JOSEPHUS and TACITUS), and now residing at Jerusalem. **Cyrenians**—Jews of Cyrene, in Libya, on the coast of Africa. **them of Cilicia**—amongst whom may have been Saul of Tarsus (ch. 7:58; 21:39). **and of Asia**—See on ch. 16:6.

10. not able to resist the wisdom and the spirit by which he spake—What he said, and the power with which he spake it, were alike resistless.

ADAM CLARKE

7. *The word of God increased.* By such preachers as the apostles and these deacons, no wonder the doctrine of God increased—became widely diffused and generally known; in consequence of which the number of the disciples must be greatly multiplied—for God will ever bless His own Word when ministered by those whom He has qualified to proclaim it. *A great company of the priests were obedient to the faith.* This was one of the greatest miracles wrought by the grace of Christ; that persons so intent on the destruction of Christ, His apostles, and His doctrine should at last espouse that doctrine is astonishing, and that they who had withstood the evidence of the miracles of Christ should have yielded to the doctrine of His death and resurrection is worthy of note. And from this we may learn that it is not by miracles that sinners are to be converted unto God, but by the preaching of Christ dying for their offenses and rising again for their justification.

8. *Stephen, full of faith and power.* Instead of *faith,* "grace" is the reading of some MSS.

9. *The synagogue . . . of the Libertines.* That Jews and proselytes from various countries had now come up to Jerusalem to bring offerings and to attend the Feast of Pentecost we have already seen, chap. ii. The persons mentioned here were foreign Jews, who appear to have had a synagogue peculiar to themselves at Jerusalem, in which they were accustomed to worship when they came to the public festivals.

10. *They were not able to resist the wisdom.* He was wise, well-exercised, and experienced in divine things; and, as appears by his defense in the following chapter, well-versed in the

MATTHEW HENRY

It is not said, They were not able to resist him, but, They were not able to resist the *wisdom and the Spirit by which he spoke*. They thought they had only disputed with Stephen; but they were disputing with the Spirit of God in him, for whom they were an unequal match.

III. At length, he sealed it with his blood. When they could not answer his arguments as a disputant, they prosecuted him as a criminal, and suborned witnesses against him, to swear blasphemy upon him. They suborned men, that is, instructed them what to say, and then hired them to swear it.

1. How they incensed both the government and the mob against him (*v.* 12): *They stirred up the people* against him, that, if the sanhedrim should still think fit to let him alone, yet they might run him down by a popular tumult; they also found means to stir up the elders and scribes against him, that, if the people should countenance him, they might prevail by authority. Thus they doubted not but to gain their point, when they had two strings to their bow.

2. How they got him to the bar: *They came upon him and caught him and brought him to the council.* They came upon him in a body, and flew upon him as a lion upon his prey; so the word signifies.

3. How they were prepared with evidence ready to produce against him. They had *heard him speak blasphemous words against Moses and against God* (*v.* 11)—against this *holy place and the law* (*v.* 13); for they heard him say what Jesus would do to their place and their customs, *v.* 14. Those who swore it against him are called *false witnesses*, because though there was something of truth in their testimony, yet they put a wrong and malicious construction upon what he had said, and perverted it. The general charge exhibited against him—that he *spoke blasphemous words*; and, to aggravate the matter, "He *ceases not to speak blasphemous words*." It intimates likewise something of contumacy and contempt of admonition. "He has been warned against it, and yet ceases not to talk at this rate." Stephen's persecutors would be thought to have a deep concern upon them for the honour of God's name, and to do this in a jealousy for that. He is said to have spoken blasphemous words *against Moses and against God*. But did Stephen blaspheme Moses? By no means. Christ, and the preachers of his gospel, never said anything that looked like blaspheming Moses. Very unjustly therefore is Stephen indicted for blaspheming Moses. How this charge is supported and made out. All they can charge him with is that *that he hath spoken blasphemous words against this holy place and the law*. Thus does the charge dwindle when it comes to the evidence. He is charged with blaspheming *this holy place*. Christ was condemned as a blasphemer for words which were thought to reflect upon the temple, even when they by their wickedness had profaned it. He is charged with blaspheming *the law*. The charge dwindles again; for all they can accuse him of is that *they had heard him say* that this *Jesus of Nazareth shall destroy this place, and change the customs which Moses delivered to us*. He could not be charged with having said anything to the disparagement either of the temple or of the law. He had said, *Jesus of Nazareth shall destroy this place*, destroy the temple, destroy Jerusalem. It is probable that he might say so; and what blasphemy was it against the holy place to say that it should not be perpetual. And is he a blasphemer, then, who tells them that Jesus of Nazareth will bring a just destruction upon their place and nation, and they may thank themselves? He had said, *This Jesus shall change the customs which Moses delivered to us. Christ came, not to destroy*, but to fulfil, the law; and, if he changed some customs it was to introduce and establish those that were much better.

IV. We are here told how God owned him (*v.* 15): *All that sat in the council, looking steadfastly on him, saw his face as it had been the face of an angel.* It is usual for judges to observe the countenance of the prisoner, which sometimes is an indication either of guilt or innocence. He looked as if he had never been better pleased in his life than he was now when he stood fair for the crown of martyrdom. Such an undisturbed serenity, such an undaunted courage, and such an unaccountable mixture of mildness and majesty, there was in his countenance, that everyone said he looked like an angel. There was a miraculous splendour and brightness upon his countenance, God designing thereby to put honour upon his faithful witness and confusion upon his persecutors and judges. *All that sat in the council saw it*, and an arrant shame it was that they could not but see by it that he was owned of God. Wisdom and holiness make a man's face to shine, and yet these will not secure men from the greatest indignities.

JAMIESON, FAUSSET, BROWN

11-14. blasphemous words against Moses—doubtless referring to the impending disappearance of the whole Mosaic system. **and against God**—This must refer to the supreme dignity and authority which he claimed for Christ, as the head of that new economy which was so speedily to supersede the old (cf. ch. 7:56, 59, 60).

ALBERT BARNES:

"Looking stedfastly on him." Fixing the eyes intently on him. Probably they were attracted by the unusual appearance of the man, his meekness, his calm and collected fearlessness, and the proofs of conscious innocence and sincerity. "The face of an angel." This expression is one evidently denoting that he manifested evidence of sincerity, gravity, fearlessness, confidence in God. It is used in the Old Testament to denote peculiar wisdom (2 Sam. 14:17; 19:27). In Gen. 23:10, it is used to denote peculiar majesty and glory, as if it were the face of God. When Moses came down from Mount Sinai, it is said that the skin of his face shone so that the children of Israel were afraid to come nigh to him (Ex. 34:29, 30; 2 Cor. 3:7, 13). The expression is used to denote the impression produced on the countenance by communion with God; the calm serenity and composure which follow a confident committing of all into his hands. It is not meant that there was anything miraculous in the case of Stephen, but it is language that denotes calmness, dignity, and confidence in God, all of which were so marked on his countenance that it impressed them with clear proofs of his innocence and piety. The language is very common in the Jewish writings. It is not unusual for deep feeling, sincerity, and confidence in God, to impress themselves on the countenance. Any deep emotion will do this; and it is to be expected that religious feeling, the most tender and solemn of all feeling, will diffuse seriousness, serenity, calmness, and peace, not affected sanctimoniousness, over the countenance.—*Popular Commentary*

15. as . . . the face of an angel—a play of supernatural radiance attesting to all who beheld his countenance the divine calm of the spirit within.

ADAM CLARKE

Jewish history. The spirit by which he spake was the Holy Spirit, and its power was irresistible.

11. *Then they suborned men.* They made "underhand" work; got associated to themselves profligate persons, who for money would swear anything.

12. *And they*—the Libertines, etc., mentioned before, *stirred up the people*—raised a mob against him, and to assist and countenance the mob got the *elders* and *scribes* to conduct it, who thus made themselves one with the basest of the people whom they collected; and then altogether, without law or form of justice, rushed on the good man, seized him, and brought him to a council who, though they sat in the seat of judgment, were ready for every evil work.

Blasphemous words against Moses, and against God. This was the most deadly charge they could bring against him. We have already seen, Matt. ix. 4, that *blasphemy*, when against *God*, signifies speaking impiously of His nature, attributes, or works; and when against *men*, it signifies speaking injuriously of their character, blasting their reputation. These false witnesses came to prove that he had blasphemed Moses by representing him as an impostor, or the like; and God, by either denying His being, His providence, or the justice of His government.

13. *Against this holy place.* The Temple, that it shall be destroyed. *And the law.* That it cannot give life, nor save from death. It is very likely that they had heard him speak words to this amount, which were all as true as the spirit from which they proceeded; but they gave them a very false coloring, as we see in the succeeding verse.

15. *Saw his face as it had been the face of an angel.* It appears that the light and power of God which dwelt in his soul shone through his face, and God gave them this proof of the falsity of the testimony which was now before them; for as the face of Stephen now shone as the face of Moses did when he came down from the mount, it was the fullest proof that he had not spoken blasphemous words either against Moses or God, else this splendor of heaven had not rested upon him.

MATTHEW HENRY

CHAPTER 7

Verses 1–16

I. The high priest calls upon him to answer for himself, *v.* 1. You hear what is sworn against you: *Are these things so? Guilty or not guilty?*

II. He begins his defence, and it is long.

1. In this discourse he appears to be a man ready and mighty in the scriptures. He was *filled with the Holy Ghost*, not so much to reveal to him new things, but to bring to his remembrance the scriptures of the Old Testament, and to teach him how to make use of them. Those that are full of the Holy Ghost will be full of the scripture, as Stephen was.

2. He quotes the scriptures according to the Septuagint translation, by which it appears he was one of the Hellenist Jews. His preface: *Men, brethren, and fathers, hearken.* He gives them, though not flattering titles, yet civil and respectful ones. They are ready to look upon him as an apostate from the Jewish church, and an enemy to them. He addresses himself to them as *men, brethren, and fathers*, resolving to look on himself as one of them, though they would not so look on him. He craves their attention: *Hearken.* His entrance upon the discourse. It is all *to the purpose*, to show them that God, as he had a church in the world many ages before that holy place was founded and the ceremonial law given, so he would have when they should both have had their period.

[1] He begins with the call of Abraham, the father of the Old Testament church. His native country was an idolatrous country, it was Mesopotamia (*v.* 2), *the land of the Chaldeans* (*v.* 4); thence God brought him. He first brought him out of the land of the Chaldeans to Charran, or Haran, and thence five years after, when his father was dead, he *removed him into* the land of *Canaan, wherein you now dwell.* From this call of Abraham we may observe, 1. That in all our ways we must acknowledge God, and attend the directions of his providence. *God removed him into this land wherein you now dwell*, and he did but follow his Leader. 2. Those whom God takes into covenant with himself must sit loose to the world, and live above it and everything in it, even that in it which is most dear to them. God's chosen must follow him with an implicit faith and obedience But let us see what this is to Stephen's case. They had charged him as a blasphemer of God, therefore he shows that he is a son of Abraham, and values himself upon his being able to say, *Our father Abraham*, and that he is a faithful worshipper of the God of Abraham, whom therefore he here calls *the God of glory.* They were proud of their being circumcised; and therefore he shows that Abraham was taken under God's guidance, and into communion with him, before he was circumcised. They had a mighty jealousy for this holy place, which may be meant of the whole land of Canaan. "Now," says Stephen, "you need not be so proud of it; for," (1) "You came originally out of *Ur of the Chaldees*, and you were not the first planters of this country. Think of the meanness of your beginnings, and how you are entirely indebted to divine grace, and then you will see boasting to be for ever excluded." (2) "God appeared in his glory to Abraham a great way off in Mesopotamia, before he came near Canaan, so that you must not think God's visits are confined to *this land.*"

[2] The unsettled state of Abraham and his seed for many ages after he was called out of Ur of the Chaldees. God did indeed promise that he would *give it to him for a possession, and to his seed after him, v.* 5. But, *First, As yet he had no child*, nor any by Sarah for many years after. *Secondly*, He himself was but a stranger and a sojourner in that land, and God *gave him no inheritance in it, no, not so much as to set his foot on*; but there he was as in a strange country. *Thirdly*, His posterity did not come to the possession of it for a long time: *After four hundred years* they shall come *and serve me in this place*, and not till then, *v.* 7. *Fourthly*, They must undergo a great deal of hardship before they shall be put into the possession of that land: they shall be brought into bondage, and ill treated in a strange land. And *at the end of four hundred years that nation to whom they shall be in bondage will I judge, saith God.* When Abraham had neither inheritance nor heir, yet he was told he should have both. God's promises, though they are slow, are sure. They will be fulfilled though perhaps not so soon as we expect. Though the people of God may be in distress and trouble for a time, yet God will at length both rescue them and reckon with those that do oppress them.

But let us see how this serves Stephen's purpose. . The Jewish nation was very inconsiderable in its

JAMIESON, FAUSSET, BROWN

CHAPTER 7

Vss. 1-60. DEFENSE AND MARTYRDOM OF STEPHEN. In this long defense Stephen takes a much wider range, and goes less directly into the point raised by his accusers, than we should have expected. His object seems to have been to show (1) that so far from disparaging, he deeply reverenced, and was intimately conversant with, the whole history of the ancient economy; and (2) that in resisting the erection of the Gospel kingdom they were but treading in their fathers' footsteps, the whole history of their nation being little else than one continued misapprehension of God's high designs towards fallen man and rebellion against them.

1-5. The God of glory—A magnificent appellation, fitted at the very outset to rivet the devout attention of his audience; denoting not that visible glory which attended many of the divine manifestations, but the glory of those manifestations themselves, of which this was regarded by every Jew as the fundamental one. It is the glory of absolutely free grace. **appeared unto our father Abraham before he dwelt in Charran, and said . . .**—Though this first call is not expressly recorded in Genesis, it is clearly implied in Genesis 15:7 and Nehemiah 9:7; and the Jewish writers speak the same language. **4. when his father was dead, he removed into this land**—Though Abraham was in Canaan before Terah's death, his settlement in it as the land of promise is here said to be after it, as being in no way dependent on the family movement, but a transaction purely between Jehovah and Abraham himself.

6-8. four hundred years—using round numbers, as in Genesis 15:13, 16 (see on Gal. 3:17). **after that shall they come forth, and serve me in this place**—Here the promise to Abraham (Gen. 15:16), and that to Moses (Exod. 3:12), are combined; Stephen's object being merely to give a rapid summary of the leading facts.

ADAM CLARKE

CHAPTER 7

1. *Are these things so?* Have you predicted the destruction of the Temple? And have you said that Jesus of Nazareth shall change our customs, abolish our religious rites and Temple service? Have you spoken these blasphemous things against Moses and against God? Here was some color of justice, for Stephen was permitted to defend himself. And in order to do this he thought it best to enter into a detail of their history from the commencement of their nation, and thus show how kindly God had dealt with them, and how ungraciously they and their fathers had requited Him. And all this naturally led him to the conclusion that God could no longer bear with a people the cup of whose iniquity had been long overflowing, and therefore they might expect to find wrath, without mixture of mercy. But how could Luke get all this circumstantial account? He might have been present and heard the whole; or, more probably, he had the account from Paul, whose companion he was, and who was certainly present when Stephen was judged and stoned, for he was consenting to his death and kept the clothes of them who stoned him. See chap. vii. 58; viii. 1; and xxii. 20.

2. *Men, brethren, and fathers.* Rather, "brethren and fathers." Literally it is "men-brethren," a very usual form in Greek. *The God of glory appeared.* As Stephen is now vindicating himself from the false charges brought against him, he shows that he had uttered no blasphemy against either God, Moses, or the Temple; but states that his accusers, and the Jews in general, were guilty of the faults with which they charged him, that they had from the beginning rejected and despised Moses and had always violated his laws. He proceeds to state that there is no blasphemy in saying that the Temple shall be destroyed—they had been without a temple till the days of David, nor does God ever confine himself to temples built by hands, seeing He fills both heaven and earth; that Jesus is the Prophet of whom Moses spoke, and whom they had persecuted, condemned, and at last put to death; that they were wicked and uncircumcised in heart and in ears, and always resisted the Holy Ghost, as their fathers did. This is the substance of Stephen's defense as far as he was permitted to make it, a defense which they could not confute, containing charges which they most glaringly illustrated and confirmed by adding the murder of this faithful disciple to that of his all-glorious Master. *Was in Mesopotamia.* In that part of it where Ur of the Chaldees was situated, near to Babel, and among the rivers (Tigris and Euphrates) which gave the name of Mesopotamia to the country. *Before he dwelt in Charran.* This is called Haran in our translation of Gen. xi. 31; this place also belonged to Mesopotamia, as well as Ur, but is placed west of it on the maps. It seems most probable that Abraham had two calls, one in Ur and the other in Haran. He left Ur at the first call and came to Haran; he left Haran at the second call and came into the Promised Land.

5. *Gave him none inheritance.* Both Abraham and Jacob had small parcels of land in Canaan; but they had them by purchase, not by God's gifts; for as Abraham was obliged to buy a burying place in Canaan, Genesis xxiii, it is obvious he had no inheritance there.

6. *That his seed should sojourn in a strange land.* See Gen. xv. 13-14. *Four hundred years.* Moses says, Exod. xii. 40, that the sojourning of the children of Israel in Egypt was 430 years. Paul has the same number, Gal. iii. 17; and so has Josephus. Stephen uses the round number of 400.

7. *Will I judge.* "I will punish," for in this sense the Greek word is frequently taken.

MATTHEW HENRY

beginnings; as their common father Abraham was fetched out of obscurity in Ur of the Chaldees, so their tribes were fetched out of servitude in Egypt. He that brought them out of Egypt can bring them into it again, and yet be no loser, while he can out of stones raise up children unto Abraham. 2. The slow steps by which the promise made to Abraham advanced towards the performance plainly show that it had a spiritual meaning, and that the land principally intended to be conveyed by it was the *better country, that is, the heavenly*. It was therefore no blasphemy to say, *Jesus shall destroy this place*, when at the same time we say, "He shall lead us to the heavenly Canaan."

[3] The building up of the family of Abraham.

First, God engaged to be a God to Abraham and his seed; and, in token of this, appointed that he and his male seed should be circumcised. He *gave him the covenant of circumcision*, and accordingly, when Abraham had a son born, he *circumcised him the eighth day* (*v.* 8). And then they began to multiply: *Isaac begat Jacob, and Jacob the twelve patriarchs*.

Secondly, Joseph, the darling and blessing of his father's house, was abused by his brethren; they *envied him* because of his dreams, and *sold him into Egypt*.

Thirdly, God owned Joseph in his troubles, and was with him by the influence of his Spirit, both on his mind, giving him comfort, and on the minds of those he was concerned with, giving him favour in their eyes. And thus at length he *delivered him out of his afflictions*.

Fourthly, Jacob was compelled to go down into Egypt by *a dearth* (which was a *great affliction*), to that degree that *our fathers found no sustenance* in Canaan, *v.* 11. But, hearing that there was *corn in Egypt* (treasured up by the wisdom of his own son), he *sent out our fathers first* to fetch corn, *v.* 12. And the *second time* that they went, Joseph made himself known to them, and it was notified to Pharaoh that they were Joseph's kindred (*v.* 13), whereupon *Joseph sent for his father Jacob to him into Egypt*, with *all his kindred and family*, to the number of *seventy-five souls*, *v.* 14.

Fifthly, Jacob and his sons died in Egypt (*v.* 15), but were carried over to be buried in Canaan, *v.* 16.

Let us now see what this is to Stephen's purpose. 1. He still reminds them of the mean beginning of the Jewish nation. It was by a miracle of mercy that they were raised up out of nothing to what they were. If they answer not the intention of their being so raised, they can expect no other than to be destroyed. Here it is urged upon them as an aggravation of their contempt of the gospel of Christ. 2. He reminds them likewise of the wickedness of those that were the patriarchs in envying their brother Joseph, and selling him into Egypt; and the same spirit was still working in them towards Christ. 3. Their holy land, which they doted so much upon, their fathers were long kept out of the possession of, and therefore let them not think it strange if, after it has been so long polluted with sin, it be at length destroyed.

Verses 17–29

I. The wonderful increase of the people of Israel in Egypt; it was by a wonder of providence that in a little time they advanced from a family into a nation. It was *when the time of the promise drew nigh*—the time when they were to be formed into a people. The notion of providence is sometimes quickest when it comes nearest the centre. God knows how to redeem the time that seems to have been lost, and, *when the year of the redeemed is at hand*, can do a double work in a single day. It was *in Egypt*, where they were oppressed. Suffering times have often been growing times with the church.

II. The extreme hardships which they underwent there, *v.* 18, 19. Stephen observes three things: 1. Their base ingratitude: They were oppressed by *another king that knew not Joseph*. Those that injure good people are very ungrateful, for they are the blessings of the age and place they live in. 2. Their hellish craft and policy: *They dealt subtly with our kindred. Come on*, said they, *let us deal wisely*, thinking thereby to secure themselves. Those are in a great mistake who think they deal wisely for themselves when they deal deceitfully or unmercifully with their brethren. 3. Their barbarous and inhuman cruelty. *They cast out their young children, to the end they might not live*. What they were now doing against the Christian church in its infancy was as impious and would be as fruitless as that was which the Egyptians did against the Jewish church in its infancy. In spite of your malice Christ's disciples will *increase and multiply*.

III. The raising up of *Moses to be their deliverer*. Moses was born when the persecution of Israel was

JAMIESON, FAUSSET, BROWN

the covenant of circumcision—i.e., the covenant of which circumcision was the token. **and so**—i.e., according to the terms of this covenant, on which Paul reasons (Gal. 3). **the twelve patriarchs**—so called as the founders of the twelve tribes of Israel. **9-16. the patriarchs, moved with envy, sold Joseph into Egypt, but God was with him**—Here Stephen gives his first example of *Israel's opposition to God's purposes, in spite of which and by means of which those purposes were accomplished.*

14. threescore and fifteen souls—according to the Septuagint version of Genesis 46:27, which Stephen follows, including the five children and grandchildren of Joseph's two sons.

17. But when—rather, 'as'—**the time of the promise**—i.e., for its fulfilment. **the people grew and multiplied in Egypt**—For more than 200 years they amounted to no more than seventy-five souls; how prodigious, then, must have been their multiplication during the latter two centuries, when 600,000 men, fit for war, besides women and children, left Egypt!

ADAM CLARKE

8. *He gave him the covenant of circumcision.* That is, he instituted the rite of circumcision as a sign of that covenant which He had made with him and his posterity. See Gen. xvii. 10. *And so Abraham begat Isaac.* "And thus," in this covenant, he begat Isaac; and as a proof that he was born under this covenant, was a true son of Abraham and inheritor of the promises, he circumcised him the eighth day.

9. *And the patriarchs.* The twelve sons of Jacob, thus called because each was chief or head of his respective family or tribe. *Moved with envy.* We translate *zelos* variously: "zeal" or "fervent affection," whether its object be good or bad, is its general meaning; and *zeloo* signifies to be "indignant, envious." See the note on chap. v. 17. The brethren of Joseph, hearing of his dreams, and understanding them to portend his future advancement, filled with envy, sold Joseph into the land of Egypt, hoping by this means to prevent his future grandeur; *but God*, from whom the portents came, *was with him*, and made their envy the direct means of accomplishing the great design.

10. *Gave him favour and wisdom in the sight of Pharaoh.* God gave him much *wisdom*, in consequence of which he had *favour* with the king of Egypt. See the whole of this remarkable history explained at large, Genesis xli—xlv.

14. *Threescore and fifteen souls.* There are several difficulties here, which it is hoped the reader will find satisfactorily removed in the note on Gen. xlvi. 20. It is well-known that in Genesis xlvi and Deut. x. 22 their number is said to be "threescore and ten"; but Stephen quotes from the Septuagint, which adds five persons to the account which are not in the Hebrew text.

16. *And were carried over to Sychem.* "It is said, Gen. l. 13, that Jacob was buried in the cave of the field of Machpelah before Mamre. And in Josh. xxiv. 32 and Exod. xiii. 19, it is said that the bones of Joseph were carried out of Egypt by the Israelites, and buried in Shechem, which Jacob bought from the sons of Hamor, the father of Shechem. As for the eleven brethren of Joseph, we are told by Josephus, *Ant.*, l. ii, c. 8, s. 2, that they were buried in Hebron, where their father had been buried. But, since the books of the Old Testament say nothing about this, the authority of Stephen (or of Luke here) for their being buried in Sychem is at least as good as that of Josephus for their being buried in Hebron."—Bishop Pearce. We have the uniform consent of the Jewish writers that all the patriarchs were brought out of Egypt and buried in Canaan, but none, except Stephen, mentions their being buried in Sychem. As Sychem belonged to the Samaritans, probably the Jews thought it too great an honor for that people to possess the bones of the patriarchs, and therefore have carefully avoided making any mention of it. *That Abraham bought for a sum of money.* Two accounts seem here to be confounded: (1) The purchase made by Abraham of the cave and field of Ephron, which was in the field of Machpelah; this purchase was made from the children of Heth, Gen. xxiii. 3, 10, 17. (2) The purchase made by Jacob, from the sons of Hamor or Emmor, of a sepulchre in which the bones of Joseph were laid; this was in Sychem or Shechem, Gen. xxxiii. 19; Josh. xxiv. 32. The word *Abraham*, therefore, in this place is certainly a mistake; and the word *Jacob*, which some have supplied, is doubtless more proper. Bishop Pearce supposes that Luke originally wrote, "which he bought for a sum of money"; i.e., which Jacob bought, who is the last person of the singular number spoken of in the preceding verse. Those who saw that the word *bought* had no nominative case joined to it, and did not know where to find the proper one, seem to have inserted *Abraham* in the text for that purpose, without sufficiently attending to the different circumstances of his purchase from that of Jacob's.

19. *The same dealt subtilly.* A word borrowed from the Septuagint, who thus translate the Hebrew, "Let us deal wisely with it"; i.e., with cunning and deceit, as the Greek word implies and which is evidently intended by the Hebrew. See Gen. xxvii. 35, "Thy brother came with

MATTHEW HENRY

at the hottest: *At that time, Moses was born* (*v.* 20), and was himself in danger of falling a sacrifice to that bloody edict. God is preparing for his people's deliverance, when their way is darkest, and their distress deepest. *He was exceedingly fair.* He was sanctified from the womb, and this made him beautiful in God's eyes. He was wonderfully preserved in his infancy, first, by the care of his tender parents, who *nourished him three months in their own house*; and then by a favourable providence that threw him *into the arms of Pharaoh's daughter, who took him up, and nourished him as her own son* (*v.* 21); for those whom God designs to make special use of he will take special care of. He became a great scholar (*v.* 22): *He was learned in all the wisdom of the Egyptians.* He became a prime minister of state in Egypt, being *mighty in words and deeds.* Though he had not a ready way of expressing himself, but stammered, yet he spoke admirably good sense, and everything he said commanded assent. Now, by all this, Stephen will make it appear that he had as high and honourable thoughts of Moses as they had.

IV. The attempts which Moses made to deliver Israel, which they spurned. This Stephen insists much upon, and it serves for a key to this story, a designed entrance upon the public service he was to be called out to (*v.* 23): *When he was full forty years old it came into his heart* (for God put it there) *to visit his brethren the children of Israel,* and to see which way he might do them any service. 1. As Israel's saviour. This he gave a specimen of in avenging an oppressed Israelite, and killing the Egyptian that abused him (*v.* 24). *Seeing one of his brethren suffer wrong, he avenged him that was oppressed, and smote the Egyptian. He supposed that his brethren would have understood that God by his hand would deliver them.* If they had but understood the signs of the times, they might have taken this for the dawning of the day of their deliverance; *but they understood not.* 2. As Israel's judge. This he gave a specimen of, *the very next day,* in offering to accommodate matters between two contending Hebrews (*v.* 26): *He showed himself to them as they strove,* and *he would have set them at one again, saying, Sirs, you are brethren, why do you wrong one to another?* For he observed that (as in most strifes) there was a fault on both sides; and therefore there must be a mutual remission and condescension. *But* the contending Israelite that was most in *the wrong thrust him away* (*v.* 27), would not bear the reproof, but was ready to fly in his face, with, *Who made thee a ruler and a judge over us?* Proud and litigious spirits are impatient of check and control. The wrong-doer was so enraged at the reproof given him that he upbraided Moses with the service he had done to their nation in killing the Egyptian: *Wilt thou kill me as thou didst the Egyptian yesterday?* (*v.* 28), charging that upon him as his crime, which was the hanging out of the flag of defiance to the Egyptians, and the banner of love and deliverance to Israel. Hereupon *Moses fled into the land of Midian.* He settled as a stranger in Midian, married, and had two sons, by Jethro's daughter, *v.* 29. How this serves Stephen's purpose. 1. They charged him with blaspheming Moses, in answer to which he retorts upon them the indignities which their fathers did to Moses, which they ought to be ashamed of, instead of picking quarrels with one that had as great a veneration for him as any of them had. 2. They persecuted him for disputing in defence of Christ and his gospel. They set up Moses and his law: "But," saith he, "you had best take heed," (1) "Lest you refuse and reject one *whom God has raised up to be to you a prince and a Saviour.* God will, by this Jesus, deliver you out of a worse slavery than that in Egypt; take heed then of thrusting him away." (2) "Lest you hereby fare as your fathers fared. You put away the gospel from you, and it will be *sent to the Gentiles*; you will not have Christ, and you shall not have him."

Verses 30–41

Stephen here proceeds in his story of Moses.

I. The vision which he saw of the glory of God at the bush (*v.* 30): *When forty years had expired,* now, at eighty years old, he enters upon that post of honour to which he was born. Where God appeared to him: *In the wilderness of Mount Sinai, v.* 30. And, when he appeared to him there, that was holy ground (*v.* 33), which Stephen takes notice of, as a check to those who prided themselves in the temple, as if there were no communion to be had with God but there. They deceive themselves if they think God is confined to places; he can bring his people into a wilderness, and there speak comfortably to them. How he appeared to him: *In a flame of fire,* and yet *the bush was not consumed.* How Moses was affected with this: (1) *He wondered at the sight, v.* 31. He had the curiosity at first to pry into it: *I will turn aside now,*

JAMIESON, FAUSSET, BROWN

20-22. In which time—of deepest depression. **Moses was born**—the destined deliverer. **exceeding fair**—lit., 'fair to God' (*Margin*), or, perhaps, divinely 'fair' (see on Heb. 11:23).

22. mighty in words—Though defective in utterance (Exod. 4:10); his recorded speeches fully bear out what is here said. **and deeds**—referring probably to unrecorded circumstances in his early life. If we are to believe JOSEPHUS, his ability was acknowledged ere he left Egypt.

23-27. In verses 23, 30, and 36, the life of Moses is represented as embracing three periods, of forty years each; the Jewish writers say the same; and though this is not expressly stated in the Old Testament, his age at death, 120 years (Deut. 34:7), agrees with it. **23. it came into his heart to visit his brethren**—his heart yearning with love to them as God's chosen people, and heaving with the consciousness of a divine vocation to set them free. **24. avenged him that was oppressed, and smote the Egyptian**—going farther in the heat of his indignation than he probably intended. **25. For he supposed his brethren would have understood . . .**—and perhaps imagined this a suitable occasion for rousing and rallying them under him as their leader; thus anticipating his work, and so running unsent. **but they understood not**—Reckoning on a spirit in them congenial with his own, he had the mortification to find it far otherwise. This furnishes to Stephen another example of *Israel's slowness to apprehend and fall in with the divine purposes of love.* **26. next day he showed himself unto them as they strove**—Here, not an Israelite and an Egyptian, but two parties in Israel itself, are in collision with each other; Moses, grieved at the spectacle, interposes as a mediator; but his interference, as unauthorized, is resented by the party in the wrong, *whom Stephen identifies with the mass of the nation* (vs. 35), just as Messiah's own interposition had been spurned.

28, 29. Wilt thou kill me, as thou didst the Egyptian yesterday?—Moses had thought the deed unseen (Exod. 2:12), but it now appeared he was mistaken. **Then fled Moses . . .**—for "when Pharaoh heard this thing, he sought to slay Moses" (Exod. 2:15).

ADAM CLARKE

subtilty." For this the Egyptians were so remarkable that "to Egyptize" signified "to act cunningly" and "to use wicked devices." *To the end they might not live.* Might not grow up and propagate, and thus build up the Hebrew nation.

20. *Moses . . . was exceeding fair.* "Was fair to God"; i.e., was divinely beautiful. See the note on Exod. ii. 2.

22. *In all the wisdom of the Egyptians.* Who were, at that time, the most intelligent and best instructed people in the universe. Philo says Moses was taught arithmetic, geometry, poetry, music, medicine, and the knowledge of hieroglyphics. In *Sohar Cadash,* fol. 46, it is said "that, of the ten portions of wisdom which came into the world, the Egyptians had nine, and that all the inhabitants of the earth had only the remaining portion." *Was mighty in words and in deeds.* This may refer to the glorious doctrines he taught and the miracles he wrought in Egypt.

23. *When he was full forty years old.* This was a general tradition among the Jews: "Moses was forty years in Pharaoh's court, forty years in Midian, and forty years he served Israel." *To visit his brethren.* Probably on the ground of trying to deliver them from their oppressive bondage. This desire seems to have been early infused into his mind by the Spirit of God; and the effect of this desire to deliver his oppressed countrymen was his refusing to be called the son of Pharoah's daughter—(see Heb. xi. 24) and thus renouncing all right to the Egyptian crown, "choosing rather to endure affliction with the people of God, than to enjoy the pleasures of sin for a season."

24. *Smote the Egyptian.* See this explained, Exod. ii. 11-12.

25. *He supposed his brethren would have understood.* He probably imagined that, as he felt from the divine influence he was appointed to be their deliverer, they would have his divine appointment signified to them in a similar way; and the act of justice which he now did in behalf of his oppressed countryman would be sufficient to show them that he was now ready to enter upon his office, if they were willing to concur.

26. *Unto them as they strove.* Two Hebrews. See on Exod. ii. 13, etc.

30. *In a flame of fire in a bush.* See this and the following verses largely explained in the notes on Exod. iii. 1-8.

F. B. MEYER:

Moses, we are here told, was "mighty in words"; that is, in eloquence as well as "in deeds." This confirms the statement of the Jewish historian, Josephus, that in the earlier part of his career, now lost in the oblivion of history, Moses led a very successful Egyptian expedition against Ethiopia. He complains to the Lord (Ex. 4:10) of being slow of speech, but that probably refers to the habit of long disuse amid the silence and loneliness of the desert.

It is clear that stung by the sense of wrong, Moses at first interfered to deliver his people. He smote the Egyptian and tried to judge between his brethren. God had to bring him into the dust by repeated failure and rejection, that he might become an emptied and a broken vessel. God will not give glory to man. The treasure must be held in an earthen vessel (2 Cor. 4:7). It is when we come to the end of ourselves that we arrive at the beginning of God. The world has ever to learn what God can do by those who are wholly emptied of self-confidence, but yielded to his hand.
—*Bible Commentary*

MATTHEW HENRY

and see this great sight; but the nearer he drew the more he was struck with amazement. (2) *He trembled, and durst not behold,* for he was soon aware that it was *the angel of the Lord.* This set him a trembling.

II. The declaration which he heard of the covenant of God (*v.* 32): *The voice of the Lord came to him; I am the God of thy fathers, the God of Abraham, the God of Isaac, and the God of Jacob;* and therefore, 1. "I am the same that I was." The covenant God made with Abraham was, *I will be to thee a God.* "Now," saith God, "that covenant is still in full force; I am, as I was, the God of Abraham." All the favours, all the honours God put upon Israel, were founded upon this covenant with Abraham. 2. "I will be the same that I am." He will be a God, (1) To their souls, which are now separated from their bodies. Our Saviour by this proves the future state, Matt. xxii. 31, 32. Abraham is dead, and yet God is still his God, therefore Abraham is still alive. Now this is that life and immortality which are brought to light by the gospel. Those therefore who stood up in defence of the gospel were so far from blaspheming Moses that they did the greatest honour imaginable to Moses. (2) To their seed, God, in declaring himself thus the God of their fathers, intimated his kindness to their seed, that they should be *beloved for the fathers' sakes.* Now the preachers of the gospel preached up this covenant, *the promise made of God unto the fathers, ch.* xxvi. 6, 7. And shall they, under colour of supporting the holy place and the law, oppose the covenant which was made with Abraham, before the law was given, and long before the holy place was built? God will have our salvation to be by promise, and not by the law; the Jews therefore who persecuted the Christians, under pretence that they blasphemed the law, did themselves blaspheme the promise.

III. The commission which God gave him to deliver Israel out of Egypt. When God had declared himself the God of Abraham he proceeded, 1. To order Moses into a reverent posture: *"Put off thy shoes from thy feet.* Be not hasty and rash in thy approaches to God; tread softly." 2. To order Moses into a very eminent service. He is commissioned to demand leave from Pharaoh for Israel to go out of his land, *v.* 34. Observe, (1) The notice God took both of their sufferings and of their sense of their sufferings: *I have seen, I have seen their affliction, and have heard their groaning.* Their deliverance takes rise from his pity. (2) The determination he fixed to redeem them by the hand of Moses: *I am come down to deliver them.* Moses is the man that must be employed: *Come, and I will send thee into Egypt:* and, if God send him, he will give him success.

IV. His acting in pursuance of this commission. 1. God put honour upon him whom they put contempt upon (*v.* 35): *This Moses whom they refused saying, Who made thee a ruler and a judge? did God send to be a ruler, and a deliverer, by the hand of the angel which appeared to him in the bush.* Now, by this example, Stephen would intimate to the council *that this Jesus whom they now refused saying, Who gave thee this authority?* has God advanced *to be a prince and a Saviour,* as the apostles had told them awhile ago (*ch.* v. 30, 31), *that the stone which the builders refused was become the headstone in the corner, ch.* iv. 11. 2. God showed favour to them by him. God might justly have refused them his service, but it is all forgotten, *v.* 36. *He brought them out after he had shown wonders and signs in the land of Egypt, in the Red Sea, and in the wilderness forty years.* So far is he from blaspheming Moses that he admires him as a glorious instrument in the hand of God. But it does not at all derogate from his just honour to say that he was but an instrument, and that he is outshone by this Jesus, whom he encourages these Jews yet to close with. The people of Israel were delivered by Moses, though they had once refused him.

V. His prophecy of Christ and his grace, *v.* 37. Moses spoke of him (*v.* 37): *This is that Moses who said unto the children of Israel, A prophet shall the Lord your God raise up unto you of your brethren.* This is spoken of as one of the greatest honours God put upon him, that by him he gave notice to the children of Israel of the great prophet that should come into the world. In asserting that Jesus should change the customs of the ceremonial law, he was so far from blaspheming Moses that really he did him the greatest honour imaginable. Christ told them himself, *If they had believed Moses, they would have believed him,* John v. 46. Moses told them that they should have a prophet raised up among them, one of their own nation, who should therefore have authority to change the customs that he had delivered, and to bring in a better hope, as *the Mediator of a better*

JAMIESON, FAUSSET, BROWN

30-34. an angel of the Lord—rather, **'the Angel of the Covenant,' who immediately calls Himself** JEHOVAH (cf. vs. 38).

35-41. This Moses whom they refused, saying, Who made thee a ruler and a judge . . .—Here, again, *"the stone which the builders refused is made the head of the corner"* (Ps. 118:22).

37. This is that Moses which said . . ., A prophet . . . him shall ye hear—This is quoted to remind his Moses-worshipping audience of the grand testimony of their faithful lawgiver, that *he himself was not the last and proper object of the Church's faith, but only a humble precursor and small model of Him to whom their absolute submission was due.*

ADAM CLARKE

36. *He brought them out, after that he had shewed wonders.* Thus the very person whom they had rejected, and in effect delivered up into the hands of Pharaoh that he might be slain, was the person alone by whom they were redeemed from their Egyptian bondage. And does not Stephen plainly say by this that the very Person, Jesus Christ, whom they had rejected and delivered up into the hands of Pilate to be crucified was the Person alone by whom they could be delivered out of their spiritual bondage and made partakers of the inheritance among the saints in light?

37. *This is that Moses, which said . . . A prophet.* This very Moses, so highly esteemed and honored by God, announced that very Prophet whom you have lately put to death.

A. T. ROBERTSON:

30. Sentence begins with genitive absolute again. "In a flame of fire in a bush" (*en phlogi puros batou*). Horeb in Ex. 3:1; but Sinai and Horeb were "probably peaks of one mountain range" (Page), Horeb "the mountain of the dried-up ground," Sinai "the mountain of the thorns." Literally, "in the flame of fire of a bush" (two genitives, *puros* and *batou* dependent on *phlogi,* flame). Descriptive genitives as in 9:15; 2 Thess. 1:8. *Batos* (bush) is the wild acacia (*mimosa nilotica*). In Ex. 3:20 it is Jehovah who speaks. Hence "angel" here with Stephen is understood to be the Angel of the Presence, the Eternal Logos of the Father, the Angel of Jehovah.

31. "The sight" (*to horama*). Used of visions in the N.T. as in Matt. 17:9. "As he drew near" (*proserchomenou autou*). Genitive absolute with present middle participle of *proserchomai.* "A voice of the Lord" (*phone kuriou*). Here the angel of Jehovah of verse 30 is termed Jehovah himself. Jesus makes powerful use of these words in his reply to the Sadducees in defense of the doctrine of the resurrection and the future life (Mark 12:26; Matt. 22:32; Luke 20:37) that God here describes himself as the God of the living. "Trembled" (*entromos genomenos*). Literally, becoming tremulous or terrified. The adjective *entromos* (*en, tromos* from *tremo,* to tremble, to quake) occurs in Plutarch and the LXX. In the N.T. only here and Acts 16:29. "Durst not" (*ouk etolma*). Imperfect active, was not daring, negative conative imperfect.

33. "Holy ground" (*ge hagia*). The priests were barefooted when they ministered in the temple. Moslems enter their mosques barefooted today (cf. Josh. 5:15). "Sandal" (*hupodema,* bound under) is here "a distributive singular" (Hackett). Even the ground near the bush was "holy," a fine example for Stephen's argument.

34. "I have surely seen" (*idon eidon*). Imitation of the Hebrew infinitive absolute (Ex. 3:7). "Seeing I saw" (Heb. 6:14). "The affliction" (*ten kakosin*). From *kakoo,* to treat evilly (from *kakos,* evil). Old word, here only in the N.T. and from Ex. 3:7. "Groaning" (*stenagmou*). Old word from *stenazo,* to sigh, to groan. In the N.T. only here and Rom. 8:26. Root *sten* in our word stentorian. "I am come down" (*kateben*). Second aorist active indicative of *katabaino,* I came down. "To deliver" (*exelesthai*). Second aorist middle infinitive of *exaireo,* to take out for myself. "I will send" (*aposteilo*). First aorist active subjunctive (hortatory of *apostello,* "Let me send").

—*Word Pictures in the New Testament*

MATTHEW HENRY

testament. He charged them to hear that prophet. This will be the greatest honour you can do to Moses and to his law, who said, *Hear you him.*

VI. The eminent services which Moses continued to do to the people of Israel, after he had been instrumental to bring them out of Egypt, *v.* 38. It was the honour of Moses, 1. That *he was in the church in the wilderness*; he presided in all the affairs of it for forty years. Many a time it had been destroyed if Moses had not been in it to intercede for it. But Christ is the president and guide of a more excellent and glorious church, and is more in it, as the life and soul of it, than Moses could be in that. 2. That *he was with the angel that spoke to him in the mount Sinai, and with our fathers. Moses was in the church in the wilderness*, but it was *with the angel that spoke to him in mount Sinai.* That angel was guide to him, else he could not have been a guide to Israel Christ is himself that angel and therefore has an authority above Moses. 3. That *he received the lively oracles to give unto them*; not only the ten commandments, but the other instructions which *the Lord spoke unto Moses.* The words of God are *oracles*, certain and infallible, by them all controversies must be determined. They are *lively oracles.* The word that God speaks is spirit and life; not that the law of Moses could give life, but it showed the way to life. Moses received them from God, and delivered nothing but what *he had first received from God.* The lively oracles which he received from God he faithfully gave to the people. He that gave them those customs by his servant Moses might change the customs by his Son Jesus, who received more lively oracles to give unto us than Moses did.

VII. The contempt that was put upon him by the people. Those that charged Stephen with speaking against Moses tread in their ancestors' steps. *They would not obey him, but thrust him from them, v.* 39. *In their hearts they turned back again into Egypt*, and preferred their garlic and onions there before the manna they had under the guidance of Moses, or the milk and honey they hoped for in Canaan. Many that pretend to be going forward towards Canaan are, at the same time, in their hearts turning back to Egypt. Now, if the customs that Moses delivered to them could not prevail to change them, wonder not that Christ comes to change the customs. *They made a golden calf*, a great indignity to Moses: for it was upon this consideration that they made the calf, because "*as for this Moses, who brought us out of the land of Egypt, we know not what is become of him.*" As if a calf were sufficient to supply the want of Moses, and as capable of going before them into the promised land. *So they made a calf in those days, and offered sacrifices unto the idol, and rejoiced in the work of their own hands.* By all this it appears that there was a great deal which the law could not do. It was therefore necessary that this law should be perfected by a better hand, and he was no blasphemer against Moses who said that Christ had done it.

Verses 42–50

I. Stephen upbraids them with the idolatry of their fathers, which God gave them up to. This was the saddest punishment of all for that sin, *that God gave them up to a reprobate mind* (*v.* 42): *Then God turned, and gave them up to worship the host of heaven.* For this he quotes a passage out of Amos v. 25. For it would be less invidious to tell them their own character and doom from an Old Testament prophet, who upbraids them,

1. For not sacrificing to their own God in the wilderness (*v.* 42): *Have you offered to me slain beasts, and sacrifices, by the space of forty years in the wilderness?* No: during all that time sacrifices to God were intermitted; they did not so much as keep the passover after the second year. This is also a check to their zeal for the customs that Moses delivered to them, and their fear of having them changed by *this Jesus*, that immediately after they were delivered these customs were for forty years together disused.

2. For sacrificing to other gods after they came to Canaan (*v.* 43): *You took up the tabernacle of Moloch* Moloch was the idol of the children of Ammon, to which they barbarously offered their own children in sacrifice; yet this unnatural idolatry they arrived at, when *God gave them up to worship the host of heaven. Yea, you took up the tabernacle of Moloch*, you submitted even to that, and to the worship of *the star of your god Remphan.* Some think *Saturn*, for that planet is called *Remphan* in the Syriac. The Septuagint puts it for *Chiun.* They had images representing the star, like the silver shrines for Diana, here called *the figures which they made to worship.* A poor thing to make an idol of, and yet better than a golden calf! Now for this it is threatened, *I will carry you away beyond Babylon.* Let it not therefore seem strange

JAMIESON, FAUSSET, BROWN

38. in the church—the collective body of God's chosen people; hence used to denote the whole body of the faithful under the Gospel, or particular sections of them. **This is he that was in the church in the wilderness, with the angel . . . and with our fathers**—alike near to the Angel of the Covenant, from whom he received all the institutions of the ancient economy, and to the people, to whom he faithfully reported the living oracles and among whom he set up the prescribed institutions. *By this high testimony to Moses, Stephen rebuts the main charge for which he was on trial.*

39. To whom our fathers would not obey . . .—Here he shows that *the deepest dishonor done to Moses came from the nation that now professed the greatest jealousy for his honor.* **in their hearts turned back . . . into Egypt**—*In this Stephen would have his hearers read the downward career on which they were themselves entering.*

42-50. gave them up—judicially. **as . . . written in the book of the prophets**—the twelve minor prophets, reckoned as one: the passage is from Amos 5:25.

42. have ye offered to me . . . sacrifices?—The answer is, Yes, but as if ye did it not; for "neither did ye offer to Me only, nor always, nor with a perfect and willing heart" [BENGEL].

43. Yea, ye took up the tabernacle of Molech . . .—Two kinds of idolatry are charged upon the Israelites: that of the golden calf and that of the heavenly bodies; Molech and Remphan being deities, representing apparently the divine powers ascribed to nature, under different aspects. **carry you beyond Babylon**—the well-known region of the captivity of Judah; while "Damascus" is used by the prophet (Amos 5:27), whither the ten tribes were carried.

ADAM CLARKE

38. *With the angel which spake to him.* Stephen shows that Moses received the law by the ministry of angels, and that he was only a mediator between the angel of God and them. *The lively oracles.* The "living oracles." The doctrines of life, those doctrines obedience to which entitled them, by the promise of God, to a long life upon earth, which spoke to them of that spiritual life which every true believer has in union with his God, and promised that eternal life which those who are faithful unto death shall enjoy with Him in the realms of glory. The Greek word which we translate *oracle* signifies a "divine revelation, a communication from God himself," and is here applied to the Mosaic law; to the Old Testament in general, Rom. iii. 2; Heb. v. 12; and to divine revelation in general, 1 Pet. iv. 11.

42. *Then God turned, and gave them up.* He left them to themselves, and then they deified and worshipped the sun, moon, planets, and principal stars. *In the book of the prophets.* As this quotation is found in Amos, chap. v. 25, by the *book of the prophets* is meant the twelve minor prophets, which in the ancient Jewish division of the sacred writings formed only one book. *Have ye offered to me slain beasts.* It is certain that the Israelites did offer various sacrifices to God while in the wilderness, and it is as certain that they scarcely ever did it with an upright heart.

43. *Ye took up the tabernacle of Moloch, and the star of your god Remphan, figures which ye made to worship them.* This is a literal translation of the place, as it stands in the Septuagint; but in the Hebrew text it stands thus: "But ye have borne the tabernacle of your Molech, and Chiun, your images, the star of your god which ye made to yourselves." This is the simple version of the place, unless we should translate "ye took Sikuth your king" (instead of "ye took up the tabernacle of your Molek"), as some have done. The place is indeed very obscure, and the two texts do not tend to cast light on each other. The rabbins say *siccuth,* which we translate "tabernacle," is the name of an idol. Molech is generally understood to mean the sun; and several persons of good judgment think that by *Remphan* or "Raiphan" is meant the planet Saturn. It will be seen above that instead of *Remphan,* or, as some of the best MSS. have it, *Rephan,* the Hebrew text has *Chiun,* which might possibly be a corruption of *Reiphan.* This emendation would bring the Hebrew, Septuagint, and the text of Luke, nearer together; but there is no authority either from MSS. or versions for this correction. However, as *Chiun* is mentioned in no other place, though *Molech* often occurs, it is the more likely that there might have been some very early mistake in the text, and that the Septuagint has preserved the true reading. It was customary for the idolaters of all nations to carry images of their gods about them in their journeys, military expeditions; and these, being very small, were enclosed in little boxes, perhaps some of them in the shape of temples, called "tabernacles"; or, as we have it, chap. xix. 24, "shrines." Such images as these I suppose the idolatrous Israelites, in imitation of their neighbors, the Moabites, Ammonites, etc., to have carried about with them; and to such the prophet appears to me unquestionably to allude. *I will carry you away beyond Babylon.* You have carried your idolatrous images about; and I will carry you into captivity, and see if the gods in whom you have trusted can deliver you from My hands. Instead of *beyond Babylon,* Amos, from whom the quotation is made, says, "I will carry you beyond Damascus." Where they were carried was into Assyria and Media, not Damascus, but beyond Babylon itself; and as Stephen knew this to be the fact, he states it here, and thus more precisely fixes the place of their captivity. The Holy Spirit, in His further revelations, has undoubted right to extend or illustrate those which He had given before. This case frequently occurs when a former prophecy is quoted in later times.

MATTHEW HENRY

to them to hear of the destruction of this place, for they had heard of it many a time from the prophets of the Old Testament.

II. He gives an answer particularly to the charge relating to the temple, *that he spoke blasphemous words against that holy place, v.* 44–50. He was accused for saying that Jesus would destroy this holy place: "And what if I did say so?" (saith Stephen) "the glory of the holy God may be preserved untouched, though this be laid in the dust"; for, 1. "It was not till our fathers came into the wilderness, that they had any fixed place of worship. He that was worshipped without a holy place in the first, and best, and purest ages of the Old Testament church, may and will be so when this holy place is destroyed." 2. The holy place was at first but a tabernacle, mean and movable, not designed to continue always. Why might not this holy place, be decently brought to its end, as well as that? 3. That tabernacle was *a tabernacle of witness*, or of testimony. This was the glory both of the tabernacle and temple, that they were erected for a testimony. 4. That tabernacle was framed *according to the fashion which Moses saw in the mount.* It had reference to good things to come. Therefore it was no diminution at all to its glory to say that this temple made with hands should be destroyed, in order to the building of *another made without hands.* 5. That tabernacle was pitched first in the wilderness; it was not a native of this land of yours, but was brought in by our fathers, into the possession of the Gentiles, *whom God drove out before the face of our fathers.* And why may not God set up his spiritual temple in those countries that were now the possession of the Gentiles? That tabernacle was brought in by those who came *with Jesus*, that is, *Joshua.* So the New-Testament Joshua should bring in the true tabernacle into the possession of the Gentiles. 6. That tabernacle continued *even to the days of David*, before there was any thought of building a temple, *v.* 45. David, having *found favour before God*, did indeed desire this further favour, to have leave to build God a constant settled tabernacle, or dwelling-place. Those who have found favour with God should show themselves forward to advance the interests of his kingdom among men. 7. God had his heart so little upon a temple that, when David desired to build one, he was forbidden to do it; God was in no haste for one. It was not he, but his son Solomon, some years after, that built him a house. 8. God often declared that temples made with hands were not his delight. Solomon acknowledged that God *dwelleth not in temples made with hands.* The whole world is his temple, in which he is everywhere present, and fills it with his glory; and what occasion has he for a temple? The one only true and living God needs no temple, for *the heaven is his throne*, in which he rests, *and the earth is his footstool*, over which he rules (*v.* 49, 50), and therefore, *What house will you build me, what is the place of my rest?* What need have I of a house, either to repose myself in or to show myself? *Hath not my hand made all these things?* And as the world is thus God's temple, wherein he is manifested, so it is God's temple in which he will be worshipped. As the earth is full of his glory, so the earth is, or shall be, full of his praise, and upon this account it is his temple. It was therefore no reflection at all upon this holy place, to say *that Jesus should destroy this temple*, and set up another, into which all nations should be admitted, *ch.* xv. 16, 17.

Verses 51–53

Stephen was going on in his discourse (as it should seem by the thread of it) to show that, as the temple, so the temple-service must come to an end. But he perceived they could not bear it. They will not so much as give him the hearing. He breaks off abruptly and by that spirit of wisdom, courage, and power, wherewith he was filled, he sharply rebuked his persecutors. If they will not admit the testimony of the gospel to them, it shall become a testimony against them.

I. They, like their fathers, were stubborn and wilful, and would not be brought upon by the various methods God took to reclaim and reform them. 1. They were *stiff-necked* (*v.* 51), and would not submit their necks to the sweet and easy yoke of God's government. They would not bow their heads, no, not to God himself, would not humble themselves before him. 2. They were *uncircumcised in heart and ears.* "In name and show you are circumcised Jews, but in heart and ears you are still uncircumcised heathens, and pay no more deference to the authority of your God than they do."

II. They were not only not influenced by the methods God took to reform them, but they were enraged and incensed against them: *You do always resist*

JAMIESON, FAUSSET, BROWN

44. Our fathers had the tabernacle of witness in the wilderness—which aggravated the guilt of that idolatry in which they indulged, with the tokens of the divine presence constantly in the midst of them.

45. which . . . our fathers that came after—rather (*Margin*) "having received it by succession," i.e., the custody of the tabernacle from their ancestors. **brought in with Jesus**—or Joshua. **into the possession**—rather, 'at the taking possession of [the territory of] the Gentiles.' **unto the days of David**—for till then Jerusalem continued in the hands of the Jebusites. But Stephen's object in mentioning David is to hasten from the tabernacle which he set up, to the temple which his son built, in Jerusalem; and this only to show, from their own Scripture (Isa. 66:1, 2), that *even that temple,* magnificent though it was, *was not the proper resting-place of Jehovah upon earth;* as his audience and the nations had all along been prone to imagine. (What that resting-place was, even *"the contrite heart, that trembleth at God's word,"* he leaves to be gathered from the prophet referred to.)

51-53. Ye stiffnecked . . . ye do always resist the Holy Ghost . . .—It has been thought that symptoms of impatience and irritation in the audience induced Stephen to cut short his historical sketch. But as little farther light could have been thrown upon Israel's obstinacy from subsequent periods of the national history on the testimony of their own Scriptures, we should view this as the *summing up,* the brief import of the whole Israelitish history—*grossness of heart, spiritual deafness, continuous resistance of the Holy Ghost, down to the very council before whom Stephen was pleading.*

ADAM CLARKE

44. *Our fathers had the tabernacle of witness in the wilderness.* That is, the Tabernacle in which the two tables of stone written by the finger of God were laid up, as a testimony that He had delivered these laws to the people, and that they had promised to obey them. As one great design of Stephen was to show the Jews that they placed too much dependence on outward privileges, and had not used the law, the Tabernacle, the Temple, nor the Temple service for the purpose of their institution, he labors to bring them to a due sense of this, that conviction might lead to repentance and conversion. And he further shows that God did not confine His worship to one place or form. He was worshipped without any shrine in the times of the patriarchs, Abraham, Isaac, Jacob. He was worshipped with a Tabernacle, or portable temple, in the wilderness. He was worshipped also in the fixed Temple projected by David but built by Solomon. He asserts farther that His infinite majesty cannot be confined to temples made by human hands; and where there is neither Tabernacle nor Temple (in any part of His vast dominions), He may be worshipped acceptably by the upright in heart. Thus he proves that neither Tabernacle nor Temple is essentially requisite for the true worship of the true God. *Speaking unto Moses.* "Who spake," as in the margin; signifying the angel of God who spake to Moses, or God himself. See Exod. xxv. 40.

45. *Brought in with Jesus.* That is, with Joshua, whom the Greek version, quoted by Stephen, always writes *Iesous,* Jesus, but which should constantly be written "Joshua" in such cases as the present, in order to avoid ambiguity and confusion. *Possession of the Gentiles.* "Of the heathens," whom Joshua conquered, and gave their land to the children of Israel.

46. *Desired to find a tabernacle.* This was in David's heart, and it met with the divine approbation; see 2 Sam. vii. 2, etc., and see the purpose, Ps. cxxxii. 2-5. But as David had been a man of war, and had shed much blood, God would not permit him to build the Temple; but he laid the plan and made provision for it, and Solomon executed the design.

48. *The most High dwelleth not in temples made with hands.* Here Stephen evidently refers to Solomon's speech, 1 Kings viii. 27. "But will God indeed dwell on the earth? behold, the heaven and heaven of heavens cannot contain thee; how much less this house that I have builded?" Both Solomon and Stephen mean that the majesty of God could not be contained, not even in the whole vortex of nature, much less in any temple which human hands could erect. *As saith the prophet.* The place referred to is Isa. lxvi. 1-2: "Thus saith the Lord, The heaven is my throne, and the earth my footstool: where is the house that ye build unto me? and where is the place of my rest?" with which the quotation by Stephen agrees.

50. *Hath not my hand made all these things?* Stephen certainly had not finished his discourse nor drawn his inferences from the facts already stated; but it is likely that, as they perceived he was about to draw conclusions unfavorable to the Temple and its ritual, they immediately raised up a clamor against him, which was the cause of the following very cutting address.

51. *Ye stiffnecked.* A metaphor taken from untoward oxen who cannot be broken into the yoke, and whose strong necks cannot be bent to the right or the left. *Uncircumcised in heart and ears.* This was a Jewish mode of speech often used by the prophets. Circumcision was instituted, not only as a sign and seal of the covenant into which the Israelites entered with their Maker, but also as a type of that purity and holiness which the law of God requires and by this cutting off, the propensity to that crime which ruins the body, debases the mind and was generally the forerunner of idolatry was happily lessened. *Ye do always resist the Holy Ghost.* Because they were uncircumcised in *heart,* they always resisted the influences of the Holy Spirit, bringing light and conviction to their minds; in consequence of which they became hardened through the deceitfulness of sin, and neither repented at the preaching of John nor credited the glad tidings told them by Christ and the apostles. Because they were

MATTHEW HENRY

the Holy Ghost. 1. They resisted the Holy Ghost speaking to them by the prophets. *Which of the prophets have not your fathers persecuted?* Their fathers resisted the Holy Ghost in the prophets, and so did they in Christ's apostles and ministers. 2. They resisted the Holy Ghost striving with them by their own consciences. There is that in our sinful hearts that always resists the Holy Ghost, but in the hearts of God's elect, this resistance is overcome, and after a struggle the throne of Christ is set up in the soul. That grace therefore which effects this change might more fitly be called *victorious* grace than *irresistible.*

III. They, like their fathers, persecuted and slew those whom God sent unto them. 1. Their fathers had been the cruel and constant persecutors of the Old Testament prophets (*v.* 52): *Which of the prophets have not your fathers persecuted?* More or less, one time or other, they had a blow at them all. That which aggravated the sin of persecuting the prophets was to *show before the coming of the just One,* to give notice of God's kind intentions to send the Messiah among them. Those that were the messengers of such glad tidings should have been courted and caressed, but, instead of this, they had the treatment of the worst of malefactors. 2. They had been the *betrayers and murderers of the just One* himself, as Peter had told them, *ch.* iii. 14, 15; v. 30. They had hired Judas to betray him, and had forced Pilate to condemn him; and therefore it is charged upon them that they were his betrayers and murderers. By slaying him, they showed they would have done if they had lived then; and thus brought upon themselves the guilt of the blood of all the prophets. To which of the prophets would those have shown any respect who had no regard to the Son of God himself?

IV. They, like their fathers, put contempt upon divine revelation. God had given, as to their fathers his law, so to them his gospel, in vain. 1. Their fathers received the law, and did not observe it, *v.* 53. God wrote to them the great things of his law, and yet they were counted by them as a strange or foreign thing. The law is said to be *received by the disposition of angels,* because angels were employed in the solemnity of giving the law, in the thunderings, lightnings, and the sound of the trumpet. But those that thus received the law yet kept it not, but by making the golden calf broke it immediately in a capital instance. 2. They received the gospel now, by the disposition not of angels, but of the Holy Ghost, and yet they did not embrace it. They were resolved not to comply with God either in his law or in his gospel.

Verses 54–60

We have here the death of the first martyr of the Christian church. Here is hell in its fire and darkness, and heaven in its light and brightness; and these serve as foils to set off each other. It is not here said that the votes of the council were taken upon his case, and that by the majority he was found guilty, and then condemned; but, it is likely, that it was not by the violence of the people, that he was put to death; for here is the usual ceremony of regular executions—he was cast out of the city, and the hands of the witnesses were first upon him.

I. See the strength of corruption in the persecutors of Stephen.

1. *When they heard these things they were cut to the heart* (*v.* 54), διεπρίοντο, the same word that is used in Heb. xi. 37, and translated *they were sawn asunder.* They were put to as much torture in their minds as ever the martyrs were put to in their bodies. They were not pricked to the heart with sorrow, as those were in *ch.* ii. 37, but cut to the heart with rage and fury, as they themselves were, *ch.* v. 33. Enmity to God is a heart-cutting thing; faith and love are heart-healing. They heard how he that *looked like an angel* before he began his discourse talked like an angel before he concluded it, and despairing to run down a cause so bravely pleaded, they yet resolved not to yield to it.

2. They *gnashed upon him with their teeth.* Great malice and rage against him. They *grinned at him* as dogs at those they are enraged at. Enmity at the saints turns men into brute beasts. Great vexation within themselves; they fretted to see in him such manifest tokens of a divine power. Gnashing with the teeth is often used to express the horror and torments of the damned. Those that have the malice of hell cannot but have with it some of the pains of hell.

3. *They cried out with a loud voice* (*v.* 57). When he said, *I see heaven opened,* they cried with a loud voice, that he might not be heard to speak. It is very common for a righteous cause to be attempted to be run down by noise and clamour; what is wanting in reason is made up in tumult.

4. They *stopped their ears* under pretence that they

JAMIESON, FAUSSET, BROWN

52. Which of . . .—*Deadly hostility to the messengers of God,* whose high office it was to tell of "the Righteous One," that well-known prophetic title of Messiah (Isa. 53:11; Jer. 23:6, etc), and this *consummated by the betrayal and murder of Messiah Himself,* on the part of those now sitting in judgment on the speaker, are the still darker features of the national character depicted in these withering words.

53. Who have received the law by the disposition—'at the appointment' or 'ordination,' i.e., by the ministry—**of angels, and have not kept it**—This closing word is designed to shut up those idolizers of the law under the guilt of high disobedience to it, aggravated by the august manner in which they had received it.

54-56. When they heard these things they were cut to the heart . . .—If they could have *answered* him, how different would have been their temper of mind!

57, 58. Then they cried out . . . and ran upon him with one accord—To men of their mould and in their temper, Stephen's last seraphic words could but bring matters to extremities, though that only revealed the diabolical spirit which they breathed.

ADAM CLARKE

uncircumcised in *ears,* they would neither hear nor obey Moses, the prophets, Christ, nor the apostles. *As your fathers did, so do ye.* They were disobedient children, of disobedient parents; in all their generations they had been disobedient and perverse. This whole people, as well as this text, are fearful proofs that the Holy Spirit, the almighty energy of the living God, may be resisted and rendered of none effect.

52. *Which of the prophets have not your fathers persecuted?* You have not only resisted the Holy Ghost, but you have *persecuted* all those who have spoken to you in His name and by His influence: thus you prove your opposition to the Spirit himself, by your opposition to everything that proceeds from Him. *They have slain them.* Isaiah, *who shewed before of the coming of* Christ, the Jews report, was sawn asunder at the command of Manasseh. *The coming of the Just One.* Meaning Jesus Christ; emphatically called the *just* or "righteous" Person, not only because of the unspotted integrity of His heart and life, but because of His plenary acquittal when tried at the tribunal of Pilate: *I find in him no fault at all.* The mention of this circumstance served greatly to aggravate their guilt. The character of *Just One* is applied to our Lord in three other places of Scripture: chap. iii. 14; xxii. 14; and Jas. v. 6. *The betrayers and murderers.* You first delivered Him up into the hands of the Romans, hoping they would have put Him to death; but when they acquitted Him, then, in opposition to the declaration of His innocence and in outrage to every form of justice, you took and murdered Him. This was a most terrible charge, and one against which they could set up no sort of defense. No wonder, then, that they were instigated by the spirit of the old destroyer, which they never resisted, to add another murder to that of which they had been so recently guilty.

53. *By the disposition of angels.* After all that has been said on this difficult passage, perhaps the simple meaning is that there were "ranks" of angels attending on the Divine Majesty when He gave the law, a circumstance which must have added greatly to the grandeur and solemnity of the occasion; and to this Ps. lxviii. 17 (marg.) seems to me most evidently to allude: "The chariots of God are twenty thousand, even many thousands of angels: the Lord is among them, as in Sinai, in the holy place." It was not then by the mouths nor by the hands of angels as prime agents that Moses, and through him the people, received the law; but God himself gave it, accompanied with many thousands of those glorious beings. As it is probable they might be assisting in this most glorious solemnity, therefore Paul might say, Gal. iii. 19, that it was "ordained by angels in the hand of a mediator." And as they were the only persons that could appear, for no man hath seen God at any time, therefore the apostle might say further (if indeed he refers to the same transaction; see the note there), "The word spoken by angels was stedfast," Heb. ii. 2.

54. *They were cut to the heart.* They were "sawn through." See the note on chap. v. 33.

They gnashed on him with their teeth. They were determined to hear him no longer; were filled with rage against him, and evidently thirsted for his blood.

MATTHEW HENRY

could not bear to hear his blasphemies. These *stopped their ears* when Stephen said, *I now see the Son of man standing in glory*. Their stopping their ears was a manifest specimen of their wilful obstinacy; they were resolved they would not hear. It was a fatal omen of that judicial hardness to which God would give them up. They stopped their ears, and then God, in a way of righteous judgment, stopped them.

5. They *ran upon him with one accord*, they all flew upon him, as beasts upon their prey. They ran upon him, one and all, hoping thereby to put him into confusion, envying him his composure and comfort in soul. They did all they could to ruffle him.

6. They *cast him out of the city, and stoned him*, to execute the law of Moses (Lev. xxiv. 16), *He that blasphemeth the name of the Lord shall surely be put to death, all the congregation shall certainly stone him*. They cast him out of the city; they treated him as the offscouring of all things. The witnesses against him were the leaders in the execution, according to the law. Thus they were to confirm their testimony. The witnesses took off their upper garments *and they laid them down at a young man's feet, whose name was Saul*. It is the first time we find mention of his name; we shall know it and love it better when we find it changed to *Paul*. This little instance of his agency in Stephen's death he afterwards reflected upon with regret (*ch.* xxii. 20): *I kept the raiment of those that slew him*.

II. See the strength of grace in Stephen. As his persecutors were full of Satan, so was he *full of the Holy Ghost*. When he was chosen to public service, he was described to be a man *full of the Holy Ghost* (*ch.* vi. 5), and now he is called out to martyrdom he has still the same character. Those that are full of the Holy Ghost are fit for anything, either to act for Christ or to suffer for him. When the followers of Christ are for his sake *killed all the day long, and accounted as sheep for the slaughter*, does this separate them from the love of Christ? Do they love him the less? No, by no means; and so it appears by this narrative.

1. Christ's gracious manifestation of himself to Stephen. When they were cut to the heart, and gnashed upon him with their teeth, then he had a view of the glory of Christ.

(1) He, *being full of the Holy Ghost, looked up steadfastly into heaven*, *v.* 55. Thus he looked above the power and fury of his persecutors, and did as it were despise them. They had their eyes fixed upon him, full of malice and cruelty; but he looked up to heaven, and never minded them. He looks up to heaven; thence only comes his help, and thitherward his way is still open. They cannot interrupt his intercourse with heaven. Thus he directed his sufferings to the glory of God, and did as it were appeal to heaven concerning them. Now that he was ready to be offered he looks up steadfastly to heaven, as one willing to offer himself. Thus he lifted up his soul with his eyes to God calling upon God for wisdom and grace to carry him through this trial. God has promised that he will be with his servants whom he calls out to suffer for him; but he will for this be sought unto. Thus he breathed after the heavenly country, to which he saw the fury of his persecutors would presently send him. It is good for dying saints to look up steadfastly to heaven: "And then, *O death! where is thy sting?*" Thus he made it to appear that he was full of the Holy Ghost. Those that are full of the Holy Ghost will look up steadfastly to heaven, for there their heart is. If we expect to hear from heaven, we must look up steadfastly to heaven.

(2) He saw the glory of God (*v.* 55); for *he saw the heavens opened*, *v.* 56. The heavens were opened, to give him a view of the happiness he was going to, that he might go cheerfully through death, so great a death. Would we by faith look up steadfastly, we might see the heavens opened by the mediation of Christ. We may also see the glory of God and the sight of this will carry us through all the terrors of sufferings and death.

(3) He *saw Jesus standing on the right hand of God* (*v.* 55), *the Son of man*, so it is, *v.* 56. When the Old Testament prophets saw the glory of God it was attended with angels. But here no mention is made of the angels. The glory of God shines brightest in the face of Jesus Christ. Here is a proof of the exaltation of Christ. He saw Jesus at the right hand of God. Whatever God's right hand gives to us, or receives from us, or does concerning us, it is by him; for he is his right hand. Stephen sees him *standing* there. He stands ready to receive him and crown him, and in the meantime to give him a prospect of the joy set before him. He sees Christ is for him, and then no matter who is against him. When our Lord Jesus

JAMIESON, FAUSSET, BROWN

58. cast him out of the city (according to Lev. 24:14; Num. 15:35; I Kings 21:13; and see Heb. 13:12. **and stoned**—'proceeded to stone' him. The actual stoning is recorded in next verse. **and the witnesses**—whose hands were to be first upon the criminal (Deut. 17:7). **laid down their clothes**—their loose outer garments, to have them taken charge of. **at a young man's feet whose name was Saul**—How thrilling is this our first introduction to one to whom Christianity—whether as developed in the New Testament or as established in the world—owes more perhaps than to all the other apostles together! Here he is, having perhaps already a seat in the Sanhedrim, some 30 years of age, in the thick of this tumultuous murder of a distinguished witness for Christ, not only "consenting unto his death" (ch. 8:1), but doing his own part of the dark deed.

55. But he, being full of the Holy Ghost, looked up steadfastly into heaven, and saw the glory of God—You who can transfer to canvas such scenes as these, in which the rage of hell grins horribly from men, as they sit condemned by a frail prisoner of their own, and see heaven beaming from his countenance and opening full upon his view—I envy you, for I find no words to paint what, in the majesty of the divine text, is here so simply told. "But how could Stephen, in the council-chamber, see heaven at all? I suppose this question never occurred but to critics of narrow soul, one of whom [MEYER] conjectures that he saw it through the window! and another, of better mould, that the scene lay in one of the courts of the temple" [ALFORD]. As the sight was witnessed by Stephen alone, the opened heavens are to be viewed as revealed to his bright beaming spirit.

and Jesus standing on the right hand of God—Why "*standing*," and not *sitting*, the posture in which the glorified Saviour is elsewhere represented? Clearly, to express the eager interest with which He watched from the skies the scene in that council chamber, and the full tide of His Spirit which He was at that moment engaged in pouring into the heart of His heroical witness, till it beamed in radiance from his very countenance. **56. I see ... the Son of man standing ...**—This is the only time that our Lord is by human lips called THE SON OF MAN after His ascension (Rev. 1:13; 14:14 are not instances). And why here? Stephen, full of the Holy Ghost, speaking now not of himself at all (vs. 55), but entirely by the Spirit, is led to repeat

ADAM CLARKE

57. *They . . . stopped their ears.* As a proof that he had uttered blasphemy, because he said he saw Jesus standing at the right hand of God. This was a fearful proof against them; for if Jesus was at the *right hand of God*, then they had murdered an innocent Person, and they must infer that God's justice must speedily avenge His death. They were determined not to suffer a man to live any longer who could say he saw the heavens opened and Jesus Christ standing at the right hand of God.

58. *Cast him out of the city, and stoned him.* They did not however wait for any sentence to be pronounced upon him; it seems they were determined to stone him first, and then prove, after it had been done, that it was done justly. For the manner of stoning among the Jews, see the note on Lev. xxiv. 23.

55. *Saw the glory of God.* The Shekinah, the splendor or manifestation of the Divine Majesty.

And Jesus standing on the right hand of God. In his official character, as Mediator between God and man.

MATTHEW HENRY

was in his agony an angel appeared to him, but Stephen had Christ himself appearing to him. Nothing so comfortable nor so animating as to see Jesus at the right hand of God; by faith we may see him there.

(4) He told those about him what he saw (*v.* 56): *Behold, I see the heavens opened.* What he saw he declared, let them make what use they pleased of it. If some were exasperated by it, others perhaps might be wrought upon to consider this Jesus, and to believe in him.

2. Stephen's pious addresses to Jesus Christ. *They stoned Stephen, calling upon God, v.* 59. Though he called upon God yet they proceeded to stone him. Though they stoned him, yet he called upon God. It is the comfort of those who are unjustly hated and persecuted by men that they have a God to go to. Men stop their ears, as they did here (*v.* 57), but God does not. Stephen was now cast out of the city, but he was not cast out from his God. He was now taking his leave of the world, and therefore calls upon God. It is good to die praying. Two short prayers Stephen offered up to God in his dying moments.

(1) Here is a prayer for himself: *Lord Jesus, receive my spirit.* Thus Christ had himself resigned his spirit immediately into the hands of the Father. We are here taught to resign ours into the hands of Christ as Mediator. The soul is the man, and our great concern, living and dying, must be about our souls. "Lord," saith he, "let my spirit be safe; let it go well with my poor soul." Our Lord Jesus is God, to whom we are to seek, and in whom we comfort ourselves living and dying. Stephen here prays to Christ, and so must we. There is no venturing into another world but under his conduct, no living comforts in dying moments but what are fetched from him. Christ's receiving our spirits at death is the great thing we are to comfort ourselves with. And, if this has been our care while we live, it may be our comfort when we come to die.

(2) Here is a prayer for his persecutors, *v.* 60. The circumstances of this prayer are observable. He *knelt down*, which was an expression of his humility in prayer. He *cried with a loud voice*, which was an expression of his importunity. In his prayer for his enemies, because that is so much against the grain of corrupt nature, it was requisite he should give proofs of his being in earnest. The prayer itself: *Lord, lay not this sin to their charge.* Herein he followed the example of his dying Master, and set an example to all following sufferers in the cause of Christ. Prayer may preach. This did so to those who stoned Stephen. *First,* What they did was a sin, a great sin. *Secondly,* Notwithstanding their malice and fury against him, he was in charity with them. Let them take notice of this, and, when their thoughts were cool, surely they would not easily forgive themselves for putting him to death who could so easily forgive them. *Thirdly,* Though the sin was very heinous, yet they must not despair of the pardon of it upon their repentance. If they would lay it to their hearts, God would not lay it to their charge.

3. His expiring with this: *When he had said this, he fell asleep.* Death is but a sleep to good people. Stephen died as much in a hurry as ever any man did, and yet, when he died, he fell asleep. He fell asleep when he was praying for his persecutors; it is expressed as if he thought he could not die in peace till he had done this. If he thus sleep, he shall do well; he shall awake again in the morning of the resurrection.

JAMIESON, FAUSSET, BROWN

the very words in which Jesus Himself, *before this same council,* had foretold His glorification (Matt. 26:64), assuring them that that exaltation of the SON OF MAN which they should hereafter witness to their dismay, was already begun and actual [ALFORD].

59, 60. calling upon God and saying, Lord Jesus . . .—An unhappy supplement of our translators is the word "God" here; as if, while addressing the Son, he was really calling upon the Father. The sense is perfectly clear without any supplement at all—"calling upon [invoking] and saying, Lord Jesus"; Christ being the Person directly invoked and addressed by name (cf. 9:14). Even GROTIUS, DE WETTE, MEYER, etc. admit this, adding several other examples of direct prayer to Christ; and PLINY, in his well-known letter to the Emperor Trajan (A.D. 110 or 111), says it was part of the regular Christian service to sing, in alternate strains, a hymn to Christ as God. **Lord Jesus, receive my spirit**—In presenting to Jesus the identical prayer which He Himself had on the cross offered to His Father, Stephen renders to his glorified Lord absolute divine worship, in the most sublime form, and at the most solemn moment of his life. In this commitment of his spirit to Jesus, Paul afterwards followed his footsteps with a calm, exultant confidence that with Him it was safe for eternity (II Tim. 1:12).

60. cried with a loud voice—with something of the gathered energy of his dying Lord (see on John 19: 16-30). **Lord**—i.e., JESUS, beyond doubt, whom he had just before addressed as Lord. **lay not this sin to their charge**—Comparing this with nearly the same prayer of his dying Lord, it will be seen how very richly this martyr of Jesus had drunk into his Master's spirit, in its divinest form.

he fell asleep—*never said of the death of Christ.* (See on I Thess. 4:14.) How bright the record of this first martyrdom for Christ, amidst all the darkness of its perpetrators; and how many have been cheered by it to like faithfulness even unto death!

ADAM CLARKE

59. *And they stoned Stephen, calling upon God.* The word *God* is not found in any MS. or version, nor in any of the primitive fathers except Chrysostom. It is not genuine, and should not be inserted here.

The whole sentence literally reads thus: "And they stoned Stephen, invoking and saying, Lord Jesus, receive my spirit!" Here is a most manifest proof that prayer is offered to Jesus Christ, and that in the most solemn circumstances in which it could be offered, viz., when a man was breathing his last. This is, properly speaking, one of the highest acts of worship which can be offered to God; and if Stephen had not conceived Jesus Christ to be God, could he have committed his soul into His hands?

60. *He kneeled down.* That he might die as the subject of his heavenly Master—acting and suffering in the deepest submission to His divine will and permissive providence; and at the same time showing the genuine nature of the religion of his Lord, in pouring out his prayers with his blood in behalf of his murderers! *Lay not this sin to their charge.* That is, do not impute it to them so as to exact punishment. How much did the servant resemble his Lord, "Father, forgive them; for they know not what they do"! This was the cry of our Lord in behalf of His murderers; and the disciple, closely copying his Master, in the same spirit and with the same meaning, varies the expression, crying with a loud voice, *Lord, lay not this sin to their charge!* Christ had given what some have supposed to be an impossible command, "Love your enemies . . . pray for them which despitefully use you, and persecute you." And Stephen shows here, in his own person, how practicable the grace of his Master had made this sublime precept. *He fell asleep.* This was a common expression among the Jews to signify death, and especially the death of good men. But this sleep is, properly speaking, not attributable to the soul, but to the body; for he had commended his spirit to the Lord Jesus, while his body was overwhelmed with the shower of stones cast on him by the mob. The first clause of the next chapter should come in here, *And Saul was consenting unto his death.* Never was there a worse division than that which separated it from the end of this chapter. This should be immediately altered, and the amputated member restored to the body to which it belongs.

MATTHEW HENRY

CHAPTER 8

Verses 1–3

I. Something more concerning Stephen and his death; how people stood affected to it. 1. Stephen's death rejoiced in by one in particular, and that was Saul, who was afterwards called Paul; he was *consenting to his death.* We have reason to think that Paul ordered Luke to insert this, for shame to himself, and glory to free grace. 2. Stephen's death bewailed by others (*v.* 2)—*devout men.* Some of the church gathered up the poor crushed and broken remains, to which they gave a decent interment. They buried him solemnly, and made great lamentation over him. It is a bad symptom if, when such men are taken away, it is not laid to heart. Those devout men paid these their last respects to Stephen, to show that they were not ashamed of the cause for which he suffered, nor afraid of the wrath of those that were enemies to it. To show the great value and esteem they had for this faithful servant of Jesus Christ. They study to do honour to him upon whom God put honour.

II. An account of this persecution of the church,

JAMIESON, FAUSSET, BROWN

CHAPTER 8

VSS. 1-4. PERSECUTION CONTINUED, IN WHICH SAUL TAKES A PROMINENT PART—HOW OVERRULED FOR GOOD—**1. Saul was consenting unto his death**—The word expresses hearty approval.

2. and devout men—pious Jews, probably, impressed with admiration for Stephen and secretly inclined to Christianity, but not yet openly declared.

ADAM CLARKE

CHAPTER 8

1. *Saul was consenting unto his death.* The word signifies "gladly consenting," being pleased with his murderous work! It has already been remarked that this clause belongs to the conclusion of the preceding chapter; so it stands in the Vulgate, and so it should stand in every version.

2. *Devout men carried Stephen to his burial.* The Greek word signifies not only to "carry," or rather to "gather up," but also to do everything necessary for the interment of the dead. Among the Jews, and indeed among most nations of the earth, it was esteemed a work of piety, charity, and mercy to bury the dead.

MATTHEW HENRY

which begins upon the martyrdom of Stephen. One would have thought Stephen's dying prayers and dying comforts should have overcome them, and melted them into a better opinion, but it seems they did not. As if they hoped to be too hard for God himself, they resolve to follow their blow.

1. Against whom this persecution was raised: It was *against the church in Jerusalem.* Christ had particularly foretold that Jerusalem would soon be made too hot for his followers, for that city had been famous for killing the prophets and stoning those that were sent to it.

2. Who was an active man in it: none so zealous, so busy, as Saul, a young Pharisee, *v.* 3. As for Saul *he made havoc of the church*; he did all he could to lay it waste and ruin it. He aimed at no less than the cutting off of the gospel Israel. Saul was bred a scholar, a gentleman, and yet did not think it below him to be employed in the vilest work of that kind. He *entered into every house.* No man could be secure in his own house, though it was his castle. He haled both men and women, without any regard to the tenderness of the weaker sex. He committed them to prison, in order to their being tried and put to death.

3. What was the effect of this persecution: *They were all scattered abroad* (*v.* 1). They, remembering our Master's rule (*when they persecute you in one city, flee to another*), dispersed themselves *throughout the regions of Judæa* and of Samaria. Their work was pretty well done in Jerusalem, and now it was time to think of the necessities of other places. Though persecution may not drive us off from our work, yet it may send us to work elsewhere. The preachers were all scattered *except the apostles.* They tarried at Jerusalem, that they might be ready to go where their assistance was most needed by the other preachers that were sent to break the ice.

Verses 4-13

Christ had said, *I am come to send fire on the earth*; and they thought, by scattering those who were kindled with that fire, to have put it out, but instead of this they did but help to spread it.

I. Here is a general account of what was done by them all (*v.* 4): *They went everywhere, preaching the word.* They went everywhere, into the way of the Gentiles, and the cities of the Samaritans, which before they were forbidden to go into. They scattered into all parts, not to take their ease, but to find out work. They were now in a country where they were no strangers, for Christ and his disciples had conversed much in the regions of Judæa; so that they had a foundation laid there for them to build upon.

II. A particular account of what was done by Philip, not Philip the apostle, but Philip the deacon. Stephen was advanced to the degree of a martyr, Philip to the degree of an evangelist.

1. What wonderful success Philip had in his preaching.

(1) The place he chose was the city of Samaria, the metropolis of that country. Some think it was the same with Sychem or Sychar, that city of Samaria where Christ was, John iv. 5. The Jews would have no dealings with the Samaritans; but Christ sent his gospel to slay all enmities.

(2) The doctrine he preached was Christ: he *preached Christ to them.* The Samaritans had an expectation of the Messiah's coming, as appears by John iv. 25. Now Philip tells them that he is come, and that the Samaritans are welcome to him.

(3) The proofs he produced were miracles, *v.* 6. The miracles were undeniable; they heard and saw the miracles which he did. He was sent to break the power of Satan; and, in token of this, unclean spirits, being charged in the name of the Lord Jesus to remove, *came out of many that were possessed with them, v.* 7. Wherever the gospel gains the admission and submission it ought to have, evil spirits are dislodged. This was signified by the casting of these unclean spirits out of the bodies of people, who came out *crying with a loud voice.* They came out with great reluctancy, but were forced to acknowledge themselves overcome by a superior power. He was sent to heal, to cure a distempered world; in token of this, *many that were taken with palsies, and that were lame, were healed.* The grace of God in the gospel is designed for the healing of those that are spiritually lame and paralytic, and cannot help themselves.

(4) The acceptance which Philip's doctrine met with in Samaria (*v.* 6): *The people with one accord gave heed to those things which Philip spoke,* induced thereto by the miracles which served at first to gain attention, and so by degrees to gain assent. The common people gave heed to Philip, *a multitude of them,* not here and there one, but with one accord;

JAMIESON, FAUSSET, BROWN

3. Saul . . . entering into every house—like as inquisitor [BENGEL]. **haling men and women . . .**—See his own affecting confessions afterwards (ch. 22:4; 26:9, 10; I Cor. 15:9; Gal. 1:13; Phil. 3:6; I Tim. 1:13).

they were all scattered abroad—all the leading Christians, particularly the preachers, agreeably to their Lord's injunctions (Matt. 10:23), though many doubtless remained, and others (as appears by ch. 9:26-30) soon returned. **except the apostles**—who remained, not certainly as being less exposed to danger, but, at whatever risk, to watch over the infant cause where it was most needful to cherish it.

they that were scattered abroad went everywhere preaching—Though solemnly enjoined to do this (Luke 24:47; ch. 1:8), they would probably have lingered at Jerusalem, but for this besom of persecution which swept them out. How often has the rage of Christ's enemies thus "turned out rather unto the furtherance of the Gospel" (see Phil. 1:12, 13).

5-25. SUCCESS OF PHILIP'S PREACHING IN SAMARIA—CASE OF SIMON MAGUS. **5. Then Philip**—not the apostle of that name, as was by some of the Fathers supposed; for besides that the apostles remained at Jerusalem, they would in that case have had no occasion to send a deputation of their own number to lay their hands on the baptized disciples [GROTIUS]. It was the deacon of that name, who comes next after Stephen in the catalogue of the seven, probably as being the next most prominent. The persecution may have been directed especially against Stephen's colleagues [MEYER]. **the city of Samaria**—or 'a city of Samaria'; but the former seems more likely. "It furnished the bridge between Jerusalem and the world" [BAUMGARTEN].

6-8. the people with one accord gave heed to . . . Philip—the way being prepared perhaps by the fruits of our Lord's sojourn, as He Himself seems to intimate (see on John 4:31-38). But "we may mark the providence of God in sending a Grecian, or a Hellenistic Jew, to a people who from national

ADAM CLARKE

3. *Saul . . . made havock of the church.* The word signifies the act of ferocious animals, such as bears, wolves, and the like, in seeking and devouring their prey. This shows with what persevering rancor this man pursued the harmless Christians, and thus we see in him what bigotry and false zeal are capable of performing. *Haling men and women.* The word signifies "dragging" them before the magistrates or dragging them to justice. *Committed them to prison.* For, as the Romans alone had the power of life and death, the Sanhedrin, by whom Saul was employed, chap. xxvi. 10, could do no more than arrest and imprison, in order to inflict any punishment short of death. It is true Paul himself says that some of them were put to death (see chap. xxvi. 10); but this was done either by Roman authority or by what was called the "judgment of zeal," i.e., when the mob took the execution of the laws into their own hands, and massacred those whom they pretended to be blasphemers of God. For these sanctified their murderous outrage under the specious name of zeal for God's glory, and quoted the example of Phineas as a precedent. Such persons as these formed a sect among the Jews, and are known in ecclesiastical history by the appellation of *Zealots* or *Sicarii.*

There was a great persecution. The Jews could not bear the doctrine of Christ's resurrection, for this point being proved demonstrated His innocence and their enormous guilt in His crucifixion. As therefore the apostles continued to insist strongly on the resurrection of Christ, the persecution against them became hot and general. *They were all scattered abroad . . . except the apostles.* Their Lord had commanded them, when persecuted in one city, to flee to another. This they did, but wherever they went they proclaimed the same doctrines, though at the risk and hazard of their lives. It is evident, therefore, that they did not flee from persecution, or the death it threatened, but merely in obedience to their Lord's command. That the apostles were not also exiled is a very remarkable fact. They continued in Jerusalem, to found and organize the infant Church, and it is marvellous that the hand of persecution was not permitted to touch them. Why this should be we cannot tell, but so it pleased the great Head of the Church.

4. *They that were scattered . . . went every where preaching.* Thus the very means devised by Satan to destroy the Church became the very instruments of its diffusion and establishment.

5. *Then Philip.* One of the seven deacons, chap. vi. 5, called afterwards "Philip the evangelist," chap. xxi. 8. *The city of Samaria.* At this time there was no city of Samaria existing; according to Josephus, *Ant.*, l. xiii, c. 10, s. 3, Hyrcanus had so utterly demolished it as to leave no vestige of it remaining. Herod the Great did afterwards build a city on the same spot of ground, but he called it *Sebaste,* i.e., *Augusta,* in compliment to the Emperor Augustus, as Josephus tells us, *Ant.*, l. xv, c. 8, s. 5; *War,* l. i, c. 2, s. 7; and by this name of *Sebaste,* or *Augusta,* that city, if meant here, would in all probability have been called. As Sychem was the very heart and seat of the Samaritan religion, and Mount Gerizim the cathedral church of that sect, it is more likely that it should be intended than any other. As the Samaritans received the same law with the Jews, as they also expected the Messiah, as Christ had preached to and converted many of that people, John iv, it was very reasonable that the earliest offers of salvation should be made to them, before any attempt was made to evangelize the Gentiles. The Samaritans, indeed, formed the connecting link between the Jews and the Gentiles; for they were a mongrel people, made up of both sorts, and holding both Jewish and pagan rites. See the account of them on Matt. x. 5.

6. *The people with one accord gave heed.* He had fixed their attention, not only with the gravity and importance of the matter of his preaching, but also by *the miracles which he did.*

MATTHEW HENRY

they were all of a mind.

(5) The satisfaction they had in attending on Philip's preaching, and the success it had with many of them (*v.* 8): *There was great joy in that city;* for (*v.* 12) *they believed Philip, and were baptized, both men and women.* [1] Philip preached *the things concerning the kingdom of God,* and he preached the name of Jesus Christ, as king of that kingdom. [2] The people not only gave heed to what he said, but at length believed it, were fully convinced that it was of God and not of men. [3] When they believed *they were baptized. Men* only were capable of being admitted into the Jewish church, but, to show that *in Jesus Christ there is neither male nor female,* the initiating ordinance is such as women are capable of, for they are numbered with God's spiritual Israel. [4] This occasioned great joy. The bringing of the gospel to any place is just matter of joy, of great joy, to that place. The gospel of Christ does not make men melancholy, but fills them with joy; for it is *glad tidings of great joy to all people,* Luke ii. 10.

2. What there was at this city of Samaria that made the success of the gospel there more than ordinarily wonderful.

(1) Simon Magus had been busy there, and had gained a great interest among the people. To unlearn that which is bad proves many times a harder task than to learn that which is good. These Samaritans had of late been drawn to follow Simon, a conjurer (for so *Magus* signifies), who had strangely *bewitched them.*

[1] How strong the delusion of Satan. He had been for a *long time, in this city, using sorceries.* Simon assumed to himself that which was considerable: *He gave out that he himself was some great one.* He had no design to reform their lives, only to make them believe that he was *some divine person.* Pride, ambition, and an affectation of grandeur, have always been the cause of abundance of mischief both to the world and to the church. The people ascribed to him what he pleased. *They all gave heed to him, from the least to the greatest. To him they had regard* (*v.* 10, 11). They said of him, *This man is the great power of God.* See how ignorant inconsiderate people mistake that which is done by the power of Satan, as if it were done by the power of God. They were brought to it by his sorceries: *He bewitched the people of Samaria* (*v.* 9), *bewitched them with sorceries* (*v.* 11). By his magic arts *he bewitched the minds of the people.* Satan, by God's permission, filled their hearts to follow Simon. When they knew no better, they were influenced by his sorceries; but, when they were acquainted with Philip's real miracles, they saw plainly that the one was real and the other a sham. When they saw the difference between Simon and Philip, they quitted Simon.

[2] How strong the power of Divine grace is. By that grace working with the word those that had been led captive by Satan *were brought into obedience to Christ.* Let us not despair of the worst, when even those whom Simon Magus had bewitched were brought to believe.

(2) Here is another thing yet more wonderful (*v.* 13): *Simon himself believed also.* He was convinced that Philip preached a true doctrine, because he saw it confirmed by real miracles, of which he was the better able to judge because he was conscious to himself of the trick of his own pretended ones. The present conviction went so far that *he was baptized.* We have no reason to think that Philip did amiss in baptizing him. Prodigals, when they return, must be joyfully welcomed home, though we cannot be sure but that they will play the prodigal again. It is God's prerogative to know the heart. The church and its ministers must go by a judgment of charity. *We must hope the best as long as we can.* The present conviction lasted so long that he continued with Philip. He that had given out himself to be some great one is content to sit at the feet of a preacher of the gospel. Even bad men, very bad, may sometimes be in a good frame, very good. The present conviction was wrought and kept up by the miracles. Many wonder at the proofs of divine truths who never experience the power of them.

Verses 14–25

The twelve kept together at Jerusalem (*v.* 1), and thither these good tidings were brought them *that Samaria had received the word of God* (*v.* 14). The word of God was not only preached to them, but received by them. *When they heard it, they sent unto them Peter and John.* Two apostles were sent, the two most eminent, to Samaria, to encourage Philip and strengthen his hands. To carry on the good work that was begun.

I. How they advanced and improved those of them that were sincere. It is said (*v.* 16), *The Holy Ghost*

JAMIESON, FAUSSET, BROWN

antipathy would have been unlikely to attend to a *native* of Judea" [WEBSTER and WILKINSON].

8. **great joy in that city**—over the change wrought on it by the Gospel, as well as the cures which attested its divine character.

9-13. **used sorcery**—magical arts. **some great one . . . the great power of God**—a sort of incarnation of divinity. **To whom all gave heed . . . because of long time he had bewitched them**—This, coupled with the rapidity with which they deserted him and attached themselves to Philip, shows the ripeness of Samaria for some religious change.

12. **were baptized, both men and women**—the detection of Simon's frauds helping to extend and deepen the effects of Philip's preaching. 13. **Then Simon himself believed also**—Left without followers, he thinks it best to join the man who had fairly outstripped him, not without a touch of real conviction. **and . . . was baptized**—What a light does this throw on what is called *Baptismal Regeneration*! **he continued with Philip**—'was in constant attendance upon' him.

14-17. **the apostles . . . sent Peter and John**—showing that they regarded Peter as no more than their own equal.

ADAM CLARKE

7. *For unclean spirits, crying with a loud voice, came out of many that were possessed.* Hence it is evident that these *unclean spirits* were not a species of diseases, as they are here distinguished from the *paralytic* and the *lame.* There is nothing more certain than that the New Testament writers mean real diabolic possessions by the terms "unclean spirits," "devils," etc., which they use.

9. *And bewitched the people of Samaria,* "Astonishing, amazing, or confounding" the judgment of the people, from *existemi,* to "remove out of a place or state, to be transported beyond oneself, to be out of one's wits."

10. *This man is the great power of God.* That is, he is invested with it and can command and use it. They certainly did not believe him to be God, but they thought him to be endued with a great supernatural power. There is a remarkable reading here in several MSS. which should not pass unnoticed. The passage reads thus, "This person is that power of God which is called the Great." This appears to be the true reading; but what the Samaritans meant by that power of God which they termed "the Great," we know not.

12. *But when they believed Philip.* So it is evident that Philip's word came with greater power than that of Simon, and that his miracles stood the test in such a way as the feats of Simon could not.

13. *Simon himself believed also.* He was struck with the doctrine and miracles of Philip—he saw that these were real; he knew his own to be fictitious. He believed therefore that Jesus was the Messiah, and was in consequence baptized. *Continued with Philip, and wondered.* He was as much "astonished" and "confounded" at the miracles of Philip as the people of Samaria were at his *legerdemain.*

14. *The word of God.* The doctrine of the Lord Jesus Christ. *They sent unto them Peter and John.* There was no individual ruler among the apostles—there was not even a president of the council; and Peter, far from being chief of the apostles, is one of those sent, with the same commission and authority as John, to confirm the Samaritans in the faith.

G. CAMPBELL MORGAN:

This man Philip, then, was the center of the wonderful movement in the city of Samaria. Jews have no dealings with Samaritans, but Christians have, and Philip came to Samaria. There he proclaimed the Messiah. In the course of this passage two great words for preaching are used in describing the work of Philip. He proclaimed the Christ—and that is the Greek word *kerusso,* which means to proclaim as a herald. We find later that Philip preached the Gospel, and that is the Greek word *euaggelizo,* which indicates the proclamation of good news. The message concerning Christ, delivered through the deacon-evangelist Philip, arrested Samaria. In Samaria the Christian preacher found a new atmosphere and a new outlook. Moreover, Samaria was at the time under the spell of Simon the sorcerer. To Samaria, driven by persecution, there came, not an apostle, but a man set apart to serve tables, in order that the apostles might be set apart to preach the Word. He proclaimed Christ, and his preaching was accompanied by mental and physical signs. Unclean spirits were cast out and men were healed. The city was full of joy, resulting from these things; and in that attitude of amazement, of surprise, and of joy, they listened. This story of Philip is but an illustration of a much wider movement. The whole Church, driven by persecution, was proceeding in power.
—*The Acts of the Apostles*

MATTHEW HENRY

was as yet fallen upon none of them, in those extraordinary powers which were conveyed by the descent of the Spirit, *only they were baptized in the name of the Lord Jesus*, and in this they had joy and satisfaction (*v.* 8). Those that are indeed given up to Christ, and have experienced the sanctifying influences of the Spirit of grace, have great reason to be thankful, and no reason to complain, though they have not those gifts that are for ornament, and would make them bright. But it is intended that they should go on to the perfection of the present dispensation. *The apostles prayed for them*, *v.* 15. The Spirit is given, not to ourselves only (Luke xi. 13), but to others also, in answer to prayer. We may take encouragement from this example in praying to God to give the renewing graces of the Holy Ghost to those whose spiritual welfare we are concerned for—for our children, for our friends, for our ministers. They laid their hands on them. Upon the use of this sign *they received the Holy Ghost.* The laying on of hands was anciently used in blessing. Thus the apostles blessed these new converts.

II. How they discovered and discarded Simon Magus.

1. The wicked proposal that Simon made, by which his hypocrisy was discovered (*v.* 18, 19): *When he saw that through laying on of the apostles' hands the Holy Ghost was given*, it gave him a notion of Christianity as no other than an exalted piece of sorcery. He was ambitious to have the honour of an apostle, but not at all solicitous to have the spirit of a Christian. He was more desirous to gain honour to himself than to do good to others. He put a great affront upon the apostles, as if they were mercenary men, would do anything for money. He put a great affront upon Christianity, as if the miracles were done by magic arts. He showed that he aimed at the rewards of divination. He showed that he had a very high conceit of himself. No less a place will serve him than to be entrusted with a power which Philip himself had not, but the apostles only.

2. The just rejection of his proposal, *v.* 20–23.

(1) Peter shows him his crime (*v.* 20): *Thou hast thought that the gift of God may be purchased with money.* He had overvalued the wealth of this world, as if it would purchase the pardon of sin, the gift of the Holy Ghost, and eternal life. He had undervalued the gift of the Holy Ghost. He thought the power of an apostle might as well be had for a good fee as the advice of a physician or a lawyer.

(2) He shows him his character, which is inferred from his crime. Peter tells him plainly, [1] That his heart was *not right in the sight of God*, *v.* 21. We are as our hearts are; if they be not right, we are wrong; and they are open in the sight of God, who knows them, judges them, and judges of us by them. Our great concern is to approve ourselves to him in our integrity, for otherwise we cheat ourselves into our own ruin. He does not aim at the glory of God nor the honour of Christ in it, but to make a hand of it for himself. [2] That he is *in the gall of bitterness, and in the bond of iniquity: I perceive that thou art* so, *v.* 23. This is plain dealing, and plain dealing is best when we are dealing about souls and eternity. *I perceive it*, saith Peter. The disguises of hypocrites many times are soon seen through; the nature of the wolf shows itself notwithstanding the cover of the sheep's clothing. Now the character here given of Simon is really the character of all wicked people. They are *in the gall of bitterness.* They are *in the bond of iniquity*—bound over to the judgment of God by the guilt of sin, and bound under the dominion of Satan by the power of sin.

(3) He reads him his doom in two things:

[1] He shall sink with his worldly wealth: *Thy money perish with thee.* Peter rejects his offer with the utmost disdain and indignation. "Away with thee and thy money too; we will have nothing to do with either." When we are tempted with money to do an evil thing, we should see what a perishing thing money is. He warns him of his danger of utter destruction if he continued in this mind: "Thy money will perish and thou wilt lose it. But this is not the worst of it: *thou wilt perish with it, and it with thee.*"

[2] He shall come short of the spiritual blessings which he undervalued (*v.* 21): "*Thou hast neither part nor lot in this matter;* thou hast nothing to do with the gifts of the Holy Ghost, for *thy heart is not right in the sight of God*, if thou thinkest that Christianity is a trade to live by in this world."

(4) He gives him good counsel, notwithstanding, *v.* 22. Though he was angry with him, yet he did not abandon him.

[1] What it is that he advises him to. He must *repent*—must see his error and retract it. His repentance must be particular: "Repent of this, own thyself guilty in this." He must not extenuate it,

JAMIESON, FAUSSET, BROWN

15, 16. prayed . . . they might receive the Holy Ghost. (For only they were baptized in the name of the Lord Jesus.)—As the baptism of adults presupposed "the renewing of the Holy Ghost" (Titus 3:5-7; I Cor. 12:13), of which the profession of faith had to be taken for evidence, this communication of the Holy Ghost by the laying on of the apostles' hands was clearly a *superadded* thing; and as it was only *occasional*, so it was invariably *attended with miraculous manifestations* (see ch. 10:44, where it followed Peter's preaching; and ch. 19:1-7, where, as here, it followed the laying on of hands). In the present case an important object was served by it—"the sudden appearance of a body of baptized disciples in Samaria, by the agency of one who was not an apostle, requiring the presence and power of apostles to perform their special part as the divinely appointed founders of the Church" [ALFORD]. Beautiful, too, was the spectacle exhibited of Jew and Samaritan, one in Christ. **18-24. offered them money**—Hence the term *simony,* to denote trafficking in sacred things, but chiefly the purchase of ecclesiastical offices. **19. that on whomsoever I lay hands, he may receive the Holy Ghost**—*Spiritual ambition* here shows itself the key to this wretched man's character.

23. in the gall of bitterness and . . . bond of iniquity—expressing both the awfulness of his condition and the captivity to it in which he was held.

20. Thy money perish with thee—i.e., 'Accursed be thou and thy money with thee.' It is the language of mingled horror and indignation, not unlike our Lord's rebuke of Peter himself (Matt. 16:23).

21. Thou hast neither part nor lot . . . thy heart is not right . . .—This is the fidelity of a minister of Christ to one deceiving himself in a very awful manner.

ADAM CLARKE

15. *When they were come down.* The very same mode of speaking, in reference to Jerusalem formerly, obtains now in reference to London. The metropolis in both cases is considered as the center; and all parts, in every direction, no matter how distant, or how situated, are represented as below the metropolis. *Prayed for them, that they might receive the Holy Ghost.* It seems evident, from this case, that even the most holy deacons, though full of the Holy Ghost themselves, could not confer this heavenly Gift on others. This was the prerogative of the apostles, and they were only instruments; but they were those alone by which the Lord chose to work. They prayed and laid their hands on the disciples, and God sent down the Gift; so the blessing came from God by the apostles, and not from the apostles to the people. But for what purpose was the Holy Spirit thus given? Certainly not for the sanctification of the souls of the people; this they had on believing in Christ Jesus, and this the apostles never dispensed. It was the miraculous gifts of the Spirit which were thus communicated.

17. *Then laid they their hands on them.* Probably only on some select persons, who were thought proper for public use in the church. They did not lay hands on *all*, for certainly no hands in this way were laid on Simon.

18. *When Simon saw.* By hearing these speak with different tongues and work miracles. *He offered them money.* Supposing that the dispensing of this Spirit belonged to them—that they could give it to whomsoever they pleased; and imagining that, as he saw them to be poor men, they would not object to taking money for their gift; and it is probable that he had gained considerably by his juggling, and therefore could afford to spare some, as he hoped to make it all up by the profit which he expected to derive from this new influence. *That the gift of God may be purchased.* Peter takes care to inform not only Simon, but all to whom these presents may come, that the Spirit of God is the Gift of God alone, and consequently cannot be purchased with money.

23. *The gall of bitterness.* A Hebraism for "excessive bitterness." Gall, wormwood, and suchlike were used to express the dreadful effects of sin in the soul: the bitter repentance, bitter regret, bitter sufferings, bitter death which it produces. In Deut. xxix. 18, idolatry and its consequences are expressed by having among them "a root that beareth gall and wormwood." And in Heb. xii. 15, some grievous sin is intended when the apostle warns them, "lest any root of bitterness springing up trouble you, and thereby many be defiled." *Bond of iniquity.* An allusion to the mode in which the Romans secured their prisoners, chaining the right hand of the prisoner to the left hand of the soldier who guarded him; as if the apostle had said, You are tied and bound by the chain of your sin; justice has laid hold upon you, and you have only a short respite before your execution, to see if you will repent.

20. *Thy money perish with thee.* This is an awful declaration, and imports thus much, that if he did not repent, he and his ill-gotten goods would perish together; his money should be dissipated and his soul go into perdition.

21. *Thou hast neither part nor lot in this matter.* You have no part among the faithful and no lot in this ministry. That the word which we translate *lot* is to be understood as implying a "spiritual portion, office," see proved in the note on Num. xxvi. 55. *Thy heart is not right.* It is not through motives of purity, benevolence, or love to the souls of men that you desired to be enabled to confer the Holy Ghost; it is through pride, vainglory, and love of money. You would now give a little money that you might, by your new gift, gain much.

22. *Repent therefore of this thy wickedness.*

MATTHEW HENRY

by calling it a mistake, or misguided zeal, but must aggravate it by calling it *wickedness.* Those that have said and done amiss must, as far as they can, unsay it and undo it again by repentance. He must *pray* that God would give him repentance, and pardon upon repentance. Penitents must pray, which implies a desire towards God, and a confidence in Christ. Simon Magus shall not be courted into the apostles' communion upon any other terms than those upon which other sinners are admitted—repentance and prayer.

[2] What encouragement he gives him to do this: *If perhaps the thought of thy heart may be forgiven thee.* There may be a great deal of wickedness in the thought of the heart, which must be repented of, or we are undone. The thought of the heart, though ever so wicked, shall be forgiven, upon our repentance. When Peter here puts a *perhaps* upon it, the doubt is of the sincerity of his repentance, not of his pardon if his repentance be sincere.

[3] Simon's request to them to pray for him, *v.* 24. *Pray you to the Lord for me, that none of the things which you have spoken come upon me. First,* Something well that he was affected with the reproof given him. This being so, he begged the prayers of the apostles for him. *Secondly,* Something wanting. He begged of them to pray for him, but did not pray for himself. His concern is more that the judgments he had made himself liable to might be prevented than that his heart, by divine grace, be made right in the sight of God.

Lastly, Here is the return of the apostles to Jerusalem, when they had finished the business they came about. There, in the city of Samaria, they were *preachers*: *They testified the word of the Lord,* confirmed what the other ministers preached. In their road home they were itinerant preachers; as they passed through many villages of the Samaritans they preached the gospel. God has a regard to the inhabitants of his villages in Israel, and so should we.

Verses 26–40

We have here the story of the conversion of an Ethiopian eunuch to the faith of Christ.

I. Philip the evangelist is directed into the road where he would meet with this Ethiopian, *v.* 26. 1. Direction given him by an angel what course to steer: *Arise, and go towards the south.* Doubtless there is a special providence of God conversant about the removes and settlements of ministers. He will direct those who sincerely desire to follow him into that way in which he will own them. Philip must *go southward, to the way that leads from Jerusalem to Gaza,* through the desert of Judah. He would never have thought of going thither, into a desert; small probability of finding work there! Yet thither he is sent. Sometimes God opens a door of opportunity to his ministers in places very unlikely. 2. His obedience to this direction (*v.* 27): *He arose and went,* without objecting.

II. An account is given of this eunuch (*v.* 27). He was a foreigner, *a man of Ethiopia.* The Ethiopians were looked upon as the meanest of the nations, blackamoors, as if nature had stigmatized them; yet the gospel is sent to them, and divine grace looks upon them. He was a person of quality, a great man in his own country, *a eunuch*—lord chamberlain or steward of the household. He was *of great authority,* and bore a mighty sway *under Candace queen of the Ethiopians.* He *had charge of all her treasure*; so great a trust did she repose in him. *Not many mighty, not many noble, are called;* but some are. He was a proselyte for *he came to Jerusalem to worship.* Some think that there were remains of the knowledge of the true God in this country, ever since the queen of Sheba's time.

III. Philip and the eunuch are brought together, and now Philip shall know the meaning of his being sent into a desert.

1. Philip is ordered to fall into company with this traveller. He had been at Jerusalem, where the apostles were preaching the Christian faith. The grace of God pursues him, overtakes him in the desert, and there overcomes him. Philip has this order by the Spirit whispering it in his ear (*v.* 29): "*Go near, and join thyself to this chariot.*" We should study to do good to those we light in company with upon the road. We should not be so shy of all strangers as some effect to be. Of those of whom we know nothing else we know this, that they have souls.

2. He finds him reading in his Bible, as he sat in his chariot (*v.* 28): He *ran to him, and heard him read, v.* 30. He not only relieved the tediousness of the journey, but redeemed time by reading the scriptures, *the book of Esaias.* It is the duty of every one of us to converse much with the holy scriptures. Persons of quality should abound more than others in the

JAMIESON, FAUSSET, BROWN

22. Repent . . . pray . . . if perhaps the thought of thine heart may be forgiven—this expression of doubt being designed to impress upon him the greatness of his sin, and the need of alarm on his part.

24. Pray ye to the Lord for me—Peter had urged him to pray for himself: he asks those wonder-working men to do it for him; having no confidence in the prayer of faith, but thinking that those men possessed some peculiar interest with heaven. **that none of these things come upon me**—not that the thought of his wicked heart might be forgiven him, but only that the evils threatened might be averted from him. While this throws great light on Peter's view of his melancholy case, it shows that Christianity, as something divine, still retained its hold of him. (Tradition represents him as turning out a great heresiarch, mingling Oriental or Grecian philosophy with some elements of Christianity.) **25. and they**—Peter and John—**when they had . . . preached**—in the city where Philip's labors had been so richly blessed—**returned . . . and preached . . . in many villages of the Samaritans**—embracing the opportunity of their journey back to Jerusalem to fulfil their Lord's commission to the whole region of Samaria (ch. 1:8).

26-40. THE ETHIOPIAN EUNUCH. "With this narrative of the progress of the Gospel among the Samaritans is connected another which points to the diffusion of the doctrine of the Cross among the remotest nations. The simplicity of the chamberlain of Meroe forms a remarkable contrast with the craft of the magician just described" [OLSHAUSEN]. **26-28. the angel of the Lord**—rather, 'an angel.' **go . . . south, the way that goeth down from Jerusalem to Gaza**—There was such a road, across Mount Hebron, which Philip might take without going to Jerusalem (as VON RAUMER'S *Palæstina* shows) **which is desert**—i.e., *the way;* not Gaza itself, which was the southernmost city of Palestine, in the territory of the ancient Philistines. To go from a city, where his hands had been full of work, so far away on a desert road, could not but be staggering to the faith of Philip, especially as he was kept in ignorance of the object of the journey. But like Paul, he "was not disobedient to the heavenly vision"; and like Abram, "he went out not knowing whither he went" (ch. 26:19; Heb. 11:8). **27. a man of Ethiopia**—Upper Egypt, Meroe. **an eunuch of great authority**—Eunuchs were generally employed for confidential offices in the East, and to some extent are still. **Candace**—the family name of the queens of Upper Egypt, like Pharaoh, Cæsar, etc. (as appears from classic authors). **had come to Jerusalem to worship**—i.e., to keep the recent feast of Pentecost, as a Gentile proselyte to the Jewish faith. (See Isa. 56:3-8, and John 12:20). **28. Was returning**—Having come so far, he not only stayed out the days of the festival, but prolonged his stay till now. It says much for his fidelity and value to his royal mistress that he had such liberty. But the faith in Jehovah and love of His worship and word, with which he was imbued, sufficiently explain this. **and sitting in his chariot, read Esaias**—Not contented with the statutory services in which he had joined, he beguiles the tedium of the journey homeward by reading the Scriptures. But this is not all; for as Philip "heard him read the prophet Esaias," he must have been reading aloud and not (as is customary still in the East) so as merely to be audible, but in a louder voice than he would naturally have used if intent on his own benefit only: evidently therefore he was *reading to his charioteer.* **29-31. the Spirit said**—by an unmistakable voice within, as in ch. 10:19; 16:6, 7. **go near and join this chariot**—This would reveal to Philip the hitherto unknown object of his journey, and encourage him to expect something.

ADAM CLARKE

Peter did not suppose his case to be utterly hopeless, though his sin, considered in its motives and objects, was of the most heinous kind.

If perhaps the thought of thine heart may be forgiven thee. His sin as yet existed only in thought and purpose; and therefore it is said, *if perhaps the thought of thine heart may be forgiven.*

24. *Pray ye to the Lord for me.* The words of Peter certainly made a deep impression on Simon's mind, and he must have had a high opinion of the apostle's sanctity and influence with God when he thus commended himself to their prayers.

26. *Gaza, which is desert.* "This is the desert" or "this is in the desert." Gaza was a town about two miles and a half from the seaside; it was the last town which a traveller passed through when he went from Phoenicia to Egypt, and was at the entrance into a wilderness. Schoettgen thinks that *desert* should be referred, not to Gaza, but to the *way,* and that it signifies a road that was less frequented. If there were two roads to Gaza from Jerusalem, as some have imagined, the eunuch might have chosen that which was desert, or less frequented, for the sake of privacy in his journeying religious exercises.

27. *An eunuch.* The term eunuch was given to persons in authority at court, to whom its literal meaning did not apply. Potiphar was probably a eunuch only as to his office, for he was a married man. See Gen. xxxvii. 36; xxxix. 1. And it is likely that this Ethiopian was of the same sort. *Of great authority.* Her treasurer, for it is here said, he *had the charge of all her treasure.* It does not appear, as some have imagined, that the Abyssinians were converted to the Christian faith by this eunuch, nor by any of the apostles, as there is strong historic evidence that they continued Jews and pagans for more than three hundred years after the Christian era. Their conversion is with great probability attributed to Frumentius, sent to Abyssinia for that purpose by Athanasius, bishop of Alexandria, about A.D 330.

28. *Sitting in his chariot, read Esaias the prophet.* He had gone to Jerusalem to worship; he had profited by his religious exercises; and even in traveling he is improving his time. God sees his simplicity and earnestness and provides him an instructor who should lead him into the great truths of the gospel, which without such a one he could not have understood. Many, after having done their duty, as they call it, in attending a place of worship, forget the errand that brought them thither, and spend their time, on their return, rather in idle conversation than in reading or conversing about the Word of God. It is no wonder that such should be always learning and never able to come to the knowledge of the truth.

29. *Then the Spirit said unto Philip.* This holy man having obeyed the first direction he received from God, and gone southward without knowing the reason why, it was requisite that he should now be informed of the object of his mission. The *Spirit said unto* him, *Go near, and join thyself.* The angel who had given him the first direction had departed, and the influence of the Holy Spirit now completed the information. It is likely that what the Spirit did in this case was by a strong impression on his mind, which left him no doubt of its being from God.

30. *Heard him read the prophet Esias.* The

MATTHEW HENRY

exercises of piety, because their example will influence many. It is wisdom for men of business to redeem time for holy duties; to fill up every minute with something that will turn to a good account. Those that are diligent in searching the scriptures are in a fair way to improve in knowledge.

3. He puts a fair question to him: *Understandest thou what thou readest?* What we read and hear of the word of God we should often ask ourselves whether we understand it or no. We cannot profit by the scriptures unless we do in some measure understand them.

4. The eunuch in a sense of his need of assistance, desires Philip's company (*v.* 31): "*How can I understand*, says he, *except someone guide me?*" He speaks as one that had very low thoughts of his own capacity. He takes the question kindly, *How can I?* Those that would learn must see their need to be taught. He speaks as one very desirous to be taught, to have someone to guide him. Though there are many things in the scriptures which are *dark and hard to be understood*, yet we must not therefore throw them by, but study them for the sake of those things that are easy. Knowledge and grace grow gradually. He invited Philip to *come up and sit with him*. In order to our right understanding of the scripture, it is requisite we should have someone to guide us; some good books, and some good men, but, above all, the Spirit of grace, to lead us into all truth.

IV. The portion of scripture which the eunuch recited, with some hints of Philip's discourse upon it.

1. The chapter he was reading was the fifty-third of Isaiah, two verses of which are here quoted (*v.* 32, 33). They are set down according to the Septuagint version, which in some things differs from the original Hebrew. The greatest variation from the Hebrew is that what in the original is, *He was taken from prison and from judgment*, is here read, *In his humiliation his judgment was taken away.* He appeared so mean and despicable in their eyes that they denied him common justice. They declared him innocent, and yet condemned him to die. He is down, and down with him. Thus *in his humiliation his judgment was taken away.* So that these verses foretold concerning the Messiah, (1) That he should die, should be *led to the slaughter*, as sheep that were offered in sacrifice. (2) That he should die wrongfully, should be hurried out of his life, and *his judgment shall be taken away.* (3) That he should die patiently. Like a *lamb dumb before the shearer*, nay, and before the butcher too, *so he opened not his mouth.* Never was there such an example of patience as our Lord Jesus. When he was accused, when he was abused, he was silent. (4) That yet he should live for ever, to ages which cannot be numbered; for so I understand those words, *Who shall declare his generation? His life is taken* only *from the earth;* in heaven he shall live to endless and innumerable ages.

2. The eunuch's question upon this is, *Of whom speaketh the prophet this? v.* 34. It is a material question he asks, and a very sensible one: "Does the prophet speak this of himself, in expectation of being used, being misused, as the other prophets were, or does he speak it *of some other man*?" He proposed this question, to draw on discourse with Philip. The way to receive good instructions is to ask good questions.

3. Philip takes this fair occasion given him to open to him the great mystery of the gospel concerning *Jesus Christ, and him crucified. He began at this scripture*, and *preached unto him Jesus*, *v.* 35. This is all the account given us of Philip's sermon. And here we have an instance of speaking of the things of God, and speaking of them to good purpose, not only as we *sit in the house*, but *as we walk by the way.*

V. The eunuch is baptized in the name of Christ, *v.* 36-38.

1. The modest proposal which the eunuch made of himself for baptism (*v.* 36): *As they went on their way* they *came unto a certain water*, the sight of which made the eunuch think of being baptized. Thus God, by hints of providence which seem casual, sometimes puts his people in mind of their duty, of which otherwise perhaps they would not have thought. The eunuch knew not how little a while Philip might be with him, and therefore, if Philip think fit, he will take the present convenience which offers itself of being baptized: "*See, here is water; what doth hinder me to be baptized?*" He does not demand baptism, does not say, "Here is water and here I am resolved I will be baptized." But he does desire it, and, unless Philip can show cause why not, he desires it now. In the solemn dedicating and devoting of ourselves to God, it is good to make haste, and not to delay; for the present time is the best time. The eunuch feared lest the good affections now working in him should cool and abate, and therefore was willing

JAMIESON, FAUSSET, BROWN

30. Understandest thou what thou readest?—To one so engaged this would be deemed no rude question, while the eager appearance of the speaker, and the question itself, would indicate a readiness to supply any want of insight that might be felt.

31. How can I, except some man guide me?—Beautiful expression at once of humility and docility; the invitation to Philip which immediately followed, to "come up and sit with him," being but the natural expression of this.

32, 33. The place . . . was this, He was led as a sheep . . .—One cannot but wonder that this, of all predictions of Messiah's sufferings in the Old Testament the most striking, should have been that which the eunuch was reading before Philip joined him. He could hardly miss to have heard at Jerusalem of the sufferings and death of Jesus, and of the existence of a continually increasing party who acknowledged Him to be the Messiah. But his question to Philip, whether the prophet in this passage meant himself or some other man, clearly shows that he had not the least idea of any connection between this prediction and those facts. **34-38. And the eunuch answered, I pray thee . . .**—The respect with which he here addresses Philip was prompted by his reverence for one whom he perceived to be his superior in divine things; his own worldly position sinking before this.

35. Then Philip opened his mouth—(See on Matt. 5:2). **began at the same scripture**—founding on it as his text. **preached unto him Jesus**—showing Him to be the glorious Burden of this wonderful prediction, and interpreting it in the light of the facts of His history.

See, here is water—more simply, 'Behold water!' as if already his mind filled with light and his soul set free, he was eagerly looking out for the first water in which he might seal his reception of the truth and be enrolled among the visible disciples of the Lord Jesus. **what doth hinder me to be baptized?**—Philip had probably told him that this was the ordained sign and seal of discipleship, but the eunuch's question was likely the first proposal of its application in this case. (Verse 37 is wanting in the principal MSS.

ADAM CLARKE

eunuch, it seems, was reading aloud, and apparently in Greek, for that was the common language in Egypt; and, indeed, almost in every place it was understood. And it appears that it was the Greek version or the Septuagint that he was reading, as the quotation below is from that version.

32. *The place of the scripture.* The "section" or "paragraph."

33. *In his humiliation his judgment was taken away.* He who was the Fountain of judgment and justice had no justice shown Him *in his humiliation*, viz., that time in which He emptied himself and appeared in the form of a servant. *Who shall declare his generation?* Answering to the Hebrew *doro*, which Bishop Lowth understands as implying his "manner of life." It was the custom among the Jews, when they were taking away any criminal from judgment to execution, to call out and inquire whether there was any person who could appear in behalf of the character of the criminal—whether there was any who, from intimate acquaintance with his manner *of life*, could say anything in his favor? In our Lord's case, this benevolent inquiry does not appear to have been made; and perhaps to this breach of justice, as well as of custom, the prophet refers.

35. *Began at the same scripture.* He did not confine himself to this one scripture, but made this his text and showed, from the general tenor of the sacred writings, that Jesus was the Christ, or Messiah; and that in His person, birth, life, doctrine, miracles, passion, death, and resurrection the scriptures of the Old Testament were fulfilled. This preaching had the desired effect, for the eunuch was convinced of the truth of Philip's doctrine and desired to be baptized in the name of Jesus.

36. *See, here is water.* He was not willing to omit the first opportunity that presented itself of his taking upon *himself* the profession of the gospel. By this we may see that Philip had explained the whole of the Christian faith to him, and the *way* by which believers were brought into the Christian Church.

MATTHEW HENRY

immediately to bind his soul unto the Lord.

2. The fair declaration which Philip made him (*v.* 37): "*If thou believest with all thy heart, thou mayest.*" He must believe with all his heart, for with the heart man believeth, not with the head only, by an assent to gospel truth in the understanding; but with the heart, by a consent of the will to gospel terms. "If thou do indeed believe with all thy heart, thou art by that united to Christ, and thou mayest by baptism be joined to the church."

3. The confession of faith which the eunuch made. It is very short, but it is comprehensive and much to the purpose: *I believe that Jesus Christ is the Son of God.* He was before a worshipper of the true God, so that all he had to do now was to *receive Christ Jesus the Lord.* He believes that Jesus is *the Christ,* the true Messiah promised. That Christ is *Jesus—a Saviour,* the only Saviour of his people from their sins. That this Jesus Christ is the *Son of God,* that he has a divine nature, as the Son is of the same nature with the Father.

4. The baptizing of him hereupon. The eunuch *commanded the chariot to stand still.* It was the best waiting place he ever met with in any of his journeys. *They went down both into the water.* Going barefoot according to the custom, they went perhaps up to the ankles or mid-leg into the water, and Philip sprinkled water upon him. Though Philip had very lately been deceived in Simon Magus, yet he did not therefore scruple to baptize the eunuch upon his profession of faith immediately. If some hypocrites crowd into the church, who afterwards prove a grief and scandal to us, yet we must not therefore make the door of admission any straiter than Christ has made it; they shall answer for their apostasy, and not we.

VI. Philip and the eunuch are separated presently; and this is as surprising as the other parts of the story. As soon as they had *come up out of the water the Spirit of the Lord caught away Philip* (*v.* 39). The working of this miracle upon Philip was a confirmation of his doctrine, as much as the working of a miracle by him would have been. He was *caught away, and the eunuch saw him no more,* but, having lost his minister, returned to the use of his Bible again.

1. How the eunuch was disposed: He *went on his way rejoicing.* Business called him home, and he must hasten to it; for it was no way inconsistent with his Christianity, which is a religion which men may and ought to carry about with them into the affairs of this life. But he went on rejoicing. He was never better pleased in all his life. He rejoiced, (1) That he himself was joined to Christ. (2) That he had these good things to bring to his countrymen, and a prospect of bringing them also into fellowship with Christ.

2. How Philip was disposed of (*v.* 40): *He was found at Azotus* or *Ashdod.* But Philip, wherever he was, would not be idle. *Passing through, he preached in all the cities,* till he came to Cæsarea, and there he settled. At Cæsarea we find him in a house of his own, *ch.* xxi. 8. He that had been faithful in working for Christ as an itinerant at length gains a settlement.

JAMIESON, FAUSSET, BROWN

and most venerable versions of the New Testament. It seems to have been added from the formularies for baptism which came into current use).

they went down both into the water, and he baptized him . . .—probably laving the water upon him, though the precise mode is neither certain nor of any consequence. **39, 40. the Spirit of the Lord caught away Philip**—To deny [as MEYER, OLSHAUSEN, BLOOMFIELD] the miraculous nature of Philip's disappearance, is vain. It stands out on the face of the words, as just a repetition of what we read of the ancient prophets, in I Kings 18:12; II Kings 2:16. And the same word (as BENGEL remarks) is employed to express a similar idea in II Corinthians 12:2, 4; I Thessalonians 4:17. **the eunuch saw him no more**—nor, perhaps, for very joy, cared to see him [BENGEL]. **and he went on his way rejoicing**—He had found Christ, and the key to the Scriptures; his soul was set free, and his discipleship sealed; he had lost his teacher, but gained what was infinitely better: He felt himself a new man, and "his joy was full." Tradition says he was the first preacher of the Gospel in Ethiopia; and how, indeed, could he choose but "tell what the Lord had done for his soul"? Yet there is no certainty as to any historical connection between his labors and the introduction of Christianity into that country. **40. Philip was found**—i.e., 'found himself,' 'made his appearance:' an expression confirming the miraculous manner of his transportation. **at Azotus**—the ancient Ashdod. **preached in all the cities**—along the coast, proceeding northward. **till he came to Cæsarea**—fifty-five miles northwest of Jerusalem, on the Mediterranean, just south of Mount Carmel; and so named by Herod, who rebuilt it, in honor of Cæsar Augustus. Henceforth we lose sight of zealous and honored Philip, as by and by we shall lose sight even of Peter. As the chariot of the Gospel rolls on, other agents are raised up, each suited to his work. But "he that soweth and he that reapeth shall rejoice together." (See on John 4:31-38).

ADAM CLARKE

37. *I believe that Jesus Christ is the Son of God.* This whole verse is omitted by several MSS.; almost all the critics declare against it as spurious.

38. *And they went down.* They "alighted from the chariot into the water." While Philip was instructing him and he professed his faith in Christ, he probably plunged himself under the water, as this was the plan which appears to have been generally followed among the Jews in their baptisms; but the person who had received his confession of faith was he to whom the baptism was attributed, as it was administered by his authority.

39. *The Spirit of the Lord caught away Philip.* Perhaps this means no more than that the Holy Spirit suggested to the mind of Philip that he should withdraw abruptly from the eunuch and thus leave him to pursue his journey, reflecting on the important incidents which had taken place.

40. *Philip was found at Azotus.* From the time he left the eunuch he was not heard of till he got to Azotus, which, according to Dr. Lightfoot, was about thirty-four miles from Gaza, and probably it was near Gaza that Philip met the eunuch. The Azotus of the New Testament is the Ashdod of the Old. It was given by Joshua to the tribe of Judah, Josh. xv. 47. It was one of the five lordships which belonged to the Philistines, and is a seaport town on the Mediterranean Sea, between Gaza on the south, and Joppa or Jaffa on the north. *Preached in all the cities, till he came to Caesarea.* This was Caesarea in Palestine, formerly called Strato's Tower, built by Herod the Great in honor of Augustus. There was an excellent harbor here made by Herod; and after the destruction of Jerusalem, it became the capital of the whole land of Judea. It must be always distinguished from Caesarea Philippi, which was an inland town not far from the springs of Jordan. Whenever the word Caesarea occurs without Philippi, the former is intended. As Philip preached in all the cities of Palestine till he came to Caesarea, he must have preached in the different cities of the Philistine country, Ashdod, Akkaron, and Jamnia. It appears, from chap. xxi. 8, that Philip settled at Caesarea, where he had a house and family, four of his unmarried daughters being prophetesses.

MATTHEW HENRY

CHAPTER 9

Verses 1-9

We found mention made of Saul twice or thrice in the story of Stephen. His name in Hebrew was *Saul—desired*; his Roman name was *Paul—little.* He was born in Tarsus, a city of Cilicia, a free city of the Romans, and himself a freeman of that city. His father and mother were both native Jews, therefore he calls himself a *Hebrew of the Hebrews*; he was of the tribe of Benjamin. His education was in the schools of Tarsus first, which was a little Athens for learning. Thence he was sent to Jerusalem, to study divinity and the Jewish law. His tutor was Gamaliel. He had extraordinary natural parts. He had likewise a handicraft trade (being bred to tent-making), which was common with those among the Jews who were bred scholars.

I. How bad he was, how very bad, before his conversion; just before he was an inveterate enemy to Christianity. In other respects he was well enough, as *touching the righteousness which is of the law, blameless,* a man of no ill morals, but a persecutor of Christians. And so ill informed was his conscience that he thought that he did God service in it.

1. His general enmity and rage against the Christian religion (*v.* 1): He *yet breathed out threatenings and slaughter against the disciples of the Lord.* The persons persecuted were the disciples of the Lord; under that character he hated and persecuted them. The matter

JAMIESON, FAUSSET, BROWN

CHAPTER 9

VSS. 1-25. CONVERSION OF SAUL, AND BEGINNINGS OF HIS MINISTRY. **1. Saul, yet breathing out threatenings and slaughter against the disciples of the Lord . . .**—The emphatic "yet" is intended to note the remarkable fact, that up to this moment his blind persecuting rage against the disciples of the Lord burned as fiercely as ever. (In the teeth of this, NEANDER and OLSHAUSEN picture him deeply impressed with Stephen's joyful faith, remembering passages of the Old Testament confirmatory of the Messiahship of Jesus, and experiencing such a violent struggle as would inwardly prepare the way for the designs of God towards him. Is not dislike, if not unconscious disbelief, of *sudden conversion* at the bottom of this?) The word "slaughter" here points to cruelties not yet recorded, but the particulars of which are supplied by himself nearly thirty years afterwards: "And I persecuted this way *unto the death*" (ch. 22:4); "and when they were *put to death,* I gave my voice [vote] against them. And I punished them oft in every synagogue, and compelled them to [did my utmost to make them] blaspheme; and being exceedingly mad against them, I persecuted them even unto strange [foreign] cities" (ch. 26:10, 11). All this was *before* his present journey.

ADAM CLARKE

CHAPTER 9

1. *Saul, yet breathing out threatenings and slaughter.* The original text is very emphatic and points out how determinate Saul was to pursue and accomplish his fell purpose of totally destroying the infant Church of Christ. The mode of speech introduced above is very frequent in the Greek writers, who often express any vehement and *hostile* affection of the mind by the verb *pneein,* to "breathe," to "pant"; so Theocritus, *Idyll.* xxii, v. 82: "They came into the assembly, breathing mutual slaughter." Euripides has the same form, *breathing out fire, and slaughter* (*Iphig. in Taur.*).

MATTHEW HENRY

of the persecution was threatenings and slaughter. There is persecution in threatenings, they terrify and break the spirit. His breathing out threatenings and slaughter intimates that it was natural to him. His very breath, like that of some venomous creatures, was pestilential. He breathed death to the Christians, wherever he came.

2. His particular design upon the Christians at Damascus. Saul cannot be easy if he knows a Christian is quiet; and therefore, hearing that the Christians in Damascus were so, he resolves to give them disturbance. He applies to the high priest for a commission (*v.* 1) to go to Damascus, *v.* 2. The high priest needed not to be stirred up to persecute the Christians, but it seems the young persecutor drove more furiously than the old one. The proselytes which the scribes and Pharisees make often prove seven times more the children of hell than themselves. Now the commission was to empower him to enquire among the synagogues at Damascus, whether there were any that inclined to favour this heresy, that believed in Christ; and if he found any such, whether men or women, to bring them up prisoners to Jerusalem. The Christians are here said to be *those of this way.* Perhaps the Christians sometimes called themselves so, from Christ *the Way.* The high priest and sanhedrim had a deference paid to their authority in matters of religion, by all their synagogues. Even the weaker sex, who might deserve excuse, or at least compassion, shall find neither with Saul. He was ordered to bring them all bound to Jerusalem as criminals. Thus was Saul employed when the grace of God wrought that great change in him. Let not us then despair of renewing grace for the conversion of the greatest sinners, nor let such despair of the pardoning mercy of God for the greatest sin; for Paul himself obtained mercy.

II. How suddenly and strangely a blessed change was wrought in him.

1. The place and time of it: *As he journeyed, he came near to Damascus;* and there Christ met with him. (1) He was in the way, travelling upon his journey. The work of conversion is not tied to the church. Some are reclaimed in travelling upon the road alone. There the Spirit may set in with us, for that wind blows where it listeth.

(2) He was near Damascus, almost at his journey's end. He who was to be the apostle of the Gentiles was converted to the faith of Christ in a Gentile country.

(3) He was in a wicked way, pursuing his design against the Christians at Damascus. Sometimes the grace of God works upon sinners when they are at the worst, which is much for the glory both of God's pity and of his power.

(4) The cruel edict and decree drew near to be put in execution; and now it was happily prevented. [1] A great kindness to the poor saints at Damascus, who had notice of his coming, as appears by what Ananias said (*v.* 13, 14). Christ has many ways of delivering the godly out of temptation, and sometimes does it by a change wrought in their persecutors. [2] It was also a very great mercy to Saul himself. It is to be valued as a signal token of the divine favour if God prevent us from prosecuting and executing a sinful purpose.

2. The appearance of Christ to him in his glory. Here it is only said that there *shone round about him a light from heaven;* but it appears from what follows (*v.* 17) that the Lord Jesus was in this light. This light shone upon him *suddenly.* Christ's manifestations of himself to poor souls are many times sudden and very surprising, and he anticipates them with the blessings of his goodness. It was a light from heaven. It was a light above the brightness of the sun (*ch.* xxvi. 13), for it was visible at midday. It shone *round about him,* not in his face only, but on every side of him. The devil comes to the soul in darkness; by this he gets and keeps possession of it. But Christ comes to the soul in light, for he is himself the light of the world. The first thing in this new creation, as in that of the world, is light.

3. The arresting of Saul: *He fell to the earth, v.* 4. It appears (*ch.* xxvi. 14) that all that were with him fell to the earth as well as he, but the design was upon him. The effect of Christ's appearing to him, and of the light which shone round about him. Christ's manifestations of himself to poor souls are humbling; they lay them very low. A step towards this intended advancement. Those whom Christ designs for the greatest honours are commonly first laid low. Those whom God will employ are first struck with a sense of their unworthiness to be employed.

4. The arraigning of Saul. He heard a voice saying to him (and it was distinguishing, to him only, for though those that were with him heard a sound (*v.* 7)

JAMIESON, FAUSSET, BROWN

2. desired . . . letters—of authorization. **to Damascus**—the capital of Syria and the great highway between eastern and western Asia, about 130 miles northeast of Jerusalem; the most ancient city perhaps in the world, and lying in the center of a verdant and inexhaustible paradise. It abounded (as appears from JOSEPHUS, Wars, II. 20, 2) with Jews, and with Gentile proselytes to the Jewish faith. Thither the Gospel had penetrated; and Saul, flushed with past successes, undertakes to crush it out. **that if he found any of this way, whether men or women**—Thrice are *women* specified as objects of his cruelty, as an aggravated feature of it (ch. 8:3; 22:4; and here).

3. he came near Damascus—so ch. 22:6. Tradition points to a bridge near the city as the spot referred to. Events which are the turning points in one's history so imprint themselves upon the memory that circumstances the most trifling in themselves acquire by connection with them something of their importance, and are recalled with inexpressible interest.

suddenly—At what time of day, it is not said; for artless simplicity reigns here. But he himself emphatically states, in one of his narratives, that it was *"about noon"* (ch. 22:6), and in the other, *"at midday"* (ch. 26:13), when there could be no deception. **there shined round about him a light from heaven**—"a great light" (he himself says) "above the brightness of the sun," then shining in its full strength.

4-6. he fell to the earth—and his companions with him (ch. 26:14), who "saw the light" (ch. 22:9).

ADAM CLARKE

Luke, who was master of the Greek tongue, chose such terms as best expressed a heart desperately and incessantly bent on accomplishing the destruction of the objects of its resentment. Such at this time was the heart of Saul of Tarsus; and it had already given full proof of its malignity, not only in the martyrdom of Stephen, but also in making havoc of the Church, and in forcibly entering every house, and dragging men and women whom he suspected of Christianity, and committing them to prison. See chap. viii. 3. *Went unto the high priest.* As the high priest was chief in all matters of an ecclesiastical nature, and the present business was pretendedly religious, he was the proper person to apply to for letters by which this virulent persecutor might be accredited. The letters must necessarily be granted in the name of the whole Sanhedrin, but the *high priest* was the proper organ through whom this business might be negotiated.

2. *Letters to Damascus to the synagogues.* Damascus, anciently called *Damask,* was once the metropolis of all Syria. It was situated at fifty miles' distance from the sea, from which it is separated by lofty mountains. It is washed by two rivers, Amara or Abara, which ran through it, and Pharpar, called by the Greeks the golden stream, which ran on the outside of its walls. It is one of the most ancient cities in the world, for it existed in the time of Abraham, Gen. xiv. 15, and how long before is not known. The city of Damascus is at present a place of considerable trade, owing to its being the rendezvous for all the pilgrims from the north of Asia on their road to and from the temple of Mecca. It is surrounded with pretty strong walls, which have *nine* gates, and is between four and five miles in circumference. In the time of Paul it was governed by Aretas, whose father, Obodas, had been governor of it under Augustus. Damascus is 112 miles south of Antioch, 130 N.N.E. of Jerusalem. The silks and linens, known by the name of "damasks," were probably first manufactured by the inhabitants of this ancient city. *Any of this way.* That is, this "religion," for so *derec* in Hebrew and *hodos* in Hellenistic Greek are often to be understood. *Derec Yehovah,* the way of the Lord, implies the whole of the worship due to Him and prescibed by himself; the way or path in which He wills men to walk, that they may get safely through life and finally attain everlasting felicity. *Whether they were men or women.* Provided they were Jews, for no converts had as yet been made among the Gentiles, nor did the power of the high priest and Sanhedrin extend to any but those who belonged to the synagogues. In every country where there were Jews and synagogues, the power and authority of the Sanhedrin and high priest were acknowledged, just as papists in all countries acknowledge the authority of the pope.

4. *And he fell to the earth.* Being struck down with the lightning. Many persons suppose he was on horseback, and painters thus represent him; but this is utterly without foundation. Painters are in almost every case wretched commentators.

MATTHEW HENRY

yet they knew not the words, *ch.* xxii. 9), *Saul, Saul, why persecutest thou me?*

(1) Saul not only saw a light from heaven, but heard a voice from heaven. God's manifestations of himself were never dumb shows, for he magnifies his word above all his name, and what was seen was always designed to make way for what was said. Saul heard a voice. Faith comes by hearing. The voice he heard was the voice of Christ. The word we hear is likely to profit us when we hear it as the voice of Christ; no voice but his can reach the heart.

(2) What he heard was very awakening.

[1] He was called by his name, and that doubled: *Saul, Saul.* His calling him by name brought the conviction home to his conscience, and put it past dispute to whom the voice spoke this. What God speaks in general is then likely to do us good when we insert our own names into the precepts and promises, as if God spoke to us by name. The doubling of it, *Saul, Saul,* intimates the tender concern that the blessed Jesus had for him, and for his recovery. He speaks as one in earnest. He speaks to him as to one in imminent danger, at the pit's brink, and just ready to drop in.

[2] The charge exhibited against him is, *Why persecutest thou me?* Before Saul was made a saint, he was made to see himself a sinner. Now he was made to see that evil in himself which he never saw before. A humbling conviction of sin is the first step towards a saving conversion from sin. He is convinced of one particular sin, which he had justified himself in. The sin he is convinced of is persecution: *Why persecutest thou me?* It is a very affectionate expostulation. 1. The person sinning: "It is thou; thou that hast good parts and accomplishments, hast the knowledge of the scriptures, which, if duly considered, would show thee the folly of it. It is worse in thee than in another." 2. The person sinned against: "It is I, who was not long since crucified for thee; must I afresh be crucified by thee?" 3. The kind and continuance of the sin. It was persecution, and he was at this time engaged in it. Those that are designing mischief are, in God's account, doing mischief. 4. The question put to him upon it: "Why dost thou do it?" (1) It is complaining language. Christ never complained so much of those who persecuted him in his own person as he did here of those who persecuted him in his followers. The sins of sinners are a very grievous burden to the Lord Jesus. (2) It is convincing language: "Why dost thou thus?" It is good for us often to ask ourselves why we do so and so, that we may discern what an unreasonable thing sin is. *Why persecutest thou me?* He thought he was persecuting only a company of poor, weak, silly people, little imagining that it was one in heaven that he was all this while insulting. Those who persecute the saints persecute Christ himself, and he takes what is done against them as done against himself.

5. Saul's question upon his indictment, and the reply to it, *v.* 5.

(1) He makes enquiry concerning Christ: *Who art thou, Lord?* He gives no direct answer to the charge preferred against him, being convicted by his own conscience. If God contend with us for our sins, we are not able to answer for one of a thousand. Convictions of sin, when they are set home with power upon the conscience, will silence all excuses and self-justifications. But he desires to know who is his judge. He who had been a blasphemer of Christ's name now speaks to him as his Lord. The question is proper: *Who art thou?* This implies his present unacquaintedness with Christ. He desired to be acquainted with him and therefore, *Lord, who art thou?* There is some hope of people when they begin to enquire after Jesus Christ.

(2) He has an answer immediately. Christ's gracious revelation of himself to him. *I am Jesus whom thou persecutest.* The name of Jesus was not unknown to him, and gladly would he bury it in oblivion. Little did he think to hear it from heaven. He said, *I am Jesus, a Saviour; I am Jesus of Nazareth,* so it is, *ch.* xxii. 8. Saul used to call him so when he blasphemed him. *"I am that Jesus whom thou persecutest."* There is nothing more effectual to awaken and humble the soul than to see sin to be against Christ. His gentle reproof of him: *It is hard for thee to kick against the pricks,* or *goads.* Those kick at the goad that stifle and smother the convictions of conscience. Those that revolt more and more when they are stricken by the word or rod of God, kick against the pricks.

6. His surrender of himself to the Lord Jesus at length, *v.* 6.

(1) The frame and temper he was in when Christ had been dealing with him. He trembled. Strong convictions, set home by the blessed Spirit, will make

JAMIESON, FAUSSET, BROWN

and heard a voice saying unto him—"in the Hebrew tongue" (ch. 26:14)—**Saul, Saul**—a reduplication full of tenderness [De Wette]. Though his name was soon changed into "Paul," we find him, in both his own narratives of the scene, after the lapse of so many years, retaining the original form, as not daring to alter, in the smallest detail, the overpowering words addressed to him.

why persecutest thou me?—No language can express the affecting character of this question, addressed from the right hand of the Majesty on high to an infuriated, persecuting mortal. (See Matthew 25:45, and that whole judgment scene.)

5. Who art thou, Lord?—"Jesus knew Saul ere Saul knew Jesus" [Bengel]. The term "Lord" here is an indefinite term of respect for some unknown but august speaker. That Saul *saw* as well as *heard* this glorious Speaker, is expressly said by Ananias (vs. 17; 22:14), by Barnabas (ch. 9:27), and by himself (ch. 26:16); and in claiming apostleship, he explicitly states that he had "*seen* the Lord" (I Cor. 9:1; 15:8), which can refer only to this scene.

I am Jesus whom thou persecutest—The "I" and "thou" here are touchingly emphatic in the original; while the term "Jesus" is purposely chosen, to convey to him the thrilling information that the hated name which he sought to hunt down—"*the Nazarene,*" as it is in ch. 22:8—was now speaking to him from the skies, "crowned with glory and honor" (see ch. 26:9). **It is hard for thee to kick against the pricks.**

ADAM CLARKE

G. CAMPBELL MORGAN:

The first phase in the apprehension of Saul was that of a great light shining round about him out of heaven, above the brightness of the sun. It was a moment fraught with tremendous issues in the whole program of Christ in the world. Then came the inquiry. A voice spoke, not in the Greek, but in the Hebrew tongue: "Saul, Saul, why persecutest thou me?" It was a voice out of heaven, out of the light, asking him, a man on the earth, why he persecuted the One who spoke. What a strange thing, what a startling thing! "Who art thou, Lord?" cried the astonished Saul. Oh, the revolution, the convulsion, the upheaval in the soul of Saul. Then came the most arresting thing. The voice replied: "I am Jesus whom thou persecutest." Then there broke upon his consciousness, dimly and indistinctly, more perfectly apprehended in after days, the great truth that Christ and the Church were one. How Paul wrought out this truth in those great letters afterward, as he insisted upon this unity of the living Lord with His people. It is as though Christ had said to him, "Those men and women whom you have haled to prison have suffered; but it is I who have suffered in their suffering, Saul. The brutal stones that you saw hurled upon Stephen, cutting into his flesh, and giving him physical pain, reached Me, hurt Me. I felt every throb of Stephen's pain."

But there was another meaning in the words. "Why persecutest thou me?" "I am above thee in the heavens; thou canst not undo My work; that against which thou art fighting is not the fanaticism of a mistaken fanatic; it is the march of God through human history." "Why persecutest thou me?" In that moment, nebulously as yet, not perfectly apprehended, the truth was breaking upon the mind of this man, and by implication, ere he knew it, he had yielded himself to the One who had spoken out of the eternal light, and who had addressed him by name. "Who art thou, Lord?" That use of the word Lord revealed a fine recognition of a trained mind, in the presence of such a manifestation of supremacy.—*The Acts of the Apostles*

5. *Who art thou, Lord?* **"Who art thou, Sir?"** He had no knowledge who it was that addressed him, and would only use the term *Kyries,* as any Roman or Greek would, merely as a term of civil respect. *I am Jesus whom thou persecutest.* "Your enmity is against Me and My religion; and the injuries which you do to My followers I consider as done to myself." The following words, making twenty in the original, and thirty in our version, are found in no Greek MS. The words are, "It is hard for thee to kick against the pricks. And he trembling and astonished said, Lord, what wilt thou have me to do? And the Lord said unto him." It is not very easy to account for such a large addition, which is not only not found in any Greek MS. yet discovered, but is wanting in the Itala, Erpen's Arabic, the Syriac, Coptic, Sahidic, and most of the Slavonian. It is found in the Vulgate; and was probably borrowed from chap. xxvi. 14, and some marginal notes. *It is hard for thee.* This is a proverbial expression, which exists, not only in substance, but even in so many words, both in the Greek and Latin writers. *Kentron* signifies an ox goad, a piece of pointed iron stuck in the end of a stick, with which the ox is urged on when drawing the plough. The origin of the proverb seems to have been this: Sometimes it happens that a restive stubborn ox kicks back against the goad and thus wounds himself more deeply; hence it has become a proverb to signify the fruitlessness and absurdity of rebelling against lawful authority, and the getting into greater difficulties by endeavoring to avoid trifling sufferings.

MATTHEW HENRY

an awakened soul to tremble. He was astonished, as one brought into a new world, that knew not where he was.

(2) His address to Jesus Christ: *Lord, what wilt thou have me to do?* This may be taken, [1] As a serious request for Christ's teachings. "Thou hast discovered sin to me, discover to me the way to pardon and peace." A serious desire to be instructed by Christ in the way of salvation is an evidence of a good work begun in the soul. Or, [2] As a sincere resignation of himself to the direction and government of the Lord Jesus. This was the first word that grace spoke in Paul, and with this began a spiritual life. *What wilt thou have me to do?* The great change in conversion is wrought upon the will, and consists in the resignation of that to the will of Christ.

(3) The general direction Christ gave him: *Arise, go into the city of Damascus, and it shall be told thee what thou must do.* It is encouragement enough to have further instruction promised him, but, [1] He must not have it yet. Let him consider awhile what he had done in persecuting Christ, and be deeply humbled for that, and then he shall be told what he has further to do. [2] He must not have it in this way, by a voice from heaven, for it is plain that he cannot bear it. He shall be told therefore what he must do by a man like himself. Christ manifests himself to his people by degrees.

7. How far his fellow travellers were affected with this. *They stood speechless*, as men in confusion, and that was all, *v.* 7. We do not find that any of them were converted, though they saw the light, and were struck dumb by it. No external means will of themselves work a change in the soul, without the Spirit and grace of God. None of them said, *Who art thou, Lord?* or, *What wilt thou have me to do?* as Paul did. *They heard a voice, but saw no man;* they heard Paul speak, but saw not him to whom he spoke, nor heard distinctly what was said to him. Thus those who came hither to be the instruments of Paul's rage against the church serve for witnesses of the power of God over him.

8. What condition Saul was in after this, *v.* 8, 9. *He arose from the earth*, when Christ commanded him. *When his eyes were opened he saw no man.* It was not so much this glaring light, but it was a sight of Christ, that had this effect upon him. Thus a believing sight of the glory of God in the face of Christ dazzles the eyes to all things here below. *They led him by the hand into Damascus.* Thus he who thought to have led the disciples of Christ prisoners and captives to Jerusalem was himself led a prisoner and a captive to Christ into Damascus. He lay *without sight, neither did eat nor drink for three days, v.* 9. He was in the dark concerning his own spiritual state, and was so wounded in spirit for sin that he could relish neither meat nor drink.

JAMIESON, FAUSSET, BROWN

6. And he, trembling and astonished, said, Lord, what wilt thou have me to do? And the Lord said—(The most ancient MSS. and versions of the New Testament lack all these words *here;* but they occur in ch. 26:14 and ch. 22:10, from which they appear to have been inserted here.) The metaphor of an ox, only driving the goad deeper by kicking against it, is a classic one, and here forcibly expresses, not only the vanity of all his measures for crushing the Gospel, but the deeper wound which every such effort inflicted upon himself. The question, What shall I do, Lord?" or, "Lord, what wilt Thou have me to do?" indicates a state of mind singularly interesting (see on ch. 2:37). Its elements seem to be these: (1) Resistless conviction that "Jesus whom he persecuted," now speaking to him, was "Christ the Lord." (See on Gal. 1:15, 16). (2) As a consequence of this, that not only all his religious views, but his whole religious character, had been an entire mistake; that he was up to that moment fundamentally and wholly wrong. (3) That though his whole future was now a blank, he had absolute confidence in Him who had so tenderly arrested him in his blind career, and was ready both to take in all His teaching and to carry out all His directions. (See more on vs. 9). **Arise, and go into the city, and it shall be told thee, . .**—See on ch. 8:26-28. **7. the men . . . stood speechless**—This may mean merely that they remained so; but if the *standing* posture be intended, we have only to suppose that though at first they "all fell to the earth" (ch. 26:14), they arose of their own accord while Saul yet lay prostrate. **hearing a**—rather 'the'—**voice**—Paul himself says, "they heard not the voice of Him that spake to me" (ch. 22:9). But just as "the people that stood by *heard"* the voice that saluted our Lord with recorded words of consolation and assurance, and yet *heard not* the articulate words, but thought "it thundered" or that some "angel spake to Him" (John 12:28, 29)—so these men heard the *voice* that spake to Saul, but heard not the *articulate words.* Apparent discrepancies like these, in the different narratives of the same scene in one and the same book of Acts, furnish the strongest confirmation both of the facts themselves and of the book which records them. **8. Saul arose . . . and when his eyes were opened, he saw no man**—after beholding the Lord, since he "could not see for the glory of that light" (ch. 22:11), he had involuntarily closed his eyes to protect them from the glare; and on opening them again he found his vision gone. "It is not said, however, that he was *blind,* for it was no punishment" [BENGEL]. **9. And he was three days without sight, and neither did eat nor drink**—i.e., according to the Hebrew mode of computation: he took no food during the remainder of that day, the entire day following, and so much of the subsequent day as elapsed before the visit of Ananias. Such a period of entire abstinence from food, in that state of mental absorption and revolution into which he had been so suddenly thrown, is in perfect harmony with known laws and numerous facts. But what three days those must have been! "Only one other space of three days' duration can be mentioned of equal importance in the history of the world" [Hows]. Since Jesus had been revealed not only to his *eyes* but to his *soul* (see on Gal. 1:15, 16), the double conviction must have immediately flashed upon him, that his whole reading of the Old Testament hitherto had been wrong, and that the system of legal righteousness in which he had, up to that moment, rested and prided himself was false and fatal. What materials these for spiritual exercise during those three days of total darkness, fasting, and solitude! On the one hand, what self-condemnation, what anguish, what death of legal hope, what difficulty in believing that in such a case there could be hope at all; on the other hand, what heartbreaking admiration of the grace that had "pulled him out of the fire," what resistless conviction that there must be a purpose of love in it, and what tender expectation of being yet honored, as a chosen vessel, to declare what the Lord had done for his soul, and to spread abroad the savor of that Name which he had so wickedly, though ignorantly, sought to destroy—must have struggled in his breast during those memorable days! Is it too much to say that all that profound insight into the Old Testament, that comprehensive grasp of the principles of the divine economy, that penetrating spirituality, that vivid apprehension of man's lost state, and those glowing views of the perfection and glory of the divine remedy, that beautiful ideal of the loftiness and the lowliness of the Christian character, that large philanthropy and burning zeal to spend and be spent through all his future life for Christ,

ADAM CLARKE

6. *Trembling.* Under a strong apprehension of meeting the judgment he deserved. *And astonished.* At the light, the thunder, and the voice. *Lord, what wilt thou have me to do?* The word *Kyrie, Lord,* is here to be understood in its proper sense, as expressing authority and dominion; in the fifth verse it appears to be equivalent to our word "sir." *Go into the city, and it shall be told thee.* Jesus could have informed him at once what was His will concerning him; but He chose to make one of those very disciples whom he was going to bring in bonds to Jerusalem the means of his salvation.

7. *Stood speechless, hearing a voice, but seeing no man.* The men were "stupefied," hearing *the voice* or thunder, but not distinguishing the words, which were addressed to Saul alone; and which were spoken out of the thunder, or in a small, still voice, after the peal had ceased. The remarkable case, 1 Kings xix. 11-13, may serve to illustrate that before us. The thunder must have been heard by all; the small, still voice by Saul alone. This consideration amply reconciles the passage in the text with that in chap. xxii. 9, where Paul says, "They that were with me saw indeed the light, and were afraid; but they heard not the voice of him that spake to me." They had heard the thunder which followed the escape of the lightning, but they heard not the *voice* of Him that spake to Saul; they did not hear the words, "I am Jesus whom thou persecutest"; but they saw and heard enough to convince them that the whole was supernatural, for they were all struck down to the earth with the splendor of the light and the sound of the thunder, which I suppose took place on this occasion. It has been a question among divines whether Jesus Christ did really appear to Saul on this occasion. Ananias, it seems, was informed that there had been a real appearance, for in addressing Saul, v. 17, he says, "The Lord . . . Jesus, that appeared unto thee in the way as thou camest." And Barnabas intimated as much when he brought him before the apostles at Jerusalem, for he "declared unto them how he had seen the Lord in the way, and that he had spoken to him." But Paul's own words, 1 Cor. ix. 1, put the subject out of dispute: "Am I not an apostle? am I not free? have I not seen Jesus Christ our Lord?" To which may be added, 1 Cor. xv. 8, "And last of all he was seen of me also, as of one born out of due time."

9. *Neither did eat nor drink.* The anxiety of his mind and the anguish of his heart were so great that he had no appetite for food; and he continued in total darkness and without food for *three days,* till Ananias proclaimed salvation to him in the name of the Lord Jesus.

MATTHEW HENRY

Verses 10–22

A good work was begun in Saul, when he was brought to Christ's feet, in that word, *Lord, what wilt thou have me to do?* And never did Christ leave any that were brought to that. He that hath convinced will comfort.

I. Ananias is here ordered to go and look after him.

1. The person employed is *Ananias, a certain disciple at Damascus,* not lately driven thither from Jerusalem, but a native of Damascus; for it is said (*ch.* xxii. 12) *that he had a good report of all the Jews who dwelt there, as a devout man according to the law.*

2. The direction given him is to go and enquire at such a house for one *Saul of Tarsus.* Christ, in a vision, called to Ananias by name, *v.* 10. Without terror or confusion, he readily answers, "*Behold I am here, Lord.*" *Go then,* saith Christ, *into the street which is called Straight, and enquire in the house of Judas for one called Saul of Tarsus.* Christ very well knows where to find out those that are his, in their distresses. They have a friend in heaven, that knows in what street, in what house, nay, and which is more, in what frame they are.

3. Two reasons are given him why he must go.

(1) Because he prays, and his coming to him must answer his prayer. This is a reason, [1] Why Ananias needed not to be afraid of him, as we find he was, *v.* 13, 14. There is no question, saith Christ, but he is a true convert, *for behold he prayeth. Behold* denotes the certainty of it. It denotes also the strangeness of it: "Behold, and wonder." But was it such a strange thing for Saul to pray? Was he not a Pharisee? Yes; but now he began to pray after another manner than he had done; then he said his prayers, now he prayed them. You may as soon find a living man without breath as a living Christian without prayer; if breathless, lifeless; and so, if prayerless, graceless. [2] Why Ananias must go to him with all speed. It is no time to linger, *for behold he prayeth.* He was under conviction of sin. Conviction should drive us to prayer. He was under a bodily affliction, blind and sick. Christ had promised him that it should be further told him what he should do (*v.* 6), and he prays that one may be sent to him to instruct him. What God has promised we must pray for.

(2) Because he hath seen in a vision such a man coming to him; and Ananias's coming to him must answer his dream, for it was of God (*v.* 12): *He hath seen in a vision a man named Ananias coming in and putting his hand on him that he might receive his sight.* Now this vision which Paul had may be considered: As an immediate answer to his prayer, and the keeping up of that communion with God which he had entered into by prayer. As designed to raise his expectations, and to make Ananias's coming more welcome to him. See what a great thing it is to bring a spiritual physician and his patient together: here were two visions in order to it.

II. Ananias objects against going to him.

1. Ananias pleads that this Saul was a notorious persecutor of the disciples of Christ, *v.* 13, 14: "*Lord, I have heard by many of this man, how much evil he hath done to thy saints in Jerusalem.* There was no man they were more afraid of. His errand to Damascus at this time is to persecute us Christians: *Here he has authority from the chief priests to bind all that call on thy name.*" Now, why does Ananias object to this? Not, "Therefore I do not owe him so much service." No, Christ has taught us another lesson, to render good for evil, and pray for our persecutors. Will it be safe for Ananias to go to him? If he thus bring himself into trouble, he will be blamed for his indiscretion. Will it be to any purpose to go to him? Can such a hard heart ever be softened?

2. Christ overrules the objection (*v.* 15, 16). "Go thy way with all speed *for he is a chosen vessel* unto me; thou needest not fear him." He was a vessel in which the gospel-treasure should be lodged, an earthen vessel (2. Cor. iv. 7), but a chosen vessel. He is designed, (1) for eminent services: *He is to bear my name before the Gentiles.* Saul must be a standard-bearer. He must bear Christ's name before kings, king Agrippa and Cæsar himself; nay, he must bear it before the children of Israel. (2) For eminent sufferings (*v.* 16): *I will show him how great things he must suffer for my name's sake.* He that has been a persecutor shall be himself persecuted. Those that bear Christ's name must expect to bear the cross for his name; and those that do most for Christ are often called out to suffer most for him. It is only like telling a soldier of a bold and brave spirit, that he shall take the field, and enter upon action, shortly. It is no discouragement to him to be told how great things he must suffer for Christ's name's sake.

JAMIESON, FAUSSET, BROWN

which distinguish the writings of this chiefest of the apostles and greatest of men, were all quickened into life during those three successive days?

10-16. a certain disciple . . . named Ananias—See on ch. 22:12. **to him said the Lord**—i.e., JESUS. (See vss. 13, 14, 17.) **11. go into the street . . . called Straight**—There is still a street of this name in Damascus, about half a mile in length, running from east to west through the city [MAUNDRELL]. **and inquire in the house of Judas for one called Saul of Tarsus**—There is something touching in the minuteness of these directions. Tarsus was the capital of the province of Cilicia, lying along the northeast coast of the Mediterranean. It was situated on the river Cydnus, was a "large and populous city" (says XENOPHON, and see ch. 21:39), and under the Romans had the privilege of self-government.

behold, he prayeth—"breathing out" no longer "threatenings and slaughter," but struggling desires after light and life in the Persecuted One. Beautiful note of encouragement as to the frame in which Ananias would find the persecutor!

12. And hath seen in a vision a man named Ananias . . .—Thus, as in the case of Cornelius and Peter afterwards, there was a mutual preparation of each for each. But we have no account of the vision which Saul had of Ananias coming unto him and putting his hands upon him for the restoration of his sight, save this interesting allusion to it in the vision which Ananias himself had.

13. Ananias answered, Lord, I have heard by many of this man . . .—"The objections of Ananias, and the removal of them by the Lord, display in a very touching manner the childlike relation of the believing soul to its Redeemer. The Saviour speaks with Ananias as a man does with his friend" [OLSHAUSEN]. **how much evil he hath done to thy saints**—"*Thy* saints," says Ananias to Christ; therefore Christ is God [BENGEL]. So, in the very next verse, Ananias describes the disciples as "those that called on Christ's name." See on ch. 7:59, 60; and cf. I Corinthians 1:2. **14. here he hath authority . . .**—so that the terror not only of the great persecutor's name, but of this commission to Damascus, had travelled before him from the capital to the doomed spot. **15. Go thy way**—Do as thou art bidden, without gainsaying. **he is a chosen vessel**—a word often used by Paul in illustrating God's sovereignty in election (Rom. 9:21-23; II Cor. 4:7; II Tim. 2:20, 21 [ALFORD]. Cf. Zech. 3:2). **16. I will show him**—(see ch. 20:23, 24; 21:11). **how great things he must suffer for my name**—i.e., Much he has done against that Name; but now, when I show him what great things he must suffer for that Name, he shall count it his honor and privilege.

ADAM CLARKE

11. *Arise, and go into the street which is called Straight.* How very particular is this direction! And it was necessary that it should be so, that he might see the whole to be a divine communication; the house was probably one in which Saul was accustomed to reside when at Damascus, and where he was known as a native of Tarsus. Tarsus was a city of Cilicia, seated on the Cydnus, and now called Tarasso. It was, at one period, the capital of all Cilicia, and became a rival to Alexandria and Athens in the arts and sciences. The inhabitants, in the time of Julius Caesar, having shown themselves friendly to the Romans, were endowed with all the privileges of Roman citizens; and it was on this account that Paul claimed the rights of a Roman citizen—a circumstance which on different occasions was to him, and the cause in which he was engaged, of considerable service. *Behold, he prayeth.* He is earnestly seeking to know My will, and to find the salvation of his soul; therefore go speedily and direct him.

12. *Hath seen in a vision.* While God prepares Ananias by a vision to go and minister to Saul, He at the same time prepares Saul by another vision to profit by this ministry.

13. *Lord, I have heard by many of this man.* This was all done in a dream, else this sort of reasoning with his Maker would have been intolerable in Ananias. *Thy saints.* That is, the Christians, or followers of Christ. *Hagioi* signifies not only holy persons but also consecrated persons; from *a*, negative, and *ge*, the "earth"; persons who are separated from all earthly uses, and consecrated to the service of God alone.

14. *And here he hath authority.* Ananias had undoubtedly heard of Saul's coming, and the commission he had received from the chief priests; and he was about to urge this as a reason why he should have no connection with so dangerous a man.

15. *Go thy way.* He was thus prevented from going further in his reasoning on this subject. *Chosen vessel.* Properly a Hebraism for an "excellent or well-adapted instrument." Every reader of the Bible must have noticed how often the word *chosen* is used there to signify excelling or eminent. So we use the word *choice*—"choice men," eminent persons; "choice things," excellent articles. So in Jer. xxii. 7; "They shall cut down thy choice cedars." Whoever considers the character of Paul, his education, attainments in natural knowledge, the distinguished part he took—first against Christianity, and afterwards, on the fullest conviction, the part he took in its favor—will at once perceive how well he was every way qualified for the great work to which God had called him. *To bear my name before the Gentiles.* To carry the ensign of the Cross among the Greeks and Romans. Hence he was emphatically called "the apostle of the Gentiles," 1 Tim. ii. 7; 2 Tim. i. 11. See also Gal. ii. 7-8 and Eph. iii. 8.

16. *How great things he must suffer.* Instead of proceeding as a persecutor and inflicting sufferings on others, I will show him how many things he himself must suffer for preaching that very doctrine which he has been hitherto employed in persecuting. Strange change indeed! And with great show of reason, as with incontrovertible strength of argument, has a noble writer, Lord Lyttleton, adduced the conversion of Saul of Tarsus and his subsequent conduct as an irrefragable proof of the truth of Christianity.

MATTHEW HENRY

III. Ananias goes on Christ's errand to Saul. He had started an objection against going to him, but he dropped it, and did not insist upon it. When difficulties are removed, what have we to do but to go on with our work, and not hang upon an objection?

1. Ananias delivered his message to Saul, *v.* 17. (1) *He put his hands on him.* Saul came to lay violent hands upon the disciples at Damascus, but here a disciple lays a helping healing hand upon him. (2) He called him *brother.* His readiness to own him as a brother intimated to him God's readiness to own him as a son, though he had been a blasphemer of God and a persecutor of his children. (3) He produces his commission. "That *same Jesus that appeared unto thee in the way as thou camest,* has now sent me to thee." *The hand that wounded heals.* His light struck thee blind, but he *hath sent me to thee that thou mightest receive thy sight.* Corrosives shall be no more applied, but lenitives. (4) He assures him that he shall not only have his sight restored, but be filled with the Holy Ghost.

2. Ananias saw the good issue of his mission. (1) In Christ's favour to Saul. At the word of Ananias, Saul was discharged from his confinement by the restoring of his sight. Saul is delivered from the spirit of bondage by his receiving sight (*v.* 18), which was signified by the falling of scales from his eyes; the cure was sudden, to show that it was miraculous. This signified the recovering of him, [1] From the darkness of his unconverted state. Christ often told the Pharisees that they were blind, and could not make them sensible of it. Saul is saved from his Pharisaical blindness, by being made sensible of it. Converting grace opens the eyes of the soul. This was what Saul was sent among the Gentiles to do, and therefore must first experience it in himself. [2] From the darkness of his present terrors. Now the scales fell from his eyes, the cloud was scattered, and the Sun of righteousness rose upon his soul, with healing under his wings. (2) In Saul's subjection to Christ: He was baptized, and thereby submitted to the government of Christ, and cast himself upon the grace of Christ. Saul is now a disciple of Christ, not only ceases to oppose him, but devotes himself entirely to his service.

IV. The good work that was begun in Saul is carried on wonderfully.

1. He received his bodily strength, *v.* 19. He had continued three days fasting, which had made him very weak; but, *when he had received meat, he was strengthened, v.* 19. The Lord is for the body, and therefore care must be taken of it that it may be fit to serve the soul in God's service.

2. He associated with the disciples that were at Damascus. He had lately *breathed out threatenings and slaughter against them,* but now breathes love and affection to them. Those that take God for their God take his people for their people. Thus he made profession of his Christian faith, and openly declared himself a disciple of Christ.

3. *He preached Christ in the synagogues, v.* 20. He was so full of Christ himself, that *the Spirit within him constrained him* to preach him to others. Where he preached—in the synagogues of the Jews. There they used to preach against Christ and to punish his disciples. There he would face the enemies of Christ where they were most daring, and openly profess Christianity. What he preached: *He preached Christ.* When he began to be a preacher, he fixed this for his principle, which he stuck to ever after: nothing but Christ, and him crucified. He preached concerning Christ, *that he is the Son of God,* in whom he is well pleased, and with us in him. How people were affected with it (*v.* 21): *All that heard him were amazed, and said, "Is not this he that destroyed those who called on this name in Jerusalem?"* Did he not come hither to seize all the Christians he could find, and *bring them bound to the chief priests*? Who would have thought then that he would ever preach Christ as he does? This miracle upon the mind of such a man outshone the miracles upon men's bodies; and giving a man such another heart was more than giving men to speak with other tongues.

4. He confuted and confounded those that opposed the doctrine of Christ, *v.* 22. He increased in strength. He became more intimately acquainted with the gospel of Christ, and his pious affections grew more strong. He grew more daring and resolute in defence of the gospel: *He increased the more* for the reflections that were cast upon him (*v.* 21), in which his new friends upbraided him as having been a persecutor, and his old friends upbraided him as being now a turncoat. He ran down his antagonists, and *confounded the Jews who dwelt in Damascus*; he silenced them, and shamed them. He was instrumental in converting many to the faith of Christ, and building up the church

JAMIESON, FAUSSET, BROWN

17-19. Ananias went his way, and putting his hands on him, said, Brother Saul—How beautifully child-like is the obedience of Ananias to "the heavenly vision!" **the Lord, even Jesus**—This clearly shows in what sense the term "Lord" is used in this book. It is JESUS that is meant, as almost invariably in the Epistles also. **who appeared unto thee in the way**—This knowledge by an inhabitant of Damascus of what had happened to Saul before entering it, would show him at once that this was the man whom Jesus had already prepared him to expect. **and be filled with the Holy Ghost**—which Ananias probably, without any express instructions on that subject, took it for granted would descend upon him; and not necessarily after his baptism [BAUMGARTEN, WEBSTER and WILKINSON]—for Cornelius and his company received it before theirs (ch. 10:44-48)—but perhaps immediately after the recovery of his sight by the laying on of Ananias' hands **18. there fell from his eyes as it were scales**—"This shows that the blindness as well as the cure was supernatural. Substances like scales would not form naturally in so short a time" [WEBSTER and WILKINSON]. And the *medical* precision of Luke's language here is to be noted. **was baptized**—as directed by Ananias (ch. 22:16).

19. when he had received meat, he was strengthened—for the exhaustion occasioned by his three days' fast would not be the less real, though unfelt during his struggles. (See on Matt. 4:2). **Then was Saul certain days with the disciples at Damascus**—making their acquaintance, in another way than either he or they had anticipated, and regaining his tone by the fellowship of the saints; but not certainly in order to learn from them what he was to teach, which he expressly disavows (Gal. 1:12, 16).

20-22. preached Christ . . . that he is the Son of God—rather, "preached Jesus," according to all the most ancient MSS. and versions of the New Testament (so vs. 21, "all that call on this name," i.e., *Jesus;* and vs. 22, "proving that this" *Jesus* "is very *Christ*").

ADAM CLARKE

17. *Brother Saul.* As he found that the Head of the Church had adopted Saul into the heavenly family, he made no scruple to give him the right hand of fellowship, and therefore said, *Brother Saul. The Lord, even Jesus.* Of what use is this intrusive word *even* here? It injures the sense. Luke never wrote it; and our translators should not have inserted it. *The Lord . . . Jesus,* the sovereign Jesus who *appeared unto thee in the way . . . hath sent me, that thou mightest receive thy sight, and be filled with the Holy Ghost.* Christ could have cured him as miraculously by His own power, without human means, as He had enlightened his heart without them; but He will honor man by making him His agent, even in working miracles. *And be filled with the Holy Ghost.* So appears that the Holy Spirit was given to him at this time, and probably by the imposition of the hands of Ananias.

18. *And arose, and was baptized.* That he was baptized by Ananias there is every reason to believe, as he appears to have been the chief Christian at Damascus.

19. *When he had received meat, he was strengthened.* His mind must have been greatly worn down under his three days' conviction of sin and the awful uncertainty he was in concerning his state, but when he was baptized and had received the Holy Ghost, his soul was divinely invigorated; and now by taking food his bodily strength, greatly exhausted by three days' fasting, was renewed also. *Then was Saul certain days with the disciples.* Doubtless under instructions relative to the doctrines of Christianity, which he must learn particularly in order to preach them successfully.

20. *Preached Christ in the synagogues.* Instead of *Christ,* "Jesus" is the reading of some MSS. The great question to be determined for the conviction of the Jews was that Jesus was the Son of God. Saul was now convinced that Jesus, whom they had crucified, and who had appeared to him on the way, was the *Son of God,* or Messiah; and therefore as such he proclaimed Him. The word *Christ* should be changed for "Jesus," as the latter is, without doubt, the genuine reading.

21. *Is not this he that destroyed them?* The verb has three acceptations in the Greek writers: (1) "To treat one as an enemy, to spoil him of his goods"; (2) "To lead away captive, to imprison"; (3) "To slay." Paul was properly "a destroyer" in all these senses. (1) He acted as the most determined enemy of the Christians: "Being exceedingly mad against them," he "persecuted them even unto strange cities," chap. xxvi. 11. (2) He shut up many of the saints in prison, chap. viii. 3; ix. 14; xxvi. 10. (3) He persecuted them unto death—gave his voice against them, that they might be destroyed, and was a principal instrument in the martyrdom of Stephen. He breathed "threatenings and slaughter." See chap. vii. 58; viii. 1; ix. 1; xxvi. 10-11. Therefore these three meanings of the original word are all exemplified in the conduct of Saul.

22. *Confounded the Jews.* Overwhelmed them so with his arguments that they were obliged to "blush" for the weakness of their own cause. *Proving that this.* This Person, viz., Jesus, is *very Christ;* "Is the Christ, or Messiah." See on v. 20.

MATTHEW HENRY

at Damascus, which he went thither to make havoc of.

Verses 23–31

Luke here makes no mention of Paul's journey into Arabia, which he tells us himself was immediately after his conversion, Gal. i. 16, 17. As soon as God *had revealed his Son in him, that he might preach him, he went not up to Jerusalem*, but he went to Arabia. Thence he returned to Damascus, and there, three years after his conversion, this happened, which is here recorded.

I. He met with difficulties at Damascus, and had a narrow escape of being killed there. What his danger was (*v.* 23): *The Jews took counsel to kill him.* He had been such a remarkable deserter, and his being a Christian was a testimony against them. It is said (*v.* 24), *The Jews watched the gates day and night to kill him.* Now Christ showed Paul *what great things he must suffer for his name* (*v.* 16). Saul was no sooner a Christian than a preacher, no sooner a preacher than a sufferer. Where God gives great grace he commonly exercises it with great trials. How he was delivered. The design against him was discovered: *Their lying in wait was known of Saul.* The disciples contrived to help him away in the night; *they let him down by the wall, in a basket*, as he himself relates it (2 Cor. xi. 33).

II. He met with difficulties at Jerusalem the first time he went thither, *v.* 26. This is thought to be that journey to Jerusalem of which he himself speaks (Gal. i. 18): *After three years I went up to Jerusalem to see Peter, and abode with him fifteen days.* But I rather incline to think that this was a journey before that, because *his coming in* and *going out, his preaching and disputing* (*v.* 28, 29), seem to be more than would consist with his fifteen days' stay. However, it might possibly be the same.

1. How shy his friends were of him (*v.* 26): *When he came to Jerusalem he assayed to join himself to the disciples.* Wherever he came, he owned himself one of that despised persecuted people. But they looked strange upon him, shut the door against him. *They were afraid of him.* The Jews had abandoned and persecuted him, and the Christians would not receive and entertain him. (1) See what was the cause of their jealousy of him: *They believed not that he was a disciple*, but that he only pretended to be so, and came among them as a spy or an informer. The disciples of Christ had need to be cautious whom they admit into communion with them. There is need of the wisdom of the serpent, to keep the mean between the extremes of suspicion on the one hand and credulity on the other; yet methinks it is safer to err on the charitable side. (2) See how it was removed (*v.* 27): *Barnabas took him to the apostles* themselves, *and he declared to them*, what Christ had done for him: *He had shown himself to him in the way* and spoken to him. What he had since done for Christ: *He had preached boldly at Damascus in the name of Jesus.* How Barnabas came to know this we are not told. Being satisfied himself, he gave satisfaction to the apostles concerning him.

2. How sharp his enemies were upon him. (1) He was admitted into the communion of the disciples. It vexed the unbelieving Jews to see Saul a trophy of Christ's victory, to see him *coming in, and going out, with the apostles* (*v.* 28). (2) He appeared vigorous in the cause of Christ, and this was yet more provoking to them (*v.* 29): *He spoke boldly in the name of the Lord Jesus.* The Grecians, or Hellenist Jews, were most offended at him, because he had been one of them; and they drew him into a dispute, in which, no doubt, he was too hard for them. That same natural quickness and fervour of spirit which made him a furious bigoted persecutor of the faith, made him a most zealous courageous defender of the faith. (3) This brought him into peril of his life: *The Grecians went about to slay him.* But notice was given of this conspiracy too, and effectual care taken to secure this young champion (*v.* 30): *When the brethren knew they brought him down to Cæsarea.* He that flies may fight again. He that fled from Jerusalem might do service at Tarsus, the place of his nativity; and thither they desired him by all means to go. Yet it was also by direction from heaven that he left Jerusalem at this time, as he tells us himself (*ch.* xxii. 17, 18), that Christ now appeared to him, and ordered him to *go quickly out of Jerusalem*, for he must be sent *to the Gentiles*, *v.* 15.

JAMIESON, FAUSSET, BROWN

23. And after many days were fulfilled, the Jews took counsel to kill him—*Had we no other record than this, we should have supposed that what is here related took place while Saul continued at Damascus after his baptism. But in Galatians* 1:17, 18 *we learn from Paul himself that he "went into Arabia, and returned again unto Damascus," and that from the time of his first visit to the close of his second, both of which appear to have been short, a period of three years elapsed;* either three full years, or one full year and part of two others. (See on Gal. 1: 16-18.) That such a blank should occur in the Acts, and be filled up in Galatians, is not more remarkable than that the flight of the Holy Family into Egypt, their stay there, and their return thence, recorded only by Matthew, should be so entirely passed over by Luke, that if we had only his Gospel, we should have supposed that they returned to Nazareth immediately after the presentation in the temple. (Indeed in one of his narratives, ch. 22: 16, 17, Paul himself takes no notice of this period.) But *wherefore this journey*? Perhaps (1) because he felt a period of repose and partial seclusion to be needful to his spirit, after the violence of the change and the excitement of his new occupation. (2) To prevent the rising storm which was gathering against him from coming too soon to a head. (3) To exercise his ministry in the Jewish synagogues, as opportunity afforded. On his return, refreshed and strengthened in spirit, he immediately resumed his ministry, but soon to the imminent hazard of his life. **24, 25. they watched the gates night and day to kill him**—The full extent of his danger appears only from his own account (II Cor. 11:32): "In Damascus, the governor under Aretas the king kept the city of the Damascenes with a garrison, desirous to apprehend me"; the exasperated Jews having obtained from the governor a military force, the more surely to compass his destruction. **25. Then the disciples . . . by night let him down** "through a window" (II Cor. 11:33) **by the wall**—Such overhanging windows in the walls of Eastern cities were common, and are to be seen in Damascus to this day.

26-31. SAUL'S FIRST VISIT TO JERUSALEM AFTER HIS CONVERSION. **26. And when Saul was come to Jerusalem**—"three years after" his conversion, and particularly "to see Peter" (Gal. 1:18); no doubt because he was the leading apostle, and to communicate to him the prescribed sphere of his labors, specially to "the Gentiles." **he assayed to join himself to the disciples**—simply as one of them, leaving his apostolic commission to manifest itself. **they were all afraid of him . . .**—knowing him only as a persecutor of the faith; the rumor of his conversion, if it ever was cordially believed, passing away during his long absence in Arabia, and the news of his subsequent labors in Damascus perhaps not having reached them. **27. But Barnabas . . . brought him to the apostles**—i.e., to Peter and James; for "other of the apostles saw I none," says he fourteen years after (Gal. 1:18, 19). Probably none of the other apostles were there at the time (ch. 4:36). Barnabas being of Cyprus, which was within a few hours' sail of Cilicia, and annexed to it as a Roman province, and Saul and he being Hellenistic Jews and eminent in their respective localities, they may very well have been acquainted with each other before this [Hows]. What is here said of Barnabas is in fine consistency with the "goodness" ascribed to him (ch. 11:24), and with the name "son of consolation," given him by the apostles (ch. 4:36); and after Peter and James were satisfied, the disciples generally would at once receive him. **how he had seen the Lord . . . and he**—the Lord—**had spoken to him**—i.e., how he had received his commission direct from the Lord Himself. **28, 29. And he was with them, coming in and going out at Jerusalem**—for fifteen days, lodging with Peter (Gal. 1:18). **29. disputed against the Grecians**—See on ch. 6:1; addressing himself specially to them, perhaps, as being of his own class, and that against which he had in the days of his ignorance been the fiercest. **they went about to slay him**—Thus was he made to feel, throughout his whole course, what he himself had made others so cruelly to feel, *the cost of discipleship.* **30. they brought him down to Cæsarea**—on the coast (see on ch. 8:40); accompanying him thus far. But Paul had another reason than his own apprehension for quitting Jerusalem so soon. "While he was praying in the temple, he was in a trance," and received express injunctions to this effect. (See on ch. 22:17-21.) **and sent him forth to Tarsus**—In Galatians 1:21 he himself says of this journey, that he "came into the regions of Syria and Cilicia";

ADAM CLARKE

23. *And after that many days were fulfilled.* What follows relates to transactions which took place about three years after his conversion, when he had come a second time to Damascus, after having been in Arabia. See Gal. i. 17-18.

24. *They watched the gates day and night to kill him.* At this time Damascus was under the government of Aretas, king of Arabia, who was now at war with Herod, his son-in-law, who had put away his daughter in order to marry Herodias, his brother Philip's wife. As Herod was supported by the Romans, Saul's enemies might intimate that he was in league with them or Herod; and as the gates of the city were constantly watched and shut, that no spy might enter and no fugitive get away, they thought it would be easy to apprehend him, and doubtless got orders for the different officers at the gates to be on the lookout that he might not be permitted to escape.

25. *Let him down by the wall.* Favored probably by a house built against or upon the wall, through the window of which they could lower him in a basket, and by this means he made his escape. His escape was something similar to that of the spies at Jericho, Josh. ii. 15.

26. *He assayed to join himself to the disciples.* "He endeavored to get closely united to them," to be in religious fellowship with them. *Believed not that he was a disciple.* They did not suppose it possible that such a person could be converted to the faith of Christ. The full power of divine grace in the conversion of the soul was not yet completely known.

27. *Barnabas . . . brought him to the apostles.* That is, to Peter and James; for others of the apostles he saw none, Gal. i. 19. It appears that he went up at this time to Jerusalem merely to see Peter, with whom he abode fifteen days, Gal. i. 18.

28. *He was with them coming in and going out.* Freely conversing and associating with them; but this seems to have continued only fifteen days. See Gal. i. 18.

29. *Disputed against the Grecians.* That is, the Hellenistic Jews, viz., those who lived in Grecian cities, spoke the Greek language, and used the Septuagint version for their Scriptures.

30. *Sent him forth to Tarsus.* This was his own city, and it was right that he should proclaim to his own countrymen and relatives that gospel through which he was become wise to salvation.

MATTHEW HENRY

III. The churches had now a comfortable gleam of liberty and peace (*v.* 31): *Then had the churches rest. Then,* when Saul was converted, those were quiet whom he used to molest. *The churches had rest.* After a storm comes a calm. This was a breathing-time allowed them, to prepare them for the next encounter. They made a good use of this lucid interval.

ALEXANDER MACLAREN:

"Being edified" sounds very theological and far away from daily life. Would it not sound more real if we read "being built up"? That is the emblem of the process that ought to go on, not only in the Christian community as a whole, but in every individual member of it. Each Christian is bound to build himself up and to help to build up other Christians; and God builds them all up by His Spirit. We have before us the picture of the rising of some stately fabric upon a firm foundation, course by course, stone by stone, each laid by a separate act of the builder's hand, and carefully bedded in its place until the whole is complete.

That is one emblem of the growth of the Christian community and of the Christian individual, and the other clause that is coupled with it in the text seems to me to give the same idea under a slightly different figure. The rising of a stately building and the advance on a given path suggest substantially the same notion of progress.—*Expositions of Holy Scripture*

They *were edified,* were built up in their most holy faith. They *walked in the fear of the Lord.* They so lived that all might say, Surely the fear of God reigns in those people. They *walked in the comfort of the Holy Ghost*—were not only faithful, but cheerful, in religion; they stuck to the ways of the Lord, and sang in those ways. They had recourse to the comfort of the Holy Ghost, and lived upon that, not only in days of trouble and affliction, but in days of rest and prosperity. When they walked *in the fear of the Lord,* then they walked *in the comfort of the Holy Ghost.* Those are most likely to walk cheerfully that walk circumspectly. God blessed it to them for their increase in number: They *were multiplied.* Sometimes the church multiplies the more for its being afflicted, yet if it were always so, the saints of the Most High would be worn out. At other times its rest contributes to its growth.

Verses 32–35

I. The visit Peter made to the churches that were newly planted, *v.* 32. 1. He *passed through all quarters.* As an apostle, he was not to be the resident pastor of any one church. He was, like his Master, always upon the remove, and *went about doing good;* but still his headquarters were at Jerusalem, for there we shall find him imprisoned, *ch.* xii. 4. *He came to the saints at Lydda.* The Christians are called *saints,* every sincere professor of the faith of Christ. These are the saints on the earth.

JAMIESON, FAUSSET, BROWN

from which it is natural to infer that instead of sailing direct for Tarsus, he landed at Seleucia, travelled thence to Antioch, and penetrated from this northward into Cilicia, ending his journey at Tarsus. As this was his first visit to his native city since his conversion, so it is not certain that he ever was there again. (See on ch. 11:25, 26.) It probably was now that he became the instrument of gathering into the fold of Christ those "kinsmen," that "sister," and perhaps her "son," of whom mention is made in ch. 23:16, etc.; Rom. 16:7, 11, 21 [Hows].

31. Flourishing State of the Church in Palestine at This Time. **31. Then had all the churches rest**—rather, 'the Church,' according to the best MSS. and versions. But this rest was owing not so much to the conversion of Saul, as probably to the Jews being engrossed with the emperor Caligula's attempt to have his own image set up in the temple of Jerusalem (Josephus, *Antiquities,* 18:8; 1, etc.).

throughout all Judea, and Galilee, and Samaria—This incidental notice of distinct churches already dotting all the regions which were the chief scenes of our Lord's ministry, and that were best able to test the facts on which the whole preaching of the apostles was based, is extremely interesting. "The fear of the Lord" expresses their holy walk; "the comfort of the Holy Ghost," their "peace and joy in believing," under the silent operation of the blessed Comforter.

32-43. Peter Heals Eneas at Lydda, and Raises Tabitha to Life at Joppa. The historian now returns to Peter, in order to introduce the all-important narrative of Cornelius (ch. 10). The occurrences here related probably took place during Saul's sojourn in Arabia. **32-35. as Peter passed throughout all quarters**—not now fleeing from persecution, but peacefully visiting the churches. **to the saints which dwelt at Lydda**—about five miles east of Joppa.

ADAM CLARKE

31. *Then had the churches rest.* Instead of *the churches,* some MSS. have "the Church." Every assembly of God's people was "a church"; the aggregate of these assemblies was "the Church." The word which we translate *rest,* and which literally signifies "peace," evidently means, in this place, "prosperity"; and in this sense both it and the Hebrew *shalom* are repeatedly used. But what was the cause of this *rest* or success? Some say, the conversion of Saul, who before made havoc of the Church; but this is not likely, as he could not be a universal cause of persecution and distress, however active and virulent he might have been during the time of his enmity to the Christian Church. Besides his own persecution, related above, shows that the opposition to the gospel continued with considerable virulence three years after his conversion; therefore it was not Saul's ceasing to be a persecutor that gave this rest to the churches. Dr. Lardner, with a greater show of probability, maintains that this rest was owing to the following circumstance: In the third year of Caligula, A.D. 39, Petronius, who was made president of Syria in the place of Vitellius, was sent by the emperor to set up his statue in the Temple at Jerusalem. This was a thunderstroke to the Jews and so occupied them that they had no time to think of anything else, apprehending that their Temple must be defiled and the national religion destroyed or themselves run the risk of being exterminated if they rebelled against the imperial decree. It appears therefore that, as these transactions took place about the time mentioned in the text, their persecution from the Romans diverted them from persecuting the Christians; and *then had the churches rest throughout all Judaea and Galilee and Samaria,* the terror occasioned by the imperial decree having spread itself through all those places.

Were edified. A metaphor taken from a building. All this is beautifully pointed out by Peter, 1 Pet. chap. ii. 4-5: "To whom [Jesus Christ] coming, as unto a living stone . . . chosen of God, and precious, ye also, as lively [living] stones, are built up a spiritual house, an holy priesthood, to offer up spiritual sacrifices . . . to God by Jesus Christ." And Paul goes through the whole figure at large, in the following inimitable words: "Ye are . . . the household of God; and are built upon the foundation of the apostles and prophets, Jesus Christ himself being the chief corner stone; in whom all the building fitly framed together groweth unto an holy temple in the Lord: in whom ye also are builded together for an habitation of God through the Spirit," Eph. ii. 19-22. *Walking in the fear of the Lord.* Keeping a continually tender conscience, abhorring all sin, having respect to every divine precept, dreading to offend Him from whom the soul has derived its being and its blessings. Without this salutary *fear* of God there never can be any circumspect walking. *In the comfort of the Holy Ghost.* In a consciousness of their acceptance and union with God, through His Spirit, by which solid peace and happiness are brought into the soul, the truly religious man knowing and feeling that he is of God by the Spirit which is given him. Nothing less can be implied in the *comfort of the Holy Ghost. Were multiplied.* No wonder that the Church of God increased when such lights as these shone among men. This is a short but full and forcible description of the righteousness, purity, and happiness of the primitive Church.

32. *As Peter passed throughout all quarters.* The churches having rest, the apostles made use of this interval of quiet to visit the different congregations, in order to build them up on their most holy faith. Of Saul we hear no more till chap. xi. 30, which is supposed to be about five years after this time—eight in all from his conversion. Peter, it seems, had continued in Jerusalem all the time that the churches were in a state of persecution throughout the whole land. Great as he was, he never evidenced that steady, determinate courage by which Paul was so eminently distinguished; nor did he ever suffer half so much for God and His truth. *To the saints.* The Jews who had been converted to Christianity. *Which dwelt at Lydda.* A town in the tribe of Ephraim, almost on the border of Judea, and nigh unto Joppa.

MATTHEW HENRY

II. The cure Peter wrought on *Æneas*, *v.* 33. His case was very deplorable: *He was sick of the palsy.* The disease was extreme, for *he kept his bed*; it was inveterate, for he kept his bed *eight years*; and we may suppose that both he himself and all about him despaired of relief for him. Christ chose such patients as this, whose disease was incurable in a course of nature. When we were without strength, as this poor man, *he sent his word to heal us.* His cure was very admirable, *v.* 34. Peter interested Christ in his case: *Æneas, Jesus Christ maketh thee whole.* Peter declares it to be Christ's act and deed, and assures him of an *immediate* cure—not, "He *will* make thee," but, "He *does* make thee whole"; and a *perfect* cure—not, "He makes thee *easy*," but "He makes thee *whole*." He ordered him to bestir himself: "*Arise and make thy bed.*" Let none say that because it is Christ that works all our works in us therefore we have no work, no duty, to do; for, though Jesus Christ makes thee whole, yet thou must arise and make use of the power he gives thee: "*Arise, and make thy bed*, to be to thee no longer a bed of sickness, but a bed of rest." Power went along with this word: he arose immediately.

III. The good influence this had upon many (*v.* 35): *All that dwelt at Lydda and Saron saw him, and turned to the Lord.* They all made enquiry into the truth of the miracle, and saw that it was a miraculous cure that was wrought upon him by the power of Christ. They all *turned to the Lord*, to the Lord Jesus. They turned themselves over to him to be ruled and taught and saved by him.

Verses 36-43

Here we have another miracle wrought by Peter—the raising of Tabitha to life.

I. The life, and death, and character of Tabitha, *v.* 36, 37. She lived at Joppa. Her name was *Tabitha*, a Hebrew name, the Greek for which is *Dorcas*, both signifying a *doe*. She was a disciple, eminent above many for works of charity. She showed her faith by her works, her good works. She was *full of good works*, as a tree that is full of fruit. Many are full of good words, who are empty and barren in good works; but Tabitha was a great doer, no great talker. She was remarkable for her *alms-deeds which she did*, not only her works of piety, but works of charity and beneficence, flowing from love to her neighbour. She is commended not only for the alms which she gave, but for the alms-deeds which she did. Those that have not estates wherewith to give in charity may yet be able to do in charity, working with their hands, or walking with their feet, for the benefit of the poor. And those who will not do a charitable deed, whatever they may pretend, if they were rich would not bestow a charitable gift. There is an emphasis upon her *doing* them, because what her hand found to do of this kind she did with all her might, and persevered in. This is the life and character of a certain disciple, and should be of all the disciples of Christ. She was removed in the midst of her usefulness (*v.* 37): *In those days she fell sick, and died.* Her friends and those about her *washed the dead body*, according to the custom. They *laid her out* in her grave-clothes *in an upper chamber*.

II. The request which her Christian friends sent to Peter to come to them with all speed, *v.* 38. The disciples at Joppa had heard that Peter was there, and that he had raised Æneas from a bed of languishing; and therefore they *sent him two men, desiring him that he would not delay to come to them.* Their friend was dead, and it was too late to send for a physician, but not too late to send for Peter.

III. The posture in which he found the survivors (*v.* 39): *Peter arose and went with them.* Let not faithful ministers grudge to be at everybody's beck, when the great apostle *made himself the servant of all.* He found the corpse laid in the upper chamber, and attended by widows.

1. Commending the deceased—a good work when it is done modestly and soberly, and without flattery. The commendation of Tabitha was like her own virtues, not in word, but in deed. *The widows showed the coats and garments which she made while she was with them.* It is much more honourable to clothe a company of decrepit widows with needful clothing, than to clothe a company of lazy footmen with rich liveries, who perhaps behind their backs will curse those that clothe them, for goodness is true greatness, and will pass better in the account shortly. Into what channel Tabitha turned much of her charity. She did, as it should seem with her own hands, *make coats and garments* for poor widows. And this is an excellent piece of charity, *If thou seest the naked, that thou cover him* (Isa. lviii. 7), and not think it enough to say, *Be ye warmed*, James ii. 15, 16. What a

JAMIESON, FAUSSET, BROWN

34. And Peter said unto him, Eneas, Jesus Christ maketh thee whole—See on ch. 3:6. **make thy bed**—See on John 5:8.

35. all that dwelt at Lydda and Saron—(or "Sharon," a rich vale between Joppa and Cæsarea). **saw him, and turned to the Lord**—i.e., there was a general conversion in consequence.

35-39. at Joppa—the modern *Jaffa*, on the Mediterranean, a very ancient city of the Philistines, afterwards and still the seaport of Jerusalem, from which it lies distant forty-five miles to the northwest. **Tabitha . . . Dorcas**—the Syro-Chaldaic and Greek names for an *antelope* or *gazelle*, which, from its loveliness, was frequently employed as a proper name for women [MEYER, OLSHAUSEN]. Doubtless the interpretation, as here given, is but an echo of the remarks made by the Christians regarding her—how well her character answered to her name. **full of good works and alms-deeds**—eminent for the activities and generosities of the Christian character.

37. when they had washed—according to the custom of civilized nations towards the dead. **in an**—rather, 'the'—**upper chamber**—(cf. I Kings 17:19). **38. the disciples sent unto Peter**—showing that the disciples generally did not possess miraculous gifts [BENGEL].

39. all the widows—whom she had clad or fed. **stood by him weeping, and showing the coats and garments which Dorcas had made**—i.e., (as the tense implies), showing these as specimens only of what she *was in the habit of making.*

ADAM CLARKE

33. *A certain man named Aeneas.* This name has been celebrated in the annals of heathen poetry in that beautiful work of the poet Virgil, called the "Aeneid," which gives an account of the misfortunes, travels, wars, of a Trojan prince of this name, after the destruction of his native city, Troy. *Had kept his bed eight years.* This was occasioned by a palsy, and now inveterate and hopeless through its long standing.

34. *Jesus Christ maketh thee whole.* Not Peter, for he had no power but what was given him from above. And, as an instrument, any man could heal with this power as well as Peter; but God chose to put honor upon those primitive preachers of His Word, that men might see that they were commissioned from heaven. *Arise, and make thy bed.* Give now full proof that Jesus Christ has made you whole by arising and by making your bed. He was at home, and therefore was not commanded, as the paralytic person, to take up his bed; but he was ordered to make it—strew it afresh, that all might see that the cure was perfect.

35. *All that dwelt in Lydda and Saron saw him.* Saron was that country that lay between Joppa and Lydda. The long affliction of this man had been well-known; and his cure, consequently, became a subject of general examination. It was found to be real. It was known to have been performed by the grace and mercy of Christ, and the consequence of all this conviction was that all these people became Christians.

36. *Now there was at Joppa.* This was a seaport town on the coast of the Mediterranean Sea, about a day's journey from Jerusalem. It is at present called Jaffa, and is still a place of considerable note. *A certain disciple named Tabitha.* This word is more properly Syriac than Hebrew. The word *tabio* and the feminine *tabitho* have the same meaning as the Greek *Dorcas*, and signify the "gazel" or "antelope"; and it is still customary in the East to give the names of beautiful animals to young women. The comparison of fine eyes to those of the antelope is continually occurring in the writings of the Arabic and Persian poets. The person in the text probably had her name in the same way. She was very beautiful, and was therefore called *Tabitha* and *Dorcas*. *This woman was full of good works.* She spent her life in acts of kindness and charity, Her soul was *full* of love to God and man, and her whole time was filled up with works of piety and mercy.

37. *She was sick, and died.* Even her holiness and usefulness could not prevent her from sickness and death. "Dust thou art, and unto dust shalt thou return," is a decree that must be fulfilled, even on the saints; for "the body is dead," sentenced to death, "because of sin," though "the Spirit is life because of righteousness." *Whom when they had washed.* Having the fullest proof that she was dead, they prepared for her interment. In most nations of the world it was customary to wash their dead before they buried them and before they laid them out to lie in state.

38. *Sent unto him . . . desiring . . . that he would not delay to come.* Tabitha died at Joppa, and Peter was at Lydda. But why did they send for Peter? We cannot tell. It is not likely that they had any expectation that he should raise her from the dead, for none of the apostles had as yet raised any; and if God did not choose to restore Stephen to life, this favor could not be reasonably expected in behalf of inferior persons. However they might hope that he who cured Aeneas at Lydda might cure Dorcas, for it is probable that they had sent for Peter before she died.

39. *Shewing the coats and garments.* These, it appears, she had made for the poor, and more particularly for poor *widows*, in whose behalf she had incessantly labored.

MATTHEW HENRY

grateful sense the poor had of her kindness: *They showed the coats*. Those are horribly ungrateful indeed who have kindness shown them and will not make at least an acknowledgement of it, by showing the kindness that is done them. Those who receive alms are not obliged so industriously to conceal it, as those are who give alms. Their showing the coats and garments which Dorcas made tended to the praise not only of her charity, but of her industry.

2. They were here lamenting the loss of her: The widows stood by Peter, weeping. They need not weep for her; *she rests from her labours and her works follow her*, but they weep for themselves and for their children, who will soon find the want of such a good woman. They take notice of what good Dorcas did *while she was with them*; but now she is gone from them, and this is their grief. The widows wept before Peter, as an inducement to him to have compassion on them, and restore one to them that used to have compassion on them. When charitable people are sick, this piece of gratitude is owing them, to pray for their recovery, that those may be spared to live who can ill be spared to die.

IV. The manner in which she was raised to life. 1. Privately: *but Peter put them all forth*. Thus Peter declined everything that looked like vainglory and ostentation; they came to see, but he did not come to be seen. 2. By prayer. In his healing Æneas there was an implied prayer, but in this greater work he addressed himself to God by solemn prayer, with the submission of a servant, and therefore he *knelt down and prayed*. 3. By the word, a quickening word. When he had prayed, he *turned to the body*, and spoke in his Master's name: "*Tabitha, arise*." Power went along with this word, and she came to life, *opened her eyes* which death had closed. When she saw Peter, she sat up (*v*. 14), *he gave her his hand and lifted her up*. Thus he would as it were welcome her to life again, and give her the right hand of fellowship among the living, from whom she had been cut off. And, *lastly*, he *called the saints and widows*, and *presented her alive* to them (*v*. 41).

V. The good effect of this miracle. 1. Many were by it convinced of the truth of the gospel, and believed in the Lord, *v*. 42. The thing was *known throughout all Joppa*, and though some never minded it many were wrought upon by it. This was the design of miracles, to confirm a divine revelation. 2. Peter was hereby induced to continue some time in this city, *v*. 43. Finding that a door of opportunity was opened for him there, he tarried there many days, till he was sent for thence upon business to another place. He took up his lodgings with one Simon a tanner. Though Peter might seem to be buried in obscurity here in the house of a poor tanner by the seaside, yet hence God fetched him to a noble piece of service.

JAMIESON, FAUSSET, BROWN

ALEXANDER MACLAREN:

When Jesus Christ went into the house of Jairus, there was the usual hubbub, the noise of the loud Eastern mourning, and He put them all forth, taking with Him only the father and mother of the damsel and Peter with James and John. When Peter goes into the upper room, where Tabitha is lying, there is the usual noise of lamentation and the clacks of many tongues, extolling the virtues of the dead woman. He remembers how Christ had gone about His miracle, and he, in his turn, "put them all forth." Mark, who was Peter's mouthpiece in his Gospel, gives us the very Aramaic words which our Lord employed when He raised the little girl, *Talitha*, the Aramaic word for "a damsel," or young girl; *cumi*, which means in that language "arise." Is it not singular and beautiful that Peter's word by the bedside of the dead Dorcas is, with the exception of one letter, absolutely identical? Christ says, *Talitha cumi*. Peter remembered the formula by which the blessing was conveyed, and he copied it. *Tabitha cumi!* Is it not clear that he is posing after his Master's attitude; that he is, consciously or unconsciously, doing what he remembered so well had been done in that other upper room, and that the miracles are both of them shaped after the pattern of the miraculous working of Jesus Christ?—*Expositions of Holy Scripture*

40-43. Peter put them all forth, and kneeled down—the one in imitation of his Master's way (Luke 8:54; and cf. II Kings 4:33); the other, in striking contrast with it. The *kneeling* became the lowly servant, but not the Lord Himself, *of whom it is never once recorded that he knelt in the performance of a miracle*.

opened her eyes, and when she saw Peter, she sat up—The graphic minuteness of detail here imparts to the narrative an air of charming reality. **41. he gave her his hand, and lifted her up**—as his Lord had done to his own mother-in-law (Mark 1:31).

43. with one Simon a tanner—a trade regarded by the Jews as half unclean, and consequently disreputable, from the contact with dead animals and blood which was connected with it. For this reason, even by other nations, it is usually carried on at some distance from towns; accordingly, Simon's house was "by the seaside" (ch. 10:6). Peter's lodging there shows him already to some extent above Jewish prejudice.

ADAM CLARKE

40. *Peter put them all forth, and kneeled down, and prayed*. It was not even known to Peter that God would work this miracle: therefore he put all the people out, that he might seek the will of God by fervent prayer and during his supplications be liable to neither distraction nor interruption, which he must have experienced had he permitted this company of weeping widows to remain in the chamber. *Said, Tabitha, arise*. During his wrestling with God he had, undoubtedly, received confidence that she would be raised at his word.

41. *Saints and widows*. In primitive times the *widows* formed a distinct part of the Christian Church.

42. *Many believed in the Lord*. That is, in Christ Jesus, in whose name and through whose power they understood this miracle to be wrought.

43. *He tarried many days in Joppa*. Taking advantage of the good impression made on the people's minds by the miracle, he preached to them the great truths of Christianity and thus established them in the faith. *Simon a tanner*. Whether the original word signifies a *tanner* or a "currier" is of little consequence. The person who dealt in the hides, whether of clean or unclean animals, could not be in high repute among the Jews. Even in Joppa the trade appears to have been reputed unclean; and therefore this Simon had his house by the sea side. See chap. x. 6.

MATTHEW HENRY — CHAPTER 10

Verses 1–8

It concerns us carefully to observe all the circumstances of the beginning of this great work, this part of the *mystery of godliness—Christ preached to the Gentiles, and believed on in the world*. The gospel was never yet designedly preached to the Gentiles, nor any of them baptized—Cornelius was the first.

I. An account given us of this Cornelius, who was the first-born of the Gentiles to Christ. We are here told that he was a great man and a good man—two characters that seldom meet. Where they do meet they put a lustre upon each other: goodness makes greatness truly valuable, and greatness makes goodness much more serviceable. 1. Cornelius was an officer of the army, *v*. 1. Here there was a band, or cohort, of the Roman army, which is here called *the Italian band*, because they were all native Romans, or Italians. Cornelius had a command in this part of the army. He was an officer of considerable rank and figure, a centurion. We read of one of that rank in our Saviour's time, of whom he gave a great commendation, Matt. viii. 10. When a Gentile must be pitched upon to receive the gospel first, it is a Gentile soldier, who is a man of more free thought; and he that truly is so, when the Christian doctrine is fairly set before him, cannot but receive it and bid it welcome. Let not soldiers and officers of the army plead that their employment may excuse them if they be not religious. It was a mortification to the Jews that not only the Gentiles were taken into the church, but that the first who was taken in was an officer of the Roman army. 2. He was a religious man. It is a very good character that is given of him, *v*. 2. He was possessed with a principle of regard to the true and living God. He was *a devout man and one*

JAMIESON, FAUSSET, BROWN — CHAPTER 10

Vss. 1-48. ACCESSION AND BAPTISM OF CORNELIUS AND HIS PARTY; OR, THE FIRST FRUITS OF THE GENTILES. We here enter on an entirely new phase of the Christian Church, the "opening of the door of faith to the Gentiles"; in other words, the recognition of Gentile, on terms of perfect equality with Jewish, discipleship without the necessity of circumcision. Some beginnings appear to have been already made in this direction (see on ch. 11: 20, 21); and Saul probably acted on this principle from the first, both in Arabia and in Syria and Cilicia. But had he been the prime mover in the admission of uncircumcised Gentiles into the Church, the Jewish party, who were never friendly to him, would have acquired such strength as to bring the Church to the verge of a disastrous schism. But on Peter, "the apostle" specially "of the circumcision," was conferred the honor of initiating this great movement, as before of the first admission of Jewish believers. (See on Matt. 16: 19.) After this, however, one who had already come upon the stage was to eclipse this "chiefest of the apostles." **1, 2. Cæsarea**—See on ch. 8:40. **the Italian band**—a cohort of Italians, as distinguished from native soldiers, quartered at Cæsarea, probably as a bodyguard to the Roman procurator who resided there. An ancient coin makes express mention of such a cohort in Syria. (AKERMAN'S *Numismatic Illustrations of the New Testament*.) **2. A devout man . . .**—an uncircumcised Gentile proselyte to the Jewish faith, of whom there were a very great number at this time; a distinguished proselyte, who had brought his whole household establishment under the hallowing influence of the

ADAM CLARKE — CHAPTER 10

1. *There was a certain man in Caesarea*. This was Caesarea of Palestine, called also Strato's Tower, as has been already noted, and the residence of the Roman procurator. *A centurion*. The chief or captain of 100 men, as both the Greek and Latin words imply. *The band called the Italian band*. The word which we translate *band* signifies the same as "cohort" or "regiment," which sometimes consisted of 555 infantry and 66 cavalry. A Roman legion consisted of 10 cohorts. When in former times the Roman legion contained 6,000, each cohort consisted of 600.

2. *A devout man*. A person who worships the true God and is no idolater. *One that feared God*. One who was acquainted with the true God, by means of His Word and laws; who respected these laws, and would not dare to

MATTHEW HENRY

that feared God. Though he was a soldier, it was no diminution of the credit of his valour to tremble before God. He kept up religion in his family. He *feared God with all his house.* He took care that not himself only, but all his, should serve the Lord. Every good man will do what he can that those about him may be good too. He was a very charitable man: He *gave much alms to the people.* He was much in prayer: He *prayed to God always.* Wherever the fear of God rules in the heart, it will appear both in works of charity and of piety.

II. The orders given him from heaven to send for Peter.

1. How, and in what way, these orders were given him. He had a vision, in which an angel delivered them to him. It was about the *ninth hour of the day.* Because it was in the temple the time of offering the evening sacrifice, it was made by devout people an *hour of prayer.* Cornelius was now at prayer: so he tells us himself, *v.* 30. An angel of God *came in to him.* He *saw him evidently* with his bodily eyes, not in a dream presented to his imagination, but in a vision presented to his sight. He called him by his name, *Cornelius,* to intimate the particular notice God took of him. This put Cornelius for the present into some confusion (*v.* 4): *When he looked on him he was afraid.* Cornelius cries, "*What is it, Lord?* What is the matter?" This he speaks as one desirous to know the mind of God, and ready to comply with it.

2. What the message was.

(1) He is assured that God accepts him (*v.* 4): *Thy prayers and thine alms are come up for a memorial before God.* Prayers and alms must go together. We must follow our prayers with alms. We must *give alms of such things as we have*; and then, behold, all things are clean to us, Luke xi. 41. And we must follow our alms with our prayers that God would graciously accept them. Cornelius prayed, and gave alms, in sincerity, as unto God; and he is here told that they were *come up for a memorial before God.* Prayers and alms are our spiritual offerings, which God is pleased to have regard to.

(2) He is appointed to enquire after a further discovery of divine grace, *v.* 5, 6. He must *send* forthwith *to Joppa, and enquire for one Simon Peter; he lodgeth at the house of one Simon a tanner; his house is by the sea side, when he comes he shall tell thee what thou oughtest to do.* Now here are two things very surprising: [1] Cornelius prays and gives alms in the fear of God, is religious himself and keeps up religion in his family, yet there is something further that he ought to do—he ought to embrace the Christian religion. Not, He may do it if he pleases. But, He must do it. He that believed the promise of the Messiah must now believe the performance of that promise. Neither our prayers nor our alms can come up for a memorial before God unless we believe in Jesus Christ. [2] Cornelius has now an angel from heaven talking to him, and yet he must not receive the gospel of Christ from this angel, but all that the angel has to say is, "Send for Peter, and he shall tell thee." And as it was an honour to the apostle that he must preach that which an angel might not, so it was a further honour that an angel was despatched to order him to be sent for. To bring a faithful minister and a willing people together is a work worthy of an angel.

III. His immediate obedience to these orders, *v.* 7, 8. He sent with all speed to Joppa, to fetch Peter to him. When he sent: As soon as ever the *angel which spoke unto him had departed.* He made haste, and delayed not, to do this commandment. In any affair wherein our souls are concerned it is good for us not to lose time. Whom he sent: *Two of his household servants, and a devout soldier, that waited on him continually.* A devout centurion had devout soldiers. A little devotion commonly goes a great way with soldiers, but there would be more of it in the soldiers if there were but more of it in the commanders. When this centurion had to choose some of his soldiers to attend his person, and to be always about him, he pitched upon such of them as were devout. What instructions he gave them (*v.* 8): *He declared all these things unto them.* He does not only tell them where to find Peter, but he tells them on what errand he was to come, that they might importune him.

Verses 9–18

Cornelius had received positive orders from heaven to send for Peter, but here is another difficulty that lies in the way of bringing them together—the question is whether Peter will come to Cornelius. It sticks at a point of conscience. He is a Gentile, he is not circumcised. Peter had not got over this stingy bigoted notion of his countrymen, and therefore will be shy of coming to Cornelius. Now, to remove this

JAMIESON, FAUSSET, BROWN

Jewish faith and the regular observance of its principal seasons of worship. **gave much alms to the people**—i.e., the *Jewish* people, on the same principle as another centurion before him (Luke 7:5); thinking it no "great thing," if they had "sown unto him spiritual things, that they should reap his carnal things" (I Cor. 9:11). **prayed to God alway**—at the stated daily seasons. (See on vs. 3.)

3-6. saw . . . evidently—'distinctly.' **the ninth hour of the day**—three o'clock, the hour of the evening sacrifice. But he had been "fasting until that hour" (vs. 30), perhaps from the sixth hour (vs. 9).

4. What is it, Lord?—language which, tremulously though it was uttered, betokened childlike reverence and humility.

Thy prayers and thine alms—The way in which both are specified is emphatic. The one denotes the spiritual outgoing of his soul to God, the other its practical outgoing to men. **are come up for a memorial before God**—i.e., as a *sacrifice* well-pleasing unto God, as an odor of a sweet smell (Rev. 8:4). **5. send to Joppa . . . for one Simon . . .**—(See on ch. 9:11).

7, 8. when the angel . . . was departed, he called—immediately doing as directed, and thereby showing the simplicity of his faith. **a devout soldier of them that waited on him continually**—of the "soldiers under him," such as the centurion at Capernaum had (Matt. 8: 9). Who this "devout soldier" was, can only be matter of conjecture. DA COSTA (*Four Witnesses*) gives a number of ingenious reasons for thinking that, having attached himself henceforth to Peter—whose influence in the composition of the second Gospel is attested by the earliest tradition, and is stamped on that Gospel itself—he is no other than the Evangelist *Mark.*

ADAM CLARKE

offend his Maker and his Judge. *With all his house.* He took care to instruct his family in the knowledge which he himself had received, and to establish the worship of God in his house. *Gave much alms.* His love to God led him to love men, and this love proved its sincerity by acts of beneficence and charity. *Prayed to God alway.* Was ever in the spirit of prayer and frequently in the act. What an excellent character is this! And yet the man was a Gentile! He was what a Jew would repute common and unclean; see v. 28.

3. *He saw in a vision evidently.* The text is as plain as it can be that an angel of God did appear to Cornelius. This was in a *vision,* i.e., "a supernatural representation"; and it was "manifestly, evidently" made, and at such a time too as precluded the possibility of his being asleep; for it was *about the ninth hour of the day,* answering to our three o'clock in the afternoon, the time of public prayer, according to the custom of the Jews, and while Peter was engaged in that sacred duty.

4. *Thy prayers and thine alms are come up for a memorial.* Being all performed in simplicity and godly sincerity, they were acceptable to the Most High. *Come up for a memorial.* This form of speech is evidently borrowed from the sacrificial system of the Jews. Pious and sincere prayers are high in God's estimation; and therefore are said to ascend to Him, as the smoke and flame of the burnt offering appeared to ascend to heaven. These prayers and alms came up for a *memorial* before God. This is a manifest allusion to the meat offering, which, in Lev. ii. 16, is said to be a memorial (speaking after the manner of men) to put God in remembrance that such a person was His worshipper and needed His protection and help.

6. *Simon a tanner.* See the note on chap. ix. 43. *He shall tell thee what thou oughtest to do.* This clause, so explanatory, is wanting in almost every MS. and version of note.

7. *And a devout soldier.* It has already been remarked that Cornelius had taken care to instruct his family in divine things, and it appears also that he had been attentive to the spiritual interests of his regiment. We do not find that it was then, even among the Romans, considered a disgrace for a military officer to teach his men lessons of morality and piety towards God, whatever it may be in some Christian countries in the present time.

8. *He sent them to Joppa.* It has been properly remarked that, from Joppa, Jonah was sent to preach to the Gentiles of Nineveh; and from the same place Peter was sent to preach the gospel to the Gentiles at Caesarea.

MATTHEW HENRY

difficulty, he has a vision here, to prepare him to receive the message sent him by Cornelius. Christ ordered them to *teach all nations*; and yet even Peter himself could not understand it, till it was here revealed by vision.

I. The circumstances of this vision.

1. It was when the messengers were now *nigh the city, v.* 9. Peter knew nothing of their approach, and they knew nothing of his praying; but he that knew both him and them was preparing things for the interview. He is pleased often to bring things to the minds of his ministers, which they had not thought of, just then when they have occasion to use them.

2. It was when *Peter went up upon the house-top to pray.* Peter was much in prayer. He prayed *about the sixth hour,* not only *morning and evening,* but *at noon.* From morning to night we should think to be too long to be without meat; yet who thinks it is too long to be without prayer? He prayed *upon the house-top.* He had this vision immediately after he had prayed. The ascent of the heart to God in prayer is an excellent preparative to receive the discoveries of the divine grace.

3. It was when he became *very hungry* (*v.* 10); and now *he would have eaten.* Now this hunger was a proper inlet to the vision about meats, as Christ's hunger in the wilderness was to Satan's temptation to turn stones into bread.

II. The vision itself. He *fell into a trance.* He quite lost himself to this world, and so had his mind entirely free for converse with divine things. The more clear we get of the world, the more near we get to heaven. He *saw heaven opened,* that he might be sure that his authority to go to Cornelius was indeed from heaven. He saw *a great sheet full of all manner of living creatures, which descended from heaven, and was let down to him to the earth.* Here were not only beasts of the earth, but fowls of the air, laid at his feet. Here were no fishes of the sea, because there were none of them in particular unclean. Some make this sheet, thus filled, to represent the church of Christ. In this we find some of all countries, without any distinction of Greek or Jew. The net of the gospel encloses all, both bad and good, those that before were clean and unclean. Or it may be applied to the bounty of the divine Providence. How should it double our comfort in the creatures, and our obligations to serve God in the use of them, to see them thus let down to us out of heaven! He was ordered by a voice from heaven to make use of this plenty and variety which God had sent him (*v.* 13): "*Rise, Peter, kill and eat.*" It might be difficult for Jews to dine and sup with a Gentile, because they would have that set before them which they were not allowed to eat. Now they might fare as they feared, and therefore might eat with them. He stuck to his principles, and would by no means hearken to the motion (*v.* 14): *Not so, Lord.* Though hunger will break through stone walls, God's laws should be to us a stronger fence than stone walls. Temptations to eat forbidden fruit must not be parleyed with, but peremptorily rejected. The reason he gives is, "*For I have never eaten anything that is common or unclean;* hitherto I have kept my integrity in this matter, and will still keep it." His conscience could witness for him that he had never gratified his appetite with any forbidden food. God, by a second voice from heaven, proclaimed the repeal of the law in this case (*v.* 15): *What God hath cleansed, that call thou not common.* He that made the law might alter it when he pleased. He has now taken off that restraint, has cleansed that which was before polluted to us. We ought to welcome it as a great mercy; not so much because hereby we gain the use of swine's flesh, hares, rabbits, and other pleasant and wholesome food for our bodies, but chiefly because conscience is hereby freed from a yoke in things of this nature. *This was done thrice, v.* 16, with the same call to him, and the same reason. The instructions given us in the things of God need to be often repeated. But at last *the vessel was received up into heaven.* Those who make this vessel to represent the church, including both Jews and Gentiles, make this very aptly to signify the admission of the believing Gentiles into the church, and into heaven too. They are such as God has cleansed.

III. The providence which explained this vision, *v.* 17, 18. *He doubted within himself what this vision which he had seen should mean.* He had no reason to doubt the truth of it, all his doubt was concerning the meaning of it. Christ reveals himself to his people by degrees, and leaves them to doubt awhile, to ruminate upon a thing, and debate it to and fro in their own minds, before he clears it up to them. Yet he was made to know presently, for *the men who were sent from Cornelius* were at *the gate enquiring whether Peter lodged there*; and by their errand it will

JAMIESON, FAUSSET, BROWN

9-16. upon the housetop—the flat roof, the chosen place in the East for cool retirement. **the sixth hour**—noon. **a trance**—differing from the "vision" of Cornelius, in so far as the things seen had not the same *objective* reality, though both were supernatural.

12. all manner of four-footed beasts . . .—i.e., the *clean* and the *unclean* (ceremonially) all mixed together.

I have never eaten anything that is common—i.e., *not sanctified* by divine permission to eat of it, and so "unclean." "The distinction of meats was a sacrament of national distinction, separation, and consecration" [WEBSTER and WILKINSON]. **15. What God hath cleansed, that call not thou common**—The ceremonial distinctions are at an end, and Gentiles, ceremonially separated from the chosen people (vs. 28), and debarred from that access to God in the visible ordinances of His Church which they enjoyed, are now on a perfect equality with them. **16. done thrice**—See Genesis 41:32.

17-24. while Peter doubted . . . what this should mean, behold, the three men . . . stood before the gate . . . and asked—'were inquiring,' i.e., in the act of doing so. The

ADAM CLARKE

9. *On the morrow, as they went on their journey.* The messengers could not have left the house of Cornelius till about two hours before sunset; therefore they must have travelled a part of the night in order to arrive at Joppa the next day, towards noon. Cornelius sent two of his household servants, by way of respect to Peter; probably the soldier was intended for their defense, as the roads in Judea were by no means safe. *Peter went up upon the house top to pray.* It has often been remarked that the houses in Judea were built with flat roofs, on which people walked, conversed, meditated, prayed. The housetop was the place of retirement, and thither Peter went for the purpose of praying to God.

10. *He became very hungry.* It seems that this happened about dinnertime, for it appears that they were making ready, "dressing the victuals" for the family. The dinner among the ancients was a very slight meal, and they had no breakfast; their supper was their principal meal. *He fell into a trance.* "An ecstasy fell upon him." A person may be said to be in an ecstasy when transported with joy or admiration, so that he is insensible to every object but that on which he is engaged.

11. *And saw heaven opened.* His mind now entirely spiritualized and absorbed in heavenly contemplation, was capable of discoveries of the spiritual world. *A great sheet knit at the four corners.* Perhaps intended to be an emblem of the universe and its various nations, to the four corners of which the gospel was to extend and to offer its blessings to all the inhabitants, without distinction of nation.

12. *All manner of fourfooted beasts.* Every species of quadrupeds, whether wild or domestic; all reptiles, and all fowls. Consequently both clean and unclean were present in this visionary representation, those that the Jewish law allowed to be sacrificed to God, or proper for food, as well as those which that law had prohibited in both cases.

13. *Rise, Peter; kill, and eat.* "Sacrifice and eat." Though this verb is sometimes used to signify the slaying of animals for food, yet as the proper notion is to slay for the purpose of sacrifice it appears to me to be better to preserve that meaning here.

14. *Common or unclean.* By *common* whatever was in general use among the Gentiles is to be understood; by *unclean,* everything that was forbidden by the Mosaic law. However the one word may be considered as explanatory of the other. The rabbins themselves, and many of the primitive fathers, believed that by the unclean animals forbidden by the law the Gentiles were meant.

15. *What God hath cleansed.* God, who made at first the distinction between Jews and Gentiles, has a right to remove it whenever and by whatever means He pleases. He, therefore, who made the distinction, for wise purposes, between the clean and the unclean now pronounces all to be clean.

16. *This was done thrice.* For the greater certainty, and to make the deeper impression on the apostle's mind. *And the vessel was received up again into heaven.* Both Jews and Gentiles came equally from God; and to Him, both, by the preaching of the gospel, shall again return.

17. *While Peter doubted . . . the men . . . stood before the gate.* In all this we find an admirable display of the economy of providence. Cornelius prays and has a vision which prepares

MATTHEW HENRY

appear what was the meaning of this vision. God knows what services are before us, and therefore how to prepare us; and we then better know the meaning of what he has taught us when we find what occasion we have to make use of it.

Verses 19–33

We have here the meeting between Peter and Cornelius. Though Paul was designed to be the apostle of the Gentiles, and Peter to be the apostle of the circumcision, yet it is ordered that Peter shall break the ice, and reap the first fruits of the Gentiles, that the believing Jews might be the better reconciled to their admission into the church, when they were first brought in by their own apostle.

I. Peter is directed by the Spirit to go along with Cornelius's messengers (*v.* 19, 20). Now the riddle is unriddled: *While Peter thought on the vision;* he was musing upon it, and then it was opened to him. Those that would be taught the things of God must think on those things. 1. Whence he had the direction. The Spirit said to him what he should do. It was not spoken to him by an angel, but spoken in him by the Spirit. 2. What the direction was. He is told that three men below want to speak with him (*v.* 19), and he must arise from his musings and go down to them, *v.* 20. Those that are searching into the meaning of the words of God, and the visions of the Almighty, should not be always poring, no, nor always praying, but should sometimes look about them. He is ordered to *go along with the messengers to Cornelius, doubting nothing*, not doubting whether he might go, no, nor whether he ought to go; for it was his duty. "*Go with them, for I have sent them.*" When we see our call clear to any service, we should not suffer ourselves to be perplexed with doubts and scruples, or a fear of men's censure.

II. He receives both them and their message: *He went down to them, v.* 21. 1. He favourably receives their message. He asks what their business is: *What is the cause wherefore you are come?* and they tell him their errand (*v.* 22): "*Cornelius*, an officer of the Roman army, *who fears God above many of good report among all the people of the Jews, was warned from God* by an angel to send for thee to his house, *and to hear words of thee.*" These words, Peter tells us more fully, are *words whereby thou and all thy house shall be saved, ch.* xi. 14. 2. He kindly entertained the messengers (*v.* 23): *He called them in, and lodged them.* What was getting ready for him (*v.* 10) they should be welcome to share in; he little thought what company he should have when he bespoke his dinner, but God foresaw it. Peter lodged them, though they were Gentiles, to show how readily he complied with the design of the vision in eating with Gentiles. Though they were two of them servants, and the other a common soldier, yet Peter thought it not below him to take them into his house.

III. He *went with them* to Cornelius. Peter was *accompanied by certain brethren from Joppa, v.* 23. Six of them went along with him, as we find, *ch.* xi. 12. This was one way in which the primitive Christians very much showed their respect to their ministers: they accompanied them in their journeys. It is a pity that those who have skill and will to do good to others by their discourse should want an opportunity for it by travelling alone. Cornelius *had got some friends together at Cæsarea.* Now when they came into the house of Cornelius Peter found, (1) That he was expected, and this was an encouragement to him. *Cornelius waited for them*, and such a guest was worth waiting for; nor can I blame him if he waited with some impatience. (2) That he was expected by many and this was a further encouragement to him. As Peter brought some with him to partake of the spiritual gift he had now to dispense, so *Cornelius had called together*, not only his own family, but *kinsmen and near friends.* We should not covet to eat our spiritual morsels alone. It ought to be both given and taken as a piece of kindness and respect to our kindred and friends to invite them to join with us in religious exercises, to go with us to hear a sermon.

IV. Here is the first interview between Peter and Cornelius. The profound respect and honour which Cornelius paid to Peter (*v.* 25): *He met him as he was coming in*, and *he fell down at his feet and worshipped him.* His worshipping a man was indeed culpable; but, considering his present ignorance, it was excusable. No wonder if, till he was better informed, he worshipped him, whom he was ordered to send for by an angel from heaven. Peter's modest refusal of this honour that was done him (*v.* 25): *He took him up saying*, "*Stand up, I myself also am a man.*" The good angels of the churches cannot bear to have the least of that honour shown to them which is due to

JAMIESON, FAUSSET, BROWN

preparations here made—of Peter for his Gentile visitors, as of Cornelius for him—are devoutly to be noted. But besides this, at the same moment, "the Spirit" expressly informs him that three men were inquiring for him, and bids him unhesitatingly go with them, as sent by Him.

21. I am he whom ye seek—This seems to have been said without any communication being made to Peter regarding the men or their errand. **22. they said, Cornelius . . . a just man . . .**—fine testimony this from his own servants. **of good report among all the nation of the Jews**—specified, no doubt, to conciliate the favorable regard of the Jewish apostle. **to hear words of thee**—See on ch. 11:14. **23. called them in and lodged them**—thus partially anticipating this fellowship with Gentiles.

Peter went . . . with them, and certain brethren—six in number (ch. 11: 12). **from Joppa**—as witnesses of a transaction which Peter was prepared to believe pregnant with great consequences. **24. Cornelius . . . called together his kinsmen and near friends**—implying that he had been long enough at Cæsarea to form relationships there and that he had intimate friends there whose presence he was not ashamed to invite to a religious meeting of the most solemn nature.

25-29. as Peter was coming in, Cornelius met him—a mark of the highest respect. **fell down at his feet, and worshipped him**—In the East this way of showing respect was customary not only to kings, but to others occupying a superior station; but among the Greeks and Romans it was reserved for the gods. Peter, therefore, declines it as due to no mortal [GROTIUS]. *"Those who claim to have succeeded Peter, have not imitated this part of his conduct"* [ALFORD] (therein only verifying II Thess. 2:4, and cf. Rev. 19:10; 22:9).

ADAM CLARKE

him to receive instruction from Peter; Peter prays and has a vision which prepares and disposes him to give instruction to Cornelius. While he is in doubts and perplexity what the full meaning of the vision might be, the messengers, who had been dispatched under the guidance of an especial providence, came to the door; and the Holy Spirit gives him information that his doubts should be all cleared up by accompanying the men who were now inquiring for him.

21. *Which were sent unto him from Cornelius.* This clause is wanting in almost every MS. of worth and in almost all the versions. *What is the cause wherefore ye are come?* He still did not know the full import of the vision; but being informed by the Holy Spirit that three men were seeking him and that he should go with them, without scruple, he instantly obeyed.

22. *Cornelius the centurion.* They gave him the simple relation which they had received from their master. *To hear words of thee.* But of what kind they could not as yet tell.

23. *Then called he them in.* They had already walked a long journey in a short time and needed refreshment; and it was thought expedient they should rest that night with Simon the tanner.

Certain brethren from Joppa. They were six in number, as we learn from chap. xi. 12. It was necessary that there should be several witnesses of the important transactions which were about to take place, as on no slight evidence would even the converted Jews believe that repentance unto life and the Holy Spirit should be granted to the Gentiles.

24. *His kinsmen and near friends.* His "relatives," and his "necessary friends." It appears that he had collected the whole circle of his intimate acquaintance, that they also might profit by a revelation which he expected to come immediately from heaven, and these amounted to many persons; see v. 27.

25. *Fell down at his feet, and worshipped him.* As Peter's coming was announced by an angel, Cornelius might have supposed that Peter himself was an angel, and of a superior order, seeing he came to announce what the first angel was not employed to declare. It was probably in consequence of this thought that he prostrated himself before Peter, offering him the highest act of civil respect; for there was nothing in the act, as performed by Cornelius, which belonged to the worship of the true God.

F. B. MEYER:

Jew and Gentile meet. It should be carefully noted that the mental impression which was produced by Peter's vision was corroborated by the fact of the knocking and inquiring group at Peter's door. This is God's invariable method. For us all, as we contemplate taking a new and important step in life, there is the urging of the Spirit, the impression or vision of duty, and the knock or appeal of outward circumstances.

Evidently Cornelius had gathered to his quarters in the barracks his kinsmen and a number of intimate friends, who were as eager as he to discover the will of God. They remained quietly waiting until the party from Joppa had completed their thirty-mile journey. Peter had taken the precaution of bringing with him six brethren, evidently with the expectation that the events of that day would not only create a new era, but would also be called into serious question.

The welcome that Cornelius gave was very significant. That a high-born Roman should prostrate himself before a Jewish evangelist was unprecedented, though it revealed the true reverence and humility of Cornelius's soul. But the noble simplicity of Peter's reply was also a revelation of the true greatness of the apostle, and ought to have more obviously influenced his would-be successors.—*Bible Commentary*

MATTHEW HENRY

God only. Christ's faithful servants could better bear to be vilified than to be deified. Let him know that Peter is a man, that *the treasure is in earthen vessels*, that he may value the treasure for its own sake.

V. The account which Peter and Cornelius give to each other, and to the company, of the hand of Heaven in bringing them together: *As he talked with him he went in, v.* 27. When he came in, *he found many that were come together*, which added solemnity, as well as opportunity of doing good, to this service.

1. Peter declares the direction God gave to him to come to those Gentiles, *v.* 28, 29. They knew it had never been allowed by the Jews, but always looked upon as an *unlawful thing for a man that is a Jew to keep company or come unto one of another nation*, an uncircumcised Gentile. It was not made so by the law of God, but by the decree of their wise men. They did not forbid them to converse or traffic with Gentiles in the street or shop, or upon the exchange, but to eat with them. They might not come into the house of a Gentile. Thus scornfully did the Jews look upon the Gentiles, who were not behindhand with them in contempt. "*But now*," saith Peter, "*God hath shown me that I should not call any man common or unclean.*" Peter, who had taught his new converts to *save themselves from the untoward generation of wicked men* (*ch.* ii. 40), is now himself taught to join himself with the towardly generation of devout Gentiles. He assures them of his readiness to do them all the good offices he could. Having now received permission, he was at their service: "*Therefore came I unto you without gainsaying, as soon as I was sent for.*" He enquires wherein he might be serviceable to them: "*I ask, therefore, for what intent you have sent for me?*"

2. Cornelius declares the directions God gave to him to send for Peter.

(1) Cornelius gives an account of the angel's appearing to him, and ordering him to send for Peter. He tells how this vision found him employed (*v.* 30): *Four days ago I was fasting until this hour. He was at the ninth hour praying in his house*, not in the synagogue, but at home. *At the ninth hour of the day*, three of the clock in the afternoon, most people were travelling or trading, working in the fields, visiting their friends, taking their pleasure, or taking a nap after dinner; yet then Cornelius was at his devotions, which shows how much he made religion his business. He describes the messenger: *There stood a man before me in bright clothing*. He repeats the message that was sent to him (*v.* 31, 32), just as we had it, *v.* 4-6. Only here it is said, *Thy prayer is heard.* We are not told what his prayer was; but if this message was an answer to it, he prayed that God would make some further discoveries of himself, and of the way of salvation to him.

(2) He declares his own and his friends' readiness to receive the message Peter had to deliver (*v.* 33): *Immediately therefore I sent to thee, and thou hast well done that thou hast come.* Faithful ministers do well to come to people that are desirous to receive instruction from them; to come when they are sent for. "*We are all here present before God. Therefore,* because thou art come to us by such a warrant, on such an errand, *we are present*, and are ready to come at a call. *We are all present.*" The whole of the man must be present; not the body here, and the heart, with the fool's eyes, in the ends of the earth. "*We are present to hear all things that are commanded thee of God.*" Peter was there to preach all things that were commanded him of God. They were ready to hear, not whatever he pleased to say, but what he was commanded of God to say. "We are ready to hear *all* that thou art commissioned to preach, though it be ever so displeasing and ever so contrary to our former notions or present secular interests. We are ready to hear all, and therefore let nothing be kept back that is profitable for us."

Verses 34-43

We have here Peter's sermon. It is intimated that he expressed himself with a great deal of solemnity and gravity, but with freedom and copiousness, in that phrase, *he opened his mouth, and spoke, v.* 34. It was a new sermon.

I. Because they were Gentiles to whom he preached. He shows that they were interested in the gospel of Christ, and entitled to the benefit of it, upon an equal footing with the Jews. He therefore lays down this as an undoubted principle, *that God is no respecter of persons*. He doth not give judgment in favour of a man for the sake of any external advantage foreign to the merits of the cause. *But in every nation he that fears God and works righteousness is accepted of him, v.* 35. God never did, nor ever will, justify and save a wicked Jew that lived and died impenitent,

JAMIESON, FAUSSET, BROWN

28. Ye know it is . . . unlawful . . . for . . . a Jew to keep company, or come unto one of another nation . . .—There was no express prohibition to this effect, and to a certain extent intercourse was certainly kept up. (See the Gospel history, towards the end.) But intimate social fellowship was not practiced, as being adverse to the spirit of the law.

29. I ask therefore . . .—The whole speech is full of dignity, the apostle seeing in the company before him a new brotherhood, into whose devout and inquiring minds he was divinely directed to pour the light of new truth.

30-33. Four days ago—the messengers being despatched on the first; on the second reaching Joppa (vs. 9); starting for Cæsarea on the third; and on the fourth arriving.

33. we are all here present before God, to hear all things that are commanded thee of God—Beautiful expression of entire preparedness to receive the expected divine teaching through the lips of this heaven-commissioned teacher, and delightful encouragement to Peter to give free utterance to what was doubtless already on his lips!

34, 35. Peter opened his mouth—See on Matthew 5:2. **Of a truth I perceive**—i.e., 'I have it now demonstrated before mine eyes.' **that God is no respecter of persons**—Not, 'I see there is no capricious *favoritism* with God,' for Peter would never imagine such a thing; but (as the next clause shows), 'I see that God has respect only to *personal character and state* in the acceptance of men, national and ecclesiastical distinctions being of no account.'

ADAM CLARKE

28. *Ye know how that it is an unlawful thing.* He addressed the whole company, among whom, it appears, there were persons well acquainted with Jewish customs. *But God hath shewed me.* He now began to understand the import of the vision which he saw at Joppa. A Gentile is not to be avoided because he is a Gentile; God is now taking down the partition wall which separated them from the Jews.

29. *I ask . . . for what intent ye have sent for me?* Peter had been informed of this by the servants of Cornelius, v. 22; but as all the company might not have been informed of the circumstances, he, as it were, invites him to tell his story afresh, that his friends might be the better prepared to receive the truth which he was about to dispense in obedience to his divine commission.

30. *Four days ago I was fasting until this hour.* The word fasting is wanting in some MSS.

31. *Thy prayer is heard.* See the note on v. 4. Cornelius prayed, fasted, and gave alms. It was in this way he looked for salvation, not to purchase it; a thought of this kind does not appear to have entered into his mind. But these were the means he used to get his soul brought to the knowledge of the truth.

33. *Are we all here present before God.* The people were all waiting for the preacher, and every heart was filled with expectation; they waited as *before God*, from whose messenger they were about to hear the words of life.

34. *God is no respecter of persons.* He does not esteem a Jew because he is a Jew; nor does he detest a Gentile because he is a Gentile. It was a long and deeply rooted opinion among the Jews that God never would extend His favor to the Gentiles, and that the descendants of Jacob only should enjoy His peculiar favor

MATTHEW HENRY

whose privileges and professions, instead of screening him from the judgment of God, will but aggravate his guilt and condemnation. He never did, nor ever will, reject or refuse an honest Gentile, who like Cornelius, fears God, and worships him, and works righteousness, who lives up to the light he has. Whatever nation he is of, that shall be no prejudice to him. God judges of men by their hearts, not by their country or parentage; and, wherever he finds an upright man, he will be found an upright God. *Fearing God, and working righteousness,* must go together. But, where these are predominant, no doubt is to be made of acceptance with God. Those that have not the knowledge of him, and therefore cannot have an explicit regard to him, may yet receive grace from God for his sake, *to fear God and to work righteousness*; and wherever God gives grace to do so, as he did to Cornelius, he will, through Christ, accept the work of his own hands. This was always a truth, before Peter perceived it, *that God respecteth no man's person.* God will not ask in the great day what country men were of, but what they were. Yet now it was made more clear than it had been. Peter is here made to perceive it, by comparing the vision which he had with that which Cornelius had.

II. Because they were Gentiles inhabiting a place within the confines of the land of Israel, he refers them to what they themselves could not but know of our Lord Jesus: for these were things the report of which spread into every corner of the nation, *v.* 37.

1. They knew, in general, *the word which God sent to the children of Israel*: *That word, I say, you know, v.* 37. Though the Gentiles were not admitted to hear it, yet they could not but hear of it. We are often told in the gospels how the fame of Christ went into all parts of Canaan. That word of power and grace, *you know.* What the purport of this word was. God by it *published the glad tidings of peace by Jesus Christ*, so it should be read. It is God himself that proclaims *peace*, who justly might have proclaimed war. To whom it was sent—to the children of Israel, in the first place.

2. They knew the several matters of fact relating to this word of the gospel sent to Israel. They knew the baptism of repentance which John preached by way of introduction to it. They knew what an extraordinary man John was, and what a direct tendency his preaching had to *prepare the way of the Lord.* They knew that immediately after John's baptism the gospel of Christ, that word of *peace, was published throughout all Judæa*, and that it took its rise from Galilee. They knew that Jesus of Nazareth *went about doing good.* They knew what a benefactor he was to that nation; how he made it his business to do good to all. He was not idle, but still doing; went about from place to place, and wherever he came he was doing good. Hereby he showed *that he was sent of God.* They knew more particularly that he *healed all that were oppressed of the devil.* He was sent to *destroy the works of the devil*; for thus he obtained many a victory over him. They knew that the Jews put him to death; they *slew* him by *hanging him on a tree.* Whom *they* slew; they, to whom he had done and designed so much good. All this they knew; but lest they should think it was only a report, Peter, for himself and the rest of the apostles, attested it (*v.* 39): *We are witnesses of all things which he did, both in the land of the Jews and in Jerusalem.*

3. They might know, by all this, that he had a commission from heaven to preach and act as he did. This Jesus *is Lord of all*; not only as *God over all blessed for evermore*, but as Mediator, *all power both in heaven and on earth* is put into his hand, and all judgment committed to him. *God anointed him with the Holy Ghost and with power*, whence he was called *Christ—the Messiah, the anointed One.* He was full of power both in preaching and working miracles, which was the seal of a divine mission. *God was with him, v.* 38. God not only sent him, but was present with him all along. Those whom God anoints he will accompany; he will himself be with those to whom he has given his Spirit.

III. Because they had had no more certain information concerning this Jesus, Peter declares to them his resurrection from the dead, and the proofs of it. Probably they had heard at Cæsarea some talk of his having risen from the dead, soon silenced by that vile suggestion of the Jews, that *his disciples came by night and stole him away.* 1. The power by which he arose is incontestably divine (*v.* 40): *Him God raised up the third day.* He did not break prison, but had a legal discharge. *God raised him up.* 2. The proofs of his resurrection were incontestably clear; for God *showed him openly.* It was such a showing of him as amounted to a demonstration of the truth

JAMIESON, FAUSSET, BROWN

But in every nation—not (observe), in every *religion;* according to a common distortion of these words. **he that feareth him, and worketh righteousness**—This being the well-known phraseology of the Old Testament in describing the truly godly man, within the pale of revealed religion, it cannot be alleged that Peter meant it to denote a merely *virtuous* character, in the heathen sense; and as Peter had learned enough, from the messengers of Cornelius and from his own lips, to convince him that the whole religious character of this Roman officer had been moulded in the Jewish faith, there can be no doubt that the apostle intended to describe exactly such saintship—in its internal spirituality and external fruitfulness—as God had already pronounced to be genuine and approved. And since to such "He giveth more grace," according to the law of His Kingdom (Jas. 4:6; Matt. 25:29), He sends Peter, not to be the instrument of his *conversion,* as this is very frequently called, but simply to "show him the way of God more perfectly," as before to the devout Ethiopian eunuch. **36-38. the word . . . sent unto the children of Israel**—for to them (he would have them distinctly know) the Gospel was first preached, even as the facts of it took place on the special theater of the ancient economy. **preaching peace by Jesus Christ**—the glorious sum of all Gospel truth (I Cor. 1:20-22). **he is Lord of all**—exalted to embrace under the canopy of His peace, Jew and Gentile alike, whom the blood of His Cross had cemented into one reconciled and accepted family of God (Eph. 2:13-18).

37. That word . . . ye know—The facts, it seems, were too notorious and extraordinary to be unknown to those who mixed so much with Jews, and took so tender an interest in all Jewish matters as they did; though, like the eunuch, they knew not the significance of them. **which was published throughout all Judea, and began from Galilee**—See Luke 4:14, 37, 44; 7:17; 9:6; 23:5. **after the baptism which John preached**—See on ch. 1:22. **38. Now God anointed Jesus of Nazareth**—rather, 'Jesus of Nazareth (as the burden of that "published word"), how God anointed Him.' **with the Holy Ghost and with power**—i.e., at His baptism, thus visibly proclaiming Him MESSIAH, "the Lord's Christ." See Luke 4:18-21. For it is not His unction for personal holiness at His incarnation that is referred to—as many of the Fathers and some moderns take it—but His investiture with the insignia of the Messianic office, in which He presented Himself after His baptism to the acceptance of the people. **went about doing good**—holding up the *beneficent* character of all His miracles, which was their predicted character (Isa. 35:5, 6, etc.). **healing all that were oppressed of the devil**—whether in the form of demoniacal possessions, or more indirectly, as in her "whom Satan had bound with a spirit of infirmity eighteen years" (Luke 13:16); thereby showing Himself the Redeemer from all evil. **for God was with him**—Thus gently does the apostle rise to the supreme dignity of Christ with which he closes, accommodating himself to his hearers. **39-43. we are witnesses of all . . . he did**—not objects of superstitious reverence, but simply *witnesses* to the great historical facts on which the Gospel is founded. **slew and hanged**—i.e., slew by hanging—**on a tree**—So ch. 5:30 (and see on Gal. 3:13). **40-41. showed him openly;**

ADAM CLARKE

and benediction. Of this opinion was Peter previously to the heavenly vision mentioned in this chapter. He was now convinced that *God is no respecter of persons,* that as all must stand before His judgment seat to be judged according to the deeds done in the body, so no one nation or people or individual could expect to find a more favorable decision than another who was precisely in the same moral state; for the phrase "respect of persons" is used in reference to unjust decisions in a court of justice, where through favor or interest or bribe a culprit is acquitted and a righteous or innocent person condemned. See Lev. xix. 15; Deut. i. 16-17; and xvi. 19.

35. *But in every nation he that feareth him.* In every nation he who, according to his light and privileges, fears God, worships Him alone (for this is the true meaning of the word), *and worketh righteousness,* abstains from all evil, gives to all their due, injures neither the body, soul, nor reputation of his neighbor, *is accepted with him.*

36. *The word which God sent.* Few verses in the New Testament have perplexed critics and divines more than this. The ancient copyists seem also to have been puzzled with it, as the great variety in the different MSS. sufficiently proves. A foreign critic makes a good sense by connecting this with the preceding verse, thus: "In every nation he that feareth him and worketh righteousness is accepted with him, according to that doctrine which God sent unto the children of Israel, by which he published peace (i.e., reconciliation between Jews and Gentiles) by Jesus Christ, who is Lord of all"; and because "Lord of all," both of Jews and Gentiles, therefore He must be impartial; and because impartial, or "no respecter of persons," therefore, "in every nation," whether Judea, Greece, or Italy, "he that feareth him [God], and worketh righteousness, is accepted with him." I believe *the word* should be translated, "that doctrine." The whole may be literally read thus: "As to the doctrine sent to the children of Israel, preaching the glad tidings of peace by Jesus Christ, He is Lord of all, ye know what was done through all Judea, beginning after the baptism which John preached. Jesus, who was from Nazareth, whom God anointed with the Holy Ghost, and with mighty power went about doing good, and healing all that were tyrannically oppressed by the devil, for God was with him."

37. *That word . . . ye know.* This account of Jesus of Nazareth you cannot be unacquainted with, because it has been proclaimed throughout all Judea and Galilee from the time that John began to preach. You have heard how He was anointed with the Holy Ghost, and of the miracles which He performed; how He went about doing good and healing all kinds of demoniacs and by these mighty and beneficent acts giving the fullest proof that God was with Him. This was the exordium of Peter's discourse, and thus he begins from what they knew to teach them what they did not know.

38. *God anointed Jesus of Nazareth.* Here the apostle refers to Christ as the promised Messiah; for as Messiah signifies "the Anointed One," and "Christ" has the same signification in Greek, and the Messiah, according to the prophets and the expectation of the Jews, was to work miracles, Peter proclaims Jesus as the Messiah, and refers to the miracles which He wrought as the proof of it. This delicate but forcible allusion is lost by most readers.

39. *We are witnesses of all.* In this speech Peter may refer not only to the twelve apostles but to the six brethren whom he had brought with him. *Whom they slew.* As the truth of the resurrection must depend on the reality of the death of Christ, it was necessary that this should be stated and shown to rest on the most indubitable evidence.

40. *Him God raised up the third day.* He lay long enough under the power of death to prove that He was dead; and not too long, lest it should be supposed that His disciples had time sufficient to practice some deceit or imposture; and to prevent this the Jews took care to have the tomb well-guarded during the whole time which He lay there.

MATTHEW HENRY

of his resurrection. He showed him not publicly indeed, but evidently; *not to all the people.* By resisting all the evidences he had given them of his divine mission, they had forfeited the favour of being eye-witnesses of this great proof of it. Those who immediately forged and promoted that lie of his being stolen away were justly given up to strong delusions to believe it. A sufficient number saw him to attest the truth of his resurrection. The resurrection of Christ was proved before sufficient witnesses. They were not so by chance, but they were *chosen before of God* to be witnesses of it. They had not a sudden and transient view of him, but a great deal of free conversation with him: *They did eat and drink with him after he rose from the dead.* This was not all; they saw him without any terror or consternation, he conversed with them so familiarly, that *they did eat and drink with him.*

IV. He concludes with an inference from all this, that therefore that which they all ought to do was to believe in this Jesus: he was sent to tell Cornelius what he must do, and it is this. One thing he lacked, he must believe in Christ.

1. Why he must believe in him. The Christian faith is *built upon the foundation of the apostles and prophets,* it is built upon the testimony given by them. By the apostles. Peter as foreman speaks for the rest, that *God commanded them to preach to the people, and to testify* concerning Christ. Their testimony is God's testimony; and they are his witnesses to the world. By the prophets of the Old Testament (*v.* 43): *To him give all the prophets witness.* Out of the mouth of these two clouds of witnesses, *this word is established.*

2. What they must believe concerning him. That we are all accountable to Christ as our Judge. This Jesus is *ordained of God to be the Judge of the quick and dead, v.* 42. He is empowered to prescribe the terms of salvation, that rule by which we must be judged. He hath assured us of this, *in that he hath raised him from the dead* (*ch.* xvii. 31), so that it is the great concern of everyone of us to make him our friend. That if we believe in him we shall all be justified by him as our righteousness, *v.* 43. The prophets did witness this, *that through his name, whosoever believeth in him shall receive remission of sins.* This is the great thing we need, without which we are undone. And the remission of sins lays a foundation for all other favours and blessings. If sin be pardoned, all is well, and shall end everlastingly well.

Verses 44–48

We have here the issue and effect of Peter's sermon. They were all brought home to Christ.

I. God's owning Peter's word, by conferring the Holy Ghost upon the hearers of it (*v.* 44): *While Peter was yet speaking these words the Holy Ghost fell on all those who heard the word,* even as he did on the apostles at first; so Peter saith, *ch.* xi. 15. When the Holy Ghost fell upon them—while Peter was preaching. Thus God bore witness to what he said, and accompanied it with a divine power. The Holy Ghost fell upon others after they were baptized, for their confirmation; but upon these Gentiles before they were baptized: to show that God is not tied to a method, nor confines himself to external signs. How it appeared that the Holy Ghost had fallen upon them (*v.* 46): *They spoke with tongues.* When they spoke with tongues, they *magnified God,* they spoke of Christ and the benefits of redemption, which Peter had been preaching. Whatever gift we are endued with, we ought to honour God with it, and particularly the gift of speaking, and all the improvements of it. What impression it made upon the believing Jews that were present (*v.* 45): *Those of the circumcision who believed were astonished,* because *upon the Gentiles also was poured out the gift of the Holy Ghost.* Had they understood the scriptures of the Old Testament it would not have been such an astonishment to them.

II. Peter's owning God's work in baptizing those on whom the Holy Ghost fell. Though they had received the Holy Ghost, yet it was requisite they should be baptized; though God is not tied to instituted ordinances, we are. Though they were Gentiles, yet, having received the Holy Ghost, they might be admitted to baptism (*v.* 47): *Can any man forbid water, that these should not be baptized, who have received the Holy Ghost as well as we?* The argument is conclusive; can we deny the sign to those who have received the thing signified? It becomes us to follow God's indications, and to take those into communion with us whom he hath taken into communion with himself. Now it appears why the Spirit was given them before they were baptized—because otherwise Peter could not have persuaded

JAMIESON, FAUSSET, BROWN

Not to all the people—for it was not fitting that He should subject Himself, in His risen condition, to a second rejection in Person.

but unto witnesses chosen before of God, . . . to us, who did eat and drink with him after he rose . . .—Not the less certain, therefore, was the fact of His resurrection, though withholding Himself from general gaze in His risen body.

he which was ordained of God to be the Judge of quick and dead—He had before proclaimed Him "Lord of all," for the dispensing of "*peace*" to all alike; now he announces Him in the same supreme lordship, for the exercise of *judgment* upon all alike. On this divine ordination, see John 5:22, 23, 27; ch. 17:31. Thus we have here all Gospel truth in brief. But, *forgiveness through this exalted One* is the closing note of Peter's beautifully simple discourse. **43. To him give all the prophets witness**—i.e., This is the burden, generally of the prophetic testimony. It was fitter thus to give the spirit of their testimony, than to quote them in detail on such an occasion. But let this apostolic statement of the evangelical import of the Old Testament writings be devoutly weighed by those who are disposed to rationalize away this element in the Old Testament. **whosoever believeth in him**—This was evidently said with special reference to the Gentile audience then before him, and formed a noble practical conclusion to the whole discourse. **44, 45. While Peter yet spake . . . , the Holy Ghost fell**—by visible and audible manifestation (vs. 46).

45. they of the circumcision . . . were astonished, . . . because that on the Gentiles also was poured out . . .—without circumcision. **46. heard them speak with tongues and magnify God**—As on the day of Pentecost it was no empty miracle, no mere speaking of foreign languages, but utterance of "the wonderful works of God" in tongues to them unknown (ch. 2:11), so here; but more remarkable in this case, as the speakers were perhaps less familiar with the Old Testament songs of praise. **46-48. Then answered Peter, Can any man forbid water . . . which have received the Holy Ghost . . .**—Mark, he does not say, They have received the Spirit, what need have they for water? but, Having the living discipleship imparted to them and visibly stamped upon them, what objection can there be to admitting them, by the seal of baptism, into the full fellowship of the Church? **who have received the Holy Ghost as well as we**—and are thus, in all that is essential to salvation, on a level with ourselves.

ADAM CLARKE

41. *Not to all the people.* In the order of divine providence the public were no longer to be instructed by Jesus Christ personally, but it was necessary those who were to preach redemption in His name should be thoroughly furnished to this good and great work; therefore the time He spent on earth after His resurrection was devoted to the instruction of His disciples. *Witnesses chosen before of God.* That is, God chose such men to attest this fact as were in every way best qualified to give evidence on the subject. The first preachers of the gospel must be the witnesses of its facts.

42. *And he commanded us to preach.* By thus assuring them that Jesus Christ was appointed to judge the world he at once showed them the necessity of subjection to Him, that they might stand in the day of His appearing. *The Judge of quick and dead.* The word *quick* we retain from our ancient mother tongue, the Saxon, "to live." By *quick and dead* we are to understand: (1) all that had lived from the foundation of the world till that time, and all that were then alive; (2) all that should be found alive at the day of judgment, as well as all that had died previously.

43. *To him give all the prophets witness.* See Isa. ix. 6; lii. 7; liii, 5-6; lix. 20; Jer. xxxi, 34; Dan. ix. 24; Mic. vii. 18, etc.; and Zech. xiii. 1. As Jesus Christ was the sum and substance of the law and the Mosaic dispensation, so all the prophets bore testimony, either directly or indirectly, to Him; and indeed without Him and the salvation He has promised there is scarcely any meaning in the Mosaic economy nor in most of the allusions of the prophets. *Remission of sins.* The phrase means simply the "taking away of sins"; and this does not refer to the guilt of sin merely, but also to its power, nature, and consequences. All that is implied in pardon of sin, destruction of its tyranny, and purification from its pollution is here intended; and it is wrong to restrict such operations of mercy to pardon alone.

44. *While Peter yet spake.* It is not very likely that the words recorded by Luke are all that the apostle spoke on this occasion; but while he continued to discourse with them on this subject, *the Holy Ghost fell on all them which heard the word,* and His descent was known by their being enabled to speak with different kinds of tongues. In what manner this gift was bestowed we cannot tell; probably it was in the same way in which it had been given on the Day of Pentecost. For as they spake with tongues, which was the effect of the descent of the Spirit as flaming tongues on the heads of the disciples on the Day of Pentecost, it is very likely that the same appearance now took place.

45. *They of the circumcision . . . were astonished.* Because it was a maxim with them that the Shekinah or divine influence could not be revealed to any person who dwelt beyond the precincts of the Promised Land. Nor did any of them believe that the Divine Spirit could be communicated to any Gentile. It is no wonder, therefore, that they were amazed when they saw the Spirit of God so liberally given as He was on this occasion.

46. *And magnify God.* They had got new hearts as well as new tongues, and having believed with the heart unto righteousness, their tongues made confession unto salvation; and God was magnified for the mercy which He had imparted.

47. *Can any man forbid water?* These had evidently received the Holy Ghost and consequently were become members of the mystical body of Christ; and yet Peter requires that they shall receive baptism by water, that they might become members of the Christian Church. In other cases they received baptism first and the Spirit afterwards by the imposition of hands; see chap. xix. 4-6, where the disciples who had received only the baptism of John were baptized again with water in the name of the Lord Jesus; and after even this the apostles prayed and laid their hands on them before they were made partakers of the Holy Ghost. So we find that Jesus Christ had His water baptism as well as John, and that even He who gave the bap-

MATTHEW HENRY

himself to baptize them. Thus is there one unusual step of divine grace taken after another to bring the Gentiles into the church. How well is it for us that the grace of a good God is so much more extensive than the charity of some good men! Peter did not baptize them himself, but *commanded them to be baptized*, v. 48. The apostles received the commission to *go and disciple all nations by baptism*. But it was to prayer and the ministry of the word that they were to *give* themselves. The business of baptizing was therefore ordinarily devolved upon the inferior ministers; these acted by the orders of the apostles.

III. Their desire for further advantage by Peter's ministry: *They prayed him to tarry certain days*. They were not willing he should go away immediately, but earnestly begged he would stay for some time among them, that they might be further instructed by him. Those who have some acquaintance with Christ cannot but covet more. Even those that have received the Holy Ghost must see their need of the ministry of the word.

CHAPTER 11

Verses 1–18

It being so great a surprise to the believing as well as the unbelieving Jews, it is worth while to enquire how it was received.

I. Intelligence was presently brought of it to the church in Jerusalem, and thereabouts. Before he himself had returned to Jerusalem *the apostles and* the *brethren* there and *in Judæa heard that the Gentiles also had received the word of God*, that the Gentiles also themselves, with whom it had hitherto been thought unlawful to hold common conversation, had *received the word of God*. The word of God was preached to them, which was a greater honour put upon them than they expected. Thus often are the prejudices of pride and bigotry held fast against the clearest discoveries of divine truth. It was entertained and submitted to by them, which was a better work wrought upon them than they expected. They looked upon them as not inclined to religion, and therefore were surprised to hear that they had received the word of the Lord. We are too apt to despair of doing good to those who yet, when they are tried, prove very tractable.

II. Offence was taken at it by the believing Jews (*v.* 2, 3): *When Peter had himself come up to Jerusalem, those that were of the circumcision contended with him*. He *went in to men uncircumcised, and did eat with them*; and thereby they think he has stained, if not forfeited, the honour of his apostleship. It is the bane and damage of the church, to monopolize it, and to exclude those from it that are not in everything as we are. Christ's ministers must not think it strange if they be censured, not only by their professed enemies, but by their professing friends. But, if we have proved our own work, we may have rejoicing in ourselves, as Peter had, whatever reflections we may have from our brethren. Those that are zealous and courageous in the service of Christ must expect to be censured by those who, under pretence of being cautious, are cold and indifferent. Those who are of catholic, generous, charitable principles, must expect to be censured by such as are conceited and strait-laced.

III. Peter gave such a full and fair account of the matter of fact as was sufficient both to justify him, and to satisfy them (*v.* 4): *He rehearsed the matter from the beginning*.

1. He takes it for granted that if they had rightly understood how the matter was they would not have contended with him. We should be moderate in our censures, because if we rightly understood that which we are so forward to run down perhaps we should see cause to run in with it.

2. He is very willing to stand right in their opinion. He is ready to *give a reason of the hope that is in him* concerning the Gentiles, and why he had receded from his former sentiments, which were the same with theirs.

(1) He was instructed by a vision no longer to keep up the distinctions which were made by the ceremonial law; he relates the vision (*v.* 5, 6), as we had it before, *ch.* x. 9, &c. The sheet which was there said to be *let down to the earth* he here says came *even to him*. We should thus see all God's discoveries of himself, coming even to us, applying them by faith to ourselves. When the sheet *came to him he fastened his eyes upon it, and considered it*, v. 6. If we would be led into the knowledge of divine things, we must fix our minds upon them, and consider them. He tells them what orders he had to eat of all sorts of meat

JAMIESON, FAUSSET, BROWN

48. he commanded them to be baptized—not doing it with his own hands, as neither did Paul, save on rare occasions (I Cor. 1:14-17; cf. ch. 2:38, and John 4:2).

prayed . . . him to tarry certain days—"golden days" [BENGEL], spent, doubtless, in refreshing Christian fellowship, and in imparting and receiving fuller teaching on the several topics of the apostle's discourse.

CHAPTER 11

VSS. 1-18. PETER VINDICATES HIMSELF BEFORE THE CHURCH IN JERUSALEM FOR HIS PROCEDURE TOWARDS THE GENTILES. **1-11. the apostles and brethren . . . in Judea**—rather, 'throughout Judea.'

2. they . . . of the circumcision—not the Jewish Christians generally, for here there were no other, but such as, from their jealousy for "the middle wall of partition" which circumcision raised between Jew and Gentile, were *afterwards* known as "they of the circumcision." They doubtless embraced apostles as well as others.

3-4. Thou wentest in . . . . But Peter rehearsed the matter . . . —These objectors scruple not to demand from Peter, though the first among the apostles, an explanation of his conduct; nor is there any insinuation on Peter's part of disrespect towards his authority in that demand—a manifest proof that such authority was unknown both to the complainers and to himself.

ADAM CLARKE

tism of the Holy Ghost required the administration of water baptism also.

48. *To be baptized in the name of the Lord*. That is, in the name of Jesus Christ, which implied their taking upon them the public profession of Christianity, and believing on Christ Jesus as their Saviour and Sovereign; for as they were baptized in His name, they professed thereby to be His disciples and followers. *Then prayed they him to tarry certain days*. They felt the necessity of further instruction, and prayed him to continue his ministry a little longer among them; and to this he no doubt consented. This was, properly speaking, the commencement of the Christian Church, as composed of Jews and Gentiles, partaking of the same baptism, united under the same Head, made partakers of the same Spirit, and associated in the same aggregate body. Now was the middle wall of partition broken down, and the Gentiles admitted to the same privileges with the Jews.

CHAPTER 11

1. *And the apostles and brethren that were in Judaea*. According to Calmet, Judea is here put in opposition to Caesarea, which, though situated in Palestine, passed for a Greek city, being principally inhabited by pagans, Greeks, or Syrians.

2. *Contended with him*. A manifest proof this that the primitive church at Jerusalem had no conception of Peter's supremacy or of his being prince of the apostles. He is now called to account for his conduct, which they judged to be reprehensible.

3. *Thou wentest in to men uncircumcised*. In a Jew, this was no small offense; and as they did not know the reason of Peter's conduct, it is no wonder they should call him to account for it, as they considered it to be a positive transgression of the law and custom of the Jews.

4. *But Peter rehearsed the matter from the beginning, and expounded it by order*. To remove their prejudice and to give them the fullest reasons for his conduct, he thought it best to give them a simple relation of the whole affair; which he did, as we have seen in the preceding chapter, with a few additional circumstances here.

MATTHEW HENRY | JAMIESON, FAUSSET, BROWN | ADAM CLARKE

without distinction, asking no questions for conscience' sake, *v.* 7. He pleads that he was as averse to the thoughts of conversing with Gentiles, as they could be, and therefore refused the liberty given him: *Not so, Lord; for nothing common or unclean has at any time entered into my mouth*, *v.* 8. But he was told that God had cleansed those persons and things which were before polluted; and therefore that he must no longer call them common (*v.* 9); so that he was not to be blamed for changing his thoughts, when God had changed the thing. And, that they might be sure he was not deceived in it, he tells them it was done three times (*v.* 10). And, further to confirm him that it was a divine vision, the things he saw did not vanish away into the air, but *were drawn up again into heaven.*

(2) He was particularly directed by the Spirit to go along with the messengers that Cornelius sent. He observes to them the time when the messengers came—immediately after he had that vision; yet, lest this should not be sufficient to clear his way, the Spirit bade him *go with the men, nothing doubting* (*v.* 11, 12). He must make no scruple of going along with them.

(3) He took some of his brethren along with him, who were of the circumcision, that they might be satisfied as well as he. He did not act separately, but with advice; not rashly, but upon due deliberation.

(4) Cornelius had a vision too (*v.* 13): *He showed us how he had seen an angel in his house*, that bade him *send to Joppa for one Simon, whose surname is Peter*. Peter is the more confirmed in the truth of his vision by Cornelius's, and Cornelius by Peter's. Here is something added in what the angel said to Cornelius; before it was, *Send for Peter, and he shall speak to thee, he shall tell thee what thou oughtest to do* (*ch.* x. 6, 32); but here it is, "*He shall tell thee words whereby thou and thy house shall be saved*" (*v.* 14). The words of the gospel are words whereby we may be eternally saved; not merely by hearing them, but by believing and obeying them. They open the way of salvation to us. Those that embrace the gospel of Christ will have salvation brought by it to their families: "*Thou and all thy house shall be saved.* Thy house shall be as welcome to the benefit of the salvation as thou thyself, even the meanest servant thou hast." Now salvation is brought to the Gentiles.

(5) That which put the matter past all dispute was the descent of the Holy Ghost upon the Gentile hearers. The fact was plain and undeniable (*v.* 15): "*As I began to speak the Holy Ghost fell on them as on us at the beginning*." Thus God attested what was done, and declared his approbation of it. Peter was hereby put in mind of a saying of his Master's: *John baptized with water; but you shall be baptized with the Holy Ghost*, *v.* 16. The Holy Ghost was the gift of Christ, and the product and performance of that great promise which he left with them when he went to heaven. It was therefore without doubt from him that this gift came. As it was promised by his mouth, so it was performed by his hand. The gift of the Holy Ghost was a kind of baptism. Comparing that promise, so worded, with this gift just now conferred, he concluded that the question was determined by Christ himself (*v.* 17): "*Forasmuch then as God gave them the like gift as he did to us*—gave it to us as *believing in the Lord Jesus Christ*, and to them upon their believing in him—*What was I, that I could withstand God?* Could I refuse to baptize them with water, whom God had baptized with the Holy Ghost?" Those take too much upon them who contrive how to exclude from their communion those whom God has taken into communion with himself.

IV. This account which Peter gave of the matter satisfied them. Some people, when they have fastened a censure upon a person, will stick to it, though afterwards it appear ever so plainly to be unjust and groundless. It was not so here. When they heard this they held their peace and said no more against what Peter had done. They not only held their peace from quarrelling with Peter, but opened their mouths to glorify God. They were thankful that God had shown more mercy to the poor Gentiles than they were inclined to show them, saying, *Then hath God also to the Gentiles granted repentance unto life!* He hath granted them the grace of repentance, in having given them his Holy Spirit, who gives a sight of sin and sorrow for it, and then a sight of Christ and joy in him. Repentance, if it be true, is unto life. Those that by repentance die unto sin thenceforward live unto God; and then, and not till then, we begin to live indeed, and it shall be to eternal life. Repentance is God's gift; it is not only his free grace that accepts it, but his mighty grace that works it in us. Wherever God designs to give life he gives repentance. God has exalted his Son Jesus not only to *give re-*

G. CAMPBELL MORGAN:

In the previous chapter (v. 29), these words occur: "Arise, and get thee down, and go with them, *nothing doubting*: for I have sent them." Such was the word of the Spirit to Peter on the housetop in Joppa. Again, in this eleventh chapter (v. 12), Peter says: "And the Spirit bade me go with them, *making no distinction.*" The verb "contended with them" is exactly the same as that translated in those two passages: "nothing doubting" and "making no distinction." The word *doubting* is an insufficient word. The Spirit of God commanded Peter to go with these men, without wavering, without discrimination, without making distinction. When he came to Jerusalem, the brethren there did this very thing. They discriminated with him, debated with him, contended with him; and he told them that the Spirit had charged him to go with these men doing nothing of the kind. It is quite evident that these men in Jerusalem were passing through the mental experience through which Peter had passed. It was perfectly natural that he should waver, that he should discriminate between Gentiles and Hebrews; but the Spirit had charged him to make no such distinction, to go without wavering or contention.—*The Acts of the Apostles*

12-18. we entered the man's house—No mention of Cornelius' name, much less of his high position, as if that affected the question. To the charge, "Thou wentest in to *men* uncircumcised," he simply speaks of the uncircumcised "*man*" to whom he had been divinely sent. **13. seen an angel**—lit., '*the* angel,' for the rumor took that definite shape.

14. Who shall tell thee words whereby thou and all thy house shall be saved—The historian makes the angel express this much more generally (ch. 10:6). So also the subsequent report of it by the deputies and by Cornelius himself to Peter (ch. 10:22, 32). But as Peter tarried with Cornelius certain days, and they doubtless talked over the wonderful scene together, perhaps this fuller and richer form of what the angel said was given to Peter; or the apostle himself may have *expressed* what the angel certainly *designed* by directing them to send for him. Observe, "salvation" is here made to hang upon "*words,*" i.e., the Gospel message concerning Christ. But on the "salvation" of Cornelius, see on ch. 10:34, 35. On that of his "house," see on Luke 19:10.

16-17. Then remembered I the word . . . John . . . baptized with water; but ye shall be baptized with the Holy Ghost. Forasmuch then . . .—i.e., 'Since God Himself has put them on a level with ourselves, by bestowing on them what the Lord Jesus pronounced the higher baptism of the Holy Ghost, would it not have been to withstand God if I had withheld from them the lower baptism of water, and kept aloof from them as still "unclean?" '

18. held their peace and glorified God—Well had it been if, when Paul afterwards adduced equally resistless evidence in justification of the same line of procedure, this Jewish party had shown the same reverential and glad submission! **Then hath God also granted to the Gentiles . . .**—rather, 'granted to the Gentiles also.' (See a similar misplacement of "also" in Heb. 12:1.) To "*grant* repentance unto life"—i.e., 'such as issues in life' (cf. II Cor. 7:10, "repentance unto salvation")—is more than to be willing to pardon upon repentance [GROTIUS]. The case of Cornelius is so manifestly one of *grace* reigning in every stage of his religious history, that we can hardly doubt that this was just the feature of it which they meant here to express. *And this is the grace that reigns in every conversion.*

12. *These six brethren.* Probably pointing to them, being present, as proper persons to confirm the truth of what he was delivering.

14. *Thou and all thy house shall be saved.* This is an additional circumstance. Before, it was said, chap. x. 6, Peter "shall tell thee what thou oughtest to do"; and, in v. 32, "who, when he cometh, shall speak unto thee." But in Peter's relation the matter is more explicitly declared: He *shall tell thee words, whereby thou and all thy house shall be saved.* He shall announce to you all the doctrine of salvation.

16. *Ye shall be baptized with the Holy Ghost.* These words are very remarkable. The words of our Lord, as quoted in chap. i. 5, to which Peter refers here, have been supposed by many to be referred to the apostles alone; but here it is evident that Peter believed they were a promise made to all Christians, i.e., to all, whether Jews or Gentiles, who should believe on Jesus Christ. Therefore when he saw that the Holy Ghost fell upon those Gentiles, he considered it a fulfillment of our Lord's promise.

17. *God gave them the like gift.* Viz., the Holy Spirit, and His various gifts and graces, in the same way and in the same measure in which He gave them to us Jews. *What was I, that I could withstand God?* It was not I who called them to salvation; it was God; and the thing is proved to be from God alone, for none other could dispense the Holy Spirit.

18. *They held their peace.* Their prejudices were confounded; they considered the subject and saw that it was from God. Then they glorified Him, because they saw that He had granted unto the *Gentiles repentance unto life.* As the word which we translate *repentance* signifies literally "a change of mind," it may be here referred to a change of religious views. And as *repentance* signifies a change of life and conduct, from evil to good, so the word may be used here to signify a change from a false religion to the true one, from idolatry to the worship of the true God. The Christians who were present were all satisfied with Peter's account and apology; but it does not appear that all were ultimately satisfied, as we know there were serious disputes in the Church afterward on this very subject. See chap. xv. 5, where Christian believers from among the Pharisees insisted that it was necessary to circumcise the converted Gentiles and cause them to keep the law of Moses. This opinion was carried much further in the church at Jerusalem afterwards as may be seen at large in chap. xxi.

MATTHEW HENRY

pentance to Israel, and the remission of sins (*ch.* v. 31), but to the Gentiles also.

Verses 19–26

We have here an account of the planting and watering of a church at Antioch, the chief city of Syria, reckoned afterwards the third most considerable city of the empire. It is suggested that Luke, the penman of this history, as well as Theophilus, to whom he dedicates it, was of Antioch, which may be the reason why he takes more particular notice of the success of the gospel at Antioch.

I. The first preachers of the gospel there were such as were dispersed from Jerusalem by persecution, that persecution which arose at the time of Stephen's death (*v.* 19): *They travelled as far as Phenice preaching the word.* Thus what was intended for the hurt of the church was made to work for its good. The enemies designed to scatter and lose them, Christ designed to scatter and use them.

1. Those that *fled from persecution* did not flee from their work. Those that persecuted the preachers of the gospel hoped thereby to prevent their carrying it to the Gentile world; but it proved that they did but hasten it the sooner. Those that were persecuted in one city fled to another; but they carried their religion along with them.

2. They pressed forward in their work. When they had preached successfully in Judæa, Samaria, and Galilee, they travelled into Phoenicia, into the island of Cyprus, and into Syria. Though the further they travelled the more they exposed themselves, yet they travelled on; *further still,* was their motto.

3. They *preached the word to none but to the Jews only* who were dispersed in all those parts. They did not yet understand that the Gentiles were to be fellow-heirs, but left the Gentiles either to turn Jews, or else remain as they were.

4. They particularly applied themselves to the Hellenist Jews, here called the Grecians. Many of the preachers were natives of Judæa and Jerusalem; but some of them were by birth of Cyprus and Cyrene, as Barnabas himself (*ch.* iv. 36), and Simon (Mark xv. 21). These, being themselves Grecian Jews, had a particular concern for those of their own denomination, and applied themselves closely to them at Antioch. To them they preached the Lord Jesus. This was the constant subject of their preaching; what else should the ministers of Christ preach, but Christ?

5. They had wonderful success in their preaching, *v.* 21. Their preaching was accompanied with a divine power. *The hand of the Lord was with them,* to bring that home to the hearts and consciences of men which they could but speak to the outward ear. These were not apostles, but ordinary ministers, yet they had the hand of the Lord with them, and did wonders. Abundance of good was done: *A great number believed, and turned unto the Lord.* They believed; they were convinced of the truth of the gospel. The effect of this was that they *turned unto the Lord.* They turned from a confidence in the righteousness of the law, to rely only upon the righteousness of Christ, the righteousness which is by faith. They turned to the Lord Jesus, and he became all in all with them. Whatever we profess or pretend, we do not really believe the gospel if we do not cordially embrace Christ offered to us in the gospel.

II. The good work thus begun at Antioch was carried on to great perfection; by the ministry of Barnabas and Saul.

1. The church at Jerusalem sent Barnabas thither.

(1) They heard the good news, that the gospel was received at Antioch, *v.* 22. *Tidings of these things came to the ears of the church that was in Jerusalem.*

(2) They despatched Barnabas to them. They *sent him forth* as an envoy from them. He must go *as far as Antioch.* It is probable that Barnabas had a particular genius for work of this kind, and, his talent lying this way, he was fittest to be employed in this work. God gives various gifts for various services.

(3) Barnabas was wonderfully pleased to find that the gospel got ground, and that some of his countrymen, men of Cyprus, were instrumental in it (*v.* 23): *When he came, and had seen the grace of God, he was glad.* He saw the grace of God among them. What we see which is good in any we must call God's grace in them. We must be glad to see the grace of God in others, and the more when we see it where we did not expect it.

(4) He did what he could to confirm those in the faith who were converted to the faith. He *exhorted them.* It is the same word with that by which the name of Barnabas is interpreted (*ch.* iv. 36)—*a son of exhortation;* his talent lay that way. Or, being *a son of consolation* (for so we render the word), he *comforted or encouraged them with purpose of heart*

JAMIESON, FAUSSET, BROWN

19-24. THE GOSPEL BEING PREACHED TO GENTILES AT ANTIOCH ALSO, BARNABAS IS SENT THITHER FROM JERUSALEM, WHO HAILS THEIR ACCESSION AND LABORS AMONG THEM. **19-24. they which were scattered abroad upon the persecution that arose about Stephen**—and who "went everywhere preaching the word" (ch. 8:4). **travelled as far as Phenice**—that part of the Mediterranean coast which, commencing a little north of Cæsarea, stretches northwards for upwards of 100 miles, halfway to Antioch. **and Cyprus**—See on ch. 4:36. An active commercial intercourse subsisted between Phenice and Cyprus. **and Antioch**—near the head of the northeast coast of the Mediterranean, on the river Orontes, and containing a large colony of Jews, to whose religion there were there numerous proselytes. "It was almost an Oriental Rome, in which all the forms of the civilized life of the empire found some representative; and through the two first centuries of the Christian era it was what Constantinople became afterwards, 'the Gate of the East' " [Hows].

20. some of them were men of Cyprus and Cyrene—(see on Luke 23:26); as Lucius, mentioned in ch. 13:1. **spake unto the Grecians**—rather, "the *Greeks,*" i.e., uncircumcised Gentiles (as the true reading beyond doubt is). The Gospel had, from the first, been preached to "the Grecians" or Greek-speaking *Jews,* and these "men of Cyprus and Cyrene" were themselves "Grecians." How, then, can we suppose that the historian would note, as something new and singular (vs. 22), that some of the dispersed Christians preached to *them?*

21. a great number believed—Thus the accession of Cornelius and his party was not the first admission of uncircumcised Gentiles into the Church. (See on ch. 10:1.) Nay, we read of no influence which the accession of Cornelius and his house had on the further progress of the Gospel among the Gentiles; whereas there here open upon us operations upon the Gentiles from quite a different quarter, and attended with ever growing success. The only great object served by the case of Cornelius was *the formal recognition of the principles which that case afterwards secured.* (See on ch. 15.)

22. sent . . . Barnabas . . . as far as Antioch—implying that even on the way to Antioch he found churches to visit [OLSHAUSEN]. It was in the first instance, no doubt, a mission of inquiry; and no one could be more suitable to inquire into the proceedings of those Cyprians and Cyrenians than one who was himself a "Grecian" of Cyprus (ch. 4:36), and "a son of consolation."

23. when he . . . had seen the grace of God—in the new converts. **was glad**—owned and rejoiced in it at once as divine, though they were uncircumcised.

ADAM CLARKE

19. *The persecution that arose about Stephen.* That is, those who were obliged to flee from Jerusalem at the time of that persecution in which Stephen lost his life. See chap. viii. 1. *Phenice.* Phoenicia, a country between Galilee and Syria, along the coast of the Mediterranean Sea, including Tyre, Sidon, etc. It is often mentioned as a part of Syria. *Cyprus.* An island of the Mediterranean Sea, over against Syria. *Antioch.* A city of Syria, built by Antiochus Seleucus, near the Orontes River, at that time one of the most celebrated cities of the East.

Unto the Jews only. For they knew nothing of the vision of Peter, and did not believe that God would open the door of faith to the Gentiles. The next verse informs us that there were others who were better instructed.

20. *Men of . . . Cyrene.* The metropolis of the Cyrenaica, a country of Africa, bounded on the north by the Mediterranean and on the south by the Sahara. *Spake unto the Grecians.* "The Hellenists." Who these were, we have already seen, chap. vi and ix. 29, viz., Jews living in Greek cities and speaking the Greek language. But instead of *Grecians,* "Greeks" is the reading of several MSS. On this evidence Griesbach has admitted it into the text, and few critics entertain any doubt of the genuineness of the reading. This intimates that, besides preaching the gospel to the Hellenistic Jews, some of them preached it to heathen Greeks.

21. *The hand of the Lord was with them.* By the *hand, arm,* and *finger* of God, in the Scripture, different displays or exertions of His power are intended. Here it means that the energy of God accompanied them and applied their preaching to the souls of all attentive hearers. *A great number believed.* That Jesus was the Christ, and that He had died for their offenses and risen again for their justification. Because the apostles preached the truth, and the hand of God was with them, therefore *a great number believed, and turned unto the Lord,* becoming His disciples.

22. *The church which was in Jerusalem.* This was the original, the mother church of Christianity, not the church of Rome. A Christian church means a company of believers in Christ Jesus, united for the purposes of Christian fellowship and edification in righteousness. *They sent forth Barnabas.* It seems, then, that the church collectively had power to commission and send forth any of its own members whom it saw God had qualified for a particular work. There must have been, even at that time, an acknowledged superiority of some members of the church beyond others. The apostles held the first rank; the deacons (probably the same as those called prophets, as being next chosen), the second; and perhaps those called evangelists, simply preachers of the truth, the third rank.

23. *Had seen the grace of God.* That is, had seen the effects produced by the grace of God. *Was glad.* Not envious because God had blessed the labors of others of his Master's servants, but rejoiced to find that the work of salvation was carried on by such instruments as God chose and condescended to use. They who cannot rejoice in the conversion of sinners because they have not been the means of it, or because such converts or their ministers have not precisely the same views of certain doctrines which they have themselves, show that they have in them little, if anything, of the mind that was in Christ. *With purpose of heart they would*

MATTHEW HENRY

to cleave to the Lord. Barnabas was glad for what he saw of the grace of God among them, and therefore was the more earnest with them to persevere. To *cleave to the Lord.* Not to fall off from following him, not to flag and tire in following him. Not only to hold him fast, but to hold fast by him. To cleave to him with purpose of heart, with an intelligent, firm, and deliberate resolution.

(5) Herein he gave a proof of his good character (*v.* 24): *He was a good man, and full of the Holy Ghost, and of faith.* He was not only a righteous man, but *a good man,* a good-tempered man. Ministers that are so recommend themselves and their doctrine very much to the good opinion of those that are without. He was a good man, that is, a charitable man; so he had approved himself, when he sold an estate, and gave the money to the poor, *ch.* iv. 37. He was richly endued with the gifts and graces of the Spirit. The goodness of his natural disposition would not have qualified him for this service if he had not been *full of the Holy Ghost.* He was full of faith, full of the grace of faith, and full of the fruits of that faith that works by love.

(6) He was instrumental to do good, by bringing in those that were without, as well as by building up those that were within: *Much people were added to the Lord.*

2. Barnabas went to fetch Saul. Barnabas takes a journey to Tarsus to tell him what a door of opportunity was opened at Antioch, and to desire him to come and spend some time with him there, *v.* 25, 26. And here also it appears that Barnabas was a good sort of a man in two things: (1) That he would take so much pains to bring an active useful man out of obscurity. It was he that brought him out of the corner into which he was driven, into a more public station. It is a very good work to fetch a candle from under a bushel, and to set it in a candlestick. (2) That he would bring in Saul at Antioch, who, being a *chief speaker* (*ch.* xiv. 12), would be likely to eclipse him there, by outshining him. Barnabas brought Saul to Antioch, though it might be the lessening of himself.

3. We are here further told,

(1) What service was now done to the church at Antioch. Paul and Barnabas continued there a whole year, presiding in their religious assemblies, and preaching the gospel, *v.* 26. *Teaching the people* is one part of the work of ministers. They are not only to be the people's mouth to God in prayer and praise, but God's mouth to the people in opening the scriptures, and teaching the good knowledge of the Lord. It is a great encouragement to ministers when they have opportunity of teaching much people, of casting the net of the gospel where there is a large shoal of fish. Preaching is not only for the conversion of those that are without, but for the instruction and edification of those that are within.

(2) What honour was now put upon the church *at Antioch: There the disciples were first called Christians.* Two such great men as Paul and Barnabas continuing there so long, being exceedingly followed, Christian assemblies made a greater figure there than anywhere, which was the reason of their being called *Christians* first there. Hitherto those who gave up their names to Christ were called *disciples, learners, scholars;* but henceforward they were called *Christians.* [1] Thus the reproachful names which their enemies had hitherto branded them with would, perhaps, be superseded. They called them *Nazarenes* (*ch.* xxiv. 5), *the men of that way, that by-way,* which had no name; and thus they prejudiced people against them. To remove the prejudice, they gave themselves a name which their enemies could not but say was proper. [2] Thus those who before their conversion had been distinguished by the names of Jews and Gentiles might after their conversion be called by one and the same name. Let not one say, "I was a *Jew*"; nor the other, "I was a *Gentile*"; when both the one and the other must now say, "I am a *Christian.*" [3] Thus they studied to do honour to their Master, and showed that they were not ashamed to own their relation to him. They took their denomination not from the name of his person, *Jesus,* but of his office, *Christ—anointed,* so putting their creed into their names, *that Jesus is the Christ.* Their enemies will turn this name to their reproach, and impute it to them as their crime, but they will glory in it. [4] Thus they now owned their dependence upon Christ. [5] Thus they laid upon themselves, and all that should ever profess that name, a strong and lasting obligation to follow the example of Christ, and to devote themselves entirely to the honour of Christ. Are we Christians? Then we ought to do nothing to the reproach of that worthy name by which we are called. And as we must look upon ourselves as Christians, and carry ourselves accordingly, so we must look upon others as

JAMIESON, FAUSSET, BROWN

exhorted them all that with purpose of heart—as opposed to a hasty and fickle discipleship—**they would cleave unto the Lord**—the Lord Jesus.

24. For he was a good man—The sense of "good" here is plainly "large-hearted," "liberal-minded," rising above narrow Jewish sectarianism, and that because, as the historian adds, he was "full of the Holy Ghost and of faith."

and much people were added unto the Lord—This proceeding of Barnabas, so full of wisdom, love, and zeal, was blessed to the great increase of the Christian community in that important city.

25, 26. Barnabas, Finding the Work in Antioch Too Much for Him, goes to Tarsus for Saul—They Labor There Together for a Whole Year with Much Success, and Antioch Becomes the Honored Birthplace of the Term CHRISTIAN. **25. Then departed Barnabas to Tarsus for to seek Saul**—Of course, this was after the hasty despatch of Saul to Tarsus, no doubt by Barnabas himself among others, to escape the fury of the Jews at Jerusalem. And as Barnabas was the first to take the converted persecutor by the hand and procure his recognition as a disciple by the brethren at Jerusalem (ch. 9:27), so he alone seems at that early period to have discerned in him those peculiar endowments by virtue of which he was afterwards to eclipse all others. Accordingly, instead of returning to Jerusalem, to which, no doubt, he sent accounts of his proceedings from time to time, finding that the mine in Antioch was rich in promise and required an additional and powerful hand to work, he leaves it for a time, takes a journey to Tarsus, "finds Saul" (seemingly implying—not that he lay hid [Bengel], but that he was engaged at the time in some preaching circuit—see on ch. 15:23), and returns with him to Antioch. Nor were his hopes disappointed. As co-pastors, for the time being, of the Church there, they so labored that the Gospel, even in that great and many-sided community, achieved for itself a name which will live and be gloried in as long as this world lasts, as the symbol of all that is most precious to the fallen family of man:—"*The disciples were called* Christians *first in Antioch.*" This name originated not within, but without, the Church; not with their *Jewish* enemies, by whom they were styled "Nazarenes" (ch. 24:5), but with the *heathen* in Antioch, and (as the form of the word shows) with the *Romans,* not the *Greeks* there [Olshausen]. It was not at first used in a good sense (as ch. 26:28, and I Pet. 4:16 show), though hardly framed out of contempt [as De Wette, Baumgarten, etc.]; but as it was a noble testimony to the light in which the Church regarded Christ—honoring Him as their only Lord and Saviour, dwelling continually on His name, and glorying in it—so it was felt to be too apposite and beautiful to be allowed to die.

ADAM CLARKE

cleave unto the Lord. These converts had begun well; they must continue and persevere. God gave them the grace, the principle of life and action; it was their business to use this. Barnabas therefore exhorted them with "determination" of heart, with "set, fixed purpose and resolution," that *they would cleave unto the Lord:* "to remain with the Lord"; to continue in union and fellowship with Him; to be faithful in keeping His truth, and obedient in the practice of it. It is absurd to talk of being children of God and of absolute, final perseverance when the soul has lost its spiritual union. There is no perseverance but in cleaving to the Lord; he who in his works denies Him does not cleave to Him.

24. *For he was a good man.* Here is a proper character of a minister of the gospel. (1) He is *a good man.* His bad heart is changed, his evil dispositions rooted out; and the mind that was in Christ implanted in him. (2) He is *full of the Holy Ghost.* He is holy, because the Spirit of holiness dwells in him. (3) He is full of *faith.* He implicitly credits his Lord; he knows that He could not lie—that His word could not fail.

25. *To Tarsus, for to seek Saul.* The persecution raised against him obliged him to take refuge in his own city, where, as a Roman citizen, his person was in safety. See chap. ix. 29-30.

26. *He brought him unto Antioch.* As this city was the metropolis of Syria and the third city for importance in the whole Roman Empire, Rome and Alexandria alone being more eminent, Barnabas might think it expedient to have for his assistance a person of such eminent talents as Saul, and who was especially appointed by Christ to proclaim the gospel to the Gentiles. Saul appears also to have been a thorough master of the Greek tongue, and consequently the better qualified to explain the gospel to the Greek philosophers, and to defend it against their cavils. Barnabas, also being a native of Cyprus, chap. iv. 36, where the Greek language was spoken, was judged to be proper for this mission, perhaps on this account, as well as on account of his disinterestedness, holiness, and zeal.

And the disciples were called Christians first in Antioch. It is evident they had the name *Christians* from *Christ,* their Master, as the Platonists and Pythagoreans had their name from their masters, Plato and Pythagoras. Now as these had their name from those great masters because they attended their teaching and credited their doctrines, so the disciples were called *Christians* because they took Christ for their Teacher, crediting His doctrines and following the rule of life laid down by Him. It has been a question, By whom was this name given to the disciples? Some think they assumed it; others that the inhabitants of Antioch gave it to them; and others, that it was given by Saul and Barnabas. The word in our common text which we translate *were called* signifies, in the New Testament, to "appoint, warn, or nominate," by divine direction. In this sense the word is used in Matt. ii. 12; Luke ii. 26; and in the preceding chapter of this book, v. 22. If, therefore, the name was given by divine appointment, it is most likely that Saul and Barnabas were directed to give it; and that therefore the name *Christian* is from God, as well as that grace and holiness which are so essentially required and implied in the character. Before this time the Jewish converts were simply called, among themselves, *disciples,* i.e., scholars; *believers, saints, the church,* or *assembly;* and, by their enemies, *Nazarenes, Galileans,* the *men of this way* or *sect;* and perhaps by other names which are not come down to us. They considered themselves as one family, and hence the appellation of *brethren* was frequent among them. A Christian, therefore, is the highest character which any human being can bear upon earth, and to receive it from God, as those appear to have done—how glorious the title! It is however worthy of remark that this name occurs in only three places in the New Testament: here, and in chap. xxvi. 28, and in 1 Pet. iv. 16.

MATTHEW HENRY

Christians, and carry ourselves towards them accordingly. A Christian should be loved and respected for his sake whose name he bears, because he belongs to Christ.

Verses 27–30

When our Lord Jesus *ascended on high he gave gifts unto men,* not only *apostles and evangelists, but prophets.*

I. A visit which some of these prophets made to Antioch (*v.* 27): *In these days came prophets from Jerusalem to Antioch.* They came from Jerusalem. Jerusalem had been infamous for *killing the prophets* and abusing them, and therefore is now justly deprived of these prophets. They came to Antioch. Barnabas came to exhort them, and they, having received the exhortation well, now have prophets sent them *to show them things to come.*

II. A particular prediction of a famine approaching, delivered by one of these prophets, his name *Agabus*; we read of him again prophesying Paul's imprisonment, *ch.* xxi. 10, 11. Here he stood up and prophesied, *v.* 28. Whence he had his prophecy. *He signified it by the Spirit, that there should be* a famine. What the prophecy was: *There should be great dearth throughout all the world,* so that many of the poor should perish for want of bread. This should be not in one particular country, but *through all the world,* that is, all the Roman empire. Christ had foretold in general *that there should be famines*; but Agabus foretells one very remarkable famine now at hand. The accomplishment of it: *It came to pass in the days of Claudius Cæsar;* it began in the second year of his reign, and continued to the fourth, if not longer. Several of the Roman historians make mention of it, as does also Josephus.

III. The good use they made of this prediction. When they were told of a famine at hand, they did not hoard up corn for themselves; but, as became Christians, laid by for charity to relieve others.

1. What they determined—that *every man, according to his ability,* should *send relief to the brethren that dwelt in Judæa, v.* 29. The persons that were recommended to them as objects of charity were *the brethren that dwelt in Judæa.* Though we must, as we have opportunity, *do good to all men,* yet we must have a special regard *to the household of faith.* No poor must be neglected, but God's poor most particularly regarded. But the communion of saints is here extended further, and provision is made by the church at Antioch for the relief of the poor in Judæa, whom they call their brethren. Now we may suppose that the greatest part of those who turned Christians in that country were the poor. If there came a famine it would go very hard with them; and, if any of them should perish for want, it would be a great reproach to the Christian profession; and therefore this early care was taken, to send them a stock beforehand, lest, if it should be deferred till the famine came, it should be too late. The agreement there was among the disciples about it, that *every man* should contribute, *according to his ability,* to this good work. Merchants find their account in sending effects to countries that lie very remote; and so should we in giving alms to those afar off that need them, which therefore we should be forward to do when we are called to it. What may be said to be *according to our ability* we must judge for ourselves, but must be careful *that we judge righteous judgment.*

2. They did as they determined (*v.* 30). *Which also they did.* They not only talked of it, but they did it. Many a good motion of that kind is made and commended, but it is not prosecuted, and so comes to nothing. The collection was made, and was so considerable that they thought it worth while *to send Barnabas and Saul to Jerusalem.* They sent it *to the elders of the churches in Judæa,* to be by them distributed according to the necessity of the receivers, as it had been contributed according to the ability of the givers. It was sent *by Barnabas and Saul.* It is no disparagement, in an extraordinary case, for ministers of the gospel to be messengers of the church's charity.

JAMIESON, FAUSSET, BROWN

27-30. By Occasion of a Famine, Barnabas and Saul Return to Jerusalem with a Contribution for the Relief of Their Suffering Brethren. **27. came prophets from Jerusalem**—inspired teachers, a class we shall afterwards frequently meet with, who sometimes, but not necessarily, foretold future events. They are classed next to apostles (I Cor. 12:28, 29; Eph. 4:11).

28. that there should be great dearth throughout all the world—the whole Roman empire. **which came to pass in the days of Claudius Cæsar**—Four famines occurred during his reign. This one in Judea and the adjacent countries took place, A.D. 41 [Josephus, *Antiquities,* 20:2, 5]. *An important date for tracing out the chronology of the Acts.* (But this subject is too difficult and extensive to admit of being handled here.)

29. Then the disciples, every man according to his ability, determined to send relief . . . .—This was the pure prompting of Christian love, which shone so bright in those earliest days of the Gospel.

30. sent it to the elders—an office well known to be borrowed from the synagogue; *after the model of which, and not at all of the temple, the Christian Churches were constituted by the apostles.* **by the hands of Barnabas and Saul**—This was Saul's second visit to Jerusalem after his conversion.

ADAM CLARKE

27. *Came prophets from Jerusalem.* Though the term prophet is used in the New Testament simply to signify a "teacher," yet here it evidently means also such as were under divine inspiration, and foretold future events. This was certainly the case with Agabus, v. 28, though perhaps his ordinary character was that of a "teacher" or "preacher." It seems from various scriptures, Romans xii; 1 Corinthians xiii and xiv, that the prophets of the New Testament were: (1) teachers or preachers in general; (2) persons who on special occasions were under the influence of the Divine Spirit, and then foretold certain future events; (3) persons who recited hymns to the honor of God in the public assemblies of the Christians; (4) persons who prayed in those assemblies, having sometimes the gift of tongues, at other times not. From Ephes. ii. 20 and iii. 5, we learn that the *prophets* of the Christian Church were inferior to the apostles; but, from v. 11 of Eph. iv, we see that they were superior to all other teachers, even to evangelists and pastors.

28. *Agabus.* This prophet, of whom we know nothing, is once more mentioned, chap. xxi. 10. He was probably a Jew, but whether converted now to Christianity we cannot tell. *Great dearth throughout all the world.* The words probably here mean the land of Judea, though sometimes by this phrase the whole Roman Empire is intended. In the former sense the disciples appear to have understood it, as the next verse informs us; for they determined to send relief to their brethren in Judea, which they could not have done had the famine been general. It does not appear that they expected it to extend even to Antioch in Syria, where they then were, else they would have thought of making provision for themselves.

It is well-known from history that there were several famines in the reign of Claudius. Dion Cassius, lib. lx, mentions a severe famine in the first and second year of the reign of Claudius, which was sorely felt in Rome itself. A second famine happened about the fourth year of this reign, which continued for several years, and greatly afflicted the land of Judea. Several authors notice this, but particularly Josephus, *Ant.,* l. xx, c. 5, s. 2, where, having mentioned Tiberius Alexander as succeeding to the procuratorship in the place of Cuspius Fadus, he says that, "during the government of these procurators, a great famine afflicted Judea." A third famine is mentioned by Eusebius, in *An. Abrahami,* which commences with the calends of October, A.D. 48, which was so powerful "in Greece that a modius [about half a bushel of grain] was sold for six drachmas." A fourth famine, which took place in the eleventh year of Claudius, is mentioned by Tacitus, *Annal.,* l. xii, s. 43, in which there was so great a dearth of provisions, and famine in consequence, that it was esteemed a divine judgment.

It may now be inquired, To which of these famines in the reign of Claudius does the prophecy of Agabus refer? Most learned men are of opinion that the famine of which Agabus prophesied was that mentioned above which took place in the fourth year of this emperor, A.D. 47. This famine is particularly mentioned by Josephus, *Ant.,* l. xx, c. 2, s. 5, who describes it as "a very great famine, in which many died for want of food."

29. *Then the disciples . . . determined to send relief.* These were probably Gentile converts; and as they considered themselves receiving the spiritual blessings, which they now so happily enjoyed, through the means of the Christians in Judea, they resolved to communicate to them a portion of their temporal goods; and every man did this *according to his ability,* i.e., he gave a certain proportion of the property with which the providence of God had entrusted him.

MATTHEW HENRY

CHAPTER 12

Verses 1–4

Ever since the conversion of Paul, we have heard no more of the agency of the priests in persecuting the saints at Jerusalem. Here the storm arises from another point. The civil power acts by itself in the persecution. But Herod, though originally of an Edomite family, yet seems to have been a proselyte to the Jewish religion; for Josephus says he was zealous for the Mosaic rites, a bigot for the ceremonies. He was not only (as Herod Antipas was) tetrarch of Galilee, but had also the government of Judæa committed to him by Claudius the emperor, and resided most at Jerusalem, where he was at this time. Three things we are here told he did:

I. He *stretched forth his hands to vex certain of the church, v.* 1. *Herod laid hands upon some of the church to afflict them,* so some read it. See how he advances gradually. He began with some of the members of the church; played first at small game, but afterwards flew at the apostles themselves. He began with vexing them only, or afflicting them. Afterwards he proceeded to greater instances of cruelty.

II. *He killed James the brother of John with the sword, v.* 2. We are here to consider, 1. Who the martyr was: it was *James the brother of John*; so called to distinguish him from the other James the brother of Joses. This who was here crowned with martyrdom was one of the first three of Christ's disciples. He was one of those whom Christ called *Boanerges—Sons of thunder*; and perhaps by his powerful awakening preaching he had provoked Herod, as John Baptist did the other Herod. He was one of those sons of Zebedee whom Christ told *that they should drink of the cup that he was to drink of, and be baptized with the baptism that he was to be baptized with,* Matt. xx. 23. And now those words of Christ were made good in him. The apostle died a martyr, to show the rest of them what they must expect. 2. What kind of death he suffered: his head was *cut off with a sword,* a more disgraceful way of being beheaded than with an axe. It is strange that we have not a more full account of the martyrdom of this great apostle, as we had of Stephen. But even this short mention is sufficient to let us know that the first preachers of the gospel were so well assured of the truth of it that they sealed it with their blood.

III. He imprisoned Peter. When he had beheaded James, *he proceeded further to take Peter also.* Blood to the bloodthirsty does but make them more so, and the way of persecution, as of other sins, is downhill; when they are in they find they must on. Those that take one bold step in a sinful way give Satan advantage against them to tempt them to take another. It is therefore our wisdom to take heed of the beginnings of sin. He did this *because he saw it pleased the Jews.* The Jews made themselves guilty of the blood of James by showing themselves well pleased with it afterwards. Those will be reckoned with as persecutors who take pleasure in others' persecuting. Though he had no reason to fear displeasing them if he did not, yet he hoped to please them by doing it, and so make amends for displeasing them in something else. Those make themselves an easy prey to Satan who make it their business to please men. *Then were the days of unleavened bread.* It was at the feast of the passover. At the passover, when *the Jews came from all parts to Jerusalem to keep the feast,* they irritated one another against the Christians, and were then more violent than at other times. Here is an account of Peter's imprisonment (*v.* 4): *When he* had laid hands on him, *he put him in prison.* He was *delivered to four quaternions of soldiers,* that is, to sixteen, who were to be a guard upon him, four at a time. Thus they thought they had him fast. Herod's design was, *after Easter, to bring him forth unto the people.* He would make a spectacle of him. Herod will gratify them with the sight of Peter in bonds, of Peter upon the block, that they may feed their eyes with such a pleasing spectacle. And very ambitious surely he was to please the people who was willing thus to please them! He would do this *after Easter—after the passover,* certainly so it ought to be read, for it is the same word that is always so rendered. After the hurry of the feast was over, and the town was empty, he would entertain them with Peter's public trial and execution. And both Herod and the people long to have the feast over, that they may gratify themselves with this barbarous entertainment.

Verses 5–19

We have here an account of Peter's deliverance out of prison.

JAMIESON, FAUSSET, BROWN

CHAPTER 12

VSS. 1-19. PERSECUTION OF THE CHURCH BY HEROD AGRIPPA I—MARTYRDOM OF JAMES AND MIRACULOUS DELIVERANCE OF PETER. **1-3. Herod the king**—grandson of Herod the Great, and son of Aristobulus. He at this time ruled over all his father's dominions. PALEY has remarked the accuracy of the historian here. For thirty years before this there was no king at Jerusalem exercising supreme authority over Judea, nor was there ever afterwards, save during the three last years of Herod's life, within which the transactions occurred.

2. killed James . . . with the sword—beheaded him; a most ignominious mode of punishment, according to the Jews. Blessed martyr! Thou hast indeed "drunk of thy Lord's cup, and hast been baptized with his baptism." (See on Mark 10:38-40.) A grievous loss this would be to the Church; for though nothing is known of him beyond what we read in the Gospels, the place which he had as one of the three whom the Lord admitted to His closest intimacy would lead the Church to look up to him with a reverence and affection which even their enemies would come to hear of. They could spring only upon one more prized victim; and flushed with their first success, they prevail upon Herod to seize him also.

3. because he saw it pleased the Jews—Popularity was the ruling passion of this Herod, not naturally so cruel as some of the family [JOSEPHUS, *Antiquities,* 19:7, 3]. **to take Peter also**—whose loss, at this stage of the Church, would have been, so far as we can see, irreparable.

Then were the days of unleavened bread—seven in number, during which, after killing and eating the Passover, no leaven was allowed in Jewish houses (Exod. 12). **4. delivered him to four quaternions of soldiers**—i.e., to four parties of four each, corresponding to the four Roman watches; two watching in prison and two at the gates, and each party being on duty for the space of one watch. **intending after Easter**—rather, after the Passover; i.e., after the whole festival was over. (The word in our King James Version is an ecclesiastical term of later date, and ought not to have been employed here.) **to bring him forth to the people**—for execution; for during "the days of unleavened bread," or the currency of any religious festival, the Jews had a prejudice against trying or putting anyone to death.

ADAM CLARKE

CHAPTER 12

1. *Herod the king.* This was Herod Agrippa, the son of Aristobulus, and grandson of Herod the Great; he was nephew to Herod Antipas, who beheaded John the Baptist, and brother to Herodias. He was made king by the Emperor Caligula, and was put in possession of all the territories formerly held by his uncle Philip and by Lysanias; viz., Iturea, Trachonitis, Abilene, with Gaulonitis, Batanaea, and Penias. To these the Emperor Claudius afterwards added Judea and Samaria; which were nearly all the dominions possessed by his grandfather, Herod the Great.

2. *He killed James the brother of John with the sword.* This was James the Greater, son of Zebedee, and must be distinguished from James the Less, son of Alphaeus. This latter was put to death by Ananias, the high priest, during the reign of Nero. This James with his brother John were those who requested to sit on the right and left hand of our Lord, see Matt. xx. 23; and our Lord's prediction was now fulfilled in one of them, who by his martyrdom drank of our Lord's cup and was baptized with His baptism. By the death of James, the number of the apostles was reduced to eleven; and we do not find that ever it was filled. The apostles never had any successors; God has continued their doctrine, but not their order. By killing with the sword we are to understand beheading. Among the Jews there were four kinds of deaths: (1) stoning; (2) burning; (3) killing with the sword, or beheading; and (4) strangling. The third was a Roman as well as a Jewish mode of punishment. Killing with the sword was the punishment which, according to the Talmud, was inflicted on those who drew away the people to any strange worship, *Sanhedr.,* fol. iii. James was probably accused of this, and hence the punishment mentioned in the text.

3. *He proceeded . . . to take Peter also.* He supposed that these two were pillars on which the infant cause rested; and that, if these were removed, the building must necessarily come down. *The days of unleavened bread.* About the latter end of March or beginning of April.

4. *Four quaternions of soldiers.* That is, sixteen, or four companies of four men each, who had the care of the prison, each company taking in turn one of the four watches of the night. *Intending after Easter to bring him forth.* "After the Passover." Perhaps there never was a more unhappy, not to say absurd, translation than that in our text. But before I come to explain the word, it is necessary to observe that our term called Easter is not exactly the same with the Jewish Passover. This festival is always held on the fourteenth day of the first vernal full moon; but the Easter of the Christians, never till the next Sabbath after said full moon. The first vernal moon is that whose fourteenth day is either on the day of the vernal equinox or the next fourteenth day after it. The vernal equinox, according to a decree of the council of Nice, is fixed to the twenty-first day of March; and therefore the first vernal moon is that whose fourteenth day falls upon the twenty-first of March or the first fourteenth day after. The earliest Paschal term being the twenty-first of March, the twenty-second of March is the earliest Easter possible; and the eighteenth of April being the latest Paschal term, the seventh day after, that is, the twenty-fifth of April, is the latest Easter possible. The term *Easter* inserted here by our translators, they borrowed from the ancient Anglo-Saxon service books or from the version of the Gospels which always translates the *to pascha* of the Greek by this term. Wycliffe used the word *paske,* i.e., Passover; but Tyndale, Coverdale, following the old Saxon mode of translation, insert *Easter* the Geneva Bible very properly renders it the Passover.

MATTHEW HENRY

I. It was a signal answer to prayer (*v.* 5): *Peter was kept in prison. But prayer was made without ceasing of the church unto God for him*, for prayers and tears are the church's arms; therewith she fights, not only against her enemies, but for her friends. The delay of Peter's trial gave them time for prayer. James must be offered upon the sacrifice and service of their faith; but Peter must be continued to them, and therefore prayer for him is stirred up, and time is given them for it, by Herod's putting off the prosecution. They were very particular in their prayers for him, that it would please God to defeat Herod's purpose. The death of James alarmed them to a greater fervency in their prayer for Peter. Though the death and sufferings of Christ's ministers may be made greatly to serve the interests of Christ's kingdom, yet it is the duty and concern of the church earnestly to pray for their life, liberty, and tranquillity. *Prayer was made without ceasing.* It was an extended prayer. Times of public distress and danger should be praying times with the church; we must pray always, but then especially.

II. Let us observe when his deliverance came. 1. It was the very night before Herod designed to bring him forth. Herod resolves he shall die, and now God opened a door of escape for him. God's time to help is when things are brought to the last extremity. 2. It was when he was *fast bound with two chains, between two soldiers*; and, besides this, to make sure work, the *keepers before the door kept the prison*, that no one might so much as attempt to rescue him. Never could the art of man do more to secure a prisoner. When men will think to be too hard for God, God will make it appear that he is too hard for them. 3. It was when he was *sleeping between the soldiers*. Not terrified with his danger. There was but a step between him and death, and yet he could lay himself down in peace, and sleep—sleep in the midst of his enemies. Even in prison, between two soldiers, God gives him sleep. Not expecting his deliverance. He did not keep awake, and was perfectly surprised with his deliverance.

III. An *angel was sent from heaven* on purpose to rescue him.

1. *The angel of the Lord came upon him; stood over him.* He seemed as one abandoned by men, yet not forgotten of his God. Gates and guards kept all his friends from him, but could not keep the angels of God from him. Wherever the people of God are they have a way open heavenward, nor can anything intercept their intercourse with God.

2. *A light shone in the prison.* Though it is a dark place, and in the night, Peter shall see his way clear.

3. The angel awoke Peter, by giving him *a blow on his side*, a gentle touch, enough to rouse him out of his sleep. When good people slumber in a time of danger, let them expect to be smitten on the side by some sharp affliction; better be raised up so than left asleep. The language of this stroke was, *Arise up quickly*.

4. *His chains fell off from his hands.* They had handcuffed him, to make him sure, but *God loosed his hands.*

5. He was ordered to dress himself immediately, and follow the angel; and he did so, *v.* 8, 9. When Peter was awake he knew not what to do but as the angel directed him. He must *gird himself.* He *must bind on his sandals*, that he might be fit to walk. He must *cast his garments about him*, and follow the angel; and he might go with a great deal of courage and cheerfulness who had a messenger from heaven for his guide and guard. He *went out, and followed him.* Those who are delivered out of a spiritual imprisonment must follow their deliverer, as Israel did; they *went out, not knowing whither they went*, but whom they followed. When Peter went out after the angel, *he knew not that it was true which was done by the angel, but thought he saw a vision.* He thought the news was too good to be true.

6. He was led safely by the angel out of danger, *v.* 10. Guards were kept at one pass and at another, which they were to make their way through, and they did so without any opposition; nay, for aught that appears, without any discovery. The angel and Peter safely *passed the first and second ward.* But still there is an iron gate, after all, that will stop them. Up to that gate they march, and it *opened to them.* They did not so much as put a hand to it, but it opened *of its own accord*, by an invisible power. When God will work salvation for his people, no difficulties in their way are insuperable; but even gates of iron are made to open of their own accord. This iron gate led him into the city out of the castle or tower, so that, when they were through this, they were got into the street. This deliverance of Peter represents to us our redemption by Christ, which is often spoken of as the setting of prisoners free, not

JAMIESON, FAUSSET, BROWN

5, 6. prayer was made without ceasing—rather (*Margin*), 'instant,' 'earnest,' 'urgent'; as in Luke 22:44; ch. 26: 7; and I Peter 4:8 (see *Greek*). **of the church unto God for him**—not in public assembly, for it was evidently not safe to meet thus; but in little groups in private houses, one of which was Mary's (vs. 12). And this was kept up during all the days of unleavened bread.

6. And when Herod would have brought him forth—'was going to bring him forth.' **the same night**—but a few hours before the intended execution. Thus long were the disciples kept waiting; their prayers apparently unavailing, and their faith, as would seem from the sequel, waxing feeble. Such, however, is the *law* of God's procedure (Deut. 32:36, and see on John 21:3). **Peter was sleeping between two soldiers, bound with two chains**—Roman prisoners had a chain fastened at one end to the wrist of their right hand, and at the other to the wrist of a soldier's left hand, leaving the right arm of the keeper free in case of any attempt to escape. For greater security the prisoner was sometimes, as here, chained to two soldiers, one on each side. (See ch. 21:23.) Ye think your prey secure, bloodthirsty priests and thou obsequious tyrant who, to "please the Jews," hast shut in this most eminent of the servants of Christ within double gates, guarded by double sentinels, while double keepers and double chains seem to defy all rescue! So thought the chief priests, who "made the sepulchre of the Lord sure, sealing the stone and setting a watch." But "He that sitteth in heaven shall laugh at you." Meanwhile, "Peter is sleeping!" In a few hours he expects a stingless death; "neither counts he his life dear unto him, so that he may finish his course with joy and the ministry which he has received of the Lord Jesus." In this frame of spirit he has dropped asleep, and lies the picture of peace. **7-11. the angel of the Lord**—rather, 'an angel'—**came upon him**—so in Luke 2:9, expressive of the unexpected nature of the visit. **smote Peter on the side . . . Arise up quickly. And his chains fell off . . . Gird thyself . . . And so he did . . . Cast thy garment**—tunic, which he had thrown off for the night—**about thee . . . follow me**—In such graphic minuteness of detail we have a charming mark of reality: while the rapidity and curtness of the orders, and the promptitude with which they were obeyed, betoken the despatch which, in the circumstances, was necessary.

9. wist not that it was true; but thought he saw a vision—So little did the apostle look for deliverance! **10. first and the second ward . . . the iron gate that leadeth unto the city**—We can only conjecture the precise meaning of all this, not knowing the position of the prison.

ADAM CLARKE

5. *Prayer was made without ceasing.* The Greek word signifies both "fervor" and "earnestness," as well as "perseverance." These prayers of the church produced that miraculous interference mentioned below, and without which Peter could not have thus escaped from the hands of this ruthless king.

6. *Sleeping between two soldiers, bound with two chains.* Two soldiers guarded his person, his right hand being bound to the left hand of one, and his left hand bound to the right hand of the other. This was the Roman method of guarding their prisoners and appears to be what is intimated in the text.

7. *Smote Peter on the side.* He struck him in such a way as was just sufficient to awake him from his sleep.

8. *Gird thyself.* It seems Peter had put off the principal part of his clothes, that he might sleep with more comfort. His resuming all that he had thrown off was a proof that everything had been done leisurely. It appears that the two soldiers were overwhelmed by a deep sleep, which fell upon them from God.

9. *He . . . wist not.* He "knew" not. He supposed himself to be in a dream.

10. *The first and the second ward.* It is supposed that ancient Jerusalem was surrounded by three walls. If so, then passing through the gates of these three walls successively is possibly what is meant by the expression in the text. The prison in which he was confined might have been that which was at the outer wall. *Iron gate.* This was the innermost wall of the three, and was strongly plated over with iron, for the greater security. Perhaps this is all that is meant by the *iron gate.* One of the quaternions of soldiers was placed at each gate. *Which opened . . . of his own accord.* Influenced by the unseen power of the angel.

MATTHEW HENRY

only the proclaiming of liberty to the captives, but the *bringing of them out of the prison-house.*

7. When this was done, *the angel departed from him,* and left him to himself. He was out of danger from his enemies, and needed no guard. He knew where he was, and how to find out his friends, and needed no guide. Miracles are not to be expected when ordinary means are to be used.

IV. Having seen how his deliverance was magnified, we are next to see how it was manifested.

1. How Peter came to himself, and so came himself to the knowledge of it, *v.* 11. So many strange and surprising things coming together upon a man just awoke out of sleep put him for the present into some confusion. At length Peter *came to himself,* and found that it was not a dream, but a real thing: "*Now I know of a surety,* now I know that it is truth, *that the Lord Jesus hath sent his angel,* and by him *hath delivered me out of the hands of Herod,* and so hath disappointed *all the expectation of the people of the Jews.*" Peter, when he recollected himself, *perceived of a truth* what great things God had done for him, which at first he could not believe for joy. Thus souls who are delivered out of a spiritual bondage are not at first aware what God has wrought in them. Many have the truth of grace that want the evidence of it. But *when the Comforter comes* he will let them know of a surety what a blessed change is wrought in them.

2. How Peter came to his friends, and brought the knowledge of it to them.

(1) He *considered the thing* (*v.* 12), considered how imminent his danger was, how great his deliverance; and now what has he to do? God's providence leaves room for the use of our prudence; and, though he has undertaken to perform and perfect what he has begun, yet he expects we should consider the thing.

(2) He went directly to a friend's house; it was the house of Mary, a sister of Barnabas, and mother of John Mark. A church in the house makes it a little sanctuary.

(3) There he found *many* that were *gathered together praying,* at the dead time of the night, praying for Peter. [1] They continued in prayer, in token of their importunity. As long as we are kept waiting for a mercy we must continue praying for it. [2] It should seem that now when the affair came near to a crisis they were more fervent in prayer than before; and it was a good sign that God intended to deliver Peter when he thus stirred up a spirit of prayer for his deliverance. [3] They gathered together for prayer. They know what an encouragement Christ gave to joint-prayer. It was always the practice of God's praying people to unite their forces in prayer. [4] They were many that were got together for this work. No doubt but there were many private Christians that knew how to pray, and to pray pertinently, and to continue long in prayer. [5] Peter came to them when they were thus employed. It was as if God should say, "You are praying that Peter may be restored to you; now here he is."

(4) He knocked at the gate, and had much ado to get them to let him in (*v.* 13–16): *Peter knocked at the door of the gate.* [1] A *damsel came to hearken*; not to open the door till she knew who was there, and what their business was. It should seem, by her being named, that she was of note among the Christians, and more zealously affected to the better part than most of her age. [2] She knew Peter's voice. But, instead of letting him in immediately out of the cold, *she opened not the gate for gladness.* Thus sometimes, in a transport of affection to our friends, we do that which is unkind. [3] She ran in and told them that Peter was certainly at the gate. But, when she spoke of Peter's being there, they said, "*Thou art mad;* it is impossible, for he is in prison." Sometimes that which we most earnestly wish for we are most backward to believe, because we are afraid of imposing upon ourselves. However, she stood to it that it was he. Then said they, *It is his angel, v.* 15. "It is a *messenger* from him, that makes use of his name"; so some take it. When the damsel was confident it was Peter, because she knew his voice, they thought it was because he that stood at the door had called himself Peter. "It is one that comes with an errand from him, and thou didst mistake as if it had been he himself. It is his *guardian angel.*" Some think that they supposed his angel to appear as a presage of his death approaching. If so, they concluded this an ill omen, and that the language of the apparition was, "Let it suffice you, Peter must die." Others think they took this to be an angel from heaven, sent to bring them a grant to their prayers.

(5) At length they let him in (*v.* 16): *He continued knocking,* and at last they admitted him. The iron gate opened of itself. The door of his friend's house

JAMIESON, FAUSSET, BROWN

passed on through one street; and forthwith the angel departed from him—when he had placed him beyond pursuit. Thus "He disappointeth the devices of the crafty, so that their heads cannot perform their enterprise" (Job 5:12).

11. when Peter was come to himself—recovered from his bewilderment, and had time to look back upon all the steps that had followed each other in such rapid succession. **Now I know of a surety, that the Lord hath sent his angel, and hath delivered me . . .**—another evidence that Peter expected nothing but to seal his testimony with his blood on this occasion.

12-17. he came to the house of Mary . . .—who "must have had a house of some pretensions to receive a large number; and, accordingly, we read that her brother Barnabas (Col. 4:10) was a person of substance (ch. 4:37). She must also have been distinguished for faith and courage to allow such a meeting in the face of persecution" [WEBSTER and WILKINSON]. To such a house it was natural that Peter should come. **mother of John . . . Mark**—so called to distinguish him from the apostle of that name, and to distinguish her from the other Marys. **where many were gathered together praying**—doubtless for Peter's deliverance, and continuing, no doubt, on this the last of the days of unleavened bread, which was their last hope, all night in prayer to God.

came to hearken—not to open; for neither was it a time nor an hour of night for that, but to listen who was there.

opened not for gladness, but ran in and told . . .—How exquisite is this touch of nature!

Thou art mad—one of those exclamations which one can hardly resist on hearing what seems far 'too good to be true.' **she constantly affirmed**—kept steadfastly affirming'—**that it was even so. Then said they, It is his angel**—his disembodied spirit, his ghost; anything, in fact, rather than himself. Though this had been the burden of their fervent prayers during all the days of unleavened bread, they dispute themselves out of it as a thing incredible. Still, it is but the unbelief of the disciples who "believed not *for joy* and wondered" at the tidings of their Lord's resurrection. How often do we pray for what we can hardly credit the bestowment of, when it comes in answer to our prayers! This, however, argues not so much hard unbelief as that kind of it incident to the best in this land of shadows, which perceives not so clearly as it might how very near heaven and earth, the Lord and His praying people, are to each other. **16. Peter continued knocking**—delay being dangerous.

ADAM CLARKE

The angel departed from him. Having brought him into a place in which he no longer needed his assistance. What is proper to God He always does; what is proper to man He requires him to perform.

11. *When Peter was come to himself.* Everything he saw astonished him; he could scarcely credit his eyes. He was in a sort of ecstasy; and it was only when the angel left him that he was fully convinced that all was real. *And . . . all the expectation of the . . . Jews.* It seems they had built much on the prospect of having him sacrificed, as they already had James.

12. *And when he had considered.* When he had weighed everything and was fully satisfied of the divine interposition, he went to the house of Mary, the mother of John Mark, the author of the Gospel, where it appears many were gathered together making prayer and supplication, probably for Peter's release.

13. *As Peter knocked.* The door was probably shut for fear of the Jews; and as most of the houses in the East have an area before the door, it might have been at this outer gate that Peter stood knocking. *A damsel came to hearken, named Rhoda.* She came to inquire who was there. Rhoda signifies a "rose"; and it appears to have been customary with the Jews to give the names of flowers and trees to their daughters.

15. *It is his angel.* It was a common opinion among the Jews that every man has a guardian angel, and in the popish church it is an article of faith. As *angelos* signifies in general "a messenger," whether divine or human, some have thought that the angel or messenger here means a servant or person which the disciples supposed was sent from Peter to announce something of importance to the brethren.

MATTHEW HENRY

that was to welcome him does not open of its own accord, but must be knocked at, long knocked at. But, *when they saw him, they were astonished,* were filled with wonder and joy in him, as much as they were but just now with sorrow and fear concerning him.

(6) Peter gave them an account of his deliverance. When he came to the company they gathered about him to congratulate him on his deliverance; and herein they were so noisy that he could not make them hear him, but was forced to *beckon to them with the hand to hold their peace,* while *he declared unto them how the Lord Jesus had brought him out of prison;* and it is very likely he did not part with them till he and they had together solemnly given thanks to God for his enlargement. What is won by prayer must be worn with praise.

(7) Peter sent the account to others of his friends: *Go, show these things to James, and to the brethren with him.* He would have James and his company to know of his deliverance, not only that they might be delivered from their fears concerning Peter, but that they might return thanks to God with him and for him. Though Herod had slain one James with the sword, yet here was another James, and that in Jerusalem too, that stood up in his room to preside among the brethren there.

(8) Peter had nothing more to do for the present than to shift for his own safety. He *departed, and went into another place.* Even the Christian law of suffering for Christ has not repealed the natural law of self-preservation, as far as God gives an opportunity of providing for it.

V. Having seen the triumph of Peter's friends in his deliverance, let us next observe the confusion of his enemies thereupon. The guards were in the utmost consternation upon it (*v.* 18): *As soon as it was day* there was *no small stir among the soldiers, what had become of Peter.* They thought themselves as sure as could be of him but last night; yet now the bird is flown. Thus have the persecutors of the gospel of Christ been often filled with vexation to see its cause conquering. Houses were searched in vain for the rescued prisoner (*v.* 19): *Herod sought for him, and found him not.* Who can find whom God hath hidden? All believers have God for *their hiding-place.* The impotent world cannot reach them. The keepers were reckoned with; *Herod examined the keepers,* and *he commanded that they should be put to death.* Herod himself retired upon it: *He went down from Judæa to Caesarea, and there abode.* He was vexed to the heart, as a lion disappointed of his prey; and the more because he had so much raised the *expectation of the people of the Jews* concerning Peter. It made him ashamed to be robbed of this boasting, and to see himself disabled to make his words good. This is such a mortification to his proud spirit that he cannot bear to stay in Judæa, but away he goes to Cæsarea.

Verses 20–25

I. The death of Herod. God reckoned with him, not only for his putting James to death, but for his design to put Peter to death; for sinners will be called to an account for the mischief they have done and the mischief they would have done.

1. How the measure of his iniquity was filled up: it was *pride* that did it. The instance of it here is very remarkable, and shows how God *resists the proud.*

(1) The men of Tyre and Sidon had offended Herod. Some very small matter would serve such a man as Herod was for a provocation. He was highly displeased with this people.

(2) The offenders truckled. They submitted and were willing upon any terms to *make peace with him.* The reason why they were desirous to have the matter accommodated: *Because their country was nourished by the king's country.* Tyre and Sidon were trading cities, and were always supplied with corn from the land of Canaan. Now if Herod should make a law to prohibit the exportation of corn to Tyre and Sidon their country would be undone. And is it not then our wisdom to make our peace with God, and humble ourselves before him, who have a much more constant and necessary dependence upon him than one country can have upon another? The method they took to prevent a rupture: *They made Blastus the king's chamberlain their friend.* Blastus had Herod's ear, and has the art of mollifying his resentments; and a time is fixed for the ambassadors of Tyre and Sidon to come and make a public submission, to beg his majesty's pardon, and promise never again to offend. That which will thus feed his pride shall serve to cool his passion.

(3) Herod appeared in all the pomp and grandeur he had: He was *arrayed in his royal apparel* (*v.* 21), *and sat upon his throne.* Foolish people value men by their outward appearance; and no better are those

JAMIESON, FAUSSET, BROWN

17. But he, beckoning . . . with his hand to hold their peace—a lively touch this. In the hubbub of joyful and wondering interrogatories there might mingle reflections, thrown out by one against another, for holding out so long against the testimony of Rhoda; while the emotion of the apostle's own spirit would be too deep and solemn to take part in such demonstrations or utter a word till, with his hand, he had signified his wish for perfect silence. **Go show these things unto James and to the brethren**—Whether James the son of Alpheus, one of the Twelve, usually known as "James the Less," and "James the Lord's brother" (Gal. 1:19), were the same person; and if not, whether the James here referred to was the former or the latter, critics are singularly divided, and the whole question is one of the most difficult. To us, it appears that there are strong reasons for thinking that they were *not* the same person, and that the one here meant, and throughout the Acts, is *the apostle* James. (But on this more hereafter.) James is singled out, because he had probably begun to take the oversight of the Church in Jerusalem, which we afterwards find him exercising (ch. 15). **And he departed, and went into another place**—according to his Lord's express command (Matt. 10:23). When told, on a former miraculous liberation from prison, to go and speak unto the people (ch. 5:20), he did it; but in this case to present himself in public would have been to tempt God by rushing upon certain destruction. **18, 19. as soon as it was day . . .**—His deliverance must have been during the fourth watch (three to six A.M.); else he must have been missed by the keepers at the change of the watch [WIES]. **examined the keepers**—who, either like the keepers of our Lord's sepulchre, had "shaken and become as dead men" (Matt. 28:4), or had slept on their watch and been divinely kept from awaking. **commanded that they should be put to death**—Impotent vengeance!

20-25. HEROD'S MISERABLE END—GROWING SUCCESS OF THE GOSPEL—BARNABAS AND SAUL RETURN TO ANTIOCH. **20. Herod was . . . displeased with them of Tyre and Sidon**—for some reason unknown; but the effect on their commercial relations made the latter glad to sue for peace.

their country was nourished by the king's country—See I Kings 5:11; Ezra 3:7; Ezekiel 27:17. Perhaps the famine (ch. 11:28) made them the more urgent for reconciliation.

ADAM CLARKE

17. *Declared . . . how the Lord had brought him out of the prison.* He still persisted in the belief that his deliverance was purely supernatural. It seems that some modern critics could have informed him of his mistake. *Shew these things unto James, and to the brethren.* That is, in one word, show them to the church, at the head of which James undoubtedly was, as we may clearly understand by the part he took in the famous council held at Jerusalem, relative to certain differences between the believing Jews and Gentiles. See chap. xv. 13-21. There is still no supremacy for Peter. He who was bishop or overseer of the church at Jerusalem was certainly at the head of the whole Church of God at this time; but James was then bishop or inspector of the church at Jerusalem, and, consequently, was the only visible head then upon earth. *He departed . . . into another place.* Where he went we know not, but it is probable that he withdrew for the present into a place of privacy, till the heat of the inquiry was over relative to his escape from the prison, for he saw that Herod was intent on his death.

19. *Commanded that they should be put to death.* He believed, or pretended to believe, that the escape of Peter was owing to the negligence of the keepers. Jailers, watchmen, etc., ordinarily suffered the same kind of punishment which should have been inflicted on the prisoner whose escape they were supposed to have favored. *He went down from Judaea to Caesarea.* How soon he went down and how long he stayed there we do not know.

20. *Highly displeased with them of Tyre.* On what account Herod was thus displeased is not related by any historian, as far as I have been able to ascertain. Josephus, who speaks of this journey of Herod to Caesarea, says nothing of it; and it is useless for *us* to conjecture. *Having made Blastus . . . their friend.* Blastus was probably a eunuch, and had considerable influence over his master, Herod; to reach the master, it is likely they bribed the chamberlain. *Desired peace.* The Tyrians and Sidonians being equally subjects of the Roman government with the inhabitants of Galilee, Herod could not go to war with them; but, being irritated against them, he might prevent their supplies. They therefore endeavored to be on peacable, i.e., friendly, terms with him. *Their country was nourished by the king's country.* That is, they had all their supplies from Galilee; for Tyre and Sidon, being places of trade and commerce, with little territory, were obliged to have all their provisions from the countries under Herod's jurisdiction. This had been the case even from the days of Solomon, as we learn from 1 Kings v. 11, where it is said that "Solomon gave Hiram twenty thousand measures of wheat for food to his household, and twenty measures of pure oil: thus gave Solomon to Hiram year by year." See also Ezek. xxvii. 17.

MATTHEW HENRY

who value themselves by the esteem of such as Herod did, who thought to make up the want of a royal heart with his *royal apparel; and sat upon his throne.*

(4) He made a speech to the men of Tyre and Sidon, a fine oration, and probably he kept them in suspense as to what their doom should be, till he made this oration to them, that the act of grace might come to them with the more pleasing surprise.

(5) The people applauded him. They *gave a shout: It is the voice of a god, and not of a man, v.* 22. It was not from any real impression made upon their minds, or any high or good thoughts they had indeed conceived of him; but they were resolved thus to curry favour with him, and strengthen the new-made peace between him and them. Thus great men are made an easy prey to flatterers if they lend an ear to them. This is a great injury to those who are thus flattered, as it makes them forget themselves, and so puffs them up with pride that they are in the utmost danger possible of falling into the condemnation of the devil.

(6) These undue praises he took to himself. This was his sin. His fault was that he said nothing, did not rebuke their flattery, nor *give God the glory* (*v.* 23); but was very willing that he should be thought a god and have divine honours paid him.

2. How his iniquity was punished: *Immediately* (*v.* 23) *the angel of the Lord smote him because he gave not God the glory; and he was eaten of worms and gave up the ghost.* Now he was reckoned with for vexing the church of Christ, killing James, imprisoning Peter, and all the other mischiefs he had done. It was no less than an angel that was the agent—*the angel of the Lord*—for those ministering spirits are the ministers either of divine justice or of divine mercy, as God is pleased to employ them. The angel smote him just at that instant when he was strutting at the applause of the people, and adoring his own shadow. The angel *smote him, because he gave not the glory to God.* It was no more than a worm that was the instrument of Herod's destruction: He was *eaten of worms—he became worm-eaten,* so it must be read; rotten he was, and he became like a piece of rotten wood. See here, What vile bodies those are which we carry about with us. We should not be proud of our bodies, we should not pamper our bodies, for this is but feeding the worms, and feeding them for the worms. See what weak and contemptible creatures God can make the instruments of his justice. See how God delights not only to bring down proud men, but to bring them down in such a way as is most mortifying. Herod is not only destroyed, but destroyed by worms, that the pride of his glory may be effectually stained.

II. The progress of the gospel after this. 1. *The word of God grew and multiplied, v.* 24. The courage and comfort of the martyrs, and God's owning them, did more to invite people to Christianity, than their sufferings did to deter them from it. After the death of Herod the word of God gained ground. 2. Barnabas and Saul returned to Antioch: *When they had fulfilled their ministry* they *returned from Jerusalem.* Though they had a great many friends there, yet at present their work lay at Antioch; and where our business is there we should be. Barnabas and Saul, when they went to *Antioch, took with them John, whose surname was Mark,* at whose mother's house they had that meeting for prayer which we read of, *v.* 12. She was sister to Barnabas. It is probable that Barnabas lodged there, and perhaps Paul with him, while they were at Jerusalem, and their intimacy in that family occasioned their taking a son of that family with them when they returned, to be trained up under them. Educating young men for the ministry, and entering them into it, is a very good work for elder ministers to take care of.

JAMIESON, FAUSSET, BROWN

21, 23. And upon a set day Herod . . . made an oration unto them—to the Tyrians and Sidonians especially. **the people gave a shout . . .** —JOSEPHUS' account of his death is remarkably similar to this (*Antiquities,* xix, 8. 2). Several cases of such deaths occur in history. Thus was this wretched man nearer his end than he of whom he had thought to make a public spectacle.

A. T. ROBERTSON:

23. "Smote him" (*epataxen auton*). Effective aorist active indicative of *patasso,* old verb, used already in verse 7 of gentle smiting of the angel of the Lord, here of a severe stroke of affliction. Like Nebuchadnezzar (Dan. 4:30) pride went before a fall. He was struck down in the very zenith of his glory. "Because" (*anth' hon*). *Anti* with the genitive of the relative pronoun, "in return for which things." He accepted the impious flattery (Hackett) instead of giving God the glory. He was a nominal Jew. "He was eaten of worms" (*genomenos skolekobrotos*). Ingressive aorist middle participle, "becoming worm-eaten." The compound verbal adjective (*skolex,* worm, *brotos,* eaten, from *bibrosko*) is a late word (2 Macc. 9:9) of the death of Antiochus Epiphanes, used also of a tree (Theophrastus), here only in the N.T. The word *skolex* was used of intestinal worms and Herodotus (IV. 205) describes Pheretima, Queen of Cyrene, as having swarms of worms which ate her flesh while still alive. Josephus (*Ant.* XIX. 8, 2) says that Herod Agrippa lingered for five days and says that the rotting of his flesh produced worms, an item in harmony with the narrative in Luke. Josephus gives further details, one a superstitious sight of an owl sitting on one of the ropes of the awning of the theater while the people flattered him, an omen of his death to him. Luke puts it simply that God smote him.—*Word Pictures in the New Testament*

24. But the word grew . . .—i.e., Not only was the royal representative ignominiously swept from the stage, while his intended victim was spared to the Church, but the cause which he and his Jewish instigators sought to crush was only furthered and glorified. How full of encouragement and consolation is all this to the Christian Church in every age! **25. Barnabas and Saul returned from Jerusalem**—where, it thus appears, they had remained during all this persecution. **when they had fulfilled their ministry**—or service; that mentioned on ch. 11:29, 30. **took with them John . . . Mark**—(See on vs. 12), not to be confounded with the second Evangelist, as is often done. As his uncle was Barnabas, so his spiritual father was Peter (I Peter 5:13).

ADAM CLARKE

21. *Upon a set day.* A day on which games were exhibited in honor of the Roman emperor. What this refers to, we learn from Josephus. "Herod, having reigned three years over all Judea (he had reigned over the tetrarchy of his brother Philip four years before this), went down to Caesarea, and there exhibited shows and games in honour of Claudius, and made vows for his health. On the second day of these shows, he put on a garment made wholly of silver, and of a contexture most truly wonderful, and came into the theatre early in the morning; at which time the silver of his garment, being illuminated by the first reflection of the sun's rays, shone out after a surprising manner, and was so resplendent as to spread a horror over those who looked intently upon him; and presently his flatterers cried out, one from one place and another from another, 'He is a god:' and they added, 'Be thou merciful to us, for although we have hitherto reverenced thee only as a man, yet shall we henceforth own thee as superior to mortal nature.' Nor did the king rebuke them, nor reject their impious flattery. But, looking up, he saw an owl on a certain rope over his head, and immediately conceived that this bird was to him a messenger of ill tidings; and he fell into the deepest sorrow; a severe pain also arose in his bowels, and he died after five days' severe illness." This is the sum of the account given by Josephus, *Ant.,* l. xix, c. 8, s. 2.

23. *The angel of the Lord smote him.* His death was most evidently a judgment from God. *Because he gave not God the glory.* He did not rebuke his flatterers, but permitted them to give him that honor that was due to God alone. *And gave up the ghost.* That is, he died of the disorder by which he was then seized, after having lingered in excruciating torments for five days, as Josephus has stated. Antiochus Epiphanes and Herod the Great died of the same kind of disease.

24. *But the word of God.* The Christian doctrine preached by the apostles *grew and multiplied*—became more evident, and had daily accessions; for the spirit of revelation rested on those men, and God was daily adding to that word as circumstances required, in order to complete that testimony of His which we now find contained in the New Testament. As there is in the original an allusion to the vegetation of grain (it *grew,* as corn grows, the stalk and the ear; it was *multiplied,* as the corn is in the full ear), there is probably a reference to the parable of the sower and his seed; for the seed is the Word of God and the doctrine of the Kingdom. It was liberally sown; it grew vigorously, and became greatly multiplied.

25. *Returned from Jerusalem.* That is, to Antioch, after the death of Herod. *When they had fulfilled their ministry.* When they had carried the alms of the Christians at Antioch to the poor saints at Jerusalem, according to what is mentioned, chap. xi. 29-30, to support them in the time of the coming famine. *And took with them John, whose surname was Mark.* This was the son of Mary, mentioned in v. 12. He accompanied the apostles to Cyprus and afterwards in several of their voyages, till they came to Perga in Pamphylia. Finding them about to take a more extensive voyage, he departed from them. See the case, chap. xiii. 13 and xv. 37-40.

MATTHEW HENRY

CHAPTER 13

Verses 1–3

We have here a divine commission to Barnabas and Saul to go and preach the gospel among the Gentiles.

I. Here is an account of the present state of the church at Antioch.

1. How well furnished it was with good ministers; there were there *certain prophets and teachers* (*v.* 1), men that were eminent for gifts, graces, and usefulness. Agabus seems to have been a prophet and not a teacher, and many were teachers who were not prophets. Antioch was a great city, and the Christians there were many; it was therefore requisite they should have many teachers.

JAMIESON, FAUSSET, BROWN

CHAPTER 13

VSS. 1-3. BARNABAS AND SAUL, DIVINELY CALLED TO LABOR AMONG THE GENTILES, ARE SET APART AND SENT FORTH BY THE CHURCH AT ANTIOCH. The first seven chapters of this book might be entitled, *The Church among the Jews;* the next five (ch. 8-12), *The Church in Transition from Jews to Gentiles;* and the last sixteen (ch. 13-28), *The Church among the Gentiles* [BAUMGARTEN]. "Though Christianity had already spread beyond the limits of Palestine, still the Church continued a stranger to *formal* missionary effort. Casual occurrences, particularly the persecution at Jerusalem (ch. 8:2), had hitherto brought about the diffusion of the Gospel. It was from Antioch that teachers were first sent forth with the definite purpose of spreading Christianity, and organizing churches,

ADAM CLARKE

CHAPTER 13

1. *Certain prophets and teachers.* It is probable that these were not distinct offices, both might be vested in the same persons. By *prophets* we are to understand, when the word is taken simply, persons who were frequently inspired to predict future events; and by *teachers,* persons whose ordinary office was to instruct the people in the Christian doctrine. These also, to be properly qualified for the office, must have been endued with the influence of the Holy Spirit; for, as but a very small portion of the Scriptures of the New Testament could have as yet been given, it was necessary that the teachers should derive much of their own teaching by immediate revelation from God.

MATTHEW HENRY

Barnabas is first named and Saul last, but afterwards the last became first. Three others are mentioned. *Simeon*, or Simon, who for distinction-sake was called *Niger, Simon the Black*; *Lucius* of Cyrene; *Manaen*, a person of some quality, as it should seem, for he was *brought up with Herod the tetrarch*, was his comrade and intimate, which gave him a fair prospect of preferment at court, and yet for Christ's sake he quitted all the hopes of it. It is better to be fellow-sufferer with a saint than fellow-persecutor with a tetrarch.

2. How well employed they were (*v.* 2): *They ministered to the Lord, and fasted.* Diligent faithful teachers do truly minister unto the Lord. Those that instruct Christians serve Christ. Ministering to the Lord, in one way or other, ought to be the stated business of churches and their teachers. Religious *fasting* is of use in our ministering to the Lord. Though it was not so much practised by the disciples of Christ, *while the bridegroom was with them*, yet, after the bridegroom was taken away, they abounded in it.

II. The orders given by the Holy Ghost. The *Holy Ghost said: Separate me Barnabas and Saul for the work whereunto I have called them.* He does not specify the work, but refers to a former call of which they themselves knew the meaning. The matter was settled between them at Jerusalem before this, that as Peter, James, and John laid out themselves among those of the circumcision, so Paul and Barnabas should *go to the heathen.* The orders were, *Separate me Barnabas and Saul.* Christ by his Spirit has the nomination of his ministers. There are some whom the Holy Ghost has separated for the service of Christ, and concerning them directions are given to those who are competent judges: *Separate* them. Christ's ministers are separated to him and to the Holy Ghost: *Separate them to me;* they are to be employed in Christ's work and under the Spirit's guidance. All that are separated to Christ as his ministers are separated to work; Christ keeps no servants to be idle. They are separated to take pains, not to take state. The work of Christ's ministers is work which all Christ's ministers hitherto have been called to.

III. Their ordination, not to the ministry in general, but to a particular service in the ministry. Simeon, and Lucius, and Manaen, *when they had fasted and prayed, laid their hands on Barnabas and Saul, and sent them away* (*v.* 3). They prayed for them. When good men are going forth about good work, they ought to be solemnly and particularly prayed for. They joined fasting with their prayers, as they did in their other ministrations, *v.* 3. They laid their hands on them. They gave them their discharge from the present service, in the church of Antioch, acknowledging that they went off not only fairly and with consent, but honourably and with a good report. They implored a blessing upon them in their present undertaking, begged that God would be with them, and give them success. They did not envy Barnabas and Saul the honour to which they were preferred, but cheerfully committed it to them, and *they sent them away* with all expedition, out of a concern for those countries where they were to break up fallow ground.

Verses 4–13

I. A general account of the coming of Barnabas and Saul to the famous island of Cyprus. Barnabas was a native of that country (*ch.* iv. 36), and he was willing they should have the first fruits of his labours. Their being sent forth by the Holy Ghost was the great thing that encouraged them in this undertaking, *v.* 4. They came to Seleucia, thence crossed the sea to Cyprus, and the first city they came to was Salamis (*v.* 5); and, when they had sown good seed there, *thence they* went onward *through the isle* (*v.* 6) till they came to Paphos. *They preached the word of God in the synagogues of the Jews;* so far were they from excluding them that they gave them the preference. They did not act clandestinely, but laid their doctrine open to the censure of the rulers of their synagogues.

They had John for their minister; not their servant in common things, but their assistant in the things of God. Such a one might be many ways of use to them, especially in a strange country.

JAMIESON, FAUSSET, BROWN

with regular institutions (ch. 14:23)" [OLSHAUSEN]. **1. there were . . . certain prophets**—see on ch. 11: 27—**and teachers; as Barnabas . . .**—implying that there were others there, besides; **but, according to** what appears the true reading, the meaning is simply that those here mentioned were in the Church at Antioch as prophets and teachers. **Simeon . . . Niger**—of whom nothing is known. **Lucius of Cyrene**—(See on ch. 2:20. He is mentioned, in Romans 16:21, as one of Paul's kinsmen. **Manaen**—or Menahem, the name of one of the kings of Israel (II Kings 15:14). **which had been brought up with**—or, the foster brother of—**Herod the tetrarch**—i.e., Antipas, who was himself "brought up with a certain private person at Rome" [JOSEPHUS, *Antiquities*, 117, 1, 3]. How differently did these two foster brothers turn out—the one, abandoned to a licentious life and stained with the blood of the most distinguished of God's prophets, though not without his fits of reformation and seasons of remorse; the other, a devoted disciple of the Lord Jesus and prophet of the Church at Antioch! But this is only what may be seen in every age: "Even so, Father, for so it seemeth good in Thy sight.' If the courtier, whose son, at the point of death, was healed by our Lord (John 4:46) was of Herod's establishment, while Susanna's husband was his steward (Luke 8:3), his foster brother's becoming a Christian and a prophet is something remarkable. **and Saul**—last of all, but soon to become first. Henceforward this book is almost exclusively occupied with him; and his impress on the New Testament, on Christendom, and on the world is paramount. **2. As they ministered to the Lord**—The word denotes the performance of *official* duties of any kind, and was used to express the priestly functions under the Old Testament. Here it signifies the corresponding ministrations of the Christian Church. **and fasted**—As this was done in other cases on special occasions (vss. 3, 14, 23), it is not improbable that they had been led to expect some such prophetic announcement at this time. **the Holy Ghost said**—through some of the prophets mentioned in vs. 1. **Separate me**—So Romans 1:1. **for the work whereunto I have called them**—by some communication, perhaps, to themselves: in the case of Saul at least, such a designation was indicated from the first (ch. 22:21). N.B. While the *personality* of the Holy Ghost is manifest from this language, His supreme *divinity* will appear equally so by comparing it with Hebrews 5:4. **3. laid their hands on them**—(See on ch. 6:6)—"recommending them to the grace of God for the work which they had to fulfil" (ch. 14:26). **sent them away**—with the double call—of *the Spirit* first, and next of *the Church.* So clothed, their mission is thus described: "They being sent forth by the Holy Ghost." Have we not here for all time the true principle of appointment to sacred offices?

4-12. ARRIVING IN CYPRUS, THEY PREACH IN THE SYNAGOGUES OF SALAMIS—AT PAPHOS, ELYMAS IS STRUCK BLIND, AND THE GOVERNOR OF THE ISLAND IS CONVERTED. **4, 5. departed unto Seleucia**—the seaport of Antioch, from which it lay nearly due west fifteen miles, and five from the Mediterranean shore, on the river Orontes. **thence sailed to Cyprus**—whose high mountain summits are easily seen in clear weather from the coast [COLONEL CHESNEY in HOWS]. "Four reasons may have induced them to turn in first to this island: (1) Its nearness to the mainland; (2) It was the native place of Barnabas, and since the time when Andrew found his brother Simon, and brought him to Jesus, and 'Jesus loved Martha, and her sister, and Lazarus,' family ties had not been without effect on the progress of the Gospel. (3) It could not be unnatural to suppose that the truth would be welcomed in Cyprus when brought by Barnabas and his kinsman Mark, to their own connections or friends. The Jews were numerous in Salamis. By sailing to that city, they were following the track of the synagogues; and though their mission was chiefly to the Gentiles, their surest course for reaching them was through the proselytes and Hellenizing Jews. (4) Some of the Cypriotes were already Christians. Indeed, no one place out of Palestine, except Antioch, had been so honorably associated with the work of successful evangelization" [HOWS]. **5. and when they were at Salamis**—the Grecian capital of the island, on the eastern side, and not many hours' sail from Seleucia. At this busy mercantile port immense numbers of Jews were settled, which accounts for what is here said, that they had more than one synagogue, in which Barnabas and Saul preached, while other cities had one only. **they had . . . John [Mark] to their minister**—'for their officer.' (See on Luke 4:20.) With what fruit they preached here

ADAM CLARKE

Barnabas. Of whom see before, chap. xi. 22-24. *Simeon . . . Niger.* Or "Simeon the Black," because of either his complexion or his hair. *Lucius of Cyrene.* See chap. xi. 20. *Manaen, which had been brought up with Herod.* Our margin has given the proper meaning of the original word "a foster-brother"; i.e., Manaen was the son of the woman who nursed Herod Antipas. Of a person whose name was Manaen or Menahem, and who was in the court of Herod, we read several things in the Jewish writers. They say that this man had the gift of prophecy, and that he told Herod, when he was but a child, that he would be king. When Herod became king he sent for him to his court, and held him in great estimation. It might have been the son of this Menahem of whom Luke here speaks.

2. *As they ministered to the Lord, and fasted.* On Mondays and Thursdays it was usual with the more pious Jews to attend the public service in their synagogues, and to fast; the former is what we are to understand by ministering to the Lord. On the Sabbaths they attended the service in the synagogue, but did not fast. The Greek word signifies "performing the office of praying, supplicating, rendering thanks." *The Holy Ghost said.* A revelation of the divine will was made to some person then present. *Separate me Barnabas and Saul.* Consecrate, or set them apart, for the particular work whereunto I have called them. How this was done we find in the next verse.

3. *And when they had fasted and prayed, and laid their hands on them.* (1) They *fasted;* this was probably done by the whole church. (2) They *prayed* that God would bless and prosper them in their work. (3) They *laid . . . hands upon them*, thus solemnly appointing them to that particular work. But was it by this fasting, praying, and imposition of hands that these men were qualified for this work? No. God had already called them to it, v. 2, and He who called them had qualified them. Both their call and their qualification came from God, but He chose that they should have also the sanction of that church of which they had been members; and therefore He said, "Separate me." The ordination of elders among the Jews was by three persons; and here we find three, Simeon, Lucius, and Manaen, ordaining two others, Barnabas and Saul. But how did the Jews ordain? Not by imposition of hands. This is strictly forbidden; see Maimon. Sanh., chap. 4. "After what manner is the ordaining of elders for ever? Not that they should lay their hands on the head of an elder; but only that they should call him Rabbi, and say to him, Behold, thou art ordained, and hast power of judging." The church at Antioch, however, did depart from this custom: they put their hands on the heads of Barnabas and Saul, thus designating them to be the persons whom they, under the direction of the Holy Spirit, sent to preach the gospel of Christ to the heathen.

4. *Being sent forth by the Holy Ghost.* By His influence, authority, and under His continual direction. Without the first, they were not qualified to go; without the second, they had no authority to go; and without the third, they could not know where to go. *Departed unto Seleucia.* Near the place where the Orontes River pours itself into the sea. *They sailed to Cyprus.* A well-known island in the Mediterranean Sea.

5. *Salamis.* The capital of the island of Cyprus, situated on the eastern part of the island. *They preached the word of God.* The doctrine of God, the Christian religion, emphatically so called. *They had also John to their minister.* This was John Mark, of whom we heard, chap. xii. 25; for their *minister*, to assist them in minor offices, as deacon or servant, that they might give themselves wholly to the doctrine of the Lord.

MATTHEW HENRY

II. A particular account of their encounter with *Elymas the sorcerer.*

1. There the *deputy,* a Gentile, *Sergius Paulus* by name, encouraged the apostles. He was governor *of the country,* under the Roman emperor. He had the character of *a prudent man,* that was ruled by reason, not passion, nor prejudice, which appeared by this, that he sent for them, *and desired to hear the word of God.* Those are wise people, however they may be ranked among the foolish of this world, who are inquisitive after the mind and will of God. If they have a message from God, let him know what it is, he is ready to receive it.

2. There Elymas, a Jew, a *sorcerer,* opposed them. This Elymas was a pretender *to the gift of prophecy, a sorcerer, a false prophet*—one that would be taken for a divine. *His name was Bar-jesus—the son of Joshua;* it signifies the *son of salvation;* but the Syriac calls him, *Bar-shoma—the son of pride; the son of inflation.* He was hanging on at court, *was with the deputy* of the country. He made it his business to withstand Barnabas and Saul. *He sought to turn away the deputy from the faith* (*v.* 8), to keep him from receiving the gospel. Satan is in a special manner busy with great men and men of power, to keep them from being religious; because he knows that their example, whether good or bad, will have an influence upon many.

Saul (who is here for the first time called Paul) fell upon him for this with a holy indignation. *Saul, who is also called Paul, v.* 9. Saul was his name as he was a Hebrew; Paul was his name as he was a citizen of Rome. Hitherto we have had him mostly conversant among the Jews, and therefore called by his Jewish name; but now, when he is sent forth among the Gentiles, he is called by his Roman name.

He was *filled with the Holy Ghost* upon this occasion; filled with power to denounce the wrath of God against him. What Paul said did not come from any personal resentment, but from the strong impressions which the Holy Ghost made upon his spirit. He *set his eyes upon him* in opposition to his wicked impudence. He gave him his true character, *v.* 10. He describes him to be, *First,* An agent for hell. This Elymas, though called *Bar-jesus—a son of Jesus*—was really a *child of the devil.* In two things he resembled the devil. In craftiness. Elymas, though void of all wisdom, was *full of all subtlety.* In malice. He was *full of all mischief*—a spiteful ill-conditioned man. A fulness of subtlety and mischief together make a man indeed a child of the devil. *Secondly,* An adversary to heaven. If he be a child of the devil, it follows of course that he is *an enemy to all righteousness.* He charged upon him his present crime: "*Wilt thou not cease to pervert the right ways of the Lord.*" The ways of the Lord are right; the only right ways to heaven and happiness. There are those who pervert these right ways, who not only wander out of these ways themselves, but mislead others, and suggest to them unjust prejudices against these ways, making them seem crooked ways. Those who pervert the right ways of the Lord are commonly so hardened in it that they will not cease to do it.

JAMIESON, FAUSSET, BROWN

is not said. Probably their feeling was what Paul afterwards expressed at Antioch in Pisidia (vs. 46). **6. when they had gone through the isle unto Paphos**—on the opposite or west side of the island, about 100 miles by land, along the south coast; the Roman capital, where the governor resided.

they found a . . . sorcerer—one of a numerous class of impostors who, at this time of general unbelief, were encouraged even by cultivated Romans. **7. Which was with the deputy**—properly, *'the proconsul.'* This name was reserved for the governors of settled provinces, which were placed under the Roman Senate, and is never given in the New Testament to Pilate, Felix, or Festus, who were but *procurators,* or subordinate administrators of unsettled, imperial, military provinces. Now as Augustus reserved Cyprus for himself, its governor would in that case have been not a proconsul, but simply a procurator, had not the emperor afterwards restored it to the Senate, as a Roman historian [DIO CASSIUS] expressly states. In most striking confirmation of this minute accuracy of the sacred historian, coins have actually been found in the island, stamped with the names of *proconsuls,* both in Greek and Latin [AKERMAN'S *Numismatic Illustrations of the New Testament*]. (GROTIUS and BENGEL, not aware of this, have missed the mark here.) **Sergius Paulus, a prudent**—intelligent—**man**—who thirsting for truth, sent for Barnabas and Saul, desiring ("earnestly desiring") to hear the Word of God. **8-12. But Elymas**—or 'the wise—**for so is his name by interpretation**—the word is from the *Arabic*—**withstood them**—perceiving, probably, how eagerly the proconsul was drinking in the word, and fearing a dismissal. (Cf. II Tim. 3:8.) **9. Then Saul . . . also . . . called Paul**—and henceforward Paul only; a softening of his former name, in accommodation to Roman ears, and (as the word signifies "little") probably with allusion as elsewhere to his insignificance of stature and appearance (II Cor. 10:1, 10) [WEBSTER and WILKINSON].

filled with the Holy Ghost—the Spirit coming mightily upon him. **set his eyes on him and said**—Henceforward Barnabas sinks into the background. The whole soul of his great colleague, now drawn out, as never before, shoots, by the lightning gaze of his eye, through the dark and tortuous spirit of the sorcerer. What a picture! **10. full of all subtlety**—referring to his magic arts. **and all malice**—The word signifies 'readiness for anything,' knavish dexterity.

thou child of the devil . . . enemy of all righteousness—These were not words of passion, for immediately before uttering them, it is said he was "filled with the Holy Ghost" [CHRYSOSTOM]. **wilt thou not cease to pervert the right ways of the Lord**—referring to his having to that hour made a trade of leading his fellow creatures astray.

ADAM CLARKE

6. *Gone through the isle.* The "whole" *isle* is added here by some MSS. *Unto Paphos.* This town, next in importance to Salamis, was situated on the western part of the isle; and having gone from Salamis to this place is a proof that they had gone through the whole island from east to west, according to the reading noticed above. There was probably no town in the universe more dissolute than Paphos. Here Venus had a superb temple; here she was worshipped with all her rites; and from this place she was named the "Paphian Venus," the "queen of Paphos." This temple and whole city were destroyed by an earthquake, so that a vestige of either does not now remain. *A certain sorcerer.* "A magician," one who used magical arts and pretended to have commerce with supernatural agents. *A false prophet.* A deceiver, one who pretended to have a divine commission, a fortune-teller. *Bar-Jesus.* That is, "the son of Jesus."

7. *The deputy of the country.* The "proconsul." In those days the Romans sent two different kinds of governors into the provinces. Some of the provinces were *imperial,* and into those they sent *propretors;* others belonged to the *senate* and people of Rome, and into those they sent *proconsuls.* Cyprus had formerly been an imperial province; but Augustus, who made the distinction, had given it to the people, whence it was governed by a proconsul. *A prudent man.* A man of "good sense," of a sound understanding, and therefore wished to hear the doctrine taught by these apostles; he did not persecute the men for their preaching, but sent for them that he might hear for himself.

8. *But Elymas the sorcerer* (*for so is his name by interpretation*). That is, Elymas is the interpretation of the word *magos,* or *sorcerer;* not of the word Bar-Jesus, as some have imagined.

9. *Saul,* (*who also is . . . Paul*). This is the first time the name Paul occurs and the last time in which this apostle is called Saul as his common or general name. *Saul, Shaül,* was the name of the first Israelitish king, and signifies "asked, sought"; from *shaal,* "he asked, inquired." *Paul, Paulus,* if derived from the Latin, signifies "little, dwarfish." It is well-known that the Jews in the apostolic age had frequently two names: one Hebrew, the other Greek or Roman. Saul was born of Jewish parents, a Hebrew of the Hebrews; he had therefore his first name from that language, *Shaül,* "asked or begged," as it is possible he might have been a child for whom his parents had addressed their fervent petitions to God. The case of Samuel is one in point. See 1 Sam. i. 9-18. As he was born in Tarsus, in Cilicia, he was consequently born a free Roman citizen; and hence his parents would naturally give him, for cognomen, some name borrowed from the Latin tongue; and Paulus, which signifies "little," might indicate that he was at his birth a small child. It is very likely that he was low in stature all his days; and that it is to this he refers himself, 2 Cor. x. 10, "For . . . his bodily presence is weak, and his speech contemptible." If he were small in stature, his voice would be naturally low and feeble; and the Greeks, who were fond of a thundering eloquence, would despise him on this very account. *Filled with the Holy Ghost.* Therefore the sentence he pronounced was not from himself, but from God. And indeed, had he not been under a divine influence, it is not likely he would have ventured thus to accost this sorcerer in the presence of the governor, who no doubt had greatly admired him.

10. *O full of all subtilty.* "Deceit," pretending to supernatural powers without possessing any, and having only cunning and deceit as their substitutes. *And . . . mischief.* From *rhadios,* "easy," and *ergon,* "a work"; one who is ready at his work; a word which excellently well defines a juggler, one who is expert at sleight of hand, though it is often employed to signify an abandoned and accomplished villain. *Child of the devil.* "Son of the devil," possessing his nature, filled with his cunning, and in consequence practicing deceit. *Enemy of all righteousness.* Opposed in your heart to all that is just, true, and good.

Wilt thou not cease to pervert? "Will you not cease perverting?" He had probably labored in this bad work from the beginning of Paul's

MATTHEW HENRY | JAMIESON, FAUSSET, BROWN | ADAM CLARKE

G. CAMPBELL MORGAN:

What was the reason for this attack upon Elymas? The very words of Paul startle the age in which we are living. We are not accustomed to such language; we never think now of addressing to any man outside or inside the Church such words as these: "O full of all guile and all villainy." Remember Paul did not say this *about* him but *to* him. He looked into his face, he fastened his eyes upon him. This is quite definite. This man Paul, contemptible of bodily presence according to his own estimate, looked into the eyes of another man, a Jew, keen, subtle, clever, occult; and looking straight into his face he said: "O full of all guile and all villainy, thou son of the devil, thou enemy of all righteousness, wilt thou not cease to pervert the right ways of the Lord?" Let us carefully bear in mind that this follows immediately upon the declaration that he was filled with the Spirit. There is no doubt that he was specially filled with the Spirit for the saying of this very thing. Why this anger? Why the fierceness of these words? The answer is that another man was involved, Sergius Paulus.
—*The Acts of the Apostles*

He denounced the judgment of God upon him, in a present blindness (*v.* 11): "*And now, behold, the hand of the Lord is upon thee; thou shalt be blind, not seeing the sun for a season.*" He shut his eyes, the eyes of his mind, against the light of the gospel, and therefore justly were the eyes of his body shut against the light of the sun; he sought to blind the deputy, and therefore is himself struck blind. Yet it was a moderate punishment. It was only *for a season*; if he will repent, and give glory to God, his sight shall be restored; nay, it should seem, though he do not, yet his sight shall be restored.

This judgment was immediately executed: *There fell on him a mist and a darkness.* Let not him any more pretend to be a guide to the deputy's conscience who is himself struck blind. *He went about seeking some to lead him by the hand;* and where now is all his skill in sorcery.

3. Notwithstanding all the endeavours of Elymas *to turn away the deputy from the faith*, he was brought to believe, and this miracle contributed to it. The deputy was a very sensible man, and observes something which intimated its divine original. In Paul's preaching: he was *astonished at the doctrine of the Lord.* The doctrine of Christ has a great deal in it that is astonishing; and the more we know of it the more reason we shall see to wonder and stand amazed at it. In this miracle: *When he saw what was done*, he believed. It is not said that he was baptized, but it is probable that he was.

III. Their departure from the island of Cyprus. They quitted the country, and *went to Perga.* Those that went were *Paul and his company.* Then John *Mark quitted them, and returned to Jerusalem*, without the consent of Paul and Barnabas. It was his fault, and we shall hear of it again.

11. the hand of the Lord is upon thee, and thou shalt be blind for a season—the judgment being mercifully designed to lead him to repentance. The tradition that it did is hardly to be depended on.

there fell on him a mist . . .—This is in Luke's *medical* style.

12. Then the deputy, when he saw what was done, believed, being astonished at the doctrine of the Lord—so marvellously attested; cf. Mark 1:27. What fruit, if any, followed this remarkable conversion, or how long after it the missionaries remained at Paphos, we know not.

13-52. AT PERGA JOHN MARK FORSAKES THEM—AT ANTIOCH, IN PISIDIA, PAUL PREACHES WITH GLORIOUS EFFECT—THE JEWS, ENRAGED, EXPEL THEM OUT OF THEIR COASTS.

13. they came to Perga in Pamphylia—The distance from Paphos to Attalia, on the Gulf of Pamphylia (see on ch. 14:25), sailing in a northwest direction, is not much greater than from Seleucia to Salamis on the east. Perga was the metropolis of Pamphylia, on the river Cestrus, and about seven miles inland from Attalia. **and John departing from them returned to Jerusalem**—As Paul afterwards peremptorily refused to take Mark with him on his second missionary journey, because he "had departed [or 'fallen off'] from them and had not gone with them to the work" (ch. 15:38), there can be no doubt that he had either wearied of it or been deterred by the prospect of the dangers which lay before him. (But see on ch. 15:37, etc.).

ministry in the place, and God in His mercy had borne with him; and no doubt the apostle had warned him, for thus much seems implied in the reproof. *The right ways of the Lord.* "The ways of the Lord, the straight ways." This saying is very emphatical. The ways of Elymas were crooked and perverse; *the ways of the Lord*, the doctrine taught by Him, plain and straight. What is here said of the conduct and teaching of Elymas, for he was a false prophet, is true of all false doctrine. It is complex, devious, and tortuous; while the doctrine of God is simple, plain, and straight, directing in the way, the sure way, that leads to present peace and everlasting happiness. From the phraseology which the apostle employs in this terrible address to Elymas we may learn, as well as from his name Bar-Jesus, that he was by birth and education a Jew. On this account he was the greater enemy to Christianity, and on this same account he was the less excusable.

11. *The hand of the Lord is upon thee.* The power of God is now about to deal with you in the way of justice. *Thou shalt be blind.* Every word here proves the immediate inspiration of Paul. He was full of the Holy Ghost when he began this address; by the light of that Spirit he discerned the state of Elymas and exposed his real character; and by the prophetic influence of that same Spirit he predicted the calamity that was about to fall upon him, while as yet there was no sign of his blindness. *Not seeing the sun for a season.* In the midst of judgment God remembers mercy. This blindness was not to be perpetual; it was intended to be the means of awakening and softening the hard heart of this poor sinner. There is an ancient tradition, and it is mentioned by both Origen and Chrysostom, that Elymas, in consequence of this, became a sincere convert to the religion of Christ. Origen says: "And Paul by a word striking him blind, who was with the proconsul, Sergius Paul, by anguish converted him to godliness." *There fell on him a mist and darkness. Achlus* is a disordered state of the eye in which the patient sees through a thick mist. This thick mist, or perturbed state of the eye, took place first; it increased, and thick, positive *darkness* was the issue. *He went about.* Not knowing how to take a right step, he groped about in great uncertainty; and not being able to find his way, he sought for some persons to lead him by the hand.

12. *The deputy . . . believed.* This was a proof that the doctrine was true; and that the power of God, from which nothing could be concealed and which nothing could resist, was with these preachers. *Being astonished.* Being struck with astonishment, as Elymas was struck with blindness.

13. *Paul and his company loosed from Paphos.* They sailed away from this island, leaving, it may be presumed, Elymas a sincere and deeply humbled penitent; and Sergius Paul, a thorough and happy believer in the doctrine of Christ. Previously to this time Luke always mentions Barnabas before Paul; but after this he mentions Paul always first, probably after seeing how God had distinguished him in the late proceedings at Cyprus, as much of the Holy Spirit now rested upon him. *They came to Perga in Pamphylia.* As Perga was not a maritime town, it is conjectured that the apostles sailed up the river Cestrus, in order to come to this place, which, according to Strabo, was situated about sixty leagues up this river, and near to which was a famous temple dedicated to Diana. *And John departing from them.* Why John Mark left his brethren at this place we are not informed; probably he went to visit his pious mother, Mary, at Jerusalem, and to see Peter, to whom he is supposed to have been much attached. It certainly was not with the approbation of Paul that he left them at this place as we learn from chap. xv. 38; yet his departure does not seem to have merited the displeasure of Barnabas. For John Mark having met these apostles at Antioch when Paul purposed to revisit the various places where they had planted the word of God, Barnabas was willing to take him with them; but Paul would not consent, because he had "departed from them from Pamphylia, and went not with them to the work," chap. xv. 35-39; and this occasioned a separation between Barnabas and Paul. It does not appear that John Mark was

MATTHEW HENRY

Verses 14–41

Perga in Pamphylia was a noted place, yet nothing at all is related of what Paul and Barnabas did there, only that *thither they came* (*v.* 13), and *thence they departed*, *v.* 14. The next place we find them in is another Antioch, in Pisidia, to distinguish it from that Antioch in Syria from which they were sent out. Abundance of Jews lived there, and to them *the gospel was to be first preached*; and Paul's sermon to them is what we have in these verses.

I. The appearance which Paul and Barnabas made in a religious assembly of the Jews at Antioch, *v.* 14. *When they came to Antioch* they applied to the Jews, which is a further proof of their good affection to them. They observed their time of worship, *on the sabbath day*, the Jewish sabbath. *The first day of the week* they observed among themselves as a Christian sabbath; but, if they will meet the Jews, it must be on the seventh-day sabbath. They met them in their place of worship, *in the synagogue*. Paul and Barnabas were strangers; but, wherever we come, we must enquire out God's faithful worshippers, and join with them. Though they were strangers, yet they were admitted into the synagogue, and to sit down there. Care should be taken in places of public worship that strangers be accommodated, even the poorest.

II. The invitation given them to preach. 1. The usual service of the synagogue was performed (*v.* 15): *The law and the prophets were read*, a portion of each, the lessons for the day. 2. When that was done, they were asked by *the rulers of the synagogue* to give them a sermon (*v.* 15): They sent a messenger to them: *Men and brethren, if you have any word of exhortation for the people, say on.* If they had not an affection to the gospel, yet they had at least the curiosity to hear Paul preach; and therefore begged the favour of him that he would speak a *word of exhortation to the people*. The bare reading of the scriptures in the public assemblies is not sufficient, but they should be expounded, and the people exhorted out of them. Those that preside, and have power, in public assemblies, should provide for a word of exhortation to the people. Sometimes a word of exhortation from a strange minister may be of great use to the people. These were more noble, more generous, than the rulers of the synagogues generally were.

III. The sermon Paul preached. He gladly embraced the opportunity given him to preach Christ to his countrymen the Jews. He *stood up and beckoned with his hand*. He waved his hand as an orator endeavouring to move affection, and to show himself in earnest. "*Men of Israel, and you that fear God, give audience.*" Everything is touched in this sermon that might convince the judgment of the Jews, to prevail with them to receive and embrace Christ as the promised Messiah.

1. He owns them to be God's favourite people, whom he had taken into special relation to himself, and for whom he had done great things.

(1) *The God of the whole earth* was, in a particular manner, *the God of this people Israel*, a God *in covenant with them*.

(2) He had *chosen their fathers* to be his friends: Abraham was called *the friend of God*. He puts them in mind of this, to let them know that the reason why God favoured them, was because he would adhere to the choice he had made of *their fathers*.

(3) He had *exalted that people*, had advanced them into a people, and raised them from nothing, *when they dwelt as strangers in the land of Egypt*. They ought to remember this, and to infer hence that God was no debtor to them. But they were debtors to him, and obliged to receive such further discoveries as he should make of his will.

(4) He had *with a high hand brought them out of Egypt*, had delivered them at the expense of a great many miracles, both of mercy to them and judgment on their oppressors.

(5) *He had suffered their manners forty years in the wilderness*, *v.* 18. God made a great deal of provision for them for forty years in the wilderness: miracles were their daily bread. He exercised a great deal of patience with them. He bore with them, suffered his anger many a time to be turned away by the prayer and intercession of Moses. So many years as we have each of us lived in this world, we must own that God has thus been as a tender father to us, has been indulgent to us, a God of pardons. We have tried his patience, and yet not tired it.

JAMIESON, FAUSSET, BROWN

14. departed from Perga—apparently without making any stay or doing any work: cf. the different language of ch. 14:25, and see immediately below. **came to Antioch in Pisidia**—usually so called, to distinguish it from Antioch in Syria, from which they had started, though it actually lies in Phrygia, and almost due north from Perga. It was a long journey, and as it lay almost entirely through rugged mountain-passes, while "rivers burst out at the base of huge cliffs, or dash down wildly through narrow ravines," it must have been a perilous one. The whole region was, and to this day is, infested by robbers, as ancient history and modern travels abundantly attest; and there can be but little doubt that to this very journey Paul many years after alludes, when he speaks amidst his "journeyings often," of his "*perils of rivers*" (as the word is), and his "*perils of robbers*" (II Cor. 11:26). If this journey were taken in May—and earlier than that the passes would have been blocked up with snow—it would account for their not staying at Perga, whose hot streets are then deserted; "men, women, and children, flocks, herds, camels, and asses, all ascending at the beginning of the hot season from the plains to the cool basin-like hollows on the mountains, moving in the same direction with our missionaries" [Hows].

15-17. Then Paul stood up, and beckoning with his hand—as was his manner on such occasions (ch. 21:40; and see ch. 26:1). **Men of Israel, and ye that fear God**—by the latter expression meaning religious proselytes, who united with the Jews in all acts of ordinary worship. **and exalted the people when they dwelt as strangers in Egypt**—by marvellous interpositions for them in their deepest depression.

18-22. forty years suffered he their manners—rather, according to what appears the true reading, 'cherished he them' (as a nurse the infant in her bosom).

ADAM CLARKE

under any obligation to accompany them any longer or any farther than he pleased. He seems to have been little else than their servant, and certainly was not divinely appointed to this work, as they were; and consequently might leave them innocently, though not kindly, if they could not readily supply his place.

14. *They came to Antioch in Pisidia.* This place is mentioned thus to distinguish it from Antioch in Syria, with which it had nothing in common but the name. There were several cities and towns in various districts of these countries called Antioch; some have reckoned up not less than twelve. *Into the synagogue on the sabbath day.* Though Paul was now on a special mission to the Gentiles, yet he availed himself of every opportunity, in every place, of making the first offer of salvation to the Jews.

15. *After the reading of the law and the prophets.* A certain portion of the *law* and another of the *prophets* were read every Sabbath, and the law was so divided as to be read over once every year. It has been a question in what language were the law and prophets read in a synagogue of Pisidia, for in that district Strabo informs us that four languages were spoken, viz., the Pisidian, the Solyman, the Greek, and the Lydian. Dr. Lightfoot conjectures, with great probability, that the Scriptures were read in the original Hebrew, and that an interpreter rendered the reading to the people in their mother tongue. *The rulers of the synagogue.* These were the persons whose business it was to read the appointed sections, to take care of the synagogue and its concerns, and to see that all was done decently and in order. *Sent unto them.* Seeing them to be Jews, they wished them to give some suitable address to the people, i.e., to the Jews who were then engaged in divine worship; for the whole of the following discourse, which greatly resembles that of Stephen, chap. vii, is directed to the Jews alone; and this was probably spoken in either Hebrew or Greek. *Ye men and brethren.* "Men brethren," a Hebraism for, "You men who are our brethren," i.e., Jews, as we ourselves are. *If ye have any word of exhortation.* "If you have any subject of consolation," any word of comfort to us, who are sojourners in this strange land, speak it. The "Consolation of Israel" was an epithet of the Messiah among the Jews, and it is probable that it was in reference to Him that the rulers of the synagogue spoke.

16. *Men of Israel*, you that are Jews by birth; *and ye that fear God*—you that are proselytes to the Jewish religion. In this discourse Paul proves that Jesus Christ is the Messiah, sent from God, for the salvation not only of the Jews, but of the whole human race. And this he does, not with the rhetorician's arts, but in a plain, simple detail of the history of Christ and the most remarkable transactions of the people of God, which referred to His manifestation in the flesh.

17. *The God of . . . our fathers.* The apostle begins his discourse with the Egyptian bondage and their deliverance from it, as points the most remarkable and striking in their history, in which the providence and mighty power of God, exerted so frequently in their behalf, were peculiarly conspicuous. *Exalted the people.* Even when they were strangers in the land and greatly oppressed, God exalted them; made them a terror to their enemies, and multiplied them greatly. *With an high arm.* A literal translation of the Hebrew phrase, "with a lifted-up arm," to protect them and destroy their enemies. The meaning of the phrase is "a manifest display of the divine power."

18. *About the time of forty years.* The space of time between their coming out of Egypt and going into the Promised Land. *Suffered he their manners.* He dealt indulgently with them; howsoever they behaved toward Him, He mercifully bore with and kindly treated them. But instead of *etropophoresen*, some MSS. read *etrophophoresen*, which signifies, "He nourished and fed them, or bore them about in His arms as a tender nurse does her child." This reading agrees excellently with the scope of the place and is a reading of at least equal value with that in the commonly received text. Both, when rightly understood, speak nearly the same sense; but the latter is the most expressive, and agrees

MATTHEW HENRY

(6) He had put them in possession of the land of Canaan (*v.* 19): *When he had destroyed seven nations in the land of Canaan, he divided their land to them by lot.*

(7) He had raised up men to deliver them out of the hands of those that oppressed them after their settlement in Canaan, *v.* 20, 21. He *gave them judges.* Though they were a provoking people, yet upon their petition a deliverer was raised up. He governed them by a *prophet, Samuel.* He *afterwards* at their request *set a king over them* (*v.* 21), *Saul, the son of Cis.* At last, he made David their king, *v.* 22. *When God had removed Saul, he raised up unto them David to be their king,* and made *a covenant of royalty with him, and with his seed.* He quotes the testimony God gave concerning him. That his choice was divine: *I have found David.* Finding implies seeking; as if God had ransacked all the families of Israel to find a man fit for his purpose, and this was he. That his character was divine: *A man after my own heart,* such a one as I would have, one on whom the image of God is stamped. That his conduct was under divine direction: *He shall fulfil all my will.* He shall desire and endeavour to do the will of God, and shall be enabled to do it. The changes of their government showed that it *made nothing perfect,* and therefore must give way to the spiritual kingdom of the Messiah, which was now in the setting up; and therefore they needed not conceive any jealousy at all of the preaching of the gospel.

2. He gives them a full account of our Lord Jesus, and shows that this Jesus is his promised Seed (*v.* 23): *Of this man's seed,* from that *man after God's own heart, hath God, according to his promise, raised unto Israel a Saviour—Jesus,* who carries salvation in his name.

(1) How welcome should the preaching of the gospel of Christ be to the Jews, and how should they embrace it, as *well worthy of all acceptation,* when it brought them the tidings of a Saviour, *a Saviour to save them from their sins,* their worst enemies. A Saviour of God's raising up. Raised up *to be a Saviour unto Israel,* to them in the first place; so far was the gospel from designing the rejection of Israel, that it designed the gathering of them. Raised up *of the seed of David,* that ancient royal family, which the people of Israel gloried so much in. Raised up *according to his promise,* the promise to David. Why then should they entertain it so coldly, now that it was brought to them?

(2) Concerning this Jesus, he tells them,

[1] That John the Baptist was his forerunner, that great man whom all acknowledged to be a prophet. Let them not say that the Messiah's coming was a surprise upon them, for they had sufficient warning by John, who *preached before his coming, v.* 24. He made way for his entrance, by preaching *the baptism of repentance to all the people of Israel.* He showed them their sins, *called them to repentance,* and *to bring forth fruits meet for repentance.* He gave notice of his approach (*v.* 25): *As he fulfilled his course.* "Now," saith he, "*Whom think you that I am?* You may be thinking that I am *the Messiah,* whom you expect; but you are mistaken, *I am not he,* but he is at the door; *behold, there cometh one* immediately *after me, whose shoes of his feet I am not worthy to loose,* and you may guess who that must be."

[2] That the rulers and people of the Jews, who should have welcomed him, were his persecutors and murderers. When the apostles preach Christ as *the Saviour,* they are so far from concealing his ignominious death, that they always *preach Christ crucified,* yea, and crucified by his own people, by *those that dwelt in Jerusalem,* and *their rulers, v.* 27. Their sin was *that though they found no cause of death in him, yet they desired Pilate that he might be slain* (*v.* 28). They compelled Pilate to crucify him, not only contrary to his inclination, but contrary to his conscience; they condemned him *to so great a death,* though they could not convict him of the least sin. Justly they might have been cut off from all benefit by the Messiah, who had thus abused him, and yet they were not; notwithstanding all this, the preaching of this gospel shall begin at Jerusalem. The reason of this was because *they knew him not, v.* 27. Christ owned this in extenuation of their crime: *They know not what they do;* and so did Peter: *I wot that through ignorance you did this, ch.* iii. 17. It was also because they knew not the voice of the prophets though they heard them read every sabbath day. They did not understand nor consider that it was foretold that the Messiah should suffer. Many that read the prophets do not know the voice of the prophets. They have the sound of the gospel in their ears, but not the sense of it in their heads. God overruled them, for the accomplishment of the prophecies of the Old

JAMIESON, FAUSSET, BROWN

20. after that he gave . . . judges . . . about the space of four hundred and fifty years—As this appears to contradict I Kings 6:1, various solutions have been proposed. Taking the words as they stand in the *Greek,* thus, 'after that, by the space of 450 years, He gave judges,' the meaning may be, that about 450 years elapsed from the time of the covenant with Abraham *until* the period of the judges; which is historically correct, the word 'about' showing that chronological exactness was not aimed at. But taking the sense to be as in our version, that it was the period of the judges itself which lasted about 450 years, this statement also will appear historically correct, if we include in it the interval of subjection to foreign powers which occurred during the period of the judges, and understand it to describe the whole period from the settlement of the tribes in Canaan to the establishment of royalty. Thus, from the Exodus to the building of the temple were 592 years [JOSEPHUS, *Antiquities,* 8. 3. 1]; deduct forty years in the wilderness; twenty-five years of Joshua's rule [JOSEPHUS, *Antiquities,* 5. 1. 29]; forty years of Saul's reign (vs. 2); forty of David's and the first four years of Solomon's reign (I Kings 6:1), and there remain, just 443 years; or, in round numbers, 'about 450 years.' **21. God gave . . . them Saul . . . of the tribe of Benjamin**—That the speaker was himself of the same name and of the same tribe, has often been noticed as in all likelihood present to the apostle's mind while speaking. **forty years**—With this length of Saul's reign (not mentioned in the Old Testament), JOSEPHUS coincides (*Antiquities* 6. 14. 9). **22. I have found David . . .**—This quotation is the substance of Psalm 89:20; I Samuel 13:14; and perhaps also of Psalm 78:70-72. **23-25. Of this man's seed hath God, according to . . . promise, raised unto Israel a Saviour, Jesus**—The emphasis on this statement lies: (1) in the *seed* from which Christ sprang—David's—and the *promise* to that effect, which was thus fulfilled; (2) on the *character* in which this promised Christ was given of God—"a SAVIOUR." His personal name "JESUS" is emphatically added, as designed to express that very character. (See on Matt. 1:21.)

26-31. children . . . of Abraham, and whosoever among you feareth God—Gentile proselytes—**to you is the word of this salvation sent**—both being regarded as one class, as "the Jew first," to whom the Gospel was to be addressed in the first instance. **27. For they that dwell at Jerusalem, and their rulers, because they knew him not . . .**—The apostle here speaks as if the more immediate guilt of Christ's death lay with the rulers and people of the metropolis, to which he fondly hoped that those residing at such a distance as Antioch would not set their seal. **28. found no cause of death**—though they *sought* it (Matt. 26:59, 60).

ADAM CLARKE

best with Paul's discourse and the history to which he alludes. See the same form of expression, Num. xi. 12; Exod. xix. 4; Isa. xlvi. 3-4; and lxiii. 9.

19. *Destroyed seven nations.* The Canaanites, Hittites, Girgasites, Amorites, Hivites, Peresites, and Jebusites.

20. *And after that he gave unto them judges about the space of four hundred and fifty years.* This is a most difficult passage. The apostle seems here to contradict the account in 1 Kings vi. 1: "And it came to pass in the four hundred and eightieth year after the children of Israel were come out of the land of Egypt, in the fourth year of Solomon's reign . . . he began to build the house of the Lord." Calmet has paraphrased these passages nearly to the same sense. The text may be thus connected; v. 19: "And having destroyed seven nations in the land of Canaan, He divided their land to them by lot, about one hundred and fifty years after. And afterwards He gave them judges, to the time of Samuel the prophet." The paraphrase of Calmet is the following: *"The God of this people of Israel chose our fathers* in the person of Abraham; he promised him the land of Canaan; and four hundred and fifty years after this promise, and the birth of Isaac, who was the son and heir of the promise, he put them in possession of that land which he had promised so long before." As this view of the subject removes all the principal difficulties, I shall not trouble my reader with other modes of interpretation.

21. *Saul the son of Cis.* In all proper names quoted from the Old Testament, we should undoubtedly follow, as nearly as possible, the same orthography: "Kish" was the name of this king's father, and so we spell it in the Old Testament. *The space of forty years.* Reckoning from the time of his anointing by Samuel to the time of his death.

22. *David . . . a man after mine own heart.* That is, a man who would rule the kingdom according to God's will.

23. *Of this man's seed hath God . . . raised . . . a Saviour.* That the Messiah was promised to come from the family of David, see **Isa. xi. 1-2** and Jer. xxiii. 5-6.

25. *As John fulfilled his course.* "As John was fulfilling his race, he said." It has been supposed that the word "course," or "race," is used here to point out the short duration of the Baptist's ministry, and the fervent zeal with which he performed it. It signifies properly his ministry, or life.

26. *Men and brethren.* This should have been translated simply "brethren." See the note on chap. vii. 2. *Children of the stock of Abraham.* All you that are Jews. *And whosoever among you feareth God.* That is, all you who are Gentiles, and are now proselytes to the Jewish religion. *The word of this salvation.* The doctrine that contains the promise of deliverance from sin and the means by which it is brought about.

27. *Because they knew him not.* A gentle excuse for the persecuting high priests. They did not know that Jesus was the Christ, because they did not know the prophets; and only did they not know the prophets which were read every Sabbath day? Because they did not desire to know His will, and therefore they knew not the doctrine of God; nor did they know that, in condemning Christ, they fulfilled those very Scriptures which were read every Sabbath day in their synagogues.

MATTHEW HENRY

Testament: *Because they knew not the voice of the prophets, they fulfilled them in condemning him.* It is possible that men may be fulfilling scripture prophecies, even when they are breaking scripture precepts. All that was foretold concerning the sufferings of the Messiah was fulfilled in Christ (*v.* 29): *When they had fulfilled all* the rest *that was written of him,* they fulfilled what was foretold concerning his being buried. They *took him down from the tree, and laid him in a sepulchre.* This is taken notice of here as that which made his resurrection the more illustrious. They laid him in a sepulchre, and thought they had him fast.

[3] That he *rose again from the dead.* This was the great truth that was to be preached; for it is the main pillar, by which the whole fabric of the gospel is supported.

First, He rose by consent (*v.* 30): *God raised him from the dead.* His enemies laid him in a sepulchre, with design he should always lay there; but God said, *No.*

Secondly, There was sufficient proof of his having risen (*v.* 31): *He was seen many days.* They *came up with him from Galilee to Jerusalem,* and *they are his witnesses unto the people.* They have attested the thing many a time, and are ready to attest it, though they were to die for the same. Paul says nothing of his own seeing him, because it was in a vision, which was more convincing to himself than it could be to others.

Thirdly, The resurrection of Christ was the performance of the promise. It was not only true news, but good news: "In declaring this, we *declare unto you glad tidings* (*v.* 32, 33), which should be in a particular manner acceptable to you Jews. The doctrine we preach, if you receive it aright, brings you the greatest satisfaction imaginable; for it is in the resurrection of Christ that *the promise which was made to your fathers is fulfilled to you.*" The great promise of the Old Testament was that of the Messiah, *in whom all the families of the earth should be blessed,* and not the family of Abraham only. It was to be the common benefit of all families that he should be raised up to them. God hath *raised up Jesus*; *raised* him *again* (so we read it), meaning *from the dead.* This is the fulfilling of the promises made to the fathers, the promise of sending the Messiah. "This is he that should come, and in him you have all that God promised in the Messiah, though not all that you promised yourselves." Paul puts himself into the number of the Jews, to whom the promise was fulfilled: *To us their children.* And the preaching of the gospel to the Gentiles, which was the great thing that the Jews found themselves aggrieved at, was so far from infringing the promise made to them that the promise itself that *all the families of the earth* should be blessed in the Messiah, could not otherwise be accomplished.

Fourthly, The resurrection of Christ was the great proof of his being the Son of God, and confirms what was written in the second Psalm. *Thou art my Son, this day have I begotten thee. He was declared to be the Son of God with power, by the resurrection from the dead.* When he was first raised up out of obscurity, God declared concerning him by a voice from heaven, *This is my beloved Son* (Matt. iii. 17), which has a plain reference to that in the second Psalm, *Thou art my Son.* Now all which was declared at Christ's baptism and again at his transfiguration, was undeniably proved by his resurrection. The decree which was so long before declared was then confirmed. "This day have I made it to appear that I have begotten thee."

Fifthly, His being raised the third day, so as not to see corruption, and to a heavenly life, so as no more to return to corruption, further confirms his being the Messiah promised. He rose to die no more. Lazarus came out of the grave with his grave-clothes on, because he was to use them again; but Christ, having no more occasion for them, left them behind. Now this makes them sure mercies indeed that he has risen to die no more. As, if Christ had died and had not risen again, so if he had risen to die again, we had come short of the sure mercies, or at least could not have been sure of them. He rose so soon after he was dead that his body did not see corruption. Now this was one of *the sure mercies of David,* for it was said to him, *Neither wilt thou suffer thy Holy One to see corruption, v.* 35. This promise could not have its accomplishment in David, but looked forward to Christ. It could not be accomplished in David himself (*v.* 36), for *David, after he had served his own generation, by the will of God, fell asleep, and was laid to his fathers, and saw corruption.* Here we have a short account of the life, death, and burial, of the patriarch David, and his continuance under the power of death. His life: *He served his own generation, by the will of God.* David was a useful good man; he did good in the world *by the will of God.* He

JAMIESON, FAUSSET, BROWN

29. they took him down . . . and laid him in a sepulchre—Though the burial of Christ was an act of honor and love to Him by the disciples to whom the body was committed, yet since His enemies looked after it and obtained a guard of soldeirs to keep watch over it as the remains of their own victim, the apostle regards this as the last manifestation on their part of enmity to the Saviour, that they might see how God laughed all their precautions to scorn by "raising Him from the dead."

31. he was seen many days of them which came up with him from Galilee to Jerusalem, . . .—i.e., by those who, having gone out and in with Him in closest intimacy during all His public ministry, which lay chiefly in Galilee, and having accompanied Him on His last journey to Jerusalem, could not possibly be mistaken as to the identity of the risen One, and were therefore unexceptionable and sufficient witnesses.

32, 33. God hath fulfilled the same— hath completely fulfilled.' **in that he hath raised up Jesus again**—lit., 'raised up'; but the meaning is (notwithstanding the contrary opinion of many excellent interpreters) *"from the dead"*; as the context plainly shows.

as it is written in the second psalm—in many MSS. 'the first Psalm'; what we call the first being regarded by the ancient Jews as only an introduction to the Psalter, which was considered to begin with the second. **this day have I begotten thee**—As the apostle in Romans 1:4 regards the resurrection of Christ merely as the *manifestation* of a prior Sonship, which he afterwards (ch. 8:32) represents as *essential,* it is plain that this is his meaning here. (Such *declarative* meaning of the verb 'to be' is familiar to every reader of the Bible.) See i.e., John 15:8, "So shall ye be," i.e., *be seen* to be "My disciples." It is against the whole sense of the New Testament to ascribe the *origin* of Christ's Sonship to His resurrection. **34-37. now no more to return to corruption**—i.e., to the grave where death reigns; and cf. Romans 6:9, "Christ being raised from the dead dieth no more, *death hath no more dominion over him.*" **I will give you the sure mercies of David**—(Isa. 55:3). The word rendered "mercies" is peculiar, denoting the *sanctity* of them, as comprehending the whole riches of the new covenant; while the other word, "sure," points to the *certainty* with which they would, through David's Seed, be at length all substantiated. See on John 1:14. But how do these words prove the resurrection of Christ? "They presuppose it; for since an eternal kingdom was promised to David, the Ruler of this kingdom could not remain under the power of death. But to strengthen the indefinite prediction by one more definite, the apostle adduces Psalm 16:10, of which Peter had given the same explanation (see on ch. 2:27, 30, 31), both apostles denying the possibility of its proper reference to David" [OLSHAUSEN]. **36. For David, after he had served his own generation by the will of God**—rather, 'served,' in his own generation, the will (or 'counsel') of God; yielding himself an instrument for the accomplishment of God's high designs, and in this respect being emphatically "the man after God's own heart."

ADAM CLARKE

30. *But God raised him from the dead.* And thus gave the fullest proof of His innocence.

31. *He was seen many days.* The thing was done but a very short time since; and many of the witnesses are still alive, and ready to attest the fact of this Resurrection in the most unequivocal manner.

32. *We declare unto you glad tidings.* We proclaim that gospel to you which is the fulfillment of the promise made unto the fathers.

33. *Thou art my Son, this day have I begotten thee.* It has been disputed whether this text should be understood of the incarnation or of the resurrection of our Lord. If understood of His incarnation, it can mean no more than this, that the human nature of our blessed Lord was begotten by the energy of the Holy Spirit in the womb of the blessed Virgin; for as to His divine nature, which is allowed to be God, it could be neither created nor begotten. But the doctrine of the eternal sonship of Christ is absolutely irreconcilable to reason and contradictory to itself. Eternity is that which has had no beginning nor stands in any reference to time; Son supposes time, generation, and Father, and time also antecedent to such a generation. Therefore the rational conjunction of these two terms, "Son" and "eternity," is absolutely impossible, as they imply essentially different and opposite ideas. If the passage in question be understood of the resurrection of Christ, it points out that the human nature, which was produced by the power of God in the womb of the Virgin and which was the Son of God, could see no corruption; and therefore, though it died for sin, must be raised from the dead before it saw corruption. Thus God owned that human nature to be peculiarly His own; and therefore Jesus Christ was "declared to be the Son of God with power . . . by the resurrection from the dead," Rom. i. 4.

34. *No more to return to corruption.* To the grave, to death, the place and state of corruption. *The sure mercies of David.* These words are quoted literatim from the Septuagint version of Isa. lv. 3, and which Paul considers as being fulfilled in the resurrection of Christ. From this application of the words it is evident that the apostle considered the word *David* as signifying the Messiah; and then the *sure* or faithful *mercies,* being such as relate to the new covenant and the various blessings promised in it, are evidently those which are sealed and confirmed to mankind by the resurrection of Christ.

MATTHEW HENRY

served his own generation so as therein to serve God. He served the good of men, but did not serve the will of men. David was a great blessing to the age wherein he lived; he was the *servant* of his generation: many are the curse, and plague, and burden of their generation. Those that will do good in the world must make themselves *servants of all.* We were not born for ourselves, but are members of communities, to which we must study to be serviceable. Yet here is the difference between David and Christ, that David was to serve only his own generation, but Christ was to serve *all* generations, must ever live to reign for all ages, as long as the sun and moon endure. His death: *He fell asleep.* Death is a sleep, a quiet rest, to those who, while they lived, laboured in the service of God and their generation. He did not fall asleep till he had done the work for which God raised him up. God's witnesses never die till they have finished their testimony; and then *the sleep of the labouring man will be sweet.* His burial: *He was laid to his fathers.* His continuance in the grave: *He saw corruption.* We are sure he did not rise again. He saw corruption, and therefore that promise could not have its accomplishment in him. It was accomplished in the Lord Jesus (*v.* 37): *He whom God raised again saw no corruption.* Of him therefore the promise must be understood, and no other. Having given them this account of the Lord Jesus, he comes to make application of it. 1. In the midst of his discourse he had told his hearers that they were concerned in all this (*v.* 26): "*To you is the word of this salvation sent.* It is sent to you for a word of salvation; if it be not so, it is your own fault." He therefore speaks to them with tenderness and respect: You are *men and brethren.* Those to whom he does here bring the *word of salvation* are, (*a*) The native Jews, Hebrews of the Hebrews, as Paul himself was: *Children of the stock of Abraham,* to you is this word of salvation sent; nay, it is therefore sent to you, to save you from your sins. It is an advantage to be of a good stock; for, though salvation does not always follow the children of godly parents, yet the word of salvation does. (*b*) The proselytes: "*Whosoever among you that feareth God, to you is the word of this salvation sent;* you need the further discoveries and directions of revealed religion, and will bid them welcome, and therefore shall certainly be welcome to take the benefit of them." 2. In the close of his discourse he applies what he had said concerning Christ to his hearers. Now they would be ready to ask, What is all this to us? And he tells them plainly what it is to them. It will be their unspeakable advantage if they embrace Jesus Christ, and believe this word of salvation. "*Be it known unto you therefore, men and brethren*—we are warranted to proclaim it to you, and you are called to take notice of it." He did not stand up to preach before them, but to preach to them, and not without hopes of prevailing with them. They are *brethren,* spoken to, and dealt with, by men like themselves; of the same nation. It is proper for the preachers of the gospel to call their hearers brethren, with an affectionate concern for their welfare, and as being equally interested with them in the gospel they preach. Let all that hear the gospel of Christ know these two things: *First,* That it is an act of indemnity granted to the children of men. It is for and in consideration of the mediation of Christ that this act of grace is passed and proclaimed (*v.* 38): "*Through this man is preached unto you the forgiveness of sins.* Your sins may be forgiven. The remission of sins is *through this man.* By his merit it was purchased, in his name it is offered. We preach to you *the forgiveness of sins.* That is the salvation we bring you." *Secondly,* That it does that for us which the law of Moses could not do. "Be it known to you that it is by Christ only that *those who believe in him* are *justified from all things from which you could not be justified by the law of Moses*" (*v.* 39); therefore they ought to entertain and embrace the gospel, and not to adhere to the law in opposition to it. The great concern of sinners is to be justified, and accepted as righteous in God's sight. Those who are truly justified are acquitted from all their guilt. It was impossible for a sinner to be justified by the law of Moses. By Jesus Christ we obtain a complete justification; for by him a complete atonement was made for sin. All that believe in Christ, and give up themselves to be ruled by him, are justified by him. It is at their utmost peril if they reject the gospel of Christ (*v.* 40, 41): '*Beware therefore.* Beware lest you not only come short of the blessings and benefits spoken of in the prophets, but fall under the doom spoken of in the prophets; *lest that come upon you which is spoken of.*" The threatenings are warnings, designed to awaken us to beware lest it should come upon us. The apostle follows the Septuagint translation, which

JAMIESON, FAUSSET, BROWN

This done, he 'fell asleep, and was gathered to his fathers, and saw corruption.' David, therefore (argues the apostle), could not be the subject of his own prediction, which had its proper fulfilment only in the resurrection of the uncorrupted body of the Son of God, emphatically God's "Holy One."

ALEXANDER MACLAREN:

Paul's yearning for his brethren's salvation is not content with proclaiming the fact of Christ's resurrection, nor with pointing to it as fulfilling prophecy; he gathers all up into a loving, urgent offer of salvation for every believing soul, and solemn warning to despisers. Here the whole man flames out. Here the characteristic evangelical teaching, which is sometimes ticketed as "Pauline" by way of stigma, is heard. Already had he grasped the great antithesis between law and gospel. Already his great word "justified" has taken its place in his terminology. The essence of the Epistles to Romans and Galatians is here. Justification is the being pronounced and treated as not guilty. Law cannot justify. "In him" we are justified. Observe that this is an advance on the previous statement that "through him" we receive remission of sins.

"In him" points, though but incidentally and slightly, to the great truth of incorporation with Jesus, of which Paul had afterward so much to write. The justifying in Christ is complete and absolute. And the sole sufficient condition of receiving it is faith. But the greater the glory of the light the darker the shadow which it casts. The broad offer of complete salvation has ever to be accompanied with the plain warning of the dread issue of rejecting it. Just because it is so free and full, and to be had on such terms, the warning has to be rung into deaf ears, "Beware therefore!" Hope and fear are legitimately appealed to by the Christian evangelist. They are like the two wings which may lift the soul to soar to its safe shelter in the Rock of Ages.
—*Expositions of Holy Scripture*

38-41. the forgiveness of sins—the first necessity of the sinner, and so the first experienced blessing of the Gospel.

39. by him all that believe are justified from all things—The sense requires that a pause in the sentence be made here: 'By him the believer is absolved from all charges of the law.' What follows—**from which ye could not be justified by the law of Moses**—is not an *exceptional* but an *explanatory* clause. The meaning is not, 'Though the law justifies from many things, it cannot justify from all things, but Christ makes up all deficiencies"; but the meaning is, 'By Christ the believer is justified from all things, whereas the law justifies from nothing.' (N.B. The deeper sense of justification, the *positive* side of it, is reserved for the Epistles, addressed to the justified themselves: and whereas it is the *resurrection* of Christ here, and throughout the Acts chiefly, which is dwelt on, because the first thing in order to bring peace to the guilty through Christ was to establish His Messiahship by His resurrection, in the Epistles to believers His *death* as the way of reconciliation is fully unfolded.) **40. Beware, therefore . . .**—By this awful warning of the Old Testament the apostle would fain "shut them up unto the faith."

ADAM CLARKE

36. *David . . . fell on sleep . . . and saw corruption.* David died, was buried, and never rose again; therefore David cannot be the person spoken of here. These words can be applied to Jesus Christ only, and in Him they are most exactly fulfilled.

38. *Be it known unto you therefore.* This is the legitimate conclusion: Seeing the word of God is true, and He has promised an endless succession to the seed of David; seeing David and all his family have failed in reference to the political kingdom, a spiritual Kingdom and a spiritual succession must be intended, that the sure covenant and all its blessings may be continued. Again: Seeing the person by whom this is to be done is to see no corruption; seeing David has died, and has seen (fallen under the power of) corruption; seeing Jesus the Christ has wrought all the miracles which the prophets said He should work; seeing He has suffered all the indignities which your prophets said He must suffer; seeing after His death He has most incontestably risen again from the dead, and has not fallen under the power of corruption—then He must be the very Person in whom all the predictions are fulfilled, and the Person through whom all the blessings of the covenant must come. *Through this man is preached unto you the forgiveness of sins.* See the notes on chap. v. 30-31. Remission of sins—the removal of the power, guilt, and pollution of sin—comes alone through this Man whom you crucified and who is risen from the dead.

39. *And by him.* On His account, and through Him, *all that believe* in His divine mission and the end for which He has been manifested, namely, to put away sin by the sacrifice of himself, *are justified from all things,* from the guilt of all transgressions committed against God, *from which ye could not be justified by the law of Moses;* because it is impossible that "the blood of bulls and of goats, and the ashes of an heifer sprinkling the unclean," or any other rite or service of this kind, could take away sin from the soul, cancel its guilt in the conscience, or make an atonement to the divine justice.

40. *Beware . . . lest that come upon you.* If you reject these benefits, now freely offered to you in this preaching of Christ crucified,

MATTHEW HENRY

reads, *Behold, you despisers* (for, *behold, you among the heathen*). Beware lest it be said to you, *Behold, you despisers*. It is the ruin of many that they despise religion, they look upon it as a thing below them, and are not willing to stoop to it. "Take heed lest the judgment come upon you which was spoken of in the prophets: that *you shall wonder and perish*." Those that will not wonder and be saved shall wonder and perish. Those that enjoyed the privileges of the church will wonder when they find that their privileges do but make their condemnation the more intolerable. Let the unbelieving Jews expect that God will *work a work in their days which you shall in no wise believe, though a man declare it unto you*. This may be understood as a prediction, either, (1) Of their sin, that they should be incredulous, that that great work of God, the redemption of the world by Christ, though it should be in the most solemn manner declared unto them, yet they would *in no wise believe it*. Those that had the honour and advantage to have this work wrought in their days had not the grace to believe it. Or, (2) Of their destruction, a work which one would not have believed should have ever been done, considering how much they had been the favourites of Heaven. Thus is there a *strange punishment to the workers of iniquity*, especially to the despisers of Christ.

Verses 42–52

The design of this story being to vindicate the apostles, especially Paul, it is here observed that he proceeded therein with all the caution imaginable.

I. There were some of the Jews that were so incensed against the preaching of the gospel that they would not bear to hear it, but *went out of the synagogue* (*v*. 42). Now this bespoke: An open infidelity. They thus publicly avowed their contempt of Christ and of his doctrine, and they thus endeavoured to beget prejudices in the minds of others. An obstinate infidelity. They went out of the synagogue to show that they did not believe the gospel, they were resolved they would not. Justly therefore was the gospel taken from them, when they first took themselves from it. For it is certainly true that God never leaves any till they first leave him.

II. The Gentiles were as willing to hear the gospel as those Jews were to get out of the hearing of it: *They besought that these words might be preached to them the next sabbath*. They begged that forgiveness of sins through Christ might be preached to them. The Jews' leavings, nay, loathings, were their longings. This justifies Paul in his preaching to them, that he was invited to it. Who could refuse to break the bread of life to those who begged so hard for it, and to give that to the poor at the door which the children at the table threw under their feet? They had heard the doctrine of Christ, but did not understand it at the first hearing, and therefore they begged it might be preached to them again. What we have heard we should desire to hear again, that it may take deep root in us, and the nail that is driven may be clenched. It aggravates the bad disposition of the Jews that the Gentiles desired to hear that often which they were not willing to hear once.

III. There were many, both of Jews and proselytes, that were wrought upon by the preaching of the gospel. *Many of the Jews and religious proselytes followed Paul and Barnabas*. They submitted to the grace of God, and were admitted to the benefit and comfort of it. They *followed Paul and Barnabas*; they became their disciples, or rather the disciples of Christ. Those that join themselves to Christ will join themselves to his ministers, and follow them. And Paul and Barnabas bade those of the Jews welcome that were willing to come under their instructions. They were exhorted and encouraged to persevere herein: *Paul and Barnabas, speaking to them, persuaded them to continue in the grace of God*. And the grace of God shall not be wanting to those who thus continue in it.

IV. The *next sabbath day* (*v*. 44): *Almost the whole city came together to hear the word of God*. This brought a vast concourse of people to the synagogue on the sabbath day. Some came out of curiosity, others longing to see what the Jews would do, and many who had heard something of the word of God came to hear more, and to hear it, *not as the word of men but as the word of God*. Now this justified Paul in preaching to the Gentiles, that he met with the most encouraging auditors among them.

V. The Jews were enraged at this; and not only would not receive the gospel themselves, but were filled with indignation at those that crowded after it (*v*. 45): *When the Jews saw the multitudes*, this *filled them with envy*. They grudged the interest the apostles had in the people. This was the same spirit that worked in the Pharisees towards Christ; they were cut to the

JAMIESON, FAUSSET, BROWN

41. ye will not believe though a man declare it unto you—i.e., even on unexceptionable testimony. The words, from Habakkuk 1:5, were originally a merciful but fruitless warning against the approaching destruction of Jerusalem by the Chaldeans and the Babylonish captivity. As such nothing could more fitly describe the more awful calamity impending over the generation which the apostle addressed.

42, 43. And when the Jews were gone out of the synagogue, the Gentiles besought that these words might be preached to them the next sabbath—rather (according to what is beyond doubt the true reading), 'Now, as they were going out [of the synagogue], they besought'—i.e., not the Gentiles, whose case comes in afterwards, but the mixed congregation of Jews and proselytes, to whom the discourse had been addressed, entreated to have another hearing of such truths; those of them, that is, who had been impressed. 'And after the breaking up of the synagogue, many of' both classes, Jews and religious proselytes, followed Paul and Barnabas (observe, from this time forward, the inverted order of these names; except ch. 14:14; 13:7; 12:25; on which see). These had evidently been won to the Gospel by what they had heard, and felt a clinging to their spiritual benefactors.

who, speaking to them—following up the discourse in the synagogue by some further words of encouragement. **persuaded them to continue in the grace of God**—which they had experienced through the Gospel. (Cf. ch. 11:23.) **44-48. the next sabbath came almost the whole city together to hear the word of God**—the intervening days having been spent in further inquiry and instruction, and the excitement reaching the Gentiles, who now for the first time crowded, along with the usual worshippers, into the synagogue.

45. But when the Jews—those zealots of exclusive Judaism—**saw the multitudes, they were filled with envy**—rather, 'indignation,' and broke out in their usual

ADAM CLARKE

you may expect such judgments from the hand of God as your forefathers experienced, when, for their rebellion and their contempt of His benefits, their city was taken, their Temple destroyed, and themselves either slain by the sword or carried into captivity. It is evident that Paul refers to Hab. i. 5-10.

41. *Behold, ye despisers*. There is a remarkable difference here between the Hebrew text in Habakkuk and that in the Septuagint, which is a little abridged here by Paul. It may now be necessary to inquire how Luke and the Septuagint should substitute *ye despisers*, for "ye among the heathen," in the Hebrew text. Without troubling myself or my readers with laborious criticisms on these words, I will simply state my opinion, that the prophet, instead of *bagoyim*, "among the heathen," wrote *bogadim*, "despisers," or *transgressors*—a word which differs only in a single letter, *daleth*, for *vau*. It seems as evident as it can be that this was the word which the Septuagint found in the copy from which they translated. Their evidence, and that of the apostle, joined to the consideration that the interchange of the two letters mentioned above might have been easily made, is quite sufficient to legitimate the reading for which I contend. The word which we translate *perish* signifies more properly "disappear, or hide yourselves"; as people, astonished and alarmed at some coming evil, betake themselves to flight, and hide themselves in order to avoid it.

42. *When the Jews were gone out*. That part of them in whom the words of the prophet were fulfilled, viz., those who, though they had the clearest relation of so interesting a history, would not believe it; they shut their eyes against the light and hardened their hearts against the truth. There were other Jews in the assembly that did believe and were saved. *The Gentiles besought*. There is some doubt whether the original should be translated *the Gentiles besought* or "they besought the Gentiles"; for the words will bear either, but the latter sense more naturally. When the Jews retired, determining not to credit what was spoken, the apostle, seeing the Gentiles of a better mind, requested them to come and hear those words, or doctrines, the next Sabbath. On this verse there is a great number of various readings: instead of, "when the Jews were going out of the synagogue," some MSS. read, "As they were going out, they entreated that these words should be preached unto them the next Sabbath." The most eminent critics approve of this reading; indeed it stands on such authority as to render it almost indubitable. We are therefore to understand the words thus: that, "as they were going out on the breaking up of the assembly, some of them desired that they might have these doctrines preached to them on the ensuing week or Sabbath." And thus all the ambiguity of the verse vanishes.

43. *Many of the Jews*. Direct descendants from some of the twelve tribes, and religious proselytes, heathens who had been converted to Judaism, and, having submitted to circumcision, had become *proselytes* of the covenant; though some think that the expression means persons who believed in one God, like the Jews, but who had not received circumcision.

44. *The next sabbath day*. The good news had spread far and wide, by means of the converted Jews and proselytes. *Almost the whole city*. Jews, proselytes, and Gentiles came together to hear "this doctrine of God," this divine teaching, by which so many of their kindred and acquaintance had become so wise and happy.

45. *The Jews . . . were filled with envy*. See on chap. v. 17. These could not bear the Gentiles, who believed in Christ, to be equal with them; and yet, according to the gospel, it was

MATTHEW HENRY

heart when they saw *the whole world go after him.* They opposed the doctrine the apostles preached: *They spoke against those things that were spoken by Paul,* finding some fault or other with everything he said, *contradicting and blaspheming.* They contradicted for contradiction-sake, and when they could find no colour of objection, they broke out into ill language against Christ and his gospel, blaspheming him and it. Commonly those who begin with contradicting end with blaspheming.

VI. The apostles hereupon solemnly declare themselves discharged from their obligation to the Jews, and at liberty to bring the word of salvation to the Gentiles. The Jews had the tender of the gospel, and did refuse it, and therefore ought not to say anything against the Gentiles having it. In declaring this, it is said (*v.* 46), *Paul and Barnabas waxed bold.* There is a time for the preachers of the gospel to show as much of the boldness of the lion as of the harmlessness of the dove. When the adversaries of Christ's cause begin to be daring, it is not for its advocates to be timid. The impudence of the enemies of the gospel, instead of frightening, should rather embolden its friends. They know in whom they had trusted to bear them out. Now Paul and Barnabas, having made the Jews a fair offer of gospel grace, here give them fair notice of their bringing it to the Gentiles. 1. They own that the Jews were entitled to the first offer: "*It was necessary that the word of God should first have been spoken to you,* to whom the promise was made, to whom Christ reckoned himself first sent." 2. They charge them with the refusal of it: *You put it from you.* If men put the gospel from them, God justly takes it from them. Herein they *judge themselves unworthy of everlasting life.* In one sense we must all judge ourselves unworthy of everlasting life, for there is nothing in us by which we can pretend to merit it, but here the meaning is, "You make it to appear, that you are not meet for eternal life. *You do,* in effect, *pass this judgment* upon yourselves, and *out of your own mouth you shall be judged*; you will not have it by Christ, by whom alone it is to be had, and so shall your doom be, you shall not have it at all." 3. Upon this they ground their preaching the gospel to the uncircumcised: "*Lo, we turn to the Gentiles.* If one will not, another will." 4. They justify themselves in this by a divine warrant (*v.* 47): "*For so hath the Lord commanded us.*" This is according to what was foretold in the Old Testament. When the Messiah, in the prospect of the Jews' infidelity, was ready to say, *I have laboured in vain,* he was told, that though *Israel were not gathered,* yet *he should be glorious.* "For *I have set thee* to be *a light of the Gentiles, that thou shouldst be for salvation unto the ends of the earth.*" He is set up to be a light; he enlightens the understanding, and so saves the soul. He is, and is to be, light and salvation to the Gentiles, to the end of the earth. All nations shall at length become his kingdom. This prophecy has had its accomplishment in part in the setting up of the kingdom of Christ in this island of ours.

VII. The Gentiles cheerfully embraced that which the Jews scornfully rejected, *v.* 48, 49. How the Gentiles welcomed this happy turn in their favour!

1. They took the comfort of it: *When they heard this they were glad.* It was good news to them. They were as welcome to the benefits of the Messiah's kingdom as the Jews themselves, and might share in their promise. When the Gentiles did but hear that the offers of grace should be made them *they were glad.* Many grieve under doubts whether they have an interest in Christ or no, when they should be rejoicing that they have an interest in him.

2. They gave God the praise of it: *They glorified the word of the Lord, the gospel;* the more they knew of it, the more they admired it. Oh! what a light, what a power, what a treasure, does this gospel bring along with it! Because now the knowledge of it was diffused, and not confined to the Jews only. It is the glory of the word of the Lord that the further it spreads the brighter it shines, which shows it to be not like the light of the candle, but like that of the sun when he goes forth in his strength. Because now the knowledge of it was brought to them. Those speak best of the honour of the word of the Lord that have themselves been subdued by its power, and comforted by its sweetness.

3. Many of them became sincerely obedient to the faith: *As many as were ordained to eternal life believed.* Those believed to whom God gave grace to believe. Those came to Christ whom the Father drew, and to whom the Spirit made the gospel call effectual. God gave this grace to believe to all those among them who were ordained to eternal life; or, *as many as were disposed to eternal life,* as many as had a concern about their eternal state, and aimed

JAMIESON, FAUSSET, BROWN

manner. **contradicting and blaspheming**—There is nothing more awful than Jewish fury and execration of the name of Jesus of Nazareth, when thoroughly roused.

46. Then Paul and Barnabas waxed bold, and said, . . .—This is in the highest style of a last and solemn protestation.

It was necessary that the word should first have been spoken to you—See the direction of Christ in Luke 24:47; also Romans 1:16. **since ye judge yourselves unworthy of everlasting life**—pass sentence upon yourselves.

47. For so hath the Lord commanded us, saying . . .—These and other predictions must have been long before this brought vividly home to Paul's mind in connection with his special vocation to the Gentiles. **I have set thee**—i.e., Messiah; from which Paul inferred that he was but following out this destination of his Lord, in transferring to the Gentiles those "unsearchable riches" which were now by the Jews rejected and despised.

48. when the Gentiles heard this, they were glad—to perceive that their accession to Christ was a matter of divine arrangement as well as apostolic effort.

and glorified the word of the Lord—by a cordial reception of it.

and as many as were ordained to eternal life believed—a very remarkable statement, which cannot, without foree, be interpreted of anything lower than this, that *a divine ordination to eternal life is the cause,* not the effect, *of any man's believing.*

ADAM CLARKE

really the case. *Contradicting.* The arguments and statements brought forward by the disciples; *and blaspheming,* speaking impiously and injuriously of Jesus Christ.

46. *Waxed bold.* Having great liberty of speech; a strong, persuasive, and overpowering eloquence. They had eternal truth for the basis of this discourse, a multitude of incontestable facts to support it, an all-persuading eloquence to illustrate and maintain what they had asserted. *Ye put it from you.* "Ye disdain" this doctrine, and consider it "contemptible"; so the word is frequently used.

47. *For so . . . the Lord commanded us.* The apostles could quote a pertinent scripture for everything they did, because the outlines of the whole gospel dispensation are founded in the law and the prophets, and they were now building the Church of God according to the pattern shown them in the mount. *I have set thee to be a light of the Gentiles.* This quotation is from Isa. xlix. 6 and was most fully in point. *For salvation unto the ends of the earth.* The very name of the Messiah, viz., Jesus, announced the design and end of His mission. He is the "Saviour," and is to be proclaimed as such to *the ends of the earth,* to all mankind.

48. *As many as were ordained to eternal life believed.* This text has been most pitifully misunderstood. Many suppose that it simply means that those in that assembly who were foreordained, or predestinated by God's decree to eternal life, believed under the influence of that decree. Now we should be careful to

MATTHEW HENRY

to make sure of eternal life, and it was the grace of God that wrought it in them.

4. When they believed they did what they could to spread the knowledge of Christ (*v.* 49): *And the word of the Lord was published throughout all the region.* Those new converts were themselves ready to communicate to others that which they were so full of themselves. Those that have become acquainted with Christ themselves will do what they can to bring others acquainted with him. Those in great and rich cities that have received the gospel should not think to engross it, but should do what they can to get it published in the country among the ordinary sort of people, who have souls to be saved as well as they.

VIII. Paul and Barnabas, having sown the seeds of a Christian church there, quitted the place, and went to do the like elsewhere. We read not anything of their working miracles here, to confirm their doctrine. Though God then did ordinarily make use of that method of conviction. Begetting faith by the immediate influence of his Spirit was itself the greatest miracle to those in whom it was wrought.

1. How *the unbelieving Jews* expelled the apostles out of that country. *They raised persecution against Paul and Barnabas.* Satan and his agents are most exasperated against the preachers of the gospel when they see them go on successfully. Thus it has been the common lot of the best men in the world to suffer ill for doing well. (1) What method the Jews took to give them trouble: *They stirred up the devout and honourable women* against them. It is sad when, under colour of devotion to God, they conceive an enmity to Christ, as those here mentioned. What! women persecutors! Can they forget the tenderness and compassion of their sex? What! honourable women! Can they thus stain their honour. But, which is strangest of all, devout women! Will they kill Christ's servants, and think therein they do God service? By these devout and honourable women they stirred up likewise *the chief men of the city*, the magistrates and the rulers, and set them against the apostles. (2) How far they carried it, so far that *they expelled them out of their coasts*; they banished them. It was not by fear, but downright violence, that they were driven out. This was a method God took to make those that were well disposed the more warmly affected towards the apostles; for it is natural to us to pity those that are persecuted, and to be the more ready to help them. The expelling of the apostles out of their coasts perhaps raised them more friends than conniving at them in their coasts would have done.

2. How the apostles abandoned and rejected the unbelieving Jews (*v.* 51): *They shook off the dust of their feet against them.* They declared that they would have no more to do with them. They expressed their detestation of their infidelity. As Jews and Gentiles, if they believe, are equally acceptable to God and good men; so, if they do not, they are equally abominable. Thus they set them at defiance, and expressed their contempt of them and their malice. Thus they left a testimony behind them that they had had a fair offer made them of the grace of the gospel. Thus Christ had ordered them to do, and for this reason, Matt. x. 14; Luke ix. 5. When *they left them, they came to Iconium*, not so much for safety, as for work.

3. What frame they left the new converts in *at Antioch* (*v.* 52): *The disciples* went on with their work. They were very cheerful. One would have expected that when Paul and Barnabas were expelled out of their coasts, the disciples would have been full of grief and full of fear. But no; *they were filled with joy* in Christ. All their fears were swallowed up in their believing joys. They were courageous, wonderfully animated with a holy resolution to cleave to Christ. The more we relish the comforts and encouragements we meet with in the power of godliness the better prepared we are to face the difficulties we meet with in the profession of godliness.

JAMIESON, FAUSSET, BROWN

49-52. And the word of the Lord was published throughout all the region—implying some stay in Antioch and missionary activity in its vicinity.

the devout and honourable women—female proselytes of distinction, jaundiced against the new preachers by those Jewish ecclesiastics to whom they had learned to look up. The potent influence of the female character both for and against the truth is seen in every age of the Church's history.

expelled them—an easier thing than to refute them.

shook off the dust of their feet against them—as directed (Matt. 10:14). **came unto Iconium**—a populous city about forty-five miles southeast from Pisidian Antioch: at the foot of Mount Taurus; on the borders of Lycaonia, Phrygia, and Pisidia; and in later times largely contributing to the consolidation of the Turkish empire.

the disciples—who, though not themselves expelled, had to endure sufferings for the Gospel, as we learn from ch. 14:22—**were filled with joy and with the Holy Ghost**—who not only raised them above shame and fear, as professed disciples of the Lord Jesus, but filled them with holy and elevated emotions.

ADAM CLARKE

examine what a word means before we attempt to fix its meaning. Whatever *tetagmenoi* may mean, which is the word we translate *ordained*, it includes no idea of *pre*ordination or *predes*tination of any kind. The verb *tasso* signifies to "place, set, order, appoint, dispose"; hence it has been considered here as implying the disposition or readiness of mind of several persons in the congregation, such as the religious proselytes mentioned in v. 43, who possessed the reverse of the disposition of those Jews who spake against those things, contradicting and blaspheming, v. 45. Though the word in this place has been variously translated, yet, of all the meanings ever put on it, none agrees worse with its nature and known signification than that which represents it as intending those who were predestinated to eternal life; this is no meaning of the term and should never be applied to it.

49. *The word of the Lord was published.* Those who had come from different parts and were converted carried the glad tidings to their respective neighborhoods.

50. *Devout and honourable women.* It is likely that these were heathen matrons who had become proselytes to the Jewish religion; and as they were persons of affluence and respectability, they had considerable influence with the civil magistracy of the place, and probably their husbands were of this order; and it is likely that they used that influence, at the instigation of the Jews, to get the apostles expelled from the place.

51. *They shook off the dust of their feet against them.* This was a very significant rite; by it they in effect said: "You are worse than the heathen; even your very land is accursed for your opposition to God, and we dare not permit even its dust to cleave to the soles of our feet; and we shake it off, in departing from your country, according to our Lord's command (Matt. x. 14), for a testimony against you, that we offered you salvation, but you rejected it and persecuted us." The Jews, when travelling in heathen countries, took care, when they came to the borders of their own, to shake off the dust of their feet, lest any of the unhallowed ground should defile the sacred land of Israel. *Came unto Iconium.* According to Strabo, Iconium was a small fortified town, the capital of Lycaonia.

52. *The disciples were filled with joy, and with the Holy Ghost.* Though in the world they had tribulation, yet in Christ they had peace. The happiness of a genuine Christian lies far beyond the reach of earthly disturbances, and is not affected by the changes and chances to which mortal things are exposed. The martyrs were more happy in the flames than their persecutors could be on their beds of down.

MATTHEW HENRY

CHAPTER 14

Verses 1–7

I. The preaching of the gospel in Iconium. As the blood of the martyrs has been the seed of the church, so the banishment of the confessors has helped to scatter that seed. They made the first offer of the gospel *to the Jews in their synagogues.* Though the Jews at Antioch had used them barbarously, yet they did not therefore decline preaching the gospel to the Jews at Iconium. Let not those of any denomination be condemned in the gross, nor some suffer for others' faults. The apostles concurred herein. *They went both together into the synagogue* to testify their unanimity and mutual affection.

II. The success of their preaching there: *They so spoke that a great multitude, both of the Jews and also of the Greeks,* that is the Gentiles, *believed.* The gospel was now preached to Jews and Gentiles together. In the close of the foregoing chapter it was preached first to the Jews, and then to the Gentiles, but here they are put together. The Jews have not so lost their preference as to be thrown behind, only the Gentiles are brought to stand upon even terms with them, and both together admitted into the church without distinction. There seems to have been something remarkable in the manner of the apostles' preaching there: *They so spoke that a great multitude believed*—so plainly, so convincingly, so warmly, so affectionately. What they spoke came from the heart and therefore was likely to reach to the heart. So boldly and courageously, that those who heard them could not but say that *God was with them of a truth.*

III. The opposition that their preaching met with there. Unbelieving Jews were the first spring of their trouble here, as elsewhere (*v.* 2): they *stirred up the Gentiles.* The influence which the gospel had upon many of the Gentiles, and their embracing it, as it provoked some of the Jews to a holy jealousy, so it provoked others of them to a wicked jealousy. Disaffected Gentiles, irritated by the unbelieving Jews, were the instruments of their trouble. The Jews, by false suggestions, made *their minds evil affected against the brethren.* They soured and embittered their spirits against both the converters and the converted. It is no wonder if those who are ill affected towards good people wish ill to them and contrive ill against them; it is all owing to ill will. *They molested* the minds of the Gentiles (so some of the critics take it); they were continually teasing them. The tools of persecutors have a dog's life, set on continually.

IV. Their continuance in their work there, and God's owning them in it, *v.* 3. We have here, 1. The apostles working for Christ. Because the minds of *the Gentiles were evil affected against them,* one would think that therefore they should have withdrawn. On the contrary, therefore *they abode there a long time, speaking boldly in the Lord.* The more they perceived the spite against the new converts, the more they were animated to go on in their work. *They spoke boldly,* and were not afraid of giving offence to the unbelieving Jews. But observe what animated them: *They spoke boldly in the Lord,* in his strength, not depending upon anything in themselves. 2. Christ working with the apostles, according to his promise, *Lo, I am with you always.* He failed not to give testimony to the word of his grace. The gospel is a word of grace, the assurance of God's goodwill to us. It is the word of Christ's grace, for it is in him alone that we find favour with God. Christ himself has attested this word of grace; he has assured us that it is the word of God. It is said particularly concerning the apostles here *that the Lord confirmed their testimony, in granting signs and wonders to be done by their hands*—in the miracles they wrought in the kingdom of nature—as well as in the greater miracles wrought on men's minds by the power of divine grace. The Lord was with them, while they were with him.

V. The division which this occasioned in the city (*v.* 4): *The multitude of the city was divided.* It seems, this business of the preaching of the gospel was so universally taken notice of that every person, even of *the multitude of the city,* was either for it or against it; none stood neuter. We may here see the meaning of Christ's prediction that he *came not to send peace upon earth, but rather division,* Luke xii. 51–53. If all would have given in unanimously into his measures, there would have been universal concord; but, disagreeing here, the breach was wide as the sea. It is better that part of the city go to heaven than all to hell. Let us not think it strange if the preaching of the gospel occasion division, it is better to be persecuted as dividers for swimming against the stream than yield ourselves to be carried down the stream

JAMIESON, FAUSSET, BROWN

CHAPTER 14

Vss. 1-7. MEETING WITH SIMILAR SUCCESS AND SIMILAR OPPOSITION AT ICONIUM, PAUL AND BARNABAS FLEE FOR THEIR LIVES TO LYSTRA AND DERBE, AND PREACH THERE. "After this detailed account of Paul's labors at Pisidian Antioch, Luke subjoins only brief notices of his further labors, partly because from the nature of the case his discourses must have embraced nearly the same topics, and partly because the consequences that resulted assumed quite a similar shape" [OLSHAUSEN]. **1. they went both together into the synagogue**—Though Paul was now the prominent speaker and actor, yet in everything Barnabas went along with him. **a . . . multitude . . . of the Greeks believed**—meaning probably the religious proselytes, as opposed to "the Gentiles" mentioned vs. 2.

ALEXANDER MACLAREN:

The usual results followed the preaching of the Gospel. The Jews were again the mischief-makers, and, with the astuteness of their race, pushed the Gentiles to the front, and this time tried a new piece of annoyance. "The brethren" bore the brunt of the attack—that is, the converts, not Paul and Barnabas. It was a cunning move to drop suspicions into the minds of influential townsmen, and so to harass, not the two strangers, but their adherents. The calculation was that that would stop the progress of the heresy by making its adherents uncomfortable, and would also wound the teachers through their disciples.

But one small element had been left out of the calculation—the sort of men these teachers were; and another factor which had not hitherto appeared came into play and upset the whole scheme. Paul and Barnabas knew when to retreat and when to stand their ground. This time they stood; and the opposition launched at their friends was the reason why they did so. "Long time *therefore* abode they." If their own safety had been in question, they might have fled; but they could not leave the men whose acceptance of their message had brought them into straits. But behind the two bold speakers stood "the Lord," Christ himself, the true worker. Men who live in Him are made bold by their communion with Him, and He witnesses for those who witness for Him.

—*Expositions of Holy Scripture*

3. Long time therefore abode they—because in spite of opposition they were meeting with so much success. **speaking boldly in the Lord**—rather, 'in dependence on the Lord,' i.e., on their glorified Head.

who gave testimony to the word of his grace—a notable definition of the Gospel, whose whole burden is GRACE. **and granted**—granting,' i.e., who confirmed the Gospel by granting miraculous attestation to it. (The "and" is wanting in the best MSS.)

ADAM CLARKE

CHAPTER 14

1. *So spake,* with such power and demonstration of the Spirit, *that a great multitude both of the Jews,* genuine descendants of one or other of the twelve tribes, *and also of the Greeks,* probably such as were proselytes, *believed,* received the Christian religion as a revelation from God, and confided in its Author for salvation, according to the apostles' preaching.

2. *Evil affected.* "Irritated or exasperated their minds against the brethren," the disciples of Christ.

3. *Long time therefore abode they.* Because they had great success, therefore they continued a long time, gaining many converts, and building up in their most holy faith those who had believed, notwithstanding the opposition they met with from both the unbelieving Jews and the heathens. *Speaking boldly.* Having great liberty of speech, a copious and commanding eloquence, springing from a consciousness of the truth which they preached.

4. *The multitude of the city was divided.* The Jews treated the apostles as false teachers, and their miracles as impositions, and many of the people held with them; while the others, who had not hardened their hearts against the truth, felt the force of it and, being without prejudice, could easily discern the miracles to be the work of God, and therefore held with the apostles.

MATTHEW HENRY

that leads to destruction.

VI. The attempt made upon the apostles by their enemies. Their evil affection against them broke out at length into violent outrages, *v.* 5. Who the plotters were: *Both the Gentiles and the Jews, with their rulers.* The Gentiles and Jews were at enmity with one another, and yet united against Christians. If the church's enemies can thus unite for its destruction, shall not its friends unite for its preservation? What the plot was. Their design was *to use the apostles despitefully*, to expose them to disgrace, and then *to stone them.*

VII. The deliverance of the apostles, *v.* 6, 7. They got away, upon notice given them of the design against them, and they made an honourable retreat (for it was not an inglorious flight) to *Lystra and Derbe.* They found safety. God has shelters for his people in a storm. They found work, and this was what they went for. To these cities they went, and there, and *in the region that lieth round about, they preached the gospel.* In times of persecution ministers may see cause to quit the spot, when yet they do not quit the work.

Verses 8–18

I. A miraculous cure wrought by Paul at Lystra upon a cripple that had been lame from his birth. The deplorable case of the poor cripple (*v.* 8): He was *impotent in his feet, disabled* (so the word is). It was well known that he had been so *from his mother's womb*, and that he *never had walked*, nor could *stand up.* The expectation that was raised in him of a cure (*v.* 9): He heard Paul preach, and, it is likely, was much affected with what he heard. This Paul was aware of, by the spirit of discerning, perhaps the aspect of his countenance did in part witness for him: *Paul perceived that he had faith to be healed.* The cure wrought: *Paul, perceiving that he had faith to be healed*, brought *the word and healed him.* Paul spoke to him with a loud voice, that the people about might take notice, and have their expectations raised of the effect. It is said (*v.* 8) *that he sat*, not that he sat begging. But we may imagine how welcome Paul's word was to him, "*Stand upright on thy feet;* help thyself, and God shall help thee." *He leaped and walked*, and not only *stood upright*, but he walked to and fro before them all. Those that by the grace of God are cured of their spiritual lameness must show it by leaping with a holy exultation and walking in a holy conversation.

II. The impression which this cure made upon the people: they were amazed at it. The working of this one miracle was enough to make them in the eyes of this people truly great and honourable, though the multitude of Christ's miracles could not screen him from the utmost contempt among the Jews. The people take them for gods (*v.* 11): *They lifted up their voices in the speech of Lycaonia, The gods are come down to us in the likeness of men.* This notion of the thing agreed well enough with the fabulous account they had of the visits which their gods made to this lower world; and proud enough they were to think that they should have a visit made to them. They carried this notion so far here that they pretended to tell which of their gods they were (*v.* 12): *They called Barnabas Jupiter;* for, if they will have him to be a god, it is as easy to make him the prince of their gods as not. And *Paul they called Mercury*, who was the messenger of the gods, for Paul was *the chief speaker.* The priest thereupon prepares *to do sacrifice to them, v.* 13. The temple of Jupiter was before the gate of their city, as its protector and guardian; and the priest, hearing the people cry out thus, thought it was time for him to do his duty. If Jupiter be among them *himself*, it concerns him to do him the utmost honours imaginable. When Christ appeared in the likeness of men, and did many, very many miracles, yet they were so far from doing sacrifice to him that they made him a sacrifice. But Paul and Barnabas, upon the working of one miracle, are immediately deified. They *brought oxen*, to be sacrificed *to them, and garlands*, with which to crown the sacrifices.

III. Paul and Barnabas protest against this, and with much ado prevent it. Many of the heathen emperors called themselves *gods*, and took a pride in having divine honours paid them: but Christ's ministers refused those honours when they were tendered. The holy indignation which Paul and Barnabas conceived at this: *When they heard this, they rent their clothes.* We do not find that they rent their clothes when the people vilified them, they could bear this without disturbance: but when they deified them, and spoke of worshipping them, they could not bear it. The pains they took to prevent it. They did not connive at it. Christ had put honour enough upon them in making them apostles, they

JAMIESON, FAUSSET, BROWN

5. an assault made . . . to stone them—rather here, 'an impetuous movement' with a view to stoning them: for in II Corinthians 11:25, Paul says, "*Once* I was stoned," and that was at Lystra, as expressly related in vs. 19. (PALEY'S remarks—*Horæ Paulinæ*—on this singular coincidence between the Epistle and the history are very striking.) **fled**—(See Matt. 10: 23). **6. unto Lystra and Derbe**—the one some twenty miles to the south, the other some sixty miles to the east of Iconium, somewhere near the bases of what are called the Black Mountains and the roots of Mount Taurus; but their exact position has not yet been discovered.

8-21. AT LYSTRA, PAUL HEALING A CRIPPLE, THE PEOPLE ARE SCARCE RESTRAINED FROM SACRIFICING TO THEM AS GODS, BUT AFTERWARDS, THEIR MINDS BEING POISONED, THEY STONE PAUL, LEAVING HIM FOR DEAD—WITHDRAWING TO DERBE, THEY PREACH AND TEACH THERE. There being no mention of the synagogue at Lystra, it is probable there were too few Jews there to form one. **8-10. there sat there a certain man . . . a cripple from his mother's womb. . . . The same heard Paul speak**—in the open air and (vs. 11) to a crowd of people. **who steadfastly beholding him**—as he did Elymas the sorcerer when about to work a miracle on him. **and perceiving that he had faith to be healed**—Paul may have been led by the sight of this cripple to dwell on the Saviour's miracles of healing, and His present power; and perceiving from the eagerness with which the patient drank in his words, that he was prepared to put his own case into the Redeemer's hands, the Spirit of the glorified Physician came all upon Paul, and "with a loud voice" he bade him "stand upright upon his feet." The effect was instantaneous—he sprang to his feet "and walked."

11-13. in the speech of Lycaonia—whether a corruption of the Greek tongue, which was well enough understood in this region, or the remains of some older tongue, is not known. **The gods are come down to us in the likeness of men**—the language of an unsophisticated people. But "that which was a superstition in Lycaonia, and for which the whole creation groaned, became a reality at Bethlehem" [WEBSTER and WILKINSON]. **they called Barnabas, Jupiter**—the father of the gods, from his commanding mien (CHRYSOSTOM thinks). **and Paul, Mercurius**—the god of eloquence and the messenger and attendant of Jupiter, in the heathen mythology. **the priest of Jupiter, which was**—i.e., whose temple stood—**before their city, brought oxen and garlands**—to crown the victims and decorate, as on festive occasions, the porches.

14-18. when . . . Barnabas and Paul heard—Barnabas is put first here, apparently as having been styled the "Jupiter" of the company—**they rent their clothes and ran in**—rather (according to the true reading), ran forth

ADAM CLARKE

5. *An assault made.* A "desperate attempt" was made by *their ruler*, i.e., by the heathen rulers of the people, and the synagogue.

9. *That he had faith to be healed.* How did this faith come to this poor heathen? Why, by hearing the Word of God preached; for it is said, *The same heard Paul speak.* And it appears that he credited the doctrine he heard, and believed that Jesus could, if He would, make him whole. Besides, he must have heard of the miracles which the apostles had wrought (see v. 3), and this would raise his expectation of receiving a cure.

10. *He leaped and walked.* Giving the fullest proof of his restoration; his leaping, however, might have been through joy of having received his cure.

12. *They called Barnabas, Jupiter; and Paul, Mercurius.* The heathens supposed that Jupiter and Mercury were the gods who most frequently assumed the human form, and Jupiter was accustomed to take Mercury with him on such expeditions. Jupiter was the supreme god of the heathens, and Mercury was by them considered the god of eloquence. As the ancients usually represented Jupiter as rather an aged man, large, noble, and majestic; and Mercury young, light, and active, the conjecture of Chrysostom is very probable, that Barnabas was a large, noble, well-made man, and probably in years; and Paul, young, active, and eloquent; on which account they termed the former Jupiter, and the latter Mercury. That Mercury was eloquent and powerful in his words is allowed by the heathens; and the very epithet that is applied here to Paul, "He was the chief or leader of the discourse," was applied to Mercury.

13. *Then the priest of Jupiter, which was before their city.* Many cities were put under the protection of a particular deity, and the image of that deity placed at the entrance, to signify that he was the guardian and protector. To this Luke, everywhere as accurate as he is circumstantial, refers. Lystra, it appears, was under the guardianship of *Jupiter Propulaius*, which Luke translates "the Jupiter that was before the city," which is another term for *Jupiter Custos*, or Jupiter the Guardian. All these deities, according to the attributes they sustained, had their peculiar priests, rites, and sacrifices. Hence we can see with what accuracy Luke wrote. The person who was going to offer them sacrifices was the priest of *Jupiter Custos*, under whose guardianship the city of Lystra was, and whom the priest supposed had visited the city in a human form. *Oxen and garlands.* That is, oxen adorned with flowers, their horns gilded, and necks bound about with fillets, as was the custom in sacrificial rites. They also crowned the gods themselves, the priests, and gates of the temples, with flowers.

MATTHEW HENRY

needed not assume either the honour of princes or the honour of gods. Let us see how they prevented it. *They ran in among the people* as soon as they heard of it. They did not stand still, expecting honours to be done them, but plainly declined them by thrusting themselves into the crowd. They reasoned with them, *crying out*, "*Sirs, why do you these things?* Why do you go about to make gods of us?"

[1] "Our nature will not admit it: *We also are men of like passions with you.* You wrong God if you give that honour to us, or to any other man, which is to be given to God only. We are not only men, but sinful men and suffering men, and therefore will not be deified.

[2] "Our doctrine is directly against it. Must we be added to the number of your gods whose business it is to abolish the gods you have? *We preach unto you that you should turn from these vanities unto the living God.*" When they preached to the Jews they had nothing to do but to preach the grace of God in Christ, and needed not to preach against idolatry; but, when they had to do with the Gentiles, they must rectify their mistakes in natural religion. See here what they preached to the Gentiles.

First, The gods which they and their fathers worshipped, and all the ceremonies of their worship of them, were *vanities*, idle things, unreasonable, unprofitable. Therefore *turn from these vanities*.

Secondly, The God to whom they would have them *turn* is *the living God*. They had hitherto worshipped dead images, that were utterly unable to help them, now they are persuaded to worship a living God, who has life in himself, and life for us, and lives for evermore.

Thirdly, This God is the creator of the world, the fountain of all being and power: "He *made heaven and earth, and the sea, and all things therein*. We call you to worship *the God that made you and all the world*; worship the true God."

Fourthly, The world owed it to his patience that he had not destroyed them long ere this for their idolatry (*v.* 16): *In times past he suffered all nations to walk in their own ways.* Your serving them was a trial of God's patience. Now that he has sent his gospel into the world, if you still continue in your idolatry, he will not bear with you as he has done. Now that God has sent a revelation into the world which is to be published to *all nations* the case is altered. Now you will no longer be excused in these vanities, but must turn from them. God's patience with us hitherto should *lead us to repentance*, and not encourage us to presume. Our having done ill while we were in ignorance will not bear us out in doing ill when we are better taught.

Fifthly, Even when they were not under the direction and correction of the word of God, yet they should have known, to do better by the works of God, *v.* 17. *He left not himself without witness;* besides *the witness* for God within them (the dictates of natural conscience), they had *witnesses* for God round about them—the bounty of common providence. Their having no scriptures did in part excuse them. This however did not wholly excuse them. There were other *witnesses* for God. God, having *not left himself without witness*, has not left us without a guide, and so has left us without excuse. The bounties of common providence witness to us that there is a God. The *rain and fruitful seasons* could not come by chance. All the powers of nature witness to us a sovereign power in the God of nature. It is not the heaven that gives us rain, but God that gives us rain from heaven. The benefits we have by these bounties witness to us that we ought to make our acknowledgments to the Creator. *He left not himself without witness in that he did good.* God seems to reckon the instances of his *goodness* to be more pregnant, cogent proofs of his title to our homage than the evidences of his *greatness*; for his goodness is his glory. Because the most sensible instance of the goodness of Providence is that of the daily provision made by it of meat and drink for us, the apostle chooses to insist upon that, and shows how God does us good, (1) In preparing it for us. He does us good in giving us rain from heaven,—rain for us to drink,—rain for our land to drink, for our meat, as well as drink we have from the rain; in giving us this, he *gives us fruitful seasons.* Of all the common operations of providence, the heathen chose to form their notion of the supreme God by that which bespeaks terror, and this was *the thunder*. But the apostle sets before us his beneficence, that we may have good thoughts of him—may love him and delight in him, as one that does good, in giving *rain from heaven and fruitful seasons.* (2) In giving us the comforts of it. It is he *that fills our hearts with food and gladness.* God is not only a benefactor, but a bountiful one. *He fills our hearts with food*, not merely for necessity,

JAMIESON, FAUSSET, BROWN

—among the people, crying out, . . . Sirs, why do ye these things?—This was something more than that abhorrence of idolatry which took possession of the Jews as a nation from the time of the Babylonish captivity: it was that delicate sensibility to everything which affects the honor of God which Christianity, giving us in God a reconciled Father, alone can produce; making the Christian instinctively feel himself to be wounded in all dishonor done to God, and filling him with mingled horror and grief when such gross insults as this are offered to him. **We . . . are men of like passions . . .**—How unlike either imposture or enthusiasm is this, and how high above all self-seeking do these men of Christ show themselves to be!

unto the living God—This is the most glorious and distinctive of all the names of God. It is the familiar phraseology of the Old Testament, which, in such contrast with all that is to be found within the literature of heathenism, is shown to be, with its sequel, the New Testament, the one Book of the true religion. **who made heaven, and earth, and the sea, and all . . . therein**—This idea of *creation*, utterly unknown alike to rude and to cultivated heathenism, would not only define what was meant by "the living God," but open up a new world to the more thoughtful part of the audience. **Who in times past suffered all nations to walk in their own ways**—i.e., without extending to them the revelation vouchsafed to the seed of Abraham, and the grace attending it; cf. ch. 17:30; I Corinthians 1:21. Yet not without guilt on their part was this privation (Rom. 1:20, etc.).

17. Nevertheless he left not himself without witness—Though the heinousness of idolatry is represented as so much less in the heathen, by how much they were outside the pale of revealed religion, he takes care to add that the heathen have divine "witness" enough to leave them "without excuse." **he did good**—scattering His beneficence everywhere and in a thousand forms. **rain from heaven, and fruitful seasons**—on which human subsistence and all human enjoyment depend. In Lycaonia, where, as ancient writers attest, rain is peculiarly scarce, this allusion would have all the greater effect.

filling our hearts with food and gladness—a natural colloquialism, the heart being gladdened by the food supplied to the body.

ADAM CLARKE

15. *We also are men of like passions with you.* This saying of the apostles has been most strangely perverted. A pious commentator, taking the word *passion* in its vulgar and most improper sense (a bad temper, an evil propensity) and supposing that these holy men wished to confess that they also had many sinful infirmities and wrong tempers, endeavors to illustrate this sense of the word by appealing to the contention of Paul and Barnabas. But the expression means no more than, "We are truly *human beings*, with the same powers and appetites as your own; need food and raiment as you do; and are all mortal like yourselves." *That ye should turn from these vanities.* That is, from these idols and false gods. How often false gods and idolatry are termed *vanity* in the Scriptures, no careful reader of the Bible needs to be told. What a bold saying was this in the presence of a heathen mob, intent on performing an act of their superstitious worship, in which they no doubt thought the safety of the state was concerned! The ancient fable related by Ovid, *Metam., l. i.* vv. 211-239, will cast some light on the conduct of the Lystrians in this case. The following is its substance: "Jupiter, having been informed of the great degeneracy of mankind, was determined himself to survey the earth. Coming to this province [*Lycaonia*], disguised in human shape, he took up his residence at the palace of *Lycaon*, then kind of that country: giving a sign of his godhead, the people worship him: Lycaon sneers, doubts his divinity, and is determined to put it to the trial. Some ambassadors from the Molossian state having just arrived, he slew one of them, boiled part of his flesh, and roasted the rest, and set it before Jupiter: the god, indignant at the insult, burnt the palace, and turned the impious king into a *wolf*." From this time, or rather from this fable, the whole province was called Lycaonia. The simple people now seeing such proofs of supernatural power, in the miracles wrought by Barnabas and Paul, thought that Jupiter had again visited them; and fearing lest they should meet with his indignation, should they neglect duly to honor him, they brought oxen and garlands, and would have offered them sacrifice, had they not been prevented by the apostles themselves. This circumstance will account for their whole conduct, and shows the reason why Jupiter was the tutelar god of the place. *The living God.* Widely different from those stocks and stones which were objects of their worship. *Which made heaven, and earth.* And as all things were made by His power, so all subsist by His providence; and to Him alone all worship, honor, and glory are due.

16. *Who in times past suffered all nations.* The words *all nations* should be rendered "all the Gentiles," merely to distinguish them from the Jewish people, who, having a revelation, were not left *to walk in their own ways.*

17. *He left not himself without witness.* Though He gave the Gentiles no revelation of His will, yet He continued to govern them by His gracious providence, doing them *good* in general, giving them rain to fertilize their grounds, and *fruitful seasons* as the result.

MATTHEW HENRY

but plenty, dainty, and variety. The Gentiles that *lived without God in the world*, yet lived upon God. Those heathen had *their hearts filled with food*; but *these things will not fill the soul*, nor will those that know how to value their own souls be satisfied with them. We must all own that God fills our hearts with food and gladness; not only *food*, that we may live, but *gladness*, that we may live cheerfully. We must thank God, not only for our food, but for our gladness. And, if *our hearts be filled with food and gladness*, they ought to be filled with love and thankfulness.

Lastly, The success of this prohibition which the apostles gave to *the people* (*v.* 18): By *these sayings*, they *restrained the people from doing sacrifice to them*. They could *scarcely* restrain them from it. Paul and Barnabas had cured a cripple, and therefore the people deified them, which should make us very cautious that we do not give that honour to another, or take it to ourselves, which is due to God only.

Verses 19-28

I. How Paul was stoned and left for dead, *v.* 19, 20. They fell upon Paul rather than Barnabas, because Paul, being the chief speaker, galled and vexed them more than Barnabas did. How the people were incensed against Paul; *there came certain Jews from Antioch*, and they incensed the people against them. See how restless the rage of the Jews was against the gospel of Christ; they could not bear that it should have footing anywhere. To what degree they were incensed by these barbarous Jews: the mob rose and *stoned Paul*, and then *drew him out of the city supposing he had been dead*. As it is with great difficulty that men are restrained from evil on one side, so it is with great ease that they are persuaded to evil on the other side. See how fickle worldly people are. Those that but the other day would have treated the apostles as more than men now treat them as worse than brutes. Today *Hosanna*, tomorrow *Crucify*; today sacrificed to, tomorrow sacrificed. Popular breath turns like the wind. How he was delivered by the power of God: When he was *drawn out of the city, the disciples stood round about him*, *v.* 20. It seems there were some here at Lystra that became disciples, and even these new converts had courage to own Paul when he was thus run down. They stood round about him, as a guard to him, stood about him to see whether he were alive or dead; and all of a sudden *he rose up*. God's faithful servants, though they may be brought within a step of death, shall not die as long as he has work for them to do.

II. How they went on with their work. All the stones they threw at Paul could not beat him off from his work: They *drew him out of the city* (*v.* 19), but he *came into the city* again. However, their being persecuted here is a known indication to them to seek for opportunities of usefulness elsewhere, and therefore for the present they quit Lystra.

1. They went to break up and sow fresh ground at *Derbe*. Thither the next day *Paul and Barnabas departed*, there they preached the gospel, there they *taught many*, *v.* 21. Nothing is recorded that happened at Derbe.

2. They returned, and went over their work again; and, having stayed as long as they thought fit at Derbe, they came back to Lystra, to Iconium, and Antioch, *v.* 21.

(1) They *confirmed the souls of the disciples*, *v.* 22. Young converts are apt to waver, and a little thing shocks them. The apostles come and tell them that *this is the true grace of God wherein they stand*, that there is no danger like that of losing their part in Christ, no advantage like that of keeping their hold of him; that, whatever their trials may be, they shall have strength from Christ to pass through them; and, whatever their losses may be, they shall be abundantly recompensed. And this *confirms the souls of the disciples*. Those that are converted need to be confirmed; those that are planted need to be rooted. Ministers' work is to establish saints as well as to awaken sinners. True confirmation is confirmation of the soul. It is the grace of God and nothing less, that can effectually *confirm the souls of the disciples*.

(2) *They exhorted them to continue in the faith*; or, *they encouraged them*. They told them it was both their duty and interest to persevere. Those that are in the faith are concerned to *continue in the faith*. And it is requisite that they should often be exhorted to do so.

(3) That which they insisted most upon was *that we must through much tribulation enter into the kingdom of God*. But is this the way to *confirm the souls of the disciples*, and to engage them to *continue in the faith?* One would think it would rather shock

JAMIESON, FAUSSET, BROWN

with these sayings scarce restrained they the people that they had not done sacrifice to them—In spite of this,and Peter's repudiation of all such honor (ch. 10:26), how soon idolatrous tendencies began to show themselves in the Christian Church, at length to be systematized and enjoined in the Church of Rome!

came thither Jews from Antioch and Iconium—Furious zeal that would travel so far to counteract the missionaries of the Cross! **persuaded the people**—'the multitudes.' **and having stoned Paul**—See on vs. 5. Barnabas they seem to have let alone; Paul, as the prominent actor and speaker, being the object of all their rage. The words seem to imply that it was the Jews who did this; and no doubt they took the lead (vs. 19), but it was the act of the instigated and fickle multitudes along with them. **drew him out of the city**—By comparing this with ch. 7:58 it will be seen that the Jews were the chief actors in this scene. **as the disciples stood round about him**—sorrowing. So his labors here had not been in vain: "Disciples" had been gathered, who now rallied around the bleeding body. And *one appears to have been gained on this occasion, of far more importance than all the rest*—TIMOTHEUS. See on ch. 16:1-3. (It could scarcely have been at the *subsequent* visit, vs. 21, for the reason given in II Timothy 3:10, 11; while at the *third* visit, ch. 16:1-3, he was already a Christian.) **he rose up**—It is possible that this recovery was natural; the insensibility occasioned by such treatment as he had received sometimes passing away of itself, and leaving the patient less hurt than appeared. But certainly the impression naturally left on the mind by the words is that the restoration was miraculous; and so the best interpreters understand the words. This is confirmed by what follows—**came into the city**—Noble intrepidity! **next day he departed with Barnabas to Derbe**—a journey for which he could hardly be fit if his recovery had been natural. (See as to Derbe, on vs. 6.) **and when they had preached . . . to that city and had taught many**—rather, "had made many disciples" (*margin*); but probably without suffering any persecution, as Derbe is not mentioned along with Antioch, Iconium, and Lystra (II Tim. 3:11).

21-28. PAUL AND BARNABAS RETRACE THEIR STEPS, RETURN TO ANTIOCH IN SYRIA, AND THUS COMPLETE THEIR FIRST MISSIONARY JOURNEY. **21, 22. they returned . . . to Lystra, Iconium, and Antioch, confirming the souls . . .**—At Derbe, Paul was not far from the well-known pass which leads down from the central tableland to Cilicia and Tarsus. But his thoughts did not center in an earthly home. He revisited the places where he had been reviled and persecuted, but where he had left as sheep in the desert the disciples whom his Master had enabled him to gather. They needed building up and strengthening in the faith, comforting in the midst of their inevitable suffering, and fencing round by permanent institutions. Undaunted therefore by the dangers that awaited them, our missionaries return to them, using words of encouragement which none but the founders of a true religion would have ventured to address to their earliest converts, that "we can only enter into the kingdom of God by passing through much tribulation" [Hows].

ADAM CLARKE

G. CAMPBELL MORGAN:

We note finally the perils threatening these men. There were the perils of opposition. Disobedience produced the spirit of opposition: hatred, plotting, stoning. But the gravest peril threatening these men was that which came to them in the hour when men suggested that they should worship them. That is the supreme peril to the Christian worker. It would have been so easy to gain power and notoriety, to take this worship and abandon the pathway of persecution and of the stones. That is the peril of the prophet. When men bring garlands to worship, when men suggest his deification, he is in extreme danger. If men would help the prophet, they should pray that he may never accept the garland or the worship of men. This was a most insidious hour. I would not suggest that there was any trembling on the part of Paul. He was not seduced, because he was living in such fellowship with his Lord that it was impossible.
—*The Acts of the Apostles*

19. *There came thither certain Jews from Antioch.* Those were, no doubt, the same who had raised up persecution against Paul and Barnabas at Iconium and Antioch before. They followed the apostles with implacable malice; and what they could not do themselves they endeavored to do by others, whose minds they first perverted, and then irritated to deeds of fell purpose. *Supposing he had been dead.* They did not leave stoning him till they had the fullest evidence that he was dead; and so, most probably, he was.

20. *The disciples stood round about him.* No doubt in earnest prayer, entreating the Author of life that his soul might again return to its battered tenement. *He rose up.* Miraculously restored, not only to life, but to perfect soundness; so that he was able to walk into the city, that his persecutors might see the mighty power of God in his restoration, and the faith of the young converts be confirmed in the truth and goodness of God.

21. *Preached the gospel to that city.* Derbe, a city in the same province.

They returned again to Lystra, and to Iconium. Behold the courage of these Christian men! They counted not their lives dear to them, and returned to do their Master's work in the very places in which they had been so grievously persecuted, and where one of them had been apparently stoned to death!

MATTHEW HENRY

them, and make them weary. No, as the matter is fairly stated it will help to confirm them. It is true they will meet with tribulation. It is so appointed. They must undergo it, there is no remedy, all that *will live godly in Christ Jesus should suffer persecution.* All that will be Christ's disciples must *take up their cross.* When we gave up our names to Jesus Christ it was what we agreed to; when we sat down and counted the cost, if we reckoned aright, it was what we counted upon. It is the lot of the leaders in Christ's army, as well as of the soldiers. It is not only *you,* but *we,* that are subject to it. As Christ did not put the apostles upon any harder service than what he underwent before them, so neither did the apostles put the ordinary christians. It is true we must count upon *much tribulation,* but this is encouraging, that we shall get through it. We shall not only get through it, but get through it *into the kingdom of God.* It is true *we must go by the cross,* but it is as true that we shall *go to the crown.*

(4) *They ordained them elders in every church.* Now at this second visit they settled them in some order, under the guidance of a settled ministry. Every church had its governors or presidents. It is requisite that every particular church should have one or more such to preside in it. Those governors were then elders, to see to the observance and execution of the laws Christ has made. These elders were *ordained.* They, having *devoted* themselves, were solemnly set *apart* to the work of the ministry. These elders were ordained to them, to their service, for their good. Those that are in the faith have need to be build up in it, and have need of the elders' help therein.

(5) *By prayer* joined with *fasting* they *commended them to the Lord on whom they believed.* Even when persons are brought to believe, ministers' care concerning them is not over. There is still that lacking in their faith which needs to be perfected. The ministers that take most care of those that believe must after all commend them to the Lord. To his custody they must commit themselves, and their ministers must commit them. It is by prayer that they must be commended to the Lord. It is a great encouragement to us that we can say, "It is he in whom they believed; we commit to him those who have committed themselves to him." It is good to join fasting with prayer, in token of our humiliation for sin, and in order to add vigour to our prayers. When we are parting with our friends, the bare farewell is to commend them to the Lord, and to leave them with him.

3. They went on preaching the gospel in other places where they had been. From Antioch they *passed through Pisidia,* thence they came into the province of *Pamphylia,* the head-city of which was *Perga,* where they had been before (*ch.* xiii. 13), and came thither again to *preach the word* (*v.* 25). Thence they *went down to Attalia,* a city of Pamphylia. They stayed not long at a place, but wherever they came endeavoured to lay a foundation which might afterwards be built upon, and to sow the seeds which would in time produce a great increase.

III. How they at length came back to Antioch in Syria, whence they had been sent forth. From Attalia they came by sea to Antioch, *v.* 26.

1. Why they came thither: because *thence they had been recommended to the grace of God.* The brethren having recommended them to the grace of God, for the work *which they fulfilled,* they thought they owed them an account of it, that they might help them by their praises, as they had been helped by their prayers.

2. What account they gave them of their negotiation (*v.* 27): They *gathered the church together.* They gave them an account of two things: (1) Of the tokens they had had of the divine presence with them in their labours: *They rehearsed all that God had done with them.* They did not tell what *they* had done, but what God had done. For it is he that not only worketh in us both to will and to do, but then worketh with us to make what we do successful. God's grace can do anything without ministers' preaching; but ministers' preaching can do nothing without God's grace. (2) Of the fruit of their labours among the heathen. They told how *God had opened the door of faith unto the Gentiles.* There is no entering into the kingdom of Christ but by the door of faith. It is God that opens the door of faith. We have reason to be thankful that God has *opened the door of faith to the Gentiles.* Thus the gospel was spread, and it shone more and more, and none was able to shut this door which God had opened.

3. How they disposed of themselves for the present: *There they abode a long time with the disciples* (*v.* 28), not because they *feared their enemies,* but because they *loved their friends.*

JAMIESON, FAUSSET, BROWN

ALBERT BARNES:

"And when they had ordained." The word "ordain" we now use in an ecclesiastical sense, to denote a setting apart to an office by the imposition of hands. But it is evident that the word here is not employed in that sense. That imposition of hands might have occurred in setting apart afterward to this office is certainly possible, but it is not implied in the word employed here, and did not take place in the transaction to which this word refers. The word occurs but in one other place in the New Testament (2 Cor. 8:19), where it is applied to Luke and translated, "who was also chosen of the church [that is, appointed or elected by suffrage by the churches] to travel with us." The verb properly denotes *to stretch out the hand*; and as it was customary to elect to office, or to vote, by stretching out or elevating the hand, so the word simply means to elect, appoint, or designate to any office. The word here refers simply to an election or appointment of the elders. It is said, indeed, that Paul and Barnabas did this. But probably all that is meant by it is that they presided in the assembly when the choice was made. It does not mean that they appointed them without consulting the church; but it evidently means that they appointed them in the usual way of appointing officers, by the suffrages of the people.—*Popular Commentary*

23, 24. when they had ordained them elders—lit., 'chosen by show of hands.' But as that would imply that this was done by the apostles' own hands, many render the word, as in our version, "ordained." Still, as there is no evidence in the New Testament that the word had then lost its proper meaning, as this is beyond doubt its meaning in II Corinthians 8:19, and as there is indisputable evidence that the concurrence of the people was required in all elections to sacred office in the earliest ages of the Church, it is perhaps better to understand the words to mean, 'when they had made a choice of elders,' i.e., superintended such choice on the part of the disciples. **and had prayed with fasting**—lit., 'fastings,' thus setting them solemnly apart. This last clause confirms our interpretation of the former. For if "ordination" was by prayer and fasting (see ch. 13:3), why should it be said they first "ordained elders," and after that "prayed with fasting"? Whereas if the first clause refer to the *choice* and the second to the *ordination,* all is natural. **they commended**—'committed'—**them**—i.e., all these churches. **to the Lord**—Jesus.

25. when they had preached the word in Perga—now doing what, for some reason, they had not done on their former visit, but probably with no visible fruit. **they went down into Attalia**—a seaport on the Gulf of Pamphylia, drawing to itself the commerce of Egypt and Syria. **26. sailed to Antioch, from whence they had been recommended**—See on ch. 13:3.

27. when they had gathered the church together, they rehearsed all that God had done with them . . .—As their call and mission had been solemn and formal, in the presence of and by the Church as well as the Holy Ghost, they dutifully, and no doubt with eager joy, convened the church and gave their report of "all that God had done with them," i.e., by and for them. **and how**—in particular—**he had opened the door of faith to the Gentiles**—to such even as before had not been proselytes. (See on ch. 11:21; and on the language, see I Cor. 16:9; II Cor. 2:12; Col. 4:3.) The ascribing directly to God of such access to the Gentiles is to be noted. **28. there they abode long time**—'no little time.' From the commencement of the mission till they left Antioch to go up to attend the council at Jerusalem, some four or five years elapsed; and as the missionary journey would probably occupy less than two years, the rest of the time would be the period of their stay at Antioch.

ADAM CLARKE

23. *When they had ordained them elders. Elder* seems to be here the name of an office. These were all young or new converts, and yet among them the apostles constitute *elders.* They appointed persons the most experienced, and the most advanced in the divine life, to watch over and instruct the rest. But what is the meaning of the word *cheirotonesantes,* which we translate *ordained?* The word *ordain* we use in an ecclesiastical sense and signify by it the appointment of a person to an office in the church by the imposition of the hands of those who are rulers in that church. But *cheirotonia* signifies the "holding up" or "stretching out the hand," as approving of the choice of any person to a particular work, whereas *cheirothesia* signifies the "imposition of hands." I believe the simple truth to be this, that in ancient times the people chose by the *cheirotonia* (lifting up of hands) their spiritual pastor; and the rulers of the church, whether apostles or others, appointed that person to his office by the *cheirothesia,* or "imposition of hands"; and perhaps each of these was thought to be equally necessary, the church agreeing in the election of the person, and the rulers of the church appointing, by imposition of hands, the person thus elected. *And had prayed with fasting.* This was to implore God's special assistance, as they well knew that without His influence even their appointment could avail nothing. *Commended them to the Lord.* To His especial care and protection.

25. *They went down into Attalia.* This was a seaport town in Pamphylia.

26. *And thence sailed to Antioch.* This was Antioch in Syria, to reach which, by sea, they were obliged to coast a part of the Mediterranean Sea, steering between Cyprus and Cilicia.

Whence they had been recommended . . . for the work which they fulfilled. The reader will recollect that it was from this Antioch they had been sent to preach the gospel to the heathen in Asia Minor (see chap. xiii. 1-2), and that they *fulfilled* that *work.*

27. *Had gathered the church together.* The church by which they had been sent on this very important, successful mission. *They rehearsed all that God had done with them.* Not what they had done themselves, but what God made them the instruments of working. *And how he had opened the door of faith.* How God by His providence and grace had made a way for preaching Christ crucified among the heathen; and how the heathen had received that gospel, which, through faith in Christ Jesus, was able to save their souls.

MATTHEW HENRY

CHAPTER 15

Verses 1–5

Even when things go on very smoothly and pleasantly it is folly to be secure; some uneasiness or other will arise, which is not foreseen. If ever there was a heaven upon earth, surely it was in the church at Antioch at this time. But here we have their peace disturbed, and differences arising.

I. A new doctrine started among them, obliging the Gentile converts to submit to circumcision and the ceremonial law, *v.* 1.

1. The persons that urged this were *certain men who came down from Judæa.* They came to Antioch, because that was the headquarters of those that preached to the Gentiles, and the rendezvous of the Gentile converts; and, if they could but make an interest there, this leaven would soon be diffused to all the churches of the Gentiles. *Yet one thing they lack,* they must be circumcised. Those that are ever so well taught have need to stand upon their guard that they be not untaught again, or ill taught.

2. The position they laid down was this, that except the Gentiles who turned Christians were *circumcised after the manner of Moses, they could not be saved.* Many of the Jews who embraced the faith of Christ, yet continued very *zealous for the law, ch.* xxi. 20. They knew it was from God and its authority was sacred, and had been bred up in the observance of it. Herein they were connived at, because the prejudices of education are not to be overcome all at once. But it did not suffice them that they were herein indulged themselves, they must have the Gentile converts brought under the same obligations. There is a strange proneness in us to make our own opinion and practice a rule and a law to everybody else, and to conclude that because we do well all do wrong that do not just as we do. Those Jews who believed that Christ was the Messiah could not get clear of the notions they had of the Messiah, that he should set up a temporal kingdom in favour of the Jewish nation; it was a disappointment to them that there was as yet nothing done towards this. But now that they hear the doctrine of Christ is received among the Gentiles, and his kingdom begins to be set up in the midst of them, they hope their point will be gained, the Jewish nation will be made as considerable as they can wish, though in another way. It is no wonder if those who have wrong notions of the kingdom of Christ take wrong measures for the advancement of it. It is observable what a mighty stress they laid upon it; they do not only say, "*You ought to be circumcised after the manner of Moses. Except you be circumcised you cannot be saved.* If you be not herein of our mind and way, you will never go to heaven, and therefore of course you must go to hell." Though otherwise good men and believers in Christ, yet they cannot be saved; salvation itself cannot save them. None are in Christ, but those that are within their pale.

II. The opposition which Paul and Barnabas gave to this schismatical notion (*v.* 2): *They had no small dissension and disputation with them.* They would by no means yield to this doctrine. As faithful servants of Christ, they would not see his truths betrayed. They knew that Christ came to free us from the yoke of the ceremonial law, and therefore could not bear to hear of circumcising the Gentile converts, when their instructions were only to baptize them. As spiritual fathers to the Gentile converts, they would not see their liberties encroached upon. They had told the Gentiles that if they believed in Jesus Christ they should be saved. And therefore the apostles set themselves against it.

III. The expedient pitched upon for preventing the mischief of this dangerous notion. They determined that Paul and Barnabas, and some others of their number, should *go to Jerusalem to the apostles and elders.* They sent the case to Jerusalem: Because those who taught this doctrine came from Jerusalem, and pretended to have directions from the apostles there. It was therefore very proper to send to Jerusalem about it, to know if they had any such direction from the church there. And it was soon found to be all wrong. It was true that these *went out from them* (*v.* 24), but they never had any such orders from them. Because those who were taught this doctrine would be the better confirmed in their opposition to it, if they were sure that *the apostles and elders at Jerusalem* were against it. Because the apostles at Jerusalem were fittest to be consulted in a point not yet fully settled; their decision would be likely to end the controversy.

IV. Their journey to Jerusalem upon this errand, *v.* 3: *They were brought on their way by the church.* Thus the church showed their favour to those who stood up for them. They did good as they went

JAMIESON, FAUSSET, BROWN

CHAPTER 15

Vss. 1-35. Council at Jerusalem to Decide on the Necessity of Circumcision for the Gentile Converts. **1, 2. certain men**—See the description of them in Galatians 2:4.

Paul and Barnabas—now the recognized heads of the Church at Antioch—**had no small dissension and disputation with them, they determined**—i.e., the church did—**that Paul and Barnabas, and certain others of them**—Titus was one (Gal. 2:1); probably as an uncircumcised Gentile convert endowed with the gifts of the Spirit. He is not mentioned in the Acts, but only in II Corinthians, Galatians, II Timothy, and the Epistle addressed to him [Alford]. **they determined that Paul and Barnabas should go up to Jerusalem . . . about this question**—That such a deputation should be formally despatched by the Church of Antioch was natural, as it might be called the mother church of Gentile Christianity.

3-6. being brought on their way by the church—a kind of official escort.

A. T. ROBERTSON:

1. "And certain men came down from Judea" (*kai tines katelthontes apo tes Ioudaias*). Evidently the party of the circumcision in the church in Jerusalem (11:2) had heard of the spread of the gospel among the Gentiles in Cyprus, Pamphylia, and South Galatia (Phrygia, Pisidia, Lycaonia). Possibly John Mark after his desertion at Perga (13:13) told of this as one of his reasons for coming home. At any rate echoes of the jubilation in Antioch in Syria would be certain to reach Jerusalem. The Judaizers in Jerusalem, who insisted that all the Gentile Christians must become Jews also, had acquiesced in the case of Cornelius and his group (11:1-18) after plain proof by Peter that it was the Lord's doing. But they had not agreed to a formal campaign to turn the exception into the rule and to make Christianity mainly Gentile with a few Jews instead of mainly Jewish with a few Gentiles. Since Paul and Barnabas did not come up to Jerusalem, the leaders among the Judaizers decided to go down to Antioch and attack Paul and Barnabas there. They had volunteered to go without church action in Jerusalem, for their activity is disclaimed by the conference (Acts 15:24). In Gal. 2:4 Paul with some heat describes these Judaizers as "false brethren, secretly introduced who sneaked in to spy out our liberty." It is reasonably certain that this visit to Jerusalem described in Gal. 2:1-10 is the same one as the Jerusalem Conference in Acts 15:5-29 in spite of the effort of Ramsay to identify it with that in 11:29.

—*Word Pictures in the New Testament*

ADAM CLARKE

CHAPTER 15

1. *Except ye be circumcised.* The persons who taught this doctrine appear to have been converts to Christianity; but supposing that the Christian religion was intended to perfect the Mosaic, and not to supersede it, they insisted on the necessity of circumcision, because by that a man was made debtor to the whole law, to observe all its rites and ceremonies. This question produced great disturbance in the apostolic Church; and, notwithstanding the decree mentioned in this chapter, the apostles were frequently obliged to interpose their authority in order to settle it; and we find a whole church, that at Galatia, drawn aside from the simplicity of the Christian faith by the subtilty of Judaizing teachers among themselves, who insisted on the necessity of the converted Gentiles being circumcised.

Ye cannot be saved. Ye can enjoy neither God's blessing in time nor His glory in eternity. Such an assertion as this, from any reputable authority, must necessarily shake the confidence of young converts.

2. *No small dissension and disputation.* Paul and Barnabas were fully satisfied that God did not design to bring the converted Gentiles under the yoke of circumcision. They knew that Jesus Christ was "the end of the law for righteousness [justification] to every one that believeth," and therefore they opposed the Judaizing teachers.

And certain other of them. If this be the journey to which Paul alludes, Gal. ii. 1-5, then he had Titus with him; and how many others went from the church of Antioch we cannot tell. This journey was fourteen years after Paul's conversion, and was undertaken by express revelation, as he informs us in Gal. ii. 2, which revelation appears to have been given to certain persons in the church of Antioch, as we learn from this verse, and not to Paul and Barnabas themselves.

3. *Being brought on their way by the church.* That is, the members of the church provided them with all necessaries for their journey.

MATTHEW HENRY

along. They visited the churches by the way; they passed through Phenice and Samaria, and as they went *declared the conversion of the Gentiles,* which *caused great joy to all the brethren.* The progress of the gospel is and ought to be a matter of great joy. *All the brethren* in Christ's family rejoice when more are born into the family; for the family will be never the poorer for the multitude of its children. In Christ and heaven there is portion enough, and inheritance enough for them all.

V. Their hearty welcome at Jerusalem, *v.* 4. The good entertainment their friends gave them: They were *received of the church, and of the apostles and elders.* They received them with all possible expressions of love and friendship. The good entertainment they gave their friends: They *declared all things that God had done with them,* gave them an account of the success of their ministry among the Gentiles. As they went they had planted, as they came back they had watered; but in both they were ready to own it was God that gave the increase.

VI. The opposition they met with from the same party at Jerusalem, *v.* 5. *There rose up certain of the sect of the Pharisees.* They believed in Christ but thought it was needful to circumcise them. Those who have been most prejudiced against the gospel yet have been captivated by it. When Christ was here upon earth, few or none of the rulers and of the Pharisees believed on him; but now there are those of the sect of the Pharisees who believed, and many of them, we hope, in sincerity. It is very hard for men suddenly to get clear of their prejudices: those that had been Pharisees, even after they became Christians, retained some of the old leaven. All did not so, witness Paul, but some did.

Verses 6–21

We have here a council called on this occasion (*v.* 6): *The apostles and presbyters came together, to consider of this matter.* They did not give their judgment rashly, but considered of this matter. Though they were clear concerning it in their own minds, yet they would take time to consider of it, and to hear what might be said by the adverse party. Here is a direction to the pastors of the churches, when difficulties arise, to come together in solemn meetings. They may know one another's mind, and strengthen one another's hands.

I. Peter's speech. He was a faithful member of this assembly, and offered that which was very much to the purpose, and which would come better from him than from another, because he had himself been the first that preached the gospel to the Gentiles. *There had been much disputing, pro and con,* upon this question, and liberty of speech allowed, as ought to be in such cases. When both sides had been heard, *Peter rose up.*

1. He put them in mind of the commission he had some time ago *to preach the gospel to the Gentiles. You know that from the beginning of the days* of the gospel *God made choice* of one to preach the gospel to the Gentiles, and I was the person chosen, *that the Gentiles by my mouth should hear the word, and believe, v.* 7. Everybody rejoiced that *God had granted to the Gentiles repentance unto life,* and nobody said a word of circumcising them. See *ch.* xi. 18. Why should the Gentiles who hear the word of the gospel by Paul's mouth be compelled to submit to circumcision, any more than those that heard it by my mouth?

2. He puts them in mind how remarkably God owned him in preaching to the Gentiles (*v.* 8): *God, who knows the hearts, bore them witness* by *giving them the Holy Ghost, even as he did unto us* apostles." See *ch.* xi. 15–17. Those to whom God *gives the Holy Ghost,* he thereby *bears witness* to that they are his; *sealed* with that Holy Spirit of promise—*marked* for God. "God has *put no difference between us and them* (*v.* 9); they, though Gentiles, are as welcome to the grace of Christ and the throne of grace as the Jews are." We ought not to make any conditions of our brethren's acceptance with us but such as God has made the conditions of their acceptance with him. Now the Gentiles were fitted for communion with God, in *having their hearts purified by faith,* and therefore why should we think them unfit for communion with us, unless they will submit to the ceremonial purifying enjoined by the law to us? *By faith the heart is purified.* The faith of all the saints is alike precious, and has like precious effects and those that by it are united to Christ are so to look upon themselves as joined to one another as that all distinctions even that between Jew and Gentile, are swallowed up in it.

3. He sharply reproves those teachers who went about to bring the Gentiles under the obligation of the law of Moses, *v.* 10: "*Now therefore, why tempt*

JAMIESON, FAUSSET, BROWN

they passed through Phenice—See on ch. 11:19. **and Samaria, declaring the conversion of the Gentiles, and they caused great joy to the brethren**—As the converts in those parts were Jewish (ch. 11:19), their spirit contrasts favorably with that of others of their nation.

And when they were come to Jerusalem—This was Paul's THIRD VISIT TO JERUSALEM after his conversion, and *on this occasion took place what is related in* Galatians 2:1-10. (See there.) **were received of the church, and the apostles and elders**—evidently at a meeting formally convened for this purpose: the deputation being one so influential, and from a church of such note. **they declared all things that God had done with them.** See on ch. 14:14-27.

6. the apostles and elders came together to consider of this—but in presence, as would seem, of the people (vss. 12, 22, 23).

7. Peter . . .—This is the last mention of him in the Acts, and one worthy of his standing, as formally pronouncing, from the divine decision of the matter already in his own case, in favor of the views which all of Paul's labors were devoted to establishing.

a good while ago—probably about fifteen years before this. **made choice . . . that the Gentiles by my mouth**—See on ch. 11:21.

8. God, which knoweth the hearts—implying that the real question for admission to full standing in the visible Church is *the state of the heart.* Hence, though that cannot be known by men, no principle of admission to church privileges which *reverses* this can be sound.

9. put no difference between us and them: purifying their hearts by faith—"Purification" here refers to "sprinkling (of the conscience by the blood of Jesus) from dead works to serve the living God." (See on I Cor. 6:11.) How rich is this brief description of the inward revolution wrought upon the genuine disciples of the Lord Jesus!

ADAM CLARKE

Declaring the conversion of the Gentiles. Much stress is laid on this. It was a miracle of God's mercy that the Gentiles should be received into the Church of God; and they had now the fullest proof that the thing was likely to become general, by the conversion of Cornelius, the conversion of the people of Antioch, of Cyprus, Pisidia, Pamphylia, Lycaonia.

4. *They were received of the church.* The whole body of Christian believers. *The apostles.* We read of none but John, Peter, and James. See Gal. ii. 9. *And elders.* Those who were officers in the church, under the apostles. *They declared.* To this council they gave a succinct account of the great work which God had wrought by them among the Gentiles. This was Paul's third journey to Jerusalem after his conversion. See an account of his first journey, chap. ix. 26, and of his second in chap. xi. 30.

5. *But there rose up certain of the sect of the Pharisees.* This verse appears to be part of the declaration made by Paul and Barnabas to this council; for, having stated how God blessed their ministry among the Gentiles, they proceed to declare how all the good work was likely to be destroyed by certain Pharisees who, having received the Christian faith, came down to Antioch and began to teach the necessity of circumcision.

6. *The apostles and elders came together.* This was the first council ever held in the Christian Church, and we find that it was composed simply of the apostles and elders.

7. *When there had been much disputing.* By those of the sect of the believing Pharisees, for they strongly contended for the circumcision. Though the apostles and elders were under the inspiration of the Almighty, and could by this inspiration have immediately determined the question, yet it was highly necessary that the objecting party should be permitted to come forward and allege their reasons for the doctrines they preached; and that these reasons should be fairly met by argument, and the thing proved to be useless in itself, inexpedient in the present case, and unsupported by any express authority from God. *Peter rose up, and said.* This was after the matters in dispute had been fully debated; and now the apostles, like judges, after hearing counsel on both sides, proceed to give judgment on the case. *A good while ago.* "From the days of old," a phrase which simply signifies "some years ago."

8. *And God, which knoweth the hearts.* We had this epithet of the Divine Being once before; see chap. i. 24, and the note there: "It occurs nowhere else in the New Testament." *Bare them witness.* Considered them as proper or fit to receive the gospel of Christ. It is properly remarked by learned men that "to bear witness to any person" signifies to "approve," to "testify in behalf of." Here it signifies that, as God evidently sent the gospel to the Gentiles and by the preaching of it conveyed the Holy Spirit to them who believed, and as He who knows all hearts and their secrets can make no improper judgment of any, therefore what He had done was right.

9. *Put no difference between us and them.* Giving them the Holy Spirit, though uncircumcised, just as He had given Him to us who were circumcised; an evident proof that, in the judgment of God, circumcision was no preparation to receive the gospel of Christ. And as the purification of the heart by the Holy Spirit was the grand object of the religion of God, and that alone by which the soul could be prepared for a blessed immortality, and the Gentiles had received that without circumcision, consequently the shadow could not be considered of any worth, now the substance was communicated.

MATTHEW HENRY

you God to put a yoke upon the neck of the disciples, a yoke which neither our fathers nor we were able to bear?" Here he shows that, (1) They offered a very great affront to God. "By calling that in question which he has already settled by no less an indication than that of the gift of the Holy Ghost; you do, in effect ask, 'Did he know what he did? Or was he in earnest in it?' " Those tempt God who prescribe to him, and say that people cannot be saved but upon such and such terms, which God never appointed. (2) They offered a very great wrong to the disciples: Christ came to proclaim *liberty to the captives*, and they go about to enslave those whom he has made free. This yoke Christ came to ease us of. Now for these teachers to go about to lay that yoke upon the neck of the Gentiles from which he came to free even the Jews was the greatest injury imaginable to them.

4. Whereas the Jewish teachers had urged that circumcision was necessary to salvation, Peter shows that both Jews and Gentiles were to be saved purely *through the grace of our Lord Jesus Christ*, and in no other way (*v.* 11): *We believe to be saved through that grace* only. "We that are circumcised believe to salvation, and so do those that are uncircumcised. We must depend upon the grace of Christ for salvation as well as they. There is not one way of salvation for the Jews and another for the Gentiles. Why should we burden them with the law of Moses, as necessary to their salvation, when it is not that, but the gospel of Christ, that is necessary both to our salvation and theirs?"

II. An account of what Barnabas and Paul said. *What miracles and wonders God had wrought among the Gentiles by them*, *v.* 12. This they had given in to the church *at Antioch* (*ch.* xiv. 27), and now again to the synod; and it was very proper to be given in here. Paul and Barnabas undertake to show, by a plain relation of matters of fact, that God owned the preaching of the pure gospel to them without the law. 1. What account they gave; they declared what signs and wonders, *God had wrought among the Gentiles by them*, what confirmation he had given by miracles wrought in the kingdom of nature, and what success by miracles wrought in the kingdom of grace. What need had they of any other advocate when God himself pleaded their cause? 2. What attention was given to them: *All the multitude kept silence, and gave audience to Paul and Barnabas;* it should seem they took more notice of their narrative than they did of all the arguments that were offered. As in natural philosophy and medicine nothing is so satisfactory as experiments, so in the things of God the best explication of the word of grace is the accounts given of the operations of the Spirit of grace. Those that fear God will most readily hear those that can tell them *what God has done for their souls*, or by their means.

III. The speech which James made to the synod. *After they had held their peace*, then James stood up. The hearing of variety of ministers may be of use when one truth does not drive out, but clench, another.

1. He addresses himself respectfully to those present: "*Men and brethren, hearken unto me.* We are all brethren, and equally concerned that nothing be done to the dishonour of Christ and the uneasiness of Christians."

2. He refers to what Peter had said concerning the conversion of the Gentiles (*v.* 14): "*Simeon hath declared how God at the first did visit the Gentiles*, in Cornelius and his friends, who were the first fruits of the Gentiles." James observes here: That the *grace of God* was the origin of it; it was God *that visited the Gentiles.* The acquaintance began on his part; he not only *visited and redeemed his people*, but visited and redeemed those that were *not a people.* That the glory of God was the end of it: it was *to take out of them a people for his name*, who should glorify him, and in whom he would be glorified. As of old he took the Jews, so now the Gentiles.

3. He confirms this with a quotation out of the Old Testament. It was foretold in the Old Testament, and therefore it must be fulfilled, *v.* 15. *To this agree the words of the prophets;* most of the Old Testament prophets spoke more or less of the calling in of the Gentiles. It was the general expectation of the pious Jews that the Messiah should be *a light to enlighten the Gentiles* (Luke ii. 32): but James waives the more illustrious prophecies of this, and pitches upon one that seemed more obscure: *It is written*, Amos ix. 11, 12, where is foretold, (1) The setting up of the kingdom of the Messiah (*v.* 16): *I will raise up the tabernacle of David, that is fallen.* This tabernacle was ruined and *fallen down*; there had not been for many ages a king of the house of David. But God *will return, and will build it again*, raise it out of its ruins, a phœnix out of its ashes;

JAMIESON, FAUSSET, BROWN

why tempt—'try,' 'provoke'—**ye God**—by standing in the way of His declared purpose. **to put a yoke upon the neck of the disciples . . .** He that was circumcised became thereby bound to keep the whole law. (See Gal. 5:1-6.) It was not then the mere yoke of burdensome ceremonies, but of an obligation which the more earnest and spiritual men became, the more impossible they felt it to fulfil. (See Rom. 3:5; Gal. 2:4, etc.).

11. through the grace of the Lord Jesus—i.e., by that only. **we shall be saved, even as they**—circumcision in our case being no advantage, and in their case uncircumcision no loss; but *grace* doing all for both, and the same for each.

12. Then all . . . gave audience to Barnabas and Paul—On this order of the names here, see on vs. 25. **declaring what miracles and signs God wrought among the Gentiles by them**—This detail of facts, immediately following up those which Peter had recalled to mind, would lead all who waited only for divine teaching to see that God had Himself pronounced the Gentile converts to be disciples in as full standing as the Jews, without circumcision; and the attesting *miracles* to which Paul here refers would tend, in such an assembly to silence opposition.

13. James answered, saying . . . .—Whoever this James was (see on Gal. 1:19), he was the acknowledged head of the church at Jerusalem, and here, as president of the assembly, speaks last, winding up the debate. His decision, though given as his own judgment only, could not be of great weight with the opposing party, from his conservative reverence for all Jewish usages within the circle of Israelitish Christianity. **14-17. Simeon**—a Hebrew variation of Simon, as in II Peter 1:1; (*Gr.*) the Jewish and family name of Peter. **hath declared how God at the first**—answering to Peter's own expression "a good while ago" (vs. 7). **did visit the Gentiles to take out of them**—in the exercise of His adorable sovereignty. **a people for**—the honor of—**his name**—or for His glory.

15. to this agree the words of the prophets—generally; but those of Amos (ch. 9:11) are specified (nearly as in the Septuagint version). The point of the passage lies in the predicted purpose of God, under the new economy, that "the heathen" or "Gentiles" should be "called by His name," or have "His name called upon them." By the "building again of the fallen tabernacle of David," or restoring its decayed splendor, is meant that only and glorious recovery which it was to experience under David's "son and Lord."

ADAM CLARKE

10. *Now therefore why tempt ye God?* As God, by giving the Holy Spirit to the Gentiles, evidently shows He does not design them to be circumcised in order to become debtors to the law, to fulfill all its precepts, why will you provoke Him to displeasure by doing what He evidently designs shall not be done? *A yoke . . . which neither our fathers nor we were able to bear.* This does not refer to the moral law—that was of eternal obligation—but to the ritual law, which, through the multitude of its sacrifices and ordinances, was exceedingly burdensome to the Jewish people.

11. *Through the grace of the Lord Jesus Christ we shall be saved.* This seems to be an answer to an objection, "Has not God designed to save us, the Jews, by an observance of the law; and them, the Gentiles, by the faith of the gospel?" No, for we Jews can be saved no other way than through the grace of the Lord Jesus Christ, and this is the way in which the Gentiles in question have been saved.

12. *Gave audience to Barnabas and Paul.* These apostles came forward next to corroborate what Peter had said, by showing the miracles and wonders which God had by them wrought among the Gentiles. Peter stated facts; Paul and Barnabas confirmed the statement.

13. *James answered.* He was evidently president of the council, and is generally called bishop of Jerusalem. The rest either argued on the subject or gave their opinion; James alone pronounced the definitive sentence. Had Peter been prince and head of the apostles, and of the Church, he would have appeared here in the character of judge, not of mere counsellor or disputant.

14. *Simeon hath declared.* It is remarkable that James does not give him even the title which he received from our Lord at the time in which he is supposed to have been made head of the Church, and vicar of Christ upon earth, so that it is evident James did not understand our Lord as giving Peter any such preeminence and therefore he does not even call him "Peter," but simply *Simeon. To take out of them a people for his name.* To form among the Gentiles, as he had among the Jews, a people called by His name and devoted to His honor.

15. *And to this agree the words of the prophets.* Peter had asserted the fact of the conversion of the Gentiles, and James shows that that fact was the fulfillment of declaration made by the prophets.

16. *After this I will return, and will build again.* These two verses, sixteenth and seven

MATTHEW HENRY

and this was now lately fulfilled, when our Lord Jesus was raised out of that family. The church of Christ may be called the tabernacle of David. This may sometimes be brought very low, and may seem to be in ruins, but it shall be built again, its withering interests shall revive. (2) The bringing in of the Gentiles as the effect and consequence of this (*v.* 17): *That the residue of men might seek after the Lord;* not the Jews only, but *the residue of men,* such as had hitherto been left out of the pale of the visible church; they must now be brought *to seek after the Lord. That the residue of men might seek* (James here adds, *after the Lord*), *and all the Gentiles upon whom my name is called.* His name shall be declared among them, and they shall be brought both to know his name and to call upon it: they shall call themselves the people of God, and he shall call them so; and thus, by consent of both parties, *his name is called upon them.* This promise now begins to be fulfilled, for it is added, *saith the Lord, who doeth all these things. He saith it who doeth it.* Though with us saying and doing are two things they are not so with God. The uniting of *Jews and Gentiles in one body,* and all those things that were done in order to it, were, [1] What God did: whatever instruments were employed in it. [2] What God was well pleased with; for he is the God of the Gentiles, as well as the Jews.

4. He resolves it into the purpose and counsel of God (*v.* 18): *Known unto God are all his works from the beginning of the world.* He not only foretold the calling of the Gentiles by the prophets, but he fore-ordained it in his eternal counsels. Whatever God does, he did before design and determine to do. He not only *does whatever he determined,* which is more than we can do (our purposes are frequently broken off, and our measures broken), but he *determined whatever he does.* What we shall do in such or such a case we cannot tell till it comes to the setting to; but *known unto God are all his works.* We are poor short-sighted creatures; the wisest men can see but a little way before them, and not at all with any certainty; but this is our comfort, that there is an infallible certainty in the divine prescience: *known unto God are all his works.*

5. He gives his advice with reference *to the Gentiles* (*v.* 19): *My sentence is: I give it as my opinion*; not as having authority over the rest, but as being an adviser with them.

(1) That circumcision and the observance of the ceremonial law be by no means imposed upon the Gentile converts. I am clearly for using them with all possible tenderness, and putting no manner of discouragement upon them—*not to give them any molestation nor disturbance.* Great care must be taken not to discourage nor disquiet young converts with matters of *doubtful disputation.* Let the essentials of religion be first impressed deeply upon them, and these will satisfy them and make them easy.

(2) That yet it would be well that in some things, which gave most offence to the Jews, the Gentiles should comply with them. It will please the Jews and, if a little thing will oblige them, better do so than cross them) if the Gentile converts abstain, [1] *From pollutions of idols, and from fornication,* which are two bad things, and always to be abstained from. Not but that the apostles were careful to warn against *pollutions of idols,* that they should have no manner of fellowship with idolaters in their idolatrous worships, and particularly not in the feasts they held upon their sacrifices. *Fornication, and all manner of uncleanness.* How large, how pressing, is Paul in his cautions against this sin! But the Jews suggested that these were things in which the Gentiles, even after conversion, allowed themselves, and the apostle of Gentiles connived at it. Now, to obviate this suggestion, James advises that they should be publicly warned *to abstain from pollutions of idols and from fornication.* [2] *From things strangled, and from blood,* which had been forbidden before the giving of the law of Moses.

6. He gives a reason for his advice—that great respect ought to be shown to the Jews, for they have been so long accustomed to the solemn injunctions of the ceremonial law that they must be borne with, if they cannot presently come off from them (*v.* 21): *For Moses hath of old those that preach him in every city, being read in the synagogues every sabbath day.* "Moses is continually preached to them, and they are called upon *to remember the law of Moses.*" Even that word of God which is written to us should also be preached. "His writings are read *in their synagogues,* and on *the sabbath day*; so that from their childhood they have been trained up in a regard to the law of Moses. This has been done *of old time*; they have received from their fathers an honour for Moses. This has been done *in every city,* so that none of them can be ignorant what stress that law laid upon these things. They cannot be

JAMIESON, FAUSSET, BROWN

ALBERT BARNES:

17. "That the residue of men." This verse is quoted literally from the Septuagint, and differs in some respects from the Hebrew. The phrase "the residue of men" here is evidently understood, both by the LXX and by James, as referring to others than Jews, to the Gentiles—the rest of the world—implying that many of them would be admitted to the friendship and favor of God. The Hebrew is, "that they may possess the remnant of Edom." This change is made in the Septuagint by a slight difference in the reading of two Hebrew words. The LXX, instead of the Hebrew "shall inherit," reads "shall seek of thee"; and instead of "Edom," they read "man," or "mankind," that is, men. Why this variation occurred cannot be explained; but the *sense* is not materially different. In the Hebrew the word *Edom* has undoubted reference to another nation than the Jewish; and the expression means that, in the great prosperity of the Jews after their return, they would extend the influence of their religion to other nations; that is, as James applies it, the Gentiles might be brought to the privileges of the children of God.—*Popular Commentary*

18, 19. Known unto God are all his works from the beginning—He who announced these things so long before, and He who had now brought them to pass, were one and the same; so that they were no novelty.

Wherefore, my sentence—or 'judgment'—**is, that we trouble not**—with Jewish obligations—**them which from among the Gentiles are turned to God**—rather, 'are turning.' The work is regarded as in progress, and indeed was rapidly advancing.

20. But . . . that they abstain from pollutions of idols—i.e., things polluted by having been offered in sacrifice to idols. The heathen were accustomed to give away or sell portions of such animals. From such food James would enjoin the Gentile converts to abstain, lest it should seem to the Jews that they were not entirely weaned from idolatry. **and from fornication**—The characteristic sin of heathendom, unblushingly practiced by all ranks and classes, and the indulgence of which on the part of the Gentile converts would to Jews, whose Scriptures branded it as an abomination of the heathen, proclaim them to be yet joined to their old idols. **and from things strangled**—which had the blood in them. **and from blood**—in every form, as peremptorily forbidden to the Jews, and the eating of which, therefore, on the part of the Gentile converts, would shock their prejudices. See on vss. 28, 29.

21. For Moses of old time hath in every city them that preach him . . . every sabbath day—thus keeping alive in every Jew those feelings which such practices would shock, and which, therefore, the Gentile converts must carefully respect if the oneness of both classes in Christ was to be practically preserved. The wisdom of these suggestions commended itself to all present.

ADAM CLARKE

teenth, are quoted from Amos ix. 11-12, nearly as they now stand in the best editions of the Septuagint, and evidently taken from that version, which differs considerably from the Hebrew text. As James quoted them as a prophecy of the calling of the Gentiles into the Church of God, it is evident the Jews must have understood them in that sense; otherwise they would have immediately disputed his application of them to the subject in question and have rejected his conclusion by denying the premises.

17. *That the residue of men might seek.* Instead of this the Hebrew has, "That they may possess the remnant of Edom." Now it is evident that in the copy from which the Seventy translated they found *yidreshu,* "they might seek," instead of *yireshu,* "they may possess," where the whole difference between the two words is the change of the *yod* for a *daleth,* which might be easily done; and *Edom,* the "Idumeans," which differs from the other letters. It shows that even in Jerusalem and in the early part of the apostolic age the Septuagint version was quoted in preference to the Hebrew text. But God was evidently preparing the way of the gospel by bringing this venerable version into general credit and use, which was to be the means of conveying the truths of Christianity to the whole Gentile world. How precious should this august and most important version be to every Chritsain, and especially to every Christian minister! A version without which no man ever did or ever can critically understand the New Testament!

18. *Known unto God are all his works from the beginning.* As if he had said, This is not a new counsel of God; He had purposed, from the time He called the Israelites, to make the Gentiles partakers of the same grace and mercy. The whole of this verse is very dubious; the principal part of it is omitted by the most ancient MSS.

19. *Wherefore my sentence is.* "Wherefore I judge." There is an authority here that does not appear in the speech of Peter; this authority was felt and bowed to by all the council, and the decree proposed by James adopted.

20. *But that we write unto them.* Four things are prohibited in this decree: (1) *Pollutions of idols;* (2) *fornication;* (3) *things strangled;* (4) *blood.* By the first, *pollutions of idols,* or as it is in v. 29, "meats offered to idols," not only all idolatry was forbidden, but eating things offered in sacrifice to idols, knowing that they were thus offered, and joining with idolaters in their sacred feasts. By the second, *fornication,* all uncleanness of every kind was prohibited; for *porneia* not only means *fornication,* but "adultery," and especially the prostitution which was so common at the idol temples. By the third, *things strangled,* we are to understand the flesh of those animals which were strangled for the purpose of keeping the blood in the body, as such animals were esteemed a greater delicacy. By the fourth, *blood,* we are to understand, not only the thing itself, but also all cruelty, manslaughter, and murder, as some of the ancient fathers have understood it.

21. *Moses of old time hath in every city.* The sense of this verse seems to be this: As it was necessary to write to the Gentiles what was strictly necessary to be observed by them, relative to these points, it was not so to the converted Jews; for they had Moses—that is, the law—preached to them, "in the city"—that is, Antioch; and by the reading of the law in the synagogues every Sabbath day they were kept in remembrance of those institutions which the Gentiles, who had not the law, could not know.

MATTHEW HENRY

blamed if they are loth to part with them, and cannot of a sudden be persuaded to look upon those things as needless and indifferent. We must therefore give them time, they must be borne with awhile, and brought on gradually." Thus does this apostle show a spirit of moderation, contriving, as much as may be, to please both sides and provoke neither.

Verses 22–35

We have here the result of the consultation. The advice which James gave was universally approved. Letters were accordingly sent by messengers of their own to the Gentile converts, which would be a great confirmation to them against the false teachers.

I. The choice of the delegates that were to be sent with Paul and Barnabas on this errand.

1. They thought fit *to send men of their own company to Antioch, with Paul and Barnabas, v.* 22. This was agreed to by *the apostles and elders, with the whole church.* To show their respect to the church at Antioch, as a sister-church, as also that they were desirous further to know their state. To encourage Paul and Barnabas, and to make their journey home the more pleasant. To put a reputation upon the letters they carried, that more regard might be paid to the message, which was likely to meet with opposition from some. To keep up *the communion of saints,* and to show *that, though they were many, yet they were one.*

2. Those they sent were not inferior persons, who might serve to carry the letters, but *they were chosen men, and chief men among the brethren.* They are here named: *Judas,* who was called *Barsabas, and Silas.*

II. The drawing up of the letters to notify the sense of the synod in this matter.

1. A very obliging preamble to this decree, *v.* 23. That which intimates the humility of the apostles, that they join *the elders and brethren* in commission with them, whom they had advised with in this case. Herein they remembered the instructions their Master gave them (Matt. xxiii. 8). That which bespeaks their respect: they *send greeting,* and call them *brethren of the Gentiles,* thereby giving them the right hand of fellowship: "You are our brethren, though Gentiles." Now that *the Gentiles are fellow-heirs and of the same body,* they are to be encouraged, and called brethren.

2. A just and severe rebuke to the judaizing teachers (*v.* 24): "*We have heard that certain who went out from us have troubled you with words.* They *went out from us* indeed, but, as for their urging the law of Moses upon you, we *gave* them *no such commandment.*" They did a great deal of wrong to the Gentile converts, in saying, *You must be circumcised, and you must keep the law.* It perplexed them: "*They have troubled you with words.* You depended upon those who told you, *If you believe in the Lord Jesus Christ you shall be saved;* and now you are startled by those that tell you *you must keep the law of Moses or you cannot be saved.* They trouble you with words —mere words—sound, but no substance." How has the church been troubled with words, by the pride of men that loved to hear themselves talk! It endangered them; they *subverted* their souls, put them into disorder, and pulled down that which had been built up.

3. An honourable testimony given of the messengers.

(1) Of Paul and Barnabas, whom these judaizing teachers had censured as having done their work by the halves, because they had brought the Gentile converts to Christianity only, and not to Judaism. "They are men that are dear to us; they are *our beloved Barnabas and Paul.*" Sometimes it is good for those that are of eminence to express their esteem. They are men *that have hazarded their lives for the name of our Lord Jesus Christ* (*v.* 26). They have ventured their all for Christ, have engaged in the most dangerous services, as good soldiers of Christ. It is not likely that such faithful confessors should be unfaithful preachers.

(2) Of Judas and Silas: *They are chosen men* (*v.* 25), and they are men that have heard our debates, and will *tell you the same things by mouth, v.* 27. What is of use to us it is good to have both in writing and by word of mouth, that we may have the advantage both of reading and of hearing it.

4. Here is the direction given what to require from the Gentile converts.

(1) The matter of the injunction, which is according to the advice given by James. They should never eat anything that they knew had been offered in sacrifice to an idol, but look upon it as thereby polluted to them. This to us is an antiquated case. *That they should not eat blood. That they should not eat anything that was strangled,* or had not the blood

JAMIESON, FAUSSET, BROWN

22, 23. Judas surnamed Barsabas—therefore not the apostle "Judas the brother of James" (ch. 1:13), surnamed "Thaddeus" (Matt. 10:3); nor can it be shown that he was a brother of "Joseph called Barsabas" (ch. 1:23). But nothing is known of him beyond what is here said. **and Silas**—the same as "Silvanus" in the Epistles. He became Paul's companion on his second missionary journey (vs. 40). **chief men among the brethren**—selected purposely as such, to express the honor in which they held the church at Antioch, and the deputies they had sent to the council, and, as the matter affected all Gentile converts, to give weight to the written decision of this important assembly. They were "prophets," vs. 32 (and see on ch. 11:27), and as such doubtless their eminence in the church at Jerusalem had been obtained. **And they wrote . . . by them**—This is the first mention in the New Testament history of *writing* as an element in its development. And the combination here of written and oral transmission of an important decision reminds us of the first occasion of writing mentioned in the Old Testament, where a similar combination occurs (Exod. 17:14). But whereas *there* it is the deep *difference* between Israel and the Gentiles which is proclaimed, *here* it is the *obliteration of that difference* through faith in the Lord Jesus [BAUMGARTEN]. **greeting**—The only other place in the New Testament where this word occurs (except in the letter of Lysias, ch. 23: 26) is James 1:1, which seems to show that both letters were drawn up by the same hand [BENGEL]. **the Gentiles in Antioch, and Syria, and Cilicia**—showing that churches then existed in Cilicia as well as Syria, which owed their existence, in all likelihood, to Paul's labors during the interval between his return to Tarsus (ch. 9:30) and his departure in company with Barnabas for Antioch (see on ch. 11:25, 26). **24-27. Forasmuch as we have heard that certain which went out from us have troubled you with words**—without authority or even knowledge of the church at Jerusalem, though they belonged to it, and probably pretended to represent its views. **subverting your souls**—Such strong language is evidently designed to express indignation at this attempt, by an unauthorized party, to bring the whole Christian Church under judicial and legal bondage. **our beloved Barnabas and Paul**—Barnabas is put first here, and in vs. 12, on account of his former superior position in the church at Jerusalem (see ch. 9:27; 11:22)—an evidence this that we have the document precisely as written, as also of the credibility of this precious history. **Men that have hazarded**—lit., 'rendered up,' as in *will* they did—**their lives for the name of our Lord Jesus Christ**—Noble testimony to those beloved men! It was doubtless prompted more immediately by the narrative they had just listened to from their own lips (vs. 12), and judiciously inserted in this letter, to give them the highest weight as the bearers of it, along with their own deputies. **Judas and Silas . . . shall tell you the same . . . by mouth**—Mark here how considerate and tender it was to send men who would be able to say of Barnabas and Paul what could not be expected to come from themselves.

ADAM CLARKE

22. *Then pleased it the apostles and elders, with the whole church.* James determined what ought to be done; and the whole assembly resolved how that should be done.

Chosen men of their own company. Paul and Barnabas were to return. They could have witnessed to the church at Antioch what was done at the council at Jerusalem; but as it was possible that their testimony might be suspected, from the part they had already taken in this question at Antioch, it was necessary that a deputation from the council should accompany them. Accordingly, Judas and Silas are sent to corroborate by their oral testimony what was contained in the letters sent from the council.

23. *Send greeting unto the brethren . . . of the Gentiles.* There was no occasion to send such a letter to the brethren which were of the Jews, because that law which had been so long read in their synagogues taught them all those things, and therefore the epistle is sent exclusively to the Gentiles. The word *greeting* is in the original *chairein,* "to be well, to be safe"—a very usual form in Greek epistles.

24. *Certain which went out from us.* So the persons who produced these doubtful disputations at Antioch had gone out from the apostles at Jerusalem and were of that church; persons zealous for the law and yet, strange to tell, so conscientiously attached to the gospel that they risked their personal safety by professing it. *To whom we gave no such commandment.* As, therefore, they went out from that church, they should have taught nothing which was not owned and taught by it; much less should they have taught in opposition to it.

27. *Judas and Silas . . . shall . . . tell you the same things.* These were proofs that the testimony of Paul and Barnabas was true, and that the letter was not forged, as they could witness the same things which the letter contained.

MATTHEW HENRY

let out. That they should be very strict in censuring those that *were guilty of fornication.* "These things are in a particular manner offensive to the Jews, and therefore do not disoblige them herein."

(2) The manner in which it is worded. They express themselves with something of authority: *It seemed good to the Holy Ghost, and to us,* that is, to us under the guidance of the Holy Ghost. They would not order anything because *it seemed good to them,* but that they knew it first *seemed good to the Holy Ghost.* They express themselves with abundance of tenderness and fatherly concern. *First,* They are afraid of burdening them: We will *lay upon you no greater burden.* They dreaded nothing so much as imposing too far upon them, so as to discourage them at their setting out. *Secondly,* They impose upon them *no other than necessary things.* Church-rulers should impose only necessary things, things which Christ has made our duty. They have not authority to make new laws, but only to see that the laws of Christ be duly executed. *Thirdly,* They enforce their order with a commendation of those that shall comply with it, rather than with the condemnation of those that shall transgress it. *"From which if you keep yourselves you will do well."* It is all sweetness and love and good humour. The difference of the style of the true apostles from that of the false is very observable. Those that were for imposing the ceremonial laws were positive and imperious: *Except you keep it, you cannot be saved* (*v.* 1). The apostles of Christ, who only recommend necessary things, are mild and gentle: *"From which if you keep yourselves, you will do well. Fare ye well;* we are hearty well-wishers to your honour and peace."

III. The delivering of the letters. *When they were dismissed they then came to Antioch;* they stayed no longer at Jerusalem than till their business was done, and then came back. As soon as they came to Antioch, *they gathered the multitude together, and delivered the epistle to them* (*v.* 30, 31), that they might all know what it was that was forbidden them. But this was not all; it was that they might know that *no more* than this was forbidden them. The people were wonderfully pleased (*v.* 31): *They rejoiced for the consolation.* That they were confirmed in their freedom from the yoke of the ceremonial law. That those who troubled their minds with an attempt to force circumcision upon them were hereby silenced. That the Gentiles were hereby encouraged to receive the gospel, and those that had received it to adhere to it. That the peace of the church was hereby restored. They got the strange ministers that came from Jerusalem to give them each a sermon, *v.* 32. Judas and Silas, *being prophets also themselves, exhorted the brethren with many words,* and *confirmed them.* Even those that had the constant preaching of Paul and Barnabas, yet were glad of the help of Judas and Silas; the diversity of the gifts of ministers is of use to the church. Observe what is the work of ministers with those that are in Christ. (1) To confirm them; to confirm their choice of Christ and their resolutions for Christ. (2) To exhort them to perseverance: to quicken them to that which is good, and direct them in it. They comforted the brethren (so it may be rendered), and this would contribute to the confirming of them; for the joy of the Lord will be our strength. One word would affect one, and another another; what they had to say might have been summed up in a few words, yet it was for the edification of the church that they used *many words.* The dismission of the Jerusalem ministers, *v.* 33. When they had *spent some time among them* they were let go in peace from the brethren at Antioch, to the apostles at Jerusalem. The continuance of Silas, together with Paul and Barnabas, at Antioch. Silas chose rather to *abide still at Antioch, v.* 34. We know not the reason that moved him to it. Paul and Barnabas, though their work lay chiefly among the Gentiles, yet continued for some time in Antioch. They continued there, not to take their pleasure, but *teaching and preaching the word of God.* It is probable there was a great resort of Gentiles thither from all parts, so that in preaching there they did in effect preach to many nations. And thus they were not only not idle at Antioch, but were serving their main intention. There were *many others also* there. The multitude of workmen in Christ's vineyard does not give us a writ of ease. There may be opportunity for us; the zeal and usefulness of others should excite us, not lay us asleep.

Verses 36-41

Here we have a private quarrel between two ministers, no less men than Paul and Barnabas, yet ending well.

I. Here is a good proposal Paul made to Barnabas to go and review their work among the Gentiles and

JAMIESON, FAUSSET, BROWN

28, 29. For it seemed good to the Holy Ghost and to us . . .—The One, inwardly guiding to and setting His seal on the decision come to; the other, the external ecclesiastical authority devoutly embracing, expressing, and conveying to the churches that decision:—a great principle this for the Church in all time. **to lay upon you no greater burden than these necessary things . . . from which if ye keep yourselves, ye shall do well**—The whole language of these prohibitions, and of vss. 20, 21, implies that they were designed as concessions to Jewish feelings on the part of the Gentile converts, and not as things which were all of unchanging obligation. The only cause for hesitation arises from "fornication" being mixed up with the other three things; which has led many to regard the whole as permanently prohibited. But the remarks on vs. 20 may clear this. The then state of heathen society in respect of all the four things seems the reason for so mixing them up.

30-33. they rejoiced for the consolation—As the same word is in the next verse properly rendered "exhorted," the meaning probably is 'rejoiced for the exhortation' (*margin*), or advice; so wise in itself and so contrary to the imposition attempted to be practiced upon them by the Judaizers.

Judas and Silas, being prophets themselves—i.e., inspired teachers—**exhorted the brethren with many words**—'much discourse'—**and confirmed them**—opening up, no doubt, the great principle involved in the controversy now settled, of gratuitous salvation, or the purification of the heart by faith alone (as expressed by Peter, vss. 9, 11), and dwelling on the necessity of harmony in principle and affection between the Gentile disciples and their Jewish brethren. **were let go in peace**—with peace, as the customary parting salutation.

34, 35. it pleased Silas—Silas determined—**to abide there still**—(The authorities against the insertion of this verse are strong. It may have been afterwards added to explain vs. 40). Doubtless the attraction to Antioch for Silas was Paul's presence there, to whom he seems to have now formed that permanent attachment which the sequel of this book and Paul's Epistles show to have existed. **Paul . . . and Barnabas continued in Antioch, teaching**—to the disciples—**and preaching**—to those without—**the word of the Lord, with many others**—other laborers—**also**—How rich must Antioch at this time have been in the ministrations of the Gospel! (*For a painful scene on this occasion between Paul and Peter, see* Gal. 2:11, etc.).

ADAM CLARKE

28. *For it seemed good to the Holy Ghost, and to us.* The whole council had met under His direction, had consulted under His influence; and gave forth their decree from His especial inspiration.

29. *Fare . . . well.* An old English form of expressing "good wishes" and "goodwill"—"Go well, go prosperously!" The Greek word *errhosthe,* here used, from "to strengthen, make strong," has nearly the same signification: "be strong, courageous, active, be in health, and be prosperous!"

31. *They rejoiced for the consolation.* It was not a matter of small moment to have a question on which such stress was laid decided by an apostolic council, over which the Spirit of God presided.

33. *They were let go.* That is, both had liberty to depart; but Silas chose to stay a little longer with the brethren.

34. *Notwithstanding it pleased Silas.* This whole verse is wanting in some MSS. It does not appear to have been originally in the text.

MATTHEW HENRY

renew it. Antioch was now a safe and quiet harbour for them; but Paul remembered that they only put in there to refit and refresh themselves, and therefore begins now to think of putting to sea again. Paul remembered that the work appointed him was afar off among the Gentiles, and therefore he is here meditating a second expedition among them; and this *some days after*, for his active spirit could not bear to be long out of work; no, nor his bold and daring spirit to be long out of danger. 1. To whom he makes this proposal—to Barnabas, his old friend and fellow-labourer. We have need one of another, and may be in many ways serviceable one to another; and therefore should be forward both to borrow and lend assistance. Every soldier has his comrade. 2. For whom the visit is designed: "Let us not begin new work, but let us take a view of the fields we have sown. *Let us go again and visit our brethren in every city where we have preached the word of the Lord.*" He calls all the Christians brethren. He has a concern for them in *every city*. Wherever we have *preached the word of the Lord*, let us go and water the seed sown. Those that have preached the gospel should visit those to whom they have preached it. As we must look after our praying, and hear what answer God gives to that; so we must look after our preaching, and see what success that has. 3. What was intended in this visit: "Let us *see how they do.*" He would visit them that he might acquaint himself with their case, as the physician visits his recovering patient, that he may prescribe what is proper for the perfecting of his cure, and the preventing of a relapse. Let us see how they do. (1) What spirit they are of, how they stand affected, and how they behave themselves. (2) What state they are in, that we may rejoice with them if they rejoice, and may weep with them if they weep, and may know the better how to pray for them.

II. The disagreement between Paul and Barnabas about an assistant. Barnabas would have his nephew John, whose surname was Mark, to go along with them, *v.* 37. He determined to take him, because he was his relation. We should suspect ourselves of partiality, and guard against it in preferring our relations. Paul opposed it (*v.* 38): *He thought not good to take him with them* who had *departed from them*, from Pamphylia (*ch.* xiii. 13), and *went not with them to the work*. He run his colours just as they were going to engage. It is probable that he promised very fair now that he would not do so again. But Paul thought it was not fit he should be thus honoured; at least, not till he had been longer tried. If a man deceive me once, it is his fault; but, if twice, it is my own, for trusting him.

III. The issue of this disagreement: they separated upon it. The contention was so sharp that they *departed asunder one from the other*. Neither would yield, and therefore there is no remedy but they must part. Now here is that which is just matter of lamentation, and yet very instructive. For we see, 1. That the best of men are but men, *subject to like passions* as we are, as these two good men had expressly owned concerning themselves (*ch.* xiv. 15), and now it appeared too true. I doubt there was (as usually there is in such contentions) a *fault on both sides*. They were certainly both in fault to be hot as to let the contention be sharp, as also each to stick resolutely to his opinion, and neither to yield. It is a pity that some friend did not interpose to prevent its coming to an open rupture. We must own it was their infirmity, not that we must make use of it to excuse our own intemperate heats and passions. No; but it must check our censures of others, and moderate them. Repentance teaches us to be severe in reflections upon ourselves; but charity teaches us to be candid in our reflections upon others. It is only Christ's example that is a copy without a blot. 2. That we are not to think it strange if there be differences among wise and good men. Even those that are united to one and the same Jesus, and sanctified by one and the same Spirit, have different opinions, different views. We shall never be all of a mind till we come to heaven. 3. That these differences often prevail so far as to occasion separations. Paul and Barnabas, who were not separated by the persecutions of the unbelieving Jews, nor the impositions of the believing Jews, were yet separated by an unhappy disagreement between themselves.

JAMIESON, FAUSSET, BROWN

36-46. DISSENSION BETWEEN PAUL AND BARNABAS—THEY PART COMPANY TO PROSECUTE SEPARATE MISSIONARY TOURS. **And some days after**—How long is a matter of conjecture. **Paul said to Barnabas, Let us go again and visit our**—the true reading is, the—**brethren in every city where we have preached . . . and see how they do**—whether they were advancing or declining, etc.: a pattern for churches and successful missionaries in every age. ("Reader, how stands it with thee?") [BENGEL]. "Paul felt that he was not called to spend a peaceful, though laborious life at Antioch, but that his true work was far off among the Gentiles." We notice here, for the first time, a trace of that tender solicitude for his converts, that earnest longing to see their faces, which appears in the letters which he wrote afterwards, as one of the most remarkable and attractive features of his character. He thought, doubtless, of the Pisidians and Lycaonians, as he thought afterwards at Athens and Corinth of the Thessalonians, from whom he had been lately "taken in presence, not in heart, night and day praying exceedingly that he might see their face and perfect that which was lacking in their faith" [Hows]. **Barnabas determined to take with them John . . . Mark**—his nephew (Col. 4:10). **But Paul thought not good to take him with them who departed from them**—i.e., who *had* departed; but the word is stronger than this—'who stood aloof' or 'turned away' from them—**from Pamphylia, and went not with them to the work**—the work yet before them. The allusion is to what is recorded in ch. 13:13 (on which see). **And the contention was so sharp between them**—such was the 'irritation,' or 'exacerbation'—**that they departed asunder one from the other**—Said they not truly to the Lystrians that they were "men of like passions with them"; (Ch. 14:15.) But *who was to blame*? (1) That John Mark had either tired of the work or shrunk from the dangers and fatigues that yet lay before them, was undeniable; and Paul concluded that what he had done he might, and probably would, do again. Was he wrong in this? (See Prov. 25:19.) But (2) To this Barnabas might reply that no rule was without exception; that one failure, in a young Christian, was not enough to condemn him for life; that if near relationship might be thought to warp his judgment, it also gave him opportunities of knowing the man better than others; and that as he was himself anxious to be allowed another trial (and the result makes this next to certain), in order that he might wipe out the effect of his former failure and show what "hardness he could now endure as a good soldier of Jesus Christ," his petition ought not to be rejected. Now, since John Mark *did* retrieve his character in these respects, and a reconciliation took place between Paul and him, so cordial that the apostle expresses more than once the confidence he had in him and the value he set upon his services (Col. 4:10, 11; II Tim. 4:11), it may seem that events showed Barnabas to be in the right, and Paul too harsh and hasty in his judgment. But, in behalf of Paul, it may well be answered, that not being able to see into the future he had only the unfavorable past to judge by; that the gentleness of Barnabas (ch. 4:36; 11:24) had already laid him open to imposition (see on Gal. 2:13), to which near relationship would in this case make him more liable; and that in refusing to take John Mark on this missionary journey he was not judging his Christian character nor pronouncing on his fitness for future service, but merely providing in the meantime against being again put to serious inconvenience and having their hands weakened by a possible second desertion. On the whole, then, it seems clear that each of these great servants of Christ had something to say for himself, in defense of the position which they respectively took up; that while Barnabas was quite able to appreciate the grounds on which Paul proceeded, Paul was not so competent to judge of the considerations which Barnabas probably urged; that while Paul had but one object in view, to see that the companion of their arduous work was one of thoroughly congenial spirit and sufficient nerve, Barnabas, over and above the same desire, might not unreasonably be afraid for the soul of his nephew, lest the refusal to allow him to accompany them on their journey might injure his Christian character and deprive the Church of a true servant of Jesus Christ; and that while both sought only the glory of their common Master, each looked at the question at issue, to some extent, through the medium of his own temperament, which grace sanctifies and refines, but does not destroy—*Paul,* through the medium of absolute devotion to the cause and kingdom of Christ, which, warm and womanly as his affections were, gave a tinge of lofty

ADAM CLARKE

36. *Let us go . . . and visit our brethren in every city.* This heavenly man projected a journey to Cyprus, Perga, Iconium, Lystra, Derbe, Antioch in Pisidia; for in all these places he had preached and founded churches in the preceding year. He saw it was necessary to water the seed he had planted; for these were young converts, surrounded with impiety, opposition, and superstition, and had few advantages among themselves.

39. *The contention was so sharp between them.* For all this sentence there is only in the Greek text: "There was therefore a paroxysm," an incitement, a stirring up. But does this imply anger or ill will on either side? Certainly not. Here, these two apostles differed, and were strenuous, each in support of the part he had adopted. "Paul," as an ancient Greek commentator has it, "being influenced only with the love of righteousness; Barnabas being actuated by love to his relative." John Mark had been tried in trying circumstances, and he failed; Paul therefore would not trust him again. The affection of Barnabas led him to hope the best, and was therefore desirous to give him another trial. Barnabas would not give up; Paul would not agree. They therefore agreed to depart from each other, and take different parts of the work. Each had an attendant and companion at hand. So Barnabas took John Mark and sailed to Cyprus; Paul took Silas, and went into Syria. To all human appearance it was best that they separated, as the churches were more speedily visited, and the work of God more widely and more rapidly spread. And why is it that this is brought in as a proof of the sinful imperfection of these holy apostles? because those who thus treat the subject can never differ with another without feeling wrong tempers; and then, as destitute of good breeding as they are of humility, they attribute to others the angry, proud, and wrathful dispositions which they feel in themselves; and because they cannot be angry and sin not, they suppose that even apostles themselves cannot. Should any man say there was sin in this contention between Paul and Barnabas, I answer, there is no evidence of this in the text. Should he say the word *paroxysm* denotes this, I answer, "It does not." And the verb is often used in a good sense. So Isocrates ad Demosth. cap. xx: "But thou wilt be the more *stirred up* to the love of good works." And such persons forget that this is the very form used by the apostle himself, Heb. x. 24: which these objectors would be highly displeased with me were I to translate, "Let us consider one another to an angry contention of love and good works." From these examples it appears that the word is used to signify "incitement" of any kind; it is taken to express a strong excitement to the love of God and man, and to the fruits by which such love can be best proved; and, in the case before us, there was certainly nothing contrary to this pure principle in either of those heavenly men.

MATTHEW HENRY

ALEXANDER MACLAREN:

Scripture narratives are remarkable for the frankness with which they tell the faults of the best men. It has nothing in common with the cynical spirit in historians, of which this age has seen eminent examples, which fastens upon the weak places in the noblest natures, like a wasp on bruises in the ripest fruit, and delights in showing how all goodness is imperfect, that it may suggest that none is genuine. Nor has it anything in common with that dreary melancholy which also has its representatives among us, that sees everywhere only failures and fragments of men, and has no hope of ever attaining anything beyond the common average of excellence. But Scripture frankly confesses that all its noblest characters have fallen short of unstained purity, and with boldness of hope as great as its frankness teaches the weakest to aspire, and the most sinful to expect perfect likeness to a perfect Lord. It is a plane mirror, giving back all images without distortion.
—*Expositions of Holy Scripture*

IV. The good that was brought out of this evil. It was strange that even the sufferings of the apostles (as Phil. i. 12), but much more strange that even the quarrels of the apostles, should tend to the *furtherance of the gospel of Christ.* God would not permit such things to be, if he knew not how to make them to serve his own purposes. 1. More places are hereby visited. Barnabas went one way; he sailed to Cyprus (*v.* 39), where they began their work (*ch.* xiii. 4), and which was *his own country, ch.* iv. 36. Paul went another way into Cilicia, which was *his own country, ch.* xxi. 39. Each seems to be influenced by his affection to his native soil, as usual. Yet God served his own purposes by it. 2. More hands are hereby employed in the ministry of the gospel among the Gentiles. John Mark, who had been an unfaithful hand, is not rejected, and, for aught we know, proves a very useful and successful hand. Silas who was a new hand is brought in.

V. We may further observe, 1. That the church at Antioch seem to countenance Paul in what he did. Barnabas sailed with his nephew to Cyprus, and no notice was taken of him. But, when Paul departed, he was *recommended by the brethren to the grace of God.* They prayed publicly for Paul, and for the success of his ministry. They transferred the matter to the grace of God, leaving it to that grace both to work upon him and to work with him. Those are happy at all times who are enabled so to carry themselves as not to forfeit their interest in the love and prayers of good people. 2. That yet Paul afterwards seems to have had, upon further trial, a better opinion of John Mark than now he had; for he writes to Timothy (2 Tim. iv. 11), *Take Mark and bring him with thee, for he is profitable to me for the ministry.* Even those whom we justly condemn we should condemn moderately, because we know not but afterwards we may see cause to think better of them, and we should so regulate our resentments that if it should prove so we may not afterwards be ashamed of them. Even those whom we have justly condemned, if afterwards they prove more faithful, we should cheerfully receive, forgive and forget, and, as there is occasion, give a good word to. 3. That Paul went on cheerfully in his work (*v.* 41): *He went through Syria and Cilicia, confirming the churches.* Ministers are well employed when they are made use of in confirming those that believe, as well as in converting those that believe not.

JAMIESON, FAUSSET, BROWN

sternness to his resolves where that seemed to be affected; *Barnabas,* through the medium of the same singleness of heart in Christ's service, though probably not in equal strength (Gal. 2:13), but also of a certain natural gentleness which, where a Christian relative was concerned, led him to attach more weight to what seemed for his spiritual good than Paul could be supposed to do. In these circumstances, it seems quite possible that they might have amicably 'agreed to differ,' each taking his own companion, as they actually did. But the 'paroxysm' (as the word is), the 'exacerbation' which is expressly given as the cause of their parting, shows but too plainly, that human infirmity amidst the great labors of the Church at Antioch at length sundered those who had sweetly and lovingly borne together the heat and burden of the day during a protracted tour in the service of Christ. "Therefore let no man glory in men" (I Cor. 3:21). As for John Mark, although through his uncle's warm advocacy of his cause he was put in a condition to dissipate the cloud that hung over him, how bitter to him must have ever afterwards been the reflection that it was his culpable conduct which gave occasion to whatever was sinful in the strife between Paul and Barnabas, and to a separation in action, though no doubt with a mutual Christian regard, between those who had till then wrought nobly together! How watchful does all this teach Christians, and especially Christian ministers and missionaries, to be against giving way to rash judgment and hot temper towards each other, especially where on both sides the glory of Christ is the ground of difference! How possible is it that in such cases both parties may, on the question at issue, be more or less in the right! How difficult is it even for the most faithful and devoted servants of Christ, differing as they do in their natural temperament even under the commanding influence of grace, to see even important questions precisely in the same light! And if, with every disposition to yield what is unimportant, they still feel it a duty each to stand to his own point, how careful should they be to do it lovingly, each pursuing his own course without disparagement of his Christian brother! And how affectingly does the Lord overrule such difference of judgment and such manifestations of human infirmity, by making them "turn out rather unto the furtherance of the Gospel"; as in this case is eminently seen in the two missionary parties instead of one, not travelling over the same ground and carrying their dispute over all the regions of their former loving labors, but dividing the field between them! **and so Barnabas took Mark, and sailed unto Cyprus; and Paul chose Silas** (see on vs. 34)—going two and two, as the Twelve and the Seventy (Mark 6:7; Luke 10:1). **and departed, being recommended . . . to the grace of God** —(no doubt by some solemn service; see ch. 13:3), as in ch. 14:26. It does not follow from the historian's silence that Barnabas was not so recommended, too; for this is the last mention of Barnabas in the history, whose sole object now is to relate the proceedings of Paul. Nor does it seem quite fair [with DE WETTE, MEYER, HOWS, ALFORD, HACKET, WEBSTER and WILKINSON, etc.] to conclude from this that the Church at Antioch took that marked way of showing their sympathy with Paul in opposition to Barnabas. **41. and he went through Syria and Cilicia, confirming the churches**—"It is very likely that Paul and Barnabas made a deliberate and amicable arrangement to divide the region of their first mission between them; Paul taking the *continental,* and Barnabas the *insular,* part of the proposed visitation. If Barnabas visited Salamis and Paphos, and if Paul (travelling westward), after passing through Derbe, Lystra, and Iconium, went as far as Antioch in Pisidia, the whole circuit of the proposed visitation was actually accomplished, for it does not appear that any converts had been made at Perga and Attalia" [HOWS]. "This second missionary tour appears to have proceeded at first solely from the desire of visiting the churches already planted. In the end, however, it took a much wider sweep, for it brought the apostle to Europe" [OLSHAUSEN].

ADAM CLARKE

G. CAMPBELL MORGAN:

The Greek word translated "contention" is the word from which we derive our word paroxysm. I am greatly comforted whenever I read this. I am thankful for the revelation of the humanity of these men. If I had never read that Paul withstood Peter to the face, and that Paul and Barnabas had a contention, I should have been afraid. These men were not angels; they were men. It is very interesting to study the differing opinions as to who was to blame. There are most eloquent defenses of Paul and of Barnabas as to who was right and who was wrong. Amid differing opinions a man may have one of his own. My own sympathy is entirely with Barnabas, notwithstanding the fact that the church at Antioch sent Paul and Silas out by the grace of God; and the account does not say that they gave a benediction to Barnabas and Mark. Perhaps they were both right. Paul was severe because Mark had failed them once, and he felt that no man could go to this work who, having put his hand to the plough, had looked back. Mark had gone away from them when their faces were set toward the difficulties of Perga and Pamphylia. He had not gone with them to the work. Barnabas felt that Mark should have another chance. Perhaps there is a sense in which Paul and Barnabas were both right. Mark profited by the actions of both. Mark sailed away to Cyprus with Barnabas, and they pass out of the story in the Acts of the Apostles. We do know something more of Mark. When he had been with Barnabas some time, he was restored to Paul's fellowship; for when Paul wrote to the Colossian Church, he spoke of him as his "fellow worker," commended him to the Church; and in his last hours besought that Timothy would bring him with him. The last thing we know about Mark, the "servant of Jesus," whom Paul for a time would not trust, but to whom Barnabas gave a second chance, is that it was he who wrote the Gospel of the perfect Servant. Perhaps his moral courage was stiffened by Paul's severity and confirmed by the tenderness of Barnabas.
—*The Acts of the Apostles*

40. *Being recommended . . . unto the grace of God.* Much stress has been laid upon this to show that Barnabas was in the wrong and Paul in the right, because "the brethren recommended Paul and Silas to the grace of God, but they did not recommend Barnabas and John Mark; this proves that the church condemned the conduct of Barnabas, but approved that of Paul." Now there is no proof that the church did not recommend Barnabas to the grace of God, as well as Paul; but as Luke had for the present dropped the story of Barnabas, and was now going on with that of Paul and Silas, he begins it at this point, viz., his being recommended by the brethren to the grace of God; and then goes on to tell of his progress in Syria, Derbe, and Lystra. See the next chapter. With this verse the following chapter should begin; and this is the division followed by the most correct copies of the Greek text.

41. *Confirming the churches.* This was the object of his journey. They were young converts, and had need of establishment; and there is no doubt that by showing them the decision made at the late council of Jerusalem their faith was greatly strengthened, their hope confirmed, and their love increased.

MATTHEW HENRY

CHAPTER 16

Verses 1–5

Paul was a spiritual father, and as such a one we have him here adopting Timothy: and in all he appears to have been a wise and tender father.

I. His taking Timothy into his acquaintance and under his tuition. And we are here accordingly told, 1. That he was a disciple, one that belonged to Christ. He took him to be brought up for Christ.

2. That his mother was a Jewess originally, *but believed in Christ*; her name was *Eunice*, his grandmother's name was *Lois*. Paul speaks of them both with great respect and commends them especially for their unfeigned faith (2 Tim. i. 5).

3. That his father was a Greek, a Gentile. Now because his father was a Greek he was not circumcised: his father being no Jew he was not obliged to circumcision, nor entitled to it, unless when he grew up he did himself desire it. Though his mother could not prevail to have him circumcised in his infancy, yet she educated him in the fear of God, that though he wanted the sign of the covenant he might not want the thing signified. 4. That he had gained a very good character among the Christians: he was *well reported of by the brethren* that were at Lystra and Iconium. He had a name for good things with good people. 5. That Paul would have him *to go forth with him*. Paul had a great love for him.

6. That Paul took him and circumcised him. This was strange. Had not Paul opposed those with all his might that were for imposing circumcision upon the Gentile converts? He had, and yet circumcised Timothy, not to oblige him to keep the ceremonial law, but only to render his ministry acceptable among the Jews that abounded in those quarters. Therefore, that they might not shun him as one unclean, because uncircumcised, he took him and *circumcised him*. He was against those who made circumcision necessary to salvation. Though he went not in this instance according to the letter of the decree, he went according to the spirit of it, which was a spirit of tenderness towards the Jews. Paul made no difficulty of taking Timothy to be his companion, though he was uncircumcised; but the Jews would not hear him if he were, and therefore Paul will humour them herein.

II. His confirming the churches which he had planted (*v.* 4, 5): *He went through the cities* where he had *preached the word of the Lord*. They delivered to them copies of the decrees of the Jerusalem synod. All the churches were concerned in that decree, and therefore it was requisite they should all have it well attested. This was of very good service to them. 1. The churches were hereby *established in the faith*, *v.* 5. They were confirmed particularly in their opinion against the imposing of the ceremonial law upon the Gentiles. When they saw the testimony, not only of the apostles and elders, but of the Holy Ghost, in them, against it, they were established. Testimonies to truth, though they may not prevail to convince those that oppose it, may be of very good use to establish those that are in doubt concerning it. And, besides, that spirit of tenderness which appeared in these letters plainly showed that the apostles and elders were herein under the guidance of him who is love itself. 2. They *increased in number daily*. The imposing of the yoke of the ceremonial law upon their converts was enough to frighten people from them. But, if they find there is no danger of being so enslaved, they are ready to embrace Christianity. And thus the church *increased in numbers daily*. And it is a joy to those who heartily wish well to the souls of men, to see such an increase.

JAMIESON, FAUSSET, BROWN

CHAPTER 16

VISITATION OF THE CHURCHES FORMERLY ESTABLISHED, TIMOTHEUS HERE JOINING THE MISSIONARY PARTY.

1-5. Then came he to Derbe and Lystra; and, behold, a certain disciple was there—i.e., at Lystra (not Derbe, as some conclude from ch. 20:4). **named Timotheus**—See on ch. 14:20. As Paul styles him "his own son in the faith" (I Tim. 1:2), he must have been gained to Christ at the apostle's first visit; and as Paul says he "had fully known his persecutions which came on him at Lystra" (II Tim. 3:10, 11), he may have been in that group of disciples that surrounded the apparently lifeless body of the apostle outside the walls of Lystra, and that at a time of life when the mind receives its deepest impressions from the spectacle of innocent suffering and undaunted courage [Hows]. His would be one of "the souls of the disciples confirmed" at the apostle's second visit, "exhorted to continue in the faith, and" warned "that we must through much tribulation enter into the kingdom of God" (ch. 14: 21, 22). **the son of a certain . . . Jewess**—"The unfeigned faith which dwelt first in his grandmother Lois" descended to "his mother Eunice," and thence it passed to this youth (II Tim. 1:5), who "from a child knew the Holy Scriptures" (II Tim. 3:15). His gifts and destination to the ministry of Christ had already been attested (I Tim. 1:18; 4:14); and though some ten years after this Paul speaks of him as still young (I Tim. 4:12), "he was already well reported of by the brethren that were at Lystra and Iconium" (vs. 2), and consequently must have been well known through all that quarter. **but his father was a Greek**—Such mixed marriages, though little practiced, and disliked by the stricter Jews in Palestine, must have been very frequent among the Jews of the dispersion, especially in remote districts, where but few of the scattered people were settled [Hows]. **Him would Paul have to go forth with him**—This is in harmony with all we read in the Acts and Epistles of Paul's affectionate and confiding disposition. He had no relative ties which were of service to him in his work; his companions were few and changing; and though Silas would supply the place of Barnabas, it was no weakness to yearn for the society of one who might become, what Mark once appeared to be, a *son* in the Gospel [Hows]. And such he indeed proved to be, the most attached and serviceable of his associates (Phil. 2:19-23; I Cor. 4:17; 16:10, 11; I Thess. 3:1-6). His double connection, with the Jews by the mother's side and the Gentiles by the father's, would strike the apostle as a peculiar qualification for his own sphere of labor. "So far as appears, Timothy is the first Gentile who after his conversion comes before us as a regular missionary; for what is said of Titus (Gal. 2:3) refers to a later period" [Wies]. But before his departure, Paul **took and circumcised him**—a rite which every Israelite might perform. **because of the Jews . . . for they knew all that his father was a Greek**—This seems to imply that the father was no proselyte. Against the wishes of a Gentile father no Jewish mother was, as the Jews themselves say, permitted to circumcise her son. We thus see why all the religion of Timothy is traced to the female side of the family (II Tim. 1:5). "Had Timothy not been circumcised, a storm would have gathered round the apostle in his farther progress. His fixed line of procedure was to act on the cities through the synagogues; and to preach the Gospel to the Jew first and then to the Gentile. But such a course would have been impossible had not Timothy been circumcised. He must necessarily have been repelled by that people who endeavored once to murder Paul because they imagined he had taken a Greek into the temple (ch. 21:29). The very intercourse of social life would have been almost impossible, for it was still 'an abomination' for the circumcised to eat with the uncircumcised" [Hows]. In refusing to compel Titus afterwards to be circumcised (Gal. 2:3) at the bidding of Judaizing Christians, as necessary to salvation, he only vindicated "the truth of the Gospel" (Gal. 2:5); in circumcising Timothy, "to the Jews he became as a Jew that he might gain the Jews." Probably Timothy's ordination took place now (I Tim. 4:14; II Tim. 1:6); and it was a service, apparently, of much solemnity—"before many witnesses" (I Tim. 6:12). **And as they went through the cities, they delivered . . . the decrees . . . . And so were the churches established in the faith, and increased in number daily**—not the churches, but the number of their members, by this visit and the written evi-

ADAM CLARKE

CHAPTER 16

1. *A certain disciple*. This Timothy was the same person to whom Paul wrote those two noble Epistles which are still extant.

His mother's name was Eunice, as we learn from 2 Tim. i. 5. What his father's name was we know not.

2. *Which was well reported of*. These words are spoken of Timothy, and not of his father. At this time Timothy must have been very young; for, several years after, when appointed to superintend the church at Crete, he appears to have been then so young that there was a danger of its operating to the prejudice of his ministry: 1 Tim. iv. 12, "Let no man despise thy youth." He had a very early religious eudcation from his godly mother, Eunice, and his not less pious grandmother, Lois; and from his religious instructions was well-prepared for the work to which God now called him.

3. *Took and circumcised him*. For this simple reason that the Jews would neither have heard him preach and would have any connection with him had he been otherwise. Besides, Paul himself could have had no access to the Jews in any place had they known that he associated with a person who was uncircumcised; they would have considered both to be unclean.

5. *And so were the churches established*. The disputations at Antioch, relative to circumcision, had no doubt spread far and wide among other churches and unhinged many. The decrees of the apostles came in good time and prevented further mischief. The people, saved from uncertainty, became established in the faith; and the Church had a daily accession of converted souls.

MATTHEW HENRY

Verses 6–15

I. Paul's travels up and down to do good. 1. He and Silas his colleague went throughout Phrygia and the region of Galatia. 2. They were forbidden at this time to preach the gospel in Asia (the country properly so called). At this time Christ would employ Paul in a piece of new work, which was to preach the gospel to a Roman colony at Philippi, for hitherto the Gentiles to whom he had preached were Greeks. The Romans were more particularly hated by the Jews than other Gentiles. It was the Holy Ghost that forbade them. The removals of ministers are in a particular manner under a divine guidance and direction. But these New Testament ministers are only forbidden to preach in one place, while they are directed to another where there is more need.

3. They would have gone into Bithynia, but were not permitted: *the Spirit suffered them not*, *v.* 7. They came to Mysia. Though their judgment and inclination were to go into Bithynia, yet they were overruled. We must now follow providence, and, if this *suffer us not* to do what we assay to do, we ought to acquiesce, and believe it for the best. *The Spirit of Jesus* suffered them not; so many ancient copies read it. The servants of the Lord Jesus ought to be always under the check and conduct of the *Spirit of the Lord Jesus.* 4. They *passed by Mysia*, or passed *through it* (so some), sowing good seed, we may suppose, as they went along; and they came down to Troas, the city of Troy. Here a church was planted; for here we find one in being, *ch.* xx. 6, 7. At Troas Luke fell in with Paul, and joined himself to his company; for henceforward, when he speaks of Paul's journeys, he puts himself into the number of his retinue, *we* went, *v.* 10.

II. Paul's particular call to Macedonia, that is, to Philippi, inhabited mostly by Romans, as appears, *v.* 21.

1. The vision Paul had, *v.* 9. An angel appeared to him, to intimate to him that it was the will of Christ he should go to Macedonia. Though he shall not go where he has a mind to go, he shall go where God has work for him to do. (1) The person Paul saw. There stood by him *a man of Macedonia.* Christ would have Paul directed to Macedonia, not as the apostles were at other times, by a messenger from heaven, to send him thither, but by a messenger thence to call him thither. Paul shall be called to Macedonia by a man of Macedonia, and by him speaking in the name of the rest. A man of Macedonia, not a magistrate of the country, much less a priest, but an ordinary inhabitant of that country, a plain man, that did not come to trifle with him, but in good earnest to importune his assistance. (2) The invitation given him. This honest Macedonian *prayed him, saying, Come over into Macedonia, and help us;* that is, "Come and preach the gospel to us. *Thou hast helped many.* O come and help us. It is thy business, and it is thy delight, to help poor souls; O come and help us. We have need of thy help, as much as any people, and therefore, O come, come with all speed among us. Do not only help us with thy prayers here; thou must come over and help us." People have great need of help for their

JAMIESON, FAUSSET, BROWN

dence laid before them of the triumph of Christian liberty at Jerusalem, and the wise measures there taken to preserve the unity of the Jewish and Gentile converts.

6-12. THEY BREAK NEW GROUND IN PHRYGIA AND GALATIA—THEIR COURSE IN THAT DIRECTION BEING MYSTERIOUSLY HEDGED UP, THEY TRAVEL WESTWARD TO TROAS, WHERE THEY ARE DIVINELY DIRECTED TO MACEDONIA—THE HISTORIAN HIMSELF HERE JOINING THE MISSIONARY PARTY, THEY EMBARK FOR NEAPOLIS, AND REACH PHILIPPI. **6-8. Now when they had gone throughout Phrygia and the region of Galatia**—proceeding in a northwesterly direction. At this time must have been formed "the churches of Galatia" (Gal. 1:2; I Cor. 16:1); founded, as we learn from the Epistle to the Galatians (particularly ch. 4:19), by the apostle Paul, and which were already in existence when he was on his *third* missionary journey, as we learn from ch. 18:23, where it appears that he was no less successful in Phrygia. *Why* these proceedings, so interesting as we should suppose, are not here detailed, it is not easy to say; for the various reasons suggested are not very satisfactory: e.g., that the historian had not joined the party [ALFORD]; that he was in haste to bring the apostle to Europe [OLSHAUSEN]; that the main stream of the Church's development was from Jerusalem to Rome, and the apostle's labors in Phrygia and Galatia lay quite out of the line of that direction [BAUMGARTEN]. **and were forbidden of the Holy Ghost**—speaking by some prophet, see on ch. 11:27. **to preach the word in Asia**—not the great Asiatic continent, nor even the rich peninsula now called Asia Minor, but only so much of its western coast as constituted the Roman province of Asia. **After they were come to Mysia**—where, as being part of Roman Asia, they were forbidden to labor (vs. 8)—**they assayed**—or attempted—**to go into**—or, towards—**Bithynia**—to the northeast. **but the Spirit**—speaking as before—**suffered them not**—probably because, (1) Europe was ripe for the labors of this missionary party; and (2) other instruments were to be honored to establish the Gospel in the eastern regions of Asia Minor, especially the apostle Peter (see I Pet. 1:1). By the end of the first century, as testified by Pliny the governor, Bithynia was filled with Christians. "This is the first time that the Holy Ghost is expressly spoken of as determining the course they were to follow in their efforts to evangelize the nations, and it was evidently designed to show that whereas hitherto the diffusion of the Gospel had been carried on in unbroken course, connected by natural points of junction, it was now to take a leap to which it could not be impelled but by an immediate and independent operation of the Spirit; and though primarily, this intimation of the Spirit was only negative, and referred but to the immediate neighborhood, we may certainly conclude that Paul took it for a sign that a new epoch was now to commence in his apostolic labors" [BAUMGARTEN]. **came down to Troas**—a city on the northeast coast of the Ægean Sea, the boundary of Asia Minor on the west; the region of which was the scene of the great Trojan war. **9, 10. a vision appeared to Paul in the night**—while awake, for it is not called a dream. **There stood a man of Macedonia, and prayed him, saying, Come over into Macedonia, and help us**—Stretching his eye across the Ægean Sea, from Troas on the northeast, to the Macedonian hills, visible on the northwest, the apostle could hardly fail to think this the destined scene of his future labors; and, if he retired to rest with this thought, he would be thoroughly prepared for the remarkable intimation of the divine will now to be given him. This visional Macedonian discovered himself by what he said. But it was a cry not of conscious *desire* for the Gospel, but of deep *need* of it and unconscious *preparedness* to receive it, not only in that region, but, we may well say, throughout all that western empire which Macedonia might be said to represent. It was a virtual confession "that the highest splendor of heathendom, which we must recognize in the arts of Greece and in the polity and imperial power of Rome, had arrived at the end of all its resources. God had left the Gentile peoples to walk in their own ways (ch. 14:2). They had sought to gain salvation for themselves; but those who had carried it farthest along the paths of natural development were now pervaded by the feeling that all had indeed been vanity. This feeling is the simple, pure result of all the history of heathendom. And Israel, going along the way which God had marked out for him, had likewise arrived at his end. At last he is in a condition to realize his original vocation, by becoming the guide

ADAM CLARKE

F. B. MEYER:

Guided to new fields. Paul had a wonderful influence over young men. Timothy, Titus, and Mark bore his impress. When circumcision was insisted upon, as in the previous chapter, no one opposed it more stoutly than Paul; when it conciliated Jewish prejudice, he was quite willing to concede it, since in itself it was a matter of perfect indifference. As the stoning of Stephen was the first step toward winning Paul, so his own stoning at Lystra on the former occasion probably gave him Timothy.

Our path through life will often be indicated by the fact that the doors which lead off the straight track are barren and bolted, so that we have no option save to go on. Paul was blocked first on the left, that he should not go into the province of Asia; then on the right, that he should not go into Bithynia. Finally he reached Troas, and stood face to face with the ocean that lay between him and Europe.

Here he had a vision which made a deep impression upon him. He saw a man of Macedonia standing in an attitude of entreaty and saying, "Come over into Macedonia, and help us." Note that phrase, "assuredly gathering" (v. 10). God often leaves us to infer our course. He does not ignore his own great gift of reason.—*Bible Commentary*

6. *Were forbidden of the Holy Ghost to preach the word in Asia.* The Asia mentioned here could not be Asia Minor in general, but it was what was called Proconsular Asia. The apostles were not suffered to visit these places at this time; but they afterwards went thither, and preached the gospel with success, for it was in this Proconsular Asia that the seven churches were situated.

7. *After they were come to Mysia.* They passed through Phrygia into Mysia, which lay between Bithynia on the north, Phrygia on the east, Aeolia on the south, and the Mediterranean on the west. *But the Spirit suffered them not.* God saw that that was not the most proper time to preach the Word at Bithynia, as He willed them to go immediately to Macedonia, the people there being ripe for the Word of Life. Instead of *the Spirit,* "the Spirit of Jesus," is the reading of some MSS. The reading is undoubtedly genuine, and should be immediately restored to the text.

8. *Came down to Troas.* The part of Phrygia Minor in which the celebrated city of Troy was formerly situated.

9. *A vision appeared to Paul in the night.* Whether this was in a dream or whether a representation made to the senses of the apostle, we cannot tell.

MATTHEW HENRY

souls, and it is their duty to look out for it and invite those among them that can help them.

2. The interpretation made of the vision (*v.* 10): They *gathered assuredly from this that the Lord had called them to preach the gospel* there. We may sometimes infer a call of God from a call of man. If a man of Macedonia says, *Come and help us*, Paul thence gathers assuredly that God says, Go and help them.

III. Paul's voyage to Macedonia hereupon: He *was not disobedient to the heavenly vision*, but followed this divine direction with more satisfaction than he would have followed any contrivance or inclination of his own. Thitherward he turned his thoughts. *Immediately we endeavoured to go into Macedonia.* Paul communicated it to his companions, and they all resolved for Macedonia. As Paul will follow Christ, so all his will follow him, or rather follow Christ with him. God's calls must be complied with immediately. Do it today, lest thy heart be hardened. They could not immediately go into Macedonia; but they immediately endeavoured to go. If we cannot be so quick as we would be in our performances, yet we may be in our endeavours. Thitherward he steered his course. They *set sail from Troas.* They *came with a straight course*, a prosperous voyage, *to Samothracia*; the *next day they came to Neapolis*; and at last they landed at *Philippi*. It is said (*v.* 12) to be *The chief city of that part of Macedonia;* or, as some read it, *the first city*. They began with the first city, because, if the gospel were received there, it would the more easily spread thence all the country over. It was a colony. The Romans not only had a garrison, but the inhabitants of the city were Romans.

IV. The cold entertainment which Paul and his companions met with at Philippi. One would have expected that having such a particular call from God thither they would have had a joyful welcome there. Where was the man of Macedonia that begged Paul to come thither with all speed? Why did not he stir up his countrymen, to go and meet him? It is a good while before any notice at all is taken of him: *We were in that city abiding certain days*. They had made all the haste they could thither, but, now that they are there, they are almost tempted to think they might as well have stayed where they were. Those eminent and useful men are not fit to live in this world that know not how to be slighted and overlooked. Let not ministers think it strange if they be first strongly invited to a place, and then looked shyly upon when they come. When they have an opportunity of preaching it is in an obscure place, *v.* 13. There was no synagogue of the Jews there. They found out a little meeting of good women. The place of this meeting is out of the city. It was a place *where prayer was wont to be made*. Those that worshipped the true God, and would not worship idols, met there to pray together. Each of them prayed apart every day, but, besides this, *they came together on the sabbath day*. Though they were but a few and discountenanced by the town, yet a solemn assembly the worshippers of God must have on the sabbath day. When we cannot do as we would we must do as we can; if we have not synagogues, we must be thankful for more private places, and resort to them. This place is said to be *by a river side*, which perhaps was chosen, as befriending contemplation. Thither Paul and Silas and Luke went, and *sat down*. They *spoke unto the women who resorted thither*, and led them on further to the knowledge of Christ.

V. The conversion of *Lydia*. In this story of *the Acts*, we have not only the conversion of places recorded, but of many particular persons; for such is the worth of souls that the reducing of one to God is a great matter. Nor have we only the conversions that were effected by miracle, as Paul's, but some that were brought about by the ordinary methods of grace, as Lydia's here.

1. Who this convert was. Four things are recorded of her:

(1) Her name, *Lydia*. It is an honour to her to have her name recorded here in the book of God. We cannot have our names recorded in the Bible, but, if God open our hearts, we shall find them *written in the book of life*.

(2) Her calling. She was *a seller of purple*. She had a calling, an honest calling, which the historian takes notice of to her praise. It was a mean calling. She was *a seller of purple*, not a wearer of purple, few such are called. Though she had a calling to mind, yet she was a worshipper of God. The business of our particular callings may be made to consist very well with the business of religion, and therefore it will not excuse us to say, We have shops to look after, and a trade to mind; for have we not also a

JAMIESON, FAUSSET, BROWN

who is to lead the Gentiles unto God, the only Author and Creator of man's redemption; and Paul is in truth the very person in whom this vocation of Israel is now a present divine reality, and to whom, by this nocturnal apparition of the Macedonian, the preparedness of the heathen world to receive the ministry of Israel towards the Gentiles is confirmed" [BAUMGARTEN]. *This voice cries from heathendom still to the Christian Church, and never does the Church undertake the work of missions, nor any missionary go forth from it, in the right spirit, save in obedience to this cry.* **and after he had seen the vision, immediately we endeavoured to go into Macedonia**—The "we," here first introduced, is a modest intimation that the historian himself had now joined the missionary party. (The modern objections to this are quite frivolous.) Whether Paul's broken health had anything to do with this arrangement for having "the beloved physician" with him [WIES], can never be known with certainty; but that he would deem himself honored in taking care of so precious a life, there can be no doubt. **11, 12. Therefore loosing from Troas, we came**—lit., 'ran'—**with a straight course**—i.e., 'ran before the wind.' **to Samothracia**—a lofty island on the Thracian coast, north from Troas, with an inclination westward. The wind must have set in strong from the south or south-southeast to bring them there so soon, as the current is strong in the opposite direction, and they afterwards took five days to what they now did in two (ch. 20:6) [HOWS]. **next day to Neapolis**—on the Macedonian, or rather Thracian, coast, about sixty-five miles from Samothracia, and ten from Philippi, of which it is the harbor. **Philippi . . . the chief**—rather, perhaps, 'the first'—**city of that part of Macedonia**—The meaning appears to be—the first city one comes to, proceeding from Neapolis. The sense given in our version hardly consists with fact. **a colony**—i.e., possessing all the privileges of Roman citizenship, and, as such, both exempted from scourging and (in ordinary cases) from arrest, and entitled to appeal from the local magistrate to the emperor. Though the Pisidian *Antioch* and *Troas* were also "colonies," the fact is mentioned in this history of Philippi only on account of the frequent references to Roman privileges and duties in the sequel of the chapter.

12-34. AT PHILIPPI, LYDIA IS GAINED AND WITH HER HOUSEHOLD BAPTIZED—AN EVIL SPIRIT IS EXPELLED, PAUL AND SILAS ARE SCOURGED, IMPRISONED, AND MANACLED, BUT MIRACULOUSLY SET FREE, AND THE JAILER WITH ALL HIS HOUSEHOLD CONVERTED AND BAPTIZED. **12, 13. we were in that city abiding certain days**—waiting till the sabbath came round: their whole stay must have extended to some weeks. As their rule was to begin with the Jews and proselytes, they did nothing till the time when they knew that they would convene for worship. **on the sabbath day**—the first after their arrival, as the words imply. **we went out of the city**—rather, as the true reading is, 'outside of the (city) gate.' **by a river-side**—one of the small streams which gave name to the place ere the city was founded by Philip of Macedon. **where prayer was wont to be made**—or a prayer meeting held. It is plain there was no synagogue at Philippi (contrast ch. 17:1), the number of the Jews being small. The meeting appears to have consisted wholly of women, and these not all Jewish. The neighbor hood of streams was preferred, on account of the ceremonial washings used on such occasions. **we sat down and spake unto the women . . .**—a humble congregation, and simple manner of preaching. *But here and thus were gathered the first fruits of Europe unto Christ, and they were of the female sex*, of whose accession and services honorable mention will again and again be made.

14, 15. Lydia—a common name among the Greeks and Romans. **a seller of purple, of the city of Thyatira**—on the confines of Lydia and Phrygia. The Lydians, particularly the inhabitants of Thyatira, were celebrated for their dyeing, in which they inherited the reputation of the Tyrians. Inscriptions to this effect, yet remaining, confirm the accuracy of our historian. This woman appears to have been in good circumstances, having an establishment at Philippi large enough to accommodate the missionary party (vs. 15), and receiving her goods from her native town.

ADAM CLARKE

10. *We endeavoured to go into Macedonia.* This is the first place that the historian Luke refers to himself: *we endeavoured.* And from this it has been supposed that he joined the company of Paul, for the first time, at Troas. *Assuredly gathering.* Drawing an inference from the vision that had appeared. *That the Lord had called us for to preach.* That is, they inferred that they were called to *preach the gospel* in Macedonia, from what the vision had said, "Come over . . . and help us"; the *help* meaning, "Preach to us the gospel." Instead of *the Lord,* meaning Jesus, several MSS. have "God."

11. *Loosing from Troas.* Setting sail from this place. *With a straight course to Samothracia.* This was an island of the Aegean Sea, contiguous to Thrace, and hence called Samothracia, or the Thracian Samos. It is about twenty miles in circumference. *And the next day to Neapolis.* There were many cities of this name, but this was a seaport town of Macedonia, a few miles eastward of Philippi. *Neapolis* signifies the "new city."

12. *And from thence to Philippi.* This was a town of Macedonia, on the confines of Thrace, situated on the side of a steep eminence. It took its name from Philip II, king of Macedon. *The chief city of that part of Macedonia.* This passage has greatly puzzled both critics and commentators. It is well-known that when Paulus Aemilius had conquered Macedonia he divided it into four parts and that he called the country that lay between the rivers Strymon and Nessus the first part and made Amphipolis its chief city or metropolis; Philippi, therefore, was not its chief city. But Bishop Pearce has, with great show of reason, argued that though Amphipolis was made the chief city of it by Paulus Aemilius, yet Philippi might have been the chief city in the days of Paul, which was 220 years after the division by P. Aemilius. Besides, as it was at this place that Augustus gained that victory which put him in possession of the whole Roman Empire, might not he have given to it that dignity which was before enjoyed by Amphipolis? *And a colony.* That is, a colony of Rome; for it appears that a colony was planted here by Julius Caesar, and afterwards enlarged by Augustus. The people, therefore, were considered as freemen of Rome and from this called themselves Romans, v. 21. The Jewish definition of *kolonia* is "a free city, which does not pay tribute."

13. *By a river side, where prayer was wont to be made.* "Where it was said there was a *proseucha.*" The *proseucha* was a "place of prayer," or a place used for worship, where there was no synagogue. It was a large building uncovered, with seats, as in an amphitheatre. Buildings of this sort the Jews had by the seaside and by the sides of rivers. *Spake unto the women.* Probably this was before the time of their public worship, and while they were waiting for the assembling of the people in general; and Paul improved the opportunity to speak concerning Christ and salvation to the women that resorted thither.

14. *Lydia, a seller of purple.* She probably had her name from the province of Lydia, in which the city of Thyatira was situated. The Lydian women have been celebrated for their beautiful purple manufactures.

MATTHEW HENRY

God to serve and a soul to look after?

(3) The place she was of—*of the city of Thyatira*, which was a great way from Philippi. Providence brings Lydia to Philippi, to be under Paul's ministry, and there, where she met with it, she made a good use of it.

(4) Her religion before the Lord opened her heart. She worshipped God according to the knowledge she had; she was one of the devout women. Sometimes the grace of God wrought upon those who, before their conversion, were very wicked and vile, sometimes it fastened upon those who were of a good character. It is not enough to be worshippers of God, but we must be believers in Jesus Christ. To them Christ would be welcome; for those that know what it is to worship God see their need of Christ. She heard the apostles. Here, where prayer was made *the word was preached.* Can we expect God should hear our prayers if we will not hearken to his word? Those that worshipped God according to the light they had looked out for further light.

2. What the work was that was wrought upon her: *Whose heart the Lord opened.* The author of this work: it was *the Lord.* Conversion-work is God's work; it is he *that works in us both to will and to do*; not as if we had nothing to do, but of ourselves, without God's grace, we can do nothing. The salvation of those that are saved must be wholly ascribed to him. The seat of this work; it is in the heart that the change is made. Conversion-work is heart-work; it is a *renewing of the heart.* The nature of the work; she had not only her heart touched, but her heart opened. An unconverted soul is shut up, and fortified against Christ. Christ, in dealing with the soul, knocked at the door that is shut against him (Rev. iii. 20); and, when a sinner is effectually persuaded to embrace Christ, *then the heart is opened for the King of glory to come in.*

3. What were the effects of this work on the heart. She took great notice of the word of God. Her heart was so *opened that she attended to the things that were spoken by Paul. She applied to herself* (so some read it) *the things that were spoken by Paul*; and then only the word does us good, when we apply it to ourselves. She gave up her name to Jesus Christ. *She was baptized*, and with her *her household* also was baptized. She was very kind to the ministers, and very desirous to be further instructed by them: *She besought us saying, "If you have judged me to be faithful to the Lord, come into my house, and abide there."* Thus she desired an opportunity to testify her gratitude to those who had been the instruments of divine grace in this blessed change that was wrought upon her. When her heart was open to Christ, her house was open to his ministers for his sake. Nay, they are not only welcome to her house, but she is extremely pressing and importunate with them: *She constrained us*; which intimates that Paul was unwilling to go. But Lydia will have no nay. She desired an opportunity of receiving further instruction. In her own house she might not only hear them, but ask them questions; and she might have them to pray with her daily, and to bless her household.

Verses 16-24

Paul and his companions now begin to be taken notice of.

I. *A damsel that had a spirit of divination* caused them to be taken notice of.

1. The account that is given of this damsel: She was *possessed with a spirit of divination* as that damsel was by whom the oracles of Apollo at Delphos were delivered. In those times of ignorance and idolatry, the devil, thus led men captive at his will; and he could not have gained such adoration from them as he had, if he had not pretended to give oracles to them. This damsel *brought her masters much gain by soothsaying*; many came to consult this witch and none came but with the rewards of divination in their hands.

2. The testimony which this damsel gave to Paul and his companions: She *met them* in the street, as they were going to prayer, *v.* 16. They went thither publicly, everybody knew whither they were going. How subtle Satan is in taking the opportunity to give us diversion when we are going about any religious exercises, and to put us out of temper when we need to be most composed. When she met with them she followed them, crying, *"These men are the servants of the most high God; they show unto us the way of salvation."*

(1) This witness is true. [1] "They are *the servants of the most high God*; they attend on him, are employed by him as servants; they come to us on his errands, the message they bring is from him. The gods we Gentiles worship are inferior beings, therefore not gods, but these men belong *to the most high*

JAMIESON, FAUSSET, BROWN

which worshipped God—i.e., was a proselyte to the Jewish faith, and as such present at this meeting.

whose heart the Lord opened—i.e., the Lord Jesus (see vs. 15; and cf. Luke 24:45; Matt. 11:27).

that she attended to the things . . . spoken by Paul—"showing that the inclination of the heart towards the truth originates not in the will of man. The first disposition to turn to the Gospel is a work of grace" [OLSHAUSEN]. Observe here the place assigned to 'giving attention' or 'heed' to the truth—that species of attention which consists in having the whole mind engrossed with it, and in apprehending and drinking it in, in its vital and saving character. **And when . . . baptized . . . and her household**—probably without much delay. The mention of baptism here for the first time in connection with the labors of Paul, while it was doubtless performed on all his former converts, indicates a special importance in this first European baptism. Here also is the first mention of a Christian *household.* Whether it included children, also in that case baptized, is not explicitly stated; but the presumption, as in other cases of household baptism, is that it did. Yet the question of infant baptism must be determined on other grounds; and such incidental allusions form only part of the historical materials for ascertaining the practice of the Church. **she besought us, saying, If ye have judged me to be faithful to the Lord**—the Lord Jesus; i.e., 'By the faith on Him which ye have recognized in me by baptism.' There is a beautiful modesty in the expression. **And she constrained us**—The word seems to imply that they were reluctant, but were overborne.

16-18. as we went to prayer—The words imply that it was *on their way to the usual place of public prayer*, by the river side, that this took place; therefore not on the same day with what had just occurred. **a . . . damsel**—a female servant, and in this case a slave (vs. 19). **possessed of a spirit of divination**—or, of Python, i.e., a spirit supposed to be inspired by the Pythian Apollo, or of the same nature. The reality of this demoniacal possession is as undeniable as that of any in the Gospel history. **These men are servants of the most high God . . .**—Glorious testimony! But see on Luke 4:41.

ADAM CLARKE

Which worshipped God. That is, she was a proselyte to the Jewish religion, as were probably all the women that resorted hither.

Whose heart the Lord opened. As she was a sincere worshipper of God, she was prepared to receive the heavenly truths spoken by Paul and his companions; and as she was faithful to the grace she had received, so God gave her more grace, and gave her now a divine conviction that what was spoken by Paul was true.

Therefore *she attended unto the things*—she believed them and received them as the doctrines of God; and in this faith she was joined by her whole family, and in it they were all baptized.

16. *As we went to prayer.* "Into the *proseucha*"; see on v. 13. The article is added here by some MSS. This makes the place more emphatic, and seems to determine the above meaning to be right—not the act of prayer or praying to God, but the place in which these proselytes assembled for the purpose of praying, reading the law and the prophets, and suchlike exercises of devotion. *Possessed with a spirit of divination.* "Having a spirit of Python." Pytho was, according to fable, a huge serpent that had an oracle at Mount Parnassus, famous for predicting future events. Apollo slew this serpent, and hence he was called *Pythius*, and became celebrated as the foreteller of future events; and all those who either could or pretended to predict future events were influenced by the spirit of Apollo Pythius. *Brought her masters much gain by soothsaying.* "By divination," or what we call telling fortunes. Our term *soothsaying* coming from the Anglo-Saxon "truth"; and "to say," i.e., "truth saying." For as it was supposed among the heathen that such persons spoke by the inspiration of their god, consequently what they said must be true.

17. *These men are the servants.* It is astonishing how such a testimony could be given in such a case; every syllable of it true, and at the same time full, clear, and distinct. But mark the deep design and artifice of this evil spirit. He well knew that the Jewish law abhorred all magic, incantations, magical rites, and dealings

MATTHEW HENRY

God, who is over all men, over all gods. They are his servants, and therefore it is our duty to hearken to them and it is at our peril if we affront them." [2] "They *show unto us the way of salvation*." Even the heathen had some notion of the miserable deplorable state of mankind, and their need of salvation. "Now," saith she, "these are the men that show us what we have in vain sought for."

(2) How came this testimony from the mouth of one that had a spirit of divination? Is Satan divided against himself? We may take it either, [1] As extorted from this spirit of divination for the honour of the gospel by the power of God; as the devil was forced to say of Christ (Mark i. 24): *I know thee who thou art, the Holy One of God*. The truth is sometimes magnified by the confession of its adversaries, in which they are witnesses against themselves. Or, [2] As designed by the evil spirit to the dishonour of the gospel. Those that were most likely to receive the apostles' doctrine were such as were prejudiced against these spirits of divination, and therefore would, by this testimony, be prejudiced against the gospel; and, as for those who regarded these diviners, the devil thought himself sure of them.

II. She continued *many days* clamouring thus (*v.* 18); and, it should seem, Paul took no notice of her; but finding perhaps that it did them a prejudice, rather than any service, he soon silenced her, by casting the devil out of her. 1. He was *grieved*. It was a disturbance to him to hear a sacred truth so profaned. Perhaps they were spoken in an ironical bantering way, and then justly might Paul be grieved, as any good man's heart would be, to hear any good truth of God bawled out in the streets in a canting, jeering way. 2. He *commanded the evil spirit to come out of her. He turned and said, I command thee in the name of Jesus Christ to come out of her;* and by this he will show *that these men are the servants of the living God*. Her silence shall demonstrate it more than her speaking could do. Power went along with the word of Christ, before which Satan could not stand, but was forced to quit his hold. *He came out the same hour*.

III. The masters of the damsel that was dispossessed caused them to be taken notice of, by bringing them before the magistrates for doing it.

1. That which provoked them was, that *her masters saw that the hope of their gain was gone*, *v.* 19. See here what evil *the love of money is the root of!* The power of Christ and the great kindness done to her in delivering her out of Satan's hand, made no impression upon them when they apprehended that they should hereby lose money.

2. The course they took with him was to incense the higher powers against them: *They caught them and dragged them into the market-place*, where public justice was administered. They brought them *to the rulers*, their justices of peace. From them they hurried them *to the magistrates*, the governors of the city.

3. The charge they exhibited against them was that they were the troublers of the land, *v.* 20. They take it for granted that these men are Jews. The general charge against them is *that they troubled the city*, sowed discord, and disturbed the public peace. If they troubled the city, it was but like the angel's troubling the water of Bethesda's pool, in order to healing. The proof of this charge is their teaching customs not proper to be admitted by a Roman colony, *v.* 21. The Romans were always very jealous of innovations in religion. Right or wrong, they would adhere to that which they had received by tradition from their fathers. No foreign nor upstart deity must be allowed.

IV. The magistrates caused them to be taken notice of.

1. By countenancing the persecution they raised the mob upon them (*v.* 22): *The multitude rose up together against them*. It has been the artifice of Satan to make God's ministers and people odious, by representing them as dangerous men, who aimed at the destruction of the constitution and the changing of the customs.

2. They further represented them as the vilest malefactors: *They rent off their clothes* in order to their being scourged. This was one of those three times that Paul was beaten with rods, according to the Roman usage, which was not under the compassionate limitation of the number of stripes not to exceed forty, which was provided by the Jewish law. It is here said that *they laid many stripes upon them* (*v.* 23), without counting how many. One would think, this might have satiated their cruelty; if they must be whipped, surely they must be discharged. No, they are imprisoned. The judges made their commitment very strict: They *charged the jailer to keep them safely*, as if they were dangerous men, that either would venture to break prison

JAMIESON, FAUSSET, BROWN

this did she many days—i.e., on many successive occasions when on their way to their usual place of meeting, or when engaged in religious services. **Paul being grieved**—for the poor victim; grieved to see such power possessed by the enemy of man's salvation, and grieved to observe the malignant design with which this high testimony was borne to Christ.

19. when her masters saw that the hope of their gains was gone, they caught Paul and Silas—as the leading persons—**and drew them into the market-place**—or Forum, where the courts were—**to the magistrates, saying . . .**—We have here a full and independent confirmation of the reality of this supernatural cure, since on any other supposition such conduct would be senseless. **20. These men, being Jews**—objects of dislike, contempt, and suspicion by the Romans, and at this time of more than usual prejudice. **do exceedingly trouble our city**—See similar charges, ch. 17:6; 24:5; 1 Kings 18:17. There is some color of truth in all such accusations, in so far as the Gospel, and generally the fear of God, as a reigning principle of human action, is in a godless world a thoroughly *revolutionary* principle. How far external commotion and change will in any case attend the triumph of this principle depends on the breadth and obstinacy of the resistance it meets with. **21. And teach customs, which are not lawful for us to receive, neither to observe, being Romans**—Here also there was a measure of truth; as the introduction of new gods was forbidden by the laws, and this might be thought to apply to any change of religion. But the whole charge was pure hypocrisy; for as these men would have let the missionaries preach what religion they pleased if they had not dried up the source of their gains, so they conceal the real cause of their rage under color of a zeal for religion, and law, and good order: so ch. 17:6,7; and 19:25, 27. **22. the multitude rose up together against them**—so ch. 19:28, 34; 21:30; Luke 23:18. **the magistrates rent off their**—Paul's and Silas'—**clothes**—i.e., ordered the lictors, or rod-bearers, to tear them off, so as to expose their naked bodies (see on vs. 37). The word expresses the roughness with which this was done to prisoners preparatory to whipping. **and commanded to beat them**—without any trial (vs. 37), to appease the popular rage. Thrice, it seems, Paul endured this indignity (II Cor. 11:25). **23, 24. when they had laid many stripes upon them**—the bleeding wounds from which they were not washed till it was done by the converted jailer (vs. 33).

ADAM CLARKE

with familiar spirits. He therefore bore what was in itself a true testimony to the apostles, that by it he might destroy their credit and ruin their usefulness.

18. *I command thee in the name of Jesus.* Jesus is the "Saviour"; Satan is Apollyon, the "destroyer." The sovereign Saviour says to the destroyer, Come out of her. *And he came out in the same hour.*

19. *When her masters saw.* It appears she was maintained by some men who received a certain pay from every person whose fortune she told. *The hope of their gains was gone.* "This hope"; viz., the spirit. So completely was this spirit cast out that the girl could divine no more, and yet she continued a heathen still, for we do not hear a word of her conversion. *Drew them into the marketplace.* This was the place of public resort, and by bringing them here they might hope to excite a general clamor against them; and probably those who are here called *the rulers* were civil magistrates, who kept offices in such public places for the preservation of the peace of the city.

20. *Brought them to the magistrates.* The "commanders of the army," who, very likely, as this city was a Roman colony, possessed the sovereign authority. The civil magistrates, therefore, having heard the case, as we shall soon find, in which it was pretended that the safety of the state was involved, would naturally refer the business to the decision of those who had the supreme command. *Exceedingly trouble our city.* They are destroying the public peace, and endangering the public safety.

21. *And teach customs.* Religious opinions and religious rites. *Which are not lawful for us to receive.* The Romans were very jealous of their national worship. Cicero, *De Legibus*, lib. ii, c. 8, says: "No person shall have any separate *gods*, nor new *ones;* nor shall he privately worship any strange *gods*, unless they be publicly allowed." It was on such laws as these that the people of Philippi pleaded against the apostles. These men bring new gods, new worship, new rites; we are Romans, and the laws forbid us to worship any new or strange god, unless publicly allowed.

22. *The multitude rose up together.* There was a general outcry against them; and the magistrates tore off their clothes, and delivered them to the mob, commanding the lictors to beat them with rods. This was the Roman custom of treating criminals.

23. *Laid many stripes upon them.* The Jews never gave more than thirty-nine stripes to any criminal, but the Romans had no law relative to this. They gave as many as they chose; and the apostles had, undoubtedly, the fullest measure. And perhaps Paul refers to this where he says, 2 Cor. xi. 23, "In stripes beyond measure."

ALBERT BARNES:

18. "But Paul, being grieved." Being molested, troubled, offended. Paul was grieved, probably, (1) because her presence was troublesome to him; (2) because it might be said that he was in alliance with her, and that his pretensions were just like hers; (3) because what she did was for the sake of gain, and was a base imposition; (4) because her state was one of bondage and delusion, and it was proper to free her from this demonaical possession; and (5) because the system under which she was acting was a part of a scheme of delusion and imposture, which had spread over a large portion of the pagan world, and which was then holding it in bondage. Throughout the Roman empire the inspiration of the priestesses of Apollo was believed in, and temples were everywhere reared to perpetuate and celebrate the delusion. Against this extensive system of imposture and fraud, Christianity must oppose itself; and this was a favorable instance to expose the delusion, and to show the power of the Christian religion over all the arts and powers of imposture. The mere fact that in a very few instances—of which this was one—they spoke the truth did not make it improper for Paul to interpose. That fact would only tend to perpetuate the delusion, and to make his interposition more proper and necessary. The expulsion of the evil spirit would also afford a signal proof of the fact that the apostles were really from God—a far better proof than her noisy and troublesome proclamation of it would furnish.—*Popular Commentary*

MATTHEW HENRY

themselves or were in confederacy with those that would attempt to rescue them. The jailer made their confinement very severe (*v.* 24): *Having received such a charge he thrust them into the inner prison.* When magistrates are cruel, it is no wonder that the officers under them are so too. *He put them into the inner prison*, the dungeon, into which none were usually put but condemned malefactors. As if this were not enough, *he made their feet fast in the stocks.* And they were not the first of God's messengers that had their feet in the stocks. Oh what hard usage have God's servants met with, as in the former days, so in the latter times!

Verses 25–34

We have here the designs of the persecutors of Paul and Silas baffled and broken.

I. The persecutors designed to dishearten and discourage the preachers of the gospel; but here we find them both hearty and heartened.

1. They were themselves hearty, wonderfully hearty. Let us consider what their case was. The many stripes they had laid upon them were very sore, and one might have expected to hear them complaining of them. Yet this was not all; they had reason to fear the axes next. In the meantime they were in the inner prison, their feet in the stocks, which hurt them; and yet, *at midnight* they *prayed and sang praises to God.* They prayed together, prayed to God to support them and comfort them in their afflictions—prayed that even their bonds and stripes might turn to the furtherance of the gospel,—prayed for their persecutors, that God would forgive them and turn their hearts. This was not at an hour of prayer, but at midnight; it was not in a house of prayer, but in a dungeon; yet it was seasonable to pray, and the prayer was acceptable. As in the dark, so out of the depths, we may cry unto God. No trouble, how grievous soever, should indispose us for prayer. *They sang praises to God.* We never want matter for praise, if we do not want a heart. And what should put the heart of a child of God out of tune for this duty if a dungeon and a pair of stocks will not do it? Nay, *they not only praised God, but they sang praises to him.* As our rule is that the afflicted should pray, and therefore, being in affliction, they prayed; so our rule is that the merry should sing psalms, and therefore, being merry in their affliction, *they sang psalms.* Notice is here taken of the circumstance that *the prisoners heard them.* If the prisoners did not hear them pray, yet *they heard them sing praises.* They sang so loud, that though they were in the dungeon, they were heard all the prison over. We should sing psalms with all our heart. Though they knew the prisoners would hear them, yet they sang aloud, as those that were not ashamed of their Master. Shall those that would sing psalms in their families plead, in excuse for their omission of the duty, that they are afraid their neighbours should hear them, when those that sing profane songs roar them out, and care not who hears them? The prisoners were made to hear the prison-songs of Paul and Silas, that they might be prepared for the miraculous favour shown to them all for the sake of Paul and Silas, when *the prison-doors were thrown open.*

2. God heartened them wonderfully by his signal appearances for them, *v.* 26. There was immediately a great earthquake; *the very foundations of the prison were shaken.* The Lord was in these earthquakes, to show his resentment of the indignities done to his servants. The prison doors were thrown open, and the prisoners' fetters were knocked off: *Every man's bands were loosed.* As afterwards God gave to Paul all *those that were in the ship with him* (*ch.* xxvii. 24), so now he gave him all those that were in the prison with him.

II. The persecutors designed to stop the progress of the gospel, but here we find converts made in the prison, the trophies of the gospel's victories erected there, and the jailer, their own servant, become a servant of Christ.

1. He is afraid he shall lose his life, and Paul makes him easy as to this care, *v.* 27, 28. (1) He *awoke out of his sleep.* It is probable that the shock of the earthquake woke him, and the prisoners' expressions of joy and amazement, when in the dark they found their bands loosed. This was enough to awaken the jailer, whose place required that he should not be hard to wake. (2) He saw the prison doors open, and supposed that the prisoners had fled; and then what would become of him? He knew the Roman law in that case. (3) In his fright *he drew his sword*, and was going *to kill himself*, to prevent a more terrible death, which he knew he was liable to for letting his prisoners escape. The philosophers generally allowed self-murder. This jailer thought there was no harm in anticipating his own death; but Christianity proves

JAMIESON, FAUSSET, BROWN

charged the jailer . . . who . . . thrust them into the inner prison—"pestilential cells, damp and cold, from which the light was excluded, and where the chains rusted on the prisoners. One such place may be seen to this day on the slope of the Capitol at Rome" [Hows]. **made their feet fast in the stocks**—an instrument of torture as well as confinement, made of wood bound with iron, with holes for the feet, which were stretched more or less apart according to the severity intended. (ORIGEN at a later period, besides having his neck thrust into an iron collar, lay extended for many days with his feet apart in the rack.) Though jailers were proverbially unfeeling, the manner in which the order was given in this case would seem to warrant all that was done.

25. And at midnight Paul and Silas prayed and sang praises—lit., 'praying, were singing praises'; i.e., while engaged in pouring out their hearts in prayer, had broken forth into singing, and were hymning loud their joy. As the word here employed is that used to denote the Paschal hymn sung by our Lord and His disciples after their last Passover (Matt. 26:30), and which we know to have consisted of Psalms 113-118, which was chanted at that festival, it is probable that it was portions of the Psalms, so rich in such matter, which our joyous sufferers chanted forth; nor could any be more seasonable and inspiring to them than those very six Psalms, which every devout Jew would no doubt know by heart. *"He giveth songs in the night"* (Job 35:10). Though their bodies were still bleeding and tortured in the stocks, their spirits, under 'the expulsive power of a new affection,' rose above suffering, and made the prison walls resound with their song. "In these midnight hymns, by the imprisoned witnesses for Jesus Christ, the whole might of Roman injustice and violence against the Church is not only set at naught, but converted into a foil to set forth more completely the majesty and spiritual power of the Church, which as yet the world knew nothing of. And if the sufferings of these two witnesses of Christ are the beginning and the type of numberless martyrdoms which were to flow upon the Church from the same source, in like manner the unparalleled triumph of the Spirit over suffering was the beginning and the pledge of a spiritual power which we afterwards see shining forth so triumphantly and irresistibly in the many martyrs of Christ who were given up as a prey to the same imperial might of Rome" [NEANDER in BAUMGARTEN]. **and the prisoners heard them**—lit 'were listening to them,' i.e., when the astounding events immediately to be related took place; not asleep, but wide awake and rapt (no doubt) in wonder at what they heard. **26-28. And suddenly there was a great earthquake**—in answer, doubtless, to the prayers and expectations of the sufferers that, for the truth's sake and the honor of their Lord, some interposition would take place. **every one's bands**—i.e., the bands of all the prisoners—**were loosed**—not by the earthquake, of course, but by a miraculous energy accompanying it. By this and the joyous strains which they had heard from the sufferers, not to speak of the change wrought on the jailer, these prisoners could hardly fail to have their hearts in some measure opened to the truth; and this part of the narrative seems the result of information afterwards communicated by one or more of these men.

the keeper . . . awaking . . . drew . . . his sword, and would have killed himself . . .—knowing that his life was forfeited in that case (ch. 12:19; and cf. 27:42).

ADAM CLARKE

24. *The inner prison.* Probably what we would call the dungeon; the darkest and most secure cell. *Made their feet fast in the stocks.* The *stocks* is supposed to mean two large pieces of wood, pierced with holes like our stocks, and fitted to each other, that when the legs were in they could not be drawn out. The holes being pierced at different distances, the legs might be separated to a great extent, which must produce extreme pain.

25. *At midnight Paul and Silas . . . sang praises.* Though these holy men felt much and had reason to fear more, yet they were undismayed and even happy in their sufferings; they were so fully satisfied that they were right and had done their duty that there was no room for regret or self-reproach. At the same time, they had such consolations from God as could render any circumstances not only tolerable but delightful. They *prayed*, first, for grace to support them, and for pardon and salvation for their persecutors; and then, secondly, *sang praises unto God*, who had called them to such a state of salvation, and had accounted them worthy to suffer shame for the testimony of Jesus. And although they were in the inner prison, they sang so loudly and so heartily that the prisoners heard them.

26. *There was a great earthquake.* Thus God bore a miraculous testimony of approbation to His servants, and by the earthquake and loosing the bonds of the prisoners showed, in a symbolical way, the nature of that religion which they preached. While it shakes and terrifies the guilty, it proclaims deliverance to the captives and the opening of the prison doors to them that are bound, and sets at liberty them that are bruised. *Every one's bands were loosed.* And yet so eminently did God's providence conduct everything that not one of the prisoners made his escape, though the doors were open and his bolts off!

27. *The keeper of the prison . . . would have killed himself.* Every jailer was made responsible for his prisoner, under the same penalty to which the prisoner himself was exposed. The jailer, awaking and finding the prison doors open, taking it for granted that all the prisoners had made their escape and that he must lose his life on the account, chose rather to die by his own hand than by that of others. For it was customary among the heathens when they found death inevitable to take away their own lives.

MATTHEW HENRY

itself to be of God by this, that it keeps us to the law of our creation, obliges us to be just to our own lives, and teaches us cheerfully to resign them to our graces, but courageously to hold them out against our corruptions. (4) Paul stopped him (*v.* 28): He *cried with a loud voice, saying, Do thyself no harm.* All the cautions of the word of God against sin have this tendency, "*Do thyself no harm.* Hurt not thyself, and then none else can hurt thee; do not sin, for nothing else can hurt thee." The jailer needs not fear being called to an account for the escape of his prisoners, for *they are all here.* It was strange that some of them did not slip away, when the prison doors were opened, and they were loosed from their bands. God showed his power in binding their spirits, as much as in loosing their feet.

2. He is afraid he shall lose his soul, and Paul makes him easy as to this care too. One concern leads him to another, and a much greater. He begins to think whither death would have brought him, and what would have become of him on the other side death.

(1) Whatever was the cause, he was put into a great consternation. The Spirit of God, that was sent to convince, in order to his being a Comforter, struck a terror upon him. *He called for a light,* and *sprang in and came trembling to Paul and Silas.* This jailer, when he was thus made to tremble, could not apply to a more proper person than to Paul, for it had once been his own case; he had been once a persecutor of good men, had cast them into prison; and therefore he was able to speak the more feelingly to the jailer.

(2) In this consternation, he applied to Paul and Silas for relief. How reverent and respectful his address to them is: *He called for a light; he fell down before them.* It is probable that he had heard what the damsel said of them, that they were *the servants of the living God, who showed to them the way of salvation.* He fell down before them, to beg their pardon, for the indignities he had done them, and to beg their advice, what he should do. He gave them a title of respect, *Sirs, lords, masters;* just now it was, *Rogues* and *villains,* and he was their master; but now, *Sirs, lords,* and they are his masters. Converting grace changes people's language. How serious his enquiry is: *What must I do to be saved? First,* His salvation is now his great concern, and lies nearest his heart, which before was the furthest thing from his thoughts. *Secondly,* He does not enquire concerning others, what they must do; but concerning himself, "What must I do?" It is his own precious soul that he is in care about. *Thirdly,* He is convinced that something must be done, and done by him too, in order to his salvation; that it is not a thing that will do itself. He asks not, "What may be done for me?" but, "What shall I do?" *Fourthly,* He is willing to do anything: "Tell me what I must do, and I am here ready to do it. Sirs, put me into the right way, though narrow, and thorny, and uphill, yet I will walk in it." Those who are thoroughly convinced of sin, and truly concerned about their salvation will be glad to have Christ upon his own terms, Christ upon any terms. *Fifthly,* He is desirous to know what he should do, and asks those that were likely to tell him. Those that set their faces Zionward must ask the way thither. We cannot know it of ourselves, but God has made it known to us by his word, has appointed his ministers to assist us, and has promised *to give his Holy Spirit to those that ask him,* to be their guide in the way of salvation. *Sixthly,* He *brought them out.* He brings them out of the dungeon, in hopes they will bring him out of a much worse.

(3) They directed him what he must do, *v.* 31. Though they are cold, and sore, and sleepy, they do not adjourn this cause to a more convenient time and place. They strike while the iron is hot, take him now when he is in a good mind, lest the conviction should wear off. Now that God begins to work, it is time for them to set in as *workers together with God.* They are as glad to show him the way to heaven as the best friend they have. They gave him the same directions they did to others, *Believe in the Lord Jesus Christ.* Here is the sum of the whole gospel, the covenant of grace in a few words: *Believe in the Lord Jesus Christ, and thou shalt be saved, and thy house.* The happiness promised: "*Thou shalt be saved;* not only rescued from eternal ruin, but brought to eternal life and blessedness. Though a persecutor, yet thy heinous transgressions shall be all forgiven; and thy hard embittered heart shall be softened and sweetened by the grace of Christ." The condition required: *Believe in the Lord Jesus Christ.* We must approve the method God has taken of reconciling the world to himself by a Mediator; and accept of Christ as he is offered to us. This is the only way and a sure way

JAMIESON, FAUSSET, BROWN

But Paul cried with a loud voice—the better to arrest the deed—**Do thyself no harm, for we are all here**—What divine calmness and self-possession! No elation at their miraculous liberation, or haste to take advantage of it; but one thought filled the apostle's mind at that moment—anxiety to save a fellow creature from sending himself into eternity, ignorant of the only way of life; and his presence of mind appears in the assurance which he so promptly gives to the desperate man, that his prisoners had none of them fled as he feared. But how, it has been asked by skeptical critics, could Paul in his inner prison know what the jailer was about to do? In many conceivable ways, without supposing any supernatural communication. Thus, if the jailer slept at the door of "the inner prison," which suddenly flew open when the earthquake shook the foundations of the building; if, too, as may easily be conceived, he uttered some cry of despair on seeing the doors open; and, if the clash of the steel, as the affrighted man drew it hastily from the scabbard, was audible but a few yards off, in the dead midnight stillness, increased by the awe inspired in the prisoners by the miracle—what difficulty is there in supposing that Paul, perceiving in a moment how matters stood, after crying out, stepped hastily to him, uttering the noble entreaty here recorded? Not less flat is the question, why the other liberated prisoners did not make their escape:—as if there were the smallest difficulty in understanding how, under the resistless conviction that there must be something supernatural in their instantaneous liberation without human hand, such wonder and awe should possess them as to take away for the time not only all desire of escape, but even all thought on the subject. **29, 30. Then he called for a light, and sprang in . . . and fell down before Paul and Silas, and brought them out and said**—How graphic this rapid succession of minute details, evidently from the parties themselves, the prisoners and the jailer, who would talk over every feature of the scene once and again, in which the hand of the Lord had been so marvellously seen. **Sirs, what must I do to be saved?**—If this question should seem in advance of any light which the jailer could be supposed to possess, let it be considered (1) that the "trembling" which came over him could not have arisen from any fear for the safety of his prisoners, for they were all there; and if it had, he would rather have proceeded to secure them again than leave them, to fall down before Paul and Silas. For the same reason it is plain that his trembling had nothing to do with any account he would have to render to the magistrates. Only one explanation of it can be given—that he had become all at once alarmed about his spiritual state, and that though, a moment before, he was ready to plunge into eternity with the guilt of self-murder on his head, without a thought of the sin he was committing and its awful consequences, his unfitness to appear before God, and his need of salvation, now flashed full upon his soul and drew from the depths of his spirit the cry here recorded. If still it be asked how it could take such definite shape, let it be considered (2) that the jailer could hardly be ignorant of the nature of the charges on which these men had been imprisoned, seeing they had been publicly whipped by order of the magistrates, which would fill the whole town with the facts of the case, including that strange cry of the demoniac from day to day—"These men are the servants of the most high God, which *show unto us the way of salvation*"—words proclaiming not only the divine commission of the preachers, but the news of salvation they were sent to tell, the miraculous expulsion of the demon and the rage of her masters. All this, indeed, would go for nothing with such a man, until roused by the mighty earthquake which made the building to rock; then despair seizing him at the sight of the open doors, the sword of self-destruction was suddenly arrested by words from one of those prisoners such as he would never imagine could be spoken in their circumstances—words evidencing something divine about them. Then would flash across him the light of a new discovery; "That was a true cry which the Pythoness uttered, "These men are the servants of the most high God, which show unto us the way of salvation! That I now must know, and from them, as divinely sent to me, must I learn that 'way of salvation!' " Substantially, this is the cry of every awakened sinner, though the degree of light and the depths of anxiety it expresses will be different in each case. **31-34. Believe on the Lord Jesus Christ, and thou shalt be saved**—The brevity, simplicity, and directness of this reply are, in the circumstances, singularly beautiful. Enough at

ADAM CLARKE

ALEXANDER MACLAREN:

The jailer behaves as such a man in his position would do. He apparently slept in a place that commanded a view of the doors; and he lay dressed, with his sword beside him, in case of riot or attempted escape. His first impulse on awaking is to look at the gates. They are open; some of his charge have broken them. His immediate thought of suicide not only shows the savage severity of punishment which he knew would fall on him, but tells a dreary tale of the desperate sense of the worthlessness of life and blank ignorance of anything beyond which then infected the Roman world. Suicide, the refuge of cowards or of pessimists, sometimes becomes epidemic. Faith must have died and hope vanished before a man can say, "I will take the leap into the dark."

—Expositions of Holy Scripture

29. *He called for a light.* That he might see how things stood and whether the words of Paul were true; for on this his personal safety depended. *Came trembling.* Terrified by the earthquake and feeling the danger to which his own life was exposed.

G. CAMPBELL MORGAN:

"Lords, what must I do to be delivered?" There was no evangelical faith in this. He did not mean, "What must I do to be eternally saved?" He had not got nearly as far as that. It was fear, panic; and his own solution of his difficulty was suicide; but the voice of the apostle said: "Do thyself no harm, for we are all here"; the prisoners have not escaped as you imagine. Then, filled with fear, he went into the presence of the men, one of whom could so speak to him, and bowing down he said: "Lords, what must I do to be delivered?" He was simply a man stricken with panic, and wondering what was the next thing. The evangelical values were coming, but they did not come out of that poor panic-stricken heart. They came in answer to its cry, from the great apostle: "Believe on the Lord Jesus, and thou shalt be saved." All the evangelical values are in that. The infinite music of the Gospel is thrilling through it like an anthem. This man did not understand it, not even then; but it was an answer to be explained. "You have called us lords; believe on the Lord Jesus Christ, the only Lord of human life. You have asked what you shall do to be saved, and your feeling is one born of fear, and desire to be saved from this hour of difficulty. Believe on this Lord, and you shall be saved from this hour, and from all hours of difficulty."

—The Acts of the Apostles

31. *Believe on the Lord Jesus.* Receive the religion of Christ, which we preach, and let your household also receive it, and all of you shall be placed in the sure way to final salvation.

MATTHEW HENRY

to salvation. No other way of salvation than by Christ, and no danger of coming short if we take this way. It is the gospel that is to be preached to every creature, *He that believes shall be saved.* The extension of this to his family: *Thou shalt be saved, and thy house.* Be they ever so many, let them believe in Jesus Christ and they shall be saved.

(4) They proceeded to instruct him and his family in the doctrine of Christ (*v.* 32): They *spoke unto him the word of the Lord.* He was, for aught that appears, an utter stranger to Christ, and therefore it is requisite he should be told who this Jesus is, that he may believe in him. Christ's ministers should have the word of the Lord so ready to them, and so richly dwelling in them, as to be able to give instructions offhand to any that desire to hear and receive them. They spoke the word to *all that were in his house.* Masters of families should take care that all under their charge partake of the means of knowledge and grace, and that the word of the Lord be spoken to them; for the souls of the poorest servants are as precious as those of their masters, and are bought with the same price.

(5) The jailer and his family were immediately baptized. He was *baptized, he and all his, straightway.* The Spirit of grace worked such a strong faith in them, all on a sudden, as superseded further debate; and Paul and Silas knew by the Spirit that it was a work of God that was wrought in them.

(6) The jailer was hereupon very respectful to Paul and Silas. He *took them the same hour of the night,* would not let them lie a minute longer in the inner prison. He *washed their stripes,* to cool them, and abate the smart of them. He *brought them into his house,* bade them welcome. Now nothing was thought good enough for them, as before nothing bad enough. He *set meat before them,* and they were welcome to it. They had broken the bread of life to him and his family; and he, having reaped so plentifully of their spiritual things, thought it was but reasonable that they should reap of his carnal things. What have we houses and tables for but as we have opportunity to serve God and his people with them?

(7) The voice of rejoicing with that of salvation was heard in the jailer's house; never was such a truly merry night kept there before: *He rejoiced, believing in God, with all his house.* His believing in Christ is called believing *in God,* which intimates that Christ is God, and that the gospel has a direct tendency to bring us to God. His faith produced joy. Those that by faith have given up themselves to God in Christ as theirs have a great deal of reason to rejoice. Believing in Christ is rejoicing in Christ. He signified his joy to all about him. One cheerful Christian should make many.

Verses 35–40

I. Orders sent for the discharge of Paul and Silas, *v.* 35, 36. The magistrates that had so basely abused them the day before gave the orders *as soon as it was day,* more in haste to give them a discharge than they were to petition for one. The magistrates sent *sergeants—those that had the rods,* those that had been employed in beating them. The order was, *Let those men go.* The jailer brought them the news (*v.* 36): *The magistrates have sent to let you go: Now therefore depart.* Not that he was desirous to part with them as his guests, but as his prisoners; they shall still be welcome to his house, but he is glad they are at liberty from his stocks.

II. Paul's insisting upon the breach of privilege which the magistrates had been guilty of, *v.* 37. Paul said to the sergeants, "*They have beaten us openly, uncondemned, being Romans, and have cast us into prison* against all law and justice, and *now do they thrust us out privily? Nay verily; but let them come themselves and fetch us out,* and own that they have done us wrong."

1. Paul did not plead this before he was beaten lest he should seem to be afraid of suffering for the truth which he had preached. He had nobler things than this to comfort himself with in his affliction.

2. He did plead it afterwards, to put an honour upon the cause he suffered for, to let the world know that the preachers of the gospel merited better treatment. He did it likewise to mollify the magistrates towards the Christians at Philippi, and beget in the people a better opinion of the Christian religion.

(1) Paul lets them know how many ways they had run themselves into a premunire. They had *beaten* those that were Romans. Roman historians give instances of cities that had their charters taken from them for indignities done to Roman citizens. To tell them they had beaten those who were the messengers of Christ would have had no influence upon them; but to tell them they have abused Roman citizens will put them into a fright: so common is it for people to

JAMIESON, FAUSSET, BROWN

that moment to have his faith directed simply to the Saviour, with the assurance that this would bring to his soul the needed and sought salvation—the *how* being a matter for after teaching. **thou shalt be saved, and thy house**—See on Luke 19:10. **And they spake unto him the word of the Lord**—unfolding now, doubtless, more fully what "the Lord Jesus Christ" was to whom they had pointed his faith, and what the "salvation" was which this would bring him. **and to all that were in his house**—who from their own dwelling (under the same roof no doubt with the prison) had crowded round the apostles, aroused first by the earthquake. (From their addressing the Gospel message "to all that were in the house" it is not necessary to infer that it contained no children, but merely that as it contained adults besides the jailer himself, so to all of these, as alone of course fit to be addressed, they preached the word.) **And he took them**—the word implies change of place—**the same hour of the night, and washed their stripes**—in the well or fountain which was within or near the precincts of the prison [HOWS]. The mention of "the same hour of the night" seems to imply that they had to go forth into the open air, which, unseasonable as the hour was, they did. These bleeding wounds had never been thought of by the indifferent jailer. But now, when his whole heart was opened to his spiritual benefactors, he cannot rest until he has done all in his power for their bodily relief. **and was baptized, he and all his, straightway**—probably at the same fountain, since it took place "straightway"; the one washing on his part being immediately succeeded by the other on theirs. **And when he had brought them into his house, he set meat before them and rejoiced, believing**—i.e., as the expression implies, 'rejoiced because he had believed'—**in God**—as a converted heathen, for the faith of a *Jew* would not be so expressed [ALFORD]. **with all his house**—the wondrous change on himself and the whole house filling his soul with joy. "This is the second house which, in the Roman city of Philippi, has been consecrated by faith in Jesus, and of which the inmates, by hospitable entertainment of the Gospel witnesses, have been sanctified to a new beginning of domestic life, pleasing and acceptable to God. The first result came to pass in consequence simply of the preaching of the Gospel; the second was the fruit of a testimony sealed and ennobled by suffering" [BAUMGARTEN].

35, 36. when it was day, the magistrates sent the sergeants, saying, Let those men go—The cause of this change can only be conjectured. When the commotion ceased, reflection would soon convince them of the injustice they had done, even supposing the prisoners had been entitled to no special privileges; and if rumor reached them that the prisoners were somehow under supernatural protection, they might be the more awed into a desire to get rid of them. **the keeper**—overjoyed to have such orders to execute—**told this . . . to Paul . . . now therefore . . . go in peace**—Very differently did Paul receive such orders. **37. Paul said unto them**—to the sergeants who had entered the prison along with the jailer, that they might be able to report that the men had departed. **They have beaten us openly**—The *publicity* of the injury done them, exposing their naked and bleading bodies to the rude populace, was evidently the most stinging feature of it to the apostle's delicate feeling, and to this accordingly he alludes to the Thessalonians, probably a year after: "Even after we had suffered before, and *were shamefully entreated* (or 'insulted') as ye know at Philippi" (I Thess. 2:2).

ADAM CLARKE

32. *And they spake unto him the word of the Lord.* Thus, by teaching him and all that were in his house the doctrine of the Lord, they plainly pointed out to them the way of salvation. And it appears that he and his whole family who were capable of receiving instructions embraced this doctrine and showed the sincerity of their faith by immediately receiving baptism.

33. *Washed their stripes.* "He washed from the stripes"; i.e., he washed the blood from the wounds.

34. *He set meat before them.* They were sufficiently exhausted, and needed refreshment; nor had the apostles any such inherent miraculous power as could prevent them from suffering through hunger, or enable them to heal their own wounds. As they were the instruments of bringing health to his soul, he became the instrument of health to their bodies.

35. *The magistrates sent the serjeants.* The original word means the *lictors,* persons who carried before the consul the *fasces,* which was a hatchet, round the handle of which was a bundle of rods tied. Why the magistrates should have sent an order to dismiss the apostles, whom they had so barbarously used the preceding evening, we cannot tell, unless we receive the reading of the Codex Bezae as genuine, viz., "And when it was day, the magistrates came together into the court, and remembering the earthquake that had happened, they were afraid, and they sent the serjeants." The Itala version of this same MS. has the same reading; so has also the margin of the later Syriac. If this MS. be correct, the cause of the dismissal of the apostles is at once evident. The earthquake had alarmed the magistrates; and taking it for granted that this was a token of the divine displeasure against them for their unprincipled conduct towards those good men, they wished to get as quietly rid of the business as they could, and therefore sent to dismiss the apostles. Whether this reading be genuine or not, it is likely that it gives the true cause of the magistrates' conduct.

37. *They have beaten us openly . . . being Romans.* Paul well knew the Roman laws, and on their violation by the magistrates he pleads. The Valerian law forbade any Roman citizen to be bound. The Porcian law forbade any to be beaten with rods. And the illegality of the proceedings of these magistrates was further evident in their condemning and punishing them unheard. This was a gross violation of a common maxim in the Roman law. Cicero: "Many who are accused of evil may be absolved, when the cause is heard; but unheard, no man can be condemned."

MATTHEW HENRY

be more afraid of Cæsar's wrath than of Christ's. They had beaten them *uncondemned*; had not calmly examined what was said against them, much less enquired what they had to say for themselves. Christ's servants would not have been abused as they have been if they and their cause might but have had an impartial trial. It was an aggravation of this that they had done it openly. They had *cast them into prison*, without showing any cause of their commitment. They now *thrust them out privily*; they had not indeed the impudence to stand by what they had done, but yet had not the honesty to own themselves in a fault.

(2) He insists upon it that they should make them an acknowledgment of their error, and give them a public discharge, as they had done them a public disgrace: "*Let them come themselves, and fetch us out*, and give a testimony that we have done nothing worthy of stripes or of bonds." It was not a point of honour that Paul stood thus stiffly upon, but a point of justice, and not to himself so much as to his cause.

III. The reversing of the judgment given against Paul and Silas, *v.* 38, 39. The magistrates were frightened when they were told that Paul was a Roman. The proceedings of persecutors have often been illegal, even by the law of nations, and often inhuman, against the law of nature, but always sinful, and against God's law. They *came and besought them* not to take advantage of the law against them; they *brought them out* of the prison, owning that they were wrongfully put into it, and desired them that they would peaceably and quietly *depart out of the city*. Yet, if the repentance of these magistrates had been sincere, they would not have desired them to depart out of their city, but would have begged of them to continue in their city, to show them the way of salvation. But many are convinced that Christianity is not to be persecuted who yet are not convinced that it ought to be embraced. They are compelled to do honour to Christ and his servants, and yet do not go so far as to have benefit by Christ.

IV. The departure of Paul and Silas from Philippi, *v.* 40. They went out of the prison when they were legally discharged. They took leave of their friends: they *went to the house of Lydia, saw the brethren*, and they *comforted them*. Young converts should have a great deal said to them to comfort them, for *the joy of the Lord will be* very much *their strength. They departed.* Paul and Silas had an extraordinary call to Philippi; and yet, when they have come thither, they see little of the fruit of their labours, and are soon driven thence. Yet they did not come in vain. They laid the foundation of a church at Philippi, which became very eminent, and had people that were more generous to Paul than any other church, as appears by his epistle to the Philippians, *ch.* i. 1; iv. 15. Let not ministers be discouraged, though they see not the fruit of their labours presently; the seed sown seems to be lost under the clods, but it shall come up again in a plentiful harvest.

JAMIESON, FAUSSET, BROWN

uncondemned—unconvicted on trial—**being Romans**—see on ch. 22:28—**and cast us into prison**—both illegal. Of Silas' citizenship, if meant to be included, we know nothing. **and now do they thrust**—hurry—**us out**—see Mark 9:38, *Greek*—**privily?**—Mark the intended contrast between the *public* insult they had inflicted and the *private* way in which they ordered them to be off. **nay verily**—no, indeed—**but let them come themselves and fetch us out**—by open and formal act, equivalent to a public declaration of their innocence. **38. they feared when they heard they were Romans**—their authority being thus imperilled; for they were liable to an action for what they had done. **39, 40. And they came**—in person—**and besought them**—not to complain of them. What a contrast this suppliant attitude of the prætors of Philippi to the tyrannical air with which they had the day before treated the preachers! (See Isa. 60:14; Rev. 3:9.) **brought them out**—conducted them forth from the prison into the street, as insisted on—**and desired**—'requested'—**them to depart out of the city**—perhaps fearing again to excite the populace. **And they went out of the prison**—Having attained their object—to vindicate their civil rights, by the infraction of which in this case the Gospel in their persons had been illegally affronted—they had no mind to carry the matter farther. Their citizenship was valuable to them only as a shield against unnecessary injuries to their Master's cause. What a beautiful mixture of *dignity* and *meekness* is this! Nothing secular, which may be turned to the account of the Gospel, is morbidly disregarded; in any other view, nothing of this nature is set store by:—an example this for all ages. **and entered into the house of Lydia**—as if to show by this leisurely proceeding that they had not been made to leave, but were at full liberty to consult their own convenience. **and when they had seen the brethren**—not only her family and the jailer's, but probably others now gained to the Gospel. **they comforted them**—rather, perhaps, 'exhorted' them, which would include comfort. "*This assembly of believers in the house of Lydia was the first church that had been founded in Europe*" [BAUMGARTEN]. **and departed**—but not all; for two of the company remained behind (see on ch. 17:14): *Timotheus*, of whom the Philippians "learned the proof" that he honestly cared for their state, and was truly likeminded with Paul, "serving with him in the Gospel as a son with his father" (Phil. 2:19-23); and *Luke*, "whose praise is in the Gospel," though he never praises himself or relates his own labors, and though we only trace his movements in connection with Paul, by the change of a pronoun, or the unconscious variation of his style. In ch. 17 the narrative is again in the *third* person, and the pronoun is not changed to the *second* till we come to ch. 20:5. The modesty with which Luke leaves out all mention of his own labors need hardly be pointed out. We shall trace him again when he rejoins Paul in the same neighborhood. His vocation as a physician may have brought him into connection with these contiguous coasts of Asia and Europe, and he may (as Mr. SMITH suggests, "Shipwreck," etc.) have been in the habit of exercising his professional skill as a surgeon at sea [HOWS].

ADAM CLARKE

Let them come themselves and fetch us out. The apostles were determined that the magistrates should be humbled for their illegal proceedings, and that the people at large might see that they had been unjustly condemned and that the majesty of the Roman people was insulted by the treatment they had received.

38. *They feared, when they heard that they were Romans.* They feared because the Roman law was so constituted that an insult offered to a citizen was deemed an insult to the whole Roman people. There is a remarkable addition here, in both the Greek and the Latin of the Codex Bezae. It is as follows: "And when they were come with many of their friends to the prison, they besought them to go out, saying: We were ignorant of your circumstances, that ye were righteous men. And, leading them out, they besought them, saying, Depart from this city, lest they again make an insurrection against you, and clamour against you."

40. *Entered into the house of Lydia.* This was the place of their residence while at Philippi; see v. 15. *They comforted them, and departed.* The magistrates were sufficiently humbled and the public at large, hearing of this circumstance, must be satisfied of the innocency of the apostles.

CHAPTER 17

Verses 1-9

Paul's two epistles to the Thessalonians give such a shining character of that church, that we cannot but be glad to meet with an account of the first founding of the church there.

I. Here is Paul's coming to Thessalonica. Paul went on with his work, notwithstanding the ill usage he had met with at Philippi. He takes notice of this in his first epistle to the church here (1 Thess. ii. 2). The opposition and persecution that he met with made him the more resolute. He could never have held out, and held on, as he did, if he had not been animated by a spirit of power from on high. 2. He did but *pass through Amphipolis and Appollonia.* We may suppose though he is said only to *pass through* these cities, yet that he stayed so long in them as to publish the gospel there, and to prepare the way for the entrance of other ministers among them.

II. His preaching to the Jews first, in their synagogue at Thessalonica. He found a synagogue of the Jews there (*v.* 1). By it he made his entry. It was always his manner to begin with the Jews, for if they received the gospel they would cheerfully embrace the new converts; if they refused it, they might thank them-

CHAPTER 17

VSS. 1-15. AT THESSALONICA THE SUCCESS OF PAUL'S PREACHING ENDANGERING HIS LIFE, HE IS DESPATCHED BY NIGHT TO BEREA, WHERE HIS MESSAGE MEETS WITH ENLIGHTENED ACCEPTANCE—A HOSTILE MOVEMENT FROM THESSALONICA OCCASIONS HIS SUDDEN DEPARTURE FROM BEREA—HE ARRIVES AT ATHENS. **1. when they had passed through Amphipolis**—thirty-three miles southwest of Philippi, on the river Strymon, and at the head of the gulf of that name, on the northern coast of the Ægean Sea. **and Apollonia**—about thirty miles southwest of Amphipolis; but the exact site is not known. **they came to Thessalonica**—about thirty seven miles due west from Apollonia, at the head of the Thermaic (or Thessalonian) Gulf, at the northwestern extremity of the Ægean Sea; the principal and most populous city in Macedonia. "We see at once how appropriate a place it was for one of the starting-points of the Gospel in Europe, and can appreciate the force of what Paul said to the Thessalonians within a few months of his departure from them: 'From you, the word of the Lord sounded forth like a trumpet, not only in Macedonia and Achaia, but in every place,' " (I Thess. 1; 8) [HOWS]. **where was a synagogue of the Jews**

CHAPTER 17

1. *Passed through Amphipolis.* This city was the metropolis of the first division of Macedonia, as made by Paulus Aemilius; see the note on chap. xvi. 10. It was built by Cimon, the Athenian general who sent 10,000 Athenians thither as a colony. It stood in an island in the river Strymon and had its name of Amphipolis because included between the two grand branches of that river where they empty themselves into the sea, the river being on "both sides of the city." *Apollonia.* This was another city of Macedonia, between Amphipolis and Thessalonica. It does not appear that Paul stopped at any of these cities, and they are only mentioned by the historian as places through which the apostles passed on their way to Thessalonica. It is very likely that in these cities there were no Jews, and that might have been the reason why the apostles did not preach the gospel there, for we find them almost constantly beginning with the Jews; and the Hellenist Jews living among the Gentiles became the medium through which the gospel of Christ was conveyed to the heathen world. *Thessalonica.* This was a celebrated city of Macedonia, situated on what was

MATTHEW HENRY

selves if the apostles carried it to those that would bid it welcome. He met them in their synagogue on the sabbath day, in their place and at their time of meeting. It is good being in the house of the Lord on his day. This was Christ's manner, and Paul's manner, and has been the manner of all the saints. He *reasoned with them out of the scriptures*. They agreed with him to receive the scriptures, so far they were of a mind. But they received the scripture, and therefore thought they had reason to reject Christ; Paul received the scripture, and therefore saw great reason to embrace Christ. It was therefore requisite that he should, by reasoning with them, convince them that his inferences from the scripture were right and theirs were wrong. The preaching of the gospel should be both scriptural preaching and rational; such Paul's was, for he *reasoned out of the scriptures*: we must reason out of them and upon them. Reason must not be set up in competition with the scripture, but it must be made use of in explaining and applying the scripture. He continued to do this *three sabbath days* successively. God waits for sinners' conversion; all the labourers come not into the vineyard at the first hour, nor are wrought upon so suddenly as the jailer. The drift and scope of his arguing was to prove that *Jesus is the Christ*; this was that which he opened and alleged, *v.* 3. He first explained his thesis, and opened the terms, and then alleged it, and laid it down. He opened it like one that knew it, and alleged it like one that believed it. It was necessary the Messiah should *suffer, and die, and rise again*, for the Old Testament prophecies concerning the Messiah made it necessary he should. Paul here alleges and makes it out undeniably, not only that it was possible he might be the Messiah, though he suffered, but that, being the Messiah, it was necessary he should suffer. He could not be made perfect but by sufferings; for, if he had not died, he could not have risen again from the dead. He must needs have suffered for us, because he could not otherwise purchase redemption for us; and he must needs have risen again because he could not otherwise apply the redemption to us. Jesus is the Messiah: "*This Jesus whom I preach unto you is Christ*, is the Christ, is he that should come. God has both by the scriptures and by miracles, borne witness to him." Gospel ministers should preach Jesus; he must be their principal subject. That which we are to preach concerning Jesus is that he is Christ.

III. The success of his preaching there, *v.* 4. Some of the Jews believed and they *consorted with Paul and Silas*. Those that believe in Jesus Christ come into communion with his faithful ministers, and associate with them. Many more of the devout Greeks, and of the chief women, embraced the gospel. These were *the worshipping Gentiles*; as in America they call those of the natives that are converted to the faith of Christ the *praying Indians*. Of these *a great multitude believed*. And not a few of the chief women of the city embraced Christianity. Particular notice is taken of this, for an example to the ladies, the chief women, to submit themselves to the commanding power of Christ's holy religion; for this intimates how acceptable it will be to God, and what great influence it may have upon many. No mention is here made of their preaching the gospel to the Gentile idolaters at Thessalonica, and yet it is certain that they did, for Paul writes to the Christians there as having *turned to God from idols* (1 Thess. i. 9), and that at the first entering in of the apostles among them.

IV. The trouble that was given to Paul and Silas at Thessalonica.

1. Who were the authors of their trouble: the *Jews who believed not, who were moved with envy*, *v.* 5. Some of the Jews believed the gospel and pitied and prayed for those that did not; while those that did not envied and hated those that did.

2. Who were the instruments of the trouble: the Jews made use of *certain lewd persons of the baser sort*. All wise and sober people looked upon them with respect, and none would appear against them but such as were the scum of the city. It is the honour of religion that those who hate it are generally the *lewd fellows of the baser sort*.

3. In what method they proceeded against them. (1) They *set the city in an uproar*. They began a riot, and then the mob was up presently. See how the devil carries on his designs; he sets cities in an uproar, sets souls in an uproar, and then fishes in troubled waters. (2) They *assaulted the house of Jason*, where the apostles lodged, *to bring them out to the people*, whom they had incensed against them. The proceedings here were altogether illegal. If men have offended, magistrates are appointed to enquire into the offence, and to judge of it; but to make the rabble judges and executioners too was to make truth

JAMIESON, FAUSSET, BROWN

implying that (as at Philippi) there was none at Amphipolis and Apollonia.

2-4. Paul, as his manner was—always to begin with the Jews. **went in unto them**—In writing to the converts but a few months after this, he reminds them of the courage and superiority to indignity, for the Gospel's sake, which this required after the shameful treatment he had so lately experienced at Philippi (I Thess. 2:2).

Opening and alleging that Christ must needs have suffered . . .—His preaching, it seems, was chiefly expository, and designed to establish from the Old Testament Scriptures (1) that the predicted Messiah was to be a suffering and dying, and therefore a rising, Messiah; (2) that this Messiah was none other than Jesus of Nazareth.

consorted—cast in their lot—**with Paul and Silas**—Cf. II Corinthians 8:5. **of the chief women**—female proselytes of distinction. From the First Epistle to the Thessalonians it appears that the converts were nearly all Gentiles; not only such as had before been proselytes, who would be gained in the synagogue, but such as up to that time had been idolaters (I Thess. 1:9, 10). During his stay, while Paul supported himself by his own labor (I Thess. 2:9; II Thess. 3:7-9), he received supplies once and again from the Philippians, of which he makes honorable acknowledgment (Phil. 4:15, 16).

5-9. the Jews . . . moved with envy—seeing their influence undermined by this stranger. **lewd fellows of the baser sort**—better, perhaps, 'worthless market-people,' i.e., idle loungers about the market place, of indifferent character.

gathered a company—rather, 'having raised a mob'—**assaulted the house of Jason**—with whom Paul and Silas abode (vs. 7), one of Paul's kinsmen, apparently (Rom. 16:21), and from his name, which was sometimes used as a Greek form of the word *Joshua* [GROTIUS], probably a Hellenistic Jew. **sought to bring them**—Jason's lodgers—**out to the people.**

ADAM CLARKE

called the Thermaic Gulf. According to Stephanus Byznatinus, it was embellished and enlarged by Philip, king of Macedon, who called it *Thessalonica*, "the victory of Thessalia," on account of the victory he obtained there over the Thessalians; but prior to this it was called Thermae. But Strabo, Tzetzes, and Zonaras say that it was called *Thessalonica* from Thessalonica, wife of Cassander and daughter of Philip.

2. *As his manner was.* He constantly offered salvation first to the Jews, and for this purpose attended their Sabbath days' meetings at their synagogues.

3. *Opening and alleging.* "Proving by citations." His method seems to have been this: (1) He collected the scriptures that spoke of the Messiah. (2) He applied these to Jesus Christ, showing that in Him all these scriptures were fulfilled, and that He was the Saviour of whom they were in expectation. He showed also that the *Christ*, or Messiah, *must needs have suffered*—that this was predicted, and was an essential mark of the true Messiah. By proving this point he corrected their false notion of a triumphant Messiah and thus removed the scandal of the Cross.

4. *The devout Greeks.* That is, Gentiles who were proselytes to the Jewish religion, so far as to renounce idolatry and live a moral life, but probably had not received circumcision.

5. *Certain lewd fellows of the baser sort.* This is not a very intelligible translation. These were probably a low kind of lawyers, or *attorneys* without principle, who gave advice for a trifle and fomented disputes and litigations among the people. They were such as always attended forensic litigations, waiting for a job and willing to defend any side of a question for money. They were wicked men of the forensic tribe. *Gathered a company, and set all the city on an uproar.* And after having made this sedition and disturbance, charged the whole on the peaceable and innocent apostles! This is precisely the same way that persecution against the truth and followers of Christ is still carried on. *Assaulted the house of Jason.* This was the place where the apostles lodged, and therefore his goods were clear spoil and his person fair game.

MATTHEW HENRY

fall in the street, to depose equity, and enthrone fury. (3) When they could not get the apostles into their hands they fall upon an honest citizen of their own, his name *Jason*, a converted Jew, and drew him out with some others of the brethren to the rulers of the city. (4) They accused them to the rulers, and represented them as dangerous persons. The crime charged upon Jason is receiving and harbouring the apostles (*v.* 7). Two very black characters are here given them: [1] That they were enemies to the public peace, and threw everything into disorder wherever they came: *Those that have turned the world upside down are come hither also*. In one sense it is true that wherever the gospel comes in its power to any place, to any soul, it works such a change there that it may be said to turn the world upside down. The love of the world is rooted out of the heart, and the way of the world contradicted in the life; so that the world is turned upside down there. They would have it thought that the preachers of the gospel were mischief makers wherever they came. Because they persuaded people to turn from idols to the living and true God, from malice and envy to love and peace, they are charged with turning the world upside down, when it was only the kingdom of the devil in the world that they thus overturned. Their enemies *set the city in an uproar*, and then laid the blame upon them. If Christ's faithful ministers be thus invidiously misrepresented, let them not think it strange; we are not better than Paul and Silas, who were thus abused. The accusers cry out, "They are *come hither also*; it is therefore time for us to bestir ourselves." [2] That they were enemies to the established government (*v.* 7): They all *do contrary to the decrees of Cæsar*, for they say: *There is another king, one Jesus*. It is true the Roman government was very jealous of any governor under their dominion taking upon him the title of king. His followers said indeed, Jesus is a king, but not an earthly king. There was nothing in the doctrine of Christ that tended to the dethroning of princes. The Jews knew this very well, and of all people it ill became the Jews to do it, who hated Cæsar and his government, and who expected a Messiah that should be a temporal prince, and overturn the thrones of kingdoms, and were therefore opposing our Lord Jesus because he did not appear under that character.

4. The great uneasiness which this gave to the city (*v.* 8): *They troubled the people and the rulers of the city, when they heard these things*. They had no ill opinion of the apostles or their doctrine, but if they be represented to them by the prosecutors as enemies to Cæsar, they will be obliged to suppress them. It troubled them to be brought under a necessity of disturbing good men.

5. The issue of this troublesome affair. The magistrates had no mind to prosecute the Christians. Care was taken to secure the apostles; they fled, and kept out of their hands; so that nothing was to be done but to discharge Jason and his friends upon bail, *v.* 9. So they *took security of Jason and the other*. Among the persecutors of Christianity, as there have been instances of the madness and rage of brutes, so there have been likewise of the prudence and temper of men; moderation has been a virtue.

Verses 10–15

I. Paul and Silas removing to Berea, and employed in preaching the gospel there, *v.* 10. They had proceeded so far at Thessalonica that the foundations of a church were laid, and therefore when the storm rose they withdrew. That command of Christ to his disciples, *When they persecute you in one city flee to another*, intends their flight to be not so much for their own safety ("flee to another, to hide there") as for the carrying on of their work ("flee to another, to preach there"). The devil was outshot in his own bow; he thought by persecuting the apostles to stop the progress of the gospel, but it was so overruled as to be made to further it. 1. The care that the brethren took of Paul and Silas. They *immediately sent them away by night to Berea*. They *sent them away by night*, under the covert of that, as if they had been evil doers. 2. The constancy of Paul and Silas in their work. Though they fled from Thessalonica, they did not flee from the service of Christ. When *they came to Berea, they went into the synagogue of the Jews*. They did not decline paying their respect to the Jews, either in revenge for the injuries they had received or for fear of what they might receive. If others will not do their duty to us, yet we ought to do ours to them.

II. The good character of the Jews in Berea (*v.* 11): *These were more noble than those in Thessalonica*. They *were more noble, better bred*.

1. They had a freer thought, were willing to hear reason, and admit the force of it, though it was contrary to their former sentiments. This was more

JAMIESON, FAUSSET, BROWN

And when they found them not, they drew Jason and certain brethren unto the rulers—lit., 'the politarchs'; the very name given to the magistrates of Thessalonica in an inscription on a still remaining arch of the city—so minute is the accuracy of this history. **crying, These that have turned the world upside down**—See on ch. 16:20.

all do contrary to the decrees of Cæsar . . .—meaning, probably, nothing but what is specified in the next words. **saying . . . there is another king, one Jesus**—See on John 19:12.

having taken security of Jason and of the other—'the others'—probably making them deposit a money pledge that the preachers should not again endanger the public peace.

10-12. the brethren immediately sent away Paul and Silas by night—for it would have been as useless as rash to attempt any further preaching at that time, and the conviction of this probably made his friends the more willing to pledge themselves against any present continuance of missionary effort. **to Berea**—fifty or sixty miles southwest of Thessalonica; a town even still of considerable population and importance.

These were more noble than those in Thessalonica—The comparison is between *the Jews* of the two places; for the triumphs of the Gospel at Thessalonica were mostly among the Gentiles. See on vss. 2-4.

ADAM CLARKE

ALEXANDER MACLAREN:

The charges are a violent distortion of the truth. Possibly the Jewish ringleaders believed what they said, but more probably they consciously twisted Paul's teachings, because they knew that no other charges would excite so much hostility or be so damning as those which they made. The mere suggestion of treason was often fatal. The wild exaggeration that the Christians had "turned the whole civilized world upside down" betrays passionate hatred and alarm, if it was genuine, or crafty determination to rouse the mob, if it was consciously trumped up. But whether the charges were believed or not by those who made them, here were Jews disclaiming their nation's dearest hope, and, like the yelling crowd at the Crucifixion, declaring they had no king but Caesar. The degradation of Israel was completed by these fanatical upholders of its prerogatives.

—*Expositions of Holy Scripture*

7. *These all do contrary to the decrees of Caesar*. Persecutors always strive to affect the lives of the objects of their hatred by accusing them of sedition or plots against the state. *That there is another king, one Jesus*. How malevolent was this saying! The apostles proclaimed Jesus as King—that is true; but never once insinuated that His kingdom was of this world.

8. *And they troubled the people and the rulers*. It is evident that there was no disposition in either the people or the rulers to persecute the apostles. But these wicked Jews, by means of the unprincipled, wicked lawyers, those "lewd fellows of the baser sort," threw the subject into the form of law, making it a state question, in which form the rulers were obliged to notice it. But they showed their unwillingness to proceed in a matter which they saw proceeded from malice by letting Jason and his companions go off on bail.

9. *Taken security*. "Having taken what was sufficient." Sufficient for the present, to prove that the apostles were upright, peaceable, and loyal men; and that Jason and his friends were the like, and would be at any time forthcoming to answer for their conduct.

10. *Sent away Paul and Silas by night*. Fearing some farther machinations of the Jews and their associates. *Berea*. This was another city of Macedonia, on the same gulf with Thessalonica, and not far from Pella, the birthplace of Alexander the Great.

11. *These were more noble than those in Thessalonica*. "Were of a better race, extraction, or birth" than those at Thessalonica; but the word refers more to their conduct as a proof of their better disposition than to their birth

MATTHEW HENRY

noble.

2. They had a better temper. As they were ready to come into a unity with those that they were brought to concur with, so they continued in charity with those that they saw cause to differ from. This was more noble. *They received the word with all readiness of mind;* they were very willing to hear it, and did not shut their eyes against the light. They did not pick quarrels with the word, nor seek occasion against the preachers of it; but bade it welcome. This was true nobility. The Jews thought themselves well-born and that they could not be better born. But they are here told who among them were the most noble and the best-bred men—those that were most disposed to receive the gospel. These were the most noble, and, if I may so say, the most gentleman-like men. *They searched the scriptures daily whether those things were so.* Their readiness of mind to receive the word was not such as that they took things upon trust. Since Paul reasoned out of the scriptures, and referred them to the Old Testament for the proof of what he said, they had recourse to their Bibles, examined whether Paul's arguments were cogent, and determined accordingly. The doctrine of Christ does not fear a scrutiny. The New Testament is to be examined by the Old. The Jews received the Old Testament, and those that did so could not but see cause sufficient to receive the New, because in it they see all the prophecies and promises of the Old fully and exactly accomplished. Those that read and receive the scriptures must *search them* (John v. 39), must study them, that they may find out the whole truth contained in them, and may have an intimate acquaintance with the mind of God revealed in them. Searching the scriptures must be our daily work. Those are truly noble, and are in a fair way to be more and more so, that make the scriptures their oracle and touchstone. Those that rightly study the scriptures, and *meditate therein day and night,* have their minds filled with noble thoughts. *These are more noble.*

III. The good effect of the preaching of the gospel at Berea, *v.* 12. Of the Jews there were many that believed. At Thessalonica there were only *some of them that believed* (*v.* 4), but at Berea, where they heard with unprejudiced minds, many believed. God gives grace to those whom he first inclines to make a diligent use of the means of grace, and particularly to search the scriptures. Of the Greeks likewise, many believed, both of *the honourable women and of men not a few,* men of the first rank, as should seem by their being mentioned with the honourable women. The wives first embraced the gospel, and then they persuaded their husbands to embrace it.

IV. The persecution that was raised against Paul and Silas at Berea. *The Jews at Thessalonica* were the mischief-makers at *Berea.* They *had notice that the word of God was preached at Berea.* They came thither *and they stirred up the people,* and incensed them against the preachers of the gospel. See how restless Satan's agents are in their opposition to the gospel of Christ and the salvation of the souls of men. This occasioned Paul's removal to Athens. So long Paul stayed at Berea, and such success he had there, that there were brethren there, and sensible active men too, which appeared by the care they took of Paul, *v.* 14. They were aware of the coming of the persecuting Jews from Thessalonica, and, fearing what it would come to, they lost no time, but *immediately sent Paul away,* while they retained Silas and Timothy there still, who might be sufficient to carry on the work without exposing him. They *sent Paul to go as it were to the sea.* He went out from Berea in that road which went to the sea, but he went by land to Athens. *Those that conducted Paul brought him to Athens.* The Spirit of God directed him to that famous city—famous of old for its power and dominion—famous afterwards for learning. Those who wanted learning went thither to get it, because those that had learning went thither to show it. It was a great university. Paul is sent thither, and is not ashamed nor afraid to show his face among the philosophers there, and there to preach Christ crucified. He ordered *Silas and Timothy to come to him to Athens,* when he found there was a prospect of doing good there; or because, there being none there that he knew, he was solitary and melancholy without them.

Verses 16–21

A scholar that is in love with the learning of the ancients would think he should be very happy if he were where Paul now was, at Athens, but Paul, though bred a scholar, does not make this any of his business at Athens. He has other work to mind: his business is, in God's name, *to turn them from the service of idols* to the *service of the true and living*

JAMIESON, FAUSSET, BROWN

in that they received the word with all readiness of mind—heard it not only without prejudice, but with eager interest, "in an honest and good heart" (Luke 8:17), with sincere desire to be taught aright (see John 7:17). Mark the "nobility" ascribed to this state of mind.

searched the scriptures daily whether those things were so—whether the *Christian* interpretation which the apostle put upon the Old Testament Scriptures was the true one. **Therefore many of them believed**—convinced that Jesus of Nazareth whom Paul preached was indeed the great Promise and Burden of the Old Testament. From this it is undeniable, (1) that *the people,* no less than the ministers of the Church, *are entitled and bound to search the Scriptures;* (2) that *they are entitled and bound to judge, on their own responsibility, whether the teaching they receive from the ministers of the Church is according to the word of God;* (3) that *no faith but such as results from personal conviction ought to be demanded, or is of any avail.* **of honourable women which were Greeks, and of men**—which were Greeks—**not a few**—"The upper classes in these European-Greek and Romanized towns were probably better educated than those of Asia Minor" [WEBSTER and WILKINSON]. **the Jews of Thessalonica . . . came thither also**—"like hunters upon their prey, as they had done before from Iconium to Lystra" [HOWS]. **13, 14. immediately the brethren**—the converts gathered at Berea. **sent away Paul**—as before from Jerusalem (ch. 9:30), and from Thessalonica (vs. 10). How long he stayed at Berea we know not; but as we know that he longed and expected soon to return to the Thessalonians (I Thess. 2:17), it is probable he remained some weeks at least, and only abandoned his intention of revisiting Thessalonica at that time when the virulence of his enemies there, stimulated by his success at Berea, brought them down thither to counterwork him. **to go as it were to the sea**—rather, perhaps, 'in the direction of the sea.' Probably he delayed fixing his next destination till he should reach the coast, and the providence of God should guide him to a vessel bound for the destined spot. Accordingly, it was only on arriving at Athens, that the convoy of Berean brethren, who had gone thus far with him, were sent back to bid Silas and Timothy follow him thither. **Silas and Timotheus abode there still**—"to build it up in its holy faith, to be a comfort and support in its trials and persecutions, and to give it such organization as might be necessary" [HOWS]. Connecting this with the apostle's leaving Timothy and Luke at Philippi on his own departure (see on ch. 16:40), we may conclude that this was his fixed plan for cherishing the first beginnings of the Gospel in European localities, and organizing the converts. Timotheus must have soon followed the apostle to Thessalonica, the bearer, probably, of one of the Philippian "contributions to his necessity" (Phil. 4:15, 16), and from thence he would with Silas accompany him to Berea **15. Silas and Timotheus to come to him with all speed**—He probably wished their company and aid in addressing himself to so new and great a sphere as Athens. Accordingly it is added that he "waited for them" there, as if unwilling to do anything till they came. That they did come, there is no good reason to doubt (as some excellent critics do). For though Paul himself says to the Thessalonians that he "thought it good to be left at Athens alone" (I Thess. 3:1), he immediately adds that he "sent Timotheus to establish and comfort them" (vs. 2); meaning, surely, that he despatched him from Athens back to Thessalonica. He had indeed sent for him to Athens; but, probably, when it appeared that little fruit was to be reaped there, while Thessalonica was in too interesting a state to be left uncherished, he seems to have thought it better to send him back again. (The other explanations which have been suggested seem less satisfactory.) Timotheus rejoined the apostle at Corinth (ch. 18: 5).

16-34. PAUL AT ATHENS. **16, 17. wholly given to idolatry**—'covered with idols'; meaning the city,

ADAM CLARKE

or any peculiar lineal nobility. It was a maxim among the Jews that "none was of a noble spirit who did not employ himself in the study of the law." It appears that the Bereans were a better educated and more polished people than those at Thessalonica.

12. *Therefore many of them believed.* From the manner in which they heard, received, and examined the Word preached to them, it was not likely they could be deceived. And as it was the truth that was proclaimed to them, it is no wonder that they apprehended, believed, and embraced it. *Of honourable women which were Greeks.* Probably mere heathens are meant; and these were some of the chief families in the place. Thus we find that the preaching of Paul at Berea was made the instrument of converting both Jews and Gentiles.

14. *To go as it were to the sea.* This passage is generally understood to mean that the disciples took Paul towards the sea, as if he had intended to embark and return to Troas, but with the real design to go to Athens. By taking a vessel at that part of the sea nearest to Berea they might have coasted it to Athens, which was quite a possible case; and as we do not hear of his stopping at any place on his journey to preach, it is very probable that he went by sea to this city. *Silas and Timotheus abode there still.* The persecution, it seems, was directed principally against Paul. Silas and Timotheus, holy men, were left behind to water the seed which Paul had planted.

15. *Brought him unto Athens.* This was one of the most celebrated cities in the world, whether we consider its antiquity, its learning, its political consequence, or the valor of its inhabitants. About thirteen or fourteen hundred years before Christ it was called Athens, from *Athene,* a name of Minerva, to whom it was dedicated and who was always considered the protectress of the city. The whole city at first was built upon a hill or rock, in the midst of a spacious plain; but in process of time the whole plain was covered with buildings, which were called the lower city, while the ancient was called Acropolis, or the upper city. In its most flourishing state this city was not less than twenty-two Roman miles in circumference. The buildings of Athens were the most superb and best executed in the world. The greatest men that ever lived, scholars, lawyers, statesmen, and warriors, were Athenians. Its institutions, laws, and literature were its own unrivalled boast and the envy of the world. The city still exists; the Acropolis in a state of comparative repair.

16. *He saw the city wholly given to idolatry.* "Full of idols." Bishop Pearce produces a most

MATTHEW HENRY

God in Christ.

I. Here is the impression which the superstition of the Athenians made upon Paul's spirit, *v.* 16. 1. The account here given of that city: it was *wholly given to idolatry.* This agrees with the account which the heathen writers give of it, that there were more idols in Athens than there were in all Greece besides. Whatever strange gods were recommended to them, they admitted them, and allowed them a temple and an altar. It is observable that there, where human learning most flourished, idolatry most abounded. *The world by wisdom knew not God,* 1 Cor. i. 21. The greatest pretenders to reason were the greatest slaves to idols: so necessary was it that there should be a divine revelation, and that centring in Christ. 2. The disturbance which the sight of this gave to Paul. *His spirit was stirred within him.* He was filled with concern for the glory of God, which he saw given to idols, and with compassion to the souls of men, which he saw thus enslaved to Satan.

II. The testimony that he bore against their idolatry, and his endeavours to bring them to the knowledge of the truth. He *went to the synagogue of the Jews,* who, though enemies to Christianity, were free from idolatry, and took the opportunity given him there of disputing for Christ, *v.* 17. He discoursed *with the Jews,* and put it to them what reason they could give why, since they expected the Messiah, they would not receive Jesus. There he met with the devout persons that had forsaken the idol temples, and he talked with these to lead them on to the Christian church, to which the Jews' synagogue was but as a porch. He entered into conversation with all that came in his way about matters of religion: *In the market he disputed daily with those that met with him,* that were heathen, and never came to the Jews' synagogue. The zealous advocates for the cause of Christ will be ready to plead it in all companies, as occasion offers.

III. The enquiries which some of the philosophers made.

1. Who they were that entered into discourse with him: *He disputed with all that met him, in the places of concourse.* Most took no notice of him, but there were some of the philosophers that thought him worth making remarks upon. (1) *The Epicureans,* who *thought God altogether such a one as themselves.* They would not own, either that God made the world or that he governs it. The Epicureans indulged themselves in all the pleasures of sense, and placed their happiness in them, in what Christ has taught us in the first place to deny ourselves. (2) *The Stoics,* who thought themselves altogether as good as God; they made their virtuous man to be no way inferior to God himself. To which Christianity is directly opposite, as it teaches us to come off from all confidence in ourselves, that Christ may be all in all.

2. What their different sentiments were of him (*v.* 18). (1) *Some called him a babbler—this scatterer of words,* that goes about, throwing here one idle word or story and there another; or, *this picker up of seeds.* The term is used for *a little sort of bird,* that is worth nothing at all, *that picks up the seeds that lie uncovered, either in the field or by the wayside, and hops here and there for that purpose.* Such a pitiful contemptible animal they took Paul to be, or supposed he went from place to place venting his notions to get money, a penny here and another there, as that bird picks up here and there a grain. They looked upon him as an idle fellow, and regarded him, as we say, no more than a ballad-singer. (2) *Others* called him *a setter forth of strange gods.* And, if he had strange gods to set forth, he could not bring them to a better market than to Athens. They thought he seemed to do so, *because he preached unto them Jesus, and the resurrection.* Though he did not call these gods, yet they thought he meant to make them so. "Jesus they took for a new god, and the resurrection, for a new goddess." As if believing in Jesus and looking for the resurrection, were the worshipping of new demons.

3. The proposal they made to give him a public hearing, *v.* 19, 20. They had heard some broken pieces of his doctrine, and are willing to have a more perfect knowledge of it. (1) They look upon it as strange and surprising. "It is a new doctrine. *Thou bringest certain strange things to our ears* which we never heard of before, and know not what to make of now." By this it should seem that, among all the learned books they had, they either had not, or heeded not, the books of Moses and the prophets. There was but one book in the world that was of divine inspiration, and that was the only book they were strangers to. (2) They desired to know more of it, only because it was new and strange: "*May we know what this new doctrine is?* We would gladly know *what these things mean.*" It was fit they should know

JAMIESON, FAUSSET, BROWN

not the inhabitants. PETRONIUS, a contemporary writer at Nero's court, says satirically that it was easier to find a god at Athens than a man. This "stirred the spirit" of the apostle. "The first impression which the masterpieces of man's taste for art left on the mind of St. Paul was a revolting one, since all this majesty and beauty had placed itself between man and his Creator, and bound him the faster to his gods, who were not God. Upon the first contact, therefore, which the Spirit of Christ came into with the sublimest creations of human art, the judgment of the Holy Ghost—through which they have all to pass—is set up as 'the strait gate,' and this must remain the correct standard for ever" [BAUMGARTEN].

therefore disputed—or, discussed—**he in the synagogue with the Jews.** The sense is not, 'Therefore went he to the Jews,' because the Gentile Athenians were steeped in idolatry; but, 'Therefore set he himself to lift up his voice to the idol-city, but, as his manner was, he began with the Jews.' **and with the devout persons**—Gentile proselytes. After that, **in the market**—the *Agora,* or place of public concourse—**daily with them that met with him**—or 'came in his way.'

18-21. certain . . . of the Epicureans—a well-known school of *atheistic materialists,* who taught that pleasure was the chief end of human existence; a principle which the more rational interpreted in a refined sense, while the sensual explained it in its coarser meaning. **and of the Stoics**—a celebrated school of *severe and lofty pantheists,* whose principle was that the universe was under the law of an iron necessity, the spirit of which was what is called the Deity: and that a passionless conformity of the human will to this law, unmoved by all external circumstances and changes, is the perfection of virtue. While therefore the Stoical was in itself superior to the Epicurean system, both were alike hostile to the Gospel. "The two enemies it has ever had to contend with are the two ruling principles of the Epicureans and Stoics—*Pleasure and Pride*" [HOWS]. **What will this babbler say?** The word, which means 'a pickerup of seeds,' birdlike, is applied to a gatherer and retailer of scraps of knowledge, a prater; a general term of contempt for any pretended teacher.

a setter forth of strange gods—'demons,' but in the Greek (not Jewish) sense of '*objects of worship.*' **because he preached Jesus and the resurrection**—Not as if they thought he made these to be two divinities: the strange gods were *Jehovah* and *the Risen Saviour,* ordained to judge the world.

ADAM CLARKE

apposite quotation from Pausanias, which confirms the observation: "There was no place where so many idols were to be seen." Petronius, who was contemporary with Paul, in his *Satyr,* chap. xvii, makes Quartilla say of Athens: "Our region is so *full of deities* that you may more frequently meet with a *god* than a *man.*"

17. *Disputed he in the synagogue with the Jews,* proving that Jesus was the Messiah; *and with the devout persons,* probably heathens, proselyted to the Jewish religion. *And in the market;* I suppose the *agora* here means some such place as our exchange, where people of business usually met and where the philosophers conversed and reasoned.

18. *Certain philosophers of the Epicureans.* These were the followers of Epicurus, who acknowledged no gods except in name, and absolutely denied that they exercised any government over the world or its inhabitants; and that the chief good consisted in the gratification of the appetities of sense. *And of the Stoicks.* These did not deny the existence of the gods, but they held that all human affairs were governed by fate. They did not believe that any good was received from the hands of their gods; and considered, as Seneca asserts, that any good and wise man was equal to Jupiter himself. Both these sects agreed in denying the resurrection of the body, and the former did not believe in the immortality of the soul. Epicurus, the founder of the Epicurean sect, was born at Athens, 341 B.C. Zeno, the founder of the Stoic sect, was born in the isle of Cyprus about thirty years before Christ. His disciples were called Stoics from the *Stoa,* a famous portico at Athens where they studied. *What will this babbler say?* The word which we translate *babbler* signifies literally "a collector of seeds," and is the "name of a small bird that lives by picking up seeds on the road." The epithet became applied to persons who collected the sayings of others, without order or method, and detailed them among their companions in the same way. *A setter forth of strange gods.* "Of strange or foreign demons." That this was strictly forbidden, at both Rome and Athens, see on chap. xvi. 21. There was a difference in the heathen theology between *god* and *demon.* The *theoi* were such as were gods by nature; the *daimonia* were men who were deified. This distinction seems to be in the mind of these philosophers when they said that the apostles seemed to be setters forth of "strange demons" because they preached unto them Jesus, whom they showed to be a man, suffering and dying, but afterwards raised to the throne of God. This would appear to them tantamount with the deification of heroes who had been thus honored for their especial services to mankind.

20. *Thou bringest . . . strange things to our ears.* The doctrine of the apostles was different from any they had ever heard. It was wholly spiritual and divine; thus it was *strange.* It was contrary to their customs and manners, and thus it was strange also. As it spoke much of the exaltation and glory of Jesus Christ, they supposed Paul to be a "setter forth of strange gods"; and therefore, on the authority of the laws which forbade the introduction of any new deities or modes of worship, he was called before the Areopagus.

MATTHEW HENRY

what this doctrine was before they embraced it; and they were so fair as not to condemn it till they had had some account of it. (3) The place they brought him to. It was to *Areopagus*, the same word that is translated (*v.* 22) *Mars' Hill*; it was the town-house, or guildhall of their city, where the magistrates met upon public business, and where learned men met to communicate their notions. The court of justice which sat here was famous for its equity. Hither they brought Paul to be tried, not as a criminal but as a candidate.

4. The general character of the people of that city (*v.* 21): *All the Athenians spent their time in nothing else but either to tell or to hear some new thing.* They were inquisitive concerning Paul's doctrine, not because it was *good*, but because it was *new.* (1) They were all for conversation. It is true that good company is of great use to a man, and will polish one that has laid a good foundation in study; but that knowledge will be very flashy and superficial which is got by conversation only. (2) They affected novelty; they were for *telling and hearing some new thing.* They were for new schemes and new notions. They were given to change. (3) They meddled in other people's business and never minded their own. Tattlers are always *busy bodies.* (4) *They spent their time in nothing else.* Time is precious and it is hastening apace into eternity, but abundance of it is wasted in unprofitable converse. To set up for newsmongers, and to spend our time in nothing else, is to lose that which is very precious for the gain of that which is worth little.

Verses 22–31

We have here St. Paul's sermon at Athens. Divers sermons we have had, which the apostles preached to the Jews, or such Gentiles as were worshippers of the true God; and all they had to do with them was to open and allege *that Jesus is the Christ*; but here we have a sermon to heathens, that worshipped false gods, and to them the scope of their discourse was quite different from what it was to the other. In the former case their business was to lead their hearers by prophecies and miracles to the knowledge of the Redeemer, and faith in him; in the latter it was to lead them by the common works of providence to the knowledge of the Creator, and the worship of him.

I. He lays down this that he aimed to bring them to *the knowledge of the only living and true God.* He is here obliged to instruct them in the first principle of all religion, that there is a God, and that God, is but one. When he preached against the gods they worshipped he had no design to draw them to atheism, but to the service of the true Deity, by declaring that he does not seek to introduce any new gods, but to reduce them *to the knowledge of one God.*

1. He shows them that they had lost the knowledge of the true God that made them, in the worship of false gods that they had made. *I perceive that in all things you are too superstitious.* The crime he charges upon them is that they feared and worshipped demons, spirits that they supposed inhabited the images. "It is time for you to be told that *there is but one God.* You easily admit everything that comes under a show of religion, but it is that which corrupts it more and more; I bring you that which will reform it." They charged Paul with setting forth new demons: "Nay," says he, "you have demons enough already; I will not add to the number of them."

2. He shows them that they themselves had given a fair occasion for the declaring of this one true God to them, by *setting up an altar, To the unknown God.* It is sad to think that at Athens, a place which was supposed to have the monopoly of wisdom, the true God was an unknown God, the only God that was unknown. There, where we are sensible we are defective and come short, and just there, the gospel takes us up, and carries us on.

(1) Various conjectures the learned have concerning this *altar dedicated to the unknown God.* Some think the meaning is, *To the God whose honour it is to be unknown*, and that they intended the God of the Jews, whose name is ineffable, and whose nature is unsearchable. The heathen called the Jews' God the God without name. *This God*, says Paul, *I now declare unto you.* Others think the meaning is, *To the God whom it is our unhappiness not to know*, that they would think it their happiness to know him.

(2) Observe, how modestly Paul mentions this. He tells them that he observed it *as he passed by, and saw their devotions.* It was public, and he could not forbear seeing it. Observe how he takes occasion from this to bring in his discourse of the true God. He tells them that the God he preached to them was one that they did already worship. He was one whom they ignorantly worshipped. "Now," says he, "I come to take away *that reproach*, that you may wor-

JAMIESON, FAUSSET, BROWN

they took him, and brought him to Areopagus—"the hill where the most awful court of judicature had sat from time immemorial to pass sentence on the greatest criminals, and to decide on the most solemn questions connected with religion. No place in Athens was so suitable for a discourse on the mysteries of religion" [Hows]. The apostle, however, was not here on his *trial*, but to expound more fully what he had thrown out in broken conversations in the Agora. **all the Athenians . . . spent their time in nothing else but to tell or hear some new thing**—lit., 'newer thing,' as if what was new becoming presently stale, they craved something still more new [Bengel]. This lively description of the Athenian character is abundantly attested by their own writers.

22. Then Paul stood . . . and said—more graphically, 'standing in the midst of Mars' hill, said." This prefatory allusion to the position he occupied shows the writer's wish to bring the situation vividly before us [Baumgarten].

I perceive that in all things ye are too superstitious—rather (with most modern interpreters and the ancient Greek ones), 'in all respects extremely reverential' or 'much given to religious worship,' a conciliatory and commendatory introduction, founded on his own observation of the symbols of devotion with which their city was covered, and from which all Greek writers, as well as the apostle, inferred the exemplary religiousness of the Athenians. (The authorized translation would imply that only *too much* superstition was wrong, and represents the apostle as repelling his hearers in the very first sentence; whereas the whole discourse is studiously courteous.)

I found an altar . . . To the—or 'an'—**unknown god**—erected, probably, to commemorate some divine interposition, which they were unable to ascribe to any known deity. That there were such altars, Greek writers attest; and on this the apostle skilfully fastens at the outset, as the text of his discourse, taking it as evidence of that dimness of religious conception which, in virtue of his better light, he was prepared to dissipate.

23. as I passed by and beheld your devotions—rather, 'the objects of your devotion,' referring, as is plain from the next words, to their works of art consecrated to religion.

ADAM CLARKE

19. *They took him, and brought him unto Areopagus.* The Areopagus was a hill not far from the Acropolis, already described, where the supreme court of justice was held—one of the most sacred and reputable courts that had ever existed in the Gentile world. It had its name, *Areopagus,* or the "Hill of Mars," or "Ares," from the circumstance, according to poetic fiction, of Mars being tried there by a court of twelve gods for the murder of Halirrhothius, son of Neptune.

21. *All the Athenians and strangers which were there.* As Athens was renowned for its wisdom and learning, it became a place of public resort for philosophers and students from different parts of the then civilized world. The flux of students was in consequence great; these, having much leisure time, would necessarily be curious to know what was passing in the world and would frequently assemble together in places of public resort to meet with strangers just come to the city, and either, as Luke says, to tell or to hear some new thing.

22. *Paul stood in the midst of Mars' hill.* That is, in the midst of the judges who sat in the Areopagus.

Ye are too superstitious. I perceive that in all respects you are greatly addicted to religious practices; and as a religious people you will candidly hear what I have to say in behalf of that worship which I practice and recommend.

To the unknown God. That there was an altar at Athens thus inscribed we cannot doubt after such a testimony, though Jerome questions it in part; for he says Paul found the inscription in the plural number, but because he would not appear to acknowledge a plurality of gods, he quoted it in the singular. This is a most foolish saying. Had Paul done so, how much would such a begging of the question have prejudiced his defense in the minds of his intelligent judges! Pausanias says that at Athens there are "altars of gods which are called, The unknown ones." Now though in these last passages both gods and altars are spoken of in the plural number, yet it is reasonable to suppose that on each or upon some one of them the inscription "To the unknown god" was actually found.

23. *Beheld your devotions.* "The objects of your worship"; the different images of their gods which they held in religious veneration, sacrificial instruments, altars, etc.

MATTHEW HENRY

ship him understandingly. And it cannot but be acceptable to have your blind devotion turned into a reasonable service, that you may not worship *you know not what*."

II. He confirms his doctrine of one living and true God, by his works of creation and providence: "The God whom I call you to the worship of, is *the God that made the world*." The Gentiles in general, and the Athenians particularly, in their devotions were governed, not by their philosophers, but by their poets, and their idle fictions. Now Paul here sets himself to give them right notions of *the one only living and true God*, and then to carry the matter further for the bringing them off from their idolatry. Observe what glorious things Paul here says of that God whom he served, and would have them to serve.

1. *He is the God that made the world, and all things therein; the Father almighty, the Creator of heaven and earth.* Paul here maintains that God by the operations of an infinite power, according to the contrivance of an infinite wisdom, made the world and all things therein, the origin of which was owing to an eternal mind.

2. He is therefore *Lord of heaven and earth.* If he created all, without doubt he has the disposing of all: and, where he gives being, he has an indisputable right to give law.

3. He is, in a particular manner, the Creator of men, of all men (*v.* 26): *He made of one blood all nations of men.* He made the first man, he makes every man. He has made the nations of men, not only all men in the nations, but as nations. He is their founder and disposed them into communities. He made them all of one blood, of one and the same nature, that hereby they might be engaged in mutual affection and assistance, as fellow-creatures and brethren. *He hath made them to dwell on all the face of the earth.* He made them not to live in one place, but to be dispersed over all the earth; one nation therefore ought not to look with contempt upon another, as the Greeks did, which proud conceit of themselves, the apostle here takes down.

4. He is the great benefactor of the whole creation (*v.* 25): *He giveth to all life, and breath, and all things.* He not only *breathed into the first man the breath of life*, but still breathes it into every man. He gave us these souls; he formed the spirit of man within him He *gives to all the children of men their life and breath*; for as the meanest of the children of men live upon him, so the greatest, the wisest philosophers and mightiest potentates, cannot live without him. *He gives to all*, not only to all the children of men, but to the inferior creatures, to all animals; they have their life and breath from him, and where he gives life and breath he gives all things needful for the support of life.

5. He is the sovereign disposer of all the affairs of the children of men (*v.* 26): *He hath determined the times before appointed, and the bounds of their habitation.* (1) The sovereignty of God's disposal concerning us: he *hath determined* every event; the disposals of Providence are incontestable and must not be disputed. (2) The wisdom of his disposals; he hath *determined* what was *before appointed.* The determinations of the Eternal Mind are not sudden resolves, but an eternal counsel. (3) The things about which his providence is conversant; these are time and place. [1] *He has determined the times* that are concerning us. *Our times are in his hand.* Whether they be prosperous times or calamitous times, it is he that has determined them. [2] He has also *determined and appointed the bounds of our habitation.* He that *appointed the earth to be a habitation for the children of men* has appointed to the children of men a distinction of habitations upon the earth. The particular habitations in which our lot is cast are of God's appointing, which is a reason why we should accommodate ourselves to the habitations we are in, and make the best of that which is.

6. *He is not far from everyone of us*, *v.* 27. He is *everywhere present.* He is an infinite Spirit, *that is not far from any of us.* He is nigh unto us, both to receive the homage we render him and to give the mercies we ask of him, wherever we are, though near no altar, image, or temple. Be we in a palace or in a cottage, in a crowd or in a corner, in a city or in a desert, in the depths of the sea or afar off upon the sea, this is certain, *God is not far from everyone of us.*

7. *In him we live, and move, and have our being*, *v.* 28. We have a necessary and constant dependence upon his providence, as the streams have upon the spring, and the beams upon the sun. (1) *In him we live.* It is not only owing to his patience that our forfeited lives are not cut off, but it is owing to his fatherly care, that our frail lives are prolonged. If he suspend the positive acts of his goodness, we die of ourselves. (2) *In him we move.* It is likewise by him that our souls move our bodies, as he is the first

JAMIESON, FAUSSET, BROWN

Whom therefore ye ignorantly worship—rather, 'Whom, therefore, knowing Him not, ye worship,' alluding to "The Unknown God." **him declare**—announce —**I unto you**—*This is like none of his previous discourses, save that to the idolaters of Lycaonia* (ch. 14:15-17). His subject is not, as in the synagogues, the Messiahship of Jesus, but THE LIVING GOD, in opposition to the materialistic and pantheistic polytheism of Greece, which subverted all true religion. Nor does he come with *speculation* on this *profound subject*—of which they had had enough from others—but an authoritative "announcement" of Him after whom they were groping; not giving Him any name, however, nor even naming the Saviour Himself, but unfolding the true character of both as they were able to receive it. **24, 25. God that made the world and all . . . therein**—The most profound philosophers of Greece were unable to conceive any real distinction between God and the universe. Thick darkness, therefore, behooved to rest on all their religious conceptions. To dissipate this, the apostle sets out with a sharp statement of the fact of *creation* as the central principle of all true religion—not less needed now, against the transcendental idealism of our day. **seeing he is Lord**—or Sovereign—**of heaven and earth**—holding in free and absolute subjection all the works of His hands; presiding in august royalty over them, as well as pervading them all as the principle of their being. How different this from the blind Force or Fate to which all creatures were regarded as in bondage! **dwelleth not in temples made with hands**—This thought, so familiar to Jewish ears (I Kings 8:27; Isa. 66:1, 2; ch. 7:48), and so elementary to Christians, would serve only more sharply to define to his heathen audience the spirituality of that living, personal God, whom he "announced" to them. **Neither is worshipped with**—ministered unto, served by—**men's hands, as though he needed anything**—No less familiar as this thought also is to us, even from the earliest times of the Old Testament (Job 35:6, 8; Ps. 16:2, 3; 50:12-14; Isa. 40:14-18), it would pour a flood of light upon any candid heathen mind that heard it. **seeing he**—He Himself—**giveth to all life, and breath, and all things**—The Giver of all cannot surely be dependent for aught upon the receivers of all (I Chron. 29:14). This is the culminating point of a pure Theism. **26, 27. and hath made of one blood all nations of men to dwell on all the face of the earth**—Holding with the Old Testament teaching, that in the blood is the life (Gen. 9:4; Lev. 17:11; Deut. 12:23), the apostle sees this lifestream of the whole human race to be one, flowing from one source [BAUMGARTEN]. **and hath determined the times before appointed, and the bounds of their habitation**—The apostle here opposes both Stoical Fate and Epicurean Chance, ascribing the *periods* and *localities* in which men and nations flourish to the sovereign will and prearrangements of a living God.

-though he be not far from every one of us—The difficulty of finding God outside the pale of revealed religion lies not in His distance from us, but in our distance from Him through the blinding effect of sin.

28. For in him we live, and move, and have our being—or, more briefly, 'exist').—This means, not merely, "Without Him we have no *life*, nor that *motion* which every inanimate nature displays, nor even *existence* itself" [MEYER], but that God is the living, immanent Principle of all these in men.

ADAM CLARKE

Whom therefore ye ignorantly worship. There is here a fine paronomasia or play on the words. The apostle tells them that (on their system) they were a very religious people—that they had an altar inscribed, *Agnosto theo*, "To the unknown God." Him therefore, says he, whom *agnoountes*, "ye unknowingly" worship, I proclaim to you—assuming it as a truth that, as the true God was *not known* by them and there was an altar dedicated "to the unkown God," this God was that God whose nature and operations he now proceeded to declare. By this fine turn he eluded the force of that law which made it a capital offense to introduce any new god into the state, and of the breach of which he was charged, v. 18; and thus he showed that he was bringing neither new god nor new worship among them, but only explaining the worship of one already acknowledged by the state, though not as yet known.

24. *God that made the world.* Paul assumes that this God could not be confined within temples made with hands, as He was the Lord or Governor of heaven and earth. That by fair consequence the gods whom they worshipped, which were shut up in their temples, could not be this God; and they must be less than the places in which they were contained. This was a strong, decisive stroke against the whole system of the Grecian idolatry.

25. *Neither is worshipped with men's hands.* This is an indirect stroke against making of images and offering of sacrifices. He is not worshipped with human hands, as if He needed anything. Nor has He required victims for His support; for it is impossible that He should need anything who himself gives being, form, and life to all creatures. *Giveth . . . life, and breath, and all things.* These words are elegantly introduced by Paul. God gives *life*, because He is the Fountain of it. He gives *breath*, the faculty of breathing or respiration, by which this life is preserved. But as much more is necessary to keep the animal machine in a state of repair, God gives all the other things which are requisite for this great and important purpose, that the end for which life was given may be fully answered.

26. *Hath made of one blood.* In some MSS. the word *blood* is omitted. *He hath made of one* (meaning Adam) *all nations of men . . . and hath determined the times before appointed.* Instead of *the times before appointed*, several MSS. read "the appointed times"; that is, the times appointed by His providence, on which the several families should go to those countries where His wisdom designed they should dwell. *And the bounds of their habitation.* Every family being appointed to a particular place, that their posterity might possess it for the purposes for which infinite wisdom and goodness gave them their being and the place of their abode. Every nation had its lot thus appointed by God, as truly as the Israelites had the land of Canaan.

28. *For in him we live, and move, and have our being.* He is the very Source of our existence. The principle of life comes from Him; the principle of motion also comes from Him—one of the most difficult things in nature to be properly apprehended, and a strong proof of the continual presence and energy of the Deity.

MATTHEW HENRY

cause, so he is the first mover. (3) *In him we have our being;* not only from him we had it at first, but in him we have it still; we were and still are of such a noble rank of beings, capable of knowing and enjoying God; and are not thrust into the meanness of brutes, nor the misery of devils.

8. Upon the whole matter we are *God's offspring.* The apostle here quotes a saying of one of the Greek poets, Aratus, a native of Cilicia, Paul's countryman, who, speaking of the heathen *Jupiter,* that is, in the poetical dialect, the supreme *God,* says this of him, *for we are also his offspring.* By this it appears not only that Paul was himself a scholar, but that human learning is both ornamental and serviceable to a gospel minister, especially for the convincing of those that are without; for it enables him to beat them at their own weapons, and to cut off Goliath's head with his own sword. How can the adversaries of truth be beaten out of their strongholds by those that do not know them? Since in him we live, we ought to live to him; since in him we move, we ought to move towards him; and since in him we have our being, we ought to consecrate our being to him.

III. From all these great truths concerning God, he infers the absurdity of their idolatry. 1. God cannot be represented by an image. If we are *the offspring of God,* then certainly he who is *the Father of our spirits* is himself a Spirit, and we ought not to think the Godhead is *like unto gold, or silver, or stone, graven by art and man's device, v.* 29. God honoured man in making his soul after his own likeness; but man dishonours God if he makes him after the likeness of his body. 2. *He dwells not in temples made with hands, v.* 24. A temple brings him never the nearer to us, nor keeps him ever the longer among us. A temple is convenient for us to come together in to worship God; but God needs not any place of rest or residence. 3. He is *not worshipped with men's hands, as though he needed anything, v.* 25. He that maintains all, cannot be benefited by any of our services, nor needs them. What need can God have of our services, or what benefit can he have by them, when he has all perfection in himself, and we have nothing that is good but what we have from him? 4. It concerns us all to enquire after God (*v.* 27): *That they should seek the Lord.* We have plain indications of God's presence among us, and his bounty to us, that we might be put upon enquiring, *Where is God our Maker.* Nothing, one would think, should be more powerful with us to convince us that there is a God, than the consideration of our own nature, especially the noble powers and faculties of our own souls. Yet so dark is this discovery, in comparison with that by divine revelation, that those who have no other could but *haply feel after God* and *find him.* It was very uncertain whether they could by this searching *find out God*; it is but a peradventure: *if haply* they might. If they did find out something of God, yet it was but some confused notions of him; they did but feel after him, as men in the dark, or blind men. It is true that by the knowledge of ourselves we may be led to the knowledge of God, but it is a very confused knowledge. We have therefore reason to be thankful that by the gospel of Christ we do not now feel after him, but *with open face behold, as in a glass, the glory of God.*

IV. He proceeds to call them all to repent of their idolatries, *v.* 30, 31. This is the practical part of Paul's sermon before the university; having declared God to them (*v.* 23), he properly presses upon them *repentance towards God.* Having shown them the absurdity of their worshipping other gods, he persuades them to return from it to the living and true God.

1. The conduct of God towards the Gentile world before the gospel came among them: *The times of this ignorance God winked at.* They were times of great ignorance. In the things of God they were grossly ignorant. Those are ignorant indeed who either know not God or worship him ignorantly; idolatry was owing to ignorance. These times of ignorance God winked at. Understand it as an act of divine patience and forbearance. He winked at these times, but gave them the gifts of his providence, *ch.* xiv. 16, 17. He was not quick and severe with them, but was long-suffering towards them, because they did it ignorantly.

2. The charge God gave to the Gentile world by the gospel: *He now commandeth all men everywhere to repent*—to change their mind and their way. It is to turn with sorrow and shame from every sin, and with cheerfulness and resolution to every duty. This is God's command. He interposes his own authority for our good, and has made that our duty which is our privilege. It is his command to *all men, everywhere.* All men have made work for repentance, and

JAMIESON, FAUSSET, BROWN

as certain also of your own poets have said, For we are also his offspring—the first half of the fifth line, word for word, of an astronomical poem of ARATUS, a Greek countryman of the apostle, and his predecessor by about three centuries. But, as he hints, the same sentiment is to be found in other Greek poets. They meant it doubtless in a *pantheistic* sense; but the truth which it expresses the apostle turns to his own purpose—to teach a pure, personal, spiritual Theism. (Probably during his quiet retreat at Tarsus, ch. 9:30, revolving his special vocation to the Gentiles, he gave himself to the study of so much Greek literature as might be turned to Christian account in his future work. Hence this and his other quotations from the Greek poets, I Cor. 15:33; Titus 1:12). **29. Forasmuch then as we are the offspring of God, we ought not to think**—*The courtesy of this language is worthy of notice*—**that the Godhead is like unto gold, or silver, or stone, graven by art and man's device**—('graven by the art or device of man'). One can hardly doubt that the apostle would here point to those matchless monuments of the plastic art, in gold and silver and costliest stone, which lay so profusely beneath and around him. The more intelligent pagan Greeks no more pretended that these sculptured gods and goddesses were real deities, or even their actual likenesses. than Romanist Christians do their images; and Paul doubtless knew this; yet here we find him condemning all such efforts visibly to represent the invisible God. How shamefully inexcusable then are the Greek and Roman churches in paganizing the worship of the Christian Church by the encouragement of pictures and images in religious service! (In the eighth century, the second council of Nicea decreed that the image of God was as proper an object of worship as God Himself.)

That they should seek the Lord--That is the high end of all these arrangements of Divine Power, Wisdom, and Love.

if haply they might feel after him—as men groping their way in the dark—**and find him**—a lively picture of the murky atmosphere of Natural Religion-

30. the times of this ignorance God winked at—literally (and far better), 'overlooked,' i.e., bore with, without interposing to punish it, otherwise than suffering the debasing tendency of such worship to develop itself (cf. ch. 14:16, and see on Rom. 1:24, etc.).

but now—that a new light was risen upon the world. **commandeth**—'That duty—all along lying upon man estranged from his Creator, but hitherto only silently recommending itself and little felt—is now peremptory.' **all men every where to repent**—(cf. Col. 1:6, 23; Titus 1:11)—a tacit allusion to the narrow precincts of favored Judaism, within which immediate and entire repentance was ever urged.

ADAM CLARKE

And have our being. "And we are"; we live in Him, move in Him, and are in Him. Without Him we not only can do nothing, but without Him we are nothing. "We are," i.e., we continue to be, because of His continued, present, all-pervading, and supporting energy. *As certain also of your own poets.* Probably he means not only Aratus, in whose poem, entitled *Phaenomena,* the words quoted by Paul are to be found literatim, but also Cleanthus, in whose "Hymn to Jupiter" the same words occur. But the sentiment is found in several others, being very common among the more enlightened philosophers. By saying *your own poets* he does not mean poets born at Athens, but merely Grecian poets, Aratus and Cleanthus being chief. Aratus was a Cilician, one of Paul's own countrymen, and with his writings Paul was undoubtedly well-acquainted, though he had flourished about three hundred years before that time.

29. *Forasmuch then as we are the offspring of God.* This inference of the apostle was very strong and conclusive, and his argument runs thus: "If we are the offspring of God, He cannot be like those images of gold, silver, and stone which are formed by the art and device of man, for the parent must resemble his offspring. Seeing therefore that we are living and intelligent beings, He from whom we have derived that being must be living and intelligent. It is necessary also that the object of religious worship should be much more excellent than the worshipper; but a man is, by innumerable degrees, more excellent than an image made out of gold, silver, or stone. And yet it would be impious to worship a man; how much more so to worship these images as gods!" Every man in the Areopagus must have felt the power of this conclusion; and, taking it for granted that they had felt it, he proceeds.

27. *That they should seek the Lord.* This is a conclusion drawn from the preceding statement. God, who is infinitely great and self-sufficient, has manifested himself as the Maker of the world, the Creator, Preserver, and Governor of men. He has assigned them their portion and dispensed to them their habitations and the various blessings of His providence, to the end that they should seek Him in all His works. *Feel after him.* That they might grope after Him, as a person does his way who is blind or blindfolded. The Gentiles, who had not a revelation, must grope after God as the principle of spiritual life, that they might find Him to be a Spirit and the Source of all intellectual happiness; and the apostle seems to state that none need despair of finding this fountain of goodness, because He is *not far from every one of us.*

30. *The times of this ignorance God winked at.* He who has an indisputable right to demand the worship of all His creatures has mercifully overlooked those acts of idolatry which have disgraced the world and debased man.

But *now,* as He has condescended to give a revelation of himself, He *commands,* as the Sovereign, *all men every where,* over every part of His dominions, *to repent,* "to change their views";

MATTHEW HENRY

have cause enough to repent, and all men are invited to repent, and shall have the benefit of it. Now the way of remission is more opened than it had been, and the promise more fully confirmed; and therefore now he expects we should all repent.

3. The great reason to enforce this command. God commands us to repent, *because he hath appointed a day in which he will judge the world in righteousness* (*v.* 31). (1) The God that made the world will judge it. The God that now governs the world will reward the faithful friends of his government and punish the rebels. (2) There is a day appointed for this general review of all that men have done in time, a day of decision, a day of recompence, a day that will put a final period to all the days of time. (3) The world will be judged in righteousness; for God is not unrighteous. (4) God will judge the world *by that man whom he hath ordained*, who can be no other than the Lord Jesus, to whom all judgment is committed. (5) God's raising Christ from the dead is the great proof of his being appointed and ordained the Judge of quick and dead. God hath *given assurance unto all men*, sufficient ground for their faith to build upon, both that there is a judgment to come and that Christ will be their Judge. Let all his enemies be assured of it, and tremble before him; let all his friends be assured of it, and triumph in him. (6) The consideration of the judgment to come, and of the great hand Christ will have in that judgment, should engage us all to repent of our sins and turn from them to God.

Verses 32–34

We have here a short account of the issue of Paul's preaching at Athens.

I. Few were the better: the gospel had as little success at Athens as anywhere. Some ridiculed Paul and his preaching. They heard him patiently till he came to speak of the resurrection of the dead (*v.* 32), and then they *mocked*. If he speak of a *resurrection of the dead*, though it be of the resurrection of Christ himself, it is altogether incredible to them. They had deified their heroes after their death, but never thought of their being raised from the dead. How can this be? This great doctrine, which is the saints' joy, is their jest. We are not to think it strange if sacred truths are made the scorn of profane wits. Others were willing to take time to consider of it; they said, *We will hear thee again of this matter*. They would not at present comply with what Paul said, nor oppose it. Thus many lose the benefit of the practical doctrine of Christianity, by wading beyond their depth into controversy. Those that would not yield to the present convictions of the word thought to get clear of them by putting them off to another opportunity. Thus the devil cozens them of all their time, by cozening them of the present time. Paul thereupon left them for the present to consider of it (*v.* 33): *He departed from amongst them*.

II. Yet there were some that were wrought upon, *v.* 34. There were certain men that adhered to him, and believed. When he departed from amongst them, they would not part with him so. Two are particularly named; one was an eminent man, *Dionysius the Areopagite*, one of that high court that sat in Aeropagus, one of those before whom Paul was summoned to appear; his judge becomes his convert. The *woman named Damaris*. Though there was not so great a harvest gathered in at Athens, yet these few being wrought upon there, Paul had no reason to say he had *laboured in vain*.

JAMIESON, FAUSSET, BROWN

The word "repentance" is here used (as in Luke 13: 3, 5; 15:10) in its most comprehensive sense of "repentance unto life." **31. Because he hath appointed a day in the which he will judge the world**—Such language beyond doubt teaches that the judgment will, in its essence, be a solemn judicial assize held upon all mankind *at once*. "Aptly is this uttered on the Areopagus, the seat of judgment" [BENGEL].

by that man whom he hath ordained—cf. John 5:22, 23, 27; ch. 10:42. **whereof he hath given assurance unto all men, in that he hath raised him from the dead**—the most patent evidence to mankind at large of the judicial authority with which the Risen One is clothed. **32-34. when they heard of the resurrection of the dead, some mocked**—As the Greek religion was but the glorification of the present life, by the worship of all its most beauteous forms, the Resurrection, which presupposes the vanity of the present life, and is nothing but life out of the death of all that sin has blighted, could have no charm for the true Greek. It gave the deathblow to his fundamental and most cherished ideas; nor until these were seen to be false and fatal could the Resurrection, and the Gospel of which it was a primary doctrine, seem otherwise than ridiculous. **So Paul departed**—Whether he would have opened, to any extent, the Gospel scheme in this address, if he had not been interrupted, or whether he reserved this for exposition afterwards to earnest inquirers, we cannot tell. Only the speech is not to be judged of as quite complete. **others said, We will hear thee again of this**—"an idle compliment to Paul and an opiate to their consciences, such as we often meet with in our own day. They probably, like Felix, feared to hear more, lest they should be constrained to believe unwelcome truths" (ch. 24:25; and cf. Matt. 13:15) [WEBSTER and WILKINSON]. **Howbeit certain men clave unto him**—Instead of mocking or politely waiving the subject, having listened eagerly, they joined themselves to the apostle for further instruction; and so they "believed." **Dionysius the Areopagite**—a member of that august tribunal. Ancient tradition says he was placed by the apostle over the little flock at Athens. "Certainly the number of converts there and of men fit for office in the Church was not so great that there could be much choice" [OLSHAUSEN]. **a woman named Damaris**—not certainly one of the apostle's audience on the Areopagus, but won to the faith either before or after. Nothing else is known of her. Of any further labors of the apostle at Athens, and how long he stayed, we are not informed. Certainly he was not driven away. But "it is a serious and instructive fact that the mercantile populations of Thessalonica and Corinth received the message of God with greater readiness than the highly educated and polished Athenians. Two letters to the Thessalonians, and two to the Corinthians, remain to attest the flourishing state of those churches. But we possess no letter written by Paul to the Athenians; and we do not read that he was ever in Athens again" [Hows].

ADAM CLARKE

because he hath appointed a day, in the which he will judge the world in righteousness. And as justice will then be done, no sinner, no persevering idolater, shall escape punishment. The word which we translate *wink at* signifies simply "to look over," and seems to be here used in the sense of passing by, not particularly noticing it. So God overlooked, or passed by, the times of heathenish ignorance.

31. *He hath appointed a day*. He has fixed the time in which He will judge the world, though He has not revealed this time to man. *By that man whom he hath ordained*. He has also appointed the Judge by whom the inhabitants of the earth are to be tried. *Whereof he hath given assurance*. "Having given to all this indubitable proof" that Jesus Christ shall judge the world, by raising Him from the dead. The sense of the argument is this: "Jesus Christ, whom we preach as the Saviour of men, has repeatedly told His followers that He would judge the world, and has described to us at large the whole of the proceedings of that awful time, Matt. xxv. 31, etc.; John v. 25. Though He was put to death by the Jews, and thus He became a Victim for sin, yet God raised Him from the dead. By raising Him from the dead, God has set His seal to the doctrines He has taught. One of these doctrines is that He shall *judge the world*. His resurrection, established by the most incontrovertible evidence, is therefore a proof, an incontestable proof, that He shall judge the world according to His own declaration."

32. *When they heard of the resurrection*. Paul undoubtedly had not finished his discourse; it is likely that he was about to proclaim salvation through Christ crucified. But on hearing of the resurrection of the body, the assembly instantly broke up—the Epicureans mocking, "began to laugh," and the Stoics saying they would take another opportunity to hear him on that subject.

33. *So Paul departed from among them*. He could not be convicted of having done anything contrary to the law, and when the assembly broke up he was permitted to go about his own business.

34. *Certain men clave unto him*. Became affectionately united to him *and believed* the doctrines he had preached. *Dionysius the Areopagite*. There can be no doubt that this man was one of the judges of this great court, but whether the president or otherwise we cannot tell. Humanly speaking his conversion must have been an acquisition of considerable importance to the Christian religion; for no person was a judge in the Areopagus who had not borne the office of *archon*, or chief governor of the city, and none bore the office of judge in this court who was not of the highest reputation among the people for his intelligence and exemplary conduct.

MATTHEW HENRY

CHAPTER 18

Verses 1–6

We do not find that Paul was much persecuted at Athens, nor that he was driven thence by any ill usage, but his reception being cold, and little prospect of doing good there, he departed from Athens, and thence he came to Corinth.

I. Paul working for his living, *v.* 2, 3. 1. Though he was bred a scholar, yet he was master of a handicraft trade. He was a tentmaker. It was the custom of the Jews to bring up their children to some trade, yea, though they gave them learning or estates. An honest trade, by which a man may get his bread, is not to be looked upon by any with contempt. Paul, having in his youth learned to make tents, did not by disuse lose the art. 2. Though he was entitled to a maintenance from the churches he had planted, yet he worked at his calling to get bread, which is more to his praise who did not ask for supplies than to theirs who did not supply him unasked. See how humble Paul was. See how industrious he was. He that had so much to do with his mind did not think

JAMIESON, FAUSSET, BROWN

CHAPTER 18

VSS. 1-22. PAUL'S ARRIVAL AND LABORS AT CORINTH, WHERE HE IS REJOINED BY SILAS AND TIMOTHY, AND, UNDER DIVINE ENCOURAGEMENT, MAKES A LONG STAY—AT LENGTH, RETRACING HIS STEPS, BY EPHESUS, CÆSAREA, AND JERUSALEM, HE RETURNS FOR THE LAST TIME TO ANTIOCH, THUS COMPLETING HIS SECOND MISSIONARY JOURNEY. **1-4. came to Corinth**—rebuilt by Julius Cæsar on the isthmus between the Ægean and Ionian Seas; the capital of the Roman province of Achaia, and the residence of the proconsul; a large and populous mercantile city, and the center of commerce alike for East and West; having a considerable Jewish population, larger, probably, at this time than usual, owing to the banishment of the Jews from Rome by Claudius Cæsar (vs. 2). Such a city was a noble field for the Gospel, which, once established there, would naturally diffuse itself far and wide.

ADAM CLARKE

CHAPTER 18

1. *Paul departed from Athens*. How long he stayed here we cannot tell; it is probable it could not be less than three months. But finding that the gospel made little progress among the Athenians, he resolved to go to Corinth. Corinth was situated on the isthmus that connects Peloponnesus to Attica, and was the capital of all Achaia. It was most advantageously situated for trade; for by its two ports, the Lecheum and Cenchreae, it commanded the commerce of both the Ionian and the Aegean Sea. It was destroyed by the Romans under Mummius about one hundred and forty-six years before Christ, in their wars with Attica; but was rebuilt by Julius Caesar, and became one of the most considerable cities of Greece. It is about forty-six miles west of Athens.

2. *Claudius had commanded all Jews to depart from Rome*. This edict of the Roman em-

MATTHEW HENRY

it below him to work with his hands. See how careful Paul was to recommend his ministry. He therefore maintained himself with his own labour that he might not make the gospel of Christ *burdensome*, 2 Cor. xi. 7, &c. 3. Though we may suppose he was master of his trade, yet he did not disdain to work at journey-work: He *wrought with Aquila and Priscilla*, who *were of that calling*, so that he got no more than day-wages, a bare subsistence. 4. Though he was himself a great apostle, yet he chose to work with Aquila and Priscilla, because he found them to be very intelligent in the things of God (*v.* 26), and he owns that they had been his *helpers in Christ Jesus*, Rom. xvi. 3. Choose to work with those that are likely to be helpers in Christ Jesus. Concerning this Aquila he was a Jew, but born in Pontus, *v.* 2. He was lately come from Italy to Corinth. The reason of his leaving Italy was because by a late edict of the emperor Claudius Cæsar all Jews were banished from Rome. Aquila, though a Christian, was banished because he had been a Jew. If Jews persecute Christians, it is not strange if heathens persecute them both.

II. We have here Paul preaching to the Jews, both the native *Jews and the Greeks*.

1. He *reasoned with them in the synagogue every sabbath*. See in what way the apostles propagated the gospel, not by force and violence, but by fair arguing. Paul was a rational as well as a scriptural preacher.

2. *He persuaded them*. It denotes the urgency of his preaching. He followed his arguments with affectionate persuasions, not to refuse the offer of salvation made to them. The good effect of his preaching. He persuaded them, that is, he prevailed with them. Some of them were convinced by his reasonings, and yielded to Christ.

3. He was yet more earnest in this matter when his fellow-labourers came up with him (*v.* 5): *When Silas and Timothy had come from Macedonia* and were ready to assist him here, then Paul was more than before *pressed in spirit*, which made him more than ever pressing in his preaching. And being thus pressed, he *testified to the Jews that Jesus is the Christ*.

III. We have him here abandoning the unbelieving Jews, and turning from them to the Gentiles, *v.* 6.

1. Many of the Jews persisted in their contradiction to the gospel of Christ; they *opposed themselves* and *blasphemed*; they *set themselves in battle array* (so the word signifies) against the gospel. They could not argue against it, but what was wanting in reason they made up in ill language: they *blasphemed*.

2. Paul hereupon declared himself discharged from them, and left them to perish in their unbelief. He that was *pressed in spirit to testify to them* (*v.* 5), was pressed in spirit to testify against them (*v.* 6); he *shook his raiment*, shaking off the dust from it for a testimony against them. Thus he cleared himself from them, but threatened the judgments of God against them. He had done his part, and was clean from the blood of their souls; he had, like a faithful watchman, given them warning, so that if they perish in their unbelief their blood is not to be required at his hands. It is very comfortable to a minister to have the testimony of his conscience for him, that he has faithfully discharged his trust by warning sinners. They would certainly perish if they persisted in their unbelief, and the blame would lie wholly upon themselves: "Your *blood be upon your own heads*." If anything would frighten them at last into a compliance with the gospel, surely this would.

3. Having given them over, yet he does not give over his work. *Henceforth I will go unto the Gentiles*. The guests that were first invited will not come; guests must be had therefore *from the highways and the hedges*. Thus the fall of the Jews became the riches of the Gentiles.

Verses 7–11

I. Paul changed his quarters. He departed out of the synagogue, and he *entered into a certain man's house, named Justus*, *v.* 7. It should seem, he went to this man's house, not to lodge, for he continued with Aquila and Priscilla, but to preach. This honest man opened his doors to him. When Paul could not have liberty to preach in the synagogue, he preached in a house. The man was next door to a Jew; he was one that *worshipped God*; he was not an idolater, though he was a Gentile. 2. The house was next door to the synagogue, it *joined close to it*. I rather think it was done in charity, to show that he would come as near to them as he could, and was ready to return to them if they were but willing to receive his message.

II. Paul presently saw the good fruit of his labours, both among Jews and Gentiles. *Crispus*, a Jew, an eminent one, *the chief ruler of the synagogue, believed on the Lord Jesus, with all his house*, *v.* 8. This would

JAMIESON, FAUSSET, BROWN

a Jew . . . Aquila . . . with his wife Priscilla—From these Latin names one would conclude that they had resided so long in Rome as to lose their Jewish family names. **born in Pontus**—the most easterly province of Asia Minor, stretching along the southern shore of the Black Sea. From this province there were Jews at Jerusalem on the great Pentecost (ch. 2:9), and the Christians of it are included among "the strangers of the dispersion," to whom Peter addressed his first Epistle (I Pet. 1:1). Whether this couple were converted before Paul made their acquaintance, commentators are much divided. They may have brought their Christianity with them from Rome [OLSHAUSEN], or Paul may have been drawn to them merely by like occupation, and, lodging with them, have been the instrument of their conversion [MEYER]. They appear to have been in good circumstances, and after travelling much, to have eventually settled at Ephesus. The Christian friendship now first formed continued warm and unbroken, and the highest testimony is once and again borne to them by the apostle. **Claudius . . .**—This edict is almost certainly that mentioned by SUETONIUS, in his life of this emperor (ch. 25). **tentmakers**—manufacturers, probably, of those hair-cloth tents supplied by the goats of the apostle's native province, and hence, as sold in the markets of the Levant, called *cilicium*. Every Jewish youth, whatever the pecuniary circumstances of his parents, was taught some trade (see on Luke 2:42), and Paul made it a point of conscience to work at that which he had probably been bred to, partly that he might not be burdensome to the churches, and partly that his motives as a minister of Christ might not be liable to misconstruction. To both these he makes frequent reference in his Epistles. **the Greeks**—i.e., Gentile proselytes; for to the heathen, as usual, he only turned when rejected by the Jews (vs. 6). **5, 6. And when Silas and Timotheus were come from Macedonia**—i.e., from Thessalonica, whither Silas had probably accompanied Timothy when sent back from Athens (see on ch. 17:15). **Paul was pressed in the spirit**—rather (according to what is certainly the true reading) 'was pressed with the word'; expressing not only his zeal and assiduity in preaching it, but some inward *pressure* which at this time he experienced in the work (to convey which more clearly was probably the origin of the common reading). What that pressure was we happen to know, with singular minuteness and vividness of description, from the apostle himself, in his first Epistles to the Corinthians and Thessalonians (I Cor. 2:1-5; I Thess. 3:1-10). He had come away from Athens, as he remained there, in a depressed and anxious state of mind, having there met, for the first time, with unwilling Gentile ears. He continued, apparently for some time, laboring alone in the synagogue of Corinth, full of deep and anxious solicitude for his Thessalonian converts. His early ministry at Corinth was colored by these feelings. Himself deeply humbled, his power as a preacher was more than ever felt to lie in demonstration of the Spirit. At length Silas and Timotheus arrived with exhilarating tidings of the faith and love of his Thessalonian children, and of their earnest longing again to see their father in Christ; bringing with them also, in token of their love and duty, a pecuniary contribution for the supply of his wants. This seems to have so lifted him as to put new life and vigor into his ministry. *He now wrote his* FIRST EPISTLE TO THE THESSALONIANS, in which the "pressure" which resulted from all this strikingly appears. (See Introduction to First Thessalonians.) Such emotions are known only to the ministers of Christ, and, even of them, only to such as "travail in birth until Christ be formed in" their hearers. **Your blood be upon your own heads . . .**—See Ezekiel 33:4, 9. **from henceforth I will go unto the Gentiles**—Cf. ch. 13: 46. **7, 8. he departed thence, and entered into a certain man's house, named Justus**—not changing his lodging, as if Aquila and Priscilla up to this time were with the opponents of the apostle [ALFORD], but merely ceasing any more to testify in the synagogue, and henceforth carrying on his labors in this house of Justus, which "joining hard to the synagogue," would be easily accessible to such of its worshippers as were still open to light. Justus, too, being probably a proselyte, would more easily draw a mixed audience than the synagogue. From this time forth conversions rapidly increased. **Crispus, the chief ruler of the synagogue, believed on the Lord with all his house**—an event felt to be so important that the apostle deviated from his usual practice (I Cor. 1:14-16) and baptized him, as well

ADAM CLARKE

peror is not mentioned by Josephus; but it is probably the same to which Suetonius refers in his life of Claudius, where he says, "He expelled the Jews from Rome, as they were making continual insurrections, under their leader Chrestus." Who this Chrestus was we cannot tell; probably Suetonius meant "Christ," but this I confess does not appear to me likely. There might have been a Jew of the name of Chrestus who had made some disturbances, and in consequence Claudius thought proper to banish all Jews from the city. But how could he intend Christ, who was never at Rome?

3. *He abode with them, and wrought*. It was a custom among the Jews, even of such as had a better education than ordinary, which was Paul's case, to learn a trade, that wherever they were they might provide for themselves in case of necessity. And though Paul in some cases lived on the bounty of his converts, yet he chose not to do so at Ephesus, chap. xx. 34; nor at Corinth or other places, 1 Cor. iv. 12; 2 Cor. ix. 8-9; 2 Thess. iii. 8; and this Paul did for a reason which he gives in 2 Cor. xi. 9-12.

4. *He reasoned in the synagogue every sabbath*. Discoursed at large concerning Jesus as the Messiah, proving this point from their own Scriptures, collated with the facts of our Lord's life. *And persuaded the Jews and the Greeks*. Many, both Jews and proselytes, were convinced of the truth of his doctrine. Among his converts was Epenetus, the firstfruit of his labor in Achaia, Rom. xvi. 5; and the family of Stephanas was the next; and then Crispus and Caius, or Gaius—all of whom the apostle himself baptized, 1 Cor. i. 14-16.

5. *When Silas and Timotheus were come*. We have seen, chap. xvii. 13, that when Paul was obliged to leave Berea because of the persecution raised up against him in that place, he left Silas and Timotheus behind, to whom he afterwards sent word to rejoin him at Athens with all speed. It appears, from 1 Thess. iii. 10, that on Timothy's coming to Athens, Paul immediately sent him, and probably Silas with him, to comfort and establish the church at Thessalonica. How long they labored here is uncertain, but they did not rejoin him till some time after he came to Corinth. It appears that he was greatly rejoiced at the account which Timothy brought of the church at Thessalonica; and it must have been immediately after this that he wrote his First Epistle to that church, which is probably the first, in order of time, of all his Epistles. *Paul was pressed in the spirit*. Or he was "constrained by the Spirit" of God, in an extraordinary manner, to testify *to the Jews that Jesus was Christ*. Instead of *in the spirit*, "in the word" is the reading of several MSS. Bishop Pearce thus paraphrases the verse: "And when Silas and Timotheus were come from Macedonia, Paul set himself, together with them, wholly *to the word*; i.e., he was fully employed, now that he had their assistance, in preaching the gospel, called *the word* in chap. iv. 6; xvi. 6, 32; and xvii. 11." This appears to be the true sense of the word, and that *to logo* is the genuine reading there can be no doubt. From this time we hear no more of Silas; probably he died in Macedonia.

6. *When they opposed*. Systematically opposing, putting themselves "in warlike order" against him; so the word implies. *He shook his raiment*. This was an action similar to that of shaking the dust off the feet; see on Matt. x. 14. *Your blood be upon your own heads*. That is, you alone are the cause of the destruction that is coming upon yourselves and upon your country. *I am clean*. "I am pure or innocent" of your death and ruin. I have proposed to you the gospel of Jesus Christ, the only means by which you can be saved, and you have utterly rejected it. I shall labor no more with you, and from henceforth shall confine my labors to the Gentiles. Paul must refer to the Jews and Gentiles of Corinth particularly, for he preached to the Jews occasionally in other places (see chap. xix. 8-9), and several were brought to the knowledge of the truth.

7. *And he departed thence*. From his former lodging, or that quarter of the city where he had dwelt before with Aquila and Priscilla; and went to lodge with *Justus*, apparently a proselyte. This person is called Titus, and Titus

MATTHEW HENRY

leave the Jews inexcusable, that the ruler of their synagogue believed the gospel, and yet they opposed and blasphemed it. Not only he but his house, believed. Many of the Corinthians, who were Gentiles, *hearing, believed, and were baptized.* Some perhaps came to hear Paul under some convictions of conscience, but it is probable that the most came only for curiosity. But, hearing, *they believed,* and, *believing,* they were *baptized,* and so fixed for Christ.

III. Paul was encouraged by a vision to go on with his work at Corinth (*v.* 9): *The Lord Jesus spoke to Paul in the night by a vision.* 1. He renewed his commission and charge to preach the gospel: "*Be not afraid of the Jews.* Be not afraid of the magistrates of the city. It is the cause of heaven thou art pleading, do it boldly. Do not speak shyly and with caution, but plainly and fully and with courage. Speak out." 2. He assured him of his presence with him, which was sufficient to put life and spirit into him: "*Be not afraid, for I am with thee,* to bear thee out, and to deliver thee from all thy fears, to work with thee, and to confirm the word by signs following." Those that have Christ with them need not to fear, and ought not to shrink. 3. He gave him a warrant of protection: "*No man shall set on thee to hurt thee.*" He does not promise that no man should set on him (for the next news we hear is that he is set upon, and *brought to the judgment-seat, v.* 12), but "*No man shall set on thee to hurt thee.* Whatever trouble they may give thee, there is no real evil in it." 4. He gave him a prospect of success: "*For I have much people in this city.* Therefore do thou go on vigorously and cheerfully in it; for there are many in this city that are to be effectually called by thy ministry." The Lord knows those that are his. "I have them, though they yet know me not, for the Father has given them to me, and of all that were given me I will lose none." *In this city,* though it be a very profane wicked city, full of impurity, and the more so for a temple of Venus there, yet in this heap, that seems to be all chaff, there is wheat; in this ore, that seems to be all dross, there is gold. Let us not despair concerning any place, when even in Corinth Christ had *much people.*

IV. Upon this encouragement he made a long stay there (*v.* 11): He *continued at Corinth a year and six months, teaching the word of God among them.* He stayed so long, 1. For the bringing in of those that were without. God works variously. The people Christ has at Corinth must be called in by degrees. Let Christ's ministers go on in their duty, though their work be not done all at once. 2. For the building up of those that were within. Those that are converted have still need to be *taught the word of God.* No sooner was the good seed sown in that field than the enemy came and sowed tares, the false apostles, of whom Paul in his epistles to the Corinthians complains so much. Soon after Paul came to Corinth, it is supposed, he wrote the first epistle to the Thessalonians, and the second epistle to the same church was written not long after. Ministers may be serving Christ by writing good letters, as well as by preaching good sermons.

Verses 12–17

We have here an account of some disturbance at Corinth, but no great harm done.

I. Paul is accused by the Jews before the Roman governor, *v.* 12, 13. The governor was *Gallio, deputy of Achaia.* This Gallio was elder brother to the famous Seneca, a man of great ingenuousness and great probity, and a man of wonderful good temper; he was called *Sweet Gallio,* and is said to have been universally beloved. How rudely Paul is apprehended, and brought before Gallio; *The Jews made insurrection with one accord against Paul.* They were the ringleaders. They were unanimous in it: they came upon him *with one accord.* They did it with violence and fury: *They made an insurrection* and hurried Paul away *to the judgment-seat.* How falsely Paul is accused before Gallio (*v.* 13): *This fellow persuades men to worship God contrary to the law.* They could not charge him with persuading men not to worship God at all, but only to worship God in a way contrary to the law. But the charge was unjust. The law relating to the temple-service those Jews at Corinth could not observe, and there was no part of their synagogue-worship which Paul contradicted. Thus when people are taught to worship God in Christ, and to worship him in the Spirit, they are ready to quarrel, as if they were taught to worship him contary to the law.

II. Gallio dismisses the cause, and will not take any cognizance of it, *v.* 14, 15. Paul was going about to make his defence, but the judge, being resolved not to pass any sentence upon this cause, would not give himself the trouble of examining it.

JAMIESON, FAUSSET, BROWN

as Caius (Gaius) and the household of Stephanas, with his own hand [Hows]. **many of the Corinthians . . . believed and were baptized**—The beginning of the church gathered there.

9-11. Then spake the Lord to Paul . . . by a vision, Be not afraid . . . no man shall set on thee to hurt thee . . .—From this it would seem that these signal successes were stirring up the wrath of the unbelieving Jews, and probably the apostle feared being driven by violence, as before, from this scene of such promising labor. He is reassured, however, from above. **I have much people in this city**—"whom in virtue of their election to eternal life He already designates as His" (cf. ch. 13:48) [Baumgarten].

continued there a year and six months—the whole period of this stay at Corinth, and not merely up to what is next recorded. *During some part of this period he wrote his* Second Epistle to the Thessalonians. (See Introduction to Second Thessalonians.)

12-17. when Gallio was the deputy—'the proconsul.' See on ch. 13:7. He was brother to the celebrated philosopher Seneca, the tutor of Nero, who passed sentence of death on both.

contrary to the—Jewish—**law**—probably in not requiring the Gentiles to be circumcised.

ADAM CLARKE

Justus, in several MSS. and versions.

8. *Crispus, the chief ruler of the synagogue.* This person held an office of considerable consequence, and therefore his conversion to Christianity must have been very galling to the Jews. It belonged to the chief or ruler of the synagogue to preside in all the assemblies, interpret the law, decide concerning things lawful and unlawful, punish the refractory, excommunicate the rebellious, solemnize marriages, and issue divorces. It is likely that, on the conversion of Crispus, Sosthenes was chosen to succeed him. *Many of the Corinthians.* Those to whom the sacred historian refers were probably Gentiles and were the fruits of the apostle's labors after he had ceased to preach among the Jews.

9. *Then spake the Lord to Paul in the night by a vision.* It is likely that Paul was at this time much discouraged by the violent opposition of the Jews, and probably was in danger of his life (see v. 10), and might have been entertaining serious thoughts of ceasing to preach, or leaving Corinth. To prevent this, and comfort him, God was pleased to give him this vision. *Be not afraid.* That this comfort and assurance were necessary himself shows us in his First Epistle to these Corinthians, chap. ii. 3: "I was with you in weakness, and in fear, and in much trembling."

10. *No man shall set on thee.* No man shall be permitted to "lay violent hands" upon you. It is very likely that the Jews had conspired his death, and his preservation was an act of the especial interposition of Divine Providence. *I have much people in this city.* "In this very city." There are many here who have not resisted My Spirit, and consequently are now under its teachings and are ready to embrace My gospel as soon as you shall declare it unto them.

11. *He continued there a year and six months.* He was now confident that he was under the especial protection of God and therefore continued *teaching the word,* "the doctrine" *of God.* It is very likely that it was during his stay here that he wrote his First Epistle to the Thessalonians, and the Second not long after.

12. *When Gallio was the deputy of Achaia.* The Romans comprehended under the name of Achaia all that part of Greece which lay between Thessaly and the southernmost coasts of Peloponnesus. Pausanias, in *Attic.* vii. 16, says that the Romans were accustomed to send a governor into that country, and that they called him the "governor of Achaia," not of Greece; because the Achaeans, when they subdued Greece, were the leaders in all the Grecian affairs. *Gallio.* This proconsul was eldest brother to the celebrated Seneca, the stoic philosopher, preceptor of Nero, and who is so well-known among the learned by his works. Gallio and Annaeus Mela, his brother, shared in the disgrace of their brother Seneca; and by this tyrant, Nero, whose early years were so promising, the three brothers were put to death. It was to this *Gallio* that Seneca dedicates his book *De Ira.* Seneca describes him as a man of the most amiable mind and manners. *And brought him to the judgment seat.* They had no power to punish any person in the Roman provinces, and therefore were obliged to bring their complaint before the Roman governor. "The powers that be are ordained of God." Had the Jews possessed the power here, Paul had been put to death!

13. *Persuadeth men to worship God contrary to the law.* This accusation was very insidious. The Jews had permission by the Romans to worship their own God in their own way; this the laws allowed. The Roman worship was also established by the law. The Jews probably intended to accuse Paul of acting contrary to both laws. "He is not a Jew, for he does not admit of circumcision; he is not a Gentile, for he preaches against the worship of the gods. He is setting up a worship of his own, in opposition to all laws, and persuading many people to join with him. He is therefore a most dangerous man, and should be put to death."

MATTHEW HENRY

1. He shows himself very ready to do the part of a judge in any matter that it was proper for him to take cognizance of. He *said to the Jews,* "*If it were a matter of wrong, or wicked lewdness,* I should think myself bound *to bear with you.*" It is the duty of magistrates to right the injured, and to animadvert upon the injurious; and if the complaint be not made with all the decorum that might be, yet they should hear it out.

2. He will by no means allow them to make a complaint to him of a thing that was not within his jurisdiction (*v.* 15): "*If it be a question of words and names, and of your law, look you to it; I will be no judge of such matters.*" And therefore *he drove them from the judgment-seat* (*v.* 16). Here was something right in Gallio's conduct, and praiseworthy—that he would not pretend to judge of things he did not understand; that he left the Jews to themselves in matters relating to their own religion, would not himself be the tool of their malice. It was certainly wrong to speak so slightly of a law and religion which he might have known to be of God, and with which he ought to have acquainted himself. He speaks as if he boasted of his ignorance of the scriptures, as if it were below him to take notice of the law of God.

III. The abuse done to Sosthenes, and Gallio's unconcernedness in it, *v.* 17. The parties put a great contempt upon the court, when *they took Sosthenes and beat him before the judgment-seat.* Many conjectures there are concerning this matter, because it is uncertain who this Sosthenes was, and who the Greeks were that abused him. It seems most probable that Sosthenes was a Christian. It is certain that there was one Sosthenes that was a friend of Paul, and well known at Corinth; Paul calls him his brother, and joins him with himself in his first epistle to the church at Corinth (1 Cor. i. 1). He is said to be a *ruler of the synagogue.* As for the Greeks that abused him, it is very probable that they were those that joined with the Jews in opposing the gospel (*v.* 4, 6). They were so enraged against Paul that they beat Sosthenes; and so enraged against Gallio, that they beat him before the judgment-seat, whereby they tell him that they cared not for him, if he would not be their executioner, they would be their own judges. The court put no less a contempt upon the cause, and the persons too. But *Gallio cared for none of these things.* If by this he meant that he cared not for the affronts of bad men, it was commendable. But, if it be meant that he concerned not himself for the abuses done to good men, it carries his indifference too far. Gallio, as a judge, ought to have protected Sosthenes, and restrained and punished the Greeks that assaulted him. Those that see and hear of the sufferings of God's people, and have no sympathy with them, nor concern for them, it being all one to them whether the interests of religion sink or swim, are of the spirit of Gallio here, who, when a good man was abused before his face, *cared for none of these things.*

Verses 18–23

We have here Paul in motion, as we have had him at Corinth for sometime at rest, but in both busy, very busy.

I. Paul's departure from Corinth, *v.* 18. 1. He did not go away till sometime after the trouble he met with there; from other places he had departed when the storm arose, but not from Corinth, because there it had no sooner risen than it fell again. *After this he tarried there yet a good while, v.* 11. While he found he laboured not in vain, he continued labouring. 2. When he went, he took leave of the brethren, solemnly, and with much affection. 3. He took *with him Priscilla and Aquila.* They seemed disposed to remove, and not inclined to stay long at a place, a disposition which may arise from a good principle, and have good effects, and therefore ought not to be condemned in others, though it ought to be suspected in ourselves. 4. At Cenchrea, the port where those that went to sea from Corinth took ship, either Paul or Aquila (for the original does not determine which) had his head shaved, to discharge himself from the vow of a Nazarite: *Having shorn his head at Cenchrea; for he had a vow.* Those that lived in Judæa were, in such a case, bound to do it at the temple: but those who lived in other countries might do it in other places. I see no harm in admitting it concerning Paul, in compliance for a time with the Jews, to whom he *became as a Jew* (1 Cor. ix. 20), *that he might win upon them.*

II. Paul's calling *at Ephesus,* which was the metropolis of the Lesser Asia. 1. *There he left Aquila and Priscilla.* They might be serviceable to the interests of the gospel at Ephesus. Paul intended shortly to settle there for some time. Aquila and Priscilla

JAMIESON, FAUSSET, BROWN

If it were a matter of wrong or wicked lewdness—any offense punishable by the magistrate.

if it be a question of words and names, and of your law . . . I will be no judge . . .—in this only laying down the proper limits of his office. **drave them . . .**—annoyed at such a case.

all the Greeks—the Gentile spectators. **took Sosthenes**—perhaps the successor of Crispus, and certainly the head of the accusing party. It is very improbable that this was the same Sosthenes as the apostle afterwards calls "his brother" (I Cor. 1:1). **and beat him before the judgment-seat**—under the very eye of the judge.

And Gallio cared for none of those things—nothing loath, perhaps, to see these turbulent Jews, for whom probably he felt contempt, themselves getting what they hoped to inflict on another, and indifferent to whatever was beyond the range of his office and case. His brother eulogizes his loving and lovable manners. Religious indifference, under the influence of an easy and amiable temper, reappears from age to age.

18. Paul . . . tarried . . . yet a good while—During his long residence at Corinth, Paul planted other churches in Achaia (II Cor. 1:1). **then took . . . leave of the brethren, and sailed . . . into**—rather, 'for'—**Syria**—to Antioch, the starting point of all the missions to the Gentiles, which he feels to be for the present concluded. **with him Priscilla and Aquila**—In this order the names also occur in vs. 26 (according to the true reading); cf. Rom. 16: 3 and II Tim. 4:19, which seem to imply that the wife was the more prominent and helpful to the Church. Silas and Timotheus doubtless accompanied the apostle, as also Erastus, Gaius, and Aristarchus (ch. 19:22, 29). Of Silas, as Paul's associate, we read no more. His name occurs last in connection with Peter and the churches of Asia Minor [WEBTER and WILKINSON]. **having shorn his head in Cenchrea**—the eastern harbor of Corinth, about ten miles distant, where a church had been formed (Rom. 16:1). **for he—Paul—had a vow**—That it was the Nazarite vow (Num. 6) is not likely. It was probably one made in one of his seasons of difficulty or danger, in prosecution of which he cuts off his hair and hastens to Jerusalem to offer the requisite sacrifice within the prescribed thirty days (JOSEPHUS, *Jewish War,* 2. 15. 1). This explains the haste with which he leaves Ephesus (vs. 21), and the subsequent observance, on the recommendation of the brethren, of a similar vow (ch. 21:24). This one at Corinth was voluntary, and shows that even in heathen countries he systematically studied the prejudices of his Jewish brethren. **19. he came to Ephesus**—the capital of the Roman province of Asia. (See Introduction to Epistle to Ephesians.) It was a sail, right across from the west to the east side of the Ægean Sea, of some eight or ten days, with a fair wind. **left them**—Aquila and Priscilla

ADAM CLARKE

14. *Paul was now about to open his mouth.* He was about to enter on his defense; but Gallio, perceiving that the prosecution was through envy and malice, would not put Paul to any further trouble, but determined the matter as follows. *If it were a matter of wrong.* Of "injustice"; anything contrary to the rights of the subject. *Or wicked lewdness.* "Destructive mischief." *Reason would that I should bear with you.* "According to reason, or the merit of the case, I should patiently hear you."

15. *But if it be a question of words.* Concerning "doctrine" *and names*—whether the person called Jesus be the Person you call the Messiah. *And of your law*—any particular nicety concerning that law which is peculiar to yourselves. *Look ye to it*—settle the business among yourselves; the Roman government does not meddle with such matters; and I will not take upon me to decide in a case that does not concern my office.

16. *And he drave them from the judgment seat.* He saw that their accusation was both frivolous and vexatious, and he ordered them to depart, and the assembly to disperse. The word which we translate *he drave* does not signify here any act of violence on the part of Gallio or the Roman officers, but simply an authoritative dismission.

17. *Then all the Greeks took Sosthenes.* As this man is termed the chief ruler of the synagogue, it is probable that he had lately succeeded Crispus in that office (see v. 8); and that he was known either to have embraced Christianity or to have favored the cause of Paul. He is supposed to be the same person whom Paul associates with himself in the First Epistle to the Corinthians, chap. i. 1. But why should *the Greeks* beat Sosthenes? I have in the above note proceeded on the supposition that this outrage was committed by the Jews; and my reason for it is this: *The Greeks* is omitted by several MSS., and it is much more likely that the Jews beat one of their own rulers through envy at his conversion than that the Greeks should do so. *And Gallio cared for none of those things.* "And Gallio did not concern himself," did not intermeddle with any of these things. It is not very likely, however, that Gallio saw this outrage; for, though it was before the judgment seat, it probably did not take place till Gallio had left the court; and though he might be told of it, he left the matter to the lictors and would not interfere. The conduct of Gallio has been, in this case, greatly censured, and I think with manifest injustice. In the business brought before his tribunal, no man could have followed a more prudent or equitable course. His whole conduct showed that it was his opinion that the civil magistrate had nothing to do with religious opinions or the concerns of conscience, in matters where the safety of the state was not implicated. He therefore refused to make the subject a matter of legal discussion.

18. *And Paul . . . tarried there yet a good while.* The persecuting Jews plainly saw from the manner in which the proconsul had conducted this business that they could have no hope of raising a state persecution against the apostles, and the laws provided so amply for the personal safety of every Roman citizen that they were afraid to proceed any further in their violence. It could not be unknown that Paul was possessed of the right of Roman citizenship, and therefore his person was sacred as long as he did nothing contrary to the laws. *Having shorn his head in Cenchrea.* But who was it that had shorn his head? Paul or Aquila? Some think the latter, who had bound himself by the Nazarite vow, probably before he became a Christian; and being under that vow, his conscience would not permit him to disregard it. There is nothing in the text that absolutely obliges us to understand this action as belonging to Paul. It seems to have been the act of Aquila alone; and therefore both Paul and Priscilla are mentioned before Aquila; and it is natural to refer the vow to the latter. Yet there are certainly some weighty reasons why the vow should be referred to Paul, and not to Aquila; I cannot help leaning to the latter opinion. *Cenchrea.* This was a port on the east side of the isthmus of Corinth, opposite to the Lecheum, which was the other port on the west. And it is

MATTHEW HENRY

might dispose the minds of many to give Paul, when he should come among them, a favourable reception. 2. There he preached *to the Jews in their synagogue. He entered into the synagogue*, not as a hearer, but as a preacher, for *there he reasoned with the Jews.* Though he had abandoned the Jews at Corinth, he did not, for their sakes, decline the synagogues of the Jews in other places, but still made the first offer of the gospel to them. We must not condemn a whole body or denomination of men, for the sake of some that conduct themselves ill. 3. The Jews at Ephesus courted his stay with them (*v.* 20): *They desired him to tarry longer with them.* These were more noble, and better bred, than those Jews at Corinth, and it was a sign that God had not quite cast away his people, but had a remnant among them. 4. Paul would not stay with them now: *He consented not; but bade them farewell.* He *must by all means keep this feast at Jerusalem.* Which of the feasts it was we are not told. 5. He intimated his purpose, after this journey, to come and spend some time at Ephesus. It is good to have opportunities in reserve, when one good work is over to have another to apply ourselves to: *I will return again to you*, but he inserts that necessary proviso, *if God will.* Our times are in God's hand; we purpose, but he disposes; and therefore we must make all our promises with submission to the will of God.

III. Paul's visit to Jerusalem; a short visit it was. He came by sea to the port that lay next to Jerusalem. *He sailed from Ephesus* (*v.* 21), *and landed at Cæsarea, v.* 22. He went *up*, *and saluted the church*, by which, I think, is plainly meant the church at Jerusalem. It was a very friendly visit that he made them, in pure kindness to testify his hearty goodwill to them. The increase of our new friends should not make us forget our old ones, but it should be a pleasure to good men, to revive former acquaintance. He took care to keep up a good correspondence with them, that they might both congratulate and wish well to one another's comfort and success. It was but a short visit. He went *up, and saluted them*, and made no stay among them. It was designed but for a transient interview. God's people are dispersed and scattered; yet it is good to see one another sometimes.

IV. His return through those countries where he had formerly preached the gospel. *He went and spent some time in Antioch*, whence he was first sent out to preach among the Gentiles, *ch.* xiii. 1. He went down to Antioch, to refresh himself with the sight of the ministers there; and a very good refreshment it is to a faithful minister to have for awhile the society of his brethren. *Thence he went over the country of Galatia and Phrygia in order*, where he had preached the gospel, and planted churches. These country churches (for such they were, Gal. i. 2, and we read not of any city in Galatia where a church was) Paul visited *in order* as they lay, watering what he had been instrumental to plant, and *strengthening all the disciples*. Paul's countenancing them was encouraging them; but that was not all: he preached that to them which strengthened them. Disciples need to be strengthened. Ministers must do what they can to strengthen them by directing them to Christ, whose strength is perfected in their weakness.

Verses 24-28

The sacred history leaves Paul upon his travels, and goes here to meet Apollos at Ephesus.

I. Here is an account of his character.

1. He was *a Jew, born at Alexandria* in Egypt, but of Jewish parents.

2. He was a man well fitted for public service. He was *an eloquent man, and mighty in the scriptures.* He had a great command of language: He *came to Ephesus*, being *mighty in the scriptures*, having an excellent faculty of expounding scripture. He was not only ready in the scriptures, able to quote texts offhand, and tell you where to find them, but he was *mighty in the scriptures.* He understood the sense and meaning of them, he knew how to make use of them and to apply them, how to reason out of the scriptures, and to reason strongly.

3. He *was instructed in the way of the Lord;* that is, he had some acquaintance with the doctrine of Christ, had obtained some general notions of the gospel and the principles of Christianity. He was taught something of Christ and the way of salvation by him. Those that are to teach others must first be themselves taught the word of the Lord, not only to talk of it, but to walk in it. It is not enough to have our tongues tuned to the word of the Lord, but we must have our feet directed into the way of the Lord.

4. Yet he *knew only the baptism of John.* He knew *the preparing of the way of the Lord*, rather than the way of the Lord itself. He had himself been baptized

JAMIESON, FAUSSET, BROWN

—there, but he himself entered into the synagogue—merely taking advantage of the vessel putting in there. **and reasoned with the Jews**—the *tense* here not being the usual one denoting *continuous* action (as in ch. 17:2; 18:4), but that expressing *a transient act.* He had been forbidden to preach the word in Asia (ch. 16:6), but he would not consider that as precluding this passing exercise of his ministry when Providence brought him to its capital; nor did it follow that the prohibition was still in force. **20. when they desired him to tarry**—The Jews seldom rose against the Gospel till the successful preaching of it stirred them up, and there was no time for that here. **21. I must . . . keep this feast**—probably Pentecost, presenting a noble opportunity of preaching the Gospel. **but I will return**—the fulfilment of which promise is recorded in ch. 19:1.

22. And when he had landed at Cæsarea—where he left the vessel. **and gone up**—i.e., to Jerusalem—**and saluted the church**—In these few words does the historian despatch the apostle's FOURTH VISIT TO JERUSALEM after his conversion. The expression "going *up*" is invariably used of a journey to the metropolis; and thence he naturally "went *down* to Antioch." Perhaps the vessel reached too late for the feast, as he seems to have done nothing in Jerusalem beyond "saluting the Church," and privately offering the sacrifice with which his vow (vs. 18) would conclude. It is left to be understood, as on his arrival from his first missionary tour, that "when he was come, and had gathered the church together, he rehearsed all that God had done with him" (ch. 14:27) on this his *second missionary journey.*

23. Ch. 21:16. PAUL'S THIRD AND LAST MISSIONARY JOURNEY—HE VISITS THE CHURCHES OF GALATIA AND PHRYGIA. **and after he had spent some time there**—but probably not long. **he departed**—little thinking, probably, he was never more to return to Antioch. **went over all . . . Galatia and Phrygia in order**—visiting the several churches in succession. See on ch. 16:6. Galatia is mentioned first here, as he would come to it first from Antioch. It was on this visitation that he ordained the weekly collection (I Cor. 16:1, 2), which has been since adopted generally, and converted into a public usage throughout Christendom. Timotheus and Erastus, Gaius and Aristarchus, appear to have accompanied him on this journey (ch. 19:22, 29; II Cor. 1: 1), and from II Corinthians we may presume, Titus also. The details of this visit, as of the former (ch. 16:6), are not given.

24-28. EPISODE CONCERNING APOLLOS AT EPHESUS AND IN ACHAIA. This is one of the most interesting and suggestive incidental narratives in this precious history. **24, 25, a . . . Jew named Apollos**—a contraction from Apollonius. **born at Alexandria**—the celebrated city of Egypt on the southeastern shore of the Mediterranean, called after its founder, Alexander the Great. Nowhere was there such a fusion of Greek, Jewish, and Oriental peculiarities, and an intelligent Jew educated in that city could hardly fail to manifest all these elements in his mental character. **eloquent**—turning his Alexandrian culture to high account. **and mighty in the scriptures**—his eloquence enabling him to express clearly and enforce skilfully what, as a Jew, he had gathered from a diligent study of the Old Testament Scriptures. **came to Ephesus**—on what errand is not known. **This man was instructed in the way of the Lord . . . knowing only the baptism of John**—He was instructed, probably, by some disciple of the Baptist, in the whole circle of John's teaching concerning Jesus, but no more: he had yet to learn the new light which the outpouring of the Spirit at Pentecost had thrown upon the Redeemer's death and resurrection; as appears from ch. 19:2, 3.

ADAM CLARKE

likely that it was at Cenchrea that Paul took shipping for Syria, as it would be more convenient for him and a shorter passage to embark at Cenchrea in order to go by the Aegean Sea to Syria than to embark at the Lecheum and sail down into the Mediterranean.

19. *He came to Ephesus.* Where it appears he spent but one Sabbath. It is supposed that Paul left Aquila and Priscilla at this place, and that he went on alone to Jerusalem, for it is certain they were at Ephesus when Apollos arrived there. See vv. 24 and 26. Ephesus was, at the time in which Paul visited it, one of the most flourishing cities of Asia Minor. It abounded with the most eminent orators and philosophers in the world, and was adorned with the most splendid buildings. Here was that famous temple of Diana, reputed one of the seven wonders of the world. This city is now under the dominion of the Turks and is in a state of almost entire ruin.

21. *I must . . . keep this feast.* Most likely the Passover, at which he wished to attend for the purpose of seeing many of his friends and having the most favorable opportunity to preach the gospel to thousands who would attend at Jerusalem on that occasion. The whole of this clause, *I must by all means keep this feast that cometh in Jerusalem,* is wanting in some MSS. Without this clause the verse will read thus: "But he bade them farewell, saying, I will return again unto you, if God will." And this he did before the expiration of that same year, chap. xix. 1, and spent three years with them, chap. xx. 31, extending and establishing the church at that place.

22. *Landed at Caesarea.* This must have been Caesarea in Palestine. *Gone up.* To Jerusalem, though the name is not mentioned; but this is a common form of speech in the Evangelists, Jerusalem being always meant when this expression was used. For the word "to go up" is often used absolutely to signify "to go to Jerusalem"; e.g., "Go ye up unto this feast: I go not up yet," John vii. 8; "But when his brethren were gone up, then went he also up unto the feast," v. 10; "There were certain Greeks . . . that came up to worship," John xii. 20. *Saluted the church.* That is, the church at Jerusalem, called emphatically *The church* because it was the first church—the mother or apostolic church; and from it all other Christian churches proceeded. *Went down to Antioch.* That is, Antioch in Syria, as the word is generally to be understood when without addition; so Caesarea is always to be understood Caesarea in Palestine when without the addition of "Philippi."

23. *In order. Kathexes,* a word peculiar to Luke. See his Gospel, chap. i. 1; viii. 1; and his history of the Acts, chap. iii. 24; xi. 4, and the place above—the only places where this word occurs in the New Testament. It properly signifies "in order, distinctly, particularly." If Paul went up to Jerusalem at this time, which we are left to infer, for Luke has not expressed it (v. 22), it was his fourth journey thither.

24. *A certain Jew named Apollos.* It is strange that we should find a Jew, not only with a Roman name, as *Aquila*, an "eagle," but with the name of one of the false gods, as *Apollos. Born at Alexandria.* This was a celebrated city of Egypt built by Alexander the Great, from whom it took its name. It was seated on the Mediterranean Sea. It was in this city that Ptolemy Soter founded the famous academy called the Museum, in which a society of learned men devoted themselves to philosophical studies. Some of the most celebrated schools of antiquity flourished here; and here was the Tower of Pharos, esteemed one of the seven wonders of the world. *An eloquent man.* Having strong rhetorical powers; highly cultivated, no doubt, in the Alexandrian schools. *Mighty in the scriptures.* Thoroughly acquainted with the law and prophets, and well skilled in the Jewish method of interpreting them.

25. *This man was instructed in the way of the Lord.* He was "catechized," initiated, in the way, the "doctrine," of Jesus as the Christ.

MATTHEW HENRY

only with the baptism of John, but was not baptized with the Holy Ghost.

II. We have here the employment and improvement of his gifts at Ephesus.

1. He there made a very good use of his gifts in public. He was willing to be employed (*v.* 25): *Being fervent in the Spirit, he spoke and taught diligently the things of the Lord.* Though he had not the miraculous gifts of the Spirit, he made use of the gifts he had. We have seen how Apollos was qualified with a good head and a good tongue: he was *an eloquent man, and mighty in the scriptures.* Let us now see what he had further to recommend him as a preacher; and his example is recommended to the imitation of all preachers. He was a lively affectionate preacher; he had a good heart; he was *fervent in Spirit.* He had in him a great deal of divine fire as well as divine light. This appeared both in his forwardness to preach when he was called to it, and in his fervency in his preaching. He preached as one in earnest, and that had his heart in his work. Many are fervent in spirit, but are weak in knowledge, and, on the other hand, many are eloquent enough, and mighty in the scriptures, but they have no life or fervency. Here was a complete *man of God*, full both of divine knowledge and of divine affections. He was an industrious laborious preacher. *He spoke and taught diligently.* He took pains in his preaching, and he did not offer that to God, or to the synagogue, that either cost nothing or cost *him* nothing. *He taught diligently, accurately, exactly;* everything he said was well-weighed. He was an evangelical preacher. Though he knew only the baptism of John, yet that was the beginning of the gospel of Christ, and to that he kept close; for he taught the things of the Lord Christ, the things that tended to make way for him. He was a courageous preacher: *He began to speak boldly in the synagogue*, as one who, having put confidence in God, did not fear the face of man. *In the synagogue*, where the Jews not only were present, but had power, there he preached the things of God.

2. He there made a good increase of his gifts. *Aquila and Priscilla expounded to him the way of God more perfectly.* Aquila and Priscilla heard him preach in the synagogue. They encouraged his ministry, by a diligent and constant attendance upon it. Thus young ministers, that are hopeful, should be countenanced by grown Christians. Finding him defective in his knowledge of Christianity, *they took him to them* and *expounded to him the way of God more perfectly.* They did not despise him themselves, or disparage him to others; did not call him a young raw preacher, not fit to come into a pulpit. They communicated what they knew to him, and gave him a clear, methodical account of those things which before he had but confused notions of. See an instance of truly Christian charity in Aquila and Priscilla. Aquila did not undertake to speak in the synagogue, because he had not such gifts for public work as Apollos had; but he furnished Apollos with matter, and then left him to clothe it with acceptable words. Instructing young Christians and young ministers privately in conversation is a piece of very good service. See an instance of great humility in Apollos. He was a very bright young man, of great parts and learning, and one mightily cried up and followed; and yet, finding that Aquila and Priscilla could speak intelligently and experimentally of the things of God, though they were but mechanics, he was glad to receive instructions from them, to be shown by them his defects and mistakes. Young scholars may gain a great deal by converse with old Christians, as young students in the law may by old practitioners. Apollos, though he *was instructed in the way of the Lord*, did not rest in the knowledge he had attained. Those that know much should covet to know more. Here is an instance of a good woman doing good with the knowledge God had given her in private converse.

III. Here is his preferment to the service of the church of Corinth. Paul had set the wheels a-going at Corinth. Many were stirred up by his preaching to receive the gospel, and they needed to be confirmed. Paul was gone and now there was a fair occasion in this vacancy for Apollos to set in, who was fitted rather to water than to plant. His call to this service. He himself inclined to do: *He was disposed to pass into Achaia.* Apollos thought there might be some work for him, and God disposed his mind that way. His friends encouraged him to go; they gave him letters of recommendation. Though those at Ephesus had a great loss of his labours, they did not grudge those in Achaia the benefit of them; but, on the contrary, used their interest in them to introduce him. His success in this service. Believers were greatly edified: *He helped those much who had believed through grace.* Those who believe in Christ, it is through grace that they believe; it is *not of themselves, it is*

JAMIESON, FAUSSET, BROWN

being fervent in the spirit—His heart warm, and conscious, probably, of his gifts and attainments, he burned to impart to others the truth he had himself received. **he spake and taught diligently**—rather, 'accurately' (it is the same word as is rendered "perfectly" in vs. 26).

26. speak boldly in the synagogue, whom when Aquila and Priscilla heard—joying to observe the extent of Scripture knowledge and evangelical truth which he displayed, and the fervency, courage, and eloquence with which he preached the truth. **they took him unto them**—privately—**and expounded unto him the way of God more perfectly**—opening up those truths, to him as yet unknown, on which the Spirit had shed such glorious light. (In what appears to be the true reading of this verse, Priscilla is put before Aquila, as in vs. 18, on which see; she being probably the more intelligent and devoted of the two.) One cannot but observe how providential it was that this couple should have been left at Ephesus when Paul sailed thence for Syria; and no doubt it was chiefly to pave the way for the better understanding of this episode that the fact is expressly mentioned by the historian in vs. 19. We see here also an example of not only *lay* agency (as it is called), but *female* agency of the highest kind and with the most admirable fruit. Nor can one help admiring the humility and teachableness of so gifted a teacher in sitting at the feet of a Christian woman and her husband.

27, 28. And when he was disposed—'minded,' 'resolved'—**to pass into Achaia**—of which Corinth, on the opposite coast (see on vs. 1), was the capital; there to proclaim that Gospel which he now more fully comprehended. **the brethren**—We had not before heard of such gathered at Ephesus. But the desire of the Jews to whom Paul preached to retain him among them for some time (vs. 20), and his promise to return to them (vs. 21), seem to indicate some drawing towards the Gospel, which, no doubt, the zealous private labors of Priscilla and Aquila would ripen into discipleship. **wrote, exhorting the disciples to receive him**—a beautiful specimen of 'letters of recommendation' (as ch. 15: 23, 25-27, and see II Cor. 3:1); by which, as well as by interchange of deputations, etc., the early churches maintained active Christian fellowship with each other. **when he was come, helped them much**—was a great acquisition to the Achaian brethren. **which believed through grace**—one of those incidental expressions which show that *faith's being a production of God's grace in the heart* was so current and recognized a truth that it was taken for granted, as a necessary consequence of the general system of grace, rather than expressly insisted on. (It is against the natural order of the words to read them, as BENGEL, MEYER, and others, do, 'helped through grace those who believed.')

ADAM CLARKE

Being fervent in the spirit. Being full of zeal to propagate the truth of God, he taught diligently, "accurately" (so the word should be translated), the things of Christ as far as he could know them through the ministry of John the Baptist; for it appears he knew nothing more of Christ than what John preached.

26. *They took him unto them.* This "eloquent man, and mighty in the scriptures," who was even a public teacher, was not ashamed to be indebted to the instructions of a Christian woman, in matters that concerned not only his own salvation but also the work of the ministry in which he was engaged.

27. *When he was disposed to pass into Achaia.* There is a very long and important addition here in the Codex Bezae, of which the following is a translation: "But certain Corinthians, who sojourned at Ephesus, and heard him, entreated him to pass over with them to their country. Then, when he had given his consent, the Ephesians wrote to the disciples at Corinth, that they should receive this man. Who, when he was come . . ."

Which had believed through grace. These words may refer either to Apollo or to the people at Corinth. It was through grace that they had believed, and it was through grace that Apollo was enabled to help them much.

TODAY'S DICTIONARY OF THE BIBLE:

Apollos, a Jew "born at Alexandria," a man well versed in the Scriptures and eloquent (Acts 18:24; NIV, "learned"). He came to Ephesus (about A.D. 49), where he spake "boldly" in the synagogue (18:26), although he did not know as yet that Jesus of Nazareth was the Messiah. Aquila and Priscilla instructed him more perfectly in "the way of God"—i.e., in the knowledge of Christ. He then proceeded to Corinth, where he met Paul (Acts 18:27; 19:1). Very useful in watering the good seed Paul had sown (1 Cor. 1:12), he was instrumental in leading many to Christ. His disciples were much attached to him (1 Cor. 3:4-7, 22). He was with Paul at Ephesus when he wrote the First Epistle to the Corinthians; and Paul makes kindly reference to him in his letter to Titus (3:13). Some have supposed that he was the author of the Epistle to the Hebrews.

MATTHEW HENRY

God's gift to them. Those who through grace do believe, yet still have need of help. Faithful ministers are capable of being in many ways helpful to those who through grace do believe, and it is their business to help them. Unbelievers were greatly mortified. Their objections were fully answered, their mouths were stopped, and their faces filled with shame (*v.* 28): *He mightily convinced the Jews, and that publicly.* He did it *earnestly*, he took pains to do it. He did it effectually and to universal satisfaction. If the Jews were but convinced of this—that Jesus is Christ, even their own law would teach them to hear him. The business of ministers is to preach Christ. The way he took to convince them was *by the scriptures*; thence he fetched his arguments. Ministers must be able not only to preach the truth, but to prove it and defend it, and to convince gainsayers with meekness and yet with power.

JAMIESON, FAUSSET, BROWN

For he mightily convinced the Jews—The word is very strong: 'stoutly bore them down in argument,' 'vigorously argued them down', and the *tense* implies that he *continued* to do it, or that this was the characteristic of his ministry. **showing by the scriptures that Jesus was Christ**—Rather, that the Christ (or Messiah) was Jesus. This expression, when compared with vs. 25, seems to imply a richer testimony than with his partial knowledge he was at first able to bear; and the power with which he bore down all opposition in argument is that which made him such an acquisition to the brethren. Thus his ministry would be as good as another visitation to the Achaian churches by the apostle himself (see I Cor. 3:6) and the more as, in so far as he was indebted for it to Priscilla and Aquila, it would have a decidedly *Pauline* cast.

ADAM CLARKE

28. *He mightily convinced the Jews.* "He vehemently confuted" the Jews; *and that publickly,* not in private conferences, but in his public preaching; *shewing by the scriptures* of the Old Testament, which the Jews received as divinely inspired, *that Jesus,* who had lately appeared among them and whom they had crucified, *was the Christ,* the promised Messiah, and that there was salvation in none other; and that they must receive Him as the Messiah in order to escape the wrath to come.

MATTHEW HENRY — CHAPTER 19

Verses 1–7

Ephesus was a city of great note in Asia, famous for a temple built there to Diana, which was one of the wonders of the world: thither *Paul came to preach the gospel while Apollos was at Corinth* (*v.* 1); while he was watering there, Paul was planting here, and went on in the new work that was cut out for him at Ephesus with the more cheerfulness and satisfaction, because he knew that such an able minister as Apollos was now at Corinth, carrying on the good work there. Paul having gone through the country of Galatia and Phrygia, having *passed through the upper coasts, came to Ephesus,* where he had left Aquila and Priscilla, and there found them. He met with some disciples there, who professed faith in Christ as the true Messiah, but were as yet in the first and lowest form in the school of Christ, under his usher John the Baptist. They were in number *about twelve* (*v.* 7).

I. How Paul catechised them.

1. They did believe in the Son of God; but Paul enquires whether they had *received the Holy Ghost,*—whether they had been acquainted with, and had admitted, this revelation? This was not all; extraordinary gifts of the Holy Ghost were conferred upon the apostles and other disciples after Christ's ascension. Had they participated in these gifts? "*Have you received the Holy Ghost since you believed?* Have you had that seal of the truth of Christ's doctrine in yourselves?" There are graces of the Spirit given to all believers, which are as earnests to them. But many are deceived in this matter, thinking they have received the Holy Ghost when really they have not. As there are pretenders to the gifts of the Holy Ghost, so there are to his graces and comforts; we should therefore strictly examine ourselves, Have we received the Holy Ghost since we believed? The tree will be known by its fruits. Do we bring forth the fruits of the Spirit? Do we walk in the Spirit?

2. They owned their ignorance in this matter: *Whether there be a Holy Ghost* is more than we know. That there is a promise of the Holy Ghost we know from the scriptures and that this promise will be fulfilled in its season we doubt not. We have not so much as heard whether the Holy Ghost be indeed yet given. The gospel light, like that of the morning, shone more and more, gradually; not only clearer and clearer, but further and further.

3. Paul enquired how they came to be baptized, if they knew nothing of the Holy Ghost. *Unto what then were you baptized?* This is strange and unaccountable. What! baptized, and yet know nothing of the Holy Ghost? Ignorance of the Holy Ghost is as inconsistent with a sincere profession of Christianity as ignorance of Christ is. Let us often consider unto what we were baptized, that we may live up to our baptism.

4. They own that they were baptized *unto John's baptism,* that is, they were baptized in the name of John, by some disciple of his, that ignorantly kept up his name as the head of a party. As it is here expressed, *unto John's baptism.*

5. Paul explains to them the true intent and meaning of John's baptism, as principally referring to Jesus Christ. Those that have been left in ignorance, or led into error, by any infelicities of their education, should be compassionately instructed and better taught, as these disciples were by Paul. He owns that John's baptism was a very good thing, as far as it went: *John verily baptized with the baptism of repentance.* He shows them that John's baptism had a further reference. They should believe on him who should come after him, that is, on Christ Jesus,—that his baptism of repentance was designed only to prepare the way of the Lord, whom he directed

JAMIESON, FAUSSET, BROWN — CHAPTER 19

Vss. 1-41. Signal Success of Paul at Ephesus. **1-3. while Apollos was at Corinth**—where his ministry was so powerful that a formidable party in the Church of that city gloried in his type of preaching in preference to Paul's (I Cor. 1:12; 3:4), no doubt from the marked infusion of Greek philosophic culture which distinguished it, and which the apostle studiously avoided (I Cor. 2:1-5). **Paul having passed through the upper coasts**—'parts,' the interior of Asia Minor, which, with reference to the seacoast, was elevated. **came to Ephesus**—thus fulfilling his promise (ch. 18:21). **finding certain disciples**—in the same stage of Christian knowledge as Apollos at first, newly arrived, probably, and having had no communication as yet with the church at Ephesus.

Have ye received the Holy Ghost since ye believed?—rather, 'Received ye the Holy Ghost when ye believed?' implying, certainly, that the one did not of necessity carry the other along with it (see on ch. 8:14-17). Why this question was asked, we cannot tell; but it was probably in consequence of something that passed between them from which the apostle was led to suspect the imperfection of their light.

We have not so much as heard whether there be any Holy Ghost—This cannot be the meaning, since the personality and office of the Holy Ghost, in connection with Christ, formed an especial subject of the Baptist's teaching. Literally, the words are, 'We did not even hear whether the Holy Ghost was (given); meaning, at the time of their baptism. That the word 'given' is the right supplement, as in John 7:39, seems plain from the nature of the case.

4. Then said Paul, John . . . baptized with the baptism of—water unto—**repentance, saying unto the people, that they should believe on him which should come after him**—i.e., who should baptize with the Holy Ghost. The point of contrast is not between John and Christ personally, but between the *water* baptism of John unto *repentance,* and the promised baptism of *the Spirit* from the hands of his coming Master unto *new life.* As to all the facts, or at least the significancy, of this baptism, which made the whole life and work of Christ another thing from what it was conceived to be before it was vouchsafed, these simple disciples were unenlightened.

ADAM CLARKE — CHAPTER 19

1. *Paul having passed through the upper coasts.* That is, through those parts of Asia Minor that lay eastward of Ephesus, such as Galatia, Phrygia, and probably Lycaonia and Lydia; and it is in reference to Ephesus that these are called the *upper* coasts.

2. *Have ye received the Holy Ghost?* It is likely that these were Asiatic Jews, who, having been at Jerusalem about twenty-six years before this, had heard the preaching of John and received his baptism, believing in the coming Christ, whom John had proclaimed; but it appears that till this time they had got no further instruction in the Christian religion. Paul, perceiving this, asked them if they had received the Holy Ghost since they believed. For it was the common privilege of the disciples of Christ to receive not only the ordinary graces but also the extraordinary gifts of the Holy Spirit, and thus the disciples of Christ differed from those of John and of all others. John baptized with water; Jesus baptized with the Holy Ghost. *We have not so much as heard whether.* That is, they had not heard that there were particular gifts and graces of the Holy Spirit to be received. They could not mean that they had not heard of the Holy Spirit; for John, in his baptism, announced Christ as about to baptize with the Holy Ghost, Matt. iii. 11; Luke iii. 16. But they simply meant that they had not heard that this Spirit, in His gifts, had been given to or received by anyone.

4. *That they should believe on him which should come after.* John baptized them with the baptism of repentance; this was common to all the baptisms administered by the Jews to proselytes. But telling them that they should believe on Him who was coming was peculiar to John's baptism.

MATTHEW HENRY

them to: *Behold the Lamb of God.* He was only the harbinger,—Christ is the Prince. His baptism was the porch which you were to pass through, not the house you were to rest in.

6. When they were thus shown the error they thankfully accepted the discovery, and *were baptized in the name of the Lord Jesus, v.* 5. When they came to understand things better, they desired to be *baptized in the name of the Lord Jesus,* and were so. It does not therefore follow hence that there was not an agreement between John's baptism and Christ's, for those that were here baptized *in the name of the Lord Jesus* had never been so baptized before.

II. How Paul conferred the extraordinary gifts of the Holy Ghost upon them, *v.* 6. Paul solemnly *prayed to God laying his hands on them.* God granted the thing he prayed for: *The Holy Ghost came upon them, and they spoke with tongues and prophesied.* They had the Spirit of prophesy, that they might understand the mysteries of the kingdom of God themselves, and the gift of tongues, that they might preach them to every nation and language. Oh, what a wonderful change was here made on a sudden in these men! those that but just now had *not so much as heard that there was any Holy Ghost* are now themselves filled with the Holy Ghost.

Verses 8–12

Paul is here very busy at Ephesus.

I. He begins, as usual, in the Jews' synagogue.

1. Where he preached to them: in their synagogue (*v.* 8). Where there were no Christian assemblies yet formed, he frequented the Jewish assemblies. Paul went into the synagogue, because there he had them together, and had them, it might be hoped, in a good frame.

2. What he preached to them: *The things concerning the kingdom of God* among men, the great things which concerned God's dominion over all men and favour to them, and men's subjection to God and happiness in God. Or, more particularly, *the things concerning the kingdom of the Messiah.* He gave them a right notion of this kingdom, and showed them their mistakes about it.

3. How he preached to them. He preached argumentatively: he disputed; gave reasons, and answered objections, that they might not only believe, but might see cause to believe. He preached affectionately: he persuaded. Paul was a moving preacher, and was master of the art of persuasion. He preached undauntedly, and with a holy resolution: he spoke boldly.

4. How long he preached to them: *For the space of three months,* which was a competent time allowed them to consider of it.

5. What success his preaching had among them. There were some that were persuaded to believe in Christ. Many continued in their infidelity, and were confirmed in their prejudices against Christianity. Now that he settled among them, and his word came more closely to their consciences, they were soon weary of him. They had an invincible aversion to the gospel of Christ themselves: they were *hardened, and believed not.* They did their utmost to raise and keep up in others an aversion to the gospel. *They spoke evil of that way before the multitude,* to prejudice them against it. Though they could not show any manner of evil in it, yet they said all manner of evil concerning it.

II. When he had carried the matter as far as it would go in the synagogue of the Jews, he left the synagogue. They drove him from them by their railing at those things which he spoke *concerning the kingdom of God*: they hated to be reformed, hated to be instructed, and therefore *he departed from them.*

1. When Paul departed from the Jews he took the disciples with him, and *separated them.* Lest they should be infected with the poisonous tongues of those blasphemers, he separated those who believed, to be the foundation of a Christian church. When Paul departed there needed no more to separate the disciples; let him go where he will, they will follow him.

2. When Paul separated from the synagogue he *disputed daily in the school of one Tyrannus.* He had by this separation a double advantage. (1) That now his opportunities were more frequent. In the synagogue he could only preach every sabbath day (*ch.* xiii. 43), but now he disputed daily. (2) That now they were more open. To the synagogue of the Jews none might come but Jews or proselytes; Gentiles were excluded. In the school of Tyrannus, both Jews and Greeks attended his ministry, *v.* 10. Some think this school of Tyrannus was a divinity-school of the Jews, and such a one they commonly had in their great cities besides their synagogue; they called it *Bethmidrash, the house of enquiry.* But

JAMIESON, FAUSSET, BROWN

5-7. When they heard this—not the mere words reported in vs. 4, but *the subject expounded* according to the tenor of those words. **they were baptized**—not however by Paul himself (I Cor. 1:14). **in the name of the Lord Jesus**—into the whole fulness of the new economy, as now opened up to their believing minds. **And when Paul had laid his hands upon them,... they spake with tongues . . .**—See on ch. 10:44, 45.

8-10. he went into the synagogue and spake boldly for . . . three months . . .—See on ch. 17:2, 3. **when divers**—'some'—**were hardened . . .**—implying that others, probably a large number, believed. **spake evil of that way before the multitude, he departed**—from the synagogue, as at Corinth (ch. 18:7). **and separated the disciples**—withdrawing to a separate place of meeting, for the sake both of the converts already made, and the unsophisticated multitude. **disputing**—'discoursing' or 'discussing'—**daily in the school**—or lecture hall—**of one Tyrannus**—probably a converted teacher of rhetoric or philosophy.

ADAM CLARKE

5. *When they heard this.* As there is no evidence in the New Testament of persons being rebaptized, unless this be one, many criticisms have been hazarded to prove that these persons were not rebaptized. I see no need of this. To be a Christian a man must be baptized in the Christian faith; these persons had not been baptized into that faith, and therefore were not Christians; they felt this, and were immediately baptized into *the name of the Lord Jesus.*

6. *They spake with tongues, and prophesied.* They received the miraculous gift of different languages, and in those languages they taught to the people the great doctrines of the Christian religion; for this appears to be the meaning of the word *prophesied,* as it is used above.

8. *Spake boldly . . . three months.* We have often remarked that Paul in every place made his first offers of salvation to the Jews, and it was only when they rejected it that he turned to the Gentiles; see chap. xviii. 6. And the same line of conduct he pursues here; he goes to the school of Tyrannus, at least a public place to which all might resort, when they obstinately rejected the gospel in the synagogue.

9. *When divers were hardened.* When "some" of them were hardened; several no doubt felt the power of divine truth, and yielded consent. Our term *divers,* one of the most bald in our language, has too general a meaning for this place.

***Separated the disciples.* Paul and those converted under his ministry had doubtless been in the habit of attending public worship in the synagogue, but on the persecuting conduct of these Jews, he and his converts wholly withdrew from the synagogue and took a place for themselves; and constantly afterwards held their own meetings at a schoolroom, which no doubt they hired for the purpose.**

***Disputing and persuading.* Holding conversations with them in order to persuade them of the truth of the doctrine of Christ.**

G. CAMPBELL MORGAN:

Mark the diversities. How did these twelve men enter into the larger life? They heard the teaching, they obeyed, they were baptized into the name of Jesus. Then Paul laid on his hands and they received the Holy Spirit. In the tenth chapter we find Peter was talking to Cornelius and he received the Spirit immediately and was baptized, not before but after receiving the Spirit. The Spirit bloweth where He listeth. We must not take any illustration in this book, and make it an abiding rule, for if so, there will be as many schools as there are stories in the Acts of the Apostles. We cannot base a doctrine of the Spirit's methods upon any one story. Upon the whole of them we can base the doctrine of the Spirit's method, and that may be stated thus. Not according to human ideas, or human laws formulated by any story; but in many ways, through the laying on of hands, and without such laying on; in answer to water baptism, before water baptism; so comes the Spirit. The important matter is that we have this Spirit, without whose presence and illumination we cannot preach this Christ, or teach Him. May it be ours to press to the highest height, and the fullest knowledge, that we may lift all those whom we teach on to this highest level.—*The Acts of the Apostles*

MATTHEW HENRY

others think it was a philosophy-school of the Gentiles, belonging to one Tyrannus. Some convenient place it was, which Paul and the disciples had the use of, either for love or money.

3. Here he continued his labours for *two years.* These two years commence from the end of the *three months* which he spent in the synagogue (*v.* 8); therefore he might justly reckon it in all three years, as he does, *ch.* xx. 31.

4. The gospel hereby spread far and near (*v.* 10): *All those that dwelt in Asia heard the word of the Lord Jesus;* not only all that dwelt in Ephesus, but all that dwelt in that large province called *Asia,* of which Ephesus was the head city. There was great resort to Ephesus from all parts of the country, which gave Paul an opportunity of sending the report of the gospel to all the towns and villages of that country. They all heard the *word of the Lord Jesus.* Some of all sects, some out of all parts both in city and country, embraced this gospel, and entertained it, and by them it was communicated to others.

III. God confirmed Paul's doctrine by miracles, *v.* 11, 12. Why did he not work miracles at Thessalonica, Berea, and Athens? Or, if he did, why are they not recorded? But here at Ephesus we have the proofs of this kind which he gave of his divine mission. They were *special miracles.* God exerted powers that were not according to the common course of nature. Or, they were not only (as all miracles are) *out of the common road,* but they were even uncommon miracles. God wrought *something above the common road of miracles.* It was not Paul that wrought them but it was God that *wrought them by the hand of Paul.* He was but the instrument.

3. He not only cured the sick that were brought to him, or to whom he was brought, but *from his body were brought to the sick handkerchiefs or aprons.* We read of one that was cured by the touch of Christ's garment when it was upon him, and he perceived that *virtue went out of him*; but here were people cured by Paul's garments when they were taken from him. Christ gave his apostles power *against unclean spirits and against all manner of sickness* (Matt. x. 1), those to whom Paul sent relief had it in both cases: *for the diseases departed from them* and the *evil spirits went out of them.*

Verses 13–20

We have here in these verses two remarkable instances of the conquest of Satan, not only in those that were violently possessed by him, but in those that were voluntarily devoted to him.

I. Here is the confusion of some of Satan's servants, some *vagabond Jews,* that were *exorcists,* who made use of Christ's name in their diabolical enchantments.

1. The general character of those who were guilty of this presumption. They were Jews, but *vagabond* Jews. They strolled about to tell people their fortunes, and pretended by spells and charms to cure diseases, and bring people to themselves that were melancholy or distracted. The superstitious Jews, to put a reputation upon these magic arts, wickedly attributed the invention of them to Solomon. And Christ seems to refer to this (Matt. xii. 27), *By whom do your children cast them out?*

2. A particular account of some at Ephesus that led this course of life. They were *seven sons of one Sceva, a Jew, and chief of the priests, v.* 14. Their father was a chief of the priests, head of one of the twenty-four courses of priests. One would think the temple would find both employment and encouragement enough for the sons of a chief priest.

3. The profaneness they were guilty of: *They took upon them to call over evil spirits the name of the Lord Jesus;* not as those who had a veneration for Christ and a confidence in his name, as we read of some who cast out devils in Christ's name and yet did not follow with his disciples (Luke ix. 49), but as those who were willing to try all methods to carry on their wicked trade. They said, *We adjure you by Jesus whom Paul preaches;* not, "whom we believe in, or depend upon," but *whom Paul preaches*; as if they had said, "We will try what that name will do."

4. The confusion they were put to in their impious operations. The evil spirit gave them a sharp reply (*v.* 15): "*Jesus I know, and Paul I know; but who are you?* What power have you to command us in his name, or who gave you any such power? What have you to do to declare the power of Jesus, seeing you hate his instructions?" *The man in whom the evil spirit was* gave them a warm reception, *leaped upon them, overcame them* and *prevailed against them,* so that *they fled out of the house,* not only *naked,* but *wounded.* A warning to all those who name the name of Christ, but do not depart from iniquity. The same enemy that overcomes them with his

JAMIESON, FAUSSET, BROWN

this continued . . . two years—in addition to the former three months. See on ch. 20:31. But during some part of this period he must have paid a second unrecorded visit to Corinth, since the one next recorded (see on ch. 20:2, 3) is twice called his *third* visit (II Cor. 12:14 13:1). See on II Corinthians 1:15, 16, which might seem inconsistent with this. The passage across was quite a short one (see on ch. 18:19). Towards the close of this long stay at Ephesus, as we learn from I Corinthians 16:8, he wrote his FIRST EPISTLE TO THE CORINTHIANS; also (though on this opinions are divided) the EPISTLE TO THE GALATIANS. (See Introduction to those Epistles.) And just as at Corinth his greatest success was after his withdrawal to a separate place of meeting (ch. 18:7-10), so at Ephesus. **so that all they which dwelt in**—the Roman province of—**Asia heard the word of the Lord Jesus, both Jews and Greeks**—This is the "great door and effectual opened unto him" while resident at Ephesus (I Cor. 16:9, which induced him to make it his headquarters for so long a period. The unwearied and varied character of his labors here are best seen in his own subsequent address to the elders of Ephesus (ch. 20:17, etc.). And thus Ephesus became the "ecclesiastical center for the entire region, as indeed it remained for a very long period" [BAUMGARTEN]. Churches arose at Colosse, Laodicea, and Hierapolis eastward, either through his own labors or those of his faithful helpers whom he sent out in different directions, Epaphras, Archippus, Philemon (Col. 1:7; 4:12-17; Philemon 23). **11, 12. God wrought special**—no ordinary—**miracles by the hands of Paul**—implying that he had not been accustomed to work such. **So that from his body were brought unto the sick handkerchiefs or aprons, . . .**—Cf. ch. 5:15, 16, very different from the magical acts practiced at Ephesus. "*God* wrought these miracles" merely "*by the hands of Paul*"; and the very exorcists (vs. 13), observing that the name of Jesus was the secret of all his miracles, hoped, by aping him in this, to be equally successful; while the result of all in the "magnifying of the Lord Jesus" (vs. 17) showed that in working them the apostle took care to hold up Him whom he *preached* as the source of all the miracles which he *wrought.*

vagabond Jews—simply, 'wandering Jews,' who went from place to place practicing exorcism, or the art of conjuring evil spirits to depart out of the possessed. That such a power did exist, for some time at least, seems implied in Matthew 12:27. But no doubt this would breed imposture; and the present case is very different from that referred to in Luke 9:49, 50.

We adjure you by Jesus whom Paul preacheth—a striking testimony to the power of Christ's name in Paul's mouth. **14-17. seven sons of . . . Sceva . . . chief of the priests**—head, possibly, of one of the 24 courts. **the evil spirit answered, Jesus I know**—'recognize'—**and Paul I know**—'know intimately,' in contrast to them, whom he altogether disowns—**but who are ye? And the man in whom the evil spirit was**—Mark the clear line of demarkation here between "*the evil spirit* which answered and said" and "*the man in whom the evil spirit was.*" The reality of such possessions could not be more clearly expressed. **leaped on them . . . so that they fled . . . naked and wounded**—This was so appalling a testimony at once against those profane impostors and in favor of Paul and the Master whom he preached, that we wonder not that it spread

ADAM CLARKE

10. *By the space of two years.* The schoolhouse of Tyrannus was Paul's regular chapel; and it is likely that in it he taught Christianity, as Tyrannus taught languages or sciences.

All they . . . in Asia heard the word. Meaning probably the Proconsular Asia. *Jews and Greeks.* For, although he ceased preaching in the synagogues of the Jews, yet they continued to hear him in the school of Tyrannus.

11. *God wrought special miracles.* Miracles of no "ordinary" kind, i.e., extraordinary miracles.

12. *Handkerchiefs or aprons.* Probably the *sudaria* were a sort of handkerchiefs, which in travelling were always carried in the hand for the convenience of wiping the face; and the *simikinthia* were either the sashes or girdles that went about the loins. These, borrowed from the apostle and applied to the bodies of the diseased, became the means in the hand of God of their restoration to health. *The diseases departed from them, and the evil spirits went out of them.* Here there is a most evident distinction made between the *diseases* and the *evil spirits;* hence they were not one and the same thing.

13. *Certain of the vagabond Jews, exorcists.* "Certain of the Jews who went about practicing exorcisms." *Vagabond* has a very bad acceptation among us; but literally *vagabundus* signifies a "wanderer," one that has no settled place of abode.

14. *Seven sons of one Sceva.* It has been often remarked that in our Lord's time there were many of the Jews that professed to cast out demons; and perhaps to this our Lord alludes, Matt. xii. 27.

15. *Jesus I know, and Paul I know.* In the answer of the demoniac, the verb is varied: I "acknowledge" Jesus, and "am acquainted with" Paul; but of whom are ye?

16. *And the man in whom the evil spirit was.* Thus we find that one man was more powerful than these seven brothers, so that he stripped them of their upper garments and beat and wounded the whole! Was not this a proof that he derived his strength from the evil spirit that dwelt in him?

MATTHEW HENRY

temptations will overcome them with his terrors. If we resist the devil by a true and lively faith in Christ, he will flee from us; but if we think to resist him by the bare using of Christ's name, as a spell or charm, he will prevail against us.

5. The general notice that was taken of this (*v.* 17): *This was known to all the Jews and Greeks also dwelling at Ephesus.* It was the common talk of the town. Men were terrified: *fear fell on them all.* In this instance they saw the malice of the devil whom they served, and the power of Christ whom they opposed. God was glorified; *the name of the Lord Jesus was the more magnified;* for now it appeared to be a name above every name.

II. Here is the conversion of others of Satan's servants.

1. Those that had been guilty of wicked practices confessed them, *v.* 18. Many that had believed and were baptized, but had not then been so particular as they might have been in the confession of their sins, came to Paul, and confessed what evil lives they had led, and what a great deal of secret wickedness their own consciences charged them with. *They showed their deeds,* took shame to themselves and gave glory to God and warning to others. Where there is true contrition for sin there will be an ingenuous confession of sin to God and to man whom we have offended when the case requires it.

2. Those that had conversed with wicked books burnt them (*v.* 19): *Many also of those who used curious arts,* that traded in the study of magic and divination. These, having their consciences more awakened than ever, *brought their books together, and burnt them before all men.* Ephesus was notorious for the use of these curious arts. It was therefore much for the honour of Christ and his gospel to have such a noble testimony borne against those *curious* arts, in a place where they were so much in vogue. Thus they showed a holy indignation at the sins they had been guilty of. Those very things were now detestable to them, as much as ever they had been delectable. Thus they showed their resolution never to return to the use of those arts. Being steadfastly resolved never to make use of them, they burnt them. Thus they put away a temptation to return to them again. Those that truly repent of sin will keep themselves as far as possible from the occasions of it. Thus they prevented their doing mischief to others. It was the safest course to commit them all to the flames. Those that are recovered from sin themselves will do all they can to keep others from falling into it. Thus they showed a contempt of the wealth of this world; for the price of the books was cast up, and it was found to be *fifty thousand pieces of silver.* Probably they had cost them so much; yet, being the devil's books, they did not think this would justify them in being so wicked as to sell them again. Thus they publicly testified their joy for their conversion from these wicked practices. These converts joined together in making this bonfire, and made it before all men. They chose to do it together, by consent, and to do it at the high cross (as we say), that Christ and his grace in them might be the more magnified.

III. Here is a general account of the progress and success of the gospel (*v.* 20): *So mightily grew the word of God, and prevailed.* It is a blessed sight to see the word of God growing and prevailing mightily. To see it grow extensively, by the addition of many to the church. When still more and more are wrought upon by the gospel, then it grows; when those that had been most stiff in their opposition to it, are brought into obedience to it, then it may be said to *grow mightily.* To see it prevail extensively. When strong corruptions are mortified, evil customs of long standing broken off, and pleasant, gainful, fashionable sins are abandoned, then it prevails mightily; and Christ in it goes on conquering and to conquer.

Verses 21–41

I. Paul is here brought into some trouble at Ephesus, just when he is forecasting to go thence.

1. How he laid his purpose of going to other places, *v.* 21, 22. He was a man of vast designs for God, and was for making his influences as widely diffusive as might be. He designed a visit to the churches of Macedonia and Achaia, *v.* 21. There he had planted churches, and now is concerned to visit them. He *purposed in the spirit,* either in his own spirit, or by the direction of the Holy Spirit, who was his guide in all his motions. He purposed to go and see how the work of God went on in those places. Thence he designed to go to Jerusalem, to visit the brethren there, and thence he intended to go to Rome, to go and *see Rome.* It was an expression people commonly used, that they would go and see Rome, would look about them there, when that which he designed

JAMIESON, FAUSSET, BROWN

to "all the Jews and Greeks at Ephesus, that fear fell on them," and that "the name of the Lord Jesus was magnified."

19, 20. many that believed came and confessed . . . their deeds—the dupes of magicians, etc., acknowledging how shamefully they had been deluded, and how deeply they had allowed themselves to be implicated in such practices. **Many of them . . . which used curious arts**—The word signifies things 'overdone'; significantly applied to arts in which laborious but senseless incantations are practiced. **brought their books**—containing the mystic formularies. **and burned them before all**—The *tense,* here used graphically, expresses progress and continuance of the conflagration.

counted the price . . . and found it fifty thousand pieces of silver—probably about $10,000 (presuming it to be the *drachma*). From their nature they would be costly, and books then bore a value above any standard we are familiar with. The scene must have been long remembered at Ephesus, as a strong proof of honest conviction on the part of the sorcerers and a striking triumph of Jesus Christ over the powers of darkness. The workers of evil were put to scorn, like Baal's priests on Carmel, and the word of God mightily grew and prevailed [Hows].

21, 22. After these things were ended—completed, implying something like a natural finish to his long period of labor at Ephesus. **Paul purposed . . . when he had passed through Macedonia and Achaia, to go to Jerusalem . . . After I have been there, I must see Rome also**—Mark here the vastness of the apostle's missionary plans. They were all fulfilled, though he "saw Rome" only as a prisoner.

ADAM CLARKE

17. *The name of the Lord Jesus was magnified.* They saw that there was a sovereign power in the name of Jesus which could not be imitated by these lying exorcists; they therefore reverenced this name, and despised those pretenders.

19. *Which used curious arts.* From the use of this word in the Greek writers we know that it signified "magical arts, sorceries, incantations." Ephesus abounded with these. *Brought their books together.* When it is said they brought their books together, we are to understand the books which treated of these curious arts. *And burned them before all.* These must have been thoroughly convinced of the truth of Christianity and of the unlawfulness of their own arts.

20. *So mightily grew the word of God and prevailed.* It is probable that it was about this time that Paul had that conflict which he mentions in 1 Cor. xv. 32, "If after the manner of men I have fought with [wild] beasts at Ephesus." See the note there. It means some severe trials not here mentioned, unless we may suppose him to refer to the ferocious insurrection headed by Demetrius, mentioned at the end of this chapter.

21. *Paul purposed in the spirit.* Previously to this he appears to have concerted a journey to Macedonia and a visit to Corinth, the capital of Achaia, where he seems to have spent a considerable time (see 1 Cor. xvi. 5-6), and afterwards to go to Jerusalem. But it is likely that he did not leave Ephesus till after Pentecost (1 Cor. xvi. 8). And he resolved if possible to see Rome, which had been the object of his wishes for a considerable time. See Rom. i. 10, 13; xvi. 23. It is generally believed that during this period, while at Ephesus, he wrote his First Epistle to the Corinthians.

MATTHEW HENRY

was to see the Christians there. The good people at Rome were the glory of the city which he longed for a sight of. He sent Timothy and Erastus into Macedonia, to give them notice of the visit he intended them. For the present he stayed in Asia.

2. How he was seconded in his purpose, and obliged to pursue it by the troubles which at length he met with at Ephesus. It was strange that he had been quiet there so long; yet it should seem he had met with trouble there not recorded in this story, for in his epistle he speaks of his having *fought with beasts at Ephesus* (1 Cor. xv. 32). And he speaks of the trouble which came to them in Asia, near Ephesus, when he *despaired of life*, 2 Cor. i, 8, 9.

II. But, in the trouble here related, he was worse frightened than hurt. In general, *there arose no small stir about that way*, *v*. 23. Let us view the particulars of it.

1. A great complaint against Paul for drawing people off from the worship of Diana, and so spoiling the trade of the silversmiths that worked for Diana's temple.

(1) The complainant is Demetrius, a silversmith. The most advantageous branch of his trade was *making silver shrines for Diana*, *v*. 24. Some think these were medals stamped with the effigies of Diana, others think they were representations of the temple, with the image of Diana in it in miniature, all of silver. Those that came from far to pay their devotions at the temple of Ephesus bought these little temples or shrines, to carry home with them. See how craftsmen, and crafty men too above the rank of silversmiths, make an advantage to themselves of people's superstition.

(2) The persons he appeals to are not the magistrates, but the mob; he called the *craftsmen* together, *with the workmen of like occupation*, and these he endeavoured to incense against Paul.

(3) His complaint and representation are very full. He lays it down for a principle that the making silver shrines for the worshippers of Diana was very necessary to be kept up (*v*. 25): "*You know that by this craft we have our wealth*." It is natural for men to be jealous for that by which they get their wealth; and many have set themselves against the gospel of Christ, because it calls men off from those crafts which are unlawful, how much wealth soever is to be obtained by them. He charges it upon Paul that he had dissuaded men from worshipping idols. He had asserted, *Those are no gods which are made with hands*, *v*. 26. Could any truth be more plain and self-evident than this, *The workman made it, therefore it is not God?* Yet this must be looked upon as an heretical and atheistical notion, and Paul as a criminal for maintaining it. The consequence of it was that not only at Ephesus, but almost throughout all Asia, he had *persuaded and turned away much people* from the worship of Diana. There are those who will stickle for that which is most grossly absurd and unreasonable, if it have but human laws, and worldly interest on its side. He reminds them of the danger which their trade was in of going to decay. "If this doctrine gains credit, we are all undone, and may even shut up shop; *this our craft will be set at nought*." He pretends a mighty zeal for Diana: *Not only this our craft is in danger*. All his care is lest *the temple of the great goddess Diana should be despised, and her magnificence should be destroyed;* and he would not see the diminution of the honour of that goddess, *whom all Asia and the world worship*. See what the worship of Diana had to plead for itself. It had pomp on its side; the magnificence of the temple was the thing that charmed them. It had numbers on its side; *All Asia and the world worship* it; and therefore it must needs be the right way of worship, let Paul say what he will to the contrary.

2. The popular resentment of this complaint. They showed, (1) A great displeasure against the gospel and the preachers of it. *They were full of wrath* (*v*. 28). The craftsmen went stark mad when they were told that their trade and their idol were both in danger. (2) A great jealousy for the honour of their goddess: *They cried out*, "*Great is Diana of the Ephesians*. Let Paul say ever so much to prove that those are no gods which are made with hands, we will abide by it that, *Great is Diana of the Ephesians*. We must and will stand up for the religion of our country." Much more should the servants of the true God do so. (3) A great disorder among themselves (*v*. 29): *The whole city was full of confusion*—the common and natural effect of an intemperate zeal for a false religion.

3. The proceedings of the mob under the power of these resentments.

(1) They laid hands on some of Paul's companions, and hurried them into the theatre (*v*. 29). Those

JAMIESON, FAUSSET, BROWN

So he sent into Macedonia . . . Timotheus and Erastus—as his pioneers, in part to bring "them into remembrance of his ways which were in Christ" (I Cor. 4:17 and I Cor. 16:10), partly to convey his mind on various matters. After a brief stay he was to return (I Cor. 16:11). It is very unlikely that this Erastus was "the chamberlain of the city" of Corinth, of that name (Rom. 16:23). **he himself stayed in**—the province of—**Asia for a season**—i.e., at Ephesus, its chief city. (Asia is mentioned in contrast with Macedonia in the previous clause.) **23. the same time**—of Paul's proposed departure. **about that**—'the'—**way**—So the new religion seemed then to be designated (ch. 9:2; 22:4; 24:14).

24-26. silver shrines for—'of'—**Diana**—small models of the Ephesian temple and of the shrine or chapel of the goddess, or of the shrine and statue alone, which were purchased by visitors as memorials of what they had seen, and were carried about and deposited in houses as a charm. (The models of the chapel of *our Lady of Loretto*, and such like, which the Church of Rome systematically encourages, are such a palpable imitation of this heathen practice that it is no wonder it should be regarded by impartial judges as *Christianity paganized*.) **gain to the craftsmen**—the master-artificers. **Whom he called together with the workmen of like occupation**—rather, 'with the workmen (or fabricators) of such articles,' meaning the artisans employed by the master-artificers, all who manufactured any kind of memorial of the temple and its worship for sale. **ye see and hear**—The evidences of it were to be seen, and the report of it was in everybody's mouth. **that not alone at Ephesus, but almost throughout all Asia, this Paul hath . . . turned away much people**—Noble testimony this to the extent of Paul's influence! **saying that they be no gods which are made with hands**—The universal belief of *the people* was that they were gods, though the more intelligent regarded them only as habitations of Deity, and some, probably, as mere aids to devotion. It is exactly so in the Church of Rome. **27. So that not only this our craft is in danger . . . but . . .**—i.e., 'that indeed is a small matter; but there is something far worse.' So the masters of the poor Pythoness put forward the *religious revolution* which Paul was attempting to effect at Philippi, as the sole cause of their zealous alarm, to cloak the self-interest which they felt to be touched by his success (ch. 16:19-21). In both cases religious zeal was the hypocritical pretext; self-interest, the real moving cause of the opposition made. **also the temple of the great goddess Diana . . . despised, and her magnificence . . . destroyed, whom all Asia and the world worshippeth**—It was reckoned one of the wonders of the world. It was built about 550 B.C., of pure white marble, and though burned by a fanatic on the night of the birth of Alexander the Great, 356 B.C., was rebuilt with more splendor than before. It was 425 feet long by 220 broad, and the columns, 127 in number, were sixty feet in height, each of them the gift of a king, and thirty-six of them enriched with ornament and color. It was constantly receiving new decorations and additional buildings, statues, and pictures by the most celebrated artists, and kindled unparalleled admiration, enthusiasm, and superstition. *Its very site is now a matter of uncertainty*. The little wooden image of Diana was as primitive and rude as its shrine was sumptuous; not like the *Greek* Diana, in the form of an imposing huntress, but quite Asiatic, in the form of a manybreasted female (emblematic of the manifold ministrations of Nature to man), terminating in a shapeless block. Like some other farfamed idols, it was believed to have fallen from heaven (vs. 35), and models of it were not only sold in immense numbers to private persons, but set up for worship in other cities [Hows]. What power must have attended the preaching of that one man by whom the deathblow was felt to be given to their gigantic and witching superstition! **28, 29. Great is Diana of the Ephesians**—the civic cry of a populace so proud of their temple that they refused to inscribe on it the name of Alexander the Great, though he offered them the whole spoil of his Eastern campaign if they would do it [STRABO in Hows]

ADAM CLARKE

22. *So he sent into Macedonia*. He desired Timothy to go as far as Corinth, 1 Cor. iv. 18, and after that to return to him at Ephesus, 1 Cor. xvi. 11; but he himself continued in Asia some time longer, probably to make collections for the poor saints in Jerusalem. *Erastus*, mentioned here for the first time, appears to have been the chamberlain of either Ephesus or Corinth; see Rom. xvi. 23. He was one of Paul's companions and is mentioned as being left by the apostle at Corinth, 2 Tim. iv. 20.

23. *No small stir about that way*. Concerning the gospel, which the apostles preached; and which is termed "this way," chap. ix. 2.

24. *Silver shrines for Diana*. It is generally known that the temple of Diana at Ephesus was deemed one of the seven wonders of the world and was a most superb building. It appears that the *silver shrines* mentioned here were small, portable representations of this temple, which were bought by strangers as matters of curiosity and probably of devotion. *Brought no small gain*. There were many made, many sold, and probably at considerable prices.

25. *By this craft we have our wealth*. The word signifies not only "wealth," but also "abundance." It was a most lucrative trade; and he plainly saw that, if the apostles were permitted to go on thus preaching, the worship of Diana itself would be destroyed, and consequently all the gain that he and his fellows derived from it would be brought to nought.

26. *This Paul hath persuaded and turned away much people*. From the mouth of this heathen we have in one sentence a most pleasing account of the success with which God had blessed the labors of the apostles: *not alone at Ephesus, but almost throughout all Asia*, they had *persuaded* and converted *much people*. For they had insisted that they could be no gods which are made with hands, and this the common sense of the people must at once perceive.

TODAY'S DICTIONARY OF THE BIBLE:

Diana—so called by the Romans; called Artemis by the Greeks—the "great" goddess worshiped among heathen nations under various modifications. Her most noted temple was that at Ephesus. It was built outside the city walls, and was one of the seven wonders of the ancient world. "First and last it was the work of 220 years; built of shining marble; 342 feet long by 164 feet broad; supported by a forest of columns, each 56 feet high; a sacred museum of masterpieces of sculpture and painting. At the center, hidden by curtains, within a gorgeous shrine, stood the very ancient image of the goddess, on wood or ebony reputed to have fallen from the sky. Behind the shrine was a treasury, where, as in 'the safest bank in Asia,' nations and kings stored their most precious things. The temple as St. Paul saw it subsisted till A.D. 262, when it was ruined by the Goths" (Acts 19:23-41).—Moule on *Ephesians; Introd.*

29. *The whole city was filled with confusion*. Thus we find the peace of the whole city was disturbed, not by an apostle preaching the gospel of Christ, but by one interested, unprincipled knave who did not even plead conscience for what he was doing; but that it was by this craft he and his fellows got their wealth, and he was afraid to lose it.

MATTHEW HENRY

whom they seized were *Gaius and Aristarchus. Gaius was of Derbe, ch.* xx. 4. *Aristarchus* is also there spoken of, and Col. iv. 10. They came with Paul *from Macedonia*, and this was their only crime, that they were Paul's companions.

(2) *Paul*, who had escaped being seized by them, when he perceived his friends in distress, for his sake *would have entered in unto the people*. It was an evidence of a generous spirit, and that he loved his neighbour as himself.

(3) He was persuaded from it by the kindness of his friends. *The disciples suffered him not*, for it better became him to offer it than it would have become them to suffer it. Others of his friends interposed, to prevent his throwing himself thus into the mouth of danger, *v.* 31. They were *certain of the chief of Asia*. Whether they were converts to the Christian faith, or whether they were only well-wishers to Paul, as an ingenuous good man, we are not told, only that they were *Paul's friends*. It is a friendly part to take more care of the lives and comforts of good men than they do themselves. Paul was overruled by his friends to obey the law of self-preservation, and has taught us to keep out of the way of danger as long as we can without going out of the way of duty. We may be called to lay down our lives, but not to throw away our lives.

(4) The mob was in a perfect confusion (*v.* 32): *Some cried one thing and some another, the assembly was confused*. The truth was *the greater part knew not wherefore they had come together*. Upon such occasions, the greatest part come only to enquire what the matter is: they follow the cry, follow the crowd, increase like a snowball, and where there are many there will be more.

(5) The Jews would have interested themselves in this tumult, but now at Ephesus they had not interest enough to raise the mob, and yet, when it was raised, they had ill will enough to set in with it (*v.* 33): *They drew Alexander out of the multitude*, called him out to speak on the behalf of the Jews against Paul and his companions: "You have heard what Demetrius and the silversmiths have to say against them, as enemies to their religion; give us leave now to tell you what we have to say against him as an enemy to our religion." *The Jews put him forward* to do this, and therefore what he designed to say is called his apologizing to the people, not for himself in particular, but for the Jews in general. Now they would have them know that they were as much Paul's enemies as they were. *Alexander beckoned with the hand*, desiring to be heard against Paul; for it had been strange if a persecution had been carried on against the Christians and there were not Jews at one end or the other of it: if they could not begin the mischief, they would help it forward. Some think this Alexander had been a Christian, but had apostatized to Judaism, and therefore was drawn out as a proper person to accuse Paul; and that he was that *Alexander the coppersmith* that did Paul so much evil (2 Tim. iv. 14), and whom he had *delivered unto Satan*, 1 Tim. i. 20.

(6) This occasioned the prosecutors to drop the prosecution of Paul's friends, and to turn it into acclamations in honour of their goddess (*v.* 34): *When they knew that he was a Jew*, and, as such, an enemy to the worship of Diana, they were resolved not to hear him, and therefore set the mob a shouting, '*Great is Diana of the Ephesians;* whoever runs her down, be he Jew or Christian, we are resolved to cry her up." This was all the cry for *two hours* together; and it was thought a sufficient confutation of Paul's doctrine, *that those are not gods which are made with hands*. Thus the most sacred truths are often run down with nothing else but noise and clamour and popular fury.

4. The suppressing and dispersing of these rioters, by the prudence and vigilence of *the town clerk*. With much ado he, at length, stilled the noise, so as to be heard, and then made a pacific speech to them.

(1) He humours them with an acknowledgment that Diana was the celebrated goddess of the Ephesians . 35. They needed not to be so loud and strenuous in asserting a truth which nobody denied. Everyone *knows that the city of the Ephesians is a worshipper of the great goddess Diana*. The temple of Diana at Ephesus was a very rich and sumptuous structure, but the *image* of Diana in the temple was had in greater veneration than the temple, for they persuaded the people that it *fell down from Jupiter*, and therefore was none of the gods that were made with men's hands. Because this image of Diana had been set up time out of mind, and nobody could tell who made it, they made the people believe it fell down from Jupiter. "Now *these things*," says the town clerk very gravely, "*cannot be spoken against*; they have obtained such universal credit that you need

JAMIESON, FAUSSET, BROWN

having caught Gaius and Aristarchus—disappointed of Paul, as at Thessalonica (ch. 17:5, 6). They are mentioned in ch. 20:4; 27:2; Rom. 16:23; I Cor. 1:14; and probably III John 1. If it was in the house of Aquila and Priscilla that he found an asylum (see I Cor. 16:9), that would explain Romans 16:3, 4, where he says of them that "for his life they laid down their own necks" [Hows]. **rushed . . . into the theatre**—a vast pile, whose ruins are even now a wreck of immense grandeur [Sir C. Fellowes, *Asia Minor,* 1839] **30-34. when Paul would have entered in**—with noble forgetfulness of self—**unto the people** —the *demos,* i.e., the people met in public assembly. **the disciples suffered him not**—The *tense* used implies only that they were *using their efforts* to restrain him; which might have been unavailing but for what follows. **And certain of the chief of Asia**—lit., 'And certain also of the Asiarchs.' These were wealthy and distinguished citizens of the principal towns of the Asian province, chosen annually, and ten of whom were selected by the proconsul to preside over the games celebrated in the month of May (the same month which Romanism dedicates to *the Virgin*). It was an office of the highest honor and greatly coveted. Certain of these, it seems, were favorably inclined to the Gospel, at least were Paul's "friends," and knowing the passions of a mob, excited during the festivals, "sent (a message) to him desiring him not to adventure himself into the theater."

they drew Alexander out of the multitude, the Jews putting him forward—rather, 'some of the multitude urged forward Alexander, the Jews thrusting him forward.' As the blame of such a tumult would naturally be thrown upon the Jews, who were regarded by the Romans as the authors of all religious disturbances, they seem to have put forward this man to clear them of all responsibility for the riot. (Bengel's conjecture, that this was Alexander the coppersmith, II Tim. 4:14, has little to support it.) **beckoned with the hand**—cf. ch. 13:16; 21:40. **would have made his defence**—'offered to speak in defense.'

But when they knew he was a Jew, all with one voice, for the space of two hours, cried out, Great is Diana . . .—The very appearance of a Jew had the opposite effect to that intended. To prevent him obtaining a hearing, they drowned his voice in one tumultuous shout in honor of their goddess, which rose to such frantic enthusiasm as took two hours to exhaust itself.

35-41. when the town-clerk—keeper of the public archives, and a magistrate of great authority. **had appeased**—'calmed'—**the people**—'the multitude'—which the very presence of such an officer would go far to do. **he said . . . what man . . . knoweth not that the city of the Ephesians is a worshipper of the great goddess Diana**—lit., 'the *neocoros* or warden.' The word means 'temple-sweeper'; then, 'temple-guardian.' Thirteen cities of Asia had an interest in the temple, but Ephesus was honored with the charge of it. (Various cities have claimed this title with reference to *the Virgin* or certain *saints*) [Webster and Wilkinson]. **and of the image which fell down from Jupiter**—'from the sky' or 'from heaven.' See on vs. 27. "With this we may compare various legends concerning images and pictures in the Romish Church, such as the traditional likenesses of Christ, which were said to be 'not made with hands'" [Webster and Wilkinson]. **Seeing that these things cannot be spoken against . . .**—Like a true

ADAM CLARKE

Rushed . . . into the theatre. The theatres, being very spacious and convenient places, were often used for popular assemblies and public deliberation, especially in matters which regarded the safety of the state.

31. *Certain of the chief of Asia*. Some of the "Asiarchs." The Asiarchs were those to whom the care and regulation of the public games were entrusted; they were a sort of high priests, and were always persons of considerable riches and influence. These could not have been Christians, but they were what the sacred text states them to have been, ***his friends;*** and foreseeing that Paul would be exposed to great danger if he went into the theatre amidst such a tumultuous assembly, they sent a message to him, entreating him not to go into danger so apparent.

32. *Some . . . cried one thing, and some another*. This is an admirable description of a tumultuous mob, gathered together without law or reason; getting their passions inflamed, and looking for an opportunity to commit outrages, without why or wherefore—principle or object.

For the assembly was confused. Ecclesia, the same word which we translate "church"; and thus we find that it signifies any assembly, and that only the circumstances of the case can determine the precise nature of the assembly to which this word is applied.

33. *They drew Alexander out of the multitude, the Jews putting him forward*. From this and the following verses it is pretty evident that this Alexander was brought forward on this occasion by the Jews, that he might make an oration to the multitude, in order to exculpate the Jews, who were often by the heathens confounded with the Christians; and cast the whole blame of the uproar upon Paul and his party. He was probably chosen because he was an able speaker; and when he beckoned with his hand to gain an audience, the Greeks, knowing that he was a Jew and consequently as much opposed to the worship of Diana as Paul was, would not hear him.

35. *When the townclerk*. Literally, the "scribe." *Is a worshipper of the great goddess Diana*. The word *neocoros*, which we translate "worshipper," signified at first, among the ancient Greeks, no more than "sweeper of the temple," and answered nearly to our "sexton." In process of time the care of the temple was entrusted to this person. At length the *neocori* became persons of great consequence, and were those who offered sacrifices for the life of the emperor. Whole cities took this appellation, as appears on many ancient coins and medals; and Ephesus is supposed to have been the first that assumed this title. *Of the image which fell down from Jupiter*. The original image of the Ephesian Diana was supposed to have descended from heaven, which intimates that it was so old that no person knew either its maker or the time in which it was formed; and it was the interest of the priests to persuade the people that this image had been sent to them as a present from Jupiter himself.

MATTHEW HENRY

not fear contradiction."

(2) He cautions them against all violent and tumultuous proceedings, which their religion did not need (*v.* 36): *You ought to be quiet, and to do nothing rashly.* A very good rule this is to be observed at all times, both in private and public affairs; not to be hasty and precipitate in our motions, but to be calm and composed, and always keep reason in the throne and passion under check. *We ought to be quiet and to do nothing rashly;* to do nothing in haste, which we may repent of at leisure.

(3) He wipes off the odium that had been cast upon Paul and his associates (*v.* 37): "*You have brought hither these men.* What can you prove upon them? They are not robbers of churches. They have offered no violence to Diana's temple or the treasures of it; nor are they *blasphemers of your goddess.* Why should you prosecute those *with all this violence* who do not inveigh with any bitterness against you? Since they are calm, why should you be hot?" It was the idol in the heart that they levelled all their force against, by reason and argument; if they can but get that down, the idol in the temple will fall of course. Those that preach against idolatrous churches have truth on their side, with meekness instructing, not with passion and foul language reproaching, those that oppose themselves; for God's truth needs not man's intemperate heat.

(4) He turns them over to the regular methods of the law. A great mercy it is to live in a country where provision is made for the keeping of the peace, and the administration of public justice, and herein we of this nation are as happy as any people. If the complaint be of a private injury, let them have recourse to the judges and courts of justice. If Demetrius and the company of the silversmiths find themselves aggrieved, let them bring their action, and the matter shall be fairly tried, and justice done: *The law is open, and there are deputies,* whose business it is to hear both sides, and in their determination all parties must acquiesce, and not be their own judges, nor appeal to the people. If the complaint be of a public grievance it must be redressed, not by a confused rabble, but by a convention of the states (*v.* 39): *If you enquire anything concerning other matters it shall be determined in a lawful assembly* called together in a regular way by those in authority. Private persons should not intermeddle in public matters, we have enough to do to mind our own business.

(5) He makes them sensible of the danger they have run themselves into by this riot (*v.* 40): "It is well if we be not *called in question for this day's uproar,* for *there is no cause whereby we may give an account of this concourse.* Let the matter go no further, for it has gone too far already." Most people stand in awe of men's judgment more than of the judgment of God. How well were it if we would thus still the tumult of our disorderly appetites and passions with the consideration of the account we must shortly give to the Judge of heaven and earth for all these disorders! We are concerned to manage ourselves *as those that must give account.*

(6) When he has thus shown them the absurdity of their riotous meeting, he advises them to separate with all speed (*v.* 41): he *dismissed the assembly.* See here how the overruling providence of God preserves the public peace, by an unaccountable power over the spirits of men. Thus the world is kept in some order, and men are restrained from being as the fishes of the sea, where the greater devour the less. Considering what an ungovernable, untameable wild beast the mob is, when it is up, we shall see reason to acknowledge God's goodness that we are not always under the tyranny of it. See how many ways God has of protecting his people. Perhaps this town clerk was no friend at all to Paul, yet his human prudence is made to serve the divine purpose.

CHAPTER 20

Verses 1–6

I. Paul's departure from Ephesus. He had tarried there longer than he had done at any one place. Now it was time to think of removing, for he must *preach in other cities also*; but after this we never find him breaking up fresh ground again, for in the close of the next chapter we find him made a prisoner, and so continued, and so left, at the end of this book. Paul left Ephesus soon after the uproar had ceased, *v.* 1. His removal might somewhat appease the rage of his adversaries, and gain better quarter for the Christians there. Some think that before he now left Ephesus he wrote *the first epistle to the Corinthians,* and that his *fighting with beasts at Ephesus,* which he mentions in that epistle, was a figurative descrip-

JAMIESON, FAUSSET, BROWN

legal man, he urges that such was notoriously the constitution and fixed character of the city, with which its very existence was all but bound up. Did they suppose that all this was going to be overturned by a set of itinerant orators? Ridiculous! What did they mean, then, by raising such a stir?

For ye have brought hither these men, which are neither robbers of churches—'temple-plunderers,' or sacrilegious persons. **nor yet blasphemers of your goddess**—This is a remarkable testimony, showing that the apostle had, in preaching against idolatry, studiously avoided (as at Athens) insulting the feelings of those whom he addressed—a lesson this to missionaries and ministers in general.

if Demetrius have a matter—of complaint—**against any man, the law is open**—rather, 'the court-days are being held.' **and there are deputies**—lit., 'proconsuls' (see on ch. 13:7); i.e., probably, the proconsul and his council, as a court of appeal. **if ye inquire**—'have any question.' **concerning other matters**—of a public nature.

For we—the public authorities—**are in danger of being called in question**—by our superiors.

CHAPTER 20

VSS. 1-12. PAUL FULFILS HIS PURPOSE OF PROCEEDING AGAIN TO MACEDONIA AND GREECE—RETURNING THENCE, ON HIS ROUTE FOR JERUSALEM, HE REVISITS PHILIPPI AND TROAS—HIS MINISTRATIONS AT TROAS. This section of the apostle's life, though peculiarly rich in material, is related with great brevity in the History. Its details must be culled from his own Epistles. **1, 2. departed**—after Pentecost (I Cor. 16:8). **to go into Macedonia**—in pursuance of the *first* part of his plan ch. 19:21). From his Epistles we learn; (1) That, as might have been expected from its position on the coast, he revisited Troas (II Cor. 2:12; see on ch. 16:8). (2) That while on his former visit he appears to have done

ADAM CLARKE

37. *These men . . . are neither robbers of churches.* "Spoilers of sacred places." As his design evidently was to appease and conciliate the people, he fixed first on a most incontrovertible fact: These men have not spoiled your temples, nor is there any evidence that they have even blasphemed your goddess.

38. *If Demetrius . . . have a matter against any man.* If it be any breach of law, in reference to Demetrius and the artists, *the law is open,* or rather, "the judges are now sitting"; so the words may be understood. *And there are deputies,* "proconsuls," appointed to guard the peace of the state, and to support every honest man in his right. *Let them implead one another;* let the one party bring forward his action of assault or trespass, and the other put in his defense; the laws are equal and impartial, and justice will be done to him who is wronged.

39. *But if ye enquire any thing concerning other matters,* in which the safety of the state or the national worship is concerned, know that such a matter is not the business of the mob; it must be heard and determined *in a lawful assembly,* one legally constituted and properly authorized to hear and determine on the subject.

40. *For we are in danger.* Popular commotions were always dreaded by the Roman government. One of the Roman laws made all such commotions of the people capital offenses against those who raised them. "He who raises a mob shall forfeit his life." If such a law existed at Ephesus—and it probably did, from this reference to it in the words of the town clerk or recorder—then Demetrius must feel himself in great personal danger, and that his own life lay now at the mercy of those whom he had accused, concerning whom he had raised such an outcry and against whom nothing disorderly could be proved.

41. *He dismissed the assembly.* Another proof that the word *ecclesia,* which we generally translate "church," signifies an *assembly* of any kind.

CHAPTER 20

1. *After the uproar was ceased.* The tumult excited by Demetrius apparently induced Paul to leave Ephesus sooner than he had intended. He had written to the Corinthians that he should leave that place after Pentecost, 1 Cor. xvi. 8; but it is very probable that he left it sooner.

MATTHEW HENRY

tion of this uproar. He did not leave them abruptly, but took leave of them solemnly: *He called unto him the disciples, and embraced them, took leave of them* (saith the Syriac) *with the kiss of love.* Loving friends know not how well they love one another till they come to part, and then it appears how near they lay to one another's hearts.

A. T. ROBERTSON:

2. "Those parts (*ta mere ekeina*). We have no way of knowing why Luke did not tell of Paul's stay in Troas (2 Cor. 2:12), nor of meeting Titus in Macedonia (2 Cor. 2:13 to 7:16), nor of Paul's visit to Illyricum (Rom. 15:19) to give time for 2 Corinthians to do its work (2 Cor. 13), one of the most stirring experiences in Paul's whole career when he opened his heart to the Corinthians and won final victory in the church by the help of Titus who also helped him round up the great collection in Achaia. He wrote 2 Corinthians during this period after Titus arrived from Corinth. The unity of 2 Corinthians is here assumed. Paul probably met Luke again in Macedonia, but all this is passed by except by the general phrase: "had given them much exhortation" (*parakalesas autous logoi polloi*). Literally, "having exhorted them [the Macedonian brethren] with much talk" (instrumental case). "Into Greece" (*eis ten Hellada*). That is, Achaia (18:12; 19:21), and particularly Corinth, whither he had at last come again after repeated attempts, pauses, and delays (2 Cor. 13:1). Now at last the coast was clear and Paul apparently had an open door in Corinth during these three months, so completely had Titus at last done away with the opposition of the Judaizers there.

—*Word Pictures in the New Testament*

II. His visitation of the Greek churches, which he had planted, and which appear to have laid very near his heart. He went first *to Macedonia* (*v.* 1), according to his purpose before the uproar (*ch.* xix. 21); there he visited the churches of Philippi and Thessalonica, and *gave them much exhortation, v.* 2. He had a great deal to say to them, and did not stint himself in time. He stayed *three months in Greece* (*v.* 2, 3), that is, *in Achaia*, for thither also he purposed to go, to Corinth, and thereabouts (*ch.* xix. 21).

III. The altering of his measures. *Paul was about to sail into Syria, to Antioch*, but he changed his mind, and resolved *to return to Macedonia*, the same way he came. The reason was because the Jews, expecting he would steer that course as usual, had waylaid him, designing to be the death of him.

IV. His companions in his travels when he went into Asia; they are here named, *v.* 4. *Sopater of Berea*, it is likely, is the same with *Sosipater*, who is mentioned Rom. xvi. 21.

JAMIESON, FAUSSET, BROWN

no missionary work there, he now went expressly "to preach Christ's Gospel," and found "a door opened unto him of the Lord" there, which he entered so effectually as to lay the foundation of a church there (6, 7). (3) That he would have remained longer there but for his uneasiness at the non-arrival of Titus, whom he had despatched to Corinth to finish the collection for the poor saints at Jerusalem (I Cor. 16:1, 2; II Cor. 8:6), but still more, that he might bring him word what effect his first Epistle to that church had produced. (He had probably arranged that they should meet at Troas.) (4) That in this state of mind, afraid of something wrong, he "took leave" of the brethren at Troas, and went from thence into Macedonia.

It was, no doubt, the city of PHILIPPI that he came to (landing at Nicopolis, its seaport, see on ch. 16: 11, 12), as appears by comparing II Corinthians 11: 9, where "Macedonia" is named, with Philippians 4:15, where it appears that Philippi is meant. Here he found the brethren, whom he had left on his former visit in circumstances of such deep interest, a consolidated and thriving church, generous and warmly attached to their father in Christ; under the superintendence, probably, of our historian, "the beloved physician" (see on ch. 16:40). All that is said by our historian of this Macedonian visit is that "he went over those parts and gave them much exhortation." (5) Titus not having reached Philippi as soon as the apostle, "his flesh had no rest, but he was troubled on every side: without were fightings, within were fears" (II Cor. 7:5). (6) At length Titus arrived, to the joy of the apostle, the bearer of better tidings from Corinth than he had dared to expect (II Cor. 7:6, 7, 13), but checkered by painful intelligence of the efforts of a hostile party to undermine his apostolic reputation there (II Cor.). (7) Under the mixed feelings which this produced, he wrote—from Macedonia, and probably Philippi—*his* SECOND EPISTLE TO THE CORINTHIANS (see Introduction to II Corinthians); despatching Titus with it, and along with him two other unnamed deputies, expressly chosen to take up and bring their collection for the poor saints at Jerusalem, and to whom he bears the beautiful testimony, that they were "the glory of Christ" (II Cor. 8:22, 23). (8) It must have been at this time that he penetrated as far as to the confines of "Illyricum," lying along the shores of the Adriatic (Rom. 15:19). He would naturally wish that his second Letter to the Corinthians should have some time to produce its proper effect ere he revisited them, and this would appear a convenient opportunity for a northwestern circuit, which would enable him to pay a passing visit to the churches at Thessalonica and Berea, though of this we have no record. On his way southward to Greece, he would preach the Gospel in the intermediate regions of Epirus, Thessaly, and Bœotia (see Rom. 15:19), though of this we have no record. **he came into Greece**—or Achaia, in pursuance of the *second* part of his plan (ch. 19:21). **3. And there abode three months**—Though the province only is here mentioned, it is the city of CORINTH that is meant, as the province of "Macedonia" (vs. 1) meant the city of Philippi. Some rough work he anticipated on his arrival at Corinth (II Cor. 10:1-8, 11; 13:1-10) though he had reason to expect satisfaction on the whole; and as we know there were other churches in Achaia besides that at Corinth (II Cor. 1:1; 11:10), he would have time enough to pay them all a brief visit during the three months of his stay there. This period was rendered further memorable by the despatch of *the* EPISTLE TO THE ROMANS, written during his stay at Corinth and sent by "Phœbe, a servant [deaconess] of the Church at Cenchrea" (see on ch. 18:3), a lady apparently of some standing and substance, who was going thither on private business. (See on Rom. 16:1 and Introduction to Epistles to Romans.) **And when the Jews laid wait for him, as he was about to sail into Syria**—He had intended to embark, probably at Cenchrea, the eastern harbor of the city, for Palestine, on his route to Jerusalem, the *third* part of his plan (ch. 19:21). But having detected some conspiracy against his life by his bitter Jewish enemies as at Damascus (ch. 9:22-25) and Jerusalem (ch. 9:29, 30), he changed his plan and determined "to return" as he had come, "through Macedonia." As he was never more to return to Corinth, so this route would bring him, for the last time, face to face with the attached disciples of *Berea, Thessalonica,* and *Philippi.* **4, 5. there accompanied him into**—the province of—**Asia, Sopater of Berea**—The true reading, beyond doubt, is, 'Sopater [the son] of Pyrrhus of Berea.' Some think this mention of his father was to distinguish him from Sosipater (the same name in fuller form),

ADAM CLARKE

A. T. ROBERTSON:

1. "After the uproar was ceased" (*meta to pausasthai ton thorubon*). Literally, after the ceasing (accusative of articular aorist middle infinitive of *pauo*, to make cease) as to the uproar (accusative of general reference). Noise and riot, already in Matt. 26:5; 27:24; Mark 5:38; 14:2; see also Acts 21:34; 24:18. Pictures the whole incident as bustle and confusion. "Took leave" (*aspamenos*). First aorist middle participle of *aspazomai*, old verb from *a* intensive and *spao*, to draw, to draw to oneself in embrace either in greeting or farewell. Here it is in farewell as in 21:6. Luke here condenses what was probably a whole year of Paul's life and work as we gather from 2 Corinthians, one of Paul's "mighty and powerful" letters as his enemies called them (2 Cor. 10:10). "This epistle more than any other is a revelation of Paul's own heart: it is his spiritual autobiography."

—*Word Pictures in the New Testament*

2. *He came into Greece.* Into "Hellas," Greece properly so called, the regions between Thessaly and Propontis, and the country of Achaia. He did not, however, go there immediately. He passed through Macedonia, v. 1, in which he informs us, 2 Cor. vii. 5-7, that he suffered much, from both believers and infidels; but was greatly comforted by the arrival of Titus, who gave him a very flattering account of the prosperous state of the church at Corinth. A short time after this, being still in Macedonia, he sent Titus back to Corinth, 2 Cor. viii. 16-17, and sent by him the Second Epistle which he wrote to that church, as Theodoret and others suppose. Some time after, he visited Corinth himself, according to his promise, 1 Cor. xvi. 5. This was his third voyage to that city, 2 Cor. xii. 14; xiii. 1.

3. *Abode three months.* Partly, as we may suppose, at Corinth; from which place he is supposed to have sent his Epistle to the Romans, because he continued longer here than at any other place, and mentions several of the Corinthians in his salutations to the believers of Rome. *When the Jews laid wait for him.* Paul had determined to go by sea to Syria, and from thence to Jerusalem. This was the first object of his journey, and this was the readiest road he could take; but, hearing that the Jews had *laid wait* for him, probably to attack his ship on the voyage, seize his person, sell him for a slave, and take the money which he was carrying to the poor saints at Jerusalem, he resolved to go as much of the journey as he conveniently could by land. Therefore he returned through Macedonia and from thence to Troas, where he embarked to sail for Syria on his way to Jerusalem. The whole of his journey is detailed in this and the following chapter.

4. *And there accompanied him.* Rather, says Bishop Pearce, "there followed him as far as to Asia"; for they were not in his company till he set sail from Philippi and came to them at Troas, in Asia, whither they had gone before and where they tarried for him, v. 5. *Into Asia.* These words are wanting in two MSS. Some think that they embarrass this place; for how these could "accompany" him into Asia, and "go before him," and "tarry for him" at Troas, v. 6, is not so very clear. Mr. Wakefield gets rid of the difficulty by reading the verse thus: "Now Sopater of Berea accompanied him; but Aristarchus and Secundus of Thessalonica, Gaius of Derbe, Timothy (of Lystra), and Tychicus and Trophimus of Asia, went before, and tarried for us at Troas."

Sopater of Berea. Sopater seems to be the same as *Sosipater*, whom Paul mentions as his kinsman, Rom. xvi. 21. Some MSS. add *Pyrrhou*, "Sopater the son of Pyrrhus." *Aristarchus* of Thessalonica. This person occurs in chap. xix. 29, and is mentioned there as a Macedonian. He attended Paul in his journey to Rome, chap. xxvii. 2, and was his fellow laborer, Philemon, v. 24, and his fellow prisoner, Col. iv. 10-11. Secundus is mentioned nowhere but in this place.

MATTHEW HENRY

Timothy is reckoned among them, for though Paul, when he departed from Ephesus (*v.* 1), left Timothy there, yet he soon followed him, and accompanied him, with others here named. Now, one would think, this was no good husbandry, to have all these worthy men accompanying Paul, but so it was ordered, 1. That they might assist him in instructing such as by his preaching were awakened and startled; wherever Paul came, the waters were stirred, and then there was need of many hands to help the cripples in. 2. That they might be trained up by him, and fitted for future service.

V. His coming to Troas. They went before, and stayed for him at Troas (*v.* 5). We should not think it hard to stay awhile for good company in a journey. Paul made the best of his way thither. Luke was now in company with him; for he says, *We sailed from Philippi* (*v.* 6), and the first time we find him in his company was here at Troas, *ch.* xvi. 11. *The days of unleavened bread* are mentioned only to describe the time. He *came to them to Troas*, by sea, *in five days*, and when he was there stayed but *seven days*. There is no remedy, but a great deal of time will unavoidably be lost in travelling to and fro, by those who go about doing good, yet it shall not be put upon the score of lost time. Paul thought it worth while to bestow *five days* in going to Troas, though it was but for an opportunity of *seven days'* stay there.

Verses 7-12

We have here an account of what passed at Troas the last of the seven days that Paul stayed there.

I. There was a solemn religious assembly of the Christians that were there. 1. *The disciples came together, v.* 7. Though they read, and meditated, and prayed, and sung psalms, apart, and thereby kept up their communion with God, yet that was not enough; they must come together to worship God in concert, and so keep up their communion with one another. There ought to be stated times for the disciples of Christ to come together; though they cannot all come together in one place, yet as many as can. 2. They *came together upon the first day of the week*, which they called *the Lord's day* (Rev. i. 10). This is here said to be the day when it was their practice to come together in all the churches. The first day of the week is to be religiously observed by all the disciples of Christ; and it is a sign between Christ and them. 3. *They were gathered together in an upper chamber* (*v.* 8); they had no capacious stately chapel, but met in a private house, in a garret. As they were few, and did not need, so they were poor, and could not build, a large meeting-place; yet they came together, in that despicable inconvenient place. It will be no excuse for our absenting ourselves from religious assemblies that the place of them is not so decent nor so commodious as we would have it to be. 4. They *came together to break bread*, that is, to celebrate the ordinance of the Lord's supper. In the breaking of the bread, not only the breaking of Christ's body for us, to be a sacrifice for our sins, is commemorated, but the breaking of Christ's body to us, to be food and a feast for our souls, is signified. It was the custom of many churches to receive the Lord's supper every Lord's day, in concert, in a solemn assembly, to testify their joint concurrence in the same faith and worship.

II. In this assembly Paul gave them a sermon, a long sermon, a farewell sermon, *v.* 7. 1. He *preached to them*. The preaching of the gospel ought to accompany the sacraments. 2. It was a farewell sermon, he being *ready to depart on the morrow*. When he was gone, they might have the same gospel preached, but not as he preached it; and therefore they must make the best use of him that they could while they had him. 3. It was a very long sermon: He *continued his speech until midnight*; for he had a great deal to say, and knew not that ever he should have another opportunity of preaching to them. There may be occasion for ministers to preach, not only in *season, but out of season*. We know some that would have reproached Paul for this as a long-winded preacher, that tired his hearers; but they were willing to hear: he saw them so, and therefore continued his speech. We wish we had the heads of this long sermon, but we may suppose it was for substance the same with his epistles. The meeting being continued till midnight, there were candles set up, *many lights* (*v.* 8). This might prevent the reproach of their enemies, who said they met in the night for works of darkness.

III. *A young man* in the congregation, that slept at sermon, was killed by a fall *out of the window, but raised to life again;* his name signifies *one that had good fortune*, and he answered his name.

1. The infirmity with which he was overtaken.

JAMIESON, FAUSSET, BROWN

mentioned in Romans 16:21. But that they were the same person seems more probable. **of the Thessalonians, Aristarchus**—See on ch. 19:29. **and Secundus**—of whom nothing else is known. **Gaius of Derbe**—Though the Gaius of ch. 19:29 is said to be of "Macedonia," and this one "of Derbe," there is no sufficient reason for supposing them different persons; on the contrary, Romans 16:23 (cf. with III John 1, where there is hardly any reason to doubt that the same Gaius is addressed) seems to show that though he spent an important part of his Christian life away from his native Derbe, he had latterly retired to some place not very far from it. **and Timotheus**—not probably of Derbe, as one might suppose from this verse, but of Lystra (see on ch. 16:1); both being so associated in his early connection with the apostle that the mention of the one in the previous clause would recall the other on the mention of his name. **and of Asia, Tychicus and Trophimus**—The latter was an Ephesian, and probably the former also. They seem to have put themselves, from this time forward, at the apostle's disposal, and to the very last been a great comfort to him (Eph. 6:21, 22; Col. 4:7, 8; ch. 21:29; II Tim. 4:12, 20). From the mention of the places to which each of these companions belonged, and still more the order in which they occur, we are left to conclude that they were deputies from their respective churches, charged with taking up and bringing on the collection for the poor saints at Jerusalem, first at Berea, next at Thessalonica, then at Philippi [Hows], *where we gather that our historian himself rejoined the party* (from the resumption at vs. 5 of the "us," dropped at ch. 16:17), by whom the Philippian collection would naturally be brought on **5, 6. These going before**—perhaps to announce and prepare for the apostle's coming. **tarried for us at Troas. And we sailed ... from Philippi after the days of unleavened bread**—(i.e., the Passover). This, compared with I Corinthians 16:8, shows that the three months spent at Corinth (vs. 3) were the winter months. **came ... to Troas**—for the third and last time. (See on ch. 16:8, and on vs. 1.) **in the five days**—As it might have been done in two days, the wind must have been adverse. The vivid style of one now present will be here again observed. **where we abode seven days**—i.e., arriving on a Monday, they stayed over the Jewish sabbath and the Lord's Day following; Paul occupying himself, doubtless, in refreshing and strengthening fellowship with the brethren during the interval. **7. upon the first day of the week, when the disciples came together**—This, compared with I Corinthians 16:2, and other similar allusions, plainly indicates that the Christian observance of the day afterwards distinctly called "the Lord's Day," was already a fixed practice of the churches.

Paul preached—discoursed. The *tense* implies continued action—'kept discoursing.'

8. there were many lights in the upper chamber—not a mere piece of graphic detail by an eyewitness [Hackett, Hows], but mentioned, probably, as increasing the heat and contributing to drowsiness [Webster and Wilkinson], as the next clause seems to show. **9. in a**—'the'—**window**—or window-seat, of recess.

ADAM CLARKE

Gaius of Derbe. This is supposed to be the same who is mentioned in chap. xix. 26, and who is there called "a man of Macedonia," of which some suppose he was a native, but descended from a family that came from Derbe; but as Gaius, or Caius, was a very common name, these might have been two distinct persons. One of this name was baptized by Paul at Corinth, 1 Cor. i. 14, and entertained him as his host while he abode there, Rom. xvi. 23. *And Timotheus*. This was the same person of whom mention is made, chap. xvi. 1, and to whom Paul wrote the two Epistles which are still extant; and who was a native of Lystra, as we learn from the above place. *Tychicus . . . of Asia*. This person was high in the confidence of Paul. He styles him "a beloved brother and faithful minister in the Lord," whom he sent to the Ephesians, that he might know their affairs, and comfort their hearts, Eph. vi. 21-22. He sent him for the same purpose, and with the same commendations, to the Colossians, Col. iv. 7-8. Paul seems also to have designed him to superintend the church at Crete in the absence of Titus; see Titus ii. 12. He seems to have been the most intimate and confidential friend that Paul had. *Trophimus*. Was an Ephesian. He accompanied Paul from Ephesus into Greece, as we see here; and from thence to Jerusalem, chap. xxi. 29. He had no doubt travelled with him on other journeys, for we find, by 2 Tim. iv. 20, that he was obliged to leave him sick at Miletus, being then, as it is likely, on his return to his own kindred at Ephesus.

6. *Days of unleavened bread*. The seven days of the Passover, in which they ate unleavened bread. See the account of this festival in the notes on Exodus xii. It is evident, from the manner in which Luke writes here, that he had not been with Paul since the time he accompanied him to Philippi, chap. xvi. 10-12; but he now embarks at Philippi with the apostle and accompanies him to Troas and continues with him through the rest of his journey.

7. *Upon the first day of the week*. What was called "the Lord's day," the Christian Sabbath, in which they commemorated the resurrection of our Lord, and which among all Christians afterwards took the place of the Jewish Sabbath. *To break bread*. To break the Eucharist, as the Syriac has it; intimating by this that they were accustomed to receive the Holy Sacrament on each Lord's day. It is likely that, besides this, they received a common meal together. Some think the *agape*, or "love feast," is intended.

Continued his speech until midnight. At what time he began to preach we cannot tell, but we hear when he concluded. He preached during the whole night, for he did not leave off till the break of the next day, v. 11, though about midnight his discourse was interrupted by the fall of Eutychus. Paul must have preached a sermon not less than six hours long. But it is likely that a good part of this time was employed in hearing and answering questions.

8. *Upper chamber*. The pious Quesnel supposes that the smoke issuing from the many lamps in this upper chamber was the cause of Eutychus falling asleep; and this, he says, the apostle mentions in charity to excuse the young man's appearing negligent.

MATTHEW HENRY

He presumptuously *sat in the window*, unglazed perhaps, and so exposed himself; whereas, if he could have been content to sit on the floor, he had been safe. He slept, nay, he *fell into a deep sleep when Paul was preaching*, which was a sign he did not duly attend to the things that Paul spoke of. The particular notice taken of his sleeping makes us willing to hope none of the rest slept, though it was sleeping time and after supper.

2. The calamity with which he was seized herein: *He fell down from the third loft, and was taken up dead*. Some think that the hand of Satan was in it, and that he designed it for a disturbance to this assembly and a reproach to Paul. Others think that God designed it for a warning to all people to take heed of sleeping when they are hearing the word preached. We must look upon it as a bad sign of our low esteem of the word of God. We must do what we can to prevent our being sleepy, get our hearts affected with the word we hear to such a degree as may drive sleep far enough.

3. The miraculous mercy shown him in his recovery *to life again, v.* 10. It proved an occasion of that which was a great confirmation to his preaching. *Paul fell on the dead body, and embraced it*, thereby expressing a great compassion to, and an affectionate concern for, this young man. Such tender spirits as Paul had are much affected with sad accidents of this kind, and are far from judging and censuring those that fall under them. As a sign it represented the descent of that divine power upon the dead body, for the putting of life into it again, which at the same time he inwardly, earnestly, and in faith prayed for. He assured them that he had returned to life. Various speculations this ill accident had occasioned in the congregation, but Paul puts an end to them all: "*Trouble not yourselves, for his life is in him.*" He returned to his work immediately after this interruption (*v.* 11): *He came up again* to the meeting, they broke bread together in a love-feast, and *they talked a long while, even till break of day*. Paul did not now go on in a continued discourse, as before, but he and his friends fell into a free conversation. They knew not when they should have Paul's company again, and therefore made the best use they could of it when they had it, and reckoned a night's sleep well lost for that purpose. Before they parted *they brought the young man alive* into the congregation, and *they were not a little comforted, v.* 12. It was matter of great rejoicing among them, not only to the relations of the young man, but to the whole society.

Verses 13–16

Paul is hastening towards Jerusalem. He had called at Troas, and now he makes a sort of coasting voyage, no doubt endeavouring to make every place he came to the better for him.

I. He sent his companions by sea to Assos, but he himself was *minded to go afoot, v.* 13. He would foot it to Assos: and, if the land-way which Paul took was the shorter way, yet it is taken notice of by the ancients as a rough way. That way Paul would take, 1. That he might call on his friends by the way. Or, 2. That he might be alone, and might have the greater freedom of converse with God and his own heart in solitude. Or, 3. That he might inure himself to hardship, and not seem to indulge his ease. We should use ourselves to deny ourselves.

II. At Assos he went on board with his friends. There they *took him in*.

III. He made the best of his way to Jerusalem. His ship passed by *Chios* (*v.* 15), touched at *Samos*, they tarried awhile at *Trogyllium*, the seaport next to Samos, *and the next day* they came *to Miletus*, the seaport that lay next to Ephesus; for (*v.* 16) he had determined not to go to Ephesus at this time, *for he hasted, if it were possible for him, to be at Jerusalem on the day of pentecost*. He had been at Jerusalem about four or five years ago (*ch.* xviii. 21, 22), and now he was going thither again to pay his continued respects to that church. He aimed to be there by the feast of pentecost because it was a time of concourse, and the feast of pentecost had been particularly made famous among the Christians by the pouring out of the Spirit. Men of business must fit themselves to set time (with submission to Providence) and strive to keep it, not suffering ourselves to be diverted from it. It is a pleasure to us to be with our friends; it diverts us, nothing more; but we must not by it be diverted from our work. When Paul has a call to Jerusalem, he will not loiter away the time in Asia, though he had more and kinder friends there.

Verses 17–35

When he came to Miletus, he went ashore, and carried there so long as to send for the elders of Ephesus to come to him thither; for if he had gone

JAMIESON, FAUSSET, BROWN

fell down from the third loft—'story'—**and was taken up dead**—"The window projected (according to the side of the room where it was situated) either over the street or over the interior court; so that in either case he fell on the hard earth or pavement below."

10-12. Paul . . . fell on him—like Elisha (II Kings 4:34).

his life is in him—now restored; cf. Mark 5:39. **broken bread and eaten**—with what a mixture of awe and joy after such an occurrence! **and eaten**—denoting a common repast, as distinguished from the breaking of the eucharistic bread. **and talked a long while, even till break of day.** How lifelike this record of dear Christian fellowship, as free and gladsome as it was solemn! ((See Eccles. 9:7.)

13-38. CONTINUING HIS ROUTE TO JERUSALEM, HE REACHES MILETUS, WHENCE HE SENDS FOR THE ELDERS OF EPHESUS—HIS FAREWELL ADDRESS TO THEM. **13, 14. we . . . sailed** (from Troas) **unto Assos; there . . . to take in Paul: for so had he appointed, minding himself to go afoot**—'to go by land.' (See on Mark 6:33.) In sailing southward from Troas to Assos, one has to round Cape Lectum, and keeping due east to run along the northern shore of the Gulf of Adramyttium, on which it lies. This is a sail of nearly forty miles; whereas by land, cutting right across, in a southeasterly direction, from sea to sea, by that excellent Roman road which then existed, the distance was scarcely more than half. The one way Paul wished his companions to take, while he himself, longing perhaps to enjoy a period of solitude, took the other, joining the ship, by appointment, at Assos. **came to Mitylene**—the capital of the beautiful and classical island of Lesbos, which lies opposite the eastern shore of the Ægean Sea, about thirty miles south of Assos; in whose harbor they seem to have lain for the night. **15, 16. came the next day over against Chios**—now Scio: one of the most beautiful of those islands between which and the coast the sail is so charming. They appear not to have touched at it. **next day we arrived**—'touched' or 'put in'—**at Samos**—another island coming quite close to the mainland, and about as far south of Chios as it is south of Lesbos. **tarried**—for the night—**at Trogyllium**—an anchorage on the projecting mainland, not more than a mile from the southern extremity of the island of Samos. **next day we came to Miletus**—on the mainland; the ancient capital of Ionia, near the mouth of the Meander. **For Paul had determined to sail by**—or 'sail past'—**Ephesus**—He was right opposite to it when approaching Chios. **because he would not spend time in Asia**—the Asian province of which Ephesus was the chief city. **for he hasted, if . . . possible . . . to be at Jerusalem the day of Pentecost**—as a suitable season for giving in the great collection from all the western churches, for keeping the feast, and clearing his apostolic position with the Church, then represented in large number at Jerusalem. The words imply that there was considerable ground to doubt if he would attain this object—for more than three of the seven weeks from Passover to Pentecost had already expired—and they are inserted evidently to explain why he did not once more visit Ephesus. **17. from Miletus he sent to Ephesus, and called the elders of**

ADAM CLARKE

9. *There sat in a window.* This was probably an opening in the wall, to let in light and air, for there was no glazing at that time; and it is likely that Eutychus fell backward through it down to the ground, on the outside.

10. *And Paul . . . fell on him.* Stretched himself upon him, in the same manner as Elisha did on the Shunammite's son, 2 Kings iv. 33-35; though the action of lying on him, in order to communicate warmth to the flesh, might not have been continued so long as in the above instance.

11. *Had broken bread.* Had taken some refreshment, in order to their journey. *And talked a long while.* Having "familiarly conversed," for this is the import of the word, which is very different from the *dielezeto*, of the seventh verse, and the *dialegonmenou,* of the ninth, which imply solemn, grave discourse.

13. *Sailed unto Assos.* Assos, according to Pausanias, *Eliac.* ii. 4, and Pliny, *Hist. Nat.* xxxvi. 27, was a maritime town of Asia. The passage by sea to this place was much longer than by land; and therefore Paul chose to go by land, while the others went by sea. *Intending to take in Paul.* "To take him in again," for it appears he had already been aboard that same vessel, probably the same that had carried them from Philippi to Troas, v. 6.

14. *Came to Mitylene.* This was a seaport town in the isle of Lesbos.

15. *Over against Chios.* This was a very celebrated island between Lesbos and Samos, famous in antiquity for its extraordinary wines. At this island the apostle did not touch. *Arrived at Samos.* This was another island of the Aegean Sea. It does not appear that they landed at Samos; they passed close by it, and anchored at Trogyllium. This was a promontory of Ionia, which gave name to some small islands in the vicinity of Samos. *Came to Miletus.* Miletus is famous for being the birthplace of Thales, one of the seven wise men of Greece. Anaximander was also born here, and several other eminent men.

16. *To sail by Ephesus.* Not to touch there at this time. *To be at Jerusalem the day of Pentecost.* That he might have the opportunity of preaching the kingdom of God to multitudes of Jews from different places, who would come up to Jerusalem at that feast; and then he no doubt expected to see there a renewal of that Day of Pentecost in which the Spirit was poured out on the disciples and in consequence of which so many were converted to God.

17. *He sent to Ephesus, and called the elders of the church.* These are called *episcopoi,*

MATTHEW HENRY

up to Ephesus, he could never have got away from them. These Paul sent for, that he might instruct and encourage them to go on in the work to which they had laid their hands.

It is a very pathetic and practical discourse with which Paul here takes leave of these elders, and has in it much of the excellent spirit of this good man.

I. He appeals to them concerning both his life and doctrine, all the time he had been in and about Ephesus (*v.* 18): "*You know after what manner I have been with you.*" They all knew him to be a man of a serious, gracious, heavenly spirit, that he was no designing self-seeking man. He could not have been carried on with so much evenness and constancy in his services and sufferings, but by the power of divine grace. The temper of his mind, and the tenor both of his preaching and conversation, were such as plainly proved that God was with him of a truth.—He likewise makes this reference to his own conduct as an instruction to them to follow his example: "*You know after what manner I have been with you;* in like manner be you with those that are committed to your charge when I am gone."

1. His spirit and conversation were excellent and exemplary. (1) He had conducted himself well all along, *from the very first day that he came into Asia.* He appeared from the first day they knew him to be a man that aimed not only to do well, but to do good. He was a man that was consistent with himself. Take him where you would he was the same at all seasons, he did not turn with the wind nor change with the weather, but as uniform like a die, which, throw it which way you will, lights on a square side. (2) He had made it his business to serve the Lord. He never served himself, nor made himself a servant of men, nor was he a time-server. (3) He had done his work *with all humility of mind.* He never took state upon him, nor kept people at a distance, but conversed as freely and familiarly with the meanest, for their good, as if he had stood upon a level with them. He was willing to stoop to any service. (4) He had always been very tender, affectionate, and compassionate, among them; he had *served the Lord with many tears.* Paul was herein like his Master; often in tears. In his preaching, what he had told him before he told them again, *even weeping,* Phil. iii. 18. So near did they lie to his heart that he *wept with those that wept,* which was very endearing. (5) He had struggled with many difficulties among them. He went on in his work in the face of much opposition, *many temptations,* trials of his patience and courage. These befell him *by the lying in wait of the Jews,* who still were plotting some mischief or other against him. Those are the faithful servants of the Lord that continue to serve him in the midst of troubles and perils, that care not what enemies they make, so that they can but approve themselves to their Master, and make him their friend.

2. His preaching was likewise such as it should be, *v.* 20, 21. (1) He was a plain preacher: delivered his message so as to be understood. This is intimated in two words, *I have shown you, and have taught you.* He did not amuse them with nice speculations, nor lose them in the clouds of lofty notions and expressions; but he showed them the plain truths of the gospel, and taught them as children are taught. (2) He was a powerful preacher, which is intimated in his *testifying* to them; he preached as one upon oath. He preached the gospel, not as a hawker proclaims news in the street (it is all one to him whether it be true or false), but as a conscientious witness gives in his evidence at the bar. (3) He was a profitable preacher. He studied that which was *profitable unto them,* which had a tendency to make them wise and good, wiser and better, to reform their hearts and lives. He preached such things as *brought with them* divine light, and heat, and power to their souls. It is not enough not to preach that which is hurtful, but we must preach that which is profitable. Paul aimed to please only in order to profit. (4) He was a painstaking preacher; he preached *publicly, and from house to house.* He was neither afraid nor ashamed to preach the gospel publicly, nor did he grudge to bestow his pains privately, among a few, when there was occasion for it. Ministers should in their private visits, and as they go from house to house, discourse of those things which they have taught publicly. And, especially, they should help persons to apply the truth to themselves and their own case. (5) He was a faithful preacher. He preached everything that he thought might be profitable, and kept back nothing. He declined not preaching whatever he thought might be profitable, though it was not fashionable, nor to some acceptable. He did not keep back reproofs, when they were necessary, for fear of offending; nor did he keep back the preaching of the cross, though he knew it was to the Jews

JAMIESON, FAUSSET, BROWN

the church—As he was now some forty miles south of Ephesus, we might think that more time would be lost by sending thus far for the elders to come to him, than by going at once to Ephesus itself, when so near it. But if unfavorable winds and stormy weather had overtaken them, his object could not have been attained, and perhaps he was unwilling to run the risk of detention at Ephesus by the state of the church and other causes. Those here called "*elders*" or "presbyters," are in vs. 28 called "*bishops.*" (See note there.) The identity of presbyters and bishops in the New Testament is beyond all reasonable dispute. **18. Ye know . . . after what manner I have been with you at all seasons**—For the Christian integrity and fidelity of his whole official intercourse with them he appeals to themselves.

19. Serving the Lord—Jesus—**with all humility . . . and many tears and temptations**—Self-exaltation was unknown to him, and ease of mind: He "sowed in tears," from anxieties both on account of the converts from whom he "travailed in birth," and of the Jews, whose bitter hostility was perpetually plotting against him, interrupting his work and endangering his life.

20. kept back—timidly withheld from fear of consequences. **nothing that was profitable**—edification directing all.

have taught you publicly, and from house to house—Did an *apostle,* whose functions were of so wide a range, not feel satisfied without *private* as well as public ministrations? How then must *pastors* feel? [BENGEL].

ADAM CLARKE

"bishops," v. 28. By the *presbyteroi,* "presbyters or elders," here we are to understand all that were in authority in the church, whether they were bishops or overseers, or seniors in years, knowledge, and experience. The *elders* were probably the first order in the church; an order which was not so properly constituted, but which rose out of the state of things. From these *presbuteroi* the *episcopoi,* overseers or superintendents, were selected. Those who were eldest in years, Christian knowledge, and experience would naturally be preferred to all others as overseers of the Church of Christ. From the Greek word come the Latin *presbyterus,* the English "presbyter," the French *prestre,* and our own term "priest"; and all, when traced up to their original, signify merely an elderly or aged person, though it soon became the name of an office rather than of a state of years. Now as these *elders* are called "bishops," in v. 28, we may take it for granted that they were the same order; or rather, that these superintendents of the Church were indifferently called either "presbyters" or "bishops."

19. *Serving the Lord with all humility.* This relates not only to his zealous and faithful performance of his apostolic functions, but also to his private walk as a Christian, and shows with what carefulness this apostle himself was obliged to walk in order to have his calling and election as a Christian ratified and made firm.

20. *I kept back nothing.* Notwithstanding the dangers to which he was exposed and the temptations he must have had to suppress those truths that were less acceptable to the unrenewed nature of man, or to the particular prejudices of the Jews and the Gentiles, he fully and faithfully, at all hazards, declared what he terms, v. 27, the whole counsel of God.

ALBERT BARNES:

"With all humility." Without arrogance, pride, or a spirit of dictation; without a desire to "lord it over God's heritage"; without being elated with the authority of the apostolic office, the variety of the miracles which he was enabled to perform, or the success which attended his labors. What an admirable model for all who are in the ministry; for all who are endowed with talents and learning; for all who meet with remarkable success in their work! The proper effect of such success and of such talent will be to produce true humility. The greatest endowments are usually connected with the most simple and childlike humility.

"And with many tears." Paul not infrequently gives evidence of the tenderness of his heart, of his regard for the souls of men, and of his deep solicitude for the salvation of sinners (Phil. 3:18; 2 Cor. 2:4). The particular thing, however, here specified as producing weeping was the opposition of the Jews. But it cannot be supposed that those tears were shed from a apprehension of personal danger. It was rather because the opposition of the Jews impeded his work, and retarded his progress in winning souls to Christ. A minister of the gospel will feel, and deeply feel for the salvation of his people. He will weep over their condition when he sees them going astray, and in danger of perishing. He will be specially affected with opposition, because it will retard his work, and prevent the progress and the triumph of the gospel. It is not because it is a personal concern, but because it is the cause of his Master. "And temptations." Trials arising from their opposition. We use the word "temptation" in a more limited sense, to denote inducements offered to one to lead him into sin. The word in the Scriptures most commonly denotes "trials" of any kind.—*Popular Commentary*

MATTHEW HENRY

a stumbling-block and to the Greeks foolishness. (6) He was a catholic preacher. He *testified both to the Jews and also to the Greeks.* Though he was born and bred a Jew, and was trained up in their prejudices against the Gentiles, yet he did not therefore confine himself to the Jews and avoid the Gentiles; but preached as readily to them as to the Jews. And, on the other hand, though he was called to be the apostle of the Gentiles, and the Jews had an implacable enmity against him upon that score, yet he did not therefore abandon them as reprobates. Ministers must preach the gospel with impartiality; for they are ministers of Christ for the universal church. (7) He was a truly Christian evangelical preacher. He did not preach philosophical notions, nor did he preach politics, but he preached faith and repentance. These he urged upon all occasions. [1] *Repentance towards God.* He preached repentance as God's great command (*ch.* xvii. 30), *that men should repent, and turn to God, and do works meet for repentance* (so he explains it, *ch.* xxvi. 20); and he preached it as Christ's gift, in order to the *remission of sins* (*ch.* v. 31). [2] *Faith towards our Lord Jesus Christ.* We must by repentance look towards God as our end; and by faith towards Christ as our way to God. Our repentance towards God is not sufficient, we must have a true faith in Christ as our Redeemer and Saviour. For there is no coming to God, as penitent prodigals to a Father, but in the strength of Jesus Christ as Mediator.

II. He declares his expectation of sufferings and afflictions in his present journey to Jerusalem, *v.* 22–24. *Now, behold, I go bound in the spirit to Jerusalem,* which may be understood either, (1) Of the certain foresight he had of trouble before him. He was in full expectation of trouble, and made it his daily business to prepare for it. Or, (2) Of the strong impulse he was under to go this journey: "*I go bound in the spirit,* that is, firmly resolved to proceed, and not from any humour or design of my own. I go led by the Spirit, and bound to follow him wherever he leads me." He does not know particularly the things that shall befall him at Jerusalem. God had not thought fit to reveal them to him. It is good to be kept in the dark concerning future events, that we may be always waiting on God and waiting for him. We know not the things that shall befall us nor what a day, or a night, or an hour, may bring forth; and therefore must refer ourselves to God, let him do with us as seemeth good in his eyes. Yet he does know in general that there is a storm before him; for the prophets in every city he passed through told him, by the Holy Ghost, that bonds and afflictions awaited him. He fixes a brave and heroic resolution to go on with his work. It was a melancholy peal that was rung in his ears in every city, that *bonds and afflictions did abide him*; yet by the grace of God he was enabled to go on with his work. Let us take it from his own mouth here (*v.* 24): "*None of these things move me.*" Paul is here an example,

(1) Of holy courage and resolution. He made nothing of them: *None of these things move me; I make no account of them.* He did not lay these things to heart, Christ and heaven lay there. They did not drive him off from his work; he did not tack about, and go back again, when he saw the storm rise, but went on resolutely. They did not deprive him of his comfort. In the midst of troubles he was as one unconcerned. Those that have their conversation in heaven can look down, not only upon the common troubles of this earth but upon the threatening rage and malice of hell itself, and say that none of these things moved them, as knowing that none of these things can hurt them.

(2) Of a holy contempt of life: *Neither count I my life dear to myself.* Life is sweet, and is naturally dear to us. *All that a man has will he give for his life.* Yet to an eye of faith it is comparatively despicable; it is not so dear but it can be cheerfully parted with for Christ.

(3) Of a holy concern to go through with the work of life, which should be much more our care than to secure either the outward comforts of it or the countenance of it. Two things this great and good man is in care about, and if he gain them it is no matter to him what becomes of life: [1] That he may be found faithful to the trust reposed in him, that he may *finish the ministry which he has received of the Lord Jesus,* may do the work, which he was sent into the world about, or, rather, which he was sent into the church about. And may not do his work by halves. The apostleship was a ministry both to Christ and to the souls of men; and those that were called to it considered more the ministry of it than the dignity or dominion of it. This ministry was *received from the Lord Jesus.* He entrusted them with it, and from him they received their charge; for him they do their

JAMIESON, FAUSSET, BROWN

21. Testifying both to Jews and . . . Greeks—laboring under a common malady, and recoverable only by a common treatment—**repentance toward God, and faith toward our Lord Jesus Christ**—See on ch. 5:31. REPENTANCE, as distinguished from *faith,* is that state of the "honest and good heart" which arises from a discovery of one's contrariety to the righteous demands of the divine law. This is said to be "*toward God,*" because seeing Him to be the party dishonored by sin, it feels all its acknowledgments and compunctions to be properly due to Him, as the great Lawgiver, and directs them to Him accordingly; condemning, humbling itself, and grieving before Him, looking also to Him as its only Hope of deliverance. FAITH is said to be "*toward our Lord Jesus Christ,*" because in that frame of mind just described it eagerly credits the testimony of relief divinely provided in Christ, gladly embraces the overtures of reconciliation in Him, and directs all its expectations of salvation, from its first stage to its last, to Him as the one appointed Medium of all grace from God to a sinful world. Thus we have here a brief summary of all Gospel preaching. And it is easy to see why repentance is here put before faith; for the former must of necessity precede the latter. There *is* a repentance subsequent to faith, the fruit of felt pardon and restoration. It was this which drew the tears with which the Saviour's feet were once so copiously moistened. (Luke 7:37, 38, 47; and cf. Ezek. 16: 63.) But that is not the light in which it is here presented. **22, 23. And now, behold, I**—"I"—is emphatic here. **bound in the spirit**—cf. ch. 19:21. This internal pressure, unattended with any knowledge of "what was to befall him there," was the result of that higher guidance which shaped all his movements.

Save that the Holy Ghost witnesseth in every city . . .—by prophetic utterances from city to city, as in ch. 11:4; 21:10, 11. Analogous premonitions of coming events are not unknown to the general method of God's providence. They would tend to season the apostle's spirit.

24. But none of these things move me, neither . . .—In this noble expression of absolute dedication to the service of Christ and preparedness for the worst that could befall him in such a cause, note (1) his jealousy for the peculiar character of his mission, as *immediately from Christ Himself,* on which all the charges against him turned; (2) the burden of that Gospel which he preached—GRACE; it was "the Gospel of the Grace of God."

ADAM CLARKE

21. *Testify both to . . . Jews, and . . . Greeks.* He always began with the *Jews;* and in this case he had preached to them alone for three months, chap. xix. 8-10, and left their synagogues only when he found, through their obstinacy, he could do them no good. *Repentance toward God.* As all had sinned against God, so all should humble themselves before Him against whom they have sinned. But humiliation is no atonement for sin; therefore repentance is insufficient unless faith in our Lord Jesus Christ accompany it. Repentance disposes and prepares the soul for pardoning mercy, but can never be considered as making compensation for past acts of transgression. This *repentance* and *faith* were necessary to the salvation of both Jews and Gentiles, for all had sinned and come short of God's glory.

22. *I go bound in the spirit.* Either meaning the strong influence of the Divine Spirit upon his mind or the strong propensity in his own will, wish, and desire to visit Jerusalem; and in this sense "to bind" is sometimes used. But it appears more consistent with the mind of the apostle, and with that influence under which we find that he constantly acted, to refer it to the influence of the Holy Ghost.

24. *None of these things move me.* I consider them as nothing; I value them not a straw; they weigh not with me.

Neither count I my life dear. I am not my own; my life and being are the Lord's. He requires me to employ them in His service; I act under His direction, and am not anxious about the issue.

Finish my course with joy. "My ministerial function." We have already met with this word in application to the same subject, chap. xiii. 25. And the apostle here adds, by way of explanation, even that "ministry, which I have received of the Lord." The words *with joy* are omitted by several MSS.

MATTHEW HENRY

work, in his name, in his strength. The work of this ministry was to *testify the gospel of the grace of God*. It is a proof of God's goodwill to us, and a means of his good work in us; it shows him gracious towards us, and tends to make us gracious, and so is the gospel of the grace of God. Paul desired not to live a day longer than he might be instrumental to spread the knowledge of this gospel. [2] That he may finish well. He cares not when the period of his life comes, nor how, so that he may but *finish his course with joy*. He looks upon his life as *a course, a race*, so the word is. This intimates that we have our labours appointed us, and our limits appointed us, for we were not sent into the world to be here always, but to pass through the world, nay, to run through it, and it is soon run through. He counts upon the finishing of his course, and speaks of it as sure and near. Dying is the end of our race, when we come off either with honour or shame. He is full of care to finish it well. He thinks nothing too much to do, nor too hard to suffer, so that he may but finish well, finish with joy. We must look upon it as the business of our life to provide for a joyful death, that we may not only die safely, but die comfortably.

III. Counting upon it that this was the last time they should see him, he appeals to their consciences concerning his integrity.

1. He tells them that he was now taking his last leave of them (*v.* 25): *I know that you all, among whom I have* been conversant *preaching the kingdom of God*, shall never see my face again. Paul here speaks it with assurance, that these Ephesians should *see his face no more*; and we cannot think that he who spoke so doubtfully of that which he was not sure of (*not knowing the things that shall befall me there, v.* 22) would speak this with so much confidence unless he had had a special warrant from the Spirit to say it. He would never have said thus solemnly, *Now, behold, I know it*, if he had not known it *for certain*. We ought often to think of it, that those who now are preaching to us the kingdom of God will shortly be removed and we shall see their faces no more. Yet a little while is their light with us; it concerns us therefore to improve it while we have it, that when we shall see their faces no more on earth, yet we may hope to look them in the face with comfort in the great day.

2. He appeals to them concerning the faithful discharge of his ministry among them (*v.* 26). (1) He challenges them to prove him unfaithful: *I am pure from the blood of all men*, the blood of souls. "You cannot say but I have given warning, and therefore no man's blood can be laid at my door." If a minister has approved himself faithful, he may have this rejoicing in himself, *I am pure from the blood of all men*. (2) He therefore leaves the blood of those that perish upon their own heads, because they had fair warning given them, but they would not take it. (3) He charges these ministers to look to it that they took care and pains, as he had done. *I take you to record this day*. As sometimes the heaven and earth are appealed to, so here this day shall be a witness, this parting day.

3. He proves his own fidelity with this (*v.* 27): *For I have not shunned to declare unto you all the counsel of God*. He had preached to them nothing but the counsel of God, and had not added any inventions of his own; "it was pure gospel, and nothing else." The gospel is the counsel of God. This counsel of God it is the business of ministers to declare as it is revealed, and not otherwise. He had preached to them the whole counsel of God. As he had preached to them the gospel pure, so he had preached it to them entire. He had not wilfully nor designedly avoided the declaring of any part of the counsel of God. He had not declined preaching upon the most difficult parts of the gospel, nor declined preaching upon the most plain and easy parts of it; he had not shunned preaching those doctrines which he knew would be provoking to the watchful enemies of Christianity, or displeasing to the careless professors of it. And thus it was that he kept himself pure from the blood of all men.

IV. He charges them as ministers to be diligent and faithful in their work.

1. He commits the care of the church at Ephesus to them, who, though doubtless they were so numerous that they could not all meet in one place, are yet called here *one flock*, because they not only agreed in one faith, but in many instances they kept up communion one with another. To these elders or presbyters the apostle here commits the government of this church, and tells them that not he, but *the Holy Ghost, had made them overseers—bishops of the flock*. "You that are presbyters are bishops of the Holy Ghost's making." Now that they begin to be fledged they must learn to fly themselves, and to

JAMIESON, FAUSSET, BROWN

25-27. I know that ye all . . . shall see my face no more—not an inspired prediction of what was certainly to be, but what the apostle, in his peculiar circumstances, fully expected. Whether, therefore, he ever did see them again, is a question to be decided purely on its own evidence.

I am pure from the blood of all men—(Ch. 18:6; and cf. I Sam. 12:3, 5; Ezek. 3:17-21; 33:8, 9).

For I have not shunned to declare . . . all the counsel of God—God's way of salvation, and His kingdom of souls saved by His Son Jesus Christ. See Luke 7:30.

28. Take heed . . . unto yourselves—Cf. I Tim. 3: 2-7; 4:16; 6:11. **and to all the flock**—Cf. Hebrews 13:17. Observe here how the *personal* is put before the *pastoral* care. **over . . . which the Holy Ghost hath made you**—Cf. John 20:22, 23; Ephesians 4:8, 11, 12; Revelation 3:1. (Ch. 14:23 shows that the apostle did not mean to exclude *human* ordination.) **overseers**—or, as the same word is *everywhere else* rendered in our version, 'bishops.' The *English Version* has hardly dealt fair in this

ADAM CLARKE

To testify. "Earnestly, solemnly, and strenuously to assert, vindicate, and prove the gospel of the grace of God," not only to be in itself what it professes to be, but to be also the power of God for salvation to everyone that believes.

25. *Ye all . . . shall see my face no more*. This probably refers simply to the persons who were now present, concerning whom he might have had a divine intimation that they should not be found in life when he should come that way again. Or it may refer only to Ephesus and Miletus. From the dangers to which he was exposed it was, humanly speaking, unlikely that he should ever return; and this may be all that is implied. But that he did revisit those parts, though probably not Miletus or Ephesus, appears likely from Phil. i. 25-27; ii. 24; Philemon 22; Heb. xiii. 19-23. But in all these places he speaks with a measure of uncertainty: he had not an absolute evidence that he should not return, but in his own mind it was a matter of uncertainty. The Holy Spirit did not think proper to give him a direct revelation on this point.

26. *I am pure from the blood of all*. If any man, Jew or Gentile, perish in his sins, his blood shall be upon him; he alone shall be accessory to his own perdition. I am blameless, because I have fully shown to both the way to escape from every evil.

27. *I have not shunned to declare*. "I have not suppressed or concealed" anything, through fear or favor, that might be beneficial to your souls. This is properly the meaning of the original word. *All the counsel of God*. All that God has "determined" and revealed concerning the salvation of man—the whole doctrine of Christ crucified, with repentance towards God, and faith in Jesus as the Messiah and great atoning Priest. In Isa. ix. 6, Jesus Christ is called the *wonderful Counsellor*, which the Septuagint translate "the messenger of the great counsel." To this the apostle may have referred, as we well know that this version was constantly under his eye. Declaring therefore to them the whole counsel of God, the whole of that counsel or design of God, was in effect declaring the whole that concerned the *Lord Jesus*, who was the *Messenger of this counsel*.

28. *Made you overseers*. "Appointed you bishops," for so we translate the original word in most places where it occurs: but "overseers"

CHARLES H. SPURGEON:

According to the verse before us the apostle regarded life as a race which he had to run. Now, the more quickly a race is run the better: certainly, length is not the object of desire. The one thought of a runner is how he can most speedily reach the winningpost. He spurns the ground beneath him: he cares not for the course he traverses except so far as it is the way over which he must run to reach his desired end. Such was life to Paul: all the energies of his spirit were consecrated to the pursuit of one object—namely, that he might everywhere bear testimony to the gospel of the grace of God; and the life which he lived here below was only valued by him as a means to that end. He also regarded the gospel, and his ministry in witnessing to it, as a sacred deposit which had been committed to him by the Lord himself. He looked upon himself "as put in trust with the gospel"; and he resolved to be faithful though it should cost him his life. He says he "desired to fulfill the ministry which he had received of the Lord Jesus Christ." Before his mind's eye he saw the Savior taking into His pierced hands the priceless casket which contains the celestial jewel of the grace of God, and saying to him, "I have redeemed thee with My blood, and I have called thee by My name, and now I commit this precious thing into thy hands, that thou mayest take care of it, and guard it even with thy heart's blood. I commission thee to go everywhere in My place and stead, and to make known to every people under heaven the gospel of the grace of God." All believers occupy a somewhat similar place. We are none of us called to the apostleship, and we may not all have been called to the public preaching of the Word of God; but we are all charged to be valiant for the truth upon the earth, and to contend earnestly for the faith once delivered to the saints. Oh, to do this in the spirit of the apostle of the Gentiles!—*The Treasury of the New Testament*

MATTHEW HENRY

act without him, for the Holy Ghost had made them overseers. The Holy Ghost in them qualified them for, and enriched them to, this great undertaking, the *Holy Ghost fell upon them, ch.* xix. 6. The Holy Ghost also directed those that called, and ordained, them to this work in answer to prayer.

2. He commanded them to mind the work to which they were called. Dignity calls for duty; if the Holy Ghost has made them *overseers of the flock*, they must be true to their trust. (1) They must take heed to themselves in the first place, must walk circumspectly. "You have many eyes upon you, some to take example by you, others to pick quarrels with you, and therefore you ought to *take heed to yourselves.*" Those are not likely to be skilful or faithful keepers of the vineyards of others that do not keep their own. (2) "*Take heed to the flock.*" Ministers must not only take heed to their own souls, but must have a constant regard to the souls of those who are under their charge. "*Take heed to all the flock*, that none of them wander from the fold or be seized by the beasts of prey; that none of them be missing." (3) They must feed the church of God, must lead the sheep of Christ into the green pastures, must lay meat before them, must feed them with wholesome doctrine, and must see that nothing is wanting that is necessary in order to their being nourished up to eternal life. There is need of pastors, not only to gather the church of God, but to *feed* it by building up those that are within. (4) They must watch (*v.* 31), as shepherds keep watch over their flocks by night; watch against everything that will be hurtful to the flock, and watch for everything that will be advantageous to it.

3. He gives them several good reasons why they should mind the business of their ministry.

(1) Let them consider the interest of their Master, and his concern for the flock, *v.* 28. It is *the church which he has purchased with his own blood.* "It is his own; you are but his servants to take care of it for him. Your carelessness and treachery are so much the worse if you neglect your work, for you wrong God. And, if it be the church of God, he expects you should show your love to him by feeding his sheep and lambs." He has purchased it. Therefore it ought to be dear to us, for it was dear to him, because it cost him dear, and we cannot better show it than by feeding his sheep and his lambs. This church of God is what he has purchased *with his own blood.* In consideration of this, therefore, *feed the church of God,* because it is purchased at so dear a rate. Did Christ lay down his life to purchase it, and shall his ministers be wanting in any care and pains to feed it?

(2) Let them consider the danger that the flock was in of being made a prey to its adversaries, *v.* 29, 30. "You are concerned to take heed both to yourselves and to it." Here are reasons for both. [1] *Take heed to the flock*, for wolves are abroad, that seek to devour (*v.* 29): *I know this, that after my departure grievous wolves shall enter in among you.* Some understand it of persecutors. They thought, because, while Paul was with them, the rage of the Jews was most against him, that, when he had gone out of the country, they would be quiet: "No," says he, "*after my departure* you will find the persecuting spirit still working." Ministers must take a more than ordinary care of the flock in times of persecution. It is rather to be understood of seducers and false teachers. Probably Paul has an eye to those of the circumcision, who preached up the ceremonial law; these he calls *grievous wolves.* While Paul was at Ephesus, they kept away, for they durst not face him; but, when he was gone, then they entered in among them. [2] *Take heed to yourselves*, for some shepherds will apostatise (*v.* 30): "*Also of your ownselves, shall men arise speaking perverse things.* They will pervert some sayings of the gospel to make them patronize their errors. But it is to *draw away disciples after them*, to make a party for themselves." Some read it, *to draw away disciples after them*—those that are already disciples of Christ draw them from him to follow them. But, though there were some such seducers in the church of Ephesus, yet it should seem by Paul's Epistle to that church that that church was not so much infested with false teachers as some other churches were; but its peace and purity were preserved by the blessing of God on the pains and vigilance of these presbyters.

(3) Let them consider the great pains that Paul had taken in planting this church (*v.* 31): "*Remember that for the space of three years I ceased not to warn everyone night and day with tears.*" Paul, like a faithful watchman, had warned them, and by the warnings he gave men, he prevailed with them to embrace Christianity. He warned everyone; besides the public warnings he gave in his preaching, he applied himself to particular persons according as he saw their

JAMIESON, FAUSSET, BROWN

case with the sacred text, in rendering the word "overseers," whereas it ought here, as in all other places, to have been 'bishops,' in order that the fact of elders and bishops having been originally and apostolically synonymous, might be apparent to the ordinary English reader, which now it is not [ALFORD]. The distinction between these offices cannot be certainly traced till the second century, nor was it established till late in that century. **to feed the church of God**—or, 'the Church of the Lord.' Which of these two readings of the text is the true one, is a question which has divided the best critics. The evidence of MSS. preponderates in favor of 'THE LORD'; some of the most ancient Versions, though not all, so read; and *Athanasius,* the great champion of the supreme Divinity of Christ early in the fourth century, says the expression 'Church of God' is unknown to the Scriptures. Which reading, then, does the *internal* evidence favor? As 'Church of God' occurs nine times elsewhere in Paul's writings, and 'Church of the Lord' nowhere, the probability, it is said, is that he used his wonted phraseology here also. But if he did, it is extremely difficult to see how so many early transcribers should have altered it into the quite unusual phrase, 'Church of the Lord'; whereas, if the apostle did use this latter expression, and the historian wrote it so accordingly, it it easy to see how transcribers might, from being so accustomed to the usual phrase, write it 'Church of God.' On the whole, therefore, we accept the *second* reading as most probably the true one. But see what follows.

which he hath purchased—'made His own,' 'acquired—**with his own blood**—'His own' is emphatic: 'That glorified Lord who from the right hand of power in the heavens is gathering and ruling the Church, and by His Spirit, through human agency, hath set you over it, cannot be indifferent to its welfare in your hands, seeing He hath given for it His own most precious blood, thus making it His own by the dearest of all ties.' The transcendent sacredness of the Church of Christ is thus made to rest on the dignity of its Lord and the consequent preciousness of that blood which He shed for it. And as the sacrificial atoning character of Christ's death is here plainly *expressed,* so His supreme dignity is *implied* as clearly by the second reading as it is *expressed* by the first. What a motive to *pastoral fidelity* is here furnished!

29, 30. after my departing shall grievous wolves enter in among you—Two classes of coming enemies are here announced, the one more external to themselves, the other bred in the bosom of their own community; both were to be teachers, but the one, "grievous wolves," not sparing, i.e., making a prey of the flock; the other, simply sectarian "perverters" of the truth, with the view of drawing a party after them. Perhaps the one pointed to that subtle poison of Oriental Gnosticism which we know to have very early infected the Asiatic churches; the other to such Judaizing tendencies as we know to have troubled nearly all the early churches. See the Epistles to the *Ephesians, Colossians,* and *Timothy,* also those to the seven churches of Asia (chs. 2 and 3). But watchfulness against *all* that tends to injure and corrupt the Church is the duty of its pastors in every age.

31. by the space of three years—speaking in round numbers; for it was nearer three than two years.

ADAM CLARKE

or "inspectors" is much more proper. The persons who examine into the spiritual state of the flock of God, and take care to lead them in and out and to find them pasture, are termed "superintendents." That "bishop" and "presbyter," or "elder," were at this time of the same order, and that the word was indifferently used of both, see noticed on v. 17. *Feed the church of God.* This verse has been the subject of much controversy, particularly in reference to the term *of God,* in this place, and concerning it there is great dissension among the MSS. and versions. Three readings exist in them, in reference to which critics and commentators have been much divided; viz., "the church of God," "of the Lord," "of the Lord and God."

F. B. MEYER:

"Take heed unto yourselves, and to all the flock." There are many lessons in this verse:

(1) The Christian worker must not neglect his own soul. He must take heed to himself, as well as to the flock. Our temptation is to neglect our close walk with God in our eagerness to save others.

(2) The overseer, elder, or bishop, is not set over the flock, but is in it. Note the force of the Greek, as given in RV: the flock in the which they are made bishops. So to the end of life the most eminent of God's servants must remember that he is but a saved sinner, needing the blood and righteousness of Christ as much as the weakest of his flock; and he also must lie down in green pastures, and be led beside still waters.

(3) The office of the minister is given by the Holy Ghost. It is He who lays on him the burden of souls, and equips him for his work. He, too, is willing to direct and use. How awful and solemn the responsibility!

(4) Notice that the Church is distinctly asserted to be God's. "Feed the church of God." We are his people and the sheep of his pasture. His by choice, by purchase, by the drawing of the Holy Ghost. We must get a right understanding of this doctrine of the Church, that she has been taken out of the world to be God's peculiar possession and delight.

(5) The purchase money of the Church is here said to be God's own blood. It is a remarkable expression. It stands alone in the Word of God, but brings out very distinctly the thought that the entire Godhead achieved man's redemption in the offering of the cross. We are dear to God, and must give Him the benefit of his great expenditure!

—Great Verses Through the Bible

29. *After my departing.* Referring most likely to his death, for few of these evils took place during his life. *Grievous wolves.* Persons professing to be teachers; Judaizing Christians, who, instead of feeding the flock, would feed themselves, even to the oppression and ruin of the church.

30. *Also of your own selves.* From out of your own assembly *shall men arise, speaking perverse things,* teaching for truth what is erroneous in itself and perversive of the genuine doctrine of Christ crucified. *To draw away disciples.* To make schisms or rents in the church, in order to get a party to themselves.

31. *Therefore watch, and remember.* The only way to abide in the truth is to *watch* against evil, and for good; and to "keep in mind" the heavenly doctrines originally received. *By the space of three years.* The Greek word here does not necessarily mean three whole years; it may be months more or less. In chap. xix. 8 and 10, we have an account of his spending "two years and three months" among them; probably this is all that is intended.

MATTHEW HENRY

case called for it. He was constant in giving warning; he *warned night and day*; his time was filled up with his work. He was indefatigable in it; he *ceased not* to warn. He warned those that were righteous not to turn from their righteousness, as he had warned them when they were wicked to turn from their wickedness. He spoke to them about their souls with a great deal of affection and concern: he *warned them with tears*. As he had served the Lord, so he had served them, *with many tears, v.* 19. Thus free had he been of his pains; and why then should they be sparing of their pains in carrying it on?

V. He recommends them to divine direction and influence (*v.* 32): "*And now, brethren, I commend you to God.*" Paul directs them to look up to God with an eye of faith, and beseeches God to look down on them with an eye of favour.

1. See here to whom he commends them. He commends them to God, begs of God to provide for them, and encourages them to cast all their care upon him: "Whatever you want, go to God. Let this be your comfort, that you have a God to go to, a God all sufficient." From whomsoever we are separated, still we have God nigh unto us. He commends them *to the word of his grace*, by which some understand Christ: he is *the word* (John i. 1). He is here called *the word of God's grace*, because *from his fulness we receive grace for grace*. Paul commends them not only to God and to his providence, but to Christ and his grace. It comes to much the same thing, if by the word of his grace we understand the gospel of Christ. "You will find much relief by acting faith on the providence of God, but much more by acting faith on the promises of the gospel." He commends them to the word of God's grace, not only as the foundation of their hope and the fountain of their joy, but as the rule of their walking: "*I commend you to God*, as your Master, *and to the word of his grace*. Observe the precepts of this word, and then live upon the promises of it."

2. See here what he commends them to the word of God's grace for. They had received the gospel of the grace of God, and were entrusted to preach it. Now he recommends them to that, for their edification: "*It is able to build you up*. Though you are already furnished with good gifts, there is that in it with which you need to be better acquainted and more affected." Ministers must aim at their own edification as well as at the edification of others. The most advanced Christians, while they are in this world, are capable of growing. For their glorification: *It is able to give you an inheritance among all those who are sanctified*. The word of God's grace gives it, not only as it gives the knowledge of it, but as it gives the promise of it, the promise of a God *that cannot lie*; and by the word, the Spirit of grace is given (*ch.* x. 44), to be the seal of the promise. Heaven is an inheritance which gives an indefeasible right to all the heirs. This inheritance is secured to all those, and those only, that are sanctified; for as those cannot be welcome guests to the holy God that are unsanctified, so really heaven would be no heaven to them; but *to all that are sanctified*, that are born again, it is as sure as almighty power and eternal truth can make it. We cannot expect to be among the glorified hereafter unless we be among the sanctified here.

VI. He recommends himself to them as an example of indifference to this world. He had recommended them to God for spiritual blessings, which are the best blessings; but what shall they do for food for their families. "As to these," Paul says, "do as I did."

1. He never aimed at worldly wealth (*v.* 33): "*I have coveted no man's silver, or gold, or apparel.*" There were many in Ephesus who were rich, and made a very good appearance. Paul was not ambitious to live like them. We may take it in this sense: *I never coveted to have so much silver and gold at command* as I see others have. I neither condemn them nor envy them. I can live comfortably and usefully without living great. *He knew how to want and how to be abased*. He was not greedy to receive from them, silver, or gold, or apparel; so far from being always craving that he was not so much as coveting. "Whose kindness have I coveted, or asked? Or to whom have I been burdensome?"

2. He had worked for his living, and taken a great deal of pains to get bread (*v.* 34): "*Yea, you yourselves know that these hands of mine have ministered to my necessities, and to those that were with me.*" Paul was sometimes reduced to necessities, and the want of the common supports of life. What an unthinking, unkind, and ungrateful world is this, that could let such a man as Paul be poor in it! He desired no more than to have his necessities supplied. When he was to earn his bread, he did it by a manual occupation. Paul had a head and a tongue that he might

JAMIESON, FAUSSET, BROWN

I ceased not to warn every one night and day with tears—What an appeal to be able to make! "And if this was an apostle's part, how much more a pastor's!" [BENGEL].

32-35. I commend you to God—the almighty Conservator of His people.

and to the word of his grace—that message of His pure grace (vs. 24) by the faith of which He keeps us (I Pet. 1:5).

which—i.e., God —**is able to build you up, and to give you an inheritance . . .**—Observe how salvation—not only in its *initial stages* of pardon and regeneration, but in all its *subsequent stages* of "up-building," even to its *consummation* in the final inheritance—is here ascribed to the "ability" of God to bestow it, as in Romans 16:25; Ephesians 3:20; particularly Jude 24; and cf. II Timothy 1:12, where *the same thing is ascribed to Christ*.

among all them which are sanctified—Sanctification is here viewed as the final character and condition of the heirs of glory, regarded as one saved company.

these hands—doubtless holding them up, as before Agrippa in chains (ch. 26:29). **have ministered unto my necessities, and to them that were with me**—See ch. 18:3; and I Corinthians 4:12; 9:6, written from Ephesus; also I Thessalonians 2:9.

ADAM CLARKE

32. *I commend you to God*. Instead of *to God*, several MSS. have "to the Lord"; neither reading makes any difference in the sense.

And to the word of his grace. The doctrine of salvation by Christ Jesus.

Being made children of God by faith in Christ Jesus, and *sanctified* by His Spirit, they have a right to the heavenly *inheritance;* for only the children of the family can possess the celestial estate. Thus we find they must be saved by grace and be made thereby children of God; be *sanctified* by His Spirit; and then, being prepared for, they are removed in due time into the heavenly inheritance.

33. *I have coveted no man's silver*. And from this circumstance they would be able to discover the grievous wolves and the perverters; for these had nothing but their own interests in view, whereas the genuine disciples of Christ neither coveted nor had worldly possessions. Paul's account of his own disinterestedness is very similar to that given by Samuel of his, 1 Sam. xii. 3-5.

34. *These hands have ministered*. It was neither "sin nor discredit" for the apostle to work to maintain himself, when the circumstances of the church were such that it could not support him. Still many eminent ministers of God are obliged to support themselves and their families, at least in part, in the same way, while indefatigably testifying the gospel of the grace of God.

MATTHEW HENRY

have got money by, but they were these hands, saith he, *that ministered to my necessities.* Paul puts these presbyters (and others in them) in mind of this, that they may not think it strange if they be thus neglected. The less encouragement they have from men, the more they shall have from God. He worked not only for himself, but for the support of those also that were with him. This was hard indeed. It had better become them to have worked for him. But so it is; those that are willing to take the labouring oar will find those about them willing they should have it.

3. Even then, when he worked for the supply of his own necessities, yet he spared something out of what he got for the relief of others; for this he here obliges them to do (*v.* 35): "*I have shown you all things, that so labouring you ought to support the weak.*" Understand it of their helping to support the sick, and the poor, and those that could not labour, because it agrees with Paul's exhortation (Eph. iv. 28): *Let him labour, working with his hands, that he may have to give to him that needeth.* We must labour in an honest employment, not only that we may be able to live, but that we may be able to give. This might seem a hard saying, and therefore Paul backs it with a saying of our Master's. An excellent saying it is, and has something of a paradox in it: *It is more blessed to give than to receive.* It is more blessed to give to others than to receive from others; not only more blessed to be rich, and so on the giving hand, than to be poor, and so on the receiving hand (everyone will own this); but more blessed to do good with what we have, be it much or little, than to increase it and make it more. The sentiment of the children of this world is contrary to this; they are afraid of giving. They are in hope of getting. Clear gain is with them the most blessed thing that can be; but Christ tells us, *It is more blessed to give than to receive.* It makes us more like to God, who gives to all, and receives from none; and to the Lord Jesus, *who went about doing good.* It is more blessed to give our pains than to receive pay for it. It is more pleasant to do good to the grateful, but it is more honourable to do good to the ungrateful, for then we have God to be our paymaster.

Verses 36–38

After the parting sermon that Paul preached to the elders of Ephesus we have here the parting prayer and tears.

I. They parted with prayer (*v.* 36): *And, when he had thus spoken, he kneeled down, and prayed with them all.* It was a joint prayer. He not only prayed for them, but prayed with them, *prayed with them all.* Public prayers are so far from being intended to supersede our own secret prayers, that they are designed to quicken and encourage them. It was a humble reverent prayer. This was expressed by the posture they used: *He kneeled down, and prayed with them,* which is significant both of adoration and of petition, especially petition for the forgiveness of sin. It was a prayer after sermon. He had committed the care of the church at Ephesus to those elders, and now he prays that God would enable them faithfully to discharge this great trust reposed in them. He prayed for the flock *that the great Shepherd of the sheep* would take care of them all, and keep them from being a prey to the grievous wolves. Thus he taught these ministers to pray for those they preached to. It was a parting prayer. It is good for friends, when they part, to part with prayer, that by praying together just at parting they may be enabled to pray the more feelingly one for another when they are separated. Paul here followed the example of Christ, who, when he took leave of his disciples, after he had preached to them, prayed with them all, John xvii. 1.

II. They parted with tears, and most affectionate embraces, *v.* 37, 38. *They all wept sorely.* He that was so often in tears while he was with them (*v.* 19, 31), no doubt shed many at parting. But the notice is taken of their tears: *They all wept sorely;* there was not a dry eye among them. These were tears of love and mutual endearment. *They fell upon Paul's neck, and kissed him.* Those that are most living are commonly best beloved. Paul, who was a most affectionate friend himself, had friends that were very affectionate to him. That which cut them to the heart thus was *that word which Paul spoke, that* he was certain *they should see his face no more.* When they are told that they shall see his face no more in this world, that it is a final farewell they are now giving and taking, this makes it a great mourning. When our friends are separated from us by death, this is the consideration with which we raise up our mourning, that we shall see their faces no more; but we complain not of this as those that have no hope. Though we shall see their faces no more in this world, we hope

JAMIESON, FAUSSET, BROWN

that so labouring—as I have done, for others, as well as myself—**ye ought to support the weak, and to remember the words of the Lord Jesus, how he**—'how Himself'—**said, It is more blessed to give than to receive**—This golden saying, snatched from oblivion, and here added to the Church's abiding treasures, is apt to beget the wish that more of what issued from those Lips which "dropped as an honeycomb," had been preserved to us. But see on John 21:25.

36-38. he kneeled down and prayed with them all . . .—Nothing can be more touching than these three concluding verses, leaving an indelible impression of rare ministerial fidelity and affection on the apostle's part, and of warm admiration and attachment on the part of these Ephesian presbyters. Would to God that such scenes were more frequent in the Church!

ADAM CLARKE

35. *I have shewed you all things.* The clause should be read thus—"I have showed you in all things." *It is more blessed to give than to receive.* That is, the giver is more "happy" than the receiver. Where or on what occasion our Lord spake these words we know not, as they do not exist in any of the four Evangelists. But that our Lord did speak them Paul's evidence is quite sufficient to prove. The sentiment is worthy of Christ.

37. *Fell on Paul's neck.* Leaned their heads against his shoulders and kissed his neck. This was not an unusual custom in the East.

38. *That they should see his face no more.* This was a most solemn meeting, and a most affecting parting. The man who had first pointed out to them the Lord Jesus Christ, by whom they had been brought into so glorious a state of salvation, is now going away, in all likelihood to be seen no more till the day in which the quick and dead shall stand before the throne of judgment.

As the disciples are stated to have come together on *the first* day *of the week,* we may learn from this that ever since the apostolic times the "Lord's day," now the Christian Sabbath, was set apart for religious exercises, such as the preaching of God's holy Word and celebrating the sacrament of the Lord's Supper.

ALBERT BARNES:

"The words of the Lord Jesus." These words are nowhere recorded by the evangelists. But they did not pretend to record all his sayings and instructions (John 21:25). There is the highest reason to suppose that many of his sayings which are not recorded would be treasured up by those who heard them; would be transmitted to others; and would be regarded as a precious part of his instructions. Paul evidently addresses the elders of Ephesus as if they had heard this before, and were acquainted with it. Perhaps he himself had reminded them of it. This is one of the Redeemer's most precious sayings; and it seems even to have a peculiar value from the fact that it is not recorded in the regular and professed histories of his life. It comes to us recovered, as it were, from the great mass of his unrecorded sayings; rescued from that oblivion to which it was hastening if left to mere tradition, and placed in permanent form in the sacred writings by the act of an apostle who had never seen the Savior before his crucifixion. It is a precious relic, and the effect of it is to make us regret that more of his words were not recovered from an uncertain tradition, and placed in a permanent form by an inspired penman. God, however, who knows what is requisite to guide us, has directed the words which are needful for the welfare of the church, and has preserved by inspiration the doctrines which are adapted to convert and bless man.

"It is more blessed to give." It is a higher privilege; it tends more to the happiness of the individual and of the world. The giver is more blessed or happy than the receiver. There is pleasure in the act of giving when it is done with pure motives. It promotes our own peace; is followed by happiness in the recollection of it; and will be followed by happiness for ever. That is the most truly happy man who is most benevolent. He is the most miserable who has never known the luxury of doing good, but who lives to gain all he can, and to hoard all he gains. Those who give from a pure motive God will bless. They will be rewarded, not only in the peace which they shall experience in this life, but in the higher bliss of heaven (Matt. 15:34-36).

We may also remark that this is a sentiment truly great and noble. It is worthy of the Son of God. It is that on which he himself acted when he came to give pardon to the guilty, comfort to the disconsolate and the mourner, peace to the anxious sinner, sight to the blind, hearing to the deaf, life to the dead, and heaven to the guilty and the lost. Acting on this, he gave his own tears to weep over human sorrows and human guilt; his own labors and toils to instruct and save man; his own life a sacrifice for sin on the cross. Loving to give, he has freely given us all things. Loving to give, he delights in the same character in his followers, and seeks that they who have wealth, and strength, and influence, should be willing to give all to save the world. Imitating his great example, and complying with his command, the church shall yet learn more and more to give its wealth to bless the poor and needy; its sons and its daughters to bear the gospel to the benighted heathen; its undivided and constant efforts to save a lost world. Here closes this speech of Paul; an address of inimitable tenderness and beauty. Happy would it be if every minister could bid such an adieu to his people, when called to part from them; and happy if, at the close of life, every Christian could leave the world with a like consciousness that he had been faithful in the discharge of his duty. Thus dying, it will be blessed to leave the world; and thus would the example of the saints live in the memory of survivors long after they themselves have ascended to their rest.—*Popular Commentary*

MATTHEW HENRY

to see them again in a better world, and to be there together for ever and with the Lord.

III. They *accompanied him unto the ship* that they might have a little more of his company and conversation, and see the last of him. Loth to part bids oft farewell. But this was a comfort to both sides, that the presence of Christ both went with him and stayed with them.

CHAPTER 21

Verses 1–7

I. How much ado Paul had to get clear from Ephesus, intimated in the first words of the chapter, *after we had gotten from them.* Paul was loth to leave them, and they were loth to part with him, but so it must be.

II. What a prosperous voyage they had thence. *They came with a straight course to Coos—the next day to Rhodes,—thence to Patara,* a famous port, the metropolis of Lycia (*v.* 1); here they very happily *found a ship sailing over into Phenicia,* the very course they were steering, *v.* 2. Providence must be acknowledged when things happen thus opportunely. This ship that was bound for Phenicia (that is, Tyre) they took the convenience of, *went on board, and set sail.* In this voyage *they discovered Cyprus,* the island that Barnabas was of, and which he took care of, and therefore Paul did not visit it, but *we left it on the left hand* (*v.* 3), *sailed* upon the coast of *Syria, and* at length *landed at Tyre, for there the ship was to unlade her burden.*

III. The halt that Paul made at Tyre.

1. *At Tyre he found disciples.* Wherever Paul came, he enquired what disciples were there, and associated with them; for we know what is the usage with birds of a feather. When Christ was upon earth, though he went sometimes into the coast of Tyre, yet he never went thither to preach the gospel there. But, after the enlarging of the gospel commission, Christ was preached at Tyre, and had disciples there.

2. Paul, *finding those disciples at Tyre, tarried there seven days.* He stayed seven days at Troas (*ch.* xx. 6), and here so many days at Tyre, that he might be sure to spend one Lord's day with them.

3. The disciples at Tyre were endowed with such gifts that they could by the Spirit foretell the troubles Paul would meet with at Jerusalem; for *the Holy Ghost witnessed it in every city, ch.* xx. 23. God saw fit to have it much prophesied of before, that people's faith, instead of being offended, might be confirmed. Foreseeing his troubles, out of love to him, they begged of him *that he would not go up to Jerusalem.* Therefore they said to him, *by the Spirit, that he should not go up.* It was not at all their fault to think so, but it was their mistake, for his trial would be for the glory of God and the furtherance of the gospel, and he knew it.

4. The disciples of Tyre, though they were none of Paul's converts, yet showed a very great respect to Paul. Though they had had but seven days' acquaintance with him, they all came together, *with their wives and children,* solemnly to take leave of him. We should pay respect, not only to our own ministers, but we must, as there is occasion, testify our love and respect to all the faithful ministers of Christ. It is good to train up children in a respect to good people and good ministers. No doubt, gracious notice was taken of the children of the disciples at Tyre, that honoured an apostle, as Christ accepted the hosannas of the little children. We should be good husbands of our opportunities, and make the utmost we can of them for the good of our souls. *They brought Paul on his way,* that they might have so much the more of his company and his prayers.

5. They parted with prayer, as Paul and the Ephesian elders had done, *ch.* xx. 36. *We kneeled down on the shore and prayed.* As he was much in prayer so he was mighty in prayer. Those that are going to sea should commit themselves to God by prayer, and put themselves under his protection, as those that hope, even when they leave the *terra firma,* to find firm footing for their faith in the providence of God. They kneeled down on the shore, though we may suppose it either stony or dirty, and there prayed. Where he lifted up his prayer, he bowed his knees. Mr. George Herbert says, *Kneeling never spoiled silk stockings.*

6. They parted at last (*v.* 6): *When we had taken our leave one of another, we took ship,* and *they returned home again.* Paul left his blessing behind him with those that returned home, and those that stayed sent their prayers after those that went to sea.

IV. Their arrival at Ptolemais (*v.* 7): *We came to*

JAMIESON, FAUSSET, BROWN

CHAPTER 21

Vss. 1-16. SAILING FROM EPHESUS, THEY LAND AT TYRE, AND THENCE SAILING TO PTOLEMAIS, THEY PROCEED BY LAND TO CÆSAREA AND JERUSALEM. **1. we were gotten**—'torn'—**from them**—expressing the difficulty and pain of the parting. **with a straight course**—running before the wind, as ch. 16:11. **unto Coos**—Cos, an island due south from Miletus, which they would reach in about six hours, and coming close to the mainland. **the day following unto Rhodes**—another island, some fifty miles to the southeast, of brilliant classic memory and beauty. **thence unto Patara**—a town on the magnificent mainland of Lycia, almost due east from Rhodes. It was the seat of a celebrated oracle of Apollo. **2. And finding a ship**—their former one going no farther, probably—**to Phœnica**—See on ch. 11:19. **went abroad**—One would almost think this extracted from a journal of the voyage, so graphic are its details. **3. when we . . . discovered**—'sighted,' as the phrase is—**Cyprus, we left it on the left hand**—i.e., steered southeast of it, leaving it on the northwest. **sailed into**—'unto'—**Syria, and landed at Tyre**—the celebrated seat of maritime commerce for East and West. It might be reached from Patara in about two days. **there the ship was to unlade her burden**—which gave the apostle time for what follows.

4-6. finding disciples—finding out the disciples,—implying some search. They would expect such, from what is recorded, ch. 11:19. Perhaps they were not many; yet there were gifted ones among them. **who said to Paul . . . that he should not go up to Jerusalem**—See on ch. 20:23; also on vss. 11-14.

they all brought us on our way with wives and children . . . and we kneeled down on the shore and prayed—See on ch. 20:36-38. Observe here that the *children* of these Tyrian disciples not only were taken along with their parents, but must have joined in this act of solemn worship. See on Ephesians 6:1.

ADAM CLARKE

Besides its being the day on which our blessed Lord rose from the dead, the practice of the apostles and the primitive Church is an additional reason why we should religiously celebrate this first day of the week. They who, professing the Christian religion, still prefer the Jewish Sabbath have little to support them in the New Testament.

CHAPTER 21

1. *Came with a straight course.* Having had, as is necessarily implied, wind and tide in their favor. *Coos.* An island in the sea. It was famous for being the birthplace of Hippocrates, the most eminent of physicians, and Apelles, the most celebrated of painters. *Rhodes.* Another island in the same sea, celebrated for its Colossus, which was one of the seven wonders of the world. This was a brazen statue of Apollo so high that ships in full sail could pass between its legs. It was the work of Chares, a pupil of Lysippus, who spent 12 years in making it. It was 106 feet high and so great that few people could fathom its thumb. It was thrown down by an earthquake about 224 years before Christ, after having stood 66 years. *Patara.* One of the chief seaport towns of Syria.

2. *Phoenicia.* A part of Syria.

3. *Cyprus.* See the note on chap. iv. 36. *Tyre.* A city of Phoenicia, one of the most celebrated maritime towns in the world. *There the ship was to unlade her burden.* The freight that she had taken in at Ephesus she was to unlade at Tyre, to which place she was bound.

4. *Who said to Paul through the Spirit.* We cannot understand this as a command from the Holy Spirit not to go up to Jerusalem, else Paul must have been highly criminal to have disobeyed it. *Through the Spirit* must either refer to their own great earnestness to dissuade him from taking a journey which they plainly saw would be injurious to him—or if it refer to the Holy Spirit, it must mean that if he regarded his personal safety he must not at this time go up to Jerusalem. The Spirit foretold Paul's persecutions, but does not appear to have forbidden his journey; and Paul was persuaded that in acting as he was about to do, whatever personal risk he ran, he should bring more glory to God by going to Jerusalem than by tarrying at Tyre or elsewhere. The purport of this divine communication was, "If you go up to Jerusalem, the Jews will persecute you, and you will be imprisoned." As he was apprised of this, he might have desisted, for the whole was conditional. Paul might or might not go to Jerusalem; if he did go, he would be persecuted and be in danger of losing his life.

5. *When we had accomplished those days.* That is, the seven days mentioned in the preceding verse. *And they all brought us on our way, with wives and children.* It is not likely that Paul, Silas, and Luke had either wives or children with them; and it is more natural to suppose that the brethren of Tyre with their wives and children are those that are meant. These, through affection to the apostles, accompanied them from their homes to the ship; and the coming out of the husbands, wives, and children shows what a general and affectionate interest the preaching and private conversation of these holy men had excited. *Kneeled down on the shore, and prayed.* As God fills heaven and earth, so He may be worshipped everywhere: as well, when circumstances require it, on the seashore as in the temple. We have already seen, in the case of Lydia, that the Jews had *proseuchas* by the riversides; and an observation in Tertullian seems to intimate that they preferred such places, and in the open air offered their petitions to God by the seashore.

6. *Taken . . . leave.* "Having given each other the kiss of peace," as the constant custom of the Jews and primitive Christians.

MATTHEW HENRY

Ptolemais. Paul begged leave to go ashore there, *to salute the brethren.* He would not pass by them without paying his respects to them, and he *abode with them one day*; better a short stay than no visit.

Verses 8–14

We have here Paul and his company arrived at length at Cæsarea, it being the place where the gospel was first preached to the Gentiles, and *the Holy Ghost fell upon them, ch.* x. 1, 44.

I. Who it was that entertained Paul and his company *at Cæsarea.* He seldom had occasion to go to a public house, but, wherever he came, some friend or other took him in, and bade him welcome. "We that were of Paul's company went where he went, and came to Cæsarea." Those that travel together through this world will separate at death, and then it will appear who are of Paul's company and who are not.

1. They were entertained by Philip the evangelist, whom we left at Cæsarea many years ago, after he had baptized the eunuch (*ch.* viii. 40), and there we now find him again. He was originally a deacon, (*ch.* vi. 5). He was now and had long been an evangelist. He had a house at Cæsarea and he bade him and them very welcome to it: *We entered into the house of Philip the evangelist, and we abode with him.*

2. This Philip *had four maiden daughters, who did prophesy, v.* 9. It intimates that they prophesied of Paul's troubles at Jerusalem, or perhaps they prophesied for his comfort and encouragement.

II. A plain and full prediction of the sufferings of Paul, by a noted prophet, *v.* 10, 11. 1. Paul and his company tarried many days at Cæsarea. What cause Paul saw to tarry so long there we cannot tell; but we are sure he did not stay either there or anywhere else to be idle. 2. *Agabus the prophet came to Cæsarea from Judæa;* this was he of whom we read before, who came *from Jerusalem to Antioch,* to foretell a general famine, *ch.* xi. 27, 28. See how God dispenseth his gifts variously. To Paul was given the word of wisdom and knowledge, by the Spirit, and the gifts of healing; Agabus, and to Philip's daughters, was given prophecy, by the same Spirit—the foretelling of things to come. So that that which was the most eminent gift of the Spirit under the Old Testament, the foretelling of things to come, was under the New Testament quite outshone by other gifts. It should seem as if Agabus came on purpose to Cæsarea, to meet Paul with this prophetic intelligence. 3. He foretold Paul's bonds at Jerusalem: By a sign, as the prophets of old did. *Agabus took Paul's girdle,* and with it *bound* first *his own hands, and then his own feet.* That which we see usually makes a greater impression upon us than that which we only hear of. By an explication of the sign: *Thus saith the Holy Ghost, So shall the Jews at Jerusalem bind the man that owneth this girdle,* and, *shall deliver him into the hands of the Gentiles.* Paul had this express warning given him of his troubles, that he might prepare for them.

III. The great importunity which his friends used with him to dissuade him from going to Jerusalem, *v.* 12. "Not only those of that place, but we that were of Paul's company, besought him with tears that he would not go up to Jerusalem." Here appeared a commendable affection to Paul. Good men that are very active sometimes need to be dissuaded from overworking themselves, and good men that are very bold need to be dissuaded from exposing themselves too far. Yet there was a mixture of infirmity, especially in those of Paul's company, who knew he undertook this journey by divine direction. But we see in them the infirmity incident to us all; when we see trouble at a distance, we can make light of it; but when it comes near we begin to shrink, and draw back.

IV. The holy bravery with which Paul persisted in his resolution, *v.* 13.

1. He reproves them for dissuading him. Here is a quarrel of love on both sides. They love him dearly, and therefore oppose his resolution; he loves them dearly, and therefore chides them for opposing it: *What mean you to weep and to break my heart?* Their weeping about him *broke his heart.* It was a temptation to him, it began to weaken his resolution. "I know I am appointed to suffering, and you ought to encourage me. You, with your tears, break my heart, and discourage me. Has not our Master told us to take up our cross? And would you have me to avoid mine?" It was a trouble to him that they should so earnestly press him to that in which he could not gratify them without wronging his conscience. As he was much in tears himself, so he had a compassionate regard to the tears of his friends. But now it breaks his heart, when he is under a necessity of denying the request of his weeping friends. It

JAMIESON, FAUSSET, BROWN

7. when we had finished our course—completing the voyage—**from Tyre, we came**—which they would do the same day—**to Ptolemais**—anciently called Accho (Judg. 1:31), now St. Jean d'Acre, or Acre. **and saluted the brethren, and abode . . .**—disciples gathered probably as at Tyre, on the occasion mentioned (ch. 11:19). **8-10. next day we [that were of Paul's company] departed**—(The words in brackets are omitted in the best MSS. They were probably added as the connecting words at the head of some church lessons.) **and came to Cæsarea**—a run along the coast, southward, of some thirty miles.

Philip the evangelist—a term answering apparently very much to our *missionary* [Hows], by whose ministry such joy had been diffused over Samaria, and the Ethiopian eunuch had been baptized (ch. 8). **one of the seven**—deacons, who had "purchased to himself a good degree" (I Tim. 3:13). He and Paul now meet for the first time, some twenty-five years after that time. **the same man had four daughters . . . which did prophesy**—fulfilling Joel 2:28 (see ch. 2:18). This is mentioned, it would seem, merely as a high distinction divinely conferred on so devoted a servant of the Lord Jesus, and probably indicates the high tone of religion in his family. **tarried there many**—'a good many'—**days**—Finding himself in good time for Pentecost at Jerusalem, he would feel it a refreshing thing to his spirit to hold Christian communion for a few days with such a family. **there came down from Judea**—the news of Paul's arrival having spread—**a certain prophet . . . Agabus**—no doubt the same as in ch. 11:28.

11-14. So shall the Jews bind the man that owneth this girdle . . .—For though the Romans did it, it was at the Jews' instigation (vs. 33; ch. 28:17). Such dramatic methods of announcing important future events would bring the old prophets to remembrance. (Cf. Isa. 20:2, etc.; Jer. 13:1, and Ezek. 5:1, etc.). This prediction and that at Tyre (vs. 4) were intended, not to prohibit him from going, but to put his courage to the test and when he stood the test, to deepen and mature it. **we and they at that place** (the Cæsarean Christians) **besought him**—even with tears, vs. 13—**not to go to Jerusalem.**

Then Paul answered, What mean ye to weep and to break mine heart—Beautiful union of manly resoluteness and womanly tenderness, alike removed from mawkishness and stoicism!

ADAM CLARKE

7. ***We came to Ptolemais.*** **This was a seaport town of Galilee, not far from Mount Carmel, between Tyre and Caesarea, where the river Belus empties itself into the sea. It was at first called Accho, and belonged to the tribe of Asher, Judg. i. 31. It was enlarged and beautified by the first of the Egyptian Ptolemies, from whom it was called *Ptolemais.* This place terminated St. Paul's voyage.**

8. ***We that were of Paul's company.*** **This clause is wanting in some MSS.**

Philip the evangelist. **One of the seven deacons, who seems to have settled here after he had baptized the eunuch. See on chap. viii. 40.**

9. ***Four daughters, virgins, which did prophesy.*** **Probably these were no more than teachers in the church, for we have already seen that this is a frequent meaning of the word *prophesy;* and this is undoubtedly one thing intended by the prophecy of Joel, quoted in chap. ii. 17-18 of this book.**

10. ***Agabus.*** **See the note on chap. xi. 28.**

11. ***Took Paul's girdle, and bound his own hands.*** **This was no doubt a *prophet* in the commonly received sense of the term; and his mode of acting was like that of the ancient prophets, who often accompanied their predictions with significant emblems. Jeremiah was commanded to bury his girdle by the river Euphrates, to mark out the captivity of the Jews, Jer. xiii. 4. For more examples of this figurative or symbolical prophesying, see Isaiah xx; Jer. xxvii. 2-3; xxviii. 4; Ezekiel iv; xii. *Into the hands of the Gentiles.* That is, the Romans, for the Jews had not, properly speaking, the power of life and death. And as Agabus said he should be delivered into the hands of the Gentiles he showed thereby that they would attempt to destroy his life. This prediction of Agabus was literally fulfilled; see v. 33.**

12. ***Besought him not to go up to Jerusalem.*** **For they all understood the prophecy to be conditional and contingent, and that it was in Paul's power to turn the scale.**

was an unkind kindness thus to torment him with their dissuasions. When our friends are called out to sufferings, we shall show our love rather by comforting them than by sorrowing for them. But observe, These Christians at Cæsarea, if they could have foreseen the particulars of that event, would have been better reconciled to it for their own sakes; for, when Paul was made a prisoner at Jerusalem, he was presently sent to Cæsarea (*ch.* xxiii. 33), and there he continued at least *two years* (*ch.* xxiv. 27), and he was a prisoner at large, as appears (*ch.* xxiv. 23). The church at Cæsarea had much more of Paul's company and help when he was imprisoned than they could have had if he had been at liberty. That which we oppose, as thinking it to operate much against us, may be overruled by the providence of God to work for us.

2. He repeats his resolution to go forward, notwithstanding: "*What mean you to weep thus? I am ready* to suffer whatever is appointed for me. I am willing to suffer, and therefore why are you unwilling that I should suffer? For my part, *I am ready.*" "I was told at first *what great things I must suffer,*" *ch.* ix. 16. "I am *prepared* for it. I can *bid it welcome.* I can, through grace, not only bear it, but rejoice in it." (1) See how far his resolution extends: I tell you, *I am ready not only to be bound, but to die at Jerusalem.* It is our wisdom to think of the worst that may befall us, and to prepare accordingly. (2) See what it is that makes him willing to suffer and die: it is *for the name of the Lord Jesus.* All that a man has will he give for his life; but life itself will Paul give for the service and honour of the name of Christ.

V. The patient acquiescence of his friends in his resolution, *v.* 14. 1. They submitted to the wisdom of a good man. "*When he would not be persuaded, we ceased* our importunity. Paul knows best his own mind, and what he has to do, and it becomes us to leave it to himself. No doubt, Paul has a good reason for his resolution, and God has gracious ends to serve in confirming him in it." It is good manners not to over-press those in their own affairs that will not be persuaded. 2. They submitted to the will of a good God: *We ceased,* saying, *The will of the Lord be done.* They did not resolve his resolution into his stubbornness, but into his willingness to suffer, and God's will that he should. This may refer, (1) To Paul's present firmness; he is inflexible, and in this they see the will of the Lord done. (2) To his approaching sufferings: "If there be no remedy the will of the Lord Jesus be done. We leave it to God, we leave it to Christ, and therefore we do, not as we will, but as he will." God is wise, and knows how to make all work for good, and therefore "welcome his holy will." Not only, "The will of the Lord must be done, and there is no remedy"; but, "Let the will of the Lord be done, for his will is his wisdom." When a trouble is come, this must allay our griefs, that the will of the Lord is done; when we see it coming, this must silence our fears, that the will of the Lord shall be done.

Verses 15–26

I. Paul's journey to Jerusalem from Cæsarea, and the company that went along with him. They *took up their carriages,* their bag and baggage, like travellers or soldiers, and were their own porters. If they could have persuaded Paul to go some other way, they would gladly have gone along with him; but if he will go to Jerusalem, they do not say, "Let him go by himself then"; but, "*Let us go and die with him.*" Thus Paul's boldness emboldened them. Certain of the disciples of Cæsarea went along with them. The less while that Paul is likely to enjoy his liberty the more industrious they are to improve every opportunity of conversation with him. They brought with them an honest old gentleman that had a house of his own at Jerusalem, in which he would gladly entertain Paul and his company, *one Mnason of Cyprus* (*v.* 16), *with whom we should lodge.* Such a great concourse of people there was to the feast that it was a hard matter to get lodgings; the public houses would be taken up by those of the better sort, and it was looked upon as a scandalous thing for those that had private houses to let their rooms out at those times. Every one then would choose his friends to be his guests, and Mnason took Paul and his company to be his lodgers. He shall be welcome to him, whatever comes of it. This Mnason is called an *old disciple*—a disciple *from the beginning.* He had been long a Christian, and was now in years. It is an honourable thing to be an old disciple of Jesus Christ, to have been enabled by the grace of God to continue long in a course of duty, steadfast in the faith. And with these old disciples one would choose to lodge; for the multitude of their years will teach wisdom.

G. CAMPBELL MORGAN:

What, then, did these men and Luke mean when they said to him: "through the Spirit, that he should not set foot in Jerusalem"? We must interpret that declaration of the fourth verse by other declarations. In the previous chapter (v. 23), Paul said that "in every city the Holy Spirit testifieth unto me, saying that bonds and afflictions abide me." In verse 11 of this chapter we find Agabus prophesying in the Spirit, not telling him that he was not to go, but declaring that if he should go, then he would be bound and imprisoned. When these men in Tyre told Paul not to go, their advice was the result of the Spirit's foretelling that if he went, he would suffer. Taking the whole story into account, we are not warranted in believing that the Spirit declared that he was not to go; but that the Spirit told him that he was going to suffering and to prison. These disciples at Tyre, when they heard it, when they were informed by the Spirit and by spiritual interpretation, of the difficulties that awaited him, urged him not to go. The Spirit said that bonds awaited Paul, and their advice was really advice to falsify the teaching of the Spirit. I do not think they meant it in that way; they had not thought the situation out. Now the Spirit could never instruct men to give advice to one which, if followed, would be an attempt to escape the very pathway of suffering that the Spirit indicated was lying ahead of him. I believe, then, that at this point Paul was true to the deepest facts, and that he was right.

There is great comfort in this chapter for us. Recognizing that such things do occur, understanding the story by our own experience, is there not a test by which we may finally decide which conviction is according to the mind of the Spirit of God? I think that there is. It is the test of motive. The motive of the conviction that took possession of the minds of all these people, Luke included, was a very high motive. It was love for Paul. Paul's motive was an infinitely higher motive. It was love for the Lord and passion for the accomplishment of His purpose. The last and final test for those who are submitted to the Spirit, who are seeking His guidance, who believe they have the light of His revelation, is always that of motive. There may be motives which in themselves are very high, which become wrong, because there ought to be the infinitely higher motive.—*The Acts of the Apostles*

I am ready not to be bound only—'If that is all, let it come.' **but to die . . .**—It was well he could add this, for he had that also to do.

15, 16, we took up our carriages—'our baggage'—**and went up to Jerusalem**—for the *fifth* time after his conversion, thus concluding *his third missionary tour,* which proved his *last,* so far as recorded; for though he accomplished the fourth and last part of the missionary plan sketched out (ch. 19:21)—"After I have been at Jerusalem, I must also see Rome"—it was as "a prisoner of Jesus Christ." **went with us . . . and brought with them**—rather, 'brought us to'.

One Mnason of Cyprus, an old disciple . . .—not an *aged* disciple, but probably 'a disciple of old standing,' perhaps one of the 3000 converted on the day of Pentecost, or, more likely still, drawn to the Saviour Himself during His lifetime. He had come, probably, with the other Cyprians (ch. 11:20), to Antioch, "preaching the Lord Jesus unto the Grecians," and now he appears settled at Jerusalem.

13. *I am ready not to be bound only.* He was resolute and determined, but was under no constraining necessity.

14. *The will of the Lord be done.* May that which is most for His glory take place! They plainly saw from the prophecy what would take place if Paul went to Jerusalem, and everyone saw that he had power to go or not to go.

15. *Took up our carriages.* We made ourselves ready, packed up our things, got our baggage in order.

16. *And brought with them one Mnason.* It is not very likely that they would bring a man *with* them with whom they were to *lodge* in Jerusalem. Therefore the text should perhaps be read as Bishop Patrick proposes: "There went with us certain of the disciples of Caesarea, bringing us to one Mnason, with whom we were to lodge." This is most likely, as the text will bear this translation. But it is possible that Mnason, formerly of Cyprus, now an inhabitant of Jerusalem, might have been down at Caesarea, met the disciples, and invited them to lodge with him while they were at Jerusalem; and having transacted his business at Caesarea, might now accompany them to Jerusalem. His being an *old disciple* may either refer to his having been a very early convert, probably one of those on the Day of Pentecost, or to his being now an old man.

MATTHEW HENRY

II. Paul's welcome at Jerusalem. 1. Many of the brethren there *received him gladly*, *v.* 17. The word here used concerning the welcome they gave to the apostles is used concerning the welcome of the apostles' doctrine, *ch.* ii. 41. They *gladly received his word.* We think if we had Paul among us we should gladly receive him; but it is a question whether we should or no if, having his doctrine, we do not gladly receive that. 2. They paid a visit to James and the elders of the church (*v.* 18): *"The day following, Paul went in unto James,* and took us with him." It should seem that James was now the only apostle that was resident at Jerusalem. They forecasted to have an apostle at Jerusalem because there was a great resort thither from all parts. James was now upon the spot, and all the elders were present. He *saluted them.* The proper signification of salutation is, wishing salvation to you. And such mutual salutations very well become Christians, in token of their love to each other and joint regard to God.

III. The account they had from him of his ministry among the Gentiles, and their satisfaction in it. He gave them a narrative of the success of the gospel in those countries where he had been employed: *He declared particularly what things God had wrought among the Gentiles by his ministry*, *v.* 19. Not what things he had wrought, but what God had wrought by his ministry. It was *not I, but the grace of God which was with me.* He declared it particularly, that the grace of God might appear the more illustrious in the circumstances of his success. Hence they took occasion to give praise to God (*v.* 20): *When they heard it, they glorified the Lord.* Paul ascribed it all to God, and to God they gave the praise of it. They gave glory to the grace of God, which was extended to the Gentiles. They did not envy him, nor were they jealous of his growing reputation, but, on the contrary, *glorified the Lord.* If God be praised, Paul is pleased.

IV. The request of James and the elders to Paul, or their advice rather, that he would gratify the believing Jews by showing some compliance with the ceremonial law, and appearing publicly in the temple to offer sacrifice. The ceremonial law, though it was by no means to be imposed upon the Gentile converts, yet it was not become unlawful as yet to those that had been bred up in the observance of it. It was dead, but not buried; dead, but not yet deadly.

1. They desired him to take notice of the great numbers there were of the Jewish converts: *Thou seest, brother, how many thousands of the Jews there are who believe.* They called him brother. Though they were conformists and he a nonconformist, yet they were brethren, and owned the relation. The number of the names at first was but one hundred and twenty, yet now many thousands. Let none therefore despise the day of small things; for, though the beginning be small, God can make the latter end greatly to increase. And this account of the success of the gospel among the Jews was, no doubt, as grateful to Paul as the account which he gave them of the conversion of the Gentiles was to them; for his heart's desire and prayer to God for the Jews was *that they might be saved.*

2. They informed him of a prevailing infirmity these believing Jews laboured under: *They are all zealous of the law.* They believe in Christ as the true Messiah, but they know the law of Moses was of God, they have found spiritual benefit in the institutions of it, and therefore they can by no means think of parting with it. This was a great weakness to be so fond of the shadows when the substance was come. But see, The power of education and long usage, and especially of a ceremonial law. The charitable allowance that must be made in consideration of these. Their being zealous of the law was capable of a good construction, which charity would put upon it; and it was capable of a good excuse.

3. They gave him to understand that these Jews were ill-affected to him, *v.* 21. Paul himself could not get the good word of all that belonged to Christ's family: *"They are informed of thee* that thou not only dost not teach the Gentiles to observe the law, but *dost teach all the Jews who are among the Gentiles to forsake Moses, not to circumcise their children nor to walk after the customs* of our nation." It was true that Paul preached the abrogation of the law of Moses, taught them that it was impossible to be justified by it. But it was false that he taught them to forsake Moses; for the religion he preached tended not to destroy the law, but to fulfil it. But even the believing Jews, having got this notion of Paul, that he was an enemy to Moses, were much exasperated against him. The elders here present, loved and honoured him, and called him brother, but the people could hardly be induced to entertain a favour-

JAMIESON, FAUSSET, BROWN

17-40. Paul Reports the Events of His Third Missionary Journey—In the Temple, Purifying Himself from a Jewish Vow, He Is Seized By a Mob and Beaten to the Danger of His Life—The Uproar Becoming Universal, the Roman Commandant Has Him Brought in Chains to the Fortress, from the Stairs of Which He Is Permitted to Address the People. The apostle was full of anxiety about this visit to Jerusalem, from the numerous prophetic intimations of danger awaiting him, and having reason to expect the presence at this feast of the very parties from whose virulent rage he had once and again narrowly escaped with his life. Hence we find him asking the Roman Christians to wrestle with him in prayer, "for the Lord Jesus Christ's sake, and for the love of the Spirit, *that he might be delivered from them that believed not in Judea,*" as well as "that his service which he had for Jerusalem (the great collection for the poor saints there) might be accepted of the saints" (Rom. 15:30, 31). **17-19. the brethren received us gladly**—the disciples generally, as distinguished from the official reception recorded in vs. 18. **Paul went in with us unto James; and all the elders were present**—to "report himself" formally to the acknowledged head of the church at Jerusalem, and his associates in office. See on ch. 15:13. Had any other of the apostles been in Jerusalem on that occasion, it could hardly fail to have been noted. **he declared particularly**—in detail—**what God had wrought among the Gentiles by his ministry**—as on previous occasions (ch. 14:27; and see Rom. 15:15); no doubt referring to the insidious and systematic efforts of the Judaizing party in a number of places to shrivel the Church of Christ into a Jewish sect, and his own counter-procedure. **20-25. they glorified the Lord . . .**—constrained to justify his course, notwithstanding the Jewish complexion of the Christianity of Jerusalem.

A. T. ROBERTSON:

There were undoubtedly a great many thousands of believers in Jerusalem and all Jewish Christians, some, alas, Judaizers (Acts 11:2; 15:1, 5). This list may include the Christians from neighboring towns in Palestine and even some from foreign countries here at the Feast of Pentecost, for it is probable that Paul arrived in time for it as he had hoped. But we do not have to count the hostile Jews from Asia (v. 27) who were clearly not Christians at all. "All zealous for the law" (*pantes zelotai tou nomou*). Zealots (substantive) rather than zealous (adjective) with objective genitive (*tou nomou*). The word zealot is from *zeloo*, to burn with zeal, to boil. The Greek used *zelotes* for an imitator or admirer. There was a party of Zealots (developed from the Pharisees), a group of what would be called "hot-heads," who brought on the war with Rome. One of this party, Simon Zelotes (Acts 1:13), was in the number of the twelve apostles. It is important to understand the issues in Jerusalem. It was settled at the Jerusalem Conference (Acts 15 and Galatians 2) that the Mosaic ceremonial law was not to be imposed upon Gentile Christians. Paul won freedom for them, but it was not said that it was wrong for Jewish Christians to go on observing it if they wished. We have seen Paul observing the passover in Philippi (Acts 20:6) and planning to reach Jerusalem for Pentecost (20:16). The Judaizers rankled under Paul's victory and power in spreading the gospel among the Gentiles and gave him great trouble in Galatia and Corinth. They were busy against him in Jerusalem also and it was to undo the harm done by them in Jerusalem that Paul gathered the great collection from the Gentile Christians and brought it with him and the delegates from the churches. Clearly, then, Paul had real ground for his apprehension of trouble in Jerusalem while still in Corinth (Rom. 15:25) when he asked for the prayers of the Roman Christians (vv. 30-32). The repeated warnings along the way were amply justified.

—Word Pictures in the New Testament

ADAM CLARKE

18. *Went in with us unto James.* This was James the Less, son of Mary and cousin to our Lord. He appears to have been bishop of the church in Jerusalem and perhaps the only apostle who continued in that city. We have already seen what a very important character he sustained in the council. See chap. xv. 13. *All the elders were present.* It appears that they had been convened about matters of serious and important moment; and some think it was relative to Paul himself, of whose arrival they had heard, and well knew how many of those that believed were disaffected towards him.

19. *Declared particularly.* He no doubt had heard that they were prejudiced against him, and by declaring what God had done by him among the Gentiles, showed how groundless this prejudice was; for were he a bad man, or doing anything that he should not do, God would not have made him such a singular instrument of so much good.

20. *How many thousands.* "How many myriads," how many times 10,000. This intimates that there had been a most extraordinary and rapid work even among the Jews; but what is here spoken is not to be confined to the Jews of Jerusalem, but to all that had come from different parts of the land to be present at this Pentecost.

They are all zealous of the law. The Jewish economy was not yet destroyed, nor had God as yet signified that the whole of its observances was done away. He continued to tolerate that dispensation which was to be in a certain measure in force till the destruction of Jerusalem, and from that period it was impossible for them to observe their own ritual. Thus God abolished the Mosaic dispensation by rendering, in the course of His providence, the observance of it impossible.

21. *Thou teachest . . . to forsake Moses.* From anything that appears in the course of this book to the contrary, this information was incorrect; we do not find Paul preaching thus to the Jews. It is true that in his Epistles, some of which had been written before this time, he showed that circumcision and uncircumcision were equally unavailable for the salvation of the soul, and that by the deeds of the law no man could be justified; but he had not yet said to any Jew, "Forsake Moses, and do not circumcise your children." He told them that Jesus Christ had delivered them from the yoke of the law; but they had, as yet, liberty to wear that yoke if

MATTHEW HENRY

able thought of him; for it is certain the least judicious are the most censorious, the weak-headed are the hot-headed.

4. They therefore desired Paul that he would by some public act make it to appear that the charge against him was false, and that he did not teach people to break the customs of the Jewish church, for he himself retained the use of them.

(1) They conclude that something of this kind must be done: "*What is it therefore?* What must be done? The *multitude will hear that thou art come* to town. When they hear thou art come, *they must needs come together*, expecting to hear thee." Now something must be done to satisfy them that Paul does not teach the people to forsake Moses, and they think it necessary, For Paul's sake, that his reputation should be cleared. For the people's sake, that they may not continue prejudiced against so good a man. For their own sake, that since they knew it was their duty to own Paul their doing it might not be turned to their reproach.

(2) They produce a fair opportunity which Paul might take to clear himself: "*Do this that we say unto thee. We have four men*, Jews who believe, and *they have a vow on them*, a vow of Nazariteship for a certain time; their time has now expired (*v.* 23), and they are to offer their offerings according to the law, when they shave the head of their separation, a he-lamb for a burnt-offering, a ewe-lamb for a sin-offering, and a ram for a peace-offering. Now Paul having so far of late complied with the law as to take upon him the vow of a Nazarite, and to signify the expiration of it by shaving his head at Cenchrea (*ch.* xviii. 18), they desire him but to go a little further, and to join with these four in offering the sacrifices of a Nazarite: "*Purify thyself with them* according to the law; and be at charges with them, in buying sacrifices for this solemn occasion, and to join with them in the sacrifice." This, they think, will effectually stop the mouth of calumny, and everyone will be convinced that Paul did not teach the Jews to forsake Moses, but that he himself kept the law.

5. They enter a protestation that this shall be no infringement at all of the decree lately made in favour of the Gentile converts (*v.* 25): "*As touching the Gentiles* who *believe, we have written and concluded that they observe no such things;* but only that they keep themselves from *things offered to idols, and from blood, and from things strangled, and from fornication.*" They knew how jealous Paul was for the preservation of the liberty of the converted Gentiles, and therefore expressly covenant to abide by that. Thus far is their proposal.

V. Here is Paul's compliance with it. Though he would not be persuaded not to go to Jerusalem, yet, when he was there, he was presuaded to do as they there did, *v.* 26. *Then Paul took the men*, and the very *next day, purifying himself with them*, and not *with multitude nor tumult*, as he himself pleads (*ch.* xxiv. 18), he *entered into the temple*, to signify the accomplishment of the days of purification to the priests. Now it has been questioned whether James and the elders did well to give Paul this advice, and whether he did well to take it. Some have blamed this occasional conformity of Paul's, as indulging the Jews too much in their adherence to the ceremonial law, and a discouragement of those who stood fast in the liberty wherewith Christ had made them free. Had it not been better to take pains with their people to convince them of their error, and to show them that they were made free from the law? To urge him to encourage them in it by his example seems to have more in it of fleshly wisdom than of the grace of God. Others think the advice was prudent and good. It was Paul's avowed principle, *To the Jews became I as a Jew, that I might gain the Jews*, 1 Cor. ix. 20. He had circumcised Timothy to please the Jews. Those that are weak in the faith are to be borne with, when those that undermine the faith must be opposed. It is true, this compliance of Paul's sped ill to him, yet this is not a sufficient ground to go upon in condemning it: Paul might do well, and yet suffer for it. Integrity and uprightness will be more likely to preserve us than sneaking compliances. And when we consider what a great trouble it must needs be to James and the presbyters, that they had by their advice brought Paul into trouble, it should be a warning to us not to press men to oblige us by doing anything contrary to their own mind.

Verses 27–40

We have here Paul brought into a captivity which we are not likely to see the end of. When we see the beginning of a trouble, we know not either how long it will last or how it will issue.

JAMIESON, FAUSSET, BROWN

we have four men—Christian Jews, no doubt. **which have a vow**—perhaps kept ready on purpose. **be at charges with them**—i.e., defray the expense of the sacrifices legally required of them, along with his own, which was deemed a mark of Jewish generosity.

touching the Gentiles . . . we have written and concluded that they observe no such things . . .—This shows that with all their conciliation to Jewish prejudice, the Church of Jerusalem was taught to adhere to the decision of the famous council held there (ch. 15).

26. to signify—i.e., announce to the priest—**the accomplishment of the days of purification . . .**—See on Numbers 6:14-21.

ADAM CLARKE

they pleased. He had shown them that their ceremonies were *useless* but not *destructive;* that they were dangerous only when they depended on them for salvation.

22. *The multitude must needs come together.* Whether this refers to a regular convocation of the church or to a tumult that would infallibly take place when it was heard that the apostle was come, we cannot pretend to say; but it is evident that James and the elders wished some prudent steps to be taken in order to prevent an evil that they had too much reason to fear.

23. *We have four men which have a vow.* From the shaving of the head, mentioned immediately after, it is evident that the four men in question were under the vow of Nazariteship, and that the days of their vow were nearly at an end, as they were about to shave their heads; for during the time of the Nazariteship the hair was permitted to grow, and shaven off only at the termination of the vow. Among the Jews it was common to make vows to God on extraordinary occasions, and that of the Nazarite appears to have been one of the most common; and it was permitted by their law for any person to perform this vow by proxy. See the law produced in my note on Num. vi. 21. "It was also customary for the richer sort to bestow their charity on the poorer sort for this purpose; for Josephus, *Ant.*, lib. xix, c. 6, s. 1, observes that Agrippa, on his being advanced from a prison to a throne by the Emperor Claudius, came to Jerusalem; and there, among other instances of his religious thankfulness shown in the Temple, *he ordered very many Nazarites to be shaven*, he furnishing them with money for the expenses of that, and of the sacrifices necessarily attending it."

24. *Be at charges with them.* Or rather, "be at charges for them"; help them to bear the expense of that vow. Eight lambs, four rams, besides oil, flour, etc., were the expenses on this occasion. See the notes on Numbers vi. *Thou . . . walkest orderly, and keepest the law.* Perhaps this advice meant no more than, Show them, by such means as are now in your power, that you are not an enemy to Moses; that you do still consider the law to be holy, and the commandment holy, just, and good. Paul did so, and bore the expenses of those who, from a scruple of conscience, had made a vow, and perhaps were not well able to bear the expense attending it. Had they done this in order to acquire justification through the law, Paul could not have assisted them in any measure with a clear conscience. But as he did assist them, it is a proof that they had vows rather referred to a sense of obligation and the gratitude due to God for mercies already received than to the procuring of future favors of any kind.

25. *As touching the Gentiles.* See the notes on chap. xv.

26. *To signify the accomplishment.* "Declaring" the accomplishment. As this declaration was made to the priest, the sense of the passage is the following, if we suppose Paul to have made an offering for himself, as well as the four men: "The next day Paul, taking the four men, began to purify, set himself apart, or consecrate himself with them. Entering into the Temple, he publicly declared to the priests that he would observe the separation of a Nazarite, and continue it for seven days, at the end of which he would bring an offering for himself and the other four men, according to what the law prescribed in that case." But it is likely that Paul made no offering for himself, but was merely at the expense of theirs. However we may consider this subject, it is exceedingly difficult to account for the conduct of James and the elders, and of Paul on this occasion. There seems to have been something in this transaction which we do not fully understand.

MATTHEW HENRY

I. We have here Paul seized.

1. He was seized in the temple, when he was there attending the days of his purifying, and the solemn services of those days, *v.* 27. It was not till *the seven days were almost ended* that he was taken notice of. In the temple, where he should have been protected, as in a sanctuary, he was most violently set upon by those who did what they could to have his blood mingled with his sacrifices. The temple did they themselves thus profane.

2. The informers against him were the Jews of Asia, not those of Jerusalem—the Jews of the dispersion, who were most exasperated against him. Those who seldom came up to worship at the temple in Jerusalem themselves, yet appeared most zealous for the temple, as if thereby they would atone for their habitual neglect of it.

3. The method they took was to raise the mob. *They stirred up all the people.* Those are fittest to be employed against Christ and Christianity that are governed least by reason and most by passion.

4. The arguments wherewith they exasperated the people against him were popular, but very false and unjust. They cried out, "*Men of Israel, help.*" The enemies of Christianity, since they could never prove it to be an ill thing, have been always very industrious to put it into an ill name, and so run it down by outrage and outcry. What is wanting in right is made up in noise.

5. They charge upon him both bad doctrine and bad practice.

(1) They charge upon him bad doctrine. Though not here at Jerusalem, yet in other places, nay in all places, he teaches all men, everywhere; as if, because he was an itinerant, he was a ubiquitary: "He spread to the utmost of his power certain damnable and heretical positions." [1] Against the people of the Jews. He had taught that Jews and Gentiles stand on the same level before God, *and neither circumcision avails anything nor uncircumcision*; nay, he had taught against the unbelieving Jews that they were rejected (and therefore had separated from them and their synagogues). Those commonly seem most jealous for the church's name that belong to it in name only. [2] Against the law. His teaching men to believe the gospel as the end of the law, and the perfection of it, was interpreted as preaching against the law. [3] Against *this place*, the temple. Because he taught men to pray everywhere, he was reproached as an enemy to the temple. Paul had himself been active in persecuting Stephen, and putting him to death for words spoken *against this holy place*, and now the same thing is laid to his charge. He that was then made use of as the tool is now set up as the butt of Jewish rage and malice.

(2) They charge upon him bad practices. They charge it upon him that he had himself polluted it. He *has brought Gentiles also into the temple*, into the inner court of the temple, which none that were uncircumcised were admitted to come into. Paul was himself a Jew, and had right to enter into the court of the Jews. And they, seeing some with him there that joined with him in his devotions, concluded that Trophimus an Ephesian, who was a Gentile, was one of them. Did they see him there? Truly no. They had seen him with him in the city, and therefore they supposed that Paul had brought him with him into the temple, which was utterly false. Innocency is no fence against calumny and false accusation. *Evil men dig up mischief*, and go far to seek proofs of their false accusations, as they did here. By such unjust and groundless suggestions have wicked men thought to justify themselves in the most barbarous outrages. Paul thought to recommend himself to their good opinion by going into the temple, and thence they take an occasion to accuse him. If he had kept further off them, he had not been so maligned by them.

II. We have Paul in danger of being pulled in pieces by the rabble. The execution shall be of a piece with the prosecution, all unjust and irregular. Therefore, as those who neither feared God nor regarded man, they resolved to knock him on the head immediately.

1. All the city was in an uproar, *v.* 30. The people heard a hue-and-cry from the temple, and were up in arms. *All the city was moved*, when they were called to from the temple, *Men of Israel, help.* Just such a zeal the Jews here show for God's temple as the Ephesians did for Diana's temple, when Paul was informed against as an enemy to that (*ch.* xix. 29): *The whole city was full of confusion.*

2. They drew Paul out of the temple, and shut the doors. In dragging him furiously out of the temple they showed a real detestation of him as one not fit to be looked upon as a member of the Jewish nation. They pretended a veneration for the temple. They condemned Paul for drawing people from the temple,

JAMIESON, FAUSSET, BROWN

27-30. the Jews . . . of Asia—in all likelihood those of *Ephesus* (since they recognized Trophimus apparently as a townsman, vs. 29, embittered by their discomfiture (ch. 19:9, etc.).

took Paul, and drew him out of the temple; and forthwith the doors were shut—that the murder they meant to perpetrate might not pollute that holy place.

ALEXANDER MACLAREN:

Note the charge against Paul. The "Jews from Asia" knew him by sight, as they had seen him in Ephesus and elsewhere; and possibly some of them had been fellow passengers with him from Miletus. No wonder that they construed his presence in the Temple into an insult to it. If Luther or John Knox had appeared in St. Peter's, he would not have been thought to have come as a worshiper. Paul's teaching may very naturally have created the impression in hot-tempered partisans, who could not draw distinctions, that he was the enemy of Temple and sacrifice.

It has always been the vice of religious controversy to treat inferences from heretical teaching, which appear plain to the critics, as if they were articles of the heretic's belief. These Jewish zealots practiced a very common method when they fathered on Paul all which they supposed to be involved in his position. Their charges against him are partly flat lies, partly conclusions drawn from misapprehension of his position, partly exaggeration, and partly hasty assumptions. He had never said a word which could be construed as "against the people." He had indeed preached that the law was not for Gentiles, and was not the perfect revelation which brought salvation, and he had pointed to Jesus as in himself realizing all that the Temple shadowed; but such teaching was not "against" either, but rather for both, as setting both in their true relation to the whole process of revelation. He had not brought "Greeks" into the Temple, not even the one Greek whom malice multiplied into many. When passion is roused, exaggerations and assumptions soon become definite assertions. The charges are a complete object lesson in the baser arts of religious partisans; and they have been but too faithfully reproduced in all ages. Did Paul remember how he had been "consenting" to the death of Stephen on the very same charges? How far he had traveled since that day!

—Expositions of Holy Scripture

ADAM CLARKE

27. *The Jews which were of Asia.* **These pursued him with the most deliberate and persevering malice in every place, and it appears that it was through them that the false reports were sent to and circulated through Jerusalem.**

28. *This is the man, that teacheth.* **As much as if they had said: This is the man concerning whom we wrote to you, who in every place endeavors to prejudice the Gentiles against the Jews, against the Mosaic law, and against the Temple and its services.**

Brought Greeks also into the temple. **This was a most deliberate and malicious untruth. Paul could accomplish no purpose by bringing any Greek or Gentile into the Temple; and their having seen Trophimus, an Ephesian, with him,** *in the city* **only, was no ground on which to raise a slander that must so materially affect both their lives. Josephus informs us,** *War***, lib. v, c. 5, s. 2, that on the wall which separated the court of the Gentiles from that of the Israelites was an inscription in Greek and Latin letters which stated that no stranger was permitted to come within the holy place on pain of death. With such a prohibition as this before his eyes, was it likely that Paul would enter into the Temple in company with an uncircumcised Greek? The calumny refutes itself.**

30. *They took Paul.* **They tumultuously seized on him;** *and drew him out of the temple,* **out of the court of the Israelites, where he was worshipping.** *And . . . the doors were shut;* **the doors of the court of the Gentiles, probably**

MATTHEW HENRY

and yet, when he himself was very devoutly worshipping in the temple, they drew him out of it. The officers of the temple shut the doors. Lest the crowd should by the running in of more to them be thrust back into the temple, and some outrage should be committed, to the profanation of that holy place.

3. They went about to kill him (*v.* 31), for they fell a beating him (*v.* 32), resolving to beat him to death. Now was Paul, like a lamb, thrown into a den of lions. No doubt, he was still of the same mind as when he said, *I am ready not only to be bound, but to die at Jerusalem.*

III. We have here Paul rescued out of the hands of his Jewish enemies by a Roman enemy. Tidings were brought of the tumult *to the chief captain of the band.* Somebody that was concerned not for Paul, but for the public peace and safety, gave this information to the colonel, who had always a jealous and watchful eye upon these tumultuous Jews, and he is the man that must be instrumental to save Paul's life, when never a friend he had was capable of doing him any service. The tribune, or chief captain, got his forces together with all possible expedition, and went to suppress the mob: *He took soldiers* and *centurions,* and *ran down to them.* He had them near at hand, and *he ran down unto the multitude*; for at such times delays are dangerous. The very sight of the Roman general frightened them from beating Paul. They were deterred from that by the the power of the Romans from which they ought to have been restrained by the justice of God. God often makes those to be a protection to his people who yet have no affection for his people. The shepherd makes use even of his dogs for the defence of his sheep. The governor takes him into custody. He rescued him, not out of a concern for him, but out of a concern for justice, because he ought not to be put to death without trial. He therefore takes Paul out of the hands of the mob into the hands of the law (*v.* 33): *He took him, and commanded him to be bound with two chains, for he demanded who he was, and what he had done.* This violent taking of him out of the hands of the multitude, they laid to the charge of the chief captain as his crime (*ch.* xxiv. 7): *The chief captain Lysias came with great violence, and took him out of our hands.*

IV. The provision which the chief captain made to bring Paul to speak for himself. One had almost as good enter into a struggle with the winds and the waves, as with such a mob; and yet Paul made a shift to get liberty of speech among them.

1. There was no knowing the sense of the people; for when the chief captain enquired concerning Paul *some cried one thing, and some another,* so that it was impossible for the chief captain to know their mind, when really they knew not either one another's mind or their own. Those that will hearken to the clamours of the multitude will know nothing for a certainty.

2. There was no quelling the rage and fury of the people; for when *the chief captain commanded that Paul should be carried into the castle,* the tower of Antonia, where the Roman soldiers kept garrison, near the temple, the soldiers themselves had much ado to get him safely thither, the people were so violent (*v.* 35): *When he came upon the stairs,* leading up to the castle, the soldiers were forced to take him up in their arms, and carry him, to keep him from the people, who would have pulled him limb from limb if they could. When they could not reach him with their cruel hands, *They followed, crying, Away with him, v.* 36. *Take him out of the land of the living* (so the ancients expound it), chase him out of the world.

3. Paul at length begged leave of the chief captain to speak to him (*v.* 37): *As he was to be led into the castle, he said unto the chief captain,* "*May I speak unto thee?*" What a humble modest question was this! Paul knew how to speak to the greatest of men, yet he humbly begs leave to speak to this commander.

4. The chief captain tells him what notion he had of him: *Canst thou speak Greek? Art not thou that Egyptian who made an uproar?* It seems, there had lately been an insurrection somewhere in that country, headed by an Egyptian. The captain here says *that he led out into the wilderness four thousand men that were murderers.* It happened in the thirteenth year of Claudius, about three years ago. The ringleader of this rebellion had made his escape, and the chief captain concluded that Paul could not be a criminal of less figure than this Egyptian. See how good men are exposed to ill will by mistake.

5. Paul rectifies his mistake concerning him, by informing him particularly what he was. *I am a man who is a Jew; I am of Tarsus, a city of Cilicia,*

JAMIESON, FAUSSET, BROWN

31. tidings came—lit., 'went up,' i.e., to the fortress of Antonia, where the commandant resided. See on vs. 32. This part of the narrative is particularly graphic. **the chief captain**—'the chiliarch,' or tribune of the Roman cohort, whose full number was 1,000 men.

33. commanded him to be bound with two chains—See on ch. 12.

34. some cried one thing—The difficulty would be so to state his crimes as to justify their proceedings to a Roman officer.

to be carried into the castle—rather, perhaps, 'the barracks,' or that part of the fortress of Antonia appropriated to the soldiers. The fort was built by Herod on a high rock at the northwest corner of the great temple area, and called after Mark Antony.

35, 36. Away with him—as before of his Lord (Luke 23:18; John 19:15).

37-40. Art not thou that Egyptian . . .—The form of the question implies that the answer is to be in the negative, and is matter of some surprise: 'Thou art not then . . . .?' **madest an uproar . . .**—The narrative is given in JOSEPHUS (*Jewish War,* ii, 8. 6; and 13. 5), though his two allusions and ours seem to refer to different periods of the rebellion.

ADAM CLARKE

to prevent Paul from getting any succor from his friends in the city, for their whole proceedings show that they purposed to murder him. They brought him out of the court of the Israelites, that court being peculiarly holy, that it might not be defiled by his blood; and they shut the court of the Gentiles, that they might have the opportunity unmolested of killing him in that place, for the court of the Gentiles was reckoned to be less holy than that of the Israelites.

31. *The chief captain of the band.* The Roman tribune, who had a troop of soldiers under him which lodged in general in the castle of Antonia, which was built at the angle where the northern and western porticoes of the outer court of the Temple were joined together. This castle was built by John Hyrcanus, high priest of the Jews. It was at first called Baris, and was the royal residence of the Asmoneans, as long as they reigned in Jerusalem. It was beautified by Herod the Great and called Antonia, in honor of his friend Mark Antony. By this castle the Temple was commanded, as it stood on higher ground. Josephus describes this castle, *War,* b. v. c. 5, s. 8, "as having four towers, from one of which the whole temple was overlooked; and that one of the towers was joined to the porticoes of the temple, and had a double pair of stairs from it, by which soldiers in the garrison were used to come down with their arms to the porticoes, on the festival days, to keep the people quiet; for, as the temple was a guard to the city, so this castle was a guard to the temple." The name of this chief captain, or tribune, was Claudius Lysias, as we learn from chap. xxiii. 26.

32. *Ran down unto them.* Ran down the stairs to the porticoes mentioned above.

33. *To be bound with two chains.* To be bound between two soldiers, his right hand chained to the left hand of the one, and his left hand to the right of the other.

36. *Away with him.* That is, Kill him; dispatch him! for so much this phrase always means in the mouth of a Jewish mob.

38. *Art not thou that Egyptian?* The history to which Claudius Lysias refers is taken from Josephus, *Ant.,* l. xx, c. 7, s. 6, and *War,* l. ii, c. 13, s. 5, and is in substance as follows: An Egyptian, whose name is not known, pretended to be a prophet, and told his followers that the walls of Jerusalem would fall down before them if they would assist him in making an attack on the city. He had address enough to raise a rabble of 30,000 men, and with these advanced as far as the Mount of Olives. But Felix, the Roman governor, came suddenly upon him with a large body of Roman troops, both infantry and cavalry. The mob was speedily dispersed, 400 killed, 200 taken prisoners, and the Egyptian himself, with some of his most faithful friends, escaped, of whom no account was ever afterwards heard. As Lysias found such an outcry made against Paul, he supposed that he must be some egregious malefactor, and probably that Egyptian who had escaped, as related above. Learned men agree that Luke refers to the same fact of which Josephus speaks; but there is a considerable difference between the numbers in Josephus and those in Luke, the former having 30,000, the latter only 4,000. The small number of killed and prisoners, only 600 in all according to Josephus, leads us to suspect that his number is greatly exaggerated, as 600 in killed and prisoners of a mob of 30,000, routed by regular infantry and cavalry, is no kind of proportion; but it is a sufficient proportion to a mob of 4,000. Dean Aldridge has supposed that the number in Josephus was originally 4,000, but that ancient copyists, mistaking the Greek delta, "four," for lambda, "thirty," wrote 30,000, instead of 4,000. There is another way of reconciling the two historians, which is this: When this Egyptian impostor at first began to make great boasts and large promises, a multitude of people, to the amount at least of 30,000 weary of the Roman yoke, from which he promised them deliverance, readily arranged themselves under his banners. As he performed nothing that he promised, 26,000 of these had melted away before he reached Mount Olivet; this remnant the Romans attacked and dispersed. Josephus speaks of the

MATTHEW HENRY

a citizen of no mean city. Whether he means Tarsus or Rome is not certain; they were neither of them mean cities, and he was a freeman of both. Though the chief captain had put him under such an invidious suspicion, he did not render railing for railing, but mildly denied the charge, and owned what he was.

6. He humbly desired a permission to speak to the people. He sues for it as a favour, which he will be thankful for: *I beseech thee, suffer me to speak to the people.* The chief captain rescued him with no other design than to give him a fair hearing. He desires he may have leave immediately to defend himself; for it needed no more than to be set in a true light.

7. He obtained leave to plead his own cause, for he needed not to have counsel assigned him, when the Spirit of the Father was ready to dictate to him, Matt. x. 20. *The chief captain gave him license* (*v.* 40). He had that justice done him by the chief captain which he could not obtain from his countrymen the Jews. This licence being obtained the people were attentive to hear: *Paul stood on the stairs.* A sorry pulpit it was, and yet better than none. There he *beckoned with the hand unto the people,* made signs to them to be quiet, and so far he gained his point that there was made a profound silence. When the cause of Christ and his gospel is to be pleaded, there ought to be a great silence, that we may *give the more earnest heed,* and all little enough. Paul addressed himself to speak: he *spoke unto them in the Hebrew tongue,* that is, in their own vulgar tongue, to which he hereby owned not only an abiding relation, but an abiding respect.

JAMIESON, FAUSSET, BROWN

a citizen of no mean city—See on ch. 16:37.

stood on the stairs—"What nobler spectacle than that of Paul at this moment! There he stood, bound with two chains, ready to make his defense to the people. The Roman commander sits by, to enforce order by his presence. An enraged populace look up to him from below. Yet in the midst of so many dangers, how self-possessed is he, how tranquil!" [CHRYSOSTOM (or in his name) in HACKET]. **a great silence**—the people awed at the permission given him by the commandant, and seeing him sitting as a listener. **in the Hebrew tongue**—the Syro-Chaldaic the vernacular tongue of the Palestine Jews since the captivity.

ADAM CLARKE

number he had in the beginning; Luke, of those that he had when he arrived at Mount Olivet. *That were murderers? Sicarii,* "assassins." They derived their name from *sica,* a sort of crooked knife, which they concealed under their garments, and privately stabbed the objects of their malice.

39. *I am a man which am a Jew.* A periphrasis for "I am a Jew." *Of Tarsus . . . no mean city.* In the notes on chap. ix. 11, I have shown that Tarsus was a city of considerable importance, and in some measure a rival to Rome and Athens; and that, because of the services rendered to the Romans by the inhabitants, Julius Caesar endowed them with all the rights and privileges of Roman citizens. When Paul calls it *no mean city* he speaks a language that was common to those who have had occasion to speak of Tarsus. Xenophon calls it "a great and flourishing city."

40. *Paul stood on the stairs.* Where he was out of the reach of the mob and was surrounded by the Roman soldiers. *Beckoned with the hand.* Waving the hand, which was the sign that he was about to address the people. *He spake unto them in the Hebrew tongue.* What was called then the Hebrew, viz., the Chaldaeo-Syriac; very well expressed by the *Codex Bezae,* "in their own dialect."

Never was there a more unnatural division than that in this chapter; it ends with a single comma! The best division would have been at the end of the twenty-fifth verse.

MATTHEW HENRY — CHAPTER 22

Verses 1, 2

I. With what an admirable composure he addresses himself to speak. There appears no fright, but his mind is sedate and composed. There appears no passion. He breaks out into no angry expressions.

II. What respectful titles he gives even to those who thus abused him: "*Men, brethren, and fathers* (*v.* 1). *To you, O men, I call;* men, that should hear reason, and be ruled by it; men, from whom one may expect humanity. You, *brethren* of the common people; you, *fathers* of the priests." Thus he lets them know that he was one of them. Though we must not give flattering titles to any, yet we ought to give titles of due respect to all; and those we would do good to we should endeavour not to provoke. Though he was rescued out of their hands, and was taken under the protection of the chief captain, yet he does not fall foul upon them. *Hear you my defence;* a just and reasonable request, for every man that is accused has a right to answer for himself.

III. The language he spoke in, which recommended what he said to the auditory: *He spoke in the Hebrew tongue,* that is, the vulgar language of the Jews, which, at this time, was not the pure Old Testament Hebrew, but the Syriac, a dialect of the Hebrew. It showed his continued respect to his countrymen, the Jews. By this it appears he is a Jew. What he said was the more generally understood. To speak in that language was indeed to appeal to the people. *When they heard that he spoke in the Hebrew tongue, they kept the more silence.* The chief captain was surprised to hear him speak Greek (*ch.* xxi. 37), the Jews were surprised to hear him speak Hebrew, and both therefore think the better of him. Many wise and good men are therefore slighted only because they are not known.

Verses 3-21

Paul here gives an account of himself not only to satisfy the chief captain that he was not that Egyptian he took him to be, but the Jews also that he was not that enemy to their law and temple they took him to be.

I. What his extraction and education were. 1. He was one of their own nation. "*I am verily a man who is a Jew.* I am a sincere friend to your nation, for I am one of it." 2. He was born in a creditable reputable place, *in Tarsus, a city of Cilicia,* and was by his birth a freeman of that city. This was, indeed, but a small matter to make any boast of, and yet it was needful to be mentioned at this time to those who insolently trampled upon him. 3. He had a learned and liberal education. He *was brought up* in Jerusalem, the principal seat of the Jewish learning, and *at the feet of Gamaliel,* and therefore he could not be ignorant of their law, nor be thought to slight it because he did not know it. 4. He was in his early days a very forward and eminent professor of the Jews' religion. (1) He was an intelligent professor

JAMIESON, FAUSSET, BROWN — CHAPTER 22

VSS. 1-30. PAUL'S DEFENSE FROM THE STAIRS OF THE FORTRESS—THE RAGE OF THE AUDIENCE BURSTING FORTH, THE COMMANDANT HAS HIM BROUGHT INTO THE FORT TO BE EXAMINED BY SCOURGING, BUT LEARNING THAT HE IS A ROMAN, HE ORDERS HIS RELEASE AND COMMANDS THE SANHEDRIM TO TRY HIM.

1, 2. when they heard . . . the Hebrew tongue—see on ch. 21:40—**they kept the more silence**—They could have understood him in Greek, and doubtless fully expected the renegade to address them in that language, but the sound of their holy mother tongue awed them into deeper silence.

3. a Jew of Tarsus, brought up in this city, at the feet—See on Luke 10: 39—**of Gamaliel**—(See on ch. 5:24); a fact of great importance in the apostle's history, standing in the same relation to his future career as Moses' education in the Egyptian court to the work for which he was destined.

ADAM CLARKE — CHAPTER 22

1. *Men, brethren, and fathers.* A Hebrew form of expression for "brethren and fathers," for two classes only are addressed.

Hear ye my defence. "This apology of mine." In this sense the word "apology" was anciently understood; hence the "Apologies" of the primitive fathers, i.e., their defenses of the Christian religion. And this is its proper literal meaning; but it is now used only as implying an excuse for improper conduct.

2. *When they heard that he spake in the Hebrew tongue.* He had probably been traduced by the Jews of Asia as a mere Gentile, distinguished only by his virulence against the Jewish religion.

3. *I am verily a man which am a Jew.* A periphrasis for "I am really a Jew." He shows that he could not be ignorant of the Jewish religion, as he had had the best instructer in it which Jerusalem could produce. *Feet of Gamaliel.* See a full account of this man in the note on chap. v. 34. It has been generally supposed that the phrase *brought up at the feet* is a reference to the Jewish custom, viz., that the disciples of the rabbins sat on low seats, or on the ground, whilst the rabbin himself occupied a lofty chair. But we rather learn, from Jewish authority, that the disciples of the rabbins stood before their teachers. Kypke therefore contends that *at the feet* means the same as "near," or "before," which is not an unfrequent mode of speech among both sacred and profane writers.

MATTHEW HENRY

of their religion. He minded his business at Gamaliel's feet, and was there *taught according to the perfect manner of the law of the fathers.* What departures he had made from the law were not owing to any confused or mistaken notions of it, for he understood it to a nicety. Paul had as great a value for antiquity, and tradition, as any of them had; and there was never a Jew of them all that understood his religion better than Paul did, or could better give an account of it. (2) He was an active professor of their religion: *I was zealous towards God, as you all are this day.* Many that are very well skilled in the theory of religion are willing to leave the practice of it to others, but Paul was as much a zealot as a rabbi. Here he compliments his hearers *that they all were this day zealous towards God; he bears them record* (Rom. x. 2) *that they have a zeal for God, but not according to knowledge.* Though this did by no means justify their rage, yet it enabled those that prayed, *Father, forgive them,* to plead, as Christ did, *For they know not what they do.*

II. What a fiery furious persecutor he had been in the beginning of his time, *v.* 4, 5. He mentions this to make it the more plainly to appear that the change which was wrought upon him, when he was converted to the Christian faith, was purely the effect of a divine power. Immediately before that sudden change was wrought in him he had the utmost antipathy imaginable to Christianity. He may have a further view in it to invite and encourage those people to repent, for he himself had been *a blasphemer, and a persecutor,* and yet obtained mercy. Let us view Paul's picture of himself when he was a persecutor. 1. He hated Christianity with a mortal enmity: *I persecuted this way unto the death.* He *breathed out slaughter against them, ch.* ix. 1. When *they were put to death, he gave his voice against them, ch.* xxvi. 10. He *persecuted it to the death,* that is, he could have been willing himself to die in his opposition to Christianity, so some understand it. He would contentedly have lost his life in defence of the laws and traditions of the fathers. 2. He did all he could to frighten people from this way, and out of it, by *binding and delivering into prison both men and women.* Now that he himself was bound, he lays a particular stress upon this part of his charge against himself, that he had bound the Christians, and carried them to prison; he likewise reflects with a special regret that he had imprisoned not only the men, but the women. 3. He was employed by the great sanhedrim, the high priest, and all the estate of the elders, in suppressing this new sect, *v.* 5. When they heard that many of the Jews at Damascus had embraced the Christian faith, they resolved to proceed against them, and could not think of a fitter person to be employed in that business than Paul. They therefore sent him, and letters by him, to the Jews at Damascus, here called *the brethren,* ordering them to be assisting to Paul in seizing those among them that had turned Christians, and bringing them up prisoners to Jerusalem, to be punished, and that they might either be compelled to retract, or be put to death for a terror to others. "Such a son," says Paul, "I was at first, just such as you now are. I know the heart of a persecutor, and therefore pity you, and pray that you may know the heart of a convert, as God soon made me to do."

III. In what manner he was converted. It was not from any natural or external causes. It was the Lord's doing, and the circumstances of the doing of it were enough to justify him in the change; and none can condemn him for it, without reflecting upon that divine energy. He relates the story of his conversion here very particularly, as we had it before (*ch.* ix), aiming to show that it was purely the act of God. 1. He was as fully bent upon persecuting the Christians just before Christ arrested him as ever. He *made his journey, and was come nigh to Damascus* (*v.* 6), and had no other thought than to execute the cruel design he was sent upon. 2. It was *a light from heaven* that first startled him, *a great light,* which *shone suddenly round about him,* and the Jews knew that God is light, and that such a light as this shining at noon, must be from God. It shone upon him in the open road, at high noon, and so strongly *that it struck him to the ground* (*v.* 7), and all *that were with him, ch.* xxvi. 14. 3. It was a *voice from heaven* that first begat in him awful thoughts of Jesus Christ. The voice called to him by name, *Saul, Saul, why persecutest thou me?* And when he asked, *Who art thou, Lord?* it was answered, *I am Jesus of Nazareth, whom thou persecutest, v.* 8. 4. Lest it should be objected, "How came this light and voice to work such a change upon him, and not upon those that journeyed with him?" he observes *that his fellow travellers saw indeed the light, and were afraid;* but, though the light made them afraid, they heard not

JAMIESON, FAUSSET, BROWN

the perfect manner of the law of the fathers—the strictest form of traditional Judaism.

zealous—'a zealot'—**toward God as ye all are this day**—his own former murderous zeal against the disciples of the Lord Jesus being merely reflected in their present treatment of himself.

4. I persecuted . . .—See on ch. 9:1, 2, 5-7.

the high priest—still alive—**doth bear me witness, and all the estate of the elders**—the whole Sanhedrim.

8. Jesus of Nazareth—the Nazarene. See on ch. 9:5.
9-11. they that were with me—See on ch. 9:7, etc.

ADAM CLARKE

According to the perfect manner. That is, according to that strict interpretation of the law, and especially the traditions of the elders, for which the Pharisees were remarkable. That it is Pharisaism that the apostle has in view when he says he was taught "according to the most exact manner" is evident; and hence, in chap. xxvi. 5, he calls Pharisaism "the most exact system," and under it he was zealous towards God, scrupulously exact in every part of his duty, accompanying this with reverence to the Supreme Being.

4. *I persecuted this way.* This doctrine, this way of worshipping God and arriving at a state of blessedness. *Binding and delivering into prisons.* See on chap. viii. 3; ix. 2.

5. *The high priest doth bear me witness.* He probably referred to the letters of authority which he had received from the high priest and the whole *estate of the elders,* "the whole of the presbytery," that is, the Sanhedrin; and it is likely that he had those letters to produce. This zeal of his against Christianity was an ample proof of his sincerity as a Pharisaical Jew.

6-13. *As I made my journey.* See the whole of this account and all the particular circumstances considered at large in the notes on chap. ix. 1, etc.

MATTHEW HENRY

the voice of him that spoke to Paul. Now faith comes by hearing, and therefore that change was wrought upon him that heard the words, and heard them directed to himself, which was not wrought upon those who only saw the light. 5. He assures them that when he was thus startled he referred himself entirely to a divine guidance: "*What shall I do, Lord?* Let the same voice from heaven that has stopped me in the wrong way guide me into the right way," *v.* 10. And immediately he had directions to go to Damascus, and *there it shall be told thee all things which are appointed for thee to do.* The extraordinary ways of divine revelation, by visions, and voices, and the appearance of angels, were designed only to introduce and establish the ordinary method by the scriptures and a standing ministry. The voice here tells not Paul what he shall do, but bids him go to Damascus, and there it shall be told him. 6. As a demonstration of the greatness of that light which fastened upon him, he tells them of the immediate effect it had upon his eyesight (*v.* 11): *I could not see for the glory of that light.* It struck him blind for the present. Condemned sinners are struck blind by the power of darkness, and it is a lasting blindness, but convinced sinners are struck blind, as Paul here was, not by darkness, but by light: but it is in order to their being enlightened. Those that were with Paul were not blinded, as he was. They, having their sight, led *Paul by the hand into the city.* Paul, being a Pharisee, was proud of his spiritual eyesight. The Pharisees said, *Are we blind also?* John ix. 40. Paul was thus struck with bodily blindness to make him sensible of his spiritual blindness.

IV. How he was confirmed in the change he had made, and further directed what he should do, by Ananias.

1. The character here given of Ananias. He was not a man that was any way prejudiced against the Jewish nation or religion, but was himself *a devout man according to the law*; and thence advanced further to the faith of Christ. He had a *good report of all the Jews that dwelt at Damascus.* This was the first Christian that Paul had any friendly communication with.

2. The cure immediately wrought by him upon Paul's eyes. He *came to him* (*v.* 13); and, to assure him that he came to him from Christ, he *stood by him, and said, Brother Saul, receive thy sight.* Power went along with this word, and *the same hour* he recovered his sight, and *looked up upon him,* ready to receive from him the instructions sent by him.

3. The declaration which Ananias makes to him of the favour which the Lord Jesus designed him above any other.

(1) In the present manifestation of himself to him (*v.* 14): *The God of our fathers has chosen thee.* This powerful call is the result of a particular choice; his calling God the God of our fathers intimates that Ananias was himself a Jew by birth. *This God of our fathers has chosen thee that thou shouldst* know his will. Those whom God hath chosen he hath chosen to know his will, and to do it. *That thou shouldst see that Just One, and shouldst hear the voice of his mouth,* and so shouldst know his will immediately from himself. It was a distinguishing favour, that he should see Christ here upon earth after his ascension into heaven. Stephen saw him *standing at the right hand of God,* but Paul saw him standing at his right hand. Stephen saw him, but we do not find that he heard the voice of his mouth, as Paul did. Christ is here called *that Just One*; for he is Jesus Christ the righteous, and suffered wrongfully. Those whom God has chosen to know his will must have an eye to Christ, and must see him, and hear the voice of his mouth.

(2) In the after-manifestation of himself by him to others (*v.* 15): "*Thou shalt be his witness unto all men,* Gentiles as well as Jews, *of that thou hast seen and heard.*" Paul so particularly relating the manner of his conversion here and *ch.* xxvi, we think that he frequently related the same narrative in his preaching for the conversion of others; he told them what God had done for his soul, to encourage them to hope that he would do something for their souls.

4. The counsel he gave him to join himself to the Lord Jesus by baptism (*v.* 16): *Arise, and be baptized.* He had in his circumcision been given up to God, but he must now by baptism be given up to God in Christ. (1) The great gospel privilege which by baptism we have sealed to us is the remission of sins: *Be baptized and wash away thy sins;* that is, "Receive the comfort of the pardon of thy sins in and through Jesus Christ, and receive power against sin," for our being washed includes our being both justified and sanctified. (2) The great gospel duty which by our baptism we are bound to is *to call on the name of*

JAMIESON, FAUSSET, BROWN

ALEXANDER MACLAREN:

The blaze struck all the company to the ground (Acts 24:14). Prone on the earth, and probably with closed eyes, their leader heard his own name twice sounded, with appeal, authority, and love in the tones. The startling question which followed not only pierced conscience, and called for a reasonable vindication of his action, but flashed a new light on it as being persecution which struck at this unknown heavenly speaker. So the first thought in Saul's mind is not about himself or his doings but about the identity of that Speaker. Awe, if not actual worship, is expressed in addressing Him as Lord. Wonder, with perhaps some foreboding of what the answer would be, is audible in the question, "Who art thou?" Who can imagine the shock of the answer to Saul's mind? Then the man whom he had thought of as a vile apostate, justly crucified and not risen as his dupes dreamed, lived in heaven, knew him, Saul, and all that he had been doing, was "apparelled in celestial light," and yet in heavenly glory was so closely identified with these poor people whom he had been hunting to death that to strike them was to hurt Him!

A bombshell had burst, shattering the foundation of his fortifications. A deluge had swept away the ground on which he had stood. His whole life was revolutionized. Its most solid elements were dissolved into vapor, and what he had thought misty nonsense was now the solid thing. To find a "why" for his persecuting was impossible, unless he had said (what in effect he did say), "I did it ignorantly." When a man has a glimpse of Jesus exalted to heaven, and is summoned by Him to give a reason for his life of alienation, that life looks very different from what it did, when seen by dimmer light. Clothes are passable by candlelight that look very shabby in sunshine. When Jesus comes to us, His first work is to set us to judge our past, and no man can muster up respectable answers to His question, "Why?" for all sin is unreasonable, and nothing but obedience to Him can vindicate itself in His sight.—*Expositions of Holy Scripture*

12. Ananias, a devout man, according to the law, having a good report of all the Jews which dwelt there—One would not know from this description of Ananias that he was a Christian at all, the apostles object being to hold him up as unexceptionable, even to the most rigid Jews.

13-15. The God of our fathers hath chosen thee—studiously linking the new economy upon the old, as but the sequel of it; both having one glorious Author. **that thou shouldest . . . see that**—'the'—**Just One**—cf. ch. 3:14; 7:52. **hear the voice of his mouth**—in order to place him on a level with the other apostles, who had "seen the [risen] Lord."

16. be baptized and wash away thy sins—This way of speaking arises from baptism being the visible seal of remission.

ADAM CLARKE

14. ***And see that Just One.*** **The Lord Jesus, called the *Just One* in opposition to the Jews, who crucified Him as a malefactor; see the note on chap. vii. 52. This is an additional proof that Jesus Christ did actually appear unto Saul of Tarsus.**

15. ***Thou shalt be his witness unto all.*** **You shall proclaim Christ crucified to both Jews and Gentiles.**

16. ***Arise, and be baptized.*** **Take now the profession of Christ's faith most solemnly upon you by being baptized in the name of Father, Son, and Holy Spirit. *Wash away thy sins.* Let this washing of your body represent to you the washing away of your sins, and know that this washing away of sin can be received only by invoking the name of the Lord.**

MATTHEW HENRY

the Lord, the Lord Jesus; to acknowledge him to be our Lord and our God, and to apply to him accordingly. We must *wash away our sins, calling on the name of the Lord*; that is, we must seek for the pardon of our sins in Christ's name. (3) We must do this quickly. *Why tarriest thou?* Our covenanting with God in Christ is needful work, that must not be deferred. Why should not that be done at the present time that must be done some time, or we are undone?

V. How he was commissioned to go and preach the gospel to the Gentiles. This was the great thing for which they were so angry at him, and therefore it was requisite he should for this produce a divine warrant. This commission he did not receive presently upon his conversion, for this was *at Jerusalem*. 1. He received his orders to do it when he was at prayer, begging of God to appoint him his work and to show him the course he should steer. He was *at prayer in the temple*, which was to be called *a house of prayer for all people*; not only in which all people should pray, but in which all people should be prayed for. Paul's praying in the temple was an evidence that he had a veneration for the temple. It would be a great satisfaction to Paul afterwards, in the execution of this commission, to reflect upon it that he received it when he was at prayer. 2. He received it in a vision. He fell *into a trance* (*v.* 17). In this trance he saw Jesus Christ (*v.* 18): *I saw him saying unto me*. 3. Before Christ gave him a commission to go to the Gentiles, he told him it was to no purpose for him to think of doing any good at Jerusalem; so that they must not blame him, but themselves, if he be sent to the Gentiles. "*Make haste*," says he, "*and get thee quickly out of Jerusalem*"; thou wilt find they *will not receive thy testimony concerning me*. As God knows before who will receive the gospel, so he knows who will reject it. 4. Paul renewed his petition because they knew what he had been before his conversion, and therefore must ascribe so great a change in him to the power of almighty grace. Thus he reasoned, both with himself and with the Lord, and thought he reasoned justly (*v.* 19, 20): "*Lord*," says he, "*they know* that I was as bitter an enemy as any of them to such as believed on thee, that I *imprisoned them* and *beat them in every synagogue*. Particularly in Stephen's case; they know that when he was stoned I was standing by, *consenting to his death*, and *kept the clothes of those that stoned him*. If I appear among them, preaching the doctrine that Stephen preached and suffered for, they will no doubt receive my testimony." "No," says Christ to him, "they will not; but will be more exasperated against thee as a deserter." 5. Paul's petition for a warrant to preach the gospel at Jerusalem is overruled (*v.* 21): *Depart, for I will send thee far hence, unto the Gentiles*. God often gives gracious answers to the prayers of his people, not in the thing itself that they pray for but, in something better. It is God that appoints his labourers both their day and their place, and it is fit they should acquiesce in his appointment, though it may cross their own inclinations. Paul hankers after Jerusalem: to be a preacher there was the summit of his ambition; but Christ designs him greater preferment. So often does Providence contrive better for us than we for ourselves. Paul shall not go to preach among the Gentiles without a commission: *I will send thee*. And, if Christ send him, his Spirit will go along with him, and give him to see the fruit of his labours. He was sent to places at a distance. Surely they would see that they had no reason to be angry with Paul for preaching among the Gentiles, for he was compelled to it, by an overruling command from heaven.

Verses 22–30

Paul was going on with his account of himself. But, whatever he designs to say, they resolve he shall say no more to them: *They gave him audience to this word*. Hitherto they had heard him with patience and some attention. But when he speaks of being sent to the Gentiles they cannot bear it. Upon the mention of this, they have no manner of patience, but forget all rules of decency and equity.

Now here we are told how furious the people were against Paul, for mentioning the Gentiles as taken into the cognizance of divine grace.

I. They interrupted him that nobody might hear a word he said. Galled consciences kick at the least touch; and those who are resolved not to be ruled by reason commonly resolve not to hear it if they can help it.

II. They clamoured against him as one that was unworthy of life. They cried out with a confused noise, "*Away with such a fellow* as this *from the earth, it is not fit that he should live*." Thus the men

JAMIESON, FAUSSET, BROWN

calling on the name of the Lord—rather, 'having called,' i.e., *after* having done so; referring to the confession of Christ which *preceded* baptism, as ch. 8:37.

17-21. it came to pass . . .—This thrilling dialogue between the glorified Redeemer and his chosen vessel is nowhere else related. **when I was come again to Jerusalem**—on the occasion mentioned in ch. 9:26-29. **while I prayed in the temple**—He thus calls their attention to the fact that after his conversion he kept up his connection with the temple as before.

get . . . quickly out of Jerusalem—cf. ch. 9:29—**for they will not receive thy testimony . . .**

And I said, Lord, they know . . .—'Can it be, Lord, that they will resist the testimony of one whom they knew so well as among the bitterest of all against Thy disciples, and whom nothing short of resistless evidence could have turned to Thee?'

Depart for I will send thee far hence unto the Gentiles—i.e., 'Enough; thy testimony is not to be thrown away upon Jerusalem; the Gentiles, afar off, are thy peculiar sphere.'

22, 23. gave him audience to this word . . . then . . . Away with such a fellow from the earth . . .—Their national prejudices lashed into fury

ADAM CLARKE

17. *When I was come again to Jerusalem*. It is likely that he refers to the first journey to Jerusalem, about three years after his conversion, chap. ix. 25-26 and Gal. i. 18. *I was in a trance*. This circumstance is not mentioned anywhere else, unless it be that to which himself refers in 2 Cor. xii. 2-4, when he conceived himself transported to the third heaven; and if the case be the same, the appearance of Jesus Christ to him and the command given are circumstances related only in this place.

19. *I imprisoned and beat in every synagogue*. This shows what an active instrument Saul of Tarsus was in the hands of this persecuting priesthood, and how very generally the followers of Christ were persecuted, and how difficult it was at this time to profess Christianity.

20. *When the blood of thy martyr Stephen was shed*. See on chap. vii. 58; viii. 1. All these things Paul alleged as reasons why he could not expect to be received by the Christians; for how could they suppose that such a persecutor could be converted?

21. *I will send thee far hence unto the Gentiles*. This was the particular appointment of Paul; he was the apostle of the Gentiles. For though he preached frequently to the Jews, yet to preach the gospel to the Gentiles and to write for the conversion and establishment of the Gentile world were his peculiar destination. Hence we find him and his companions travelling everywhere. None of the apostles travelled, none preached, none labored as this man; and, we may add, none was so greatly owned of God. Next to Jesus Christ, Paul is the glory of the Christian Church. Jesus is the Foundation; Paul, the master builder.

22. *They gave him audience unto this word*. Namely, that God had sent him to the Gentiles. Not that they refused to preach the law to the

MATTHEW HENRY

that have been the greatest blessings of their age have been represented not only as the burdens of the earth, but the plague of their generation. The ungodly Jews here say of Paul that it was not fit he should live; and therefore he must be removed, that the world may be eased of the burden of him.

III. They went stark mad against Paul, and against the chief captain (*v.* 23); as men whose reason was quite lost in passion, they cried out and howled; they *cast off their clothes.* They thus showed how ready they were to stone him; those that stoned Stephen threw off their clothes, *v.* 20. Or, they *rent their clothes,* as if he had spoken blasphemy; and *threw dust into the air,* in detestation of it. All they intended was to make the chief captain sensible how much they were enraged and exasperated at Paul.

IV. The chief captain took care for his safety, by ordering him to be brought into the castle, *v.* 24. A prison sometimes has been a protection to good men from popular rage. Paul's hour was not yet come, and therefore God raised up one that took care of him.

V. He ordered him the torture. *He ordered that he should be examined by scourging,* that *he might know wherefore they cried so against him.* Herein he did not proceed fairly; he should have singled out some of the complainants, and should have examined them, what they had to lay to the charge of a man that could give so good an account of himself. It was proper to ask them, but not at all proper to ask Paul, *wherefore they cried so against him.* No man is bound to accuse himself, though he be guilty, much less ought he to be compelled to accuse himself when he is innocent. Is this a fair or just occasion to scourge Paul, that a rude tumultuous mob cry out against him, but cannot tell why or wherefore?

VI. Paul pleaded his privilege as a Roman citizen, by which he was exempted from all trials and punishments of this nature (*v.* 25): *As they bound him with thongs* he made no outcry against the injustice of their proceedings against an innocent man, but let them understand the illegality of their proceedings against him as a citizen of Rome. He *said to the centurion that stood by, "Is it lawful for you to scourge a man that is a Roman, and uncondemned?"* The manner of his speaking plainly intimates what a holy security and serenity of mind this good man enjoyed, not disturbed either with anger or fear in the midst of all those indignities that were done him, and the danger he was in.

VII. The chief captain was surprised at this, and put into a fright. He had taken Paul to be a vagabond Egyptian. How many men of great worth and merit are despised because they are not known! The chief captain had centurions, under-officers, attending him, *ch.* xxi. 32. One of these reports this matter to the chief captain (*v.* 26): *Take heed what thou doest, for this man is a Roman.* They all knew what a value was put upon this privilege of the Roman citizens. The chief captain would be satisfied of the truth of this from his own mouth (*v.* 27): "*Tell me, art thou a Roman?* Art thou entitled to the privileges of a Roman citizen?" "Yes," says Paul, "*I am.*" The chief captain compares notes with him upon this matter, and it appears that the privilege Paul had as a Roman citizen was more honourable than the colonel's; for the colonel owns that his was purchased: "I am a freeman of Rome; but *with a great sum obtained I this freedom.*" Says Paul, "*I was free-born.*" He pleads it for his own preservation, for which end not only we may but we ought to use all lawful means. This put an immediate stop to Paul's trouble. Those that were appointed to examine him by scourging *departed from him* (*v.* 29). The colonel himself was afraid when he heard he was a Roman, because he had bound him in order to his being beaten. Thus many are restrained from evil practices by the fear of man who would not be restrained from them by the fear of God. See here the benefit of human laws and magistracy, and what reason we have to be thankful to God for them. By the general support of equity and fair dealing between man and man, they have served to check the rage of wicked men. Therefore this service we owe to all in authority, to pray for them, because this benefit we have reason to expect from them. The governor, the next day, brought Paul before the Sanhedrim, *v.* 30. He first *loosed him from his bands,* and then summoned the chief priests and all their council to come together to take cognizance of Paul's case, for he found it to be a matter of religion. This Roman, who was a military man, kept Paul in custody, and appealed from the rabble to the general assembly. We may hope that hereby he intended Paul's safety, as thinking the chief priests and elders

JAMIESON, FAUSSET, BROWN

at the mention of a mission to the Gentiles, they would speedily have done to him as they did to Stephen, but for the presence and protection of the Roman officer.

24-26. examined by scourging—according to the Roman practice. **that he might know wherefore they cried so**—Paul's speech being to him in an unknown tongue, he concluded from the horror which it kindled in the vast audience that he must have been guilty of some crime.

Paul said to the centurion that stood by—to superintend the torture and receive the confession expected to be wrung from him. **Is it lawful for you to scourge a man that is a Roman . . .**—See on ch. 16:37.

27-29. art thou a Roman?—showing that this being of Tarsus, which he had told him before (ch. 21:39) did not necessarily imply that he was a Roman citizen. **With a great sum obtained I this freedom**—Roman citizenship was bought and sold in the reign of Claudius, we know, at a high price: at a subsequent date, for next to nothing. But to put in a false claim to this privilege was a capital crime. **I was** [free] **born**—born to it, by purchase, or in reward of services, on the part of his father or some ancestor. **chief captain feared . . .**—See on ch. 16: 38.

30. commanded the chief priests and all their council to appear—i.e., the Sanhedrim to be formally convened. Note here the power to order a Sanhedrim to try this case, assumed by the Roman officers and acquiesced in on their part.

ADAM CLARKE

Gentiles and make them proselytes, for this they were fond of doing, so that our Lord says they compassed sea and land to make a proselyte; but they understood the apostle as stating that God had rejected *them* and called the Gentiles to be His peculiar people in their place, and this they could not bear. *Away with such a fellow.* According to the law of Moses, he who attempted to seduce the people to any strange worship was to be stoned, Deut. xiii. 15. The Jews wished to insinuate that the apostle was guilty of this crime and that therefore he should be stoned, or put to death.

23. *Cast off their clothes.* Bishop Pearce supposes that shaking their upper garments is all that is meant here, and that it was an ancient custom for men to do so when highly pleased or greatly irritated; but it is likely that some of them were now actually throwing off their clothes, in order to prepare to stone Paul. *Threw dust into the air.* In sign of contempt and by way of execration. Shimei acted so in order to express his contempt of David, 2 Sam. xvi. 13, where it is said he "cursed [him] as he went, and threw stones at him"; or, as the margin, he "dusted him with dust." Their throwing dust in the air was also expressive of extraordinary rage and vindictive malice. The apostle, being guarded by the Roman soldiers, was out of the power of the mob; and their throwing dust in the air not only showed their rage, but also their vexation that they could not get the apostle into their power.

24. *Examined by scourging.* As the chief captain did not understand the Hebrew language, he was ignorant of the charge brought against Paul and ignorant also of the defense which the apostle had made. As he saw that they grew more and more outrageous, he supposed that Paul must have given them the highest provocation; and therefore he determined to put him to the torture, in order to find out the nature of his crime.

25. *And as they bound him.* They were going to tie him to a post, that they might scourge him. *Is it lawful?* The Roman law absolutely forbade the binding of a Roman citizen.

28. *With a great sum obtained I this freedom.* So it appears that the freedom, even of Rome, might be purchased and that it was sold at a very high price. *But I was free born.* It has been generally believed that the inhabitants of Tarsus, born in that city, had the same rights and privileges as Roman citizens in consequence of a charter or grant from Julius Caesar. Pliny tells us that Tarsus was a free city. And Appian says that Antony "made the people of Tarsus free, and discharged them from paying tribute." These testimonies are of weight sufficient to show that Paul, by being born at Tarsus, might have been *free born* and a Roman.

29. *After he knew that he was a Roman.* He who was going to scourge him durst not proceed to the torture when Paul declared himself to be a *Roman.* A passage from Cicero throws the fullest light on this place: "Whosoever he might be whom thou wert hurrying to the rack, were he even unknown to thee, if he said that he was a Roman citizen, he would necessarily obtain from thee, the Praetor, by the simple mention of Rome, if not an escape, yet at least a delay of his punishment."

30. *He . . . commanded . . . all their council to appear.* Instead of "to come," which we translate, *to appear,* "to assemble," or "meet together" is the reading of several MSS.; this reading is most probably the true one. As the chief captain wished to know the certainty of the matter, he desired the Jewish council, or Sanhedrin, to assemble and examine the business thoroughly, that he might know of what the apostle was accused. As the law would not permit him to proceed against a Roman in any judicial way but on the clearest evidence, and as he understood that the cause of their enmity was something that concerned their religion, he considered the Sanhedrin to be the most proper judge and therefore commanded them "to assemble."

MATTHEW HENRY

would do him justice, and clear him; for their court governed by rules of equity. That which he is here said to aim at is the gratifying of his own curiosity: He *would have known the certainty wherefore he was accused of the Jews.*

CHAPTER 23

Verses 1–5

Perhaps he thought if he were brought before the sanhedrim at Jerusalem he should be able to deal with them to some good purpose, and yet we do not find that he works at all upon them.

I. Paul's protestation of his own integrity. Paul appeared here,

1. With a good courage. He was not at all put out of countenance upon his being brought before such an august assembly, but *he earnestly beheld the council.* When Stephen was brought before them, they thought to have faced him down, but could not, such was his holy confidence. Now that Paul was brought before them he thought to have faced them down, but could not, such was their wicked impudence.

2. With a good conscience. He said, "*Men and brethren, I have lived in all good conscience before God unto this day.*" He had always been a man inclined to religion; always put a difference between moral good and evil. He was no designing man, who cared not what he did, so he could but compass his own ends. Even when he persecuted the church of God, he thought he ought to do it. Though his conscience was misinformed, yet he acted according to the dictates of it. He seems rather to speak of the time since his conversion, since he fell under their displeasure. "Even *to this day,* I have *lived in all good conscience before God.*" He had aimed at nothing but to please God and do his duty. See here the character of an honest man. He sets God before him, and lives as in his sight. He makes conscience of what he says and does, though he may be under some mistakes. He is universally conscientious; and those that are not so are not at all truly conscientious. He continues so, and perseveres in it: "I have lived so *until this day.*" Whatever changes pass over him, he is still the same, strictly conscientious.

II. The outrage of which Ananias the high priest was guilty: he *commanded those that stood by to smite him on the mouth* (*v.* 2). The high priest was highly offended at Paul. His protestation of his integrity was provocation enough to one who was resolved to run him down. When he could charge him with no crime, he thought it was crime enough that he asserted his own innocency. In his rage he ordered him to be smitten, and to be smitten, on the mouth as having offended with his lips, and in token of his enjoining him silence. If therefore we see such indignities done to good men, nay, if they be done to us for well doing and well saying, we must not think it strange: Christ will give those the *kisses of his mouth* (Song. i, 2) who for his sake receive blows on the mouth.

III. The denunciation of the wrath of God against the high priest; *God shall smite thee, thou whited wall, v.* 3. Paul did not speak this in any sinful heat or passion, but in a holy zeal against the high priest's abuse of his power, not at all with a spirit of revenge. He gives him his due character: *Thou whited wall;* that is, thou hypocrite—a mud-wall, trash and dirt and rubbish underneath, but plastered over, or white-washed. Those that daubed with untempered mortar failed not to daub themselves over with something that made them look not only clean, but gay. He reads him his just doom: "*God shall smite thee,* shall bring upon thee his sore judgments, especially spiritual judgments." He assigns a good reason for that doom: "For *sittest thou* pretending *to judge me after the law,* and yet *commandest me to be smitten* before any crime is proved upon me, which is *contrary to the law?*" It is against all law, human and divine, natural and positive, to hinder a man from making his defence, and to condemn him unheard. It is inexcusable in a high priest that is appointed to judge according to the law.

IV. The offence which was taken at this bold word of Paul's (*v.* 4): *Those that stood by said, Revilest thou God's high priest?* See here then, What a hard game Paul had to play, when his enemies were abusive to him, and his friends were ready to find fault with his management. These were disgusted at Paul for giving him his due.

V. The excuse that Paul made for what he had said, because he found it was a stumbling-block. Though he had taken the liberty to tell the high priest his fault, yet, when he found it gave offence,

JAMIESON, FAUSSET, BROWN

CHAPTER 23

VSS. 1-10. PAUL'S DEFENSE BEFORE THE SANHEDRIM DIVIDES THE RIVAL FACTIONS, FROM WHOSE VIOLENCE THE COMMANDANT HAS THE APOSTLE REMOVED INTO THE FORTRESS.

1. Paul, earnestly beholding the council—with a look of conscious integrity and unfaltering courage, perhaps also recognizing some of his early fellow pupils. **I have lived in all good conscience before God until this day**—The word has an indirect reference to the 'polity' or "commonwealth of Israel," of which he would signify that he had been, and was to that hour, an honest and God-fearing member.

2. the high priest . . . commanded . . . to smite him on the mouth—a method of silencing a speaker common in the East to this day [HACKET]. But for a judge thus to treat a prisoner on his trial, for merely prefacing his defense by a protestation of his integrity, was infamous.

3, 4. God shall smite thee—as indeed He did; for he was killed by an assassin during the Jewish war (JOSEPHUS, *Jewish War,* ii. 17. 9). **thou whited wall**—i.e., hypocrite (Matt. 23:27). This epithet, however correctly describing the man, must not be defended as addressed to a judge, though the remonstrance which follows—"for sittest thou . . ."—ought to have put him to shame.

ADAM CLARKE

This chapter should end with the twenty-ninth verse, and the following should begin with the thirtieth; this is the most natural division, and is followed by some of the most correct editions of the original text.

CHAPTER 23

1. *I have lived in all good conscience.* Some people seem to have been unnecessarily stumbled with this expression. What does the apostle mean by it? Why, that, while he was a Jew, he was one from principle of conscience; that what he did while he continued Jew, he did from the same principle; that when God opened his eyes to see the nature of Christianity he became a Christian because God persuaded his conscience that it was right for him to become one—that, in a word, he was sincere through the whole course of his religious life and his conduct had borne the most unequivocal proofs of it.

2. *The high priest Ananias.* There was a high priest of this name who was sent a prisoner to Rome by Quadratus, governor of Syria, to give an account of the part he took in the quarrel between the Jews and the Samaritans; see Joseph., *Antiq.,* l. xx, c. 6, s. 8. Krebs has proved that this very Ananias, on being examined at Rome, was found innocent, returned to Jerusalem, and was restored to the high priesthood; see Joseph., *Antiq.,* l. xx, c. 9, s. 2. *To smite him on the mouth.* Because he professed to have a good conscience, while believing on Jesus Christ and propagating His doctrine.

3. *God shall smite thee, thou whited wall.* Thou hypocrite! who sittest on the seat of judgment, pretending to hear and seriously weigh the defense of an accused person, who must in justice and equity be presumed to be innocent till he is proved to be guilty; and instead of acting according to the law, *commandest me to be smitten contrary to the law,* which always has the person of the prisoner under its protection.

MATTHEW HENRY

he cried, *I have done wrong*. He wished he had not done it. He excuses it with this, that he did not consider when he said it to whom he spoke (*v.* 5): *I wist not, brethren, that he was the high priest.* "I did not just then think of the dignity of his place, or else I would have spoken more respectfully to him." But, says he, I did not consider it. But the Jews acknowledged that prophets might use a liberty in speaking of rulers which others might not. He takes care that what he had said should not be drawn into a precedent, to the weakening of the obligation of that law in the least: *For it is written, Thou shalt not speak evil of the ruler of thy people.* It is for the public good that the honour of magistracy should be supported, and not suffer for the miscarriages of those who are entrusted with it. Not as if great men may not hear of their faults, and public grievances be complained of by proper persons, but there must be a particular tenderness for the honour of those in authority because the law of God requires a particular reverence to be paid to them, as God's vicegerents.

Verses 6–11

And now he finds that he who has delivered does and will deliver. He that delivered him from the tumult of the people here delivers him from that of the elders.

I. His own prudence and ingenuity contribute much to his escape. Paul's greatest honour, and that upon which he most valued himself, was that he was a Christian, and an apostle of Christ; and yet he had sometimes occasion to make use of his other honours. His being a citizen of Rome saved him from his being scourged by the chief captain, and here his being a Pharisee saved him from being condemned by the sanhedrim. It will consist very well with our willingness to suffer for Christ to use all lawful methods, both to prevent suffering and to extricate ourselves out of it. The honest policy Paul used here for his own preservation was to divide his judges, and, by incensing one part of them more against him, to engage the contrary part for him.

1. The great council was made up of Sadducees and Pharisees, and Paul perceived it (*v.* 6): *One part were Sadducees and the other Pharisees.* Now these differed very much from one another, and yet they ordinarily agreed well enough to do the business of the council together. The Pharisees were bigots, zealous for the ceremonies, but at the same time they were very orthodox in the faith of the Jewish church concerning the world of spirits, the resurrection of the dead, and the life of the world to come. The Sadducees were deists—no friends to the scripture, or divine revelation. The books of Moses they admitted as containing a good history and a good law, but had little regard to the other books of the Old Testament. They *deny the resurrection*; not only the return of the body to life, but a future state of rewards and punishments. They denied the existence of angels and spirits, and allowed of no being but matter. They thought that God himself was corporeal. When they read of angels in the Old Testament, they supposed that they were impressions on the fancies of those they were sent to, and no real existences—that they were this, or that, or anything rather than what they were. And, as for the souls of men, they denied their existence in a state of separation from the body, and any difference between the soul of a man and of a beast. These, no doubt, pretended to be free-thinkers, but really thought as meanly as possible. It is strange how men of such wicked principles could have a place in the great sanhedrim; but many of them were of quality and estate, and they complied with the public establishment, and so got in and kept in. But how degenerate was the character of the Jewish church, when such profane men as these were among their rulers!

2. In this matter of difference between the Pharisees and Sadducees Paul openly declared himself to be on the Pharisees' side against the Sadducees (*v.* 6): He *cried out*, "*I am a Pharisee*, the *son of a Pharisee. I hope for the resurrection of the dead*, and this is it for which I am now *called in question*." Paul owns himself a Pharisee, so far as the Pharisees were in the right. Though as Pharisaism was opposed to Christianity he set himself against it, yet, as it was opposed to Sadducism, he adhered to it. We must never think the worse of any truth of God, for its being held by men otherwise corrupt. He might truly say that being persecuted, as a Christian, this was the thing he was called in question for. He might truly say he was called in question for the hope of the resurrection of the dead, as he afterwards pleaded, *ch.* xxiv. 15, and *ch.* xxvi. 6, 7.

3. This occasioned a division in the council. There

JAMIESON, FAUSSET, BROWN

5. **I wist not . . . that he was the high priest**—All sorts of explanations of this have been given. The high priesthood was in a state of great confusion and constant change at this time (as appears from JOSEPHUS), and the apostle's long absence from Jerusalem, and perhaps the manner in which he was habited or the seat he occupied, with other circumstances to us unknown, may account for such a speech. But if he was thrown off his guard by an insult which touched him to the quick, "what can surpass the grace with which he recovered his self-possession, and the frankness with which he acknowledged his error? If his conduct in yielding to the momentary impulse was not that of Christ Himself under a similar provocation (John 18:22, 23), certainly the manner in which he atoned for his fault was *Christlike*" [HACKET].

6-9. **when Paul perceived**—from the discussion which plainly had by this time arisen between the parties—**that the one part were Sadducees, and the other Pharisees, he cried out**—raising his voice above both parties-

the Sadducees say . . . there is no resurrection, neither angel, nor spirit—See on Luke 20:37.

—I am a Pharisee, the son of a Pharisee—The true reading seems to be, 'the son of Pharisees,' i.e., belonging to a family who from father to son had long been such—**of the hope and resurrection of the dead**—i.e., not the vague hope of immortality, but the definite expectation of the resurrection—**I am called in question**—By this adroit stroke, Paul engages the whole Pharisaic section of the council in his favor; the doctrine of a resurrection being common to both, though they would totally differ in their *application* of it. This was, of course, quite warrantable, and the more so as it was already evident that no impartiality in trying his cause was to be looked for from such an assembly.

ADAM CLARKE

5. *I wist not, brethren, that he was the high priest.* After all the learned labor that has been spent on this subject, the simple meaning appears plainly to be this: Paul did not know that Ananias was high priest. He had been long absent from Jerusalem; political changes were frequent; the high priesthood was no longer in succession, and was frequently bought and sold; the Romans put down one high priest and raised up another as political reasons dictated. As the person of Ananias might have been wholly unknown to him, as the hearing was very sudden, and there was scarcely any time to consult the formalities of justice, it seems very probable that Paul, if he ever had known the person of Ananias, had forgotten him. And as in a council or meeting of this kind the presence of the high priest was not indispensably necessary, he did not know that the person who presided was not the *sagan*, or high priest's deputy, or some other person put in the seat for the time being. *Thou shalt not speak evil of the ruler of thy people.* If I had known he was the high priest, I should not have publicly pronounced this execration, for respect is due to his person for the sake of his office. I do not see that Paul intimates that he had done anything through inadvertence, nor does he here confess any fault. He states two facts: (1) That he did not know him to be the high priest; (2) That such a one, or any ruler of the people, should be reverenced. But he neither recalls or makes an apology for his words; he had not committed a trespass, and he did not acknowledge one.

8. *The Sadducees say that there is no resurrection.* It is strange, since these denied a future state, that they observed the ordinances of the law; for they also believed the five books of Moses to be a revelation from God. Yet they had nothing in view but temporal good, and they understood the promises in the law as referring to these things alone.

6. *I am a Pharisee, the son of a Pharisee.* Instead of "of a Pharisee," some MSS. have "of the Pharisees"; which, if acknowledged to be the genuine reading, would alter the sense thus, "I am a Pharisee, and a disciple of the Pharisees," for so the word *son* is frequently understood. *Of the hope and resurrection.* Concerning the hope of the resurrection. Paul had preached the resurrection of the dead, on the foundation and evidence of the resurrection of Christ. For this he and the apostles were some time before imprisoned by the high priest and elders, chap. iv. 1-3 and v. 17, because they preached through Jesus the resurrection of the dead. This they could not bear; for if Jesus Christ rose from the dead, their malice and wickedness in putting Him to death were incontrovertibly established.

MATTHEW HENRY

arose a *dissension between the Pharisees and the Sadducees* (*v.* 7), for this word of Paul's made the Sadducees more warm and the Pharisees more cool in the prosecution of him; so that *the multitude was divided.* All the cry had been against Paul, but now there arose a great cry against one another, *v.* 9. Everything was done with clamour and noise; and in such a tumultuous manner were the great principles of their religion stickled for. Gainsayers may be convinced by fair reasoning, but never by a great cry.

4. The Pharisees hereupon (would one think it?) took Paul's part (*v.* 9): *They strove, saying, We find no evil in this man.* He had given a good account of himself, and had now declared himself orthodox in the great principles of religion, and therefore they cannot see that he has *done anything worthy of death or of bonds.* Nay, they go further, "*If a spirit or an angel hath spoken to him* we ought not to oppose him, *lest we be found fighting against God*"; as Gamaliel, who was himself a Pharisee, had argued, *ch.* v. 39. We may observe, to the honour of the gospel, that it was witnessed to even by its adversaries, and confessions, not only of its innocency, but of its excellency, were extorted sometimes by the power of truth even from those that persecuted it. Pilate found no fault in Christ though he put him to death; and the Pharisees here supposed it possible that Paul might have a commission sent him from heaven by an angel to do what he did; and yet it should seem, they after this joined with the high priest in prosecuting him, *ch.* xxiv. 1. They sinned against the knowledge which they not only had, but sometimes owned. We will hope that some of them at least did henceforward conceive a better opinion of Paul than they had had, and were favourable to him. And then it must be observed to their honour that their zeal for the traditions of the elders was so far swallowed up in a zeal for the fundamental doctrines of religion, that if he will heartily join with them against the Sadducees, and adhere to the hope of the resurrection of the dead, they will charitably hope that he walks according to the light God has given him, and are so far from persecuting him that they are ready to patronize and protect him.

II. The chief captain's care and conduct stand him in more stead; for when he has thrown this bone of contention between the Pharisees and Sadducees he is never the nearer, but is in danger of being pulled in pieces by them. The chief captain is forced to come with his soldiers and rescue him, as he had done, *ch.* xxi. 32, and *ch.* xxii. 24. Paul's danger. Between his friends and his enemies he had like to have been pulled to pieces, the one hugging him to death, the other crushing him to death. His deliverance: *The chief captain ordered his soldiers to go down* and *to take him by force from among them,* and *to bring him into the castle.*

III. Divine consolations stood him in most stead of all. The chief captain had rescued him out of the hands of cruel men, but still he had him in custody. The castle was indeed a protection to him, but withal it was a confinement; and, as it was now his preservation from so great a death, it might be his reservation for a greater. Perhaps, in the night following, Paul was full of thoughts and cares what should become of him, and how his present troubles might be turned to answer some good purpose. Then did the Lord Jesus make him a kind visit (*v.* 11): *The Lord stood by him,* came to his bedside. Whoever is against us, we need not fear if the Lord stand by us. Christ bids him have a good heart upon it: "*Be of good cheer, Paul;* be not discouraged." It is the will of Christ that his servants who are faithful should be always cheerful. Christ, by his word, satisfies him that God approved of his conduct. It is a strange argument which he makes use of to encourage him: *As thou hast testified of me in Jerusalem, so must thou bear witness also at Rome.* One would think this was but cold comfort, and yet this was designed to encourage him. He had been serving Christ as a witness for him in what he had hitherto endured. He was still going on with his work. He had not yet finished his testimony, but was only reserved for further service. Nothing disheartened Paul so much as the thought of being taken off from doing service to Christ and good to souls: *Fear not,* says Christ, *I have not done with thee.* Paul seems to have had a particular fancy to go to Rome, to preach the gospel there. Being a citizen of Rome, he longed for a journey thither, and had designed it (*ch.* xix. 21): *After I have been at Jerusalem, I must also see Rome.* Now he was ready to conclude that this had broken his measures, and he should never see Rome; but even in that Christ tells him he should be gratified.

JAMIESON, FAUSSET, BROWN

the scribes . . . of the Pharisees' part . . . strove, saying, We find no evil in this man, but—as to those startling things which he brings to our ears—**if a spirit or an angel hath spoken to him**—referring, perhaps, to his trance in the temple, of which he had told them (ch. 22:17). They put this favorable construction upon his proceedings for no other reason than that they had found him one of their own party. They care not to inquire into the *truth* of what he alleged, over and above their opinions, but only to explain it away as something not worth raising a noise about. (The following words, "Let us not fight against God," seem not to belong to the original text, and perhaps are from ch. 5:39. In this case, either the meaning is, 'If he has had some divine communication, *what of that?*' or, the conclusion of the sentence may have been drowned in the hubbub, which the next verse shows to have been intense).

10. the chief captain, fearing lest Paul should have been pulled to pieces . . . commanded the soldiers to go down and take him by force . . .—This shows that the commandant was not himself present, and further, that instead of the Sanhedrim trying the cause, the proceedings quickly consisted in the one party attempting to seize the prisoner, and the other to protect him.

11-35. IN THE FORTRESS PAUL IS CHEERED BY A NIGHT VISION—AN INFAMOUS CONSPIRACY TO ASSASSINATE HIM IS PROVIDENTIALLY DEFEATED, AND HE IS DESPATCHED BY NIGHT WITH A LETTER FROM THE COMMANDANT TO FELIX AT CÆSAREA, BY WHOM ARRANGEMENTS ARE MADE FOR A HEARING OF HIS CAUSE. **11. the night following**—his heart perhaps sinking, in the solitude of his barrack ward, and thinking perhaps that all the predictions of danger at Jerusalem were now to be fulfilled in his death there. **the Lord**—i.e., Jesus—**stood by him . .**

Be of good cheer, Paul; for as thou hast testified of me in Jerusalem, so must thou . . . also at Rome—i.e., 'Thy work in Jerusalem is done, faithfully and well done; but thou art not to die here; thy purpose next to "see Rome" (ch. 19:21) shall not be disappointed, and there also must thou bear witness of Me.' As this vision was not unneeded now, so we shall find it cheering and upholding him throughout all that befell him up to his arrival there.

ADAM CLARKE

7. *And the multitude was divided.* Paul, perceiving the assembly to consist of Sadducees and Pharisees, and finding he was not to expect any justice, thought it best thus to divide the council by introducing a question on which the Pharisees and Sadducees were at issue. He did so; and the Pharisees immediately espoused his side of the question, because in opposition to the Sadducees, whom they abhorred as irreligious men.

9. *The scribes . . . arose, and strove.* They "contended forcibly"—they came to an open rupture with the Sadducees; and in order to support their own party against them, they even admitted as truth Paul's account of his miraculous conversion, and therefore they said, *If a spirit or an angel hath spoken to him.* He had previously mentioned that Jesus Christ had appeared to him when on his way to Damascus; and though they might not be ready to admit the doctrine of Christ's resurrection, yet they could, consistently with their own principles, allow that the soul of Christ might appear to him. They immediately caught at this, as furnishing a strong proof against the doctrine of the Sadducees, who neither believed in angel nor spirit, while the Pharisees confessed both. *Let us not fight against God.* These words are wanting in some MSS.

10. *The chief captain . . . commanded the soldiers to go down.* It appears that the chief captain was present during these transactions, and that he had a body of soldiers in readiness in the castle of Antonia; and it was from this that he commanded them to "come down," for the rescue and preservation of Paul.

11. *Be of good cheer, Paul.* It is no wonder if, with all these trials and difficulties, Paul was much dejected in mind; and especially as he had not any direct intimation from God what the end of the present trials would be. To comfort him and strengthen his faith, God gave him this vision. *So must thou bear witness also at Rome.* This was pleasing intelligence to Paul, who had long desired to see that city and preach the gospel of Christ there. He appears to have had an intimation that he should see it; but how, he could not tell. This vision satisfied him that he should be sent thither by God himself. This would settle every fear and scruple concerning the issue of the present persecution.

MATTHEW HENRY

Verses 12-35

We have here the story of a plot against the life of Paul.

I. How this plot was laid. They found they could gain nothing by popular tumult, or legal process, and therefore have recourse to the barbarous method of assassination.

1. Who they were that formed this conspiracy. They were *certain Jews, v.* 12. *And they were more than forty* that were in the design, *v.* 13.

2. When the conspiracy was formed: *When it was day.* In the night Christ appeared to Paul to protect him, and, when it was day, here were forty men appearing against him to destroy him; they were not up so soon but Christ was up before them.

3. What the conspiracy was. These men *banded together*; they engaged to stand by one another, and everyone, to his power, to be aiding and assisting to murder Paul. What a monstrous idea must these men have formed of Paul, before they could be capable of forming such a monstrous design against him! What laws of truth and justice so sacred, so strong, which malice and bigotry will not break through!

4. How firm they made it: *They bound themelves under an anathema*, imprecating the heaviest curses upon themselves if they did not kill Paul, and so quickly *that they would not eat nor drink till they had done it.* What a complication of wickedness is here! To design to kill an innocent man that had done them no harm, was *going in the way of Cain*; yet, as if this had been a small matter, they bound themselves to it. To incline to do evil, and intend to do it, is bad; but to engage to do it is much worse. This is entering into covenant with the devil; it is leaving no room for repentance. They bound one another to it, and did all they could, not only to secure the damnation of their own souls, but of theirs whom they drew into the association. They showed a great contempt of the providence of God to do such a thing within so short a time. When we say, *Tomorrow we will do this or that*, we must add, *If the Lord will.* But with what face could they insert a proviso for the permission of God's providence when what they were about was directly against the prohibitions of God's word? What a woeful dilemma did they throw themselves upon! God certainly meets them with his curse if they do go on in it, and they desire he would if they do not! Such language of hell those speak that wish God to damn them, and the devil to take them, if they do not do so and so. They showed a most eager desire to compass this matter.

5. What method they took to bring it about. There is no getting near Paul in the castle. Therefore the chief priests and elders must desire the governor of the castle to let Paul come to them, to be further examined, and then, in his passage from the castle to the council, they would put an end to all disputes about Paul by killing him, *v.* 14, 15. They come to the principal members of the great sanhedrim. They are so confident of their approbation of this villainy, that they are not ashamed to own to them *that they have bound themselves under a great curse, that they will eat nothing till they have killed Paul.* They design to breakfast the next morning upon his blood. They doubt not but the chief priests will lend them a helping hand, and be their tools, pretending to *the chief captain that they would enquire something more perfectly concerning him.* What an ill opinion had they of their priests, when they could apply to them on such an errand as this! The priests and elders consented to it without boggling at it in the least. Instead of reproving them, they bolstered them up in it, because it was against Paul whom they hated.

II. How the plot was discovered. Providence so ordered it that it was brought to light, and brought to nought.

1. How it was discovered to Paul, *v.* 16. There was a youth that was related to Paul, *his sister's son*; and somehow or other *he heard of their lying in wait*, and *he went into the castle*, and *he told Paul* what he heard. God has many ways of bringing *to light the hidden works of darkness.*

2. How it was discovered to the chief captain. Paul had got a good interest in the officers that attended, by his peaceable deportment. He could call one of the centurions to him and he was ready to come at his call (*v.* 17); and he desired that he would introduce this young man to the chief captain, to give in an information. The centurion very readily gratified him, *v.* 18. He went himself to recommend his errand to the chief captain: "*Paul the prisoner* (this was his title now) *called me to him, and prayed me to bring this young man to thee; he has something to say to thee.*" It is true charity to poor prisoners to act for them as well as to give to them. "*I was sick*

JAMIESON, FAUSSET, BROWN

ALBERT BARNES:

"And bound themselves under a curse." The Greek is, "they anathematized themselves"; that is, they bound themselves by a solemn oath. They invoked a curse on themselves, or devoted themselves to destruction, if they did not do it. Lightfoot remarks, however, that they could be absolved from this vow by the Rabbins if they were unable to execute it. Under various pretenses, they could easily be freed from such oaths, and it was common to take them; and if there was any difficulty in fulfilling them, they could easily apply to their religious teachers and be absolved.

"That they would neither eat nor drink." That is, that they would do it as soon as possible. This was a common form of an oath, or curse, among the Jews. Sometimes they only vowed abstinence from particular things, as from meat or wine. But in this case, to make the oath more certain and binding, they vowed abstinence from all kinds of food and drink till they had killed him. Who these were—whether they were Sadducees or not—is not mentioned by the sacred writer. It is evident, however, that the minds of the Jews were greatly inflamed against Paul; and as they saw him in the custody of the Roman tribune, and as there was no prospect that he would punish him, they resolved to take the matter into their own hands. It is needless to remark that this was a most wicked oath. It was a deliberate purpose to commit murder; and it shows the desperate state of morals among the Jews at that time, and the infuriated malice of the people against the apostle that such an oath could have been taken.—*Popular Commentary*

12-14. bound themselves under a curse . . . that they would neither eat . . . till they had killed Paul—Cf. II Samuel 3:35; I Samuel 14:24.

15. Now . . . ye with the council signify to the chief captain . . . as though . . .—That these high ecclesiastics fell in readily with this infamous plot is clear. What will not unscrupulous and hypocritical religionists do under the mask of religion? The narrative bears unmistakable internal marks of truth. **or ever he come near**—Their plan was to assassinate him on his way down from the barracks to the council. The case was critical, but He who had pledged His word to him that he should testify for Him at Rome provided unexpected means of defeating this well-laid scheme.

16-22. Paul's sister's son—See on ch. 9:30. If he was at this time residing at Jerusalem for his education, like Paul himself, he may have got at the schools those hints of the conspiracy on which he so promptly acted.

Then Paul called one of the centurions—Though divinely assured of safety, he never allows this to interfere with the duty he owed to his own life and the work he had yet to do. (See on ch. 27:22-25, 31.)

ADAM CLARKE

12. *That they would neither eat nor drink.* These forty Jews were no doubt of the class of the *sicarii* mentioned before (similar to those afterwards called "assassins"), a class of fierce zealots, who took justice into their own hand, and who thought they had a right to dispatch all those who, according to their views, were not orthodox in their religious principles. If these were in their bad way conscientious men, must they not all perish through hunger, as God put it out of their power to accomplish their vow? No, for the doctrine of sacerdotal absolution was held among the Jews as among the Papists. Hence it is said, in *Hieros. Avodah Zarah*, fol. 40: "He that hath made a vow not to eat any thing, woe to him, if he eat; and woe to him, if he do not eat. If he eat, he sinneth against his vow; and if he do not eat, he sinneth against his life." What must such a man do in this case? Let him go to the wise men, and they will loose him from his vow, as it is written in Prov. xii. 18: "The tongue of the wise is health." When vows were so easily dispensed with, they might be readily multiplied.

15. *And we, or ever he come near, are ready to kill him.* We shall lie in weight and dispatch him before he can reach the chief captain. The plan was well and deeply laid, and nothing but an especial providence could have saved Paul.

16. *Paul's sister's son.* This is all we know of Paul's family.

17. *Bring this young man unto the chief captain.* Though Paul had the most positive assurance from divine authority that he should

MATTHEW HENRY

and in prison, and you went on an errand for me," will pass as well in the account as, "*I was sick and in prison, and you came unto me.*" Those that have acquaintance and interest should be ready to use them for the assistance of those that are in distress. This centurion helped to save Paul's life by this piece of civility. Those that cannot give a good gift to God's prisoners may yet speak a good word for them. The chief captain received the information with a great deal of tenderness, *v.* 19. He *took the young man by the hand* to encourage him, that he might not be put out of countenance, but might be assured of a favourable audience. The notice that is taken of this circumstance should encourage great men to make themselves easy of access. This familiarity to which this Roman tribune admitted Paul's nephew is here upon record to his honour. Let no man think he disparages himself by his humility or charity. He *went with him aside privately and asked him,* "*What is it that thou hast to tell me?*" The young man delivered his errand to the chief captain very readily (*v.* 20, 21): "*The Jews have agreed to desire thee that thou wouldst bring down Paul tomorrow into the council; but do not thou yield unto them, for there lie in wait for him of them more than forty men*, who have sworn to be the death of him, *and now are they ready looking for a promise from thee.*" The captain dismissed the young man with a charge of secrecy: *See that thou tell no man that thou hast shown these things unto me, v.* 22. Those that cannot keep counsel are not fit to be employed in business.

III. How the plot was defeated: The chief captain, finding how restless they were in their designs to do him a mischief, and how near he was to become himself accessory to it, resolved to send him away with all speed out of their reach. He seemed afraid lest, if he should detain Paul in his castle here, they would find some way or other to compass their end. Whatever came of it, he would protect Paul, because he did not deserve such treatment. What a melancholy observation is it, that the Jewish *chief priests*, when they knew of this assassination-plot, should countenance it, while a Roman *chief captain*, purely from a natural sense of justice and humanity, sets himself to baffle it.

1. He orders a considerable detachment of the Roman forces under his command *to go to Cæsarea* with all expedition, and to bring Paul thither *to Felix the governor*. I see not but the chief captain might have set Paul at liberty, and given him leave to shift for his own safety. He himself owns *that nothing was laid to his charge worthy of bonds* (*v.* 29), and he ought to have had the same tenderness for his liberty that he had for his life; but he feared that this would have incensed the Jews too much against him. *Two centurions* are employed in this business, *v.* 23, 24. They must *get ready two hundred soldiers to go to Cæsarea*; and with these *seventy horse, and two hundred spearmen* besides. (1) The chief captain designed hereby to expose the Jews, as a headstrong tumultuous people, that needed to be awed by such a train as this. He thought less would not serve to defeat their attempt. (2) God designed hereby to encourage Paul. Yet Paul did not desire such a guard because he trusted in God's all-sufficiency; it was owing, however, to the governor's own care. But he was also made considerable; thus his *bonds in Christ* were made manifest all the country over (Phil. i. 13); and so great a preacher made so great a prisoner. When his enemies hate him, and I doubt his friends neglect him, then does a Roman tribune carefully provide, [1] For his ease: *Let them provide beasts, that they set Paul on.* Had his Jewish persecutors ordered his removal to Cæsarea, they would have made him run on foot, or dragged him thither in a cart. But the chief captain treats him like a gentleman, and orders him a good horse to ride upon. [2] For his security. They have a strict charge given them *to bring him safely to Felix the governor*, who was supreme in all civil affairs among the Jews, as this chief captain was in military affairs. The Roman historians speak much of this Felix, as a man of mean extraction, but that raised himself by his shifts to be governor of Judæa. To the judgment of such a man as this is poor Paul turned over; and yet better so than in the hands of *Ananias the high priest*!

2. The chief captain orders that he be taken away at *the third hour of the night*, three hours after sunset, that they might have the cool of the night to march in.

3. *He writes a letter to Felix the governor* of this province, by which he leaves the whole matter with Felix. This letter is here inserted *verbatim*, *v.* 25.

(1) The compliments he passes upon *the governor*, *v.* 26. He is *the most excellent governor Felix*, this title being given him of course. He sends him *greeting*.

(2) The just and fair account which he gives him

JAMIESON, FAUSSET, BROWN

took him by the hand—This shows that he must have been quite in his boyhood, and throws a pleasing light on the kind-hearted impartiality of this officer.

and now are they ready, looking for a promise from thee—Thus, as is so often the case with God's people, not till the last moment, when the plot was all prepared, did deliverance come.

23, 24. two hundred soldiers—a formidable guard for such an occasion; but Roman officials felt their honor concerned in the preservation of the public peace, and the danger of an attempted rescue would seem to require it. The force at Jerusalem was large enough to spare this convoy.

the third hour of the night—nine o'clock. **beasts . . . set Paul on**—as relays, and to carry baggage. **unto Felix, the governor**—the procurator. See on ch. 24:24, 25. **25-30. Claudius**—the Roman name he would take on purchasing his citizenship. **Lysias**—his Greek family name. **the most excellent governor**—an honorary title of office.

ADAM CLARKE

be preserved, yet he knew that the divine providence acts by reasonable and prudent means; and that if he neglected to use the means in his power, he could not expect God's providence to work in his behalf. He who will not help himself, according to the means and power he possesses, has neither reason nor revelation to assure him that he shall receive any assistance from God.

F. B. MEYER:

Would-be murderers baffled. The Lord had told his servant that he was needed in Rome, but the conspirators said that he should not leave Jerusalem. There is only one conclusion when such a collision occurs—God's Word must stand, to the discomfiture of those who have sworn that they will neither eat nor drink till they have perpetrated their plan to the contrary.

These high ecclesiastics fell in with an infamous plot. What will not unscrupulous men do under cover of religion! It is a pleasing trait that the Roman officer took Paul's nephew by the hand and led him aside for a private audience. How proudly would the boy recount the whole story to his mother when he emerged from those grim walls. At nine o'clock that night there was a clattering of horses' hooves as 70 horsemen and 200 soldiers went through the stone-paved streets on their way to Caesarea. Already Paul had begun his journey to Rome. Often afterward, when it seemed as though his life would be forfeited, he must have rested on the Master's words, "So must thou bear witness also at Rome." What a lifebuoy that promise was! And if God had saved him from the mob at Jerusalem and given him the friendship of Lysias, what could God not do for him in the future!—*Bible Commentary*

23. *Two hundred soldiers.* "Infantry or foot soldiers." *Horsemen threescore and ten.* There was always a certain number of horse, or cavalry, attached to the foot. *Spearmen.* Persons who held a spear or javelin in their hand, from "taking or holding a thing in the right hand." *The third hour of the night.* About 9:00 p.m., for the greater secrecy, and to elude the cunning, active malice of the Jews.

24. *Provide them beasts.* One for Paul and some others for his immediate keepers. *Felix the governor.* This Felix was a freed man of the Emperor Claudius and brother of Pallas, chief favorite of the emperor. Tacitus calls him Antonius Felix, and gives us to understand that he governed with all the authority of a king and the baseness and insolence of a slave. Drusilla, the sister of Agrippa, was his wife at this time; see chap. xxiv. 22. He was an unrighteous governor; a base, mercenary, and bad man; see chap. xxiv. 2.

25. *He wrote a letter after this manner.* It appears that this was not only the substance of the letter, but the letter itself. The whole of it is so perfectly formal as to prove this, and in this simple manner are all the letters of the ancients formed. In this also we have an additional proof of Luke's accuracy.

MATTHEW HENRY

of Paul's case: [1] He was one that the Jews had a pique against: *They had taken him*, and would *have killed him;* and perhaps Felix did not think much the worse of him for that, *v.* 27. [2] He had protected him because he was a Roman: "When they were about to kill him, *I came with an army and rescued him*"; which action for a citizen of Rome would recommend him to the Roman governor. [3] He could not understand the merits of his cause. He took the proper method to know: he *brought him forth into their council* (*v.* 28), to be examined there, but he found *that he was accused of questions of their law* (*v.* 29), about *the hope of the resurrection of the dead*, *v.* 6. The Romans allowed the nations they conquered the exercise of their own religion, and never offered to impose theirs upon them; yet, as conservators of the public peace, they would not suffer them, under colour of their religion, to abuse their neighbours. [4] Thus far he understood, that there was *nothing laid to his charge worthy of death or of bonds.*

(3) His referring Paul's case to Felix (*v.* 30): "*When it was told me that the Jews laid wait for the man,* to kill him, *I sent straightway to thee*, and let *his accusers* go after him, and *say before thee what they have against him*, for, being bred a soldier, I will never pretend to be a judge, and so *farewell.*"

4. Paul was accordingly conducted to Cæsarea; the soldiers got him safely out of Jerusalem by night, and left the conspirators to consider whether they should eat and drink or no. If they would not repent of the wickedness of their oath they were now at leisure to repent to the rashness of it. If any of them did starve themselves to death, they fell unpitied. Paul was conducted to *Antipatris*, which was about the midway to Cæsarea, *v.* 31. Thence *the two hundred foot-soldiers*, and *the two hundred spearmen returned* to their quarters in *the castle*. There needed not so strong a guard, but *the horsemen* might serve to bring him to Cæsarea, and would do it with more expedition.

5. He was delivered into the hands of Felix, *v.* 33. The officers *presented the letter*, and *Paul with it, to Felix*. Paul had never affected acquaintance or society with great men, yet Providence overrules his sufferings so as by them to give him an opportunity of witnessing to Christ before great men. *The governor* enquired *of what province* the prisoner originally was, and was told *that he was a native of Cilicia*, *v.* 34. He promises him a speedy trial (*v.* 35): "*I will hear thee when thine accusers have come.*" He ordered him into custody, that he should *be kept* a prisoner *in Herod's judgment-hall.*

JAMIESON, FAUSSET, BROWN

came I with an army—rather, 'with the military.' **perceived to be accused of questions of their law . . .**—Amidst all his difficulty in getting at the charges laid against Paul, enough, no doubt, come out to satisfy him that the whole was a question of religion, and that there was no case for a civil tribunal.

gave commandment to his accusers . . . to say before thee—This was not done when he wrote, but would be before the letter reached its destination.

31, 32. brought him . . . to Antipatris—nearly forty miles from Jerusalem, on the way to Cæsarea; so named by Herod in honor of his father, Antipater. **On the morrow they**—the infantry—**left the horsemen**—themselves no longer needed as a guard. The remaining distance was about twenty-five or twenty-six miles.

34, 35. asked of what province he was—the letter describing him as a Roman citizen. **I will hear thee**—The word means, 'give thee a full hearing.' **to be kept in Herod's judgment hall**—'prætorium,' the palace built at Cæsarea by Herod, and now occupied by the Roman procurators; in one of the buildings attached to which Paul was ordered to be kept.

ADAM CLARKE

30. *I sent straightway to thee.* As the proper person before whom this business should ultimately come, and by whom it should be decided. *Farewell.* "Be in good health."

31. *Antipatris.* This place was rebuilt by Herod the Great and denominated *Antipatris* in honor of his father, Antipater. It was situated between Joppa and Caesarea, on the road from Jerusalem to this latter city. The distance between Jerusalem and Caesarea was about seventy miles.

32. *On the morrow they left the horsemen.* Being now so far from Jerusalem, they considered Paul in a state of safety from the Jews and that the 70 horsemen would be a sufficient guard; 400 footmen therefore returned to Jerusalem, and the horsemen went on to Caesarea with Paul. We need not suppose that all this troop reached Antipatris on the same night in which they left Jerusalem; therefore, instead of "They brought him by night to Antipatris," we may understand the text thus—"Then the soldiers took Paul by night, and brought him to Antipatris." And the thirty-second verse need not to be understood as if the footmen reached the castle of Antonia the next day (though all this was possible) but that, having reached Antipatris and refreshed themselves, they set out the same day on their march to Jerusalem. *On the morrow they . . . returned;* that is, they began their march back again to the castle. See on chap. xxiv. 1.

33. *Who.* That is, the seventy horsemen mentioned above.

35. *I will hear thee.* "I will give you a fair, full, and attentive hearing *when thine accusers are also come*, in whose presence you shall be permitted to defend yourself. *In Herod's judgment hall.* "In Herod's praetorium," so called because it was built by Herod the Great. The praetorium was the place where the Roman *praetor* had his residence; and it is probable that in or near this place there was a sort of guardroom where state prisoners were kept. Paul was lodged here till his accusers should arrive.

MATTHEW HENRY — CHAPTER 24

Verses 1–9

We must suppose *that Lysias, the chief captain*, gave notice to the chief priests that they must follow him to Cæsarea, and there they would find a judge ready to hear them.

I. We have here the cause followed against Paul. Here is no time lost, for they are ready for a hearing *after five days*. He says here (*v.* 11) *that it was but twelve days since he came up to Jerusalem*, and he had *spent seven in his purifying in the temple.* Those who had been his judges do themselves appear here as his prosecutors. *Ananias* himself *the high priest*, now stands to inform against him. One would wonder, That he should thus disparage himself, and forget the dignity of his place. That he should thus discover himself and his enmity against Paul! Ananias is not ashamed to own himself a sworn enemy to Paul. *The elders* attended him, to signify their concurrence with him. The pains that evil men take in an evil matter, and their unwearied industry, should shame us out of our coldness, and our indifference in that which is good.

II. We have here the cause pleaded against Paul. The prosecutors brought *with them a certain orator named Tertullus*, a Roman, and therefore fittest to be employed in a cause before *the Roman governor*, and most likely to gain favour. The high priest, and elders, though they had their own hearts spiteful enough, did not think their own tongues sharp enough. Paul is set to the bar before Felix the governor: *He was called forth*, *v.* 2. Tertullus's business is, on the behalf of the prosecutors, to open the information against him. His speech is made up of flattery and falsehood; it calls evil good, and good evil.

1. One of the worst of men is here applauded as one of the best of benefactors, only because he was the judge. Felix is represented by the historians of his own nation, as well as by Josephus the Jew,

JAMIESON, FAUSSET, BROWN — CHAPTER 24

Vss. 1-27. Paul, Accused by a Professional Pleader before Felix, Makes His Defense, and Is Remanded for a Further Hearing. At a Private Interview Felix Trembles under Paul's Preaching, but Keeps Him Prisoner for Two Years, when He Was Succeeded by Festus. **1. after five days**—or, on the fifth day from their departure from Jerusalem. **Ananias . . . with the elders**—a deputation of the Sanhedrim.

a certain orator—one of those Roman advocates who trained themselves for the higher practice of the metropolis by practicing in the provinces, where the Latin language, employed in the courts, was but imperfectly understood and Roman forms were not familiar. **informed . . . against Paul**—'laid information,' i.e., put in the charges.

ADAM CLARKE — CHAPTER 24

1. *After five days.* These days are to be reckoned from the time in which Paul was apprehended at Jerusalem, and twelve days after he had arrived in that city; see v. 11. Calmet reckons the days thus: Luke says that Paul was apprehended at Jerusalem when the seven days of his vow were nearly ended, chap. xxi. 27; that is, at the end of the fifth day after his arrival. The next day, which was the sixth, he was presented before the Sanhedrin. The night following he was taken to Antipatris. The next day, the seventh, he arrived at Caesarea. Five days afterwards, that is, the twelfth day after his arrival at Jerusalem, the high priest and the elders, with Tertullus, came down to accuse him before Felix.

A certain orator named Tertullus. This was probably a Roman proselyte to Judaism, yet he speaks everywhere as a Jew. Roman orators, advocates, were found in different provinces of the Roman Empire and they, in general, spoke both the Greek and Latin languages; and being well acquainted with the Roman laws and customs, were no doubt very useful.

MATTHEW HENRY

as a very bad man, who allowed himself in all manner of wickedness, was a great oppressor, very cruel, and very covetous. And yet Tertullus here, in the name of the high priest and elders, compliments him, and extols him to the sky, as if he were so good a magistrate as never was the like. To engage him to gratify their malice against Paul they magnify him as the greatest blessing to their church and nation that ever came among them.

(1) They are very ready to own it (*v.* 2): "*By thee we enjoy great quietness and very worthy deeds are done to the whole nation of the Jews, by thy providence.*" To give him his due, he had been instrumental to suppress the insurrection of that Egyptian of whom the chief captain spoke (*ch.* xxi. 38). The unhappiness of great men is to have their services magnified beyond measure, and never to be faithfully told of their faults. Hereby they are hardened and encouraged in evil. The policy of bad men, by flattering princes in what they do amiss is to draw them in to do worse.

(2) They promise to retain a grateful sense of it (*v.* 3): "*We accept it always, and in all places, most noble Felix, with all thankfulness.*" And, if it had been true that he was such a governor, it had been just that they should thus accept his good offices with all thankfulness. The benefits which we enjoy by government, especially by the administration of wise and good governors, are what we ought to be thankful for both to God and man.

(3) They therefore expect his favour in this cause, *v.* 4. They pretend a great care not to intrench upon his time: We will *not be further tedious to thee*; *I pray thee that thou wouldest hear us of thy clemency a few words.* They were so conscious to themselves that it would soon appear to have more malice than matter in it that they found it necessary thus to insinuate themselves into his favour. Everybody knew that the high priest and the elders hated Felix; and yet, to gain their ends against Paul, they show him all this respect. Princes cannot always judge of the affections of their people by their applauses; flattery is one thing, and true loyalty is another.

2. One of the best of men is here accused as one of the worst of malefactors. After a flourish of flattery he comes to his business. This part of his discourse is as nauseous for its raillery as the former part is for its flattery. As I cannot but be sorry that a man of wit and sense should have such a saleable tongue (as one calls it), so I cannot but be angry at those dignified men that put such words into his mouth. Two things Tertullus here complains of to Felix.

(1) The peace of the nation was disturbed by Paul. They could not have baited Christ's disciples if they had not first dressed them up in the skins of wild beasts. Innocence, nay excellence and usefulness, are no fence against calumny, no, nor against the impressions of calumny upon the minds both of magistrates and multitudes. Be the representation ever so unjust, when it is enforced, as here it was, with gravity, with assurance, something will stick. They do not say, "We suspect him to be a dangerous man," but, as if the thing were past dispute, "*We have found him* to be so", as if he were a traitor and rebel already convicted. Paul was a useful man, and a great blessing to his country, and yet he is here called *a pestilent fellow* (*v.* 5): "*We have found him the plague* of the nation, a walking pestilence." They would have it thought that he had done more mischief in his time than a plague could do,—that the mischief he did was spreading and infectious,—that it was of as fatal consequence as the plague is,—that it was as much to be dreaded and guarded against as a plague is. Paul was a peace-maker; he lived peaceably and quietly himself, and taught others to do so too, and yet is here represented as *a mover of sedition among all the Jews throughout all the world.* The Jews were disaffected to the Roman government. This Felix knew. Now they would fain make him believe that this Paul was the man that made them so. They moved sedition in all places where he came, and then cast the blame unjustly upon him. Paul was a man of catholic charity, who made himself the servant of all for their good; and yet he is here charged as being a *ringleader of the sect of the Nazarenes.* Now it was true that Paul was an active leading man in propagating Christianity. But, *First,* It was utterly false that this was a sect. True Christianity establishes that which is of common concern to all mankind, publishes goodwill to men, and therefore cannot be thought to take its rise from such narrow opinions as sects owe their origin to. True Christianity has a direct tendency to the uniting of the children of men, and, as far as it obtains its just influence upon the minds of men, will make them peaceable and loving, and therefore is far from being a sect. True Christianity aims at no worldly benefit

JAMIESON, FAUSSET, BROWN

2-4. Seeing that by thee we enjoy great quietness . . .—In this fulsome flattery there was a semblance of truth: nothing more. Felix acted with a degree of vigor and success in suppressing lawless violence [JOSEPHUS, *Antiquities* xx. 8. 4; confirmed by TACITUS, *Ann.* xii. 54]. **by thy providence**—a phrase applied to the administration of the emperors.

5-8, a pestilent fellow—a plague, or pest—**and a mover of sedition among all the Jews**—by exciting disturbances among them—**throughout the world**—See on Luke 2:1. This was the *first* charge; and true only in the sense explained on ch. 16:20.

a ringleader of the sect of the Nazarenes—the *second* charge; and true enough.

G. CAMPBELL MORGAN:

Let us carefully consider the indictment. What was the charge against Paul? They first of all described him as "a pestilent fellow." That in itself was a very serious charge. It was intended to be a declaration of the character of Paul, and was employed in order to prejudice his case in the minds of the Roman governor and the court. No word could have been used by Tertullus in the presence of Felix more calculated to suggest that Paul was a man of the very basest morals. The translation hardly carries the offensiveness of the description.

Introducing him thus as "a pestilent fellow," the charges were three: first, that he was "a mover of insurrections among all the Jews throughout all the world." The only ground there could have been for any such charge might have been that the account of the uproar in Ephesus, and at Philippi, had reached Jerusalem. The second charge and the real one, so far as the enmity of his enemies was concerned, was uttered when Tertullus said that he was "a ringleader of the sect of the Nazarenes." The third charge was of the nature of an illustration in proof of both these earlier charges, and was expressed in the words: "Who moreover assayed to profane the temple." Had this been true, then by such profanation Paul would have violated the Hebrew law, and run the risk of stirring up insurrection in Jerusalem itself. This general examination of the accusation shows that it consisted of a truth objectionably stated. This, then, was the charge preferred against Paul as he was arraigned before Felix.

—*The Acts of the Apostles*

ADAM CLARKE

2. *Tertullus began to accuse him.* There are three parts in this oration of Tertullus: (1) the exordium, (2) the proposition, (3) the conclusion. The exordium contains the praise of Felix and his administration, merely for the purpose of conciliating his esteem, vv. 2-4. The proposition is contained in v. 5. The narration and conclusion, in vv. 6-8. *By thee we enjoy great quietness.* As bad a governor as Felix most certainly was, he rendered some services to Judea. The country had long been infested with robbers; and a very formidable banditti of this kind, under one Eliezar, he entirely suppressed (Joseph., *Antiq.*, l. xx, c. 6; *Bell.*, l. ii, c. 22). He also suppressed the sedition raised by an Egyptian impostor who had seduced 30,000 men; see on chap. xxi. 38. He had also quelled a very afflictive disturbance which took place between the Syrians and the Jews of Caesarea. On this ground Tertullus said, "By you we enjoy great quietness, and illustrious deeds are done to this nation by your prudent administration." This was all true; but notwithstanding this, he is well-known from his own historians and from Josephus to have been not only a very bad man, but also a very bad governor. He was mercenary, oppressive, and cruel; and of all these the Jews brought proofs to Nero, before whom they accused him; and had it not been for the interest and influence of his brother Pallas, he had been certainly ruined.

3. *We accept it always, and in all places.* We have at all times a grateful sense of your beneficent administration, and we talk of it in all places, not only before your face, but behind your back.

4. *Hear us of thy clemency.* Give us this further proof of your kindness by hearkening to our present complaint. The whole of this exordium was artful enough, though it was lame. The orator had certainly a very bad cause, of which he endeavored to make the best. Felix was a bad man and bad governor, and yet he must praise him to conciliate his esteem. Paul was a very good man and nothing amiss could be proved against him, and yet he must endeavor to blacken him as much as possible in order to please his unprincipled and wicked employers. His oration has been blamed as weak, lame, and imperfect; and yet perhaps few with so bad a cause could have made better of it.

5. *For we have found this man.* Here the proposition of the orator commences. He accuses Paul, and his accusation includes four particulars: (1) He is a pest, an exceedingly bad and wicked man. (2) He excites disturbances and seditions against the Jews. (3) He is the chief of the sect of the Nazarenes, who are a very bad people and should not be tolerated. (4) He has endeavored to pollute and profane the Temple, and we took him in the fact. *A pestilent fellow.* The word *loimos, pestis*—the plague or pestilence—is used by both Greek and Roman authors to signify a very bad and profligate man; we have weakened the force of the word by translating the substantive adjectively. Tertullus did not say that Paul was a *pestilent fellow,* but he said that he was the very pestilence itself. *A mover of sedition.* Instead of *sedition,* some MSS. read "commotions," which is probably the true reading. *Among all the Jews.* Bishop Pearce contends that the words should be understood thus—"one that stirreth up tumults against all the Jews"; for if they be understood otherwise, Tertullus may be considered as accusing his countrymen as if they, at Paul's instigation, were forward to make insurrections everywhere. On the contrary, he wishes to represent them as a persecuted and distressed people by means of Paul and his Nazarenes. *A ringleader.* This is a military phrase, and signifies the "officer who stands on the right of the first rank"; the "captain of the front rank" of the sect of the Nazarenes; "of the heresy of the Nazarenes." This word is used six times by Luke; viz., in this verse, and in v. 14, and in chap. v. 17; xv. 5; xxvi. 5; and xxviii. 22. But in none of them does it appear necessarily to include that bad sense which we generally assign to the word "heresy." See the note on chap. v. 17, where the subject is largely considered; and see further on v. 14.

MATTHEW HENRY

or advantage, and therefore must by no means be called a sect. Those that espouse a sect aim at wealth and honour; but the professors of Christianity expose themselves thereby to the loss of all that is dear to them in this world. *Secondly*, It is invidiously called *the sect of the Nazarenes*, by which Christ was represented as of Nazareth, whence no good thing was expected to arise; whereas he was of Bethlehem, where the Messiah was to be born. *Thirdly*, It was false that Paul was the author or standard-bearer of this sect; for he did not draw people to himself, but to Christ. Paul had a veneration for the temple, and had lately himself with reverence attended the temple-service; and yet it is here charged upon him that he went about to *profane the temple*, *v.* 6.

(2) The course of justice against Paul was obstructed by the chief captain. They pleaded that they *took him, and would have judged him according to their law*. This was false; they did not go about to judge him according to their law, but went about to *beat him to death* or to *pull him to pieces*, to throw him into the hands of ruffians that lay in wait to destroy him. It is easy for men, when they know what they should have done, to say, this they would have done, when they meant something else. They reflected upon the chief captain. *The chief captain Lysias came upon us and with great violence took him out of our hands*, *v.* 7. See how persecutors are enraged at their disappointments, which they ought to be thankful for. These cruel men justify themselves, and reckon him their enemy who kept them from shedding blood with their own hands. They referred the matter to Felix and his judgment, the chief captain having obliged them to it (*v.* 8): "He *commanded his accusers to come to thee*, that thou mightest hear the charge. He has left it to thee to examine him, and try what thou canst get out of him."

III. The assent of the Jews to this charge (*v.* 9): *They confirmed it, saying that those things were so.* Some think this expresses the proof of their charge by witnesses upon oath. It rather seems to intimate the approbation which the high priest and the elders gave to what Tertullus said. Those that have not the wit and parts to do mischief with that some others have, yet make themselves guilty of the mischiefs others do, by assenting to that which others do. Many that have not learning enough to plead for Baal yet have wickedness enough to vote for Baal.

Verses 10–21

We have here Paul's defence of himself, and there appears in it an accomplishment of Christ's promise to his followers that when they were before governors and kings, for his sake, it should be *given them in that same hour what they should speak.* Though Tertullus had said a great many provoking things, yet Paul did not interrupt him, but let him go on to the end of his speech. And when he had done he waited for a permission from the judge to speak in his turn, and had it. The *governor beckoned to him to speak*, *v.* 10. He made no reflections at all upon Tertullus, and levelled his defence against those that employed him.

I. He addressed himself very respectfully to the governor. Here are no such flattering compliments as Tertullus soothed him up with, but a profession that he *answered for himself cheerfully before him*, looking upon him as one that would be fair and impartial. It was likewise the language of one that was conscious to himself of his own integrity. He did not stand trembling at the bar; he was very cheerful when he had one to be his judge that was not a party, but an indifferent person. Nay, when he considers who his judge is, *I the more cheerfully answer for myself*, because *I know thou hast been many years a judge to this nation;* and this was very true. He could say of his own knowledge that there had not formerly been any complaints against Paul. He never had Paul brought before him till now; and therefore he was not so dangerous a criminal as he was represented to be. He was well acquainted with the Jewish nation. He knew what furious zealots they were against all that did not comply with them, and therefore would make allowances for that. Though he did not know him, he knew his prosecutors, and by this might guess what manner of man he was.

II. He denies the facts that he was charged with, upon which their character of him was grounded. *Moving sedition*, and *profaning the temple*, were the crimes for which he stood indicted, crimes which they knew the Roman governors were not accustomed to enquire into. But Paul desires that though he would not enquire into the crimes he would protect one that was unjustly charged with them. Now he would have him to understand.

JAMIESON, FAUSSET, BROWN

hath gone about—attempted—**to profane the temple**—the *third* charge; and entirely false.

we . . . would have judged according to our law. But . . . Lysias came upon us, and with great violence took him out of our hands—a wilful falsehood and calumnious charge against a public officer. He had commanded the Sanhedrim to meet for no other purpose than to "judge him according to their law"; and only when, instead of doing so, they fell to disputing among themselves, and the prisoner was in danger of being "pulled in pieces of them" (ch. 23:10)—or as his own letter says "killed of them" (ch. 23:27)—did he rescue him, as was his duty, "by force" out of their hands. **Commanding his accusers to come unto thee**—Here they insinuate that, instead of troubling Felix with the case, he ought to have left it to be dealt with by the Jewish tribunal; in which case his life would soon have been taken. **by examining whom**—Lysias, as would seem (vs. 22)—**thyself mayest . . .**—referring all, as if with confidence, to Felix. **the Jews assented . . .**—See on ch. 23:15.

10. thou hast been many years a judge to this nation—He had been in this province for six or seven years, and in Galilee for a longer period. Paul uses no flattery, but simply expresses his satisfaction at having to plead before one whose long official experience of Jewish matters would enable him the better to understand and appreciate what he had to say.

ADAM CLARKE

6. *Hath gone about to profane the temple.* This was a heavy charge, if it could have been substantiated, because the Jews were permitted by the Romans to put any person to death who profaned their Temple. This charge was founded on the gross calumny mentioned in chap. xxi. 28-29; for as they had seen Trophimus, an Ephesian, with Paul in the city, they pretended that Paul had brought him into the Temple. *Would have judged according to our law.* He pretended that they would have tried the case fairly had not the chief captain taken him violently out of their hands; whereas, had not Lysias interfered, they would have murdered him on the spot.

7. *With great violence.* I rather think means "with an armed force." Tertullus intimates that Lysias interfered contrary to law and brought soldiers to support him in his infringement on their constitution. This is what he seems to say and complain of, for the Jews were vexed with Lysias for rescuing the apostle from their hands.

8-9. *Commanding his accusers to come.* Here Tertullus closes his opening and statement of the case, and now he proceeds to call and examine his witnesses; and they were no doubt examined one by one, though Luke sums the whole up in one word—*The Jews also assented, saying that these things were so.*

10. *Then Paul . . . answered.* The apostle's defense consists of two parts: (I) The exordium, which has for its object the praise of his judge, whose qualifications to discern and decide on a question of this nature he fully allows, and expects from this circumstance to have a favorable hearing. (II) The tractation, which consists of two parts: (*a*) Refutation: (1) of the charge of polluting the Temple, (2) of stirring up sedition, (3) of being a leader of any sect who had a different worship from the God of their fathers; (*b*) Affirmation: (1) that he had lived so as to preserve a good conscience towards God and towards men; (2) that so far from polluting the Temple, he had been purified in it, and was found thus worshipping according to the law of God; (3) that what Tertullus and his companions had witnessed was perfectly false; and he defied them to produce a single proof, and appealed to those who had been witnesses of his conduct in Jerusalem, who should have been there could they have proved anything against him. *Thou hast been of many years a judge.* Cumanus and Felix were, for a time, joint governors of Judea. But after the condemnation of Cumanus the government fell entirely into the hands of Felix; and from Josephus we learn that this was now the sixth or seventh year of his administration, which might be called *many years* when the very frequent removals of the governors of the provinces are considered. *A judge*—The same here in signification as the Hebrew *shophet,* which means a "ruler" or "governor." This was the title of the ancient governors of Israel. *The more cheerfully.* With a "better heart or courage" because, as your long residence among us has brought you to a thorough acquaintance with our customs, I may expect a proper decision in my favor, my cause being perfectly sound.

MATTHEW HENRY

1. That he came up to Jerusalem on purpose to worship God in peace and holiness. He came to keep up his communion with the Jews, not to put any affront upon them.

2. That it was but twelve days since he came up to Jerusalem, and he had been six days a prisoner; and it could not be supposed that in so short a time he could do the mischief they charged upon him.

3. That he had demeaned himself at Jerusalem very quietly and peaceably. If it had been true that he was a *mover of sedition among all the Jews*, surely he would have been industrious to make a party at Jerusalem: but he did not do so. He was in the temple, attending the public service there. He was in the synagogues where the law was read and opened. He went about in the city among his relations and friends. They could not charge him with offering anything either against the faith or against the peace of the Jewish church. (1) He had nothing in him of a contradicting spirit, as the movers of sedition have. They never found him *disputing with any man.* He was ready, if asked, to give a reason of his own hope, and to give instruction to others; but he never picked a quarrel with any man about his religion. (2) He had nothing in him of a turbulent spirit: "They never found me *raising up the people*." He behaved as became a Christian with love and quietness, and due subjection to lawful authority. Nor did he ever mention or think of such a thing as taking up arms for the propagating of the gospel.

4. That as to what they had charged him with, of moving sedition in other countries, he was wholly innocent, and they could not make good the charge (*v.* 13): *Neither can they prove the things whereof they now accuse me.* He maintains his own innocency. He was no enemy to the public peace. He bemoans his own calamity, that he was accused of those things which could not be proved against him. And it has often been the lot of very worthy good men to be thus injured, to have things laid to their charge which they abhor the thought of. He shows the iniquity of his prosecutors, who said that which they knew they could not prove, and thereby did him wrong, and did the judge wrong too, in imposing upon him. He appeals to the equity of his judge. The judge must give sentence *according to that which is not only alleged but proved.*

III. He gives a fair and just account of himself, which does intimate what was the true reason of their prosecuting him.

1. He acknowledged himself to be one whom they looked upon as a heretic. The chief captain had observed, and the governor now cannot but observe, an uncommon violence and fury in his prosecutors. Guessing at the crime by the cry, he must needs have been a very bad man. Now Paul here unriddles the matter: *In the way which they call heresy*—or a *sect, so worship I the God of my fathers.* It is no new thing for the right way of worshipping God to be called heresy. Let us therefore never be driven off from any good way by its being put into an ill name.

2. He vindicates himself from this imputation. They call Paul a heretic, but he is not so.

(1) He *worships the God of his fathers*, and therefore is right in the object of his worship. He worships the God of Abraham, Isaac, and Jacob, the God who took them into covenant with himself. Paul adheres to that covenant, and sets up no other in opposition to it. *I worship* the same God that all my fathers worshipped. His religion gloried in its antiquity, and in an uninterrupted succession of its professors. It is very comfortable in our worshipping God to have an eye to him as the God of our fathers. He approved himself theirs, and therefore, if we serve him as they did, he will be ours.

(2) He *believed all things which are written in the law and the prophets*, and therefore is right in the rule of his worship. He received the scriptures entire, and he receives them pure. He sets not up any other rule of faith or practice but the scriptures. Divine revelation, as it is in the scripture, is that which he resolves to live and die by, and therefore he is not a heretic.

(3) He has his eye upon a future state, and therefore is right in the end of his worship. Those that turn aside to heresy have a regard to this world, but Paul aims to make heaven of his religion, and neither more nor less (*v.* 15): "*I have hope towards God;* my hope is towards God and not towards the world. I depend upon God and upon his power, that *there shall be a resurrection of the dead*, of all, both *the just and unjust*." There shall be a resurrection of the dead, of all men from the beginning to the end of time. We have not only another life to live when our present life is at an end, but there is to be another world. It shall be a resurrection *both of the just and of the unjust*, of those that did well, and to them

JAMIESON, FAUSSET, BROWN

11. thou mayest understand—canst easily learn—**that there are yet but twelve days since I went up to Jerusalem**—viz., 1. The day of his arrival in Jerusalem (ch. 21:15-17); 2. The interview with James (ch. 21:18-26); 3. The assumption of the vow (ch. 21:26); 4, 5, 6. Continuance of the vow, interrupted by the arrest (ch. 21: 27, etc); 7. Arrest of Paul (ch. 21:27); 8. Paul before the Sanhedrim (ch. 22:30; 23:1-10); 9. Conspiracy of the Jews and defeat of it (ch. 23:12-24), and despatch of Paul from Jerusalem on the evening of the same day (ch. 22:23, 31); 10, 11, 12, 13. The remaining period referred to (ch. 24:1) [MEYER]. This short period is mentioned to show how unlikely it was that he should have had time to do what was charged against him. **for to worship**—a very different purpose from that imputed to him.

12, 13. they neither found me . . . Neither can they prove the things . . .—After specifying several particulars, he challenges proof of any one of the charges brought against him. So much for the charge of *sedition.*

14, 15. But this I confess to thee—in which Felix would see no crime—**that after the way they call heresy**—literally, and better, 'a sect'—**so worship I the God of my fathers**—the ancestral God. Two arguments are contained here: (1) Our nation is divided into what they call *sects*—the sect of the Pharisees, and that of the Sadducees—all the difference between them and me is, that I belong to neither of these, but to another sect, or religious section of the nation, which from its Head they call *Nazarenes:* for this reason, and this alone, am I hated. (2) The Roman law allows every nation to worship its own deities; I claim protection under that law, worshipping the God of my ancestors, even as they, only of a different sect of the common religion.

believing all . . .—Here, disowning all opinions at variance with the Old Testament Scriptures, he challenges for the Gospel which he preached the authority of the God of their fathers. So much for the charge of *heresy.*

And have hope . . . as they themselves . . . allow, that there shall be a resurrection . . .—This appeal to the faith of his accusers shows that they were chiefly of the *Pharisees,* and that the favor of that party, to which he owed in some measure his safety at the recent council (ch. 23:6-9), had been quite momentary.

ADAM CLARKE

11. *There are yet but twelve days.* This is his reply to their charge of sedition, the improbability of which is shown from the short time he had spent in Jerusalem, quite insufficient to organize a sedition of any kind; nor could a single proof be furnished that he had attempted to seduce any man or unhinge any person from his allegiance by subtle disputations, in either the Temple, the synagogues, or the city. So that this charge necessarily fell to the ground self-confuted unless they could bring substantial proof against him, which he challenges them to do.

14. *That after the way which they call heresy.* See the explanation of this word in the note on chap. v. 17, and see before, v. 5, where what is here translated *heresy* is there rendered "sect." At this time the word had no bad acceptation in reference to religious opinions. The Pharisees themselves, the most respectable body among the Jews, are called a "sect"; for Paul, defending himself before Agrippa, says that he lived a Pharisee according to the strictest sect. And Josephus, who was a Pharisee, speaks of "the sect of the Pharisees," *Life*, chap. xxxviii. Therefore it is evident that the word heresy had no bad meaning among the Jews; it meant simply a "religious sect." Why then did they use it by way of degradation to Paul? This seems to have been the cause. They had already two accredited sects in the land, the Pharisees and Sadducees. The interests of each of these were pretty well balanced, and each had a part in the government, for the council, or Sanhedrin, was composed of both Sadducees and Pharisees; see chap. xxiii. 6. They were afraid that the Christians, whom they called Nazarenes, should form a new sect and divide the interests of both the preceding; and what they feared, that they charged them with. On this account the Christians had both the Pharisees and the Sadducees for their enemies. *So worship, I the God of my fathers.* I bring in no new object of worship, no new religious creed. I believe all things as they profess to believe; I acknowledge *the law* and *the prophets* as divinely inspired books, and have never in the smallest measure detracted from the authority or authenticity of either.

15. *And have hope toward God.* I not only do not hold anything by which the general creed of this people might be altered, in reference to the present state, but also I hold nothing different from their belief in reference to a future state; for if I maintain the doctrine of the resurrection of the dead, it is what themselves allow.

MATTHEW HENRY

our Saviour has told us that it will be a *resurrection of life*; and of those that did evil, he has said to them it will be a resurrection of condemnation. This implies that it will be a resurrection to a final judgment. The just shall rise by virtue of their union with Christ as their head; the unjust shall rise by virtue of Christ's dominion over them as their Judge. God is to be depended upon for the resurrection of the dead: I have *hope towards God* that there shall be a resurrection; it shall be effected by the almighty power of God. The resurrection of the dead is a fundamental article of our creed, as it was also of that of the Jewish church. It is what *they themselves also allow*, but it is more clearly revealed by the gospel. In all our religion we ought to serve God with a confidence in him *that there will be a resurrection of the dead*, expecting our recompence in that.

(4) His conversation is of a piece with his devotion (*v.* 16): *And herein do I exercise myself, to have always a conscience void of offence towards God and towards men.* This protestation of Paul's is to the same purport with that which he made before the high priest (*ch.* xxiii. 1): *I have lived in all good conscience.* [1] What was Paul's aim and desire: To *have a conscience void of offence*. Either, *First*, "A conscience not offending; not informing me wrong, nor in anything misleading me." Or, *Secondly*, A conscience, not offended. "This is what I am ambitious of, to keep upon good terms with my own conscience. I am as careful not to offend my conscience as I am not to offend a friend with whom I daily converse." [2] What was his care and endeavour, in pursuance of this: "*I exercise myself.* I make it my constant business" (those that did so were called *ascetics*, from the word here used), "that I may keep peace with my own conscience." [3] The extent of this care: *First*, To all times: *To have always a conscience void of offence.* Paul was conscious to himself that he *had not yet attained perfection*, and the evil that he would not do yet he did. Sins of infirmity are uneasy to conscience, but they do not wound it as presumptuous sins do; and, though offence may be given to conscience, yet care must be taken that it be not an abiding offence. This however we must always exercise ourselves in. *Secondly*, To all things: *Both towards God, and towards man.* His conscientious care extended itself to the whole of his duty, and he was afraid of breaking the law of love either to God or his neighbour. We must be very cautious that we do not think, or speak, or do anything amiss, either against God or man. [4] The inducement to it: *Herein, for this cause;* so it may be read. "Because I look for the resurrection of the dead and the life of the world to come, therefore I thus exercise myself."

IV. Having made confession of his faith, he gives a plain account of his case, and of the wrong done him by his persecutors. He challenges them to prove him guilty.

1. In the temple. Here they fell furiously upon him as an enemy to their nation and the temple, *ch.* xxi. 28. (1) It was very hard to accuse him as an *enemy to their nation*, when he came to *bring alms to his nation*, for the relief of the poor at Jerusalem. He had no malice to that people and was ready to do them all good offices. (2) It was very hard to accuse him of having profaned the temple when he brought offerings and was himself at charges therein (*ch.* xxi. 24), and was found *purifying himself in the temple*, according to the law (*v.* 18), *neither with multitude nor with tumult*. They were Jews from Asia, his enemies; they had no pretence to make a tumult and raise a multitude against him, for he had neither for him. He challenges them to prove it (*v.* 19): "Those Jews of Asia ought to have been *here before thee*, that they might have been examined, whether *they had aught against me*."

2. In the council. "Let *these same* that are *here* say whether they have *found any evil doing in me when I stood before the council* (*v.* 20). When I was there all I said was, *Touching the resurrection of the dead I am called in question by you this day* (*v.* 21), which gave no offence to anyone but the Sadducees. I stuck to that which is the faith of the whole Jewish church, excepting those whom they themselves call heretics."

Verses 22–27

I. Felix adjourned the cause (*v.* 22): He *had a more perfect knowledge of that way* than the high priest and the elders thought he had. He had got a notion of Christianity, that it was not such an evil thing as it was represented. Therefore he put off the prosecutors with an excuse: "*When the chief captain shall come down I will know the uttermost of your matter*, I shall know the truth. Either Paul deserves to be punished for raising the tumult, or you do for doing

JAMIESON, FAUSSET, BROWN

G. CAMPBELL MORGAN:

He dismissed the Hebrew description of his religion with a touch of satire. They had spoken of it as a sect; but he said: "I confess unto thee, that after the Way which they call a sect, so serve I the God of our fathers." Everything he subsequently said on that matter was in denial of their statements. His claim was that his religion was their religion; carried to its ultimate conclusion. In effect he claimed that they had profaned their own religion, and violated its intention by stopping short at a point when they should have gone on. He claimed that his religion was according to Hebrew religion: "So serve I the God of our fathers." He argued that this Way was "according to the law," and in harmony with that which was "written in the prophets." He declared that it was according to the spiritual hope of resurrection, which was at the heart of the Hebrew religion. Finally he maintained that it was his religion according to personal conviction.—*The Acts of the Apostles*

16. And herein—On this account, accordingly; i.e., looking forward to that awful day (cf. II Cor. 5:10). **I exercise myself**—The "I" here is emphatic; 'Whatever they do, this is my study.' **to have always a conscience void of offence . . .**—See ch. 23:1; II Corinthians 1:12; 2:17, etc.; i.e., 'These are the great principles of my life and conduct—how different from turbulence and sectarianism!'

17. Now after many—several—**years**—absence from Jerusalem—**I came to bring alms to my nation**—referring to the collection from the churches of Macedonia and Greece, which he had taken such pains to gather. This only allusion in the Acts to what is dwelt upon so frequently in his own Epistles (Rom. 15:25, 26; I Cor. 16:1-4; II Cor. 8:1-4), throws a beautiful light on the truth of this History. (See PALEY'S *Horæ Paulinæ*.) **and offerings**—connected with his Jewish vow: see next verse. **18-21. found me purified in the temple**—not polluting it, therefore, by my own presence, and neither gathering a crowd nor raising a stir: If then these Asiatic Jews have any charge to bring against me in justification of their arrest of me, why are they not here to substantiate it? **Or else let these . . . here say**—'Or, passing from all that preceded my trial, let those of the Sanhedrim here present say if I was guilty of aught there.' No doubt his hasty speech to the high priest might occur to them, but the provocation to it on his own part was more than they would be willing to recall. **Except . . . this one voice . . . Touching the resurrection . . .**—This would recall to the Pharisees present their own inconsistency, in befriending him then and now accusing him.

22, 23. having more perfect knowledge of that—'the'—**way**—See on ch. 19:23; and on vs. 10. **When Lysias . . . shall come . . . I will know . . .**—Felix might have dismissed the case as a tissue of unsupported charges. But if from his interest in the matter he really wished to have the presence of Lysias and others involved, a brief delay was not unworthy of him as a judge. Certainly, so far as recorded, neither Lysias nor any other parties

ADAM CLARKE

16. *And herein do I exercise myself.* And this very tenet is a pledge for by good behavior; for as I believe there will be a resurrection, "both of the just and unjust," and that every man shall be judged for the deeds done in the body, so *I exercise myself* day and night that I may have *a conscience void of offence toward God, and toward men. Toward God.* In entertaining no opinion contrary to His truth and in offering no worship contrary to His dignity, purity, and excellence. *Toward men.* In doing nothing to them that I would not, on a change of circumstances, they would do to me, and in withholding nothing by which I might comfort and serve them.

17. *Now after many years.* And as a full proof that I act according to the dictates of this divine and beneficent creed, far from coming to disturb the peace of society or to injure any person, I have brought *alms to my nation,* the fruits of my own earning and influence among a foreign people, and *offerings* to my God and His temple, proving hereby my attachment to my country and my reverence for the worship of my country's God.

18. *Found me purified in the temple.* And the Jews of Asia, who stirred up the persecution against me in Jerusalem, found me purified in the Temple, regularly performing the religious vow into which I had entered, giving no cause for suspicion; for I made no *tumult,* nor had I any number of people with me by whom I could have accomplished any seditious purpose.

20. *Any evil doing in me, while I stood before the council.* The Jews of Asia, the most competent witnesses, though my declared enemies, and they who stirred up the persecution against me, should have been here. Why are they kept back? Because they could prove nothing against me. Let these therefore who are here depose, if they have found any evil in me or proved against me by my most virulent adversaries when examined before them in their council at Jerusalem.

21. *Except it be for this one voice.* The Sadducees who belong to that council, and who deny the resurrection of the dead, may indeed blame me for professing my faith in this doctrine. But as this is a doctrine credited by the nation in general, and as there can be nothing criminal in such a belief, and they can bring no accusation against me relative to anything else, this of course is the sum of all the charges to which I am called to answer before you this day.

22. *And when Felix heard these things.* There is considerable difficulty in this verse. Translators greatly vary concerning the sense, and the MSS. themselves read variously. Wakefield's translation appears to be as proper as most: "Now Felix, upon hearing these things, put them off by saying, When Lysias the captain is come down, after I have gained a more exact knowledge of this doctrine, I will inquire fully into your business."

MATTHEW HENRY

it yourselves. I will hear what he says, and determine accordingly between you." It was a disappointment to the high priest and the elders that Paul was not condemned, or remitted to their judgment. But thus sometimes God restrains the wrath of his people's enemies by the agency, not of their friends, but of such as are strangers to them. It was an injury to Paul that he was not released. But he was a judge that neither feared God nor regarded man, and what good could be expected from him?

II. He detained the prisoner in custody. Felix thought a man of such a public character as Paul was had many friends, and he might have an opportunity of obliging them, or making a hand of them. He continued him a prisoner, commanded a centurion to keep him, *v.* 23. Yet he took care he should be *a prisoner at large*, his keeper must let him have liberty, make his confinement as easy to him as possible. The high priest and the elders grudged him his life, but Felix generously allowed him a sort of liberty. He also gave orders that none of his friends should be hindered from coming to him; and a man's prison is as it were his own house if he has but his friends about him.

III. He had frequent conversation with him afterwards in private, *v.* 24, 25.

1. With what design *Felix sent for Paul.* He had a mind to have some talk with him *concerning the faith in Christ.* Felix had a mind to talk with Paul more freely than he could in open court *concerning the faith of Christ*; and this only to satisfy his curiosity, or rather the curiosity of *his wife Drusilla, who was a Jewess*, daughter of Herod Agrippa. Being educated in the Jewish religion, she was more inquisitive concerning the Christian religion. But it was no great matter what religion she was of; for, whatever it was, she was a reproach and scandal to it—a Jewess, but an adulteress; and was noted for an impudent woman. Many are fond of new notions and speculations in religion who yet hate to come under the power and influence of religion.

2. What the account was which Paul gave him of the Christian religion. He expected to be amused with a mystical divinity, but he is alarmed with a practical divinity. Paul, being asked *concerning the Christ, reasoned* concerning *righteousness, temperance, and judgment to come.* He discoursed with clearness and warmth *of righteousness, temperance, and judgment to come.* Faith in Christ is designed to enforce upon the children of men the great laws of justice and temperance. Justice and temperance were celebrated virtues among the heathen moralists; if the doctrine Paul preaches will but free him from an obligation to these, he will readily embrace it. "It is so far from doing so that it strengthens the obligations of those sacred laws." *Paul reasoned of righteousness and temperance*, to convince Felix of his unrighteousness and intemperance, that, seeing the odiousness of them, he might enquire concerning the faith of Christ, with a resolution to embrace it. By the doctrine of Christ is discovered to us the judgment to come. Men have their day now, Felix hath his; but God's day is coming. From this account of the heads of Paul's discourse we may gather, [1] Paul in his preaching had no respect to persons, for the word of God has not. [2] Paul in his preaching aimed at the consciences of men and led them to a sight of their sins. [3] Paul preferred the serving of Christ, and the saving of souls, before his own safety. [4] Paul was willing to run hazards, in his work, even where there was little probability of doing good. Felix and Drusilla were such hardened sinners that it was not at all likely they should be brought to repentance by Paul's preaching, and yet Paul deals with them as one that did not despair of them. Let the watchman give fair warning, and then they have delivered their own souls, though they should not prevail to deliver the souls they watch for.

3. What impressions Paul's discourse made upon this great but wicked man: *Felix trembled, being put into a fright.* Paul never trembled before him, but he was made to tremble before Paul. We do not find that Drusilla trembled, though she was equally guilty. See here, The power of the word of God. It is searching, it is startling, it can strike a terror into the heart of the most proud and daring sinner. The workings of natural conscience; when it is startled and awakened, it fills the soul with horror and amazement. A prospect of the judgment to come is enough to make the stoutest heart to tremble.

4. How Felix struggled to get clear of these impressions. He did by them as he did by Paul's prosecutors (*v.* 25), *he deferred them*; he said, *Go thy way for this time, when I have a convenient season I will call for thee.* He trembled and that was all. Many are startled by the word of God who are not effectually changed by it. Many are in fear of the

JAMIESON, FAUSSET, BROWN

appeared again in the case. Verse 23, however, seems to show that *at that time* his prepossessions in favor of Paul were strong.

24, 25. Felix . . . with his wife Drusilla . . . a Jewess—This beautiful but infamous woman was the third daughter of Herod Agrippa I, who was eaten of worms (see on ch. 12: 1), and a sister of Agrippa II, before whom Paul pleaded, ch. 26. She was "given in marriage to Azizus, king of the Emesenes, who had consented to be circumcised for the sake of the alliance. But this marriage was soon dissolved, after this manner: When Festus was procurator of Judea, he saw her, and being captivated with her beauty, persuaded her to desert her husband, transgress the laws of her country, and marry himself" [JOSEPHUS, *Antiquities*, xx. 7. 1. 2]. Such was this "wife" of Felix. **he sent for Paul and heard him concerning the faith in Christ**—Perceiving from what he had heard on the trial that the new sect which was creating such a stir was represented by its own advocates as but a particular development of the Jewish faith, he probably wished to gratify the curiosity of his Jewish wife, as well as his own, by a more particular account of it from this distinguished champion. And no doubt Paul would so far humor this desire as to present to them the great leading features of the Gospel. But from vs. 25 it is evident that his discourse took an entirely practical turn, suited to the life which his two auditors were notoriously leading. **And as he reasoned of righteousness**—with reference to the *public* character of Felix—**temperance**—with reference to his immoral life—**and judgment to come**—when he would be called to an awful account for both-

-**Felix trembled**—and no wonder. For, on the testimony of TACITUS, the Roman Annalist (vs. 9; xii. 54), he ruled with a mixture of cruelty, lust, and servility, and relying on the influence of his brother Pallas at court, he thought himself at liberty to commit every sort of crime with impunity. How noble the fidelity and courage which dared to treat of such topics in such a presence, and what withering power must have been in those appeals which made even a Felix to tremble! **Go thy way for this time; and when I have a convenient season I will call for thee**—Alas for Felix! This was his golden opportunity, but—*like multitudes still*—he missed it. Convenient seasons in abundance he found to call for Paul, but never again to "hear him concerning the faith in Christ," and writhe under the terrors of the wrath to come. Even in those moments of terror he had

ADAM CLARKE

23. *He commanded a centurion to keep Paul.* He gave him into the custody of a captain, by whom he was most likely to be well used. *And to let him have liberty;* he freed him from the chains with which he was bound to the soldiers, his keepers. *And that he should forbid none of his acquaintance,* of his "own people," his fellow apostles, and the Christians in general, *to minister or come unto him;* to furnish him with any of the conveniences and comforts of life, and visit him as often as they pleased. This was an ample proof that Felix found no evil in him; and he would certainly have dismissed him but for two reasons: (1) He wanted to please the Jews, who, he knew, could depose grievous things against his administration. (2) He hoped to get money from the apostle or his friends as the purchase of his liberty.

24. *His wife Drusilla.* Felix was thrice married. Two of his wives were named Drusilla; one was a Roman, the niece or granddaughter of Antony and Cleopatra, mentioned by Tacitus, l. v, c. 9. The other, the person in the text, was a Jewess, daughter of Herod Agrippa the Great. When she was but six years of age she was affianced to Epiphanes, son of Antiochus, king of Comagene, who had promised to embrace Judaism on her account. But as he did not keep his word, her brother Agrippa (mentioned in chap. xxv. 13) refused to ratify the marriage. About the year of our Lord 53 he married her to Azizus, king of the Emesenes, who received her on condition of being circumcised. Felix, having seen her, fell desperately in love with her and by means of a pretended Jewish magician, a native of Cyprus, persuaded her to leave her husband, on which Felix took her to wife. She appears on the whole to have been a person of indifferent character, though one of the finest women of that age. It is said that she and a son she had by Felix were consumed in an eruption of Mount Vesuvius. See Josephus, *Antiq.*, l. xx, c. 7. *Heard him concerning the faith in Christ.* For the purpose mentioned in the note on v. 21, that he might be the more accurately instructed in the doctrines and views of the Christians.

25. *As he reasoned of righteousness.* The principles and requisitions of justice and right between God and man, and between man and his fellows in all relations and connections of life. *Temperance.* "Chastity; self-government or moderation" with regard to a man's appetites, passions, and propensities of all kinds. *And judgment to come.* The day of retribution in which the unjust, intemperate, and incontinent must give account of all the deeds done in the body.

This discourse of Paul was most solemnly and pointedly adapted to the state of the person to whom it was addressed. Felix was tyrannous and oppressive in his government; lived under the power of avarice and unbridled appetites; and his incontinence, intemperance, and injustice appear fully in depriving the king of Emesa of his wife and in his conduct towards Paul and the motives by which that conduct was regulated. *Go thy way for this time.* His conscience had received as much terror and alarm as it was capable of bearing; and probably he wished to hide, by privacy, the confusion and dismay which by this time were fully evident in his countenance.

MATTHEW HENRY

consequences of sin, and yet continue in love and league with sin. He did not fight against his convictions. He artfully shifted off his convictions by putting off the prosecution of them to another time. Like a sorry debtor, he begs a day; Paul has spent himself, and has tired him and his lady, and therefore, "*Go thy way for this time, when I have a convenient season I will call for thee.*" Many lose all the benefit of their convictions for want of striking while the iron is hot. By dropping his convictions now, he lost them for ever, and himself with them. In the affairs of our souls, delays are dangerous. The matter is adjourned to some more convenient season, and then convictions cool and wear off. Felix put off this matter to a more convenient season, but we do not find that this more convenient season ever came. The present season is, without doubt, the most convenient season.

IV. He detained him a prisoner, and left him so, when two years after he was removed from the government, *v.* 26, 27. He was convinced in his conscience that Paul had done *nothing worthy of death or of bonds*, and yet had not the honesty to release him. Here we are told what principles he was governed by herein. 1. The love of money. He would not release Paul because he hoped that at length his friends would make a purse to purchase his liberty. He cannot find in his heart to do his duty as a judge, unless he can get money by it: *He hoped that money would have been given him of Paul.* In hopes of this, he detains him a prisoner, and *sends for him the oftener, and communes with him.* He sends for him to feel his pulse, and gives him an opportunity to ask what he would take to release him. And now we see what became of his promise both to Paul and to himself, that he would hear more of Christ at some other convenient season. All his business now is to get money by Paul. Paul was but a poor man, but Felix knew there were those who wished well to him who were able to assist him. Though Paul is to be commended that he would not offer money to Felix, yet I know not whether his friends are to be commended in not doing it for him. I ought not to bribe a man to do an unjust thing, but, if he will not do me justice without a fee, it is but doing myself justice to give it to him; and, if they might do it, it was a shame they did not do it. The Christians here at Cæsarea had parted with their tears to prevent his going to the prison (*ch.* xxi. 13), and could they not find in their hearts to part with their money to help him out? However, this will not excuse Felix. The judge that will not do right without a bribe will no doubt do wrong for a bribe. 2. Men-pleasing. Felix was recalled from his government about *two years after this*, and Porcius Festus was put in his place. He *left Paul bound*, and the reason here given is because he was *willing to do the Jews a pleasure.* He would continue him a prisoner rather than offend them; and he did it in hope thereby to atone for the many offences he had done against them. Thus those who do some base things are tempted to do more to screen themselves. But, when he had done it, it seems he did not gain his point. The Jews, notwithstanding this, accused him to the emperor. Those that aim to please God by doing good will have what they aim at; but so will not those that seek to please men by doing evil.

JAMIESON, FAUSSET, BROWN

no thought of submission to the Cross or a change of life. The Word discerned the thoughts and intents of his heart, but that heart even then clung to its idols; even as Herod, who "did many things and heard John gladly," but in his best moments was enslaved to his lusts. How many Felixes have appeared from age to age!

26. He hoped . . . that money should have been given him . . . wherefore he sent for him the oftener, and communed with him—Bribery in a judge was punishable by the Roman law, but the spirit of a slave (to use the words of TACITUS) was in all his acts, and his "communing with Paul"—as if he cared for either him or his message—simply added hypocrisy to meanness. The position in life of Paul's Christian visitors might beget the hope of extracting something from them for the release of their champion; but the apostle would rather lie in prison than stoop to this!

27. after two years—What a trial to this burning missionary of Christ, to suffer such a tedious period of inaction! How mysterious it would seem! But this repose would be medicine to his spirit; he would not, and could not, be entirely inactive, so long as he was able by pen and message to communicate with the churches; and he would doubtless learn the salutary truth that even he was not essential to his Master's cause. That Luke wrote his Gospel during this period, under the apostle's superintendence, is the not unlikely conjecture of able critics. **Porcius Festus**—Little is known of him. He died a few years after this [JOSEPHUS, *Antiquities*, xx. 8. 9, to 9. 1]. **came into Felix' room**—He was recalled, on accusations against him by the Jews of Cæsarea, and only acquitted through the intercession of his brother at court [JOSEPHUS, *Antiquities*, xx. 8, 10]. **Felix, willing to show the Jews a pleasure**—'to earn the thanks of the Jews,' which he did not. **left Paul bound** (ch. 26:29)—which does not seem to have been till then.

ADAM CLARKE

A. T. ROBERTSON:

26. "He hoped withal" (*hama kai elpizon*). "At the same time also hoping." Paul had mentioned the "alms" (24:17) and that excited the avarice of Felix for "money" (*chremata*). Roman law demanded exile and confiscation for a magistrate who accepted bribes, but it was lax in the provinces. Felix had doubtless received them before. Josephus (*Ant.* XX. 8, 9) represents Felix as greedy for money. "The oftener" (*puknoteron*). Comparative adverb of *puknos*, old word, in N.T. only here and Luke 5:33 and 1 Tim. 5:23. Paul kept on not offering a bribe, but Felix continued to have hopes (present tense *elpizon*), kept on sending for him (present tense *metapempomenos*), and kept on communing. But he was doomed to disappointment. He was never terrified again.

—*Word Pictures in the New Testament*

26. *He hoped also that money should have been given him.* Bishop Pearce asks, "How could St. Luke know this?" To which I answer: From the report of Paul, with whom Felix had frequent conferences and to whom he undoubtedly expressed this wish.

27. *After two years.* That is, from the time that Paul came prisoner to Caesarea.

MATTHEW HENRY

CHAPTER 25

Verses 1–12

We commonly say, "New lords, new laws, new customs"; but here was a new governor, and yet Paul had the same treatment from him. Festus, like Felix, does not release him.

I. The pressing application which the high priest and other Jews used with the governor to abandon Paul. See how speedy they were in their applications to Festus. As soon as ever he *had come into the province*, within *three days he went up to Jerusalem.* The priests were upon him to proceed against Paul. He stayed *three days at Cæsarea*, where Paul was a prisoner. As soon as ever he comes up to Jerusalem the priests are in all haste with him against Paul. See how spiteful they were in their application. They *informed the governor against Paul* (*v.* 2) before he was brought upon a fair trial, that so they might make him a party who was to be the judge. But this artifice, though base enough, they could not confide in. They form another project much more base, and that is to assassinate Paul before he came upon his trial. See how specious the pretence was. Now that *the governor was himself at Jerusalem they desired he would send for Paul thither*, and try him there. He was charged with having profaned the

JAMIESON, FAUSSET, BROWN

CHAPTER 25

Vss. 1-2. FESTUS, COMING TO JERUSALEM, DECLINES TO HAVE PAUL BROUGHT THITHER FOR JUDGMENT, BUT GIVES THE PARTIES A HEARING ON HIS RETURN TO CÆSAREA—ON FESTUS ASKING THE APOSTLE IF HE WOULD GO TO JERUSALEM FOR ANOTHER HEARING BEFORE HIM, HE IS CONSTRAINED IN JUSTICE TO HIS CAUSE TO APPEAL TO THE EMPEROR. **1-3. Festus . . . after three days . . . ascended . . . to Jerusalem**—to make himself acquainted with the great central city of his government without delay. **Then the high priest**—a successor of him before whom Paul had appeared (ch. 23:2). **and the chief of the Jews**—and "the whole multitude of the Jews" (vs. 24) clamorously—**informed him against Paul . . .**

ADAM CLARKE

CHAPTER 25

1. *Now when Festus was come into the province.* By the province is meant Judea; for after the death of Herod Agrippa, Claudius thought it imprudent to trust the government in the hands of his son Agrippa, who was then but seventeen years of age; therefore Cuspius Fadus was sent to be procurator. And when afterwards Claudius had given to Agrippa the tetrarchate of Philip, that of Batanea and Abila, he nevertheless kept the province of Judea more immediately in his own hands, and governed it by procurators sent from Rome (Joseph., *Ant.*, l. xx, c. 7, s. 1). Felix being removed, Porcius Festus is sent in his place; and having come to Caesarea, where the Roman governor generally had his residence, after he had tarried three days he went up to Jerusalem to acquaint himself with the nature and complexion of the ecclesiastical government of the Jews; no doubt, for the purpose of the better administration of justice among them.

2. *The high priest . . . informed him against Paul.* They supposed that as Felix, to please them, on the resignation of his government had

MATTHEW HENRY

temple at Jerusalem, and it is usual for criminals to be tried in the court where the fact was committed; but that which they designed was to way-lay him and to murder him upon the road. *They desired favour against Paul.* The business of prosecutors is to demand justice against one that they suppose to be a criminal. To desire favour against a prisoner, and from the judge, too, who ought to be of counsel for them, is a very impudent thing. The favour ought to be for the prisoner, but here they desire it against him.

II. The governor's resolution that Paul shall take his trial at Cæsarea, *v.* 4, 5. He gave orders *that Paul should be kept at Cæsarea.* Whatever was his reason for refusing it, God made use of it as a means of preserving Paul out of the hands of his enemies. God does not bring it to light, yet he finds another way to bring it to nought, by inclining the heart of the governor, not to remove Paul to Jerusalem. God is not tied to one method, in working out salvation for his people. Yet he will do them the justice to hear what they have to say against Paul, if they will go down to Cæsarea: "*Let those among you who are able go down with me, and accuse this man.* Let them go and give in their evidence." Festus will not take it for granted that there is wickedness in him, till it is proved upon him. If he be guilty, it lies upon them to prove him so.

III. Paul's trial before Festus. Festus stayed *at Jerusalem about ten days,* and then *went down to Cæsarea.* Since they are so eager in the prosecution, he is willing this cause should be first called; he will despatch it *the next day.* 1. The court set, and the prisoner called to the bar. Festus *sat in the judgment-seat,* and he *commanded Paul to be brought, v.* 6. 2. The prosecutors exhibiting their charges against the prisoner (*v.* 7): *The Jews stood round about,* which intimates that they were many. They *stood round about,* if possible, to frighten the judge into a compliance with their malicious design, or, at least, to frighten the prisoner; but in vain: he had too just and strong an assurance to be frightened by them. *When they stood round about him, they brought many and grievous accusations against Paul,* so it should be read. They represented him to the court as black and odious as their wit and malice could contrive; but when they came to the evidence, there they failed: *they could not prove* **what they alleged against** him, for it was all false. It is no new thing for the most excellent ones of the earth to have all manner of evil said against them falsely, even *before the judgment-seat.* 3. The prisoner's insisting upon his own vindication, *v.* 8. He insisted upon his general plea, Not guilty: *Neither against the law of the Jews, nor against the temple, nor yet against Cæsar, have I offended anything at all.* He had not violated the law of the Jews. *He established the law.* Preaching Christ, *the end of the law,* was no offence against the law. He had not profaned the temple. He had not offended against Cæsar, nor his government. By this it appears that they had charged him with some instances of disaffection to the present higher powers, which obliged him to purge himself as to that matter.

IV. Paul's appeal to the emperor. This gave the cause a new turn. God puts it into his heart to do it, for the bringing about of that which he had said to him, *that he must bear witness to Christ at Rome.*

1. The proposal which Festus made to Paul to go and take his trial at Jerusalem, *v.* 9. *Festus was willing to do the Jews a pleasure,* inclined to gratify the prosecutors rather than the prisoner, and asked him whether he would be willing to go up to Jerusalem and clear himself there. He would not offer to turn him over to the high priest and the sanhedrim, but, *Wilt thou go thither, and be judged of these things before me?* The president might have ordered him thither, but he would not do it without his own consent.

2. Paul's refusal to consent to it, and his reasons for it. (1) As a citizen of Rome, it was most proper for him to be tried in that which was properly his court, which sat at Cæsarea: *I stand at Cæsar's judgment-seat, where I ought to be judged.* The court being held in Cæsar's name, and by his authority and commission, before one that was delegated by him, it might well be said to be his judgment seat. Paul's owning that he ought to be judged at Cæsar's judgment seat plainly proves that Christ's ministers are not exempted from the jurisdiction of the civil powers, and, if they be guilty, of a real crime, to submit to their censure; if innocent, yet to submit to their enquiry. (2) As a member of the Jewish nation, he had done nothing to make himself obnoxious to them: *To the Jews have I done no wrong, as thou very well knowest.* It very well becomes those that are innocent to plead their innocency, and to

JAMIESON, FAUSSET, BROWN

desired favour—in vs. 15, "judgment"—**against him**—It would seem that they had the insolence to ask him to have the prisoner executed even without a trial (vs. 16). **laying wait . . . to kill him**—How deep must have been their hostility, when two years after the defeat of their former attempt, they thirst as keenly as ever for his blood! Their plea for having the case tried at Jerusalem, where the alleged offense took place, was plausible enough; but from vs. 10 it would seem that Festus had been made acquainted with their causeless malice, and that in some way which Paul was privy to. **4-6. answered that Paul should be kept**—rather, 'is in custody'—**at Cæsarea, and . . . himself would depart shortly thither. Let them . . . which among you are able, go down**—'your leading men.'

7. the Jews . . . from Jerusalem—clamorously, as at Jerusalem; see vs. 24. **many and grievous complaints against Paul**—From his reply, and Festus' statement of the case before Agrippa, these charges seem to have been a jumble of political and religious matter which they were unable to substantiate, and vociferous cries that he was unfit to live. Paul's reply, not given in full, was probably little more than a challenge to prove any of their charges, whether political or religious.

9, 10. Festus, willing to do the Jews a pleasure—to ingratiate himself with them—**said, Wilt thou go up to Jerusalem, and . . . be judged . . . before me**—or, 'under my protection'. If this was meant in earnest, it was temporizing and vacillating. But, possibly, anticipating Paul's refusal, he wished merely to avoid the odium of refusing to remove the trial to Jerusalem.

Then said Paul, I stand at Cæsar's judgment seat—i.e., I am already before the proper tribunal. This seems to imply that he understood Festus to propose handing him over to the Sanhedrim for judgment (and see on vs. 11), with a mere promise of protection from him. But from going to Jerusalem at all he was too well justified in shrinking, for there assassination had been quite recently planned against him.

to the Jews have I done no wrong, as thou knowest very well—lit., 'better,' i.e., (perhaps), better than to press such a proposal.

ADAM CLARKE

left Paul bound, so Festus, on the assumption of it, would, to please them, deliver him into their hand. But as they wished this to be done under the color of justice, they exhibited a number of charges against Paul, which they hoped would appear to Festus a sufficient reason why a new trial should be granted, and he be sent to Jerusalem to take this trial. Their motive is mentioned in the succeeding verse.

4. *Festus answered, that Paul should be kept at Caesarea.* It is truly astonishing that Festus should refuse this favor to the heads of the Jewish nation, which to those who were not in the secret must appear so very reasonable; and especially as, on his coming to the government, it might be considered an act that was likely to make him popular—and he could have no interest in denying their request. But God had told Paul that he should testify of Him at Rome, and He disposed the heart of Festus to act as he did, and thus disappointed the malice of the Jews and fulfilled His own gracious design. *He . . . would depart shortly.* So had the providence of God disposed matters that Festus was obliged to return speedily to Caesarea, and thus had not time to preside in such a trial at Jerusalem. And this reason must appear sufficient to the Jews; especially as he gave them all liberty to come and appear against him who were able to *prove* the alleged charges.

5. *Let them . . . which among you are able.* "Those who have authority"; for so is this word often used by good Greek authors, and by Josephus.

6. *When he had tarried . . . more than ten days.* The strangeness of this mode of expression suggests the thought that our printed text is not quite correct in this place, and this suspicion is confirmed by an examination of MSS and versions. "Not more than eight or ten days" is the reading of several MSS.

7. *The Jews . . . laid many and grievous complaints against Paul.* As they must have perceived that the Roman governors would no intermeddle with questions of their law, they no doubt invented some new charges, such as sedition and treason, in order to render the mind o the governor evil affected towards Paul. Bu their malicious designs were defeated, for assertion would not go for proof before a Romar tribunal; this court required proof, and th bloodthirsty persecutors of the apostle could produce none.

8. *While he answered for himself.* In thi instance Luke gives only a general accoun both of the accusations and of Paul's defense But from the words in this verse the charge appear to have been threefold: (1) that he ha broken the law, (2) that he had defiled th Temple, (3) that he dealt in treasonable prac tices; to all of which he no doubt answere particularly, though we have nothing furthe here than this, *Neither against the temple, nor yet agains Caesar, have I offended any thing at all.*

9. *Willing to do the Jews a pleasure.* Thi was merely to please them and conciliate thei esteem; for he knew that, as Paul was Roma citizen, he could not oblige him to take a ne trial at Jerusalem.

10. *I stand at Caesar's judgment seat.* Ever procurator represented the person of the em peror in the province over which he presided and as the seat of government was at Caesare and Paul was now before the tribunal on whic the emperor's representative sat, he could say with the strictest propriety, that he stood befor *Caesar's judgment seat,* where, as a freeman o Rome, he should be tried. *As thou very we knowest.* The record of this trial before Feli was undoubtedly left for the inspection of Fe tus; for, as he left the prisoner to his successo he must also leave the charges against him ar the trial which he had undergone. Beside Festus must be assured of his innocence fro the trial through which he had just now passed.

11. *For if I be an offender.* If it can b proved that I have broken the laws, so as expose me to capital punishment, I do not wi to save my life by subterfuges. I am before t only competent tribunal; here my busine should be ultimately decided.

MATTHEW HENRY

insist upon it. (3) He was willing to abide by the rules of the law, and to let that take its course, *v.* 11. If he be guilty of any capital crime that deserves death, he will neither flee from justice nor fight with it: "I refuse not to die." If he be innocent, as he protests he is, "*If there be none of these things whereof these accuse me, no man may deliver me unto them,* no, not the governor himself; for it is his business as much to protect the innocent as to punish the guilty"; and he claims his protection.

3. His appealing to court. Since he is continually in danger of the Jews, and one attempt made after another to get him into their hands, since he cannot have justice done him in any other way: "*I appeal unto Cæsar.* Rather than be delivered to the Jews let me be delivered to Nero." It is a hard case that a son of Abraham must be forced to appeal to a Nero, from those who call themselves the seed of Abraham, and shall be safer in Rome than in Jerusalem.

V. The judgment given upon the whole matter. His enemies hoped the cause would be ended in his death; his friends hoped it would be ended in his deliverance; they are both disappointed, the thing is left as it was. It is an instance of the slow steps which Providence sometimes takes, by which we are often made ashamed both of our hopes and of our fears, and are kept still waiting on God. The president takes advice upon the matter: *He conferred with the council*—not with the council of the Jews, but with his own counsellors. He determines to send him to Rome. A Roman citizen might appeal at any time to a superior court, even to the supreme. *Hast thou appealed unto Cæsar? Unto Cæsar thou shalt go.* In our judgment before God those that by justifying themselves appeal to the law, to the law they shall go, and it will condemn them; but those that by repentance and faith appeal to the gospel, to the gospel they shall go, and it will save them.

Verses 13–27

We have here the preparation that was made for another hearing of Paul before king Agrippa, only to gratify his curiosity.

I. The friendly visit which king Agrippa made to Festus, now upon his coming into the government in that province (*v.* 13): *After certain days, king Agrippa came to Cæsarea.*

1. Who the visitants were. (1) King Agrippa, the son of that Herod (surnamed *Agrippa*) who killed James the apostle, and was himself eaten of worms; and great grandson of Herod the Great, under whom Christ was born. (2) Bernice came with him. She was his own sister, the widow of his uncle Herod, after whose death she lived with this brother of hers; after she was a second time married to Polemon, king of Cilicia, she got to be divorced from him, and returned to her brother king Agrippa. Tacitus and Suetonius speak of a criminal intimacy afterwards between her and Titus Vespasian. Drusilla, the wife of Felix, was another sister. Such lewd people were the great people generally in those times!

2. What the design of this visit was: they *came to salute Festus,* to compliment him upon his accession to the government. But it is probable they came as much to divert themselves as to show respect to him, and to share in the entertainments of his court.

II. The account which Festus gave to king Agrippa of Paul and his case.

1. To entertain him. It would be particularly acceptable to Agrippa, not only because he was a judge, and there were some points of law and practice in it well worth his notice, but much more as he was a Jew, and there were some points of religion in it much more deserving his cognizance.

2. To have his advice. *Festus* was but newly come to be a judge, and therefore was willing to have the counsel of those that were older and more experienced. The particular account he gives to king Agrippa concerning Paul, *v.* 14–21.

(1) He found him a prisoner when he came into the government of this province: *There is a certain man left in bonds by Felix;* and therefore, if there were anything amiss in the first taking of him into custody, Festus is not to answer for that.

(2) The Jewish sanhedrim were extremely set against him: "The *chief priests and the elders informed me* against him as a dangerous man, and desired he might therefore be condemned to die."

JAMIESON, FAUSSET, BROWN

if there be none of these things . . . no man may deliver me unto them—The word signifies to 'surrender in order to gratify' another.

I appeal to Cæsar—The right of appeal to the supreme power, in case of life and death, was secured by an ancient law to every Roman citizen, and continued under the empire. Had Festus shown any disposition to pronounce final judgment, Paul, strong in the consciousness of his innocence and the justice of a Roman tribunal, would not have made this appeal. But when the only other alternative offered him was to give his own consent to be transferred to the great hotbed of plots against his life, and to a tribunal of unscrupulous and bloodthirsty ecclesiastics whose vociferous cries for his death had scarcely subsided, no other course was open to him. **12. Festus**—little expecting such an appeal, but bound to respect it—**having conferred with the council**—his assessors in judgment, as to the admissibility of the appeal—**said, Hast thou**—for 'thou hast.' **to Cæsar shalt thou go**—as if he would add perhaps 'and see if thou fare better.'

13-27. Herod Agrippa II, on a Visit to Festus, Being Consulted by Him on Paul's Case, Desires to Hear the Apostle, Who Is Accordingly Brought Forth. **13. King Agrippa**—great grandson of Herod the Great, and Drusilla's brother (see on ch. 24:24). On his father's awful death (ch. 12:23), being thought too young (17) to succeed, Judea, was attached to the province of Syria. Four years after, on the death of his uncle Herod, he was made king of the northern principalities of Chalcis, and afterwards got Batanea, Iturea, Trachonitis, Abilene, Galilee, and Perea, with the title of king. He died A.D. 100, after reigning fifty-one years. **and Bernice**—his sister. She was married to her uncle Herod, king of Chalcis, on whose death she lived with her brother Agrippa—not without suspicion of incestuous intercourse, which her subsequent licentious life tended to confirm. **came to salute Festus**—to pay his respects to him on his accession to the procuratorship.

14, 15. when there many—'several'—**days, Festus declared Paul's cause**—taking advantage of the presence of one who might be presumed to know such matters better than himself; though the lapse of "several days" ere the subject was touched on shows that it gave Festus little trouble.

ADAM CLARKE

No man may deliver me unto them. The words of the apostle are very strong and appropriate. The Jews asked as a "favor," *charin,* from Festus, that he would send Paul to Jerusalem, v. 3. Festus, willing to do the Jews *charin,* this "favor," asked Paul if he would go to Jerusalem, and there be judged, v. 9. Paul says, I have done nothing amiss, either against the Jews or against Caesar. Therefore no man "can make a present of me to them"; that is, favor them so far as to put my life into their hands, and thus gratify them by my death. Festus, in his address to Agrippa, v. 16, admits this, and uses the same form of speech: "It is not the custom of the Romans gratuitously to give up anyone." Much of the beauty of this passage is lost by not attending to the original words. *I appeal unto Caesar.* A freeman of Rome who had been tried for a crime and sentence passed on him had a right to appeal to the emperor if he conceived the sentence to be unjust; but even before the sentence was pronounced, he had the privilege of an appeal, in criminal cases, if he conceived that the judge was doing anything contrary to the laws. This law was so very sacred and imperative that, in the persecution under Trajan, Pliny would not attempt to put to death Roman citizens who were proved to have turned Christians. Hence, in his letter to Trajan, l. x, Ep. 97, he says, "There were others guilty of similar folly, whom, finding them to be Roman citizens, I have determined to send to the city." Very likely these had appealed to Caesar.

12. *Conferred with the council.* From this circumstance we may learn that the appeal of Paul to Caesar was conditional, else Festus could not have deliberated with his council whether it should be granted; for he had no power to refuse to admit such an appeal. We may, therefore, understand Paul thus: "I now stand before a tribunal where I ought to be judged; if you refuse to hear and try this cause, rather than go to Jerusalem, I appeal to Caesar." Festus therefore consulted with the council, whether he should proceed to try the cause or send Paul to Rome; and it appears that the majority were of opinion that he should be sent to Caesar. *Hast thou appealed unto Caesar?* Rather, "Thou hast appealed unto Caesar, and to Caesar thou shalt go." The Jews were disappointed of their hope, and Festus got his hand creditably drawn out of a business with which he was likely to have been greatly embarrassed.

13. *King Agrippa.* This was the son of Herod Agrippa, who is mentioned in chap. xii. 1. Upon the death of his father's youngest brother, Herod, he succeeded him in the kingdom of Chalcis, by the favor of the Emperor Claudius (Jos., *Antiq.,* l. xx, c. 4, s. 2; and *Bell.,* l. ii, c. 12, s. 1. Afterwards Claudius removed him from that kingdom to a larger one, giving him the tetrarchy of Philip, which contained Trachonitis, Batanea, and Gaulonitis. He gave him, likewise, the tetrarchy of Lysanias, and the province which Varus had governed (Jos., *Antiq.,* l. xx, c. 6, s. 1; *Bell.,* l. ii, c. 12, s. 8. Nero made a further addition, and gave him four cities: Abila, Julias in Peraea, Tarichaea, and Tiberias in Galilee (Jos., *Antiq.,* l. xx, c. 7, 2. 4; *Bell.,* l. ii, c. 13, s. 2. Claudius gave him the power of appointing the high priest among the Jews (Joseph., *Antiq.,* l. xx, c. 1, s. 3); and instances of his exercising this power may be seen in Joseph., *Antiq.,* l. xx, c. 7, s. 8, 11. This king was strongly attached to the Romans and did everything in his power to prevent the Jews from rebelling against them; and when he could not prevail, he united his troops to those of Titus and assisted in the siege of Jerusalem. He survived the ruin of his country several years. Bernice, or as she is sometimes called, Berenice, was sister of this Agrippa and of the Drusilla mentioned in chap. xxiv. She was at first married to her uncle Herod, king of Chalcis (Joseph., *Antiq.,* l. xix, c. 9, s. 1); and on his death went to live with her brother Agrippa, with whom she was violently suspected to lead an incestuous life.

14. *Declared Paul's cause unto the king.* Festus knew that Agrippa was better acquainted with such matters than he, and he wished in some sort to make him a party in this business.

15. *Desiring to have judgment against him.* Instead of *judgment,* "condemnation, sentence of

MATTHEW HENRY	JAMIESON, FAUSSET, BROWN	ADAM CLARKE

(3) He had insisted upon the Roman law in favour of the prisoner, and would not condemn him unheard (*v.* 16): "*It is not the manner of the Romans* to *deliver any man to die before the accused has the accusers face to face.*" *Hear the other side* had become a proverb among them. We must not give men bad characters, nor condemn their words and actions, till we have heard what is to be said in their vindication.

(4) He had brought him upon his trial, according to the duty of his place, *v.* 17. He had been expeditious in it *as soon as ever they had come, without any delay, on the morrow,* he had brought on the cause. He had likewise tried him in the most solemn manner: He *sat on the judgment-seat.* He called a great court on purpose for the trial of Paul, that the sentence might be definitive, and the cause ended.

(5) He was extremely *disappointed* in the charge they brought against him (*v.* 18, 19): *When the accusers stood up against him they brought no accusations of such things as I supposed.* He supposed by the eagerness of their prosecution, and their urging it thus upon the Roman governors one after another, That they had something to accuse him of that was dangerous either to private property or the public peace. Such were the outcries against the primitive Christians, so loud, so fierce, that the standers-by could not but conclude them the worst of men; and to represent them so was the design of that clamour, as it was against our Saviour. That they had something to accuse him of that was cognizable in the Roman courts, and which the governor was properly the judge of, as Gallio expected (*ch.* xviii. 14). But he finds the matter is not so; they had *certain questions against him,* instead of proofs and evidences against him. And they were questions *of their own superstition,* so he calls their religion. The Romans protected their religion according to their law, but not their superstition. But the great question, it seems, was *concerning one Jesus that was dead, whom Paul affirmed to be alive.* See how slightly this Roman speaks of Christ, and of his death and resurrection, and of the great controversy between the Jews and the Christians whether he were the Messiah promised or no, and the great proof of his being the Messiah, his resurrection from the dead. What Paul affirmed concerning Jesus, that he is alive, is a matter of such vast importance that if it be not true we are all undone.

(6) He had proposed to Paul that the cause might be adjourned to the Jewish courts, as best able to take cognizance of an affair of this nature (*v.* 20): "*Because I doubted of such manner of questions I asked him whether he would go to Jerusalem and there be judged of these matters.*"

(7) Paul had chosen rather to remove his cause to Rome than to Jerusalem: "He *appealed to be reserved to the hearing of Augustus* (*v.* 21), and therefore I *commanded him to be kept till I might send him to Cæsar.*"

III. The bringing of him before Agrippa.

1. The king desired it (*v.* 22): "*I would also hear the man myself.*" Agrippa knows more of this matter than Festus does; he has heard of Paul. Nothing would oblige him more than to hear Paul. Agrippa would not for all the world have gone to a meeting to hear Paul preach, any more than Herod to hear Jesus; and yet they are both glad to have them brought before them, only to satisfy their curiosity.

2. Festus granted it: *Tomorrow thou shalt hear him.* There was a good providence in this, for the encouragement of Paul, who seemed buried alive in his imprisonment, and deprived of all opportunities of doing good. This gives him an opportunity of preaching Christ to a great congregation, and (which is more) to a congregatoin of great ones. Felix heard him in private concerning the faith of Christ. But Agrippa and Festus agree he shall be heard in public.

3. Great preparation was made for it (*v.* 23): *The next day* there was a great appearance *in the place of hearing.*

(1) Agrippa and Bernice took this opportunity to show themselves in state; *they came with great pomp.* They came *with great fancy,* so the word is. Great pomp is but great fancy. It neither adds any real excellency, nor gains any real respect, but feeds a vain humour. It is but a show, a dream, a fantastical thing (so the word signifies). The pomp which Agrippa and Bernice appeared in was, [1] Stained by their lewd characters, and all the beauty of it sullied, and all virtuous people that knew them could not but contemn them in the midst of all this pomp as vile persons. [2] Outshone by the real glory of the poor prisoner at the bar. His bonds in so good a cause were more glorious than their chains of gold. Who would be fond of worldly pomp that here sees so bad a woman loaded with it and so good a man

16-21. to deliver any man to die—See on the word "deliver up," vs. 11.

as I supposed—'suspected'—crimes punishable by civil law.

questions . . . of their own superstition—rather 'religion' (see on ch. 17:22). It cannot be supposed that Festus would use the word in any discourteous sense in addressing his Jewish guest. **one Jesus**—"Thus speaks this miserable Festus of Him to whom every knee shall bow" [BENGEL]. **whom Paul affirmed**—kept affirming'—**was alive**—showing that the resurrection of the Crucified One had been the burden, as usual, of Paul's pleading. The insignificance of the whole affair in the eyes of Festus is manifest.

because I doubted of such manner of questions—The "I" is emphatic—I, as a Roman judge, being at a loss how to deal with such matters. **the hearing of Augustus**—the imperial title first conferred by the Roman Senate on Octavius.

22-27. I would also hear—'should like to hear'—**the man myself**—No doubt Paul was right when he said, "The king knoweth of these things . . . for I am persuaded that none of these things are hidden from him; for this thing was not done in a corner" (ch. 26:26). Hence his curiosity to see and hear the man who had raised such commotion and was remodelling to such an extent the whole Jewish life.

when Agrippa was come, and Bernice, with great pomp—in the same city in which their father, on account of his pride, had perished, eaten up by worms [WETST].

death" is the reading of several MSS., which is probably genuine. This is evidently the meaning of the place, whichever reading we prefer. Nothing could satisfy these men but the death of the apostle. It was not justice they wanted, but his destruction.

16. *It is not the manner of the Romans to deliver any man to die.* "To make a present of any man"; gratuitously to give up the life of any man, through favor or caprice. Here is a reference to the subject discussed on v. 11. *Before that he which is accused have the accusers face to face.* For this righteous procedure the Roman laws were celebrated over the civilized world. Appian says: "It is not their custom to condemn men before they have been heard."

19. *Questions . . . of their own superstition.* "Questions concerning their own religion." *Superstition* meant something as bad among the Romans as it does among us; and is it likely that Festus, only a procurator, should thus speak to Agrippa, a king, concerning his own religion? He could not have done so without offering the highest insult. The word must therefore simply mean "religion."

20. *I doubted of such manner of questions.* Such as whether he had broken their law, defiled their Temple; or whether this Jesus, who was dead, was again raised to life.

21. *Unto the hearing of Augustus.* "To the discrimination of the emperor."

22. *I would also hear the man myself.* A spirit of curiosity, similar to that of Herod, Luke xxiii. 8.

23. *With great pomp.* "With much phantasy," great splendor, great parade, superb attendance or splendid retinue; in this sense the Greek word is used by the best writers. *The place of hearing.* A sort of audience chamber, in the palace of Festus. This was not a trial of Paul, there were no Jews present to accuse him, and he could not be tried but at Rome, as he had appealed to Caesar. These grandees wished to hear the man speak of his religion, and in his own defense, through a principle of curiosity.

MATTHEW HENRY

loaded with the reverse of it?

(2) The chief captains and principal men of the city took this opportunity to pay their respects to Festus and to his guests. I am apt to think that those who were to appear in pomp perplexed themselves more with care about their clothes than Paul, who was to appear as a prisoner, did with care about his cause.

IV. The speech with which Festus introduced the cause. He addressed himself respectfully to the company: "*King Agrippa, and all men who are here present with us.*" He speaks *to all the men* as if he intended a tacit reflection upon Bernice. The word used is that which signifies men in distinction from women; what had Bernice to do here? He represents the prisoner as one that the Jews had a very great spite against. *The multitude of them, both at Jerusalem and here at Cæsarea,* cry out *that he ought not to live any longer.* He confesses the prisoner's innocency (*v.* 25): *I found that he had committed nothing worthy of death.* Upon a full hearing of the case his own conscience brought in Paul *not guilty.* And why did he not discharge him then, for he stood upon his deliverance? Why, truly, because he was so much clamoured against, and he feared the clamour would turn upon himself if he should release him. It is a pity but every man that has a conscience should have courage to act according to it. He acquaints them with the present state of the case, that the prisoner had appealed to the emperor himself, and that he had admitted his appeal: *I have determined to send him.* And thus the cause now stood. He desires their assistance in examining the matter calmly and impartially, that he might have at least such an insight into the cause as was necessary to his stating it to the emperor, *v.* 36, 27. He thought it *unreasonable to send a prisoner and not withal to signify the crimes laid against him,* that the matter might be put in a readiness for the emperor's determination. He could not as yet write *anything certain* concerning Paul; so confused were the informations that were given in against him, that Festus could make nothing at all of them. He therefore desired Paul might thus be publicly examined, that he might be advised by them what to write.

JAMIESON, FAUSSET, BROWN

with the chief captains—See on ch. 21:32. JOSEPHUS (*Jewish War,* iii. 4. 2) says that five cohorts, whose full complement was 1000 men, were stationed at Cæsarea. **principal men of the city**—both Jews and Romans. "This was the most dignified and influential audience Paul had yet addressed, and the prediction (ch. 9:15) was fulfilled, though afterwards still more remarkably at Rome (ch. 27:24; II Tim. 4:16, 17" [WEBSTER and WILKINSON].

I have no certain—'definite'—**thing to write to my lord**—Nero. "The writer's accuracy should be remarked here. It would have been a mistake to apply this term ('lord') to the emperor a few years earlier. Neither Augustus nor Tiberius would let himself be so called, as implying the relation of master and slave. But it had now come (rather, was coming) into use as one of the imperial titles" [HACKET].

ADAM CLARKE

26. *I have no certain thing to write.* Nothing alleged against him has been substantiated. *Unto my lord.* The title *Kyrios, Dominus, Lord,* both Augustus and Tiberius had absolutely refused; and forbade, even by public edicts, the application of it to themselves. Tiberius himself was accustomed to say that he was lord only of his slaves, emperor or general of the troops, and prince of the senate. The succeeding emperors were not so modest; they affected the title. Nero, the then emperor, would have it; and Pliny the younger is continually giving it to Trajan in his letters.

27. *For it seemeth to me unreasonable.* Every reader must feel the awkward situation in which Festus stood. He was about to send a prisoner to Rome to appear before Nero, though he had not one charge to support against him; and yet he must be sent, for he had appealed to Caesar. He hopes therefore that Agrippa, who was of the Jewish religion, would be able to discern more particularly the merits of this case; and might, after hearing Paul, direct him how to draw up those letters which, on sending the prisoner, must be transmitted to the emperor.

This chapter ends as exceptionably as the twenty-first. It should have begun at v. 13, and have been continued to the end of the twenty-sixth chapter, or both chapters have been united in one.

MATTHEW HENRY — CHAPTER 26

Verses 1–11

Agrippa was the most honourable person in the assembly, having the title of king bestowed upon him, and, though not here superior, yet senior, to Festus. Festus having opened the cause, Agrippa intimates to Paul a licence given him to *speak for himself,* v. 1. This was a favour which the Jews would not allow him, but Agrippa freely gives it to him. Notice is taken of his gesture: He *stretched forth his hand,* as one that had perfect freedom and command of himself.

I. Paul addressed himself with a very particular respect to Agrippa, *v.* 2, 3. He answered cheerfully before Felix, because he knew he had been *many years a judge to that nation, ch.* xxiv. 10. But his opinion of Agrippa goes further. Being accused of the Jews, and having many base things laid to his charge, he is glad he has an opportunity of clearing himself. Since he is forced to answer for himself, he is glad it is before king Agrippa, who, being himself a proselyte to the Jewish religion, understood all matters relating to it better than the other Roman governors did: *I knew thee to be expert in all customs and questions which are among the Jews.* It seems, Agrippa was expert in the customs of the Jewish religion. He was expert also in the questions that arose upon those customs. Agrippa was well versed in the scriptures of the Old Testament, and therefore could make a better judgment upon the controversy concerning Jesus being the Messiah than another could. It is an encouragement to a preacher to have those to speak to that are intelligent, and can discern things that differ. He therefore begs that he would *hear him patiently.* Paul designs a long discourse, and begs that Agrippa will hear him out, and not be weary; he designs a plain discourse, and begs that he will hear him with mildness, and not be angry. Surely the least we can expect, when we preach the faith of Christ, is to be heard patiently.

II. He professes that though he was branded as an apostate, yet he still adhered to all that good which he was first trained up in.

1. See here what his religion was in his youth: His *manner of life was well known, v.* 4, 5. He was not indeed born among his own nation, but he was bred among them at Jerusalem. His education was neither foreign nor obscure; it was among his own

JAMIESON, FAUSSET, BROWN — CHAPTER 26

VSS. 1-32. PAUL'S DEFENSE OF HIMSELF BEFORE KING AGRIPPA, WHO PRONOUNCES HIM INNOCENT, BUT CONCLUDES THAT THE APPEAL TO CÆSAR MUST BE CARRIED OUT. This speech, though in substance the same as that from the fortress stairs of Jerusalem (ch. 22), differs from it in being less directed to meet the charge of apostasy from the Jewish faith, and giving more enlarged views of his remarkable change and apostolic commission, and the divine support under which he was enabled to brave the hostility of his countrymen. **1-3. Agrippa said**—Being a king he appears to have presided. **Paul stretched forth the hand**—chained to a soldier (vs. 29, and see on ch. 12:6).

I know thee to be expert . . .—His father was zealous for the law, and he himself had the office of president of the temple and its treasures, and the appointment of the high priest [JOSEPHUS, *Antiquities,* 20. 1. 3]. **hear me patiently**—The idea of 'indulgently' is also conveyed.

ADAM CLARKE — CHAPTER 26

1. *Then Paul stretched forth the hand.* This act, as we have already seen on chap. xxi. 40, was merely to gain attention; it was no rhetorical flourish, nor designed for one. From knowing, partly by descriptions and partly by ancient statues, how orators and others who address a concourse of people stood, we can easily conceive the attitude of Paul. When the right hand was stretched out, the left remained under the cloak, which being thrown off the right shoulder, to give the arm the fuller liberty, it then rested on the left. Under these circumstances, the hand could be stretched out gracefully.

2. *I think myself happy.* As if he had said, This is a peculiarly fortunate circumstance in my favor that I am called to make my defense before a judge so intelligent and so well acquainted with the laws and customs of our country. This Agrippa was king of Trachonitis, a region which lay on the north of Palestine, on the east side of Jordan, and south of Damascus.

4. *My manner of life.* The apostle means to state that, though born in Tarsus, he had a regular Jewish education, having been sent up to Jerusalem for that purpose, but at what age does not appear; probably about twelve, for at this age the male children were probably brought to the annual solemnities.

MATTHEW HENRY

nation at Jerusalem. Those that *knew him from the beginning* could testify for him that he was a Pharisee, that he was of the *most strict sect of that religion.* He was not only called a Pharisee, but he *lived a Pharisee.* And he was of the better sort of Pharisees; for he was brought up at the feet of Gamaliel, who was an eminent rabbi of the school or house of Hillel. Now if Paul was a Pharisee, and lived a Pharisee, then he was a scholar, a man of learning; the Pharisees knew the law, and were well versed in it. It was a reproach to the other apostles that they had not had an academical education, but were bred fishermen, *ch.* iv. 13. Here is an apostle raised up that had sat at the feet of their most eminent doctors. Then he was a moralist, a man of virtue, and not a rake or loose debauched young man. He was, *as touching the righteousness which is in the law, blameless.* As he could not be thought to have deserted his religion because he did not know it (for he was a learned man), so he could not be thought to have deserted it because he did not love it. Then he was orthodox, sound in the faith. He was a Pharisee, in opposition to a Sadducee. They could not say, He quitted his religion for want of a due regard to divine revelation; no, he always had a veneration for the ancient *promise made of God unto the fathers.*

Now though Paul knew very well that all this would not justify him before God, yet he knew it was for his reputation among the Jews, and an argument, *such as Agrippa would feel,* that he was not such a man as they represented him to be. Though he counted it but loss that he might win Christ, yet he mentioned it when it might serve to honour Christ. He reflects upon it with some satisfaction that he had before his conversion *lived in all good conscience before God.*

2. See here what his religion is. He has not indeed such a zeal for the ceremonial law as he had in his youth. But for the main principles of his religion he is as zealous as ever.

(1) His religion is built upon the *promise made of God unto the fathers.* It is built upon divine revelation; it is built upon divine grace, and that grace manifested and conveyed by promise. The promise of God is the guide and ground of his religion, the promise *made to the fathers,* which was more ancient than the ceremonial law. Christ and heaven are the two great doctrines of the gospel—that *God has given to us eternal life, and this life is in his Son.* Now these two are the matter of the *promise made unto the fathers.*

(2) His religion consists in the hopes of this promise. He places it not, as they did, in meats and drinks, but in a believing dependence upon God's grace in the covenant, and upon the promise. He had hope in Christ as the promised seed; he hoped to be blessed in him. He had hopes of heaven. Paul had no confidence in the flesh, but in Christ.

(3) Herein he concurred with all the pious Jews. "*Our twelve tribes, instantly serving God day and night,* hope to *come to this promise.* Now all the Israelites profess to believe in this promise, both of Christ and heaven. They all hope for a Messiah to come, and we that are Christians hope in a Messiah already come; so that we all agree to build upon the same promise. They look for the *resurrection of the dead,* and this is what I look for. Why should I be looked upon as an apostate from the faith and worship of the Jewish church, when I agree with them in this fundamental article? I hope to come to the same heaven at last that they hope to come to; and, if we expect to meet so happily in our end, why should we fall out so unhappily by the way?" *Paul instantly serves God day and night* in the gospel of his Son; the twelve tribes by their representatives do so in the law of Moses, but he and they do it in hope of the same promise. Much more should Christians, who hope in the same Jesus, for the same heaven, though differing in the modes and ceremonies of worship, live together in holy love. Those only can upon good grounds hope for eternal life that are diligent and constant in the service of God; and the prospect of that eternal life should engage us to diligence and constancy in all religious exercises. And of those that *instantly serve God day and night,* though not in our way, we ought to judge charitably.

(4) This was what he was now suffering for: *I am judged for the hope of the promise made unto the fathers.* He stuck to the promise, against the ceremonial law, while his persecutors stuck to the ceremonial law, against the promise. It is common for men to hate and persecute the power of that religion in others which yet they pride themselves in the form of. Paul's hope was what *they themselves also allowed* (*ch.* xxiv. 15), and yet they were thus

JAMIESON, FAUSSET, BROWN

4, 5. from my youth, which was at the first . . . at Jerusalem, know all the Jews; which knew me from the beginning—plainly showing that he received his education, even from early youth, at Jerusalem. See on ch. 22:3. **if they would**—'were willing to'—**testify**—but this, of course, they were not, it being a strong point in his favor. **after the most straitest**—'the strictest'—**sect**—as the Pharisees confessedly were. This was said to meet the charge, that as a Hellenistic Jew he had contracted among the heathen lax ideas of Jewish peculiarities.

6, 7. I . . . am judged for the hope of the promise made . . . to our fathers—'for believing that the promise of Messiah, the Hope of the Church (ch. 13:32; 28:20) has been fulfilled in Jesus of Nazareth risen from the dead.'

Unto which promise—the fulfilment of it—**our twelve tribes**—James 1:1; and see on Luke 2:36. **instantly**—'intently'; see on ch. 12:5. **serving God**—in the sense of religious worship; see on "ministered," ch. 13:2. **day and night, hope to come**—The apostle rises into language as catholic as the thought—representing his despised nation, all scattered thought it now was, as twelve great branches of one ancient stem, in all places of their dispersion offering to the God of their fathers one unbroken worship, reposing on one great "promise" made of old unto their fathers, and sustained by one "hope" of "coming" to its fulfilment; the single point of difference between him and his countrymen, and the one cause of all their virulence against him, being, that his hope had found rest in One already come, while theirs still pointed to the future.

For which hope's sake, King Agrippa, I am accused of the Jews—'I am accused of Jews, O king' (so the true reading appears to be); of all quarters the most surprising for such a charge to come from. The charge of *sedition* is not so much as alluded to throughout this speech. It was indeed a mere pretext.

ADAM CLARKE

5. *After the most straitest sect.* That is, the Pharisees; who were reputed the strictest in their doctrines and in their moral practices of all the sects then among the Jews. The sects were the Pharisees, Sadducees, and Essenes.

6. *For the hope of the promise.* This does not appear to mean the hope of the Messiah, as some have imagined, but the hope of the resurrection of the dead, to which the apostle referred in chap. xxiii. 6, where he says to the Jewish council, "Of the hope and resurrection of the dead I am called in question."

ALBERT BARNES:

7. "Unto which" promise. To the fulfillment of which promise they hope to come; that is, they hope and believe that the promise will be fulfilled, and that they will partake of its benefits. "Our twelve tribes." This was the name by which the Jews were designated. The ancient Jewish nation had hoped to come to that promise; it had been the hope and expectation of the nation. Long before the coming of the Messiah, ten of the twelve tribes had been carried captive to Assyria, and had not returned, leaving but the two tribes of Benjamin and Judah. But the name, "the twelve tribes," as used to designate the Jewish people, would still be retained (James 1:1). Paul here says that the hope referred to had been that of the Jewish nation. Except the comparatively small portion of the nation, the Sadducees, the great mass of the nation had held to the doctrine of a future state. This Agrippa would well know.

"Instantly." Constantly: with intensity; with zeal. This was true, for amidst all the sins of the nation they observed with punctuality and zeal the outward forms of the worship of God. "Serving" God. In the ordinances and observances of the temple. As a nation they did not serve him in their hearts, but they kept up the outward forms of religious worship. "Day and night." With unwearied zeal; with constancy and ardor (Luke 2:37). The ordinary Jewish services and sacrifices were in the morning and evening, and might be said to be performed day and night. Some of their services, as the Paschal supper, were prolonged usually till late at night. The main idea is, that they kept up the worship of God with constant and untiring zeal and devotion. "For which hope's sake." On account of my cherishing this hope in common with the great mass of my countrymen. If Paul could convince Agrippa that the main point of his offense was that which had been the common belief of his countrymen, it would show to his satisfaction that he was innocent. And on this ground he put his defense—that he held only that which the mass of the nation had believed, and that he maintained this in the only consistent and defensible manner—that God had, in fact, raised up the Messiah, and had thus given assurance that the dead would rise.

—Popular Commentary

MATTHEW HENRY

enraged against him for practising according to that hope.

(5) This was what he would persuade all that heard him cordially to embrace (*v.* 8): *Why should it be thought a thing incredible with you that God should raise the dead?* He explained the *promise made to the fathers* to be the promise of the resurrection and eternal life, and proved that he was in the right way because he believed in Christ who had *risen from the dead*, which was a pledge and earnest of that resurrection which the fathers hoped for. Now many of his hearers were Gentiles, Festus particularly, and we may suppose, when they heard him speak so much of Christ's resurrection, and of the resurrection from the dead, that they mocked. If it be above the power of nature, yet it is not above the power of the God of nature. Do we not see a kind of resurrection in nature, at the return of every spring? Has the sun such a force to raise dead plants, and should it seem incredible to us that God should raise dead bodies?

III. He acknowledges that while he continued a Pharisee he was a bitter enemy to Christians and Christianity, and thought he ought to be so. His becoming a Christian and a preacher was not the result of any previous inclination that way. He did not reason himself into Christianity, but was brought into the highest degree of an assurance of it, immediately from the highest degree of prejudice against it. His conversion in such a miraculous way was not only to himself, but to others also, a convincing proof of the truth of Christianity. Perhaps he designs it for an excuse of his prosecutors. Paul himself once thought he did what he ought to do when he persecuted the disciples of Christ, and he charitably thinks they laboured under the like mistake. Observe,

(1) What a fool he was in his opinion (*v.* 9): He *thought with himself that he ought to do many things contrary to the name of Jesus of Nazareth.* Because it agreed not with the notion he had of the kingdom of the Messiah, he was for doing all he could against it. He thought he did God good service in persecuting those who called on the name of Jesus Christ. It is possible for those to be confident they are in the right who yet are evidently in the wrong.

2. What a fury he was in his practice, *v.* 10, 11. There is not a more violent principle in the world than conscience misinformed. He gives an account of what he did and aggravates it as one that was truly penitent for it. He filled the jails with Christians. *Many of the saints did I shut up in prison* (*ch.* xxvi. 10), *both men and women, ch.* viii. 3. He made himself the tool of the chief priests. Herein from them he *received authority* and proud enough he was to be a man in authority for such a purpose. He was very officious to vote the putting of Christians to death, particularly Stephen, to whose death Saul was consenting (*ch.* viii. 1). He brought them under punishments of an inferior nature, *in the synagogues*, where they were *scourged* as transgressors of the rules of the synagogue. He not only punished them for their religion, but he forced them to abjure their religion, by putting them to the torture: "*I compelled them to blaspheme* Christ." Nothing will lie heavier upon persecutors than forcing men's consciences. His rage swelled so against Christians and Christianity that Jerusalem itself was too narrow a stage for it to act upon, but, being *exceedingly mad against them, he persecuted them even to strange cities.* He was mad at them, mad to see them multiply the more for their being afflicted. He was *exceedingly mad*; the stream of his fury would admit no banks, no bounds. Persecutors are mad men, and some of them *exceedingly mad.* There is not a more restless principle than malice, especially that which pretends conscience.

This was Paul's character, and this his manner of life in the beginning of his time. All imaginable external objections lay against his being a Christian.

Verses 12–23

All who believe a God must acknowledge that those who speak and act by his direction are not to be opposed; for that *is fighting against God.* Now Paul here makes it out that he had an immediate call from heaven to preach the gospel of Christ to the Gentile world.

I. He was made a Christian by a divine power. He was brought into it on a sudden by the hand of heaven, by a divine and spiritual energy, by a revelation of Christ from above: and this when he was in the full career of his sin, going to Damascus. Nor was he tempted to give it up by the failing of his friends, for he had at this time as ample an *authority and commission from the chief priests* to persecute Christianity as ever he had. Two things bring about this surprising change, a vision from heaven and a voice from heaven.

JAMIESON, FAUSSET, BROWN

8. Why should it be thought a thing incredible . . . that God should raise the dead?—rather, 'Why is it judged a thing incredible if God raises the dead?' the case being viewed as an accomplished *fact.* No one dared to call in question the overwhelming evidence of the resurrection of Jesus, which proclaimed Him to be the Christ, the Son of God; the only way of getting rid of it, therefore, was to pronounce it incredible. But *why,* asks the apostle, *is it so judged?* Leaving this pregnant question to find its answer in the breasts of his audience, he now passes to his personal history.

9-15. See on ch. 9:1, etc. and cf. ch. 22:4, etc.

ALBERT BARNES:

10. "And when they were put to death." In the history of those transactions, there is no account of any Christian being put to death except Stephen. But there is no improbability in supposing that the same thing which had happened to Stephen had occurred in other cases. Stephen was the first martyr, and as he was a prominent man his case is particularly recorded. "I gave my voice." Paul was not a member of the Sanhedrin, but this does not mean that he voted. It simply means that he joined in the persecution; he approved it; he assented to the putting of the saints to death. The Syriac renders it, "I joined with those who condemned them." It is evident, also, that Paul instigated them in this persecution, and urged them on to deeds of blood and cruelty.

11. "And compelled them to blaspheme." To blaspheme the name of Jesus by denying that he was the Messiah, and by admitting that he was an impostor. This was the object which they had in view in the persecution. It was not to make them blaspheme or reproach God, but to deny that Jesus was the Messiah, and to reproach him as a deceiver and an impostor. It is not necessarily implied in the expression, "and compelled them to blaspheme," that he succeeded in doing it, but that he endeavored to make them apostatize from the Christian religion and deny the Lord Jesus. It is certainly not impossible that a few might thus have been induced by the authority of the Sanhedrin and by the threats of Paul to do it, but it is certain that the great mass of Christians adhered firmly to their belief that Jesus was the Messiah.

"And being exceedingly mad." Nothing could more forcibly express his violence against the Christians. He raged like a madman; he was so ignorant that he laid aside all appearance of reason; with the fury and violence of a maniac, he endeavored to exterminate them from the earth. None but a madman will persecute men on account of their religious opinions; and all persecutions have been conducted like this, with the violence, the fury, and the ungovernable temper of maniacs.

—Popular Commentary

ADAM CLARKE

8. *That God should raise the dead.* As Agrippa believed in the true God, and knew that one of His attributes was omnipotence, he could not believe that the resurrection of the dead was an impossible thing. To this belief of his the apostle appeals, and the more especially because the Sadducees denied the doctrine of the resurrection, though they professed to believe in the same God. *Two* attributes of God stood pledged to produce this resurrection: His truth, on which His promise was founded; and His power, by which the thing could be easily affected, as that power is unlimited. Some of the best critics think this verse should be read thus: "What! should it be thought a thing incredible with you, if God should raise the dead?"

10. *Many of the saints.* From what is said in this verse it seems that Paul, before his conversion, was invested with much power. He imprisoned the Christians; punished many in various synagogues; compelled them to blaspheme—to renounce and perhaps to execrate Christ, in order to save their lives; and *gave* his voice, exerted all his influence and authority, against them, in order that they might be put to death. And from this it would seem that there were other persons put to death besides Stephen, though their names are not mentioned.

12. *Whereupon as I went to Damascus.* See the whole account of the conversion of Saul of Tarsus explained at large in the notes on chap. ix. 2, etc.

MATTHEW HENRY

1. He saw a heavenly vision; it was without doubt a divine appearance. He *saw a great light, a light from heaven,* such as could not be produced by any art *at midday*; it was not in a house where tricks might have been played with him, but it was *in the way,* in the open air; it was such a light as was *above the brightness of the sun,* and this could not be the product of Paul's own fancy, for it *shone round about those that journeyed with him*: made the sun itself to be in their eyes a less light. They all fell to the earth upon the sight of it, such a mighty consternation did it put them into. In the creation of grace, as of the world, the first thing created is light, 2 Cor. iv. 6. Christ himself appeared to him (*v.* 16): *I have appeared to thee for this purpose.* Christ was in this light, though those that travelled with Paul saw the light only, and not Christ in the light.

2. He heard a heavenly voice *speaking to him*; it is here said to be *in the Hebrew tongue,* his native language. He called him by his name, and repeated it (*Saul, Saul*). He convinced him of sin, the sin of persecuting the Christians. He interested himself in the sufferings of his followers: *Thou persecutest me* (*v.* 14), and again, It is *Jesus whom thou persecutest, v.* 15. Little did Paul think, when he was trampling upon those that he looked upon as the blemishes of this earth, that he was insulting one that was so much the glory of heaven. He checked him for his wilful resistance of those convictions: *It is hard for thee to kick against the pricks.* Christ made himself known to him. Paul asked (*v.* 15), "*Who art thou, Lord?*" And he said, "*I am Jesus;* he whom thou hast despised, and hated." Paul thought Jesus was buried in the earth, and, though stolen out of his own sepulchre, yet laid in some other. All the Jews were taught to say so, and therefore he is amazed to hear him speak from heaven, to see him surrounded with all this glory. This convinced him that the doctrines of Jesus were divine and heavenly, and not to be opposed, but to be cordially embraced: and this is enough to make him a Christian immediately.

II. He was made a minister by a divine authority: *That the same Jesus that appeared to him in that glorious light* ordered him *to go and preach the gospel to the Gentiles.* What is said of his being an apostle is here joined immediately to that which was said to him by the way. He puts the two together for brevity-sake: *Rise, and stand upon thy feet.* He must stand up, for Christ has work for him to do: *I have appeared to thee to make thee a minister.* Christ has the making of his own ministers. Christ will manifest himself to all those whom he makes his ministers; for how can those preach him who do not know him? And how can those know him to whom he does not by his spirit make himself known?

1. The office to which Paul is appointed: he is made a minister, to attend on Christ, and act for him, as a witness. Christ appeared to him that he might appear for Christ before men.

2. The matter of Paul's testimony: he must give an account to the world, *Of the things which he had seen.* He saw these things that he might publish them, and he did take all occasions to publish them, as here, and before, *ch.* xxii. *Of those things in which he would appear to him.* Paul at first had but confused notions of the gospel, till Christ appeared to him and gave him fuller instructions. *The gospel he preached he received from Christ* immediately (Gal. i. 12); but he received it gradually. Christ often appeared to Paul and still taught him.

3. The spiritual protection he was taken under (*v.* 17), *delivering thee from the people of the Jews and from the Gentiles.* Christ had shown Paul at this time *what great things he must suffer* (*ch.* ix. 16), and yet tells him here he will *deliver him from the people.* Great sufferings are reconcilable to the promise of the deliverance of God's people. Sometimes God delivers them into the hands of their persecutors that he may have the honour of delivering them out of their hands.

4. The special commission given him to go among the Gentiles; it was some years after Paul's conversion before he was *sent to the Gentiles.*

(1) There is great work to be done among the Gentiles, and Paul must be instrumental in doing it. A world that sits in darkness must be enlightened. He is *sent to open their eyes, and to turn them from darkness to light.* He shall open their eyes, which before were shut against the light, and they shall be willing to understand. Christ opens the heart by opening the eyes, does not lead men blindfold, but gives them to see their own way. He is sent not only to open their eyes for the present, but to keep them open, *to turn them from darkness to light,* that is, from following false and blind guides, to follow a divine revelation of unquestionable certainty and

JAMIESON, FAUSSET, BROWN

A. T. ROBERTSON:

13. "At midday" (*hemeras meses*). Genitive of time and idiomatic use of *mesos,* in the middle of the day, more vivid than *mesembrian* (22:6). "Above the brightness of the sun" (*huper ten lamproteta tou heliou*). Here alone, not in Acts 9 or 22, though implied in 9:3 and 22:6, "indicating the supernatural character of the light" (Knowling). Luke makes no effort to harmonize the exact phrases here with those in the other accounts and Paul here (v. 16) blends together what Jesus said to him directly and the message of Jesus through Ananias (9:15). The word *lamprotes,* old word, is here alone in the N.T. "Shining round about me" (*perilampsan me*). First aorist active participle of *perilampo,* common *Koine* verb, in N.T. only here and Luke 2:9.

14. "When we were all fallen" (*panton katapesonton hemon*). Genitive absolute with second aorist active participle of *katapipto.* "In the Hebrew language" (*tei Ebraidi dialektoi*). Natural addition here, for Paul is speaking in Greek, not Aramaic as in 22:2. "It is hard for thee to kick against the goad" (*skleron soi pros kentra laktizein*). Genuine here, but not in chapters 9 and 22. A common proverb as Aeschylus *Ag.* 1624: *Pros kentra me laktize.* "It is taken from an ox that being pricked with a goad kicks and receives a severer wound" (Page). Compare the parables of Jesus (Matt. 13:35). Blass observes that Paul's mention of this Greek and Latin proverb is an indication of his culture. Besides, he mentions (not invents) it here rather than in chapter 22 because of the culture of this audience. *Kentron* means either sting as of bees (2 Macc. 14:19) and so of death (1 Cor. 15:55) or an iron goad in the ploughman's hand as here (the only two N.T. examples). Note plural here (goads) and *laktizein* is present active infinite so that the idea is "to keep on kicking against goads." This old verb means to kick with the heel (adverb *lax,* with the heel), but only here in the N.T. There is a papyrus example of kicking (*laktizo*) with the feet against the door.
—*Word Pictures in the New Testament*

16-18. But rise . . .—Here the apostle appears to condense into one statement various sayings of his Lord to him in visions at different times, in order to present at one view the grandeur of the commission with which his Master had clothed him [ALFORD].

a minister . . . both of these things which thou hast seen—putting him on a footing with those "eye-witnesses and ministers of the word" mentioned in Luke 1:2. **and of those in which I will appear to thee**—referring to visions he was thereafter to be favored with; such as ch. 18:9, 10; 22:17-21; 23:11; II Corinthians 12, etc. (Gal. 1:12).

Delivering thee from the people—(the Jews) and from the Gentiles. He was all along the object of Jewish malignity, and was at that moment in the hands of the Gentiles; yet he calmly reposes on his Master's assurances of deliverance from both, at the same time taking all precautions for safety and vindicating all his legal rights.

unto whom now I send thee—The emphatic "I" here denotes the authority of the Sender [BENGEL]. **To open their eyes, and to turn them from darkness to light**—rather, 'that they may turn' (as in vs. 20), i.e., as the effect of their eyes being opened. The whole passage leans upon Isaiah 61: 1 (Luke 4:18).

ADAM CLARKE

16. *But rise.* The particulars mentioned here and in the following two verses are not given in chap. ix nor in chap. xxiii, where he gives an account of his conversion. He has detailed the different circumstances of that important event, as he saw it necessary; and perhaps there were several others which then took place that he had no opportunity of mentioning, because there was nothing in succeeding occurrences which rendered it necessary to produce them. *To make thee a minister.* "An under-rower"; that is, one who is under the guidance and authority of another; an assistant, or servant. So Paul was to act solely under the authority of Jesus Christ. *And a witness. Martyra,* a "martyr." Though this word literally means a *witness,* yet we apply it only to such persons as have borne testimony to the truth of God at the hazard and expense of their lives. In this sense also ancient history states Paul to have been a *witness;* for it is said he was beheaded at Rome, by the command of Nero. *In the which I will appear.* Here Christ gives him to understand that he should have further communications from himself; and this may refer either to those interpositions of divine providence by which he was so often rescued from destruction, or to those encouragements which he received in dreams, visions, trances, or to that general inspiration under which he was enabled to apprehend and reveal the secret things of God for the edification of the Church.

17. *Delivering thee from the people.* From the Jews—*and from the Gentiles,* put here in opposition to the Jews; and both meaning mankind at large, wheresoever the providence of God might send him. But he was to be delivered from the malice of the Jews, that he might be sent with salvation to the Gentiles.

18. *To open their eyes.* To be the instrument of informing their understanding in the things of God. *To turn them from darkness to light.* From heathenism and superstition to the knowledge and worship of the true God.

MATTHEW HENRY

truth. This was turning them from darkness to light, from the ways of darkness to those on which the light shines. The great design of the gospel is to rectify the mistakes of those who are in error, that things may be set and seen in a true light. A world that lies in wickedness, must be reformed; it is not enough for them to have their eyes opened, they must have their hearts renewed. Satan rules by the power of darkness, and God by the convincing evidence of light. Sinners are under the power of Satan; converting grace turns them from under the dominion of Satan, and brings them into subjection to God. When gracious dispositions are strong in the soul (as corrupt and sinful dispositions had been), it is then turned from the power of Satan unto God.

(2) There is a great happiness designed for the Gentiles by this work—*that they may receive forgiveness of sins, and inheritance among those who are sanctified;* they are turned from the slavery of Satan to the service of God. That they may be restored to his favour, which by sin they have forfeited: *That they may receive forgiveness of sins.* They are persuaded to lay down their arms, and return to their allegiance, that they may have the benefit of the act of indemnity. That they may be happy in the fruition of him, *that they may have an inheritance among those who are sanctified by faith that is in me.* Heaven is an inheritance, it descends to all the children of God; for, *if children, then heirs. That they may have a right,* so some read it; not by merit, but purely by grace. All that are effectually turned from sin to God are not only pardoned, but preferred. All that shall be saved hereafter are sanctified now. None can be happy that are not holy; nor shall any be saints in heaven that are not first saints on earth. We need no more to make us happy than to have our lot among those that are sanctified, to fare as they fare. Those who are sanctified shall be glorified. Let us therefore now cast in our lot among them. We are sanctified and saved by faith in Christ. Some refer it to the word next before, *sanctified by faith,* for faith purifies the heart. Others refer it to the receiving of both pardon and the inheritance. It comes all to one; for it is by faith that we are justified, sanctified, and glorified. *By faith, that faith which is in me;* it is emphatically expressed. That faith which in a particular manner fastens upon Jesus Christ and his mediation, by which we rely upon Christ, and resign ourselves to him.

III. He had discharged his ministry by divine aid and under divine direction and protection.

1. God gave him a heart to comply with the call (*v.* 19): *I was not disobedient to the heavenly vision.* If Paul had conferred with flesh and blood, and been swayed by his secular interest, he would have done as Jonah did, gone anywhere rather than upon this errand. He accepted his commission and he applied himself to act accordingly.

2. God enabled him to go through a great deal of work, though in it he grappled with a great deal of difficulty, *v.* 20. He applied himself to the preaching of the gospel with all vigour. He began at Damascus, where he was converted. When he came to Jerusalem, where he had his education, he there witnessed for Christ, where he had most furiously set himself against him. He preached *throughout all the coasts of Judæa;* he made the first offer of the gospel to the Jews, as Christ had appointed, and did not leave them till they had wilfully thrust the gospel from them. He turned to the Gentiles.

3. His preaching was all practical. He showed them that they ought, (1) *To repent of their sins,* to be sorry for them, and enter into covenant against them. They ought to change their mind and change their way. (2) *To turn to God.* They must not only conceive an antipathy to sin, but they must come into a conformity to God; they must turn to God, in love and affection, and return to God in duty and obedience, and turn and return from the world and the flesh. (3) *To do works meet for repentance.* This was what John preached, who was the first gospel preacher, Matt. iii. 8. Those that profess repentance must practise it, must live a life of repentance. It is not enough to speak penitent words, but we must do works agreeable to those words. Now what fault could be found with such preaching as this?

4. The Jews had no quarrel with him but upon this account, that he did all he could to persuade people to be religious, and to bring them to God by bringing them to Christ (*v.* 21): It was for these causes, and no other, *that the Jews caught me in the temple, and went about to kill me;* and let anyone judge whether these were crimes worthy of death or of bonds. They caught him in the temple worshipping God, and there they set upon him, as if the

JAMIESON, FAUSSET, BROWN

and from the power of Satan—Note the connection here between being "turned from darkness" and "from the power of Satan," whose whole power over men lies in keeping them *in the dark:* hence he is called "the ruler of the darkness of this world." See on II Corinthians 4:

4. **that they may receive forgiveness . . . and inheritance among the sanctified by faith that is in me**—Note: *Faith* is here made the instrument of salvation at once in its first stage, *forgiveness,* and its last, *admission to the home of the sanctified;* and the faith which introduces the soul to all this is emphatically declared by the glorified Redeemer to *rest upon Himself*—"FAITH, even THAT WHICH IS IN ME." And who that believes this can refrain from casting his crown before Him or resist offering Him supreme worship?

19-21. Whereupon, O King Agrippa, I was not disobedient unto the heavenly vision—This musical and elevated strain, which carries the reader along with it, and doubtless did the hearers, bespeaks the lofty region of thought and feeling to which the apostle had risen while rehearsing his Master's communications to him from heaven. **showed . . . to them of Damascus, and at Jerusalem**—omitting Arabia; because, beginning with the Jews, his object was to mention first the places where his former hatred of the name of Christ was best known: the mention of the Gentiles, so unpalatable to his audience, is reserved to the last.

repent and return to God, and do works meet for repentance—a brief description of conversion and its proper fruits, suggested, probably, by the Baptist's teaching (Luke 3:7, 8).

ADAM CLARKE

From the power of Satan unto God. From the "authority" and domination of Satan; for as the kingdom of darkness is his kingdom, so those who live in this darkness are under his dominion, and he has authority and right over them.

And inheritance. By remission of sins, i.e., the removal of the guilt and pollution of sin, they become children of God; and, if children, then heirs. And as the inheritance is said to be *among them which are sanctified,* this is a further proof that *aphesis hamartion* signifies, not only the forgiveness of sins, but also the purification of the heart. *By faith that is in me.* By believing on Christ Jesus, as dying for their offenses and rising again for their justification. Thus we see not only that this salvation comes through Christ, but that it is to be received by faith; and consequently neither by the merit of works nor by that of suffering.

F. B. MEYER:

To us also the heavenly visions come. On our summer holidays, rising between us and some soaring Alp, or meeting us in our walk beside the gently breaking sea; on beds of pain and in chambers of watching; visions of the risen Lord; visions of his infinite grief and pain which we have caused; visions of the possibilities of our life as a minister and witness of the things which we have seen; visions of results far down the vista wherein dark souls should become light, slaves emancipated, the defiled saintly. Ah, visions of God! ye leave an indelible impression that molds and ennobles all after-years! Pitiable the soul to which visions of a holier, sweeter life never come, or, if they come, are never seen.

The one important matter is our treatment of them. We may indolently refuse to follow the beckoning hand and obey the voice that calls. We may return to our evil courses and follow the devices and desires of our own hearts. We may cling to the prison cell, instead of following the angel that strikes us on our side and bids us go forth into freedom. And if so, like Balaam, we shall become spiritually blind and fail to see visions that the dumb creatures recognize, and that would fain arrest us in our perilous career.

On the other hand, if we will obey the vision, we shall not only retain the impression and feel its prolonged and enthralling power, but shall receive still further manifestations of the will of God. "A witness both of the thing wherein thou hast seen Me, and of the things wherein I will appear unto thee." To those who love and obey Him, He is ever drawing near with fresh and deeper thoughts of the Father.

—*Great Verses Through the Bible*

20. *That they should repent.* Be deeply humbled for their past iniquities, *and turn to God* as their Judge and Saviour, avoiding all idolatry and all sin, and thus *do works meet for repentance;* that is, show by their conduct that they had contrite hearts and that they sincerely sought salvation from God alone. For the meaning of the word *repentance,* see the note on Matt. iii. 2.

21. *For these causes the Jews . . . went about to kill me.* These causes may be reduced to four heads: (1) He had maintained the resurrection of the dead; (2) The resurrection of Christ, whom they had crucified and slain; (3) That this Jesus was the promised Messiah; (4) He had offered salvation to the Gentiles as well as to the Jews.

MATTHEW HENRY

better place the better deed.

5. He had no help but from heaven (*v.* 22): "*Having therefore obtained help of God, I continue unto this day.* I have stood to what I said, and have not been afraid nor ashamed to persist in it." What was it that bore him up? Not any strength of his own resolutions, but *having obtained help of God.* He could not have gone on in it, but by help obtained of God. Those who are employed in work for God shall obtain help from God. Our continuance to this day must be attributed to help obtained of God. The preachers of the gospel could never have done as they did, if they had not had immediate help from heaven.

6. He preached no doctrine but what agreed with the scriptures of the Old Testament: He *witnessed both to small and great.* It was an evidence of the grace of the gospel that it was witnessed to the meanest, and the poor were welcome to the knowledge of it; and of the incontestable truth of it that it was neither afraid nor ashamed to show itself to the greatest. The enemies of Paul objected against him that he preached something more than *that men should repent, and turn to God, and do works meet for repentance.* Besides these, he had preached Christ, and his death, and his resurrection, and this was what they quarrelled with him for. "And so I did," says Paul, "and so I do, but therein also I say *no other than that which Moses and the prophets said should come*; and what greater honour can be done to them than to show that what they foretold is accomplished?" Three things they prophesied, and Paul preached: (1) *That Christ should suffer*, that the Messiah should be a *sufferer.* His ignominious death should be not only consistent with, but pursuant of, his undertaking. The cross of Christ was a stumbling-block to the Jews; but Paul stands to it that, in preaching that, he preached the fulfilling of the Old Testament predictions. (2) *That he should be the first that should rise from the dead; that he should be the chief of the resurrection, the head, or principal one.* He was the first that rose from the dead to die no more. (3) *That he should show light unto the people, and to the Gentiles*, to the people of the Jews in the first place. To them he showed light by himself, and then to the Gentiles by the ministry of his apostles. In this Paul refers to his commission (*v.* 18), *To turn them from darkness to light.* He rose from the dead on purpose that he might show light to the people. This also was foretold by the Old Testament prophets, *that the Gentiles should be brought to the knowledge of God by the Messiah;* and what was there in all this that the Jews could justly be displeased at?

Verses 24–32

We have reason to think that Paul had a great deal more to say. He had just fallen upon that which was the life of the cause—the death and resurrection of Jesus Christ. Lead him but to this subject and he will never know when to conclude; for the power of Christ's death, and the fellowship of his sufferings, are with him inexhaustible subjects. It was a thousand pities then that he should be interrupted, and that, being permitted to speak for himself (*v.* 1), he should not be permitted to say all he designed.

I. Festus, the Roman governor, is of opinion that the poor man is crazed. He takes him to be a lunatic, a distracted man, that should be pitied, but at the same time should not be heeded. He thinks he has found out an expedient to excuse himself both from condemning Paul as a prisoner and from believing him as a preacher; for, if he be not *compos mentis—in his senses*, he is not to be either condemned or credited.

1. What it was that Festus said of him (*v.* 24): *He said with a loud voice* that he might oblige Paul to break off his discourse, and might divert the auditors from attending to it: "*Paul, thou art beside thyself. Much learning hath made thee mad*, thou hast cracked thy brains with studying." This he speaks, not so much in anger, as in scorn and contempt. He did not understand what Paul said; it was all a riddle to him, and therefore he imputes it all to a heated imagination. He owns Paul to be a scholar, and a man of learning. The apostles, who were fishermen, were despised because they had no learning; Paul who was a university-man, is despised as having too much learning. Thus the enemies of Christ's ministers will always have something or other to upbraid them with. He reproaches him as a madman. John Baptist and Christ were represented as having a devil, as being crazed. Festus put this invidious character upon him, which perhaps never a one in the company but himself thought of.

2. How Paul cleared himself from this invidious imputation. He denies the charge, protesting that

JAMIESON, FAUSSET, BROWN

22, 23. having obtained help—'succor.' **from God**—'that [which cometh] from God.' **I continue**—'stand,' 'hold my ground'

—unto this day, witnessing . . .—i.e., This life of mine, so marvellously preserved, in spite of all the plots against it, is upheld for the Gospel's sake; therefore I "witnessed . . . "

That Christ should suffer . . .—The construction of this sentence implies that in regard to the question 'whether the Messiah is a suffering one, and whether, rising first from the dead, he should show light to the (Jewish) people and to the Gentiles,' he had only said what the prophets and Moses said should come.

24. Festus said with a loud voice—surprised and bewildered. **Paul, thou art beside thyself, much learning doth make thee mad**—'is turning thy head.' The union of flowing Greek, deep acquaintance with the sacred writings of his nation, reference to a resurrection and other doctrines to a Roman utterly unintelligible, and, above all, lofty religious earnestness, so strange to the cultivated, cold-hearted skeptics of that day—may account for this sudden exclamation.

ADAM CLARKE

ALBERT BARNES:

"Witnessing." Bearing testimony to what he had seen, according to the command of Christ (v. 16). "To small." To those in humble life; to the poor, the ignorant, and the obscure. Like his Master, he did not despise them, but regarded it as his duty and privilege to preach the gospel to them. "And great." The rich and noble; to kings, princes, and governors. He had thus stood on Mars' Hill at Athens; he had declared the same gospel before Felix, Festus, and now before Agrippa. He offered salvation to all. He passed by none because they were poor; and he was not deterred by the fear of the rich and the great from making known their sins and calling them to repentance. What an admirable illustration of the proper duties of a minister of the gospel! "Saying none other thing." Delivering no new doctrine, but maintaining only that the prophecies had been fulfilled. As he had done this only, there was no reason for the opposition and persecution of the Jews. "Should come." Should come to pass, or should take place. Paul here evidently means to say that the doctrine of the atonement, and of the resurrection of Christ, is taught in the Old Testament.
—Popular Commentary

23. *That Christ should suffer.* That "the Christ," or "Messiah," should suffer. This, though fully revealed in the prophets, the prejudices of the Jews would not permit them to receive. They expected their Messiah to be a glorious secular prince; and, to reconcile Isaiah 53 with their system, they formed the childish notion of two Messiahs—*Messiah ben David,* who should reign, conquer, and triumph; and *Messiah ben Ephraim,* who should suffer and be put to death. As the apostle says, he preached "none other things than those which the prophets and Moses did say should come"; therefore he understood that both Moses and the prophets spoke of the resurrection of Christ. *That he should be the first that should rise from the dead.* That is, that He should be the first who should rise from the dead so as to die no more; and to give, in His own person, the proof of the resurrection of the human body, no more to return under the empire of death. In no other sense can Jesus Christ be said to be the first that rose again from the dead, for Elisha raised the son of the Shunammite. A dead man, put into the sepulchre of the Prophet Elisha, was restored to life as soon as he touched the prophet's bones. Christ himself had raised the widow's son at Nain; and He had also raised Lazarus and several others. All these died again; but the human nature of our Lord was raised from the dead, and can die no more. Thus He was the first who rose again from the dead to return no more into the empire of death. *And should shew light unto the people.* Should give the true knowledge of the law and the prophets to the Jews, for these are meant by the term *people,* as in v. 17. *And to the Gentiles,* who had no revelation, and who sat in the valley of the shadow of death. That the Messiah should be the Light of both the Jews and the Gentiles, the prophets had clearly foretold. See Isa. lx. 1: "Arise, shine [or be illuminated]; for thy light is come, and the glory of the Lord is risen upon thee." And again, Isa. xlix. 6: "I will also give thee for a light to the Gentiles, that thou mayest be my salvation unto the end of the earth." With such sayings as these Agrippa was well acquainted, from his education as a Jew.

24. *Paul, thou art beside thyself.* "Thou art mad, Paul!" "Thy great learning hath turned thee into a madman."

MATTHEW HENRY

there was neither ground nor colour for it (*v.* 25): "*I am not mad, most noble Festus.* I do not ramble, *but speak the words of truth and soberness.*" He gives him all possible respect, compliments him with his title of honour, *most noble Festus,* to teach us not to render railing for railing, but to speak civilly to those who speak slightly of us. He appeals to Agrippa concerning what he spoke (*v.* 26): *For the king knows of these things.* He therefore *spoke freely before him,* who knew something of them, and therefore would be willing to know more: *For I am persuaded that none of these things are hidden from him. This thing was not done in a corner;* all the country rang of it, and therefore it was unreasonable to censure him as a distracted man for relating it, much more for speaking of the death and resurrection of Christ, which was so universally spoken of. Agrippa could not be ignorant of it, and it was a shame for Festus that he was so.

II. Agrippa is so far from thinking him a madman that he thinks, he never heard a man talk more to the purpose.

1. Paul applies himself closely to Agrippa's conscience. He will speak to those who understand him, and whom he is likely to fasten something upon, and therefore still addresses *Agrippa*: "*King Agrippa, believest thou the prophets?*" He does not stay for an answer, but, in compliment to Agrippa, takes it for granted: *I know that thou believest;* for everyone knew that Agrippa professed the Jews' religion, and therefore both knew the writings of the prophets and gave credit to them. It is good dealing with those who have acquaintance with the scriptures and believe them; for such one has some hold of.

2. Agrippa owns there was a great deal of reason in what Paul said (*v.* 28): *Almost thou persuadest me to be a Christian.* Some understand this as spoken ironically, *Wouldest thou in so little a time persuade me to be a Christian?* But, taking it so, it is an acknowledgment that Paul spoke very much to the purpose. Others take it as spoken seriously. He is as near being persuaded to believe in Christ as Felix, when he trembled, was to leave his sins. Many are almost persuaded to be religious who are not quite persuaded; they are under strong convictions, but yet are overruled by some external inducements, and do not pursue their convictions.

3. Paul concludes with a pious wish that all his hearers were Christians, and this wish turned into a prayer: *I pray to God for it* (*v.* 29). *That not only thou but all that hear me this day were both almost, and altogether, such as I am, except these bonds.* He professes his resolution to cleave to his religion. In wishing that they were all as he was, he does in effect declare against ever being as they were, how much soever it might be to his worldly advantage. He intimates his satisfaction not only in the truth, but in the benefit and advantage of Christianity. He could not wish better to the best friend he had in the world than to wish him a faithful zealous disciple of Jesus Christ. He intimates his trouble and concern that Agrippa went no further than being almost a Christian (what good would that do?). He intimates that it would be the unspeakable happiness of every one of them to become *true Christians*—that there is grace enough in Christ for all, be they ever so many. He intimates the hearty goodwill he bore to them all; he wishes them, (1) As well as he wished his own soul. (2) Better than he now was as to his outward condition. He wishes they might all be comforted Christians as he was, but not persecuted Christians as he was. When he wished them in bonds to Christ, he desired they might never be in bonds for Christ. Nothing could be said more tenderly nor with a better grace.

III. They all agree that Paul is an innocent man. The court broke up with some precipitation (*v.* 30): *When he had spoken* the king was afraid he would say something yet more moving. The king himself found his own heart begin to yield, and durst not trust himself to hear more, but, like Felix, dismissed Paul for this time. *The king rose up, and the governor, and Bernice and those that sat with them.* They all concurred in an opinion of Paul's innocency, *v.* 31. The court withdrew to consult, and *they talked among themselves,* all to the same purport, *that this man does nothing worthy of death;* nay, he *does nothing worthy of bonds.* Thus was he made manifest in the consciences of those who yet would not receive his doctrine; and the clamours of the hot-headed Jews, who cried out, *Away with him, it is not fit he should live,* were shamed by the moderate counsels of this court. *Agrippa* gave his judgment *that he might have been set at liberty, if he had not himself appealed to Cæsar* (*v.* 32), but by that appeal he had put a bar in his own door. Agrippa, who was but almost

JAMIESON, FAUSSET, BROWN

25, 26. I am not mad, most noble Festus, but . . . Can anything surpass this reply, for readiness, self-possession, calm dignity? Every word of it refuted the rude charge, though Festus, probably, did not intend to hurt the prisoner's feelings. **the king knoweth . . .**—See on vss. 1-3.

27-29. believest thou the prophets? I know that thou believest—The courage and confidence here shown proceeded from a vivid persuasion of Agrippa's knowledge of the *facts* and faith in the *predictions* which they verified; and the king's reply is the highest testimony to the correctness of these presumptions and the immense power of such bold yet courteous appeals to conscience. **Almost**—or, 'in a little time'—**thou persuadest me to be a Christian**—Most modern interpreters think the ordinary translation inadmissible, and take the meaning to be, 'Thou thinkest to make me with little persuasion (or small trouble) a Christian—but I am not to be so easily turned. But the apostle's *reply* can scarcely suit any but the sense given in our authorized version, which is that adopted by CHRYSOSTOM and some of the best scholars since. The objection on which so much stress is laid, that the word "Christian" was at that time only a term of contempt, has no force except on the other side; for taking it in that view, the sense is, 'Thou wilt soon have me one of that despised sect.' **I would to God . . .**—What unequalled magnanimity does this speech breathe! Only his Master ever towered above this. **not only . . . almost . . . but altogether**—or, 'whether soon or late,' or 'with little or much difficulty. **except these bonds**—doubtless holding up his two chained hands (see on ch. 12:6): which in closing such a noble utterance must have had an electrical effect.

30-32. when he had thus spoken, the king rose—not over-easy, we may be sure.

This man might have been set at liberty if he had not appealed to Cæsar—It would seem from this that such appeals, once made, behooved to be carried out.

ADAM CLARKE

25. *I am not mad, most noble Festus.* The title *most noble,* or "most excellent," which he gives to Festus, shows at once that he was far above indulging any sentiment of anger or displeasure at Festus, though he had called him a madman. "Most excellent" was merely a title which belonged to the office of Festus. Paul hereby acknowledges him as the governor. *Speak forth the words of truth and soberness.* Words of "truth and of mental soundness."

26. *Before whom also I speak freely.* This is a further judicious apology for himself and his discourse. As if he had said: Conscious that the king understands all these subjects well, being fully versed in the law and the prophets, I have used the utmost freedom of speech, and have mentioned the tenets of my religion in their own appropriate terms. *This thing was not done in a corner.* The preaching, miracles, passion, death, and resurrection of Jesus Christ were most public and notorious; and of them Agrippa could not be ignorant. And indeed it appears from his own answer that he was not, but was now more fully persuaded of the truth than ever, and almost led to embrace Christianity.

27. *Believest thou the prophets?* Having made his elegant compliment and vindication to Festus, he turns to Agrippa; and with this strong appeal to his religious feeling, says, *Believest thou the prophets?*—and immediately anticipates his reply, and with great address speaks for him, *I know that thou believest.* The inference from this belief necessarily was: "As you believe the prophets, and I have proved that the prophets have spoken about Christ, as suffering and triumphing over death, and that all they say of the Messiah has been fulfilled in Jesus of Nazareth, then you must acknowledge that my doctrine is true."

28. *Almost thou persuadest me to be a Christian.* This declaration was almost the necessary consequence of the apostle's reasoning and Agrippa's faith. If he believed the prophets, see vv. 22-23, and believed that Paul's application of their words to Christ Jesus was correct, he must acknowledge the truth of the Christian religion; but he might choose whether he would embrace and confess this truth or not. However, the sudden appeal to his religious faith extorts from him the declaration, "Thou hast nearly persuaded me to embrace Christianity." How it could have entered into the mind of any man who carefully considered the circumstances of the case to suppose that these words of Agrippa are spoken ironically is to me unaccountable.

29. *I would to God.* So fully am I persuaded of the infinite excellence of Christianity and so truly happy am I in possession of it that "I most ardently wish that not only you, but this whole council, were not only almost, but altogether, such as I am, these chains excepted."

32. *Then said Agrippa.* The king himself, who had participated in the strongest emotions on the occasion, feels himself prompted to wish the apostle's immediate liberation; but this was now rendered impracticable because he had appealed to Caesar. The appeal was no doubt registered, and the business must now proceed to a full hearing. Bishop Pearce conjectures, with great

MATTHEW HENRY

persuaded to be a Christian, proves no better than if he had not been at all persuaded. And now I cannot tell whether Paul repented of his having appealed to Cæsar, now he saw that was the only thing that hindered his discharge. What we think is for our welfare often proves to be a trap; such short-sighted creatures are we. Or whether, notwithstanding this, he was satisfied in what he had done, and believed there was a providence in it, and it would issue well at last. And besides, he was told in a vision that he must *bear witness at Rome, ch.* xxiii. 11. And it is all one to him whether he goes thither a prisoner or at his liberty.

ADAM CLARKE

probability, that Agrippa, on his return to Rome, represented Paul's case so favorably to the emperor, or his ministers of state, that he was soon set at liberty there, as may be concluded from chap. xxviii. 30, that he dwelt two whole years in his own hired place. And to the same cause it seems to have been owing that Julius, who had the care of Paul as a prisoner in the ship, treated him courteously; see chap. xxvii. 3, 43. And the same may be gathered from chap. xxviii. 14, 16. So that this defense of the apostle before Agrippa, Bernice, and Festus was ultimately serviceable to his important cause.

MATTHEW HENRY

CHAPTER 27

Verses 1–11

I. How Paul was shipped off for Italy: a long voyage, but there is no remedy. He has appealed to Cæsar, and to Cæsar he must go: *It was determined that we should sail into Italy.* It was determined by the counsel of God, before it was determined by the council of Festus, that Paul should go to Rome; for God had work for him to do there. Whose custody he was committed to—to *one named Julius, a centurion of Augustus's band.* He had soldiers under him, who were a guard upon Paul. What bottom he embarked in: they went on board a ship of Adramyttium (*v.* 2), a sea-port of Africa. What company he had in this voyage; there were some prisoners who were committed to the custody of the same centurion. Paul was linked with these, as Christ with the thieves that were crucified with him, and was obliged to take his lot with them in this voyage; and we find (*v.* 42) that for their sakes he had like to have been killed, but for his sake they were preserved. But he had also some of his friends with him, Luke particularly, for he puts himself in all along, *We* sailed into Italy, and, *We* launched, *v.* 2. Aristarchus, a Thessalonian, is particularly named, as being now in his company. It was a comfort to Paul to have the society of some of his friends in this tedious voyage. Those that go long voyages at sea have need of wisdom, that they may do good to the bad company they are in, may make them better, or at least be made never the worse by them.

II. What course they steered, and what places they touched at. They touched at Sidon, thither they came *the next day. Julius the centurion* was extraordinarily civil to Paul. It is probable that he was one of the *chief captains, or principal men,* that heard him plead his own cause before Agrippa (*ch.* xxv. 23), and was convinced of his innocency. Though Paul was committed to him as a prisoner, he treated him as a friend, as a gentleman. He *gave him liberty to go among his friends to refresh himself.* Julius herein gives an example to those in power to be respectful to those whom they find worthy of their respect. God herein encourages those that suffer for him to trust in him; for he can put it into the hearts of those to befriend them from whom they least expect it. And it is likewise an instance of Paul's fidelity. He did not go about to make his escape. If the centurion is so civil as to take his word, he is so just and honest as to keep his word. They thence *sailed under Cyprus, v.* 4. If the wind had been fair, they had left Cyprus on the right hand; but, the wind not favouring them, they were driven to sailing with a side wind, and left it on the left hand. Sailors must do as they can, when they cannot do as they would, and make the best of their wind, whatever point it is in; so must we all in our passage over the ocean of this world. At a port called Myra they changed their ship. They went on board a vessel of Alexandria bound for Italy, *v.* 5, 6. Great trading there was between that city and Italy; from Alexandria they carried corn to Rome, and the East-India goods and Persian which they imported at the Red Sea they exported again, especially to Italy. And it was a particular favour shown to the Alexandrian ships in the ports of Italy that they were not obliged to strike sail, when they came into port. With much ado they made *The Fair Havens,* a port of the island of Crete, *v.* 7, 8. They *sailed slowly many days.* It was a great while before they made the point of Cnidus, and were forced to sail under Crete, as before under Cyprus; much difficulty they met with in passing by Salmone, a promontory on the eastern shore of the island of Crete. Though the voyage hitherto was not tempestuous, yet it was very tedious. Thus many that are not driven backward in their affairs by cross providences, yet sail slowly, and do not get forward by favourable providences. The place they came to was called *The Fair Havens.* It is known to this day by the same name, and answers the name from the pleasantness

JAMIESON, FAUSSET, BROWN

CHAPTER 27

VSS. 1-44. THE VOYAGE TO ITALY—THE SHIPWRECK AND SAFE LANDING AT MALTA. **1. we should sail . . .**—The "we" here reintroduces the historian as one of the company. Not that he had left the apostle from the time when he last included himself—ch. 21:18—but the apostle was parted from him by his arrest and imprisonment, until now, when they met in the ship. **delivered Paul and certain other prisoners**—State prisoners going to be tried at Rome; of which several instances are on record. **Julius**—who treats the apostle throughout with such marked courtesy (vss. 3, 43; ch. 28:16), that it has been thought [BENGEL] he was present when Paul made his defense before Agrippa (see ch. 25:23), and was impressed with his lofty bearing. **a centurion of Augustus' band**—the Augustan cohort, an honorary title given to more than one legion of the Roman army, implying, perhaps, that they acted as a bodyguard to the emperor or procurator, as occasion required. **2. a ship of**—belonging to—**Adramyttium**—a port on the northeast coast of the Ægean Sea. Doubtless the centurion expected to find another ship, bound for Italy, at some of the ports of Asia Minor, without having to go with this ship all the way to Adramyttium; and in this he was not disappointed. See on vs. 6. **meaning to sail by the coasts**—'places'—**of Asia**—a coasting vessel, which was to touch at the ports of proconsular Asia. **[one] Aristarchus, a Macedonian of Thessalonica, being with us**—rather, 'Aristarchus the Macedonian . . .' The word "one" should not have been introduced here by our translators, as if this name had not occurred before; for we find him seized by the Ephesian mob as a "man of *Macedonia* and Paul's companion in travel" (ch. 19:29) and as a *"Thessalonian"* accompanying the apostle from Ephesus on his voyage back to Palestine (ch. 20:4). Here both these places are mentioned in connection with his name. After this we find him at Rome with the apostle (Col. 4:10; Philemon 24). **3. next day we touched at Sidon**—To reach this ancient and celebrated Mediterranean port, about seventy miles north from Cæsarea, in one day, they must have had a fair wind. **Julius courteously**—(see on vs. 1)—**gave him liberty to go to his friends**—no doubt disciples, gained, it would seem, by degrees, all along the Phœnician coast since the first preaching there (see on ch. 11:19; and 21:4). **to refresh himself**—which after his long confinement would not be unnecessary. Such small personal details are in this case extremely interesting. **4. when we had launched**—'set sail'—**from thence, we sailed under Cyprus, because the winds were contrary**—The wind blowing from the westward, probably with a touch of the north, which was adverse, they sailed *under the lee* of Cyprus, keeping it on their *left,* and steering between it and the mainland of Phœnicia. **5. when we had sailed over the Sea of Cilicia and Pamphylia**—coasts with which Paul had been long familiar, the one, perhaps, from boyhood, the other from the time of his first missionary tour—**we came to Myra, a city of Lycia**—a port a little east of Patara (see on ch. 21:1). **6. there . . . found a ship of Alexandria, sailing into Italy, and he put us therein**—(See on vs. 2). As Egypt was the granary of Italy, and this vessel was laden with wheat (vs. 35), we need not wonder it was large enough to carry 276 souls, passengers and crew together (vs. 37). Besides, the Egyptian merchantmen, among the largest in the Mediterranean, were equal to the largest merchantmen in our day. It may seem strange that on their passage from Alexandria to Italy they should be found at a Lycian port. But even still it is not unusual to stand to the north towards Asia Minor, for the sake of the current. **7. sailed slowly many days**—owing to contrary winds—**and scarce**—'with difficulty'—**were come over against Cnidus**—a town on the promontory of the peninsula of that name, hav-

ADAM CLARKE

CHAPTER 27

1. *And when it was determined.* That is, when the governor had given orders to carry Paul to Rome, according to his appeal, together with other prisoners who were bound for the same place. *We should sail.* By this it is evident that Luke was with Paul, and it is on this account that he was enabled to give such a circumstantial account of the voyage. *Julius, a centurion of Augustus' band.* Lipsius has found the name of this cohort on an ancient marble; see Lips. in *Tacit. Hist.,* l. ii. The same cohort is mentioned by Suetonius in his life of Nero, 20.

2. *A ship of Adramyttium.* There were several places of this name; and in different MSS. the name is variously written. The port in question appears to have been a place in Mysia, in Asia Minor. *Aristarchus, a Macedonian.* We have seen this person with Paul at Ephesus, during the disturbances there, chap. xix. 29, where he had been seized by the mob and was in great personal danger. He afterwards attended Paul to Macedonia, and returned with him to Asia, chap. xx. 4. Now, accompanying him to Rome, he was there a fellow prisoner with him, Col. iv. 10, and is mentioned in Paul's Epistle to Philemon, v. 24, who was probably their common friend. Luke and Aristarchus were certainly not prisoners at this time, and seem to have gone with Paul merely as his companions, through affection to him, and love for the cause of Christianity. How Aristarchus became his fellow prisoner, as is stated in Col. iv. 10, we cannot tell, but it could not have been at this time.

6. *A ship of Alexandria.* It appears, from v. 38, that this ship was laden with wheat, which she was carrying from Alexandria to Rome. We know that the Romans imported much corn from Egypt, together with different articles of Persian and Indian merchandise.

7. *Sailed slowly many days.* Partly because the wind was contrary and partly because the vessel was heavy-laden. *Over against Cnidus.* This was a city or promontory of Asia, opposite

MATTHEW HENRY

of its situation and prospect. It was not the harbour they were bound for; it was a fair haven, but it was not their haven. It was not a *commodious haven to winter in, v.* 12. Every fair haven is not a safe haven; nay, there may be most danger where there is most pleasure.

III. What advice Paul gave them—it was to be content to winter where they were. They had lost a deal of time while they were struggling with contrary winds. Sailing was now dangerous, because *the fast was already past,* that is, the famous yearly fast of the Jews, the day of atonement, which was on the tenth day of the seventh month; it was about the 20th of our September. But (which is strange) we never have any mention made in all the scripture history of the observance of it, unless it be meant here, where it serves only to describe the season of the year. Michaelmas is reckoned by mariners as bad a time of the year to be at sea in as any other. Paul put them in mind of it, and gave them notice of their danger (*v.* 10): "*I perceive* that *this voyage will be with hurt and damage.*" There were some good men in the ship, and many more bad men: but in things of this nature *all things come alike to all.* If both be in the same ship, they both are in the same danger. They would not be advised by Paul in this matter, *v.* 11. They thought him impertinent in interposing in an affair of this nature, and the centurion to whom it was referred to determine it, takes upon him to overrule. The centurion gave more regard to the opinion of the master and owner of the ship than to Paul's; for every man is to be credited in his own profession. The centurion was very civil to Paul (*v.* 3), and yet would not be governed by his advice.

Verses 12–20

I. The ship putting to sea again, at first with a promising gale. What induced them to leave the fair havens: it was because they thought the harbour not *commodious to winter in.* They ran upon a mischief to avoid an inconvenience, as we often do. Some of the ship's crew were for staying there. It is better to be safe in an incommodious harbour than to be lost in a tempestuous sea. But they were outvoted, and the *greater part advised to depart thence also*; yet they aimed not to go far, but only to another port of the same island, here called *Phenice.* It is here described to lie towards the south-west and north-west. Probably the haven was between two promontories, one of which pointed to the north-west and the other to the south-west, by which it was guarded against the east winds. In vain had nature provided for us the waters to sail on, if it had not likewise provided for us natural harbours to take shelter in. What encouragement they had at first to pursue their voyage. They set out with a fair wind (*v.* 13), the *south wind blew softly,* upon which they flattered themselves with hope that they should gain their point, and so they sailed close by the coast of Crete. Those who put to sea with ever so fair a gale know not what storms they may yet meet with, and therefore must not be secure.

II. The ship in a storm presently, a dreadful storm. They imagined that because the south wind now blew softly it would always blow so; in confidence of this, they ventured to sea, but were soon made sensible of their folly in giving more credit to a smiling wind than to the word of God in Paul's mouth.

1. What their danger and distress was. There *arose against them a tempestuous wind.* This wind the sailors called *Euroclydon,* a north-east wind, which upon those seas was in a particular manner troublesome and dangerous. The ship was *exceedingly tossed* (*v.* 18); it was kicked like a football from wave to wave. The ship could not possibly *bear up into the wind,* and therefore they folded up their sails, which in such a storm would endanger them rather than do them any service, and so *let the ship drive.* It is probable that they were very near the haven of Phenice, and thought they should presently be in a quiet haven, and lo, of a sudden, they are in this distress. The use of the loadstone for the direction of sailors not being then found out (so that they had no guide at all, when they could see neither sun nor stars) made the case the more hazardous. Thus melancholy sometimes is the condition of the people of God upon a spiritual account. Thus it may be with them, and yet light is sown for them. They had abundance of winter-weather: *No small tempest,* so that they were ready to perish for cold; and all this continued many days. See what hardships those often undergo who are much at sea, besides the hazards of life they run; and yet to get gain there are still those who make nothing of all this; and it is an instance of divine Providence that it disposes some to this employment, notwithstanding the difficulties that attend

JAMIESON, FAUSSET, BROWN

ing the island of Coos (see on ch. 21:1) to the west of it. But for the contrary wind they might have made the distance from Myra (130 miles) in one day. They would naturally have put in at Cnidus, whose larger harbor was admirable, but the strong westerly current induced them to run south. **under**—the lee of—**Crete**—See on Titus 1:5. **over against Salmone**—the cape at the eastern extremity of the island. **8. And hardly passing it**—'with difficulty coasting along it,' from the same cause as before, the westerly current and head winds. **came to . . . the Fair Havens**—an anchorage near the center of the south coast, and a little east of Cape Matala, the southern most point of the island. **nigh whereunto was the city Lasea**—identified by the REV. GEORGE BROWN [SMITH'S *Voyages and Shipwreck of St. Paul,* App. iii., 2d Ed., 1856. To this invaluable book commentators on this chapter, and these notes, are much indebted]. **9, 10. when much time was spent**—since leaving Cæsarea. But for unforeseen delays they might have reached the Italian coast before the stormy season. **and when sailing**—the navigation of the open sea—**was now dangerous, because the fast was now . . . past**—that of the day of atonement, answering to the end of *September* and beginning of *October,* about which time the navigation is pronounced unsafe by writers of authority. Since all hope of completing the voyage during that season was abandoned, the question next was, whether they should winter at Fair Havens, or move to Port Phenice, a harbor about forty miles to the westward. Paul assisted at the consultation and strongly urged them to winter where they were. **Sirs, I perceive, that this voyage will be with hurt and much damage . . .**—not by any divine communication, but simply in the exercise of a good judgment aided by some experience. The event justified his decision. **11. Nevertheless the centurion believed the master and owner . . . more than . . . Paul**—He would naturally think them best able to judge, and there was much to say for their opinion, as the bay at Fair Havens, being open to nearly one-half of the compass, could not be a good winter harbor. **12. Phenice**—'Phenix,' now called *Lutro*—**which lieth toward the southwest and northwest**—If this means that it was open to the west, it would certainly not be good anchorage. It is thought therefore to mean that a *wind from* that quarter would lead into it, or that it lay in an *easterly* direction from such a wind [SMITH]. The next verse seems to confirm this.

13. when the south wind blew softly, supposing they had attained their purpose—With such a wind they had every prospect of reaching their destination in a few hours.

14, 15. a tempestuous—'typhonic'—**wind**—i.e., like a *typhon* or tornado, causing a whirling of the clouds, owing to the meeting of opposite currents of air. **called Euroclydon**—The true reading appears to be *Euro-aquilo,* or east-northeast, which answers all the effects here ascribed to it. **could not bear up into**—'face'—**the wind, we let her drift**—before the gale.

ADAM CLARKE

to Crete, at one corner of the peninsula of Caria. Some think that this was an island between Crete and a promontory of the same name.

8. *The fair havens.* This port still remains, and is known by the same name; it was situated towards the northern extremity of the island.

9. *Sailing was now dangerous, because the fast was now already past.* It is generally allowed that the fast mentioned here was that of the great Day of Atonement, which was always celebrated on the tenth day of the seventh month, which would answer to the latter end of our September; see Lev. xvi. 29; xxiii. 27, etc. As this was about the time of the autumnal equinox, when the Mediterranean Sea was sufficiently tempestuous, we may suppose this feast alone to be intended. To sail after this feast was proverbially dangerous among the ancient Jews.

10. *I perceive that this voyage will be with hurt.* Paul might either have had this intimation from the Spirit of God or from his own knowledge of the state of this sea after the autumnal equinox, and therefore gave them this prudent warning.

11. *The centurion believed the master.* The "pilot"; *and the owner of the ship,* the "captain" and "proprietor." This latter had the command of the ship and the crew; the pilot had the guidance of the vessel along those dangerous coasts, under the direction of the captain; and the centurion had the power to cause them to proceed on their voyage or to go into port, as he pleased, as he had other state prisoners on board and probably the ship itself was freighted for government. Paul told them, if they proceeded, they would be in danger of shipwreck. The pilot and captain said there was no danger; and the centurion, believing them, commanded the vessel to proceed on her voyage.

12. *Might attain to Phenice.* It appears that the Fair Havens were at the eastern end of the island, and they wished to reach Phoenice, which lay farther towards the west. *Toward the south west and north west.* The *libs* certainly means the southwest, called *libs,* from Libya, from which it blows towards the Aegean Sea. The *chorus* means a northwest wind.

13. *When the south wind blew softly.* Though this wind was not very favorable, yet because it blew softly they supposed they might be able to make their passage. *They sailed close by Crete.* Kept as near the coast as they could.

14. *A tempestuous wind, called Euroclydon.* The reading of the Codex Alexandrinus is *eurakylon,* the "northeast" wind, which is the same with the *euro-aquilo* of the Vulgate.

15. *And when the ship was caught.* The ship was violently hurried away before this strong *levanter;* so that it was impossible for her to "face the wind," to "turn her prow to it," so as to shake it out, as I have heard sailors say, and have seen them successfully perform in violent tempests and squalls. *We let her drive.* We were obliged to let her go right before this tempestuous wind, whithersoever it might drive her.

MATTHEW HENRY

it. Perhaps Christ therefore chose ministers from among seafaring men, because they had been used to endure hardness.

2. What means they used for their own relief. When they could not make head against the wind, they let the ship run adrift. When it is fruitless to struggle, it is wisdom to yield. They nevertheless did what they could to avoid the present danger; there was a little island called Clauda. They took care to prevent their shipwreck, and therefore so ordered their matters that they did not run against the island, but quietly ran under it, *v.* 16. When they were afraid they should scarcely save the ship, they were busy to save the boat. They had *much work to come by the boat* (*v.* 16), but at last they took it up, *v.* 17. They used means which were proper enough in those times; they *undergirded the ship*, *v.* 17. They bound the ship under the bottom of it with strong cables, to keep it from bulging in the extremity of the tempest. For fear of falling *into the quicksands* they *struck sail*, and then let the ship go as it would. It is strange how a ship will live at sea (so they express it), even in very stormy weather, if it have but sea-room. The next day they lightened the ship of its cargo, threw the goods and merchandise overboard. See what the wealth of this world is; the time may come when it will be a burden, not only too heavy to be carried safe of itself, but heavy enough to sink him that has it. But see the folly of the children of this world, they can be thus prodigal of their goods when it is for the saving of their lives, and yet how sparing of them in works of piety and charity, and in suffering for Christ. Any man will rather make shipwreck of his goods than of his life; but many will rather make *shipwreck of faith and a good conscience* than of their goods. The third day they *cast out the tacklings of the ship*.

3. The despair which at last they were brought to (*v.* 20): *All hope that we should be saved was then taken away*. The storm continued, and they saw no symptoms of its abatement. The means they had used were ineffectual, so that they were at their wits' end; and they had no heart either to eat or drink. They had provision enough on board (*v.* 38), but such bondage were they under, through fear of death, that they could not admit the supports of life.

Verses 21-44

We have here the issue of the distress of Paul and his fellow-travellers; they escaped with their lives and that was all. We are here told (*v.* 37) what number there were on board—in all two hundred and seventy-six souls, and one Paul among them worth more than all the rest. We left them in despair, giving up themselves for gone. Paul among these seamen was not, like Jonah, the cause of the storm, but the comforter in the storm.

I. The encouragement Paul gave them, by assuring them that their lives should all be saved. Paul rescued them from their despair first, that they might not die of that, and then they were in a fair way to be rescued from their distress. *After long abstinence, Paul stood forth in the midst of them.* During the distress hitherto Paul was one of the crowd, helping with the rest to *throw out the tackling* (*v.* 19), but now though a prisoner, he undertook to be their counsellor and comforter.

1. He reproves them for not taking his advice (*v.* 8): "*You should have hearkened to me and not have loosed from Crete*, and then we should not have *gained this harm and loss*." They did not hearken to Paul when he warned them of their danger, and yet he will speak comfort and relief to them now that they are in danger, so compassionate is God to those that are in misery, though they bring themselves into it by their own wilfulness. Paul, before administering comfort, will first make them sensible of their sin in not hearkening to him. That which they are blamed for is their loosing from Crete, where they were safe. Most people bring themselves into inconvenience, because they do not know when they are well off, by aiming against advice to better themselves.

2. He assures them that though they should lose the ship yet they should none of them lose their lives. "Your case is sad, but it is not desperate, now, *I exhort you to be of good cheer*." Thus we say to sinners that are convinced of their sin and folly, "*You should have hearkened unto us*, and should have had nothing to do with sin; yet now we *exhort you to be of good cheer*: though you would not take our advice when we said, *Do not presume*, yet take it now when we say, *Do not despair*." They would use no further means, because *all hope that they should be saved was taken away*. Now Paul quickens them to bestir themselves. If they would resume their vigour they should secure their lives. They must

JAMIESON, FAUSSET, BROWN

16, 17. under—the lee of—**a certain**—'small'—**island . . . Clauda**—southwest of Crete, now called *Gonzo;* about twenty-three miles to leeward. **we had much work to come by**—i.e., to hoist up and secure—**the boat**—now become necessary. But why was this difficult? Independently of the gale, raging at the time, the boat had been towed between twenty and thirty miles after the gale sprang up, and could scarcely fail to be filled with water [SMITH]. **undergirding the ship**—i.e., passing four or five turns of a cable-laid rope round the hull or frame of the ship, to enable her to resist the violence of the seas, an operation rarely resorted to in modern seamanship. **fearing lest they should fall into the quicksands**—'be cast ashore' or 'stranded upon the Syrtis,' the *Syrtis Major,* a gulf on the African coast, southwest of Crete, the dread of mariners, owing to its dangerous shoals. **they strake**—'struck'—**sail**—This cannot be the meaning, for to strike sail would have driven them directly towards the Syrtis. The meaning must be, 'lowered the gear' (appurtenances of every kind); here, perhaps, referring to the lowering of the heavy mainyard with the sail attached to it [SMITH]. **18-20. cast out with our own hands**—passengers and crew together—**the tackling of the ship**—whatever they could do without that carried weight. This further effort to lighten the ship seems to show that it was now in a *leaking* condition, as will presently appear more evident. **neither sun nor stars appeared in many**—'several'—**days**—probably most of the fourteen days mentioned in vs. 27. This continued thickness of the atmosphere prevented their making the necessary observations of the heavenly bodies by day or by night; so that they could not tell where they were. **all hope that we should be saved was taken away**—"Their exertions to subdue the leak had been unavailing; they could not tell which way to make for the nearest land, in order to run their ship ashore, the only resource for a sinking ship: but unless they did make the land, they must founder at sea. Their apprehensions, therefore, were not so much caused by the fury of the tempest, as by the state of the ship" [SMITH]. From the inferiority of ancient to modern naval architecture, leaks were sprung much more easily, and the means of repairing them were fewer than now. Hence the far greater number of shipwrecks from this cause.

21-26. But after long abstinence—See on vs. 33. "The hardships which the crew endured during a gale of such continuance, and their exhaustion from laboring at the pumps and hunger, may be imagined, but are not described" [SMITH] **Paul stood forth in the midst of them, and said, Sirs, ye should have hearkened to me . . .**—not meaning to reflect on them for the past, but to claim their confidence for what he was now to say . . . .

ADAM CLARKE

16. *A certain island . . . called Clauda.* Called also *Gaudos;* situated at the southwestern extremity of the island of Crete. *Much work to come by the boat.* It was likely to have been washed overboard; or if the boat was in tow, at the stern of the vessel, which is probable, they found it very difficult to save it from being staved or broken to pieces.

17. *Undergirding the ship.* This method has been used even in modern times. It is called frapping the ship. A stout cable is slipped under the vessel at the prow, which they can conduct to any part of the ship's keel and then fasten the two ends on the deck, to keep the planks from starting; as many rounds as they please may be thus taken about the vessel. *The quicksands.* "Into the syrt." There were two famous *Syrts*, or quicksands, on the African coast: one called the *syrtis major*, lying near the coast of Cyrene; and the other, the *syrtis minor*, not far from Tripoli. Both these were proverbial for their multitude of shipwrecks.

18. *Lightened the ship.* Of what, we know not; but it was probably cumbrous wares, by which the deck was thronged, and which were prejudicial to the due trim of the vessel.

19. *The tackling of the ship.* All supernumerary anchors, cables, baggage, etc.

20. *Neither sun nor stars in many days appeared.* And consequently they could make no observation; and, having no magnetical needle, could not tell in what direction they were going.

ALEXANDER MACLAREN:

That was the last attempt to save themselves, and after it there was nothing to do but to wait the apparently inevitable hour when they would all go down together. Idleness feeds despair, and despair nourishes idleness. Food was scarce, cooking it was impossible, appetite there was none. The doomed men spent the long idle days—which were scarcely days, so thick was the air with mist and foam and tempest—crouching anywhere for shelter, wet, tired, hungry, and hopeless. So they drifted "for many days," almost losing count of the length of time they had been thus. It was a gloomy company, but there was one man there in whom the lamp of hope burned when it had gone out in all others. Sun and stars were hidden, but Paul saw a better light, and *his* sky was clear and calm.

—*Expositions of Holy Scripture*

21. *Have gained this harm and loss.* It seems strange to talk of gaining a loss, but it is a correct rendering of the original which expresses the idea of "acquisition," whether of good or evil.

MATTHEW HENRY

count upon the loss of the ship. Their ship shall be wrecked. *Not a life shall be lost*. This would be good news to those that were ready to die for fear of dying.

3. He tells them what ground he had for this assurance, he has a divine revelation for it. An angel of God appeared to him in the night, and told him that for his sake they should all be preserved (*v*. 23-25). They should have it not only by providence, but by promise, and as a particular favour to Paul.

(1) The solemn profession Paul makes of relation to God. It is he *whose I am, and whom I serve*. He looks upon God, as his rightful owner, who has a sovereign incontestable title to him, and dominion over him: *Whose I am*. We are more his than our own. As his sovereign ruler and master, who has right to give him law: *Whom I serve*. Because his we are, therefore we are bound to serve him. He does not say, "Whose *we* are, and whom we serve," for most that were present were strangers to him. This he tells the company, that they might thereby be drawn in to take him for their God, and to serve him likewise.

(2) The account he gives of the vision he had: *There stood by me this night an angel of God*. Though he was *afar off upon the sea* (Ps. lxv. 5), yet this could not intercept his communion with God. Thence he can direct a prayer to God, and thither God can direct an angel to him. The *ship is tossed* with winds and waves, and yet the angel finds a way into it. No storms nor tempests can hinder the communications of God's favour to his people, for he is a very present help. We may suppose that Paul, being a prisoner, had not a cabin of his own in the ship, but was put down into the hold (any dark or dirty place was thought good enough for him in common with the rest of the prisoners), and yet there the angel of God stood by him. Meanness and poverty set none at a distance from God and his favour. Paul had this vision but *this last night*. He has this fresh vision to assure him of the safety of those with him.

(3) The encouragements that were given him in the vision, *v*. 14. [1] He is forbidden to fear. Though all about him are at their wits' end, and lost in despair, yet, *Fear not, Paul*. Let not the saints be afraid, no, not at sea, in a storm; for *the Lord of hosts is with them*. [2] He is assured that he shall come safely to Rome: *Thou must be brought before Cæsar*. The rage of the most stormy sea, cannot prevail against God's witnesses till they have finished their testimony. This is comfortable for the faithful servants of God in straits and difficulties, that as long as God has any work for them to do their lives shall be prolonged. [3] For his sake all that were in the ship with him should be delivered too: *God hath given thee all those that sail with thee*. God chooses by preserving them all for his sake, to show what great blessings good men are to the world. Paul here delivers a whole ship's crew, almost three hundred souls. God often spares wicked people for the sake of the godly. The good people are hated and persecuted in the world as if they were not worthy to live in it, yet really it is for their sakes that the world stands. It was a great favour to Paul, and he looked upon it to be so, that others were saved for his sake: *They are given thee*. There is no greater satisfaction to a good man than to know that he is a public blessing.

4. He comforts them (*v*. 25): "*Wherefore, sirs, be of good cheer, for I believe God, that it shall be even as it was told me*." He would not require them to give credit to that to which he did not himself give credit; and therefore solemnly professes that he believes it himself. And shall it be as God hath said? Then be of good cheer, be of good courage. If with God saying and doing are not two things, then with us believing and enjoying should not be.

5. He gives them a sign, telling them particularly what this tempestuous voyage would issue in (*v*. 26): "*We must be cast upon a certain island*, and that will both break the ship and save the passengers." Providence undertakes to bring them to an island that shall be a refuge for them.

II. Their coming at length to an anchor upon an unknown shore, *v*. 27-29. They had been a full fortnight in the storm, continually expecting death: *The fourteenth night they came near land;* they were *that night driven up and down in Adria*, in the Adriatic Sea, a part of the Mediterranean, extending to the African shore; and knew not whereabouts they were. *About midnight the mariners apprehended that they drew near to some shore*. To try whether it was so or no, *they sounded*; the water would be shallower as they drew near to shore; by the first experiment *they found they drew twenty fathoms deep of water*, and by *the next fifteen fathoms*, which was a demonstration that they were near some shore. They took the hint, and, fearing rocks near the shore, *they cast anchor, and wished for the day*. When they had

JAMIESON, FAUSSET, BROWN

whose I am—I Cor. 6:19, 20—**and whom I serve**—in the sense of *worship* or *religious consecration* (see on ch. 13:2).

there stood by me this night the angel of God—as in ch. 16:9 and 23:11).

saying, Fear not, Paul: thou must be brought before Cæsar and, lo, God hath given thee all . . . that sail with thee—While the crew were toiling at the pumps, Paul was wrestling in prayer, not for himself only and the cause in which he was going a prisoner to Rome, but with true magnanimity of soul for all his shipmates; and God heard him, "giving him" (remarkable expression!) all that sailed with him. "When the cheerless day came he gathered the sailors (and passengers) around him on the deck of the laboring vessel, and raising his voice above the storm" [HOWS], reported the divine communication he had received; adding with a noble simplicity, "*for I believe God* that it shall be even as it was told me," and encouraging all on board to "be of good cheer" in the same confidence. What a contrast to this is the speech of Cæsar in similar circumstances to his pilot, bidding him keep up his spirit because he carried Cæsar and Cæsar's fortune! [PLUTARCH.] The Roman general knew no better name for the Divine Providence, by which he had been so often preserved, than *Cæsar's fortune* [HUMPHRY]. From the explicit particulars—that the ship would be lost, but not one that sailed in it, and that they "must be cast on a certain island"—one would conclude a visional representation of a total wreck, a mass of human beings struggling with the angry elements, and one and all of those whose figures and countenances had daily met his eye on deck, standing on some unknown island shore. From what follows, it would seem that Paul from this time was regarded with a deference akin to awe. **27-29. when the fourteenth night was come**—from the time they left Fair Havens—**as we were driven**—drifting—**up and down in Adria**—the *Adriatic*, that sea which lies between Greece and Italy. **about midnight the shipmen deemed**—no doubt from the peculiar sound of the breakers—**that they drew near some country**—'that some land was approaching them.' This nautical language gives a graphic character to the narrative. **they cast four anchors out of the stern**—The ordinary way was to cast the anchor, as now, from the *bow:* but ancient ships, built with both ends alike, were fitted with hawseholes in the stern, so that in case of need they could anchor either way. And when the fear was, as here, that they might fall on the rocks *to leeward*, and the intention was to run the ship ashore as soon as daylight enabled them to fix upon a safe spot, the very best thing they could do was to anchor by the stern [SMITH]. In stormy weather two anchors were used, and we have instances of four being employed, as here. **and wished**—'anxiously' or 'devoutly wished'—**for day**—the remark this of one

ADAM CLARKE

22. *There shall be no loss of . . . life*. That must be joyous news to those from whom "all hope that we should be saved was . . . taken away," v. 20.

F. B. MEYER:

Yes, the angels of God can find their way through the murkiest air, and alight on the most weather-beaten vessel that ever ploughed its difficult way through the stormy seas. Wheresoever thou art, O child of God, God's angels have their eyes fixed lovingly on thee; and in a moment, if it were God's will to give thee eyes, thou wouldest behold them.

But if, like Paul, we would have the angel ministry, with their assurances against fear, like him we must be able to comply with two conditions—of being owned and being loyal.

Whose I am. We are his by creation, by purchase, by consecration. That sentiment of being owned, which in the case of slaves is inimical to the highest development, is the elementary condition of our truest growth and well-being. We belong to One who is infinitely worthy. We cannot do as we would with ourselves. We may not take our own course.

Whom I serve. The word rendered serve is the deepest and most expressive term that Paul could employ of the prostration of the soul at the feet of God. It is employed of the glorified, who serve him day and night in his temple, and of whom it is said that his servants shall do him service. The heavenly life begins here; and following its course, angels minister to us, and the stars in their courses fight for us.

—*Great Verses Through the Bible*

26. *We must be cast upon a certain island*. The angel which gave him this information did not tell him the name of the island. It turned out to be Melita, on which, by the violence of the storm, they were wrecked some days after.

28. *And sounded*. "Heaving the lead." *Twenty fathoms*. About forty yards in depth.

29. *Cast four anchors out of the stern*. By this time the storm must have been considerably abated, though the agitation of the sea could not have subsided much. The anchors were cast out of the stern to prevent the vessel from drifting ashore, as they found that, the farther they stood in, the shallower the water grew; therefore they dropped the anchor astern, as even one ship's length might be of much consequence.

MATTHEW HENRY

light, there was no land to be seen. Now they had no light to see by; no marvel then they wished for day. When those that fear God *walk in darkness, and have no light*, let them do as these mariners did, cast anchor, and wish for the day, and be assured that the day will dawn.

III. The defeating of the sailors' attempt to quit the ship. 1. The treacherous design of the seamen, and that was to leave the sinking ship (*v.* 30): *They were about to flee out of the ship*, and to save themselves, and leave all the rest to perish. They pretended they would *cast anchors out of the fore-ship*, and in order to this *they let down the boat*, and were *going into it*. Paul had, in God's name, assured them that they should come safely to land, but they will rather trust their own refuge of lies than God's word and truth. 2. Paul's discovery of it, *v.* 31. Paul saw through it, and gave notice to the centurion and the soldiers concerning it, and told them plainly, *Except these abide in the ship, you cannot be saved*. Now the greatest difficulty of all was before them, and therefore the seamen were now more necessary than ever yet. Now that they are near land, they must use their art to bring the ship to it. When God has done that for us which we could not, we must then in his strength help ourselves. God, who appointed the end, *that they should be saved*, appointed the means, that they should be saved by the help of these seamen. Duty is ours, events are God's; and we do not trust God, but tempt him, when we do not use proper means, such as are within our power, for our own preservation. 3. The effectual defeat of it by the soldiers, *v.* 32. It was no time to stand arguing the case with the seamen, and therefore they made no more ado, *but cut the ropes of the boat to let it fall off*. And now the seamen, being forced to stay in the ship, are forced likewise to work for the safety of the ship, because if the rest perish they must perish with them.

IV. The new life which Paul put into the company. Happy they who had such a one as Paul in their company. The day was coming on. The dawning of the day revived them a little, and then Paul got them together. He chid them for their neglect of themselves: *This is the fourteenth day that you have tarried, and continued fasting, having taken nothing*, *v.* 33. They ate very little, next to nothing. "*You have continued fasting*, that is, you have lost your stomach; you have had no appetite at all to your food, nor any relish of it, through prevailing fear and despair." What folly it is to die for fear of dying! He courts them to their food (*v.* 34): "*Wherefore I pray you to take some meat*. We have a hard struggle before us; if our bodies be weak through fasting, we shall not be able to help ourselves." Paul will have these people eat, or otherwise the waves will be too hard for them: *I pray you* take some nourishment; *for this is for your health*, or rather *your preservation, or safety, at this time*. You cannot without nourishment have strength to shift for your lives. As *he that will not labour, let him not eat;* so he that means to labour must eat. Weak and trembling Christians, that give way to doubts and fears, continue fasting from the Lord's supper, and fasting from divine consolations, and then complain they cannot go on in their spiritual work: and it is owing to themselves. If they would feed and feast as they ought, they would be strengthened, and it would be for their souls' health and salvation. He assured them of their preservation: *There shall not a hair fall from the head of any of you*. "You cannot eat for fear of dying; I tell you, you are sure of living, and therefore eat." He himself spread their table for them: *When he had thus spoken, he took bread*. They were not reduced to short allowance, they had plenty, but what good did that do them, when they had no stomach? We have reason to be thankful to God that we have not only food to our appetite, but appetite to our food. He was chaplain to the ship, and they had reason to be proud of their chaplain. *He gave thanks to God in presence of them all*. Whether he had before this prayed with the whole company promiscuously is not certain. Now *he gave thanks to God, in presence of them all*, that they were alive, and that they had a promise that their lives should be preserved; he gave thanks for the provision they had, and begged a blessing upon it. We must *in everything give thanks*; and must particularly have an eye to God in receiving our food. *He gave thanks in presence of them all*, not only to show that he served a Master he was not ashamed of, but to invite them into his service too. If we crave a blessing upon our meat, and give thanks for it in a right manner, we shall credit our profession, and recommend it to the good opinion of others. He set them a good example: *When he had given thanks, he broke the bread* (it was sea-biscuit) and *he began to eat*. Whether they would be encouraged or no, he

JAMIESON, FAUSSET, BROWN

present, and with all his shipmates alive to the horrors of their condition. "The ship might go down at her anchors, or the coast to leeward might be iron-bound, affording no beach on which they could land with safety. Hence their anxious longing for day, and the ungenerous but natural attempt, not peculiar to ancient times, of the seamen to save their own lives by taking to the boat" [SMITH]. **30. as the shipmen were about to flee out of the ship**—under cover of night—**when they had let down the boat . . . as though they would . . . cast anchors out of the foreship**—'bow'—rather, 'carry out' anchors, to hold the ship fore as well as aft. "This could have been of no advantage in the circumstances, and as the pretext could not deceive a seaman, we must infer that the officers of the ship were parties to the unworthy attempt, which was perhaps detected by the nautical skill of St. Luke, and communicated by him to St. Paul" [SMITH]. **31. Paul said to the centurion and to the soldiers**—the only parties now to be trusted, and whose own safety was now at stake. **except ye abide in the ship ye cannot be saved**—The soldiers and passengers could not be expected to possess the necessary seamanship in so very critical a case. The flight of the crew, therefore, might well be regarded as certain destruction to all who remained. *In full assurance of ultimate safety, in virtue of a* DIVINE *pledge, to all in the ship, Paul speaks and acts throughout this whole scene in the exercise of a sound judgment as to the indispensable* HUMAN *conditions of safety;* and as there is no trace of any feeling of inconsistency between these two things in his mind, so even the centurion, under whose orders the soldiers acted on Paul's views, seems never to have felt perplexed by the twofold aspect, divine and human, in which the same thing presented itself to the mind of Paul. *Divine agency and human instrumentality are in all the events of life quite as much as here*. The only difference is that the one is for the most part shrouded from view, while the other is ever naked and open to the senses. **32. Then the soldiers cut off the ropes of the boat**—already lowered—**and let her fall off**—let the boat drift away. **33-37. while day was coming on**—'until it should be day'; i.e., in the interval between the cutting off of the boat and the approach of day, which all were "anxiously looking for" (vs. 29).

Paul—now looked up to by all the passengers as the man to direct them—**besought them all to take meat**—'partake of a meal'—**saying, This is the fourteenth day ye have tarried**—'waited for a breathingtime.' **having eaten nothing**—i.e., taken no regular meal. The impossibility of cooking, the occupation of all hands to keep down leakage, etc., sufficiently explain this, which is indeed a common occurrence in such cases.

I pray you to take some meat, for this is for your health, for there shall not a hair fall from . . . any of you—On this beautiful union of confidence in the divine pledge and care for the whole ship's health and safety see on vs. 31. **when he had thus spoken he took bread**—assuming the lead

—and gave thanks to God in presence of them all—an impressive act in such circumstances, and fitted to plant a testimony for the God he served in the breasts of all. **when he had broken it, he began to eat**—not understood by the Christians in the ship as a lovefeast, or celebration of the Lord's Supper, as some think, but a meal to recruit exhausted nature, which Paul shows them by his own example how a Christian partakes of.

ADAM CLARKE

30. *The shipman*, the sailors, *let down the boat*. Having lowered the boat from the deck into the sea, they pretended that it was necessary to carry some anchors ahead to keep her from being carried in a dangerous direction by the tide, but with the real design to make for shore, and so leave the prisoners and the passengers to their fate. This was timely noticed by the pious and prudent apostle, who, while simply depending on the promise of God, was watching for the safety and comfort of all.

31. *Except these abide in the ship, ye cannot be saved*. God, who has promised to save your lives, promises this on the condition that you make use of every means He has put in your power to help yourselves.

32. *The soldiers cut off the ropes*. These were probably the only persons who dared to oppose the will of the sailors; this very circumstance is an additional proof of the accuracy of Luke.

33. *While the day was coming on*. It was then apparently about daybreak.

This day is the fourteenth day that ye have . . . continued fasting. You have not had one regular meal for these fourteen days past. Indeed we may take it for granted that during the whole of the storm very little was eaten by any man; for what appetite could men have for food who every moment had death before their eyes?

34. *An hair fall from the head*. A proverbial expression for "You shall neither lose your lives nor suffer any hurt in your bodies, if you follow my advice."

35. *Gave thanks to God*. Who had provided the food, and preserved their lives and health to partake of it.

MATTHEW HENRY

would. He would eat his meat, and be thankful. The most effectual way of preaching is by example. It had a happy influence upon them all (*v.* 36): *Then were they all of good cheer.* They then ventured to believe the message God sent them by Paul when they plainly perceived that Paul believed it himself. It is an encouragement to people to commit themselves to Christ as their Saviour when those who invite them to do so make it to appear that they do so themselves. It is here that the number of the persons is set down: *they were in all two hundred threescore and sixteen souls.* See how many may be influenced by the good example of one. *They did all eat,* nay, *they did all eat enough* (*v.* 38). They once more lightened the ship. They had before thrown *the wares and the tackle overboard,* and now *the wheat*; better they should sink the food than that it should sink them. We may ourselves be under a necessity of throwing that away to save our lives which we had gathered and laid up for the support of our lives.

V. Their putting to shore, and the staving of the ship in the adventure. When it was quite day they began to look about them. *They knew not where they were;* they could not tell what country it was they were now upon the coast of. It is probable that these seamen had often sailed this way, and yet here they were at a loss. *They observed a creek with a level shore, into which they hoped to thrust the ship, v.* 39. Though they knew not what country it was, nor whether the inhabitants were civil or barbarous, they determined to cast themselves upon their mercy; it was dry land, which would be very welcome to those that had been so long at sea. It was a pity but they had had some help from the shore. Those who live on the sea-coast have often opportunity of succouring those who are in distress at sea, and of saving precious lives, and they ought to do their utmost in order to it. They made straight to the shore (*v.* 40): *They took up the anchors. They then committed themselves to the sea,* and *they loosed the rudder-bands,* which were fastened during the storm for the greater steadiness of the ship, but, now that they were *putting into the port, were loosed,* that the pilot might steer with the greater freedom; *they then hoisted up the main-sail to the wind, and made towards shore.* When they saw the shore they hastened to it as fast as they could, and perhaps made more haste than good speed. And should not a poor soul that has long been struggling with winds and tempests in this world long to put into the safe and quiet haven of everlasting rest? And should it not hoist up the main-sail of faith to the wind of the Spirit, and so with longing desires make to shore? They made a shift among them *to run the ship aground,* in a shelf or bed of sand, or an isthmus, or neck of land, washed with the sea on both sides, and therefore two seas are said to meet upon it, and *there the forepart stuck fast. The hinder part* would soon be broken *by the violence of the waves.* The ship, that had strangely weathered the storm in the vast ocean, where it had room to roll, is dashed to pieces when it sticks fast. Thus if the heart fixes in the world it is lost. Satan's temptations beat against it, and it is gone; but, as long as it keeps above the world, though it be tossed with its cares and tumults, there is hope of it. They had the shore in view, and yet suffered shipwreck in the harbour, to teach us never to be secure.

VI. A particular danger that Paul and the rest of the prisoners were in. In this critical moment *the soldiers advised the killing of the prisoners* whom they were to give an account of, *lest any of them should swim out and escape, v.* 42. There was no great danger of that, for they could not escape far, weak and weary as they were; and, under the eye of so many soldiers that had the charge of them, it was not likely they should attempt it. But it was so much the worse that they were thus prodigal of other people's lives when without a miracle of mercy they must lose their own. The centurion, for Paul's sake, quashed this motion. Paul, who was his prisoner, had found favour with him. Julius, though he despised Paul's advice (*v.* 11), yet, being *willing to save Paul,* he prevented the execution of that bloody project. As God had saved all in the ship for Paul's sake, so here the centurion saves all the prisoners for his sake; such a diffusive good is a good man.

VII. The saving of the lives of all the persons in the ship. Some were saved by swimming: *The centurion commanded his soldiers, as many of them as could swim, to get to land* first, and to be ready to receive the prisoners, and prevent their escape. The rest with much ado scrambled to the shore, some on boards, and others on the *broken pieces of the ship,* and the more busy because they were assured their labour should not be in vain; but *so it came to pass* that through the good providence of God they *escaped*

JAMIESON, FAUSSET, BROWN

Then were they all of good cheer, and they also took some meat—'took food'; the first full meal since the commencement of the gale. Such courage in desperate circumstances as Paul here showed is wonderfully infectious. **38-40. when they had eaten enough . . .**—With fresh strength after the meal, they make a third and last effort to lighten the ship, not only by pumping, as before, but by throwing the whole cargo of wheat into the sea (see on vs. 6). **when it was day they knew not the land**—This has been thought surprising in sailors accustomed to that sea. But the scene of the wreck is remote from the great harbor, and possesses no marked features by which it could be recognized, even by a native if he came unexpectedly upon it [SMITH], not to speak of the rain pouring in torrents (ch. 28:2), which would throw a haze over the coast even after day broke. Immediately on landing they knew where they were (ch. 28:1). **discovered a creek with a shore**—Every creek of course, must have a shore; but the meaning is, a *practicable* shore, in a nautical sense, i.e., one with a smooth beach, in contradistinction to a rocky coast (as vs. 41 shows). **into which they were minded, if . . . possible, to thrust the ship**—This was their one chance of safety.

taken up the anchors, they committed themselves to the sea—The *Marg.* is here evidently right, 'cut the anchors (away), they left them in the sea.' **loosed the rudder bands**—Ancient ships were steered by two large paddles, one on each quarter. When anchored by the stern in a gale, it would be necessary to lift them out of the water and secure them by lashings or rudder bands, and to loose these when the ship was again got under way [SMITH]. **hoised up the mainsail**—rather, 'the foresail,' the best possible sail that could be set in the circumstances. How necessary must the crew have been to execute all these movements, and how obvious the foresight which made their stay indispensable to the safety of all on board (see on vs. 31)! **41. falling into a place where two seas met**—SMITH thinks this refers to the channel, not more than 100 yards broad, which separates the small island of Salmone from Malta, forming a communication between the sea inside the bay and that outside. **the fore part stuck fast, and remained immovable**—"The rocks of Malta disintegrate into extremely minute particles of sand and clay, which, when acted upon by the currents or surface agitation, form a deposit of tenacious clay; but, in still waters, where these causes do not act, mud is formed; but it is only in creeks, where there are no currents, and at such a depth as to be undisturbed by the waves, that the mud occurs. A ship, therefore, impelled by the force of a gale, into a creek, with such a bottom, would strike a bottom of mud, graduating into tenacious clay, into which the fore part would fix itself, and be held fast, while the stern was exposed to the force of the waves" [SMITH]. **hinder part was broken**—The *continued action* denoted by the tense here is to be noted—'was fast breaking,' going to pieces. **42-44. the soldiers' counsel was to kill the prisoners, lest any . . . should escape**—Roman cruelty, which made the keepers answerable for their prisoners with their own lives, is here reflected in this cruel proposal. **the centurion . . .**—Great must have been the influence of Paul over the centurion's mind to produce such an effect. All followed the swimmers in committing themselves to the deep, and according to the divine pledge and Paul's confident assurance given them, every soul got safe to land—yet without miracle. (While the graphic minuteness of this narrative of the shipwreck puts it beyond doubt that the narrator was himself on board, the great number of *nautical phrases,* which all critics have noted, along with the *unprofessional* air which the whole narrative wears, agrees singularly with all we know and have reason to believe of "the beloved physician"; see on ch. 16:40.)

ADAM CLARKE

38. *They lightened the ship.* They hoped that by casting out the lading the ship would draw less water, in consequence of which they could get nearer the shore.

39. *They knew not the land.* And therefore knew neither the nature of the coast nor where the proper port lay. *A . . . creek with a shore.* A bay, with a shore; a neck of land perhaps on either side, running out into the sea, and this little bay or gulf between them—though some think it was a tongue of land running out into the sea, having the sea on both sides, at the point of which these "two seas met," v. 41. There is such a place as this in the island of Malta, where tradition says Paul was shipwrecked, and which is called la Cale de St. Paul.

40. *Taken up the anchors.* Weighed all the anchors that they had cast out of the stern. Some think the meaning of the word is they slipped their cables, and so left the anchors in the sea. *Loosed the rudder bands.* Or the bands of the rudders; for large vessels in ancient times had two or more rudders, one at the side, and another at the stern, and sometimes one at the prow. The bands were some kind of fastenings by which the rudders were hoisted some way out of the water; for as they could be of no use in the storm, and should there come fair weather, the vessel could not do without them, this was a prudent way of securing them from being broken to pieces by the agitation of the waves. These bands being loosed, the rudders would fall down into their proper places, and serve to steer the vessel into the creek which they now had in view. *Hoised up the mainsail.* Not the *mainsail,* but the *jib,* or triangular sail which is suspended from the foremast to the bowsprit; with this they might hope both to steer and to carry in the ship.

41. *Where two seas met.* The tide running down from each side of the tongue of land, mentioned in v. 39, and meeting at the point. *Ran the ship aground.* In striving to cross at this point of land they had not taken a sufficiency of sea room, and therefore ran aground. *The forepart stuck fast.* Got into the sands; and perhaps the shore here was very bold or steep, so that the stem of the vessel might be immersed in the quicksands, which would soon close round it, while the stern, violently agitated with the surge, would soon be broken to pieces.

43. *Willing to save Paul.* Had one fallen, for the reasons those cruel and dastardly soldiers gave, so must all the rest. The centurion saw that Paul was not only an innocent but an extraordinary and divine man, and therefore for his sake he prevented the massacre; and, unloosing every man's bonds, he commanded those that could to swim ashore and escape. It is likely that all the soldiers escaped in this way, for it was one part of the Roman military discipline to teach the soldiers to swim.

44. *And the rest.* That could not swim. *Some on boards,* planks, spars, etc., got *safe to land;* manifestly by an especial providence of God.

MATTHEW HENRY

all safely to land. They were rescued from the dreaded sea, and brought to the desired haven. Though there be great difficulty in the way of the promised salvation, yet it shall without fail be accomplished; and even the wreck of the ship may furnish out means for the saving of the lives, and, when all seems to be gone, all proves to be safe, though it be *on boards, and broken pieces of the ship.*

CHAPTER 28

Verses 1-10

What a great variety of places and circumstances do we find Paul in! He was a planet, and not a fixed star. An ill wind indeed it is that blows nobody any good; this ill wind blew good to the island of Melita; for it gave them Paul's company, who was a blessing to every place he came to.

I. The kind reception which the inhabitants of this island gave (*v.* 2): *The barbarous people showed us no little kindness.* Providence continues its care of them, and what benefits we receive by the hand of man must be acknowledged to come from the hand of God. As he can make enemies to be at peace, so he can make strangers to be friends, friends in need, and those are friends indeed. 1. The general notice taken of the kindness which the natives of Malta showed. They are called *barbarous people,* because they did not, in language and customs, conform either to the Greeks or Romans, who looked upon all but themselves as barbarians, though otherwise civilized enough, and perhaps in some cases more civil than they. These barbarous people were full of humanity: They *showed us no little kindness.* So far were they from making a prey of this shipwreck that they laid hold of it as an opportunity of showing mercy. It is written for our imitation, that we may hence learn to be compassionate to those that are in distress and misery, and to relieve and succour them to the utmost of our ability. If Providence hath so *appointed the bounds of our habitation* as to give us an opportunity of being frequently serviceable to persons at a loss, we should not place it among the inconveniences of our lot, but the advantages of it. 2. A particular instance of their kindness: *They kindled a fire,* and *they received us every one*—made room for us about the fire, and bade us all welcome. Waters from above met those from below, and it rained so hard that this would wet them to the skin presently; and *it was a cold rain too,* so that they wanted nothing so much as a good fire *to warm them, and dry their clothes. Be you warmed,* is as necessary as, *Be you filled.*

II. The further danger that Paul was in by a viper's fastening on his hand.

1. When the fire was to be made, and to be made bigger, Paul was as busy as any of them in gathering sticks, *v.* 3. Paul was an industrious active man, and loved to be doing when anything was to be done, and would stoop to anything by which he might be serviceable, even to the gathering of sticks to make a fire of. We should be willing to condescend to the meanest offices for the good of our brethren. Those that receive benefit by the fire should help to carry fuel to it.

2. It happened there was a viper among them, that lay as dead till it came to the heat, and then revived, and flew at him that unawares threw it into the fire, and *fastened upon his hand, v.* 3. As there is a snake under the green grass, so there is often under the dry leaves. See how many perils human life is exposed to, and what danger we are in from the inferior creatures. We often meet with that which is mischievous where we expect that which is beneficial; and many come by hurt when they are honestly employed, and in the way of their duty.

3. The barbarous people concluded that this viper was sent by divine justice to be the avenger of blood. *When they saw the venomous animal hang on his hand,* they concluded, "*No doubt this man is a murderer* and therefore, *though he has escaped the sea, yet* divine *vengeance* pursues him, and will *not suffer him to live.*"

(1) Some of the discoveries of natural light. They were barbarous people and yet they knew naturally, That there is a God that governs the world and that things do not come to pass by chance but by divine direction. That evil pursues sinners, that there are good works which God will reward and wicked works which he will punish. That murder is a heinous crime, and which shall not long go unpunished. Those that think they shall go unpunished in any evil way will be judged out of the mouth of these barbarians. Learn from these illiterate people that, though malefactors have escaped the vengeance of

JAMIESON, FAUSSET, BROWN

CHAPTER 28

Vss. 1-31. THE WINTERING AT MALTA, AND NOTABLE OCCURRENCES THERE—PROSECUTION OF THE VOYAGE TO ITALY AS FAR AS PUTEOLI, AND LAND JOURNEY THENCE TO ROME—SUMMARY OF THE APOSTLE'S LABORS THERE FOR THE TWO FOLLOWING YEARS. **1. knew the island was called Melita**—See on ch. 27:39. The opinion that this island was not Malta to the south of Sicily, but Meleda in the Gulf of Venice—which till lately had respectable support among competent judges—is now all but exploded; examination of all the places on the spot, and of all writings and principles bearing on the question, by gentlemen of the highest qualification, particularly SMITH (see on ch. 27:41), having set the question, it may now be affirmed, at rest. **2. the barbarous people**—so called merely as speaking neither the Greek nor the Latin language. They were originally Phœnician colonists. **showed us no little**—'no ordinary'—**kindness,** **for they kindled a fire, and received us every one, because of the present rain**—'the rain that was on us'—not now first falling, but then falling heavily—**and because of the cold**—welcomed us all, drenched and shivering, to these most seasonable marks of friendship. In this these "barbarians" contrast favorably with many since, bearing the Christian name. The lifelike style of the narrative here and in the following verses gives it a great charm. **3. when Paul had gathered a bundle of sticks**—'a quantity of dry sticks.' The vigorous activity of Paul's character is observable in this comparatively trifling action [WEBSTER and WILKINSON]. **and laid them on the fire,** **there came a viper out of the heat**—Having laid itself up among the sticks on the approach of the cold winter season, it had suddenly recovered from its torpor by the heat. **and fastened**—its fangs—**on his hand**—Vipers dart at their enemies sometimes several feet at a bound. They have now disappeared from Malta, owing to the change which cultivation has produced.

4-6. No doubt this man is a murderer—His chains, which they would see, might strengthen the impression. **whom . . . vengeance suffereth not to live**—They believed in *a Supreme, Resistless, Avenging Eye and Hand,* however vague their notions of *where* it resided.

ADAM CLARKE

CHAPTER 28

1. *They knew that the island was called Melita.* Now called Malta. It is about fifty miles from the coast of Sicily; twenty miles long, twelve miles in its greatest breadth; and about sixty miles in circumference. It is one immense rock of white, soft freestone, with about one foot depth of earth on an average. It produces cotton, excellent fruits, and fine honey, from which it appears the island originally had its name; for *meli,* and in the genitive case, *melitos,* signifies "honey." Others suppose that it derived its name from the Phoenicians, who established a colony in it, and made it a place of "refuge" when they extended their traffic to the ocean, because it was furnished with excellent harbors. Hence in their tongue it would be called *Meliteh,* "escape or refuge."

2. *The barbarous people.* This island was peopled by the Phoenicians or Carthaginians. Their ancient language was no doubt in use among them at that time, though mingled with some Greek and Latin terms; and this language must have been unintelligible to the Romans and the Greeks. With these, as well as with other nations, it was customary to call those *barbarians* whose language they did not understand. Paul himself speaks after this manner in 1 Cor. xiv. 11: "If I know not the meaning of the voice, I shall be unto him that speaketh a barbarian, and he that speaketh shall be a barbarian unto me."

Because of the present rain, and . . . of the cold. This must have been sometime in October; and when we consider the time of the year, the tempestuousness of the weather, and their escaping to shore on planks, spars, etc., wet of course to the skin, they must have been very *cold,* and have needed all the kindness that these well-disposed people showed them.

4. *The venomous beast.* The venomous animal; for *theria* is a general name among the Greek writers for serpents, vipers, scorpions, wasps, and suchlike creatures. *Vengeance suffereth not to live.* These heathens had a general knowledge of retributive justice, and they thought that the stinging of the serpent was a proof that Paul was a murderer.

MATTHEW HENRY

the sea, yet there is no outrunning divine justice.

(2) Some of the mistakes of natural light. In two things their knowledge was defective: [1] They thought all wicked people were punished in this life. The day of vengeance is to come in the other world, though some are made examples of in this world, to prove that there is a God, yet many are left unpunished, to prove that there is a judgment to come. [2] They thought all who were remarkably afflicted in this life were wicked people. Divine revelation sets this matter in a true light—that all things come ordinarily alike to all, that good men are oftentimes greatly afflicted in this life, for the exercise of their faith and patience.

4. When he shook off the viper from his hand they expected *that he would have swollen*, or *that he would have fallen down dead suddenly*. See how apt men are, when once they have got an ill opinion of a man, to abide by it, and to think that God must necessarily confirm their peevish sentence.

III. Paul's deliverance from the danger, and the undue construction the people put upon this. It does not appear that it put him into any fright or confusion at all. He did not shriek or start. Such a wonderful presence of mind he had as no man could have upon such a sudden accident, but by the special aids of divine grace. He *shook off the viper into the fire*. Thus, in the strength of the grace of Christ, believers shake off the temptations of Satan. When we despise the censures and reproaches of men, having the testimony of conscience for us, then we do, as Paul here, *shake off the viper into the fire*. It does us no harm. He was none the worse. Those that thought it would have been his death *looked a great while, but saw no harm at all come to him*. God hereby intended to make way for the entertainment of the gospel among them. They then magnified him as much as before they had vilified him: *They changed their minds, and said that he was a god*; for they thought it impossible that a mortal man should have a viper hang on his hand so long and be never the worse. See the uncertainty of popular opinion, how it turns with the wind, and how apt it is to run into extremes both ways.

IV. The miraculous cure of an old gentleman that was ill of a fever, and of others, by Paul. The kind entertainment which *Publius, the chief man of the island*, gave to these distressed strangers; he *received them and lodged them three days very courteously*. It is happy when God gives a large heart to those to whom he has given a large estate. It became him, who was the chief man of the island, the richest man, to be rich in good works. The illness of *the father of Publius*: He *lay sick of a fever and a bloody flux*. Providence ordered it that he should be ill just at this time, that the cure of him might be a present recompence to Publius for his generosity, and a recompence particularly for his kindness to Paul. His cure: Paul took cognizance of his case. He entered in, not as a physician to heal him by medicines, but as an apostle to heal him by miracle; and he prayed for his cure, and then laid his hands on him, and he was perfectly well in an instant. Though he must needs be in years, yet he recovered his health. The cure of many others. If he can heal diseases so effectually, he shall soon have patients enough; and he *bade them all welcome*. He did not plead that he was a stranger there, thrown accidentally among them, and waiting to be gone by the first opportunity, and therefore might be excused. No, a good man will endeavour to do good wherever the providence of God casts him. Paul thanked God for an opportunity of being useful among them. Hereby he did in effect discharge his quarters, which should encourage us to entertain strangers, for some thereby have entertained angels and some apostles unawares. God will not be behind-hand with any for kindness shown to his people in distress. Never were any people so enriched by a shipwreck on their coasts as these Maltese were.

V. The grateful acknowledgment made of the kindness Paul had done them, *v*. 10. They *honoured us with many honours*. They showed them all possible respect. They justly thought nothing too much by which they might testify the esteem they had for them. *When we departed, they loaded us with such things as were necessary*; they put on board such things as we had occasion for. Paul accepted the kindness of the good people of Melita, not as a fee for his cures (freely he had received, and freely he gave), but as the relief of his wants, and theirs that were with him.

Verses 11–16

We have here the progress of Paul's voyage towards Rome, and his arrival there at length. After a storm comes a calm: the latter part of his voyage was easy and quiet.

F. B. MEYER:

Accidents are not punishments. The clinging of the viper to Paul's hand was not an evidence of the anger of God, but was permitted in order to give these simplehearted people an evidence which they would appreciate of God's care for his own.

How changeable is human opinion, shifting in a moment from the highest to the lowest estimate of our fellows, and basing that estimate solely on the favorable or unfavorable aspect of outward circumstances! Let us not judge by appearance, but righteously. Because Paul cast off the viper, they accounted him divine; if he had died, they would have thought him a felon. Let us also shake off temptation. We cannot prevent its attacking us, but we need not take the viper into our heart.

Paul's unfailing influence for good shows what a blessing even one Christian man can be wherever he goes if he lives in the power of God.—*Bible Commentary*

JAMIESON, FAUSSET, BROWN

shook off the beast and felt no harm—See Mark 16:18. **they looked**—'continued looking'—**when he should have swollen or fallen down dead**—familiar with the effects of such bites—**and saw no harm come to him, they changed their minds, and said . . . he was a god**—from "a murderer" to "a god," as the Lycaonian greeting of Paul and Silas from "sacrificing to them" to "stoning them" (ch. 14:13, 19). What has not the Gospel done for the uncultivated portion of the human family, while its effects on the educated and refined, though very different, are not less marvellous! Verily it is God's chosen restorative for the human spirit, in all the multitudinous forms and gradations of its lapsed state. **7, 8. possessions of the chief man**—'the first man'—**of the island**—He would hardly be so styled in the lifetime of his father, if his distinction was that of the *family*. But it is now ascertained that this was the proper *official* title of the Maltese representative of the Roman prætor to Sicily, to whose province Malta belonged; two inscriptions having been discovered in the island, one in Greek, the other in Latin, containing the same words which Luke here employs. **who received us**—of Paul's company, but doubtless including the "courteous" Julius—**and lodged us three days courteously**—till proper winter lodgings could be obtained for them. **the father of Publius lay sick of a fever**—'fevers.' The word was often thus used in the plural number, probably to express *recurring attacks*. **and of a bloody flux**—'of dysentery.' (The *medical* accuracy of our historian's style has been observed here.) **to whom Paul entered in, and prayed**—thereby precluding the supposition that any charm resided in himself. **and laid his hands on him, and healed him**—Thus, as our Lord rewarded Peter for the use of his boat (Luke 5:3, 4, etc.), so Paul richly repays Publius for his hospitality. Observe the fulfilment here of two things predicted in Mark 16:18—the "taking up serpents," and "recovering of the sick by laying hands on them." **9. this . . . done, others . . . came and were healed**—'kept coming to [us] and getting healed,' i.e., during our stay, not all at once [Webster and Wilkinson].

10. who also honoured us . . . and when we departed they laded us . . .—This was not taking hire for the miracles wrought among them (Matt. 10:8), but such grateful expressions of feeling, particularly in providing what would minister to their comfort during the voyage, as showed the value they set upon the presence and labors of the apostle among them, and such as it would have hurt their feelings to refuse. Whether any permanent effects of this three months' stay of the greatest of the apostles were left at Malta, we cannot certainly say. But though little dependence is to be placed upon the tradition that Publius became bishop of Malta and afterwards of Athens, we may well believe the accredited tradition that the beginnings of the Christian Church at Malta sprang out of this memorable visit.

ADAM CLARKE

6. *When he should have swollen*. When he should have been "inflamed." *Said that he was a god*. As Hercules was one of the gods of the Phoenicians, and was worshipped in Malta under the epithet of the "dispeller of evil," they probably thought that Paul was Hercules; and the more so because Hercules was famous for having destroyed, in his youth, two serpents that attacked him in his cradle.

7. *The chief man of the island*. The term *chief*, used here by Luke, was the ancient title of the governor of this island, as is evident from an inscription found in Malta. This title is another proof of the accuracy of Luke, who uses the very epithet by which the Roman governor of that island was distinguished.

8. *The father of Publius lay sick of a fever* and dysentery. *Paul . . . prayed*. That God would exert His power; *and laid his hands on him*, as the means which God ordinarily used to convey the energy of the Holy Spirit, *and healed him*, God having conveyed the healing power by this means.

9. *Others . . . which had diseases*. Luke was a physician, yet we do not find him engaging in these cures. As a medical man, he might have been of use to the father of Publius, but he is not even consulted on the occasion.

10. *Honored us with many honors*. The word is often used to signify a pecuniary "recompense" or "present." In the sense of a pecuniary recompense, or price, paid for anything, the word is met with in I Cor. vi. 20 and vii. 23. *Such things as were necessary*. They had before given them many presents, and now they gave them a good sea stock, all that was necessary for their passage.

MATTHEW HENRY

I. Their leaving Malta. When they are refreshed they must put to sea again. The difficulties and discouragements we have met with in our Christian course must not hinder us from pressing forward. The time of their departure: *After three months*, the three winter months. Better lie by than go forward while the season was dangerous. Paul had warned them against venturing to sea in winter weather, and they would not take the warning; but, now he needed not to warn them. Experience is therefore called the mistress of fools, because those are fools that will not learn till experience has taught them. The ship in which they departed. It was in a ship of Alexandria. This ship had *wintered in that isle*, and was safe. Here were two ships, both of Alexandria, but one is wrecked there and the other is saved. Events are thus varied, that we may learn both how to want and how to abound. The sign of the ship, which probably gave it its name: it was *Castor and Pollux*. They hoped they should have better sailing under this badge than they had had before.

II. Their landing in or about Italy, and the pursuing of their journey towards Rome. They landed first at Syracuse in Sicily, the chief city of that island. There they *tarried three days*. From Syracuse they came to Rhegium, a city in Italy. There, it seems, they stayed one day. It does not appear that they did so much as go ashore, but only came to an anchor in the road. From Rhegium they came to Puteoli, a sea-port town not far from Naples. The ship of Alexandria was bound for that port, and therefore there Paul, and the rest that were bound for Rome, were put ashore, and went the remainder of their way by land. At Puteoli they *found brethren*. Who brought the knowledge of Christ hither we are not told, but here it was, so wonderfully did the leaven of the gospel diffuse itself. God has many that serve and worship him in places where we little think he has. Though it is probable there were but few brethren in Puteoli, yet Paul found them out. As it were by instinct they got together. Brethren in Christ should find out one another, as those of the same country do in a foreign land. They desired Paul and his companions to *tarry with them seven days*, that is, to forecast to stay at least one Lord's day with them. Paul was willing to allow them so much of his time; and the centurion agreed to stay one week there, to oblige Paul. From Puteoli they went forward towards Rome. This was their last stage.

III. The meeting which the Christians at Rome gave to Paul.

1. The great honour they did to Paul. They had heard much of his fame and what eminent service he had done to the kingdom of Christ. They had heard of his sufferings, and how God had owned him in them, and therefore thought themselves obliged to show him all possible respect. He had some time ago written a long epistle to them in return for which they showed him this respect. They *went to meet him*, that they might bring him in state, though he was a prisoner. Some of them went as far as *Appiforum*, which was fifty-one miles from Rome; others to a place called the *Three Taverns*. They were so far from being ashamed of him, because he was a prisoner, that for that very reason they counted him worthy of double honour.

2. The great comfort Paul had in this. Now that he was drawing near to Rome he began to have some melancholy thoughts about his appeal to Caesar, and the consequences of it. What things might befall him here he could not tell; but he began to grow dull upon it, till he met with these good people that came from Rome, and *when he saw them*, (1) He *thanked God*. If our friends be kind to us, it is God that makes them so, and we must give him the glory of it. When he saw so many Christians that were of Rome, he thanked God that the gospel of Christ had had such wonderful success there in the metropolis of the empire. When we go abroad into the world, and meet with those, even in strange places, that bear up Christ's name, and fear God, we should lift up our hearts to heaven in thanksgiving; blessed be God that there are so many excellent ones on this earth, bad as it is. (2) He *took courage*. It put new life into him, and now he can enter Rome a prisoner as cheerfully as ever he had entered Jerusalem at liberty. He finds there are those there who love and value him. It is an encouragement to those who are travelling towards heaven to meet with their fellow travellers. When we see the numerous and serious assemblies of good Christians, we should not only give thanks to God, but take courage to ourselves.

IV. The delivering of Paul into custody at Rome, *v.* 16. He is now come to his journey's end. He is still a prisoner. He had longed to see Rome, but, when he comes there, he is delivered to the *captain*

JAMIESON, FAUSSET, BROWN

11. we departed in a ship of Alexandria—(see on ch. 27:6)—**which had wintered in the isle**—no doubt driven in by the same storm which had wrecked on its shores the apostle's vessel—an incidental mark of consistency in the narrative. **whose sign**—or 'figurehead'; the figure, carved or painted on the bow, which gave name to the vessel. Such figureheads were anciently as common as now. **was Castor and Pollux**—the tutelar gods of mariners, to whom all their good fortune was ascribed. St. Anthony is substituted for them in the modern superstitions of Mediterranean (Romanist) sailors. They carry his image in their boats and ships. It is highly improbable that two ships of Alexandra should have been casually found, of which the owners were able and willing to receive on board such a number of passengers (ch. 27:6). We may then reasonably conceive that it was compulsory on the owners to convey soldiers and state travellers [WEBSTER and WILKINSON]. **12, 13. landing at Syracuse**—the ancient and celebrated capital of Sicily, on its eastern coast, about eighty miles, or a day's sail, north from Malta. **we tarried there three days**—probably from the state of the wind. Doubtless Paul would wish to go ashore, to find out and break ground among the Jews and proselytes whom such a mercantile center would attract to it; and if this was allowed at the outset of the voyage (ch. 27:3), much more readily would it be now when he had gained the reverence and confidence of all classes with whom he came in contact. At any rate we cannot wonder that he should be regarded by the Sicilians as the founder of the Church of that island. **from thence we fetched a compass**—i.e., proceeded circuitously, or *tacked*, working to windward probably, and availing themselves of the sinuosities of the coast, the wind not being favorable [SMITH]. What follows confirms this. **and came to Rhegium**—now *Reggio*, a seaport on the southwest point of the Italian coast, opposite the northeast point of Sicily, and at the entrance of the narrow straits of Messina. **after one day the south wind blew**—a south wind having sprung up'; being now favored with a fair wind, for want of which they had been obliged first to stay three days at Syracuse, and then to tack and put in for a day at Rhegium. **the next day to Puteoli**—now *Pozzuoli*, situated on the northern part of the magnificent bay of Naples about 180 miles north of Rhegium, a distance which they might make, running before their "south wind," in about twenty-six hours. The Alexandrian corn ships enjoyed a privilege peculiar to themselves, of not being obliged to strike their topsail on landing. By this they were easily recognized as they hove in sight by the crowds that we find gathered on the shore on such occasions [HOWS]. **14, 15. Where we found brethren**—not "*the* brethren" (see on ch. 21:4), from which one would conclude they did not expect to find such [WEBSTER and WILKINSON]. **and were desired**—'requested'—**to tarry with them seven days**—If this request came from Julius, it may have proceeded partly from a wish to receive instructions from Rome and make arrangements for his journey thither, partly from a wish to gratify Paul, as he seems studiously and increasingly to have done to the last. One can hardly doubt that he was influenced by both considerations. However this may be, the apostle had thus an opportunity of spending a Sabbath with the Christians of the place, all the more refreshing from his long privation in this respect, and as a seasoning for the unknown future that lay before him at the metropolis. **so we went toward Rome. And from thence, when the brethren**—of Rome—**heard of us**—by letter from Puteoli, and probably by the same conveyance which took Julius' announcement of his arrival. **they came to meet us as far as Appii Forum**—a town forty-one miles from Rome. **and the Three Taverns**—thirty miles from Rome. Thus they came to greet the apostle in two parties, one stopping short at the nearer, the other going on to the more distant place. **whom when Paul saw, he thanked God**—for such a welcome. How sensitive he was to such Christian affection all his Epistles show (Rom. 1:9, etc.). **and took courage**—his long-cherished purpose to "see Rome" (ch. 19:21), there to proclaim the unsearchable riches of Christ, and the divine pledge that in this he should be gratified (ch. 23:11), being now about to be auspiciously realized. **16. when we came to Rome**—the renowned capital of the ancient world, situated on the Tiber. **the centurion delivered the prisoners to the captain of the guard**—the *Prætorian Prefect*, to whose custody, as commander of the Prætorian guard, the highest military authority in the city, were committed all who were to come before the

ADAM CLARKE

11. *After three months*. Supposing that they had reached Malta about the end of October, as we have already seen, then it appears that they left it about the end of January or the beginning of February; and, though in the depth of winter, not the worst time for sailing, even in those seas, the wind being then generally more steady and, on the whole, the passage more safe. *Whose sign was Castor and Pollux*. These were two fabulous semi-deities, reported to be the sons of Jupiter and Leda, who were afterwards translated to the heavens, and made the constellation called *Gemini*, or the "Twins." This constellation was deemed propitious to mariners; and, as it was customary to have the images of their gods on both the head and the stern of their ships, we may suppose that this Alexandrian ship had these on either her prow or stern, and that these gave name to the ship.

12. *Landing at Syracuse*. In order to go to Rome from Malta, their readiest course was to keep pretty close to the eastern coast of Sicily, in order to pass through the straits of Rhegium and get into the Tyrrhenian Sea. *Syracuse* is one of the most famous cities of antiquity; it is the capital of the island of Sicily, and was built about 730 years before the Christian era. This was the birthplace of the illustrious Archimedes, who, when the city was besieged by the Romans, under Marcellus, about 212 years before Christ, defended the place with his powerful engines against all the valor and power of the assailants. He beat their galleys to pieces by huge stones projected from his machines.

13. *We fetched a compass*. "Whence we coasted about." *Rhegium*. A city and promontory in Italy, opposite to Sicily. It is now called *Reggio*. It had its name, *Rhegium*, from the Greek "to break off," because it appears to have been broken off from Sicily. *The south wind blew*. This was the fairest wind they could have from Syracuse, to reach the straits of Rhegium. *The next day to Puteoli*. This place, now commonly called Pozzuoli, is an ancient town of Naples.

14. *Where we found brethren*. That is, Christians; for there had been many in Italy converted to the faith of Christ some considerable time before this, as appears from Paul's Epistle to the Romans, written some years before this voyage. *We went toward Rome*. One of the most celebrated cities in the universe, the capital of Italy, and once of the whole world, situated on the river Tiber. This famous city was founded by Romulus, 753 years before the Christian era.

15. *When the brethren heard of us*. By whom the gospel was planted at Rome is not known; it does not appear that any apostle was employed in this work. It was probably carried thither by some of those who were converted to God on the Day of Pentecost; for there were then at Jerusalem, not only "devout men," proselytes to the Jewish religion, "from every nation under heaven," Acts ii. 5, but there were "strangers of Rome" also, v. 10. And it is most reasonable to believe, as we know of no other origin, that it was by these that Christianity was planted at Rome. *As far as Appii forum*. About fifty-two miles from Rome; a long way to come on purpose to meet the apostle! The Appii Forum, or "Market of Appius," was a town on the Appian Way, a road paved from Rome to Campania by the consul Appius Claudius. It was near the sea and was a famous resort for sailors and peddlers. *And The three taverns*. This was another place on the same road, and about thirty-three miles from Rome. Some of the Roman Christians had come as far as Appii Forum; others, to the Three Taverns. *Thanked God, and took courage*. He had longed to see Rome (see Rom. i. 9-15); and finding himself brought through so many calamities, and now so near the place that he was met by a part of that church to which, some years before, he had written an Epistle, he gave thanks to God, who had preserved him; and took fresh courage in the prospect of bearing there a testimony for his Lord and Master.

16. *The captain of the guard*. This word properly means the "commander of a camp"; but it signifies the prefect, or commander of the pretorian cohorts, or emperor's guards. *With a soldier that kept him*. That is, the soldier to

MATTHEW HENRY

of the guard, and can see no more of Rome than he will permit him. How many great men had made their entry into Rome, crowned and in triumph, who really were the plagues of their generation! But here a good man makes his entry into Rome, chained and triumphed over as a poor captive. This thought is enough to put one for ever out of conceit with this world. Yet he has some favour shown him. He is a prisoner, but not a close prisoner: *Paul was suffered to dwell by himself*, and a soldier was appointed to be his guard, who, we hope, let him take all the liberty that could be allowed to a prisoner. This may encourage God's prisoners, that he can give them favour in the eyes of those that carry them captive. If he either makes it easy to them or them easy under it, they have reason to be thankful.

Verses 17–22

Paul must call his own cause; and here he represents it to the chief of the Jews at Rome, these *chief of the Jews* were the most distinguished men of that religion. *Paul called them together* that there might be a good understanding between him and them.

I. What account he gave them of his cause. 1. He professes his own innocency: "I have *committed nothing against the people* of the Jews; nor have I committed anything *against the customs of our fathers*." Paul did not impose the customs of the fathers upon the Gentiles: they were never intended for them. But it is as true that he never opposed them in the Jews, but did himself conform to them. 2. He complains of the hard usage he had met with—*he was delivered prisoner from Jerusalem into the hands of the Romans*. If he had spoken the whole truth in this matter, it would have looked worse upon the Jews, for they would have murdered him if the Romans had not protected him; but, however, they accused him as a criminal, before Felix the governor, in effect, delivering him prisoner into the hands of the Romans. 3. He declares the judgment of the Roman governors concerning him, *v.* 18. They examined him, enquired into his case. The chief captain examined him, so did Felix, and Festus, and Agrippa, and they could find no cause of death in him; but, on the contrary, would have let him go. Those who most carefully examined his case acquitted him, and none condemned him but unheard, and such as were prejudiced against him. 4. He pleads the necessity he was under to remove his cause to Rome; and that it was only in his own defence, and not with any design to recriminate (*v.* 19): *When the Jews spoke against it* he was *constrained to appeal unto Caesar*. This was all he aimed at in this appeal; not to accuse his nation, but only to vindicate himself. It is an invidious thing to accuse, especially to accuse a nation. Paul made intercession for them, but never against them. The Roman government had at this time an ill opinion of the Jewish nation, and it had been an easy thing to have exasperated the emperor. But Paul would not for ever so much do such a thing; he was for making the best of everybody, and not making bad worse. 5. He puts his sufferings upon the true footing (*v.* 20): "*For this cause I have called for you*, not to quarrel with you but to *see you and speak with you* as my countrymen, because *for the hope of Israel I am bound with this chain*." He carried the mark of his imprisonment about with him, and probably was chained to the soldier that kept him. He preached that the Messiah was come, he whom Israel hoped for. "Do not all the Jews agree in this, that the Messiah will be the glory of his people Israel? This Messiah I preach, and prove he is come. I preach such a hope in a Messiah already come as must produce a joy in him." He preached that the resurrection of the dead would come. This also was the hope of Israel. "They would have you still expect a Messiah that would free you from the Roman yoke, and make you great and prosperous upon earth. This is what they hate me for,—because I would take you off from the nation of a temporal Messiah, and lead you to that which is the true and real hope of Israel, a spiritual kingdom of holiness and love set up in the hearts of men, to be the pledge of, and preparative for, the joyful resurrection of the dead and the life of the world to come."

II. What was their reply. They own, 1. That they had nothing to say in particular against him; nor had any instructions either by letter or word of mouth (*v.* 21): "*We have neither received letters out of Judæa concerning thee nor have any of the brethren shown or spoken any harm of thee*." This was very strange, that that restless rage of the Jews which had followed Paul wherever he went should not follow him to Rome. Some think they told a lie here, and had orders to prosecute him, but durst not own it. But I am apt to think that what they said was true, and

JAMIESON, FAUSSET, BROWN

emperor for trial. Ordinarily there were two such prefects; but from A.D. 51 to 62, one distinguished general—*Burrus Afranius*, who had been Nero's tutor—held that office; and as our historian speaks of "*the* captain," as if there were but one, it is thought that this fixes the apostle's arrival at Rome to be not later than the year 62 [WIES]. But even though there had been two when Paul arrived, he would be committed only to one of them, who would be "*the* captain" who got charge of him. (At most, therefore, this can furnish no more than confirmation to the chronological evidence otherwise obtained.) **but Paul was suffered to dwell by himself with a**—'the'—**soldier that kept**—'guarded'—**him**—(See on ch. 12:6). This privilege was allowed in the case of the better class of prisoners, not accused of any flagrant offense, on finding security—which in Paul's case would not be difficult among the Christians. The extension of this privilege to the apostle may have been due to the terms in which Festus wrote about him; but far more probably it was owing to the high terms in which Julius spoke of him, and his express intercession in his behalf. It was overruled, however, for giving the fullest scope to the labors of the apostle compatible with confinement at all. As the soldiers who kept him were relieved periodically, he would thus make the personal acquaintance of a great number of the Prætorian guard; and if he had to appear before the Prefect from time to time, the truth might thus penetrate to those who surrounded the emperor, as we learn, from Philippians 1:12, 13, that it did.

17-20. Paul called the chief of the Jews together—Though banished from the capital by Claudius, the Jews enjoyed the full benefit of the toleration which distinguished the first period of Nero's reign, and were at this time in considerable numbers, wealth, and influence settled at Rome. We have seen that long before this a flourishing Christian Church existed at Rome, to which Paul wrote his Epistle (see on ch. 20:3), and the first members of which were probably Jewish converts and proselytes. (See Introduction to Epistle to Romans.) **yet was I delivered prisoner from Jerusalem into the hands of the Romans**—the Roman authorities, Felix and Festus.

I was constrained to appeal . . . not that I had aught to accuse my nation of—'I am here not as their accuser, but as my own defender, and this not of choice but necessity.' His object in alluding thus gently to the treatment he had received from the Jews was plainly to avoid whatever might irritate his visitors at the first; especially as he was not aware whether any or what information against him had reached their community. **For this cause . . . have I called for you . . . because . . . for the hope of Israel**—see on 26:6, 7—**I am bound with this chain**—'This cause is not so much mine as yours; it is the nation's cause; all that is dear to the heart and hope of Israel is bound up with this case of mine.' From the touching allusions which the apostle makes to his chains, before Agrippa first, and here before the leading members of the Jewish community at Rome, at his first interview with them, one would gather that his great soul felt keenly his being in such a condition; and it is to this keenness of feeling, under the control of Christian principle, that we owe the noble use which he made of it in these two cases.

21, 22. We neither received letters out of Judea concerning thee . . .—We need not suppose (with THOLUCK and others) that there was any dishonest concealment here. The distinction made between himself, against whom they heard nothing, and his "sect," as "everywhere spoken against," is a presumption in favor of their sincerity; and there is ground to think that as the case took an

ADAM CLARKE

whom he was chained, as has been related before, chap. xii. 6.

17. *Paul called the chief of the Jews together*. We have already seen, in chap. xviii. 2, that Claudius had commanded all Jews to depart from Rome, but it seems they were permitted to return very soon; and from this verse it appears that there were then chiefs, probably of synagogues, dwelling at Rome. *I have committed nothing*. Lest they should have heard and received malicious reports against him, he thought it best to state his own case.

20. *For the hope of Israel I am bound*. As if he had said: This, and this alone, is the cause of my being delivered into the hands of the Romans. I have proclaimed Jesus as the Messiah; have maintained that though He was crucified by the Jews, yet He rose again from the dead; and, through Him, I have preached the general resurrection of mankind. This all Israel professes to hope for, and yet it is on this account that the Jews persecute *me*. Both the Messiah and the Resurrection might be said to be the hope of Israel; and it is hard to tell which of them is here meant. See chap. xxiii. 6; xxiv. 15, 21; and xxvi. 6.

21. *We neither received letters*. This is very strange, and shows us that the Jews knew their cause to be hopeless, and therefore did not send it forward to Rome. They wished for an opportunity to kill Paul; and when they were frustrated by this appeal to the emperor, they permitted the business to drop.

MATTHEW HENRY

Paul now found he had gained the point he aimed at in appealing to Caesar, which was to remove his cause into a court to which they durst not follow it. 2. That they desired to know particularly concerning the religion he took so much pains to propagate in the face of so much opposition (*v.* 22): *We desire to hear of thee what thou thinkest.* Though we know little else of Christianity, we know *it is a sect everywhere spoken against.* This was all they knew concerning the Christian religion, that it was a *sect everywhere spoken against.* They put it into an ill name, and then ran it down. They looked upon it to be a sect, and this was false. True Christianity establishes that which is of common concern to all mankind, and is not built upon such narrow opinions as sects commonly owe their original to. All its gains are spiritual and eternal. It has a direct tendency to the uniting of the children of men, and not the dividing of them. They said it was everywhere spoken against, and this was too true. It is, and always has been, the lot of Christ's holy religion to be everywhere spoken against.

Verses 23–29

We have here a short account of a long conference which Paul had with the Jews at Rome about the Christian religion. They were willing to give it a hearing, which was more than the Jews at Jerusalem would do.

I. We are here told how Paul managed this conference. The Jews appointed the time, a day was set for this dispute, *v.* 23. Those Jews seemed well disposed to receive conviction, and yet it did not prove that they all were so.

1. There were *many got together to Paul.* Though he was a prisoner yet they were willing to come to him to his lodging. And the confinement he was now under, instead of prejudicing them against his doctrine, ought to confirm it to them; for it was a sign that he thought it worth suffering for. One would visit such a man as Paul in his prison rather than not have instruction from him.

2. He was very full in his discourse with them, seeking their conviction more than his own vindication. He expounded the kingdom of God to them,—showed them the nature of that kingdom, that it is heavenly and spiritual, and shines not in external pomp, but in purity of heart and life. Let but that be expounded to them, and set in a true light, and they will be brought into obedience to it. He not only expounded the kingdom of God, but he testified it,—plainly declared it to them, and confirmed it by incontestable proofs. He attested the extraordinary powers in the kingdom of grace by which it was set up, and the miracles in the kingdom of nature by which it was confirmed. He bore his testimony to it from his own experience of its power. He not only expounded and testified the kingdom of God, but he pressed them with all earnestness to embrace the kingdom of God. He followed his doctrine with a warm and lively applicaton to his hearers. He persuaded them concerning Jesus. The design and tendency of his whole discourse were to bring them to Christ, to convince them of his being the Messiah. He urged upon them *the things concerning Jesus, out of the law of Moses and out of the prophets,* and showed how they had all had their accomplishment in this Jesus. He dealt with them out of the scriptures of the Old Testament.

3. He was very long; for he continued his discourse from *morning till evening.* The subject was curious—he was full of it—it was of vast importance—he was in good earnest—he knew not when he should have such another opportunity, and therefore, he kept them all day.

II. What was the effect of this discourse. One would have thought that so good a cause and managed by such a skilful hand as Paul's, could not but carry the day. But it did not prove so: the child Jesus is set for the fall of some and the rising again of others, a foundation stone to some and a stone of stumbling to others. *They did not agree among themselves, v.* 25. His hearers could not agree about the sense and evidence of what he preached. *Some believed the things that were spoken, and some believed not, v.* 24. Some are wrought upon by the word, and others hardened; some receive the light, and others shut their eyes against it. So it was among Christ's hearers, some believed and some blasphemed.

III. The awakening word which Paul said to them at parting. He perceived by what they muttered that there were many among them, that were obstinate, and would not yield. "Hold," says Paul, "take one word with you before you go. What do you think will be the effect of your obstinate infidelity? What will it come to?"

1. "You will by the righteous judgment of God be

JAMIESON, FAUSSET, BROWN

unexpected turn by Paul's appealing to Cæsar, so no information on the subject would travel from Jerusalem to Rome in advance of the apostle himself. **we desire**—'deem it proper'—**to hear of thee what thou thinkest**—what are thy sentiments, views, etc. The apparent freedom from prejudice here expressed may have arisen from a prudent desire to avoid endangering a repetition of those dissensions abuut Christianity to which, probably, SUETONIUS alludes, and which had led to the expulsion of the Jews under Claudius [HUMPHRY]. See on ch. 18:2.

23, 24. there came many—'considerable numbers'—**into his lodging**—The word denotes one's place of stay as a *guest* (Philemon 22), not "his own hired house," mentioned in vs. 30. Some Christian friends—possibly Aquila and Priscilla, who had returned to Rome (Rom. 16:3), would be glad to receive him, though he would soon find himself more at liberty in a house of his own. **to whom he expounded and testified the kingdom of God**—opening up the great spiritual principles of that kingdom in opposition to the contracted and secular views of it entertained by the Jews.

persuading them concerning Jesus—as the ordained and predicted Head of that kingdom. **out of the law . . . and the prophets**—drawing his materials and arguments from a source mutually acknowledged. **from morning till evening**—"Who would not wish to have been present?" exclaims BENGEL; but virtually we *are* present while *listening* to those Epistles which he *dictated* from his prison at Rome, and to his other epistolary expositions of Christian truth against the Jews. **and some believed . . . some not**—What simplicity and candor are in this record of a result repeated from age to age where the Gospel is presented to a promiscuous assemblage of sincere and earnest inquirers after truth, frivolous worldlings, and prejudiced bigots! **25-29. when they**—the Jews—**agreed not among themselves**—the discussion having passed into one between the two parties into which the visitors were now divided, respecting the arguments and conclusions of the apostle.

they departed—the material of discussion being felt by both parties to be exhausted.

ADAM CLARKE

22. *For as concerning this sect.* See the note on chap. xxiv. 14. A saying of Justin Martyr casts some light on this saying of the Jews. He asserts that the Jews not only cursed them in their synagogues, but they sent out chosen men from Jerusalem to acquaint the world, and particularly the Jews everywhere, that the Christians were an atheistical and wicked sect, which should be detested and abhorred by all mankind (Justin Martyr, *Dial.,* p. 234).

23. *To whom he expounded . . . the kingdom of God.* To whom he showed that the reign of the Messiah was to be a spiritual reign; and that Jesus, whom the Jewish rulers had lately crucified, was the true Messiah, who should rule in this spiritual Kingdom. These two points were probably those on which he expatiated from morning to evening, proving both out of the law and out of the prophets.

24. *Some believed.* His message was there treated as his gospel is to the present day. Some believe and are converted; others continue in obstinate unbelief and perish. Could the Jews then have credited the spiritual nature of the Messiah's kingdom, they would have found little difficulty to receive Jesus Christ as the Messiah.

25. *Agreed not among themselves.* It seems that a controversy arose between the Jews themselves, in consequence of some believing and others disbelieving, and the two parties contested together; and in respect to the unbelieving party, the apostle quoted the following passage from Isa. vi. 9.

MATTHEW HENRY

sealed up under unbelief. Turn to that scripture (Isa. vi. 9, 10), and tremble lest the case there described should prove to be your case." As there are in the Old Testament gospel promises, which will be accomplished in all that believe, so there are gospel threatenings of spiritual judgments, which will be fulfilled in those that believe not. Isaiah the prophet is sent to make those worse that would not be made better. *Well spoke the Holy Ghost by* Esaias *the prophet unto our fathers.* Though what is there said had in it much of terror to the people and of grief to the prophet, yet it is here said to be well spoken. *He that believes not shall be damned* is gospel, as well as, *He that believes shall be saved,* Mark xvi. 16. "*Well did Esaias prophesy of you.* The Holy Ghost said to your fathers, that which would be fulfilled in you, *Hearing you shall hear, and shall not understand.*" (1) "That which was their great sin against God is yours. *Your eyes you have closed,*" *v.* 27. "As your fathers would not see God's hand lifted up against them in his judgments, so you will not see God's hand stretched out to you in gospel grace." They did not see, because they were resolved they would not, and none so blind as those that will not see. They have purposely *closed their eyes, lest they should see with their eyes* the great things which belong to their everlasting peace; will not receive the evidence of them, *lest they should hear with their ears.* And that which they are afraid of in shutting up their eyes and ears, is, *lest they should understand with their heart, and should be converted, and I should heal them.* They kept their mind in the dark, or at least in a constant confusion and tumult. God's method is to bring people first to see and hear, and so to understand with their hearts, and then to bow their wills, and so heal them, which is the regular way of dealing with a rational soul; and therefore Satan prevents the conversion of souls to God by blinding the mind and darkening the understanding. And the case is very sad when the sinner joins with him herein, and puts out his own eyes. They are in love with their disease, and are afraid lest God should heal them. This was the sin. (2) "That which was the great judgment of God upon them for this sin is his judgment upon you, and that is, you shall be blind. *Hearing you shall hear—but you shall not understand* it; because you will not give your minds to understand it, God will not give you strength and grace to understand it. *Seeing you shall see but you shall not perceive.*" What with their resisting the grace of God and rebelling against the light, and God's withdrawing and withholding his grace and light from them,—what with their not receiving the love of the truth, and God's giving them up for that to strong delusions, to believe a lie, *the heart of this people is waxed gross, and their ears are dull of hearing.* No physic that can be given them operates upon them, and therefore their disease must be adjudged incurable. And how should those be healed that will not be converted to the use of the methods of cure? And how should those be converted that will not be convinced either of their disease or of their remedy? And how should those be convinced that *shut their eyes and stop their ears*? When once they are thus given up to hardness of heart, they are already in the suburbs of hell.

2. "Your unbelief will justify God in sending the gospel to the Gentile world (*v.* 28): therefore seeing you put the grace of God away from you, and will not submit to the power of divine truth and love, *be it known unto you that the salvation of God is sent unto the Gentiles.* They will hear it, and receive it, and be happy in it." Now Paul designs hereby, (1) To abate their displeasure at the preaching of the gospel to the Gentiles, by showing them the absurdity of it. They were angry that the salvation of God was sent to the Gentiles, but, if they thought that salvation of so small a value as not to be worthy of their acceptance, surely they could not grudge it to the Gentiles. The salvation of God was sent into the world, the Jews had the first offer of it, they would not accept the invitation which was given to them first to the wedding-feast and therefore must thank themselves if other guests be invited. (2) To improve their displeasure at the favour done to the Gentiles to their advantage, and to bring good out of that evil. The Jews have rejected the gospel of Christ, but it is not yet too late to repent of their refusal; they may say No, and take it, as the elder brother in the parable, Matt. xxi. 29. Is the gospel sent to the Gentiles? Let us go after it rather than come short of it. And will they hear it, who are thought to be out of hearing? And shall not we hear it, whose privilege it is to have God so nigh to us in all that we call upon him for? Thus he would have them shamed into the belief of the gospel by the welcome it met with among the

JAMIESON, FAUSSET, BROWN

after Paul had spoken one word—one solemn parting testimony, from those Scriptures regarded by both alike as "the Holy Ghost speaking" to Israel. **Hearing, ye shall hear . . .**—See on Matthew 13:13-15; and John 12:38-40. With what pain would this stern saying be wrung from him whose "heart's desire and prayer to God for Israel was that they might be saved," and who "had great heaviness and continual sorrow in his heart" on their account (Rom. 10:1; 9:2)!

the salvation of God is sent to the Gentiles, and they will hear—See on ch. 13:44-48. "This 'departure to the Gentiles' he had intimated to the perverse Jews at *Antioch* (ch. 13:46), and at *Corinth* (ch. 18:6); now at *Rome:* thus in *Asia, Greece,* and *Italy*" [BENGEL].

ADAM CLARKE

26. *Hearing ye shall hear.* See the notes on Matt. xiii. 14 and John xii. 39-40.

28. *The salvation of God is sent unto the Gentiles.* Paul had spoken to this effect twice before, chap. xiii. 46 and chap. xviii. 6, where see the notes. But here he uses a firmer tone, being out of the Jewish territories and under the protection of the emperor. By *the salvation of God,* all the blessings of the kingdom of Christ are intended. This salvation God could have sent unto the Gentiles independently of the Jewish disobedience; but He waited till they had rejected it, and then reprobated them, and elected the Gentiles. Thus the elect became reprobate, and the reprobate elect. *They will hear it.* That is, they will obey it; for *akouein* signifies not only "to hear" but also "to obey."

G. CAMPBELL MORGAN:

This whole book of the Acts is the story of God's final striving with the Hebrew people. In the life of our Lord He came first to the Hebrew, the Jew. He said upon one occasion to a woman who asked His help: "It is not meet to take the children's bread, and cast it to the dogs." That little incidental word revealed the fact that He came first to the Hebrew people. They rejected Him. They had their new opportunity beyond his rejection at Pentecost, and yet another in that period in which this man had stood in Jerusalem. Jerusalem finally rejected Christ when it rejected Paul. After that Paul strove to reach them in every city. He went first to the synagogue, first to the Hebrew. The word of Paul in Rome was the final word. Before very many years had gone, after a period of oppression, tyranny, and suffering, the Roman eagles were carried through Jerusalem, and the nation was swept out. It was the occasion of the last and solemn abandonment of the people, this word spoken by Paul to the Hebrew rulers in that city of Rome, the central city of the world.

The words he quoted were words which had been spoken to Isaiah in that great vision, the record of which we have in the sixth chapter, when his whole ministry was changed. Our Lord quoted these very words in the thirteenth chapter of Matthew, in the course of the parables of the Kingdom. When He was showing why the Kingdom was to be taken from the Jewish people, He quoted the same words. John also quoted exactly the same word in the twelfth chapter of his Gospel, where he was giving the last things in the presentation of the Kingdom to Israel. Mark these occurrences of these words in the Bible: Isaiah, Jesus, John, and Paul. If we say that Paul quoted them from Isaiah, we shall say that which is correct, but do not forget that they were not the words of Isaiah, but the words of Jehovah spoken to Isaiah about these people. The declaration is that they themselves had closed their eyes because they would not see; and therefore God had made them blind; that they themselves had hardened their heart because they would not yield; and therefore God handed them over to their own hardness of heart. But it is interesting and solemn to remember that here in Rome, the city to whose yoke the Hebrew people had bowed the neck anew, in order to encompass the death of Christ, Paul's final word of excommunication was spoken.—*The Acts of the Apostles*

MATTHEW HENRY

Gentiles. And, if it had not that effect upon them, it would aggravate their condemnation.

IV. The breaking up of the assembly, as it should seem, in some disorder. They turned their backs upon Paul. *When Paul had said these words*, he had said enough for them, and *they departed*, no more affected, either with those terrible words in the close of his discourse or all the comfortable words he had spoken before, than the seats they sat on. They set their faces one against another; for they had great disputes among themselves. Those that agreed to depart from Paul, yet agreed not in the reasons why they departed, but had *great reasoning among themselves*. Many have great reasoning who yet do not reason right. Nor will men's reasoning among themselves convince them, without the grace of God to open their understandings.

Verses 30, 31

We are here taking our leave of the history of blessed Paul. We should carefully take notice of every particular of the circumstances in which we must here leave him.

I. It cannot but be trouble to us that we must leave him in bonds for Christ. *Two whole years* of that good man's life are here spent in confinement. He appealed to Cæsar, in hope of a speedy discharge from his imprisonment, and yet he is detained a prisoner. Then his bonds in Christ were manifest in Cæsar's court, as he says, Phil. i. 13. During these two years' imprisonment he wrote his epistles to the Ephesians, Philippians, Colossians, and to Philemon. How or by what means he obtained his liberty we are not told, only that two years he was a prisoner. Tradition says that after his discharge he went from Italy to Spain, thence to Crete, and so with Timothy into Judæa, and thence went to visit the churches in Asia, and at length came a second time to Rome, and there was beheaded in the last year of Nero. It would grieve one to think that such a useful man as Paul was should be so long in restraint. Two years he was a prisoner under Felix (*ch.* xxiv. 27), and he is here two years more a prisoner under Nero. How many churches might Paul have planted if he had been at liberty! But God will show that he is no debtor to the most useful instruments he employs, but will carry on his own interest, both without their services and by their sufferings. Even Paul's bonds fell out *to the furtherance of the Gospel*, Phil. i. 12–14. Yet even Paul's imprisonment was in some respects a kindness to him, for these *two years he dwelt in his own hired house*, and that was more, for aught I know, than ever he had done before. Such a retirement as this would be a refreshment to one who had been all his days an itinerant. Now he lived for two years in the same house; so that the bringing of him into this prison was like Christ's call to his disciples *to come into a desert place, and rest awhile*, Mark vi. 31. When he was at liberty, he was in continual fear by reason of *the lying in wait of the Jews* (*ch.* xx. 19), but now his prison was his castle.

II. Yet it is a pleasure to us that, though we leave him in bonds for Christ, yet we leave him at work for Christ. His prison becomes a temple, a church, and then it is to him a palace. Thanks be to God, his mouth is not stopped; a faithful zealous minister can better bear any hardship than being silenced. He is bound, but the word of the Lord is not bound. He was glad *to see some of them* (*v.* 15), but it would not be half his joy unless he could impart to them some spiritual gift, which here he has an opportunity to do.

1. To whom he preached. Whoever would had liberty to come to his house to hear, and they were welcome. Ministers' doors should be open to such as desire to receive instruction from them. When we cannot do what we would in the service of God we must do what we can. *He received all that came to him*, and was not afraid of the greatest, nor ashamed of the meanest. He might hope the better to speed because *they came in unto him*, which supposed a desire to be instructed and a willingness to learn, and where these are it is probable that some good may be done.

2. What he preached. He is God's ambassador, and therefore *preaches the kingdom of God*. He meddles not with the affairs of the kingdoms of men; let those treat of them whose work it is. He preaches the kingdom of God among men; the same that he defended in his public disputes, *testifying the kingdom of God* (*v.* 23), he enforced in his public preaching, as that which will make us all wise and good, wiser and better, which is the end of preaching. He is an agent for Christ, and therefore *teaches those things which concern the Lord Jesus Christ*—the whole history of Christ, all that relates to the mystery of godliness. Paul stuck still to his principle—to know and preach *nothing but Christ*; *and him crucified.*

JAMIESON, FAUSSET, BROWN

the Jews departed, and had great—'much'—**reasoning among themselves**—"This verse is wanting in many MSS. [and omitted by several recent editors], but certainly without reason. Probably the words were regarded as superfluous, as they seem to tell us what we were told before, that Paul 'departed' (see vs. 25). But in vs. 25 it is the breaking off of the discourse that is meant, here the final departure from the house" [OLSHAUSEN]. **30. in his own hired house**—(see on vs. 23), yet still in custody, for he only "received all that *came to him*"; and it is not said that he went to the synagogue or anywhere else. **with all confidence, no man forbidding him**—enjoying, in the uninterrupted exercise of his ministry, all the liberty of a *guarded* man.

Thus closes this most precious monument of the beginnings of the Christian Church in its march from east to west, among the Jews first, whose center was Jerusalem; next among the Gentiles, with Antioch for its headquarters; finally, its banner is seen waving over imperial Rome, foretokening its universal triumphs. That distinguished apostle whose conversion, labors, and sufferings for "the faith which once he destroyed" occupy more than half of this History, it leaves a prisoner, unheard, so far as appears, for two years. His accusers, whose presence was indispensable, would have to await the return of spring before starting for the capital, and might not reach it for many months; nor, even when there, would they be so sanguine of success—after Felix, Festus, and Agrippa had all pronounced him innocent—as to be impatient of delay. And if witnesses were required to prove the charge advanced by Tertullus, that he was "a mover of sedition among all the Jews throughout the [Roman] world" (ch. 24:5), they must have seen that unless considerable time was allowed them the case would certainly break down. If to this be added the capricious delays which the emperor himself might interpose, and the practice of Nero to hear but one charge at a time, it will not seem strange that the historian should have no proceedings in the case to record for two years. Begun, probably, before the apostle's arrival, its progress at Rome under his own eye would furnish exalted employment, and beguile many a tedious hour of his two years' imprisonment. Had the case come on for hearing during this period, much more if it had been disposed of, it is hardly conceivable that the History should have closed as it does. But if, at the end of this period, the Narrative only wanted the decision of the case, while hope deferred was making the heart sick (Prov. 13:12), and if, under the guidance of that Spirit whose seal was on it all, it seemed of more consequence to put the Church at once in possession of this History than to keep it back indefinitely for the sake of what might come to be otherwise known, we cannot wonder that it should be wound up as it is in its two concluding verses. All that we know of the apostle's proceedings and history beyond this must be gathered from the *Epistles of the Imprisonment*—Ephesians, Philippians, Colossians, and Philemon—written during this period, and the *Pastoral Epistles*—to Timothy and Titus, which, in our judgment, are of subsequent date. From the former class of Epistles we learn the following particulars: (1) That the trying restraint laid upon the apostle's labors by his imprisonment had only turned his influence into a new channel; the Gospel having in consequence penetrated even into the palace, and pervaded the city, while the preachers of Christ were emboldened; and though the Judaizing portion of them, observing his success among the Gentiles, had been led to inculcate with fresh zeal their own narrower Gospel, even this had done much good by extending the truth common to both (see on Phil. 1:12-18; 4:22); (2) That as in addition to all his other labors, "the care of all the churches pressed upon him from day to day" (II Cor. 11:28), so with these churches he kept up an active correspondence by means of letters and messages, and on such errands he lacked not faithful and beloved brethren enough ready to be employed—*Luke; Timotheus; Tychicus;* (John) *Mark; Demas; Aristarchus; Epaphras; Onesimus; Jesus,* called Justus; and, for a short time, *Epaphroditus.* (See on Col. 4:7, 9-12, 14; Philemon 23, 24; and Introduction to Ephesians, Philippians, and Philemon.) That the apostle suffered martyrdom under Nero at Rome has never been doubted. But that the appeal which brought him to Rome issued in his liberation, that he was at large for some years thereafter and took some wide missionary circuits, and that he was again arrested, carried to Rome, and then executed—was the undisputed belief of the early Church, as expressed by CHRYSOSTOM, JE-

ADAM CLARKE

30. *Paul dwelt two whole years in his own hired house.* As a state prisoner, he might have had an apartment in the common prison; but peculiar favor was showed him, and he was permitted to dwell alone, with the soldier that guarded him, v. 16. Finding now an opportunity of preaching the gospel, he hired a house for the purpose. Here he received all that came unto him, and preached the gospel with glorious success; so that his bonds became the means of spreading the truth, and he became celebrated even in the palace of Nero, Phil. i. 12-13; and we find that there were several saints even in Caesar's household, Phil. iv. 22. While he was in captivity, the church at Philippi, to which he was exceedingly dear, sent him some pecuniary assistance by the hands of their minister, Epaphroditus, who, it appears, risked his life in the service of the apostle, and was taken with a dangerous malady. When he got well, he returned to Philippi and, it is supposed, carried with him that Epistle which is still extant. From it we learn that Timothy was then at Rome with Paul, and that he had the prospect of being shortly delivered from his captivity. See Phil. i. 12-13; ii. 25; iv. 15-16, 18, etc.

31. *Preaching the kingdom of God.* Showing the spiritual nature of the true Church, under the reign of the Messiah. *Those things which concern the Lord.* The Redeemer of the world was to be represented as the Lord, as Jesus, and as the Christ. As *the Lord*, the sole Potentate, the Maker and Upholder of all things, and the Judge of all men. As *Jesus*—the "Saviour"; He who saves, delivers, and preserves; and especially He who saves His people from their sins. As *Christ*—the same as Messiah, both signifying the "anointed"; He who was appointed by the Lord to this great and glorious work, who had the Spirit without measure, and who anoints, communicates the gifts and graces of that Spirit to all true believers. Paul taught the *things which concerned* or belonged to *the Lord Jesus Christ.* He proved Him to be the Messiah foretold by the prophets and expected by the Jews; he spoke of what He does as the Lord, what He does as Jesus, and what He does as Christ. *With all confidence.* "Liberty of speech"; perfect freedom to say all he pleased, and when he pleased. He had the fullest toleration from the Roman government to preach as he pleased and what he pleased, and the unbelieving Jews had no power to prevent him. It is supposed that it was during this residence at Rome he converted Onesimus, and sent him back to his master, Philemon, with the Epistle which is still extant. And it is from vv. 22 and 24 of that Epistle that we learn that Paul had then with him Epaphras, Marcus, Aristarchus, Demas, and Luke.

MATTHEW HENRY

3. With what liberty he preached. Divine grace gave him a liberty of spirit. He preached *with all confidence*. He was *not ashamed of the gospel of Christ.* Divine Providence gave him a liberty of speech: *No man forbidding him.* The Jews that used to forbid him to speak to the Gentiles had no authority here; and the Roman government as yet took no cognizance of the profession of Christianity as a crime. It set bounds to the rage of persecutors; there were many, both Jews and Gentiles, in Rome, that hated Christianity; and yet so it was that Paul though a prisoner was connived at in preaching the gospel. Though there were so many that had it in their power to forbid Paul's preaching, yet God so ordered it, *that no man did forbid him.* See God here providing comfort for the relief of the persecuted. Though it was not a wide door that was opened to him, yet it was kept open, and it was to many an effectual door, so that there were saints even in Cæsar's household, Phil. iv. 22. When the city of our solemnities is thus made a quiet habitation at any time, we must give thanks to God for it, still longing for that holy mountain in which there shall never be any pricking brier nor grieving thorn.

JAMIESON, FAUSSET, BROWN

ROME, and EUSEBIUS, in the fourth century, up to CLEMENT of Rome, the "fellow laborer" of the apostle himself (Phil. 4:3), in the first century. The strongest possible confirmation of this is found in the Pastoral Epistles, which bear marks throughout of a more advanced state of the Church, and more matured forms of error, than can well have existed at any period before the appeal which brought the apostle to Rome; which refer to movements of himself and Timothy that cannot without some straining (as we think) be made to fit into any prior period; and which are couched in a manifestly riper style than any of his other Epistles. (See Introduction to Timothy and Titus, and *Notes*.) All this has been called in question by modern critics of great research and acuteness [PETAVIUS, LARDNER, DE WETTE, WIESELER, DAVIDSON, and others]. But those who maintain the ancient view are of equal authority and more numerous, while the weight of argument appears to us to be decidedly on their side.

ADAM CLARKE

Here Luke's account of Paul's travels and sufferings ends, and it is probable that this history was written soon after the end of the two years mentioned in v. 30. That the apostle visited many places after this, suffered much in the great cause of Christianity, and preached the gospel of Jesus with amazing success, is generally believed. How he came to be liberated we are not told; but it is likely that, having been kept in this sort of confinement for about two years, and none appearing against him, he was released by the imperial order. Concerning the time, place, and manner of his death we have little certainty. It is commonly believed that, when a general persecution was raised against the Christians by Nero, about A.D. 64, under pretense that they had set Rome on fire, both Paul and Peter then sealed the truth with their blood, the latter being crucified with his head downward, the former being beheaded, in either A.D. 64 or 65.

THE EPISTLE TO THE ROMANS

I. Introduction (1:1-15)
A. The address (1:1-7)
B. Personal interest (1:8-13)
C. The reason of the letter (1:14-15)

II. The Gospel—unto salvation (1:16-11:36)
A. Fundamental affirmation (1:16-17)
B. Condemnation—the Gospel needed (1:18-3:20)
1. The Gentile condemned (1:18-32)
2. The Jew condemned (2:1-3:8)
3. The whole world guilty (3:9-20)

C. Salvation—the Gospel message (3:21-8:39)
1. Justification (3:21-5:21)
2. Sanctification (6:1-8:17)
3. Glorification (8:18-39)

D. Objections discussed (9:1-11:36)
1. Election (9:1-33)
2. Rejection (10:1-21)
3. Restoration (11:1-36)

III. The transformation—by salvation (12:1-15:13)
A. Final appeal (12:1, 2)
B. Simplicity—personal life (12:3-21)
1. The character of humility (12:3)
2. The consciousness of communion (12:4-8)
3. The conduct of simplicity (12:9-21)

C. Submission—relative life (13:1-14)
1. Definition (13:1-10)
2. Inspiration (13:11-14)

D. Sympathy—relative life (14:1-15:13)
1. Sympathy as toleration (14:1-12)
2. Sympathy as edification (14:13-23)
3. Sympathy as hospitality (15:1-13)

IV. Conclusion (15:14-16:27)
A. Personal matters (15:14-16:24)
B. Closing doxology (16:25-27)

In the Old Testament David's Psalms, and in the New Testament Paul's Epistles, are stars of the first magnitude. We have upon record several particular epistles, more of Paul's than of any other. His apprehension was quick and piercing; his expressions were fluent and copious; his affections very warm and zealous, and his resolutions no less bold and daring: this made him, before his conversion, a very keen and bitter persecutor. He became the most skillful zealous preacher; never any better fitted to win souls, nor more successful.

This epistle to the Romans is placed first, not because of the priority if its date, but because of the superlative excellency of the epistle, it being one of the longest and fullest of all. It is gathered from some passages in the epistle that it was written A.D. 56, from Corinth. Paul was now going to Jerusalem with the money that was given to the poor saints there; and of that he speaks (15:26). The great mysteries treated of in this epistle must needs produce many things dark and hard to be understood (2 Pet. 3:16). The former part of it doctrinal, in the first eleven chapters; the latter part practical, in the last five.

I. The doctrinal part of the epistle instructs us—
1. Concerning the way of salvation.
2. Concerning the persons saved, such as belong to the election of grace, Gentiles and Jews. Two things the Jews then stumbled at—justification by faith without the works of the law, and the admission of the Gentiles into the chruch; and therefore both these he studied to clear and vindicate.

II. The practical part follows.

III. As he draws toward a conclusion, he makes an apology for writing to them, sends particular salutations to many friends there, adds the salutations of his friends with him, and ends with a benediction to them and a doxology to God.

CHAPTER 1

Verses 1–7

I. The person who writes the epistle described (*v.* 1): *Paul, a servant of Jesus Christ;* this is his title of honour, which he glories in, a servant. *Called to be an apostle.* Christ sought him to make an apostle of him, Acts ix. 15. He here builds his authority upon his call; he did not run without sending. *Called an apostle,* as if this were the name he would be called by, though he acknowledged himself not meet to be called so, 1 Cor. xv. 9. *Separated to the gospel of God.* The Pharisees had their name from separation, because they *separated themselves to the study of the law,* such a one Paul had formerly been; but now he had changed his studies, was a gospel Pharisee, separated by the counsel of God (Gal. i. 15), *separated from his mother's womb.* He was an entire devotee to the gospel of God.

CHAPTER 1

Vss. 1-17. INTRODUCTION. **1. Paul**—see on Acts 13:9—**a servant of Jesus Christ**—The word here rendered "servant" means 'bond-servant,' or one subject to the will and wholly at the disposal of another. In this sense it is applied to the disciples of Christ at large (I Cor. 7:21-23), as in the Old Testament to all the people of God (Isa. 66:14). But as, in addition to this, the prophets and kings of Israel were *officially* "the servants of the Lord" (Josh. 1:1; Ps. 18, title), the apostles call themselves, in the same official sense, "the servants of Christ" (as here, and Phil. 1:1; Jas. 1:1; II Pet. 1:1; Jude 1), expressing such absolute subjection and devotion to the Lord Jesus as they would never have yielded to a mere creature. (See on vs. 7; and on John 5:22, 23.) **called to be an apostle**—when first he "saw the Lord"; the indispensable qualification for apostleship. (See on Acts 9:5; 22:14; I Cor. 9:1.) **separated unto the**—preaching of the—**gospel**—neither so late as when "the Holy Ghost said, *Separate* me Barnabas and Saul" (Acts 13:2), nor so early as when "*separated* from his mother's womb" (see on Gal. 1:15). He was called at one and the same time to the faith and the apostleship of Christ (Acts 26:16-18). **of God**—i.e,, the Gospel of which God is the glorious Author. (So ch. 15: 16; I Thess. 2:2, 8, 9; I Pet. 4:17.) **2. Which he**

CHAPTER 1

1. *Paul, a servant of Jesus Christ.* The word here translated *servant* properly means a "slave," one who is the entire property of his master, and is used here by the apostle with great propriety. He felt he was not his own, and that his life and powers belonged to his heavenly Owner, and that he had no right to dispose of or employ them but in the strictest subserviency to the will of his Lord. In this sense, and in this spirit, he is the willing slave of Jesus Christ; and this is, perhaps, the highest character which any soul of man can attain on this side of eternity. *Called to be an apostle.* The word *apostle,* from *apostellein,* "to send," signifies simply a "messenger" or "envoy"; one sent on a confidential errand. But here it means an extraordinary messenger, one sent by God himself to deliver the most important message on behalf of his Maker—in a word, one sent by the divine authority to preach the gospel to the nations. The word *kletos, called,* signifies here the same as "constituted," and should be joined with *apostolos,* as it is in the Greek, and translated thus: "Paul, a servant of Jesus Christ, constituted an apostle." This sense the word *called* has in many places of the sacred writings; e.g., "Behold, what manner of love the Father hath bestowed on us, that we should be called [constituted, or made] the sons of God." As it is likely that no apostle had been employed in founding the church at Rome, and there was need of much authority to settle the matters that were there in dispute, it was necessary he should show them that he derived his authority from God, and was immediately delegated by Him to preach and write as he was now doing. *Separated unto the gospel.* Set apart and appointed to this work, and to this only; as the Israelites were separate from all the people of the earth, to be the servants of God.

2. *Which he had promised afore.* Both in the

MATTHEW HENRY

II. Having mentioned the gospel of God, he digresses, to give us an encomium of it.

1. The antiquity of it. It was *promised before* (*v.* 2); it was of ancient standing in the promises and prophecies of the Old Testament.

2. The subject-matter of it: it is concerning Christ, *v.* 3, 4. The prophets and apostles all bear witness to him. When Paul mentions Christ, how he heaps up his names and titles, *his Son Jesus Christ our Lord.* He cannot go on in his discourse without some expression of love and honour, as here, where in one person he shows us his two distinct natures. (1) His human nature: *Made of the seed of David* (*v.* 3), that is, born of the virgin Mary, who was of the house of David (Luke i. 27). (2) His divine nature: *Declared to be the Son of God* (*v.* 4), *according to the Spirit of holiness. According to the flesh*, that is, his human nature, *he was of the seed of David;* but, *according to the Spirit of holiness*, that is, the divine nature, he is the Son of God. The great proof or demonstration of this is *his resurrection from the dead.* Those that would not be convinced by that would be convinced by nothing. So that we have here a summary of the gospel doctrine concerning Christ's two natures in one person.

3. The fruit of it (*v.* 5): *By whom we have received grace and apostleship.* Paul reckons the apostleship a favour. We may justly reckon it a great favour to be employed in any work or service for God. This apostleship was received *for obedience to the faith*, that is, to bring people to that obedience. Paul's was for this obedience *among all nations*, for he was the *apostle of the Gentiles.* Observe the description here given of the Christian profession: it is *obedience to the faith.* It does not consist in a notional knowledge, much less does it consist in perverse disputings, but in obedience. The act of faith is the obedience of the understanding to God revealing, and the product of that is the obedience of the will to God commanding. He here speaks of Christianity as an obedience. Christ has a yoke. "*Among whom are you*, *v.* 6. You Romans in this stand upon the same level with other Gentile nations of less fame and wealth; you are all one in Christ." No respect of persons with God. *The called of Jesus Christ;* all those, and those only, are brought to an obedience of the faith that are effectually called of Jesus Christ.

III. The persons to whom it is written (*v.* 7): *To all that are in Rome, beloved of God, called to be saints;* that is, to all the professing Christians that were in Rome, bond or free, learned or unlearned. Rich and poor meet together in Christ Jesus. The privilege of Christians: They are *beloved of God.* He hath a common love to all mankind and a peculiar love for true believers. The duty of Christians; and that is to be holy, for hereunto are they called, *called to be saints.* Saints, and only saints, are beloved of God with a special and peculiar love. *Called saints*, saints in profession; it were well if all that are called saints were saints indeed. It will be of little avail at the great day to have been called saints, if we be not really so.

IV. The apostolical benediction (*v.* 7): *Grace to you and peace.* It hath not only the affection of a good wish, but the authority of a blessing. The favours desired: *Grace and peace.* The Old Testament salutation was, *Peace be to you;* but now grace is prefixed—*grace*, that is, the favour of God towards us. All gospel blessings are included in these two: *grace and peace. Peace*, that is, all good. The fountain of those favours, *from God our Father, and the Lord Jesus Christ.* All good comes, From God as a Father. We are taught, when we come for grace and peace, to call him our Father. *From the Lord Jesus Christ*, as Mediator. We have them from his fulness, peace from the fulness of his merit, grace from the fulness of his Spirit.

Verses 8–15

I. His thanksgiving for them (*v.* 8): *First, I thank my God.* It is good to begin everything with blessing God. He speaks this with delight and triumph. *Through Jesus Christ.* All our duties and performances are pleasing to God only through Jesus Christ, praises as well as prayers.—*For you all.* We must express our love to our friends, not only by praying for them, but by praising God for them. When some of the Roman Christians met him (Acts xxviii. 15), he thanked God for them, and took courage; but here his true catholic love extends itself further, and he *thanks God for them all.—That your faith is spoken of.* Wherever he came he heard great commendations of the Christians at Rome, which he mentions, not to make them proud, but to quicken them to answer the general character people gave of them. The greater reputation a man hath for religion, the more careful he should be to preserve it.—*Throughout the whole world*, that is, the Roman

JAMIESON, FAUSSET, BROWN

had promised afore . . . in the holy scriptures—Though the Roman Church was Gentile by nation (see on vs. 13), yet as it consisted mostly of proselytes to the Jewish faith (see *Introduction* to this Epistle), they are here reminded that in embracing Christ they had not cast off, but only the more profoundly yielded themselves to, Moses and the prophets (Acts 13:32, 33). **3, 4. Concerning his Son Jesus Christ our Lord**—the grand burden of this "Gospel of God." **made of the seed of David**—as, according to "the holy scriptures," He behooved to be. (See on Matt. 1:1.) **according to the flesh**—i.e., in His *human* nature (cf. ch. 9:5, and John 1:14); implying, of course, that He had *another* nature, of which the apostle immediately proceeds to speak. **And declared**—lit., 'marked off,' 'defined,' 'determined,' i.e., 'shown,' or 'proved.' **to be the Son of God**—Observe how studiously the language changes here. He "*was* MADE [says the apostle] of the seed of David, according to the flesh"; but He was *not* made, He was only "*declared* [or proved] *to* BE the Son of God." So John 1:1, 14, "In the beginning WAS the Word . . . and the Word *was* MADE flesh"; and Isaiah 9:6, "Unto us *a Child* is BORN, unto us *a Son is* GIVEN." Thus the Sonship of Christ is in no proper sense a *born* relationship to the Father, as some, otherwise sound divines, conceive of it. By His birth in the flesh, that Sonship, which was essential and uncreated, merely effloresced into palpable manifestation. (See on Luke 1:35; Acts 13:32, 33.) **with power**—This may either be connected with "declared," and then the meaning will be 'powerfully declared' [LUTHER, BEZA, BENGEL, FRITZSCHE, ALFORD, etc.]; or (as in our version, and as we think rightly) with "the Son of God," and then the sense is, 'declared to be the Son of God in possession of that "power" which belonged to Him as the only-begotten of the Father, no longer shrouded as in the days of His flesh, but "by His resurrection from the dead" gloriously displayed and henceforth to be for ever exerted in this nature of ours" [VULGATE, CALVIN, HODGE, PHILIPPI, MEHRING, etc.]. **according to the spirit of holiness**—If "according to the flesh" means here, 'in His human nature,' this uncommon expression must mean 'in His *other* nature,' which we have seen to be that "of the Son of God"—an eternal, uncreated nature. This is here styled the "*spirit*," as an impalpable and immaterial nature (John 4:24), and "the spirit of *holiness*," probably in absolute contrast with that "likeness, of sinful flesh" which He assumed. One is apt to wonder that if this be the meaning, it was not expressed more simply. But if the apostle had said 'He was declared to be the Son of God according to *the Holy Spirit*,' the reader would have thought he meant '*the Holy Ghost*'; and it seems to have been just to avoid this misapprehension that he used the rare expression, "the spirit of holiness." **5. By whom**—as the ordained channel—**we have received grace**—the whole "grace that bringeth salvation"—**and apostleship**—for the publication of that "grace," and the organization of as many as receive it into churches of visible discipleship. (We prefer thus taking them as two distinct things, and not, with some good interpreters, as one—'the grace of apostleship.') **for obedience to the faith**—rather, 'for the obedience of faith'—i.e., in order to men's yielding themselves to the belief of God's saving message, which is the highest of all obedience. **for his name**—that He might be glorified. **6. Among whom are ye also**—i.e., along with others; for the apostle ascribes nothing special to the Church of Rome (cf. I Cor. 14:36) [BENGEL]. **the called**—see on ch. 8:30—**of Christ Jesus**—i.e., either called '*by* Him' (John 5:25), or the called '*belonging* to Him'; 'Christ's called ones.' Perhaps this latter sense is best supported, but one hardly knows which to prefer. **7. beloved of God**—(Cf. Deut. 33:12; Col. 3:12). **Grace . . .** (See on John 1:14). **and peace**—the peace which Christ made through the blood of His cross (Col. 1:20), and which reflects into the believing bosom . . . "the peace of God which passeth all understanding" (Phil. 4:7). **from God our Father, and the Lord Jesus Christ**—"Nothing speaks more decisively for the divinity of Christ than these juxtapositions of Christ with the eternal God, which run through the whole language of Scripture, and the derivation of purely divine influences from Him also. The name of no man can be placed by the side of the Almighty. He only, in whom the Word of the Father who is Himself God became flesh, may be named beside Him; for men are commanded to honor Him even as they honor the Father (John 5:23)" [OLSHAUSEN]. **8. your faith is spoken of throughout the whole world**—This was quite practicable through the frequent visits paid to the capital from all the provinces; and

ADAM CLARKE

law and in the prophets God showed His purpose to introduce into the world a more perfect and glorious state of things; which state was to take place by and under the influence of the Messiah, who should bring life and immortality to light by His gospel.

3. *Concerning his Son.* That is, the gospel relates everything concerning the conception, birth, preaching, miracles, passion, death, resurrection, and ascension of Jesus Christ, who was of the seed-royal, being, as far as His humanity was considered, the Son of David, and then the only rightful Heir to the Israelitish throne.

4. *And declared to be the Son of God.* The word which we render "declared" comes from *horizo*, to "bound, define, determine, or limit," and hence our word "horizon," the line that determines the farthest visible part of the earth, in reference to the heavens. In this place the word signifies such a manifest and complete exhibition of the subject as to render it indubitable. The resurrection of Christ from the dead was such a manifest proof of our Lord's innocence, the truth of His doctrine, and the fulfillment of all that the prophets had spoken, as to leave no doubt on any considerate and candid mind. *With power.* With a miraculous display of divine energy; for how could His body be raised again but by the miraculous energy of God?

According to the spirit of holiness. There are many differences of sentiment relative to the meaning of this phrase in this place; some supposing that the spirit of holiness implies the divine nature of Jesus Christ; others, His immaculate sanctity; etc. To me it seems that the apostle simply means that the Person called Jesus, lately crucified at Jerusalem, and in whose name salvation was preached to the world, was the Son of God, the very Messiah promised before in the Holy Scriptures; and that He was this Messiah was amply demonstrated. (1) By His resurrection from the dead, the irrefragable proof of His purity, innocence, and the divine approbation. (2) He was proved to be the Son of God, the promised Messiah, by the Holy Spirit (called here *the spirit of holiness*).

5. *Grace and apostleship.* The peculiar influence and the essential qualifications which such an office requires. *For obedience to the faith.* That by this office, which I have received from God, and the power by which it is accompanied, I might proclaim the *faith*, the gospel of Jesus; and show all nations the necessity of believing in it, in order to their salvation.

6. *Ye are also the called.* You Romans are all invited to believe in Christ Jesus, for the salvation of your souls; and to you, with the rest, my apostolical mission extends. This appears to be the most obvious sense of the word *called* in this place—to be called by the gospel is to be invited to believe in Christ Jesus, and become His disciples. The word sometimes means "constituted," or "made," as in v. 1.

7. *Called to be saints.* Invited to become holy persons, by believing the gospel and receiving the gifts of the Holy Ghost. Or, here, the word may have the meaning of "made" or "constituted," as above. *Grace to you.* May you be partakers of the divine favor, the source whence every blessing is derived. *And peace.* The same as *shalom* in Hebrew, generally signifying all kinds of blessing, but especially harmony and unity, and the bond of such unity. *From God our Father.* The apostle wishes them all the blessings which can flow from God, as the Fountain of grace, producing in them all the happiness which a heart filled with the peace of God can possess; all of which are to be communicated to them through the Lord Jesus Christ.

8. *First, I thank my God.* From this to the end of v. 17 belongs to the preface, in which the apostle endeavors to conciliate the good opinion of the Christians at Rome, and to prepare their

MATTHEW HENRY

empire. This was indeed a good name, a name for good things with God and good people. It is a desirable thing to be famous for faith. Rome was a city upon a hill, everyone took notice of what was done there. Thus those who have many eyes upon them have need to walk circumspectly, for what they do, good or bad, will be spoken of.

II. His prayer for them, *v.* 9. Though a famous flourishing church, yet they had need to be prayed for. One of the greatest kindnesses we can do our friends, and sometimes the only kindness that is in the power of our hands, is, by prayer to recommend them to the loving-kindness of God. From Paul's example here we may learn, Constancy in prayer: *Always without ceasing.* Charity in prayer: *I make mention of you.* He made express mention of them. It is not unfit sometimes to be express in our prayers for particular churches and places; not to inform God, but to affect ourselves. We are likely to have the most comfort in those friends that we pray most for. He makes a solemn appeal to the searcher of hearts: *For God is my witness.* It is very comfortable to be able to call God to witness to our constancy in the discharge of a duty. God is particularly a witness to our secret prayers. *God, whom I serve with my spirit.* Those that serve God with their spirits may, with a humble confidence, appeal to him; hypocrites who rest in bodily exercise cannot. His particular prayer was that he might have an opportunity of paying them a visit (*v.* 10): *Making request, if by any means,* &c. The expressions here used intimate that he was very desirous of such an opportunity: *if by any means;* that he had long and often been disappointed: *now at length;* and yet that he submitted it to the divine Providence: *a prosperous journey by the will of God.* Our journeys are prosperous or otherwise according to the will of God, comfortable or not as he pleases.

III. His great desire to see them, with the reasons of it, *v.* 11–15. Fruitful Christians are as much the joy as barren professors are the grief of faithful ministers. Accordingly, he *often purposed to come, but was let hitherto* (*v.* 13), for man purposeth, but God disposeth. Paul was for doing that first, not which was most pleasant (then he would have gone to Rome), but which was most needful.

1. That they might be edified (*v.* 11): *That I may impart unto you.* He received, that he might communicate. *To the end you may be established.* That as they grew upward in the branches they might grow downward in the root. The best saints have need to be more and more established.

2. That he might be comforted, *v.* 12. What he heard of their flourishing in grace was so much a joy to him that it must needs be much more so to behold it.—*By the mutual faith both of you and me.* It is very comfortable when there is a mutual confidence between minister and people, they confiding in him as a faithful minister, and he in them as a faithful people. It is very refreshing to Christians to compare notes about their spiritual concerns.—*That I might have some fruit, v.* 13. The more good he did the greater would his reward be.

3. That he might discharge his trust as the apostle of the Gentiles (*v.* 14): *I am a debtor.* His receivings made him a debtor. We should think of this when we covet great things, that all our receivings put us in debt; we are but stewards of our Lord's goods. His office made him a debtor. Paul had improved his talent, and laboured in his work, and done as much good as ever any man did, and yet, he still writes himself debtor.—*Debtor to the Greeks, and to the barbarians, to the wise and to the unwise.* The Greeks fancied themselves to have the monopoly of wisdom, and looked upon all the rest of the world as barbarians. Paul was a debtor to both, and looked upon himself as obliged to do all the good he could both to the one and to the other. Accordingly, we find him paying his debt, doing good *both to Greeks and barbarians.* For these reasons he was ready, if he had an opportunity, *to preach the gospel at Rome, v.* 15. Paul was ready to run the risk at Rome, if called to it: *I am ready.* It denotes a great readiness of mind. What he did was not for filthy lucre, but of a ready mind.

Verses 16–18

Paul here enters upon a large discourse of justification, describing the deplorable condition of the Gentile world. He was ready to preach the gospel at Rome, *for, I am not ashamed of it, v.* 16. There is a great deal in the gospel which such a man as Paul might be tempted to be ashamed of, especially that he whose gospel it was is a man hanged upon a tree. Yet Paul was not ashamed to own it. I reckon him a Christian indeed that is neither ashamed of the gospel nor a shame to it.

JAMIESON, FAUSSET, BROWN

the apostle, having an eye to the influence they would exercise upon others, as well as their own blessedness, given thanks for such faith to "his God through Jesus Christ," as being the source, according to his theology of faith, as of all grace in men.

9. For God . . . whom I serve—the word denotes religious service—**with my spirit**—from my inmost soul—**in the gospel of his Son**—to which Paul's whole religious life and official activity were consecrated—**is my witness, that without ceasing I make mention of you always in my prayers**—so for the Ephesians (Eph. 1:15, 15); so for the Philippians (Phil. 1:3, 4); so for the Colossians (Col. 1:3, 4); so for the Thessalonians (I Thess. 1:2, 3). What catholic love, what all-absorbing spirituality, what impassioned devotion to the glory of Christ among men!

10. Making request, if by any means now at length I may have a prosperous journey by the will of God, to come to you—Though long anxious to visit the capital, he met with a number of providential hindrances (vs. 13; ch. 15:22; and see on Acts 19:21; 23:11, 28:15); insomuch that *nearly a quarter of a century* elapsed, after his conversion, ere his desire was accomplished, and that only as "a prisoner of Jesus Christ." Thus taught that his whole future was in the hands of God, he makes it his continual prayer that at length the obstacles to a happy and prosperous meeting might be removed.

11, 12. For I long to see you, that I may impart to you some spiritual gift—not any supernatural gift, as the next clause shows, and cf. I Corinthians 1:7. **to the end that ye may be established; That is, that I may be comforted together with you by the mutual faith both of you and me**—"Not wishing to 'lord it over their faith,' but rather to be a 'helper of their joy,' the apostle corrects his former expressions: my desire is to instruct you and do you good, that is, for us to instruct and do one another good: in giving I shall also receive" [JOWETT]. "Nor is he insincere in so speaking, for there is none so poor in the Church of Christ who may not impart to us something of value: it is only our malignity and pride that hinder us from gathering such fruit from every quarter" [CALVIN]. How "widely different is the apostolic style from that of the court of Papal Rome!" [BENGEL.] **13. oftentimes I purposed to come unto you, but was let**—hindered—**hitherto**—chiefly by his desire to go first to places where Christ was not known (ch. 15:20-24). **that I might have some fruit**—of my ministry—**among you also, even as among other Gentiles**—The GENTILE origin of the Church at Rome is here so explicitly stated, that those who conclude, merely from the Jewish strain of the argument, that they must have been mostly Israelites, decide in opposition to the apostle himself. (But see *Introduction* to this Epistle.) **14, 15. I am debtor both to the**—cultivated—**Greeks and to the**—rude—**Barbarians . . . So, as much as in me is, I am ready to preach the gospel to you that are at Rome also**—He feels himself under an all-subduing obligation to carry the gospel to all classes of mankind, as adapted to and ordained equally for all (I Cor. 9:16).

16. For I am not ashamed of the gospel—(The words, "of Christ," which follow here, are not found in the oldest and best MSS.) This language implies that it required some courage to bring to 'the mistress of the world' what "to the Jews was a stumbling block and to the Greeks foolishness." But its inherent glory, as God's life-giving message to a dying world, so filled his soul, that, like his blessed Master, he "despised the shame."

ADAM CLARKE

minds for his reproofs and exhortations. *Your faith is spoken of,* is celebrated, *throughout the whole world*—in every place where the Christian religion is professed, through all parts of the Roman dominions; for in this sense we should understand the words *the whole world.*

9. *Whom I serve with my spirit.* Whom "I worship with the profoundest religious reverence," for so the original certainly means. I not only employ all the powers of my body in this service, but all those of my soul, being thoroughly convinced of the absolute truth of the religion I preach.

10. *Making request.* By this we see how earnestly the apostle longed to see Rome. It had long been a subject of continual prayer to God that he might have *a prosperous journey* to, or rather "meeting" with, them.

11. *Some spiritual gift.* This probably means some of the extraordinary gifts of the Holy Spirit, which, being given to them, might tend greatly to establish their faith in the gospel of Christ. It is very likely that such gifts were conferred only by means of apostles; and as the apostle had not yet been at Rome, consequently the Roman Christians had not yet received any of these miraculous gifts, and thus they differed widely from all the other churches which had been raised by the apostle's ministry.

13. *But was let hitherto.* The word *let,* from the Anglo-Saxon, *lettan,* to "hinder," signifies impediment or hindrance of any kind. But it is likely that the original word, "I was forbidden," refers to a divine prohibition; he would have visited them long before, but God did not see right to permit him.

14. *I am debtor both to the Greeks, and to the Barbarians.* All the nations of the earth, themselves excepted, were termed *Barbarians* by the Greeks.

15. *I am ready to preach.* I have a ready mind. I was prevented only by the providence of God from visiting you long ago.

16. *I am not ashamed of the gospel of Christ.* This text is best illustrated by Isa. xxviii. 16; xlix. 23, quoted by the apostle, chap. x. 11: "For the scripture saith, Whosoever believeth on him shall not be confounded nor disappointed of their hope.

MATTHEW HENRY

I. The proposition, *v.* 16, 17. It reveals to us,

1. The salvation of believers as the end: *It is the power of God unto salvation.* Paul is not ashamed of the gospel; it shows us *the way of salvation. It is through the power of God;* without that power the gospel is but a dead letter. It is to those, and those only, that believe. The medicine prepared will not cure the patient if it be not taken.—*To the Jew first. The lost sheep of the house of Israel* had the first offer made them, both by Christ and his apostles. Upon their refusal the apostles turned to the Gentiles, Acts xiii. 46. Jews and Gentiles now stand upon the same level, both equally welcome to the Saviour. The long-expected Messiah proves *a light to enlighten the Gentiles,* as well as *the glory of his people Israel.*

2. The justification of believers as the way (*v.* 17): *For therein is the righteousness of God revealed.* That which will show us the way of salvation must needs show us the way of justification. The gospel makes known a righteousness. There is such a righteousness *revealed in the gospel.* This evangelical righteousness, (1) Is called the *righteousness of God*; it is of God's appointing. It is so called to cut off all pretensions to a righteousness resulting from the merit of our own works. It is the righteousness of Christ. (2) It is said to be *from faith to faith.* From the first faith, by which we are put into a justified state, to after faith, by which we live; from faith engrafting us into Christ, to faith deriving virtue from him as our root: both implied in the next words, *The just shall live by faith. Just by faith,* there is faith justifying us; *live by faith,* there is faith maintaining us. Faith is all in all, both in the beginning and progress of a Christian life. It is increasing, continuing, persevering faith. To show that this is no novel upstart doctrine, he quotes for it that famous scripture in the Old Testament: *The just shall live by faith.* Being justified by faith he shall live by it both the life of grace and of glory. Thus is the evangelical righteousness from faith to faith—from Old Testament faith in a Christ to come to New Testament faith in a Christ already come.

A. T. ROBERTSON:

"A righteousness of God" (*dikaiosune theou*). Subjective genitive, "a God kind of righteousness," one that each must have and can obtain in no other way save "from faith unto faith" (*ek pisteos eis pistin*), faith the starting point and faith the goal (Lightfoot). "Is revealed" (*apokaluptetai*). It is a revelation from God, this God kind of righteousness, that man unaided could never have conceived or still less attained. In these words we have Paul's statement in his own way of the theme of the Epistle, the content of the gospel as Paul understands it. Every word is important: *soterian* (salvation), *euaggelion* (gospel), *apokaluptetai* (is revealed), *dikaiosune theou* (righteousness of God), *pistis* (faith), and *pisteuonti* (believing). He grounds his position on Hab. 2:4 (quoted also in Gal. 3:11). By "righteousness" we shall see that Paul means both "justification" and "sanctification." It is important to get a clear idea of Paul's use of *dikaiosune* here, for it controls the thought throughout the Epistle. Jesus set up a higher standard of righteousness (*dikaiosune*) in the Sermon on the Mount than the scribes and Pharisees taught and practiced (Matt. 5:20) and proves it in various items. Here Paul claims that in the gospel, taught by Jesus and by himself, there is revealed a God kind of righteousness with two ideas in it (the righteousness that God has and that He bestows). It is an old word for quality from *dikaios*, a righteous man, and that from *dike*, right or justice (called a goddess in Acts 28:4), and that allied with *deiknumi*, to show, to point out.

—*Word Pictures in the New Testament*

JAMIESON, FAUSSET, BROWN

for IT IS THE POWER OF GOD UNTO SALVATION TO EVERY ONE THAT BELIEVETH—Here and in the next verse the apostle announces the great theme of his ensuing argument; SALVATION, the one overwhelming necessity of perishing men; this revealed IN THE GOSPEL MESSAGE; and that message so *owned and honored of God as to carry,* in the proclamation of it, GOD'S OWN POWER TO SAVE EVERY SOUL THAT EMBRACES IT, Greek and Barbarian, wise and unwise alike. **17. For therein is the righteousness of God revealed**—that is (as the whole argument of the Epistle shows), GOD'S JUSTIFYING RIGHTEOUSNESS. **from faith to faith**—a difficult clause. Most interpreters (judging from the sense of such phrases elsewhere) take it to mean, 'from one degree of faith to another.' But this agrees ill with the apostle's design, which has nothing to do with the progressive stages of faith, but solely with faith itself as the appointed way of receiving God's "righteousness." We prefer, therefore, to understand it thus: 'The righteousness of God is in the gospel message, revealed (to be) from (or "by") faith to (or "for") faith,' that is, 'in order to be by faith received.' (So substantially, MELVILLE, MEYER, STUART, BLOOMFIELD, etc.). **as it is written**—Habakkuk 2:4—**The just shall live by faith**—This golden maxim of the Old Testament is thrice quoted in the New Testament—here; Galatians 3:11; Hebrews 10:38—showing that the gospel way of 'LIFE BY FAITH,' so far from disturbing, only continued and developed the ancient method. On the foregoing verses, note (1) What manner of persons ought the ministers of Christ to be, according to the pattern here set up: absolutely subject and officially dedicated to the Lord Jesus; separated unto the gospel of God, which contemplates the subjugation of all nations to the faith of Christ: debtors to all classes, the refined and the rude, to bring the gospel to them all alike, all shame in the presence of the one, as well as pride before the other, sinking before the glory which they feel to be in their message; yearning over all faithful churches, not lording it over them, but rejoicing in their prosperity, and finding refreshment and strength in their fellowship! (2) The peculiar features of the gospel here brought prominently forward should be the devout study of all who preach it, and guide the views and the taste of all who are privileged statedly to hear it: that it is "the gospel of God," as a message from heaven, yet not absolutely new, but on the contrary, only the fulfilment of Old Testament promise, that not only is Christ the great theme of it, but Christ in the very nature of God as His own Son, and in the nature of men as partaker of their flesh—the Son of God now in resurrection-power and invested with authority to dispense all grace to men, and all gifts for the establishment and edification of the Church, Christ the righteousness provided of God for the justification of all that believe in His name; and that in this glorious Gospel, when preached as such, there resides the very power of God to save Jew and Gentile alike who embrace it. (3) While Christ is to be regarded as the ordained *Channel* of all grace from God to men (vs. 8), let none imagine that His proper divinity is in any respect compromised by this arrangement, since He is here expressly associated with "God the Father," in prayer for "grace and peace" (including all spiritual blessings) to rest upon this Church (vs. 7). (4) While this Epistle teaches, in conformity with the teaching of our Lord Himself, that all salvation is suspended upon *faith,* this is but half a truth, and will certainly minister to self-righteousness, if dissociated from another feature of the same truth, here explicitly taught, that this faith is *God's own gift*—for which accordingly in the case of the Roman believers, he "thanks his God through Jesus Christ" (vs. 8). (5) Christian fellowship, as indeed all real fellowship, is a mutual benefit; and as it is not possible for the most eminent saints and servants of Christ to impart any refreshment and profit to the meanest of their brethren without experiencing a rich return into their bosoms, so just in proportion to their humility and love will they feel their need of it and rejoice in it.

ADAM CLARKE

It is the power of God unto salvation. The almighty power of God accompanies this preaching to the souls of them that believe; and the consequence is they are saved; and what but the power of God can save a fallen, sinful soul? *To the Jew first.* Not only the Jews have the first offer of this gospel, but they have the greatest need of it; being so deeply fallen, and having sinned against such glorious privileges, they are much more culpable than the Gentiles, who never had the light of a divine revelation. *And also to the Greek.* Though the salvation of God has hitherto been apparently confined to the Jewish people, yet it shall be so no longer; for the gospel of Christ is sent to the Gentiles as well as the Jews, God having put no difference between them, and Jesus Christ having tasted death for every man.

17. *For therein.* In the gospel of Christ. *Is the righteousness of God.* God's method of saving sinners. *Revealed from faith to faith.* Shown to be by *faith,* and not by the works of any law. That *righteousness* signifies God's method of saving mankind by faith in Christ is fully evident from the use of the term in chap. ix. 30: "The Gentiles, which followed not after righteousness"—who had no knowledge, by revelation, of God's method of justifying and saving sinners, "have attained to righteousness"—have had imparted to them God's method of salvation by faith in Christ. V. 31: "But Israel," the Jews, "which followed after the law of righteousness"—that law, the end or object of which is Christ, and through Him justification to all that believe (chap. x. 4)—"hath not attained to the law of righteousness"—have not found out the genuine plan of salvation, even in that law which so strongly and generally proclaims justification by faith. And why have they not found it? V. 32: "Because they sought it not by faith, but as it were by the works of the law"—they did not discern that even its works or prescribed religious observances were intended to lead to faith in that glorious Mediator of whom they were the types and representatives; but the Jews trusted in the observances themselves, hoping to acquire justification and final salvation by that means. "For they stumbled at that stumblingstone"—at the doctrine of Christ crucified as the only sure ground on which the expectation of future salvation can be founded. Therefore, "being ignorant of God's righteousness"—God's method of saving sinners—"and going about to establish their own righteousness"—their own method of salvation, by the observance of those rites and ceremonies which should have led them by faith to Christ—they did not submit "themselves unto the righteousness of God"—they would not submit to be saved in God's way, and therefore rejected, persecuted, and crucified the Lord Jesus; see chap. x. 3. This collation of passages most evidently shows that the word *righteousness* here means simply God's method of saving sinners, or God's way of salvation, in opposition to the ways and means invented by the fancies or prejudices of men. There are few words in the sacred writings which are taken in a greater variety of acceptations than the word *tsedakah* in Hebrew, and *dikaiosyne* in Greek, both of which we generally translate *righteousness.* Our English word was originally "rightwiseness," and thus the righteous man was a person who was allowed to understand the claims of justice and right, and who, knowing them, acted according to their dictates. Such a man is thoroughly wise; he aims at the attainment of the best end by the use of the best means. This is a true definition of wisdom, and the righteous man is he that knows most and acts best. The Hebtew *tsadak,* in its ideal meaning, contains the notion of a beam or scales in equipoise, what we call "even balance." *The just shall live by faith.* This has been understood two ways: (1) That the just or righteous man cannot live a holy and useful life without exercising continual faith in our Lord Jesus—which is strictly true. (2) It is contended by some able critics that the words of the original text should be: "The just by faith, shall live"; that is, he alone that is justified by faith shall be saved—which is also true, as it is impossible to get salvation in any other way. This last meaning is probably the true one, as the original text in Hab. ii. 4 speaks of those who believed the declarations of God when the Chaldeans besieged Jerusalem, and, having acted con-

MATTHEW HENRY

II. The proof of this proposition. Justification must be either by faith or works. It cannot be by works, and therefore he concludes it must be by faith. The apostle, like a skilful surgeon, before he applies the plaster, searches the wound—endeavours first to convince of guilt and wrath, and then to show the way of salvation. This makes the gospel the more welcome. In general (*v.* 18), *the wrath of God is revealed.* The light of nature and the light of the law reveal the wrath of God from sin to sin. It is well for us that the gospel reveals the justifying righteousness of God from faith to faith.

1. The sinfulness of man described; he reduceth it to two heads, *ungodliness and unrighteousness.*

2. The cause of that sinfulness, and that is, *holding the truth in unrighteousness.* Some ideas they had of the difference of good and evil; but they held them in unrighteousness. They held the truth as a captive or prisoner, that it should not influence them. An unrighteous wicked heart is the dungeon in which many a good truth is detained and buried.

3. The displeasure of God against it: *The wrath of God is revealed from heaven;* not only in the written word, but in the providences of God, his judgments executed upon sinners. They are a revelation from heaven. Or *wrath from heaven is revealed*; it is not the wrath of a man like ourselves, *but wrath from heaven,* therefore the more terrible.

Verses 19–32

I. The means and helps they had to come to the knowledge of God. Among them *he left not himself without witness* (Acts xiv. 17).

1. What discoveries they had: *That which may be known of God is manifest among them;* that is, there were some even among them that had the knowledge of God. *That which may be known,* which implies that there is a great deal which may not be known. The being of God may be apprehended, but cannot be comprehended. Finite understandings cannot perfectly know an infinite being; but, there is that which may be known.

2. Whence they had these discoveries: *God hath shown it to them.* Those common natural notions which they had of God were imprinted upon their hearts by the God of nature himself.

3. By what means these discoveries were confirmed, namely, by the work of creation (*v.* 20): *For the invisible things of God,* &c.

(1) Observe what they knew: *The invisible things of him, even his eternal power and Godhead.* The power and Godhead of God are invisible things, and yet are clearly seen in their products. He works in secret but manifests what he has wrought, and therein makes known his power and Godhead. They did come to the knowledge of the Godhead, at least so much knowledge as was sufficient to have kept them from idolatry. This was that truth which they held in unrighteousness.

(2) How they knew it: *By the things that are made,* which could not make themselves; and therefore must have been produced by some first cause or intelligent agent, which first cause could be no other than an eternal powerful God. The workman is known by his work. The concurrence of all the parts to the good and beauty of the whole, do abundantly prove a Creator and his eternal power and Godhead. Thus did the light shine in the darkness. And *this from the creation of the world.* To evince this truth, we have recourse to the great work of creation. The date of the discovery. It is as old as the creation of the world. These notices concerning God are ancient truths. The way of the acknowledgment of God is a good old way; it was from the beginning. Truth got the start of error.

II. Their gross idolatry, *v.* 21–23, 25. We shall the less wonder at the inefficacy of these natural discoveries to prevent the idolatry of the Gentiles if we remember how prone even the Jews were to idolatry; so miserably are the degenerate sons of men plunged in the mire of sense.

1. The inward cause of their idolatry, *v.* 21, 22. They are therefore without excuse, in that they did know God. Though some have greater light and means of knowledge than others, yet all have enough to leave them inexcusable. They *glorified him not as God.* To glorify him as God is to glorify him only; but they did not so glorify him, for they set up a multitude of other deities. To glorify him as God is to worship him with spiritual worship; but they made images of him. Not to glorify God as God is in effect not to glorify him at all. *Neither were they thankful.* Insensibleness of God's mercies is at the bottom of our sinful departures from him. *But they became vain in their imaginations, in their reasonings,* in their practical inferences. They had a great deal of knowledge of general truths (*v.* 19), but no prudence to

JAMIESON, FAUSSET, BROWN

18. WHY THIS DIVINELY PROVIDED RIGHTEOUSNESS IS NEEDED BY ALL MEN. **For the wrath of God**—His holy displeasure and righteous vengeance against sin—**is revealed from heaven**—in the consciences of men, and attested bv innumerable outward evidences of a moral government. **against all ungodliness**—i.e., their whole *irreligiousness,* or their living without any conscious reference to God, and proper feelings towards Him. **and unrighteousness of men**—i.e., all their *deviations from moral rectitude* in heart, speech, and behavior. (So these terms must be distinguished when used together, though, when standing alone, either of them includes the other.)

18-32. THIS WRATH OF GOD, REVEALED AGAINST ALL INIQUITY, OVERHANGS THE WHOLE HEATHEN WORLD. **18. who hold**—rather, 'hold down,' 'hinder,' or 'keep back'—**the truth in unrighteousness**—The apostle, though he began this verse with a comprehensive proposition regarding men in general, takes up in the end of it only one of the two great divisions of mankind, to whom he meant to apply it; thus gently sliding into his argument. But before enumerating their actual iniquities, he goes back to the origin of them all, their stifling the light which still remained to them. As darkness overspreads the mind, so impotence takes possession of the heart, when the "still small voice" of conscience is first disregarded, next thwarted, and then systematically deadened. Thus "the truth" which God left with and in men, instead of having free scope and developing itself, as it otherwise would, was obstructed (cf. Matt. 6:22, 23; Eph. 4:17, 18). **19. Because that which may be**—rather, 'which is'—**known of God is manifest in them; for God hath showed it unto them**—The sense of this pregnant statement the apostle proceeds to unfold in the next verse.

20. For the invisible things of him from—or 'since'—**the creation of the world are clearly seen**—the mind brightly beholding what the eye cannot discern—**being understood by the things that are made**—Thus, the outward creation is not the *parent* but the *interpreter* of our faith in God. That faith has its primary sources within our own breast (vs. 19); but it becomes *an intelligible and articulate conviction* only through what we observe around us ("by the things which are made," vs. 20). And thus are the inner and the outer revelation of God the complement of each other, making up between them one universal and immovable conviction *that God is.* (With this striking apostolic statement agree the latest conclusions of the most profound speculative students of Theism.) **even his eternal power and Godhead**—both that there *is* an Eternal Power, and that this is not a mere blind force, or pantheistic 'spirit of nature,' but the power of a living *Godhead.* **so that they are without excuse**—all their degeneracy being a voluntary departure from truth thus brightly revealed to the unsophisticated spirit.

21. Because that, when they knew God—that is, while still retaining some real knowledge of Him, and ere they sank down into the state next to be described—**they glorified him not as God, neither were thankful**—neither yielded the *adoration* due to Himself, nor rendered the *gratitude* which His beneficence demanded—**but became vain**—(cf. Jer. 2:5)—**in their imaginations**—thoughts, notions, speculations, regarding God; cf. Matt. 15:19; Luke 2:35; I Cor. 3:20, Greek—**and their foolish**—'senseless,' 'stupid'—**heart**—i.e., their whole inner man—**was darkened**—How instructively is the downward progress of the human soul here traced!

ADAM CLARKE

formably to them, escaped with their lives.

18. *For the wrath of God is revealed.* The apostle has now finished his preface, and comes to the grand subject of the Epistle; namely, to show the absolute need of the gospel of Christ, because of the universal corruption of mankind, which was so great as to incense the justice of God and call aloud for the punishment of the world. (1) He shows that all the heathen nations were utterly corrupt, and deserved this threatened punishment. And this is the subject of the first chapter, from v. 18 to the end. (2) He shows that the Jews, notwithstanding the greatness of their privileges, were no better than the Gentiles: and therefore the wrath of God was revealed against them also. This subject he treats in chap. ii. and chap. iii. 1-19. (3) He returns, as it were, on both, chap. iii. 20-31, and proves that, as the Jews and Gentiles were equally corrupt, they could not be saved by the deeds of any law; that they stood equally in need of that salvation which God had provided; that both were equally entitled to that salvation, for God was the God of the Gentiles as well as of the Jews. By *the wrath of God* we are not to understand any uneasy passion in the Divine Being; but the displeasure of His righteousness, which is expressed by the punishments inflicted on the ungodly, those who retain not God in their knowledge; and the unrighteous, those whose lives are profligate. As in the gospel the righteousness of God is *revealed* for the salvation of the ungodly, so is the wrath of God *revealed* against the workers of iniquity. Those who refuse to be saved in the way revealed by His mercy must be consumed in the way revealed by His justice. *Ungodliness.* Probably intended here to express atheism, polytheism, and idolatry of every kind. *Unrighteousness.* Everything contrary to strict morality; all viciousness and profligacy of conduct. *Who hold the truth in unrighteousness.* Some contend that the word here does not signify to *hold,* but to "hinder"; and that the place should be translated, "who through maliciousness hinder the truth"; i.e., prevent it from taking hold of their hearts, and from governing their conduct. This is certainly a very usual acceptation of the verb.

20. *The invisible things of him.* His invisible perfections are manifested by His visible works, and may be apprehended by what He has made; their immensity showing His omnipotence; their vast variety, His omniscience; and their adaptation to the most beneficent purposes, His infinite goodness. *His eternal power.* That all-powerful energy that ever was and ever will exist; so that, ever since there was a creation to be surveyed, there have been intelligent beings to make that survey. *And Godhead.* His acting as God in the government and support of the universe. His works prove His being.

21. *Because that, when they knew God.* When they thus acquired a general knowledge of the unity and perfections of the divine nature, *they glorified him not as God*—they did not proclaim Him to the people, but shut up His glory (as Bishop Warburton expresses it) in their mysteries, and gave the people, in exchange for an incorruptible God, an image made like to corruptible man. *They glorified him not.* They did not give Him that worship which His perfections required. *Neither were thankful.* They manifested no gratitude for the blessings they received from His providence but *became vain in their imagination,* "in their reasonings." This certainly refers to the foolish manner in which even the wisest of their philosophers discoursed about the divine nature, not excepting Socrates, Plato, or Seneca.

MATTHEW HENRY

apply them to particular cases. They soon disputed themselves into a thousand vain and foolish fancies. When truth is forsaken, errors multiply. *And their foolish heart was darkened.* The foolishness and practical wickedness of the heart cloud and darken the intellectual powers and faculties. *Professing themselves to be wise, they became fools, v.* 22. Those that had the most luxuriant fancy, in framing to themselves the idea of a God, fell into the most gross and absurd conceits. Thus the *world by wisdom knew not God.* A proud conceit of wisdom is the cause of a great deal of folly. Paul's preaching was no where so laughed at and ridiculed as among the learned Athenians—*conceiting themselves* to be wise. The plain truth of the being of God would not content them; they thought themselves above that, and so fell into the greatest errors.

2. The outward acts of their idolatry, *v.* 23–25. (1) Making images of God (*v.* 23), by which they *changed the glory of the incorruptible God.* It was the greatest honour God did to man that he made man in the image of God; but it is the greatest dishonour man has done to God that he has made God in the image of man. This is called (*v.* 25) *changing the truth of God into a lie.* Idols are called lies, for they belie God, as if he had a body, whereas he is a Spirit. (2) Giving divine honour to the creature: *Worshipped and served the creature, besides the Creator.* They did in effect disown him by the worship they paid to the creature; for God will be all or none. Or, *above* the Creator, thinking the supreme God inaccessible. The sin itself was their worshipping the creature at all; but this is mentioned as an aggravation of the sin, that they worshipped the creature more than the Creator. This was the general wickedness of the Gentile world. Even the wise men among them, who knew and owned a supreme God and were convinced of the nonsense and absurdity of their polytheism and idolatry, yet did as the rest of their neighbours did. I mention this because methinks it doth fully explain that of the apostle here (*v.* 18): *Who hold the truth in unrighteousness.* Upon the mention of the dishonour done to God by the idolatry of the Gentiles the apostle expresses himself in an awful adoration of God: *Who is blessed for ever. Amen.* When we see or hear of any contempt cast upon God or his name, we should think and speak highly and honourably of him. In this as in other things, the worse others are, the better we should be.

III. The judgments of God upon them for this idolatry; not many temporal judgments but spiritual judgments, giving them up to the most brutish and unnatural lusts. *He gave them up;* it is thrice repeated here, *v.* 24, 26, 28. Spiritual judgments are of all judgments the sorest. By whom they were given up. God gave them up, in a way of righteous judgment, leaving them to themselves—letting them alone; for his grace is his own, he may give or withhold his grace at pleasure. This we are sure of that it is no new thing for God to give men up to their own hearts' lusts. And yet God is not the author of sin, for, though the greatest wickedness follow upon this giving up, the fault of that is to be laid upon the sinner's wicked heart. If the patient will not submit to the methods prescribed, but wilfully does that which is prejudicial to him, the physician is not to be blamed. The fatal symptoms that follow are not to be imputed to the physician, but to the disease itself and to the folly of the patient. To what they were given up.

1. *To uncleanness and vile affections, v.* 24, 26, 27. It is (as it is said here) *through the lusts of their own hearts*—there all the fault is to be laid. Those who dishonoured God were given up to dishonour themselves. A man cannot be delivered up to a greater slavery than to be given up to his own lusts. The particular instances of their uncleanness and vile affections are their unnatural lusts, for which many of the heathen, even of those among them who passed for wise men, were infamous. Perhaps the apostle especially refers to the abominations that were committed in the worship of their idol-gods. Dunghill service for dunghill gods. See what wickedness there is in the nature of man. How much are we beholden to the restraining grace of God! For, were it not for this, man, who was made but little lower than the angels, would make himself a great deal lower than the devils. This is said to be that *recompence of their error which was meet.*

JAMIESON, FAUSSET, BROWN

23. **Professing themselves**—'boasting,' or 'pretending to be—**wise, they became fools**—"It is the invariable property of error in morals and religion, that men take credit to themselves for it and extol it as wisdom. So the heathen" (I Cor. 1:21) [THOLUCK]. **and changed** —or 'exchanged'—**the glory of the uncorruptible God into**—or 'for'—**an image . . . like to corruptible man**—The allusion here is doubtless to the *Greek* worship, and the apostle may have had in his mind those exquisite chisellings of the human form which lay so profusely beneath and around him as he stood on Mars' Hill; and "beheld their devotions." (See on Acts 17:29.) But as if that had not been a deep enough degradation of the living God, there was found 'a lower deep' still. **and to birds, and four-footed beasts, and to creeping things**—referring now to the *Egyptian* and *Oriental* worship. In the face of these plain declarations of the *descent* of man's religious belief from loftier to ever lower and more debasing conceptions of the Supreme Being, there are expositors of this very Epistle (as REICHE and JOWETT), who, believing neither in any fall from primeval innocence, nor in the noble traces of that innocence which lingered even after the fall and were only by degrees obliterated by wilful violence to the dictates of conscience, maintain that man's religious history has been all along a struggle to *rise,* from the lowest forms of nature worship, suited to the childhood of our race, into that which is more rational and spiritual.

25. **Who changed the truth of God into a lie**—i.e., the truth concerning God into idol falsehood. **and worshipped and served the creature more than the Creator**—Professing merely to worship the Creator *by means of* the creature, they soon came to lose sight of the Creator *in* the creature. How aggravated is the guilt of the Church of Rome, which, under the same flimsy pretext, does shamelessly what the heathen are here condemned for doing, and with light which the heathen never had! **who is blessed for ever! Amen**—By this doxology the apostle instinctively relieves the horror which the penning of such things excited within his breast; an example to such as are called to expose like dishonor done to the blessed God.

Wherefore God also—in righteous retribution—**gave them up**—This divine abandonment of men is here strikingly traced in three successive stages, at each of which the same word is used (vs. 24; vs. 26; and vs. 28, where the word is rendered "gave over"). "As they deserted God, God in turn deserted them; not giving them divine (i.e., supernatural) laws, and suffering them to corrupt those which were human; not sending them prophets, and allowing the philosophers to run into absurdities. He let them do what they pleased, even what was in the last degree vile, that those who had not honored God, might dishonor themselves" [GROTIUS].

26, 27. **For this cause God gave them up**—See on vs. 24. **for even their women**—that sex whose priceless jewel and fairest ornament is modesty, and which, when that is once lost, not only becomes more shameless than the other sex, but lives henceforth only to drag the other sex down to its level. **did change . . .**—The practices here referred to, though too abundantly attested by classic authors, cannot be further illustrated, without trenching on things which "ought not to be named among us as become the saints." But observe how vice is here seen consuming and exhausting itself. When the passions, scourged by violent and continued indulgence in *natural* vices, became impotent to yield the craved enjoyment, resort was had to artificial stimulants by the practice of *unnatural* and monstrous vices. How early these were in full career, in the history of the world, the case of Sodom affectingly shows; and because of such abominations, centuries after that, the land of Canaan "spued out" its old inhabitants. Long before this chapter was penned, the Lesbians and others throughout refined Greece had been luxuriating in such debasements; and as for the Romans, TACITUS, speaking of the emperor Tiberius, tells us that new words had then to be coined to express the newly invented stimulants to jaded passion. No wonder that, thus sick and dying as was this poor humanity of ours under the highest earthly culture, its many-voiced cry for the balm in Gilead, and the Physician there, "Come over and help us," pierced the hearts of the missionaries of the Cross, and made them "not ashamed of the Gospel of Christ!" **and receiving in themselves that recompense of their error which was meet**—alluding to the many physical and moral ways in which, under the righteous government of God, vice was made self-avenging.

ADAM CLARKE

22. *Professing themselves to be wise.* This is most strikingly true of all the ancient philosophers, whether Greeks or Romans, as their works, which remain, sufficiently testify. The word signifies not merely the *professing* but the "assumption" of the philosophic character.

23. *They changed the glory.* The finest representation of their deities was in the human figure, and on such representative figures the sculptors spent all their skill. And when they had formed their gods according to the human shape, they endowed them with human passions. *And to birds.* As the eagle of Jupiter among the Romans, and the ibis and hawk among the Egyptians, which were all sacred animals. *Four-footed beasts.* As the ox among the Egyptians, from which the idolatrous Israelites took their golden calf. The goat, the monkey, and the dog were also sacred animals among the same people. *Creeping things.* Such as the crocodile and *scarabeus,* or beetle, among the Egyptians.

25. *Changed the truth of God into a lie.* In the place of the true worship of God, they established idolatry. In various places of Scripture idols are termed *lies,* Isa. xliv. 20; Jer. x. 14; and xiii. 25. The true God was known among the primitive inhabitants of the earth. Those who first became idolaters literally changed the truth of God into a lie; they did know the true God, but they put idols in His place.

24. *God . . . gave them up.* They had filled up the measure of their iniquities, and God, by permitting them to plunge into all manner of irregularities, thus, by one species of sin, inflicted punishment on another. *Dishonour their own bodies.* Probably alluding here to what is more openly expressed in vv. 26-27. *Between themselves.* "Of themselves," of their own free accord.

26. *For this cause God gave them up.* Their system of idolatry necessarily produced all kinds of impurity. How could it be otherwise, when the highest objects of their worship were adulterers, fornicators, and prostitutes of the most infamous kind, such as Jupiter, Apollo, Mars, Venus?

MATTHEW HENRY

2. To a reprobate mind in these abominations, *v.* 28. (1) They *did not like to retain God in their knowledge.* The blindness of their understandings was caused by the wilful aversion of their wills and affections. They would neither know nor do anything but just what pleased themselves. There are many that have God in their knowledge, but they do not retain him there. Because it thwarts their lusts; they do not like it. There is a difference between the *knowledge* and the *acknowledgment* of God; the pagans knew God, but would not acknowledge him.

(2) Answerable to this wilfulness of theirs God gave them over to a wilfulness in the grossest sins, here called a *reprobate mind.* See whither a course of sin leads, and into what a gulf it plunges the sinner at last. This reprobate mind was a blind seared conscience, past feeling, Eph. iv. 19. Thus wilful hardness is justly punished with judicial hardness.—*To do those things which are not convenient.* And here he subjoins a black list of those unbecoming things which the Gentiles were guilty of. No wickedness, so contrary to the light of nature, but a reprobate mind will comply with it. By the histories of those times it appears that these sins here mentioned were reigning national sins. No fewer than twenty-three several sorts of sins and sinners are here specified, *v.* 29–31. It was time to have the gospel preached among them, for the world had need of reformation.

First, Sins against the first table: *Haters of God.* Here is the devil in his own colours, sin appearing sin. Every sin has in it a hatred of God. *Proud men and boasters* put those crowns upon their own heads which must be cast before his throne.

Secondly, Sins against the second table. In general here is a charge of unrighteousness. This is put first, for every sin is unrighteousness. It is especially put for second-table sins, doing as we would not be done by. Against the fifth commandment: *Disobedient to parents,* and *without natural affection.* Disobedient children are justly punished with unnatural parents; and unnatural parents with disobedient children. Against the sixth commandment: *Wickedness* (doing mischief for mischief's sake), *maliciousness, envy, murder, debate, malignity, despiteful, implacable, unmerciful;* all expressions of that hatred of our brother which is heart-murder. Against the seventh commandment: *Fornication.* Against the eighth commandment: *Unrighteousness, covetousness.* Against the ninth commandment: *Deceit, whisperers, back-biters, covenant-breakers, inventors of evil things, and without understanding;* wise to do evil, and yet having no knowledge to do good. So quick of invention in sin, and yet without understanding (stark fools) in the thoughts of God. Every heart by nature has in it the seed and spawn of all these sins.

F. B. MEYER:

From gross sins of the flesh. Few men knew as much as did Paul of the unutterableness of human need. In terrible words he enumerates its various aspects. Truth would enter human hearts from God's work in nature and from conscience; yet men pull down the blind and close the curtain. It is not that they do not know, but that they refuse to have God in their knowledge. They shun the thought of God (Ps. 10:4). They will not lift their happy faces toward him with filial confidence. Thus a heavy darkness steals over them and veils his presence.

The next downward step is uncleanness; and when once men have deliberately chosen the downward path, there is nothing to stop them. They go headlong from one point to another in their descent into darkness. When our hearts turn from the purifying presence of God, they become the haunt of every foul bird and noisome reptile. What a marvel it is that out of such material God can even create saints!

—*Bible Commentary*

JAMIESON, FAUSSET, BROWN

gave them over—or 'up'—see on vs. 24). **to do those things which are not convenient**—in the old sense of that word, i.e., 'not becoming,' 'indecorous,' 'shameful.' **haters of God**—The word usually signifies 'God-hated,' which some here prefer, in the sense of 'abhorred of the Lord'; expressing the detestableness of their character in His sight (cf. Prov. 22:14; Ps. 73:20). But the active sense of the word, adopted in our version and by the majority of expositors, though rarer, agrees perhaps better with the context. **32. Who knowing**—from the voice of conscience, ch. 2:14, 15—**the judgment of God**—the stern law of divine procedure—**that they which commit such things are worthy of death**—here used in its widest known sense, as the uttermost of divine vengeance against sin: see Acts 28:4. **not only do the same**—which they might do under the pressure of temptation and in the heat of passion. **but have pleasure in them that do them**—deliberately set their seal to such actions by encouraging and applauding the doing of them in others. This is the climax of our apostle's charges against the heathen; and certainly, if the things are in themselves as black as possible, this settled and unblushing satisfaction at the practice of them, apart from all the blinding effects of present passion, must be regarded as the darkest feature of human depravity.—On this section, note, (1) "The wrath of God" against sin has all the dread reality of a "revelation from heaven" sounding in the consciences of men, in the self-inflicted miseries of the wicked, and in the vengeance which God's moral government, sooner or later, takes upon all who outrage it; so this "wrath of God" is not confined to high-handed crimes, or the grosser manifestations of human depravity, but is "revealed" against all violations of divine law of whatever nature—"against all ungodliness" as well as "unrighteousness of men," against all disregard of God in the conduct of life as well as against all deviations from moral rectitude; and therefore, since no child of Adam can plead guiltless either of "ungodliness" or of "unrighteousness," to a greater or less extent, it follows that every human being is involved in the awful sweep of "the wrath of God" (vs. 18). The apostle places this terrible truth in the forefront of his argument on justification by faith, that upon the basis of *universal condemnation* he might rear the edifice of a free, world-wide salvation; nor can the Gospel be scripturally preached or embraced, save as the good news of salvation to those that are all equally "lost." (2) We must not magnify the supernatural revelation which God has been pleased to make of Himself, through Abraham's family to the human race, at the expense of that older, and, in itself, lustrous revelation which He has made to the whole family of man through the medium of their own nature and the creation around them. Without the latter, the former would have been impossible, and those who have not been favored with the former will be without excuse, if they are deaf to the voice and blind to the glory of the latter (vss. 19, 20). (3) Wilful resistance of light has a retributive tendency to blunt the moral perceptions and weaken the capacity to apprehend and approve of truth and goodness; and thus is the soul prepared to surrender itself, to an indefinite extent, to error and sin (vs. 21, etc.). (4) Pride of wisdom, as it is a convincing evidence of the want of it, so it makes the attainment of it impossible (vs. 22; and cf. Matt. 11:25; I Cor. 3:18-20). (5) As idolatry, even in its most plausible forms, is the fruit of unworthy views of the Godhead, so its natural effect is to vitiate and debase still further the religious conceptions; nor is there any depth of degradation too low and too revolting for men's ideas of the Godhead to sink to, if only their natural temperament and the circumstances they are placed in be favorable to their unrestrained development (vss. 23, 25). The apostle had Greece and Egypt in his eye when he penned this description. But all the paganisms of the East at this day attest its accuracy, from the more elaborate idolatry of India and the simpler and more stupid idolatry of China down to the childish rudiments of nature worship prevalent among the savage tribes. Alas! Christendom itself furnishes a melancholy illustration of this truth; the constant use of material images in the Church of Rome and the materialistic and sensuous character of its entire service (to say nothing of the less offensive but more stupid service of the Greek Church,) debasing the religious ideas of millions of nominal Christians, and lowering the whole character and tone of Christianity as represented within their immense pale. (6) Moral corruption invariably follows religious debasement. The grossness of pagan idolatry is only equalled by the revolting

ADAM CLARKE

28. *They did not like to retain God.* It would, perhaps be more literal to translate, "They did not search to retain God in their knowledge." They did not examine the evidences before them (vv. 19-20) of His being and attributes; therefore *God gave them over to a reprobate mind,* to an "unsearching or undiscerning" mind, for it is the same word in both places. They did not reflect on the proofs they had of the divine nature, and God abandoned them to the operations of a mind incapable of reflection.

29. *Being filled with all unrighteousness.* Every vice contrary to justice and righteousness. *Fornication.* All commerce between the sexes out of the bounds of lawful marriage. Some of the best MSS. omit this reading. *Wickedness.* "Malignity," that which is oppressive to its possessor and to its object. *Covetousness.* The intense love or lust of gain, the determination to be rich, the principle of a dissatisfied and discontented soul. *Maliciousness.* "Malice, ill-will"; what is radically and essentially vicious. *Full of envy.* "Pain felt and malignity conceived at the sight of excellence or happiness in another." *Murder.* Taking away the life of another by any means; mortal hatred, for he that hates his brother in his heart is a murderer. *Debate.* "Contention, discord." Of this vile passion the Greeks made a goddess. *Deceit.* "Lying, falsity, prevarication, imposition." *Malignity.* Bad customs, founded in corrupt sentiment, producing evil habits, supported by general usage. It is generally interpreted a malignity of mind which leads its possessor to put the worst construction on every action, ascribing to the best deeds the worst motives. *Whisperers.* Secret detractors; those who, under pretended secrecy, carry about accusations against their neighbors, whether true or false, blasting their reputation by clandestine tittle-tattle. This word should be joined to the succeeding verse. The whispering is well expressed by the Greek word *psithuristas.*

30. *Backbiters.* Those who speak against others; false accusers, slanderers. *Haters of God.* Atheists, contemners of sacred things, maligners of providence, scorners. All profligate deists are of this class; and it seems to be the finishing part of a diabolic character. *Despiteful.* Stormy, boisterous; abusing both the characters and persons of those over whom they can have any power. *Proud.* They who are continually exalting themselves and depressing others, magnifying themselves at the expense of their neighbors. *Boasters.* Self-assuming, vainglorious, and arrogant men. *Inventors of evil things.* Those who have invented destructive customs, rites, fashions; such as the different religious ceremonies among the Greeks and Romans—the orgies of Bacchus, the mysteries of Ceres. Multitudes of which evil things, destructive and abominable ceremonies, are to be found in every part of the heathen worship. *Disobedient to parents.* Though filial affection was certainly more recommended and cultivated than many other virtues, yet there are many instances on record of the grossest violation of this great branch of the law of nature.

31. *Without understanding.* Persons incapable of comprehending what was spoken; destitute of capacity for spiritual things. *Covenantbreakers.* Persons who could be bound by no oath because, properly speaking, they had no God to witness or avenge their misconduct. As every covenant or agreement is made as in the presence of God, so he that opposes the being and doctrine of God is incapable of being bound by any covenant; he can give no pledge for his conduct. *Without natural affection.* Without that attachment which nature teaches the young of all animals to have to their mothers, and the mothers to have for their young. The heathen, in general, have made no scruple to expose the children they did not think proper to bring up, and to dispatch their parents when they were grown old or past labor. *Implacable.* The word here shows a deadly enmity, the highest pitch of an unforgiving spirit; in a word, persons who would not make reconciliation to either God or man. *Unmerciful.* Those who were incapable, through the deep-rooted wickedness of their own nature, of showing mercy to an enemy when brought under their power.

MATTHEW HENRY

In the close he mentions the aggravations of the sins, *v.* 32. 1. They *knew the judgment of God.* They knew the law. They knew the penalty. They knew *that those who commit such things were worthy of death*; their own consciences could not but suggest this to them. It is a great aggravation of sin when it is committed against knowledge. It is daring presumption to run upon the sword's point. 2. They *not only do the same, but have pleasure in those that do them.* To be pleased with other people's sins is to love sin for sin's sake: it is joining in a confederacy for the devil's kingdom. Our own sins are much aggravated by our concurrence with the sins of others.

Now lay all this together, and then say whether the Gentile world could be justified before God by any works of their own.

JAMIESON, FAUSSET, BROWN

character and frightful extent of the immoralities which it fostered and consecrated (vss. 24, 26, 27). And so strikingly is this to be seen in all its essential features in the East at this day, that (as HODGE says) the missionaries have frequently been accused by the natives of having forged the whole of the latter part of this chapter, as they could not believe that so accurate a description of themselves could have been written eighteen centuries ago. The kingdoms of Israel and Judah furnish a striking illustration of the inseparable connection between religion and morals. Israel corrupted and debased the worship of Jehovah, and the sins with which they were charged were mostly of the grosser kind—intemperance and sensuality: the people of Judah, remaining faithful to the pure worship, were for a long time charged mostly with formality and hypocrisy; and only as they fell into the idolatries of the heathen around them, did they sink into their vices. And may not a like distinction be observed between the two great divisions of Christendom, the Popish and the Protestant? To test this, we must not look to Popery, surrounded with, and more or less influenced by, the presence and power of Protestantism; nor to Protestantism under every sort of disadvantage, internal and external. But look at Romanism where it has unrestrained liberty to develop its true character, and see whether impurity does not there taint society to its core, pervading alike the highest and the lowest classes; and then look at Protestantism where it enjoys the same advantages, and see whether it be not marked by a comparatively high standard of social virtue. (7) To take pleasure in what is sinful and vicious for its own sake, and knowing it to be such, is the last and lowest stage of human recklessness (vs. 32). But (8) this knowledge can never be wholly extinguished in the breast of men. So long as reason remains to them, there is still a small voice in the worst of men, protesting, in the name of the Power that implanted it, "that they which do such things are worthy of death" (vs. 32).

ADAM CLARKE

32. *Who, knowing the judgment of God.* The grand rule of right which God has revealed to every man, the knowledge of which He has, more or less, given to every nation of the world, relative to honoring parents, taking care of their own offspring, keeping engagements. In the worst states of heathenism this great principle has been acknowledged; but through the prevalence of corruption in the heart, this law, though acknowledged, was not obeyed; and the corruption increased so that those were highest in repute who had cast off all restraints of this kind; so that they even delighted in them; highly applauded, and gladly associated with those transgressors—which argues the very highest pitch of moral depravity.

MATTHEW HENRY

CHAPTER 2

Verses 1–16

The apostle had represented the state of the Gentile world to be as bad and black as the Jews were ready enough to pronounce it. Designing to show that the state of the Jews was very bad too, he sets himself to show that God would proceed upon equal terms of justice with Jews and Gentiles.

I. He arraigns them for their censoriousness and self-conceit (*v.* 1): *Thou art inexcusable, O man, whosoever thou art that judgest.* He intends especially the Jews, and to them particularly he applies this general charge, *Thou who teachest another teachest thou not thyself?* The Jews looked with a great deal of contempt upon the poor Gentiles; while in the meantime they were themselves as bad and immoral—though not idolaters. *Therefore thou art inexcusable.* If the Gentiles, who had but the light of nature, were inexcusable, much more the Jews, who had the light of the law.

II. He asserts the invariable justice of the divine government, *v.* 2, 3. He here shows what a righteous God that is with whom we have to do. The *judgment of God is according to truth,* according to the heart, and not according to the outward appearance, according to the works, and not with respect to persons, for he would not be God if he were not just; but it behoves those especially to consider it who condemn others for those things which they themselves are guilty of, and so think to bribe the divine justice by protesting against sin. As if preaching against sin would atone for the guilt of it. But observe how he puts it to the sinner's conscience (*v.* 3): *Thinkest thou this, O man?* The case is so plain that we may venture to appeal to the sinner's own thoughts: "Canst thou think that *thou shalt escape the judgment of God?* Can the heart-searching God be imposed upon by formal pretences, the righteous Judge of all so bribed?"

III. He draws up a charge against them (*v.* 4, 5), consisting of two branches:

1. Slighting the goodness of God (*v.* 4), *the riches of his goodness.* The more light we sin against the more love we sin against. There is in every wilful sin an interpretative contempt of the goodness of God, particularly the goodness of his patience, taking occasion thence to be so much the more bold in sin. *Not knowing* that *the goodness of God leadeth thee to repentance.* What method God takes to bring sinners to repentance. He leads them, not drives them like beasts, allures them; and it is goodness that leads, bands of love. The consideration of the goodness of God, his common goodness to all, should be

JAMIESON, FAUSSET, BROWN

CHAPTER 2

VSS. 1-29. THE JEW UNDER LIKE CONDEMNATION WITH THE GENTILE. From those *without,* the apostle now turns to those *within* the pale of revealed religion, the self-righteous Jews, who looked down upon the uncovenanted heathen as beyond the pale of God's mercies, within which they deemed themselves secure, however inconsistent their life may be. Alas! what multitudes wrap themselves up in like fatal confidence, who occupy the corresponding position in the Christian Church!

4. the goodness of God leadeth thee to repentance—i.e., is designed and adapted to do so.

ADAM CLARKE

CHAPTER 2

1. *That judgest.* "The judger"; you assume the character of a judge, and in that character condemn others who are less guilty than yourself.

2. *We are sure that the judgment of God.* God is impartial, and will punish sin wheresoever He finds it. Transgression in a Jew is not less criminal than iniquity in a Gentile.

4. *Or despisest thou the riches of his goodness?* Will you render of none effect that marked benevolence of God towards you which has given so many superior advantages, and that *forbearance* which has tolerated your many miscarriages, and that *longsuffering* which, after repeated provocations, still continues to bear with you? *Not knowing.* Not "acknowledging" that this goodness of God, which has so long manifested itself in forbearance and long-suffering, *leadeth thee to repentance*—was designed to accomplish this blessed end, which your want of consideration and acknowledgment has rendered, hitherto, ineffectual. This was a maxim among the Jews themselves; for, in *Synopsis Sohar,* it is said: "The holy blessed God delays his anger against the wicked, to the end that they may repent and be converted."

MATTHEW HENRY

effectual to bring us all to repentance.

2. Provoking the wrath of God, *v.* 5. The rise of this provocation is a *hard and impenitent heart.* To sin is to walk in the way of the heart; and when that is a hard and impenitent heart, how desperate must the course needs be! The provocation is expressed by *treasuring up wrath.* A treasure denotes abundance. It is a treasure that will be spending to eternity, and yet sinners are still adding to it as to a treasure. A treasure denotes secrecy. It denotes reservation to some further occasion. These treasures will be broken open. They are treasured up *against the day of wrath.* Though the present day be a day of patience towards sinners, yet there is a day of wrath coming. And that day of wrath will be *the day of the revelation of the righteous judgment of God.* The wrath of God is not like our wrath, a heat and passion: but it is a righteous judgment, his will to punish sin. This righteous judgment of God is now many times concealed in the prosperity of sinners, but shortly it will be manifested before all the world.

IV. Having mentioned the righteous judgment of God in *v.* 5, he here illustrates that judgment, and the righteousness of it.

1. He will *render to every man according to his deeds* (*v.* 6).

(1) In dispensing his favours; and this is mentioned twice here, both in *v.* 7 and *v.* 10. For he delights to show mercy. The objects of his favour: *Those who by patient continuance,* &c. Those whom the righteous God will reward are, *First,* Such as fix to themselves the right end, that *seek for glory, and honour, and immortality.* There is a holy ambition which is at the bottom of all practical religion, This is looking in our desires and aims as high as heaven, and resolved to take up with nothing short of it. This seeking implies a loss, desire to retrieve it, and pursuits and endeavours consonant to those desires. *Secondly,* Such as having fixed the right end, adhere to the right way: *A patient continuance in well-doing.* There must be well-doing, *v.* 10. It is not enough to know well, and promise well, but we must do well. A continuance in well doing. Not for a fit and a start, like the morning cloud and the early dew; it is perseverance that wins the crown. A patient continuance. This patience respects not only the length of the work, but the difficulties of it. Those that will do well and continue in it must put on a great deal of patience. The product of his favour. He will render to such eternal life. Heaven is life, eternal life, and it is called (*v.* 10) *glory, honour, and peace.* Those that seek for the vain glory and honour of this world often miss of them; but those that seek for immortal glory and honour shall have them, and not only *glory and honour,* but *peace.* Heavenly glory and honour have peace with them, undisturbed everlasting peace.

(2) In dispensing his frowns (*v.* 8, 9). The objects of his frowns. *Such as are contentious and do not obey the truth.* Contentious against God. Every wilful sin is a quarrel with God. *Contentious, and do not obey the truth.* The truths of religion are not only to be known, but to be obeyed. Disobedience to the truth is interpreted a striving against it. *But obey unrighteousness.* Those that refuse to be the servants of truth will soon be the slaves of unrighteousness. The products of these frowns: *Indignation and wrath, tribulation and anguish.* These are the wages of sin. And this *upon the soul*; souls are the vessels of that wrath. Sin qualifies the soul for this wrath. Hell is eternal tribulation and anguish, the product of wrath and indignation. This comes of contending with God. Those that will not bow to his golden sceptre will certainly be broken by his iron rod.

2. *There is no respect of persons with God, v.* 11. As to the spiritual state, there is a respect of persons; but not as to outward relation or condition. God does not save men with respect to their external privileges, but according as their state and disposition really are. In dispensing both his frowns and favours it is both to Jew and Gentile. If to *the Jews first,* who had greater privileges, yet *also to the Gentiles,* whose want of such privileges will neither excuse them from the punishment of their ill-doing nor bar them out from the reward of their well-doing.

V. He proves the equity of his proceedings with all (*v.* 12–16). Three degrees of light are revealed to the children of men:

1. The light of nature. This the Gentiles have, and by this they shall be judged: *As many as have sinned without law shall perish without law;* that is, the unbelieving Gentiles, who had no other guide but natural conscience, shall not be reckoned with for the transgression of the law they never had. They shall be judged by the law of nature. The light of nature was to the Gentiles instead of a written law.

JAMIESON, FAUSSET, BROWN

5. treasurest up unto thyself wrath against—rather 'in'—**the day of wrath**—i.e., wrath to come on thee in the day of wrath. What an awful idea is here expressed—that the sinner himself is amassing, like hoarded treasure, an ever accumulating stock of divine wrath, to burst upon him in "the day of the revelation of the righteous judgment of God!" And this is said not of the reckless, but of those who boasted of their purity of faith and life.

7-10. To them who . . .—The substance of these verses is that the final judgment will turn upon *character* alone. **by patient continuance in well-doing . . .**—Cf. Luke 8:15: "That on the good ground are they, which in an honest and good heart, having heard the word, keep it, and bring forth fruit *with patience*"; denoting the *enduring* and *progressive* character of the new life.

But unto them that are contentious, and do not obey the truth . . .—referring to such keen and determined resistance to the Gospel as he himself had too painfully witnessed on the part of his own countrymen. (See Acts 13: 44-46; 17:5, 13; 18:6, 12; and cf. I Thess. 2:15, 16.) **indignation and wrath**—in the bosom of a sin-avenging God. **Tribulation and anguish**—the *effect* of these in the sinner himself.**to the Jew first**—first in perdition if unfaithful; but if obedient to the truth, first in salvation (vs. 10).

11, 12. For as many as have sinned—not 'as many as have sinned *at all,*' but, 'as many as are *found in sin*' at the judgment of the great day (as the whole context shows). **without law**—i.e., without the advantage of a positive Revelation. **shall also perish without law**—exempt from the charge of rejecting or disregarding it.

ADAM CLARKE

5. *But after thy hardness.* Occasioned by your long course of iniquity. *And impenitent heart*—produced by your hardness, through which you are callous to the calls and expostulations of conscience. *Treasurest up*—continue to increase your debt to the divine justice, which will infallibly inflict *wrath,* punishment, in *the day of wrath*—the judgment day, in which He will render to every man according to his works. The word *treasure* the Hebrew uses to express any kind of store or collection. So treasures of gold, silver, corn, wine, oil, etc., mean collections or an abundance of such things; the word is used by the Greek writers precisely in the same sense. By *wrath* we are to understand "punishment," as in chap. 1. 18; and it is used so by the very best Greek writers. The *treasure of wrath,* in this verse, is opposed to the *riches of goodness,* in the preceding. As surely as you despise or neglect to improve the riches of God's goodness, so surely you shall share in the treasures of His wrath. The punishment shall be proportioned to the mercy you have abused.

6. *Who will render.* Who, in the day of judgment, will reward and punish every man according as his life and conversation have been.

7. *To them.* In this manner will God, in the great day, dispense punishments and rewards: (1) He will give eternal life to them who, in all the trials and difficulties of the present state, have persevered *in well doing*—seeking for and expecting *glory, honour,* and *immortality.*

10. *But glory, honour, and peace.* While the finally impenitent Jew and Gentile shall experience the fullest effects of the righteous indignation of the supreme Judge, every man that *worketh good*—that lives in a conscientious obedience to the known will of God—whether he be Jew or Gentile, shall have *glory, honour,* and *peace;* i.e., eternal blessedness.

8. *But unto them.* (2) He will manifest His *indignation,* and inflict *wrath*—punishment, on all who are *contentious*—who obstinately dispute against the truth, and *obey unrighteousness*—who act under the influence of the principle of sin, and not under the influence of the Spirit of God.

9. *Tribulation and anguish.* Misery of all descriptions, without the possibility of escape, will this righteous Judge inflict upon every impenitent sinner. The Jew first, as possessing greater privileges, and having abused greater mercies; and also on the Gentile, who, though he had not the same advantages, had what God saw was sufficient for his state; and, having sinned against them, shall have punishment proportioned to his demerit.

11. *For there is no respect of persons with God.* The righteous Judge will not act according to any principle of partiality; the character and conduct alone of the persons shall weigh with Him. He will take no wicked man to glory, let his nation or advantages be what they may; and He will send no righteous man to perdition, though brought up in the very bosom of Gentilism.

12. *For as many as have sinned without law.* They, viz., the Gentiles, who shall be found to have transgressed against the mere light of nature, or rather, "that true Light, which lighteth every man that cometh into the world," John i. 9, shall not come under the same rule with those, the Jews, who have in addition to this enjoyed an extraordinary revelation, but they shall be dealt with according to the inferior dispensation under which they lived, while those, the Jews, who have *sinned in the law*—the positive, divine revelation granted to them, *shall be judged by the law,* and punished proportionably to the abuse of such an extraordinary advantage.

13. *For not the hearers of the law.* It does not follow, because one people are favored with a divine revelation, that therefore they shall be saved; while the others who have not had that revelation shall finally perish; this is not God's procedure. Where He has given a *law,* a divine revelation, He requires obedience to that law; and only those who have been *doers* of that *law,* who have lived according to the light and privileges granted in that revelation, *shall be justified*—shall be finally acknowledged to be such as are fit for the kingdom of God.

14. *For when the Gentiles, which have not the law.* Nor does it follow that the Gentiles, who

MATTHEW HENRY

He had said (*v.* 12) they had *sinned without law*, which looks like a contradiction; for where there is no law there is no transgression. But, says he, though they had not the written law, they had that which was equivalent. They *had the work of the law*. The work of the law is to direct us what to do, and to examine us what we have done. (1) They had that which directed them what to do by the light of nature. They apprehended a clear and vast difference between good and evil. They *did by nature the things contained in the law*. They had a sense of justice and equity, honour and purity, love and charity. Thus they were a *law unto themselves*. (2) They had that which examined them as to what they had done: *Their conscience also bearing witness*. They had that within them which approved what was well done and which reproached them for what was done amiss. Conscience is a witness, and first or last will bear witness, testifying of that which is most secret; and their *thought accusing or excusing*, passing a judgment upon the testimony of conscience. Conscience is that candle of the Lord which was not quite put out, no, not in the Gentile world. Their *thoughts the meanwhile*. According as they observed or broke these natural laws and dictates, their consciences did either acquit or condemn them. All this did evince that they had that which was to them instead of a law. So that the guilty Gentiles are left without excuse. God is justified in condemning them. They cannot plead ignorance.

2. The light of the law. This the Jews had, and by this they shall be judged (*v.* 12): *As many as have sinned in the law shall be judged by the law*. They sinned in the face and light of so pure and clear a law. These shall be judged *by the law*; their punishment shall be, as their sin is, so much the greater for their having the law. *The Jew first*, *v.* 9. The apostle shows (*v.* 13) that their having, and hearing, and knowing the law, would not justify them, but their doing it. It was a great privilege that they had the law, but not a saving privilege, unless they lived up to the law they had. We may apply it to the gospel: it is not hearing, but doing that will save us.

3. The light of the gospel: and according to this those that enjoyed the gospel shall be judged (*v.* 16): *According to my gospel;* the gospel in general, called Paul's because he was a preacher of it. Some refer those words, *according to my gospel*, to what he says of the day of judgment. It is good for us to get acquainted with what is revealed concerning that day. There is a day set for a general judgment. The judgment of that day will be put into the hands of Jesus Christ. Nothing speaks more terror to sinners, or more comfort to saints, than this, that Christ shall be the Judge. The secrets of men shall then be judged. That will be the great discovering day.

Verses 17–29

He had said (*v.* 13) that not the hearers but the doers of the law are justified; and he here applies that great truth to the Jews.

I. He allows their profession (*v.* 17–20), that they might see he did not condemn them out of ignorance. He knew the best of their cause.

1. They were a peculiar people, having the written law and the special presence of God among them. *Thou art called a Jew*. It was a very honourable title. Salvation was of the Jews; and this they were very proud of, and yet many that were so called were the vilest of men. It is no new thing for the worst practices to be shrouded under the best names. *And restest in the law*. They were mightily puffed up with this privilege, and thought this enough to bring them to heaven, though they did not live up to the law. It is a dangerous thing to rest in external privileges, and not to improve them. *And makest thy boast of God*. A believing, humble, thankful glorying in God, is the summary of all religion. Boasting in God, and in the outward profession of his name, is the summary of all hypocrisy. Spiritual pride is of all kinds of pride the most dangerous.

JAMIESON, FAUSSET, BROWN

and as many as have sinned in the law—within the pale of a positive, written Revelation. **shall be judged by the law**—tried and condemned by the higher standard of that written Revelation.

13-15. For not the hearers . . .—As touching the Jews, in whose ears the written law is continually resounding, the condemnation of as many of them as are found sinners at the last involves no difficulty; but even as respects the heathen, who are strangers to the law in its positive and written form—since they show how deeply it is engraven on their moral nature, which witnesses within them for righteousness and against iniquity, accusing or condemning them according as they violate or obey its stern dictates—their condemnation also for all the sin in which they live and die will carry its dreadful echo in their own breasts.

their thoughts the meanwhile accusing or else excusing—i.e., perhaps by turns doing both.

16. In the day . . .—Here the unfinished statement of vs. 12 is resumed and closed. **shall judge the secrets of men**—here specially referring to the unfathomed depths of hypocrisy in the self-righteous whom the apostle had to deal with. (See Eccles. 12:14; I Cor. 4:5.) **according to my gospel**—to my teaching as a preacher of the Gospel.

Behold—'But if' is, beyond doubt, the true reading here. (It differs but in a single letter from the received reading, and the sense is the same.)

ADAM CLARKE

have not had a divine revelation, shall either perish because they had it not or their unrighteous conduct pass unpunished because not having this revelation might be considered as an excuse for their sins. *Do by nature the things contained in the law*. Do, without this divine revelation, through that light which God imparts to every man, *the things contained in the law*—act according to justice, mercy, temperance, and truth, the practice of which the revealed law so powerfully enjoins; *these . . . are a law unto themselves*—they are not accountable to any other law, and are not to be judged by any dispensation different from that under which they live.

15. *Which shew the work of the law*. In acting according to justice, mercy, temperance, and truth they show that the great object of the law, which was to bring men from injustice, cruelty, intemperance, and falsity, is accomplished so far in them; *their conscience also bearing witness*—that faculty of the soul, where that divine light dwells and works, shows them that they are right; and thus they have a comfortable testimony in their own souls of their own integrity. *Their thoughts the mean while accusing or else excusing one another;* or rather, "their reasonings between one another accusing or answering for themselves." As if the apostle had said: And this point, that they have a law and act according to it, is further proved from their conduct in *civil* affairs; and from that correct sense which they have of *natural justice* in their *debates*, either in their *courts of law* or in their *treatises on morality*. All these are ample proofs that God has not left them without light; and that, seeing they have such correct notions of right and wrong, they are accountable to God for their conduct in reference to these notions and principles. This seems to be the true meaning of this difficult clause. See below. Much stress has been laid on the words *by nature*, in v. 14, as if the apostle designed to intimate that nature, independently of the influence of divine grace, possessed such principles as were sufficient to guide a man to glory. But certainly the term cannot be so understood here. I rather think that "certainly, truly" is its sense here: "For when the Gentiles, which have not the law, *truly*, or in effect, *do* the things contained in the law." This seems to be its sense in Gal. iv. 8: "When ye knew not God, ye did service unto them which certainly are no gods"; i.e., are false gods. The passage in v. 15, *Their thoughts . . . accusing or else excusing one another*, certainly does not refer to any expostulations or operations of *conscience*, for this is referred to in the preceding clause. The words *accusing* and *excusing*, "answering or defending one another among themselves," are all forensic or law terms, and refer to the mode of conducting suits of law in courts of justice, where one is plaintiff, who produces his accusation; another is defendant, who rebuts the charge and defends himself; and then the business is argued before the judges. This process shows that they have a law of their own, and that to this law it belongs to adjust differences—to right those who have suffered wrong, and to punish the guilty. As to the phrase *written in their hearts*, it is here opposed to the Jewish laws, which were written on tables of stone. The Jews drew the maxims by which their conduct was regulated from a divine revelation; the Gentiles drew theirs from what God, in the course of His providence and gracious influence, had shown them to be right, useful, and necessary. And with them this law was "well known and affectionately regarded"; for this is one meaning of the phrase *written in their hearts*.

17. *Behold, thou art called a Jew*. What the apostle had said in the preceding verses being sufficient to enforce conviction on the conscience of the Jew, he now openly argues with him in the most plain manner, asserting that his superior knowledge, privileges, and profession served only to aggravate his condemnation. *And restest in the law*. You trust in it for your endless salvation. The word implies the strongest confidence of safety and security. You "repose your whole trust and confidence" in this law. *And makest thy boast of God*. That you know His nature and attributes, which are not known to the Gentiles. The word implies the idea of "exulting" in anything, as being a proper object

MATTHEW HENRY

2. They were a knowing people (*v.* 18) *and knowest his will.* The world will then be set to rights, when God's will is the only will, and all other wills are melted into it. The will of God, that which he would have them do. *And approvest the things that are more excellent.* A good apprehension in *the things of God,* reading it thus, *Thou discernest things that differ,* knowest how to distinguish between good and evil. Good and bad lie sometimes so near together that it is not easy to distinguish them; but the Jews were, or at least thought they were, able to distinguish, to cleave the hair in doubtful cases. Or, we may, understand *controversies.* A man may be well skilled in the controversies of religion, and yet a stranger to the power of godliness. A warm affection to the things of God, as we read it, *Approvest the things that are excellent.* There may be a consent of the practical judgment *to the law, that it is good,* and yet that consent overpowered by the lusts of the flesh, and of the mind:

I see the better, but pursue the worse.

They got this acqaintance with that which is good, by being *instructed out of the law.* It was the custom of the Jews to take a great deal of pains in teaching their children, and all their lessons were *out of the law;* it were well if Christians were but as industrious to teach their children *out of the gospel.* Now this is called (*v.* 20), *The form of knowledge, and of the truth in the law.* A form of knowledge produces but a form of godliness, 2 Tim. iii. 5. A form of knowledge may deceive men, but cannot impose upon the heart-searching God.

3. They were a teaching people, or at least thought themselves so (*v.* 19, 20): *And art confident that thou thyself art a guide of the blind.* Apply it, (1) To the Jews in general. They thought themselves guides to the poor blind Gentiles that sat in darkness. All other nations must come to school to them, to learn what is good. (2) To their rabbis, and doctors. The apostle expresses this in several terms, *a guide of the blind, a light of those who are in darkness, an instructor of the foolish, a teacher of babes,* the better to set forth their proud conceit. This was a string they loved to be harping upon. The best work, when it is prided in, is unacceptable to God. It is good to instruct the foolish, but considering our own inability to make these teachings successful without God, there is nothing in it to be proud of.

II. He aggravates their provocations (*v.* 21-24) from two things:

1. They sinned against their knowledge, did that themselves which they taught others to avoid: *Thou that teachest another, teachest thou not thyself?* Teaching is a piece of that charity which begins at home, though it must not end there. The Pharisees pulled down with their lives what they built up with their preaching. The greatest obstructors of the success of the word are those whose bad lives contradict their good doctrine, who in the pulpit preach so well that it is a pity they should ever come out, and out of the pulpit live so ill that it is a pity they should ever come in. He specifies three particular sins that abound among the Jews: (1) Stealing. (2) Adultery, *v.* 22. Many of the Jewish rabbin are said to have been notorious for this sin. (3) Sacrilege, and this is charged upon those that professed to abhor idols. It was in the latter days of the Old Testament church that they were charged *with robbing God in tithes and offerings* (Mal. iii. 8, 9), converting that to their own use which was set apart for God. And this is almost equivalent to idolatry.

2. They dishonoured God by their sin, *v.* 23, 24. While God and his law were an honour to them, which they boasted of, they were a dishonour to God and his law, by giving occasion to those that were without to reflect upon their religion. *As it is written, v.* 24. He does not mention the place, because he wrote this to those that were instructed in the law. The great evil of the sins of professors is the dishonour done to God and religion by their profession. "*Blasphemed through you.* The reproaches you bring upon yourselves reflect upon your God, and religion is wounded through your sides." A good caution to professors to walk circumspectly.

III. He asserts the utter insufficiency of their profession to clear them from the guilt of these provocations (*v.* 25-29): *Circumcision verily profiteth, if thou keep the law;* that is, obedient Jews shall not lose the reward of their obedience. He is here speaking to the Jews, whose Judaism would benefit them, if they would but live up to the laws of it; but if not "*thy circumcision is made uncircumcision.* Thou wilt be no more justified than the uncircumcised Gentiles, but more condemned for sinning against greater light."

1. He shows that the uncircumcised Gentiles, if

JAMIESON, FAUSSET, BROWN

approvest the things that are excellent—*Margin,* 'triest the things that differ.' Both senses are good, and indeed the former is but the result of the latter action. (See on Phil. 1:10.)

hast the form of knowledge and of the truth in the law—not being left, as the heathen are, to vague conjecture on divine things, but favored with definite and precise information from heaven.

thou that abhorrest idols—as the Jews did ever after their captivity, though bent on them before—**dost thou commit sacrilege?**—not, as some excellent interpreters, 'dost thou rob idol-temples?' but more generally, as we take it, 'dost thou profane holy things?' (as in Matt. 21:12, 13, and in other ways). **as it is written**—(See *Marginal reference.*) **25-29. For circumcision**—i.e., One's being within the covenant of which circumcision was the outward sign and seal. **verily profiteth, if thou keep the law**—if the inward reality correspond to the outward sign. **but if . . .**—i.e., 'Otherwise, thou art no better than the uncircumcised heathen.' **Therefore if the uncircumcision keep the . . . law . . .**—Two mistaken interpretations, we think, are given of these words: *First,* that the case here supposed is an impossible one, and put merely for illustration [HALDANE, CHALMERS, HODGE]; *second* that it is the case of the heathen who may and do please God when they act, as has been and is done, up to the light of nature [GROTIUS, OLSHAUSEN, etc.]. The first interpretation is, in our judgment, unnatural; the second, opposed to the apostle's own teaching. But the case here put is, we think, such as that of Cornelius (Acts 10), who, though outside the *external* pale of God's covenant, yet having come to the knowledge of the truths contained in it, do manifest the grace of the covenant without the seal of it, and exemplify the character and walk of Abraham's children, though not called by the name of Abraham. Thus, this is but another way of announcing that God was about to show the insufficiency of the mere badge of the Abrahamic covenant, by calling from among the Gentiles a seed of Abraham that had never received the seal of circumcision (see on Gal. 5:6); and this interpretation is confirmed by all that follows.

ADAM CLARKE

of hope and dependence; and when referred to God, it points out that He is the sure Cause of hope, dependence, joy, and happiness; and that it is the highest honor to be called to know His name, and be employed in His service. As if the apostle had said: You rejoice in God as the Object of your hope and dependence; you praise and magnify Him; you account it your greatest honor that He is your God, and that you worship Him.

18. *Knowest his will.* Have been favored with a revelation of His own will, immediately from himself. *The things that are more excellent.* "The things that differ"—that revelation which God has given of himself makes the nicest distinctions between right and wrong, between vice and virtue; showing how you should walk so as to please God, and, consequently, acquire the most excellent portion that human spirits can have on this side of heaven. For all these blessings you acknowledge to receive from your law, *being instructed,* being "catechized," from your infancy in the knowledge of divine things.

19. *And art confident.* In consequence of all these religious advantages, you believe that you are able to teach others, and to be guides and lights to the bewildered, darkened Gentiles, who may become proselytes to your religion.

20. *An instructor of the foolish.* You believe the Gentiles to be babes and fools when compared with yourselves; that you alone possess the only true knowledge; that you are the only favorites of Heaven; and that all nations must look up to you as possessing the only *form of knowledge,* the grand scheme and draught of all true science, of everything that is worthy to be learned: the system of eternal truth, derived from the law.

21. *Thou therefore.* That the Jewish priesthood was exceedingly corrupt in the time of the apostle, and that they were so long before, is fully evident from the sacred writings and from Josephus. The high priesthood was bought and sold like other commodities.

24. *For the name of God is blasphemed.* In *Debarim rabba* it is said: "The rulers destroy the influence of their own words among the people; and this is done when a rabbin, sitting and teaching in the academy, says, Do not take usury, and himself takes it; do not commit rapine, and himself commits it; do not steal, and himself steals." That they were exceedingly lax in their morals, the following fact proves: "Rabbi Ilai said, If a man see that his evil propensities are likely to prevail against him, let him go to some place where he is not known, and let him put on black clothes, and cover his head with a black veil; and then let him do whatsoever he pleases, lest the name of God should be publicly profaned."

25. *For circumcision verily profiteth.* It is a blessing to belong to the Church of God and wear the sign of the covenant, provided the terms of the covenant are complied with. *But if thou be a breaker of the law.* If you do not observe the conditions of the covenant, the outward sign is both without meaning and without effect. This was a maxim of the rabbins themselves; for they allowed that an apostate or ungodly Israelite must go to hell, notwithstanding his circumcision.

26. *Therefore if the uncircumcision.* If the Gentile be found to act according to the spirit and design of the law, his acting thus uprightly, according to the light which God has afforded him, will be reckoned to him as if he were circumcised and walked agreeably to the law.

MATTHEW HENRY

they live up to the light they have, stand upon the same level with the Jews; if *they keep the righteousness of the law* (*v.* 26), *fulfil the law* (*v.* 27); that is, by submitting sincerely to the conduct of natural light, perform the matter of the law. It seems to be meant of such an obedience as some of the Gentiles did attain to. Doubtless, there were many such instances: and *they were the uncircumcision, that kept the righteousness of the law.* They were accepted with God. *Their uncircumcision was counted for circumcision.* Their obedience was a great aggravation of the disobedience of the Jews, *v.* 27. *Judge thee,* who *by the letter and circumcision dost transgress.* To carnal professors the law is but the letter; they read it as a bare writing, but are not ruled by it as a law. External privileges, if they do not do us good, do us hurt. The obedience of those that enjoy less means, and make a less profession, will help to condemn those that enjoy greater means, and make a greater profession, but do not live up to it.

2. He describes the true circumcision, *v.* 28, 29. It is *not that which is outward in the flesh and in the letter.* This is not to drive us off from the observances of external institutions (they are good in their place), but from trusting to them and taking up with a name to live, without being alive indeed. *He is not a Jew.* To be Abraham's children is to do the works of Abraham. It is *that which is inward, of the heart, and in the spirit.* It is the heart that God looks at. The praise thereof, though it be *not of men,* who judge according to outward appearance, yet it is *of God,* for *he seeth not as man seeth.* Fair pretences and a plausible profession may deceive men: but God sees through shows to realities. This is alike true of Christianity. He is not a Christian that is one outwardly, nor is that baptism which is outward in the flesh.

JAMIESON, FAUSSET, BROWN

he is not a Jew which is one outwardly . . .—In other words, the name of "Jew" and the rite of "circumcision" were designed but as outward symbols of a separation from the irreligious and ungodly world unto holy devotedness in heart and life to the God of salvation. Where this is realized, the signs are full of significance; but where it is not, they are worse than useless. Note, (1) It is a sad mark of depravity when all that is designed and fitted to melt only hardens the heart (vs. 4, and cf. II Pet. 3:9; Eccles. 8:11). (2) Amidst all the inequalities of religious opportunity measured out to men, and the mysterious bearing of this upon their character and destiny for eternity, the same great principles of judgment, in a form suited to their respective discipline, will be applied to all, and perfect equity will be seen to reign throughout every stage of the divine administration (vss. 11-16). (3) "The law written on the heart" (vss. 14, 15)—or the Ethics of Natural Theology—may be said to be the one deep foundation on which all revealed religion reposes; and see on ch. 1:19, 20, where we have what we may call its other foundation—the Physics and Metaphysics of Natural Theology. The testimony of these two passages is to the theologian invaluable, while in the breast of every teachable Christian it wakens such deep echoes as are inexpressibly solemn and precious. (4) High religious professions are a fearful aggravation of the inconsistencies of such as make them (vss. 17-24). See II Samuel 12:14. (5) As no external privileges, or badge of discipleship, will shield the unholy from the wrath of God, so neither will the want of them shut out from the kingdom of heaven such as have experienced without them that change of heart which the seals of God's covenant were designed to mark. In the sight of the great Searcher of hearts, the Judge of quick and dead, the renovation of the character in heart and life is all in all. In view of this, have not all baptized, sacramented disciples of the Lord Jesus, who "profess that they know God, but in works deny Him," need to tremble—who, under the guise of friends, are "the enemies of the cross of Christ"?

ADAM CLARKE

27. *And shall not uncircumcision which is by nature?* And shall not the Gentile, who is according to the custom of his country—who is by birth not obliged to be circumcised? *If it fulfil the law.* If such a person act according to the spirit and design of the law. *Judge,* "condemn" *thee,* who, while you enjoy the letter, the written law, and bear in your body the proof of the circumcision which it requires, *dost transgress the law.*

28. *For he is not a Jew,* a genuine member of the Church of God, who has only an outward profession. *Neither is that circumcision.* Circumcision is a rite which represents a spiritual thing, viz., the change and purification of the heart, as may be seen from Jer. iv. 4, 6, 10; ix. 26; Ezek. xliv. 7, 9.

29. *But he is a Jew.* A true member of the Church of God. *Which is one inwardly.* Who has his heart purified, according to what God has uniformly prescribed by His prophets. For *circumcision is . . . of the heart, in the spirit,* "by the Spirit" of God, who is the Author of all spiritual affections and holy purposes; or everything here is to be understood spiritually, and not literally; for without holiness none can please God, and without holiness none can see Him. *Whose praise is not of men.* It has, with great probability, been conjectured that the apostle may here refer to the signification of the name Jew, or Judah, *Yehudah,* "Praise." Such a one is a true Israelite, who walks in a conformity to the spirit of his religion. His countrymen may praise him because he is a steady professor of the Jewish faith; but God praises him because he has entered into the spirit and design of the covenant made with Abraham, and has got the end of his faith, the salvation of his soul.

MATTHEW HENRY — CHAPTER 3

Verses 1–18

I. Here the apostle answers several objections. Divine truths must be cleared from cavil.

Object. 1. If Jew and Gentile stand so much upon the same level before God, *what advantage then hath the Jew?* Now does not this levelling doctrine deny them all prerogatives, and reflect dishonour upon the ordinance of circumcision.

Answer. The Jews are, notwithstanding this, a people greatly privileged and honoured (*v.* 2): *Much every way.* The door is open to the Gentiles as well as the Jews, but the Jews have a fairer way up to this door. He reckons up many of the Jews' privileges Rom. ix. 4, 5; here he mentions but one *that unto them were committed the oracles of God,* that is, the scriptures of the Old Testament. The scriptures are the oracles of God: they are a divine revelation. We must have recourse to the law and to the testimony, as to an oracle. Now these oracles were committed to the Jews. The Old Testament was deposited in their hands, to be carefully preserved pure and uncorrupt. The Jews were entrusted with that sacred treasure for their own use and benefit in the first place, and then for the advantage of the world. The Jews had the means of salvation, but they had not the monopoly of salvation. Now this he mentions with a *chiefly,* this was their prime and principal privilege. The enjoyment of God's word and ordinances is the chief happiness of a people.

Object. 2. To what purpose were the oracles of God committed to them, when so many of them continued strangers to Christ, and enemies to his gospel? *Some did not believe, v.* 3.

Answer. But shall their unbelief make the faith of God without effect? The apostle startled at such a thought: *God forbid!* The obstinacy of the Jews could not invalidate those prophecies of the Messiah which were contained in the oracles committed to them. Christ will be glorious. God's words shall be accomplished, though there be a generation that by their unbelief go about to make God a liar. *Let God be true but every man a liar;* let us abide by this principle, that God is true to every word which he has spoken. Better question the credit of all the men in the world than doubt of the faithfulness of God. All men are liars, compared with God. It is very comfortable, when we find every man a liar (no faith in man), that God is faithful. He quotes Ps.

JAMIESON, FAUSSET, BROWN — CHAPTER 3

Vss. 1-8. JEWISH OBJECTIONS ANSWERED. **1, 2. What advantage then hath the Jew?**—i.e., 'If the final judgment will turn solely on the state of the heart, and this may be as good in the Gentile *without,* as in the Jew *within,* the sacred enclosure of God's covenant, what better are we Jews for all our advantages?

Answer: **Much every way; chiefly, because**—(rather, 'first, that')—**unto them were committed the oracles of God**—This remarkable expression, denoting 'divine communications' in general, is transferred to the Scriptures to express their *oracular,* divine, authoritative character.

3, 4. For what if some did not believe?—It is the unbelief of the great body of the nation which the apostle points at; but as it sufficed for his argument to put the supposition thus gently, he uses this word "some" to soften prejudice. **shall their unbelief make the faith**—or, faithfulness—**of God of none effect?**—'nullify,' 'invalidate' it. **God forbid**—lit., *'Let it not be,'* i.e., 'Away with such a thought'—a favorite expression of our apostle, when he would not only repudiate a supposed consequence of his doctrine, but express his abhorrence of it. "The Scriptures do not authorize such a use of God's name as must have been common among the English translators of the Bible" [HODGE]. **yea, let God be**—held—**true, and every man a liar**—i.e., even though it should follow from this that every man is a liar. **when thou art judged**—so in Psalm 51:4, according to the LXX; but in the *Hebrew* and in our version, 'when thou judgest.' The general sentiment, however, is the same in both—that we are to vindicate the righteousness of God, at whatever expense to ourselves.

ADAM CLARKE — CHAPTER 3

As the first nine verses are a dialogue between the apostle and a Jew, I shall prefix the speakers to their respective questions and answers, to make the whole the more intelligible to the reader.

1. JEW. *What advantage then hath the Jew? or what profit is there of circumcision?* As if he had said: You lately allowed (chap. ii. 25) that "circumcision verily profiteth." But if circumcision, or our being in covenant with God, raises us no higher in the divine favor than the Gentiles; if the virtuous among them are as acceptable as any of us; nay, and condemn our nation too, as no longer deserving the divine regards; pray tell me, wherein lies the superior honor of the Jew; and what benefit can arise to him from his circumcision, and being vested in the privileges of God's peculiar people?

2. APOSTLE. *Much every way.* The Jews, in reference to the means and motives of obedience, enjoy many advantages beyond the Gentiles; and, principally, because *unto them were committed the oracles of God*—that revelation of His will to Moses and the prophets, containing a treasure of excellencies with which no other part of the world has been favored.

3. JEW. *For what?* "What then, *if some did not believe?"* If some of the Jewish nation have abused their privileges, and acted contrary to their obligations, shall their wickedness annul the promise which God made to Abraham that He would, by an everlasting covenant, be a God to him and to his seed after him? Gen. xvii. 7. Shall God, therefore, by stripping the Jews of their peculiar honor, as you intimate He will, falsify His promise to the nation, because some of the Jews are bad men?

4. APOSTLE. *God forbid.* "Let it not be, far from it, by no means." *Yea, let God be true, but every man a liar.* We must ever maintain that God is true, and that if, in any case, His promise appear to fail, it is because the condition on which it was given has not been complied with; which is the sense of what is written, Ps. li. 3: I acknowledge my sin, and condemn myself that the truth of Thy promise (2 Sam. vii. 15-16) to establish my house and throne forever may

MATTHEW HENRY

li. 4, *That thou mightest be justified*, to show, 1. That God will preserve his own honour in the world, notwithstanding the sins of men. 2. That it is our duty to justify God and to assert and maintain his justice, truth, and goodness, however it goes. Thus is God justified in his sayings, and cleared when *he is judged*, as it is here rendered.

Object. 3. Carnal hearts might hence take occasion to encourage themselves in sin. If all our sin be so far from overthrowing God's honour that it commends it, and his ends are secured, is it not unjust for God to punish our sin and unbelief so severely? *If our unrighteousness commend the righteousness of God, what shall we say? v*. 5. What inference may be drawn from this? *Is God unrighteous, who taketh vengeance? I speak as a man*, that is, it is suggested like a man.

Answer. *God forbid*. Suggestions that reflect dishonour upon God and his justice and holiness are rather to be startled at than parleyed with. *For then how shall God judge the world? v*. 6. The sin has never the less of malignity in it though God bring glory to himself out of it. It is only accidentally that sin commends God's righteousness. No thanks to the sinner for that. It is not for us to arraign the proceedings of such an absolute Sovereign. The sentence of the supreme court, whence lies no appeal, is not to be called in question.

Object. 4. The former objection is repeated (*v*. 7, 8). But his setting off the objection in its own colours is sufficient to answer it: *If the truth of God has more abounded through my lie*, why *should I be judged as a sinner, and not rather* thence take encouragement to go on in my sin, that grace may abound? *Let us do evil that good may come* is oftener in the heart than in the mouth of sinners, so justifying themselves in their wicked ways. There were those who charged such doctrines as this upon Paul and his fellow-ministers: Some affirm that we say so. It is no new thing for the best of God's people and ministers to be charged with holding and teaching such things as they do most detest, and it is not to be thought strange, when our Master himself was said to be in league with Beelzebub. It is an old artifice of Satan thus to cast dirt upon Christ's ministers—*Lay slander thickly on, for some will be sure to stick*.

Answer. He says no more by way of confutation but that the damnation of those is just. Those who deliberately do evil that good may come of it will be so far from escaping, under the shelter of that excuse, that it will rather justify their damnation. Sinning upon such a surmise, and in such a confidence, argues a great deal both of the wit and of the will in the sin. Their damnation is just; and, whatever excuses of this kind they may now please themselves with, they will none of them stand good in the great day, but God will be justified in his proceedings.

II. Paul next revives his assertion of the general guilt of mankind, both of Jews and Gentiles, *v*. 9–18. "*Are we better than they*, we Jews, or will this justify us? No, by no means." or, Are we Christians (Jews and Gentiles) so much better than the unbelieving part as to have merited God's grace? Alas! no. They *are all under sin*. Under the guilt of sin. We are guilty before God, *v*. 19. And this he had proved. It is a law term: *We have charged them with it*, and have made good our charge. This charge and conviction he here further illustrates by several scriptures out of the Old Testament. The 10th, 11th, and 12th verses are taken from Ps. xiv. 1–3. The rest that follows here is found in the Septuagint translation of the 14th Psalm. What is said in Ps. xiv is expressly spoken of *all the children of men*. The *Lord looked down*, as upon the old world. He who, when he himself had made all, looked upon everything that he had made, and behold all was very good, now that man had marred all, looked, and behold all was very bad. Observe,

1. That which is habitual, which is twofold:

(1) An habitual defect of everything that is good. *There is none righteous*, none that has an honest good principle of virtue, *no, not one;* implying that, if there had been but one, God would have found him out. When all the world was corrupt, God had his eye upon one righteous Noah. No righteousness is born with us. *There is none that understandeth, v*. 11. The fault lies in the corruption of the understanding. Religion and righteousness have so much reason on their side that if people had but any understanding they would be better and do better. Sinners are fools. *None that seeketh after God*, that is, none that has any desire after him. *They are together become unprofitable, v*. 12. Those that have forsaken God soon grow good for nothing. *There is none that doeth good;* no, not a just man upon the earth, that doeth good, and sinneth not.

(2) An habitual defection to everything that is

JAMIESON, FAUSSET, BROWN

5, 6. But if . . .—Another objection: 'It would appear, then, that the more faithless we are, so much the more illustrious will the fidelity of God appear; and in that case, for Him to take vengeance on us for our unfaithfulness would be (to speak as men profanely do) unrighteousness in God.' *Answer:* **God forbid; for then how shall God judge the world?**—i.e., 'Far from us be such a thought; for that would strike down all future judgment.

7, 8. For if the truth of God . . .—A further illustration of the same sentiment: i.e., 'Such reasoning amounts to this—which indeed we who preach salvation by free grace are slanderously accused of teaching—that the more evil we do, the more glory will redound to God; a damnable principle.' (Thus the apostle, instead of refuting this principle, thinks it enough to hold it up to execration, as one that shocks the moral sense.)—On this brief section, Note (1) Mark the place here assigned to the Scriptures. In answer to the question, "What advantage hath the Jew?" or, "What profit is there of circumcision?" those holding Romish views would undoubtedly have laid the stress upon the *priesthood*, **as the** glory of the Jewish economy. But in the apostle's esteem, "the oracles of God" were the jewel of the ancient Church (vss. 1, 2). (2) God's eternal purposes and man's free agency, as also the doctrine of salvation by grace and the unchanging obligations of God's law, have ever been subjected to the charge of inconsistency by those who will bow to no truth which their own reason cannot fathom. But amidst all the clouds and darkness which in this present state envelop the divine administration and many of the truths of the Bible, such broad and deep principles as are here laid down, and which shine in their own luster, will be found the sheet-anchor of our faith. "Let God be true, and every man a liar"; and as many advocates of salvation by grace as say, "Let us do evil that good may come," "their damnation is just."

9-20. THAT THE JEW IS SHUT UP UNDER LIKE CONDEMNATION WITH THE GENTILE IS PROVED BY HIS OWN SCRIPTURE. **9. are we better than they?**—'do we excel them?' **No, in no wise**—Better off the Jews certainly were, for having the oracles of God to *teach* them better; but as they *were* no better, that only aggravated their guilt. **10-12. As it is written . . .**—(Ps. 14:1-3; 53:1-3). These statements of the Psalmist were indeed suggested by particular manifestations of human depravity occurring under his own eye; but as this only showed what man, when unrestrained, is in his present condition, they were quite pertinent to the apostle's purpose.

ADAM CLARKE

be vindicated when Thou shalt execute that dreadful threatening (2 Sam. xii. 10) that the sword shall never depart from my house, which I own I have brought upon myself by my own iniquity. Should any man say that the promise of God had failed toward him, let him examine his heart and his ways, and he will find that *he* has departed out of that way in which alone God could, consistently with His holiness and truth, fulfill the promise.

5. JEW. *But if our unrighteousness commend the righteousness of God*. May we not suppose that our unrighteousness may serve to commend and illustrate the mercy of God in keeping and fulfilling to us the promise which He made to our forefathers? The more wicked we are, the more His faithfulness to His ancient promise is to be admired. And if so, would not God appear unjust in taking vengeance and casting us off? *I speak as a man*. I feel for the situation of both myself and my countrymen, and it is natural for one to speak as I do.

6. APOSTLE. *God forbid*. "By no means." God cannot be unjust; were He unjust, He could not be qualified to judge the world, nor inflict that punishment on the unfaithful Jews to which I refer.

7. JEW. *For if the truth of God*. But to resume my reasoning (see v. 5): If the faithfulness of God in keeping His promise made to our fathers is, through our unfaithfulness, made far more glorious than it otherwise would have been, why should we then be blamed for that which must redound so much to the honor of God?

8. APOSTLE. *And not rather*. And why do you not say, seeing you assume this ground, that in all cases we should do wickedly, because God, by freely pardoning, can so glorify His own grace? This is a most impious sentiment, but it follows from your reasoning; it has, indeed, been most injuriously laid to the charge of us apostles, who preach the doctrine of free pardon, through faith, without the merit of works; but this is so manifest a perversion of the truth that a just punishment may be expected to fall on the propagators of such a slander.

9. JEW. *What then?* After all, have not we Jews a better claim to the privileges of the kingdom of God than the Gentiles have?

APOSTLE. *No, in no wise*. For I have already proved that both Jews and Gentiles are under the guilt of sin; that they are equally unworthy of the blessings of the Messiah's kingdom; and that they must both, equally, owe their salvation to the mere mercy of God. From this, to the end of the twenty-sixth verse, the apostle proceeds to prove his assertion that both Jews and Gentiles were all under sin; and, that he might enforce the conviction upon the heart of the Jew, he quotes his own Scriptures, which he acknowledged had been given by the inspiration of God, and consequently true.

10. *As it is written*. See Ps. xiv. 1-3, from which this and the following two verses are taken. *There is none righteous*. This is true, not only of the Jews, but of the Gentiles—of every soul of man, considered in his natural and practical state, previously to his receiving the mercy of our Lord Jesus Christ. There is no righteous principle in them, and consequently no righteous act can be expected from them; see on v. 12. God himself is represented as looking down from heaven to see if there were any that feared and sought after Him; and yet He, who cannot be deceived, could find none!

12. *They are all gone out of the way*. They have all "diverged" from the right way; they have either abandoned or corrupted the worship of God: the Jews, in forsaking the law and the prophets; and the Gentiles, in acting contrary to the law which God had written on their hearts. And the departure of both from the truth proves the evil propensity of human nature in general. *They are together become unprofitable*. They are "useless," good for nothing; or, as the Hebrew has it, "they are putrid." He views the whole mass of mankind as slain and thrown together, to putrefy in heaps. This is what is termed the corruption of human nature. *There is none that doeth good*. In v. 10 it is said, "There is none righteous"; here, *There is none that doeth good*. The first may refer to the want of a righteous principle; the second, to the necessary consequence of the absence of

MATTHEW HENRY

evil: *They are all gone out of the way.* God made man in the way, set him in right, but he hath forsaken it.

2. That which is actual.

(1) In their words (*v.* 13, 14), in three things particularly: [1] Cruelty: *Their throat is an open sepulchre,* waiting an opportunity to do mischief. And when they do not vent it publicly, yet they are underhand intending mischief: the *poison of asps is under their lips,* the most venomous and incurable poison, with which they blast the good name of their neighbours. [2] Cheating: *With their tongues they have used deceit.* Herein they show themselves the devil's children. They *have used* it: it intimates that they make a trade of lying. [3] Cursing: reflecting upon God, and blaspheming his holy name; wishing evil to their brethren: *Their mouth is full of cursing and bitterness.* How many, who are called Christians, do by these sins evince that they are still under the reign and dominion of sin.

(2) In their ways (*v.* 15–17): *Their feet are swift to shed blood.* Wherever they go, *destruction and misery* go along with them; these are their companions—destruction and misery to themselves at last. Destruction and misery are in their ways; their sin is its own punishment: a man needs no more to make him miserable than to be a slave to his sins. —*And the way of peace have they not known.* They are strangers to all true peace; they know not the things that belong to their peace.

(3) The root of all this we have: *There is no fear of God before their eyes, v.* 18. The fear of God is here put for all practical religion. Wicked people have not this before their eyes; they are governed by other rules, aim at other ends. Where no fear of God is, no good is to be expected. When once fear is cast off, prayer is restrained, and then all goes to wreck and ruin quickly. So that we have here a short account of the general depravity and corruption of mankind.

Verses 19–31

From all this Paul infers that it is in vain to look for justification by the works of the law, and that it is to be had only by faith, which he lays down (*v.* 28) as the summary of his discourse. *We conclude that a man is justified by faith, without the deeds of the law.* Man, under the power of such corruption, could never, by any works of his own, gain acceptance with God; but it must be resolved purely into the free grace of God, given through Jesus Christ. There are two things from which the apostle here argues: the guiltiness of man, to prove that we cannot be justified by the works of the law, and the glory of God, to prove that we must be justified by faith.

I. He argues from man's guiltiness. The argument is very plain: we can never be justified and saved by the law that we have broken. Now concerning the guiltiness of man,

1. He fastens it particularly upon the Jews (*v.* 19). *This that the law says, it says to those who are under the law;* this conviction belongs to the Jews as well as others, for it is written in their law. "The law convicts and condemns you—you see it does." That *every mouth may be stopped.* Those that are justified have their mouths stopped by a humble conviction; those that are condemned have their mouths stopped too, for they shall at last be convinced.

2. He extends it in general to all the world: *That all the world may become guilty before God. May become guilty;* that is, may be proved guilty. They must all plead guilty. Guilty before God is a dreadful word. All are guilty, and therefore all have need of a righteousness wherein to appear before God. *For all have sinned* (*v.* 23), and *have come short of the glory of God*—have failed of that which is the chief end of man. *Come short,* as the archer comes short of the mark, as the runner comes short of the prize; so come short, as not only not to win, but to be great losers. (1) Come short of glorifying God. *They glorified him not as God.* Man by sin comes short of this, and, instead of glorifying God, dishonours him. (2) Come short of glorying *before God.* There is no boasting of innocency: if we go about to glory before God we have all sinned, and this will silence us. We may glory before men, who cannot search our hearts, but

JAMIESON, FAUSSET, BROWN

13-18. Their . . .—From generals, the apostle here comes to particulars, culling from different parts of Scripture passages which speak of depravity as it affects *the different members of the body;* as if to show more affectingly how "from the sole of the foot even to the head there is no soundness" in us. **Their throat is an open sepulchre**—(Ps. 5:9); i.e., 'What proceeds out of their heart, and finds vent in speech and action through the throat, is like the pestilential breath of an open grave.' **with their tongues they have used deceit**—(Ps. 5:9); i.e., 'That tongue which is man's glory (Ps. 16:9; 57:8) is prostituted to the purposes of deception.' **the poison of asps is under their lips**—(Ps. 140:3): i.e., 'Those lips which should "drop as an honey-comb," and "feed many," and "give thanks unto His name" (Canticles 4:11; Prov. 10:21; Heb. 13:15), are employed to secrete and to dart deadly poison.' **Whose mouth . . .**—(Ps. 10:7): i.e., 'That mouth which should be "most sweet" (Canticles 5:16), being "set on fire of hell" (Jas. 3:6), is filled with burning wrath against those whom it should only bless.' **Their feet are swift to shed blood**—(Prov. 1:16; Isa. 59:7): i.e., 'Those feet, which should "run the way of God's commandments" (Ps. 119:32), are employed to conduct men to deeds of darkest crime.' **Destruction and misery are in their ways; and the way of peace have they not known**—This is a supplementary statement about men's *ways,* suggested by what had been said about the "feet," and expresses the mischief and misery which men scatter in their path, instead of that peace which, as strangers to it themselves, they cannot diffuse. **There is no fear of God before their** EYES—(Ps. 36:1): i.e., 'Did the eyes but "see Him who is invisible" (Heb. 11:27), a reverential awe of Him with whom we have to do would chasten every joy and lift the soul out of its deepest depressions; but to all this the natural man is a stranger.' How graphic is this picture of human depravity, finding its way through each several organ of the body into the life: but how small a part of the "desperate wickedness" that is *within* (Jer. 17:9) "proceedeth *out of* the heart of man!" (Mark 7:21-23; Ps. 19:12.) **Therefore we conclude . . .** —It is the unavoidable tendency of dependence upon our own works, less or more, for acceptance with God, to beget a spirit of "boasting." But that God should encourage such a spirit in sinners, by any procedure of His, is incredible. This therefore stamps falsehood upon every form of 'justification by works,' whereas the doctrine that.

Our faith *receives* a righteousness
That makes the sinner just,

manifestly and entirely excludes "boasting"; and this is the best evidence of its truth. Inference second: *This and no other way of salvation is adapted alike to Jew and Gentile.*

19. Now we know that what . . . the law—i.e., the Scriptures, considered as a law of duty—**saith, it saith to them that are under the law**—of course, therefore, to the Jews. **that every mouth**—opened in self-justification—**may be stopped, and all the world may become**—i.e., be seen to be, and own itself—**guilty**—and so condemned—**before God.**

for all have sinned—Though men differ greatly in the *nature* and *extent* of their sinfulness, there is absolutely no difference between the best and the worst of men, in the *fact* that "all have sinned," and so underlie the wrath of God. **and come short of the glory**—or 'praise'—**of God**—i.e., 'have failed to earn His approbation' (cf. John 12:43, *Greek*). the best interpreters.

ADAM CLARKE

such a principle. If there be no righteousness within, there will be no acts of goodness without.

13. *Their throat is an open sepulchre.* This and all the following verses to the end of v. 18 are found in the Septuagint, but not in the Hebrew text. The verses in question, however, are not found in the Alexandrian MS. But they exist in the Vulgate, the Aethiopic, and the Arabic. As the most ancient copies of the Septuagint do not contain these verses, some contend that the apostle has quoted them from different parts of Scripture; and later transcribers of the Septuagint, finding that the tenth, eleventh, and twelfth verses were quoted from Psalm xiv, imagined that the rest were found originally there too, and so incorporated them in their copies from the apostle's text. *Their throat is an open sepulchre*—By their malicious and wicked words they bury, as it were, the reputation of all men. The whole of this verse appears to belong to their habit of lying, defamation, slandering, by which they wounded, blasted, and poisoned the reputation of others.

14. *Whose mouth is full of cursing.* They never speak but in profane oaths, blasphemies, and malice.

15. *Their feet are swift to shed blood.* They make use of every means in their power to destroy the reputation and lives of the innocent.

16. *Destruction and misery are in their ways. Destruction* is their work, and *misery* to themselves and to the objects of their malice is the consequence of their impious and murderous conduct.

17. *And the way of peace have they not known.* They neither have peace in themselves nor do they suffer others to live in quiet; they are brooders and fomenters of discord.

18. *There is no fear of God before their eyes.* This completes their bad character; they are downright atheists, at least practically such. They fear not God's judgments, although His eye is upon them in their evil ways. There is not one article of what is charged against the Jews and Gentiles here that may not be found justified by the histories of both, in the most ample manner. And what was true of them in those primitive times is true of them still. With very little variation, these are the evils in which the vast mass of mankind delight and live.

28. *Therefore we conclude.* Seeing these things cannot be denied, viz., that all have sinned; that all are guilty; that all are helpless; that none can deliver his own soul; and that God, in His endless mercy, has opened "a new and living way" to the holiest by the blood of Jesus, Heb. x. 19-20; therefore we, apostles and Christian teachers, *conclude,* prove by fair, rational consequence, that *a man,* any man, *is justified,* has his sins blotted out, and is received into the divine favor, *by faith* in Christ's blood, *without the deeds of the law,* which never could afford, to either Jew or Gentile, a ground for justification; because both have sinned against the law which God has given them, and consequently forfeited all right and title to the blessings which the obedient might claim.

19. *What things soever the law saith.* That the word *law* here does not mean the Pentateuch is evident from the preceding quotations, not one of which is taken from that work. The term *law* must here mean either the Jewish writings in general or that rule of moral conduct which God had given to both Jews and Gentiles: to the former in their own Scriptures; to the latter in that law written in their hearts by His own Spirit, and acknowledged in their written codes, and in their pleading in every civil case. Now, according to this great law, this rule of moral conduct, whether given in a written revelation, as to the Jews, or by the secret inspiration of His Spirit, as in certain cases to the Gentiles, *every mouth may be stopped, and all the world,* both Jews and Gentiles, stand convicted *before God;* for all mankind have sinned against this law.

23. *For all have sinned.* And consequently are equally helpless and guilty; and, as God is no respecter of persons, all human creatures being equally His offspring, and there being no reason why one should be preferred before another, therefore His endless mercy has embraced all. *And come short of the glory of God.* These words

MATTHEW HENRY

there is no glorying before God. (3) Come short of being glorified by God. Come short of justification, which is glory begun—come short of sanctification, which is the glorious image of God upon man. It is impossible now to get to heaven in the way of spotless innocency. That passage is blocked up.

3. Further to drive us off from expecting justification by the law, he ascribes this conviction to the law (*v.* 20): *For by the law is the knowledge of sin.* That law which convicts and condemns us can never justify us. It is the proper use and intendment of the law to open our wound, and therefore not likely to be the remedy. That which is searching is not sanative. Paul makes this use of the law, *ch.* vii. 9, *Therefore by the deeds of the law shall no flesh be justified in his sight.* (1) *No flesh shall be justified.* The corruption that remained in our nature will for ever obstruct any justification by our own works. (2) Not justified in his sight. As the conscience stands in relation to God, *in his sight*, we cannot be justified by the deeds of the law.

II. He argues from God's glory to prove that justification must be expected only by faith in Christ's righteousness. Is there no hope? Is the wound become incurable because of transgression? No, blessed be God, it is not (*v.* 21, 22); there is another way laid open for us, *the righteousness of God without the law is manifested* now under the gospel. This is called *the righteousness of God*, righteousness of his ordaining, and providing, and accepting,—righteousness which he confers upon us.

1. Now concerning this righteousness of God. It is manifested. The gospel-way of justification is a highway, it is laid open for us. It is *without the law.* The righteousness that Christ hath brought in is a complete righteousness. Yet *it is witnessed by the law and the prophets.* The law is so far from justifying us that it directs us to another way of justification, points at Christ as our righteousness, to whom bear all the prophets witness. It is by the *faith of Jesus Christ*, that faith which hath Jesus Christ for its object. It is by this that we become interested in that righteousness which God has ordained, and which Christ has brought in. It is *to all, and upon all, those that believe.* Jews and Gentiles are alike welcome to God through Christ; *for there is no difference.* It is *to all*, the gospel excludes none that do not exclude themselves; but it is *upon all that believe*, not only tendered to them, but put upon them as a crown, as a robe.

2. But now how is this for God's glory?

(1) It is for the glory of his grace (*v.* 24): *Justified freely by his grace.* It is *by his grace.* And, to make it the more emphatic, he says it is *freely by his grace.* The grace of God comes *freely, freely*; nothing in us to deserve such favours: no, it is all *through the redemption that is in Jesus Christ.* It comes freely to us, but Christ bought it, and paid dearly for it. Christ's purchase is no bar to the freeness of God's grace; for grace provided and accepted this vicarious satisfaction.

(2) It is for the glory of his justice and righteousness (*v.* 25, 26): *Whom God hath set forth to be a propitiation*, &c. [1] Jesus Christ is the great propitiation. He is our throne of grace, in and through whom atonement is made for sin. He is all in all in our reconciliation, not only the maker, but the matter of it. God was in Christ, reconciling the world unto himself. [2] *God hath set him forth.* God, the party offended, makes the first overtures towards a reconciliation. *Fore-ordained* him to this, in the counsels of his love form eternity, and has exhibited him to a guilty world as their propitiation. [3] *By faith in his blood* we become interested in this propitiation. There is the healing plaster provided. Faith is the applying of this plaster to the wounded soul. And this faith hath a special regard to *the blood of Christ.* Without blood there should be no remission, and no blood but this would do it effectually. [4] All who by faith are interested in this propitiation have *the remission of their sins that are past.* It was for this that Christ was set forth to be a propitiation. *Through the forbearance of God.* Divine patience has kept us out of hell, that we might have space to repent, and get to heaven. *Past through the forbearance of God.* It is owing to the divine forbearance that we were not taken in the very act of sin. It is owing to the master's goodness and the dresser's mediation that barren trees are let alone in the vineyard. It is owing to Christ that there is ever a sinner on this side hell. [5] God does in all this *declare his righteousness.* This he insists upon with a great deal of emphasis: *To declare, I say, at this time his righteousness.* He declares his righteousness, *First*, In the propitiation itself. It appears that he hates sin, when nothing less than the blood of Christ would satisfy for it. Finding sin, though but imputed, upon his own Son, he did not spare him, because he had

JAMIESON, FAUSSET, BROWN

20. Therefore by the deeds of—obedience to—**the law there shall no flesh be justified**—i.e., be held and treated as righteous; as is plain from the whole scope and strain of the argument. **in his sight**—at His bar (Ps. 143:2). **for by the law is the knowledge of sin**—See on ch. 4:15; 7:7; I John 3:4).—Note: How broad and deep does the apostle in this section lay the foundations of his great doctrine of Justification by free grace—in the disorder of man's whole nature, the consequent universality of human guilt, the condemnation, by reason of the breach of divine law, of the whole world, and the impossibility of justification before God by obedience to that violated law! Only when these humiliating conclusions are accepted and felt, are we in a condition to appreciate and embrace the grace of the Gospel, next to be opened up.

21-26. God's Justifying Righteousness, through Faith in Jesus Christ, Alike Adapted to Our Necessities and Worthy of Himself. **21-23. But now the righteousness of God**—see on ch. 1:17—**without the law**—i.e., a righteousness to which our obedience to the law contributes nothing whatever (vs. 28; Gal. 2:16). **is manifested, being witnessed**—attested—**by the law and the prophets**—the Old Testament Scriptures. Thus this justifying righteousness, though *new*, as only now fully disclosed, is an *old* righteousness, predicted and foreshadowed in the Old Testament. **by faith of**—i.e., in—**Jesus Christ unto all and upon all them that believe**—i.e., perhaps, brought nigh "*unto* all" men the Gospel, and actually "*upon* all" believing men, as theirs in possession [Luther and others]; but most interpreters understand both statements of believers as only a more emphatic way of saying that all believers, without distinction or exception, are put in possession of this gratuitous justification, purely by faith in Christ Jesus. **for there is no difference;**

24. justified freely—without anything done on our part to deserve—**by his grace**—His free love—**through the redemption that is in Christ Jesus**—a most important clause; teaching us that though justification is quite gratuitous, it is not a mere *fiat* of the divine will, but based on a "Redemption," i.e., 'the payment of a Ransom,' in Christ's death. That this is the sense of the word 'redemption,' when applied to Christ's death, will appear clear to any impartial student of the passages where it occurs. **25, 26. Whom God hath set forth to be a propitiation**—or 'propitiatory sacrifice'—**through faith in his blood**—Some of the best interpreters, observing that "faith *upon*" is the usual phrase in Greek, not "faith *in*" Christ, would place a comma after "faith," and understand the words as if written thus: "to be a propitiation, in His blood, through faith." But "faith *in* Christ" is used in Galatians 3:26 and Ephesians 1:15; and "faith in His blood" is the natural and appropriate meaning here. **to declare his righteousness for the remission**—rather, 'pretermission' or 'passing by'—**of sins**—'the sins'—**that are past**—not the sins committed by the believer before he embraces Christ, but the sins committed under the old economy, before Christ came to "put away sin by the sacrifice of Himself." **through the forbearance of God**—God not *remitting* but only *forbearing* to punish them, or passing them by, until an adequate atonement for them should be made. In thus not imputing them, God *was* righteous, but He was not *seen* to be so; there was no "manifestation of His righteousness" in doing so under the ancient economy. But now that God can "set forth" Christ as a "propitiation for sin through faith in His blood," the righteousness of His procedure in passing by the sins of believers before, and in now remitting them, is "manifested," declared, brought fully out to the view of the whole world. (Our translators have unfortunately missed this glorious truth, taking "the sins that are past" to mean the past sins of believers—committed before faith—and rendering, by the word "remission," what means only a 'passing by'; thus making it appear that "remission of sins" is "through the forbearance of God," which it certainly is not.) **To declare . . . at this time**—now for the first time, under the Gospel—**his righteousness: that he might be just, and the justifier of him that believeth in Jesus**—Glorious paradox! 'Just in punishing,' and 'merciful in pardoning,' men can understand; but 'just in justifying the guilty,' startles them. But the propitiation through faith in Christ's blood resolves the paradox and harmonizes the discordant elements. For in that "God hath made Him to be sin for us who knew no sin," *justice* has full satisfaction; and in that "we are made the righteousness of God in Him," *mercy* has her heart's delight!—Note (1) One way of a sinner's justifica-

ADAM CLARKE

have been variously translated. "Failed of attaining the glory of God"; stand in need of the glory, that is, the mercy of God." The simple meaning seems to be this: that all have sinned, and none can enjoy God's glory but they that are holy; consequently both Jews and Gentiles have failed in their endeavors to attain it, as by the works of any law no human being can be justified.

20. *Therefore by the deeds of the law.* On the score of obedience to this moral law, *there shall no flesh,* "no human being," *be justified:* none can be accepted in the sight of God. And why? Because *by the law is the knowledge of sin.* It is that which ascertains what sin is, shows how men have deviated from its righteous demands, and sentences them to death because they have broken it.

21. *But now the righteousness of God.* God's method of saving sinners is now shown by the gospel to be through His own mere mercy, by Christ Jesus; *without the law*—without any right or claim which might result from obedience to the law; and is evidently that which was intended by God from the beginning, for it is *witnessed by the law and the prophets*—the rites and ceremonies of the one, and the preachings and predictions of the others, all bearing testimony to the great design of God, and to the absolute necessity there was for the sacrifice and salvation which God has provided.

22. *Even the righteousness of God.* That method of saving sinners which is not of works, but by faith in Christ Jesus; and it is not restrained to any particular people, as the law and its privileges were, but is unto all mankind in its intention and offer, and becomes effectual to them that believe; for God hath now made *no difference* between the Jews and the Gentiles.

24. *Being justified freely by his grace.* So far from being able to attain the glory of God by their obedience, they are all guilty; and to be saved must be freely pardoned by God's grace, which is shown to them who believe, through the redemption, the "ransom price," which is in the sacrifice of Christ Jesus. The original properly means the price laid down for the redemption of a captive.

25. *Whom God hath set forth.* Appointed and published to be a *propitiation,* the "mercy seat," or "place of atonement"; because the blood of the sacrifice was sprinkled on and before that, in order to obtain remission of sin. The mercy seat was the lid or cover of the ark of the covenant, where God was manifest in the symbol of His presence between the cherubim; therefore the atonement that was made in this place was properly made to God himself. *Through faith in his blood.* This shows what we are to understand both by the *redemption* and by the *propitiation;* viz., that they refer to the sacrificial death of Jesus Christ, as the atonement made, and the *price* paid down, for the redemption of the souls of men. *To declare his righteousness.* "For the manifestation of His righteousness"; His mercy in saving sinners, by sending Jesus Christ to make an atonement for them; thereby declaring His readiness to remit all past transgressions committed by both Jews and Gentiles, during the time in which His merciful forbearance was exercised towards the world. And this applies to all who hear the gospel now; to them is freely offered remission of all *past sins.*

26. *To declare, I say, at this time.* To manifest now, by the dispensation of the gospel, *his righteousness,* His infinite mercy; and to manifest it in such a way that He might still appear to be the *just* God, and yet *the justifier,* the Pardoner, *of him which believeth in Jesus.* Here we learn that God designed to give the most evident displays of both His justice and mercy: of His justice, in requiring a sacrifice, and absolutely refusing to give salvation to a lost world in any other way; and of His mercy, in providing the sacrifice which His justice required. Thus, because Jesus was an Atonement, a Ransom Price, for the sin of the world, therefore God can, consistently with His justice, pardon every soul that believeth in Jesus. This is the full discovery of God's righteousness, of His wonderful method of magnifying His law and making it honorable; of showing the infinite purity of His justice, and of saving a lost world. Hitherto, from the ninth verse, the apostle had gone on without interruption, proving that Jew

MATTHEW HENRY

made himself sin for us. *Secondly,* In the pardon upon that propitiation. *That he might be just, and the justifier of him that believeth.* It is now become not only an act of grace and mercy, but an act of righteousness, in God, to pardon the sins of penitent believers, having accepted the satisfaction that Christ by dying made to his justice for them. He is just, that is, faithful to his word.

(3) It is for God's glory; for boasting is thus excluded, *v.* 27. Now, if justification were by the works of the law, boasting would not be excluded. If we were saved by our own works, we might put the crown upon our own heads. But the *law of faith* doth for ever exclude boasting; for faith is a depending, self-emptying, self-denying grace, and casts every crown before the throne. He speaks of *the law of faith.* Believers are not left lawless: faith is a law, it is a working grace.

From all this he draws this conclusion (*v.* 28): *That a man is justified by faith without the deeds of the law.*

III. He shows the extent of this privilege of justification by faith, and that it is not the peculiar privilege of the Jews, but pertains to the Gentiles also; for he had said (*v.* 22) that there is no difference. He asserts and proves it (*v.* 29, 30): *Is he the God of the Jews only?*

It is one God of grace that *justifies the circumcision by faith, and the uncircumcision through faith.* However the Jews, in favour of themselves, will needs fancy a difference, really there is no more difference than between *by* and *through.* He obviates an objection (*v.* 31), as if this doctrine did nullify the law. "No," says he, "though we do say that the law will not justify us, yet we do not therefore say that it was given in vain.

We establish the right use of the law, and secure its standing, by fixing it on the right basis. Though we cannot be saved by it as a covenant, yet we own it, and submit to it, as a rule in the hand of the Mediator, subordinate to the law of grace; and so are so far from overthrowing that we establish the law."

JAMIESON, FAUSSET, BROWN

tion is taught in the Old Testament and in the New alike: only more dimly during the twilight of Revelation; in unclouded light under its perfect day (vs. 21). (2) As there is no difference in the *need,* so is there none in the *liberty to appropriate* the provided salvation. The best need to be saved by faith in Jesus Christ; and the worst only need that. On this common ground all saved sinners meet here, and will stand for ever (vss. 22-24). (3) It is on the atoning blood of Christ, as the one propitiatory sacrifice which God hath set forth to the eye of the guilty, that the faith of the convinced and trembling sinner fastens for deliverance from wrath. Though he knows that he is "justified freely, by God's grace," it is only because it is "through the *redemption* that is in Christ Jesus" that he is able to find peace and rest even in this (vs. 25). (4) The strictly accurate view of believers under the Old Testament is not that of a company of *pardoned* men, but of men whose sins, put up with and passed by in the meantime, awaited a *future expiation* in the fulness of time (vss. 25, 26; see on Luke 9:31; and on Heb. 9:15; and 11:39, 40).

27-31. Inferences from the Foregoing Doctrines, and an Objection Answered. Inference first: *Boasting is excluded by this, and no other way of justification.* **27, 28. Where is boasting then? . . . excluded. By what law?**—on what principle or scheme?—**of works? Nay; but by the law of faith.**

29. Is he the God of the Jews only? . . .—The way of salvation must be one equally suited to the whole family of fallen man: but the doctrine of justification by faith is the only one that lays the basis of a Universal Religion; this therefore is another mark of its truth.

30. it is one God who shall justify—'has unchangeably fixed that He shall justify'—**the circumcision by**—'of'—**faith, and the uncircumcision through faith**—probably this is but a varied statement of the same truth for greater emphasis (see on vs. 22); though Bengel thinks that the justification of the Jews, as the born heirs of the promise, may be here purposely said to be "*of* faith," while that of the Gentiles, previously "strangers to the covenants of promise," may be said to be "*through* faith," as thus admitted into a new family. *Objection.* **31. Do we then make void the law through faith?**—'Does this doctrine of justification by faith, then, dissolve the obligation of the law? If so, it cannot be of God. But away with such a thought, for it does just the reverse.' **God forbid: yea, we establish the law**—It will be observed here, that, important as was this objection, and opening up as it did so noble a field for the illustration of the peculiar glory of the Gospel, the apostle does no more here than indignantly repel it, intending at a subsequent stage of his argument (ch. 6) to resume and discuss it at length.—Note (1) It is a fundamental requisite of all true religion that it tend to humble the sinner and exalt God; and every system which breeds self-righteousness, or cherishes boasting, bears falsehood on its face (vss. 27, 28). (2) The fitness of the Gospel to be a universal religion, beneath which the guilty of every name and degree are invited and warranted to take shelter and repose, is a glorious evidence of its truth (vss. 29, 30). (3) The glory of God's law, in its eternal and immutable obligations, is then only fully apprehended by the sinner, and then only is it enthroned in the depths of his soul, when, believing that "He was made sin for him who knew no sin," he sees himself "made the righteousness of God in Him." Thus do we not make void the law through faith: yea, we establish the law. (4) This chapter, and particularly the latter part of it, "is the proper seat of the Pauline doctrine of Justification, and the grand proof-passage of the Protestant doctrine of the Imputation of Christ's righteousness and of Justification not on account of, but through faith alone" [Philippi]. To make good this doctrine, and reseat it in the faith and affection of the Church, was worth all the bloody struggles that it cost our fathers, and it will be the wisdom and safety, the life and vigor of the churches, to "stand fast in this liberty wherewith Christ hath made them free, and not be again entangled"—in the very least degree—"with the yoke of bondage."

ADAM CLARKE

and Gentile were in a state of guilt and condemnation, and that they could be saved only by the redemption that is in Christ Jesus. The Jew, finding his boasted privileges all at stake, interrupts him, and asks:

27. Jew. *Where is boasting then?* "This glorying" of ours. Have we nothing in which we can trust for our acceptance with God? No merit of our own? Nothing accruing to us from our circumcision and being in covenant with God?

Apostle. *It is excluded.* "It is shut out"; the door of heaven is shut against everything of this kind.

Jew. *By what law?* By what rule, doctrine, or reason is it shut out? by the law *of works?* The rule of obedience, which God gave to us, and by which obedience we are accepted by Him?

Apostle. *Nay.* Not by the law of works; glorying is not cut off or shut out by that; it stands in full force as the rule of life. But you have sinned and need pardon. The law of works grants no pardon; it requires obedience, and threatens the disobedient with death. But all glorying in the expectation of salvation through your own obedience is excluded by the law; the doctrine of faith, faith alone, in the mercy of God, through the propitiation made by the blood of Jesus (v. 25), is that by which you can be justified, pardoned, and taken into the divine favor.

29. *Is he the God of the Jews only?* Do not begin to suppose that because you cannot be justified by the works of the law, and God has in His mercy found out a new method of saving you, that therefore this mercy shall apply to the Jews exclusively. Is not God the Maker, Preserver, and Redeemer *also of the Gentiles? Yes, of the Gentiles also,* as much as of the Jews. For all have equally sinned and there is no reason, if God be disposed to show mercy at all, that He should prefer the one to the other; since they are all equally guilty, sinful, and necessitous.

30. *Seeing it is one God.* This has been rendered, "Seeing God is one." It however makes little difference in the sense. The apostle's meaning most evidently is, It is one and the same God who made both Jews and Gentiles, who shall *justify,* pardon, *the circumcision,* the believing Jews, *by faith,* and the *uncircumcision,* the believing Gentiles, by the same faith; as there is but one Saviour and one atonement provided for the whole. It is fanciful to suppose that the apostle has one meaning when he says, *by faith,* and a different meaning when he says, *through faith.* Both the prepositions are to be understood in precisely the same sense; only the addition of the article in the last case extends and more pointedly ascertains the meaning. It is one and the same God who shall justify the believing Jews by faith and the believing Gentiles "by that same faith."

31. *Do we then make void the law through faith?* (1) By *law* here we may understand the whole of the Mosaic law, in its rites and ceremonies, of which Jesus Christ was the Subject and the End. (2) We may understand also the moral law, that which relates to the regulation of the manners or conduct of men. This law also was established by the doctrine of salvation by faith, because this faith works by love, and love is the principle of obedience: and whosoever receives salvation through faith in Christ receives power to live in holy obedience to every moral precept.

MATTHEW HENRY

CHAPTER 4

Verses 1–8

Here the apostle proves that Abraham was justified not by works, but by faith. He appeals to the case of Abraham their father, and puts his own name to the relation, being a Hebrew of the Hebrews: *Abraham our Father*. Now *what has he found?* All the world is seeking; but none can be truly reckoned to have found, but those who are justified before God; and thus Abraham found this one pearl of great price. What has he found *as pertaining to the flesh*, that is, by circumcision and his external privileges? Was he justified by them? Was it the merit of his works that recommended him to God's acceptance? No, by no means.

I. If he had been justified by works, room would have been left for boasting. If so, *he hath whereof to glory* (*v.* 2). "But was not his name made great, and then might not he glory?" Yes, but not before God; he might deserve well of men, but he could never merit of God. Paul himself had *whereof to glory before men*, and we have him sometimes glorying in it, but nothing to glory in before God. Man must not pretend to glory in anything before God; no, not Abraham.

II. It is expressly said that Abraham's faith was counted to him for righteousness. *What saith the scripture? v.* 3. In all controversies in religion this must be our question. It is not what this great man, and the other good man, say, but *What saith the scripture?* Now the scripture saith that *Abraham believed, and this was counted to him for righteousness* (Gen. xv. 6); therefore he had not whereof to glory before God, it being purely of free grace that it was so imputed. It is mentioned in Genesis, upon occasion of a very signal act of faith concerning the promised seed, and it followed upon a grievous conflict he had had with unbelief. It is not the perfect faith that is required to justification, but the prevailing faith, the faith that has the upper hand of unbelief.

III. If he had been justified by works, the reward would have been *of debt, and not of grace*. This is his argument (*v.* 4, 5): Abraham's reward was God himself; so he had told him but just before (Gen. xv. 1), *I am thy exceeding great reward.* Now, if Abraham had merited this by the perfection of his obedience, it had not been an act of grace in God. God will have free grace to have all the glory. And therefore *to him that worketh not*—that can pretend to no such merit, but casts himself wholly upon the free grace of God in Christ, by a lively, active, obedient faith—to such a one *faith is counted for righteousness. Him that justifieth the ungodly*, that is, him that was before ungodly. His former ungodliness was no bar to his justification upon his believing. No room therefore is left for despair; though God clears not the impenitent guilty; yet through Christ he justifies the ungodly.

IV. He further illustrates this by a passage out of the Psalms, where David speaks of the remission of sins, as constituting the blessedness of a man, pronouncing blessed, not the man who has no sin, but *the man to whom the Lord imputeth not sin.* 1. The nature of forgiveness. It is the remission of a debt, it is the covering of sin. God is said *to cast sin behind his back, to hide his face from it*, which implies that the ground of our blessedness is not our innocency, but God's not laying it to our charge. It is God's *not imputing sin* (*v.* 8), which makes it wholly a gracious act of God. The acceptance and the reward cannot be expected as debts; and therefore Paul infers (*v.* 6) that it is the imputing of righteousness without works. 2. The blessedness of it: *Blessed are they.* It is said, *Blessed are those whose iniquities are forgiven*, to show what that blessedness is, and what is the ground of it. Pardoned people are the only blessed people. Oh, how much therefore is it our interest to make it sure to ourselves that our sins are pardoned! For this is the foundation of all other benefits.

Verses 9–17

St. Paul observes in this paragraph when and why Abraham was thus justified.

I. It was before he was circumcised, *v.* 10. His faith was counted to him for righteousness while he was in uncircumcision. It was imputed. Now this the apostle takes notice of in answer to the question (*v.* 9), *Cometh this blessedness then on the circumcision only, or on the uncircumcision also?* Abraham was pardoned and accepted in uncircumcision. Here are two reasons why Abraham was justified by faith in circumcision:

JAMIESON, FAUSSET, BROWN

CHAPTER 4

VSS. 1-25. THE FOREGOING DOCTRINE OF JUSTIFICATION BY FAITH ILLUSTRATED FROM THE OLD TESTAMENT. First: *Abraham was justified by faith.* **1-3. What shall we say then that Abraham, our father as pertaining to the flesh, hath found?**—i.e., (as the order in the original shows), 'hath found, as pertaining to ("according to," or "through") the flesh'; meaning, 'by all his natural efforts or legal obedience.' **For if Abraham were justified by works, he hath whereof to glory; but not before God**—'If works were the ground of Abraham's justification, he would have matter for boasting; but as it is perfectly certain that he hath none in the sight of God, it follows that Abraham could not have been justified by works.' And to this agree the words of Scripture.

For what saith the Scripture? Abraham believed God, and it—his faith—**was counted to him for righteousness**—Gen. 15.6. Romish expositors and Arminian Protestants make this to mean that God accepted Abraham's act of believing as a substitute for complete obedience. But this is at variance with the whole spirit and letter of the apostle's teaching. Throughout this whole argument, *faith* is set in direct opposition to *works,* in the matter of justification—and even in the next two verses. The meaning, therefore, cannot possibly be that the mere act of believing—which is as much a work as any other piece of commanded duty (John 6:29; I John 3:23)—was counted to Abraham for all obedience. The meaning plainly is that Abraham believed in the promises which embraced Christ (Gen. 12:3; 15:5, etc.), as we believe in Christ Himself; and in both cases, faith is merely the instrument that puts us in possession of the blessing gratuitously bestowed. **4, 5. Now to him that worketh**—as a servant for wages—**is the reward not reckoned of grace**—as a matter of favor—**but of debt**—as a matter of right. **But to him that worketh not**—who, despairing of acceptance with God by "working" for it the work of obedience, does not attempt it—**but believeth on him that justifieth the ungodly**—casts himself upon the mercy of Him that justifieth those who deserve only condemnation. **his faith . . .**—See on vs. 3. Second: *David sings of the same justification.*

6-8. David also describeth—'speaketh,' 'pronounceth'—**the blessedness of the man unto whom the Lord imputeth righteousness without works**—whom, though void of all good works, He, nevertheless, regards and treats as righteous. **Saying, Blessed . . .**—(Ps. 32:1, 2). David here sings in express terms only of "transgression forgiven, sin covered, iniquity not imputed"; but as the negative blessing necessarily includes the positive, the passage is strictly in point.

9-12. Cometh this blessedness then . . .—i.e., 'Say not, All this is spoken of the *circumcised,* and is therefore no evidence of God's *general* way of justifying men; for Abraham's justification took place long before he was circumcised, and so could have no dependence upon that rite: nay, "the sign of circumcision" was given to Abraham as "a seal" (or token) of the (justifying) righteousness which he had *before* he was circumcised; in order that he might stand forth to every age as *the parent believer*—the model man of justification by faith—after whose type, as the first public example of it, all were to be moulded, whether Jew or Gentile, who should thereafter believe to life everlasting.'

ADAM CLARKE

CHAPTER 4

1. JEW. *What shall we then say that Abraham, our father as pertaining to the flesh, hath found?* The *pertaining to the flesh* must here refer to the sign in Abraham's flesh, viz., his circumcision, on which the Jew would found his right to peculiar blessings.

2. *For if Abraham were justified by works.* The JEW proceeds: I conclude, therefore, that Abraham was *justified by works,* or by his obedience to the law of circumcision; and, consequently, he has cause for glorying, to "exult" in something which he has done to entitle him to these blessings. Now it is evident that he has this glorying, and consequently that he was justified by works.

APOSTLE. *But not before God.* These seem to be the apostle's words, and contain the beginning of his answer to the arguments of the Jew, as if he had said: Allowing that Abraham might glory in being called from heathenish darkness into such marvellous light, and exult in the privileges which God had granted to him, yet this glorying was not before God as a reason why those privileges should be granted, the glorying itself being a consequence of these very privileges.

3. *For what saith the scripture?* The scriptural account of this transaction, Gen. xv. 6, is decisive; for there it is said, Abraham "believed" God, and it was counted, it was reckoned "to him for righteousness," for justification.

4. *Now to him that worketh is the reward not reckoned of grace, but of debt.* Therefore if Abraham had been justified by works, the blessings he received would have been given to him as a reward for those works, and consequently his believing could have had no part in his justification, and his faith would have been useless.

5. *But to him that worketh not.* Which was the case with Abraham, for he was called when he was ungodly, i.e., an idolater; and, on his believing, was freely justified. And as all men have sinned, none can be justified by works; and, therefore, justification, if it take place at all, must take place in behalf of the ungodly, forasmuch as all mankind are such. It is necessary to observe here, in order to prevent confusion and misapprehension, that although the verb *dikaioo* has a variety of senses in the New Testament, yet here it is to be taken as implying the "pardon of sin," "receiving a person into the favor of God." It is also necessary to observe that our translators render the verb *logizomai* differently in different parts of this chapter. It is rendered "counted," vv. 3, 5; "reckoned," vv. 4, 9-10; "imputed," vv. 6, 8, 11, 22-24. "Reckoned" is probably the best sense in all these places.

6. *Even as David also.* David, in Ps. xxxii. 1-2, gives us also the true notion of this way of justification, i.e., by faith, without the merit of works, where he says—

7. *Blessed are they whose iniquities are forgiven.* That is, the man is truly "happy" whose iniquities, whose transgressions of the law, are forgiven; for by these he was exposed to the most grievous punishment. *Whose sins,* his innumerable deviations from the strict rule of truth and righteousness, *are covered*—entirely removed out of sight, and thrown into oblivion.

8. *Blessed is the man to whom the Lord will not impute sin.* That man is truly happy to whose charge God does not reckon sin; that is, they alone are happy who are redeemed from the curse of the law and the consequence of their ungodly life, by having their sins freely forgiven, through the mercy of God.

9. *Cometh this blessedness . . . upon the circumcision only?* The word *only* is very properly supplied by our translators, and is here quite necessary to complete the sense. If this pardon, granted in this way, be essential to "happiness"—and David says it is so—then is it the privilege of the Jews exclusively? This cannot be; for it is by the mere mercy of God, through faith. But if God offer it to the circumcision, not because they have been obedient, for they also have sinned, but because of His mere mercy, then of course the same blessedness may be offered to the Gentiles who believe in the Lord Jesus. And this is evident; *for we say,* following our own Scriptures, *that faith was*

MATTHEW HENRY

1. That circumcision might be *a seal of* the *righteousness of faith*, *v.* 11. For the confirmation of Abraham's faith God was pleased to appoint a sealing ordinance, and Abraham received it as a special favour, *the sign of circumcision*, &c. (1) The nature of sacraments in general; they are signs and seals. They are signs of absolute grace and favour; they are seals of the conditional promises. God does in the sacraments seal to us to be to us a God, and we do therein seal to him to be to him a people. (2) The nature of circumcision in particular: it was the initiating sacrament of the Old Testament. *A sign*—a sign of that original corruption which we are all born with, and which is cut off by spiritual circumcision. It was *an outward and sensible sign of an inward and spiritual grace signified thereby. A seal of the righteousness of the faith.* In general, it was a seal of the covenant of grace, particularly of justification by faith. Now if infants were then capable of receiving a seal of the covenant of grace, which proves that they then were within the verge of that covenant, how they come to be now cast out of the covenant, those are concerned to make out that reject the baptism of the seed of believers.

2. *That he might be the father of all those that believe.* In him commenced a much clearer and fuller dispensation of the covenant of grace than any that had been before extant; and therefore he is called *the father of all that believe. The father of all those that believe;* that is, a standing *pattern of faith*, as parents are examples to their children; and a standing precedent of justification by faith, as the liberties of the fathers descend to their children. (1) The father of believing Gentiles, *though they be not circumcised.* Abraham being himself uncircumcised when he was justified by faith, uncircumcision can never be a bar. Thus were the doubts and fears of the poor Gentiles anticipated. (2) The father of believing Jews because they *are not of the circumcision only, but walk in the steps of that faith*—not only are of Abraham's family, but follow the example of Abraham's faith. See here who are the genuine children of those that were the church's fathers. Those that tread in their steps; this is the line of succession. Those have most reason to call Christ Father, not that bear his name in being Christians in profession, but that tread in his steps.

II. It was before the giving of the law, *v.* 13–16.

1. What that promise was—*that he should be the heir of the world.* The meek are said to *inherit the earth*, and the world is theirs. Though Abraham had so little of the world in possession, yet he was heir of it all. Or, rather, it points at Christ, the seed here mentioned *To thy seed, which is Christ.* Now Christ is the heir of the world, and it is in him that Abraham was so.

2. How it was made to him: *Not through the law, but through the righteousness of faith. Not through the law;* it was upon his trusting God, in his leaving his own country when God commanded him. Now, being by faith, it could not be by the law (*v.* 14, 15): *If those who are of the law be heirs*, then *faith is made void*; for, if it were requisite that there should be a perfect performance of the whole law, then the promise can never take its effect, since the way to life by perfect obedience to the law, and spotless sinless innocency, is wholly blocked up, and the law in itself opens no other way. This he proves, *v.* 15. *The law worketh wrath*—wrath in us to God; as the damming up of a stream makes it swell—wrath in God against us. Now it is certain that we can never expect the inheritance by a law that worketh wrath. How the law works wrath he shows in the latter part of the verse: *Where no law is there is no transgression* (an acknowledged maxim).

3. Why the promise was made to him by faith; for three reasons, *v.* 16. (1) *That it might be by grace and not by the law; by grace, and not of debt, not of merit.* Faith hath particular reference to grace granting, as grace hath reference to faith receiving. God will have every crown thrown at the feet of grace, free grace. (2) *That the promise might be sure.* The first covenant was not sure: but, through man's failure, the benefits designed by it were cut off. The more effectually to ensure the conveyance of the new covenant, there is another way found out, *not by works but by faith*, which received all from Christ, in whose keeping it is safe. (3) *That it might be sure to all the seed.* If it had been by the law, it had been limited to the Jews. It was by faith that Gentiles as well as Jews might become interested in it, the spiritual as well as the natural seed of faithful Abraham. God would contrive the promise in such a way as might comprehend all true believers, and for this (*v.* 17) he refers us to Gen. xvii. 5, where the reason of the change of his name from *Abram—a high father*, *to Abraham—the high father of a multitude*,

JAMIESON, FAUSSET, BROWN

ALBERT BARNES:

11. "And he received the sign." A sign is that by which anything is shown, or represented. And circumcision thus showed that there was a covenant between Abraham and God (Gen. 17:1-10). It became the public mark or token of the relation which he sustained to God. "A seal." A seal is that mark of wax or other substance, which is attached to an instrument of writing, as a deed, to confirm, ratify it, or to make it binding. Sometimes instruments were sealed, or made authentic, by stamping on them some word, letter, or device, which had been engraved on silver or on precious stones. The seal or stamp was often worn as an ornament on the finger (Esther 8:8; Gen. 41:42; 38:18; Ex. 28:11, 36; 29:6). To affix the seal, whether of wax or otherwise, was to confirm a contract or an engagement. In allusion to this, circumcision is called a seal of the covenant which God had made with Abraham. That is, he appointed this as a public attestation to the fact that he had previously approved of Abraham, and had made important promises to him.

"Which he had, yet being uncircumcised." He believed (Gen. 15:5); was accepted, or justified; was admitted to the favor of God, and favored with clear and remarkable promises (Gen. 15:18-21; 17:1-9), before he was circumcised. Circumcision, therefore, could have contributed neither to his justification, nor to the promises made to him by God. "That he might be the father." All this was done that Abraham might be held up as an example, or a model, of the very doctrine which the apostle was defending. The word "father" here is used evidently in a spiritual sense, as denoting that he was the ancestor of all true believers; that he was their model and example. They are regarded as his children because they are possessed of his spirit, are justified in the same way, and are imitators of his example. In this sense the expression occurs in Luke 19:9; John 8:33; Gal. 3:7, 29.

—*Popular Commentary*

13-15. For the promise . . .—This is merely an enlargement of the foregoing reasoning, applying to the *law* what had just been said of *circumcision*. **that he should be the heir of the world**—or, that "all the families of the earth should be blessed in him." **was not to Abraham or to his seed through the law**—in virtue of obedience to the law—**but through the righteousness of faith**—in virtue of his simple faith in the divine promises. **For if they which are of the law be heirs**—If the blessing is to be earned by obedience to the law. **faith is made void**—the whole divine method is subverted. **Because the law worketh wrath**—has nothing to give to those who break is but condemnation and vengeance. **for where there is no law, there is no transgression**—It is just the law that makes transgression, in the case of those who break it; nor can the one exist without the other. **16, 17. Therefore . . .**—A general summary: 'Thus justification is by *faith*, in order that its purely *gracious* character may be seen, and that all who follow in the steps of Abraham's faith—whether of his natural seed or no—may be assured of the like justification with the parent-believer.'

ADAM CLARKE

reckoned to Abraham for righteousness. He had no merit; he was an idolater. But he believed in God, and his faith was reckoned to him "in reference to his justification."

10. *How was it then reckoned?* In what circumstances was Abraham when this blessing was bestowed upon him? When he was circumcised, or before? *Not in circumcision, but in uncircumcision.* Faith was reckoned to Abraham for justification, as we read in Gen. xv. 6, but circumcision was not instituted till about fourteen or fifteen years after, Gen. xvii. 1, etc.; for faith was reckoned to Abraham for righteousness or justification at least one year before Ishmael was born; compare Genesis xv and xvi. At Ishmael's birth he was eighty-six years of age, Gen. xvi. 16; and at the institution of circumcision, Ishmael was thirteen, and Abraham ninety-nine years old.

11. *And he received the sign of circumcision, a seal.* So far was obedience to the law of circumcision from being the reason of his justification that he not only received this justification before he was circumcised, but he received the *sign* of circumcision as a *seal* of the pardon which he had before actually received. And thus he became the *father*, the great head and representative, of all them that believe; particularly the Gentiles, who are now in precisely the same state in which Abraham was when he received the mercy of God. The whole of the apostle's argument in this fourth chapter to the Romans proves that we believing Gentiles are the seed of Abraham, to whom, as well as to himself, the promise was made; and that the promise made to him is the same in effect as that promise which is now made to us. There is nothing more common in the Jewish writers than the words *sign* and *seal* as signifying the mark in the flesh by the rite of circumcision.

12. *And the father of circumcision.* He is also the head and representative of all the circumcision of all the Jews *who also walk in the steps of that faith;* who seek for justification by faith only, and not by the works of the law—for this was the faith that Abraham had before he received circumcision.

13. *For the promise, that he should be the heir of the world.* This promise intimated that he should be the medium through whom the mercy of God should be communicated to the *world*, to both Jews and Gentiles; and the manner in which he was justified, be the rule and manner according to which all men should expect this blessing. Abraham is here represented as having all the world given to him as his inheritance, because in him all nations of the earth are blessed.

14. *For if they which are of the law be heirs.* If the Jews only be heirs of the promise made to Abraham, and that on the ground of prior obedience to the law, then *faith is made void*, is entirely useless; *and the promise*, which was made to faith, is *made of none effect.*

15. *Because the law worketh wrath.* For *law*, any law, or rule of duty. No law makes provision for the exercise of mercy, for it *worketh wrath*, "punishment," for the disobedient. *Law* necessarily subjects the transgressor to punishment. But the Jews have a law, which they have broken, and now they are exposed to the penal sanctions of that law; and if the promises of pardon without the works of the law do not extend to them, they must be finally miserable, because they have all broken the law, and the law exacts punishment. This was a home stroke, and the argument is unanswerable.

16. *Therefore it is of faith, that it might be by grace.* On this account the promise is mercifully grounded, not on obedience to a law, but on the infinite goodness of God; and thus the promise is *sure to all the seed*—to all, both Jews and Gentiles, who, believing in Christ Jesus, have a right to all the blessings contained in the Abrahamic covenant. *All the seed* necessarily comprehends all mankind.

MATTHEW HENRY

is thus rendered: *For a father of many nations have I made thee;* that is, all believers should take Abraham for their pattern, and call him *father.*

Verses 17–22

I. Whom he believed: *God who quickeneth.* It is God himself that faith fastens upon. Now observe what in God Abraham's faith had an eye to. 1. *God who quickeneth the dead.* It was promised that he should be *the father of many nations,* when he and his wife were now as good as dead (Heb. xi. 11, 12), and therefore he looks upon God as a God that could breathe life into dry bones. He that quickeneth the dead can do anything, can give a child to Abraham when he is old, can bring the Gentiles, who are *dead in trespasses and sins,* to a divine and spiritual life, Eph. ii. 1. 2. *Who calleth things which are not as though they were.* The justification and salvation of sinners, the espousing of the Gentiles that had not been a people, were a gracious calling of things which are not as though they were. This expresses the sovereignty of God and his absolute power and dominion, a mighty stay to faith when all other props sink and totter. It is faith indeed to build upon the all-sufficiency of God for the accomplishment of that which is impossible to anything but that all-sufficiency. Thus Abraham became *the father of many nations before him whom he believed.* It is by faith in God that we become accepted of him.

II. How he believed. *Against hope, he believed in hope, v.* 18. There was a hope against him, a natural hope. All the arguments of sense, and reason, and experience, which in such cases usually beget and support hope, were against him. But, against all those inducements to the contrary, he believed; for he had a hope for him: *He believed in hope,* which arose, as his faith did, from the consideration of God's all-sufficiency. *That he might become the father of many nations.* Therefore God, by his almighty grace, enabled him thus to believe against hope. It was fit that he who was to be the father of the faithful should have something more than ordinary in his faith. This was that which he believed, when it was counted to him for righteousness. *Being not weak in faith, he considered not his own body, v.* 19. His own body was now dead—become utterly unlikely to beget a child. When God intends some special blessing for his people, he commonly puts a sentence of death upon the blessing itself. But Abraham did not consider this, *he did not dwell in his thoughts upon it.* His faith thought of nothing but the faithfulness of the promise, and this kept up his faith. Though it may seem to be the wisdom of carnal reason, yet it is the weakness of faith, to look into the bottom of all the difficulties that arise against the promise. *He staggered not at the promise of God through unbelief* (*v.* 20). *He disputed not;* he did not hold any self-consultation about it, did not take time to consider whether he should close with it or no, but by a resolute act of his soul, with a holy boldness, ventured all upon the promise. He took it not for a point that would admit of argument or debate. He *staggered not through unbelief.* Unbelief is at the bottom of all our staggerings at God's promises. It is not the promise that fails, but our faith that fails when we stagger. He *was strong in faith, giving glory to God, he was strengthened* in faith, his faith *got ground by exercise.* Though weak faith shall not be rejected, yet strong faith shall be commended and honoured. The strength of his faith appeared in the victory it won over his fears. Abraham's faith gave God the glory, especially of his faithfulness. Abraham gave glory to God by trusting him. We never hear our Lord Jesus commending anything so much as great faith (Matt. viii. 10 and xv. 28): therefore God gives honour to faith, great faith, because faith, great faith, gives honour to God. He was *fully persuaded that what God had promised he was able to perform—was carried on with the greatest confidence* and assurance; it is a metaphor taken from ships that come into the harbour with full sail. Abraham saw the storms of doubts, and fears, and temptations likely to rise against the promise. But Abraham, having taken God for his pilot, and the promise for his card and compass, like a bold adventurer sets up all his sails, regards neither winds nor clouds, but trusts to the wisdom and faithfulness of his pilot, and bravely makes to the harbour, and comes home an unspeakable gainer. Such was his full persuasion, built on the omnipotence of God: *He was able.* Our waverings rise mainly from our distrust of the divine power. It is requisite we believe not only that he is faithful, but that he is able. *And therefore it was imputed to him for righteousness, v.* 22. Because he ventured his all in the divine promise, God graciously accepted him, and not only answered, but out-did, his expectation, and justified him. This shows why faith

JAMIESON, FAUSSET, BROWN

As it is written . . .—(Gen. 17:5). This is quoted to justify his calling Abraham the "father of us all," and is to be viewed as a parenthesis. **before**—i.e., 'in the reckoning of' —**him whom he believed**—i.e., 'Thus Abraham, in the reckoning of Him whom he believed, is the father of us all, in order that all may be assured, that doing as he did, they shall be treated as he was.' **even God, quickeneth the dead**—The nature and greatness of that faith of Abraham which we are to copy is here strikingly described. What he was required to believe being above nature, his faith had to fasten upon God's power to surmount physical incapacity, and call into being what did not then exist. But God having made the promise, Abraham believed Him in spite of those obstacles. This is still further illustrated in what follows.

18-22. Who against hope—when no ground for hope appeared. **believed in hope**—i.e., cherished the believing expectation. **that he might become the father of many nations, according to that which was spoken, So**—i.e., Such "as the stars of heaven," Gen. 15:5—**shall thy seed be . . .**

he considered not . . .—paid no attention to those physical obstacles, both in himself and in Sarah, which might seem to render the fulfilment hopeless.

He staggered—hesitated—**not . . . but was strong in faith, giving glory to God**—as able to make good His own word in spite of all obstacles.

And being fully persuaded . . .—i.e., the glory which Abraham's faith gave to God consisted in this, that, firm in the persuasion of God's ability to fulfil his promise, no difficulties shook him.

And therefore it was imputed . . .—'Let all then take notice that this was not because of anything meritorious in Abraham, but merely because he so *believed.*'

ADAM CLARKE

17. *As it is written, I have made thee a father.* That Abraham's being a father of many nations has relation to the covenant of God made with him may be seen, Gen. xvii. 4-5: "Behold my covenant is with thee, and thou shalt be a father of many nations. Neither shall thy name any more be called Abram, but thy name shall be Abraham; for a father of many nations have I made thee"; i.e., he was constituted the head of many nations, the Gentile world, by virtue of the covenant which God made then with him. *God, who quickeneth the dead.* God is the most proper Object of trust and dependence; for being almighty, eternal, and unchangeable, He can even raise the dead to life, and call *those things which be not as though they were.* He is the Creator; He gave being when there was none. He can as infallibly assure the existence of those things which are not as if they were already actually in being. And, on this account, He can never fail of accomplishing whatsoever He has promised.

19. *He considered not his own body now dead.* He showed at once the correctness and energy of his faith: God cannot lie; Abraham can believe. It is true that, according to the course of nature, he and Sarah were so old that they could not have children; but God is almighty, and can do whatsoever He will, and will fulfill His promise. This was certainly a wonderful degree of faith; as the promise stated that it was in *his posterity* that all the nations of the earth were to be blessed; that he had, as yet, no child by Sarah; that he was one hundred years old; that Sarah was ninety; and that, added to the utter improbability of her bearing at that age, she had ever been barren before. All these were so many reasons why he should not credit the promise; yet he believed. Therefore it might be well said, v. 20, that *he staggered not at the promise,* though everything was unnatural and improbable; *but was strong in faith,* and, by this almost inimitable confidence, gave *glory to God.* It was to God's honor that His servant put such unlimited confidence in Him; and he put this confidence in Him on the rational ground that God was *fully able* to perform what He had promised.

21. *And being fully persuaded.* His soul was "full of confidence" that the truth of God bound Him to fulfil His promise, and His power enabled Him to do it.

22. *And therefore it was imputed to him for righteousness.* Abraham's strong faith in the promise of the coming Saviour, for this was essential to his faith, was reckoned to him for justification. For it is not said that any righ-

MATTHEW HENRY

is chosen to be the prime condition of our justification, because it is a grace that of all others gives glory to God.

Verses 23–25

In the close of the chapter, he applies all to us. He here concludes that his justification was to be the pattern of ours: *It was not written for his sake alone.* It was not intended only for an historical commendation of Abraham, or a relation of something peculiar to him. The accounts we have of the Old Testament saints were not intended for histories only, but for precedents to direct us, for ensamples (1 Cor. x. 11) for *our learning, ch.* xv. 4. And this particularly concerning Abraham was written *for us also*, to assure us what that righteousness is which God requireth. For us on whom the ends of the world are come, as well as for the patriarchs; for the grace of God is the same yesterday, today, and for ever.

I. Our common privilege; it shall be imputed to us, that is, righteousness shall. *It shall be imputed;* he uses a future verb, to signify the continuation of this mercy in the church, that as it is the same now so it will be while God has a church in the world. There is a fountain opened that is inexhaustible.

II. Our common duty, the condition of this privilege, and that is believing. The proper object of this believing is a divine revelation. The revelation to Abraham was concerning a Christ to come; the revelation to us is concerning a Christ already come, which difference in the revelation does not alter the case. Now we are to believe on him that raised up Christ; not only believe his power, but depend upon his grace. So he explains it, *v.* 25. He was *delivered for our offences.* He died indeed as a malefactor, because he died for sin; but it was not his own sin. He died to make atonement for our sins. He was *raised again for our justification.* By the merit of his death he paid our debt, in his resurrection he took out our acquittance. The apostle puts a special emphasis on Christ's resurrection; it is Christ that died, *yea, rather, that has risen again, ch.* viii. 34. So that upon the whole matter it is very evident that we are not justified by the merit of our own works, but by dependence upon Jesus Christ and his righteousness, which was the truth that Paul in this and the foregoing chapter had been fixing as the great spring and foundation of all our comfort.

JAMIESON, FAUSSET, BROWN

23-25. Now . . .—Here is the application of this whole argument about Abraham: These things were not recorded as mere historical facts, but as illustrations for all time of God's method of justification by faith. **to whom it shall be imputed, if we believe in him that raised up Jesus our Lord from the dead**—in Him that *hath* done this, even as Abraham believed that God *would* raise up a seed in whom all nations should be blessed. **Who was delivered for**—'on account of'—**our offences**—i.e., in order to expiate them by His blood. **and raised again for**—'on account of,' i.e., in order to—**our justification**—As His resurrection was the divine assurance that He had "put away sin by the sacrifice of Himself," and the crowning of His whole work, our justification is fitly connected with that glorious act. *Note,* (1) The doctrine of justification by works, as it generates self-exaltation, is contrary to the first principles of all true religion (vs. 2; and see on ch. 3:21-26, *Note* 1). (2) The way of a sinner's justification has been the same in all time, and the testimony of the Old Testament on this subject is one with that of the New (vs. 3, etc., and see on ch. 3:27-31, *Note* 1). (3) Faith and works, in the matter of justification, are opposite and irreconcilable, even as grace and debt (vss. 4, 5; and see on ch. 11:6). If God "justifies the ungodly," works cannot be, in any sense or to any degree, the ground of justification. For the same reason, the first requisite, in order to justification, must be (under the conviction that we are "ungodly") to despair of it by works; and the next, to "believe in Him that justifieth the ungodly"—that hath a justifying righteousness to bestow, and is ready to bestow it upon those who deserve none, and to embrace it accordingly. (4) The sacraments of the Church were never intended, and are not adapted, to *confer* grace, or the blessings of salvation, upon men. Their proper use is to set a divine *seal* upon *a state already existing,* and so, they *presuppose,* and do not *create* it (vss. 8-12). As circumcision merely "sealed" Abraham's already existing acceptance with God, so with the sacraments of the New Testament. (5) As Abraham is "the heir of the world," all nations being blessed in him, through his Seed Christ Jesus, and justified solely according to the pattern of his faith, so the transmission of the true religion and all the salvation which the world will ever experience shall yet be traced back with wonder, gratitude, and joy, to that morning dawn when "the God of glory appeared unto our father Abraham, when he was in Mesopotamia, before he dwelt in Charran," Acts 7: 2 (vs. 13). (6) Nothing gives more glory to God than simple faith in His word, especially when all things seem to render the fulfilment of it hopeless (vss. 18-21). (7) All the Scripture examples of faith were recorded on purpose to beget and encourage the like faith in every succeeding age (vss. 23, 24; and cf. ch. 15:4). (8) *Justification,* in this argument, cannot be taken—as Romanists and other errorists insist—to mean a change upon men's *character;* for besides that this is to confound it with *Sanctification,* which has its appropriate place in this Epistle, the whole argument of the present chapter—and nearly all its more important clauses, expressions, and words—would in that case be unsuitable, and fitted only to mislead. Beyond all doubt it means exclusively a change upon men's *state* or *relation to God;* or, in scientific language, it is an *objective,* not a *subjective* change—a change from guilt and condemnation to acquittal and acceptance. And the best evidence that this is the key to the whole argument is, that it opens all the wards of the many-chambered lock with which the apostle has enriched us in this Epistle.

ADAM CLARKE

teousness, either his own or that of another, was imputed or reckoned to him for justification; but *it,* i.e., his faith in God.

23. *Now it was not written for his sake alone.* The fact of Abraham's believing and receiving salvation through that faith is not recorded as a mere circumstance in the patriarch's life, intended to do him honor.

24. *But for us also.* The mention of this circumstance has a much more extensive design than merely to honor Abraham. It is recorded as the model according to which God will save both Jews and Gentiles.

25. *Who was delivered for our offences.* Who was delivered up to death as a Sacrifice for our sins; for in what other way or for what other purpose could He, who is innocence itself, be *delivered for our offences? And was raised again for our justification.* He was raised that we might have the fullest assurance that the death of Christ had accomplished the end for which it took place, viz., our reconciliation to God. (1) From a careful examination of the divine oracles it appears that the death of Christ was an atonement or expiation for the sin of the world. (2) And as His death was an atonement for our sins, so His resurrection was the proof and pledge of our eternal life. (3) The doctrine of justification by faith, which is so nobly proved in the preceding chapter, is one of the grandest displays of the mercy of God to mankind. It is so very plain that all may comprehend it, and so free that all may attain it. (4) The doctrine of the imputed righteousness of Christ, as held by many, will not be readily found in this chapter, where it has been supposed to exist in all its proofs. It is repeatedly said that faith is imputed for righteousness, but in no place here that Christ's obedience to the moral law is imputed to any man. The truth is, the moral law was broken, and did not now require obedience. It required this before it was broken; but after it was broken, it required death. Either the sinner must die or someone in his stead; but there was none whose death could have been an equivalent for the transgressions of the *world* but Jesus Christ. Jesus therefore died for man; and it is through His blood, the merit of His passion and death, that we have redemption, and not by His obedience to the moral law in our stead. (5) This doctrine of the imputed righteousness of Christ is capable of great abuse. To say that Christ's personal righteousness is imputed to every true believer is not scriptural. To say that He has fulfilled all righteousness for us, or in our stead, if by this is meant His fulfillment of all moral duties, is neither scriptural nor true. That He has died in our stead is a great, glorious, and scriptural truth; that there is no redemption but through His blood is asserted beyond all contradiction in the oracles of God. But there are a multitude of duties which the moral law requires which Christ never fulfilled in our stead, and never could—in the relation of parents, husbands, wives, etc.

MATTHEW HENRY

CHAPTER 5

Verses 1–5

The precious benefits and privileges which flow from justification are such as should quicken us all to give diligence to make it sure to ourselves. The fruits of this tree of life are exceedingly precious.

I. *We have peace with God, v.* 1. It is sin that breeds the quarrel between us and God. Justification takes away the guilt, immediately upon the removing of that obstacle, the peace is made. By faith we lay hold of God's arm and of his strength, and so are at peace. There is more in this peace than barely a cessation of enmity, there is friendship and loving-kindness, for God is either the worst enemy or the best friend. Christ has called his disciples *friends,* John xv. 13–15. And surely a man needs no more to make him happy than to have God his friend! But this is *through our Lord Jesus Christ*—through him as

JAMIESON, FAUSSET, BROWN

CHAPTER 5

Vss. 1-11. THE BLESSED EFFECTS OF JUSTIFICATION BY FAITH. The *proof* of this doctrine being now concluded, the apostle comes here to treat of its *fruits,* reserving the full consideration of this topic to another stage of the argument (ch. 8). **1. Therefore being**—'having been'—**justified by faith, we have peace with God . . .**—If we are to be guided by MS. authority, the true reading here, beyond doubt, is, 'Let us have peace'; a reading, however, which most reject, because they think it unnatural to exhort men to *have* what it belongs to God to *give,* because the apostle is not here giving exhortations, but stating matters of fact. But as it seems hazardous to set aside the decisive testimony of MSS., as to what the apostle *did* write, in favor of what we merely think he *ought* to have written, let us pause and ask—If it be the privilege of the justi-

ADAM CLARKE

CHAPTER 5

1. *Therefore being justified by faith.* The apostle takes it for granted that he has proved that justification is by faith, and that the Gentiles have an equal title with the Jews to salvation by faith. And now he proceeds to show the effects produced in the hearts of the believing Gentiles by this doctrine. We are justified, have all our sins pardoned by faith, as the instrumental cause; for, being sinners, we have no works of righteousness that we can plead. *We have peace with God.* Before, while sinners, we were in a state of enmity with God, which was sufficiently proved by our rebellion against his authority, and our transgression of his laws; but now, being reconciled, we have peace with God. *Peace* is generally the firstfruits of our

MATTHEW HENRY

the great peacemaker, *the Mediator between God and man*, not only the maker, but the matter and maintainer, of our peace.

II. *We have access by faith into this grace wherein we stand*, *v.* 2. This is a further privilege, not only peace, but grace. The saints' happy state. It is a state of grace, God's loving-kindness to us and our conformity to God. Into this grace we have access: we were not born in this state, but we are brought into it. We could not have got into it of ourselves, but we are led into it as blind, or lame, or weak people are led. *We have had access.* Paul, in his conversion, had this access; then he was made nigh. It was Christ that introduced and led him by the hand into this grace. *By whom we have access by faith.* By Christ as the author, by faith as the means of this access. Their happy standing in this state: *Wherein we stand.* Not only wherein we are, but wherein we stand. The phrase denotes also our progress; while we stand, we are going. We must not lie down, as if we had already attained, but stand as those that are pressing forward, stand as servants attending on Christ our master. The phrase denotes, further, our perseverance: we stand firmly and safely; stand as soldiers stand, that keep their ground. It is not in the court of heaven as in earthly courts, where high places are slippery places.

III. *We rejoice in hope of the glory of God.* Besides the happiness in hand, there is a happiness in hope, *the glory of God.* Those that have access by faith into the grace of God now may hope for the glory of God hereafter. Grace is glory begun, the earnest and assurance of glory. Those who hope for the glory of God hereafter, have enough to rejoice in now.

IV. *We glory in tribulations also;* not only notwithstanding our tribulations, but even in our tribulations. What a growing increasing happiness the happiness of the saints is: *Not only so. We glory in tribulations also*, especially tribulations for righteousness' sake. This being the hardest point, he sets himself to show the grounds and reasons of it. Tribulations, by a chain of causes, greatly befriend hope, which he shows in the method of its influence. *Tribulation worketh patience*, the powerful grace of God working in and with the tribulation. It proves, and by proving improves, patience, as steel is hardened by the fire. That which worketh patience is matter of joy; for patience does us more good than tribulations can do us hurt. Tribulation in itself worketh impatience; but, as it is sanctified to the saints, it worketh patience. *Patience experience*, *v.* 4. It works an experience of God, the patient sufferers have the greatest experience of the divine consolations. It works an experience of ourselves. It is by tribulation that we make an experiment of our own sincerity. It works *an approbation*, as he is approved that has passed the test. *Experience hope.* He who, being thus tried, comes forth as gold, will thereby be encouraged to hope. Experience of God is a prop to our hope. Experience of ourselves helps to evidence our sincerity. This *hope maketh not ashamed*, will not deceive us. Nothing confounds more than disappointment. It maketh not ashamed of our sufferings. It is in a good cause, for a good Master, and in good hope; and therefore we are not ashamed. *Because the love of God is shed abroad.* This hope will not disappoint us, because it is sealed with the Holy Spirit as a Spirit of love. *The love of God*, that is, the sense of God's love to us, drawing out love in us to him again. The ground of all our comfort and holiness, and perseverance in both, is laid in the *shedding abroad of the love of God in our hearts.* Sense of God's love to us will make us not ashamed, either of our hope in him or our sufferings for him.

Verses 6–21

The apostle here describes the fountain and foundation of justification, laid in the death of the Lord Jesus. He enlarges upon this instance of the love of God which is shed abroad. 1. The persons he died for, *v.* 6–8. 2. The precious fruits of his death, *v.* 9–11. 3. The parallel he runs between the communication of sin and death by the first Adam and of righteousness and life by the second Adam, *v.* 12, to the end.

I. The character we were under when Christ died for us.

1. *We were without strength* (*v.* 6), in a sad condition; altogether unable to help ourselves out of that condition. Therefore, our salvation is here said to come *in due time.* God's time to help and save is when those that are to be saved are without strength. It is the manner of God to help at a dead lift.

2. *He died for the ungodly;* not only helpless creatures, and therefore likely to perish, but guilty sinful creatures, and therefore deserving to perish. Being ungodly, they had need of one to die for them.

JAMIESON, FAUSSET, BROWN

fied to "*have* peace with God," why might not the apostle begin his enumeration of the fruits of justification by calling on believers to 'realize' this peace as belonged to them, or cherish the joyful consciousness of it as their own? And if this is what he has done, it would not be necessary to continue in the same style, and the other fruits of justification might be set down simply as matters of fact. This "peace" is first a change in God's relation to us; and next, as the consequence of this, a change on our part towards Him. God, on the one hand, has "reconciled us to Himself by Jesus Christ" (II Cor. 5:18); and we, on the other hand, setting our seal to this, "are reconciled to God" (II Cor. 5:20). The "propitiation" is the meeting-place; there the controversy on both sides terminates in an honorable and eternal "peace." **2. By whom also we have**—'have had'—**access by faith into this grace**—favor with God—**wherein we stand**—i.e., 'To that same faith which *first* gave us "peace with God" we owe our introduction into that *permanent standing* in the favor of God which the justified enjoy.' As it is difficult to distinguish this from the peace first mentioned, we regard it as merely an additional phase of the same [MEYER, PHILIPPI, MEHRING], rather than something new [BEZA, THOLUCK, HODGE]. **and rejoice**—'glory,' 'boast,' 'triumph'—'rejoice' is not strong enough. **in hope of the glory of God**—See on "hope," vs. 4. **3, 4. we glory in tribulation also; knowing that tribulation worketh patience**—Patience is the quiet endurance of what we cannot but wish removed, whether it be the withholding of promised good (ch. 8:25), or the continued experience of positive ill (as here). There is indeed a patience of unrenewed nature, which has something noble in it, though in many cases the offspring of pride, if not of something lower. Men have been known to endure every form of privation, torture, and death, without a murmur and without even visible emotion, merely because they deemed it unworthy of them to sink under unavoidable ill. But this proud, stoical hardihood has nothing in common with the *grace* of patience—which is either the meek endurance of ill because it is of God (Job 1:21, 22; 2:10), or the calm waiting for promised good till His time to dispense it come (Heb. 10:36); in the full persuasion that such trials are divinely appointed, are the needed discipline of God's children, are but for a definite period, and are not sent without abundant promises of "songs in the night." If such be the "patience" which "tribulation worketh," no wonder that **patience worketh experience**—rather 'proof,' as the same word is rendered in II Corinthians 2:9; 13:3; Philippians 2:22; i.e., experimental *evidence* that we have "believed through grace." **and experience**—'proof'—**hope**—"of the glory of God," as prepared for us. Thus have we hope in two distinct ways, and at two successive stages of the Christian life: *first,* immediately on believing, along with the sense of peace and abiding access to God (vs. 1); *next,* after the reality of this faith has been "proved," particularly by the patient endurance of trials sent to test it. We first get it by looking *away from ourselves* to the Lamb of God; next by looking *into* or *upon ourselves* as transformed by that "looking unto Jesus." In the one case, the mind acts (as they say) *objectively;* in the other, *subjectively.* The one is (as divines say) the *assurance of faith;* the other, the *assurance of sense.* **5. And hope maketh not ashamed**—putteth not to shame, as empty hopes do—**because the love of God**—i.e., not 'our love to God,' as the Romish and some Protestant expositors (following some of the Fathers) represent it; but clearly 'God's love to us'—as most expositors agree. **is shed abroad**—lit., 'poured forth,' i.e., copiously diffused (cf. John 7:38; Titus 3:6). **by the Holy Ghost which is**—rather 'was'—**given unto us**—i.e., at the great Pentecostal effusion, which is viewed as the formal donation of the Spirit to the Church of God, for all time and for each believer. (*The Holy Ghost is here first introduced in this Epistle.*) It is as if the apostle had said, 'And how can this hope of glory, which as believers we cherish, put us to shame, when we feel God Himself, by His Spirit given to us, drenching our hearts in sweet, all-subduing sensations of His wondrous love to us in Christ Jesus?" This leads the apostle to expatiate on the amazing character of that love. **6-8. For when we were yet without strength**—i.e., powerless to deliver ourselves, and so ready to perish. **in due time**—at the appointed season—**Christ died for the ungodly**—Three signal properties of God's love are here given: First, "Christ died *for the ungodly*," whose character, so far from meriting any interposition in their behalf, was altogether repulsive to the eye of God; second,

ADAM CLARKE

justification. *Through our Lord Jesus Christ.* His passion and death being the sole cause of our reconciliation to God.

2. *By whom also.* We are not only indebted to our Lord Jesus Christ for the free and full pardon which we have received, but our continuance in a justified state depends upon His gracious influence in our hearts and His intercession before the throne of God. *We have access.* "We have received this access." It was only through Christ that we could at first approach God, and it is only through Him that the privilege is continued to us. And this access to God, or "introduction" to the Divine Presence, is to be considered as a lasting privilege. We are not brought to God for the purpose of an interview, but to remain with Him. *Into this grace.* This state of favor and acceptance. *Wherein we stand.* Having firm footing, and a just title through the blood of the Lamb to the full salvation of God. *And rejoice.* Have solid happiness, from the evidence we have of our acceptance with Him.

3. *And not only so.* We are not only happy from being in this state of communion with our God, and the prospect of being eternally with Him. *But we glory in tribulations also.* All the sufferings we endure for the testimony of our Lord are so sanctified to us by His grace that they become powerful instruments of increasing our happiness. *Tribulation worketh patience.* "Endurance" under trials, without sustaining loss or deterioration. It is a metaphor taken from refining metals. We do not speak thus from any sudden raptures or extraordinary sensations we may have of spiritual joy; for we find that the tribulations through which we pass are the means of exercising and increasing our patience, our meek forbearance of injuries received, or persecutions experienced, on account of the gospel.

4. *And patience, experience.* "Full proof, by trial," of the truth of our religion, the solidity of our Christian state, and the faithfulness of our God. In such cases we have the opportunity of putting our religion to the test; and by every such test it receives the deeper sterling stamp. The apostle uses here also a metaphor taken from the purifying, refining, and testing of silver and gold. *Experience, hope.* For we thus calculate, that He who has supported us in the past will support us in those which may yet come; and as we have received so much spiritual profiting by means of the sufferings through which we have already passed, we may profit equally by those which are yet to come. This *hope* prevents us from dreading coming trials; we receive them as means of grace, and find that all things work together for good to them that love God.

5. *And hope maketh not ashamed.* A hope that is not rationally founded will have its expectation cut off, and then shame and confusion will be the portion of its possessor. *Because the love of God is shed abroad in our hearts.* We have the most solid and convincing testimony of God's love to us by that measure of it which He has communicated to our hearts. There it is "poured out" and diffused abroad, filling, quickening, and invigorating all our powers and faculties. The *Holy Ghost* comes with it; by His energy it is diffused and pervades every part.

6. *For when we were yet without strength.* The apostle, having pointed out the glorious state of the believing Gentiles, takes occasion to contrast this with their former state, and the means by which they were redeemed from it. Their former state he points out in four particulars, which may be applied to men in general. (1) They were *without strength;* in a weak, dying state; neither able to resist sin nor *do* any good; utterly devoid of power to extricate themselves from the misery of their situation. (2) They were *ungodly;* without either the worship or knowledge of the true God; they had not God in them; and, consequently, were not partakers of the divine nature. Satan lived in, ruled, and enslaved their hearts.

MATTHEW HENRY

This he illustrates (*v.* 7, 8) as an unparalleled instance of love; herein God's thoughts and ways were above ours. (1) One would hardly *die for a righteous man*, that is, one that is unjustly condemned; everybody will pity such a one, but few will hazard their own in his stead. (2) One might perhaps be persuaded *to die for a good man*, who is more than barely a righteous man. Many that are good themselves yet do but little good to others; but those that are useful commonly get themselves well beloved. And yet observe how he qualifies this: it is but some that would do so, after all, it is but a *peradventure*. (3) *But Christ died for sinners* (*v.* 8), neither righteous nor good; not only such as were useless, but such as were guilty. Now herein *God commended his love*, not only proved but magnified it and made it illustrious, not only put it past dispute, but rendered it the object of the greatest wonder and admiration. *Commendeth his love* in order to the shedding abroad of his love in our hearts by the Holy Ghost. *While we were yet sinners*. He died to save us, not in our sins, but from our sins; but we were yet sinners when he died for us. (4) Nay, which is more, *we were enemies* (*v.* 10), not only malefactors, but traitors and rebels. And that for such as these Christ should die is such a mystery, such an unprecedented instance of love, that it may well be our business to eternity to admire and wonder at it. Justly might he who had thus loved us make it one of the laws of his kingdom that we should love our enemies.

II. The precious fruits of his death.

1. Justification and reconcilation are the fruit of the death of Christ: *We are justified by his blood* (*v.* 9), *reconciled by his death*, *v.* 10. Sin is pardoned, the enmity slain, an end made of iniquity, and an everlasting righteousness brought in. Immediately upon our believing, we are actually put into a state of justification and reconciliation. *Justified by his blood*. Our justification is ascribed to the blood of Christ because *without blood there is no remission*, Heb. ix. 22. In all the propitiatory sacrifices, the sprinkling of the blood was of the essence of the sacrifice.

2. Hence results salvation from wrath: *Saved from wrath* (*v.* 9), *saved by his life*, *v.* 10. If God justified and reconciled us when we were enemies, much more will be save us when we are justified and reconciled. He that has done the greater, which is of enemies to make us friends, will certainly do the less, which is when we are friends to use us friendly and to be kind to us. The apostle, once and again, speaks of it with a *much more*. *We shall be saved from wrath*. It is the wrath of God that is the fire of hell. *Reconciled by his death, saved by his life*. His life here spoken of is not to be understood of his life in the flesh, but his life in heaven. We are reconciled by Christ humbled, we are saved by Christ exalted. The dying Jesus laid the foundation in satisfying for sin, and slaying the enmity, but it is the living Jesus that perfects the work. Christ dying was the testator, who bequeathed us the legacy; but Christ living is the executor, who pays it.

3. All this produces, as a further privilege, our *joy in God*, *v.* 11. God is now so far from being a terror to us that he is our *joy*. *We are reconciled and saved from wrath*. *And not only so*, there is more in it yet, a constant stream of favours; not only get into the harbour, but come in with full sail: *We joy in God*, solacing ourselves in his love. And all this (which he repeats as a string he loved to be harping upon) by virtue of the atonement, for by him we *received the atonement*. To *receive the atonement* is, (1) To give our consent to the atonement, being willing and glad to be saved in a gospel way and upon gospel terms. (2) To take the comfort of the atonement. Now *we joy in God*, now we do indeed *receive the atonement*, *glorying* in it.

JAMIESON, FAUSSET, BROWN

He did this "when they were *without strength*"—with nothing between them and perdition but that self-originating divine compassion; third, He did this "*at the due time*," when it was most fitting that it should take place (cf. Gal. 4:4). The two former of these properties the apostle now proceeds to illustrate. **For scarcely for a righteous man**—a man of simply *unexceptionable* character—**will one**—'any one'—**die: yet peradventure for a good man**—a man who, besides being unexceptionable, is *distinguished for goodness*, a benefactor to society—**some**—'some one'—**would**—rather 'doth'—**even dare to die**—"Scarce an instance occurs of selfsacrifice for one merely upright; though for one who makes himself a blessing to society there *may* be found an example of such noble surrender of life" [So BENGEL, OLSHAUSEN, THOLUCK, ALFORD, PHILIPPI]. (To make the "righteous" and the "good" man here to mean the same person, and the whole sense to be that "though rare, the case may occur, of one making a sacrifice of life for a worthy character" [as CALVIN, BEZA, FRITZSCHE, JOWETT], is extremely flat. **But God commendeth**—'setteth off,' 'displayeth'—in glorious contrast with all that men will do for each other. **his love toward us, in that, while we were yet sinners**—i.e., in a state not of positive "goodness," nor even of negative "righteousness," but on the contrary, "sinners," a state which His soul hateth. **Christ died for us**—Now comes the overpowering inference, emphatically redoubled. **9, 10. Much more then, being**—'having been'—**now justified by his blood, we shall be saved from wrath through him. For if, when we were enemies, we were reconciled to God by the death of his Son, much more, being now**—'having now been'—**reconciled, we shall be saved by his life**—i.e., 'If that part of the Saviour's work which cost Him His blood, and which had to be wrought for persons incapable of the least sympathy either with His love or His labors in their behalf—even our "justification," our "reconciliation"—is already completed; how much more will He do all that remains to be done, since He has it to do, not by death-agonies any more, but in untroubled "life," and no longer for enemies, but for friends—from whom, at every stage of it, He receives the grateful response of redeemed and adoring souls?' To be "saved from wrath through Him," denotes here the whole work of Christ towards *believers*, from the moment of justification, when the wrath of God is turned away from them, till the Judge on the great white throne shall discharge that wrath upon them that "obey not the Gospel of our Lord Jesus Christ"; and that work may all be summed up in "keeping them from falling, and presenting them faultless before the presence of His glory with exceeding joy" (Jude 24): thus are they "saved from wrath through Him." **11. And not only so, but we also joy**—rather, 'glory'—**in God through our Lord Jesus Christ, by**—'through'—**whom we have now received the atonement**—rather, 'the reconciliation' (*Margin*), as the same word is rendered in vs. 10 and in II Corinthians 5:18, 19. (In fact, the earlier meaning of the English word 'atonement' was "the *reconciliation* of two estranged parties") [TRENCH]. The foregoing effects of justification were all benefits to ourselves, calling for gratitude; this last may be termed a purely disinterested one. Our first feeling towards God, after we have found peace with Him, is that of clinging gratitude for so costly a salvation; but no sooner have we learned to cry, Abba, Father, under the sweet sense of reconciliation, than "gloriation" in Him takes the place of dread of Him, and now He appears to us "altogether lovely!"—On this section, *note* (1) How gloriously does the Gospel evince its divine origin by basing all acceptable obedience on "peace with God," laying the foundations of this peace in a righteous "justification" of the sinner "through our Lord Jesus Christ," and making this the entrance to a permanent standing in the divine favor, and a triumphant expectation of future glory! (vss. 1, 2). Other peace, worthy of the name, there is none; and as those who are strangers to it rise not to the enjoyment of such high fellowship with God, so they have neither any taste for it nor desire after it. (2) As only believers possess the true secret of patience under trials, so, although "not joyous but grievous" in themselves (Heb. 12:17), when trials divinely sent afford them the opportunity of evidencing their faith by the grace of patience under them, they should "count it all joy" (vss. 3, 4; and see Jas. 1:2, 3). (3) "Hope," in the New Testament sense of the term, is not a lower degree of faith or assurance (as many now say, I *hope* for heaven, but am not *sure* of it); but invariably means 'the confident expectation of future good.' It

ADAM CLARKE

(3) They were *sinners*, v. 8, aiming at happiness, but constantly "missing the mark," which is the ideal meaning of the Hebrew *chata* and the Greek *hamartano*. (4) They were *enemies*, v. 10, from *echthos*, "hatred, enmity," persons who hated God and holiness; and acted in continual hostility to both. What a gradation is here! *Died for the ungodly*. "He died instead of the ungodly"; see also v. 8; so Luke xxii. 19. The body of Christ, "which is given for you"; i.e., the life that is laid down in your stead. In this way the preposition *hyper* is used by the best Greek writers.

7. *For scarcely for a righteous man will one die*. The Jews divide men, as to their moral character, into four classes. The first class consists of those who say, "What is mine, is my own; and what is thine, is thy own." These may be considered the just, who render to every man his due; or rather, they who neither give nor take. The second class is made up of those who say, "What is mine, is thine; and what is thine, is mine." These are they who accommodate each other, who borrow and lend. The third class is composed of those who say, "What is mine, is thine; and what is thine, let it be thine." These are the pious, or good, who give up all for the benefit of their neighbor. The fourth class are those who say, "What is thine, is mine; and what is thine, shall be mine." These are the impious, who take all, and give nothing. Now, for one of the first class, who would die? *Peradventure for a good man some would even dare to die*. This is for one of the third class, who gives all he has for the good of others. This is the truly benevolent man, whose life is devoted to the public good; for such a person, peradventure, some who have had their lives perhaps preserved by his bounty would even dare to die.

8. *But God commendeth his love*. God "hath set" this act of infinite mercy in the most conspicuous light, so as to recommend it to the notice and admiration of all. *While we were yet sinners*. We were neither righteous nor good, but impious and wicked.

9. *Much more then, being now justified*. If Jesus Christ, in His endless compassion towards us, gave His life for ours, while we were yet enemies; being now justified *by his blood*, by His death on the Cross, and thus reconciled to God, *we shall be saved from wrath*, from "punishment" for past transgression, *through him*, by what He has thus suffered for us.

10. *We were reconciled*. The enmity existing before rendered the reconciliation necessary. In every human heart there is a measure of enmity to holiness, and consequently to the Author of it. *We shall be saved by his life*. For, (1) as He died for our sins, so He rose again for our justification; and His resurrection to *life* is the grand proof that He has accomplished whatever He had purposed in reference to the salvation of man. (2) This may be also understood of His life of intercession: for it is written, "He ever liveth to make intercession for them," Heb. vii. 25. Through this life of intercession at the right hand of God we are spared and blessed. (3) And it will not be amiss to consider that, as our salvation implies the renovation of our nature, and our being restored to the image of God, so [it] may be rendered: "We shall be saved in His life." (4) The example also of the life of Christ is a means of salvation. He hath left us "an example" that we "should follow his steps"; and he that followeth Him "shall not walk in darkness, but shall have the light of life," John viii. 12.

11. *We also joy*, "we exult," or "glory" *in God*. We now feel that God is reconciled to us, and we are reconciled to Him. The enmity is removed from our souls; and He, for Christ's sake, through *whom we have received the atonement*, "the reconciliation," has remitted the wrath, the punishment which we deserved; and now, through this reconciliation, we expect an eternal glory. It was certainly improper to translate here *atonement*, instead of "reconciliation"; as *katallasso* signifies to "reconcile," and is so rendered by our translators in all the places where it occurs. It does not mean the *atonement* here, as we generally understand that word, viz., the sacrificial death of Christ, but

MATTHEW HENRY

III. The parallel that the apostle runs between the communication of sin and death by the first Adam and of righteousness and life by the second Adam (*v.* 12, to the end), showing a correspondence between our fall and our recovery.

1. A general truth laid down as the foundation of his discourse—that Adam was a type of Christ (*v.* 14): *Who is the figure of him that was to come.* God dealt with Adam and Adam acted as a common father, of and for all his posterity. Jesus Christ, the Mediator, acted as the head of all the elect, dealt with God for them, as their father, died for them, rose for them, entered within the veil for them, did all for them.

2. A more particular explication of the parallel. (1) How Adam communicated sin and death to all his posterity (*v.* 12): *By one man sin entered.* We see the world under a deluge of sin and death, full of iniquities and full of calamities. It was *by one man,* and he the first man. [1] By him *sin entered.* When God pronounced all very good (Gen. i. 31) there was no sin in the world. It never entered into the world of mankind till Adam sinned. Then entered the guilt of Adam's sin imputed to posterity, and a general depravedness of nature. *For that* (so we read it), rather *in whom, all have sinned.* Sin entered into the world by Adam, for in him we all sinned. God, as the author of nature, had made this the law of nature, that man should beget in his own likeness. In Adam therefore, as in a common receptacle, the whole nature of man was reposited. Adam therefore sinning and falling, the nature became guilty and corrupt. Thus in him all have sinned. [2] *Death by sin,* for death is the wages of sin. When sin came, of course death came with it. [3] *So death passed, passed through* all men, as an infectious disease passes through a town, so that none escape it. It is the universal fate, without exception. *Death reigned, v.* 14. None are exempted from its sceptre. It is the last enemy, 1 Cor. xv. 26. He shows that sin did not commence with the law of Moses, but was *in the world until,* or *before,* that law. Sin was in the world before the law; witness Cain's murder, the apostasy of the old world, the wickedness of Sodom. His inference hence is, Therefore there was a law; for *sin is not imputed where there is no law.* Original sin is a want of conformity to, and actual sin is a transgression of, the law of God: therefore all were under some law. His proof of it is, *Death reigned from Adam to Moses, v.* 14. This proves that sin was in the world before the law, and original sin, for death reigned over those that had not sinned any actual sin, that *had not sinned after the similitude of Adam's transgression.*

JAMIESON, FAUSSET, BROWN

presupposes faith; and what faith *assures* us will be ours, hope accordingly *expects.* In the nourishment of this hope, the soul's look *outward* to Christ for the ground of it, and *inward* upon ourselves for evidence of its reality, must act and react upon each other (vs. 2 and vs. 4 compared). (4) It is the proper office of the Holy Ghost to beget in the soul the full conviction and joyful consciousness of the love of God in Christ Jesus to sinners of mankind, and to ourselves in particular; and where this exists, it carries with it such an assurance of final salvation as cannot deceive (vs. 5). (5) The *justification* of sinful men is not in virtue of their amendment, but of "the *blood* of God's Son"; and while this is expressly affirmed in vs. 9, our *reconciliation* to God by the "*death* of His Son," affirmed in vs. 10, is but a variety of the same statement. In both, the blessing meant is the *restoration of the sinner to a righteous standing* in the sight of God; and in both, the meritorious ground of this, which is intended to be conveyed, is the *expiatory sacrifice* of God's Son. (6) Gratitude to God for redeeming love, if it could exist without delight in God Himself, would be a selfish and worthless feeling; but when the one rises into the other—the transporting sense of eternal "reconciliation" passing into "gloriation in God" Himself—then the lower is sanctified and sustained by the higher, and each feeling is perfective of the other (vs. 11).

12-21. Comparison and Contrast between Adam and Christ in Their Relation to the Human Family. (This profound and most weighty section has occasioned an immense deal of critical and theological discussion, in which every point, and almost every clause, has been contested. We can here but set down what appears to us to be the only tenable view of it as a whole and of its successive clauses, with some slight indication of the grounds of our judgment). **12. Wherefore**—i.e., Things being so; referring back to the whole preceding argument. **as by one man**—Adam. **sin**—considered here in its guilt, criminality, penal desert. **entered into the world, and death by**—as the penalty of—**sin; and so death passed upon all men, for that all have sinned**—rather, 'all sinned,' i.e., in that one man's first sin. Thus death reaches every individual of the human family, as the penalty due to *himself.* [So, in substance, Bengel, Hodge, Philippi.] Here we should have expected the apostle to finish his sentence, in some such way as this: 'Even so, by one man righteousness has entered into the world, and life by righteousness.' But, instead of this, we have a digression, extending to five verses, to illustrate the important statement of vs. 12; and it is only at vs. 18 that the comparison is resumed and finished. **13-14. For until the law sin was in the world**—i.e., during all the period from Adam "until the law" of Moses was given, God continued to treat men as sinners. **but sin is not imputed where there is no law**—'There must therefore have been a law during that period, because sin *was* then imputed'; as is now to be shown. **Nevertheless death reigned from Adam to Moses, even over them that had not sinned after the similitude of Adam's transgression**—But who are they?—a much contested question. *Infants* (say some), who being guiltless of *actual sin,* may be said not to have sinned in the way that Adam did [Augustin, Beza, Hodge]. But why should infants be specially connected with the period "from Adam to Moses," since they die alike in every period? And if the apostle meant to express here the death of infants, why has he done it so enigmatically? Besides, the death of infants is comprehended in the universal mortality on account of the first sin, so emphatically expressed in vs. 12; what need then to specify it here? and why, if not necessary, should we presume it to be meant here, unless the language unmistakably point to it—which it certainly does not? The meaning then must be, that 'death reigned from Adam to Moses, even over those that had not, like Adam, transgressed against a positive commandment, threatening death to the disobedient.' (So most interpreters.) In this case, the particle "even," instead of specifying one particular class of those who lived "from Adam to Moses" (as the other interpretation supposes), merely explains what it was that made the case of those who died from Adam to Moses worthy of special notice—namely, that 'though unlike Adam and all since Moses, those who lived between the two had no positive threatening of death for transgression, "nevertheless, death reigned *even over them.*"' **who is the figure**—or, 'a type'—**of him that was to come**—Christ. **"This clause is inserted on the first** mention of the name 'Adam, the *one man* of whom he is speaking, to recall the purpose for which he is

ADAM CLARKE

rather the effect of that atonement, the removal of the enmity, and by this, the change of our condition and state; from *kata,* intensive, and *allasso,* "to change"—the thorough change of our state from enmity to friendship. God is reconciled to us and we are reconciled to Him by the death of His Son, and thus there is a glorious change from enmity to friendship; and we can exult in God through our Lord Jesus Christ, by whom we have received this "reconciliation."

12. *Wherefore, as by one man sin entered into the world.* From this verse to the conclusion of the chapter the apostle produces a strong argument to prove that, as all mankind stood in need of the grace of God in Christ to redeem them from their sins, so this grace has been afforded equally to all, both Jews and Gentiles. The order in which the apostle handles this argument is this: (1) He affirms that death passed upon all men by Adam's one transgression, v. 12. (2) He proves this, vv. 13-14. (3) He affirms there is a correspondence between Adam and Christ, or between the "offence" and the "free gift," v. 14. (4) This correspondence, so far as the two opposite parts answer to each other, is justly expressed in vv. 18-19; and there we have the main or fundamental position of the apostle's argument, in relation to the point which he has been arguing from the beginning of the Epistle, namely, the extensiveness of the grace of the gospel, that it actually reaches to all men, and is not confined to the Jews. (5) But before he laid down this position, it was necessary that he should show that the correspondence between Adam and Christ, or between the "offence" and the "gift," is not to be confined strictly to the bounds specified in the position, as if the gift reached no further than the consequences of the offense, when in reality it extends vastly beyond them, vv. 15-17. (6) Having settled these points, as previously necessary to clear his fundamental position and fit to his argument, he then lays down that position in a diversified manner of speech, vv. 18-19, just as in 1 Cor. xv. 20-21, and leaves us to conclude, from the premises laid down, vv. 15-17, that the gift and the grace in their utmost extent are as free to all mankind who are willing to accept of them as this particular instance, the resurrection from the dead. They *shall* all be raised from the dead hereafter; they *may* all be quickened by the Spirit here. (7) Having thus shown the extensiveness of the divine grace, in opposition to the dire effects of the law under which Adam was, that the Jews might not overlook what he intended they should particularly observe, he puts them in mind that the law given to Adam, Transgress and die, was introduced into the Jewish constitution by the ministry of Moses; and for this end, that "the offence," with the penalty of death annexed to it, "might abound," v. 20. But to illustrate the divine grace by setting it in contrast to the law, he immediately adds: Where sin, subjecting to death, "abounded, grace did much more abound"; that is, in blessings bestowed, it has stretched far beyond both Adam's transgression and the transgressions under the law of Moses, vv. 20-21. *Sin entered into the world.* There was neither sin nor death before the offense of Adam; after that there were both. Adam's transgression was therefore the cause of both. *And death by sin.* Natural evil is evidently the effect of moral evil; if man had never sinned, he had never suffered. *Death passed upon all men.* Hence we see that all human beings partook in the consequences of Adam's sin. *For that all have sinned.* All are born with a sinful nature; and the seeds of this evil soon vegetate, and bring forth corresponding fruits.

13. *For until the law sin was in the world.* As death reigned from Adam to Moses, so also did *sin.* Now, as there was no written *law* from Adam to that given to Moses, the death that prevailed could not be the breach of that law; for sin, so as to be punished with temporal death, *is not imputed when there is no law,* which shows the penalty of sin to be death. Therefore men are not subjected to death for their own personal transgressions, but for the sin of Adam, as through his transgression all come into the world with the seed of death and corruption in their own nature, superadded to their moral depravity.

14. *Who is the figure of him that was to come.*

MATTHEW HENRY

[2] Wherein the communication of grace and love by Christ goes beyond the communication of guilt and wrath by Adam, *v.* 15–17. It is designed for the magnifying of Christ's love, and for the comfort of believers. *First,* If guilt and wrath be communicated much more shall grace and love. *Much more the grace of God, and the gift by grace.* God's goodness is, of all his attributes, in a special manner his glory. We know that God is rather inclined to show mercy; punishing is his strange work. *Secondly,* If there was so much power and efficacy in the sin of a man, to condemn us, much more are there power and efficacy in the righteousness and grace of Christ, to justify and save us. Surely Adam could not propagate so strong a poison but Jesus Christ could propagate as strong an antidote, and much stronger.

Thirdly, It is but the guilt of one single offence of Adam's that is laid to our charge: *The judgment was by one,* that is, by one offence, *v.* 16, 17. But from Jesus Christ we receive and derive an *abundance of grace, and of the gift of righteousness.* The stream of grace and righteousness is deeper and broader than the stream of guilt. God in Christ forgives all trespasses.

Fourthly, By Adam's sin *death reigned*; but by Christ's righteousness believers are preferred to *reign in life, v.* 17. We are by Christ and his righteousness entitled to, and instated in, more and greater privileges than we lost by the offence of Adam. The plaster is wider than the wound, and more healing than the wound is killing.

JAMIESON, FAUSSET, BROWN

treating of him, as *the figure of Christ*" [ALFORD]. The point of analogy intended here is plainly the *public character* which both sustained, neither of the two being regarded in the divine procedure towards men as mere *individual* men, but both alike as *representative* men. (Some take the proper supplement here to be "Him [that is] to come"; understanding the apostle to speak from his own time, and to refer to Christ's second coming [FRITZSCHE, DE WETTE, ALFORD]. But this is unnatural, since the analogy of the second Adam to the first has been in full development ever since "God exalted Him to be a Prince and a Saviour," and it will only remain to be consummated at His second coming. The simple meaning is, as nearly all interpreters agree, that Adam is a type of Him who was to come after him in the same public character, and so to be "the second Adam.") **15. But**–'Yet,' 'Howbeit'–**not as the offence**–'trespass'–**so also is the free gift**–or 'the gracious gift,' 'the gift of grace.' The two cases present points of contrast as well as resemblance. **For if . . .**–rather, 'For if through the offense of the one the many died (i.e., in that one man's first sin), much more did the grace of God, and the free gift by grace, even that of the one man, Jesus Christ, abound unto the many.' By "the many" is meant the *mass* of mankind represented respectively by Adam and Christ, as opposed, not to *few,* but to "the one" who represented them. By "the free gift" is meant (as in vs. 17) the glorious gift of *justifying righteousness;* this is expressly distinguished from "the grace of God," as the *effect* from the *cause;* and both are said to "abound" towards us in Christ–in what sense will appear in the next two verses. And the "much more," of the one case than the other, does not mean that we get much more of good by Christ than of evil by Adam (for it is not a case of quantity at all); but that we have much more reason to expect, or it is much more agreeable to our ideas of God, that the many should be benefited by the merit of one, than that they should suffer for the sin of one; and if the latter has happened, *much more* may we assure ourselves of the former [PHILIPPI, HODGE]. **16. And not as it was by one that sinned, so is the gift**–'Another point of contrast may be mentioned.' **for the judgment**–'sentence'–**was by one**–rather, 'was of one,' meaning not 'one man, but, as appears from the next clause, 'one offense'–**to condemnation, but the free gift**–'gift of grace'–**is of many offences unto justification**–a glorious point of contrast. 'The condemnation by Adam was for *one sin;* but the justification by Christ is an absolution not only from the guilt of that first offense, mysteriously attaching to every individual of the race, but from the *countless offenses* into which, as a germ lodged in the bosom of every child of Adam, it unfolds itself in his life.' This is the meaning of "grace *abounding* towards us in the *abundance of the gift* of righteousness." It is a grace not only rich in its *character,* but rich in *detail;* it is a "righteousness" not only rich in *a complete justification* of the guilty, condemned sinner; but rich in the *amplitude of the ground* which it covers, leaving no one sin of any of the justified uncancelled, but making him, though loaded with the guilt of myriads of offenses, "the righteousness of God in Christ." **17. For if by**–'the'–**one man's offence death reigned by one**–'through the one'–**much more shall they which receive**–'the'–**abundance of grace and of the gift of**–justifying–**righteousness . . . reign in life by one**–'through the one'–**Jesus Christ**–We have here the two ideas of vs. 15 and vs. 16 sublimely combined into one, as if the subject had grown upon the apostle as he advanced in his comparison of the two cases. Here, for the first time in this section, he speaks of that LIFE which springs out of justification, in contrast with the death which springs from sin and follows condemnation. The proper idea of it therefore is, 'Right to live'–'Righteous life'–life possessed and enjoyed with the good will, and in conformity with the eternal law, of "Him that sitteth on the Throne"; life therefore in its widest sense–life in the whole man and throughout the whole duration of human existence, the life of blissful and loving relationship to God in soul and body, for ever and ever. It is worthy of note, too, that while he says death "reigned over" us through Adam, he does not say Life "reigns over us" through Christ; lest he should seem to invest this new life with the very attribute of death–that of fell and malignant tyranny, of which we were the hapless victims. Nor does he say Life reigns *in* us, which would have been a scriptural enough idea; but, which is much more pregnant, "*We* shall reign in life." While *freedom* and *might* are implied in the figure of "reigning," "life" is represented as the

ADAM CLARKE

Adam was the *figure, typos,* the "type, pattern, or resemblance" *of him that was to come;* i.e., of the Messiah. The correspondence between them appears in the following particulars: (1) Through him, as its spring and fountain, sin became diffused through the world, so that every man comes into the world with sinful propensities. Through Christ, as its Spring and Fountain, righteousness becomes diffused through the earth, so that every man is made partaker of a principle of grace and truth. (2) "As in Adam all die, even so in Christ shall all be made alive," I Cor. xv. 22. "For since by man came death, by man came also the resurrection of the dead," v. 21. (3) As in or through Adam guilt came upon all men, so, through Christ, "the free gift came upon all men unto justification of life," v. 18. These alone seem to be the instances in which a similitude exists between Adam and Christ.

15. *For if through the offence of one many be dead.* That "the many" of the apostle here means all mankind needs no proof to any but that person who finds himself qualified to deny that all men are mortal. And if "the many"—that is, all mankind—have died through the offense of one, certainly the *gift by grace* which abounds unto "the many" by Christ Jesus must have reference to every human being. If the consequences of Christ's incarnation and death extend only to a few, or a select number of mankind, then the consequences of Adam's sin have extend only to a few, or a select number of mannumber; and if only many and not all have fallen, only that many had need of a Redeemer. For it is most evident that the same persons are referred to in both clauses of the verse. *Hath abounded unto many.* That is, Christ Jesus died for every man; salvation is free for all; saving grace is tendered to every soul; and a measure of the divine light is actually communicated to every heart, John i. 9. And as the grace is offered, so it may be received; and hence the apostle says, v. 17: "They which receive abundance of grace and of the gift of righteousness shall reign in life by . . . Jesus Christ." By receiving is undoubtedly meant not only the act of receiving, but retaining and improving the grace which they receive; and as all may receive, so all may improve and retain the grace they do receive; and, consequently, all may be eternally saved. But of multitudes Christ still may say, "They will not come unto Me, that they might have life."

16. *And not as it was by one that sinned.* That is, the judicial act that followed Adam's sin (the sentence of death pronounced upon him, and his expulsion from paradise) took its rise from his one offense alone, and terminated in condemnation; but the free gift of God in Christ takes its rise also from the *many offences* which men, in a long course of life, have personally committed; and the object of this grace is to justify them freely, and bring them to eternal life.

17. *Death reigned by one.* Death is here personified, and is represented as reigning over the human race. *Shall reign in life.* Those who receive, retain, and improve the abundant grace offered by Jesus Christ shall be redeemed from the empire of death and exalted to the throne of God, to live and reign with Him ever, world without end. See Rev. i. 5-6; ii. 7, 10-11; iii. 21. If we carefully compare v. 15 with v. 17, we shall find that there is a correspondence between the abounding, v. 17, and *hath abounded,* v. 15; between the *gift of righteousness,* i.e., "justification," v. 17, and *the gift by grace,* v. 15. Therefore, if we understand the abounding of grace and the gift of justification, v. 17, we shall understand *the grace of God, and the gift by grace, which . . . hath abounded unto many,* v. 15. But the abounding of grace, and the gift of justification, v. 17, are that *grace* and *gift* which are received by those who shall *reign in* (eternal) *life.* Reigning in life is the consequence of receiving the grace and gift. Therefore receiving the grace is a necessary qualification on our part for reigning in life; and this necessarily implies our believing in Christ Jesus as having died for our offenses, receiving the grace so freely offered us, using the means in order to get more grace, and bringing forth the fruits of the Spirit.

MATTHEW HENRY

(2) How, in correspondence to this, Christ communicates righteousness and life to all true believers. He shows not only wherein the resemblance holds, but wherein the communication of grace and love by Christ *goes beyond* the communication of guilt and wrath by Adam.

[1] Wherein the resemblance holds, *v.* 18, 19.

First, By the offence and disobedience of one many were made sinners, and judgment came upon all men to condemnation. Adam's sin was disobedience. The thing he did was therefore evil because it was forbidden, this opened the door to other sins. The malignity and poison of sin are very strong and spreading, else the guilt of Adam's sin would not have reached so far. Who would think there should be so much evil in sin? By Adam's sin many are made sinners: *many*, that is, all his posterity. *Made sinners*, It denotes the making of us such by a judicial act. Judgment is come upon all those that by Adam's disobedience were made sinners. All the race of mankind lie under a sentence, like an attainder upon a family.

Secondly, In like manner, *by the righteousness and obedience of one are many made righteous*, and so the *free gift comes upon all.* 1. The nature of Christ's righteousness, how it is brought in; it is by his obedience. The disobedience of the first Adam ruined us, the obedience of the second Adam saves us. By his obedience he wrought out a righteousness for us, satisfied God's justice. 2. The fruit of it. There is a *free gift come upon all men.* The salvation wrought is a *common salvation*; whoever will may come, and take of these waters of life. This free gift is *unto justification of life*. It is not only a justification that frees from death, but that entitles to life. *Many shall be made righteous, shall be constituted* righteous, as by letters patent.

F. B. MEYER:

We are here taught the unity of the race, not only in Adam, but in Christ. Adam's sin has affected the standing of every man; but the grace and the obedience of the "one man," Jesus Christ, have secured for all men the offer of the free gift. The guilt that lay upon the race by the sin of Adam has been removed from the race by the obedience of the Son of man to the cross. None, therefore, is condemned on account of that first transgression or doomed for that primal fall. In a sense, all are made righteous; that is, all stand before God on the basis of their individual, rather than their racial, responsibility. We are not condemned with Adam, but will be condemned if we refuse to avail ourselves of the grace of Jesus Christ. All that sin forfeited is put within our reach. Nay, we may reach higher heights than Adam if we will only receive the abundance of the grace of Christ.—*Bible Commentary*

JAMIESON, FAUSSET, BROWN

glorious territory or atmosphere of that reign. And by recurring to the idea of vs. 16, as to the "many offenses" whose complete pardon shows "the abundance of grace and of the gift of righteousness," the whole statement is to this effect: 'If one man's one offense let loose against us the tyrant power of Death, to hold us as its victims in helpless bondage, "much more," when we stand forth enriched with God's "abounding grace" and in the beauty of a complete absolution from countless offenses, shall we expatiate in a life divinely owned and legally secured, "reigning" in exultant freedom and unchallenged might, through that other matchless "One," Jesus Christ!' (On the import of the *future* tense in this last clause, see on vs. 19, and on ch. 6. 5.) **18. Therefore**—now at length resuming the unfinished comparison of vs. 12, in order to give *formally* the concluding member of it, which had been done once and again *substantially*, in the intermediate verses. **as by the offence of one judgment came**—or, more simply, 'it came'—**upon all men to condemnation; even so by the righteousness of one the free gift came**—rather, 'it came'—**upon all men to justification of life**—[So CALVIN, BENGEL, OLSHAUSEN, THOLUCK, HODGE, PHILIPPI]. But better, as we judge: 'As through one offense it [came] upon all men to condemnation; even so through one righteousness [it came] upon all men to justification of life'—[So BEZA, GROTIUS, FERME, MEYER, DE WETTE, ALFORD, REVISED VERSION]. In this case, the apostle, resuming the statement of vs. 12, expresses it in a more concentrated and vivid form—suggested no doubt by the expression in vs. 16, "through one offense," representing Christ's whole work, considered as the ground of our justification, as "ONE RIGHTEOUSNESS." (Some would render the peculiar word here employed, 'one righteous act' [ALFORD, etc.]; understanding by it Christ's *death* as the one redeeming act which reversed the one undoing act of Adam. But this is to limit the apostle's idea too much; for as the same word is properly rendered "righteousness" in ch. 8:4, where it means "the righteousness of the law as fulfilled by us who walk not after the flesh, but after the Spirit," so here it denotes Christ's whole "obedience unto death," considered as the one meritorious ground of the reversal of the condemnation which came by Adam. But on this, and on the expression, "all men," see on vs. 19. The expression "justification of life," is a vivid combination of two ideas already expatiated upon, meaning 'justification entitling to and issuing in the rightful possession and enjoyment of life'). **19. For . . .**—better, 'For as by the one man's disobedience the many were made sinners, even so by the obedience of the One shall the many be made righteous.' On this great verse observe: *First,* By the "obedience" of Christ here is plainly not meant more than what divines call His *active* obedience, as distinguished from His sufferings and death; it is the entire work of Christ in its *obediential* character. Our Lord Himself represents even His death as His great act of obedience to the Father: "This commandment (i.e., to lay down and resume His life) have I received of My Father" (John 10:8). *Second,* The significant word twice rendered "*made*," does not signify to *work a change upon* a person or thing, but to *constitute* or *ordain,* as will be seen from all the places where it is used. Here, accordingly, it is intended to express that *judicial act* which holds men, in virtue of their connection with Adam, as sinners; and, in connection with Christ, as righteous. *Third,* The change of *tense* from the past to the future—"as through Adam we *were* made sinners, so through Christ we *shall be* made righteous"—delightfully expresses the enduring character of the act, and of the economy to which such acts belong, in contrast with the for-ever-past ruin of believers in Adam. (See on ch. 6:5.) *Fourth,* The "all men" of vs. 18 and the "many" of vs. 19 are the same party, though under a slightly different aspect. In the latter case, the contrast is between the *one* representative (Adam—Christ) and the *many* whom he represented; in the former case, it is between the one *head* (Adam—Christ) and the *human race,* affected for death and life respectively by the actings of that one. Only in this latter case it is the redeemed family of man that is alone in view; it is *humanity* as actually lost, but also as actually saved, as ruined and recovered. Such as refuse to fall in with the high purpose of God to constitute His Son a "second Adam," the Head of a new race, and as impenitent and unbelieving finally perish, have no place in this section of the Epistle, whose sole object is to show how God repairs in the second Adam the evil done by the first. (Thus the doctrine of *universal restoration* has no place here. Thus

ADAM CLARKE

18. *Therefore as by the offence of one.* Literally, "Therefore, as by one offense unto all men, unto condemnation; so likewise, by one righteousness unto all men, to justification of life." This is evidently an elliptical sentence, and its full meaning can be gathered only from the context. He who had no particular purpose to serve would most probably understand it, from the context, thus: "Therefore as by one sin all men came into condemnation, so also by one righteous act all men came unto justification of life."

ALBERT BARNES:

18. "Therefore." This is properly a summing up, a recapitulation of what had been stated in the previous verses. The apostle resumes the statement or proposition made in verse 12, and after the immediate explanation, in the parenthesis (vv. 13-17), in this verse and the following sums up the whole subject. The explanation, therefore, of the previous verses is designed to convey the real meaning of verses 18, 19. "As by the offence of one." Admitting this as an undisputed and everywhere apparent fact, a fact which no one can call in question. "Judgment came." This is not in the Greek, but it is evidently implied and is stated in verse 16. The meaning is, that all have been brought under the reign of death by one man. "Upon all men." The whole race. This explains what is meant by "the many" in verse 15. "To condemnation," verse 16.

"Even so." In the manner explained in the previous verses. With the same certainty and to the same extent. The apostle does not explain the mode in which it was done, but simply states the fact. "By the righteousness of one." This stands opposed to the "one offence" of Adam, and must mean, therefore, the holiness, obedience, purity of the Redeemer. The *sin* of one man involved men in ruin; the *obedience unto death* of the other (Phil. 2:8) restored them to the favor of God. Came "upon all men." Was with reference to all men; was *originally adapted* to the race. As the sin of Adam was of such a nature in the relation in which he stood as to affect all the race, so the work of Christ, in the relation in which he stood was adapted also to all the race. As the tendency of the one was to involve the race in condemnation, so the tendency of the other was to restore them to acceptance with God. There was an *original applicability* in the work of Christ to all men—a richness, a fullness of the atonement fitted to meet the sins of the entire world, and restore the race to favor. "Unto justification of life." With reference to that justification which is connected with eternal life. That is, his work is *adapted* to produce acceptance with God, to the same extent as the crime of Adam has affected the race by involving them in sin and misery. The apostle does not affirm that in fact as many will be affected by the one as by the other; but that it is fitted to meet all the consequences of the Fall; to be as widespread in its effects; and to be as salutary as that had been ruinous. This is all that the argument requires. Perhaps there could not be found a more striking declaration anywhere, that the work of Christ had *an original applicability* to all men; or that it is in its own nature fitted to save all. The course of argument here leads inevitably to this; nor is it possible to avoid it without doing violence to the obvious and fair course of the discussion. It does not prove that all will in fact be saved, but that the plan is *fitted* to meet all the evils of the Fall.

—*Popular Commentary*

MATTHEW HENRY

IV. *The law entered that the offence might abound.* Not to make sin to abound the more in itself, but to discover the abounding sinfulness of it. The glass discovers the spots, but does not cause them. The letting of a clearer light into a room discovers the dust and filth which were there before, but were not seen.

That grace might much more abound—that the terrors of the law might make gospel-comforts so much the sweeter. The greater the strength of the enemy, the greater the honour of the conqueror. This abounding of grace he illustrates, *v.* 21. *Sin reigned unto death;* it was a cruel bloody reign.

But *grace reigns* to life, *eternal life*, and this *through righteousness* by *Jesus Christ our Lord*, through the power and efficacy of Christ.

JAMIESON, FAUSSET, BROWN

too the forced interpretation by which the "justification of all" is made to mean a justification merely in *possibility* and *offer* to all, and the "justification of the many" to mean the *actual* justification of as many as believe [ALFORD, etc.], is completely avoided. And thus the harshness of comparing a *whole* fallen family with a recovered *part* is got rid of. However true it be in *fact* that part of mankind is not saved, this is not the *aspect* in which the subject is here presented. It is *totals* that are compared and contrasted; and it is the *same total* in two successive conditions—namely, *the human race* as ruined in Adam and recovered in Christ). **20, 21. Moreover the law**—'The law, however.' The Jew might say, If the whole purposes of God towards men center in Adam and Christ, where does "the law" come in, and what was the use of it? *Answer:* **It entered**—But the word expresses an important idea besides 'entering.' It signifies, 'entered incidentally,' or 'parenthetically.' (In Galatians 2: 4 the same word is rendered, 'came in *privily*.') The meaning is, that the promulgation of the law at Sinai was no primary or essential feature of the divine plan, but it was "added" (Gal. 3:19) for a subordinate purpose—the more fully to reveal the evil occasioned by Adam, and the need and glory of the remedy by Christ. **that the offence might abound**—(or, 'be multiplied'). But what offense? Throughout all this section 'the offense' (four times repeated besides here) has one definite meaning, namely, 'the one first offense of Adam'; and this, in our judgment, is its meaning here also: 'All our multitudinous breaches of the law are nothing but *that one first offense,* lodged mysteriously in the bosom of every child of Adam as an *offending principal,* and *multiplying itself* into myriads of particular offenses in the life of each.' What was one *act* of disobedience in the head has been converted into a vital and virulent *principle* of disobedience in all the members of the human family, whose every act of wilful rebellion proclaims itself the child of the original transgression. **But where sin abounded**—or, 'was multiplied'—**grace did much more abound**—rather, 'did exceedingly abound,' or 'superabound.' The comparison here is between the multiplication of one offense into countless transgressions, and such an overflow of grace as more than meets that appalling case. **That as sin** —Observe, the word "offense" is no more used, as that had been sufficiently illustrated; but—what better befitted this comprehensive summation of the whole matter—the great general term *sin.* **hath reigned unto death**—rather, 'in death,' triumphing and (as it were) revelling in that complete destruction of its victims. **even so might grace reign**—In vss. 14, 17 we had the reign of *death* over the guilty and condemned in Adam; here it is the reign of the mighty *causes* of these—of SIN which clothes Death a Sovereign with venomous *power* (I Cor. 15:56) and with awful *authority* (ch. 6:23), and of GRACE, the grace which originated the scheme of salvation, the grace which "sent the Son to be the Saviour of the world," the grace which "made Him to be sin for us who knew no sin," the grace which "makes us to be the righteousness of God in Him," so that "we who receive *the abundance of grace* and of the gift of righteousness do reign in life by One, Jesus Christ!" **through righteousness**—not *ours* certainly ('the obedience of Christians,' to use the wretched language of GROTIUS) nor yet exactly 'justification' [STUART, HODGE]; but rather, 'the (justifying) righteousness of Christ' [BEZA, ALFORD, and in substance, OLSHAUSEN, MEYER]; the same which in vs. 19 is called His "obedience," meaning His whole mediatorial work in the flesh. This is here represented as the *righteous medium* through which grace reaches its objects and attains all its ends, the stable throne from which Grace as a Sovereign dispenses its saving benefits to as many as are brought under its benign sway. **unto eternal life**—which is salvation in its highest form and fullest development for ever. **by Jesus Christ our Lord**—Thus, on that "Name which is above every name," the echoes of this hymn to the glory of "Grace" die away, and "Jesus is left alone."

ADAM CLARKE

20. *The law entered, that the offence might abound.* After considering various opinions concerning the true meaning of this verse, I am induced to prefer my own as being the most simple. By *law* I understand the Mosaic law. By entering in, or, rather, "coming in privily," see Gal. ii. 4 (the only place where it occurs besides), I understand the temporary or limited use of that law, which was, as far as its rites and ceremonies are considered, confined to the Jewish people, and to them only till the Messiah should come. But considered as the moral law, or rule of conscience and life, it has in its spirit and power been slipped in, introduced into every conscience, that sin might abound, that the true nature, deformity, and extent of sin might appear; for by the law is the knowledge of sin. For how can the finer deviations from a straight line be ascertained without the application of a known straightedge? Without this rule of right, sin can be known only in a sort of general way.

But where sin abounded. Whether in the world or in the heart of the individual, being discovered by this most pure and righteous law, *grace did much more abound;* not only pardon for all that is past is offered by the gospel, but also the Holy Spirit, in the abundance of His gifts and graces, is communicated, so as to prepare the receiver for an "exceeding and eternal weight of glory." Thus the grace of the gospel not only redeems from death and restores to life, but brings the soul into such a relationship with God, and into such a participation of eternal glory, as we have no authority to believe ever would have been the portion even of Adam himself had he even eternally retained his innocence.

21. *That as sin hath reigned unto death.* As extensively, as deeply, as universally, as *sin,* whether implying the act of transgression or the impure principle from which the act proceeds, or both. *Hath reigned,* subjected the whole earth and all its inhabitants; the whole soul, and all its powers and faculties. *Unto death,* temporal of the body, spiritual of the soul, and eternal of both. *Even so,* as extensively, deeply, and universally, *might grace reign*—filling the whole earth, and pervading, purifying, and refining the whole soul. *Through righteousness*—through this doctrine of free salvation by the blood of the Lamb, and by the principle of holiness transfused through the soul by the Holy Ghost.

Unto eternal life—the proper object of an immortal spirit's hope, the only sphere where the human intellect can rest, and be happy in the place and state where God is. *By Jesus Christ our Lord*—as the Cause of our salvation, the Means by which it is communicated, and the Source whence it springs. Thus we find that the salvation from sin here is as extensive and complete as the guilt and contamination of sin.

MATTHEW HENRY

CHAPTER 6

Verses 1–23

The apostle's transition, which joins this discourse with the former: "*What shall we say then?* (*v.* 1). *Shall we continue in sin that grace may abound?*" Shall we hence take encouragement to sin because the more sin we commit the more will the grace of God be magnified in our pardon? The apostle startled at the thought of it (*v.* 2): "*God forbid.*" Those opinions that give any countenance to sin are to be rejected with the greatest abhorrence. The apostle is very full in pressing the necessity of holiness in this chapter, which may be reduced to two heads: His exhortations to holiness, and his arguments to enforce those exhortations.

I. For the first, we may hence observe the nature of sanctification. It has two things in it, mortification and vivification—dying to sin and living to righteousness.

1. Mortification, putting off the old man. (1) We must *live no longer in sin* (*v.* 2). Though there are none that live without sin, yet there are those that do not live in sin.

(2) In particular, being *baptized into Jesus Christ, we were baptized into his death*, *v.* 3. Baptism binds us to Christ. Particularly, we were baptized into his death. As Christ died for sin, so we should die to sin. This was the profession and promise of our baptism, and we do not do well if we do not answer this profession, and make good this promise.

We are buried with him by baptism, *v.* 4. Our conformity is complete. We are in profession quite cut off from all commerce and communion with sin. Thus must we be, as Christ was, separate from sin and sinners. We are sealed to be the Lord's, therefore to be cut off from sin. As Christ was buried, that he might rise again to a new and more heavenly life, so we are in baptism buried, that we may rise again to a new life of faith and love.

Vivification, or living to righteousness. It is to *walk in newness of life*, *v.* 4. Newness of life supposes newness of heart; there is no way to make the stream sweet but by making the spring so. Walk by new rules. Make a new choice of the way. Choose new paths to walk in, new leaders to walk after, new companions to walk with.

JAMIESON, FAUSSET, BROWN

CHAPTER 6

Vss. 1-11. The Bearing of Justification by Grace upon a Holy Life. **1. What . . .**—The subject of this *third* division of our Epistle announces itself at once in the opening question, "Shall we (or, as the true reading is, 'May we,' 'Are we to') continue in sin, that grace may abound?" Had the apostle's doctrine been that salvation depends *in any degree* upon our good works, no such objection to it could have been made. Against the doctrine of a purely gratuitous justification, the objection is plausible; nor has there ever been an age in which it has not been urged. That it *was* brought against the apostles, we know from ch. 3: 8; and we gather from Galatians 5:13; I Peter 2:16; Jude 4, that some did give occasion to the charge; but that it was a total perversion of the doctrine of Grace the apostle here proceeds to show. **2. God forbid**—'That be far from us'; the instincts of the new creature revolting at the thought. **How shall we, that are dead . . .**—lit., and more forcibly, 'We who died to sin (as presently to be explained), how shall we live any longer therein?' **3. Know ye not, that so many of us as were baptized into Jesus Christ**—cf. I Corinthians 10:2—**were baptized into his death?**—sealed with the seal of heaven, and as it were formally entered and articled, to all the *benefits* and all the *obligations* of Christian discipleship in general, and of His *death* in particular. And since He was "made sin" and "a curse for us" (II Cor. 5:21; Gal. 5:13), "bearing our sins in His own body on the tree," and "rising again for our justification" (ch. 4:25; I Pet. 2:24), our whole sinful case and condition, thus taken up into His Person, has been brought to an end in His death. Whoso, then, has been baptized into Christ's death has formally surrendered the whole state and life of sin, as in Christ a dead thing. He has sealed himself to be not only "the righteousness of God in Him," but "a new creature"; and as he cannot be in Christ to the one effect and not to the other, for they are one thing, he has bidden farewell, by baptism into Christ's death, to his entire connection with sin. "How," then, "can he live any longer therein?" The two things are as contradictory in the fact as they are in the terms. **4. Therefore we are**—rather, 'were' (it being a past act, completed at once). **buried with him, by baptism into death**—(The *comma* we have placed after "him" will show what the sense is. It is not, 'By baptism we are buried with Him into death,' which makes no sense at all; but, 'By *baptism with Him into death* we are buried with Him'; in other words, 'By the same baptism which publicly enters us into His *death*, we are made partakers of His *burial* also). To leave a dead body unburied is represented, alike in heathen authors as in Scripture, as the greatest indignity (Rev. 11:8, 9). It was fitting, therefore, that Christ, after "dying for our sins according to the Scriptures," should "descend into the lower parts of the earth" (Eph. 4:9). As this was the last and lowest step of His humiliation, so it was the honorable dissolution of His last link of connection with that life which He laid down for us; and we, in being "buried with Him by our baptism into His death," have by this public act severed our last link of connection with that whole sinful condition and life which Christ brought to an end in His death. **that like as Christ was raised from the dead by the glory of the Father**—i.e., by such a forthputting of the Father's *power* as was the effulgence of His whole glory—**even so we also**—as risen to a new life with Him—**should walk in newness of life**—But what is that "newness?" Surely if our *old* life, now dead and buried with Christ, was wholly sinful, the *new*, to which we rise with the risen Saviour, must be altogether a holy life; so that every time we go back to "those things whereof we are now ashamed" (vs. 21), we belie our resurrection with Christ to newness of life, and "forget that we have been purged from our old sins" (II Pet. 1:9). Whether the mode of baptism by immersion be alluded to in this verse, as a kind of symbolical burial and resurrection, does not seem to us of much consequence. Many interpreters think it is, and it may be so. But as it is not clear that baptism in apostolic times was exclusively by immersion (see on Acts 2:41), so *sprinkling* and *washing* are indifferently used in the New Testament to express the cleansing efficacy of the blood of Jesus. And just as the woman with the issue of blood got virtue out of Christ by simply *touching* Him, so the essence of baptism seems to lie in the simple *contact* of the element with the body, symbolizing living contact with Christ crucified; the mode and extent of suffusion being indifferent and variable with climate and circum-

ADAM CLARKE

CHAPTER 6

The apostle, having proved that salvation, to both Jew and Gentile, must come through the Messiah, and be received by faith only, proceeds in this chapter to show the obligations under which both were laid to live a holy life, and the means and advantages they enjoyed for that purpose. This he does, not only as a thing highly and indispensably necessary in itself—for without holiness none can see the Lord—but to confute a calumny which appears to have been gaining considerable ground even at that time, viz., that the doctrine of justification by faith alone, through the grace of Christ Jesus, rendered obedience to the moral law useless; and that the more evil a man did, the more the grace of God would abound to him in his redemption from that evil. That this calumny was then propagated we learn from chap. iii. 8; and the apostle defends himself against it in the thirty-first verse of the same by asserting that his doctrine, far from making void the law, served to establish it. But in this and the following two chapters he takes up the subject in a regular, formal manner, and shows both Jews and Gentiles that the principles of the Christian religion absolutely require a holy heart and a holy life and make the amplest provisions for both.

1. *Shall we continue in sin?* It is very likely that these were the words of a believing Gentile, who—having as yet received but little instruction, for he is but just brought out of his heathen state to believe in Christ Jesus—might imagine, from the manner in which God had magnified His mercy, in blotting out his sin on his simply believing on Christ, that, supposing he even gave way to the evil propensities of his own heart, his transgressions could do him no hurt now that he was in the favor of God.

2. *God forbid.* "Let it not be; by no means; far from it; let not such a thing be mentioned!" —any of these is the meaning of the Greek phrase, which is a strong expression of surprise and disapprobation; and is not properly rendered by our *God forbid!* for, though this may express the same thing, yet it is not proper to make the sacred name so familiar on such occasions. *How shall we, that are dead to sin?* The phraseology of this verse is common among Hebrews, Greeks, and Latins. To die to a thing or person is to have nothing to do with it or him, to be totally separated from them; and to live to a thing or person is to be wholly given up to them, to have the most intimate connection with them.

3. *Know ye not?* Every man who believes the Christian religion, and receives baptism as the proof that he believes it, and has taken up the profession of it, is bound thereby to a life of righteousness. To be *baptized into Jesus Christ* is to receive the doctrine of Christ crucified, and to receive baptism as a proof of the genuineness of that faith, and the obligation to live according to its precepts. *Baptized into his death.* That, as Jesus Christ in His crucifixion died completely, so that no spark of the natural or animal life remained in His body, so those who profess His reliigon should be so completely separated and saved from sin that they have no more connection with it, nor any more influence from it, than a dead man has with or from his departed spirit.

4. *We are buried with him by baptism into death.* It is probable that the apostle here alludes to the mode of administering baptism by immersion, the whole body being put under the water, which seemed to say, The man is drowned, is dead; and when he came up out of the water, he seemed to have a resurrection to life. The man is risen again; he is alive! *Raised up from the dead by the glory of the Father.* From this we learn that, as it required the *glory of the Father*, that is, His glorious energy, to raise up from the grave the dead body of Christ, so it requires the same glorious energy to quicken the dead soul of a sinner and enable him to walk in newness of life.

MATTHEW HENRY

Our conformity to the resurrection of Christ obliges us to rise again to newness of life. Christ was raised up *from the dead by the glory of the Father*. Now in baptism we are obliged to conform to that pattern, to be planted in the *likeness of his resurrection* (*v.* 5), to *live with him*, *v.* 8. Conversion is the first resurrection from the death of sin to the life of righteousness; and this resurrection is conformable to Christ's resurrection. We have all risen with Christ.

Our conformity to the death of Christ obliges us to die unto sin. Thus we are here said to be *planted together in the likeness of his death* (*v.* 5), as the engrafted stock is planted together into the likeness of the shoot, of the nature of which it doth participate. We are planted in the vineyard in a likeness to Christ, which likeness we should evidence in sanctification. Our creed concerning Jesus Christ is, among other things, that he was *crucified, dead, and buried*; now baptism is a sacramental conformity to him in each of these. *First, Our old man is crucified with him, v.* 6. The death of the cross was a slow death; but it was a sure death. Such is the mortification of sin in believers. It was a cursed death. Sin dies as a malefactor, devoted to destruction. *Crucified with him.* The crucifying of Christ for us has an influence upon the crucifying of sin in us. *Secondly*, We are dead with Christ, *v.* 8. Christ was obedient to death: when he died, we might be said to die with him. Baptism signifies and seals our union with Christ, so that we are dead with him, and engaged to have no more to do with sin than he had. *Thirdly, The body of sin must be destroyed, v.* 6. The corruption that dwelleth in us is the body of sin. This is the root to which the axe must be laid. We must not only cease from the acts of sin, but we must get the vicious habits and inclinations weakened and destroyed. *That henceforth we should not serve sin.* It is the body of sin that sways the sceptre; destroy this, and the yoke is broken.

To show the necessity of sanctification. There is such an antipathy in our hearts by nature to holiness that it is no easy matter to bring them to submit to it: it is the Spirit's work.

Our baptism carries in it a great reason why we should die to sin, and live to righteousness. Observe this reasoning.

In general, we are *dead to sin.* Our baptism signifies our cutting off from the kingdom of sin. We are dead to sin by our union with Christ, in and by whom it is killed. All this is in vain if we persist in sin; we return to that to which we were dead, like walking ghosts. For (*v.* 7) *he that is dead is freed from sin*; he that is dead to it is freed from the rule and dominion of it. Now shall we be such fools as to return to that slavery from which we are discharged?

In two things we must conform to the resurrection of Christ: *First*, He rose to die no more, *v.* 9. Over Christ *death has no more dominion*; he was dead indeed, but he is alive, and so alive that he lives for evermore. Thus we must rise from the grave of sin never again to return to it. *Secondly*, He rose to live unto God (*v.* 10), to live a heavenly life. He rose again to leave the world. *Now I am no more in the world*, John xvii. 11. He rose to *live to God.* Thus must we rise to live to God: this is what he calls *newness of life* (*v.* 4), to live by other rules, with other aims, than we have done. A life devoted to God is a new life; before, self was the chief and highest end, but now God.

JAMIESON, FAUSSET, BROWN

stances). **5. For if we have been planted together**—lit., 'have become formed together.' (The word is used here only.) **in the likeness of his death, we shall be also in the likeness of his resurrection**—i.e., 'Since Christ's death and resurrection are inseparable in their efficacy, union with Him in the one carries with it participation in the other, for privilege and for duty alike.' The *future* tense is used of participation in His resurrection, because this is but partially realized in the present state. (See on ch. 5:19.)

6, 7. Knowing this . . .—The apostle now grows more definite and vivid in expressing the sin-destroying efficacy of our union with the crucified Saviour. **that our old man**—'our old selves'; i.e., '*all that we were* in our old unregenerate condition, before union with Christ' (cf. Col. 3:9, 10; Eph. 4:22-24; Gal. 2:20; 5:24; 6:14). **is**—rather, 'was'—**crucified with him**—in order—**that the body of sin**—not a figure for 'the *mass* of sin'; nor the '*material body*,' considered as the seat of sin, which it is not; but (as we judge) for 'sin as it dwells in us in our present *embodied* state, under the law of the fall.' **might be destroyed**—(in Christ's death)—to the end—**that henceforth we should not serve**—'be in bondage to'—**sin.**

For he that is dead—rather, 'hath died'—**is freed**—'hath been set free'—**from sin**—lit., 'justified,' 'acquitted,' 'got his discharge from sin.' As death dissolves all claims, so the whole claim of sin, not only to "reign unto death," but to keep its victims in sinful bondage, has been discharged once for all, by the believer's penal death in the death of Christ; so that he is no longer a "*debtor* to the flesh to live after the flesh" (ch. 8:12).

8. Now if we be dead—'if we died'—**with Christ . . .**—See on vs. 5. **9-11. Christ being raised from the dead dieth no more; death hath no more dominion over him**—Though Christ's death was in the most absolute sense a voluntary act (Jas. 10:17, 18; Acts 2:24), that voluntary surrender gave death such rightful "dominion over *Him*" as dissolved its dominion over *us*. But this once past, "death hath," even in that sense, "dominion over Him no more." **For in that he died, he died unto**—i.e., in obedience to the claims of—**sin once**—for all—**but in that he liveth, he liveth unto**—in obedience to the claims of—**God**—There never, indeed, was a time when Christ did not "live unto God." But in the days of His flesh He did so under the continual burden of sin "laid on Him" (Isa. 53:6; II Cor. 5:21); whereas, now that He has "put away sin by the sacrifice of Himself," He "liveth unto God," the acquitted and accepted Surety, unchallenged and unclouded by the claims of sin. **Likewise**—even as your Lord Himself—**reckon ye also yourselves to be dead indeed**—'dead

ADAM CLARKE

5. *For if we have been planted together.* When the seed or plant is inserted in the ground, it derives from that ground all its nourishment and all those juices by which it becomes developed; by which it increases in size, grows firm, strong, and vigorous and puts forth its leaves, blossoms, and fruit. The *death* of Jesus Christ is represented as the cause whence His fruitfulness as the Author of eternal salvation to mankind is derived; and genuine believers in Him are represented as being *planted . . . in . . . his death*, and growing out of it; deriving their growth, vigor, firmness, beauty, and fruitfulness from it.

6. *Our old man is crucified with him.* This seems to be a further extension of the same metaphor. When a seed is planted in the earth, it appears as if the whole body of it perished. The *body* dies that the germ may live. How is the principle of life which Jesus Christ has implanted in us to be brought into full effect, vigor, and usefulness? By the destruction of the *body of sin.* Our *old man*, our wicked, corrupt, and fleshly self, is to be crucified, to be as truly slain as Christ was crucified, that our souls may as truly be raised from a death of sin to a life of righteousness as the body of Christ was raised from the grave, and afterwards ascended to the right hand of God. But how does this part of the metaphor apply to Jesus Christ? Plainly and forcibly. Jesus Christ took on Him a body, a body "in the likeness of sinful flesh," chap. viii. 3, and gave up that body to death; through which death alone an atonement was made for sin, and the way laid open for the vivifying Spirit to have the fullest access to, and the most powerful operation in, the human heart. Here the body of Christ dies that He may be a quickening Spirit to mankind. Our *body of sin* is destroyed by this quickening Spirit, that henceforth we should live unto Him who died and rose again. Thus the metaphor, in all its leading senses, is complete, and applies most forcibly to the subject in question. We find that the *old man*, used here and in Eph. iv. 22 and Col. iii. 9, is the same as "the flesh with the affections and lusts," Gal. v. 24; and "the body of the sins of the flesh," Col. ii. 11; and the very same which the Jewish writers term the "old Adam" and which they interpret by "evil concupiscence"; the same which we mean by indwelling sin, or the infection of our nature, in consequence of the Fall. From all which we may learn that the design of God is to counterwork and destroy the very spirit and soul of sin, that we shall no longer serve it, no longer be its slaves.

7. *He that is dead is freed from sin.* Literally, is "justified" from sin, or is freed or delivered from it. Does not this simply mean that the man who has received Christ Jesus by faith, and has been, through believing, made a partaker of the Holy Spirit, has had his "old man," all his evil propensities, destroyed; so that he is not only justified freely from all sin, but wholly sanctified unto God? The context shows that this is the meaning. Every instance of violence is done to the whole scope and design of the apostle by the opinion that "this text is a proof that believers are not fully saved from sin in this life, because only he that is dead is freed from sin." Then death is his justifier and deliverer! So then, the death of Christ and the influences of the Holy Spirit were only sufficient to depose and enfeeble the tyrant sin; but our death must come in to effect his total destruction! Thus our death is, at least partially, our Saviour; and thus, that which was an effect of sin (for sin entered into the world, and death by sin) becomes the means of finally destroying it! The divinity and philosophy of this sentiment are equally absurd. It is the blood of Christ alone that cleanses from all unrighteousness; and the sanctification of a believer is no more dependent on death than his justification.

9. *Christ being raised from the dead dieth no more.* So we, believing in Christ Jesus, and having a death unto sin and a life unto righteousness, should sin no more.

10. *He died unto sin once.* From the whole scope of the apostle's discourse it is plain that he considers the death of Christ is a death or sacrifice for sin, a sin offering. In this sense no man has ever died for sin, or ever can die.

11. *Reckon ye also yourselves to be dead.*

MATTHEW HENRY

It is to be *alive unto God through Jesus Christ our Lord, v.* 11. To converse with God, to have a regard to him, a delight in him, this is to be alive to God. It is to have the affections and desires alive towards God. Or, *living* (our life in the flesh) *unto God,* to his honour and glory as our end, by his word and will as our rule; this is to live unto God.—*Through Jesus Christ our Lord.* Christ is our spiritual life; there is no living to God but through him. He is the Mediator; no intercourse between sinful souls and a holy God, but by the mediation of the Lord Jesus. In living to God, Christ is all in all. *We must be dead indeed unto sin, v.* 11. As the death of the oppressor is a release, so much more is the death of the oppressed. Thus must we be dead to sin, fulfil its will no more. He that is dead is separated from his former company. Death makes a mighty change; such a change doth sanctification make in the soul, it cuts off all correspondence with sin.

Sin must not reign in our mortal bodies that we should obey it, v. 12. Though sin may remain as an outlaw, yet let it not reign as a king. Let it not make laws, so that we should obey it. Though we may be sometimes overtaken and overcome by it, yet let us never be obedient to it. *In the lusts thereof.* Sin lies very much in the gratifying of the body. And there is a reason implied in the phrase *your mortal body.* It was sin that made our bodies mortal, and therefore do not yield obedience to such an enemy.

We must not *yield our members as instruments of unrighteousness, v.* 13. The members of the body are made use of by the corrupt nature as tools, but we must not consent to that abuse. One sin begets another; it is like the letting forth of water, therefore leave it before it be meddled with. The members of the body may perhaps be forced to be instruments of sin; but do not yield them to be so, do not consent to it. This is one branch of sanctification, the mortification of sin.

It is to *yield ourselves to God, as those that are alive from the dead, v.* 13. The very life and being of holiness lie in the dedication of ourselves to the Lord, giving our own selves to the Lord. "Not yield your estates to him, but yield yourselves; nothing less than your whole selves. Not only submit to him, but comply with him; be always ready to serve him. Yield yourselves to him as wax to the seal, to take any impression, to be, and have, and do, what he pleases." *As those that are alive from the dead.* To yield a dead carcase to a living God is not to please him, but to mock him: "Yield yourselves as those that are alive and good for something, a *living sacrifice, ch.* xii. 1. The surest evidence of our spiritual life is the dedication of ourselves to God. It is to yield *our members as instruments of righteousness to God.* The members of our bodies, when withdrawn from the service of sin, are not to lie idle, but to be made use of in the service of God. The body must be always ready to serve the soul in the service of God.

2. He argues from the precious promises of the new covenant, *v.* 14. It might be objected that we cannot subdue sin, it is unavoidably too hard for us: "No," says he, "you wrestle with an enemy that may be dealt with and subdued; it is an enemy that is already foiled and baffled. *Sin shall not have dominion.*" Sin may struggle in a believer, and may create him a great deal of trouble, it may vex him, but shall not rule over him. *For we are not under the law, but under grace,* not under the law of sin and death, but under the law of the spirit of life, which is in Christ Jesus. New lords, new laws. Or, not under the covenant of works, which requires brick, and gives no straw, but under the covenant of grace, which accepts sincerity as our gospel perfection, which requires nothing but what it promises strength to perform. It does not leave our salvation in our own keeping, but lays it up in the hands of the Mediator, who undertakes for us that sin shall not have dominion over us, who hath himself condemned it, and will destroy it. Christ rules by the golden sceptre of grace. We are under grace, grace which accepts the willing mind, which leaves room for repentance, which promises pardon upon repentance. Shall we sin against so much goodness, abuse such love? See how the apostle starts at such a thought (*v.* 15): *Shall we sin because we are not under the law, but under grace? God forbid.*

3. This will be evidence of our state, for us, or against us (*v.* 16): *To whom you yield yourselves servants to obey, his servants you are.* All the children of men are either the servants of God, or the servants of sin. We must enquire to which of these masters we yield obedience. Our obeying the laws of sin will be an evidence against us that we belong to that family on which death is entailed. Our obeying the laws of Christ will evidence our relation to Christ's family.

JAMIESON, FAUSSET, BROWN

on the one hand')—**unto sin, but alive unto God through Jesus Christ**—(The words, "our Lord," at the close of this verse, are wanting in the best MSS.) Note (1) "Antinomianism is not only an error; it is a falsehood and a slander" [HODGE]. That "we should continue in sin that grace may abound," not only is never the deliberate sentiment of any real believer in the doctrine of Grace, but is abhorrent to every Christian mind, as a monstrous abuse of the most glorious of all truths (vs. 1). (2) As the death of Christ is not only the expiation of guilt, but the death of sin itself in all who are vitally united to Him; so the resurrection of Christ is the resurrection of believers, not only to acceptance with God, but to newness of life (vss. 2-11). (3) In the light of these two truths, let all who name the name of Christ "examine themselves whether they be in the faith."

12-23. WHAT PRACTICAL USE BELIEVERS SHOULD MAKE OF THEIR DEATH TO SIN AND LIFE TO GOD THROUGH UNION TO THE CRUCIFIED SAVIOUR. Not content with showing that his doctrine has no tendency to relax the obligations to a holy life, the apostle here proceeds to enforce these obligations. **12. Let not sin therefore**—as a Master—**reign**—(The reader will observe that wherever in this section the words "Sin," "Obedience," "Righteousness," "Uncleanness," "Iniquity," are figuratively used, to represent a *Master,* they are here printed in capitals, to make this manifest to the eye, and so save explanation.) **in your mortal body, that ye should obey it**—sin—**in the lusts thereof**—"the lusts of the body," as the *Greek* makes evident. (The other reading, perhaps the true one, 'that ye should obey the lusts thereof,' comes to the same thing.) The "body" is here viewed as the instrument by which all the sins of the heart become facts of the outward life, and as itself the seat of the lower appetites; and it is called "our *mortal* body," probably to remind us how unsuitable is this reign of sin in those who are "alive from the dead." But the reign here meant is the unchecked dominion of sin *within* us. Its outward acts are next referred to. **13. Neither yield ye your members instruments of unrighteousness unto Sin, but yield yourselves**—this is the great surrender—**unto God as those that are alive from the dead, and**—as the fruit of this—**your members**—till now prostituted to sin—**instruments of righteousness unto God**—But what if indwelling sin should prove too strong for us? The reply is: But it will not.

14. For Sin shall not have dominion over you—as the slaves of a tyrant lord—**for ye are not under the law, but under grace**—The force of this glorious assurance can only be felt by observing the grounds on which it rests. To be "under the law" is, first, to be under its claim to entire obedience; and so, next under its curse for the breach of these. And as all power to obey can reach the sinner only through *Grace,* of which the law knows nothing, it follows that to be "under the law" is, finally, to be shut up under an *inability to keep it,* and consequently to be the *helpless slave of sin.* On the other hand, to be "under grace," is to be under the glorious canopy and saving effects of that "grace which reigns through righteousness unto eternal life through Jesus Christ our Lord" (see on ch. 5:20, 21). The curse of the law has been completely lifted from off them; they are made "the righteousness of God in Him"; and they are "alive unto God through Jesus Christ." So that, as when they were "under the law," Sin *could not but* have dominion over them, so now that they are "under grace," Sin *cannot* but be subdued under them. If before, Sin resistlessly triumphed, Grace will now be more than conqueror. **15, 16. What then? . . . Know ye not**—it is a dictate of common sense—**that to whom ye yield yourselves servants to obey**—with the view of obeying him—**his servants ye are to whom ye obey**—to whom ye yield that obedience—**whether of Sin unto death**—i.e., 'issuing in death,' in the awful sense of ch. 8:6, as the sinner's final condition—**or of Obedience unto righteousness**—i.e., obedience resulting in a righteous character, as the enduring condition of the servant of new Obedience (I John 2:17; John 8:34; II Pet. 2:19; Matt. 6:24).

ADAM CLARKE

Die as truly unto sin as He died for sin. Live as truly *unto* God as He lives *with* God. This seems to be the spirit of the apostle's meaning.

12. *Let not sin therefore reign.* This is a personification. Sin is represented as a king, ruler, or tyrant, who has the desires of the mind and the members of the body under his control, so that by influencing the passions he governs the body. Do not let sin reign, do not let him work; that is, let him have no place, no being in your souls; because, wherever he is he governs, less or more.

13. *Neither yield ye your members.* Do not yield to temptation. It is no sin to be tempted; the sin lies in yielding. While the sin exists only in Satan's solicitation, it is the devil's sin, not ours. When we yield, we make the devil's sin our own; then we enter into temptation. "Resist the devil, and he will flee from you." *Yield yourselves unto God.* Let God have your wills; keep them ever on His side. There they are safe, and there they will be active. Satan cannot force the will, and God will not. Indeed it would cease to be will were it forced by either; it is essential to its being that it be free. *And your members as instruments.* Let soul and body be employed in the service of your Maker; let Him have your hearts, and with them your heads, your hands, your feet. Think and devise what is pure; speak what is true, and to the use of edifying; work that which is just and good; and walk steadily in the way that leads to everlasting felicity. Be holy within and holy without.

14. *Sin shall not have dominion over you.* God delivers you from it; and if you again become subject to it, it will be the effect of your own choice or negligence. *Ye are not under the law.* That law which exacts obedience without giving power to obey, that condemns every transgression and every unholy thought without providing for the extirpation of evil or the pardon of sin. *But under grace.* You are under the merciful and beneficent dispensation of the gospel, that, although it requires the strictest conformity to the will of God, affords sufficient power to be thus conformed; and in the death of Christ has provided pardon for all that is past, and grace to help in every time of need.

15. *Shall we sin, because we are not under the law?* Shall we abuse our high and holy calling because we are not under that law which makes no provision for pardon, but are under that gospel which has opened the fountain to wash away all sin and defilement? Shall we sin because grace abounds? Shall we do evil that good may come of it? This be far from us!

16. *To whom ye yield yourselves.* Can you suppose that you should continue to be the *servants* of Christ if you give way to *sin?* Is he not the master who exacts the service, and to whom the service is performed? *Sin* is the service of Satan; *righteousness,* the service of Christ. If you sin, you are the servants of Satan, and not the servants of God. The word which we translate *servants* properly signifies "slaves"; and a slave among the Greeks and Romans was considered as his master's property, and he might dispose of him as he pleased. Under a bad master, the lot of the slave was most oppressive and dreadful: his ease and comfort were never consulted; he was treated worse than a beast; and in many cases his life hung on the mere caprice of the master. This state is the state of every poor, miserable sinner; he is the slave of Satan, and his own evil lusts and appetites are his most cruel taskmasters. The same word is applied to the servants of Christ, the more forcibly to show that they are their Master's property; and that, as He is infinitely good and benevolent, therefore His service must be perfect freedom. Indeed, He exacts no obedience from them which He does not turn to their eternal advantage, for this Master has no self-interest to secure.

MATTHEW HENRY

4. He argues from their former sinfulness, *v.* 17–21.

(1) What they had been and done formerly. *You were the servants of sin.* Those that are now the servants of God would do well to remember the time when they were the servants of sin, to keep them humble, and to quicken them in the service of God. It is a reproach to the service of sin that so many thousands have quitted the service; and never any that sincerely deserted it, and gave up themselves to the service of God, have returned to the former drudgery. "*God be thanked that you were so.* God be thanked that we can speak of it as a thing past."

(2) How the blessed change was made, and wherein it did consist.

[1] *You have obeyed from the heart that form of doctrine which was delivered to you, v.* 17. This describes conversion, it is our conformity to, and compliance with, the gospel—*Margin. Whereto you were delivered. First,* The rule of grace, *that form of doctrine.* The gospel is the great rule both of truth and holiness; it is the stamp, grace is the impression of that stamp. *Secondly,* Our conformity to that rule. It is to *obey from the heart.* The gospel is a doctrine to be obeyed, and that from the heart; not in profession only, but in power—from the heart, the commanding part of us. It is to be *delivered into it,* as into a mould, as the wax is cast into the impression of the seal, answering it line for line.

You have yielded your members servants to uncleanness, and to iniquity unto iniquity, v. 19. It is the misery of a sinful state that the body is made a drudge to sin. *You have yielded.* Sinners are voluntary in the service of sin. The devil could not force them into the service, if they did not yield themselves to it. *To iniquity unto iniquity.* To iniquity as the work unto iniquity as the wages. Sow the wind, and reap the whirlwind; growing worse and worse, more and more hardened. This he speaks *after the manner of men. You were free from righteousness* (*v.* 20); not free by any liberty given, but by a liberty taken, which is licentiousness. But a freedom from righteousness is the worst kind of slavery. Thus (*v.* 19), "*Yield your members servants to righteousness unto holiness.* Let them be under the conduct and at the command of the righteous law of God." *Righteousness unto holiness,* which intimates growth, and progress, and ground obtained. As every sinful act confirms the sinful habit, and makes the nature more and more prone to sin, so every gracious act confirms the gracious habit. One duty fits us for another; and the more we do the more we may do for God.

(3) What apprehensions they now had of their former way. He appeals to themselves (*v.* 21), whether they had not found the service of sin, [1] An unfruitful service: "*What fruit had you then?* Did you ever get anything by it?" Besides the future losses, which are infinitely great, the very present gains of sin are not worth mentioning. *What fruit?* Nothing that deserves the name of fruit. [2] An unbecoming service; it is that of which we *are now ashamed.* Shame came into the world with sin, and is still the certain product of it. Who would wilfully do that which sooner or later he is sure to be ashamed of?

5. He argues from the end of all these things. To persuade us from sin to holiness here are good and evil, life and death, set before us; and we are put to our choice. The end of sin is death (*v.* 21): *The end of those things is death.* Though the way may seem pleasant and inviting, yet it will be bitterness in the latter end.

Being made free from sin, you became servants of righteousness (*v.* 18), *servants to God, v.* 22. Conversion is, *First,* A freedom from the service of sin. *Secondly,* A resignation of ourselves to the service of God. When we are made free from sin, it is not that we may live as we list, and be our own masters. We cannot be made the servants of God till we are freed from the power and dominion of sin; we cannot serve two masters.

JAMIESON, FAUSSET, BROWN

17. But God be thanked, that ye were the servants of Sin—i.e., that this is a state of things now past and gone. **but ye have obeyed from the heart that form of doctrine which was delivered you**—rather (*Margin*), 'whereunto ye were delivered,' or cast, as in a mould. The idea is, that the teaching to which they had heartily yielded themselves had stamped its own impress upon them. **18. Being then**—'And being'; it is the continuation and conclusion of the preceding sentence; not a new one—**made free from Sin, ye became the servants of**—'servants to'—**Righteousness**—The case is one of emancipation from entire servitude to one Master to entire servitude to another, whose property we are (see on ch. 1:1). There is no middle state of personal independence; for which we were never made, and to which we have no claim. When we would not that God should reign over us, we were in righteous judgment "sold under Sin"; now being through grace "made free from Sin," it is only to become "servants to Righteousness," which is our true freedom. **19. I speak after the manner of men**—descending, for illustration, to the level of common affairs. **because of the infirmity of your flesh**—the weakness of your spiritual apprehension. **for as ye have yielded**—'as ye yielded,' the thing being viewed as now past—**your members servants to Uncleanness and to Iniquity unto**—the practice of—**iniquity; even so now yield your members servants to Righteousness unto holiness**—rather, 'unto (the attainment of) sanctification,' as the same word is rendered in II Thessalonians 2:13; I Corinthians 1:30; I Peter 1:2: —i.e., 'Looking back upon the *heartiness* with which ye served Sin, and the *lengths* ye went to be stimulated now to like zeal and like exuberance in the service of a better Master.' **20. For when ye were the servants**—'were servants'—**of Sin, ye were free from**—rather, 'in respect of'—**Righteousness**—Difficulties have been made about this clause where none exist. The import of it seems clearly to be this:—'Since no servant can serve "two masters," much less where their interests come into deadly collision, and each demands the whole man, so, while ye were in the service of Sin ye were in no proper sense the servants of Righteousness, and never did it one act of real service: whatever might be your conviction of the claims of Righteousness, your real services were all and always given to Sin: Thus had ye full proof of the nature and advantages of Sin's service.' The searching question with which this is followed up, shows that this is the meaning. **21. What fruit had ye then in those things whereof ye are now ashamed? for the end of those things is death**—What permanent *advantage,* and what abiding *satisfaction,* have those things yielded? The apostle answers his own question:—'Abiding satisfaction, did I ask? They have left only a sense of "*shame.*" Permanent advantage? "The end of them is *death.*"' By saying they were "*now* ashamed," he makes it plain that he is not referring to that disgust at themselves, and remorse of conscience by which those who are the most helplessly "sold under sin" are often stung to the quick; but that ingenuous feeling of self-reproach, which pierces and weighs down the children of God, as they think of the dishonor which their past life did to His name, the ingratitude it displayed, the violence it did to their own conscience, its deadening and degrading effects, and the death—"the second death"—to which it was dragging them down, when mere Grace arrested them. (On the sense of "death" here, see on ch. 5:12-21, *Note* 3, and on vs. 16: see also Rev. 21:8—The change proposed in the pointing of this verse: 'What fruit had ye then? things whereof ye are now ashamed" [LUTHER, THOLUCK, DE WETTE, PHILIPPI, ALFORD, etc.], seems unnatural and uncalled for. The ordinary pointing has at least powerful support [CHRYSOSTOM, CALVIN, BEZA, GROTIUS, BENGEL, STUART, FRITZSCHE]). **22. But now**—as if to get away from such a subject were unspeakable relief—**being made free from Sin, and become servants to God**—in the absolute sense intended throughout all this passage—**ye have**—not 'ought to have,' but 'do have,' in point of fact—**your fruit unto holiness**—'sanctification,' as in vs. 19; meaning that *permanently holy state and character* which is built up out of the whole "fruits of righteousness," which believers successively bring forth. They "have their fruit" *unto* this, i.e., all *going towards* this blessed result. **and the end everlasting life**—as the final state of the justified believer; the beatific experience not only of complete exemption from the fall with all its effects, but of the perfect life of acceptance with God, and conformity to His likeness, of unveiled access to Him, and ineffable fellowship

ADAM CLARKE

17. *But God be thanked, that ye were the servants of sin.* This verse should be read thus: "But thanks be to God that, although you were the servants of sin, nevertheless you have obeyed from the heart that form of doctrine that was delivered unto you"; or, "that mold of teaching into which you were cast." The apostle does not thank God that they were sinners; but that, although they were such, they had now received and obeyed the gospel. The Hebrew phrase, Isa. xii. 1, is exactly the same as that of the apostle here: "In that day thou shalt say . . . I will praise thee . . . [for] thou wast angry with me": that is, "Although Thou wast angry with me, Thou hast turned away Thy wrath." *That form of doctrine.* Christianity is represented under the notion of a "mold," or "die," into which they were cast, and from which they took the impression of its excellence. The figure upon this die is the image of God, righteousness and true holiness, which was stamped on their souls in believing the gospel and receiving the Holy Ghost. The words may be literally translated, "into which mold of doctrine ye have been cast."

18. *Being then made free from sin.* A term that refers to the manumission of a slave. They were redeemed from the slavery of sin, and became the servants of righteousness. Both *sin* and *righteousness* are personified: *sin* can enjoin no good and profitable work; *righteousness* can require none that is unjust or injurious.

19. *I speak after the manner of men.* This phrase is often used by the Greek writers to signify what was easy to be comprehended; what was level with common understandings, delivered in a popular style; what was different from the high flights of the poets and the studied, sublime obscurity of the philosophers. *Because of the infirmity of your flesh.* As if he had said: I make use of metaphors and figures connected with well-known natural things. *Servants to uncleanness.* These different expressions show how deeply immersed in and enslaved by sin these Gentiles were before their conversion to Christianity. Several of the particulars are given in the first chapter of this Epistle.

20. *Ye were free from righteousness.* These two servitudes are incompatible; if we cannot serve God and mammon, surely we cannot serve Christ and Satan. We must be either sinners or saints, God's servants or the devil's slaves.

21. *What fruit had ye then in those things?* God designs that every man shall reap benefit by his service. What benefit have you derived from the service of sin? *Whereof ye are now ashamed.* You blush to remember your former life. It was scandalous to yourselves, injurious to others, and highly provoking to God. *The end of those things is death.* Whatever sin may promise of pleasure or advantage, the end to which it necessarily tends is the destruction of body and soul.

22. *But now being made free from sin.* As being free from righteousness is the finished character of a sinner, so being *made free from sin* is the finished character of a genuine Christian. *And become servants to God.* They were transferred from the service of one master to that of another; they were freed from the slavery of sin, and engaged in the service of God. *Fruit unto holiness.* Holiness of heart was the principle, and righteousness of life the fruit.

MATTHEW HENRY

The wages of sin is death, v. 23. Death is as due to a sinner as wages are to a servant. All that are sin's servants and do sin's work must expect to be thus paid. If the fruit be unto holiness the end will be everlasting life—a very happy end!—Though the way be up-hill, yet everlasting life at the end of it is sure. So, *v.* 23, *The gift of God is eternal life.* Heaven is life, and it is eternal life, no infirmities attending it, no death to put a period to it. This is the gift of God. The death is the wages of sin; but the life is a gift. Sinners merit hell, but saints do not merit heaven. We must thank God, and not ourselves, if ever we get to heaven. And this gift is *through Jesus Christ our Lord.* It is Christ that purchased it, prepares us for it, preserves us to it.

CHARLES H. SPURGEON:

Let us notice that *eternal life is imparted by grace through faith.* When it first enters the soul, it comes as God's free gift. The dead cannot earn life; the very supposition is absurd. Eternal life enjoyed on earth comes to us as a gift. "What!" saith one, "do you mean to say that eternal life comes into the soul here?" I say yes, here, or else never. Eternal life must be our possession now; for if we die without it, it will never be our possession in the world to come, which is not the state of probation, but of fixed and settled reward. When the flame of eternal life first drops into a man's heart, it is not as the result of any good works of his which preceded it, for there were none; nor as the result of any feelings of his, for good feelings were not there till the life came. Both good works and good feelings are the fruit of heavenly life which enters the heart.

"Eternal life is the gift of God in Jesus Christ." By faith we come consciously into Christ. We trust Him, we rest upon Him, we become one with Him, and thus eternal life manifests itself. Has He not said, "I give unto my sheep eternal life"; and again, "He that believeth in him hath everlasting life"? O beloved, you that have been quickened by the Spirit of God, I am sure you trace that first quickening to the grace of God. Whatever your doctrinal views may be, you are all agreed in the experimental acknowledgment that by the grace of God, you are what you are. How could you, being dead, give yourself life? How could you, being the slave of sin, set yourself free? But the Lord in mercy visited you as surely as the Lord Jesus Christ visited the tomb of Lazarus; and He spoke with His almighty voice and bade you to come to life, and you arose and came to life at His bidding. You remember well the change that came upon you. If any man here could have been literally dead, and then could have been made to live, what a wonderful experience his would have been! We should go a long way to hear the story of a man who had been dead and then was made alive again. But I tell you, his experience, if he could tell it, would not be any more wonderful than our experience as quickened from death in sin; for we have suffered the pains and come through the entrance of life into the soul, and we know the joys which afterward come of it.

—The Treasury of the New Testament

JAMIESON, FAUSSET, BROWN

with Him through all duration. **23. For the wages of sin is death; but the gift of God is eternal life through—'in'—Jesus Christ our Lord**—This concluding verse—as pointed as it is brief—contains the marrow, the most fine gold, of the Gospel. As the laborer is worthy of his hire, and feels it to be his due—his own of right— so is death the due of sin, the wages the sinner has well wrought for, his own. But "eternal life" is in no sense or degree the wages of our righteousness; we do nothing whatever to earn or become entitled to it, and never can: it is therefore, in the most absolute sense, "THE GIFT OF GOD." Grace reigns in the bestowal of it in every case, and that "in Jesus Christ our Lord," as the righteous Channel of it. In view of this, who that hath tasted that the Lord is gracious can refrain from saying, "Unto Him that loved us, and washed us from our sins in His own blood, and hath made us kings and priests unto God and His Father, to Him be glory and dominion for ever and ever. Amen!" (Rev. 1:5, 6). Note (1) As the most effectual refutation of the oft-repeated calumny, that the doctrine of Salvation by grace encourages to continue in sin, is the holy life of those who profess it, let such ever feel that the highest service they can render to that Grace which is all their hope, is to "yield themselves unto God, as those that are alive from the dead, and their members instruments of righteousness unto God" (vss. 12, 13). By so doing they will "put to silence the ignorance of foolish men," secure their own peace, carry out the end of their calling, and give substantial glory to Him that loved them. (2) The fundamental principle of Gospel-obedience is as original as it is divinely rational; that 'we are set free from the law in order to keep it, and are brought graciously under servitude to the law in order to be free' (vss. 14, 15, 18). So long as we know no principle of obedience but the terrors of the law, which condemns all the breakers of it, and knows nothing whatever of grace, either to pardon the guilty or to purify the stained, we are shut up under a moral impossibility of genuine and acceptable obedience: whereas when Grace lifts us out of this state, and through union to a righteous Surety, brings us into a state of conscious reconciliation, and loving surrender of heart to a God of salvation, we immediately feel the glorious *liberty to be holy,* and the assurance that "Sin shall not have dominion over us" is as sweet to our renewed tastes and aspirations as the ground of it is felt to be firm, "because we are not under the Law, but under Grace." (3) As this most momentous of all transitions in the history of a man is wholly of God's free grace, the change should never be thought, spoken, or written of but with lively thanksgiving to Him who so loved us (vs. 17). (4) Christians, in the service of God, should emulate their former selves in the zeal and steadiness with which they served sin, and the length to which they went in it (vs. 19). (5) To stimulate this holy rivalry, let us often "look back to the rock whence we were hewn, the hole of the pit whence we were digged," in search of the enduring advantages and permanent satisfactions which the service of Sin yielded; and when we find to our "shame" only gall and wormwood, let us follow a godless life to its proper "end," until, finding ourselves in the territories of "death," we are fain to hasten back to survey the service of Righteousness, that new Master of all believers, and find Him leading us sweetly into abiding "holiness," and landing us at length in "everlasting life" (vss. 20-22). (6) Death and life are before all men who hear the Gospel: the one, the natural issue and proper reward of sin; the other, the absolutely free "GIFT OF GOD" to sinners, "in Jesus Christ our Lord." And as the one is the *conscious* sense of the hopeless loss of all blissful existence, so the other is the conscious possession and enjoyment of all that constitutes a rational creature's highest "life" for evermore (vs. 23). Ye that read or hear these words, "I call heaven and earth to record this day against you, that I have set before you life and death, blessing and cursing, therefore choose life, that both thou and thy seed may live!" (Deut. 30:19).

ADAM CLARKE

23. *For the wages of sin is death.* The second death, everlasting perdition. Every sinner earns this by long, sore, and painful service. Oh, what pains do men take to get to hell! *But the gift of God is eternal life.* A man may merit hell, but he cannot merit heaven. The apostle does not say that the wages of righteousness is eternal life: no, but that this eternal life, even to the righteous, is the gracious "gift of God." And even this gracious gift comes *through Jesus Christ our Lord.* He alone has procured it; and it is given to all those who find redemption in His blood. A sinner goes to hell because he deserves it; a righteous man goes to heaven because Christ has died for him, and communicated that grace by which his sin is pardoned and his soul made holy. The word *wages* signified the daily pay of a Roman soldier. So every sinner has a daily pay, and this pay is death; he has misery because he sins. Sin constitutes hell; the sinner has a hell in his own bosom; all is confusion and disorder where God does not reign. Every indulgence of sinful passions increases the disorder, and consequently the misery, of a sinner. If men were as much in earnest to get their souls saved as they are to prepare them for perdition, heaven would be highly peopled, and devils would be their own companions.

The apostle, having in the preceding chapter shown the converted Gentiles the obligations they were under to live a holy life, addresses himself here to the Jews who might hesitate to embrace the gospel, lest by this means they should renounce the law, which might appear to them as a renunciation of their allegiance to God. As they rested in the law as sufficient for justification and sanctification, it was necessary to convince them of their mistake. That the law was insufficient for their justification the apostle had proved, in chapters iii, iv, and v; that it is insufficient for their sanctification he shows in this chapter; and introduces his discourse by showing that a believing Jew is discharged from his obligations to the law, and is at liberty to come under another and much happier constitution, viz., that of the gospel of Christ, 1-4. In the fifth verse he gives a general description of the state of a Jew, in servitude to sin, considered as under mere law. In the sixth verse he gives a summary account of the state of a Christian, or believing Jew, and the advantages he enjoys under the gospel. Upon the fifth verse he comments, from verse 7 to the end of the chapter; and upon the sixth verse he comments, chap. viii. 1-11.

In explaining his position in the fifth verse he shows: (1) That the law reaches to all the branches and latent principles of sin, v. 7. (2) That it subjected the sinner to death, vv. 8-12, without the expectation of pardon. (3) He shows the reason why the Jew was put under it, v. 13. (4) He proves that the law, considered as a rule of action, though it was spiritual, just, holy, and good in itself, yet was insufficient for sanctification, or for freeing a man from the power of inbred sin. For, as the prevalency of sensual appetites cannot wholly extinguish the voice of reason and conscience, a man may acknowledge the law to be holy, just, and good, and yet his passions reign within him, keeping him in the most painful and degrading servitude, while the law supplies no power to deliver him from them, vv. 14-24, as that power can be supplied only by the grace of Jesus Christ, v. 25.

MATTHEW HENRY — CHAPTER 7

Verses 1–6

Among other arguments to persuade us against sin, and to holiness, this was one (*v.* 14), that *we are not under the law*; and this argument is here further insisted upon (*v.* 6): *We are delivered from the law.* 1. We are delivered from that power of the law which condemns us for the sin committed by us. The law

JAMIESON, FAUSSET, BROWN — CHAPTER 7

Vss. 1-25. SAME SUBJECT CONTINUED. **1-6.** *Relation of Believers to the Law and to Christ.* Recurring to the statement of ch. 6:14, that believers are "not under the law but under grace," the apostle here shows *how* this change is brought about, and what holy consequences follow from it. **1. I speak to them that know the law**—of Moses to whom,

ADAM CLARKE — CHAPTER 7

1. *For I speak to them that know the law.* This is a proof that the apostle directs this part of his discourse to the Jews. *As long as he liveth.* Or "as long as it liveth"; law does not extend its influence to the dead, nor do abrogated laws bind. It is all the same whether we understand these words as speaking of a law

MATTHEW HENRY

saith, *The soul that sins shall die;* but we are delivered from the law. 2. We are delivered from that power of the law which provokes the sin that dwelleth in us. This the apostle seems especially to refer to (*v.* 5): *The motions of sins which were by the law.* The law, by threatening, corrupt and fallen man, but offering no grace to cure, did but stir up the corruption. We being lamed by the fall, the law comes and directs us, but provides nothing to heal and help our lameness. We are under grace, which promises strength to do what it commands, and pardon upon repentance when we do amiss. The difference between a law-state and a gospel-state he had before illustrated by the similitude of serving a new master; now here under the similitude of being married to a new husband.

I. Our first marriage was to the law. The law of marriage is binding till the death of one of the parties, no matter which, and no longer. For this he appeals to themselves, as persons knowing the law (*v.* 1): *I speak to those that know the law.* Many of the Christians at Rome had been Jews, and so were well acquainted with the law. One has some hold of knowing people. *The law hath power over a man as long as he liveth;* in particular, the law of marriage hath power. The obligation of laws extends no further. The condemnation of laws extends no further; death is the finishing of the law. The severest laws could but kill the body, and after that there is no more that they can do. Thus while we were alive to the law we were under the power of it. Such is the law of marriage (*v.* 2), the woman is bound to her husband during life, she cannot marry another; if she do, she shall be reckoned an adulteress, *v.* 3.

II. Our second marriage is to Christ.

1. We are freed, by death, from our obligation to the law as a covenant, *v.* 3. *You are become dead to the law, v.* 4. He does not say, "The law is dead," but, which comes all to one, *You are dead to the law.* It is dead, it has lost its power; and this (*v.* 4) *by the body of Christ,* that is, by the sufferings of Christ in his body, by his crucified body. We are dead to the law by our union with the mystical body of Christ, but have no more to do with it than the dead servant hath to do with his master's yoke.

2. We are married to Christ. We enter upon a life of dependence on him and duty to him: *Married to another, even to him who is raised from the dead.* As our dying to sin and the law is in conformity to the death of Christ, and the crucifying of his body, so our devotedness to Christ in newness of life is in conformity to the resurrection of Christ. We are married to the raised exalted Jesus. Now we are thus married to Christ, (1) *That we should bring forth fruit unto God, v.* 4. One end of marriage is fruitfulness. Now the great end of our marriage to Christ is our fruitfulness in love, and grace, and every good work. As our old marriage to sin produced fruit unto death, so our second marriage to Christ produces fruit unto God. Good works are the children of the new nature. Whatever our professions and pretensions may be, there is no fruit brought forth to God till we are married to Christ. This distinguishes the good works of believers from the good works of hypocrites and self-justifiers that they are done in union with Christ. Thus were we married to the law (*v.* 5): *When we were in the flesh,* then *the motions of sins which were by the law did work in our members,* we were carried down the stream of sin, and the law was but as an imperfect dam, which made the stream to swell the higher. Our desire was towards sin, and sin ruled over us. We were under a law of sin and death, as the wife under the law of marriage; and the product of this marriage was fruit brought forth unto death. Lust, having conceived by the law, *bringeth forth sin, and sin, when it is finished, bringeth forth death,* Jam. i. 15. This is the posterity that springs from this marriage to sin and the law. This comes of the motions of sin working in our members.

JAMIESON, FAUSSET, BROWN

though not themselves Jews (see on ch. 1:13), the Old Testament was familiar. **2, 3. if her husband be dead**–'die' So vs. 3. **she be married**–'joined.' So vs. 4.

4. Wherefore . . . ye also are become dead–rather, 'were slain'–**to the law by the body of Christ**–through His slain body. The apostle here departs from his usual word "died," using the more expressive phrase 'were slain,' to make it clear that he meant their being "crucified with Christ" (as expressed in ch. 6:3-6, and Gal. 2:20. **that ye should be married to another, even to him that is**–'was'–**raised from the dead**–to the intent–**that we should bring forth fruit unto God**–It has been thought that the apostle should here have said that 'the *law* died to us,' not 'we to the law,' but that he purposely inverted the figure, to avoid the harshness to Jewish ears of *the death of the law* [CHRYSOSTOM, CALVIN, HODGE, PHILIPPI, etc.]. But this is to mistake the apostle's design in employing this figure, which was merely to illustrate the general principle that '*death dissolves legal obligation.*' It was essential to his argument that *we,* not the law, should be the dying party, since it is we that are "crucified with Christ," and not the law. This death dissolves our marriage obligation to the law, leaving us at liberty to contract a new relation–to be joined to the Risen One, in order to spiritual fruitfulness, to the glory of God [BEZA, OLSHAUSEN, MEYER, ALFORD, etc.]. The confusion, then, is in the expositors, not the text; and it has arisen from not observing that, like Jesus Himself, believers are here viewed as having a double life–the old sin-condemned life, which they lay down with Christ, and the new life of acceptance and holiness to which they rise with their Surety and Head; and all the issues of this new life, in Christian obedience, are regarded as the "fruit" of this blessed union to the Risen One. How such holy fruitfulness was impossible before our union to Christ, is next declared. **5. For when we were in the flesh**–in our unregenerate state, as we came into the world. See on John 3:6; and ch. 8:5-9. **the motions**–'passions' (*Margin*), 'affectious' (as in Gal. 5:24), or 'stirrings.' **of sins**–i.e., 'prompting to the commission of sins.' **which were by the law**–by occasion of the law, which fretted, irritated our inward corruption by its prohibitions. See on vss. 7-9.

did work in our members–the members of the body, as the instruments by which these inward stirrings find vent in action, and become facts of the life. See on ch. 6: 6. **to bring forth fruit unto death**–death in the sense of ch. 6:21. Thus hopeless is all holy fruit before union to Christ.

ADAM CLARKE

abrogated, so that it cannot command, or of its objects being dead, so that it has none to bind. In either case the law has no force.

2. *For the woman which hath an husband.* The apostle illustrates his meaning by a familiar instance. A married woman is bound to her husband while he lives; but when her husband is dead, she is discharged from the law by which she was bound to him alone.

3. *So then if, while her husband liveth.* The object of the apostle's similitude is to show that each party is equally bound to the other, but that the death of either dissolves the engagement. *So . . . she is no adulteress, though she be married to another.* And do not imagine that this change would argue any disloyalty in you to your Maker; for as He has determined that this law of ordinances shall cease, you are no more bound to it than a woman is to a deceased husband, and are as free to receive the gospel of Christ as a woman in such circumstances would be to remarry.

4. *Wherefore, my brethren.* This is a parallel case. You were once under the law of Moses and were bound by its injunctions, but now you are become dead to that law—a modest, inoffensive mode of speech, for "the law, which was once your husband, is dead." God has determined that it shall be no longer in force; so that now, as a woman whose husband is dead is freed from the law of that husband, or from her conjugal vow, and may legally be married to another, so God, who gave the law under which you have hitherto lived, designed that it should be in force only till the advent of the Messiah. That advent has taken place; the law has consequently ceased, and now you are called to take on you the yoke of the gospel, and lay down the yoke of the law; and it is the design of God that you should do so. *That ye should be married to another . . . who is raised from the dead.* As "Christ is the end of the law for righteousness to every one that believeth," the object of God in giving the law was to unite you to Christ; and as He has died, He has not only abolished that law which condemns every transgressor to death, but He has also made that atonement for sin by His own death, which is represented in the sacrifices prescribed by the law. And as Jesus Christ is risen again from the dead, He has thereby given the fullest proof that by His death He has procured the resurrection of mankind and made that atonement required by the law. *That we should bring forth fruit unto God*—we, Jews, who believe in Christ, have, in consequence of our union with Him, received the gifts and graces of the Holy Spirit; so that we bring forth that fruit of holiness unto God which, without this union, it would be impossible for us to produce.

5. *For when we were in the flesh.* When we were without the gospel, in our carnal and unregenerated state, though believing in the law of Moses and performing the rites and offices of our religion. *The motions of sins, which were by the law.* "The passions of sins, the evil propensities to sins." To every particular sin there is a propensity; one propensity does not excite to all kinds of sinful acts. Hence the apostle uses the plural number, "the passions or propensities of sins," sins being not more various than their propensities in the unregenerate heart which excite to them. These "propensities" constitute the fallen nature; they are the disease of the heart, the pollution and corruption of the soul. *Did work in our members.* The evil propensity acts in the whole nervous and muscular system, applying that stimulus to every part which is necessary to excite them to action. *To bring forth fruit unto death.* To produce those acts of transgression which subject the sinner to death, temporal and eternal. When the apostle says the *motions of sins, which were by the law,* he points out a most striking and invariable characteristic of sin, viz., its rebellious nature; it ever acts against law, and the most powerfully against known law. Because the law requires obedience, therefore it will transgress. The law is equally against evil passions and evil actions, and both these exert themselves against it. So these motions which were by the law became roused into the most powerful activity by the prohibitions of the law. They were comparatively dormant till the law said, "Thou shalt not do this; thou shalt do

MATTHEW HENRY

We are *delivered from the law* (*v.* 6); our obligation to it is as a husband is made void. And then he speaks of the law being dead as far as it was a law of bondage to us: *That being dead wherein we were held.*

(2) *That we should serve in newness of spirit, and not in the oldness of the letter, v.* 6. Still we must serve, but it is a service that is perfect freedom, whereas the service of sin was a perfect drudgery. There must be a renovation of our spirits wrought by the spirit of God, and in that we must serve. *Not in the oldness of the letter;* that is, we must not rest in mere external services. The letter is said to kill with its bondage and terror, but we are delivered from that yoke that we may serve God without fear, in holiness and righteousness, Luke i. 74, 75. It becomes us to worship within the veil, and no longer in the outward court.

Verses 7–14

What shall we say then? Is the law sin? He had said so much of the influence of the law that it might easily be misinterpreted as a reflection upon the law, to prevent which he shows the great excellency of it as a guide.

The great advantage that he had found by the law. 1. It was discovering: *I had not known sin but by the law, v.* 7. As that which is straight discovers that which is crooked, so there is no way of coming to that knowledge of sin which is necessary to repentance, but by comparing our hearts and lives with the law.

JAMIESON, FAUSSET, BROWN

6. But now—See on the same expression in ch. 6:22, and cf. James 1:15. **we are delivered from the law**—The word is the same which, in ch. 6:6 and elsewhere, is rendered "destroyed," and is but another way of saying (as in vs. 4) that "we were *slain* to the law by the body of Christ"; language which, though harsh to the ear, is designed and fitted to impress upon the reader the *violence* of that death of the Cross, by which, as by a deadly wrench, we are "delivered from the law." **that being dead wherein we were held**—It is now universally agreed that the true reading here is, 'being dead to that wherein we were held.' The received reading has no authority whatever, and is inconsistent with the strain of the argument; for the death spoken of, as we have seen, is not the *law's,* but ours, through union with the crucified Saviour. **that we should**—'so as to' or 'so that we'—**serve in newness of spirit**—'in the newness of the spirit' **and not in the oldness of the letter**—not in our old way of literal, mechanical obedience to the divine law, as a set of external rules of conduct, and without any reference to the state of our hearts; but in that new way of spiritual obedience which, through union to the risen Saviour, we have learned to render (cf. ch. 2:29; II Cor. 3:6).

7-25. *False Inferences regarding the Law Repelled.* And first, vss. 7-13, In the case of the UNREGENERATE. **7, 8. What . . . then? Is the law sin? God forbid!**—'I have said that when we were in the flesh the law stirred our inward corruption, and was thus the occasion of deadly fruit: Is then the law *to blame* for this? Far from us be such a thought.' **Nay**—'On the contrary' (as in ch. 8:37; I Cor. 12:22; *Greek*).

I had not known sin but by the law—It is important to fix what is meant by "*sin*" here. It certainly is not 'the general nature of sin' [ALFORD, etc.], though it be true that this is learned from the law; for such a sense will not suit what is said of it in the following verses, where the meaning is the same as here. The only meaning which suits all that is said of it in this place is 'the *principle* of sin in the heart of fallen man.' The sense, then, is this: 'It was by means of the law that I came to know what a virulence and strength of sinful propensity I had within me.' The *existence* of this it did not need the law to reveal to him; for even the heathens recognized and wrote of it. But the dreadful nature and desperate power of it the law alone discovered—in the way now to be described.

ADAM CLARKE

that"; then the rebellious principle in the evil propensity became roused, and acts of transgression and omissions of duty were the immediate consequences.

6. *But now we are delivered from the law.* We who have believed in Christ Jesus are delivered from that yoke by which we were bound, which sentenced every transgressor to perdition, but provided no pardon even for the penitent and no sanctification for those who are weary of their inbred corruptions. *That being dead wherein we were held.* To us believers in Christ this commandment is abrogated; we are transferred to another constitution. That law which kills ceases to bind us; it is dead to us who have believed in Christ Jesus, who is "the end of the law" for justification and salvation to everyone that believes. *That we should serve in newness of spirit.* We are now brought under a more spiritual dispensation; now we know the spiritual import of all the Mosaic precepts. We see that the law referred to the gospel, and can be fulfilled only by the gospel. *The oldness of the letter.* The merely literal rites, ceremonies, and sacrifices are now done away; and the *newness of spirit,* the true intent and meaning of all, are now fully disclosed; so that we are got from an imperfect state into a state of perfection and excellence. We sought justification and sanctification, pardon and holiness, by the law, and have found that the law could not give them; we have sought these in the gospel scheme, and we have found them. We serve God now, not according to the old, literal sense, but in the true spiritual meaning.

7. *Is the law sin?* The apostle had said, v. 5: "The motions of sins, which were by the law, did . . . bring forth fruit unto death"; and now he anticipates an objection, "Is therefore the law sin?" To which he answers, as usual, "By no means." Law is only the means of disclosing this sinful propensity, not of producing it, as a bright beam of the sun introduced into a room shows millions of motes which appear to be dancing in it in all directions. But these were not introduced by the light; they were there before, only there was not light enough to make them manifest. So the evil propensity was there before, but there was not light sufficient to discover it. *I had not known sin, but by the law.* Mr. Locke and Dr. Taylor have properly remarked the skill used by Paul in dexterously avoiding, as much as possible, the giving offense to the Jews: and this is particularly evident in his use of the word *I* in this place. In the beginning of the chapter, where he mentions their knowledge of the law, he says "ye"; in the fourth verse he joins himself with them, and says "we"; but here, and so to the end of the chapter, where he represents the power of sin and the inability of the law to subdue it, he appears to leave them out, and speaks altogether in the first person, though it is plain he means all those who are under the law. So, chap. iii. 7, he uses the singular pronoun, "Why . . . am I . . . judged as a sinner?" when he evidently means the whole body of unbelieving Jews. There is another circumstance in which his address is peculiarly evident: his demonstrating the insufficiency of the law under color of vindicating it. He knew that the Jew would take fire at the least reflection on the law, which he held in the highest veneration; and therefore he very naturally introduces him catching at that expression, v. 5, "the motions of sins, which were by the law," or notwithstanding the law. "What!" says this Jew, "do you vilify the law, by charging it with favoring sin?" By no means, says the apostle; I am very far from charging the law with favoring sin. "The law is holy, and the commandment holy, and just, and good," v. 12. Thus he writes in vindication of the law; and yet at the same time shows: (1) That the law requires the most extensive obedience, discovering and condemning sin in all its most secret and remote branches, v. 7. (2) That it gives sin a deadly force, subjecting every transgression to the penalty of death, vv. 8-14. And yet, (3) supplies neither help nor hope to the sinner, but leaves him under the power of sin, and the sentence of death, v. 14. While the human heart is its own measure, it will rate its workings according to its own propensities, for itself is its highest rule. But when God gives a true insight of His own

A. B. SIMPSON:

First, we have the effect of the law in revealing him himself, and convicting him of sin. He says, "I had not known sin but by the law; I had not known lust, except the law had said, Thou shalt not covet. But sin taking occasion by the commandment wrought in me all manner of concupiscence, for without the law sin was dead." And then he goes on to tell us how the consiousness of sin was developed. "I was alive without the law once." That is, I felt happy and right, and free from condemnation, and even from the workings of sin. But there came a change, the commandment came forbidding him to do the things that he was doing, and then, like a torrent checked, or a wild beast at bay, all the strength of his evil nature asserted itself. Then he adds, "Sin revived and I died," that is, he became conscious of all the force of evil in his heart and gave up his hope and comfort in despair.

Is not this the experience usually of the young disciple? His early experience is cloudless and delightful. He has not yet seen the depths of his own evil heart, and thinks, perhaps, that there are no such depths of sin in him. But suddenly! some great sacrifice is demanded, some cherished thing is to be cut out of the life, some difficult obedience is to be performed, some secret sin is revealed, and then the whole strength of the will concentrates upon that issue, and the battle is a sharp and decisive one.—*Christ in the Bible*

MATTHEW HENRY

Particularly he came to the knowledge of the sinfulness of lust. By lust he means sin dwelling in us. This he came to know when the law said, *Thou shalt not covet*. The law spoke in the spiritual sense and meaning of it. By this he knew that lust was sin and a very sinful sin. Paul had a very quick and piercing judgment, and yet never attained the right knowledge of indwelling sin till the Spirit by the law made it known to him. There is nothing about which the natural man is more blind than about original corruption. Thus *the law is a schoolmaster, to bring us to Christ*.

III. The ill use that his corrupt nature made of the law. *Sin, taking occasion by the commandment, wrought in me all manner of concupiscence, v.* 8. Paul had in him all manner of concupisence, as touching the righteousness of the law, blameless, and yet sensible of all manner of concupiscence. And it was sin that wrought it, indwelling sin, and it took occasion by the commandment. The corrupt nature would not have swelled and raged so much if it had not been for the restraints of the law. Ever since Adam ate forbidden fruit, we have all been fond of forbidden paths.

Without the law sin was dead, as a snake in winter, which the sunbeams of the law quicken and irritate.

It was humbling (*v.* 9): *I was alive*. He thought himself in a very good condition, very secure and confident of the goodness of his state. Thus he was *once, in times past*, when he was a Pharisee; and the reason was he was then *without the law*. Though brought up at the feet of Gamaliel, a doctor of the law, though himself a strict observer of it, yet *without the law*. He had the letter of the law, but he had not the spiritual meaning of it —the shell, but not the kernel. He had the law in his hand and in his head, but he had it not in his heart. *But when the commandment came* (not to his eyes only, but to his heart), *sin revived*, as the dust in a room rises when the sunshine is let into it. Paul then saw that in sin which he had never seen before—sin in its consequences, sin with death at the heels of it, sin and the curse entailed upon it. "The Spirit, by the commandment, convinced me that I was in a state of sin, and in a state of death because of sin." Of this excellent use is the law; it is a lamp and a light; it opens the eyes, prepares the way of the Lord.

JAMIESON, FAUSSET, BROWN

for I had not known lust, except . . .—Here the same Greek word is unfortunately rendered by three different English ones —"lust"; "covet"; "concupiscence"—which obscures the meaning. By using the word "lust" only, in the wide sense of all 'irregular desire,' or every outgoing of the heart towards anything forbidden, the sense will best be brought out; thus, 'For I had not known lust, except the law had said, Thou shalt not lust; But sin, taking ('having taken') occasion by the commandment (that one which forbids it), wrought in me all manner of lusting.' This gives a deeper view of the tenth commandment than the mere words suggest. The apostle saw in it the prohibition not only of desire after *certain things there specified*, but of 'desire after *everything divinely forbidden*'; in other words, all 'lusting' or 'irregular desire.' It was this which "he had not known but by the law." The law forbidding all such desire so stirred his corruption that it wrought in him "all manner of lusting"—desire of every sort after what was forbidden.

For without the law—i.e., before its extensive demands and prohibitions come to operate upon our corrupt nature. **sin was** —rather, 'is'—**dead**—i.e., the sinful principle of our nature lies so dormant, so torpid, that its virulence and power are unknown, and to our feeling it is as good as "dead."

9. For I was alive without the law once—'In the days of my ignorance, when, in this sense, a stranger to the law, I deemed myself a righteous man, and, as such, entitled to life at the hand of God.' **but when the commandment came** —forbidding all irregular desire; for the apostle sees in this the spirit of the whole law. **sin revived**— 'came to life'; in its malignity and strength it unexpectedly revealed itself, as if sprung from the dead. **and I died**—'saw myself, in the eye of a law never kept and not to be kept, a dead man.'

10, 11. And—thus—**the commandment, which was . . .**— designed—**to**—give—**life**—through the keeping of it

ADAM CLARKE

perfections, to be applied as a rule of both passion and practice, then sin is discovered, and discovered too to be exceedingly sinful. So strong propensities, because they appear to be inherent in our nature, would have passed for natural and necessary operations, and their sinfulness would not have been discovered if the law had not said, *Thou shalt not covet;* and thus determined that the propensity itself, as well as its outward operations, is sinful.

8. *Sin, taking occasion by the commandment*. I think the pointing, both in this and in the eleventh verse, to be wrong; the comma should be after *occasion*, and not after *commandment*. "But sin, taking occasion, wrought in me by this commandment all manner of concupiscence." There are different opinions concerning the meaning of the word *occasion*. Dr. Waterland translates the clause, "Sin, taking advantage." Dr. Taylor contends that all commentators have mistaken the meaning of it, and that it should be rendered "having received force." For this acceptation of the word I can find no adequate authority except in its etymology. The word appears to signify, in general, whatsoever is necessary for the completion or accomplishment of any particular purpose. There is a personification in the text; sin is represented as a murderer watching for life, and snatching at every means and embracing every opportunity to carry his fell purpose into effect. The miserable sinner has a murderer, sin, within him; this murderer can destroy life only in certain circumstances. Finding that the law condemns the object of his cruelty to death, he takes occasion from this to work in the soul all manner of concupiscence, evil and irregular desires and appetites of every kind, and by thus increasing the evil, exposes the soul to more condemnation; and thus it is represented as being slain, v. 11. That is, the law, on the evidence of those sinful dispositions and their corresponding practices, condemns the sinner to death, so that he is dead in law. Thus the very prohibition, as we have already seen in the preceding verse, becomes the instrument of exciting the evil propensity; for, although a sinner has the general propensity to do what is evil, yet he seems to feel most delight in transgressing known law. *For without the law sin was dead.* Where there is no law there is no transgression, "for sin is the transgression of the law"; and no fault can be imputed unto death where there is no statute by which such a fault is made a capital offense. Dr. Taylor thinks that *without the law* means the time before the giving of the law from Mount Sinai, which took in the space of 430 years, during which time the people were under the Abrahamic covenant of grace; and *without the law* that was given on Mount Sinai, the sting of death, which is sin, had not power to slay the sinner; the law was not reenacted till it was given by Moses, chap. v. 13. The Jew was then *alive*, v. 9, because he was not under the law subjecting him to death for his transgressions; *but when the commandment came*, with the penalty of death annexed, *sin revived*, and the Jew died. *All manner of concupiscence*. It showed what was evil and forbade it; and then the principle of rebellion, which seems essential to the very nature of sin, rose up against the prohibition, and he was the more strongly incited to disobey in proportion as obedience was enjoined. Thus the apostle shows that the law had authority to prohibit, condemn, and destroy; but no power to pardon sin, root out enmity, or save the soul. The word which we render *concupiscence* signifies simply "strong desire" of any kind; but in the New Testament it is generally taken to signify irregular and unholy desires. Sin in the mind is the desire to do, or to be, what is contrary to the holiness and authority of God. *For without the law sin was dead*. This means, according to Dr. Taylor's hypothesis, the time previous to the giving of the law. But it seems also consistent with the apostle's meaning to interpret the place as implying the time in which Paul, in his unconverted Jewish state, had not the proper knowledge of the law—while he was unacquainted with its spirituality. He felt evil desire, but he did not know the evil of it.

10. *And the commandment*, meaning the law in general. *Which was ordained to life*, the rule of righteousness teaching those statutes "which

MATTHEW HENRY

Thus the commandment, which was ordained to life, proved unto death, *v.* 10. The same word which to some is an occasion of life unto life is to others an occasion of death unto death. The same sun that makes the garden of flowers more fragrant makes the dunghill more noisome. The way to prevent this mischief is to bow our souls to the commanding authority of the law of God.

It *deceived me.* Sin puts a cheat upon the sinner, and it is a fatal cheat, *v.* 11. *By it slew me.* It deceived and slew him.

I. The great excellency of the law in itself. Far be it from Paul to reflect upon the law. It is *holy, just, and good, v.* 12. Laws are as the law-makers are. God, the great lawgiver, is holy, just, and good, therefore his law must needs be so. The ways of the Lord are right. It is good in the design of it; it was given for the good of mankind. It makes the observers of it good. Wherever there is true grace there is an assent to this—that the law is holy, just, and good. It *wrought death in me by that which is good, v.* 13. Nothing so good but a corrupt and vicious nature will pervert it, and make it an occasion of sin. Now in this sin appears sin. The worst thing that sin does is the perverting of the law. Thus sin by the commandment does appear sin (*v.* 13); it appears in its own colours. Thus by the commandment it becomes *exceedingly sinful*; that is, it appears to be so.

The law is spiritual (*v.* 14), not only in regard to the effect of it, but in regard to the extent of it; it reaches our spirits. It is given to man, whose principal part is spiritual; the soul is the best part, and therefore the law to the man must needs be a law to the soul. Herein the law of God is above all other laws, that it is a spiritual law. The law of God takes notice of the iniquity regarded in the heart. *We know this.* Wherever there is true grace there is an experimental knowledge of the spirituality of the law of God.

Verses 14–25

Here is a description of the conflict between grace and corruption in the heart, and it is applicable two ways: 1. To the struggles that are in a convinced soul, but yet unregenerate, in the person of whom it is supposed, by some, that Paul speaks. 2. To the struggles that are in a renewed sanctified soul, but yet in a state of imperfection, as other apprehend. And a great controversy there is of which of these we are to understand the apostle here.

I. Apply it to the struggles that are felt in a convinced soul, that is yet in a state of sin, knows his Lord's will, but does it not, continues a slave to his reigning lusts. The apostle had said (*ch.* vi. 14), *Sin shall not have dominion, because you are not under the law, but under grace,* for the proof of which he here shows that a man under the law, and not under grace, may be under the dominion of sin. The law may discover sin, and convince of sin, but it cannot conquer and subdue sin. It discovers the defilement but will not wash it off. It makes a man weary and heavy laden (Matt. xi. 28), burdens him with his sin;

JAMIESON, FAUSSET, BROWN

—I found to be unto death—through breaking it.

For sin—my sinful nature—**taking occasion by the commandment, deceived me**—or 'seduced me'—drew me aside into the very thing which the commandment forbade. **and by it slew me**—'discovered me to myself to be a condemned and gone man' (cf. vs. 9, "I *died*").

12, 13. Wherefore—'So that'—**the law is**—'is indeed'—**good, and the commandment**—that one so often referred to, which forbids all lusting—**holy, and just, and good. Was then that which is good made**—'Hath then that which is good become'—**death unto me? God forbid**—i.e., 'Does the *blame* of my death lie with the good law? Away with such a thought.' **But sin**—became death unto me, to the end—**that it might appear sin**—that it might be seen in its true light—**working death in**—rather, 'to'—**me by that which is good, that sin by the commandment might become exceeding sinful**—'that its enormous turpitude might stand out to view, through its turning God's holy, just, and good law into a provocative to the very things which is forbids.' So much for *the law in relation to the unregenerate,* of whom the apostle takes himself as the example; first, in his ignorant, self-satisfied condition; next, under humbling discoveries of his inability to keep the law, through inward contrariety to it; finally, as self-condemned, and already, in law, a dead man. Some inquire to what period of his recorded history these circumstances relate. But there is no reason to think they were wrought into such conscious and explicit discovery at any period of his history before he "met the Lord in the way"; and though, "amidst the multitude of his thoughts within him" during his memorable three day's blindness immediately after that, such views of the law and of himself would doubtless be tossed up and down till they *took shape* much as they are here described (see on Acts 9:9) we regard this whole description of his inward struggles and progress rather as the *finished result* of all his past recollections and subsequent reflections on his unregenerate state, which he throws into historical form only for greater vividness. But now the apostle proceeds to repel false inferences *regarding the law,* secondly: vss. 14-25, In the case of the REGENERATE; taking himself here also as the example. **14. For we know that the law is spiritual**—in its demands. **but I am carnal**—fleshly (see on vs. 5), and as such, incapable of yielding spiritual obedience. **sold under sin**—enslaved to it. The "I" here, though of course not the *regenerate,* is neither the *unregenerate,* but the sinful principle of the renewed man, as is expressly stated in vs. 18.

ADAM CLARKE

if a man do, he shall live in them," Lev. xviii. 5. *I found,* by transgressing it, *to be unto death;* for it only presented the duty and laid down the penalty, without affording any strength to resist sin or subdue evil propensities.

11. *Sin, taking occasion.* Sin, deriving strength from the law, threatening death to the transgressor, *deceived me,* drew me aside to disobedience, promising me gratification, honor, independence, as it promised to Eve; for to her history the apostle evidently alludes, and uses the very same expression, *deceived me.* See the Septuagint, Gen. iii. 13. *And by it slew me.* Subjected me to that death which the law denounced against transgressors, and rendered me miserable during the course of life itself. It is well-known to scholars that the verb signifies not only "to slay" or "kill," but also to "make wretched." Every sinner is only exposed to death because he has sinned, and must sooner or later die; but he is miserable in both body and mind by the influence and the effects of sin. He lives a dying life, or a living death.

12. *Wherefore the law is holy.* As if he had said, to soothe his countrymen, to whom he had been showing the absolute insufficiency of the law either to justify or save from sin: I do not intimate that there is anything improper or imperfect in the law as a rule of life. It prescribes what is *holy, just,* and *good;* for it comes from a holy, just, and good God. The *law,* which is to regulate the whole of the outward conduct, is holy; and the *commandment,* "Thou shalt not covet," which is to regulate the heart, is not less so. All is excellent and pure; but it neither pardons sin nor purifies the heart; and it is because it is holy, just, and good that it condemns transgressors to death.

13. *Was then that which is good made death unto me?* This is the question of the Jew, with whom the apostle appears to be disputing. "Do you allow the law to be good, and yet say it is the cause of our death?" The apostle answers: *God forbid.* "By no means." It is not the law that is the cause of your death, but sin. It was sin which subjected us to death by the law, justly threatening sin with death, which law was given that sin might appear—might be set forth in its own colors—when we saw it subjected us to death by a law perfectly holy, just, and good; that sin, by the law, might be represented what it really is, an exceeding great and deadly evil.

14. *For we know that the law is spiritual.* This is a general proposition, and probably, in the apostle's autograph, concluded the above sentence. The law is not to be considered as a system of external rites and ceremonies, nor even as a rule of moral action. It is a spiritual system; it reaches to the most hidden purposes, thoughts, dispositions, and desires of the heart and soul; and it reproves and condemns everything, without hope of reprieve or pardon, that is contrary to eternal truth and rectitude. *But I am carnal, sold under sin.* This was probably, in the apostle's letter, the beginning of a new paragraph. I believe it is agreed, on all hands, that the apostle is here demonstrating the insufficiency of the law in opposition to the gospel; that by the former is the knowledge, by the latter the cure, of sin. Therefore by *I* here he cannot mean himself, nor any Christian believer. If the contrary could be proved, the argument of the apostle would go to demonstrate the insufficiency of the gospel as well as the law. It is difficult to conceive how the opinion could have crept into the Church, or prevailed there, that "the apostle speaks here of his *regenerate state;* and that what was, in such a state, true of himself, must be true of all others in the same state." This opinion has, most pitifully and most shamefully, not only lowered the standard of Christianity, but destroyed its influence and disgraced its character. It requires but little knowledge of the spirit of the gospel, and of the scope of this Epistle, to see that the apostle is here either personating a Jew under the law and without the gospel or showing what his own state was when he was deeply convinced that by the deeds of the law no man could be justified, and had not as yet heard those blessed words: "Brother Saul, the Lord . . . Jesus, that appeared unto thee in the way . . . hath sent me, that thou mightest receive thy sight, and

MATTHEW HENRY

and yet it yields no help towards the shaking off of that burden; this is to be had only in Christ. The law may make a man cry out, *O wretched man that I am! who shall deliver me?* and yet leave him thus fettered. Now a soul advanced thus far by the law is in a fair way towards a state of liberty by Christ, though many rest here and go no further. It is possible for a man to go to hell with his eyes open, and to carry about with him a self-accusing conscience, even in the service of the devil. He may *consent to the law that it is good,* may have that within him that witnesses against sin and for holiness; and yet all this overpowered by the reigning love of sin. Drunkards and unclean persons have some faint desires to leave off their sins, and yet persist in them. Of such as these there are many that will needs have all this understood. It is very hard to imagine why, if the apostle intended this, he should speak all along in his own person; and not only so, but in the present tense.

II. It seems rather to be understood of the struggles that are maintained between grace and corruption in sanctified souls. That there are remainders of indwelling corruption, even where there is a living principle of grace, is past dispute. If we say that we have no sin, we deceive ourselves, 1 John i. 8, 10. That true grace strives against these sins and corruptions is likewise certain (Gal. v. 17): *The flesh lusteth against the spirit, and the spirit against the flesh; and these are contrary the one to the other, so that you cannot do the things that you would.* And his design is further to open the nature of sanctification, that it does not attain to a sinless perfection in this life. That which we do sincerely strive against, shall not be laid to our charge, and through grace the victory is sure at last.

1. What he complains of—the remainder of indwelling corruptions. The law is insufficient to justify even a regenerate man, which is not the fault of the law, but of our own corrupt nature, which cannot fulfil the law. Observe the particulars of this complaint. (1) *I am carnal, sold under sin, v.* 14. Even where there is spiritual life there are remainders of carnal affections, and so far a man may be *sold under sin.*

(2) *What I would, that I do not; but what I hate, hat do I, v.* 15. And to the same purport, *v.* 19, 21, *Vhen I would do good, evil is present with me.* He vas pressing forward towards perfection, yet he cknowledges that he had not already attained, either was already perfect, Phil. iii. 12. Fain he vould perfectly do the will of God, but his corrupt ature drew him another way: it was like the bias a bowl, which, when it is thrown straight, yet raws it aside.

JAMIESON, FAUSSET, BROWN

ALBERT BARNES:

"We know." We admit. It is a conceded, well-understood point. "That the law is spiritual." This does not mean that the law is designed to control the spirit, in contradistinction from the body, but it is a declaration showing that the evils of which he was speaking were not the fault of the law. That was not, in its nature, sensual, corrupt, earthly, carnal; but was pure and spiritual. The *effect* described was not the fault of the law, but of the man, who was sold under sin. The word spiritual is often thus used to denote that which is pure and holy, in opposition to that which is fleshly or carnal (8:5, 6; Gal. 5:16-23). The *flesh* is described as the source of evil passions and desires; the *spirit* as the source of purity, or as that which is agreeable to the proper influences of the Holy Spirit. "But I am." The present tense shows that he is describing himself as he was at the time of writing. This is the natural and obvious construction, and if this be not the meaning, it is impossible to account for his having changed the past tense (v. 7) to the present. "Carnal." Fleshly; sensual; opposed to spiritual. This word is used because in the Scriptures the *flesh* is spoken of as the source of sensual passions and propensities (Gal. 5:19-21). The sense is, that these corrupt passions still retained a strong and withering and distressing influence over the mind. The renewed man is exposed to temptations from his strong native appetites; and the power of these passions, strengthened by long habit before he was converted, has traveled over into religion, and they continue still to influence and distress him. It does not mean that he is *wholly* under their influence; but that the tendency of his natural inclinations is to indulgence.

"Sold under sin." This expression is often adduced to show that it cannot be of a renewed man that the apostle is speaking. The argument is, that it cannot be affirmed of a Christian that he is sold under sin. A sufficient answer to this might be, that in fact, this is the very language which Christians often now adopt to express the strength of that native depravity against which they struggle, and that no language would better express it. It does not mean that they choose or prefer sins. It strongly implies that the prevailing bent of their mind is against it, but that such is its strength that it brings them into slavery to it. The expression here used, "sold under sin," is "borrowed from the practice of selling captives taken in war, as slaves" (Stuart). It hence means to deliver into the power of anyone, so that he shall be dependent on his will and control (Schleusner). The emphasis is not on the word *sold,* as if any act of selling had taken place, but the *effect* was as if he had been sold; i.e. he was subject to it, and under its control; and it means that sin, contrary to the prevailing inclination of his mind (vv. 15-17), had such an influence over him as to lead him to commit it, and thus to produce a state of conflict and grief (vv. 19-24). The verses which follow this are an explanation of the sense and of the manner in which he was "sold under sin."—*Popular Commentary*

15,
16. For . . .—better, 'For that which I do I know not'; i.e., 'In obeying the impulses of my carnal nature I act the slave of another will than my own as a renewed man? **for . . .** rather, 'for not what I would (wish, desire) that do I, but what I hate that I do. But if wat I would not that I do, I consent unto the law that it is good—the judgment of my inner man going along with the law.'

ADAM CLARKE

be filled with the Holy Ghost," Acts ix. 17. In this and the following verses he states the contrariety between himself, or any Jew while without Christ, and the law of God. Of the latter he says, "It *is spiritual";* of the former, *I am carnal, sold under sin.* Of the carnal man, in opposition to the spiritual, never was a more complete or accurate description given. The expressions "in the flesh" and "after the flesh," in v. 5 and in chap. viii. 5, 8-9, etc., are of the same import with the word *carnal* in this verse. To be "in the flesh," or to be "carnally minded," solely respects the unregenerate. While unregenerate, a man is in a state of death and enmity against God, chap. viii. 6-9. This is Paul's own account of a carnal man. Those who are of another opinion maintain that by the word *carnal* here the apostle meant that corruption which dwelt in him after his conversion. But this opinion is founded on a very great mistake; for although there may be, after justification, the remains of the carnal mind, which will be less or more felt till the soul is completely sanctified, yet the man is never denominated from the inferior principle, which is under control, but from the superior principle which habitually prevails. Whatever epithets are given to corruption or sin in Scripture, opposite epithets are given to grace or holiness. By these different epithets are the unregenerate and regenerate denominated. From all this it follows that the epithet *carnal,* which is the characteristic designation of an unregenerate man, cannot be applied to Paul after his conversion; nor, indeed, to any Christian in that state. [But cf. I Cor. 3:3—ED.] But the word *carnal,* though used by the apostle to signify a state of death and enmity against God, is not sufficient to denote all the evil of the state which he is describing; hence he adds, expressions which the Spirit of God uses in Scripture to describe the full depravity of fallen man. It implies a willing slavery; Ahab had sold himself to work evil, I Kings xxi. 20. And of the Jews it is said, in their utmost depravity, "Behold, for your iniquities have you sold yourselves," Isa. l. 1. Now if the word *carnal* in its strongest sense had been sufficiently significant of all he meant, why add to this charge another expression still stronger? We must therefore understand the phrase *sold under sin* as implying that the soul was employed in the drudgery of sin; that it was "sold over" to this service, and had no power to disobey this tyrant, until it was redeemed by another. And if a man be actually sold to another, and he acquiesce in the deed, then he becomes the legal property of that other person. This state of bondage was well-known to the Romans. The sale of slaves they saw daily, and could not misunderstand the emphatical sense of this expression. Sin is here represented as a person, and the apostle compares the dominion which sin has over the man in question to that of a master over his legal slave. Universally through the Scriptures man is said to be in a state of bondage to sin until the Son of God make him free, but in no part of the sacred writings is it ever said that the children of God are sold under sin.

15. *For that which I do I allow not.* The first clause of this verse is a general assertion concerning the employment of the person in question in the state which the apostle calls *carnal* and *sold under sin.* The Greek word which is here translated *I do* means a work which the agent continues to perform till it is finished, and is used by the apostle, Phil. ii. 12, to denote the continued employment of God's saints in His service to the end of their lives, "Work out your own salvation." The word here denotes an employment of a different kind; and therefore the man who now feels the galling dominion of sin says, What I am continually laboring at *I allow not.* "I do not acknowledge" to be right, just, holy, or profitable. *But what I hate, that do I.* I am a slave, and under the absolute control of my tyrannical master; I hate his service, but am obliged to work his will. Who, without blaspheming, can assert that the apostle is speaking this of a man in whom the Spirit of the Lord dwells? From v. 7 to this one the apostle, says Dr. Taylor, denotes the Jew in the flesh by a single *I;* here he divides that *I* into two *I's,* or figurative persons, representing two different and opposite principles which were in him. The

ALBERT BARNES:

"For what I would." That which I approve; and which is my prevailing and established desire. What I would wish always to do. "But what I hate." What I disapprove of; what is contrary to my judgment, my prevailing inclination, my established principles of conduct. "That do I." Under the influence of sinful propensities, and carnal inclinations and desires. This represents the strong native propensity to sin; and even the power of corrupt propensity under the restraining influence of the gospel.

On this remarkble and important passage we may observe: (1) That the prevailing propensity, the habitual fixed inclination of the mind of the Christian, is to do right. The evil course is hated, the right course is loved. This is the characteristic of a pious mind. It distinguishes a holy man from a sinner. (2) That the evil which is done is disapproved; is a source of grief; and the habitual desire of the mind is to avoid it, and be pure. This also distinguishes the Christian from the sinner. (3) That there is no need of being embarrassed here with any metaphysical difficulties or inquiries how this can be. It is in fact the experience of all Christians. The habitual, fixed inclination and desire of their minds is to serve God. They have a fixed abhorrence of sin; and yet they are conscious of imperfection, and error, and sin, which is the source of uneasiness and trouble. The strength of natural passion may in an unguarded moment overcome them. The power of long habits, of previous thoughts, may annoy them. A man who was an infidel before his conversion, and whose mind was filled with skepticism, and cavils, and blasphemy, will find the effect of his former habits of thinking lingering in his mind and annoying his peace for years. These thoughts will start up with the rapidity of lightning. Thus it is with every vice and every opinion. It is one of the effects of habit. "The very passage of an impure thought through the mind leaves pollution behind it"; and where sin has been long indulged, it leaves its withering, desolating effect on the soul long after conversion, and produces that state of conflict with which every Christian is familiar. An effect somewhat similar is felt by all men. All are conscious of doing that, under the excitement of passion and prejudice, which their conscience and better judgment disapprove.—*Popular Commentary*

His conscience witnessed for him that he had a good principle ruling and prevailing in him, notwithstanding. The rule of this good principle which he had was the law of God, to which he here speaks of having a threefold regard. [1] *I consent unto the law that it is good, v.* 16. Here is the approbation of the judgment. Wherever there is grace there is not only a dread of the severity of the law, but a consent to the goodness of the law. This is a sign that the law is written in the heart. The sanctified judgment not only concurs to the equity of the law, but to the excellency of it.

The fault lay in that corruption of his nature which he did really bewail and strive against: *It is no more I that do it, but sin that dwelleth in me.* This he mentions twice (*v.* 17, 20), not as an excuse for the guilt of sin, but that he might not sink in despair, but take comfort from the covenant of grace, which accepts the willingness of the spirit, and has provided pardon for the weakness of the flesh. He here professes his dissent from the law of sin. "It is not I; it is against my mind that it is done."

In me, that is in my flesh, dwelleth no good, v. 18. There is no good to be expected, any more than one would expect good corn growing upon a rock. As the new nature cannot commit sin (1 John iii. 9), so the flesh, the old nature, cannot perform a good duty. How should it? For the flesh serveth the law of sin (*v.* 25).

17. Now then it is no more I—*my renewed self*—**that do it**—'that work it' —**but sin which dwelleth in me**—that principle of sin that still has its abode in me. To explain this and the following statements, as many do [even BENGEL and THOLUCK], of the sins of unrenewed men against their better convictions, is to do painful violence to the apostle's language, and to affirm of the unregenerate what is untrue. That coexistence and mutual hostility of "flesh" and "spirit" in the same renewed man, which is so clearly taught in ch. 8:4, etc., and in Galatians 5:16, etc., is the true and only key to the language of this and the following verses. (It is hardly necessary to say that the apostle means not to disown the blame of yielding to his corruptions, by saying, "it is not he that does it, but sin that dwelleth in him." Early heretics thus abused his language; but the whole strain of the passage shows that his sole object in thus expressing himself was to bring more vividly before his readers the conflict of two opposite principles, and how entirely, as a new man—honoring from his inmost soul the law of God—he condemned and renounced his corrupt nature, with its affections and lusts, its stirrings and its outgoings, root and branch). **18. For . . .**—better, 'For I know that there dwelleth not in me, that is in my flesh, any good.' **for to will**—'desire' —**is present with me; but to perform that which is good**—the supplement "how," in our version, weakens the statement—**I find not**—Here, again, we have the *double self* of the renewed man; 'In me dwelleth no good; but this corrupt self is not my true self; it is but sin dwelling in my real self, as a renewed man.'

19, 21. For . . .—The conflict here graphically described between a self that 'desires' to do good and a self that in spite of this does evil, cannot be the struggles between conscience and passion in the *un-*

one *I*, or principle, assents to the law that it is good, and wills and chooses what the other does not practice, v. 16. This principle he expressly tells us, v. 22, is the "inward man"; "the law of my mind," v. 23; the "mind," or rational faculty, v. 25; for he could find no other inward man, or law of the mind, but the rational faculty, in a person who was carnal and sold under sin. The other *I*, or principle, transgresses the law, v. 23, and does those things which the former principle allows not. This principle he expressly tells us, v. 18, is the "flesh," the "law in my members," or sensual appetite, v. 23; and he concludes in the last verse that these two principles, residing and counteracting each other in the same person, are reason and lust, or sin that dwells in us. And it is very easy to distinguish these two *I's*, or principles. For instance, v. 17: "Now then it is no more I that do it, but sin that dwelleth in me." The *I* he speaks of here is opposed to indwelling or governing sin; and therefore plainly denotes the principle of reason, the "inward man," or "law of my mind"; in which, I add, a measure of the light of the Spirit of God shines, in order to show the sinfulness of sin. These two different principles he calls, one "flesh," and the other "Spirit," Gal. v. 17, where he speaks of their contrariety in the same manner that he does here. And we may give a probable reason why the apostle dwells so long upon the struggle and opposition between these two principles; it appears intended to answer a tacit but very obvious objection. The Jew might allege: "But the law is holy and spiritual; and I assent to it as good, as a right rule of action, which ought to be observed. Yea, I esteem it highly; I glory and rest in it, convinced of its truth and excellency. And is not this enough to constitute the law a sufficient principle of sanctification?" The apostle answers, "No; wickedness is consistent with a sense of truth. A man may assent to the best rule of action, and yet still be under the dominion of lust and sin, from which nothing can deliver him but a principle and power proceeding from the fountain of life."

16. *If then I do that which I would not,* knowing that the law condemns it and that therefore it must be evil, *I consent unto the law;* I show by this circumstance that I acknowledge the law to be good.

17. *Now then it is no more I.* It is not that *I* which constitutes reason and conscience. *But sin*—corrupt and sensual inclinations—*that dwelleth in me*—that has the entire domination over my reason, darkening my understanding, and perverting my judgment; for which there is condemnation in the law, but no cure. So we find here that there is a principle in the unregenerate man stronger than reason itself; a principle which is, properly speaking, not of the essence of the soul, but acts in it, as its lord or as a tyrant. This is inbred and indwelling sin, the seed of the serpent, by which the whole soul is darkened, confused, perverted, and excited to rebellion against God.

18. *For I know that in me.* I have learned by experience that in an unregenerate man there is *no good.* There is no principle by which the soul can be brought into the light, no principle by which it can be restored to purity; fleshly appetities alone prevail, and the brute runs away with the man. *For to will is present with me.* When the apostle says, *To will is present with me,* he shows that the will is on the side of God and truth, so far that it consents to the propriety and necessity of obedience. There has been a strange clamor raised up against this faculty of the soul, as if the very essence of evil dwelt in it, whereas the apostle shows throughout this chapter that the will was regularly on God's side, while every other faculty appears to have been in hostility to Him. The truth is, men have confounded the will with the passions, and laid to the charge of the former what properly belongs to the latter. The will is right, but the passions are wrong. It discerns and approves, but is without ability to perform it has no power over sensual appetites; in these the principle of rebellion dwells.

19. *For the good that I would I do not.* Here again is the most decisive proof that the will is on the side of God and truth. *But the evil which I would not.* And here is equally decisive proof

MATTHEW HENRY	JAMIESON, FAUSSET, BROWN	ADAM CLARKE

regenerate, because the description given of this "desire to do good" in the verse immediately following is such as cannot be ascribed, with the least show of truth, to any but the *renewed.*

that the will is against or opposed to evil. It is not the will that leads men astray, but the corrupt passions which oppose and oppress the will. The plain state of the case is this: the soul is so completely fallen that it has no power to do good till it receive that power from on high. But it has power to see good, to distinguish between that and evil; to acknowledge the excellence of this good, and to will it, from a conviction of that excellence; but further it cannot go. Yet in various cases it is solicited and consents to sin; and because it is will, that is, because it is a free principle, it must necessarily possess this power; and although it can do no good unless it receive grace from God, yet it is impossible to force it to sin. Even Satan himself cannot do this; and before he can get it to sin, he must gain its consent. Thus God in His endless mercy has endued this faculty with a power in which, humanly speaking, resides the salvability of the soul; and without this the soul must have eternally continued under the power of sin, or been saved as an inert, absolutely passive machine. But does not this arguing destroy the doctrine of free grace? No! it establishes that doctrine. (1) It is through the grace, the unmerited kindness, of God that the soul has such a faculty, and that it has not been extinguished by sin. (2) This will, though a free principle, yet, properly speaking, has no power by which it can subjugate the evil or perform the good. We know that the eye has a power to discern objects, but without light this power is perfectly useless, and no object can be discerned by it. So of the person represented here by the apostle it is said, *To will is present with me,* v. 18; "To will is ever in readiness, it is ever at hand, it lies constantly before me"; *but how to perform that which is good I find not;* that is, the man is unregenerate, and he is seeking justification and holiness from the law. The law was never designed to give these—it gives the knowledge, not the cure, of sin. Here, then, the free agency of man is preserved, without which he could not be in a salvable state; and the honor of the grace of Christ is maintained, without which there can be no actual salvation.

20. *It is no more I.* My will is against it; my reason and conscience condemn it. *But sin that dwelleth in me*—the principle of sin, which has possessed itself of all my carnal appetites and passions, and thus subjects my reason and domineers over my soul. Thus I am in perpetual contradiction to myself. Two principles are continually contending in me for the mastery: my reason, on which the light of God shines, to show what is evil; and my passions, in which the principle of sin works, to bring forth fruit unto death.

21. *I find then a law.* I am in such a condition and state of soul, under the power of such habits and sinful propensities, *that when I would do good*—when my will and reason are strongly bent on obedience to the law of God and opposition to the principle of sin—*evil is present with me,* "evil is at hand; it lies constantly before me." As the will to do good is constantly at hand, v. 18, so the principle of rebellion exciting me to sin is equally present; but as the one is only will, wish, and desire, without power to do what is willed, to obtain what is wished, or to perform what is desired, sin continually prevails. The word *law* in this verse must be taken as implying any strong or confirmed habit, under the influence of which the man generally acts; and in this sense the apostle most evidently uses it in v. 23.

22. *I delight in the law of God after the inward man.* Every Jew, and every unregenerate man, who receives the Old Testament as a revelation from God must acknowledge the great purity, excellence, and utility of its maxims, though he will ever find that without the grace of our Lord Jesus he can never act according to those heavenly maxims; and without the mercy of God, can never be redeemed from the curse entailed upon him for his past transgressions. To say that the *inward man* means the regenerate part of the soul is supportable by no argument. If it be said that it is impossible for an unregenerate man to *delight in the law of God,* the experience of millions contradicts the assertion. Every true penitent admires the moral law, longs most earnestly for a conformity to it, and feels that he can never be satisfied till he

A. B. SIMPSON:

"I delight in the law of God after the inward man." This inward man which delights in the law of God is undoubtedly the new man, the regenerated soul, born from above. Notwithstanding our corruptions and struggles, let us never give up the confidence of our salvation. We are the Lord's children, although we may be full of fault and blame. The nugget is genuine gold, although it is mixed with much rough rock and native ore. In due time the great Refiner will cleanse it from the dross; but be careful and do not throw it away because it still has some dross.

We see the honest struggle between these two natures. The new and heaven-born heart is opposed by the old natural heart, and a terrible struggle ensues in which the good is often defeated by the evil, yet never yields its consent. "I see another law in my members, warring against the law of my mind, and bringing me into captivity to the law of sin which is in my members." Now, this is the struggle in which so many Christian lives spend all their earthly experience. It is an honest and earnest conflict, and God gives full credit for the intent, but looks with sorrow upon the failure which is so needless and vain.

What is the struggling soul to do? To continue the fight forever? What did Paul do? Listen, "O wretched man that I am! who shall deliver me from the body of this death?" When we can do nothing else, we can at least give a good cry. When it came to the worst, Paul just lifted up his voice and called for help. With his little ship sinking in the rough waters, he shouted for aid. And such a cry is never heard in vain. God heard him, and a moment later, lo! the vision beyond the surf of the white sails of the lifeboat coming to his aid with Jesus in the prow, waving His hand in encouragement and victory, while Paul answers back with a shout of triumph, "Thank God through Jesus Christ our Lord." And now the lifeboat is quickly attached to the sinking ship and quickly bears it across the rough waters into the open sea of peace and grace and glory into which we pass in the following chapter.

The seventh chapter of Romans is the hopeless struggle of the new heart with the old heart in a saved man. The eighth chapter of Romans is the victory of the same man over his old enemy and all others, when something is added to his life—the indwelling presence and power of Jesus Christ and the Holy Ghost to fill him and keep him in triumph over all his foes. Rom. 7:25 gives us the key to the whole chapter in the words, "I myself"; it is the story of what I myself can do; it is the best that the good self is able to accomplish, while the eighth chapter is the best that Christ in us is able to accomplish, and the key to the chapter is, "In Christ, and Christ in us."

I myself can choose the right and struggle for it, but cannot fully accomplish it. With the mind I can serve the law of God, but with the flesh I will still often serve the law of sin. But when I come into the higher place of union with Christ, then "the law of the Spirit of life in Christ Jesus hath made me free from the law of sin and death."

In the fifth chapter of Galatians, the same conflict is described, "The flesh lusteth against the Spirit, and the Spirit against the flesh." Usually we spell the word "spirit" with a small "s" and that keeps us in the seventh chapter of Romans, our spirit struggling against our flesh. The true way to spell it is with a capital "S," and this takes us into the eighth chapter of Romans, and this makes the struggle no longer between our spirit and our flesh, but rather between the divine Spirit and our flesh. The battle is not ours, but God's, and the victory is sure and complete, and so the apostle says in Galatians, "This I say then, Walk in the Spirit, and ye shall not fulfil the lust of the flesh."
—*Christ in the Bible*

[2] *I delight in the law of God after the inward man, v.* 22. **He delighted not only in the promises of the word, but in the precepts and prohibitions of the word. All that are born again do truly delight in the law of God, never better pleased than when heart and life are in the strictest conformity to the law and will of God.** *After the inward man; First,* The mind or rational faculties. The soul is the inward man, and that is the seat of gracious delights, which are therefore sincere and serious, but secret. *Secondly,* The new nature. The new man is called the *inner man* (Eph. iii. 16).

22. For I delight in the law of God after the inward man—'from the bottom of my heart.' The word here rendered "delight" is indeed stronger than "consent" in vs. 16; but both express a state of mind and heart to which the unregenerate man is a stranger.

MATTHEW HENRY

I see another law in my members warring against the law of my mind, v. 23. Christ having set up his throne in his heart, it was only the rebellious members of the body that were the instruments of sin—all that corrupt nature which is the seat not only of sensual but of more refined lusts. This wars against the law of the mind, the new nature, to which corrupt disposition and inclination are as great a burden and grief as the worst drudgery and captivity could be. *It brings me into captivity.*

ALBERT BARNES:

"The body of this death." Marg., "this body of death." The word "body" here is probably used as equivalent to "flesh," denoting the corrupt and evil propensities of the soul. It is thus used to denote the law of sin in the members as being that with which the apostle was struggling, and from which he desired to be delivered. The expression "body of this death" is a Hebraism, denoting a body deadly in its tendency; and the whole expression may mean the corrupt principles of man; the carnal, evil affections that lead to death or to condemnation. The expression is one of vast strength, and strongly characteristic of the apostle Paul. It indicates that it was near him, attending him, and was distressing in its nature. And it indicates an earnest wish to be delivered from it. Some have supposed that he refers to a custom practiced by ancient tyrants, of binding a dead body to a captive as a punishment, and compelling him to drag the cumbersome amd offensive burden with him wherever he went. I do not see any evidence that the apostle had this in view. But such a fact may be used as a striking and perhaps not improper illustration of the meaning of the apostle here. No strength of words could express deeper feeling; none more feelingly indicate the necessity of the grace of God to accomplish that to which the unaided human powers are incompetent.
—*Popular Commentary*

His general complaint we have *v.* 24, *O wretched man that I am! who shall deliver me from the body of this death?* The thing he complains of is a body of death; either the body of flesh, which is a mortal dying body, or the body of sin, the corrupt nature, which tends to death. It was as troublesome to Paul as if he had had a dead body tied to him. This made him cry out, *O wretched man that I am!* Had I been required to speak of Paul, I should have said, "O blessed man that thou art." But in his own account he was a wretched man, because of the corruption of nature. *Who shall deliver me?* He speaks like one that was sick of it. The remainders of indwelling sin are a very grievous burden to a gracious soul.

JAMIESON, FAUSSET, BROWN

23. But I see another—it should be 'a different'—**law in my members**—see on vs. 5—**warring against the law of my mind, and bringing me into captivity to the law of sin which is in my members**—In this important verse, observe, first, that the word "law" means *an inward principle of action, good or evil, operating with the fixedness and regularity of a law.* The apostle found two such laws within him; the one "the law of sin in his members," called (in Gal. 5:17, 24) "the flesh which lusteth against the spirit," "the flesh with the affections and lusts," i.e., the sinful principle in the regenerate; the other, "the law of the mind," or the holy principle of the renewed nature. Second, when the apostle says he "sees" the one of these principles "warring against" the other, and "bringing him into captivity" to itself, *he is not referring to any actual rebellion going on within him while he was writing, or to any captivity to his own lusts then existing.* He is simply describing the two conflicting principles, and pointing out what it was the inherent property of each to aim at bringing about. Third, when the apostle describes himself as *"brought into captivity"* by the triumph of the sinful principle of his nature, he clearly speaks in the person of a *renewed man.* Men do not feel themselves to be in captivity in the territories of their own sovereign and associated with their own friends, breathing a congenial atmosphere, and acting quite spontaneously. But here the apostle describes himself, when drawn under the power of his sinful nature, as forcibly seized and reluctantly dragged to his enemy's camp, from which he would gladly make his escape. This ought to settle the question, whether he is here speaking as a regenerate man or the reverse.

O wretched man that I am! who shall deliver me from the body of this death?—The apostle speaks of the "body" here with reference to "the law of sin" which he had said was "in his members," but merely as the instrument by which the sin of the heart finds vent in action, and as itself the seat of the lower appetites (see on ch. 6:6, and on vs 5); and he calls it "the body of *this* death," as feeling, at the moment when he wrote, the horrors of that death (ch. 6:21, and vs. 5) into which it dragged him down. But the language is not that of a sinner newly awakened to the sight of his lost state; it is the cry of a living but agonized believer, weighed down under a burden which is not himself, but which he longs to shake off from his renewed self. Nor does the question imply ignorance of the way of relief at the time referred to. It was designed only to prepare the way for that outburst of thankfulness for the divinely provided remedy which immediately follows. **25. I thank God**—the Source—**through Jesus Christ**—the Channel of deliverance. **So then**—to sum up the whole matter—**with the mind**—the mind indeed—**I myself serve the law of God, but with the flesh the law of sin**—'Such then is the unchanging character of these two principles within me. God's holy law is dear to my renewed mind, and has the willing service of my new man; although that corrupt nature which still remains in me listens to the dictates of sin.' Note (1) This whole chapter was of essential service to the Reformers in their contendings with the Church of Rome. When the divines of that corrupt church, in a Pelagian spirit, denied that the sinful principle in our fallen nature, which they called 'Concupiscence,' and which is commonly called 'Original Sin,' had the nature of *sin* at all, they were triumphantly answered from this chapter, where—both in the first section of it, which speaks of it in the unregenerate, and in the second, which treats of its

ADAM CLARKE

awakes up after this divine likeness; and he hates himself because he feels that he has broken it, and that his evil passions are still in a state of hostility to it.

23. *But I see another law in my members.* Though the person in question is more or less under the continual influence of reason and conscience, which offer constant testimony against sin, yet as long as help is sought only from the law, and the grace of Christ in the gospel is not received, the remonstrances of reason and conscience are rendered of no effect by the prevalence of sinful passions; which, from repeated gratifications, have acquired all the force of habit, and now *give law* to the whole carnal man. *Warring against the law of my mind.* There is an allusion here to the case of a city besieged, at last taken by storm, and the inhabitants carried away into captivity; carrying on a system of warfare; laying continual siege to the soul; repeating incessantly its attacks; harassing, battering, and storming the spirit; and, by all these assaults, reducing the man to extreme misery. Never was a picture more impressively drawn and more effectually finished; for the next sentence shows that this spiritual city was at last taken by storm, and the inhabitants who survived the sackage led into the most shameful, painful, and oppressive captivity. *Bringing me into captivity to the law of sin.* He does not here speak of an occasional advantage gained by sin; it was a complete and final victory gained by corruption, which, having stormed and reduced the city, carried away the inhabitants with irresistible force into captivity. This is the consequence of being overcome; he was now in the hands of the foe, as the victor's lawful captive. This is the import of the original word, and is the very term used by our Lord when speaking of the final ruin, dispersion, and captivity of the Jews. He says, "They . . . shall be led away captive into all nations," Luke xxi. 24. When all this is considered, who, in his right mind, can apply it to the holy soul of the apostle of the Gentiles? Is there anything in it that can belong to his gracious state? Surely nothing. The basest slave of sin, who has any remaining checks of conscience, cannot be brought into a worse state than that described here by the apostle. Sin and corruption have a final triumph; and conscience and reason are taken prisoners, laid in fetters, and sold for slaves. Can this ever be said of a man in whom the Spirit of God dwells, and whom the law of the Spirit of life in Christ Jesus has made free from the law of sin and death? See chap. viii. 2.

24. *O wretched man that I am!* This affecting account is finished more impressively by the groans of the wounded captive. Having long maintained a useless conflict against innumerable hosts and irresistible might, he is at last wounded and taken prisoner; and to render his state more miserable, is not only encompassed by the slaughtered, but chained to a dead body; for there seems to be here an allusion to an ancient custom of certain tyrants, who bound a dead body to a living man, and obliged him to carry it about, till the contagion from the putrid mass took away his life! Virgil paints this in all its horrors in the account he gives of the tyrant Mezentius. We may naturally suppose that the cry of such a person would be, "Wretched man that I am, who shall deliver me from this dead body?" And how well does this apply to the case of the person to whom the apostle refers! A *body*—a whole mass of sin and corruption, was bound to his soul with chains which he could not break; and the mortal contagion, transfused through his whole nature, was pressing him down to the bitter pains of an eternal death. He now finds that the law can afford him no deliverance, and he despairs of help from any human being. But while he is emitting his last or almost expiring groan, the redemption by Christ Jesus is proclaimed to him; and, if the apostle refers to his own case, Ananias unexpectedly accosts him with—"Brother Saul, the Lord . . . Jesus, that appeared unto thee in the way . . . hath sent me [unto thee], that thou mightest receive thy sight, and be filled with the Holy Ghost." He sees then an open door of hope, and he immediately, though but in the prospect of this deliverance, returns God thanks for the well-grounded hope

MATTHEW HENRY

His great comfort lay in Jesus Christ (*v.* 25) *I thank God, through Jesus Christ our Lord.* In the midst of his complaints he breaks out into praises. It is a special remedy against fears and sorrows to be much in praise: many a poor, drooping soul hath found it so. *Who shall deliver me?* says he (*v.* 24), as one at a loss for help. At length he finds an all-sufficient friend, even Jesus Christ. If it were not for Christ, this iniquity that dwells in us would certainly be our ruin. It is Christ that has purchased deliverance for us in due time. *Blessed be God that giveth us this victory through our Lord Jesus Christ!*

With the mind I myself serve the law of God, v. 25. It is not enough to consent to the law, and to delight in the law, but we must serve the law. Thus it was with Paul's mind; this it is with every sanctified renewed mind.

To the same purport (*v.* 25). *With the flesh I serve the law of sin*, the unregenerate part, is continually working towards sin.

JAMIESON, FAUSSET, BROWN

presence and actings in believers—it is explicitly, emphatically, and repeatedly called *"sin."* As such, they held it to be *damnable.* (See the Confessions both of the Lutheran and Reformed churches.) In the following century, the orthodox in Holland had the same controversy to wage with 'the Remonstrants' (the followers of Arminius), and they waged it on the field of this chapter. (2) Here we see that *Inability* is consistent with *Accountability.* (See vs. 18; Gal. 5:17.) "As the Scriptures constantly recognize the truth of these two things, so are they constantly united in Christian experience. Everyone feels that he cannot do the things that he would, yet is sensible that he is guilty for not doing them. Let any man test his power by the requisition to love God perfectly at all times. Alas! how entire our inability! Yet how deep our self-loathing and self-condemnation!" [HODGE]. (3) If the first sight of the Cross by the eye of faith kindles feelings never to be forgotten, and in one sense never to be repeated—like the first view of an enchanting landscape—the experimental discovery, in the latter stages of the Christian life, of its power to beat down and mortify inveterate corruption, to cleanse and heal from longcontinued backslidings and frightful inconsistencies, and so to triumph over all that threatens to destroy those for whom Christ died, as to bring them safe over the tempestuous seas of this life into the haven of eternal rest—is attended with yet more heart-affecting wonder draws forth deeper thankfulness, and issues in more exalted adoration of Him whose work Salvation is from first to last (vss. 24, 25). (4) It is sad when such topics as these are handled as mere questions of biblical interpretation or systematic theology. Our great apostle could not treat of them apart from personal experience, of which the facts of his own life and the feelings of his own soul furnished him with illustrations as lively as they were apposite. When one is unable to go far into the investigation of indwelling sin, without breaking out into an, "O wretched man that I am!" and cannot enter on the way of relief without exclaiming "I thank God through Jesus Christ our Lord," he will find his meditations rich in fruit to his own soul, and may expect, through Him who presides in all such matters, to kindle in his readers or hearers the like blessed emotions (vss. 24, 25). So be it even now, O Lord!

ADAM CLARKE

which he has of salvation "through Jesus Christ our Lord."

25. *I thank God through Jesus Christ.* Instead of *I thank God,* several excellent MSS., with the Vulgate, some copies of the Itala, and several of the fathers, read "the grace of God," or "the grace of our Lord Jesus Christ"; this is an answer to the almost despairing question in the preceding verse. The whole, therefore, may be read thus: "O wretched man that I am! who shall deliver me from the body of this death?" ANSWER—"The grace of God through our Lord Jesus Christ." Thus we find that a case of the kind described by the apostle in the preceding verses, whether it were his own before he was brought to the knowledge of Christ, particularly during the three days that he was at Damascus, without being able to eat or drink, in deep penitential sorrow, or whether he personates a Pharisaic yet conscientious Jew deeply concerned for his salvation—I say, we find that such a case can be relieved by the gospel of Christ only; or, in other words, that no scheme of redemption can be effectual to the salvation of any soul, whether Jew or Gentile, but that laid down in the gospel of Christ. *So then with the mind I myself serve the law of God.* That this clause contains the inference from the preceding train of argumentation appears evident from the *therefore* with which the apostle introduces it. As if he had said: "To conclude, the sum of what I have advanced concerning the power of sin in the carnal man and the utter insufficiency of all human means and legal observances to pardon sin and expel the corruption of the heart is this: that the very same person, the 'the same I,' while without the gospel, under the killing power of the law, will find in himself two opposite principles, the one subscribing to and approving the law of God and the other, notwithstanding, bringing him into captivity to sin. His 'inward man,' his rational powers and conscience, will assent to the justice and propriety of the requisitions of the law; and yet, notwithstanding this, his fleshly appetites, the 'law in his members,' will 'war against the law of his mind,' and continue, till he receives the gospel of Christ, to keep him in the galling captivity of sin and death."

CHAPTER 8 (MATTHEW HENRY)

Verses 1–9

I. The apostle here begins with one signal privilege of true Christians, and describes the character of those to whom it belongs: *There is therefore now no condemnation to those that are in Christ Jesus, v.* 1. This is his triumph after that melancholy complaint and conflict. The complaint he takes to himself, but humbly transfers the comfort to all true believers. It is the unspeakable privilege of all those that are in Christ Jesus that there is therefore now no condemnation to them. He does not say, "There is no accusation against them", for this there is; but the accusation is thrown out. He does not say, "There is nothing in them that deserves condemnation", for this there is, and they see it, and own it; but it shall not be their ruin. He does not say, "There is no cross, no affliction to them", for this there may be; but *no condemnation.* Now this arises from their being in Christ Jesus; by virtue of their union with him through faith they are thus secured. It is the undoubted character of all those who are so in Christ Jesus that *they walk not after the flesh but after the Spirit.* The character is given from their walk, not from any one particular act.

CHAPTER 8 (JAMIESON, FAUSSET, BROWN)

VSS. 1-39. CONCLUSION OF THE WHOLE ARGUMENT —THE GLORIOUS COMPLETENESS OF THEM THAT ARE IN CHRIST JESUS. In this surpassing chapter the several streams of the preceding argument meet and flow in one "river of the water of life, clear as crystal, proceeding out of the throne of God and of the Lamb," until it seems to lose itself in the ocean of a blissful eternity.

FIRST: *The Sanctification of Believers* (vss. 1-13). **1. There is therefore now . . .**—referring to the immediately preceding context [OLSHAUSEN, PHILIPPI, MEYER, ALFORD, etc.]. The subject with which ch. 7 concludes is still under consideration. The scope of the four opening verses is to show how "the law of sin and death" is deprived of its power to bring believers again into bondage, and how the holy law of God receives in them the homage of a living obedience [CALVIN, FRASER, PHILIPPI, MEYER, ALFORD, etc.]. **no condemnation to them which are in Christ Jesus**—As Christ, who "knew no sin," was, to all legal effects, "made sin for us," so are we, who believe in Him, to all legal effects, "made the righteousness of God in Him" (II Cor. 5:21); and thus, one with Him in the divine reckoning, there is to such "NO CONDEMNATION." (Cf. John 3:18; 5:24; ch. 5:18, 19.) But this is no mere legal *arrangement:* it is a union in *life;* believers, through the indwelling of Christ's Spirit in them, having one life with Him, as truly as the head and the members of the same body have one life. **who walk not after the flesh, but after the Spirit**—The evidence of MSS. seems to show that this clause formed no part of the original text of this verse, but that the first part of it was early introduced, and the second later, from vs. 4, probably as an explanatory comment, and to make the transition to vs. 2 easier.

CHAPTER 8 (ADAM CLARKE)

1. *There is therefore now no condemnation.* To do justice to Paul's reasoning, this chapter must be read in the closest connection with the preceding. There we have seen the unavailing struggles of an awakened Jew, who sought pardon and holiness from that law which he was conscious he had broken; and in which he could find no provision for pardon, and no power to sanctify. This conviction having brought him to the very brink of despair, and being on the point of giving up all hope, he hears of redemption by Jesus Christ, thanks God for the prospect he has of salvation, applies for and receives it, and now magnifies God for the unspeakable gift of which he has been made a partaker. Those who restrain the word *now,* so as to indicate by it the gospel dispensation only, do not take in the whole of the apostle's meaning. The apostle has not been dealing in general matters only, but also in those which are particular. He has not been pointing out merely the difference between the two dispensations, the Mosaic and the Christian; but he marks out the state of a penitent under the former and that of a believer under the latter. The last chapter closed with an account of his salvation. The *now,* therefore, in the text must refer more to the happy transition from darkness to light, from condemnation to pardon, which this believer now enjoys, than to the Christian dispensation taking the place of the Jewish economy. *Who walk not after the flesh.* In this one verse we find the power and virtue of the gospel scheme. It pardons and sanctifies; the Jewish law could do neither. By faith in our Lord Jesus Christ the penitent, condemned by the law, is pardoned; the carnal man, laboring under the overpowering influence of the sin of his nature, is sanctified. He is first freely justified; he feels no condemnation. He is fully sanctified; he walks not after the flesh, but after the spirit. This last clause is wanting in the principal MSS.,

MATTHEW HENRY

II. How we come by this great privilege, and how we may answer this character.

1. How we come by these privileges—the privilege of justification, the privilege of sanctification. The law could not do it, *v.* 3. It could neither justify nor sanctify. The law made nothing perfect: *It was weak.* Yet that weakness was not through any defect in the law, but *through the flesh,* through the corruption of human nature. In case of failure, the law, as a covenant of works, made no provision, and so left us as it found us. *The law of the Spirit of life in Christ Jesus* does it, *v.* 2. The covenant of grace in Christ is a treasury of merit and grace, and thence we receive pardon and a new nature, *are freed from the law of sin and death,* both from the guilt and power of sin. We are under another covenant, under the *law of the Spirit,* the law that gives the Spirit, spiritual life to qualify us for eternal.

The foundation of this freedom is laid in Christ's undertaking for us, of which he speaks, *v.* 3, *God sending his own Son.* When the law failed, God provided another method. Christ comes to do that which the law could not do.

The best exposition of this verse we have Heb. x. 1-10. (1) How Christ appeared: *In the likeness of sinful flesh.* Not sinful, but in the likeness of that flesh. He took upon him that nature which was corrupt, though perfectly abstracted from the corruptions of it. It was great condescension that he who was God should be made in the likeness of flesh; but much greater that he who was holy should be made in the likeness of sinful flesh. *And for sin.* God sent him *in the likeness of sinful flesh, and as a sacrifice for sin.*

(2) What was done by this appearance of his: Sin *was condemned.* For all that are Christ's both the damning and the domineering power of sin is broken. Though it live and remain, its life in the saints is still but like that of a condemned malefactor. The condemning of sin saved the sinner from condemnation. Christ was made sin for us (2 Cor. v. 21). When he was condemned, sin was condemned in the flesh of Christ. So was satisfaction made to divine justice, and way made for the salvation of the sinner.

JAMIESON, FAUSSET, BROWN

2. For the law of the Spirit of life in Christ Jesus hath made me free—rather, 'freed me'—referring to the time of his conversion, when first he believed—**from the law of sin and death**—It is the Holy Ghost who is here called "the Spirit of *life,*" as opening up in the souls of believers a fountain of spiritual life (see on John 7:38, 39); just as He is called "the Spirit of truth," as "guiding them into all truth" (John 16:13), and "the Spirit of counsel and might, the spirit of knowledge and the fear of the Lord" (Isa. 11:2), as the inspirer of these qualities. And He is called "the Spirit of life *in Christ Jesus,*" because it is as members of Christ that He takes up His abode in believers, who in consequence of this have one life with their Head. And as the word "*law*" here has the same meaning as in ch. 7:23, namely, 'an inward principle of action, operating with the fixedness and regularity of a law,' it thus appears that "*the law of the Spirit of life in Christ Jesus*" here means, 'that new principle of action which the Spirit of Christ has opened up within us —the law of our new being.' This "*sets us free,*" as soon as it takes possession of our inner man, "from the law of sin and death" i.e., from the enslaving power of that corrupt principle which carries death in its bosom. The "strong man armed" is overpowered by the "stronger than he"; the weaker principle is dethroned and expelled by the more powerful; the principle of spiritual life prevails against and brings into captivity the principle of spiritual death—"leading captivity captive." If this be the apostle's meaning, the whole verse is to this effect: That the triumph of believers over their inward corruption, through the power of Christ's Spirit in them, *proves* them to be in Christ Jesus, and as such absolved from condemnation. But this is now explained more fully. **3, 4. For what the law could not do . . .**—a difficult and much controverted verse. But it is clearly, we think, the law's inability to *free us from the dominion of sin* that the apostle has in view; as has partly appeared already (see on vs. 2), and will more fully appear presently. The law could irritate our sinful nature into more virulent action, as we have seen in ch. 7:5, but it could not secure its own fulfilment. How that is accomplished comes now to be shown. **in that it was weak through the flesh**—i.e., having to address itself to us through a corrupt nature, too strong to be influenced by mere commands and threatenings. **God . . .**—The sentence is somewhat imperfect in its structure, which occasions a certain obscurity. The meaning is, that *whereas* the law was powerless to secure its own fulfilment for the reason given, God took the method now to be described for attaining that end. **sending**—'having sent'—**his own Son**—This and similar expressions plainly imply that Christ was God's "OWN SON" *before* He was sent—that is, in His own proper Person, and independently of His mission and appearance in the flesh (see on ch. 8:32; Gal. 4:4); and if so, He not only has the *very nature* of God, even as a son of his father, but is essentially *of* the Father, though in a sense too mysterious for any language of ours properly to define (see on ch. 1-4). And this peculiar relationship is put forward here to *enhance the greatness* and *define the nature* of the relief provided, as coming *from beyond the precincts of sinful humanity altogether,* yea, *immediately from the Godhead itself.* **in the likeness of sinful flesh**—lit., "of the flesh of sin"; a very remarkable and pregnant expression. He was made in the reality of our flesh, but only in the *likeness* of its sinful condition. He took our nature as it is in us, compassed with infirmities, with nothing to distinguish Him as man from sinful men, save that He was without sin. Nor does this mean that He took our nature with all its properties save one; for sin is *no property of humanity at all,* but only the disordered state of our souls, as the fallen family of Adam; a disorder affecting, indeed, and overspreading our entire nature, but still purely *our own.* **and for sin**—lit., 'and about sin'; i.e., 'on the business of sin.' The expression is purposely a general one, because the design was not to speak of Christ's mission to *atone* for sin, but in virtue of that atonement to *destroy its dominion* and *extirpate it altogether* from believers. We think it wrong, therefore, to render the words (as in *Margin*) 'by a sacrifice for sin' (suggested by the language of the LXX and approved by CALVIN, etc.); for this sense is too definite, and makes the idea of *expiation* more prominent than it is. **condemned sin**—'condemned it to *lose its power* over men [BEZA, BENGEL, FRASER, MEYER, THOLUCK, PHILIPPI, ALFORD]. In this glorious sense our Lord says of His approaching death (John 12:31), "Now is the *judgment* of this world; now shall the prince of this world be *cast out*", and

ADAM CLARKE

versions, and fathers. It was probably to make the thing more obvious that this explanatory clause was added by some copyist, for it does not appear to have made an original part of the text; and it is most likely that it was inserted here from the fourth verse.

2. *For the law of the Spirit of life.* The gospel of the grace of Christ, which is not only a law or rule of life, but affords that sovereign energy by which guilt is removed from the conscience, the power of sin broken, and its polluting influence removed from the heart. Most people allow that Paul is here speaking of his own state; and this state is so totally different from that described in the preceding chapter that it is absolutely impossible that they should have been the state of the same being at one and the same time.

3. *For what the law could not do.* The law could not pardon; the law could not sanctify; the law could not dispense with its own requisitions; it is the rule of righteousness, and therefore must condemn unrighteousness. This is its unalterable nature. Had there been perfect obedience to its dictates, instead of condemning, it would have applauded and rewarded; but as the *flesh,* the carnal and rebellious principle, had prevailed, and transgression had taken place, it was rendered *weak,* inefficient to undo this work of the flesh, and bring the sinner into a state of pardon and acceptance with God.

God sending his own Son in the likeness of sinful flesh. Did that which the law could not do; i.e., purchased pardon for the sinner, and brought every believer into the favor of God. And this is effected by the incarnation of Christ. He in whom dwelt the fullness of the Godhead bodily took upon Him the *likeness of sinful flesh,* that is, a human body like ours, but not sinful as ours; *and for sin,* "and as a sacrifice for sin" (this is the sense of the word in a multitude of places); *condemned sin in the flesh*—condemned that to death and destruction which had condemned us to both.

Condemned sin in the flesh. The design and object of the incarnation and sacrifice of Christ was to condemn sin, to have it executed and destroyed; not to tolerate it as some think, or to render it subservient to the purposes of His grace, as others; but to annihilate its power, guilt, and being in the soul of a believer.

MATTHEW HENRY

(3) The happy effect of this upon us (*v.* 4): *That the righteousness of the law might be fulfilled in us.* A righteousness of satisfaction for the breach of the law is fulfilled by the imputation of Christ's perfect righteousness. A righteousness of obedience to the law is fulfilled in us, when by the Spirit the law of love is written upon the heart, and that love is the fulfilling of the law, *ch.* xiii. 10. *Us who walk not after the flesh, but after the Spirit.* This is the description of all those that are interested in this privilege.

2. How we may answer to this character, *v.* 5, &c. (1) By looking to our minds. By examining what we mind, the things of the flesh or the things of the spirit. The favour of God, the welfare of the soul, the concerns of eternity, are the things of the Spirit. The man is as the mind is. The mind is the forge of thoughts. Which way do the thoughts move with most pleasure? The mind is the seat of wisdom. Whether are we more wise for the world or for our souls? *They savour the things of the flesh;* so the word is rendered, Matt. xvi. 23. It is a great matter what truths, what tidings, what comforts, we do most relish. Now, to caution us against this carnal-mindedness, he shows the great misery of it, and compares it with the unspeakable comfort of spiritual-mindedness. [1] It is death, *v.* 6. It is the death of the soul; for it is its alienation from God, in union and communion with whom the life of the soul consists. A carnal soul is a dead soul, dead as a soul can die. Death includes all misery; carnal souls are miserable souls. But to be *spiritually minded* is *life and peace.* A sanctified soul is a living soul, and that life is peace; it is a very comfortable life. It is life and peace in the other world, as well as in this. Spiritual-mindedness is eternal life and peace begun. [2] It is enmity to God (*v.* 7) and this is worse than the former. The former speaks the carnal sinner a dead man, but this speaks him a devil of a man. It is not only the alienation of the soul from God, but the opposition of the soul against God. To prove this, he urges that *it is not subject to the law of God, neither indeed can be.* The holiness of the law of God, and the unholiness of the carnal mind, are as irreconcilable as light and darkness. The carnal man may, by the power of divine grace, be made subject to the law of God, but the *carnal mind* never can; this must be broken and expelled. Hence he infers (*v.* 8), *Those that are in the flesh cannot please God.* Pleasing God is our highest end, of which those that are in the flesh cannot but fall short; they cannot please him, nay, they cannot but displease him.

(2) By enquiring whether we have the Spirit of God and Christ, or not (*v.* 9): *You are not in the flesh, but in the Spirit.* It denotes our being overcome and subdued by one of these principles. Now the great question is whether we are in the flesh or in the Spirit; and how may we come to know it? Why, by enquiring whether the Spirit of God dwell in us. The Spirit visits many that are unregenerate; but in all that are sanctified he dwells. Shall we put this question to our own hearts, Who dwells, who rules, who keeps house, here? To this he subjoins a general rule of trial: *If any man has not the Spirit of Christ, he is none of his.* To be Christ's is a privilege and honour which many pretend to that have no part nor lot in the matter. None are his but those that have his Spirit; that are spirited as he was spirited. The frame and disposition of our souls must be conformable to Christ's pattern. That are actuated and guided by the Holy Spirit of God. Having the Spirit of Christ is the same with having the Spirit of God to dwell in us. All that are actuated by the Spirit of God as their rule are conformable to the spirit of Christ as their pattern.

Two more excellent benefits, which belong to true believers.

I. Life. The happiness is not barely a negative happiness, not to be condemned; but it is positive (*v.* 10, 11): *If Christ be in you.* Now we are here told what becomes of the bodies and souls of those in whom Christ is.

1. We cannot say but that *the body is dead*; it is a frail, mortal, dying body. In the midst of life we are in death: be our bodies ever so strong, they are as good as dead, and this *because of sin.* It is sin that kills the body. Methinks, were there no other argument, love to our bodies should make us hate sin, because it is such an enemy to our bodies.

2. But the spirit, that is life. The life of the saint lies in the soul, while the life of the sinner goes no further than the body. When the body dies *the spirit is life.* Death to the saints is but the freeing of the heaven-born spirit from the clog and load of this body, that it may be fit to partake of eternal life. And this *because of righteousness.* The righteousness

JAMIESON, FAUSSET, BROWN

again (see on John 16:11), "When He (the Spirit) shall come, He shall convince the world of . . . judgment, because the prince of this world is *judged,*" i.e., condemned to let go his hold of men, who, through the Cross, shall be emancipated into the liberty and power to be holy. **in the flesh**—i.e., in human nature, henceforth set free from the grasp of sin. **That the righteousness of the law**—'the righteous demand', 'the requirement' [ALFORD], or 'the precept' of the law; for it is not precisely the word so often used in this Epistle to denote 'the righteousness which justifies' (ch. 1:17; 3:21; 4:5, 6; 5:17, 18, 21), but another form of the same word, intended to express the *enactment* of the law, meaning here, we believe, the practical obedience which the law calls for. **might be fulfilled in us**—or, as we say, '*realized* in us.' **who walk**—the most ancient expression of *the bent of one's life,* whether in the direction of good or of evil (Gen. 48:15; Ps. 1:1; Isa. 2:5; Mic. 4:5; Eph. 4:17; I John 1:6, 7). **not after**—i.e., according to the dictates of—**the flesh, but after the spirit**—From vs. 9 it would seem that what is more immediately intended by "the spirit" here is *our own mind* as renewed and actuated by the Holy Ghost. **5. For they that are after the flesh**—i.e., under the influence of the fleshly principle—**do mind**—give their attention to (Phil. 3:19)—**the things of the flesh . . .**—Men must be under the predominating influence of one or other of these two principles, and, according as the one or the other has the mastery, will be the complexion of their life, the character of their actions. **6. For**—a mere particle of transition here [THOLUCK], like 'but' or 'now.' **to be carnally minded**—lit., 'the mind' or 'minding of the flesh' (*Margin*); i.e., the pursuit of fleshly ends. **is death**—not only 'ends in' [ALFORD, etc.], but even now 'is'; carrying death into its bosom, so that such are "dead while they live" (I Tim. 5:6; Eph. 2:1, 5) [PHILIPPI]. **but to be spiritually minded**—'the mind' or 'minding of the spirit'; i.e., the pursuit of spiritual objects. **is life and peace**—not "life" only, in contrast with the "death" that is in the other pursuit, but "peace"; it is the very element of the soul's deepest repose and true bliss. **7. Because the carnal mind is enmity against God**—The desire and pursuit of carnal ends is a state of enmity to God, wholly incompatible with true life and peace in the soul. **for it is not subject**—'doth not submit itself'—**to the law of God, neither indeed can be**—In such a state of mind there neither is nor can be the least subjection to the law of God. Many things may be done which the law requires, but nothing either is or can be done *because* God's law requires it, or purely to please God. **8. So then**—nearly equivalent to 'And so.' **they that are in**—and, therefore, under the government of—**the flesh cannot please God**—having no obediential principle, no desire to please Him. **9. But ye are not in the flesh, but in the spirit, if so be that the Spirit of God dwell in you**—This does not mean, 'if the *disposition* or *mind* of God dwell in you; but 'if *the Holy Ghost* dwell in you' (see I Cor. 6:11, 19; 3:16, etc.). (It thus appears that to be "in the spirit" means here to be under the dominion of *our own renewed mind;* because the indwelling of God's Spirit is given as the evidence that we are "in the spirit.") **Now**—'But'—**if any man have not the Spirit of Christ**—Again, this does not mean 'the *disposition* or *mind* of Christ,' but the Holy Ghost; here called "the Spirit of Christ," just as He is called "the Spirit of life in Christ Jesus" (see on vs. 2). It is as "the Spirit of Christ" that the Holy Ghost takes possession of believers, introducing into them all the gracious, dovelike disposition which dwelt in Him (Matt. 3:16; John 3:34). Now if any man's heart be void, not of such dispositions, but of the blessed Author of them, "the Spirit of Christ"—**he is none of his**—even though intellectually convinced of the truth of Christianity, and in a general sense influence by its spirit. Sharp, solemn statement this! **10, 11. And if Christ be in you**—by His indwelling Spirit in virtue of which we have *one life* with him. **the body**—'the body indeed.' **is dead because of**—'by reason of'—**sin; but the spirit is life because**—or, 'by reason'—**of righteousness**—The word 'indeed,' which the original requires, is of the nature of a concession—'I grant you that the body is dead . . . and so far redemption is incomplete, *but . . .*'; i.e., 'If Christ be in you by His indwelling Spirit, though your "bodies" have to pass through the stage of "death" in consequence of the first Adam's "sin," your spirit is instinct with new and undying "life," brought in by the "righteousness" of the second Adam' [THOLUCK, MEYER, and ALFORD in part, but only HODGE entirely]. **But**—'And'—**if the Spirit of him that raised up Jesus from the dead dwell in you**—i.e., 'If He

ADAM CLARKE

4. *That the righteousness of the law might be fulfilled in us.* That the guilt might be pardoned through the merit of that sacrifice; and that we might be enabled, by the power of His own grace and Spirit, to walk in newness of life; loving God with all our heart, soul, mind, and strength, and our neighbor as ourselves. And thus the righteousness, the spirit, design, and purpose of the law are fulfilled in us, through the *strength of the Spirit of Christ,* which is here put in opposition to *the weakness of the law through the flesh.*

5. *For they that are after the flesh.* Here is the great distinction between Jews and genuine Christians: the former are *after the flesh,* are under the power of the carnal, rebellious principle; and consequently *mind,* "relish," *the things of the flesh,* the things which appertain merely to the present life, having no relish for spiritual and eternal things. *But they that are after the Spirit.* They who are regenerated, who are born of the Spirit, being redeemed from the influence and law of the carnal mind; these relish *the things of the Spirit*—they are spiritually minded, and pass through things temporal, so as not to lose the things which are eternal.

6. *For to be carnally minded is death.* To live under the influence of the carnal mind is to live in the state of condemnation, and consequently liable to death eternal; whereas, on the contrary, he who is *spiritually minded* has the *life* and *peace* of God in his soul, and is in full prospect of life eternal.

7. *Because the carnal mind is enmity against God.* Because it is a *carnal mind,* and relishes earthly and sinful things, and lives in opposition to the pure and holy law of God, therefore, it *is enmity against God;* it is irreconcilable and implacable hatred. *It is not subject to the law of God.* It will come under no obedience, for it is sin, and the very principle of rebellion; and therefore it cannot be subject, nor subjected, for it is essential to sin to show itself in rebellion; and when it ceases to rebel, it ceases to be sin. From this we learn that the design of God in the economy of the gospel is not to weaken, curtail, or lay the carnal principle in bonds, but to destroy it. As it is *not subject,* and cannot be subject, *to the law of God,* it must be destroyed, else it will continue to rebel against God.

8. *So then.* Because this carnal mind is enmity against God, *they that are in the flesh,* who are under the power of the workings of this carnal mind (which every soul is that has not received redemption in the blood of the Lamb), *cannot please God,* because of the rebellious workings of this principle of rebellion and hatred. And if they cannot *please* God, they must be displeasing to Him, and consequently in the broad road to final perdition.

9. *But ye are not in the flesh.* You Christians, who have believed in Christ Jesus as the Sin Offering which has condemned sin in the flesh, and having been justified by faith and made partakers of the Holy Spirit, are enabled to walk in newness of life. *If so be that the Spirit of God dwell in you.* Or "seeing that" the Spirit of God dwelleth in you. The *flesh,* the sinful principle, dwelt in them before, and its motions were the proofs of its indwelling; but now the Spirit dwells in them, and His testimony in their conscience and His powerful operations in their hearts are the proofs of His indwelling.

10. *And if Christ be in you.* This is the criterion by which you may judge of the state of grace in which you stand. If Christ dwell in your hearts by faith, *the body is dead because of sin,* "in reference to sin"; the members of your body no more perform the work of sin than the body of a dead man does the functions of natural life. Or the apostle may mean that although *because of sin* the life of man is forfeited and the sentence, "Dust thou art, and unto dust shalt thou return," must be fulfilled on every human being, until the judgment of the great day, yet their souls being quickened by the indwelling Spirit of Christ, which enables them to live a life of righteousness, they receive a full assurance that their bodies, which are now condemned to death because of sin, shall be raised again to a life of immortal glory.

MATTHEW HENRY

of Christ imputed to them secures the soul from death; the righteousness of Christ inherent in them, preserves it, and at death elevates it, and makes it meet to partake of the inheritance of the saints in light.

3. There is a life reserved too for the poor body at last: *He shall also quicken your mortal bodies, v.* 11. The body shall be reunited to the soul, and clothed with a glory agreeable to it. Two great assurances of the resurrection of the body are mentioned: (1) The resurrection of Christ: He *that raised up Christ from the dead shall also quicken.* Christ rose as the forerunner of all the saints, 1 Cor. xv. 20. It is in the virtue of Christ's resurrection that we shall rise. (2) The indwelling of the Spirit. The same Spirit that raiseth the soul now will raise the body shortly: *By his Spirit that dwelleth in you.* The Spirit, breathing upon dead and dry bones, will make them live, and the saints even in their flesh shall see God. Hence the apostle infers how much it is our duty to walk not after the flesh, but after the Spirit, *v.* 12, 13. Two motives he mentions here: [1] We are not debtors to the flesh. We are indeed bound to clothe, and feed, and take care of the body, as a servant to the soul in the service of God, but no further. We are not debtors to it. We are debtors to Christ and to the Spirit: there we owe our all. See 1 Cor. vi. 19, 20. [2] Consider what will be at the end of the way. *If you live after the flesh, you shall die;* that is, die eternally. Dying indeed is the soul's dying: the death of the saints is but a sleep. But, on the other hand, *You shall live,* that is the true life: *If you through the Spirit mortify the deeds of the body.* We cannot do it without the Spirit working it in us, and the Spirit will not do it without our doing our endeavour. We are put upon this dilemma, either to displease the body or destroy the soul.

II. The *Spirit of adoption v.* 14–16.

1. All that are Christ's are taken into the relation of children to God, *v.* 14. (1) Their property: They are *led by the Spirit of God,* not driven as beasts, but led as rational creatures. It is the undoubted character of all true believers that they are led by the Spirit of God. They do in their obedience follow that guidance, and are sweetly led into all truth and all duty. (2) Their privilege: *They are the sons of God,* owned and loved by him as his children.

2. And those that are the sons of God have the Spirit,

(1) To work in them the disposition of children. *You have not received the spirit of bondage again to fear, v.* 15. Understand it, *First,* Of that spirit of bondage which the Old Testament church was under, by reason of the darkness of that dispensation. You are not under that dispensation, you have not received that spirit. *Secondly,* Of that spirit of bondage which many of the saints themselves were under at their conversion. Then the Spirit himself was to the saints a spirit of bondage: "But," says the apostle, "with you this is over."

JAMIESON, FAUSSET, BROWN

dwell in you as the Spirit of the Christ-raising One,' or, 'in all the *resurrection-power* which He put forth in raising Jesus.' **he that raised up Christ from the dead**—Observe the change of name from JESUS, as the historical Individual whom God raised from the dead, to CHRIST, the same Individual, considered as the Lord and Head of all His members, or of redeemed Humanity [ALFORD]. **shall also quicken**—rather, 'shall quicken even'—**your mortal bodies by**—the true reading appears to be 'by reason of'—**his Spirit that dwelleth in you**—; 'Your bodies indeed are not exempt from the death which sin brought in; but your spirits even now have in them an undying life, and if the Spirit of Him that raised up Jesus from the dead dwell in you, even these bodies of yours, though they yield to the last enemy and the dust of them return to the dust as it was, shall yet experience the same resurrection as that of their living Head, in virtue of the indwelling of the same Spirit in you that quickened Him.' **12, 13. Therefore, brethren, we are debtors, not to the flesh, to live after the flesh**—'Once we were sold under sin (ch. 7:14); but now that we have been set free from that hard master and become servants to Righteousness (ch. 6:22), we owe nothing to the flesh, we disown its unrighteous claims and are deaf to its imperious demands.' Glorious sentiment! **For if ye live after the flesh, ye shall die**—in the sense of ch. 6:21—**but if ye through the Spirit do mortify the deeds of the body**—see on ch. 7:23—**ye shall live**—in the sense of ch. 6:22. The apostle is not satisfied with assuring them that they are under no *obligations* to the flesh, to hearken to its suggestions, without reminding them where it will end if they do; and he uses the word "mortify" (put to death) as a kind of play upon the word "die" just before. 'If *ye* do not kill sin, *it* will kill you. But he tempers this by the bright alternative, that if they do, through the Spirit, mortify the deeds of the body, such a course will infallibly terminate in "life" everlasting. And this leads the apostle into a new line of thought, opening into his final subject, the "glory" awaiting the justified believer. Note (1) "There can be no safety, no holiness, no happiness, to those who are out of Christ: No *safety,* because all such are under the condemnation of the law (vs. 1); no *holiness,* because such only as are united to Christ have the spirit of Christ (vs. 9); no *happiness,* because to be 'carnally minded is death' (vs. 6)' [HODGE]. (2) The sanctification of believers, as it has its whole foundation in the atoning death, so it has its living spring in the indwelling of the Spirit of Christ (vss. 2-4). (3) "The bent of the thoughts, affections, and pursuits, is the only decisive test of character (vs. 5)" [HODGE]. (4) No human refinement of the carnal mind will make it spiritual, or compensate for the absence of spirituality. "Flesh" and "spirit" are essentially and unchangeably opposed; nor can the carnal mind, as such, be brought into real subjection to the law of God (vss. 5-7). Hence (5) the estrangement of God and the sinner is mutual. For as the sinner's state of mind is "enmity against God" (vs. 7), so in this state he "cannot please God" (vs. 8). (6) Since the Holy Ghost is, in the same breath, called indiscriminately "the Spirit of God," "the Spirit of Christ," and "Christ" Himself (as an indwelling life in believers), the *essential unity* and yet Personal *distinctness* of the Father, the Son, and the Holy Ghost, in the one adorable Godhead must be believed, as the only consistent explanation of such language (vss. 9-11). (7) The consciousness of spiritual life in our renewed souls is a glorious assurance of resurrection life in the body also, in virtue of the same quickening Spirit whose inhabitation we already enjoy (vs. 11). (8) Whatever professions of spiritual life men may make, it remains eternally true that "if we live after the flesh we shall die," and only "if we through the Spirit do mortify the deeds of the body we shall live" (vs. 13, and cf. Gal. 6:7, 8; Eph. 5:6; Phil. 3:18, 19; I John 3:7, 8).

SECOND: *The Sonship of Believers--Their future Inheritance—The Intercession of the Spirit for Them* (vss. 14-27). **14. For as many as are led by the Spirit of God, they . . .**—'these are sons of God'. Hitherto the apostle has spoken of the Spirit simply as a *power* through which believers mortify sin: now he speaks of Him as a gracious, loving *Guide,* whose "leading"—enjoyed by all in whom is the Spirit of God's dear Son—shows that they also are "sons of God." **15. For . . .**—'For ye received not (at the time of your conversion) the spirit of bondage,' i.e., 'The spirit ye received was not a spirit of bondage.' **again**—gendering—**to fear**—as under the law which "worketh wrath", i.e., 'Such was your condition before ye believed, living in legal bondage, haunted with incessant forebodings under a

ADAM CLARKE

11. *But if the Spirit.* **This verse confirms the** sense given to the preceding. He who here receives the grace and Spirit of Christ, and continues to live under its influence a life of obedience to the divine will, shall have a resurrection.

12. *Therefore, brethren.* Dr. Taylor is of opinion that the apostle, having spoken separately to both Jews and Gentiles concerning holiness and the obligations to it, now addresses himself to both conjointly, and, (1) Draws the general conclusion from all his arguments upon this subject, v. 12. (2) Proves the validity of their claims to eternal life, vv. 14-17. (3) And as the affair of suffering persecution was a great stumbling block to the Jews, and might very much discourage the Gentiles, he introduces it to the best advantage, v. 17, and advances several arguments to fortify their minds under all trials: as (*a*) That they suffered with Christ; (*b*) In order to be glorified with Him in a manner which will infinitely compensate all sufferings, vv. 17-18. (*c*) All mankind are under various pressures, longing for a better state, vv. 19-22. (*d*) Many of the most eminent Christians are in the same distressed condition, v. 23. (*e*) According to the plan of the gospel, we are to be brought to glory after a course of patience exercised in a variety of trials, vv. 24-25. (*f*) The Spirit of God will supply patience to every upright soul under persecution and suffering, vv. 26-27. (*g*) All things, even the severest trials, shall work together for their good, v. 28. And this he proves by giving us a view of the several steps which the wisdom and goodness of God have settled in order to our complete salvation, vv. 29-30. Thence he passes to the affair of our perseverance, concerning which he concludes, from the whole of his preceding arguments, that as we are brought into a state of pardon by the free grace of God, through the death of Christ, who is now our Mediator in heaven, no possible cause, providing we continue to love and serve God, shall be able to pervert our minds or separate us from His love in Christ Jesus, vv. 31-39. *Therefore* is the grand inference from all that he has been arguing in relation to sanctity of life, both to the Gentiles, chap. vi, and to the Jews, chaps. vii and viii to this verse, where I suppose he begins to address himself to both, in a body, to the end of the chapter.

13. *But if ye through the Spirit*—if you seek that grace and spiritual help which the gospel of Christ furnishes—resist, and, by resisting, *mortify the deeds of the* flesh, against which the law gave you no assistance, *ye shall live* a life of faith, love, and holy obedience here, and a life of glory hereafter.

14. *For as many as are led by the Spirit.* No man who has not divine assistance can either find the way to heaven or walk in it when found. As Christ by His sacrificial offering has opened the kingdom of God to all believers, and as a Mediator transacts the concerns of their Kingdom before the throne, so the Spirit of God is the great Agent here below to enlighten, quicken, strengthen, and guide the true disciples of Christ; and all that are born of this Spirit are led and guided by Him, and none can pretend to be the children of God who are not thus guided.

15. *Ye have not received the spirit of bondage.* All that were under the law were under **bondage to its rites and ceremonies; and as,** through the prevalence of that corrupt nature with which every human being is polluted, and to remove which the law gave no assistance, they were often transgressing, consequently they had forfeited their lives, and were continually, through fear of death, subject to bondage, Heb. ii. 15. The believers in Christ Jesus were brought from under that law and from under its condemnation, and consequently were freed from its bondage.

MATTHEW HENRY

But you *have received the Spirit of adoption*. It is God's prerogative, when he adopts, to give a spirit of adoption—the nature of children. A sanctified soul bears the image of God, as the child bears the image of the father.

Whereby we cry, Abba, Father. Praying is here called *crying*. Children that cannot speak vent their desires by crying. Now, the Spirit teaches us in prayer to come to God as a Father. And why both, *Abba, Father?* Because Christ said so in prayer (Mark xiv. 36), *Abba, Father*. It denotes an affectionate endearing importunity. Little children, begging of their parents, can say little but *Father, Father*, and that is rhetoric enough. It also denotes that the adoption is common both to Jews and Gentiles.

(2) To witness to the relation of children, *v.* 16. *Beareth witness with our spirit*. Many speak peace to themselves to whom the God of heaven does not speak peace. But those that are sanctified have God's Spirit witnessing with their spirits. This testimony is always agreeable to the written word, and is therefore always grounded upon sanctification. The Spirit witnesses to none the privileges of children who have not the nature and disposition of children.

Verses 17-25

A fourth happiness of believers, namely, a title to the future glory. *If children, then heirs*, *v.* 17. In earthly inheritances this rule does not hold, only the first-born are heirs. Heaven is an inheritance that all the saints are heirs to. They do not come to it by any merit of their own; but as heirs, purely by the act of God. Their present state is a state of education and preparation for the inheritance. 1. *Heirs of God*. The Lord himself is the portion of the saints' inheritance. The vision of God and the fruition of God make up the inheritance the saints are heirs to. 2. *Joint-heirs with Christ*. True believers *shall inherit all things*. Those that now partake of the Spirit of Christ, as his brethren, shall partake of his glory. Lord, what is man, that thou shouldst thus magnify him! Now this future glory is the reward of present sufferings, the accomplishment of present hopes.

JAMIESON, FAUSSET, BROWN

sense of unpardoned sin. But it was not to perpetuate that wretched state that ye received the Spirit.'

but ye have received—'ye received'—**the spirit of adoption. whereby**—rather, 'wherein'—**we cry, Abba, Father**—The word "cry" is emphatic, expressing the spontaneousness, the strength, and the exuberance of the final emotions. In Galatians 4:6 this cry is said to proceed from *the Spirit* in us, drawing forth the filial exclamation in our hearts. Here, it is said to proceed from *our own hearts* under the vitalizing energy of the Spirit, as the very element of the new life in believers (cf. Matt. 10:19, 20; and see on vs. 4). "Abba" is the *Syro-Chaldaic* word for "Father"; and the *Greek* word for that is added, not surely to tell the reader that both mean the same thing, but for the same reason which drew both words from the lips of Christ Himself during his agony in the garden (Mark 14:36). He, doubtless, loved to utter His Father's name in both the accustomed forms; beginning with His cherished mother tongue, and adding that of the learned. In this view the use of both words here has a charming simplicity and warmth.

16. The Spirit itself—It should be 'Himself' (see on vs. 26). **beareth witness with our spirit, that we are the children**—'are children'—**of God**—The testimony of our own spirit is borne in that cry of *conscious sonship*, "Abba, Father"; but we are not therein alone; for the Holy Ghost within us, yea, even in that very cry which it is His to draw forth, sets His own distinct seal to ours; and thus, "in the mouth of two witnesses" the thing is established. The apostle had before called us "*sons* of God," referring to our *adoption*; here the word changes to "children," referring to our *new birth*. The one expresses the *dignity* to which we are *admitted;* the other the *new life* which we *receive*. The latter is more suitable here; because a son by *adoption* might not be heir of the property, whereas a son by *birth* certainly is, and this is what the apostle is now coming to.

17. And if children, then heirs—'heirs also'. **heirs of God**—of' our Father's kingdom. **and joint-heirs with Christ**—as the "First-born among many brethren" (vs. 29), and as "Heir of all things."

ADAM CLARKE

But ye have received the Spirit of adoption. You are brought into the family of God by adoption; and the Agent that brought you into this family is the Holy Spirit; and this very Spirit continues to witness to you the grace in which you stand, by enabling you to call God your Father, with the utmost filial confidence and affection. *The Spirit of adoption*. Adoption was an act frequent among the ancient Hebrews, Greeks, and Romans, by which a person was taken out of one family and incorporated with another. Persons of property, who had no children of their own, adopted those of another family. The child thus adopted ceased to belong to his own family and was in every respect bound to the person who had adopted him, as if he were his own child, and in consequence of the death of his adopting father he possessed his estates. If a person after he had adopted a child happened to have children of his own, then the estate was equally divided between the adopted and real children. The Romans had regular forms of law by which all these matters were settled. *Whereby we cry, Abba, Father*. It has been remarked that slaves were not permitted to use the term *Abba*, father, or *Imma*, mother, in accosting their masters and mistresses. And from this some suppose that the apostle intimates that being now brought from under the spirit of bondage, in which they durst not call God their *Father*, they are not only brought into a new state, but have got that language which is peculiar to that state. Some have supposed that the apostle, by using the Syriac and Greek words which express *Father*, shows the union of Jewish and Gentile believers in those devotions which were dictated by a filial spirit. Others have thought that these were the first words which those generally uttered who were made partakers of the Holy Spirit. It is enough to know that it was the language of their sonship; and that it expressed the clear assurance they had of being received into the divine favor, the affection and gratitude they felt for this extraordinary blessing and their complete readiness to come under the laws and regulations of the family, and to live in the spirit of obedience.

16. *The Spirit itself beareth witness with our spirit*. "That same Spirit," the Spirit of adoption; that is, the Spirit who witnesses this adoption; which can be no other than the Holy Ghost himself, and certainly cannot mean any disposition or affection of mind which the adopted person may feel. *With our spirit*. In our understanding, the place or recipient of light and information, and the place or faculty to which such information can properly be brought. This is done that we may have the highest possible evidence of the work which God has wrought. As the window is the proper medium to let the light of the sun into our apartments, so the understanding is the proper medium of conveying the Spirit's influence to the soul. We therefore have the utmost evidence of the fact of our adoption which we can possibly have; we have the word and Spirit of God, and the word sealed on our spirit by the Spirit of God. And this is not a momentary influx. If we take care to walk with God and not grieve the Holy Spirit, we shall have an abiding testimony; and while we continue faithful to our adopting Father, the Spirit that witnesses that adoption will continue to witness it, and hereby we shall know that we are of God by the Spirit which He giveth us.

17. *And if children, then heirs*. For the legitimate children alone can inherit the estate. This is not an estate to which they succeed in consequence of the death of a former possessor; it is like the Promised Land, given by God himself, and divided among the children of the family. *Heirs of God*. It is neither an earthly portion nor a heavenly portion, but GOD himself, who is to be their Portion. It is not heaven they are to inherit; it is GOD, who is infinitely greater and more glorious than heaven itself. *Joint-heirs with Christ*. Partaking of the same eternal glory with the glorified human nature of Christ. *If so be that we suffer with him*. Observe, says Dr. Taylor, how prudently the apostle advances to the harsh affair of suffering. He does not mention it till he has raised up their thoughts to the highest object of joy and pleasure —the happiness and glory of a joint inheritance

MATTHEW HENRY

I. The reward of the saints' present sufferings. *If so be that we suffer with him* (*v.* 17), or *forasmuch as we suffer with him.* The state of the church in this world always is an afflicted state. He tells them that they suffered with Christ, and should be glorified with him. Though we may be losers for him, we shall not be losers by him in the end. This the gospel is filled with the assurances of. He holds the balance (*v.* 18), in a comparison between the two. 1. In one scale he puts the *sufferings of this present time.* The sufferings of the saints last no longer than the present time (2 Cor. iv. 17), light affliction, and but for a moment. So that on the sufferings he writes *tekel,* weighed in the balance and found light. 2. In the other scale he puts the glory, and finds that an exceeding and eternal weight: *Glory that shall be revealed.* In our present state we come short, not only in the enjoyment, but in the knowledge of that glory: it shall be revealed. It surpasses all that we have yet seen and known. There is something to come, something behind the curtain, that will outshine all. *Shall be revealed in us;* not only revealed to us, to be seen, but revealed in us, to be enjoyed. He concludes the sufferings *not worthy to be compared with the glory.* They cannot merit that glory; and, if suffering for Christ will not merit, much less will doing. The sufferings are small and short, and concern the body only; but the glory is rich and great, and concerns the soul, and is eternal. This he reckons as an arithmetician that is balancing an account. He first sums up what is disbursed for Christ in the sufferings of this present time, and finds they come to very little; he then sums up what is secured to us by Christ in the glory that shall be revealed, and this he finds to be an infinite sum. And who would be afraid then to suffer for Christ, who as he is beforehand with us in suffering, so he will not be behind-hand with us in recompence? He could reckon not by art only, but by experience, for he knew both. And, upon the view of both, he gives this judgment here. The reproach of Christ appears riches to those who have respect to the recompence of reward.

II. The accomplishment of the saints' present hopes and expectations, *v.* 19, &c. As the saints are suffering for it, so they are waiting for it. He will establish that word unto his servants on which he has caused them to hope. If hope deferred makes the heart sick, surely when the desire comes it will be a tree of life. Now he observes an expectation of this glory.

1. In the creatures, *v.* 19–22. That must needs be a great, a transcendent glory, which all the creatures are so earnestly expecting and longing for. By the *creature* here we understand the whole frame of nature, the whole creation. The sense of the apostle in these four verses we may take in the following observations: (1) There is a present vanity to which the creature, by reason of the sin of man, is made subject, *v.* 20. When man sinned, the ground was cursed for man's sake, and with it all the creatures. *Under the bondage of corruption, v.* 21. The creation is sullied and stained, much of the beauty of the world gone. And it is not the least part of their bondage that they are used, or abused rather, by men as instruments of sin. And this *not willingly,* not of their own choice. All the creatures desire their own perfection. When they are made instruments of sin it is not willingly. They are thus captivated, not for any sin of their own, but for man's sin: *By reason of him who hath subjected the same.* And this yoke (poor creatures) they bear in hope that it will not be so always. We have reason to pity the poor creatures that for our sin have become subject to vanity. (2) The creatures *groan and travail in pain* together under this vanity and corruption, *v.* 22. Sin is a burden to the whole creation. There is a general outcry of the whole creation aganst the sin of man. (3) The creature shall be *delivered from this bondage into the glorious liberty of the children of God* (*v.* 21)—they shall no more be subject to vanity and corruption. This lower world shall be renewed: when there will be new heavens there will be a new earth. (4) The creature doth therefore earnestly expect the *manifestation of the children of God, v.* 19. Now the saints are God's hidden ones, the wheat seems lost in a heap of chaff; but then they shall be manifested. The children of God shall appear in their own colours. And this redemption of the creature is reserved till then. This the whole creation longs for; and it may serve as a reason why now a good man should be merciful to his beast.

JAMIESON, FAUSSET, BROWN

if so be that we suffer—'provided we be suffering with Him' —**that we may be also glorified together**—with Him. This necessity of conformity to Christ in suffering in order to participate in His glory, is taught alike by Christ Himself and by His apostles (John 12:24-26; Matt. 16:24, 25; II Tim. 2:12).

18. For I reckon that the sufferings of this present time are not worthy to be compared with the glory which shall be revealed in us—i.e., 'True, we must suffer with Christ, if we would partake of His glory; but what of that? For if such sufferings are set over against the coming glory, they sink into insignificance.' **19-22. For . . .**—'The apostle, fired with the thought of the future glory of the saints, pours forth this splendid passage, in which he represents the whole creation groaning under its present degradation, and looking and longing for the revelation of this glory as the end and consummation of its existence' [HODGE]. **the earnest expectation**—(cf. Phil. 1:20). **of the creature**—rather, 'the creation.'

ALEXANDER MACLAREN:

"The unveiling of the sons of God." That unveiling is represented as coming along with the glory which shall be revealed to usward, and as being contemporaneous with the deliverance of the creation itself from the bondage of corruption, and its passing into the liberty of the glory of the children of God. It coincides with the vanishing of the pain in which the whole creation now groans and travails, and with the adoption—that is, the redemption of our body. Then hope will be seen and will pass into still fruition. All this points to the time when Jesus Christ is revealed, and His servants are revealed with Him in glory. That revelation brings with it of necessity the manifestation of the sons of God for what they are—the making visible in the life of what God sees them to be.

That revelation of the sons of God is the result of the entire dominion and transforming supremacy of the Spirit of God in them. In the whole sweep of their consciousness there will in that day be nothing done from other motives; there will be no sidelights flashing in and disturbing the perfect illumination from the candle of the Lord set on high in their being; there will be no contraditions in the life.

—Expositions of Holy Scripture

waiteth for the manifestation—'is waiting for the revelation.' **of the sons of God**—i.e., "for the redemption of their bodies" from the grave (vs. 23), which will reveal their sonship, now hidden (cf. Luke 20:36; Rev. 21:7). **For the creature**—'the creation'—**was made subject to vanity, not willingly**—i.e., through no natural principle of decay. The apostle, personifying creation, represents it as only submitting to the vanity with which it was smitten, on man's account, in obedience to that superior power which had mysteriously linked its destinies with man's. And so he adds—**but by reason of him who hath subjected the same**—'who subjected it'—**in hope; because**—or 'in hope that'—**the creature itself also**—'even the creation itself'—**shall be delivered from the bondage of corruption**—its bondage to the principle of decay—**into the glorious liberty**—rather, 'the liberty of the glory'—**of the children of God**—i.e., the creation itself shall, in a glorious sense, be delivered into that freedom from debility and decay in which the children of God, when raised up in glory, shall expatiate: into this freedom from corruptibility the creation itself shall, in a glorious sense, be delivered [So CALVIN, BEZA, BENGEL, THOLUCK, OLSHAUSEN, DE WETTE, MEYER, PHILIPPI, HODGE, ALFORD, etc.]. If for man's sake alone the earth was cursed, it cannot surprise us that it should share in his recovery. And if so, to represent it as sympathizing with man's miseries, and as looking forward to his complete redemption as the period of its own emancipation from its present sin-blighted condition, is a beautiful thought, and in harmony with the general teaching of Scripture on the subject. (See on II Pet. 3:13.)

ADAM CLARKE

with the ever-blessed Son of God. We are *heirs; heirs of God, and joint-heirs with Christ; if so be that we suffer with him.* This, with the additional consideration that we suffer with Christ, or as He himself suffered, would greatly qualify the transitory afflictions of this world, and dispose them to attend to the other arguments He had to offer.

18. *For I reckon that the sufferings.* If the glory that is to be revealed be the enjoyment of God himself, then the sufferings of this life, which, when compared with eternity, are but as for a moment, are not worthy to be put in competition with this glory which shall be revealed in us.

19. *For the earnest expectation of the creature.* There is considerable difficulty in this and the following four verses, and the difficulty lies chiefly in the meaning of the word which we translate *the creature,* and *creation.* Some think that by it the brute creation is meant; others apply it to the Jewish people; others, to the godly; others, to the Gentiles; others, to the good angels; and others, to the fallen spirits, both angelic and human. Dr. Lightfoot's mode of explanation appears to me to be the best, on the whole. "There is," says he, "a twofold key hanging at this place, which may unlock the whole, and make the sense plain and easy. (1) The first is the phrase which we render 'the whole creation,' v. 22, and with which we meet twice elsewhere in the New Testament. Mark xvi. 15: 'Preach the gospel to every creature'; and Col. i. 23: The gospel 'was preached to every creature.' Now it is sufficiently apparent what is meant in both these places, viz. 'all nations.' For that which in Mark is, 'Preach the gospel to every creature,' is, in Matthew, 'Go . . . and teach all nations.' (2) The second key is the word, v. 20, which is not unfitly rendered *vanity;* but then this vanity is improperly applied to the vanishing, dying, changing state of the creation. For *vanity* does not so much denote the vanishing condition of the outward state as it does the inward vanity or emptiness of the mind. So the apostle, speaking of the Gentiles concerning whom he speaks here, tells us, They 'became vain in their imaginations,' chap. i. 21; and again, The 'Gentiles walk, in the vanity of their mind,' Eph. iv. 17. Throughout this whole place the apostle seems to allude to the bondage of the Israelites in Egypt and their deliverance from it, with a comparison made betwixt the Jewish and the Gentile church. When God would deliver Israel from his bondage, He challenges him for His Son, and His firstborn, Exod. iv. 22. And in like manner the Gentiles earnestly expect and wait for such a kind of manifestation of the sons of God within and among themselves. The Romans to whom the apostle writes knew well how many predictions and promises it had pleased God to publish by His prophets concerning gathering together and adopting sons to himself among the Gentiles; the *manifestation* of which *sons* the whole Gentile world with a 'neck' as it were 'stretched out,' as the word implies, doth now wait for."

20. *For the creature was made subject to vanity.* The Gentile world was subject to vanity of mind; but how? *Not willingly, but by reason of him who hath subjected the same.* May we not say it became vain willingly, but was made subject to vanity unwillingly?

21. *Because the creature.* This and the preceding verse should be thus connected: "in hope that the creature itself also shall be delivered." The word *phthora* denotes, very frequently, "sinful corruption." So 2 Pet. i. 4: "Corruption . . . through lust." 2 Cor. xi. 3: "Lest your minds should be corrupted." I Cor. xv. 33: "Evil communications corrupt good manners." The sense, therefore, of the apostle in this place seems to be: The Gentile world shall, in time, be delivered from the bondage of their "sinful corruption" (i.e., the bondage of their lusts and vile affections), and be brought into such a noble liberty as the sons of God enjoy.

22. *The whole creation groaneth and travaileth.* If it be inquired how the Gentile world groaned and travailed in pain, let them who explain this of the fabric of the material world tell us how that groans and travails. They must needs own it to be a borrowed and allusive

MATTHEW HENRY

2. In the saints, who are new creatures, *v.* 23–25. (1) The grounds of this expectation in the saints. It is our having received *the first-fruits of the spirit.* Grace is the first-fruits of glory, it is glory begun. We, having received such clusters in this wilderness, cannot but long for the full vintage in the heavenly Canaan. *Not only they*—not only the creatures, but even we cannot but long for something more and greater. In having the first-fruits of the Spirit we have that which is very precious, but we have not all we would have. *We groan within ourselves* with silent groans, which pierce heaven soonest of all. Or, *We groan among ourselves.* It is the unanimous vote of the whole church. Present receivings and comforts are consistent with a great many groans; as the throes of a woman in travail—groans that are symptoms of life, not of death. (2) The object of this expectation. *The adoption, to wit, the redemption of our body.* The resurrection is here called *the redemption of the body.* It shall then be rescued from the power of death and the grave. It shall be made like that glorious body of Christ, Phil. iii. 21; 1 Cor. xv. 42. This is called *the adoption.* It is the adoption manifested before all the world, angels and men. As Christ was, so the saints will be, declared to be the sons of God with power, by the resurrection from the dead, *ch.* i. 4. It is the adoption perfected and completed. The children of God have bodies as well as souls; and, till those bodies are brought into the glorious liberty of the children of God, the adoption is not perfect. (3) The agreeableness of this to our present state, *v.* 24, 25. Our happiness is not in present possession: *We are saved by hope.* Our reward is out of sight. Those that will deal with God must deal upon trust. Faith respects the promise, hope the thing promised. Faith is the evidence, hope the expectation, of things not seen. Faith is the mother of hope. *We do with patience wait.* In hoping for this glory we have need of patience. Our way is rough and long, though he seem to tarry, it becomes us to wait for him.

Verses 26–28

Two privileges more to which true Christians are entitled:

I. The help of the Spirit in prayer.

1. Our weakness in prayer: *We know not what we should pray for as we ought.* As to the matter of our requests, we know not what to ask. We are short-sighted. We are like foolish children, that are ready to cry for fruit before it is ripe and fit for them. As to the manner, we know not how to pray as we ought. The apostle speaks of this in the first person: *We know not.* He puts himself among the rest. If so great a saint as Paul knew not what to pray for, what little reason have we to go forth about that duty in our own strength!

2. The assistances which the Spirit gives us. He *helps our infirmities,* meant especially of our praying infirmities. The Spirit in the word helps. The Spirit in the heart helps; for this end the Holy Ghost was poured out. *Helpeth, heaves with us, over against us,* helps as we help one that would lift up a burden, by lifting over against him at the other end. We must not sit still, and expect that the Spirit should do all; when the Spirit goes before us we must bestir ourselves. We cannot without God, and he will not without us. The *Spirit itself makes intercession for us.* Christ intercedes for us in heaven, the Spirit intercedes for us in our hearts; so graciously has God provided for the encouragement of the praying remnant. Now this intercession which the Spirit makes is, (1) *With groanings that cannot be uttered.* There may be praying in the Spirit where there is not a word spoken. It is not the rhetoric and eloquence, but the faith and fervency, of our prayers, that the Spirit works, in us. *Cannot be uttered;* we know not what to say, nor how to express ourselves. When we can but cry, *Abba, Father,* with a holy humble boldness, this is the work of the Spirit. (2) *According to the will of God, v.* 27. The Spirit interceding in us evermore melts our wills into the will of God.

3. The sure success of these intercessions: *He that searches the heart knoweth what is the mind of the Spirit, v.* 27. To a hypocrite, all whose religion lies in his tongue, nothing is more dreadful than that God searches the heart. To a sincere Christian, who makes heart-work of his duty, nothing is more comfortable. He will hear and answer those desires which we want words to express. He knows what we have need of before we ask. Christ had said, "Whatever you ask the Father according to his will he will give you." But how shall we learn to ask according to his will. Why, the Spirit will teach us that.

JAMIESON, FAUSSET, BROWN

23. And not only they, but ourselves also—or 'not only [so], but even we ourselves'—i.e., besides the inanimate creation. **which have the first-fruits of the Spirit**—or, 'the Spirit as the first-fruits' of our full redemption (cf. II Cor. 1:22), moulding the heart to a heavenly frame and attempering it to its future element. **even we ourselves**—though we have so much of heaven already within us. **groan within ourselves**—under this "body of sin and death," and under the manifold "vanity and vexation of spirit" that are written upon every object and every pursuit and every enjoyment under the sun. **waiting for the**—manifestation of our—**adoption, to wit, the redemption of our body**—from the grave: "not (be it observed) the deliverance of ourselves from the body, but the redemption of the body itself from the grave" [BENGEL]. **24. For we are saved by hope**—rather, 'For in hope we are saved'; i.e., it is more a salvation in hope than as yet in actual possession. **but hope that is seen is not hope**—for the very meaning of hope is, the expectation that something now *future* will become *present.* **for what a man seeth, why doth he yet hope for?**—the latter ending when the other comes. **25. But if we hope for that we see not, then do we with patience wait for it**—i.e., then, patient waiting for it is our fitting attitude. **26, 27. Likewise the Spirit also . . .**—or, 'But after the like manner doth the Spirit also help . . . **our infirmities**—rather (according to the true reading), 'our infirmity'; not merely the one infirmity here specified, but *the general weakness of the spiritual life* in its present state, of which one example is here given. **for we know not what we should pray for as we ought**—It is not the proper *matter* of prayer that believers are at so much loss about, for the fullest directions are given them on this head: but to ask for the right things "as they ought" is the difficulty. This arises partly from the dimness of our spiritual vision in the present veiled state, while we have to "walk by faith, not by sight" (see on I Cor. 13:9; and on II Cor. 5:7), and the large admixture of the ideas and feelings which spring from the fleeting objects of sense that there is in the very best views and affections of our renewed nature; partly also from the necessary imperfection of all human language as a vehicle for expressing the subtle spiritual feelings of the heart. In these circumstances, how can it be but that much uncertainty should surround all our spiritual exercises, and that in our nearest approaches and in the freest outpourings of our hearts to our Father in heaven, doubts should spring up within us whether our *frame* of mind in such exercises is altogether befitting and well pleasing to God? Nor do these anxieties subside, but rather deepen, with the depth and ripeness of our spiritual experience. **But the Spirit**—rather, 'Himself.' (See end of vs. 27)—**maketh intercession for us with groanings which cannot be uttered**—i.e., which cannot be expressed in articulate language. Sublime and affecting ideas, for which we are indebted to this passage alone! 'As we struggle to express in articulate language the desires of our hearts and find that our deepest emotions are the most inexpressible, we "groan" under this felt inability. But not in vain are these groanings. For "the Spirit Himself" is in them, giving to the emotions which He Himself has kindled the only language of which they are capable; so that though on our part they are the fruit of impotence to utter what we feel, they are at the same time the intercession of the Spirit Himself in our behalf.' **And**—rather, 'But,' inarticulate though these groanings be—**he that searcheth the hearts knoweth what is the mind of the Spirit, because he**—the Spirit—**maketh intercession for the saints according to the will of God**—As the Searcher of hearts, He watches the surging emotions of them in prayer, and knows perfectly what the Spirit means by the groanings which He draws forth within us, because that blessed Intercessor pleads by them only for what God Himself designs to bestow. Note (1) Are believers "led by the Spirit of God" (vs. 14)? How careful then should they be not to "grieve the Holy Spirit of God" (Eph. 4:30)! Cf. Psalm 32:8, 9: "I will . . . *guide* thee with Mine eye. *Be not* (then) *as the horse, or as the mule . . .*" (2) "The spirit of bondage," to which many Protestants are "all their lifetime subject," and the 'doubtsome faith' which the Popish Church systematically inculcates, are both rebuked here, being in direct and painful contrast to that "spirit of adoption," and that witness of the Spirit, along with our own spirit, to the fact of our sonship, which it is here said the children of God, as such, enjoy (vss. 15, 16). (3) As suffering with Christ is the ordained preparation for participating in this glory, so the insignificance of the one

ADAM CLARKE

phrase; but in the sense above given, the very literal construction may be admitted.

23. *And not only they, but ourselves also.* Neither the Gentiles only, but we Jews also, to whom God hath granted *the firstfruits of the Spirit.* We sigh among ourselves for their sakes, *waiting for the adoption;* that is, *the redemption of our* mystical *body,* whereof the Gentiles make a very great part.

24. *For we are saved by hope.* We are supported and are comfortable in the expectation we have of receiving from the hand of our God all the good we need in the troubles and adversities of this life, and of having our bodies raised from corruption and death at the general resurrection. *Hope that is seen is not hope.* As hope signifies "the expectation of future good," so it necessarily supposes that the object of it is not *seen,* i.e., not "enjoyed"; for to see in Scripture language sometimes signifies to enjoy, as in Job vii. 7: "Mine eye shall no more see [margin, 'enjoy'] good." The *hope that is seen,* that is, "enjoyed," is no longer hope; it is fruition; and a man cannot hope for that which he has in his possession.

25. *But if we hope for that we see not.* If we have a well-grounded expectation of our resurrection and final glorification, knowing that such things are necessarily future and must for a certain time be delayed, then do we patiently wait for them, continue patiently to endure the common ills of life and whatever tribulations we may be exposed to in consequence of our Christian profession.

26. *The Spirit also helpeth our infirmities.* The same Spirit mentioned before as bearing witness with ours that we are the children of God; and consequently it is not a disposition or frame of mind, for the disposition of our mind surely cannot help the infirmities of our minds. The word *synantilambanetai* is very inadequately expressed by *helpeth.* It is compounded of *syn,* "together," *anti,* "against," and *lambanomai,* "to support or help," and signifies such assistance as is afforded by any two persons to each other who mutually bear the same load or carry it between them. He who prays receives help from the Spirit of God; but he who prays not receives no such help. *For we know not what we should pray for as we ought.* And should therefore be liable to endless mistakes in our prayers if suitable desires were not excited by the Holy Spirit and power received to bring these desires, by prayer, before the throne of grace. *But the Spirit itself,* "the same Spirit," viz., the Spirit that witnesses of our adoption and sonship, vv. 15-16, *maketh intercession for us.* Surely if the apostle had designed to teach us that he meant our own sense and understanding by the *Spirit,* he never could have spoken in a manner in which plain common sense was never likely to comprehend his meaning.

27. *He maketh intercession for the saints.* The word *entynchano* signifies to apply oneself to a person in behalf of another, to "intercede" or "negotiate for." Our Lord makes intercession for us by negotiating and managing, as our Friend and Agent, all the affairs pertaining to our salvation. And the Spirit of God makes intercession for the saints, not by supplication to God on their behalf, but by directing and qualifying their supplications in a proper manner by His agency and influence upon their hearts; which, according to the gospel scheme, is the peculiar work and office of the Holy Spirit. *According to the will of God.* According to the mind, intention, or design of God. And thus the prayers which we offer up, and the desires which subsist in the unutterable groanings, are all such as are pleasing in the sight of God. So that God, whose is the Spirit, and who is acquainted with the mind of the Spirit, knows what He means when He leads the saints to express themselves in words, desires, groans, sighs, or tears. In each, God reads the language of the Holy Ghost, and prepares the answer according to the request.

MATTHEW HENRY

ALBERT BARNES:

28. "And we know." This verse introduces another source of consolation and support, drawn from the fact that all things are under the direction of an infinitely wise Being, who has purposed the salvation of the Christian, and who has so appointed all things that they shall contribute to it.

"All things." All our afflictions and trials; all the persecutions and calamities to which we are exposed. Though they are numerous and long continued, yet they are among the means that are appointed for our welfare.

"Work together for good." They shall cooperate; they shall mutually contribute to our good. They take off our affections from this world; they teach us the truth about our frail, transitory, and dying condition; they lead us to look to God for support, and to heaven for a final home; and they produce a subdued spirit, a humble temper, a patient, tender, and kind disposition. This has been the experience of all saints; and at the end of life they have been able to say it was good for them to be afflicted (Ps. 119:67, 71; Jer. 31:18, 19; Heb. 12:11).

"For good." For our real welfare; for the promotion of true piety, peace, and happiness in our hearts.

"To them that love God." This is a characteristic of true piety. To them, afflictions are a blessing; to others, they often prove otherwise. On others, they are sent as chastisements; and they produce murmuring instead of peace; rebellion instead of submission; and anger, impatience, and hatred instead of calmness, patience, and love. The Christian is made a better man by receiving afflictions as they should be received, and by desiring that they should accomplish the purpose for which they are sent; the sinner is made more hardened by resisting them, and refusing to submit to their obvious intention and design.—*Popular Commentary*

II. The concurrence of all providences for the good of those that are Christ's, *v.* 28. Notwithstanding all these privileges, we see believers compassed about with manifold afflictions, but in this the Spirit's intercession is always effectual, that all this is working together for their good.

1. The character of the saints, who are interested in this privilege. *They love God.* Those that love God make the best of all he does, and take all in good part. *They are the called according to his purpose,* not according to any merit or desert of ours, but according to God's own gracious purpose.

2. The privilege of the saints, that *all things work together for good to them.* All the providences of God are theirs—merciful providences, afflicting providences. They are all for good; perhaps for temporal good, at least, for spiritual and eternal good. Either directly or indirectly, every providence has a tendency to the spiritual good of those that love God. *They work together,* as several ingredients in a medicine concur to answer the intention. *He worketh all things together for good;* so some read it. All this *we know*—know it for a certainty, from the word of God, from our own experience, and from the experience of all the saints.

Verses 29, 30

The apostle, having reckoned up so many ingredients of the happiness of true believers, comes here to represent the ground of them all, which he lays in predestination. He here sets before us the order of the causes of our salvation, a golden chain, which cannot be broken. There are four links of it:

I. *Whom he did foreknow he also did predestinate to be conformed to the image of his Son.* All that God designed for glory and happiness as the end he decreed to grace and holiness as the way. God's foreknowledge of the saints is the same with that everlasting love wherewith he is said to have loved them. *Whom he did foreknow,* that is, whom he designed for

JAMIESON, FAUSSET, BROWN

as compared with the other cannot fail to lighten the sense of it, however bitter and protracted (vss. 17, 18). (4) It cannot but swell the heart of every intelligent Christian to think that if external nature has been mysteriously affected for evil by the fall of man, it only awaits his completed recovery, at the resurrection, to experience a corresponding emancipation from its blighted condition into undecaying life and unfading beauty (vss. 19-23). (5) It is not when believers, through sinful "quenching of the Spirit," have the fewest and faintest glimpses of heaven, that they sigh most fervently to be there; but, on the contrary, when through the unobstructed working of the Spirit in their hearts, "the first-fruits" of the glory to be revealed are most largely and frequently tasted, then, and just for that reason, is it that they "groan within themselves" for full redemption (vs. 23). For thus they reason: If such be the drops, what will the ocean be? If thus "to see through a glass darkly" be so very sweet, what will it be to "see face to face?" If when "my Beloved stands behind our wall, looking forth at the windows, showing Himself through the lattice" (Canticles 2:9)—that thin veil which parts the seen from the unseen—if He is even thus to me "Fairer than the children of men," what shall He be when He stands confessed before my undazzled vision, the Only-begotten of the Father in my own nature, and I shall be like Him, for I shall see Him as He is? (6) "The patience of hope" (I Thess. 1:3) is the fitting attitude for those who with the joyful consciousness that they are already *"saved"* (II Tim. 1:9; Titus 3:5), have yet the painful consciousness that they are saved but *in part:* or, "that being justified by His grace, they are made (in the present state) heirs according to the hope (only) of eternal life," Titus 3:7 (vss. 24, 25). (7) As prayer is the breath of the spiritual life, and the believer's only effectual relief under the "infirmity" which attaches to his whole condition here below, how cheering is it to be assured that the blessed Spirit, cognizant of it all, comes in aid of it all; and in particular, that when believers, unable to articulate their case before God, can at times do nothing but lie "groaning" before the Lord, these inarticulate groanings are the Spirit's own vehicle for conveying into "the ears of the Lord of Sabaoth" their whole case; and come up before the Hearer of prayer as the Spirit's own intercession in their behalf, and that they are recognized by Him that sitteth on the Throne, as embodying only what His own "will" determined before to bestow upon them (vss. 26, 27)! (8) What a view do these two verses (vss. 26, 27) give of the relations subsisting between the Divine Persons in the economy of redemption, and the harmony of their respective operations in the case of each of the redeemed!

THIRD: *Triumphant Summary of the Whole Argument* (vss. 28-39). **28. And**—or, 'Moreover,' or 'Now'; noting a transition to a new particular. **we know . . .**—The order in the original is more striking: "We know that to them that love God" (cf. I Cor. 2:9; Eph. 6:24; Jas. 1:12; 2:5) "all things work together for good [even] to them who are the called (rather, 'who are called') according to His (eternal) purpose." Glorious assurance! And this, it seems, was a "household word," a "known" thing, among believers. This working of all things for good is done quite naturally to "them that love God", because such souls, persuaded that He who gave His own Son for them cannot but mean them well in all His procedure, learn thus to take in good part whatever He sends them, however trying to flesh and blood: and to them who are the called, according to "His purpose," all things do in the same intelligible way "work together for good"; for, even when "He hath His way in the whirlwind," they see "His chariot paved with love" (Canticles 3:10). And knowing that it is in pursuance of an eternal *"purpose"* of love that they have been *"called* into the fellowship of His Son Jesus Christ" (I Cor. 1:9), they naturally say within themselves, 'It cannot be that He "of whom, and through whom, and to whom are all things," should suffer that purpose to be thwarted by anything really adverse to us, or that He should not make all things, dark as well as light, crooked as well as straight, to co-operate to the furtherance and final completion of His high design.' **29. For**—as touching this "calling according to his purpose"—**whom he did foreknow he also did predestinate**—foreordain. In what sense are we to take the word "foreknow" here? 'Those who He foreknew would repent and believe,' say *Pelagians* of every age and every hue. But this is to thrust into the text what is contrary to the whole spirit, and even letter, of the apostle's teaching (see ch. 9:11; II Tim. 1:9). In ch. 11:2, and Psalm 1:6,

ADAM CLARKE

ALBERT BARNES:

"To them who are the called." Christians are often represented as called of God. The word is sometimes used to denote an external invitation, offer, or calling (Matt. 20:16; 22:14). But excepting in these places, it is used in the New Testament to denote those who had *accepted* the call, and were true Christians (Rom. 1:6, 7; 1 Cor. 1:2, 24; Rev. 17:14). It is evidently used in this sense here—to denote those who were true Christians. The connection as well as the usual meaning of the word requires us thus to understand it. Christians are said to be called because God has invited them to be saved, and has sent into their heart such an influence as to make the call effectual to their salvation. In this way their salvation is to be traced entirely to God.

"According to his purpose." The word here rendered "purpose" means properly a *proposition,* or a laying down anything in view of others; and is thus applied to the bread that was laid on the table of showbread (Matt 12:4; Mark 2:26; Luke 6:4). Hence it means, when applied to the mind, a plan or purpose of mind. It implies that God had a plan, purpose, or intention in regard to all who became Christians. They are not saved by chance or haphazard. God does not convert men without design; and his designs are not new, but are eternal. What he does, he always meant to do. What it is right for him to do, it was right always to intend to do. What God always meant to do is his purpose or plan. That he has such a purpose in regard to the salvation of his people is often affirmed (Rom. 9:11; Eph. 1:11; 3:11; 2 Tim. 1:9; Jer. 51:29).

This purpose of saving his people is: (1) one over which a creature can have no control; it is according to the counsel of his own will (Eph. 1:11); (2) without any merit on the part of the sinner—a purpose to save him by grace (2 Tim. 1:9); (3) eternal (Eph. 3:11); (4) such as should excite lively gratitude in all who have been inclined by the grace of God to accept the offers of eternal life. They owe it to the mere mercy of God, and they should acknowledge him as the fountain and source of all their hopes of heaven. —*Popular Commentary*

28. *And we know that all things work together for good to them that love God.* To understand this verse aright, let us observe: (1) That the persons in whose behalf all things work for good are they who *love God* and, consequently, who live in the spirit of obedience. (2) It is not said that all things *shall* work for good, but that they work now in the behalf of him who loveth now, for both verbs are in the present tense. (3) All these things *work together;* while they are working, God's providence is working, His Spirit is working, and they are working together with Him. *To them who are the called according to his purpose.* Dr. Taylor translates *the called,* "the invited," and observes that it is a metaphor taken from inviting guests or making them welcome to a feast. Our being *called* or "invited," according to God's purpose, proves that all things work for our good, on the supposition that we love God, and not otherwise. How is it evident and unquestionable that we are *called?* From our being in the Visible Church and professing the faith of the gospel. For always, in the apostolic writings, all that are in the Visible Church and profess the faith of the gospel are numbered among the *called* or "invited"; i.e., among the persons who are invited to feast on the covenant sacrifice.

MATTHEW HENRY

his friends and favourites. Now those whom God thus foreknew he did predestinate to be conformed to Christ. 1. Holiness consists in our conformity to the image of Christ. This takes in the whole of sanctification. Christ is the express image of his Father, and the saints are conformed to the image of Christ. Thus it is that we have God's love restored to us and God's likeness renewed upon us. 2. All that God hath from eternity foreknown with favour he hath predestinated to this conformity. It is not we that can conform ourselves to Christ. None can know their election but by their conformity to the image of Christ; for all that are chosen are chosen to sanctification.

3. That which is herein chiefly designed is the honour of Jesus Christ, that he might be the *first-born among many brethren*; that is, that Christ might have the honour of being the great pattern, might have pre-eminence. And blessed be God that there are many brethren; though they seem but a few in one place at one time, yet, when they come all together, they will be a great many. In spite of all the opposition of the powers of darkness, Christ will be the first-born among many, very many brethren.

II. *Whom he did predestinate those he also called*, not only with the external call, but with the internal and effectual call. The former comes to the ear only, but this to the heart. The call is then effectual when we come at the call; and we then come at the call when the Spirit draws us, persuades and enables us to embrace Christ in the promises. It is an effectual call from self and earth to God, and Christ—from sin and vanity to grace, and holiness. This is the gospel call. *Them he called*, that the purpose of God, according to election, might stand.

III. *Whom he called those he also justified.* All that are effectually called are accepted as righteous through Jesus Christ. They are no longer dealt with as criminals, but owned and loved as friends and favourites.

IV. *Whom he justified those he also glorified.* The power of corruption being broken in effectual calling, and the guilt of sin removed in justification, nothing can come between that soul and glory. It is spoken of as a thing done: *He glorified*, because of the certainty of it; he *hath* saved us. God's design of love has its full accomplishment. This was what he aimed at all along—to bring them to heaven. Are they chosen? It is to salvation. Called? It is to his kingdom and glory. Begotten again? It is to an inheritance incorruptible. Afflicted? It is to work for them this exceeding and eternal weight of glory. The author of all these is the same. God himself hath undertaken the doing of it from first to last. This is a mighty encouragement to our faith and hope.

Verses 31–39

The apostle closes with a holy triumph, in the name of all the saints. *What shall we then say to these things?* What use shall we make of all that has been said? He speaks as one wondering at the height and depth, and length and breadth, of the love of Christ, which passeth knowledge. The more we know of other things the less we wonder at them; but the further we are led into an acquaintance with gospel mysteries the more we are affected with the admiration of them. If ever Paul rode in a triumphant chariot on this side of heaven, here it was. He here makes a challenge, dares all the enemies of the saints to do their worst: *If God be for us, who can be against us?* This includes all, that *God is for us.* All that he is, and has, and does, is for his people. And, if so, *who can be against us*, so as to prevail against us? Be they ever so strong, ever so many, what can they do? While God is for us, and we keep in his love, we may defy all the powers of darkness. Let Satan do his worst, he is chained. Who then dares fight against us, while God himself is fighting for us? And this we say to these things.

I. We have supplies ready in all our wants (*v.* 32): *He that spared*, &c. Who can cut off our streams, while we have a fountain to go to? 1. What God has done for us, on which our hopes are built: *He spared not his own Son.* Now we may know that he loves us, in that he hath not withheld his Son. If nothing less will save man, rather than man shall perish let him go.

JAMIESON, FAUSSET, BROWN

God's "knowledge" of His people cannot be restricted to a mere foresight of future events, or acquaintance with what is passing here below. Does "whom He did foreknow," then, mean 'whom He foreordained?' Scarcely, because both 'foreknowledge' and 'foreordination' are here mentioned, and the one as the *cause* of the other. It is difficult indeed for our limited minds to distinguish them as states of the Divine Mind towards men; especially since in Acts 2:23 "the counsel" is put *before* "the foreknowledge of God," while in I Peter 1:2 "election" is said to be "*according to* the foreknowledge of God." But probably God's foreknowledge of His own people means His *peculiar, gracious, complacency in them,* while His "predestinating" or "foreordaining" them signifies His fixed *purpose*, flowing from this, to "save them and call them with an holy calling" (II Tim. 1:9). **to be conformed to the image of his Son**—i.e., to be His sons after the pattern, model, or image of *His* Sonship in our nature. **that he might be the first-born among many brethren**—"The First-born," the Son by nature; His "many brethren," sons by adoption: He, in the Humanity of the Only-begotten of the Father, bearing our sins on the accursed tree; they in that of mere men ready to perish by reason of sin, but redeemed by His blood from condemnation and wrath, and transformed into His likeness: He "the First-born from the dead"; they "that sleep in Jesus," to be in due time "brought with Him"; "The First-born," now "crowned with glory and honor"; His "many brethren," "when He shall appear, to be like Him, for they shall see Him as He is." **30. Moreover**—'And,' or 'Now'; explanatory of the foregoing verse—'In "predestinating us to be conformed to the image of His Son" in final glory, He settled all the successive steps of it. Thus—**whom he did predestinate, them he also called**—The word "called" (as Hodge and others truly observe) is never in the Epistles of the New Testament applied to those who have only the *outward invitation* of the Gospel (as in Matt. 20:16; 22:14). It always means '*internally, effectually, savingly called.*' It denotes the *first great step* in personal salvation and answers to "conversion." Only the word *conversion* expresses the *change of character* which then takes place, whereas this "calling" expresses the *divine authorship* of the change, and the *sovereign power* by which we are summoned, Matthew-like, Zaccheus-like, out of our old, wretched, perishing condition, into a new, safe, blessed life. **and whom he**—thus—**called, them he also justified**—brought into the definite state of reconciliation already so fully described. **and whom he justified, them he also glorified**—brought to final glory (vss. 17, 18). Noble climax, and so rhythmically expressed! And all this is viewed as past; because, starting from the past decree of "predestination to be conformed to the image of God's Son" of which the other steps are but the successive unfoldings—all is beheld as one entire, eternally completed salvation. **31. What shall we then say to these things?**—'We can no farther go, think, wish' [BENGEL]. This whole passage, to vs. 34, and even to the end of the chapter, strikes all thoughtful interpreters and readers, as transcending almost every thing in language, while OLSHAUSEN notices the 'profound and colossal' character of the thought. **If God be for us, who can be against us?** If God be *resolved* and *engaged* to bring us through, all *our* enemies must be *His;* and "Who would set the briers and thorns against Him in battle? He would go through them. He would burn them together" (Isa. 27:4). What strong consolation is here! Nay, but the great Pledge of all has already been given; for, **32. He**—rather, 'He surely.' (It is a pity to lose the emphatic particle of the original.) **that spared not**—'withheld not,' 'kept not back.' This expressive phrase, as well as the whole thought, is suggested by Genesis 22:12, where Jehovah's touching commendation of Abraham's conduct regarding his son Isaac seems designed to furnish something like a glimpse into the spirit of His own act in *surrendering* His own Son. "Take now (said the Lord to Abraham) thy *son,* thine *only, whom thou lovest,* and . . . offer him for a burnt offering" (Gen. 22:2); and only when Abraham had all but performed that loftiest act of self-sacrifice, the Lord interposed, saying, "Now I know that thou fearest God, seeing thou HAST NOT WITHHELD THY SON, THINE ONLY SON, from Me." In the light of this incident, then, and of this language, our apostle can mean to convey nothing less than this, that in "not sparing His own Son, but delivering Him up," or surrendering Him, God exercised, in His *Paternal* character, a mysterious act of *Self-sacrifice,* which, though involving none of the *pain* and none of the *loss* which are

ADAM CLARKE

29. *The firstborn among many brethren.* That He might be the Chief or Head of all the redeemed; for His human nature is the first-fruits of the resurrection from the dead; and He is the first human being that, after having passed through death, was raised to eternal glory.

30. *Whom he did predestinate.* The Gentiles, whom He determined to call into His Church with the Jewish people, *he called*—He invited by the preaching of the gospel, to believe on His Son, Jesus Christ. *He also justified.* Pardoned the sins of all those who with hearty repentance and true faith turned unto Him. *He also glorified.* He has honored and dignified the Gentiles with the highest privileges, and He has already taken many of them to the Kingdom of glory and many more are on their way thither; and all who love Him and continue faithful unto death shall inherit that glory eternally. Though the terms are here used in a more general sense, yet if we take them more restrictedly, we must consider that in the work of justification sanctification is implied, justification being the foundation and beginning of that work. From all this we learn that none will be *glorified* who have not been sanctified and *justified.* The word *doxa,* which we render "glory," and *doxazo,* to "glorify," both mean to "render illustrious, eminent," in various parts of the New Testament; and in this sense the verb is used in John xi. 4; xii. 23, 28; xiii. 31-32; xiv. 13; xv. 8; xxi. 19; Acts iii. 13; and in chap. xi. 13—in none of which places eternal beatification can be intended. Here it seems to mean that those whom God had called into a state of justification He had rendered illustrious by innumerable gifts, graces, and privileges, in the same manner as He had done to the Israelites of old. The whole of the preceding discourse will show that everything here is conditional, as far as it relates to the ultimate salvation of any person professing the gospel of Christ; for the promises are made to character, and not to persons, as some have most injudiciously affirmed. The apostle insists upon a character all along from the beginning of the chapter. V. 1: "There is . . . no condemnation to them which are in Christ Jesus, who walk not after the flesh, but after the Spirit." V. 13: "If ye live after the flesh, ye shall die." The absolute necessity of holiness to salvation is the very subject of his discourse; this necessity he positively affirms, and establishes by the most solid arguments.

31. *What shall we then say to these things?* What conclusion should we draw from the above premises—from all that was already laid down in the preceding chapters, but especially in the preceding verses, from vv. 28 to 30 inclusive? As if he had said: What comfort may we derive from these doctrines? God has called us all to holiness, and to love to Him, which is the principle of holiness. *If God be for us, who can be against us?* He who is infinitely wise has undertaken to direct us; He who is infinitely powerful has undertaken to protect us; He who is in-

MATTHEW HENRY

Thus did he *deliver him up for us all*, not only for our good, but in our stead, to be a propitiation for sin. He did not *spare his own Son that served him*, that he might spare us. 2. What we may therefore expect he will do: He will *with him freely give us all things*. It is implied that he will give us Christ, for other things are bestowed with him. He will with him freely give us all things, all good things, and more we should not desire. Freely, without reluctancy; and freely, without recompence. *How shall he not?* Can it be imagined that he should give so great a gift for us when we were enemies, and should deny us any good thing, now that we are friends and children? He that hath prepared a crown and kingdom for us will be sure to give us enough to bear our charges in the way to it.

II. We have an answer ready to all accusations and a security against all condemnations (*v.* 33, 34): *Who shall lay anything?* This is enough, *It is God that justifieth*. If God justifies, this answers all. We may challenge all our accusers to come and put in their charge. This overthrows them all; it is God, the righteous faithful God, that justifieth. *Who is he that condemneth?* Though they cannot make good the charge, yet they will be ready to condemn; but we have a plea ready which cannot be overruled. *It is Christ that died*, &c. It is by Christ, and our union with him, that we are thus secured. 1. His death: *It is Christ that died*. By the merit of his death he paid our debt. 2. His resurrection: *Yea, rather, that has risen again*. This is a much greater encouragement. Therefore the apostle mentions it with a *yea, rather*. If he had died, and not risen again, we had been where we were. 3. His sitting at the right hand of God: He is *even at the right hand of God* a mighty encouragement to us in reference to all accusations, that we have a friend, such a friend, in court. Our friend is himself the judge. 4. The intercession which he makes there. He is there, not unconcerned about us, not forgetful of us, but *making intercession*. And is not this abundant matter for comfort? What room is left for doubting and disquietment? Some understand the accusation and condemnation here spoken of as that which the suffering saints met with from men. The primitive Christians had many black crimes laid to their charge. For these the ruling powers condemned them: "But no matter for that" (says the apostle); "while we stand right at God's bar it is of no great moment how we stand at men's."

III. We have good assurance of our preservation and continuance in this blessed state, *v.* 35, to the end. The fears of the saints lest they should lose their hold of Christ are often very discouraging and disquieting, but here is that which may silence their fears, that nothing can separate them.

1. A daring challenge to all the enemies of the saints to separate them, if they could, from the love of Christ. *Who shall?* None shall, *v.* 35–37. God having manifested his love in giving his own Son for us, can we imagine that anything else should divert or dissolve that love?

(1) The present calamities of Christ's beloved ones

JAMIESON, FAUSSET, BROWN

inseparable from the very idea of self-sacrifice on our part, was not less real, but, on the contrary, as far transcended any such acts of ours as His nature is above the creature's. But this is inconceivable if Christ be not God's "own (or proper) Son," partaker of His very nature, as really as Isaac was of his father Abraham's. In that sense, certainly, the Jews charged our Lord with making Himself "equal with God" (see on John 5:18), which He in reply forthwith proceeded, not to disown, but to illustrate and confirm. Understand Christ's Sonship thus, and the language of Scripture regarding it is intelligible and harmonious; but take it to be an *artificial* relationship, ascribed to Him in virtue either of His miraculous birth, or His resurrection from the dead, or the grandeur of His works, or all of these together—and the passages which speak of it neither explain of themselves nor harmonize with each other. **delivered him up**—not to *death* merely (as many take it), for that is too narrow an idea here, but 'surrendered Him' in the most comprehensive sense; cf. John 3:16, "God so loved the world that He GAVE His only-begotten Son." **for us all**—i.e., for all believers alike; as nearly every good interpreter admits must be the meaning here. **how shall he not**—how can we conceive that He should not. **with him also**—rather, 'also with Him.' (The word "also" is often so placed in our version as to obscure the sense; see on Heb. 12:1.) **freely give us all things?**—all other gifts being not only immeasurably *less* than this Gift of gifts, but virtually *included in it*. **33, 34. Who shall lay anything to the charge of**—or, 'bring any charge against.' **God's elect?**—the first place in this Epistle where believers are styled "the *elect*." In what sense this is meant will appear in next chapter. **yea rather, that is risen again**—to make good the purposes of His death. Here, as in some other cases, the apostle delightfully corrects himself (see Gal. 4:9; and on ch. 1:12); not meaning that the resurrection of Christ was of more saving value than His death, but that having "put away sin by the sacrifice of Himself"—which though precious to us was to Him of unmingled bitterness—it was incomparably more delightful to think that He was again *alive*, and living to see to the efficacy of His death in our behalf. **who is even**—'also'—**at the right hand of God**—The right hand of the king was anciently the seat of honor (cf. I Sam. 20:25; I Kings 2:19; Ps. 45:9), and denoted participation in the royal power and glory (Matt. 20:21). The classical writings contain similar allusions. Accordingly Christ's sitting at the right hand of God—predicted in Psalm 110:1, and historically referred to in Mark 16:19; Acts 2:33; 7:56; Ephesians 1:20; Colossians 3:1; I Peter 3:22; Revelation 3:21—signifies the *glory* of the exalted Son of man, and the *power* in the government of the world in which He participates. Hence it is called "sitting on the right hand of *Power*" (Matt. 26:64), and "sitting on the right hand of the *Majesty* on high" (Heb. 1:3) [PHILIPPI]. **who also maketh intercession for us**—using all His boundless *interest* with God in our behalf. This is the top of the climax. "His *Session* at God's right hand denotes His *power* to save us; His *Intercession*, His *will* to do it" [BENGEL]. But how are we to conceive of this intercession? Not certainly as of one pleading 'on bended knees and with outstretched arms,' to use the expressive language of CALVIN. But yet, neither is it merely a figurative intimation that the power of Christ's redemption is continually operative [THOLUCK], or merely to show the fervor and vehemence of His love for us [CHRYSOSTOM]. It cannot be taken to mean less than this: that the glorified Redeemer, conscious of His claims, expressly *signifies His will* that the efficacy of His death should be made good to the uttermost, and signifies it in some such royal style as we find Him employing in that wonderful Intercessory Prayer which He spoke *as from within the veil* (see on John 17:11, 12): "Father, I WILL that they also whom Thou hast given Me be with Me where I am" (see on John 17:24). But *in what form* this will is expressed is as undiscoverable as it is unimportant. **35, 36. Who shall separate us from the love of Christ?** This does not mean 'our love to Christ,' as if, Who shall hinder us from loving Christ? but 'Christ's love to us,' as is clear from the closing words of the chapter, which refer to the same subject. Nor would the other sense harmonize with the scope of the chapter, which is to exhibit the ample ground of the believer's confidence in Christ. "It is no ground of confidence to assert, or even to feel, that we will never forsake Christ; but it is the strongest ground of assurance to be convinced that His love will never change" [HODGE]. **shall tribulation . . .** 'None of these, nor all together, how ter-

ADAM CLARKE

finitely good has undertaken to save us. What cunning, strength, or malice can prevail against His wisdom, power, and goodness?

32. *He that spared not his own Son.* And can we, His sincere followers, doubt of the safety of our state, or the certainty of His protection? No; for if He loved us, Gentiles and Jews, so intensely as to deliver up to death His own Son *for us all*, can He withhold from us any minor blessing? Nay, will He not, on the contrary, *freely give us all things?*

33. This and the following two verses contain a string of questions, most appropriately introduced and most powerfully urged, tending to show the safety of the state of those who have believed the gospel of the grace of God. I shall lay these verses down as they are pointed by the best Greek critics: "Who shall lay anything to the charge of God's elect?—God, who justifieth? Who is he that condemneth?—Christ, who died? or, rather, who is risen again? He who is at the right hand of God? He who maketh intercession for us? Who shall separate us from the love of Christ?—Tribulation? or distress? or persecution? or famine? or nakedness? or peril? or sword?" In all these questions the apostle intimates that if neither God nor Christ *would* bring any charge against them who love Him, none else *could*. And as God justifies through Christ, who died, consequently no charge can lie against these persons, as God alone could produce any; and He, so far from doing this, has justified them—freely forgiven their trespasses.

34. *Who is even at the right hand of God.* To which He has exalted our human nature, which He took in conjunction with His divinity; and there he *maketh intercession for us*—manages all the concerns of His own kingdom in general, and of every member of His Church in particular.

35. *Who shall separate us from the love of Christ?* I do think that this question has been generally misunderstood. The apostle is referring to the persecutions and tribulations to which genuine Christians were exposed through their attachment to Christ, and the gracious provision God had made for their support and final salvation. As in this provision God had shown His infinite love to them in providing Jesus Christ as their Sin Offering, and Jesus Christ had shown His love in suffering death upon the Cross for them, so, here, he speaks of the love of the followers of God to that Christ

MATTHEW HENRY

supposed—that they meet with *tribulation*, are in *distress*, are followed with *persecution* from an angry malicious world that always hated those whom Christ loved, pinched with *famine*, and starved with *nakedness*, exposed to the greatest *perils*, the *sword* of the magistrate drawn against them. Can a case be supposed more black and dismal? It is illustrated (*v.* 36) by a passage quoted from Ps. xliv. 22, *For thy sake we are killed all the day long*, that is, continually exposed to and expecting the fatal stroke. *Accounted as sheep for the slaughter;* they make no more of killing a Christian than of butchering a sheep.

(2) The inability of all these things to separate us from the love of Christ. All this will not cut the bond of love and friendship that is between Christ and true believers. [1] Christ doth not, will not, love us the less for all this. They are neither a cause nor an evidence of the abatement of his love. These things separate us from the love of other friends. When Paul was brought before Nero all men forsook him, but then the Lord stood by him, 2 Tim. iv. 16, 17. Whatever persecuting enemies may rob us of, they cannot rob us of the love of Christ, and therefore, let them do their worst, they cannot make a true believer miserable. [2] We do not, will not, love him the less for this, because we do not think that he loves us the less. A true Christian loves Christ never the less though he suffer for him, thinks never the worse of Christ though he lose all for him.

(3) The triumph of believers in this (*v.* 37): *Nay, in all these things we are more than conquerors.*

[1] We are conquerors. A strange way of conquering, but it was Christ's way. It is a surer and a nobler way of conquest by faith and patience than by fire and sword. The enemies have sometimes confessed themselves baffled and overcome by the invincible courage and constancy of the martyrs.

[2] We are more than conquerors. Those are more than conquerors that conquer, *First*, With little loss. Many conquests are dearly bought; but what do the suffering saints lose? Why, they lose that which the gold loses in the furnace, nothing but the dross. *Secondly*, With great gain. The spoils are exceedingly rich; glory, honour, and peace, a crown of righteousness that fades not away. In this the suffering saints have triumphed. As afflictions abound, consolations much more abound, 2 Cor. i. 5. Those that have gone smiling to the stake, and stood singing in the flames—these were more than conquerors.

[3] It is only *through Christ that loved us.* We are conquerors, not in our own strength, but in the grace that is in Christ Jesus. We are conquerors by virtue of Christ's victory. We have nothing to do but to pursue the victory, and to divide the spoil, and so are more than conquerors.

2. A direct and positive conclusion of the whole matter: *For I am persuaded, v.* 38, 39. And here he enumerates all those things which might separate between Christ and believers, and concludes that it could not be done. (1) *Neither death nor life*, neither the fear of death nor the hope of life. We shall not be separated from that love either in death or in life. (2) *Nor angels, nor principalities, nor powers.* The good angels will not, the bad shall not; and neither can. The good angels are engaged friends, the bad are restrained enemies. (3) *Nor things present, nor things to come*—neither the sense of troubles present nor the fear of troubles to come. Time shall not separate us, eternity shall not, from the love of Christ, whose favour is twisted in with both present things and things to come. (4) *Nor height, nor depth*—neither the height of prosperity, nor the depth of adversity, nothing from heaven above, nothing on earth below. (5) *Nor any other creature*—anything than can be named or thought of. It will not, it cannot, separate us from the love of God, which is in Christ Jesus our Lord. Nothing does it, can do it, but sin. This is the ground of the steadfastness of the love, because Jesus Christ, in whom he loves us, is the same yesterday, today and for ever.

JAMIESON, FAUSSET, BROWN

rible soever to the flesh, are tokens of God's wrath, or the least ground for doubt of His love.' From whom could such a question come better than from one who had himself for Christ's sake endured so much? (See II Cor. 11:11-33; I Cor. 4:10-13.) The apostle says not (remarks CALVIN nobly) 'What,' but "Who," just as if all creatures and all afflictions were so many gladiators taking arms against the Christians [THOLUCK]. **As it is written, For thy sake . . .**—Psalm 44:22—quoted as descriptive of what God's faithful people may expect from their enemies *at any period* when their hatred of righteousness is roused, and there is nothing to restrain it (see Gal. 4:29). **37. Nay, in all these things we are more than conquerors, through him that loved us**—not, "We are so far from being conquered by them, that they do us much good" [HODGE]; for though this be true, the word means simply, 'We are pre-eminently conquerors.' See on ch. 5:20. And so far are they from "separating us from Christ's love," that it is just "through Him that loved us" that we are victorious over them. **38, 39. For I am persuaded, that neither death, nor life, nor angels, nor principalities, nor powers**—whether good or bad. But as the bad are not called "angels," or "principalities," or "powers," save with some addition to show that such are meant (Matt. 25:41; Col. 2:15; Eph. 6: 12; II Pet. 2:4—except perhaps I Cor. 6:3), probably the *good* are meant here, but merely as the same apostle *supposes* an angel from heaven to preach a false gospel. (So the best interpreters.) **nor things present, nor things to come**—no condition of the present life and none of the unknown possibilities of the life to come. **nor any other creature**—rather, 'created thing'—any other thing in the whole created universe of God—**shall be able to separate us . . .**—"All the terms here are to be taken in their most general sense, and need no closer definition. The indefinite expressions are meant to denote all that can be thought of, and are only a rhetorical paraphrase of the conception of *allness*" [OLSHAUSEN]. **from the love of God, which is in Christ Jesus our Lord**—Thus does this wonderful chapter, with which the argument of the Epistle properly closes, leave us who are "justified by faith" in the arms of everlasting Love, whence no hostile power or conceivable event can ever tear us. "Behold what manner of love is this?" And "what manner of persons ought we to be," who are thus "blessed with all spiritual blessings in Christ?"—Note (1) There is a glorious consistency between the eternal purposes of God and the free agency of men, though the link of connection is beyond human, perhaps created, apprehension (vs. 28). (2) How ennobling is the thought that the complicated movements of the divine government of the world are all arranged in expressed furtherance of the "good" of God's chosen (vs. 28)! (3) To whatever conformity to the Son of God in dignity and glory, believers are or shall hereafter be raised, it will be the joy of everyone of them, as it is most fitting, "that in all things He should have the pre-eminence" (Col. 1:18), (vs. 29). (4) "As there is a beautiful harmony and necessary connection between the several doctrines of grace, so must there be a like harmony in the character of the Christian. He cannot experience the joy and confidence flowing from his election without the humility which the consideration of its being gratuitous must produce; nor can he have the peace of one who is justified without the holiness of one who is saved" (vss. 29, 30) [HODGE]. (5) However difficult it may be for finite minds to comprehend the emotions of the Divine Mind, let us never for a moment doubt that in "not sparing His own Son, but delivering Him up for us all," God made a real sacrifice of all that was dearest to His heart, and that in so doing He meant for ever to assure His people that all other things which they need—inasmuch as they are nothing to this stupendous gift, and indeed but the necessary sequel of it—will in due time be forthcoming (vs. 32). (6) In return for such a sacrifice on God's part, what can be considered too great on ours? (7) If there could be any doubt as to the meaning of the all-important word "JUSTIFICATION" in this Epistle—whether, as the Church of Rome teaches, and many others affirm, it means '*infusing* righteousness into the unholy, so as to *make* them righteous,' or, according to Protestant teaching, '*absolving, acquitting,* or *pronouncing righteous* the guilty' vs. 33 ought to set such doubt entirely at rest. For the apostle's question in this verse is, "Who shall *bring a charge against* God's elect?" In other words, 'Who shall *pronounce*' or '*hold them guilty?*' seeing that "God *justifies*" them: showing beyond all doubt, that to "justify" was intended to express precisely the op-

ADAM CLARKE

who had first loved them. Therefore the question is not, Who shall separate the love of Christ from us? or prevent Christ from loving us? but, Who shall separate *us* from the love of Christ? Who or what shall be able to remove *our affection* from Him? And the questions that immediately follow show that this is the sense of the passage; for the *tribulation, distress*, etc., which he enumerates are things by which *they* might be affected, but by which *Christ* could not be affected. *Shall tribulation? Thlipsis*, grievous affliction, or distress of any kind; from *thlibo*, to "compress, oppress, straiten"; anything by which a man is rendered miserable. *Or distress?* A word of nearly the same import with the former, but more intense in its signification. It signifies "straitness," being hemmed in on every side, without the possibility of getting out or escaping. *Or persecution? Diogmos* from *dioko*, to "pursue, press upon, prosecute," signifies such pursuing as an enemy uses in order to overtake the object of his malice that he may destroy him. *Or famine?* The total want of bread, and all the necessaries of life. *Or peril?* A state of extreme and continued danger, perplexing and distressing with grievous forebodings and alarms. *Or sword?* "Slaughter"; the total destruction of life, and especially beheading, and suchlike, done by the order of the civil magistrate; for the word is used in this Epistle, chap. xiii. 4, to signify the authority and power which he has of judicially terminating life; i.e., of inflicting capital punishment.

36. *As it is written.* And these are no more than we may naturally expect from the present constitution of the world, and the positive predictions of the prophet, Ps. xliv. 22, who foresaw that a wicked world would always persecute and oppress the true followers of God.

37. *Nay.* As the prophet adds in the same place, "All this is come upon us; yet have we not forgotten thee, neither have we dealt falsely in thy covenant," vv. 17-18. So all these things may happen unto us, but *in all these things we are more than conquerors.* We abide faithful in the new covenant of our God; and He is faithful who has promised to support and make us more than conquerors; i.e., to give us a complete triumph over sin, and death, and hell, not leaving one enemy unsubdued.

38. *For I am persuaded*, after the blessed experience we have had of support by the grace and Spirit of Him that loved us, that neither fear of *death*, nor hope of *life*, nor evil *angels, nor principalities, nor powers*, persecuting us for Christ's sake; nor the *things* we endure at *present, nor* the *things to come*, whatever tribulation we may be called to suffer in future.

39. *Nor height* of honor, *nor depth* of ignominy, *nor any other creature* (nor any other thing whatever), *shall be able to separate us* who love God *from the love of God, which* He has vouchsafed to us *in Christ Jesus.*

MATTHEW HENRY

ALEXANDER MACLAREN:

In that great ocean of the divine love we live and move and have our being, floating in it like some sea flower which spreads its filmy beauty and waves its long tresses in the depths of mid-ocean. The sound of its waters is ever in our ears; and above, beneath, around us, its mighty currents run evermore. We need not cower before the fixed gaze of some stony god, looking on us unmoved like those Egyptian deities that sit pitiless with idle hands on their laps, and wide-open lidless eyes gazing out across the sands. We need not fear the Omnipresence of love, nor the Omniscience which knows us altogether, and loves us even as it knows. Rather we shall be glad that we are ever in His presence, and desire, as the height of all felicity and the power for all goodness, to walk all the day long in the light of His countenance till the day come when we shall receive the crown of our perfecting in that we shall be "ever with the Lord."

—*Expositions of Holy Scripture*

JAMIESON, FAUSSET, BROWN

posite of 'holding guilty'; and consequently (as CALVIN triumphantly argues) that it means *'to absolve from the charge of guilt.'* (8) If there could be any reasonable doubt in what light the *death* of Christ is to be regarded in this Epistle, vs. 34 ought to set that doubt entirely at rest. For there the apostle's question is, Who shall *"condemn"* God's elect, since "Christ *died*" for them; showing beyond all doubt (as PHILIPPI justly argues) that it was the *expiatory* (character of that death which the apostle had in view. (9) What an affecting view of the love of Christ does it give us to learn that His greatest *nearness* to God and most powerful *interest* with Him—as "seated on His right hand"—is employed in behalf of His people here below (vs. 34)! (10) "The whole universe, with all that it contains, so far as it is good, is the friend and ally of the Christian; and, so far as it is evil, is more than a conquered foe" (vss. 35-39), [HODGE]. (11) Are we who "have tasted that the Lord is gracious," both "kept by the *power* of God through faith unto salvation" (I Pet. 1:5), and embraced in the arms of Invincible *Love?* Then surely, while "building ourselves up on our most holy faith," and "praying in the Holy Ghost," only the more should we feel constrained to *"keep ourselves in the love of God,* looking for the mercy of our Lord Jesus Christ unto eternal life" (Jude 20,21).

ADAM CLARKE

ALEXANDER MACLAREN:

The recognition of this triumphant sovereignty of love over all these real and supposed antagonists makes us, too, lords over them, and delivers us from the temptations which some of them present us to separate ourselves from the love of God. They all become our servants and helpers, uniting us to that love. So we are set free from the dread of death and from the distractions incident to life. So we are delivered from superstitious dreads of an unseen world, and from craven fear of men. So we are emancipated from absorption in the present and from careful thought for the future. So we are at home everywhere, and every corner of the universe is to us one of the many mansions of our Father's house. "All things are yours, . . . and ye are Christ's; and Christ is God's."

—*Expositions of Holy Scripture*

MATTHEW HENRY — CHAPTER 9

Verses 1–5

The apostles' solemn profession of a great concern for the nation and people of the Jews—that he was heartily troubled that so many of them were enemies to the gospel. For this he had *great heaviness and continual sorrow.* It is wisdom as much as may be to mollify those truths which sound harshly: dip the nail in oil, it will drive the better. He introduces his discourse with this affectionate profession, that they might not think he triumphed over the rejected Jews. Paul was so far from desiring it that he most pathetically deprecates it.

I. He asserts it with a solemn protestation (*v.* 1): *I say the truth in Christ,* "I speak it as one of God's people, children that will not lie. I appeal to Christ concerning it." He appeals likewise to his own conscience. That which he was going to assert was a secret; it was concerning a sorrow in his heart to which none was a capable competent witness but God and his own conscience.—*That I have great heaviness, v.* 2. The very mention of it was unpleasant.

II. He backs it with a very serious imprecation out of love to the Jews. *I could wish;* he does not say, I do wish, for it was no proper means appointed for such an end; but, if it were, *I could wish that myself were accursed from Christ for my brethren*—a very high pang of zeal and affection for his countrymen. Love is apt to be thus bold, and venturous, and self-denying. Because the glory of God's grace in the salvation of many is to be preferred before the welfare and happiness of a single person, Paul would be content to forego all his own happiness to purchase theirs. 1. He would be content to be cut off from the land of the living, as an anathema. They thirsted for his blood, persecuted him as the most obnoxious person in the world. "I am willing to bear all this, and a great deal more, for your good. Your unbelief and rejection create in my heart a heaviness so much greater than all these troubles can that I could look upon them not only as tolerable, but as desirable, rather than this rejection." 2. He would be content to be excommunicated from the society of the faithful if that would do them any good. He could wish himself no more remembered among the saints. He would be content to have his name buried in oblivion or reproach, for the good of the Jews. 3. He could be content to be cut off from all his share of happiness in Christ, if that might be a means of their salvation.

III. He gives us the reason of this affection and concern.

1. Because of their relation to them: *My brethren, my kinsmen, according to the flesh.* Though they were very bitter against him upon all occasions, thus respectfully does he speak of them. It shows him to be a man of forgiving spirit. *My kinsmen.* Paul was a Hebrew of the Hebrews. We ought to be in a special manner concerned for the spiritual good of our relations. Concerning them, and our usefulness to them, we must in a special manner give account.

2. Especially because of their relation to God (*v.* 4, 5): *Who are Israelites,* distinguished by visible church privileges, many of which are here mentioned: (1) *The adoption;* not that which is saving, and which entitles to eternal happiness, but that which was external. (2) *And the glory.* The many tokens of the

JAMIESON, FAUSSET, BROWN — CHAPTER 9

VSS. 1-33. THE BEARING OF THE FOREGOING TRUTHS UPON THE CONDITION AND DESTINY OF THE CHOSEN PEOPLE—ELECTION—THE CALLING OF THE GENTILES. Too well aware that he was regarded as a traitor to the dearest interests of his people (Acts 21:33; 22:22; 25:24), the apostle opens this division of his subject by giving vent to his real feelings with extraordinary vehemence of protestation. **1, 2. I say the truth in Christ**—as if steeped in the spirit of Him who wept over impenitent and doomed Jerusalem (cf. ch. 1:9; II Cor. 12:19; Phil. 1:8). **my conscience bearing me witness in the Holy Ghost**—'my conscience as quickened, illuminated, and even now under the direct operation of the Holy Ghost.' **That I have . . .**—'That I have great grief (or, sorrow) and unceasing anguish in my heart'—the bitter hostility of his nation to the glorious Gospel, and the awful consequences of their unbelief, weighing heavily and incessantly upon his spirit. **3. For I could wish that myself were accursed from Christ for**—'in behalf of'—**my brethren, my kinsmen according to the flesh**—In proportion as he felt himself severed from his nation, he seems to have realized all the more vividly their natural relationship. To explain away the wish here expressed, as too strong for any Christian to utter or conceive, some have rendered the opening words, 'I *did* wish,' referring it to his former unenlightened state; a sense of the words too tame to be endured: others unwarrantably soften the sense of the word "accursed." But our version gives the true import of the original; and if it be understood as the language rather of "strong and indistinct emotions than of definite ideas" [HODGE], expressing passionately how he felt his whole being swallowed up in the salvation of his people, the difficulty will vanish, and we shall be reminded of the similar idea so nobly expressed by Moses (Exod. 32:32). **4. Who are Israelites**—See ch. 11:1; II Corinthians 11:22; Philippians 3:5. **to whom pertaineth**—'whose is'—**the adoption**—It is true that, compared with the new economy, the old was a state of minority and pupilage, and so far that of a bond-servant (Gal. 4:1-3); yet, compared with the state of the surrounding heathen, the choice of Abraham and his seed was a real separation of them to be a *Family of God* (Exod. 4:22; Deut. 32:6; Isa. 1:2; Jer. 31:9; Hos. 11:1; Mal. 1:6). **and the glory**—that "glory of the Lord," or 'visible token of the Divine Presence in the midst of them,' which rested on the ark and filled the tabernacle during all their wanderings in the wilderness; which in Jerusalem continued to be seen in the tabernacle and temple, and only disappeared when, at the Captivity, the temple was demolished, and the sun of the ancient economy began to go down. This was what the Jews called the *"Shekinah."* **and the covenants**—"the covenants of promise" to which the Gentiles before Christ were "strangers" (Eph. 2:12); meaning the *one covenant* with Abraham in its successive *renewals* (see Gal. 3:16, 17). **and the giving of the law**—from Mount Sinai, and the possession of it thereafter, which the Jews justly deemed their peculiar honor (Deut. 26:18, 19; Ps. 147:19, 20; ch. 2:17). **and the service of God**—or, of the sanctuary,

ADAM CLARKE — CHAPTER 9

1. *I say the truth in Christ, I lie not.* This is one of the most solemn oaths any man can possibly take. He appeals to Christ as the Searcher of hearts that he tells the truth; asserts that his conscience was free from all guile in this matter, and that the Holy Ghost bore him testimony that what he said was true.

3. *For I could wish that myself were accursed from Christ.* Very few passages in the New Testament have puzzled critics and commentators more than this. Every person saw the perfect absurdity of understanding it in a literal sense, as no man in his right mind could wish himself eternally damned in order to save another, or to save even the whole world. And the supposition that such an effect could be produced by such a sacrifice was equally absurd and monstrous. The Greek word *anathema* properly signifies anything devoted to God, so as to be destroyed; it answers to the Hebrew *cherem,* which the Septuagint translate by it, and means either a "thing or person separated from its former state or condition, and devoted to destruction." In this sense it is used, Deut. vii. 25-26; Josh. vi. 17-18; vii. 12. It is certain that the word, among both Hebrews and Greeks, was used to express a person devoted to destruction for the public safety. This one circumstance is sufficient to explain the word in this place. Paul desired to be devoted to destruction, as the Jews then were, in order to redeem his countrymen from this most terrible excision. He was willing to become a sacrifice for the public safety, and to give his life to redeem theirs.

4. *Who are Israelites.* Descendants of Jacob, a man so highly favored of God, and from whom he received his name *Israel*—"a prince of God," Gen. xxxii. 28, from which name his descendants were called *Israelites,* and separated unto God for His glory and praise. Their very name of *Israelites* implied their very high dignity; they were a royal nation, princes of the most high God. *The adoption.* The Israelites were all taken into the family of God, and were called His sons and firstborn, Exod. iv. 22; Deut. xiv. 1; Jer. xxxi. 9; Hos. xi. 1; and this adoption took place when God made the covenant with them at Horeb. *The glory.* The manifestation of God among them; principally by the cloud and pillar, and the Shekinah, or Divine Presence, appearing between the cherubim over the mercy seat. These were peculiar to the Jews; no other nation was ever thus favored. *The covenants.* The covenants made with Abraham, both that which relates to the spiritual seed and that which was peculiar to his natural descendants, Gal. iii. 16-17; which covenants were afterwards renewed by Moses, Deut. xxix. 1. *The giving of the law.* The revelation of God by God himself, containing a system of moral and political precepts. This was also peculiar to the Jews, for to no other nation had He ever given a revelation of His

MATTHEW HENRY

divine presence and guidance, the cloud, the Shechinah, the distinguishing favours conferred upon them—these were the glory. (3) *And the covenants*—the covenant made with Abraham, and often renewed with his seed upon divers occasions. Still these pertained to Israel. (4) *And the giving of the law*. It is a great privilege to have the law of God among us, and it is to be accounted so. (5) *And the services of God*. They had the ordinances of God's worship among them—the temple, the altars, the priests, the sacrifices, the feasts. While other nations were worshipping and serving stocks, and stones, and devils, and they knew not what of other idols their own invention, the Israelites were serving the true God in the way of his own appointment. (6) *And the promises*—promises relating to the Messiah and the gospel state. The comfort of the promises is to be had in obedience to that law and attendance upon that service. (7) *Whose are the fathers* (*v.* 5), Abraham, Isaac, and Jacob, that stood so high in the favour of God. It was for the fathers' sake that they were taken into covenant. (8) But the greatest honour of all was that *of them as concerning the flesh, Christ came*. This was the great privilege of the Jews, that Christ was of kin to them. Mentioning Christ, he interposes a very great word concerning him, that he is *over all, God blessed for ever*. It is a very full proof of the Godhead of Christ; he is not only over all, as Mediator, but he is God blessed for ever. It was likewise the honour of the Jews that, seeing God blessed for ever would be a man, he would be a Jew.

Verses 6–13

The rejection of the Jews, by the establishment of the gospel dispensation, did not at all invalidate the word of God's promise to the patriarchs: *Not as though the word of God hath taken no effect* (*v.* 6). We are not to ascribe inefficacy to any word of God: nothing that he has spoken does or can fall to the ground; see Isa. lv. 10, 11. This is to be understood especially of the promise of God, which may be to a wavering faith very doubtful; but it is not, it cannot be, made of no effect.

Now the difficulty is to reconcile the rejection of the unbelieving Jews with the word of God's promise. This he does in four ways: 1. By explaining the true meaning and intention of the promise, *v.* 6–13. 2. By asserting the absolute sovereignty of God, *v.* 14–24. 3. By showing how this rejection of the Jews, and the taking in of the Gentiles, were foretold in the Old Testament, *v.* 25–29. 4. By fixing the true reason of the Jews' rejection, *v.* 30, to the end.

In this paragraph the apostle explains the true meaning and intention of the promise. When we misunderstand the promise, no marvel if we are ready to quarrel with God about the accomplishment. When God said he would be *a God to Abraham, and to his seed*, he did not mean it of all his seed according to the flesh. He intended it with a limitation. And as from the beginning it was appropriated to Isaac and not to Ishmael, to Jacob and not to Esau, and yet for all this the word of God was not made of no effect; so now the same promise is appropriated to believing Jews that embrace Christ, and, though it throws off multitudes that refuse Christ, yet the promise is not therefore invalidated.

I. He lays down this proposition—that *they are not all Israel who are of Israel* (*v.* 6), *neither because they are*, &c., *v.* 7. They are not all really Israel that are so in name and profession. Grace does not run in the blood.

II. He proves this by instances. Some of Abraham's seed were chosen, and others not; God therein wrought according to the counsel of his own will.

1. He specifies the case of Isaac and Ishmael, both of them the seed of Abraham; and yet Isaac only taken into covenant with God, and Ishmael rejected. For this he quotes Gen. xxi. 12, *In Isaac shall thy seed be called*, because the covenant was to be established with Isaac, Gen. xvii. 19. The blessings wrapt up in that great word, being communicated by God as a benefactor, he was free to determine on what head they should rest, and accordingly entailed them upon Isaac. This he explains further (*v.* 8, 9). The children of the flesh, as such, are not therefore the children of God, for then Ishmael had put in a good claim. This remark comes home to the unbelieving Jews. They had confidence in the flesh. Ishmael was a child of the flesh, representing those that expect justification and salvation by their own strength and righteousness. The *children of the promise are counted for the seed*. Those that have the happiness of being counted for the seed have it not for the sake of any merit of their own, but purely by virtue of the promise. Isaac was a child of promise; this he proves, *v.* 9. He was also con-

JAMIESON, FAUSSET, BROWN

meaning the whole divinely instituted religious service, in the celebration of which they were brought so nigh unto God. **and the promises**—the great Abrahamic promises, successively unfolded, and which had their fulfilment only in Christ; (see Heb. 7:6; Gal. 3:16, 21; Acts 26:6, 7). **5. Whose are the fathers**—here, probably, the three great fathers of the covenant—Abraham, Isaac, and Jacob—by whom God condescended to name Himself (Exod. 8:6, 13; Luke 20:37). **and**—most exalted privilege of all, and as such, reserved to the last—**of whom as concerning the flesh**—see on ch. 1:3—**Christ came**—or, 'is Christ'—**who is over all, God**—rather, 'God over all.' **blessed for ever. Amen**—To get rid of the bright testimony here borne to the supreme divinity of Christ, various expedients have been adopted: (1) To place a period, either after the words "concerning the flesh Christ came," rendering the next clause as a doxology to the Father—"God who is over all be blessed for ever"; or after the word "all"-thus, "Christ came, who is over all: God be blessed . . . ." [ERASMUS, LOCKE, FRITZSCHE, MEYER, JOWETT, etc.]. But it is fatal to this view, as even *Socinus* admits, that in other Scripture doxologies the word "Blessed" *precedes* the name of God on whom the blessing is invoked (thus: "Blessed be God," Ps. 68:35; "Blessed be the Lord God, the God of Israel," Ps. 72:18). Besides, any such doxology here would be 'unmeaning and frigid in the extreme'; the sad subject on which he was entering suggesting anything but a doxology, even in connection with Christ's Incarnation [ALFORD]. (2) To transpose the words rendered 'who is'; in which case the rendering would be, 'whose (i.e., the fathers') is Christ according to the flesh' [CRELLIUS, WHISTON, TAYLOR, WHITBY]. But this is a desperate expedient, in the face of all MS. authority; as is also the conjecture of GROTIUS and others, that the word "God" should be omitted from the text. It remains then, that we have here no doxology at all, but a naked statement of fact, that while Christ is "of" the Israelitish nation *"as concerning the flesh,"* He is *in another respect* "God over all, blessed for ever." (In II Cor. 11:31 the very Greek phrase which is here rendered "who is," is used in the same sense; and cf. ch. 1:25, *Greek*.) In this view of the passage, as a testimony to the supreme divinity of Christ, besides all the orthodox fathers, some of the ablest modern critics concur [BENGEL, THOLUCK, STUART, OLSHAUSEN, PHILIPPI, ALFORD, etc.] **6. Not as though the word of God had taken none effect**—'hath fallen to the ground,' i.e., failed: cf. Luke 16:17, *Greek*. **for they are not all Israel which are of Israel**—better, 'for not all they which are of Israel are Israel.' *Here the apostle enters upon the profound subject of* ELECTION, the treatment of which extends to the end of ch. 11—'Think not that I mourn over the total loss of Israel; for that would involve the failure of God's word to Abraham; but not all that belong to the natural seed, and go under the name of "Israel," are *the* Israel of God's irrevocable choice.' The difficulties which encompass this subject lie not in the apostle's teaching, which is plain enough, but in the truths themselves, the evidence for which, taken by themselves, is overwhelming, but whose perfect harmony is beyond human comprehension in the present state. The great source of error here lies in hastily inferring [as THOLUCK and others], from the apostle's taking up, at the close of this chapter, the calling of the Gentiles in connection with the rejection of Israel, and continuing this subject through the two next chapters, that the Election treated of in the body of this chapter is *national*, not *personal* Election, and consequently is Election merely to *religious advantages*, not to *eternal salvation*. In that case, the argument of vs. 6, with which the subject of Election opens, would be this: 'The choice of Abraham and his seed has not failed; because though Israel has been rejected, *the Gentiles* have taken their place; and God has a right to choose what nation He will to the privileges of His visible kingdom.' But so far from this, the Gentiles are not so much as mentioned at all till towards the close of the chapter; and the argument of this verse is, that 'all Israel *is not* rejected, but only a portion of it, the remainder being *the* "Israel" whom God has chosen in the exercise of His sovereign right.' And that this is a choice not to mere external privileges, but to eternal salvation, will abundantly appear from what follows. **7-9. Neither, because they are the seed of Abraham, are they all children**—'Not in the line of mere fleshly descent from Abraham does the election run; else Ishmael, Hagar's child, and even Keturah's children, would be included, which they were not.' **but**—the true election are such of Abraham's seed as God unconditionally

ADAM CLARKE

will. *The service*. The particular ordinances, rites, and ceremonies of their religious worship, and especially the sacrificial system, so expressive of the sinfulness of sin and the holiness of God. *The promises*. The land of Canaan, and the blessings of the Messiah and His kingdom, which promises had been made and often repeated to the patriarchs and to the prophets.

5. *Whose are the fathers*. Abraham, Isaac, Jacob, Joseph, the twelve patriarchs, Moses, Joshua, Samuel, David, etc., without controversy, the greatest and most eminent men that ever flourished under heaven. From these, in an uninterrupted and unpolluted line, the Jewish people had descended, and it was no small glory to be able to reckon, in their genealogy, persons of such incomparable merit and excellency. *And of whom as concerning the flesh Christ came*. These ancestors were the more renowned as being the progenitors of the human nature of the Messiah Christ; the Messiah "according to the flesh" sprang from them. But this Messiah was more than man; He is *God over all*; the very Being who gave them being, though He appeared to receive a being from them. Here the apostle most distinctly points out the two-fold nature of our Lord—His eternal Godhead and His humanity.

6. *Not as though the word of God hath taken none effect*. A Jew might have objected, as in chap. iii. 3: "Is not God bound by His faithfulness to continue the Jews as His peculiar church and people, notwithstanding the infidelity of the major part of them?" To which it may be answered: This awful dispensation of God towards the Jews is not inconsistent with the veracity of the divine promise; for even the whole body of natural-born Jews are not the whole of the Israelites comprehended in the promise. Abraham is the father of many nations; and his seed is not only that which is of the *law*, but that also which is "of the faith of Abraham," chap. iv. 16-17. The Gentiles were included in the Abrahamic covenant as well as the Jews, and therefore the Jews have no exclusive right to the blessings of God's kingdom.

7. *Neither because they are the seed of Abraham*. Nor can they conclude, because they are the natural descendants of Abraham, that therefore they are all of them, without exception, the children in whom the promise is to be fulfilled. *But, In Isaac shall thy seed be called*. The promise is not confined to immediate natural descent, but may be accomplished in any part of Abraham's posterity. For Abraham had several sons besides Isaac, Gen. xxv. 1-2, particularly Ishmael, who was circumcised before Isaac was born, and in whom Abraham was desirous that the promise should be fulfilled, Gen. xvii. 18. In him God might have fulfilled the promise had He so pleased; and yet He said to Abraham, Gen. xxi. 12: Not in Ishmael, but "in Isaac shall thy seed be called."

8. *That is, They which are the children of the flesh*. Whence it appears that not the children who descend from Abraham's loins, nor those who were circumcised as he was, nor even those whom he might expect and desire, are therefore the Church and people of God; but those who are made children by the good pleasure and promise of God, as Isaac was, are alone to be accounted for the seed with whom the covenant was established.

9. *For this is the word of promise*. That is, this is evidently implied in the promise recorded in Gen. xviii. 10: "At this time I will come," saith God, "and exert My divine power, and Sarah, though fourscore and ten years old, shall have a son"; which shows that it is the

MATTHEW HENRY

ceived and born by virtue of the promise, and so a proper type of those who are now counted for the seed, even true believers, who are born, not of the will of the flesh, nor of the will of man, but of God.

2. The case of Jacob and Esau (*v.* 10–13), which is much stronger. There was a previous difference between Ishmael and Isaac, before Ishmael was cast out: Ishmael was of a fierce disposition, and had mocked or persecuted Isaac. But, in the case of Jacob and Esau, they were both the sons of Isaac by one mother. The difference was made between them by the divine counsel before they were born, or had done any good or evil. Both lay struggling alike in their mother's womb, when it was said, *The elder shall serve the younger, that the purpose of God according to election might stand*—that this great truth may be established, that God chooses some and refuses others by his own absolute and sovereign will. This difference that was put between Jacob and Esau he further illustrates by a quotation from Mal. i. 2, 3, where it is said, not of Jacob and Esau, but the Edomites and Israelites their posterity, *Jacob have I loved, and Esau have I hated.* The people of Israel were taken into the covenant, while the Edomites were rejected. Such a difference did God put between those two nations, that both descended from the loins of Abraham and Isaac, as at first there was a difference put between Jacob and Esau. (1) Some understand it of the election and rejection of conditions or qualifications. As God chose Isaac and Jacob, and rejected Ishmael and Esau, so he might and did choose faith to be the condition of salvation and reject the works of the law. (2) Others understand it of the election and rejection of particular persons—some loved, and others hated, from eternity. But the apostle speaks of Jacob and Esau, not in their own persons, but as ancestors. Nor does God condemn any merely because he will do it, without any reason taken from their own deserts. (3) Others therefore understand it of the election and rejection of people considered complexly. His design is to justify God, and his mercy and truth, in calling the Gentiles, while he suffered the obstinate part of the Jews to persist in unbelief. The choosing of Jacob the younger, and preferring him before Esau the elder (so crossing hands), were to intimate that the Jews, though the natural seed of Abraham, should be laid aside; and the Gentiles, who were as the younger brother, should be taken in in their stead. The Jews had for many ages been the favourites of heaven. Now that the gospel was preached, Christian churches (and in process of time Christian nations), become their successors in the divine favour.

Verses 14–24

The apostle comes here to maintain the absolute sovereignty of God, in disposing of the children of men. God is to be considered as an owner and benefactor, giving to the children of men such grace and favour as he has determined in and by his secret and eternal will.

Now this part of his discourse is in answer to two objections.

I. It might be objected, *Is there unrighteousness with God?* This the apostle startles at the thought of: *God forbid!* Far be it from us to think such a thing. He denies the consequences, and proves the denial.

1. In respect of those to whom he shows mercy, *v.* 15, 16. He quotes that scripture to show God's sovereignty in dispensing his favours (Exod. xxxiii. 19): *I will be gracious to whom I will be gracious.* All God's reasons of mercy are taken from within himself. He dispenses his gifts to whom he will, without giving us any reason. The expression is very emphatic, and the repetition makes it more so: *I will have mercy on whom I will have mercy*, he will do what he will. Therefore God's mercy endures for ever, because the reason of it is fetched from within himself; therefore his gifts and callings are without repentance.

JAMIESON, FAUSSET, BROWN

chooses, as exemplified in that promise. **In Isaac shall thy seed be called**—(Gen. 21:12). **10-13. And not only so; but when Rebecca . . .**—It might be thought that there was a natural reason for preferring the child of Sarah, as being Abraham's true and first wife, both to the child of Hagar, Sarah's maid, and to the children of Keturah, his second wife. But there could be no such reason in the case of Rebecca, Isaac's only wife; for the choice of her son Jacob was the choice of one of two sons by the same mother and of the younger in preference to the elder, and before either of them was born, and consequently before either had done good or evil to be a ground of preference: and all to show that the sole ground of distinction lay in the unconditional choice of God—*"not of works, but of Him that calleth."*

ALBERT BARNES:

13. "As it is written." Mal. 1:2, 3. That is, the distribution of favors is on the principle advanced by the prophet, and is in accordance with the declaration that God had in fact loved the one and hated the other.

"Jacob." This refers, doubtless, to the posterity of Jacob. "Have I loved." I have shown affection for that people; I have bestowed on them great privileges and blessings as proofs of attachment. I have preferred Jacob to Esau.

"Esau." The descendants of Esau, the Edomites (see Mal. 1:4). "Have I hated." This does not mean any positive hatred, but that he had preferred Jacob, and had withheld from Esau those privileges and blessings which he had conferred on the posterity of Jacob. This is explained in Mal. 1:3, "And I hated Esau, and laid his mountains and heritage waste for the dragons of the wilderness" (cf. Jer. 49:17, 18; Ezek. 35:6). It was common among the Hebrews to use the terms *love* and *hatred* in this comparative sense, where the former implied strong positive attachment, and the latter, not positive hatred, but merely a less love, or the withholding of the expressions of affection. "He that spareth his rod *hateth* his son; but he that *loveth* him chasteneth him betimes" (Prov. 13:24); "No man can serve two masters, for either he will *hate* the one and *love* the other" (Matt. 6:24); "If any man come to me, and *hate* not his father and mother" (Luke 14:26).
—*Popular Commentary*

14. What shall we say then? Is there unrighteousness with God? God forbid—This is the first of two objections to the foregoing doctrine, that God chooses one and rejects another, not on account of their works, but purely in the exercise of His own good pleasure: '*This doctrine is inconsistent with the justice of God.*' The answer to this objection extends to vs. 19, where we have the second objection.

15. For he saith to Moses—Exod. 33:19—**I will have mercy on whom I will have**—'on whom I have'—**mercy, and I will have compassion on whom I will have**—'on whom I have'—**compassion**—'There can be no unrighteousness in God's choosing whom He will, for to Moses He expressly claims the right to do so.' Yet it is worthy of notice that this is expressed in the positive rather than the negative form: not, 'I will have mercy on *none but* whom I will'; but, 'I will have mercy on *whomsoever* I will.'

ADAM CLARKE

sovereign will and act of God alone which singles out and constitutes the peculiar seed that was to inherit the promise made to Abraham.

11. *For the children being not yet born.* As the word *children* is not in the text, the word "nations" would be more proper; for it is of nations that the apostle speaks, as the following verses show, as well as the history to which he refers. *Neither having done any good.* To merit the distinction of being made the peculiar people of God. *Or evil*, to deserve to be left out of this covenant, and the distinguishing national blessings which it conferred. *That the purpose of God according to election might stand*—that such distinctions might appear to depend on nothing but God's free choice. *Not of works*, or any desert in the people or nations thus chosen; but of the mere purpose *of him that calleth* any people He pleases, to make them the depositories of His especial blessings, and thus to distinguish them from all others.

12-13. *The elder shall serve the younger.* These words, with those of Malachi, *Jacob have I loved, but Esau have I hated*, are cited by the apostle to prove, according to their typical signification, that the "purpose of God according to election" does and will stand, "not of *works*, but of *him that calleth*"; that is, that the purpose of God, which is the ground of that election which He makes among men, unto the honor of being Abraham's seed, might appear to remain unchangeable in Him, and to be even the same which He had declared unto Abraham. That these words are used in a *national* and not in a *personal* sense is evident from this: that, taken in the latter sense they are not true, for Jacob never did exercise any power over Esau, nor was Esau ever subject to him. Jacob, on the contrary, was rather subject to Esau, and was sorely afraid of him; and, first, by his messengers, and afterwards personally, acknowledged his brother to be his lord, and himself to be his servant; see Gen. xxxii. 4; xxxiii. 8, 13. And hence it appears that neither Esau nor Jacob, nor even their posterities, are brought here by the apostle as instances of any *personal* reprobation from eternity. For it is very certain that very many, if not the far greatest part, of Jacob's posterity were wicked, and rejected by God; and it is not less certain that some of Esau's posterity were partakers of the faith of their father Abraham. (1) It incontestably appears from these passages that the prophet does not speak at all of the *person* of Jacob or Esau, but of their respective *posterities.* (2) If neither the prophet nor the apostle speaks of the persons of Jacob or Esau, but of their posterity, then it is evident that neither the love of God to Jacob nor the hatred of God to Esau were such according to which the eternal states of men, in either happiness or misery, are to be determined; nor is there here any scriptural or rational ground for the decree of unconditional personal election and reprobation, which comparatively modern times have endeavored to build on these scriptures.

14. *What shall we say then?* To what conclusion shall we come on the facts before us? Shall we suggest that God's bestowing peculiar privileges in this unequal manner on those who otherwise are in equal circumstances is inconsistent with justice and equity? "By no means." Whatever God does is right, and He may dispense His blessings to whom and on what terms He pleases.

15. *For he saith to Moses, I will have mercy.* The words of God to Moses, Exod. xxxiii. 19, show that God has a right to dispense His blessings as He pleases; for, after He had declared that He would spare the Jews of old and continue them in the relation of His peculiar people, when they had deserved to have been cut off for their idolatry, He said: "I will make all my goodness pass before thee, and I will proclaim the name of the Lord before thee . . . and will shew mercy on whom I will shew mercy"; and I will have compassion on whom I will have compassion. As if He had said: I will make such a display of My perfections as shall convince you that My nature is kind and beneficent; but know that I am a debtor to none of My creatures. I will give My salvation in My own way and on My own terms. "He that believeth not shall be damned." This

MATTHEW HENRY

Hence he infers (*v.* 16), *It is not of him that willeth.* It is not to be ascribed to the most generous desire, nor to the most industrious endeavour, of man, but only and purely to the free grace and mercy of God. In Jacob's case it was *not of him that willeth, nor of him that runneth*; but only the mercy and grace of God. The reason why the unworthy, undeserving Gentiles are called, while the greatest part of the Jews are left to perish in unbelief, is not because those Gentiles were better deserving or better disposed for such a favour, but because of God's free grace that made that difference. Such is the method of God's grace towards all that partake of it, for he is found of those that sought him not (Isa. lxv. 1).

2. In respect of those who perish, *v.* 17. God's sovereignty is here discovered in the instance of Pharaoh. What God did with Pharaoh. He raised him up. Thus doth God raise up sinners in outward prosperity, external privileges. What he designed in it: *That I might show my power in thee.* God would, by all this, serve the honour of his name, and manifest his power.

His conclusion concerning both these we have, *v.* 18. *He hath mercy on whom he will have mercy, and whom he will he hardeneth.* The various dealings of God must be resolved into his absolute sovereignty. He is debtor to no man, his grace is his own; we have none of us deserved it, nay, we have all justly forfeited it a thousand times. Those who are saved must thank God only, and those who perish must thank themselves only. We are bound to do our utmost for the salvation of all we have to do with; but God is bound no further than he has been pleased to bind himself; and that is that he will receive, and not cast out, those that come to Christ. Had he mercy on the Gentiles? It was because he would have mercy on them.

II. It might be objected, *Why doth he yet find fault? For who hath resisted his will?* (*v.* 19). He might well find fault if people refused to come up to the terms on which such a salvation is offered; the salvation being so great, the terms could not be hard. If God, while he gives effectual grace to some, denies it to others, why doth he find fault with those to whom he denies it? This objection he answers at large,

1. By reproving the objector (*v.* 20): *Nay but, O man.* This is not an objection fit to be made by the creature against his Creator, by man against God. Observe how contemptibly he speaks of man, when he comes to argue with God his Maker: "*Who art thou,* thou that art so foolish, so incompetent a judge of the divine counsels? art thou able to fathom such a depth." *That repliest against God.* It becomes us to submit to him, not to reply against him; not to fly in his face, nor to charge him with folly.

2. By resolving all into the divine sovereignty. We are the thing formed, and he is the former; and it does not become us to arraign his wisdom in ordering and disposing of us into this or that shape of figure. God's sovereignty over us is fitly illustrated by the power that the potter hath over the clay; compare Jer. xviii. 6.

(1) He gives us the comparison, *v.* 21. The potter, out of the same lump, may make either a fashionable vessel, or a contemptible vessel, and herein he acts arbitrarily.

(2) The application of the comparison, *v.* 22–24. Two sorts of vessels God forms out of the great lump of fallen mankind: *Vessels of wrath.* In these God is willing to show his wrath. God will make it appear that he hates sin. He will likewise make his power known. In order to this, God *endured them with much long-suffering*—exercised a great deal of patience towards them, and so they became *fitted for destruction,* fitted by their own sin and self-hardening. The reigning corruptions and wickedness of the soul are its preparedness for hell.

JAMIESON, FAUSSET, BROWN

16. So then it is not of him that willeth—hath the inward *desire*—**nor of him that runneth**—maketh active *effort*—(cf. I Cor. 9:24, 26; Phil. 2:16; 3:14). Both these are indispensable to salvation, yet salvation is owing to neither, but is purely "of God that showeth mercy." See on Philippians 2: 12, 13, "Work out your own salvation with fear and trembling: for it is God which, *out of His own good pleasure,* worketh in you both to *will* and to *do.*" **17. For the scripture saith to Pharaoh**—observe here the light in which the Scripture is viewed by the apostle. **Even for this same**—'this very'—**purpose have I raised**—'raised I'—**thee up . . .**—The apostle had shown that God claims the right to choose whom He will: here he shows by an example that God punishes whom He will. But "God did not make Pharaoh wicked; He only forbore to make him good, by the exercise of special and altogether unmerited grace" [HODGE]. **that I might**—'may'—**show my power in thee**—It was not that Pharaoh was worse than others that he was so dealt with, but "in order that he might become a monument of the penal justice of God, and it was with a view to this that God provided that the evil which was in him should be manifested in this definite form" [OLSHAUSEN]. **and that my name might**—'may'—**be declared**—'proclaimed'—**in all the earth**—"This is the principle on which all punishment is inflicted, that the true character of the Divine Lawgiver should be known. This is of all objects, where God is concerned, the highest and most important; in itself the most worthy, and in its results the most beneficent" [HODGE]. **18. Therefore hath he**—'So then he hath.' The result then is that He hath—**mercy on whom he will have mercy, and whom he will he hardeneth**—by judicially abandoning them to the hardening influence of sin itself (Ps. 81:11, 12; ch. 1:24, 26, 28; Heb. 3:8, 13), and of the surrounding incentives to it (Matt. 24:12; I Cor. 15:38; II Thess. 2:17). **19.** *Second objection* to the doctrine of Divine Sovereignty: **Thou shalt say then unto me, Why**—'Why then' is the true reading—**doth he yet find fault? for who hath resisted**—'Who resisteth'—**his will?**—i.e., '*This doctrine is incompatible with human responsibility';* If God chooses and rejects, pardons and punishes, whom He pleases, why are those blamed who, if rejected by Him, cannot help sinning and perishing? This objection shows quite as conclusively as the former the real nature of the doctrine objected to—that it is Election and Non-election to eternal salvation prior to any difference of personal character; this is the only doctrine that could suggest the objection here stated, and to this doctrine the objection *is* plausible. What now is the apostle's answer? It is twofold. *First:* 'It is irreverence and presumption in the creature to arraign the Creator.' **20, 21. Nay but, O man, who art thou that repliest against God? Shall the thing formed say to him that formed it, Why hast thou made**—'didst thou make'—**me thus**—(Isa. 45:9)? **Hath not the potter power over the clay; of the same lump to make one vessel unto honour, and another to dishonour?**—"The objection is founded on ignorance or misapprehension of the relation between God and His sinful creatures; supposing that He is under obligation to extend His grace to all, whereas He is under obligation to none. All are sinners, and have forfeited every claim to His mercy; it is therefore perfectly competent to God to spare one and not another, to make one vessel to honor and another to dishonor. But it is to be borne in mind that Paul does not here speak of God's right over His creatures *as creatures,* but *as sinful creatures:* as he himself clearly intimates in the next verses. It is the cavil of a sinful creature against his Creator that he is answering, and he does so by showing that God is under no obligation to give His grace to any, but is as sovereign as in fashioning the clay" [HODGE]. But, *Second:* 'There is nothing unjust in such sovereignty.' **22, 23. What if God, willing to show**—'designing to manifest'—**his wrath**—His holy displeasure against sin—**and to make his power**—to punish it—**known, endured with much long-suffering the vessels of wrath**—i.e., 'destined to wrath'; just as "vessels of mercy," in the next verse, mean 'vessels destined to mercy'; compare Ephesians 2:3, "children of wrath." **fitted for destruction**—It is well remarked by STUART that the "difficulties which such statements involve are not to be got rid of by softening the language of one text, while so many others meet us which are of the same tenor; and even if we give up the Bible itself, so long as we acknowledge an omnipotent and omniscient God we cannot abate in the least degree from any of the difficulties which such texts make." Be it observed, however, that if God, as the apostle teaches, expressly "designed to manifest His wrath, and to make His

ADAM CLARKE

is God's ultimate design; this purpose He will never change, and this He has fully declared in the everlasting gospel. This is the grand decree of reprobation and election.

16. *So then it is not of him that willeth.* I conclude, therefore, from these several instances, that the making or continuing any body of men as the peculiar people of God is righteously determined, not by the judgment, hopes, or wishes of men, but by the will and wisdom of God alone.

17. *For the scripture saith unto Pharaoh.* Instead of showing the Israelites mercy, He might justly have suffered them to go on in sin, till He should have signalized His wisdom and justice in their destruction; as appears from what God in His Word declares concerning His dealings with Pharaoh and the Egyptians, Exod. ix. 15-16: "For now I had stretched forth my hand [in the plague of boils and blains], and I had smitten thee and thy people with the pestilence; and thou hadst [by this plague] been cut off from the earth [as thy cattle were by the murrain]; *but in very deed for this cause have I raised thee up*"—I have restored you to health by removing the boils and blains, and by respiting your deserved destruction to a longer day, that I may, in your instance, give such a demonstration of My power in your final overthrow that all mankind may learn that I am God, the righteous Judge of all the earth, the Avenger of wickedness.

18. *Therefore hath he mercy on whom he will.* This is the apostle's conclusion from the facts already laid down: that God, according to His own will and wisdom, in perfect righteousness, bestows *mercy*—that is to say, His blessings—upon one part of mankind (the Jews of old and the Gentiles of the present time) while He suffers another part (the Egyptians of old and the Jews of the present day) to go on in the abuse of His goodnsss and forbearance, hardening themselves in sin, till He brings upon them a most just and exemplary punishment, unless this be prevented by their deep repentance and general return to God through Jesus, the promised, the real *Messiah.*

19. *Why doth he yet find fault?* The question here is: If God's glory be so highly promoted and manifested by our obstinacy, and He suffers us to proceed in our hardness and infidelity, why does He find fault with us, or punish us for that which is according to His good pleasure?

20. *Nay but, O man, who art thou?* As if he had said: Weak, ignorant man, dare you retort on the infinitely good and righteous God? God has made, created, *formed* the Jewish nation, and shall the thing formed, when it hath corrupted itself, pretend to correct the wise and gracious Author of its being, and say, *Why hast thou made me thus?*

21. *Hath not the potter power over the clay?* The apostle continues his answer to the Jew. Has not God shown by the parable of the potter, Jer. xviii. 1 ff., that He may justly dispose of nations and of the Jews in particular according as He in His infinite wisdom may judge most right and fitting; even as the potter has a right, out of the same lump of clay, to make one vessel to a more honorable and another to a less honorable use, as his own judgment and skill may direct? The reference to this parable shows most positively that the apostle is speaking of men, not *individually,* but *nationally;* and it is strange that men should have given his words any other application with this scripture before their eyes.

22. *What if God, willing to shew his wrath?* The apostle refers here to the case of Pharaoh and the Egyptians, and to which he applies Jeremiah's parable of the potter, and from them to the then state of the Jews. Pharaoh and the Egypians were *vessels of wrath*—persons deeply guilty before God; and by their obstinate refusal of His grace and abuse of His goodness they had fitted themselves for that destruction which the *wrath,* the vindictive justice of God, inflicted, after He had *endured* their obstinate rebellion *with much longsuffering;* which is a most absolute proof that the hardening of their hearts and their ultimate punishment were the consequences of their obstinate refusal of His grace and abuse of His goodness, as the history in Exodus sufficiently shows. As the Jews of

MATTHEW HENRY

Vessels of mercy. The happiness bestowed upon the saved remnant is the fruit, not of their merit, but of God's mercy. Vessels of honour must to eternity own themselves vessels of mercy. What he designs in them: *To make known the riches of his glory*, that is, of his goodness; for God's goodness is his greatest glory. God makes known his glory, this goodness of his, in the preservation and supply of all the creatures: the earth is full of his goodness, but when he would demonstrate the riches of his goodness, he does it in the salvation of the saints. What he does for them: he does before *prepare them to glory*. This is God's work. We can destroy ourselves fast enough, but we cannot save ourselves. Sinners fit themselves for hell, but it is God that prepares saints for heaven. And would you know who these *vessels of mercy are*? Those whom he hath called (*v.* 24); for whom he did predestinate those he also called with an effectual call: and these not of the Jews only, but of the Gentiles. The question is not now whether of the seed of Abraham or no, but whether or no called according to his purpose.

Verses 25–29

The apostle here shows how the rejection of the Jews, and the taking in of the Gentiles, were foretold in the Old Testament. The Jews would, no doubt, willingly refer it to the Old Testament. Now he shows how this was there spoken of.

I. By the prophet Hosea. The Gentiles had not been the people of God: "But," says he, "*I will call them my people*, make them such and own them as such, notwithstanding all their unworthiness." Former badness is no bar to God's present grace and mercy.—*And her beloved which was not beloved.* Those whom God calls his people he calls beloved: he loves those that are his own. *In the place where it was said, &c., there shall they be called.* Wherever they are scattered over the face of the earth, there will God own them. Behold, what manner of love! This honour have all his saints.

II. By the prophet Isaiah, who speaks of the casting off of many of the Jews, in two places:

1. One is Isa. x. 22, 23, which speaks of the saving of a remnant, that is, but a remnant. It is no strange thing for God to abandon to ruin a great many of the seed of Abraham, and yet maintain his word of promise to Abraham in full force. This is intimated in the supposition that the number of children of Israel was as the sand of the sea. And yet only a remnant shall be saved; for many are called, but few are chosen. In this salvation of the remnant we are told (*v.* 28) from the prophet, (1) That he will complete the work: *He will finish the work.* When God begins he will make an end, whether in ways of judgment or of mercy. As for God, his work is perfect. Margin, *He will finish the account.* God has taken an account of the children of men: and he will finish the account, call in as many as belong to the election of grace, and then the account will be finished. (2) That he will finish it quickly. Now he will *cut it short*, and make a short work upon the earth. But he will cut it short *in righteousness.* Men, when they cut short, do amiss; but, when God cuts short, it is always in righteousness. *The work* (*the word*, the law) was under the Old Testament very long. Our duty is now, under the gospel, summed up in much less room than it was under the law; religion is brought into a less compass. With us contractions are apt to darken things, but it is not so in this case. Though it be cut short, it is clear and plain; and, because short, the more easy.

2. Another is quoted from Isa. i. 9, where the prophet is showing how God would preserve a seed. It was no strange thing for God to leave the greatest part of the people of the Jews to ruin, and to reserve to himself only a small remnant: and they must not wonder if he did so now. What God is. He is *the Lord of sabaoth*, that is, the Lord of hosts. When God secures a seed to himself he acts as Lord of sabaoth. It is an act of almighty power and infinite sovereignty. What his people are; they are a *seed*, a small number. But they are a useful number. It is a wonder of divine power and mercy that there are any saved; for even those that are left to be a seed, if God had dealt with them according to their sins, had perished with the rest.

Verses 30–33

The true reason of the reception of the Gentiles, and the rejection of the Jews. There was a difference in the way of their seeking, and therefore there was that different success. He concludes like an orator, *What shall we say then?*

I. Concerning the Gentiles. 1. How they had been alienated from righteousness: they followed not after

JAMIESON, FAUSSET, BROWN

power (in the way of wrath) known," it could only be by punishing some, while He pardons others; and if the choice between the two classes was not to be founded, as our apostle also teaches, on their own doings but on God's good pleasure, the decision behooved ultimately to rest with God. Yet, even in the necessary punishment of the wicked, as HODGE observes, so far from proceeding with undue severity, the apostle would have it remarked that God "endures with much long-suffering" those objects of His righteous displeasure. **and that he might make known the riches of his glory on the vessels of mercy**—that 'glorious exuberance of Divine mercy' which was manifested in choosing and eternally arranging for the salvation of sinners. **24. even us, whom he hath called . . .** —rather, 'Whom he hath also called, even us . . . , in not only "*afore preparing*," but in due time effectually "*calling* us." **not of the Jews . . .** —better, 'not from among Jews only, but also from among Gentiles.' *Here for the first time in this chapter the calling of the Gentiles is introduced;* all before having respect, not to the substitution of the called Gentiles for the rejected Jews, but to the choice of one portion and the rejection of another of the same Israel. Had Israel's rejection been total, God's promise to Abraham would *not* have been fulfilled by the substitution of the Gentiles in their room; but Israel's rejection being only partial, the preservation of a "remnant," in which the promise was made good, was but "according to the election of grace." And now, for the first time, the apostle tells us that along with this elect remnant of *Israel*, it is God's purpose to "take out of the *Gentiles* a people for His name" (Acts 28:14); and that subject, thus introduced, is now continued to the end of ch. 11. **25. As he saith also in Osee**—'Hosea.' **I will call them my people, which were not my people; and her beloved, which was not beloved**—quoted, though not quite to the letter, from Hosea 2:23, a passage relating immediately, not to the heathen, but to the kingdom of the ten tribes; but since they had sunk to the level of the heathen, who were "not God's people," and in that sense "not beloved," the apostle legitimately applies it to the heathen, as "aliens from the commonwealth of Israel and strangers to the covenants of promise" (so I Pet. 2:10). **26. And**—another quotation from Hosea 1:10—**it shall come to pass, that in the place where it was said unto them, Ye are not my people; there shall they be called the children**—'called sons'—**of the living God**—The expression, 'in the place where . . . there,' seems designed only to give greater emphasis to the gracious change here announced, from divine exclusion to divine admission to the privileges of the people of God. **27-29. Esaias also crieth**—('But Isaiah crieth')—an expression denoting a solemn testimony openly borne (John 1:15; 7:28, 37; 12:44; Acts 23:6; 24:41). **concerning Israel, Though the number of the children**—'sons'—**of Israel be as the sand of the sea, a**—'the'—**remnant**—i.e., the elect remnant *only*—**shall be saved: For he will finish the work, and cut**—'is finishing the reckoning, and cutting'—**it short in righteousness; because a short work**—'reckoning'—**will the Lord make upon the earth**—Isaiah 10:22, 23, as in the LXX. The sense given to these words by the apostle may seem to differ from that intended by the prophet. But the sameness of sentiment in both places will at once appear, if we understand those words of the prophet, "the consumption decreed shall overflow with righteousness," to mean that while a remnant of Israel should be graciously spared to return from captivity, "the decreed consumption" of the impenitent majority should be "replete with righteousness," or illustriously display God's righteous vengeance against sin. The "short reckoning" seems to mean the speedy completing of His word, both in cutting off the one portion and saving the other. **And as Esaias said**—'hath said'—**before**—i.e., probably in an earlier part of his book, namely, Isaiah 1:9. **Except the Lord of Sabaoth**—i.e., 'The Lord of Hosts': the word is *Hebrew*, but occurs so in the Epistle of James (ch. 5:4), and has thence become naturalized in our Christian phraseology. **had left us a seed**—meaning a 'remnant'; small at first, but in due time to be a seed of plenty (cf. Ps. 22:30, 31; Isa. 6:12, 13). **we had been**—'become'—**as Sodom . . .**—But for this precious seed, the chosen people would have resembled the cities of the plain, both in degeneracy of character and in merited doom. **30, 31. What shall we say then?**—'What now is the result of the whole?' The result is this—very different from what one would have expected—**That the Gentiles, which followed not after righteousness, have attained**—'attained'—**to righteousness, even the righteousness of faith**—As we have seen that "the righteousness of

ADAM CLARKE

the apostle's time had sinned after the similitude of the Egyptians, hardening their hearts and abusing His goodness after every display of His long-suffering kindness, being now fitted for destruction, they were ripe for punishment; and that *power*, which God was making *known* for their salvation, having been so long and so much abused and provoked, was now about to show itself in their destruction as a nation. But even in this case there is not a word of their final damnation; much less that either they or any others were by a sovereign decree reprobated from all eternity; and that their very sins, the proximate cause of their punishment, were the necessary effect of that decree which had from all eternity doomed them to endless torments.

23. *And that he mght make known.* God "endured with much longsuffering the *vessels of wrath*": (1) "To *shew his wrath*, and to make his power known"; and also (2) *That he might make known the riches of his glory on the vessels of mercy.*

24. *Even us, whom he hath called.* All the Jews and Gentiles who have been "invited" by the preaching of the gospel to receive justification by faith in our Lord Jesus Christ, and have come to the gospel feast on this invitation.

25. *As he saith also in Osee.* It is a cause of not a little confusion that a uniformity in the orthography of the proper names of the Old and New Testaments has not been preserved. What stranger to our sacred books would suppose that the *Osee* above meant the Prophet Hosea, from whom, chap. ii. 23, this quotation is taken: "I will have mercy on her that had not obtained mercy; and I will say to them which were not my people, Thou art my people"? The apostle shows that this calling of the Gentiles was no fortuitous thing, but a firm purpose in the divine mind, which He had largely revealed to the prophets; and by opposing the calling of the Gentiles, the Jews in effect renounced their prophets and fought against God.

26. *And it shall come to pass.* These quotations are taken out of Hosea, chap. i. 10: "Yet the number of the children of Israel shall be as the sand of the sea, which cannot be measured nor numbered; and it shall come to pass, that in the place where it was said unto them, Ye are not my people, there it shall be said unto them, Ye are the sons of the living God." As if he had said: The decrease of numbers in the Church, by God's utterly taking away the ten tribes (v. 6) shall be well supplied by what shall afterwards come to pass by calling the Gentiles into it.

28. *For he will finish the work, and cut it short.* These appear to be forensic terms, and refer to the conclusion of a judicial proceeding; the Lord has tried and found them guilty, and will immediately execute upon them the punishment due to their transgressions.

29. *And as Esaias said before.* What God designs to do with the Jews at present, because of their obstinacy and rebellion, is similar to what He has done before, to which the same prophet refers, chap. i. 9: "Except the Lord of hosts had left unto us a very small remnant, we should have been as Sodom, and we should have been like unto Gomorrah"; i.e., had not God, who commands and overrules all the powers in heaven and earth, in mercy preserved a very small remnant, to keep up the name and being of the nation, it had been quite cut off and extinct, as were Sodom and Gomorrah.

MATTHEW HENRY

it. God was *found of those that sought him not*, Isa. lxv. 1. Thus doth God delight to dispense grace in a way of sovereignty and absolute dominion. 2. How they attained to righteousness, notwithstanding: *By faith;* by embracing Christ, and believing in Christ. They attained to that by the short cut of believing sincerely in Christ for which the Jews had been long in vain beating about the bush.

II. Concerning the Jews. 1. How they missed their end: they *followed after the law of righteousness* (*v.* 31). As many as stuck to their old Jewish principles and ceremonies, embracing the shadows now that the substance was come, these fell short of acceptance with God. 2. How they mistook their way, which was the cause of their missing the end, *v.* 32, 33. They sought, but not in the right way. *Not by faith*, not by depending upon the merit of Christ, and submitting to the terms of the gospel, which were the very life and end of the law. But they sought by the *works of the law.* This was the *stumbling-stone at which they stumbled.* They could by no means be reconciled to the doctrine of Christ, which brought them to expect justification through the merit of another. Christ himself is to some a stone of stumbling, for which he quotes Isa. viii. 14; xxviii. 16. It is sad that Christ should be set for the fall of any, and yet it is so (Luke ii. 34). So he is to multitudes; so he was to the unbelieving Jews. But still there is a remnant that do believe on him; and they *shall not be ashamed*, their hopes and expectations of justification by him shall not be disappointed, as theirs are who expect it by the law. The unbelieving Jews have no reason to quarrel with God for rejecting them; they had a fair offer made to them upon gospel terms, which they did not like. If they perish, they may thank themselves.

MARTIN LUTHER:

33. "He who believes in him will not be put to shame." The Hebrew text reads: "He who believes shall not make haste." This can be reconciled by interpreting it to mean that he who believes in Christ is secure in his conscience and righteous and, as the Scripture says, "bold as a lion" (Prov. 28:1). And again, "Whatever befalls the righteous man will not disturb him' (Prov. 12:21), while, according to Prov. 28:1, "The wicked flee when no one pursues," and again in Isa. 57:20: "The wicked are like the tossing sea, for it cannot rest." "There is no peace, says my God, for the wicked" (Isa. 57:21). And in Ps. 1:4 we read: "The wicked are not so, but are like chaff which the wind drives away"; in Lev. 26:36: "The sound of a driven leaf shall put them to flight"; and in Isa. 30:15 ff.: "For thus said the Lord God, the Holy One of Israel, In returning and rest you shall be saved; in quietness and in trust shall be your strength. And you would not, but you said, No! We will speed upon horses, therefore you shall speed away; and, We will ride upon swift steeds, therefore your pursuers shall be swift. A thousand shall flee at the threat of one ..." And this is the meaning, that he who believes in Christ will not be in a hurry, will not flee, will not be terrified, for he fears nothing, he stands quiet and secure, established on the solid rock, as our Lord taught in Matt. 7:24.—*Luther's Works*

JAMIESON, FAUSSET, BROWN

faith" is the righteousness which *justifies* (see on ch. 3:22, etc.), this verse must mean that 'the Gentiles, who while strangers to Christ were quite indifferent about acceptance with God, having embraced the Gospel as soon as it was preached to them, experienced the blessedness of a justified state.' **but Israel, which followed**—'following'—**after the law of righteousness, hath not attained**—'attained not'—**unto the law of righteousness**—The word "law" is used here, we think, in the same sense as in ch. 7:23, to denote 'a principle of action'; i.e., 'Israel, though sincerely and steadily aiming at acceptance with God, nevertheless missed it.' **32, 33. Wherefore? Because they sought it not by faith, but as it were**—rather simply, 'as'—**by the works of the law**—as if it were thus attainable, which justification is not: Since, therefore, it is attainable only by faith, they missed it. **for**—it is doubtful if this particle was originally in the text—**they stumbled at that stumbling stone**—better, 'against the stone of stumbling,' meaning *Christ.* But in this they only did—**as it is written**—Isa. 8:14; 28:16)—**Behold . . .** —Two Messianic predictions are here combined, as is not unusual in quotations from the Old Testament. Thus combined, the prediction brings together both the classes of whom the apostle is treating: those to whom Messiah should be only a stone of stumbling, and those who were to regard Him as the Cornerstone of all their hopes. Thus expounded, this chapter presents no serious difficulties, none which do not arise out of the subject itself, whose depths are unfathomable; whereas on every other view of it the difficulty of giving it any consistent and worthy interpretation is in our judgment insuperable. Note, (1) To speak and act "in Christ," with a conscience not only illuminated, but under the present operation of the Holy Ghost, is not peculiar to the supernaturally inspired, but is the privilege, and ought to be the aim, of every believer (vs. 1). (2) Grace does not destroy, but only intensify and elevate, the feelings of nature; and Christians should study to show this (vss. 2, 3). (3) To belong to the visible Church of God, and enjoy its high and holy distinctions, is of the sovereign mercy of God, and should be regarded with devout thankfulness (vss. 4, 5). (4) Yet the most sacred external distinctions and privileges will avail nothing to salvation without the heart's submission to the righteousness of God (vss. 31-33). (5) What manner of persons ought "God's elect" to be—in *humility*, when they remember that He hath saved them and called them, not according to their works, but according to His own purpose and grace, given them in Christ Jesus before the world began (II Tim. 1:9); in *thankfulness*, for "Who maketh thee to differ, and what hast thou that thou didst not receive?" (I Cor. 4:7); in *godly jealousy* over themselves; remembering that "God is not mocked," but "whatsoever a man soweth that shall he also reap" (Gal. 6:7); in *diligence* "to make our calling and election sure" (II Pet. 1:10); and yet in calm *confidence* that "whom God predestinates, and calls, and justifies, them (in due time) He also glorifies" (ch. 8:30). (6) On all subjects which from their very nature lie beyond human comprehension, it will be our wisdom to set down what God says in His word, and has actually done in His procedure towards men, as indisputable, even though it contradict the results at which in the best exercise of our limited judgment we may have arrived (vss. 14-23). (7) Sincerity in religion, or a general desire to be saved, with assiduous efforts to do right, will prove fatal as a ground of confidence before God, if unaccompanied by implicit submission to His revealed method of salvation (vss. 31-33). (8) In the rejection of the great mass of the chosen people, and the inbringing of multitudes of estranged Gentiles, God would have men to see a law of His procedure, which the judgment of the great day will more vividly reveal-that "the last shall be first and the first last" (Matt. 20:16).

ADAM CLARKE

31. *But Israel, which followed after.* But the Jews, who have hitherto been the people of God, though they have been industrious in observing a rule by which they supposed they could secure the blessings of God's peculiar kingdom, yet have not come up to the true and only rule by which those blessings can be secured.

32. *Wherefore?* And where lies their mistake? Being ignorant of God's righteousness, of His method of saving sinners by faith in Christ, they went about to establish their own righteousness—their own method of obtaining everlasting salvation. They attend not to the Abrahamic covenant, which stands on the extensive principles of grace and faith; but they turn all their regards to the law of Moses. They imagine that their obedience to that law gives them a right to the blessings of the Messiah's kingdom. But finding that the gospel sets our special interest in God and the privileges of His Church on a different footing, they are offended, and refuse to come into it.

33. *As it is written, Behold, I lay in Sion.* Christ, the Messiah, is become "a stone of stumbling" to them, and thus what is written in the prophecy of Isaiah is verified in their case, Isa. viii. 14; xxviii. 16: *Behold, I lay in Sion*, i.e., I shall bring in My Messiah. But He shall be a widely different Person from him whom the Jews expect; for whereas they expect the Messiah to be a mighty secular prince, and to set up a secular kingdom, He shall appear "a man of sorrows, and acquainted with grief"; and redeem mankind, not by His sword or secular power, but by His humiliation, passion, and death. Therefore they will be offended at Him and reject Him, and think it would be reproachful to trust in such a Person for salvation. *And whosoever believeth on him.* But so far shall any be from confusion or disappointment who believes in Christ that, on the contrary, every genuine believer shall find salvation—the remission of sins here, and eternal glory hereafter.

MATTHEW HENRY

CHAPTER 10

Verses 1–11

The scope of the apostle in this part of the chapter is to show the great pre-eminence of the righteousness of faith above that of the law; that he might persuade the Jews to believe in Christ.

I. Paul here professes his good affection to the Jews (*v.* 1, 2), where he gives them a good wish, and a good witness.

1. A good wish (*v.* 1), a wish that they might be saved. Though Paul preached against them, yet he prayed for them. This, he says, was *his heart's desire and prayer*. The strength and sincerity of his desire. It was *his heart's desire*; it was not a formal compli-

JAMIESON, FAUSSET, BROWN

CHAPTER 10

Vss. 1-21. Same Subject Continued—How Israel Came to Miss Salvation, and the Gentiles to Find It. **1. Brethren, my heart's desire**—The word here expresses 'entire complacency,' that in which the heart would experience full satisfaction. **and prayer**—'supplication'—**to God for Israel**—'for them' is the true reading; the subject being continued from the close of the preceding chapter. **is, that they may be saved**—'for their salvation.' Having before poured forth the anguish of his soul at the general unbelief of his nation and its dreadful consequences (ch. 9:1-3), he here expresses in the most emphatic terms his desire and prayer for

ADAM CLARKE

CHAPTER 10

1. *My heart's desire.* Though the apostle knew that the Jews were now in a state of rejection, yet he knew also that they were in this state through their own obstinacy, and that God was still waiting to be gracious, and consequently that they might still repent and turn to Him. Of his concern for their salvation he had already given ample proof, when he was willing to become a sacrifice for their welfare; see chap. ix. 3.

2. *They have a zeal of God.* They believe their law to have come immediately from God himself, and are jealous of its glory and ex-

MATTHEW HENRY

ment, as good wishes are with many from the teeth outward, but a real desire. The soul of prayer is the heart's desire. Cold desires do but beg denials. The offering up of this desire to God. It was his prayer. There may be desires in the heart, and yet no prayer. Wishing and woulding, if that be all, are not praying.

2. A good witness, as a reason of his good wish (*v.* 2): *I bear them record that they have a zeal of God.* The unbelieving Jews were the most bitter enemies Paul had in the world, and yet Paul gives them as good a character as the truth would bear. Charity teaches us to put the best construction upon words and actions that they will bear. We should take notice of that which is commendable even in bad people. *They have a zeal of God.* Their opposition to the gospel is from a principle of respect to the law. There is such a thing as a blind misguided zeal: such was that of the Jews.

II. He here shows the fatal mistake that the unbelieving Jews were guilty of. Their zeal was *not according to knowledge.* It is true God gave them that law for which they were so zealous; but they might have known that, by the appearance of the promised Messiah, an end was put to it. He gave the most convincing evidence that could be of his being the Messiah; and yet they would not own him, but shut their eyes against the clear light, so that their zeal for the law was blind. This he shows further, *v.* 3.

1. The nature of their unbelief. They *have not submitted themselves to the righteousness of God.* Unbelief is a non-submission to the righteousness of God. *Have not submitted.* In true faith, there is need of a great deal of submission.

2. The causes of their unbelief, and these are two: (1) Ignorance of God's righteousness. They did not consider what need we have of a righteousness wherein to appear before him; if they had, they would never have expected justification by their own works, as if they could satisfy God's justice. (2) A proud conceit of their own righteousness: *Going about to establish their own*—a righteousness of their own working out, by the merit of their works. They thought they needed not to be beholden to the merit of Christ.

III. He here shows the folly of that mistake.

1. The subserviency of the law to the gospel (*v.* 4): *Christ is the end of the law for righteousness.* The design of the law was to lead people to Christ. The use of the law was to direct people for righteousness to Christ. (1) Christ is the end of the ceremonial law, because he is the perfection of it. (2) Christ is the end of the moral law in that he did what the law could not do (*ch.* viii. 3). The end of the law was to bring men to perfect obedience, and so to obtain justification. The law is not destroyed, but, full satisfaction being made by the death of Christ for our breach of the law, the end is attained, and we are put in another way of justification. Christ is thus the end of the law; but it is only to *everyone that believeth.*

2. The excellency of the gospel above the law.

(1) What is the righteousness which is of the law? This he shows, *v.* 5. The tenor of it is, *Do, and live.* It owneth nothing as a righteousness sufficient to justify a man but that of perfect obedience. For this he quotes that scripture (Lev. xviii. 5), *You shall therefore keep my statutes and my judgments, which if a man do, he shall live in them.* The doing supposed must be perfect and sinless, without the least breach or violation. Now, was it not extreme folly in the Jews to adhere so closely to this way of justification and salvation, when there was a new and a living way opened?

(2) What is that righteousness which is of faith, *v.* 6, &c. This he describes in the words of Moses, in Deuteronomy. He quotes it from Deut. xxx. 11–14, and shows,

[1] That it is not at all hard or difficult. The way of justification and salvation has in it no such depths or knots as may discourage us, no insuperable difficulties attending it. *First,* We need not go to heaven to enquire into the secrets of the divine counsel. It is true Christ is in heaven; but we may be justified and saved without going thither. *Secondly,* We need not go to the deep, to fetch Christ out of the grave: *Into the deep, to bring up Christ from the dead.* It is true that Christ was in the grave, and it is as true that he is now in heaven; but we need not perplex ourselves with fancied difficulties. No, salvation is not put at so vast a distance from us.

[2] But it is very plain and easy: *The word is nigh thee.* Christ is nigh thee, for the word is nigh thee.

JAMIESON, FAUSSET, BROWN

their salvation. **2. For I bear them record**—or, 'witness,' as he well could from his own sad experience—**that they have a zeal of**—'for'—**God, but not according to knowledge**—(Cf. Acts 22:3; 26:9-11; Gal. 1:13, 14). He alludes to this well-meaning of his people, notwithstanding their spiritual blindness, not certainly to excuse their rejection of Christ and rage against His saints, but as some ground of hope regarding them. (See I Tim. 1:13).

3. For they being ignorant of God's righteousness—i.e., for the justification of the guilty (see on ch. 1:17)—**and going about**—'seeking'—**to establish their own righteousness, have not submitted themselves to the righteousness of God**—The apostle views the general rejection of Christ by the nation as one act.

For Christ is the end—the object or aim—**of the law for**—justifying—**righteousness to every one that believeth**—i.e., contains within Himself all that the law demands for the justification of such as embrace Him, whether Jew or Gentile (Gal. 3:24).

5-10. For Moses describeth the righteousness which is of the law, That the man that doeth—'hath done'—**those things**—which it commands—**shall live in them**—(Lev. 28:5). This is the one way of justification and life—by "the righteousness which is of (or, by our own obedience to) the law."

But the—justifying—**righteousness which is of faith speaketh on this wise**—'speaketh thus'—its language or import is to this effect (quoting in substance Deut. 30:13, 14). **Say not in thine heart, Who shall ascend into heaven? that is, to bring Christ down . . .** —i.e., 'Ye have not to sigh over the impossibility of attaining to justification; as if one should say, oh! if I could but get someone to mount up to heaven and fetch me down Christ, there might be some hope, but since that cannot be, mine is a desperate case.' **or, Who shall descend . . .** —another case of impossibility, suggested by Proverbs 30:4, and perhaps also Amos 9:2—probably proverbial expressions of impossibility (cf. Ps. 139:7-10; Prov. 24:7, etc.).

But what saith it? It saith—continuing the quotation from Deuteronomy 30:14—**The word is nigh thee**—easily accessible.

ADAM CLARKE

cellence; they conscientiously observe its rites and ceremonies, but they do not consider the object and end of those rites. They sin more through ignorance than malice; and this pleads in their excuse. By this fine apology for them, the apostle prepares them for the harsher truths which he was about to deliver.

3. *For . . . being ignorant of God's righteousness*—not knowing God's method of saving sinners, which is the only proper and efficient method. *And going about to establish their own righteousness*—seeking to procure their salvation by means of their own contriving. They *have not submitted*—they have not bowed to the determinations of the Most High, relative to His mode of saving mankind, viz., through faith in Jesus Christ as the only available Sacrifice for sin, the end to which the law pointed.

4. *For Christ is the end of the law.* Where the law ends, Christ begins. The law ends with representative sacrifices; Christ begins with the real offering. The law is our schoolmaster to lead us to Christ; it cannot save, but it leaves us at His door, where alone salvation is to be found. Christ as an atoning Sacrifice for sin was the grand Object of the whole sacrificial code of Moses; His passion and death were the fulfillment of its great object and design. Separate this sacrificial death of Christ from the law, and the law has no meaning, for it is impossible that the blood of bulls and goats should take away sins. God never designed that the sacrifices of the law should be considered the atonement for sin, but a type or representative of that atonement; and that the atonement was the sacrifice offered by Christ. Thus He was *the end of the law,* in respect to its sacrifices.

5. *For Moses describeth the righteousness which is of the law.* The place to which the apostle refers seems to be Lev. xviii. 5: "Ye shall therefore keep my statutes, and my judgments; which if a man do, he shall live in them." These words seem to be spoken in answer to an objection which might be made by a Jew: "Did not Moses give us a law, the observance of which would secure our salvation?" Such a law Moses undoubtedly gave, and that law promises life to those who perform it precepts; but who can plead for life on this ground who rejects that Christ who is "the end of the law"? No man ever did, nor ever can, fulfill that law so as to merit salvation by the performance of it. For as "all have sinned, and come short of the glory of God," they are all under the curse of the law, which says: "Cursed is every one that continueth not in all things which are written in the book of the law to do them," Deut. xxvii. 26; Gal. iii. 10. Therefore by the deeds of this law none can be justified, because all are in a state of condemnation for transgressions already committed against it.

6-7. *But the righteousness which is of faith.* As it is most evident that there can be no justification by works, as all are sinful and all in a guilty state, if God will grant salvation at all, it must be by *faith.* But faith must have an object and a reason for its exercise. The Object is Jesus Christ; the reason is the infinite merit of His passion and death. *Who shall ascend into heaven?* As Christ is "the end of the law" for justification to everyone that believes, no observance of the law can procure Him. Who by the practice of the law can bring Christ down from heaven? or, when brought down, and crucified and buried, as a Sacrifice for sin, who can bring Him up again from the dead? And both His death and resurrection are essentially necessary for the salvation of a lost world. Or the sense of the apostle may be this: They who will not believe in Christ crucified must in effect be seeking another Messiah to come down from heaven with a different revelation; or they who will not credit the doctrine that we preach concerning His resurrection seem in effect to say, Christ yet remains to be raised from the dead, and reign over the Jews as a mighty secular Sovereign, subjecting the Gentile world to the sway of His righteous sceptre.

8. *But what saith it? The word is nigh thee.* There is no occasion to seek high or low for the saving power; the word of reconciliation is nigh.

MATTHEW HENRY

It is *in thy mouth, and in thy heart*. The work thou hast to do lies within thee. All that which is to be done for us is already done to our hands. Those that were under the law were to do all themselves, *Do this, and live;* but the gospel discovers the greatest part of the work done already, and what remains cut short in righteousness, salvation, brought to our door, as it were. It is in our mouth—we are reading it daily; it is in our heart—we are, or should be, thinking of it daily. Even *the word of faith*. Now what is this word of faith? We have the tenor of it, *v.* 9, 10. What is promised to us: *Thou shalt be saved*. It is salvation that the gospel exhibits and tenders which Christ is the author of, a Saviour to the uttermost. Upon what terms. Two things are required as conditions of salvation: (*a*) *Confessing the Lord Jesus*—openly professing relation to him and dependence on him, standing by him in all weathers. Our Lord Jesus lays a great stress upon this confessing of him before men; see Matt. x. 32, 33. It was a very great thing, especially, when the profession of Christ and Christianity hazarded life, and all that is dear in this world, which was the case in the primitive times. (*b*) *Believing in the heart that God raised him from the dead*. The profession of faith with the mouth, if there be not the power of it in the heart, is but a mockery; especially concerning his resurrection, which is the fundamental article of the Christian faith. This is further illustrated (*v.* 10), and the order inverted, because there must first be faith in the heart before there can be an acceptable confession with the mouth. Concerning faith: It is *with the heart that man believeth*, which implies more than an assent of the understanding, and takes in the consent of the will. This is *unto righteousness*. There is the righteousness of justification and the righteousness of sanctification. Faith is to both. Concerning profession: It is with *the mouth that confession is made*—confession to God in prayer and praise, confession to men by owning the ways of God before others. And this is said to be *unto salvation*, because it is the performance of the condition of that promise, Matt. x. 32. Justification by faith lays the foundation of our title to salvation; but by confession we build upon that foundation. So that we have here a brief summary of the terms of salvation, that we must give up, to God, our souls and our bodies—our souls in believing with the heart, and our bodies in confessing with the mouth. For this (*v.* 11) he quotes Isa. xlv. 17, *Whosoever believeth on him shall not be ashamed*. He will not be ashamed to own that Christ in whom he trusts; he that believes in the heart will not be ashamed to confess with the mouth. He shall not be ashamed of his hope in Christ. He shall never have cause to repent his confidence in reposing such a trust in the Lord Jesus.

Verses 12–21

There is no difference between Jews and Gentiles, but they stand upon the same level in point of acceptance with God. In Jesus Christ there is neither Greek nor Jew, Col. iii. 11. *There is no difference*.

I. God is the same to all: *The same Lord over all is rich unto all*. There is not one God to the Jews who is more kind, and another to the Gentiles who is less kind; but he is the same to all. When he proclaimed his name, *The Lord, the Lord God, gracious and merciful*, he thereby signified not only what he was to the Jews, but what he is and will be to all his creatures that seek unto him: liberal and bountiful in dispensing his favours *to all that call upon him*. Something must be done by us, and it is as little as can be, we must call upon him. We have nothing to do but to draw out by prayer.

II. The promise is the same to all (*v.* 13): *Whoever shall call*. Calling upon the name of the Lord is here put for all practical religion. What is the life of a Christian but a life of prayer? He that thus calls upon him shall be saved. It is but ask and have; what would we have more? For the further illustration of this he observes,

1. How necessary it was that the gospel should be preached to the Gentiles, *v.* 14, 15. This was what the Jews were so angry with Paul for. He shows how needful it was to bring them within the reach of the promise. *They cannot call on him in whom they have not believed*. Except they believe that he is God, they will not call upon him by prayer. The grace of faith is absolutely necessary to the duty of prayer; we cannot pray aright without it. He that comes to God by prayer must believe, Heb. xi. 6. *They cannot believe in him of whom they have not heard*. Some way or other the divine revelation must be made known to us, before we can receive it and assent to it; it is not born with us. *They cannot hear without a preacher*. Somebody must tell them what they are to believe. *They cannot preach except they be sent*. How shall

JAMIESON, FAUSSET, BROWN

in thy mouth—when thou confessest Him. **and in thine heart**—when thou believest on Him. Though it is of *the law* which Moses more immediately speaks in the passage quoted, yet it is of the law as Israel shall be brought to look upon it when the Lord their God shall circumcise their heart "to love the Lord their God with all their heart" (vs. 6); and thus, in applying it, the apostle (as OLSHAUSEN truly observes) is not merely appropriating the language of Moses, but keeping in the line of his deeper thought. **that is, the word of faith, which we preach**—i.e., the word which men have to believe for salvation (cf. I Tim. 4:6). **That if thou shalt . . .** —So understanding the words, the apostle is here giving the language of the true method of justification; and this sense we prefer [with CALVIN, BEZA, FERME, LOCKE, JOWETT]. But able interpreters render the words, 'For,' or 'Because if thou shalt . . . , [VULGATE, LUTHER, DE WETTE, STUART, PHILIPPI, ALFORD, REVISED VERSION]. In this case, these are the apostle's own remarks, confirming the foregoing statements as to the simplicity of the gospel method of salvation. **confess with thy mouth the Lord Jesus**—i.e., probably, 'If thou shalt confess Jesus [to be] the Lord,' which is the proper manifestation or evidence of faith (Matt. 10:32; I John 4:15). This is put first merely to correspond with the foregoing quotation—"in thy mouth and in thine heart." So in I Pet. 1:10 the "calling of believers" is put before their "election," as that which is first "made sure," although in point of time it comes after it. **and shalt believe in thine heart that God hath raised**—'that God raised'—**him from the dead . . .** —See on ch. 4:25. In the next verse the two things are placed in their natural order. **For with the heart man believeth unto**—justifying—**righteousness; and with the mouth confession is made unto salvation**—This confession of Christ's name, especially in times of persecution, and whenever obloquy is attached to the Christian profession, is an indispensable test of discipleship.

11-13. For the scripture saith—in Isaiah 28:16, a glorious Messianic passage. **Whosoever believeth on him shall not be ashamed**—Here, as in ch. 9:33, the quotation is from the LXX, which renders those words of the original, "shall not make haste" i.e., fly for escape, as from conscious danger), 'shall not be put to shame,' which comes to the same thing.

For there is no difference—or 'distinction'—**between Jew and Greek; for the same Lord over all**—i.e., not *God* [as CALVIN, GROTIUS, OLSHAUSEN, HODGE], but *Christ*, as will be seen, we think, by comparing vss. 9, 12, 13 and observing the apostle's usual style on such subjects. [So CHRYSOSTOM, MELVILLE, BENGEL, MEYER, DE WETTE, FRITZSCHE, THOLUCK, STUART, ALFORD, PHILIPPI.] **is rich**—a favorite Pauline term to express the exuberance of that saving grace which is in Christ Jesus. **unto all that call upon him**—This confirms the application of the preceding words to *Christ;* since to call upon the name of the Lord Jesus is a customary expression. (See Acts 7:59, 60; 9:14, 21; 22:16; I Cor. 1:2; II Tim. 2:22). **For saith the scripture whosoever**—The expression is emphatic, 'Everyone whosoever'—**shall call upon the name of the Lord shall be saved**—Joel 2:32; quoted also by Peter, in his great Pentecostal sermon (Acts 2:21), with evident application to Christ.

14, 15. How then shall they call on him in whom they have not believed? and . . . believe in him of whom they have not heard? and . . . hear without a preacher?

ADAM CLARKE

The way of salvation is now both plain and easy. By the preaching of the gospel the doctrine of salvation is *nigh thee*, and the saving influence is at hand. It is *in thy mouth*, easy to be understood, easy to be professed; *and in thy heart*, if you are upright before God, sincerely desiring to be saved on His own terms.

9. *That if thou shalt confess*. Acknowledge the Lord Jesus Christ as the only Saviour. *Believe in thine heart* that He who died for your offenses has been raised for your justification, and depend solely on Him for that justification, and *thou shalt be saved*.

10. *For with the heart man believeth*. And be sincere in this. *For with the heart*, duly affected with a sense of guilt and of the sufficiency of the sacrifice which Christ has offered, *man believeth unto righteousness*, believes to receive "justification"; for this is the proper meaning of the term here, and in many other parts of this Epistle. *And with the mouth confession is made unto salvation*. He who believes aright in Christ Jesus will receive such a full conviction of the truth, and such an evidence of his redemption, that his mouth will boldly confess his obligation to his Redeemer, and the blessed persuasion he has of the remission of all his sins through the blood of the Cross.

11. *For the scripture saith*. And however the Jews may despise this gospel, because it comes not unto them with pomp and ceremony, it puts those who receive it into possession of every heavenly blessing; and this is according to the positive declarations of the prophets, for it is written, Isa. xxviii. 16; xlix. 23: *Whosoever believeth on him shall not be ashamed*. He shall neither be disappointed of his hope nor ashamed of his confidence, because he has that faith which is "the evidence of things not seen," the subsistence "of things hoped for," Heb. xi. 1.

12. *For there is no difference between the Jew and the Greek*. All are equally welcome to this salvation. Here the Jew has no exclusive privilege, and from this the Greek is not rejected. One simple way of being saved is proposed to all, viz., faith in the Lord Jesus Christ.

13. *For whosoever shall call*. Nor shall anyone who hears this doctrine of salvation and credits it as he is commanded be permitted to pray or supplicate the throne of grace in vain. For the Prophet Joel hath declared, chap. ii. 32: *Whosoever shall call upon*, invoke, *the name of the Lord* Jesus Christ, the Saviour of sinners, *shall be saved*—shall have his guilt pardoned, his heart purified; and if he abide in the faith, rooted and grounded in Him, showing forth the virtues of Him who has called him out of darkness into His marvellous light, he shall be saved with all the power of an eternal life. It is evident that Paul understood the text of Joel as relating to our blessed Lord; and therefore his word *Kyrios* must answer to the prophet's word *Yehovah*, which is no mean proof of the Godhead of Jesus Christ.

MATTHEW HENRY

a man act as an ambassador, unless he have both his credentials and his instructions from the prince that sends him? It is God's prerogative to send ministers. He only can qualify men for, and incline them to, the work of the ministry. But the competency of that qualification, and the sincerity of that inclination, must not be left to the judgment of every man for himself. This must needs be submitted to the judgment of those who are presumed the most able judges, and who are empowered to set apart such as they find so qualified and inclined. And those that are thus set apart, not only may, but must preach, as those that are sent.

2. How welcome the gospel ought to be to those to whom it was preached, because it showed the way to salvation, *v.* 15. For this he quotes, Isa. lii. 7. What the gospel is: It is *the gospel of peace*. Peace is put in general for all good; so it is explained here; it is *glad tidings of good things*. The things of the gospel are good things indeed, the best things; the best news that ever came from heaven to earth. What the work of ministers is: To *bring these glad tidings*; to *evangelize peace* (so the original is). Every preacher is in this sense an evangelist. How acceptable they should therefore be for their work's sake: *How beautiful are the feet*, that is, how welcome are they! Those that preach the gospel of peace should see to it that their feet (their life and conversation) be beautiful: the holiness of ministers' lives is the beauty of their feet. *How beautiful!* namely, in the eyes of those that hear them. Those that welcome the message cannot but love the messengers.

3. He answers an objection against all this (*v.* 16): *But they have not all obeyed the gospel.* All the Jews have not, all the Gentiles have not; far the greater part of both remain in unbelief and disobedience. The gospel is given us not only to be known and believed, but to be obeyed. It is no strange thing, but it is a very sad and uncomfortable thing, for the ministers of Christ to bring the report of the gospel, and not to be believed in it. He shows that the word preached is the ordinary means of working faith (*v.* 17): *So then*, though many that hear do not believe, yet those that believe have first heard. *Faith cometh by hearing.* The beginning, progress, and strength of faith, are by hearing. The word of God is therefore called *the word of faith*. God gives faith, but it is by the word as the instrument. *Hearing* is *by the word of God*. It is not hearing the enticing words of man's wisdom, but hearing the word of God, that will befriend faith. Those who would not believe the report of the gospel, yet, having heard it, were thereby left inexcusable, *v.* 18, *to the end.*

(1) The Gentiles have heard it (*v.* 18): *Have they not heard?* They have either heard the gospel, or at least heard of it. *Their sound went into all the earth;* not only a confused sound, but their *words* are *gone unto the ends of the world.* The commission which the apostles received runs thus: *Go you into all the world —preach to every creature—disciple all nations;* and they did with indefatigable industry and wonderful success pursue that commission. It was in order to this that the gift of tongues was poured so plentifully upon the apostles.

(2) The Jews have heard it too, *v.* 19–21. For this he appeals to two passages of the Old Testament. *Did not Israel know* that the Gentiles were to be called in? They might have known it from Moses and Isaiah.

First, One is taken from Deut. xxxii. 21, *I will provoke you to jealousy.* The Jews not only had the offer; they had the refusal. In all places where the apostles came still the Jews had the first offer, and the Gentiles had but their leavings. If one would not, another would. Now this provoked them to jealousy. The Gentiles are here called *no people*, and *a foolish nation.* How much soever there be of the wit and wisdom of the world, those that are not the people of God are a foolish people. Such was the state of the Gentile world, who yet were made the people of God, and Christ to them the wisdom of God. What a provocation it was to the Jews to see the Gentiles taken into favour we may see, especially Acts xxii. 22. It was an instance of the great wickedness of the Jews that they were thus enraged. God often makes people's sin their punishment. A man needs no greater plague than to be left to the impetuous rage of his own lusts.

Secondly, Another is taken from Isa. lxv. 1, 2, and in it Esaias is very bold. Those that will be found faithful have need to be very bold. Those that are resolved to please God must not be afraid to displease any man. Now Esaias speaks boldly and plainly, Of the preventing grace and favour of God in the reception of the Gentiles (*v.* 20): *I was found of those that sought me not.* The prescribed method is, Seek and find; this is a rule for us, not a rule for

JAMIESON, FAUSSET, BROWN

and . . . preach except . . . sent?—i.e., 'True, the same Lord over all is rich unto all alike that call upon Him. But this calling implies believing, and believing hearing, and hearing preaching, and preaching *a mission to preach:* Why, then, take ye it so ill, O children of Abraham, that in obedience to our heavenly mission (Acts 26:16-18) we preach among *the Gentiles* the unsearchable riches of Christ?' **as it is written**—(Isa. 52:7). **How beautiful are the feet of them that preach the gospel of peace . . .**—The whole chapter of Isaiah from which this is taken, and the three that follow, are so richly Messianic, that there can be no doubt "the glad tidings" there spoken of announce a more glorious release than of Judah from the Babylonish captivity, and the very feet of its preachers are called "beautiful" for the sake of their message. **16, 17. But they have not all obeyed the gospel**—i.e., the Scripture hath prepared us to expect this sad result. **For Esaias saith, Lord, who hath believed our report?**—i.e.,'Where shall one find a believer?' The prophet speaks as if next to none would believe: The apostle softens this into "They have not all believed." **So then faith cometh by hearing, and hearing by the word of God**—'This is another confirmation of the truth that faith supposes the hearing of the Word, and this a commission to preach it.' **18. But I say, Have they not heard?**—'Did they not hear?' Can Israel, through any region of his dispersion, plead ignorance of these glad tidings? **Yes, verily, their sound went**—'their voice went out'—**into all the earth, and their words unto the end of the world**—These beautiful words are from Psalm 19:4. Whether the apostle quoted them as in their primary intention applicable to his subject [as OLSHAUSEN, ALFORD, etc.], or only "used scriptural language to express his own ideas, as is done involuntarily almost by every preacher in every sermon" [HODGE], expositors are not agreed. But though the latter may seem the more natural since "the rising of the Sun of righteousness upon the world" (Mal. 4:2), "the Day-spring from on high visiting us, giving light to them that sat in darkness, and guiding our feet into the way of peace" (Luke 1:78, 79), must have been familiar and delightful to the apostle's ear, we cannot doubt that the irradiation of the world with the beams of a better Sun by the universal diffusion of the Gospel of Christ, must have a mode of speaking quite natural, and to him scarcely figurative. **19. But I say, Did not Israel know?**—know, from their own Scriptures, of God's intention to bring in the Gentiles? **First**—i.e., First in the prophetic line [DE WETTE]. **Moses saith . . .**—'I will provoke you to jealousy ('against') [them that are] not a nation, and against a nation without understanding will I anger you' (Deut. 32:21). In this verse God warns His ancient people that because they had (that is, in aftertimes would) moved Him to jealousy with their "no-gods," and provoked Him to anger with their vanities, He in requital would move them to jealousy by receiving into His favor a "no-people," and provoke them to anger by adopting a nation void of understanding. **20. But Esaias is very bold, and saith**—i.e., is still plainer, and goes even the length of saying—**I was found of them that sought me not**—until I sought them—**I was made**—'became'—**manifest unto them that asked not after me**—until the invitation from Me came to them. That the calling of the Gentiles was meant by these words of the prophet (Isa. 65:1) is manifest from what immediately follows, "I said, Behold Me, behold Me, unto a nation that was not called by My name." **21. But to**—rather, 'with regard to'—**Israel he saith, All day**—'All the day'—**long I have stretched out**—'did I stretch forth'—**my hands**—the attitude of gracious entreaty. **unto a disobedient and gainsaying people**—These words, which immediately follow the announcement just quoted of the calling of the Gentiles, were enough to forewarn the Jews both of God's purpose to eject them from their privileges, in favor of the Gentiles, and of the cause of it on their own part.—Note, (1) Mere sincerity, and even earnestness in religion—though it may be some ground of hope for a merciful recovery from error—is no excuse, and will not compensate, for the deliberate rejection of saving truth, when in the providence of God presented for acceptance (vss. 1-3; and see on ch. 9, *Note* 7). (2) The true cause of such rejection of saving truth, by the otherwise sincere, is the prepossession of the mind by some false notions of its own. So long as the Jews "sought to set up their own righteousness," it was in the nature of things impossible that they should "submit themselves to the righteousness of God"; the one of these two methods of acceptance being in the teeth of the other (vs. 3). (3) The es-

ADAM CLARKE

16. *But they have not all obeyed the gospel.* This seems to be the objection of a Jew; as if he had said: A divine mission would be attended with success, whereas there are numbers who pay no attention to the glad tidings you preach. To this the apostle answers that the Spirit of God by Isaiah, chap. liii. 1, foretold it would be so, even in the case of the Jews themselves, when he said, *Lord, who hath believed our report?* For although God brings the message of salvation to men, He does not oblige them to embrace it.

17. *So then faith cometh by hearing.* Preaching the gospel is the ordinary means of salvation; faith in Christ is the result of hearing the *word*, the "doctrine" of God preached.

18. *But I say, Have they not heard?* But to return to the objection: You say they have not all believed; I ask: Have they not all heard? Have not the means of salvation been placed within the reach of every Jew in Palestine, and within the reach of all those who sojourn in the different Gentile countries where we have preached the gospel, as well to the Jews as to the Gentiles themselves? Yes; for we may say of the preaching of the gospel what the Psalmist has said (Ps. xix. 4) of the heavenly bodies: *Their sound went into all the earth, and their words unto the ends of the world.* As the celestial luminaries have given testimony of the eternal power and Godhead of the Deity to the habitable world, the gospel of Christ has borne testimony to His eternal goodness and mercy to all the land of Palestine, and to the whole Roman Empire.

19. *But I say, Did not Israel know?* You object to this preaching among the Gentiles; but is not this according to the positive declaration of God? He, foreseeing your unbelief and rebellion, said by Moses, Deut. xxxii. 21, *I will provoke you to jealousy by them that are no people, and by a foolish nation I will anger you.* As you have provoked Me to jealousy with worshipping those that are no gods, I will provoke you to jealousy by those which are *no people*. This most evidently refers to the calling or inviting of the Gentiles to partake of the benefits of the gospel, and plainly predicts the envy and rage which would be excited in the Jews in consequence of those offers of mercy made to the Gentiles.

20. *But Esaias* (the Greek orthography for Isaiah) *is very bold.* Speaks out in the fullest manner and plainest language, chap. lxv. 1, notwithstanding the danger to which such a declaration exposed him among a crooked, perverse, and dangerous people: *I was found of them that sought me not;* I put my salvation in the way of those (the Gentiles) who were not seeking for it, and knew nothing of it; thus the "Gentiles, which followed not after righteousness, have attained to [the law of] righteousness," chap. ix. 30, and they have found that redemption which the Jews have rejected.

21. *But to Israel he saith.* In the very next verse (Isa. lxv. 2), *All day long have I stretched forth my hands,* manifesting the utmost readiness and willingness to gather them all together under My protecting care; but I stretched forth My hands in vain, for they are a disobedient and gainsaying people. They not only disobey My command, but they gainsay and contradict My prophets. Thus the apostle proves, in answer to the objection made, v. 16, that the infidelity of the Jews was the effect of their own obstinacy; that the opposition which they are now making to the gospel was foretold

MATTHEW HENRY

God, who is often found of those that do not seek. Thus he manifested himself to the Gentiles, by sending the light of the gospel among them. Was not this our own particular case? Did not God begin in love, and manifest himself to us when we did not ask after him? And was not that a time of love indeed, to be often remembered with a great deal of thankfulness? Of the obstinacy and perverseness of Israel, *v.* 21. God's great goodness to them: *All day long I have stretched forth my hands.* (*a*) His offers: *I have stretched forth my hands*, offering them life and salvation. Stretching forth the hands is the gesture of those that require audience, or desire acceptance. Christ was crucified with his hands stretched out. *Stretched forth my hands* as offering reconciliation—come let us shake hands and be friends; and our duty is to give the hand to him. (*b*) His patience in making these offers: *All day long.* He waits to be gracious. He bears long, but he will not bear always. Their great badness to him. They were a *disobedient gainsaying people*, not only disobedient to the call, but gainsaying, and quarrelling with it. The Jews contradicted and blasphemed. It is a wonder of mercy in God that his goodness is not overcome by man's badness; and it is a wonder of wickedness in man that his badness is not overcome by God's goodness.

JAMIESON, FAUSSET, BROWN

sential terms of salvation have in every age been the same: "Whosoever will" is invited to "take of the water of life freely," Revelation 22:17 (vs. 13). (4) How will the remembrance of the simplicity, reasonableness, and absolute freeness of God's plan of salvation overwhelm those that perish from under the sound of it (vss. 4-13). (5) How piercingly and perpetually should that question—"HOW SHALL THEY HEAR WITHOUT A PREACHER?"—sound in the ears of all churches, as but the apostolic echo of their Lord's parting injunction, "PREACH THE GOSPEL TO EVERY CREATURE" (Mark 16:15), and how far below the proper standard of love, zeal, and self-sacrifice must the churches as yet be, when with so plenteous a harvest the laborers are yet so few (Matt. 9:37, 38), and that cry from the lips of pardoned, gifted, consecrated men—"Here am I, send me" (Isa. 6:8), is not heard everywhere (vss. 14, 15)! (6) The blessing of a covenant relation to God is the irrevocable privilege of no people and no Church; it can be preserved only by fidelity, on our part, to the covenant itself (vs. 19). (7) God is often found by those who apparently are the farthest from Him, while He remains undiscovered by those who think themselves the nearest (vss. 20, 21). (8) God's dealings even with reprobate sinners are full of tenderness and compassion; all the day long extending the arms of His mercy even to the disobedient and gainsaying. This will be felt and acknowledged at last by all who perish, to the glory of God's forbearance and to their own confusion (vs. 21).

ADAM CLARKE

and deplored 700 years before; and that their opposition, far from being a proof of the insufficiency of the gospel, proved that this was the grand means which God had provided for their salvation; and having rejected this, they could expect no other.

MATTHEW HENRY

CHAPTER 11

Verses 1–32

The apostle proposes here a plausible objection, which might be urged against the divine conduct (*v.* 1): "*Hath God cast away his people?*" Is the rejection total and final? Will he have no more a peculiar people to himself? He shows that there was a great deal of goodness and mercy expressed along with this seeming severity: 1. That, though some of the Jews were cast off, yet they were not all so. 2. That, though the body of the Jews were cast off, yet the Gentiles were taken in. And, 3. That, though the Jews were cast off at present, yet in God's due time they should be taken into his church again.

I. The Jews, it is true, were many of them cast off, but not all. The supposition of this he introduces with a *God forbid.*

1. There was a chosen remnant of believing Jews, that obtained righteousness and life by faith in Jesus Christ, *v.* 1–7. These are said to be such as he *foreknew* (*v.* 2), whom he thus foreknew he did predestinate. Here lies the ground of the difference. They are called the *election* (*v.* 7). Believers are the *election*, all those and those only whom God hath chosen. He shows that he himself was one of them: *For I also am an Israelite.* Paul was a chosen vessel (Acts ix. 15), and yet he was of the *seed of Abraham.* He suggests that as in Elias's time, so now, this chosen remnant was really more and greater than one would think it was. (1) His mistake concerning Israel; as if he himself was the only faithful servant God had in the world. He refers to 1 Kings xix. 14, where (it is here said) *he maketh intercession to God against Israel.* A strange kind of intercession! *He deals with God against Israel;* so it may be read. In prayer we deal with God. It is said of Elijah (Jas. v. 17) that he *prayed in praying.* We are then likely to pray in praying, when we pray as those that are dealing with God. Elijah in this prayer spoke as if there were none left faithful in Israel but himself. See to what a low ebb the profession of religion may sometimes be brought. The powers of Israel were then persecuting powers: They have *killed thy prophets, and digged down thine altars*, and they *seek my life.* The multitude of Israel were then idolatrous: *I am left alone.* Thus those few that were faithful to God were not only lost in the crowd of idolaters, but crushed and driven into corners. *Digged down thine altars.* When altars were set up for Baal, it is no wonder if God's altars were pulled down; they could not endure that standing testimony against their idolatry. This was his intercession *against Israel.* It is a very sad thing for any person or people to have the prayers of God's people against them, for God espouses, and sooner or later will visibly own, the cause of his praying people. (2) The rectifying of this mistake (*v.* 4): *I have reserved.* Things are often much better with the church of God than wise and good men think they are. In times of general apostasy, there is usually a remnant that keep their integrity—all do not go one way. When there is a remnant who keep their integrity it is God that reserves to himself that remnant. It is his free and almighty grace that

JAMIESON, FAUSSET, BROWN

CHAPTER 11

VSS. 1-36. SAME SUBJECT CONTINUED AND CONCLUDED—THE ULTIMATE INBRINGING OF ALL ISRAEL, TO BE, WITH THE GENTILES, ONE KINGDOM OF GOD ON THE EARTH. **1. I say then, Hath**—'Did'—**God cast away his people?**

God forbid—Our Lord did indeed announce that "the kingdom of God should be *taken from* Israel" (Matt. 21:41); and when asked by the Eleven, after His resurrection, if He would at that time "*restore* the kingdom to Israel," His reply is a virtual admission that Israel was in some sense already out of covenant (Acts 1:9). Yet here the apostle teaches that, in two respects, Israel was *not* "cast away"; First, Not *totally;* Second, Not *finally*. FIRST, Israel is not *wholly* cast away. **for I also am an Israelite**—See Phil. 3:5, and so a living witness to the contrary. **of the seed of Abraham**—of pure descent from the father of the faithful. **of the tribe of Benjamin**—Phil. 3:5), that tribe which, on the revolt of the ten tribes, constituted, with Judah, the one faithful kingdom of God (I Kings 12:21), and after the captivity was, along with Judah, the kernel of the Jewish nation (Ezra 4:1; 10:9). **2-4. God hath**—'did'—**not cast away his people**—i.e., *wholly.* **which he foreknew**—On the word "foreknew," see on ch. 8:29. **Wot**—i.e., 'Know'—**ye not that the scripture saith of**—lit., 'in,' i.e., in the section which relates to—**Elias? how he maketh intercession**—'pleadeth'—**against Israel**—(The word "saying," which follows, as also the particle "and" before "digged down," should be omitted, as without MSS. authority.) **and I am left alone**—'I only am left.'

ADAM CLARKE

CHAPTER 11

1. *I say then, Hath God cast away his people?* Has He utterly and finally rejected them? for this is necessarily the apostle's meaning, and is the import of the Greek word which signifies to "thrust" or "drive away." Has He thrust them off, and driven them eternally from Him?

God forbid—"By no means." This rejection is neither *universal* nor *final.*

For I also am an Israelite—I am a regular descendant from Abraham, through Israel or Jacob, and by his son Benjamin. And I stand in the Church of God, and in the peculiar covenant; for the rejection is only of the obstinate and disobedient; those who believe on Christ, as I have done, are continued in the Church.

2. *God hath not cast away his people which he foreknew.* God has not finally and irrecoverably rejected a people whom He has "loved (or approved) so long," for this is evidently the meaning of the word in this place. *Wot ye not what the scripture saith?* "Do you not know what the Scripture saith?" The reference is to 1 Kings xix. 10, 14. And the apostle's answer to the objecting Jew is to the following effect: God has not universally thrust away His people, for whom in the promise to Abraham He intended, and to whom decreed, to grant His special favor and blessing; but the case is now much as it was in the days of Elijah. That prophet, in his addresses to God, made his complaint against Israel thus:

3. *Lord, they have killed thy prophets.* They will not permit any person to speak unto them in Thy name; and they murder those who are faithful to the commission which they have received from Thee. *Digged down thine altars.* They are profligate and profane beyond example, and retain not the slightest form of religion. *I am left alone.* There is no prophet besides myself left, and they seek to destroy me.

MATTHEW HENRY

makes the difference between them and others.—*Seven thousand:* a competent number, and yet, compared with the many thousands of Israel, a very small number. Now the description of this remnant is that *they had not bowed the knee to the image of Baal.* In court, city, and country, Baal had the ascendant; and the generality of people, more or less, paid their respect to Baal. The best evidence of integrity is to swim against the stream when it is strong. This is thankworthy, not to bow to Baal when everybody bows. Sober singularity is commonly the badge of true sincerity.

(3) The application of this instance to the case in hand: *Even so at this present time, v.* 5–7. As it has been, so it is. In Elijah's time there was a remnant, and so there is now. *A remnant*, a few of many, a remnant of believing Jews. This is called *a remnant according to the election of grace.* If the difference between them and others be made purely by the grace of God, as certainly it is (*I have reserved them*, saith he, *to myself*), then it must needs be according to the election.

Now concerning this remnant we may observe, *First,* Whence it takes its rise, from the free grace of God (*v.* 6), that grace which excludes works. Election is purely according to the good pleasure of his will, Eph. i. 5. Paul's heart was so full of the freeness of God's grace that he turns aside to make this remark. *If of grace, then not of works.*

Secondly, What it obtains: that which Israel in vain sought for (*v.* 7): *Israel hath not obtained that which he seeketh for,* that is, justification, and acceptance with God, but the *election have obtained it.* In them the promise of God has its accomplishment, and God's ancient kindness for that people is remembered. They were the persons whom God had in his eye in the counsels of his love.

2. *The rest were blinded, v.* 7. Some are chosen and called. But others are left to perish in their unbelief. The gospel, which to those that believed was the savour of life unto life, to the unbelieving was the savour of death unto death. The same sun softens wax and hardens clay. *They were blinded; they were hardened;* so some. They could neither see the light nor feel the touch, of gospel grace. Blindness and hardness are expressive of the same senselessness and stupidity of spirit. This seemed harsh doctrine: to qualify it, therefore, he vouches two witnesses out of the Old Testament.

(1) Isaiah, who spoke of such a judgment in his day, *ch.* xxix. 10; vi. 9. The *spirit of slumber.* They are under the power of a prevailing unconcernedness, like people that are slumbering and sleeping. *Eyes, that they should not see, and ears, that they should not hear.* They had the faculties, but in the things that belonged to their peace they had not the use of those faculties. They saw Christ, but they did not believe in him; they heard his word, but they did not receive it. It was all one as if they had neither seen nor heard—*Unto this day.* Ever since Esaias prophesied, this hardening work has been in the doing; some among them have been blind and senseless. It is still true concerning multitudes of them, even to this day in which we live.

(2) David (*v.* 9, 10), quoted from Ps. lxix. 22, 23, where David having foretold the sufferings of Christ from his own people the Jews, particularly that of their giving him *vinegar to drink*, foretells the dreadful judgments of God upon them for it: *Let their table become a snare,* which the apostle here applies to the present blindness of the Jews, and the offence they took at the gospel. He speaks here, [1] Of the ruin of their comforts: *Let their table be made a snare,* that is, as the psalmist explains it, Let that which should be for their welfare be a trap to them. The

JAMIESON, FAUSSET, BROWN

seven thousand, that have not bowed the knee to Baal—not "the image of Baal," according to the supplement of our version.

5. Even so at this present time—'in this present season'; this period of Israel's rejection. (See Acts 1:7, *Greek.*) **there is**—'there obtains,' or 'hath remained.' **a remnant according to the election of grace**—, 'As in Elijah's time the apostasy of Israel was not so universal as it seemed to be, and as he in his despondency concluded it to be, so now, the rejection of Christ by Israel is not so appalling in extent as one would be apt to think: There is now, as there was then, a faithful remnant; not however of persons naturally better than the unbelieving mass, but of persons graciously chosen to salvation.' (See I Cor. 4:7; II Thess. 2:13.) This establishes our view of the argument on Election in ch. 9, as not being an election of Gentiles in the place of Jews, and merely to religious advantages, but a sovereign choice of some of Israel itself, from among others, to believe and be saved. (See on ch. 9:6.)

6. And . . .—better, 'Now if it (the election) be by grace, it is no more of works; for [then] grace becomes no more grace: but if it be of works . . .' (The authority of ancient MSS. against this latter clause, as superfluous and not originally in the text, though strong, is not sufficient, we think, to justify its exclusion. Such seeming redundancies are not unusual with our apostle). The general position here laid down is of vital importance: That there are but two possible sources of salvation—men's works, and God's grace; and that these are so essentially distinct and opposite, that salvation cannot be of any combination or mixture of both, but must be wholly either of the one or of the other.

7-10. What then?—How stands the fact? **Israel hath not obtained that which he seeketh for**—better, 'What Israel is in search of (i.e., Justification, or acceptance with God—see on ch. 9:31); this he found not; but the election (the elect remnant of Israel) found it, and the rest were hardened,' or judicially given over to the 'hardness of their own hearts.'

as it is written—Isa. 29:10, and Deut. 29: 4—**God hath given**—'gave'—**them the spirit of slumber**—'stupor'. **unto this**—'this present'—**day. And David saith**—Psalm 69:23, which in such a Messianic psalm must be meant of the rejecters of Christ. **Let their table . . .**—i.e., Let their very blessings prove a curse to them, and their enjoyments only sting and take vengeance on them.

ADAM CLARKE

4. *But what saith the answer of God?* The answer which God made assured him that there were *seven thousand,* that is, several or many thousands; for so we must understand the word *seven,* a certain for an uncertain number. These had continued faithful to God; but, because of Jezebel's persecution, they were obliged to conceal their attachment to the true religion; and God, in His providence, preserved them from her sanguinary rage. *Who have not bowed the knee.* Baal was the god of Jezebel; or, in other words, his worship was then the worship of the state. But there were several thousands of pious Israelites who had not acknowledged this idol, and did not partake in the idolatrous worship.

5. *Even so then at this present time.* As in the present day the irreligion of the Jews is very great, yet there is a remnant, a considerable number, who have accepted of the grace of the gospel. *According to the election of grace.* And these are saved just as God has saved all believers from the beginning. They are chosen by His *grace,* not on account of any worth or excellence in themselves, but through His goodness are they chosen to have a place in His Church, and continue to be His people, entitled to all the privileges of the new covenant. The *election of grace* simply signifies God's gracious design in sending the Christian system into the world, and saving under it all those who believe in Christ Jesus, and none else. Thus the believers in Christ are chosen to inherit the blessings of the gospel, while those who seek justification by the works of the law are rejected.

6. *And if by grace.* And let this very remnant of pious Jews who have believed in Christ Jesus know that they are brought in in precisely the same way as God has brought in the Gentiles, the one having no more worthiness to plead than the other, both being brought in and continued in by God's free grace, and not by any observance of the Mosaic law. And this is done according to the election of grace, or the rule of choosing any persons to be the people of God upon the footing of grace, which takes in all that believe in His Son, Jesus Christ. Some of the Jewish people did so believe; therefore those believing Jews are "a remnant according to the election of grace." They are saved in that way in which alone God will save mankind. *And if by grace.* Then let these very persons remember that their election and interest in the covenant of God has no connection with their old Jewish works; for were it of works, grace would lose its proper nature, and cease to be what it is—a free, undeserved gift. *But if it be of works.* On the other hand, could it be made to appear that they are invested in these privileges of the kingdom of Christ only by the observance of the law of Moses, then *grace* would be quite set aside; and if it were not, *work,* or the merit of obedience, would lose its proper nature, which excludes favor and free gift.

7. *What then?* What is the real state of the case before us? *Israel,* the body of the Jewish people, have not obtained that which they so earnestly desire, i.e., to be continued, as they have been hitherto, the peculiar people of God; *but the election hath obtained it*—as many of them as have believed in Jesus Christ and accepted salvation through Him. This is the grand scheme of the election by grace; God chooses to make those His peculiar people who believe in His Son, and none other shall enjoy the blessings of His kingdom. Those who would not receive Him are *blinded;* they have shut their eyes against the light, and are in the very circumstances of those mentioned by the Prophet Isaiah, chap. xxix. 10.

8. *God hath given them the spirit of slumber.* As they had willfully closed their eyes against the light, so God has, in judgment, given them up to the *spirit of slumber.*

9. *And David saith, Let their table.* And from their present disposition it is reasonable to conclude that the same evils will fall upon them as fell upon the disobedient in former times, as predicted by David, Ps. lxix. 22-23, that their very blessings should become curses to them, and their temporal mercies be their only recompense; and yet even these earthly blessings, by not being enjoyed in the Lord, should

MATTHEW HENRY

curse of God will turn meat into poison. Their very food, that should nourish them, shall choke them. [2] Of the ruin of their powers and faculties (*v.* 10), their eyes darkened, their backs bowed down, that they can neither find the right way, nor, if they could, are they able to walk in it. *They mind earthly things.* We have our eyes darkened if we are bowed down in worldly-mindedness.

II. Another thing which qualified this doctrine of the rejection of the Jews was that though they were cast off, yet the Gentiles were taken in (*v.* 11–14), which he applies by way of caution to the Gentiles, *v.* 17–22.

1. The Jews' leavings were a feast for the poor Gentiles (*v.* 11): "*Have they stumbled that they should fall?* Had God no other end in rejecting them than their destruction?" He startled at this as usually he does when anything is suggested which seems to reflect upon the wisdom, or righteousness, or goodness of God: *God forbid!* no, *through their fall salvation is come to the Gentiles.* By the divine appointment it was so ordered that the gospel should be preached to the Gentiles upon the Jews' refusal of it. And so it was in the history (Acts xiii. 46): *It was necessary that the word of God should first have been spoken to you; but, seeing you put it from you, lo, we turn to the Gentiles.* The Jews had the refusal, and so the tender came to the Gentiles. See how Infinite Wisdom brings light out of darkness, good out of evil. To the same purport he says (*v.* 12), *The fall of them was the riches of the world.* The riches of the Gentiles was the multitude of converts among them. True believers are God's jewels. To the same purport (*v.* 15): *The casting away of them is the reconciling of the world.* God's displeasure towards them made way for his favour towards the Gentiles. God was in Christ *reconciling the world,* 2 Cor. v. 19. In every nation he that feared God and wrought righteousness should be accepted of him.

2. The use that the apostle makes of this doctrine.

(1) As a kinsman to the Jews, here is a word of exhortation to them, to stir them up to receive the gospel offer. This God intended in his favour to the Gentiles, to provoke the Jews to jealousy (*v.* 11), and Paul endeavours to enforce it accordingly (*v.* 14): *If by any means I might provoke to emulation those who are my flesh.* "Shall the despised Gentiles run away with all the comforts and privileges of the gospel, and shall not we repent of our refusal, and now at last put in for a share?" There is a commendable emulation in the affairs of our souls; why should not we be as holy and happy as any of our neighbours? The blessings are not lessened by the multitudes of the sharers.—*And might save some of them.* See what was Paul's business, to save souls; and yet the utmost he promises himself is but to save some. Of the many he dealt with he could but save some. Ministers must think their pains well bestowed if they can but be instrumental to save some.

(2) As an apostle to the Gentiles, here is a word of caution for them: "*I speak to you Gentiles.* You believing Romans, you hear what riches of salvation are come to you by the fall of the Jews, but take heed lest you do anything to forfeit it." Paul takes this, as other occasions, to apply his discourse to the Gentiles, because he was the apostle of the Gentiles. This was the purport of his extraordinary mission, Acts xxii. 21, *I will send thee far hence unto the Gentiles.* It ought to be our great and special care to do good to those that are under our charge: we must particularly mind that which is our own work. The Gentile world was a wider province; and the work to be done in it required a very able, courageous workman. God calls those to special work whom he either sees or makes fit for it.—*I magnify my office.* There were those that vilified it, and him because of it. It is a sign of true love to Jesus Christ to reckon that service for him truly honourable which the world looks upon with scorn. The office of the ministry is an office to be *magnified.* Ministers are stewards of the mysteries of God, and for their work's sake are to be esteemed highly in love.—*My office, my ministry,* my service. It was not the dignity but the work, of an apostle, that Paul was so much in love with. Now two things he exhorts the Gentiles to,

[1] To have a respect for the Jews, and to desire their conversion. The advantage that would accrue to the church by their conversion, *v.* 12, 15. It would be as life from the dead; and therefore they must long for the receiving of them in again.

JAMIESON, FAUSSET, BROWN

Let their eyes be darkened . . . and bow down their back alway—expressive either of the *decrepitude,* or of the *servile condition,* to come on the nation through the just judgment of God. The apostle's object in making these quotations is to show that what he had been compelled to say of the then condition and prospects of his nation was more than borne out by their own Scriptures. But, SECONDLY, God has not cast away His people *finally.* The illustration of this point extends from vs. 11 to vs. 31.

11. I say then, Have they stumbled—'Did they stumble'—**that they should fall? God forbid; but**—the supplement "rather" is better omitted—**through their fall**—lit., 'trespass,' but here best rendered 'false step' [DE WETTE]; not "fall," as in our version. **salvation is come to the Gentiles, to provoke them to jealousy**—Here, as also in ch. 10:19 (quoted from Deut. 32: 21), we see that emulation is a legitimate stimulus to what is good.

12. Now if the fall of them—'But if their trespass,' or 'false step'—**be the riches of the**—Gentile—**world**—as being the occasion of their accession to Christ. **and the diminishing of them**—i.e., the reduction of the *true* Israel to so small a remnant

—**the riches of the Gentiles; how much more their fulness!**—i.e., their full recovery (see on vs. 26); i.e., 'If an event so untoward as Israel's fall was the occasion of such unspeakable good to the Gentile world, of how much greater good may we expect an event so blessed as their full recovery to be productive?'

13. I speak—'am speaking'—**to you Gentiles**—another proof that this Epistle was addressed to Gentile believers. (See on ch. 1:13.)

I magnify—'glorify'—**mine office**—The clause beginning with "inasmuch" should be read as a parenthesis. **If . . . I may provoke . . .** (See on vs. 11). **my flesh**—Cf. Isa. 58:7.

15. For if the casting away of them—The apostle had denied that they were cast away (vs. 1); here he affirms it. But both are true; they *were* cast away, though neither totally nor finally, and it is of this partial and temporary rejection that the apostle here speaks. **be the reconciling of the**—Gentile—**world, what shall the receiving of them be, but life from the dead?**—The reception of

ADAM CLARKE

be a stumbling block over which they should fall, and, instead of being a blessing, should be the means of their punishment.

10. *Let their eyes be darkened.* All these words are declarative, and not imprecatory. God declares what will be the case of such obstinate unbelievers; "their table," their common providential blessings, will become "a snare, and a trap, and a stumblingblock," and the means of their punishment. Their eyes will be more and more darkened as they persist in their unbelief, and their "back shall be bowed down always." Far from becoming a great and powerful nation, they shall continue ever in a state of abject slavery and oppression, till they acknowledge Jesus as the promised Messiah, and submit to receive redemption in His blood.

11. *Have they stumbled that they should fall?* Have the Jews, now for their disobedience and unbelief rejected, so sinned against God as to be forever put out of the reach of His mercy? "By no means." Are they, as a nation, utterly irrecoverable? This is the sense of the place, and here the prophecy of the restoration of the Jewish nation commences. *But rather through their fall salvation is come.* The Church of God cannot fail; if the Jews have broken the everlasting covenant, Isa. xxiv. 5, the Gentiles shall be taken into it; and this very circumstance shall be ultimately the means of exciting them to seek and claim a share in the blessings of the new covenant. This is what the apostle terms provoking *them to jealousy,* i.e., exciting them to emulation, for so the word should be understood. We should observe here that the *fall* of the Jews was not in itself the cause or reason of the calling of the Gentiles. Whether the Jews had stood or fallen, whether they had embraced or rejected the gospel, it was the original purpose of God to take the Gentiles into the Church, for this was absolutely implied in the covenant made with Abraham; and it was in virtue of that covenant that the Gentiles were now called, and not because of the unbelief of the Jews.

12. *Now if the fall of them.* The English reader may imagine that because *fall* is used in both these verses the original word is the same. But *their fall* and *the fall of them* are *parastoma,* the same word which we render "offence," chap. v. 15, 17-18, and might be rendered "lapse." Whereas *that they should fall* (v. 11) is *hina pesosi.* Now *pipto,* "to fall," is used in a sense so very emphatical as to signify "being slain." It is well-known that to *fall* in battle means to be "killed." It is in such a sense as this that Paul used the word *fall* when he says, "Have they stumbled that they should fall?" *The riches of the world.* If in consequence of their unbelief the riches of God's grace and goodness be poured out on the whole Gentile world, how much more shall that dispensation of grace and mercy enrich and aggrandize the Gentiles, which shall bring the whole body of the Jews to the faith of the gospel! Here the apostle supposes, or rather predicts, that such a dispensation shall take place, and that therefore the Jews have not so stumbled as to be finally irrecoverable.

13. This and the following verse should be read in a parenthesis. Paul, as the apostle of the Gentiles, wished to show them the high pitch of glory and blessedness to which they had been called, that they might have a due sense of God's mercy in calling them to such a state of salvation, and that they might be jealous over themselves, lest they should fall as the Jews had done before them; and he dwells particularly on the greatness of those privileges which the Gentiles had now received, that he might stir up the minds of his countrymen to emulation, and might be the means of saving some of them, as he states in the following verse. *I magnify mine office.* Literally, "I honor this my ministry."

14. *Might save some of them.* And yet all these were among the reprobate, or rejected; however, the apostle supposed that none of them were irrecoverably shut out from the divine favor and that *some* of them, by his preaching, might be disposed to receive salvation by Christ Jesus.

15. *But life from the dead.* If the rejection of the Jews became the occasion of our receiving the gospel, so that we can even glory in our tribulations, though they themselves be-

MATTHEW HENRY

What it is grounded upon, and what reason we have to look for it.

Because of the holiness of the first-fruits and the root, *v.* 16. A good beginning promises a good ending. By the first-fruits understand the same with the root, namely, the patriarchs, Abraham, Isaac, and Jacob. Now, if they were holy—if they were in the covenant—then we have reason to conclude that God hath a kindness for the *lump*—the body of that people; and for the *branches*—the particular members of it. *If the root be holy, so are the branches.* Though a wise man does not beget a wise man, yet a free man begets a free man. Though grace does not run in the blood, yet external privileges do (till they are forfeited). The Jewish branches are reckoned holy, because the root was so.

[2] To take heed to themselves, lest they should stumble and fall, as the Jews had done, *v.* 17-22.

First, The privilege which the Gentiles had by being taken into the church. They were grafted in (*v.* 17), as a branch of a wild olive into a good olive, which is contrary to the custom of the husbandman, who grafts the good olive into the bad; but those that God grafts into the church he finds wild and barren, and good for nothing. Men graft to mend the tree; but God grafts to mend the branch. The church of God is an olive-tree, flourishing and fruitful, the fruit useful. Those that are out of the church are as wild olive-trees not only useless, but what they do produce is sour and unsavoury: *Wild by nature*, *v.* 24. It is the natural state of everyone of us to be wild by nature. Conversion is the grafting in of wild branches into the good olive. Those that are grafted into the good olive-tree partake of the root and fatness of the olive. All that are by a lively faith grafted into Christ partake of him as the branches of the root. The Gentiles, being grafted into the church, partake of the same privileges that the Jews did, *the root and fatness.* Christ only is the root. Now the believing Gentiles partake of this root.

Secondly, A caution not to abuse these privileges. 1. "Be not proud (*v.* 18): *Boast not against the branches.*" Grace is given, not to make us proud, but to make us thankful. The law of faith excludes all boasting either of ourselves or against others. "Do not say (*v.* 19): *They were broken off that I might be grafted in;* that is, do not think that thou didst merit more at the hand of God than they. But remember, *thou bearest not the root, but the root thee.* Though thou art grafted in, thou art still but a branch borne by the root; nay, and an engrafted branch, brought into the good olive *contrary to nature* (*v.* 24), not free-born, but by an act of grace. Therefore, *if thou boast*, know (this word must be supplied to clear the sense) *thou bearest not the root but the root thee.*" 2. "Be not secure (*v.* 20): *Be not high-minded, but fear.* Be not too confident of your own strength and standing." A holy fear is an excellent preservative against high-mindedness: happy is the man that thus feareth always. *Fear* what? "Why fear lest thou lose the privileges thou now enjoyest, as they have lost theirs." The evils that befall others should be warnings to us. The patent which churches have of their privileges is not for a certain term, but it runs as long as they carry themselves well, and no longer. Consider, (1) "How they were broken off. It was not undeservedly, but *because of unbelief.*" They did by this cut themselves off.

JAMIESON, FAUSSET, BROWN

the whole family of Israel, scattered as they are among all nations under heaven, and the most inveterate enemies of the Lord Jesus, will be such a stupendous manifestation of the power of God upon the spirits of men, and of His glorious presence with the heralds of the Cross, as will not only kindle devout astonishment far and wide, but so change the dominant mode of thinking and feeling on all spiritual things as to seem like a *resurrection from the dead.*

16. **For**—'But'—**if the first fruit be holy, the lump is also holy; and if the root . . ., so the branches**—The Israelites were required to offer to God the first fruits of the earth—both in their raw state, in a sheaf of newly reaped grain (Lev. 23:10, 11), and in their prepared state, made into cakes of dough (Num. 15:19-21)—by which the whole produce of that season was regarded as *hallowed.* It is probable that the latter of these offerings is here intended, as to it the word "lump" best applies; and the argument of the apostle is, that as the separation unto God of Abraham, Isaac, and Jacob, from the rest of mankind, as the parent stem of their race, was as real an offering of first fruits as that which hallowed the produce of the earth, so, in the divine estimation, it was as real a separation of the mass or "lump" of that nation in all time to God. The figure of the "root" and its "branches" is of like import—the consecration of the one of them extending to the other,

17, 18. **And if**—rather, 'But if'; i.e., 'If notwithstanding this consecration of Abraham's race to God. **some of the branches**—The mass of the unbelieving and rejected Israelites are here called "some," not, as before, to meet Jewish prejudice (see on ch. 3:3, and on "not all" in ch. 10:16), but with the opposite view of checking Gentile pride. **and thou, being a wild olive, wert**—'wast'—**graffed in among them**—Though it is more usual to graft the superior cutting upon the inferior stem, the opposite method, which is intended here, is not without example. **and with them partakest**—'wast made partaker,'—along with the branches left, the believing remnant—**of the root and fatness of the olive tree**—the rich grace secured by covenant to the true seed of Abraham—**boast not against the**—rejected—**branches. But if thou**—'do'—**boast**—remember that—**thou bearest not**—'it is not thou that bearest'—**the root, but the root thee**—'If the branches may not boast over the root that bears them, then may not the Gentile boast over the seed of Abraham; for what is thy standing, O Gentile, in relation to Israel, but that of a branch in relation to the root? From Israel hath come all that thou art and hast in the family of God; for "salvation is of the Jews" (John 4:22).

19-21. **Thou wilt say then**—as a plea for boasting—**The branches were broken off, that I might be graffed in. Well**—'Be it so, but remember that'—**because of unbelief they**

ADAM CLARKE

came chief instruments of our sufferings, yet so far must we feel from exulting over them that we should esteem their full conversion to God as great and choice a favor as we would the restoration of a most intimate friend to life, who had been at the gates of death. The restoration of the Jews to a state of favor with God to which the apostle refers, and which is too plainly intimated by the spirit of prophecy to admit of a doubt, will be a most striking event. Their being preserved as a distinct people is certainly a strong collateral proof that they shall once more brought into the Church of God; and their conversion to Christianity will be an incontestable proof of the truth of divine revelation, and doubtless will become the means of converting multitudes of deists, who will see the prophecies of God, which had been delivered so long before, so strikingly fulfilled in this great event. We need not wonder if a whole nation should then be born as in a day.

16. *For if the firstfruit be holy.* As consecrating the firstfruits to God was the means of drawing down His blessing upon the rest, so the conversion of Abraham to the true faith. and the several Jews who have now embraced Christianity, are pledges that God will, in process of time, admit the whole Jewish nation into His favor again, so that they shall constitute a part of the Visible Church of Christ. *If the root be holy, so are the branches.* The word *holy* in this verse is to be taken in that sense which it has so frequently in the Old and New Testaments, viz., "consecrated, set apart to sacred uses." It must not be forgotten that the first converts to Christ were from among the Jews; these formed the *root* of the Christian Church. These were *holy,* "consecrated" to God, and those who among the Gentiles were converted by their means were also "consecrated." But the chief reference is to the ancestors of the Jewish people, Abraham, Isaac, and Jacob; and as these were devoted to God and received into His covenant, all their posterity, the *branches* which proceeded from this *root,* became entitled to the same privileges; and as the *root* still remains, and the *branches* also, the descendants from that root still remain. They still have a certain title to the blessings of the covenant, though because of their obstinate unbelief these blessings are suspended, as they cannot, even on the ground of the old covenant, enjoy these blessings but through faith; for it was when Abraham believed God that it was accounted to him for righteousness, and thus he became an heir of the righteousness which is by faith.

17. *And if some of the branches*—if the present nation of the Jews, because of their unbelief, are cut off from the blessings of the Church of God, and the high honor and dignity of being His peculiar people. *And thou, being a wild olive*—ye Gentiles, being without the knowledge of the true God, and consequently bringing forth no fruits of righteousness. *Wert grafted in among them*—are now inserted in the original stock, having been made partakers of the faith of Abraham, and consequently of his blessings; and enjoy, as the people did who sprang from him, *the fatness of the olive tree,* the promises made to the patriarchs, and the spiritual privileges of the Jewish church.

18. *Boast not against the branches.* While you are ready to acknowledge that you were included in the covenant made with Abraham, and are now partakers of the same blessings with him, do not "exult over," much less insult, *the branches,* his present descendants, whose place you now fill up, according to the election of grace. For remember, you are not the *root,* nor do you bear the root, but the root bears you. You have not been the means of deriving any blessing on the Jewish people; but through that very people, which you may be tempted to despise, all the blessing and excellencies which you enjoy have been communicated to you.

19. *Thou wilt say then.* You may think that you have reason to exult over them, because it is a fact that God has been displeased with them, and therefore has *broken* them *off;* has cast them out of the Church and taken you into it in their place.

20. *Well; because of unbelief.* This statement is all true; but then, consider, why is it that

MATTHEW HENRY

They were *natural branches* (*v.* 21), yet, when they sunk into unbelief, God did not spare them. Prescription, long usage, the faithfulness of their ancestors, would not secure them. It was in vain to plead, though they insisted much upon it, that they were Abraham's seed. This is called here *severity*, *v.* 22. Severity is a word that sounds harshly; and I do not remember that it is anywhere else in scripture ascribed to God. God is most severe towards those that have been in profession nearest to him, if they rebel against him. Of all judgments, spiritual judgments are the sorest; for of these he is here speaking, *v.* 8. (2) "How thou standest, thou that are engrafted in." "By what means thou standest: *By faith*, which is a depending grace. Thou dost not stand in any strength of thy own: thou art no more than the free grace of God makes thee. That which ruined them was unbelief, and by faith thou standest." On what terms (*v.* 22): "*Towards thee goodness, if thou continue in his goodness*, that is, continue in a dependence upon the free grace of God." The condition of our happiness, is to keep ourselves in the love of God.

III. Another thing that qualifies this doctrine of the Jews' rejection is that the rejection is not final.

1. How this conversion of the Jews is here described. It is said to be their fulness (*v.* 12), that is, the addition of them to the church. This would be the enriching of the world with a great deal of light and strength and beauty. It is called the receiving of them. They shall be received into the love of Christ. And this will be as *life from the dead*—so strange and surprising, and yet withal so welcome and acceptable. It is called the *grafting of them in again* (*v.* 23). That which is grafted in receives sap and virtue from the root; so does a soul that is truly grafted into the church receive life, and strength, and grace from Christ the quickening root. They shall be *grafted into their own olive-tree* (*v.* 24) to retrieve those privileges which they had so long enjoyed, but have now sinned away and forfeited by their unbelief. It is called the *saving of all Israel*, *v.* 26. The adding of them to the church is the saving of them.

Because of the power of God (*v.* 23): *God is able to graft them in again.* Our comfort is that God is able to work a change, able to graft those in that have been long cast out and withered. *If they abide not still in unbelief.* So that nothing is to be done but to remove that unbelief, and God is able to take that away, though nothing less than an almighty power will do it.

Because of the grace of God manifested to the Gentiles. This is his argument (*v.* 24): "If thou wast grafted into a good olive, that was wild by nature, much more shall these that were the natural branches." This is a suggestion very proper to check the insolence of those Gentile Christians that looked with disdain upon the rejected Jews.

JAMIESON, FAUSSET, BROWN

were broken off, and thou standest—not as a Gentile, but solely—**by faith**—But as faith cannot live in those "whose soul is lifted up" (Hab. 2:4)—**Be not high-minded, but fear**—(Prov. 28:14; Phil. 2:12):

for if God spared not the natural branches—sprung from the parent stem—**take heed lest he also spare not thee**—a mere wild graft. The former might, beforehand, have been thought very improbable; but, after that, no one can wonder at the latter.

22, 23. Behold therefore the goodness and severity of God: on them that fell, severity—in rejecting the chosen seed—**but toward thee, goodness**—'God's goodness' is the true reading' i.e., His sovereign goodness in admitting thee to a covenant standing who before wert a "stranger to the covenants of promise" (Eph. 2:12-20). **if thou continue in his goodness**—in believing dependence on that pure goodness which made thee what thou art.

otherwise . . . And they also—'Yea, and they'—**if they abide not still in unbelief, shall be graffed in: for God is able to graff them in again**—This appeal to the *power* of God to effect the recovery of His ancient people implies the vast difficulty of it—which all who have ever labored for the conversion of the Jews are made depressingly to feel. That intelligent expositors should think that this was meant of *individual* Jews, reintroduced from time to time into the family of God on their believing on the Lord Jesus, is surprising; and yet those who deny the *national* recovery of Israel must and do so interpret the apostle. But this is to confound the two things which the apostle carefully distinguishes. Individual Jews have been at all times admissible, and have been admitted, to the Church through the gate of faith in the Lord Jesus. This is the "remnant, *even at this present time,* according to the election of grace," of which the apostle, in the first part of the chapter, had cited himself as one. But here he manifestly speaks of something *not* then existing, but to be looked forward to as a great future event in the economy of God, the reingrafting of *the nation as such,* when they "abide not in unbelief." And though this is here spoken of merely as a supposition (if their unbelief shall cease)—in order to set it over against the other supposition, of what will happen to the Gentiles if they shall not abide in the faith—the supposition is turned into an explicit prediction in the verses following. **24. For if thou wert cut**—'wert cut off'—**from the olive tree, which is wild by nature, and wast graffed contrary to nature into a good olive tree; how much more shall these . . .**—This is just the converse of vs. 21: 'As the excision of the merely *engrafted* Gentiles through unbelief is a thing much more to be expected than was the excision of the *natural* Israel, before it happened; so the restoration of Israel, when they shall be brought to believe in Jesus, is a thing far more in the line of what we should expect, than the admission of the Gentiles to a standing which they never before enjoyed.'

25. For I would not . . . that ye should be ignorant of this mystery—The word "mystery," so often used by our apostle, does not mean (as with us) something incomprehensible, but 'something before kept secret, either wholly or for the most part, and now only fully disclosed' (cf. ch. 16:25; I Cor. 2:7-10; Eph. 1:9, 10; 3:3-6, 9, 10).

lest ye should be wise in your own conceits—as if

ADAM CLARKE

they were cast out? Was it not because of their unbelief? And you stand by *faith;* you were made partakers of these blessings by faith. *Be not highminded;* let this humble, not exalt you in your own estimation.

21. *For if God spared not the natural branches.* If He, in His infinite justice and holiness, could not tolerate sin in the people whom He foreknew, whom He had so long loved, cherished, miraculously preserved, and blessed, *take heed lest he also spare not thee.* Be convinced that the same righteous principle in Him will cause Him to act towards you as He has acted towards them, if you sin after the similitude of their transgression; and to this, self-sufficiency and self-confidence will soon lead you.

22. *Behold therefore the goodness.* The exclamation, *Behold the goodness of God!* is frequent among the Jewish writers when they wish to call the attention of men to particular displays of God's mercy, especially towards those who are singularly unworthy. *And severity of God.* As *goodness* signifies the essential quality of the divine nature, the fountain of all good to men and angels, so *severity* signifies that particular exercise of His goodness and holiness which leads Him to sever from His mystical body whatsoever would injure, corrupt, or destroy it. The apostle, having adopted this metaphor as the best he could find to express that act of God's justice and mercy by which the Jews were rejected and the Gentiles elected in their stead, and in order to show that though the Jewish tree was cut down, or its branches lopped off, yet it was not rooted up, he informs the Gentile believers that, as it is customary to insert a good scion in a bad or useless stock, they who were bad, contrary to the custom in such cases, were grafted in a good stock, and their growth and fruitfulness proclaimed the excellence and vegetative life of the stock in which they were inserted. This was the *goodness* of the heavenly Gardener to them; but it was *severity*, an act of "excision," to the Jews.

23. *If they abide not still in unbelief.* So we find that their rejection took place in consequence of their willful obstinacy, and that they may return into the fold, the door of which still stands open. *For God is able to graff them in again.* Fallen as they are and degraded, God can, in the course of His providence and mercy, restore them to all their forfeited privileges; and this will take place if *they abide not still in unbelief*, which intimates that God has furnished them with all the power and means necessary for faith, and that they may believe on the Lord Jesus whenever they will.

24. *The olive tree which is wild by nature.* Which is "naturally" wild and barren; for that the wild olive bore no fruit is sufficiently evident from the testimony of the authors who have written on the subject. Hence the proverb, "More unfruitful than the wild olive." *And wert graffed contrary to nature.* "Contrary to all custom"; for a scion taken from a barren or useless tree is scarcely ever known to be grafted into a good stock; but here the Gentiles, a fruitless and sinful race, are grafted on the ancient patriarchal stock. Now if it was possible to effect such a change in the state and disposition of the Gentiles, who were (Eph. ii. 12) "without God [atheists] in the world," how much more possible is it, speaking after the manner of men, to bring about a similar change in the Jews, who acknowledge the one, only, and true God, and receive the law and the prophets as a revelation from Him! This seems to be the drift of the apostle's argument.

25. *I would not . . . that ye should be ignorant of this mystery.* Mystery signifies anything that is hidden or covered, or not fully made manifest. In the New Testament it signifies, generally, "any thing or doctrine that has not, in former times, been fully known to men"; or "something that has not been heard of, or which is so deep, profound, and difficult of comprehension that it cannot be apprehended without special direction and instruction." Here it signifies the doctrine of the future restoration of the Jews, not fully known in itself, and not at all known as to the time in which it will take place. In chap. xvi. 25, it means the Christian religion, not known till the advent of Christ. *Lest ye should be wise in your own conceits.*

MATTHEW HENRY

3. The time and extent of this conversion, when and where it is to be expected. It is called a mystery (*v.* 25), that which was not obvious, and which one would not expect upon the view of the present state of that people. The case of the rejected Jews seemed as bad now as that of the Gentiles had been. Now he would have them know so much of this mystery as to keep them humble: lest *you be wise in your own conceit.* Ignorance is the cause of our self-conceitedness. (1) Their present state: *Blindness, in part, is happened to Israel, v.* 25. It is but in part; there is a remnant that see the things which belong to their peace, *v.* 7, 8.

(2) When this blessed change should be: when the *fulness of the Gentiles shall come in,* when the gospel has had its intended success, and made its progress in the Gentile world. The Jews shall continue in blindness, till God hath performed his whole work among the Gentiles. God's taking them again was not because he had need of them, but of his own free grace.

(3) The extent of it: *All Israel shall be saved, v.* 26. He will *have mercy upon all, v.* 32. They should be brought to believe in Christ the true Messiah whom they crucified, and become one sheep-fold with the Gentiles under Christ the great Shepherd. Some think it is done already, when before, and in, and after, the destruction of Jerusalem by the Romans, multitudes of the Jews were convinced, and turned Christians. Others think that it is yet to have its accomplishment towards the end of the world.

(4) Because of the promises and prophecies of the Old Testament. He quotes a very remarkable one, *v.* 26, from Isa. lix. 20, 21. [1] The coming of Christ promised: *There shall come out of Zion the deliverer.* Jesus Christ is the great deliverer. In Isaiah it is, *the Redeemer shall come to Zion.* There he is called the Redeemer; here the deliverer; he delivers in a way of redemption, by a price. There he is said to come to Zion, because when the prophet prophesied he was yet to come into the world. When the apostle wrote this, he had come, and he is speaking of the fruits of his appearing, which shall come *out of Zion.* [2] The purpose of this coming: *He shall turn away ungodliness from Jacob.* Christ's errand into the world was to turn away ungodliness, that iniquity might not be our ruin, and that it might not be our ruler. Especially to turn it away from Jacob. What greater kindness could he do them than to turn away ungodliness from them, and then make way for all good? In Isaiah it is, *The Redeemer shall come to Zion, and unto those that turn from transgression in Jacob,* those only that leave their sins and turn to God; to them Christ comes as a Redeemer.—*For this is my covenant with them*—this, that the deliverer shall come to them—this, that my Spirit shall not depart from them. The apostle adds, *When I shall take away their sins.* Pardon of sin is laid as the foundation. *For I will be merciful.*

JAMIESON, FAUSSET, BROWN

ye alone were in all time coming to be the family of God. **that blindness**—'hardness'—**in part is happened to**—'hath come upon'—**Israel**—i.e., hath come partially, or upon a portion of Israel.

until the fulness of the Gentiles be—'have'—**come in**—i.e., not the general conversion of the world to Christ, as many take it; for this would seem to contradict the latter part of this chapter, and throw the national recovery of Israel too far into the future: besides, in vs. 15, the apostle seems to speak of the receiving of Israel, not as following, but as contributing largely to bring about the general conversion of the world—but, 'until the Gentiles have had their *full* time of the visible Church all to themselves while the Jews are out, which the Jews had till the Gentiles were brought in.' (See Luke 21:24.)

26, 27. And so all Israel shall be saved—To understand this great statement, as some still do, merely of such a gradual inbringing of *individual* Jews, that there shall at length remain none in unbelief, is to do manifest violence both to it and to the whole context. It can only mean the ultimate ingathering of Israel as a *nation,* in contrast with the present "remnant." [So THOLUCK, MEYER, DE WETTE, PHILIPPI, ALFORD, HODGE]. Three confirmations of this now follow: two from the prophets, and a third from the Abrahamic covenant itself. *First,* **as it is written, There shall come out of Sion the Deliverer, and shall**—or, according to what seems the true reading, without the "and"—'He shall"—**turn away ungodliness from Jacob**—The apostle, having drawn his illustrations of man's *sinfulness* chiefly from Psalm 14 and Isaiah 59, now seems to combine the language of the same two places regarding Israel's *salvation* from it [BENGEL]. In the one place the Psalmist longs to see the "salvation of Israel coming *out of Zion*" (Ps. 14:7); in the other, the prophet announces that "the Redeemer (or, "Deliverer") shall come *to* (or *for*) Zion" (Isa. 59:20). But as all the glorious manifestations of Israel's God were regarded as issuing out of Zion, as the seat of His manifested glory (Ps. 20:2; 110:2; Isa. 31:9), the turn which the apostle gives to the words merely adds to them that familiar idea. And whereas the prophet announces that He "shall come *to* (or, '*for*') them that turn from transgression in Jacob," while the apostle makes Him say that He shall come "to turn away ungodliness *from* Jacob," this is taken from the LXX version, and seems to indicate a different reading of the original text. The sense, however, is substantially the same in both. *Second,* **For**—rather, 'and' (again); introducing a new quotation. **this is my covenant with them**—lit., 'this is the covenant from me unto them." **when I shall take away their sins**—This, we believe, is rather a brief summary of Jeremiah 31:31-34 than the express words of any prediction, Those who believe that there are no predictions regarding the literal Israel in the Old Testament, that stretch beyond the end of the Jewish economy, are obliged to view these quotations by the apostle as mere adaptations of Old Testament language to express his own predictions [ALEXANDER on Isaiah, etc.]. But how forced this is, we shall presently see.

28, 29. As concerning the Gospel they are enemies for your sakes—i.e., they are regarded and treated as enemies (in a state of exclusion through unbelief, from the family of God) for the benefit of you Gentiles; in the sense of vss. 11, 15. **but as touching the election**—of Abraham and his seed

ADAM CLARKE

It seems from this, and from other expressions in this Epistle, that the converted Gentiles had not behaved toward the Jews with that decorum and propriety which the relation they bore to them required. In this chapter the apostle strongly guards them against giving way to such a disposition. *Blindness in part is happened to Israel.* Partial blindness, or blindness to a part of them; for they were not all believers. Several thousands of them had been converted to the Christian faith; though the body of the nation, and especially its rulers, civil and spiritual, continued opposed to Christ and His doctrine. *Until the fulness of the Gentiles be come in.* And this blindness will continue till the Church of the Gentiles be fully completed—till the gospel be preached through all the nations of the earth, and multitudes of heathens everywhere embrace the faith. By the *fulness* a "great multitude" may be intended, which should be so dilated on every hand as to fill various regions. The apostle, therefore, seems to give this sense of the mystery—that the Jews will continue in a state of blindness till such time as a "multitude of nations," or Gentiles, shall be converted to the Christian faith; and the Jews, hearing of this, shall be excited, by a spirit of emulation, to examine and acknowledge the validity of the proofs of Christianity and embrace the faith of our Lord Jesus Christ.

26. *And so all Israel shall be saved.* Shall be brought into the way of salvation by acknowledging the Messiah, for the word certainly does not mean eternal glory; for no man can conceive that a time will ever come in which every Jew then living shall be taken to the Kingdom of glory. The term *saved* as applied to the Israelites in different parts of the Scripture signifies no more than their being gathered out of the nations of the world, separated to God, and possessed of the high privilege of being His peculiar people. And we know that this is the meaning of the term by finding it applied to the body of the Israelites when this alone was the sum of their state. *As it is written.* The apostle supports what he advances on this head by a quotation from Scripture, which in the main is taken from Isa. lix. 20: *The Deliverer* shall come out of Zion, and *turn away ungodliness from Jacob.* Now this cannot be understood of the manifestation of Christ among the Jews or of the multitudes which were converted before, at, and for some time after, the Day of Pentecost; for these times were all past when the apostle wrote this Epistle. And as no remarkable conversion of that people has since taken place, therefore the fulfillment of this prophecy is yet to take place. In what manner Christ is to *come out of Sion,* and in what way or by what means He is to "turn away transgression from Jacob," we cannot tell; and to attempt to conjecture, when the time, occasion, means, etc., are all in mystery, would be more than reprehensible.

27. *For this is my covenant unto them, when I shall take away their sins.* The reader, on referring to Isa. lix. 20-21, will find that the words of the original are here greatly abridged. They are the following: "And the Redeemer shall come to Zion, and unto them that turn from transgression in Jacob, saith the Lord. As for me, this is my covenant with them, saith the Lord, My Spirit that is upon thee, and my words which I have put in thy mouth, shall not depart out of thy mouth, nor out of the mouth of thy seed, nor out of the mouth of thy seed's seed, saith the Lord, from henceforth and for ever."

It may not be amiss to subjoin here a collection of those texts in the Old Testament that seem to point out a restoration of the Jewish commonwealth to a higher degree of excellence than it has yet attained: Isa. ii. 2-5; xix. 24-25; xxv. 6 ff.; xxx. 18-19, 26; lx throughout; lxv. 17 to the end; Jer. xxxi. 10-12; xlvi. 27-28; Ezek. xx. 34, 40 ff.; xxviii. 25-26; xxiv. 20 ff.; xxxvi. 8-16; xxxvii. 21-28; xxxix. 25 ff.; Joel iii. 1-2, 17, 20-21; Amos ix. 9 to the end; Obad. vv. 17, 21; Mic. iv. 3-7; vii. 18-20; Zeph. iii. 19-20.

28. *As concerning the gospel.* The unbelieving Jews, with regard to the *gospel* which they have rejected, are at present *enemies* to God, **and aliens from His kingdom,** under His Son, Jesus Christ. But with regard to the original purpose of *election,* whereby they were chosen

MATTHEW HENRY

This is expressed more plainly (*v.* 28): *They are beloved for the fathers' sakes.* And the same love would revive their privileges for still the ancient loving-kindness is remembered. Though, as concerning the gospel, they are enemies to it *for your sakes*, that is, for the sake of the Gentiles, against whom they have such an antipathy; yet, when God's time shall come, this will wear off, and God's love to their fathers will be remembered. Many fare the better for the sake of their godly ancestors. It is upon this account that the church is called their own *olive-tree*, which is some encouragement to us to hope that there may be room for them in it again, for old acquaintance-sake. That which hath been may be again. Now from all this he infers that certainly God had great mercy in store for that people, and he proves his inference (*v.* 29) by this truth: *For the gifts and callings of God are without repentance.* Those gifts and callings are immutable; whom he so loves, he loves to the end. We never find God repenting that he had given a man grace, or effectually called him.

This is his argument (*v.* 30, 31): *As you in times past have not*, &c. It is good for those that have found mercy with God to be often thinking what they were in time past, and how they obtained that mercy. He argues further from the occasion of the Gentiles' call: "*You have obtained mercy through their unbelief;* much more shall they obtain mercy through your mercy. *That through your mercy they might obtain mercy*, that is, that they may be beholden to you, as you have been to them." True grace hates monopolies. Those that have found mercy themselves should endeavour that through their mercy others also may obtain mercy.

To the same purport (*v.* 32): *God has concluded them all in unbelief*, shut them up as in a prison. They all stand before God convicted of unbelief. They would not believe. "Why then," saith God, "you shall not."

Verses 33–36

The apostle having insisted so largely upon reconciling the rejection of the Jews with the divine goodness, he concludes here with the acknowledgment of the divine wisdom in all this.

I. The secrecy of the divine counsels: *O the depth!* in general, the whole mystery of the gospel, which we cannot fully comprehend.—*The riches of the wisdom and knowledge of God*, a depth which the angels pry into, 1 Pet. i. 12. Much more may it puzzle any human understanding. He confesses himself at a loss in the contemplation, and, despairing to find the bottom, he humbly sits down at the brink, and adores the depth. Those that know most in this state of imperfection cannot but be most sensible

JAMIESON, FAUSSET, BROWN

—**they are beloved**—*even in their state of exclusion*—**for the fathers' sakes. For the gifts and calling**—'and the calling'—**of God are without repentance**—'not to be,' or 'cannot be repented of.' By the "*calling* of God," in this case, is meant that sovereign act by which God, in the exercise of His free choice, "called" Abraham to be the father of a peculiar people; while "the *gifts* of God" here denote the articles of the covenant which God made with Abraham, and which constituted the real distinction between his and all other families of the earth. Both these, says the apostle, are irrevocable; and as the point for which he refers to this at all is the *final destiny* of the Israelitish nation, it is clear that *the perpetuity through all time of the Abrahamic covenant* is the thing here affirmed. And lest any should say that though Israel, *as a nation*, has no destiny at all under the Gospel, but as a people disappeared from the stage when the middle wall of partition was broken down, yet the Abrahamic covenant still endures in the *spiritual* seed of Abraham, made up of Jews and Gentiles in one undistinguished mass of redeemed men under the Gospel—the apostle, as if to preclude that supposition, expressly states that the very Israel who, as concerning the Gospel, are regarded as "enemies for the Gentiles' sakes," are "*beloved for the fathers' sakes*"; and it is in proof of this that he adds, "For the gifts and the calling of God are without repentance." But in what sense are the now unbelieving and excluded children of Israel "beloved for the fathers' sakes"? Not merely from ancestral *recollections*, as one looks with fond interest on the child of a dear friend for that friend's sake [DR. ARNOLD]—a beautiful thought, and not foreign to Scripture, in this very matter (see II Chron. 20:7; Isa. 41:8)—but it is from ancestral *connections* and *obligations*, or their lineal descent from and oneness in covenant with the fathers with whom God originally established it. In other words, the natural Israel—not "the *remnant* of them according to the election of grace," but THE NATION, sprung from Abraham according to the flesh—are still an elect people, and as such, "beloved." The very same love which chose the fathers, and rested on the fathers as a parent stem of the nation, still rests on their descendants at large, and will yet recover them from unbelief, and reinstate them in the family of God. **30, 31. For as ye in times past have not believed**—or, 'obeyed'—**God**—that is, yielded not to God "the obedience of faith," while strangers to Christ. **yet now have obtained mercy through**—by occasion of—**their unbelief**—(See on vss. 11, 15, 28). **even so have these**—the Jews—**now not believed**—or, 'now been disobedient'—**that through your mercy**—the mercy shown to you—**they also may obtain mercy**—Here is an entirely new idea. The apostle has hitherto dwelt upon the unbelief of the Jews as making way for the faith of the Gentiles—the exclusion of the one occasioning the reception of the other; a truth yielding to generous, believing Gentiles but mingled satisfaction. Now, opening a more cheering prospect, he speaks of the mercy shown to the Gentiles as a means of Israel's recovery; which seems to mean that it will be by the instrumentality of believing Gentiles that Israel as a nation is at length to "look on Him whom they have pierced and mourn for Him," and so to "obtain mercy." (See II Cor. 3:15, 16.) **32. For God hath concluded them all in unbelief**—'hath shut them all up to unbelief'—**that he might have mercy upon all**—i.e., those "all" of whom he had been discoursing; the Gentiles first, and after them the Jews [FRITZSCHE, THOLUCK, OLSHAUSEN, DE WETTE, PHILIPPI, STUART, HODGE]. Certainly it is not 'all mankind individually' [MEYER, ALFORD]; for the apostle is not here dealing with individuals, but with those great divisions of mankind, Jew and Gentile. And what he here says is that God's purpose was to shut each of these divisions of men to the experience first of an humbled, condemned state, without Christ, and then to the experience of His mercy in Christ. **33. Oh, the depth . . .**—The apostle now yields himself up to the admiring contemplation of the grandeur of that divine plan which he had sketched out. **of the riches both of the wisdom and knowledge of God**—Many able expositors render this, 'of the riches and wisdom and knowledge . . .' [ERASMUS, GROTIUS, BENGEL, MEYER, DE WETTE, THOLUCK, OLSHAUSEN, FRITZSCHE, PHILIPPI, ALFORD, REVISED VERSION]. The words will certainly bear this sense, "the depth of God's riches." But "the riches of God" is a much rarer expression with our apostle than the riches of this or that perfection of God; and the words immediately following limit our attention to the unsearchableness of God's "*judgments*," which probably

ADAM CLARKE

and separated from all the people of the earth to be the peculiar people of God, *they are beloved for the fathers' sakes;* He has still favor in store for them on account of their forefathers, the patriarchs.

29. *For the gifts and calling of God.* The *gifts* which God has bestowed upon them, and the *calling*—the invitation—with which He has favored them, He will never revoke. In reference to this point there is no "change of mind" in Him; and therefore the possibility and certainty of their restoration to their original privileges, of being the people of God, of enjoying every spiritual blessing with the fullness of the Gentiles, may be both reasonably and safely inferred. *Repentance*, when applied to God, signifies simply "change of purpose" relative to some declarations made subject to certain conditions.

30. *For as ye in times past.* The apostle pursues his argument in favor of the restoration of the Jews. *As ye*, Gentiles, *in times past*, for many ages back. *Have not believed.* Were in a state of alienation from God, yet not so as to be totally and forever excluded, *Have now obtained mercy.* For you are now taken into the kingdom of the Messiah; through *their unbelief*—by that method which, in destroying the Jewish peculiarity, and fulfilling the Abrahamic covenant, has occasioned the unbelief and obstinate opposition of the Jews.

31. *Even so have these also.* In like manner the Jews are, through their infidelity, shut out of the kingdom of God. *That through your mercy.* This exclusion will not be everlasting; but this will serve to open a new scene, when, through further displays of mercy to you Gentiles, *they also may obtain mercy*—shall be received into the kingdom of God again; and this shall take place whenever they shall consent to acknowledge the Lord Jesus, and see it their privilege to be fellow heirs with the Gentiles of the grace of life. As sure, therefore, as the Jews were once in the Kingdom, and the Gentiles were not; as sure as the Gentiles are now in the Kingdom, and the Jews are not; so surely will the Jews be brought back into that Kingdom.

32. *For God hath concluded them all in unbelief.* God hath "shut" or "locked" them all up under unbelief. This refers to the guilty state of both Jews and Gentiles. They had all broken God's law—the Jews, the written law; the Gentiles, the law written in their hearts. See chap. i. 19-20 and ii. 14-15. They are represented here as having been accused of their transgressions; tried at God's bar; found guilty on being tried; condemned to the death they had merited; remanded to prison, till the sovereign will relative to their execution should be announced; "shut" or "locked up," under the jailer, *unbelief;* and there both continued in the same state, awaiting the execution of their sentence. But God, in His own compassion, moved by no merit in either party, caused a general pardon by the gospel to be proclaimed to *all.* The Jews have refused to receive this pardon on the terms which God has proposed it, and therefore continue locked up under unbelief. The Gentiles have welcomed the offers of grace, and are delivered out of their prison. But as the offers of mercy continue to be made to all indiscriminately, the time will come when the Jews, seeing the vast accession of the Gentile world to the kingdom of the Messiah, and the glorious privileges which they in consequence enjoy, shall also lay hold on the hope set before them, and thus become with the Gentiles one flock under one Shepherd and Bishop of all their souls. The same figure is used in Gal. iii. 22-23. "But the scripture hath concluded [locked up] all under sin, that the promise by faith of Jesus Christ might be given to them that believe. But before faith came, we were kept [we were guarded as in a stronghold] under the law, shut up [locked up together] unto the faith which should afterwards be revealed." It is a fine and well-chosen metaphor in both places, and forcibly expresses the guilty, helpless, wretched state of both Jews and Gentiles.

33. *O the depth of the riches both of the wisdom and knowledge of God!* This is a very proper conclusion of the whole preceding dis-

MATTHEW HENRY

of their own weakness and short-sightedness.—*The depth of the riches.* Men's riches are shallow, you may soon see the bottom; but God's riches are deep. There is not only depth in the divine counsels, but riches too, and that passing knowledge.—*Riches of the wisdom and knowledge of God.* His seeing all things—that all is naked and open before him: there is his knowledge. His ruling and ordering all things and bringing about his own purposes in all; this is his *wisdom.—How unsearchable are his judgments!* that is, his counsels and purposes: and his *ways,* that is, the execution of these counsels and purposes. We know not what he has in view; it is *past finding out.* Secret things belong not to us. What he does we know not now, John xiii. 7. We cannot give a reason of God's proceedings. The judgments of his hands, and the ways of his providence, are dark and mysterious, which therefore we must not pry into, but silently adore. The apostle speaks this especially with reference to that strange turn, the casting off of the Jews, and the entertainment of the Gentiles, with a purpose to take in the Jews again in due time. These are methods unaccountable, concerning which we must say, *O the depth!—Past finding out, cannot be traced.* God leaves no prints nor footsteps behind him, but his paths of providence are new every morning. He does not go the same way so often as to make a track of it. It follows (*v.* 34), *For who hath known the mind of the Lord?* Is there any creature made of his cabinet-council? Is there any to whom he has imparted his counsels, to know the way that he takes? The apostle makes the same challenge (1 Cor. ii. 16): *For who hath known the mind of the Lord?* And yet there he adds, *But we have the mind of Christ.* He that knew the mind of the Lord has declared him, John i. 18. And so, though we know not the mind of the Lord, yet if we have the mind of Christ, we have enough.—*Or who has been his counsellor?* It is nonsense for any man to prescribe to God, or to teach him how to govern the world.

II. The sovereignty of the divine counsels. In all these things God does what he will, because he will, and yet there is no unrighteousness with him.

1. He challenges any to prove God a debtor to him (*v.* 35): *Who hath first given to him?* Who is there of all the creatures that can prove God is beholden to him? *Of thine own we have given thee.* All the duties we can perform are not requitals, but rather restitutions. The apostle here proclaims, in God's name, that payment is ready: *It shall be recompenced to him again.* It is certain God will let nobody lose by him; but never anyone yet durst make a demand of this kind. This is here suggested, (1) To silence the clamours of the Jews. When God took away their visible church-privileges from them, he did but take his own. (2) To silence the insultings of the Gentiles. When God sent the gospel among them, it was not because he owed them so much favour, but of his own good pleasure.

2. He resolves all into the sovereignty of God (*v.* 36): *For of him, and through him, and to him, are all things,* that is, God is all in all. Of God as the spring and fountain of all, through Christ, as the conveyance, to God as the ultimate end. If all be of him and through him, there is all the reason in the world that all should be to him and for him. To do all to the glory of God is to make a virtue of necessity; for all shall in the end be to him, whether we will or no. And so he concludes with a short doxology: *To whom be glory for ever, Amen.* Paul had been discoursing at large of the counsels of God concerning man, but, after all, he concludes with the acknowledgment of the divine sovereignty, as that into which all these things must be ultimately resolved. Especially when we come to talk of the divine counsels and actings, it is best for us to turn our arguments into awful and serious adorations.

JAMIESON, FAUSSET, BROWN

means His decrees or plans (Ps. 119:75), and of "His *ways,*" or the method by which He carries these into effect. [So LUTHER, CALVIN, BEZA, HODGE, etc.] Besides, all that follows to the end of the chapter seems to show that while the *Grace* of God to guilty men in Christ Jesus is presupposed to be the whole theme of this chapter, that which called forth the special admiration of the apostle, after sketching at some length the divine purposes and methods in the bestowment of this grace, was "the depth of the riches of God's *wisdom and knowledge*" in these purposes and methods. The "knowledge," then, points probably to the vast sweep of divine comprehension herein displayed; the "wisdom" to that fitness to accomplish the ends intended, which is stamped on all this procedure. **34, 35. For who hath known the mind of the Lord?**—See Job 15:8; Jeremiah 23:18. **or who hath been his counsellor**—See Isaiah 40:13, 14. **or who hath first given to him, and it shall be recompensed to him**—'and shall have recompense made to him—**again**—see Job 35:7, and 41:11. These questions, it will thus be seen, are just quotations from the Old Testament, as if to show how familiar to God's ancient people was the great truth which the apostle himself had just uttered, that God's plans and methods in the dispensation of His Grace have a reach of comprehension and wisdom stamped upon them which finite mortals cannot fathom, much less could ever have imagined, before they were disclosed. **36. For of him, and through him, and to him, are all things: to whom**—'to Him'—**be glory for ever. Amen**—Thus worthily—with a brevity only equalled by its sublimity—does the apostle here sum up this whole matter. "OF Him are all things," as their eternal Source: "THROUGH HIM are all things," inasmuch as He brings all to pass which in His eternal counsels He purposed: "To Him are all things," as being His own last End; the manifestation of the glory of His own perfections being the ultimate, because the highest possible, design of all His procedure from first to last.—On this rich chapter, Note (1) It is an unspeakable consolation to know that in times of deepest religious declension and most extensive defection from the truth, the lamp of God has never been permitted to go out, and that a faithful remnant has ever existed—a remnant larger than their own drooping spirits could easily believe (vss. 1-5). (2) The preservation of this remnant, even as their separation at the first, is all of mere grace (vss. 5, 6). (3) When individuals and communities, after many fruitless warnings, are abandoned of God, they go from bad to worse (vss. 7-10). (4) God has so ordered His dealings with the great divisions of mankind, "that no flesh should glory in His presence." Gentile and Jew have each in turn been "shut up to unbelief," that each in turn may experience the "mercy" which saves the chief of sinners (vss. 11-32). (5) As we are "justified by faith," so are we "kept by the power of God through faith"—faith alone—unto salvation (vss. 20-32). (6) God's covenant with Abraham and his natural seed is a perpetual covenant, in equal force under the Gospel as before it. Therefore it is, that the Jews as a nation still survive, in spite of all the laws which, in similar circumstances, have either extinguished or destroyed the identity of other nations. And therefore it is that the Jews as a nation will yet be restored to the family of God, through the subjection of their proud hearts to Him whom they have pierced. (7) Thus has the Christian Church the highest motive to the establishment and vigorous prosecution of *missions to the Jews;* God having not only promised that there shall be a remnant of them gathered in every age, but pledged Himself to the final ingathering of the whole nation assigned the honor of that ingathering to the Gentile Church, and assured them that the event, when it does arrive, shall have a life-giving effect upon the whole world (vss. 12-16, 26-31). (8) Those who think that in all the evangelical prophecies of the Old Testament the terms "Jacob," "Israel," etc., are to be understood solely of *the Christian Church,* would appear to read the Old Testament differently from the apostle, who, from the use of those very terms in Old Testament prophecy, draws arguments to prove that God has mercy in store for *the natural Israel* (vss. 26, 27). (9) Mere intellectual investigations into divine truth in general, and the sense of the living oracles in particular, as they have a hardening effect, so they are a great contrast to the spirit of our apostle, whose lengthened sketch of God's majestic procedure towards men in Christ Jesus ends here in a burst of *admiration,* which loses itself in the still loftier frame of *adoration* (vss. 33-36).

ADAM CLARKE

course. *Wisdom* may here refer to the designs of God; *knowledge,* to the means which He employs to accomplish these designs.

34. *For who hath known the mind of the Lord?* Who can pretend to penetrate the counsels of God, or fathom the reasons of His conduct? His designs and His counsels are like himself, infinite; and consequently, inscrutable.

35. *Or who hath first given to him?* Who can pretend to have any demands upon God? To whom is He indebted? Have either Jews or Gentiles any right to His blessings? May not He bestow His favors as He pleases, and to whom He pleases? Does He do any injustice to the Jews in choosing the Gentiles? And was it because He was under obligation to the Gentiles that He has chosen them in the place of the Jews? Let him who has any claim on God prefer it, and he shall be compensated.

36. *For of him.* This is far from being the case, *for of him,* as the original Designer and Author; *and through* (by) *him,* as the prime and efficient Cause; *and to him,* as the ultimate End for the manifestation of His eternal glory and goodness, *are all things* in universal nature, through the whole compass of time and eternity. *To whom be glory.* And let Him have the praise of all His works, from the hearts and mouths of all His intelligent creatures, *for ever*—throughout all the generations of men. *Amen*—"So be it!" Let this be established forever!

F. B. MEYER:

This verse reminds us of those lagoons of perfectly still clear water, of which travelers tell. So clear that it is easily possible to look into their translucent depths to where the submarine foliage waves! So deep that the ordinary measuring line fails to plumb them! All these words are monosyllables. A child just learning to read could easily spell them out. But who shall exhaust their meaning?

"Of Him." The entire scheme of redemption; the marvelous history of the chosen people, with which this chapter is occupied; the universe of matter—all are included in the all things that have emanated out of God. No one has been his counselor, or given aught to Him. From all created things, which are as the stream, let us climb to Him, who is their fountain, source, and origin; and in Him let us learn to fill our own souls to the very brim.

"Through Him." Through Jesus Christ, the Mediator, God has poured the entire grace and wealth of his nature to bless and help us. There is no good thing that does not come to us through the mediation of the Second Person of the Holy Trinity. Through Him He made the worlds. Through Him we have received the reconciliation. Through Him, also, all grace is made to abound toward us. Never forget to magnify the Lord Jesus as the source of all your supply.

"To Him." Creation, providence, and redemption are all tending back to God. The tide is setting in toward the throne. A revenue of glory shall yet accrue from all that has happened within the parenthesis of time. Every whit in the great temple shall one day say "Glory!"

—*Great Verses Through the Bible*

MATTHEW HENRY

CHAPTER 12

Verses 1–21

I. Concerning our duty to God. We see what is godliness.

1. It is to surrender ourselves to God, and so to lay a good foundation. This is here pressed as the spring of all duty and obedience, *v.* 1, 2.

(1) The body must be presented to him, *v.* 1. The exhortation is here introduced very pathetically: *I beseech you, brethren.* Though he was a great apostle, yet he calls the meanest Christians *brethren*, a term of affection and concern. He uses entreaty; this is the gospel way. This is to insinuate the exhortation, that it might come with the more pleasing power. Many are sooner wrought upon if they be accosted kindly, are more easily led than driven.

[1] The duty pressed—to present our *bodies a living sacrifice. Your bodies*—your whole selves. Our bodies and spirits are intended. Sacrifice is here taken for whatsoever is by God's own appointment dedicated to himself. Christ, who was once offered to bear the sins of many, is the only sacrifice of atonement; but our persons and performances, tendered to God through Christ, are as sacrifices of acknowledgment to the honour of God. Presenting them denotes a voluntary act. It must be a free-will offering. The presenting of the body to God implies not only the avoiding of the sins that are committed with or against the body, but the using of the body as a servant of the soul in the service of God. It is to yield the members of our bodies as instruments of righteousness, *ch.* vi. 13. Though bodily exercise alone profits little, yet in its place it is a proof of the dedication of our souls to God. *First,* Present them a living sacrifice. A Christian makes his body a sacrifice to God. A body sincerely devoted to God is a living sacrifice. It is Christ living in the soul by faith that makes the body a living sacrifice. Holy love kindles the sacrifices, puts life into the duties. *Alive,* that is, to God, *v.* 11. *Secondly,* They must be holy. There must be that real holiness which consists in an entire rectitude of heart and life, our bodies must not be made the instruments of sin and uncleanness, but set apart for God, and put to holy uses. It is the soul that is the proper subject of holiness; but a sanctified soul communicates a holiness to the body. That is holy which is according to the will of God; when the bodily actions are so, the body is holy.

[2] The arguments to enforce this, which are three: *First,* Consider the mercies of God: *I beseech you by the mercies of God.* This is an argument most sweetly cogent. There is the mercy that is in God and the mercy that is from God—mercy in the spring and mercy in the streams: both are included here. God is a merciful God, therefore let us present our bodies to him; he will be sure to use them kindly. We receive from him every day the fruits of his mercy, particularly mercy to our bodies: he made them, he maintains them, be bought them. The greatest mercy of all is that Christ hath made not his body only, but his soul, an offering for sin. Let us render ourselves as an acknowledgment of all these favours—all we are, all we have, all we can do; and, after all, it is but very poor returns, and yet, because it is what we have, *Secondly,* It is *acceptable to God.* These living sacrifices are acceptable to God. If the presenting of ourselves will but please him, we may easily conclude that we cannot bestow ourselves better. *Thirdly,* It is our *reasonable service.* There is an act of reason in it; for it is the soul that presents the body. Our God must be served in the spirit and with the understanding. God does not impose upon us anything hard or unreasonable, but that which is altogether agreeable to the principles of right reason. That is a reasonable service which we are able and ready to give a reason for.

(2) The mind must be renewed for him. This is pressed (*v.* 2): "*Be you transformed by the renewing of your mind.*" Conversion and sanctification are the renewing of the mind, a change not of the substance, but of the qualities of the soul. The man is not what he was—old things are passed away, all things are become new. The renewing of the mind is the renewing of the whole man, for out of it are the *issues of life.* The progress of sanctification, dying to sin more and more and living to righteousness more and more, is the carrying on of this renewing work. This is called the *transforming* of us. The same word is used 2 Cor. iii. 18, where we are said to be *changed into the same image from glory to glory.* Not that we can work such a change ourselves: we could as soon make a new world as make a new heart by any power of our own; it is God's work. "Use the means which God hath appointed and ordained for it." It is God that turns us, and then we are turned. "Lay your souls under the changing transforming influences of

JAMIESON, FAUSSET, BROWN

CHAPTER 12

Vss. 1-21. Duties of Believers, General and Particular. The doctrinal teaching of this Epistle is now followed up by a series of exhortations to practical duty. And *first,* the all-comprehensive duty. **1. I beseech you therefore**—in view of all that has been advanced in the foregoing part of this Epistle.

that ye present—See on ch. 6:13, where we have the same exhortation and the same word there rendered "yield" (as also in vss. 16, 19). **your bodies**—i.e., 'yourselves in the body,' considered as the organ of the inner life. As it is through the body that all the evil that is in the unrenewed heart comes forth into palpable manifestation and action, so it is through the body that all the gracious principles and affections of believers reveal themselves in the outward life. Sanctification extends to the whole man (I Thess. 5:23, 24).

a living sacrifice—in glorious contrast to the legal sacrifices, which, save as they were *slain,* were no sacrifices at all. The death of the one "Lamb of God, taking away the sin of the world," has swept all dead victims from off the altar of God, to make room for the redeemed themselves as "living sacrifices" to Him who made "Him to be sin for us"; while every outgoing of their grateful hearts in praise, and every act prompted by the love of Christ, is itself a sacrifice to God of a sweet-smelling savor (Heb. 13:15, 16). **holy**—As the Levitical victims, when offered without blemish to God, were regarded as holy, so believers, "yielding themselves to God as those that are alive from the dead, and their members as instruments of righteousness unto God, are, in His estimation, not ritually but really "holy," and so—

by the mercies of God—those mercies, whose free and unmerited nature, glorious Channel, and saving fruits have been opened up at such length.

acceptable—'wellpleasing'—**unto God**—not as the Levitical offerings, merely as appointed symbols of spiritual ideas, but objects, intrinsically, of divine complacency, in their renewed character, and endeared relationship to Him through His Son Jesus Christ. **which is your reasonable**—rather, 'rational' —**service**—in contrast, not to the senselessness of idol worship, but to the offering of irrational victims under the law. In this view the presentation of ourselves, as living monuments of redeeming mercy, is here called "our rational service"; and surely it is the most rational and exalted occupation of God's reasonable creatures. So II Peter 1:5, "to offer up *spiritual sacrifices,* acceptable to God through Jesus Christ." **but be ye transformed**—or, 'transfigured' (as in Matt. 17:2; and II Cor. 3:18, *Greek*). **by the renewing of your mind** —not by a mere outward disconformity to the ungodly world, many of whose actions in themselves may be virtuous and praiseworthy; but by such an inward spiritual transformation as makes the whole life new—new in its motives and ends, even where the actions differ in nothing from those of the world —new, considered as a whole, and in such a sense as to be wholly unattainable save through the constraining power of the love of Christ.

ADAM CLARKE

CHAPTER 12

The apostle, having now finished the *doctrinal* part of this Epistle, proceeds to the *practical.*

1. *I beseech you therefore, brethren.* This address is probably intended for both the Jews and the Gentiles; though some suppose that the Jews are addressed in the first verse, the Gentiles in the second.

That ye present your bodies. A metaphor taken from bringing sacrifices to the altar of God. The person offering picked out the choicest of his flock, brought it to the altar, and presented it there as an atonement for his sin. They are exhorted to give themselves up in the spirit of sacrifice; to be as wholly the Lord's property as the whole burnt offering was, no part being devoted to any other use.

A living sacrifice. In opposition to those dead sacrifices which they were in the habit of offering while in their Jewish state; and that they should have the lusts of the flesh mortified, that they might live to God. *Holy.* Without spot or blemish, referring still to the sacrifice required by the law.

By the mercies of God. "By the tender mercies or compassions of God," such as a tender father shows to his refractory children; who, on their humiliation, is easily persuaded to forgive their offenses. *Acceptable unto God.* The sacrifice being perfect in its kind, and the intention of the offerer being such that both can be *acceptable* and well pleasing to God, who searches the heart. All these phrases are sacrificial, and show that there must be a complete surrender of the person—the *body,* the whole man, mind and flesh, to be given to God; and that he is to consider himself no more his own, but the entire property of his Maker. *Your reasonable service.* Nothing can be more consistent with reason than that the work of God should glorify its Author. We are not our own; we are the property of the Lord by the right of creation and redemption, and it would be as unreasonable as it would be wicked not to live to His glory, in strict obedience to His will. The *reasonable service* of the apostle may refer to the difference between the Jewish and Christian worship. The former religious service consisted chiefly in its sacrifices, which were of irrational creatures. The Christian service or worship is "rational," because performed according to the true intent and meaning of the law, the heart and soul being engaged in the service. He alone lives the life of a fool and a madman who lives the life of a sinner against God; for in sinning against his Maker he wrongs his own soul, loves death, and rewards evil unto himself.

Be ye transformed. "Be ye metamorphosed, transfigured," appear as new persons, and with new habits; as God has given you a new form of worship, so that you serve in the newness of the spirit, and not in the oldness of the letter. The word implies a radical, thorough, and universal change, both outward and inward. *By the renewing of your mind.* Let the inward change produce the outward. Where the spirit, the temper, and disposition of the *mind,* Eph. iv. 23, are not renewed, an outward change is of but little worth, and but of short standing.

MATTHEW HENRY

the blessed Spirit." Though the new man be created of God, yet we must put it on (Eph. iv. 24), and be pressing forward towards perfection.

[1] What is the great enemy to this renewing; and that is, conformity to this world: *Be not conformed to this world.* All the disciples and followers of the Lord Jesus must be nonconformists to this world. *Do not fashion yourselves* according to the world. We must not conform to the things of the world. We must not conform to the men of the world, we must not follow a multitude to do evil. If sinners entice us, we must not consent to them, but in our places witness against them. True Christianity consists much in a sober singularity. Yet we must take heed of the extreme of affected rudeness and moroseness, which some run into. The rule of the gospel is a rule of direction, not a rule of contrariety.

[2] What is the great effect of this renewing: *That you may prove what is that good, and acceptable, and perfect will of God.* By the will of God, here we are to understand his revealed will concerning our duty, that will which we pray may be done by us as it is done by the angels. *First,* The will of God is *good, and acceptable, and perfect*; three excellent properties of a law. It is good in itself. It is good for us. It is acceptable, it is pleasing to God. The only way to attain his favour as the end is to conform to his will as the rule. It is perfect, to which nothing can be added. *Secondly,* It concerns Christians to prove what is that will of God which is good, and acceptable, and perfect; to know it experimentally, to know the excellency of the will of God by the experience of a conformity to it. It is to approve *things that are excellent* (Phil. i. 10). It is to be *of quick understanding in the fear of the Lord,* Isa. xi. 3. *Thirdly,* Those are best able to prove what is the good, and acceptable, and perfect will of God, who are transformed by the renewing of their mind. It disposes the soul to receive the revelations of the divine will. The promise is (John vii. 17), *If any man will do his will, he shall know of the doctrine.* A good wit can dispute about the will of God; while an honest, humble heart loves it.

2. When this is done, to serve him (*v.* 11, 12), *Serving the Lord.* To be religious is to serve God. (1) We must make a business of it, and not be slothful in that business. *Not slothful in business.* We must not drive on slowly in religion. Slothful servants will be reckoned with as wicked servants. (2) We must be *fervent in spirit, serving the Lord.* God must be served with the spirit under the influences of the Holy Spirit. And there must be fervency in the spirit —a holy zeal, and warmth, as those that love God not only with the heart and soul, but with all our hearts, and with all our souls. This is the holy fire that kindles the sacrifice and carries it up to heaven, an offering of a sweet-smelling savour. (3) *Rejoicing in hope.* God is honoured by our hope and trust in him, especially when we rejoice in that hope. (4) *Patient in tribulation.* Thus also God is served, not only by working for him when he calls us to work, but by sitting still quietly when he calls us to suffer. Those that rejoice in hope are likely to be patient in tribulation. (5) *Continuing instant in prayer.* Prayer is a friend to hope and patience, and we do in it serve the Lord.

II. Concerning our duty which respects ourselves; this is sobriety.

1. A sober opinion of ourselves, *v.* 3. *I say, through the grace given unto me.* It is said to everyone of us, one as well as another. Pride is a sin that is bred in the bone of all of us. *Not to think of himself more highly than he ought to think.* We must take heed of having too great an opinion of ourselves. We must not be self-conceited, nor esteem too much our own wisdom. There is a high thought of ourselves which we may and must have to think ourselves too good to be the slaves of sin and drudges to this world. We should think soberly, that is, we must have a modest opinion of ourselves and our own abilities, according to what we have received from God, and not otherwise. The words will bear yet another sense agreeable enough. *Of himself* is not in the original; therefore it may be read, *That no man be wise above what he ought to be wise, but be wise unto sobriety.* There is a knowledge that puffs up. We must take heed of this, and labour after that knowledge which tends to sobriety. To this head refers also that exhortation (*v.* 16), *Be not wise in your own conceits.* It is good to be wise, but it is bad to think ourselves so; for there is more hope of a fool than of him that is wise in his own eyes. It was an excellent thing for Moses to have his face shine and not know it. Now the reasons are these:

(1) Because whatever we have that is good, *God hath dealt* it to us. The best and most useful man in the world is no more, no better, than what the free grace of God makes him every day. When we are

JAMIESON, FAUSSET, BROWN

2. And be ye not conformed to this world—Cf. Eph. 2:2; Gal. 1:4, *Greek.*

that ye may prove—i.e., experimentally. (See on the word "experience" in ch. 5:4, and cf. I Thess. 5:10, where the sentiment is the same.) **what is that**—'the'—**good, and acceptable**—'well pleasing'—**and perfect, will of God**—We prefer this rendering [with CALVIN] to that which many able critics [THOLUCK, MEYER, DE WETTE, FRITZSCHE, PHILIPPI, ALFORD, HODGE] adopt—'that ye may prove,' or 'discern the will of God, [even] what is good, and acceptable, and perfect.' God's will is *"good,"* as it demands only what is essentially and unchangeably good (ch. 7:10); it is *"well pleasing,"* in contrast with all that is arbitrary, as demanding only what God has eternal complacency in (cf. Mic. 6:8, with Jer. 9:24); and it is *"perfect,"* as it required nothing else than the perfection of God's reasonable creature, who, in proportion as he attains to it, reflects God's own perfection. Such then is the great general duty of the redeemed—SELF-CONSECRATION, in our whole spirit and soul and body to Him who hath called us into the fellowship of His Son Jesus Christ. Next follow specific duties, chiefly social; beginning with Humility, the chiefest of all the graces—but here with special reference to spiritual gifts.

11. not slothful in business—The word rendered "business" means 'zeal,' 'diligence,' 'purpose'; denoting the energy of action. **serving the Lord**—i.e., the Lord Jesus (see Eph. 6:5-8). Another reading—'serving the time,' or 'the occasion'—which differs in form but very slightly from the received reading, has been adopted by good critics [LUTHER, OLSHAUSEN, FRITZSCHE, MEYER]. But as MS. authority is decidedly against it, so is internal evidence; and comparatively few favor it. Nor is the sense which it yields a very Christian one. **12. rejoicing . . .**—Here it is more lively to retain the order and the verbs of the original: 'In hope, rejoicing; in tribulation, enduring; in prayer, persevering.' Each of these exercises helps the other. If our "hope" of glory is so assured that it is a rejoicing hope, we shall find the spirit of "endurance in tribulation" natural and easy; but since it is "prayer" which strengthens the faith that begets hope and lifts it up into an assured and joyful expectancy, and since our patience in tribulation is fed by this, it will be seen that all depends on our "perseverance in prayer."

For I say—authoritatively—**through the grace given unto me**—as an apostle of Jesus Christ; thus exemplifying his own precept by modestly falling back on that office which both warranted and required such plainness towards all classes. **to every man that is among you, not to think . . .**—It is impossible to convey in good English the emphatic play, so to speak, which each word here has upon another: 'not to be high-minded above what he ought to be minded, but so to be minded as to be sober-minded [CALVIN, ALFORD]. This is merely a strong way of characterizing all undue self-elevation.

ADAM CLARKE

2. *And be not conformed to this world.* By *this world* may be understood that present state of things among both the Jews and the Gentiles; the customs and fashions of the people who then lived, the Gentiles particularly, who had neither the power nor the form of godliness. The world that now is, this present state of things, is as much opposed to the spirit of genuine Christianity as the world then was.

That ye may prove. That you may have practical proof and experimental knowledge of the *will of God*—of His purpose and determination, which is *good* in itself, infinitely so. *Acceptable,* "well pleasing to and well received by" every mind that is renewed and transformed. *And perfect.* Finished and complete. When the mind is renewed, and the whole life changed, then the will of God is perfectly fulfilled; for this is its grand design in reference to every human being.

11. *Not slothful in business.* That God who forbade working on the seventh day has, by the same authority, enjoined it on the other six days. He who neglects to labor during the week is as culpable as he is who works on the Sabbath. An idle, slothful person can never be a Christian. *Fervent in spirit.* Do nothing at any time but what is to the glory of God, and do everything as unto Him; and in everything let your hearts be engaged. Be always in earnest, and let your heart ever accompany your hand. *Serving the Lord.* Ever considering that His eye is upon you, and that you are accountable to Him for all that you do, and that you should do everything so as to please Him. In order to this there must be simplicity in the intention and purity in the affections.

12. *Rejoicing in hope.* Of that glory of God that to each faithful follower of Christ shall shortly be revealed. *Patient in tribulation.* Remembering that what you suffer as Christians you suffer for Christ's sake; and it is to His honor, and the honor of your Christian profession, that you suffer it with an even mind. *Continuing instant in prayer.* Making the most fervent and intense application to the throne of grace for the light and power of the Holy Spirit; without which you can neither abhor evil, do good, love the brethren, entertain a comfortable hope, nor bear up patiently under the tribulations and ills of life.

3. *Through the grace given unto me.* By the grace given, Paul most certainly means his apostolic office, by which he had the authority, not only to preach the gospel, but also to rule the Church of Christ. This is the meaning of the word in Eph. iii. 8: "Unto me, who am less than the least of all saints, is this grace given [is conceded this office or employment immediately by God himself], that I should preach among the Gentiles the unsearchable riches of Christ." *Not to think . . . more highly.* "Not to act proudly"; to arrogate nothing to himself on account of any grace he had received, or of any office committed to him. *But to think soberly.* The reader will perceive here a sort of *paronomasia,* or play upon words: *phronein,* from *phren,* the "mind," signifies to "think, mind, relish, to be of opinion"; and *sophronein* signifies to be of a sound mind, to "think discreetly, modestly, humbly." Let no man think himself more or greater than God has made him; and let him know that whatever he is or has of good or excellence, he has it from God; and that the glory belongs to the Giver, and not to him who has received the gift.

MATTHEW HENRY

thinking of ourselves, we must remember to think not how we have attained; but think how kind God hath been to us.

(2) Because God deals out his gifts in a certain measure: According to *the measure of faith.* The measure of spiritual gifts he calls the measure of faith, for this is the radical grace. What we have and do that is good is so far right and acceptable as it is founded in faith. Christ had the Spirit given him without measure. But the saints have it by measure. Christ, who had gifts without measure, was meek and lowly; and shall we, that are stinted, be proud and self-conceited?

(3) Because God has dealt out gifts to others as well as to us: *Dealt to every man.* Had we the monopoly of the Spirit there might be some pretence for this conceitedness of ourselves; but others have their share as well as we. Therefore it ill becomes us to lift up ourselves, and to despise others, as if we only were the people in favour with Heaven. This reasoning he illustrates by a comparison taken from the members of the natural body. *As we have many members in one body,* &c., *v.* 4, 5. [1] All the saints make up one body in Christ, who is the head of the body. Believers lie not in the world as a confused disorderly heap, but are organized and knit together. [2] Particular believers are members of this body, deriving life and spirits from the head. Some members in the body are bigger and more useful than others, and each received according to its proportion. If the little finger should receive as much nourishment as the leg, how unseemly and prejudicial would it be! We must remember that we are not the whole; we are but parts. [3] All *the members have not the same office* (*v.* 4), but each hath its respective place and work assigned it. So in the mystical body, some are called to one sort of work; others are called to another sort of work. [4] Each member hath its place and office, for the good of the whole, and of every other member. We are not only members of Christ, but we are *members one of another, v.* 5. We are engaged to do all the good we can one to another. Whatever we have we received it not for ourselves, but for the good of others.

2. A sober use of the gifts that God hath given us. As we must not on the one hand be proud of our talents, so on the other hand we must not bury them. We must not say, "I am nothing, therefore I will sit still, and do nothing"; but, "I am nothing in myself, and therefore I will lay out myself to the utmost in the strength of the grace of Christ." *Having gifts,* let us use them. *Gifts differing.* The immediate design is different, though the ultimate tendency of all is the same. *According to the grace.* It is grace that appoints the office, qualifies and inclines the person. Seven particular gifts he specifies (*v.* 6-8), which seem to be meant of so many distinct offices. There are two general ones here expressed by prophesying and ministering, the former the work of the bishops, the latter the work of the deacons. The five latter will therefore be reduced to the two former.

(1) *Prophecy. Whether prophecy, let us prophesy according to the proportion of faith.* It is not meant of the extraordinary gifts of foretelling things to come, but the ordinary office of preaching the word. The work of the Old Testament prophets was not only to foretell future things, but to warn the people concerning sin and duty. And thus gospel preachers are prophets. Those that preach the word must do it *according to the proportion of faith,* [1] As to the manner of our prophesying, it must be according to the proportion of the grace of faith. Let him that preaches set all the faith he hath on work, to impress the truths he preaches upon his own heart in the first place. As people cannot hear well, so ministers cannot preach well, without faith. And we must remember the proportion of faith—that, though all men have not faith, yet a great many have besides ourselves. "*Hast thou faith? Have it to thyself;* and do not make it a ruling rule to others, remembering that thou hast but thy proportion." [2] As to the matter of our prophesying, it must be according to the proportion of the doctrine of faith. There are some staple-truths, as I may call them, plainly and uniformly taught in the scripture, which are the touchstone of preaching, by which we must *prove all things,* and then *hold fast that which is good,* 1 Thess. v. 20, 21. Truths that are more dark must be examined by those that are more clear, for it is certain one truth can never contradict another. Seo here what ought to be the great care of preachers—to preach sound doctrine. It is necessary that it be according to the proportion of faith: for it is the word of faith that we preach. Now there are two particular works which he that prophesieth hath to mind—teaching and exhorting. *First,* Let him that teacheth wait on teaching. Teaching is the bare explaining and proving

JAMIESON, FAUSSET, BROWN

according as God hath dealt to every man the measure of faith—Faith is here viewed as the inlet to all the other graces, and so, as the receptive faculty of the renewed soul—i.e., 'as God hath given to each his particular capacity to take in the gifts and graces which He designs for the general good.'

4, 5. For as we have many members . . .—The same diversity and yet unity obtains in the body of Christ, whereof all believers are the several members, as in the natural body.

6-8. Having then gifts differing according to the grace given to us—Here, let it be observed, all the gifts of believers alike are viewed as communications of mere *grace.*

whether—we have the gift of—**prophecy**—i.e., of inspired teaching (as in Acts 15:32). Anyone speaking with divine authority—whether with reference to the past, the present, or the future—was termed a prophet (Exod. 7:1).

let us prophesy according to the proportion of faith—rather, 'of our faith.' Many Romish expositors and some Protestant (as CALVIN and BENGEL, and, though, hesitatingly, BEZA and HODGE), render this 'the analogy of faith,' understanding by it 'the general tenor' or 'rule of faith,' divinely delivered to men for their guidance. But this is against the context, whose object is to show that, as all the gifts of believers are according to their respective capacity for them, they are not to be puffed up on account of them, but to use them purely for their proper ends.

or he that teacheth—Teachers are expressly distinguished from prophets, and put after them, as exercising a lower function (Acts 13:1; I Cor. 12:28,

ADAM CLARKE

Measure of faith. It is very likely that the *faith* here used means the Christian religion; and the *measure,* the degree of knowledge and experience which each had received in it, and the power this gave him of being useful in the Church of God.

4. *For as we have many members.* As the human body consists of many parts, each having its respective office, and all contributing to the perfection and support of the whole; each being indispensably necessary in the place which it occupies, and each equally useful though performing a different function.

5. *So we, being many.* We who are members of the Church of Christ, which is considered the body of which He is the Head, have various offices assigned to us, according to the measure of grace, faith, and religious knowledge which we possess; and although each has a different office, and qualifications suitable to that office, yet all belong to the same body, and each has as much need of the help of another as that other has of his. Therefore let there be neither pride on the one hand, nor envy on the other.

6. *Having then gifts differing.* As the goodness of God, with this view of our mutual subserviency and usefulness, has endowed us with different gifts and qualifications, let each apply himself to the diligent improvement of his particular office and talent, and modestly keep within the bounds of it, not exalting himself or despising others. *Whether prophecy.* That *prophecy* in the New Testament often means the gift of "exhorting, preaching, or of expounding the Scriptures," is evident from many places in the Gospels, Acts, and Paul's Epistles; see 1 Cor. xi. 4-5; and especially 1 Cor. xiv. 3: "He that prophesieth speaketh unto men to edification, and exhortation, and comfort." This was the proper office of a preacher; and it is to the exercise of this office that the apostle refers in the whole of the chapter from which the above quotations are made. I think the apostle uses the term in the same sense here—Let every man who has the gift of preaching and interpreting the Scriptures do it in proportion to the grace and light he has received from God and in no case arrogate to himself knowledge which he has not received; let him not esteem himself more highly on account of this gift, or affect to be wise above what is written, or indulge himself in fanciful interpretations of the Word of God. *The proportion of faith,* which some render the "analogy of faith," signifies in grammar "the similar declension of similar words"; but in scriptural matters it has been understood to mean the general and consistent plan or scheme of doctrines delivered in the Scriptures, where everything bears its due relation and proportion to another. Thus the death of Christ is commensurate in its merits to the evils produced by the fall of Adam. The doctrine of justification by faith bears the strictest analogy or proportion to the grace of Christ and the helpless, guilty, condemned state of man.

Or he that teacheth. The teacher was a person whose office it was to instruct others, whether by catechizing or simply explaining the grand truths of Christianity.

MATTHEW HENRY

of gospel truths, without practical application. Now he that has a faculty of teaching, and has undertaken that province, let him stick to it. It is a good gift, let him use it, and give his mind to it. *Secondly*, Let him that *exhorteth* wait *on exhortation*. Let him give himself to that. This is the work of the pastor, to apply gospel truths and rules more closely to the people, and to press upon them that which is more practical. Many that are very accurate in teaching may yet be very cold and unskilful in exhorting; and on the contrary. The one requires a clearer head, the other a warmer heart. To wait on our work is to bestow the best of our time and thoughts upon it, and to study not only to do it, but to do it well.

(2) *Ministry*. If a man hath *the office of a deacon* let him use that office well. It includes all those offices which concern *the outward business of the house of God. Serving tables*, Acts vi. 2. Now let him on whom this care of ministering is devolved attend to it with faithfulness and diligence. [1] *He that giveth, let him do it with simplicity*. Those church-officers that were the stewards of the church's alms. Let them do it *liberally* and faithfully, with all sincerity and integrity, having no other intention in it than to glorify God and do good. He that hath wherewithal, let him give, and give plentifully and liberally. God loves a cheerful bountiful giver. [2] *He that ruleth with diligence*. It should seem, he means those that were assistants to the pastors in exercising church-discipline. Now such must do it with diligence. The word denotes both care and industry to discover what is amiss to keep the church pure. [3] *He that showeth mercy with cheerfulness*. Some think it is meant in general of all that in anything show mercy; Let them be willing to do it, and take a pleasure in it. But it seems to be meant of some particular church-officers, whose work it was to take care of the sick and strangers. Now this must be done with cheerfulness. A pleasing countenance in acts of mercy is a great relief and comfort to the miserable; when they see it is not done grudgingly and unwillingly, but with pleasant looks and gentle words. Those that have to do with such as are sick and sore, and commonly cross and peevish, have need to put on not only patience, but cheerfulness.

III. Concerning that part of our duty which respects our brethren. Now all our duty towards one another is summed up in one word, and that a sweet word, *love*. Therefore the apostle mentions this first: *Let love be without dissimulation;* not in compliment and pretence, but in reality. There is a love owing to our friends, and to our enemies. He specifies both.

1. To our friends. There is a mutual love that Christians owe, and must pay.

(1) An affectionate love (*v*. 10): *Be kindly affectioned one to another, with brotherly love*—it signifies not only love, but a readiness and inclination to love, kindness flowing out as from a spring. It properly denotes the love of parents to their children. Such must our love be to one another, and such it will be where there is a new nature and the law of love is written in the heart. *One to another*. This may recommend the grace of love to us, that, as it is made our duty to love others, so it is as much their duty to love us. And what can be sweeter on this side heaven than to love and be beloved?

(2) A respectful love: *In honour preferring one another*. Let us be forward to give to others the pre-eminence. We should be forward to take notice of the gifts, and graces, and performances of our brethren, and value them accordingly, be more pleased to hear another praised than ourselves; *going before*, or *leading one another in honour;* so some read it: not in taking honour, but in giving honour. Though we must prefer others (as our translation reads it) as more capable and deserving than ourselves, yet we must not make that an excuse for doing nothing, nor under a pretence of honouring others, indulge ourselves in ease and slothfulness. Therefore he immediately adds (*v*. 11), *Not slothful in business*.

JAMIESON, FAUSSET, BROWN

29). Probably it consisted mainly in opening up the evangelical bearings of Old Testament Scripture; and it was in this department apparently that Apollos showed his power and eloquence (Acts 18:24). **or he that exhorteth**—Since all preaching, whether by apostles, prophets, or teachers, was followed up by exhortation (Acts 11:23; 14:22; 15:32, etc.), many think that no specific class is here in view. But if liberty was given to others to exercise themselves occasionally in exhorting the brethren, generally, or small parties of the less instructed, the reference may be to them.

Or ministry, let us wait on—be occupied with'—**our ministering**—The word here used imports any kind of service, from the dispensing of the word of life (Acts 6:4) to the administering of the temporal affairs of the Church (Acts 6:1-3). The latter seems intended here, being distinguished from "prophesying," "teaching," and "exhorting."

he that giveth—in the exercise of private benevolence probably, rather than in the discharge of diaconal duty. **with simplicity**—so the word probably means. But as simplicity seems enjoined in the next clause but one of this same verse, perhaps the meaning here is, 'with liberality,' as the same word is rendered in II Corinthians 8:2; 9:11. **he that ruleth**—whether in the Church or his own household. See I Timothy 3:4, 5, where the same word is applied to both. **with diligence**—with earnest purpose. **he that showeth mercy, with cheerfulness**—not only without grudging either trouble or pecuniary relief, but feeling it to be "more blessed to give than to receive," and to help than be helped.

9. Let love be without dissimulation—'Let your love be unfeigned' (as in II Cor. 6:6; I Pet. 2:22; and see I John 3:18). **Abhor that which is evil; cleave to that which is good**—What a lofty tone of moral principle and feeling is here inculcated! It is not, Abstain from the one, and do the other; nor, Turn away from the one, and draw to the other; but, Abhor the one, and cling, with deepest sympathy, to the other.

10. Be . . .—better, 'In brotherly love be affectionate one to another; in [giving, or showing] honor, outdoing each other.' The word rendered "prefer" means rather 'to go before,' 'take the lead,' i.e., 'show an example.' How opposite is this to the reigning morality of the heathen world! and though Christianity has so changed the spirit of society, that a certain beautiful disinterestedness and self-sacrifice shines in the character of not a few who are but partially, if at all under the transforming power of the Gospel, it is only those whom "the love of Christ constrains to live not unto themselves," who are capable of thoroughly acting in the spirit of this precept.

ADAM CLARKE

8. *Or he that exhorteth*. The person who admonished and reprehended the unruly or disorderly; and who supported the weak and comforted the penitents, and those who were under heaviness through manifold temptations.

7. *Or ministry. Diakonia* simply means the office of a deacon.

He that giveth. He who distributeth the alms of the church. *With simplicity*, being influenced by no partiality, but dividing to each according to the necessity of his case. *He that ruleth*. He that presides over a particular business; but as the verb also signifies to "defend or patronize," it is probably used here to signify receiving and providing for strangers, and especially the persecuted who were obliged to leave their own homes, and were destitute, afflicted, and tormented. It might also imply the persons whose business it was to receive and entertain the apostolical teachers who travelled from place to place, establishing and confirming the churches. *He that sheweth mercy*. Let the person who is called to perform any act of compassion or mercy to the wretched do it, not grudgingly nor of necessity, but from a spirit of pure benevolence and sympathy. The poor are often both wicked and worthless; and if those who are called to minister to them as stewards, overseers, etc., do not take care, they will get their hearts hardened with the frequent proofs they will have of deception, lying, idleness, etc. If whatever is done in this way be not done unto the Lord, it can never be done with *cheerfulness*.

9. *Let love be without dissimulation*. Have no "hypocritical" love; let not your love wear a mask; make no empty professions. *Abhor that which is evil*. Hate sin as you would hate that hell to which it leads. *Stygeo* signifies to "hate or detest with horror"; the preposition greatly strengthens the meaning. Styx was a feigned river in hell by which the gods were wont to swear, and if any of them falsified this oath he was deprived of his nectar and ambrosia for a hundred years; hence the river was reputed to be hateful, and *stygeo* signified "to be as hateful as hell." *Cleave to that which is good*. "Be cemented or glued to that which is good"; so the word literally signifies. Have an unalterable attachment to whatever leads to God and contributes to the welfare of your fellow creatures.

10. *Be kindly affectioned one to another with brotherly love*. It is difficult to give a simple translation of the original. The word *philadelphia* signifies that affectionate regard which every Christian should feel for another, as being members of the same mystical body; hence it is emphatically termed the "love of the brethren." When William Penn, of deservedly famous memory, made a treaty with the Indians in North America, and purchased from them a large woody tract, which, after its own nature and his name, he called Pennsylvania, he built a city on it, and peopled it with Christians of his own denomination, and called the city from the word in the text *Philadelphia*. The word *philostorgos*, which we translate *kindly affectioned*, signifies that tender and indescribable affection which a mother bears to her child, and which almost all creatures manifest towards their young. "Love a brother Christian with the affection of a natural brother." *In honour preferring one another*. The meaning appears to be this: Consider all your brethren as more worthy than yourself; and let neither grief nor envy affect your mind at seeing another honored and yourself neglected. This is a hard lesson, and very few persons learn it thoroughly. If we wish to see our brethren honored, still it is with the secret condition in our own minds that we be honored more than they. We have no objection to the elevation of others, providing we may be at the head. But who can bear even to be what he calls neglected? I once heard the following conversation between two persons. "I know not," said one, "that I neglect to do anything in my power to promote the interest of true religion in this place, and yet I seem to be held in very little repute, scarcely any person even noticing me." To which the other replied: "My good friend, set yourself down for nothing, and if any person takes you for something it will be all clear gain."

MATTHEW HENRY

(3) A liberal love (*v.* 13): *Distributing to the necessities of saints.* It is but a mock love which rests in the verbal expressions of kindness and respect, while the wants of our brethren call for real supplies, and it is in the power of our hands to furnish them. It is no strange thing for saints in this world to want necessaries for the support of their natural life. Surely the things of this world are not the best things; if they were, the saints would not be put off with so little of them. It is the duty of those who have wherewithal to *distribute*, or (as it might better be read) to *communicate* to those necessities. It is not enough to draw out the soul, but we must draw out the purse, to the hungry. *Communicating.* Our poor brethren have a kind of interest in that which God hath given us; and our relieving them should come from a fellow-feeling of their wants. The charitable benevolence of the Philippians to Paul is called their communicating with his affliction, Phil. iv. 14. We are in a special manner bound to communicate to the saints. There is a common love owing to our fellow-creatures, but a special love owing to our fellow-christians. He mentions another branch of this bountiful love: *Given to hospitality.* As there is occasion, we must welcome strangers. *I was a stranger, and you took me in*, is mentioned as one instance of the mercifulness of those that shall obtain mercy. It intimates, not only that we must take opportunity, but that we must seek opportunity, thus to show mercy.

(4) A sympathizing love (*v.* 15): *Rejoice with those that do rejoice, and weep with those that weep.* True love will interest us in the sorrows and joys of one another, and teach us to make them our own. Some rejoicing, and others weeping for the trial, as of other graces, so of brotherly love and Christian sympathy. Not that we must participate in the sinful mirths or mournings of any. Not envying those that prosper, but rejoicing with them; not despising those that are in trouble, but concerned for them, and ready to help them.

(5) A united love: "*Be of the same mind one towards another* (*v.* 16). Agree in affection; endeavour to be all one; *wishing the same good* to others that you do to yourselves"; so some understand it. This is to love our brethren as ourselves.

(6) A condescending love: *Mind not high things, but condescend to men of low estate, v.* 16. True love cannot be without lowliness. To love one another aright is to be willing to stoop to the meanest offices of kindness for the good of one another. Love is a condescending grace. *Mind not high things.* We must not be ambitious of honour and preferment. The Romans, living in the imperial city, were perhaps ready to take occasion thence to think the better of themselves. Therefore the apostle so often cautions them against high-mindedness; compare *ch.* xi. 20. *Condescend to men of low estate.* It may be meant of *mean things*, to which we must condescend. If our condition in the world be poor and low, yet we must bring our minds to it, and acquiesce in it. So the margin: *Be contented with mean things.* Be reconciled to the place which God in his providence hath put us in. We must account nothing below us but sin. It may be meant of *mean persons*; so we read it (I think both are to be included): *Condescend to men of low estate.* We need not be ashamed to converse with the lowly, while the great God overlooks heaven and earth to look at such. True love values grace in rags as well as in scarlet. A jewel is a jewel, though it lie in the dirt. *Condescend;* that is, suit yourselves to them, stoop to them for their good. He adds, *Be not wise in your own conceits;* to the same purport with *v.* 3. We shall never find in our hearts to condescend to others while we find there so great a conceit of ourselves: and therefore this must needs be mortified. "*Be not wise by yourselves*, be not confident of the sufficiency of your own wisdom, nor be shy of communicating what you have to others. It is the merchandise of wisdom that we profess; now merchandise consists in commerce, receiving and returning."

(7) A love that engages us, as much as lies in us, *to live peaceably with all men, v.* 18. Even those with whom we cannot live intimately and familiarly, yet we must with such live peaceably. Thus must we labour to preserve the peace, that it be not broken, and to piece it again when it is broken. It is not expressed so as to oblige us to impossibilities: *If it be possible, as much as lies in you.* Study the things that make for peace.—*If it be possible.* It is not possible to preserve the peace when we cannot do it without offending God and wounding conscience. The wisdom that is from above is first pure and then peaceable, Jas. iii. 17. Peace without purity is the peace of the devil's palace.—*As much as lieth in you.* There must be two words to the bargain of peace. We may be unavoidably striven with. Our care

JAMIESON, FAUSSET, BROWN

13. given to hospitality—i.e., the entertainment of strangers. In times of persecution, and before the general institution of houses of entertainment, the importance of this precept would be at once felt. In the East, where such houses are still rare, this duty is regarded as of the most sacred character [HODGE]. **15. Rejoice with them that rejoice; weep**—the "and" should probably be omitted—**with them that weep**—What a beautiful spirit of sympathy with the joys and sorrows of others is here inculcated! But it is only one charming phase of the unselfish character which belongs to all living Christianity. What a world will ours be when this shall become its reigning spirit! Of the two, however, it is more easy to sympathize with another's sorrows than his joys, because in the one case he *needs* us; in the other not. But just for this reason the latter is the more disinterested, and so the nobler. **16. Be**—'Being'—**of the same mind one toward another**—The feeling of the common bond which binds all Christians to each other, whatever diversity of station, cultivation, temperament, or gifts may obtain among them, is the thing here enjoined. This is next taken up in detail. **Mind not**—'not minding'—**high things**—i.e., Cherish not ambitious or aspiring purposes and desires. As this springs from selfish severance of our own interests and objects from those of our brethren, so it is quite incompatible with the spirit inculcated in the preceding clause.

but condescend—'condescending'—**to men of low estate**—or (as some render the words), 'inclining unto the things that be lowly.' But we prefer the former.

Be not wise in your own conceits—This is just the application of the caution against high-mindedness to the estimate we form of our own mental character.

18. If it be possible—i.e., If others will let you—**as much as lieth in you**—or, 'dependeth on you'—**live peaceably**—or, 'be at peace'—**with all men**—The impossibility of this in some cases is hinted at, to keep up the hearts of those who, having done their best unsuccessfully to live in peace, might be tempted to think the failure was *necessarily* owing to themselves. But how emphatically expressed is the injunction to let nothing on our part prevent it! Would that Christians were guiltless in this respect!

ADAM CLARKE

13. ***Distributing to the necessity of saints.*** **Relieve your poor brethren according to the power which God has given you. Do good unto all men, but especially to them which are of the household of faith.**

Given to hospitality. **"Pursuing hospitality," or the duty of entertaining strangers. A very necessary virtue in ancient times, when houses of public accommodation were exceedingly scarce. This exhortation might have for its object the apostles, who were all itinerants; and in many cases the Christians, flying before the face of persecution.**

15. ***Rejoice with them that do rejoice.*** **Take lively interest in the prosperity of others. Let it be a matter of rejoicing to you when you hear of the health, prosperity, or happiness of any brother.** ***Weep with them that weep.*** **Labor after a compassionate or sympathizing mind. Let your heart feel for the distressed; enter into their sorrows, and bear a part of their burdens.**

16. ***Be of the same mind.*** **Live in a state of continual harmony and concord, and pray for the same good for all which you desire for yourselves.** ***Mind not high things.*** **Be not ambitious; affect nothing above your station; do not court the rich nor the powerful; do not pass by the poor man to pay your court to the great man; do not affect titles or worldly distinctions, much less sacrifice your conscience for them. The attachment to high things and high men is the vice of little, shallow minds.**

But condescend to men of low estate. **Be a companion of the humble, and pass through life with as little noise and show as possible. Let the poor, godly man be your chief companion; and learn from his humility and piety to be humble and godly. The term which we translate** ***condescend*** **signifies "to be led, carried, or dragged away to prison with another"; and points out the state in which the primitive Christians were despised and rejected of men, and often led forth to prison and death.**

Be not wise in your own conceits. **Be not puffed up with an opinion of your own consequence, for this will prove that the consequence itself is imaginary.** ***Be not wise*** **"by yourselves"—do not suppose that wisdom and discernment dwell alone with you. Believe that you stand in need of both help and instruction from others.**

18. ***If it be possible.*** **To live in a state of peace with one's neighbors, friends, and even family, is often very difficult. But the man who loves God must labor after this, for it is indispensably necessary even for his own sake. A man cannot have broils and misunderstandings with others without having his own peace very materially disturbed: he must, to be happy, be at peace with all men, whether they will be at peace with him or not.**

MATTHEW HENRY

must be that nothing be wanting on our parts to preserve the peace.

2. To our enemies. Those that embrace religion have reason to expect to meet with enemies in a world whose smiles seldom concur with Christ's. Now Christianity teaches us how to behave towards our enemies; and it quite differs from all other rules and methods, which generally aim at victory and dominion; but this at inward peace. Whoever are our enemies, our rule is to do them all the good we can.

(1) To do them no hurt (*v.* 17): *Recompence to no man evil for evil.* We have so learned God, who does so much for his enemies (Matt. v. 45), much more have we so learned Christ, who died for us when we were enemies (*ch.* v. 8, 10).—"*To no man;* not to one that has been thy friend, for by recompencing evil for evil thou wilt certainly lose him; not to one that has been thine enemy, for by not recompencing evil for evil thou mayest perhaps gain him." To the same purport, *v.* 19, *Dearly beloved, avenge not yourselves.* He addresses himself to such in this endearing language, to mollify them. Anything that breathes love sweetens the blood. Would you pacify a brother offended? Call him dearly beloved. Such a soft word may be effectual to turn away wrath. *Avenge not yourselves.* It forbids private revenge, which flows from anger and ill-will. See how strict the law of Christ is in this matter, Matt. v. 38-40. It is forbidden not only to take it into our own hands to avenge ourselves, but to thirst after even that judgment in our case which the law affords, for the satisfying of a revengeful humour. This is a hard lesson to corrupt nature; and therefore he subjoins, [1] A remedy against it: *Rather give place unto wrath.* Not to our own wrath; to give place to this is to give place to the devil. We must resist and suppress this. *First,* To the wrath of our enemy. "Give place to it; do not answer wrath with wrath, but with love rather." When men's passions are up, and the stream is strong, let it have its course, lest it be made to rage and swell the more. When others are angry, let us be calm. *Secondly,* Many apply it to the wrath of God: "Give place to this, and let him alone to deal with thine adversary." [2] A reason against it: *For it is written, Vengeance is mine.* God is the sovereign King, the righteous Judge, and to him it belongs to administer justice. Some of this power he hath trusted in the hands of the civil magistrates; their legal punishments therefore are to be looked upon as a branch of God's revengings. If vengeance be God's we may not do it. We step into the throne of God if we do. We need not do it. For God will, if we meekly leave the matter with him.

(2) We must not only not do hurt to our enemies, but do them all the good we can. It is a command peculiar to Christianity: *Love your enemies,* Matt. v. 44. We are here taught to show that love to them both in word and deed.

[1] In word: *Bless those who persecute you, v.* 14. It has been the common lot of God's people to be persecuted. Now we are here taught to bless those that so persecute us. *Bless* them; "Speak well of them. Speak respectfully to them, not rendering railing for railing." We must wish well to them. We must offer up that desire to God, by prayer for them. We can testify our goodwill by praying for them.—*Bless and curse not.* It denotes a thorough goodwill; not, "Bless them when you are at prayer, and curse them at other times"; but, "Bless them always, and curse not at all." Cursing ill becomes the mouths of those whose work it is to bless God.

[2] In deed (*v.* 20): "*If thine enemy hunger* be ready to show him any kindness, and be never the less forward for his having been thine enemy, that thou mayest thereby testify the sincerity of thy forgiveness of him." *First,* What we must do. We must do good to our enemies. "*If he hunger,* do not say, Now God is avenging me of him. But *feed him. Then,* when he has need of thy help, and thou hast an opportunity of starving him, *feed him* (a significant word)—feed him abundantly; feed him, as we do children and sick people, with much tenderness. Contrive to do it so as to express thy love. *If he thirst, give him drink:* in token of reconciliation and friendship. So confirm your love to him." *Secondly,* Why we must do this. *Thou shalt heap coals of fire on his head;* that is, "Thou shalt either," 1. "Melt him into repentance and friendship" (alluding to those who melt metals; they not only put fire under them, but heap fire upon them) "thou wilt win a friend by it, and if thy kindness have not that effect then," 2. "It will make his malice against thee the more inexcusable." Not that this must be our intention in showing him kindness, but such will be the effect. Those that revenge are the conquered, and those that forgive are the conquerors. (1) "*Be not overcome of evil.*

JAMIESON, FAUSSET, BROWN

17. **Recompense**—'Recompensing' . . .—see on vs. 14. **Provide**—'Providing'—**things honest**—'honorable'—**in the sight of all men**—The idea (which is from Prov. 3:4) is the care which Christians should take so to demean themselves as to command the respect of all men.

19-21. **avenge not . . .**—see on vs. 14. **but rather give place unto wrath**—This is usually taken to mean, 'but give room or space for wrath to spend itself.' But as the context shows that the injunction is to leave vengeance to God, "wrath" here seems to mean, not the *offense,* which we are tempted to avenge, but the *avenging wrath* of God (see II Chron. 24:18), which we are enjoined to await, or give room for. (So the best interpreters).

14. **Bless**—i.e., Call down by prayer a blessing on—**them which persecute you . . .**—This is taken from the Sermon on the Mount, which, from the allusions made to it, seems to have been the storehouse of Christian morality among the churches.

if thine enemy hunger . . .—This is taken from Proverbs 25:21, 22, which without doubt supplied the basis of those lofty precepts on that subject which form the culminating point of the Sermon on the Mount.

in so doing thou shalt heap coals of fire on his head—As the heaping of "coals of fire" is in the Old Testament the figurative expression of divine vengeance (Ps. 140:10; 11:6. etc.), the true sense of these words seems to be, 'That will be the most effectual vengeance—a vengeance under which he will be fain to bend [So ALFORD, HODGE, etc.]. The next verse confirms this.

ADAM CLARKE

17. *Recompense.* Do not take notice of every little injury you may sustain. Beware of too nice a sense of your own honor; intolerable pride is at the bottom of this. *Provide things honest.* Be prudent, be cautious; neither eat, drink, nor wear, but as you pay for everything.

19. *Dearly beloved, avenge not yourselves.* You are the children of God, and He loves you; and because He loves you He will permit nothing to be done to you that He will not turn to your advantage. Never take the execution of the law into your own hands; rather suffer injuries. The Son of Man is come, not to destroy men's lives, but to save; be of the same spirit. When He was reviled, He reviled not again. It is the part of a noble mind to bear up under unmerited disgrace; little minds are litigious and quarrelsome. *Give place unto wrath.* Leave room for the civil magistrate to do his duty; he holds the sword for this purpose; and if he be unfaithful to the trust reposed in him by the state, leave the matter to God, who is the righteous Judge; for by avenging yourselves you take your cause both out of the hands of the civil magistrate and out of the hands of God. I believe this to be the meaning of *give place unto wrath,* "punishment"; the penalty which the law, properly executed, will inflict. *Vengeance is mine.* This fixes the meaning of the apostle, and at once shows that the exhortation, *Rather give place unto wrath,* or "punishment," means, Leave the matter to the judgment of God; it is His law that in this case is broken, and to Him the infliction of deserved punishment belongs. *I will repay.* In My own time and in My own way. But He gives the sinner space to repent, and this long-suffering leads to salvation.

14. *Bless them which persecute you.* Give good words, or pray for them that give you bad words, who make dire imprecations against you. *Bless* them, pray for them, and on no account curse them, whatever the provocation may be. Have the loving, forgiving mind that was in your Lord.

20. *If thine enemy hunger, feed him.* Do not withhold from any man the offices of mercy and kindness. You have been God's enemy, and yet God fed, clothed, and preserved you alive; do to your enemy as God has done to you. If your enemy be hungry, feed him; if he be thirsty, give him drink—so has God dealt with you. And has not a sense of His goodness and long-suffering towards you been a means of melting down your heart into penitential compunction, gratitude, and love towards Him? How know you that a similar conduct towards your enemy may not have the same gracious influence on him towards you? Your kindness may be the means of begetting in him a sense of his guilt; and, from being your fell enemy, he may become your real friend. This I believe to be the sense of this passage, which many have encumbered with difficulties of their own creating. The whole is a quotation from Prov. xxv. 21-22, in the precise words of the Septuagint; and it is very likely that the latter clause of this verse, *Thou shalt heap coals of fire on his head,* is a metaphor taken from smelting metals. The ore

MATTHEW HENRY

Let not the evil of any provocation that is given you have such a power over you as to disturb your peace, to destroy your love, or to bring you to study or attempt any revenge." He that cannot quietly bear an injury is perfectly conquered by it. (2) "*But overcome evil with good*, with the good of patience and forbearance, nay, and of kindness and beneficence to those that wrong you." He that hath this rule over his spirit is better than the mighty.

3. There remain two exhortations which recommend all the rest as good in themselves, and of good report.

(1) As good in themselves (*v.* 9): *Abhor that which is evil, cleave to that which is good.* We must not only not do evil, but we must *abhor that which is evil.* We must hate sin with an utter and irreconcilable hatred. We must not only do that which is good, but we must cleave to it. It denotes a deliberate choice of, a sincere affection for, and a constant perseverance in, that which is good.

(2) As of good report (*v.* 17): "*Provide things honest in the sight of all men;* study and take care to do, that which recommends religion to all with whom you converse."

JAMIESON, FAUSSET, BROWN

Be not overcome of evil—for then you are the conquered party. **but overcome evil with good**—and then the victory is yours; you have subdued your enemy in the noblest sense.

ADAM CLARKE

is put into the furnace, and fire put both under and over, that the metal may be liquefied, and leaving the dross, may fall down pure to the bottom of the furnace. It is most evident from the whole connection of the place and the apostle's use of it that the heaping of the coals of fire upon the head of the enemy is intended to produce, not an evil, but the most beneficial effect; and the following verse is an additional proof of this.

21. *Be not overcome of evil.* Do not, by giving place to evil, become precisely the same character which you condemn in another. *Overcome evil with good*—however frequently he may grieve and infuriate you, always repay him with kindness; your goodwill, in the end, may overcome his evil.

MATTHEW HENRY — CHAPTER 13

Verses 1–6

We are here taught how to conduct ourselves towards magistrates, and those that are in authority over us, called here the *higher powers*, intimating their authority (they are powers), and their dignity (they are higher powers). The just power which they have must be submitted to and obeyed.

I. The duty enjoined: *Let every soul be subject.* Every soul—every person, one as well as another, not excluding the clergy.—*Every soul.* Not that our consciences are to be subjected to the will of any man. It is God's prerogative to make laws immediately to bind conscience. Our subjection must be free and voluntary, sincere and hearty. The subjection of soul here required includes inward honour and outward reverence and respect, both in speaking to them and in speaking of them. "They are *higher powers;* be content they should be so, and submit to them accordingly." Now there was good reason for the pressing of this duty, 1. Because of the reproach which the Christian religion lay under in the world, as an enemy to public peace, order, and government. Our Lord Jesus was so reproached, though he told them his kingdom was not of this world: no marvel, then, if his followers have been loaded in all ages with the like calumnies, called *facetious, seditious,* and *turbulent.* The apostle therefore shows that obedience to civil magistrates is one of the laws of Christ, whose religion helps to make people good subjects. 2. Because of the temptation which the Christians lay under to be otherwise affected to civil magistrates. The apostle enjoins obedience to civil government, which was the more necessary to be pressed now because the magistrates were heathens and unbelievers, which yet did not destroy their civil power and authority.

II. The reasons to enforce this duty.

1. For *wrath's sake.* Magistrates bear the sword; it is to no purpose to contend with him that bears the sword. The least show of resistance in a Christian would be very prejudicial to the whole society; and therefore they had more need than others to be exact in their subjection. To this head must that argument be referred (*v.* 2), *Those that resist shall receive to themselves damnation:* they shall be called to an account for it. God will reckon with them for it, because the resistance reflects upon him. The magistrates will reckon with them for it. So it follows (*v.* 3), *Rulers are a terror.* This is a good argument, but it is low for a Christian.

2. We must be subject, *not only for wrath, but for conscience' sake;* not so much *from the fear of punishment,* as *from the love of virtue.* Now to oblige conscience to this subjection he argues, *v.* 1-4, 6,

(1) From the institution of magistracy: *There is no power but of God.* God as the ruler of the world hath appointed the ordinance of magistracy, so that all civil power is derived from him. The usurpation of power and the abuse of power are not of God, but the power itself is. The most unjust and oppressive princes in the world have no power but what is given them from above (John xix. 11). It is an instance of God's wisdom, power, and goodness, in the management of mankind, that he has disposed them into such a state as distinguishes between governors and governed, and has not left them like the fishes of the sea, where the greater devour the less.—*The powers that be:* whatever the particular form and method of government are. It is an ordinance of God, and it is

JAMIESON, FAUSSET, BROWN — CHAPTER 13

VSS. 1-14. SAME SUBJECT CONTINUED—POLITICAL AND SOCIAL RELATIONS—MOTIVES.

1, 2. Let every soul—every man of you—**be subject unto the higher powers**—or, 'submit himself to the authorities that are above him.'

Whosoever therefore resisteth the power—'So that he that setteth himself against the authority'—**resisteth the ordinance of God; and they that resist shall receive to themselves damnation**—or, 'condemnation,' according to the old sense of that word; that is, not from the magistrate, but from God, whose authority in the magistrate's is resisted.

For there is no power—'no authority'—**but of God: the powers that be are**—'have been' —**ordained of God.**

ADAM CLARKE — CHAPTER 13

1. *Let every soul be subject unto the higher powers.* This is a very strong saying, and most solemnly introduced; and we must consider the apostle as speaking, not from his own private judgment, or teaching a doctrine of present expediency, but declaring the mind of God on a subject of the utmost importance to the peace of the world; a doctrine which does not exclusively belong to any class of people, order of the community, or official situations, but to every soul; and, on the principles which the apostle lays down, to every soul in all possible varieties of situation, and on all occasions. And what is this solemn doctrine? Let every man be obedient to the civil government under which the providence of God has cast his lot.

2. *Whosoever . . . resisteth the power.* "He who sets himself in order against this order" of God; and *they who resist,* they who obstinately, and for no right reason, oppose the ruler, and strive to unsettle the constitution, and to bring about illegal changes, *shall receive to themselves damnation.* "Condemnation"; shall be condemned by both the spirit and the letter of that constitution, which, under pretense of defending or improving, they are indirectly laboring to subvert.

For there is no power but of God. As God is the Origin of power, and the supreme Governor of the universe, He delegates authority to whomsoever He will; and though in many cases the governor himself may not be of God, yet civil government is of Him. For without this there could be no society, no security, no private property; all would be confusion and anarchy, and the habitable world would soon be depopulated.

MATTHEW HENRY

to be received and submitted to accordingly.—*Ordained of God.* Hence it follows (*v.* 2) that whosoever *resisteth the power resisteth the ordinance of God.* Magistracy is from God as an ordinance, that is, it is a great law, and it is a great blessing. And those who spurn at their power reflect upon God himself. Magistrates are here again and again called God's ministers. He is the *minister of God, v.* 4, 6. Magistrates are in a more peculiar manner God's servants; the dignity they have calls for duty. Though they are lords to us, they are servants to God.

(2) From the intention of magistracy: *Rulers are not a terror to good works, but to the evil,* &c. Magistracy was designed to be,

[1] A terror to evil works and evil workers. They bear the sword; not only the sword of war, but the sword of justice. Such is the power of sin and corruption that many will not be restrained from the greatest enormities by any regard to the law of God and nature; but only by the fear of temporal punishments. Laws with penalties for the lawless and disobedient (1 Tim. i. 9) must be constituted in Christian nations, and are agreeable with, and not contradictory to, the gospel. In this work the magistrate is the *minister of God, v.* 4. He acts as God's agent, and therefore must take heed of infusing into his judgments any private personal resentments of his own.—*To execute wrath upon him that doeth evil.* The judicial processes of the most vigilant faithful magistrates yet come far short of the judgment of God: they reach only to the evil act, on him that *doeth* evil.—*He beareth not the sword in vain.* It is not for nothing that God hath put such a power into the magistrate's hand. And therefore, "*If thou do that which is evil, be afraid;* for civil powers have quick eyes and long arms." It is a good thing when the punishment of malefactors is managed as an ordinance of God. As a holy God, that hates sin. As King of nations, and the God of peace and order. As the protector of the good. As one that by the punishment of some would terrify others, and so prevent the like wickedness.

[2] A praise to those that do well. "Do that which is good (*v.* 3), and thou needest not be *afraid of the power,* nay, thou shalt have praise of it." This is the intention of magistracy, and therefore we must, for conscience' sake, be subject to it, as a constitution designed for the public good. But pity it is that ever this gracious intention should be perverted. Yet even then the blessing and benefit of a common protection, and a face of government and order, are such that it is our duty rather to submit to persecution for well-doing, than by any irregular and disorderly practices to attempt a redress. Better a bad government than none at all.

(3) From our interest in it: "He is *the minister of God to thee for good.*" Protection draws allegiance. By upholding the government, we keep up our own hedge. This subjection is likewise consented to by the tribute we pay (*v.* 6): "*For this cause pay you tribute,* as a testimony of your submission, and an acknowledgment that in conscience you think it to be due. By your paying tribute you not only own the magistrate's authority, but the blessing of that authority to yourselves. Honour is a burden: and, if he do as he ought, *he is attending continually upon this very thing,* in consideration of which fatigue, we pay tribute." He does not say, "You give it as an alms," but, "You pay it as a just debt." This is the lesson the apostle teaches, and it becomes all Christians to learn and practise it, that the godly in the land may be found (whatever others are) the quiet and the peaceable in the land.

Verses 7–10

We are here taught a lesson of justice and charity.

I. Of justice (*v.* 7): *Render therefore to all their dues.* What we have we have as stewards; others have an interest in it, and must have their dues. Render to all their dues; and that readily and cheerfully, not tarrying till you are by law compelled to it. Due taxes: *Tribute to whom tribute is due, custom to whom custom.* He wrote this to the Romans, who, as they were rich, so they were drained by taxes and impositions, to the just and honest payment of which they are here pressed by the apostle. Our Lord was born when his mother went to be taxed; and he enjoined the payment of tribute to Cæsar. Many, who in other things seem to be just, yet make no conscience of this, but pass it off with a false ill-favoured maxim, that it is no sin to cheat the king. Due respect: *Fear to whom fear, honour to whom honour.* This sums up the duty which we owe not only to magistrates, but to all that are over us in the Lord, according to the fifth commandment: *Honour thy father and mother.* Where there is not this respect in the heart to our superiors, no other duty will be paid aright. Due

JAMIESON, FAUSSET, BROWN

3, 4. For rulers are not a terror to good works—'to the good work,' as the true reading appears to be—**but to the evil . . . he beareth not the sword in vain**—i.e., the symbol of the magistrate's authority to punish. **5. Wherefore ye must needs be subject, not only for wrath**—for fear of the magistrate's vengeance—**but also for conscience' sake**—from reverence for God's authority. It is of *Magistracy in general,* considered as a divine ordinance, that this is spoken: and the statement applies equally to all forms of government, from an unchecked despotism—such as flourished when this was written, under the Emperor Nero—to a pure democracy. The inalienable right of all subjects to endeavor to alter or improve the form of government under which they live is left untouched here. But since Christians were constantly charged with turning the world upside down, and since there certainly were elements enough in Christianity of moral and social revolution to give plausibility to the charge, and tempt noble spirits, crushed under misgovernment, to take redress into their own hands, it was of special importance that the pacific, submissive, loyal spirit of those Christians who resided at the great seat of political power, should furnish a visible refutation of this charge.

6, 7. For, for this cause pay ye—rather, 'ye pay'—**tribute also**—i.e., "This is the reason why ye pay the contributions requisite for maintaining the civil government." **for they are God's ministers, attending continually upon**—'to'—**this very thing.**

Render therefore to all their dues—From magistrates the apostle now comes to other officials, and from them to men related to us by whatever tie. **tribute**—land tax. **custom**—mercantile tax. **fear**—reverence for superiors. **honour**—the respect due to persons of distinction.

ADAM CLARKE

3. *For rulers are not a terror to good works.* Here the apostle shows the civil magistrate what he should be: he is clothed with great power, but that power is entrusted to him, not for the terror and oppression of the upright man, but to overawe and punish the wicked. It is, in a word, for the benefit of the community, and not for the aggrandizement of himself, that God has entrusted the supreme civil power to any man. *Wilt thou then not be afraid of the power?* If you would not live in fear of the civil magistrate, live according to the laws. You may expect that he will rule according to the laws; and consequently instead of incurring blame, you will have *praise.* This is said on the supposition that the ruler is himself a good man. Such the laws suppose him to be; and the apostle, on the general question of obedience and protection, assumes the point that the magistrate *is* such.

4. *For he is the minister of God to thee for good.* Here the apostle puts the character of the ruler in the strongest possible light. *He is the minister of God*—the office is by divine appointment. *He beareth not the sword in vain.* His power is delegated to him for the defense and encouragement of the good, and the punishment of the wicked; and he has authority to punish capitally, when the law so requires. This the term *sword* leads us to infer. *For he is the minister of God, a revenger.* "For he is God's vindictive minister." *To execute wrath;* to inflict "punishment" upon the transgressors of the law; and this according to the statutes of that law, for God's civil ministers are never allowed to pronounce or inflict punishment according to their own minds or feelings, but according to the express declarations of the law.

5. *Ye must needs be subject.* There is a necessity that you should be subject, not only for wrath, "on account of the punishment" which will be inflicted on evildoers, *but also for conscience sake;* not only to avoid punishment, but also to preserve a clear conscience.

6. *For this cause pay ye tribute also.* Because civil government is an order of God, and the ministers of state must be at considerable expense in providing for the safety and defense of the community, it is necessary that those in whose behalf these expenses are incurred should defray that expense; and hence nothing can be more reasonable than an impartial and moderate taxation, by which the expenses of the state may be defrayed and the various officers, whether civil or military, who are employed for the service of the public be adequately remunerated. By *God's ministers* are not meant here the ministers of religion, but the civil officers in all departments of the state.

7. *Render therefore to all their dues.* This is an extensive command. Be rigidly just; withhold from neither the king nor his ministers, nor his officers of justice and revenue, nor from even the lowest of the community, what the laws of God and your country require you to pay. *Tribute to whom tribute.* This word probably means such taxes as were levied on persons and estates. *Custom to whom custom.* This word probably means such duties as were laid upon goods, merchandise, etc., on imports and exports; what we commonly call *custom. Fear to whom fear.* It is likely that the word which we translate *fear* signifies that "reverence" which produces obedience. Treat all official characters with respect, and be obedient to your superiors. *Honour to whom honour.* The word may here mean that "outward respect" which the principle of reverence, from which it springs, will generally produce. Never behave rudely to any person; but behave respectfully to men in office. If you cannot even respect the man—for an important office may be filled by an unworthy person—respect the office, and the man on account of his office. If a man habituate himself to disrespect official characters, he will soon find himself disposed to pay little respect or obedience to the laws themselves.

MATTHEW HENRY

payment of debts (*v.* 8): "*Owe no man anything;* do not continue in anyone's debt, while you are able to pay it." Many that are very sensible of the trouble think little of the sin of being in debt.

II. Of charity: *Owe no man anything.* "Whatever you owe, it is eminently summed up in this debt of love. But to *love one another*, this is a debt that must be always in the paying, and yet always owing." Love is a debt. Love *is the fulfilling of the law;* not perfectly, but it is a good step towards it. It is inclusive of all the duties of the second table, which he specifies, *v.* 9, and these suppose the love of God. If the love be sincere, it is accepted as the *fulfilling of the law.* Surely we serve a good master, that has summed up all our duty in one word, and that a short word and a sweet word—*love*, the beauty and harmony of the universe. Loving and being loved is all the pleasure, joy, and happiness, of an intelligent being. *God is love* (1 John iv. 16), and love is his image upon the soul. Now, to prove that love is the fulfilling of the law, he gives us, 1. An induction of particular precepts, *v.* 9. He specifies the last five of the ten commandments, which he observes to be all summed up in this royal law, *Thou shalt love thy neighbour as thyself.* On this is built that golden rule of doing as we would be done by. Were there no restraints of human laws in these things the law of love would of itself be effectual to keep peace and good order among us. The apostle puts the seventh before the sixth, and mentions this first, *Thou shalt not commit adultery;* for though this commonly goes under the name of love (pity it is that so good a word should be so abused) yet it is really as great a violation of it as killing and stealing. He that tempts others to sin, though he may pretend the most passionate love does really hate them. 2. A general rule concerning the nature of brotherly love: *Love worketh no ill* (*v.* 10)—he that walks in love *worketh no ill to his neighbour*, to anyone that he has anything to do with. Love intends and designs no ill to anybody. More is implied than is expressed; it not only worketh no ill, but it worketh all the good that may be. Love is a living active principle of obedience to the whole law. The whole law is written in the heart, if the law of love be there.

Verses 11–14

We are here taught a lesson of sobriety and godliness in ourselves. Four things we are here taught, as a Christian's directory for his day's work: when to awake, how to dress ourselves, how to walk, and what provision to make.

I. When to awake: *Now it is high time to awake* (*v.* 11). We have need to be often excited and stirred up to awake. The word of command to all Christ's disciples is, *Watch.* "*Awake*—be concerned about your souls and your eternal interest. Considering," 1. "The time we are cast into: *Knowing the time.* Consider what time of day it is with us, and you will see it is high time to awake. It is gospel time, it is a time when more is expected than was in the times of that ignorance which God winked at, when people sat in darkness. It is high time to awake; for the sun has been up a great while, and shines in our faces. It is high time to awake; for others are awake and up about us. Know the time to be a busy time; we have a great deal of work to do. Know the time to be a perilous time. We are in the midst of enemies and snares. It is time to awake, for we have slept enough." 2. "The salvation we are upon the brink of: *Now is our salvation nearer than when we believed.* The eternal happiness we chose for our portion is now nearer to us than it was when we became Christians. Let us mind our way and mend our pace. The nearer we are to our centre the quicker should our motion be. Is there but a step between us and heaven, and shall we be so very slow and dull in our Christian course?"

II. How to dress ourselves. This is the next care, when we are awake and up: "The *night is far spent, the day is at hand;* therefore it is time to dress ourselves." Clearer discoveries will be quickly made of gospel grace than have been yet made, as light gets ground.

1. "What we must put off; our night-clothes, which it is a shame to appear abroad in: *Cast off the works of darkness.*" Sinful works are works of darkness. Let us therefore, who are of the day, cast them off, and have no more to do with them.

2. "What we must put on." Our care must be *wherewithal we shall be clothed*, how shall we dress our souls? (1) *Put on the armour of light.* Christians are soldiers in the midst of enemies, therefore their array must be armour. A Christian may reckon himself undressed if he be unarmed. The graces of the Spirit are this armour, to secure the soul from Satan's temptations. This is called the armour of light.

JAMIESON, FAUSSET, BROWN

8. Owe no man anything, but to love one another—"Acquit yourselves of all obligations except love, which is a debt that must remain ever due" [HODGE].

for he that loveth another hath fulfilled the law—[or the law itself is but love in manifold action, regarded as matter of duty.

9. For this, . . .—better thus: 'For the [commandments], Thou shalt not kill, Thou shalt not commit adultery, Thou shalt not steal, Thou shalt not covet, and whatever other commandment [there may be], it is summed up . . . (The clause, "Thou shalt not bear false witness," is wanting in all the most ancient MSS.) The apostle refers here only to the second table of the law, as love to our neighbor is what he is treating of.

10. Love worketh no ill to his—or, 'one's'—**neighbour: therefore . . .**—As love, from its very nature, studies and delights to please its objects, its very existence is an effectual security against our wilfully injuring him. Next follow some general motives to the faithful discharge of all these duties.

11. And that—rather, 'And this' [do]—**knowing the time, that now it is high time**—lit., 'the hour has already come.' **to awake out of sleep**—of stupid, fatal indifference to eternal things.

for now is our salvation—rather, 'the salvation,' or simply 'salvation'—**nearer than when we**—first—**believed**—This is in the line of all our Lord's teaching, which represents the decisive day of Christ's second appearing as at hand, to keep believers ever in the attitude of wakeful expectancy, but without reference to the *chronological* nearness or distance of that event.

12. The night—of evil—**is far spent, the day**—of consummated triumph over it—**is at hand:**

let us therefore cast off—as a dress—**the works of darkness**—all works holding of the kingdom and period of darkness, with which, as followers of the risen Saviour, our connection has been dissolved. **and let us put on the armour of light**—described at length in Ephesians 6:11-18.

ADAM CLARKE

8. *Owe no man any thing, but to love one another.* In the preceding verses the apostle has been showing the duty, reverence, and obedience which all Christians, from the highest to the lowest, owe to the civil magistrate, whether he be emperor, king, proconsul, or other state officer; here he shows them their duty to each other. But this is widely different from that which they owe to the civil government. To the first they owe subjection, reverence, obedience, and tribute; to the latter they owe nothing but mutual love, and those offices which necessarily spring from it. Therefore the apostle says, *Owe no man;* as if he had said: You owe to your fellow brethren nothing but mutual love, and this is what the law of God requires, and in this the law is fulfilled.

9. *For this, Thou shalt not commit adultery.* He that loves another will not deprive him of his wife, of his life, of his property, of his good name; and will not even permit a desire to enter into his heart which would lead him to wish to possess anything that is the property of another; for the law, the sacred Scripture, has said: *Thou shalt love thy neighbour as thyself.* It is remarkable that *thou shalt not bear false witness* is missing from several MSS. The generality of the best critics think it a spurious reading.

10. *Love worketh no ill.* As he that loves another will act towards that person as, on a reverse of circumstances, he would that his neighbor should act towards him, therefore this love can never work ill towards another; and on this head, i.e., the duty we owe to our neighbor, *love is the fulfilling of the law.*

11. *And that, knowing the time.* Some think the passage should be understood thus: We have now many advantages which we did not formerly possess. *Salvation* is *nearer*—the whole Christian system is more fully explained, and the knowledge of it more easy to be acquired than formerly; on which account a greater progress in religious knowledge and in practical piety is required of us, and we have for a long time been too remiss in these respects.

12. *The night is far spent.* If we understand this in reference to the heathen state of the Romans, it may be paraphrased thus: *The night is far spent*—heathenish darkness is nearly at an end. *The day is at hand*—the full manifestation of the Sun of Righteousness, in the illumination of the whole Gentile world, approaches rapidly. The manifestation of the Messiah is regularly termed by the ancient Jews *day*, because previously to this all is *night. Cast off the works of darkness*—prepare to meet this rising light, and welcome its approach, by throwing aside superstition, impiety, and vice of every kind; and *put on the armour of light*—fully receive the heavenly teaching, by which your spirits will be as completely armed against the attacks of evil as your bodies could be by the best weapons and impenetrable armor. This sense seems most suitable to the following verses, where the vices of the Gentiles are particularly specified; and they are exhorted to abandon them, and to receive the gospel of Christ. The common method of explanation is this: *The night is far spent*—our present imperfect life, full of afflictions, temptations, and trials, is almost run out; *the day* of eternal blessedness *is at hand*—is about to dawn on us in our glorious resurrection unto eternal life. Therefore, *let us . . . cast off*—let us live as candidates for this eternal glory. But this sense cannot at all comport with what is said below, as the Gentiles are most evidently intended.

MATTHEW HENRY

The graces of the Spirit are suitable splendid ornaments. (2) *Put on the Lord Jesus Christ, v.* 14. This stands in opposition to a great many base lusts, mentioned, *v.* 13. *Rioting and drunkenness* must be cast off. "*Put on Christ*, this includes all. Put on the righteousness of Christ for justification; be found in him (Phil. iii. 9) as a man is found in his clothes. Put on the spirit and grace of Christ for sanctification; put on the *new man* (Eph. iv. 24)." Jesus Christ is the best clothing for Christians to adorn themselves with, to arm themselves with. All other things are filthy rags. By baptism we have in profession put on Christ. Let us do it in truth and sincerity. *The Lord Jesus Christ.* "Put him on as Lord to rule you, as Jesus to save you, and in both as Christ, appointed by the Father to this ruling saving work."

III. How to walk. When we are up and dressed, we are not to sit still. What have we good clothes for, but to appear abroad in them?—*Let us walk.* Christianity teaches us how to walk so as to please God. Our conversation must be as becomes the gospel. *Walk honestly; decently* and becomingly. Christians should be careful to conduct themselves well in those things wherein men have an eye upon them, and to study that which is lovely and of good report. We must not walk in *rioting and drunkenness*; we must abstain from all excess in eating and drinking. We must not give the least countenance to revelling. *Not in chambering and wantonness;* not in any of those lusts of the flesh, those works of darkness—whatsoever transgresseth the pure and sacred law of chastity and modesty. Not in *strife and envying*. These are also works of darkness; for, though the acts and instances of strife and envy are very common, yet none are willing to acknowledge themselves envious and contentious. To strive and to envy ill becomes the disciples and followers of the peaceable and humble Jesus. Where there are riot and drunkenness, there usually are chambering and wantonness, and strife and envy.

IV. What provision to make (*v.* 14): "*Make not provision for the flesh.* Be not careful about the body." Our great care must be to provide for our souls; but must we take no care about our bodies? Two things are here forbidden: 1. Perplexing ourselves with an inordinate care; do not stretch your wits, nor set your thoughts upon the tenter-hooks, in making this provision. It forbids an anxious encumbering care. 2. Indulging ourselves in an irregular desire. The necessities of the body must be considered, but the lusts of it must not be gratified. Natural desires must be answered but wanton appetites must be checked and denied.

JAMIESON, FAUSSET, BROWN

13. Let us walk honestly—'becomingly,' 'seemingly'—**as in the day**—'Men choose the night for their revels, but our night is past, for we are all the children of the light and of the day (I Thess. 5:5): let us therefore only do what is fit to be exposed to the light of such a day.' **not in rioting and drunkenness**—varied forms of intemperance; denoting revels in general, usually ending in intoxication. **not in chambering and wantonness**—varied forms of impurity; the one pointing to definite acts, the other more general. **not in strife and envying**—varied forms of that venomous feeling between man and man which reverses the law of love.

14. But—to sum up all in one word—**put ye on the Lord Jesus Christ**—in such wise that Christ only may be seen in you (see II Cor. 3:3; Gal. 3:27; Eph. 4:24). **and make no provision**—'take no forethought'—**for the flesh, to fulfil the lust [thereof]**—'Direct none of your attention to the cravings of your corrupt nature, how you may provide for their gratification.'—Note, (1) How gloriously adapted is Christianity for human society in all conditions! As it makes war directly against no specific forms of government, so it directly recommends none. While its holy and benign principles secure the ultimate abolition of all iniquitous government, the reverence which it teaches for magistracy, under whatever form, as a divine institution, secures the loyalty and peaceableness of its disciples, amid all the turbulence and distractions of civil society, and makes it the highest interest of all states to welcome it within their pale, as in this as well as every other sense—"the salt of the earth, the light of the world" (vss. 1-5). (2) Christianity is the grand specific for the purification and elevation of all the social relations; inspiring a readiness to discharge all obligations, and most of all, implanting in its disciples that love which secures all men against injury from them, inasmuch as it is the fulfilling of the law (vss. 6-10). (3) The rapid march of the kingdom of God, the advanced stage of it at which we have arrived, and the ever-nearing approach of the perfect day—nearer to every believer the longer he lives—should quicken all the children of light to redeem the time, and, seeing that they look for such things, to be diligent, that they may be found of Him in peace, without spot and blameless (II Pet. 3:14). (4) In virtue of 'the expulsive power of a new and more powerful affection,' the great secret of persevering holiness in all manner of conversation will be found to be "Christ IN US, the hope of glory" (Col. 1:27), and Christ ON US, as the character in which alone we shall be able to shine before men (II Cor. 3:8) (vs. 14).

ADAM CLARKE

13. *Let us walk honestly, as in the day.* "Let us walk decently." Let our deportment be decent, orderly, such as we shall not be ashamed of in the eyes of the whole world. *Not in rioting and drunkenness. Rioting,* according to Hesychius, signifies "unclean and dissolute songs," banquets, and suchlike. *Methais* signifies "drunken festivals," such as were celebrated in honor of their gods, when after they had sacrificed they drank to excess, accompanied with abominable acts of every kind. *Not in chambering.* This is no legitimate word, and conveys no sense till, from its connection in this place, we force a meaning upon it. The original word signifies "whoredoms" and prostitution of every kind. *And wantonness.* All manner of "uncleanness." *Not in strife and envying.* Not in contentions and furious altercations, which must be the consequence of such practices as are mentioned above. Can any man suppose that this address is to the Christians at Rome? That they are charged with practices almost peculiar to the heathens? And practices of the most abandoned and dissolute sort? If those called Christians at Rome were guilty of such acts, there could be no difference, except in profession, between them and the most abominable of the heathens. But it is impossible that such things should be spoken to the followers of Christ, for the very grace that brings repentance enables the penitent to cast aside and abominate all such vicious and abominable conduct. The advices to the Christians may be found in the preceding chapter; those at the conclusion of this chapter belong solely to the heathens.

14. *Put ye on the Lord Jesus.* This is in reference to what is said, v. 13: "Let us put on decent garments"—let us make a different profession, unite with other company, and maintain that profession by a suitable conduct. Putting on or being clothed with Jesus Christ signifies receiving and believing the gospel; and consequently taking its maxims for the government of life, having the mind that was in Christ. The ancient Jews frequently use the phrase putting on the Shekinah, or divine majesty, to signify the soul's being clothed with immortality and rendered fit for glory. "To be clothed with a person" is a Greek phrase signifying to "assume the interests" of another—to enter into his views, to imitate him, and be wholly on his side. Chrysostom particularly mentions this as a common phrase, "such a one hath put on such a one"; i.e., he closely follows and imitates him. The mode of speech itself is taken from the custom of stage players; they assumed the name and garments of the person whose character they were to act, and endeavored as closely as possible to imitate him in their spirit, words, and actions. *And make not provision for the flesh.* By *flesh* we are here to understand not only the body, but all the irregular appetities and passions which led to the abominations already recited. No provision should be made for the encouragement and gratification of such a principle as this. *To fulfil the lusts thereof.* "In reference to its lusts"; such as the rioting, drunkenness, prostitutions, and uncleanness, mentioned in v. 13, to make provision for which the Gentiles lived and labored, and bought and sold, and schemed and planned; for it was the whole business of their life to gratify the sinful lusts of the flesh. Their philosophers taught them little else; and the whole circle of their deities, as well as the whole scheme of their religion, served only to excite and inflame such passions and produce such practices.

MATTHEW HENRY

CHAPTER 14

Verses 1–23

I. An account of the unhappy contention which had broken out in the Christian church.

1. There was a difference among them about the distinction of meats and days. The members of the Christian church at Rome were some of them originally Gentiles, and others of them Jews. Now those that had been Jews were trained up in the observance of the ceremonial appointments touching meats and days, and therefore retained the ceremonial institutions, while other Christians made no such difference.

JAMIESON, FAUSSET, BROWN

CHAPTER 14

VSS. 1-23. SAME SUBJECT CONTINUED—CHRISTIAN FORBEARANCE. The subject here, and on to ch. 15: 13, *is the consideration due from stronger Christians to their weaker brethren;* which is but the great law of love (treated of in ch. 13) in one particular form.

ADAM CLARKE

CHAPTER 14

It seems very likely, from this and the following chapter, that there were considerable misunderstandings between the Jewish and Gentile Christians at Rome relative to certain customs which were sacredly observed by the one and disregarded by the other. The principal subject of dispute was concerning *meats* and *days*. The converted Jew, retaining a veneration for the law of Moses, abstained from certain meats and was observant of certain days; while the converted Gentile, understanding that the Christian religion laid him under no obligations to such ceremonial points, had no regard to either. It

MATTHEW HENRY

2. It was not so much the difference itself that did the mischief as the mismanagement of the difference, making it a bone of contention. Those who were strong, and knew their Christian liberty, despised the weak, who did not. They should have pitied them, and helped them. So apt are those who have knowledge to be puffed up with it, and to look disdainfully and scornfully upon their brethren. Those who were weak, and durst not use their Christian liberty, judged and censured the strong, who did, as if they were loose Christians. They judged them as breakers of the law. Well, this was the disease, and we see it remaining in the church to this day.

II. We have proper suggestions laid down for allaying this contention. Not by excommunicating, suspending, and silencing either side, but by persuading them both to a mutual forbearance: reasoning the case with the strong that they should not be so scornful, and with the weak that they should not be so censorious. Let us observe the rules he gives, some to the strong and some to the weak, and some to both.

1. Those who are weak must be *received, but not to doubtful disputations, v.* 1. Spend your zeal in those things wherein you and all the people of God are agreed. *Receive him, take him to you, lend him your hand,* to help him. Receive him into your company. Receive him: not to quarrel with him, and to argue about uncertain points that are in controversy. Let not your Christian friendship be disturbed with such vain janglings and strifes of words.—*Not to judge his doubtful thoughts* (so the margin). Receive him, not to expose him, but to instruct and strengthen him.

Concerning meats (*v.* 2): *One believeth that he may eat all things*—he is well satisfied that every creature of God is good, and nothing to be refused; nothing *unclean of itself, v.* 14. This the strong Christian is clear in, and practises accordingly, eating what is set before him. On the other hand, *another, who is weak,* is dissatisfied in this point; he will eat no flesh at all, but *eateth herbs,* contenting himself with only the fruits of the earth.

2. Those who are strong must by no means despise the weak; nor those who are weak judge the strong, *v.* 3. This is levelled directly against the fault of each party. It is seldom that any such contention exists but there is a fault on both sides. We must not despise nor judge our brethren. Why so?

(1) Because God hath received them. Strong believers and weak believers, if they be true believers, are accepted of God. "Nay, God doth not only receive him, but *hold him up* (*v.* 4). If they have true faith, they shall be held up—the one in his integrity, and the other in his comfort. This hope is built upon the power of God, for *God is able to make him stand.*"

(2) Because they are servants to their own master (*v.* 4): *Who art thou that judgest another man's servant?* We reckon it a piece of ill manners to meddle with other people's servants. Weak and strong Christians are indeed our brethren, but they are not our servants. We make ourselves our brethren's masters, and do in effect usurp the throne of God, when we take upon us thus to judge them. God sees not as man sees; and he is their master, and not we. If we must needs be judging, let us exercise our faculty upon our own hearts and ways.—*To his own master he stands or falls.* How well for us is it that we are not to stand nor fall by the judgment one of another, but by the judgment of God. Concerning days, *v.* 5. Those who thought themselves still under some kind of obligation by the ceremonial law esteemed *one day above another*—kept up a respect to the times of the passover, pentecost, new moons, and feast of tabernacles. Those who knew that all these things were abolished by Christ's coming esteemed every day alike. We must understand it with an exception of the Lord's day, which all Christians unanimously observed. The apostle seems willing to let the ceremonial law wither by degrees, and to let it have an honourable burial.

JAMIESON, FAUSSET, BROWN

1. Him that is weak in the faith—rather, 'in faith'; i.e., not 'him that is weak in the truth believed' [CALVIN, BEZA, ALFORD, etc.], but (as most interpreters agree), 'him whose faith wants that firmness and breadth which would raise him above small scruples.' (See on vss. 22, 23.) **receive ye**—to cordial Christian fellowship—**but not to doubtful disputations**—rather, perhaps, 'not to the deciding of doubts,' or 'scruples;' i.e., not for the purpose of arguing him out of them: which indeed usually does the reverse; whereas to receive him to full brotherly confidence and cordial interchange of Christian affection is the most effectual way of drawing them off. Two examples of such scruples are here specified, touching Jewish *meats* and *days.* "The strong," it will be observed, are those who knew these to be abolished under the Gospel; "the weak" are those who had scruples on this point. **2. one believeth that he may eat all things**—See Acts 10:16. **another, who is weak, eateth herbs**—restricting himself probably to a vegetable diet, for fear of eating what might have been offered to idols, and so would be unclean. (See I Cor. 8.)

3. Let not him that eateth despise—look down superciliously upon—**him that eateth not; and let not him that eateth not judge**—sit in judgment censoriously upon—**him that eateth: for God hath received him**—as one of His dear children, who in this matter acts not from laxity, but religious principle.

4. Who art thou that judgest another man's—rather, 'another's'—**servant?** —i.e., CHRIST'S, as the whole context shows, especially vss. 8, 9. **Yea . . .**—'But he shall be made to stand, for God is able to make him stand'; i.e., to make good his standing, not at the day of judgment, of which the apostle treats in vs. 10, but in the true fellowship of the Church *here,* in spite of thy censures.

5. One man esteemeth one day above another: another esteemeth every day—The supplement "alike" should be omitted, as injuring the sense.

ADAM CLARKE

appears further that mutual censures and uncharitable judgments prevailed among them, and that brotherly love and mutual forbearance did not generally prevail. The apostle in this part of his Epistle exhorts that in such things, not essential to religion and in which both parties, in their different way of thinking, might have an honest meaning and serious regard to God, difference of sentiments might not hinder Christian fellowship and love; but that they would mutually forbear each other, make candid allowance, and especially not carry their gospel liberty so far as to prejudice a weak brother, a Jewish Christian, against the gospel itself, and tempt him to renounce Christianity.

1. *Him that is weak in the faith.* By this the apostle most evidently means the converted Jew, who must indeed be weak in the faith if he considered this distinction of meats and days essential to his salvation. *Receive ye.* Associate with him; receive him into your religious fellowship; but when there, let all religious altercations be avoided. *Not to doubtful disputations.* Do not reject any from your Christian communion because of their particular sentiments on things which are in themselves indifferent.

2. *One believeth that he may eat all things.* He believes that whatsoever is wholesome and nourishing, whether herbs or flesh, whether enjoined or forbidden by the Mosaic law, may be safely and conscientiously used by every Christian. *Another, who is weak, eateth herbs.* Certain Jews lately converted to the Christian faith and having as yet little knowledge of its doctrines believe the Mosaic law relative to clean and unclean meats to be still in force; and therefore when they are in a Gentile country, for fear of being defiled, avoid flesh entirely and live on vegetables.

3. *Let not him that eateth,* the Gentile, who eats flesh, *despise him,* the Jew, who *eatest not* flesh but herbs. *And let not him,* the Jew, *which eateth not* indiscriminately, *judge*—condemn—*him,* the Gentile, *that eateth* indiscriminately flesh or vegetables. *For God hath received him.* Both being sincere and upright, and acting in the fear of God, are *received* as heirs of eternal life, without any difference on account of these religious scruples or prejudices.

4. *Who art thou that judgest another man's servant?* Who has ever given you the right to condemn the servant of another man, in things pertaining to his own master? *To his own master he standeth or falleth.* He is to judge him, not you; your intermeddling in this business is both rash and uncharitable. *Yea, he shall be holden up.* He is sincere and upright, and *God,* who *is able to make him stand,* will uphold him, and so teach him that he shall not essentially err. And it is the will of God that such upright though scrupulous persons should be continued members of His Church.

5. *One man esteemeth one day above another.* Perhaps the word *day* is here taken for "time, festival," and suchlike, in which sense it is frequently used. Reference is made here to the Jewish institutions and especially their festivals, such as the Passover, Pentecost, Feast of Tabernacles, new moons, jubilee. The converted Jew still thought these of moral obligation; the Gentile Christian not having been bred up in this way had no such prejudices. And as those who were the instruments of bringing him to the knowledge of God gave him no such injunctions, consequently he paid to these no religious regard. *Another.* The converted Gentile *esteemeth every day*—considers that all time is the Lord's, and that each day should be devoted to the glory of God, and that those festivals are not binding on him. We add here *alike,* and make the text say what I am sure was never intended, viz., that there is no distinction of days, not even of the Sabbath; and that every Christian is at liberty to consider even this day to be holy or not holy, as he happens to be persuaded in his own mind. That the Sabbath is of lasting obligation may be reasonably concluded from its institution (see the note on Gen. ii. 3) and from its typical reference. All allow that the Sabbath is a type of that rest in glory which remains for the people of God. Now all types are intended to continue in full force till the antitype or thing

MATTHEW HENRY

(3) Because both the one and the other, if they be true believers, have an eye to God, and do approve themselves to God in what they do, *v.* 6. He *that regards the day*—it is well. We have reason to think, because in other things he conducts himself like a good Christian, that *he regardeth it unto the Lord*; and God will accept of his honest intention. The sincerity and uprightness of the heart were never rejected for the weakness and infirmity of the head: so good a master do we serve. On the other hand, he *that regards not the day*, but esteems every day alike—he does not do it out of a spirit of contradiction, or contempt of his brother. If he be a good Christian we charitably conclude that to the *Lord he does not regard it*. He makes no such difference of days only because he knows God hath made none; and therefore intends his honour in endeavouring to dedicate every day to him. So for the other instance: *He that eateth* whatever is set before him he *eateth to the Lord*. He understands the liberty that God has granted him, and uses it to the glory of God. He *giveth God thanks* for the variety of food he has, and the liberty he has to eat it. On the other hand, *he that eateth not, to the Lord he eateth not*. It is for God's sake, because he is afraid of offending God by eating that which he is sure was once prohibited; and he *giveth God thanks too* that there is enough besides. Thus, while both approve themselves to him in their integrity, why should either of them be judged or despised? Whether we eat flesh, or eat herbs, it is a thankful regard to God, the author and giver of all our mercies, that sanctifies and sweetens it. It appears by this that *saying grace* (as we commonly call it), before and after meat was the common known practice of the church. Blessing the creatures in the name of God before we use them, and blessing the name of God for them after, are both included. Observe his description of true Christians, taken from their end and aim (*v.* 7, 8), and the ground of it, *v.* 9.

[1] Our end and aim: not self, but the Lord. If we would know what way we walk in, we must enquire what end we walk towards. *First*, Not to self. We have learned to deny ourselves: *None of us liveth to himself*. This is a thing in which all the people of God are one, however they differ in other things. Not one that hath given up his name to Christ is allowedly a self-seeker; it is contrary to the foundation of true Christianity. We neither *live to ourselves nor die to ourselves*. The business of our lives is not to please ourselves, but to please God. When we come to die it is to the Lord, that we may depart and be with Christ. *Secondly*, But *to the Lord* (*v.* 8), to the Lord Christ. Christ is the gain we aim at, living and dying. We live to glorify him; we die to glorify him, and to go to be glorified with him. Christ is the centre, in which all the lines of life and death do meet. So that, *whether we live or die, we are the Lord's*. Though some Christians are weak and others strong, yet they are all the Lord's, and are accordingly owned and accepted of him. Is it for us then to judge or despise them, as if we were their masters?

[2] The ground of this, *v.* 9. It is grounded upon Christ's absolute sovereignty, the fruit and end of his death and resurrection. *To this end he both died, and rose, and revived, that he might be Lord both of dead and living*. He is head over all things to the church. He is Lord of those that are living to rule them, of those that are dead to receive them and raise them up. We must consider that Christ is Lord of the dead, as well as of the living. If they are dead, they have already given up their account, and let that suffice. And this leads to another reason against judging and despising.

(4) Because both the one and the other must shortly give an account, *v.* 10–12. *Why dost thou* that are weak *judge thy brother* that is strong? And *why dost thou* that art strong *set at nought thy brother* that is weak? Why is all this clashing, and contradicting, and censuring, among Christians? *We shall all stand before the judgment-seat of Christ*. Christ will be the Judge, and before him we shall stand as persons to be tried. To illustrate this (*v.* 11), he quotes a passage out of the Old Testament, which speaks of Christ's universal sovereignty and dominion, and that established with an oath: *As I live* (saith the Lord), *every knee shall bow to me*. It is a prophecy, in general, of Christ's dominion. Here is a proof of Christ's Godhead. Divine honour is due to him, and must be paid. The bowing of the knee to him, and the confession made with the tongue, are but outward expressions of inward adoration and praise. *Every knee* and *every tongue*, either freely or by force.

[1] All his friends do it freely. Bowing to him—the understanding bowed to his truths, the will to his laws, the whole man to his authority; and this expressed by the bowing of the knee, the posture of

JAMIESON, FAUSSET, BROWN

6. He that regardeth the day, regardeth it to the Lord—the Lord CHRIST, as before—

and he . . . not, to the Lord he doth not—each doing what he believes to be the Lord's will.

He that eateth, eateth to the Lord, for he giveth God thanks; and he that eateth not, to the Lord he eateth not, and giveth God thanks—The one gave thanks to God for the flesh which the other scrupled to use; the other did the same for the herbs to which, for conscience' sake, he restricted himself. From this passage about the observance of days, ALFORD unhappily infers that such language could not have been used if the *sabbath law* had been in force under the Gospel in any form. Certainly it could not, if the sabbath were merely one of the Jewish festival days; but it will not do to take this for granted merely because it was observed *under* the Mosaic economy. And certainly, if the sabbath was more ancient than Judaism; if, even under Judaism, it was enshrined among the eternal sanctities of the Decalogue, uttered, as no other parts of Judaism were, amidst the terrors of Sinai; and if the Lawgiver Himself said of it when on earth, "The Son of man is LORD EVEN OF THE SABBATH DAY" (see Mark 2:28)—it will be hard to show that the apostle must have meant it to be ranked by his readers among those vanished Jewish festival days, which only "weakness" could imagine to be still in force—a weakness which those who had more light ought, out of love, merely to bear with. **7, 8. For none of us—Christians—liveth to himself**—(See II Cor. 5:14, 15), to dispose of himself or shape his conduct after his own ideas and inclinations. **and no man**—'and none'—of us Christians—**dieth to himself. For whether we live, we live unto the Lord**—the Lord CHRIST; see next verse—**and whether we die, we die unto the Lord; whether we live therefore, or die, we are the Lord's**—Nothing but the most vivid explanation of these remarkable words could make them endurable to any Christian ear, if Christ were a *mere creature*. For Christ is here—in the most emphatic terms, and yet in the most unimpassioned tone—held up as the supreme Object of the Christian's life, and of his death too; and that by the man whose horror of creature-worship was such, that when the poor Lycaonians would have worshipped him, he rushed forth to arrest the deed, directing them to "the living God," as the only legitimate Object of worship (Acts 14:15). Nor does Paul *teach* this here, but rather *appeals* to it as a known and recognized fact, of which he had only to remind his readers. And since the apostle, when he wrote these words, had never been at Rome, he could only know that the Roman Christians would assent to this view of Christ, because it was *the common teaching of all the accredited preachers of Christianity, and the common faith of all Christians*. **9. For to this end Christ both . . .**—The true reading here is, To this end Christ died and lived ['again']—**that he might be Lord both of the dead and**—'and of the'—**living**—The grand object of His death was to *acquire* this absolute Lordship over His redeemed, both in their living and in their dying, as His of right. **10. But why . . .**—The original is more lively:—'But thou (the weaker believer), why judgest thou thy brother? And thou again (the stronger), why despisest thou thy brother?' **for we shall all**—the strong and the weak together—**stand before the judgment seat of Christ**—All the most ancient and best MSS. read here, 'the judgment seat of God.' The present reading doubtless crept in from II Corinthians 5:10, where "the judgment seat of *Christ*" occurs. But here "the judgment seat of *God*" seems to have been used, with reference to the quotation and the inference in the next two verses. **11, 12. For it is written**—Isaiah 45:23—**As I live, saith the Lord**—*Hebrew*, JEHOVAH—**every knee shall bow to me, and every tongue shall confess to God**—consequently, shall bow to the award of God upon their character and actions.

ADAM CLARKE

signified take place; consequently the Sabbath will continue in force till the consummation of all things. The word *alike* should not be added, nor is it acknowledged by any MS. or ancient version.

6. *He that regardeth the day*. A beautiful apology for mistaken sincerity and injudicious reformation. Do not condemn the man for what is indifferent in itself; if he keep these festivals, his purpose is to honor God by the religious observance of them. On the other hand, he who finds that he cannot observe them in honor of God, not believing that God has enjoined them, does not observe them at all. In like manner, he that eateth any creature of God which is wholesome and proper food gives thanks to God as the Author of all good. And he who cannot eat of all indiscriminately, but is regulated by the precepts in the Mosaic law relative to clean and unclean meats, also *giveth God thanks*. Both are sincere, both upright; both act according to their light. God accepts both, and they should bear with each other.

7. *None of us liveth to himself*. The Greek writers use the phrase to signify acting according to one's own judgment, following one's own opinion. Christians must act in all things according to the mind and will of God, and not follow their own wills. The apostle seems to intimate that in all the above cases each must endeavor to please God, for he is accountable to Him alone for his conduct in these indifferent things. God is our Master; we must live to Him, as we live under His notice and by His bounty; and when we cease to live among men, we are still in His hand. Therefore what we do, or what we leave undone, should be in reference to that eternity which is ever at hand.

9. *Christ both died, and rose*. That we are not our own, but are the Lord's in both life and death, is evident from this—that Christ lived, and died, and rose again, *that he might be Lord of the dead and living; for* His power extends equally over both worlds. Separate, as well as embodied, spirits are under His authority; and He it is who is to raise even the dead to life, and thus all throughout eternity shall live under His dominion. The clause *and rose* is wanting in several reputable MSS., and certainly is not necessary to the text.

10. *But why dost thou*, Christian Jew, observing the rites of the Mosaic law, *judge*, condemn, *thy brother*, the Christian Gentile, who does not think himself bound by this law? *Or why dost thou*, Christian Gentile, *set at nought* your Christian Jewish brother, as if he were unworthy of your regard, because he does not yet believe that the gospel has set him free from the rites and ceremonies of the law? ***We shall all stand before the judgment seat of Christ.*** Why should we then judge and condemn each other? We are accountable to God for our conduct, and shall be judged at His bar; and let us consider that whatever measure we mete, the same shall be measured unto us again.

MATTHEW HENRY

adoration and prayer. Confessing to him—acknowledging his glory, grace, and greatness—acknowledging our own meanness and vileness, confessing our sins to him.

[2] All his foes shall be constrained to do it. Hence he concludes (*v.* 12), *Everyone of us shall give account of himself to God.* We must not give account for others, nor they for us; but everyone for himself. We have little to do to judge others, for they are not accountable to us, nor are we accountable for them. They must give account to their own master, and not to us; if we can in anything be helpers of their joy, it is well; but we have not dominion over their faith. We have the more to do to judge ourselves. We have an account of our own to make up. Let this take up his thoughts, and he that is strict in judging himself will not be apt to judge and despise his brother.

(5) Because the stress of Christianity is not to be laid upon these things, nor are they at all essential to religion. Why should you spend your zeal either for or against those things which are so minute and inconsiderable in religion? *The kingdom of God is not meat,* &c. Observe here,

[1] The nature of true Christianity. It is here called, *The kingdom of God;* it is a religion intended to rule us. *First,* It is *not meat and drink*: it does not consist either in using or in abstaining from such and such meats and drinks. Christianity gives no rule in that case. The matter is left at large. Every *creature of God is good,* 1 Tim. iv. 4. It is not being of this party and persuasion, of this or the other opinion in minor things, that will recommend us to God. But it will be asked, "Who feared God and worked righteousness, and who did not?" *Secondly, It is righteousness, and peace, and joy in the Holy Ghost.* These are some of the essentials of Christianity in the pursuit of which we must spend our zeal. Righteousness, peace, and joy, are very comprehensive words. As to God, our great concern is *righteousness,* for the righteous Lord loveth righteousness. As to our brethren, it is *peace*—to live in peace and love, and charity with them. Christ came into the world to be the great peacemaker. As to ourselves, it is *joy in the Holy Ghost.* Next to our compliance with God, to delight ourselves always in the Lord. Surely we serve a good Master, who makes peace and joy so essential to our religion. *Thirdly,* It is in these things to *serve Christ* (*v.* 18), to do all this out of respect to Christ himself as our Master, to his will as our rule and to his glory as our end. What is Christianity but the serving of Christ?

[2] The advantages of it. He that duly observeth these things is acceptable to God. He has the love and favour of God, and we need no more to make us happy. Those are most pleasing to God that are best pleased with him. He is approved of men—of all wise and good men, and the opinion of others is not to be regarded. The approbation of men is not to be slighted; for we must provide things honest in the sight of all men: but the acceptance of God is to be aimed at in the first place.

3. In these doubtful things everyone not only may, but must, walk according to the light that God hath given him. This is laid down, *v.* 5, *Let every man be fully persuaded in his own mind;* that is, "Practise according to your own judgment in these things, and leave others to do so too. If your sober sentiments be otherwise, do not make their practice a rule to you, any more than you must prescribe yours as a rule to them. First be persuaded that what you do is lawful, before you venture to do it." In doubtful things, it is good keeping on the sure side of the hedge. To this purport he argues, *v.* 14 and 23, which two verses give us a rule not to act against the dictates,

(1) Of a mistaken conscience, *v.* 14. If we really think it a sin to do it it is to us a sin, because we act against our consciences, though mistaken and misinformed.

[1] His own clearness in this matter. "*I know and am persuaded*—I am fully persuaded that there *is nothing unclean of itself,* that is, no kind of meat that lies under any ceremonial uncleanness, nor is forbidden to be eaten." Sin had brought a curse upon the whole creation. Now that Christ has removed the curse the matter is set at large again. Therefore Paul says that he was persuaded by the Lord Jesus, not only as the author of that persuasion, but as the ground of it. So that now there is nothing unclean of itself, every creature of God is good; nothing *common*; nothing profane; in this sense the Jews used the word *common.* This was Paul's own clearness, and he practised accordingly.

[2] But here is a caution: *To him that esteemeth anything to be unclean, to him it is unclean.* He who does a thing which he verily believes to be unlawful, however the thing be in itself, to him it is a sin. Our wills, in all their choices should follow the dictates of our under-

JAMIESON, FAUSSET, BROWN

So then—infers the apostle—**every one of us shall give account of himself to God**—Now, if it be remembered that all this is adduced quite incidentally, to show that CHRIST is the absolute Master of all Christians, to rule their judgments and feelings towards each other while "living," and to dispose of them "dying," the testimony which it bears to the absolute Divinity of Christ will appear remarkable. On any other view, the quotation to show that we shall all stand before the judgment seat of *God* would be a strange proof that Christians are all amenable to *Christ.*

For the kingdom of God—or, as we should say, Religion; i.e., the proper business and blessedness for which Christians are formed into a community of renewed men in thorough subjection to God (cf. I Cor. 4:20). **is not meat and drink**—'eating and drinking'—**but righteousness, and peace, and joy in the Holy Ghost**—a beautiful and comprehensive division of living Christianity. The first—"righteousness"—has respect to *God,* denoting here 'rectitude,' in its widest sense (as in Matt. 6:33); the second—"peace"—has respect to *our neighbors,* denoting 'concord' among brethren (as is plain from vs. 19; cf. Eph. 4:3; Col. 3:14, 15); the third—"joy in the Holy Ghost"—has respect to *ourselves.* This phrase, 'joy in the Holy Ghost,' represents Christians as so thinking and feeling under the workings of the Holy Ghost, that their joy may be viewed rather as that of the blessed Agent who inspires it than their own (cf. I Thess. 1:6). **18. For he that in these things**—'in this,' meaning this threefold life. **serveth Christ**—Here again observe how, though we do these three things as a "kingdom of *God,*" yet it is "*Christ*" that we serve in so doing; the apostle passing here from God to Christ as naturally as before from Christ to God—in a way to us inconceivable, if Christ had been viewed as a mere creature (cf. II Cor. 8:21). **is acceptable to God, and approved of men**—these being the things which God delights in, and men are constrained to approve. (Cf. Prov. 3:4; Luke 2:52; Acts 2:47; 19:20.)

Let every man be fully persuaded in his own mind—be guided in such matters by conscientious conviction.

14, 15. I know, and am persuaded by—or rather, 'in'—**the Lord Jesus**—as "having the mind of Christ" (I Cor. 2:16). **that there is nothing unclean of itself**—Hence it is that he calls those "the strong" who believed in the abolition of all ritual distinctions under the Gospel. (See Acts 10:15.)

but—'save that'—**to him that esteemeth anything to be unclean, to him it is unclean**—'and therefore, though *you* can eat of it without sin, *he cannot.*'

ADAM CLARKE

12. *Every one of us shall give account of himself.* We shall not, at the bar of God, be obliged to account for the conduct of each other—each shall give account of himself; and let him take heed that he be prepared to give up his accounts with joy.

17. *For the kingdom of God.* That holy religion which God has sent from heaven, and which He intends to make the instrument of establishing a counterpart of the Kingdom of glory among men. *Is not meat and drink.* It consists not in these outward and indifferent things. *But righteousness.* Pardon of sin, and holiness of heart and life. *And peace.* In the soul, from a sense of God's mercy; peace regulating, ruling, and harmonizing the heart. *And joy in the Holy Ghost.* Solid spiritual happiness, a joy which springs from a clear sense of God's mercy, the love of God being shed abroad in the heart by the *Holy Ghost.* In a word, it is happiness brought into the soul by the Holy Spirit, and maintained there by the same influence. This is a genuine counterpart of heaven: *righteousness* without sin, *peace* without inward disturbance, *joy* without any kind of mental agony or distressing fear.

18. *For he that in these things.* The man, whether Jew or Gentile, who *in these things*—"righteousness, and peace, and joy in the Holy Ghost"—*serveth Christ,* acts according to His doctrine, is *acceptable to God.* For he has not only the form of godliness in thus serving Christ, but he has the power, the very spirit and essence of it, in having "righteousness, and peace, and joy in the Holy Ghost"; and therefore the whole frame of his mind, as well as his acts, must be acceptable to God. *And approved of men;* for although religion may be persecuted, yet the righteous man who is continually laboring for the public good will be generally esteemed.

Let every man be fully persuaded. With respect to the propriety or non-propriety of keeping the above festivals let every man act from the plenary conviction of his own mind. There is a sufficient latitude allowed; all may be fully satisfied.

14. *I know, and am persuaded by the Lord Jesus.* After reasoning so long and so much with these contending parties on the subject of their mutual misunderstandings, without attempting to give any opinion, but merely to show them the folly and uncharitableness of their conduct, he now expresses himself fully and tells them that *nothing is unclean of itself,* and that he has the inspiration and authority of Jesus Christ to say so; for to such an inspiration he must refer in such words as *I know, and am persuaded by the Lord Jesus.* And yet, after having given them this decisive judgment, through respect to the tender, mistaken conscience of weak believers, he immediately adds: *But to him that esteemeth any thing to be unclean, to him it is unclean;* because if he act contrary to his conscience, he must necessarily contract guilt. For he who acts in opposition to his conscience in one case may do it in another, and thus even the plain declarations of the Word of God may be set aside on things of the utmost importance, as well as the erroneous though well-intentioned dictates of his conscience on matters which he makes of the last consequence, though others who are better taught know them to be indifferent. It is dangerous to trifle with conscience,

MATTHEW HENRY

standings. This order is broken if the understanding (though misguided) tells us that such a thing is a sin, and yet we will do it. This is a *will* to do evil; there is the same corruption of the will in the doing of it as if really it were a sin. It must be understood likewise with this proviso, though men's judgments and opinions may make that which is good in itself to become evil to them, yet they cannot make that which is evil in itself to become good.

4. Another rule here prescribed is to those who know their Christian liberty, yet to take heed of using it so as to give offence to a weak brother. This is laid down *v.* 13, *Let us not judge one another any more.* "*Judge this rather*, instead of censuring the practice of others, let us look to our own, that no *man put a stumbling-block, or an occasion to fall, in his brother's way.*" We must take heed of saying or doing anything which may occasion our brother to stumble or fall; which may be an occasion,

(1) Of grief to our brother, "One that is weak, and thinks it unlawful to eat such and such meats, will be greatly troubled to see thee eat them." Christians should take heed of grieving one another, and of saddening the hearts of Christ's little ones.

(2) Of guilt to our brother. The former is a *stumbling-block*, that gives our brother a great shake; but this is an *occasion to fall.* "If thy weak brother, purely by thy example and influence, be drawn to act against his conscience and to walk contrary to the light he has, and so to contract guilt upon his soul, thou art to be blamed for giving the occasion." To the same purport (*v.* 21) he recommends it to our care not to give offence by the use of lawful things: *It is good neither to eat flesh nor to drink wine;* these are things not necessary to the support of human life, and therefore we must deny ourselves in them, rather than give offence. *It is good*—pleasing to God, profitable to our brother, and no harm to ourselves. This is to be extended to all things whereby thy brother stumbleth, or is offended, is involved either in sin or in trouble: or *is made weak*—his graces weakened, his comforts weakened, his resolutions weakened. Observe the motives to enforce this caution.

[1] Consider the royal law of Christian love and charity, which is hereby broken (*v.* 15): *If thy brother be grieved with thy meat.* Possibly thou art ready to say, "Now he talks foolishly and weakly." We are apt, in such a case, to lay all the blame on that side. But the reproof is here given to the stronger: *Now walkest thou not charitably.* Thus the apostle takes part with the weakest, and condemns the defect in love on the one side more than the defect in knowledge on the other side. Charity to the souls of our brethren is the best charity. True love would make us tender of their peace and purity, and beget a regard to their consciences as well as to our own. Christ deals gently with those that have true grace, though they are weak in it.

[2] Consider the design of Christ's death: *Destroy not him with thy meat for whom Christ died, v.* 15. *First,* Drawing a soul to sin threatens the destruction of that soul. It denotes an utter destruction. *Secondly,* The consideration of the love of Christ in dying for souls should make us very tender of the happiness and salvation of souls. Did Christ quit a life for souls, such a life, and shall not we quit a morsel of meat for them? Did he think it worth while to deny himself so much for them as to die for them, and shall not we think it worth while to deny ourselves so little for them?—*With thy meat.* Thou pleadest that it is thy own meat, but remember that, though the meat is thine, the brother offended by it is Christ's.

JAMIESON, FAUSSET, BROWN

13. Let us not therefore judge—'assume the office of judge over'—**one another; but judge this rather . . .**—a beautiful sort of play upon the word 'judge,' meaning, 'But let this be your judgment, not to put a stumbling block. . . .'

21. It is good not to eat flesh, nor to drink wine, nor any thing—'nor to do any thing'—**whereby**—'wherein'—**thy brother stumbleth, or is offended, or is made weak**—rather, 'is weak.' These three words, it has been remarked, are each intentionally weaker than the other:—'Which may cause a brother to stumble, or even be obstructed in his Christian course, nay—though neither of these may follow—wherein he continues weak; unable wholly to disregard the example, and yet unprepared to follow it.' But this injunction to abstain from *flesh,* from *wine,* and from *whatsoever* may hurt the conscience of a brother, must be properly understood. Manifestly, the apostle is treating of the regulation of the Christain's conduct with reference simply to the prejudices of the weak in faith; and his directions are to be considered not as *prescriptions for one's entire lifetime,* even to promote the good of men on a large scale, but simply as cautions against the too free use of Christian liberty in matters where other Christians, through weakness, are not persuaded that such liberty is divinely allowed. How far the *principle* involved in this may be legitimately extended, we do not inquire here; but ere we consider that question, it is of great importance to fix how far it is here actually expressed, and what is the precise nature of the illustrations given of it.

But if thy brother be grieved—has his weak conscience hurt—**with thy meat**—rather, 'because of meat.' The word "meat" is purposely selected as something contemptible in contrast with the tremendous risk run for its sake. Accordingly, in the next clause, that idea is brought out with great strength.

Destroy not him with—'by'—**thy meat for whom Christ died**—"The worth of even the poorest and weakest brother cannot be more emphatically expressed than by the words, 'for whom Christ died' " [OLSHAUSEN]. The same sentiment is expressed with equal sharpness in I Corinthians 8:11. *Whatever tends to make anyone violate his conscience tends to the destruction of his soul; and he who helps, whether wittingly or no, to bring about the one is guilty of aiding to accomplish the other.*

ADAM CLARKE

even when erroneous; it should be borne with and instructed; it must be won over, not taken by storm. Its feelings should be respected because they ever refer to God, and have their foundation in His fear. He who sins against his conscience in things which everyone else knows to be indifferent will soon do it in those things in which his salvation is most intimately concerned. It is a great blessing to have a well-informed conscience; it is a blessing to have a tender conscience; and even a sore conscience is infinitely better than none.

13. *Let us not therefore judge one another any more.* Let us abandon such rash conduct. It is dangerous; it is uncharitable. Judgment belongs to the Lord. *That no man put a stumblingblock.* Let both the converted Jew and Gentile consider that they should labor to promote each other's spiritual interests, and not be a means of hindering each other in their Christian course; or of causing them to abandon the gospel, on which, and not on questions of rites and ceremonies, the salvation of their soul depends.

21. *It is good neither to eat flesh.* The spirit and self-denying principles of the gospel teach us that we should not only avoid everything in eating or drinking which may be an occasion of offense or apostasy to our brethren, but even to lay down our lives for them should it be necessary. *Whereby thy brother stumbleth. Proskoptei* from *pros,* "against," and *kopto,* "to strike, to hit the foot against a stone in walking, so as to halt, and be impeded in one's journey." It here means, spiritually, anything by which a man is so perplexed in his mind as to be prevented from making due progress in the divine life, anything by which he is caused to halt, to be undecisive, and undetermined; and under such an influence no man has ever yet grown in grace and in the knowledge of Jesus Christ. *Or is offended. Scandalizetai* from *scandalon,* a "stumbling block"; anything by which a person is caused to fall, especially into a snare, trap, or gin. Originally the word signified the piece of wood or key in a trap which, being trodden on, caused the animal to fall into a pit or the trap to close upon him. In the New Testament it generally refers to total apostasy from the Christian religion, and this appears to be its meaning in this place. *Or is made weak.* Without mental vigor; without power sufficiently to distinguish between right and wrong, good and evil, lawful and unlawful. The last two terms are omitted by two excellent MSS. and by some of the primitive fathers. It is very likely that they were added by some early hand by way of illustration.

15. *If thy brother be grieved.* If he thinks that you do wrong, and he is in consequence stumbled at your conduct. *Now walkest thou not charitably.* "According to love," for "love worketh no ill to his neighbour"; but by your eating some particular kind of meat on which neither your life nor well-being depends, you work ill to him by grieving and distressing his mind; and therefore you break the law of God in reference to him, while pretending that your Christian liberty raises you above his scruples. *Destroy not him with thy meat, for whom Christ died.* This puts the uncharitable conduct of the person in question in the strongest light, because it supposes that the weak brother may be so stumbled as to fall and perish finally, even the man *for whom Christ died.* To injure a man in his circumstances is bad; to injure him in his person is worse; to injure him in his reputation it still worse; and to injure his soul is worst of all. No wickedness, no malice, can go further than to injure and destroy the soul. Your uncharitable conduct may proceed thus far; therefore you are highly criminal before God. From this verse we learn that a man for whom Christ died may perish, or have his soul destroyed, and destroyed with such a destruction as implies perdition; the original is very emphatic. Christ died in his stead; do not destroy his soul. The sacrificial death is as strongly expressed as it can be, and there is no word in the New Testament that more forcibly implies eternal ruin than the verb *apollyo,* from which is derived that most significant name of the devil, Apollyon, the "Destroyer," the great universal murderer of souls.

MATTHEW HENRY

[3] Consider the work of God (*v.* 20): "*For meat destroy not the work of God.*" Do not undo that which God hath done. You should work together with God, do not countermine his work. The work of grace and peace is the work of God. The same for whom Christ died (*v.* 15) are here called the work of God; besides the work that is wrought for us there is a work to be wrought in us. Every saint is God's workmanship. We must be very careful to do nothing which tends to the destruction of this work, either in ourselves or others. We must deny ourselves rather than obstruct and prejudice our own or others' grace and peace. Many do for meat and drink destroy the work of God in themselves, so likewise in others. Think what thou destroyest—*the work of God*; think for what thou destroyest it—*for meat*, which was but for the belly, and the belly for it.

[4] Consider the evil of giving offence. He grants that *all things indeed are pure*. But, if we abuse this liberty, it turns into sin to us: *It is evil to him that eats with offence*. Lawful things may be done unlawfully. It is observable that the apostle directs his reproof most against those who gave the offence. He directs his speech to the strong, because they were better able to bear the reproof, and to begin the reformation. For the further pressing of this rule, we may here observe two directions.—*First, Let not then your good be evil spoken of* (*v.* 16)—take heed of doing any thing which may give occasion to others to speak evil, either of the Christian religion in general, or of your Christian liberty in particular. It is true we cannot hinder loose and ungoverned tongues from speaking evil of us, and of the best things we have; but we must not (if we can help it) give them any occasion to do it. We must deny ourselves in many cases for the preservation of our credit and reputation, forbearing to do that which we rightly know we may lawfully do, when our doing it may be a prejudice to our good name. In such a case we must rather cross ourselves than shame ourselves. We should manage all our good duties in such a manner that they may not be evil spoken of. As we tender the reputation of the good we profess and practise, let us so order it that it may not be evil spoken of. *Secondly, Hast thou faith? Have it to thyself before God*, *v.* 22. "Art thou satisfied that thou mayest eat all meats, and observe all days (except the Lord's day) alike? *Have it to thyself*, and do not trouble others by the imprudent use of it." In these indifferent things, though we must never contradict our persuasion, yet we may sometimes conceal it, when the avowing of it will do more hurt than good. A rule to thyself (not to be imposed upon others, or made a rule to them), or a rejoicing to thyself. Paul had faith in these things: *I am persuaded that there is nothing unclean of itself;* but he had it to himself, so as not to use his liberty to the offence of others. In things necessary let there be unity, in things unnecessary let there be liberty, and in both let there be charity.—*Have it to thyself before God.* The end of such knowledge is that we may have a conscience void of offence towards God. Those are right indeed that are so in God's sight.

It is a dangerous thing to put a force upon conscience, though it be under a mistake (*v.* 22). *Happy is he that condemns not himself in that thing which he allows.* Many a one allows himself in practice to do that which yet in his judgment and conscience he condemns himself for. Whilst he does it his own heart gives him the lie, and his conscience condemns him for it. Now, happy is the man who so orders his conversation as not to expose himself to the reproaches of his own conscience. He is happy that has peace and quietness within.

5. There is one rule more laid down here: *Let us therefore follow after the things which make for peace, and things wherewith one may edify another*, *v.* 91. We must study mutual peace. Many wish for peace, and talk loudly for it, that do not follow the things that make for peace. Meekness, humility, self-denial, and love, are the springs of peace, the things that make for our peace. We are not always so happy as to obtain peace; there are so many that delight in war: but the God of peace will accept us if we follow after the things that make for peace. We must study mutual edification. We cannot edify one another, while we are quarrelling and contending. We are God's building, God's temple, and have need to be edified. None so strong but they may be edified; none so weak but may edify.

Nor must we act against the dictates of a doubting conscience. He *that doubteth is damned if he eat* (*v.* 23), that is, it turns into sin to him; *he is condemned* of his own conscience, because he *eateth not of faith*, because he does that which he is not fully persuaded he may lawfully do. Here his own

JAMIESON, FAUSSET, BROWN

For—'For the sake of'—**meat destroy not the work of God**—See on vs. 15. The apostle sees in whatever tends to violate a brother's conscience the *incipient* destruction of God's work (for every converted man is such)—on the same principle as "he that hateth his brother is a murderer" (I John 3:15).

All things indeed are pure—'clean'; the ritual distinctions being at an end. **but it is evil to that man**—there is criminality in the man—**who eateth with offence**—i.e., so as to stumble a weak brother.

16, 17. Let not then your good—i.e., this liberty of yours as to Jewish meats and days, well founded though it be—**be evil spoken of**—for the evil it does to others.

22. Hast thou faith—on such matters? **have it to thyself**—within thine own breast—**before God**—a most important clause. It is not mere *sincerity*, or a private *opinion*, of which the apostle speaks; it is conviction as to what is the truth and will of God. If thou hast formed this conviction in the sight of God, keep thyself in this frame before Him. Of course, this is not to be over-pressed, as if it were wrong to discuss such points at all with our weaker brethren. All that is here condemned is such a zeal for small points as endangers Christian love.

Happy is he that condemneth not himself in that which he alloweth—allows himself to do nothing, about the lawfulness of which he has scruples; does only what he neither knows nor fears to be sinful.

19. the things . . .—more simply, 'the things of peace, and the things of mutual edification.'

23. And—rather, 'But'—**he that doubteth is damned**—See on the word "damnation," ch. 13:2. **if he eat, because he eateth not of faith**—See on the meaning of "faith" here, vs. 22.

ADAM CLARKE

20. *For meat destroy not the work of God.* Do not hinder the progress of the gospel either in your own souls or in those of others by contending about lawful or unlawful meats. And do not destroy the soul of your Christian brother, v. 15, by offending him so as to induce him to apostatize.

All things indeed are pure. This is a repetition of the sentiment delivered in v. 14, in different words. Nothing that is proper for aliment is unlawful to be eaten; *but it is evil for that man who eateth with offence*—the man who either eats contrary to his own conscience or so as to grieve and stumble another does an evil act; and however lawful the thing may be in itself, his conduct does not please God.

16. *Let not then your good be evil spoken of.* Do not make such a use of your Christian liberty as to subject the gospel itself to reproach. Whatsoever you do, do it in such a manner, spirit, and time as to make it productive of the greatest possible good. There are many who have such an unhappy method of doing their good acts as not only to do little or no good by them but a great deal of evil. It requires much prudence and watchfulness to find out the proper time of performing even a good action.

22. *Hast thou faith?* The term *faith* seems to signify in this place a "full persuasion in a man's mind that he is right," that what he does is lawful, and has the approbation of God and his conscience. *Happy is he that condemneth not.* That man only can enjoy peace of conscience who acts according to the full persuasion which God has given him of the lawfulness of his conduct, whereas he must be miserable who allows himself in the practice of anything for which his conscience upbraids and accuses him. This is a most excellent maxim, and every genuine Christian should be careful to try every part of his conduct by it. If a man have not peace in his own bosom, he cannot be happy; and no man can have peace who sins against his conscience. If a man's passions or appetite allow or instigate him to a particular thing, let him take good heed that his conscience approve what his passions allow, and that he live not the subject of continual self-condemnation and reproach. Even the man who has the too scrupulous conscience had better, in such matters as are in question, obey its erroneous dictates than violate this moral feeling and live only to condemn the actions he is constantly performing.

19. *Let us therefore follow.* Far from contending about meats, drinks, and festival times, in which it is not likely that the Jews and Gentiles will soon agree, let us endeavor to the utmost of our power to promote peace and unanimity, that we may be instrumental in edifying each other, in promoting religious knowledge and piety instead of being stumbling blocks in each other's way.

23. *And he that doubteth.* This verse is a necessary part of the preceding, and should be read thus: "But he that doubteth is condemned if he eat, because he eateth not of faith." The meaning is sufficiently plain. He that feeds on any kind of meats prohibited by the Mosaic law with the persuasion in his mind that he may be wrong in so doing is condemned by his conscience for doing that which he has reason to think God has forbidden. *For whatsoever is not of faith is sin.* Whatever he does, without a full persuasion of its lawfulness (see v. 22), is to him *sin*, for he does it under a conviction that

MATTHEW HENRY

heart cannot but condemn him as a transgressor.—*For whatsoever is not of faith is sin.* Whatever is done while we are not clearly persuaded of the lawfulness of it, is a sin against conscience. He that will venture to do that which his own conscience suggests to him to be unlawful, when it is not so in itself, will by a like temptation be brought to do that which his conscience tells him is unlawful when it is really so.

CHAPTER 15

Verses 1–4

The apostle here lays down two precepts, showing the duty of the strong Christian to consider the weakest.

I. We must *bear the infirmities of the weak, v.* 1. We all have our infirmities; but the weak are more subject to them than others. We must bear with their infirmities, and not have our affections alienated from them. Thus Christ bore with his weak disciples. We must also bear their infirmities by sympathizing with them, ministering strength to them. This is bearing one another's burdens.

II. We must not please ourselves, but our neighbour, *v.* 1, 2.

1. Christians must not please themselves. It is good for us to cross ourselves sometimes, and then we shall the better bear others crossing of us. We shall be spoiled if we be always humoured. The first lesson we have to learn is to deny ourselves, Matt. xvi. 24.

2. Christians must please their brethren. Christians should study to be pleasing. How amiable and comfortable a society would the church of Christ be if Christians would study to please one another!—*Please his neighbour,* not in everything, but *for his good,* especially for the good of his soul. *To edification,* that is, not only for his profit, but for the profit of others, to edify the body of Christ. The closer the stones lie, and the better they are squared to fit one another, the stronger is the building. *For even Christ pleased not himself.* The self-denial of our Lord Jesus is the best argument against the selfishness of Christians.

(1) Christ pleased not himself. He did not consult his own worldly credit, ease, safety, nor pleasure; he emptied himself, and made himself of no reputation: and all this for our sakes, and to set us an example. His whole life was a self-denying, self-displeasing life.

(2) Herein the scripture was fulfilled: *As it is written, The reproaches of those that reproached thee fell on me.* It is quoted to show that Christ was so far from pleasing himself that he did in the highest degree displease himself. In his humiliation the content and satisfaction of natural inclination were altogether crossed and denied. He preferred our benefit before his own ease and pleasure. This the apostle chooses to express in scripture language. The shame of those reproaches, which Christ underwent. Whatever dishonour was done to God was a trouble to the Lord Jesus. Christ also did himself endure the greatest indignities; there was much of reproach in his suffering. The sin of those reproaches. Every sin is a kind of reproach to God. Now the guilt of these fell upon Christ, when he was made a sin-offering for us. Nothing could be more contrary to him, nor more against him, than to be made sin and a curse for us, and to have the reproaches of God fall upon him. We must not please ourselves, for Christ pleased not himself; we must bear the infirmities of the weak, for Christ bore the reproaches of those that reproached God. He bore the guilt of sin and the curse for it; we are only called to bear a little of the trouble of it. He bore the presumptuous sins of the wicked; we are called only to bear the infirmities of the weak.—*Even Christ.* Even he pleased not himself, even he bore

JAMIESON, FAUSSET, BROWN

for whatsoever is not of faith is sin—a maxim of unspeakable importance in the Christian life.—

CHAPTER 15

Vss. 1-13. Same Subject Continued and Concluded. **1. We then that are strong**—on such points as have been discussed, the abolition of the Jewish distinction of meats and days under the Gospel. See on ch. 14:14, 20.

ought . . . not to please ourselves—ought to think less of what we may lawfully do than of how our conduct will affect others.

2,

3. Let every one of us—lay himself out to—**please his neighbour**—not indeed for his mere gratification, but—**for his good**—with a view—**to his edification. For even Christ pleased not**—lived not to please—**himself;**

but, as it is written—(Ps. 69:9)—**The reproaches . . .** —see Mark 10:42-45.

ADAM CLARKE

he may be wrong in so doing. Therefore if he makes a distinction in his own conscience between different kinds of meats, and yet eats of all indifferently, he is a sinner before God. There are few readers who have not remarked that the last three verses of this Epistle (chap. xvi. 25-27) appear to stand in their present place without any obvious connection, and apparently after the Epistle is concluded. And it is well-known to critics that a number of MSS. and versions add those verses at the end of the fourteenth chapter. These words certainly connect better with the close of the fourteenth chapter and the beginning of the fifteenth than they do with the conclusion of the sixteenth, where they are now generally found. But I shall defer my observations upon them till I come to that place, with only this remark, that the *stablishing* mentioned in chap. xvi. 25 corresponds well with the *doubting* of chap. xiv. 23; and indeed the whole matter of these verses agrees so well with the subject so largely handled in the preceding chapter that there can be very little doubt of their being in their proper place if joined to the end of this chapter, as they are in some MSS. and versions.

CHAPTER 15

1. *We then that are strong.* The sense of this verse is supposed to be the following: We Gentile Christians who perfectly understand the nature of our gospel liberty not only lawfully may, but are bound in duty to, bear any inconveniences that may arise from the scruples of the weaker brethren, and to ease their consciences by prudently abstaining from such indifferent things as may offend and trouble them, and not take advantage from our superior knowledge to make them submit to our judgment.

2. *Let every one of us please his neighbour.* For it should be a maxim with each of us to do all in our power to please our brethren, and especially in those things in which their spiritual edification is concerned. Though we should not indulge men in mere whims and caprices, yet we should bear with their ignorance and their weakness, knowing that others had much to bear with from us before we came to our present advanced state of religious knowledge.

3. *For even Christ pleased not himself.* Christ never acted as One who sought His own ease or profit. He not only bore with the weakness, but with the insults, of His creatures; as it is written in Ps. lxix. 9: *The reproaches of them that reproached thee fell on me*—I not only bore their insults, but bore the punishment due to them for their vicious and abominable conduct. That this psalm refers to the Messiah and His sufferings for mankind is evident, not only from the quotation here, but also from John xix. 28-29, when our Lord's receiving the vinegar during His expiatory suffering is said to be a fulfilling of the scripture, viz., of v. 21 of this very psalm; and His cleansing the Temple, John ii. 15-17, is said to be a fulfillment of v. 9, "For the zeal of thine house hath eaten me up," the former part of which verse the apostle quotes here.

MATTHEW HENRY

our sins. And should not we be humble, and self-denying, and ready to consider one another.

(3) Therefore we must go and do likewise: *For whatsoever things were written aforetime were written for our learning.* [1] That which is written of Christ, is *written for our learning*; he hath left us an example. The example of Christ is recorded for our imitation. [2] That which is written in the scriptures of the Old Testament is written for our learning. What happened to the Old Testament saints happened to them for ensample. They are *written*, that they might remain for our use and benefit. *First*, For our learning. We must therefore labour, not only to understand the literal meaning of the scripture, but to learn out of it that which will do us good. Practical observations are more necessary than critical expositions. *Secondly*, *That we through patience and comfort of the scriptures might have hope.* The scripture was written that we might know what to hope for from God. Now the way of attaining this hope is *through patience and comfort of the scripture*. Patience and comfort suppose trouble and sorrow; such is the lot of the saints in this world. But both these befriend that hope which is the life of our souls. Patience works experience, and experience hope, which maketh not ashamed, *ch.* v. 3–5. The more patience we exercise under troubles the more hopefully we may look through our troubles; nothing more destructive to hope than impatience. And the *comfort of the scriptures*, that comfort which springs from the word of God is likewise a great stay to hope, as it is an earnest in hand of the good hoped for.

Verses 5, 6

The apostle, having delivered two exhortations, intermixes here a prayer for the success of what he had said.

I. The title he gives to God: *The God of patience and consolation.* He gives the grace of patience; he confirms and keeps it up as the God of consolation. When he comes to beg the pouring out of the spirit of love and unity he addresses himself to God as the God of patience and consolation. 1. As a God that bears with us and comforts us, is not extreme to mark what we do amiss—to teach us so to testify our love to our brethren. Or, 2. As a God that gives us patience and comfort. He had spoken (*v.* 4) of patience and comfort of the scriptures; it comes through the scripture as the conduit-pipe, but from God as the fountain-head. Nothing breaks the peace more than an impatient, and peevish, melancholy temper.

II. The mercy he begs of God: *Grant you to be like-minded one towards another, according to Christ Jesus.* The foundation of Christian love and peace is laid in likemindedness. This like-mindedness must be *according to Christ Jesus*, according to the precept of Christ, the royal law of love, according to the pattern and example of Christ, which he had propounded to them for their imitation, *v.* 3. The method of our prayer must be first for truth, and then for peace; for such is the method of the wisdom that is from above: *it is first pure, then peaceable.* This is to be like-minded according to Christ Jesus. Like-mindedness among Christians, according to Christ Jesus, is the gift of God. We are taught to pray that the will of God may be done on earth as it is done in heaven: now there it is done unanimously, among the angels; and our desire must be that the saints on earth may do so too.

III. The end of his desire: that God may be glorified, *v.* 6. We should have the glory of God in our eye in every prayer. Like-mindedness among Christians is in order to our glorifying God, 1. *With one mind and one mouth.* It will not suffice that there be one mouth, but there must be one mind; nay, there will hardly be one mouth where there is not one mind. 2. As *the Father of our Lord Jesus Christ.* God must be glorified as he has now revealed himself in the face of Jesus Christ, in whom he is our Father. The unity of Christians glorifies *God as the Father of our Lord Jesus Christ.*

Verses 7–12

He had exhorted the strong to receive the weak (*ch.* xiv. 1), here, *Receive one another;* for sometimes the prejudices of the weak Christian make him shy of the strong, as much as the pride of the strong Christian makes him shy of the weak, neither of which ought to be. Let there be a mutual embracing among Christians. Now the reason why Christians must receive one another is taken, as before, from the condescending love of Christ to us: *As Christ also received us, to the glory of God.* Has Christ been so kind to us, and shall we be so unkind to those that are his? Christ has received us into the nearest and dearest relations to himself. He has received us

JAMIESON, FAUSSET, BROWN

4. For whatsoever things were written aforetime were written for our learning—'instruction'-

-**that we through . . .** —'through the comfort and the patience of the Scriptures'—**might have hope**—i.e., 'Think not that because such portions of Scripture relate immediately to Christ, they are inapplicable to you; for though Christ's sufferings, as a Saviour, were exclusively His own, the *motives* that prompted them, the *spirit* in which they were endured, and the *general principle* involved in His whole work—self-sacrifice for the good of others—furnish our most perfect and beautiful model; and so all Scripture relating to these is for our instruction; and since the duty of *forbearance,* the strong with the weak, requires "patience," and this again needs "comfort," all those Scriptures which tell of *patience* and *consolation,* particularly of the patience of Christ, and of the consolation which sustained Him under it, are our appointed and appropriate nutriment, ministering to us "*hope*" of that blessed day when these shall no more be needed.' See on ch. 4, *Note* 7. (For the same connection between "patience and hope" see on ch. 12:12, and I Thess. 1:3). **5, 6. Now the God of patience and consolation**—Such beautiful names of God are taken from the graces which He inspires: as "the God of hope" (vs. 13), "the God of peace" (vs. 33).-

-**grant you to be like minded**—'of the same mind'—**according to Christ Jesus**—It is not mere unanimity which the apostle seeks for them; for unanimity in evil is to be deprecated. But it is "*according to Christ Jesus*"—after the sublimest model of Him whose all-absorbing desire was to do, "not His own will, but the will of Him that sent Him" (John 6:38). *That* . . . —rather, 'that with one accord ye may with one mouth glorify the God and Father of our Lord Jesus Christ'; the mind and the mouth of all giving harmonious glory to His name. What a prayer! And shall this never be realized on earth?

7. Wherefore—returning to the point—**receive ye one another . . . to the glory of God**—If Christ received us, and bears with all our weaknesses, well may we receive and compassionate one with another, and by so doing God will be glorified.

ADAM CLARKE

4. *For whatsoever things were written aforetime.* This refers not only to the quotation from Psalms 69, but to all the Old Testament scriptures; for it can be to no other scriptures that the apostle alludes. And from what he says here of them, we learn that God had not intended them merely for those generations in which they were first delivered, but for the instruction of all the succeeding generations of mankind.

That we through patience and comfort of the scriptures—that we, through those remarkable examples of *patience* exhibited by the saints and followers of God, whose history is given in those scriptures, and the *comfort* which they derived from God in their patient endurance of sufferings brought upon them through their faithful attachment to truth and righteousness—*might have hope* that we shall be upheld and blessed as they were, and our sufferings become the means of our greater advances in faith and holiness, and consequently our hope of eternal glory be the more confirmed. Some think that the word which we translate *comfort* should be rendered "exhortation"; but there is certainly no need here to leave the usual acceptation of the term, as the word comfort makes a regular and consistent sense with the rest of the verse.

5. *Now the God of patience and consolation.* May that God who endued them with *patience,* and gave them the *consolation* that supported them in all their trials and afflictions,

grant you to be likeminded—give you the same mode of thinking and the same power of acting towards each other, *according* to the example of *Christ.*

6. *That ye*—Jews and Gentiles—*may with one mind.* Thinking the same things, and bearing with each other, after the example of Christ. *And one mouth,* in all your religious assemblies, without jarring or contentions. *Glorify God* for calling you into such a state of salvation, and showing himself to be your loving, compassionate Father, as he is *the Father of our Lord Jesus Christ.* It is very likely that the apostle refers here to religious acts in public worship which might have been greatly interrupted by the dissensions between the converted Jews and the converted Gentiles. These differences he labors to compose; and after having done all that was necessary in the way of instruction and exhortation, he now pours out his soul to God, who alone could rule and manage the heart, that He would enable them to think the same things, to be of the same judgment, and that all, feeling their obligation to Him, might join in the sweetest harmony in every act of religious worship.

7. *Wherefore receive ye one another.* Have the most affectionate regard for each other, and acknowledge each other as the servants and children of God Almighty.

As Christ also received us. In the same manner and with the same cordial affection as Christ has received us into communion with himself, and has made us partakers of such inestimable blessings,

MATTHEW HENRY

(though we were strangers and enemies, and had played the prodigal) into fellowship and communion with himself. Those words, *to the glory of God*, may refer both to Christ's receiving us, which is our pattern, and to our receiving one another, which is our practice according to that pattern.

I. Christ hath received us to the glory of God. The end of our reception by Christ is that we might glorify God in this world, and be glorified with him in that to come. We are called to an eternal glory by Christ Jesus, John xvii. 24.

II. We must receive one another to the glory of God. This must be our great end in all our actions, that God may be glorified; and nothing more conduces to this than the mutual love and kindness of those that profess religion; compare *v.* 6, *That you may with one mind and one mouth glorify God.* He shows how Jesus Christ has received both Jews and Gentiles; in him they are both one, *one new man*, Eph. ii. 14–16. Those that agree in Christ may well afford to agree among themselves.

1. He received the Jews, *v.* 8. Let not any think hardly or scornfully therefore of those that were originally Jews. (1) Jesus Christ was a *minister of the circumcision.* He was a *minister—a servant.* Christ blessed them, looked upon himself as primarily sent to the *lost sheep of the house of Israel, laid hold of the seed of Abraham* (Heb. ii. 16, margin), and by them, as it were, caught at the whole body of mankind. Christ's personal ministry was appropriated to them. (2) He was so for the truth of God. That is, to make good the promises given to the patriarchs concerning the special mercy God had in store for their seed.—*To confirm the promises made unto the fathers.* The best confirmation of promises is the performance of them. When Messiah the Prince appeared in the fulness of time, as a minister of the circumcision, all these promises were confirmed. In Christ all the promises of God are Yea, and in him Amen.

2. He received the Gentiles likewise. This he shows, *v.* 9–12.

(1) Christ's favour to the Gentiles. One design of Christ was that the Gentiles likewise might be converted. A good reason why they should not think the worse of any Christian for his having been formerly a Gentile; for Christ has received him. *That the Gentiles might glorify God for his mercy.* They shall have matter for praise, even the mercy of God. Considering the miserable and deplorable condition that the Gentile world was in, the receiving of them appears more as an act of mercy than the receiving of the Jews. The greatest mercy of God to any people is the receiving of them into covenant with himself. They shall have a heart for praise. They shall glorify God for his mercy. God intended to reap a harvest of glory from the Gentiles, who had been so long turning his glory into shame.

(2) The fulfilling of the scriptures in this. The favour of God to the Gentiles was not only mercy, but truth. Though there were not promises directly given to them, yet there were many prophesies concerning them, which related to the calling of them, some of which he mentioned. Thus, by referring them to the Old Testament, he labours to qualify their dislike of the Gentiles. [1] It was foretold that the Gentiles should have the gospel preached to them: "*I will confess to thee among the Gentiles* (*v.* 9), thy name shall be known and owned in the Gentile world." Christ, in and by his apostles and ministers, whom he sent to disciple all nations, did confess to God among the Gentiles. Christ's declaring God's name to his brethren is called *his praising God in the midst of the congregation*, Ps. xxii. 22. When David's psalms are read and sung among the Gentiles, to the praise and glory of God, it may be said that David is *confessing to God among the Gentiles, and singing to his name.* He that was the sweet psalmist of Israel is now the sweet psalmist of the Gentiles. Converting grace makes people greatly in love with David's psalms. If any confess to God among the Gentiles, and sing to his name, it is not they, but Christ and his grace in them. [2] The Gentiles should *rejoice with his people*, *v.* 10. Those Jews that retain a prejudice against the Gentiles will by no means admit them to any of their joyful festivities. But, the partition-wall being taken down, the Gentiles are welcome to rejoice with his people. [3] They should praise God (*v.* 11): *Praise the Lord, all ye Gentiles.* Converting grace sets people praising God. The Gentiles had been, for many ages, praising their idols of wood and stone, but now they are brought to praise the Lord. [4] They should believe in Christ (*v.* 12), quoted from Isa. xi. 10. *First,* The revelation of Christ, as the Gentiles' king. He is here called *the root of Jesse.* Christ, as God, was David's root; Christ, as man, was David's offspring.—*And he that shall rise to reign over the Gentiles.* When Christ rose from the dead, when he

JAMIESON, FAUSSET, BROWN

8-12. Now—'For' is the true reading: the apostle is merely assigning an additional motive to Christian forbearance. **I say that Jesus Christ was**—'hath become'—**a minister of the circumcision**—a remarkable expression, meaning 'the Father's Servant for the salvation of the circumcision (or, of Israel).' **for the truth of God**—to make good the veracity of God towards His ancient people. **to confirm the**—Messianic—**promises made unto the fathers**—To cheer the Jewish believers, whom he might seem to have been disparaging, and to keep down Gentile pride, the apostle holds up Israel's salvation as the primary end of Christ's mission.

But next after this, Christ was sent—**that the Gentiles might glorify God for his mercy**—A number of quotations from the Old Testament here follow, to show that God's plan of mercy embraced, from the first, the Gentiles along with the Jews.

as it is written—(Ps. 18:49)—**I will confess to**—i.e., glorify—**thee among the Gentiles . . .**

And again—(Deut. 32:43, though there is some difficulty in the *Heb.*)—**Rejoice, ye Gentiles**—along— **with his people**—Israel. **And again**—(Ps. 117:1)—**Praise the Lord, all ye Gentiles; and laud him, all ye people**—'peoples'—the various nations outside the pale of Judaism.

And again, Esaias saith—(Isa. 11:10)—**There shall be a**—'the'—**root of Jesse**—meaning, not 'He from whom Jesse sprang,' but 'He that is sprung from Jesse' (i.e., Jesse's son David)—see Revelation 22:16. **and he that shall rise . . .** —So the LXX in substantial, though not verbal, agreement with the original.

ADAM CLARKE

condescending to be present in all our assemblies. And as Christ has received us thus to the glory of God, so should we, Jews and Gentiles, cordially receive each other, that God's glory may be promoted by our harmony and brotherly love.

8. *Jesus Christ was a minister of the circumcision.* To show the Gentiles the propriety of bearing with the scrupulous Jews, he shows them here that they were under the greatest obligations to his people; to whom, in the days of His flesh, Jesus Christ confined His ministry, giving the world to see that He allowed the claim of the Jews as having the first right to the blessings of the gospel. And He confined His ministry thus to the Jews to *confirm the truth of God* contained in the *promises* made unto the patriarchs; for God had declared that thus it should be; and Jesus Christ, by coming according to the promise, has fulfilled this truth by making good the promises. Therefore salvation is of the Jews, as a kind of right conveyed to them through the promises made to their fathers. But this salvation was not exclusively designed for the Jewish people, as God by His prophets had repeatedly declared.

9. *And that the Gentiles might glorify God for his mercy.* As the Jews were to glorify God for His *truth,* so the Gentiles were to glorify God for His *mercy.* The Jews received the blessings of the gospel by right of promise, which promise God had most punctually and circumstantially fulfilled. The Gentiles had received the same gospel as an effect of God's mere mercy, having no right in consequence of any promise or engagement made with any of their ancestors, though they were originally included in the covenant made with Abraham.

I will confess to thee among the Gentiles. This quotation is taken from Ps. xviii. 49, and shows that the Gentiles had a right to glorify God for His mercy to them.

MATTHEW HENRY

ascended on high, it was to reign over the Gentiles. *Secondly*, The recourse of the Gentiles to him: *In him shall the Gentiles trust*. The prophet has it, *to him shall the Gentiles seek*. The method of faith is first to seek unto Christ, as to one proposed to us for a Saviour; and, finding him able and willing to save, then to trust in him. Those that know him will trust in him. This seeking to him is the effect of a trust in him. We shall never seek to Christ till we trust in him. Trust is the mother; diligence in the use of means the daughter. Jews and Gentiles being thus united in Christ's love, why should they not be united in one another's love?

Verse 13

Here is another prayer directed to God, as the God of hope.

I. He addresses himself to God, as the *God of hope*. He is the foundation on which our hope is built, and he is the builder that doth himself raise it: he is both the object of our hope, and the author of it. That hope is but fancy, which is not fastened upon God and which is not of his working in us.

II. What he asks of God, not for himself, but for them.

1. *That they might be filled with all joy and peace in believing*. Joy and peace are two of those things in which the kingdom of God consists, *ch*. xiv. 17. (1) How desirable this joy and peace are; they are filling. Carnal joy puffs up the soul, but cannot fill it. True, heavenly, spiritual joy is filling to the soul; it has a satisfaction in it, answerable to the soul's vast and just desires. Nothing more than this joy, only more of it, even the perfection of it in glory, is the desire of the soul that hath it. (2) How it is attainable. By prayer. Prayer fetches in spiritual joy and peace. By believing. True substantial joy is the fruit of faith. It is owing to the weakness of our faith that we are so much wanting in joy and peace. Only believe; believe the goodness of Christ, the love of Christ, and the result must needs be joy and peace. It is *all* joy and peace—all sorts of true joy and peace. When we come to God by prayer we must enlarge our desires. Ask for all joy.

2. That they might *abound in hope through the power of the Holy Ghost*. What is laid out upon them is but little, compared with what is laid up for them; therefore the more hope they have the more joy and peace they have. Christians should desire and labour after an abundance of hope, such hope as will not make ashamed. This is through the power of the Holy Ghost. Our own power will never reach it; and therefore where this hope is, and is abounding, the blessed spirit must have all the glory.

Verses 14-16

I. He commends these Christians. He began his epistle with their praises (*ch*. i. 8), *Your faith is spoken of throughout the world*. Because sometimes he had reproved them sharply, he now concludes with the like commendation, to part friends. It was not a piece of idle flattery, but a due acknowledgment of their worth, and of the grace of God in them. We must be forward to observe and commend in others that which is excellent and praiseworthy. Paul had no personal acquaintance with these Christians, and yet he says he was persuaded of their excellencies, though he knew them only by hearsay. As we must not, on the one hand, be so simple as to believe every word; so, on the other hand, we must not be so sceptical as to believe nothing; but especially we must be forward to believe good concerning others. It is safer to err on this side. They *were full of goodness*; therefore the more likely to take in good part what he had written, and to account it a kindness; and not only so, but to put it in practice, especially that which relates to the healing of their differences. A good understanding of one another, and a goodwill to one another, would soon put an end to strife. *Filled with all knowledge*. Goodness and knowledge together! A very rare and an excellent conjunction; the head and the heart of the new man. *Able to admonish one another*. Those that have goodness and knowledge should communicate what they have. "You that excel so much in good gifts may think you have no need of any instructions of mine." How gladly would ministers leave off their admonishing work, if people were able and willing to admonish one another! Would to God that all the Lord's people were prophets.

II. He clears himself from the suspicion of intermeddling needlessly with that which did not belong to him, *v*. 15. Observe how affectionately he speaks to them: *My brethren* (*v*. 14), and again, *brethren*, *v*. 15. He had himself, and taught others, the art of obliging. He acknowledges he had written *boldly in some sort*.

JAMIESON, FAUSSET, BROWN

13. Now . . .—This seems a concluding prayer, suggested by the whole preceding subject matter of the epistle. **the God of hope**—(see on vs.

—**fill you with all joy and peace in believing**—the native truth of that *faith* which is the great theme of this epistle (cf. Gal. 5:22).

that ye may abound in hope—"of the glory of God." (See on ch. 5:1.) **through the power of the Holy Ghost**—to whom, in the economy of redemption, it belongs to inspire believers with all gracious affections.—On the foregoing portion, note, (1) No Christian is at liberty to regard himself as an isolated disciple of the Lord Jesus, having to decide questions of duty and liberty solely with reference to himself. As Christians are one body in Christ, so the great law of love binds them to act in all things with tenderness and consideration for their brethren in "the common salvation" (vss. 1, 2). (2) Of this unselfishness CHRIST is the perfect model of all Christians (vs. 3). (3) Holy Scripture is the divine storehouse of all furniture for the Christian life, even in its most trying and delicate features (vs. 4). (4) The harmonious glorification of the God and Father of our Lord Jesus Christ by the whole body of the redeemed, as it is the most exalted fruit of the scheme of redemption, so it is the last end of God in it (vss. 5-7).

14-33. CONCLUSION: IN WHICH THE APOSTLE APOLOGIZES FOR THUS WRITING TO THE ROMAN CHRISTIANS, EXPLAINS WHY HE HAD NOT YET VISITED THEM, ANNOUNCES HIS FUTURE PLANS, AND ASKS THEIR PRAYERS FOR THE COMPLETION OF THEM.

14, 15. And . . .—rather, 'Now I am persuaded, my brethren, even I myself, concerning you'—**that ye also yourselves are full of goodness**—of inclination to all I have been enjoining on you-

-filled with all knowledge—of the truth expounded—**and able**—without my intervention—**to admonish one another.**

Nevertheless, I have written the more boldly unto you in some sort—'measure'—**as putting you in mind,**

ADAM CLARKE

13. ***Now the God of hope*****. "May the God of this hope"—that God who caused both Jews and Gentiles to hope that the gracious promises which He made to them should be fulfilled; and who, accordingly, has fulfilled them in the most punctual and circumstantial manner.** ***Fill you with all joy*****. Give you true spiritual happiness:** ***peace*** **in your own hearts, and unity among yourselves;** ***in believing*** **not only the promises which He has given you, but believing in Christ Jesus, in whom all the promises are yea and amen.**

CHARLES H. SPURGEON:

The apostle attributes the power to be filled with joy and peace in believing, and the power to abound in hope, to the Holy Ghost. But, then, I wanted also to show you that the power of the church outside, that with which she is to be aggressive and work upon the world for the gathering out of God's elect from among men, is also this same energy of the Holy Spirit. Hence I have taken the nineteenth verse, for the apostle there says that God had through him made "the Gentiles obedient by word and deed, through mighty signs and wonders, by the power of the Spirit of God." So you see, dear friends, that first of all to keep the church happy and holy within herself there must be a manifestation of the power of the Holy Spirit, and secondly, that for the church to invade the territories of the enemy and to conquer the world for Christ, she must be clothed with the self-same sacred energy. We may then go further and say that the power of the church for external work will be proportionate to the power which dwells within herself. Gauge the energy of the Holy Spirit in the hearts of believers and you may fairly calculate their influence upon unbelievers. Only let the church be illuminated by the Holy Spirit and she will reflect the light and become to onlookers "fair as the moon, clear as the sun, and terrible as an army with banners."

—*The Treasury of the New Testament*

14. ***And I . . . am persuaded of you*****. This is supposed to be an address to the Gentiles, and it is managed with great delicacy. He seems to apologize for the freedom he had used in writing to them, which he gives them to understand proceeded from the authority he had received by his apostolical office, the exercise of which office respected them particularly.**

15. ***Nevertheless . . . I have written*****. Notwithstanding I have this conviction of your extensive knowledge in the things of God, I have**

MATTHEW HENRY

1. He did it only as their remembrancer: *As putting you in mind.* People commonly excuse themselves from hearing the word with this, that the minister can tell them nothing but what they knew before. Yet have they not need to know it better, and to be put in mind of it?

2. He did it as the apostle of the Gentiles. It was in pursuance of his office: *Because of the grace given to me of God*, to be the minister *of Jesus Christ to the Gentiles, v.* 16. He thus laid out himself among the Gentiles, that he might not receive that grace of God in vain. Christ received that he might give; so did Paul; so have we talents which must not be buried. Paul was a minister. Whose minister he was: the *minister of Jesus Christ*; his we are, and him we serve. To whom: to the Gentiles. These Romans were Gentiles: "Now," says he, "I do not thrust myself upon you, I am appointed to it: my commission is my warrant. What he ministered: the *gospel of God—ministering as about holy things* (so the word signifies). For what end: *that the offering up of the Gentiles might be acceptable.* Paul laid out himself thus to bring about something that might be acceptable to God. It is the *offering up of the Gentiles*; *the oblation of the Gentiles*, in which the Gentiles are looked upon either, (1) As the priests, offering the oblation of prayer and praise. Long had the Jews been the holy nation, the kingdom of priests, but now the Gentiles are made priests unto God. Or, (2) The Gentiles are themselves the sacrifice offered up to God by Paul. Paul gathered in souls by his preaching, not to keep them to himself, but to offer them up to God. And it is an acceptable offering, *being sanctified by the Holy Ghost.* That which made them sacrifices to God was their sanctification; and this was not his work, but the work of the Holy Ghost. None are acceptably offered to God but those that are sanctified.

Verses 17–21

He goes on further to magnify his office in the efficacy of it, and to mention to the glory of God the wonderful things that God had done by him. Though, compared with the multitude of their idolatrous neighbours, they were but a little flock, yet, there were many that were their companions in the kingdom and patience of Jesus Christ. It was likewise a great confirmation of the truth of the Christian doctrine that it had such strange success. Therefore Paul gives them this account, which he makes the matter of his glorying; not vain glory, but holy gracious glorying; it is *through Jesus Christ.* Thus does he centre all his glorying in Christ. And it is *in those things which pertain to God. Whereof I may glory.* I would rather read it thus: *Therefore I have a rejoicing in Christ Jesus concerning the things of God.* Paul would have them to rejoice with him in the efficacy of his ministry, of which he speaks not only with the greatest deference possible to the power of Christ, but with a protestation of the truth of what he said (*v.* 18): *I will not dare to speak of any of those things which Christ hath not wrought by me.* He would not take the praise of another man's work, for (says he) I dare not do it.

I. His unwearied diligence and industry in his work.

1. He preached in many places: *From Jerusalem* and *round about unto Illyricum.* We have in the book of the Acts an account of Paul's travels. There we find him, after he was sent forth to preach to the Gentiles (Acts xiii), labouring in Seleucia, Cyprus, Pamphylia, Pisidia, and Lycaonia (Acts xiii, xiv), afterwards travelling through Syria and Cilicia, Phrygia, Galatia, Mysia, Troas, and thence called over to Macedonia, and so into Europe, Acts xv, xvi. Then we find him very busy at Thessalonica, Berea, Athens, Corinth, Ephesus, and the parts adjacent. Now it might be suspected that if Paul undertook so much work, surely he did it by the halves. "No," says he, "*I have fully preached the Gospel of Christ*—have given them a full account of the truth and terms of the gospel, have not shunned to declare the whole counsel of God."

2. He preached in places that had not heard the gospel before, *v.* 20, 21. He broke up the fallow ground, and introduced Christianity where nothing had reigned for many ages but idolatry and witchcraft. Paul broke the ice, and therefore must needs meet with the more difficulties and discouragements in his work. Paul was called out to the hardest work. He was a bold man that made the first attack upon the palace of the strong man armed in the Gentile world, and Paul was that man who ventured the first onset in many places, and suffered greatly for it. He mentions this as a proof of his apostleship; for the office of the apostles was especially to bring in those that were without. He principally laid himself

JAMIESON, FAUSSET, BROWN

because of the grace that is given to me of God—as an apostle of Jesus Christ. **16. that I should be the**—rather, 'a'—**minister**—The word here used is commonly employed to express the office of the priesthood, from which accordingly the figurative language of the rest of the verse is taken. **of Jesus Christ**—'Christ Jesus,' according to the true reading —**to the Gentiles**—a further proof that the Epistle was addressed to a *Gentile* church. (See on ch. 1: 13.)

ministering the gospel of God—As the word here is a still more priestly one, it should be rendered, 'ministering as a priest in the Gospel of God.' **that the offering up of the Gentiles**—as an oblation to God, in their converted character—

might be acceptable, being sanctified by the Holy Ghost—the end to which the ancient offerings typically looked.

17. I have therefore whereof I may glory—or (adding the article, as the reading seems to be), 'I have my glorying.' **through**—'in'—**Christ Jesus in those things which pertain to God**—the things of the ministry committed to me of God.

18-22. For I will not dare to speak of any—'to speak aught'—**of those things which Christ hath not wrought by me**—a modest, though somewhat obscure form of expression, meaning, 'I will not dare to go beyond what Christ *hath* wrought by me'—in which form accordingly the rest of the passage is expressed. Observe here how Paul ascribes all the success of his labors to the activity of the living Redeemer, working in and by him. **so that from Jerusalem, and round about unto**—'as far as'—**Illyricum**—to the extreme northwestern boundary of Greece. It corresponds to the modern Croatia and Dalmatia (II Tim. 4:10). See Acts 20:1, 2.

I have fully preached the gospel of Christ. Yea . . .—rather, 'Yet making it my study (cf. II Cor. 5:9; I Thess. 4:11, *Greek*) so to preach the Gospel, not where Christ was [already] named, that I might not build upon another man's foundation: but (might act) as it is written, To whom no tidings of Him came, they shall see . . .,

ADAM CLARKE

made bold to write to you *in some sort*, "to a party" among you, as some learned men translate the words, who stand more in need of such instructions than the others; and I do this *because of the grace*—because of the "office"—which I have received from God, namely, to be the apostle of the Gentiles.

16. *Ministering the gospel of God.* "Acting as a priest." Here is a plain allusion, says Dr. Whitby, to the Jewish sacrifices offered by the priest, and *sanctified* or made acceptable by the *libamen* offered with them; for he compares himself, in preaching the gospel, to the priest performing his sacred functions—preparing his sacrifice to be offered. The Gentiles, converted by him and dedicated to the service of God, are his sacrifices and oblation. The Holy Spirit is the *libamen* poured upon this sacrifice, by which it was sanctified and rendered *acceptable* to God. The words of Isa. lxvi. 20, "And they shall bring all your brethren for an offering unto the Lord out of all nations," might have suggested the above idea to the mind of the apostle.

17. *I have therefore whereof I may glory.* Being sent of God on this most honorable and important errand, I have matter of great exultation, not only in the honor which He has conferred upon me, but in the great success with which He has crowned my ministry.

18. *For I will not dare to speak.* If the thing were not as I have stated it, I would not dare to arrogate to myself honors which did not belong to me. But God has made me the apostle of the Gentiles; and the conversion of the Gentiles is the fruit of my ministry, Christ having *wrought by me* for this purpose.

Round about unto Illyricum. It is a country of Europe, extending from the Adriatic gulf to Pannonia. From Jerusalem the apostle went round the eastern coast of the Mediterranean Sea.

I have fully preached the gospel. "I have successfully preached"—I have not only proclaimed the Word, but made converts and founded churches.

MATTHEW HENRY

out for the good of those that sat in darkness. He was in care not to *build upon another man's foundation.* He quotes a scripture for this out of Isa. lii. 15, *To whom he was not spoken of, they shall see.* The transition from darkness to light is more sensible than the after-growth and increase of that light. And commonly the greatest success of the gospel is at its first coming to a place; afterwards most people become sermon-proof.

II. The great success that he had in his work: It was effectual to *make the Gentiles obedient.* The design of the gospel is to bring people to be *obedient.* This Paul aimed at in all his travels. Now how was this great work wrought? Christ was the principal agent. He does not say, "which I worked," but "which Christ wrought by me," *v.* 18. Whatever good we do, it is not we, but Christ by us, that does it. Paul takes all occasions to own this. Paul was a very active instrument: *By word and deed,* that is, by his preaching, and by the miracles he wrought, or his preaching and his living. Those ministers are likely to win souls that preach both by word and deed. This is according to Christ's example, who began both to do and teach.—*Through mighty signs and wonders.* These made the preaching of the word so effectual. The *power of the Spirit of God* made this effectual, *v.* 19. (1) The power of the Spirit in Paul, as in the other apostles, for the working of those miracles. Miracles were wrought by the power of the Holy Ghost. Or, (2) The power of the Spirit in the hearts of those who saw the miracles. Paul himself could not make one soul obedient further than the power of the Spirit of God accompanied his labours. This is an encouragement to faithful ministers, who labour under the sense of great weakness and infirmity. The same almighty Spirit that wrought with Paul often perfects strength in weakness. The converted nations were his joy and crown of rejoicing: and he tells them of it, that they might rejoice with him.

Verses 22–29

St. Paul here declares his purpose to come and see the Christians at Rome. The manner of his expression is gracious, and for our imitation. Even our common discourse should have an air of grace; by this it will appear what country we belong to. It should seem that Paul's company was very much desired at Rome. Should the apostle of the Gentiles be a stranger at Rome, the metropolis of the Gentile world? He promises to come shortly, and gives a good reason why he could not come now.

I. He excuses it that he never came yet. 1. He assures them that he had a great desire to see them; **not to see Rome, but** *to come unto you* (*v.* 3), a company of poor despised saints in Rome. These were **the men that Paul was ambitious of an acquaintance with at Rome. And he had a special desire to see** them, because of the great character they had in all the churches for faith and holiness. This desire Paul had had for many years, and yet could never compass it. God's dearest servants are not always gratified in everything that they have a mind to. 2. He tells them that the reason why he could not come to them was because he had so much work cut out for him elsewhere. *For which cause* he was so much *hindered.* God had opened a wide door for him in other places, and so turned him aside. (1) The gracious providence of God about his ministers, casting their lot, not according to their contrivance, but according to his own purpose. Man purposes but God disposes. The gospel does not come by chance to any place, but by the will and counsel of God. (2) The gracious prudence of Paul, in bestowing his time and pains where there was most need. Had Paul consulted his own honour, the greatness of the work would never have hindered him from seeing Rome. Paul sought the things of Christ more than his own things. There was now a gale of opportunity, the fields were white unto the harvest; such a season slipped might never be retrieved. It concerns us all to do that first which is most needful. This Paul mentions as a sufficient satisfying reason. We must not take it ill of our friends if they prefer necessary work, which is pleasing to God, before unnecessary visits and compliments.

II. He promised to come and see them shortly, *v.* 23, 24, 29. *Having no more place in these parts,* namely, in Greece, where he then was. He had driven the chariot of the gospel to the sea-coast, and having thus conquered Greece he is ready to wish there were another Greece to conquer.

1. How he forecasted his intended visit. His project was to see them in his way to Spain. It appears by this that Paul intended a journey into Spain. But it is not certain whether ever he fulfilled his purpose, and went to Spain. He did indeed come to

JAMIESON, FAUSSET, BROWN

by word and deed—by preaching and working; which latter he explains in the next clause.

through mighty—lit., 'in the power of'—**signs and wonders**—i.e., glorious miracles. **by the power of the Spirit of God**—'the Holy Ghost,' as the true reading seems to be. This seems intended to explain the efficacy of the word preached, as well as the working of the miracles which attested it.

For which cause—'Being so long occupied with this missionary work, I have been much (or, 'for the most part') hindered . . . , (See on ch. 1:9-11.)

23, 24. But now having no more place—'no longer having place,'—i.e., unbroken ground, where Christ has not been preached—**and having a great desire**—'a longing'—**these many years to come unto you**—(see, as before, on ch. 1:9-11)—**whensoever I take my journey into Spain**—Whether this purpose was ever accomplished has been much disputed, as no record of it nor allusion to it anywhere occurs. Those who think our apostle was never at large after his first imprisonment at Rome will of course hold

ADAM CLARKE

20. ***So have I strived to preach the gospel.*** **For I have considered it my "honor" to preach the gospel where that gospel was before unknown. This is the proper import of the word; from** ***philos,*** **a "friend," and** ***time,*** **"honor."**

21. ***But as it is written.*** **These words, quoted from Isa. lii. 15, the apostle applies to his own conduct; not that the words themselves predicted what Paul had done, but that he endeavored to fulfill such a declaration by his manner of preaching the gospel to the heathen.**

By word and deed. **These words may refer to the doctrines which he taught and to the miracles which he wrought among them. So they became obedient to the doctrines, on the evidence of the miracles with which they were accompanied.**

19. ***Through mighty signs and wonders.*** **This more fully explains the preceding clause. Through the power of the Holy Ghost he was enabled to work among the Gentiles** ***mighty signs and wonders,*** **so that they were fully convinced that both his doctrine and mission were divine; and therefore they cheerfully received the gospel of the Lord Jesus.**

22. ***For which cause.*** **My considering it a point of honor to build on no other man's foundation; and, finding that the gospel has been long ago planted at Rome, I have been prevented from going thither, purposing rather to spend my time and strength in preaching where Christ has not yet been proclaimed.**

23. ***But . . . having no more place in these parts.*** **Having nothing further at present that I can do—for** ***topon echein*** **signifies not merely "to have a place of residence," or the like, but "convenience, opportunity," which is a frequent meaning of the phrase among the best Greek writers—having no large place or city where Christianity has not yet been planted, in which I can introduce the gospel. The apostle was then at Corinth; and having evangelized all**

A. B. SIMPSON:

Again and again, in Paul's missionary work, God put His hand upon the work. Look at him at Derby and Lystra, beaten by the mob, and left for dead. He simply rose upon his feet, taking strength from the living One, and went forth to his work as if nothing had happened. On his way to Rome, standing on the rocking deck of the little ship bravely triumphing over the angry storm and the terror of the captain and the crew, leading them by his triumphant faith to the shore. Or, again, on the shores of Malta, flinging from his hand the viper that threatened his life, and then going forth throughout the island, to pour into other hearts the blessing which he himself had received.

This was the way Paul did his mission work, turning every curse into a blessing and every assault into a victory.

This is the very way God still wants to send forth His workers, and seal their labors with His mighty hand. But you must first know His power in your own life, and then it will be easy to claim it for the lives of others, and as the seal of your work. There is nothing God will not do for you if you will first let Him do it in you.

The greatest need of foreign work today, both at home and abroad—a mighty baptism of the Holy Ghost. This will produce missionary enthusiasm, the consecration of means, the calling of true workers, the preparation of the power that you most need. And this will open the hearts of the heathen, will break the barriers and bars of brass asunder, and will give the triumphs of the Gospel in the face of idolatry and opposition.—*Christ in the Bible*

MATTHEW HENRY

Rome, but he was brought thither a prisoner, and there was detained two years; and whither he went after is uncertain. The grace of God often with favour accepts the sincere intention, when the providence of God in wisdom prohibits the execution. Now, in his way to Spain he proposed to come to them. *I trust to see you:* not, "I am resolved I will," but, "I hope I shall." We must purpose all our purposes in like manner with a submission to the divine providence.

2. What he expected in his intended visit. (1) What he expected from them. He expected they would bring him on his way towards Spain. It was not a stately attendance but a loving attendance, such as friends give, that Paul expected. They might be helpful to Paul in his voyage thither; and it was not barely their accompanying him part of the way, but their furthering him in his expedition, that he counted upon. (2) What he expected in them: to *be somewhat filled with their company.* That which Paul desired was their company and conversation. Paul was himself a man of great attainments in knowledge and grace, and yet see how he pleased himself with the thoughts of good company. He intended to make some stay with them, for he would be filled with their company; not just look at them, and away. It is but somewhat filled, he thought he should leave them with a desire of more of their company. The satisfaction we have in communion with the saints in this world is but partial. It is partial compared with our communion with Christ. That will fill the soul. It is partial compared with the communion we hope to have with the saints in the other world. (3) What he expected from God with them, *v.* 29. He expected to come *in the fulness of the blessing of the gospel of Christ.* Concerning what he *expected* from *them* he speaks doubtfully: *I trust to be brought on my way, and to be filled with your company.* Paul had learnt not to be too confident of the best. These very men slipped from him afterwards, *At my first answer, no man stood by me;* none of the Christians at Rome. But concerning what he expected from God he speaks confidently. *I am sure when I do come I shall come in the fulness,* &c. We cannot expect too little from man, nor too much from God. Now Paul expected that God would bring him to them, loaded with blessings. Compare *ch.* i. 11, *That I may impart unto you some spiritual gift.* The blessing of the gospel of Christ is the best and most desirable blessing. There is then a happy meeting between people and ministers, when they are both under the fulness of the blessing. When ministers are fully prepared to give out, and people fully prepared to receive, this blessing, both are happy.

III. He gives them a good reason why he could not come and see them now. He must first make a journey to Jerusalem, *v.* 25–28. He was going to Jerusalem, as the messenger of the church's charity.

1. Concerning this charity itself. And he speaks of that probably to excite the Roman Christians to do the like. Examples are moving, and Paul was very ingenious at begging, not for himself, but for others. (1) For whom it was intended: *For the poor saints which are at Jerusalem, v.* 26. It is no strange thing for saints to be poor. Riches are not the best things, nor is poverty a curse. It seems, the saints at Jerusalem were poorer than other saints because the famine that was over all the world in the days of Claudius Cæsar did in a special manner prevail in Judæa. This was the occasion of that contribution mentioned, Acts xi. 28–30. Though the saints at Jerusalem were at a great distance from them, yet they thus extended their bounty to them, to teach us to stretch out the hand of our charity to all that are of the household of faith, though in places distant from us. We must extend our bounty, as the sun his beams. (2) By whom it was collected: *By those of Macedonia* (the chief of whom were the Philippians) *and Achaia* (the chief of whom were the Corinthians). It seems those of Macedonia and Achaia were rich and wealthy, while those at Jerusalem were poor and needy, so that some should have what others want, and so this mutual dependence of Christians one upon another might be maintained.—*It pleased them.* This intimates how ready they were to it, and how cheerful they were in it.—*To make a certain contribution; a communication,* in token of the communion of saints, as in the natural body one member communicates to the relief of another, as there is occasion. Time was when the saints at Jerusalem were on the giving hand, when they laid their estates at the apostles' feet for charitable uses, and took special care that the Grecian widows should not be neglected in the daily ministration. And now that the providence of God had turned the scale, and made them necessitous, they found the Grecians kind to them; for the merciful shall obtain mercy. (3) What reason there was for it (*v.* 27): *And their*

JAMIESON, FAUSSET, BROWN

that it never was; while those who are persuaded, as we are, that he underwent a second imprisonment, prior to which he was at large for a considerable time after his first, incline naturally to the other opinion. **I will come to you**—If these words were not originally in the text, and there is weighty evidence against them, they must at least be inserted as a necessary supplement. **in my journey . . .**—'as I pass through by you, to be set forward on my journey thither, if first I be somewhat filled with your company': i.e., 'I should indeed like to stay longer with you than I can hope to do, but I must, to some extent at least, have my fill of your company.'

And I am sure—'I know'—**that . . . I shall come in the fulness of the blessing of Christ**—Such, beyond all doubts, is the true reading, the words "of the gospel" being in hardly any MSS. of antiquity and authority. Nor was the apostle mistaken in this confidence, though his visit to Rome was in very different circumstances from what he expected. See Acts 28:16-31.

25-27. But now I go to Jerusalem to minister—'ministering'—**to the saints**—in the sense immediately to be explained. **For . . .**—better, 'For Macedonia and Achaia have thought good to make a certain contribution for the poor of the saints which are at Jerusalem.' (See Acts 24: 17.) 'They have thought it good; and their debtors verily they are'; i.e., 'And well they may, considering what the Gentile believers owe to their Jewish brethren.'

For if the Gentiles have been made partakers of their spiritual things, their duty is also—'they owe it also'—**to minister unto them in carnal things**—(Cf. I Cor. 9:11; Gal. 6:6; and see Luke 7:4; Acts 10:2).

ADAM CLARKE

those parts, he had no opportunity of breaking up any new ground.

24. *Whensoever I take my journey into Spain.* Where it is very likely the gospel had not yet been planted. *I will come to you.* These words are wanting in almost every MS. of note. If the first clause of this verse be read in connection with the latter clause of the preceding, it will fully appear that this rejected clause is useless. "Having a great desire these many years to come unto you whensoever I take my journey into Spain: for I trust to see you in my journey."

Somewhat filled with your company. The word which we translate *filled* would be better rendered "gratified"; for it signifies to be "satisfied, to be gratified, and to enjoy." The apostle, though he had not the honor of having planted the church at Rome, yet expected much gratification from the visit which he intended to pay them.

29. *In the fulness of the blessing of the gospel of Christ.* The words *of the gospel* are wanting in almost every MS. of importance. There is no doubt they should be omitted. "The fulness of the blessing of Christ" is really more than "the fulness of the blessing of the gospel of Christ."

25. *Now I go unto Jerusalem.* From this and the following two verses we learn that the object of his journey to Jerusalem was to carry a contribution made among the Gentile Christians of Macedonia and Achaia for the relief of the poor Jewish Christians at Jerusalem. About this affair he had taken great pains, as appears from 1 Cor. xvi. 1-4; 2 Corinthians vii and ix. His design in this affair is very evident from 2 Cor. ix. 12-13. The apostle was in hopes that this liberal contribution sent by the Gentile Christians who had been converted by Paul's ministry would engage the affections of the Jewish Christians, who had been much prejudiced against the reception of the Gentiles into the Church without being previously obliged to submit to the yoke of the law. He wished to establish a coalition between the converted Jews and Gentiles, being sensible of its great importance to the spread of the gospel; and his procuring this contribution was one laudable device to accomplish this good end. This shows why he so earnestly requests the prayers of the Christians at Rome, that his service which he had for Jerusalem might be accepted of the saints.

27. *For if the Gentiles have been made partakers.* It was through and by means of the Jews that the Gentiles were brought to the knowledge of God and the gospel of Christ. These were the *spiritual things* which they had received, and the pecuniary contribution was the *carnal things* which the Gentiles were now returning.

MATTHEW HENRY

debtors they are. The Gentiles were greatly beholden to the Jews, and were bound in gratitude to be very kind to them. From the stock of Israel came Christ himself; out of the same stock came the prophets, and apostles, and first preachers of the gospel. The Jews, having had the lively oracles committed to them, were the Christians' library-keepers. They were cut off, that the Gentiles might be admitted in. Thus did the Gentiles partake of their spiritual things, and receive the gospel of salvation as it were at secondhand from the Jews; and therefore *their duty is to minister unto them in carnal things*: it is the least they can do.

2. Concerning Paul's agency in this business. He *ministered unto the saints* (*v.* 25) by stirring up others, receiving what was gathered, and transmitting it to Jerusalem. Many good works of that kind stand at a stay for want of some one active person to lead in them, and to set the wheels going. Besides this, Paul had other business in this journey, to visit and confirm the churches. Paul was one that laid out himself to do good every way, like his Masfer, to the bodies as well as to the souls of people. This Paul had undertaken, and therefore he resolves to go through with it, before he fell upon other work (*v.* 28): *When I have sealed to them this fruit.* He calls the alms *fruit*, for it is one of the fruits of righteousness; it sprang from a root of grace in the givers. And his sealing it intimates his great care about it. Paul was very solicitous to approve himself faithful in the management of this matter.

Verses 30–33

I. St. Paul's desire of a share in the prayers of the Romans for him, expressed very earnestly, *v.* 30–32. He had prayed much for them, and this he desires as the return of his kindness. Interchanging prayers is an excellent token of the interchanging of loves. How careful should we be lest we do anything to forfeit our interest in the love and prayers of God's praying people!

1. Why they must pray for him. *I beseech you*, "*For the Lord Jesus Christ's sake.* You love Christ, and own Christ; for his sake then do me this kindness. *For the love of the Spirit.* As a proof of that love which the Spirit works in the hearts of believers one to another, pray for me. If ever you experienced the Spirit's love to you, and would be found returning your love to the Spirit, be not wanting in this office of kindness."

2. How they must pray for him: *That you strive together.* That *you strive in prayer.* We must put forth all that is within us in that duty; pray with fixedness, faith, and fervency. This not only when we are praying for ourselves, but when we are praying for our friends. True love to our brethren should make us as earnest for them as sense of our own need makes us for ourselves. "*Strive together with me*, who am wrestling with God daily, upon my own and my friends' account." He would have them to ply the same oar. Those who are put far asunder by the disposal of God's providence may yet meet together at the throne of his grace.

3. What they must beg of God for him. In praying both for ourselves and for our friends, it is good to be particular. He recommends himself to their prayers, with reference to three things: (1) The dangers which he was exposed to: *That I may be delivered from those that do not believe in Judæa.* Some prospect he had of trouble from them in this journey; and therefore they must pray that God would deliver him. We may, and must, pray against persecution. (2) His services: *Pray that my service which I have for Jerusalem may be accepted of the saints.* Why, was there any danger that it would not be accepted? Paul was the apostle of the Gentiles, and as the unbelieving Jews looked spitefully at him, which was their wickedness, so those that believed were shy of him, which was their weakness. "Pray that it may be accepted." As God must be sought unto for the restraining of the ill will of our enemies, so also for the preserving and increasing of the goodwill of our friends. (3) His journey to them. To engage their prayers for him, he interests them in his concerns (*v.* 32): *That I may come unto you with joy.* If he should not do good, and prosper, in one visit, he thought he should have small joy of the next: may *come with joy, by the will of God.* All our joy depends upon the will of God.

II. Here is another prayer of the apostle for them (*v.* 33): *Now the God of peace be with you all, Amen.* He describes God under this title here, because of the divisions among them; if God be the God of peace, let us be men of peace. Those who have the fountain cannot want any of the streams. *With you all;* both weak and strong. Those who are united in the blessing of God should be united in affection one to another.

JAMIESON, FAUSSET, BROWN

28, 29. When therefore I have . . . sealed—i.e., delivered over safely—**to them this fruit**—of the faith and love of the Gentile converts—**I will come**—'come back,' or 'return'—**by you into Spain**—See on vs. 24. **30. Now I beseech you, brethren, for the Lord Jesus Christ's sake, and for the love of the Spirit**—or, 'by the Lord Jesus Christ, and by the love of the Spirit'—not the love which the Spirit bears to us, but that love which He kindles in the hearts of believers towards each other; i.e. 'By that Saviour whose name is alike dear to all of us and whose unsearchable riches I live only to proclaim, and by that love one to another which the blessed Spirit diffuses through all the brotherhood, making the labors of Christ's servants a matter of common interest to all—I beseech you'—**that ye strive together with me in your prayers to God for me**—implying that he had his grounds for anxious fear in this matter. **31. That I may be delivered from them that do not believe**—'that do not obey,' i.e., the truth, by believing it; as in ch. 2:8. **in Judea**—He saw the storm that was gathering over him in Judea, which, if at all, would certainly burst upon his head when he reached the capital; and the event too clearly showed the correctness of these apprehensions. **and that my service which I have for Jerusalem**—See on vss. 25-28. **may be accepted by**—'prove acceptable to'—**the saints**—Nor was he without apprehension lest the opposition he had made to the narrow jealousy of the Jewish converts against the free reception of their Gentile brethren, should make this gift of theirs to the poor saints at Jerusalem less welcome than it ought to be. He would have the Romans therefore to join him in wrestling with God that this gift might be gratefully received, and prove a cement between the two parties. But further. **32. That I may come unto you with**—'in'—**joy by the will of God** (Acts 18:21; I Cor. 4:19; 16:7; Heb. 6:3; Jas. 4:15—**and may with you be refreshed**—rather, 'with you refresh myself,' after all his labors and anxieties, and so be refitted for future service. **33. Now the God of peace be with you all. Amen**—The peace here sought is to be taken in its widest sense: the peace of reconciliation to God, first, "through the blood of the everlasting covenant" (Heb. 13:20; I Thess. 5:23; II Thess. 3:16; Phil. 4:9); then the peace which that reconciliation diffuses among all the partakers of it (I Cor. 14:33; II Cor. 13:11; and see on ch. 16:20); more widely still, that peace which the children of God, in beautiful imitation of their Father in Heaven, are called and privileged to diffuse far and wide through this sin-distracted and divided world (ch. 22:18; Matt. 5:9; Heb. 12:14; Jas. 3:18).—*Note,* (1) Did "the chiefest of the apostles" apologize for writing to a Christian church which he had never seen, and a church that he was persuaded was above the need of it, save to "stir up their pure minds by way of remembrance" (II Pet. 1:13; 3:1); and did he put even this upon the sole plea of apostolic responsibility (vss. 14-16)? What a contrast is thus presented to hierarchical pride, and in particular to the affected humility of the bishop of this very Rome! How close the bond which the one spirit draws between ministers and people—how wide the separation produced by the other! (2) There is in the Christian Church no real priesthood, and none but figurative sacrifices. Had it been otherwise, it is inconceivable that the 16th verse of this chapter should have been expressed as it is. Paul's only priesthood and sacrificial offerings lay, first, in ministering to them as "the apostle of the Gentiles," not the sacrament with the 'real presence' of Christ in it, or the sacrifice of the mass, but "the Gospel of God," and then, when gathered under the wing of Christ, presenting them to God as a grateful offering, "being sanctified [not by sacrificial gifts, but] by the Holy Ghost." (See Heb. 13:9-16.) (3) Though the debt we owe to those by whom we have been brought to Christ can never be discharged, we should feel it a privilege when we render them any lower benefit in return (vss. 26, 27). (4) Formidable designs against the truth and the servants of Christ should, above all other ways of counteracting them, be met by combined prayer to Him who rules all hearts and controls all events; and the darker the cloud, the more resolutely should all to whom Christ's cause is dear "strive together in their prayers to God" for the removal of it (vss. 30, 31). (5) Christian fellowship is so precious that the most eminent servants of Christ, amid the toils and trials of their work, find it refreshing and invigorating; and it is no good sign of any ecclesiastic, that he deems it beneath him to seek and enjoy it even amongst the humblest saints in the Church of Christ (vss. 24, 32).

ADAM CLARKE

28. *When therefore I have performed this* service, *and have sealed,* faithfully delivered up, *to them this fruit,* of the success of my ministry and of your conversion to God, *I will come by you into Spain.* This was in his desire; he had fully purposed it, if God should see meet to permit him; but it does not appear that he ever went.

30. *For the love of the Spirit.* By that love of God which the Holy Spirit sheds abroad in your hearts. *That ye strive together.* "That you agonize with me." He felt that much depended on the success of his present mission to the Christians at Jerusalem, and their acceptance of the charitable contribution which he was bringing with him, in order to conciliate them to the reception of the Gentiles into the Church of God without obliging them to submit to circumcision.

31. *That I may be delivered from them that do not believe.* He knew that his countrymen who had not received the gospel lay in wait for his life; and no doubt they thought they should do God service by destroying him, not only as an apostate, in their apprehension, from the Jewish religion, but as one who was laboring to subvert and entirely destroy it. *And that my service.* But several eminent MSS. read "the gift which I bear." This probably was a gloss, which in many MSS. subverted the word in the text; for *service* in its connection here could refer to nothing else but the contribution which he was carrying to the poor saints at Jerusalem.

32. *That I may come unto you with joy.* That his apprehensions of ill usage were not groundless, and the danger to which his life was exposed real, we have already seen in the account given of this visit, Acts xxi—xxiv; and that he had such intimations from the Holy Spirit himself appears from Acts xx. 23; xxi. 11; and xx. 38. Should his journey to Jerusalem be prosperous and his service accepted, so that the converted Jews and Gentiles should come to a better understanding, he hoped to see them at Rome with great joy; and if he got his wishes gratified through their prayers, it would be the full proof that this whole business had been conducted according to the will of God.

33. *The God of peace be with you.* The whole object of the Epistle is to establish peace between the believing Jews and Gentiles, and to show them their mutual obligations, and the infinite mercy of God to both; and now he concludes with praying that the God of peace—He from whom it comes and by whom it is preserved—may be forever with them. The word *Amen* at the end does not appear to have been written by the apostle; it is wanting in some of the most ancient MSS.

MATTHEW HENRY

CHAPTER 16

Verses 1–16

I. Here is the recommendation of a friend, by whom (as some think) this epistle was sent—one *Phebe, v.* 1, 2. It should seem that she was a person of quality and estate, who had business which called her to Rome, where she was a stranger; and therefore Paul recommends her to the acquaintance of the Christians there. Courtesy and Christianity agree well together.

1. He gives a very good character of her. (1) As a sister to Paul: *Phebe our sister;* not in nature, but in grace. Both Christ and his apostles had some of their best friends among the devout (and upon that account honourable) women. (2) As a *servant to the church at Cenchrea*: a servant by office, not to preach the word (that was forbidden to women), but in acts of charity and hospitality. Phebe seems to have been a person of some account; and yet it was no disparagement to her to be a servant to the church. Everyone in his place should strive to serve the church, for therein he serves Christ. Cenchrea was a small sea-port town adjoining to Corinth. (3) As a *succourer of many*, and particularly of Paul, *v.* 2. She relieved many that were in want and distress. Her bounty was extensive, she was a succourer of many. Observe the gratitude of Paul in mentioning her particular kindness to him: *And to myself also.* Acknowledgment of favours is the least return we can make.

2. He recommends her to their care. "*Receive her in the Lord*. Entertain her; bid her welcome, as a servant and friend of Christ." *As it becometh saints* to receive, who love Christ, and therefore love all that are his for his sake; or, as *becometh saints* to be received, with love and honour. *Assist her in whatsoever business she has need of you.* Being a woman, a stranger, a Christian, she had need of help: and Paul engaged them to be assistant to her. It becomes Christians to be helpful one to another in their affairs, especially to be helpful to strangers; for we are members one of another. Paul bespeaks help for one that had been so helpful to many.

II. Here are commendations to some particular friends among those to whom he wrote. Though the care of all the churches came upon Paul daily, enough to distract an ordinary head, yet he could retain the remembrance of so many; and his heart was so full of love and affection as to send salutations to each of them. *Greet* them, *salute* them; it is the same word, "Let them know that I remember them."

1. Concerning Aquila and Priscilla, a famous couple, that Paul had a special kindness for. They were originally of Rome, but were banished thence by the edict of Claudius, Acts xviii. 2. At Corinth, Paul became acquainted with them, wrought with them at the trade of tent-making; after some time, they returned to Rome. He calls them his *helpers in Christ Jesus*. Nay, they did not only do much, but they ventured much, for Paul: They have *for my life laid down their own necks*. They exposed themselves to secure Paul, hazarded their own lives for the preservation of his. Paul was in a great deal of danger at Corinth; but they sheltered him. It was a good while ago that they had done Paul this kindness; and yet he speaks as feelingly of it as if it had been but yesterday. *To whom not only I give thanks, but also all the churches of the Gentiles;* who were all beholden to these good people for helping to save the life of him that was the apostle of the Gentiles. He sends likewise greeting to the *church in their house, v.* 5. Religion reigning in a family, will turn a house into a church. It had a good influence upon this that Priscilla the good wife of the family was so very eminent and forward in religion, so eminent that she is often named first. When Priscilla and Aquila were at Ephesus, though but sojourners there, yet there also they had a church in their house, 1 Cor. xvi. 19. A truly godly man will be careful to take religion along with him wherever he goes.

2. Concerning Epenetus, *v.* 5. He calls him his *well-beloved.* Endearing language should pass among Christians to express love, and to engage love. So he calls Amplias, *beloved in the Lord*; and Stachys, his *beloved.* Of Epenetus it is further said that he was the *first-fruit of Achaia unto Christ*: one that was offered up to God by Paul, as the first-fruits of his ministry there; an earnest of a great harvest; for in Corinth, the chief city of Achaia, God had much people, Acts xviii. 10. Special respect is to be paid to those that set out early, and come to work in the vineyard at the first hour.

3. Concerning Mary, and some others. *Mary,* who *bestowed much labour on us.* True love never sticks at labour, but rather takes a pleasure in it;

JAMIESON, FAUSSET, BROWN

CHAPTER 16

VSS. 1-27. CONCLUSION, EMBRACING SUNDRY SALUTATIONS AND DIRECTIONS, AND A CLOSING PRAYER. **1. I commend unto you Phœbe our sister, which is a servant**—or 'deaconess'—**of the church which is at Cenchrea**—The word is Cenchreæ, the eastern part of Corinth (Acts 18:18). That in the earliest churches there were deaconesses, to attend to the wants of the female members, there is no good reason to doubt. So early at least as the reign of Trajan, we learn from PLINY's celebrated letter to that emperor—A.D. 110, or 111—that they existed in the Eastern churches. Indeed, from the relation in which the sexes then stood to each other, something of this sort would seem to have been a necessity. Modern attempts, however, to revive this office have seldom found favor; either from the altered state of society, or the abuse of the office, or both.

2. Receive her in the Lord—i.e., as a genuine disciple of the Lord Jesus. **as**—'so as'—**becometh saints**—so as saints should receive saints. **assist her in whatsoever business she hath**—'may have'—**need of you**—some private business of her own. **for she hath been a succourer of many, and of myself also**—(See Ps. 41:1-3; II Tim. 1:16-18).

3-5. Salute Priscilla—The true reading here is 'Prisca' (as in II Tim. 4:19), a contracted form of Priscilla, as "Silas" of "Silvanus." **and Aquila my helpers**—The wife is here named before the husband (as in Acts 18:18, and vs. 26, according to the true reading; also in II Tim. 4:19), probably as being the more prominent and helpful to the Church. **who have for my life laid down**—'who did for my life lay down'—**their own necks**—i.e., risked their lives; either at Corinth (Acts 18:6, 9, 10), or more probably at Ephesus (Acts 19:30, 31; and cf. I Cor. 15:32). They must have returned from Ephesus (where we last find them in the history of the Acts) to Rome, whence the edict of Claudius had banished them (Acts 18:2); and doubtless, if not the principal members of that Christian community, they were at least the most endeared to our apostle. **unto whom not only I give thanks, but also all the churches of the Gentiles**—whose special apostle this dear couple had rescued from imminent danger. **5. Likewise the church that is in their house**—The Christian assembly that statedly met there for worship. "From his occupation as tent-maker, he had probably better accommodations for the meetings of the church than most other Christians" [HODGE]. Probably this devoted couple had written to the apostle such an account of the stated meetings at their house, as made him feel at home with them, and include them in this salutation, which doubtless would be read at their meetings with peculiar interest. **Salute my well beloved Epænetus, who is the first fruits**—i.e., the first convert—**of Achaia unto Christ**—The true reading here, as appears by the MSS., is, 'the first fruits of Asia unto Christ'—i.e., Proconsular Asia (see Acts 16:6). In I Corinthians 16:15 it is said that "the household of Stephanas was the first fruit of Achaia"; and though if Epænetus was one of that family, the two statements might be reconciled according to the received text, there is no need to resort to this supposition, as that text is in this instance without authority. Epænetus, as the first believer in that region called Proconsular Asia, was dear to the apostle. (See Hos. 9:10; and Mic. 7:1). None of the names mentioned from vss. 5-15 are otherwise known. One wonders at the number of them, considering that the writer had never been at Rome. But as Rome was then the center of the civilized world, to and from which journeys were continually taken to the remotest parts, there is no great difficulty in supposing that so active a travelling missionary as Paul would, in course of time, make the acquaintance of a considerable number of the Christians then residing at Rome. **6. Greet**—or 'salute'—**Mary, who bestowed much labour on us**—labor, no doubt, of a womanly kind.

ADAM CLARKE

CHAPTER 16

1. *I commend unto you Phebe.* As the apostle had not been at Rome previously to his writing this Epistle, he could not have had a personal acquaintance with those members of the church there to whom he sends these friendly salutations. It is likely that many of them were his own converts, who in different parts of Asia Minor and Greece had heard him preach the gospel and afterwards became settlers at Rome. Phoebe is here termed a *servant,* "a deaconess" *of the church . . . at Cenchrea.* There were deaconesses in the primitive Church, whose business it was to attend the female converts at baptism; to instruct the catechumens, or persons who were candidates for baptism; to visit the sick, and those who were in prison; and, in short, perform those religious offices for the female part of the Church which could not with propriety be performed by men. They were chosen in general out of the most experienced of the Church, and were ordinarily widows who had borne children. Some ancient constitutions required them to be forty, others fifty, and others sixty years of age. It is evident that they were ordained to their office by the imposition of the hands of the bishop, and the form of prayer used on the occasion is extant in the apostolical constitutions. In the tenth or eleventh century the order became extinct in the Latin church, but continued in the Greek church till the end of the twelfth century. *Cenchrea* was a seaport on the east side of the isthmus which joined the Morea to Greece, as Lechaeum was the seaport on the west side of the same isthmus.

2. *Succourer of many.* One who probably entertained the apostles and preachers who came to minister at Cenchrea, and who was remarkable for entertaining strangers.

3. *Greet Priscilla and Aquila.* This pious couple had been obliged to leave Rome, on the edict of Claudius, see Acts xviii. 2, and take refuge in Greece. It is likely that they returned to Rome at the death of Claudius, or whenever the decree was annulled. It seems they had greatly contributed to assist the apostle in his important labors. Instead of "Priscilla," the principal MSS. and versions have "Prisca," which most critics suppose to be the genuine reading.

4. *Who have for my life laid down their own necks.* What transaction this refers to we know not; but it appears that these persons had on some occasion hazarded their own lives to save that of the apostle, and that the fact was known to all the churches of God in that quarter, who felt themselves under the highest obligations to these pious persons for the important service which they had thus rendered.

5. *The church that is in their house.* In these primitive times no such places existed as those which we now term churches; the word always signifying the "congregation" or "assembly" of believers, and not the place they assembled in.

Epaenetus . . . the firstfruits of Achaia. In 1 Cor. xvi. 15, the house or family of Stephanas is said to be the firstfruits of Achaia. How then can it be said here that Epenetus was the firstfruits, or first person who had received the gospel in that district? *Ans.*—Epenetus might have been one of the family of Stephanas; for it is not said that Stephanas was the firstfruits, but his house or family; and there can be no impropriety in supposing that one of that house or family was called Epenetus; and that this person, being the only one of the family now at Rome, might be mentioned as the firstfruits of Achaia. This would rationally account for the apparent difficulty were we sure that *of Achaia* was the true reading; but this is more than doubtful, for *of Asia* is the reading of several MSS.

6. *Greet Mary, who bestowed much labour on us.* Who this *Mary* was or what the *labour* was which she bestowed upon the apostles, we know

MATTHEW HENRY

where there is much love there will be much labour. He says of Tryphena and Tryphosa that they laboured in the Lord (*v.* 12), and of the beloved Persis, that she laboured much in the Lord, abounding more in the work of the Lord.

4. Concerning Andronicus and Junia, *v.* 7. Some take them for a man and his wife. They were Paul's *cousins*, akin to him; so was Herodion, *v.* 11. Religion does not take away, but sanctifies, and improves, our respect to our kindred, engaging us to rejoice in them the more, when we find them related to Christ by faith. They were his fellow-prisoners. Partnership in suffering sometimes does much towards the union of souls and the knitting of affections. They were *of note among the apostles*. They were eminent for knowledge, and gifts, and graces, which made them famous among the apostles.

Who also were in Christ before me. In time they had the start of Paul. How ready was Paul to acknowledge in others any kind of precedency!

5. Concerning Apelles, who is here said to be *approved in Christ* (*v.* 10), a high character! One that had been tried; his friends and enemies had tried him, and he was as gold, a man that one might trust and repose a confidence in.

6. Concerning Aristobulus and Narcissus; notice is taken of their household, *v.* 10, 11. Those of their household who *are in the Lord* (as it is limited, *v.* 11), that were Christians. How studious was Paul to leave none out of his salutations that he had any knowledge of or acquaintance with!

7. Concerning Rufus (*v.* 13), *chosen in the Lord*. He was a choice Christian, whose gifts and graces evinced that he was eternally chosen in Christ Jesus.

—*And his mother and mine*, his mother by nature and mine by Christian love. This good woman, upon some occasion, or other, had been as a mother to Paul, and Paul here gratefully owns it.

JAMIESON, FAUSSET, BROWN

7. Andronicus and Junia—or, as it might be, 'Junias,' a contracted form of 'Junianus'; in this case, it is a man's name. But if, as is more probable, the word be, as in our version, "Junia," the person meant was no doubt either the wife or the sister of Andronicus. **my kinsmen**—or, 'relatives.' **and my fellow prisoners**—on what occasion, it is impossible to say, as the apostle elsewhere tells us that he was "in prisons more frequent" (II Cor. 11:23). **which are of note among the apostles**—Those who think the word "apostle" is used in a lax sense, in the Acts and Epistles, take this to mean 'noted apostles' [CHRYSOSTOM, LUTHER, CALVIN, BENGEL, OLSHAUSEN, THOLUCK, ALFORD, JOWETT]; others, who are not clear that the word "apostle" is applied to any without the circle of the Twelve, save where the connection or some qualifying words show that the literal meaning of 'one sent' is the thing intended, understand by the expression used here, 'persons esteemed by the apostles' [BEZA, GROTIUS, DE WETTE, MEYER, FRITZSCHE, STUART, PHILIPPI, HODGE]. And of course, if "Junia" is to be taken for a woman, this latter must be the meaning. **who also were in Christ before me**—The apostle writes as if he envied them this priority in the faith. And, indeed, if to be "in Christ" be the most enviable human condition, the earlier the date of this blessed translation, the greater the grace of it. This latter statement about Andronicus and Junia seems to throw some light on the preceding one. Very possibly they may have been among the first fruits of Peter's labors, gained to Christ either on the day of Pentecost or on some of the succeeding days. In that case they may have attracted the special esteem of those apostles who for some time resided chiefly at Jerusalem and its neighborhood; and our apostle, though he came late in contact with the other apostles, if he was aware of this fact, would have pleasure in alluding to it. **8. Amplias**—a contracted form of 'Ampliatus' —**my beloved in the Lord**—an expression of dear Christian affection. **9, 10. Urbane**—rather, 'Urbanus.' It is a man's name. **our helper**—'fellow labourer'—**in Christ. Salute Apelles approved**—'the approved'—**in Christ**—or, as we should say, 'that tried Christian'; a noble commendation. **Salute them which are of Aristobulus' household**—It would seem, from what is said of Narcissus in the following verse, that this Aristobulus himself had not been a Christian; but that the Christians of his household simply were meant; very possibly some of his slaves. **11. Salute Herodion, my kinsman**—(See on vs. 7), **Greet them that be of the household of Narcissus, which are in the Lord**—which implies that others in his house, including probably himself, were not Christians. **12. Salute Tryphena and Tryphosa, who labour in the Lord**—two active women. **Salute the beloved Persis**—another woman—**which laboured much in the Lord**—referring probably, not to official services, such as would fall to the deaconesses, but to such higher Christian labors—yet within the sphere competent to woman—as Priscilla bestowed on Apollos and others (Acts 18:18). **13. Salute Rufus, chosen**—'the chosen'—**in the Lord**—meaning, not 'who is one of the elect,' as every believer is, but 'the choice' or 'precious one' in the Lord. (See I Pet. 2:4; II John 13.) We read in Mark 15:21 that Simon of Cyrene, who was compelled to bear our Lord's cross, was "the father of Alexander and Rufus." From this we naturally conclude that when Mark wrote his Gospel, Alexander and Rufus must have been well known as Christians among those by whom he expected his Gospel to be first read; and, in all likelihood, this was that very "Rufus"; in which case our interest is deepened by what immediately follows about his mother. **and**—salute —**his mother and mine**—The apostle calls her "his own mother," not so much as our Lord calls every elderly woman believer His mother (Matt. 12:49, 50), but in grateful acknowledgment of her motherly attentions to himself, bestowed no doubt for his Master's sake, and the love she bore to his honored servants. To us it seems altogether likely that the conversion of Simon the Cyrenian dated from that memorable day when "passing [casually] by, as he came from the country" (Mark 15:21), "they compelled him to bear the" Saviour's cross. Sweet compulsion, if what he thus beheld issued in his *voluntarily* taking up his own cross! Through him it is natural to suppose that his wife would be brought in, and that this believing couple, now "heirs together of the grace of life" (I Peter 3:7), as they told their two sons, Alexander and Rufus, what honor had unwittingly been put upon their father at that hour of deepest and dearest moment to all Christians, might be blessed to the inbringing of both of them to Christ. In this case, sup-

ADAM CLARKE

not. Her works, though hidden from man, are with God and her name is recorded with honor in this book of life.

7. *Andronicus and Junia, my kinsmen*. As the word signifies "relatives," whether male or female, and as *Junia* may probably be the name of a woman, the wife of Andronicus, it would be better to say "relatives" than *kinsmen*. But probably Paul means no more than that they were Jews; for in chap. ix. 3 he calls all the Jews his "kinsmen according to the flesh." *My fellowprisoners*. As Paul was in prison often, it is likely that these persons shared this honor with him on some occasion, which is not distinctly marked. *Of note among the apostles*. Whether this intimates that they were noted apostles or only highly reputed by the apostles is not absolutely clear, but the latter appears to me the most probable. They were well-known not only to Paul but also to the rest of the apostles. *In Christ before me*. That is, they were converted to Christianity before Paul was; probably at the Day of Pentecost, or by the ministry of Christ himself, or by that of the seventy disciples.

8. *Amplias my beloved in the Lord*. One who is my "particular friend," and also a genuine Christian.

9. *Urbane, our helper*. Who this Urbanus was we know not; what is here stated is that he had been a fellow laborer with the apostles. *Stachys my beloved*. One of my "particular friends."

10. *Apelles approved in Christ*. A man who, on different occasions, had given the highest proofs of the sincerity and depth of his religion. Some suppose that *Apelles* was the same with Apollos. Whoever he was, he had given every demonstration of being a genuine Christian. *Of Aristobulus' household*. It is doubted whether this person was converted, as the apostle does not salute him, but his *household;* or as the margin reads, "his friends." He might have been a Roman of considerable distinction who, though not converted himself, had Christians among his servants or his slaves. But whatever he was, it is likely that he was dead at this time, and therefore only those of his household are referred to by the apostle.

11. *Herodion my kinsman*. Probably another converted Jew. See on v. 7. *Of the household of Narcissus*. Probably dead also, as we have supposed Aristobulus to have been at this time. *Which are in the Lord*. This might intimate that some of this family were not Christians, those only of that family that were converted to the Lord being saluted.

12. *Tryphena and Tryphosa*. Two holy women, who it seems were assistants to the apostle in his work, probably by exhorting, visiting the sick, etc. *Persis* was another woman who it seems excelled the preceding; for of her it is said, She *laboured much in the Lord*. We learn from this that Christian women as well as men labored in the ministry of the Word. In those times of simplicity all persons, whether men or women, who had received the knowledge of the truth believed it to be their duty to propagate it to the uttermost of their power.

13. *Rufus chosen in the Lord*. One of great excellence in Christianity; a "choice" man, as we would say. So the word often signifies. *His mother and mine*. It is not likely that the mother of Rufus was the mother of Paul; but while she was the natural mother of the former, she acted as a mother to the latter. We say of a person of this character that she is a "motherly" woman. Among the ancients, he or she who acted a kind, instructing, and indulgent part to another was styled the "father" or "mother" of such a one.

MATTHEW HENRY

8. Concerning the rest, he salutes the *brethren who are with them* (*v.* 14), and the *saints who are with them* (*v.* 15). It is the good property of saints to delight in being together; and Paul thus joins them together in his salutations to endear them one to another. In Christian congregations there should be smaller societies linked together in love and converse.

Lastly, He concludes with the recommendation of them to the love and embraces one of another: *Salute one another with a holy kiss.* Mutual salutations, as they express love, so they increase and strengthen love. Paul here encourages the use of them, and only directs that they may be holy. He adds, in the close, a general salutation to them all, in the name of the churches of Christ (*v.* 16): "*The churches of Christ salute you;* that is, the churches which I am with desire me to testify their affection to you and good wishes for you." This is one way of maintaining the communion of saints.

Verses 17–20

A caution to take heed of those whose principles and practices were destructive to Christian love.

I. The caution itself: *I beseech you, brethren.* He does not will and command, but for love's sake beseeches. He teaches them, 1. To see their danger: *Mark those who cause divisions and offences.* Our Master had himself foretold that divisions and offences would come, and against such we are here cautioned. Those who burden the church with dividing and offending impositions cause divisions and offences, contrary to, or different from, the *doctrine which we have learned.* If truth be once deserted, unity and peace will not last long. Now, *mark* those that thus cause divisions. There is need of a piercing watchful eye to discern the danger we are in from such people; for commonly the pretences are plausible, when the projects are very pernicious. A danger discovered is half prevented. 2. To shun it: "*Avoid them.* Shun all unnecessary communion and communication with them, lest you be leavened and infected by them.—*Their word will eat as doth a canker.*" Some think he especially warns them to take heed of the judaizing teachers.

II. The reasons to enforce this caution.

1. Because of the pernicious policy of these seducers, *v.* 18. His description of them, in two things: (1) The master they serve: not *our Lord Jesus Christ.* Though they call themselves Christians, they do not serve Christ, whatever they pretend. But they *serve their own belly.* It is some base lust or other that they are pleasing. Their *God is their belly*, Phil. iii. 19. What a base master do they serve, and how unworthy to come in competition with Christ. (2) The method they take to compass their design: *By good words and fair speeches they deceive the hearts of the simple.* Their words and speeches have a show of holiness and zeal for God (it is an easy thing to be godly from the teeth outward), and a show of kindness and love to those into whom they instil their corrupt doctrines. We have great need therefore to keep our hearts with all diligence.

2. Because of the peril we are in: "For *your obedience has come abroad unto all men*—you are noted in all the churches for a willing, tractable, complying people." (1) Therefore, because it was so, these seducing teachers would be the more apt to assault them. "The false teachers hear that you are an obedient people, and therefore they will be likely to come among you, to see if you will be obedient to them." (2) Though it were so, yet they were in danger from these seducers. This Paul suggests, not as one suspicious of them, but as one solicitous for them: "Your *obedience has come abroad unto all men; I am glad therefore on your behalf.*" Thus does he insinuate their commendation, the better to make way for the caution. "You must not be secure: *I would have you wise unto that which is good, and simple concerning evil.*" A pliable temper is good when it is under good government; but otherwise it may be very ensnaring. Two general rules: [1] To be *wise unto that which is good.* There is need of a great deal of wisdom in our adherence to good truths, and good duties, and good people, lest in any of these we be imposed upon and deluded. [2] To be *simple concerning evil*—so wise as not to be *deceived, and* yet so simple as not to be deceivers. The wisdom of the serpent becomes Christians, but not the subtlety of the old serpent. That is a wisely simple man that knows not how to do anything against the truth. Now Paul was the more solicitous for the Roman church, because it was so famous; it was a city upon a hill, and many eyes were upon the Christians there.

3. Because of the promise of God, that we shall have victory at last (*v.* 20): *The God of peace shall bruise Satan under your feet.*

JAMIESON, FAUSSET, BROWN

posing the elder of the two to have departed to be with Christ ere this letter was written, or to have been residing in some other place, and Rufus left alone with his mother, how instructive and beautiful is the testimony here borne to her! **14, 15. Salute Asyncritus . . .**—These have been thought to be the names of ten less notable Christians than those already named. But this will hardly be supposed if it be observed that they are divided into two pairs of five each, and that after the first of these pairs it is added, "and the brethren which are with them," while after the second pair we have the words, "and all the saints which are with them." This perhaps hardly means that each of the five in both pairs had "a church at his house," else probably this would have been more expressly said. But at least it would seem to indicate that they were each a center of some few Christians who met at his house—it may be for further instruction, for prayer, for missionary purposes, or for some other Christian objects. These little peeps into the rudimental forms which Christian fellowship first took in the great cities, though too indistinct for more than conjecture, are singularly interesting. Our apostle would seem to have been kept minutely informed as to the state of the church at Rome, both as to its membership and its varied activities, probably by Priscilla and Aquila. **16. Salute one another with an holy kiss**—So I Corinthians 16:20; I Thessalonians 5:26; I Peter 5:14. The custom prevailed among the Jews, and doubtless came from the East, where it still obtains. Its adoption into the Christian churches, as the symbol of a higher fellowship than it had ever expressed before, was probably as immediate as it was natural. In this case the apostle's desire seems to be that on receipt of his epistle, with its salutations, they should in this manner expressly testify their Christian affection. It afterwards came to have a fixed place in the church service, immediately after the celebration of the Supper, and continued long in use. In such matters, however, the state of society and the peculiarities of different places require to be studied. **The churches of Christ salute you**—The true reading is, 'All the churches'; the word "all" gradually falling out, as seeming probably to express more than the apostle would venture to affirm. But no more seems meant than to assure the Romans in what affectionate esteem they were held by the churches generally; all that knew he was writing to Rome having expressly asked their own salutations to be sent to them. (See vs. 19.) **17. Now I beseech you, brethren, mark them which cause divisions and offences contrary to the doctrine which ye have learned**—'which ye learned'—**and avoid them**—The fomentors of "divisions" here referred to are probably those who were unfriendly to the truths taught in this epistle, while those who caused "offenses" were probably those referred to in ch. 14:15 as haughtily disregarding the prejudices of the weak. The direction as to both is, first, to "mark" such, lest the evil should be done ere it was fully discovered; and next, to "avoid" them (cf. II Thess. 3:6, 14), so as neither to bear any responsibility for their procedure, nor seem to give them the least countenance. **18. For they that are such serve not our Lord Jesus Christ**—'our Lord Christ' appears to be the true reading. **but their own belly**—not in the grosser sense, but as 'living for low ends of their own' (cf. Phil. 3:19). **and by good words and fair speeches deceive the simple**—the unwary, the unsuspecting. (See Prov. 14:15.) **19. For your obedience**—i.e., tractableness—**is come abroad unto all. I am glad therefore on your behalf**—'I rejoice therefore over you,' seems the true reading. **but yet I would have you wise unto that which is good, and simple**—'harmless,' as in Matthew 10:16, from which the warning is taken—**concerning**—'unto'—**evil**—'Your reputation among the churches for subjection to the teaching ye have received is to me sufficient ground of confidence in you; but ye need the serpent's wisdom to discriminate between transparent truth and plausible error, with that guileless simplicity which instinctively cleaves to the one and rejects the other.'

20. And the God of peace shall bruise Satan under your feet shortly—The apostle encourages the Romans to persevere in resisting the wiles of the devil

ADAM CLARKE

14. *Salute Asyncritus . . .* Who these were we know not. *Hermas* was probably the same to whom a work called the Shepherd is attributed; a work with this title is still extant, and may be found among the writings of the apostolical fathers. But it is in vain to look for identity of persons in similarity of names, for among the Greeks and Romans at this time there were many persons who bore the same names mentioned in this chapter.

15. *Salute Philologus.* Of these several persons, though much has been conjectured, nothing certain is known. Even the names of some are so ambiguous that we know not whether they were men or women. They were persons well-known to Paul, and undoubtedly were such as had gone from different places where the apostle had preached to sojourn or settle at Rome. One thing we may remark, that there is no mention of Peter, who, according to the Roman and papistical catalogue of bishops, must have been at Rome at this time. If he were not now at Rome, the foundation stone of Rome's ascendancy, of Peter's supremacy, and of the uninterrupted succession is taken away, and the whole fabric falls to the ground. But if Peter were at Rome at this time, Paul would have sent his salutations to him in the first place.

16. *Salute one another with an holy kiss.* In those early times the *kiss*, as a token of peace, friendship, and brotherly love, was frequent among all people; and the Christians used it in their public assemblies, as well as in their occasional meetings. This was at last laid aside, not because it was abused, but because, the Church becoming very numerous, the thing was impossible. In some countries the kiss of friendship is still common; and in such countries it is scarcely ever abused, nor is it an incentive to evil because it is customary and common. Shaking of hands is now substituted for it in almost all Christian congregations. *The churches of Christ salute you.* The word *all* is added here by some of the most reputable MSS. and principal versions. Paul must mean, here, that all the churches in Greece and Asia, through which he had passed, in which the faith of the Christians at Rome was known, spoke of them affectionately and honorably; and probably knowing the apostle's design of visiting Rome, desired to be kindly remembered to the church in that city.

18. *They . . . serve not our Lord Jesus.* They profess to be apostles, but they are not apostles of Christ; they neither do His will nor preach His doctrine. They serve *their own belly*—they have intruded themselves into the Church of Christ that they might get a secular support; it is for worldly gain alone that they take up the profession of the ministry. They have no divine credentials; they convert not the heathen nor the ungodly, for they have no divine unction. But *by good words and fair speeches* (for they have no miraculous nor saving powers) *deceive the hearts of the simple*, perverting Christian converts, that they may get their property, and thus secure a maintenance for themselves.

19. *For your obedience is come abroad.* The apostle gives this as a reason why they should continue to hear and heed those who had led them into the path of truth, and avoid those false teachers whose doctrines tended to the subversion of their souls. *Yet I would have you wise.* I would wish you carefully to discern the good from the evil, and to show your wisdom by carefully avoiding the one and cleaving to the other.

20. *The God of peace.* Who neither sends nor favors such disturbers of the tranquility of His Church. *Shall bruise Satan.* Shall give you the

MATTHEW HENRY

(1) The titles he gives to God: *The God of peace.* When we come to God for spiritual victories, we must not only eye him as the Lord of hosts, whose all power is, but as the God of peace, a God at peace with us, creating peace for us. Victory comes from God more as the God of peace than as the God of war.

(2) The blessing he expects from God—a victory over Satan. Satan tempting and troubling, acting as a deceiver and as a destroyer, the *God of peace* will *bruise under our feet.* "Though you cannot overcome in your own strength and wisdom, yet the God of peace will do it for you." [1] The victory shall be complete: *He shall bruise Satan under your feet,* plainly alluding to the first promise the Messiah made in paradise (Gen. iii. 15). Christ hath overcome for us, and we have nothing to do but to pursue the victory. Let this quicken us to our spiritual conflict, to fight the good fight of faith. [2] The victory shall be speedy: He shall do it *shortly.* It will encourage soldiers when they know the war will be at an end quickly, in such a victory. It is the victory which all the saints shall have over Satan when they come to heaven, together with the present victories which through grace they obtain in earnest of that. Hold out therefore, faith and patience, yet a little while! *The grace of our Lord Jesus Christ be with you.* If the grace of Christ be with us, who can be against us so as to prevail? Paul, not only as a friend, but as an apostle, thus with authority blesses them, and repeats it, *v.* 24.

Verses 21–24

He here adds an affectionate remembrance of them from some particular persons who were now with him. 1. Some that were his particular friends. *Timotheus my work-fellow.* Paul sometimes calls Timothy his son; but here he styles him his work-fellow, as one equal with him. *Lucius,* probably Lucius of Cyrene, a noted man in the church of Antioch (Acts xiii. 1). *Sosipater,* supposed to be the same with Sopater of Berea, mentioned Acts xx. 4. These Paul calls his kinsmen. It is a very great comfort to see the holiness and usefulness of our kindred. 2. One that was Paul's amanuensis (*v.* 22): *I Tertius, who wrote this epistle.* Paul made use of a scribe because he wrote a bad hand, which was not very legible, which he excuses, when he writes to the Galatians with his own hand (Gal. vi. 11). The least piece of service done to the church shall not pass without a remembrance and a recompence. 3. Some others that were of note among the Christians (*v.* 23): *Gaius my host.* Paul commends him for his great hospitality; not only my host, but of the *whole church.*

Erastus, the chamberlain of the city, is another; he means the city of Corinth. It seems he was a person of honour and account, one in public place. Not many mighty, not many noble, are called, but some are.

Quartus is likewise mentioned, and called a brother.

JAMIESON, FAUSSET, BROWN

with the assurance that, as good soldiers of Jesus Christ, they are "shortly" to receive their discharge, and have the satisfaction of "putting their feet upon the neck" of that formidable enemy—symbol familiar, probably, in all languages to express not only the completeness of the defeat, but the abject humiliation of the conquered foe. (See Josh. 10:24; II Sam. 22:41; Ezek. 21:29; Ps. 91:13.) Though the apostle here styles Him who is thus to bruise Satan, the God of peace," with special reference to the "divisions" (vs. 17) by which the church at Rome was in danger of being disturbed, this sublime appellation of God has here a wider sense, pointing to the whole "purpose for which the Son of God was manifested, to destroy the works of the devil" (I John 3:8); and indeed this assurance is but a reproduction of the first great promise, that the Seed of the woman should bruise the Serpent's head (Gen. 3:15). **The grace of our Lord Jesus Christ be with you. Amen**—The "Amen" here has no MS. authority. What comes after this, where one would have expected the epistle to close, has its parallel in Philippians 4:20, etc., and being in fact common in epistolary writings, is simply a mark of genuineness. **21. Timotheus, my work-fellow**—'my fellow labourer'; see Acts 16:1-5. The apostle mentions him here rather than in the opening address to this church, as he had not been at Rome [BENGEL]. **and Lucius**—not Luke, for the fuller form of 'Lucas' is not 'Lucius' but 'Lucanus.' The person meant seems to be "Lucius of Cyrene," who was among the "prophets and teachers" at Antioch with our apostle, before he was summoned into the missionary field (Acts 13:1). **and Jason**—See Acts 17:5. He had probably accompanied or followed the apostle from Thessalonica to Corinth. **Sosipater**—See Acts 20:4. **22. I, Tertius, who wrote this**—'the'—**epistle**—as the apostle's amanuensis, or penman—**salute you in the Lord**—So usually did the apostle dictate his epistles, that he calls the attention of the Galatians to the fact that to them he wrote with his own hand (Gal. 6:11). But this Tertius would have the Romans to know that, far from being a mere scribe, his heart went out to them in Christian affection; and the apostle, by giving his salutation a place here, would show what sort of assistants he employed. **23. Gaius mine host, and**—the host—**of the whole church**—See Acts 20:4. It would appear that he was one of only two persons whom Paul baptized with his own hand (cf. III John 1). His Christian hospitality appears to have been something uncommon.

Erastus the chamberlain—'treasurer'—**of the city**—doubtless of Corinth. (See Acts 19:22; II Tim. 4:20.)

Quartus a brother—rather, 'the' or 'our brother'; as Sosthenes and Timothy are called (I Cor. 1:1, and II Cor. 1:1 *(Greek).* Nothing more is known of this Quartus.

24. The grace, . . .—a repetition of the benediction precisely as in vs. 20, save that it is here invoked on them "all."

ADAM CLARKE

dominion over the great adversary of your souls, and over all his agents who, through his influence, endeavor to destroy your peace and subvert your minds. Several critics suppose that the word *Satan* is a sort of collective term here, by which all opposers and adversaries are meant, and especially those false teachers to whom he refers above. *The grace of our Lord.* That you may be truly wise, simple, obedient, and steady in the truth, may the favor or gracious influence of our Lord Jesus Christ be with you—without which you cannot be preserved from evil, nor do anything that is good.

Here the apostle appears to have intended to conclude his Epistle; but afterwards he added a postscript, if not two, as we shall see below. Several ancient MSS. omit the whole of this clause, probably thinking that it had been borrowed from v. 24. But on the ground that the apostle might have added a postscript or two, not having immediate opportunity to send the Epistle, there is no need for this supposition.

21. *Timotheus my workfellow.* This is on all hands allowed to be the same Timothy to whom Paul directs the two Epistles which are still extant. *Lucius.* This was probably Luke, the Evangelist, and writer of the book called the Acts of the Apostles. *Jason.* It is likely that this is the same person mentioned in Acts xvii. 7, who at Thessalonica received the apostles into his house, and befriended them at the risk of both his property and life. *Sosipater.* He was a Berean, the son of one Pyrrhus, a Jew by birth, and accompanied Paul from Greece into Asia, and probably into Judea. See Acts xx. 4.

22. *I Tertius, who wrote this epistle.* It appears that Paul dictated it to him, and he wrote it down from the apostle's mouth, and here introduces himself as joining with Paul in affectionate wishes for their welfare. *Salute you in the Lord.* I wish you well in the name of the Lord: or, I feel for you that affectionate respect which the grace of the Lord Jesus inspires. It is not clear whether the following two verses be the words of Tertius or of Paul.

23. *Gaius mine host. Gaius* in Greek is the same as *Caius* in Latin, which was a very common name among the Romans. Luke (Acts xix. 29) mentions one "Gaius of Macedonia," who was exposed to much violence at Ephesus in the tumult excited by Demetrius the silversmith against Paul and his companions; and it is very possible that this was the same person. He is here called not only the *host,* the "entertainer" of Paul, or Tertius (if he wrote this and the following verse), but also of *the whole church;* that is, he received and lodged the apostles who came from different places, as well as the messengers of the churches. *Erastus the chamberlain of the city.* "Treasurer of the city" of Corinth, from which Paul wrote this Epistle. This is supposed to be the same person as is mentioned in Acts xix. 22. He was one of Paul's companions, and, as appears from 2 Tim. iv. 20, was left about this time by the apostle at Corinth. He is called the *chamberlain,* which signifies the same as "treasurer," he to whom the receipt and expenditure of the public money were intrusted. Such persons were in very high credit; and if Erastus was at this time treasurer, it would appear that Christianity was then in considerable repute in Corinth. But if the Erastus of the Acts was the same with the Erastus mentioned here, it is not likely that he now held the office, for this could not at all comport with his travelling with Paul. Hence several, both ancients and moderns, who believe the identity of the persons, suppose that Erastus was not now treasurer, but that having formerly been so, he still retained the title. Chrysostom thought that he still retained the employment. *Quartus a brother.* Whether the brother of Erastus or of Tertius we know not; probably nothing more is meant than that he was a Christian—one of the heavenly family, a *brother* in the Lord.

24. *The grace of our Lord.* This is the conclusion of Tertius, and is similar to what Paul used above. Hence it is possible that Tertius wrote the whole of the twenty-second, twenty-third, and twenty-fourth verses without receiving any particular instructions from Paul, except the bare permission to add his own salutations with those of his particular friends. There is a great deal of disagreement among the

MATTHEW HENRY

Verses 25–27

Here the apostle solemnly closes his epistle with a magnificent ascription of glory to the blessed God. He does, as it were, breathe out his soul to these Romans in the praise of God.

I. A description of the gospel of God, which comes in in a parenthesis. *To establish you according to my gospel.* Paul calls it his gospel, because he was the preacher of it. Paul had his head and heart so full of the gospel that he could scarcely mention it without a digression to set forth the nature and excellency of it.

1. It is the *preaching of Jesus Christ.* The sum and substance of the whole gospel is Jesus Christ and him crucified. We preach not ourselves, says Paul, but Christ Jesus the Lord. That which establishes souls is the plain preaching of Jesus Christ.

2. *It is the revelation of the mystery which was kept secret since the world began, and by the scriptures of the prophets made known.* The subject-matter of the gospel is a mystery. Blessed be God, there is as much of this mystery made plain as will suffice to bring us to heaven, if we do not wilfully neglect so great salvation.

(1) This mystery was kept secret since the world began: It was *wrapped up in silence from eternity*; so some. Before the foundation of the world was laid, the mystery was hid in God, Eph. iii. 9. Or, *since the world began*, so we translate it. During all the times of the Old Testament this mystery was comparatively kept secret. Thus it was hid from ages and generations, even among the Jews, much more among the Gentiles. Even the disciples of Christ themselves, before his resurrection and ascension, were very much in the dark about the mystery of redemption.

(2) It is now made manifest. The shadows of the evening are done away, and the Sun of righteousness has risen upon the world. But how is it made manifest by the scriptures of the prophets? Surely, because now the event has given the best exposition to the prophecies of the Old Testament. Being accomplished, they are explained. The Old Testament does not only borrow light from, but return light to, the revelation of the New Testament. Now Christ appears to have been the treasure hid in the field of the Old Testament. To him bear *all the prophets witness.* See Luke xxiv. 27.

(3) It is manifested *according to the commandment of the everlasting God.* Lest any should object, "Why was this mystery kept secret so long, and why made manifest now?"—he resolves it into the will of God. *The everlasting God.* He is from everlasting. He is to everlasting. We must never look for any new revelation, but abide by this, for this is according to the commandment of the everlasting God. Christ, in the gospel, is the same yesterday, today, and for ever.

(4) It is *made known to all nations for the obedience of faith.* The extent of this revelation he often takes notice of. Christ is salvation to the ends of the earth, to all nations. And the design of it is very observable; it is for the obedience of faith. The gospel is revealed, not to be talked of, and disputed about, but to be submitted to. See here what is the right faith—even that which works in obedience; and what is the right obedience—even that which springs from faith; and what is the design of the gospel—to bring us to both.

II. A doxology to that God whose gospel it is, ascribing glory to him for ever (*v.* 27).

1. The matter of this praise. In thanking God, we fasten upon his favours, to us; in praising and adoring God, we fasten upon his perfections in himself. Two of his principal attributes are here taken notice of: (1) His power (*v.* 25): *To him that is of power to establish you.* It is no less than a divine power that establishes the saints. In giving God the glory of this power we may, and must, take to ourselves the comfort of it—that whatever our doubts, and difficulties, and fears, may be, our God, whom we serve, is of power to establish us. (2) His wisdom (*v.* 27): *To God only wise.* Power to effect without wisdom to contrive, and wisdom to contrive without power to effect, are alike vain and fruitless; but both together, and both infinite, make a perfect being. He is only perfectly and infallibly wise. He is the spring and fountain of all the wisdom of the creatures. With him are strength and wisdom.

2. The Mediator of this praise: *Through Jesus Christ. To God only wise through Jesus Christ;* so some. It is in and through Christ that God is manifested to the world as the only wise God. Or rather, as we read it, *glory through Jesus Christ.* All the glory that passes from fallen man to God must go through the hands of the Lord Jesus. As he is the Mediator of all our prayers, so he is, and I believe will be to eternity, the Mediator of all our praises.

JAMIESON, FAUSSET, BROWN

25. Now to him that is of power—more simply, as in Jude 24, 'to Him that is able'—**to stablish**—confirm, or uphold—**you, according to my gospel, and the preaching of Jesus Christ**—i.e., in conformity with the truths of that Gospel which I preach, and not I only, but all to whom has been committed "the preaching of Jesus Christ."

—according to the revelation of the mystery—see on ch. 11:25—**which was kept secret since the world began**—lit., 'which hath been kept in silence during eternal ages'.

26. But is now made manifest—The reference here is to that peculiar feature of the Gospel economy which Paul himself was specially employed to carry into practical effect and to unfold by his teaching—the introduction of the Gentile believers to an equality with their Jewish brethren, and the new, and, to the Jews, quite unexpected form which this gave to the whole Kingdom of God (cf. Eph. 3:1-10, etc.). This the apostle calls here a mystery hitherto undisclosed, in what sense the next verse will show, but now fully unfolded; and his prayer for the Roman Christians, in the form of a doxology to Him who was able to do what he asked, is that they might be established in the truth of the Gospel, not only in its essential character, but specially in that feature of it which gave themselves, as Gentile believers, their whole standing among the people of God.

and by the scriptures of the prophets, according to the commandment of the everlasting God, made known to all nations for—in order to—**the obedience of faith**—Lest they should think, from what he had just said, that God had brought in upon his people so vast a change on their condition without giving them any previous notice, the apostle here adds that, on the contrary, "the Scriptures of the prophets" contain all that he and other preachers of the Gospel had to declare on these topics, and indeed that the same "everlasting God," who "from eternal ages" had kept these things hid, had given "commandment'" that they should now, according to the tenor of those prophetic Scriptures, be imparted to every nation for their believing acceptance.

27. to God, . . .—'To the only wise God through Jesus Christ, be'—lit., 'to whom be'; i.e., 'to Him, I say, be the glory for ever. Amen.' At its outset, this is an ascription of glory to the *power* that could do all this; at its close it ascribes glory to the *wisdom* that planned and that presides over the gathering of a redeemed people out of all nations. The apostle adds his devout "Amen," which the reader—if he has followed him with the astonishment and delight of him who pens these words—will fervently echo.

ADAM CLARKE

MSS. and versions relative to this verse, some rejecting it entirely, and some of those which place the following verses at the end of chap. xiv inserting it at the end of the twenty-seventh verse in that place.

25. *Now to him.* In the note at the end of chap. xiv I have shown that this and the following verses are by the most reputable MSS. and versions placed at the end of that chapter, which is supposed by most critics to be their proper place. *Of power to stablish you.* To that God without whom nothing is wise, nothing strong; who is as willing to teach as He is wise, as ready to help as He is strong. *According to my gospel.* That gospel which explains and publishes God's purpose of taking the Gentiles to be His people under the Messiah, without subjecting them to the law of Moses. This is what he here calls the preaching of Jesus Christ.

Which was kept secret. This purpose of calling the Gentiles, and giving them equal privileges to the Jews without obliging them to submit to circumcision.

26. *But now is made manifest.* Now, under the New Testament dispensation, and by my preaching. *By the scriptures of the prophets.* Hints relative to this important work being scattered up and down through all their works, but no clear revelation that the Gentiles, who should be admitted into the Church, should be admitted without passing under the yoke of the Mosaic law. This was the point which was kept secret. As to the calling of the Gentiles, this was declared in general terms by the prophets, and the apostle quotes and makes a most important use of their predictions; but the other was a point on which the prophets gave no information, and it seems to have been peculiarly revealed to Paul, who received *the commandment of the everlasting God* to make it known to all the Gentiles—all the people of the earth that were not of Jewish extraction. And it was to be made known *for the obedience of faith*, that they might believe its doctrines and obey its precepts; its universal voice requiring repentance towards God, faith in our Lord Jesus Christ, and circumcision of the heart, in the place of all Jewish rites and ceremonies.

27. *To God only wise.* This comes in with great propriety. He alone who is the Fountain of wisdom and knowledge had all this mystery in himself; and He alone who knew the times, places, persons, and circumstances could reveal the whole; and He has revealed all in such a way as not only to manifest His unsearchable wisdom, but also His infinite goodness. Therefore to Him be *glory* for His wisdom in devising this most admirable plan, and His goodness in sending Christ Jesus to execute it; to Him, through Christ Jesus, be glory *for ever*—because this plan is to last forever, and is to have no issue but in eternal glory. *Written to the Romans from Corinthus.* That this Epistle was written from Corinth is almost universally believed. That *Phebe* was a deaconess of the church at Cenchrea, we have seen in the first verse of this chapter; and that the Epistle might have been sent by her to Rome is possible. This subscription, however, stands on very questionable grounds. It is wanting in almost all the ancient MSS.; and even of those which are more modern, few have it entirely, as in our common editions. The subscriptions to the sacred books are of little or no authority, all having been added in latter times, and frequently by injudicious hands. The word *Amen* was seldom added by the inspired writers, and here it is wanting in almost all the ancient MSS. As this was a word in frequent use in religious services, pious people would naturally employ it in finishing the reading or copying of this Epistle, as they would thereby express their conviction of the truth of its contents, and their desire that the promises contained in it might be fulfilled to them and to the Church at large.

THE FIRST EPISTLE TO THE CORINTHIANS

I. Introduction (1:1-8)
A. The writers (1:1)
1. Paul (1:1a)
2. Sosthenes (1:1b)
B. The Church (1:2-8)
1. Nature (1:2, 3)
2. Character (1:4)
3. Equipment (1:5-8)

II. Corrective—the carnalities (1:9-11:34)
A. Fundamental proposition (1:9)
B. Divisions (1:10-4:21)
1. The wisdom of words and the word of the cross (1:10-2:16)
2. Causative carnality corrected (3:1-4:21)
C. Derelictions (5:1-6:20)
1. Discipline (5:1-13)
2. Disputes (6:1-11)
3. Desecration (6:12-20)
D. Difficulties (7:1-11:34)
1. Concerning marriage (7:1-40)
2. Concerning things sacrificed to idols (8:1-11:1)
3. Concerning women (11:2-16)
4. Concerning the Lord's Supper (11:17-34a)
5. Conclusion (11:34b)

III. Constructive—the spiritualities (12:1-15:58)
A. The unifying Spirit (12:1-31)
1. The creation of unification (12:1-3)
2. The administration of unification (12:4-7)
3. The realization of unification (12:8-31)
B. The unfailing law (13:1-14:40)
1. The law (13:1-13)
2. The law at work (14:1-40)
C. The ultimate triumph (15:1-57)
1. The Gospel of Christ's resurrection (15:1-11)
2. The importance of Christ's resurrection (15:12-34)
3. Intellectual difficulties (15:35-50)
4. The assurance and challenge (15:51-57)
D. Final injunction (15:58)

IV. Illustrative conclusion (16:1-24)
A. Concerning the collection (16:1-4)
B. Paul the worker (16:5-9)
C. Timothy the worker (16:10, 11)
D. Apollos the worker (16:12)
E. Injunctions to workers (16:13, 14)
F. Interrelation of workers (16:15-18)
G. Salutations (16:19-24)

Corinth was a principal city of Greece. It was situated on the isthmus that joined Peloponnesus to the rest of Greece, and had two ports adjoining, one called Lechaeum, not far from the city, whence they traded to Italy and the west, the other, called Cenchrea, at a more remote distance, whence they traded to Asia. From this situation, it is no wonder that Corinth should be a place of great trade and wealth; and neither is it to be wondered at if a place so famous for wealth and arts should be infamous for vice. Yet in this lewd city did Paul plant and raise a Christian church, chiefly among the Gentiles. "You know that you were Gentiles, carried away to those dumb idols even as you were led," though it is not improbable that many Jewish converts might be also among them, for we are told that "Crispus, the chief ruler of the synagogue, believed on the Lord, with all his house" (Acts 18:8). He continued in this city nearly two years, being encouraged by a divine vision assuring him God "had much people in that city" (Acts 18:9, 10).

Some time after he left them he wrote this epistle to them, to water what he had planted and rectify some gross disorders which during his absence had been introduced. Pride, avarice, luxury, lust, with all these either the body of this people or some particular persons among them are here charged by the apostle. Their pride discovered itself in their parties and factions. And this vice was not wholly fed by their wealth, but by the insight they had into the Greek learning and philosophy. Their avarice was manifest in their lawsuits before heathen judges. Their luxury appeared in more instances than one—in their dress, in their debauching themselves even at the Lord's table. Their lust broke out in a most flagrant and infamous instance—that a man should have his father's wife. And it is plain from other passages of the epistle that they were not so entirely free from their former lewd inclinations as not to need very strict cautions against fornication. The pride of their learning had also carried many of them so far as to disbelieve or dispute the doctrine of the resurrection.

It is manifest that there was much that deserved reprehension, and needed correction, in this church. And the apostle sets himself to do both with all wisdom and faithfulness, and with a due mixture of tenderness and authority. After a short introduction he first blames them for their discord and factions, and prescribes humility as a remedy for the evils that abounded among them. This he does through the first four chapters. In the fifth he treats the case of the incestuous person. In the sixth chapter he blames them for their lawsuits, carried on before heathen judges, and in the close of the chapter warns them against the sin of fornication. In the seventh chapter he gives advice upon a case of conscience about marriage. He gives also some directions here about virgins. In the eighth he directs them about meats offered to idols. From this he also takes occasion, in the ninth chapter, to expatiate a little on his own conduct. In the tenth chapter he dissuades them against having communion with idolaters, by eating of their sacrifices, inasmuch as they could not be at once partakers of the Lord's table and the table of devils. In the eleventh chapter he gives direction about their habit in public worship, blames them for their gross irregularities and scandalous disorders in receiving the Lord's Supper. In the twelfth chapter he enters on the consideration of spiritual gifts, which were poured forth in great abundance on this church. Toward the close he informs them that he could recommend to them something far more excellent, upon which he breaks out, in the thirteenth chapter, into the commendation and characteristics of charity. And then, in the fourteenth, he directs them how to keep up decency and order in the churches in the use of their spiritual gifts. The fifteenth chapter is taken up in confirming and explaining the great doctrine of the resurrection. The last chapter consists of some particular advices and salutations.

CHAPTER 1

Verses 1–9
We have here the apostle's preface to his whole epistle.

I. The inscription. It is an epistle from Paul to the church of Corinth, which he himself had planted, though there were some among them that now questioned his apostleship (*ch.* ix. 1, 2). The most faithful and useful ministers are not secure from this contempt. *Paul, called to be an apostle of Jesus Christ, through the will of God.* He had not taken this honour to himself, but had a divine commission for it. It was necessary at this time, to assert his character, and magnify his office, when false teachers made a merit of running him down. It was not pride in Paul, but

CHAPTER 1

Vss. 1-31. The Inscription; Thanksgiving for the Spiritual State of the Corinthian Church; Reproof of Party Divisions: His own Method of Preaching Only Christ. 1. called to be—Found in some, not in others, of the oldest MSS. Possibly inserted from Romans 1:1; but as likely to be genuine. Translate, lit., "a called apostle" [Conybeare and Howson]. through the will of God—not because of my own merit. Thus Paul's call as "an apostle by the will of God," while constituting the ground of the authority he claims in the Corinthian Church (cf. Gal. 1:1), is a reason for humility on his own part (ch. 15:8, 10) [Bengel]. In assuming the ministerial office a man should see he

CHAPTER 1

1. *Paul, called to be an apostle.* The word *called* may be here used, as in some other places, for "constituted." As the apostle had many irregularities to reprehend in the Corinthian church, it was necessary that he should be explicit in stating his authority. *Through the will of God.* By a particular appointment from God alone; for, being an extraordinary messenger, he derived no part of his authority from man.

MATTHEW HENRY

faithfulness to his trust to maintain his apostolical character and authority. He joins Sosthenes with him in writing. Paul, and Sosthenes his brother, once a ruler of the Jewish synagogue, afterwards a convert to Christianity. He speaks, through the rest of the epistle, in his own name, and in the singular number.

TODAY'S DICTIONARY OF THE BIBLE:

Sosthenes—*safe in strength*—the chief ruler of the synagogue at Corinth, who was seized and beaten by the mob in the presence of Gallio, the Roman governor, when he refused to proceed against Paul at the instigation of the Jews (Acts 18:12-17). The motives of this assault against Sosthenes are not recorded, nor is it mentioned whether it was made by Greeks or Romans. Some identify him with one whom Paul calls "Sosthenes our brother," a convert to the faith (1 Cor. 1:1).

The persons to whom this epistle was directed were *the church of God that was at Corinth, sanctified in Christ Jesus, and called to be saints*. All Christians are thus far sanctified in Christ Jesus, that they are by baptism dedicated and devoted to him. If they be not truly holy, it is their own fault and reproach. It is the design of Christianity to sanctify us in Christ.

He directs the epistle *to all that in every place call on the name of Christ Jesus our Lord, both theirs and ours*. God hath a remnant in all places; and we should have a common concern for and hold communion with all that call on Christ's name.

II. The apostolical benediction. *Grace be to you, and peace, from God our Father, and from the Lord Jesus Christ*. Grace and peace—the favour of God, and reconciliation to him. It is indeed the summary of all blessings. This advantage we have by the gospel, 1. That we are directed how to obtain that peace from God: it is in and by Christ. 2. We are told what must qualify us for this peace; namely, grace: first grace, and then peace.

III. The apostle's thanksgiving to God on their behalf. Paul begins most of his epistles with thanksgiving to God for his friends and prayer for them. He gives thanks, 1. For their conversion to the faith of Christ: *For the grace which was given you through Jesus Christ, v.* 4. Those who are united to him by faith, are the objects of divine favour. God loves them. 2. For the abundance of their spiritual gifts. They did not come behind any of the churches in any gift, *v.* 7. He specifies *utterance and knowledge, v.* 5. Many have the flower of utterance that have not the root of knowledge, and their converse is barren. Many have the treasure of knowledge, and want utterance to employ it for the good of others, and then it is in a manner wrapped up in a napkin. But, where God gives both, a man is qualified for eminent usefulness. These gifts were a confirmation of the testimony of Christ among them, *v.* 6. So that the

JAMIESON, FAUSSET, BROWN

does so not of his own impulse, but by the will of God (Jer. 23:21); Paul if left to his own will would never have been an apostle (Rom. 9:16). **Sosthenes**
Associated by Paul with himself in the inscription, either in modesty, Sosthenes being his inferior [CHRYSOSTOM], or in order that the name of a "brother" of note in Corinth (Acts 18:17) might give weight to his Epistle and might show, in opposition to his detractors that he was supported by leading *brethren*. Gallio had driven the Jews who accused Paul from the judgment seat. The Greek mob, who disliked Jews, took the opportunity then of beating Sosthenes the ruler of the Jewish synagogue, while Gallio looked on and refused to interfere, being secretly pleased that the mob should second his own contempt for the Jews. Paul probably at this time had showed sympathy for an adversary in distress, which issued in the conversion of the latter. So Crispus also, the previous chief ruler of the synagogue had been converted. Saul the persecutor turned into Paul the apostle, and Sosthenes the leader in persecution against that apostle, were two trophies of divine grace that, side by side, would appeal with double power to the Church at Corinth [BIRKS]. **2. the church of God**—He calls it so notwithstanding its many blots. Fanatics and sectaries vainly think to anticipate the final sifting of the wheat and tares (Matt. 13:27-30). It is a dangerous temptation to think there is no church where there is not apparent perfect purity. He who thinks so, must at last separate from all others and think himself the only holy man in the world, or establish a peculiar sect with a few hypocrites. It was enough for Paul in recognizing the Corinthians as a church, that he saw among them evangelical doctrine, baptism, and the Lord's Supper" [CALVIN]. It was the Church *of God*, not of this or of that favorite leader [CHRYSOSTOM]. **at Corinth**—a church at dissolute Corinth—what a paradox of grace! **sanctified**—*consecrated*, or *set apart as holy to God in* (by union with) *Christ Jesus*. In the *Greek* there are no words "to them that are"; translate simply, "men sanctified." **called to be saints**—rather, "called saints"; saints by calling: applied by Paul to *all* professing members of the Church. As "sanctified in Christ" implies the fountain sources of holiness, the believer's original sanctification in Christ (ch. 6:11; Heb. 10:10, 14; I Pet. 1:2) in the purposes of God's grace, so "called saints" refers to their actual *call* (Rom. 8:30), and the end of that call that they should be holy (I Pet. 1:15). **with all that in every place call upon . . . Christ**—The Epistle is intended for these also, as well as for the Corinthians. The true CATHOLIC CHURCH (a term first used by IGNATIUS, *ad Smyrnæos*, c. 8): not consisting of those who call themselves from Paul, Cephas, or any other eminent leader (vs. 12), but of all, wherever they be, who call on Jesus as their Saviour in sincerity (cf. II Tim. 2:22). Still a general unity of discipline and doctrine in the several churches is implied in ch. 4:17; 7:17 11-16; 14-33, 36. The worship due to God is here attributed to Jesus (cf. Joel 2:32; Matt. 4:10; Acts 9:14). **both theirs and ours**—"in every place which is their home . . . and our home also"; this is added to include the Christians throughout Achaia, not residing in Corinth, the capital (II Cor. 1:1). Paul feels the home of his converts to be also his own. Cf. a similar phrase in Romans 16:13 [CONYBEARE and HOWSON]. "Ours" refers to Paul and Sosthenes, and the Corinthians' home [ALFORD]. BEZA better explains, "Both their Lord and our Lord." All believers have one and the same Lord (ch. 8:6; Eph. 4:5); a virtual reproof of the divisions of the Corinthians, as if Christ were divided (vs. 13). **3. peace**—peculiarly needed in the Corinthian church, on account of its dissensions. On this verse see Romans 1:7. **4. He puts the** causes for praise and hope among them in the foreground, not to discourage them by the succeeding reproof, and in order to appeal to their better selves. **my God**—(Rom. 1:8; Phil. 1:3). **always**—(Cf. Phil. 1:4). **the grace . . . given you**—(Cf. vs. 7). **by . . . Christ**—lit., IN *Jesus Christ* given you as members in Christ. **5. utterance**—ALFORD from MENOCHIUS translates, "doctrine." Ye are rich in *preachers* or the *preaching* of the word, and rich in *knowledge* or *apprehension* of it: lit. (the) *word* (preached).' *English Version* (as in II Cor. 8:7) is better: for Paul, purposing presently to dwell on the *abuse* of the two gifts on which the Corinthians most prided themselves, *utterance* (speech) and *knowledge* (ch. 1:20; 3:18; 4:19; ch. 13 and 14), previously gains their goodwill by congratulating them on *having* those gifts. **6. According as the testimony of (of,** and concerning) Christ (who is both the object and author of this testimony [BENGEL]; ch. 2:1; I Tim.

ADAM CLARKE

Sosthenes our brother. Probably the same person mentioned in Acts xviii. 17.

2. *The church of God which is at Corinth*. This church was planted by the apostle himself.

Sanctified in Christ Jesus. "Separated" from the corruptions of their place and age. *Called to be saints*. "Constituted saints," or "invited" to become such; this was the design of the gospel, for Jesus Christ came to save men from their sins.

With all that in every place. All who profess Christianity, both in Corinth, Ephesus, and other parts of Greece or Asia Minor; and by this we see that the apostle intended that this Epistle should be a general property of the universal Church of Christ, though there are several matters in it that are suited to the state of the Corinthians only.

4. *For the grace . . . which is given you*. Not only their calling to be saints, and to be sanctified in Christ Jesus, but for the various spiritual gifts which they had received, as specified in the succeeding verses.

5. *Ye are enriched*—"ye abound." *In all utterance*. "In all doctrine"; for so the word should certainly be translated and understood.

6. *As the testimony of Christ*. The testimony of Christ is the gospel which the apostle had preached, and which had been confirmed by various gifts of the Holy Spirit and miracles wrought by the apostle.

MATTHEW HENRY

more plentifully they were poured forth on any church the more confirming evidence they had of their divine mission.

And it is no wonder that when they had such a foundation for their faith they should live in expectation of the coming of their Lord Jesus Christ, *v.* 7. It is the character of Christians that they wait for Christ's second coming. And the more confirmed we are in the Christian faith the more earnest our expectation of it.

IV. The encouraging hopes the apostle had of them for the time to come, founded on the power and love of Christ, and the faithfulness of God, *v.* 8, 9. He who had begun a good work in them, would not leave it unfinished. Those that wait for the coming of our Lord Jesus Christ will be kept by him, and those that are so *will be blameless in the day of Christ.* How glorious are the hopes of such a privilege, whether for ourselves or others! O glorious expectation, especially when the faithfulness of God comes in to support our hopes! Those that come at his call shall never be disappointed in their hopes in him. If we approve ourselves faithful to God, we shall never find him unfaithful to us.

Verses 10–13

Here the apostle enters on his subject.

I. He exhorts them to unity and brotherly love, and reproves them for their divisions. He had received an account from some that wished them well of some unhappy differences among them. He writes to them in a very engaging way: "*I beseech you, brethren, by the name of our Lord Jesus Christ;* be unanimous. *Speak all the same thing;* avoid *divisions* or *schisms. Be perfectly joined together in the same mind.* In the great things of religion be of a mind: but, when there is not a unity of sentiment, let there be a union of affections."

II. He hints at the origin of these contentions. Pride lay at the bottom, and this made them factious. They quarrelled about their ministers. Those who were disposed to be contentious broke into parties, and set their ministers at the head of their several factions: some cried up Paul, others cried up Apollos, some Cephas, or Peter, and some were for none of them, but Christ only. So liable are the best things in the world to be corrupted, and the gospel and its institutions, which are at perfect harmony with themselves and one another, to be made the engines of variance, discord, and contention. How far will pride carry Christians in opposition to one another! Even so far as to set Christ and his own apostles at variance, and make them rivals and competitors.

JAMIESON, FAUSSET, BROWN

2:6; II Tim. 1:8) was confirmed *among* [ALFORD] you; i.e., by God, through my preaching and through the miracles accompanying it (ch. 12:3; Mark 16:20; II Cor. 1:21, 22; Gal. 3:2, 5; Eph. 4:7, 8; Heb. 2:4). God *confirmed* (cf. Phil. 1:7; Heb. 2:3), or gave effect to the Gospel among (or better as *English Version,* "in") the Corinthians *by their accepting it* and setting their seal to its truth, through the inward power of His Spirit, and the outward gifts and miracles accompanying it [CALVIN]. **7. ye come behind**–are inferior to other Christians elsewhere [GROTIUS]. **in no gift**–not that all had all gifts, but different persons among them had different gifts (ch. 12. 4, etc.). **waiting for . . . coming of . . . Christ**–The crowning proof of their "coming behind in no gift." *Faith, hope,* and *love,* are all exercised herein (cf. II Tim. 4:8; Titus 2:13). "Leaving to others their MEMENTO MORI (remember death), do thou earnestly cherish this joyous expectation of the Lord's coming" [BENGEL]. The *Greek* verb implies, "to expect constantly, not only for a certain time, but even to the end till the expected event happens" (Rom. 8:19, [TITTM., *Synonyms*]. **8. Who**–God, vs. 4 (not Jesus Christ, vs. 7, in which case it would be "in *His* day"). **unto the end**–viz., "the coming of Christ." **blameless in the day of . . . Christ**–(I Thess. 5:23). After that day there is no danger (Eph. 4:30; Phil. 1: 6). Now is our day to work, and the day of our enemies to try us: then will be the day of Christ, and of His glory in the saints [BENGEL]. **9. faithful**–to His promises (Phil. 1:6; I Thess. 5:24). **called**–according to His purpose (Rom. 8:28). **unto . . . fellowship of . . . Jesus**–to be fellow heirs with Christ (Rom. 8:17-28), like Him sons of God and heirs of glory (Rom. 8:30; II Thess. 2:14; I Pet. 5:10; I John 1:3). CHRYSOSTOM remarks that the name of Christ is oftener mentioned in this than in any other Epistle, the apostle designing thereby to draw them away from their party admiration of particular teachers to Christ alone. **10. Now**–Ye already have *knowledge, utterance,* and *hope,* maintain also *love.* **brethren**–The very title is an argument for *love.* **by . . . Christ**–whom Paul wishes to be all in all to the Corinthians, and therefore names Him so often in this chapter. **speak . . . same thing**–not speaking different things as ye do (vs. 12), in a spirit of variance. **divisions**–lit., "splits," "breaches." **but**–"but rather." **perfectly joined together**–the opposite word to "divisions." It is applied to *healing a wound,* or *making whole a rent.* **mind . . . judgment**–the view taken by the *understanding,* and the *practical decision* arrived at [CONYBEARE and HOWSON], as to what is to be done. The *mind,* within, refers to things to be believed: the *judgment* is displayed outwardly in things to be done [BENGEL]. *Disposition–opinion* [ALFORD]. **11.** (Ch. 11:18.) **by them . . . of . . . house of Chloe**–They seem to have been alike in the confidence of Paul and of the Corinthians. The Corinthians "wrote" to the apostle (ch. 7:1), consulting him concerning certain points; marriage, the eating of things offered to idols, the decorum to be observed by women in religious assemblies. But they said not a syllable about the enormities and disorders that had crept in among them. *That* information reached Paul by other quarters. Hence his language about those evils is, "It hath been declared unto me . . ."; "It is reported commonly" (ch. 5:1, 2). All this he says *before* he refers to their *letter,* which shows that the latter did not give him any intimation of those evils. An undesigned proof of genuineness [PALEY's *Horæ Paulinæ*]. Observe his prudence: He names the family, to let it be seen that he made his allegation not without authority: he does not name the individuals, not to excite odium against them. He tacitly implies that the information ought rather to have come to him directly from their presbyters, as they had consulted him about matters of less moment. **contentions**–not so severe a word as "divisions," lit., schisms (*Margin,* vs. 10). **12. this I say**–this is what *I mean* in saying "contentions" (vs. 11). **every one of you saith**–Ye say severally, "glorying in men" (vs. 31; ch. 3:21, 22), one, I am of Paul; another, I am of Apollos. . . . Not that they formed *definite* parties, but they individually betrayed the *spirit* of party in contentions under the name of different favorite teachers. Paul will not allow himself to be flattered even by those who made his name their party cry, so as to connive at the dishonor thereby done to Christ. These probably were converted under his ministry. Those alleging the name of Apollos, Paul's successor at Corinth (Acts 18:24, etc), were persons attracted by his rhetorical style (probably acquired in Alexandria, ch. 3:6), as contrasted with the "weak bodily presence" and "contemptible

ADAM CLARKE

7. *So that ye come behind in no gift.* Every gift and grace of God's Spirit was possessed by the members of that church, some having their gifts after this manner, others after that. *Waiting for the coming of our Lord.* It is difficult to say whether the apostle means the final judgment or our Lord's coming to destroy Jerusalem and make an end of the Jewish polity. (See 1 Thess. iii. 13.)

8. *Who shall . . . confirm you.* As the testimony of Christ was *confirmed* among you, so, in conscientiously believing and obeying, God will *confirm* you through that testimony. (See v. 6.) *In the day of our Lord Jesus.* In the day that He comes to judge the world, according to some; but in the day in which He comes to destroy the Jewish polity, according to others. While God destroys them who are disobedient, He can save you who believe.

9. *God is faithful.* The faithfulness of God is a favorite expression among the ancient Jews, and by it they properly understand the integrity of God in preserving whatever is entrusted to Him. *Unto the fellowship.* Into the communion or participation of Christ, in the graces of His Spirit and the glories of His future kingdom. God will continue to uphold and save you if you entrust your bodies and souls to Him. But can it be said that God will keep what is either not entrusted to Him or, after being entrusted, is taken away?

10. *Now I beseech you, brethren.* The apostle having finished his introduction comes to his second point, exhorting them to abstain from dissensions, that they might be of the same heart and mind, striving together for the hope of the gospel. *By the name of our Lord Jesus.* By His authority, and in His place, and on account of your infinite obligations to His mercy in calling you into such a state of salvation. *That ye all speak the same thing.* The members of the Church of God should labor to be of the *same mind,* and to *speak the same thing,* in order to prevent divisions, which always hinder the work of God. On every essential doctrine of the gospel all genuine Christians agree; why then need religious communion be interrupted?

11. *By them which are of the house of Chloe.* This was doubtless some very religious matron at Corinth whose family were converted to the Lord, some of whom were probably sent to the apostle to inform him of the dissensions which then prevailed in the church at that place. *Contentions.* "Altercations"; produced by the "divisions," mentioned above. When once they had divided, they must necessarily have contended, in order to support their respective parties.

12. *Every one of you saith.* It seems from this expression that the whole church at Corinth was in a state of dissension. The converts at Corinth were partly Jews and partly Greeks. The Gentile part, as Dr. Lightfoot conjectures, might boast the names of Paul and Apollos; the Jewish, those of Cephas and Christ. But these again might be subdivided; some probably considered themselves disciples of Paul, he being the immediate instrument of their conversion, while others might prefer Apollos for his extraordinary eloquence.

MATTHEW HENRY

III. He expostulates with them upon their discord and quarrels: "*Is Christ divided?* No, there is but one Christ, and therefore Christians should be of one heart. *Was Paul crucified for you?* Was he your sacrifice and atonement?

Or, *were you baptized in the name of Paul?* Were you devoted to my service, or engaged to be my disciples, by that sacred rite?" Ministers, however instrumental they are of good to us, are not to be put in Christ's stead. And happy were it for the churches if there were no name of distinction among them, as Christ is not divided.

Verses 14–16

Here the apostle gives an account of his ministry among them. He thanks God he had baptized but a few among them, *Crispus*, who had been a ruler of a synagogue at Corinth (Acts xviii. 8), *Gaius, and the household of Stephanas*, besides whom, he says, he did not remember that he had baptized any. He is not to be understood in such a sense as if he were thankful for not having baptized at all, but for not having done it in present circumstances. He left it to other ministers to baptize, while he filled up his time with preaching the gospel. This, he thought, was more his business. In this sense he says, *Christ sent him not to baptize, but to preach the gospel*—not so much to baptize as to preach. Ministers should consider themselves set apart more especially to that service in which Christ will be most honoured and the salvation of souls promoted, and for which they are best fitted. The principal business Paul did among them was to preach *the gospel* (*v.* 17), *the cross* (*v.* 18), *Christ crucified*, *v.* 23. He did not preach his own fancy, but the gospel. Christ crucified is the foundation of all our hopes and the fountain of all our joys. By his death we live. This is what Paul preached, what all ministers should preach, and what all the saints live upon.

Verses 17–31

I. The manner in which Paul preached the gospel, and the cross of Christ: *Not with the wisdom of words* (*v.* 17), *the enticing words of man's wisdom* (*ch.* ii. 4), lest *the cross of Christ should be of no effect*, lest the success should be ascribed to the force of art, and not of truth; not to the plain doctrine of a crucified Jesus, but to the powerful oratory of those who spread it. He preached a crucified Jesus in plain language, and told the people that that Jesus who was crucified at Jerusalem was the Son of God and Saviour of men, and that all who would be saved must repent of their sins, and believe in him. This truth needed no artificial dress; it shone out with the greatest majesty in its own light, and prevailed in the world by its divine authority, without any human helps. The plain preaching of a crucified Jesus was more powerful than all the oratory and philosophy of the heathen world.

II. We have the different effects of this preaching: To those who perish it is foolishness, *but to those who are saved it is the power of God*, *v.* 18.

JAMIESON, FAUSSET, BROWN

speech" of the apostle. Apollos, doubtless, did not willingly foster this spirit of undue preference (ch. 4:6, 8); nay, to discourage it, he would not repeat his visit just then (ch. 16:12). **I of Cephas**—probably Judaizers, who sheltered themselves under the name of Peter, the apostle of the circumcision ("Cephas" is the *Hebrew*, "Peter" the *Greek* name; John 1:42; Gal. 2:11, etc.): the subjects handled in chs. 7-9 were probably suggested as matters of doubt by them. The church there began from the Jewish synagogue, Crispus the chief ruler, and Sosthenes his successor (probably), being converts. Hence some Jewish leaven, though not so much as elsewhere, is traceable (II Cor. 11:22). *Petrism* afterwards sprang up much more rankly at Rome. If it be wrong to boast "I am of Peter," how much more so to boast "I am of the Pope!" [BENGEL]. **I of Christ**—A fair pretext used to slight the ministry of Paul and their other teachers (ch. 4:8; II Cor. 10:7-11). **13. Is Christ divided?**—into various parts (one under one leader, another under another) [ALFORD]. The unity of His body is not to be cut in pieces, as if all did not belong to Him, the One Head. **was Paul crucified for you?**—In the *Greek* the interrogation implies that a strong negative answer is expected: "Was it Paul (*surely you will not say so*) that was crucified for you?" In the former question the majesty of "CHRIST" (the Anointed One of God) implies the impossibility of His being "divided." in the latter, *Paul's* insignificance implies the impossibility of his being the head of redemption, "crucified for" them, and giving his name to the redeemed. This, which is true of Paul the *founder* of the Church of Corinth, holds equally good of Cephas and Apollos, who had not such a claim as Paul in the Corinthian Church. **crucified . . . baptized**—The cross claims us for Christ, as redeemed by Him; baptism, as dedicated to Him. **in the name**—rather, "*into* the name" (Gal. 3:27), implying the *incorporation* involved in the idea of baptism. **14. I thank God's providence now, who** so ordered it that I baptized none of you but Crispus (the former ruler of the synagogue, Acts 18:8) and Gaius (written by the Romans *Caius*, the host of Paul at Corinth, and of the church, Rom. 16:23; a person therefore in good circumstances). Baptizing was the office of the deacons (Acts 10:48) rather than of the apostles, whose office was that of establishing and superintending generally the churches. The deacons had a better opportunity of giving the necessary *course of instruction preparatory to baptism.* Crispus and Gaius were probably among the first converts, and hence were baptized by Paul himself, who founded the church. **15. Lest**—not that Paul had this reason at the time, but God so arranged it that none might say [ALFORD]. **16. household of Stephanas**—"The first fruits of Achaia," i.e., among the first converted there (ch. 16:15, 17). It is likely that such "households" included infants (Acts 16:33). The history of the Church favors this view, as infant baptism was the usage from the earliest ages. **17.** Paul says this not to depreciate baptism; for he exalts it most highly (Rom. 6:3). He baptized some first converts; and would have baptized more, but that his and the apostles' peculiar work was to preach the Gospel, to found by their autoptic testimony particular churches, and then to superintend the churches in general. **sent me**—lit., "as an apostle." **not to baptize**—even in Christ's name, much less in my own. **not with wisdom of words**—or *speech; philosophical reasoning* set off with *oratorical language* and secular learning, which the Corinthians set so undue a value upon (vs. 5; ch. 2:1, 4) in Apollos, and the want of which in Paul they were dissatisfied with (II Cor. 10:10). **cross of Christ**—the sum and substance of the Gospel (vs. 23; ch. 2:2), Christ crucified. **be made of none effect**—lit., "be made void" (Rom. 4:14); viz., by men thinking more of the human reasonings and eloquence in which the Gospel was set forth, than of the Gospel itself of Christ crucified, the sinner's only remedy, and God's highest exhibition of love. **18. preaching . . .**—lit., "the word," or speech as to the cross; in contrast to the "wisdom of *words*" (so called), vs. 17. **them that perish**—rather, "them that are perishing", viz., by preferring human "wisdom of words" to the doctrine of the "cross of Christ." It is not the final state that is referred to; but, "them that are in the way of perishing." So also in II Corinthians 2:15, 16. **us which are saved**—In the *Greek* the collocation is more modest, "to them that are being saved (that are in the way of salvation) as," i.e., to which class *we* belong. **power of God**—which includes in it that it is the wisdom of God" (vs. 24). God's powerful instrument of salvation; the highest exhibition of God's power (Rom. 1:16). **What seems**

ADAM CLARKE

13. *Is Christ divided?* Can He be split into different sects and parties? Has He different and opposing systems? Or is the Messiah to appear under different persons? *Was Paul crucified for you?* As the gospel proclaims salvation through the *crucified* only, has Paul poured out his blood as an atonement for you? This is impossible, and therefore your being called by my name is absurd; for His disciples you should be, alone, who has bought you by His blood. *Were ye baptized in the name of Paul?* To be *baptized in*, or "into," the *name* of one implied that the baptized was to be the disciple of him into whose name, religion, etc., he was baptized. As if he said: Did I ever attempt to set up a new religion, one founded on my own authority, and coming from myself? On the contrary, have I not preached Christ crucified for the sin of the world; and called upon all mankind, both Jews and Gentiles, to believe on Him?

14. *I thank God that I baptized none of you.* None of those who now live in Corinth, except *Crispus*, the ruler of the synagogue, Acts xviii. 8. *And Gaius*, the same person probably with whom Paul lodged, Rom. xvi. 23, where see the notes.

15. *Lest any should say.* He was careful not to baptize, lest it should be supposed that he wished to make a party for himself; because superficial observers might imagine that he baptized them into his own name, to be his followers, though he baptized them into the name of Christ only. Instead of *I had baptized* the Codex Alexandrinus, the Codex Ephraim, and several others read "ye were baptized." And if we read "so that," instead of *lest*, the sentence will stand thus: "So that no one can say that ye were baptized into my name." This appears to be the true reading.

16. *The household of Stephanas.* From Rom. xvi. 15 we learn that the family of Stephanas were the first converts in Achaia, probably converted and baptized by the apostle himself. *I know not whether I baptized any other.* I do not recollect that there is any person now residing in Corinth, or Achaia, besides the abovementioned, whom I have baptized. It is strange that the doubt here expressed by the apostle should be construed so as to affect his inspiration! What, does the inspiration of prophet or apostle necessarily imply that he must understand the geography of the universe, and have an intuitive knowledge of all the inhabitants of the earth, and how often and where they may have changed their residence! Nor was that inspiration ever given so to work on a man's memory that he could not forget any of the acts which he had performed during life. Inspiration was given to the holy men of old that they might be able to write and proclaim the mind of God in the things which concern the salvation of men.

17. *For Christ sent me not to baptize.* It appears sufficiently evident that baptizing was considered to be an inferior office; and though every minister of Christ might administer it, yet apostles had more important work. Preparing these adult heathens for baptism by the continual preaching of the Word was of much greater consequence than baptizing them when thus prepared to receive and profit by it. *Not with wisdom of words.* In several places in the New Testament the term *logos* is taken not only to express a word, a speech, a saying, etc., but "doctrine," or the matter of teaching. Here, and in 1 Thess. i. 5, and several other places, it seems to signify "reason," or that mode of rhetorical argumentation so highly prized among the Greeks. The apostle was sent not to pursue this mode of conduct, but simply to announce the truth; to proclaim Christ crucified for the sin of the world; and to do this in the plainest and simplest manner possible, lest the numerous conversions which followed might be attributed to the power of the apostle's eloquence, and not to the demonstration of the Spirit of God.

18. *For the preaching of the cross.* "The doctrine of the Cross," or the doctrine that is of or concerning the Cross; that is, the doctrine that proclaims salvation to a lost world through the crucifixion of Christ. *Is to them that perish foolishness.* There are, properly speaking, but two classes of men known where the gospel is

MATTHEW HENRY

III. We have here the triumphs of the cross over human wisdom, according to the ancient prophecy (Isa. xxix. 14): *I will destroy the wisdom of the wise, and bring to nothing the understanding of the prudent. Where is the wise? Where is the scribe? Where is the disputer of this world? Hath not God made foolish the wisdom of this world?* (*v.* 19, 20). All the valued learning of this world was confounded by the Christian revelation and the glorious triumphs of the cross.

When God would save the world, he took a way by himself; and good reason, for *the world by wisdom knew not God*, *v.* 21. All the boasted science of the heathen world did not, could not, effectually bring home the world to God.

Men were puffed up by their imaginary knowledge, and therefore *it pleased him, by the foolishness of preaching, to save those that believe.*

1. The thing preached was foolishness in the eyes of worldly-wise men. Our living through one who died, our being blessed by one who was made a curse, our being justified by one who was himself condemned, was all folly.

2. The manner of preaching the gospel was foolishness to them too. None of the famous men for wisdom or eloquence were employed. A few fishermen were called out, and sent upon this errand. These were commissioned to disciple the nations. The proud pretenders to learning and wisdom despised the doctrine for the sake of those who dispensed it.

It is to the Jews a stumbling-block, and to the Greeks foolishness; but unto those who are called, both Jews and Greeks, Christ the power of God and the wisdom of God, *v.* 23, 24. 1. Christ crucified is a stumbling-block to the Jews. They despised him, and looked upon him as execrable, because he did not gratify them with a sign to their mind, though his divine power shone out in innumerable miracles. The Jews require a sign, *v.* 22. 2. He was to the Greeks foolishness. They laughed at the story of a crucified Saviour. They sought for wisdom. There was nothing in the plain doctrine of the cross to suit their taste: they entertained it therefore with scorn and contempt. What, hope to be saved by one that could not save himself! And trust in one who was condemned and crucified as a malefactor, a man of mean birth and poor condition in life! This was what the pride of human reason and learning could not relish. It is just with God to leave those to themselves who pour such proud contempt on divine wisdom and grace. 3. To those who are saved *he is the wisdom of God, and the power of God.* Those who are enlightened by the Spirit of God, discern more glorious discoveries of God's wisdom and power in the doctrine of Christ crucified than in all his other works.

JAMIESON, FAUSSET, BROWN

to the world "weakness" in God's plan of salvation (vs. 25), and in its mode of delivery by His apostle (ch. 2:3) is really His mighty "power." What seems "foolishness" because wanting man's "wisdom of words" (vs. 17), is really the highest "wisdom of God" (vs. 24). **19. I will destroy**—slightly altered from the LXX, Isaiah 29:14. The *Hebrew* is, "The wisdom of the wise shall perish, and the understanding of their prudent men shall be hid." Paul by inspiration gives the sense of the Spirit, by making GOD the cause of their *wisdom perishing*, etc., "*I* will destroy," etc. **understanding of the prudent**—lit., "of the understanding ones." **20. Where**—nowhere; for God "brings them to naught" (vs. 19). **the wise**—generally. **the scribe**—Jewish [ALFORD]. **the disputer**—Greek [ALFORD]. Cf. the Jew and Greek of this world contrasted with the godly wise, vss. 22, 23. VITRINGA thinks the reference is to the Jewish discourses in the synagogue, *daraschoth*, from a *Hebrew* root "to dispute." Cf. "questions," Acts 26:3; Titus 3:9. If so, "wise" refers to *Greek* wisdom (cf. vs. 22). Paul applies Isaiah 33:18 here in a higher sense; there the primary reference was to temporal deliverance, here to external; vs. 22, which is in threefold opposition to vs. 18 there, sanctions this higher application; the Lord in the threefold character being the sole ground of glorying to His people. **of this world . . . of this world**—rather, "dispensation (or *age*) . . ., world"; the *Greek* words are distinct. The former is here *this age* or *worldly order of things* in a moral point of view, as opposed to the Christian dispensation or order of things. The latter is the *world* viewed externally and cosmically. **made foolish**—shown the world's philosophy to be folly, because it lacks faith in Christ crucified [CHRYSOSTOM]. Has treated it as folly, and not used its help in converting and saving men (vss. 26, 27) [ESTIUS]. **21. after that**—rather, "whereas." **in the wisdom of God**—in the wise arrangement of God. **world by wisdom**—rather, "by *its* wisdom," or *its philosophy* (John 1:10; Rom. 1:28). **knew not God**—whatever other knowledge it attained (Acts 17:23, 27). The deistic theory that man can by the light of nature discover his duty to God, is disproved by the fact that man *has* never discovered it without revelation. All the stars and moon cannot make it day; that is the prerogative of the sun. Nor can nature's highest gifts make the moral day arise; that is the office of Christ. Even the Jew missed this knowledge, in so far as he followed after mere carnal *world* wisdom. **it pleased God**—Paul refers to Jesus' words (Luke 10:21). **by the foolishness of preaching**—by that preaching which the world (unbelieving Jews and Gentiles alike) deem *foolishness*. **save them that believe**—(Rom. 1:16). **22. For**—lit., "Since", seeing that. This verse illustrates how the "preaching" of Christ crucified came to be deemed "foolishness" (vs. 21). **a sign**—The oldest MSS. read "signs." The *singular* was a later correction from Matthew 12:38; 16:1; John 2:18. The signs the Jews craved for were not mere miracles, but direct tokens from heaven that Jesus was Messiah (Luke 11:16). **Greeks seek . . . wisdom**—viz., a philosophic demonstration of Christianity. Whereas Christ, instead of *demonstrative* proof, demands *faith* on the ground of *His word*, and of a reasonable amount of evidence that the alleged revelation is His word. Christianity begins not with solving intellectual difficulties, but with satisfying the heart that longs for forgiveness. Hence not the refined Greeks, but the theocratic Jews were the chosen organ for propagating revelation. Again, intellectual Athens (Acts 17:18-21, etc.) received the Gospel less readily than commercial Corinth. **23. we**—Paul and Apollos. **Christ crucified**—The *Greek* expresses not the mere fact of His crucifixion, but the *permanent character* acquired by the transaction, whereby He is now a Saviour (Gal. 3:1) [GREEN]. A Messiah (Christ) crucified was the stone on which the Jews stumbled (Matt. 21:44). The opposition of Jew and Gentile alike shows that a religion so seemingly contemptible in its origin could not have succeeded if it had not been divine. **unto the Greeks**—the oldest MSS. read "unto the *Gentiles*." **24. called**—(cf. vs. 26). The same class as the "us which are (being) saved" (vs. 18); the elect, who have obeyed the call; called effectually (Rom. 8:28, 30). **Christ**—"Crucified" is not here added, because when the offense of the cross is overcome, "Christ" is received in all His relations, not only in His cross, but in His life and His future kingdom. **power**—so meeting all the reasonable requirements of the Jews who sought "a sign." The cross (the death of a slave), which to the Jews (looking for a temporal Messiah) was a "stumbling block," is really "the power of God" to the salvation of all who believe. **wisdom of God**—

ADAM CLARKE

preached: the unbelievers and gainsayers, who are perishing; and the obedient believers, who are in a state of salvation.

19. *For it is written.* The place referred to is Isa. xxix. 14.

20. *Where is the wise . . . the scribe . . . the disputer of this world?* These words most manifestly refer to the Jews, as the places (Isa. xxix. 14; xxxiii. 18; and xliv. 25) to which he refers cannot be understood of any but the Jews. The *wise* man of the apostle is the *chakam* of the prophet, whose office it was to teach others. The *scribe* of the apostle is the *sopher* of the prophet; this signifies any man of learning, as distinguished from the common people, especially any master of the traditions. The *disputer* answers to the *derosh*, or *darshan*, the "propounder of questions"; the seeker of allegorical, mystical, and cabalistical senses from the Holy Scriptures. Now as all these are characters well-known among the Jews, and as the words *of this world* are a simple translation of *olam hazzeh*, which is repeatedly used to designate the Jewish republic, there is no doubt that the apostle has the Jews immediately in view.

21. *For after that in the wisdom of God.* The plain meaning of this verse is that the wise men of the world, especially the Greek philosophers, who possessed every advantage that human nature could have independently of a divine revelation, and who had cultivated their minds to the uttermost, could never, by their learning, wisdom, and industry, find out God; nor had the most refined philosophers among them just and correct views of the divine nature, nor of that in which human happiness consists. *By the foolishness of preaching.* By the preaching of Christ crucified, which the Gentiles termed *foolishness*, in opposition to their own doctrines, which they termed *wisdom*. It was not by the foolishness of preaching, literally, nor by the foolish preaching, that God saved the world; but by that gospel which they called *foolishness;* which was, in fact, *the wisdom of God*, and also the power of God to the salvation of them that believed.

22. *For the Jews require a sign.* Instead of *a sign*, several MSS., with many of the fathers, have "signs"; which reading, as undoubtedly genuine, Griesbach has admitted into the text. *And the Greeks seek after wisdom.* Such wisdom, or philosophy, as they found in the writings of Cicero, Seneca, Plato, etc., which was called philosophy, and which came recommended to them in all the beauties and graces of the Latin and Greek languages.

23. *But we.* Apostles, differing widely from these Gentile philosophers. *Preach Christ crucified.* Call on men, both Jews and Gentiles, to believe in Christ, as having purchased their salvation by shedding His blood for them. *Unto the Jews a stumblingblock.* Because Jesus came meek, lowly, and impoverished; not seeking worldly glory, nor affecting worldly pomp; whereas they expected the Messiah to come as a mighty prince and conqueror. Because Christ did not come so, they were offended at Him. *Unto the Greeks foolishness.* Because they could not believe that proclaiming supreme happiness through a man that was crucified at Judea as a malefactor could ever comport with reason and common sense; for both the matter and manner of the preaching were opposite to every notion they had formed of what was dignified and philosophic.

24. *But unto them which are called.* Those, of both Jews and Greeks, who were by the preaching of the gospel *called* or "invited" to the marriage feast, and have accordingly believed in Christ Jesus. The *called*, or "invited," is a title of genuine Christians, and is frequently used in the New Testament. "Saints" is used in the same sense.

MATTHEW HENRY

And yet *the foolishness of God is wiser than men, v.* 25. "*You see your calling, brethren, how that not many wise men after the flesh, not many mighty, not many noble, are called,*" *v.* 26, &c. There is a great deal of meanness and weakness in the outward appearance of our religion. Few of distinguished character in any of these respects were chosen for the work of the ministry. Not the wise men after the flesh. Not the mighty and noble. But God seeth not as man seeth. He hath chosen the foolish things of the world, the weak things of the world, the base and despicable things of the world, men of mean birth, of low rank, of no liberal education, to be the preachers of the gospel. He is a better judge than we what instruments and measures will best serve the purposes of his glory. Few of distinguished rank and character were called to be Christians. As the preachers were poor and mean, so generally were the converts. Few of the wise, and mighty, and noble, embraced the doctrine of the cross. Yet what glorious discoveries are there of divine wisdom in the whole scheme of the gospel.

IV. We have an account how admirably all is fitted, 1. To beat down the pride and vanity of men. God hath chosen *the foolish things of the world to confound the wise, the weak things of the world to confound the mighty, and base things, and things which are despised, and things which are not, to bring to nought* (*to abolish*) *things that are*; the conversion of the Gentiles was to open a way to the abolishing of that constitution upon which they valued themselves so much. It is common for the Jews to speak of the Gentiles under this character, as *things that are not.*

The gospel is fitted to bring down the pride of both Jews and Greeks, *that no flesh should glory in his presence* (*v.* 29), that there might be no pretence for boasting. Divine wisdom alone had the contrivance of the method of redemption; divine grace alone revealed it, and made it known. It lay, in both respects, out of human reach. The gospel dispensation is a contrivance to humble man. 2. It is as admirably fitted to glorify God. The hand of the Lord went along with the preachers, and was mighty in the hearts of the hearers; and Jesus Christ was made both to ministers and Christians what was truly great and honourable. All we have we have from God as the fountain, and in and through Christ as the channel of conveyance. He is made of God to us *wisdom, righteousness, sanctification, and redemption* (*v.* 30). We are foolishness and he is made wisdom to us. We are guilty and he is made righteousness. We are depraved and corrupt; and he is made sanctification. We are in bonds, and he is made redemption to us.

And what is designed in all is *that all flesh may glory in the Lord, v.* 31. Man is humbled, and God glorified by the whole scheme.

JAMIESON, FAUSSET, BROWN

so really exhibiting, and in the highest degree (if they would but see it), that which the Greeks sought after—*wisdom* (Col. 2:3). **25. foolishness of God** —i.e., God's plan of salvation which men deem "foolishness." **weakness of God**—Christ "crucified through weakness" (II Cor. 13:4, the great *stumbling block* of the Jews), yet "living by the *power* of God." **So He** *perfects strength* **out of the** *weakness* **of His servants (ch. 2:3; II Cor. 12:9). 26. ye see**—rather, from the prominence of the verb in the *Greek*, "see" or "consider" (imperative) [ALFORD from VULGATE and IRENÆUS]. **your calling . . .** *are called*—Instead of the words in italics, supplied by *English Version*, supply, "were your callers." What Paul is dwelling on (cf. vss. 27, 28) is the weakness of the instrumentality which the Lord employed to convert the world [HINDS and WHATELY; so ANSELM]. However, *English Version* accords well with vs. 24. "The whole history of the expansion of the Church is a progressive victory of the ignorant over the learned, the lowly over the lofty, until the emperor himself laid down his crown before the cross of Christ" [OLSHAUSEN]. **wise . . . after the flesh**—the wisdom of this world acquired by human study without the Spirit. (Contrast Matt. 16:17.) **27. the foolish things**—a general phrase for *all persons and things foolish.* Even *things* (and those, too, *foolish things*) are chosen by God to confound *persons,* (and those too persons who are *wise*). This seems to me the force of the change from neuter to masculine. **to confound**—The *Greek* is stronger, "*that* He might confound (or put to shame)." God confounds the wise by effecting through His instruments, without human wisdom, that the worldly wise, with it, cannot effect, viz., to bring men to salvation. **chosen . . . chosen**—The repetition indicates the gracious deliberateness of God's purpose (Jas. 2:5). **28.** *yea,* **and things which are not**—*Yea* is not in the *Greek.* Also some of the oldest MSS. omit "and." Thus the clause, "things which are not" (are regarded as naught), is in apposition with "foolish . . . weak . . . base (i.e., lowborn) and despised things." God has chosen all four, though regarded as *things that are not,* to bring to naught things that are. **29. no flesh . . . glory**—For they who try to glory (boast) because of human greatness and wisdom, are "confounded" or *put to shame* (vs. 27). Flesh, like "the flower of the field," is beautiful, but frail (Isa. 40:6). **in his presence**—We are to glory not *before* Him, but in Him [BENGEL]. **30. But . . . ye**—in contrast to them that "glory" in worldly wisdom and greatness. **of him are**—not of yourselves (Eph. 2:8), but of Him (Rom. 11:36). *From* Him ye are (i.e., have spiritual life, who once were spiritually among the "things which are not." vs. 28). **in Christ**—by living union with Him. Not "in the flesh" (vss. 26, 29). **of God**—*from* God; emanating *from* Him and sent by Him. **is made unto us**—*has been made* to us, to our eternal gain. **wisdom**—unattainable by the worldly mode of seeking it (vss. 19, 20; contrast Col. 2:3; Prov. 8; Isa. 9:6). By it we become "wise unto salvation," owing to His *wisdom* in originating and executing the plan, whereas once we were "fools." **righteousness**—the ground of our justification (Jer. 23:5, 6; Rom. 4:25; II Cor. 5:21); whereas once we were "weak" (Rom. 5:6). Isaiah 42:21; 45:24. **sanctification**—by His Spirit; whereas formerly we were "base." Hereafter our righteousness and sanctification alike shall be both perfect and inherent. Now the righteousness wherewith we are justified is perfect, but not inherent; that wherewith we are sanctified is inherent, but not perfect [HOOKER]. Now sanctification is perfect in principle, but not in attainment. These two are joined in the *Greek* as forming essentially but *one* thing, as distinguished from the "wisdom" in *devising* and executing the plan for us ("abounded toward us in all wisdom," Eph. 1:8), and "redemption," the *final completion* of the scheme in the deliverance of the body (the position of "redemption" last shows that this limited sense is the one intended here). Luke 21:28; Romans 8:23; Ephesians 1:14; 4:30. **redemption**—whereas once we were "despised." **31. glory in . . Lord**—(Jer. 9:23, 24)—in opposition to "flesh glorying in His presence" (vs. 29). In contrast to morbid slavish self-abasement, Paul joins with humility the elevating consciousness of our true dignity in Christ. He who glories is to glory in the Lord, not in the flesh, nor in the world.

ADAM CLARKE

25. *The foolishness of God is wiser.* The meaning of these strong expressions is that the things of God's appointment which seem to men *foolishness* are infinitely beyond the highest degree of human wisdom; and those works of God which appear to superficial observers weak and contemptible surpass all the efforts of human power. The means which God has appointed for the salvation of men are so wisely imagined and so energetically powerful that all who properly use them shall be infallibly brought to the end—final blessedness—which He has promised to them who believe and obey.

26. *Ye see your calling.* The state of grace and blessedness to which you are invited. I think *blepo* should be read in the imperative: "Take heed to, or consider, your calling, brethren; that not many of you are wise after the flesh, not many mighty, not many noble." *Men* is not in the original, and Paul seems to allude to the Corinthian believers in particular. This seems to have been said in opposition to the high and worldly notions of the Jews, who assert that the Divine Spirit never rests upon any man unless he be wise, powerful, and rich. Now this Divine Spirit did rest upon the Christians at Corinth, and yet these were, in the sense of the world, neither wise, rich, nor noble. We spoil, if not corrupt, the apostle's meaning by adding *are called,* as if God did not send His gospel to the wise, the powerful, and the noble, or did not will their salvation. The truth is, the gospel has an equal call to all classes of men; but the *wise,* the *mighty,* and the *noble* are too busy or too sensual to pay any attention to an invitation so spiritual and so divine; and therefore there are few of these in the Church of Christ in general.

27. *But God hath chosen the foolish things.* God has chosen by means of men who are esteemed rude and illiterate to confound the greatest of the Greek philosophers and overturn their systems; and by means of men *weak,* without secular power or authority, to confound the scribes and Pharisees; and in spite of the exertions of the Jewish sanhedrin, to spread the doctrine of Christ crucified all over the land of Judea, and by such instruments as these to convert thousands of souls to the faith of the gospel.

28. *And base things . . . and things which are despised.* It is very likely that the apostle refers here to the Gentiles and to the Gentile converts, who were considered base and despicable in the eyes of the Jews, who counted them no better than dogs, and who are repeatedly called the *things that are not.* By these very people, converted to Christianity, God has brought *to nought* all the Jewish pretensions.

29. *That no flesh should glory.* God does His mighty works in such a way as proves that, though He may condescend to employ men as instruments, yet they have no part either in the contrivance or energy by which such works are performed.

30. *But of him are ye in Christ Jesus.* Even the good which you possess is granted by God, for it is by and through Him that, Christ Jesus comes, and all the blessings of the gospel dispensation. *And righteousness.* "Justification," as procuring for us that remission of sins which the law could not give, Gal. ii. 21; iii. 21. *And sanctification.* As procuring for and working in us not only an external and relative holiness, as was that of the Jews, but true and eternal holiness, Eph. iv. 24, wrought in us by the Holy Spirit.

31. *According as it is written.* In Jer. ix. 23-24: "Thus saith the Lord, Let not the wise man glory in his wisdom, neither let the mighty man glory in his might, let not the rich man glory in his riches: but let him that glorieth glory in this, that he understandeth and knoweth me, that I am the Lord which exercise lovingkindness, judgment, and righteousness, in the earth." So then, as all good is of and from God, let him that has either wisdom, strength, riches, pardon, holiness, or any other blessing, whether temporal or spiritual, acknowledge that he was nothing but what he has received.

MATTHEW HENRY

CHAPTER 2

Verses 1–5

The apostle reminds the Corinthians how he acted when he first preached the gospel among them.

I. As to the matter or subject he tells us (*v.* 2), *He determined to know nothing among them but Jesus Christ and him crucified.* Christ, in his person and offices, is the sum and substance of the gospel, and ought to be the great subject of a gospel minister's preaching. Anyone that heard Paul preach found him to harp so continuously on this string that he would say he knew nothing but Christ and him crucified.

II. The manner wherein he preached Christ. Negatively. *He came not among them with excellency of speech or wisdom, v.* 1. *His speech and preaching were not with enticing words of man's wisdom, v.* 4. He did not set himself to captivate the ear by eloquent expressions, nor to entertain the fancy with lofty flights. Divine wisdom needed not to be set off with such human ornaments. Positively. He came among them *declaring the testimony of God, v.* 1. He published a divine revelation. Ornaments of speech and philosophical skill and argument could add no weight to what came recommended by such authority. *He was also among them in weakness and fear, and in much trembling;* and yet *his speech and preaching were in demonstration of the Spirit and of power, v.* 3, 4. His enemies in the church of Corinth spoke very contemptuously of him: *His bodily presence, say they, is weak, and his speech contemptible,* 2 Cor. x. 10. Possibly he had a little body, and a low voice; but, it is plain that he was no mean speaker. Nor did he want courage nor resolution, he was *in nothing terrified by his adversaries.* Yet he was no boaster. He did not proudly vaunt himself, like his opposers. None know the fear and trembling of faithful ministers; and a deep sense of their own weakness is the occasion of this fear and trembling. They know how insufficient they are. Yet he spoke with authority: *In the demonstration of the Spirit and of power.* He preached the truths of Christ in their native dress, with plainness of speech. He laid down the doctrine as the Spirit delivered it; and left the Spirit to demonstrate the truth of it.

III. Here is the end mentioned for which he preached Christ crucified: *That your faith should not stand in the wisdom of man, but the power of God* (*v.* 5)—that they might not be drawn by human motives, nor overcome by mere human arguments. When nothing but Christ crucified was plainly preached, the success must be entirely attributed to a divine power.

The apostle shows them that he had communicated to them a treasure of the truest and the highest wisdom: *We speak wisdom among those who are perfect* (*v.* 6). Those that receive the doctrine as divine, and have looked well into it, discover true wisdom in it. Though what we preach is foolishness to the world, it is wisdom to them.

JAMIESON, FAUSSET, BROWN

CHAPTER 2

Vss. 1-16. PAUL'S SUBJECT OF PREACHING, CHRIST CRUCIFIED, NOT IN WORLDLY, BUT IN HEAVENLY, WISDOM AMONG THE PERFECT. **1. And I**—"So I" [CONYBEARE] as one of the "foolish, weak, and despised" instruments employed by God (ch. 1:27, 28); "glorying in the Lord," not in man's wisdom (ch. 1:31). Cf. ch. 1:23, "We." **when I came**—(Acts 18:1, etc.). Paul might, had he pleased, have used an ornate style, having studied secular learning at Tarsus of Cilicia, which Strabo preferred as a school of learning to Athens or Alexandria; here, doubtless, he read the *Cilician* Aratus' poems (which he quotes, Acts 17:28), and Epimenides (Titus 1:12), and Menander (I Cor. 15:33). Grecian intellectual development was an important element in preparing the way for the Gospel, but it failed to regenerate the world, showing that for this a superhuman power is needed. Hellenistic (Grecizing) Judaism at Tarsus and Alexandria was the connecting link between the schools of Athens and those of the Rabbis. No more fitting birthplace could there have been for the apostle of the Gentiles than Tarsus, free as it was from the warping influences of Rome, Alexandria, and Athens. He had at the same time *Roman citizenship,* which protected him from sudden violence. Again, he was reared in the *Hebrew divine law* at Jerusalem. Thus, as the three elements, Greek cultivation, Roman polity (Luke 2:1), and the divine law given to the Jews, combined just at Christ's time, to prepare the world for the Gospel, so the same three, by God's marvellous providence, met together in the apostle to the Gentiles [CONYBEARE and HOWSON]. **testimony of God**—"the testimony *of Christ"* (ch. 1:6); therefore Christ is God. **2.** The *Greek* implies, "The only definite thing that I made it my business to know among you, was to know Jesus Christ (His person) and Him crucified (His office)" [ALFORD], not exalted on the earthly throne of David, but executed as the vilest malefactor. The historical fact of Christ's crucifixion had probably been put less prominently forward by the seekers after human wisdom in the Corinthian church, to avoid offending learned heathens and Jews. Christ's *person* and Christ's *office* constitute the sum of the Gospel. **3. I**—the *preacher:* as vs. 2 describes the *subject,* "Christ crucified," and vs. 4 the *mode* of preaching: "my speech . . . not with enticing words," "but in demonstration of the Spirit." **weakness**—personal and bodily (II Cor. 10:10; 12:7, 9; Gal. 4:13). **trembling**—(cf. Phil. 2:12). Not *personal fear,* but a *trembling anxiety to perform a duty;* anxious conscientiousness, as proved by the contrast to "eye service" (Eph. 6:5) [CONYBEARE and HOWSON]. **4. my speech**—in private. **preaching**—in public [BENGEL]. ALFORD explains it, *My discourse* on doctrines, and *my preaching* or announcement of facts. **enticing**—rather, "persuasive." **man's wisdom**—"man's" is omitted in the oldest authorities. Still "wisdom" does refer to *man's* wisdom. **demonstration of . . . Spirit . . .**—*Persuasion* is man's means of moving his fellow man. God's means is *demonstration,* leaving no doubt, and inspiring implicit faith, by the powerful working of the Spirit (then exhibited both outwardly by miracles, and inwardly by working on the heart, now in the latter and the more important way only, (Matt. 7:29; Acts 6:10; Heb. 4:12; cf. also Rom. 15:19). The same simple power accompanies divine truth now, producing certain persuasion and conversion, when the Spirit demonstrates by it. **5. stand in . . . wisdom of men**—rest on it, owe its origin and continuance to it. **6, 7.** Yet the Gospel preaching, so far from being at variance with true "wisdom," is a wisdom infinitely higher than that of the wise of the world. **we speak**—resuming "we" (preachers, I, Apollos, etc.) from "we preach" (ch. 1:28), only that here, "we speak" refers to something less public (cf. vss. 7.13, "mystery" "hidden") than "we preach," which is public. For "wisdom" here denotes not the whole of Christion doctrine, but its sublimer and deeper principles. **perfect**—Those *matured in Christian experience and knowledge* alone can understand the true superiority of the Christian wisdom which Paul preached. Distinguished not only from *worldly* and *natural* men, but also from *babes,* who though "in Christ" retain much that is "carnal" (ch. 3:1, 2), and cannot therefore understand the deeper truths of Christianity (ch. 14:20; Phil. 3:15; Heb. 5:14). Paul does not mean by the "mystery" or "hidden wisdom (vs. 7) some *hidden tradition distinct from the Gospel* (like the Church of Rome's *disciplina arcani* and doctrine of reserve), but the *unfolding* of the treasures of knowledge, once hidden in God's counsels, but *now* announced to all, which would be in-

ADAM CLARKE

CHAPTER 2

1. *When I came to you.* Acting suitably to my mission, which was to preach the gospel, but not with human eloquence, chap. i. 17.

I declared to you the *testimony,* the gospel, *of God, not with excellency of speech,* not with arts of rhetoric, used by your own philosophers, where the excellence of the speech recommends the matter, and compensates for the want of solidity and truth. On the contrary, the testimony concerning Christ and His salvation is so supremely excellent as to dignify any kind of language by which it may be conveyed.

2. *I determined not to know any thing among you.* Satisfied that the gospel of God could alone make you wise unto salvation, I determined to cultivate no other knowledge, and to teach nothing but *Jesus Christ, and him crucified,* as the foundation of all true wisdom, piety, and happiness.

3. *I was with you in weakness.* It is very likely that Paul had not only something in his speech very unfavorable to a ready and powerful elocution, but also some infirmity of body that was still more disadvantageous to him. A fine appearance and a fine voice cover many weaknesses and defects, and strongly and forcibly recommend what is spoken, though not remarkable for depth of thought or solidity of reasoning. Many popular orators have little besides their persons and their voice to recommend them. *In fear, and in much trembling.* An eminent divine has said that it requires three things to make a good preacher: study, temptation, and prayer. The latter, no man that lives near to God can neglect; the former, no man who endeavors rightly to divide "the word of truth" will neglect; and with the second every man will be more or less exercised whose whole aim is to save souls. Those of a different cast the devil permits to pass quietly on in their own indolent and prayerless way.

4. *And my speech.* My "doctrine"; the matter of my preaching. *And my preaching.* "My proclamation." *Was not with enticing words of man's wisdom.* "With persuasive doctrines of human wisdom"; in every case I left man out, that God might become the more evident. I used none of the means of which great orators avail themselves in order to become popular, and thereby to gain fame. *But in demonstration of the Spirit.* In the "manifestation." The doctrine that he preached was revealed by the Spirit. That it was a revelation of the Spirit, the holiness, purity, and usefulness of the doctrine rendered manifest; and the overthrow of idolatry and the conversion of souls, by the power and energy of the preaching, were the demonstration that all was divine. The greater part of the best MSS., versions, and fathers leave out the adjective *man's* before *wisdom.*

5. *That your faith should not stand.* That the illumination of your souls and your conversion to God might appear to have nothing human in it. Your belief, therefore, of the truths which have been proposed to you is founded, not in human wisdom, but in divine power.

6. *We speak wisdom among them that are perfect.* By *among them that are perfect* we are to understand Christians of the highest knowledge and attainments, those who were fully instructed in the knowledge of God through Christ Jesus. Nothing, in the judgment of Paul, deserved the name of *wisdom* but this. And though he apologizes for his not coming to them with excellency of speech or wisdom, yet he means what was reputed wisdom among the Greeks, and which, in the sight of God, was mere folly when compared with that wisdom that came from above.

MATTHEW HENRY

Those who are wise themselves are the only proper judges of what is wisdom: *not* indeed *the wisdom of this world, nor of the princes of this world,* but *the wisdom of God in a mystery* (*v.* 6, 7); not worldly wisdom, but divine; not such as the men of this world could have discovered, nor such as worldly men, destitute of the Spirit of God, can receive. How different is the judgment of God from that of the world! The wisdom he teaches is of a quite different kind from what passes under that notion in the world. *But the wisdom of God in a mystery, the hidden wisdom of God.* The depth of which, now it is revealed, none but himself can fathom. Now, concerning this wisdom, observe,

I. The rise and origin of it: *It was ordained of God, before the world, to our glory, v.* 7. It was ordained of God; he had determined long ago to make it known; and that to our glory, *the glory of us,* either us apostles or us Christians. It was a great honour put upon the apostles, to be entrusted with the revelation of this wisdom. It was a great privilege for Christians to have this glorious wisdom discovered to them. And the wisdom of God taught by the gospel prepares for our everlasting glory and happiness in the world to come. What honour does he put on his saints!

II. The ignorance of the great men of the world about it: *Which none of the princes of this world knew* (*v.* 8). The Roman governor, and the rulers of the Jewish nation, seem to be the persons here chiefly meant. Jesus Christ is the Lord of glory, and the reason why he was hated was because he was not known. Had his crucifiers known him, known who and what he was, they would have withheld their impious hands. Thus he pleaded with his Father for their pardon: *Father, forgive them, for they know not what they do,* Luke xxiii. 34.

III. It is such wisdom as could not have been discovered without a revelation, according to what the prophet Isaiah says (Isa. lxiv. 4), *Eye hath not seen, nor ear heard, nor have entered into the heart of man the things which God hath prepared for those that love him*—*for him that waiteth for him,* that waiteth for his mercy, so the LXX. Waiting upon God is an evidence of love to him. There are things which God hath prepared for those that love him, and wait for him. But the apostle speaks here of the divine revelation under the gospel. The great truths of the gospel are things lying out of the sphere of human discovery: *Eye hath not seen, nor ear heard them, nor have they entered into the heart of man.* Were they objects of sense there had been no need of a revelation. But, lying out of the sphere of nature, we cannot discover them but by the light of revelation.

IV. By whom this wisdom is discovered to us: *God hath revealed them to us by his Spirit, v.* 10.

JAMIESON, FAUSSET, BROWN

telligently comprehended in proportion as the hearer's inner life became perfectly transformed into the image of Christ. Cf. instances of such "mysteries," i.e., deeper Christian truths, not preached at Paul's first coming to Corinth, when he confined himself to the fundamental elements (vs. 2), but now spoken to the "perfect" (ch. 15:51; Rom. 11:25; Eph. 3:5, 6). "Perfect" is used not of *absolute perfection,* but relatively to "babes," or those less ripe in Christian growth (cf. Phil. 3:12, 15, with I John 2:12-14). "God" (vs. 7) is opposed to the world, the apostles to "the princes [great and learned men] of this world" (vs. 8; cf. ch. 1:20) [BENGEL]. **come to naught**—nothingness (ch. 1:28). They are transient, not immortal. Therefore, their wisdom is not real [BENGEL]. Rather, translate with ALFORD, "Which *are being brought* to naught," viz., by God's choosing the "things which are not (the *weak and despised things of the Gospel*), to bring to naught (the same verb as here) things that are" (ch. 1:28). **7. wisdom of God**—emphatically contrasted with the wisdom *of men* and *of this world* (vss. 5, 6). **in a mystery**—connected in construction with "we speak": We speak as dealing with a mystery; i.e. not something *to be kept hidden,* but what heretofore was so, but is *now revealed.* Whereas the pagan mysteries were revealed only to a chosen few, the Gospel mysteries were made known to all who would obey the truth. "If our Gospel be *hid,* it is hid to them that are *lost*" (II Cor. 4:3), "whom the God of this world hath *blinded.*" Ordinarily we use "mystery" in reference to those from whom the knowledge is *withheld;* the apostles, in reference to those to whom it is *revealed* [WHATELY]. It is hidden before it is brought forward, and when it is brought forward it still remains hidden to those that are imperfect [BENGEL]. **ordained**—lit., "foreordained" (cf. vs. 9), "prepared for them that love Him." **before the world**—rather, "before *the ages*" (of time), i.e., from eternity. This infinitely antedates worldly wisdom in antiquity. It was before not only the wisdom of the world, but eternally before the world itself and its ages. **to our glory**—ours both now and hereafter, from "the Lord of *glory*" (vs. 8), who *brings to naught* "the princes of this world." **8. Which**—wisdom. The strongest proof of the natural man's destitution of heavenly wisdom. **crucified . . . Lord of glory**—implying the inseparable connection of Christ's humanity and His divinity. The Lord of glory (which He had in His own right before the world was, John 17:4, 24) was crucified. **9. But**—(it has happened) as it is written. **Eye hath not seen . . .**—ALFORD translates, "The things which eye saw not, . . . the things which God prepared . . ., to us God revealed through His Spirit." Thus, however, the "but" of vs. 10 is ignored. Rather construe, as ESTIUS, "('We speak,' supplied from vs. 8), things which eye saw not (heretofore), . . . things which God prepared. . . . But God revealed them to us . . . ." The quotation is not a verbatim one, but an inspired *exposition* of the "wisdom" (vs. 6, from Isa. 64:4). The exceptive words, "O God, *beside* (i.e., except) Thee," are not quoted directly, but are virtually expressed in the exposition of them (vs. 10), "None *but thou,* O God, seest these mysteries, and *God hath revealed them to us by His Spirit.*" **entered**—lit., "come up into the heart." A Hebraism (cf. *Margin,* Jer. 3:16). In Isaiah 64 it is "Prepared (lit., 'will do') for him that *waiteth for* Him"; here, "for them that *love* Him." For Isaiah spake to them who *waited for* Messiah's appearance as future; Paul, to them *who love Him* as having actually appeared (I John 4:19); cf. vs. 12, "the things that are freely given to us of God" [BENGEL]. **10. revealed . . . by . . . Spirit**—The inspiration of thoughts (so far as truth essential to salvation is concerned) makes the *Christian* (ch. 3:16; 12:3; Matt. 16:17; John 16:13; I John 2:20, 27); that of *words,* the PROPHET (II Sam. 23:1, 2; I Kings 13:1, 5), "by the *word* of the Lord" (vs. 13; John 20:30, 31; II Pet. 1:21). The secrets of revelation are secret to some, not because those who know them will not reveal them (for indeed, the very notion of *revelation* implies an unveiling of what had been veiled), but because those to whom they are announced have not the will or power to comprehend them. Hence the Spirit-taught alone know these secrets (Ps. 25:14; Prov. 3:32; John 7:17; 15:15). **unto us**—the "perfect" or fully matured in Christian experience (vs. 6). Intelligent men may understand the outline of doctrines; but without the Holy Spirit's revelation to the heart, these will be to them a mere outline—a skeleton, correct perhaps, but wanting life [*Cautions for the Times,* xiv.], (Luke 10:21). **the Spirit searcheth**—working in us and with our spirits (cf. Rom. 8:16, 26, 27). The Old

ADAM CLARKE

7. *The wisdom of God in a mystery.* The gospel of Jesus Christ, which had been comparatively *hidden* from the foundation of the world (the settling of the Jewish economy, as this phrase often means), though appointed from the beginning to be revealed in the fullness of time.

8. *Which none of the princes of this world knew.* Here it is evident that *this world* refers to the Jewish state, and to the degree of knowledge in that state, and the rulers, the priests, rabbins, etc., who were principally concerned in the crucifixion of our Lord. *The Lord of glory.* Or the "glorious Lord," infinitely transcending all the rulers of the universe, whose is eternal glory.

9. *But, as it is written.* The quotation is taken from Isa. lxiv. 4. The sense is continued here from verse the seventh, and "we speak" is understood—We do not speak or preach the wisdom of this world; but that mysterious wisdom of God, of which the prophet said: *Eye hath not seen, nor ear heard, neither have entered into the heart of man, the things which God hath prepared for them that love him.* These words have been applied to the state of glory in a future world; but they certainly belong to the present state, and express merely the wondrous light, life, and liberty which the gospel communicates to them that believe in the Lord Jesus Christ in that way which the gospel itself requires.

10. *But God hath revealed them unto us.* A manifest proof that the apostle speaks here of the glories of the gospel, and not of the glories of the future world.

MATTHEW HENRY

The scripture is given by inspiration of God. And the apostles spoke by inspiration of the same Spirit. What he taught was revealed of God by his Spirit, *that Spirit that searches all things, yea, the deep things of God, and knows the things of God, as the spirit of a man that is in him knows the things of a man, v.* 11. A double argument in proof of the divinity of the Holy Ghost: 1. Omniscience is attributed to him: *He searches all things, even the deep things of God.* He enters into the very depths of God, penetrates into his most secret counsels. Now who can have such a thorough knowledge of God but God? 2. This allusion seems to imply that the Holy Spirit is as much in God as a man's mind is in himself. He is as much and as intimately one with God as the man's mind is with the man. The Spirit of God knows the things of God because he is one with God. Neither can we know the secret counsels and purposes of God till they are made known to us by his Holy Spirit. And it was by this Spirit that the apostles had received the *wisdom of God in a mystery.* "*Now we have received not the spirit of the world, but the Spirit which is of God, that we might know the things freely given to us of God* (*v.* 12). We have what we deliver in the name of God by inspiration from him; and it is by his gracious illumination that *we know the things freely given to us of God* unto salvation" —that is, "the great privileges of the gospel." Though these things are given to us, we cannot know them to any saving purpose till we have the Spirit.

V. In what manner this wisdom was taught: *Which things we speak, not in the words which man's wisdom teaches, but which the Holy Ghost teaches, v.* 13. They had received the wisdom they taught from the Spirit of God. Nor did they put a human dress on it, but plainly declared the doctrine of Christ, in terms also taught them by the Holy Spirit. The truths of God need no garnishing by human skill or eloquence, but look best in the words which the Holy Ghost teaches. *Comparing spiritual things with spiritual*—one part of revelation with another. Spiritual things, when brought together, will help to illustrate one another; but, if the principles of human art and science are to be made a test of revelation, we shall certainly judge amiss concerning it. The language of the Spirit of God is the most proper to convey his meaning.

VI. How this wisdom is received.

1. *The natural man receiveth not the things of God, for they are foolishness to him, neither can he know them, because they are spiritually discerned, v.* 14. Either, (1) The man under the power of corruption, and never yet illuminated by the Spirit of God. Men unsanctified receive not the things of God. The truths of God are foolishness to such a mind. Evil inclinations and wicked principles render the man unwilling to enter into the mind of God. It is the quickening beams of the Spirit of truth and holiness that must help the mind to discern their excellency. Thus the natural man cannot know them, because they are spiritually discerned. Or, (2) The natural man, that is, the wise man of the world (*ch.* i. 19, 20), one who hath the wisdom of the world, man's wisdom (*ch.* ii. 4–6), a man that would receive nothing by faith, nor own any need of supernatural assistance. This was very much the character of the philosophy and the Grecian learning and wisdom in that day. Such a man receives not the things of the Spirit of God. Revelation is not with him a principle of science; he looks upon it as the extravagant thought of some deluded dreamer. For that reason he can have no knowledge of things revealed, because they are only spiritually discerned.

2. *But he that is spiritual judgeth all things, yet he himself is judged of no man, v.* 15. He who is sanctified is capable of judging about matters of human wisdom, and has also a relish and savour of

JAMIESON, FAUSSET, BROWN

Testament shows us God (the Father) for us. The Gospels, God (the Son) with us. The Acts and Epistles, God (the Holy Ghost) in us [MONOD], (Gal. 3:14). **deep things of God**—(Ps. 92:5). His divine nature, attributes, and counsels. The Spirit delights to explore the infinite depths of His own divine mind, and then reveal them to us, according as we are capable of understanding them (Deut. 29: 29). This proves the personality and Godhead of the Holy Ghost. Godhead cannot be separated from the Spirit of God, as manhood cannot be separated from the Spirit of man [BENGEL]. **11. what man . . .**—lit., "who of *men* knoweth the things of a *man,* save the spirit of that man?" **things of God knoweth no man**—rather, "*none* knoweth," not angel or man. This proves the impossibility of any knowing the things of God, save by the Spirit of God (who alone knows them, since even in the case of man, so infinitely inferior in mind to God, none of his fellow men, but his own spirit alone knows the things hidden within him). **12. we . . . received, not . . . spirit of . . . world**—the personal evil "spirit that now worketh in the children of disobedience" (Eph. 2:2). This spirit is natural in the unregenerate, and needs not to be *received.* **Spirit which is of God**—i.e., which comes from God. We have received it only by the *gift* of God, whose Spirit it is, whereas our own spirit is the spirit that is in us men (vs. 11). **that we might know . . . things . . . freely given . . . of God**—present experimental knowledge, to our unspeakable comfort, of His deep mysteries of wisdom, and of our future possession of the good "things which God hath prepared for them that love Him" (vs. 9). **13. also**—We not only *know* by the Holy Ghost, but *we also speak* the "things freely given to us of God" (vs. 12). **which the Holy Ghost teacheth**—The old MSS. read "the Spirit" simply, without "Holy." **comparing spiritual things with spiritual**—expounding the Spirit-inspired Old Testament Scripture, by comparison with the Gospel which Jesus by the same Spirit revealed [GROTIUS]; and conversely illustrating the Gospel mysteries by comparing them with the Old Testament types [CHRYSOSTOM]. So the *Greek* word is translated, "comparing" (II Cor. 10:12). WAHL (*Clavis*) translates, "*explaining* (as the *Greek* is translated, Gen. 40:8, LXX) to spiritual (i.e., Spirittaught) men, spiritual things (the things which we ourselves are taught by the Spirit)." Spirit-taught men alone can comprehend spiritual truths. This accords with vss. 6, 9, 10, 14, 15; ch. 3:1. ALFORD translates, "Putting together (combining) spirituals with spirituals"; i.e., attaching spiritual *words* to spiritual *things,* which we should not do, if we were to use words of worldly wisdom to expound spiritual things (so vss. 1, 4; I Pet. 4:11). Perhaps the generality of the neuters is designed to comprehend these several notions by implication. Comparing, or combining, spirituals with spirituals; implying both that spiritual things are only suited to spiritual persons (so "things" comprehended *persons,* ch. 1:27), and also that spiritual truths can only be combined with spiritual (not worldly-wise) words; and lastly, spirituals of the Old and New Testaments can only be understood by mutual comparison or combination, not by combination with worldly "wisdom," or natural perceptions (ch. 1:21, 22; 2:1, 4-9; cf. Ps. 119:18). **14. natural man**—lit., "a man of animal soul." As contrasted with the *spiritual* man, he is governed by the animal soul, which overbears his *spirit,* which latter is without the Spirit of God (Jude 19). So the *animal* (*English Version,* "natural") body, or body led by the lower animal nature (including both the mere human fallen *reason* and *heart*), is contrasted with the Spiritquickened body (ch. 15:44-46). The *carnal* man (the man led by bodily appetites, and also by a self-exalting spirit, estranged from the divine life) is closely akin; so too the "earthly." "Devilish," or "demon-like"; "led by an evil spirit," is the awful character of such a one, in its worst type (Jas. 3:15). **receiveth not**—though they are offered to him, and are "worthy of being *received* by all men" (I Tim. 1:15). **they are foolishness unto him**—whereas he seeks "wisdom" (ch. 1: 22). **neither can he**—Not only *does* he not, but he *cannot* know them, and therefore has no wish to "receive" them (Rom. 8:7). **15. He that is spiritual**—lit., "*the* spiritual (man)." In vs. 14, it is "*A* [not '*the,*' as *English Version*] natural man." *The spiritual* is *the* man distinguished above his fellow men, as he in whom the Spirit rules. In the unregenrate, the spirit which ought to be the organ of the Holy Spirit (and which is so in the regenerate), is overridden by the animal soul, and is in abeyance, so that such a one is never called "spiritual." **judgeth all things**—and persons, by their true standard (cf.

ADAM CLARKE

Yea, the deep things of God. It is only the Spirit of God who can reveal the counsels of God. These are the purposes which have existed in His infinite wisdom and goodness from eternity; and particularly what refers to creation, providence, redemption, and eternal glory, as far as men and angels are concerned in these purposes. The apostles were so fully convinced that the scheme of redemption proclaimed by the gospel was divine that they boldly asserted that these things infinitely surpassed the wisdom and comprehension of man. The apostles were as truly conscious of their own inspiration as they were that they had consciousness at all; and what they spoke, they spoke as they were moved by the Holy Ghost.

12. *Now we have received, not the spirit of the world.* We who are the genuine apostles of Christ have received this Spirit of God, by which we know the deep things of God; and through the teaching of that Spirit we preach Christ crucified. We have not therefore *received . . . the spirit of the world*—of the Jewish teachers, who are all looking for a worldly kingdom and a worldly Messiah, and interpret all the scriptures of the Old Testament which relate to Him in a carnal and worldly sense. *That we might know the things.* It is evident that, as the apostle means by "princes of the world" the rulers of the Jews, vv. 6-8, so by *spirit of the world* he here means Jewish wisdom, or their carnal mode of interpreting the sacred oracles and their carnal expectation of a worldly kingdom under the Messiah.

13. *Which things also we speak.* We dare no more use the language of the Jews and the Gentiles in speaking of those glorious things than we can indulge their spirit. The Greek orators affected a high and florid language, full of tropes and figures, which dazzled more than it enlightened. The rabbins affected obscurity, and were studious to find out cabalistical meanings, which had no tendency to make the people wise unto salvation. The apostles could not follow any of these; they spoke the things of God in the words of God. *Comparing spiritual things with spiritual.* This is commonly understood to mean comparing the spiritual things under the Old Testament with the spiritual things under the New, but this does not appear to be the apostle's meaning. The word which we translate *comparing* rather signifies "conferring, discussing, or explaining"; and the word *pneumatikois* should be rendered "to spiritual men," and not be referred to *spiritual things.* The passage therefore should be thus translated: "Explaining spiritual things to spiritual persons." And this sense the following verse absolutely requires.

14. *But the natural man.* The animal man—the man who is in a mere state of nature, and lives under the influence of his animal passions. The person in question is not only one who either has had no spiritual teaching or has not profited by it, but one who lives for the present world, having no respect to spiritual or eternal things. This "animal man" is opposed to the "spiritual man"; and as this latter is one who is under the influence of the Spirit of God, so the former is one who is without that influence. *But the natural man*—The apostle appears to give this as a reason why he explained those deep spiritual things to spiritual men: because the "animal man"; the man who is in a state of nature, without the regenerating grace of the Spirit of God, *receiveth not the things of the Spirit*—neither apprehends nor comprehends them. He has no relish for them; he considers it the highest wisdom to live for this world.

15. *But he that is spiritual judgeth all things.* He who has the mind of Christ discerns and judges of all things spiritual, yet he himself is not discerned by the mere animal man. Some suppose that the word should be understood thus: "He examines, scrutinizes, convinces, reproves," which it appears to mean in chap. xiv. 24; and they read the verse thus: The *spiritual* man, the well-taught Christian, convinces, i.e.,

MATTHEW HENRY

divine truths. It is the sanctified mind that must discern the real beauties of holiness; but they do not lose their power of discerning about common and natural things. The spiritual man may judge of all things, natural and supernatural, human and divine. But he himself is judged or discerned of no man. The carnal man knows no more of a spiritual man than he does of other spiritual things. The spiritual man does not lie open to his observation. *He that is spiritual* can judge both of common things and things divine. He does not lose the power of reasoning by founding his religion on revelation. But *he himself is judged of no man*—can be judged, so as to be confuted, by no man. He who founds all his knowledge upon principles of science, and the mere light of reason, can never be a judge of the truth or falsehood of what is received by revelation.

For who hath known the mind of the Lord, that he may instruct him (*v.* 16), that is, the *spiritual man*? Who can enter so far into the mind of God as to instruct him who has the Spirit of God, and is under his inspiration? Very few have known anything of the mind of God by a natural power. *But*, adds the apostle, *we have the mind of Christ*: and the mind of Christ is the mind of God. It is the great privilege of Christians that they have the mind of Christ.

CHAPTER 3

Verses 1–4

Here, I. Paul blames the Corinthians for their weakness. Those who are renewed to a spiritual life may yet in many things be defective. The apostle tells *them he could not speak to them as unto spiritual* men, *but as unto carnal* men, *as to babes in Christ*, *v.* 1. It was but too evident they were much under the command of carnal and corrupt affections. They were still mere babes in Christ. They had received some of the first principles of Christianity, but had not grown up to maturity. He had communicated no more of the deep things of it to them.

They could not bear such food, they needed to be fed with milk, not with meat, *v.* 2. It is the duty of a faithful minister of Christ to consult the capacities of his hearers and teach them as they can bear. And yet it is natural for babes to grow up to men; and babes in Christ should endeavour to grow in stature, and become men in Christ. Christians are utterly to blame who do not endeavour to grow in grace and knowledge.

II. He blames them for their carnality, and mentions their contention and discord about their ministers as evidence of it: *For you are yet carnal; for whereas there are among you envyings, and strifes, and divisions, are you not carnal, and walk as men?* (*v.* 3). *While one said, I am of Paul;* and *another, I am of Apollos*, *v.* 4. Contentions and quarrels about religion are sad evidences of remaining carnality. True religion makes men peaceable and not contentious. *Do not you walk as men?* It is to be lamented that many who should walk as Christians, above the common rate of men, do indeed walk as men, live and act too much like other men.

JAMIESON, FAUSSET, BROWN

ch. 6:2-4; I John 4:1), in so far as he is spiritual. "Discerneth . . . is discerned," would better accord with the translation of the same *Greek* (vs. 14). Otherwise for "discerned," in vs. 14, translate, "judged of," to accord with the translation, "judgeth . . . is judged" in this 15th verse. He has a practical insight into the verities of the Gospel, though he is not infallible on all theoretical points. If an individual may have the Spirit without being infallible, why may not the Church have the Spirit, and yet not be infallible (a refutation of the plea of Rome for the Church's infallibility, from Matt. 28: 20; John 16:13)? As the believer and the Church have the Spirit, and are yet not therefore impeccable, so he and the Church have the Spirit, and yet are not infallible or impeccable. He and the Church are both infallible and impeccable, only in proportion to the *degree* in which they are led by the Spirit. The Spirit leads into all truth and holiness; but His influence on believers and on the Church is as yet partial. Jesus alone, who had the Spirit without measure (John 3:34), is both infallible and impeccable. Scripture, because it was written by men, who while writing were infallibly inspired, is unmixed truth (Prov. 28:5; I John 2:27). **16. For**—proof of vs. 15, that the spiritual man "is judged of no man." In order to judge the spiritual man, the ordinary man must "know the mind of the Lord." But "who of ordinary men knows" that? **that he may instruct him**—i.e., so as to be able to set Him right as His counsellor (quoted from Isa. 40:13, 14). So the LXX translates the *Greek* verb, which means to "prove," in Acts 9:22. Natural men who judge spiritual men, living according to the mind of God ("We have the mind of Christ"), are virtually wishing to instruct God, and bring Him to another mind, as counsellors setting to right their king. **we have the mind of Christ**—in our degree of capability to apprehend it. Isaiah 40 refers to JEHOVAH: therefore, as it is applied here to *Christ*, He is Jehovah.

CHAPTER 3

Vss. 1-23. PAUL COULD NOT SPEAK TO THEM OF DEEP SPIRITUAL TRUTHS, AS THEY WERE CARNAL, CONTENDING FOR THEIR SEVERAL TEACHERS; THESE ARE NOTHING BUT WORKERS FOR GOD, TO WHOM THEY MUST GIVE ACCOUNT IN THE DAY OF FIERY JUDGMENT. THE HEARERS ARE GOD'S TEMPLE, WHICH THEY MUST NOT DEFILE BY CONTENTIONS FOR TEACHERS, WHO, AS WELL AS ALL THINGS, ARE THEIRS, BEING CHRIST'S. **1. And I**—i.e., as the natural (animal) man cannot receive, so *I also could not speak unto you* the deep things of God, *as* I would *to the spiritual; but* I was compelled to speak to you *as* I would *to* MEN OF FLESH. The oldest MSS. read this for "carnal." The former (lit., "fleshy") implies men wholly *of flesh*, or *natural. Carnal*, or *fleshly*, implies not they were *wholly natural* or unregenerate (ch. 2:14), but that they had much of a *carnal tendency;* e.g., their divisions. Paul had to speak to them *as* he would to men *wholly natural*, inasmuch as they are *still carnal* (vs. 3) in many respects, notwithstanding their conversion (ch. 1:4-9). **babes**—contrasted with the *perfect* (fully matured) *in Christ* (Col 1:28; cf. Heb. 5:13, 14). This implies they were not men wholly *of flesh*, though carnal in tendencies. They had life in Christ, but it was weak. He blames them for being still in a degree (not *altogether*, cf. ch. 1:5, 7; therefore he says "*as*") *babes* in Christ, when by this time they ought to have "come unto a perfect man, unto the measure of the stature of the fulness of Christ" (Eph. 4:13). In Romans 7:14, also the oldest MSS. read, "I am a man *of flesh*." **2.** (Heb. 5:12.) **milk**—the elementary "principles of the doctrine of Christ." **3. envying**—jealousy, *rivalry*. As this refers to their *feelings*, "strife" refers to their *words*, and "divisions" to their *actions* [BENGEL]. There is a gradation, or ascending climax: *envying* had produced *strife*, and strife *divisions* (factious parties) [GROTIUS]. His language becomes severer now as He proceeds; in ch. 1:11 he had only said "contentions," he now multiplies the words (cf. the stronger term, ch. 4:6, than in ch. 3:21). **carnal**—For "strife" is a "work of the flesh" (Gal. 5:20). The "flesh" includes all feelings that aim not at the glory of God, and the good of our neighbor, but at gratifying self. **walk as men**—as unregenerate men (cf. Matt. 16:23). "After the flesh, not after the Spirit" of God, as becomes you as regenerate by the Spirit (Rom. 8:4; Gal. 5:25, 26). **4.** (Ch. 1:12.) **are ye not carnal**—The oldest MSS. read, "Are ye not *men?*" i.e., "walking as men" unregenerate (vs. 3). **5. Who then**—Seeing then that ye severally strive so for your favorite teachers,

ADAM CLARKE

can easily convict, all men, every animal man, of error and vice; yet he himself is convicted of no man. His mind is enlightened and his life is holy, and therefore the animal man cannot convict him of sin. This is a good sense, but the first appears the most natural.

16. *For who hath known the mind of the Lord?* Who that is still an animal man can know the mind of God? so as to *instruct him*, viz., the spiritual man, the same that is spoken of in v. 15. But the words may be better understood thus: How can the animal man know the mind of the Lord? And how can any man communicate that knowledge which he has never acquired, and which is foolishness to him, because it is spiritual and he is animal? This quotation is made from Isa. xl. 13. *But we have the mind of Christ.* He has endowed us with the same disposition, being born again by His Spirit; therefore we are capable of knowing His mind and receiving the teachings of His Spirit. The words *that he may instruct him* should be translated "that he may teach it"; that is, the mind of God—not instruct God, but teach His mind to others.

CHAPTER 3

1. *I, brethren, could not speak unto you as unto spiritual.* This is a continuation of the preceding discourse. *But as unto carnal.* Persons under the influence of fleshly appetites, coveting and living for the things of this life. *Babes in Christ.* Just beginning to acquire some notion of the Christian religion, but as yet very incapable of judging what is most suitable to yourselves, and consequently utterly unqualified to discern between one teacher and another; so that your making the distinctions which you do make, so far from being a proof of mature judgment, is on the contrary a proof that you have no right judgment at all; and this springs from your want of knowledge in divine things.

2. *I have fed you with milk.* I have instructed you in the elements of Christianity—in its simplest and easiest truths; because from the low state of your minds in religious knowledge, you were incapable of comprehending the higher truths of the gospel; and in this state you will still continue. The apostle thus exposes to them the absurdity of their conduct in pretending to judge between preacher and preacher while they had but a very partial acquaintance even with the first principles of Christianity.

3. *There is among you envying, and strife, and divisions.* There are three things here worthy of note: these people were wrong in *thought, word,* and *deed. Envying* refers to the state of their souls; they had inward grudgings and disaffection towards each other. *Strife* or "contention" refers to their words; they were continually disputing and contending whose party was the best, each endeavoring to prove that he and his party were alone in the right. *Divisions* refers to their conduct; as they could not agree, they contended till they separated from each other, and thus rent the Church of Christ. Thus the *envying* and grudging led to *strife* and evil speaking, and this led to *divisions* and fixed parties. In this state well might the apostle say, *Are ye not carnal, and walk as men?* You act just as the people of the world, and have no more of the spirit of religion than they.

4. *For while one saith, I am of Paul.* It was notorious that both Paul and Apollos held the same creed; between them there was not the slightest difference. When, therefore, the dissentients began to prefer the one to the other, it

MATTHEW HENRY

Verses 5–10

Here the apostle instructs them how to cure this humour.

I. By reminding them that the ministers about whom they contended were but ministers: *Who then is Paul, and who is Apollos, but ministers by whom you believed? Even as the Lord gave to every man, v.* 5, mere instruments used by the God of all grace. We should take care not to deify ministers, nor put them into the place of God. All the gifts and powers that even apostles discovered and exerted in the work of the ministry were from God. They were intended to manifest their mission and doctrine to be divine. *Paul had planted and Apollos had watered, v.* 6. Both were useful, one for one purpose, the other for another. Paul was fitted for planting work, and Apollos for watering work, but God gave the increase.

The success of the ministry must be derived from the divine blessing: *Neither he that planteth is anything, nor he that watereth, but God who giveth the increase, v.* 7. Even apostolical ministers can do nothing with efficacy and success unless God give the increase. Paul and Apollos are nothing at all in their own account, but God is all in all.

II. By representing to them the unanimity of Christ's ministers: *He that planteth and he that watereth are one* (*v.* 8), employed by one Master, busied in one work, in harmony with one another, however they may be set in opposition to each other by factious party-makers. All the faithful ministers of Christ are one in the great business and intention of their ministry. All such may expect a glorious recompence of their fidelity, and in proportion to it: *Every man shall receive his own reward, according to his own labour.* Those that work hardest shall fare best. Those that are most faithful shall have the greatest reward.

They are labourers with God, fellow-labourers (*v.* 9). They are engaged in his business. They are working together with God, and he who knows their work will take care they do not labour in vain. The judgment of God is according to truth. He ever rewards in proportion to the diligence and faithfulness of his servants. They are always under his eye, employed in his husbandry and building; and therefore, to be sure, he will carefully look over them: "*You are God's husbandry, you are God's building;* and therefore are neither of Paul nor of Apollos. It is all for God that we have been doing among you." *According to the grace of God which is given unto me, as a wise master-builder, I have laid the foundation, and another buildeth thereon.* It was honourable to be a master-builder in the edifice of God; but it added to his character to be a wise one. But, though he gives himself such a character, it is not to gratify his own pride, but to magnify divine grace. He was a wise master-builder, but the grace of God made him such. Spiritual pride is abominable. But to take notice of the favours of God to promote our gratitude to him, and to speak of them to his honour, is but a proper expression of the duty and regard we owe him. Ministers should not be proud of their gifts or graces; but the better qualified they are for their work, and the more success they have in it, the more thankful should they be to God. *I have laid the foundation, and another buildeth thereon.* It was Paul that laid the foundation of a church among them. He would derogate from none that had done service among them, nor would he be robbed of his own honour and respect. Faithful ministers may and ought to have a concern for their own reputation. Their usefulness depends much upon it. *But let every man take heed how he buildeth thereon.* There may be very indifferent building on a good foundation. Nothing must be laid upon it but what the foundation will bear, and what is of a piece with it. Gold and dirt must not be mingled together. Ministers of Christ should take great care that they do not build their own fancies or false reasonings on the foundation of divine revelation.

Verses 11–15

Here the apostle informs us what foundation he had laid. *Other foundation can no man lay besides what is laid—even Jesus Christ.* The doctrine of our Saviour and his mediation is the principal doctrine of Christianity. It lies at the bottom, and is the foundation, of all the rest. But of those that hold the foundation there are two sorts:

JAMIESON, FAUSSET, BROWN

"Who is (of what intrinsic power and dignity) Paul?" If so great an apostle reasons so of himself, how much more does humility, rather than self-seeking, become ordinary ministers! **Paul... Apollos**—The oldest MSS. read in the reverse order, "Apollos"... "Paul." He puts Apollos before himself in humility. **but ministers...**—The oldest MSS. have no "but." "Who is Apollos... Paul? (mere) ministers (a lowly word appropriate here, *servants*), by whom (not '*in whom*'; *by whose ministrations*) ye believed." **as... Lord gave to every man**—i.e., to the several hearers, for it was GOD that "gave the increase" (vs. 6). **6. I... planted, Apollos watered**—(Acts 18:1; 19:1). Apollos at his own desire (Acts 18:27) was sent by the brethren to Corinth, and there followed up the work which Paul had begun. **God gave the increase**—i.e., the growth (vs. 10; Acts 18:27). "Believed through *grace*." Though ministers are nothing, and God all in all, yet God works by instruments, and promises the Holy Spirit in the faithful use of means. This is the dispensation of the Spirit, and ours is the ministry of the Spirit. **7. neither is he that... anything... but God**—viz., is all in all. "God" is emphatically last in the *Greek*. "He that giveth the increase (namely), GOD." Here follows a parenthesis from vs. 8 to vs. 21, where "Let no man glory in men" stands in antithetic contrast to "God" here. **8. one**—essentially in their aim they are *one*, engaged in one and the same ministry; therefore they ought not to be made by you the occasion of forming separate parties. **and every man**—rather "*but* every man." Though in their service or ministry, they are essentially "one," yet every minister is separately responsible in "*his own*" work, and "shall receive *his own* (emphatically repeated) reward, according to *his own* labor." The *reward* is something over and above personal salvation (vss. 14, 15; II John 8). He shall be rewarded according to, not his success or the amount of work done, but "according to his own labor." It shall be said to him, "Well done, thou good and (not *successful*, but) *faithful* servant, enter thou into the joy of thy Lord" (Matt. 25:23). **9.** Translate, as the *Greek* collocation of words, and the emphasis on "God" thrice repeated, requires, "For (in proof that "each shall receive reward according to his own labor," viz., from God) it is of God that we are the fellow workers (laboring *with*, but *under*, and *belonging to* Him as His servants, II Cor. 5:20; 6:1; cf. Acts 15:4; *Note*, I Thess. 3:2) of God that ye are the field (or tillage), of God that ye are the building" [ALFORD]. "Building" is a new image introduced here, as suited better than that of husbandry, to set forth the different kinds of teaching and their results, which he is now about to discuss. "To edify" or "build up" the Church of Christ is similarly used (Eph. 2:21, 22; 4:29). **10. grace... given unto me**—Paul puts this first, to guard against seeming to want humility, in pronouncing himself "a WISE master builder," in the clause following [CHRYSOSTOM]. The "grace" is that "given" to him in common with all Christians (vs. 5), only proportioned to the work which God had for him to do [ALFORD]. **wise**—i.e., skilful. His *skill* is shown in his *laying a foundation*. The unskilful builder lays none (Luke 6:49). Christ is the foundation (vs. 11). **another**—who ever comes after me. He does not name *Apollos;* for he speaks generally of *all successors*, whoever they be. His warning, "Let every man (every *teacher*) take heed how..." refers to other successors rather than Apollos, who doubtless did not, as they, build wood, hay, etc., on the foundation (cf. ch. 4: 15). "I have done my part, let them who follow me see (so the *Greek* for "take heed") to theirs" [BENGEL]. **how**—with what material [ALFORD]. How far *wisely*, and in builder-like style (I Pet. 4: 11). **buildeth thereupon**—Here the *building* or *superstructure* raised *on* Christ the "foundation," laid by Paul (ch. 2:2) is not, as in Ephesians 2:20, 21, the Christian Church made up of believers, the "lively stones" (I Peter 2:5), but *the doctrinal and practical teaching* which the teachers who succeeded Paul, superadded to his first teaching; not that they taught what was false, but their teaching was subtle and speculative reasoning, rather than solid and simple truth. **11.** (Isa. 28:16; Acts 4:12; Eph. 2:20.) **For**—my warning ("take heed..." vs. 10) is as to the superstructure ("buildeth *thereupon*"), not as to *the foundation:* "For other *foundation* can no man lay, than that which has (already) been laid (by God) Jesus Christ," the person, not the mere abstract doctrine about Him, though the latter also is included;*Jesus*, GOD-SAVIOUR; *Christ*, MESSIAH or ANOINTED. **can**—A man *can* not lay any other, since the only one recognized by God

ADAM CLARKE

was the fullest proof of their carnality, because in the doctrines of these apostles there was no difference, so that what the people were captivated by must be something in their outward manner, Apollos being probably more eloquent than Paul. Their preferring one to another on such an account proved that they were *carnal* —led by their senses and mere outward appearances, without being under the guidance of either reason or grace.

5. *Ministers by whom ye believed.* The different apostles who have preached unto you the word of life are the means which God has used to bring you to the knowledge of Christ. No one of those has either preached or recommended himself; they all preach and recommend Christ Jesus the Lord.

6. *I have planted.* I first sowed the seed of the gospel at Corinth, and in the region of Achaia. *Apollos watered.* Apollos came after me, and by his preachings and exhortations watered the seed which I had sowed. *But God gave the increase.* The seed has taken root, has sprung up, and borne much fruit; but this was by the especial blessing of God.

7. *So then neither is he that planteth any thing.* God alone should have all the glory, as the seed is His, the ground is His, the laborers are His, and the produce all comes from himself.

8. *He that planteth and he that watereth are one.* Both Paul and Apollos have received the same doctrine, preach the same doctrine, and labor to promote the glory of God in the salvation of your souls. Why should you be divided with respect to Paul and Apollos while these apostles are intimately one in spirit, design, and operation? *According to his own labour.* God does not reward His servants according to the success of their labor, because that depends on himself; but He rewards them according to the quantum of faithful labor which they bestow on His work.

9. *For we are labourers together with God.* It would perhaps be more correct to translate, "We are fellow laborers of God"; i.e., we labor together in the work of God. Far from being divided among ourselves, we jointly labor, as oxen in the same yoke, to promote the honor of our Master. *Ye are God's husbandry, ye are God's building.* The word which we translate *husbandry* signifies properly an "arable field"; so Prov. xxiv. 30: "I went by the field of the slothful"; and chap. xxxi. 16: The wise woman "considereth a field, and buyeth it." It would be more literal to translate it, "You are God's farm." *Ye are God's building.* You are not only the field which God cultivates, but you are the house which God builds, and in which He intends to dwell. As no man in viewing a fine building extols the quarryman that dug up the stones, the hewer that cut and squared them, the mason that placed them in the wall, the woodman that hewed down the timber, the carpenter that squared and jointed it, but the architect who planned it, and under whose direction the whole work was accomplished; so no man should consider Paul or Apollos or Cephas anything but as persons employed by the great Architect to form a building which is to become a habitation of himself through the Spirit, and the design of which is entirely His own.

10. *As a wise masterbuilder.* The design or plan of the building is from God; all things must be done according to the pattern which He has exhibited. But the execution of this plan was entrusted chiefly to Paul; he was the wise or "experienced architect" which God used in order to lay the foundation; to ascertain the essential and immutable doctrines of the gospel—those alone which came from God, and which alone He would bless to the salvation of mankind. *Let every man take heed how he buildeth thereupon.* Let him take care that the doctrines which he preaches be answerable to those which I have preached; let him also take heed that he enjoin no other practice than that which is suitable to the doctrine, and in every sense accords with it.

11. *Other foundation can no man lay.* I do not speak particularly concerning the *foundation* of this spiritual building; it can have no other foundation than Jesus Christ. There cannot be

MATTHEW HENRY

I. Some build upon this foundation *gold, silver, and precious stones* (*v.* 12), namely, those who hold nothing but the *truth as it is in Jesus*, and preach nothing else. This is building well upon a good foundation.

II. Others *build wood, hay, and stubble*, on this foundation; that is, though they adhere to the foundation, they depart from the mind of Christ in many particulars, and build upon the good foundation what will not abide the test when the day of trial shall come. There is a time coming when a discovery will be made of what men have built on this foundation: *Every man's work shall be made manifest.* Every man's work shall be made manifest to himself, and made manifest to others, both those that have been misled by him and those that have escaped his errors. There is a day coming that will show us ourselves, and show us our actions in the true light, without covering or disguise: *For the day shall declare it* (that is, every man's work), *because it shall be revealed by fire;* and the *fire shall try every man's work, of what sort it is*, *v.* 13. The day shall declare and make it manifest, the last day, the great day of trial; see *ch.* iv. 5. There is a day coming that will distinguish one man from another, and one man's work from another's, as the fire distinguishes gold from dross, or metal that will bear the fire from other materials that will be consumed in it.

Some men's works will *abide the trial.* It will appear that they not only held the foundation, but that they built regularly and well upon it. The foundation and the superstructure were all of a piece. And such a builder shall not, cannot fail of a reward. He will have praise and honour in that day, and eternal recompence after it. Fidelity in the ministers of Christ will meet with a full and ample reward in a future life. And, Lord, how great! how much exceeding their deserts! There are others *whose works shall be burnt* (*v.* 15). The great day will pluck off all disguises, and make things appear as they are: *He whose work shall be burnt will suffer loss.* If he have built upon the right foundation wood and hay and stubble, he will suffer loss, though he may in the general have been an honest and an upright Christian. This part of his work will be lost, though he himself may be saved. Those who hold the foundation of Christianity, though they build hay, wood, and stubble, upon it, may be saved. This may help to enlarge our charity. Nothing will damn men but wickedness. He shall be saved, *yet so as by fire*, saved out of the fire. God will have no mercy on their works, though he may pluck them as brands out of the burning.

Verses 16, 17

Here the apostle resumes his argument, founding it on his former allusion, *You are God's building*, *v.* 9. *Know you not that you are the temple of God, and the Spirit of God dwelleth in you? If any man defile* (corrupt and destroy) *the temple of God, him shall God destroy* (the same word is in the original in both clauses), *for the temple of God is holy, which temple you are.* It looks from other parts of the epistle (see *ch.* vi. 13-20), as if the false teachers among the Corinthians were not only loose livers, but taught licentious doctrines. Such doctrine was not to be reckoned among hay and stubble, which would be consumed while the person who laid them on the foundation escaped the burning. Those who spread principles of this sort would provoke God to destroy them. *Know you not that you are the temple of God, and that the Spirit of God dwelleth in you?* Christian

JAMIESON, FAUSSET, BROWN

has been already laid. **12. Now**—rather, "But." The image is that of a building on a solid foundation, and partly composed of durable and precious, partly of perishable, materials. The "gold, silver, precious stones," which all can withstand fire (Rev. 21:18, 19), are *teachings* that will stand the fiery test of judgment; "wood, hay, stubble," are those which cannot stand it; not positive heresy, for that would destroy the foundation, but teaching mixed up with human philosophy and Judaism, curious rather than useful. Besides the *teachings*, the superstructure represents also the *persons* cemented to the Church by them, the reality of whose conversion, through the teachers' instrumentality, will be tested at the last day. Where there is the least grain of real gold of faith, it shall never be lost (I Pet. 1:7; cf. ch. 4:12). On the other hand, the lightest straw feeds the fire [BENGEL] (Matt. 5:19). **13. Every man's work**—each teacher's superstructure on the foundation. **the day**—of the Lord (ch. 1:8; Heb. 10:25; I Thess. 5:4). The article is emphatic, "*The* day," i.e., the great day of days, the long expected day. **declare it**—old English for "make it clear" (ch. 4:4). **it shall be revealed by fire**—it, i.e., "every man's work." Rather, "*He,*" the Lord, whose day it is (II Thess. 1:7, 8). Translate lit., "*is being revealed* (the present in the *Greek* implies the *certainty* and *nearness* of the event, Rev. 22:10, 20) *in* fire" (Mal. 3:3; 4:1). The *fire* (probably *figurative* here, as the *gold, hay,* etc.) is not *purgatory* (as Rome teaches, i.e., *purificatory* and *punitive*), but *probatory*, not restricted to those dying in "venial sin"; the supposed *intermediate class* between those entering heaven at once, and those dying in mortal sin who go to hell, but *universal*, testing the godly and ungodly alike (II Cor. 5:10; cf. Mark 9:49). This fire is not till the *last* day, the supposed fire of purgatory begins *at death.* The fire of Paul is to try the *works*, the fire of purgatory the *persons*, of men. Paul's fire causes "loss" to the sufferers; Rome's purgatory, great gain, viz., heaven at last to those purged by it, if only it were true. Thus this passage, quoted by Rome for, is altogether against, purgatory. "It was not this doctrine that gave rise to prayers for the dead; but the practice of praying for the dead [which crept in from the affectionate but mistaken solicitude of survivors] gave rise to the doctrine" [WHATELY]. **14. abide**—abide the testing fire (Matt. 3:11, 12). **which he hath built thereupon**—which he built *on the foundation.* **reward**—*wages*, as a builder, i.e., teacher. His converts built on Christ the foundation, through his faithful teaching, shall be his "crown of rejoicing" (II Cor. 1:14; Phil. 2:16; I Thess. 2:19). **15. If . . . be burnt**—if any *teacher's* work consist of such materials as the fire will destroy [ALFORD]. **suffer loss**—i.e., forfeit the special "reward"; not that he shall lose salvation (which is altogether a *free gift*, not a "reward" or wages), for he remains still on the foundation (vs. 12; II John 6). **saved; yet so as by fire**—rather, "so as *through* fire" (Zech. 3:2; Amos 4:11; Jude 23). "Saved, yet *not without* fire" (Rom. 2:27) [BENGEL]. As a builder whose building, not the foundation, is consumed by fire, escapes, but with the loss of his work [ALFORD]; as the shipwrecked merchant, though he has lost his merchandise, is saved, though having to pass *through* the waves [BENGEL]. Malachi 3:1, 2; and 4:1, give the key to explain the imagery. The "Lord suddenly coming to His temple" in flaming "fire," all the parts of the building which will not stand that fire will be consumed; the builders will escape with personal salvation, but with the loss of their work, through the midst of the conflagration [ALFORD]. Again, a distinction is recognized between minor and fundamental doctrines (if we regard the superstructure as representing the *doctrines* superadded to the elementary essentials); a man may err as to the former, and yet be saved, but not so as to the latter (cf. Phil. 3:15). **16. Know ye not**—It is no new thing I tell you, in calling you "God's building"; ye know and ought to remember, ye are the noblest kind of building, "the temple of God." **ye**—all Christians form together one vast temple. The expression is not, "ye are *temples,*" but "ye are *the temple*" collectively, and "lively stones" (I Pet. 2:5) individually. **God . . . Spirit**—God's indwelling, and that of the Holy Spirit, are one; therefore the Holy Spirit is God. No literal "temple" is recognized by the New Testament in the Christian Church. The only one is the spiritual temple, the whole body of believing worshippers in which the Holy Spirit dwells (ch. 6: 19; John 4:23, 24). The *synagogue*, not the temple, was the model of the Christian house of worship. The temple was the *house of sacrifice*, rather than of prayer. Prayers in the temple were silent

ADAM CLARKE

two opinions on this subject among the true apostles of our Lord. The only fear is lest an improper use should be made of this heavenly doctrine, lest a bad superstructure should be raised on this Foundation.

12. *If any man build . . . gold, silver.* By *gold, silver*, and *precious stones* the apostle certainly means pure and wholesome doctrines; by *wood, hay*, and *stubble*, false doctrines, such as at that time prevailed in the Corinthian church.

13. *The day shall declare it, because it shall be revealed by fire.* There is much difference of opinion relative to the meaning of the terms in this and the following two verses. That the apostle refers to the approaching destruction of Jerusalem I think very probable; and when this is considered, all the terms and metaphors will appear clear and consistent. The *day* is the time of punishment coming on this disobedient and rebellious people. And this day being *revealed by fire* points out the extreme rigor and totally destructive nature of that judgment. *And the fire shall try every man's work.* If the apostle refers to the Judaising teachers and their insinuations that the law, especially circumcision, was of eternal obligation, then the day of fire—the time of vengeance—which was at hand, would sufficiently disprove such assertions as, in the judgment of God, the whole Temple service should be destroyed; and the people, who fondly presumed on their permanence and stability, should be dispossessed of their land and scattered over the face of the whole earth.

14. *If any man's work abide.* Perhaps there is here an allusion to the purifying of different sorts of vessels under the law. All that could stand the fire were to be purified by the fire; and those which could not resist the action of the fire were to be purified by water, Num. xxxi. 23. The "gold," "silver," and "precious stones" could stand the fire; but the "wood," "hay," and "stubble" must be necessarily consumed. So, in that great and terrible day of the Lord, all false doctrine, as well as the system that was to pass away, should be made sufficiently manifest; and God would then show that the gospel, and that alone, was that system of doctrine which He should bless and protect, and none other.

15. *If any man's work shall be burned, he shall suffer loss.* If he have preached the necessity of incorporating the law with the gospel, or proclaimed as a doctrine of God anything which did not proceed from heaven, *he shall suffer loss*—all his time and labor will be found to be uselessly employed and spent. *But he himself shall be saved.* If he have sincerely and conscientiously believed what he preached, and yet preached what was wrong, not through malice or opposition to the gospel, but through mere ignorance, *he shall be saved.* God in His mercy will pass by his errors, and he shall not suffer punishment because he was mistaken. Yet, as in most erroneous teachings there is generally a portion of willful and obstinate ignorance, the salvation of such erroneous teachers is very rare; and is expressed here, *yet so as by fire*, i.e., with great difficulty. The apostle obviously refers to the case of a man who, having builded a house and begun to dwell in it, the house happens to be set on fire, and he has warning of it just in time to escape with his life, losing at the same time his house, his goods, his labor, and almost his own life. So he who, while he holds the doctrine of Christ crucified as the only foundation on which a soul can rest its hopes of salvation, builds at the same time on that foundation Antinomianism or any other erroneous or destructive doctrine, he shall lose all his labor, his own soul scarcely escape everlasting perdition; nor even this unless sheer ignorance and inveterate prejudice, connected with much sincerity, be found in his case.

16. *Ye are the temple of God.* The apostle resumes here what he had asserted in v. 9: "Ye are God's building." As the whole congregation of Israel were formerly considered as the temple and habitation of God, because God dwelt among them, so here the whole church of Corinth is called *the temple of God*, because all genuine believers have the *Spirit* of God to dwell in them; and Christ has promised to be

MATTHEW HENRY

churches are temples of God. He dwells among them by his Holy Spirit. Every Christian is a living temple of the living God. Christ by his Spirit dwells in all true believers. The temple was set apart from every common to a holy use, to the immediate service of God. So all Christians are separated from common uses, and set apart for God and his service. They are sacred to him. Christians are holy by profession, and should be pure and clean both in heart and conversation.

Here he prescribes humility for the remedy of the irregularities in the Church of Corinth: "*Let no man deceive himself* (*v.* 18). Do not be led away from the truth and simplicity of the gospel." We are in great danger of deceiving ourselves when we have too high an opinion of human wisdom and arts. But *he who seems to be wise must become a fool that he may be wise.* He must be sensible of his own ignorance, and lament it; he must distrust his own understanding, and not lean on it. The person who resigns his own understanding, that he may follow the instruction of God, is in the way to true and everlasting wisdom. He that has a low opinion of his own knowledge and powers will submit to better information; but the proud man, conceited of his own wisdom and understanding, will undertake to correct even divine wisdom itself. We must abase ourselves before God if we would be either truly wise or good: *For the wisdom of this world is foolishness with God, v.* 19. There can be no more comparison between his wisdom and ours than between his power and being and ours. There is no common measure by which to compare finite and infinite. And much more is the wisdom of man foolishness with God when set in competition with his. How justly does he despise, how easily can he baffle and confound it! *He knows the thoughts of the wise, that they are vain* (*v.* 20). God has a perfect knowledge of the thoughts of men, their most secret counsels and purposes. And he knows them to be vanity. And should not all this teach us modesty, and a deference to the wisdom of God? He who would be wise indeed must learn of God, and not set his own wisdom up in competition with God's.

Verses 21–23

An exhortation against over-valuing their teachers. They had an equal interest in all their ministers: *Therefore let no man glory in men* (*v.* 21)—forget that their ministers are men, or pay that deference to them that is due only to God, set them at the head of parties. The only way to avoid this mischief is to have a due sense of the common weakness of human understanding, and an entire deference to the wisdom of God. Ministers are not to be set up in competition with one another. They were appointed of Christ, for the common benefit of the church: "*Paul, and Apollos, and Cephas, are all yours.* All are to be valued and used for your own spiritual benefit." Upon this occasion also he gives in an inventory of the church's possessions, the spiritual riches of a true believer: "*All is yours.* Nay, the world itself is yours. *Life is yours*, that you may prepare for the life of heaven; and *death is yours*, that you may go to the possession of it. It is the kind messenger that will fetch you to your Father's house. *Things present* are yours, for your support on the road; *things to come* are yours, to enrich you for ever at your journey's end." All is ours, time and eternity, earth and heaven, life and death. But it must be remembered, at the same time, *that we are Christ's*. All things are ours, upon no other ground than our being Christ's. Those that would be safe for time, and happy to eternity, must be Christ's. *And Christ is God's*. He is the Christ of God, anointed of God, and commissioned by him. God in Christ reconciling a sinful world to himself, and shedding abroad the riches of

JAMIESON, FAUSSET, BROWN

and individual (Luke 1:10; 18:10-13), not joint and public, nor with reading of Scripture, as in the synagogue. The temple, as the name means (from a *Greek* root "to dwell"), was the earthly *dwelling place of God,* where alone He put His name. The synagogue (as the name means an *assembly*) was the place for assembling men. God now too has His earthly temple, not one of wood and stone, but the congregation of believers, the "living stones" on the "spiritual house." Believers are all spiritual priests in it. Jesus Christ, our High Priest, has the only literal priesthood (Mal. 1:11; Matt. 18:20; I Pet. 2: 5) [VITRINGA]. **17. If any . . . defile . . . destroy**—rather as the *Greek* verb is the same in both cases, "*destroy* . . . destroy." God repays in kind by a righteous retaliation. The destroyer shall himself be destroyed. As temporal death was the penalty of marring the material temple (Lev. 16:2; Dan. 5: 2, 3, 30), so eternal death is the penalty of marring the spiritual temple—the Church. The *destroyers* here (vss. 16, 17), are distinct from the *unwise* or unskilful builders (vss. 12, 15); the latter held fast the "foundation" (vs. 11), and, therefore, though they lose their work of superstructure and the special reward, yet they are themselves saved; the destroyers, on the contrary, assailed with false teaching the foundation, and so subvert the temple itself, and shall therefore be destroyed. (See *Note*, vs. 10), [ESTIUS and NEANDER]. I think Paul passes here from the teachers to all the members of the Church, who, by profession, are "priests unto God" (Exod. 19:6; I Pet. 2:9; Rev. 1:6). As the Aaronic priests were doomed to die if they violated the old temple (Exod. 28:43), so any Christian who violates the sanctity of the spiritual temple, shall perish eternally (Heb. 12:14: 10:26, 31). **holy**—inviolable (Hab. 2:20). **which** *temple* **ye are**—rather, "the which (i.e., holy) are ye" [ALFORD], and, therefore, want of holiness on the part of any of you (or, as ESTIUS, "to tamper with *the foundation* in *teaching* you") is a violation of the temple, which cannot be let to pass with impunity. GROTIUS supports *English Version*. **18. seemeth**—i.e., *is, and is regarded by* himself and others. **wise in this world**—wise in mere worldly wisdom (ch. 1:20). **let him become a fool**—by receiving the Gospel in its unworldly simplicity, and so *becoming a fool in the world's sight* [ALFORD]. Let him *no longer think* himself wise, but seek the true wisdom from God, bringing his understanding into captivity to the obedience of faith [ESTIUS]. **19. with God**—*in the judgment of* God. **it is written**—in Job 5:13. The formula of quoting SCRIPTURE used here, establishes the canonicity of Job. **He taketh . . . wise in . . . own craftiness**—proving the "foolishness" of the world's wisdom, since it is made by God the very snare to catch those who think themselves so wise. Lit., "He who taketh . . ." the whole of the sentence not being quoted, but only the part which suited Paul's purpose. **20.** Quotation from Psalm 94:11. There it is *of men;* here it is "of the wise." Paul by inspiration states the class of men whose "thoughts" (or rather, "reasonings," as suits the *Greek* and the sense of the context) the Spirit designated in the Psalm, "vanity," viz., the "proud" (vs. 2) and worldly-wise, whom God in vs. 8 calls "fools," though they "boast themselves" of their *wisdom* in pushing their interests (vs. 4). **21. let no man glory in men**—resuming the subject from vs. 4; cf. ch. 1:12 and 31, where the true object of glorying is stated: "He that glorieth, let him glory in THE LORD." Also ch. 4:6, "That no one of you be puffed up for one against another." **For all things**—not only *all men*. For you to glory thus in men, is lowering yourselves from your high position as heirs of *all things*. All men (including your teachers) belong to Christ, and therefore to you, by your union with Him; He makes them and all things work together for your good (Romans 8:28). Ye are not for the sake of them, but they for the sake of you (II Cor. 4:5, 15). They belong to you, not you to them. **22.** Enumeration of some of the "all things." The teachers, in whom they gloried, he puts first (ch. 1:12). He omits after "Cephas" *or Christ* (to whom exclusively some at Corinth, ch. 1:12, professed to belong); but, instead, substitutes "ye are Christ's" (vs. 23). **world . . . life . . . death . . . things present . . . things to come**—Not only shall they not "separate you from the love of God in Christ" (Rom 8:38, 39), but they "all are yours," i.e., are for you (Rom. 8:28), and belong to you, as they belong to Christ your Head (Heb. 1:2). **things present**—"things *actually* present" [ALFORD]. **23. ye are Christ's**—not Paul's, or Apollos', or Cephas' (ch. 11:3; Matt. 23: 8-10). "Neither be ye called masters; for one is your Master, even Christ" (Rom. 14:8). Not merely a particular section of you, but

ADAM CLARKE

always in the midst even of two or three who are gathered together in His name. Therefore where God is, there is His temple.

17. *If any man defile the temple.* "If any man destroy the temple of God, him will God destroy." The verb is the same in both clauses. If any man injure, corrupt, or destroy the church of God by false doctrine, God will destroy him—will take away his part out of the book of life.

18. *If any man among you seemeth to be wise.* "If any pretend or affect to be wise." This seems to refer to some individual in the church of Corinth who had been very troublesome to its peace and unity. *Let him become a fool.* Let him divest himself of his worldly wisdom, and be contented to be called a *fool,* and esteemed one, that he may become wise unto salvation, by renouncing his own wisdom and seeking that which comes from God. But probably the apostle refers to him who, pretending to great wisdom and information, taught doctrines contrary to the gospel.

19. *The wisdom of this world,* whether it be the pretended deep and occult wisdom of the rabbins or the wire-drawn speculations of the Grecian philosophers, *is foolishness with God;* for as folly consists in spending time, strength, and pains to no purpose, so these may be fitly termed fools who acquire no saving knowledge by their speculations. *He taketh the wise in their own craftiness.* This is a quotation from Job. v. 13, and powerfully shows what the wisdom of this world is. It is a sort of craft, a subtle trade, which they carry on to wrong others and benefit themselves; and they have generally too much cunning to be caught by men, but God often overthrows them with their own devisings.

20. *The Lord knoweth the thoughts of the wise.* They are always full of schemes and plans for earthly good; and God knows that all this is *vain,* "empty," and unsatisfactory, and will stand them in no stead when He comes to take away their souls. This is a quotation from Ps. xciv. 11. What is here said of the vanity of human knowledge is true of every kind of wisdom that leads not immediately to God himself.

22. *Whether Paul, or Apollos.* As if he had said: God designs to help you by all things and persons; every teacher sent from Him will become a blessing to you if you abide faithful to your calling. *Or the world.* The word *cosmos* here means rather the inhabitants of the world than what we commonly understand by the world itself; and this is its meaning in John iii. 16-17; vi. 33; xiv. 31; xvii. 21. See particularly John xii. 19. The apostle's meaning evidently is: Not only Paul, Apollos, and Cephas are yours—appointed for and employed in your service—but every person besides with whom you may have any intercourse or connection, whether Jew or Greek, whether enemy or friend. *Or life,* with all its trials and advantages; every hour of it, every tribulation in it, the whole course of it, as the grand state of your probation, is a general blessing to you. *Or death.* That solemn hour, so dreadful to the wicked, and so hateful to those who live without God—that is yours. *Death* is your servant. He comes a special messenger from God for you; he comes to undo a knot that now connects body and soul, which it would be unlawful for yourselves to untie. He comes to take your souls to glory; and he cannot come before his due time to those who are waiting for the salvation of God. *Or things present.* Every occurrence in providence in the present life, for God rules in providence as well as in grace. *Or things to come.* The whole order and economy of the eternal world; all in heaven and all in earth are even now working together for your good.

23. *And ye are Christ's.* "You are of Christ"; all the light and life which you enjoy you have received through and from Him, and He has bought you with His blood. *And Christ is God's.* "And Christ is of God." Christ, the

MATTHEW HENRY

his grace on a reconciled world, is the sum and substance of the gospel.

CHAPTER 4

I. The apostle challenges the respect due to him on account of his character and office. *Let a man so account of us as of the ministers of Christ, and stewards of the mysteries of God* (*v.* 1). In our opinion of ministers we should be careful to avoid extremes. Apostles themselves were, 1. Not to be overvalued, for they were ministers, not masters. They were servants of Christ, and no more. They had no authority to propagate their own fancies, but to spread Christian faith. 2. Apostles were not to be undervalued; for, they were ministers of Christ. They are not stewards of the common things of the world, but of divine mysteries. They did not set up for masters, but they deserved respect and esteem in this honourable service. Especially,

II. When they did their duty in it. *It is required in stewards that a man be found faithful* (*v.* 2), trustworthy. The stewards in Christ's family must appoint what he hath appointed. They must teach what he hath commanded.

When they have the testimony of a good conscience, and the approbation of their Master, they must slight the opinions and censures of their fellow-servants: *But with me*, saith the apostle, *it is a small thing that I should be judged of you, or of man's judgment*, *v.* 3. Indeed, reputation and esteem among men are a good step towards usefulness in the ministry. But he that would make it his chief endeavour to please men would hardly approve himself a faithful servant of Christ, Gal. i. 10. He that would be faithful to Christ must despise the censures of men for his sake. The best of men are too apt to judge rashly, and harshly. It is a comfort that men are not to be our final judges. Nay, we are not thus to judge ourselves: "*Yea, I judge not myself. For though I know nothing by myself*, cannot charge myself with unfaithfulness, *yet am I not thereby justified; but he that judgeth me is the Lord.* It is his judgment that must determine me. Such I am as he shall find and judge me to be."

III. The apostle takes occasion hence to caution the Corinthians against censoriousness: *Therefore judge nothing before the time, until the Lord come*, *v.* 5. It is judging out of season, judging persons' future state, or the secret springs and principles of their actions. To judge in these cases is to assume the seat of God. How bold a sinner is the forward and severe censurer! How ill-timed and arrogant are his censures! But there is one who will judge the censurer, and those he censures. This should make them now cautious of judging others, and careful in judging themselves. There is a time coming when *the Lord will bring to light the hidden things of darkness, and make manifest the counsels of the hearts.* There is a day coming that will fetch men's secret sins into open day and discover the secrets of their hearts. The Lord Jesus Christ will manifest the counsels of the heart, of all hearts. The Lord Jesus Christ must have the knowledge of the counsels of the heart, else

JAMIESON, FAUSSET, BROWN

ye all are Christ's (ch. 1:12). **Christ is God's**—(ch. 11:3). God is the ultimate end of all, even of Christ, His co-equal Son (ch. 15:28; Phil. 2:6-11).

CHAPTER 4

Vss. 1-21. TRUE VIEW OF MINISTERS: THE JUDGMENT IS NOT TO BE FORESTALLED; MEANWHILE THE APOSTLES' LOW STATE CONTRASTS WITH THE CORINTHIANS' PARTY PRIDE, NOT THAT PAUL WOULD SHAME THEM, BUT AS A FATHER WARN THEM; FOR WHICH END HE SENT TIMOTHY, AND WILL SOON COME HIMSELF. **1. account . . . us**—Paul and Apollos. **ministers of Christ**—not heads of the Church in whom ye are severally to glory (ch. 1:12); the headship belongs to Christ alone; we are but His servants ministering to you (ch. 1:13; 3:5, 22). **stewards**—(Luke 12:42; I Pet. 4:10). Not the depositories of grace, but dispensers of it ("rightly dividing" or *dispensing it*), so far as God gives us it, to others. The chazan, or *overseer*, in the synagogue answered to the *bishop* or "angel" of the Church, who called seven of the synagogue to read the law every sabbath, and *oversaw* them. The parnasin of the synagogue, like the ancient "deacon" of the Church, took care of the poor (Acts 6) and subsequently preached in subordination to the presbyters or bishops, as Stephen and Philip did. The Church is not the appendage to the priesthood; but the minister is the steward of God to the Church. Man shrinks from too close contact with God; hence he willingly puts a priesthood between, and would serve God by deputy. The pagan (like the modern Romish) priest was rather to conceal than to explain "the mysteries of God." The minister's office is to "preach" (lit., "proclaim as a herald," Matt. 10:27) the deep truths of God ("mysteries," heavenly truths, only known by revelation), so far as they have been revealed, and so far as his hearers are disposed to receive them. JOSEPHUS says that the Jewish religion made known to all the people the mysteries of their religion, while the pagans concealed from all but the "initiated" few, the mysteries of theirs. **2. Moreover**—The oldest MSS. read, "Moreover here" (i.e., on earth). The contrast thus is between man's usage as to stewards (vs. 2), and God's way (vs. 3). Though *here* below, *in the case of stewards, inquiry is made, that one man be found* (i.e., proved to be) faithful; yet God's steward awaits no such *judgment* of man, in man's day, but the Lord's judgment in His great day. Another argument against the Corinthians for their partial preferences of certain teachers for their gifts: whereas what God requires in His stewards is *faithfulness* (I Sam. 3:20; Heb. 3:5; *Margin*); as indeed is required in earthly stewards, but with this difference (vs. 3), that God's stewards await not man's judgment to test them, but the testing which shall be in the day of the Lord. **3. it is a very small thing**—lit., "it amounts to a very small matter"; not that I despise *your* judgment, but as compared with God's, it almost comes to nothing. **judged . . . of man's judgment**—lit., "man's *day*," contrasted with the day (ch. 3:13) of the Lord (vs. 5; I Thess. 5:4). "The day of man" is here put before us as a *person* [WAHL]. All days previous to the day of the Lord *are man's days.* EMESTI translates the thrice recurring *Greek* for "judged . . . judge . . . judgeth" (vs. 4), thus: To me for my part (though capable of being found faithful) it is a very small matter that I should *be approved of* by man's judgment; yea, I do not even *assume the right of judgment and approving* myself—but He that *has the right, and is able to* judge on my case (the Dijudicator), is the Lord. **4. by myself**—Translate, "I am conscious to myself of no (ministerial) unfaithfulness." BENGEL explains the *Greek* compound, "*to decide in judgments on* one in relation to others," not simply to *judge.* **am I not hereby justified**—Therefore conscience is not an infallible guide. Paul did not consider his so. This verse is directly against the judicial power claimed by the priests of Rome. **5.** Disproving the judicial power claimed by the Romish priesthood in the confessional. **Therefore**—as the Lord is the sole Decider or Dijudicator. **judge**—not the same *Greek* word as in vss. 3, 4, where the meaning is to *approve of*, or *decide on*, the merits of one's case. **Here all judgments in general are forbidden, which would, on our part, presumptuously forestall God's prerogative of final *judgment*. Lord**—Jesus Christ, whose "ministers" we are (vs. 1), and who is to be the judge (John 5:22, 27; Acts 10:42; 17:31). **manifest . . . hearts**—Our judgments now (as those of the Corinthians respecting their teachers) are necessarily defective; as we only see the outward *act*, we

ADAM CLARKE

Messiah, is the Gift of God's eternal love and mercy to mankind.

CHAPTER 4

1. *Let a man so account of us.* This is a continuation of the subject in the preceding chapter, and should not have been divided from it. The fourth chapter would have begun better at v. 6, and the third should have ended with the fifth verse. *As of the ministers of Christ.* The word means an "under-rower," or one who, in the trireme, quadrireme, or quinquereme galleys, rowed in one of the undermost benches; but it means also, as used by the Greek writers, any inferior officer or assistant. By the term here the apostle shows the Corinthians that, far from being heads and chiefs, he and his fellow apostles considered themselves only as inferior officers, employed under Christ; from whom alone they received their appointment, their work, and their recompense. *Stewards of the mysteries of God.* "Economists" of the divine mysteries. The steward was the master's deputy in regulating the concerns of the family, providing food for the household, seeing it served out at the proper times and seasons, and in proper quantities. He received all the cash, expended what was necessary for the support of the family, and kept exact accounts, which he was obliged at certain times to lay before the master. The *mysteries*, the doctrines of God, relative to the salvation of the world by the passion and death of Christ; and the inspiration, illumination, and purification of the soul by the Spirit of Christ, constituted a principal part of the divine treasure intrusted to the hands of the stewards by their heavenly Master.

3. *It is a very small thing that I should be judged of you.* Those who preferred Apollos or Cephas before Paul would of course give their reasons for this preference; and these might, in many instances, be very unfavorable to his character as a man, a Christian, or an apostle. Of this he was regardless, as he sought not his own glory, but the glory of God in the salvation of their souls. *Or of man's judgment.* Literally, "or of man's day": any day set apart by a judge or magistrate to try a man on. *I judge not mine own self.* I leave myself entirely to God, whose I am, and whom I serve.

4. *For I know nothing by myself.* I am not conscious that I am guilty of any evil, or have neglected to fulfill faithfully the duty of a steward of Jesus Christ. The import of the verb is "to be conscious of guilt." *Yet am I not hereby justified.* I do not pretend to say that though I am not conscious of any offense towards God I must therefore be pronounced innocent. No. I leave those things to God; He shall pronounce in my favor, not I myself. By these words the apostle, in a very gentle yet effectual manner, censures those rash and precipitate judgments which the Corinthians were in the habit of pronouncing on both men and things—a conduct than which nothing is more reprehensible and dangerous.

5. *Judge nothing before the time.* God, the righteous Judge, will determine everything shortly; it is His province alone to search the heart, and *bring to light the hidden things of darkness.*

MATTHEW HENRY

he could not make them manifest. We should be very careful how we censure others, when we have to do with a Judge from whom we cannot conceal ourselves. When he shall come to judge, *every man shall have praise of God. Every man*, that is, everyone qualified for it. Christians may well be patient under unjust censures, when they know such a day as this is coming. But how fearful should they be of loading any with reproaches now whom their common Judge shall hereafter commend.

IV. The apostle here lets us into the reason why he had used his own name and that of Apollos in this discourse of his. He had done *it in a figure*, and *he had done it for their sakes.* He chose rather to mention his own name, and the name of a faithful fellow-labourer, than the names of any heads of factions among them, that hereby he might avoid what would provoke. *That they might learn not to think of men above what is written, nor be puffed up for one against another* (*v.* 6). Apostles were not to be esteemed other than servants of Christ. We must be very careful not to transfer the honour and authority of the Master to his servant. We must not think of them above what is written. Pride commonly lies at the bottom of these quarrels. We shall not be puffed up for one against another if we remember that they are all instruments employed by God in his husbandry and building, and endowed by him with their various talents and qualifications.

Verses 7–13

Here the apostle improves the foregoing hint to a caution against pride and self-conceit.

I. He cautions them against pride; all the distinction made among them was owing to God: *Who maketh thee to differ? And what hast thou that thou didst not receive?* (*v.* 7). Here the apostle turns his discourse to the ministers who set themselves at the head of these factions. What had they to glory in, when all their peculiar gifts were from God? But it may be taken as a general maxim: We have no reason to be proud of our attainments, or performances; all that we have, or are, or do, that is good, is owing to the free and rich grace of God. Boasting is for ever excluded. Those who receive all should be proud of nothing. Due attention to our obligations to divine grace would cure us of arrogance and self-conceit.

II. He presses the duty of humility upon them by a very smart irony: "*You are full, you are rich, you have reigned as kings without us.* You have not only a sufficiency, but an affluence, of spiritual gifts; nay, you can make them the matter of your glory *without us.*" There is a very elegant gradation from sufficiency to wealth, and thence to royalty, to intimate how much the Corinthians were elated by the abundance of their wisdom and spiritual gifts. "*You have reigned as kings,*" says the apostle, "that is, in your own conceit; and *I would to God you did reign, that we also might reign with you.* I wish you had as much of the true glory of a Christian church upon you as you arrogate to yourselves." Those do not commonly know themselves best who think best of themselves. The Corinthians might have reigned, and the apostle with them, if they had not been blown up with an imaginary royalty. Pride is a great prejudice to our improvement. He is stopped from growing wiser or better who thinks himself at the height; not only full, but rich, nay, a king.

III. He comes to set forth his own circumstances and those of the other apostles, and compares them with theirs. 1. To set forth the case of the apostles: *For I think it hath pleased God to set forth us the apostles last, as it were appointed to death. For we are made a spectacle to the world, and to angels, and to men.* Never were any men in this world so hunted and worried. An allusion is made to some of the bloody spectacles in the Roman amphitheatres, where the victor did not escape with his life, but was only reserved for another combat, so that such wretched criminals might very properly be called *persons devoted or appointed to death.* They are said to be set forth last, because those who combated one another in the after-part of the day, were most exposed, being obliged to fight naked. The general meaning is that the apostles were exposed to continual danger of death. God had set them forth. The apostles were shown to manifest the power of divine grace, to confirm the truth of their mission and doctrine. These were ends worthy of God—noble views, fit to animate them to the combat. The office of an apostle was, as an honourable, so a hard and hazardous one: "*For we are made a spectacle to the world, and to angels, and to men, v.* 9. A *show.* Angels and men are witnesses to our persecutions, patience, and magnanimity. They all see that we suffer for our fidelity to Christ. How sharp our sufferings, and how patiently we endure them, by the power of divine

JAMIESON, FAUSSET, BROWN

cannot see the *motives* of "hearts." "Faithfulness" (vs. 2) will hereby be estimated, and the "Lord" will "justify," or the reverse (vs. 4), according to the state of the *heart.* **then shall every man have praise**—(ch. 3:8; I Sam. 26:23; Matt. 25:21, 23; 28). Rather, "*his due* praise," not exaggerated praise, such as the Corinthians heaped on favorite teachers; "the praise" (so the *Greek*) due for acts estimated by the motives. "Then," not before: therefore wait till *then* (Jas. 5:7). **6. And**—"Now," marking transition. **in a figure transferred to myself**—i.e., I have represented under the persons of Apollos and myself what really holds good of all teachers, making us two a *figure* or *type* of all the others. I have mentioned us two, whose names have been used as a party cry; but under our names I mean others to be understood, whom I do not name, in order not to shame you [ESTIUS]. **not to think . . .**—The best MSS. omit "think." Translate, "That in us (as your example) ye might learn (this), not (to go) beyond what is written." Revere the *silence* of Holy Writ, as much as its *declarations:* so you will less dogmatize on what is not expressly revealed (Deut. 29:29). **puffed up for one**—viz., "for one (favorite minister) against another." The *Greek* indicative implies, "That ye be not puffed up *as ye are.*" **7.** Translate, "Who distinguisheth thee (above another)?" Not thyself, but God. **glory, as if thou hadst not received it**—as if it was to thyself, not to God, thou owest the receiving of it. **8.** Irony. Translate, "*Already* ye are filled full (with spiritual food), *already* ye are rich, ye have seated yourselves upon your throne as kings, without us." The emphasis is on "already" and "without us"; ye act as if ye needed no more to "hunger and thirst after righteousness," and as if already ye had reached the "kingdom" for which Christians have to strive and suffer. Ye are so puffed up with your favorite teachers, and your own fancied spiritual attainments in knowledge through them, that ye feel like those "filled full" at a feast, or as a "rich" man priding himself in his riches: so ye feel ye can now do "without us," your first spiritual fathers (vs. 15). They forgot that before the "kingdom" and the "*fulness* of joy," at the marriage feast of the Lamb, must come the cross, and suffering, to every true believer (II Tim. 2:5, 11, 12). They were like the self-complacent Laodiceans (Rev. 3:17; cf. Hosea 12:8). *Temporal* fulness and riches doubtless *tended* in some cases at Corinth, to generate this spiritual self-sufficiency; the contrast to the apostle's literal "hunger and thirst" (vs. 11) proves this. **I would . . . ye did reign**—Translate, "I would *indeed* . . ." I would truly it were so, and that your kingdom had really begun. **that we also might reign with you**—(II Cor. 12:14). "I seek not yours, but you." Your spiritual prosperity would redound to that of us, your fathers in Christ (ch. 9: 23). When you reach the kingdom, you shall be our "crown of rejoicing, in the presence of our Lord Jesus" (I Thess. 2:19). **9. For**—assigning the reason for desiring that the "reign" of himself and his fellow apostles with the Corinthians were come; viz., the present afflictions of the former. **I think**—The Corinthians (ch. 3:18) "seemed" to (lit., as here, "thought") themselves "wise in this world." Paul, in contrast, "thinks" that God has sent forth him and his fellow ministers "last," i.e., the lowest in this world. The apostles fared worse than even the prophets, who, though sometimes afflicted, were often honored (II Kings 1:10; 5:9; 8:9, 12). **set forth**—as a spectacle or gazing-stock. **us the apostles**—Paul includes Apollos with the apostles, in the broader sense of the word; so Romans 16:7; II Corinthians 8:23 (*Greek* for "messengers," *apostles*). **as it were appointed to death**—as criminals condemned to die. **made a spectacle**—lit., "a theatrical spectacle." So the *Greek* in Hebrews 10: 33, "made a *gazing-stock* by reproaches and afflictions." Criminals "condemned to die," in Paul's time, were exhibited as a gazing-stock to amuse the populace in the amphitheater. They were "set forth last" in the show, to fight with wild beasts. This explains the imagery of Paul here. (Cf. TERTULLIAN, *de Pudicitia*, ch. 14.) **the world**—to the whole world, including "both angels and men"; "the whole family in heaven and earth" (Eph. 3: 15). As Jesus was "seen of angels" (I Tim. 3:16), so His followers are a spectacle to the holy angels who take a deep interest in all the progressive steps of redemption (Eph. 3:10; I Pet. 1:12). Paul tacitly implies that though "last" and lowest in the world's judgment, Christ's servants are deemed by angels a spectacle worthy of their most intense regard [CHRYSOSTOM]. However, since "the world" is a comprehensive expression, and is applied in this Epistle to the evil especially (ch. 1:27, 28), and since

ADAM CLARKE

If you are so pure and upright in your conduct, if what you have been doing in these divisions, etc., is right in His sight, then shall you *have praise* for the same; if otherwise, yourselves are most concerned. Some refer the praise to Paul and his companions: "Then shall every one of us apostles have praise of God."

6. *These things.* Which I have written, chap. iii. 5, etc. *I have in a figure transferred to myself and to Apollos.* I have written as if myself and Apollos were the authors of the sects which now prevail among you; although others, without either our consent or knowledge, have proclaimed us heads of parties.

7. *For who maketh thee to differ?* It is likely that the apostle is here addressing himself to some one of those *puffed up* teachers, who was glorying in his gifts, and in the knowledge he had of the gospel, etc. As if he had said: If you have all that knowledge which you profess to have, did you not receive it from myself or some other of my fellow helpers who first preached the gospel at Corinth? Have you a particle of light that you have not received from our preaching? Why then do you glory, boast, and exult, as if God had first spoken by you, and not by us?

8. *Now we* (Corinthians) *are full* of secular wisdom; *now ye are rich,* in both wealth and spiritual gifts (chap. xiv. 26). *Ye have reigned as kings,* flourishing in the enjoyment of these things, in all tranquillity and honor, *without* any want of *us;*

and I would to God ye did reign, in deed, and not in conceit only, *that we also,* poor, persecuted, and despised apostles, *might reign with you.*—Whitby. Though this paraphrase appears natural, yet I am of opinion that the apostle here intends a strong irony; and one which, when taken in conjunction with what he had said before, must have stung them to the heart. It is not an unusual thing for many people to forget, if not despise, the men by whom they were brought to the knowledge of the truth; and take up with others to whom, in the things of God, they owe nothing.

9. *God hath set forth us the apostles last.* Seneca speaks thus, Epist. vii: "In the morning men are exposed to lions and bears; at mid-day to their spectators; those that kill are exposed to one another; the victor is detained for another slaughter; the conclusion of the fight is death. The former fighting compared to this was mercy; now it is mere butchery: they have nothing to cover them; their whole body is exposed to every blow, and every stroke produces a wound." *We are made a spectacle.* We are exhibited on the "theatre" to the world; we are lawful booty to all mankind, and particularly to the men of the world, who have their portion in this life. *Angels* are astonished at our treatment, and so are the more considerate part of *men.* Who at that time would have coveted the apostolate?

MATTHEW HENRY

grace. Ours is hard work, but honourable; it is hazardous, but glorious. The world cannot but see and wonder at our undaunted resolution, our invincible patience." 2. He compares his own case with that of the Corinthians: "*We are fools for Christ's sake, but you are wise in Christ; we are weak, but you are strong; you are honourable, but we are despised, v.* 10. We can pass for fools in the world, and be despised as such, so that the honour of the gospel may by this means be secured and displayed. *But you are wise in Christ.* You have the fame of being wise and learned Christians, and you do not a little value yourselves upon it. *We are weak, but you are strong.* We are suffering for Christ's sake when you are in easy and flourishing circumstances." All Christians are not alike exposed. The standard-bearers in an army are most struck at. So ministers in a time of persecution are commonly the first and greatest sufferers. Those are not always the greatest proficients in Christianity who think thus of themselves, or pass for such upon others. The Corinthians may think themselves, and be esteemed by others, as wiser and stronger men in Christ than the apostles themselves. But O! how gross is the mistake!

IV. He enters into some particularities of their sufferings: *Even to this present hour; we hunger and thirst, and are naked, and are buffeted, and have no certain dwelling-place, and labour, working with our own hands, v.* 11, 12. Nay, they were *made as the filth of the world, and the off-scouring of all things, v.* 13. Poor circumstances indeed, for the prime ministers of our Saviour's kingdom to have no house nor home, and to be destitute of food and raiment! But yet no poorer than his who had not *where to lay his head,* Luke ix. 58. But O glorious charity and devotion, that would carry them through all these hardships! How ardently did they love God. They thought they had a rich amends for all the outward good things they wanted, if they might but serve Christ and save souls. Nay, though they *were made the filth of the world, and the off-scouring of all things.* They were treated as men not fit to live. And apostles could not meet with better usage. They suffered in their persons and characters as the very worst and vilest men. Nay, as the *off-scouring of all things.* To be the off-scouring of anything is bad, but what is it to be the off-scouring of all things! How much did the apostles resemble their Master! They suffered for him, and they suffered after his example. Those may be very dear to God, and honourable in his esteem, whom men may think unworthy to live, and use and scorn as the very dirt and refuse of the world.

V. We have here the apostles' behaviour under all: *Being reviled, we bless; being persecuted, we suffer it; being defamed, we entreat, v.* 12, 13. They returned blessings for reproaches, and were patient under the sharpest persecutions. The disciples of Christ, and especially his ministers, should hold fast their integrity, and keep a good conscience. They must be content, with him and for him, to be despised and abused.

Verses 14-16

Here Paul challenges their regard to him as their father. 1. What he had written was not for their reproach, but admonition (*v.* 14): *I write not to shame you, but as my beloved children I warn you.* Reproofs that expose commonly do but exasperate, when those that kindly and affectionately warn are likely to reform; to lash like an enemy or executioner will provoke and render obstinate. To expose to open shame is but the way to render shameless.

2. He shows them upon what foundation he called them his sons. He was their father: *for in Christ Jesus he had begotten them by the gospel, v.* 15. They were made Christians by his ministry. He was the instrument of their new birth, and therefore claimed the relation of a father to them. There commonly is, and always ought to be, an endeared affection between faithful ministers and those they beget in Christ Jesus through the gospel. They should love like parents and children.

JAMIESON, FAUSSET, BROWN

the spectators (in the image drawn from the amphitheater gaze at the show with savage delight, rather than with sympathy for the sufferers, I think *bad* angels are included, besides *good* angels. ESTIUS makes the bad *alone* to be meant. But the generality of the term "angels," and its frequent use in a good sense, as well as Ephesians 3:10; I Peter 1:12, incline me to include *good* as well as *bad* angels, though, for the reasons stated above, the bad may be principally meant. **10.** Irony. How much your lot (*supposing it real*) is to be envied, and ours to be pitied. **fools**—(ch. 1:21; 3:18; cf. Acts 17:18; 26:24.) **for Christ's sake . . . in Christ** —Our connection with Christ only entails on us the lowest ignominy, "ON ACCOUNT OF," or, "FOR THE SAKE OF" Him, as "fools"; yours gives you full fellowship IN Him as "wise" (i.e., *supposing you really are all you seem,* ch. 3:18). **we . . . weak . . . ye . . . strong**—(ch. 2:3; II Cor. 13:9). **we . . . despised**—(II Cor. 10:10) because of our "weakness," and our not using worldly philosophy and rhetoric, on account of which ye Corinthians and your teachers are (seemingly) so "honorable." Contrast with "despised" the "ye (*Galatians*) despised not my temptation . . . in my flesh." **11.** (IICor. 11:23-27.) **naked**—i.e., insufficiently clad (Rom. 8:35). **buffeted**—as a *slave* (I Pet. 2:20), the reverse of the state of the Corinthians, "reigning as *kings*" (Acts 23:2). So Paul's master before him was "buffeted" as a slave, when about to die a slave's death (Matt. 26:67). **12. working with our own hands**—viz., "even unto this present hour" (vs. 11). This is not stated in the *narrative* of Paul's proceedings *at Ephesus,* from which city he wrote this Epistle (though it is expressly stated of him *at Corinth,* cf. Acts 18:3, and 19). But in his *address* to the Ephesian elders at Miletus (Acts 20:34), he says, "Ye yourselves know that these hands have ministered unto my necessities . . . ." The undesignedness of the coincidence thus indirectly brought out is incompatible with forgery. **13. defamed,** we **entreat**—viz., God for our defamers, as Christ enjoined (Matt. 5:10, 44) [GROTIUS]. We reply gently [ESTIUS]. **filth**—"the refuse" [CONYBEARE and HOWSON], the *sweepings* or *rubbish* thrown out after a cleaning. **of all things**—not of the "world" only.

14. warn—rather, **"admonish" as a father** uses "admonition" to "beloved sons," not provoking them to wrath (Eph. 6:4). The Corinthians might well be "ashamed" at the disparity of state between the father, Paul, and his spiritual children themselves.

15. ten thousand—implying that the Corinthians had more of them than was desirable. **instructors**—*tutors* who had the care of rearing, but had not the rights, or peculiar affection, of the father, who alone had begotten them spiritually. **in Christ**—Paul admits that these "instructors" were not mere legalists, but *evangelical* teachers. He uses, however, a stronger phrase of himself in begetting them spiritually, "In Christ Jesus," implying both the Saviour's *office and person.* As Paul was the means of spiritually *regenerating* them, and yet "baptized none of them save Crispus, Gaius, and the household of Stephanas," regeneration cannot be inseparably *in* and *by* baptism (ch. 1:14-17).

ADAM CLARKE

10. *We are fools for Christ's sake.* Here he still carries on the allusion to the public spectacles among the Romans, where they were accustomed to hiss, hoot, mock, and variously insult the poor victims. To this Philo alludes, speaking of the treatment which the Jews received at Rome: "For, as if exhibited upon a theatre, we are hissed, most outrageously hooted, and insulted beyond all bounds." *Ye are wise in Christ.* Surely all these expressions are meant ironically. The apostles were neither *fools,* nor *weak,* nor contemptible; nor were the *Corinthians,* morally speaking, *wise,* and *strong,* and *honourable.* Change the persons, and then the epithets will perfectly apply.

11. *We both hunger, and thirst.* Who would then have been an apostle of Christ, even with all its spiritual honors and glories, who had not a soul filled with love to both God and man, and the fullest conviction of the reality of the doctrine he preached, and of that spiritual world in which alone he could expect rest? *Have no certain dwellingplace.* We are mere itinerant preachers, and when we set out in the morning know not where or whether we shall or not get a night's lodging.

12. *Working with our own hands.* They were obliged to labor in order to supply themselves with the necessaries of life while preaching the gospel to others. *Being reviled, we bless.* What a most amiable picture does this exhibit of the power of the grace of Christ! Man is naturally a proud creature, and his pride prompts him always to avenge himself in whatever manner he can, and repay insult with insult. It is only the grace of Christ that can make a man patient in bearing injuries, and render blessing for cursing, beneficence for malevolence. Blaspheming against men is anything by which they are injured in their persons, characters, or property.

13. *We are made as the filth of the world, and are the offscouring of all things.* The Greek word which we render *filth* is a "purgation, or lustrative sacrifice"; that which we translate *offscouring* is "a redemption sacrifice." To understand the full force of these words as applied by the apostle in this place we must observe that he alludes to certain customs among the heathens, who, in the time of some public calamity, chose out some unhappy men of the most abject and despicable character to be a public *expiation* for them. These they maintained a whole year at the public expense; and then they led them out, crowned with flowers, as was customary in sacrifices; and, having heaped all the curses of the country upon their heads, and whipped them seven times, they burned them alive, and afterwards their ashes were thrown into the sea, while the people said these words: "Be thou our propitiation." The apostle therefore means that he and his fellows were treated like those wretched beings who were judged to be fit for nothing but to be expiatory victims to the infernal gods, for the safety and redemption of others. Our words *filth* and *offscouring* convey no legitimate sense of the original.

14. *I write not these things to shame you.* It is not by way of finding fault with you for not providing me with the necessaries of life that I write thus; but I do it to warn you to act differently for the time to come; and be not so ready to be drawn aside by every pretender to apostleship, to the neglect of those to whom, under God, you owe your salvation.

15. *For though ye have ten thousand instructors.* "Myriads of leaders," that is, an indefinite multitude; for so the word is often used. The *paidagogos,* from which we have our word "pedagogue," which we improperly apply to a "schoolmaster," was, among the Greeks, the person or servant who attended a child, had the general care of him, and who led him to school for the purpose of being instructed by the teacher. It seems there were many at Corinth who offered their services to instruct this people, and who were not well-affected towards the apostle. *Not many fathers.* Many offer to instruct you who have no parental feeling for you; and how can they? You are not their spiritual children; you stand in this relation to me alone. *For in Christ Jesus*—by the power and unction of His Spirit—*I have begotten you*—I was the means of bringing you into a

MATTHEW HENRY

3. We have here the special advice he urges on them: *Wherefore I beseech you be you followers of me, v.* 16. This he elsewhere explains and limits (*ch.* xi. 1): "*Be you followers of me, as I also am of Christ.* Follow me as far as I follow Christ. I would not have you be my disciples, but his." Ministers should so live that their people may live after their copy. They should guide them by their lives as well as their lips, go before them in the way to heaven, and not content themselves with pointing it out.

Verses 17–21

I. He tells them of his having sent Timothy to them, *to bring them into remembrance of his ways in Christ, as he taught everywhere in every church* (*v.* 17). Those who have had ever so good teaching are apt to forget and need to have their memories refreshed. He had not one doctrine for one place and people, and another for another. He therefore taught the same things in every church, and lived after the same manner in all times and places. The truth of Christ is one and invariable. What one apostle taught at one time and in one place, he taught at all times and in all places. To render their regard to Timothy the greater, he gives them his character. He was *his beloved son*, a spiritual child of his, as well as themselves. The children of one father should have one heart. But he adds, "*He is faithful in the Lord*—trustworthy, as one that feared the Lord." It is a great commendation of any minister that he is faithful in the Lord; this must go a great way in procuring regard to his message.

II. He rebukes those who imagined he would not come to them, by letting them know this was his purpose: "*I will come to you shortly*." But he adds, *if the Lord will*. All our purposes must be formed with a dependence on Providence.

III. He lets them know what would follow upon his coming to them: *I will know, not the speech of those that are puffed up, but the power, v.* 19. He would bring the great pretenders among them to a trial, would know what they were by the authority and efficacy of what they taught, and whether it was accompanied with divine influences and saving effects on the minds of men. For, adds he, *the kingdom of God is not in word, but in power*, the powerful influence of divine truth on the minds and manners of men. It is a good way in the general to judge of a preacher's doctrine, to see whether the effects of it upon men's hearts be truly divine. That is most likely to come from God which in its own nature is most fit, and in event is found to produce most likeness to God.

IV. He puts it to their choice how he should come among them, *whether with a rod or in love and the spirit of meekness* (*v.* 21); that is, according as they were they would find him. Stubborn offenders must be used with severity. In families, in Christian communities, paternal pity and tenderness, Christian love and compassion, will sometimes force the use of the rod. But this is far from being desirable, if it may be prevented. *Or in love and the spirit of meekness.* As much as if he had said, "Take warning, cease your unchristian feuds, and you shall find me as gentle and benign as you can wish. I had rather come and display the tenderness of a father among you than assert his authority." It is a happy temper in a minister to have the spirit of love and meekness predominant, and yet to maintain his just authority.

JAMIESON, FAUSSET, BROWN

16. be ye followers of me—lit., "imitators," viz., in my ways, which be in Christ (vs. 17; ch. 11:1), not in my crosses (vss. 8-13; Acts 26:29; Gal. 4:12).

17. For this cause—that ye may the better "be followers of me" (vs. 16), through his admonitions. **sent . . . Timotheus**—(ch. 16:10; Acts 19:21, 22). "Paul purposed . . . when he had passed through Macedonia and *Achaia,* to go to Jerusalem. So he sent into Macedonia Timotheus and Erastus." Here it is not expressly said that he sent Timothy into Achaia (of which Corinth was the capital), but it is *implied,* for he sent him with Erastus *before him.* As he therefore purposed to go into Achaia himself, there is every probability they were to go thither also. They are said only to have been sent into Macedonia, because it was the country to which they went immediately from Ephesus. The undesignedness of the coincidence establishes the genuineness of both the Epistle and the history. In both, Timothy's journey is closely connected with Paul's own (cf. vs. 19). Erastus is not specified in the Epistle, probably because it was Timothy who was charged with Paul's orders, and possibly Erastus was a Corinthian, who, in accompanying Timothy, was only returning home. The seeming discrepancy at least shows that the passages were not taken from one another [PALEY'S *Horæ Paulinæ*]. **son**—i.e., converted by me (cf. vs. 14, 15; Acts 14:6, 7; with 16:1, 2; I Tim. 1:2, 18; II Tim. 1:2). Translate, "My son, beloved and faithful in the Lord." **bring you into remembrance**—Timothy, from his spiritual connection with Paul, as converted by him, was best suited to *remind* them of the apostle's walk and teaching (II Tim. 3:10), which they in some respects, though not altogether (ch. 11:2), had forgotten. **as I teach . . . in every church**—an argument implying that what the Spirit directed Paul to teach "everywhere" else, must be necessary at Corinth also (ch. 7:17). **18. some . . . as though I would not come**—He guards against some misconstruing (as by the Spirit he foresees they will, when his letter shall have arrived) his sending Timothy, "as though" he "would not come" (or, "were not coming") himself. A *puffed-up* spirit was the besetting sin of the Corinthians (cf. ch. 1:11; 5:2). **19. ALFORD translates, "But come I will"**; an emphatical negation of their supposition (vs. 18). **shortly**—after Pentecost (ch. 16:8). **if the Lord will**—a wise proviso (Jas. 4:15). He does not seem to have been able to go as soon as he intended. **and will know**—take cognizance of. **but the power**—I care not for their high-sounding "speech," "but" what I desire to know is "their power," whether they be really powerful in the Spirit, or not. The predominant feature of Grecian character, a love for power of *discourse,* rather than that of godliness, showed itself at Corinth. **20. kingdom of God is not in word**—Translate, as in vs. 19, to which the reference is "speech." Not empty "speeches," but the manifest "power" of the Spirit attests the presence of "the kingdom of God" (the *reign of the Gospel* spiritually), in a church or in an individual (cf. ch. 2:1, 4; I Thess. 1:5). **21. with a rod, or in love**—The *Greek* preposition is used in both clauses; must I come IN displeasure to exercise the *rod,* or IN love, and the Spirit of meekness (Isa. 11:4; II Cor. 13:3)?

ADAM CLARKE

state of salvation, so that you have been born again. You are my children alone in the gospel.

16. *Wherefore, I beseech you, be ye followers of me.* It should rather be translated, "Be ye imitators of me"; *mimetai,* from which we have our word "mimic," which, though now used only in a bad or ludicrous sense, simply signifies an imitator of another person, whether in speech, manner, habit, or otherwise. As children should imitate their parents in preference to all others, he calls on them to imitate him, as he claims them for his children.

17. *For this cause.* That you imitate me, and know in what this consists. *I sent unto you Timotheus.* The same person to whom he wrote the two Epistles that are still extant under his name, and whom he calls here his *beloved son,* one of his most intimate disciples, and whom he had been the means of bringing to God through Christ.

My ways which be in Christ. This person will also inform you of the manner in which I regulate all the churches, and show to you that what I require of you is no other than what I require of all the churches of Christ which I have formed, as I follow the same plan of discipline in every place.

18. *Some are puffed up.* Some of your teachers act with great haughtiness, imagining themselves to be safe, because they suppose that I shall not revisit Corinth.

19. *But I will come to you shortly.* God being my Helper, I fully purpose to visit you; and then I shall put those proud men to the proof, not of their *speech*—eloquence, or pretensions to great knowledge and influence—but of their *power*—the authority they profess to have from God, and the evidences of that authority in the works they have performed.

20. *For the kingdom of God.* The religion of the Lord Jesus is *not in word*—in human eloquence, excellence of speech, or even in doctrines; *but in power,* in the mighty energy of the Holy Spirit, enlightening, quickening, converting, and sanctifying believers.

21. *Shall I come unto you with a rod, or in love?* Here he alludes to the case of the teacher and father, mentioned in v. 15. Shall I come to you with the authority of a teacher, and use the *rod* of discipline? or shall I come in the tenderness of a father, and entreat you to do what I have authority to enforce? Among the Jews, those who did not amend, after being faithfully admonished, were whipped, either publicly or privately, in the synagogue.

CHAPTER 5 (MATTHEW HENRY)

Verses 1–6

I. One of their community was guilty of fornication, *v.* 1. It was told in all places, to their dishonour. The heinous sins of professed Christians are quickly noted and noised abroad. We should walk circumspectly, for many eyes are upon us. This was not a common instance of fornication, but *such as was not so much as named among the Gentiles, that a man should have his father's wife.* Not that there were no such instances of incestuous marriages among the heathens; but, whenever they happened, they gave a shock to every man of virtue and probity among them. They could not mention them without detestation. Yet such a horrible wickedness was committed by one in the church of Corinth. The best churches are, in this state of imperfection, liable to very great corruptions.

CHAPTER 5 (JAMIESON, FAUSSET, BROWN)

VSS. 1-13. THE INCESTUOUS PERSON AT CORINTH: THE CORINTHIANS REPROVED FOR CONNIVANCE, AND WARNED TO PURGE OUT THE BAD LEAVEN. QUALIFICATION OF HIS FORMER COMMAND AS TO ASSOCIATION WITH SINNERS OF THE WORLD. **1. commonly**—rather, "actually" [ALFORD]. Absolutely [BENGEL]. "It is reported," implies, that the Corinthians, though they "wrote" (ch. 7:1) to Paul on other points, gave him no information on those things which bore against themselves. These latter matters reached the apostle indirectly (ch. 1:11). **so much as named**—The oldest MSS. and authorities omit "named": "Fornication of such a gross kind as (exists) not even among the heathen, so that one (of you) hath (in concubinage) his father's wife," i.e., his stepmother, while his father is still alive (II Cor. 7:12; cf. Lev. 18:8). She was perhaps a heathen, for which reason he does not direct his rebuke against her (cf. vss. 12, 13). ALFORD thinks "have" means *have in marriage:* but the connection is called "fornication," and neither Christian nor Gentile *law* would have sanctioned such a *marriage,* however Corinth's notorious profligacy might wink at the concubinage.

CHAPTER 5 (ADAM CLARKE)

1. *There is fornication among you.* The word which we translate *fornication* in this place must be understood in its utmost latitude of meaning as implying all kinds of impurity; for that the Corinthians were notoriously guilty of every species of irregularity and debauch we have already seen, and it is not likely that in speaking on this subject, in reference to a people so very notorious, he would refer to only one species of impurity. *That one should have his father's wife.* Commentators and critics have found great difficulties in this statement. One part of the case is sufficiently clear, that a man who professed Christianity had illegal connections with his father's wife. But the principal question is, Was his father alive or dead? Most think the father was alive, and imagine that to this the apostle refers, 2 Cor. vii. 12, where, speaking of the person who did the wrong, he introduces also him who had suffered the wrong; which must mean the father, and the father then alive. After all that has been said on this subject, I think it most natural to conclude that

MATTHEW HENRY

II. He greatly blames them for their own conduct hereupon: *They were puffed up* (*v.* 2), *they gloried.* Perhaps on account of this very scandalous person. He might be a man very greatly esteemed. Instead of mourning for his fall, and their own reproach upon his account, they continued to applaud him and pride themselves in him. Pride or self-esteem often lies at the bottom of our immoderate esteem of others, and this makes us as blind to their faults as to our own. Or else some of the opposite party were puffed up. It is a very wicked thing to glory over the miscarriages and sins of others. Probably this was one effect of the divisions among them. The opposite party made their advantage of this scandalous lapse, and were glad of the opportunity. The sins of others should be our sorrow.

III. We have the apostle's direction to them how they should now proceed with this scandalous sinner. He would have him excommunicated and delivered to Satan (*v.* 3–5); *as absent in body, yet present in spirit, he had judged already as if he had been present.* He says this to let them know that, though he was at a distance, he did not pass an unrighteous sentence, nor judge without having as full cognizance of the case as if he had been on the spot. The apostle adds, *him who hath so done this deed.* He had so committed the evil as to heighten the guilt by the manner of doing it. In dealing with scandalous sinners, not only are they to be charged with the fact, but the aggravating circumstances of it.

Paul had judged that *he should be delivered to Satan* (*v.* 5), and this was to be done *in the name of Christ*, and in a full assembly, where the apostle would be also present in spirit. Some think that this is to be understood of mere ordinary excommunication, and that delivering him to Satan is only meant of disowning him, that by this means he might be brought to repentance, and his flesh might be mortified. Those that live in sin, when they profess relation to Christ, belong to another master, and by excommunication should be delivered up to him; and this in the name of Christ. It was to be done also *when they were gathered together.* The more public the more solemn, and the more solemn the more likely to have a good effect on the offender. Others think the apostle is not to be understood of mere excommunication, but of a miraculous power or authority they had of delivering a scandalous sinner into the power of Satan, which is the meaning of the *destruction of the flesh.* In this sense the destruction of the flesh has been a happy occasion of the salvation of the spirit. The great end of church-censures is the good of those who fall under them. It is that their spirit may be saved in the day of the Lord Jesus, *v.* 5.

IV. He hints the danger of contagion from this example: *Your glorying is not good. Know you not that a little leaven leaveneth the whole lump?* The bad example of a man in rank and reputation is very mischievous, spreads the contagion far and wide. A little leaven will quickly spread the ferment through a great lump.

Verses 7, 8

Here the apostle exhorts them to purity.

I. The advice itself, addressed either, 1. To the church in general; and so purging out the old leaven, that they might be a new lump, refers to the *putting away from themselves that wicked person, v.* 13. Or, 2. To each particular member of the church. And so it implies that they should purge themselves from all impurity of heart and life. Christians should be careful to keep themselves clean, as well as purge polluted members out of their society. They were also to purge themselves from malice and wickedness. This is leaven that sours the mind to a great degree. Christians should be careful to keep free from malice and mischief. Love is the very essence and life of the Christian religion. It is the fairest image of God, *for God is love* (1 John iv. 16), and therefore it is no wonder if it be the greatest beauty and ornament of a Christian.

JAMIESON, FAUSSET, BROWN

2. puffed up—with your own wisdom and knowledge, and the eloquence of your favorite teachers: at a time when ye ought to be "mourning" at the scandal caused to religion by the incest. Paul *mourned* because they did not mourn (II Cor. 2:4). We ought to *mourn* over the transgressions of others, and *repent* of our own (II Cor. 12:21) [BENGEL]. **that**—ye have not felt such mourning as would lead to the result *that* .... **taken away from among you**—by excommunication. The incestuous person was hereby brought to bitter repentance, in the interval between the sending of the first and second Epistles (II Cor. 2:5-10). Excommunication in the Christian Church corresponded to that in the Jewish synagogue, in there being a lighter and heavier form: the latter an utter separation from church fellowship and the Lord's house, the former exclusion from the Lord's Supper only but not from the Church. **3. as absent**—The best MSS. read, "being absent." **present in spirit**—(II Kings 5:26; Col. 2:5). **so done**—rather, "perpetrated," as the *Greek* word here is stronger than that for "done" in vs. 2. "So," i.e., so scandalously while called a brother. **4. In the name of our Lord Jesus Christ**—By His authority and as representing His *person* and will (II Cor. 2:10). Join this with "to deliver such a one unto Satan" (vs. 5). The clause, "When ye have been gathered together and my spirit (wherein I am 'present,' though 'absent in body,' (vs. 3), with the power of our Lord Jesus," stands in a parenthesis between. Paul speaking of himself uses the word "spirit"; of Christ, "power." Christ's power was promised to be present with HIS Church "gathered together in His name" (Matt. 18: 18-20): and here Paul by inspiration gives a special promise of his apostolic spirit, which in such cases was guided by the Holy Spirit, ratifying their decree passed according to his *judgment* ("I have judged," vs. 3), as though he were present in person (John 20:21-23; (II Cor. 13:3-10). This power of infallible judgment was limited to the apostles; for they alone had the power of working miracles as their credentials to attest their infallibility. Their successors, to establish their claim to the latter, must produce the former (II Cor. 12:2). Even the apostles in ordinary cases, and where not specially and consciously inspired, were fallible (Acts 8:13, 23; Gal. 2:11-14). **5.** Besides excommunication (of which the Corinthians themselves had the power), Paul delegates here to the Corinthian Church *his own* special power as an apostle, of inflicting corporeal disease or death in punishment for sin ("to deliver to Satan such an one," i.e., so heinous a sinner). For instances of this power, see Acts 5:1-11; 13:11; I Tim. 1:20. As Satan receives power at times to try the godly, as Job (Job 2:4-7) and Paul (II Cor. 12:7; cf. also as to Peter, Luke 22:31), much more the ungodly. Satan, the "accuser of the brethren" (Rev. 12:10) and the "adversary" (I Pet. 5:8), demands the sinner for punishment on account of sin (Zech. 3:1). When God lets Satan have his way, He is said to "deliver the sinner unto Satan" (cf. Ps. 109:6). Here it is not finally; but for the affliction of the body with disease, and even *death* (ch. 11:30, 32), so as to *destroy fleshly lust.* He does not say, "for the destruction of the *body,*" for *it* shall share in redemption (Rom. 8:23); but of the corrupt "flesh" which "cannot inherit the kingdom of God," and the lusts of which had prompted this offender to incest (Rom. 7:5; 8:9, 10). The "destruction of the flesh" answers to "*mortify* the deeds of the *body*" (Rom. 8:13), only that the latter is done by one's self, the former is effected by chastisement from God (cf. I Pet. 4:6). **the spirit ... saved**—the spiritual part of man, in the believer the organ of the Holy Spirit. Temporary affliction often leads to permanent salvation (Ps. 83:16). **6.** Your glorying in your own attainments and those of your favorite teachers (ch. 3:21; 4:19; 5:2), while all the while ye connive at such a scandal, is quite unseemly. **a little leaven leaveneth ... whole lump**—(Gal. 5:9), viz., with *present* complicity in the guilt, and the danger of future contagion (ch. 15:33; II Tim. 2:17). **7. old leaven**—The remnant of the "old" (Eph. 4:22-24) heathenish and natural corruption. The image is taken from the extreme care of the Jews in searching every corner of their houses, and "purging out" every particle of leaven from the time of killing the lamb before the Passover (Deut. 16:3, 4). So Christians are continually to search and purify their hearts (Ps. 139:23, 24). **as ye are unleavened**—normally, and as far as your Christian calling is concerned: free from the leaven of sin and death (ch. 6:11). Paul often grounds exhortations on the assumption of Christian professors' *normal* state as realized (Rom. 6:3, 4) [ALFORD]. Regarding the

ADAM CLARKE

the person in question had married the wife of his deceased father, not his own mother, but stepmother, then a widow. The word *named* is wanting in almost every MS. and version of importance and certainly makes no part of the text. The words should be read, "and such fornication as is not amongst the Gentiles," i.e., not allowed.

2. *Ye are puffed up.* Ye are full of strife and contention relative to your parties and favorite teachers, and neglect the discipline of the church. Had you considered the greatness of this crime, you would have rather *mourned,* and have put away this flagrant transgressor from among you. *Taken away from among you.* This is supposed by some to refer to the punishment of death, by others to excommunication. The Christian Church was at this time too young to have those forms of excommunication which were practiced in succeeding centuries. Probably no more is meant than a simple disowning of the person, accompanied with the refusal to admit him to the sacred ordinances, or to have any intercourse or connection with him.

3. *Absent in body, but present in spirit.* Perhaps Paul refers to the gift of the discernment of spirits, which it is very likely the apostles in general possessed on extraordinary occasions. He had already seen this matter so clearly that he had determined on that sort of punishment which should be inflicted for this crime.

4. *In the name of our Lord Jesus.* Who is the Head of the Church, and under whose authority every act is to be performed. *And my spirit.* My apostolical authority derived from Him; *with the power,* with the miraculous energy *of the Lord Jesus,* which is to inflict the punishment that you pronounce.

5. *To deliver such an one unto Satan.* There is no evidence that delivering to Satan was any form of excommunication known among either the Jews or the Christians. It was a species of punishment administered in extraordinary cases, in which the body and the mind of an incorrigible transgressor were delivered by the authority of God into the power of Satan, to be tortured with diseases and terrors as a warning to all. But while the body and mind were thus tormented, the immortal spirit was under the influence of the divine mercy; and the affliction, in all probability, was in general only for a season; though sometimes it was evidently unto death, as the *destruction of the flesh* seems to imply. But the soul found mercy at the hand of God.

6. *Your glorying is not good.* You are triumphing in your superior knowledge, and busily employed in setting up and supporting your respective teachers, while the church is left under the most scandalous corruptions—corruptions which threaten its very existence if not purged away. *Know ye not?* With all your boasted wisdom, do you not know and acknowledge the truth of a common maxim, *A little leaven leaveneth the whole lump?* If this *leaven,* the incestuous person, be permitted to remain among you; if his conduct be not exposed by the most formidable censure, the floodgates of impurity will be opened on the church, and the whole state of Christianity ruined in Corinth.

7. *Purge out therefore the old leaven.* As it is the custom of the Jews previously to the Passover to search their houses in the most diligent manner for the old leaven, and throw it out, sweeping every part clean, so act with this incestuous person.

MATTHEW HENRY

II. The reason with which this advice is enforced: *For Christ our passover is sacrificed for us, v.* 7. The Jews, after they had killed the passover, kept the feast of unleavened bread. So must we; not for seven days only, but all our days. The whole life of a Christian must be a feast of unleavened bread.

He must purge out the old leaven, and keep the feast of unleavened bread of sincerity and truth. He must be without guilt in his conduct towards God and man. The sacrifice of our Redeemer is the strongest argument with a gracious heart for purity and sincerity. Heinous evil could not be expiated but with the blood of the Son of God! And shall a Christian love the murderer of his Lord? God forbid.

Verses 9–13

Here the apostle advises them to shun the company of scandalous professors.

I. The advice itself: *I wrote to you in a letter not to company with fornicators, v.* 9. Some think this was an epistle written to them before, which is lost. Some think it is to be understood of this very epistle, but thought it needful now to be more particular.

And therefore he tells them that if any man called a brother, and being a member of a Christian church, were *a fornicator, or covetous, or an idolater, or a railer,* that they should not *keep company with him, not so much as eat with such a one.* They were to avoid all familiarity with him; but, that they might shame him, and bring him to repentance, must disclaim and shun him. They may call themselves *brethren in Christ,* but they are not Christian brethren. They are only fit companions for their brethren in iniquity.

II. How he limits this advice. He does not forbid their eating nor conversing with the *fornicators of this world,* &c. They know no better. They profess no better. "*You must needs go out of the world* if you will have no conversation with such men. It is impossible, as long as you are in the world, but you must fall into their company. This cannot be wholly avoided."

JAMIESON, FAUSSET, BROWN

Corinthian Church as the Passover "unleavened lump" or mass, he entreats them to correspond in fact with this their normal state. "For Christ our Passover (Exod. 12:5-11, 21-23; John 1:29) *has been* (*English Version,* "is") sacrificed for us"; i.e., as the Jews *began* the days of unleavened bread with the slaying of the Passover lamb, so, Christ our Passover *having been already slain,* let there be no leaven of evil in you who are the "unleavened lump." Doubtless he alludes to the Passover which had been two or three weeks before kept by the Jewish Christians (ch. 16:8): the Gentile Christians probably also refraining from leavened bread at the love feasts. Thus the Jewish Passover naturally gave place to our Christian Easter. The time however, of *keeping feast* (metaphorical; i.e., *leading the Christian life of joy* in Christ's finished work, cf. Prov. 15:15) among us Christians, corresponding to the Jewish Passover, is not limited, as the latter, to one season, but is ALL our time; for the transcendent benefits of the once-for-all completed sacrifice of *our* Passover Lamb extends to all the time of our lives and of this Christian dispensation; in no part of our time is the leaven of evil to be admitted. **For even**—an additional reason, besides that in vs. 6, and a more cogent one for purging out every leaven of evil; viz., that Christ has been already sacrificed, whereas the old leaven is yet unremoved, which ought to have been long ago purged out. **8. not . . . old leaven**—of our unconverted state as Jews or heathen. **malice**—the opposite of "sincerity," which allows no leaven of evil to be mixed up with good (Matt. 16:6). **wickedness**—the opposite of "truth," which allows not evil to be mistaken for good. The *Greek* for "malice" means the evil *habit* of mind; "wickedness," the *outcoming* of the same in word and deed. The *Greek* for "sincerity" expresses literally, a thing which, when examined *by the sun's light,* is found pure and unadulterated. **9. I wrote . . . in an epistle**—rather, "in the Epistle": a former one not now extant. That Paul does not refer to the *present* letter is proved by the fact that no direction "not to company with fornicators" occurs in the previous part of it; also the words, "in an (or *the*) epistle," could not have been added if he meant, "I have just written" (II Cor. 10:10). *"His letters"* (*plural;* not applying to merely *one*) confirm this. II Corinthians 7:8 also refers to our *first* Epistle, just as here a *former* letter is referred to by the same phrase. Paul probably wrote a former brief reply to inquiries of the Corinthians: *our* first Epistle, as it enters more fully into the same subject, has superseded the former, which the Holy Spirit did not design for the guidance of the Church in general, and which therefore has not been preserved. See my *Introduction.* **10.** Limitation of the prohibition alluded to in vs. 9. As in dissolute Corinth to "company with no fornicators . . ." would be almost to company with none in the (unbelieving) world; ye need not *utterly* ("altogether") forego intercourse with fornicators, etc., of the unbelieving world (cf. ch. 10:27; John 17:15; I John 5:18, 19). As "fornicators" sin against themselves, so "extortioners" against their neighbors, and "idolaters" against God. The attempt to get "out of the world," in violation of God's will that believers should remain in it but keep themselves from its evil, led to monasticism and its consequent evils. **11. But now I have written**—"Now" does not express *time,* but *"the case being so,"* viz., that to avoid fornicators, etc., *of the world,* you would have to leave the world altogether, which would be absurd. So "now" is used in Hebrews 11:16. Thus we avoid making the apostle *now* retract a command which he had before given. **I have written**—i.e., my meaning in the letter I wrote was . . . . **a brother**—contrasted with a "fornicator, etc., *of the world*" (vs. 10). There is less danger in associating with open worldlings than with carnal professors. Here, as in Ephesians 5:3, 5, "covetousness" is joined with "fornication": the common fount of both being "the fierce and ever fiercer longing of the creature, which has turned from God, to fill itself with the inferior objects of sense" [TRENCH, *Syn. New Testament*]. Hence "idolatry" is associated with them: and the covetous man is termed an "idolater" (Num. 25:1, 2). The Corinthians did not fall into open idolatry, but ate things offered to idols, so making a compromise with the heathen; just as they connived at fornication. Thus this verse prepares for the precepts in ch. 8:4, etc. Cf. the similar case of fornication, combined with a similar idolatrous compromise, after the pattern of Israel with the Midianites (Rev. 2:14). **no not to eat**—not to sit at the same table with such; whether at the love feasts (*agapæ*) or in private intercourse, much more at

ADAM CLARKE

8. *Therefore let us keep the feast.* It is very likely that the time of the Passover was now approaching, when the Church of Christ would be called to extraordinary acts of devotion, in commemorating the passion, death, and resurrection of Christ; and of this circumstance the apostle takes advantage in his exhortation to the Corinthians. *Not with old leaven.* Under the Christian dispensation we must be saved equally from Judaism, heathenism, and sin of every kind. *Malice* and *wickedness* must be destroyed; and *sincerity* and *truth,* inward purity and outward holiness, take their place. *Sincerity,* such purity of affections and conduct that even the light of God shining upon them discovers no flaw, and *truth*—inwardly as well as outwardly what they profess to be.

10. *For then must ye needs go out of the world.* What an awful picture of the general corruption of manners does this exhibit! The Christians at Corinth could not transact the ordinary affairs of life with any others than with fornicators, covetous persons, extortioners, railers, drunkards, and idolaters because there were none others in the place! How necessary was Christianity in that city!

11. *But now I have written.* I not only write this, but I add more: If anyone who *is called a brother,* i.e., professes the Christian religion, be a *fornicator, covetous, idolater, railer, drunkard, or extortioner,* not even to *eat* with such—have no communion with such a one, in things either sacred or civil. You may transact your worldly concerns with a person that knows not God and makes no profession of Christianity, whatever his moral character may be; but you must not even thus far acknowledge a man professing Christianity who is scandalous in his conduct. Let him have this extra mark of your abhorrence of all sin; and let the world see that the Church of God does not tolerate iniquity.

MATTHEW HENRY

III. The reason of this limitation is here assigned. Christians must have gone out of the world to avoid the company of loose heathens. But the dread of sin wears off by familiar converse with the wicked. Besides, heathens were such as Christians had nothing to do to judge and censure, and avoid upon a censure passed; for *they are without* (*v.* 12), and must be left to *God's judgment*, *v.* 13. But, as to members of the church, they are within, are professedly bound by the laws and rules of Christianity, and not only liable to the judgment of God, but to the censures of the fellow-members of the same body, when they transgress those rules. They are to be punished, by having this mark of disgrace put upon them, that they may be shamed, and, if possible, reclaimed thereby. Though the church has nothing to do with those without, it must endeavour to keep clear of the guilt and reproach of those within.

IV. How he applies the argument to the case before him: "*Therefore put away from among yourselves that wicked person*, *v.* 13. Cast him out of your fellowship."

CHAPTER 6

Verses 1–8

Here the apostle reproves them for going to law with one another before heathen judges for little matters; and therein blames all *vexatious law-suits.*

I. The fault he blames them for. *Brother went to law with brother* (*v.* 6). The bonds of fraternal love were broken through. Christians should not contend with one another, for they are brethren. They brought the matter before the heathen magistrates: *they went to law before the unjust, not before the saints* (*v.* 1), brought the controversy before unbelievers (*v.* 6). This tended much to the reproach of Christianity. And therefore, says the apostle, "*Dare any of you*, having a controversy with another, go to law before the unjust?" Here is at least an intimation that they went to law for trivial matters, for the apostle blames them that they did not suffer wrong rather than go to law (*v.* 7). Christians should be of a forgiving temper. And it is more for their honour to suffer small injuries than seem to be contentious.

II. He lays before them the aggravations of their fault: *Do you not know that the saints shall judge the world* (*v.* 2), *shall judge angels?* (*v.* 3).

And are they unworthy *to judge the smallest matters, the things of this life?* It was a dishonour to their Christian character, as saints, for them to carry little matters, about the things of life, before heathen magistrates. When they were to judge the world, nay, to judge angels, it is unaccountable that they could not determine little controversies among one another. They are not partners in their Lord's commission, but see his proceeding against the wicked world, and approve it. Others understand it as condemning the world by their faith and practice. The first sense seems to be most natural. "Shall Christians have the honour to sit with the sovereign Judge, and are they not worthy to judge of the trifles about which you contend before heathen magistrates? Cannot they make up your mutual differences?

JAMIESON, FAUSSET, BROWN

the Lord's table: at the last, too often now the guests "are not as children in one family, but like a heterogeneous crowd of strangers in an inn" [BENGEL] (cf. Gal. 2:12; II John 10:11). **12. what have I to do**—You might have easily understood that my concern is not with unbelievers *outside* the Church, but that I referred to those within it. **also**—Implying, *Those within* give me enough to do without those outside. **do not ye . . .**—Ye judge your fellow citizens, not strangers: much more should I [BENGEL]. Rather, Is it not *your duty* to judge them that are within? *God* shall judge them that are without: do you look at home [GROTIUS]. God is the Judge of the salvation of the heathen, not we (Rom. 2:12-16). Paul here gives an anticipatory censure of their going to law with saints before heathen tribunals, instead of judging such causes among themselves within. **13. put away from among yourselves that wicked**—Sentence of excommunication in language taken from Deuteronomy 24:7.

CHAPTER 6

VSS. 1-11. LITIGATION OF CHRISTIANS IN HEATHEN COURTS CENSURED: ITS VERY EXISTENCE BETRAYS A WRONG SPIRIT: BETTER TO BEAR WRONG NOW, AND HEREAFTER THE DOERS OF WRONG SHALL BE SHUT OUT OF HEAVEN. **1. Dare**—This word implies treason against Christian brotherhood [BENGEL]. **before the unjust**—The Gentile judges are here so termed by an epithet appropriate to the subject in question, viz., one concerning *justice.* Though all Gentiles were not altogether *unjust,* yet in the highest view of justice which has regard to God as the Supreme Judge, they are so: Christians, on the other hand, as regarding God as the only Fountain of justice, should not expect justice from them. **before . . . saints**—The Jews abroad were permitted to refer their disputes to Jewish *arbitrators* (JOSEPHUS, *Antiquities,* 14:10, 17). So the Christians were allowed to have Christian arbitrators. **2. Do ye not know**—as a truth universally recognized by Christians. Notwithstanding all your glorying in your "knowledge," ye are acting contrary to it (ch. 1:4, 5; 8:1). The oldest MSS. have "Or" before "know ye not"; i.e., "What! (expressing surprise) know ye not . . . ." **saints . . . judge**—i.e., "rule," including *judgment:* as assessors of Christ. Matthew 19:28, "judging," i.e., "ruling over." (Cf. Ps. 49:14; Dan. 7:22, 27; Rev. 2:26; 3:21; 20:4.) There is a distinction drawn by able expositors between the saints who *judge* or *rule,* and the world which is ruled by them: as there is between the elected (Matt. 20:23) twelve apostles who sit on thrones judging, and the twelve tribes of Israel that are judged by them. To *reign,* and to be *saved,* are not necessarily synonymous. As Jehovah employed angels to carry the law into effect when He descended on Sinai to establish His throne in Israel, so at His coming the saints shall administer the kingdom for, and under, Him. The nations of the earth, and Israel the foremost, in the flesh, shall, in this view, be the *subjects* of the rule of the Lord and His saints in glorified bodies. The mistake of the Chiliasts was that they took the merely carnal view, restricting the kingdom to the terrestrial part. This part shall have place with the accession of spiritual and temporal blessings such as Christ's presence must produce. Besides this earthly glory, there shall be the heavenly glory of the saints reigning in transfigured bodies, and holding such blessed intercourse with mortal men, as angels had with men of old, and as Christ, Moses, and Elias, in glory had with Peter, James, and John, in the flesh at the transfiguration (II Tim. 2:12; II Pet. 1:16-18). But here the "world" seems to be the unbelieving world that is to be "condemned" (ch. 11:22), rather than the whole world, including the subject nations which are to be brought under Christ's sway; however, it may include *both* those to be condemned, with the bad angels, and those about to be brought into obedience to the sway of Christ with His saints. Cf. Matthew 25:32, 40, "all nations," "these my brethren" on the thrones with Him. The event will decide the truth of this view. **judged by you**—or, *before* you (cf. ch. 3:22). **smallest matters**—The weightiest of earthly questions at issue are infinitely *small* compared with those to be decided on the judgment day. **3. judge angels**—viz., *bad* angels. We who are now "a spectacle to angels" shall then "judge angels." The

ADAM CLARKE

12. *For what have I to do to judge them also that are without?* The term *without* signifies those who were not members of the church. The word *also,* which greatly disturbs the sense here, is wanting in several MSS. The sentence I think, with the omission of *also,* should stand thus: "Does it belong to me to pass sentence on those which are without"—which are not members of the church? "By no means. You pass sentence on them which are within"—which are members of the church: "those which are without"—which are not members of the church, "God will pass sentence on," in that way in which He generally deals with the heathen world. "But put away the evil from among yourselves." This is most evidently the apostle's meaning, and renders all comments unnecessary. In the last clause there appears to be an allusion to Deut. xvii. 7, where the like directions are given to the congregation of Israel, relative to a person found guilty of idolatry: "Thou shalt put the evil away from among you"—where the version of the Septuagint is almost the same as that of the apostle.

CHAPTER 6

1. *Dare any of you?* From the many things that are here reprehended by the apostle, we learn that the Christian church at Corinth was in a state of great imperfection, notwithstanding there were very many eminent characters among them. Divided as they were among themselves, there was no one person who possessed any public authority to settle differences between man and man; therefore, as one party would not submit to the decisions of another, they were obliged to carry their contentions before heathen magistrates; and probably these very subjects of litigations arose out of their ecclesiastical divisions. *Before the unjust, and not before the saints.* The heathen judges were termed *dikastai* from their presumed righteousness in the administration of justice. Here the apostle, by a paronomasia, calls them *adikoi,* unrighteous persons; and it is very likely that at Corinth, where such corruption of manners reigned, there was a great perversion of public justice; and it is not to be supposed that matters relative to the Christians were fairly decided. The Christians the apostle terms *saints,* which they were all by profession; and doubtless many were so in spirit and in truth.

2. *The saints shall judge the world.* Nothing can be more evident than that the writers of the New Testament often use *ho cosmos, the world,* to signify the Jewish people; and sometimes the Roman Empire, and the Jewish state. In the former sense it is often used by our Lord. "When the Son of man shall sit in the throne of his glory, ye also shall sit upon twelve thrones, judging the twelve tribes of Israel," Matt. xix. 28. It is supposed that He refers to the same subject as that mentioned here—the saints judging the world; and that Paul has His words in view in what he says here to the Corinthians. By "judging the twelve tribes of Israel" some have imagined that having authority in the Church is merely intended; but Dr. Lightfoot contends that the words referred to the coming of our Lord to execute judgment on the Jews, and to destroy their state; and that the doctrine of the apostles, not themselves, was to judge and condemn that most disobedient people. I think, with Dr. Lightfoot, that these words of the apostle refer to the prediction of Dan. chap. vii. 18, 27, and such like prophecies, where the kingdoms of the earth are promised to the saints of the Most High; that is, that a time shall come when Christianity shall so far prevail that the civil government of the world shall be administered by Christians, which, at that time, was administered by heathens.

MATTHEW HENRY

Must you, about *the affairs of this life, set those to judge who are of no esteem in the church?*" i.e., *heathen* magistrates (so some read, and perhaps most properly, *v.* 4). "Must those be called in to judge in your controversies of whom you ought to entertain so low an opinion? Is not this shameful?" *v.* 5. Some who read it as our translators make it an ironical speech: "If you have such controversies depending, set those to judge who are of least esteem among yourselves. They are trifles not worth contending about. *Bear and forbear*, and the men of meanest skill among you may end your quarrels. *I speak it to your shame*," *v.* 5.

III. He puts them on a method to remedy this fault. 1. By referring it to some to make it up: "*Is it so that there is no wise man among you, no one able to judge between his brethren?* (*v.* 5). You who value yourselves so much upon your wisdom and knowledge, is there none among you that has wisdom enough to judge in these differences? Must brethren quarrel, and the heathen magistrate judge, in a church so famous as yours for knowledge and wisdom?" 2. By suffering wrong rather than taking this method to right themselves: *It is utterly a fault among you to go to law in this matter:* it is always a fault of one side to go to law, except in a case where the title is indeed dubious, and there is a friendly agreement of both parties to refer it to the judgment of those learned in the law to decide it. *Should you not rather take wrong, rather suffer yourselves to be defrauded?* A Christian should rather put up with a little injury than tease himself, and provoke others, by a litigious contest. The peace of his own mind, and the calm of his neighbourhood, are of more worth than victory in such a contest. But the apostle tells them they were so far from bearing injuries *that they actually did wrong, and defrauded, and that their brethren.* It is utterly a fault to wrong and defraud any; but it is an aggravation of this fault to defraud our Christian brethren.

Verses 9–11

Here he takes occasion to warn them against many heinous evils, to which they had been formerly addicted.

I. He puts it to them as a plain truth, that such sinners should not inherit the kingdom of God. The meanest among them must know this much, that *the unrighteous shall not inherit the kingdom of God* (*v.* 9). He specifies several sorts of sins: against the first and second commandments, as *idolaters*; against the seventh, as *adulterers, fornicators, effeminate*, and *Sodomites*; against the eighth, as *thieves* and *extortioners*; against the ninth, as *revilers*; and against the tenth, as *covetous* and *drunkards*. Heaven could never be intended for these. The scum of the earth are no ways fit to fill the heavenly mansions.

II. Yet he warns them against deceiving themselves: *Be not deceived.* Those who cannot but know the fore-mentioned truth are but too apt not to attend to it. Men are very much inclined to flatter themselves that they may live in sin and yet die in Christ, may lead the life of the devil's children and yet go to heaven with the children of God. But this is all a gross cheat. We cannot hope to sow to the flesh and yet reap everlasting life.

III. He puts them in mind what a change the gospel and grace of God had made in them: *Such were some of you* (*v.* 11). Some that are eminently good after their conversion have been as remarkably wicked before. *How glorious a change does grace make!* It changes the vilest of men into saints and the children of God. You are not what you were. *You are washed, you are sanctified, you are justified in the name of Christ, and by the Spirit of our God. The washing of regeneration* can purge away all guilt and defilement. *You are sanctified, you are justified.* None are cleansed from the guilt of sin, and reconciled to God through Christ, but those who are also sanctified by his Spirit. All who are made righteous in the sight of God are made holy by the grace of God.

Verses 12–20

The twelfth verse and former part of the thirteenth seem to relate to that early dispute among Christians about the distinction of meats, and yet to be prefatory to the caution that follows against fornication. The connection seems plain enough if we attend to the famous determination of the apostles, Acts xv, where the prohibition of certain foods was joined with that of fornication. Now some among the Corinthians seem ready to say, even in the case of fornication, *All things are lawful for me.* This pernicious conceit

JAMIESON, FAUSSET, BROWN

saints shall join in approving the final sentence of the Judge on them (Jude 6). Believers shall, as administrators of the kingdom under Jesus, put down all rule that is hostile to God. Perhaps, too, *good* angels shall then receive from the Judge, with the approval of the saints, higher honors. **4. judgments**—i.e., cases for judgment. **least esteemed**—lit., "those of no esteem." Any, however low in the Church, rather than the heathen (ch. 1:28). Questions of earthly property are of secondary consequence in the eyes of true Christians, and are therefore delegated to those in a secondary position in the Church. **5. your shame**—Thus he checks their *puffed-up* spirit (ch. 5:2; cf. ch. 15:34). To shame you out of your present unworthy course of litigation before the heathen, I have said (vs. 4), "Set the least esteemed in the Church to judge." Better even this, than your present course. **Is it so?**—Are you in such a helpless state that . . . ? **not a wise man**—though ye admire "wisdom" so much on other occasions (ch. 1:5, 22). Paul alludes probably to the title, "cachain," or *wise man*, applied to each Rabbi in Jewish councils. **no, not one**—not even one, amidst so many reputed among you for wisdom (ch. 3:18; 4:6). **shall be able**—when applied to. **brethren**—lit., "brother"; i.e., judge between brother and brother. As each case should arise, the arbitrator was to be chosen from the body of the church, such a wise person as had the charism, or gift, of church government. **6. But**—emphatically answering the question in the end of vs. 5 in the negative. Translate, "Nay . . . ." **7. utterly a fault**—lit., "a shortcoming" (not so strong as *sin*). Your going to law at all is a falling short of your high privileges, not to say your doing so *before unbelievers*, which aggravates it. **rather take wrong**—(Prov. 20:22; Matt. 5:39, 40); i.e., "suffer yourselves to be wronged." **8. ye**—emphatic. *Ye*, whom your Lord commanded to return good for evil, *on the contrary*, "do wrong (by taking away) and defraud" (by retaining what is entrusted to you; or "defraud" marks the *effect* of the "wrong" done, viz., the *loss* inflicted). Not only do ye not bear, but ye inflict wrongs. **9. unrighteous**—Translate, "Doers of wrong": referring to vs. 8 (cf. Gal. 5:21). **kingdom of God**—which is a kingdom of *righteousness* (Rom. 14:17). **fornicators**—alluding to ch. 5; also below, vss. 12-18. **effeminate**—self-polluters, who submit to unnatural lusts. **11. ye are washed**—The Greek middle voice expresses, "Ye have had yourselves washed." This washing implies the admission to the *benefits of Christ's salvation* generally; of which the parts are; (1) *Sanctification*, or the setting apart from the world, and adoption into the Church: so "sanctified" is used ch. 7:14; John 17:19. Cf. I Pet. 1:2, where it rather seems to mean the *setting apart* of one as *consecrated by the Spirit in the eternal purpose of God.* (2) *Justification* from condemnation through the righteousness of God in Christ by faith (Rom. 1:17). So PARÆUS. The order of *sanctification* before *justification* shows that it must be so taken, and not in the sense of *progressive* sanctification. "Washed" precedes both, and so must refer to the Christian's outward new birth of water, the sign of the inward setting apart to the Lord by the inspiration of the Spirit as the seed of new life (John 3:5; Eph. 5:26; Titus 3:5; Heb. 10:22). Paul (cf. the Church of England Baptismal Service), in charity, and faith in the ideal of the Church, presumes that baptism realizes its original design, and that those outwardly baptized inwardly enter into vital communion with Christ (Gal. 3:27). He presents the grand ideal which those alone realized in whom the inward and the outward baptism coalesced. At the same time he recognizes the fact that this in many cases does not hold good (vss. 8-10), leaving it to God to decide who are the really "washed," while he only decides on broad general principles. **in the name of . . . Jesus, and by the Spirit**—rather, "in the Spirit," i.e., by His *in*-dwelling. Both clauses belong to the three—"washed, sanctified, justified." **our God**—The "our" reminds them that amidst all his reproofs God is still the common God of himself and them.

12-20. REFUTATION OF THE ANTINOMIAN DEFENSE OF FORNICATION, AS IF IT WAS LAWFUL BECAUSE MEATS ARE SO. **12. All things are lawful unto me**—These, which were Paul's own words on a former occasion (to the Corinthians, cf. ch. 10:23, and Gal. 5:23), were made a pretext for excusing the eating of meats offered to idols, and so of what was generally connected with idolatry (Acts 15:29), "fornication" (perhaps in the letter of the Corinthians to Paul, ch. 7:1). Paul's remark had referred only to things *indifferent:* but they wished to treat fornication as such, on the ground that the

ADAM CLARKE

4. *Things pertaining to this life.* They could examine all civil cases among themselves, which they were permitted to determine without any hindrance from the heathen governments under which they lived. *Who are least esteemed in the church.* Those who were in the lowest order of judges.

5. *Is it so, that there is not a wise man among you?* Have you none among yourselves that can be arbitrators of the differences which arise, that you go to the heathen tribunals?

6. *Brother goeth to law with brother.* One Christian sues another at law! This is almost as great a scandal as can exist in a Christian society. Those in a religious community who will not submit to a proper arbitration, made by persons among themselves, should be expelled from the Church of God.

7. *There is utterly a fault among you.* There is a most manifest "defect" among you: (1) Of peaceableness; (2) Of brotherly love; (3) Of mutual confidence; and (4) Of reverence for God, and concern for the honor of His cause. *Why do ye not rather take wrong?* Better suffer an injury than take a method of redressing yourselves which must injure your own peace and greatly dishonor the cause of God.

8. *Nay, ye do wrong.* Far from suffering, you are the aggressors; and defraud your pious, long-suffering brethren, who submit to this wrong rather than take those methods of redressing their grievances which the spirit of Christianity forbids. Probably the apostle refers to him who had taken his father's wife.

9. *The unrighteous shall not inherit the kingdom.* The unrighteous, those who act contrary to right, cannot *inherit*, for the inheritance is by right. He who is not a child of God has no right to the family inheritance, for that inheritance is for the children. "If children, then heirs; heirs of God, and joint-heirs with Christ," Rom. viii. 17. There are here ten classes of transgressors which the apostle excludes from the kingdom of God; and any man who is guilty of any one of the evils mentioned above is thereby excluded from this Kingdom, whether it imply the Church of Christ here below or the state of glory hereafter.

11. *And such were some of you.* It was not with the prospect of collecting saints that the apostles went about preaching the gospel of the Kingdom. None but sinners were to be found over the face of the earth; they preached that sinners might be converted unto God, made saints, and constituted into a church; and this was the effect as well as the object of their preaching. *But ye are washed.* Several suppose that the order in which the operations of the grace of God take place in the soul is here inverted, but I am of a very different mind. Everything will appear here in its order when we understand the terms used by the apostle. *Ye are washed;* you have been baptized into the Christian faith, and you have promised in this baptism to put off all filthiness of the flesh and spirit; the washing of your bodies is emblematical of the purification of your souls. *Ye are sanctified.* From *a*, privative, and *ge*, "the earth"; you are separated from earthly things to be connected with spiritual. You are separated from time to be connected with eternity. You are separated from idols to be joined to the living God. Separation from common, earthy, or sinful uses, to be wholly employed in the service of the true God, is the ideal meaning of this word, in both the Old and New Testaments. It was in consequence of their being separated from the world that they became a church of God. You were formerly workers of iniquity, and associated with workers of iniquity; but now you are separated from them, and united together to work out your salvation with fear and trembling before God. *Ye are justified.* You have been brought into a state of favor with God, your sins having been blotted out through Christ Jesus, the Spirit of God witnessing the same to your conscience, and carrying on by His energy the great work of regeneration in your hearts.

12. *All things are lawful unto me.* It is likely that some of the Corinthians had pleaded that the offense of the man who had his father's wife, as well as the eating the things offered to

MATTHEW HENRY

Paul here sets himself to oppose: he tells them that many things lawful in themselves were not expedient. Christians should not barely consider what is in itself lawful to be done, but what is fit for them to do. They should be very careful that by carrying this maxim too far they be not brought into bondage, either to a crafty deceiver or a carnal inclination. *All things are lawful for me*, says he, *but I will not be brought under the power of any*, *v.* 12. There is a liberty wherewith Christ has made us free, in which we must stand fast. But surely he would never carry this liberty so far as to put himself into the power of any bodily appetite. He would not become a glutton nor a drunkard. And much less would he abuse the maxim of lawful liberty to countenance the sin of fornication. He would not abuse this maxim about eating and drinking to encourage any intemperance, nor indulge a carnal appetite: "*Though meats are for the belly and the belly for meats* (*v.* 13). If I am in danger of being subjected to my belly and appetite, I will abstain. *But God shall destroy both it and them.*" There is a time coming when the need and use of food shall be abolished. The transition to his arguments against fornication seems very natural: *But the body is not for fornication, but for the Lord, and the Lord for the body*, *v.* 13. Meats and the belly are for one another; not so fornication and the body.

I. The body is not for fornication, but for the Lord. This is the first argument he uses against this sin, for which the heathen inhabitants of Corinth were infamous. The *body is not for fornication*; it was never formed for any such purpose, *but for the Lord.* It is to be a member of Christ, and therefore must not be made the member of a harlot, *v.* 15. And *the Lord is for the body*, that is, as some think, Christ is to be Lord of the body, to have property in it and dominion over it. We must take care that we do not use what belongs to Christ as if it were our own, and much less to his dishonour.

II. Some understand this last passage, *The Lord is for the body*, thus: He is for its resurrection and glorification, according to what follows, *v.* 14, which is a second argument against this sin, the honour intended to be put on our bodies: *God hath both raised up our Lord, and will raise us up by his power* (*v.* 14). It will be an honour to our bodies that they will be raised. Let us not abuse those bodies by sin which, if they be kept pure, shall be made like to *Christ's glorious body*.

III. A third argument is the honour already put on them: *Know you not that your bodies are the members of Christ? v.* 15. If the soul be united to Christ by faith, the whole man is become a member of his mystical body. The body is in union with Christ as well as the soul. *But now*, says the apostle, *shall I take the members of Christ, and make them the members of a harlot? God forbid.* Would it not be dishonouring Christ, and dishonouring ourselves to the very last degree? What, make Christ's members the members of a harlot? God forbid. *Know you not that he who is joined to a harlot is one body* with hers? *For two*, says he, *shall be one flesh. But he who is joined to the Lord is one spirit, v.* 16, 17. He is joined to the Lord in union with Christ, and made partaker by faith of his Spirit. How shall one in so close a union with Christ as to be one spirit with him yet be so united to a harlot as to become one flesh with her? Can anything be more inconsistent with our profession or relation? It is no wonder therefore that the apostle should say, "*Flee fornication*" (*v.* 18). *Other vices may be conquered in fight, this only by flight;* so speak many of the fathers.

IV. A fourth argument is that it is a sin against our own bodies. *Every sin that a man does is without the body; he that committeth fornication sinneth against his own body* (*v.* 18); every sin, that is, every external act of sin besides, is without the body.

JAMIESON, FAUSSET, BROWN

existence of bodily appetites proved the *lawfulness* of their gratification. **me**—Paul giving himself as a sample of Christians in general. **but I**—whatever others do, *I will not* . . . . **lawful . . . brought under the power**—The *Greek* words are from the same root, whence there is a play on the words: All things *are in* my *power*, but I will not be *brought under the power of any* of them (the "all things"). He who commits "fornication," steps aside from his own legitimate power or liberty, and is "brought under the power" of an harlot (vs. 15; cf. ch. 7:4). The "power" ought to be in the hands of the *believer*, not in the *things which he uses* [BENGEL]; else his liberty is forfeited; he ceases to be his own master (John 8:34-36; Gal. 5:13; I Pet. 2:16; II Pet. 2:19). Unlawful things ruin thousands; "lawful" things (unlawfully used), ten thousands. **13.** The argument drawn from the indifference of meats (ch. 8:8; Rom. 14:14, 17; cf. Mark 7:18; Col. 2:20-22) to that of fornication does not hold good. Meats doubtless are indifferent, since both they and the "belly" for which they are created are to be "destroyed" in the future state. But "the body is not (created) for fornication, but for the Lord, and the Lord for the body" (as its Redeemer, who hath Himself assumed the body): "And God hath raised up the Lord, and will also raise up us" (i.e., our bodies): therefore the "body" is not, like the "belly," after having served a temporary use, to be destroyed: Now "he that committeth fornication, sinneth against his own body (vs. 18). Therefore fornication is not indifferent, since it is a sin against one's own body, which, like the Lord for whom it is created, is not to be destroyed, but to be raised to eternal existence. Thus Paul gives here the germ of the three subjects handled in subsequent sections: (1) The relation between the sexes. (2) The question of meats offered to idols. (3) The resurrection of the body. **shall destroy**—at the Lord's coming to change the natural bodies of believers into spiritual bodies (ch. 15:44, 52). There is a real essence underlying the superficial phenomena of the present temporary organization of the body, and this essential germ, when all the particles are scattered, involves the future resurrection of the body incorruptible. **14.** (Rom. 8:11.) **raised up**—rather, "raised," to distinguish it from "will raise *up* us"; the *Greek* of the latter being a compound, the former a simple verb. Believers shall be raised up *out of* the rest of the dead (*Note*, Phil. 3:11); the first resurrection (Rev. 20:5). **us**—Here he speaks of the possibility of his being found in the grave when Christ comes; elsewhere, of his being possibly found alive (I Thess. 4:17). In either event, the Lord's coming rather than death is the great object of the Christian's expectation (Rom. 8:19). **15.** Resuming the thought in vs. 13, "the body is for the Lord" (ch. 12:27; Eph. 4:12, 15, 16; 5:30). **shall I then**—such being the case. **take**—spontaneously alienating them from Christ. For they cannot be at the same time "the members of an harlot," and "of Christ" [BENGEL]. It is a fact no less certain than mysterious, that moral and spiritual ruin is caused by such sins; which human wisdom (when untaught by revelation) held to be actions as blameless as eating and drinking [CONYBEARE and HOWSON]. **16.** Justification of his having called fornicators "members of an harlot" (vs. 15). **joined**—by carnal intercourse; lit., "cemented to": cleaving to. **one body**—with her. **saith he**—GOD speaking by Adam (Gen. 2:24; Matt. 19:5). "He which made them at the beginning said . . ." (Eph. 5:31). **17. one spirit**—with Him. In the case of union with a harlot, the fornicator becomes one "body" with her (not one "spirit," for the spirit which is normally the organ of the Holy Spirit in man, is in the carnal so overlaid with what is sensual that it is ignored altogether). But the believer not only has his body sanctified by union with Christ's body, but also becomes "one spirit" with Him (John 15:1-7; 17:21; II Pet. 1:4; cf. Eph. 5:23-32, and John 3:6). **18. Flee**—The only safety in such temptations is *flight* (Gen. 39:12; Job 31:1). **Every sin**—The *Greek* is forcible. "*Every sin whatsoever* that a man doeth." Every *other* sin; even gluttony, drunkenness, and selfmurder are "without," i.e., comparatively external to the body (Mark 7:18; cf. Prov. 6: 30-32). He certainly injures, but he does not alienate the body itself; the sin is not terminated in the body; he rather sins against the perishing accidents of the body (as the "belly," and the body's present temporary organization), and against the soul than against the body in its permanent essence, designed "for the Lord." "But" the fornicator alienates that body which is the Lord's, and makes it one with a harlot's body, and so "sinneth against his own body," i.e., against the *verity* and *nature*

ADAM CLARKE

idols, was not contrary to the law, as it then stood. To this the apostle answers: Though such a thing be lawful, yet the case of fornication, mentioned in chap. v. 1, is not expedient—it is not agreeable to propriety, decency, order, and purity. It is contrary to the established usages of the best and most enlightened nations, and should not be tolerated in the Church of Christ.

13. *Meats for the belly.* God has provided different kinds of aliments for the appetite of man, and among others those which are generally offered to idols; and He has adapted the appetite to these aliments, and the aliments to the appetite.

But God shall destroy both it and them; none of these is eternal; all these lower appetites and sensations will be destroyed by death and have no existence in the resurrection body. *Now the body is not for fornication.* Though God made an appetite for food, and provided food for that appetite, yet He has not made the body for any uncleanness nor indulgence in sensuality; but He has made it for Christ. And Christ was provided to be a Sacrifice for this body as well as for the soul, by taking our nature upon Him; so that now, as human beings, we have an intimate relationship to the Lord; and our bodies are made not only for His service but to be His temples.

14. *And God hath both raised up the Lord.* He has raised up the human nature of Christ from the grave, as a pledge of our resurrection; and will also raise us up by His own power, that we may dwell with Him in glory forever.

15. *Know ye not that your bodies are the members of Christ?* Because He has taken your nature upon Him, and thus, as believers in Him, you are the members of Christ. *Shall I then take?* Shall we who profess to be members of His body, of His flesh, and of His bones, connect ourselves with harlots, and thus dishonor and pollute the bodies which are members of Christ?

17. *Is one spirit.* He who is united to God, by faith in Christ Jesus, receives His Spirit, and becomes a partaker of the divine nature. Who can change such a relationship for communion with a harlot, or for any kind of sensual gratification?

18. *Flee fornication.* Abominate, detest, and escape from every kind of uncleanness. Some sins, or solicitations to sin, may be reasoned with; in the above cases, if you parley you are undone; reason not but fly! *Sinneth against his own body.* Though sin of every species has a tendency to destroy life, yet none are so mortal as those to which the apostle refers; they strike immediately at the basis of the constitution. By the just judgment of God, all these irregular and sinful connections are married to death.

MATTHEW HENRY

This sin is in a peculiar manner styled uncleanness, pollution, because no sin has so much external turpitude in it, especially in a Christian. He sins against his own body; he defiles it, he degrades it. He casts vile reproach on what his Redeemer has dignified to the last degree by taking it into union with himself. We should not make our present vile bodies more vile by sinning against them.

V. The fifth argument against this sin is that the bodies of Christians are *the temples of the Holy Ghost which is in them, and which they have of God, v.* 19. He that is joined to Christ is one spirit. He is yielded up to him and is hereupon possessed, and inhabited, by his Holy Spirit. This is the proper notion of a temple—a place where God dwells, and sacred to his use. Such temples real Christians are of the Holy Ghost.

Hence we are not our own. We are possessed by and for God; nay, and this in virtue of a purchase made of us: *You are bought with a price.* In short, our bodies were made for God, they were purchased for him. And shall we desecrate his temple, and offer it up to the use and service of a harlot? The temple of the Holy Ghost must be kept holy. Our bodies must be kept as his whose they are, and fit for his use and residence.

VI. The apostle argues from the obligation we are under *to glorify God both with our body and spirit, which are his, v.* 20. He made both, he bought both. They must be kept as vessels fitted for our Master's use. We must look upon our whole selves as holy to the Lord. We are to honour *him with our bodies and spirits, which are his.* Body and spirit are to be kept clean, that God may be honoured by both. But God is dishonoured when either is defiled by so beastly a sin. Therefore flee fornication, nay, and every sin. Use your bodies for the glory and service of their Lord and Maker.

JAMIESON, FAUSSET, BROWN

of his body; not a mere *effect* on the body from without, but a *contradiction* of the truth of the body, wrought *within itself* [ALFORD]. **19.** Proof that "he that fornicates sinneth against his own **body" (vs. 18). your body**—not "bodies." As in ch. 3:17, he represented the whole company of believers (souls and bodies), i.e., the Church, as "the temple of God," the Spirit; so here, the *body* of each individual of the Church is viewed as the ideal "temple of the Holy Ghost." So John 17:23, which proves that not only the Church, but also each member of it, is "the temple of the Holy Ghost." Still though many the several members form one temple, the whole collectively being that which each is in miniature individually. Just as the Jews had one temple only, so in the fullest sense all Christian churches and individual believers form one temple only. Thus "YOUR [*plural*] body" is distinguished here from "HIS OWN [*particular* or *individual*] body" (vs. 18). In sinning against the latter, the fornicator sins against "your (ideal) body," that of "Christ," whose "members your bodies" are (vs. 15). In this consists the sin of fornication, that it is a sacrilegious desecration of God's temple to profane uses. The unseen, but much more efficient, Spirit of God in the spiritual temple now takes the place of the visible Shekinah in the old material temple. The whole man is the temple; the soul is the inmost shrine; the understanding and heart, the holy place; and the body, the porch and exterior of the edifice. Chastity is the guardian of the temple to prevent anything unclean entering which might provoke the indwelling God to abandon it as defiled [TERTULLIAN *de cultu fœminarum*]. None but God can claim a temple; here the Holy Ghost is assigned one; therefore the Holy Ghost is God. **not your own**—The fornicator treats his body as if it were "his own," to give to a harlot if he pleases (vs. 18; cf. vs. 20). But we have no right to alienate our body which is the Lord's. In ancient servitude the person of the servant was wholly the property of the master, not his own. *Purchase* was one of the ways of acquiring a slave. Man has *sold himself* to sin (I Kings 21:20; Rom. 7:14). Christ buys him to Himself, to serve Him (Rom. 6:16-22). **20. bought with a price**—Therefore Christ's blood is strictly a ransom paid to God's justice by the love of God in Christ for our redemption (Matt. 20:28; Acts 20:28; Gal. 3:13; Heb. 9:12; I Pet. 1:18, 19; II Pet. 2:1 Rev. 5:9). While He thus took off our obligation to punishment, He laid upon us a new obligation to obedience (ch. 7:22, 23). If we accept Him as our Prophet to reveal God to us, and our Priest to atone for us, we must also accept Him as our King to rule over us as wholly His, presenting every token of our fealty (Isa. 26:13). **in your body**—as "in" a temple (cf. John 13:32; Rom. 12:1; Phil. 1:20). **and in your spirit, which are God's**—not in the oldest MSS. and versions, and not needed for the sense, as the context refers *mainly* to the "body" (vss. 16, 18, 19). The "spirit" is *incidentally* mentioned in vs. 17, which perhaps gave rise to the interpolation, at first written in the margin, afterwards inserted in the text.

ADAM CLARKE

19. *Your body is the temple of the Holy Ghost.* What an astonishing saying is this! As truly as the living God dwelt in the Mosaic Tabernacle and in the Temple of Solomon, so truly does the Holy Ghost dwell in the souls of genuine Christians; and as the Temple and all its utensils were holy, separated from all common and profane uses and dedicated alone to the service of God, so the bodies of genuine Christians are holy, and all their members should be employed in the service of God alone.

And ye are not your own. You have no right over yourselves, to dispose of either your body or any of its members as you may think proper or lawful; you are bound to God, and to Him you are accountable.

20. *Ye are bought with a price.* As the slave who is purchased by his master for a sum of money is the sole property of that master, so you, being bought with the price of the blood of Christ, are not your own; you are His property. As the slave is bound to use all his skill and diligence for the emolument of his master, so you should employ body, soul, and spirit in the service of your Lord; promoting, by every means in your power, the honor and glory of your God, whom you must also consider as your Lord and Master. *And in your spirit, which are God's* is wanting in some MSS. and in several of the primitive fathers. Almost every critic of note considers them to be spurious.

MATTHEW HENRY

CHAPTER 7

Verses 1–9

The apostle comes now to answer some cases of conscience which the Corinthians had proposed to him. They were *things whereof they wrote to him, v.* 1. The apostle was as ready to resolve as they were to propose their doubts. In the former chapter, he warns them to avoid fornication; here he gives some directions about marriage.

I. It was good to abstain from marriage altogether: *It is good for a man not to touch a woman* (not to take her to wife), by good here not understanding what is so conformable to the mind of God as if to do otherwise were sin, an extreme into which many of the ancients have run in favour of celibacy and virginity. *At this juncture* it would be a convenience for Christians to keep themselves single, provided they can keep themselves chaste.

II. He informs them that marriage, and the comforts and satisfactions of that state, are by divine wisdom prescribed for preventing fornication (*v.* 2).

JAMIESON, FAUSSET, BROWN

CHAPTER 7

VSS. 1-40. REPLY TO THEIR INQUIRIES AS TO MARRIAGE; THE GENERAL PRINCIPLE IN OTHER THINGS IS, ABIDE IN YOUR STATION, FOR THE TIME IS SHORT. **1.** The Corinthians in their letter had probably asked questions which tended to disparage marriage, and had implied that it was better to break it off when contracted with an unbeliever. **good**—i.e., "expedient," because of "the present distress"; i.e., the unsettled state of the world, and the likelihood of persecutions tearing rudely asunder those bound by marriage ties. Hebrews 13: 4, in opposition to ascetic and Romish notions of superior *sanctity* in celibacy, declares, "Marriage is HONORABLE IN ALL." Another reason why in some cases celibacy may be a matter of Christian *expediency* is stated in vss. 34, 35, "that ye may attend upon the Lord without distraction." But these are exceptional cases, and in exceptional times, such as those of Paul. **2.** Here the general rule is given *to avoid* **fornication**—More lit., "*on account of fornications,*" to which as being very prevalent at Corinth, and not even counted sins among the heathen, unmarried persons might be tempted. The *plural,* "fornications," marks irregular lusts, as contrasted with the *unity* of the marriage relation [BENGEL]. **let every man have**—a positive command to all who have not the gift of continency, in fact to the great majority of the world (vs. 5). The dignity of marriage is set forth by Paul (Eph. 5:25-

ADAM CLARKE

CHAPTER 7

1. *The things whereof ye wrote unto me.* It is sufficiently evident that the principal part of this Epistle was written in answer to some questions which had been sent to the apostle in a letter from the Corinthian church; and the first question seems to be this: "Is it proper for a man to marry in the present circumstances of the church?" The question concerning the expediency or inexpediency of marriage was often agitated among the ancient philosophers; and many, though inclined to decide against it, because of the troubles and cares connected with it, tolerated it in their opinions because, though an evil, it was judged to be a necessary evil. But this was not the common opinion; the Jews absolutely required that every man should marry, and reputed those as murderers who did not. By the laws of Lycurgus unmarried persons were prohibited from seeing the public games. By the laws of the Spartans bachelors were punished. And Plato declares all such unworthy of any honor.

2. *Let every man have his own wife.* Let every man have one woman, *his own;* and every woman one man, *her own.* Here, plurality of wives and husbands is most strictly forbidden; and they are commanded to marry for the purpose of procreating children.

MATTHEW HENRY

And, when they are married, let each render the other *due benevolence* (*v.* 3).

ALBERT BARNES:

3. "Let them not imagine that there is any virtue in living separate from each other, as if they were in a state of celibacy."—*Doddridge.* They are bound to each other; in every way they are to evince kindness, and to seek to promote the happiness and purity of each other. There is a great deal of delicacy used here by Paul, and his expression is removed as far as possible from the grossness of heathen writers. His meaning is plain; but instead of using a word to express it which would be indelicate and offensive, he uses one which is not indelicate in the slightest degree. The word which he uses (*benevolence*) denotes kindness, goodwill, affection of mind. And by the use of the word "due," he reminds them of the sacredness of their vow, and of the fact that in person, property, and in every respect, they belong to each other. It was necessary to give this direction, for the contrary might have been regarded as proper by many who would have supposed there was special virtue and merit in living separate from each other (facts have shown that many have imbibed such an idea). It was not possible to give the rule with more delicacy than Paul has done. Many mss., however, instead of "due benevolence," read "a debt" or "that which is owed"; and this reading has been adopted by Griesbach in the text. Homer, with a delicacy not unlike the apostle Paul, uses the word "friendship" to express the same idea. —*Popular Commentary*

And therefore they should not defraud one another of the use of their bodies, except it be *with mutual consent* (*v.* 5) and *for a time* only, while they employ themselves in some extraordinary duties of religion, *or give themselves to fasting and prayer.* Seasons of deep humiliation require abstinence from lawful pleasures.

III. The apostle limits what he had said (*v.* 2). Paul did not bind every man to marry. No, he *could wish all men were as himself* (*v.* 7). Natural constitutions vary.

JAMIESON, FAUSSET, BROWN

32), in the fact that it signifies the mystical union between Christ and the Church. **3, 4.** *The duty of cohabitation on the part of the married.* **due benevolence**—The oldest MSS. read simply, "her due"; i.e., the conjugal cohabitation *due* by the marriage contract (cf. vs. 4).

4. A paradox. She *hath not power over* her body, and yet it is *her own.* The *oneness of body* in which marriage places husband and wife explains this. The one complements the other. Neither without the other realizes the perfect ideal of man.

5. Defraud . . . not—viz., of the conjugal duty "due" (vs. 3; cf. LXX, Exod. 21:10). **except it be**—"unless perchance" [ALFORD]. **give yourselves to**—lit., "be at leisure for"; be *free from interruptions for;* viz., on some *special "season,"* as the *Greek* for "time" means (cf. Exod. 19:15; Joel 2:16; Zech. 7:3). **fasting and prayer**—The oldest MSS. omit "fasting and"; an interpolation, evidently, of ascetics. **come together**—The oldest MSS. read, "be together," viz., in the regular state of the married. **Satan**—who often thrusts in his temptations to unholy thoughts amidst the holiest exercises. **for your incontinency**—*because of* your inability to "contain" (vs. 9) your natural propensities, which Satan would take advantage of.

6. by permission . . . not of commandment—not *by God's permission to me to say it:* but, "by way of permission to you, not as a commandment." "This" refers to the directions vss. 2-5.

7. even as I—having the gift of continence (Matt. 19:11, 12). This wish does not hold good absolutely, else the extension of mankind and of the Church would cease; but relatively to "the present distress" (vs. 26).

8. to the unmarried—in general, of both sexes (vss. 10, 11). **and widows**—in particular. **even as I**—unmarried (ch. 9:5).

ADAM CLARKE

3. *Let the husband render unto the wife due benevolence.* Though our version is no translation of the original, yet few persons are at a loss for the meaning, and the context is sufficiently plain. Some have rendered the words, not unaptly, the "matrimonial debt" or "conjugal duty"—that which a wife owes to her husband, and the husband to his wife; and which they must take care mutually to render, else alienation of affection will be the infallible consequence, and this in numberless instances has led to adulterous connections. In such cases the wife has to blame herself for the infidelity of her husband, and the husband for that of his wife. What miserable work has been made in the peace of families by a wife or a husband pretending to be wiser than the apostle, and too holy and spiritual to keep the commandments of God!

4. *The wife hath not power.* Her person belongs to her husband; her husband's person belongs to her. Neither of them has any authority to refuse what the other has a matrimonial right to demand. The woman that would act so is either a knave or a fool. It would be trifling to attribute her conduct to any other cause than weakness or folly. She does not love her husband; or she loves someone else better than her husband; or she makes pretensions to a fancied sanctity unsupported by Scripture or common sense.

5. *Defraud ye not one the other.* What you owe thus to each other never refuse paying, unless by mutual consent; and let that be only for a certain time, when prudence dictates the temporary separation, or when some extraordinary spiritual occasion may render it mutually agreeable, in order that you may fast and pray, and derive the greatest possible benefit from these duties by being enabled to wait on the Lord without distraction. *That Satan tempt you not for your incontinency.* It is most evident that the separations permitted by the apostle, for he enjoins none, are only for a season, on extraordinary occasions; and that the persons may *come together again,* lest Satan, taking advantage of their matrimonial abstinence, might tempt either party to illicit commerce. *Incontinency,* "want of strength" to regulate one's desires or appetities; from *a,* negative, and *kratos,* "strength." It is remarkable that the apostle supposes that even this temporary continence might produce incontinence; and universal observation confirms the supposition.

6. *I speak this by permission.* It was a constant custom of the more conscientious rabbins to make a difference between the things which they enjoined on their own judgment and those which they built on the authority of the law. Thus Rabbi Tancum: "The washing of hands before meat is in our own power; washing after meat is commanded." We may understand the apostle here as saying that the directions already given were from his own judgment, and not from any divine inspiration; and we may take it for granted that where he does not make this observation he is writing under the immediate afflatus of the Holy Spirit.

7. *For I would that all men.* He wished that all that were then in the Church were, like himself, unmarried; but this was in reference to the necessities of the Church, or what he calls, v. 26, the "present distress." For it never could be his wish that marriage should cease among men, and that human beings should no longer be propagated upon earth. Nor could he wish that the Church of Christ should always be composed of single persons; this would have been equally absurd. But as the Church was then in straits and difficulties, it was much better for its single members not to encumber themselves with domestic embarrassments. *Every man hath his proper gift of God.* Continence is a state that cannot be acquired by human art or industry; a man has it from God, or not at all.

8. *The unmarried and widows.* It is supposed that the apostle speaks here of men who had been married but were now widowers; as he does of women who had been married, in the word *widows.* And when he says *even as I,* he means that he himself was a widower; for several of the ancients rank Paul among the married apostles.

MATTHEW HENRY

IV. He sums up (*v.* 9, 10): Marriage, with all its inconveniences, is much better than to burn with impure and lustful desires.

Verses 10–16

The apostle gives them direction in a case which must have been frequent in that age of the world, whether they were to live with heathen relatives in a married state. Moses's law permitted divorce. This might move a scruple in many minds.

I. Marriage, by Christ's command, is for life. The wife *must not depart from the husband* (*v.* 10), nor the *husband put away his wife*, *v.* 11. The Lord himself had forbidden such separations, Matt. v. 32. They must not separate for any other cause than what Christ allows. Husbands and wives should not quarrel at all, or should be quickly reconciled. They are bound to each other for life. They cannot throw off the burden, and therefore should set their shoulders to it, and endeavour to make it as light to each other as they can.

II. The case of such as had an unbelieving mate (*v.* 12). It does not mean that the apostle decided this case by his own wisdom. He closes this subject with a declaration to the contrary (*v.* 40).

1. The advice itself, that if an unbelieving husband or wife were pleased to dwell with a Christian relative, the other should not separate, *v.* 12, 13. The Christian calling did not dissolve the marriage covenant, but bind it the faster. Yet, if the unbelieving relative desert the believer, in such *a case a brother or sister is not in bondage* (*v.* 15). In such a case the deserted person must be free to marry again. The apostle says (*v.* 11), *If the woman depart from her husband let her remain unmarried.*

2. The reasons of this advice. (1) The relation is sanctified by the holiness of either party (*v.* 14). The apostle tells them that, though they were yoked with unbelievers, yet, if they themselves were holy, marriage was to them a holy state. He is sanctified for the wife's sake. She is sanctified for the husband's sake. *Else were your children unclean, but now are they holy* (*v.* 14). The children born to Christians, though married to unbelievers, are not to be reckoned as part of the world, but of the church.

A. T. ROBERTSON:

14. "Is sanctified in the wife" (*hegiastai en tei gunaiki*). Perfect passive indicative of *hagiazo*, to set apart, to hallow, to sanctify. Paul does not, of course, mean that the unbelieving husband is saved by the faith of the believing wife, though Hodge actually so interprets him. Clearly he only means that the marriage relation is sanctified so that there is no need of a divorce. If either husband or wife is a believer and the other agrees to remain, the marriage is holy and need not be set aside. This is so simple that one wonders at the ability of men to get confused over Paul's language. "Else were your children unclean" (*epei ara ta tekna akatharta*). The common ellipse of the condition with *epei*: "since, accordingly, if it is otherwise, your children are illegitimate (*akatharta*)." If the relations of the parents be holy, the child's birth must be holy also (not illegitimate). "He is not assuming that the child of a Christian parent would be baptized; that would spoil rather than help his argument, for it would imply that the child was not *hagios* till it was baptized. The verse throws no light on the question of infant baptism" (Robertson and Plummer).

—Word Pictures in the New Testament

JAMIESON, FAUSSET, BROWN

9. if they cannot contain—i.e., "have not continency." **burn**—with the secret flame of lust, which lays waste the whole inner man. [Cf. AUGUSTINE, *de Sancta Virginitate*.] The dew of God's grace is needed to stifle the flame, which otherwise would thrust men at last into hell-fire. **10. not I, but the Lord**—(Cf. vss. 12, 25, 40). In ordinary cases he writes on *inspired apostolic authority* (ch. 14:37); but here on the *direct* authority of the *Lord Himself* (Mark 10:11, 12). In both cases alike the things written are inspired by the Spirit of God "but not all for all time, nor all on the primary truths of the faith" [ALFORD]. **Let not the wife depart**—lit., "be separated from." Probably the separation on either side, whether owing to the husband or to the wife, is forbidden. **11. But and if she depart**—or "be separated." If the sin of separation has been committed, that of a new marriage is not to be added (Matt. 5:32). **be reconciled**—by appeasing her husband's displeasure, and recovering his good will. **let not . . . husband put away . . . wife**—In Matthew 5:32 the only exception allowed is, "saving for the cause of fornication." **12. to the rest**—the other classes (besides "the married," vs. 10, where both husband and wife are believers) about whom the Corinthians had inquired, viz., those involved in mixed marriages with unbelievers. **not the Lord**—by any direct command spoken by Him. **she be pleased**—*Greek*, "consents": implying his wish in the first instance, with which hers *concurs*. **13. the woman**—a believer. **let her not leave him**—"her husband," instead of "him," is the reading of the oldest MSS. The *Greek* for "leave" is the same as in vs. 12, "put away"; translate, "Let her not *put away* [i.e., part with] her husband." The wife had the power of effecting a divorce by Greek and Roman law. **14. sanctified**—Those inseparably connected with the people of God are *hallowed* thereby, so that the latter may retain the connection without impairing their own sanctity (cf. I Tim. 4:5); nay, rather imparting to the former externally some degree of their own hallowed character, and so preparing the way for the unbeliever becoming at last sanctified inwardly by faith. **by . . . by**—rather, "in . . . in"; i.e., in virtue of the marriage tie between them. **by the husband**—The oldest MSS. read, "by the brother." It is the fact of the husband being a "brother," i.e., a *Christian*, though the wife is not so, that sanctifies or hallows the union. **else . . . children unclean**—i.e., beyond the hallowed pale of God's people: in contrast to "holy," i.e., all that is within the consecrated limits [CONYBEARE and HOWSON]. The phraseology accords with that of the Jews, who regarded the heathen as "unclean," and all of the elect nation as "holy," i.e., partakers of the holy covenant. Children were included in the covenant, as God made it not only with Abraham, but with his "seed after" him (Gen. 17:7). So the faith of one Christian parent gives to the children a near relationship to the Church, just as if both parents were Christians (cf. Rom. 11:16). Timothy, the bearer of this Epistle, is an instance in point (Acts 16:1). Paul appeals to the Corinthians as recognizing the principle, that the infants of heathen parents would not be admissible to Christian baptism, because there is no faith on the part of the parents; but where one parent is a believer, the children are regarded as not aliens from, but admissible even in infancy as sharers in, the Christian covenant: for the Church presumes that the believing parent will rear the child in the Christian faith. Infant baptism tacitly superseded infant circumcision, just as the Christian Lord's day gradually superseded the Jewish sabbath, without our having any express command for, or record of, transference. The setting aside of circumcision and of sabbaths in the case of the Gentiles was indeed expressly commanded by the apostles and Paul, but the substitution of infant baptism and of the Lord's day were tacitly adopted, not expressly enacted. No explicit mention of it occurs till Irenæus in the third century; but no society of Christians that we read of disputed its propriety till 1500 years after Christ. Anabaptists would have us defer baptism till maturity as the child cannot understand the nature of it. But a child may be made heir of an estate: it is *his*, though incapable at the time of using or comprehending its advantage; he is not hereafter *to acquire the title and claim* to it. he will hereafter understand his claim, and be capable of employing his wealth: he will then, moreover, become responsible for the use he makes of it [ARCHBISHOP, WHATELY]. **15. if . . . depart**—i.e., wishes for separation. Translate, "separateth himself": offended with her Christianity, and refusing to live with her unless she renounce it. **brother or**

ADAM CLARKE

9. *But if they cannot contain.* If they find it inconvenient and uncomfortable to continue as widowers and widows, let them remarry.

10. *I command, yet not I, but the Lord.* I do not give my own private opinion or judgment in this case; for the Lord Jesus commands that man shall not put asunder them whom God hath joined, Matt. v. 32; xix. 6. And God has said the same, Gen. ii. 24.

11. *But and if she depart.* He puts the case as probable, because it was frequent, but lays it under restrictions. *Let her remain unmarried.* She departs at her own peril, but she must not marry another; she must either continue unmarried or be reconciled to her husband. *And let not the husband put away his wife.* Divorces cannot be allowed but in the case of fornication. An act of this kind dissolves the marriage vow, but nothing else can.

12. *But to the rest speak I, not the Lord.* As if he had said: For what I have already spoken I have the testimony of the Lord by Moses, and of my own Lord and Master, Christ; but for the directions which I am now about to give there is no written testimony, and I deliver them now for the first time. These words do not intimate that the apostle was not now under the influences of the divine Spirit, but that there was nothing in the sacred writings which bore directly on this point. *If any brother,* a Christian man, *hath a wife that believeth not,* i.e., who is a heathen, not yet converted to the Christian faith, *and she be pleased to dwell with him,* notwithstanding his turning Christian since their marriage, *let him not put her away* because she still continues in her heathen superstition.

13. *And the woman,* converted from heathenism to the Christian faith, *which hath an husband,* who still abides in heathenism; *if he be pleased to dwell with her,* notwithstanding she has become a Christian since their marriage, *let her not leave him* because he still continues a heathen.

14. *The unbelieving husband is sanctified by the wife.* Or rather, is to be reputed as sanctified on account of his wife. She being a Christian woman and he, though a heathen, being by marriage one flesh with her, her sanctity, as far as it refers to outward things, may be considered as imputed to him so as to render their connection not unlawful. The case is the same when the wife is a heathen and the husband a Christian. The word sanctification here is to be applied much more to the Christian state than to any moral change in the persons, for "saints" is a common term for Christians. *Else were your children unclean.* If this kind of relative sanctification were not allowed, the children of these persons could not be received into the Christian Church, nor enjoy any rights or privileges as Christians; but the Church of God never scrupled to admit such children as members, just as well as she did those who had sprung from parents both of whom were Christians. The Jews considered a child as born "out of holiness" whose parents were not proselytes at the time of the birth, though afterwards they became proselytes. On the other hand, they considered the children of heathens born "in holiness" provided the parents became proselytes before the birth. All the children of the heathens were reputed unclean by the Jews, and all their own children holy. This shows clearly what the apostle's meaning is.

15. *But if the unbelieving depart.* Whether husband or wife, if such obstinately depart and utterly refuse all cohabitation, *a brother or a sister,* a Christian man or woman, *is not*

MATTHEW HENRY

(2) Another reason is that *God hath called Christians to peace, v.* 15.

(3) It is possible for the believing relative to be an instrument of the other's salvation (*v.* 16). Should a Christian desert a mate, when an opportunity offers to give the most glorious proof of love? Endeavour to save a soul. It is not impossible. *What know I but I may save his soul?* should move me to attempt it.

Verses 17–24

I. He lays down this rule in general—*as God hath distributed to everyone.* And again, *As the Lord hath called everyone, so let him walk.* In every state a man may live so as to be a credit to it. The apostle adds that this was a general rule, to be observed in all places: *So ordain I in all churches.*

II. He specifies particular cases: 1. That of circumcision. It matters not whether a man be a Jew or Gentile (*v.* 19). External observances without internal piety are as nothing. Therefore let every man abide *in the calling* (the state) *wherein he was called, v.* 20. 2. That of servitude and freedom. "Now," says the apostle, "*art thou called being a servant? Care not for it.* It is not inconsistent with thy duty, profession, or hopes, as a Christian. *Yet, if thou mayest be made free, use it rather," v.* 21. There are many conveniences in a state of freedom above that of servitude. But men's outward condition does neither hinder nor promote their acceptance with God. He who is a slave may yet be a Christian freeman; he who is a freeman may yet be Christ's servant. He must not be so the servant of men, that Christ's will is not obeyed, and regarded, more than his master's. The servants of Christ should be at the absolute command of no other master besides himself.

JAMIESON, FAUSSET, BROWN

a sister is not under bondage—is not bound to renounce the faith for the sake of retaining her unbelieving husband [HAMMOND]. So Deuteronomy 13:6; Matthew 10:35-37; Luke 14:26. **The believer does not lie under the same obligation in the case of a union with an unbeliever, as in the case of one with a believer. In the former case he is not bound not to separate, if the unbeliever separate or "depart," in the latter nothing but "fornication" justifies separation** [PHOTIUS in *Æcumenius*]. **but God hath called us to peace**—Our Christian calling is one that tends to "peace" (Rom. 12:18), not quarrelling; therefore the believer should not ordinarily depart from the unbelieving consort (vss. 12-14), on the one hand; and on the other, in the exceptional case of the unbeliever desiring to depart, the believer is not bound to force the other party to stay in a state of continual discord (Matt. 5:32). Better still it would be not to enter into such unequal alliances at all (vs. 40; II Cor. 6:14). **16. What knowest thou but that by staying with thy unbelieving partner thou mayest save him or her?** Enforcing the precept to stay with the unbelieving consort (vss. 12-14). So Ruth the Moabitess became a convert to her husband's faith: and Joseph and Moses probably gained over their wives. So conversely the unbelieving husband may be won by the believing wife (I Pet. 3:1) [CALVIN]. Or else (vs. 15), if thy unbelieving consort wishes to depart, let him go, so that thou mayest live "in peace": for *thou canst not be sure of converting him,* so as to make it obligatory on thee at all costs to stay with him against his will [MENOCHIUS and ALFORD]. **16. save**—be the instrument of salvation to (Jas. 5:20). **17. But**—*Greek,* "If not." "Only." Caution that believers should not make this direction (vs. 16; as ALFORD explains it) a ground for separating *of themselves* (vss. 12-14). Or, *But if* there be *no* hope of gaining over the unbeliever, still let the general principle be maintained, "As *the Lord* hath allotted to each, as *God* hath called each, so let him walk" (so the *Greek* in the oldest reading); let him walk in the path allotted to him and wherein he was called. The heavenly calling does not set aside our earthly callings. **so ordain I in all churches**—Ye also therefore should obey. **18. not become uncircumcised**—by surgical operation (I Maccabees 1:15; JOSEPHUS, *Antiquities,* 12. 5. 1). Some Christians in excess of anti-Jewish feeling might be tempted to this. **let him not be circumcised**—as the Judaizing Christians would have him (Acts 15; Gal. 5:2). **19. Circumcision . . . nothing, but . . . keeping of . . . commandments of God**—viz., is all in all. In Galatians 5:6 this "keeping of the commandments of God" is defined to be "faith which worketh by love"; and in Galatians 6:15, "a new creature." Circumcision was a commandment of God: but not for ever, as "love." **20. the same calling**—i.e., the *condition* from which he is called a Jew, a Greek, a slave, or a freeman. **21. care not for it**—Let it not be a trouble to thee that thou art a servant or slave. **use it rather**—Continue rather in thy state as a servant (vs. 20; Gal. 3:28; I Tim. 6:2). The *Greek,* "But if *even* thou mayest be made free, *use* it," and the context (vss. 20, 22) favors this view [CHRYSOSTOM, BENGEL, and ALFORD]. This advice (if this translation be right) is not absolute, as the spirit of the Gospel is against slavery. What is advised here is, contentment under one's existing condition (vs. 24), though an undesirable one, since in our union with Christ all outward disparities of condition are compensated (vs. 22). Be not unduly impatient to cast off "*even*" thy condition as a servant *by unlawful means* (I Pet. 2:13-18); as, e.g., Onesimus did by fleeing (Philemon 10-18). The precept (vs. 23), "Become not (so the *Greek*) the servants of men," implies plainly that slavery is abnormal (cf. Lev. 25:42). "Men stealers," or slave dealers, are classed in I Timothy 1:10, with "murderers" and "perjurers." NEANDER, GROTIUS, etc., explain, "If called, being a slave, to Christianity, be content—but yet, if *also* thou canst be free (as a still *additional* good, which if thou canst not attain, be satisfied without it; but which, if offered to thee, is not to be despised), *make use of the opportunity of becoming free, rather than* by neglecting it to remain a slave." I prefer this latter view, as more according to the tenor of the Gospel, and fully justified by the *Greek.* **22. the Lord's freeman**—(Philemon 16)—rather, "freedman." Though a slave externally, spiritually *made free* by the Lord: from sin, John 8:36; from the law, Romans 8:2; from "circumcision," vs. 19; Galatians 5:1. **Christ's servant**—(ch. 9:21). Love makes Christ's service perfect freedom (Matt. 11:29,30; Gal. 5:13; I Peter 2:16). **23. be not ye**—*Greek,* "become not ye." Paul here changes from "thou" (vs. 21) to "ye."

ADAM CLARKE

under bondage to any particular laws, so as to be prevented from remarrying. Such, probably, the law stood then; but it is not so now, for the marriage can be dissolved only by death or by the ecclesiastical court. *God hath called us to peace.* The refractory and disagreeing party should not be compelled to fulfill such matrimonial engagements as would produce continual jarring and discord. At the same time each should take care that he give no cause for disagreements and separations, for the Author of the Christian religion is the Author of *peace,* and has *called* us to it.

16. *For what knowest thou, O wife?* You that are Christians, and who have heathen partners, do not give them up because they are such, for you may become the means of saving them unto eternal life. Bear your cross and look up to God, and He may give your unbelieving husband or wife to your prayers.

17. *But as God hath distributed to every man.* Let every man fulfill the duties of the state to which God in the course of His providence has called him. *So ordain I in all churches.* I do not lay on you a burden which others are not called to bear; this is the general rule which, by the authority of God, I impose on every Christian society.

18. *Is any man called being circumcised?* Is any man who was formerly a Jew converted to Christianity? *Let him not become uncircumcised.* Let him not endeavor to abolish the sign of the old covenant, which he bears in his flesh. *Let him not be circumcised.* Let no man who, being a Gentile, has been converted to the Christian faith submit to circumcision as something necessary to his salvation.

19. *Circumcision is nothing.* Circumcision itself, though commanded of God, is nothing of itself, it being only a sign of the justification which should be afterwards received by faith. At present, neither it nor its opposite either hinders or furthers the work of grace; and *keeping* the commandments of God, from His love shed abroad in a believing heart, is the sum and substance of religion.

20. *Let every man abide in the same calling.* As both the circumcised and uncircumcised, in Christ, have the same advantages, and to their believing the same facilities, so any situation of life is equally friendly to the salvation of the soul, if a man be faithful to the grace he has received. Therefore in all situations a Christian should be content, for all things work together for good to him who loves God.

21. *Art thou called being a servant?* Are you converted to Christ while you are a "slave"—the property of another person, and bought with his money? *Care not for it*—this will not injure your Christian condition. But if you can obtain your liberty, *use it rather,* prefer this state for the sake of freedom, and the temporal advantages connected with it.

22. *For he that is called.* The man who, being a "slave," is converted to the Christian faith is the Lord's freeman; his condition as a slave does not vitiate any of the privileges to which he is entitled as a Christian. On the other hand, all free men who receive the grace of Christ must consider themselves the "slaves of the Lord," i.e., His real property, to be employed and disposed of according to His godly wisdom, who, notwithstanding their state of subjection, will find the service of their Master to be perfect freedom.

MATTHEW HENRY

III. He sums up his advice (*v.* 24). He should quietly abide in the condition in which he is; and this he may well do, when he may abide therein with God. The presence and favour of God are not limited to any outward condition. He who is bound may have it as well as he who is free. The favour of God is not bound.

Verses 25–35

The apostle here gives directions to virgins how to act.

I. The manner wherein he introduces them, *v.* 25. Though Christ had before delivered no universal law about that matter, he now gives direction by an inspired apostle.

III. He is very careful to satisfy them that he does not condemn marriage, nor declare it unlawful. Though he says, "If thou *art loosed from a wife do not seek a wife,*" yet he adds, "*If thou art bound to a wife, do not seek to be loosed.* It is thy duty to continue in the married relation." Duty must be done, and God trusted with events. Marrying is not in itself a sin, but marrying at that time was likely to add to the calamities of the times.

JAMIESON, FAUSSET, BROWN

YE ALL are "bought" with the blood of Christ, whatever be your earthly state (ch. 6:20). "Become not servants to men," either externally, or spiritually; the former sense applying to the free alone: the latter to Christian freemen and slaves alike, that they should not be servile adherents to their party leaders at Corinth (ch. 3:21, 22; Matt. 23:8-10; II Cor. 11:20); nor indeed slaves to men generally, so far as their condition admits. The external and internal conditions, so far as is attainable, should correspond, and the former be subservient to the latter (cf. vss. 21, 32-35). **24. abide with God**—being chiefly careful of the footing on which he stands towards God rather than that towards men. This clause, "with God," limits the similar precept in vs. 20. A man may cease to "abide in the calling wherein he was called," and yet not violate the precept here. If a man's calling be not favorable to his "abiding with God" (retaining holy fellowship with Him), he may use lawful means to change from it (cf. *Note,* vs. 21).

25. no commandment of the Lord: yet . . . my judgment—I have no *express revelation* from the Lord *commanding* it, but I give my *judgment* (opinion); viz., under the ordinary inspiration which accompanied the apostles in all their canonical writings (cf. vs. 40; ch. 14:37; I Thess. 4:15). The Lord inspires me in this case to give you only a *recommendation,* which you are free to adopt or reject—not a positive *command.* In the second case (vss. 10, 11) it was a positive command; for the Lord had already made known His will (Mal. 2: 14, 15; Matt. 5:31, 32). In the third case (vs. 12), the Old Testament commandment of God to put away strange wives (Ezra 10:3), Paul by the Spirit revokes. **mercy of the Lord**—(I Tim. 1:13). He attributes his apostleship and the gifts accompanying it (including inspiration) to God's grace alone. **faithful**—in dispensing to you the inspired directions received by me from the Lord. **26. I suppose**—"I consider." **this**—viz., "for a man so to be," i.e., in the same state in which he is (vs. 27). **for**—by reason of. **the present distress**—the distresses to which believers were then beginning to be subjected, making the married state less desirable than the single; and which would prevail throughout the world before the destruction of Jerusalem, according to Christ's prophecy (Matt. 24:8-21; cf. Acts 11:28).

27. Illustrating the meaning of "so to be," vs. 26. Neither the married (those "bound to a wife") nor the unmarried (those "loosed from a wife") are to "seek" a change of state (cf. vss. 20, 24).

28. trouble in the flesh—Those who marry, he says, shall incur "trouble in the flesh" (i.e., in their outward state, by reason of the present distress), not *sin,* which is the trouble of the *spirit.* **but I spare you**—The emphasis in the *Greek* is on "I." *My* motive in advising you so is, to "spare you" such trouble in the flesh. So ALFORD after CALVIN, BENGEL, and others. ESTIUS from AUGUSTINE explains it, "I spare you further details of the inconveniences of matrimony, lest even the incontinent may at the peril of lust be deterred from matrimony: thus I have regard for your infirmity." The antithesis in the *Greek* of "I . . . you" and "such" favors the former. **29. this I say**—A summing up of the whole, wherein he draws the practical inference from what precedes (ch. 15:50). **the time**—the *season* (so the *Greek*) of this present dispensation up to the coming of the Lord (Rom.

ADAM CLARKE

23. *Ye are bought with a price.* As truly as your bodies have become the property of your masters, in consequence of their paying down a price for you, so sure you are now the Lord's property, in consequence of your being purchased by the blood of Christ. Some render this verse interrogatively: "Are you bought with a price" from your slavery? "Do not again become slaves of men." Never sell yourselves; prefer and retain your liberty now that ye have acquired it.

24. *Let every man . . . abide with God.* Let him live to God in whatever station he is placed by Providence. If he be a slave, God will be with him even in his slavery, if he be faithful to the grace which he has received. It is very likely that some of the slaves at Corinth, who had been converted to Christianity, had been led to think that their Christian privileges absolved them from the necessity of continuing slaves or, at least, brought them on a level with their Christian masters. A spirit of this kind might have soon led to confusion and insubordination, and brought scandals into the church. It was therefore a very proper subject for the apostle to interfere in; and to his authority the persons concerned would doubtless respectfully bow.

25. *Now concerning virgins.* This was another subject on which the church at Corinth had asked the advice of the apostle. The word virgin we take to signify a "pure, unmarried young woman"; but it is evident that the word in this place means young unmarried persons of either sex, as appears from vv. 26-27, 32-34, and from Rev. xiv. 4. The word is frequently applied to men as well as to women. *I have no commandment of the Lord.* There is no thing in the sacred writings that directly touches this point. *Yet I give my judgment.* As every way equal to such commandments had there been any, seeing I have received the teaching of His own Spirit, and have obtained *mercy of the Lord to be faithful* to this heavenly gift, so that it abides with me to lead me into all truth. In this way I think the apostle's words may be safely understood.

26. *This is good for the present distress.* The word signifies "necessity, distress, tribulation, and calamity," as it does in Luke xxi. 23; 2 Cor. vi. 4; and xii. 10. In such times, when the people of God had no certain dwelling place, when they were lying at the mercy of their enemies without any protection from the state—the state itself often among the persecutors—he who had a family to care for would find himself in very embarrassed circumstances, as it would be much more easy to provide for his personal safety than to have the care of a wife and children. On this account it was much better for unmarried persons to continue for the present in their celibacy.

27. *Art thou bound unto a wife?* I.e., married; for the marriage contract was considered in the light of a bond. *Seek not to be loosed.* Neither regret your circumstances, notwithstanding the present distress, nor seek on this account for a dissolution of the marriage contract. But if you are under no matrimonial engagements, do not for the present enter into any.

28. *But and if thou marry.* As there is no law against this, even in the present distress, you have not sinned, because there is no law against this; and it is only on account of prudential reasons that I give this advice. *And if a virgin marry.* Both the man and the woman have equal privileges in this case; either of them may marry without sin. It is probable, as there were many sects and parties in Corinth, that there were among them those who forbade to marry, 1 Tim. iv. 3. *Trouble in the flesh.* From the simple circumstance of the incumbrance of a family while under persecution, because of the difficulty of providing for its comfort and safety while flying before the face of persecution. *But I spare you.* The evil is coming, but I will not press upon you the observance of a prudential caution which you might deem too heavy a cross.

29. *The time is short.* These persecutions and distresses are at the door, and life itself will soon be run out. Even then Nero was plotting those grievous persecutions with which he not only afflicted but devastated the Church of Christ.

MATTHEW HENRY

IV. General rules to all Christians to carry themselves with a holy indifference towards the world. Those *that had wives must be as though they had none.* They know not how soon they shall have none. Those that have children should be as though they had none. Those that are their comfort now may prove their greatest cross. *Those that weep must be as though they wept not.* Even in sorrow the heart may be joyful, and the end of our grief may be gladness. *Those that rejoice should be as though they rejoiced not.* Here is not their rest, nor are these things their portion. *Those that buy must be as though they possessed not.* Buying and possessing should not too much engage our minds. They hinder many people altogether from minding the better part. *Those that use this world as not abusing it, v.* 31. The world may be used, but must not be abused. It is abused when, instead of being oil to the wheels of our obedience, it is made fuel to lust. We must keep the world out of our hearts, that we may not abuse it when we have it in our hands.

V. Two reasons, *v.* 29. We have but little time to continue in this world. Therefore do not set your hearts on worldly enjoyments. Do not be overwhelmed with worldly cares and troubles (*v.* 31). It is not so much a world as the appearance of one. All is show with nothing solid in it; and it is transient show too, and will quickly be gone.

VI. The embarrassment of worldly cares, *v.* 32. A wise concern about worldly interests is a duty; but to be careful, full of care, is a sin.

II. A state of celibacy was preferable. It is worded with modesty, but delivered with apostolical authority. Ministers do not lose their authority by prudent condescensions. The married state would bring more care and cumber along with it (*v.* 33, 34), and would therefore make persecution more terrible.

God must *be attended upon without distraction, v.* 35. But how is this possible when the mind is swallowed up of the cares of this life? This is the general maxim by which the apostle would have Christians govern themselves. In the application of it Christian prudence must direct. The unmarried man and woman mind the things of the Lord, that they may please the Lord, and be holy both in body and spirit, *v.* 32, 34. Not but the married person may be holy both in body and spirit too. It is the constant care of those in that relation to please each other. At that season, therefore, the apostle advises that those who were single should abstain from marriage. And the very same rule must determine persons for marriage, if in the unmarried state persons are likely to be more distracted in the service of God than if they were married. That condition of life should be chosen by the Christian in which it is most likely he will have the best helps, and the fewest hindrances, in the service of God.

Verses 36–38

Advice about the disposal of children in marriage. It was in that age reckoned a disgrace for a woman to remain unmarried past a certain number of years. "Now," says the apostle, "if any man thinks he behaves unhandsomely towards his daughter, he may use his pleasure. It is no sin in him to dispose of her to a suitable mate. But if a man has deter-

JAMIESON, FAUSSET, BROWN

13:11). He uses the *Greek* expression which the Lord used in Luke 21:8; Mark 13:33. **short**—lit., "contracted." **it remaineth**—The oldest MSS. read, "The time (season) is shortened *as to what remains,* in order that both they . . ."; i.e., the effect which the shortening of the time ought to have is, "that for the remaining time (henceforth), both they . . ." The clause, "as to what remains," though in *construction* belonging to the previous clause, in *sense* belongs to the following. However, CYPRIAN and *Vulgate* support *English Version.* **as though they had none**—We ought to consider nothing as our own in real or permanent possession. **30. they that weep . . . wept not**—(Cf. II Cor. 6:10). **they that buy . . . possessed not**—(Cf. Isa. 24:1, 2). Christ specifies as the condemning sin of the men of Sodom not merely their open profligacy, but that "they bought, they sold," etc., as men whose all was in this world (Luke 17:28). "Possessed" in the *Greek* implies a *holding fast of a possession;* this the Christian will not do, for his "enduring substance" is elsewhere (Heb. 10:34). **31. not abusing it**—not abusing it by an *overmuch using* of it. The meaning of "abusing" here is, not so much *perverting,* as *using it to the full* [BENGEL]. We are to use it, not to *take our fill* of its pursuits as our chief aim (cf. Luke 10:40-42). As the planets while turning on their own axis, yet revolve round the sun; so while we do our part in our own worldly sphere, God is to be the center of all our desires. **fashion**—the present fleeting *form.* Cf. Psalm 39:6, "vain show"; Psalm 73:20, "a dream"; James 4:14, "a vapor." **passeth away**—not merely *shall pass away,* but *is* now actually *passing away.* The image is drawn from a *shifting* scene in a play represented on the stage (I John 2:17). Paul inculcates not so much the outward denial of earthly things, as the inward spirit whereby the married and the rich, as well as the unmarried and the poor, would be ready to sacrifice all for Christ's sake. **32. without carefulness**—I would have you to be not merely "without trouble," but "without distracting cares" (so the *Greek*). **careth**—if he uses aright the advantages of his condition.

34. difference also—Not merely the unmarried and the married *man* differ in their respective duties, but *also* the *wife* and the *virgin.* Indeed a woman undergoes a greater change of condition than a man in contracting marriage.

35. for your own profit—not to display *my* apostolic authority. **not . . . cast a snare upon you**—image from *throwing a noose* over an animal in hunting. Not that by hard injunctions I may entangle you with the fear of committing sin where there is no sin. **comely**—*befitting* under present circumstances. **attend upon**—lit., "assiduously wait on"; *sitting down* to the duty. Cf. Luke 10:39, Mary; Luke 2:37, "Anna . . . a widow, who departed not from the temple, but served God with fastings and prayers night and day" (I Tim. 5:5). **distraction**—the same *Greek* as "cumbered" (Luke 10:40, Martha).

behaveth . . . uncomely—is not treating his daughter well in leaving her unmarried beyond the flower of her age, and thus debarring her from the lawful gratification of her natural feeling as a marriageable woman. **need so require**—if the exigencies of the case require it; viz., regard to the feelings and welfare of his daughter. Opposed to "having no ne-

ADAM CLARKE

They that have wives. Let none begin to think of any comfortable settlement for his family; let him sit loose to all earthly concerns, and stand ready prepared to escape for his life or meet death, as the providence of God may permit. The husband will be dragged from the side of his wife to appear before the magistrates and be required to either abjure Christ or die.

30. *They that weep.* There will shortly be such a complete system of distress and confusion that private sorrows and private joys will be absorbed in the weightier and more oppressive public evils. Yet let every man still continue in his calling; let him buy and sell and traffic as usual, though in a short time, either by the coming persecution or by the levelling hand of death, he that had earthly property will be brought into the same circumstances with him who had none.

31. *And they that use this world.* Let them who have earthly property or employments discharge conscientiously their duties, from a conviction of the instability of earthly things. Make a right use of everything, and pervert nothing from its *use.* To *use* a thing is to employ it properly in order to accomplish the end to which it refers. To *abuse* a thing signifies to pervert it from that use. Pass through things temporal so as not to lose those which are eternal. *For the fashion of this world.* The present state or constitution of things; the frame of the world, that is, the world itself. But often the term *world* is taken to signify the Jewish state and polity; the destruction of this was then at hand, and this the Holy Spirit might then signify to the apostle.

32. *Without carefulness.* Though all these things will shortly come to pass, yet do not be anxious about them. *He that is unmarried careth for the things that belong to the Lord.* He has nothing to do with a family, and therefore can give his whole time to the service of his Maker, having Him alone to please.

33. *But he that is married.* He has a family to provide for, and his wife to please, as well as to fulfill his duty to God and attend to the concerns of his own soul. The single man has nothing to attend to but what concerns his own salvation; the married man has all this to attend to, and besides to provide for his wife and family, and take care of their eternal interests also.

34. *There is a difference also between a wife and a virgin.* That is: There is this difference between a married and an unmarried woman. *The unmarried . . . careth* (only) *for the things of the Lord,* having no domestic duties to perform. *That she may be holy*—separated to divine employments, *both in body and in spirit.* Whereas *she that is married careth* (also) *for the things of the world, how she may please her husband,* having many domestic duties to fulfill, her husband being obliged to leave to her the care of the family and all other domestic concerns.

35. *This I speak for your own profit.* The advices belong to yourselves alone, because of the peculiar circumstances in which you are placed. Nothing spoken here was ever designed to be of general application; it concerned the church at Corinth alone, or churches in similar circumstances. *Not that I may cast a snare upon you.* Here is a manifest allusion to the retiarius among the Romans, who carried a small casting net, which he endeavored to throw over the head of his adversary and thus entangle him; or to a similar custom among the Persians, who made use of a noose called the *camand,* which they employed in the same way. The apostle therefore intimates that what he says was not intended absolutely to bind them, but to show them the propriety of following an advice which in the present case would be helpful to them in their religious connections, that they might *attend upon the Lord without distraction,* which they could not do in times of persecution, when, in addition to their own personal safety, they had a wife and children to care for.

36. *Uncomely towards his virgin.* Different meanings have been assigned to this verse. I shall mention three of the principal. (1) "In those early times, both among the Hebrews and Christians, the daughters were wholly in the power of the father, so that he might give or not give them in marriage as he chose; and might

MATTHEW HENRY

mined in himself to keep her a virgin with her consent, he does well."

ALBERT BARNES:

37. "Nevertheless." But. The apostle in this verse states some instances where it would not be proper to give a daughter in marriage. The verse is a kind of summing up of all that he had said on the subject.

"That standeth steadfast in his heart." Most commentators have understood this of the father of the virgin, and suppose that it refers to his purpose of keeping her from the marriage connection. The phrase to stand steadfast is opposed to a disposition that is vacillating, unsettled, and denotes a man who has command of himself, who adheres to his purpose, a man who has hitherto adhered to his purpose, and to whose happiness and reputation it is important that he should be known as one who is not vacillating or easily moved.

"Having no necessity." Where there is nothing in *her* disposition or inclination that would make marriage necessary, or when there is no engagement or obligation that would be violated if she did not marry. "But hath power over his own will." Hath power to do as he pleases; is not bound in the case by another. When there is no engagement, or contract, made in childhood, or promise made in early life that would bind him. Often daughters were espoused or promised when they were very young, and in such a case a man would be bound to adhere to his engagement; and much as he might desire the reverse, and her celibacy, yet he would not have power over his own will or be at liberty to withhold her. "And hath so decreed in his heart." Has so judged, determined, resolved. "That he will keep his virgin." His daughter in an unmarried state. He has power and authority to do it, and if he does it he will not sin. "Doeth well." In either of these cases, he does well. If he has a daughter and chooses to retain her in an unmarried state, he does well or right.

—*Popular Commentary*

Verses 39, 40

Advice to widows. Death only can annul the bond. Second marriages are not unlawful. She has such a liberty only with a limitation that *she marry in the Lord, v.* 40. It will be much more for the peace and quiet of such, and give them less hindrance in the service of God, to continue unmarried.

JAMIESON, FAUSSET, BROWN

cessity" (vs. 37). **let them marry**—the daughter and her suitor. **37. steadfast**—not to be turned from his purpose by the obloquy of the world. **having no necessity**—arising from the natural inclinations of the daughter. **power over his . . . will**—when, owing to his daughter's will not opposing his will, he has power to carry into effect his will or wish. **decreed**—determined.

38. *her*—The oldest MSS. have "his own virgin daughter." **but**—The oldest MSS. have "and."

39. bound by the law—The oldest MSS. omit "by the law." **only in the Lord**—Let her marry *only a Christian* (II Cor. 6:14).

40. happier—(vss. 1, 28, 34, 35). **I think also**—"I also think"; just as you Corinthians and your teachers *think* much of your opinions, *so I also give my opinion* by inspiration; so in vs. 25, "my judgment" or opinion. *Think* does not imply doubt, but often a matter of well-grounded assurance (John 5:39).

ADAM CLARKE

bind them to perpetual celibacy if he thought proper; and to this case the apostle alludes. If the father had devoted his daughter to perpetual virginity, and he afterwards found that she had fixed her affections upon a person whom she was strongly inclined to marry, and was now getting past the prime of life; he, seeing from his daughter's circumstances that it would be wrong to force her to continue in her state of celibacy, though he had determined before to keep her single, yet he might in this case alter his purpose without sin, and let her and her suitor marry." (2) "The whole verse and its context speaks of young women dedicated to the service of God, who were called *virgins* in the primitive Church. And a case is put here, 'that circumstances might occur to render the breach of even a vow of this kind necessary, and so no sin be committed.'" (3) "The apostle does not mean a virgin, but the 'state of virginity' or celibacy, whether in man or woman." This last opinion seems to be the true sense of the apostle.

38. *Instead of he that giveth her in marriage,* I purpose to read "he who marrieth," which is the reading of the Codex Alexandrinus, the Codex Vaticanus, and of some others. *His own virgin* is added after the above by several very ancient and reputable MSS., but it seems so much like a gloss that Griesbach has not made it even a candidate for a place in the text. "He then who marrieth," though previously intending perpetual virginity, doeth well, as this is agreeable to laws both divine and human; and he "who marrieth not," *doeth better,* because of the present distress.

39. *The wife is bound by the law.* This seems to be spoken in answer to some other question of the Corinthians to this effect: "May a woman remarry whose husband is dead, or who has abandoned her?" To which he replies, in general, that as long as her husband is living the law binds her to him alone; but, if the husband die, she is free to remarry, but *only in the Lord.* That is, she must not marry a heathen nor an irreligious man; and she should not only marry a genuine Christian, but one of her own religious sentiments; for, in reference to domestic peace, much depends on this.

40. *But she is happier if she so abide.* If she continue in her widowhood because of the present distress. *After my judgment.* According to the view I have of the subject, which view I take by the light of the divine Spirit, who shows me the tribulations which are coming on the Church. *I think . . . I have the Spirit of God.* Might be translated, "I am certain that I have the Spirit of God." Ulpian, on Demosthen., *Olynth.* 1, says, "The word *dokein* is used by the ancients, not always to express what is doubtful, but often to express what is true and certain." The apostle cannot be understood as expressing any doubt of his being under the inspiration of the divine Spirit, as this would have defeated his object in giving the above advices; for if they were not dictated by the Spirit of God, can it be supposed that, in the face of apparent self-interest and the prevalence of strong passions, they could have been expected to have become rules of conduct to this people? They must have understood him as asserting that he had the direction of the Spirit of God in giving those opinions, else they could not be expected to obey.

MATTHEW HENRY — CHAPTER 8

Verses 1-3

Things that had been offered to idols. It was a custom among the heathens to make feasts of their sacrifices. These were usually kept in the temple, where the sacrifice was offered (*v.* 10). What remained, after all, belonged to the priests, who sometimes sold it in the markets. See *ch.* x. 25. It was accounted a very profane thing among them to eat at their private tables any meat whereof they had not first sacrificed. What should Christians do if anything that had been sacrificed should be set before them? What, if they should be invited to feast with them in their temples?

JAMIESON, FAUSSET, BROWN — CHAPTER 8

VSS. 1-13. ON PARTAKING OF MEATS OFFERED TO IDOLS. **1.** Though to those knowing that an idol has no existence, the question of eating meats offered to idols (referred to in the letter of the Corinthians, cf. ch. 7:1) might seem unimportant, it is not so with some, and the infirmities of such should be respected. The portions of the victims not offered on the altars belonged partly to the priests, partly to the offerers; and were eaten at feasts in the temples and in private houses and were often sold in the markets; so that Christians were constantly exposed to the temptation of receiving them, which was forbidden (Num. 25:2; Ps. 106:28). The apostles forbade it in their decree issued from Jerusalem (Acts 15, and 21:25); but Paul does not allude here to that decree, as he rests his precepts rather on his own independent apostolic authority. **we know**

ADAM CLARKE — CHAPTER 8

1. *As touching things offered unto idols.* This was another subject on which the Corinthians had asked the apostle's advice.

MATTHEW HENRY

The Corinthians had an opinion that even this might be done, because they knew an idol was nothing in the world, *v.* 4. Paul says, "We who abstain know as much of the vanity of idols, and that they are nothing. *Knowledge puffeth up, but charity edifieth*," *v.* 1. The preference of charity to conceited knowledge. There is no evidence of ignorance more common than a conceit of knowledge. He that knows most best understands his own ignorance. He that imagines himself a knowing man has reason to suspect that he knows nothing aright. Much may be known when nothing is known to any good purpose.

But, adds the apostle, *if any man love God, the same is known* of God. He shall be approved of God; he will accept him and have pleasure in him. The charitable person is most likely to have God's favour. How much better is it to be approved of God than to have a vain opinion of ourselves!

Verses 4–6

The vanity of idols. Heathen idols have no divinity in them. They are merely imaginary gods. The gods of the heathen have nothing of real godhead belonging to them; for there is no other God but one. We Christians well know there is but one God. All things are of him, and we, and all things else, are for him. It is the great privilege of us Christians that we know the true God, and true Mediator between God and man.

Verses 7–13

Their inference was not just, namely, that therefore they might go into the idol-temple and feast there with their heathen neighbours. He does not so much insist upon the unlawfulness as the mischief such freedom might do to weaker Christians.

I. Every Christian man, at that time, was not so fully convinced that an idol was nothing. Weak Christians may be ignorant, or have but a confused knowledge of the greatest and plainest truths. *So their conscience, being weak, was defiled.* They were weak in their understanding, and, while they ate what was sacrificed contracted the guilt of idolatry and so greatly polluted themselves. We should be careful to do nothing that may occasion weak Christians to defile their consciences.

JAMIESON, FAUSSET, BROWN

that we all have knowledge—The Corinthians doubtless had referred to their "knowledge" (viz., of the indifference of meats, as in themselves having no sanctity or pollution). Paul replies, "We are aware that we all have [speaking *generally*, and so far as Christian *theory* goes; for in vs. 7 he speaks of some who *practically* have *not*] this knowledge." **Knowledge puffeth up**—when without "love." Here a parenthesis begins; and the main subject is resumed in the same words, vs. 4. "As concerning [touching] therefore the eating . . . ." "Puffing up" is to please self. "Edifying" is to please one's neighbor. Knowledge only says, All things are lawful for me; Love adds, But all things do not edify [BENGEL], (ch. 10:23; Rom. 14:15). **edifieth**—tends to *build up* the spiritual temple (ch. 3:9; 6:19). **2. And**—omitted in the oldest MSS. The absence of the connecting particle gives an emphatical sententiousness to the style, suitable to the subject. The first step to knowledge is to know our own ignorance. Without love there is only the *appearance* of knowledge. **knoweth**—The oldest MSS. read a *Greek* word implying *personal experimental acquaintance*, not merely *knowledge of a fact*, which the *Greek* of "we know" or *are aware* (vs. 1) means. **as he ought to know**—experimentally and in the way of "love." **3. love God**—the source of love to our neighbor (I John 4:11, 12, 20; 5:2). **the same**—lit., "this man"; he who loves, not he who "thinks that he knows," not having "charity" or love (vss. 1, 2). **is known of him**—is known with the knowledge of approval and is acknowledged by God as His (Ps. 1:6; Gal. 4:9; II Tim. 2:19). Contrast, "I never knew you" (Matt. 7:23). To love God is to know God; and he who thus knows God has been first known by God (cf. ch. 13:12; I Pet. 1:2). **4. As concerning . . .**—resuming the subject begun in vs. 1, "As touching . . . ." **idol is nothing**—has no true being at all, the god it represents is not a living reality. This does not contradict ch. 10:20, which states that they who worship idols, worship *devils;* for here it is the GODS *believed by the worshippers to be represented by the idols* which are denied to have any existence, not the devils which really under the idols delude the worshippers. **none other God**—The oldest MSS. omit the word "other"; which gives a clearer sense. **5.** "For even supposing there are (exist) gods so called (II Thess. 2:4), whether in heaven (as the sun, moon, and stars) or in earth (as deified kings, beasts, etc.), as there be (a recognized fact, Deut. 10:17; Ps. 135: 5; 136:2) gods many and lords many." Angels and men in authority are termed *gods* in Scripture, as exercising a divinely delegated power under God (cf. Exod. 22:9, with vs. 28; Ps. 82:1, 6; John 10:34, 35). **6. to us**—believers. **of whom**—from whom as Creator all things derive their existence. **we in him**—rather "we *for* Him," or "*unto* Him." God the FATHER is the end *for* whom and for whose glory believers live. In Colossians 1:16 all things are said to be created (not only "*by*" Christ, but also) "*for* Him" (CHRIST). *So entirely are the Father and Son one* (cf. Rom. 11: 36; Heb. 2:10). **one Lord**—contrasted with the **"many lords" of heathendom (vs. 5). by whom**—(John 1:3; Heb. 1:2). **we by him**—as all things are "*of*" the Father by creation, so they (we believers especially) are restored *to* Him by the new creation (Col. 1:20; Rev. 21:5). Also, as all things are *by* Christ by creation, so they (we especially) are restored *by* Him by the new creation. **7. Howbeit**—Though to us who "have knowledge" (vss. 1, 4-6) all meats are indifferent, yet "this knowledge is not in all" in the same degree as we have it. Paul had admitted to the Corinthians that "we all have knowledge" (vs. 1), i.e., so far as Christian *theory* goes; but *practically* some have it not in the same degree. **with conscience**—an ancient reading; but other very old MSS. read "association" or "habit." In either reading the meaning is: Some Gentile Christians, whether from old *association* of ideas or misdirected *conscience*, when they ate such meats, ate them with some feeling as if the idol were something real (vs. 4), and had changed the meats by the fact of the consecration into something either holy or else polluted. **unto this hour**—after they have embraced Christianity; an implied censure, that they are not further advanced by this time in Christian "knowledge." **their conscience . . . is defiled**—by their eating it "as a thing offered to idols." If they ate it unconscious at the time that it had been offered to idols, there would be no defilement of conscience. But conscious of what it was, and not having such knowledge as other Corinthians boasted of, viz., that an idol is nothing and can therefore neither pollute nor sanctify meats, they by eating them sin against conscience (cf. Rom. 14:15-23). It was on the ground of Christian ex-

ADAM CLARKE

We know that we all have knowledge. I am inclined to think that these are not Paul's words, but a quotation from the letter of the Corinthians to him, and a proof of what the apostle says below, *Knowledge puffeth up. Knowledge puffeth up, but charity edifieth.* This knowledge is very nearly allied to pride; it *puffeth up* the mind with vain conceit, makes those who have it bold and rash, and renders them careless of the consciences of others.

2. *He knoweth nothing yet.* The person who acts in this rash, unfeeling way, from the general knowledge which he has of the vanity of idolatry and the liberty which the gospel affords from Jewish rites, with all his knowledge does not know this, that though the first and greatest commandment says, "Thou shalt love the Lord thy God with all thy heart," yet the second is like unto it: "Thou shalt love thy neighbour as thyself." He then that can torment his neighbors' weak or tender conscience with his food or his conduct does not love him as himself, and therefore knows nothing as he ought to know.

3. *But if any man love God,* in that way which the commandment requires, which will necessarily beget love to his neighbor, *the same is known of him,* is approved of God, and acknowledged as His genuine follower.

5. *There be that are called gods.* There are many images that are supposed to be representations of divinities. But these divinities are nothing, the figments of mere fancy; and these images have no corresponding realities. *Whether in heaven or in earth.* As the sun, moon, planets, stars, the ocean, rivers, trees, etc. And thus there are, nominally, *gods many, and lords many.*

6. *But to us there is but one God, the Father.* Who produced all things, himself uncreated and unoriginated. *And we in him,* "and we for Him," all intelligent beings having been created for the purpose of manifesting His glory by receiving and reflecting His wisdom, goodness, and truth. *And one Lord Jesus.* Only one visible Governor of the world and the Church. *By whom are all things.* Who was the Creator, as He is the Upholder, of the universe. *And we by him,* being brought to the knowledge of the true God by the revelation of Jesus Christ; for it is the only begotten Son alone that can reveal the Father. The "gods" of whom the apostle speaks were their divinities, or objects of religious worship; the "lords" were the rulers of the world, such as emperors, who were considered next to gods, and some of them were deified. In opposition to those "gods" he places *God, the Father,* the Fountain of plenitude and being; and in opposition to the "lords" he places *Jesus Christ,* who made and who governs all things.

7. *There is not in every man that knowledge.* This is spoken in reference to what is said, v. 4: "We know that an idol is nothing in the world." *For some with a conscience of the idol,* viz., that it is something, *eat it*—the flesh that was offered to the idol—as a thing thus offered, considering the feast as a sacred banquet by which they have fellowship with the idol. *And their conscience being weak,* not properly instructed in divine things, *is defiled*—he performs what he does as an act of religious worship, and thus his conscience contracts guilt through this idolatry.

MATTHEW HENRY

II. He tells them that mere eating and drinking had nothing in them virtuous nor criminal, *v.* 8. Some of the Corinthians made a merit of their eating what had been offered to idols, and that in their very temples too (*v.* 10), because it plainly showed that they thought the idols nothing. Eating this food, and forbearing that, have nothing in them to recommend a person to God.

III. He cautions them against abusing their liberty. Even upon the supposition that they had such power, they must be cautious how they use it; it might be a *stumbling-block to the weak* (*v.* 9).

We must deny ourselves rather than occasion their stumbling, and endanger their souls (*v.* 11): *Through thy knowledge shall thy weak brother perish, for whom Christ died?* If he had such compassion as to die for them, we should have so much compassion for them as to deny ourselves, for their sakes. That man has very little of the spirit of the Redeemer who had rather his brother should perish than himself be abridged of his liberty.

The hurt done to them Christ takes as done to himself, *v.* 12. Injuries done to Christians are injuries to Christ. Shall we be void of compassion for those to whom Christ has shown so much? Shall we sin against Christ who suffered for us?

IV. His own example (*v.* 13). We must not rigorously claim our own rights, to the hurt and ruin of a brother's soul, and so to the injury of our Redeemer, who died for him. And, if we must be so careful not to occasion other men's sins, how careful should we be to avoid sin ourselves!

JAMIESON, FAUSSET, BROWN

pediency, not to cause a stumbling block to "weak" brethren, that the Jerusalem decree against partaking of such meats (though indifferent *in themselves*) was passed (Acts 15). Hence he here vindicates it against the Corinthian asserters of an inexpedient liberty. **8.** Other old MSS. read, "Neither if we do not eat, are we the better: neither if we eat are we the worse": the language of the eaters who justified their eating thus [LACHMANN]. In *English Version* Paul admits that "meat neither *presents* [so the *Greek* for 'commendeth'] us as commended nor as disapproved before God": it does not affect our standing before God (Rom. 14:6). **9. this liberty of yours**—the watchword for lax Corinthians. The very indifference of meats, which I concede, is the reason why ye should "take heed" not to tempt weak brethren *to act against their conscience* (which constitutes sin, Rom. 14:22, 23).

10. if any man—being weak. **which hast knowledge**—The very knowledge which thou pridest thyself on (vs. 1), will lead the weak after thy example to do that against his conscience, which thou doest without any scruple of conscience; viz., to eat meats offered to idols. **conscience of him which is weak**—rather, "His conscience, *seeing he* is weak" [ALFORD and others]. **emboldened**—lit., "built up." You ought to have *built up* your brother in good: but by your example your *building* him *up* is the emboldening him to violate his conscience. **11. shall . . . perish**—The oldest MSS. read "perisheth." A single act seemingly unimportant may produce everlasting consequences. The weak brother loses his faith, and if he do not recover it, his salvation [BENGEL] (Rom. 14:23). **for whom Christ died**—and for whose sake we too ought to be willing to die (I John 3:16). And yet professing Christians at Corinth virtually tempted their brethren to their damnation, so far were they from sacrificing aught for their salvation. Note here, that it is no argument against the dogma that *Christ died for all, even for those who perish,* to say that thus He would have died *in vain* for many. Scripture is our rule, not our suppositions as to consequences. More is involved in redemption than the salvation of man: the *character of God* as at once just and loving is vindicated even in the case of the lost for they might have been saved, and so even in their case Christ has not died in vain. So the mercies of God's providence are not in vain, though many abuse them. Even the condemned shall manifest God's love in the great day, in that they too had the offer of God's mercy. It shall be the most awful ingredient in their cup that they might have been saved but would not: Christ died to redeem even them. **12. wound their weak conscience**—lit., "*smite* their conscience, being (as yet) *in a weak state.*" It aggravates the cruelty of the act that it is committed on the weak, just as if one were to *strike an invalid.* **against Christ**—on account of the sympathy between Christ and His members (Matt. 25:40; Acts 9:4, 5). **13. meat**—Old English for "food" in general. **make . . . to offend**—*Greek,* "is a stumbling block to." **no flesh**—In order to ensure my avoiding flesh offered to idols, I would abstain from *all kinds of flesh,* in order not *to be a stumbling block* to my brother.

ADAM CLARKE

8. *Meat commendeth us not to God.* No such feasts as these can be a recommendation of our souls or persons to the Supreme Being. As to the thing considered in itself, the eating gives us no spiritual advantage, and the eating not is no spiritual loss.

9. *But take heed.* Lest by frequenting such feasts and eating things offered to idols, under the conviction that an idol is nothing and that you may eat those things innocently, this liberty of yours should become a means of grievously offending a weak brother who has not your knowledge or inducing one who respects you for your superior knowledge to partake of these things with the conscience, the persuasion and belief, that an idol is something, and to conclude that, as you partake of such things, so he may also, and with safety. He is not possessed of your superior information on this point, and he eats to the idol what you take as a common meal.

10. *If any man see thee which hast knowledge.* Of the true God, and who are reputed for your skill in divine things. *Sit at meat in the idol's temple.* Is it not strange that any professing the knowledge of the true God should even enter one of those temples? And is it not more surprising that any Christian should be found to feast there? But by all this we may see that the boasted knowledge of the Corinthians had very little depth in things purely spiritual. *Be emboldened to eat.* Be "built up"—be confirmed and established in that opinion which before he doubtingly held, that on seeing you eat he may be led to think there is no harm in feasting in an idol temple nor in eating things offered to idols.

11. *Shall the weak brother perish?* Being first taught by thy conduct that there was no harm in thus eating, he grieves the Spirit of God, becomes again darkened and hardened, and sliding back into idolatry, dies in it, and so finally perishes. *For whom Christ died.* So we learn that a man may perish for whom Christ died; this admits of no quibble. If a man *for whom Christ died,* apostatizing from Christianity (for he is called a *brother* though *weak*), returning again to and dying in idolatry, cannot go to heaven, then a man for whom Christ died may perish everlastingly. And if it were possible for a believer, whether strong or weak, to retrace his steps back to idolatry and die in it, surely it is possible for a man who had escaped the pollutions that are in the world to return to it, live and die in its spirit, and perish everlastingly also.

12. *But when ye sin so against the brethren.* Against Christians, who are called by the gospel to abhor and detest all such abominations. *Ye sin against Christ.* By sending to perdition, through your bad example, a soul for whom He shed His blood, and so far defeating the gracious intentions of His sacrificial death.

13. *Wherefore.* Rather than give any occasion to a Christian to sin against and so to harden his conscience that he should return to idolatry and perish, I would not only abstain from all meats offered to idols, but I would eat *no flesh,* should I exist through the whole course of time, but live on the herbs of the field, rather than cause my brother to stumble, and thus fall into idolatry and final ruin. The greater our reputation for knowledge and sanctity, the greater mischief we shall do by our influence and example if we turn aside from the holy commandment delivered unto us. Every man should walk so as either to light or lead his brother to heaven.

MATTHEW HENRY — CHAPTER 9

Verses 1, 2

Paul not only met with opposition from those without, but discouragement from those within. Some among the Corinthians questioned, if they did not disown, his apostolical character. He asserts his apostolical mission and character: *Am I not an apostle? Have I not seen Jesus Christ our Lord?* To be a witness of his resurrection was one great branch of the apostolical charge. *"Am I not free?"* It was not because he had no right to live of the gospel that he maintained himself with his own hands.

JAMIESON, FAUSSET, BROWN — CHAPTER 9

VSS. 1-27. HE CONFIRMS HIS TEACHING AS TO NOT PUTTING A STUMBLING BLOCK IN A BROTHER'S WAY (ch. 8:13) BY HIS OWN EXAMPLE IN NOT USING HIS UNDOUBTED RIGHTS AS AN APOSTLE, SO AS TO WIN MEN TO CHRIST. **1. Am I not an apostle? am I not free?**—The oldest MSS. read the order thus, "Am I not free? am I not an apostle?" He alludes to ch. 8:9, "this liberty of yours": If you claim it, I appeal to yourselves as the witnesses, have not I also it? "Am I not free?" If you be so, much more I. For "am I not an apostle?" so that I can claim not only Christian, but also apostolic, liberty. **have I**

ADAM CLARKE — CHAPTER 9

1. *Am I not an apostle?* It is sufficiently evident that there were persons at Corinth who questioned the apostleship of Paul; and he was obliged to walk very circumspectly that they might not find any occasion against him. *Am I not an apostle? am I not free?* These questions are all designed as assertions of the affirmative: "I am an apostle, and I am free"—possessed of all the rights and privileges of an apostle. *Have I not seen Jesus Christ?* From whom in His personal appearance to me I have received my apostolic commission. This was judged es-

MATTHEW HENRY

He offers the success of his ministry among them as a proof of his apostleship. He justly upbraids the Corinthians with their disrespect, *v.* 2. "You, above all others, should own my character, and not call it in question." It was aggravated ingratitude for this people to call in question his authority.

Verses 3–14

He proceeds to claim the rights belonging to his office.

I. These he states, *v.* 3–6.

II. He proceeds to prove his claim, from the common practice of mankind.

F. B. MEYER:

Rights and their surrender. Paul's claim to an equality with Peter and the other apostles was violently disputed by his enemies at Corinth, because in several matters he differed from them. Unlike Peter, he had no wife to support; and he worked for his livelihood instead of being supported by the churches. In this chapter he strongly asserts his rights in this particular; but he is equally strong in saying that he had refused to avail himself of his right, that he might influence a wider circle of men. He was a soldier, a vineyard keeper, a shepherd, and could claim his maintenance. But he desired to be free from the slightest imputation of self-seeking. He knew that jealous critics were watching his every action and seeking to weigh his secret motives. These were the very men he desired to win, and for their sakes he voluntarily surrendered his undoubted rights.

What a lesson for all of us and especially for those who are called to be ministers of Christ's gospel! We must be above suspicion. If we do or permit anything that might prove a hindrance to the acceptance of Christ by others, we must forego it, though reasonable in itself, that we may win them to our Savior.

—Bible Commentary

Those who give themselves up to any way of business in the world expect to live out of it (*v.* 7–9). It is very reasonable for ministers to expect a livelihood out of their labours, *v.* 8. It is also consonant to the old law.

JAMIESON, FAUSSET, BROWN

not seen Jesus—*corporeally,* not in a mere vision: cf. ch. 15:8, where the fact of the resurrection, which he wishes to prove, could only be established by an actual bodily appearance, such as was vouchsafed to Peter and the other apostles. In Acts 9:7, 17 the contrast between "the men with him seeing *no man,*" and "Jesus that appeared unto thee in the way," shows that Jesus actually appeared to him in going to Damascus. His vision of Christ in the temple (Acts 22:17) was "in a trance." To be a witness of Christ's resurrection was a leading function of an apostle (Acts 1:22). The best MSS. omit "Christ." **ye my work in the Lord**—Your conversion is His workmanship (Eph. 2:10) through my instrumentality: the "seal of mine apostleship" (vs. 2). **2. yet doubtless**—*yet at least* I am such to you. **seal of mine apostleship**—Your conversion by my preaching, accompanied with miracles ("the signs of an apostle," Rom. 15:18, 19; II Cor. 12:12), and your gifts conferred by me (ch. 1:7), vouch for the reality of my apostleship, just as a seal set to a document attests its genuineness (John 3:33; Rom. 4:11). **3. to them that . . . examine me**—i.e., who call in question mine apostleship. **is this**—viz., that you are the seal of mine apostleship. **4. Have we not power**—*Greek,* "right," or lawful power, equivalent to "liberty" claimed by the Corinthians (ch. 8:9). The "we" includes with himself his colleagues in the apostleship. The *Greek* interrogative expresses, "You surely *won't* say (will you?) that we have *not* the power or right. . . ." **eat and drink**—without laboring with our hands (vss. 11, 13, 14). Paul's not exercising this right was made a plea by his opponents for insinuating that he was himself conscious he was no true apostle (II Cor. 12:13-16). **5. lead about a sister, a wife**—i.e., "a sister *as a wife*"; "a sister" by faith, which makes all believers brethren and sisters in the one family of God: "a wife" by marriage covenant. Paul implies he did not exercise his undoubted right to marry and "lead about" a believer, for the sake of Christian expediency, as well to save the Church the expense of maintaining her in his wide circuits, as also that he might give himself more undistractedly to building up the Church of Christ (ch. 7:26, 32, 35). Contrast the Corinthians' want of self-sacrifice in the exercise of their "liberty" at the cost of destroying, instead of edifying, the Church (ch. 8: 9, 10; *Margin,* 11-13). **as other apostles**—implying that some of them had availed themselves of the power which they all had, of marrying. We know from Matthew 8:14, that Cephas (Peter) was a married man. A confutation of Peter's self-styled followers, the Romanists, who exclude the clergy from marriage. CLEMENS ALEXANDRINUS (*Stromata* or *Miscellanies,* 7. sec. 63) records a tradition that he encouraged his wife when being led to death by saying, "Remember, my dear one, the Lord." Cf. EUSEBIUS, *E. H.* 3. 30. **brethren of the Lord**—held in especial esteem on account of their relationship to Jesus (Acts 1:14; Gal. 1:9). James, Joses, Simon, and Judas. Probably *cousins* of Jesus: as cousins were termed by the Jews "brethren." ALFORD makes them literally *brothers* of Jesus by Joseph and Mary. **Cephas**—probably singled out as being a name carrying weight with one partisan section at Corinth. "If your favorite leader does so, surely so may I" (ch. 1:12; 3:22). **6. Barnabas**—long the associate of Paul, and, like him, in the habit of self-denyingly forbearing to claim the maintenance which is a minister's right. So Paul supported himself by tent-making (Acts 18:3; 20:34; I Thess. 2: 9; II Thess. 3:8). **7.** The minister is spiritually a soldier (II Tim. 2:3), a vine-dresser (ch. 3:6-8; Song of Sol. 1:6), and a shepherd (I Pet. 5:2, 4). **of the fruit**—The oldest MSS. omit "of." **8. as a man**—I speak thus not merely *according to human judgment,* but with the sanction of the divine law also. **9. ox . . . treadeth . . . corn**—(Deut. 25:4). In the East to the present day they do not after reaping carry the sheaves home to barns as we do, but take them to an area under the open air to be threshed by the oxen treading them with their feet, or else drawing a threshing instrument over them (cf. Mic. 4:13). **Doth God . . . care for oxen?**—rather, "Is it for the oxen that God careth?" Is the animal the ultimate object for whose sake this law was given? No. God does care for the lower animal (Ps. 36:6; Matt. 10:29), but it is with the ultimate aim of the welfare of *man,* the head of animal creation. In the humane consideration shown for the lower animal, we are to learn that still more ought it to be exercised in the case of man, the ultimate object of the law; and that the human (spiritual as well as temporal) laborer is worthy of his hire. **10. altogether**—Join this with "saith." "Does he (the divine lawgiver) by all means say it for our sakes?"

ADAM CLARKE

sentially necessary to constitute an apostle. See Acts xxii. 14-15; xxvi. 16. *Are not ye my work?* Your conversion from heathenism is the proof that I have preached with the divine unction and authority.

2. *If I be not an apostle unto others.* If there be other churches which have been founded by other apostles, yet it is not so with you. *The seal of mine apostleship are ye.* Your conversion to Christianity is God's *seal* to my apostleship. Had not God sent me, I could not have profited your souls. The *seal* was a figure cut in a stone, and that set in a ring, by which letters of credence and authority were stamped. The ancients, particularly the Greeks, excelled in this kind of engraving. *In the Lord.* The apostle shows that it was by the grace and influence of God alone that he was an apostle, and that they were converted to Christianity.

3. *Mine answer to them.* This is my defense against those who examine me. The words are forensic; and the apostle considers himself as brought before a legal tribunal, and questioned so as to be obliged to answer as upon oath. His defense therefore was this, that they were converted to God by his means. This verse belongs to the preceding two verses.

4. *Have we not power to eat and to drink?* Have we not "authority," or "right," to expect sustenance while we are laboring for your salvation? Meat and drink, the necessaries, not the superfluities, of life, were what those primitive messengers of Christ required; it was just that they who labored in the gospel should live by the gospel. They did not wish to make a fortune or accumulate wealth; a living was all they desired.

5. *Have we not power to lead about a sister, a wife?* When the apostle speaks of leading about a sister, a wife, he means, first, that he and all other apostles, and consequently all ministers of the gospel, had a right to marry. For it appears that our Lord's brethren, James and Jude, were married; and we have infallible evidence that Peter was a married man, not only from this verse, but from Matt. viii. 14, where his mother-in-law is mentioned as being cured of a fever by our Lord. And secondly, we find that their wives were persons of the same faith, for less can never be implied in the word *sister.*

6. *Or I only and Barnabas?* Have we alone of all the apostles no right to be supported by our converts? It appears from this: (1) That the apostles did not generally support themselves by their own labor; (2) That Paul and Barnabas did thus support themselves. Some of the others probably had not a business at which they could conveniently work, but Paul and Barnabas had a trade at which they could conveniently labor wherever they came.

7. *Who goeth a warfare . . . at his own charges?* These questions, which are all supposed from the necessity and propriety of the cases to be answered in the affirmative, tend more forcibly to point out that the common sense of man joins with the providence of God in showing the propriety of every man living by the fruits of his labor. The first question applies particularly to the case of the apostle. Does a soldier provide his own victuals? *Opsonion* is used by the Greek writers to express the military pay or wages, for the Roman soldiers were paid not only in money but in victuals.

8. *Say I these things as a man?* Is this only human reasoning? or does not God say in effect the same things?

9. *Thou shalt not muzzle the mouth of the ox.* See Deut. xxv. 4. *Doth God take care for oxen?* This question is to be understood thus: Is it likely that God should be solicitous for the comfort of oxen and be regardless of the welfare of man? In this divine precept the kindness and providential care of God are very forcibly pointed out. He takes care of oxen; He wills them all that happiness of which their nature is susceptible; and can we suppose that He is unwilling that the human soul shall have that happiness which is suited to its spiritual and eternal nature?

MATTHEW HENRY

But this law was not chiefly given out of God's regard to oxen, but to teach mankind that all due encouragement should be given to those who are labouring for our good—that the labourers should taste of the fruit of their labours, *v.* 10. Those that lay themselves out to do our souls good should not have their mouths muzzled. He argues from common equity. What they had sown was much better than they expected to reap. They had been instruments of conveying to them the greater spiritual blessings; and had they no claim to a share in their carnal things? What, get so much good by them, and yet grudge to do so little good to them! He argues from the maintenance they afforded others. Who has so just a claim as I from the church of Corinth? Who has laboured so much for your good? He renounced his right, rather than by claiming it he would hinder his success, but asserted his right lest his self-denial should prove prejudicial to the ministry.

He argues from the old Jewish establishment: "*Do you not know that those who minister about holy things live of the things of the temple, and those who wait at the altar are partakers with the altar?* (*v.* 13). He asserts it to be the institution of Christ: "*Even so hath the Lord ordained that those who preach the gospel should live of the gospel*" (*v.* 14). But those transgress an appointment of Christ who deny or withhold it.

Verses 15–18

I. He had neglected to claim his right in times past, *v.* 15. Nor did he write this to make his claim now.

II. He would not have his glorying made void, *v.* 15, to have it justly said that he preferred his wages to his work. It is the glory of a minister to deny himself, that he may serve Christ, and save souls.

III. This self-denial yielded him much more content than his preaching did, *v.* 16. This is a duty expressly bound upon him. Those who are set apart to the office of the ministry have it in charge to preach the gospel. Woe be to them if they do not. But it is not given in charge to all, nor any preacher of the gospel, to do his work gratis. It may be his duty to preach under some circumstances, without receiving a maintenance for it; but he has a right to it. It may sometimes be his duty to insist on his maintenance for so doing, and whenever he forbears he parts with his right.

JAMIESON, FAUSSET, BROWN

It would be untrue, that God saith it *altogether* (in the sense of *solely*) for *our* sakes. But it is true, that He *by all means saith it* for our sakes as the ultimate object in the lower world. GROTIUS, however, translates, "mainly" or "especially," instead of *altogether*. **that**—"meaning that" [ALFORD]; lit., "because." **should plough**—*ought* to plough in hope. The obligation rests with the people not to let their minister labor without remuneration. **he that thresheth in hope should be partaker of his hope**—The oldest MS. versions and Fathers read, "He that thresheth (*should* or *ought to thresh*) in the hope of partaking" (viz., *of the fruit of his threshing*). "He that plougheth," spiritually, is the first planter of a church in a place (cf. ch. 3:6, 9); "he that thresheth," the minister who tends a church already planted. **11. we . . . we**—emphatical in the *Greek*. WE, the same persons who have sown to you the infinitely more precious treasures of the *Spirit*, may at least claim in return what is the only thing *you* have to give, viz., the goods that nourish the *flesh* ("*your* carnal things"). **12. others**—whether true apostles (vs. 5) or false ones (II Cor. 11:20). **we rather**—considering our greater labors for you (II Cor. 11:23). **suffer all things**—without complaining of it. We desire to *conceal* (lit., "hold as a water-tight vessel") any distress we suffer from straitened circumstances. The same *Greek* is in ch. 13:7. **lest we . . . hinder . . . gospel**—not to *cause a hindrance to* its progress by giving a handle for the imputation of self-seeking, if we received support from our flock. The less of incumbrance and expense caused to the Church, and the more of work done, the better for the cause of the Gospel (II Tim. 2:4). **13. minister about holy things**—the Jewish priests and Levites. The *Greek* especially applies to the former, the priests *offering sacrifices*. **partakers with the altar**—a part of the victims going to the service of the altar, and the rest being shared by the priests (Lev. 7:6; Num. 18:6, etc.; Deut. 18:1, etc.). **14. Even so**—The only inference to be drawn from this passage is, not that the Christian ministry is of a sacrificial character as the Jewish priesthood, but simply, that as the latter was supported by the contributions of the people, so should the former. The stipends of the clergy were at first from voluntary offerings at the Lord's Supper. At the love feast preceding it every believer, according to his ability, offered a gift; and when the expense of the table had been defrayed, the bishop laid aside a portion for himself, the presbyters, and deacons; and with the rest relieved widows, orphans, confessors, and the poor generally [TERTULLIAN, *Apology*, ch. 39]. The stipend was in proportion to the dignity and merits of the several bishops, presbyters, and deacons [CYPRIAN, c. 4, ep. 6]. **preach . . . gospel**—plainly marked as the duty of the Christian minister, in contrast to the *ministering about sacrifices* (*Greek*) *and waiting at the altar* of the Jewish priesthood and Levites (vs. 13). If the Lord's Supper were a *sacrifice* (as the Mass is supposed to be), this 14th verse would certainly have been worded so, to answer to vs. 13. Note the same Lord Christ "ordains" the ordinances in the Old and in the New Testaments (Matt. 10:10; Luke 10:7). **15.** Paul's special gift of continency, which enabled him to abstain from marriage, and his ability to maintain himself without interrupting seriously his ministry, made that expedient to him which is ordinarily inexpedient; viz., that the ministry should not be supported by the people. What to him was a duty, would be the opposite to one, for instance, to whom God had committed a family, without other means of support. **I have used none of these things**—none of these "powers" or rights which I might have used (vss. 4-6, 12). **neither**—rather, "*Yet* I have *not* written." **so done unto me**—lit., "in my case": as is done in the case of a soldier, a planter, a shepherd, a ploughman, and a sacrificing priest (vss. 7, 10, 13). **make my glorying void**—deprive me of my privilege of preaching the Gospel without remuneration (II Corinthians 11:7-10). Rather than hinder the progress of the Gospel by giving any pretext for a charge of interested motives (II Cor. 12. 17, 18), Paul would "die" of hunger. Cf. Abraham's similar disinterestedness (Gen. 14:22, 23). **16. though I preach . . . I have nothing to glory of**—i.e., If I preach the Gospel, and do so not gratuitously, I have no matter for "glorying." For the "necessity" that is laid on me to preach (cf. Jer. 20:9, and the case of Jonah) does away with ground for "glorying." The sole ground for the latter that I have, is my preaching *without charge* (vs. 18): since there is no necessity laid on me as to the latter, it is my voluntary act for the Gospel's sake. **17.** Translate, "If I be doing this (i.e., preaching) of my own accord (which I am

ADAM CLARKE

10. *And he that thresheth in hope should be partaker of his hope.* Many of the best MSS. and versions read the passage thus: "And he who thresheth in hope of partaking."

11. *If we have sown unto you spiritual things.* If we have been the means of bringing you into a state of salvation by the divine doctrines which we have preached unto you, is it too much for us to expect a temporal support when we give ourselves up entirely to this work? Every man who preaches the gospel has a right to his own support and that of his family while thus employed.

12. *If others be partakers of this power.* If those who in any matter serve you have a "right" to a recompense for that service, surely we who have served you in the most essential matters have a right to our support while thus employed in your service. *We have not used this power.* Though we had this "right," we have not availed ourselves of it, but have worked with our hands to bear our own charges, lest any of you should think that we preached the gospel merely to procure a temporal support, and so be prejudiced against us, and thus prevent our success in the salvation of your souls.

13. *They which minister about holy things.* All the officers about the Temple, whether priests, Levites, Nethinim, etc., had a right to their support while employed in its service. The priests partook of the sacrifices; the others had their maintenance from tithes, firstfruits, and offerings made to the Temple, for it was not lawful for them to live on the sacrifices. Hence the apostle makes the distinction between those who *minister about holy things* and those who *wait at the altar.*

14. *Even so hath the Lord ordained.* This is evidently a reference to our Lord's ordination, Matt. x. 10: "The workman is worthy of his meat." And Luke x. 7: "For the labourer is worthy of his hire." And in both places it is the preacher of the gospel of whom he is speaking.

15. *Neither have I written.* Though I might plead the authority of God in the law, of Christ in the gospel, the common consent of our own doctors, and the usages of civil society, yet I have not availed myself of my privileges; nor do I now write with the intention to lay in my claims.

16. *For though I preach the gospel.* I have cause of glorying that I preach the gospel free of all charges to you; but I cannot glory in being a preacher of the gospel, because I am not such by either my own skill or power. I have received from God both the office and the grace by which I execute the office.

MATTHEW HENRY

IV. *If I do this thing willingly, I have a reward.* Indeed, it is willing service only that is capable of reward from God. Leave the heart out of our duties, and God abhors them: they are but the carcasses, without the life and spirit, of religion. Ministers have a dispensation of the gospel committed to them. Christ's willing servants shall not fail of a recompence, and his slothful and unwilling servants shall all be called to an account.

V. *What is my reward then?* (*v.* 18). *That when I preach the gospel I may make it without charge, that I abuse not my power in the gospel.* It is an abuse of power to employ it against the very ends for which it is given. And the apostle would never use his so as to frustrate the ends of it, but would willingly and cheerfully deny himself.

Verses 19–23

I. He asserts his liberty (*v.* 19). He was free-born, a citizen of Rome. He was in bondage to none, *yet he made himself a servant to all, that he might gain the more.* He made himself a servant, that they might be made free.

II. He accommodated himself to all sorts of people. *To the Jews, and those under the law, he became a Jew.* He submitted to it, that he might prevail with them and win them over to Christ.

To those that are without the law, as without law, that is, to the Gentiles. In innocent things he could comply with people's usages for their advantage. He behaved among them as one that was not under the bondage of the Jewish laws. He did not stand on privileges and punctilios.

To the weak he became as weak, that he might gain the weak, v. 22. He did not despise nor judge them, but became as one of them. He denied himself for their sakes, that he might gain their souls. The rights of God he could not give up, but he might resign his own, and he very often did so for the good of others.

III. His reason for acting in this manner (*v.* 23): *This I do for the gospel's sake, and that I may be partaker thereof with you.* A heart warmed with zeal for God, and breathing after the salvation of men, will not plead and insist upon rights and privileges.

Verses 24–27

He had a glorious prize, an incorruptible crown, in view. "*Know you not that those who run in a race run all, but one obtaineth the prize?*" (*v.* 24).

JAMIESON, FAUSSET, BROWN

not, for the "necessity" is laid on me which binds a servant to obey his master), I have a reward; but if (as is the case) involuntarily (Acts 9:15; 22:15; 26: 16; not of my own natural will, but by the constraining grace of God; Romans 9:16; I Tim. 1:13-16), I have had a dispensation (of the Gospel) entrusted to me" (and so can claim no "reward," seeing that I only "have done that which was my duty to do," Luke 17:10, but incur the "woe," vs. 16, if I fail in it). **18. What is my reward?**—The answer is in vs. 19; viz., that by making the Gospel without charge, where I might have rightfully claimed maintenance, I might "win the more." **of Christ**—The oldest MSS and versions omit these words. **abuse** –rather "that *I use* not *to the full* my power." This is his matter for "*glorying*"; the "*reward*" ultimately aimed at is the gaining of the more (vs. 19). The former, as involving the latter, is verbally made the answer to the question, "What is my reward?" But really the "reward" is that which is the ultimate aim of his preaching without charge, viz., that he may gain the more; it was for this end, not to have matter of glorying, that he did so. **19. free from all men**—i.e., from the power of all men. **gain the more**—i.e., *as many of them* ("all men") *as possible.* "Gain" is an appropriate expression in relation to a "reward" (I Thess. 2:19, 20); he therefore repeats it frequently (vss. 20-22). **20. I became as a Jew**—in things not defined by the *law,* but by Jewish usage. Not Judaizing in essentials, but in matters where there was no compromise of principle (cf. Acts 16:3; 21:20-26); an undesigned coincidence between the history and the Epistle, and so a sure proof of genuineness. **to them that are under the law, as under the law**—in things defined by *the law;* such as ceremonies not then repugnant to Christianity. Perhaps the reason for distinguishing this class from the former is that Paul himself belonged *nationally* to "the Jews," but did not in *creed* belong to the class of "them that are under the law." This view is confirmed by the reading inserted here by the oldest MSS., versions, and Fathers, "not being (i.e., parenthetically, 'not that I am') myself under the law." **21. To them . . . without law**—i.e., without *revealed* law: the heathen (cf. Rom. 2:12 with vs. 15). **as without law**—not urging on them the ceremonies and "works of the law," but "the hearing of faith" (Gal. 3:2). Also discoursing in their own manner, as at Athens, with arguments from their own poets (Acts 17:28). **being not without law to God**—"While thus conforming to others in matters indifferent, taking care not to be *without law* in relation to God, but *responsible to law* (lit., IN LAW) in relation to Christ." This is the Christian's true position in relation to the world, to himself, and to God. Everything develops itself according to its proper law. So the Christian, though no longer subject to the literal law as constraining him from without, is subject to an inward principle or law, the spirit of faith in Christ acting from within as the germ of a new life. He does not in the *Greek* (as in *English Version*) say "*under the law* (as he does in vs. 20) to Christ"; but uses the milder term, "in . . . law," *responsible to law.* Christ was responsible to the law for us, so that we are no longer responsible to it (Gal. 3:13, 24), but to Him, as the members to the Head (ch. 7:22; Rom. 8:1-4; I Pet. 2:16). Christians serve Christ in newness of spirit, no longer in oldness of the letter (i.e., the old *external* law *as such*), Romans 7:4-6. To Christ, as man's Head, the Father has properly delegated His authority (John 5:22, 27); whence here he substitutes "Christ" for "God" in the second clause, "not without law to *God,* but under the law to *Christ.*" The law of Christ is the law of love (Gal. 6:2; cf. 5:13). **22. gain the weak** –i.e., establish, instead of being a stumbling block to inexperienced Christians (ch. 8:7). Romans 14: 1, "Weak in the faith." ALFORD thinks the "weak" are not Christians at all, for these have been already "won"; but those outside the Church, who are yet "without strength" to believe (Rom. 5:6). But when "weak" *Christians* are by the condescending love of stronger brethren kept from falling from faith, they are well said to be "gained" or won. **by all means . . . some**—The gain of even "*some*" is worth the expenditure of "all means." He conformed himself to the feelings of each in the several classes, that out of them *all* he might *gain some.* **23. partaker thereof**—*Greek,* "*fellow partaker*": of the Gospel blessings promised at Christ's coming: "with" (not as *English Version,* "you": but) *them,* viz., with those thus "gained" by me to the Gospel. **24. Know ye not**—The Isthmian games, in which the foot race was a leading one, were of course well known, and a subject of patriotic pride to the Corinthians, who lived in the immediate neighborhood.

ADAM CLARKE

17. *For if I do this thing willingly.* If I be a cordial cooperator with God, *I have a reward,* an incorruptible crown, v. 25. Or, if I freely preach this gospel without being burdensome to any, I have a special reward. But if I do not, I have simply an office to fulfill, into which God has put me, and may fulfill it conscientiously, and claim my privileges at the same time; but then I lose that special reward which I have in view by preaching the gospel without charge to any.

18. *That I abuse not my power.* I am inclined to think that *katachresasthai* is to be understood here, not in the sense of abusing, but of "using to the uttermost"—exacting everything that a man can claim by law.

19. *For though I be free.* Although I am under no obligation to any man, yet I act as if every individual had a particular property in me, and as if I were the "slave" of the public.

20. *Unto the Jews I became as a Jew.* In Acts xvi. 3, we find that for the sake of the unconverted Jews he circumcised Timothy. *To them that are under the law.* To those who considered themselves still under obligation to observe its rites and ceremonies, though they had in the main embraced the gospel, he became as if under the same obligations; and therefore purified himself in the Temple, as we find related in Acts xxi. 26. After the first clause, *to them that are under the law, as under the law,* the following words, "not being myself under the law," are added by several MSS.

21. *To them that are without law.* The Gentiles, who had no written law, though they had the law written in their hearts; see on Rom. ii. 15. *Being not without law to God.* Instead of *to God* and *to Christ,* the most important MSS. and versions have "of God" and "of Christ"; being not without the law of God, but under the law of Christ.

22. *To the weak became I as weak.* Those who were conscientiously "scrupulous," even in respect to lawful things. *I am made all things to all men.* I assumed every shape and form consistent with innocency and perfect integrity; giving up my own will, my own way, my own ease, my own pleasure, and my own profit, that I might save the souls of all. Let those who plead for the system of accommodation on the example of Paul attend to the end he had in view and the manner in which he pursued that end. It was not to get money, influence, or honor, but to save souls! It was not to get ease, but to increase his labors. It was not to save his life, but rather that it should be a sacrifice for the good of immortal souls!

23. *And this I do for the gospel's sake.* Instead of *this,* "all things" (I do all things for the gospel's sake), is the reading of many MSS. Several of the fathers have the same reading, and there is much reason to believe it to be genuine. *That I might be partaker thereof with you.* That I might attain to the reward of eternal life which it sets before me; and this is in all probability the meaning of *to evangelion,* which we translate "the gospel," and which should be rendered here "prize" or "reward"; this is a frequent meaning of the original word: "I do all this for the sake of the prize, that I may partake of it with you."

24. *They which run in a race run all.* It is sufficiently evident that the apostle alludes to the athletic exercises in the games which were celebrated every fifth year on the isthmus which joins the Peloponnesus to the mainland, and were thence termed the "Isthmian games."

MATTHEW HENRY

I. It is quite otherwise in the Christian race than in your races; where only one wins the prize. You may all run so as to obtain. You cannot fail if you run well. And it is a glorious contest who shall get first to heaven.

II. He directs them in their course, by setting more fully to view his own example. 1. Those that ran in their games were kept to a set diet, *v.* 23. "The fighters and wrestlers in your exercises are kept to strict diet and discipline. They use a very spare diet and deny themselves much; so do I; so should you." 2. They were not only temperate, but inured themselves to hardships. Those who fought with one another prepared themselves by beating the air, as the apostle calls it. There is no room for any such exercise in the Christian warfare. Christians are ever in close combat. One enemy the apostle here mentions, namely, the body; this must be kept under, beaten black and blue.

III. The apostle presses this advice by proper arguments drawn from the same contenders. Those who conquered in these games were crowned only with the withering leaves or boughs of trees, of olive, bays, or laurel. But Christians have an incorruptible crown in view. Can they expose their bodies to so much hardship who have no more in view than the trifling huzzas of a giddy multitude, or a crown of leaves? And shall not Christians, who hope for a crown of glory, exert themselves in beating down their fleshly inclinations? All run, but one receives the prize, *v.* 24.

But the Christian racer is at no such uncertainty. Everyone may run here so as to obtain; but then he must keep to the path of duty prescribed, which is the meaning of *running not as uncertainly, v.* 26. And would the Grecian racers exert themselves to the very last, when one only could win? And shall not Christians be much more vigorous when all are sure of a crown?

The danger of yielding to fleshly inclinations: *I keep my body under, lest by any means, when I have preached to others, I myself should be a castaway* (*v.* 27), *rejected,* one to whom the *judge* or *umpire,* will not decree the crown. A preacher of salvation may yet miss it. He may show others the way to heaven, and never get thither himself. A holy fear of himself was necessary to preserve the fidelity of an apostle; and how much more necessary is it to our preservation?

JAMIESON, FAUSSET, BROWN

These periodical games were to the Greeks rather a passion than a mere amusement: hence their suitableness as an image of Christian earnestness. **in a race**—*Greek,* "in a race course." **all . . . one**—Although we knew that one alone could be saved, still it would be well worth our while to run [BENGEL]. Even in the Christian race not "all" who enter on the race win (ch. 10:1-5). **So run, that ye may obtain**—said parenthetically. These are the words in which the instructors of the young in the exercise schools (*gymnasia*) and the spectators on the race course exhorted their pupils to stimulate them to put forth all exertions. The *gymnasium* was a prominent feature in every Greek city. Every candidate had to take an oath that he had been ten months in training, and that he would violate none of the regulations (II Timothy 2:5; cf. I Tim. 4:7, 8). He lived on a strict self-denying diet, refraining from wine and pleasant foods, and enduring cold and heat and most laborious discipline. The "prize" awarded by the judge or umpire was a chaplet of green leaves; at the Isthmus, those of the indigenous pine, for which parsley leaves were temporarily substituted (vs. 25). The *Greek* for "obtain" is *fully obtain.* It is in vain to begin, unless we persevere to the end (Matt. 10:22; 24:13; Rev. 2:10). The "so" expresses, Run *with such perseverance* in the heavenly course, as "all" the runners exhibit in the earthly "race" just spoken of: *to the end that* ye may attain the prize. **25. striveth**—in wrestling: a still more severe contest than the foot race. **is temperate**—So Paul exercised self-denial, abstaining from claiming sustenance for the sake of the "reward," viz., to "gain the more" (vss. 18, 19). **corruptible**—*soon withering,* as being only of fir leaves taken from the fir groves which surrounded the Isthmian race course or stadium. **incorruptible**—(I Pet. 1:4; 5:4; Rev. 2:10). "Crown" here is not that of a king (which is expressed by a different *Greek* word, viz., "diadem"), but a *wreath* or *garland.* **26. I**—Paul returns to his main subject, *his own* self-denial, and his motive in it. **run, not as uncertainly**—not as a runner uncertain of the goal. Ye Corinthians gain no end in your entering idol temples or eating idol meats. But *I,* for my part, in all my acts, whether in my becoming "all things to all men," or in receiving no sustenance from my converts, have a definite end in view, viz., to "gain the more." I know what I aim at, and how to aim at it. He who runs with a clear aim, looks straightforward to the goal, makes it his sole aim, casts away every encumbrance (Heb. 12:1, 2), is indifferent to what the bystanders say, and sometimes even a fall only serves to rouse him the more [BENGEL]. **not as one that beateth the air**—instead of beating the adversary. Alluding to the *sciamachia* or *sparring in the school in sham-fight* (cf. ch. 14:9), wherein they struck out into the air as if at an imaginary adversary. The real adversary is Satan acting on us through the flesh. **27. keep under**—lit., "bruise the face under the eyes," so as to render it black and blue; so, to *chastise* in the most sensitive part. Cf. "*mortify* the deeds of the body," Romans 8:13; also I Pet. 2:11. It is not ascetic fasts or macerations of the body which are here recommended, but the *keeping under* of our natural self-seeking, so as, like Paul, to lay ourselves out entirely for the great work. **my body**—the old man and the remainders of lust in my flesh. "My body," so far as by the *flesh* it opposes the *spirit* [ESTIUS] (Gal. 5:17). Men may be severe to their bodies and yet indulge their lust. Ascetic "neglect of the body" may be all the while a more subtile "satisfying of the flesh" (Col. 2:23). Unless the soul keep the body under, the body will get above the soul. The body may be made a good servant, but is a bad master. **bring it into subjection**—or bondage, as a *slave* or servant *led away captive;* so the *Greek.* **preached**—lit., "heralded." He keeps up the image from the races. The *heralds* summoned the candidates for the foot race into the race course [PLATO, *Legg.* 8. 833], and placed the crowns on the brows of the conquerors, announcing their names [BENGEL]. They probably proclaimed also the laws of the combat; answering to the *preaching* of the apostles [ALFORD]. The *Christian* herald is also a *combatant,* in which respect he is distinguished from the herald at the games. **a castaway**—failing shamefully of the prize myself, after I have *called* others to the contest. *Rejected* by God, the Judge of the Christian race, notwithstanding my having, by my preaching, led others to be accepted. Cf. the equivalent term, "reprobate," Jeremiah 6:30; II Corinthians 13:6.

ADAM CLARKE

But one receiveth the prize. The apostle places the Christian race in contrast to the Isthmian games; in them, only one received the prize, though all ran; in this, if all run, all will receive the prize. Therefore he says, *So run, that ye may obtain.* Be as much in earnest to get to heaven as others are to gain their prize; and, although only one of them can win, all of you may obtain.

25. *Is temperate in all things.* All those who contended in these exercises went through a long state and series of painful preparations. To this exact discipline Epictetus refers, cap. 35: "Do you wish to gain the prize at the Olympic games?—Consider the requisite preparations and the consequences: you must observe a strict regimen; must live on food which you dislike; you must abstain from all delicacies; must exercise yourself at the necessary and prescribed times both in heat and in cold; you must drink nothing cooling; take no wine as formerly; in a word, you must put yourself under the directions of a pugilist, as you would under those of a physician, and afterwards enter the lists. Here you may get your arm broken, your foot put out of joint, be obliged to swallow mouthfuls of dust, to receive many stripes, and after all be conquered." *They do it to obtain a corruptible crown.* The *crown* won by the victor in the Olympian games was made of the wild olive. These were all *corruptible,* for they began to wither as soon as they were separated from the trees or plucked out of the earth. In opposition to these, the apostle says, he contended for an incorruptible crown, the heavenly inheritance.

26. *I therefore so run, not as uncertainly.* In the foot-course in those games, how many soever ran, only one could have the prize, however strenuously they might exert themselves; therefore all ran uncertainly. But it was widely different in the Christian course; if everyone ran as he ought, each would receive the prize. *Not as one that beateth the air.* Kypke observes that there are three ways in which persons were said to beat the air: (1) When in practicing for the combat they threw their arms and legs about in different ways, thus practicing the attitudes of offense and defense. (2) Sometimes boxers were to aim blows at their adversaries which they did not intend to take place, and which the others were obliged to exert themselves to prevent as much as if they had been really intended. (3) Pugilists were said to beat the air when they had to contend with a nimble adversary, who, by running from side to side, stooping, and various contortions of the body, eluded the blows of his antagonist; who spent his strength on the air, frequently missing his aim, and sometimes overturning himself in attempting to hit his adversary, who by his agility had been able to elude the blow.

27. *But I keep under my body.* This is an allusion, not only to boxers, but also to wrestlers in the same games, as we learn from the word *hypopiazo,* which signifies to "hit in the eyes"; and *doulagogo,* which signifies to trip, and give the antagonist a fall, and then keep him down when he was down, and having obliged him to acknowledge himself conquered, make him a slave. The apostle considers his body as an enemy with which he must contend; he must mortify it by self-denial, abstinence, and severe labor. It must be the slave of his soul, and not the soul the slave of the body, which in all unregenerate men is the case. *Lest . . . when I have preached to others.* The word which we translate "having preached" refers to the office of the "herald" at these games, whose business it was to proclaim the conditions of the games, display the prizes, exhort the combatants, excite the emulation of those who were to contend, declare the terms of each contest, pronounce the name of the victors, and put the crown on their heads. *Should be a castaway.* The word signifies such a person as the judges of the games reject as not having deserved the prize. So Paul himself might be rejected by the great Judge; and to prevent this he ran, he contended, he denied himself, and brought his body into subjection to his spirit, and had his spirit governed by the Spirit of God.

MATTHEW HENRY

CHAPTER 10

Verses 1–5

He sets before them the example of the Jews. They enjoyed great privileges, but they fell under very grievous punishments.

I. The providence of God towards them, and what happened to them ought to be warnings to us.

II. He specifies some of their privileges. 1. Their deliverance from Egypt. They were miraculously conducted through the Red Sea, where the pursuing Egyptians were drowned: it was a lane to them, but a grave to these. They were very dear to God when he would work such miracles for their deliverance.

2. They had sacraments like ours. *They were all baptized unto Moses in the cloud, and in the sea* (*v.* 2).

A. B. SIMPSON:

1. The first great type held forth is the cloud, which led them through the wilderness and covered them as a pavilion from their enemies. It is here spoken of as a divine baptism which came upon them as they passed through the sea. The account of that cloud is very striking and beautiful. First, it preceded and guided them as they went forth out of the land of bondage. So the Holy Spirit leads us out of the world and sin into Christ, going before us at first, while we follow somewhat at a distance. But when at last they came to the deep, dark flood and went down into the death of which it was a symbol, then that cloud that had gone before them gently turned backward, and passing through the camp baptized them into its very substance, covered them over as a pavilion, wrapped itself around them as a garment, penetrated their very being as the element of their living and breathing, and then passed behind and stood above them as a wall of majestic protection from their enemies and a glorious light to shine upon their pathway as they marched on before.

So, after we have followed the Holy Spirit in His earlier leadings, and have come to the place of surrender and death to self and sin, then He comes nearer, passes through our very being, baptizes us into himself and then passes through all our life and becomes our reward, gathering up our past, protecting us as a mighty Providence from all evil, and guarding and guiding all our future way. Beautiful, majestic symbol of the presence of God with His people and the baptism of the Holy Ghost!

2. The next type was the sea. "They were all baptized unto Moses in the sea." There is no doubt that primarily the sea represented our baptism by water. We know the Red Sea represented the idea of their death to the old life of Egypt, and we know that baptism is the symbol of death, for "as many of us as were baptized into Christ were baptized into his death."

But it represents much more than the ceremony of baptism. It is a vivid figure of that real death to self and sin in which all true life must begin. This is the first goal to which the Holy Ghost is ever leading us—the grave. It was of this the Master said, "I have a baptism to be baptized with and how am I straitened until it be accomplished," and every true servant must follow Him by the same steps, by the same death. Is it not our deepest need? Is it not the secret of all our failures, all our sorrows, all our defeats? Is it not our deepest desire that we may be dead indeed unto self and sin? Oh, let us go forth with Him to the cross. Let us follow the pillar of cloud and fire down into the very bottom of the sea, and when we reach its depths and all seems lost, then the heavenly cloud will meet us and will enfold us in the bosom of God and baptize us into all His glorious fullness.

—*Christ in the Bible*

JAMIESON, FAUSSET, BROWN

CHAPTER 10

Vss. 1-33. Danger of Fellowship with Idolatry Illustrated in the History of Israel: Such Fellowship Incompatible with Fellowship in the Lord's Supper. Even Lawful Things Are to Be Forborne, so as Not to Hurt Weak Brethren. **1. Moreover**—The oldest MSS. read "for." Thus the connection with the foregoing chapter is expressed. Ye need to exercise self-denying watchfulness notwithstanding all your privileges, lest yc be castaways. For the Israelites with all their privileges were most of them castaways through want of it. **ignorant**—with all your boasted "knowledge." **our fathers**—The Jewish Church stands in the relation of parent to the Christian Church. **all**—Arrange as the *Greek,* "Our fathers were *all* under the *cloud*"; giving the "all" its proper emphasis. Not so much as one of so great a multitude was detained by force or disease (Ps. 105:37) [Bengel]. Five times the "all" is repeated, in the enumeration of the five favors which God bestowed on Israel (vss. 1-4). Five times, correspondingly, they sinned (vss. 6-10). In contrast to the "all" stands "many (rather, 'the most') of them" (vs. 5). *All* of them had great privileges, yet *most* of them were castaways through lust. Beware you, having greater privileges, of sharing the same doom through a similar sin. Continuing the reasoning (ch. 9:24), "They which run in a race, run *all,* but *one* receiveth the prize." **under the cloud**—were continually *under the defense* of the pillar of cloud, the symbol of the divine presence (Exod. 13:21, 22; Ps. 105: 39; cf. Isa. 4:5). **passed through the sea**—by God's miraculous interposition for them (Exod. 14:29). **2. And**—"And so" [Bengel]. **baptized unto Moses**—the servant of God and representative of the Old Testament covenant of the law: as Jesus, the Son of God, is of the Gospel covenant (John 1:17; Heb. 3:5, 6). The people were led to believe in Moses as God's servant by the miracle of the cloud protecting them, and by their being conducted under him safely through the Red Sea; therefore they are said to be "baptized unto" him (Exod. 14:31). "Baptized" is here equivalent to "*initiated*": it is used in accommodation to Paul's argument to the Corinthians; they, it is true, have been "baptized," but so also virtually were the Israelites of old; if the virtual baptism of the latter availed not to save them from the doom of lust, neither will the actual baptism of the former save them. There is a resemblance between the symbols also: for the cloud and sea consist of water, and as these took the Israelites out of sight, and then restored them again to view, so the water does to the baptized [Bengel]. Olshausen understands "the cloud" and "the sea" as symbolizing the *Spirit* and *water* respectively (John 3:5; Acts 10:44-47). Christ is the pillar-cloud that screens us from the heat of God's wrath. Christ as "the light of the world" is our "pillar of fire" to guide us in the darkness of the world. As the rock when smitten sent forth the waters, so Christ, having been once for all smitten, sends forth the waters of the Spirit. As the manna bruised in mills fed Israel, so Christ, when "it pleased the Lord to bruise Him," has become our spiritual food. A strong proof of inspiration is given in this fact, that the *historical* parts of Scripture, without the consciousness even of the authors, are covert prophecies of the future. **3. same spiritual meat**—As the Israelites had the water from the rock, which answered to *baptism,* so they had the manna which corresponded to the other of the two Christian sacraments, the Lord's Supper. Paul plainly implies the *importance* which was attached to these two sacraments by all Christians in those days: "an inspired protest against those who lower their dignity, or deny their necessity" [Alford]. Still he guards against the other extreme of thinking the mere external possession of such privileges will ensure salvation. Moreover, had there been seven sacraments, as Rome teaches, Paul would have alluded to them, whereas he refers to only the two. He does not mean by "the same" that *the Israelites and we Christians* have the "same" sacrament; but that *believing and unbelieving* Israelites alike had "the same" spiritual privilege of the manna (cf. vs. 17). It was "*spiritual* meat" or food; because given by the power of God's spirit, not by human labor [Grotius and Alford]. Galatians 4:29, "born after the Spirit," i.e., supernaturally. Psalm 78:24, "corn of heaven" (Ps. 105:40). Rather, "spiritual" in its *typical* signification, Christ, the true Bread of heaven, being signified (John 6:32). Not that the Israelites clearly understood the signification; but believers among them would feel that in the type something more was meant; and their implicit and

ADAM CLARKE

CHAPTER 10

1. *I would not that ye should be ignorant.* It seems as if the Corinthians had supposed that their being made partakers of the ordinances of the gospel, such as baptism and the Lord's Supper, would secure their salvation, notwithstanding they might be found partaking of idolatrous feasts; as long, at least, as they considered an idol to be nothing in the world. To remove this destructive supposition, which would have led them to endless errors in both principle and practice, the apostle shows that the Jews had sacramental ordinances in the wilderness, similar to those of the Christians; and that, notwithstanding they had the typical baptism from the cloud, and the typical eucharist from the paschal lamb, and the manna that came down from heaven, yet, when they joined with idolaters and partook of idolatrous feasts, God was not only displeased with them but signified this displeasure by pouring out His judgments upon them, so that in one day 23,000 of them were destroyed.

2. *And were all baptized unto Moses.* Rather "into Moses", into the covenant of which Moses was the mediator; and by this typical baptism they were brought under the obligation of acting according to the Mosaic precepts, as Christians receiving Christian baptism are said to be baptized "into Christ," and are thereby brought under obligation to keep the precepts of the gospel.

3. *Spiritual meat.* The manna which is here called *spiritual:* (1) Because it was provided supernaturally; and, (2) Because it was a type of Christ Jesus, John vi. 31.

MATTHEW HENRY

They did all eat of the same spiritual meat, and drink of the same spiritual drink. These were great privileges. One would think that this should have saved them.

Yet was it otherwise, *v.* 5. Men may enjoy many and great spiritual privileges in this world, and yet come short of eternal life. Let none presume upon their great privileges.

Verses 6–14

I. Several of their sins are specified as cautions to us. We should shun inordinate desires after carnal objects, *v.* 6. God fed them with manna, but they must have flesh, Num. xi. 4. Carnal desires get head by indulgence. If once they prevail, and bear sway in us, we know not whither they will carry us.

He warns against idolatry (*v.* 7). The apostle is speaking to the case of the Corinthians, who were tempted to feast on the heathen sacrifices.

He cautions against fornication, a sin to which the inhabitants of Corinth were in a peculiar manner addicted. How needful was a caution against fornication to those who lived in so corrupt a city! Let us fear the sins of Israel, if we would shun their plagues.

He warns us against *tempting Christ* (*as some of them tempted, and were destroyed of serpents, v.* 9), or provoking him to jealousy, *v.* 22. For which reason God sent fiery serpents among them (Num. xxi. 5, 6). And it is but just to fear that such as tempt Christ under the present dispensation will be left by him in the power of the old serpent.

JAMIESON, FAUSSET, BROWN

reverent, though indistinct, faith was counted to them for justification, of which the manna was a kind of sacramental seal. "They are not to be heard which feign that the old fathers did look only for transitory promises" (Article vii, Church of England), as appears from this passage (cf. Heb. 4: 2). **4. drink**–(Exod. 17:6). In Numbers 20:8, "the beasts" also are mentioned as having drunk. The literal water typified "*spiritual* drink," and is therefore so called. **spiritual Rock that followed them**–rather, "*accompanied* them." Not the literal rock (or its water) "followed" them, as ALFORD explains, as if Paul sanctioned the Jews' tradition (Rabbi Solomon on Num. 20:2) that the rock itself, or at least the stream from it, followed the Israelites from place to place (cf. Deut. 9:21). But Christ, the "Spiritual Rock" (Ps. 78:20, 35; Deut. 32:4, 15, 18, 30, 31, 37; Isa. 28:16; I Pet. 2:6), accompanied them (Exod. 33:15). "Followed" implies His *attending on* them to *minister to* them; thus, though mostly going *before* them, He, when occasion required it, *followed "behind"* (Exod. 14:19). He satisfied all alike as to their bodily thirst whenever they needed it; as on three occasions is expressly recorded (Exod. 15:24, 25; 17:6; Num. 20:8); and this drink for the body symbolized the spiritual drink from the Spiritual Rock (cf. John 4:13, 14; see *Note,* vs. 3). **5. But**–though they had so many tokens of God's presence. **many of them**–rather, "the majority of them"; "the whole part." All except Joshua and Caleb of the first generation. **not**–in the *Greek* emphatically standing in the beginning of the sentence: "Not," as one might have naturally expected, "with the more part of them was . . . ." **God**–whose judgment alone is valid. **for**–the event showed, they had not pleased God. **overthrown**–lit., "strewn in heaps." **in the wilderness**–far from the land of promise. **6. were**–*Greek,* "came to pass as." **our examples**–samples to us of what will befall us, if we also with all our privileges walk carelessly. **lust**–the fountain of all the four other offenses enumerated, and therefore put first (Jas. 1:14, 15; cf. Ps. 106: 14). A particular case of lust was that after flesh, when they pined for the fish, leeks, etc., of Egypt, which they had left (Num. 11:4, 33, 34). These are included in the "evil things," not that they are so in themselves, but they became so to the Israelites when they lusted after what God withheld, and were discontented with what God provided. **7. idolaters**–A case in point. As the Israelites *sat down* (a deliberate act), *ate,* and *drank* at the idol feast to the calves in Horeb, so the Corinthians were in danger of idolatry by a like act, though not professedly worshipping an idol as the Israelites (ch. 8: 10, 11; 10:14, 20, 21; Exod. 32:6). He passes here from the first to the second person, as they alone (not he also) were in danger of idolatry, etc. He resumes the first person appropriately at the 16th verse. **some**–The multitude follow the lead of some bad men. **play**–with lascivious dancing, singing, and drumming round the calf (cf. "rejoiced," Acts 7:41). **8. fornication**–lit., Fornication was generally, as in this case (Num. 25), associated at the idol feasts with spiritual fornication, i.e., idolatry. This all applied to the Corinthians (ch. 5:1, 9; 6:9, 15, 18; ch. 8:10). Balaam tempted Israel to both sins with Midian (Rev. 2:14). Cf. ch. 8:7, 9, "stumbling block," "eat . . . thing offered unto . . . idol." **three and twenty thousand**–in Numbers 25:9 "twenty and four thousand." If this were a real discrepancy, it would militate rather against inspiration of the *subject matter* and *thought,* than against *verbal* inspiration. The solution is: Moses in Numbers includes all who died "in the plague"; Paul, all who died "*in one day*"; 1000 more may have fallen the next day [KITTO, *Biblical Cyclopædia*]. Or, the real number may have been between 23,000 and 24,000, say 23,500, or 23,600; when writing generally where the exact figures were not needed, one writer might quite veraciously give one of the two round numbers near the exact one, and the other writer the other [BENGEL]. Whichever be the true way of reconciling the seeming discrepant statements, at least the ways given above prove they are not really irreconcilable. **9. tempt Christ**–So the oldest *versions,* Irenæus (264), and *good* MSS. read. Some of the *oldest* MSS. read "Lord"; and one MS. only "God." If "Lord" be read, it will mean *Christ.* As "Christ" was referred to in one of the five privileges of Israel (vs. 4), so it is natural that He should be mentioned here in one of the five corresponding sins of that people. In Numbers 21:5 it is "spake against *God*" (whence probably arose the alteration in the one MS., I Cor. 10:9, "God," to harmonize it with Num. 21:5). As either "Christ" or "Lord" is the

ADAM CLARKE

4. *Spiritual drink.* By the *spiritual meat* and *spiritual drink* the apostle certainly means both meat and drink which were furnished to the Israelitish assembly miraculously, as well as typically. *The spiritual Rock that followed them.* It appears that the apostle does not speak about the rock itself, but of Him whom it represented; namely, Christ. This was the *Rock that followed them,* and ministered to them; and this view of the subject is rendered more probable by what is said, v. 9, that they tempted Christ, and were destroyed by serpents.

5. *They were overthrown in the wilderness.* And yet all these persons were "under the cloud," "all passed through the sea," all were "baptized unto Moses in the cloud and in the sea," all ate "the same spiritual meat," all drank "the same spiritual drink," for they were made partakers of the spiritual Rock, Christ. Nothing can be a more decisive proof than this that people who have every outward ordinance and are made partakers of the grace of our Lord Jesus may so abuse their privileges and grieve the Spirit of God as to fall from their state of grace and perish everlastingly.

6. *These things were our examples.* The punishments which God inflicted on them furnish us with evidences of what God will inflict upon us if we sin after the similitude of those transgressors. *We should not lust after evil things.* It is most evident that the apostle refers here to the history in Num. xi. 4, etc: "And the mixed multitude . . . fell a lusting . . . and said, Who shall give us flesh to eat?" Into the same spirit the Corinthians had most evidently fallen; they lusted after the flesh in the idol feasts, and therefore frequented them to the great scandal of Christianity. The apostle shows them that their sin was of the same nature as that of the murmuring, rebellious Israelites whom God so severely punished; and if He did not spare the natural branches, there was no likelihood that He should spare *them.*

7. *Neither be ye idolaters.* The apostle considers partaking of the idolatrous feasts as being the flesh to their gods considered them as feeding invisibly with them on the flesh thus offered, and that everyone that partook of the feast was a real participator with the god to whom the flesh or animal had been offered in sacrifice.

Rose up to play. The Jews generally explain this word as implying idolatrous acts only. I have considered it as implying acts of impurity, with which idolatrous acts were often accompanied. It also means those dances which were practiced in honor of their gods.

8. *Fell in one day three and twenty thousand.* In Num. xxv. 9 the number is 24,000; and allowing this to be the genuine reading (and none of the Hebrew MSS. exhibit any various reading in the place), Moses and the apostle may be thus reconciled: In Num. xxv. 4, God commands Moses to "take all the heads [the rulers] of the people, and hang them up before the Lord against the sun"; these possibly amounted to 1,000, and those who fell by the plague were 23,000, so that the whole amounted to 24,000.

9. *Neither let us tempt Christ.* Instead of *Christ* several MSS. and a few versions have "the Lord."

MATTHEW HENRY

He warns against murmuring (*v.* 10). When they met with discouragements in the way to Canaan, they were very apt to fly in the face of their leaders. Something like this seems to have been the case of the Corinthians; they murmured against Paul, and in him against Christ.

II. The apostle subjoins to these particular cautions a more general one (*v.* 11). Their sins against God were typical of the infidelity of many under the gospel. God's judgments on them were types of spiritual judgments now. Their history was written, to be a standing monitor to the church. Nothing in scripture is written in vain, and it is our wisdom and duty to receive instruction from it.

A caution (*v.* 12). Others have fallen, and so may we. God has not promised to keep us from falling, if we do not look to ourselves: his protection supposes our own care.

III. He adds a word of comfort, *v.* 13. Though it is displeasing to God for us to presume, it is not pleasing to him for us to despair. Either our trials will be proportioned to our strength, or strength will be supplied in proportion to our temptations. Others have the like temptations; what they bear up under, and break through, we may also. Men may be false, and the world may be false; but God is faithful, and our strength and security are in him. He is wise as well as faithful. He knows what we can bear. He will take care that we be not overcome, if we rely upon him. *He will make a way to escape.* There is no valley so dark but he can find a way through it.

IV. "*Flee idolatry;* shun it." Idolatry is the most heinous affront to the true God. "Seeing you have such encouragement to trust God, be not shaken by any discouragements. God will help you in your trials, and help you out of them." We cannot fall by a temptation if we cleave fast to him.

Verses 15–22

The apostle urges the general caution against idolatry.

I. An appeal to their own reason and judgment: "*I speak to wise men, judge you what I say,*" *v.* 15.

JAMIESON, FAUSSET, BROWN

genuine reading, "Christ" must be "God." Cf. "Why do ye tempt the Lord?" (Exod. 17:2, 7. Cf. Rom. 14:11, with Isa. 45:22, 23). Israel's discontented complainings were temptings of Christ especially, the "Angel" of the covenant (Exod. 23:20, 21; 32:34; Isa. 63:9). Though they drank of "that Rock . . . Christ" (vs. 4), they yet complained for want of water (Exod. 17:2, 7). Though also eating the same spiritual meat (Christ, "the true manna," "the bread of life"), they yet murmured, "Our soul loatheth this light bread." In this case, being punished by the fiery serpents, they were saved by the brazen serpent, the emblem of *Christ* (cf. John 8:56; Heb. 11:26). The *Greek* for "tempt" means, *tempt* or *try, so as to wear out* the long-suffering of Christ (cf. Ps. 95:8, 9; Num. 14:22). The Corinthians were in danger of provoking God's long-suffering by walking on the verge of idolatry, through overweening confidence in their knowledge. **10. some of them . . . murmured**—upon the death of Korah and his company, who themselves were murmurers (Num. 16:41, 49). Their murmurs against Moses and Aaron were virtually murmurs against God (cf. Exod. 16:8, 10). Paul herein glances at the Corinthian murmurs against himself, the apostle of Christ. **destroyed**—14,700 perished. **the destroyer**—THE same destroying angel sent by God as in Exodus 12:23, and II Samuel 24:16. **11. Now . . . these things . . . ensamples**—resuming the thread of vs. 6. The oldest MSS. read, "by way of example." **the ends of the world**—lit., "of the ages"; the New Testament dispensation in its successive phases (*plural*, "ends") being the winding up of all former "ages." No new dispensation shall appear till Christ comes as Avenger and Judge; till then the "ends," being many, include various successive periods (cf. Heb. 9:26). As we live in the last dispensation, which is the consummation of all that went before, our responsibilities are the greater; and the greater is the guilt, Paul implies, to the Corinthians, which they incur if they fall short of their privileges. **12. thinketh he standeth**—stands and thinks that he stands [BENGEL]; i.e., stands "by faith" "well pleasing" to God; in contrast to vs. 5, "with many of them God was not well pleased" (Rom. 11:20). **fall**—from his place in the Church of God (cf. vs. 8, "fell"). Both temporally and spiritually (Rom. 14:4). Our security, so far as relates to God, consists in faith; so far as relates to ourselves, it consists in fear. **13.** Consolation to them, under their temptation; it is none but such as is "common to man," or "such as man can bear," "adapted to man's powers of endurance" [WAHL]. **faithful**—(Ps. 125:3; Isa. 27:3, 8; Rev. 3:10). "God is faithful" to the covenant which He made with you in calling you (I Thess. 5:24). To be *led into* temptation is distinct from *running* into it, which would be "tempting God" (vs. 9; Matt. 4:7). **way to escape**—(Jer. 29:11; II Pet. 2:9). The *Greek* is, "*the* way of escape"; the appropriate way of escape in each particular temptation; not an immediate escape, but one in due time, after patience has had her perfect work (Jas. 1:2-4,12). He "makes" the way of escape simultaneously with the temptation which His providence permissively aranges for His people. **to bear it**—*Greek*, "to bear up under it," or "against it." Not, He will take it away (II Cor. 12:7-9). **14.** Resuming the argument, vs. 7; ch. 8: 9, 10. **flee**—Do not tamper with it by doubtful acts, such as eating idol meats on the plea of Christian liberty. The only safety is in *wholly shunning* whatever borders on idolatry (II Cor. 6:16, 17). The Holy Spirit herein also presciently warned the Church against the idolatry, subsequently transferred from the idol feast to the Lord's Supper itself, in the figment of transubstantiation. **15.** Appeal to their own powers of *judgment* to weigh the force of the argument that follows: viz., that as the partaking of the Lord's Supper involves a partaking of the Lord Himself, and the partaking of the Jewish sacrificial meats involved a partaking of the altar of God, and, as the heathens sacrifice to devils, to partake of an idol feast is to have fellowship with devils. We cannot divest ourselves of the responsibility of "judging" for ourselves. The weakness of private judgment is not an argument against its use, but its abuse. We should the more take pains in searching the infallible word, with every aid within our reach, and above all with humble prayer for the Spirit's teaching (Acts 17:11). If Paul, an inspired apostle, not only permits, but urges, men to *judge* his sayings by Scripture, much more should the fallible ministers of the present visible Church do so. **To wise men**—refers with a mixture of irony to the Corinthian boast of "wisdom" (ch. 4:40; II Cor. 11:19). Here you have an opportunity of exercising your "wisdom" in judging "what I say."

ADAM CLARKE

10. *Neither murmur ye.* It appears from what the apostle says here that the Corinthians were murmuring against God and His apostle for prohibiting them from partaking of the idolatrous feasts, just as the Israelites did in the wilderness in reference to a similar subject. *Destroyed of the destroyer.* The Jews suppose that God employed destroying angels to punish those rebellious Israelites; they were five in number, and one of them they call *the destroyer.*

11. *Upon whom the ends of the world are come.* The end of the times included within the whole duration of the Mosaic economy. For although the word *aion* means in its primary sense "endless being" or duration, yet in its accommodated sense it is applied to any round or duration that is complete in itself; and here it evidently means the whole duration of the Mosaic economy. We are to consider the apostle's words as referring to the end of the Jewish dispensation and the commencement of the Christian, which is the last dispensation which God will vouchsafe to man in the state of probation.

12. *Let him that thinketh he standeth.* "Let him who most confidently standeth"—him who has the fullest conviction in his own conscience that his heart is right with God, and that his mind is right in the truth—take heed lest he fall from his faith, and from the state of holiness in which the grace of God has placed him. I have already shown that the verb *dokein,* which we render "to seem, to think, to suppose," is used by the best Greek writers, not to lessen or weaken the sense, but to render it stronger and more emphatic. In a state of probation everything may change; while we are in this life we may stand or fall. Our standing in the faith depends on our union with God, and that depends on our watching unto prayer and continuing to possess that faith that worketh by love. The highest saint under heaven can stand no longer than he depends upon God and continues in the obedience of faith. He that ceases to do so will fall into sin and get a darkened understanding and a hardened heart, and he may continue in this state till God comes to take away his soul. Therefore "let him who most assuredly standeth take heed lest he fall"; not only partially, but finally.

13. *But such as is common to man.* Chrysostom has properly translated this word "small, short, moderate." Your temptations or trials have been but trifling in comparison of those endured by the Israelites; they might have been easily resisted and overcome. Besides, God will not suffer you to be tried above the strength He gives you; but as the trial comes, He will provide you with sufficient strength to resist it; as the trial comes in, He will make your way out. The words are very remarkable, "He will, with the temptation, make the deliverance, or way out." Satan is never permitted to block up our way without the providence of God making a way through the wall.

14. *Wherefore . . . flee from idolatry.* This is a trial of no great magnitude; to escape from so gross a temptation requires but a moderate portion of grace and circumspection.

15. *I speak as to wise men.* The Corinthians valued themselves not a little on their wisdom and various gifts; the apostle admits this and draws an argument from it against themselves. As you are so wise, surely you can see the propriety of abominating idolatry of every kind; for an idol is nothing in the world and can do nothing for you and nothing against you.

MATTHEW HENRY

II. He lays down his argument from the Lord's supper. Is not this sacred rite a token whereby we professedly hold communion with Christ? Thus to partake of the Lord's table is to profess ourselves his guests and covenant people; and this in conjunction with all true Christians, with whom we have communion also in this ordinance (*v.* 17).

III. He confirms this from the Jewish worship and customs. Those who were admitted to eat of the offerings were reckoned to partake of the sacrifice itself, and therefore surely to worship God.

IV. He applies this to the argument against feasting with idolaters on their sacrifices. An idol was nothing. What was sacrificed to idols was nothing. But the eating of it as a part of a heathen sacrifice was, (1) A partaking with them in their idolatry, just as he who eats the Lord's supper is supposed to partake in the Christian sacrifice. "Therefore do not feast on their sacrifices. I would not have you be in communion with devils." (2) It was a virtual renouncing of Christianity, *v.* 21. Communion with Christ, and communion with devils, could never be had at once. One must be renounced, if the other was maintained. How much reason have we to look to it that every sin and idol be renounced by us, when we eat and drink at the Lord's table.

JAMIESON, FAUSSET, BROWN

16. The cup of blessing—answering to the Jewish "cup of blessing," over which thanks were offered in the Passover. It was in doing so that Christ instituted this part of the Lord's Supper (Matt. 26. 27; Luke 22:17, 20). **we bless**—"we," not merely ministers, but also the congregation. The minister "blesses" (i.e., *consecrates with blessing*) the cup, not by any priestly transmitted authority of his own, but as representative of the congregation, who virtually through him bless the cup. The consecration is the corporate act of the whole Church. The act of *joint blessing* by him and them (not "the cup" itself, which, as also "the bread," in the *Greek* is in the accusative), and the consequent drinking of it together, constitute the communion, i.e., the joint participation "of the blood of Christ." Cf. vs. 18, "They who eat . . . are partakers" (joint communicants). "Is" in both cases in this verse is literal, not *represents.* He who with faith partakes of the cup and the bread, partakes really but spiritually of the blood and body of Christ (Eph. 5:30, 32), and of the benefits of His sacrifice on the cross (cf. vs. 18). In contrast to this is to have "fellowship with devils" (vs. 20). ALFORD explains, "The cup . . . is the [joint] participation (i.e., that whereby the act of participation takes place) of the blood . . . ." It is the seal of our living union with, and a means of our partaking of, Christ as our Saviour (John 6:53-57). It is not said, "The cup . . . is *the blood,*" or "the bread . . . is *the body,*" but "is the *communion* [joint-participation] of the blood . . . body." If the bread be changed into the literal body of Christ, where is the sign of the sacrament? Romanists eat Christ "*in remembrance* of Himself." To drink literal *blood* would have been an abomination to Jews, which the first Christians were (Lev. 17:11, 12). *Breaking the bread* was part of the act of consecrating it, for thus was represented the crucifixion of Christ's body (I Cor. 11:24). The distinct specification of the bread and the wine disproves the Romish doctrine of concomitancy, and exclusion of the laity from the cup. **17. one bread**—rather, "loaf." One loaf alone seems to have been used in each celebration. *and* **one body**—Omit "and"; "one loaf [that is], one body." "We, *the many* (viz., believers assembled; so the *Greek*), are one bread (by our partaking of the same loaf, which becomes assimilated to the substance of all our bodies; and so we become), one body" (with Christ, and so with one another). **we . . . all**—*Greek*, "the whole of us." **18. Israel after the flesh**—the literal, as distinguished from the spiritual, Israel (Rom. 2: 29; 4:1; 9:3; Gal. 4:29). **partakers of the altar**—and so *of God,* whose is the altar; they have fellowship in God and His worship, of which the altar is the symbol. **19, 20. What say I then?**—The inference might be drawn from the analogies of the Lord's Supper and Jewish sacrifices, that an idol is *really what the heathen thought it to be, a god,* and that in eating idol meats they had fellowship with the god. This verse guards against such an inference: "What would I say then? that a thing sacrificed to an idol is any real thing (in the sense that the heathen regard it), or that an idol is any real thing?" (The oldest MSS. read the words in this order. Supply *"Nay";*) "But [I say] that the things which the Gentiles sacrifice, they sacrifice to devils" (demons). Paul here introduces a new fact. It is true that, as I said, an idol has no reality in the sense that the heathen regard it, but it has a reality in another sense; heathendom being under Satan's dominion as "prince of this world," *he* and *his demons* are in fact the powers worshipped by the heathen, whether they are or are not conscious of it (Deut. 32:17; Lev. 17:7; II Chron. 11:15; Ps. 106. 37; Rev. 9:20). "Devil" is in the *Greek* restricted to Satan; "demons" is the term applied to his subordinate evil spirits. Fear, rather than love, is the motive of heathen worship (cf. the English word "panic," from PAN, whose human form with horns and cloven hoofs gave rise to the vulgar representations of Satan which prevail now); just as fear is the spirit of Satan and his demons (Jas. 2:19). **I would not that ye . . . have fellowship with devils**—by partaking of idol feasts (ch. 8:10). **21. Ye cannot . . .**—really and spiritually; though ye may outwardly (I Kings 18:21). **cup of devils**—in contrast to *the cup of the Lord.* At idol feasts libations were usually made from the cup to the idol first, and then the guests drank; so that in drinking they had fellowship with the idol. **the Lord's table**—The Lord's Supper is a feast on a *table,* not a sacrifice on an altar. Our only altar is the cross, our only sacrifice that of Christ once for all. The Lord's Supper stands, however, in the same relation, analogically, to Christ's sacrifice, as the Jews' sacrificial feasts did to their sacrifices (cf. Mal. 1:7, "altar . . .

ADAM CLARKE

16. *The cup of blessing.* The apostle speaks here of the Eucharist, which he illustrates by *the cup of blessing,* over which thanks were expressed at the conclusion of the Passover.

The communion of the blood of Christ. We who partake of this sacred cup in commemoration of the death of Christ are made partakers of His body and blood and thus have fellowship with Him, as those who partake of an idol feast thereby, as much as they can, participate with the idol to whom the sacrifice was offered.

17. *For we being many are one bread.* The original would be better translated thus: "Because there is one bread, or loaf, we, who are many, are one body." As only one loaf was used at the Passover, and those who partook of it were considered to be one religious body, so we who partake of the eucharistical bread and wine, in commemoration of the sacrificial death of Christ, are one spiritual society, because we are all made partakers of that one Christ whose blood was shed for us to make an atonement for our sins, as the blood of the paschal lamb was shed and sprinkled in reference to this of which it was the type.

18. *Behold Israel after the flesh.* The Jews not yet converted to Christianity, the latter being Israel after the Spirit. As the design of the apostle was to withdraw his converts at Corinth from all temptations to idolatry, he produces two examples to show the propriety of his endeavors. (1) All who join together in celebrating the Lord's Supper, and are partakers of that one bread, give proof by this that they are Christians and have fellowship with Christ. (2) All the Israelites who offer sacrifice and partake of those sacrifices give proof thereby that they are Jews, and are in fellowship with the object of their worship. So they who join in idol festivals and eat things which have been offered to idols give proof that they are in communion with those idolaters, and that they have fellowship with the demons they worship.

19. *What say I then?* A Jewish phrase for, "I conclude." And this is his conclusion: that although an idol is nothing, has neither power nor influence, nor are things offered to idols anything the worse for being thus offered, yet, as the things sacrificed by the Gentiles are sacrificed to demons and not to God, those who partake of them have fellowship with demons. Those who profess Christianity cannot have fellowship with both Christ and the devil.

21. *Ye cannot drink the cup of the Lord.* It is in vain that you who frequent these idol festivals profess the religion of Christ and commemorate His death and passion in the holy Eucharist; for you cannot have that fellowship with Christ which this ordinance implies while you are partakers of the table of demons.

MATTHEW HENRY

V. He warns them that God is a jealous God (*v.* 22). Those who have fellowship with other gods provoke him to jealousy. And, before this be done, persons should consider whether they are stronger than he. It is a dangerous thing to provoke God's anger, unless we could withstand his power. Shall we rouse almighty wrath? Are we a match for God?

Verses 23–33

In what instances Christians might lawfully eat what had been sacrificed to idols.

I. That may be lawful which is not expedient, which will not edify. He must be concerned not to hurt his neighbour, nay, he must be concerned to promote his welfare. Those who allow themselves in everything not plainly sinful in itself will often run into what is evil by accident. The welfare of others, as well as our own convenience, must be consulted in many things we do.

II. He tells them that what was *sold in the shambles they might eat without asking questions.* They need not be so scrupulous as to ask the butcher whether the meat he sold had been offered to an idol? It was there sold as common food, and as such might be bought and used; *for the earth is the Lord's, and the fulness thereof* (*v.* 26).

III. If they were invited by any heathen acquaintances to a feast, *they might go, and eat what was set before them, without asking questions* (*v.* 27). There is a civility owing even to infidels and heathens. Anything fit to be eaten, that was set before them, they might lawfully eat. It is to be understood of civil feasting, not religious. At a common feast they might expect common food.

IV. Yet, if any should say it was a thing that had been offered to idols, they should refrain. They should refrain for his sake who suggested this to them, and for conscience' sake, out of regard to conscience. Christians should be very cautious of doing what may thus prejudice the consciences of others.

V. He urges them to refrain where they will give offence. Christians should take care not to use their liberty to the hurt of others, nor their own reproach.

JAMIESON, FAUSSET, BROWN

table of the Lord"), and the heathen idol feasts to their idolatrous sacrifices (Isa. 65:11). The heathen sacrifices were offered to idol nonentities, behind which Satan lurked. The Jews' sacrifice was but a shadow of the substance which was to come. Our one sacrifice of Christ is the only substantial reality; therefore, while the partaker of the Jew's sacrificial feast partook rather "of the altar" (vs. 18) than of GOD manifested fully, and the heathen idol-feaster had fellowship really with demons, the communicant in the Lord's Supper has in it a real communion of, or fellowship in, the body of Christ once sacrificed, and now exalted as the Head of redeemed humanity. **22. Do we provoke the Lord to jealousy?**—by dividing our fellowship between Him and idols (Ezek. 20:39). Is it our wish to provoke Him to assert His power? Deuteronomy 32:21 is before the apostle's mind [ALFORD], (Exod. 20:5). **are we stronger?**—that we can risk a contest with Him. **23. All things are lawful for me . . .**—Recurring to the Corinthian plea (ch. 6:12), he repeats his qualification of it. The oldest MSS. omit both times "for me." **edify not**—tend not to *build up* the spiritual temple, the Church, in faith and love. Paul does not appeal to the apostolic decision (Acts 15), which seems to have been not so much regarded outside of Palestine, but rather to the broad principle of true Christian freedom, which does not allow us to be governed by external things, as though, because we *can* use them, we *must* use them (ch. 6:12). Their use or non-use is to be regulated by regard to *edification.* **24.** (Vs. 33; ch. 13:5; Rom. 15:1, 2.) **25. shambles**—butchers' stalls; the flesh-market. **asking no question**—whether it has been offered to an idol or not. **for conscience' sake**—If on asking you should hear it had been offered to idols, a scruple would arise in your conscience which was needless, and never would have arisen had you asked no questions. **26.** The ground on which such eating without questioning is justified is, the earth and all its contents ("the fulness thereof," Ps. 20:1; 50:12), including all meats, belong to the Lord, and are appointed for our use; and where conscience suggests no scruple, all are to be eaten (Rom. 14:14, 20; I Tim. 4:4, 5; cf. Acts 10:15). **27. ye be disposed to go**—tacitly implying, they would be as well not to go, but yet not forbidding them to go (vs. 9) [GROTIUS]. The feast is not an idol feast, but a general entertainment, at which, however, there might be meat that had been offered to an idol. **for conscience' sake**—See *Note,* vs. 25. **28. if any man**—a weak Christian at table, wishing to warn his brother. **offered in sacrifice unto idols**—The oldest MSS. omit "unto idols." At a heathen's table the expression, offensive to him, would naturally be avoided. **for conscience' sake**—not to cause a stumbling block to the conscience of thy weak brother (ch. 8:10-12). **for the earth is the Lord's, . . .**—not in the oldest MSS. **29. Conscience . . . of the other**—the weak brother introduced in vs. 28. **for why is my liberty judged of another man's conscience?**—Paul passes to the first person, to teach his converts by putting himself as it were in their position. The *Greek* terms for "the other" and "another" are distinct. *"The other" is the one with whom Paul's and his Corinthian converts' concern is; "another" is any other with whom he and they have no concern.* If a guest know the meat to be idol meat while I know it not, I have "liberty" to eat without being condemned by his "conscience" [GROTIUS]. Thus the "for . . ." is an argument for vs. 27, "Eat, asking no questions." Or, Why should I give occasion by the rash use of my liberty that another should condemn it [ESTIUS], or that my liberty should cause the destruction of my weak brother?" [MENOCHIUS.] Or, the words are those of the Corinthian objector (perhaps used in their letter, and so quoted by Paul), "Why is my liberty judged by another's conscience?" Why should not I be judged only by my own, and have liberty to do whatever it sanctions? Paul replies in vs. 31, Your doing so ought always to be limited by regard to what most tends "to the glory of God" [VATABLUS, CONYBEARE and HOWSON]. The first explanation is simplest; the "for . . ." in it refers to "not thine own" (i.e., "not *my* own," in Paul's change to the first person); I am to abstain only in the case of liability to offend *another's* conscience; in cases where *my own* has no scruple, I am not bound, in God's judgment, by any other conscience than my own. **30. For**—The oldest MSS. omit "For." **by grace**—rather, "thankfully" [ALFORD]. **I . . . be partaker**—I partake of the food set before me. **evil spoken of**—by him who does not use his liberty, but will eat nothing without scrupulosity and questioning whence the meat comes. **give thanks**—which con-

ADAM CLARKE

22. *Do we provoke the Lord to jealousy?* All idolatry is represented as a sort of spiritual adultery. It is giving that heart to Satan that should be devoted to God; and He is represented as being jealous because of the infidelity of those who have covenanted to give their hearts to Him. *Are we stronger than he?* As He has threatened to punish such transgressors and will infallibly do it, can we resist His omnipotence? A sinner should consider, while he is in rebellion against God, whether he be able to resist that power whereby God will inflict vengeance.

23. *All things are lawful for me.* I may lawfully eat all kinds of food, *but all things are not expedient.* It would not be "becoming" in me to eat of all, because I should by this offend and grieve many weak minds.

24. *Let no man seek his own.* Let none for his private gratification or emolument disturb the peace or injure the soul of another. Let every man live, not for himself, but for every part of the great human family with which he is surrounded.

25. *Whatsoever is sold in the shambles, that eat.* The case to which the apostle refers is simply this: It was customary to bring the flesh of the animal to market, the blood of which had been poured out in sacrifice to an idol. Or, taken more particularly, the case was this: One part of the sacrifice was consumed on the altar of the idol; a second part was dressed and eaten by the sacrificer; and a third belonged to the priest, and was often sold in the shambles. To partake of the second share, or to feast upon the sacrifice, Paul absolutely forbids, because this was one part of the religious worship which was paid to the idol; it was sitting down as guests at his table, in token that they were in fellowship with him. This was utterly incompatible with receiving the sacrament of the Lord's Supper, which was the communion of the body and blood of Christ. But as to the third share, the apostle leaves them at liberty either to eat of it or forbear—except that, by eating, their weak brethren should be offended; in that case, though the thing was lawful, it was their duty to abstain.

26. *For the earth is the Lord's.* And because God made the earth and its fullness, all animals, plants, and vegetables, there can be nothing in it or them impure or unholy, because all are the creatures of God.

27. *If any . . . bid you to a feast.* The apostle means any common meal, not an idol festival; for to such no Christian could lawfully go. Whatsoever is set before you, eat. Do not act as the Jews generally do, torturing both themselves and others with questions.

28. *This is offered in sacrifice unto idols.* While they were not apprized of this circumstance they might lawfully eat; but when told that the flesh set before them had been offered to an idol, then they were not to eat, for the sake of his weak conscience who pointed out the circumstance. For the apostle still takes it for granted that even the flesh offered in sacrifice to an idol might be eaten innocently at any private table, as in that case they were no longer in danger of being partakers with devils, as this was no idol festival. *For the earth is the Lord's, and the fulness thereof.* This whole clause, which appears also in v. 26, is wanting here in a number of MSS. and in several of the fathers. It has scarcely any authority to support it.

29-30. *For why is my liberty judged of another man's conscience?* Though in the case of flesh offered to idols and other matters connected with idolatry (on which it appears there was much of a tender conscience among some of the Corinthians) it was necessary to sacrifice something to an overscrupulous conscience, yet the gospel of Christ did not lay any man under this general burden, that he must do nothing at which any weak brother might feel hurt or be stumbled; for the liberty of the gospel must not take for its rule the scrupulosity of any conscience. For if a man, by grace—by the allowance or authority of the gospel—partake of anything that God's bounty has sent and which the gospel has not forbidden and give thanks to God for the blessing, no man has right or

MATTHEW HENRY

VI. The apostle takes occasion from this discourse to lay down a general rule for Christians' conduct (*v.* 31, 32). In all we do, we should aim at the glory of God. And therefore nothing should be done by us to offend any, *whether Jew, or Gentile, or the church, v.* 32. Our own humour and appetite must not determine our practice, but the honour of God and the good and edification of the church.

VII. He presses all upon them by his own example, *v.* 33. A preacher may press his advice home with boldness and authority when he can enforce it with his own example. And it is highly commendable in a minister to neglect his own advantage that he may promote the salvation of his hearers.

CHAPTER 11

Verses 1–16

Be ye followers of me, as I also am of Christ (*v.* 1). It is plain that Paul not only preached such doctrine as they ought to believe, but led such a life as they ought to imitate. Ministers are likely to preach most to the purpose when they can press their hearers to follow their example. Yet would not Paul be followed blindly. He would be followed himself no further than he followed Christ. Christ's pattern is a copy without a blot; so is no man's else. He passes next to reprehend an indecency among them, of which the women were more especially guilty.

I. A commendation of what was praiseworthy in them (*v.* 2). When we reprove what is amiss in any, it is very prudent and fit to commend what is good in them.

II. The superiority of the man over the woman. Christ is at the head of mankind. In this high office he has a superior, God being his head. And as God is the head of Christ, and Christ the head of the whole human kind, so the man is the head of the two sexes: and the woman should be in subjection ,and not usurp the man's place. The women of the church of Corinth prayed and prophesied even in their assemblies, *v.* 5. It is indeed an apostolical canon, that the women *should keep silence in the churches* (*ch.* xiv. 34; 1 Tim. ii. 12). The apostle does not in this place prohibit the thing, but reprehend the manner of doing it. The manner of doing a thing enters into the morality of it. We must not only be concerned to do good, but that the good we do be well done.

III. The thing he reprehends is the woman's praying or prophesying uncovered, or the man's doing either covered, *v.* 4, 5.

JAMIESON, FAUSSET, BROWN

secrates all the Christian's acts (Rom. 14:6; I Tim. 4:3, 4).

31. Contrast Zechariah 7:6; the picture of worldly men. The godly may "eat and drink," and it shall be well with him (Jer. 22:15, 16). **to the glory of God**–(Col. 3:17; I Pet. 4:11)–which involves our having regard to the edification of our neighbor.

32. Give none offence–in things indifferent (ch. 8:13; Rom. 14:13; II Cor. 6:3); for in all essential things affecting Christian doctrine and practice, even in the smallest *detail,* we must not swerve from principle, whatever offense may be the result (ch. 1:23). Giving offense is unnecessary, if our own spirit cause it; necessary, if it be caused by the truth. **33. I please**–I try to please (ch. 9:19, 22; Rom. 15:2). **not seeking mine own**–(vs. 24). **many**–rather as *Greek,* "THE many."

CHAPTER 11

Vss. 1-34. CENSURE ON DISORDERS IN THEIR ASSEMBLIES: THEIR WOMEN NOT BEING VEILED, AND ABUSES AT THE LOVE-FEASTS. **1.** Rather belonging to the end of ch. 10, than to this chapter. **followers**–*Greek,* "imitators." **of Christ**–who did not please Himself (Rom. 15:3); but gave Himself, at the cost of laying aside His divine glory, and dying as man, for us (Eph. 5:2; Phil. 2:4, 5). We are to follow Christ first, and earthly teachers only so far as they follow Christ. **2.** Here the chapter ought to begin. **ye remember me in all things**–in your *general* practice, though in the *particular* instances which follow ye fail. **ordinances**–*Greek,* "traditions," i.e., apostolic directions given by word of mouth or in writing (vs. 23; ch. 15:3; II Thess. 2:15). The reference here is mainly to *ceremonies:* for in vs. 23, as to the LORD'S SUPPER, which is not a mere ceremony, he says, not merely, "I *delivered* unto you," but also, "I received of the Lord"; here he says only, "I delivered to you." Romanists argue hence for oral traditions. But the difficulty is to know *what is a* genuine apostolic tradition intended for all ages. Any that can be *proved* to be such ought to be observed; any that cannot, ought to be rejected (Rev. 22:18). Those preserved in the written word alone can be proved to be such. **3.** The Corinthian women, on the ground of the abolition of distinction of sexes in Christ, claimed equality with the male sex, and, overstepping the bounds of propriety, came forward to pray and prophesy without the customary headcovering of females. The Gospel, doubtless, did raise women from the degradation in which they had been sunk, especially in the East. Yet, while on a level with males as to *the offer of, and standing in grace* (Gal. 3:28), their subjection in point of *order, modesty,* and *seemliness,* is to be maintained. Paul reproves here their unseemliness as to *dress:* in ch. 14:34, as to the retiring *modesty in public* which becomes them. He grounds his reproof here on the subjection of woman to man in the order of creation. **the head**–an appropriate expression, when he is about to treat of woman's appropriate *headdress* in public. **of every man . . . Christ**–(Eph. 5:23). **of . . . woman . . . man**–(*V.*8; Gen. 3:16; I Tim. 2:11, 12; I Pet. 3:1, 5, 6). **head of Christ is God**–(ch. 3: 23; 15:27, 28; Luke 3:22, 38; John 14:28; 20:17; Eph. 3:9). "Jesus, therefore, must be of the same essence as God: for, since the man is the head of the woman, and since the head is of the same essence as the body, and God is the head of the Son, it follows the Son is of the same essence as the Father" [S. CHRYSOSTOM]. "The woman is of the essence of the man, and not made by the man; so, too, the Son is not made by the Father, but of the essence of the Father" [THEODORET, t. 3, p. 171]. **4. praying**–in public (vs. 17). **prophesying**–preaching in the Spirit (ch. 12:10). **having**–i.e., if he were to have: a supposed case to illustrate the impropriety in the *woman's* case. It was the Greek custom (and so that at Corinth) for men in worship to be uncovered; whereas the Jews wore the Talith, or veil, to show reverence before God, and their unworthiness to look on Him (Isa. 6:2); however,

ADAM CLARKE

authority to condemn such a person. This seems to be the meaning of these two verses; and they read a lesson of caution to rash judges, and to those who are apt to take offense.

31. *Whether therefore ye eat, or drink.* As no general rule can be laid down in reference to the above particulars, there is one maxim of which no Christian must lose sight—that whether he eats or drinks of this or the other kind of aliments, or whatever else he may do, he must do it so as to bring glory to God. This is a sufficient rule to regulate every man's conscience and practice in all indifferent things, where there are no express commands or prohibitions.

32. *Give none offence.* Scrupulously avoid giving any cause of offense either to the unconverted *Jews* or to the unconverted *Gentiles,* so as to prejudice them against Christianity; *nor to the church of God,* made up of converts from the above parties.

33. *Even as I please all men.* Act as I do. Forgetting myself, my own interests, convenience, ease, and comfort, I labor for the welfare of others, and particularly that they may be saved. How blessed and amiable were the spirit and conduct of this holy man!

CHAPTER 11

1. *Be ye followers of me.* This verse certainly belongs to the preceding chapter, and is here out of all proper place and connection.

2. *That ye remember me in all things. It* appears that the apostle had previously given them a variety of directions relative to the matters mentioned here; that some had paid strict attention to them, and that others had not; and that contentions and divisions were the consequences, which he here reproves and endeavors to rectify.

3. *The head of every man is Christ.* The apostle is speaking particularly of Christianity and its ordinances. Christ is the Head or Author of this religion and is the Creator, Preserver, and Lord of every man. The man also is the lord or head of the woman; and the Head or Lord of Christ, as Mediator between God and man, is God the Father. Here is the order—God sends His Son, Jesus Christ, to redeem man; Christ comes and lays down His life for the world; every man who receives Christianity confesses that Jesus Christ is Lord, to the glory of God the Father; and every believing woman will acknowledge, according to Gen. iii. 16, that God has placed her in a dependence on the subjection to the man. So far there is no difficulty in this passage.

4. *Praying or prophesying.* Any person who engages in public acts in the worship of God, whether prayer, singing, or exhortation; for we learn from the apostle himself that "to prophesy" signifies to speak "unto men to edification, and exhortation, and comfort," chap. xiv. 3. And this comprehends all that we understand by exhortation, or even preaching. *Having his head*

MATTHEW HENRY

IV. The reasons on which he grounds his reprehension. *The man that prays or prophesies with his head covered dishonoureth his head,* namely, Christ, the head of every man (*v.* 3).

The woman who prays or prophesies with her head uncovered dishonoureth her head, namely, the man, *v.* 3. She appears in the dress of her superior, and throws off the token of her subjection. The sexes should not affect to change places. The woman should keep to the rank God has chosen for her.

A. T. ROBERTSON:

5. "With her head unveiled" (*akatakaluptoi tei kephalei*). Associative instrumental case of manner and the predicative adjective (compound adjective and feminine form same as masculine), "with the head unveiled." Probably some of the women had violated this custom. "Amongst Greeks only the *hetairai*, so numerous in Corinth, went about unveiled; slave women wore the shaven head—also a punishment of the adulteress" (Findlay). "One and the same thing as if she were shaven" (*hen kai to auto tei exuremenei*). Literally, "One and the same thing with the one shaven" (associative instrumental case again, Robertson, *Grammar*, p. 530). Perfect passive articular participle of the verb *xurao*, later form for the old *xureo*. It is public praying and prophesying that the Apostle here has in mind. He does not here condemn the act, but the breach of custom which would bring reproach. A woman convicted of adultery had her hair shorn (Isa. 7:20). The Justinian code prescribed shaving the head for an adulteress whom the husband refused to receive after two years. Paul does not tell Corinthian Christian women to put themselves on a level with courtesans.

—Word Pictures in the New Testament

The man is the image and glory of God. It is the man who is set at the head of this lower creation, and therein he bears the resemblance of God. The woman, on the other hand, *is the glory of the man* (*v.* 7).

JAMIESON, FAUSSET, BROWN

Maimonides (*Mishna*) excepts cases where (as in Greece) the custom of the place was different. **dishonoureth his head**—not as ALFORD, "Christ" (vs. 3): but literally, as "his head" is used in the beginning of the verse. *He dishonoreth his head* (the principal part of the body) by wearing a covering or veil, which is a mark of subjection, and which makes him look downwards instead of upwards to his Spiritual Head, Christ, to whom alone he owes subjection. Why, then, ought not man to wear the covering in token of his subjection to Christ, as the woman wears it in token of her subjection to man? "Because Christ is not seen: the man is seen; so the covering of him who is under Christ is not seen; of her who is under the man, is seen" [BENGEL]. (Cf. vs. 7.) **5. woman . . . prayeth . . . prophesieth**—This instance of women speaking in public worship is an extraordinary case, and justified only by the miraculous gifts which such women possessed as their credentials; for instance, Anna the prophetess and Priscilla (so Acts 2:18). The ordinary rule to them is: silence in public (ch. 14:34, 35; I Tim. 2:11, 12). Mental receptivity and activity in family life are recognized in Christianity, as most accordant with the destiny of woman. This passage does not necessarily sanction women speaking in public. even though possessing miraculous gifts; but simply records what took place at Corinth, without expressing an opinion on it, reserving the censure of it till ch. 14:34, 35. Even those women endowed with prophecy were designed to exercise their gift, rather in other times and places, than the public congregation. **dishonoureth . . . head**—in that she acts against the divine ordinance and the modest propriety that becomes her: in putting away the veil, she puts away the badge of her subjection to man, which is her true "honor"; for through him it connects her with Christ, the head of the man. Moreover, as the *head-covering* was the emblem of maiden modesty before man (Gen. 24:65), and conjugal chastity (Gen. 20:16); so, to *uncover the head* indicated withdrawal from the *power* of the husband, whence a suspected wife had her head *uncovered* by the priest (Num. 5:18). ALFORD takes "her head" to be man, her symbolical, not her literal head; but as it is literal in the former clause, it must be so in the latter one. **all one as if . . . shaven**—As woman's hair is given her by nature, as her covering (vs. 15), to cut it off like a man, all admit, would be indecorous: therefore, to put away the head-covering, too, like a man, would be similarly indecorous. It is *natural* to her to have long hair for her covering: she ought, therefore, to add the other (the wearing of a head-covering) to show that she does of *her own will* that which *nature* itself teaches she ought to do, in token of her subjection to man. **6.** A woman would not like to be "shorn" or (what is worse) "shaven"; but if she chooses to be uncovered (unveiled) in front, let her be so also behind, i.e., "shorn." **a shame**—an unbecoming thing (cf. vss. 13-15). Thus the shaving of nuns is "a shame." **7-9.** Argument, also, from man's more immediate relation to God, and the woman's to man. **man . . . image . . . glory of God**—being created in God's "image," *first* and *directly:* the woman, *subsequently,* and *indirectly,* through the mediation of man. Man is the representative of God's "glory" this ideal of man being realized most fully in the Son of man (Ps. 8:4, 5; cf. II Cor. 8:23). Man is declared in Scripture to be both the "image," and in the "likeness," of God (cf. Jas. 3:9). But "image" alone is applied to the Son of God (Col. 1:15; cf. Heb. 1:3). "Express image," *Greek,* "the impress." The Divine Son is not merely "*like*" God, He is God of God, "being of one substance (essence) with the Father." [NICENE CREED]. **woman . . . glory of . . . man**—He does not say, also, "*the image* of the man." For the sexes differ: moreover, the woman is created in the *image of God,* as well as the man (Gen. 1:26, 27). But as the moon in relation to the sun (Gen. 37:9), so woman shines not so much with light direct from God, as with light derived from man, i.e., *in her order in creation;* not that she does not *in grace* come individually into *direct* communion with God; but even here much of her knowledge is mediately given her through man, on whom she is naturally dependent. **8. is of . . . of**—*takes his being from* ("out of") . . . *from:* referring to woman's original creation, "taken out of man" (cf. Gen. 2:23). The woman was made by God mediately through the man, who was, as it were, a veil or medium placed between her and God, and therefore, should wear the veil or head-covering in public worship, in acknowledgement of this subordination to man in the order of creation. The man being made immediately by God as His glory, has no veil between him-

ADAM CLARKE

covered, with his cap or turban on, *dishonoureth his head,* because the head being covered was a sign of subjection; and while he was employed in the public ministration of the Word he was to be considered as a representative of Christ, and on this account his being veiled or covered would be improper. This decision of the apostle was in point-blank hostility to the canons of the Jews; for they would not suffer a man to pray unless he was veiled, for which they gave this reason: "He should veil himself to show that he is ashamed before God, and unworthy with open face to behold Him."

5. *But every woman that prayeth.* Whatever may be the meaning of praying and prophesying in respect to the man, they have precisely the same meaning in respect to the woman. So that some women at least, as well as some men, might speak to others to edification, and exhortation, and comfort. And this kind of prophesying or teaching was predicted by Joel, ii. 28, and referred to by Peter, Acts ii. 17. And had there not been such gifts bestowed on women, the prophecy could not have had its fulfillment. The only difference marked by the apostle was, the man had his head uncovered, because he was the representative of Christ; the woman had hers covered, because she was placed by the order of God in a state of subjection to the man, and because it was a custom, among both the Greeks and the Romans, and among the Jews an express law, that no woman should be seen abroad without a veil. This was a common custom through all the East, and none but public prostitutes went without veils. And if a woman should appear in public without a veil, she would dishonor, *her head*—her husband. And she must appear like to those women who had their hair shorn off as the punishment of whoredom, or adultery.

6. *For if the woman be not covered.* If she will not wear a veil in the public assemblies, *let her . . . be shorn*—let her carry a public badge of infamy; *but if it be a shame*—if to be shorn or shaven would appear, as it must, a badge of infamy, *then let her be covered*—let her by all means wear a veil.

7. *A man indeed ought not to cover his head.* He should not wear his cap or turban in the public congregation, for this was a badge of servitude, or an indication that he had a conscience overwhelmed with guilt; and besides, it was contrary to the custom that prevailed, among both the Greeks and the Romans. *He is the image and glory of God.* He is God's vicegerent in this lower world; and by the authority which he has received from his Maker he is His representative among the creatures and exhibits, more than any other part of the creation, the glory and perfections of the Creator. *But the woman is the glory of the man.* As the man is, among the creatures, the representative of the glory and perfections of God, so that the fear of Him and the dread of Him are on every beast of the field, etc., so the woman is, in the house and family, the representative of the power and authority of the man. I believe this to be the meaning of the apostle; and that he is speaking here principally concerning power and authority, and skill to use them. It is certainly not the moral image of God, nor His celestial glory, of which he speaks in this verse.

8. *For the man is not of the woman.* His meaning is that the man does not belong to the woman, as if she were the principal; but the woman belongs to the man in that view.

MATTHEW HENRY

She is the image of God, inasmuch as she is the image of the man, *v.* 8. *The woman was made for the man, and not the man for the woman.* And she should do nothing that looks like an affectation of equality.

She ought to have power on her head, because of the angels. Power, that is, a veil, the token that she is under the power of her husband. Jews and Christians have had an opinion that these ministering spirits are present in their assemblies.

V. A caution lest the inference be carried too far (*v.* 11, 12). They were made to be a mutual comfort and blessing, not one a slave and the other a tyrant. As it is the will of God that the woman know her place, so it is his will also that the man abuse not his power.

VI. The woman's hair is a natural covering; to wear it long is a glory to her; but for a man to have long hair is a token of softness and effeminacy.

VII. He sums up all by referring to the usages and customs of the churches, *v.* 16. The common practice of the churches is what he would have them govern themselves by.

JAMIESON, FAUSSET, BROWN

self and God [FABER STAPULENSIS *in Bengel*]. **9. Neither**—rather, "For also"; *Another argument: The immediate object of woman's creation.* "The man was not created for the sake of the woman; but the woman for the sake of the man" (Gen. 2:18, 21, 22). Just as the Church, the bride, is made for Christ; and yet in both the natural and the spiritual creations, the bride, while made for the bridegroom, in fulfilling that end, attains her own true "glory," and brings "shame" and "dishonor" on herself by any departure from it (vss. 4, 6). **10. power on her head**—the kerchief: French *couvre-chef, head-covering, the emblem* of "power on her head"; the sign of her being under man's power, and exercising delegated authority under him. Paul had before his mind the root-connection between the *Hebrew* terms for "veil" (*radid*), and subjection (*radad*). **because of the angels**—who are present at our Christian assemblies (cf. Ps. 138:1, "gods," i.e., *angels*), and delight in the orderly subordination of the several ranks of God's worshippers in their respective places, the outward demeanor and dress of the latter being indicative of that inward humility which angels know to be most pleasing to their common Lord (ch. 4:9; Eph. 3:10; Eccles. 5:6). HAMMOND quotes Chrysostom, "Thou standest with angels; thou singest with them; thou hymnest with them; and yet dost thou stand laughing?" BENGEL explains, "As the angels are in relation to God, so the woman is in relation to man. God's face is uncovered; angels in His presence are veiled (Isa. 6:2). Man's face is uncovered; woman in His presence is to be veiled. For her not to be so, would, by its indecorousness, offend the angels (Matt. 18: 10, 31). She, by her weakness, especially needs their ministry; she ought, therefore, to be the more careful not to offend them." **11.** Yet neither sex is insulated and independent of the other in the Christian life [ALFORD]. The one needs the other in the sexual relation; and in respect to Christ ("in the Lord"), the man and the woman together (for neither can be dispensed with) realize the ideal of redeemed humanity represented by the bride, the Church. **12.** As the woman was formed *out of* (from) the man, even so is man born *by means* of woman; but all things (including both man and woman) are *from* God as their source (Rom. 11:36; II Cor. 5:18). They depend mutually each on the other, and both on him. **13.** Appeal to their own sense of decorum. **a woman . . . unto God**—By rejecting the emblem of subjection (the head-covering), she passes at one leap in praying publicly beyond both the *man* and *angels* [BENGEL]. **14.** The fact that nature has provided woman, and not man, with long hair, proves that man was designed to be uncovered, and woman covered. The Nazarite, however, wore long hair lawfully, as being part of a vow sanctioned by God (Num. 6:5). Cf. as to Absalom, II Samuel 14:26, and Acts 18:18. **15. her hair . . . for a covering**—Not that she does not need additional covering. Nay, her long hair shows she ought to cover her head as much as possible. The will ought to accord with nature [BENGEL]. **16.** A summary close to the argument by appeal to the universal custom of the churches. **if any . . . seem**—The *Greek* also means "*thinks*" (fit) (cf. Matt. 3:9). If any man *chooses* (still after all my arguments) to be contentious. If any be contentious and *thinks* himself *right* in being so. A reproof of the Corinthians' self-sufficiency and disputatiousness (ch. 1:20). **we**—apostles: or we of the Jewish nation, from whom ye have received the Gospel, and whose usages in all that is good ye ought to follow: Jewish women veiled themselves when in public, according to Tertullian [ESTIUS]. The former explanation is best, as the Jews are not referred to in the context: but he often refers to himself and his fellow apostles, by the expression, "we—us" (ch. 4:9, 10). **no such custom**—as that of women praying uncovered. Not as CHRYSOSTOM, "that of being contentious." The *Greek* term implies a *usage*, rather than a *mental habit* (John 18:39). The usage of true "churches (plural: not, as Rome uses it, 'the Church,' as an abstract entity; but '*the churches*, as a number of *independent witnesses*) of God" (the churches which God Himself recognizes), is a valid argument *in the case of external rites*, especially, *negatively*, e.g., Such rites were not received among them, therefore, ought not to be admitted among us: but in questions of *doctrine*, or the *essentials of worship*, the argument is not valid [SCLATER] (ch. 7:17; 14: 33). **neither**—nor yet. Catholic usage is not an infallible test of *truth*, but a general test of *decency*. **17. in this**—which follows. **I declare**—rather, "I enjoin"; as the *Greek* is always so used. The oldest MSS. read literally "This I enjoin (you) not

ADAM CLARKE

9. *Neither was the man created.* For the man was not created upon the woman's account. The reason is plain from what is mentioned above; and from the original creation of woman she was made for the man, to be his proper or suitable helper.

10. *For this cause ought the woman to have power on her head because of the angels.* "And because of this superiority in the man, I conclude that the woman should have on her head a veil, the mark of her husband's power over her, especially in the religious assemblies, where the angels are supposed to be invisibly present." The custom of the Nazarite may cast some light upon this place. As Nazarite means one who has separated himself by vow to some religious austerity, wearing his own hair, etc., so a married woman was considered a Nazarite for life, i.e., separated from all others, and joined to one husband, who is her lord. And hence the apostle, alluding to this circumstance, says, *The woman ought to have power on her head*, i.e., wear her hair and veil; for her hair is a proof of her being a Nazarite, and of her subjection to her husband, as the Nazarite was under subjection to the Lord, according to the rule or law of his order.

11. *Neither is the man without the woman.* The apostle seems to say: I do not intimate any disparagement of the female sex, by insisting on the necessity of her being under the power or authority of the man, for they are both equally dependent on each other.

12. *For as the woman is of the man.* For as the woman was first formed out of the side of man, man has ever since been formed out of the womb of the woman; but they, as all other created things, are of God.

13. *Judge in yourselves.* Consider the subject in your own common sense, and then say whether it be decent for a woman to pray in public without a veil on her head. The heathen priestesses prayed or delivered their oracles bareheaded or with dishevelled hair; to be conformed to them would be very disgraceful to Christian women. And in reference to such things as these the apostle appeals to their sense of honor and decency.

14. *Doth not even nature itself teach you that if a man have long hair?* Nature certainly teaches us, by bestowing it, that it is proper for women to have long hair; and it is not so with men. The hair of the male rarely grows like that of a female, unless art is used, and even then it bears but a scanty proportion to the former. Hence it is truly womanish to have long hair, and it is a shame to the man who affects it. In ancient times the people of Achaia, the province in which Corinth stood, and the Greeks in general, were noted for their long hair; and hence called by Homer, in a great variety of places, "the long-haired Greeks." Long hair was certainly not in repute among the Jews. The Nazarites let their hair grow, but it was as a token of humiliation; and it is possible that Paul had this in view. There were consequently two reasons why the apostle should condemn this practice: (1) Because it was a sign of humiliation; (2) Because it was womanish. After all, it is possible that Paul may refer to dressed, frizzled, and curled hair, which shallow and effeminate men might have affected in that time, as they do in this.

15. *But if a woman have long hair.* The Author of their being has given a larger proportion of hair to the head of women than to that of men; and to them it is an especial ornament, and may in various cases serve as a veil.

16. *But if any man seem to be contentious.* If any person sets himself up as a wrangler, put himself forward as a defender of such points —that a woman may pray or teach with her head uncovered. and that a man may, without reproach, have long hair—let him know that we have no such custom as either, nor are they sanctioned by any of the churches of God, whether among the Jews or among the Gentiles.

17. *Now in this . . . I praise you not.* In the beginning of this Epistle the apostle did praise them for their attention in general to the rules he had laid down; see v. 2. But here he is

MATTHEW HENRY

Verses 17–22

The apostle sharply rebukes them for much greater disorders in their partaking of the Lord's supper.

I. Such scandalous disorders as they were guilty of, called for a sharp reprehension. The ordinances of Christ, if they do not make us better, will be very apt to make us worse; if they do not melt and mend, they will harden.

II. His charge against them. Upon coming together, they fell into *divisions.* They fell a quarrelling with one another. The apostle had heard a report of the Corinthians' divisions, and he tells them he had too much reason to believe it.

There must be heresies also. No marvel there should be breaches of Christian love in the churches, when such offences will come. Such offences must come. God permits them, that those who are approved (such honest hearts as will bear the trial) may be set to view, and appear faithful. The wisdom of God can make the wickedness of others a foil to the integrity of the saints.

III. The apostle lays the blame of this conduct closely on them. 1. Their conduct perfectly destroyed the purpose and use of such an institution, *v.* 20. They might as well have stayed away.

He charges them with scandalous disorder, *v.* 21. They would not stay for one another. Thus some wanted, while others had more than enough. The poor were deprived of the food prepared for them, and the rich turned a feast of charity into a debauch.

2. Their conduct carried in it a contempt of the church, *v.* 22. If they had a mind to feast, they might do it at home in their own houses. Religious feasts should be attended religiously.

Verses 23–34

The apostle sets the sacred institution here to view.

I. He tells us how he came by the knowledge of it. *He had received from the Lord what he delivered to them, v.* 23.

JAMIESON, FAUSSET, BROWN

praising (you)." **that**—*inasmuch as: in that* you . . . Here he qualifies his praise (vs. 2). "I said that I praised you for keeping the ordinances delivered to you; but I must now give injunction in the name of the Lord, on a matter in which I praise you not; viz., as to the Lord's Supper (vs. 23; ch. 14:37). **not for the better**—not so as to progress to what is better. **for the worse**—so as to retrograde to what is worse. The result of such "coming together" must be "condemnation" (vs. 34). **18. first of all**—In the first place. The "divisions" (*Greek, "schisms"*) meant, are not merely those of opinion (ch. 1:10), but in outward acts at the lovefeasts (*Agapæ*), (vs. 21). He does not follow up the expression, "in the first place," by "in the second place." But though not expressed, a *second* abuse was in his mind when he said, "In the first place," viz., THE ABUSE OF SPIRITUAL GIFTS, *which also created disorder in their assemblies* [ALFORD], (ch. 12:1; 14:23, 26, 33, 40). **in the church**—not the place of worship; for Isidore of Pelusium denies that there were such places specially set apart for worship in the apostles' times (*Epistle* 246.2). But, "in the assembly" or "congregation"; in convocation for worship, where especially love, order, and harmony should prevail. The very ordinance instituted for uniting together believers in one body, was made an occasion of "divisions" (schisms). **partly**—He hereby excepts the innocent. "I am unwilling to believe *all* I hear, but *some* I cannot help believing" [ALFORD]: while my love is unaffected by it [BENGEL]. **19. heresies**—Not merely "schisms" or "divisions" (vs. 18), which are "*recent* dissensions of the congregation through differences of opinion" [AUGUSTINE, *Con. Crescon. Don.* 2. 7, quoted by *French Synonyms, New Testament*], but also "heresies," i.e., "schisms which have now become *inveterate*"; "Sects" [CAMPBELL, vol. 2, pp. 126, 127]: so Acts 5:17; 15:5 translate the same *Greek.* At present there were dissensions at the love-feasts; but Paul, remembering Jesus' words (Matt. 18:7; 24:10, 12; Luke 17:1) foresees "there must be (come) also" *matured separations,* and established parties in secession, as separatists. The "must be" arises from sin in professors necessarily bearing its natural fruits: these are overruled by God to the probation of character of both the godly and the ungodly, and to the discipline of the former for glory. "Heresies" had not yet its technical sense ecclesiastically, referring to doctrinal errors: it means *confirmed schisms.* St. Augustine's rule is a golden rule as regards questions of heresy and catholicity: "In doubtful questions, liberty; in essentials, unity; in all things, charity." **that . . . approved may be made manifest**—through the *disapproved* (reprobates) becoming manifested (Luke 2:35; I John 2:19). **20. When . . . therefore**—Resuming the thread of discourse from vs. 18. *this* **is not to**—rather, "there is no such thing as eating the LORD'S Supper"; *it is not possible* where each is greedily intent only on devouring "HIS OWN supper," and some are excluded altogether, not having been waited for (vs. 33), where some are "drunken," while others are "hungry" (vs. 21). The lovefeast usually preceded the Lord's Supper (as eating the Passover came before the Lord's Supper at the first institution of the latter). It was a club-feast, where each brought his portion, and the rich, extra portions for the poor; from it the bread and wine were taken for the Eucharist; and it was at it that the excesses took place, which made a *true* celebration of the Lord's Supper during or after it, with true discernment of its solemnity, out of the question. **21. one taketh before** *other*—the rich "before" the poor, who had no supper of their own. Instead of "tarrying for one another" (vs. 33); hence the precept (ch. 12: 21, 25). **his own supper**—"His own" belly is his God (Phil. 3:19); "the *Lord's* Supper," the spiritual feast, never enters his thoughts. **drunken**—The one has more than is good for him, the other less [BENGEL]. **22. What!**—*Greek,* "For." **houses**—(cf. vs. 34)—"at home." That is the place to satiate the appetite, not the assembly of the brethren [ALFORD]. **despise ye the church of God**—*the congregation* mostly composed of the poor, whom "GOD hath chosen," however ye show contempt for them (Jas. 2:5); cf. "of God" here, marking the true honor of the Church. **shame them that have not**—viz., *houses* to eat and drink in, and who, therefore, ought to have received their portion at the lovefeasts from their wealthier brethren. **I praise you not**—resuming the words (vs. 17). **23.** His object is to show the unworthiness of such conduct from the dignity of the holy supper. **23. I**—Emphatic in the *Greek.* It is not *my own* invention, but the Lord's institution. **received of the Lord**—by immediate revelation (Gal. 1:12; cf. Acts 22:17, 18;

ADAM CLARKE

obliged to condemn certain irregularities which had crept in among them, particularly relative to the celebration of the Lord's Supper. Through some false teaching which they had received, in the absence of the apostle, they appear to have celebrated it precisely in the same way the Jews did their Passover. That, we know, was a regular meal, only accompanied with certain peculiar circumstances and ceremonies. Two of these ceremonies were eating bread, solemnly broken, and drinking a cup of wine called the cup of blessing. Now it is certain that our Lord has taken these two things and made them expressive of the crucifixion of His body and the shedding of His blood as an atonement for the sins of mankind. The teachers which had crept into the Corinthian church appear to have perverted the whole of this divine institution, for the celebration of the Lord's Supper appears to have been made among them a part of an ordinary meal. The people came together and it appears brought their provisions with them. Some had much; others had less. Some ate to excess; others had scarcely enough to suffice nature. One was hungry, and the other was drunken, "was filled to the full"; this is the sense of the word in many places of Scripture.

18. *There be divisions among you.* They had "schisms" among them; the old parties were kept up, even in the place where they assembled to eat the Lord's Supper.

19. *There must be also heresies.* Not a common consent of the members of the church either in the doctrines of the gospel or in the ceremonies of the Christian religion. Their difference in religious opinion led to a difference in their religious practice, and thus the church of God, that should have been one body, was split into sects and parties. The divisions and the heresies sprang out of each other.

20. *This is not to eat the Lord's supper.* They did not come together to eat the Lord's Supper exclusively, which they should have done and not have made it a part of an ordinary meal.

21. *Every one taketh before . . . his own supper.* They had a grand feast, though the different sects kept in parties by themselves; but all took as ample a supper as they could provide (each bringing his own provisions with him) before they took what was called the Lord's Supper.

22. *Have ye not houses to eat and to drink in?* They should have taken their ordinary meal at home, and have come together in the church to celebrate the Lord's Supper. *Despise ye the church of God?* You render the sacred assembly and the place contemptible by your conduct, and you show yourselves destitute of that respect which you owe to the place set apart for divine worship. *And shame them that have not.* "Them that are poor"; not them who had not victuals at that time, but those who are so poor as to be incapable of furnishing themselves as others had done.

23. *I have received of the Lord.* It is possible that several of the people at Corinth did receive the bread and wine of the Eucharist as they did the paschal bread and wine, as a mere

MATTHEW HENRY

II. He gives us a more particular account of the institution than we meet with elsewhere.

1. The author—our Lord Jesus Christ.

2. The time of the institution: *It was the very night wherein he was betrayed;* just as he was entering on his sufferings which are therein to be commemorated.

3. The institution itself. Our Saviour took bread, and when he had given thanks, *he broke, and said, Take, eat; this is my body, broken for you; this do in remembrance of me. And in like manner he took the cup, when he had supped, saying, This cup is the New Testament in my blood; this do, as oft as you drink it, in remembrance of me, v.* 24, 25.

(1) The materials of this sacrament, [1] The visible signs; these are bread and the cup. What is eaten is called bread, though it is at the same time said to be *the body of the Lord.* Bread and the cup are both made use of, because it is a holy feast. The cup is put for what was in it, without once specifying what the liquor was. [2] The things signified by these outward signs: they are Christ's body and blood, his body broken, his blood shed.

(2) The sacramental actions. Our Saviour did, at the institution, deliver his body and blood, with all the benefits procured by his death, to his disciples, and continues to do the same every time the ordinance is administered to true believers. They are to take him as their Lord and life, yield themselves up to him, and live upon him.

(3) An account of the ends of this institution. It was appointed to be done *in remembrance of Christ,* to keep fresh in our minds his dying for us, as well as to remember an absent friend, even Christ interceding for us. The motto on this ordinance, and the very meaning of it, is, *When this you see, remember me.* It was *to show forth Christ's death.* It is not barely in remembrance of Christ, but to commemorate his glorious condescension and grace in our redemption. We own before the world, by this very service, that we are the disciples of Christ, who trust in him alone for salvation and acceptance with God.

(4) It should be frequent. Our bodily meals return often. And it is fit that this spiritual diet should be taken often too. It must be perpetual. It is to be celebrated *till the Lord shall come.* The Lord's supper is not a temporary, but a standing and perpetual ordinance.

JAMIESON, FAUSSET, BROWN

II Cor. 12:1-4). The renewal of the institution of the Lord's Supper by special revelation to Paul enhances its solemnity. The similarity between Luke's and Paul's account of the institution, favors the supposition that the former drew his information from the apostle, whose companion in travel he was. Thus, the undesigned coincidence is a proof of genuineness. **night**—the time fixed for the Passover (Exod. 12:6): though the time for the Lord's Supper is not fixed. **betrayed**—With the traitor at the table, and death present before His eyes, He left this ordinance as His last gift to us, to commemorate His death. Though about to receive such an injury from man, He gave this pledge of His amazing love to man. **24. brake**—The *breaking* of the bread involves its *distribution* and reproves the Corinthian mode at the love-feast, of "every one taking before other his own supper." **my body . . . broken for you**—"given" (Luke 22:19) for you (*Greek,* "in your behalf"), and "broken," so as to be distributed among you. The oldest MSS. omit "broken," leaving it to be supplied from "brake." The two old versions, Memphitic and Thebaic, read from Luke, "given." The literal "body" could not have been meant; for Christ was still sensibly present among His disciples when He said, "This is My body." They *could* only have understood Him symbolically and analogically: As this bread is to your bodily health, so My body is to the spiritual health of the believing communicant. The words, Take, eat," are not in the oldest MSS. **25. when he had supped**—*Greek,* "after the eating of supper," viz., the Passover supper which preceded the Lord's Supper, as the love-feast did subsequently. Therefore, you Corinthians ought to separate common meals from the Lord's Supper [BENGEL]. **the new testament**—or "covenant." The cup is the parchment-deed, as it were, on which My new covenant, or last will is written and sealed, making over to you all blessings here and hereafter. **in my blood**—ratified by MY blood: "not by the blood of goats and calves" (Heb. 9:12).—**as oft as**—*Greek,* "as many times soever": implying that it is an ordinance *often* to be partaken of. **in remembrance of me**—Luke expresses this, which is understood by Matthew and Mark. Paul twice records it as suiting his purpose. The old sacrifices brought *sins* continually to remembrance (Heb. 10:1, 3). The Lord's Supper brings to remembrance *Christ* and His sacrifice once for all for the full and final *remission of sins.* **26. For**—in proof that the Lord's Supper is "in remembrance" of Him. **show**—*announce publicly.* The *Greek* does not mean to dramatically *represent,* but "ye publicly profess each of you, the Lord has died FOR ME" [WAHL]. This word, as "is" in Christ's institution (vss. 24, 25), implies not *literal* presence, but a *vivid realization, by faith,* of Christ in the Lord's Supper, as a living person, not a mere abstract dogma, "bone of our bone, and flesh of our flesh" (Eph. 5:30; cf. Gen. 2:23); and ourselves "members of His body, of His flesh, and of His bones," "our sinful bodies made clean by His body (once for all offered), and our souls washed through His most precious blood" [*Church of England Prayer Book*]. "Show," or "announce," is an expression applicable to *new* things; cf. "show" as to the Passover (Exod. 13:8). So the Lord's death ought always to be fresh in our memory; cf. in heaven, Revelation 5:6. That the Lord's Supper is in *remembrance* of Him, implies that He is bodily absent, though spiritually present, for we cannot be said to commemorate one absent. The fact that we not only show the Lord's death in the supper, but *eat* and *drink* the pledges of it, could only be understood by the Jews, accustomed to such feasts after propitiatory sacrifices, as implying our *personal appropriation* therein of the benefits of that death. **till he come**—when there shall be no longer need of symbols of His body, the body itself being manifested. The *Greek* expresses the *certainly* of His coming. Rome teaches that we eat Christ present corporally, "till He come" corporally; a contradiction in terms. The shewbread, lit., "bread of the presence," was in the sanctuary, but not in the Holiest Place (Heb. 9:1-8); so the Lord's Supper in heaven, the antitype to the Holiest Place, shall be superseded by Christ's own bodily presence; then the wine shall be drunk "anew" in the Father's kingdom, by Christ and His people together, of which heavenly banquet, the Lord's Supper is a spiritual foretaste and specimen (Matt. 26:29). Meantime, as the shewbread was placed *new,* every sabbath, on the table before the Lord (Lev. 24:5-8); so the Lord's death was *shown,* or announced *afresh* at the Lord's table the first day of every week in the primitive Church. We are now "priests unto God" in the dispensation of

ADAM CLARKE

commemoration of an event. And as our Lord had by this institution consecrated that bread and wine, not to be the means of commemorating the deliverance from Egypt and their joy on the account, but their deliverance from sin and death by His passion and cross, therefore the apostle states that he had received from the Lord what he delivered; viz., that the eucharistic bread and wine were to be understood of the accomplishment of that of which the paschal lamb was the type—the body broken for them, the blood shed for them.

ALEXANDER MACLAREN:

"Do this" is the true meaning of the words, not "in remembrance of me," but something far more sweet and pathetic—"do this for the *remembering* of me." The former expression is equal to: "Do this because you remember." The real meaning of the words is, "Do this in case you forget"; do this in order that you may recall to memory what the slippery memory is so apt to lose—the impression of even the sweetest sweetness, of the most loving love, and the most self-abnegating sacrifice, which He offered for us.

There is something to me infinitely pathetic and beautiful in looking at the words not only as the commandment of the Lord, but as the appeal of the Friend, who wished, as we all do, not to be utterly forgotten by those whom He cared for and loved; and who, not only because their remembrance was their salvation, but because their forgetfulness pained His heart, brings to their hearts the plaintive appeal: "Do not forget Me when I am gone away from you; and even if you have no better way of remembering Me, take these poor symbols, to which I am not too proud to entrust the care of My memory, and do this, lest you forget Me."

"In remembrance of me"—Jesus Christ, then, takes up an altogether unique and solitary position here, and into the sacredest hours of devotion and the loftiest moments of communion with God, intrudes His personality and says, "When you are most religious, remember Me; and let the highest act of your devout life be a thought turned to myself."

—*Expositions of Holy Scripture*

26. *Ye do shew the Lord's death.* As in the Passover they showed forth the bondage they had been in and the redemption they had received from it, so in the Eucharist they showed forth the sacrificial death of Christ and the redemption from sin derived from it.

MATTHEW HENRY

III. The danger of receiving unworthily and using it to the purposes of feasting and faction. 1. They shall *be guilty of the body and blood of the Lord* (*v.* 27). Instead of being cleansed by his blood, they are guilty of his blood.

IV. The duty of those who would come to the Lord's table (*v.* 28). Such self-examination is necessary to a right attendance at this holy ordinance. Those should have the wedding-garment on who would be welcome at this marriage-feast—grace in habit, and grace in exercise, *v.* 31. To be exact and severe on ourselves is the most proper way not to fall under the just severity of our heavenly Father. We must not judge others, lest we be judged (Matt. vii. 1); but we must judge ourselves, to prevent our being judged and condemned by God.

They eat and drink judgment to themselves, v. 29. They provoke God, and are likely to bring down punishment on themselves. But fearful believers should not be discouraged from attending at this holy ordinance by the sound of these words. The Holy Spirit never indited this to deter serious Christians from their duty, though the devil has often made this advantage of it, and robbed good Christians of their choicest comforts. The Corinthians came to the Lord's table *not discerning the Lord's body*—not making a distinction between that and common food.

For this cause many are weak and sickly among you, and many sleep. Even those who were thus punished were in a state of favour with God: *They were chastened of the Lord, that they should not be condemned with the world, v.* 32. He frequently punishes those whom he tenderly loves. It is kindness to use the rod to prevent the child's ruin. They were punished by him out of fatherly goodwill, punished now that they might not perish for ever.

V. A caution against the irregularities of which they were guilty (*v.* 33, 34). They were to eat for hunger and pleasure only at home. Our holy duties, through our own abuse, may prove matter of condemnation. Holy things are to be used in a holy manner, or else they are profaned.

JAMIESON, FAUSSET, BROWN

Christ's spiritual presence, antitypical to the HOLY PLACE: the perfect and eternal dispensation, which shall not begin till Christ's coming, is antitypical to the HOLIEST PLACE, which Christ our High Priest alone in the flesh as yet has entered (Heb. 9:6, 7); but which, at His coming, we, too, who are believers, shall enter (Rev. 7:15; 21:22). The supper joins the two closing periods of the Old and the New dispensations. The first and second comings are considered as *one* coming, whence the expression is not "return," but "come" (cf., however, John 14:3). **27. eat and drink**—So one of the oldest MSS. reads. But three or four equally old MSS., the *Vulgate* and Cyprian, read, "or." Romanists quote this reading in favor of communion in one kind. This consequence does not follow. Paul says, "Whosoever is guilty of unworthy conduct, *either* in eating the bread, *or* in drinking the cup, is guilty of the body and blood of Christ." Impropriety in only *one* of the two elements, vitiates true communion in *both.* Therefore, in the end of the verse, he says, not "body *or* blood," but "body and blood." Any who takes the bread without the wine, *or* the wine without the bread, *"unworthily"* communicates, and so "is guilty of Christ's body and blood"; for he disobeys Christ's express command to partake of both. If we do not partake of the sacramental symbol of the Lord's death worthily, we share in the guilt of that death. (Cf. "crucify to themselves the Son of God afresh," Heb. 6:6.) *Unworthiness in the person,* is not what ought to exclude any, but *unworthily communicating:* However unworthy we be, if we examine ourselves so as to find that we penitently believe in Christ's Gospel, we may worthily communicate. **28. examine**—*Greek,* "prove" or "test" his own state of mind in respect to Christ's death, and his capability of "discerning the Lord's body" (vss. 29, 31). Not auricular confession to a priest, but self-examination is necessary. **so**—after due self-examination. **of . . . of**—In vs. 27, where the receiving was *unworthily,* the expression was, "eat this bread, drink . . . cup" without "of." Here the "of" implies due circumspection in communicating [BENGEL]. **let him eat**—His self-examination is not in order that he may stay away, but that he may eat, i.e., communicate. **29. damnation**—A mistranslation which has put a stumbling block in the way of many in respect to communicating. The right translation is "judgment." The *judgment* is described (vss. 30-32) as temporal. **not discerning**—*not duty judging: not distinguishing in judgment* (so the *Greek:* the sin and its punishment thus being marked as corresponding) from common food, the sacramental pledges of the Lord's body.Most of the oldest MSS. omit "Lord's" (see vs. 27). Omitting also "unworthily," with most of the oldest MSS, we must translate, "He that eateth and drinketh, eateth and drinketh judgment to himself, IF he discern not the body" (Heb. 10:29). The Church is "the body of *Christ*" (ch. 12:27). The Lord's body is *His literal body* appreciated and discerned by the soul in the faithful receiving, and not present in the elements themselves. **30. weak . . . sickly**—He is "weak" who has *naturally* no strength: "sickly," who has *lost his strength* by disease [TITTM. *Synonyms*]. **sleep**—are being lulled in death: not a violent death; but one the result of sickness, sent as the Lord's chastening for the individual's salvation, the mind being brought to a right state on the sick bed (vs. 31). **31. if we would judge ourselves**—Most of the oldest MSS, read "But," not "For." Translate also literally "If we duly judged ourselves, we should not be (or *not have been*) judged," i.e., we should escape (or *have escaped*) our present judgments. In order to *duly judge* or "discern [appreciate] the Lord's body," we need to "duly judge ourselves." A prescient warning against the dogma of priestly absolution after full confession, as the necessary preliminary to receiving the Lord's Supper. **32. chastened**—(Rev. 3:19). **with the world**—who, being bastards, are without chastening (Heb. 12:8). **33. tarry one for another**—In contrast to vs. 21. The expression is not, "Give a share to one another," for all the viands brought to the feast were *common* property, and, therefore, they should "tarry" till all were met to partake together of the common feast of fellowship [THEOPHYL]. **34. if any . . . hunger**—so as not to be able to "tarry for others," let him take off the edge of his hunger at home [ALFORD] (vs. 22). **the rest**—"the other questions you asked me as to the due celebration of the Lord's Supper." Not other questions in *general;* for he does subsequently set in order other general questions in this Epistle.

ADAM CLARKE

27. *Whosoever shall eat . . . and drink . . . unworthily.* To put a final end to controversies and perplexities relative to these words and the context, let the reader observe that to *eat* and *drink* the bread and wine in the Lord's Supper *unworthily* is to eat and drink as the Corinthians did, who ate it, not in reference to Jesus Christ's sacrificial death, but rather in such a way as the Israelites did the Passover, which they celebrated in remembrance of their deliverance from Egyptian bondage. Likewise these mongrel Christians at Corinth used it as a kind of historical commemoration of the death of Christ and did not, in the whole institution, discern the Lord's body and blood as a sacrificial offering for sin; and besides, in their celebration of it they acted in a way utterly unbecoming the gravity of a sacred ordinance. *Shall be guilty of the body and blood of the Lord.* If he use it irreverently, if he deny that Christ suffered unjustly (for of some such persons the apostle must be understood to speak), then he in effect joins issue with the Jews in their condemnation and crucifixion of the Lord Jesus, and renders himself guilty of the death of our blessed Lord. Some, however, understand the passage thus: is guilty, i.e., eats and drinks unworthily, and brings on himself that punishment mentioned in v. 30.

28. *Let a man examine himself.* Let him try whether he has proper faith in the Lord Jesus, and whether he discerns the Lord's body, and whether he duly considers that the bread and wine point out the crucified body and spilt blood of Christ.

29. *Eateth and drinketh damnation.* "Judgment, punishment"; and yet this is not unto *damnation,* for the judgment or punishment inflicted upon the disorderly and the profane was intended for their emendation; for in v. 32 it is said, when we are "judged," we are chastened, corrected as a father does his children, "that we should not be condemned with the world."

30. *For this cause.* That they partook of this sacred ordinance without discerning the Lord's body. *Many are weak and sickly.* It is hard to say whether these words refer to the consequences of their own intemperance or to some extraordinary disorders inflicted immediately by God himself. That there were disorders of the most reprehensible kind among these people at this sacred supper, the preceding verses sufficiently point out; and after such excesses, many might be *weak* and *sickly* among them, and *many* might *sleep,* i.e., "die"; for continual experience shows us that many fall victims to their own intemperance. However, acting as they did in this solemn and awful sacrament, they might have "provoked God to plague them with divers diseases and sundry kinds of death."

31. *If we would judge ourselves.* If, having acted improperly, we condemn our conduct and humble ourselves, we shall not be *judged,* i.e., "punished" for the sin we have committed.

33. *When ye come together to eat* (the Lord's Supper), *tarry one for another*—do not eat and drink in parties as ye have done heretofore, and do not connect it with any other meal.

34. *And if any man hunger,* let him not come to the house of God to eat an ordinary meal; *let him eat at home*—take that in his own house which is necessary for the support of his body before he comes to that sacred repast, where he should have the feeding of his soul alone in view. *That ye come not together unto condemnation.* That you may avoid the curse that must fall on such worthless communicants as those above mentioned, and that you may get that especial blessing which everyone that discerns the Lord's body in the Eucharist must receive. *The rest will I set in order.* All the other matters relative to this business to which you have referred in your letter I will regulate when I come to visit you, as, God permitting, I fully design. The apostle did visit them about one year after this, as is generally believed.

MATTHEW HENRY

CHAPTER 12

Verses 1–11

Of spiritual gifts. Where grace is given it is for the salvation of those who have it. Gifts are bestowed for the advantage and salvation of others. And there may be great gifts where there is not a dram of grace. This church was rich in gifts, but there were many things scandalously out of order in it.

I. Gifts come from God, and are to be used for him.

II. He puts them in mind of the sad state out of which they had been recovered, *v.* 2. Their former character: they *were Gentiles.* Not God's peculiar people, but of the nations whom he had in a manner abandoned. What a change was here! Christian Corinthians were once Gentiles. It is of great use to the Christian, and a proper consideration to stir him up both to duty and thankfulness, to think what once he was. The conduct they were under: *Carried away to these dumb idols, even as you were led.* Miserable abjectness of mind! And those who despised these gross conceptions of the vulgar yet countenanced them by their practice. Could the Spirit of God be among such stupid idolaters?

III. How they might discern those gifts that were from the Spirit of God: *No man, speaking by the Spirit, calls Jesus accursed.* Thus did both Jews and Gentiles: they blasphemed him as an imposter, and execrated his name. None could act under the influence, nor by the power of the Spirit of God, who disowned and blasphemed Christ: for the Spirit of God could never so far contradict itself as to declare him accursed. No man can call Christ *Lord,* with a believing dependence upon him, unless that faith be wrought by the Holy Ghost.

IV. The same giver may bestow various gifts, *v.* 4.

JAMIESON, FAUSSET, BROWN

CHAPTER 12

Vss. 1-31. The Use and the Abuse of Spiritual Gifts, Especially Prophesying and Tongues. This is the *second* subject for correction in the Corinthian assemblies: the "*first*" was discussed (ch. 11: 18-34). **1. spiritual gifts**—the signs of the Spirit's continued efficacious presence in the Church, which is Christ's body, the complement of His incarnation, as the body is the complement of the head. By the love which pervades the whole, the gifts of the several members, forming reciprocal complements to each other, tend to the one object of perfecting the body of Christ. The ordinary and permanent gifts are comprehended together with the extraordinary, without distinction specified, as both alike flow from the divine indwelling Spirit of life. The extraordinary gifts, so far from making professors more peculiarly *saints* than in our day, did not always even *prove* that such persons were in a safe state at all (Matt. 7:22). They were needed at first in the Church: (1) as a pledge to Christians themselves who had just passed over from Judaism or heathendom, that God was in the Church; (2) for the propagation of Christianity in the world; (3) for the edification of the Church. Now that we have the whole *written* New Testament (which they had not) and Christianity established as the result of the miracles, we need no further miracle to attest the truth. So the pillar of cloud which guided the Israelites was withdrawn when they were sufficiently assured of the Divine Presence, the manifestation of God's glory being thenceforward enclosed in the Most Holy Place [Archbishop Whately]. Paul sets forth in order: I. The unity of the body (vss. 1-27). II. The variety of its members and functions (vss. 27-30). III. The grand principle for the right exercise of the gifts, viz., love (vs. 31, and ch. 13). IV. The comparison of the gifts with one another (ch. 14). **I would not have you ignorant**—with all your boasts of "knowledge" at Corinth. If ignorant now, it will be your own fault, not mine (ch. 14:38). **2.** (Eph. 2:11.) **that ye were**—The best MSS. read, "That when ye were"; thus "ye were" must be supplied before "carried away"—Ye were blindly transported hither and thither at the will of your false guides. **these dumb idols**—*Greek,* "*the* idols which are dumb"; contrasted with the living God who "speaks" in the believer by His Spirit (vs. 3, etc.). This gives the reason why the Corinthians needed instruction as to spiritual gifts, viz., their past heathen state, wherein they had no experience of intelligent spiritual powers. When blind, ye went to the *dumb.* **as ye were led**—The *Greek* is, rather, "as ye might (happen to) be led," viz., on different occasions. The heathen oracles led their votaries at random, without any definite principle. **3.** The negative and positive criteria of inspiration by the Spirit—the rejection or confession of Jesus as Lord [Alford] (I John 4:2; 5:1). Paul gives a test of truth against the Gentiles; John, against the false prophets. **by the Spirit**—rather, as *Greek,* "in the Spirit"; that being the power pervading him, and the element *in* which he speaks [Alford], (Matt. 16:17; John 15:26). **of God . . . Holy**—The same Spirit is called at one time "the Spirit of God"; at another, "the Holy Ghost," or "Holy Spirit." Infinite *Holiness* is almost synonymous with *Godhead.* **speaking . . . say**—"Speak" implies the act of utterance; "say" refers to that which is uttered. Here, "say" means a *spiritual* and *believing* confession of Him. **Jesus**—not an abstract doctrine, but the historical, living God-man (Rom. 10:9). **accursed**—as the Jews and Gentiles treated Him (Gal. 3:13). Cf. "to curse Christ" in the heathen Pliny's letter (*Ep.* 10. 97). The spiritual man feels Him to be the Source of all blessings (Eph. 1:3) and to be severed from Him is to be accursed (Rom. 9:3). **Lord**—acknowledging himself as His servant (Isa. 26:13). "Lord" is the LXX *translation* for the incommunicable Hebrew name Jehovah. **4. diversities of gifts**—i.e., varieties of spiritual endowments peculiar to the several members of the Church: cf. "dividing to every man severally" (vs. 11). **same Spirit**—The Holy Trinity appears here: the *Holy Spirit* in this verse; *Christ* in vs. 5; and *the Father* in vs. 6. The terms "gifts," "administrations," and "operations," respectively correspond to the Divine Three. *The Spirit* is treated of in vs. 7, etc.; *the Lord,* in vs. 12, etc.; *God,* in vs. 28. (Cf. Eph. 4:4-6.) **5, 6.** "Gifts" (vs. 4), "administrations" (the various *functions* and *services* performed by those having the gifts, cf. vs. 28), and "operations" (the actual *effects* resulting from both the former, through the universally operative power of the one Father who is "above all, through all, and in us all"), form an ascending climax [Henderson, *Inspir-*

ADAM CLARKE

CHAPTER 12

1. *Now concerning spiritual gifts.* This was a subject about which they appear to have written to the apostle, and concerning which there were probably some contentions among them. The words may as well be translated "concerning spiritual persons" as *spiritual gifts,* and indeed the former agrees much better with the context.

I would not have you ignorant. I wish you fully to know whence all such gifts come, and for what end they are given, that each person may serve the church in the capacity in which God has placed him, that there may be no misunderstandings and no schism in the body.

2. *Ye were Gentiles.* Previously to your conversion to the Christian faith, you were heathens, *carried away,* not guided by reason or truth, but hurried by your passions into a senseless worship, the chief part of which was calculated only to excite and gratify animal propensities. *Dumb idols.* Though often supplicated, could never return an answer; so that not only the image could not speak, but the god or demon pretended to be represented by it could not speak—a full proof that an idol was nothing in the world.

3. *No man speaking by the Spirit of God.* It was granted on all hands that there could be no religion without divine inspiration, because God alone could make His will known to men. Hence heathenism pretended to this inspiration; Judaism had it in the law and the prophets; and it was the very essence of the Christian religion. Both Judaism and heathenism were full of expectations of a future teacher and deliverer; and to this person, especially among the Jews, the Spirit in all the prophets gave witness. This was the Messiah, who was manifested in the person of Jesus of Nazareth; and Him the Jews rejected, though He proved His divine mission both by His doctrines and by His miracles. But as the Holy Spirit through all the law and the prophets gave testimony to the Messiah, and as Jesus proved himself to be the Christ by both His miracles and His doctrines, no man under the inspiration of the divine Spirit could say to Him, "Anathema"—Thou art a deceiver, and a person worthy of death, etc., as the Jews did. Therefore the Jews were no longer under the inspiration of the Spirit of God. *And that no man can say that Jesus is the Lord.* Nor can we demonstrate this person to be the Messiah and the Saviour of men but by the Holy Ghost, He attesting the truth of our doctrines to them that hear, by enlightening their minds, changing their hearts, and filling them with the peace and love of God.

4. *There are diversities of gifts.* "Gracious endowments," leading to miraculous results.

5. *Differences of administrations.* Various offices in the Church, such as apostle, prophet, and teacher; the qualifications for such offices, as well as the appointments themselves, coming immediately from the one Lord Jesus Christ.

MATTHEW HENRY

There are different offices, and officers to discharge them (see *v.* 28–30), but the same Lord, who appointed all, *v.* 6. *There are diversities of operations* (*v.* 10), *but it is the same God that worketh all in all.* However different they may be in themselves, in this they agree; all are from God. And several of the kinds are here specified, *v.* 8–10.

V. The end for which these gifts were bestowed, *v.* 7. They were not distributed for the advantage of those who had them, but for the benefit of the church. Whatever gifts God confers on any man, he confers them that he may do good with them. They are a trust put into his hands. They are not given for show, but for service.

To one was given the *word of wisdom*; a knowledge of the mysteries of the gospel, and ability to explain them.

To another the word of knowledge, by the same Spirit; that is, say some, the knowledge of mysteries (*ch.* ii. 13): say others, a skill and readiness to give advice and counsel in perplexed cases.

To another faith, by the same Spirit, whereby they were enabled to trust God in any emergency.

To another the gift of healing, by the same Spirit; that is, healing the sick. *To another the working of miracles.*

To another prophecy; to explain scripture by a peculiar gift of the Spirit.

To another the discerning of spirits, power to distinguish between true and false prophets. *To another divers kinds of tongues,* or ability to speak languages by inspiration. *To another the interpretation of tongues,* or ability to render foreign languages.

VI. *All these worketh one and the same Spirit, dividing to every man as he will.* Shall not the Spirit of God do what he will with his own? It is not as men will, nor as they may think fit, but as the Spirit pleases.

JAMIESON, FAUSSET, BROWN

ation]. **same Lord**—whom the Spirit glorifies by these *ministrations* [BENGEL]. **6. operations**—(Cf. vs. 10). **same God . . . worketh**—by His Spirit *working* (vs. 11). **all in all**—all of them (the "gifts") in all the persons (who possess them). **7. But**—Though all the gifts flow from the *one* God, Lord, and Spirit, the "manifestation" by which the Spirit acts (as He is hidden in Himself), varies in each individual. **to every man**- *to each* of the members of the Church *severally.* **to profit withal**—*with a view to the profit* of the whole body. **8-10.** Three classes of gifts are distinguished by a distinct Greek word for "another" (*a distinct class*), marking the three several *genera: allo* marks the species, *hetero* the genera (cf. *Greek,* ch. 15:39-41). I. Gifts of intellect, viz., (1) wisdom; (2) knowledge. II. Gifts dependent on a special *faith,* viz., that of miracles (Matt. 17:20): (1) healings; (2) workings of miracles; (3) prophecy of future events; (4) discerning of spirits, or the divinely given faculty of distinguishing between those really inspired, and those who pretended to inspiration. III. Gifts referring to the *tongues:* (1) diverse kinds of tongues; (2) interpretation of tongues. The catalogue in vs. 28 is not meant strictly to harmonize with the one here, though there are some particulars in which they correspond. The three genera are summarily referred to by single instances of each in ch. 13:8. The first genus refers more to believers; the second, to unbelievers. **by . . . by . . . by**—The first in *Greek* is, "By means of," or "through the operation of"; the second is, "according to" the disposing of (cf. vs. 11); the third is, "in," i.e., *under the influence of* (so the *Greek,* Matt. 22:43; Luke 2:27). **word of wisdom**—the ready *utterance of* (for imparting to others, Eph. 6:19) *wisdom,* viz., new revelations of the divine wisdom in redemption, as contrasted with human philosophy (ch. 1:24; 2:6, 7; Eph. 1:8; 3:10; Col. 2:3). **word of knowledge**—ready *utterance supernaturally* imparted of truths ALREADY REVEALED (in this it is distinguished from "the word of wisdom," which related to NEW revelations). Cf. ch. 14:6, where "revelation" (answering to "wisdom" here) is distinguished from "knowledge" [HENDERSON]. *Wisdom* or *revelation* belonged to the "prophets"; *knowledge,* to the "teachers." *Wisdom* penetrates deeper than *knowledge. Knowledge* relates to things that are to be done. *Wisdom,* to things eternal: hence, *wisdom* is not, like *knowledge,* said to "pass away" (ch. 13:8), [BENGEL]. **9. faith**—not of doctrines, but of miracles: confidence in God, by the impulse of His Spirit, that He would enable them to perform any required miracle (cf. ch. 13:2; Mark 11:23; Jas. 5:15). Its nature, or principle, is the same as that of saving faith, viz., reliance on God; the producing cause, also, in the same, viz., a power altogether supernatural (Eph. 1:19, 20). But the objects of faith differ respectively. Hence, we see, saving faith does not save by its instrinsic merit, but by the merits of Him who is the object of it. **healing**—*Greek* plural, "healings"; referring to different kinds of disease which need different kinds of healing (Matt. 10:1). **10. working of miracles**—As "healings" are miracles, those here meant must refer to miracles of special and extraordinary POWER (so the *Greek* for "miracles" means); e.g., healings might be effected by human skill in course of time; but the raising of the dead, the infliction of death by a word, the innocuous use of poisons, etc., are *miracles of special power.* Cf. Mark 6:5; Acts. 19:11. **prophecy**—Here, probably, not in the wider sense of public teaching by the Spirit (ch. 11:4, 5; 14:1-5, 22-39); but, as its position between "miracles" and a "discerning of spirits" implies, *the inspired disclosure of the future* (Acts 11:27, 28; 21:11; I Tim. 1:18), [HENDERSON]. It depends on "faith" (vs. 9; Rom. 12:6). The *prophets* ranked next to the *apostles* (vs. 28; Eph. 3:5; 4:11). As *prophecy* is part of the whole scheme of redemption, an inspired insight into the obscurer parts of the existing Scriptures, was the necessary preparation for the miraculous foresight of the future. **discerning of spirits**—discerning between the operation of God's Spirit, and the evil spirit, or unaided human spirit (ch. 14: 29; cf. I Tim. 4:1; I John 4:1). **kinds of tongues**—the power of speaking *various languages:* also a *spiritual language unknown to man, uttered in ecstasy* (ch. 14:2-12). This is marked as a distinct genus in the *Greek,* "To another and a *different* class." **interpretation of tongues**—(ch. 14:13, 26, 27). **11. as he will**—(vs. 18; Heb. 2:4).

ADAM CLARKE

6. *Diversities of operations.* Miraculous influences exerted on others, such as the expulsion of demons, inflicting extraordinary punishments (as in the case of Ananias and Sapphira, Elymas the sorcerer, etc.), the healing of different diseases, raising the dead, etc. All these proceeded from God the Father, as the Fountain of all goodness and power, and the immediate Dispenser of every good and perfect gift.

In the preceding three verses we find more than an indirect reference to the doctrine of the sacred Trinity. Gifts are attributed to the Holy Spirit, v. 4; administrations to the Lord Jesus, v. 5; operations to God the Father, v. 6.

7. *The manifestation of the Spirit.* This is variably understood by the fathers, some of them rendering "illumination," others "demonstration," and others "operation." The apostle's meaning seems to be this: Whatever gifts God has bestowed, or in what various ways soever the Spirit of God may have manifested himself, it is all for the common benefit of the Church. God has given no gift to any man for his own private advantage or exclusive profit. He has it for the benefit of others as well as for his own salvation.

8. *Word of wisdom.* In all these places I consider that the proper translation of *logos* is "doctrine," as in many other places of the New Testament. It is very difficult to say what is intended here by the different kinds of gifts mentioned by the apostle; they were probably all supernatural, and were necessary at that time only for the benefit of the Church. By "doctrine of wisdom" we may understand the mystery of our redemption, in which the wisdom of God was most eminently conspicuous. By "the doctrine of knowledge" we may understand either a knowledge of the types, etc., in the Old Testament or what are termed "mysteries": the calling of the Gentiles, the recalling of the Jews, the mystery of iniquity, of the beast, etc., and especially the mystical sense or meaning of the Old Testament, with all its types, rites, ceremonies.

9. By *faith* we are to understand that miraculous faith by which they could remove mountains, chap. xiii. 2. *Gifts of healing* simply refers to the power which at particular times the apostles received from the Holy Spirit to cure diseases.

10. *The working of miracles.* This seems to refer to the same class as the "operations," v. 6, as the words are the same; and to signify those powers by which they were enabled at particular times to work miraculously on others, ejecting demons, inflicting punishments or judgments, as in the cases mentioned under v. 6. *Prophecy.* This seems to import two things: (1) The predicting future events such as then particularly concerned the state of the Church and the apostles—as the dearth foretold by Agabus, Acts xi. 28; and the binding of Paul, and delivering him to the Romans, Acts xxi. 10; and Paul's foretelling his own shipwreck on Malta, Acts xxvii. 25; and (2) As implying the faculty of teaching or expounding the Scriptures, which is also a common acceptation of the word. *Discerning of spirits.* A gift by which the person so privileged could discern a false miracle from a true one, or a pretender to inspiration from him who was made really partaker of the Holy Ghost. It probably extended also to the discernment of false professors from true ones as appears in Peter in the case of Ananias and his wife. *Divers kinds of tongues.* "Different languages," which they had never learned, and which God gave them for the immediate instruction of people of different countries who attended their ministry. *Interpretation of tongues.* It was necessary that while one was speaking the deep things of God in a company where several were present who did not understand, though the majority did, there should be a person who could immediately interpret what was said to that part of the congregation that did not understand the language. This power to interpret was also an immediate gift of God's Spirit and is classed here among the miracles.

11. *But all these worketh that one and the selfsame Spirit.* All these gifts are miraculously bestowed. They cannot be acquired by human art or industry, the different languages excepted; but they were given in such a way, and

MATTHEW HENRY

Verses 12–26

The apostle puts the gifted men among the Corinthians in mind of their duty, by comparing the church of Christ to a human body.

I. One body may have many members, the many members of the same body make but one body (*v.* 12). All the members are *baptized into the same body, and made to drink of the same Spirit, v.* 13. Christians become members of this body by baptism: they are baptized into one body. And by communion at the other ordinance we are sustained by drinking into one Spirit. It is baptism by the Spirit, it is internal renovation and drinking into one Spirit that makes us true members of Christ's body. All who have the spirit of Christ are the members of Christ, whether Jew or Gentile, bond or free.

II. Each member has its particular form, place, and use. The meanest member makes a part of the body. The foot and ear are less useful, perhaps, than the hand and eye; shall they say, therefore, that they do not belong to the body? *v.* 15, 16. So every member of the body mystical cannot have the same place and office. The meanest member of his body is as much a member as the noblest. All his members are dear to him. There must be a distinction of members in the body: *They are many members, and yet are but one body, v.* 20. So it is in the body of Christ. Variety in the members of the body contributes to the beauty of it. So it is for the beauty and good appearance of the church that there should be diversity of gifts. The disposal of members and their situation, are as God pleases, *v.* 18. So is it also in the members of Christ's body. We should be doing the duties of our own place, and not quarrelling with others, that we are not in theirs. All the members of the body are useful and necessary to each other. Those members of the body *which seem to be more feeble are necessary* (*v.* 21, 22). Every member serves some good purpose or other. Nor is there a member of the body of Christ but ought to be useful to his fellow-members, and in some cases, is needful to them. Those who excel in any gift cannot say that they have no need of those who in that gift are their inferiors, while perhaps, in other gifts, they exceed them. The eye has need of the hand, and the head of the feet. Such is the man's concern for his whole body that *on the less honourable members more abundant honour is bestowed, and our uncomely parts have more abundant comeliness, v.* 24. So should the members of Christ's body behave towards their fellow-members. Divine wisdom has ordered things in this manner that the members of the body should not be schismatics. That *there might be no schism in the body* (*v.* 25). The members of the natural body are made to have a care and concern for each other. So should it be in Christ's body. Christian sympathy is a great branch of Christian duty.

Verses 27–31

I. Here the apostle applies this similitude to the church of Christ.

1. The relation wherein Christians stand to Christ and one another. *Now you are the body of Christ, and members in particular.* All have a common relation to one another.

JAMIESON, FAUSSET, BROWN

12, 13. Unity, not unvarying uniformity, is the law of God in the world of grace, as in that of nature. As the many members of the body compose an organic whole and none can be dispensed with as needless, so those variously gifted by the Spirit, compose a spiritual organic whole, the body of Christ, into which all are baptized by the one Spirit. **of that one body**—Most of the oldest MSS. omit "one." **so also** *is* **Christ**—i.e, the whole Christ, *the head and body.* So Psalm 18:50, "His anointed (Messiah or Christ), David (the antitypical David) and His seed." **by . . . Spirit . . . baptized**—lit., "in"; in virtue of; through. The *designed* effect of baptism, which is realized when not frustrated by the unfaithfulness of man. **Gentiles**—lit., "Greeks." **all made to drink into one Spirit**—The oldest MSS. read, "Made to drink of one Spirit," omitting "into" (John 7:37). There is an indirect allusion to the Lord's Supper, as there is a direct allusion to baptism in the beginning of the verse. So the "Spirit, the water, and the blood" (I John 5:8), similarly combine the two outward signs with the inward things signified, the Spirit's grace. **are . . . have been**—rather as *Greek,* "were . . . were" (the past tense). **14.** Translate, "For the body *also.*" The analogy of the body, not consisting exclusively of one, but of many members, illustrates the mutual dependence of the various members in the one body, the Church. The well-known fable of the belly and the other members, spoken by Menenius Agrippa, to the seceding commons [LIVY, 2. 32], was probably before Paul's mind, stored as it was with classical literature. **15.** The humbler members ought not to disparage themselves, or to be disparaged by others more noble (vss. 21, 22). **foot . . . hand**—The humble speaks of the more honorable member which most nearly resembles itself: so the "ear" of the "eye" (the nobler and more commanding member, Num. 10: 31), (vs. 16). As in life each compares himself with those whom he approaches nearest in gifts, not those far superior. The *foot* and *hand* represent men of active life; the *ear* and *eye,* those of contemplative life. **17.** Superior as the *eye* is, it would not do if it were the sole member to the exclusion of the rest. **18. now**—as the case really is. **every one**—each severally. **19. where were the body**—which, by its very idea, "hath many members" (vss. 12, 14), [ALFORD]. **20. now**—as the case really is: in contrast to the supposition (vs. 19; cf. vs. 18). **many members**—mutually dependent. **21.** The higher cannot dispense with the lower members. **22. more feeble**—more susceptible of injury: e.g., the brain, the belly, the eye. Their very feebleness, so far from doing away with the need for them, calls forth our greater care for their preservation, as being felt "necessary." **23. less honourable**—"We think" the feet and the belly "less honorable," though not really so in the nature of things. **bestow . . . honour**—*putting* shoes *on* (*Margin*) the feet, and clothes to cover the belly. **uncomely parts**—the secret parts: the poorest, though unclad in the rest of the body, cover these. **24. tempered . . . together**—on the principle of mutual compensation. **to that part which lacked**—to the deficient part [ALFORD], (vs. 23).

25. no schism (cf. vs. 21)—no disunion; referring to the "divisions" noticed (ch. 11:18). **care one for another**—i.e., *in behalf of* one another.

26. And—Accordingly. **all . . . suffer with it**—"When a thorn enters the heel, the whole body feels it, and is concerned: the back bends, the belly and thighs contract themselves, the hands come forward and draw out the thorn, the head stoops, and the eyes regard the affected member with intense gaze" [CHRYSOSTOM]. **rejoice with it**—"When the head is crowned, the whole man feels honored, the mouth expresses, and the eyes look, gladness" [CHRYSOSTOM]. **27. members in particular**—i.e., severally members of it. Each church is in miniature what the whole aggregate of churches is collectively, "the body of Christ" (cf. ch. 3:16): and its individual components are members, every one in his assigned place.

ADAM CLARKE

in such circumstances, as sufficiently proved that they also were miraculous gifts.

12. *For as the body is one.* Though the human body have many members and though it be composed of a great variety of parts, yet it is but one entire system, every part and member being necessary to the integrity or completeness of the whole. *So also is Christ.* That is, So is the Church the body of Christ, being composed of the different officers already mentioned, and especially those enumerated, v. 28, apostles, prophets, teachers, etc. It cannot be supposed that Christ is composed of many members, and therefore the term Church must be understood; unless we suppose, which is not probable, that the term *Christ* is used to express the Church or whole body of Christian believers.

13. *For by one Spirit are we all baptized.* As the body of man, though composed of many members, is informed and influenced by one soul, so the Church of Christ, which is His body, though composed of many members, is informed and influenced by one Spirit, the Holy Ghost; actuating and working by His spiritual body, as the human soul does in the body of man. *To drink into one Spirit.* We are to understand being made partakers of the gifts and graces of the Holy Ghost agreeably to the words of our Lord, John vii. 37, etc.: "If any man thirst, let him come unto me, and drink . . . this spake he of the Spirit, which they that believe on him should receive."

14. *For the body is not one member.* The mystical body, the Church, as well as the natural body, is composed of many members.

15. *If the foot shall say.* As all the members of the body are necessarily dependent on each other, and minister to the general support of the system, so is it in the Church.

21. *And the eye cannot say unto the hand, I have no need of thee.* The apostle goes on, with his principal object in view, to show that the gifts and graces with which their different teachers were endowed were all necessary for their salvation, and should be collectively used. For not one of them was unnecessary, nor could they dispense with the least of them; the body of Christ needed the whole for its nourishment and support.

22. *Those members . . . which seem to be more feeble.* These, and the less honorable and uncomely, mentioned in the next verses, seem to mean the principal viscera, such as the heart, lungs, stomach, and intestinal canal. These, when compared with the arms and limbs, are comparatively weak and some of them, considered in themselves, uncomely and less honorable; yet these are more essential to life than any of the others. A man may lose an eye by accident, and an arm or a leg may be amputated, and yet the body live and be vigorous; but let the stomach, heart, lungs, or any of the viscera be removed, and life becomes necessarily extinct.

25. *That there should be no schism in the body.* That there should be no unnecessary and independent part in the whole human machine, and that every part should contribute something to the general proportion, symmetry, and beauty of the body.

26. *And whether one member suffer.* As there is a mutual exertion for the general defense, so there is a mutual sympathy. If the eye, the hand, the foot be injured, the whole man grieves; and if by clothing, or anything else, any particular member or part is adorned, strengthened, or better secured, it gives a general pleasure to the whole man.

27. *Now ye are the body of Christ.* As the members in the human body, so the different members of the mystical body of Christ. All are intended by Him to have the same relation to each other, to be mutually subservient to each other, to mourn for and rejoice with each other. He has also made each necessary to the beauty, proportion, strength, and perfection of the whole. Not one is useless; not one, unnecessary. Paul, Apollos, Cephas, etc., with all their variety of gifts and graces, are "for the perfecting of the saints, for the work of the ministry, for the edifying to the body of Christ," Eph. iv. 12. Hence no teacher should be exalted above or opposed to another.

MATTHEW HENRY

2. The variety of offices instituted by Christ, and gifts or favours dispensed by him (*v.* 28). Observe, (1) The plenteous variety of these gifts and offices. He was no niggard of his benefits and favours. They had no want, but a store—all that was necessary, and even more. (2) Observe the order of these offices and gifts. Those of most value have the first place. God does, and we should, value things according to their real worth. What holds the last and lowest rank in this enumeration is diversity of tongues. It is by itself the most useless and insignificant of all these gifts. The Corinthians valued themselves exceedingly on this gift. How proper a method it is to beat down pride to let persons know the true value of what they pride themselves in! It is but too common a thing for men to value themselves most on what is least worth.

(3) The various distribution of these gifts. All members and officers had not the same endowments (*v.* 29, 30). The Spirit distributes to everyone as he will. We must be content with our own rank and share. All are to minister to one another, and promote the good of the body in general.

II. He closes this chapter with an advice and a hint. An advice to covet the best gifts. We should desire that most which is best, and most worth. Grace is therefore to be preferred before gifts. But some read this passage, not as an advice, but a charge: *You are envious* at each other's gifts. You quarrel and contend about them. It was a quarrel about precedency; and it is no wonder that a quarrel about precedency should extinguish charity. When all would stand in the first rank, no wonder if they jostle. To have the heart glow with mutual love is vastly better than to glare with the most pompous titles, offices, or powers.

JAMIESON, FAUSSET, BROWN

28. set . . . in the church—as He has "set the members . . . in the body" (vs. 18). **first apostles**—above even the *prophets.* Not merely the *Twelve,* but others are so called, e.g., Barnabas, etc. (Rom. 16:7). **teachers**—who taught, for the most part, truths already revealed; whereas. the *prophets* made new revelations and spoke all their prophesyings under the Spirit's influence. As the teachers had the "word of knowledge," so the prophets "the word of wisdom" (vs. 8). Under "teachers" are included "evangelists and pastors." **miracles**—lit., "powers" (vs. 10): ranked below "teachers," as the function of *teaching* is more edifying, though less dazzling than working miracles. **helps, governments**—lower and higher departments of "ministrations" (vs. 5); as instances of the former, deacons whose office it was to *help* in the relief of the poor, and in baptizing and preaching, subordinate to higher ministers (Acts 6:1-10; 8:5-17); also, others who *helped* with their time and means, in the Lord's cause (cf. ch. 13:3; Num. 11:17). The Americans similarly use "helps" for *"helpers."* And, as instances of the latter, *presbyters,* or *bishops,* whose office it was to *govern* the Church (I Tim. 5:17; Heb. 13:17, 24). These officers, though now ordinary and permanent, were originally specially endowed with the Spirit for their office, whence they are here classified with other functions of an inspired character. Government (lit., *guiding the helm* of affairs), as being occupied with external things, notwithstanding the outward status it gives, is ranked by the Spirit with the lower functions. Cf. "He that giveth (answering to 'helps')—he that ruleth" (answering to "governments") (Rom. 12:8). Translate, lit., "Helpings, governings" [ALFORD]. **diversities of tongues**—(vs. 10). *"Divers* kinds of tongues." **29. Are all?**—Surely not. **31. covet earnestly**—*Greek,* "emulously desire." Not in the spirit of *discontented* "coveting." The Spirit "divides to every man severally *as He will"* (vs. 1); but this does not prevent men *earnestly seeking,* by prayer and watchfulness, and cultivation of their faculties, the *greatest* gifts. BEZA explains, "Hold in the highest estimation"; which accords with the distinction in his view (ch. 14:1) between *"follow after* charity—*zealously esteem* spiritual gifts"; also with (vss. 11, 18) the sovereign will with which the Spirit distributes the gifts, precluding individuals from desiring gifts not vouchsafed to them. But see the *Note,* ch. 14:1. **the best gifts**—Most of the oldest MSS. read, "the *greatest gifts."* **and yet**—*Greek,* "and *moreover."* *Besides* recommending your zealous desire for the greatest gifts, I am about to show you a something still more excellent (lit., "a way most waylike") to desire, "the way of love" (cf. ch. 14:1). This love, or "charity," includes both "faith" and "hope" (ch. 13:7), and bears the same fruits (ch. 13) as the ordinary and permanent fruits of the Spirit (Gal. 5:22-24). Thus "long-suffering," cf. vs. 4; "faith," vs. 7; "joy," vs. 6; "meekness," vs. 5; "goodness," vs. 5; "gentleness," vs. 4 (the *Greek* is the same for "is kind"). It is the work of the Holy Spirit, and consists in love to God, on account of God's love in Christ to us, and as a consequence, love to man, especially to the brethren in Christ (Rom. 5:5; 15:30). This is more to be desired than gifts (Luke 10:20).

ADAM CLARKE

28. *God hath set some in the church.* As God has made evident distinctions among the members of the human body, so that some occupy a more eminent place than others, so has He in the Church. And to prove this, the apostle enumerates the principal offices, and in the order in which they should stand. *First apostles.* Persons immediately designated by Christ, and sent by Him to preach the gospel to all mankind. *Secondarily prophets.* A person who, under divine inspiration, predicts future events; but the word is often applied to those who preach the gospel. *Thirdly teachers.* Persons whose chief business it was to instruct the people in the elements of the Christian religion, and their duty to each other. *Miracles.* Persons endued with miraculous gifts. *Gifts of healings.* Such as laying hands upon the sick, and healing them. *Helps.* Dr. Lightfoot conjectures that these were the apostles' helpers; persons who accompanied them, baptized those who were converted by them, and were sent by them to such places as they could not attend to, being otherwise employed. The Levites are termed by the Talmudists "helps of the priests." The word occurs in Luke i. 54; Rom. viii. 26. *Governments.* Dr. Lightfoot contends that this word does not refer to the power of ruling, but to the case of a person endued with a deep and comprehensive mind, who is profoundly wise and prudent. *Diversities of tongues.* "Kinds of tongues"; that is, different kinds. The power to speak, on all necessary occasions, languages which they had not learned.

29. *Are all apostles?* That is: All are not apostles, all are not prophets, etc. God has distributed His various gifts among various persons, each of whom is necessary for the complete edification of the body of Christ.

31. *But covet earnestly.* To *covet* signifies to "desire earnestly." Some think that this verse should be read affirmatively, "You earnestly contend about the best gifts; but I show unto you a more excellent way"; i.e., get your hearts filled with love to God and man—love, which is the principle of obedience, which works no ill to its neighbor, and which is the fulfilling of the law. This is a likely reading, for there were certainly more contentions in the church of Corinth about the gifts than about the graces of the Spirit.

MATTHEW HENRY

CHAPTER 13

Verses 1–3

Here the apostle shows what more excellent way he meant, *charity,* or *love*: love in its fullest meaning, true love to God and man. Without this the most glorious gifts are nothing.

JAMIESON, FAUSSET, BROWN

CHAPTER 13

VSS. 1-13. CHARITY OR LOVE SUPERIOR TO ALL GIFTS. The New Testament psalm of love, as the 45th Psalm (see its title) and Canticles in the Old Testament.

ADAM CLARKE

CHAPTER 13

1. *Though I speak.* At the conclusion of the preceding chapter the apostle promised to show the Corinthians a "more excellent way" than that in which they were now proceeding. They were so distracted with contentions, divided by parties, and envious of each other's gifts that unity was nearly destroyed. This was a full proof that love to God and man was wanting, and that without this their numerous gifts and other graces were nothing in the eyes of God; for it was evident that they did not love one another, which is a proof that they did not love God, and consequently that they had not true religion. Before I proceed to the consideration of the different parts of this chapter, it may be necessary to examine whether the word *agape* be best translated by charity or "love." Wycliffe, translating from the Vulgate, has the word *charity;* and him our Authorized Version follows. But Coverdale, Matthews, Cranmer, and the Geneva Bible have "love," which is adopted by recent translators and commentators in general, among whom are Dodd and Wesley. All these strenuously contend that the word *charity,* which is now confined to "alms-

MATTHEW HENRY

1. The gift of tongues (*v.* 1). It is the charitable heart, not the voluble tongue, that is acceptable with God.

TODAY'S DICTIONARY OF THE BIBLE:

Tongues, Gift of, granted on the day of Pentecost (Acts 2:4), in fulfillment of a promise Christ made to his disciples (Mark 16:17). What this gift actually was has been a subject of much discussion. Some have argued that it was merely an outward sign of the presence of the Holy Spirit among the disciples, typifying his manifold gifts, and showing that salvation was to be extended to all nations. But the words of Luke (Acts 2:9) clearly show that the various people in Jerusalem at the time of Pentecost did really hear "the wonderful works of God" being spoken in their own special language with which they were naturally acquainted (comp. Joel 2:28, 29).

Among the gifts of the Spirit the apostle enumerates in 1 Cor. 12:10; 14:1-28, "divers kinds of tongues" and the "interpretation of tongues."

2. Prophecy, and the understanding of mysteries, and all knowledge. This without charity is as nothing, *v.* 2. A clear and deep head is of no signification, without a benevolent and charitable heart. It is not great knowledge that God sets a value upon, but true and hearty devotion and love. 3. Miraculous faith. Moving mountains is a great achievement in the account of men; but one dram of charity is, in God's account, of much greater worth than all the faith of this sort in the world. Saving faith is ever in conjunction with charity, but the faith of miracles may be without it.

4. The outward acts of charity, *v.* 3. There may be an open and lavish hand, where there is no liberal and charitable heart. If we give away all we have, while we withhold the heart from God, it will not profit.

5. Even sufferings, *v.* 3. Should we sacrifice our lives for the faith of the gospel; this will stand us in no stead without charity. True charity is the very heart and spirit of religion. If we feel none of its sacred heat in our hearts, it will profit nothing, though we be burnt to ashes for the truth.

Verses 4–7

Some of the properties and effects of charity.

I. *It is long suffering.* It can endure evil and provocation, without being filled with resentment or revenge. It will put up with many slights from the person it loves, and wait long to see the kindly effects of such patience on him.

II. *It is kind. The law of kindness is in her lips.* It seeks to be useful; and not only seizes on opportunities of doing good, but searches for them.

III. *It envieth not;* it is not grieved at the good of others. Envy is the effect of ill-will. The mind which is bent on doing good to all can never wish ill to any.

JAMIESON, FAUSSET, BROWN

1. tongues—from these he ascends to "prophecy" (vs. 2); then, to "faith"; then to benevolent and self-sacrificing deeds: a climax. He does not except even himself, and so passes from addressing *them* ("unto you," ch. 12:31, to putting the case in his own person, "Though I . . ." **speak with the tongues**—with the eloquence which was so much admired at Corinth (e.g., Apollos, Acts 18:24; cf. ch. 1:12; 3:21, 22), and with the command of various languages, which some at Corinth abused to purposes of mere ostentation (ch. 14:2, etc.). **of angels**—higher than men, and therefore, it is to be supposed, speaking a more exalted language. **charity**—the principle of the ordinary and more important gifts of the Spirit, as contrasted with the extraordinary gifts (ch. 12). **sounding . . . tinkling**—*sound* without soul or feeling: such are "tongues" without *charity*. **cymbal**—Two kinds are noticed (Ps. 150:5), the loud or *clear,* and the *highsounding* one: hand cymbals and finger cymbals, or castanets. The sound is sharp and piercing.

2. mysteries—(Rom. 11:25 16:25). *Mysteries* refer to the deep counsels of God hitherto secret, but now revealed to His saints. *Knowledge,* to truths long known. **faith . . . remove mountains**—(Matt. 17:20; 21:21). The practical power of the will elevated by faith [NEANDER]; confidence in God that the miraculous result will surely follow the exercise of the will at the secret impulse of His Spirit. Without "love" prophecy, knowledge, and faith, are not what they seem (cf. ch. 8:1, 2; Matt. 7:22; Jas. 2:41, cf. vs. 8), and so fail of the heavenly reward (Matt. 6:2). Thus Paul, who teaches justification by faith only (Rom. 3:4, 5; Gal. 2:16; 3:7-14), is shown to agree with James, who teaches (Jas. 2:24) "by works" (i.e., by LOVE, which is the "spirit" of faith, Jas. 2:26) a man is justified, "and not by faith only." **3. bestow . . . goods . . . poor**—lit., "dole out in food" all my goods; one of the highest functions of the "helps" (ch. 12:28).

give . . . body to be burned lit., "to such a degree as that I should be burned." As the three youths did (Dan. 3:28), "yielded their bodies" (cf. II Cor. 12:15). These are most noble exemplifications of love in giving and in suffering. Yet they may be without love; in which case the "goods" and "body" are given, but not the *soul,* which is the sphere of love. Without the soul God rejects all else, and so rejects the man, who is therefore "profited" nothing (Matt. 16:26; Luke 9:23-25). Men will fight for Christianity, and die for Christianity, but not live in its spirit, which is *love.*

suffereth long—under provocations of *evil from* others. The negative side of *love.*

is kind—the positive side. Extending *good* to others. Cf. with love's features here those of the "wisdom from above" (Jas. 3:17). **envieth**—The *Greek* includes also *jealousy.*

ADAM CLARKE

giving," is utterly improper, and that the word "love" alone expresses the apostle's sense. *The tongues of men.* All human languages, with all the eloquence of the most accomplished orator. *And of angels.* I.e., though a man knew the language of the eternal world so well that he could hold conversation with its inhabitants, and find out the secrets of their Kingdom. Or probably the apostle refers to a notion that was common among the Jews that there was a language by which angels might be invoked, adjured, collected, and dispersed; and by the means of which many secrets might be found out, and curious arts and sciences known. *Sounding brass.* That is, like a trumpet made of brass. *Tinkling cymbal.* Though I possessed the knowledge of all languages, and could deliver even the truth of God in them in the most eloquent manner, and had not a heart full of love to God and man, my religion is no more to my salvation than the sounds emitted by the brazen trumpet, or the jingling of the cymbals could contribute intellectual pleasure to the instruments which produce them; and, in the sight of God, I am of no more moral worth than those sounds are. I will quote Josiah Gregory: "People of little religion are always noisy; he who has not the love of God and man filling his heart is like an empty wagon coming violently down a hill: it makes a great noise, because there is nothing in it."

2. *And though I have the gift of prophecy.* Though I should have received from God the knowledge of future events, so that I could correctly foretell what is coming to pass in the world and in the Church; *and understand all mysteries.* The meaning of all the types and figures in the Old Testament, and all the unexplored secrets of nature; *and all knowledge*—every human art and science; *and though I have all faith*—such miraculous faith as would enable me even to remove mountains, or had such powerful discernment in sacred things that I could solve the greatest difficulties; *and have not charity*—this love to God and man, as the principle and motive of all my conduct, the characteristics of which are given in the following verses; *I am nothing*—nothing in myself, nothing in the sight of God, nothing in the Church, and good for nothing to mankind. Balaam and several others not under the influence of this love of God prophesied.

3. *And though I bestow all my goods to feed the poor.* This is a proof that *charity,* in our sense of the word, is not what the apostle means; for surely almsgiving can go no further than to give up all that a man possesses in order to relieve the wants of others. The word which we translate *to feed the poor* signifies to "divide into morsels, and put into the mouth," which implies carefulness and tenderness in applying the bounty thus freely given. *And though I give my body to be burned.* Mr. Wakefield renders this clause thus: "And though I give up my body so as to have cause of boasting"; in vindication of which he first refers to Dan. iii. 28; Acts xv. 26; Rom. viii. 32; Phil. i. 20. "That I may boast" is the reading of the Aethiopic and Coptic, and of the Codex Alexandrinus; several Greek and Latin MSS. referred to by Jerome; and of Jerome himself. who translates the passage thus: "If I deliver up my body that I may glory, or have cause of boasting." The charity or love which God recommends, the apostle describes in sixteen particulars, which are the following:

4. (1) *Charity suffereth long.* "Has a long mind"; to the end of which neither trials, adversities, persecutions, nor provocations can reach. The love of God, and of our neighbor for God's sake, is patient towards all man. It suffers all the weakness, ignorance, errors, and infirmities of the children of God, and all the malice and wickedness of the children of this world; and all this, not merely for a time, but *long,* without end. (2) *Is kind.* It is tender and compassionate in itself, and *kind* and obliging to others; it is mild, gentle, and benign; and if called to suffer, inspires the sufferer with the most amiable sweetness and the most tender affection. It is also submissive to all the dispensations of God, and creates trouble to no one. (3) *Charity envieth not.* Is not grieved because another possesses a greater portion of earthly, intellectual, or spiritual blessings. Those who have this pure love rejoice as much at

MATTHEW HENRY

IV. *It vaunteth not itself, is not puffed up*, is not bloated with self-conceit. True love will give us an esteem of our brethren, and this will limit our esteem of ourselves. The word rendered in our translation *vaunteth itself* bears other significations, but in every sense and meaning true charity stands in opposition to it. The Syriac renders it—*does not raise tumults* and disturbances. Charity calms the angry passions, instead of raising them. Others render it—*It does not act insidiously*, does not seek to ensnare them. It is not froward nor apt to be cross and contradictory. Some understand it of dissembling and flattery. Charity abhors such falsehood and flattery.

V. *It behaveth not unseemly*. It does nothing out of place or time; but behaves with courtesy and good-will towards all men.

VI. Charity is an utter enemy to selfishness: *Seeketh not its own*. Indeed self-love, in some degree, is natural to all men. And a reasonable love of self is by our Saviour made the measure of our love to others. *Thou shalt love thy neighbour as thyself*. But charity never seeks its own to the hurt of others. It often neglects its own for the sake of others.

VII. *It is not exasperated*. Where the fire of love is kept in, the flames of wrath will not easily kindle, nor long keep burning. Anger cannot rest in the bosom where love reigns. It is hard to be angry with those we love.

JAMIESON, FAUSSET, BROWN

vaunteth not—in words, even of gifts which it really possesses; an indirect rebuke of those at Corinth who used the gift of tongues for mere display.

not puffed up—with party zeal, as some at Corinth were (ch. 4:6).

5. not . . . unseemly—*is not uncourteous*, or inattentive to civility and propriety.

ALBERT BARNES:

5. "Doth not behave itself unseemly." It means to conduct improperly, or disgracefully, or in a manner to deserve reproach. Love seeks that which is proper or becoming in the circumstances and relations of life in which we are placed. It prompts to the due respect for superiors, producing veneration and respect for their opinions; and it prompts to a proper regard for inferiors, not despising their rank, their poverty, their dress, their dwellings, their pleasures, their view of happiness; it prompts to the due observance of all the relations of life, as those of a husband, wife, parent, child, brother, sister, son, daughter, and produces a proper conduct and deportment in all these relations. The proper idea of the phrase is that it prompts to all that is fit and becoming in life; and would save from all that is unfit and unbecoming. There may be included in the word also the idea that it would prevent anything that would be a violation of decency or delicacy.

"Seeketh not her own." There is, perhaps, not a more striking or important expression in the New Testament than this; or one that more beautifully sets forth the nature and power of that love which is produced by true religion. Its evident meaning is that it is not selfish; it does not seek its own happiness exclusively or mainly; it does not seek its own happiness to the injury of others. This expression is not, however, to be pressed as if Paul meant to teach that a man should not regard his own salvation. But it is not simply or mainly that he may be happy that he is to seek it. It is, that he may thus glorify God his Savior, and accomplish the great design which his Maker has had in view in his creation and redemption.

It is the *characteristic* of the man, not that he promotes his own worth, health, happiness, or salvation, but that he lives to do good to others. Love to others will prompt to that, and that alone. There is not a particle of selfishness in true love. It seeks the welfare of others, and of all others. That true religion will produce this, is evident everywhere in the New Testament; and especially in the life of the Lord Jesus, whose whole biography is comprehended in one expressive declaration, "who went about doing good" (Acts 10:38).

"Is not easily provoked." This word occurs in the New Testament in only one other place. Acts 17:16, "His spirit *was stirred* within him when he saw the city wholly given to idolatry." The word properly means to sharpen by, or with, or on anything (from "sharp"), and may be applied to the act of sharpening a knife or sword; then it means to sharpen the mind, temper, courage of anyone; to excite or impel. Here it means evidently to rouse to anger; to excite to indignation or wrath. Tindal renders it, "is not provoked to anger."

—Popular Commentary

ADAM CLARKE

the happiness, the honor, and comfort of others as they can do in their own. They are ever willing that others should be preferred before them. (4) *Charity vaunteth not itself*. This word is variously translated; "acteth not rashly, insolently; is not inconstant." There is a phrase in our own language that expresses what I think to be the meaning of the original, does not "set itself forward"—does not desire to be noticed or applauded, but wishes that God may be All in All. (5) *Is not puffed up*. Is not "inflated" with a sense of its own importance; for it knows it has nothing but what it has received, and that it deserves nothing that it has got. Every man whose heart is full of the love of God is full of humility; for there is no man so humble as he whose heart is cleansed from all sin. True humility arises from a sense of the fullness of God in the soul; abasement from a sense of corruption is a widely different thing.

5. (6) *Doth not behave itself unseemly*. Love never acts out of its place or character; observes due decorum and good manners; is never rude, bearish, or brutish; and is ever willing to become all things to all men, that it may please them for their good to edification. No ill-bred man, or what is termed rude or unmannerly, is a Christian. A man may have a natural bluntness, or be a clown, and yet there be nothing boorish or hoggish in his manner. I must apologize for using such words; they best express the evil against which I wish both powerfully and successfully to declaim. I never wish to meet with those who affect to be called "blunt, honest men"; who feel themselves above all the forms of respect and civility, and care not how many they put to pain, or how many they displease. But let me not be misunderstood; I do not contend for ridiculous ceremonies and hollow compliments. There is surely a medium, and a sensible Christian man will not be long at a loss to find it out. (7) *Seeketh not her own*. Is not desirous of her own spiritual welfare only, but of her neighbor's also. For the writers of the Old and New Testaments do almost everywhere, agreeably to their Hebrew idiom, express a preference given to one thing before another by an affirmation of that which is preferred, and a negative of that which is contrary to it. Love is never satisfied but in the welfare, comfort, and salvation of all. That man is no Christian who is solicitous for his own happiness alone, and cares not how the world goes, so that himself be comfortable. (8) *Is not easily provoked*. "Is not provoked, is not irritated, is not made sour or bitter." How the word *easily* got into our translation it is hard to say; but, however it got in, it is utterly improper, and has nothing in the original to countenance it. The New Testament, printed in 1547, the first year of Edward VI, in English and Latin, has simply, "is not provokeed to angre." The edition published in English in the following year, 1548, has the same rendering, but the orthography better: "is not provoked to anger." The Bible in folio, with notes, published the next year, 1549, by Edmund Becke, preserves nearly the same reading, "is not provoketh to anger." The large folio printed by Richard Cardmarden, at Rouen, 1566, has the same reading. The translation made and printed by the command of King James I, in 1611, departs from all these, and improperly inserts the word *easily*, which might have been His Majesty's own. And yet this translation was not followed by some subsequent editions; for the quarto Bible printed at London four years after, 1615, not only retains this original and correct reading, "it is not provoked to anger," but has the word "love" everywhere in this chapter instead of *charity*, in which all the preceding versions and editions agree. In short, this is the reading of Coverdale, Matthews, Cranmer, the Geneva, and others; and our own Authorized Version is the only one which I have seen where this false reading appears. The apostle's own words in v. 7 are a sufficient proof that love of which he speaks can never be provoked. When the man who possesses this love gives way to provocation, he loses the balance of his soul and grieves the Spirit of God. In that instant he ceases from loving God with all his soul, mind, and strength; and surely if he get embittered against his neighbor, he does not love him as himself. (9) *Thinketh no evil*. "Believes no evil where

MATTHEW HENRY

VIII. Charity *thinks no evil.* It cherishes no malice, nor gives way to revenge: so some understand it. It is not soon, nor long, angry. It does not suspect evil of others. It will hide faults that appear, instead of hunting and raking out those that lie covered and concealed.

IX. The matter of its joy and pleasure is here suggested. *It rejoiceth not in iniquity.* It wishes ill to none, much less will it make this the matter of its delight, or rejoice in doing harm and mischief. The sins of others stir all its compassion, but can give it no entertainment. *It rejoiceth in the truth.* It gives it much satisfaction to see truth and justice prevail among men, and mutual faith and trust established.

X. *It beareth all things, it endureth all things.* Some read the first, *covers all things.* It is not for blazing nor publishing the faults of a brother. Though such a man be free to tell his brother his faults in private, he is very unwilling to expose him by making them public. Thus we do by our own faults, and thus charity would teach us to do by the faults of others.

XI. *Believeth all things; hopeth all things.* Indeed charity does by no means destroy prudence. Wisdom may dwell with love, and charity be cautious. But it is apt to believe well of all. All charity is apt to make the best of everything; it will judge well, and believe well. And, when in spite of inclination, it cannot believe well of others, it will yet hope well. How lovely a mind is that which is tinctured throughout with such benevolence! Happy the man who has this heavenly fire glowing in his heart!

Or, it *beareth all things*—will be patient upon provocation, and long patient. What a fortitude and firmness fervent love will give the mind! What cannot a lover endure for the beloved and for his sake!

Verses 8–13

How much it is preferable to the gifts on which the Corinthians were so apt to pride themselves.

I. *Charity never faileth.* It is a permanent and perpetual grace, lasting as eternity.

Prophecy must fail. Tongues will cease. There will be but one language in heaven. There is no confusion of tongues in the region of perfect tranquillity. And *knowledge will vanish away.* Not that holy and happy souls shall be unknowing: it is a very poor happiness that can consist with utter ignorance. The apostle is here setting the grace of charity in opposition to supernatural gifts. And it is more valuable, because more durable; *it* shall enter into heaven, where *they* will have no place.

II. *We know in part, and we prophesy in part, v.* 9. How little a portion of God was heard even by apostles and inspired men! These gifts were fitted to the present imperfect state of the church, whereas charity was to last for ever.

JAMIESON, FAUSSET, BROWN

thinketh no evil—*imputeth not evil* [ALFORD]; lit., "*the* evil" which actually is there (Prov. 10:12; I Pet. 4:8). Love makes allowances for the falls of others, and is ready to put on them a charitable construction. Love, so far from devising evil against another, excuses "*the* evil" which another inflicts on her [ESTIUS]; *doth not meditate upon evil* inflicted by another [BENGEL]; and in doubtful cases, takes the more charitable view [GROTIUS].

6. rejoiceth in the truth—rather, "rejoiceth *with* the truth." Exults not at the perpetration of iniquity (unrighteousness) by others (cf. Gen. 9:22, 23), but rejoices when the truth rejoices; sympathizes with it in its triumphs (II John 4). See the opposite (II Tim. 3:8), "Resist the truth." So "the truth" and "unrighteousness" are contrasted (Rom. 2:8). "The truth" is the Gospel truth, the inseparable ally of love (Eph. 4:15; II John 12). The false charity which compromises "the truth" by glossing over "iniquity" or unrighteousness is thus tacitly condemned (Prov. 17:15). **7. Beareth all things**—without speaking of what it has to bear. The same *Greek* verb as in ch. 9:12. It *endures without divulging* to the world personal distress. Literally said of *holding fast* like a watertight vessel; so the charitable man *contains himself* in silence from giving vent to what selfishness would prompt under personal hardship.

believeth all things—unsuspiciously believes all that is not palpably false, all that it can with a good conscience believe to the credit of another. Cf. James 3:17, "easy to be entreated"; *Greek,* "easily persuaded." **hopeth**—what is good of another, even when others have ceased to hope.

endureth—persecutions in a patient and loving spirit.

8. never faileth—never is to be out of use; it always holds its place.

shall fail . . . vanish away—The same *Greek* verb is used for both; and that different from the *Greek* verb for "faileth." Translate, "Shall be done away with," i.e., shall be dispensed with at the Lord's coming, being superseded by their more perfect heavenly analogues; for instance, *knowledge* by *intuition.* Of "tongues," which are still more temporary, the verb is "shall *cease.*" A primary fulfilment of Paul's statement took place when the Church attained its maturity; then "tongues" entirely "ceased," and "prophesyings" and "knowledge," so far as they were supernatural gifts of the Spirit, were superseded as no longer required when the ordinary preaching of the word, and the Scriptures of the New Testament collected together, had become established institutions. **9, 10. in part**—partially and imperfectly. Cf. a similar contrast to the "perfect man," "the measure of the stature of the fulness of Christ" (Eph. 4:11-13). **that which is in part**—fragmentary and isolated.

ADAM CLARKE

no evil seems." Never supposes that a good action may have a bad motive; gives every man credit for his profession of religion, uprightness, godly zeal, while nothing is seen in his conduct or in his spirit inconsistent with this profession. His heart is so governed and influenced by the love of God that he cannot think of evil but where it appears. The original implies that he does not "invent or devise" any evil, or does not "reason" on any particular act or word so as to infer evil from it, for this would destroy his love to his brother; it would be ruinous to charity and benevolence.

6. (10) *Rejoiceth not in iniquity.* "Rejoiceth not in falsehood." but on the contrary, *rejoiceth in the truth.* (11) *But rejoiceth in the truth.* Everything that is opposite to falsehood and irreligion. Those who are filled with the love of God and man rejoice in the propagation and extension of divine truth.

7. (12) *Beareth all things.* This word is also variously interpreted; to "endure, bear, sustain, cover, conceal, contain." But the true import must be found either in "cover" or "contain." Love conceals everything that should be concealed; betrays no secret; retains the grace given; and goes on to continual increase. A person under the influence of this love never makes the sins, follies, faults, or imperfections of any man the subject of either censure or conversation. He covers them as far as he can; and if alone privy to them, he retains the knowledge of them in his own bosom as far as he ought. (13) *Believeth all things.* Is ever ready to believe the best of every person, and will credit no evil of any but on the most positive evidence. (14) *Hopeth all things.* When there is no place left for believing good of a person, then love comes in with its hope, where it could not work by its faith; and begins immediately to make allowances and excuses, as far as a good conscience can permit; and further, anticipates the repentance of the transgressor, and his restoration to the good opinion of society and his place in the Church of God, from which he had fallen. 15) *Endureth all things.* Bears up under all persecutions and maltreatment from open enemies, and professed friends; bears adversities with an even mind, as it submits with perfect resignation to every dispensation of the providence of God; and never says of any trial, affliction, or insult, "This cannot be endured."

8. (16) *Charity never faileth.* "This love never falleth off," because it bears, believes, hopes, and endures all things; and while it does so it cannot fail. It is the means of preserving all other graces; indeed, properly speaking, it includes them all; and all receive their perfection from it. Love to God and man can never be dispensed with. It is essential to social and religious life; without it no communion can be kept up with God, nor can any man have a preparation for eternal glory whose heart and soul are not deeply imbued with it. *Prophecies, they shall fail.* Whether the word imply predicting future events or teaching the truths of religion to men, all such shall soon be rendered useless. Though the accurate prophet and the eloquent, persuasive preacher be useful in their day, they shall not be always so, nor shall their gifts fit them for glory; nothing short of the love above described can fit a soul for the kingdom of God. *Tongues, they shall cease.* The miraculous gift of different languages shall also cease, as being unnecessary. *Knowledge, it shall vanish away.* All human arts and sciences, as being utterly useless in the eternal world, though so highly extolled and useful here.

9. *For we know in part.* We have here but little knowledge even of earthly, and much less of heavenly, things. He that knows most knows little in comparison of what is known by angels and the spirits of just men made perfect. And as we know so very little, how deficient must we be if we have not much love! *We prophesy in part.* Even the sublimest prophets have been able to say but little of the heavenly state, and the best preachers have left the Spirit of God very much to supply. When you have learned all you can from your ministers, remember you have much to learn from God; and for this you should diligently wait on Him by the reading of His Word and by incessant prayer.

10. *But when that which is perfect.* The state of eternal blessedness. *Then that which is in*

MATTHEW HENRY

III. How much better it will be with the church hereafter (*v.* 10). When the end is once attained, the means will of course be abolished. Then the church will be in a state of perfection, complete both in knowledge and holiness. God will be known then clearly. What confused and indistinct notions of things, have children, in comparison of grown men! And how naturally do men despise and relinquish their infant thoughts!

The things to be known will be open to our eyes; and our knowledge will be free from all obscurity and error. God is to be seen *face to face*; and we *are to know him* as *we are known by him.* O glorious change! To pass from darkness to light, from clouds to the clear sunshine of our Saviour's face, and in God's own light to see light! It is at best but twilight while we are in this world; there it will be perfect and eternal day.

IV. Faith, hope, and love, are the three principal graces, of which charity is the chief. Faith fixes on the divine revelation, and assents to that: hope fastens on future felicity, and waits for that. But love fastens on the divine perfections themselves. These will all shine forth in the most glorious splendours in another world, and there will love be made perfect; there we shall perfectly love God. And there shall we perfectly love one another. When faith and hope are at an end, true charity will burn for ever with the brightest flame. Where God is to be seen as he is, and face to face, there charity is in its greatest height—there, and there only, will it be perfected.

JAMIESON, FAUSSET, BROWN

11. When . . . a child—(ch. 3:1; 14:20). **I spake**—alluding to "tongues." **understood**—or, "had the sentiments of." Alluding to "prophecy." **I thought**—*Greek* "reasoned" or "judged"; alluding to "knowledge." **when I became . . . I put away**—rather, "now that I am become a man, I have done away with the things of the child." **12. now**—in our present state. **see**—an appropriate expression, in connection with the "prophets" of *seers* (I Sam. 9:9). **through a glass**—i.e., in a mirror; the reflection *seeming* to the eye to be behind the mirror, so that we see it *through* the mirror. Ancient mirrors were made of polished brass or other metals. The contrast is between the inadequate knowledge of an object gained by seeing it reflected in a dim mirror (such as ancient mirrors were), compared with the perfect idea we have of it by seeing itself directly. **darkly**—lit., "in enigma." As a "mirror" conveys an image to the *eye,* so an "enigma" to the *ear.* But neither "eye nor ear" can fully represent (though the believer's soul gets a small revelation now of) "the things which God hath prepared for them that love Him" (ch. 2:9). Paul alludes to Numbers 12:8, "not in *dark* speeches"; LXX, "not in *enigmas.*" Compared with the *visions* and *dreams* vouchsafed to other prophets, God's communications with Moses were "not in enigmas." But compared with the intuitive and direct vision of God hereafter, even the revealed word now is "a dark discourse," or a shadowing forth *by enigma* of God's reflected likeness. Cf. II Pet. 1:19, where the "light" or *candle* in a dark place stands in contrast with the "day" dawning. God's word is called a *glass* or mirror also in II Corinthians 3:18. **then**—"when that which is perfect is come" (vs. 10). **face to face**—not merely "mouth to mouth" (Num. 12:8). Genesis 32:30 was a type (John 1:50, 51). **know . . . known**—rather as *Greek, "fully* know . . . *fully* known." Now we *are known by,* rather than *know,* God (ch. 8:3; Gal. 4:9). **13. And now**—Translate, *"But* now." "In this present state" [HENDERSON]. Or, "now" does not express time, but *opposition,* as in ch. 5:11, "the case being so" [GROTIUS]; whereas *it is the case that* the *three* gifts, "prophecy," "tongues," and "knowledge" (cited as specimens of the whole class of gifts) "fail" (vs. 8), *there abide* permanently only *these three—faith, hope, charity.* In one sense *faith* and *hope* shall be done away, faith being superseded by sight, and hope by actual fruition (Rom. 8:24; II Cor. 5:7); and charity, or love, alone never faileth (vs. 8). But in another sense, "faith and hope," as well as "charity," ABIDE; viz., after the extraordinary gifts have ceased; for those three are *necessary and sufficient for salvation at all times,* whereas the extraordinary gifts are not at all so; cf. the use of "abide," ch. 3:14. *Charity,* or love, is connected specially with the Holy Spirit, who is the bond of the loving union between the brethren (Rom. 15:30; Col. 1:8). *Faith* is towards God. *Hope* is in behalf of ourselves. *Charity* is love to God creating in us love towards our neighbor. In an unbeliever there is more or less of the three opposites—unbelief, despair, hatred. Even hereafter *faith* in the sense of *trust in God* "abideth"; also "hope," in relation to ever new joys in prospect, and at the anticipation of ever increasing blessedness, sure never to be disappointed. But love alone in every sense "abideth"; it is therefore "the greatest" of the three, as also because it presupposes "faith," which without "love" and its consequent "works" is dead (Gal. 5:6; Jas. 2:17, 20). **but**—rather, "and"; as there is not so strong opposition between charity and the other two, faith and hope, which like it also "abide."

ADAM CLARKE

part, that which is imperfect, *shall be done away;* the imperfect as well as the probationary state shall cease forever.

11. *When I was a child.* This future state of blessedness is as far beyond the utmost perfection that can be attained in this world as our adult state of Christianity is above our state of natural infancy, in which we understand only as children understand.

12. *Now we see through a glass, darkly.* Of these words some literal explanation is necessary. The word which we translate *a glass* literally signifies a mirror or reflector, and among the ancients mirrors were made of fine polished metal. The word here may signify anything by which the image of a person is reflected, as in our "looking, or look-in, glass." The word is not used for a glass to look through, nor would such an image have suited with the apostle's design. The word which we render *darkly* will help us to the true meaning of the place. "Now, in this life, we see by means of a mirror reflecting the images of heavenly and spiritual things, in an enigmatical manner, invisible things being represented by visible, spiritual by natural, eternal by temporal; but then, in the eternal world, face-to-face, everything being seen in itself, and not by means of a representative or similitude." *Now I know in part.* Though I have an immediate revelation from God concerning His great design in the dispensation of the gospel, yet there are lengths, breadths, depths, and heights of this design which even that revelation has not discovered; nor can they be known and apprehended in the present imperfect state. Eternity alone can unfold the whole scheme of the gospel. *As also I am known.* In the same manner in which disembodied spirits know and understand.

13. *And now* (in the present life) *abideth faith, hope, charity.* These three supply the place of that direct vision which no human embodied spirit can have; these abide or "remain" for the present state. *Faith,* by which we apprehend spiritual blessings, and walk with God. *Hope,* by which we view and expect eternal blessedness, and pass through things temporal so as not to lose those which are eternal. *Charity* or "love," by which we show forth the virtues of the grace which we receive by faith in living a life of obedience to God and of goodwill and usefulness to man. *But the greatest of these is charity.* Without *faith* it is impossible to please God; and without it, we cannot partake of the grace of our Lord Jesus. Without *hope* we could not endure as seeing Him who is invisible, nor have any adequate notion of the eternal world, nor bear up under the afflictions and difficulties of life. But great and useful and indispensably necessary as these are, yet *charity* or "love" is greater; "love is the fulfilling of the law"; but this is never said of faith or hope. *Love* is properly the image of God in the soul; for "God is love." By *faith* we receive from our Maker; by *hope* we expect a future and eternal good; but by love we resemble God, and by it alone are we qualified to enjoy heaven and be one with Him throughout eternity. *Faith,* says one, is the foundation of the Christian life and of good works; *hope* rears the superstructure; but *love* finishes, completes, and crowns it in a blessed eternity. *Faith* and *hope* respect ourselves alone; *love* takes in both God and man. *Faith* helps, and *hope* sustains us; but *love* to God and man makes us obedient and useful. This one consideration is sufficient to show that love is greater than either faith or hope. Some say *love* is the greatest because it remains throughout eternity, whereas *faith* and *hope* proceed only through life; hence we say that there faith is lost in sight, and hope in fruition. But does the apostle say so? Or does any man inspired by God say so? I believe not. *Faith* and *hope* will as necessarily enter into eternal glory as *love* will. The perfections of God are absolute in their nature, infinite in number, and eternal in their duration. However high, glorious, or sublime the soul may be in that eternal state, it will ever, in respect to God, be limited in its powers, and must be improved and expanded by the communications of the Supreme Being. Hence it will have infinite glories in the nature of God to apprehend by *faith,* to anticipate by *hope,* and enjoy by *love.*

MATTHEW HENRY

CHAPTER 14

Verses 1–5

He teaches them, among spiritual gifts, which they should prefer.

I. An exhortation to charity (*v.* 1). See you do not miss this, the principal of all graces.

II. He directs them which spiritual gift to prefer: "*Desire spiritual gifts, but rather that you may prophesy.*" Gifts are fit objects of our desire and pursuit, in subordination to grace and charity.

III. The reasons of this preference. He only compares prophesying with speaking with tongues. This was more ostentatious than the plain interpretation of scripture, but less fit to pursue the purposes of Christian charity. He that spoke with tongues must wholly speak between God and himself, *v.* 2.

What cannot be understood can never edify. But he that prophesies speaks to the advantage of his hearers. They may be exhorted and comforted by it, *v.* 3.

He that speaks with tongues may edify himself, *v.* 4, others can reap no benefit from his speech. Whereas the end of speaking in the church is to edify the church (*v.* 4), to which prophesying is immediately adapted. That is the best gift which does most good.

Every gift of God is a favour from God, but then those are to be most valued that are most useful. Greater is he who interprets scripture to edify the church than he who speaks tongues to recommend himself. That makes most for the honour of a minister which is most for the church's edification, not that which shows his gifts to most advantage.

Verses 6–14

If I come to you speaking with tongues, what will it profit you, unless I speak to you by revelation, or by knowledge, or by prophesying, or by doctrine? (*v.* 6).

JAMIESON, FAUSSET, BROWN

CHAPTER 14

Vss. 1-25. SUPERIORITY OF PROPHECY OVER TONGUES. **1. Follow after charity**—as your first and chief aim, seeing that it is "the greatest" (ch. 13:13). **and desire**—Translate, "Yet (as a *secondary* aim) desire zealously (*Note,* ch. 12:31) spiritual gifts." **but rather**—"*but chiefly* that ye may prophesy" (speak and exhort under inspiration) (Prov. 29: 18; Acts 13:1; I Thess. 5:20), whether as to future events, i.e., strict *prophecy,* or explaining obscure parts of Scripture, especially the prophetical Scriptures or illustrating and setting forth questions of Christian doctrine and practice. Our modern *preaching* is the successor of *prophecy,* but without the inspiration. Desire zealously this (prophecy) *more* than any other spiritual gift; or *in preference to* "tongues" (vs. 2, etc.) [BENGEL].

2. speaketh . . . unto God—who alone understands *all* languages. **no man understandeth**—generally speaking; the few who have the gift of interpreting tongues are the exception. **in the spirit**—as opposed to "the understanding" (vs. 14). **mysteries**—unintelligible to the hearers, exciting their wonder, rather than instructing them. Corinth, being a mart resorted to by merchants from Asia, Africa, and Europe, would give scope amidst its mixed population for the exercise of the gift of tongues; but its legitimate use was in an audience understanding the tongue of the speaker, not, as the Corinthians abused it, in mere display. **3. But**—on the other hand. **edification**—of which the two principal species given are "exhortation" to remove *sluggishness,* "comfort" or *consolation* to remove *sadness* [BENGEL]. Omit "to."

4. edifieth himself—as he understands the meaning of what the particular "tongue" expresses; but "the church," i.e., the congregation, does not.

Translate, "Now I wish you all to speak with tongues (so far am I from thus speaking through having any objection to tongues), but rather IN ORDER THAT (as my ulterior and higher wish for you) ye should prophesy." Tongues must therefore mean *languages,* not ecstatic, unintelligible rhapsodie (as NEANDER fancied): for Paul could never "wish" for the latter in their behalf.

greater—because *more useful.* **except he interpret**—the unknown tongue which he speaks, "that the Church may receive edifying" (*building up*).

6. Translate, "*But* now"; seeing there is no edification without interpretation. **revelation . . . prophesying**—corresponding one to the other; "revelation" being the supernatural *unveiling* of divine truths to man,

ADAM CLARKE

CHAPTER 14

1. *Follow after charity.* Most earnestly labor to be put in possession of that love which beareth, believeth, hopeth, and endureth all things. It may be difficult to acquire and difficult to retain this blessed state, but it is essential to your present peace and eternal happiness. This clause belongs to the preceding chapter. *Desire spiritual gifts.* You are very intent on getting those splendid gifts which may add to your worldly consequence and please your carnal minds; but labor rather to get the gifts of God's Spirit, by which you may grow in grace and be useful to others; and particularly desire *that ye may prophesy*—that you may be able to teach and instruct others in the things of their salvation.

2. *For he that speaketh in an unknown tongue.* This chapter is crowded with difficulties. It is not likely that the Holy Spirit should in the church suddenly inspire a man with the knowledge of some foreign language which none in the church understood but himself; and lead him to treat the mysteries of Christianity in that language, though none in the place could profit by his teaching. Dr. Lightfoot's mode of reconciling these difficulties is the most likely I have met with. He supposes that by the unknown *tongue* the Hebrew is meant, and that God restored the true knowledge of this language when He gave the apostles the gift of tongues. As the Scriptures of the Old Testament were contained in this language, and it has beauties, energies, and depths in it which no verbal translation can reach, it was necessary, for the proper elucidation of the prophecies concerning the Messiah and the establishment of the Christian religion, that the full meaning of the words of this sacred language should be properly understood. *Speaketh not unto men, but unto God.* None present understanding the language, God alone knowing the truth and import of what he says. *In the spirit he speaketh mysteries.* Though his own mind (for so *pneumati* is understood here by many eminent critics) apprehends the mysteries contained in the words which he reads or utters; but if by *the spirit* we understand the Spirit of God, it only shows that it is by that Spirit that he is enabled to speak and apprehend these mysteries.

3. *But he that prophesieth.* The person who has the gift of teaching is much more useful to the church than he is who has only the gift of tongues, because he speaks to the profit of men: viz., to their *edification,* by the Scriptures he expounds; to their *exhortation,* by what he teaches; and to their *comfort,* by his revelation.

4. *He that speaketh in an unknown tongue*—in the Hebrew, for instance. The knowledge of the depth and power of which he has got by a divine revelation *edifieth himself* by that knowledge. *But he that prophesieth.* Has the gift of preaching. *Edifieth the church.* Speaketh unto men to edification, exhortation, and comfort, v. 3.

5. *I would that ye all spake with tongues.* The word *thelo* does not so much imply a wish or desire as a command or permission. As if he had said: I do not restrain you to prophesying or teaching, though I prefer that; but I give you full permission to speak in Hebrew whenever it is proper, and when one is present who can interpret for the edification of the church, provided yourselves have not that gift, though you understand the language. The apostle said "tongue," in the singular number, vv. 2, 4, because he spoke of a single man; now he says *tongues,* in the plural number, because he speaks of many speaking. But he has the same meaning in both places. *Greater is he that prophesieth.* A useful, zealous preacher, though unskilled in learned languages, is much *greater* in the sight of God, and in the eye of sound common sense, than he who has the gift of those learned tongues, *except he interpret;* and we seldom find great scholars good preachers. This should humble the scholar, who is too apt to be proud of his attainments and despise his less learned but more useful brother.

6. *Speaking with tongues.* Without interpreting. *What shall I profit you?* I.e., I shall not profit you, *except I shall speak to you either by revelation* of some secret thing; *or by knowledge* of some mystery; *or by prophesying,* fore-

MATTHEW HENRY

It would signify nothing to utter any of these in an unknown tongue.

I. Unintelligible language is like piping or harping without distinction of sounds: it gives no more direction than a pipe with but one stop or a harp with but one string can direct a dancer how he should order his steps, *v.* 7.

A trumpet giving an *uncertain sound.* If, instead of sounding an onset, it sounded a retreat, or sounded one knew not what, who would prepare for the battle? Words without a meaning can convey no notion nor instruction to the mind; and words not understood have no meaning. He compares the speaking in an unknown tongue to the gibberish of barbarians.

There are (*v.* 10) many kinds of voices in the world, none of which is without its proper signification. But whatever proper signification the words of any language may have to those who understand them, they are perfect gibberish to men of another language. In this case, speaker and hearers are barbarians to each other (*v.* 11), they talk and hear only sounds without sense. To speak in the church in an unknown tongue is to talk gibberish.

II. Be chiefly desirous of those gifts that are most for the church's edification, *v.* 12. "Covet those gifts most that will do the best service to men's souls." If they did speak a foreign language, they should beg of God the gift of interpreting it, *v.* 13. The church must understand, that it might be edified. The sum is that they should perform all religious exercises in their assemblies so that all might join in them and profit by them. He enforces this advice. His own mind might be devoutly engaged, *but his understanding would be unfruitful* (*v.* 14), he would not be understood, nor therefore would others join with him in his devotions. Language that is most obvious and easy to be understood is the most proper for public devotion.

Verses 15–20

The apostle,

I. Directs them how they should sing and pray in public (*v.* 15). He would have them perform both so as to be understood by others, that others might join with them. Public worship should be performed so as to be understood.

II. He enforces the argument with several reasons.

1. Otherwise the unlearned could not say Amen to their prayers or thanksgivings, could not join in the worship, for they did not understand it, *v.* 16. All should say *Amen* inwardly; and it is not improper to testify this inward concurrence in public prayers and devotions, by an audible *Amen.* Now, how should

JAMIESON, FAUSSET, BROWN

"prophesying" the enunciation to men of such revelations. So "knowledge" corresponds to "doctrine," which is the gift of *teaching* to others our knowledge. As the former pair refers to specially *revealed mysteries,* so the latter pair refers to the *general obvious truths of salvation,* brought from the common storehouse of believers. **7.** Translate, "And things without life-giving sound, whether pipe or harp, YET (*notwithstanding their giving sound*) if they give not a distinction in the tones (i.e., notes) how . . .?" **what is piped or harped**—i.e., what tune is played on the pipe or harp.

8. Translate, "For if *also,*" an *additional* step in the argument. **uncertain sound**—having no definite meaning: whereas it ought to be so marked that one succession of notes on the trumpet should summon the soldiers to attack; another, to retreat; another, to some other evolution.

9. So . . . ye—who have life; as opposed to "things without life" (vs. 7). **by the tongue**—the language which ye speak in. **ye shall speak**—Ye will be speaking into the air, i.e., *in vain* (ch. 9:26). **10. it may be**—i.e., perhaps, speaking by conjecture. "It may chance" (ch. 15: 37). **so many**—as may be enumerated by investigators of such matters. Cf. "so much," used generally for a definite number left undefined (Acts 5:8; also II Sam. 12:8). **kinds of voices**—kinds of articulate speech. **without signification**— *without articulate voice* (i.e., distinct meaning). *None is without its own voice,* or mode of speech, *distinct* from the rest. **11. Therefore**—seeing that none is without meaning. **a barbarian**—a foreigner (Acts 28:2). Not in the depreciatory sense as the term is now used, but one *speaking a foreign language.*

zealous—emulously desirous. **spiritual** *gifts*—lit., "spirits"; i.e., emanations from the one Spirit. **seek that ye may excel to**—Translate, "Seek *them,* that ye may abound *in them* to the edifying. . . ." **13.** Explain, "Let him who speaketh with a tongue [unknown] *in his prayer* (or, *when praying*) *strive* that he may interpret" [ALFORD]. This explanation of "pray" is needed by its logical connection with "prayer in an unknown tongue" (vs. 14). Though his words be unintelligible to his hearers, let him in them pray that he may obtain the gift of interpreting, which will make them "edifying" to "the church" (vs. 12). **14. spirit**—my higher being, the *passive* object of the Holy Spirit's operations, and the instrument of prayer in the unknown tongue, distinguished from the "understanding," the *active* instrument of thought and reasoning; which in this case must be "unfruitful" in edifying others, since the vehicle of expression is unintelligible to them. On the distinction of *soul* or *mind* and *spirit,* see Ephesians 4:23; Hebrews 4:12.

15. What is it then? —What is my determination thereupon? **and**—rather as *Greek,* "but"; I will not only pray with my spirit, which (vs. 14) might leave the understanding unedified, BUT with the understanding also [ALFORD and ELLICOTT]. **pray with the understanding also**—and, by inference, I will keep silence altogether if I cannot pray with the understanding (so as to make myself understood by others). A prescient warning, *mutatis mutandis,* against the Roman and Greek practice of keeping liturgies in dead languages, which long since have become unintelligible to the masses; though their forefathers spoke them at a time when those liturgies were framed for *general* use.

16. Else . . . thou—He changes from the *first* person, as he had just expressed *his own* resolution, "*I* will pray with the understanding," whatever "thou" doest. **bless**—the highest kind of prayer. **occupieth the room of the unlearned**—one who, whatever other gifts he may possess, yet, as wanting the gift of interpretation, is reduced by the speaking in an unknown tongue to the position of one unlearned, or "a private person." **say Amen**—Prayer is not a vicarious duty done by others *for*

ADAM CLARKE

telling some future event; *or by doctrine,* instructing you what to believe and practice.

7. *And even things without life.* As if he had said, I may illustrate this further by referring to a *pipe* or *harp;* if these were to utter mere *sounds* without order, harmony, or melody, though every tone of music might be in the sounds, surely no person could discern a tune in such sounds nor receive pleasure from such discords. Even so is the person who speaks in an unknown tongue, but does not interpret. His speech tends no more to edification than those discordant and unmeaning sounds do to pleasure and delight.

8. *If the trumpet give an uncertain sound.* If, when the soldier should prepare himself for the battle, the trumpet should give a different sound to that which is ordinarily used on such occasions, the soldier is not informed of what he should do, and therefore does not arm himself; consequently that vague, unintelligible sound of the trumpet is of no use.

9. *Likewise ye.* If you do not speak in the church so as to be understood, your labor is useless. *Ye shall speak into the air*—your speech will be lost and dissipated in the air, without conveying any meaning to any person; there will be a noise or sound, but nothing else.

10. *There are, it may be.* "For example." *So many kinds of voices.* So many different languages, each of which has its distinct articulation, pronunciation, emphasis, and meaning; or there may be so many different nations, each possessing a different language.

11. *If I know not the meaning of the voice.* The "power" and signification of the language. *I shall be unto him that speaketh a barbarian.* I shall appear to him, and he to me, as a person who had no distinct and articulate sounds which can convey any kind of meaning. This observation is very natural. When we hear persons speaking in a language of which we know nothing, we wonder how they can understand each other, as in their speech there appears to us no regular distinction of sounds or words.

12. *Forasmuch as ye are zealous.* Seeing you affect so much to have spiritual gifts, seek that you may get those by which you may excel in edifying the church.

13. *Pray that he may interpret.* Let him who speaks or reads the prophetic declarations in the Old Testament, in that tongue in which they were originally spoken and written, pray to God that he may so understand them himself and receive the gift of interpretation that he may be able to explain them in all their depth and latitude to others.

14. *For if I pray in an unknown tongue.* If my prayers are composed of sentences and sayings taken out of the prophets and in their own language, *my spirit prayeth,* my heart is engaged in the work, and my prayers answer all the purpose of prayers to myself; *but my understanding is unfruitful* to all others, because they do not understand my prayers, and I either do not or cannot interpret them.

15. *I will pray with the spirit.* I will endeavor to have all my prayers influenced and guided by the Spirit of God, and to have my own heart deeply affected in and by the work. *And I will pray with the understanding also.* I will endeavor so to pray that others may understand me, and thus be edified and improved by my prayers. And therefore I will pray in a language in the public congregation that may be understood by all present, so that all may join not only in the act but in the spirit of devotion. *I will sing with the spirit.* It does appear that singing psalms or spiritual hymns was one thing that was implied in what is termed "prophesying" in the Old Testament, as is evident from 1 Sam. x. 5-6, 10. And when this came through an immediate afflatus or inspiration of God, there is no doubt that it was exceedingly edifying, and must have served greatly to improve and excite the devotional spirit of all who were present.

16. *He that occupieth the room of the unlearned.* One who is not acquainted with the language in which you speak, sing, or pray. *Say Amen.* Give his assent and ratification to what he does not understand. It was very frequent in primitive times to express their approbation in

MATTHEW HENRY

the people say *Amen* to what they did not understand? The intention of public devotions is therefore entirely destroyed if they are performed in an unknown tongue. Others are not, cannot be, edified (*v.* 17) by what they understand not.

2. He alleges his own example, to make the greater impression. (1) He did not come behind any of them in this spiritual gift. It was not envy that made Paul depreciate what they so highly valued and so much vaunted of; he surpassed them all in this very gift of tongues. There was more ground for them to envy him upon this head than for him to envy them. When we beat down men's unreasonable value for themselves, we should let them see that this does not proceed from an envious and grudging spirit.

(2) He had rather *speak five words with understanding than ten thousand words in an unknown tongue*, *v.* 19. A truly Christian minister will value himself much more upon doing good to men's souls than upon procuring the greatest applause.

3. The fondness then discovered for this gift was but too plain an indication of the immaturity of their judgment, *v.* 20. Children are apt to be struck with novelty and strange appearances. Do not you act like them, and prefer noise and show to worth and substance; be like children in nothing but an innocent and inoffensive disposition. Christians should have wisdom and knowledge that are ripe and mature.

Verses 21–25

The apostle pursues the argument.

I. Tongues, as the Corinthians used them, were rather a token of judgment from God than mercy to any people (*v.* 21). It is an evidence that a people are abandoned of God when he gives them up to the discipline of those who speak in another language. They can never be benefited by such teaching as this; and, when they are left to it, it is a sad sign that God gives them over as past cure. Yet thus did the Corinthian preachers who would always deliver their inspirations in an unknown tongue.

II. Tongues were rather a sign to unbelievers than to believers, *v.* 22. The gift of tongues was necessary to spread Christianity. It was proper and intended to convince unbelievers; interpreting scripture in their own language, as most for the edification of such as did already believe. That gifts may be rightly used, it is proper to know the ends which they are intended to serve. To go about the conversion of infidels had been a vain undertaking without the gift of tongues, but, in an assembly of Christians it would be perfectly impertinent.

JAMIESON, FAUSSET, BROWN

us; as in Rome's liturgies and masses. We must join *with* the leader of the prayers and praises of the congregation, and say aloud our responsive "A-men" in assent, as was the usage of the Jewish (Deut. 27:15-26; Neh. 8:6) and Christian primitive churches [JUSTIN MART., *Apol.* 2. 97]. **17. givest thanks**—The prayers of the synagogue were called "eulogies," because to each prayer was joined a *thanksgiving*. Hence the prayers of the Christian Church also were called *blessings* and *giving of thanks*. This illustrates Colossians 4:2; I Thessalonians 5:17, 18. So the *Kaddisch* and *Keduscha*, the synagogue formulæ of "hallowing" the divine "name" and of prayer for the "coming of God's kingdom," answer to the Church's Lord's Prayer, repeated often and made the foundation on which the other prayers are built [TERTULLIAN, *de Oratione*]. **18. tongues**—The oldest MSS. have the singular, "in a tongue [foreign]."

19. I had rather—The *Greek* verb more literally expresses this meaning, "I WISH to speak five words with my understanding (rather) than ten thousand words in an unknown tongue"; even the two thousandth part of ten thousand. The *Greek* for "I would rather," would be a different verb. Paul would NOT wish at all to speak "ten thousand words in an unknown tongue."

20. Brethren—an appellation calculated to conciliate their favorable reception of his exhortation. **children in understanding**—as preference of gifts abused to nonedification would make you (cf. ch. 3:1; Matt. 10:16; Rom. 16:19; Eph. 4: 14). The *Greek* for "understanding" expresses the will of one's *spirit*, Romans 8:6 (it is not found elsewhere); as the "heart" is the will of the "soul." The same *Greek* is used for "minded" in Romans 8:6. **men**—full-grown. Be childlike, not childish.

In the law—as the whole Old Testament is called, being all of it the law of God. Cf. the citation of the Psalms as the "law," John 10:34. Here the quotation is from Isaiah 28:11, 12, where God virtually says of Israel, This people hear Me not, though I speak to them in the language with which they are familiar; I will therefore speak to them in other tongues, namely, those of the foes whom I will send against them; but even then they will not hearken to Me; which Paul thus applies, Ye see that it is a penalty to be associated with men of a strange tongue, yet ye impose this on the Church [GROTIUS]; they who speak in foreign tongues are like "children" just "weaned from the milk" (Isa. 28:9), "with stammering lips" speaking unintelligibly to the hearers, appearing ridiculous (Isa. 28:14), or as babbling drunkards (Acts 2:13), or madmen (vs. 23).

22. Thus from Isaiah it appears, reasons Paul, that "tongues" (unknown and uninterpreted) are not a sign mainly intended for believers (though at the conversion of Cornelius and the Gentiles with him, tongues were vouchsafed to him and them to confirm their faith), but mainly to be a *condemnation* to those, the majority, who, like Israel in Isaiah's day, reject the sign and the accompanying message. Cf. "yet . . . will they not hear Me" (vs. 21). "Sign" is often used for a *condemnatory* sign (Ezek. 4:3, 4; Matt. 12:39-42). Since they *will* not understand, they *shall* not understand. **prophesying . . . not for them that believe not, but . . . believe**—i.e., prophesying has no effect on them that are radically and obstinately like Israel (Isa. 28:11,

ADAM CLARKE

the public assemblies by *Amen*. This practice, soberly and piously conducted, might still be of great use in the Church of Christ.

17. *Thou verily givest thanks well*. Because he felt gratitude and, from a sense of his obligation, gave praise to God; but because this was in an unknown tongue, those who heard him received no edification.

18. *I speak with tongues more than ye all*. He understood more languages than any of them did; and this was indispensably necessary, as he was the apostle of the Gentiles in general, and had to preach to different provinces where different dialects, if not languages, were used. In the Hebrew, Syriac, Greek, and Latin, he was undoubtedly well-skilled from his education; and how many he might understand by miraculous gift we cannot tell. But even literally understood, it is very probable that he knew more languages than any man in the church of Corinth.

19. *Yet in the church*. As the grand object of public worship is the edification of those who attend, *five words* spoken so as to convey edification were of much more consequence than *ten thousand* which, not being understood, could convey none. By the word *tongue*, to which we add *unknown*, I suppose the apostle always means the Hebrew, for the reasons offered in the note on v. 1.

20. *Be not children in understanding*. There are three words here to which we must endeavor to affix the proper sense: (1) *paidia* signifies "children" in general, but particularly such as are grown up, so as to be fit to send to school in order to receive instruction; (2) *nepios* signifies an "infant," one that cannot yet speak, and is in the lowest stage of infancy; (3) *teleioi*, from *teleo*, "I complete or perfect," signifies those who are arrived at perfect maturity, of both growth and understanding. We shall now see the apostle's meaning: *Brethren, be not* as "little children" just beginning to go to school, in order to learn the first elements of their mother tongue, and with an understanding sufficient only to apprehend those elements. *In malice*. "In wickedness be as infants," who neither speak, do, nor purpose evil. *But in understanding*. "Be perfect men," whose vigor of body and energy of mind show a complete growth and a well-cultivated understanding.

21. *In the law it is written*. But the passage quoted is in Isa. xxviii. 11. Here is no contradiction, for the term *torah*, law, was frequently used by the Jews to express the whole Scriptures, law, prophets, and hagiographa; and they used it to distinguish these sacred writings from the words of the scribes. *With men of other tongues*. Bishop Pearce paraphrases this verse as follows: "With the tongues of foreigners and with the lips of foreigners will I speak to this people; and yet, for all that, will they not hear me, saith the Lord." To enter into the apostle's meaning we must enter into that of the prophet. The Jewish people were under the teaching of the prophets who were sent from God; these instructed, reproved, and corrected them by this divine authority. They however became so refractory and disobedient that God purposed to cast them off, and abandon them to the Babylonians: then they had a people to teach, correct, and reprove them whose language they did not understand. The discipline that they received in this way was widely different from that which they received while under the teaching of the prophets and the government of God; and yet for all this they did not humble themselves before their Maker, that this affliction might be removed from them.

22. *Wherefore tongues are for a sign*. The miraculous gift of tongues was never designed for the benefit of those who have already believed, but for the instruction of unbelievers, that they might see from such a miracle that this is the work of God, and so embrace the gospel. But as in the times of the prophet the strange Babylonish tongues came in the way of punishment and not in the way of mercy, take heed that it be not the case now; that by dwelling on the gift ye forget the Giver, and what was designed for you as a blessing may prove to you to be a curse. For it, because you have the gift of tongues, you will choose for your own aggrandizement to use them in the

MATTHEW HENRY

III. The credit and reputation of their assemblies required them to prefer prophesying before speaking with tongues. If their ministers, or all employed in public worship, should talk unintelligible language, and infidels should drop in, they would conclude them to be mad. What sort of religion is that which leaves out sense and understanding? Would not this make Christianity ridiculous to a heathen? If, instead of speaking with tongues, those who minister plainly interpret scripture, a heathen or unlearned person, coming in, will probably be convinced, and become a convert to Christianity (*v.* 24, 25); and so will be brought to confess his guilt, to pay his homage to God, and own that he is indeed among you. Prophesying would certainly edify the church, and might probably convert infidels. The ministry was not instituted to make ostentation of gifts and parts, but to save souls.

Verses 26–33

I. He blames them for the confusion they introduced into the assembly (*v.* 26). "You are apt to confound the several parts of worship"; or else, "You are apt to be confused if you do not stay for one another. Can this be edifying? *Let all things be done to edifying.*"

II. He corrects their faults. 1. As to speaking in an unknown tongue, he orders that no more than two or three should do it at one meeting, and this one after another. And even this was not to be done unless there were someone to interpret (*v.* 27, 28). But, if there were none to interpret, he was to be silent in the church, and only exercise his gift between God and himself (*v.* 28).

2. As to prophesying he orders, (1) That two or three only should speak at one meeting (*v.* 29). There might be false prophets, and the true prophets were to judge of these and discover who was divinely inspired and who was not. (2) He orders that, if any assistant prophet had a revelation, while another was prophesying, the other should hold his peace, be silent (*v.* 30). He who had the new revelation might claim liberty of speech in his turn.

The reason annexed (*v.* 31): *That all might prophesy*, one after another. Divine inspirations are not, like the diabolical possessions of heathen priests, violent and ungovernable; but are sober and calm, and capable of regular conduct. The man inspired by the Spirit of God may still observe the rules of natural order and decency in delivering his revelations.

JAMIESON, FAUSSET, BROWN

12), unbelievers, but on them that are either in receptivity or in fact believers; it makes believers of those not wilfully unbelievers (vs. 24, 25; Rom. 10: 17), and spiritually nourishes those that already believe. **23. whole . . . all . . . tongues**—The more there are assembled, and the more that speak in unknown tongues, the more will the impression be conveyed to strangers "coming in" from curiosity ("unbelievers"), or even from a better motive ("unlearned"), that the *whole* body of worshippers is a mob of fanatical "madmen"; and that "the Church is like the company of builders of Babel after the confusion of tongues, or like the cause tried between two deaf men before a deaf judge, celebrated in the Greek epigram" [GROTIUS]. **unlearned**—having some degree of faith, but not gifts [BENGEL]. **24. all**—one by one (vs. 31). **prophesy**—speak the truth by the Spirit intelligibly, and not in unintelligible tongues. **one**—"anyone." Here *singular;* implying that this effect, viz., *conviction by all,* would be produced on *anyone,* who might happen to enter. In vs. 23 the *plural* is used; "unlearned or unbelievers"; implying that however many there might be, not one would profit by the tongues; yea, their being many would confirm them in rejecting the sign, as many unbelieving men together strengthen one another in unbelief; individuals are more easily won [BENGEL]. **convinced**—convicted in conscience; said of the "one that believeth not" (John 16:8, 9). **judged**—His secret character is opened out. "Is searched into" [ALFORD]. Said of the "one unlearned" (cf. ch. 2:15). **25. And thus**—omitted in the oldest MSS. and versions. **secrets of his heart made manifest**—He sees his own inner character opened out by the sword of the Spirit (Heb. 4:12; Jas. 1:23), the word of God, in the hand of him who prophesieth. Cf. the same effect produced on Nebuchadnezzar (Dan. 2:30 and end of verse 47). No argument is stronger for the truth of religion than its manifestation of men to themselves in their true character. Hence hearers even now often think the preacher must have aimed his sermon particularly at them. **and so**—convicted at last, judged, and manifested to himself. Cf. the effect on the woman of Samaria produced by Jesus' unfolding of her character to herself (John 4:19, 29). **and report**—to his friends at home, as the woman of Samaria did. Rather, as the *Greek* is, "He will worship God, *announcing,*" i.e., openly avowing then and there, "that God is in you of a truth," and by implication that the God who is in you is of a truth the God.

26-40. RULES FOR THE EXERCISE OF GIFTS IN THE CONGREGATION. **26. How is it then?**—rather, "*What then* is the true rule to be observed as to the use of gifts?" Cf. vs. 15, where the same *Greek* occurs. **a psalm**—extemporary, inspired by the Spirit, as that of Mary, Zechariah, Simeon, and Anna (Luke 1 and 2). **a doctrine**—to impart and set forth to the congregation. **a tongue . . . a revelation**—The oldest MSS. transpose the order: "revelation . . . tongue"; "interpretation" properly following "tongue" (vs. 13). **Let all things be done unto edifying**—The general rule under which this particular case falls; an answer to the question at the beginning of this verse. Each is bound to obey the ordinances of his church not adverse to Scripture. See Article XXXIV, Church of England Prayer Book. **27. let it be by two**—at each time, in one assembly; not more than two or three might speak with tongues at each meeting. **by course**—in turns. **let one interpret**—one who has the gift of interpreting tongues; and not more than one. **28. let him**—the speaker in unknown tongues. **speak to himself, and to God**—(cf. vss. 2, 4)—privately and not in the hearing of others. **29. two or three**—at one meeting (he does not add "at the most," as in vs. 27, lest he should seem to "quench prophesyings," the most edifying of gifts), and these "one by one," in turn (vs. 27, "by course," and vs. 31). Paul gives here similar rules to the prophets, as previously to those speaking in unknown tongues. **judge**—by their power of "discerning spirits" (ch. 12:10), whether the person prophesying was really speaking under the influence of the Spirit (cf. ch. 12:3; I John 4:1-3). **30. If any thing**—Translate, "*But* if any thing." **another that sitteth by**—a hearer. **let the first hold his peace**—Let him who heretofore spoke, and who came to the assembly furnished with a previous ordinary (in those times) revelation from God (vs. 26), give place to him who at the assembly is moved to prophesy by a sudden revelation from the Spirit. **31. For ye may**—rather, "For ye *can* [if ye will] all prophesy one by one," giving way to one another. The "for" justifies the precept (vs. 30), "let the first hold his peace." **32. And**—following up the assertion in vs. 31, "Ye can (if ye will) prophesy one

ADAM CLARKE

public congregation where none understands them, God may curse your blessings. *Prophesying.* Teaching the things of God in a known language is of infinitely more consequence than speaking in all the foreign tongues in the universe.

23. *Will they not say that ye are mad?* So they well might, finding a whole assembly of people talking languages which those who had most need of instruction could not understand.

24. *But if all prophesy.* If all those who teach do it in the tongue which all understand, if an unbeliever, or one who knows nothing of the sacred language, come in and hear things just suited to his own state, he is convicted by all and *he is judged* by all.

25. *And thus are the secrets of his heart.* As these who were the prophets or teachers had often the discernment of spirits, they were able in certain cases, and probably very frequently, to tell a man the *secrets* of his own heart; and where this was not directly the case, God often led His ministers to speak those things that were suitable to the case before them, though they themselves had no particular design. The sinner, therefore, convinced that God alone could uncover the secrets of his heart, would be often obliged to fall *down on his face,* abashed and confounded, and acknowledge that God was truly among them.

26. *How is it . . . every one of you hath a psalm?* When the whole church came together, among whom there were many persons with extraordinary gifts, each of them wished to put himself forward and occupy the time and attention of the congregation; hence confusion must necessarily take place, and perhaps not a little contention. This was contrary to that edifying which was the intention of these gifts.

27. *Speak in an unknown tongue.* The Hebrew, as has already been conjectured. Let it be *by two, or at the most by three, and that by course.* Let only two or three in one assembly act in this way, that too much time may not be taken up with one exercise; and let this be done *by course,* the one after the other, that two may not be speaking at the same time; *and let one interpret* for all that shall thus speak.

28. *But if there be no interpreter.* If there be none present who can give the proper sense of this Hebrew reading and speaking, then let him keep silence and not occupy the time of the church by speaking in a language which only himself can understand.

29. *Let the prophets.* Those who have the gift of speaking to men "to edification, and exhortation, and comfort," v. 3. *Two or three.* As prophesying implied psalmody, teaching, and exhortation, Dr. Lightfoot thinks that the meaning of the place is this: Let one sing who has a psalm; let another teach who has a doctrine; and let a third exhort, or comfort, who has a gift of that kind. *And let the other judge.* The other prophets or qualified persons judge of the propriety of what had been spoken; or let them "discern" how the revelation under the new covenant confirmed and illustrated the revelation granted under the Old Testament. It appears to have been taken for granted that a man might pretend to this spirit of prophecy who was not sent of God; and therefore it was the duty of the accredited teachers to examine whether what he spoke was according to truth and the analogy of faith.

30. *Be revealed to another that sitteth by.* Probably those who were teachers sat on a particular seat, or place, from which they might most readily address the people; and this may be the meaning of sitting by. If such a person could say, I have just received a particular revelation from God, then let him have the liberty immediately to speak it, as it might possibly relate to the circumstances of that time and place.

31. *For ye may all prophesy one by one.* The gifts which God grants are given for the purpose of edification, but there can be no edification where there is confusion; therefore let them speak one by one.

32. *And the spirits of the prophets.* Let no one interrupt another; let all be ready to prefer others before themselves, and let each feel a

MATTHEW HENRY

III. The apostle gives the reasons of these regulations. They would be for the church's benefit, their instruction and consolation. Divine inspiration should by no means throw Christian assemblies into confusion. If they are managed in a tumultuous and confused manner, what a notion must this give of the God who is worshipped! Does it look as if he were the God of peace and order, and an enemy to confusion? Things were thus orderly managed in all the other churches. And it would be perfectly scandalous for them, who exceeded most churches in spiritual gifts, to be more disorderly than any in the exercise of them.

Verses 34, 35

Here the apostle, 1. Enjoins silence on their women in public assemblies, who must not ask questions for their own information in the church, but ask their husbands at home. There is indeed an intimation (*ch.* xi. 5) as if the women sometimes did pray and prophesy in their assemblies. But here he seems to forbid all public performances of theirs. They are not permitted to speak (*v.* 34) in the church. Nor must she therefore be allowed to teach in a congregation; nor so much as to ask questions in the church, but learn in silence there; and, if difficulties occurred, *ask their own husbands at home.* As it is the woman's duty to learn in subjection, it is the man's duty to keep up his superiority, by being able to instruct her. If it be a shame for her to speak in the church, where she should be silent, it is a shame for him to be silent when he should speak, and not be able to give an answer, when she asks him at home. 2. The apostle concludes it was a shame for women to speak in the church. Shame is the mind's uneasy reflection on having done an indecent thing. And what more indecent than for a woman to quit her rank. The woman was made subject to the man, and she should keep her station and be content with it.

Verses 36–40

A just rebuke of the Corinthians for their extravagant pride and self-conceit. Are you the only church favoured with divine revelations. How intolerably assuming is this behaviour!

JAMIESON, FAUSSET, BROWN

by one," i.e., restrain yourselves from speaking all together; "and the spirits of the prophets," i.e., their own spirits, acted on by the Holy Spirit, are not so hurried away by His influence, as to cease to be under their own control; they can if they will hear others, and not demand that they alone should be heard uttering communications from God. **33.** In all the churches of the saints God is a God of peace; let Him not among you be supposed to be a God of confusion [ALFORD]. Cf. the same argument in ch. 11:16. LACHMANN and others put a full stop at "peace," and connect the following words thus: "As in all churches of the saints, let your women keep silence in your churches."

34. (I Tim. 2:11, 12.) For women to speak in public would be an act of independence, as if they were not subject to their husbands (cf. ch. 11:3; Eph. 5:22 Titus 2:5; I Pet. 3:1). For "under obedience," translate, "in *subjection*" or "*submission,*" as the *Greek* is translated (Eph. 5:21, 22, 24). **the law**—a term applied to the whole Old Testament; here, Genesis 3:16. **35.** Anticipation of an objection. Women may say, "But if we do not understand something, may we not 'ask' a question publicly so as to 'learn'? Nay, replies Paul, if you want information, 'ask' not in public, but 'at home'; ask not other men, but 'your own particular (so the *Greek*) husbands.' " **shame**—indecorous. **36. What!**—*Greek,* "Or." Are you about to obey me? *Or,* if you set up your judgment above that of other churches. I wish to know, do you pretend that your church is the first church FROM which the gospel word came, that you should give the law to all others? Or are you the only persons UNTO whom it has come?

A. T. ROBERTSON:

34. "Keep silence in the churches" (*en tais ekklesiais sigatosan*). The same verb used about the disorders caused by speakers in tongues (v. 28) and prophets (v. 30). For some reason some of the women were creating disturbance in the public worship by their dress (11:2-16) and now by their speech. There is no doubt at all as to Paul's meaning here. In church the women are not allowed to speak (*lalein*) nor even to ask questions. They are to do that "at home" (*en oikoi*). He calls it a shame (*aischron*) as in 11:6 (cf. Eph. 5:12; Titus 1:11). Certainly women are still in subjection (*hupotassesthosan*) to their husbands (or ought to be). But somehow modern Christians have concluded that Paul's commands on this subject, even 1 Tim. 2:12, were meant for specific conditions that do not apply wholly now. Women do most of the teaching in our Sunday schools today. It is not easy to draw the line. The daughters of Philip were prophetesses. It seems clear that we need to be patient with each other as we try to understand Paul's real meaning here.
—*Word Pictures in the New Testament*

ADAM CLARKE

spirit of subjection to his brethren. God grants no ungovernable gifts.

33. *For God is not the author of confusion.* Let not the persons who act in the congregation in this disorderly manner say that they are under the influence of God; for He is not the Author of confusion. But two, three, or more praying or teaching in the same place at the same time is *confusion,* and God is not the Author of such work; and let men beware how they attribute such disorder to the God of order and peace. The apostle calls such conduct "tumult, sedition"; and such it is in the sight of God and in the sight of all good men. How often is a work of God marred and discredited by the folly of men! For nature will always, and Satan too, mingle themselves as far as they can in the genuine work of the Spirit, in order to discredit and destroy it. Nevertheless in great revivals of religion it is almost impossible to prevent wildfire from getting in among the true fire, but it is the duty of the ministers of God to watch against and prudently check this; but if themselves encourage it, then there will be confusion and every evil work.

34. *Let your women keep silence in the churches.* This was a Jewish ordinance; women were not permitted to teach in the assemblies, or even to ask questions. This was their condition till the time of the gospel, when, according to the prediction of Joel, the Spirit of God was to be poured out on the women as well as the men, that they might "prophesy," i.e., teach. And that they did prophesy or teach is evident from what the apostle says, chap. xi. 5, where he lays down rules to regulate this part of their conduct while ministering in the church. But does not what the apostle says here contradict that statement and show that the words in chap. xi should be understood in another sense? For here it is expressly said that they should *keep silence in the churches;* for it was *not permitted* to a woman *to speak.* Both places seem perfectly consistent. It is evident from the context that the apostle refers here to asking questions, and what we call "dictating" in the assemblies. It was permitted to any man to ask questions, to object, altercate, attempt to refute, etc., in the synagogue; but this liberty was not allowed to any woman. Paul confirms this in reference also to the Christian church. He orders them to *keep silence;* and, if they wished to "learn any thing, let them ask of their husbands at home," because it was perfectly indecorous for women to be contending with men in public assemblies, on points of doctrine, cases of conscience, etc. But this by no means intimated that when a woman received any particular influence from God to enable her to teach that she was not to obey that influence; on the contrary, she was to obey it, and the apostle lays down directions in chap. xi for regulating her personal appearance when thus employed. All that the apostle opposes here is their questioning, finding fault, disputing, in the Christian church, as the Jewish men were permitted to do in their synagogues; together with the attempts to usurp any authority over the men by setting up their judgment in opposition to them, for the apostle has in view especially acts of disobedience, arrogance, etc., of which no woman would be guilty who was under the influence of the Spirit of God. *But . . . to be under obedience, as also saith the law.* This is a reference to Gen. iii. 16: "Thy desire shall be to thy husband, and he shall rule over thee." From this it is evident that it was the disorderly and disobedient that the apostle had in view, and not any of those on whom God had poured out his Spirit.

35. *For it is a shame for women to speak in the church.* The Jews would not suffer a woman to read in the synagogue, though a servant or even a child had this permission; but the apostle refers to irregular conduct, such conduct as proved that they were not under obedience, v. 34.

36. *Came the word of God out from you?* Was it from you that other churches received the gospel? Are you the mother church, that you should have rules, and orders, and customs, different from all others; and set yourselves up for a model to be copied by all the churches of Christ? *Or came it unto you only?* Are you the only church of God? Are there not many others founded before you that have no such

MATTHEW HENRY

What he said to them was the command of God; nor durst any true prophet deny it (*v.* 37). "If their revelations contradict mine, they do not come from the same Spirit; either I or they must be false prophets.

But if any continue after all, uncertain or ignorant whether they or I speak by the Spirit of God, they must be left under the power of this ignorance." It is just with God to leave those to the blindness of their own minds who wilfully shut out the light. Though they should not despise the gift of tongues, yet they should prefer prophesying. It was the more useful gift. He charges them to let all things be done decently and in order (*v.* 40). They must do nothing that was manifestly childish (*v.* 20), or that would give occasion to say they were mad (*v.* 23), nor must they act so as to breed confusion, *v.* 33. All parts of divine worship should be carried on in a composed and orderly manner.

JAMIESON, FAUSSET, BROWN

37. prophet—the species. **spiritual**—the genus: spiritually endowed. The followers of Apollos prided themselves as "spiritual" (ch. 3:1-3; cf. Gal. 6:1). Here *one capable of discerning spirits* is specially meant. **things that I write ... commandments of the Lord**—a direct assertion of inspiration. Paul's words as an apostle are Christ's words. Paul appeals not merely to one or two, but *to a body of men*, for the reality of three facts about which no body of men could possibly be mistaken: (1) that his having converted them was not due to mere eloquence, but to the "demonstration of the Spirit and of power"; (2) that part of this demonstration consisted in the communication of miraculous power, which they were then exercising so generally as to require to be corrected in the irregular employment of it; (3) that among these miraculous gifts was one which enabled the "prophet" or "spiritual person" to decide whether Paul's Epistle was Scripture or not. He could not have written so, unless the facts were *notoriously true:* for he takes them for granted, as consciously known by the whole body of men whom he addresses [HINDS *on Inspiration*]. **38. if any man be ignorant**—wilfully; not wishing to recognize these ordinances and my apostolic authority in enjoining them. **let him be ignorant**—I leave him to his ignorance: it will be at his own peril; I feel it a waste of words to speak anything further to convince him. An argument likely to have weight with the Corinthians, who admired "knowledge" so much. **39. covet**—earnestly desire. Stronger than "forbid not"; marking how much higher he esteemed "prophecy" than "tongues." **40. Let ...**—The oldest MSS. read, "*But* let. . . ." This verse is connected with vs. 39, "But (while *desiring prophecy*, and *not forbidding tongues*) let all things be done decently." "Church government is the best security for Christian liberty" [J. NEWTON]. (Cf. vss. 23, 26-33.)

ADAM CLARKE

customs and permit no such disorders?

37. *If any man think himself to be a prophet.* He who is really a *spiritual* man, under the influence of the Spirit of God and capable of teaching the divine will, he will acknowledge that what I now say is from the same Spirit; and that the things which I now write are the *commandments* of God, and must be obeyed on pain of His displeasure.

38. *But if any man be ignorant.* If he affect to be so, or pretend that he is ignorant, *let him be ignorant*—let him be so at his peril.

39. *Covet to prophesy.* Let it be your endeavor and prayer to be able to teach the way of God to the ignorant; this is the most valuable, because the most useful, gift of the Spirit. *And forbid not to speak with tongues.* Let every gift have its own place and operation; let none envy another; nor prevent him from doing that part of the work to which God, by giving the qualification, has evidently called him.

40. *Let all things be done decently.* In their proper forms with becoming reverence, according to their dignity and importance. Everything in the Church of God should be conducted with gravity and composure, suitable to the importance of the things, the infinite dignity of the object of worship, and the necessity of the souls in behalf of which those religious ordinances are instituted. *And in order.* Everything in its place, everything in its time, and everything suitably. *Let all things be done decently and in order* is a direction of infinite moment in all the concerns of religion, and of no small consequence in all the concerns of life. How much pain, confusion, and loss would be prevented were this rule followed!

MATTHEW HENRY

CHAPTER 15

Verses 1–11

It is the apostle's business in this chapter to establish the doctrine of the resurrection of the dead, which some of the Corinthians flatly denied, *v.* 12. And they disowned a future state of recompences, by denying the resurrection of the dead. He begins with an epitome of the gospel. Now concerning the gospel observe,

I. What a stress he lays upon it (*v.* 1, 2). It was what he constantly preached. The doctrine which Paul had heretofore taught, he still taught. It was what they had received. It was no strange doctrine. It was that very gospel in which they had hitherto stood, and must continue to stand. The doctrine of Christ's death and resurrection is at the foundation of Christianity. Remove this foundation, and the whole fabric falls. It was that alone by which they could hope for salvation (*v.* 2). There is no salvation in his name, but upon supposition of his death and resurrection. These are the saving truths of our holy religion. They must be retained in mind, they must be held fast. We believe in vain, unless we continue and persevere in the faith of the gospel. We shall be never the better for a temporary faith. And in vain is it to profess faith in Christ, if we deny the resurrection. Take away this, you make nothing of Christianity.

II. What this gospel is. It was that doctrine which he had received, and delivered to them, *among the first, the principal.* It was a doctrine of the first rank, a most necessary truth. Christ's death and resurrection are the very sum and substance of evangelical truth.

III. This truth is confirmed,

1. By Old Testament predictions. He died for our sins; he was buried, and rose from the dead, according to the scripture-prophecies. It is a great confirmation of our faith of the gospel to see how it corresponds with ancient prophecies.

JAMIESON, FAUSSET, BROWN

CHAPTER 15

VSS. 1-58. THE RESURRECTION PROVED AGAINST THE DENIERS OF IT AT CORINTH. Christ's resurrection rests on the evidence of many eyewitnesses, including Paul himself, and is the great fact preached as the groundwork of the Gospel: they who deny the resurrection in general, must deny that of Christ, and the consequence of the latter will be, that Christian preaching and faith are vain. **1. Moreover**—"Now" [ALFORD and ELLICOTT]. **I declare**—lit., "I make known": it implies some degree of reproach that it should be now necessary to make it known to them afresh, owing to some of them "not having the knowledge of God" (vs. 34). Cf. Galatians 1: 11. **wherein ye stand**—wherein ye now take your stand. This is your present actual privilege, if ye suffer not yourselves to fall from your high standing. **2. ye are saved**—rather, "ye are being saved." **if ye keep in memory what I preached unto you**—Able critics, BENGEL and others, prefer connecting the words thus, "I declare unto you the Gospel (vs. 1) in what words I preached it unto you." Paul reminds them, or rather makes known to them, as if anew, not only the fact of the Gospel, but also *with what words,* and *by what arguments,* he preached it to them. Translate in that case, "if ye hold it fast." I prefer arranging as *English Version,* "By which ye are saved, if ye hold fast (in memory and personal appropriation) *with what speech* I preached it unto you." **unless**—which is impossible, your faith is vain, in resting on Christ's resurrection as an objective reality. **3. I delivered unto you**—A short creed, or summary of articles of faith, was probably even then existing; and a profession in accordance with it was required of candidates for baptism (Acts 8:37). **first of all**—lit., "among the foremost points" (Heb. 6:2). The atonement is, in Paul's view, of primary importance. **which I ... received**—from Christ Himself by special revelation (cf. ch. 11:23). **died for our sins**—i.e., to atone FOR them; *for* taking away *our sins* (I John 3:5; cf. Gal. 1:4): "gave Himself for our sins" (Isa. 53:5; II Cor. 5:15; Titus 2:14). The "for" here does not, as in some passages, imply vicarious substitution, but "in behalf of" (Heb. 5:3; I Pet. 2:24). It does not, however, mean merely "on account of," which is expressed by a different *Greek* word (Rom. 4:25), (though in *English Version* translated similarly, "for"). **according to the scriptures**—which "cannot be broken." Paul puts the testimony of *Scripture* above that of those who saw the Lord after His resurrection [BENGEL]. So our Lord quotes Isaiah 53:12, in Luke 22:37; cf. Psalm 22:15, etc.; Daniel 9:26. **4. buried ... rose**

ADAM CLARKE

CHAPTER 15

It appears from this chapter that there were some false apostles at Corinth who denied the resurrection (see v. 12), in consequence of which Paul discusses three questions in this chapter: (1) Will there be a resurrection of the dead? vv. 1-35; (2) What will be the nature of the resurrection bodies? vv. 35-51; (3) What will become of those who are found alive in the day of judgment? vv. 51-57.

1. *The gospel which I preached unto you.* This gospel is contained in Christ dying for our sins, being buried, and rising again the third day.

2. *If ye keep in memory.* Your future salvation, or being brought finally to glory, will now depend on your faithfulness to the grace that you have received.

3. *For I delivered unto you first of all.* "As the chief things," or matters of the greatest importance; fundamental truths. *That which I also received.* By revelations from God himself, and not from man. *That Christ died for our sins.* The death of Jesus Christ, as a vicarious Sacrifice for sin, is among the things that are of chief importance, and is essential to the gospel scheme of salvation. *According to the scriptures.* It is not said anywhere in the Scriptures, in express terms, that Christ should rise on the third day; but it is fully implied in His types, as in the case of Jonah, who came out of the belly of the fish on the third day; but particularly in the case of Isaac, who was a very expressive type of Christ; for, as his being brought to the Mount Moriah, bound, and laid on the wood, in order to be sacrificed, pointed out the death of Christ, so his being brought alive on the third day from the mount was a figure of Christ's resurrection.

MATTHEW HENRY

2. By the testimony of many eye-witnesses, who saw Christ after he had risen from the dead. How uncontrollably evident was Christ's resurrection from the dead, when so many eyes saw him at so many different times.

ALBERT BARNES:

6. "Above five hundred brethren at once." More than five hundred Christians or followers of Jesus at one time. This was probably in Galilee, where the Lord Jesus had spent the greater part of his public ministry and where he had made most disciples. The place, however, is not designated, and, of course, cannot be known. It is remarkable that this fact is omitted by all the evangelists; but why they should have omitted so remarkable a proof of the resurrection of the Lord Jesus is unknown. There is a slight circumstance hinted at in Matt. 28:10, which may throw some light on this passage. After his resurrection, Jesus said to the women who were at the sepulchre, "Go tell my brethren that they go into Galilee, and there shall they see me." And in verse 16 it is said, "The eleven disciples went away into Galilee, into a mountain where Jesus had appointed them." Jesus had spent most of his public ministry in Galilee. He had made most of his disciples there. It was proper, therefore, that those disciples, who would, of course, hear of his death, should have some public confirmation of the fact that he had risen. It is very probable, also, that the eleven who went down into Galilee after he rose would apprize the brethren there of what had been said to them, that Jesus would meet them on a certain mountain; and it is morally certain that they who had followed him in so great numbers in Galilee would be drawn together by the report that the Lord Jesus who had been put to death was about to be seen there again alive.

—Popular Commentary

Even Paul himself was last of all favoured with the sight of him. The Lord Jesus appeared to him by the way to Damascus, Acts ix. 17. He was highly favoured of God, but he always endeavoured to keep up a mean opinion of himself. So he does here, by observing, (1) That he was *one born out of due time* (*v.* 8). He was not matured for the apostolic function, as the others were, who had personal converse with our Lord. He was out of time for it.

(2) By owning himself inferior to the other apostles. The least and not worthy to be called an apostle, because he had been *a persecutor of the church of God*, *v.* 9. A humble spirit, in the midst of high attainments, is a great ornament to any man. What kept Paul low was the remembrance of his former wickedness, his raging zeal against Christ and his members. How easily God can bring a good out of the greatest evil! When sinners are by divine grace turned into saints, he makes the remembrance of their former sins very serviceable, to make them humble, and diligent, and faithful. (3) By ascribing all that was valuable in him to divine grace. We are nothing but what God makes us. Though he was conscious of his own zeal, and service, he thought himself so much more the debtor to divine grace. *Yet not I, but the grace of God which was with me.* The more he laboured, and the more good he did, the more humble he was and the more disposed to own the favour of God towards him. The apostle tells them (*v.* 11) that he not only preached the same gospel himself at all times, and in all places, but that all the apostles preached the same. All agreed in this that Jesus Christ, and him crucified and slain, and then rising from the dead, was the very sum and substance of Christianity. By this faith they live. In this faith they die.

Verses 12–19

If Christ be preached that he rose from the dead, how say some among you that there is no resurrection of the dead? (*v.* 12). The apostle produces an incontestable fact, namely, the resurrection of Christ.

JAMIESON, FAUSSET, BROWN

again—His burial is more closely connected with His resurrection than His death. At the moment of His death, the power of His inextinguishable life exerted itself (Matt. 27:52). The grave was to Him not the destined receptacle of corruption, but an apartment fitted for entering into life (Acts 2:26-28) [BENGEL]. **rose again**—*Greek,* "hath risen": the state thus begun, and its consequences, still continue. **5. seen of Cephas**—Peter (Luke 24:34). **the twelve**—The round number for "the Eleven" (Luke 24:33, 36). "The Twelve" was their ordinary appellation, even when their number was not full. However, very possibly Matthias was present (Acts 1:22, 23). Some of the oldest MSS. and versions read, "the Eleven": but the best on the whole, "the Twelve." **6. five hundred**—This appearance was probably on the mountain (Tabor, according to tradition), in Galilee, when His most solemn and public appearance, according to His special promise, was vouchsafed (Matt. 26:32; 28:7, 10, 16). He "appointed" this place, as one remote from Jerusalem, so that believers might assemble there more freely and securely. ALFORD'S theory of *Jerusalem* being the scene, is improbable; as such a multitude of believers could not, with any safety, have met in one place in the metropolis, after His crucifixion there. The number of disciples (Acts 1:15) at Jerusalem shortly after, was one hundred and twenty, those in Galilee and elsewhere not being reckoned. Andronicus and Junius were, perhaps, of the number (Rom. 16:7): they are said to be "among the apostles" (who all were witnesses of the resurrection, Acts 1:22). **remain unto this present**—and, therefore, may be sifted thoroughly to ascertain the trustworthiness of their testimony. **fallen asleep**—in the sure hope of *awaking* at the resurrection (Acts 7:60). **7. seen of James**—the Less, the brother of our Lord (Gal. 1:19). The Gospel according to the Hebrews, quoted by JEROME (*Catalogus Scriptorum Ecclesiasticorum,* p. 170 D.), records that "James swore he would not eat bread from the hour that he drank the cup of the Lord, till he should see Him rising again from the dead." **all the apostles**—The term here includes many others besides "the Twelve" already enumerated (vs. 5): perhaps the seventy disciples (Luke 10) [CHRYSOSTOM]. **8. one born out of due time**—*Greek,* "the one abortively born": the abortion in the family of the apostles. As a child *born before the due time* is puny, and though born alive, yet not of the proper size, and scarcely worthy of the name of man, so "I am *the least* of the apostles," scarcely "meet to be called an apostle"; a supernumerary taken into the college of apostles out of regular course, not led to Christ by long instruction, like a natural birth, but by a sudden power, as those prematurely born [GROTIUS]. Cf. the similar image from childbirth, and by the same spiritual power, the resurrection of Christ (I Pet. 1:3). *"Begotten again* by the *resurrection* of Jesus." Jesus' appearance to Paul, on the way to Damascus, is the one here referred to. **9. least**—The name, "Paulus," in Latin, means *least.* **I persecuted the church**—Though God has forgiven him, Paul can hardly forgive himself at the remembrance of his past sin. **10. by . . . grace . . . and his grace**—The repetition implies the prominence which God's *grace* had in his mind, as the sole cause of his marvellous conversion and subsequent labors. Though "not meet to be called an apostle," grace has given him, in Christ, the meetness needed for the office. Translate as the *Greek,* "His grace which was (showed) *towards* me." **what I am**—occupying the honorable office of an apostle. Contrast with this the self-sufficient prayer of another Pharisee (Luke 18:11). **but I laboured**—by God's grace (Phil. 2:16). **than they all**—than any of the apostles (vs. 7). **grace of God . . . with me**—Cf. "the Lord working *with* them" (Mark 16:20). The oldest MSS. omit "which was." The "not I, but grace," implies, that though the human will concurred *with* God when brought by His Spirit into conformity with His will, yet "grace" so preponderated in the work, that his own co-operation is regarded as nothing, and grace as virtually the sole agent. (Cf. ch. 3:9; Matt. 10:20; II Cor. 6:1; Phil. 2:12, 13.) **11. whether it were I or they**—(the apostles) who "labored more abundantly" (vs. 10) in preaching, such was the substance of our preaching, viz., the truths stated in vss. 3, 4. **12. if**—Seeing that it is an admitted fact that Christ is announced by us eyewitnesses as having risen from the dead, how is it that some of you deny that which is a necessary consequence of Christ's resurrection, viz., the general resurrection? **some**—Gentile reasoners (Acts 17:32; 26:8) who would not believe it because they did not see "how" it could be (vss. 35, 36). **13.** If there be no general resur-

ADAM CLARKE

5. *That he was seen of Cephas, then of the twelve.* This refers to the journey to Emmaus, Luke xxiv. 13 and 34, and to what is related Mark xvi. 14. *Then of the twelve.* Perhaps the term *twelve* is used here merely to point out the society of the apostles, who, though at this time they were only eleven, were still called the *twelve* because this was their original number, and a number which was afterward filled up. See John xx. 24.

6. *Above five hundred brethren at once.* This was probably in Galilee, where our Lord had many disciples. See Matt. xxviii. 16. What a remarkable testimony is this to the truth of our Lord's resurrection! *Five hundred* persons saw Him at one time, the greater part of whom were alive when the apostle wrote, and he might have been confronted by many if he had dared to assert a falsity.

7. *After that, he was seen of James.* But where, and on what occasion, we are not told. But one thing is sufficiently evident from what is here said, that this James, of whom the apostle speaks, was still alive; for the apostle's manner of speaking justifies this conclusion.

8. *And last of all . . . of me also.* It seems that it was essential to the character of a primitive apostle that he had seen and conversed with Christ; and it is evident, from the history of Saul's conversion, Acts ix. 4-7, that Jesus Christ did appear to him; and he pleaded this ever after as a proof of his call to the apostleship. And it does not appear that, after this time, Jesus ever did make any personal discovery of himself to anyone. *As of one born out of due time.* The apostle considers himself as coming after the time in which Jesus Christ personally conversed with His disciples; and that therefore, to see Him at all, he must see Him in this extraordinary way. The words signify not merely one *born out of due time,* but one born before his time; and consequently, not bidding fair for vigor, usefulness, or long life. But it is likely that the apostle had a different meaning; and that he refers to the original institution of the twelve apostles, in the rank of whom he never stood, being appointed, not to fill up a place among the twelve, but as an extra and additional apostle.

9. *I am the least of the apostles.* This was literally true in reference to his being chosen last, and chosen not in the number of the twelve, but as an extra apostle. How much pains do some men take to make the apostle contradict himself, by attempting to show that he was the very greatest of the apostles, though he calls himself the least! Taken as a man and a minister of Christ, he was greater than any of the twelve; taken as an apostle he was less than any of the twelve, because not originally in that body. *Am not meet to be called an apostle.* None of the twelve had ever persecuted Christ nor withstood His doctrine: Saul of Tarsus had been, before his conversion, a grievous persecutor; and therefore he says, "I am not proper to be called an apostle, because I persecuted the Church of God," i.e., of Christ, which none of the apostles ever did.

10. *But by the grace of God I am what I am.* God, by His mere grace and goodwill, has called me to be an apostle, and has denominated me such. *And his grace.* Nor have I been unfaithful to the divine call. I used the grace which He gave me; and when my labors, travels, and sufferings are considered, it will be evident that I have labored more abundantly than the whole twelve. This was most literally true. *Yet not I, but the grace of God.* It was not through my own power or wisdom that I performed these things, but through the divine influence which accompanied me.

11. *Whether it were I or they.* All the apostles of Christ agree in the same doctrines. We all preach one and the same thing; and, as we preached, *so ye believed,* having received from us the true apostolical faith, that Jesus died for our sins, and rose again for our justification, and that His resurrection is the pledge and proof of ours.

12. *Now if Christ be preached.* Seeing it is true that we have thus preached Christ, and you have credited this preaching, *how say some among you,* who have professed to receive

MATTHEW HENRY

I. It was foretold in ancient prophecies that he should rise; and it has been proved by multitudes of eye-witnesses that he has risen.

II. This supposition decried, would destroy the principal evidence of Christianity; and so, 1. Make preaching vain. "*We* apostles should *be found false witnesses of God.* Would not our labour be wholly in vain? If Christ be not raised, the gospel is a jest; it is chaff and emptiness."

2. It would make the faith of Christians vain because it is through his death and sacrifice for sin alone that forgiveness is to be had. Had he remained under the power of death, how could he have delivered us from its power? And how vain a thing would faith in him be. There had been no justification nor salvation if Christ had not risen.

III. They took death to be the destruction and extinction of the man, and not merely of the bodily life. "Upon supposition there is no resurrection, no after-state and life, then dead Christians are quite lost. How vain a thing were our faith and religion upon this supposition!" And this,

IV. Would infer that Christ's ministers and servants were *of all men most miserable*, as having *hope in him in this life only* (*v.* 19). If there be no resurrection, or state of future recompence, and, if all their hopes in Christ lie within the compass of this life, they are in a much worse condition than the rest of mankind. Better be anything than a Christian upon these terms. They fare much harder than other men in this life, and yet have no further nor better hopes. The Christian is by his religion crucified to this world, and taught to live upon the hope of another.

Verses 20-34

The apostle establishes the truth of the resurrection of the dead, the dead in Christ.

I. On the resurrection of Christ. He has truly risen himself, as the first-fruits of those who sleep in him. As he has risen, they shall rise. Christ's resurrection is a pledge and earnest of ours. This is the first argument used by the apostle in confirmation of the truth: and it is illustrated by a parallel between the first and second Adam, *v.* 21. All who die die through the sin of Adam; all who are raised, rise through the merit and power of Christ. But the meaning is not that, as all men died in Adam, so all men, without exception, shall be made alive in Christ.

Christ rose as the first-fruits; therefore *those that are Christ's* (*v.* 23) shall rise too. All who thus rise, rise in virtue of Christ's resurrection, and so, as by man came death, by man came deliverance. He states that there will be an order observed in their resurrection. What that precisely will be we are nowhere told. It is only here said that the first-fruits are supposed to rise first, and afterwards all who are Christ's, when he shall come again.

JAMIESON, FAUSSET, BROWN

rection, which is the consequent, then there can have been no resurrection of Christ, which is the antecedent. The head and the members of the body stand on the same footing: what does not hold good of them, does not hold good of Him either: His resurrection and theirs are inseparably joined (cf. vss. 20-22; John 14:19). **14. your faith . . . vain**—(vs. 11). The *Greek* for "vain" here is, *empty, unreal:* in vs. 17, on the other hand, it is, *without use, frustrated.* The principal argument of the first preachers in support of Christianity was that God had raised Christ from the dead (Acts 1:22; 2:32; 4: 10, 33; 13:37; Rom. 1:4). If this fact were false, the faith built on it must be false too. **15. testified of God**—i.e., concerning God. The rendering of others is, "against God" [*Vulgate,* ESTIUS, GROTIUS]: the *Greek* preposition with the genitive implies, not direct antagonism (as the accusative would mean), but *indirect* to *the dishonor of* God. *English Version* is probably better. **if so be**—as they assert. It is not right to tell untrue stories, though they are told and seem for the glory of God (Job 13:7). **16.** The repetition implies the unanswerable force of the argument. **17. vain**—Ye are, by the very fact (supposing the case to be as the skeptics maintained), *frustrated* of all which "your faith" appropriates: Ye are still under the everlasting condemnation of your sins (even in the *disembodied* state which is here referred to), from which Christ's resurrection is our justification (Rom. 4:25): "saved *by his life*" (Rom. 5:10). **18. fallen asleep in Christ**—in communion with Christ as His members. "In Christ's case the term used is *death,* to assure us of the reality of His suffering; in our case, *sleep,* to give us consolation: In His case, His resurrection having actually taken place, Paul shrinks not from the term death; in ours, the resurrection being still only a matter of hope, he uses the term *falling asleep*" [PHOTIUS, *Quæstiones Amphilochiæ,* 197]. **perished**—Their souls are lost; they are in misery in the unseen world. **19.** If our hopes in Christ were limited to this life only, we should be, of all men, most to be pitied; viz., because, while others live unmolested, we are exposed to every trial and persecution, and, after all, are doomed to bitter disappointment in our most cherished hope; for all our hope of salvation, even of the soul (not merely of the body), hangs on the resurrection of Christ, without which His death would be of no avail to us (Eph. 1:19, 20; I Pet. 1:3). The heathen are "without hope" (Eph. 2:12; I Thess. 4:13). We should be even worse, for we should be also without present enjoyment (ch. 4:9). **20. now**—as the case really is. **and become**—omitted in the oldest MSS. **the first fruits**—the earnest or pledge, that the whole resurrection harvest will follow, so that our faith is not vain, nor our hope limited to this life. The time of writing this Epistle was probably about the Passover (ch. 5:7); the day after the Passover sabbath was that for offering *the first fruits* (Lev. 23: 10, 11), and the same was the day of Christ's resurrection: whence appears the appropriateness of the image. **21. by man . . . by man**—The first fruits are of the same nature as the rest of the harvest; so Christ, the bringer of life, is of the same nature as the race of men to whom He brings it; just as Adam, the bringer of death, was of the same nature as the men on whom he brought it. **22. in Adam all**—in union of nature with Adam, as representative head of mankind in their fall. **in Christ . . . all**—in union of nature with Christ, the representative head of mankind in their recovery. The life brought in by Christ is co-extensive with the death brought in by Adam. **23. But every man in his own order**—rather, "rank": the *Greek* is not in the abstract, but concrete: image from troops, "each in his own regiment." Though all shall rise again, let not any think all shall be saved; nay, each shall have his proper place, Christ first (Col. 1:18), and after Him the godly who die in Christ (I Thess. 4:16), in a separate band from the ungodly, and then "the end," i.e., the resurrection of the rest of the dead. Christian churches, ministers, and individuals seem about to be judged first "at His coming" (Matt. 25: 1-30); then "all the nations" (Matt. 25:31-46). Christ's own flock shall share His glory "at His coming," which is not to be confounded with "the end," or general judgment (Rev. 20:4-6, 11-15). The latter is not in this chapter specially discussed, but only the first resurrection, viz., that of the saints: not even the judgment of Christian hollow professors (Matt. 25:1-30) at His coming, is handled, but only the glory of them "that are Christ's," who alone in the highest sense "obtain the resurrection from the dead" (Luke 14:14; 20:35, 36; Phil. 3:11, see *Note*). The second coming of Christ is not a mere *point* of time, but a *period* beginning with the

ADAM CLARKE

this doctrine from us, *that there is no resurrection of the dead,* though we have shown that His resurrection is the proof and pledge of ours? That there was some false teacher, or teachers, among them, who was endeavoring to incorporate Mosaic rites and ceremonies with the Christian doctrines, and even to blend Sadduceeism with the whole, appears pretty evident. To confute this mongrel Christian and overturn his bad doctrine the apostle writes this chapter.

13. *If there be no resurrection of the dead.* As Christ was Partaker of the same flesh and blood with us, and He promised to raise mankind from the dead through His resurrection, if the dead rise not, then Christ has had no resurrection. There seem to have been some at Corinth who, though they denied the resurrection of the dead, admitted that Christ had risen again. The apostle's argument goes therefore to state that, if Christ was raised from the dead, mankind may be raised; if mankind cannot be raised from the dead, then the body of Christ was never raised.

14. *Then is our preaching vain.* Our whole doctrine is useless and false.

15. *False witnesses.* As having testified the fact of Christ's resurrection, as a matter which ourselves had witnessed, when we knew that we bore testimony to a falsehood. But could 500 persons agree in this imposition? And if they did, is it possible that someone would not discover the cheat, when he could have no interest in keeping the secret, and might greatly promote his secular interest by making the discovery? Such a case never occurred, and never can occur. The testimony, therefore, concerning the resurrection of Christ is incontrovertibly true.

17. *Ye are yet in your sins.* If Christ has not risen from the dead, there is a presumption that He has been put to death justly; and if so, consequently He has made no atonement; and *ye are yet in your sins*—under the power, guilt, and condemnation of them.

18. *They also which are fallen asleep.* All those who, by either martyrdom or natural death, have departed in the faith of our Lord Jesus Christ, *are perished;* their hope was without foundation, and their faith had not reason and truth for its object.

19. *If in this life only we have hope.* It would be better to translate and point this verse as follows: "And if in this life we have hoped in Christ only, we are more to be pitied than all men." If in this life we have no other hope and confidence but in Christ (and if He be still dead, and not yet risen), we are more to be pitied than any other men; we are sadly deceived.

20. *But now is Christ risen.* On the contrary, Christ is raised from the dead, and is become the *firstfruits of them that slept.* His resurrection has been demonstrated, and our resurrection necessarily follows; as sure as the firstfruits are the proof that there is a harvest, so surely the resurrection of Christ is a proof of ours.

21. *For since by man came death.* Mortality came by Adam, immortality by Christ; so sure as all have been subjected to natural death by Adam, so sure shall all be raised again by Christ Jesus.

MATTHEW HENRY

II. He argues from the continuance of the mediatorial kingdom till all Christ's enemies are destroyed, the last of which is death, *v.* 24–26.

1. This argument implies: (1) That our Saviour rose from the dead to have all power put into his hands. (2) That this mediatorial kingdom is to have an end, *v.* 24. (3) That it is not to have an end till all opposing power be put down, *v.* 24, 25. (4) That, among other enemies, death must be destroyed (*v.* 26). Therefore the saints must rise, else death and the grave would have power over them. When saints shall live again, and die no more, then, and not till then, will death be abolished.

2. Our Saviour, as man and mediator between God and man, has a delegated royalty. As man, all his authority must be delegated. As Mediator, a middle person between God and man, partaking of both natures, he was to reconcile both parties, God and man. Upon his ascension, he was made head over all things to the church, had power given him to govern and protect it against all its enemies, and in the end destroy them and complete the salvation of all that believe in him. This delegated royalty must at length *be delivered up to the Father*, from whom it was received (*v.* 24);

for it is a power received for particular ends (*v.* 25, 26). The Redeemer must reign till his enemies be destroyed, and, when this end is attained, then will he deliver up the power. The Redeemer shall certainly reign till the last enemy of his people be destroyed, till death itself be abolished. He shall have all power in heaven and earth till then. What support should this be to his saints in every hour of distress and temptation!

When this is done, *and all things are put under his feet*, *v.* 28, then the man Christ Jesus shall appear upon giving it up to be a subject of the Father. And it will appear to the divine glory, that God may be all in all, that the accomplishment of our salvation may appear altogether divine. Though the human nature must be employed in the work of our redemption, yet God was all in all in it.

III. He argues for the resurrection, from the case of those who were baptized for the dead (*v.* 29).

JAMIESON, FAUSSET, BROWN

resurrection of the just at His appearing, and ending with the general judgment. The ground of the universal resurrection is the union of all mankind in nature with Christ, their representative Head, who has done away with death, by His own death in their stead: the ground of the resurrection of believers is not merely this, but their personal union with Him as *their* "Life" (Col. 3:4), effected *causatively* by the Holy Spirit, and *instrumentally* by faith as the *subjective*, and by ordinances as the *objective* means. **24. Then**—after that: next in the succession of "orders" or "ranks." **the end**—the general resurrection, and final judgment and consummation (Matt. 25:46). **delivered up . . . kingdom to . . . Father**—(Cf. John 13:3). Seeming at variance with Daniel 7:14, "His dominion is an *everlasting* dominion which *shall not pass away*." *Really*, His giving up of the *mediatorial* kingdom to the Father, when the end for which the mediatorial economy was established has been accomplished, is altogether in harmony with its continuing everlastingly. The change which shall then take place, shall be in the *manner* of administration, not in the *kingdom* itself; God shall then come into *direct* connection with the earth, instead of mediatorially, when Christ shall have fully and finally removed everything that severs asunder the holy God and a sinful earth (Col. 1:20). The glory of God is the final end of Christ's mediatorial office (Phil. 2:10, 11). His co-equality with the Father is independent of the latter, and prior to it, and shall, therefore, continue when its function shall have ceased. His manhood, too, shall everlastingly continue, though, as now, subordinate to the Father. The *throne of the Lamb* (but no longer mediatorial) as well as *of* God, shall be in the heavenly city (Rev. 22:3; cf. 3: 21). The unity of the Godhead, and the unity of the Church, shall be simultaneously manifested at Christ's second coming. Cf. Zephaniah 3:9; Zechariah 14:9; John 17:21-24. The oldest MSS. for "*shall have* delivered up," read, "*delivereth* up," which suits the sense better. It is "when He *shall have* put down all rule," that "He *delivereth* up the kingdom to the Father." **shall have put down all rule**—the effect produced during the millenary reign of Himself and His saints (Ps. 110:1; 8:6; 2:6-9), to which passages Paul refers, resting his argument on the two words, "all" and "until," of the Psalmist: a proof of verbal inspiration of Scripture (cf. Rev. 2: 26, 27). Meanwhile, He "rules in the midst of His enemies" (Ps. 110:2). He is styled "the King" when He takes His great power (Matt. 25:34; Rev. 11:15, 17). The *Greek* for "put down" is, "*done away with*," or "brought to naught." "All" must be subject to Him, whether openly opposed powers, as Satan and his angels, or kings and angelic principalities (Eph. 1:21). **25. must**—because Scripture foretells it. **till**—There will be no further need of His mediatorial kingdom, its object having been realized. **enemies under his feet**—(Luke 19:27; Eph. 1:22). **26. shall be**—*Greek*, "*is* done away with" (Rev. 20:14; cf. 1:18). It is to believers especially this applies (vss. 55-57); even in the case of unbelievers, death is done away with by the general resurrection. Satan brought in *sin*, and *sin* brought in *death!* So they shall be destroyed (rendered utterly powerless) in the same order (vs. 56; Heb. 2: 14; Rev. 19:20; 20:10, 14). **27. all things**—including death (cf. Eph. 1:22; Phil. 3:21; Heb. 2:8; I Pet. 3:22). It is said, "*hath* put," for what God has said is the same as if it were already done, so sure is it. Paul here quotes the 8th Psalm in proof of his previous declaration, "For (it is written), '*He hath put all things under His feet.*' " **under his feet**—as His footstool (Ps. 110:1). In perfect and lasting subjection. **when he**—viz., God, who by His Spirit inspired the Psalmist. **28. Son . . . himself . . . subject**—not as the creatures are, but as a Son *voluntarily subordinate* to, though co-equal with, the Father. In the mediatorial kingdom, the Son had been, in a manner, distinct from the Father. Now, His kingdom shall merge in the Father's, with whom He is one; not that there is thus any derogation from His honor; for the Father Himself wills "that all should honor the Son, as they honor the Father" (John 5:22, 23; Heb. 1:6). **God . . . all in all**—as Christ is all in all (Col. 3:11; cf. Zech. 14:9). *Then*, and not till then, "*all* things," without the least infringement of the divine prerogative, shall be subject to the Son, and the Son subordinate to the Father, while co-equally sharing His glory. Contrast Psalm 10:4; 14:1. Even the saints do not fully realize God as their "all" (Ps. 73:25) now, through desiring it; then each shall feel, *God is all to me*. **29. Else**—if there be no resurrection. **what shall they do?**—How wretched is their lot! **they . . . which are baptized for the dead**—third person; a

ADAM CLARKE

24. *When he shall have delivered up the kingdom.* The mediatorial Kingdom, which comprehends all the displays of His grace in saving sinners and all His spiritual influence in governing the Church.

All rule and all authority and power. As the apostle is here speaking of *the end* of the present system of the world, the rule, authority, and power may refer to all earthly governments, emperors, kings, princes, etc.; though angels, principalities, and powers, and the rulers of the darkness of this world, and all spiritual wickedness in high places may be also intended. Our Lord Jesus is represented here as administering the concerns of the Kingdom of grace in this lower world during the time that this divine economy lasts; and when *the end*—the time determined by the wisdom of God—comes, then, as there is no longer any need of this administration, the Kingdom is delivered up unto the Father: an allusion to the case of Roman viceroys or governors of provinces, who, when their administration was ended, delivered up their kingdoms or governments into the hands of the emperor.

25. *For he must reign.* This is according to the promise, Ps. cx. 1: "The Lord said unto my Lord, Sit thou at my right hand, until I make thine enemies thy footstool." Therefore the Kingdom cannot be given up till all rule and government be cast down. So that while the world lasts, Jesus, as the Messiah and Mediator, must reign; and all human beings are properly His subjects, are under His government, and are accountable to Him.

26. *The last enemy*, Death, shall be destroyed; shall be "counterworked, subverted," and finally "overturned." But death cannot be *destroyed* by there being simply no further death; death can be destroyed and annihilated only by a general resurrection.

27. *For he hath put all things under his feet.* The Father hath put all things under the feet of Christ according to the prophecy, Psalms cx. *He is excepted.* I.e., The Father, who hath put all things under Him, the Son. This observation seems to be introduced by the apostle to show that he does not mean that the divine nature shall be subjected to the human nature. Christ, as Messiah, and Mediator between God and man, must ever be considered inferior to the Father; and His human nature, however dignified in consequence of its union with the divine nature, must ever be inferior to God. The whole of this verse should be read in a parenthesis.

28. *The Son also himself be subject.* When the administration of the Kingdom of grace is finally closed; when there shall be no longer any state of probation, and consequently no longer need of a distinction between the Kingdom of grace and the Kingdom of glory; then the Son, as being man and Messiah, shall cease to exercise any distinct dominion; and *God* shall *be all in all.*

29. *Else what shall they do which are baptized for the dead?* This is certainly the most difficult verse in the New Testament; for, notwith-

MATTHEW HENRY

But what is this baptism for the dead? Some understand the passage of the martyrs: Why do they suffer martyrdom for their religion? This is sometimes called the baptism of blood by the ancients. Some understand it of a custom that was observed among many who professed the Christian name in the first ages, of baptizing some in the name and stead of catechumens dying without baptism. But whether this be the meaning, or whatever else be, doubtless the apostle's argument was good and intelligible to the Corinthians. And his next is as plain to us.

IV. He argues from the absurdity of his own conduct and that of other Christians.

1. It would be a foolish thing for them to run so many hazards (*v.* 30). Christianity were a foolish profession if it proposed no hopes beyond this life, required men to risk all the blessings and comforts of this life, and to face and endure all the evils of it, without any future prospects.

And must he not fix this character on it if he give up his future hopes, and deny the resurrection of the dead? "*I die daily,*" *v.* 31. He was in continual danger of death, and carried his life, as we say, in his hand. He had encountered very great difficulties and fierce enemies; he had *fought with beasts at Ephesus* (*v.* 32), and was in danger of being pulled to pieces by an enraged multitude (Acts xix. 24, &c.). I take it that this fighting with beasts is a figurative expression, that the beasts intended were men of a fierce and ferine disposition. "Now," says he, "what advantage have I from such contests, if the dead rise not? *If I am to perish by death,* and expect nothing after it, could anything be more weak?" Was Paul so senseless? Could anything but the sure hopes of a better life after death have extinguished the love of life in him to this degree? "*What advantageth it me, if the dead rise not?*" It is very lawful and fit for a Christian to propose advantage to himself by his fidelity to God. Thus did Paul.

2. It would be a much wiser thing to take the comforts of this life (*v.* 32). Let us even live like beasts, if we must die like them. This would be a wiser course, if there were no resurrection. If there were no hopes after death, would not every wise man prefer an easy comfortable life, and endeavour to enjoy the comforts of life as fast as possible, because the continuance of it is short? Nothing but the hopes of better things hereafter can enable a man to forgo all the comforts and pleasures here.

V. The apostle closes his argument with a caution, exhortation, and reproof. 1. A caution against men of loose lives and principles, *v.* 33. Possibly, some of those who said that there was no resurrection of the dead were men of loose lives, and had that speech often in their mouths *Let us eat and drink, for tomorrow we die.* He now warns the Corinthians how dangerous such men's conversation must prove. They would probably be corrupted by them, and fall in with their course of life Those who would keep their innocence must keep good company Error and vice are infectious. 2. Here is an exhortation to break off their sins, and lead a more holy and righteous life (*v.* 34): "Rouse yourselves, break off your sins. Do not, by sloth and stupidity, be led away into such conversation as will sap your Christian hopes." The disbelief of a future state destroys all virtue and piety. If there will be a resurrection and a future life, we should live and act as those who believe it. 3. Here is a reproof to some at least among them. It is a shame in Christians not to have the knowledge of God. Those who profess this religion reproach

JAMIESON, FAUSSET, BROWN

class distinct from that in which the apostle places himself, "we" (vs. 30); first person. ALFORD thinks there is an allusion to a practice at Corinth of baptizing a living person *in behalf of* a friend who died unbaptized; thus Paul, without giving the least sanction to the practice, uses an *ad hominem* argument from it against its practicers, some of whom, though using it, denied the resurrection: "What account can they give of their practice; why are they at the trouble of it, if the dead rise not?" [So Jesus used an *ad hominem* argument, Matthew 12:27.] But if so, it is strange there is no direct censure of it. Some Marcionites adopted the practice at a later period, probably from taking this passage, as ALFORD does; but, generally, it was unknown in the Church. BENGEL translates, "over (immediately upon) the dead," i.e., who will be gathered to the dead *immediately after* baptism. Cf. Job 17:1, "the graves are ready for me." The price they get for their trouble is, that they should be gathered to the dead for ever (vss. 13, 16). Many in the ancient Church put off baptism till near death. This seems the better view; though there may have been some rites of symbolical baptism at Corinth, now unknown, perhaps grounded on Jesus' words (Matt. 20:22, 23), which Paul here alludes to. The best punctuation is, "If the dead rise not at all, why are they then baptized *for them*" (so the oldest MSS. read the last words, instead of "for the dead")? **30. we**—apostles (vs. 9; ch. 4:9). A gradation from those who could only for a little time enjoy this life (i.e., those baptized at the point of death), to *us,* who could enjoy it longer, if we had not renounced the world for Christ [BENGEL]. **31. by your rejoicing**—*by the glorying which I have concerning you,* as the fruit of my labors in the Lord. Some of the earliest MSS. and fathers read "our," with the same sense. BENGEL understands "your rejoicing," to be the *enjoyable state of the Corinthians,* as contrasted with his dying daily to give his converts *rejoicing* or *glorying* (ch. 4:8; II Cor. 4:12, 15; Eph. 3:13; Phil. 1:26). But the words, "which I have," favor the explanation—'*the rejoicing which I have over you.*' Many of the oldest MSS. and *Vulgate* insert "brethren" here. **I die daily**—This ought to stand first in the sentence, as it is so put prominently forward in the *Greek.* I am day by day in sight of death, exposed to it, and expecting it (II Cor. 4:11, 12; 1:8, 9; 11:23). **32.** Punctuate thus: "If after the manner of men I have fought with beasts at Ephesus, what advantageth it me? If the dead rise not, let us eat and drink . . ." [BENGEL]. If "*merely as a man*" (with the mere human hope of the present life; not with the Christian's hope of the resurrection; answering to "If the dead rise not," the parallel clause in the next sentence), I have fought with men resembling savage beasts. Heraclitus, of Ephesus, had termed his countrymen "wild beasts" 400 years before. So Epimenides called the Cretians (Titus 1:12). Paul was still at Ephesus (ch. 16:8), and there his life was daily in danger (ch. 4:9; cf. II Cor. 1:8). Though the tumult (Acts 19:29, 30) had *not yet taken place* (for after it he set out *immediately* for Macedonia), this Epistle was written evidently just before it, when the storm was gathering; "many adversaries" (ch. 16:9) were already menacing him. **what advantageth it me?**—seeing I have renounced all that, "*as a mere man,*" might compensate me for such sufferings, gain, fame, etc. **let us eat . . .**—Quoted from LXX, (Isa. 22:13), where the prophet describes the reckless self-indulgence of the despisers of God's call to mourning, Let us enjoy the good things of life now, for it soon will end. Paul imitates the language of such skeptics, to reprove both their theory and practice. "If men but persuade themselves that they shall die like the beasts, they soon will live like beasts too" [SOUTH]. **33. evil communications corrupt good manners**—a current saying, forming a verse in Menander, the comic poet, who probably took it from Euripides (SOCRATES, *Historia Ecclesiastica,* 3. 16). "Evil communications" refer to intercourse with those who deny the resurrection. Their notion seems to have been that the resurrection is merely spiritual, that sin has its seat solely in the body, and will be left behind when the soul leaves it, if, indeed, the soul survive death at all. **good**—not only *good-natured,* but *pliant.* Intimacy with the profligate society around was apt to corrupt the principles of the Corinthians. **34. Awake**—lit., "*out of the sleep*" of carnal intoxication into which ye are thrown by the influence of these skeptics (vs. 32; Joel 1:5). **to righteousness**—in contrast with "sin" in this verse, and *corrupt manners* (vs. 33). **sin not**—Do not give yourselves up to sinful pleasures. The *Greek* expresses a continued state of abstinence from sin. Thus, Paul implies that

ADAM CLARKE

standing the greatest and wisest men have labored to explain it, there are to this day nearly as many different interpretations of it as there are interpreters. The sum of the apostle's meaning appears to be this: If there be no resurrection of the dead, those who, in becoming Christians, expose themselves to all manner of privations, crosses, severe sufferings, and a violent death, can have no compensation, nor any motive sufficient to induce them to expose themselves to such miseries. But as they receive baptism as an emblem of "death" in voluntarily going under the water, so they receive it as an emblem of the resurrection unto eternal life in coming up out of the water; thus they are *baptized for the dead,* in perfect faith of the resurrection. The following three verses seem to confirm this sense.

30. *And why stand we in jeopardy every hour?* Is there any reason why we should voluntarily submit to so many sufferings, and every hour be in danger of losing our lives, if the dead rise not? On the conviction of the possibility and certainty of the resurrection, we are thus baptized for the dead. We have counted the cost, despise sufferings, and exult at the prospect of death, because we know we shall have a resurrection unto eternal life.

31. *I protest by your rejoicing.* "By your exultation or boasting." *I die daily.* A form of speech for "I am continually exposed to death."

32. *If after the manner of men.* Much learned criticism has been employed on this verse, to ascertain whether it is to be understood literally or metaphorically. Does the apostle mean to say that he had literally fought with wild beasts at Ephesus? or, that he had met with brutish, savage men, from whom he was in danger of his life? That Paul did not fight with wild beasts at Ephesus may be argued: (1) From his own silence on this subject, when enumerating his various sufferings, 2 Cor. xi. 23 ff; (2) From the silence of his historian, Luke, who in the acts of this apostle gives no intimation of this kind; and it certainly was too remarkable a circumstance to be passed over, either by Paul in the catalogue of his own sufferings or by Luke in his history; (3) From similar modes of speech which are employed metaphorically and are so understood; (4) From the improbability that a Roman citizen, as Paul was, should be condemned to such a punishment when in other cases, by pleading his privilege, he was exempted from being scourged; and (5) From the positive testimony of Tertullian and Chrysostom, who deny the literal interpretation. *What advantageth it me, if the dead rise not?* I believe the common method of pointing this verse is erroneous; I propose to read it thus: "If, after the manner of men, I have fought with beasts at Ephesus, what doth it advantage me? If the dead rise not, let us eat and drink, for tomorrow we die."

What the apostle says here is a regular and legitimate conclusion from the doctrine that there is no resurrection: For if there be no resurrection, then there can be no judgment—no future state of rewards and punishments. Why, therefore, should we bear crosses, and keep ourselves under continual discipline? Let us eat and drink, take all the pleasure we can, for tomorrow we die; and there is an end of us forever. The words, *Let us eat and drink; for tomorrow we die,* are taken from Isa. xxii. 13, as they stand now in the Septuagint; and are a pretty smooth proverbial saying, which might be paralleled from the writings of several Epicurean heathens.

33. *Be not deceived.* Do not impose on yourselves, and do not permit others to do it. *Evil communications corrupt good manners.* There are many sayings like this among the Greek poets; but this of the apostle is generally supposed to have been taken from Menander's *lost* comedy of *Thais*: "Bad company good morals doth corrupt."

34. *Awake to righteousness.* Shake off your slumber; awake fully, thoroughly, "as ye ought to do"; so the word should be rendered, not *awake to righteousness. Sin not.* For this will lead to the destruction of both body and soul. Life is but a moment; improve it. Heaven has blessings without end.

MATTHEW HENRY

themselves, by remaining without the knowledge of God; for it must be owing to their own sloth. It must be ignorance of God that leads men into the disbelief of a resurrection and future life. Those who know God know that he is not unfaithful nor unkind, to forget their labour and patience, their faithful services and cheerful sufferings, or let their *labour be in vain.* Those who own a God and observe how unequal the distributions of the present life are, and how frequently the best men fare worst, can hardly doubt an after state, where everything will be set to rights.

Verses 35–50

A plausible objection against doctrine of the resurrection of the dead, *v.* 35. The objection is plainly twofold. *How are they raised up?* that is, "By what means? What power is equal to this effect?" The other part of the objection is about the quality of their bodies: "*With what body will they come?*" The former objection is that of those who opposed the doctrine, the latter the enquiry of curious doubters.

I. To the former the apostle replies by telling them this was to be brought about by divine power, that very power which they had all observed to do something very like it, year after year, in the death and revival of the corn, *v.* 36. It not only sprouts after it is dead, but it must die that it may live. It is a foolish thing to question the divine power to raise the dead, when we see it every day quickening and reviving things that are dead.

II. But he is longer in replying to the second enquiry.

1. There is a change made in the grain that is sown. God gives it such a body as he will. Every seed sown has its *proper body.* It is certain the grain undergoes a great change, so will the dead, when they rise again.

JAMIESON, FAUSSET, BROWN

they who live in sinful pleasures readily persuade themselves of what they wish, viz., that there is to be no resurrection. **some**—the same as in vs. 12. **have not the knowledge of God**—*and so know not His power* in the resurrection (Matt. 22:29). Stronger than "are ignorant of God." An habitual *ignorance:* wilful, in that they prefer to keep their sins, rather than part with them, in order to *know God* (cf. John 7:17; I Pet. 2:15). **to your shame**—that you Corinthian Christians, who boast of your *knowledge,* should have among you, and maintain intercourse with, those so practically ignorant of God, as to deny the resurrection. **35. How**—It is folly to deny a fact of REVELATION, because we do not know the "*how.*" Some measure God's power by their petty intelligence, and won't admit, *even on His assurance,* anything which they cannot explain. Ezekiel's *answer of faith* to the question is the truly wise one (Ezek. 37:3). So Jesus argues not on principles of philosophy, but wholly from "the power of God," as declared by the Word of God (Matt. 19:26; Mark 10:27; 12:23; Luke 18:27). **come**—The dead are said to *depart,* or to be *deceased:* those rising again to *come.* The objector could not understand *how* the dead are to rise, and with *what kind of a body* they are to come. Is it to be the same body? If so, how is this, since the resurrection bodies will not eat or drink, or beget children, as the natural bodies do? Besides, the latter have mouldered into dust. *How* then can they rise again? If it be a different body, how can the personal identity be preserved? Paul answers, In one sense it will be the same body, in another, a distinct body. It will be a body, but a spiritual, not a natural, body. **36. fool**—with all thy boasted philosophy (Ps. 14:1). **that which thou**—"thou," emphatical: appeal to the objector's *own* experience: "The seed which *thou thyself* sowest." Paul, in this verse and in vs. 42, answers the question of vs. 35, "How?" and in vss. 37-41 and 43, the question, "With *what kind* of body?" He converts the very objection (the death of the natural body) into an argument. Death, so far from preventing *quickening,* is the necessary prelude and prognostication of it, just as the seed "is not quickened" into a new sprout with increased produce, "except it die" (except a dissolution of its previous organization takes place). Christ by His death for us has not given us a reprieve from death as to the life which we have from Adam; nay, He permits the law to take its course on our fleshly nature; but He brings from Himself new spiritual and heavenly life out of death (vs. 37). **37. not that body that shall be**—a *body* beautiful and no longer a "bare grain" [BENGEL]. No longer without stalk or ear, but clothed with blade and ears, and yielding many grains instead of only one [GROTIUS]. There is not an identity of all the particles of the old and the new body. For the perpetual transmutation of matter is inconsistent with this. But there is a hidden germ which constitutes the identity of body amidst all outward changes: the outward accretions fall off in its development, while the germ remains the same. Every such germ ("seed," vs. 38) "shall have its own body," and be instantly recognized, just as each plant now is known from the seed that was sown (see *Note,* ch. 6:13). So Christ by the same image illustrated the truth that His death was the necessary prelude of His putting on His glorified body, which is the ground of the regeneration of the many who believe (John 12:24). Progress is the law of the spiritual, as of the natural world. Death is the avenue not to mere *revivification* or *reanimation,* but to *resurrection* and *regeneration* (Matt. 19:28; Phil. 3:21). Cf. "*planted,*" etc., Romans 6:5. **38. as it hath pleased him**—at creation, when He gave *to each of the* (kinds of) *seeds* (so the *Greek* is for "to every seed") *a body of its own* (Gen. 1:11, "after its kind," suited to its species). So God can and will give to the blessed at the resurrection *their own* appropriate *body,* such *as it pleases Him,* and such as is suitable to their glorified state: a body peculiar to the individual, substantially the same as the body sown. **39-41.** Illustrations of the suitability of bodies, however various, to their species: the flesh of the several species of animals; bodies celestial and terrestrial; the various kinds of light in the sun, moon, and stars, respectively. **flesh**—animal organism [DE WETTE]. He implies by the word that our resurrection bodies shall be in some sense really flesh, not mere phantoms of air [ESTIUS]. So some of the oldest creeds expressed it, "I believe in the resurrection of the *flesh.*" Cf. as to Jesus' own resurrection body, Luke 24:39; John 20:27; to which *ours shall be made like,* and therefore shall be *flesh,* but not of animal organism (Phil. 3:21) and liable to corrup-

ADAM CLARKE

Some have not the knowledge of God. The original is very emphatic: "Some have an ignorance of God"; they do not acknowledge God. To have an ignorance of God—a sort of substantial darkness, that prevents the light of God from penetrating the soul—is a worse state than to be simply in the dark or without the divine knowledge. The apostle probably speaks of those who were once enlightened, once had good morals, but were corrupted by bad company.

35. *But some man will say.* It is very likely that the apostle by *some man* means particularly the false apostle or teacher at Corinth who was chief in the opposition to the pure doctrine of the gospel, and to whom, in this covert way, he often refers. The second part of the apostle's discourse begins at this verse. What shall be the nature of the resurrection body? (1) The question is stated, v. 35. (2) It is answered: first, by a similitude, vv. 36-38; secondly, by an application, vv. 39-41; and thirdly, by explication, vv. 42-50.

36. *Thou fool.* If this be addressed, as it probably is, to the false apostle, there is a peculiar propriety in it, as this man seems to have magnified his own wisdom and set it up against both God and man; and none but a *fool* could act so. At the same time, it is folly in any to assert the impossibility of a thing because he cannot comprehend it. *That which thou sowest is not quickened, except it die.* A grain of wheat is composed of the body and the germ. The latter forms an inconsiderable part of the mass of the grain; the body forms nearly the whole. This body dies—becomes decomposed—and forms a fine earth, from which the germ derives its first nourishment; by the nourishment thus derived the germ is *quickened,* receives its first vegetable life, and through this means is rendered capable of deriving the rest of its nourishment and support from the grosser earth in which the grain was deposited. Whether the apostle would intimate here that there is a certain germ in the present body which shall become the seed of the resurrection body, this is not the place to inquire.

37. *Thou sowest not that body that shall be.* This is decomposed and becomes the means of nourishing the whole plant.

38. *But God giveth it a body.* And is there any other way of accounting for it by the miraculous working of God's power? For out of that one bare grain are produced a system of roots, a tall and vigorous stalk, with all its appendages of leaves, besides the full corn in the ear, the whole making several hundred times the quantum of what was originally deposited. There are no proofs that what some call "nature" can effect this; it will ever be a philosophical as well as a scriptural truth that *God giveth it a body as it hath pleased* [*pleaseth*] *him;* and so doth He manage the whole of the work that every seed shall have its *own body:* that the wheat germ shall never produce barley; nor the rye, oats.

39. *All flesh is not the same flesh.* Though the organization of all animals is in its general principles the same, yet there are no two different kinds of animals that have flesh of the same flavor, whether the animal be beast, fowl, or fish. And this is precisely the same with vegetables.

MATTHEW HENRY

2. There is a great deal of variety among other bodies. (1) In bodies of flesh (*v.* 39). (2) In bodies celestial and terrestrial there is also a difference.

(3) There is a variety of glory among heavenly bodies themselves, *v.* 41. The bodies of the dead, when they rise, will be so far changed that there will be a variety of glories. It must be as easy to divine power to raise the dead, as out of the same materials to form so many different kinds of flesh and plants, and celestial bodies as well as terrestrial ones. And can he, out of the same materials, form such various beings, and yet not be able to raise the dead?

3. *So also*, says he, *is the resurrection of the dead.* Burying the dead is like sowing them; it is like committing the seed to the earth, that it may spring out of it again. When we rise, they will be out of the power of the grave, and never more be liable to corruption. Ours is at present a vile body, Phil. iii. 21. But at the resurrection it will be made like the glorious body of our Saviour, and shine out with a splendour resembling his. It is laid in the earth, a poor helpless thing, wholly in the power of death. But when we arise our bodies will have heavenly life and vigour infused into them. When we rise our body will rise spiritual. We shall at the resurrection have bodies made fit to be perpetual associates of spirits made perfect. And why should it not be in the power of God to raise incorruptible spiritual bodies as first to make matter out of nothing, and then produce such variety of beings, both in earth and heaven? *To God all things are possible.*

4. He illustrates this by a comparison of the first and second Adam. (1) As we have our natural body, from the first Adam, we expect our spiritual body from the second. (2) *The first Adam was made a living soul*, such a being as ourselves. The *second Adam is a quickening Spirit*; he is the resurrection

JAMIESON, FAUSSET, BROWN

tion. But vs. 50 below implies, it is not "flesh and blood" in the animal sense we now understand them; for these "shall not inherit the kingdom of God." **not the same**—not flesh of the same nature and excellency. As the kinds of flesh, however widely differing from one another, do not cease to be flesh, so the kinds of bodies, however differing from one another, are still bodies. All this is to illustrate the difference of the new celestial body from its terrestrial seed, while retaining a substantial identity. **beasts**—quadrupeds. **another of fishes . . . another of birds**—Most of the oldest MSS. read thus, "another FLESH of *birds* . . . another of *fishes*": the order of nature. **40. celestial bodies**—not the sun, moon, and stars, which are first introduced in vs. 41, but *the bodies of angels*, as distinguished from the bodies of earthly creatures. **the glory of the celestial**—(Luke 9:26). **glory of . . . terrestrial**—(Matt. 6:28, 29; I Pet. 1:24).

41. one glory of . . . sun . . . another . . . of . . . moon—The analogy is not to prove different degrees of glory among the blessed (whether this may be, or not, *indirectly* hinted at), but this: As the various fountains of *light*, which is so similar in its aspect and properties, differ (the sun from the moon, and the moon from the stars; *and even* one star from another star, though all seem so much alike); so there is nothing unreasonable in the doctrine that *our present bodies* differ from *our resurrection bodies*, though still continuing *bodies*. Cf. the same simile, appropriate especially in the clear Eastern skies (Dan. 12:3; Matt. 13:43). Also that of *seed* in the same parable (Matt. 13:24; Gal. 6:7, 8). **42. sown**—Following up the image of *seed*. A delightful word instead of *burial*. **in corruption**—*liable to corruption: corruptible:* not merely a prey *when dead* to corruption; as the contrast shows, "raised in incorruption," i.e., *not liable to corruption, incorruptible*. **43. in dishonour**—answering to "our *vile* body" (Phil. 3:21); lit., "our body of humiliation": liable to various humiliations of disease, injury, and decay at last. **in glory**—the garment of incorruption (vss. 42, 43) like His glorious body (Phil. 4:21), which we shall put on (vss. 49, 53; II Cor. 5:2-4). **in weakness**—liable to infirmities (II Cor. 13:4). **in power**—answering to a "spiritual body" (vs. 44; cf. Luke 1:17, "Spirit and power"). Not liable to the weaknesses of our present frail bodies (Isa. 33:24; Rev. 21:4). **44. a natural body**—lit., *"an animal body,"* a body moulded in its organism of "flesh and blood" (vs. 50) to suit the animal soul which predominates in it. The Holy Spirit *in the spirit* of believers, indeed, is an earnest of a superior state (Rom. 8:11), but meanwhile *in the body* the animal soul preponderates; hereafter the Spirit shall predominate, and the animal soul be duly subordinate. **spiritual body**—a body wholly moulded by the Spirit, and its organism not conformed to the lower and animal (Luke 20:35, 36), but to the higher and spiritual, life (cf. ch. 2:14; I Thess. 5:23). **There is . . .**—The oldest MSS. read, "IF there is a natural (or *animal-souled*) body, there is *also* a spiritual body." It is no more wonderful a thing, that there should be a body fitted to the capacities and want of man's highest part, his spirit (which we see to be the case), than that there should be one fitted to the capacities and wants of his subordinate part, the animal soul [ALFORD]. **45. so**—in accordance with the distinction just mentioned between the natural or *animal-souled* body and the *spiritual* body. **it is written**—(Gen. 2:7)—"Man became (was made to become) a living soul," i.e., endowed with *an animal soul*, the living principle of his body. **the last Adam**—the LAST Head of humanity, who is to be fully manifested in *the last day*, which is *His* day (John 6:39). He is so called in Job 19:25; see my *Note* there (cf. Rom. 5:14). In contrast to "the last," Paul calls "man" (Gen. 2:7) "the FIRST Adam." **quickening**—not only living, but *making alive* (John 5:21; 6:33, 39, 40, 54, 57, 62, 63; Rom. 8:11). As the *natural* or *animal-souled* body (vs. 44) is the fruit of our union with the first Adam, an *animal-*

ADAM CLARKE

40. *There are also celestial bodies, and bodies terrestrial.* The apostle certainly does not speak of *celestial* and *terrestrial* bodies in the sense in which we use those terms. We invariably mean by the former the sun, moon, planets, and stars; by the latter, masses of inanimate matter. But the apostle speaks of human beings, some of which were clothed with *celestial*, others with *terrestrial*, bodies. It is very likely, therefore, that he means by the *celestial bodies* such as those refined human bodies with which Enoch, Elijah, and Christ himself appear to the realms of glory; to which we may add the bodies of those saints which arose after our Lord's resurrection and, after having appeared to many, doubtless were taken up to paradise. By *terrestrial* bodies we may understand those in which the saints now live. *But the glory of the celestial is one.* The *glory*—the excellence, beauty, and perfection. Even the present frail human body possesses an indescribable degree of contrivance, art, economy, order, beauty, and excellence; but the *celestial* body, that in which Christ now appears. and according to which ours shall be raised (Phil. iii. 21), will exceed the excellence of this beyond all comparison. A *glory* or "splendor" will belong to that which does not belong to this. Here there is a *glory* of excellence, for the bodies of the saints shall shine like "the sun in the kingdom of their Father." See Matt. xiii. 43.

41. *There is one glory of the sun.* As if he had said: This may be illustrated by the present appearance of the celestial bodies which belong to our system. The *sun* has a greater degree of splendor than the *moon;* the moon, than the planets; and the planets, than the *stars.*

42. *So also is the resurrection of the dead.* That is, the bodies of the dead, though all immortal, shall possess different degrees of splendor and glory, according to the state of holiness in which their respective souls were found. *It is sown in corruption.* The body is buried in a state of degradation, decay, and corruption. The apostle uses the word *sown* to intimate that the body shall rise again, as a seed springs up that has been sown in the earth. *It is raised in incorruption.* Being no more subject to corruption, dissolution, and death.

43. *It is sown in dishonour.* Being now stripped of all the glory it had as a machine, fearfully and wonderfully made by the hands of God, and also consigned to death and destruction because of sin. This is the most dishonorable circumstance. *It is raised in glory.* It is raised a glorious body, because immortal, and forever redeemed from the empire of death. *It is sown in weakness.* The principles of dissolution, corruption, and decay have prevailed over it; disease undermined it; and death made it his prey. *It is raised in power.* To be no more liable to weakness through labor, decay by age, wasting by disease, and dissolution by death.

44. *It is sown a natural body.* An "animal body." *It is raised a spiritual body.* One perfect in all its parts, no longer dependent on natural productions for its support, being built up on indestructible principles, and existing in a region where there shall be no more death. The body is spiritual and has a spiritual existence and spiritual support. As the seed which is sown in the earth rots. and out of the germ contained in it God in His providence produces a root, stalk, leaves, ear, and a great numerical increase of grains, is it not likely that God, out of some essential parts of the body that now is, will produce the resurrection body; and will then give the soul a body as it pleaseth Him; and so completely preserve the individuality of every human being, as He does of every grain, giving to each its own body (v. 38)? So that as surely as the grain of wheat shall produce wheat after it is cast in the earth, corrupts, and dies, so surely shall our bodies produce the same bodies as to their essential individuality.

45. *The first man Adam was made a living soul.* These forms of expression are common among the Jews; hence we find "Adam the first" and "Adam the last." The apostle says this is written: *The first man Adam was made a living soul.* This is found in Gen. ii. 7, in the words "the breath of life," which the apostle translates *a living soul. The last Adam was*

MATTHEW HENRY

and the life. If the first Adam could communicate to us natural and animal bodies, cannot the second Adam make our bodies spiritual ones?

ALBERT BARNES:

47. "The first man." Adam. "Is of the earth." Was made of the dust (see Gen. 2:7). "Earthy." Partaking of the earth; he was a mass of animated clay, and could be appropriately called "dust" (Gen. 3:19). Of course, he must partake of a nature that was low, mean, mortal, and corruptible.

"The second man." Christ. He is called the second man, as being the second who sustained a relation to men that was materially to affect their conduct and destiny; the second and the last (v. 45), who should sustain a peculiar headship to the race.

"The Lord from heaven." Called in chapter 2:8 the "Lord of glory." This expression refers to the fact that the Lord Jesus had a heavenly origin, in contradistinction from Adam, who was formed from the earth. The Latin Vulgate renders this, "The second man from heaven is heavenly"; and this idea seems to accord with the meaning in the former member of the verse. The sense is, evidently, that as the first man had an earthly origin, and was, therefore, earthy, so the second man being from heaven, as his proper home, would have a body adapted to that abode; unlike that which was earthy, and which would be fitted to his exalted nature, and to the world where he would dwell. And while, therefore, the phrase "from heaven" refers to his heavenly origin, the essential idea is that he would have a body that was adapted to such an origin and such a world—a body unlike that which was earthy. That is, Christ had a glorified body to which the bodies of the saints must yet be made like.—*Popular Commentary*

(3) We must first have natural bodies from the first Adam before we can have spiritual bodies from the second (*v.* 49). It is as certain that we shall have spiritual bodies as it is now that we have natural or animal ones. We are as certainly intended to bear the one as we have borne the other.

5. The reason of this change (*v.* 50). Corruption cannot inherit incorruption. The bodies of the saints, when they shall rise again, will be greatly changed from what they are now, and much for the better. They are now corruptible; they will be then incorruptible, glorious, and spiritual bodies, fitted to the celestial world, where they are ever afterwards to have their eternal inheritance.

Verses 51–57

I. He here tells them that all the saints would not die, but all would be changed.

JAMIESON, FAUSSET, BROWN

souled man, so the *spiritual* body is the fruit of our union with the second Adam, who is the quickening Spirit (II Cor. 3:17). As He became representative of the whole of humanity in His union of the two natures, He exhausted in His own person the sentence of death passed on all men, and giveth spiritual and everlasting life to whom He will. **46. afterward**—Adam had a soul not necessarily mortal, as it afterwards became by sin, but "a *living* soul," and destined to live for ever, if he had eaten of the tree of life (Gen. 3:22); still his body was but an *animal-souled* body, not a *spiritual* body, such as believers shall have; much less was he a "life-giving spirit," as Christ. His soul had the germ of the Spirit, rather than the fulness of it, such as man shall have when restored "body, soul, and spirit," by the second Adam (I Thess. 5:23). As the first and lower Adam came before the second and heavenly Adam, so the animal-souled body comes first, and must die before it be changed into the spiritual body (i.e., that in which the Spirit predominates over the animal soul). **47. of the earth**—inasmuch as being sprung from the earth, he is "earthy" (Gen. 2:7; 3. 19, "dust thou art"); i.e., not merely earthly or born *upon* the earth, but *terrene*, or *of earth;* lit., "of *heaped* earth" or clay. Adam means *red earth.* **the Lord**—omitted in the oldest MSS. and versions. **from heaven**—(John 3:13, 31). Humanity in Christ is generic. In Him man is impersonated in his true ideal as God originally designed him. Christ is the representative man, the federal head of redeemed man. **48. As is the earthy**—viz., Adam. **they . . . that are earthy**—All Adam's posterity in their *natural* state (John 3:6, 7). **the heavenly**—Christ. **they . . . that are heavenly**—His people in their regenerate state (Phil. 3:20, 21). As the former precedes the latter state, so the *natural bodies* precede the *spiritual bodies.* **49. as**—*Greek,* "even as" (see Gen. 5:3). **we shall also bear**—or wear as a garment [BENGEL]. The oldest MSS. and versions read, "We must also bear," or "let us also bear." It implies the divine appointment (cf. "must," vs. 53) and faith assenting to it. An exhortation, and yet implying a promise (so Rom. 8:29). The conformity to the image of the heavenly Representative man is to be begun here in our souls, in part, and shall be perfected at the resurrection in both bodies and souls. **50.** (See *Notes,* vss. 37, 39.) "Flesh and blood" of the same animal and corruptible nature as our present (vs. 44) *animal-souled* bodies, cannot inherit the kingdom of God. Therefore the believer acquiesces gladly in the unrepealed sentence of the holy law, which appoints the death of the present body as the necessary preliminary to the resurrection body of glory. Hence he "dies daily" to the flesh and to the world, as the necessary condition to his regeneration here and hereafter (John 3:6; Gal. 2:20). As the being *born of the flesh* constitutes a child of Adam, so the being *born of the Spirit* constitutes a child of God. **cannot**—Not merely is the change of body *possible,* but it is *necessary.* The spirit extracted from the dregs of wine does not so much differ from them, as the glorified man does from the mortal man [BENGEL] of mere animal flesh and blood (Gal. 1:16). The resurrection body will be still a body though spiritual, and substantially retaining the personal identity; as is proved by Luke 24:39; John 20:27, compared with Philippians 3:21. **the kingdom of God**—which is not at all merely animal, but altogether spiritual. *Corruption* doth not *inherit,* though it is the way to, *incorruption* (vss. 36, 52, 53). **51. Behold**—Calling attention to the "mystery" heretofore hidden in God's purposes, but now revealed. **you**—emphatical in the *Greek;* I show (*Greek,* "tell," viz., *by the word of the Lord,* I Thess. 4:15) YOU, who think you have so much knowledge, "a mystery" (cf. Rom. 11:25) which your reason could never have discovered. Many of the old MSS. and Fathers read, "We shall all sleep, but we shall not all be changed"; but this is plainly a corrupt reading, inconsistent with I Thessalonians 4:15, 17, and with the apostle's argument here, which is that a *change* is necessary (vs. 53). *English Version* is supported by some of the oldest MSS. and Fathers. The *Greek* is literally "We all shall not sleep, but . . . ." The putting off of the corruptible body for an incorruptible by an instantaneous *change* will, in the case of "the quick," stand as equivalent to death, appointed to all men (Heb. 9:27); of this Enoch and Elijah are types and forerunners. The "we" implies that Christians in that age and every successive age since and hereafter were designed to stand waiting, as if Christ might come again in their time, and as if they might be found among "the quick." **52. the last trump**—at the sounding of the trumpet *on the last day*

ADAM CLARKE

made a quickening spirit. This is also said to be *written;* but where? In the very same verse, and in these words: "And man [Adam] became a living soul," which the apostle translates a "quickening or life-giving spirit."

46. *That was not first which is spiritual.* The *natural* or "animal" body, described in v. 44, was the *first;* it was the body with which Adam was created. The *spiritual* body is the last, and is that with which the soul is to be clothed in the resurrection.

47. *The first man is of the earth.* That is, Adam's body was made out of the dust of the earth, and hence the apostle says he was "of the dust." *The second man is . . . from heaven.* The resurrection body shall be of a heavenly nature, and not subject to decay or death. What is formed of earth must live after an earthly manner, must be nourished and supported by the earth. What is from heaven is of a spiritual nature, and shall have no further connection with, nor dependence upon, earth. I conceive both these clauses to relate to man, and to point out the difference between the animal body and the spiritual body, or between the bodies which we now have and the bodies which we shall have in the resurrection. But can this be the meaning of the clause, *the second man is the Lord from heaven?* In the quotation I have omitted "the Lord," on the basis of many authorities. Some of the most eminent of modern critics leave out the word, and Tertullian says that it was put in by the heretic Marcion. I do think that the word is not legitimate in this place. The verse is read by the MSS., versions, and fathers referred to, thus: "The first man is of the earth, earthy; the second man is of heaven, heavenly." The *first man* and the *second man* of this verse are the same as the "first Adam" and the "second Adam" of v. 45, and it is not clear that Christ is meant in either place.

48. *As is the earthy.* As Adam was, who was formed from the earth, so are all his descendants: frail, decaying, and subject to death. *As is the heavenly.* As is the heavenly state of Adam and all glorified beings, so shall be the state of all those who at the resurrection are found fit for glory.

49. *And as we have borne the image of the earthy.* As being descendants from Adam we have all been born in his likeness and subject to the same kind of corruption, disgrace, and death, we shall also be raised to a life immortal such as he now enjoys in the kingdom of God. This interpretation proceeds on the ground that what is here spoken belongs to Adam in his twofold state, viz., of mortality and immortality, of disgrace and honour, of earth and heaven.

50. *Flesh and blood cannot inherit the kingdom.* This is a Hebrew periphrasis for "man," and man in his present state of infirmity and decay. Man in his present state cannot inherit the kingdom of God; his nature is not suited to that place; he could not, in his present weak state, endure an exceeding great and eternal weight of glory. Therefore it is necessary that he should die, or be changed, that he should have a celestial body suited to the celestial state.

51. *I shew you a mystery.* That is, a thing which you have never known before. But what is this *mystery?* Why, that *we shall not all sleep*—we shall not all die; *but we shall all be changed.* Of this the Jews had not distinct notions. For as flesh and blood cannot inherit glory, and all shall not be found dead at the day of judgment, then all must be *changed*—undergo such a change that their bodies may become spiritual, like the bodies of those who shall be raised from the dead.

52. *In a moment.* "In an atom"; that is, an indivisible point of time. *In the twinkling of an eye,* as soon as a man can wink, which expressions show that this mighty work is to be done by the almighty power of God, as He does all His works. The resurrection of all the dead from the foundation of the world to that time and the change of all the living then upon earth shall be the work of a single moment. *At the last trump.* This, as well as all the rest of the

MATTHEW HENRY

It will not be without changing from corruption to incorruption, *v.* 52. Changed they must be as well as the dead, because flesh and blood cannot inherit the kingdom of God. The apostle here makes known a truth unknown before, which is that the saints living at our Lord's second coming will not die, but be changed, that this change will be made in a moment, in the twinkling of an eye, and *at the sound of the last trump.* At this summons the graves shall open, the dead saints shall rise incorruptible, and the living saints be changed to the same incorruptible state, *v.* 52.

II. The reason of this change (*v.* 53). This corruptible body must be made incorruptible, this mortal body must be changed into immortal. What is sown must be quickened.

III. What will follow upon this change of the living and dead in Christ: *Then shall be brought to pass that saying, Death is swallowed up in victory.* Christ hinders it from swallowing his saints when they die; but, when they rise again, death shall be swallowed for ever.

1. They will glory over death as a vanquished enemy: "*O death! where is thy sting?* We fear no further mischiefs from thee, but defy thy power. *O grave! where is thy victory?* Once we were thy prisoners, but the prison-doors are burst open, and we are for ever released. Captivity is taken captive. Thy triumphs, grave, are at an end."

2. The foundation for this triumph, (1) Whence death had its power to hurt: *The sting of death is sin.* This gives venom to his dart. Sin is the parent of death, and gives it all its hurtful power. It is its cursed progeny and offspring. (2) The victory saints obtain over it through Jesus Christ, *v.* 56. *The sting of death is sin;* but Christ, by dying, has taken out this sting. It may hiss therefore, but it cannot hurt. *The strength of sin is the law;* but the curse of the law is removed by our Redeemer's *becoming a curse for us,* so that sin is deprived of its strength and sting, through Christ. There is a day coming when the grave shall open, the dead saints revive, and become immortal, and put out of the reach of death for ever. They often rejoice beforehand, in the hope of this victory; and, when they arise glorious from the grave, they will boldly triumph over death. It is altogether owing to the grace of God in Christ that sin is pardoned and death disarmed. This triumph of the saints over death should issue in thanksgiving to God: *Thanks be to God, who giveth us the victory through Christ Jesus, our Lord* (*v.* 57). Then only do we enjoy our blessings and honours when God has his revenue of glory out of it. And this really improves and exalts our satisfaction. We are conscious at once of having done our duty and enjoyed our pleasure. Those who remain under the power of death can have no heart to praise; but such conquests and triumphs will certainly tune the tongues of the saints to thankfulness and praise. With what acclamations will saints rising from the dead applaud him! *Thanks be to God* will be the burden of their song; and angels will join the chorus, and declare their consent with a loud Amen, Hallelujah.

I. An exhortation, and this threefold: 1. That they should be steadfast, fixed in the faith of the gospel. "Do not let your belief of these truths be shaken. They are most certain, and of the last importance." Christians should be steadfast believers of this great article of the resurrection of the dead. A disbelief of a future life will open a way to all manner of licentiousness. It will be easy and natural to infer hence that we may live like beasts, and eat and drink, for tomorrow we die. 2. He exhorts them to be *immovable* in their expectation of being raised incorruptible and immortal. Christians should not be moved away from this hope of the gospel (Col. i. 23). This hope should be an anchor to their souls, firm and sure, Heb. vi. 19, 3. He exhorts them *to abound in the work of the Lord,* and that *always.* What vigour and resolution, what constancy and patience, should those hopes inspire!

JAMIESON, FAUSSET, BROWN

[VATABLUS] (Matt. 24:31; I Thess. 4:16). Or the Spirit by Paul hints that the other trumpets mentioned subsequently in the Apocalypse shall precede, and that this shall be the *last* of all (cf. Isa. 27:13; Zech. 9:14). As the law was given with the sound of a trumpet, so the final judgment according to it (Heb. 12:19; cf. Exod. 19:16). As the Lord ascended "with the sound of a trumpet" (Ps. 47:5), so He shall descend (Rev. 11:15). The trumpet was sounded to convoke the people on solemn feasts, especially on the first day of the seventh month (the type of the *completion* of time; *seven* being the number for *perfection;* on the tenth of the same month was the atonement, and on the fifteenth the feast of tabernacles, commemorative of completed salvation out of the spiritual Egypt, cf. Zech. 14:18, 19); cf. Ps. 50:1-7. Cf. His calling forth of Lazarus from the grave "with a loud voice," John 11:43, with 5:25, 28. **and**—immediately, in consequence. **53. this**—pointing to *his own* body and that of those whom he addresses. **put on**—as a garment (II Cor. 5:2, 3). **immortality**—Here only, besides I Timothy 6:16, the word "immortality" is found. Nowhere is the immortality of the *soul,* distinct from the body, taught; a notion which many erroneously have derived from heathen philosophers. Scripture does not contemplate the anomalous state brought about by death, as the consummation to be earnestly looked for (II Cor. 5:4), but the resurrection. **54. then**—not before. Death has as yet *a sting* even to the believer, in that his *body* is to be under its power till the resurrection. But then the sting and power of death shall cease for ever. **Death is swallowed up in victory**—In *Hebrew* of Isaiah 25:8, from which it is quoted, "*He* (Jehovah) *will swallow up* death in victory"; i.e., *for ever:* as "in victory" often means in *Hebrew* idiom (Jer. 3:5; Lam. 5:20). Christ will swallow it up *so altogether victoriously* that it shall never more regain its power (cf. Hos. 6:2; 13:14; II Cor. 5:4; Heb. 2:14, 15; Rev. 20:14; 21:4). **55.** Quoted from Hos. 13:14, substantially; but freely used by the warrant of the Spirit by which Paul wrote. The *Hebrew* may be translated, "O death, where are thy plagues? Where, O Hades, is thy destruction?" The LXX, "Where is thy victory (lit., *in a lawsuit*), O death? Where is thy sting, O Hades?" "Sting" answers to the *Hebrew* "plagues," viz., a poisoned *sting* causing *plagues.* Appropriate, as to the old serpent (Gen. 3; Num. 21:6). "Victory" answers to the *Hebrew* "destruction." Cf. Isaiah 25:7, "*destroy* . . . veil . . . over all nations," viz., *victoriously destroy* it; and to "in victory" (vs. 54), which he triumphantly repeats. The "where" implies their past victorious destroying power and sting, now gone for ever; obtained through Satan's triumph over man in Eden, which enlisted God's law on the side of Satan and death against man (Rom. 5:12, 17:21). The souls in Hades being freed by the resurrection, death's sting and victory are gone. For "O grave," the oldest MSS .and versions read, "O death," the second time. **56.** If there were no sin, there would be no death. Man's transgression of the law gives death its lawful power. **strength of sin is the law**—Without the law sin is not perceived or imputed (Rom. 3:20; 4:15; 5:13). The law makes sin the more grievous by making God's will the clearer (Rom. 7:8-10). Christ's people are no longer "under the law" (Rom. 6:14).

57. to God—The victory was in no way due to ourselves (Ps. 98:1). **giveth**—a present certainty. **the victory**—which death and Hades ("the grave") had aimed at, but which, notwithstanding the opposition of them, as well as of the law and sin, we have gained. The repetition of the word (vss. 54, 55) is appropriate to the triumph gained.

58. beloved—Sound doctrine kindles Christian *love.* **steadfast**—not turning aside from the faith of the resurrection *of yourselves.* **unmovable**—not turned aside *by others* (vs. 12; Col. 1:23). **the work of the Lord**—the promotion of Christ's kingdom (Phil. 2:30).

ADAM CLARKE

peculiar phraseology of this chapter, is merely Jewish. *For the trumpet shall sound.* By this the apostle confirms the substance of the tradition that there shall be the sound of a trumpet on this great day; and this other scriptures teach. See Zech. ix. 14; Matt. xxiv. 31; John v. 25; 1 Thess. iv. 16, in which latter place the apostle treats this subject among the Thessalonians as he does here among the Corinthians. *Shall be raised incorruptible.* Fully clothed with a new body, to die no more. *We shall be changed.* That is, those who shall then be found alive.

53. *For this corruptible.* Because flesh and blood cannot inherit glory, therefore there must be a refinement by death, or a change without it.

54. *Death is swallowed up in victory.* These words are a quotation from Isa. xxv. 8, where the Hebrew is: "He [God] hath swallowed up death in victory"; or "forever." These words in the Septuagint are thus translated: "Death having prevailed, or conquered, hath swallowed up." But in the version of Theodotion, the words are the same with those of the apostle. The Hebrew *lanetsach* the Septuagint sometimes translate "in victory," but most commonly "forever." Death is here personified and represented as a devouring being, swallowing up all the generations of men; and by the resurrection of the body and the destruction of the empire of death, God is represented as swallowing him up; or that eternity gulps him down, so that he is endlessly lost and absorbed in its illimitable waste.

55. *O death, where is thy sting? O grave, where is thy victory?* These words are generally supposed to be taken from Hos. xiii. 14, where the Hebrew stands thus: "O death, I will be thy plagues; O grave, I will be thy destruction"; and which the Septuagint translate very nearly as the apostle, "O death, where is thy revenge, or judicial process? O grave, where is thy sting?" Both Death and Hades are here personified. Death is represented as having a *sting,* "dagger, or goad," by which, like the driver of oxen, he is continually irritating and urging on (these irritations are the diseases by which men are urged on till they fall into Hades, the empire of Death;); to Hades, *victory* is attributed, having overcome and conquered all human life, and subdued all to its own empire. Hades, which we here translate *grave,* is generally understood to be the place of separate spirits.

56. *The sting of death is sin.* The apostle explains himself particularly here. Death could not have entered into the world if sin had not entered first; it was *sin* that not only introduced *death,* but has armed him with all his destroying force. The goad or dagger of death is sin; by this both body and soul are slain. *The strength of sin is the law.* The law of God forbids all transgression, and sentences those who commit it to temporal and eternal death. Sin has its controlling and binding power from the law. The law curses the transgressor and provides no help for him; and if nothing else intervene, he must, through it, continue ever under the empire of death.

57. *But thanks be to God.* What the law could not do, because it is law (and law cannot provide pardon), is done by the gospel of our Lord Jesus Christ. He has died to slay Death; He has risen again to bring mankind from under the empire of Hades. All this He has done through His mere unmerited mercy; and eternal thanks are due to God for this unspeakable gift. He has given us the *victory* over sin, Satan, death, the grave, and hell.

58. *Be ye stedfast.* "Be settled"; confide in the truth of this doctrine of the resurrection, and everything that pertains to it, as confidently as a man sits down on a seat which he knows to be solid, firm, and safe, and on which he has often sat. *Always abounding in the work of the Lord.* The *work of the Lord* is obedience to His holy Word; every believer in Christ is a workman of God. He that works not to bring glory to God and good to man is not acknowledged as a servant of Christ; and if he be not a servant, he is not a son; and if not a son, then not an heir. And he must not only work, but abound in that work, ever exceeding his former self; and this, not for a time, but *always;* beginning, continuing, and ending every act of

MATTHEW HENRY

II. They have the best grounds in the world to build upon. As surely as Christ is risen, they shall rise. The labour of Christians will not be lost labour; they may lose for God, but they will lose nothing by him. He will never be found unjust to forget their labour of love. Nay, he will do exceedingly abundantly above what they can now ask or think. Those who serve God have good wages; they cannot do too much nor suffer too much for so good a Master. If they serve him now, they shall see him hereafter; they shall rise again from the dead, be crowned with glory, honour, and immortality, and inherit eternal life.

CHAPTER 16

Verses 1–4

In this chapter Paul closes this long epistle. He begins with directing them about a charitable collection on a particular occasion, the distresses and poverty of Christians in Judæa.

I. How he introduces his direction. He had given similar *orders to the churches of Galatia, v.* 1. He desired them only to conform to the same rules which he had given to other churches on a similar occasion. He also prudently mentions these orders of his to the churches of Galatia, to excite emulation, and stir them up to be liberal. Those who exceeded most churches in spiritual gifts, surely would not suffer themselves to come behind any in their bounty to their afflicted brethren. It is becoming a Christian not to bear to be outdone by a fellow-christian in anything virtuous and praise-worthy, provided this consideration only makes him exert himself, not envy others. The church of Corinth should not be outdone in this service of love by the churches of Galatia.

The time when this is to be done: *The first day of the week*, the Lord's day. It is a day of holy rest; and the more vacation the mind has from worldly cares and toils the more disposition has it to show mercy: and the other duties of the day should stir us up to the performance of this; works of charity should always accompany works of piety. Works of mercy are the genuine fruits of true love to God, and therefore are a proper service on his own day.

JAMIESON, FAUSSET, BROWN

not in vain—as the deniers of the resurrection would make it (vss. 14, 17). **in the Lord**—applying to the whole sentence and its several clauses: Ye, as being in the Lord by faith, know that your labor in the Lord (i.e., labor according to His will) is not to be without its reward in the Lord (through His merits and according to His gracious appointment).

CHAPTER 16

VSS. 1-24. DIRECTIONS AS TO THE COLLECTION FOR THE JUDEAN CHRISTIANS: PAUL'S FUTURE PLANS: HE COMMENDS TO THEM TIMOTHY, APOLLOS, ETC. SALUTATIONS AND CONCLUSIONS. **1. collection for the saints**—at Jerusalem (Rom. 15:26) and in Judea (Acts 11:29, 30; 24:17; cf. II Cor. 8:4; 9:1, 12). He says "saints" rather than "the poor," to remind the Corinthians that in giving, it is to *the Lord's people*, their own *brethren in the faith*. Towards the close of the national existence of the Jews, Judea and Jerusalem were harassed with various troubles, which in part affected the Jewish Christians. The community of goods which existed among them for a time gave temporary relief but tended ultimately to impoverish all by paralyzing individual exertion (Acts 2:44), and hence was soon discontinued. A beautiful fruit of grace it was, that he who had by persecutions robbed many of their all (Acts 26:10), should become the foremost in exertions for their relief. **as I have given**—rather, "*gave* order," viz., during my journey through Galatia, that mentioned in Acts 18:23. The churches of Galatia and Phrygia were the last which Paul visited before writing this Epistle. He was now at Ephesus, and came thither immediately from visiting them (Acts 18:23; 19:1). That he had not been silent in Galatia on contributions for the poor, appears from the hint let fall in his Epistle to that church (Gal. 2:10): an undesigned coincidence and mark of genuineness [PALEY'S *Horæ Paulinæ*]. He proposes the Galatians as an example to the Corinthians, the Corinthians to the Macedonians, the Corinthians and Macedonians to the Romans (Rom 15:26, 27; II Cor. 9:2). There is great force in example. **2. first day of . . . week**—already kept sacred by Christians as the day of the Lord's resurrection, the beginning day both of the physical and of the new spiritual creations: it gradually superseded the Jewish sabbath on the seventh day (Ps. 118:22-24; John 20:19, 26; Acts 20:7; Rev. 1:10). So the beginning of the year was changed from autumn to spring when Israel was brought out of Egypt. Three annual feasts, all typical of Christian truths, were directed to be kept on the first day of the week: the feast of the wave offering of the first sheaf, answering to the Lord's resurrection; Pentecost, or the feast of weeks, typical of the fruits of the resurrection in the Christian Church (Lev. 23: 11, 15, 16, 36); the feast of tabernacles at harvest, typical of the ingathering of the full number of the elect from one end of heaven to the other. Easter was directed to be kept as a holy sabbath (Exod. 12:16). The Christian Sabbath commemorates the respective works of the Three Persons of the Triune God—creation, redemption (the resurrection), and sanctification (on Pentecost the Holy Ghost being poured out). Jesus came to fulfil the Spirit of the Law, not to cancel it, or to lower its standard. The primary object of the sabbath is *holiness*, not merely rest: "Remember that thou keep *holy* the sabbath day." Cf. Genesis 2:3, "God *blessed* and *sanctified* it, because . . in it He had rested . . . ." The word "Remember" implies that it was in existence *before* the giving of the law from Sinai, and refers to its institution in Paradise (cf. Exod. 16:22, 23, 26, 30). "Six days shalt thou labor": the *spirit* of the command is fulfilled whether the six days' labor be on the last six days or on the first. A perpetual sabbath would doubtless be the highest Christian ideal; but living in a world of business where the Christian ideal is not yet realized, if a law of definite

ADAM CLARKE

life to God's glory and the good of his fellows. *Your labour is not in vain.* "Your labor in the Lord is not in vain"; you must not only work, but you must *labour*—put forth all your strength; and you must work and labor *in the Lord*—under His direction, and by His influence; for without Him ye can do nothing. And this labor cannot be *in vain;* you shall have a resurrection unto eternal life—not because you have labored, but because Christ died and gave you grace to be faithful. One remark I cannot help making: The doctrine of the resurrection appears to have been thought of much more consequence among the primitive Christians than it is now! How is this? The apostles were continually insisting on it, and exciting the followers of God to diligence, obedience, and cheerfulness through it. There is not a doctrine in the gospel on which more stress is laid, and there is not a doctrine in the present system of preaching which is treated with more neglect!

CHAPTER 16

1. *The collection for the saints.* The Christians living at Jerusalem, we may naturally suppose, were greatly straitened, as the enmity of their countrymen to the gospel of Christ led them to treat those who professed it with cruelty and spoil them of their goods (see Heb. x. 34; and Rom. xv. 26); and the apostle hereby teaches that it was the duty of one Christian congregation to help another when in distress.

2. *Upon the first day of the week.* It appears from the whole that *the first day of the week,* which is the Christian Sabbath, was the day on which their principal religious meetings were held in Corinth and the churches of Galatia, and consequently in all other places where Christianity had prevailed. This is a strong argument for the keeping of the Christian Sabbath. We may observe that the apostle follows here the rule of the synagogue; it was a regular custom among the Jews to make their collections for the poor on the Sabbath day, that they might not be without the necessaries of life, and might not be prevented from coming to the synagogue.

MATTHEW HENRY

II. The direction itself.

1. The manner in which the collection was to be made: *Everyone was to lay by in store* (*v.* 2). He should lay by as he could spare from time to time. It is a good thing to lay up in store for good uses. The best way in the world for them to get a treasury for this purpose is to lay by from time to time, as they can afford. "Every little," as the proverb says, "would make a mickle." We may cheerfully give when we know that we can spare, and that we have been laying by in store that we may.

2. The measure in which they are to lay by: *As God hath prospered them.* All our business and labour are that to us which God is pleased to make them. It is not the diligent hand that will make rich by itself, without the divine blessing. It is his bounty and blessing to which we owe all we have. And what argument more proper to excite us to charity to the people of God than to consider all we have as his gift? When his bounty flows forth upon us we should not confine it to ourselves, but let it stream out to others. The more good we receive from God the more we should do good to others. They were to lay by as God had blessed them. God expects that our beneficence to others should hold some proportion to his bounty to us. The greater ability he gives, the more enlarged should our hearts be, and the more open our hands; but, where the ability is less, the hands cannot be as open, however willing the mind and however large the heart; nor does God expect it.

The apostle would have everything ready against his coming. As to the disposal of it, he would leave it much to themselves. Paul no more pretended to lord it over the purses of his hearers than over their faith; he would not meddle with their contributions without their consent. They should give letters of credence, and send messengers of their own with their liberality, *v.* 3. This would be a proper testimony of their respect and brotherly love to their distressed brethren. It would argue that they were very hearty in this service, when they should send some of their own body on so long and hazardous a journey to convey their liberality. We should not only charitably relieve our poor fellow-christians but do it in such a way as will best signify our compassion to them. He offers to go with their messengers, if they think proper, *v.* 4. Ministers are doing their proper business when they are promoting or helping in works of charity.

Verses 5–9

The apostle notifies his purpose of visiting them. 1. His purpose: he intended to pass out of Asia, and to go through Macedonia, and to stay some time with them, and perhaps the winter, *v.* 5, 6. He had long laboured in this church, and done much good among them. The heart of a truly Christian minister must be much towards that people among whom he has long laboured, and with remarkable success. Though some among this people made a faction against him, doubtless there were many who loved him tenderly. And is it any wonder that he should be willing to visit them, and stay with them? It is plain that he hoped for some good effect, because he says he intended to stay, *that they might bring him on his journey whithersoever he went* (*v.* 6); not that they might accompany him a little way on the road, but help and encourage him to it, and provide him for it. His stay among them, he hoped, would cure their factious humour.

2. His excuse for not seeing them now (*v.* 7). He would not see them because he could not stay with them. Such a visit would give neither him nor them any satisfaction. He loved them so much that he longed for an opportunity to take up his abode among them for some length of time. This would be more pleasing to himself, and more serviceable to them, than a cursory visit in his way. 3. We have the limitation of this purpose: *I trust to tarry awhile with you, if the Lord permit*, *v.* 7. Concerning all our purposes it is fit we should say, "We will execute them if the Lord permit." It is not in us to effect our own designs, without the divine leave. It is by God's power and permission. 4. We have his purpose expressed of staying at Ephesus for the present. He says he would stay there till pentecost, *v.* 8. It is very probably that at the time of writing this epistle he was in Ephesus, from this passage, compared with *v.* 19, where he says, *The churches of Asia salute you.* 5. We have the reason given for his staying at Ephesus for the present, *v.* 9. God gave him great success among them. For this reason he determined to stay awhile at Ephesus. Success, and a fair prospect of more, was a just reason to determine an apostle to stay and labour in a

JAMIESON, FAUSSET, BROWN

times was necessary in Paradise, it is still more so now. **every one of you**—even those in limited circumstances. **lay by him**—though there be not a weekly *public* collection, each is *privately* to set apart *a definite proportion of his weekly income* for the Lord's cause and charity. **in store**—abundantly: the earnest of a better store *laid up* for the giver (I Tim. 6:19). **as** *God* **hath prospered him**—lit., "whatsoever he may be prospered in," or "may by prosperity have acquired" [ALFORD], (Matt. 25:15-29; II Cor. 8:12). **that there be no gatherings when I come**—that they may not *then* have to be made, when your and my time ought to be employed in more directly spiritual things. When men give once for all, not so much is given. But when each *lays by* something every Lord's day, more is collected than one would have given at once [BENGEL]. **3. approve by your letters**—rather translate, "Whomsoever ye shall approve, them will I send *with* letters": viz., letters to several persons at Jerusalem, which would be their credentials. There could be no need of letters *from them* before Paul's coming, if the persons recommended were *not to be sent off before it.* Lit., "by letters"; an abbreviated expression for "I will send, recommending them by letters" [GROTIUS]. If *English Version* be retained, the sense will be, "When I come, I will send those whom by your letters, *then to be given them,* ye shall approve." But the antithesis (opposition or contrast) to Paul himself (vs. 4) favors GROTIUS' view. So "by" means *with* (Rom. 2:27); and the *Greek* for "by" is translated, with (II Cor. 2:4). **liberality**—lit., *gracious or free gift* (II Cor. 8:4). **4. meet**—"worth while." If your collections be large enough to be *worth* an apostle's journey (a stimulus to their liberality), I will accompany them *myself* instead of giving them *letters* credential (vs. 3; cf. Acts 20:1-4). **with me**—to guard against all possible suspicion of evil (II Cor. 8:4, 19-21). **5-7.** His first intention had been (II Cor. 1:15, 16) to pass through them (Corinth) to Macedonia, and again return to them from Macedonia, and so to Judea; this he had announced in the lost epistle (ch. 5:9); now having laid aside this intention (for which he was charged with levity, II Cor. 1:17, etc., whereas it was through lenity, II Cor. 1:23; 2:1), he announces his second plan of "not seeing them now by the way," but "passing through Macedonia" first on his way to them, and then "tarrying a while," and even "abiding and wintering with them." **for I do pass**—as much as to say, "This is what I at last *resolve upon*" (not as the erroneous subscription of the Epistle represents it, as if he was THEN at Philippi, *on his way through* Macedonia); implying that there had been some previous communication upon the subject of the journey, and also that there had been some indecisiveness in the apostle's plan [PALEY]. In accordance with his second plan, we find him in Macedonia when II Corinthians was written (II Cor. 2:13; 8:1; 9:2, 4), and on his way to Corinth (II Cor. 12:14; 13:1; cf. Acts 20:1, 2). "Pass through" is opposed to "abide" (vs. 6). He was *not yet* in Macedonia (as vs. 8 shows), but at Ephesus; but he was *thinking* of *passing through* it (not *abiding* as he purposed to do at Corinth). **6.** He did "abide and even winter" for the three WINTER months in Greece (Corinth), Acts 20:3, 6; from which passage it seems that Paul probably left Corinth about a month before the "days of unleavened bread" or the Passover (so as to allow time to touch at Thessalonica and Berea, from which cities two of his companions were; as we read he did at Philippi); so that thus the three months at Corinth would be December, January, and February [BIRKS, *Horæ Apostolicæ*]. **ye**—emphatical in the *Greek.* **whithersoever I go**—He purposed to go to Judea (II Cor. 1:16) from Corinth, but his plans were not positively fixed as yet (*Note,* vs. 4; cf. Acts 19:21). **7. I will not see you now by the way**—lit., "I do not wish to see you this time in passing"; i.e., to pay you now what would have to be a merely passing visit as I did in the second visit (II Cor. 12:14). In contrast to "a while," i.e., *some time,* as the *Greek* might better be translated. **but**—The oldest MSS. read "for." **8. at Ephesus**—whence Paul writes this Epistle. Cf. vs. 19, "Asia," wherein Ephesus was. **until Pentecost**—He seems to have stayed as he here purposes: for just when the tumult which drove him away broke out, he was already intending to leave Ephesus (Acts 19:21, 22). Combined with ch. 5:7, 8, this verse fixes the date of this Epistle to a few weeks before Pentecost, and very soon after the Passover. **9. door**—(II Cor. 2:12). An *opening* for the extension of the Gospel. Wise men are on the watch for, and avail themselves of, *opportunities.* So "*door* of hope," Hosea 2:15. "Door of faith," Acts 14:27. "An

ADAM CLARKE

3. *Whomsoever ye shall approve by your letters.* Why should Paul require *letters* of approbation in behalf of certain persons when he himself should be among them and could have their characters *viva voce?* It is probable that he refers here to letters of recommendation which they had sent to him while he was away; and he now promises that, when he shall come to Corinth, he would appoint these persons whom they had recommended to carry the alms to Jerusalem. Some MSS. and several versions join *by letters* to the following words, and read the verse thus: "When I come, those whom ye shall approve I will send with letters to bring your liberality to Jerusalem." This seems most natural.

4. *And if it be meet.* If it be a business that requires my attendance, and it be judged proper for me to go to Jerusalem, I will take those persons for my companions.

5. *I will come unto you, when I shall pass through Macedonia.* Paul was now at Ephesus; for almost all allow, in opposition to the subscription at the end of this Epistle that states it was written from Philippi, that it was written from Ephesus. This is supported by many strong arguments; and the eighth verse here seems to put it past all question: "I will tarry at Ephesus"; i.e., I am in Ephesus, and here I purpose to remain until Pentecost. Though Macedonia was not in the direct way from Ephesus to Corinth, yet the apostle intended to make it in his way. And it was because it was not in the direct road, but lay at the upper end of the Aegean Sea, and very far out of his direct line, that he says, *I do pass through Macedonia*—I have purposed to go thither before I go to Corinth.

6. *Yea, and winter with you.* He purposed to stay till Pentecost at Ephesus; after that to go to Macedonia, and probably to spend the summer there; and come in the autumn to Corinth, and there spend the winter. *That ye may bring me on my journey.* That you may furnish me with the means of travelling. It appears that in most cases the different churches paid his expenses to other churches; where this was not done, then he labored at his business to acquire the means of travelling.

7. *I will not see you now by the way.* From Ephesus to Corinth was merely across the Aegean Sea, and a comparatively short passage.

8. *I will tarry at Ephesus.* And it is very probable that he did so, and that all these journeys were taken as he himself had projected.

9. *A great door and effectual is opened.* "A great and energetic door is opened to me"; that is, God has made a grand opening to me in those parts, which I perceive will require much

MATTHEW HENRY

particular place. And there were many adversaries. Great success in the work of the gospel commonly creates many enemies. The devil opposes those most who most heartily set themselves to destroy his kingdom. There were many adversaries; and therefore the apostle determined to stay. True courage is whetted by opposition. The opposition of adversaries only animated his zeal. Adversaries and opposition do not break the spirits of faithful ministers, but only enkindle their zeal. To labour in vain is heartless and discouraging. This damps the spirits, and breaks the heart. But success will give life and vigour to a minister. It is not the opposition of enemies, but the hardness of his hearers, and the backslidings of professors, that damp a faithful minister, and break his heart.

Verses 10–12

I. He recommends Timothy to them, *v.* 10. Timothy was sent by the apostle to correct the abuses which had crept in among them; and not only to direct, but to reprove, those who were culpable. No doubt the mutual strife and hatred ran very high among them. Proud spirits cannot easily bear reproof. It was reasonable therefore to think young Timothy might be roughly used. It was their duty to behave themselves well towards him, and not dishearten him in his Lord's work. They should not fly out into resentment at his reproof.

He warns them against despising him, *v.* 11. He was but a young man, and his own youthful face and years commanded but little reverence. Pride was a reigning sin among the Corinthians, and such a caution was but too necessary. Christians should be very careful not to pour contempt on any, but especially on ministers. He tells them they should use him well while he was with them; and they should send him away in friendship, and well prepared for his journey back again to Paul. This is the meaning of bringing him on his journey in peace, *v.* 11.

II. The reasons why they should behave thus towards Timothy. He was employed in the same work as Paul, and acted in it by the same authority, *v.* 10. He did not come on Paul's errand among them, nor to do his work, but the work of the Lord. Those who work the work of the Lord should be treated with all tenderness and respect. Pastors and teachers, as well as apostles and evangelists, are to be treated with honour and respect. As they were to esteem him for his work's sake, so also for Paul's sake, who had sent him to Corinth (*v.* 11). "I am expecting his return and shall judge by your conduct towards him what your regard and respect for me will be." They would hardly dare to send back Timothy with a report that would grieve or provoke the apostle.

III. He informs them of Apollos's purpose to see them. He himself had greatly desired him to come to them, *v.* 12. Though one party among them had declared for Apollos against Paul, yet Paul did not hinder Apollos from going to Corinth in his own absence. Faithful ministers are not apt to entertain jealousies of each other. True charity and brotherly love think no evil. Apollos could not be prevailed on for the present to come. He would not go to be set at the head of a party. When this had subsided he might conclude a visit would be more proper. Apostles did not vie with each other, but consulted each other's comfort and usefulness. Apollos shows his respect to Paul by declining the journey till the Corinthians were in better temper.

JAMIESON, FAUSSET, BROWN

open door," Revelation 3:8. "A door of utterance," Colossians 4:3. "Great," i.e., extensive. "Effectual," i.e., *requiring great labors* [ESTIUS]; or *opportune for effecting great results* [BEZA]. **many adversaries**—who would block up the way and prevent us from entering the open door. Not here false teachers, but open adversaries: both Jews and heathen. After Paul, by his now long-continued labors at Ephesus, had produced effects which threatened the interests of those whose gains were derived from idolatry, "many adversaries" arose (Acts 19:9-23). Where great good is, there evil is sure to start up as its antagonist. **10. Now**—rather, "But." Therefore Timothy was not the *bearer* of the Epistle; for it would not then be said, "IF Timothy come." He must therefore have been *sent* by Paul from Ephesus *before* this Epistle was written, to accord with ch. 4:17-19; and yet the passage here implies that Paul did not expect him to arrive at Corinth till *after* the letter was received. He tells them how to treat him "if" he should arrive. Acts 19:21, 22 clears up the difficulty: Timothy, when sent from Ephesus, where this Epistle was written, did not proceed direct to Corinth, but *went first to Macedonia;* thus though sent before the letter, he might not reach Corinth till after it was received in that city. The undesigned coincidence between the Epistle and the history, and the clearing up of the meaning of the former (which does not mention the journey to Macedonia at all) by the latter, is a sure mark of genuineness [PALEY'S *Horæ Paulinæ*]. It is not certain that Timothy actually reached Corinth; for in Acts 19:22 only *Macedonia* is mentioned; but it does not follow that though Macedonia was the immediate object of his mission, Corinth was not the ultimate object. The "IF Timothy come," implies uncertainty. II Corinthians 1:1 represents him with Paul in *Macedonia;* and II Corinthians 12:18, speaking of *Titus* and others sent to Corinth, does not mention Timothy, which it would have probably done, had one so closely connected with the apostle as Timothy was, stayed as his delegate at Corinth. The mission of Titus then took place, when it became uncertain whether Timothy could go forward from Macedonia to Corinth, Paul being anxious for *immediate* tidings of the state of the Corinthian Church. ALFORD argues that if so, Paul's adversaries would have charged him with fickleness in this case also (II Cor. 1:17), as in the case of his own change of purpose. But Titus was sent *directly* to Corinth, so as to arrive there before Timothy could by the route through Macedonia. Titus' presence would thus make amends for the disappointment as to the intended visit of Timothy and would disarm adversaries of a charge in this respect (II Cor. 7:6, 7). **without fear**—Referring perhaps to a nervous timidity in Timothy's character (I Tim. 3:15; 5:22, 24). His *youth* would add to this feeling, as well as his country, Lystra, likely to be despised in refined Corinth. **11. despise**—This charge is not given concerning any other of the many messengers whom Paul sent. I Timothy 4:12 accounts for it (cf. Ps. 119:141). He was a *young man,* younger probably than those usually employed in the Christian missions; whence Paul apprehending lest he should, on that account, be exposed to contempt, cautions him, "Let no man despise thy youth" [PALEY'S *Horæ Paulinæ*]. **conduct**—set him on his way with every mark of respect, and with whatever he needs (Titus 3:13). **in peace**—(Acts 15:33; Heb. 11:31). "Peace" is the salutation of kindness and respect in the East; and so it stands for every blessing. Perhaps here there is too a contrast between "peace" and the "contentions" prevalent at Corinth (ch. 1:11). **I look for him**—He and Titus were appointed to meet Paul in Troas, whither the apostle purposed proceeding from Ephesus (II Cor. 2:12, 13). Paul thus claims their respect for Timothy as one whom he felt so necessary to himself as "look for" to him [THEOPHYL]. **with the brethren**—Others besides Erastus accompanied Timothy to Macedonia (cf. vs. 12; Acts 19:22). **12. Apollos, I greatly desired . . . to come unto you**—He says this lest they should suspect that he from jealousy prevented Apollos' coming to them; perhaps they had expressly requested Apollos to be sent to them. Apollos was not at Ephesus when Paul wrote (cf. vs. 19, and ch. 1:1). Probably Apollos' unwillingness to go to Corinth at this time was because, being aware of the undue admiration of his rhetorical style which led astray many at Corinth, he did not wish to sanction it (ch. 1:12, 3:4). Paul's noble freedom from all selfish jealousy led him to urge Apollos to go; and, on the other hand, Apollos, having heard of the abuse of his name at Corinth to party purposes, perseveringly refused to go. Paul,

ADAM CLARKE

labor; and besides, I shall have *many adversaries* to oppose me. *Door* often signifies occasion or opportunity; but here the apostle may allude to the throwing open of the great doors of the Circus Maximus before the chariot races began, and the *many adversaries* may refer to the numerous competitors in those races.

10. *Now if Timotheus come.* Of Timothy we have heard before, chap. iv. 17. And we learn from Acts xix. 22 that Paul sent him with Erastus from Ephesus to Macedonia. It is evident therefore, in opposition to the very exceptionable subscription at the end of this Epistle, that the Epistle itself was not sent by Timothy, as there stated.

That he may be with you without fear. That he may be treated well, and not perplexed and harassed with your divisions and jealousies; *for he worketh the work of the Lord*—he is divinely appointed, as I also am.

11. *Let no man . . . despise him.* Let none pretend to say that he has not full authority from God to do the work of an evangelist.

But conduct him forth in peace. I believe, with Bishop Pearce, that this clause should be translated and pointed thus: Accompany him upon his journey, *that he may come unto me* in peace, "in safety," as the word is used in Mark v. 34 and Luke vii. 50. *For I look for him with the brethren.* This clause should not be understood as if Paul was expecting certain brethren with Timothy, but it was the brethren that were with Paul that were looking for him; "I, with the brethren, am looking for him."

12. *As touching our brother Apollos.* It appears from this that the "brethren" of whom the apostle speaks in the preceding verse were then with him at Ephesus; "I, with the brethren, greatly desired to come." *But his will was not at all to come.* As there had been a faction set up in the name of Apollos at Corinth, he probably thought it not prudent to go thither at this time, lest his presence might be the means of giving it either strength or countenance.

MATTHEW HENRY

Verses 13–18

I. Some general advices. They should watch (*v.* 13). The Corinthians were in manifest danger upon many accounts: their feuds ran high, the irregularities among them were very great, there were deceivers among them. In such dangerous circumstances it was their concern to watch. If a Christian would be secure, he must be on his guard. He advises them to *stand fast in the faith.* A Christian should be fixed in the faith of the gospel. It is by this faith alone that he will be able to keep his ground in an hour of temptation; it is by this that we must overcome the world (1 John v. 4), both when it fawns and when it frowns. He advises them to act like men and be strong. "Show yourselves men in Christ, by your steadiness, by your sound judgment and firm resolution." Christians should be manly and firm in defending their faith.

He advises them to do everything in charity, *v.* 14. When the apostle would have us play the man for our faith or religion, he puts in a caution against playing the devil for it. Christians should be careful that charity not only reign in their hearts, but shine out in their lives. Christianity never appears to so much advantage as when the charity of Christians is most conspicuous, when they can bear with their mistaken brethren, and oppose the open enemies of their holy faith in love.

II. Particular directions how they should behave towards some that had been eminently serviceable among them.

1. He gives us their character. (1) The household of Stephanas is mentioned by him. They were the first-fruits of Achaia. It is an honourable character to any man to be early a Christian, betimes in Christ. But they had moreover addicted themselves to the ministry of the saints, to serve the saints. It is not meant of the ministry of the word properly, but of serving them in other respects, and assisting them upon all occasions.

(2) He mentions Stephanas, and Fortunatus, and Achaicus, as coming to him from the church of Corinth. They supplied the deficiencies of the church towards him, and by so doing *refreshed his spirit and theirs, v.* 17, 18. They gave him a more perfect account of the state of the church by word of mouth than he could acquire by their letter. Report had made their cause much worse than it was in fact; but he had been made more easy by converse with them. They came to him as peace-makers. It is a great refreshment to the spirit of a faithful minister to hear better of a people by wise and good men of their own body than by common report. It is a grief to him to hear ill of those he loves; it gladdens his heart to hear the report thereof is false.

2. He directs how they should behave towards them. He would have them acknowledged (*v.* 11), that is, owned and respected. They deserve it for their good offices. Those who discover so good a spirit cannot easily be over-valued, *v.* 16. They were persons to whom they owed peculiar respect, and whom they should have in veneration.

JAMIESON, FAUSSET, BROWN

of course, could not state in his letter particularly these reasons in the existing state of division prevalent there. He calls Apollos "brother" to mark the unity that was between the two. **with the brethren**—who bear this letter (vs. 17). (See subscription added to the Epistle.) CONYBEARE thinks Titus was one of the bearers of this first letter (II Cor. 8:6, 16-24; 12:18). ALFORD thinks "the brethren" here may be the same as in vs. 11. **convenient time**—Apollos did return to Corinth when their divisions were moderated [JEROME], and so it was a more seasonable time. **13.** He shows that they ought to make their hopes of salvation to depend not on Apollos or any other teacher; that it rests with themselves. "Watch ye": for ye are slumbering. "Stand": for ye are like men tottering. "Quit you like men; be strong": for ye are effeminate (vs. 14).

"Let all your things be done with charity" (ch. 8:1; 13:1): not with strifes as at present [CHRYSOSTOM]. "In the faith" which was assailed by some (ch. 15:1, 2, 12-17). **15. first fruits of Achaia**—the first Achæan converts (cf. Rom. 16:5). The image is from the *first fruits* offered to the Lord (Lev. 23:10; cf. ch. 15:20). The members of this family had been baptized by Paul himself (ch. 1:16). **addicted themselves to the ministry of the saints**—Translate, "Set themselves, (i.e., voluntarily) to minister unto the saints" (cf. II Cor. 8:4). **16. That ye**—Translate, "That ye also," viz., in your turn . . . in return for their self-devotion [ALFORD]. **helpeth with**—them. **laboureth**—by himself.

17. Fortunatus . . . Achaicus—probably of Stephanas' household. **that . . . lacking on your part**—So far as you were unable *yourselves* to "*refresh* my spirit," in that you are absent from me, "they have supplied" by coming to me from you, and so supplying the means of intercourse between you and me. They seem to have carried this letter back; see the subscription below: hence the exhortations, vss. 16, 18, as though they would be at Corinth when the Epistle arrived.

18. refreshed my spirit and yours—"yours" will be refreshed on receiving this letter, by knowing that "my spirit is refreshed" by their having come to me from you; and (perhaps) by the good report they gave of many of you (ch. 1:4-8); *my refreshment of spirit* redounds to *yours,* as being my disciples (II Cor. 7:13; cf. Zech. 6:8). **acknowledge**—render them due acknowledgments by a kind reception of them: I Thessalonians 5:12, "know" them in their true worth and treat them accordingly.

ADAM CLARKE

13. *Watch ye.* You have many enemies; be continually on your guard. Be always circumspect: (1) Watch against evil; (2) Watch for opportunities to receive good; (3) Watch for opportunities to do good; (4) Watch over each other in love; (5) Watch that none may draw you aside from the belief and unity of the gospel. *Stand fast in the faith.* Hold in conscientious credence what you have already received as the truth of God, for it is the gospel by which you shall be saved and by which you are now put into a state of salvation. *Quit you like men.* Be not like "children, tossed to and fro . . . with every wind of doctrine." Let your understanding receive the truth; let your judgment determine on the absolute necessity of retaining it; and give up life rather than give up the testimony of God. *Be strong.* Put forth all the vigor and energy which God has given you in maintaining and propagating the truth, and your spiritual strength will increase by usage. The terms in this verse are all military. *Watch ye.* Watch, and be continually on your guard, lest you be surprised by your enemies; keep your scouts out, and all your sentinels at their posts, lest your enemies steal a march upon you. See that the place you are in be properly defended, and that each be alert to perform his duty. *Stand fast in the faith.* Keep in your ranks; do not be disorderly; be determined to keep your ranks unbroken; keep close together. On your unity your preservation depends; if the enemy succeed in breaking your ranks, and dividing one part of this sacred army from another, your rout will be inevitable. *Quit* yourselves *like men.* When you are attacked, do not flinch; maintain your ground; resist; press forward; strike home; keep compact; conquer. *Be strong.* If one company or division be opposed by too great a force of the enemy, strengthen that division and maintain your position; if an attack is to be made on any part or intrenchment of the foe, summon up all your courage, sustain each other. Fear not, for fear will enervate you. Your cause is good; it is *the faith,* the religion of Jesus. He is your Captain in the field; and should you even die in the contest, the victory is yours.

14. *Let all your things be done with charity.* Let "love" to God, to man, and to one another be the motive of all your conduct.

15. *Ye know the house of Stephanas.* You know that Stephanas and his "family" have addicted themselves to the help of the followers of Christ; they have been the chief instruments of supporting the work of God in Achaia, of which work they themselves have been the firstfruits.

16. *That ye submit yourselves unto such.* That you have due regard to them, and consider them as especial instruments in the hand of God for countenancing and carrying on His great work. The submission here recommended does not imply obedience, but kind and courteous demeanor.

17. *I am glad of the coming of Stephanas.* It was by these that the Corinthians had sent that letter to the apostle to answer which was a main part of the design of Paul in this Epistle. *Fortunatus.* This man is supposed to have survived Paul; to be the same mentioned by Clement in his epistle to the Corinthians, sec. 59, as the bearer of that epistle from Clement at Rome to the Christians at Corinth. *For that which was lacking on your part.* This may refer either to additional communications besides those contained in the letter which the Corinthians sent to the apostle—which additional circumstances were furnished by the persons above; and from them Paul had a fuller account of their spiritual state than was contained in the letter—or to some contributions on their part for the support of the apostle in his peregrinations and labors.

18. *They have refreshed my spirit and yours.* They have been a means of contributing greatly to my comfort, and what contributes to my comfort must increase yours. This is probably the meaning of the apostle. *Therefore acknowledge ye them.* Pay them particular respect, and let all be held in esteem in proportion to their work and usefulness. When this is made the rule of respect and esteem, then foolish and capricious attachments will have no place. A

MATTHEW HENRY

The apostle closes his epistle,

I. With salutations to the church of Corinth, first from those of Asia, from *Priscilla* and *Aquila* (who seem to have been at this time inhabitants of Ephesus), *with the church in their house* (*v.* 19), and from *all the brethren* (*v.* 20) at Ephesus. Paul could find room in an epistle treating of very important matters to send the salutations of friends. Religion should promote a courteous and obliging temper towards all. Those misrepresent and reproach it who would take any encouragement from it to be sour and morose.

Some of these *salute them much in the Lord.* Christian salutations are attended with hearty recommendations to the divine grace and blessing. We read also of a church in a private family, *v.* 19. Every Christian family should in some respects be a Christian church. Wherever two or three are gathered together, and Christ is among them, there is a church. He subjoins, 1. An advice, that *they should greet one another with a holy kiss* (*v.* 20), or with sincere goodwill, a tacit reproof of their feuds and factions. The love of the brethren should be a powerful incentive to mutual love. 2. His own salutation: *The salutation of me Paul with my own hand*, *v.* 21. At the close it was fit that himself should sign it, that they might know it to be genuine. So he wrote in every epistle which he did not wholly pen, as he did that to the Galatians, Gal. vi. 11.

II. With a very solemn warning to them, *v.* 22. We sometimes need words of threatening, that we may fear. Holy fear is a very good friend both to holy faith and holy living. 1. The person described. who is liable to this doom: *He that loveth not the Lord Jesus Christ.* It stands here as a warning to the Corinthians and a rebuke of their criminal behaviour. Professed Christians will, by contempt of Christ, and revolt from him, bring upon themselves the most dreadful destruction. Many who have his name much in their mouths have no true love to him in their hearts. And none love him in truth who do not love his laws and keep his commandments. What, not love the most glorious lover in the world! What had we a power of loving for, if we are unmoved with such love as this, and without affection to such a Saviour? 2. The doom of the person described: "*Let him be Anathema, Maran-atha*, lie under the heaviest and most dreadful curse." *Maran-atha* is a Syriac phrase, and signifies *The Lord cometh.* That very Lord whom they do not love is coming to execute judgment. Those who fall under his condemning sentence must perish. True faith in Christ will evermore be productive of sincere love to him. Those who love him not cannot be believers in him.

III. With his good wishes for them and expressions of goodwill to them. 1. With his good wishes, *v.* 23. The grace of our Lord Jesus Christ comprehends in it all that is good, for time or eternity. We can wish them nothing more, and we should wish them nothing less. The most solemn warnings are the result of the tenderest affection and the greatest goodwill. And therefore it is no wonder that the apostle should close all, 2. With the declaration of his love to them in Christ Jesus, *v.* 24. He parts with them in love. His heart would be with them, and he would bear them dear affection as long as their hearts were with Christ. We should be cordial lovers of all who are in Christ. Not but we should love all men, but *those* must have our dearest affection who are dear to Christ, and lovers of him. May our love be with all those who are in Christ Jesus! Amen.

JAMIESON, FAUSSET, BROWN

19. Asia—not all Asia Minor, but *Lydian Asia* only, of which Ephesus was the capital. **much**—with especial affection. **Aquila . . . Priscilla**—(Cf. Acts 18:2; Rom. 16:3, 4). Originally driven out of Italy by Claudius, they had come to Corinth (whence their salutation of the Corinthians is appropriate here), and then had removed with Paul from Corinth to Ephesus (Acts 18:2, 18, 19, 26); here, as at Rome subsequently, they set up a Church (or assembly of believers) at their house (Rom. 16: 3, 5). A pattern to Christian husbands and wives. Their Christian self-devoting love appears wherever they were (Rom. 16:3, 4). Even the gifted Apollos, so highly admired at Corinth, owed much of his knowledge to them (Acts 18:24-26). In vs. 20, "All the brethren" (i.e., the whole Church) seem to be distinguished from "the church that is in their house," which was but a partial and private assembly out of the general Church at Corinth. NEANDER thinks Romans 16:23 refers to *"the whole Church" meeting at the house of Gaius* (cf. Col. 4: 15). "Synagogue" implies an assembly in general, without reference to the character or motives of its members. "Church," like the *Hebrew Kahal*, implies an assembly *legally* convened; as, for instance, the Jews met as a body politic to receive the law (hence Stephen calls it "the *Church* in the wilderness," Acts 7:38), and having a legal bond of union. Christ's followers when dispersed from one another cease to be a *congregation* (synagogue), but still are a *Church*, having the common bond of union to the same Head by the same faith and hope [VITRINGA, *Synagogue and Temple*]. From this we may explain Paul's entering *"into every house* and haling men and women": he would in searching for Christians go to their several "houses" of prayer. **in the Lord**—They pray for all blessings on you from *the Lord*, the source of every good [GROTIUS]. ALFORD explains, "in a Christian manner," as mindful of your common Lord. "In the Lord" seems to me to refer to *their union together in Christ*, their prayers for one another's good being in virtue of that union. **20. holy kiss**—the token of the mutual love of Christians, especially at the Lord's Supper (cf. Rom. 16:16; I Thess. 5:26), "in which all the dissensions of the Corinthians would be swallowed up" [BENGEL]. **21. salutation . . . with mine own hand**—He therefore dictated all the rest of the Epistle. **22.** A solemn closing warning added *in his own hand* as in Ephesians 6:24; Colossians 4:18. **22. the Lord**—who ought to be "loved" above Paul, Apollos, and all other teachers. Love to one another is to be in connection with love to Him above all. IGNATIUS (*Epistola ad Romanos* 7) writes of Christ, "My love has been crucified" (cf. Song of Solomon 2:7). **Jesus Christ**—omitted in the oldest MSS. **let him be Anathema**—*accursed* with that curse which the Jews who call Jesus "accursed" (ch. 12:3) are bringing righteously on their own heads [BENGEL]. So far from "saluting" him, I bid him be *accursed.* **Maranatha**—*Syriac* for, "the Lord cometh." A motto or watchword to urge them to preparedness for the Lord's coming; as in Philippians 4:5, "The Lord is at hand."

23. The grace . . .—This is the salutation meant in vs. 21; and from which unbelievers (vs. 22; cf. II John 10:11) are excluded [BENGEL]. **24. My love . . .**—After having administered some severe rebukes, he closes with expressions of "love": his very rebukes were prompted by *love*, and therefore are altogether in harmony with the profession of love here made: it was *love in Christ Jesus*, and therefore embraced *"all"* who loved Him.

The subscription represents the Epistle as written from *Philippi.* Verse 8 shows it was written *at Ephesus.* BENGEL conjectures that perhaps, however, it was *sent* from Philippi (vs. 5), because the deputies of the Corinthians had accompanied Paul thither. From Ephesus there was a road to Corinth above Philippi.

ADAM CLARKE

man will then be honored in proportion to his merit, and his merit will be estimated by his usefulness among men.

19. *The churches of Asia salute you.* I.e., The churches in Asia Minor. *Aquila and Priscilla.* Of these eminent persons we have heard before; see Acts xviii. 2, 18, 26; and Rom. xvi. 3. *With the church that is in their house.* That is, the company of believers who generally worshipped there. There were no churches or chapels built at that time, and the assemblies of Christians were necessarily held in private houses. It appears that Aquila and Priscilla devoted their house to this purpose. The house of Philemon was of the same kind; Philemon v. 2. So was likewise the house of Nymphas, Col. iv. 15.

20. *With an holy kiss.* The ancient patriarchs, and the Jews in general, were accustomed to kiss each other whenever they met; and this was a token of friendship and peace with them, as shaking of hands is with us. The primitive Christians naturally followed this example of the Jews.

21. *The salutation of me Paul with mine own hand.* This should be rendered: "The salutation is written by the hand of me Paul." It is very likely that the apostle wrote this and the following verses with his own hand. The rest, though dictated by him, was written by an amanuensis.

22. *If any man love not the Lord Jesus.* This is directed immediately against the Jews. From chap. xii. 3, we find that the Jews, who pretended to be under the Spirit and teaching of God, called Jesus "accursed"; i.e., a person who should be devoted to destruction. In this place the apostle retorts the whole upon themselves, and says: *If any man love not the Lord Jesus Christ, let him be Anathema,* "accursed" and "devoted to destruction." This is not said in the way of a wish or imprecation, but as a prediction of what would certainly come upon them if they did not repent, and of what did come on them because they did not repent. It is generally allowed that the apostle refers here to some of the modes of excommunication among the Jews, of which there were three, viz.: *Niddui*, which signifies a simple separation or exclusion of a man from the synagogue, and from his wife and family, for thirty days. *Cherem*, which was inflicted on him who had borne the *niddui*, and who had not, in the thirty days, made proper compensation, in order to be reconciled to the synagogue. This was inflicted with dire execrations, which he was informed must all come upon him if he did not repent. *Shammatha.* This was the direst of all, and cut off all hope of reconciliation and repentance, after which the man was neither reconcilable to the synagogue nor acknowledged as belonging even to the Jewish nation. *Anathema, Maran-atha.* "Let him be accursed; our Lord cometh." I cannot see the reason why these words were left untranslated. The former is Greek, and has been already explained; the latter is Syriac, *maran-atha*, "Our Lord is coming"; i.e., to execute the judgment denounced. Does not the apostle refer to the last verse in their Bible? "Lest I come and smite the land with a curse"? And does he not intimate that the Lord was coming to smite the Jewish land with that curse? Which took place a very few years after. What the apostle has said was prophetic, and indicative of what was about to happen to that people. God was then coming to inflict punishment upon them; He came, and they were broken and dispersed.

23. *The grace of our Lord Jesus.* May the favor, influence, mercy, and salvation procured by Jesus Christ be *with you*—prevail among you, rule in you, and be exhibited by you, in your life and conversation!

24. *Amen.* So be it. But this word is wanting in most MSS. of repute, and certainly was not written by the apostle.

THE SECOND EPISTLE TO THE CORINTHIANS

I. Introduction (1:1-11)
A. Salutation (1:1, 2)
1. The authoritative note (1:1a)
2. The inclusive note (1:1b)
3. The salutation (1:2)
B. Thanksgiving (1:3-11)
1. The values of an experience of suffering (1:3-7)
2. The experience from which the values came (1:8-11)

II. The ministry (1:12-7:16)
A. Personal vindication (1:12-2:11)
1. A defence of principle (1:12-22)
2. An explanation of action (1:23-2:4)
3. Parenthesis (2:5-11)
B. Concerning the ministry (2:12-5:21)
1. Its power (2:12-4:6)
2. Its tribulation (4:7-12)
3. Its hope (4:13-5:10)
4. Its impulse (5:11-19)
5. Its aim (5:20, 21)
C. The consequent appeal (6:1-7:16)
1. For consistency (6:1-10)
2. For consecration (6:11-7:1)
3. For continued fellowship (7:2-16)

III. The collection for the saints (8:1-9:15)
A. The example of the Macedonians (8:1-5)
B. The deputation (8:6-9:5)
C. The results to follow (9:6-15)

IV. Paul's coming to Corinth (10:1-13:10)
A. His authority (10:1-18)
1. His appeal to them to be obedient (10:1-6)
2. His answer to the criticism of the Christ party (10:7-11)
3. The claim to divine authority (10:12-18)
B. His apostleship (11:1-12:18)
1. His apology for boasting (11:1-4)
2. His boasting (11:5-12:10)
3. His apology for boasting (12:11-18)
C. His program (12:19-13:10)
1. The real purpose of his writing (12:19-21)
2. His procedure on arrival (13:1-10)

V. Conclusion—words of cheer (13:11-14)

The apostle had signified his intentions of "coming to Corinth, as he passed through Macedonia" (1 Cor. 16:5), but, being providentially hindered, he writes this second epistle to them. There seem to be these two urgent occasions: (1) The case of the incestuous person. This therefore he gives directions about (ch. 2), and afterward (ch. 7) he declares the satisfaction he had upon their good behavior in that affair. (2) There was a contribution now making for the poor saints at Jerusalem, in which he exhorts the Corinthians to join (chs. 8, 9).

Other things very observable in this epistle are (1) the account the apostle gives of his labors and success in preaching the gospel in several places (ch. 2); (2) the comparison he makes between the Old and New Testament dispensation (ch. 3); (3) the manifold sufferings that he and his fellow laborers met with (chs. 4, 5); (4) the caution he gives the Corinthians against mingling with unbelievers (ch. 6); (5) the way in which he justifies himself and his apostleship (chs. 10-12).

MATTHEW HENRY

CHAPTER 1

Verses 1, 2

I. The inscription. The apostleship itself was ordained by Jesus Christ, according to the will of God; and Paul was called to it by Jesus Christ, according to the will of God. He joins Timotheus with himself in writing this epistle. His dignifying Timothy with the title of *brother* shows the humility of this great apostle, and his desire to recommend Timothy to the esteem of the Corinthians. The persons to whom this epistle was sent, *the church of God at Corinth*: and also *to all the saints in all Achaia*, that is, to all the Christians who lived in the region round about.

II. The salutation. Therein the apostle desires the two great and comprehensive blessings, grace and peace, for those Corinthians. These two benefits are fitly joined together, because there is no good and lasting peace without true grace; and both of them come *from God our Father, and from the Lord Jesus Christ*.

Verses 3–6

The apostle begins with the narrative of God's goodness to him and his fellow-labourers in their manifold tribulations, which he speaks of by way of thanksgiving to God (*v.* 3–6).

I. The object of the apostle's thanksgiving, the blessed God. 1. *The God and Father of our Lord Jesus Christ*. In the New Testament God is styled *the God and Father of our Lord Jesus Christ*, to denote his covenant-relation to the Mediator and his spiritual seed. 2. *The Father of mercies*. All mercies are from God originally: mercy is his genuine offspring and his delight. 3. *The God of all comfort;* from him proceedeth the COMFORTER. All our comforts come from God.

JAMIESON, FAUSSET, BROWN

CHAPTER 1

Vss. 1-24. THE HEADING; PAUL'S CONSOLATIONS IN RECENT TRIALS IN ASIA; HIS SINCERITY TOWARDS THE CORINTHIANS; EXPLANATION OF HIS NOT HAVING VISITED THEM AS HE HAD PURPOSED. **1. Timothy our brother**—When writing *to* Timothy himself, he calls him "my son" (I Tim. 1:18). Writing *of* him, "brother," and "my beloved son" (I Cor. 4:17). He had been sent before to Macedonia, and had met Paul at Philippi, when the apostle passed over from Troas to Macedonia (cf. ch. 2:12, 13; *Notes,* I Cor. 16:10, 11). **in all Achaia**—comprising Hellas and the Peloponese. The Gentiles themselves, and Annæus Gallio, the proconsul (Acts 18), strongly testified their disapproval of the accusation brought by the Jews against Paul. Hence, the apostle was enabled to labor in the whole province of Achaia with such success as to establish several churches there (I Thess. 1:8; II Thess. 1:4), where, writing from Corinth, he speaks of the "churches," viz., not only the Corinthian, but others also—Athens, Cenchrea, and, perhaps, Sicyon, Argos, etc. He addresses "the Church in Corinth," *directly*, and all "the saints" in the province, *indirectly*. In Galatians 1:2 all the "*churches*" are addressed *directly* in the same circular Epistle. Hence, here he does not say, *all the churches,* but "all the saints." **3.** This thanksgiving for his late deliverance forms a suitable introduction for conciliating their favorable reception of his reasons for not having fulfilled his promise of visiting them (vss. 15-24). **Father of mercies**—i.e., the SOURCE of all mercies (cf. Jas. 1:17; Rom. 12:1). **comfort**—which flows from His "mercies" experienced. Like a true man of faith, he mentions "mercies" and "comfort," before he proceeds to speak of *afflictions* (vss. 4, 5, 6). The "tribulation" of believers is not inconsistent with God's mercy, and does not beget in them suspicion of it; nay, in the end they feel that He is "the God of ALL comfort," i.e., who imparts *the only true and perfect* comfort *in every*

ADAM CLARKE

CHAPTER 1

1. *Paul, an apostle.* Paul, commissioned immediately by Jesus Christ himself, according to *the will of God,* to preach the gospel to the Gentiles. See on 1 Cor. i. 1.

In all Achaia. The whole of the Peloponnesus, or that country separated from the mainland by the Isthmus of Corinth. From this we may learn that this Epistle was sent not only to the church at Corinth, but to all the churches in that country.

2. *Grace be to you and peace.* See Rom. i. 7.

3. *Blessed be God.* Let God have universal and eternal praise: (1) Because he is the *Father of our Lord Jesus Christ,* who is the Gift of His endless love to man, John i. 16. (2) Because He is *the Father of mercies,* the Source whence all mercy flows, whether it respect the body or the soul, time or eternity; the Source of "tender mercy," for so the word implies. See on Rom. xii. 1. And (3) Because he is *the God of all comfort*—the Fountain whence all consolation, happiness, and bliss flow to angels and to men.

MATTHEW HENRY

II. The reasons of the apostle's thanksgivings.

1. The benefits that he himself and his companions had received from God, *v.* 4. In the world they had trouble, but in Christ they had peace.

2. The advantage which others might receive (*v.* 4). What favours God bestows on us are intended not only to make us cheerful ourselves, but also that we may be useful to others.

Their sufferings called *the sufferings of Christ* (*v.* 5), did abound, but their consolation by Christ did abound also. Then we speak best of God and his goodness when we speak from our own experience, and, in telling others, tell God also what he has done for our souls.

Verses 7–11

The apostle speaks for the encouragement of the Corinthians; and tells them (*v.* 7) of his steadfast hope that they should receive benefit by the troubles he and his companions had met with. What their sufferings had been (*v.* 8). It is not certain what particular troubles in Asia are here referred to, for the apostle was in deaths often. This however is evident, that they were great tribulations.

They *despaired even of life* (*v.* 8). And they were brought to this extremity in order *that they should not trust in themselves but in God*, *v.* 9. God often brings his people into great straits, that they may be induced to place their trust and hope in his all-sufficiency. Our extremity is God's opportunity. We may safely trust in *God, who raiseth the dead*, *v.* 9. He that can do this can do anything, and is worthy to be trusted in at all times. What the deliverance was that they had obtained. Their hope and trust were not in vain.

JAMIESON, FAUSSET, BROWN

instance (Ps. 146:3, 5, 8; Jas. 5:11). **4. us**–idiomatic for *me* (I Thess. 2:18). **that we may . . . comfort them which are in any trouble**–Translate, as the *Greek* is the same as before, "tribulation." The apostle lived, not to himself, but to the Church; so, whatever graces God conferred on him, he considered granted not for himself alone, but that he might have the greater ability to help others [CALVIN]. So participation in all the afflictions of man peculiarly qualified Jesus to be man's comforter in all his various afflictions (Isa. 50:4-6; Heb. 4:15). **5. sufferings**–standing in contrast with "salvation" (vs. 6); as "tribulation" (distress of mind), with *comfort* or "consolation." **of Christ**–Cf. Colossians 1:24. The *sufferings* endured, whether by Himself, or by His Church, with which He considers Himself identified (Matt. 25:40, 45; Acts 9:4; I John 4:17-21). Christ calls His people's sufferings His own suffering: (1) because of the sympathy and mystical union between Him and us (Rom. 8:17; I Cor. 4:10); (2) They are borne for His sake; (3) They tend to His glory (Eph. 4:1; I Pet. 4:14, 16). **abound in us**–*Greek*, "abound *unto* us." The order of the *Greek* following words is more forcible than in *English Version*, "Even so through Christ aboundeth also our comfort." The *sufferings* (plural) are many; but the *consolation* (though singular) swallows up them all. Comfort preponderates in this Epistle above that in the first Epistle, as now by the effect of the latter most of the Corinthians had been much impressed. **6. we . . . afflicted . . . for your consolation**–exemplifying the communion of saints. Their hearts were, so to speak, mirrors reflecting the likenesses of each other (Phil. 2:26, 27) [BENGEL]. Alike the afflictions and the consolations of the apostle tend, as in him so in them, as having communion with him, to their consolation (vs. 4 and ch. 4:15). The *Greek* for "afflicted" is the same as before, and ought to be translated, "Whether we *be in tribulation*." **which is effectual**–lit., worketh effectually. **in the enduring . . .**–i.e., in enabling you to endure "the same sufferings which we also suffer." Here follows, in the oldest MSS. (not as *English Version* in the beginning of vs. 7), the clause, And our hope is steadfast on your behalf." **7. so** *shall ye be*–rather, "So *are* ye." He means, there *is* a community of consolation, as of suffering, between me and you. **8, 9.** Referring to the imminent risk of life which he ran in Ephesus (Acts 19:23-41) when the whole multitude were wrought up to fury by Demetrius, on the plea of Paul and his associates having assailed the religion of Diana of Ephesus. The words (vs. 9), "we had the sentence of death in ourselves," mean, that *he looked upon himself as a man condemned to die* [PALEY]. ALFORD thinks the danger at Ephesus was comparatively so slight that it cannot be supposed to be the subject of reference here, without exposing the apostle to a charge of cowardice, very unlike his fearless character; hence, he supposes Paul refers to some deadly *sickness* which he had suffered under (vss. 9, 10). But there is little doubt that, had Paul been found by the mob in the excitement, he would have been torn in pieces; and probably, besides what Luke in Acts records, there were other dangers of an equally distressing kind, such as, "lyings in wait of the Jews" (Acts 20:19), his ceaseless foes. They, doubtless, had incited the multitude at Ephesus (Acts 19:9), and were the chief of the "many adversaries" and "[wild] beasts," which he had to fight with there (I Cor. 15:32; 16:9). His weak state of health at the time combined with all this to make him regard himself as all but dead (ch. 11:29; 12:10). What makes my supposition probable is, that the very cause of his not having visited Corinth directly as he had intended, and for which he proceeds to apologize (vss. 15-23), was, that there might be time to see whether the evils arising there not only from Greek, but from *Jewish* disturbers of the Church (ch. 11:29), would be checked by his first Epistle; there not being fully so was what entailed on him the need of writing this second Epistle. His not specifying this here *expressly* is just what we might expect in the outset of this letter; towards the close, when he had won their favorable hearing by a kindly and firm tone, he gives a more distinct reference to Jewish agitators (ch. 11:22). **above strength**–i.e., ordinary, natural powers of endurance. **despaired**–as far as human help or hope from man was concerned. But in respect to help from God we were "not in despair" (ch. 4:8). **9. But**–"Yea." **in God which raiseth the dead**–We had so given up all thoughts of life, that our only hope was fixed on the coming resurrection; so in I Corinthians 15:32 his hope of the resurrection was what buoyed him up in contending

ADAM CLARKE

4. *Who comforteth us.* Who shows himself to be the God of tender mercy, by condescending to notice us, who have never deserved any good at His hand; and also the God of all consolation, by comforting *us in all our tribulation*—never leaving us a prey to anxiety, carking care, persecution, or temptation; but, by the comforts of his Spirit, bearing us up in, through, and above all our trials and difficulties. *That we may be able to comfort them.* Even spiritual comforts are not given us for our use alone; they, like all the gifts of God, are given that they may be distributed, or become the instruments of help to others.

5. *The sufferings of Christ.* Suffering endured for the cause of Christ: such as persecutions, hardships, and privations of different kinds. *Our consolation also aboundeth.* We stood as well, as firmly, and as easily in the heaviest trial as in the lightest, because the consolation was always proportioned to the trial and difficulty. Hence we learn that he who is upheld in a slight trial need not fear a great one; for if he be faithful, his consolation shall abound as his sufferings abound. Is it not as easy for a man to lift 100 pounds' weight as it is for an infant to lift a few ounces? The proportion of strength destroys the comparative difficulty.

6. *And whether we be afflicted.* See on v. 4. *Which is effectual.* There is a strange and unusual variation in the MSS. and versions in this passage. Perhaps the whole should be read thus: *For if we be afflicted, it is for your encouragement and salvation; and if we be comforted, it is also for your encouragement, which exerted itself by enduring the same sufferings which we also suffer.* This transposition of the middle and last clauses is authorized by the best MSS. and versions. The meaning seems to be this: While you abide faithful to God, no suffering can be prejudicial to you; on the contrary, it will be advantageous, God having your comfort and salvation continually in view by all the dispensations of His providence; and while you patiently endure, your salvation is advanced, sufferings and consolations all becoming energetic means of accomplishing the great design, for all things work together for good to them that love God.

8. *Our trouble which came to us in Asia.* To what part of his history the apostle refers we know not. Some think it is to the Jews' lying in wait to kill him, Acts xx. 3; others, to the insurrection raised against him by Demetrius and his fellow craftsmen, Acts xix. 23; others, to his fighting with beasts at Ephesus, 1 Cor. xv. 32, which they understand literally; and others think that there is a reference here to some persecution which is not recorded in any part of the apostle's history.

We were pressed out of measure, above strength. The original is exceedingly emphatic; we were weighed down beyond what any natural strength could support.

9. *We had the sentence of death in ourselves.* The tribulation was so violent and overwhelming that he had no hope of escaping death. *That we should not trust in ourselves.* The tribulation was of such a nature as to take away all expectation of help but from God alone.

MATTHEW HENRY

God had delivered them, and did still deliver them, *v.* 10. What use they made of this deliverance. Past experiences are great encouragements to faith and hope. We reproach our experiences if we distrust God in future straits, who hath delivered as in former troubles. What was desired of the Corinthians upon this account (*v.* 11). He desires the help of others' prayers. If we thus help one another by our prayers, we may hope for an occasion of *giving thanks by many* for answer of prayer.

Verses 12–14

The apostle attests their integrity by the sincerity of their conversation.

I. He appeals to the testimony of conscience with rejoicing (*v.* 12). The witness appealed to, namely, conscience. This is God's deputy in the soul, and the voice of conscience is the voice of God. They rejoiced in the testimony of conscience. The testimony of conscience for us will be matter of rejoicing at all times and in all conditions. The testimony this witness gave. Conscience witnessed, (1) Concerning their conversation, their constant course of life: by that we may judge of ourselves, and not by this or that single act. (2) Concerning the manner of their conversation; that it was in simplicity and godly sincerity. This blessed apostle was a man of plain dealing; you might know where to have him. He was not a man who seemed to be one thing and was another, but a man of sincerity. (3) Concerning the principle they acted from in all their conversation, and that was not fleshly wisdom, but it was the grace of God.

II. He appeals to the knowledge of the Corinthians with hope and confidence, *v.* 13, 14. They never found anything in him unbecoming an honest man. This they had acknowledged in part already, and he doubted not but they would still do so to the end. And so there would be mutual rejoicing in one another.

Verses 15–24

The apostle here vindicates himself from the imputation of levity and inconstancy, in that he did not hold his purpose of coming to them at Corinth.

I. He avers the sincerity of his intention (*v.* 15–17), and he does this in confidence of their good opinion of him. He assured them he *was minded to come* to them that they might receive a *second benefit.*

JAMIESON, FAUSSET, BROWN

with foes, savage as wild beasts. Here he touches only on the doctrine of the resurrection, taking it for granted that its truth is admitted by the Corinthians, and urging its bearing on their practice. **10. doth deliver**—The oldest MSS. read, "will deliver," viz., as regards *immediately imminent* dangers. "In whom we trust that He will also (so the *Greek*) yet deliver us," refers to the *continuance* of God's delivering help *hereafter.* **11. helping together by prayer for us**—rather, "helping together on our behalf by your *supplication*"; the words "for us" in the *Greek* following "helping together," not "prayer." **that for the gift . . .**—lit., "That on the part of many persons the gift (lit., gift of grace; the mercy) bestowed *upon us* by means of (i.e., through the prayers of) many may be offered thanks for (may have thanks offered for it) on our behalf." **12. For**—reason why he may confidently look for their prayers for him. **our rejoicing**—*Greek,* "our glorying." Not that he glories in the testimony of his conscience, as something *to boast of;* nay, this testimony is itself the thing *in which* his glorying consists. **in simplicity**—Most of the oldest MSS. read, "in holiness." *English Version* reading is perhaps a gloss from Ephesians 6:5 [ALFORD]. Some of the oldest MSS. and versions, however, support it. **godly sincerity**—lit., "sincerity of God"; i.e., sincerity as in the presence of God (I Cor. 5:8). We *glory* in this in spite of all our adversities. *Sincerity* in *Greek* implies the non-admixture of any foreign element. He had no sinister or selfish aims (as some insinuated) in failing to visit them as he had promised: such aims belonged to his adversaries, not to him (ch. 2:17). "Fleshly wisdom" suggests tortuous and insincere courses; but the "grace of God," which influenced him by God's gifts (Rom. 12:3; 15:15), suggests holy straightforwardness and sincere faithfulness to promises (vss. 17-20), even as God is faithful to His promises. The prudence which subserves selfish interests, or employs unchristian means, or relies on human means more than on the Divine Spirit, is "fleshly wisdom." **in the world**—even in relation to the world at large, which is full of disingenuousness. **more abundantly to you-ward**—(Ch. 2:4). His greater love to them would lead him to manifest, especially to them, proofs of his sincerity, which his less close connection with *the world* did not admit of his exhibiting towards it. **13.** We write none other things (in this Epistle) than what ye read (in my former Epistle [BENGEL]; *present,* because the Epistle *continued still* to be read in the Church as an apostolic rule). CONYBEARE and HOWSON think Paul had been suspected of writing privately to some individuals in the Church in a different strain from that of his public letters; and translates, "I write nothing else to you but what ye read *openly* (the *Greek* meaning, "ye *read aloud,*" viz., when Paul's Epistles were publicly read in the congregation, I Thess. 5:27); yea, and what you acknowledge *inwardly*." **or acknowledge**—*Greek,* "or even acknowledge." The *Greek* for "read" and for "acknowledge" are words kindred in sound and root. I would translate, "None other things than what ye know by reading (by comparing my former Epistle with my present Epistle), or even know as a matter of fact" (viz., the consistency of my acts with my words). **even to the end**—of my life. Not excluding reference to *the day of the Lord* (end of vs. 14; I Cor. 4:5). **14. in part**—In contrast to "even to the end": the testimony *of his life* was not yet completed [THEOPHYL and BENGEL]. Rather, "in part," i.e., some of you, not all [GROTIUS, ALFORD]. So in ch. 2:5; Romans 11:25. The majority at Corinth had shown a willing compliance with Paul's directions in the first Epistle: but some were still refractory. Hence arises the difference of tone in different parts of this Epistle. See *Introduction.* **your rejoicing**—your subject of *glorying* or *boast.* "Are" (not merely *shall be*) implies the present recognition of one another as a subject of mutual *glorying:* that *glorying* being about to be realized in its fulness "in the day (of the coming) of the Lord Jesus." **15. in this confidence**—of my character for sincerity being "acknowledged" by you (vss. 12-14). **was minded**—I was intending. **before**—"to come unto you before" visiting Macedonia (where he now was). Cf. *Note,* I Corinthians 16: 5; also 4:18, which, combined with the words here, implies that the insinuation of some at Corinth, that he would not come at all, rested on the fact of his having thus *disappointed* them. His change of intention, and ultimate resolution of going through Macedonia first, took place **before** his sending Timothy from Ephesus into **Macedonia**, and therefore (I Cor. 4:17) before his writing the first Epistle. Cf. Acts 19:21, 22 (the order there is "Macedonia

ADAM CLARKE

11. *Ye also helping together by prayer.* Even an apostle felt the prayers of the Church of God necessary for his comfort and support. What innumerable blessings do the prayers of the followers of God draw down on those who are the objects of them! *The gift bestowed . . . by the means of many persons.* The blessings communicated by means of their prayers. *Thanks may be given by many.* When they who have prayed hear that their prayers are so particularly answered, then all that have prayed will feel themselves led to praise God for His gracious answers. Thus the prayers of many obtain the *gift,* and the thanksgivings of many acknowledge the mercy. The *gift* which the apostle mentions was his deliverance from the dangers and deaths to which he was exposed.

12. *For our rejoicing is this.* Our "boasting, exultation, subject of glorying." *The testimony of our conscience.* That testimony or witness which conscience, under the light and influence of the Spirit of God, renders to the soul of its state, sincerity, safety. *In simplicity.* Not compounded, having one end in view, having no sinister purpose. In *godly sincerity.* "The sincerity of God"; that is, such a sincerity as comes from His work in the soul. "Sincerity" comes from the "splendor, or bright shining of the sun"; and here signifies such simplicity of intention and purity of affection as can stand the test of the light of God shining upon it, without the discovery being made of a single blemish or flaw. *Not with fleshly wisdom.* The cunning and duplicity of man who is uninfluenced by the Spirit of God and has his secular interest, ease, profit, pleasure, and worldly honor in view. *But by the grace of God.* Which alone can produce the simplicity and godly sincerity before mentioned and inspire the wisdom that comes from above. *We have had our conversation.* We have conducted ourselves. The word properly refers to the whole tenor of a man's life—all that he does, says, and intends; and the object or end he has in view, and in reference to which he speaks, acts, and thinks; and is so used by the best Greek writers. The word *conversation* is not an unapt Latinism for the Greek terms, as *conversatio* comes from *con,* "together," and *verto,* "I turn"; and is used by the Latins in precisely the same sense as the other is by the Greeks, signifying the whole of a man's conduct, the tenor and practice of his life. *In the world.* Both among Jews and Gentiles have we always acted as seeing Him who is invisible. *More abundantly to you-ward.* That is, We have given the fullest proof of this in our "conduct" towards you. You have witnessed the holy manner in which we have always acted; and God is Witness of the purity of the motives by which we have been actuated; and our conscience tells us that we have lived in uprightness before Him.

13. *Than what ye read.* Viz., in the First Epistle which he had sent them. *Or acknowledge.* To be the truth of God; and which he hoped they would continue to acknowledge, and not permit themselves to be turned aside from the hope of the gospel.

14. *Have acknowledged us in part.* May signify here not *in part,* but "some of you"; and it is evident, from the distracted state of the Corinthians and the opposition raised there against the apostle, that it was only a part of them that did acknowledge him and receive and profit by his Epistles and advice. *We are your rejoicing.* You boast of us as the ministers of Christ through whom you have believed, as we boast of you as genuine converts to the Christian faith and worthy members of the Church of God.

15. *And in this confidence.* Under the conviction or persuasion that this is the case; that you exult in us, as we do in you. *I was minded.* I had purposed *to come unto you before,* as he had intimated, 1 Cor. xvi. 5; for he had intended to call on them in his way from Macedonia, but this purpose he did not fulfill; and he gives the reason, v. 23.

MATTHEW HENRY

He tells them that he had not herein *used lightness* (*v.* 17), for his purpose was not *according to the flesh.* It was for some weighty reasons that he had altered his purpose; with him there was not yea yea, and nay nay, *v.* 17.

II. He would not have the Corinthians to infer that his gospel was false or uncertain, *v.* 18, 19.

For *God is true,* and *the Son of God, Jesus Christ,* is true. Jesus Christ is not *yea* and *nay,* but in him was *yea* (*v.* 19), nothing but infallible truth. And the promises of God in Christ are not yea and nay, but yea and amen, *v.* 20. There is an inviolable constancy and certainty in all the parts of the gospel of Christ. The promises of the gospel covenant stand firm and inviolable. Bad men are false; good men are fickle; but *God is true,* neither fickle nor false. 1. They are the promises of the God of truth (*v.* 20). 2. They are made in Christ Jesus (*v.* 20), the Amen, the true and faithful witness.

3. They are confirmed by the Holy Spirit. He is given *as an earnest in their hearts, v.* 21, 22. An earnest secures the promise, and is part of the payment. And the accomplishment of them shall be to the *glory of God* (*v.* 20).

JAMIESON, FAUSSET, BROWN

and Achaia," not *Achaia, Macedonia*); 20:1, 2. **that ye might have a second benefit**—one in going to, the other in returning from, Macedonia. The "benefit" of his visits consisted in the grace and spiritual gifts which he was the means of imparting (Rom. 1:11, 12). **16.** This intention of visiting them *on the way* to Macedonia, as well as after having passed through it, must have reached the ears of the Corinthians in some way or other—perhaps in the lost Epistle (I Cor. 4:18; 5:9). The sense comes out more clearly in the *Greek* order, "By you to pass into Macedonia, and from Macedonia to come again unto you." **17. use lightness**—Was I guilty of levity? viz., by promising more than I performed. **or . . . according to the flesh, that with me there should be yea, yea . . . nay, nay?**—The "or" expresses a different alternative: Did I act with levity, or (on the other hand) do I purpose what I purpose like worldly (fleshly) men, so that my "yea" must at all costs be yea, and my "nay" nay [BENGEL, WINER, CALVIN], (Matt. 14:7, 9)? The repetition of the "yea" and "nay" hardly agrees with ALFORD's view, "What I purpose do I purpose according to the changeable purposes of the fleshly (worldly) man, that there may be with me the yea yea, and the nay nay (i.e., both affirmation and negation concerning the same thing)? The repetition will thus stand for the single yea and nay, as in Matthew 5:37; James 5:12. But the latter passage implies that the double "yea" here is not equivalent to the single "yea": BENGEL's view, therefore, seems preferable. **18.** He adds this lest they might think his DOCTRINE was changeable like his *purposes* (the change in which he admitted in vs. 17, while denying that it was due to "lightness," and at the same time implying that *not* to have changed, where there was good reason, would have been to imitate the *fleshly-minded* who at all costs obstinately hold to their purpose). **true**—*Greek,* "faithful" (I Cor. 1:9). **our word**—the *doctrine* we preach. **was not**—The oldest MSS. read "*is not.*" **yea and nay**—i.e., inconsistent with itself. **19.** Proof of the unchangeableness of the doctrine from the unchangeableness of the subject of it, viz., Jesus Christ. He is called "the Son of God" to show the impossibility of change in One who is co-equal with God himself (cf. I Sam. 15:29; Mal. 3:6). **by me . . . Silvanus and Timotheus**—The Son of God, though preached by different preachers, was one and the same, unchangeable. *Silvanus* is contracted into *Silas* (Acts 15:22; cf. I Pet. 5:12). **in him was yea**—*Greek,* "*is made* yea in Him"; i.e., our preaching of the Son of God is confirmed as true in Him (i.e., *through* Him; through the miracles wherewith He has confirmed our preaching) [GROTIUS]; or rather, by the witness of the Spirit which He has given (vss. 21, 22) and of which miracles were only one, and that a subordinate manifestation. **20.** Rather, How many soever be the promises of God, in Him is the "yea" ("*faithfulness in His word*": contrasted with the "yea and nay," vs. 19, i.e., *inconstancy as to one's word*). **and in him Amen**—The oldest MSS. read, "*Wherefore through* Him is *the* Amen"; i.e., In Him is *faithfulness* ("yea") to His word, "wherefore through Him" is the immutable verification of it ("Amen"). As "yea" is His *word,* so "Amen" is His *oath,* which makes our assurance of the fulfilment doubly sure. Cf. "two immutable things (viz., His word and His oath) in which it was impossible for God to lie" (Heb. 6:18; Rev. 3:14). The whole range of Old Testament and New Testament promises are secure in their fulfilment for us in Christ. **unto the glory of God by us**—*Greek,* "for glory unto God by us" (cf. ch. 4:15), i.e., by our ministerial labors; by us His promises, and His unchangeable faithfulness to them, are proclaimed. CONYBEARE takes the "Amen" to be the Amen at the close of thanksgiving: but then "by us" would have to mean what it cannot mean here, "by us *and you.*" **21. stablisheth us . . . in Christ**—i.e., in the faith of Christ—in believing in Christ. **anointed us**—As "Christ" is the "Anointed" (which His name means), so "He hath *anointed* (*Greek, chrisas*) us, ministers and believing people alike, with the Spirit (vss. 22; I John 2:20, 27). Hence we become "a sweet savor of Christ" (ch. 2:15). **22. sealed**—A *seal* is a token assuring the possession of property to one; "sealed" here answers to "stablisheth us" (vs. 21; I Cor. 9:2). **the earnest of the Spirit**—i.e., the Spirit as the earnest (i.e., money given by a purchaser as a pledge for the full payment of the sum promised). The Holy Spirit is given to the believer now as a first instalment to assure him his full inheritance as a son of God shall be his hereafter (Eph. 1:13, 14). "*Sealed* with that Holy Spirit of promise which is the *earnest* of our inheritance until the redemption of the purchased possession"

ADAM CLARKE

A second benefit. He had been with them once, and they had received an especial blessing in having the seed of life sown among them by the preaching of the gospel; and he had purposed to visit them again that they might have a *second* blessing, in having that seed watered.

17. *Did I use lightness?* When I formed this purpose, was it without due consideration? and did I abandon it through fickleness of mind? *That with me there should be yea.* That I should act as carnal men, who change their purposes and falsify their engagements according as may seem best to their secular interest?

18. *But as God is true.* Setting the God of truth before my eyes, I could not act in this way; and as sure as He is true, so surely were my purposes sincere; and it was only my uncertainty about your state that induced me to postpone my visit. See v. 23.

19. *For the Son of God.* If I could have changed my purpose through carnal or secular interest, then I must have had the same interest in view when I first preached the gospel to you, with Silvanus and Timotheus. But did not the whole of our conduct prove that we neither had nor could have such interest in view?

20. *For all the promises of God.* Had we been light, fickle, worldly-minded persons, persons who could be bound by our engagements only as far as comported with our secular interest, would God have confirmed our testimony among you? Did we not lay before you the promises of God? And did not God fulfill those promises by us—by our instrumentality, to your salvation and His own glory? *In him are yea, and in him Amen.* All the promises which God has made to mankind are *yea,* true in themselves, and *Amen,* faithfully fulfilled to them who believe in Christ Jesus. The *promises* are all made in reference to Christ; for it is only on the gospel system that we can have promises of grace, for it is only on that system that we can have mercy. Therefore the promise comes originally by Christ, and is *yea;* and it has its fulfillment through Christ, and is *Amen;* and this is to *the glory of God,* by the preaching of the apostles. From what the apostle says here, and the serious and solemn manner in which he vindicates himself, it appears that his enemies at Corinth had made a handle of his not coming to Corinth, according to his proposal, to defame his character and to depreciate his ministry; but he makes use of it as a means of exalting the truth and the mercy of God through Christ Jesus; and of showing that the promises of God not only come by him, but are fulfilled through him.

21. *Now he which stablisheth us with you.* It is God that has brought both us and you to this sure state of salvation through Christ; and He has anointed us, giving us the extraordinary influences of the Holy Ghost, that we might be able effectually to administer this gospel to your salvation. Through this unction we know and preach the truth, and are preserved by it from dissimulation and falsity of every kind.

22. *Who hath also sealed us.* Not only deeply impressed His truth and image upon our hearts but, by the miraculous gifts of the Holy Spirit, attested the truth of our extraordinary unction or calling to the ministry. *And given the earnest of the Spirit.* From this unction and sealing we have a clear testimony in our souls, the Divine Spirit dwelling constantly in us, of our acceptance with God, and that our ways please Him. The *arrabon* of the apostle is the same as the *erabon* of Moses, Gen. xxxviii. 17-18, 20, which we there translate "pledge." The word properly signifies an *earnest* of something promised; a "part of the price" agreed for between a buyer and seller, by giving and receiving of which the bargain was ratified; or a "deposit," which was to be restored when the thing promised was given. From the use of the term in Genesis, which the apostle puts here in Greek letters, we may at once see his meaning above and in Eph. i. 14, the Holy Spirit being an *earnest* in the *hearts;* and an "earnest of the promised inheritance" means a security given in hand for the fulfillment of all God's promises relative to grace and eternal life. We may learn from this that eternal life will be given in the great day to all who can produce the "pledge." He who is found then with the earnest of God's

MATTHEW HENRY

III. The apostle gives a good reason why he did not come to Corinth, *v.* 23. It was that he might spare them. He knew there were things amiss among them, and such as deserved censure, but was desirous to show tenderness. He assures them that this is the true reason.

He adds that he did not pretend to have any dominion over their faith, *v.* 24. Christ only is the Lord of our faith. He reveals to us what we must believe. Paul, and Apollos, were *but ministers by whom they believed* (1 Cor. iii. 5), and so the *helpers of their joy*, even the joy of faith. Our strength and ability are owing to faith, and our comfort and joy must flow from faith.

JAMIESON, FAUSSET, BROWN

(Rom. 8:23). The Spirit is the pledge of the fulfilment of "all the promises" (vs. 20). **23. Moreover I**—*Greek,* "But *I* (for my part)," in contrast to GOD who hath assured us of *His* promises being hereafter fulfilled certainly (vss. 20-22). **call God**—the all-knowing One, who avenges wilful unfaithfulness to promises. **for a record upon my soul**—As a witness *as to* the secret purposes of my soul, and a witness *against* it, if I lie (Mal. 3:5). **to spare you**—in order not to come in a rebuking spirit, as I should have had to come to you, if I had come *then.* **I came not as yet**—*Greek,* "no longer"; i.e., I *gave up my purpose of then* visiting Corinth. He wished to give them time for repentance, that he might not have to use severity towards them. Hence he sent Titus before him. Cf. ch. 10:10, 11, which shows that his detractors represented him as threatening what he had not courage to perform (I Cor. 4:18, 19).

24. Not for that—i.e., Not that. *"Faith"* is here emphatic. He had "dominion" or a right to control them in matters of *discipline,* but in matters of *"faith"* he was only a *"fellow helper* of their joy" (viz., in believing, Rom. 15:13; Phil. 1:25). The *Greek* is, "Not that we *lord it* over your faith." This he adds to soften the magisterial tone of vs. 23. His desire is to cause them not *sorrow* (ch. 2:1, 2), but *"joy."* The *Greek* for "helpers" implies a mutual leaning, one on the other, like the mutually supporting buttresses of a sacred building. "By faith (Rom. 11:20) ye stand"; therefore it is that I bestow such pains in "helping" your faith, which is the source of all true "joy" (Rom. 15:13). I want nothing more, not to *lord it over your faith.*

ADAM CLARKE

Spirit in his heart shall not only be saved from death but have that eternal life of which it is the pledge, the earnest, and the evidence.

23. *I call God for a record upon my soul.* The apostle here resumes the subject which he left in v. 16, and in the most solemn manner calls God to witness, and consequently to punish, if he asserted anything false, that it was through tenderness to them that he did not visit Corinth at the time proposed. As there were so many scandals among them, the apostle had reason to believe that he should be obliged to use the severe and authoritative part of his function in the excommunication of those who had sinned, and delivering them over to Satan for the destruction of the flesh; but to give them space to amend, and to see what effect his Epistle might produce (not having heard as yet from them), he proposed to delay his coming.

24. *Not for that we have dominion over your faith.* I will not come to exercise my apostolical authority in punishing them who have acted sinfully and disorderly, for this would be to several of you a cause of distress, the delinquents being friends and relatives; but I hope to come to promote your *joy,* to increase your spiritual happiness, by watering the seed which I have already sowed. This I think to be the meaning of the apostle. It is certain that the *faith* which they had already received was preached by the apostles; and therefore in a certain sense, according to our meaning of the term, they had a right to propound to them the articles which they ought to believe; and to forbid them, in the most solemn manner, to believe anything else as Christianity which was opposed to those articles. In that sense they had *dominion over their faith;* and this dominion was essential to them as apostles.

MATTHEW HENRY

CHAPTER 2

Verses 1–4

An account of the reason why he did not come to Corinth. He was unwilling to grieve them, or be grieved by them, *v.* 1,

2. If he had made them sorry, that would have been a sorrow to himself, for there would have been none to have made him glad.

He tells them it was to the same intent that he wrote his former epistle, *v.* 3, 4. The particular thing referred to was the case of the incestuous person. He assures them that he did not design to grieve them.

JAMIESON, FAUSSET, BROWN

CHAPTER 2

Vss. 1-17. REASON WHY HE HAD NOT VISITED THEM ON HIS WAY TO MACEDONIA; THE INCESTUOUS PERSON OUGHT NOW TO BE FORGIVEN; HIS ANXIETY TO HEAR TIDINGS OF THEIR STATE FROM TITUS, AND HIS JOY WHEN AT LAST THE GOOD NEWS REACHES HIM. **1. with myself**—in contrast to "you" (ch. 1: 23). The same antithesis between Paul and them appears in vs. 2. **not come again . . . in heaviness**—"sorrow"; implying that he had *already* paid them *one* visit *in sorrow* since his coming for the first time to Corinth. At that visit he had warned them "he would not spare if he should come again" (*Notes,* ch. 13:2; cf. ch. 12:14; 13:1). See *Introduction* to the first Epistle. The "in heaviness" implies *mutual* pain; they grieving him, and he them. Cf. vs. 2, "I make you sorry," and vs. 5, "If any have caused grief (sorrow)." In this verse he accounts for having postponed his visit, following up ch. 1:23. **2. For**—proof that he shrinks from causing them *sorrow* ("heaviness"). **if I**—The "I" is emphatic. Some detractor may say that *this* (vs. 1) is not my reason for not coming as I proposed; since I showed no scruple in causing "heaviness," or *sorrow,* in my Epistle (the first Epistle to the Corinthians). But I answer, If *I* be the one to cause you sorrow, it is not that I have any pleasure in doing so. Nay, my object was that he "who was made sorry by me" (viz., *the Corinthians in general,* vs. 3; but with tacit reference to *the incestuous person in particular)* should repent, and so "make me glad," as has actually taken place; "for . . . who is he then that . . . ?" **3. I wrote this same unto you**—viz., that I would not come to you *then* (vs. 1), as, if I were to come then, it would have to be "in heaviness" (causing *sorrow* both to him and them, owing to their impenitent state). He refers to the first Epistle (cf. I Cor. 16:7; cf. 4:19, 21; 5:2-7, 13) **sorrow from them of whom I ought to rejoice**—i.e., *sorrow* from their impenitence, when he ought, on the contrary, to have *joy* from their penitent obedience. The latter happy effect was produced by his first Epistle, whereas the former would have been the result, had he *then* visited them as he had originally proposed. **having confidence . . . that my joy is the joy of you all**—trusting that you, too, would feel that there was sufficient reason for the postponement, if it interfered with our mutual joy [ALFORD]. The communion of saints, he feels confident in them "ALL" (his charity overlooking, for the moment the small section of his detractors at Corinth, I Cor. 13:7), will make *his joy* (vs. 2) *their joy.* **4.** So far from my change of purpose being due to "lightness" (ch. 1:17), I wrote my letter to

ADAM CLARKE

CHAPTER 2

1. *But I determined this.* The apostle continues to give further reasons why he did not visit them at the proposed time. Because of the scandals that were among them he could not see them comfortably; and therefore he determined not to see them at all till he had reason to believe that those evils were put away.

2. *For if I make you sorry.* Should he have come and used his apostolical authority in inflicting punishment upon the transgressors, this would have been a common cause of distress. And though he might expect that the sound part of the church would be a cause of consolation to him, yet as all would be overwhelmed with trouble at the punishment of the transgressors, he could not rejoice to see those whom he loved in distress.

3. *And I wrote this same unto you.* This I particularly marked in my First Epistle to you; earnestly desiring your reformation, lest, if I came before this had taken place, I must have come with a rod and have inflicted punishment on the transgressors. See 1 Corinthians v.

MATTHEW HENRY

He wrote to them with much *anguish and affliction* in his own heart, and with great affection to them.

The apostle treats concerning the incestuous person. He tells them that the punishment which had been inflicted upon this offender was sufficient, *v.* 6. The desired effect was obtained.

He therefore directs them, with all speed, to receive him again to their communion, *v.* 7, 8. He beseeches them to forgive him. They must also confirm their love to him; show that their reproofs proceeded from love to his person, as well as hatred to his sin. He was in danger of being *swallowed up with over-much sorrow, v.* 7. He was in danger of falling into despair. When sorrow is excessive it does hurt; and even sorrow for sin is too great when it drives men to despair. He would have them comply with his desire to restore him, *v.* 9.

He mentions his readiness to concur with them in this matter, *v.* 10. And this he would do for their sakes, and for Christ's sake, in conformity to his doctrine and example, which are so full of kindness and tender mercy towards all those who truly repent.

Not only was there danger lest Satan should get an advantage against the penitent, by driving him to despair; but against the apostles or ministers of Christ, by representing them as too rigid and severe. Satan is a subtle enemy, and we should not be *ignorant of his devices*: he is also a watchful adversary, ready to take all advantages against us.

JAMIESON, FAUSSET, BROWN

you (vs. 3) "out of much affliction (*Greek,* 'trouble') and anguish of heart, and with many tears." **not that ye should be grieved**—Translate, "be made sorry," to accord with the translation, vs. 2. My ultimate and main object was, "not that ye might be made sorry," but that through sorrow you might be led to repentance, and so to joy, redounding both to you and me (vss. 2, 3). I made you sorry before going to you, that when I went it might not be necessary. He is easily made sorry, who is admonished by a friend himself weeping [BENGEL]. **that ye might know the love**—of which it is a proof to rebuke sins openly and in season [ESTIUS], (Ps. 141:5; Prov. 27:6). "Love" is the source from which sincere reproof springs; that the Corinthians might ultimately recognize this as his motive, was the apostle's aim. **which I have more abundantly unto you**—who have been particularly committed to me by God (Acts 18:10; I Cor. 4:15; 9:2). **5. grief . . . grieved**—Translate as before, "sorrow . . . made sorry." The "any" is a delicate way of referring to the incestuous person. **not . . . me, but in part**—He has grieved me only in part (cf. ch. 1:14; Rom. 11:25), i.e., *I am not the sole party aggrieved;* most of *you,* also, were aggrieved. **that I may not overcharge**—that I may not unduly lay the weight of the charge on you all, which I should do, if I made myself to be the sole party aggrieved. ALFORD punctuates, "He hath not made sorry me, but in part (that I press not too heavily; viz., on him) you all." Thus "you all" is in contrast to "me"; and "*in part*" is explained in the parenthetical clause. **6. Sufficient**—without increasing it, which would only drive him to despair (vs. 7), whereas the object of the punishment was, "that (his) spirit might be saved" in the last day. **to such a man**—a milder designation of the offender than if he had been *named* [MEYER]. Rather, it expresses estrangement from *such a one* who had caused such grief to the Church, and scandal to religion (Acts 22:22; I Cor. 5:5). **this punishment**—His being "delivered to Satan for the destruction of the flesh"; not only excommunication, but bodily disease (*Notes,* I Cor. 5:4, 5). **inflicted of many**—rather, "by the majority" (the more part of you). Not by an individual priest, as in the Church of Rome, nor by the bishops and clergy alone, but by the whole body of the Church. **7. with overmuch sorrow**—*Greek,* "with HIS overmuch sorrow." **8. confirm your love toward him**—by giving effect in act, and showing in deeds your love; viz., by restoring him to your fellowship and praying for his recovering from the sickness penally inflicted on him. **9. For**—Additional reason why they should restore the offender, viz., as a "proof" of their obedience "in all things"; now in *love,* as previously in *punishing* (vs. 6), at the apostle's desire. Besides his other reasons for deferring his visit, he had the further view, though, perhaps, unperceived by them, of making an experiment of their fidelity. This accounts for his deferring to give, in his Epistle, the *reason* for his change of plan (resolved on before writing it). This full discovery of his motive comes naturally from him now, in the second Epistle, after he had seen the success of his measures, but would not have been a seasonable communication before. All this accords with reality, and is as remote as possible from imposture [PALEY'S *Horæ Paulinæ*]. The interchange of feeling is marked (vs. 4), "I wrote . . . that *ye* might know the love . . .": here, "I did write, that *I* might know the proof of *you.*" **10.** Another encouragement to their taking on themselves the responsibility of restoring the offender. They may be assured of Paul's apostolic sanction to their doing so. **for if I forgave anything, to whom I forgave it**—The oldest MSS. read, "For even what I have forgiven, if I have forgiven anything." **for your sakes** ***forgave*** **I it**—He uses the past tense, as of a thing already determined on; as in I Corinthians 5:3, "I have judged already"; or, as speaking generally of forgiveness granted, or to be granted. It is for your sakes I have forgiven, and do forgive, that the Church (of which you are constituent members) may suffer no hurt by the loss of a soul, and that ye may learn leniency as well as faithfulness. **in the person of Christ**—representing Christ, and acting by His authority: answering to I Corinthians 5:4, "In the name of our Lord Jesus Christ . . . my spirit, with the power of our Lord Jesus Christ." **11.** Lit., "That we may have no advantage gained over us by Satan," viz., by letting one of our members be lost to us through despair, we ourselves furnishing Satan with the weapon, by our repulsive harshness to one now penitent. The loss of a single sinner is a common loss; therefore, in vs. 10, he said, "for your sakes." Paul had "delivered" the offender "to Satan for the destruction of the flesh

ADAM CLARKE

4. *For out of much affliction.* It is very likely that the apostle's enemies had represented him as a harsh, austere, authoritative man, who was better pleased with inflicting wounds than in healing them. But he vindicates himself from this charge by solemnly asserting that this was the most painful part of his office, and that the writing of his First Epistle to them cost him *much affliction* and anguish of heart and *many tears.*

5. *But if any have caused grief.* Here he seems to refer particularly to the cause of the incestuous person. *Grieved me, but in part.* I cannot help thinking that the *ek merous* and *apo merous,* which we render *in part,* and which the apostle uses so frequently in these Epistles, are to be referred to the people. A *part* of them had acknowledged the apostle, chap. i. 14; and here, a *part* of them had given him cause of grief; and therefore he immediately adds, *that I may not overcharge you all.* As only a part of you have put me to pain (viz., the transgressor and those who had taken his part), it would be unreasonable that I should "load you all" with the blame which attaches to that party alone.

6. *Sufficient to such a man is this punishment.* That is, the man has already suffered sufficiently. Here he gives a proof of his parental tenderness towards this great transgressor. He had been disowned by the church; he had deeply repented; and now the apostle pleads for him.

7. *Ye ought rather to forgive him.* He had now suffered enough, for the punishment inflicted had answered the end for which it was inflicted; and there was some danger that, if this poor culprit were not restored to the bosom of the church, his distress and anguish would destroy his life or drive him to despair.

8. *That ye would confirm your love toward him.* You do love him, notwithstanding the reproach he has brought on the gospel; and notwithstanding your love to him, you were obliged to cut him off for the credit of the gospel. Now that he has repented, I beseech you to confirm, to "ratify," by a public act of the church, your love to him; give him the fullest proof that you do love him, by forgiving him and restoring him to his place in the church.

10. *To whom ye forgive any thing.* Here he further shows them that his sole object in the punishment inflicted on the transgressor was his amendment and therefore promises to ratify, in the name and authority of Christ, the free pardon which he exhorts them to dispense. *In the person of Christ.* As I believe Christ acts towards his penitent soul, so do I. Christ forgives his sin, and takes him to His favor; let us forgive him his offense against the church and restore him to its communion.

11. *Lest Satan should get an advantage.* If the man who has given sufficient proof of the sincerity of his repentance be not restored, he may be overwhelmed with sorrow and sink into despair; and then the discipline of the church will be represented, not as emendatory, but as leading to destruction. Of this our enemies would most gladly avail themselves, as they wish to

MATTHEW HENRY

I. Paul's unwearied labour and diligence in his work, *v.* 12, 13. He went to Troas from Philippi by sea (Acts xx. 6), and thence he went to Macedonia. He was prevented in his design as to the place of working, yet he was unwearied in his work.

The apostle makes a long digression, to give the Corinthians an account of his travels and labours, declaring at the same time how he *had no rest in his spirit*, when he found not Titus at Troas (*v.* 13). And we find afterwards (*ch.* vii. 5–7) that when the apostle had come into Macedonia he was comforted by the coming of Titus.

II. His success in his work, *v.* 12. God *made manifest the savour of his knowledge* by him in every place where he came. The apostle speaks of this as a matter of thankfulness to God. In ourselves we are weak, and have neither joy nor victory; but in Christ we may rejoice and triumph.

W. E. VINE:

THRIAMBEUO denotes to lead in triumph, used of a conqueror with reference to the vanquished (2 Cor. 2:14). Theodoret paraphrases it, "He leads us about here and there and displays us to all the world." This is in agreement with evidences from various sources. Those who are led are not captives exposed to humiliation, but are displayed as the glory and devoted subjects of Him who leads (see the context). This is so even if there is a reference to a Roman "triumph." On such occasions the general's sons, with various officers, rode behind his chariot (Livy, xlv. 40). But there is no necessary reference here to a Roman "triumph" (Field, in *Notes on the Trans. of the N.T.*). The main thought is that of the display, "in Christ" being the sphere; its evidences are the effects of gospel testimony.

In Col. 2:15 the circumstances and subjects are quite different, and relate to Christ's victory over spiritual foes at the time of His death; accordingly the reference may be to the triumphant display of the defeated.

—Vine's Expository Dictionary

JAMIESON, FAUSSET, BROWN

that the Spirit might be saved" (I Cor. 5:5). Satan sought to destroy the spirit also: to let him do so, would be to give him an advantage, and let him *overreach* us. **not ignorant of his devices**—"Ignorant" and "devices" are words akin in sound and root in *Greek:* we are not without *knowledge* of his *knowing* schemes. **12.** Paul expected to meet Titus at Troas, to receive the tidings as to the effect of his first Epistle on the Corinthian Church; but, disappointed in his expectation *there,* he passed on to Macedonia, where he met him at last (ch. 7:5, 6, 7) The *history* (Acts) does not record his passing through Troas, in going from Ephesus *to* Macedonia; but it does in coming *from* that country (Acts 20:6); also, that he had disciples there (Acts 20:7), which accords with the *Epistle* (ch. 2:12, "a door was opened unto me of the Lord"). An undesigned coincidence marking genuineness [PALEY'S *Horæ Paulinæ*]. Doubtless Paul had fixed a time with Titus to meet him at Troas; and had desired him, if detained so as not to be able to be at Troas at that time, to proceed at once to Macedonia to Philippi, the next station on his own journey. Hence, though a wide door of Christian usefulness opened to him at Troas, his eagerness to hear from Titus the tidings from Corinth, led him not to stay longer there when the time fixed was past, but he hastened on to Macedonia to meet him there [BIRKS]. **to** *preach*—lit., "for the Gospel." He had been at Troas before, but the vision of a man from Macedonia inviting him to come over, prevented his remaining there (Acts 16:8-12). On his return to Asia, after the longer visit mentioned here, he stayed seven days (Acts 20:6). **and**—i.e., *though* Paul would, under ordinary circumstances, have gladly stayed in Troas. **door . . . opened . . . of the Lord**—*Greek,* "*in* the Lord," i.e., in His work, and by His gracious Providence. **13. no rest in my spirit** —rather, "no rest *for* my spirit" (Gen. 8:9). As here his "spirit" had no rest; so in ch. 7:5, his "flesh." His "spirit" under the Holy Spirit, hence, concluded that it was not necessary to avail himself of the "door" of usefulness at Troas any longer. **taking . . . leave of them**—the disciples at Troas. **14. Now**—*Greek,* "But." Though we left Troas disappointed in not meeting Titus there, and in having to leave so soon so wide a door, "thanks be unto God," we were triumphantly blessed in both the good news of you from Titus, and in the victories of the Gospel everywhere in our progress. The cause of triumph cannot be restricted (as ALFORD explains) to the former; for "always," and "in every place," show that the latter also is intended. **causeth us to triumph**—The *Greek,* is rather, as in Colossians 2:15, "triumphs over us": "leadeth us in triumph." Paul regarded himself as a signal trophy of God's victorious power in Christ. His Almighty Conqueror was leading him about, through all the cities of the Greek and Roman world, as an illustrious example of His power at once to subdue and to save. The foe of Christ was now the servant of Christ. As to be led in triumph by man is the most miserable, so to be led in triumph by God is the most glorious, lot that can befall any [TRENCH]. Our only true triumphs are God's triumphs over us. His defeats of us are our only true victories [ALFORD]. The image is taken from the triumphal procession of a victorious general. The *additional* idea is perhaps included, which distinguishes God's triumph from that of a human general, that the captive is brought into *willing* obedience (ch. 10:5) to Christ, and so *joins in the triumph:* God "leads him in triumph" as one not merely *triumphed over,* but also as one *triumphing over* God's foes with God (which last will apply to the apostle's triumphant missionary progress under the leading of God). So BENGEL: "*Who shows us in triumph,* not [merely] as conquered, but as the ministers of His victory. Not only the victory, but the open 'showing' of the victory is marked: for there follows, *Who maketh manifest.*" **savour**—retaining the image of a triumph. As the approach of the triumphal procession was made known by the *odor* of incense scattered far and wide by the incense-bearers in the train, so God "makes manifest by us" (His now at once triumphed over and triumphing captives, cf. Luke 5:10, "Catch," lit., "Take captive so as to preserve alive") the sweet savor of the knowledge of Christ, the triumphant Conqueror (Col. 2:15), everywhere. As the *triumph* strikes the eyes, so the savor the nostrils; thus every sense feels the power of Christ's Gospel. This *manifestation* (a word often recurring in his Epistles to the Corinthians, cf. I Cor. 4:5) refutes the Corinthian suspicions of his *dishonestly,* by reserve, *hiding* anything from them (vs. 17; ch. 4:2). **15.** The order is in *Greek,* "For (it is)

ADAM CLARKE

discredit this ministry; and there is always at hand a devil to suggest evil and prompt men to do it, for in this respect we have thorough acquaintance with *his devices.* Let us therefore be careful to remove, from both Satan and his partisans, all those occasions which might turn to the disadvantage or disparagement of the gospel of Christ.

12. *When I came to Troas.* After having written the former Epistle, and not having heard what effect it had produced on your minds, though the Lord had opened me a particular door to preach the gospel, in which I so especially rejoice and glory.

13. *I had no rest in my spirit.* I was so concerned for you, through the love I bear you, that I was greatly distressed because I did not find Titus returned to give me an account of your state. *But taking my leave of them.* I went thence into Macedonia, expecting to find him there; and thither he did come, and gave me a joyous account of your state. See chap. viii. 6-7.

14. *Now thanks be unto God.* His coming dispelled all my fears, and was the cause of the highest satisfaction to my mind; and filled my heart with gratitude to God, who is the Author of all good, and *who always causeth us to triumph in Christ;* not only gives us the victory, but such a victory as involves the total ruin of our enemies. A triumph among the Romans, to which the apostle here alludes, was a public and solemn honor conferred by them on a victorious general by allowing him a magnificent procession through the city. This was not granted by the senate unless the general had gained a very signal and decisive victory—conquered a province, etc. On such occasions the general was usually clad in a rich purple robe interwoven with figures of gold, setting forth the grandeur of his achievements; his buskins were beset with pearls; and he wore a crown, which at first was of laurel, but was afterwards of pure gold. In one hand he had a branch of laurel, the emblem of victory; and in the other, his truncheon. He was carried in a magnificent chariot, adorned with ivory and plates of gold, and usually drawn by two white horses. Musicians led up the procession, and played triumphal pieces in praise of the general; and these were followed by young men, who led the victims which were to be sacrificed on the occasion, with their horns gilded, and their heads and necks adorned with ribbons and garlands. Next followed carts loaded with the spoils taken from the enemy, with their horses and chariots. These were followed by the kings, princes, or generals taken in the war, loaded with chains. Immediately after these came the triumphal chariot, before which, as it passed, the people strewed flowers and shouted, *"Io, triumphe!"* The triumphal chariot was followed by the senate; and the procession was closed by the priests and their attendants, with the different sacrificial utensils, and a white ox, which was to be the chief victim. They then passed through the triumphal arch, along the *via sacra* to the capitol, where the victims were slain. During this time all the temples were opened, and every altar smoked with offerings and incense.

The people at Corinth were sufficiently acquainted with the nature of a *triumph.* About two hundred years before this, Lucius Mummius, the Roman consul, had conquered all Achaia, destroyed Corinth, Thebes, and Chalcis; and, by order of the senate, had a grand triumph, and was surnamed "Achaicus." Paul had now a *triumph* (but of a widely different kind) over the same people; his triumph was in Christ, and to Christ he gives all the glory. His sacrifice was that of thanksgiving to his Lord; and the incense offered on the occasion caused the *savor* of the knowledge of Christ to be manifested in every place. As the smoke of the victims and incense offered on such an occasion would fill the whole city with their perfume, so the odor of the name and doctrine of Christ filled the whole of Corinth and the neighboring regions; and the apostles appeared as triumphing in and through Christ over devils, idols, superstition, ignorance, and vice, wherever they came.

MATTHEW HENRY

III. The comfort that the apostle found, even when the gospel was not successful to the salvation of some who heard it, *v.* 15–17.

1. The success is different; for some are saved by it, while others perish under it. (1) Unto some it is a *savour of death unto death,* as men dislike an ill savour, and therefore they are blinded and hardened by it. They reject the gospel, to their ruin, even to spiritual death. (2) Unto others the gospel is a *savour of life unto life.* To humble and gracious souls the preaching of the word is most delightful and profitable. As it quickened them at first, *when they were dead in trespasses and sins,* so it will end in eternal life.

2. The awful impressions this matter made upon the apostle, *v.* 16. Who is *worthy* to be employed in such weighty work? Who is able to perform such a difficult work? The work is great and our strength is small; *all our sufficiency is of God.*

3. The comfort which the apostle had. (1) Because faithful ministers shall be accepted of God, whatever their success be (*v.* 15), in those who are saved and in those also who perish. Ministers shall be accepted, and recompensed, not according to their success, but according to their fidelity. (2) Because his conscience witnessed to his faithfulness, *v.* 17. Though many *did corrupt the word of God,* yet the apostle's conscience witnessed to his fidelity. His aim was to approve himself to God; he therefore spoke and acted always as in the sight of God, and therefore in sincerity.

JAMIESON, FAUSSET, BROWN

of Christ (that) we are a sweet savor unto God"; thus, the "for" justifies his previous words (vs. 14), "the savor of His (Christ's) knowledge." We not only scatter the savor, but "we *are* the sweet savor" itself (Song of Sol. 1:3; cf. John 1:14, 16; Eph. 5:2; I John 2:27). **in them that are saved**—rather, "that *are being* saved . . . that are perishing" (*Note,* I Cor. 1:18). As the light, though it blinds in darkness the weak, is for all that still light; and honey, though it taste bitter to the sick, is in itself still sweet; so the Gospel is still of a sweet savor, though many perish through unbelief [Chrysostom, *Homilies,* 5. 467]. (ch. 4:3, 4, 6). As some of the conquered foes led in triumph were put to death when the procession reached the capitol, and to them the smell of the incense was the "savor of death unto death," while to those saved alive, it was the "savor of life," so the Gospel was to the different classes respectively. **in them**—in the case of them. "Those being saved" (ch. 3:1, to 4:2): "Those that are perishing" (ch. 4:3-5). **16. savour of death unto death . . . of life unto life**—*an odor* arising *out of death* (a mere announcement of a *dead* Christ, and a virtually lifeless Gospel, in which light unbelievers regard the Gospel message), *ending* (as the just and natural consequence) *in death* (to the unbeliever); (but to the believer) *an odor* arising *out of life* (i.e., the announcement of a risen and *living* Saviour), *ending in life* (to the believer) (Matt. 21:44; Luke 2:34; John 9:39). **who is sufficient for these things?**—viz., for diffusing aright everywhere the savor of Christ, so diverse in its effects on believers and unbelievers. He here prepares the way for one purpose of his Epistle, viz., to vindicate his apostolic mission from its detractors at Corinth, who denied his sufficiency. The *Greek* order puts prominently foremost the momentous and difficult task assigned to him, "For these things, who is sufficient?" He answers his own question (ch. 3:5, 6), "Not that we are *sufficient* of ourselves, but our *sufficiency* is of God, who hath made us *able* (*Greek,* 'sufficient') ministers . . . ." **17. not as many**—(ch. 11:18; Phil. 2:21). Rather, "*the* many," viz., *the* false teachers of whom he treats (chs. 10-12, especially ch. 11:13; I Thess. 2:3). **which corrupt**—*Greek,* "adulterating, as hucksters do wine for gain" (ch. 4:2; Isa. 1:22; II Pet. 2:3, "Make *merchandise* of you"). **as of sincerity . . . as of God**—as one speaking from (out of) sincerity, as from (i.e., by the command of, and so in dependence on) God. **in Christ**—as united to Him in living membership, and doing His work (cf. ch. 12:19). The *whole* Gospel must be delivered such as it is, without concession to men's corruptions, and without selfish aims, if it is to be blessed with success (Acts 20:27).

ADAM CLARKE

15. *For we are unto God a sweet savour of Christ.* The apostle still alludes to the case of a triumph. The conqueror always represented the person of Jupiter, as even the heathens supposed that God alone could give the victory; and as the punishment of death was inflicted on some of the captives, who had often rebelled and broken leagues and covenants, so others were spared, made tributaries, and often became allies. Alluding to this, the apostle says: We are a *sweet savour* to God—we have fulfilled His will in faithfully proclaiming the gospel and fighting against sin. And as He has determined that those who believe shall be saved and those who believe not shall perish, we are equally acceptable to Him though we unsuccessfully preach the gospel to some who obstinately reject it and so *perish,* as we are in preaching to others who believe and are *saved.*

16. *To the one we are the savour of death unto death.* There are several sayings among the ancient Jewish writers similar to this. In *Debarim Rabba,* sec. i. fol. 248, it is said: "As the bee brings home honey to its owner, but stings others; so it is with the words of the law; They are a savour of lives to the Israelites: and a savour of death to the people of this world." The apostle's meaning is plain: Those who believe and receive the gospel are saved; those who reject it perish. *Who is sufficient for these things?* Is it the false apostle that has been laboring to pervert you? Or is it the men to whom God has given an extraordinary commission, and sealed it by the miraculous gifts of the Holy Ghost? That this is the apostle's meaning is evident from the following verse.

17. *For we are not as many, which corrupt the word of God.* God has made us sufficient for these things by giving us His own pure doctrine, the ministry of reconciliation, which we conscientiously preserve and preach; and we act, not like many among you, who, having received that doctrine, *corrupt* it, mingling with it their own inventions and explaining away its force and influence, so as to accommodate it to men of carnal minds. The word *kapelenontes,* from *kapelos,* a "tavern keeper," signifies acting like an unprincipled vintner; for this class of men have ever been notorious for adulterating their wines, mixing them with liquors of no worth, that thereby they might increase their quantity; and thus the mixture was sold for the same price as the pure wine. See Isa. i. 22. "Your vintners mix your wine with water"; that is, Your false prophets and corrupt priests adulterate the Word of God and render it of none effect by their explanations and traditions. The word has been used, among both the Greeks and the Latins, to signify a prostitution of what was right and just, for the sake of gain.

MATTHEW HENRY — CHAPTER 3

Verses 1–5

I. The apostle makes an apology for seeming to commend himself. He neither needed nor desired any verbal commendation to them, nor letters testimonial from them, as some others did, meaning the false apostles or teachers, *v.* 1.

The Corinthians themselves were his real commendation, *v.* 2. They were written *in his heart; known and read of all men.*

JAMIESON, FAUSSET, BROWN — CHAPTER 3

Vss. 1-18. The Sole Commendation He Needs to Prove God's Sanction of His Ministry He Has in His Corinthian Converts: His Ministry Excels the Mosaic, as the Gospel of Life and Liberty Excels the Law of Condemnation. **1. Are** we beginning again to recommend ourselves (ch. 5:12) (as some of them might say he had done in his first Epistle; or, a reproof to "some" who had *begun* doing so)! **commendation**—recommendation. (Cf. ch. 10:18.) The "some" refers to particular persons of the "many" (ch. 2:17) teachers who opposed him, and who came to Corinth with letters of recommendation from other churches; and when leaving that city obtained similar letters from the Corinthians to other churches. The 13th canon of the Council of Chalcedon (A.D. 451) ordained that "clergymen coming to a city where they were unknown, should not be allowed to officiate without letters commendatory from their own bishop." The history (Acts 18:27) confirms the existence of the custom here alluded to in the Epistle: "When Apollos was disposed to pass into Achaia [Corinth], *the brethren* [of Ephesus] *wrote,* exhorting the disciples to receive him." This was about two years before the Epistle,and is probably *one* of the instances to which Paul refers, as many at Corinth boasted of their being followers of Apollos (I Cor. 1:12). **2. our epistle**—of recommendation. **in our hearts**—not letters borne merely *in the hands.* Your conversion through my instrumentality, and your faith which is "known of all men" by widespread report (I Cor. 1:4-7), and which is written

ADAM CLARKE — CHAPTER 3

1. *Do we begin again to commend ourselves?* By speaking thus of our sincerity, divine mission, etc., is it with a design to conciliate your esteem or ingratiate ourselves in your affections? By no means. *Or need we . . . epistles of commendation.* Are we so destitute of ministerial abilities and divine influence that we need, in order to be received in different churches, to have letters of recommendation? Certainly not. God causes us to triumph through Christ in every place, and your conversion is such an evident seal to our ministry as leaves no doubt that God is with us. *Letters of commendation* were frequent in the primitive Church; and were also in use in the apostolic Church, as we learn from this place. But these were, in all probability, not used by the apostles. Their helpers, successors, and those who had not the miraculous gifts of the Spirit needed such letters; and they were necessary to prevent the churches from being imposed on by false teachers. But when apostles came, they brought their own testimonials, the miraculous gifts of the Holy Spirit.

2. *Ye are our epistle.* I bear the most ardent love to you. I have no need to be put in remembrance of you by any Epistles or other means; *ye are . . . written in our hearts*—I have the most affectionate remembrance of you.

MATTHEW HENRY

A. B. SIMPSON:

His credentials are the lives that have been transformed through his ministry by the power of the Holy Spirit. What better monument can any Christian worker desire? It is said of the famous Sir Christopher Wren that he was rescued as a foundling child on the very site of that glorious cathedral that he afterward built in the city of London, St. Paul's. At the close of an honored life, his dust was buried beneath its foundations, and by his own directions a plain slab covered his tomb with the simple inscription on it, "If you seek my monument, look around you." That splendid building was his sufficient monument. His work was the memorial of his life. Are we transcribing ourselves, or, better, our Master's image on the hearts and lives of men? Paul did not mean that he despised letters of introduction. They possess a certain value, and we all need to be prudent in guarding against imposters. But he had something better. His work was his highest witness. Can we say it is ours? True character will always discover itself to the world, like a spice ship sailing into the harbor, by the fragrance it diffuses all around it.—*Christ in the Bible*

II. The apostle is careful to ascribe all the praise to God. He says they were the *epistle of Christ, v.* 3. The apostle and others were but instruments. This epistle was not written with *ink, but with the Spirit of the living God;*

nor was it written in *tables of stone,* but on the *heart,* upon the *fleshy* (not *fleshly,* as fleshliness denotes sensuality) *tables of the heart,* that is, upon hearts that are softened by divine grace.

He utterly disclaims the taking of any praise to themselves, and ascribes all the glory to God, *v.* 5. *All our sufficiency is of God;* to him therefore are owing all the praise and glory of that good which is done. The best are no more than what the grace of God makes them.

Verses 6–11

The apostle makes a comparison between the Old Testament and the New and values himself and his fellow-labourers by this, that *they were able ministers of the New Testament,* that God had made them so, *v.* 6.

JAMIESON, FAUSSET, BROWN

by memory and affection on my inmost heart and is borne about wherever I go, is my letter of recommendation (I Cor. 9:2). **known and read**—words akin in root, sound, and sense (so ch. 1: 13). "Ye are *known* to be my converts by general knowledge: then ye are *known* more particularly by your reflecting my doctrine in your Christian life." The handwriting is first "known," then the Epistle is "read" [GROTIUS] (ch. 4:2; I Cor. 14:25). There is not so powerful a sermon in the world, as a consistent Christian life. The eye of the world takes in more than the ear. Christians' lives are the only religious books the world reads. IGNATIUS (*ad Ephesum,* ch. 10) writes, "Give unbelievers the chance of believing through you. Consider yourselves employed by God; your lives the form of language in which He addresses them. Be mild when they are angry, humble when they are haughty; to their blasphemy oppose prayer without ceasing; to their inconsistency, a steadfast adherence to your faith." **3. declared**—The letter is written so legibly that it can be "read by all men" (vs. 2). Translate, "Being manifestly shown to be an Epistle of Christ'; a letter coming manifestly from Christ, and "ministered by us," i.e., carried about and presented by us as its (ministering) bearers to those (the world) for whom it is intended: Christ is the Writer and the Recommender, ye are the letter recommending us. **written not with ink, but with the Spirit of the living God**—Paul was the ministering pen or other instrument of writing, as well as the ministering bearer and presenter of the letter. "Not with ink" stands in contrast to the letters of commendation which "some" at Corinth (vs. 1) used. "Ink" is also used here to include all outward materials for writing, such as the Sinaitic tables of stone were. These, however, were not written with ink, but "graven" by "the finger of God" (Exod. 31:18; 32:16). Christ's Epistle (His believing members converted by Paul) is better still: it is written not merely with the *finger,* but with the *"Spirit* of the *living God";* it is not the "ministration of death" as the law, but of the *"living* Spirit" that "giveth life" (vss. 6-8). **not in**—not *on* tables (tablets) of stone, as the ten commandments were written (vs. 7). **in fleshy tables of the heart**—ALL the best MSS. read, "On [your] *hearts* [which are] tables of flesh." Once your hearts were spiritually what the tables of the law were physically, tables of stone, but God has "taken away the stony heart out of your flesh, given you a heart of flesh" (*fleshy,* not *fleshly,* i.e., carnal; hence it is written, "out of your *flesh*" i.e., your *carnal* nature), Ezek. 11:19; 36:26. Cf. vs. 2, "As ye are our Epistle written in our hearts," so Christ has in the first instance made you "His Epistle written with the Spirit in (on) your hearts." I bear on my heart, as a testimony to all men, that which Christ has by His Spirit written in your heart [ALFORD]. (Cf. Prov. 3:3; 7:3; Jer. 31:31-34). This passage is quoted by PALEY (*Horæ Paulinæ*) as illustrating one peculiarity of Paul's style, viz., his *going off at a word into a parenthetic reflection:* here it is on the word "Epistle." So "savor," ch. 2:14-17. **4. And**—*Greek,* "But." "Such confidence, however (viz., of our 'sufficiency,' vss. 5, 6; ch. 2:16 [to which he reverts after the parenthesis], as ministers of the New Testament, 'not fainting,' ch. 4:1), we have through Christ (not through ourselves, cf. vs. 18) toward God" (i.e., **in our relation** to God and His work, the ministry committed by Him to us, for which we must render an account to Him). Confidence toward God is solid and real, as looking to Him for the strength needed now, and also for the reward of grace to be given hereafter. Cf. Acts 24:15, "hope toward God." Human confidence is unreal in that it looks to man for its help and its reward. **5.** The *Greek* is, "Not that we are (even yet after so long experience as ministers) sufficient to think anything OF ourselves as (coming) FROM ourselves; but our sufficiency is (derived) FROM God." *"From"* more definitely refers to the *source* out of which a thing comes; "of" is more general. **to think**—*Greek,* to "reason out" or "devise"; *to attain to* sound preaching *by our reasonings* [THEODORET]. The "we" refers here to *ministers* (II Pet. 1:21). **anything**—even the least. We cannot expect too little from man, or too much from God. **6. able**—rather, as the *Greek* is the same, corresponding to vs. 5, translate, *"sufficient* as ministers" (Eph. 3:7; Col. 1:23). **the new testament**—"the new *covenant*" as contrasted with the *Old* Testament or covenant (I Cor. 11:25; Gal. 4:24). He reverts here again to the contrast between the law on "tables of stone," and that "written by the Spirit on fleshly tables of the heart" vs. 3). **not of the letter**—joined with "ministers"; ministers not of *the mere literal precept,* in which the old law, as then understood,

ADAM CLARKE

Known and read of all men. For wherever I go I mention you, speak of your various gifts and graces, and praise your knowledge in the gospel.

3. *Manifestly declared to be the epistle of Christ.* You are in our hearts, and Christ has written you there; but yourselves are the *epistle of Christ.* The change produced in your hearts and lives, and the salvation which you have received, are as truly the work of Christ as a letter dictated and written by a man in his work. *Ministered by us.* You are the writing, but Christ used me as the pen. Christ dictated, and I wrote; and the divine characters are not made with *ink, but with the Spirit of the living God,* for the gifts and graces that constituted the mind that was in Christ are produced in you by the Holy Ghost.

Not in tables of stone. Where men engrave contracts or record events; *but in fleshy tables of the heart*—the work of salvation taking place in all your affections, appetites, and desires, working that change within that is so signally manifested without.

5. *Not that we are sufficient of ourselves.* We do not arrogate to ourselves any power to enlighten the mind or change the heart; we are only instruments in the hand of God.

6. *Who . . . hath made us able ministers.* This is a more formal answer to the question, "Who is sufficient for these things?" chap. ii. 16. God, says the apostle, has made us *able ministers;* He has made us sufficient for these things; for the reader will observe that he uses the same word in both places. We apostles execute, under the divine influence, what God himself has devised. We are ministers of the new covenant; of this new dispensation of truth, light, and life, by Christ Jesus; a system which not only proves itself to have come from God, but necessarily implies that God himself by His own Spirit is a continual Agent in it, ever bringing its mighty purposes to pass. *Not of the letter, but of the spirit.* The apostle does not

MATTHEW HENRY

I. He distinguishes between the letter and the spirit even of the New Testament, *v.* 6. They were ministers not merely of the letter, but they were ministers of the Spirit also. The *letter killeth*, but the Spirit of the gospel giveth life eternal.

II. He shows the excellency of the gospel above the law. The Old Testament dispensation was the *ministration of death* (*v.* 7), whereas that of the New Testament is the *ministration of life*.

The law was the *ministration of condemnation*, but the gospel is the *ministration of righteousness*. This reveals the grace and mercy of God through Jesus Christ, for obtaining the remission of sins and eternal life. The gospel therefore so much exceeds in glory that in a manner it eclipses the glory of the legal dispensation, *v.* 10.

JAMIESON, FAUSSET, BROWN

consisted; "but of the Spirit," i.e., *the spritual holiness* which lay under the old law, and which the new covenant brings to light (Matt. 5:17-48) with new *motives* added, and a new *power* of obedience imparted, viz., the Holy Spirit (Rom. 7:6). Even in *writing the letter* of the New Testament, Paul and the other sacred writers were ministers *not of the letter, but of the spirit.* No piety of spirit could exempt a man from the yoke of the letter of each legal ordinance under the Old Testament; for God had appointed this as the way in which He chose a devout Jew to express his state of mind towards God. Christianity, on the other hand, makes the spirit of our outward observances everything, and the letter a secondary consideration (John 4:24). Still the moral law of the ten commandments, being written by the finger of God, is as obligatory now as ever; but put more on the Gospel spirit of "love," than on the letter of a servile obedience, and in a deeper and fuller spirituality (Matt. 5:17-48; Rom. 13:9). No literal precepts could fully comprehend the wide range of holiness which LOVE, the work of the Holy Spirit, under the Gospel, suggests to the believer's heart instinctively from the word understood in its deep spirituality. **letter killeth**—by bringing home the knowledge of guilt and its punishment, *death;* vs. 7, "ministration of death" (Rom. 7:9). **spirit giveth life**—The spirit of the Gospel when brought home to the heart by the Holy Spirit, gives new spiritual life to a man (Rom. 6.4, 11). This "spirit of life" is for us in Christ Jesus (Rom. 8:2, 10), who dwells in the believer as a "quickening" or "life-giving Spirit" (I Cor. 15:45). Note, the spiritualism of rationalists is very different. It would admit no "stereotyped revelation," except so much as man's own inner instrument of revelation, the conscience and reason, can approve of: thus making the conscience judge of the written word, whereas the apostles make the written word the judge of the conscience (Acts 17:11; I Pet. 4:1). True spirituality rests on the whole written word, applied to the soul by the Holy Spirit as the only infallible interpreter of its far-reaching spirituality. The *letter* is nothing without the *spirit*, in a subject essentially spiritual. The *spirit* is nothing without the *letter*, in a record substantially historical. **7. the ministration of death**—the legal dispensation, summed up in the Decalogue, which denounces *death* against man for transgression. **written** *and* **engraven in stones**—There is no "and" in the *Greek.* The literal translation is, "The ministration of death *in letters,"* of which "engraven on stones" is an explanation. The preponderance of oldest MSS. is for the *English Version* reading. But one (perhaps the oldest existing MS.) has "in the letter," which refers to the preceding words (vs. 6), *"the letter* killeth," and this seems the probable reading. Even if we read as *English Version*, "The ministration of death (written) in letters," alludes to *the literal precepts* of the law as only bringing us the knowledge of sin and *"death,"* in contrast to *"the Spirit"* in the Gospel bringing us *"life"* (vs. 6). The opposition between "the letters" and "the Spirit" (vs. 8) confirms this. This explains why the phrase in *Greek* should be "in letters," instead of the ordinary one which *English Version* has substituted, "written *and."* **was glorious**—lit., "was made (invested) *in glory,"* glory was the atmosphere with which it was encompassed. **could not steadfastly behold**—lit., "fix their eyes on." Exodus 34:30, "The skin of his face shone; and they were AFRAID *to come nigh him."* "Could not," therefore means here, *for* FEAR. The "glory of Moses' countenance" on Sinai passed away when the occasion was over: a type of the transitory character of the dispensation which he represented (vs. 11), as contrasted with the permanency of the Christian dispensation (vs. 11). **8. be rather glorious**—lit., "be rather (i.e., still more, invested) in glory." "Shall be," i.e., shall be found to be in part now, but fully when the glory of Christ and His saints shall be revealed. **9. ministration of condemnation**—the law regarded in the "letter" which "killeth" (vs. 6; Rom. 7:9-11). The oldest existing MS. seems to read as *English Version.* But most of the almost contemporary MSS., versions, and Fathers, read, "If to the ministration of condemnation there be glory." **the ministration of righteousness**—the Gospel, which especially reveals the righteousness of God (Rom. 1:17), and imputes righteousness to men through faith in Christ (Rom. 3:21-28; 4:3, 22-25), and imparts righteousness by the Spirit (Rom. 8:1-4). **exceed**—"abound." **10.** *For even* the ministration of condemnation, the law, vs. 7 (*which has been glorified* at Sinai in Moses' person), *has* now (*English Version* translates less fitly, *"was made* . . . had") *lost its glory in this respect by reason of the surpassing glory* (of the

ADAM CLARKE

mean here, as some have imagined, that he states himself to be a minister of the New Testament, in opposition to the Old, and that it is the Old Testament that kills and the New that gives life; but that the New Testament gives the proper meaning of the Old, for the old covenant had its *letter* and its *spirit*, its "literal" and its "spiritual" meaning. The law was founded on the very supposition of the gospel; and all its sacrifices, types, and ceremonies refer to the gospel. The Jews rested in the *letter,* which not only afforded no means of life, but killed, by condemning every transgressor to death. They did not look at the *spirit,* did not endeavor to find out the spiritual meaning; and therefore they rejected Christ, who was "the end of the law" for justification, and so for redemption from death to everyone that believes. Every institution has its *letter* as well as its *spirit,* as every word must refer to something of which it is the sign or significator. The gospel has both its *letter* and its *spirit;* and multitudes of professing Christians, by resting in the letter, receive not the life which it is calculated to impart. Water, in baptism, is the *letter* that points out the purification of the soul; they who rest in this letter are without this purification; and dying in that state, they die eternally. Bread and wine in the sacrament of the Lord's Supper are the *letter;* the atoning efficacy of the death of Jesus and the grace communicated by this to the soul of a believer are the *spirit.* Multitudes rest in this *letter,* simply receiving these symbols without reference to the atonement or to their guilt, and thus lose the benefit of the atonement and the salvation of their souls.

7. *The ministration of death.* Here the apostle evidently intends the law. It was a ministration or "service" of *death.* It was the province of the law to ascertain the duty of man, to assign his duties, to fix penalties for transgressions. As man is prone to sin, and is continually committing it, this law was to him a continual *ministration of death.* Yet this *ministration of death* (the Ten Commandments, written on stones; a part of the Mosaic institutions being put for the whole) *was glorious*—was full of splendor; for the apostle refers to the thunderings, and lightnings, and luminous appearances which took place in the giving of the law, so that the very body of Moses partook of the effulgence in such a manner that the children of Israel could not look upon his face; and he, to hide it, was obliged to use a veil. All this was intended to show the excellency of that law as an institution coming immediately from God: and the apostle gives it all its heightenings, that he may compare it to the gospel, and thereby prove that, glorious as it was, it had no glory that could be compared with that of the gospel; and that even the glory it had was a glory that was to be *done away*—to be absorbed, as the light of the stars, planets, and moon, is absorbed in the splendor of the sun.

8. *The ministration of the spirit.* The gospel dispensation, which gives the true spiritual sense of the law. *Be rather glorious.* Forasmuch as the thing signified is of infinitely more consequence than that by which it is signified.

9. *The ministration of condemnation.* The law, which ascertained sin, and condemned it to just punishment. *The ministration of righteousness.* The gospel, the grand business of which was to proclaim the doctrine "of justification," and to show how God could be just and yet the Justifier of him who believes in Jesus.

10. *For even that which was made glorious.* The law, which was exhibited for a time in great glory and splendor, partly when it was given and partly by the splendor of God in the Tabernacle and first Temple. But all this ceased and was done away; was intended to give place

MATTHEW HENRY

The law is done away, but the gospel does and shall *remain*, *v.* 11. That dispensation was only to continue for a time; whereas the gospel shall remain to the end of the world.

Verses 12–18

I. The duty of the ministers of the gospel to use great clearness of speech. The gospel is a more clear dispensation than the law. Though the Israelites could not look *steadfastly to the end* of what was commanded, yet we may.

II. The privilege of those who enjoy the gospel, above those who lived under the law. Those who lived under the legal dispensation had their minds blinded (*v.* 14), and there was a *veil upon their hearts*, *v.* 15.

There is a time coming when this *veil also shall be taken away*, and *when it* (the body of that people) *shall turn to the Lord*, *v.* 16.

JAMIESON, FAUSSET, BROWN

Gospel): as the light of the stars and moon fades in the presence of the sun. **11. was glorious**—lit., "was with glory"; or "marked *by glory*." **that which remaineth**—abideth (Rev. 14:6). Not "the ministry," but the Spirit, and His accompaniments, life and righteousness. **is glorious**—lit., "is *in glory*." The *Greek* "with" or "by" is appropriately applied to that of which the glory was *transient*. "In" to that of which the glory is permanent. The contrast of the Old and New Testaments proves that Paul's chief opponents at Corinth were Judaizers. **12. such hope**—of the future glory, which shall result from the ministration of the Gospel (vss. 8, 9). **plainness of speech**—openness; without reserve (ch. 2:17; 4:2). **13.** We use no disguise, "as Moses put a veil over his face, that the children of Israel might not look steadfastly upon the end of that which was to be done away" [ELLICOTT and others]. The view of Exodus 34:30-35, according to LXX is adopted by Paul, that Moses in going in to speak to God *removed the veil till* he came out *and had spoken to the people*; and then *when he had done speaking*, he put on the veil *that they might not look on the end*, or the fading, *of that transitory glory*. The veil was the symbol of *concealment*, put on directly after Moses' speaking; so that God's revelations by him were interrupted by intervals of concealment [ALFORD]. But ALFORD's view does not accord with vs. 7; the Israelites "could not look steadfastly on the face of Moses for the glory of his countenance". Plainly Moses' veil was put on *because of* their not having been able to "look steadfastly at him." Paul here (vs. 13) passes from the literal fact to the truth symbolized by it, the blindness of Jews and Judaizers to the ultimate end of the law: stating that Moses *put on the veil that they might not look steadfastly at* (Christ, Rom. 10:4) *the end of that* (law) *which* (like Moses' glory) *is done away*. Not that *Moses* had this *purpose;* but often God attributes to His prophets the purpose which He has Himself. Because the Jews *would not see*, God judicially gave them up *so as not to see*. The glory of Moses' face is antitypically Christ's glory shining behind the veil of legal ordinances. The veil which has been taken off to the believer is left on to the unbelieving Jew, so that he should not see (Isa. 6: 10; Acts 28:26, 27). He stops short at the letter of the law, not seeing the end of it. The evangelical glory of the law, like the shining of Moses' face, cannot be borne by a carnal people, and therefore remains veiled to them until the Spirit comes to take away the veil (vss. 14-17) [CAMERON]. **14-18.** Parenthetical: *Of Christians in general*. He resumes the subject of *the ministry*, ch. 4:1. **14 minds**—*Greek*, "mental perceptions"; "understandings." **blinded**—rather, "hardened." The opposite to "looking steadfastly at the end" of the law (vs. 13). *The veil on Moses' face* is further typical of *the veil that is on their hearts*. **untaken away . . . which** *veil*—rather, "the same veil . . . remaineth untaken away [lit., *not unveiled*], so that they do not see THAT it (not the *veil* as *English Version*, but 'THE OLD TESTAMENT,' or covenant of legal ordinances) is done away (vss. 7, 11, 13) in Christ" or, as BENGEL, "Because it is done away in Christ," i.e., it is not done away save in Christ: the veil *therefore* remains untaken away from them, *because* they will not come to Christ, who does away, with the law as a mere letter. If they once saw that the law is done away in Him, the veil would be no longer on their hearts in reading it publicly in their synagogues (so "reading" means, Acts 15: 21). I prefer the former. **15. the veil is**—rather, "*a* veil *lieth* upon their *heart*" (Their understanding, affected by the corrupt will, John 8: 43; I Cor. 2:14). The Tallith was worn in the synagogue by every worshipper, and to this veil hanging over the breast there may be an indirect allusion here (*Note*, I Cor. 11:4): the apostle making it symbolize the spiritual veil on their heart. **16.** Moses took off the veil on entering into the presence of the Lord. So as to the Israelites whom Moses represents, "whensoever their heart (it) *turns* (not as *English Version*, 'shall turn') to the Lord, the veil is [by the very fact] (not as *English Version*, '*shall be*') taken away." Exodus 34:34 is the allusion; not Exodus 34:30, 31, as ALFORD thinks. Whenever the Israelites turn to the Lord, who is the Spirit of the law, the veil is taken off their hearts in the presence of the Lord: as the literal veil was taken off by Moses in going before God: no longer resting on the dead letter, *the veil*, they by the Spirit commune with God and with the inner spirit of the Mosaic covenant (which answers to the glory of *Moses' face unveiled* in God's presence). **17. the Lord**—Christ (vss. 14, 16; ch. 4:5). **is that Spirit**—is THE Spirit, viz., *that Spirit* spoken of in vs. 6,

ADAM CLARKE

to the gospel, and has actually given place to that system, so that now in no part of the world is that law performed, even by the people who are attached to it and reject the gospel. *The glory that excelleth*. The gospel dispensation, giving supereminent displays of the justice, holiness, goodness, mercy, and majesty of God.

11. *For if that which is done away*. Here is another striking difference between the law and the gospel. The former is termed that which is "counterworked and abolished"; the latter, that which "continues," which is not for a particular time, place, and people, as the law was, but for all times, all places, and all people.

12. *Seeing . . . we have such hope*. Such glorious prospects as those blessings which the gospel sets before us. *We use great plainness of speech*. We speak not only with all confidence, but with all imaginable *plainness*.

13. *And not as Moses*. The splendor of Moses' countenance was so great that the Israelites could not bear to look upon his face, and therefore he was obliged to veil his face. This, it appears, he did typically, to represent the types and shadows by which the whole dispensation of which he was the minister was covered. So that the Israelites *could not stedfastly look*—could not then have the full view or discernment of that in which the Mosaic dispensation should issue and terminate.

14. *But their minds were blinded*. By resting in the letter, shutting their eyes against the light that was granted to them, they contracted a hardness or stupidity of heart. And the veil that was on the face of Moses, which prevented the glory of his face from shining out, may be considered as emblematical of the veil of darkness and ignorance that is on their hearts, and which hinders the glory of the gospel from shining in. *In the reading of the old testament*. Here is an evident allusion to the conduct of the Jews in their synagogues. When they read the law they cover the whole head with a veil, which they term the *tallith*, "veil," from *talal*, "to cover"; and this voluntary usage of theirs, the apostle tells us, is an emblem of the darkness of their hearts while they are employed even in sacred duties. *Which veil is done away in Christ*. It is only by acknowledging *Christ* that the darkness is removed, and the end and spiritual meaning of the law discerned.

16. *When it shall turn to the Lord*. When the Israelitish nation shall turn to the Lord Jesus, the veil shall be taken away; the true light shall shine, and they shall see all things clearly. There is an evident allusion here to the case of Moses, mentioned in Exod. xxxiv. 34. When he came from the Lord and spoke to the Israelites, he put the veil over his face; but when he returned to speak with the Lord, then he took off the veil. So when the Israelitish nation shall return to speak with and pray to the Lord Jesus, the veil of darkness and ignorance shall be taken away from their hearts; but never before that time. The words seem to imply: (1) That there will be a conversion of the Jews to Christianity; and (2) That this conversion will be en masse; that a time will come when the whole nation of the Jews, in every place, shall turn to Christ; and then the Gentiles and Jews make one fold, under one Shepherd and Bishop of all souls.

17. *Now the Lord is that Spirit*. In vv. 6 and 8 the word *spirit* evidently signifies the gospel; so called because it points out the spiritual nature and meaning of the law, because it produces spiritual effects, and because it is especially the dispensation of the Spirit of God. Here Jesus Christ is represented as that *Spirit*, because He is "the end of the law" for justification to everyone that believes; and because the residue of the Spirit is with Him, and He is the Dispenser of all its gifts, graces, and influences.

MATTHEW HENRY

The condition of those who believe the gospel is much more happy. They have liberty (*v.* 17).

They have *light*; for with *open face we behold the glory of the Lord*, *v.* 18.

It was the peculiar privilege of Moses for God to converse with him face to face; but now all true Christians see him with open face. This light and liberty *are transforming* (*v.* 18), till grace here be consummated in glory for ever.

CHAPTER 4

Verses 1–7

In this chapter his design is to vindicate their ministry from the accusation of false teachers. He tells them how they believed, and how they showed their value for their office as ministers of the gospel.

I. Their constancy and perseverance in their work are declared (*v.* 1). And this their steadfastness was owing to the *mercy of God.* The best men in the world would faint in their work, and under their burdens, if they did not receive mercy from God. Their sincerity in their work is avouched (*v.* 2). They had no base and wicked designs covered with fair and specious pretences of something that was good. Nor did they in their preaching *handle the word of God deceitfully*; but they used *great plainness of speech.*

They *manifested the truth to every man's conscience*, declaring nothing but what in their own conscience they believed to be true. And all this they did *as in the sight of God*, desirous thus to commend themselves to God, and to the consciences of men.

JAMIESON, FAUSSET, BROWN

and here resumed after the parenthesis (vss. 7-16): Christ is the Spirit and "end" of the Old Testament, who giveth life to it, whereas "the letter killeth" (I Cor. 15:45; Rev. 19:10, end). **where the Spirit of the Lord is**—in a man's "heart", vs. 15; Rom. 8:9, 10). **there is liberty**—(John 8:36). "There," and *there only.* Such cease to be slaves to the letter, which they were while the veil was on their heart. They are free to serve God in the Spirit, and rejoice in Christ Jesus (Phil. 3:3): they have no longer the spirit of bondage, but of free sonship (Rom. 8:15; Gal. 4:7). "Liberty" is opposed to the letter (of the legal ordinances), and to the veil, the badge of slavery: also to the *fear* which the Israelites felt in beholding Moses' *glory unveiled* (Exod. 34:30; I John 4:18). **18. But we all**—Christians, as contrasted with the Jews who have a *veil* on their hearts, answering to Moses' veil on his face. He does not resume reference to *ministers* till ch. 4:1. **with open face**—Translate, "with *unveiled* face" (the *veil* being removed at conversion): contrasted with "hid" (ch. 4:3).

as in a glass—in a mirror, viz., the Gospel which reflects the glory of God and Christ (ch. 4: 4; I Cor. 13:12; Jas. 1:23, 25). **are changed into the same image**—viz., the image of Christ's glory, spiritually now (Rom. 8:29; I John 3:3); an earnest of the bodily change hereafter (Phil. 3:21). However many they be, believers all reflect the *same* image of Christ more or less: a proof of the truth of Christianity. **from glory to glory**—from one degree of glory to another. As Moses' face caught a reflection of God's glory from being in His presence, so believers are changed into His image by beholding Him. **even as . . .**—Just such a transformation "*as*" was to be expected from "the Lord the Spirit" (not as *English Version,* "the Spirit of the Lord") [ALFORD] (vs. 17): "who receives of the things of Christ, and shows them to us" (John 16:14; Rom. 8:10, 11). (Cf. as to hereafter, Ps. 17:15; Rev. 22:4.)

CHAPTER 4

Vss. 1-18. HIS PREACHING IS OPEN AND SINCERE, THOUGH TO MANY THE GOSPEL IS HIDDEN; for he preaches Christ, not himself: the human vessel is frail that God may have the glory; yet, though frail, faith and the hope of future glory sustain him amidst the decay of the outward man. **1. Therefore**—*Greek,* "For this cause": Because we have the liberty-giving Spirit of the Lord, and with unveiled face behold His glory (ch. 3:17, 18). **seeing we have this ministry**—"The ministration of the Spirit" (ch. 3:8, 9): the ministry of such a spiritual, liberty-giving Gospel: resuming ch. 3:6, 8. **received mercy**—from God, in having had *this ministry* conferred on us (ch. 3:5). The sense of "mercy" received from God, makes men active for God (I Tim. 1:11-13). **we faint not**—in boldness of speech and action, and patience in suffering (vss. 2, 8-16, etc.). **2. renounced**—lit., "bid farewell to." **of dishonesty**—rather, "of shame." "I am not *ashamed* of the Gospel of Christ" (Rom. 1:16). Shame would lead to *hiding* (vs. 3); whereas "we use great plainness of speech" (ch. 3:12; "by *manifestation* of the truth." Cf. ch. 3:3, "*manifestly declared.*" He refers to the disingenuous artifices of "many" teachers at Corinth (ch. 2:17; 3:1; 11:13-15). **handling . . . deceitfully**—so "corrupt" or *adulterate* "the word of God" (ch. 2:17; cf. I Thess. 2:3, 4).

commending—recommending ourselves: recurring to ch. 3:1. **to**—to the verdict of. **every man's conscience**—(ch. 5:11). Not to men's carnal judgment, as those alluded to (ch. 3:1). **in the sight of God**—(ch. 2:17; Gal. 1: 10).

ADAM CLARKE

And where the Spirit of the Lord is. Wherever this gospel is received, there the Spirit of the Lord is given; and wherever that Spirit lives and works, there is *liberty,* not only from Jewish bondage, but from the slavery of sin—from its power, its guilt, and its pollution.

18. *But we all, with open face.* The Jews were not able to look on the face of Moses, the mediator of the old covenant, and therefore he was obliged to veil it. But all we Christians, with face uncovered, behold, as clearly as we can see our own natural face in a "mirror," the glorious promises and privileges of the gospel of Christ; and while we contemplate, we anticipate them by desire and hope, and apprehend them by faith, and *are changed* from the glory there represented to the enjoyment of the thing which is represented, even the glorious image—righteousness and true holiness—of the God of glory. *As by the Spirit of the Lord.* By the energy of that Spirit of Christ which gives life and being to all the promises of the gospel; and thus we are made partakers of the divine nature and escape all the corruptions that are in the world. This appears to me to be the general sense of this verse; its peculiar terms may be more particularly explained. The word *katoptrizomenoi,* which we translate *beholding . . . in a glass,* comes from *kata,* "against," and *optomai,* "I look"; and properly conveys the sense of looking into a mirror, or discerning by reflected light. Now as mirrors, among the Jews, Greeks, and Romans, were made of highly polished metal (see the note on 1 Cor. xiii. 12), it would often happen, especially in strong light, that the face would be greatly illuminated by this strongly reflected light; and to this circumstance the apostle seems here to allude. So by earnestly contemplating the gospel of Jesus and believing on Him who is its Author, the soul becomes illuminated with His divine splendor, for this sacred mirror reflects back on the believing soul the image of Him whose perfections it exhibits; and thus we see the glorious form after which our minds are to be fashioned. And by believing and receiving the influence of His Spirit our form is *changed into the same image,* which we behold there; and this is the image of God, lost by our fall, and now recovered and restored by Jesus Christ.

CHAPTER 4

1. *Seeing we have this ministry.* The gospel, of which he gave that noble account which we read in the preceding chapter. *We faint not.* We meet with many tribulations, but are supported in and through all by the grace of the gospel. Instead of *ouk ekkakoumen, we faint not, enkakoumen,* "we act not wickedly," is the reading of some MSS. Wakefield thinks it the genuine reading; it certainly makes very good sense with what goes before and what follows. If we follow this reading the whole verse may be read thus: "Wherefore, as we have obtained mercy, or been graciously entrusted, with this ministry, we do not act wickedly, but have renounced the hidden things of dishonesty."

2. *But have renounced.* We have disclaimed *the hidden things of dishonesty;* "the hidden things of shame." *Not walking in craftiness.* In "subtlety" and "clever cunning," as the false teachers did. *Nor handling the word of God deceitfully.* Not using the doctrines of the gospel to serve any secular or carnal purpose; not explaining away their force so as to palliate or excuse sin; not generalizing its precepts so as to excuse many in particular circumstances from obedience, especially in that which most crossed their inclinations. There were deceitful handlers of this kind in Corinth, and there are many of them still in the garb of Christian ministers; persons who disguise that part of their creed which, though they believe it is of God, would make them unpopular; affecting moderation in order to procure a larger audience and more extensive support; not attacking prevalent and popular vices; calling dissipation of mind "relaxation," and worldly and carnal pleasures "innocent amusements." *Commending ourselves to every man's conscience.* Speaking so that every man's conscience shall bear its testimony that we proclaim the truth of God. This is one characteristic of divine truth: even

MATTHEW HENRY

II. An objection is obviated. "How then does it come to pass, that the gospel is hid, as to some who hear it?" The true reasons of this are, 1. *Those are lost souls* to whom the gospel is hid, *v.* 3. 2. *The god of this world hath blinded their minds, v.* 4. They are under the influence of the devil, who is here called *the god of this world,* because of the great interest he has in this world. And as he is the prince of darkness, and ruler of the darkness of this world, so he darkens the understandings of men. Christ's design by his gospel is to make a glorious discovery of God to the minds of men. The design of the devil is to keep men in ignorance.

III. A proof of their integrity is given, *v.* 5. They made it their business to preach Christ and not themselves. But they *preached Christ Jesus the Lord,* as being Christ's servants. All the lines of Christian doctrine centre in Christ; and in preaching Christ we preach all we should preach. Ministers should not be of proud spirits who are servants to the souls of men: yet, at the same time, they must avoid becoming the servants of the humours or the lusts of men. Why they should preach Christ. For by gospel light we have the *knowledge of the glory of God,* which shines in the *face of Jesus Christ, v.* 6. It is a pleasant thing for the eye to behold the sun in the firmament; but it is more pleasant and profitable when the gospel shines in the heart.

Why they should not preach themselves: because they were but earthen vessels. The ministers of the gospel are weak and frail creatures; they are mortal, and soon broken in pieces. And God has so ordered it that the weaker the vessels are the stronger his power may appear to be, that the treasure itself should be valued the more.

Verses 8–18

I. How their sufferings, and patience under them, are declared, *v.* 8–12. "*We are troubled on every side, yet not distressed,*" *v.* 8. We can see help in God, and help from God.

JAMIESON, FAUSSET, BROWN

3. But if—Yea, even if (as I grant is the case). **hid**—rather (in reference to ch. 3:13-18), "veiled." "Hid" (*Greek,* Col. 3:3) is said of that withdrawn from view altogether. "Veiled," of a thing within reach of the eye, but *covered* over so as not to be seen. So it was in the case of Moses' face. **to them**—in the case only of them: for *in itself* the Gospel is quite plain. **that are lost**—rather, "that are perishing" (I Cor. 1:18). So the same cloud that was "light" to the people of God, was "darkness" to the Egyptian foes of God (Exod. 14:20). **4. In whom**—Translate, "In whose case." **god of this world**—The worldly *make him their God* (Phil. 3:19). He is, *in fact,* the prince of the power of the air, *the spirit that ruleth in the children of disobedience*" (Eph. 2:2). **minds**—"understandings": "mental perceptions," as in ch. 3:14. **them which believe not**—the same as "them that are lost" (or "are perishing"). Cf. II Thessalonians 2:10-12. SOUTH quaintly says, "when the malefactor's eyes are covered, he is not far from his execution" (Esther 7:8). Those perishing unbelievers are not merely *veiled,* but blinded (ch. 3:14, 15): *Greek,* not "blinded," but "*hardened.*" **light of the glorious gospel of Christ**—Translate, "The illumination (*enlightening:* the *propagation* from those already enlightened, to others *of the light*) of the Gospel of the glory of Christ." "The glory of Christ" is not a mere *quality* (as "glorious" would express) of the Gospel; it is its very *essence and subject matter.* **image of God**—implying identity of nature and essence (John 1:18; Col. 1:15; Heb. 1:3). He who desires to see "the glory of God," may see it "in the face of Jesus Christ" (vs. 6; I Tim. 6:14-16). Paul here recurs to ch. 3:18. Christ is "the image of God," into which "same image" we, looking on it in the mirror of the Gospel, are changed by the Spirit; but this image is not visible to those blinded by Satan [ALFORD]. **5. For**—Their blindness is not our fault, as if we had selfseeking aims in our preaching. **preach . . . Christ . . . the Lord**—rather, "Christ *as Lord,*" and ourselves as your servants. . . . "*Lord,*" or *Master,* is the correlative term to "servants." **6. For**—proof that we are true servants of Jesus unto you. **commanded the light**—*Greek,* "By speaking the word, commanded light" (Gen. 1:3). **hath shined**—rather, *as Greek,* "*is He who* shined." (It *is God*) *who commanded light,* etc., *that shined,* etc., (Job 37:15): Himself our Light and Sun, as well as the Creator of light (Mal. 4:2; John 8:12). The physical world answers to the spiritual. **in our hearts**—in themselves dark. **to give the light**—i.e., to propagate *to others* the light, etc., *which is in us* (cf. *Note,* vs. 4). **the glory of God**—answering to "the glory of Christ" (*Note,* vs. 4). **in the face of Jesus Christ**—Some of the oldest MSS. retain "Jesus." Others omit it. Christ is the manifestation of the glory of God, as His image (John 14:9). The allusion is still to the brightness on Moses' "face." The only true and full manifestation of God's brightness and glory is "in the face of Jesus" (Heb. 1:3). **7.** "Lest any should say, How then is it that we continue to enjoy *such unspeakable glory* in a mortal body? Paul replies, this very fact is one of the most marvellous proofs of God's power, that an earthen vessel could bear such splendor and keep *such a treasure*" [CHRYSOSTOM, *Homilies,* 8. 496, A.]. The treasure or "the light of the knowledge of the glory of God." The fragile "earthen vessel" is the *body,* the "outward man" (vs. 16; cf. vs. 10), liable to afflictions and death. So the light in Gideon's pitchers, the type (Judg. 7:16-20, 22). The ancients often kept their treasures in jars or vessels of earthenware. "There are earthen vessels which yet may be clean; whereas a golden vessel may be filthy" [BENGEL]. **that the excellency of the power . . .**—that the *power* of the ministry (the Holy Spirit), in respect to its surpassing "excellency," exhibited in winning souls (I Cor. 2:4) and in sustaining us ministers, might be ascribed solely to God, we being weak as earthen vessels. God often allows the vessel to be chipped and broken, that the excellency of the treasure contained, and of the power which that treasure has, may be all His (vss. 10, 11; John 3:30). **may be of God . . . not of us**—rather, as *Greek,* "may be *God's* (may be seen and be thankfully (vs. 15) acknowledged to *belong* to God), and not (to come) *from* us." The power not merely comes *from* God, but *belongs to* Him continually, and is to be ascribed to him. **8.** *Greek,* "BEING hard pressed, yet not inextricably straitened; reduced to inextricable straits" (nominative to "we have,' vs. 7). **on every side**—*Greek,* "in every respect" (cf. vs. 10, "always"; ch. 7:5). This verse expresses *inward* distresses; next verse, *outward* distresses (ch. 7:5). "*Without* were fightings; *within* were fears." The first clause in each member of the series of con-

ADAM CLARKE

every man's *conscience* will acknowledge it, though it speak decidedly against his own practices.

3. *But if our gospel be hid.* "Veiled"; he refers to the subject that he had treated so particularly in the conclusion of the preceding chapter. If there be a veil on the gospel, it is only to the willfully blind; and if any man's heart be veiled that hears this gospel, it is a proof that he is among the *lost.* The word does not necessarily imply those that will perish eternally, but is a common epithet to point out a man without the gospel and without God in the world. Christ commands His disciples in preaching the gospel to go "to the lost sheep of the house of Israel," Matt. x. 6; for himself says, Matt. xviii. 11 and Luke xix. 10: "The Son of man is come to seek and to save that which was lost." The word more properly signifies, not those who are *lost,* but those who "are perishing"; and will perish, if not sought and saved.

5. *For we preach not ourselves.* We proclaim neither our own wisdom nor our own power; we have nothing but what we have received; we do not wish to establish our own authority nor to procure our own emolument. *But Christ Jesus the Lord.* We proclaim the Author of this glorious gospel as Christ, the same as *hammashiach,* the Messiah, the "Anointed One"; Him of whom the prophets wrote; and who is the Expectation, as He is the Glory, of Israel. We proclaim Him as Jesus, *Yehoshua,* the "Saviour" and "Deliverer," who saves men from their sins. And further, we proclaim this Jesus, the Messiah, to be the Lord, the great Ruler who has all power in heaven and earth, who made and governs the world, and who can save to the uttermost all that come to God through Him. *And ourselves your servants.* Laboring as fervently and as faithfully for your eternal interests as your most trusty slaves can do for your secular welfare. And we do this for Christ's sake. For although we by our labor show ourselves to be your *servants,* yea, your "slaves," yet it is a voluntary service; and we are neither employed by you nor receive our wages from you. We belong to Jesus; and are your servants on His account, and by His order.

6. *For God, who commanded the light to shine out of darkness.* The apostle refers here to Gen. i. 3. For when God created the heavens and the earth, "darkness was upon the face of the deep. . . . And God said, Let there be light: and there was light." Thus He caused *the light to shine out of darkness. Hath shined in our hearts.* He has given our *hearts* the glorious light of the gospel, as He has given the world the glorious light of the sun. It is in the "appearance" and "person" of Jesus Christ that these blessings are communicated to us.

7. *But we have this treasure in earthen vessels.* The original signifies more literally *vessels* made of shells, which are very brittle. The word *ostracon* not only signifies a shell, or vessel made of shell, but also *earthen vessels* which have been burnt in the kiln, and earthen vessels or pottery in general.

That the excellency of the power may be of God, and not of us. God keeps us continually dependent upon himself. The good therefore that is done is so evidently from the power of God that none can pretend to share the glory with Him.

8. *We are troubled on every side.* We have already seen, in the notes on the ninth chapter of the preceding Epistle, that Paul has made several allusions to those public games which were celebrated every fifth year at the Isthmus of Corinth. In this and the following three verses the apostle makes allusion to the contests at those games, and the terms which he employs in

MATTHEW HENRY

"We are *perplexed, yet not in despair* (*v.* 8), knowing that God is able to support us, and to deliver us. We are *persecuted*; yet *not forsaken* of God," *v.* 9. "We are *cast down*; yet we are *not destroyed*," *v.* 9. Still they were preserved, and kept their heads above water. Whatever condition the children of God may be in. in this world they have a "*but not*" to comfort themselves with. The apostle speaks of their sufferings as a counterpart of the sufferings of Christ, *v.* 10.

Thus did they *bear about the dying of the Lord Jesus* in their body, *that the life of Jesus might also be made manifest*, though they were always *delivered to death* (*v.* 11), and though *death worked in them* (*v.* 12). *Death worketh in us; but life in you*, *v.* 12.

II. What it was that kept them from sinking and fainting under their sufferings, *v.* 13–18.

1. Faith kept them from fainting (*v.* 13). The grace of faith is a sovereign cordial against fainting-fits in troublous times. As the apostle had David's example to imitate, who said (Ps. cxvi. 10), *I have believed, and therefore have I spoken*, so he leaves us his example to imitate: *We also believe*, says he, *and therefore speak*.

2. Hope of the resurrection kept them from sinking, *v.* 14. Their hope was firm, being well grounded, that he who raised up Christ the head will also raise up all his members. What reason has a good Christian to fear death, that dies in hope of a joyful resurrection?

3. The consideration of the benefit of the church kept them from fainting, *v.* 15. We may well afford to bear sufferings patiently when we see others are the better for them.

JAMIESON, FAUSSET, BROWN

trasted participles, implies the *earthiness* of the *vessels;* the second clause, *the excellency of the power*. **perplexed, but not in despair**—*Greek*, "*not utterly* perplexed." As *perplexity* refers to the future, so "troubled" or "hard pressed" refers to the present. **9. not forsaken**—by God and man. Jesus was forsaken by both; so much do His sufferings exceed those of His people (Matt. 27:46). **cast down**—or "struck down"; not only "persecuted," i.e., *chased* as a deer or bird (I Sam. 26:20), but actually *struck* down as with a dart in the chase (Heb. 11:35-38). The *Greek* "always" in this verse means, "throughout the whole time"; in vs. 11 the *Greek* is different, and means, "at every time," "in every case when the occasion occurs." **bearing about in the body the dying of the Lord Jesus**—i.e., having my body exposed to being put to death in the cause of Jesus (the oldest MSS. omit "the Lord"), and having in it the marks of such sufferings, I thus bear about wheresoever I go, an image of the suffering Saviour in my own person (vs. 11; ch. 1:5; cf. I Cor. 15:31). Doubtless, Paul was exposed to more dangers than are recorded in Acts (cf. ch. 7:5; 11:26). The *Greek* for "the dying" is lit., "the being made a *corpse*", such Paul regarded his body, yet a corpse which shares in the life-giving power of Christ's resurrection, as it has shared in His dying and death. **that the life also of Jesus might be made manifest in our body**—rather, "may be." The name "Jesus," by itself is often repeated here as Paul seems, amidst sufferings, peculiarly to have felt its sweetness. In vs. 11 the same words occur with the variation, "in our *mortal flesh*." The fact of a dying, corpse-like body being sustained amidst such trials, manifests that "the (resurrection) life also," as well as the dying, "of Jesus," exerts its power in us. I thus bear about in my own person an image of the risen and *living*, as well as of the suffering, Saviour. The "our" is added here to "body," though not in the beginning of the verse. "For the body is *ours* not so much in death, as in life" [BENGEL]. **11. we which live**—in the power of Christ's "life" manifested in us, in our whole man, body as well as spirit (Rom. 8:10, 11; *Note*, vs. 10; cf. ch. 5:15). Paul regards his preservation amidst so many exposures to "death," by which Stephen and James were cut off, as a standing miracle (ch. 11:23). **delivered unto**——not by chance; by the ordering of Providence, who shows "the excellency of His power" (vs. 7), in *delivering unto* DEATH His living saints, that He may manifest LIFE also in their dying flesh. "Flesh," the very element of decay (not merely their "body"), is by Him made to manifest *life*. **12.** The "*death*" of Christ manifested in the continual "perishing of our outward man" (vs. 16), works peculiarly in us, and is the means of working *spiritual* "*life*" in you. The *life* whereof we witness in our bodily *dying*, extends beyond ourselves, and is brought by our very dying to you. **13.** Translate as *Greek*, "BUT having..." i.e., not withstanding the trials just mentioned, we having... **the same spirit of faith, according as it...**—Cf. Romans 8:15, on the usage of "spirit of..." The Holy Spirit acting on our spirit. Though "death worketh in us, and life in you" (vs. 12), yet *as we have the same spirit of faith as you*, we therefore [believingly] look for the same immortal *life* as you [ESTIUS], and *speak* as we believe. ALFORD not so well translates, "The *same* ... faith *with that described* in the Scriptures" (Ps. 116:10). The balance of the sentence requires the parallelism to be this, "According to that which is written, I believed, and therefore have I spoken; we also believe, and therefore speak," viz., without fear, amidst "afflictions" and "deaths" (vs. 17). **14. Knowing**—by faith (ch. 5:1). **shall raise up us also**—at the resurrection (I Cor. 6:13, 14). **by Jesus**—The oldest MSS. have "*with* Jesus." **present us**—vividly picturing the scene before the eyes (Jude 24). **with you**—(ch. 1:14; I Thess. 2:19, 20; 3:13). **15. For**—Confirming his assertion "with you" (vs. 14), and "life ... worketh in you" (vs. 12). **all things**—whether the afflictions and labors of us ministers (vss. 8-11), or your prosperity (vs. 12; I Cor. 3:21, 22; 4:8-13). **for your sakes**—(II Tim. 2:10). **abundant grace...**—rather, "That grace (*the* grace which preserves us in trials and works life in you), being made the greater (multiplied), by means of the greater number (of its recipients), may cause the thanksgiving to abound to..." [CHRYSOSTOM] (ch. 1:11; 9:11, 12). The *Greek* is susceptible also of this translation, "That grace, being made the greater (multiplied) on account of the thanksgiving of the greater number (for grace already received), may abound (abundantly redound) to..." Thus the *Greek* for "abound" has not to be taken in an active sense, but in its ordinary neuter sense, and so the other *Greek* words. Thanksgiving invites more

ADAM CLARKE

these verses cannot be understood but in reference to those agonistical exercises to which he alludes. Dr. Hammond has explained the whole on this ground, and I shall here borrow his help. There are four pairs of expressions taken from the customs of the *agones*: (1) *Troubled on every side, yet not distressed.* (2) *Perplexed, but not in despair.* (3) *Persecuted, but not forsaken.* (4) *Cast down, but not destroyed.* Three of these pairs belong to the customs of wrestling; the fourth, to that of running in the race. *Troubled on every side.* The word *thlibesthai* belongs clearly to expressions wrestling. *Perplexed, but not in despair.* The word "to be in perplexity" is fit for the wrestler, who being puzzled by his antagonist's skill knows not what to do.

9. *Persecuted, but not forsaken.* The *pursued* (*diokomenoi*) is peculiar to the race, when one being foremost others pursue, and get up close after him, endeavoring to outstrip him, but cannot succeed. This is the meaning of not "outstripped," or "outgone," as the word implies. *Cast down, but not destroyed.* This also belongs to wrestlers, where he that throws the other first is conqueror. And then, the being not *destroyed* signifies that, although they were "thrown down"—cast into troubles and difficulties—yet they rose again, and surmounted them all.

10. *Always bearing about in the body.* Being every moment in danger of losing our lives in the cause of truth, as Jesus Christ was. There is probably an allusion here to the marks, wounds, and bruises which the contenders in those games got, and continued to carry throughout life.

11. *For we which live.* And yet, although we are preserved alive, we are in such continual dangers that we carry our life in our hands, and are constantly in the spirit of sacrifice. But the *life*, the preserving power, of Christ is manifest in our continual support.

12. *Death worketh in us.* We apostles are in continual danger, and live a dying life, while you who have received this gospel from us are in no danger.

13. *We having the same spirit of faith.* As David had when he wrote Ps. cxvi. 10: "I believed, therefore have I spoken." *We also believe* that we shall receive the fulfillment of all God's promises; and being fully convinced of the truth of the Christian religion, we *speak* and testify that our deliverance is from God.

14. *Knowing that he which raised up the Lord.* And though we shall at last seal this truth with our blood, we fear not, being persuaded that as the body of Christ was raised from the dead by the power of the Father, so shall our bodies be raised, and that we shall have an eternal life with Him in glory.

15. *For all things are for your sakes.* We proclaim all these truths and bear all these sufferings for your sakes. *That the abundant grace.* The "abounding benefit"—the copious outpouring of the gifts and graces of the Holy Spirit, by which you have been favored and enriched, may *through the thanksgiving of many redound to the glory of God;* i.e., that the gratitude of the multitudes which have been converted may keep pace with the blessings which they have received, and "abound," as these blessings have abounded.

MATTHEW HENRY

4. The thoughts of the advantage their souls would reap kept them from fainting, *v.* 16. It is our happiness if when the body is sick the soul is vigorous. The best of men have need of further renewing of the inward man, even day by day. As in wicked men things grow every day worse and worse, so in godly men they grow better and better.

5. The prospect of eternal life and happiness kept them from fainting. The apostle and his fellow-sufferers saw their afflictions working towards heaven, and that they would end at last (*v.* 17), whereupon they weighed things aright in the balance of the sanctuary. They found afflictions to be light, and the glory of heaven to be *a far more exceeding weight*. That which sense was ready to pronounce heavy and long, faith perceived to be light and short, and but for a moment. Their faith enabled them to make this right judgment of things, *v.* 18. Unseen things are eternal, seen things but temporal. By faith we not only discern these things, and the great difference between them, but by this also we take our aim at unseen things.

JAMIESON, FAUSSET, BROWN

abundant grace (II Chron. 20:19-22; Ps. 18:3; 50: 23). **16. we faint not**—notwithstanding our sufferings. Resuming vs. 1. **outward man**—the body, the flesh. **perish**—"is wearing away"; "is wasted away" by afflictions. **inward man**—our spiritual and true being, the "life" which even in our mortal bodies (vs. 11) "manifests the life of Jesus." **is renewed**—"is being renewed," viz., with fresh "grace" (vs. 15), and "faith" (vs. 13), and hope (vss. 17, 18). **17. which is but for a moment**—"Our PRESENT light (burden of) affliction" (so the *Greek;* cf. Matt. 11:30), [ALFORD]. Cf. "*now for a season* . . . in heaviness" (I Pet. 1:6). The contrast, however, between this and the "ETERNAL weight of glory" requires, I think, the translation, "Which is but for *the present passing moment.*" So WAHL. "The *lightness* of affliction" (he does not *express* "burden" after "light"; the *Greek* is "the light of affliction") contrasts beautifully with the "*weight* of the glory." **worketh**—rather, "worketh out." **a far more exceeding and**—rather, "in a surpassing and still more surpassing manner" [ALFORD]; "more and more exceedingly" [ELLICOTT, TRENCH, and others]. *Greek,* "in excess and to excess." The glory exceeds beyond all measure the affliction. **18. look not at**—as our aim. **things . . . seen**—"earthly things" (Phil. 3:19). We mind not the things seen, whether affliction or refreshment come, so as to be seduced by the latter, or deterred by the former [CHRYSOSTOM]. **things . . . not seen**—not "the invisible things" of Romans 1:20, but the things which, though not seen now, shall be so hereafter. **temporal**—rather, "for a time"; in contrast to eternal. *English Version* uses "temporal" for *temporary.* The *Greek* is rightly translated in the similar passage, "the pleasures of sin *for a season.*"

ADAM CLARKE

16. *For which cause we faint not.* See on v. 1. Here we have the same various reading, "We do no wickedness"; and it is supported by a member of MSS. The common reading, *faint not,* appears to agree best with the apostle's meaning. *But though our outward man.* That is, our bodies, that part of us that can be seen, heard, and felt. *Perish*—be slowly consumed by continual trials and afflictions, and be martyred at last. *Yet the inward man.* Our soul, that which cannot be felt or seen by others, *is renewed,* is "revived," and receives a daily increase of light and life from God.

17. *For our light affliction.* "It is everywhere visible what influence Paul's Hebrew had on his Greek: *cabad* signifies to be 'heavy,' and to be 'glorious'; the apostle in his Greek unites these two significations, and says, *weight of glory.*"

18. *While we look not at the things which are seen.* While we "aim not" at the things which are seen, do not make them our object, are not striving to obtain them; for they are not worthy the pursuit of an immortal spirit, because they are seen, they are "temporary," they are to have a short duration. But the things which we make our scope and aim are *not seen;* they are spiritual, and therefore invisible to the eye of the body; and besides, they are *eternal,* things that are permanent, that can have no end. Afflictions may be means of preparing us for glory if, during them, we receive grace to save the soul; but afflictions of themselves have no spiritual nor saving tendency. On the contrary, they sour the unregenerated mind and cause murmurings against the dispensations of divine providence.

CHAPTER 5

MATTHEW HENRY

Verses 1–11

I. He mentions their expectation, and desire, and assurance, of eternal happiness, *v.* 1–5.

1. The believer's expectation of eternal happiness after death, *v.* 1. "We know that we have a building of God, we have a firm expectation of the future felicity." (1) What heaven is in the eye and hope of a believer. He looks upon it as a house, or habitation, our Father's house, and our everlasting home. It is a house in the heavens. It is a building of God. It is eternal in the heavens, not like the earthly tabernacles, the poor cottages of clay in which our souls now dwell.

(2) When it is expected this happiness shall be enjoyed—so soon as *our house of this earthly tabernacle is dissolved.* Then comes the house not made with hands. Such as have walked with God here shall dwell with God for ever.

JAMIESON, FAUSSET, BROWN

Vss. 1-21. THE HOPE (ch. 4:17, 18) OF ETERNAL GLORY IN THE RESURRECTION BODY. Hence arises his ambition to be accepted at the Lord's coming judgment. Hence, too, his endeavor to deal openly with men, as with God, in preaching; thus giving the Corinthians whereof to boast concerning him against his adversaries. His constraining motive is the transforming love of Christ, by whom God has wrought reconciliation between Himself and men, and has committed to the apostle the ministry of reconciliation. **1. For**—Assigning the reason for the statement (ch. 4:17), that *affliction* leads to *exceeding glory.* **we know**—assuredly (ch. 4:14; Job 19:25). **if**—For *all* shall not die; many shall be "changed" without "dissolution" (I Cor. 15:51-53). If this daily *delivering unto death* (ch. 3:11) should end in actual death. **earthly**—not the same as *earthy* (I Cor. 15:47). It stands in contrast to "in the heavens." **house of *this* tabernacle**—rather, "house of the tabernacle." "House" expresses more *permanency* than belongs to the body; therefore the qualification, "of the tabernacle" (implying that it is *shifting,* not stationary), is added (cf. Job 4:19; II Pet. 1:13, 14). It thus answers to the tabernacle in the wilderness. Its wooden frame and curtains wore out in course of time when Israel dwelt in Canaan, and a fixed temple was substituted for it. The temple and the tabernacle in all essentials were one; there was the same ark, the same cloud of glory. Such is the relation between the "earthly" body and the resurrection body. The Holy Spirit is enshrined in the believer's body as in a sanctuary (I Cor. 3:16). As the ark went first in taking down the wilderness tabernacle, so the soul (which like the ark is sprinkled with blood of atonement, and is the sacred deposit in the inmost shrine, II Tim. 1:12) in the dissolution of the body; next the coverings were removed, answering to the flesh; lastly, the framework and boards, answering to the bones, which are last to give way (Num. 4). Paul, as a *tentmaker,* uses an image taken from his trade (Acts 18:3). **dissolved**—a mild word for death, in the case of believers. **we have**—in *assured* prospect of possession, as certain as if it were in our hands, laid up "in the heavens" for us. The tense is *present* (cf. John 3:36; 6:47, "*hath*"). **a building of God**—rather "*from* God." A solid *building,* not a temporary *tabernacle* or *tent.* "*Our*" body stands in contrast to "*from God.*" For though our present body be also *from God,* yet it is not fresh and perfect from His hands, as our resurrection body shall be. **not made with hands**—contrasted with houses erected by *man's* hands (I Cor. 15:44-49). So Christ's body is designated, as contrasted with the tabernacle reared by Moses (Mark 14:58; Heb. 9:11). This "house" can only be the *resurrection*

ADAM CLARKE

1. *If our earthly house of this tabernacle.* By *earthly house* the apostle most evidently means the body in which the soul is represented as dwelling or sojourning for a time, and from which it is to be liberated at death. The apostle also alludes here to the ancient Jewish Tabernacle, which, on all removals of the congregation, was *dissolved* and taken in pieces; and the ark of the covenant, covered with its own curtains, was carried by itself; and when they came to the place of rest, then the dissolved parts of the Tabernacle were put together as before.

When we consider this simile in connection with the doctrine of the resurrection, then we shall see that he intends to convey the following meaning: that as the Tabernacle was taken down in order to be again put together, so the body is to be *dissolved,* in order to be reedified; that as the ark of the covenant subsisted by itself, while the Tabernacle was down, so can the soul when separated from the body; that as the ark had then its own veil for its covering, Exod. xl. 21, so the soul is to have some vehicle in which it shall subsist till it receives its body at the resurrection.

MATTHEW HENRY

2. The believer's earnest desire after this future blessedness—*we groan.* (1) A groaning of sorrow under a heavy load, *v.* 2. *We that are in this tabernacle groan, being burdened, v.* 4. Believers groan because burdened with a body of sin. (2) There is a groaning of desire after the happiness of another life; and thus believers groan. The believer is *willing rather to be absent from the body, that he may be present with the Lord* (*v.* 8), to put off these rags of mortality that he may put on the robes of glory. Gracious souls are not found naked in the other world; no, they are clothed with garments of praise.

3. The believer's assurance of this future blessedness, from the experience of the grace of God, making him meet for this blessedness, *v.* 5. All who are designed for heaven hereafter are wrought or prepared for heaven while they are here; the stones of that spiritual building above are squared and fashioned here below. No hand less than the hand of God can work us for this thing. The *earnest of the Spirit* gave them this assurance.

II. An inference for the comfort of believers in their present state in this world, *v.* 6-8. What their present state is: they *are absent from the Lord* (*v.* 6).

God is with us here, yet we are not with him as we hope to be: *For we walk by faith, not by sight, v.* 7. Faith is for this world, and sight is reserved for the other world. How comfortable and courageous we ought to be in the hour of death (*v.* 6) and again (*v.* 8). They should be willing rather to die than live, when it is the will of God that they should *put off this tabernacle,* to close their eyes to all things in this world, and open them in a world of glory. Faith will be turned into sight.

JAMIESON, FAUSSET, BROWN

body, in contrast to the "earthly house of the tabernacle," our present body. The intermediate state is not *directly* taken into account. A comma should separate "eternal," and "in the heavens." **2. For in this**—*Greek,* "For *also* in this"; "herein" (ch. 8: 10). ALFORD takes it, "in this" tabernacle. Verse 4, which seems parallel, favors this. But the parallelism is sufficiently exact by making "in this we groan" refer generally to what was just said (vs. 1), viz., that we cannot obtain our "house in the heavens" except our "earthly tabernacle" be first dissolved by death. **we groan** (Rom. 8:23) under the body's weaknesses now and liability to death. **earnestly desiring to be clothed upon**—translate, "earnestly *longing* to *have ourselves clothed upon* . . ," viz., by being found *alive* at Christ's coming, and so to escape *dissolution* by death (vss. 1, 4), and to have our heavenly body put on over the earthly. The groans of the saints prove the existence of the longing desire for the heavenly glory, a desire which cannot be planted by God within us in vain, as doomed to disappointment. **our house**—different *Greek* from that in vs. 1; translate, "our habitation," "our domicile"; it has a more distinct reference to the *inhabitant* than the general term "house" (vs. 1) [BENGEL]. **from heaven**—This domicile is "*from heaven*" in its origin, and is to be brought to us by the Lord at His coming again "from heaven" (I Thess. 4:16). Therefore this "habitation" or "domicile" is not heaven itself. **3. If so be . . .**—Our "desire" holds good, should the Lord's coming find us alive. Translate, "If so be that having ourselves clothed (with our natural body, cf. vs. 4) we shall not be found naked" (stripped of our present body). **4. For**—resuming vs. 2. **burdened; not for that**—rather, "*in that* we desire *not* to have ourselves unclothed (of our present body), but clothed upon" (with our heavenly body). **that mortality . . .**—rather, "that what is mortal (our mortal part) may be swallowed up of (absorbed and transformed into) life." Believers shrink from, not the *consequences,* but the mere *act* of dying; especially as believing in the possibility of their being found alive at the Lord's coming (I Thess. 4:15), and so of having their mortal body absorbed into the immortal without death. Faith does not divest us of all natural feeling, but subordinates it to higher feeling. Scripture gives no sanction to the contempt for the body expressed by philosophers. **5. wrought us**—framed us by redemption, justification, and sanctification. **for the selfsame thing**—"unto" it; viz., unto what is mortal of us being swallowed up in life (vs. 4). **who also**—The oldest MSS. omit "also." **earnest of the Spirit**—(*Note,* ch. 1:22). It is the Spirit (as "the first fruits") who creates in us the groaning desire for our coming deliverance and glory (Rom. 8:23). **6.** Translate as *Greek,* "Being therefore always confident and knowing . . . ." He had intended to have made the verb to this nominative, "we are willing" (rather, "well content"), but digressing on the word "confident" (vss. 6, 7), he resumes the word in a different form, viz., as an assertion: "We are confident and well content." "Being confident . . . . we are confident" may be the *Hebraic* idiom of emphasis; as Acts 7:34, *Greek,* "Having seen, I have seen," i.e., I have *surely seen.* **always**—under all trials. BENGEL makes the contrast between "*always* confident" and "confident" especially at the prospect of being "absent from the body." We are confident as well *at all times,* as also most of all in the hope of a blessed departure. **whilst . . . at home . . . absent**—Translate as *Greek,* "While we sojourn *in our home* in the body, we are *away from our home* in the Lord." The image from a "house" is retained (cf. Phil. 3:20; Heb. 11: 13-16; 13:14). **7. we walk**—in our Christian course here on earth. **not by sight**—*Greek,* "not by appearance." Our life is governed by faith in our immortal hope; not by the outward specious *appearance* of present things [TITTM. *Synonyms*]. Cf. "apparently," LXX, "by appearance," Numbers 12:8. WAHL supports *English Version.* Ch. 4:18 also confirms it (cf. Rom. 8:24; I Cor. 13:12, 13). God has appointed in this life *faith* for our great duty, and in the next, vision for our reward [SOUTH] (I Pet. 1:8). **8. willing**—lit., "well content." Translate also, "To go (lit., *migrate*) from our home in the body, and to come to our home with the Lord." We should prefer to be found alive at the Lord's coming, and to be clothed upon with our heavenly body (vss. 2-4). But feeling, as we do, the sojourn in the body to be a separation from our true home "with the Lord," we prefer even dissolution by death, so that *in the intermediate disembodied state* we may go to be "with the Lord" (Phil. 1:23). "To be with Christ" (the disembodied state) is distinguished from Christ's coming to take us to *be with*

ADAM CLARKE

2. *For in this we groan.* While in this state and in this body, we are encompassed with many infirmities and exposed to many trials.

When the apostle says that they earnestly desired *to be clothed upon with our house which is from heaven,* he certainly means that the great concern of all the genuine followers of God was to be fully prepared to enjoy the beatific vision of their Maker and Redeemer.

3. *If so be that being clothed.* That is, fully prepared in this life for the glory of God; *we shall not be found naked.* Destitute in that future state of that divine image which shall render us capable of enjoying an endless glory.

4. *For we that are in this tabernacle.* We who are in this state of trial and difficulty *do groan, being burdened: not for that we would be unclothed.* We do not desire death; nor to die, even with the full prospect of eternal glory before our eyes, an hour before that time which God in His wisdom has assigned. *But clothed upon.* To have the fullest preparation for eternal glory. *That mortality might be swallowed up of life.* Being fully prepared for the eternal state, we shall scarcely be said to die, all that is mortal being absorbed and annihilated by immortality and glory.

5. *Now he that hath wrought us for the selfsame thing.* God has given us our being and our body for this very purpose, that both might be made immortal and both be glorified together. Or God himself has given us this insatiable hungering and thirsting after righteousness and immortality.

6. *We are always confident.* We are always "full of courage"; we never despond; we know where our help lies; and, having the earnest of the Spirit, we have the full assurance of hope. *Whilst we are at home in the body.* The original words in this sentence are very emphatic: *endemein* signifies to "dwell among one's own people"; *ekdemein,* to "be a sojourner among a strange people." Heaven is the home of every genuine Christian, and is claimed by them as such; see Phil. i. 23. Yet while here below, the body is the proper home of the soul. We see plainly that the apostle gives no intimation of an intermediate state between being at home in the body and being present with the Lord. There is not the slightest intimation here that the soul sleeps.

7. *For we walk by faith.* While we are in the present state *faith* supplies the place of direct vision. In the future world we shall have *sight.*

8. *We are confident.* We are "of good courage," notwithstanding our many difficulties; because we have this earnest of the Spirit, and the unfailing testimony of God. And notwithstanding this, we are *willing rather to be absent from the body*—we certainly prefer a state of glory to a state of suffering, and the enjoyment of the beatific vision to even the anticipation of it by faith and hope; but, as Christians, we cannot desire to die before our time.

MATTHEW HENRY

III. An inference to quicken himself and others to duty, *v.* 9–11. Well-grounded hopes of heaven will be far from giving the least encouragement to sloth, *v.* 9. *We are ambitious.* The apostle was thus ambitious to *be accepted of him,* the Lord (*v.* 9). It was the summit of ambition. Further quickening motives from the consideration of the judgment to come, *v.* 10, 11. The certainty of this judgment, for we must appear; the universality of it, for we must all appear; the great Judge before whose judgment-seat we must appear, the Lord Jesus Christ; the recompence to be then received, for things done in the body.

The apostle calls this awful judgment *the terror of the Lord* (*v.* 11), and was excited to persuade men to repent, and live a holy life, that, when Christ shall appear terribly, they may appear before him comfortably.

Verses 12–15

I. The apostle makes an apology for seeming to commend himself and his fellow-labourers (*v.* 13). The true reason was this, to put an argument in their mouths wherewith to answer his accusers.

II. He gives good reasons for their great zeal and diligence. The apostle tells them, 1. It was for the glory of God, and the good of the church, that he was thus zealous and industrious, *v.* 13. 2. *The love of Christ constrained them, v.* 14. Love has a constraining virtue to excite ministers and private Christians in their duty. Our love to Christ will have this virtue; and Christ's love to us will have this effect upon us.

JAMIESON, FAUSSET, BROWN

Him in soul and body (I Thess. 4:14-17, "with the Lord"). Perhaps the disembodied spirits of believers have fulness of communion *with Christ* unseen; but not the mutual recognition of one another, until clothed with their visible bodies at the resurrection (cf. I Thess. 4:13-17), when they shall with joy recognize Christ's image in each other perfect. **9. Wherefore**—with such a sure "confidence" of being blessed, whether we die before, or be found alive at Christ's coming. **we labour**—lit., "make it our ambition"; the only lawful ambition. **whether present or absent**—whether we be found at His coming present in the body, or absent from it. **accepted**—*Greek,* "well-pleasing." **10. appear**—rather, "be made manifest," viz., in our true character. So "appear," *Greek,* "be manifested" (Col. 3:4; cf. I Cor. 4:5). We are at all times, even now, manifest to God; *then* we shall be so to the assembled intelligent universe and to ourselves: for the judgment shall be not only in order to assign the everlasting portion to each, but to vindicate God's righteousness, so that it shall be manifest to all His creatures, and even to the conscience of the sinner himself. **receive**—His reward of grace proportioned to "the things done . ." (ch. 9:6-9; II John 8). Though salvation be of grace purely, independent of works, the saved may have a greater or less *reward,* according as he lives to, and labors for, Christ more or less. Hence there is scope for the holy "ambition" (*Note,* vs. 9; Heb. 6:10). This verse guards against the Corinthians supposing that *all* share in the house . . . "from heaven" (vss. 1, 2). There shall be a searching judgment which shall sever the bad from the good, according to their respective deeds, the *motive* of the deeds being taken into account, not the mere external act; faith and love to God are the sole motives recognized by God as sound and good (Matt. 12:36, 37; 25:35-45), **done in his body**—The *Greek* may be, "by the instrumentality of the body"; but *English Version* is legitimate (cf. *Greek,* Rom. 2:27). Justice requires that *substantially the same* body which has been the instrument of the unbelievers' sin, should be the object of punishment. A proof of the essential identity of the natural and the resurrection body. **11. terror of the Lord**—the coming judgment, so full of terrors to unbelievers [ESTIUS]. ELLICOTT and ALFORD, after GROTIUS and BENGEL, translate, "The fear of the Lord" (ch. 7:1; Eccl. 12:13; Acts 9:31; Rom. 3:18; Eph. 5:21). **persuade**—Ministers should use the terrors of the Lord to *persuade* men, not to rouse their enmity (Jude 23). BENGEL, ESTIUS, and ALFORD explain: "Persuade men" (by our whole lives, vs. 13), viz., of our integrity as ministers. But this would have been expressed after "persuade," had it been the sense. The connection seems as follows: He had been accused of seeking to please and win men, he therefore says (cf. Gal. 1:10), "It is as knowing the terror (or *fear*) of the Lord that we persuade men; but (whether *men* who hear our preaching recognize our sincerity or not) we are made manifest unto God as acting on such motives (ch. 4:2); and I trust also in your consciences." Those so "manifested" need have no "terror" as to their being "manifested (*English Version,* appear) before the judgment seat" (vs. 10). **12. For**—the reason why he leaves the manifestation of his sincerity in preaching to their consciences (ch. 3:1), viz., his not wishing to "commend" himself again. **occasion to glory**—(ch. 1:14), viz., as to our sincerity. **in appearance**—*Greek,* "face" (cf. I Sam. 16: 7). The false teachers gloried in their *outward appearance,* and in external recommendations (ch. 11: 18) their learning, eloquence, wisdom, riches, not in vital religion in their *heart.* Their conscience does not attest their inward sincerity, as mine does (ch. 1:12). **13. be**—rather as *Greek,* "have been." The contrast is between the single act implied by the past tense, "If we *have ever been* beside ourselves," and the habitual state implied by the present, "Or whether we *be* sober," i.e., *of sound mind.* **beside ourselves**—The accusation brought by Festus against him (Acts 26:24). The holy enthusiasm with which he spake of what God effected by His apostolic ministry, seemed to many to be *boasting madness.* **sober**—humbling myself before you, and not using my apostolic power and privileges. **to God . . . for your cause**—The glorifying of his office was not for his own, but for God's glory. The abasing of himself was in adaptation to their infirmity, to gain them to Christ (I Cor. 9:22). **14. For**—Accounting for his being "beside himself" with enthusiasm: the love of Christ towards us (in His death for us, the highest proof of it, Rom. 5:6-8), producing in turn love in us to Him, and not mere "terror" (vs. 11). **constraineth us**—with irresistible power *limits* us to the one great object

ADAM CLARKE

9. *Wherefore we labour.* From *philos,* "loving," and *time,* "honor." We act at all times on the principles of honor; we are, in the proper sense of the word, ambitious to do and say everything consistently with our high vocation. *We may be accepted of him.* "To be pleasing to Him." Through the love we have to God, we study and labor to please Him.

10. *For we must all appear before the judgment seat.* We labor to walk so as to please Him, because we know that we shall have to give a solemn account of ourselves before the judgment seat of Christ.

That every one may receive the things. That "each may receive to himself, into his own hand," his own reward and his own wages.

The things done in his body. That is, while he was in this lower state; for in this sense the term body is taken often in this Epistle. We may observe also that the soul is the grand agent; the body is but its instrument.

11. *Knowing therefore the terror of the Lord.* This, I think, is too harsh a translation; should be rendered, "knowing therefore the fear of the Lord"; which, strange as it may at first appear, often signifies the "worship" of the Lord, or that religious reverence which we owe to Him. As we know therefore what God requires of man, because we are favored with His own revelation, *we persuade men* to become Christians, and to labor to be acceptable to Him, because they must all stand before the judgment seat. *But we are made manifest unto God.* God, who searches the heart, knows that we are upright in our endeavors to please Him; and because we are fully persuaded of the reality of eternal things, therefore we are fully in earnest to get sinners converted to Him. *Manifest in your consciences.* We have reason to believe that you have had such proof of our integrity and disinterestedness, that your consciences must acquit us of every unworthy motive and of every sinister view.

12. *For we commend not ourselves.* I do not say these things to bespeak your good opinion, to procure your praise; but to *give you occasion to glory,* to exult on our behalf; and to furnish you with an answer to all those who either malign us or our ministry, and who only *glory in appearance.* Paul probably speaks here concerning the false apostle, who had been dividing the church and endeavoring to raise a party to himself by vilifying both the apostle and his doctrine.

13. *Beside ourselves.* Probably he was reputed by some to be deranged. Festus thought so: "Paul, thou art beside thyself; [too] much learning doth make thee mad." And his enemies at Corinth might insinuate not only that he was deranged, but attribute his derangement to a less worthy cause than intense study and deep learning. *It is to God.* If we do appear, in speaking of the glories of the eternal world, to be transported beyond ourselves, it is through the good hand of our God upon us, and we do it to promote His honor. *Whether we be sober,* speak of divine things in a more cool and dispassionate manner, it is that we may the better instruct and encourage you.

14. *For the love of Christ constraineth us.* We have the love of God shed abroad in our hearts, and this causes us to love God intensely, and to love and labor for the salvation of men. And it is the effect produced by this love which

MATTHEW HENRY

(1) What we must have continued to be, had not Christ died for us, *v.* 14. *If one died for all, then were all dead;* dead in sins and trespasses, spiritually dead.

(2) What such should do, for whom Christ died; they should live to him. They should not live *to themselves, v.* 15. Then do we live as we ought to live when we live to Christ, who died for us.

Verses 16–21

Two things that are necessary in order to our living to Christ: regeneration and reconciliation.

I. Regeneration. 1. Weanedness from the world, *v.* 16. The love of Christ is in our hearts, and the world is under our feet. *Yea, though we have known Christ after the flesh, yet,* says the apostle, *we know him no more.* We must live upon his spiritual presence and the comfort it affords.

2. A thorough change of the heart: *He is a new creature, v.* 17. Some read it, *Let him be a new creature,* not only that they wear a new livery, but that they have a new heart and new nature. *Old things are passed away,* and *all* these *things must become new.*

JAMIESON, FAUSSET, BROWN

to the exclusion of other considerations. The *Greek* implies *to compress forcibly* the energies into one channel. Love is *jealous* of any rival object engrossing the soul (ch. 11:1-3). **because we thus judge**—lit., (as) "having judged thus"; implying a judgment formed at conversion, and ever since regarded as a settled truth. **that if**—i.e., that *since.* But the oldest MSS. omit "if." "That one died for all" (*Greek,* "in behalf of all"). Thus the following clause will be, "Therefore all (lit., '*the* all,' viz., for whom He 'died') died." *His* dying is just the same as if *they all died;* and in their so dying, they died to sin and self, that they might live to God their Redeemer, whose henceforth they are (Rom. 6:2-11; Gal. 2:20; Col. 3:3; I Pet. 4:1-3). **15. they which live**—in the present life (ch. 4:11, "we which live") [ALFORD]; or, they who are thus indebted to Him for life of soul as well as body [MENOCHIUS]. **died for them**—He does not add, "rose again for them," a phrase not found in Paul's language [BENGEL]. He died *in their stead,* He arose again *for their good, "for* (*the effecting of*) their justification" (Rom. 4:25), and that He might be their Lord (Rom. 14:7-9). ELLICOTT and ALFORD join "for them" with both "died" and "rose again"; as Christ's death is *our death,* so His resurrection is *our resurrection; Greek, "*Who for them died and rose again." **not henceforth**—*Greek,* "no longer"; viz., now that His death for them has taken place, and that they know that His death saves them from death eternal, and His resurrection life brings spiritual and everlasting life to them. **16. Wherefore**—because of our settled *judgment* (vs. 14), **henceforth**—since our knowing Christ's constraining love in His death for us. **know we no man after the flesh**—i.e., according to his mere worldly and external relations (ch. 11:18; John 8:15; Phil. 3:4), as distinguished from what he is *according to the Spirit,* as a "new creature" (vs. 17). For instance, the outward distinctions of Jew or Gentile, rich or poor, slave or free, learned or unlearned, are lost sight of in the higher life of those who are dead in Christ's death, and alive with Him in the new life of His resurrection (Gal. 2:6; 3:28). **yea, though**—The oldest MSS. read, "if even." **known Christ after the flesh**—Paul when a Jew had looked for a temporal reigning, not a spiritual, Messiah. (He says "Christ," not *Jesus:* for he had not known personally Jesus in the days of His flesh, but he had looked for Christ or the Messiah.) When once he was converted he no longer "conferred with flesh and blood" (Gal. 1:16). He had this advantage over the Twelve, that as one born out of due time he had never known Christ save in His heavenly life. To the Twelve it was "expedient that Christ should go away" that the Comforter should come, and so they might know Christ in the higher spiritual aspect and in His new life-giving power, and not merely "after the flesh," in the carnal aspect of Him (Rom. 6:9-11; I Cor. 15:45; I Pet. 3:18; 4:1, 2). Doubtless Judaizing Christians at Corinth prided themselves on the mere fleshly (ch. 11:18) advantage of their belonging to Israel, the nation of Christ, or on their having seen Him in the flesh, and thence claimed superiority over others as having a nearer connection with Him (vs. 12; ch. 10:7). Paul here shows the true aim should be to know Him spiritually as new creatures (vss. 15, 17), and that outward relations towards Him profit nothing (Luke 18:19-21; John 16:7, 22; Phil. 3:3-10). This is at variance with both Romish Mariolatry and transubstantiation. Two distinct *Greek* verbs are used here for "know"; the first ("*know* we no man") means "to be personally acquainted with"; the latter ("known Christ . . . know . . . more") is to *recognize,* or estimate. Paul's *estimate* of Christ, or the expected Messiah, was carnal, but is so now no more. **17. Therefore**—connected with the words in vs. 16, "We know Christ no more after the flesh." As Christ has entered on His new heavenly life by His resurrection and ascension, so all who are "in Christ" (i.e., united to Him by faith as the branch is IN the vine) are new creatures (Rom. 6:9-11). "New" in the *Greek* implies a new nature quite different from anything previously existing, not merely *recent,* which is expressed by a different *Greek* word (Gal. 6:15). **creature**—lit., "creation," and so the *creature* resulting from the creation (cf. John 3:3, 5; Eph. 2:10; 4:23; Col. 3:10, 11). As we are "in Christ," so "God was in Christ" (vs. 19): hence He is Mediator between God and us. **old things**—selfish, carnal views (cf. vs. 16) of ourselves, of other men, and of Christ. **passed away**—spontaneously, like the snow of early spring [BENGEL] before the advancing sun. **behold**—implying an allusion to Isaiah 43:19, and 65:17. **18. all**—THE, *Greek*—**things**—all our privileges in this new crea-

ADAM CLARKE

"bears us away with itself," which causes us to love after the similitude of that love by which we are influenced; and as God so loved the world as to give His Son for it, and as Christ so loved the world as to pour out His life for it, so we, influenced by the very same love, desire to spend and be spent for the glory of God and the salvation of immortal souls. *If one died for all, then were all dead.* The first position the apostle takes for granted; viz., that Jesus Christ died for all mankind. The second position he infers from the first, and justly too; for if all had not been guilty, and consigned to eternal death because of their sin, there could have been no need of His death.

15. *And that he died for all, that they which live.* This third position he draws from the preceding: If all were dead, and in danger of endless perdition; and if He died for all, to save them from that perdition; then it justly follows that they are not their own, that they are bought by His blood; and *should not . . . live unto themselves,* for this is the way to final ruin; *but unto him which died for them,* and thus made an atonement for their sins, *and rose again* for their justification.

16. *Know we no man after the flesh.* As we know that "all have sinned, and come short of the glory of God," therefore we esteem no man on account of his family relations or the stock whence he proceeded.

Yea, though we have known Christ after the flesh. We know that the Jews valued themselves much in having Abraham for their father, and some of the Judaizing teachers at Corinth might value themselves in having seen Christ in the flesh, which certainly Paul did not; hence he takes occasion to say here that this kind of privilege availed nothing.

17. *If any man be in Christ, he is a new creature.* It is vain for a man to profess affinity to Christ according to the flesh while he is unchanged in his heart and life, and dead in trespasses and sins; for he that is in Christ, **that is, a genuine Christian, having Christ dwelling in his heart by faith, is a** ***new creature.*** **His old state is changed. He was a child of Satan; he is now a child of God. He was a slave of sin; he is now made free from sin.** *Behold, all things are become new.* **The man is not only mended, but he is new-made; he is** *a new creature,* **a "new creation."**

18. *And all things are of God.* As the thorough conversion of the soul is compared to a

MATTHEW HENRY

II. Reconciliation.

1. An unquestionable privilege, *v.* 18, 19. Reconciliation supposes a quarrel, or breach of friendship. Yet, behold, there may be a reconciliation. He has reconciled us to himself by Jesus Christ, *v.* 18.

F. B. MEYER:

"All things are of God." "Of" here is equivalent to "out of." All the precious contents of the Gospel have emanated from the heart of God; so that we may say with the psalmist, "All my springs are in thee."

That we have a building, a house not made with hands, eternal in the heavens, to which to go when the earthly house of this tabernacle is broken up; that it is possible for the mortal to be swallowed up in the descending glory of the Second Advent; that we have received the Spirit as earnest of our future glory; that we shall be one day at home with the Lord; that One died for all that the dominion of the self-life should be destroyed, and that they should henceforth live, not to themselves, but to Him; that it is possible to become a new creation in Christ; that God is already reconciled to the world of men, and is only waiting for them to be reconciled to Him; that He hath committed to men the ministry of reconciliation and commissioned them to be his ambassadors; that it is possible for us to be the righteousness of God in Jesus—all these things have issued from his heart of love.

Oh, for a soul as wide as the utmost circle of the highest heaven that containeth all, to contain his love! Oh, world's wonder! Oh, what a sight to be up in heaven, in "the fair orchard of Paradise!" But the very greatness of his provisions will make our doom the greater if we refuse or ignore them. The men who made light of the king's invitation had their city burnt. This is the terror of the Lord; and our duty is to beseech men not to put away the reconciliation which God offers. Let the "all things" of our life be of God's direction, impulse, and inspiration.—*Great Verses Through the Bible*

All things relating to our reconciliation by Jesus Christ are of God, who by the mediation of Jesus Christ has reconciled the world to himself. He has appointed the *ministry of reconciliation, v.* 18. He has appointed the office of the ministry, which is a *ministry of reconciliation.*

2. Our indispensable duty, *v.* 20. As God is willing to be reconciled to us, we ought to be reconciled to God. Though God can be no loser by the quarrel, nor gainer by the peace, yet by his ministers he beseeches sinners that they would be reconciled to him.

JAMIESON, FAUSSET, BROWN

tion (vss. 14, 15). **reconciled us**—i.e., *restored us* ("the world," vs. 19) *to His favor* by satisfying the claims of justice against us. Our position judicially considered in the eye of the law is altered, not as though the mediation of Christ had made a change in God's character, nor as if the love of God was produced by the mediation of Christ; nay, the mediation and sacrifice of Christ was the provision of God's love, not its moving cause (Rom. 8:32). Christ's blood was the price paid at the expense of God Himself, and was required to reconcile the exercise of mercy with justice, not as separate, but as the eternally harmonious attributes in the one and the same God (Rom. 3:25, 26). The *Greek* "reconcile" is *reciprocally* used as in the *Hebrew* Hithpahel conjugation, *appease, obtain the favor of.* Matthew 5:24, "Be reconciled to thy brother"; i.e., take measures that he be reconciled to thee, as well as thou to him, as the context proves. *Diallagethi,* however (Matt. 5:24), implying *mutual* reconciliation, is distinct from *Katallagethi* here, the latter referring to the *change* of status wrought in *one* of the two parties. The manner of God reconciling the world to Himself is implied (vs. 19), viz., by His "not imputing their trespasses to them." God not merely, as subsequently, reconciles the world by inducing them to lay aside their enmity, but in the first instance, does so by satisfying His own justice and righteous enmity against sin (Ps. 7:11). Cf. I Sam. 29:4, "Reconcile himself unto his master"; not remove his own anger against his master, but his master's against him [ARCHBISHOP MAGEE, *Atonement*]. The reconciling of *men to God* by their laying aside their enmity is the consequence of God laying aside His just enmity against their sin, and follows at vs. 20). **to us**—ministers (vss. 19, 20). **19. God was in Christ, reconciling**—i.e., God was BY Christ (*in virtue of Christ's intervention*) reconciling. . . . "Was reconciling" implies the time when the act of reconciliation was being carried into effect (vs. 21), viz., when "God made Jesus, who knew no sin, to be sin for us." The compound of "was" and the participle "reconciling," instead of the imperfect (*Greek*), may also imply the *continuous* purpose of God, from before the foundation of the world, to reconcile man to Himself, whose fall was foreseen. The expression "IN Christ" for "*by* Christ" may be used to imply *additionally* that God was IN Christ (John 10:38; 14: 10), and so *by* Christ (the God-man) was reconciling. . . . The *Greek* for "by" or *through* Christ (the best MSS. omit "Jesus"), vs. 18, is different. "In" must mean here *in the person of* Christ. The *Greek Katallasson* implies "changing" or *altering* the judicial status from one of condemnation to one of justification. The*atonement* (*at-one-ment*), or *reconciliation,* is the removal of the bar to peace and acceptance with a holy God, which His righteousness interposed against our sin. The first step towards restoring peace between us and God was on God's side (John 3:16). The *change* therefore *now* to be effected must be on the part of offending man, God the offended One being already reconciled. It is man, not God, who now needs to be reconciled, and to lay aside his enmity against God (Rom. 5:10, 11). ("We have *received the atonement*" [*Greek,* "reconciliation"], cannot mean "We have received the laying aside of *our own* enmity.") Cf. Romans 3:24, 25. **the world**—all men (Col. 1:20; I John 2: 2). The *manner* of the reconciling is by His "not imputing to men their trespasses," but imputing them to Christ the Sin-bearer. There is no incongruity that a father should be offended with that son whom he loveth, and at that time offended with him when he loveth him. So, though God loved men whom He created, yet He was offended with them when they sinned, and gave His Son to suffer for them, that through that Son's obedience He might be reconciled to them [reconcile them to Himself, i.e., restore them WITH JUSTICE to His favor] [BISHOP PEARSON, *Creed*]. **hath committed unto us**—*Greek,* "hath put into our hands." "Us," i.e., ministers. **20. for Christ . . . in Christ's stead**—The *Greek* of both is the same: translate in both cases "on Christ's behalf." **beseech . . . pray**—rather, "entreat [plead with you] . . . beseech." Such "beseeching" is uncommon in the case of "ambassadors," who generally stand on their dignity (cf. ch. 10:2; I Thess. 2: 6, 7). **be ye reconciled to God**—*English Version* here inserts "ye," which is not in the original, and which gives the wrong impression, as if it were emphatic thus: *God* is reconciled to you, be *ye* reconciled to God. The *Greek* expresses rather, God was the RECONCILER in Christ . . . let this reconciliation then have its designed effect. *Be reconciled to God,* i.e., let God reconcile you to Himself (vss. 18, 19). **21. For**—omitted in the oldest MSS. The

ADAM CLARKE

new creation, and creation is the proper work of an all-wise, almighty Being; then this total change of heart, soul, and life, which takes place under the preaching of the gospel, is effected by the power and grace of God. *The ministry of reconciliation.* The "office or function" of this reconciliation; called, v. 19, "the word"; the "doctrine of this reconciliation." *Reconciliation* comes from "to change thoroughly"; and the grand object of the gospel is to make a complete change in men's minds and manners; but the first object is the removal of enmity from the heart of man, that he may be disposed to accept of the salvation God has provided for him, on the terms which God has promised. The enmity in the heart of man is the grand hindrance to his salvation.

19. *That God was in Christ.* This is the doctrine which this ministry of reconciliation holds out, and the doctrine which it uses to bring about the reconciliation itself.

ALBERT BARNES:

"That God was in Christ." That God was "by" Christ, by means of Christ; "by" the agency or mediatorship of Christ. Or it may mean that God was united to Christ and manifested himself by him. Christ was the mediator by means of whom God designed to accomplish the great work of reconciliation.

"Reconciling the world unto himself." The "world" here evidently means the human race generally, without distinction of nation, age, or rank. The whole world was alienated from him, and he sought to have it reconciled. This is one incidental proof that God designed that the plan of salvation should be adapted to all men. It may be observed further, that *God* sought that the world should be reconciled. Man did not seek it. He had no plan for it. He did not desire it. He had no way to effect it. It was the *offended* party, not the *offending,* that sought to be reconciled; and this shows the strength of his love. It was love for enemies and alienated beings, and love evinced to them by a most earnest desire to become their friend, and to be at agreement with them. Tindal renders this very accurately, "For God was in Christ, and made agreement between the world and himself, and imputed not their sins unto them."
—*Popular Commentary*

20. *We are ambassadors for Christ.* "We execute the function of ambassadors in Christ's stead." He came from the Father to mankind on this important embassy. He has left the world, and appointed us in His place. *As though God did beseech you by us.* What we say to you we say on the authority of God; our entreaties are His entreaties; our warm love to you, a faint reflection of His infinite love. We pray you to return to God; it is His will that you should do so. We promise you remission of sins; we are authorized to do so by God himself. In Christ's stead we pray you to lay aside your enmity and *be reconciled to God.*

MATTHEW HENRY

And for our encouragement so to do the apostle subjoins what should be well known by us (*v.* 21). The purity of the Mediator: *He knew no sin.* The sacrifice he offered: *He was made sin;* that is, a sin-offering, a sacrifice for sin.

That *we might be made the righteousness of God in him.* As Christ, who knew no sin of his own, was made sin for us, so we, who have no righteousness of our own, are made the righteousness of God in him.

JAMIESON, FAUSSET, BROWN

grand reason why they should be reconciled to God, viz., the great atonement in Christ provided by God, is stated without the "for" as being part of *the message of reconciliation* (vs. 19). **he**—God. **sin**—not *a sin offering,* which would destroy the antithesis to "righteousness," and would make "sin" be used in different senses in the same sentence: not *a sinful person,* which would be untrue, and would require in the antithesis "righteous men," not "righteousness"; but "sin," i.e., the representative *Sin-bearer* (vicariously) of *the aggregate sin* of all men past, present, and future. The sin of the world is *one,* therefore the *singular,* not the *plural,* is used; though its *manifestations* are manifold (John 1:29). "Behold the Lamb of God, that taketh away the SIN of the world." Cf. "made a curse for us," Galatians 3:13. **for us**—*Greek,* "in our behalf." Cf. John 3:14, Christ being represented by the brazen *serpent,* the *form,* but not the *substance,* of the old serpent. At His death on the cross the sin-bearing for us was consummated. **knew no sin**—by personal experience (John 8:46) [ALFORD]. Hebrews 7:26; I Peter 2:22; I John 3:5.

might be made—not the same *Greek* as the previous "made." Rather, "might become." **the righteousness of God**—Not merely righteous, but *righteousness* itself; not merely righteousness, but the *righteousness of God,* because Christ is God, and what He is we are (I John 4:17), and He is "made of God unto us righteousness." As our sin is made over to Him, so His righteousness to us (in His having fulfilled all the righteousness of the law for us all, as our representative (Jer. 23:6; I Cor. 1:30). The innocent was punished voluntarily as if guilty, that the guilty might be gratuitously rewarded as if innocent (I Peter 2:24). "Such are we in the sight of God the Father, as is the very Son of God himself" [HOOKER]. **in him**—by virtue of our standing in Him, and in union with Him [ALFORD].

ADAM CLARKE

21. *For he hath made him to be sin for us.* "He made Him who knew no sin (who was innocent) a Sin Offering for us." The word *hamartia* occurs here twice. In the first place it means *sin,* i.e., transgression and guilt; and of Christ it is said, "He knew no sin," i.e., was innocent; for not to know sin is the same as to be conscious of innocence. In the second place it signifies a "sin offering," or "sacrifice for sin," and answers to the *chattaah* and *chattath* of the Hebrew text; which signifies both "sin" and "sin offering" in a great variety of places in the Pentateuch. The Septuagint translate the Hebrew word by *hamartia* in ninety-four places in Exodus, Leviticus, and Numbers, where a "sin offering" is meant; and where our version translates the word, not "sin," but an "offering for sin." Had our translators attended to their own method of translating the word in other places where it means the same as here, they would not have given this false view of a passage which has been made the foundation of a most blasphemous doctrine; viz., that our sins were imputed to Christ, and that He was a proper Object of the indignation of divine justice, because He was blackened with imputed sin; and some have proceeded so far in this blasphemous career as to say that Christ may be considered as the greatest of sinners, because all the sins of mankind, or of the elect, as they say, were imputed to Him, and reckoned as His own. Thus they have confounded sin with the punishment due to sin. Christ suffered in our stead, died for us, bore our sins (the punishment due to them) in His own body upon the tree, for the Lord laid upon Him the iniquities of us all; that is, the punishment due to them; explained by making "his soul," His life, "an offering for sin," and healing us by His stripes. *That we might be made the righteousness of God in him. The righteousness of God* signifies here the "salvation" of God, as comprehending justification through the blood of Christ, and sanctification through His Spirit; or as the mountains of God, the hail of God, the wind of God mean exceeding high mountains, extraordinary hail, and most tempestuous wind, so here the righteousness of God may mean a thorough righteousness, complete justification, complete sanctification such as none but God can give, such as the sinful nature and guilty conscience of man require, and such as is worthy of God to impart. And all this righteousness, justification, and holiness we receive in, by, for, and through Him.

MATTHEW HENRY

CHAPTER 6

Verses 1–10

An account of the apostle's general errand and exhortation to all to whom he preached.

I. The errand or exhortation itself, *v.* 1. As it is the duty of the ministers of the gospel to exhort their hearers to accept of grace and mercy, so they are honoured with this high title of *co-workers with* God. They are workers with God, yet under him. If they be faithful, they may hope to find God working with them, and their labour will be effectual. Observe the way of the gospel: it is not with roughness and severity, but with all mildness and gentleness, to beseech and entreat.

II. The arguments and method which the apostle used.

1. The present time is the only proper season to accept of the grace that is offered: Now *is the accepted time,* NOW *is the day of salvation, v.* 2. The morrow is none of ours: we know not what will be on the morrow.

JAMIESON, FAUSSET, BROWN

CHAPTER 6

VSS. 1-18. HIS APOSTOLIC MINISTRY IS APPROVED BY FAITHFULNESS IN EXHORTATION, IN SUFFERINGS, IN EXHIBITION OF THE FRUITS OF THE HOLY GHOST: HIS LARGENESS OF HEART TO THEM CALLS FOR ENLARGEMENT OF THEIR HEART TO HIM. EXHORTATIONS TO SEPARATION FROM POLLUTION. **1. workers together**—with God (Acts 15:4; I Cor. 3:9). Not only as "ambassadors." **beseech**—entreat (ch. 5:20). He is describing his ministry, not exhorting directly. **you also**—rather, "WE ALSO (as well as God, ch. 5:20) beseech" or "entreat you": vss. 14, 15, on to ch. 7:1, is part of this entreaty or exhortation. **in vain**—by making the grace of God a ground for continuance in sin (vs. 3). By a life of sin, showing that the word of reconciliation has been *in vain,* so far as you are concerned (Heb. 12:15; Jude 4). "The grace of God" here, is "the reconciliation" provided by God's love (ch. 5:18, 19; cf. Gal. 2:2). **2. For**—God's own promise is the ground of our exhortation. **he saith**—*God the Father* saith to God the Son, and so to all believers who are regarded as one with Him. **heard thee**—In the eternal purposes of my love I have hearkened to thy prayer for the salvation of thy people (cf. John 17:9, 15, 20, 24). **accepted . . . accepted**—The *Greek* of the latter is more emphatic, "well-accepted." What was "*an accepted* time" in the prophecy (Isa. 49:8, *Hebrew,* "in the season of grace") becomes "*the wellaccepted* time" in the fulfilment (cf. Ps. 69:13). As it is *God's* time of *receiving* sinners, *receive ye* His grace: *accept* (vs. 1) the word of reconciliation in His *accepted* time. **in the day of salvation**—"in *a* day of salvation" (Luke 4:18, 19, 21; 19:42; Heb. 3:7).

ADAM CLARKE

CHAPTER 6

1. *We then, as workers together with him.* The last two words, *with him,* are not in the text, and some supply the place thus: "We then, as workers together with you." For my own part I see nothing wanting in the text if we only suppose the term "apostles"; *we* (i.e., apostles), "being fellow workers, also entreat you not to receive the grace of God in vain." By the *grace of God,* this grace or benefit of God, the apostle certainly means the grand sacrificial offering of Christ for the sin of the world, which He had just before mentioned in speaking of the ministry of reconciliation. We learn, therefore, that it was possible to *receive the grace of God* and not ultimately benefit by it; or in other words, to begin in the Spirit and end in the flesh.

2. *For he saith.* That is, God hath said it, by the prophet Isaiah, chap. xlix. 8; which place the apostle quotes *verbatim et literatim* from the Septuagint. And from this we may at once see what is *the accepted time,* and what *the day of salvation.* The advent of the Messiah was the time of God's pleasure or benevolence, of which all the faithful were in expectation; and the *day of salvation* was the time in which this salvation should be manifested and applied. I rather think that this second verse should be read immediately after the last verse of the preceding chapter, as where it now stands it greatly disturbs the connection between the first and the third verses. I will set down the whole in the order in which I think they should stand. "Now then we are ambassadors for Christ, as though God did beseech you by us: we pray you in Christ's stead, be ye reconciled to God.

MATTHEW HENRY | JAMIESON, FAUSSET, BROWN | ADAM CLARKE

ALBERT BARNES:

3. "Giving no offence in any thing." We the ministers of God (v. 1). The word rendered "offence" means, properly, "stumbling"; then offence, or cause of offence, a falling into sin. The meaning here is, "giving no occasion for rejecting the gospel." The idea of Paul is that he and his fellow apostles so labored as that no one who saw or knew them should have occasion to reproach the ministry or the religion which they preached; but so that in their pure and self-denying lives, the strongest argument should be seen for embracing it (cf. Matt. 10:16; 1 Cor. 8:13; 10:32, 33). How they conducted so as to give no offence he states in the following verses.

"That the ministry be not blamed." The phrase, "the ministry," refers here not merely to the ministry of Paul; that is, it does not mean merely that *he* would be subject to blame and reproach, but that the *ministry itself* which the Lord Jesus had established would be blamed, or would be reproached by the improper conduct of anyone who was engaged in that work. The idea is, that the misconduct of one minister of the gospel would bring a reproach upon the profession itself and would prevent the usefulness and success of others, just as the misconduct of a physician exposes the profession to reproach, or the bad conduct of a lawyer reflects itself in some degree on the entire profession.—*Popular Commentary*

2. What caution they used not to give offence that might hinder the success of their preaching, *v.* 3. When others are too apt to take offence, we should be cautious lest we give offence; and ministers especially should be careful.

3. Their constant aim in all things to approve themselves faithful, as became the ministers of God, *v.* 4. His great desire was to be the servant of God, and to approve himself so. (1) By much patience in afflictions.

He was a great sufferer, and met with many afflictions, but he exercised much patience in all, *v.* 4, 5. Those who would approve themselves to God must approve themselves faithful in trouble as well as in peace, not only in doing the work of God diligently, but also in bearing the will of God patiently.

(2) By acting from good principles. What his principles were (*v.* 6, 7); namely, pureness; and there is no piety without purity. Knowledge was another principle; and zeal without this is but madness. He also acted with *long-suffering and kindness,* bearing with the hardness of men's hearts, and hard treatment from their hands. He acted under the influence of the Holy Ghost, from the noble principle of unfeigned love, according to the rule of the word of truth, under the power of God, having on the armour of righteousness, which is the best defence against the temptations of prosperity on the right hand, and of adversity on the left.

3. Resuming the connection with vs. 1, interrupted by the parenthetical vs. 2. "Giving no offense" (cf. I Cor. 10:33), "approving ourselves," and all the other participles down to vs. 10, are nominatives to "we also entreat you" (vs. 1), to show the pains he took to enforce his exhortation by example, as well as precept [ALFORD]. "Offense" would be given, if we were without "patience" and the other qualifications which he therefore subjoins (cf. Rom. 14:13). **4.** Translate, to mark the true order of the *Greek* words, "in everything, as God's ministers recommending ourselves," i.e., that our hearers may give our *message* a favorable hearing, through our consistency in every respect, not that they may glorify us. Alluding to ch. 3:1, he implies, *We commend ourselves,* not like them by word, but by deed. **patience**—(ch. 12:12). Put first. "Pure-minded" follows (vs. 6). Three triplets of trials exercising the "patience" (patient endurance) follow: Afflictions (or "tribulations"), necessities, distresses (or "straits"); stripes, imprisonments, tumults; labors, watchings, fastings. The first triplet expresses afflictions generally; the second, those in particular arising from the violence of men; the third, those *which* he brought on himself directly or indirectly.

5. stripes—(ch. 11:23, 24; Acts 16:23). **imprisonments**—(ch. 11:23). He had been, doubtless, elsewhere imprisoned besides at Philippi when he wrote this Epistle. **tumults**—(Acts 13:50; 14:5, 19; 16:22; and recently 19:23-41). **labours**—in the cause of Christ (ch. 11:23; Rom. 16:12). **watchings**—(ch. 11:27). Sleepless nights. **fastings**—The context here refers to his *trials,* rather than *devotional exercises* (cf. ch. 11:27). Thus "foodlessness" would seem to be the sense (cf. I Cor. 4:11, Phil. 4:12). But the usual sense of the *Greek* is *fasts,* in the strict sense; and in ch. 11:27 it is spoken of independently of "hunger and thirst." (Cf. Luke 2:37; Acts 10:30; 14:23.) However, Matthew 15:32; Mark 8:3, justify the sense, more favored by the context, *foodlessness,* though a rare use of the word. GAUSSEN remarks "The apostles combine the highest offices with the humblest exterior: as everything in the Church was to be cast in the mould of death and resurrection, the cardinal principle throughout Christianity."

6. By . . . by . . .—rather, as *Greek,* "In . . . in," implying not the instrument, but the sphere or element in which his ministry moved. **knowledge**—spiritual: in Gospel mysteries, unattainable by mere reason (I Cor. 2:6-16; II Cor. 3:6, 17, 18). **long-suffering . . . kindness**—associated with "charity" or "*love*" (I Cor. 13:4), as here. **by the Holy Ghost**—in virtue of His influences which produce these graces, and other gifts, "love unfeigned" being the foremost of them.

7. By the word of truth, by the power of God—rather, "IN . . . in. . . ." As to "the word of truth" (cf. ch. 4:2; Col. 1:5), and "the (miraculous) power of God" (ch. 4:7); I Corinthians 2:4, "in demonstration of the Spirit and of power." **by the armour**—*Greek,* "through" or "by means of the armor." "Righteousness," which is the *breastplate* alone in Ephe-

For he hath made him . . . [a] sin [offering] for us, who knew no sin; that we might be made the righteousness of God in him. For he saith, I have heard thee in a time accepted, and in the day of salvation have I succoured thee: behold, now is the accepted time; behold, now is the day of salvation." Immediately after this, the sixth chapter will very properly commence, and we shall see that the connection will be then undisturbed: "We then, as fellow workers, beseech you also that ye receive not this grace of God in vain, giving no offence in any thing, that this ministry be not blamed." This change of the place of the second verse, which everyone allows must, if it stand here, be read in a parenthesis, preserves the whole connection of the apostle's discourse and certainly sets his argument before us in a stronger light.

3. *Giving no offence.* The word signifies a "stumbling block" in general, or anything over which a man stumbles or falls; and here means any transgression or scandal that might take place among the ministers, or the Christians themselves, whereby either Jews or Gentiles might take occasion of offense and vilify the gospel of Christ.

4. *But in all things approving ourselves.* The apostle now proceeds to show how conscientiously himself and his fellow laborers acted in order to render the ministry of reconciliation effectual to the salvation of men. They not only gave no offense in anything, but they labored to manifest themselves to be the genuine ministers of God, *in much patience,* bearing calmly up under the most painful and oppressive afflictions. *In afflictions.* This may signify the series of persecutions and distresses in general, the state of cruel suffering in which the Church of God and the apostles then existed. *In necessities.* "Straits" and "difficulties," including all that want and affliction which arose from the impoverished state of the Church. *In distresses.* Such straits and difficulties as were absolutely unavoidable and insurmountable. The word implies "being reduced to a narrow place, driven to a corner, hemmed in on every side," as the Israelites were at the Red Sea—the sea before them, Pharaoh and his host behind them, and Egyptian fortresses on either hand. God alone could bring them out of such difficulties, when their enemies themselves saw that the wilderness had shut them in. So was it often with the apostles; all human help failed, and their deliverance came from God alone.

5. *In stripes, in imprisonments.* Of these the history of the Acts of the Apostles gives ample testimony; and there were doubtless many instances of persecution in various forms which are not on record. *In tumults.* "Insurrections" raised against them because of the gospel. It is more natural to understand the word thus than of agitations or tossings to and fro in consequence of their unsettled state of life; or because of persecution, which obliged them to flee from place to place. *In labours.* Both with our own hands to provide for ourselves the necessaries of life, that we might not be chargeable to others, and in labors to spread the gospel of God through all countries where His providence opened our way. *In watchings.* Passing many nights without sleep or rest. *In fastings.* Partly constrained through want of food and partly voluntary, as a means of obtaining an increase of grace both for ourselves and for the churches.

6. *By pureness.* In "simplicity" of intention, and "purity" of affection, together with that chastity and holinsss of life which the gospel enjoins. *By knowledge.* Of the divine mysteries. *By longsuffering.* Under all provocations. *By kindness.* To our most virulent persecutors, and to all men. *By the Holy Ghost.* The constant indwelling of the Holy Spirit, and with it the various gifts of the Holy Spirit by which he was enabled to work miracles. *By love unfeigned.* "Love without hypocrisy."

7. *By the word of truth.* The doctrine of truth received immediately from God, and faithfully and affectionately preached to men. *By the power of God.* Confirming this doctrine, not only by the miracles which we were enabled to work, but also by the application of that truth to the souls of the people by the energy of God. *By the armour of righteousness.* Such

MATTHEW HENRY

(3) By a due temper and behaviour under all the variety of conditions, *v.* 8–10. The apostles met with honour and dishonour, good report and evil report. We stand in need of the grace of God to arm us against the temptations of honour on the one hand, so as to bear good report without pride, and of dishonour on the other hand, so as to bear reproaches without recrimination. Some represented them as the best, and others as the worst, of men: by some they were counted deceivers, by others as true. They were slighted by the men of the world as unknown, not worth taking notice of; yet in all the churches of Christ they were well known, and of great account: they were looked upon as dying, "and yet behold, we live." They were chastened, and often fell under the lash of the law, yet not killed:

and though it was thought that they were sorrowful, a company of mopish and melancholy men, yet they were always rejoicing in God. They were despised as poor, and yet they made many rich, by preaching the unsearchable riches of Christ. They were thought to have nothing, yet they possessed all things. They had nothing in themselves, but possessed all things in Christ. Such a paradox is a Christian's life.

Verses 11–18

The apostle cautions them against mingling with unbelievers.

I. The caution is introduced with a profession of the most tender affection to them, *v.* 11–13. He seemed to want words to express the warm affections he had for these Corinthians. *Our mouth is open unto you, and our heart is enlarged unto* you.

"You are not," says he, *"straitened in us;* we would gladly do you all the service we can, and if it be otherwise, the fault is in yourselves; it is because you are straitened in yourselves. All we desire as a recompence is only that you would be proportionably affected towards us, as children should love their father."

II. The caution itself, not to mingle with unbelievers, not to be *unequally yoked* with them, *v.* 14. It is wrong for good people to join in affinity with the wicked and profane. There is more danger that the bad will damage the good than hope that the good will benefit the bad. We should not yoke ourselves in friendship with wicked men and unbelievers. We should never choose them for our bosom-friends. Much less should we join in religious communion with them. It is a very great absurdity, *v.* 14, 15.

JAMIESON, FAUSSET, BROWN

sians 6:13-17, here is made the *whole* Christian panoply (cf. ch. 10:4). **on . . . right . . . and . . . left** –i.e., guarding on every side. **8.** Translate, *"Through glory* and dishonor" (disgrace), viz., from *those in authority,* and accruing to us *present.* "By," or *"through* evil report and good report," from *the multitude,* and affecting us *absent* [BENGEL]. Regarded "as deceivers" by those who, *not knowing* (vs. 9), *dishonor* and give us an *evil report;* "as true," by those who "know" (vs. 9) us in the real "glory" of our ministry. In proportion as one has more or less of *glory* and *good report,* in that degree has he more or less of *dishonor* and *evil report.* **9. unknown . . . yet well known**–"unknown" in our true character to those who "evil report" of us, "well known" to those who hold us in "good report" (vs. 8). CONYBEARE explains, "Unknown by men, yet *acknowledged by God"* (I Cor. 13:12). Perhaps *both God and men* (believers) are intended as knowing him (ch. 5:11, and 11:6). **dying . . . live** –(ch. 1:9; 4:10, 11; 11:23). Cf. GAUSSEN'S remark, *Note,* vs. 5. "Behold" calls attention to the fact as something beyond all expectation. **chastened . . . not killed**–realizing Psalm 118:18.

10. The "as" no longer is used to express the opinion of his adversaries, but the real state of him and his fellow laborers. **making many rich**–Spiritually (I Cor. 1:5), after the example of our Lord, who "by His poverty made many rich" (ch. 8:9). **having nothing**–Whatever of earthly goods we have, and these are few, we have as though we had not; as tenants removable at will, not owners (I Cor. 7:30). **possessing all things**–The *Greek* implies *firm possession, holding fast in possession* (cf.I Cor. 3:21, 22). The things both of the present and of the future are, in the truest sense, the believer's in possession, for he possesses them all in Christ, his lasting possession, though the full *fruition* of them is reserved for the future eternity. **11. mouth . . . open unto you**–I use no concealment, such as some at Corinth have insinuated (ch. 4:2). I use all freedom and openness of speech to you as to beloved friends. Hence he introduces here, "O Corinthians" (cf. Phil. 4:15). The *enlargement* of his *heart* towards them (ch. 7:3) produced his *openness* of *mouth,* i.e., his unreserved expression of his inmost feelings. As an unloving man is *narrow* in heart, so the apostle's heart is *enlarged* by love, so as to take in his converts at Corinth, not only with their graces, but with their many shortcomings (cf. I Kings 4:29; Ps. 119:32; Isa. 60:5). **12.** Any constraint ye feel towards me, or narrowness of heart, is not from want of largeness of heart on my part towards you, but from want of it on your part towards me; "bowels," i.e., affections (cf. ch. 12:15). **not straitened in us**–i.e., for want of room in our hearts to take you in. **13.** Translate, "As a recompense in the same kind . . . be enlarged also yourselves" [ELLICOTT]. "In the same way" as my heart is enlarged towards you (vs. 11), and "as a recompense" for it (Gal. 4:12). **I speak as unto my children**–as children would naturally be expected to *recompense* their parents' love with similar love. **14. Be not**–*Greek, "Become* not." **unequally yoked**–"yoked with one alien in spirit." The image is from the symbolical precept of the law (Lev. 19: 19), "Thou shalt not let thy cattle gender with a diverse kind"; or the precept (Deut. 22:10), "Thou shalt not plough with an ox and an ass together." Cf. Deuteronony 7:3, forbidding marriages with the heathen; also I Corinthians 7:39. The believer and unbeliever are utterly *heterogeneous.* Too close intercourse with unbelievers in other relations also is included (vs. 16; I Cor. 8:10; 10:14).

ADAM CLARKE

as that described by the apostle, Eph. vi. 13-17, which he calls there "the whole armour of God." *On the right hand and on the left.* Particularly the shield and the sword; the former on the left arm, the latter in the right hand.

8. *By honour and dishonour.* By going through both; sometimes respected, sometimes despised. *By evil report and good report.* Sometimes praised, at other times calumniated. *As deceivers.* Said to carry about a false doctrine for our secular emolument. *And yet true.* Demonstrated by the nature of the doctrine, as well as by our life and conversation, that we are true men, having nothing in view but God's glory and the salvation of the world.

9. *As unknown.* Persons who are to be suspected as harboring dark designs; persons of neither birth, parentage, nor respectable connections in life. *And yet well known.* Proved by our whole conduct to have no such designs, and demonstrated to be holy, upright, and useful. *As dying.* Through continual dangers, fatigues, and persecutions. *And, behold, we live.* We are preserved by the mighty power of God in the greatest dangers and deaths. *As chastened.* As though we were disobedient children. *And not killed.* Though we continue in the very same line of conduct that is supposed to bring on us those chastisements, and which, if it were criminal, would justly expose us to death for incorrigible obstinacy; but our preservation is a proof that we please God.

10. *As sorrowful.* Considerate men supposing from our persecuted state and laborious occupation (often destitute of the necessaries of life; seldom enjoying its conveniences, and scarcely ever its comforts) that we must be the most miserable of all men. *Yet always rejoicing.* Having the consolation of God's Spirit at all times, and a glorious prospect of a blessed immortality. *As poor.* Destitute of all worldly good and secular interest. *Yet making many rich.* By dispensing to them the treasures of salvation; making them rich in faith, and heirs of the Kingdom. *As having nothing.* Being the most abject of the poor. *And yet possessing all things* that are really necessary to the preservation of our lives. For the wants under which we labor for a time are supplied again by a bountiful Providence. The man who possesses a contented spirit possesses *all things,* for he is satisfied with every dispensation of the providence of God; and "a contented mind is a continual feast."

11. *O ye Corinthians, our mouth is open unto you.* I speak to you with the utmost freedom and fluency because of my affection for you. *Our heart is enlarged.* It is expanded to take you and all your interests in, and to keep you in the most affectionate remembrance.

12. *Ye are not straitened in us.* That is, You have not a narrow place in our affections. The metaphor here is taken from the case of a person pent up in a small or narrow place, where there is scarcely room to breathe. *Ye are straitened in your own bowels.* I have not the same place in your affections which you have in mine. The *bowels* are used in Scripture to denote the most "tender affections."

13. *Now for a recompense in the same.* That you may, in some sort, repay me for my affection towards you. *I speak* to you *as unto my children,* whom I have a right to command. *Be ye also enlarged;* love me as I love you.

14-15. *Be ye not unequally yoked together with unbelievers.* This is a military term: keep in your own ranks; do not leave the Christian community to join in that of the heathens. The verb signifies to leave one's own rank, place, or order, and go into another; and here it must signify not only that they should not associate with the Gentiles in their idolatrous feasts, but that they should not apostatize from Christianity; and the questions which follow show that there was a sort of fellowship that some of the Christians had formed with the heathens which was both wicked and absurd, and if not speedily checked would infallibly lead to final apostasy. Some apply this exhortation to pious persons marrying with those who are not decidedly religious and converted to God. That the exhortation may be thus applied I grant, but it is certainly not the meaning of the apostle in this place. Nevertheless common

MATTHEW HENRY

Believers are righteous; but unbelievers are unrighteous. Believers are made light in the Lord, but unbelievers are in darkness; and what comfortable communion can these have together? Christ and Belial are contrary one to the other.

It is a dishonour to the Christian's profession (*v.* 16); for Christians are the *temples of the living God.* Now there can be no agreement between *the temple of God and idols.*

There is a great deal of danger in communicating with unbelievers, danger of being defiled and of being rejected; therefore the exhortation is (*v.* 17) *to come out from among them, to be separate,* as one would avoid the society of those who have the leprosy or the plague, and not *to touch the unclean thing.* Who can touch pitch, and not be defiled by it? We must take care not to defile ourselves by converse with those who defile themselves with sin.

It is base ingratitude to God for all the favours he has bestowed upon believers and promised to them, *v.* 18. God has promised to be a Father to them, and that they shall be his sons and his daughters; and is there a greater honour or happiness than this?

JAMIESON, FAUSSET, BROWN

fellowship—lit., "share," or "participation." **righteousness**—the state of the believer, justified by faith. **unrighteousness**—rather, as always translated elsewhere, "iniquity"; the state of the unbeliever, the fruit of unbelief. **light**—of which believers are the children (I Thess. 5:5). **15. Belial**—*Hebrew,* "worthlessness, unprofitableness, wickedness." As Satan is opposed to God, and Antichrist to Christ; Belial being here opposed to Christ, must denounce all manner of Antichristian uncleanness [BENGEL]. **he that believeth with an infidel**—Translate, "a believer with an unbeliever." **16. agreement**—accordance of sentiments (cf. I Kings 18:21; Eph. 5:7, 11). **the temple of God**—i.e., you believers (I Cor. 3:16; 6:19). **with idols**—Cf. Dagon before the ark (I Sam. 5:24). **as**—"*even as* God said." Quotation from Leviticus 26:12; Jeremiah 31:33; 32:38; Ezekiel 37:26, 27; cf. Matthew 28:20; John 14:23. **walk in them**—rather, *among* them." As "dwell" implies the divine *presence,* so "walk," the divine *operation.* God's dwelling in the body and soul of saints may be illustrated by its opposite, demoniacal possession of body and soul. **my people**—rather, "they shall be *to me* a people." **17.** Quoted from Isaiah 52:11, with the freedom of one inspired, who gives variations sanctioned by the Holy Spirit. **be ye separate**—"be separated" (Hos. 4:17). **touch not the unclean thing**—rather, "*anything* unclean" (ch. 7:1; Mic. 2:10). *Touching* is more polluting, as implying participation, than seeing. **receive you**—The *Greek* implies, "to myself"; as persons heretofore out of doors, but now admitted *within* (ch. 5:1-10). With this accords the clause, "Come *out from among* them," viz., so as to be received to me. So Ezekiel 20:41, "I will accept you"; and Zephaniah 3:19, "gather her that was driven out." "The intercourse of believers with the world should resemble that of angels, who, when they have been sent a message from heaven, discharge their office with the utmost promptness, and joyfully fly back home to the presence of God" (I Cor. 7:31; 5:9, 10). **18.** Translate, "I will be to you *in the relation of* a Father, and ye shall be *to me in the relation of* sons. . . ." This is a still more endearing relation than (vs. 16), "I will be their *God,* and they . . . My *people.*" Cf. the promise to Solomon (I Chron. 28:6; Isa. 43:6; Rev. 21:3, 7; Jer. 31:1, 9). **Lord Almighty**—*The Lord the Universal Ruler:* nowhere else found but in Revelation. The greatness of the Promiser enhances the greatness of the promises.

ADAM CLARKE

sense and true piety show the absurdity of two such persons pretending to walk together in a way in which they are not agreed. A very wise and very holy man has given his judgment on this point: "A man who is truly pious, marrying with an unconverted woman, will either draw back to perdition, or have a cross during life." The same may be said of a pious woman marrying an unconverted man. Such persons cannot say this petition of the Lord's Prayer, "Lead us not into temptation." They plunge into it of their own accord. *For what fellowship?* As *righteousness* cannot have communion with *unrighteousness,* and *light* cannot dwell with *darkness,* so *Christ* can have no concord with *Belial,* nor can he that *believeth* have any with an *infidel.* All these points were self-evident; how then could they keep up the profession of Christianity, or pretend to be under its influence, while they associated with the unrighteous, had communion with darkness, concord with Belial, and partook with infidels?

16. *What agreement hath the temple of God with idols?* Nothing could appear more abominable to a Jew than an idol in the Temple of God. Here, then, could be no agreement; the worship of the two is wholly incompatible. *Ye are the temple of the living God.* God intends to make the heart of every believer His own house. *I will dwell in them, and walk in* them. The words are very emphatic: "I will inhabit in them." *I will be their God.* They shall have no other God, they shall have none besides Me; and if they take Me for their God, I will be to them all that an infinite, eternal, and self-sufficient Being can be to His intelligent offspring. *They shall be my people.* If they take Me for their God, their supreme and eternal Good, I will take them for My people; and instruct, enlighten, defend, provide for, support, and bless them, as if I had none else to care for in the creation.

17. *Wherefore come out from among them.* Is it not plain from this and the following verse that God would be their God only on the ground of their taking Him for such, and that this depended on their being separated from the works and workers of iniquity?

18. *Will be a Father unto you.* I will act towards you as the most affectionate father can act towards his most tender and best beloved child. *And ye shall be my sons and daughters.* You shall all be of the household of God, the family of heaven; you shall be holy, happy, and continually safe. *Saith the Lord Almighty.* The Lord, the Governor of all things. Earthly fathers, however loving and affectionate, may fail to provide for their children because not everything is at their disposal; they may frequently lack both the power and the means, though to will may be present with them. But the Lord who made and who governs all things can never lack will, power, nor means. The promise is sure to the children, and the children are those who take the Almighty for their God. For the promise belongs to no soul that is not separate from sinful ways, works, and men. Those who touch the unclean thing, i.e., who do what God forbids, and hold communion with unrighteousness, can never stand in the endearing relation of children to God Almighty: and this is most forcibly stated by God himself in these verses, and in the beginning of the following chapter, the first verse of which should conclude this.

CHAPTER 7 (MATTHEW HENRY)

Verses 1–4

These verses contain a double exhortation:

I. To make a progress in holiness, *v.* 1. 1. The dying unto sin. We must *cleanse ourselves from all filthiness of flesh and spirit.* There are sins of the flesh, that are committed with the body, and sins of the spirit; and we must cleanse ourselves from the filthiness of both.

CHAPTER 7 (JAMIESON, FAUSSET, BROWN)

Vss. 1-16. SELF-PURIFICATION THEIR DUTY RESULTING FROM THE FOREGOING. HIS LOVE TO THEM, AND JOY AT THE GOOD EFFECTS ON THEM OF HIS FORMER EPISTLE, AS REPORTED BY TITUS. **1. cleanse ourselves**—This is the conclusion of the exhortation (ch. 6:1, 14; I John 3:3; Rev. 22:11). **filthiness**—"the unclean thing" (ch. 6:17). **of the flesh**—for instance, *fornication,* prevalent at Corinth (I Cor. 6:15-18). **and spirit**—for instance, *idolatry,* direct or indirect (I Cor. 6:9; 8:1, 7; 10:7, 21, 22). The spirit (Ps. 32:2) receives pollution through the flesh, the instrument of uncleanness.

CHAPTER 7 (ADAM CLARKE)

1. *Having therefore these promises.* The promises mentioned in the last three verses of the preceding chapter, to which this verse should certainly be joined. *Let us cleanse ourselves.* Let us apply to Him for the requisite grace of purification; and avoid everything in spirit and practice which is opposite to the doctrine of God, and which has a tendency to pollute the soul. *Filthiness of the flesh.* The apostle undoubtedly means drunkenness, fornication, adultery, and all such sins as are done immediately against the body; and by *filthiness of the . . . spirit,* all impure desires, unholy thoughts, and polluting imaginations. If we avoid and abhor evil inclinations, and turn away our eyes from beholding vanity, incentives

MATTHEW HENRY

2. The living unto righteousness and holiness. We must be still perfecting holiness, and not be contented with sincerity (which is our gospel perfection), without aiming at sinless perfection. This we must do in the *fear of God*; there is no holiness without it.

II. To show a due regard to the ministers of the gospel: *Receive us, v.* 2. If the ministers of the gospel are thought contemptible because of their office, there is danger lest the gospel itself be contemned also. He had done nothing to forfeit their esteem (*v.* 2).

He did not herein reflect upon them for want of affection to him, *v.* 3. He assures them again of his great affection to them, insomuch that he could spend his last breath at Corinth, and *live and die with them.*

It was his great affection to them that made him use such *boldness* of *speech towards them*, and caused him to *glory*, or make his boast of them.

Verses 5–11

I. How he was distressed, *v.* 5. He was troubled when he did not meet with Titus at Troas, and afterwards when for some time he did not meet with him in Macedonia. There were *fightings without* and there were *fears within.*

JAMIESON, FAUSSET, BROWN

perfecting holiness —The *cleansing away* impurity is a positive step towards holiness (ch. 6:17). It is not enough to begin; the end crowns the work (Gal. 3:3; 5:7; Phil. 1:6). **fear of God**—often conjoined with the consideration of the most glorious promises (ch. 5:11; Heb. 4:1). Privilege and promise go hand in hand.

2. Receive us—with *enlarged* hearts (ch. 6:13). **we have wronged . . . corrupted . . . defrauded no man**—(cf. vs. 9). This is the ground on which he asks their reception of (making room for) him in their hearts. We *wronged* none by an undue exercise of apostolic authority; vs. 13 gives an instance in point. We have corrupted none, viz., by beguilements and flatteries, while preaching "another Gospel," as the false teachers did (ch. 11:3, 4). We have defrauded none by "making a gain" of you (ch. 12:17). Modestly he leaves them to supply the *positive* good which he had done; suffering all things himself that they might be benefited (vss. 9, 12; ch. 12:13).

3. In excusing myself, I do not accuse you, as though you suspected me of such things [MENOCHIUS], or as though you were guilty of such things; for I speak only of the false apostles "ESTIUS and *Greek commentators*]. Rather, "as though you were ungrateful and treacherous" [BEZA]. **I . . . said before**—in ch. 6:11, 12; cf. Phil. 1:7. **die and live with you** —the height of friendship. I am ready to die and live with you and for you (Phil. 1:7, 20, 24; 2:17, 18). Cf. as to Christ, John 10:11.

4. boldness of speech—(cf. ch. 6:11). **glorying of you**—Not only do I speak with unreserved openness *to you*, but I *glory* (boast) *greatly to others in your behalf*, in speaking *of you*. **filled with comfort**—at the report of Titus (vss. 6, 7, 9, 13; ch. 1:4). **exceeding joyful** —*Greek*, I *overabound* with joy (vss. 7, 9, 16).

our tribulation—described in vs. 5; also in ch. 4:7, 8; 6: 4, 5.

5. *Greek*, "For also" (for "*even*"). This verse is thus connected with ch. 2:12, 13, "When I came to Troas, I had no rest in my *spirit*"; so "*also*" now, when I came to Macedonia, my "*flesh*" had no rest (he, by the term "flesh," excepts his *spiritual* consolations) from "fightings with adversaries "without" (I Cor. 5:12), and from fears for the Corinthian believers "within" the Church, owing to "false brethren" (ch. 11:26). Cf. ch. 4:8; Deuteronomy 32:25, to which he seems to allude.

ADAM CLARKE

to evil being thus lessened (for the eye affects the heart), there will be the less danger of our falling into outward sin. And if we avoid all outward occasions of sinning, evil propensities will certainly be lessened. All this is our work under the common aids of the grace of God. We may turn away our eyes and ears from evil, or we may indulge both in what will infallibly beget evil desires and tempers in the soul. How can those expect God to purify their hearts who are continually indulging their eyes, ears, and hands in what is forbidden, and in what tends to increase and bring into action all the evil propensities of the soul? *Perfecting holiness.* Getting the whole mind of Christ brought into the soul. This is the grand object of a genuine Christian's pursuit. The means of accomplishing this are: (1) Resisting and avoiding sin, in all its inviting and seducing forms. (2) Setting the *fear of God* before our eyes, that we may dread His displeasure, and abhor whatever might excite it, and whatever might provoke Him to withhold His manna from our mouths.

2. *Receive us.* This address is variously understood. *Receive us* into your affections—love us as we love you. *Receive us* as your apostles and teachers; we have given you full proof that God has both sent and owned us. *Receive,* "comprehend," what we now say to you, and carefully mark it. *We have wronged no man.* We have never acted contrary to the strictest justice. *We have corrupted no man.* With any false doctrine or pernicious opinion. *We have defrauded no man.* Of any part of his property. But what have your false teachers done? They have beguiled you from the simplicity of the truth, and thus corrupted your minds, chap. xi. 3. They have brought you into bondage; they have taken of you, devoured you, exalted themselves against you, and you have patiently suffered all this, chap. xi. 20. It is plain that he refers here to the false apostle or teacher which they had among them.

3. *I speak not this to condemn* you. I do not speak to reproach but to correct you. I wish you to open your eyes and see how you are corrupted, spoiled, and impoverished by those whom you have incautiously preferred to the true apostles of Jesus Christ. *I have said before, that ye are in our hearts.* He has in effect and substance said this in chap. i. 6-8; ii. 4, 12; iii. 2; and v. 13. *To die and live with you.* An expression which points out the strongest affection, as in cases where love blinds us to the faults of those whom we love, and causes us to prefer them to all others.

4. *Great is my boldness of speech.* He seems to refer to the manner in which he spoke of them to others. *Great is my glorying of you.* They had probably been very loving and affectionate previously to the time in which they were perverted by their false apostle. He therefore had boasted of them in all the churches. *I am filled with comfort.* My affection for you has still the most powerful ascendancy in my soul. Here we may see the affection of the most tender father to his children. *I am exceeding joyful.* "I superabound in joy"; I have a joy beyond expression—an extremely rare verb. I have not met with it in any Greek author; and it occurs nowhere in the New Testament but here and in Rom. v. 20. *In all our tribulation.* Perhaps *epi* here should be rendered "under" instead of *in*, as it signifies, Mark ii. 26; Luke iii. 2; Acts xi. 28. "Under all our tribulations, I feel inexpressible joy on your account."

5. *When we were come into Macedonia.* Paul, having left Ephesus, came to Troas, where he stopped some time; afterwards he came to Macedonia, whence he wrote this Epistle. *Our flesh had no rest.* So exceedingly anxious was he to know the success of his First Epistle to them. *Without were fightings.* The oppositions of pagans, Jews, and false brethren. *Within were fears.* Uncertain conjectures relative to the success of his Epistle; fears lest the severity of it should alienate their affections utterly from him; fears lest the party of the incestuous person should have prevailed; fears lest the teaching of the false apostle should have perverted their minds from the simplicity of the truth. All was uncertainty, all apprehension; and the Spirit of God did not think proper to remove the causes of these apprehensions in any ex-

MATTHEW HENRY

II. How he was comforted, *v.* 6, 7. The very coming of Titus was some comfort to him. The good news which Titus brought concerning the Corinthians was matter of greater consolation. He found Titus to be comforted in them; and this filled the apostle with comfort. He ascribes all his comfort to God as the author. It was God who comforted him by the coming of Titus, *v.* 6.

III. How greatly he rejoiced at their repentance. The apostle was sorry that it was needful he should make those sorry whom he would rather have made glad, *v.* 8.

But now he rejoiced, when he found they had *sorrowed to repentance, v.* 9. The effect of it (*repentance unto salvation, v.* 10), made him rejoice.

1. The antecedent of true repentance is godly sorrow. It was a godly sorrow, because a sorrow for sin. Godly sorrow will end in salvation; but worldly sorrow worketh death. The sorrows of worldly men for worldly things will bring down grey hairs the sooner to the grave. Humiliation and godly sorrow are previously necessary in order to repentance, and both of them are from God, the giver of all grace.

2. The happy fruits and consequences of true repentance are mentioned (*v.* 11). Where the heart is changed, the life and actions will be changed too. It wrought indignation at sin; it wrought fear, a fear of reverence, an awful fear of God, a cautious fear of sin, and a jealous fear of themselves. It wrought vehement desires after a thorough reformation of what had been amiss. It wrought zeal, a mixture of love and anger, a zeal for duty, and against sin. And thus *in all things had they approved themselves to be clear in that matter.* They were penitent, and therefore clear of guilt before God, who would pardon and not punish them.

JAMIESON, FAUSSET, BROWN

Translate in the order required by the *Greek,* "But he that comforteth those that are cast down, even God." Those that are of an high spirit are not susceptible of such comfort. **7. when he told us**—*Greek,* "telling us." We shared in the comfort which Titus felt in recording your desire (vs. 13). *He* rejoiced in telling the news; *we* in hearing them [ALFORD]. **earnest desire**—*Greek,* "longing desire," viz., *to see me* [GROTIUS]; or, in general, *towards me, to please me.* **mourning**—over your own remissness in not having immediately punished the sin (I Cor. 5:1, etc.) which called forth my rebuke. **fervent mind**—*Greek,* "zeal" (cf. vs. 11; John 2:17). **toward me**—*Greek,* "for me"; for my sake. They *in Paul's behalf* showed the zeal against the sin which Paul would have shown had he been present. **rejoiced the more**—more than before, at the mere coming of Titus. **8. with a letter**—*Greek,* "in the letter" viz., the first Epistle to the Corinthians. **I do not repent, though I did repent**—Translate, "I do not *regret* it, though I did *regret* it." The *Greek* words for *regret* and *repent* are distinct. Paul was almost regretting, through parental tenderness, his having used rebukes calculated to grieve the Corinthians; but now that he has learned from Titus the salutary effect produced on them, he no longer regrets it. **for I perceive . . .**—This is explanatory of "I did repent" or "regret it," and is parenthetical ("for I perceive that *that* Epistle did make you sorry, though it was but for a season"). **9. Now I rejoice**—Whereas "I did repent" or regret having made you sorry by my letter, I rejoice NOW, not that ye were caused sorrow, but that your sorrow resulted in your repentance. **ye sorrowed**—rather, as before, "ye were made sorry." **after a godly manner**—lit., "according to God," i.e., your sorrow having regard to God, and rendering your mind conformable to God (Rom. 14:22; I Pet. 4:6). **that**—Translate in *Greek* order, "*to the end that* (cf. ch. 11:9) ye might in nothing receive damage from us," which ye would have received, had your sorrow been other than that "after a godly manner" (vs. 10). **10. worketh . . . worketh**—In the best *Greek* reading the translation is, "worketh (simply) . . . worketh *out.*" "Sorrow" is not repentance, but, where it is "godly," "worketh" it; i.e., *contributes* or *tends to* it (the same *Greek* word is in Rom. 13:10). The "sorrow of the world" (i.e., such as is felt by the worldly) "worketh *out,*" as its *result at last,* (eternal) death (the same *Greek* verb is in ch. 4:17, where see the *Note*). **repentance . . . not to be repented of**—There is not in the *Greek* this play on words, so that the word qualified is not "repentance" merely, but "repentance unto salvation"; this, he says, *none will ever regret,* however attended with "sorrow" at the time. "*Repentance*" implies a *coming to a right mind;* "regret" implies merely uneasiness of feeling at the past or present, and is applied even to the *remorse* of Judas (Matt. 27:3; *Greek,* "stricken with remorse," not as *English Version,* "repented himself"); so that, though always accompanying repentance, it is not always accompanied by repentance. "Repentance" removes the impediments in the way of "salvation" (to which "death," viz., of the soul, is opposed). "The sorrow of the world" is not at the *sin* itself, but at its *penal consequences:* so that the tears of pain are no sooner dried up, than the pleasures of ungodliness are renewed. So Pharaoh, Exodus 9:27, 28-30; and Saul, I Sam. 15: 23-30. Cf. Isaiah 9:13; Revelation 16:10, 11. Contrast David's "godly sorrow," II Samuel 12:13, and Peters, Matthew 26:75. **11.** Confirmation of vs. 10 from the Corinthians' own experience. **carefulness**—solicitude, lit., "diligence"; opposed to their past negligence in the matter. **in you**—*Greek* "for you." **yea**—not only "carefulness" or *diligence,* but also "clearing of yourselves," viz., to me by Titus: anxiety to show you disapproved of the deed. **indignation**—against the offender. **fear**—of the wrath of God, and of sinning any more [SCLATER and CALVIN]; fear of Paul [GROTIUS], (I Cor. 4:2, 19-21). **vehement desire**—longing for restoration to Paul's approval [CONYBEARE and HOWSON]. "Fear" is in spite of one's self. "Longing desire" is spontaneous, and implies strong love and an aspiration for correction [CALVIN]. "Desire" *for the presence of Paul,* as he had given them the hope of it (I Cor. 4:19; 16:5) [GROTIUS and ESTIUS]. **zeal**—for right and for God's honor against what is wrong. Or, "for the good of the soul of the offender" [BENGEL]. **revenge**—*Translate,* "Exacting of punishment" (I Cor. 5:2, 3). Their "carefulness" was exhibited in the six points just specified: "clearing of themselves," and "indignation" in relation to themselves; "fear" and "vehement desire" in respect to the apostle; "zeal" and "revenge" in respect to the offender [BENGEL]; (cf. vs. 7). **In all**—the respects

ADAM CLARKE

traordinary way.

6. *Comforted us by the coming of Titus.* Who brought him a most satisfactory account of the success of his Epistle, and the good state of the Corinthian church.

7. *He told us your earnest desire.* To see me, and correct what was amiss among yourselves. *Your mourning.* Because you had sinned. *Your fervent mind.* The zeal you felt to testify your affectionate regard for me.

8. *I do not repent, though I did repent.* Though I had many doubts in my mind concerning the success of my letter, and though I grieved that I was obliged to write with so much severity, the case absolutely requiring it, yet now I am not sorry that I have written that letter, because I find it has completely answered the end for which it was sent.

9. *Ye sorrowed to repentance.* You had such a sorrow as produced a complete change of mind and conduct. We see that a man may sorrow and yet not repent. *Made sorry after a godly manner.* It was not a sorrow because you were found out, but a sorrow because you had sinned against God. *Damage by us in nothing.* Your repentance prevented that exercise of my apostolic duty which would have consigned your bodies to destruction, that your souls might be saved in the day of the Lord Jesus.

10. *For godly sorrow.* That which has the breach of God's holy law for its object. *Worketh repentance,* a thorough "change of mind" *unto salvation,* because the person who feels it cannot rest till he finds pardon through the mercy of God. *But the sorrow of the world worketh death.* Sorrow for lost goods, lost friends, death of relatives, when it is poignant and deep, produces diseases, increases those that already exist, and often leads men to lay desperate hands on themselves. This sorrow leads to destruction, the other leads to salvation; the one leads to heaven, the other to hell.

11. *What carefulness it wrought in you.* Carefulness of obeying my directions, v. 15; *yea, what clearing of yourselves* from guilt by inflicting censures on the guilty person, and putting away evil from among you, 1 Cor. xv. 18; *yea, what indignation* against him who had dishonored his profession, and defiled the church; *yea, what fear* of my displeasure, and the rod which I threatened, 1 Cor. iv. 21; *yea, what vehement desire* to rectify what was amiss in this matter, v. 7;

yea, what zeal for me; *yea, what revenge* in punishing the delinquent!

In all things. In the whole of your conduct in this affair since you have received my letter, *ye have approved yourselves to be clear;* not only to be clear of contumacy and obstinate persistence in your former conduct, but to have done all in the compass of your power to rectify the abuses which had crept in among you.

MATTHEW HENRY

Verses 12–16

The apostle endeavours to comfort the Corinthians. He had a good design in his former epistle, which might be thought severe, *v.* 12. It was not chiefly *for his cause that did the wrong*, nor was it merely *for his cause that suffered wrong*, but it was also to manifest his sincere concern and *care for them.*

Titus was rejoiced, and his spirit refreshed, with their comfort, and this comforted and rejoiced the apostle also (*v.* 13); and, as Titus was comforted while he was with them, so when he remembered his reception among them, the thought of these things increased his affections to them, *v.* 15. Great comfort and joy follow upon godly sorrow. Paul was glad, and Titus was glad, and the Corinthians were comforted. Well may all this joy be on earth, when there is joy in heaven over one sinner that repenteth. He was not ashamed of his boasting concerning them to Titus (*v.* 14);

for he was not disappointed in his expectation concerning them, and he could now with great joy declare what confidence he still had in them as to all things.

JAMIESON, FAUSSET, BROWN

just stated. **clear**—*Greek,* "pure," viz., from complicity in the guilty deed. "Approved yourselves," *Greek,* "commended yourselves." Whatever suspicion of complicity rested on you (I Cor. 5:2, 6) through your former remissness, you have cleared off by your present strenuousness in reprobating the deed. **12. though I wrote unto you**—"making you sorry with my letter" (vs. 8). **his cause that suffered wrong**—the father of the incestuous person who had his father's wife (I Cor. 5:1). The father, thus it seems, was alive. **that our care for you . . .**—Some of the oldest MSS. read thus, "That YOUR care for US might be made manifest unto you. . . ." But the words, "unto you," thus, would be rather obscure; still the obscurity of the genuine reading may have been the very reason for the change being made by correctors into the reading of *English Version.* ALFORD explains the reading: "He wrote in order to bring out their zeal on his behalf (i.e., to obey his command), and make it manifest *to themselves* in God's sight, i.e., to bring out *among them* their zeal to regard and obey him." But some of the oldest MSS. and versions (including the *Vulgate* and old *Italian*) support *English Version.* And the words, "to you," suit it better than the other reading. Ch. 2:4, "I wrote . . . that ye might know the love which *I* have more abundantly *unto you,"* plainly accords with it, and disproves ALFORD'S assertion that *English Version* is *inconsistent with the fact* as to the purpose of his letter. His writing, he says, was not so much for the sake of the individual offender, or the individual offended, but from his "earnest care" or concern for the welfare of the Church. **13.** The oldest MSS. read thus, "Therefore (*Greek,* "for this *cause,"* viz., because our aim has been attained) we have been (*English Version,* "were," is not so accurate) comforted; yea (*Greek,* "but"), in OUR comfort we exceedingly the more joyed for the joy of Titus . . ." (cf. vs. 7). **14. anything**—i.e., at all. **I am not ashamed**—"I am not put to shame," viz., by learning from Titus that you did not realize the high character I gave him of you. **as . . . all things . . . in truth, even so our boasting . . . is found a truth**—As our speaking *in general* to you was true (ch. 1:18), so our *particular* boasting to Titus *concerning you* is now, by his report, proved to be truth (cf. ch. 9:2). Some oldest MSS. read expressly, "concerning you"; this in either reading is the *sense.* **15. his inward affection**—lit., bowels (cf. ch. 6:12; Phil. 1:8; 2:1; Col. 3:12). **obedience**—(ch. 2:9).

fear and trembling—with trembling anxiety to obey my wishes, and fearful lest there should be aught in yourselves to offend him and me (vs. 11; cf. I Cor. 2:3).

16. therefore—omitted in the oldest MSS. The conclusion is more emphatical without it. **that I have confidence in you in all things**—rather, as *Greek,* "that in everything I *am of good courage concerning* (lit., in the case of) you," as contrasted with my former doubts concerning you.

ADAM CLARKE

The Corinthians were not *clear,* i.e., innocent or void of blame in the fact, but they were clear of all blame in their endeavors to remove the evil.

12. *Not for his cause that had done the wrong.* Viz., the incestuous person. *Nor for his cause that suffered wrong.* Some think the apostle means himself; others, that he means the church at Corinth, the singular being put for the plural; others, the family of the incestuous person; and others, the father of the incestuous person. If this latter opinion be adopted, it would seem to intimate that the father of this person was yet alive, which would make the transgression more flagrant; but these words might be spoken in reference to the father, if dead, whose cause should be vindicated; as his injured honor might be considered, like Abel's blood, to be crying from the earth. *But that our care for you . . . might appear.* It was not to get the delinquent punished, nor merely to do justice to those who had suffered in this business, that the apostle wrote his Epistle to them, but that they might have the fullest proof of his fatherly affection for them, and his concern for the honor of God.

13. *For the joy of Titus.* Titus, who had now met Paul in Macedonia, gave him the most flattering accounts of the improved state of the Corinthian church; and indeed their kind usage of Titus was a full proof of their affection for Paul.

14. *For if I have boasted.* The apostle had given Titus a very high character of this church, and of their attachment to himself, and doubtless this was the case previously to the evil teacher coming among them, who had succeeded in changing their conduct, and changing in a great measure their character also. But now they return to themselves, so that the good character which the apostle gave them before, and which they had for a time forfeited, is now as applicable to them as ever. Therefore his boasting of them is still found a truth.

15. *Whilst he remembereth the obedience of you all.* This is a very natural picture; he represents Titus as overjoyed even while he is delivering his account of the Corinthian church. He expatiated on it with extreme delight, and thereby showed at once both his love for Paul and his love for them. He loved them because they so loved the apostle; and he loved them because they had shown such kindness to himself; and he loved them because he found so many excellent and rare gifts, joined to so much humility, producing such an exemplary and holy life. *With fear and trembling ye received him.* You reverenced his authority; you were obedient to his directions; and you dreaded lest anything should be undone or ill done which he had delivered to you in the name of God.

16. *I have confidence in you in all things.* It appears that the apostle was now fully persuaded, from the accounts given by Titus, that every scandal had been put away from this church; that the faction which had long distracted and divided them was nearly broken; that all was on the eve of being restored to its primitive purity and excellence; and that their character was now so firmly fixed that there was no reason to apprehend that they should be again tossed to and fro with every wind of doctrine.

MATTHEW HENRY — CHAPTER 8

Verses 1–6

I. The apostle takes occasion from the good example of the churches of Macedonia to exhort the Corinthians to the good work of charity.

1. He acquaints them with their great liberality, *v.* 1. It is great grace and favour from God, if we are made useful to others.

JAMIESON, FAUSSET, BROWN — CHAPTER 8

VSS. 1-24. THE COLLECTION FOR THE SAINTS; THE READINESS OF THE MACEDONIANS A PATTERN TO THE CORINTHIANS; CHRIST THE HIGHEST PATTERN; EACH IS TO GIVE WILLINGLY AFTER HIS ABILITY; TITUS AND TWO OTHERS ARE THE AGENTS ACCREDITED TO COMPLETE THE COLLECTION. **1. we do you to wit**—*we make known to you.* **the grace of God bestowed on the churches of Macedonia**—Their liberality was not of themselves naturally, but of God's grace bestowed on them, and enabling them to be the instrument of God's "grace" to others (vss. 6, 19). The importance given in this Epistle to the collection, arose as well from Paul's engagement (Gal. 2:10), as also chiefly from his hope to conciliate the Judaizing Christians at Jerusalem to himself and the Gentile believers, by such an act of love on the part of the latter towards their

ADAM CLARKE — CHAPTER 8

1. *Moreover, brethren, we do you to wit.* In all our dignified version very few ill-constructed sentences can be found; however here is one, and the worst in the book. *We do you to wit* is in the original, "We made known unto you." This is plain and intelligible, the other is not so; and the form is now obsolete. *The grace of God bestowed.* The charitable contribution made by the churches in Macedonia, to which they were excited by the grace or influence of God upon their hearts; not *bestowed on,* but "given in." That *charis* means "liberality" appears from v. 6: "We desired Titus, that as he had begun, so he would also finish" this charitable contribution. And v. 7: That "ye abound" in this liberal contribution. And v. 19: "Who was also chosen of the churches to

MATTHEW HENRY

2. He commends the charity of the Macedonians. They were themselves in distress, yet they contributed to the relief of others, *v.* 2. As they had abundance of joy in the midst of tribulation, they abounded in their liberality; they gave out of a little, trusting in God to provide for them. They gave very largely, with *the riches of liberality* (*v.* 2); it was *according to*, yea *beyond, their power* (*v.* 3), as much as could well be expected from them, if not more. *They were willing of themselves* (*v.* 3), and were so far from needing that Paul should urge and press them that they *prayed him with much entreaty to receive the gift, v.* 4. Their charity was founded in true piety (*v.* 5). They solemnly made a fresh surrender of themselves, and all they had, unto the Lord Jesus Christ, sanctifying their contributions to God's honour, by first giving themselves to the Lord. We should give ourselves to God; we cannot bestow ourselves better. What we give or bestow for charitable uses will not be accepted of God, unless we first give ourselves to the Lord.

II. The apostle tells them that Titus was desired to go and make a collection among them (*v.* 6). Titus had already begun this work among them, therefore he was desired to finish it. When so good a work had already prospered in so good a hand, it would be a pity if it should not proceed and be finished. The work of charity will often succeed the best when the most proper persons are employed to solicit contributions and dispose of them.

Verses 7–15

I. He urges upon them the consideration of their eminence in other gifts and graces, and would have them excel in this of charity also, *v.* 7. When he would persuade the Corinthians to this good thing, he commends them for other good things. Most people love to be complimented, especially when we ask a gift of them; and it is a justice we owe to those in whom God's grace shines to give them their due commendation. What it was that the Corinthians abounded in. Faith is mentioned first, for that is the root. Those who abound in faith will abound in other graces and good works also. To their faith was added utterance. Many have faith who want utterance. With their utterance there appeared knowledge. They abounded also in all diligence. Those who have great knowledge and ready utterance are not always the most diligent Christians. Great talkers are not always the best doers. And further, they had abundant love to their ministers. Now to all these good things the apostle desires them to add this grace also, to abound in charity to the poor. He takes care to prevent any misapprehensions, and tells them (*v.* 8) he does not speak by commandment. I give *my advice, v.* 10. Many a thing which is good for us to do, yet cannot be said to be, by express and indispensable commandment, our duty at this or that time.

II. Another argument is taken from the consideration of the grace of our Lord Jesus Christ. And *you know,* saith the apostle, *the grace of our Lord Jesus Christ* (*v.* 9), *that though he was rich, yet for your sakes he became poor;* that ye thereby might be made rich, rich in the love of God, rich in the blessings of the new covenant, rich in the hopes of eternal life. We should be charitable to the poor out of what we have, because we ourselves live upon the charity of the Lord Jesus Christ.

JAMIESON, FAUSSET, BROWN

Jewish brethren.

2. trial of affliction—The *Greek* expresses, "in affliction (or, "tribulation") which *tested* them"; lit., "in a great testing of affliction." **abundance of their joy**—The greater was the depth of their poverty, the greater was the abundance of their joy. A delightful contrast in terms, and triumph, in fact, of spirit over flesh. **their deep poverty**—*Greek,* "their poverty down to the death of it." **abounded unto the riches . . .**—another beautiful contrast in terms: their *poverty* had the effect, not of producing stinted gifts, but of "abounding in the *riches* of liberality" (not as *Margin,* "simplicity"; though the idea of *singleness* of motive to God's glory and man's good, probably enters into the idea); (cf. Rom. 12:8, and *Margin;* ch. 9:11, *Note,* 13; Jas. 1:5). **3-5. they were willing**—rather, supply from vs. 5, the ellipsis thus, "According to their power . . . yea, and beyond their power, THEY GAVE." **of themselves**—not only not being besought, but themselves beseeching us. **4. that we would receive**—omitted in the oldest MSS. Translate therefore, "Beseeching of us . . . the grace and fellowship of (i.e., to grant them *the favor of sharing in*) the ministering unto the saints." The Macedonian contributions must have been from Philippi, because Philippi was the only church that contributed to Paul's support (Phil. 4:10, 15, 16). **5. And** *this they did,* **not as we hoped**—Translate, "And not as we hoped (i.e., far beyond our hopes), but their own selves gave they first to the Lord." "First," not indicating priority of time, but first of all, *above all in importance.* The giving of themselves takes precedency of their other gifts, as being the motive which led them to the latter (Rom. 15: 16). **by the will of God**—not *"according to* the will of God," but *"moved by* the will of God, who made them willing" (Phil. 2:13). It is therefore called (vs. 1), "the grace of God." **6. Insomuch that**—As we saw the Macedonians' alacrity in giving, we could not but exhort Titus, that as we collected in Macedonia, so he in Corinth should complete the work of collecting which he had already begun there, lest ye, the wealthy people of Corinth, should be outdone in liberality by the poor Macedonians. **as he had begun**—*Greek, "previously* begun," viz., the collection at Corinth, *before* the Macedonians began to contribute, during the visit to Corinth from which he had just returned. **finish in you the same grace**—complete among you this act of grace or beneficence on your part. **also**—as well as other things which he had to do among them [ALFORD]. **7. in faith**—(ch. 1:24). **utterance**—(*Note,* I Cor. 1: 5). Not as ALFORD, "doctrine" or "word." **knowledge**—(I Cor. 8:1). **diligence**—in everything that is good. **your love to us**—lit., "love from you (i.e., on your part) in us" (i.e., which has us for its object; which is felt *in the case of* us). **8. not by commandment**—"not by way of commandment." **by the occasion of the forwardness of others, and . . .**—rather, "But by (mention of) the forwardness of others (as an inducement to you), and to prove (lit., proving) the sincerity of your love." The *Greek* is *"by means of,"* not *"on account of* the forwardness . . . ." BENGEL, ELLICOTT, and others translate, *"By means of* the forwardness of others, proving the sincerity of your love ALSO." The former is the simpler construction in the *Greek.* **9. ye know the grace**—the act of gratuitous love whereby the Lord emptied Himself of His previous heavenly glory (Phil. 2:6, 7) for your sakes. **became poor**—Yet this is not demanded of you (vs. 14); but merely that, without impoverishing yourselves, you should relieve others with your abundance. If the Lord did so much more, and at so much heavier a cost, for your sakes; much more may you do an act of love to your brethren at so little a sacrifice of self. **might be rich**—in the heavenly glory which constitutes His riches, and all other things, so far as is really good for us (cf. I Cor. 3: 21, 22). **10. advice**—Herein he does not (as some misinterpret the passage) disclaim inspiration for the advice he gives; but under the Spirit, states that it is his "opinion" [ALFORD] or "judgment" [ELLICOTT, and others], not a *command,* that so their

ADAM CLARKE

travel with us" with this charitable contribution, "which is administered," which is to be dispensed, "by us." This charity is styled the *grace of God,* either from its exceeding greatness (as the "cedars of God" and "mountains of God" signify great cedars and great mountains, Ps. xxxvi. 6; lxxx. 10); or rather, it is called so as proceeding from God, who is the Dispenser of all good, and the Giver of this disposition; for the motive of charity must come from Him. *The churches of Macedonia.* These were Philippi, Thessalonica, Berea.

2. *In a great trial of affliction.* The sense of this verse is the following: The Macedonians, though both poor and persecuted, rejoiced exceedingly that an opportunity was afforded them of doing good to their more impoverished and more persecuted brethren.

3. *For to their power.* In their liberality they had no rule but their ability; they believed they were bound to contribute all they could; and even this rule they transgressed, for they went *beyond their power*—they deprived themselves for a time of the necessaries of life, in order to give to others who were destitute even of necessaries.

4. *Praying us with much intreaty.* We had not to solicit them to this great act of kindness; they even entreated us to accept their bounty, and to take on ourselves the administration or application of it to the wants of the poor in Judea.

5. *Not as we hoped.* They far exceeded our expectations, for they consecrated themselves entirely to the work of God, giving themselves and all they possessed first unto the Lord; and then, as they saw that it was the will of God that they should come especially forward in this charitable work, they gave themselves to us to assist to the uttermost in providing relief for the suffering Christians in Judea.

6. *That we desired Titus.* Titus had probably laid the plan of this contribution when he was before at Corinth, according to the direction given by the apostle, 1 Cor. xvi. 1. *The same grace.* Liberality. See the note on v. 1.

7. *As ye abound in every thing. In faith,* crediting the whole testimony of God; in *utterance,* "in doctrine," knowing what to teach; *knowledge* of God's will, and prudence to direct you in teaching and doing it; in *diligence,* to amend all that is wrong among you, and to do what is right; *and in your love to us,* whom now you prize the apostles of the Lord, and your pastors in Him. *Abound in this grace also.* Be as eminent for your charitable disposition as you are for your faith, doctrine, knowledge, diligence, and love.

8. *I speak not by commandment.* I do not positively order this; I assume no right or authority over your property; what you devote of your substance to charitable purposes must be your own work, and a freewill offering. *The forwardness of others.* Viz., the churches of Macedonia, which had already exerted themselves so very much in this good work. And the apostle here intimates that he takes this opportunity to apprise them of the zeal of the Macedonians, lest those at Corinth, who excelled in every other gift, should be outdone in this.

9. *For ye know the grace of our Lord Jesus Christ.* This was the strongest argument of all; and it is urged home by the apostle with admirable address. *Ye know.* You are acquainted with God's ineffable love in sending Jesus Christ into the world; and you know the *grace*—the infinite benevolence of Christ himself. *That, though he was rich.* The Possessor, as He was the Creator, of the heavens and the earth. *For your sakes he became poor.* He emptied himself, and "made himself of no reputation, and took upon him the form of a servant, and . . . humbled himself . . . unto death, even the death of the cross." *That ye through his poverty*—through His humiliation and death, *might be rich*—might regain your forfeited inheritance, and be enriched with every grace of His Holy Spirit, and brought at last to His eternal glory.

10. *Herein I give my advice.* For I speak not by way of commandment, v. 8. *For this is expedient for you.* It is necessary you should do this to preserve a consistency of conduct; for

MATTHEW HENRY

III. Another argument is taken from their forwardness to begin this good work. It was expedient for them to finish what they had begun, *v.* 10, 11. Good purposes, indeed, are good things; they are like buds and blossoms, pleasant to behold, and give hopes of good fruit; but they are lost, and signify nothing, without performances which would be acceptable to God (*v.* 12). When men purpose that which is good, and endeavour to perform also, God will accept of what they can do, and not reject them for what is not in their power to do. This scripture will by no means justify those who think good meanings are enough.

IV. Another argument is taken from the distribution of the things of this world, and the mutability of human affairs, *v.* 13–15. Those who have a greater *abundance may supply those who are in want*, that there may be room for charity. It is the will of God that, by our mutually supplying one another, there should *be some sort of equality*.

All should think themselves concerned to supply those who are in want. This is illustrated by the instance of gathering and distributing manna in the wilderness: *he that had gathered much* had nothing over.

Verses 16–24

I. He commends Titus for his earnest care for them. This is mentioned with thankfulness to God (*v.* 16), and it is cause of thankfulness if God hath put it into the hearts of any to do us or others any good. He commends him for his readiness to this present service, *v.* 17. Asking charity for the relief of others is looked upon as a thankless office; yet it is a good office.

II. He commends another brother, who was sent with Titus. It is generally thought that this was Luke. He is commended as a man whose *praise was in the gospel through all the churches*, *v.* 18.

JAMIESON, FAUSSET, BROWN

offering might be free and spontaneous. **this**—my giving you an *advice*, not a command. **who have begun before**—"*seeing that* ye have begun *before*" *the Macedonian churches;* "a year ago" should be connected with this clause. **not only to do, but also to be forward**—There were three steps: (1) the *forwardness*, more literally, "the will"; (2) the *setting about* it, lit., "doing it"; (3) *completion* of it [ALFORD]. In the two former, not only the *act*, but the *intention*, the Corinthians *preceded the Macedonians*. BENGEL explains, "Not only to do" FOR THE PAST YEAR, "but also to be forward" or *willing* FOR THIS YEAR. ELLICOTT translates, "already," instead of "before": "Ye began already a year ago, not only to do, but also to be forward." It appears hence, that something had been done in the matter a year before; other texts, however, show the collection was not yet paid (cf. vs. 11 and ch. 9:5, 7). This agrees with one, and only one. supposition, viz., that every man had laid by in store the fund from which he was afterwards to contribute, the very case which is shown by I Cor. 16:2 to have existed [PALEY's *Horæ Paulinæ*]. **11. perform**—"complete the doing also" (*Note*, vs. 10). **a readiness to will**—*Greek, "the* readiness *of* will"; referring to vs. 10, where the *Greek* for "to be forward," ought to be translated as here, "to will." **performance**—"completion" [ALFORD]. The godly should show the same zeal to finish, as well as to begin well, which the worldly exhibit in their undertakings (Jer. 44:25). **12. For**—Following up the rule "out of that which ye have" (vs. 11), and no more. **a willing mind**—rather, as *Greek*, "the readiness," viz., to will, referring to vs. 11. **accepted**—*Greek* "favorably accepted." **according to that a man hath**—The oldest MSS. omit "a man." Translate, "According to whatsoever it have"; the *willing mind*, or "readiness" to will, is personified [ALFORD]. Or better, as BENGEL, "*He is* accepted according to whatsoever he have"; so ch. 9:7, The Lord loveth a cheerful *giver*." Cf. as to David, I Kings 8:18. God accepts the will for the deed. He judges not according to what a man has the opportunity to do, but according to what he would do if he had the opportunity (cf. Mark 14:8; and the widow's mite, Luke 21:3, 4). **13. For**—Supply from vs. 8, "I speak." My aim is not that others (viz., the saints at Jerusalem) may be relieved at the cost of your being "distressed" (so the *Greek* for "burdened"). The golden rule is, "Love thy neighbour *as thyself*," not *more* than thyself. **14. by an equality**—"by the rule of equality" [ALFORD]: lit., "out of equality." **now at this time**—*Greek*, "at the present juncture" or season. **that their abundance also**—The *Greek* being distinct from the previous "that," translate, "in order that," viz., *at another season*, when your relative circumstances may be reversed. The reference is solely to *temporal* wants and supplies. Those, as BENGEL, who quote Romans 15:27 for interpreting it of spiritual supplies from the Jews to the Gentiles, forget that Romans 15:27 refers to the *past* benefit spiritually, which the Jews have conferred on the Gentiles, as a motive to *gratitude* on the part of the latter, not to a *prospective* benefit to be looked for from the former, which the text refers to. **15.** Exodus 16:18; LXX. As God gave an equal portion of manna to all the Israelites, whether they could gather much or little; so Christians should promote by liberality an equality, so that none should need the necessaries of life while others have superfluities. "Our luxuries should yield to our neighbor's comforts; and our comforts to his necessities" [J. HOWARD]. **16, 17.** Returning to the subject of vs. 6. **for you**—Translate, "Which put the same earnest care for you into the heart of Titus," as was in myself. My care for you led me to "*desire*" him (vss. 6 and 17, "*exhortation*," the same *Greek*); but Titus had of himself the same care, whence he "accepted (gladly) my exhortation" (vs. 17) to go to you (vs. 6). **being more forward**—more earnest than to need such exhortation. **he went**—*Greek*, "went forth." *We* should say, *he is going* forth; but the ancients put the *past* tense in letterwriting, as the things will have been past by the time that the correspondent, receives the letter. "Of his own accord," i.e., it is true he has been exhorted by me to go, but he shows that he has anticipated my desires, and already, "of his own accord," has desired to go. **18. the brother, whose praise is in the gospel**—whose praise is known in connection with the Gospel: *Luke* may be meant; **not that "the Gospel" here refers to his *written*** Gospel; but the language implies some one well known throughout the churches, and at that time with Paul, as Luke then was (Acts 20:6). Not a Macedonian, as appears from ch. 9:4. Of all Paul's "companions in travel" (vs. 19; Acts 19:29),

ADAM CLARKE

you began this work a year ago, and it is necessary that you should complete it as soon as possible. *Not only to do, but also to be forward.* Literally, "to do and to will"; but as the will must be before the deed, *thelein* must be taken here in the sense of "delight," as it frequently means in the Old and New Testaments. *A year ago.* It was about a year before this that the apostle, in his First Epistle, chap. xvi. 2, had exhorted them to make this contribution; and there is no doubt that they, in obedience to his directions, had begun to lay up in store for this charitable purpose. He therefore wishes them to complete this good work, and thus show that they were not led to it by the example of the Macedonians, seeing they themselves had been first movers in this business.

11. *A readiness to will, so there may be a performance.* You have willed and purposed this; now perform it. *Out of that which ye have.* Give as God has enabled you; and give as God has disposed you. He requires each man to do as he can, and accepts the will where the means are wanting to perform the deed.

12. *According to that a man hath.* According to his real property; not taking that which belongs to his own family, and is indispensably necessary for their support; and not taking that which belongs to others, viz., what he owes to any man.

13. *That other men be eased.* I do not design that you should impoverish yourselves in order that others may live affluently.

14. *But by an equality.* That you may do to those who are distressed now as, on a change of circumstances, you would wish them to do to you. And I only wish that of your *abundance* you would now minister to their wants; and it may be that *their abundance* may yet *supply* your wants; for so liable are all human affairs to change that it is as possible that you rich Corinthians should need the charitable help of others as it is that those Jews, who once had need of nothing, should now be dependent on your bounty. *That there may be equality.* That you may exert yourselves so in behalf of those poor people that there may be between you an *equality* in the necessaries of life, your abundance supplying them with that of which they are utterly destitute.

15. *He that had gathered much had nothing over.* On the passage to which the apostle alludes, Exod. xvi. 18, I have stated that, probably, every man gathered as much manna as he could, and when he brought it home and measured it by the omer (for this was the measure for each man's eating), if he had a surplus it went to the supply of some other family that had not been able to collect enough; the family being large, and the time in which the manna might be gathered, before the heat of the day, not being sufficient to collect a supply for so numerous a household, several of whom might be so confined as not to be able to collect for themselves. Thus there was an *equality* among the Israelites in reference to this thing, and in this light these words of Paul lead us to view the passage. To apply this to the present case: The Corinthians, in the course of God's providence, had gathered more than was absolutely necessary for their own support; by giving the surplus to the persecuted and impoverished Christian Jews there would be an *equality.*

16. *But thanks be to God.* He thanks God, who had already disposed the heart of Titus to attend to this business; and, with his usual address, considers all this as done in the behalf of the Corinthian church.

17. *He accepted the exhortation.* I advised him to visit you and excite you to this good work, and I found that he was already disposed in his heart to do it; God put this "earnest care into the heart of Titus for you," v. 16.

18. *The brother, whose praise is in the gospel.* Who this *brother* was we cannot tell; some suppose it was Luke, who wrote a Gospel, and who was the companion of Paul in several of his travels; others think it was Silas; others, Barnabas; others, Mark; and others, Apollos. Neither ancients nor moderns agree in either; but Luke, John, and Mark seem to have the most probable opinions in their favor. Whoever the person was, he was sufficiently known to the Corinthians, as we learn by what the apostle

MATTHEW HENRY

As one chosen of the churches (*v.* 19). This was done, it is most likely, at the request of Paul himself; *that no man might blame him in that abundance which was administered by him* (*v.* 20). He would not give occasion to any to accuse him of partiality, and thought it to be his duty, *to provide for things honest, not only in the sight of the Lord, but also in the sight of men.* We live in a censorious world, and should cut off occasion from those who seek occasion to speak reproachfully.

III. He commends also another brother. This brother is thought to be Apollos. Whoever he was, he had *approved himself diligent in many things*; and therefore was fit to be employed in this affair.

IV. He concludes with a general good character of them all (*v.* 23). Wherefore, he exhorts them to show their liberality that these messengers of the churches, and the churches themselves, might see a full *proof of their love,* and that it was with good reason the apostle had even *boasted on their behalf, v.* 24.

JAMIESON, FAUSSET, BROWN

Luke was the most prominent, having been his companion in preaching the Gospel at his first entrance into Europe (Acts 16:10). The fact that the person here referred to was "chosen of the churches" as their trustee to travel with Paul in conveying the contribution to Jerusalem, implies that he had resided among them some time before: this is true of Luke, who after parting from Paul at Philippi (as he marks by the change from "we" to "they," Acts 16) six years before, is now again found in his company in Macedonia. In the interim he had probably become so well known that "his praise was throughout all the churches." Cf. ch. 12:18; Philemon 24. He who is faithful in the Gospel will be faithful also in matters of inferior importance [BENGEL]. **19. not** *that* **only**—not only praised in all the churches. **chosen**—by vote: so the *Greek.* **of the churches**—therefore these companions of Paul are called "messengers of the churches" (vs. 23). **to travel**—to Jerusalem. **with this grace**—*Greek, "in the case of* this grace," or "*gift.*" **to the glory of the same Lord**—The oldest MSS. omit "same." **declaration of your ready mind**—The oldest MSS. read, "our," not *your.* This and the previous clause, "to the glory of the same Lord," do not follow "administered by us," but "chosen of the churches to travel . . . ." The union of the brother with Paul in this affair of the collection was done to guard against suspicions injurious "to the glory" of the Lord. It was also done in order to produce a "readiness" on the part of Paul and the brother to undertake the office which each, by himself, would have been less ready to undertake, for fear of suspicions arising (vs. 20) as to their appropriation of any of the money. **20. Avoiding**—taking precautions against this. **in this abundance**—*in the case of this abundance.* **21.** LXX (Prov. 3:4; Rom. 12:17). The oldest MSS. read, "For we provide." **honest things**—"*things* honorable" **22.** This *second* brother, BIRKS supposes to be Trophimus: for a Macedonian is not meant (ch. 9:4) probably the same as was sent before with Titus (ch. 12:18); and therefore sent from Ephesus, and probably an Ephesian: all this is true of Trophimus. **oftentimes . . . in many things**—Join and translate as in the *Greek,* "many times in many things." **upon the great confidence which I have in you**—"through the great confidence WHICH HE HAS towards you" [ALFORD]. BENGEL better supports *English Version,* **"We have sent . . . through the** confidence WHICH WE FEEL in regard to your liberality." **23. fellow helper concerning you**—*Greek,* "fellow worker towards you." **our brethren**—the two mentioned in vss. 18 and 22. **messengers**—rather, as the *Greek,* "apostles": in the less strict sense (Acts 14:14). **of the churches**—sent by the churches, as we are by the Lord (Phil. 2:25). There was in the synagogue an ecclesiastical officer, called "the angel of the Church," whence the title seems derived (cf. Rev. 2:1). **24.** The oldest MSS. read "[continue] *manifesting* to them in the face of the churches the manifestation of your love, and of our boasting on your behalf."

ADAM CLARKE

says of him in this place.

19. *Chosen of the churches to travel with us.* Appointed by a "show of hands." This appointment, by the suffrage of the churches, seems to refer more to Luke than anyone else. *With this grace.* Liberal contribution. See on v. 1. *Your ready mind.* Your willingness to relieve them. But, instead of *your,* "our" is the reading of almost all the best MSS. and all the versions. This is doubtless the true reading.

20. *Avoiding this, that no man should blame us.* Taking this prudent caution to have witnesses of our conduct, and such as were chosen by the churches themselves, that we might not be suspected of having either embezzled or misapplied their bounty.

21. *Providing for honest things.* Taking care to act so as not only to be clear in the sight of God, but also to be clear in the sight of all men, avoiding even the appearance of evil.

22. *We have sent with them.* Titus and probably Luke. *Our brother,* probably Apollos. *Now much more diligent.* Finding that I have the fullest confidence in your complete reformation and love to me, he engages in this business with alacrity, and exceeds even his former diligence.

23. *Whether any do enquire of Titus.* Should it be asked, "Who is this Titus?" I answer, He is my companion, and my fellow laborer in reference to you; chap. ii. 13; vii. 6-7. Should any inquire, Who are these *brethren,* Luke and Apollos? I answer, *They are "apostles" of the churches,* and intensely bent on promoting *the glory of Christ.*

24. *Wherefore shew ye to them, and before the churches.* Seeing they are persons every way worthy in themselves, and coming to you on such an important occasion, and so highly recommended, receive them affectionately; and let them thus see that the very high character I have given of you is not exaggerated, and that you are as ready in every work of charity as I have stated you to be. Act in this for your honor.

MATTHEW HENRY

CHAPTER 9

Verses 1–5

I. It was needless to press them with further arguments to afford relief to their poor brethren (*v.* 1). *He knew their forwardness* to every good work, and how they had begun this good work a year ago. He had boasted of their zeal to the Macedonians, and this had provoked many of them to do as they had done. As they had begun well, they would go on well.

II. He sends Titus and the other brethren to them, that, having this timely notice, they might be fully ready (*v.* 3), when he should come to them. When we would have others to do that which is good we must give them time. Another reason was that he might not be ashamed of his boasting concerning them, if they should be found unready, *v.* 3, 4. Some from Macedonia might *haply come with him*: and, if the collection should not then be made, this would make him, not to say them, ashamed.

JAMIESON, FAUSSET, BROWN

CHAPTER 9

Vss. 1-15. REASONS FOR HIS SENDING TITUS. THE GREATER THEIR BOUNTIFULNESS, THE MORE SHALL BE THE RETURN OF BLESSING TO THEM, AND THANKSGIVING TO GOD. **1. For**—connected with ch. 8:16: "Show love to the messengers of the churches; for as concerns the ministration for the saints, it is superfluous for me to write to you who are so forward already." **write**—emphatical: It is superfluous to *write,* for you will have witnesses present [BENGEL]. **2. ready a year ago**—to send off the money, owing to the apostle's former exhortation (I Cor. 16:1, 2). **your zeal**—*Greek,* "the zeal from you," i.e., on your part; propagated from you to others. **provoked**—i.e., stimulated. **very many**—*Greek,* "the greater number," viz., of the Macedonians. **3. have I sent**—we should say, **"I send"; whereas the** ancients put it in the past, the time which it would be by the time that the letter arrived. **the brethren**—(ch. 8:18, 22)—Titus and the two others. **should be in vain in this behalf**—"should be proved futile *in this particular,*" however true in general (ch. 7:4). A tacit compliment, softening the sharp monition. **as I said**—as I was saying (vs. 2). **4. if they of Macedonia**—rather as *Greek,* "if Macedonians." **unprepared**—with your collection; see vs. 2, "ready," *Greek,* "prepared." **we, not to say ye**—*Ye* would naturally feel more ashamed for yourselves, than we (who boasted of you) would for you. **confident boasting**—The oldest MSS. read simply "confi-

ADAM CLARKE

CHAPTER 9

1. *It is superfluous for me to write to you.* I need not enlarge, having already said enough. See the preceding chapter.

2. *I know the forwardness of your mind.* You have already firmly purposed to contribute to the support of the poor and suffering saints. *That Achaia was ready a year ago.* The apostle means not only Corinth but other churches in different parts about Corinth; we know there was a church at Cenchrea, one of the ports on the Corinthian Isthmus. *Your zeal hath provoked very many.* Hearing that the Corinthians were so intent on the relief of the sufferers in Palestine, other churches, and especially they of Macedonia, came forward the more promptly and liberally.

3. *Yet have I sent the brethren.* Titus and his companions, mentioned in the preceding chapter. *That, as I said, ye may be ready.* And he wished them to be ready, that they might preserve the good character he had given them. This was for their honor; and if they did not take care to do so, he might be reputed a liar; and thus both they and himself be *ashamed* before the Macedonians, should any of them at this time accompany him to Corinth.

MATTHEW HENRY

Verses 6–16

I. Proper directions to be observed about the right manner of bestowing charity. It should be bountifully. Men who expect a good return at harvest are not wont to pinch and spare in sowing their seed.

It should be deliberately: *Every man, according as he purposes in his heart, v.* 7. Works of charity, like other good works, should be done with thought and design. It should be freely given: *Not grudgingly, nor of necessity,* but cheerfully, *v.* 7. Persons sometimes will give merely to satisfy the importunity of those who ask their charity, and what they give is in a manner squeezed or forced from them, and this unwillingness spoils all they do.

II. Good encouragement to perform this work of charity.

1. They themselves would be no losers by what they gave in charity. What is given to the poor is far from being lost; as the precious seed which is cast into the ground is not lost, for it will spring up, and bear fruit; the sower shall receive it again with increase, *v.* 6. God loveth a cheerful giver (*v.* 7). Can a man be a loser by doing that with which God is pleased? God is able to make our charity redound to our advantage, *v.* 8. We have no reason to distrust the goodness of God; he is *able to make all grace abound.* The honour of it is lasting, the reward of it eternal.

A prayer to God that they might be gainers, and not losers, *v.* 10, 11. To whom the prayer is made—to God, *who ministereth seed to the sower,* who giveth such an increase of the fruits of the earth that we have not only bread sufficient to eat for one year, but enough to sow again for a future supply.

For what he prayeth. That they may have *bread for their food,* always a competency for themselves—that God will *multiply their seed sown,* that they may still be able to do more good—and that there may be *an increase of the fruits of righteousness,* so as to be *enriched in everything to all bountifulness* (*v.* 11). Works of charity are so far from impoverishing us that they are the proper means truly to enrich us, or make us truly rich.

2. While they would be no losers, the poor would be gainers, *v.* 12.

JAMIESON, FAUSSET, BROWN

dence," viz., in your liberality. **5. that they would go before**—Translate, "that they *should* . . . ." **whereof ye had notice before**—rather, "promised before"; "long announced by me to the Macedonians" (vs. 2) [BENGEL]. "Your promised bounty" [ELLICOTT and others]. **not as** *of* **covetousness**—Translate, "not as matter of covetousness," which it would be, if you gave niggardly.

6. *I say*—ELLICOTT and others supply the ellipsis thus: "But *remember* this." **bountifully**—lit., "*with*," or "*in blessings*." The word itself implies a *beneficent spirit in the giver* (cf. vs. 7, end), and the *plural* implies the *abundance* and liberality of the gifts. "The reaping shall correspond to the proportions and spirit of the sowing" [BENGEL]. Cf. Ezekiel 34:26, "Showers of blessing."

7. according as he purposeth in his heart—Let the full consent of the free will go with the gift [ALFORD]. Opposed to "of necessity," as "grudgingly" is opposed to "a *cheerful* giver" (Prov. 22:9; 11:25; Isa. 32:8).

8. all grace—even in external goods, and even while ye bestow on others [BENGEL]. **that**—"in order that." God's gifts are bestowed on us, not that we may have them to ourselves, but that we may the more "abound in good works" to others. **sufficiency**—so as not to need the help of others, having yourselves from God "bread for your food" (vs. 10). **in all** *things*—*Greek,* "in everything." **every good work**—of charity to others, which will be "your seed sown" (vs. 10). **9. As it is written**—realizing the highly blessed character portrayed in Psalm 112:9. **He**—the "good man" (Ps. 112:5). **dispersed**—as seed sown with full and open hand, without anxious thought in what direction each grain may fall. It is implied also that he *has* always what he may disperse [BENGEL]. So in Psalm 112:9. **the poor**—The *Greek* word is found here only in New Testament, "one in straitened circumstances, who earns his bread by labor." The word usually employed means "one so poor as to live by begging." **his righteousness**—Here "beneficence": the evidence of his being *righteous* before God and man. Cf. Deuteronomy 24:13; Matthew 6:1, "alms"; *Greek,* "righteousness." **remaineth**—unexhausted and unfailing. **10.** Translate, as in Isaiah 55:10, "He that ministereth (supplieth) seed to the sower and bread for food" (lit., "bread for *eating*"). **minister**—rather future, as the oldest MSS., "*Shall* minister (supply) and multiply." **your seed**—your means for liberality.

the fruits of your righteousness—the heavenly rewards for your Christian charity (Matt. 10:42). Righteousness shall be itself the reward, even as it is the thing rewarded (Hos. 10:12; Matt. 5:6; 6:33).

11. Cf. vs. 8. **bountifulness**—*Greek,* "single-minded liberality." Translated "simplicity," Romans 12:8. **causeth through us**—lit., "worketh through us"; i.e., through our instrumentality as the distributors. **thanksgiving**—on the part of the recipients. **12.** *Greek,* "The *ministration* of this *public* service (on your part) is not only *still further* supplying the wants of the saints (besides the supplies from other quarters), but is abounding also (viz., in respect to relieving the necessities of others in poverty through many thanksgivings to God."

ADAM CLARKE

5. *Whereof ye had notice before.* Instead of "spoken of before," several MSS. and several of the fathers have "what was promised before." The sense is not very different; probably the latter reading was intended to explain the former. *Bounty, and not as of covetousness.* Had they been backward, strangers might have attributed this to a covetous principle.

6. *He which soweth sparingly.* This is a plain maxim; no man can expect to reap but in proportion as he has sowed. And here almsgiving is represented as a seed sown, which shall bring forth a crop. If the sowing be liberal and the seed good, the crop shall be so too. Sowing is used among the Jews to express almsgiving; so they understand Isa. xxxii. 20: "Blessed are ye that sow beside all waters"; i.e., who are ready to help everyone that is in need. And Hos. x. 12, they interpret: "Sow to yourselves almsgiving, and ye shall reap in mercy"—if you show mercy to the poor, God will show mercy to you.

7. *Not grudgingly, or of necessity.* The Jews had in the Temple two chests for alms: the one was of what was necessary, i.e., what the law required; the other was of the freewill offerings. To escape perdition some would grudgingly give what necessity obliged them; others would give cheerfully, for the love of God, and through pity to the poor. Of the first, nothing is said; they simply did what the law required. Of the second much is said; God loves them. The benefit of almsgiving is lost to the giver when he does it with a grumbling heart.

8. *God is able to make all grace abound.* We have already seen, chap. viii. 1, that the word *charis,* in the connection in which the apostle uses it in these chapters, signifies a "charitable gift"; here it certainly has the same meaning. God is able to give you, in His mercy, abundance of temporal good; that, having a sufficiency, you may abound in every good work. This refers to the sowing plenteously; those who do so shall reap plenteously—they shall have an abundance of God's blessings.

9. *He hath dispersed abroad.* Here is still the allusion to the sower. He sows much, not at home merely, or among those with whom he is acquainted, but *abroad,* among the strangers, whether of his own or of another nation. The quotation is taken from Ps. cxii. 9. *He hath given to the poor.* This is the interpretation of "he hath scattered abroad"; and therefore it is said, *his righteousness remaineth for ever*—his good work is had in remembrance before God. By *righteousness* we have already seen that the Jews understand "almsgiving."

10. *Now he that ministereth seed to the sower.* The *sower,* as we have already seen, is he that gives alms of what he hath; and God, who requires him to give these alms, is here represented as providing him with the means. The word *he that ministereth* is very emphatic; it signifies "he who leads up the chorus"; it means also to "join to, associate, to supply or furnish one thing after another" so that there be no want or chasm. Thus God is represented, in the course of His providence, associating and connecting causes and effects; keeping everything in its proper place and state of dependence on another, and all upon himself; so that summer and winter, heat and cold, seedtime and harvest, regularly succeed each other. Thus God leads up this grand chorus of causes and effects. *The fruits of your righteousness.* Your beneficence.

11. *Being enriched in every thing.* Observe, Why does God give riches? That they may be applied to His glory and the good of men. Why does He increase riches? That those who have them may exercise all bountifulness. And if they be *enriched in every thing,* what will be the consequence if they do not exercise *all bountifulness?* Why, God will curse their blessings; the rust shall canker them, and the moth shall consume their garments. But if, on the other hand, they do thus apply them, then they cause *thanksgiving to God.* The ninth and tenth verses should be read in a parenthesis, for this verse connects with the eighth.

12. *For the administration of this service.* The poor are relieved, see the hand of God in this relief, and give God the glory for His grace.

MATTHEW HENRY

3. This would redound to the praise and glory of God. All who wished well to the gospel would *glorify God for this* proof *of subjection to the gospel of Christ*, and true love to all men, *v.* 13.

4. Those whose wants were supplied would make the best return they were able, by sending up many prayers to God for those who had relieved them, *v.* 14. As this is the only recompence the poor can make, so it is often greatly for the advantage of the rich.

Lastly, The apostle concludes this whole matter with this doxology, *Thanks be to God for his unspeakable gift*, *v.* 15. He means Jesus Christ, who is indeed the unspeakable gift of God unto this world.

JAMIESON, FAUSSET, BROWN

13. by—through occasion of. **experiment**—Translate, "the experience" [ELLICOTT and others]. Or, "the experimental proof" of your Christian character, afforded by "this ministration." **they**—the recipients. **for your professed subjection**—*Greek*, "for the subjection of your profession"; i.e., your subjection in accordance with your profession, in relation to the Gospel. Ye yield yourselves in willing subjection to the Gospel precepts, evinced in acts, as well as in profession. *your* **liberal distribution**—*Greek*, "the liberality of your contribution in relation to them . . . ." **14.** Translate, "Themselves also with prayer for you, longing after you on account of the exceeding grace of God (resting) upon you." *English Version* is, however, good sense: They glorify God (vs. 13) by the experimental proof, etc., "and by their prayer for you." But the *Greek* favors the former.

15. his unspeakable gift—the gift of His own Son, which includes all other inferior gifts (ch. 8:9; Rom. 8:32). If we have received from God "His unspeakable gift," what great thing is it, if we give a few perishing gifts for His sake?

ADAM CLARKE

13. *By the experiment of this ministration.* In this, and in the preceding and following verses, the apostle enumerates the good effects that would be produced by their liberal almsgiving to the poor saints at Jerusalem. (1) The wants of the saints would be supplied. (2) Many thanksgivings would thereby be rendered unto God. (3) The Corinthians would thereby give proof of their subjection to the gospel. And, (4) The prayers of those relieved will ascend up to God in behalf of their benefactors.

14. *The exceeding grace of God in you.* By the "superabounding" or "transcending grace" of God, which was in them, the apostle most evidently means the merciful and charitable disposition which they had towards the suffering saints.

15. *Thanks be unto God for his unspeakable gift.* Some contend that Christ only is here intended; others, that the almsgiving is meant. After all the difference of commentators and preachers, it is most evident that the *unspeakable gift* is precisely the same with the "superabounding grace or benefit" of the preceding verse. If therefore Jesus Christ, the Gift of God's unbounded love to man, be the meaning of the *unspeakable gift* in this verse, He is also intended by the superabounding grace in the preceding. But it is most evident that it is the work of Christ in them, and not Christ himself, which is intended in the fourteenth verse; and consequently that it is the same work, not the operator, which is referred to in this last verse.

MATTHEW HENRY

CHAPTER 10

Verses 1–6

I. He addresses them in a very mild and humble manner, *v.* 1. In the midst of the greatest provocations he shows mildness.

How humbly also does this great apostle speak of himself, as *one in presence base among them*! So his enemies spoke of him with contempt. He is desirous that no occasion may be given to use severity, *v.* 2. *He beseeches them* to give no occasion for him to be bold, or to exercise his authority against them in general.

JAMIESON, FAUSSET, BROWN

CHAPTER 10

Vss. 1-18. HE VINDICATES HIS APOSTOLIC AUTHORITY AGAINST THOSE WHO DEPRECIATED HIM FOR HIS PERSONAL APPEARANCE. HE WILL MAKE HIS POWER FELT WHEN HE COMES. HE BOASTS NOT, AS THEY, BEYOND HIS MEASURE. **1. I Paul myself**—no longer "we," "us," "our" (ch. 9:11): *I* who am represented by depreciators as "base," I, the same Paul, *of my own accord* "beseech you"; or rather "entreat," "exhort" you *for your sake.* As "I beseech you" (a distinct *Greek* verb, vs. 2) *for my sake.* **by the meekness and gentleness of Christ**—He mentions these graces of Christ especially (Ps. 18:35; Matt. 11:29), as on account of his imitation of them in particular he was despised [GROTIUS]. He entreats them by these, in order to show that though he must have recourse to more severe measures, he is naturally inclined to gentle ones after Christ's example [MENOCHIUS]. "Meekness" is more in the mind internally; "gentleness" in the external behavior, and in relation to others; for instance, the condescending *yieldingness* of a superior to an inferior, the former not insisting on his strict rights [TRENCH]. BENGEL explains it, "By the meekness and gentleness *derived by me from Christ,*" not from my own nature: he objects to understanding it of *Christ's* meekness and gentleness, since nowhere else is "gentleness" attributed to Him. But though the exact *Greek* word is not applied to Him, the idea expressed by it is (cf. Isa. 40:11; Matt. 12:19, 20). **in presence**—in personal appearance when present with you. **base**—*Greek*, "lowly"; timid, humbly diffident: opposed to "bold." "Am" stands here by ironical concession for "am reputed to be" (cf. vs. 10). **2. I beseech you**—Intimating that, as he can *beseech* in letters, so he can be severe in their presence. **that I may not be**—that I may not *have to* be bold . . . . **with that confidence**—*that authoritative sternness.* **I think**—I *am minded* to be. **as if we walked according to the flesh**—His Corinthian detractors judged of him by themselves, as if he were influenced by fleshly motives, the desire of favor or fear of giving offense, so as not to exercise his authority when present. **3. For**—Reason why they should regard him "beseeching" them (vs. 2) not to oblige him to have recourse to "bold" and stern exercise of authority. "We walk IN the flesh," and so *in weakness:* but not "ACCORDING TO the flesh" (vs. 2). **Moreover, though we WALK in it, we do not WAR according to it.** A double contrast or antithesis. "They who accuse us of walking after the flesh, shall find [to their cost] that we do not *war* after the flesh; therefore compel us not to use our weapons" [ALFORD]. **4.** A confutation of those who try to propagate their creed by force and persecution (cf. Luke 9:54-56). **weapons**—for punishing offending members (vs. 6; I Cor. 4:21; 5:5, 13); boldness of speech, ecclesiastical discipline (vs. 8; ch. 13:10), the power of the word,

ADAM CLARKE

CHAPTER 10

1. *I Paul myself beseech you by the meekness.* Having now finished his directions and advices relative to the collection for the poor, he resumes his argument relative to the false apostle, who had gained considerable influence by representing Paul as despicable in his person, his ministry, and his influence. Under this obloquy the apostle was supported by the meekness and gentleness of Christ; and through the same heavenly disposition he delayed inflicting that punishment which, in virtue of his apostolical authority, he might have inflicted on him who had disturbed and labored to corrupt the Christian Church. *Who in presence am base among you, but being absent am bold toward you.* He seems to quote these as the words of his calumniator, as if he had said: "This apostle of yours is a mere braggadocio; when he is among you, you know how base and contemptible he is; when absent, see how he brags and boasts." The word which we render *base* signifies "lowly," and, as some think, "short of stature." The insinuation is that, when there was danger or opposition at hand, Paul acted with great obsequiousness, fearing for his person and authority, lest he should lose his secular influence.

2. *Some, which think of us as if we walked according to the flesh.* As it is customary for cowards and overbearing men to threaten the weak and the timid when present, to bluster when absent, and to be very obsequious in the presence of the strong and courageous. This conduct they appear to have charged against the apostle, which he calls here walking after *the flesh*—acting as a man who had worldly ends in view and would use any means in order to accomplish them.

3. *Though we walk in the flesh.* That is: Although I am in the common condition of human nature, and must live as a human being, yet I do *not war after the flesh*—I do not act the coward, as they insinuate.

4. *The weapons of our warfare.* The apostle often uses the metaphor of a *warfare* to represent the life and trials of a Christian minister. See Eph. vi. 10-17; 1 Tim. i. 18; 2 Tim. ii. 3-5.

MATTHEW HENRY

II. He asserts the power of his preaching and his power to punish offenders.

1. The power of his preaching, *v.* 3, 5. The work of the ministry is a warfare, not *after the flesh* indeed, for it is a spiritual warfare, with spiritual enemies and for spiritual purposes. The doctrines of the gospel are the weapons. Outward force, therefore, is not the method of the gospel, but strong persuasions. People must be persuaded to God and their duty, not driven by force of arms. What opposition is made against the gospel by the powers of sin and Satan in the hearts of men, but these strongholds are pulled down by the gospel, through the grace and power of God.

ALEXANDER MACLAREN:

The first effect of any real contact with Christ and His Gospel is to reveal a man to himself, to shatter his delusive estimates of what he is, and to pull down about his ears the lofty fortress in which he has ensconced himself. It seems strange work for what calls itself a Gospel to begin by forcing a man to cry out with sobs and tears, "Oh, wretched man that I am!" But no man will ever reach the heights to which Christ can lift him, who does not begin his upward course by descending to the depths into which Christ's Gospel begins its work by plunging him. Unconsciousness of sin is sure to lead to indifference to a Savior, and unless we know ourselves to be miserable and poor and blind and naked, the offer of gold refined by fire and white garments that we may clothe ourselves will make no appeal to us. The fact of sin makes the need for a Savior; our individual sense of sin makes us sensible of our need of a Savior.

Paul believed that the weapons of his warfare were mighty enough to cast down the strongest of all strongholds in which men shut themselves up against the humbling Gospel of salvation by the mercy of God.

—Expositions of Holy Scripture

2. The apostle's power to punish offenders is asserted in *v.* 6. Though the apostle showed meekness and gentleness, yet he would not betray his authority.

Verses 7–11

"*Do you,*" says he, "*look on things after the outward appearance?* (*v.* 7). Is this a fit rule to make an estimate of things or persons by?" In outward appearance, Paul was mean and despicable with some. But there are often false appearances.

I. His relation to Christ, *v.* 7. Now the apostle reasons thus with the Corinthians: "Suppose it to be so, allowing what they say to be true, yet they ought also to allow this to us, that *we also are Christ's.*" There is room in Christ for many; and those who differ much from one another may yet be one in him. It would help to heal the differences that are among us if we would remember that those who differ from us may belong to Christ too. We must not think that we are the people, and that none belong to Christ but ourselves. This we may plead for ourselves, against those who judge us and despise us that, how weak soever we are, yet, as they are Christ's, so are we.

II. His authority from Christ as an apostle. The *Lord had given it to him*, and it was more than his adversaries could justly pretend to. It was certainly what he should not be ashamed of, *v.* 8. The nature of his authority: it was for *edification, and not for destruction.*

JAMIESON, FAUSSET, BROWN

and of the sacraments, the various extraordinary gifts of the Spirit. **carnal**—Translate, "fleshly," to preserve the allusion to vss. 2, 3. **mighty through God**—*Greek*, "mighty to God," i.e., mighty before God: not humanly, but divinely powerful. The power is not ours, but God's. Cf. "fair to God," i.e., divinely fair (*Margin*, Acts 7:20). Also above (ch. 2:15), "*unto God* a sweet savor." "The efficacy of the Christian religion proves its truth" [BENGEL]. **pulling down**—As the *Greek* is the same as in vs. 5, translate, "casting down." Cf. Jeremiah 1:10: the inspired servants of God inherit the commission of the Old Testament prophets. **strongholds**—(Prov. 21:22)—viz., in which sinners entrench themselves against reproof; all that opposes itself to Christ; the learning, and eloquence, and philosophical subtleties on which the Corinthians prided themselves. So Joshua's trumpet blast was "mighty" under God to overthrow the walls of Jericho. **5. imaginations**—rather, "reasonings." Whereas "thought" expresses men's own *purpose* and determination of living after their own pleasure [TITTM]. **high thing**—So it ought to be translated (Rom. 8:39). A distinct *Greek* word from that in Ephesians 3:18, "height," and Revelation 21:16, which belongs to God and heaven from whence we receive nothing hurtful. But "high thing" is not so much "height" as *something made high*, and belongs to those regions of air where the powers of darkness "exalt themselves" against Christ and us (Eph. 2:2; 6:12; II Thess. 2:4). **exalteth itself**—II Thessalonians 2:4 supports *English Version* rather than the translation of ELLICOTT, etc., "is lifted up." Such were the *high towers* of Judaic self-righteousness, philosophic speculations, and rhetorical sophistries, the "knowledge" so much prized by many (opposed to "the knowledge of God"), which endangered a section of the Corinthian Church. **against the knowledge of God**—True knowledge makes men humble. Where there is exaltation of self, there knowledge of God is wanting [BENGEL]. Arrange the words following thus: "Bringing every thought (i.e., *intent of the mind or will*) into captivity to the obedience of Christ," i.e., to obey Christ. The three steps of the apostle's spiritual warfare are: (1) It demolishes what is opposed to Christ; (2) It leads captive; (3) It brings into obedience to Christ (Rom. 1:5; 16:26). The "reasonings" (*English Version*, "imaginations") are utterly "cast down." The "mental intents" (*English Version*, "thoughts") are taken willing captives, and tender the voluntary obedience of faith to Christ the Conqueror. **6.** Translate, "Having ourselves (i.e., *being*) in readiness to exact punishment for all disobedience . . . ." We have this in store for the disobedient: it will be brought into action in due time. **when your obedience . . .**—He charitably assumes that most of the Corinthian Church will act obediently; therefore he says "YOUR obedience." But perhaps some will act otherwise; in order, therefore, to give all an opportunity of joining the obedient, he will not prematurely exact punishment, but wait until the full number of those gathered out to Christ has been "completed," and the remainder have been proved incorrigible. He had acted already so at Corinth (Acts 18:6-11; cf. Exod. 32:34; Matt. 13:28-30). **7.** Do ye regard mere outward appearance (mere external recommendations, personal appearance, voice, manner, oratory of teachers *present face to face,* such as they admired in the false teachers to the disparagement of Paul, vs. 10; *Note*, ch. 5:12)? Even in *outward bearing* when I shall be *present* with you (in contrast to "by *letters*," vs. 9) I will show that I am more really armed with the authority of Christ, than those who arrogate to themselves the title of being peculiarly "Christ's" (I Cor. 1:12). A Jewish emissary seems to have led this party. **let him of himself think this again**—He may "of himself," without needing to be taught it in a more severe manner, by "thinking again," arrive at "this" conclusion, "that even as . . . ." Paul modestly demands for himself only an equal place with those whom he had begotten in the Gospel [BENGEL]. **8.** "For even if I were to boast somewhat more exceedingly (than I do, vss. 3-6) of our (apostolic) authority (vs. 6; ch. 13:10) . . . I should not be put to shame (by the fact; as I should be if my authority proved to be without foundation: my threats of punishment not being carried into effect). **for edification . . . not for . . . destruction**—*Greek*, "for building up . . . not for . . . CASTING DOWN" (the same *Greek* as in vs. 5): the image of a building as in vss. 4, 5. Though we "cast down reasonings," this is not in order to destroy, but really to *build up* ("edify"), by removing those things which are hindrances to edification, and testing what is unsound, and putting together all that

ADAM CLARKE

Are not carnal. Here he refers to the means used by the false apostle in order to secure his party. *But mighty through God.* Our doctrines are true and pure. They come from God and lead to Him, and He accompanies them with His mighty power to the hearts of those who hear them; and the *strong holds*—the apparently solid and cogent reasoning of the philosophers—we, by these doctrines, pull down.

5. *Casting down imaginations.* "Reasonings" or "opinions." The Greek philosophers valued themselves especially on their ethic systems, in which their reasonings appeared to be very profound and conclusive; but they were obliged to assume principles which were either such as did not exist or were false in themselves. *Every high thing.* Even the pretendedly sublime doctrines, for instance, of Plato, Aristotle, and the Stoics in general, fell before the simple preaching of Christ crucified. *The knowledge of God.* The doctrine of the unity and eternity of the divine nature, which was opposed by the plurality of their idols, and the generation of their gods, and their man-made deities. *The obedience of Christ.* Subjection to idols was annihilated by the progress of the gospel among the heathen.

6. *And having in a readiness to revenge all disobedience.* I am ready through this mighty armor of God to punish those opposers of the doctrine of Christ and the disobedience which has been produced by them. *When your obedience is fulfilled.* When you have in the fullest manner discountenanced those men, and separated yourselves from their communion. All the terms in these two verses are military. Allusion is made to a strongly fortified city, where the enemy had made his last stand: entrenching himself about the walls; strengthening all his redoubts and ramparts; raising castles, towers, and various engines of defense and offense upon the walls; and neglecting nothing that might tend to render his stronghold impregnable. The army of God comes against the place and attacks it; the "strong holds," all the "fortified places," are carried. The "imaginations," engines, and whatever the imagination or skill of man could raise, are speedily taken and destroyed. Every "high thing"—all the castles and towers are sapped, thrown down and demolished; the walls are battered into breaches; and the besieging army, carrying everything at the point of the sword, enter the city, storm and take the citadel. Everywhere defeated, the conquered submit, and are brought "into captivity," "are led away captives."

7. *Do ye look on things after the outward appearance?* Do not be carried away with appearances; do not be satisfied with show and parade. *If any man trust to himself that he is Christ's.* Here, as in several other places of this and the preceding Epistle, the *any,* or "certain," person most evidently refers to the false apostle who made so much disturbance in the church. And this man trusted to himself—assumed to himself that he was Christ's messenger. *Let him of himself.* Without any authority, certainly, from God; but as he arrogates to himself the character of a minister of Christ, let him acknowledge that even so we are Christ's ministers; and that I have, by my preaching and the miracles which I have wrought, given the fullest proof that I am especially commissioned by Him.

8. *For though I should boast.* I have a greater authority and spiritual power than I have yet shown, both to edify and to punish; but I employ this for your *edification* in righteousness, and not for the *destruction* of any delinquent.

MATTHEW HENRY

The caution with which he speaks of his authority, professing that his design was not to terrify them with big words, nor by angry letters, *v.* 9.

The apostle declares he did not intend to frighten those who were obedient. He would have his adversaries *know this* (*v.* 11), that he would, by the exercise of his apostolical power make it appear to have a real efficacy.

Verses 12–18

I. The apostle refuses to justify himself as the false apostles did, *v.* 12. He plainly intimates that they took a wrong method to commend themselves. They were pleased, and did pride themselves, in their own attainments. We should be pleased and thankful for what we have of gifts or graces, but never pride ourselves therein, as if there were none to be compared with us. The apostle would not be of the number of such vain men.

II. He fixes a better rule for his conduct, *v.* 13. He would not go beyond the line prescribed to him, which the false apostles did, while they *boasted of other men's labours.*

III. He acted according to this rule, *v.* 14. He acted according to this rule in preaching at Corinth, for he came thither by divine direction. In boasting of them as his charge, he boasted not of *other men's labours, v.* 15.

IV. He declares his success in observing this rule. His hope was that their faith was increased, and that others would embrace the gospel also.

JAMIESON, FAUSSET, BROWN

is true in the building [CHRYSOSTOM]. **9.** I say this lest I should seem to be terrifying you, as children, with empty threats [BENGEL]. ESTIUS explains, "I might boast more of my authority, *but I forbear to do so,* that I may not seem as if . . . ." But this ellipsis is harsh: and vss. 10, 11 confirm BENGEL'S view. **10. letters**—implying that there had been already more letters of Paul received by the Corinthians than the one we have, viz., I Corinthians; and that they contained strong reproofs. **say they**—*Greek,* "says one," "such a one" (vs. 11) seems to point to some definite individual. Cf. Galatians 5: 10; a similar slanderer was in the Galatian Church. **weak**—(ch. 12:7; I Cor. 2:3). There was nothing of majesty or authority in his manner; he bore himself tremblingly among them, whereas the false teachers spoke with authoritative bearing and language.

11. think this—"consider this." **such** *will we be*—or "are," in general, not merely shall we be at our next visit. **12.** "We do not presume (irony) to judge ourselves among, or in comparison with, some of them that commend themselves." The charge falsely brought against him of *commending himself* (ch. 3:1; 5:12), really holds good of the false teachers. The phrase, "judge ourselves of the number," is drawn from the testing of athletes and senators, the "approved" being set down on the roll [WAHL]. **measuring themselves by themselves**—"*among* themselves": to correspond to the previous verb, "judge ourselves *among* them." Instead of measuring themselves by the public standard, they measure themselves by one made by themselves: they do not compare themselves with others who excel them, but with those like themselves: hence their high self-esteem. The one-eyed is easily king among the blind. **are not wise**—with all their boasted "wisdom" (I Cor. 1:19-26), they are anything but "wise." **13. not boast . . . without . . . measure**—*Greek,* "to unmeasured bounds." There is no limit to a man's high opinion of himself, so long as he measures himself by himself (vs. 13) and his fellows, and does not compare himself with his superiors. It marks the *personal* character of this Epistle that the word "boast" occurs twenty-nine times in it, and only twenty-six times in all the other Epistles put together. Undeterred by the charge of vanity, he felt he must vindicate his apostolic authority by facts [CONYBEARE and HOWSON]. It would be to "boast of things without our measure," were we to boast of conversions made by "other men's labors" (vs. 15). **distributed**—apportioned [ALFORD]. **a measure**—as a measure [ALFORD]. **to reach**—"that we should reach as far as even to you": not that he meant to go no further (vs. 16; Rom. 15:20-24). Paul's "measure" is the *apportionment* of his sphere of Gospel labors *ruled* for him by God. A "rule" among the so-called "apostolic canons" subsequently was, that no bishop should appoint ministers beyond his own limits. At Corinth no minister ought to have been received without Paul's sanction, as Corinth was *apportioned* to him by God as *his apostolic sphere.* The Epistle here incidentally, and therefore undesignedly, confirms the independent history, the Acts, which represents Corinth as the extreme limit as yet of his preaching, *at which he had stopped,* after he had from Philippi passed southward successively through Amphipolis, Apollonia, Thessalonica, Berea, and Athens [PALEY'S *Horæ Paulinæ*]. **14.** "We are not stretching ourselves beyond our measure, *as* (we should be) *if* we did not reach unto you: (but we do), for as far as even to you have we come in preaching the Gospel." **15.** "Not boasting to unmeasured bounds (i.e., not exceeding our own bounds by boasting) of (lit., "in") other men's labors." **when**—"AS your faith goes on increasing." The cause of his not yet reaching with the Gospel the regions beyond Corinth, was the weakness as yet of their faith. He desired not to leave the Corinthians before the proper time, and yet not to put off preaching to others too long. **enlarged by you**—*Greek,* "in your case." Our success in your case will give us an important step towards further progress beyond you (vs. 16). **according to our rule**—according to our divinely assigned apportionment of the area or sphere of our work; for "we stretch not ourselves beyond our measure" (vs. 14). **abundantly**—*Greek,* "unto exceeding abundance": so as to exceed the limits we have yet reached (vs. 16).

ADAM CLARKE

9. *That I may not seem.* This is an elliptical sentence, and may be supplied thus: "I have not used this authority; nor will I add any more concerning this part of the subject, lest I should seem, as my adversary has insinuated, to wish to terrify you by my letters.

10. *For his letters, say they, are weighty and powerful.* He boasts of high powers, and that he can do great things. See on vv. 1-2. *But his bodily presence is weak.* When you behold the man, you find him a feeble, contemptible mortal; and when you hear him speak, *his speech,* probably his "doctrine," is good for nothing. If we can credit some ancient writers, such as Nicephorus, we shall find the apostle thus described: "Paul was a little man, crooked, and almost bent like a bow; with a pale countenance, long and wrinkled; a bald head; his eyes full of fire and benevolence; his beard long, thick, and interspersed with grey hairs, as was his head." Perhaps there is not one of these statements correct. As to Nicephorus, he is a writer of the fourteenth century, weak and credulous, and worthy of no regard. That Paul could be no such diminutive person we may fairly presume from the office he filled under the high priest, in the persecution of the Church of Christ; and that he had not an impediment in his speech, but was a graceful orator, we may learn from his whole history, and especially from the account we have, Acts xiv. 12, where the Lycaonians took him for Mercury, the god of eloquence, induced thereto by his powerful and persuasive elocution.

11. *Such as we are in word.* A threatening of this kind would doubtless alarm the false apostle; and it is very likely that he did not await the apostle's coming, as he would not be willing to try the fate of Elymas.

12. *We dare not make ourselves.* As if he had said: I dare neither associate with, nor compare myself to, those who are full of self-commendation. *But they measuring themselves by themselves.* As they dare not compare themselves with the true apostles of Christ, they compare themselves with each other; and, as they have no perfect standard, they can have no excellence.

13. *Things without our measure.* By the *measure* mentioned here, it seems as if the apostle meant the commission he received from God to preach the gospel to the Gentiles; *a measure* or "district" that extended through all Asia Minor and Greece, down to Achaia, where Corinth was situated, *a measure to reach even unto you.* But the expressions in these verses are all agonistical, and taken from the stadium or racecourse in the Olympic and Isthmian games. The *measure* was the length of the course; the rule or line, vv. 15 and 16, was probably the same with the white line which marked out the boundaries of the stadium; and the verbs "reach unto," "stretch out," etc., are all references to the exertions made to win the race.

14. *For we stretch not ourselves beyond.* We have not proceeded straight from Macedonia through Thessaly, and across the Adriatic Gulf into Italy, which would have led us *beyond* you westward; but knowing the mind of our God, we left this direct path, and came southward through Greece, down into Achaia, and there we planted the gospel. The false apostle has therefore got into our province, and entered into our labors, and there boasts as if the conversion of the heathen Achaians had been his own work.

15. *Not boasting of things without our measure.* We speak only of the work which God has done by us; for we have never attempted to enter into other men's labors, and we study to convert those regions assigned to us by the Holy Spirit. We enter the course lawfully, and run according to rule. *When your faith is increased.* When you receive more of the life and power of godliness, and when you can better spare me to go to other places. *We shall be enlarged by you.* Probably signifies here to be "praised" or "commended"; and the sense would be this: We hope that shortly, on your gaining an increase of true religion, after your long distractions and divisions, you will plainly see that we are the true messengers of God to you; and that in all your intercourse with your neighbors, or foreign parts, you will speak of this gospel preached by us as a glorious system of saving

MATTHEW HENRY

V. He seems to check himself as if he had spoken too much in his own praise. He is afraid of boasting, or taking any praise to himself, *v.* 17.

Ministers in particular must be careful not to glory in their performances, but must give God the glory of their work, and the success thereof, *v.* 18. Of all flattery, self-flattery is the worst. Instead of praising or commending ourselves, we should strive to approve ourselves to God, and his approbation will be our best commendation.

CHAPTER 11

Verses 1–4

1. The apology the apostle makes for going about to commend himself, *v.* 1. As much against the grain as it is with a proud man to acknowledge his infirmities, so much is it against the grain with a humble man to speak in his own praise.

2. The reasons for what the apostle did. To preserve the Corinthians from being corrupted by the insinuations of the false apostles, *v.* 2, 3. *He was jealous over them with godly jealousy.* He had *espoused them to one husband,* and he was desirous to *present them as a chaste virgin*—pure, and spotless, and faithful, not having *their minds corrupted* by false teachers. To vindicate himself against the false apostles.

JAMIESON, FAUSSET, BROWN

16. To—i.e., *so as to* preach . . . beyond you (and) not to boast . . . . **in another man's line of things made ready to our hand**—Do not connect "line of things . . ."; but "boast of things . . ." To make this clearer, arrange the words thus, "Not to boast as to things (already made by the preaching of others) ready to our hand in another man's line (i.e., within the line, or sphere of labor, apportioned by God to another)." **17. glorieth**—Translate, to accord with vs. 16, "boasteth." In contrast to his opponents' practice of boasting in another's line or sphere, Paul declares the only true boasting is in the Lord (I Cor. 1:31; 15:10).

18. (Prov. 27:2.) **whom the Lord commendeth**—to whom the Lord has given as His "Epistle of commendation," the believers whom he has been the instrument of converting: as was Paul's case (ch. 3:1-3). **is approved**—can stand the test of the final trial. A metaphor from testing metals (Rom. 16:10; I Cor. 11:19). So on the other hand those finally rejected by the Lord are termed "*reprobate* silver" (Jer. 6:30).

CHAPTER 11

Vss. 1-33. Through Jealousy over the Corinthians, Who Made More Account of the False Apostles than of Him, He Is Obliged to Commend Himself as in Many Respects Superior. **1. Would to God**—Translate as *Greek,* "I would that." **bear with me**—I may ask not unreasonably to be borne with; not so the false apostles (vss. 4, 20). **my**—not in the oldest MSS. **folly**—The *Greek* is a milder term than that for "foolishness" in I Corinthians 3:19; Matthew 5:22; 25:2. The *Greek* for "folly" here implies *imprudence;* the *Greek* for "foolishness" includes the idea of *perversity* and *wickedness.* **and indeed bear**—A request (so vs. 16). But the *Greek* and the sense favor the translation, "But indeed (I need not wish it, for) ye *do* bear with me"; still I wish you to bear with me further, while I enter at large into self-commendations. **2. For I am jealous**—The justification of his self-commendations lies in his zealous care lest they should fall from Christ, to whom he, as "the friend of the Bridegroom" (John 3:29), has espoused them; in order to lead them back from the false apostles to Christ, he is obliged to boast as an apostle of Christ, in a way which, but for the motive, would be "folly." **godly jealousy**—lit., "jealousy of God" (cf. ch. 1:12, "godly sincerity," lit., "sincerity of God"). "If I am immoderate, I am immoderate to God" [Bengel]. A jealousy which has God's honor at heart (I Kings 19:10). **I . . . espoused you**—Paul uses a *Greek* term applied properly to *the bridegroom,* just as he ascribes to himself "jealousy," a feeling properly belonging to the husband; so entirely does he identify himself with Christ. **present** *you as* **a chaste virgin to Christ**—at His coming, when the heavenly *marriage* shall take place (Matt. 25:6; Rev. 19:7, 9). What Paul here says he desires to do, viz., "present" the Church as "a chaste virgin" to Christ, *Christ Himself* is said to do in the fuller sense. Whatever ministers do effectively, is really done by Christ (Eph. 5:27-32). The *espousals* are going on now. He does not say "chaste virgins"; for not individual members, but the whole body of believers conjointly constitute the Bride. **3. I fear**—(ch. 12:20)—not inconsistent with love. His source of fear was their yielding character. **subtilty**—the utter foe of the "simplicity" which is intent on one object, Jesus, and seeks none "other," and no "other" and different Spirit (vs. 4); but loves him with tender singleness of affection. Where Eve first gave way, was in mentally harboring for a moment the possibility insinuated by the serpent, of God not having her truest interests at heart, and of this "other" professing friend being more concerned for her than God. **corrupted**—so as to lose their virgin purity through seducers (vs. 4). The same *Greek* stands for "minds" as for "thoughts" (ch. 10:5, where see *Note*); *intents of the will,* or *mind.* The oldest MSS., after "simplicity," add, "and the purity" or "chastity." **in Christ**—rather, "that is *towards*

ADAM CLARKE

truth; and that, in consequence, the heathen countries around you will be the better prepared to receive our message, and thus our rule or district will be abundantly extended. This interpretation agrees well with the following verse.

16. *To preach the gospel in the regions beyond you.* He probably refers to those parts such as Sparta, that lay southward of them; and to Italy, which lay on the west. *Not to boast in another man's line.* So very scrupulous was the apostle not to build on another man's foundation that he would not even go to those places where other apostles were laboring.

17. *He that glorieth, let him glory in the Lord.* Instead of boasting or exulting even in your own success in preaching the gospel, as none can be successful without the especial blessing of God, let God, who gave the blessing, have the glory.

18. *Not he that commendeth himself.* Not the person who makes a parade of his own attainments; who preaches himself, and not Christ Jesus the Lord; and, far from being your servant for Christ's sake, affects to be your ruler—not such a one shall be approved of God by an especial blessing on his labors, *but whom the Lord commendeth,* by giving him the extraordinary gifts of the Holy Spirit and converting the heathen by his ministry. These were qualifications to which the false apostle at Corinth could not pretend.

CHAPTER 11

1. *Would to God ye could bear with me.* As the word *God* is not mentioned here, it would have been much better to translate the passage literally thus: "I wish ye could bear a little with me." The too frequent use of this sacred name produces a familiarity with it that is not at all conducive to reverence and godly fear. *In my folly.* In my seeming folly, for being obliged to vindicate his ministry, it was necessary that he should speak much of himself, his sufferings, and his success. And as this would appear like boasting, and boasting is always the effect of an empty, foolish mind, those who were not acquainted with the necessity that lay upon him to make this defense might be led to impute it to vanity.

2. *That I may present you as a chaste virgin.* There seems to be a reference to Lev. xxi. 14, that the high priest must not marry anyone that was not a pure virgin. Here then Christ is the High Priest, the Spouse or Husband; the Corinthian church, the pure virgin to be espoused; the apostle and his helpers had educated and prepared this virgin for her husband and espoused her to him.

3. *As the serpent beguiled Eve through his subtilty.* This is a strong reflection on the false apostle and his teaching. He was subtle, and by his subtlety he was enabled to corrupt the minds of the people from the simplicity of the gospel of Christ; or, to follow the metaphor, he had seduced the pure, chaste, well-educated virgin from her duty, affection, and allegiance to her one only true Husband, the High Priest, Jesus Christ.

MATTHEW HENRY

They could not pretend they had another Jesus, or another Spirit, or another gospel, to preach to them, *v.* 4. But seeing there is but one Jesus, one Spirit, and one gospel preached to them and received by them, what reason could there be why the Corinthians should be prejudiced against him, who first converted them to the faith?

Verses 5–15

I. His equality with the other apostles, *v.* 5. This he expresses very modestly: *I suppose so.* He might have spoken very positively.

He speaks modestly of himself, and humbly owns his personal infirmity, that he was *rude in speech.* However, he was not rude *in knowledge*; much less was he ignorant of the mysteries of the kingdom of heaven.

II. His equality with the false apostles in this particular. They ought to acknowledge he had been a good friend to them. He had preached the gospel to them freely, *v.* 7–10.

He says he himself had *taken wages of other churches* (*v.* 8), so that he had a right to have asked and received from them: yet he waived his right, and chose rather to abase himself. He chose rather to be supplied from Macedonia than to be chargeable unto them.

JAMIESON, FAUSSET, BROWN

Christ." **4. if . . .**—which in *fact* is impossible. However, if it were possible, ye might then bear with them (see *Note*, vs. 1). But there can be no *new Gospel;* there is but the *one* which I first preached; therefore it ought not to be "borne" by you, that the false teachers should attempt to supersede me. **he that cometh**—the high-sounding title assumed by the false teachers, who arrogated Christ's own peculiar title (**Greek,** Matt. 11:3, and Heb. 10:37), "He that is coming." Perhaps he was leader of the party which assumed peculiarly to be "Christ's" (ch. 10:7; I Cor. 1:12); hence his assumption of the title. **preacheth . . . receive**—is preaching . . . ye are receiving. **Jesus**—the "Jesus" of Gospel *history.* He therefore does not say "Christ," which refers to the *office.* **another . . . another**—*Greek,* "another Jesus . . . a *different* Spirit . . . a *different* Gospel." *Another* implies a distinct individual of the same kind; *different* implies one quite distinct in kind. **which ye have not received**—from us. **spirit . . . received . . . gospel . . . accepted**—The will of man is passive in RECEIVING the "Spirit"; but it is actively concurrent with the will of God (which goes before to give the good will) in ACCEPTING the "Gospel." **ye might well bear with him**—There would be an excuse for your conduct, though a bad one (for ye ought to give heed to no Gospel other than what ye have already heard from me, Gal. 1:6, 7); but the false teachers do not even pretend they have "another Jesus" and a "different Gospel" to bring before you; they merely try to supplant me, your accredited Teacher. Yet ye not only "bear with" them, but prefer them. **5. For**—My claim is superior to that of the false teachers, "For . . . ." **I suppose**—I reckon [ALFORD]. **I was not**—*Greek,* "That I have not been, and am not." **the very chiefest apostles**—James, Peter, and John, the witnesses of Christ's transfiguration and agony in Gethsemane. Rather, "those overmuch apostles," those *surpassers of the apostles* in their own esteem. This sense is proved by the fact that the context contains no comparison between him and the apostles, but only between him and the false teachers; vs. 6 also alludes to these, and not to the apostles; cf. also the parallel phrase, "false apostles" (*Note,* vs. 13, and ch. 12:11) [ALFORD]. **6. rude**—*Greek,* "a common man"; a "laic"; not rhetorically trained; unskilled in finish of diction. I Corinthians 2:1-4, 13; ch. 10:10, 11, shows his *words* were not without *weight,* though his "speech" was deficient in oratorical artifice. "Yet I am not so in my knowledge" (ch. 12:1-5; Eph. 3:1-5). **have been . . . made manifest**—Read with the oldest MSS., "We have made things (Gospel truths) manifest," thus showing our "knowledge." *English Version* would mean, I leave it to yourselves to decide whether I be rude in speech . . .: for we have been thoroughly (lit., "in everything") made manifest among you (lit., "in respect to you"; "in relation to you"). He had not by reserve kept back his "knowledge" in divine mysteries from them (ch. 2:17; 4:2; Acts 20:20, 27). **in all things**—The *Greek* rather favors the translation, "among all men"; the sense then is, we have manifested the whole truth among all men with a view to your benefit [ALFORD]. But the *Greek* in Philippians 4:12, "In each thing and in all things," sanctions *English Version,* which gives a clearer sense. **7. Have I**—lit., "OR have I?" Connected with last verse, "Or will any of you make it an objection that I have preached to you gratuitously?" He leaves their good feeling to give the answer, that this, so far from being an objection, was a decided superiority in him above the false apostles (I Cor. 9:6-15). **abasing myself**—in my mode of living, waiving my right of maintenance, and earning it by manual labor; perhaps with slaves as his fellow laborers (Acts 18:3; Phil. 4:12). **ye . . . exalted**—spiritually, by your admission to Gospel privileges. **because**—"in that." **gospel of God**—"of God" implies its divine glory to which they were admitted. **freely**—"without charge." **8. I robbed**—i.e., took from them in order to spare you more than what was their fair share of contribution to my maintenance, e.g., the Philippian Church (Phil. 4:15, 16). **wages**—"subsidy." **to do you service**—*Greek,* "with a view to ministration to you"; cf. "supplied" (*Greek,* "*in addition*"), vs. 9, implying, he *brought with him* from the Macedonians, supplies towards his maintenance at Corinth; and (vs. 9) *when those resources failed* ("when I wanted") he received a *new supply,* while there, from the same source. **9. wanted**—"was in want." **chargeable**—*Greek,* "burdensome," lit., "to torpify," and so to *oppress.* JEROME says it is a Cilician word (ch. 12:14, 16). **the brethren which came**—rather, as *Greek,* "the brethren *when they came.*" Perhaps Timotheus and Silas (Acts 8:

ADAM CLARKE

4. *For if he that cometh.* The false apostle who came after Paul had left Corinth. *Preacheth another Jesus.* Who can save more fully and more powerfully than that Jesus whom I have preached. *Or if ye receive another spirit.* And if in consequence of believing in this new saviour you receive another *spirit,* the gifts, graces, and consolations of which are greater than those which you have received from the Holy Ghost, who has been given to you on your believing on the Christ whom we preached. *Or another gospel.* Containing more privileges, spiritual advantages, and stronger excitements to holiness than that which we have preached and which you have accepted, *ye might well bear with him.* This would be a sufficient reason why you should not only *bear with him,* but prefer him to me.

5. *I was not . . . behind the very chiefest apostles.* That is: The most eminent of the apostles have not preached Christ, ministered the Spirit, explained and enforced the doctrines of the gospel in a more powerful and effectual manner than I have done.

6. *But though I be rude in speech.* Though I speak like a common, unlettered man, in plain, unadorned phrase, studying none of the graces of eloquence, yet I am not unskilled in the most profound *knowledge* of God, of spiritual and eternal things, of the nature of the human soul, and the sound truths of the gospel system. You yourselves are witnesses of this, as in all these things I have been thoroughly manifested among you.

7. *Have I committed an offence in abasing myself?* Have I transgressed in laboring with my hands that I might not be chargeable to you? and getting my deficiencies supplied by contributions from other churches, while I was employed in laboring for your salvation? Does your false apostle insinuate that I have disgraced the apostolic office by thus descending to servile labor for my support? Well, I have done this that you *might be exalted*—that you might receive the pure doctrines of the gospel, and be exalted to the highest pitch of intellectual light and blessedness. And will you complain that I preached the gospel gratis to you? Surely not. The whole passage is truly ironical.

8. *I robbed other churches.* This part of the sentence is explained by the latter, *taking wages . . . to do you service.* The word signifies the pay of money and provisions given daily to a Roman soldier. As if he had said: I received food and raiment, the bare necessaries of life, from other churches while laboring for your salvation. Will you esteem this a crime?

9. *And when I was present with you.* The particle which we translate *and* should be rendered "for" in this place: "For when I was with you, and was in want, *I was chargeable to no man.*" I preferred to be, for a time, even without the necessaries of life, rather than be a burden to you. To whom was this a reproach, to me or to you? *The brethren which came from*

MATTHEW HENRY

He informs them of the reason. It was not because *he did not love them* (*v.* 11), but it was to avoid offence. He would not give occasion for any to accuse him of worldly designs in preaching the gospel, or that he intended to enrich himself, *v.* 12.

III. The false apostles are charged *as deceitful workers* (*v.* 13), and though they were the ministers of Satan, would seem to be the *ministers of righteousness.* Hypocrisy is a thing not to be much wondered at in this world, especially when we consider the great influence Satan has. As he can turn himself into any shape, and look sometimes *like an angel of light,* in order to promote his kingdom of darkness, so he will teach his instruments to do the same. But it follows, *Their end is according to their works* (*v.* 15).

Verses 16–21

Let no man think me a fool, v. 16. Boasting of ourselves is usually not only a sign of a proud mind, but a mark of folly also, *v.* 17. He would not have them think that boasting of ourselves is a thing commanded by the Lord in general unto Christians. It is the duty and practice of Christians rather to humble and abase themselves; yet prudence must direct in what circumstances it is needful to speak of what God has wrought for us, and in us, and by us too, *v.* 18. But he gloried in his infirmities, as he tells them afterwards.

JAMIESON, FAUSSET, BROWN

1, 5). Cf. Philippians 4:15, 16, which refers to donations received from the Philippians (who were in Macedonia) at two distinct periods ("once and again"), one at Thessalonica, the other after his departure from Macedonia, that is, when he came into Achaia to Corinth (from the church in which city he would receive no help); and this "in the beginning of the Gospel," i.e., at its first preaching in these parts. Thus all three, the two Epistles and history, mutually, and no doubt undesignedly, coincide; a sure test of genuineness. **supplied**–*Greek,* "supplied in addition," viz., in addition to their former contributions; or as BENGEL, in addition to the supply obtained by my own manual labor. **10.** *Greek,* "There is (the) truth of Christ in me that . . ." (Rom. 9:1). **no man shall stop me of**–The oldest MSS. read, "This boasting shall not *be shut* (i.e., stopped) *as regards me.*" "Boasting is as it were personified . . . shall not have its mouth stopped as regards me" [ALFORD]. **11.** Love is often offended at its favors being not accepted, as though the party to whom they are offered wished to be under no obligation to the offerer. **12. I will do**–I will *continue* to decline help. **occasion**–*Greek, "the* occasion," viz., of misrepresenting my motives, which would be afforded to my detractors, if I accepted help. **that wherein they glory, they may be found even as we**–BENGEL joins this clause with "the occasion," viz., *of glorying* or *boasting;* the occasion "that they may be found (a point wherein they glory) even as we," i.e., quite as disinterested, or virtually, quite as gain-seeking and self-seeking. It cannot mean that the false teachers taught gratuitously even as Paul (cf. vs. 20; I Cor. 9:12). ALFORD less clearly explains by reference to vs. 18, etc., where the "glorying" here is taken up and described as "glorying after the flesh"; thus it means, that in the matters of which they boast they may be found even as we, i.e., we may be on a fair and equal footing; that there may be no *adventitious* comparisons made between us, arising out of *misrepresentations* of my course of procedure, but that in every matter of boasting we may be fairly compared and judged by *facts;* FOR (vs. 13) realities they have none, no weapons but misrepresentation, being *false apostles.* **13. For**–reason why he is unwilling they should be thought like him [BENGEL]. **such**–they and those like them. **false apostles**–those "overmuch apostles" (*Note,* vs. 5) are no apostles at all. **deceitful workers**–pretending to be "workmen" for the Lord, and really seeking their own gain. **14. is transformed**–rather, "transforms himself" (cf. Job 1:6); habitually; the first occasion of his doing so was in tempting Eve. "Himself" is emphatical: If their master *himself,* who is the "prince of darkness," the most alien to light, does so, it is less marvellous in the case of them who are his servants (Luke 22:54; Eph. 6:12). **15. no great thing**–no difficult matter. **if his ministers also**–as well as himself. **righteousness**–answering to "light" (vs. 14); the manifestation wherewith God reveals Himself in Christ (Matt. 6:33; Rom. 1:17). **end**–The test of things is *the* end which strips off every specious *form* into which Satan's agents may now "transform" themselves (ch. Phil. 3:19, 21). **according to their works**–not according to their pretensions. **16. I say again**–again taking up from vs. 1 the anticipatory apology for his boasting. **if otherwise**–but if ye will not grant this; if ye will think me a fool. **yet as a fool**–"yet even as a fool receive me"; grant me the indulgent hearing conceded even to one suspected of folly. The *Greek* denotes one who does not rightly use his mental powers; not having the idea of blame necessarily attached to it; one deceived by foolish vanities, yet boasting himself [TITTM.], (vss. 17, 19). **that I**–The oldest MSS. read, "that I, *too,*" viz., *as well as they,* may boast myself. **17. not after the Lord**–*By inspired guidance* he excepts this "glorying" or "boasting" from the inspired authoritativeness which belongs to all else that he wrote; even this boasting, though undesirable in itself, was permitted by the Spirit, taking into account its aim, viz., to draw off the Corinthians from their false teachers to the apostle. Therefore this passage gives no proof that any portion of Scripture is uninspired. It merely guards against his boasting being made a justification of boasting in general, which is not ordinarily "after the Lord," i.e., consistent with Christian humility. **foolishly**–*Greek,* "in foolishness." **confidence of boasting**–(ch. 9:4). **18. many**–including the "false teachers." **after the flesh**–as fleshly men are wont to boast, viz., of external advantages, as their birth, doings, etc. (cf. vs. 22). **I will glory also**–i.e., I also will boast of such fleshly advantages, to show you that even in these I am not their inferiors, and therefore ought not to

ADAM CLARKE

Macedonia. He probably refers to the supplies which he received from the church at Philippi, which was in Macedonia; of which he says, that "in the beginning of the gospel . . . no church communicated with me as concerning giving and receiving, but ye only. For even in Thessalonica ye sent once and again unto my necessity," Phil. iv. 15-16.

10. *As the truth of Christ is in me.* That is: I speak as becomes a Christian man, and as influenced by the gospel of Christ. It is a solemn form of asseveration, if not to be considered in the sense of an oath. *In the regions of Achaia.* The whole of the Peloponnesus, in which the city of Corinth stood. From this it appears that he had received no help from any of the other churches in the whole of that district.

11. *Wherefore.* Why have I acted thus? and why do I propose to continue to act thus? is it *because I love you not,* and will not permit you to contribute to my support? *God knoweth* the contrary; I do most affectionately love you.

12. *But what I do.* I act thus *that I may cut off occasion* of glorying, boasting, or calumniating *from them*—the false prophets and his partisans, "who seek occasion"—who would be glad that I should become chargeable to you, that it might in some sort vindicate them who exact much from you; for they "bring you into bondage" and "devour you," v. 20. Nothing could mortify these persons more than to find that the apostle did take nothing and was resolved to take nothing, while they were fleecing the people.

13. *For such are false apostles.* Persons who pretend to be apostles but have no mission from Christ. *Deceitful workers.* They do preach and labor, but they have nothing but their own emolument in view. *Transforming themselves.* Assuming as far as they possibly can, consistently with their sinister views, the habit, manner, and doctrine of the apostles of Christ.

14. *And no marvel.* And no wonder; it need not surprise you what the disciples do, when you consider the character of the master. *Satan himself is transformed into an angel of light.* As in v. 3 the apostle had the history of the temptation and fall of man particularly in view, it is very likely that here he refers to the same thing. In whatever form Satan appeared to our first mother, his pretensions and professions gave him the appearance of a good angel; and by pretending that Eve should get a great increase of light, that is, wisdom and understanding, he deceived her, and led her to transgress. It is generally said that Satan has three forms under which he tempts men: (1) the subtle serpent, (2) the roaring lion, (3) the angel of light. He often, as the angel of light, persuades men to do things under the name of religion which are subversive of it.

15. *Whose end shall be according to their works.* A bad way leads to a bad end. The way of sin is the way to hell.

16. *Let no man think me a fool.* See the note on v. 1. As the apostle was now going to enter into a particular detail of his qualifications, natural, acquired, and spiritual, and particularly of his labors and sufferings, he thinks it necessary to introduce the discourse once more as he did in v. 1.

17. *I speak it not after the Lord.* Were it not for the necessity under which I am laid to vindicate my apostleship, my present glorying would be inconsistent with my Christian profession of humility and knowing no one after the flesh.

18. *Seeing that many glory after the flesh.* Boast of external and secular things.

MATTHEW HENRY

These words, *You suffer fools gladly seeing you yourselves are wise* (*v.* 19), may be ironical.

"Notwithstanding all your wisdom, you willingly suffer yourselves to be *brought into bondage*, or suffer others to lord it over you; nay, even to *smite you on the face*, or impose upon you to your very faces" (*v.* 20).

The circumstances of the case were such as made it needful that *whereinsoever any were bold* he should be *bold also*, *v.* 21.

Verses 22–33

I. The privilege of his birth (*v.* 22). He was a Hebrew of the Hebrews; of a family among the Jews that never intermarried with the Gentiles. He was also an Israelite, and was also of the seed of Abraham.

II. He makes mention also of his apostleship, *v.* 23. They had found full proofs of his ministry: *Are they ministers of Christ? I am more so.*

III. He chiefly insists upon this, that he had been an extraordinary sufferer for Christ, *v.* 23. When the apostle would prove himself an extraordinary minister, he proves that he had been an extraordinary sufferer.

ALBERT BARNES:

23. "Are they ministers of Christ?" Though Jews by birth yet they claimed to be the ministers of the Messiah. "I speak as a fool." As if he had said, "Bear in mind, in what I am now about to say, that he who speaks is accused of being a fool in boasting. Let it not be deemed improper that I should act in this character, and since you regard me as such, let me speak like a fool." His frequent reminding them of this charge was eminently fitted to humble them that they had ever made it, especially when they were reminded by an enumeration of his trials, of the character of the man against whom the charge was brought.

"I am more." Paul was not disposed to deny that they were true ministers of Christ. But he had higher claims to the office than they had. He had been called to it in a more remarkable manner, and he had shown by his labors and trials that he had more of the true spirit of a minister of the Lord Jesus than they had. He therefore goes into detail to show what he had endured in endeavoring to diffuse the knowledge of the Savior; trials which he had borne probably while they had been dwelling in comparative ease and in a comfortable manner, free from suffering and persecution.

—*Popular Commentary*

JAMIESON, FAUSSET, BROWN

be supplanted by them in your esteem; though these are not what I desire to glory in (ch. 10:17). **19. gladly**—willingly. Irony. A plea why they should "bear with" (vs. 1) him in his folly, i.e., boasting; ye are, in sooth, so "wise" (I Cor. 4:8, 10; Paul's real view of their wisdom was very different, I Cor. 3:1-4) yourselves that ye can "bear with" the folly of others more complacently. Not only *can* ye do so, but ye *are actually* doing this and more. **20. For**—Ye may well "bear with" fools; *for* ye even "bear with" oppressors. Translate, "Ye bear with them." **a man**—as the false apostles do. **bring you into bondage**—to himself. Translate "brings," not "bring"; for the case is not merely a supposed case, but a case actually then occurring. Also "devours" (viz., by exactions, Matt. 23:24; Ps. 53: 4), "takes," "exalts," "smites." **take** *of you*—So the *Greek* for "take" is used for "take away from" (Rev. 6:4). ALFORD translates, as in ch. 12:16, "*catches* you." **exalt himself**—under the pretext of apostolic dignity. **smite you on the face**—under the pretext of divine zeal. The height of insolence on their part, and of servile endurance on yours (I Kings 22:24; Neh. 13:25; Luke 22:64; Acts 23:2; I Tim. 3:3). **21. as concerning reproach**—rather, "by way of dishonor (i.e., *self-disparagement*) I say it." **as though we . . . weak**—in not similarly (vs. 20) showing our *power* over you. "An ironical reminiscence of his own abstinence when among them from all these acts of self-exaltation at their expense" (as if such abstinence was weakness) [ALFORD]. The "we" is emphatically contrasted with the false teachers who so oppressively displayed their power. I speak so as though WE had been weak when with you, because we did not show our power this way. Howbeit (we are not really weak; for), whereinsoever any is bold . . . , I am bold also. **22. Hebrews . . . Israelites . . . the seed of Abraham**—A climax. "Hebrews," referring to the *language* and *nationality;* "Israelites," to the *theocracy* and *descent from Israel,* the "prince who prevailed with God" (Rom. 9:4); "the seed of Abraham," to the *claim to a share in the Messiah* (Rom. 11:1; 9:7). Cf. Philippians 3:5, "An Hebrew of the Hebrews," not an Hellenist or Greekspeaking Jew, but a Hebrew in tongue, and sprung from Hebrews.

23. I speak as a fool—rather, as *Greek*, "I speak as if *beside myself*"; stronger than "as a fool." **I am more**—viz., in respect to the credentials and manifestations of my ministry, more faithful and self-denying; and richer in tokens of God's recognition of my ministry. Old authorities read the order thus, "In prisons above measures, in stripes more abundantly" (*English Version*, less accurately, "more frequent"). Acts 16:23-40 records one case of his imprisonment with stripes. CLEMENT (I *Epistle to Corinthians*) describes him as having suffered bonds seven times. **in death oft**—(ch. 4:10; Acts 9:23; 13:50; 14:5, 6, 19; 17:5, 13).

24. Deuteronomy 25:3 ordained that not more than forty stripes should be inflicted. To avoid exceeding this number, they gave one short of it: thirteen strokes with a treble lash [BENGEL]. This is one of those minute agreements with Jewish usage, which a forger would have not been likely to observe.

ADAM CLARKE

19. *Ye suffer fools gladly, seeing ye yourselves are wise.* A very fine irony. You are so profoundly *wise* as to be able to discern that I am a fool. Well, it would be dishonorable to you as *wise* men to fall out with a fool; you will therefore gladly bear with his impertinence and foolishness because of your own profound wisdom.

20. *For ye suffer.* As you are so meek and gentle as to submit to be brought into *bondage,* to have your property devoured, your goods taken away, yourselves laid in the dust, so that others may *exalt* themselves over you—yea, and will bear from those the most degrading indignity—then of course you will bear with one who has never insulted, defrauded, devoured, taken of you, exalted himself against you, or offered you any kind of indignity; and who only wishes you to bear his confident boasting concerning matters which he can substantiate. The expressions in this verse are some evidence that the false apostle was a Judaizing teacher. *Ye suffer,* says the apostle, *if a man bring you into bondage,* probably meaning to the Jewish rites and ceremonies, Gal. iv. 9; v. 1. *If* he *devour you;* as the Pharisees did the patrimony of the widows, and for a pretense made long prayers; *if a man take of you,* exact different contributions, pretendedly for the Temple at Jerusalem. *If* he *exalt himself,* pretending to be of the seed of Abraham, infinitely higher in honor and dignity than all the families of the Gentiles; *if* he *smite you on the face,* treat you with indignity, as the Jews did the Gentiles, considering them only as dogs, and not fit to be ranked with any of the descendants of Jacob.

22. *Are they Hebrews?* Speaking the sacred language, and reading in the congregation from the Hebrew Scriptures? The same is my own language. *Are they Israelites?* Regularly descended from Jacob, and not from Esau? I am also one. *Are they the seed of Abraham?* Circumcised, and in the bond of the covenant? *So am I.* I am no proselyte, but I am a Hebrew of the Hebrews by both father and mother; and can trace my genealogy through the tribe of Benjamin, up to the father of the faithful.

23. *Are they ministers of Christ?* So we find that these were professors of Christianity; and that they were genuine Jews, and such as endeavored to incorporate both systems, and no doubt to oblige those who had believed to be circumcised; and this appears to have been the bondage into which they had brought many of the believing Christians. *I am more.* More of a minister of Christ than they are, and have given fuller proofs of it. I have suffered persecution for the cross of Christ, and of the Jews too; and had I preached up the necessity of circumcision, I should have been as free from opposition as these are. *In labours more abundant.* Far from sitting down to take my ease in a church already gathered into Christ, I travel incessantly, preach everywhere and at all risks, in order to get the heathen brought from the empire of darkness into the kingdom of God's beloved Son. *In stripes above measure.* Being beaten by the heathen, who had no particular rule according to which they scourged criminals; and we find, from Acts xvi. 22-23, that they beat Paul unmercifully with many stripes. *In prisons more frequent.* See Acts xxi. 11 and the whole of the apostle's history; and his long imprisonment of at least two years at Rome, Acts xxviii. It does not appear that there is any one instance of a false apostle having been imprisoned for the testimony of Christ; this was a badge of the true apostles. *In deaths oft.* That is, in the most imminent dangers. See 1 Cor. xv. 31; 2 Cor. iv. 11.

24. *Of the Jews five times received I forty stripes save one.* That is, he was five times scourged by the Jews, whose law (Deut. xxv. 3) allowed forty stripes; but they, pretending to be lenient, and to act within the letter of the law, inflicted but thirty-nine. To except one stripe from the forty was a very ancient canon among the Jews, as we learn from Josephus, *Antiq.*, l. iv, c. viii, s. 21, who mentions the same thing: "forty stripes, excepting one." The Mishna gives this as a rule, Mish., *Maccoth*, fol. 22, 10: "How often shall he, the culprit, be smitten? Ans. forty stripes, wanting one; i.e., with the number which is nighest to forty." They also thought

MATTHEW HENRY	JAMIESON, FAUSSET, BROWN	ADAM CLARKE

F. B. MEYER:

It has been truly said that this enumeration represents a life which up to that hour had been without precedent in the history of the world. Self-devotion at particular moments or for some special cause had been often witnessed before; but a self-devotion involving such sacrifices and extending over at least fourteen years, in the interests of mankind at large, was up to that time a thing unknown. The lives of missionaries and philanthropists in later times may have paralleled his experiences; but Paul did all this, and was the first to do it.

The biography of the apostle, as told by Luke, comes greatly short of this marvelous description. Of the facts alluded to, only two—the stoning and one of the Roman scourgings—are mentioned in the book of the Acts; from which we gather that the book is, after all, but a fragmentary record, and that the splendid deeds of the disciples and apostles of that first age will be known only when the Lamb himself recites them from his Book. But even this enumeration omits all that the apostle suffered after the writing of this epistle, including, of course, the sufferings between his arrest and his appearance before Nero.—*Bible Commentary*

Bonds and imprisonments were familiar to him. He says that *thrice he suffered shipwreck*. *A night and a day he had been in the deep* (*v.* 25). Wherever he went, he went in perils.

If he journeyed by land, or voyaged by sea, he was in perils of robbers; his own countrymen sought to kill him; the heathen were not more kind to him, for among them he was in peril. If he was in the city, or in the wilderness, still he was in peril. He was in peril not only among avowed enemies, but among those also who called themselves brethren, but were false brethren, *v.* 26. He was in *watchings often*, and exposed to *hunger and thirst*; in *fastings often*; and endured *cold and nakedness*, *v.* 27. Thus he was used as if he had been the burden of the earth, and the plague of his generation.

As an apostle, the *care of all the churches* lay on him, *v.* 28. He mentions this last, as if this lay the heaviest upon him, *v.* 29. There was not a weak Christian with whom he did not sympathize, nor any one scandalized, but he was affected therewith.

25. The beating by Roman magistrates at Philippi (Acts 16:23) is the only one recorded in Acts, which does not profess to give a complete journal of his life, but only a sketch of it in connection with the design of the book, viz., to give an outline of the history of the Gospel Church from its foundation at Jerusalem, to the period of its reaching Rome, the capital of the Gentile world. **once was I stoned**—(Acts 14:19). **thrice . . . shipwreck**—before the shipwreck at Melita (Acts 27). Probably in some of his voyages from Tarsus, where he stayed for some time after his conversion, and from which, as being a seafaring place, he was likely to make missionary voyages to adjoining places (Acts 9:30; 11:25; Gal. 1:21). **a night and a day . . . in the deep**—probably in part swimming or in an open boat. **26. In**—rather, "By": connected with vs. 23, but now not with "in," as there, and as in vs. 27, where again he passes to the idea of surrounding circumstances or environments [ALFORD, ELLICOTT and others]. **waters**—rather, as *Greek*, "rivers," viz., perils by the flooding of rivers, as on the road often traversed by Paul between Jerusalem and Antioch, crossed as it is by the torrents rushing down from Lebanon. So the traveller Spon lost his life. **robbers**—perhaps in his journey from Perga to Antioch in Pisidia. Pisidia was notorious for robbers; as indeed were all the mountains that divided the high land of Asia from the sea. **the heathen**—Gentiles. **in the city**—Damascus, Acts 9:24, 25; Jerusalem, Acts 9:29; Ephesus, Acts 19:23.

false brethren—(Gal. 2:4). **27. fastings**—*voluntary*, in order to kindle devotions (Acts 13:2, 3; 14:23; I Cor. 9:27); for they are distinguished from "hunger and thirst," which were *involuntary* [GROTIUS]. See, however, *Note*, ch. 6: 5. The context refers solely to *hardships*, not to self-imposed devotional mortification. "Hunger and thirst" are not synonymous with "foodlessness" (as the *Greek* of "fasting" means), but are its consequences. **cold . . . nakedness**—"cold" resulting from "nakedness," or insufficient clothing, as the *Greek* often means: as "hunger and thirst" result from "foodlessness." (Cf. Acts 28:2; Rom. 8:35.) "When we remember that he who endured all this was a man constantly suffering from infirm health (II Cor. 4:7-12; 12:7-10; Gal. 4:13, 14), such heroic self-devotion seems almost superhuman [CONYBEARE and HOWSON]. **28. without**—"Beside" trials falling on me *externally*, just recounted, there is "that which cometh upon me (lit., *the impetuous concourse to me* of business; properly, *a crowd rising up against one again and again, and ready to bear him down*), the care of all the churches" (including those not yet seen in the flesh, Col. 2:1): an *internal* and more weighty anxiety. But the oldest MSS., for "that which cometh," read, "the *pressure*": "the *pressing care-taking*" or "inspection that is upon me daily." ALFORD translates, "Omitting what is BESIDES"; viz., those other trials *besides* those recounted. But the *Vulgate*, ESTIUS, and BENGEL, support *English Version*. **the care**—The *Greek* implies, "my *anxious solicitude* for all the churches." **29. I . . . weak**—in condescending sympathy with the weak (I Cor. 9:22). "*Care* generates sympathy, which causes the minister of Christ personally to enter into the feelings of all his people, as if he stood in their position, so as to accommodate himself to all" [CALVIN].

it right to stop under forty, lest the person who counted should make a mistake, and the criminal get more than forty stripes, which would be injustice, as the law required only forty. The manner in which this punishment was inflicted is described in the Mishna, fol. 22, 2: "The two hands of the criminal are bound to a post, and then the servant of the synagogue either pulls or tears off his clothes till he leaves his breast and shoulders bare. A stone or block is placed behind him on which the servant stands; he holds in his hands a scourge made of leather, divided into four tails. He who scourges lays one third on the criminal's breast, another third on his right shoulder, and another on his left. The man who receives the punishment is neither sitting nor standing, but all the while stooping; and the man smites with all his strength, with one hand."

25. *Thrice was I beaten with rods*. This was under the Roman government, as their lictors beat criminals in this way. We hear of the apostle's being treated thus once, namely, at Philippi, Acts xvi. 22. *Once was I stoned*. Namely, at Lystra, Acts xiv. 19, etc. *A night and a day I have been in the deep*. To what this refers we cannot tell; it is generally supposed that in some shipwreck not on record the apostle had saved himself on a plank, and was a whole day and night on the sea, tossed about at the mercy of the waves.

26. *In journeyings often*. He means the particular journeys which he took to different places, for the purpose of propagating the gospel. *In perils of waters*. Exposed to great dangers in crossing rivers; for of "rivers" the original must be understood. *Of robbers*. Judea itself, and perhaps every other country, was grievously infested by bandits of this kind; and no doubt the apostle in his frequent peregrinations was often attacked; but being poor and having nothing to lose, he passed unhurt, though not without great danger. *In perils by mine own countrymen*. The Jews had the most rooted antipathy to him, because they considered him an apostate from the true faith, and also the means of perverting many others. There are several instances of this in the Acts; and a remarkable conspiracy against his life is related, Acts xxiii. 12, etc. *In perils by the heathen*. In the heathen provinces whither he went to preach the gospel. Several instances of these perils occur also in the Acts. *In perils in the city*. The different seditions raised against him; particularly in Jerusalem, to which Ephesus and Damascus may be added. *Perils in the wilderness*. Uninhabited countries through which he was obliged to pass in order to reach from city to city. In such places it is easy to imagine many dangers from bandits, wild beasts, cold, starvation, etc. *Perils in the sea*. The different voyages he took in narrow seas, such as the Mediterranean, about dangerous coasts, and without compass. *False brethren*. Persons who joined themselves to the Church, pretending faith in Christ, but intending to act as spies, hoping to get some matter of accusation against him. He not doubt suffered much also from apostates.

27. *In weariness and painfulness*. Tribulations of this kind were his constant companions.

28. *Beside those things that are without*. Independently of all these outward things, I have innumerable troubles and mental oppressions. *Which cometh upon me*. This continual press of business; this insurrection of cases to be heard, solved, and determined, relative to the doctrine, discipline, state, persecution, and supply of all the churches. All his perils were little in comparison of what he felt relative to the peace, government, and establishment of all the churches among the Gentiles; for as he was the apostle of the Gentiles, the government of all the churches among these fell in some sort on him, whether they were of his own planting or of the planting of others. See Col. ii. 1. None but a conscientious minister, who has at heart the salvation of souls, can enter into the apostle's feelings in this place.

29. *Who is weak?* What church is there under persecution with which I do not immediately sympathize? or who from his weakness in the faith and scrupulousness of conscience is likely to be turned out of the way, to whom I do not

MATTHEW HENRY

Nor was he ashamed of all this; it was what he accounted his honour, *v.* 30.

He mentions one particular part of his sufferings out of its place, as if he had forgotten it before, namely, the danger he was in at Damascus, soon after he was converted. This was his first great danger and difficulty, and the rest of his life was of a piece with this. The apostle confirms this narrative with a solemn oath, *v.* 31. It is a great comfort to a good man that *the God and Father of our Lord Jesus Christ* knows the truth of all he says, and knows all he does and all he suffers for his sake.

JAMIESON, FAUSSET, BROWN

offended—by some stumbling block put in his way by others: the "weak" is most liable to be "offended." **I burn not**—The "I" in the *Greek* is emphatic, which it is not in the former clause, "I am not weak." I not only enter into the feeling of the party offended, but *I* burn with indignation at the offender, *I myself* taking up his cause as my own. "Who meets with a stumbling block and I am not disturbed even more than himself" [NEANDER]. **30. glory of . . . infirmities**—A striking contrast! *Glorying* or *boasting of* what others make matter of shame, viz., *infirmities;* for instance, his humbling mode of escape in a basket (vs. 33). A character utterly incompatible with that of an enthusiast (cf. ch. 12:5, 9, 10).

31. This solemn asseveration refers to what follows. The persecution at Damascus was one of the first and greatest, and having no human witness of it to adduce to the Corinthians, as being a fact that happened long before and was known to few, he appeals to God for its truth. Luke (Acts 9:25) afterwards recorded it (cf. Gal. 1:20), [BENGEL]. It may ALSO refer to the revelation in ch. 12:1, standing in beautiful contrast to his humiliating escape from Damascus. **32. governor**—*Greek,* "Ethnarch": a Jewish officer to whom heathen rulers gave authority over Jews in large cities where they were numerous. He was in this case under Aretas, king of Arabia. Damascus was in a Roman province. But at this time, A.D. 38 or 39, three years after Paul's conversion, A.D. 36, Aretas, against whom the Emperor Tiberius as the ally of Herod Agrippa had sent an army under Vitellius, had got possession of Damascus on the death of the emperor, and the consequent interruption of Vitellius' operations. His possession of it was put an end to immediately after by the Romans [NEANDER]. Rather, it was granted by Caligula (A.D. 38) to Aretas, whose predecessors had possessed it. This is proved by our having no Damascus coins of Caligula or Claudius, though we do have of their immediate imperial predecessors and successors [ALFORD].

ADAM CLARKE

condescend, and whose burden I do not bear? *Who is offended,* or likely to be turned out of the way, *and I burn not* with zeal to restore and confirm him?

30. *I will glory . . . which concern mine infirmities.* I will not boast of my natural or acquired power, neither in what God has done by me; but rather in what I have suffered for Him. Many persons have understood by *infirmities* what they call the indwelling sin of the apostle, and say that "he gloried in this, because the grace of Christ was the more magnified in his being preserved from ruin, notwithstanding this indwelling adversary." And to support this most unholy interpretation they quote those other words of the apostle, chap. xii. 9: "Most gladly therefore will I rather glory in my infirmities," my indwelling corruptions, "that the power of Christ," in chaining the fierce lion, "may rest upon me." But it would be difficult to produce a single passage in the whole New Testament where the word which we translate infirmity has the sense of sin or moral corruption.

31. *The God and Father of our Lord.* Here is a very solemn asseveration, an appeal to the ever blessed God for the truth of what he asserts. It is something similar to his asseveration or oath in v. 10 of this chapter; see also Rom. ix. 5 and Gal. i. 20.

32. *In Damascus the governor under Aretas.* For a description of Damascus see the note on Acts ix. 2. And for the transaction to which the apostle refers see Acts ix. 23. As to King Aretas, there were three of this name. The first is mentioned in 2 Maccab. v. 8; the second, by Josephus. The third, who is the person supposed to be referred to here, was the father-in-law of Herod Antipas, of whom see the notes, Acts ix. 23 ff. *The governor.* Who this ethnarch was we cannot tell. The word ethnarch signifies the governor of a province, under a king or emperor. *Desirous to apprehend me.* The enemies of the apostle might have represented him to the governor as a dangerous spy, employed by the Romans.

33. *Through a window in a basket.* Probably the house was situated on the wall of the city. See the notes on this history, Acts ix. 23-25.

CHAPTER 12

Verses 1-10

I. The narrative the apostle gives of the favours God had shown him, for doubtless he himself is the man in Christ of whom he speaks.

The modest manner in which the apostle mentions this matter, *v.* 1. He therefore did not mention this till *above fourteen years* after, *v.* 2.

CHAPTER 12

VSS. 1-21. REVELATIONS IN WHICH HE MIGHT GLORY: BUT HE RATHER GLORIES IN INFIRMITIES, AS CALLING FORTH CHRIST'S POWER: SIGNS OF HIS APOSTLESHIP: HIS DISINTERESTEDNESS: NOT THAT HE IS EXCUSING HIMSELF TO THEM; BUT HE DOES ALL FOR THEIR GOOD, LEST HE SHOULD FIND THEM NOT SUCH AS HE DESIRED, AND SO SHOULD HAVE TO BE SEVERE AT HIS COMING. **1.** He proceeds to illustrate the "glorying in infirmities" (ch. 11:30). He gave one instance which might expose him to ridicule (ch. 11:33); he now gives another, but this one connected with a glorious revelation of which it was the sequel: but he dwells not on the glory done to himself, but on the *infirmity* which followed it, as displaying Christ's power. The oldest MSS. read, "I MUST NEEDS boast (or glory) though it be not expedient; *for* I will come." The "for" gives a proof that it is "not expedient to boast": I will take the case of revelations, in which if anywhere boasting might be thought harmless. "Visions" refers to things *seen:* "revelations," to things heard (cf. I Sam. 9:15) or *revealed* in any way. In "visions" their signification was not always vouchsafed; in "revelations" there was always an unveiling of truths before hidden (Dan. 2:19, 31). All parts of Scripture alike are matter of *inspiration;* but not all of *revelation.* There are degrees of revelation; but not of inspiration. **of**—i.e., *from* the Lord; Christ, vs. 2. **2.** Translate, "I know," not "I knew." **a man**—meaning *himself.* But he purposely thus distinguishes between the *rapt and glorified* person of vss. 2, 4, and *himself* the infirmity-laden victim of the "thorn in the flesh" (vs. 7). Such glory belonged not to *him,* but the *weakness* did. Nay, he did not even know whether he was in or out of the body when the glory was put upon him, so far was the glory from being *his* [ALFORD]. His spiritual self was his highest and truest self: the flesh with its infirmity merely his temporary self (Rom. 7:25). Here, however, the latter is the prominent thought. **in Christ**—a Christian (Rom. 16:7). **above**—rather, simply "fourteen

CHAPTER 12

1. *It is not expedient for me.* There are several various readings on this verse which are too minute to be noticed here; they seem in effect to represent the verse thus: "If it be expedient to glory (which does not become me), I will proceed to visions," etc. The plain meaning of the apostle, in this and the preceding chapter, in reference to glorying is that, though to boast in any attainments or in what God did by him was in all possible cases to be avoided, as being contrary to the humility and simplicity of the gospel, yet the circumstances in which he was found in reference to the Corinthian church and his detractors there rendered it absolutely necessary; not for his personal vindication, but for the honor of the gospel, the credit of which was certainly at stake. *I will come to visions.* Symbolical representations of spiritual and celestial things, in which matters of the deepest importance are exhibited to the eye of the mind by a variety of emblems, the nature and properties of which serve to illustrate those spiritual things. *Revelations.* A manifestation of things not before known, and such as God alone can make known, because they are a part of His own inscrutable counsels.

2. *I knew a man in Christ.* I knew a Christian, or a Christian man. *Fourteen years ago.* On what occasion or in what place this transaction took place we cannot tell; there are many conjectures among learned men concerning it, but of what utility can they be when everything is so palpably uncertain?

MATTHEW HENRY

He was *caught up into the third heaven, v.* 2. When this was we cannot say, much less can we pretend to say *how* this was. In some sense he was caught up into the *third heaven.*

This third heaven is called paradise (*v.* 4). The apostle does not mention what he saw in the third heaven or paradise, but tells us that *he heard unspeakable words*: nor was it lawful to utter those words.

Again, his humility appears by the check he seems to put upon himself (*v.* 6). It is an excellent thing to have a lowly spirit in the midst of high advancements; and those who abase themselves shall be exalted.

II. The methods God took to prevent his *being lifted up above measure.* When God's people communicate their experiences, let them always remember to take notice of what God has done to keep them humble.

1. The apostle was pained with a thorn in the flesh, and buffeted with a messenger of Satan, *v.* 7. We are much in the dark what this was. Some think it was an acute bodily pain or sickness. This is certain, that what the apostle calls a thorn in his flesh was for a time very grievous to him: but the thorns Christ wore for us, sanctify and make easy all the thorns in the flesh we may at any time be afflicted with.

JAMIESON, FAUSSET, BROWN

years ago." This Epistle was written A.D. 55-57. Fourteen years before will bring the vision to A.D. 41-43, the time of his second visit to Jerusalem (Acts 22:17). He had long been intimate with the Corinthians, yet had never mentioned this revelation before: it was not a matter lightly to be spoken of. **I cannot tell**—rather as *Greek,* "I know not." If *in the body,* he must have been caught up bodily; if *out of the body,* as seems to be Paul's *opinion,* his spirit must have been caught up out of the body. At all events he recognizes the possibility of conscious receptivity in disembodied spirits. **caught up**—(Acts 8:39). **to the third heaven**—*"even to...."* These *raptures* (note the *plural,* "visions," "revelations") had two degrees: first he was *caught up* "to the third heaven," and from thence to "Paradise" (vs. 4) [CLEMENS ALEXANDRINUS, *Stromata* 5. 427], which seems to denote an inner recess of the third heaven [BENGEL] (Luke 23:43; Rev. 2:7). Paul was permitted not only to "hear" the things of Paradise, but to *see* also in some degree the things of the third heaven (cf. "visions," vs. 1). The occurrence TWICE of "whether in the body . . . , I know not, God knoweth," and of "lest I should be exalted above measure," marks two stages in the revelation. "Ignorance of the *mode* does not set aside the certain knowledge of the *fact.* The apostles were ignorant of many things" [BENGEL]. The first heaven is that of the clouds, the *air;* the second, that of the stars, *the sky;* the third is spiritual (Eph. 4:10). **3.** Translate, "I *know.*" **out of**—Most of the oldest MSS. read "apart from." **4. unspeakable**—not in themselves, otherwise Paul could not have heard them; but as the explanation states, "which it is not lawful . . . to utter" [ALFORD]. They were designed for Paul's own consolation, and not for communication to others. Some heavenly words are communicable (Exod. 34: 6; Isa. 6:3). These were not so. Paul had not the power adequately to utter; nor if he had, would he have been permitted; nor would earthly men comprehend them (John 3:12; I Cor. 2:9). A man may hear and know more than he can speak.

5. of myself—concerning myself. Self is put in the background, except in respect to his infirmities. His glorying in his other self, to which the revelations were vouchsafed, was not in order to give glory to his fleshly self, but to bring out in contrast the "infirmities" of the latter, that Christ might have all the glory. **6. For**—Not but that I might glory as to "myself" (vs. 5); "FOR if I should desire to glory, I shall not be a fool"; for I have things to glory, or boast of which are good matter for glorying of (not mere external fleshly advantages which when he gloried in (ch. 11) he termed such glorying "folly," ch. 11:1, 16, 17). **think of me**—*Greek,* "form his estimate respecting me." **heareth of me**—*Greek,* "heareth aught from me." Whatever haply he heareth from me in person. If on account of healing a cripple (Acts 14:12, 13), and shaking off a viper (Acts 28), the people thought him a god, what would they have not done, if he had disclosed those revelations? [ESTIUS.] I wish each of you to estimate me by "what he sees" my *present* acts and "hears" my teaching to be; not by my boasting of *past* revelations. They who allow themselves to be thought of more highly than is lawful, defraud themselves of the honor which is at God's disposal [BENGEL] (John 5:44; 12: 43). **7. exalted above measure**—*Greek,* "overmuch uplifted." How dangerous must self-exaltation be, when even the apostle required so much restraint! [BENGEL]. **abundance**—*Greek,* "the excess"; exceeding greatness. **given . . . me**—viz., by God (Job 5:6; Phil. 1:29). **thorn in the flesh**—(Num. 33. 55; Ezek. 28:24). ALFORD thinks it to be the same bodily affliction as in Galatians 4:13, 14. It certainly was something personal, affecting him individually, and not as an apostle: causing at once *acute pain* (as "thorn" implies) and *shame* ("buffet": as slaves are *buffeted,* I Pet. 2:20).

ADAM CLARKE

Whether in the body, I cannot tell. That the apostle was in an ecstasy or trance, something like that of Peter, Acts x. 9, etc., there is reason to believe; but we know that being carried literally into heaven was possible to the Almighty. *Caught up to the third heaven.* He appeared to have been carried up to this place; but whether bodily he could not tell, or whether the spirit were not separated for the time and taken up to the third heaven he could not tell. *The third heaven*—The Jews talk of seven heavens, and Mohammed has received the same from them; but these are not only fabulous but absurd. In the sacred writings three heavens only are mentioned. The first is the atmosphere, what appears to be intended by *rekia,* the firmament or expansion, Gen. i. 6. The second, the starry heaven; where are the sun, moon, planets, and stars; but these two are often expressed under the one term *shamayim,* the two heavens, or expansions; and in Gen. i. 17 they appear to be both expressed by *rekia hashshamayim,* the "firmament of heaven." And, thirdly, the place of the blessed, or the throne of the divine glory, probably expressed by the words *hashshamayim,* the "heavens of heavens." But on these subjects the Scripture affords us but little light, and on this distinction the reader is not desired to rely.

4. *Caught up into paradise.* The Jewish writers have no less than four paradises, as they have seven heavens: but it is needless to wade through their fables. Among Christian writers it generally means the place of the blessed, or the state of separate spirits. *Which it is not lawful for a man to utter.* The Jews thought that the divine name, the Tetragrammaton *Yehovah,* should not be uttered, and that it is absolutely unlawful to pronounce it; indeed they say that the true pronunciation is utterly lost, and cannot be recovered without an express revelation. Not one of them, to the present day, ever attempts to utter it; and when they meet with it in their reading always supply its place with *Adonai,* Lord. It is probable that the apostle refers to some communication concerning the divine nature and the divine economy, of which he was only to make a general use in his preaching and writing. No doubt what he learned at this time formed the basis of all his doctrines.

5. *Of such an one will I glory.* Through modesty he does not mention himself, though the account can be understood of no other person; for did he mean any other, the whole account would be completely irrelevant.

6. *I shall not be a fool.* Who that had received such honor from God would have been fourteen years silent on the subject? *I will say the truth.* I speak nothing but truth; and the apostle seems to have intended to proceed with something else of the same kind, but, finding some reason probably occurring suddenly, says, *I forbear*—I will say no more on this subject. *Lest any man should think of me above.* The apostle spoke of these revelations for two purposes: first, lest his enemies might suppose they had cause to think meanly of him; and, secondly, having said thus much, he forbears to speak any further of them, lest his friends should think too highly of him. It is a rare gift to discern when to speak and when to be silent; and to know when enough is said on a subject, neither too little nor too much.

7. *And lest I should be exalted.* There were three evils to be guarded against: (1) the contempt of his gifts and call by his enemies, (2) the overweening fondness of his friends, and (3) self-exultation. *A thorn in the flesh.* The word signifies a "stake." Whatever it was, it was *in the flesh,* i.e., of an outward kind. It was neither sin nor sinfulness, for this could not be given him to prevent his being exalted above measure; for sin never had and never can have this tendency. What this *thorn in the flesh* might be has given birth to a multitude of conjectures: Tertullian thought it the earache; *Chrysostom,* the headache; *Cyprian,* many and grievous bodily torments. I believe the apostle to refer simply to the distresses he had endured through the opposition he met with at Corinth; which were as painful and grievous to him as *a thorn in his flesh,* or his being bound to a stake; for if he could have devoted himself to destruction, Rom. ix. 3, for his rebellious and

MATTHEW HENRY

2. The design of this was to keep the apostle humble, *v.* 7. If God loves us, he will hide pride from us, and keep us from being exalted above measure. This thorn in the flesh is said to be a messenger of Satan, which he did not send with a good design, but with ill intentions. But God overruled it for good.

3. The apostle prayed earnestly to God for the removal of this sore grievance. If an answer be not given to the first prayer, nor to the second, we must hold on, and hold out, till we receive an answer. As troubles are sent to teach us to pray, so they are continued to teach us to continue instant in prayer.

4. *My grace is sufficient for thee.* Though God accepts the prayer of faith, yet he does not always answer it in the letter; as he sometimes grants in wrath, so he sometimes denies in love. It is a great comfort to us, whatever thorns in the flesh we are pained with, that God's grace is sufficient for us. Grace signifies two things: (1) The goodwill of God towards us, and this is sufficient to strengthen and comfort us. (2) The good work of God in us. Christ Jesus will proportion the remedy to our malady.

III. The use which the apostle makes of this dispensation: *He gloried in his infirmities* (*v.* 9), and took pleasure in them for Christ's sake, *v.* 10. They were fair opportunities for Christ to manifest the power and sufficiency of his grace resting upon him. When we are weak in ourselves, then we are strong in the grace of our Lord Jesus Christ.

Verses 11-21

I. He blames them that they had not stood up in his defence. They compelled him to commend himself, *v.* 11. They in particular had good reason to speak well of him. It is a debt we owe to good men to stand up in the defence of their reputation. How much soever we are esteemed by others, we ought always to think humbly of ourselves. See an example of this in this great apostle, who thought himself to be nothing, though in truth he was not behind the greatest apostles.

JAMIESON, FAUSSET, BROWN

messenger of Satan—who is permitted by God to afflict His saints, as Job (Job 2:7; Luke 13:16). **to buffet me**—In *Greek, present:* to buffet me even now continuously. After experiencing the state of the blissful angels, he is now exposed to the influence of an evil angel. The chastisement from hell follows soon upon the revelation from heaven. As his *sight* and *hearing* had been ravished with heavenly "revelations," so his *touch* is pained with the "thorn in the flesh."

8. For—"concerning this thing." **thrice**—To his first and second prayer no answer came. To his third the answer came, which satisfied his faith and led him to bow his will to God's will. So Paul's master, Jesus, *thrice* prayed on the Mount of Olives, in resignation to the Father's will. The thorn seems (from vs. 9, and *Greek,* vs. 7, "that he *may* buffet me") to have continued with Paul when he wrote, lest still he should be "overmuch lifted up." **the Lord**—Christ. Escape from the cross is not to be sought even indirectly from Satan (Luke 4:7). "Satan is not to be asked to spare us" [BENGEL].

9. said—lit., "He hath said," implying that His answer is enough [ALFORD]. **is sufficient**—The trial must endure, but the grace shall also endure and never fail thee [ALFORD], (Deut. 33:25). The Lord puts the words into Paul's mouth, that following them up he might say, "O Lord, Thy grace is sufficient for me" [BENGEL]. **my strength**—*Greek,* "power." **is made perfect**—has its most perfect manifestation. **in weakness**—Do not ask for sensible strength, FOR My power is perfected in man's "strengthlessness" (so the *Greek*). The "for" implies, thy "strengthlessness" (the same *Greek* as is translated "weakness"; and in vs. 10, "infirmities") is the very element in which My "power" (which moves coincident with "My grace") exhibits itself more perfectly. So that Paul instead of desiring the infirmity to "depart," "rather" henceforth "*glories* in infirmities, that the power of Christ may rest (*Greek,* 'tabernacle upon', cover my infirmity all over as with a tabernacle; cf. *Greek,* John 1:12) upon" him. This effect of Christ's assurance on him appears, ch. 4:7; I Corinthians 2:3, 4; cf. I Peter 4:14. The "My" is omitted in some of the oldest MSS.; the sense is the same, "power" (referring to God's power) standing absolutely, in contrast to "weakness" (put absolutely, for man's weakness). Paul often repeats the word "weakness" or "infirmity" (chs. 11, 12, and 13) as being Christ's own word. The Lord has more need of our weakness than of our strength: our strength is often His rival; our weakness, His servant, drawing on His resources, and showing forth His glory. Man's extremity is God's opportunity; man's security is Satan's opportunity. God's way is not to take His children out of trial, but to give them strength to bear up against it (Ps. 88:7; John 17:15). **10. take pleasure in**—too strongly. Rather as the *Greek,* "I am well contented in." **infirmities**—the *genus.* Two pairs of *species* follow, partly coming from "Satan's messenger," partly from men. **reproaches**—"insults." **when**—in all the cases just specified. **then**—then especially. **strong**—"*powerful*" in "the *power of Christ*" (vs. 9; ch. 13:4; Heb. 11:34).

11. in glorying—omitted in the oldest MSS. "I am become a fool." He sounds a retreat [BENGEL]. **ye**—emphatic. "It is YE who have compelled me; for I ought to have been commended by you," instead of having to commend myself. **am I behind**—rather as *Greek,* "was I behind" when I was with you? **the very chiefest**—rather, as in ch. 11:5, "those overmuch apostles." **though I be nothing**—in myself (I Cor. 15:9, 10).

ADAM CLARKE

unbelieving countrymen, what must he have suffered on account of an eminent church being perverted and torn to pieces by a false teacher? God permitted this to keep the apostle humble, and at last completely delivered the church out of the hands and influence of this deceiver; none, not even the incestuous person, having been turned finally out of the way by the false doctrines there preached. *The messenger of Satan.* Another mode of expressing what he calls the *thorn in the flesh;* and he seems most plainly to refer to the false apostle at Corinth. The apostle himself was, as he styles himself to this church, chap. i. 1, the "apostle of Jesus Christ." The person in question is styled here "the apostle or angel of Satan." It is almost impossible to mistake the apostle's meaning and reference. Jesus Christ sent Paul to proclaim His truth, and found a church at Corinth. Satan, the adversary of God's truth, sent a man to preach lies at the same place, and turn the church of God into his own synagogue; and by his teaching lies and calumnies the apostle was severely buffeted.

8. *I besought the Lord.* That is, Christ, as the next verse absolutely proves, and the Socinians themselves confess. And if Christ be an object of prayer in such a case as this, or indeed in any case, it is a sure proof of His divinity; for only an omniscient Being can be made an object of prayer. *Thrice.* It is worthy of remark that our Lord in His agony acted in the same way. At three different times He applied to God that the cup might depart from Him; and in each application He spoke the same words, Matt. xxvi. 39-44. There is, therefore, a manifest allusion to our Lord's conduct in these words of the apostle.

9. *My grace is sufficient for thee.* Thou shalt not be permitted to sink under these afflictions. Your enemies shall not be able to prevail against you. *My strength is made perfect in weakness.* The more, and the more violently, you are afflicted and tried, being upheld by My power and prospered in all your labors, the more eminently will My power be seen and acknowledged. For the weaker the instrument I use, the more the power of My grace shall be manifested. *Will I rather glory in my infirmities.* Therefore his *infirmities* do not mean his corruptions, or sins, or sinfulness of any kind; for it would be blasphemous for any man to say, I will rather glory that God leaves my corruptions in me than that He should take them away. *That the power of Christ may rest upon me.* That it may "overshadow me as a tent" or tabernacle, affording me shelter, protection, safety, and rest. This expression is like that, John i. 14: "And the Word was made flesh," and made His tabernacle among us, "full of grace and truth." The same eternal Word promised to make His tabernacle with the apostle, and gives him a proof that He was still the same, "full of grace and truth," by assuring him that His grace should be sufficient for him. Paul, knowing that the promise of grace could not fail, because of the divine truth, says: *Most gladly therefore will I rather glory in my afflictions,* that such a power of Christ may overshadow and defend me. The words are also similar to those of the Prophet Isaiah, chap. iv. 5: "Upon all the glory shall be a defence."

10. *Therefore I take pleasure.* I not only endure them patiently, but am pleased when they occur; for I do it *for Christ's sake,* on His account; for on His account I suffer. *For when I am weak,* most oppressed with trials and afflictions, *then am I strong,* God supporting my mind with His most powerful influences, causing me to rejoice with joy unspeakable and full of glory.

11. *I am become a fool in glorying.* It is not the part of a wise or gracious man to boast; but *ye have compelled me*—I have been obliged to do it, in order to vindicate the cause of God. *I ought to have been commended of you.* You should have vindicated both myself and my ministry against the detractors that are among you. *Though I be nothing.* Though I have been thus set at nought by your false apostle, and though in consequence of what he has said some of you have been ready to consider me as nothing—what we call good for nothing.

12. *The signs of an apostle were wrought*

MATTHEW HENRY

ALBERT BARNES:

12. "Truly the signs of an apostle." Such "signs" or evidences that they were divinely commissioned (Mark 16:17; Acts 2:22; Rom. 15:19). "Were wrought among you." That is, by me (1 Cor. 9:2). "In all patience." I performed those works notwithstanding the opposition which I met with. I patiently persevered in furnishing the evidence of my divine commission. There was a succession of miracles demonstrating that I was from God, notwithstanding the unreasonable opposition which I met with, until I convinced you that I was called to the office of an apostle. "In signs and wonders." In working miracles (Acts 2:22). What these miracles at Corinth were we are not distinctly informed. They probably, however, were similar to those wrought in other places, in healing the sick—the most benevolent as it was one of the most decisive proofs of the divine power.
—Popular Commentary

II. His behaviour and kind intentions towards them. He says (*v.* 13) he had not been burdensome to them, for the time past, and tells them (*v.* 14) he would not be burdensome to them when he should come to them. He spared their purses to save their souls. Those who aim at clothing themselves with the fleece of the flock, and take no care of the sheep, are hirelings, and not good shepherds.

He would gladly spend and be spent for them (*v.* 15); so spend as to be spent, and be like a candle, which consumes itself to give light to others. He did not abate in his love to them, *v.* 15. He was careful not only that he himself should not be burdensome, but that none he employed should.

He was a man who did all things for edifying, *v.* 19. He would not shrink from his duty. Therefore he was resolved to be faithful in reproving sin, *v.* 20. Faithful ministers must not fear offending the guilty by sharp reproofs as they are needful, in public and in private.

JAMIESON, FAUSSET, BROWN

12. Truly . . .—There is understood some such clause as this, "And yet I have not been commended by you." **in all patience, in signs . . .**—The oldest MSS. omit "in." "Patience" is not one of the "signs," but the element IN which they were wrought: endurance of opposition which did not cause me to leave off working [ALFORD]. Translate, "IN . . . patience, BY signs . . . ." His mode of expression is modest, putting himself, the worker, in the background, "were wrought," not "*I* wrought." As the *signs* have not been transmitted to us, neither has the apostleship. The apostles have no literal successors (cf. Acts 1:21, 22). **mighty deeds**—palpable works of divine omnipotence. The silence of the apostles in fourteen Epistles, as to miracles, arises from the design of those Epistles being hortatory, not controversial. The passing allusions to miracles in seven Epistles prove that the writers were not enthusiasts to whom *miracles* seem the most important thing. *Doctrines* were with them the important matter, save when convincing adversaries. In the seven Epistles the mention of miracles is not *obtrusive,* but marked by a calm air of assurance, as of facts *acknowledged on all hands,* and therefore unnecessary to dwell on. This is a much stronger proof of their reality than if they were formally and obtrusively asserted. Signs and wonders is the regular formula of the Old Testament, which New Testament readers would necessarily understand of supernatural works. Again, in the Gospels the miracles are so inseparably and congruously tied up with the history, that you cannot deny the former without denying the latter also. And then you have a greater difficulty than ever, viz., *to account for the rise of Christianity;* so that the infidel has something infinitely more difficult to believe than that which he rejects, and which the Christian more rationally accepts. **13. wherein you were inferior**—i.e., were treated with less consideration by me than were other churches. **I myself**—*I made a gain of you* neither *myself,* nor *by* those others *whom I sent, Titus* and others (vss. 17, 18). **wrong**—His declining support from the Corinthians might be regarded as the denial to them of a privilege, and a mark of their spiritual inferiority, and of his looking on them with less confidence and love (cf. ch. 11:9, 11). **14. the third time**—See *Introduction* to First Corinthians. His *second* visit was probably a short one (I Cor. 16:7), and attended with humiliation through the scandalous conduct of some of his converts (cf. vs. 21; ch. 2:1). It was probably paid during his three years' sojourn at Ephesus, from which he could pass so readily by sea to Corinth (cf. ch. 1:15, 16; 13:1, 2). The context here implies nothing of a *third preparation* to come; but, "I am coming, and the third time, and will not burden you this time any more than I did at my *two previous visits*" [ALFORD]. **not yours, but you**—(Phil. 4:17). **children . . . parents**—Paul was their spiritual father (I Cor. 4:14, 15). He does not, therefore, seek earthly *treasure* from them, but *lays up* the best *treasure* (viz., spiritual) "for their souls" (vs. 15). **15. I will . . . spend**—all I have. **be spent**—all that I am. This is more than even natural parents do. They "lay up *treasures* for their children." But I spend not merely my treasures, but *myself.* **for you**—*Greek,* "for your souls"; not for your mere bodies. **the less I be loved**—Love rather descends than ascends [BENGEL]. Love him as a true friend who seeks your good more than your good will. **16. I did not burden you**—The "I" in the *Greek* is emphatic. A possible insinuation of the Corinthians is hereby anticipated and refuted: "But, you may say, granted that *I* did not burden you *myself;* nevertheless, being crafty, I caught you (in my net) with guile"; viz., made a gain of you *by means of others* (I Thess. 2:3). **17.** Paul's reply: You know well I did not. My associates were as distinterested as myself. An important rule to all who would influence others for good. **I desired Titus**—viz., to go unto you. Not the mission mentioned ch. 8:6, 17, 22; but a mission previous to this Epistle, probably that from which he had just returned announcing to Paul their penitence (ch. 7:6-16). **a brother**—rather "OUR (lit., "the") brother"; one well known to the Corinthians, and perhaps a Corinthian; probably one of the two mentioned in ch. 8:18, 22. **same spirit**—inwardly. **steps**—outwardly. **19. Again**—The oldest MSS. read, "*This long time* ye think that we are excusing ourselves unto you? (Nay.) It is *before God* (as opposed to 'unto you') that we speak in Christ" (ch. 2:17). *English Version Greek* text was a correction from ch. 3:1; 5:12. **20. For**—Assigning cause why they needed to be thus spoken to "for their edification"; viz., his fear that at his coming he

ADAM CLARKE

among you. Though I have been reputed as nothing, I have given the fullest proof of my divine mission by various signs, wonders, and miracles, and by that patience which I have manifested towards you; though I had power from God to inflict punishment on the transgressors, I have in every case forborne to do it.

13. *For what is it wherein ye were inferior?* This is a fine, forcible, yet delicate stroke. It was your duty and your interest to have supported your apostle; other churches have done so. I did not require this from you; in this respect all other churches are superior to you. I am the cause of your inferiority, by not giving you an opportunity of ministering to my necessities; *forgive me* the *wrong* I have done you. It is the privilege of the churches of Christ to support the ministry of His gospel among them. Those who do not contribute their part to the support of the gospel ministry either care nothing for it or derive no good from it.

14. *The third time I am ready.* That is, this is the third time that *I am ready*—have formed the resolution—to visit you. He had formed this resolution twice before, but was disappointed. See 1 Cor. xvi. 5 and 2 Cor. i. 15-16. He now formed it a third time, having more probability of seeing them now than he had before. See chap. xiii. 2. *I seek not yours, but you.* I seek your salvation; I desire not your property. Others have sought your property, but not your salvation. *For the children ought not to lay up for the parents.* You may have many teachers, but you have but one Father; "for in Christ Jesus I have begotten you through the gospel"; see 1 Cor. iv. 15.

15. *And I will very gladly spend and be spent for you.* I will continue to act as a loving father, who spends all he has upon his children, and expends his own strength and life in providing for them the things necessary for their preservation and comfort. *Though the more abundantly I love you.* I will then act towards you with the most affectionate tenderness, though it happen to me, as it often does to loving fathers, that their disobedient children love them less in proportion as their love to them is increased. Does it not frequently happen that the most disobedient child in the family is that one on which the parents' tenderness is more especially placed? See the parable of the prodigal son. It is in the order of God that it should be so, else the case of every prodigal would be utterly deplorable. The shepherd feels more for the lost sheep than for the ninety-nine that have not gone astray.

16. *But be it so, I did not burden you.* That is: You grant that I did not burden you, that I took nothing from you, but preached to you the gospel freely. But you say that, being crafty, *I caught you with guile;* i.e., getting from you, by means of others, what I pretended to be unwilling to receive immediately from yourselves.

17. *Did I make a gain of you?* Did any person I ever sent to preach the gospel to you or help you in your Christian course ever get anything from you for me? Produce the proof if you can.

18. *I desired Titus.* I never sent any to you but Titus and another brother; chap. viii. 6, 18. And *did Titus make a gain of you?* Did he get anything from you, either for himself or for me? You know he did not. He was actuated by *the same spirit* and he *walked in the same steps.*

19. *Think ye that we excuse ourselves?* That we "make an apology" for our conduct; or that I have sent Titus and that brother to you because I was ashamed or afraid to come myself? *We speak before God in Christ.* I have not done so. I speak the truth before God; He is Judge whether I was actuated in this way by any sinister or unworthy motive. *For your edifying.* Whatever I have done in this or any other way I have done for your *edifying,* not for any emolument to myself or friends.

20. *I fear, lest, when I come.* I think the present time is used here for the past; the apostle seems most evidently to be giving them the reason why he had not come to them according to his former purposes, and why he sent Titus and his companion. He was afraid to come at that time lest he should find them

MATTHEW HENRY

He was grieved at the apprehension that he should find scandalous sins among them not duly repented of. This would be the cause of great humiliation and lamentation. We have reason to *bewail many that have sinned, and have not repented, v.* 21. Those who love God, and love them, should mourn for them.

CHAPTER 13

I. The apostle threatens to be severe against obstinate sinners when he should come.

He was not hasty in using severity, but gave a first and second admonition (*v.* 1), referring to his first and second epistles, by which he admonished them, as if he were present with them, though in person he was absent, *v.* 2. We should go, or send, to our brother, once and again, to tell him of his fault. Now he tells them to exercise severity. The threatening itself: *That he would not spare* such as were impenitent. Though it is God's gracious method to bear long with sinners, yet he will not bear always.

II. Why he would be thus severe, *v.* 3. It was the design of the false teachers to make the Corinthians call this matter into question, of which yet they had not weak, but strong and mighty proofs (*v.* 3).

JAMIESON, FAUSSET, BROWN

should find them "not such as he would," and so he should be found by them "such as they would not" like, viz., severe in punishing misconduct.

debates—*Greek*, "strifes," "contentions." **envyings**—The oldest MSS. read "envying," *singular*. **strifes**—"factions," "intrigues," "factious schemes" [WAHL]. *Ambitious self-seeking;* from a *Greek* root, *"to work for hire."* **backbitings, whisperings**—*open* "slanderings," and "whispering backbitings" (Gal. 5:20). **swellings**—arrogant elation; puffing up of yourselves. Jude 16, "great swelling words" (II Pet. 2:18).

21. my God—*his* God, however trying the humiliation that was in store for him. **will humble me**—The indicative implies that the supposition *will actually be so.* The faithful pastor is "humbled" at, and "bewails" the falls of his people, as though they were his own. **sinned already**—before my last coming [BENGEL], i.e., before the second visit which he paid, and in which he had much at Corinth to rebuke. **have not repented**—shall not have repented [ALFORD]. **uncleanness**—for example, of married persons (I Thess. 4:7). **fornication**—among the unmarried.

CHAPTER 13

VSS. 1-14. HE THREATENS A SEVERE PROOF OF HIS APOSTOLIC AUTHORITY, BUT PREFERS THEY WOULD SPARE HIM THE NECESSITY FOR IT. **This is the third time I am coming to you**—not merely *preparing* to come to you. This proves an *intermediate visit* between the two recorded in Acts 18:1; 20:2. **In the mouth of two or three witnesses shall every word be established**—Quoted from Deuteronomy 19:15, LXX. "I will judge not without examination, nor will I abstain from punishing upon due evidence" [CONYBEARE and HOWSON]. I will no longer be among you "in all patience" towards offenders (ch. 12:12). The apostle in this case, where ordinary testimony was to be had, does not look for an immediate revelation, nor does he order the culprits to be cast out of the church before his arrival. Others understand the "two or three witnesses" to mean *his two or three visits* as establishing either (1) the truth of the facts alleged against the offenders, or (2) the reality of his threats. I prefer the first explanation to either of the two latter. **2.** Rather, "I have already said (at my second visit), and tell you (now) beforehand, AS (I did) WHEN I WAS PRESENT THE SECOND TIME, so also now in my absence (the oldest MSS. omit the 'I write,' which here wrongly follows in *English Version Greek* text) to them which heretofore have sinned (viz., before my second visit, ch. 12:21), and to all others" (who have sinned since my second visit, or are in danger of sinning). The *English Version, "as if I were* present the *second* time," viz., this next time, is quite inconsistent with vs. 1, "this is the *third* time I am coming to you," as Paul could not have called the same journey at once "the second" and "the third time" of his coming. The antithesis between "the second time" and "now" is palpable. **if I come again . . .**—i.e., *whensoever I come again* (Acts 20:2). These were probably the very words of his former threat which he now repeats again. **3. Since**—The reason why he will not spare: Since ye challenge me to give a "proof" that Christ speaks in me. It would be better if ye would "*prove* your own selves" (vs. 5). This disproves the assertion of some that Scripture nowhere asserts the infallibility of its writers when writing it. **which**—"who" (Christ.) **is not weak**—in relation to you, by me and in this very Epistle, in exercising upon you strong discipline. **mighty in you**—has given many proofs of His power in miracles, and even in punishing offenders (ch. 5:11, 20, 21). Ye have no need to put me to the proof in this, as long ago Christ has exhibited great proofs of His power by me among you (ch. 12:12) [GROTIUS]. It is therefore not me, but Christ, whom ye wrong: it is His

ADAM CLARKE

perverted from the right way, and be obliged to make use of his apostolical rod, and punish the offenders. But, feeling towards them the heart of a tender father, he was unwilling to use the rod; and sent the First Epistle to them, and the messengers above mentioned, being reluctant to go himself till he had satisfactory evidence that their divisions were ended and that they had repented for and put away the evils that they had committed. *Debates, envyings.* From these different expressions, which are too plain to need interpretation, we see what a distracted and divided state the church at Corinth must have been in. Brotherly love and charity seem to have been driven out of this once heavenly assembly. These *debates,* etc., are precisely the opposites to that love which the apostle recommends and explains by its different properties in the thirteenth chapter of his First Epistle.

21. *Lest, when I come again.* And even after all that has been done for you, I fear that when I do come—when I pay you my second visit, *my God will humble me*—will permit me to be affected with deep sorrow through what I may see among you, as I have been by the buffetings of the apostle of Satan who has perverted you. Humiliation is repeatedly used for "affliction." *Have sinned already.* "Who have sinned before"; who were some of the first offenders, and have not yet repented. *Of the uncleanness.* There must have been a total relaxation of discipline, else such abominations could not have been tolerated in the Christian Church. And although what is here spoken could be the case of only a few, yet the many were ill disciplined, else these must have been cast out.

CHAPTER 13

1. *This is the third time I am coming to you.* These words are nearly the same with those in chap. xii. 14, and probably refer to the purpose which he had twice before formed of seeing them. But the latter clause seems to attach a different meaning to the passage; at least so it has been understood by some learned men.

3. *Since ye seek a proof of Christ.* The conversion of the Corinthians was to themselves a solid proof that Christ spoke by the apostle; and therefore he could, with great propriety, say that this power of Christ, far from being *weak,* was *mighty* among them.

MATTHEW HENRY

Even as Christ himself *was crucified through weakness but liveth by the power of God* (*v.* 4), so the apostles did yet manifest the power of God, and particularly the power of his grace, in converting the world to Christianity.

He puts them upon proving their Christianity (*v.* 5). If Jesus Christ was in them, this was a proof that Christ spoke in him.

If therefore they could prove themselves *not to be reprobates, he trusted they would know that he was not a reprobate* (*v.* 6). We should examine whether we be in the faith; *prove our own selves* whether Christ be in us, or not.

Verses 7–10

I. The apostle's prayer to God on the behalf of the Corinthians, *v.* 7. We are more concerned to pray that we may not do evil than that we may not suffer evil.

II. The reasons why the apostle put up this prayer to God, *v.* 7. The best way to adorn our holy religion is *to do that which is honest*, and of good report.

Further that they might be free from all blame when he should come to them. This is intimated in *v.* 8. If therefore they did not do evil the apostle had no power to punish them (*v.* 9), "Though we are weak through persecutions and contempt, we bear it joyfully, while we see that you are strong and persevering in well-doing."

He desired their perfection (*v.* 9). He not only desired that they might be kept from sin, but also that they might grow in grace. This was the great end of his writing this epistle.

JAMIESON, FAUSSET, BROWN

patience that ye try in despising my admonitions, and derogating from my authority [CALVIN]. **4. though**—omitted in some of the oldest MSS.; then translate, "For He was even crucified . . ." **through weakness**—*Greek*, "from weakness"; i.e., His assumption of our weakness was the source, or necessary condition, *from* which the possibility of His crucifixion flowed (Heb. 2:14; Phil. 2:7, 8). **by**—*Greek*, "from"; "owing to." **the power of God**—the Father (Rom. 1:4; 6:4; Eph. 1:20). **weak in him**—i.e., in virtue of our union with Him, and after His pattern, weakness predominates in us for a time (exhibited in our "infirmities" and weak "bodily presence," ch. 10:10; 12:5, 9, 10; and also in our not putting into immediate exercise our power of punishing offenders, just as Christ for a time kept in abeyance His power). **we shall live with him**—not only hereafter with Him, free from our present infirmities, in the resurrection life (Phil. 3:21), but presently in the exercise of our apostolic authority against offenders, which flows to us *in respect to you* from *the power of God*, however "weak" we now seem to you. "With Him," i.e., even as He now exercises His power in His glorified resurrection life, after His weakness for a time. **5. Examine**—*Greek*, "Try (make trial of) yourselves." **prove your own selves**—This should be your first aim, rather than "seeking a proof of Christ speaking *in me*" (vs. 3). **your own selves**—I need not speak much in proof of Christ being in me, your minister (vs. 3), for if ye try *your own selves* ye will see that Christ is also in you [CHRYSOSTOM], (Rom. 8:10). Finding Christ dwelling in yourselves by faith, ye may well believe that He speaks in me, by whose ministry ye have received this faith [ESTIUS]. To doubt it would be the sin of Israel, who, after so many miracles and experimental proofs of God's presence, still cried (Exod. 17:7), "Is the Lord among us or not?" (Cf. Mark 8:11). **except ye be reprobates**—The *Greek* softens the expression, "*somewhat* reprobates," i.e., not *abiding the "proof"* (alluding to the same word in the context); *failing when tested*. Image from metals (Jer. 6:30; Dan. 5:27; Rom. 1:28). **6. we . . . not reprobates**—not *unable to abide the "proof"* to which ye put us (vs. 6). "I trust that" your own Christianity will be *recognized* by you (observe, "ye shall *know*," answers to "*know* your own selves," vs. 5) as sufficient "proof" that ye are not reprobates, but that "Christ speaks in me," without needing a proof from me more trying to yourselves. If ye doubt my apostleship, ye must doubt your own Christianity, for ye are the fruits of my apostleship. **7. I pray**—The oldest MSS. read, "we pray." **not that we should appear approved**—not to gain credit for ourselves, your ministers, by your Christian conduct; but for your good [ALFORD]. The antithesis to "reprobates" leads me to prefer explaining with BENGEL, "We do *not* pray *that* we may appear *approved*," by restraining you when ye do evil; "but that ye should do what is *right*" (*English Version*, "honest"). **though we be as reprobates**—though we be thereby deprived of the occasion for exercising our apostolic power (viz., in punishing), and so may appear "as reprobates" (*incapable of affording proof* of Christ speaking in us).

8. Our apostolic power is given us that we may use it not against, but for the furtherance of, the truth. Where you are free from fault, there is no scope for its exercise: and this I desire. Far be it from me to use it against the innocent, merely in order to increase my own power (vs. 10).

9. are glad—*Greek*, "rejoice." **when we are weak**—having no occasion for displaying our power; and so seeming "weak," as being compassed with "infirmities" (ch. 10:10; 11:29, 30). **ye . . . strong**—"mighty" in faith and the fruits of the Spirit. **and**—not in the oldest MSS. **we wish**—*Greek*, "pray for." **your perfection**—lit., "perfect restoration"; lit., that of a dislocated limb. Cf. vs. 11, "Be perfect," the same *Greek* word; also in I Corinthians 1:10, "perfectly joined together"; Eph. 4:12, "the perfecting of the saints."

ADAM CLARKE

4. *For though he was crucified through weakness.* It is true Christ was crucified, and His crucifixion appeared to be the effect of His *weakness;* yet even this was not so. He gave up His life; none could take it away from Him. And in His last struggle, had He even been deficient in power, He could have had more than twelve legions of angels to support Him against the high priest's mob, Matt. xxvi. 53; but how then could the Scripture be fulfilled? And had He not died, how could the human race have been saved? *We also are weak in him.* Because we are on Christ's side we appear to you as weak as He did to the Jews; but it is not so, for *we . . . live with him,* under the same influence and partaking of the same life, manifesting by our preaching and miracles the *power of God toward you.* While I do not use the rod, I appear to you weak; I will use it, and then you shall find me to be strong.

5. *Examine yourselves, whether ye be in the faith.* "Try yourselves"; pierce your hearts; try yourselves by what I have written, and see whether you retain the true faith of the gospel. *Prove your own selves.* "Put yourselves to the test," as you would try gold or silver suspected of adulteration. No more take that for gospel which is not so than you would take adulterated money for sterling coin. This is a metaphor taken from testing or assaying adulterated metals. *Know ye not your own selves?* Are you not full of wisdom and understanding? And is it not as easy to find out a spurious faith as it is to detect a base coin? There is an assay and touchstone for both. Does Jesus Christ dwell in you? You have His Spirit, His power, His mind, if you are Christians; and the Spirit of Christ bears witness with your spirit that you are the children of God. And this is the case *except ye be reprobates;* "base counterfeit coin"; mongrel Christians.

6. *Ye shall know that we are not reprobates.* You have had, and you shall have, the fullest proof that I have preached the true faith among you, and that God has confirmed it by His testimony; and thus that I am proved and manifested to be what I ought to be, and shown to be approved of God.

7. *I pray to God that ye do no evil.* That you do not persist in that course which will oblige me to use the power of Christ, with which I am endued, to punish you. *Not that we should appear approved.* We do not wish to give this proof that we are approved of God, by inflicting this punishment on the transgressors. *But that ye should do that which is honest.* That you may do that which is "right" and "seemly," *though we* should *be,* in consequence of that, *as reprobates*—as persons "not approved" of God; because your reformation will prevent the exercise of this power which would otherwise have given an awful proof that we are approved of God.

8. *For we can do nothing against the truth, but for the truth.* As we are the apostles of God, we cannot bring to you any false doctrine; and as we profess to be under the influence of God's Spirit, we cannot do anything that is opposed to that truth, or which might be prejudicial to it. On the contrary, what we say and do is *for* that *truth,* to propagate and establish it.

9. *For we are glad, when we are weak.* It will give me indescribable pleasure that I should still appear to be poor, despicable, and destitute of this extraordinary power with which God has clothed me, so that you be strong in all the gifts and graces of the Holy Spirit. *And this also we wish, even your perfection.* We cannot be satisfied that persons with such eminent endowments and who have once received the truth as it is in Jesus should be deficient in any of the graces that constitute the mind of Christ, such as brotherly love, charity, harmony, unity, and order. I have given the above paraphrase to this verse because of the last term, *perfection.* It signifies the reducing of a dislocated limb to its proper place; and hence, as Beza says on this passage: "The apostle's meaning is, that whereas the members of the church were all, as it were, dislocated and out of joint, they should be joined together in love; and they should endeavor to make perfect what was amiss among them, either in faith or morals."

MATTHEW HENRY

ALBERT BARNES:

Even "your perfection." The word here used occurs nowhere else in the New Testament, though the verb from which it is derived occurs often (Matt. 4:21; 21:16; Mark 1:19; Luke 6:40; Rom. 9:22; 1 Cor. 1:10; 2 Cor. 13:11; Gal. 6:1; 1 Thess. 3:10). On the meaning of the word, see Rom. 9:22. The idea of restoring, putting in order, fitting, repairing, is involved in the word always, and hence the idea of making perfect; i.e. of *completely restoring* anything to its proper place. Here it evidently means that Paul wished their *entire* reformation—so that there should be no occasion for exercising discipline. Doddridge renders it "perfect good order"; Macknight, "restoration." For this restoration of good order Paul has diligently labored in these epistles; and this was an object near to his heart.—*Popular Commentary*

Verses 11–14

I. A valediction.

1. He gives them several good exhortations. To be perfect, or to be knit together in love. To be of good comfort. To be of one mind, for the more easy we are with our brethren the more ease we shall have in our own souls. He exhorts them to live in peace, that difference in opinion should not cause an alienation of affections.

2. He encourages them with the promise of God's presence among them, *v.* 11. God is the God of love and peace. God will be with those who live in love and peace. He will love those who love peace.

3. He gives directions to them to salute each other, and sends kind salutations to them from those who were with him, *v.* 12, 13.

II. The apostolical benediction (*v.* 14). Thus the apostle concludes his epistle. This is a very solemn benediction, and we should give all diligence to inherit this blessing.

JAMIESON, FAUSSET, BROWN

10. Therefore—because I wish the "sharpness" to be in my *letters* rather than in *deeds* [CHRYSOSTOM]. **edification . . . not to destruction**—*for building up . . . not for casting down.* To "use sharpness" would seem to be *casting down,* rather than *building up;* therefore he prefers not to have to use it.

11. farewell—meaning in *Greek* also "rejoice"; thus in bidding farewell he returns to the point with which he set out, "we are helpers of your *joy*" (ch. 1:24; Phil. 4:4). **Be perfect**—Become perfect by filling up what is lacking in your Christian character (Eph. 4:13). **be of good comfort**—(ch. 1:6; 7:8-13; I Thess. 4:18).

The benediction which proves the doctrine of the Divine Trinity in unity. "The grace of Christ" comes first, for it is only by it we come to "the love of God" the Father (John 14:6). The variety in the order of Persons proves that "in this Trinity none is afore or after other" [ATHANAS, *Creed*].

communion—joint fellowship, or participation, in the same Holy Ghost, which joins in one catholic Church, His temple, both Jews and Gentiles. Whoever has "the fellowship of the Holy Ghost," has also "the grace of our Lord Jesus Christ," and "the love of God"; and vice versa. For the three are inseparable, as the three Persons of the Trinity itself [CHRYSOSTOM]. The doctrine of the Trinity was not revealed clearly and fully till Christ came, and the whole scheme of our redemption was manifested in Him, and we know the Holy Three in One more *in their relations to us* (as set forth summarily in this benediction), than in their *mutual relations to one another* (Deut. 29:29). **Amen**—omitted in the oldest MSS. Probably added subsequently for the exigencies of public joint worship.

ADAM CLARKE

It is a metaphor, also, taken from a building; the several stones and timbers being all put in their proper places and situations, so that the whole building might be "complete," and be a proper habitation for the owner. The same figure, though not in the same terms, the apostle uses, Eph. ii. 20-22. The *perfection* or "rejointing" which the apostle wishes is that which refers to the state of the church in its fellowship, unity, order, etc. And *perfection* in the soul is the same, in reference to it, as perfection in the church is to its order and unity. The perfection or rejointing of the soul implies its purification, and placing every faculty, passion, and appetite in its proper place; so that the original order, harmony, unity, and purity of the soul may be restored; and the whole builded up to be a habitation of God through the Spirit, Eph. ii. 22.

10. *Therefore I write these things.* I only threaten you now, by this Epistle, to put you on your guard, and lead you to reformation before I visit you; that I may not then have to use *sharpness,* "a cutting off," employing thus my apostolical authority to inflict punishment—a *power* which God has given me rather to be employed in your *edification* than in your *destruction.*

11. *Finally.* All that "remains" for me now to write is to wish you all manner of happiness, and so to take my leave. *Farewell.* A good wish; go on prosperously! *Be perfect.* "Be compact"; get into joint again; let unity and harmony be restored. *Be of good comfort.* "Receive admonition," that you may receive *comfort.* If you take my advice, you shall have consolation; if you do not, you will have nothing but misery and woe. *Be of one mind.* "Think the same"; let there be not dissensions among you. *Live in peace.* "Cultivate peace"; or, as he says elsewhere, "Follow peace," and pursue it, Heb. xii. 14. Cultivate a peaceable disposition, and neither say nor do anything which has a tendency to irritate each other. *And the God of love and peace shall be with you.* While you are full of contentions, dissensions, and discord, *peace* can have no place among you; and as to *love,* the fulfilling of the law, that worketh no ill to its neighbor, it has necessarily taken its flight. *Love* cannot live, neither exist, where there are brawls, contentions, and divisions. And where neither *peace* nor *love* is to be found, there God cannot be.

12. *Greet one another with an holy kiss.* Use every means by which a good understanding may be brought about. Let the spirit of friendship live among you, and encourage its continuance by every friendly act. See the note on Rom. xvi. 16.

13. *All the saints.* The Christians of Macedonia or Philippi, from which he wrote this Epistle. In the primitive Church a saint and a Christian were the same thing, for the Christian religion calls every man to be holy.

14. *The grace of the Lord Jesus Christ.* All the "favor" and "beneficence" that come from and through the Redeemer of the world; as the *Lord,* the Ruler and Governor of all things; as *Jesus,* the "Saviour" of all men by His passion and death; as *Christ,* the Distributer of all the divine unction which enlightens, comforts, harmonizes, and purifies the mind. May this most exalted, glorious, and all-sufficient Saviour be ever with you! *And the love of God.* God, your Maker, in that infinite love which induced Him to create the world, and form man in His own image and in His own likeness, that he might be capable of knowing, loving, and enjoying Him forever; and God in the fullest manifestations of that love which caused Him to give His only begotten Son, to the end that they who believe on Him should not perish but have everlasting life. May this God of love, and this *love of God,* be ever with you! *And the communion of the Holy Ghost.* May that Holy Spirit, that divine and eternal Energy which proceeds from the Father and the Son; that heavenly Fire that gives light and life, that purifies and refines, sublimes and exalts, comforts and invigorates, make you all "partakers" with himself! *Koinonia,* which we translate "fellowship" and *communion,* signifies properly "participation," having things in common, partaking with each other.

THE EPISTLE TO THE GALATIANS

I. Introduction (1:1-10)
A. Personal introduction (1:1-5)
1. Direct (1:1a, 2)
2. Parenthetical (1:1b)
3. Salutation (1:3-5)
B. The occasion of the epistle (1:6-10)
1. Another gospel (1:6, 7)
2. The anathema (1:8, 9)
3. The apostolic passion (1:10)

II. An apology—defense of the Gospel (1:11-2:21)
A. The authority of Paul's gospel (1:11-24)
1. Received directly (1:11, 12)
2. Obeyed without consultation (1:13-17)
3. Rejoiced in by the Church of Judea (1:18-24)
B. Authority confirmed by conference (2:1-10)
1. The reason of the going to Jerusalem (2:1-5)
2. The happenings at Jerusalem (2:6-10)
C. Authority maintained in conflict with Peter (2:11-21)
1. The dissimulation of Cephas (2:11-13)
2. The resistance of Paul (2:14-21)

III. An argument—declaration of the Gospel (3:1-5:1)
A. Justification is by faith (3:1-14)
1. An appeal to Galatian experience (3:1-5)
2. Faith the reason of Abraham's blessing (3:6-9)
3. Law cannot justify (3:10-12)
4. The cross of Christ the basis of faith (3:13, 14)
B. The relation of the law (3:15-29)
1. The promise (3:15-18)
2. The law (3:19-24)
3. The faith (3:25-29)
C. Illustrative enforcements of the truth (4:1-31)
1. Childhood and sonship (4:1-10)
2. A personal appeal (4:11-20)
3. Ishmael and Isaac (4:21-5:1)

IV. An appeal—demands of the Gospel (5:1-6:10)
A. Freedom must be maintained (5:1-12)
1. The law of liberty (5:1)
2. The alternatives (5:2-6)
3. The appeal (5:7-12)
B. Freedom is to realization (5:13-26)
1. Not fleshly license (5:13-15)
2. Life in the Spirit is victory over the flesh (5:16-26)
C. Freedom is mutual (6:1-10)
1. One another's burdens (6:1, 2)
2. His own burden (6:3-5)
3. Liberality (6:6-10)

V. Conclusion (6:11-18)
A. The conclusion in "large letters" (6:11)
B. A summary contrasting teachers (6:12-16)
1. "They" (6:12, 13)
2. "We" (6:14-16)
C. The Apostle's credential (6:17)
D. The benediction (6:18)

While he was with them, they had expressed the greatest esteem and affection both for his person and ministry. Some judaizing teachers got in among them. That which these false teachers chiefly aimed at was to draw them off from the truth as it is in Jesus, particularly in the great doctrine of justification, asserting the necessity of joining the observance of the law of Moses with faith in Christ in order to it. They did all they could to lessen the character and reputation of the apostle, representing him as one who, if he was to be owned as an apostle, yet was much inferior to others, and particularly who deserved not such a regard as Peter, James, and John. In both these attempts they had but too great success. This was the occasion of his writing this epistle, wherein he expresses his great concern that they had suffered themselves to be so soon turned aside, vindicates his own character and authority as an apostle, and shows he was not "behind the very chief of the apostles." He then sets himself to assert and maintain the great gospel doctrine of justification by faith without the works of the law, and he exhorts them to stand fast in the liberty wherewith Christ had made them free, gives them several very needful counsels and directions and then concludes the epistle.

MATTHEW HENRY

CHAPTER 1

Verses 1-5

I. The person or persons from whom this epistle is sent—from Paul *an apostle, &c., and all the brethren that were with him.* 1. He gives a general account both of his office and of the manner in which he was called to it. As to his office, he was an apostle. He acquaints them how he was called to this office, and assures them that his commission to it was wholly divine.

He was an apostle *by Jesus Christ*, he had his commission immediately from him, and consequently from *God the Father*. Furthermore his call to the apostleship was after Christ's resurrection from the dead. He had his call from him when in heaven.

JAMIESON, FAUSSET, BROWN

CHAPTER 1

VSS. 1-24. SUPERSCRIPTION. GREETINGS. THE CAUSE OF HIS WRITING IS THEIR SPEEDY FALLING AWAY FROM THE GOSPEL HE TAUGHT. DEFENSE OF HIS TEACHING: HIS APOSTOLIC CALL INDEPENDENT OF MAN.

1. apostle—in the earliest Epistles, the two to the Thessalonians, through humility, he uses no title of authority; but associates with him "Silvanus and Timotheus"; yet here, though "brethren" (vs. 2) are with him, he does not *name* them but puts his own name and apostleship prominent; evidently because his apostolic commission needs now to be vindicated against deniers of it. **of**—*Greek,* "from." Expressing the *origin* from which his mission came, "not from *men,*" but from Christ and the Father (understood) as the source. "By" expresses the immediate operating agent in the call. Not only was the call *from* God as its ultimate source, but *by* Christ and the Father as the immediate agent in calling him (Acts 22:15, and 26:16-18). The laying on of Ananias' hands (Acts 9:17) is no objection to this; for that was but a sign of the fact, not an assisting cause. So the Holy Ghost calls him specially (Acts 13:2, 3); he was an apostle *before* this special mission. **man**—singular; to mark the contrast to "Jesus Christ." The opposition between "Christ" and "man," and His name being put in closest connection with God the Father, imply His Godhead. **raised him from the dead**—implying that, though he had not seen Him in His humiliation as the other apostles (which was made an objection against him), he had seen and been *constituted an*

ADAM CLARKE

CHAPTER 1

1. *Paul, an apostle, (not of men).* Not commissioned by any assembly or council of the apostles.

***Neither by man.* Nor by any one of the apostles; neither by James, who seems to have been president of the apostolic council at Jerusalem; nor by Peter, to whom, in a particular manner, the keys of the Kingdom were entrusted. *But by Jesus Christ.* Having his mission immediately from Christ himself, and *God the Father, who raised him from the dead,* see Acts xxii. 14-15, and commanded him to go both to the Jews and to the Gentiles.**

MATTHEW HENRY

2. He joins all the brethren that were with him in the inscription of the epistle. Hereby it would appear that he had their concurrence with him in the doctrine which he had preached, and was now about to confirm.

II. To whom this epistle is sent. It should seem that all of them were more or less corrupted through the arts of those seducers who had crept in among them.

III. The apostolical benediction, *v.* 3. Grace includes God's goodwill towards us and his good work upon us; and peace implies in it all that inward comfort or outward prosperity which is really needful for us. Both these the apostle wishes for these Christians. First grace, and then peace, for there can be no true peace without grace. Having mentioned the Lord Jesus Christ, he cannot pass without enlarging upon his love (*v.* 4). This present world is an evil world: it has become so by the sin of man. Jesus Christ has died to deliver us from this present evil world, not to remove his people out of it, but to rescue them from the power of it.

This, the apostle informs us, he has done *according to the will of God and our Father.* Hence we have encouragement to look upon God as our Father. As he is the Father of our Lord Jesus, so in and through him he is also the Father of all true believers.

The apostle concludes this preface with a solemn ascription of praise and glory to him (*v.* 5).

That they were *so soon removed.* In a very little time they lost that esteem of this grace of Christ which they seemed to have. This, as it was an instance of their weakness, so it was a further aggravation of their guilt.

JAMIESON, FAUSSET, BROWN

apostle by Him in His resurrection power (Matt. 28:18; Rom. 1:4, 5). Cf. as to the ascension, the consequence of the resurrection, and the cause of His giving "apostles," Ephesians 4:11. He rose again, too, for our *justification* (Rom. 4:25); thus Paul prepares the way for the prominent subject of the Epistle, justification in Christ, not by the law. **2. all the brethren**—I am not alone in my doctrine; all my colleagues in the Gospel work, travelling with me (Acts 19:29, Gaius and Aristarchus at Ephesus; Acts 20:4, Sopater, Secundus, Timotheus, Tychicus, Trophimus, some, or all of these), join with me. Not that these were *joint authors* with Paul of the Epistle; but joined him in the *sentiments* and *salutations.* The phrase, "all the brethren," accords with a date when he had many travelling companions, he and they having to bear jointly the collection to Jerusalem [CONYBEARE and HOWSON]. **the churches**—Pessinus and Ancyra were the principal cities; but doubtless there were many other churches in Galatia (Acts 18:23; I Cor. 16:1). He does not attach any honorable title to the churches here, as elsewhere, being displeased at their Judaizing. See I Corinthians; I Thessalonians, etc. The first Epistle of Peter is addressed to Jewish Christians sojourning in Galatia (I Pet. 1:1), among other places mentioned. It is interesting thus to find the apostle of the circumcision, as well as the apostle of the uncircumcision, once at issue (ch. 2:7-15), co-operating to build up the same churches. **3. from . . . from**—Omit the second "from." The *Greek* joins God the Father and our Lord Jesus Christ in closet union, by there being but the one preposition. **4. gave himself**—(ch. 2:20)—unto death, as an offering. Found only in this and the Pastoral Epistles. The *Greek* is different in Ephesians 5:25 (*Note*). **for our sins**—which enslaved us to the present evil world. **deliver us from this**—*Greek,* "out of the . . ." The Father and Son are each said to "deliver us. . . ." (Col. 1:13): but the Son, not the Father, "*gave Himself for*" *us* in order to do so, and make us citizens of a better world (Phil. 3:20). The Galatians in desiring to return to legal bondage are, he implies, renouncing the *deliverance* which Christ wrought for us. This he more fully repeats in ch. 3:13. "Deliver" is the very word used by the Lord as to His deliverance of Paul himself (Acts 26:17): an undesigned coincidence between Paul and Luke. **world**—*Greek,* "age"; *system* or *course* of the world, regarded from a religious point of view. The present *age* opposes the "glory" (vs. 5) of God, and is under the authority of the Evil One. The "ages of ages" (*Greek,* vs. 5) are opposed to "the present evil age." **according to the will of God and our Father**—*Greek,* "of Him who is at once God [the sovereign Creator] and our Father" (John 6:38, 39; 10:18, end). Without merit of ours. His sovereignty as "GOD," and our filial relation to Him as "OUR FATHER," ought to keep us from blending our own legal notions (as the Galatians were doing) with His will and plan. This paves the way for his argument. **5. be glory**—rather, as Greek, "be *the* glory"; the glory which is peculiarly and exclusively His. Cf. Ephesians 3:21, *Note.* **6.** Without the usual expressions of thanksgiving for their faith, etc., he vehemently plunges into his subject, zealous for "the glory" of God (vs. 5), which was being disparaged by the Galatians falling away from the pure Gospel of the "grace" of God. **I marvel**—implying that he had hoped better things from them, whence his sorrowful surprise at their turning out so different from his expectations. **so soon**—after my last visit; when I hoped and thought you were untainted by the Judaizing teachers. If this Epistle was written from Corinth, the interval would be a little more than three years, which would be "soon" to have fallen away, if they were apparently sound at the time of his visit. Ch. 4:18, 20 may imply that he saw no symptom of unsoundness *then,* such as he hears of in them *now.* **removed**—Translate, "are being removed," i.e., ye are *suffering yourselves so soon* (whether from the time of my last visit, or from the time of the first temptation held out to you) [PARÆUS] *to be removed* by Jewish seducers. Thus he softens the censure by implying that the Galatians were tempted by seducers from without, with whom the chief guilt lay: and the present, "ye are *being* removed," implies that their seduction was only in process of being effected, not that it was actually effected. WAHL, ALFORD, and others take the *Greek* as middle voice. "ye are removing" or "passing over." "Shifting your ground" [CONYBEARE and HOWSON]. But thus the point of Paul's oblique reference to their misleaders is lost; and in Hebrews 7:12 the *Greek* is used passively, justifying its being taken so here. On the impulsiveness and fickleness of the Gauls

ADAM CLARKE

2. *And all the brethren which are with me.* It is very likely that this refers to those who were his assistants in preaching the gospel, and not to any private members of the church.

Churches of Galatia. Galatia was a region or province of Asia Minor; there was neither city nor town of this name. But as in this province Paul had planted several churches, he directs the Epistle to the whole of them; for it seems they were all pretty nearly in the same state and needed the same instructions.

4. *Who gave himself for our sins.* Who became a Sin Offering to God in behalf of mankind, that they might be saved from their sins.

5. *To whom be glory for ever.* Let Him have the glory to whom alone it is due, for having delivered us from the present evil world, and from all bondage to Mosaic rites and ceremonies.

6. *I marvel that ye are so soon removed.* It was a matter of wonder to the apostle that a people so soundly converted to God should have so soon made shipwreck of their faith.

MATTHEW HENRY

Verses 6–9

I. How much he was concerned at their defection. There were several things by which their defection was greatly aggravated: 1. That they were *removed from him that had called them;* not only from the apostle, but from God himself. They had been guilty of a great abuse of his kindness and mercy towards them. 2. They had been called to partake of the greatest blessings and benefits. In proportion to the greatness of the privilege they enjoyed, such were their sin and folly in deserting it.

That they were removed to *another gospel, which yet was not another.* You will find it to be no gospel at all, but the perverting of the gospel of Christ. Those who go about to establish any other way to heaven than what the gospel of Christ has revealed will find themselves wretchedly mistaken.

II. The gospel he had preached to them was the only true gospel. He pronounced an anathema upon those who pretended to preach any other gospel (*v.* 8). "If you have any other gospel preached to you under our name, or under colour of having it from an angel himself, you must conclude that you are imposed upon: and whoever preaches another gospel lays himself under a curse."

Verses 10–24

What Paul had said in the preface of this epistle he now proceeds to enlarge upon. There he had declared himself to be an apostle of Christ; and here he comes more directly to support his claim to that character and office.

I. From the scope and design of his ministry. As he professed to act by a commission from God, so that which he chiefly aimed at was to promote his glory, by recovering sinners into a state of subjection to him. He did not accommodate himself to the humours of persons, but his great care was to approve himself to God. No man could serve two such masters, and therefore he dare not allow himself to gratify men at the expense of his faithfulness to Christ. Thus, he proves that he was truly an apostle of Christ. The great end which ministers of the gospel should aim at is to bring men to God. They must not be solicitous to please men, if they would approve themselves faithful servants to Christ.

JAMIESON, FAUSSET, BROWN

(another form of Kel-t-s, the progenitors of the Erse, Gauls, Cymri, and Belgians), whence the Galatians sprang, see *Introduction* and CÆSAR, B. G. 3. 19. **from him that called you**—God the Father (vs. 15; ch. 5:8; Rom. 8:30; I Cor. 1:9; I Thess. 2:12; 5:24). **into**—rather, as *Greek,* "IN the grace of Christ," as the *element in* which, and the *instrument by* which, God calls us to salvation. Cf. *Note,* I Corinthians 7:15; Romans 5:15, "the gift by (*Greek,* 'in') grace (*Greek, 'the grace'*) of (the) one man." "The grace of Christ," is Christ's gratuitously purchased and bestowed justification, reconciliation, and eternal life. **another**—rather, as *Greek,* "a second and *different* gospel," i.e., into a *so-called* gospel, different altogether from the only true Gospel. **7. another**—A distinct *Greek* word from that in vs. 6. Though I called it a gospel (vs. 6), it is not really so. There is really but *one* Gospel, and no *other* gospel, **but**—Translate, "Only that there are some that trouble you . . ." (ch. 5:10, 12). All I meant by the "different gospel" was nothing but a perversion by "some" of the one Gospel of Christ. **would pervert**—*Greek,* "wish to pervert"; they could not really pervert the Gospel, though they could pervert Gospel professors (cf. ch. 4:9, 17, 21; 6:12, 13; Col. 2:18). Though acknowledging Christ, they insisted on circumcision and Jewish ordinances and professed to rest on the authority of other apostles, viz., Peter and James. But Paul recognizes no gospel, save the pure Gospel. **8. But**—however weighty they may seem "who trouble you." Translate as *Greek,* "Even though we," viz., I and the brethren with me, weighty and many as we are (vss. 1, 2). The *Greek* implies a case supposed which never has occurred. **angel**—in which light ye at first received me (cf. ch. 4:14; I Cor. 13:1), and whose authority is the highest possible next to that of God and Christ. A new revelation, even though seemingly accredited by miracles, is not to be received if it contradict the already existing revelation. For God cannot contradict Himself (Deut. 13:1-3; I Kings 13:18; Matt. 24:24; II Thess. 2:9). The Judaizing teachers sheltered themselves under the names of the great apostles, James, John, and Peter: "Do not bring these names up to me, for even if an *angel*. . . ." Not that he means, the apostles really supported the Judaizers; but he wishes to show, when the truth is in question, respect of persons is inadmissible [CHRYSOSTOM]. **preach**—i.e., "should preach." **any other gospel . . . than**—The *Greek* expresses not so much "any other gospel *different* from what we have preached," as, "any gospel BESIDE that which we preached." This distinctly opposes the traditions of the Church of Rome, which are at once *besides* and *against* (the *Greek* includes both ideas) the written Word, our only *attested rule.* **9. said before**—when we were visiting you (so "before" means, II Cor. 13:2). Cf. ch. 5:2, 3, 21. Translate, "If any man *preacheth* unto you any gospel BESIDE that which. . . ." Observe the indicative, not the subjunctive or conditional mood, is used, "preacheth," lit., "furnisheth you with any gospel." The *fact* is assumed, not merely supposed as a contingency, as in vs. 8, "preach," or "should preach." This implies that he had already observed (viz., during his last visit) the machinations of the Judaizing teachers: but his *surprise* (vs. 6) *now* at the Galatians being misled by them, implies that they had not apparently been so *then.* As in vs. 8 he had said, "which we preached," so here, with an augmentation of the force, "which ye received"; acknowledging that they had truly *accepted it.* **accursed**—The opposite appears in ch. 6:16. **10. For**—accounting for the strong language he has just used. **do I *now***—resuming the "now" of vs. 9. "Am I *now* persuading men?" [ALFORD], i.e., conciliating. Is what I have *just now* said a sample of men-pleasing, of which I am accused? His adversaries accused him of being an interested flatterer of men, "becoming all things to all men," to make a party for himself, and so observing the law among the Jews (for instance, circumcising Timothy), yet persuading the Gentiles to renounce it (ch. 5:11) (in order to flatter those, really keeping them in a subordinate state, not admitted to the full privileges which the circumcised alone enjoyed). NEANDER explains the "now" thus: Once, when a Pharisee, I was actuated only by a regard to human authority and to please men (Luke 16:15; John 5:44), but NOW I teach as responsible to God alone (I Cor. 4:3). **or God?**—Regard is to be had to God alone. **for if I yet pleased men**—The oldest MSS. omit "for." "If I were still pleasing men . . ." (Luke 6:26; John 15:19; I Thess. 2:4; Jas. 4:4; I John 4:5). On "yet," cf. ch. 5:11. **servant of Christ**—and so pleasing Him in all things (Titus 2:9; Col. 3:22). **11. certify**—I made known to you as to the Gospel which was

ADAM CLARKE

From him that called you. The apostle seems here to mean himself. He called them *into the grace of Christ;* and they not only abandoned that grace, but their hearts became greatly estranged from him; so that, though at first they would have plucked out their eyes for him, they at last counted him their enemy, chap. iv. 14-16.

7. *Which is not another.* It is not gospel, i.e., "good tidings," for it loads you again with the burdens from which the genuine gospel had disencumbered you. Instead of giving you peace, it troubles you; instead of being a useful supplement to the gospel of Christ, it perverts that gospel. You have gained nothing but loss and damage by the change.

8. *But though we, or an angel.* That gospel which I have already preached to you is the only true gospel; were I to preach *any other,* I should incur the curse of God. If your false teachers pretend, as many in early times did, that they received their accounts by the ministry of an angel, let them be accursed; separate them from your company, and have no religious communion with them.

9. *Let him be accursed.* Perhaps this is not designed as an imprecation, but a simple direction; for the word here may be understood as implying that such a person should have no countenance in his bad work, but let him, as Theodoret expresses it, "be separated from the communion of the church." This, however, would also imply that unless the person repented the divine judgments would soon follow.

10. *Do I now persuade men, or God?* The words may be rendered to "court or solicit the favor of God," as the after clause sufficiently proves. While the apostle was a persecutor of the Christians, he was the servant of men and *pleased men.* When he embraced the Christian doctrine, he became the *servant* of God, and pleased Him.

11. *But I certify you, brethren.* I wish you fully to comprehend that the gospel which I

MATTHEW HENRY

II. From the manner wherein he received the gospel which he preached to them (*v.* 11, 12). One thing peculiar in the character of an apostle was that he had been called to, and instructed for, this office immediately by Christ himself. He had his knowledge of the gospel, as well as his authority to preach it, directly from the Lord Jesus.

1. He tells them what his conversation in time past had been, *v.* 13, 14. It must be something very extraordinary which had made so great a change in him, and brought him not only to profess, but to preach, that doctrine, which he had before so vehemently opposed.

2. In how wonderful a manner he was brought to the knowledge and faith of Christ, and appointed to the office of an apostle, *v.* 15, 16. There was something peculiar in the case of Paul, both in the suddenness and in the greatness of the change wrought in him, and also in the manner wherein it was effected. He had Christ *revealed in him.* It will but little avail us to have Christ revealed to us if he is not also revealed in us. It pleased God *to reveal his Son in him* that he should preach him among the heathen. So that he was both a Christian and an apostle by revelation.

3. How he behaved himself hereupon, from *v.* 16. *He conferred not with flesh and blood.* So that it could not well be pretended that he was indebted to any other either for his knowledge of the gospel or his authority to preach it.

JAMIESON, FAUSSET, BROWN

preached by me, that it is not after man, i.e., not *of by*, or *from* man (vss. 1, 12). It is *not according* to man; not influenced by mere human considerations, as it would be, if it were of human origin. **brethren**—He not till now calls them so. **12.** Translate, "For *not even* did I *myself* (any more than the other apostles) receive it from man, *nor* was I taught it (by man)." "Received it," implies the absence of labor in acquiring it. "Taught it," implies the labor of learning. **by the revelation of Jesus Christ**—Translate, "by revelation of [i.e., from] Jesus Christ." By His revealing it to me. Probably this took place during the three years, in part of which he sojourned in Arabia (vss. 17, 18), in the vicinity of the scene of the giving of the law; a fit place for such a revelation of the Gospel of grace, which supersedes the ceremonial law (ch. 4:25). He, like other Pharisees who embraced Christianity, did not at first recognize its independence of the Mosaic law, but combined both together. Ananias, his first instructor, was universally esteemed for his legal piety and so was not likely to have taught him to sever Christianity from the law. This severance was partially recognized after the martyrdom of Stephen. But Paul received it by special revelation (I Cor. 11: 23; 15:3; I Thess. 4:15). A vision of the Lord Jesus is mentioned (Acts 22:18), at his first visit to Jerusalem (vs. 18); but this seems to have been subsequent to the revelation here meant (cf. vss. 15-18), and to have been confined to giving a particular command. The vision "fourteen years before" (II Cor. 12:1) was in A.D. 43, still later, six years after his conversion. Thus Paul is an independent witness to the Gospel. Though he had recived no instruction from the apostles, but from the Holy Ghost, yet when he met them his Gospel exactly agreed with theirs. **13. heard**—even before I came among you. **conversation**—"my former way of life." **Jews' religion**—The term, "Hebrew," expresses the *language;* "Jew," the *nationality*, as distinguished from the Gentiles; "Israelite," the highest title, the religious privileges, as a member of the theocracy. **the church**—Here singular, marking its unity, though constituted of many particular churches, under the one Head, Christ. **of God**—added to mark the greatness of his sinful alienation from God (I Cor. 15:19). **wasted**—laid it waste: the opposite of "building it up." **14. profited**—*Greek,* "I was becoming a proficient"; "I made progress." **above**—beyond. **my equals**—*Greek,* "Of mine own age, among my countrymen." **traditions of my fathers**—viz., those of the Pharisees, Paul being "a Pharisee, and son of a Pharisee" (Acts 23:6; 26:5). "MY fathers," shows that it is not to be understood generally of the traditions *of the nation.* **15. separated**—"set me apart": in the purposes of His electing love (cf. Acts 9:15; 22:14), in order to show in me *His "pleasure,"* which is the farthest point that any can reach in inquiring the causes of his salvation. The actual "separating" or "setting apart" to the work marked out for him, is mentioned in Acts 13:2; Romans 1:1. There is an allusion, perhaps, in the way of contrast, to the derivation of Pharisee from *Hebrew, pharash,* "separated." I was once a socalled Pharisee or *Separatist,* but God had *separated* me to something far better. **from . . . womb**—Thus merit in me was out of the question, in assigning causes for His call (Rom. 9:11). Grace is the sole cause (Ps. 22:9; 71: 6; Isa. 49:1, 5; Jer. 1:5; Luke 1:15). **called me**—on the way to Damascus (Acts 9). **16. reveal his Son in me**—within me, in my inmost soul, by the Holy Spirit (ch. 2:20). Cf. II Corinthians 4:6, "shined in our hearts." The revealing of His Son by me to the Gentiles (so translate for "heathen") was impossible, unless He had first revealed His Son *in me;* at first on my conversion, but especially at the subsequent revelation from Jesus Christ (vs. 12), whereby I learned the Gospel's independence of the Mosaic law. **that I might preach**—the present in the *Greek,* which includes the idea "that I *may* preach Him," implying an office still *continuing.* This was the main commission entrusted to him (ch. 2:7, 9). **immediately**—connected chiefly with "I went into Arabia" (vs. 17). It denotes the sudden fitness of the apostle. So Acts 9:20, "*Straightway* he preached Christ in the synagogue." **I conferred not**—*Greek,* "I had not further (viz., in addition to revelation) recourse to . . . for the purpose of consulting." The divine revelation was sufficient for me [BENGEL]. **flesh and blood**—(Matt. 16:17). **17. went I up**—Some of the oldest MSS. read, "went away." **to Jerusalem**—the seat of the apostles. **into Arabia**—This journey (not recorded in Acts) was during the whole period of his stay at Damascus, called by Luke (Acts 9:23), "many [*Greek,* a

ADAM CLARKE

preached to you is not after man; there is not a spark of human invention in it, nor the slightest touch of human cunning.

12. *I neither received it of man.* By means of any apostle, as was remarked on v. 1. No man taught me what I have preached to you. *But by the revelation of Jesus Christ.* Being commissioned by himself alone, receiving the knowledge of it from Christ crucified.

13. *Ye have heard of my conversation.* "My manner of life," the mode in which I conducted myself. *Beyond measure I persecuted the church.* For proofs of this the reader is referred to Acts ix. 1-2; xxii. 4. The apostle tells them that they had heard this, because, being Jews, they were acquainted with what had taken place in Judea relative to these important transactions.

14. *And profited in the Jews' religion.* The apostle does not mean that he became more exemplary in the love and practice of the pure law of God than any of his countrymen, but that he was more profoundly skilled in the *traditions* of the *fathers* than most of his contemporaries.

15. *Who separated me from my mother's womb.* Him whom I acknowledge as the God of grace; who preserved me by His providence when I was a helpless infant, and saved me by His grace when I was an adult persecutor.

16. *To reveal his Son in me.* To make me know Jesus Christ, and the power of His resurrection.

That I might preach him among the heathen. For it was to the Gentiles, and the dispersed Jews among the Gentiles, that Paul was especially sent. Peter was sent more particularly to the Jews in the land of Judea; Paul, to those in the different Greek provinces. *I conferred not with flesh and blood.* I did not take counsel with men; "flesh and blood" is a periphrasis for "man," any man.

17. *Neither went I up to Jerusalem.* The aim of the apostle is to show that he had his call so immediately and pointedly from God himself that he had no need of the concurrence even of the apostles, being appointed by the same

MATTHEW HENRY

ALBERT BARNES:

"And abode with him fifteen days." Why he departed then is unknown. Beza supposes that it was on account of the plots of the Grecians against him and their intention to destroy him (Acts 9:29); but this is not assigned by Paul himself as a reason. It is probable that the purpose of his visit to Peter would be accomplished in that time, and he would not spend more time than was necessary with him. It is clear that in the short space of two weeks he could not have been very extensively taught by Peter the nature of the Christian religion, and probably the time is mentioned here to show that he had not been under the teaching of the apostles.

19. "Save James the Lord's brother." That the James here referred to was an apostle is clear. The whole construction of the sentence demands this supposition. In the list of the apostles in Matt. 10:2, 3, two of this name are mentioned, James the son of Zebedee and brother of John, and James the son of Alpheus. From the Acts of the Apostles, it is clear that there were two of this name in Jerusalem. Of these, James the brother of John was slain by Herod (Acts 12:2), and the other continued to reside in Jerusalem (Acts 15:13; 21:13). This latter James was called James the Less (Mark 15:40) to distinguish him from the other James, probably because he was the younger. It is probable that this was the James referred to here, as it is evident from the Acts of the Apostles that he was a prominent man among the apostles in Jerusalem. Commentators have not been agreed as to what is meant by his being the brother of the Lord Jesus. Doddridge understands it as meaning that he was "the near kinsman" to Jesus, for he was, says he, the son of Alpheus and Mary, the sister of the virgin; and if there were but two of this name, this opinion is undoubtedly correct. In the Apostolical Constitution, three of this name are mentioned as apostles or eminent men in Jerusalem; and hence many have supposed that one of them was the son of Mary the mother of the Lord Jesus. It is said (Matt. 8:55) that the brothers of Jesus were James and Joses, and Simon, and Judas; and it is remarkable that three of the apostles bear the same names: James the son of Alpheus, Simon Zelotes, and Judas (John 14:22). It is indeed possible, as Bloomfield remarks, that three brothers of our Lord and three of his apostles might bear the same names, and yet be different persons; but such a coincidence would be very remarkable and not easily explained. But if it were not so, then the James here was the son of Alpheus, and consequently a cousin of the Lord Jesus. The word "brother" may, according to scripture usage, be understood as denoting a "near kinsman."—*Popular Commentary*

This account being of importance, to establish his claim to this office, he confirms it by a solemn oath (*v.* 20), which, though it will not justify us in solemn appeals to God upon every occasion, yet shows that, in matters of weight and moment, this may sometimes not only be lawful, but duty.

JAMIESON, FAUSSET, BROWN

considerable number of] days." It is curiously confirmatory of the legitimacy of taking "many days" to stand for "three years," that the same phrase exactly occurs in the same sense in I Kings 2: 38, 39. This was a country of the *Gentiles;* here doubtless he preached as he did before and after (Acts 9:20, 22) at Damascus: thus he shows the independence of his apostolic commission. He also here had that comparative retirement needed, after the first fervor of his conversion, to prepare him for the great work before him. Cf. Moses (Acts 7:29, 30). His familiarity with the scene of the giving of the law, and the meditations and revelations which he had there, appear in ch. 4:24, 25; Hebrews 12:18. See *Note*, vs. 12. The Lord from heaven communed with him, as He on earth in the days of His flesh communed with the other apostles. **returned**—*Greek* "returned back again." **18. after three years**—dating from my conversion, as appears by the contrast to "immediately" (vs. 16). This is the same visit to Jerusalem as in Acts 9:26, and at this visit occurred the vision (Acts 22:17, 18). The incident which led to his leaving Damascus (Acts 9: 25; II Cor. 11:33) was not the main *cause* of his going *to Jerusalem*. So that there is no discrepancy in the statement here that he went "to see Peter"; or rather, as *Greek,* "to make the acquaintance of"; "to become personally acquainted with." The two oldest MSS. read, "Cephas," the name given Peter elsewhere in the Epistle, the *Hebrew* name; as *Peter* is the *Greek* (John 1:42). Appropriate to the view of him here as the apostle especially of the Hebrews. It is remarkable that Peter himself, in his Epistles, uses the *Greek* name *Peter,* perhaps to mark his antagonism to the Judaizers who would cling to the Hebraic form. He was prominent among the apostles, though James, as bishop of Jerusalem, had the chief authority there (Matt. 16:18). **abode**—or "tarried" [ELLICOTT]. **fifteen days**—only fifteen days; contrasting with the long period of *three years,* during which, previously, he had exercised an independent commission in preaching: a fact proving on the face of it, how little he owed to Peter in regard to his apostolical authority or instruction. The *Greek* for "to see," at the same time implies *visiting a person important to know,* such as Peter was. The plots of the Jews prevented him staying longer (Acts 9:29). Also, the vision directing him to depart to the Gentiles, for that the people of Jerusalem would not receive his testimony (Acts 22:17, 18). **19.** Cf. Acts 9:27, 28, wherein Luke, as an historian, describes more generally what Paul, the subject of the history, himself details more particularly. The history speaks of "apostles"; and Paul's mention of a *second* apostle, besides Peter, reconciles the Epistle and the history. At Stephen's martyrdom, and the consequent persecution, the other ten apostles, agreeably to Christ's directions, seem to have *soon* (though not *immediately,* Acts 8:14) left Jerusalem to preach elsewhere. James remained in charge of the mother church, as its bishop. Peter, the apostle of the circumcision, was present during Paul's fifteen days' stay; but he, too, presently after (Acts 9:32), went on a circuit through Judea. **James, the Lord's brother**—This designation, to distinguish him from James the son of Zebedee, was appropriate while that apostle was alive. But before Paul's second visit to Jerusalem (ch. 2:1; Acts 15), he had been beheaded by Herod (Acts 12:2). Accordingly, in the subsequent mention of James here (ch. 2:9, 12), he is not designated by this distinctive epithet: a minute, undesigned coincidence, and proof of genuineness. James was the Lord's brother, not in our strict sense, but in the sense, "cousin," or "kinsman" (Matt. 28:10; John 20:17). His brethren are never called "sons of Joseph," which they would have been had they been the Lord's brothers strictly. However, cf. Psalm 69:8, "I am an alien to *my mother's children."* In John 7:3, 5, the "brethren" who believed not in Him may mean His *near relations,* not including the two of His brethren, i.e., relatives (James and Jude) who were among the Twelve apostles. Acts 1:14, "His brethren," refer to Simon and Joses, and others (Matt. 13:55) of His kinsmen, who were not apostles. It is not likely there would be two pairs of brothers named alike, of such eminence as James and Jude; the likelihood is that the apostles James and Jude are also the writers of the Epistles, and the brethren of Jesus. James and Joses were sons of Alpheus and Mary, sister of the Virgin Mary. **20.** Solemn asseveration that his statement is true that his visit was but for fifteen days and that he saw no apostle save Peter and James. Probably it had been reported by Judaizers that he had received a long course of instruction from the apostles in Jerusalem from the

ADAM CLARKE

authority and fitted to the work by the same grace and Spirit as they were. *But I went into Arabia.* That part of Arabia which was contiguous to Damascus, over which Aretas was then king. Of this journey into Arabia we have no other account. As Luke was not then with him, it is not inserted in the Acts of the Apostles.

18. *After three years I went up to Jerusalem to see Peter.* These three years may be reckoned either from the departure of Paul from Jerusalem or from his return from Arabia to Damascus. *To see Peter.* To become "personally acquainted" with Peter; for this is the proper import of the verb from which we have the word "history," which signifies a "relation of things from personal knowledge and actual acquaintance.

And abode with him fifteen days. It was not, therefore, to get religious knowledge from him that he paid him this visit. He knew as much of the Jewish religion as Peter did, if not more; and as to the gospel, he received that from the same source and had preached it three years before this.

19. *James the Lord's brother* is mentioned thus to distinguish him from James the brother of John.

20. *Before God, I lie not.* This he speaks in reference to having seen only Peter and James at Jerusalem; and consequently to prove that he had not learned the gospel from the assembly of the apostles at Jerusalem, nor consequently received his commission from them.

MATTHEW HENRY

ALBERT BARNES:

21. "Afterwards I came." In this account he has omitted a circumstance recorded by Luke (Acts 9:29), of the controversy which he had with the Grecians or Hellenists. It was not material to the purpose which he has here in view, which is to state that he was not indebted to the apostles for his knowledge of the doctrines of Christianity. He therefore merely states that he left Jerusalem soon after he went there, and traveled to other places.

22. "And was unknown by face." Paul had visited Jerusalem only and he had formed no acquaintance with any of the churches in the other parts of Judea. He regarded himself at the first as called to preach particularly to the Gentiles, and he did not remain even to form an acquaintance with the Christians in Judea. "The churches of Judea." Those which were out of Jerusalem. Even at the early period of the conversion of Paul there were doubtless many churches in various parts of the land. "Which were in Christ." United to Christ; or which were Christian churches. The design of mentioning this is to show that he had not derived his views of the gospel from any of them. He had neither been instructed by the apostles nor was he indebted to the Christians in Judea for his knowledge of the Christian religion.

—*Popular Commentary*

He had no communication at that time with the *churches of Christ in Judæa,* they had not so much as *seen his face.* The very report of this mighty change in him, as it filled them with joy, so it excited them to give glory to God on the account of it.

JAMIESON, FAUSSET, BROWN

first; hence his earnestness in asserting the contrary facts. **21. I came into ... Syria and Cilicia**—"preaching the faith" (vs. 23), and so, no doubt, founding the churches in Syria and Cilicia, which he subsequently confirmed in the faith (Acts 15:23, 41). He probably went first to Cæsarea, the main seaport, and thence by sea to Tarsus of Cilicia, his native place (Acts 9:30), and thence to Syria; Cilicia having its geographical affinities with Syria, rather than with Asia Minor, as the Tarsus mountains separate it from the latter. His placing "Syria" in the order of words before "Cilicia," is due to Antioch being a more important city than Tarsus, as also to his longer stay in the former city. Also "Syria and Cilicia," from their close geographical connection, became a generic geographical phrase, the more important district being placed first [CONYBEARE and HOWSON]. This sea journey accounts for his being "unknown by face to the churches of Judea" (vs. 22). He passes by in silence his *second* visit, with alms, to Judea and Jerusalem (Acts 11:30); doubtless because it was for a limited and special object, and would occupy but a few days (Acts 12:25), as there raged at Jerusalem at the time a persecution in which James, the brother of John, was martyred, and Peter was in prison, and James seems to have been the only apostle present (Acts 12:17); so it was needless to mention this visit, seeing that he could not at such a time have received the instructions which the Galatians alleged he had derived from the primary fountains of authority, the apostles. **22.** So far was I from being a disciple of the apostles, that I was even *unknown in the churches of Judea* (excepting Jerusalem, Acts 9:26-29), which were the chief scene of their labors. **23.** Translate as *Greek,* "They were hearing": tidings were brought them from time to time [CONYBEARE and HOWSON]. **he which persecuted us in times past**—"our former persecutor" [ALFORD]. The designation by which he was known among Christians still better than by his name "Saul." **destroyed**—*Greek,* "was destroying." **24. in me**—"in my case." "Having understood the entire change, and that the former wolf is now acting the shepherd's part, they received occasion for joyful thanksgiving to God in respect to me" [THEODORET]. How different, he implies to the Galatians, *their* spirit from *yours!*

ADAM CLARKE

22. *And was unknown by face.* I was not personally acquainted with any of the churches of Judea; I was converted in another place, and had not preached the gospel in any Christian congregation in that country. I knew only those at Jerusalem.

23. *They had heard only.* As a persecutor of the Church of Christ, I was well-known; and as a convert to Christ I was not less so. The fame of both was great, even where I was personally unknown.

24. *They glorified God in me.* Hearing now that I preached that faith which before I had persecuted and endeavored to destroy, they glorified God for the grace which had wrought my conversion. I owe nothing to them; I owe all to God—and they themselves acknowledge this. I received all from God, and God has all the glory.

MATTHEW HENRY — CHAPTER 2

Verses 1–10

From the very first preaching of Christianity there was a difference of apprehension between those Christians who had first been Jews and those who had first been Gentiles. Peter was the apostle of the circumcision. But Paul was the apostle of the Gentiles. He informs us of another journey which he took to Jerusalem, *v.* 1–10.

I. It was not till *fourteen years* after the former (mentioned *ch.* i. 18). It was some evidence that he had no dependence upon the other apostles, that he had been so long absent from them, and was all the while employed in preaching pure Christianity, without being called into question by them for it. *He went up with Barnabas, and took with him Titus also.* If the journey here spoken of was the same with that recorded Acts xv, then we have a plain reason why Barnabas went along with him; for he was chosen by the Christians at Antioch to be his companion and associate. Though Titus had now become not only a convert to the Christian faith, but a preacher of it too, yet he was by birth a Gentile and uncircumcised, and therefore, by making him his companion, it appeared that their doctrine and practice were of a piece. *He went up by revelation.* It was a privilege with which this apostle was often favoured to be under a special divine direction. It should teach us to endeavour to see our way made plain before us, and to commit ourselves to the guidance of Providence.

II. An account of his behaviour while he was at Jerusalem.

1. *He there communicated the gospel to them, which he preached among the Gentiles, but privately,* &c. Observe both the faithfulness and prudence of our great apostle. (1) His faithfulness in giving them a fair account of the doctrine which he had all along preached among the Gentiles, and was still resolved to preach. (2) He uses prudence and caution herein. He chooses rather to do it in a more private than in a public way. The reason of this his caution was lest he should stir up opposition against himself and thereby either the success of his past labours should be lessened, or his future usefulness be obstructed. It was enough to his purpose to have his doctrine

JAMIESON, FAUSSET, BROWN — CHAPTER 2

VSS. 1-21. HIS CO-ORDINATE AUTHORITY AS APOSTLE OF THE CIRCUMCISION RECOGNIZED BY THE APOSTLES. PROVED BY HIS REBUKING PETER FOR TEMPORIZING AT ANTIOCH: HIS REASONING AS TO THE INCONSISTENCY OF JUDAIZING WITH JUSTIFICATION BY FAITH. **1.** Translate, "After fourteen years"; viz., from Paul's conversion inclusive [ALFORD]. In the fourteenth year from his conversion [BIRKS]. The same visit to Jerusalem as in Acts 15 (A.D. 50), when the council of the apostles and Church decided that Gentile Christians need not be circumcised. **Titus ... also**—specified on account of what follows as to him, in vs. 3. Paul and Barnabas, *and others,* were deputed by the Church of Antioch (Acts 15:2) to consult the apostles and elders at Jerusalem on the question of circumcision of Gentile Christians. **2. by revelation**—not from being absolutely dependent on the apostles at Jerusalem, but by independent divine "revelation." Quite consistent with his at the same time, being a deputy from the Church of Antioch, as Acts 15:2 states. He by this *revelation* was led to suggest the sending of the deputation. Cf. the case of Peter being led by vision, and at the same time by Cornelius' messengers, to go to Cæsarea, Acts 10. **I ... communicated unto them**—viz., "to the apostles and elders" (Acts 15:2): to the apostles in particular (vs. 9). **privately**—that he and the apostles at Jerusalem might decide previously on the principles to be adopted and set forward before the public council (Acts 15). It was necessary that the Jerusalem apostles should know beforehand that the Gospel Paul preached to the Gentiles was the same as theirs, and had received divine confirmation in the results it wrought on the Gentile converts. He and Barnabas related to the *multitude,* not the nature of the doctrine they preached (as Paul did privately to the apostles), but only the miracles vouchsafed in *proof* of God's sanctioning their preaching to the Gentiles (Acts 15: 12). **to them ... of reputation**—James, Cephas, and John, and probably some of the "elders"; vs. 6, "those who seemed to be somewhat." **lest ...**—"lest I should be running, or have run, in vain"; i.e., that they might see that I am not running, and have

ADAM CLARKE — CHAPTER 2

1. *Then fourteen years after.* There is a considerable difference among critics concerning the time specified in this verse; the apostle is however generally supposed to refer to the journey he took to Jerusalem about the question of circumcision, mentioned in Acts xv. 4. Others contend that the journey of which the apostle speaks is that mentioned in Acts xi. 27, when Barnabas and Saul were sent by the church of Antioch with relief to the poor Christians in Judea.

2. *I went up by revelation.* This either means that he went up at that time by an express *revelation* from God that it was his duty to do so, made either to the church of Antioch to send these persons to Jerusalem or to these persons to go according to the directions of that church, or the apostle here wishes to say that, having received the gospel *by revelation* from God, to preach Christ among the Gentiles, he went up "according" to that revelation, and told what God had done by him among the Gentiles. Or it may refer to the revelation made to "certain prophets" who came to Antioch, and particularly "Agabus," who signified by the Spirit that there would be a dearth, in consequence of which the disciples purposed to send relief to their poor brethren at Jerusalem. See Acts xi. 27-30. *But privately to them which were of reputation.* To the "chief men"; those who were highest in reputation among the apostles, "the honorable." With these the apostle intimates that he had some private conferences.

Lest by any means. And he held these private conferences with those more eminent men to give them information how, in consequence of

MATTHEW HENRY

owned by those who were of greatest authority, whether it was approved by others or not.

2. In his practice he firmly adhered to the doctrine which he had preached. Though he had Titus with him, who was a Greek, yet he would not suffer him to be circumcised. It does not appear that the apostles at all insisted upon this; they were not for imposing it upon the Gentiles. But there were others who did, *false brethren, unawares brought in*, to *spy out their liberty which they had in Christ Jesus*. Their design herein was *to bring them into bondage*. Had they prevailed with Paul to have circumcised Titus, they would easily have imposed circumcision upon other Gentiles, and so have brought them under the bondage of the Law of Moses. But Paul would not *give place by subjection, no, not for an hour, that the truth of the gospel might continue with them*. He would not yield to those who were for the Mosaic rites and ceremonies, but would stand fast in the liberty wherewith Christ hath made us free.

3. Though he conversed with the other apostles, yet he did not receive any addition to his knowledge or authority from them, *v*. 6. That they were apostles first was no prejudice to his being equally an apostle with them. They told him nothing but what he before knew by revelation, nor could they except against the doctrine which he communicated to them.

4. The other apostles were fully convinced of his divine mission and authority, and accordingly acknowledged him as their fellow-apostle, *v*. 7–10. They justly concluded *that the gospel of the uncircumcision was committed to Paul, as the gospel of the circumcision was to Peter*.

JAMIESON, FAUSSET, BROWN

not run, in vain. Paul does not *himself* fear lest he be running, or had run, in vain; but lest he should, if he gave them no explanation, *seem* so *to them*. His race was the swift-running proclamation of the Gospel to the Gentiles (cf. "run," *Margin*, for "Word . . . *have free course*," II Thess. 3:1). His running would have been in vain, had circumcision been necessary, since he did not require it of his converts. **3. But**—So far were they from regarding me as running in vain, that "*not even* Titus who was with me, who was a Greek (and therefore uncircumcised), was compelled to be circumcised." So the *Greek* should be translated. The "false brethren," vs. 4 ("certain of the sect of the Pharisees which believed," Acts 15:5), demanded his circumcision. The apostles, however, constrained by the firmness of Paul and Barnabas (vs. 5), did not compel or insist on his being circumcised. Thus they virtually sanctioned Paul's course among the Gentiles and admitted his independence as an apostle: the point he desires to set forth to the Galatians. Timothy, on the other hand, as being a proselyte of the gate, and son of a Jewess (Acts 16: 1), he circumcised (Acts 16:3). Christianity did not interfere with Jewish usages, regarded merely as social ordinances, though no longer having their religious significance, in the case of Jews and proselytes, while the Jewish polity and temple still stood; after the overthrow of the latter, those usages naturally ceased. To have insisted on Jewish usages for *Gentile* converts, would have been to make them essential parts of Christianity. To have rudely violated them at first in the case of *Jews*, would have been inconsistent with that charity which (in matters indifferent) is made all things to all men, that by all means it may win some (I Cor. 9:22; cf. Rom. 14:1-7, 13-23). Paul brought Titus about with him as a living example of the power of the Gospel upon the uncircumcised heathen. **4. And that**—i.e., What I did concerning Titus (viz., by not permitting him to be circumcised) was not from contempt of circumcision, but "on account of the false brethren" (Acts 15:1, 24) who, had I yielded to the demand for his being circumcised, would have perverted the case into a proof that I deemed circumcision necessary. **unawares**—"in an underhand manner brought in." **privily**—stealthily. **to spy out**—as foes in the guise of friends, wishing to destroy and rob us of—**our liberty**—from the yoke of the ceremonial law. If they had found that we circumcised Titus through fear of the apostles, they would have made that a ground for insisting on imposing the legal yoke on the Gentiles. **bring us into bondage**—The *Greek* future implies the *certainty* and *continuance* of the bondage as the result. **5.** *Greek*, "To whom not even for an hour did we yield by subjection." ALFORD renders the *Greek* article, "*with* THE subjection required of us." The sense rather is, We would willingly have yielded for *love* [BENGEL] (if no principle was at issue), but not in the way of *subjection*, where "the truth of the Gospel" (vs. 14; Col. 1:5) was at stake (viz., the fundamental truth of justification by faith only, without the works of the law, contrasted with another Gospel, ch. 1:6). Truth precise, unaccommodating, abandons nothing that belongs to itself, admits nothing that is inconsistent with it [BENGEL]. **might continue with you**—Gentiles. We defended for your sakes your true faith and liberties, which *you* are now renouncing. **6.** *Greek*, "From those who . . . ." He meant to complete the sentence with "I derived no special advantage"; but he alters it into "they . . . added nothing to me." **accepteth**—so as to show any partiality; "respecteth no man's person" (Eph. 6:9). **seemed to be somewhat**—i.e., not that they *seemed* to be what they *were not*, but "*were reputed as persons of some consequence*"; not insinuating a doubt but that they were justly so reputed. **in conference added**—or "imparted"; the same *Greek* as in ch. 1:16, "I conferred not with flesh and blood." As I did not by conference impart to them aught at my conversion, so they now did not impart aught additional to me, above what I already knew. This proves to the Galatians his independence as an apostle. **7. contrariwise**—on the contrary. So far from *adding any* new light to ME, THEY gave in THEIR adhesion to the new path on which Barnabas and I, by independent revelation, had entered. So far from censuring, they gave a hearty approval to my independent course, viz., the innovation of preaching the Gospel without circumcision to the Gentiles. **when they saw**—from the effects which I showed them, were "wrought" (vs. 8; Acts 15:12). **was committed unto me**—*Greek*, "I was entrusted with . . . , as Peter was with . . . . **gospel of the uncircumcision**—i.e., of the Gentiles, who were to be converted without circumcision be-

ADAM CLARKE

his divine call, he had preached the gospel to the Gentiles, and the great good which God had wrought by his ministry; but they, not knowing the nature and end of his call, might be led to suppose he had acted wrong, and thus labored in vain. It was necessary, therefore, that he should give the apostolic council the fullest information that he had acted according to the divine mind in every respect, and had been blessed in his deed.

3. *But neither Titus, who was with me*. The apostle proceeds to state that his account was so satisfactory to the apostles that they not only did not require him to insist on the necessity of circumcision among the Gentiles, but did not even require him to have Titus, who was a Greek, circumcised; though that might have appeared expedient, especially at Jerusalem, to prevent false brethren from making a handle of his uncircumcision, and turning it to the prejudice of the gospel in Judea.

4. *To spy out our liberty*. The Judaizing brethren got introduced into the assembly of the apostles, in order to find out what was implied in the *liberty* of the gospel, that they might know the better how to oppose Paul and his fellows in their preaching Christ to the Gentiles and admitting them into the Church without obliging them to observe circumcision and keep the law.

5. *To whom we gave place by subjection*. So fully satisfied was he with his divine call, and that he had in preaching among the Gentiles acted in strict conformity to it, that he did not submit in the least to the opinion of those Judaizing teachers; and therefore he continued to insist on the exemption of the Gentiles from the necessity of submitting to Jewish rites. *That the truth of the gospel*—this grand doctrine that the Gentiles are admitted by the gospel of Christ to be fellow heirs with the Jews—*might continue;* and thus the same doctrine is continued with you Gentiles.

6. *These who seemed to be somewhat*. "Those who were of acknowledged reputation." The verb *dokein*, "to seem," is repeatedly used by the best Greek writers, not to call the sense in question or to lessen it, but to deepen and extend it. See the note on Luke viii. 18. Perhaps this verse had best be translated thus: "But there is no difference between those who were of acknowledged reputation and myself; God accepts no man's person; but in the conferences which I held with them they added nothing to me"—gave me no new light; did not attempt to impose on me any obligation, because they saw that God had appointed me my work, and that His counsel was with me.

7. *But contrariwise*. They were so far from wishing me to alter my plan, or to introduce anything new in my doctrine to the Gentiles, that they saw plainly that my doctrine was the same as their own, coming immediately from the same source; and therefore gave to me and to Barnabas the right hand of fellowship. *The gospel of the uncircumcision*. They saw to their utmost satisfaction that I was as expressly sent by God to preach the gospel to the Gentiles as Peter was to preach it to the Jews.

MATTHEW HENRY

ALBERT BARNES:

9. "And when James, Cephas, and John, who seemed to be pillars." That is, pillars or supports in the church. The word rendered "pillars" means properly firm support; then persons of influence and authority, as in a church, or that support a church as a pillar or column does an edifice. In regard to James, see Acts 15:13. Cephas, or Peter, was the most aged of the apostles and regarded as the head of the apostolical college. John was the beloved disciple, and his influence in the church must of necessity have been great. Paul felt that if he had the countenance of these men, it would be an important proof to the churches of Galatia that he had a right to regard himself as an apostle. Their countenance was expressed in the most full and decisive manner. "Perceived the grace that was given unto me." That is, the favor that had been shown to me by the great Head of the church in so abundantly blessing my labors among the Gentiles. "They gave unto me and Barnabas the right hand of fellowship." The right hand in token of fellowship or favor. They thus publicly acknowledged us as fellow laborers and expressed the utmost confidence in us. To give the right hand with us is a token of friendly salutation, and it seems that it was a mode of salutation not unknown in the time of the apostles. They were thus recognized as associated with the apostles in the great work of spreading the gospel around the world. Whether this was done in a public manner is not certainly known; but it was probably in the presence of the church, or possibly at the close of the council referred to in Acts 15.

"That we should go unto the heathen." To preach the gospel and to establish churches. In this way the whole matter was settled, and settled as Paul desired it to be. A delightful harmony was produced between Paul and the apostles at Jerusalem; and the result showed the wisdom of the course which he had adopted. There had been no harsh contention or strife. No jealousies had been suffered to arise. Paul had sought an opportunity of a full statement of his views to them in private (v. 2), and they had been entirely satisfied that God had called him and Barnabas to the work of making known the gospel among the heathen. Instead of being jealous at their success, they had rejoiced in it; and instead of throwing any obstacle in their way, they cordially gave them the right hand.—*Popular Commentary*

They gave unto him and Barnabas the right hand of fellowship, and agreed that *these should go to the heathen, while they continued to preach to the circumcision.* And thus this meeting ended in an entire harmony and agreement; they approved both Paul's doctrine and conduct, and had nothing further to add, *only that they would remember the poor*, which of his own accord *he was very forward to do.* Herein he has given us an excellent pattern of Christian charity and we should by no means confine it to those who are just of the same sentiments with us, but be ready to extend it to all whom we have reason to look upon as the disciples of Christ.

Verses 11–21

I. He acquaints them with another interview which he had with the apostle Peter at Antioch, and what passed between them there, *v.* 11–14. In their other meeting, there had been good harmony and agreement. But in this Paul finds himself obliged to oppose Peter.

JAMIESON, FAUSSET, BROWN

ing required. **circumcision . . . unto Peter**—Peter had originally opened the door to the Gentiles (Acts 10 and 15:7). But in the ultimate apportionment of the spheres of labor, the Jews were assigned to him (cf. I Pet. 1:1). So Paul on the other hand wrote to the Hebrews (cf. also Col. 4:11), though his main work was among the Gentiles. The non-mention of Peter in the list of names, presciently through the Spirit, given in Romans 16, shows that Peter's residence at Rome, much more primacy, was *then* unknown. The same is palpable from the sphere here assigned to him. **8. he**—God (I Cor. 12:6). **wrought effectually**—i.e., made the preached word efficacious to conversion, not only by sensible miracles, but by the secret mighty power of the Holy Ghost. **in Peter**—ELLICOTT and others, translate, "*For* Peter." GROTIUS translates as *English Version.* **to**—with a view to. **was mighty**—Translate as before, the *Greek* being the same, "wrought effectually." **in me**—"for (or 'in') me *also.*" **9. James**—placed first in the oldest MSS., even before Peter, as being bishop of Jerusalem, and so presiding at the council (Acts 15). He was called "the Just," from his strict adherence to the law, and so was especially popular among the Jewish party though he did not fall into their extremes; whereas Peter was somewhat estranged from them through his intercourse with the Gentile Christians. To each apostle was assigned the sphere best suited to his temperament: to James, who was tenacious of the law, the Jerusalem Jews; to Peter, who had opened the door to the Gentiles but who was Judaically disposed, the Jews of the dispersion; to Paul, who, by the miraculous and overwhelming suddenness of his conversion, had the whole current of his early Jewish prejudices turned into an utterly opposite direction, the Gentiles. Not separately and individually, but collectively the apostles together represented Christ, the One Head, in the apostleship. The twelve foundation stones of various colors are joined together to the one great foundation stone on which they rest (I Cor. 3:11; Rev. 21: 14, 19, 20). John had got an intimation in Jesus' lifetime of the admission of the Gentiles (John 12: 20-24). **seemed**—i.e., *were reputed to be* (*Note*, vss. 2, 6) pillars, i.e., weighty supporters of the Church (cf. Prov. 9:1; Rev. 3:12). **perceived the grace . . . given unto me**—(II Pet. 3:15). **gave to me and Barnabas the right hands of fellowship**—recognizing me as a *colleague* in the apostleship, and that the Gospel I preached by special revelation to the Gentiles was the same as theirs. Cf. the phrase, Lamentations 5:6; Ezekiel 17:18. **heathen**—the Gentiles. **10. remember the poor**—of the *Jewish* Christians in Judea, then distressed. Paul and Barnabas had already done so (Acts 11:23-30). **the same**—the very thing. **I . . . was forward**—or "zealous" (Acts 24:17; Rom. 15:25; I Cor. 16:1; II Cor. 8 and 9). Paul was zealous for good works, while denying justification by them. **11. Peter**—"Cephas" in the oldest MSS. Paul's withstanding Peter is the strongest proof that the former gives of the independence of his apostleship in relation to the other apostles, and upsets the Romish doctrine of Peter's supremacy. The apostles were not always inspired; but were so always in *writing* the Scriptures. If then the inspired men who *wrote* them were not invariably at other times infallible, much less were the uninspired men who kept them. The Christian fathers may be trusted generally as witnesses to facts, but not implicitly followed in matters of opinion. **come to Antioch**—then the citadel of the Gentile Church: where first the Gospel was preached to *idolatrous Gentiles*, and where the name "Christians" was first given (Acts 11:20, 26), and where Peter is said to have been subsequently bishop. The question at Antioch was not whether the Gentiles were admissible to the Christian covenant without becoming circumcised—that was the question settled at the Jerusalem council just before—but whether the Gentile Christians were to be admitted to *social intercourse with the Jewish Christians* without conforming to the Jewish institution. The Judaizers, soon after the council had passed the resolutions recognizing the equal rights of the Gentile Christians, repaired to Antioch, the scene of the gathering in of the Gentiles (Acts 11: 20-26), to witness, what to Jews would look so extraordinary, the receiving of men to communion of the Church without circumcision. Regarding the proceeding with prejudice, they explained away the force of the Jerusalem decision; and probably also desired to watch whether the *Jewish* Christians among the Gentiles violated the law, which that decision did not verbally sanction *them* in doing, though giving the Gentiles latitude (Acts 15:19). **to be blamed**—rather, "(self)-condemned"; his act

ADAM CLARKE

8. *For he that wrought effectually.* "He who wrought powerfully with Peter wrought powerfully also with me." He gave us both those talents which were suited to our work, and equal success in our different departments.

9. *James, Cephas, and John, who seemed to be pillars.* "Who were known to be very eminent, and acknowledged as chief men" among the apostles. Among the Jews, persons of great eminence and importance are represented as "pillars" and "foundations" of the world. *The right hands of fellowship.* Giving the right hand to another was the mark of confidence, friendship, and fellowship.

10. *Only they would that we should remember the poor.* they saw plainly that God had as expressly called Barnabas and me to go to the Gentiles as He had called them to preach to the Jews, and they did not attempt to give us any new injunctions, only wished us to remember the poor in Judea; but this was a thing to which we were previously disposed.

11. *When Peter was come to Antioch.* There had been a controversy whether Peter here should not be read "Kephas"; and whether this Kephas was not a different person from Peter the apostle. Instead of *Peter*, several MSS. and versions and several of the Greek fathers read *Kephas.* That Peter the apostle is meant, the most sober and correct writers of antiquity maintain.

MATTHEW HENRY

1. Peter's fault. When he came among the Gentile churches, he complied with them, and did eat with them. But, when there came some Jewish Christians from Jerusalem, *he withdrew, and separated himself.* His fault herein had a bad influence upon others.

Barnabas himself, one of the apostles of the Gentiles, *was carried away with their dissimulation.* Here note, (1) The weakness and inconstancy of the best of men, and how apt they are to falter in their duty to God, out of an undue regard to the pleasing of men. (2) The great force of bad examples, especially the examples of great men and good men.

2. The rebuke which Paul gave him. When he observes him thus behaving he is not afraid to reprove him for it. Paul adhered resolutely to his principles, when others faltered in theirs. He was as good a Jew as any and the Gentiles must comply with the Jews, or else not be admitted into Christian communion.

II. He takes occasion to speak of that great fundamental doctrine of the gospel—That justification is only by faith in Christ, and not by the works of the law. This was the doctrine which Paul had preached among the Galatians, to which he still adhered, and which it is his great business in this epistle to confirm.

JAMIESON, FAUSSET, BROWN

at one time condemning his contrary acting at another time. **2. certain**—men: perhaps James' view (in which he was not infallible, any more than Peter) was that the Jewish converts were still to observe Jewish ordinances, from which he had decided with the council the *Gentiles* should be free (Acts 15:19). NEANDER, however, may be right in thinking these self-styled delegates from James were not really from him. Acts 15:24 favors this. "Certain from James," may mean merely that they came from the Church at Jerusalem under James' bishopric. Still James' leanings were to legalism, and this gave him his influence with the Jewish party (Acts 21:18-26). **eat with . . . Gentiles**—as in Acts 10:10-20, 48, according to the command of the vision (Acts 11:3-17). Yet after all, this same Peter, through fear of man (Prov. 29:25), was faithless to his own so distinctly avowed principles (Acts 15:7-11). We recognize the same old nature in him as led him, after faithfully witnessing for Christ, yet for a brief space, to deny Him. "Ever the first to recognize, and the first to draw back from great truths" [ALFORD]. An undesigned coincidence between the Gospels and the Epistle in the consistency of character as portrayed in both. It is beautiful to see how earthly misunderstandings of Christians are lost in Christ. For in II Peter 3:15, Peter praises the very Epistles of Paul which he knew contained his own condemnation. Though apart from one another and differing in characteristics, the two apostles were one in Christ. **withdrew**—*Greek*, "*began* to withdraw . . . ." This implies a *gradual drawing back;* "separated," *entire severance.* **13. the other**—*Greek*, "the rest." **Jews**—Jewish Christians. **dissembled likewise**—*Greek*, "joined in hypocrisy," viz., in living as though the law were necessary to justification, through fear of man, though they knew from God their Christian liberty of eating with Gentiles, and had availed themselves of it already (Acts 11:2-17). The case was distinct from that in I Corinthians chs. 8-10; Romans 14. It was not a question of liberty, and of bearing with others' infirmities, but one affecting the essence of the Gospel, whether the Gentiles are to be virtually "compelled to live as do the Jews," in order to be justified (vs. 14). **Barnabas also**—"Even Barnabas": one least likely to be led into such an error, being with Paul in first preaching to the idolatrous Gentiles: showing the power of bad example and numbers. In Antioch, the capital of Gentile Christianity and the central point of Christian missions, the controversy first arose, and in the same spot it now broke out afresh; and here Paul had first to encounter the party that afterwards persecuted him in every scene of his labors (Acts 15:30-35). **14. walked not uprightly**—lit., "straight": "were not walking with straightforward steps." Cf. ch. 6:16. **truth of the gospel**—which teaches that justification by legal works and observances is inconsistent with redemption by Christ. Paul alone here maintained the truth against Judaism, as afterwards against heathenism (II Tim. 4:16, 17). **Peter**—"Cephas" in the oldest MSS. **before . . . all**—(I Tim. 5:20). **If thou . . .**—"If thou, although being a Jew (and therefore one who might seem to be more bound to the law than the Gentiles), livest (habitually, without scruple and from conviction, Acts 15:10, 11) as a Gentile (freely eating of every food, and living in other respects also as if legal ordinances in no way justify, vs. 12), and not as a Jew, *how* (so the oldest MSS. read, for "why") is it that thou art compelling (virtually, by thine example) the Gentiles to live as do the Jews?" (lit., *to Judaize*, i.e., to keep the ceremonial customs of the Jews: What had been formerly obedience to the law, is now mere *Judaism*). The high authority of Peter would constrain the Gentile Christians to regard Judaizing as necessary to all, since Jewish Christians could not consort with Gentile converts in communion without it. **15, 16.** Connect these verses together, and read with most of the oldest MSS. "But" in the beginning of vs. 16: "We (I and thou, Peter) by nature (not by proselytism), Jews, and not sinners as (Jewish language termed the Gentiles) from among the Gentiles, YET (lit., BUT) knowing that . . . even we (resuming the 'we' of vs. 15, 'we also,' as well as the Gentile sinners; casting away trust in the law), have believed . . . ." **not justified by the works of the law**—as the GROUND of justification. "The works of the law" are those which have the law for their object—which are wrought to fulfil the law [ALFORD]. **but by**—Translate, "But only (in no other way save) *through* faith *in* Jesus Christ," as the MEAN and instrument of justification. **Jesus Christ**—In the second case, read with the oldest MSS., "Christ Jesus," the *Messiahship* coming into prominence in the case of *Jewish* believers,

ADAM CLARKE

12. *Before that certain came from James, he did eat with the Gentiles.* Here was Peter's fault. He was convinced that God had pulled down the middle wall of partition that had so long separated the Jews and Gentiles, and he acted on this conviction, associating with the latter and eating with them. But when certain Jews came from James, who it appears considered the law still to be in force, lest he should place a stumbling block before them he withdrew from all commerce with the converted Gentiles, and acted as if he himself believed the law to be still in force, and that the distinction between the Jews and the Gentiles should still be kept up.

13. *And the other Jews dissembled likewise.* That is: Those who were converted to Christianity from among the Jews, and who had also been convinced that the obligation of the Jewish ritual had ceased, seeing Peter act this part, and also fearing them that were of the circumcision, separated themselves from the converted Gentiles and acted so as to convince the Jews that they still believed the law to be of moral obligation; and so powerful was the torrent of such an example that the gentle, loving-hearted *Barnabas also was carried away with their dissimulation,* "with their hypocrisy," feigning to be what they really were not.

14. *That they walked not uprightly.* They did not walk "with a straight step"—they did not maintain a firm footing. *According to the truth of the gospel.* According to that true doctrine, which states that "Christ is the end of the law" for justification "to every one that believeth"; and that such are under no obligation to observe circumcision and the other peculiar rites and ceremonies of the law. *If thou, being a Jew, livest.* This was a cutting reproof. He was a Jew and had been circumstantially scrupulous in everything relative to the law; and it required a miracle to convince him that the Gentiles were admitted on their believing in Christ to become members of the same Church and fellow heirs of the hope of eternal life; and in consequence of this he went in with the Gentiles and ate with them; i.e., associated with them as he would with Jews. But now, fearing them of the circumcision, he withdrew from this fellowship. *Why compellest thou the Gentiles?* You once considered that they were not under such an obligation, and now you act as if you did consider the law in full force; but you are convinced that the contrary is the case, yet act differently! This is "hypocrisy."

15. *We who are Jews by nature.* We who belong to the Jewish nation—who have been born, bred, and educated Jews. *And not sinners of the Gentiles.* Not without the knowledge of God, as they have been. Among the nations or Gentiles many Jews sojourned, who in Scripture are known by the name of Hellenists, and these were distinguished from those who were termed *sinners of the Gentiles*—"heathens."

MATTHEW HENRY

1. The practice of the Jewish Christians themselves: "What did we believe in Christ for? Was it not that we might be justified by the faith of Christ? And, if so, is it not folly to go back to the law?"

To give the greater weight to this he adds (*v.* 17), "*But if, while we seek to be justified by Christ, we ourselves also are found sinners, is Christ the minister of sin?* Will it not follow that he is so, if he engage us to receive a doctrine by which we are so far from being justified that we remain impure sinners?" But he rejects it with abhorrence: "*God forbid*," says he, "that thereby he should direct us into a way of justification that is defective and ineffectual.

For," says he (*v.* 18), "*if I build again the things which I destroyed I make myself a transgressor;* I own myself to remain under the guilt of sin, notwithstanding my faith in Christ."

2. What his own judgment and practice were. (1) He was dead to the law, *through the law itself.* He saw that justification was not to be expected by the works of it and that there was now no further need of the sacrifices since they were done away in Christ, by his offering up himself a sacrifice for us. But, though he was thus *dead to the law*, yet he did not look upon himself as *without law.* He was dead to the law, *that he might live unto God.* The doctrine of the gospel, instead of weakening the bond of duty, did but the more strengthen and confirm it; and therefore, though he was dead to the law, yet it was only in order to his living a new and better life to God.

JAMIESON, FAUSSET, BROWN

as "Jesus" does in the first case, referring to the general proposition. **justified by the faith of Christ**—i.e., by Christ, the object of faith, as the ground of our justification. **for by the works of the law shall no flesh be justified**—He rests his argument on this as an axiom in theology, referring to Psalm 143:2, "Moses and Jesus Christ; The law and the promise; Doing and believing; Works and faith; Wages and the gift; The curse and the blessing—are represented as diametrically opposed" [BENGEL]. The moral law is, in respect to justification, *more legal* than the ceremonial, which was an elementary and preliminary Gospel: So "Sinai" (ch. 4:24), which is more famed for the Decalogue than for the ceremonial law, is made pre-eminently the type of legal bondage. Thus, justification by the law, whether the moral or ceremonial, is excluded (Rom. 3:20). **17.** *Greek,* "But if, seeking to be justified IN (i.e., *in* believing *union with*) Christ (who has in the Gospel theory fulfilled the law for us), we (you and I) ourselves also *were* found (in *your* and *my former* communion with Gentiles) sinners (such as from the Jewish standpoint that now we resume, we should be regarded, since we have cast aside the law, thus having put ourselves in the same category as the Gentiles, who, being without the law, are, in the Jewish view, 'sinners," vs. 15), is therefore Christ, the minister of sin?" (Are we to admit the conclusion, in this case inevitable, that Christ having failed to justify us by faith, so has become to us the minister of sin, by putting us in the position of "sinners," as the Judaic theory, if correct, would make us, along with all others who are "without the law," Romans 2:14; I Corinthians 9:21; and with whom, by eating with them, we have identified ourselves?) The Christian mind revolts from so shocking a conclusion, and so, from the theory which would result in it. The whole sin lies, not with Christ, but with him who would necessitate such a blasphemous inference. But his false theory. though "*seeking*" from Christ, we have not "found" salvation (in contradiction to Christ's own words, Matt. 7:7), but "have been ourselves also (like the Gentiles) *found*" to be "sinners," by having entered into communion with Gentiles (vs. 12). **18.** *Greek,* "For if the things which I overthrew (by the faith of Christ), those very things I build up again (viz., legal righteousness, by subjecting myself to the law), I prove myself (lit., 'I commend myself') a transgressor." Instead of commending yourself as you sought to do (vs. 12, end), you merely commend yourself as a transgressor. The "I" is intended by Paul for *Peter* to take to himself, as it is *his* case, not Paul's own, that is described. A "transgressor" is another word for "sinner" (in vs. 17), for "sin is the *transgression* of the law." You, Peter, by now asserting the law to be obligatory, are proving yourself a "sinner," or "transgressor," in your having set it aside by living as the Gentiles, and with them. Thus you are debarred by transgression from justification by the law, and you debar yourself from justification by Christ, since in your theory He becomes a minister of sin. **19.** Here Paul seems to pass from his *exact words* to Peter, to the *general purport* of his argument on the question. However, his direct address to the Galatians seems not to be resumed till ch. 3:1, "O foolish Galatians . . . ." **For**—But I am not a "transgressor" by forsaking the law. "For . . . ." Proving his indignant denial of the consequence that "Christ is the minister of sin" (vs. 17), and of the premises from which it would follow. Christ, so far from being the minister of sin and death, is the establisher of righteousness and life. I am entirely in Him [BENGEL]. **I**—here emphatical. *Paul himself,* not *Peter,* as in the "I" (vs. 18). **through the law**—which was my "schoolmaster to bring me to Christ" (ch. 3:24); both by its terrors (ch. 3:13; Rom. 3:20) driving me to Christ, as the refuge from God's wrath against sin, and, when spiritually understood, teaching that itself is not permanent, but must give place to Christ, whom it prefigures as its scope and end (Rom. 10:4); and drawing me to Him by its promises (in the prophecies which form part of the Old Testament law) of a better righteousness, and of God's law written in the heart (Deut. 18:15-19; Jer. 31:33; Acts 10:43). **am dead to the law**—lit., "I died to the law," and so *am* dead to it, i.e., am passed from under its power, in respect to non-justification or condemnation (Col. 2:20; Rom. 6:14; 7:4, 6); just as a woman, once married and bound to a husband, ceases to be so bound to him when death interposes, and may be lawfully married to another husband. So by believing union to Christ in His death, we, being considered dead with Him, are severed from the law's past power over us (cf. ch. 6:14; I Cor. 7:39; Rom. 6:6-11; I Pet. 2:24). **live unto God**—(Rom. 6:11;

ADAM CLARKE

16. *Knowing that a man is not justified.* Neither the works of the Jewish law, nor of any other law, could justify any man.

17. *But if, while we seek to be justified.* If, while we acknowledge that we must be justified by faith in Christ, *we ourselves also are found sinners,* enjoining the necessity of fulfilling the law, which is impossible, we thus constitute ourselves *sinners. Is therefore Christ the minister of sin?*—Christ, who has taught us to renounce the law, and expect justification through His death? *God forbid* that we should either act so or think so.

18. *For if I build again the things which I destroyed.* If I act like a Jew and enjoin the observance of the law on the Gentiles, which I have repeatedly asserted and proved to be abolished by the death of Christ, then I "build up what I destroyed" and thus *make myself a transgressor* by not observing the law in that way in which I appear to enjoin the observance of it upon others.

19. *For I through the law am dead to the law.* In consequence of properly considering the nature and requisitions of the law, I am dead to all hope and expectation of help or salvation from the law, and have been obliged to take refuge in the gospel of Christ.

MATTHEW HENRY

(2) As he was dead to the law, so he was alive unto God through Jesus Christ (*v.* 20). He is crucified, and yet he lives; the old man is crucified, but the new man is living. Sin is mortified, and grace quickened. *I live, and yet not I.* He has the comforts and the triumphs of grace; and yet that grace is not from himself, but from another. *He is crucified with Christ,* and yet *Christ lives in him.* He is interested in the death of Christ, so as to die unto sin; and yet interested in the life of Christ, so as to live unto God.

He lives in the flesh, and yet *lives by faith*; to outward appearance he lives as other people do, yet he has a higher and nobler principle that supports him, that of faith in Christ. Those who have true faith live by that faith.

Lastly, By the doctrine of justification by faith in Christ, without the works of the law, he avoided two great difficulties. 1. *He did not frustrate the grace of God. If it be of works, it is no more of grace.* 2. He did not frustrate the death of Christ; for, if we look for salvation by the law of Moses, then we render the death of Christ needless.

JAMIESON, FAUSSET, BROWN

II Cor. 5:15; I Pet. 4:1, 2). **20. I am crucified**—lit., "I have been crucified with Christ." This more particularizes the foregoing. "I am dead" (vs. 19; Phil. 3:10). **nevertheless I live; yet not I**—*Greek,* "nevertheless I live, no longer (indeed) I." Though crucified I live; (and this) no longer that old man such as I once was (cf. Rom. 7:17). No longer Saul the Jew (ch. 5:24; Col. 3:11, but "another man"; cf. I Sam. 10:6). ELLICOTT and others translate, "*And* it is no longer I that live, but Christ that liveth in me." But the plain antithesis between "crucified" and "live," requires the translation, "nevertheless." **the life which I now live**—as contrasted with my life before conversion. **in the flesh**—My life seems to be a mere animal life "in the flesh," but this is not my true life; "it is but the mask of life under which lives another, viz., Christ, who is my true life" [LUTHER]. **I live by the faith . . .**—*Greek,* "IN faith (viz.), that of (i.e., which rests on) the Son of God." "In faith," answers by contrast to "in the flesh." *Faith,* not *the flesh,* is the real element in which I live. The phrase, "the Son of God," reminds us that His Divine Sonship is the source of His life-giving power. **loved me**—His eternal gratuitous **love** is the link that unites me to the Son of God, and His "giving Himself for me," is the strongest proof of that love. **21. I do not frustrate the grace of God**—I do not *make* it *void,* as thou, Peter, art doing by Judaizing. **for**—justifying the strong expression "frustrate," or "make void." **is dead in vain**—*Greek,* "Christ died needlessly," or "without just cause." Christ's having died, shows that the law has no power to justify us; for if the law can justify or make us righteous, the death of Christ is superfluous [CHRYSOSTOM].

ADAM CLARKE

20. *I am crucified with Christ.* The death of Christ on the Cross has showed me that there is no hope of salvation by the law; I am therefore as truly dead to all expectation of justification by the law as Christ was dead when He gave up the ghost upon the Cross. *Yet not I.* It is not of my natural life I speak, nor of any spiritual things which I myself have procured; *but Christ liveth in me.*

But this *life* I have *by the faith of the Son of God*—by believing on Christ as a Sacrifice for sin; for he *loved me,* and because He did so He *gave himself for me*—made himself a Sacrifice unto death, that I might be saved from the bitter pains of death eternal.

21. *I do not frustrate.* I do not "contemn, despise, or render useless" *the grace of God*—the doctrine of Christ crucified, which I must do if I preach the necessity of observing the law. *For if righteousness.* If "justification" and salvation *come by* an observance of *the law, then Christ is dead in vain.* His death is useless if an observance of the law can save us; but no observance of the law can save us, and therefore there was an absolute necessity for the death of Christ.

MATTHEW HENRY — CHAPTER 3

Verses 1–5

The apostle is here dealing with those who, having embraced the faith of Christ, still continued to seek for justification by the works of the law.

He reproves them, *v.* 1. He asks, *Who hath bewitched you?* They did not adhere to the gospel way of justification, wherein they had been taught. It is not enough to know the truth, and to say we believe it, but we must obey it too. Several things proved the folly of these Christians.

1. *Jesus Christ had been evidently set forth as crucified among them;* they had had the doctrine of the cross preached to them, and the sacrament of the Lord's supper administered among them, in both which Christ crucified had been set before them.

2. He appeals to the experiences they had had of the working of the Spirit upon their souls (*v.* 2). He desires to know how they came by these gifts and graces: Was it *by the works of the law*? Or was it by the *hearing of faith.* The latter, if they would say the truth, they were obliged to own.

3. He calls upon them to consider their past and present conduct (*v.* 3, 4). They had begun well; but now they were turning to the law, and expected to be advanced to higher degrees of perfection by adding the observance of it to faith in Christ, in order to their justification. This, instead of being an improvement upon the gospel, was really a perversion of it; they were so far from being more perfect Christians that they were more in danger of becoming no Christians at all.

JAMIESON, FAUSSET, BROWN — CHAPTER 3

VSS. 1-29. REPROOF OF THE GALATIANS FOR ABANDONING FAITH FOR LEGALISM. JUSTIFICATION BY FAITH VINDICATED: THE LAW SHOWN TO BE SUBSEQUENT TO THE PROMISE: BELIEVERS ARE THE SPIRITUAL SEED OF ABRAHAM, WHO WAS JUSTIFIED BY FAITH. THE LAW WAS OUR SCHOOLMASTER TO BRING US TO CHRIST, THAT WE MIGHT BECOME CHILDREN OF GOD BY FAITH. **1. that ye should not obey the truth**—omitted in the oldest MSS. **bewitched**—fascinated you so that you have lost your wits. THEMISTIUS says the Galatians were naturally very acute in intellect. Hence, Paul wonders they could be so misled in this case. **you**—emphatical. "YOU, before whose eyes Jesus Christ hath been graphically set forth (lit., *in writing,* viz., by vivid *portraiture* in preaching) among you, crucified" (so the sense and *Greek* order require rather than *English Version*). As Christ was "crucified," so ye ought to have been by faith "*crucified* with Christ," and so "dead to the law" (ch. 2:19, 20). Reference to the "eyes" is appropriate, as *fascination* was supposed to be exercised through the eyes. The sight of Christ crucified ought to have been enough to counteract all fascination. **2.** "Was it by the works of the law that ye received the Spirit (manifested by outward miracles, vs. 5; Mark 16:17; Heb. 2:4; and by spiritual graces, vs. 14; Gal. 4:5, 6; Eph. 1:13), or by the hearing of faith?" The "only" implies, "I desire, omitting other arguments, to rest the question on *this alone*"; I who was your *teacher,* desire now to "learn" this one thing from you. The epithet "Holy" is not prefixed to "Spirit" because that epithet is a joyous one, whereas this Epistle is stern and reproving [BENGEL]. **hearing of faith**—Faith consists not in *working,* but in *receiving* (Rom. 10:16, 17). **3. begun**—the Christian life (Phil. 1:6). **in the Spirit**—Not merely was Christ crucified "graphically set forth" in my preaching, but also "the Spirit" confirmed the word preached, by imparting His spiritual gifts. "Having thus begun" with the receiving His *spiritual* gifts, "are ye now *being* made perfect" (so the *Greek*), i.e., are ye *seeking* to be made perfect with *fleshly* ordinances of the law? [ESTIUS.] Cf. Romans 2:28; Philippians 3:3; Hebrews 9:10. Having begun in the Spirit, i.e., the Holy Spirit ruling your spiritual life as its "essence and active principle" [ELLICOTT], in contrast to "the flesh," the element in which the law works [ALFORD]. Having begun your Christianity in the Spirit, i.e., in the divine life that proceeds from faith, are ye seeking after something higher still (the perfecting of your Christianity) in the sensuous and the earthly, which cannot possibly elevate the inner life of the Spirit, viz., outward ceremonies? [NEANDER.] No doubt the Galatians thought that they were going more deeply into the Spirit; for the flesh may be easily mistaken for the Spirit, even by those who have made prog-

ADAM CLARKE — CHAPTER 3

1. *O foolish Galatians.* O infatuated people, you make as little use of reason as those who have none; you have acted in this business as those do who are "fascinated"—they are led blindly and unresistingly on to their own destruction. *That ye should not obey the truth.* This clause is wanting in some MSS., and in the most important of the Greek and Latin fathers. Of the clause Professor White says, "It should certainly be expunged." There are several various readings on this verse, from which it appears that the verse in the best ancient MSS. and versions was read thus: "O foolish Galatians, who hath bewitched you? Before whose eyes Jesus Christ crucified hath been plainly set forth." *Among you* is wanting in some MSS. and in several of the fathers. The words appear to disturb the sense.

2. *Received ye the Spirit by the works of the law.* This may refer to the miraculous gifts of the Spirit, which were very common in the apostolic Church. Did you receive these extraordinary gifts in consequence of your circumcision and observing the Mosaic precepts? or was it by the *hearing* of the gospel, prescribing *faith* in Christ crucified? It may also refer to the spirit of adoption, and consequently to their sonship.

3. *Having begun in the Spirit.* Having received a spiritual religion which refined and purified your hearts; and having received the Holy Spirit of God, by whom you were endued with various miraculous influences; and the spirit of adoption, by which you were assured of the remission of sins and incorporation with the family of God. *Are ye now made perfect by the flesh?* Are you seeking to complete that spiritual religion, and to perfect these spiritual gifts, by the carnal rite of circumcision? It appears that by the *Spirit,* here, not only the Holy Spirit, but His gifts, are to be understood; and by the *flesh,* by a metonymy, "circumcision" itself.

MATTHEW HENRY

They had not only embraced the Christian doctrine, but suffered for it too; and therefore their folly would be the more aggravated, if now they should desert it.

4. They had *ministered the Spirit to them, and wrought miracles among them*: and he appeals to them whether they did it *by the works of the law or by the hearing of faith.* They very well knew that it was not the former, but the latter; and therefore must needs be inexcusable in forsaking a doctrine which had been so signally owned and attested.

Verses 6–18

He largely proves the doctrine which he had reproved them for rejecting.

I. From the example of Abraham's justification (*v.* 6). His faith fastened upon the promise of God, and upon his believing he was owned and accepted of God as a righteous man.

Those who are of faith are the children of Abraham (*v.* 7). Abraham was justified by faith, and so are they (*v.* 8).

God would justify the heathen world in the way of faith; and therefore in Abraham, that is, in the seed of Abraham, which is Christ, not the Jews only, but the Gentiles also, should be blessed as Abraham was, being justified as he was. It was through faith in the promise of God that he was blessed, and it is only in the same way that others obtain this privilege.

II. We cannot be justified but by faith fastening on the gospel, because the law condemns us. If we put ourselves upon trial in that court, we are certainly lost and undone, *v.* 10.

JAMIESON, FAUSSET, BROWN

ress, unless they continue to maintain a pure faith [BENGEL]. **4. Have ye suffered so many things**—viz., persecution from Jews and from unbelieving fellow countrymen, incited by the Jews, at the time of your conversion. **in vain**—*fruitlessly, needlessly,* since ye might have avoided them by professing Judaism [GROTIUS]. Or, shall ye, by falling from grace, lose the reward promised for all your sufferings, so that they shall be "in vain" (ch. 4:11; I Cor. 15:2, 17-19, 29-32; II Thess. 1:5-7; II John 8)? **yet** rather, "If it be *really* (or 'indeed') in vain" [ELLICOTT]. "If, as it must be, what I have said, 'in vain,' is really the fact" [ALFORD]. I prefer understanding it as a mitigation of the preceding words. I hope better things of you, for I trust you will return from legalism to grace; if *so,* as I confidently expect, you will not have "suffered so many things in vain" [ESTIUS]. For "God has given you the Spirit and has wrought mighty works among you" (vs. 5; Heb. 10:32-36) [BENGEL]. **5. He . . . that ministereth**—or "supplieth," God (II Cor. 9:10). He who *supplied and supplies* to you the Spirit *still,* to the present time. These miracles do not prove grace to be in the heart (Mark 9:38, 39). He speaks of these miracles as a matter of *unquestioned notoriety* among those addressed; an undesigned proof of their genuineness (cf. I Cor. 12). **worketh miracles among you**—rather, "IN you," as ch. 2:8; Matthew 14:2; Ephesians 2:2; Philippians 2:13; at your conversion and since [ALFORD]. **doeth he it by the works of the law**—i.e., as a consequence *resulting from* (so the *Greek*) the works of the law (cf. vs. 2). This cannot be because the law was then unknown to you when you received those gifts of the Spirit. **6.** The answer to the question in vs. 5 is here taken for granted, *It was by the hearing of faith:* following this up, he says, "Even as Abraham *believed . . .*" (Gen. 15:4-6; Rom. 4:3). God supplies unto you the Spirit as the result of faith, not works, just as Abraham obtained justification by faith, not by works (vss. 6, 8, 16; ch. 4:22, 26, 28). Where justification is, there the Spirit is, so that if the former comes *by faith,* the latter must also. **7. they which are of faith**—as the source and starting point of their spiritual life. The same phrase is in the *Greek* of Romans 3:26. **the same**—*these, and these alone,* to the exclusion of all the other descendants of Abraham. **children**—*Greek,* "sons" (vs. 29). **8. And**—*Greek,* "Moreover." **foreseeing**—One great excellency of Scripture is, that in it all points liable ever to be controverted, are, with prescient wisdom, decided in the most appropriate language. **would justify**—rather, "justifieth." Present indicative. It is now, and at all times, God's *one* way of justification. **the heathen**—rather, "the Gentiles"; or "the nations," as the same *Greek* is translated at the end of the verse. God justifieth the *Jews,* too, "by faith, not by works." But he specifies *the Gentiles* in particular here. as it was *their* case that was in question, the Galatians being Gentiles. **preached before the gospel**—"announced beforehand the Gospel." For the "promise" was substantially the Gospel by anticipation. Cf. John 8:56; Hebrews 4:2. A proof that "the old fathers did not look only for transitory promises" (Article VII, Church of England). Thus the Gospel, in its essential germ, is older than the law though the full development of the former is subsequent to the latter. **In thee**—not "in thy seed," which is a point not here raised; but strictly "in thee," as followers of thy faith, it having first shown the way to justification before God [ALFORD]; or "in thee," as Father of the promised seed, viz., Christ (vs. 16), who is the Object of faith (Gen. 22:18; Ps. 72:17), and imitating thy faith (see *Note,* vs. 9). **all nations**—or as above, "all *the Gentiles*" (Gen. 12:3; 18:18; 22:18). **be blessed**—an act of grace, not something earned by works. The blessing of justification was to Abraham by faith in the promise, not by works. So to those who follow Abraham, the father of the faithful, the blessing, i.e., justification, comes purely by faith in Him who is the subject of the promise. **9. they**—and they alone. **of faith**—*Note,* vs. 7, beginning. **with**—together with. **faithful**—implying what it is in which they are "blessed together with him," viz., faith, the prominent feature of his character, and of which the result to all who like him have it, is justification. **10.** Confirmation of vs. 9. They who depend on the works of the law cannot share the blessing, for they are under the curse "written," Deuteronomy 27:26, LXX. PERFECT *obedience* is required by the words, "in all things." CONTINUAL *obedience* by the word, "continueth." No man renders this obedience (cf. Rom. 3:19, 20). It is observable, Paul quotes Scripture to the Jews who were conversant with it, as in Epistle to the He-

ADAM CLARKE

4. *Have ye suffered so many things in vain?* Have you received and lost so much good? The verb signifies to "suffer pain or loss" or to "possess and enjoy." Though it is possible that the Galatians had *suffered* some persecution for the truth of Christ, yet it is as likely that the apostle refers to the benefits which they had received. You have received faith, the pardon of your sins, the gift of the Holy Spirit, and with it many extraordinary gifts and graces. Have you received all these *in vain? if . . . yet in vain*—if it be credible that you have sacrificed so many excellent benefits for an imaginary good.

5. *He therefore that ministereth to you the Spirit.* The apostle means himself; he had been the means of conveying the Holy Spirit to them, and by that *Spirit* he wrought miracles among them. And he did all this, not as a Jew (for as such he had no power), but he did all as a believer in Christ. The word which we translate *ministereth* is very emphatic and signifies "leading up the chorus," bringing up one after another, adding grace to grace, benefit to benefit; so that it appears that they had not only some, but many, benefits, God by means of His apostle having greatly enriched them with various spiritual blessings.

6. *Abraham believed God.* This is quoted from Gen. xv. 6; and Paul produces it, Rom. iv. 3-5. Abraham, while even uncircumcised, believed in God, and his faith was reckoned to him for justification; and Abraham is called the "father of the faithful" or "of believers." If then he was justified by faith long before the law was given, the law is not necessary to salvation. It is remarkable that the Jews themselves maintained that Abraham was saved by faith. Mehilta, in *Yalcut Simeoni,* p. 1, fol. 69, makes this assertion: "It is evident that Abraham could not obtain an inheritance either in this world or in the world to come but by faith."

8. *The scripture, foreseeing.* See the notes on Rom. iv. 3-16.

As God intended to justify the heathen through faith, He *preached the gospel* that contains the grand display of the doctrine of salvation by faith, *before,* to *Abraham,* while he was in his heathen state; and thus he is called "the father of believers." Therefore it must refer to them who shall believe the same gospel among the Gentiles, consequently the promise was fulfilled: *In thee shall all nations* [*of the earth*] *be blessed.*

9. *They which be of faith.* All who believe, as Abraham has believed, are made partakers of Abraham's blessings.

10. *As many as are of the works of the law.* All that seek salvation by the performance of the works of the law are under the curse, because it is impossible for them to come up to the spiritual meaning and intent of the law; and the law pronounces them *cursed* that *continueth not in all things which are written in the book of the law to do them.* Hence every Jew is necessarily under the curse of God's broken law; and every sinner is under the same curse, though he be not a Jew, who does not take refuge in the salvation provided for him by the gospel.

MATTHEW HENRY

III. The apostle alleges the express testimony of the Old Testament, *v.* 11. *The just shall live by faith.* It is only through faith that persons become righteous, and as such obtain this life and happiness. *The law is not of faith,* but the language of it is, *The man that doeth them shall live in them.* It requires perfect obedience as the condition of life, and therefore now can by no means be the rule of our justification.

The condition of life, by the law, is perfect, personal, and perpetual obedience; the language of it is as *v.* 12. Unless our obedience be universal, and unless it be perpetual too, we fall under the curse of the law. If, as transgressors of the law, we are under the curse of it, it must be a vain thing to look for justification by it. Yet the apostle afterwards acquaints us that there is a way open to our escaping this curse, through faith in Christ (as he says, *v.* 13). A strange method it was which Christ took to redeem us from the curse of the law; it was *by his being himself made a curse for us.*

MARTIN LUTHER:

Not only my sins and yours, but the sins of the entire world, past, present, and future, attack Him, try to damn Him, and do in fact damn Him. But because in the same Person, who is the highest, the greatest, and the only sinner, there is also eternal and invincible righteousness, therefore these two converge: the highest, the greatest, and the only sin; and the highest, the greatest, and the only righteousness. Here one of them must yield and be conquered, since they come together and collide with such a powerful impact. Thus the sin of the entire world attacks righteousness with the greatest possible impact and fury. What happens? Righteousness is eternal, immortal, and invincible. Sin, too, is a very powerful and cruel tyrant, dominating and ruling over the whole world, capturing and enslaving all men. In short, sin is a great and powerful god who devours the whole human race, all the learned, holy, powerful, wise, and unlearned men. He, I say, attacks Christ and wants to devour Him as he has devoured all the rest. But he does not see that He is a person of invincible and eternal righteousness. In this duel, therefore, it is necessary for sin to be conquered and killed, and for righteousness to prevail and live. Thus in Christ all sin is conquered, killed, and buried; and righteousness remains the victor and the ruler eternally.

Thus also death, which is the almighty empress of the entire world, killing kings, princes, and all men in general, clashes against life with full force and is about to conquer it and swallow it; and what it attempts, it accomplishes. But because life was immortal, it emerged victorious when it had been conquered, conquering and killing death in turn. The Prince of life, who died, is alive and reigns. Through Christ, therefore, death is conquered and abolished in the whole world, so that now it is nothing but a picture of death. Now that its sting is lost, it can no longer harm believers in Christ, who has become the death of death, as Hosea sings (13:14): "O death, I shall be your death!"

—*Luther's Works*

JAMIESON, FAUSSET, BROWN

brews, as *said* or *spoken;* but to the Gentiles, as *written.* So Matthew, writing for Jews, quotes it as *said,* or *spoken;* Mark and Luke, writing for Gentiles, as *written* (Matt. 1:22; Mark 1:2; Luke 2: 22, 23) [Townson]. **11. by the law**—*Greek,* "IN the law." Both *in* and *by* are included. The syllogism in this verse and vs. 12, is, according to Scripture, "The just shall live by faith." But the law is not of faith, but of doing, or works (i.e., does not make faith, but works, the conditional ground of justifying). Therefore "in," or "by the law, no man is justified before God" (whatever the case may be *before men,* Rom. 4:2),—not even if he could, which he cannot, keep the law, because the Scripture element and conditional mean of justification is *faith.* **The just shall live by faith**—(Rom. 1:17; Hab. 2:4). Not as Bengel and Alford, "He who is just by faith shall live." The *Greek* supports *English Version.* Also the contrast is between "live *by faith*" (viz., as the ground and source of his justification), and "live *in them,*" viz., in his doings or works (vs. 12), as the *conditional element wherein* he is justified. **12. doeth**—Many depended on the law although they did not keep it; but without doing, saith Paul, it is of no use to them (Rom. 2:13, 17, 23; 10: 5). **13.** Abrupt exclamation, as he breaks away impatiently *from* those who would involve us again in the curse of the *law,* by seeking justification in it, *to "Christ,"* who "has redeemed us from its curse." The "us" refers primarily to the Jews, to whom the law principally appertained, in contrast to "the Gentiles" (vs. 14; cf. ch. 4:3, 4). But it is not *restricted* solely to the Jews, as Alford thinks; for these are the representative people of the world at large, and their "law" is the embodiment of what God requires of the whole world. The curse of its non-fulfilment affects the Gentiles through the Jews; for the law represents that righteousness which God requires of all, and which, since the Jews failed to fulfil, the Gentiles are equally unable to fulfil. Verse 10, "As many as are of the works of the law, are under the curse," refers plainly, not to *the Jews only,* but to all, even Gentiles (as the Galatians), who seek justification by the law. The Jews' law represents the universal law which condemned the Gentiles, though with less clear consciousness on their part (Rom. 2). The revelation of God's "wrath" by the law of conscience, in some degree prepared the Gentiles for appreciating redemption through Christ when revealed. The curse had to be removed from off the heathen, too, as well as the Jews, in order that the blessing, through Abraham, might flow to them. Accordingly, the "we," in "that *we* might receive the promise of the Spirit," plainly refers to both Jews and Gentiles. **redeemed us**—*bought us off* from our former bondage (ch. 4:5), and "from the curse" under which all lie who trust to the law and the works of the law for justification. The Gentile Galatians, by putting themselves under the law, were involving themselves in the curse from which Christ has redeemed the Jews primarily, and through them the Gentiles. The ransom price He paid was His own precious blood (I Pet. 1:18, 19; cf. Matt. 20:28; Acts 20:28; I Cor. 6:20; 7:23; I Tim. 2:6; II Peter 2:1; Rev. 5:9). **being made**—*Greek,* "having become." **a curse for us**—Having become what we were, *in our behalf,* "a curse," that we might cease to be a curse. Not merely *accursed* (in the concrete), but *a curse* in the abstract, *bearing the universal curse of the whole human race.* So II Corinthians 5:21, "Sin for us," not *sinful,* but bearing the whole sin of our race, regarded as *one* vast aggregate of sin. See *Note* there. "Anathema" means "set apart to God," to His glory, but to the person's own destruction. *"Curse,"* an execration. **written**—Deuteronomy 21:23. Christ's bearing the *particular* curse of hanging on the tree, is a sample of the *general* curse which He representatively bore. Not that the Jews put to death malefactors by hanging; but *after* having put them to death otherwise, in order to brand them with peculiar ignominy, they *hung* the bodies on a tree, and such malefactors were accursed by the law (cf. Acts 5:30; 10:39). God's providence ordered it so that to fulfil the prophecy of the curse and other prophecies, Jesus should be crucified, and so *hang* on the tree, though that death was not a Jewish mode of execution. The Jews accordingly, in contempt, call Him "the *hanged* one," *Tolvi,* and Christians, "worshippers of the hanged one"; and make it their great objection that He died the accursed death [Trypho, in *Justin Martyr,* p. 249; I Pet. 2:24]. Hung between heaven and earth as though unworthy of either! **14.** The intent of "Christ becoming a curse for us"; "To the end that upon the Gentiles the blessing of Abraham (i.e., *promised to*

ADAM CLARKE

11. *But that no man is justified by the law,* by the observance of the law, suppose he had even continued in all things that are written in it to do them, *is evident;*

for the Prophet Habakkuk, chap. ii. 4, has declared, under the direct influence of the Spirit of God, *The just shall live by faith;* or, "He who is just by faith shall live." Therefore this justification comes not by works, or the observance of the law, but by faith.

12. *And the law is not of faith.* It promises no forgiveness to believing, but requires obedience. It is not, What do you believe? but, What have you done? *The man that doeth them* perfectly at all times, and in all places, *he shall live in them;* but if in any case he fails, he forfeits his life.

13. *Christ hath redeemed us.* "Hath bought us with a price"; viz., His blood, or life.

Being made a curse for us. Being made an Atonement for our sins; for whatever was offered as an atonement for sin was considered as bearing the punishment due to sin, and the person who suffered for transgression was considered as bearing the curse in his body. Therefore in the same day in which a criminal was executed it was ordered that his body should be buried, that the land might not be polluted; because he that was hanged, which was the case with every heinous culprit, was considered accursed of God, Deut. xxi. 22-23.

MATTHEW HENRY

The design of this was *that the blessing of Abraham might come on the Gentiles through Jesus Christ*—that all who believed on Christ might become heirs of Abraham's blessing, and particularly of that great promise of the Spirit. Hence it appeared that it was not by putting themselves under the law, but by faith in Christ, that they became the people of God and heirs of the promise.

IV. The apostle urges the stability of the covenant which God made with Abraham, which was not disannulled by the giving of the law to Moses, *v.* 15, &c. Faith had the precedence of the law, for Abraham was justified by faith. God entered into covenant with Abraham (*v.* 8). The original word signifies both a covenant and a testament.

If it should be said that a testament may be defeated for want of persons to claim the benefit of it (*v.* 16), he shows that there is no danger of that. Abraham is dead, and the prophets are dead, but the covenant is made with Abraham and his seed.

Says the apostle, "It points at a single person—*that seed is Christ.*" So that the covenant is still in force; for Christ abideth for ever.

JAMIESON, FAUSSET, BROWN

Abraham, viz., justification by faith) might come in Christ Jesus" (cf. vs. 8). **that we might receive the promise of the Spirit**—the promised Spirit (Joel 2: 28, 29; Luke 24:49). This clause follows not the clause immediately preceding (for *our receiving the Spirit* is not the result of the *blessing of Abraham coming on the Gentiles*), but "Christ hath redeemed us . . ." **through faith**—not by works. Here he resumes the thought in vs. 2. "The Spirit from without, kindles within us some spark of faith whereby we lay hold of Christ, and even of the Spirit Himself, that He may dwell within us" [FLACIUS]. **15. I speak after the manner of men**—I take an illustration from a merely human transaction of everyday occurrence. **but a man's covenant**—whose purpose it is far less important to maintain. **if it be confirmed**—when once it hath been ratified. **no man disannulleth**—"none setteth aside," not even the author himself, much less any second party. None does so who acts in common equity. Much less would the righteous God do so. *The law* is here, by personification, regarded as a second person, distinct from, and subsequent to, *the promise of God. The promise* is everlasting, and more peculiarly belongs to God. *The law* is regarded as something extraneous, afterwards introduced, exceptional and temporary (vss. 17-19, 21-24). **addeth**—None addeth new conditions "making" the covenant "of none effect" (vs. 17). So legal Judaism could make no alteration in the fundamental relation between God and man, already established by the promises to Abraham; it could not add as a new condition the observance of the law, in which case the fulfilment of the promise would be attached to a condition impossible for man to perform. The "covenant" here is one of free grace, a *promise* afterwards carried into effect in the Gospel. **16.** This verse is parenthetical. The covenant of promise was not "spoken" (so *Greek* for "made") to Abraham alone, but "to Abraham and his seed"; to the latter especially; and this means Christ (and that which is inseparable from Him, the *literal Israel*, and *the spiritual*, His body, the Church). Christ not having come when the law was given, the covenant could not have been then fulfilled, but awaited the coming of Him, the Seed, to whom it was spoken. **promises**—plural, because the same promise was often repeated (Gen. 12:3, 7; 15:5, 18; 17:7; 22:18), and because it involved many things; earthly blessings to the literal children of Abraham in Canaan, and spiritual and heavenly blessings to his spiritual children; but both promised to Christ, "the Seed" and representative Head of the literal and spiritual Israel alike. In the spiritual seed there is no distinction of Jew or Greek; but to the literal seed, the promises still in part remain to be fulfilled (Rom. 11:26). The covenant was not made with "many" seeds (which if there had been, a pretext might exist for supposing there was one seed before the law, another under the law; and that those sprung from one seed, say the Jewish, are admitted on different terms, and with a higher degree of acceptability, than those sprung from the Gentile seed), but with the one seed; therefore, the promise that in Him "all the families of the earth shall be blessed" (Gen. 12:3), joins in this one Seed, Christ, Jew and Gentile, as fellow heirs on the same terms of acceptability, viz., by grace through faith (Rom. 4:13); not to some by promise, to others by the law, but to all alike, circumcised and uncircumcised, constituting but one seed in Christ (Rom. 4:16). The law, on the other hand, contemplates the Jews and Gentiles as distinct seeds. God makes a covenant, but it is one of promise; whereas the law is a covenant of works. Whereas the law brings in a mediator, a third party (vss. 19, 20), God makes His covenant of promise with the one seed, Christ (Gen. 17:7), and embraces others only as they are identified with, and represented by, Christ. **one . . . Christ**—not in the exclusive sense, the man Christ *Jesus*, but "Christ" (*Jesus* is not added, which would limit the meaning), including *His people* who are *part of Himself*, the Second Adam, and Head of redeemed humanity. Verses 28, 29 prove this, "Ye are all ONE in Christ Jesus" (Jesus is added here as the person is indicated). "And *if* ye be Christ's, ye are Abraham's SEED, heirs according to *the promise*." **17. this I say**—"this is what I mean," by what I said in vs. 15. **confirmed . . . of God**—"*ratified by* God" (vs. 15). **in Christ**—rather, "unto Christ" (cf. vs. 16). However, *Vulgate* and the old *Italian* versions translate as *English Version*. But the oldest MSS. omit the words altogether. **the law which was**—*Greek*, "which came into existence 430 years after" (Exod. 12:40, 41). He does not, as in the case of "the covenant," add "enacted *by God*" (John

ADAM CLARKE

14. *That the blessing of Abraham.* That is, justification or the pardon of sin, with all other blessings consequent on it, such as peace with God, spiritual life, and eternal glory. *Might come on the Gentiles through Jesus Christ.* So we find that He was made a curse for us that the blessings promised to Abraham might be given to them who believe on Him, as having been made a curse; i.e., an expiatory Victim for them. *The promise of the Spirit.* The spirit of adoption, sonship with God; and *Spirit* of God to attest that sonship. All this was *through faith.* Hence, from the beginning God had purposed that salvation should be *through faith,* and never expected that any soul of man should be justified by the works of the law; and gave that law only that the exceeding sinfulness of sin might appear, and that man might be prepared to welcome the gospel, which proclaimed salvation to a lost world through the atoning passion and death of Christ.

15. *I speak after the manner of men.* I am about to produce an example taken from civil transactions. *If it be confirmed*—if an agreement or bond be signed, sealed, and witnessed. *No man disannulleth.* It stands under the protection of the civil law, and nothing can be legally erased or added.

16. *Now to Abraham and his seed.* The promise of salvation by faith was made to Abraham and his posterity.

He saith not, And to seeds. It was one particular kind of posterity which was intended: *but as of one . . . which is Christ;* i.e., to the spiritual Head, and all believers in Him, who are children of Abraham, because they are believers, v. 7. But why does the apostle say, Not of *seeds, as of many?* To this it is answered that Abraham possessed in his family two seeds: one natural, viz., the members of his own household; and the other spiritual, those who were like himself because of their faith. The promises were not of a temporal nature. Had they been so, they would have belonged to his natural seed. But they did not; therefore they must have belonged to the spiritual posterity.

17. *Confirmed before of God in Christ.* I.e., the promise of justification made to believers in Christ Jesus, who are the spiritual seed of Christ, as they are children of Abraham from the similitude of their faith. Abraham believed in God and it was reckoned to him for justification; the Gentiles believed in Christ and received justification. *Four hundred and thirty*

MATTHEW HENRY

MARTIN LUTHER:

A great emphasis, or rather irony, is concealed in Paul's explicit reference to four hundred and thirty years. It is as though he were saying: "If you understand arithmetic, count on your fingers what the interval is between the giving of the promise and the Law. Certainly there was a promise a long time ago, even while there was no Law (that is, for four hundred and thirty years)." Therefore this is a rather vigorous argument based on a specific interval.—*Luther's Works*

The subsequent law could not disannul the previous covenant or promise (*v.* 18). If the inheritance was given to Abraham by promise, we may be sure that God would not retract that promise; for he is not a man that he should repent.

Verses 19–29

Why did God give the law by Moses?

I. The law *was added because of transgressions, v.* 19. The Israelites were sinners as well as others, and therefore the law was given to convince them of their sin. And it was also intended to restrain them from the commission of sin.

The law was given for this purpose *till the seed should come to whom the promise was made.* The law was added because of transgressions, till this fulness of time should come. But when a fuller discovery of divine grace in the promise was made, then the law, as given by Moses, was to cease. And though the law, considered as the law of nature, is always in force, yet we are now no longer under the bondage and terror of that legal covenant. The law then was only to lead men to see their need of the promise, by showing them the sinfulness of sin, and to point them to Christ. Whereas the promise was given immediately by God himself, the law was given *by the ministry of angels, and the hand of a mediator.*

Hence it appeared that the law could not be designed to set aside the promise; for (*v.* 20), *God is one,* and therefore it is not to be supposed that he should make void a promise which he had long before made to Abraham. This would not have been consistent with his truth and faithfulness. Moses was only a mediator, and therefore the law that was given by him could not affect the promise.

JAMIESON, FAUSSET, BROWN

1:17). The dispensation of "the promise" began with the call of Abraham from Ur into Canaan, and ended on the last night of his grandson Jacob's sojourn in Canaan, the *land of promise.* The dispensation of the law, which engenders bondage, was beginning to draw on from the time of his entrance into Egypt, the land of bondage. It was to Christ in him, as in his grandfather Abraham, and his father Isaac, not to him or them as persons, the promise was spoken. On the day following the last repetition of the promise orally (Gen. 46: 1-6), at Beersheba, Israel passed into Egypt. It is from the end, not from the beginning of the dispensation of promise, that the interval of 430 years between it and the law is to be counted. At Beersheba, after the covenant with Abimelech, Abraham called on the everlasting God, and the well was confirmed to him and his seed as an everlasting possession. Here God appeared to Isaac. Here Jacob received the promise of the blessing, for which God had called Abraham out of Ur, repeated for the last time, on the last night of his sojourn in the land of promise. **cannot**—*Greek,* "doth not disannul." **make . . . of none effect**—The promise would become so, if the power of conferring the inheritance be transferred from it to the law (Rom. 4:14). **18. the inheritance**—all the blessings to be inherited by Abraham's literal and spiritual children, according to the promise made to him and to his Seed, Christ, justification and glorification (ch. 4:7; Rom. 8:17; I Cor. 6:9). **but God . . .**—The *Greek* order requires rather, "But to Abraham it was by promise that God hath given it." The conclusion is, *Therefore the inheritance is not of, or from, the law* (Rom. 4:14). **19.** "Wherefore then serveth the law?" as it is of no avail for justification, is it either useless, or contrary to the covenant of God? [CALVIN.] **added**—to the original covenant of promise. This is not inconsistent with vss. 15, "No man addeth thereto"; for there the kind of *addition* meant, and therefore denied, is one that would add *new conditions,* inconsistent with the grace of the covenant of promise. The law, though misunderstood by the Judaizers as doing so, was really added for a different purpose, viz., "because of (or as the *Greek,* 'for the sake of') the transgressions," i.e., to bring out into clearer view *the transgressions* of it (Rom. 7:7-9); to make men more fully conscious of their *sins,* by being perceived as *transgressions of the law,* and so to make them long for the promised Saviour. This accords with vss. 23, 24; Romans 4:15. The meaning can hardly be "*to check* transgressions," for the law rather stimulates the corrupt heart to disobey it (Rom. 5:20; 7:13). **till the seed**—*during the period up to the time when the* seed came. The law was a preparatory dispensation for the Jewish nation (Rom. 5:20; *Greek,* "the law came in *additionally* and *incidentally*"), intervening between the promise and its fulfilment in Christ. **come**—(Cf. "faith *came,*" vs. 23). **the promise**—(Rom. 4:21). **ordained**—*Greek,* "constituted" or "disposed." **by angels**—as the *instrumental enactors* of the law [ALFORD] God delegated the law to angels as something rather alien to Him and severe (Acts 7:53; Heb. 2:2, 3; cf. Deut. 33:2, "He came with ten thousands of saints," i.e., angels, Ps. 68:17). He reserved "the promise" to Himself and dispensed it according to His own goodness. **in the hand of a mediator**—viz., Moses. Deuteronomy 5:5, "I stood *between* the Lord and you": the very definition of a mediator. Hence the phrase often recurs, "By the hand of Moses." In the giving of the law, the "angels" were representatives of God; Moses, as mediator, represented the people. **20.** "Now a mediator cannot be of one (but must be of *two* parties whom he mediates between); but God is one" (not two: owing to His essential *unity* not admitting of an intervening party between Him and those to be blessed; but as the ONE Sovereign, His own representative, giving the blessing *directly* by *promise* to Abraham, and, in its fulfilment, to Christ, "the Seed," without new condition, and without a mediator such as the law had). The conclusion understood is, *Therefore a mediator cannot appertain to God;* and consequently, the law, with its inseparable appendage of a mediator, cannot be the normal way of dealing of God, the one, and unchangeable God, who dealt with Abraham by *direct* promise, as a sovereign, not as one forming a compact with another party, with conditions and a mediator attached thereto. God would bring man into immediate communion with Him, and not have man separated from Him by a mediator that keeps back from access, as Moses and the legal priesthood did (Exod. 19:12, 13, 17, 21-24; Heb. 12:19-24). The law that thus interposed a mediator and conditions between man

ADAM CLARKE

years after. God made a covenant with Abraham that the Messiah should spring from his posterity. This covenant stated that justification should be obtained by faith in the Messiah. The law was given 430 years after the covenant with Abraham; therefore the law could not possibly annul the Abrahamic covenant.

19. *Wherefore then serveth the law?* If the law does not annul the Abrahamic covenant, and cannot confer salvation on its votaries, why did God give it? This was a very natural objection, and must arise in the mind of any Jew who had paid attention to the apostle's reasoning. *It was added because of transgressions.* It was given that we might know our sinfulness, and the need we stood in of the mercy of God.

Till the seed should come. The law was to be in force till the advent of the Messiah. After that it was to cease.

It was ordained by angels. The ministry of angels was certainly used in giving the law; see Ps. lxviii. 17; Acts vii. 53; and Heb. ii. 2; but they were only instruments for transmitting. Moses was the mediator between God and the people, Deut. v. 5.

20. *A mediator is not a mediator of one.* As a mediator signifies a "middle person," there must necessarily be two parties between whom he stands and acts in reference to both, as he is supposed to have the interests of both equally at heart. Though Moses was the mediator between God and the Israelites, yet he was not the mediator between God and that one seed which was to come; viz., the Gentiles who should believe in Christ. *But God is one.* He is the one God, who is the Father of the spirits of all flesh, the God of the Gentiles as well a the God of the Jews. That this is Paul's meaning is evident from his use of the same words in other places, 1 Tim. ii. 5: "For there is one God, and one mediator between God and man"; that is, There is only one God and one Mediator for the whole human race. The sense of the whole is: Moses was the mediator of one part of Abraham's seed, viz., the Israelites; but of the other seed, the Gentiles, he was certainly not the mediator; for the Mediator of that seed,

MATTHEW HENRY

II. The law was given to convince men of the necessity of a Saviour (*v.* 21). The law is by no means inconsistent with the promise. The design of it is to discover men's transgressions, and to show them the need they have of a better righteousness than that of the law.

The scripture hath concluded all under sin (*v.* 22). The law discovered their wounds, but could not afford them a remedy.

The great design of it was *that the promise by faith of Jesus Christ might be given to those that believe*, that being convinced of the insufficiency of the law to effect a righteousness for them, they might be persuaded to believe on Christ, and so obtain the benefit of the promise.

III. The law was designed for *a schoolmaster, to bring men to Christ, v.* 24. They were shut up, held under the terror and discipline of it, as prisoners in a state of confinement. Hereby they might be disposed more readily to accept Christ when he came into the world. It was proper to convince them of their lost and undone condition in themselves, and to let them see the weakness and insufficiency of their own righteousness. And thus it was their schoolmaster, to instruct and govern them in their state of minority, their *servant*, to lead and conduct them to Christ (as children were wont to be led to school by those servants who had the care of them); that they might be more fully instructed by him as their schoolmaster, in the true way of justification and salvation, which is only by faith in him.

The apostle adds (*v.* 25) *after faith has come, we are no longer under a schoolmaster*—we have no such need of the law to direct us to him as there was then.

JAMIESON, FAUSSET, BROWN

and God, was an exceptional state limited to the Jews, and parenthetically preparatory to the Gospel, God's normal mode of dealing, as He dealt with Abraham, viz., *face to face directly;* by *promise* and *grace,* and not conditions; *to all nations united* by faith *in the one seed* (Eph. 2:14, 16, 18), and not to one people to the exclusion and severance from the ONE common Father, of all other nations.

21. "Is the *law* (which involves a mediator) against the promises of God (which are without a mediator, and *rest on God* alone and immediately)? God forbid." **life**—The law, as an externally prescribed rule, can never internally impart spiritual life to men naturally dead in sin, and change the disposition. If the law had been a law capable of giving *life,* "verily (in very reality, and not in the mere fancy of legalists) righteousness would have been by the law" (for where life is, there righteousness, its *condition,* must also be). But the law does not *pretend* to give life, and therefore not righteousness; so there is no opposition between the law and the promise. Righteousness can only come through the promise to Abraham, and through its fulfilment in the Gospel of grace. **22. But**—as the law cannot give life or righteousness [ALFORD]. Or the "But" means, So far is *righteousness* from being of the law, that the *knowledge of sin* is rather what comes of the law [BENGEL]. **the scripture**—which began to be written after the time of the promise, at the time when the law was given. The *written* letter was needed so as PERMANENTLY to convict man of disobedience to God's command. Therefore he says, "the Scripture," not the "Law." Cf. vs. 8, "Scripture," for "the God of the Scripture." **concluded**—"shut up," under condemnation, as in a prison. Cf. Isaiah 24: 22, "As prisoners gathered in the pit and shut up in the prison." Beautifully contrasted with "the liberty wherewith Christ makes free," which follows, vss. 7, 9, 25, 26; ch. 5:1; Isaiah 61:1. **all**—*Greek* neuter, "the universe of things": the whole world, man, and all that appertains to him. **under sin**—(Rom. 3:9, 19; 11:32). **the promise**—*the inheritance promised* (vs. 18). **by faith of Jesus Christ**—i.e., which is by faith in Jesus Christ. **might be given**—The emphasis is on "given": that it might be a free *gift;* not something earned by the works of the law (Rom. 6:23). **to them that believe**—to them that have "the faith of (in) Jesus Christ" just spoken of. **23. faith**—viz., that just mentioned (vs. 22), of which Christ is the object. **kept**—*Greek,* "kept in ward": the effect of the "shutting up" (vs. 22; ch. 4:2; Rom. 7:6). **unto**—"with a view to the faith . . . ." We were, in a manner, morally forced to it, so that there remained to us no refuge but faith. Cf. the phrase, Psalm 78:50; *Margin,* 31:8. **which should afterwards . . .**—"which was afterwards to be revealed." **24.** "*So that* the law *hath been* (i.e., hath *turned out to be*) our schoolmaster (or "tutor," lit., "pedagogue": this term, among the Greeks, meant a faithful servant entrusted with the care of the boy from childhood to puberty, to keep him from evil, physical and moral, and accompany him to his amusements and studies) to guide us unto Christ," with whom we are no longer "shut up" in bondage, but are freemen. "Children" (lit., *infants*) need such *tutoring* (ch. 4:3). **might be**—rather, "that we *may* be justified by faith"; which we could not be till Christ, the object of faith, had come. Meanwhile the law, by outwardly checking the sinful propensity which was constantly giving fresh proof of its refractoriness—as thus the consciousness of the power of the sinful principle became more vivid, and hence the sense of need both of forgiveness of sin and freedom from its bondage was awakened—the law became a "schoolmaster to guide us unto Christ" [NEANDER]. The *moral* law shows us what we ought to do, and so we learn our inability to do it. In the *ceremonial* law we seek, by animal sacrifices, to answer for our not having done it, but find dead victims no satisfaction for the sins of living men, and that outward purifying will not cleanse the soul; and that therefore we need an infinitely better Sacrifice, the antitype of all the legal sacrifices. Thus delivered up to the *judicial* law, we see how awful is the doom we deserve: thus the law at last leads us to Christ, with whom we find righteousness and peace. *"Sin, sin!* is the word heard again and again in the Old Testament. Had it not there for centuries rung in the ear, and fastened on the conscience, the joyful sound, 'grace for grace,' would not have been the watchword of the New Testament. This was the end of the whole system of sacrifices" [THOLUCK]. **25.** "But *now that* faith is come . . . ." Moses the lawgiver cannot bring us into the heavenly Canaan though he can bring us to the border of it. At that point he is

ADAM CLARKE

according to the promise of God and covenant made with Abraham, is Christ.

21. *Is the law then against the promises of God?* Is it possible that the intervention of the law, in reference to one part of the Abrahamic seed, should annul the promise made to the other? It is impossible. *For if there had been a law.* If any *law* or "rule" of life could have been found out that would *have given life*—saved sinners from death, and made them truly happy—then *righteousness,* "justification," *should have been by the law.*

22. *But the scripture hath concluded.* All the writings of the prophets have uniformly declared that men are all sinners, and the law declares the same by the continual sacrifices which it prescribes. All therefore have sinned and come short of the glory of God; and being tried and found guilty, "the Scripture hath shut them up"—put them in prison, and locked them up, till the time should come in which the sentence of the law should be executed upon them.

23. *But before faith came.* Before the gospel was published. *We were kept under the law, shut up.* "We were kept as in a stronghold, locked up, unto the faith," the religion of the Lord Jesus, *which should afterwards be revealed.*

24. *The law was our schoolmaster.* "The law was our pedagogue into Christ." The pedagogue is not the *schoolmaster,* but the servant who had the care of the children to lead them to and bring them back from school, and had the care of them out of school hours. Thus the law did not teach us the living, saving knowledge; but by its rites and ceremonies, and especially by its sacrifices, it directed us to Christ, that we might be justified by faith. This is a beautiful metaphor and highly illustrative of the apostle's doctrine.

25. *But after that faith is come.* When Christ was manifested in the flesh and the gospel was preached, we were no longer under the pedagogue; we came to Christ, learned of Him, be-

MATTHEW HENRY

1. The goodness of God to his people of old, in giving the law to them. It furnished them with sufficient helps both to direct them in their duty to God and to encourage their hopes in him.

2. The great fault and folly of the Jews, in mistaking the design of the law. They expected to be justified by the works of it, whereas it was never designed to be the rule of their justification, but only a means of convincing them of their guilt and of their need of a Saviour.

3. The great advantage of the gospel state above the legal. We are not now treated as children in a state of minority, but as sons grown up to a full age.

(1) *We are the children of God by faith in Christ Jesus, v.* 26. The great privilege which real Christians enjoy under the gospel: They are no longer accounted servants, but *sons.* They are admitted into the number, and have a right to all the privileges of his children. How they come to obtain this privilege *by faith in Christ Jesus.* This faith in Christ, whereby they became the children of God (*v.* 27), was what they professed in baptism. Having thus become the members of Christ, they were owned as the children of God. Baptism is now the solemn rite of our admission into the Christian church. *Those who are baptized into Christ have put on Christ;* under the gospel baptism comes in the room of circumcision. Being baptized into Christ, we are baptized into his death, that as he died and rose again, so we should die unto sin, and walk in newness of life; it would be of great advantage to us did we oftener remember this.

(2) This privilege of being the children of God is now enjoyed in common by all real Christians. The law indeed made a difference between Jew and Greek, between *bond and free*, and between *male and female.* But it is not so now; they all stand on the same level, *and are all one in Christ Jesus.* All who sincerely believe on Christ, of what nation, or sex, or condition, soever they be, are accepted of him, and become the children of God through faith in him.

(3) *Being Christ's, we are Abraham's seed, and heirs according to the promise.* "You therefore become the true *seed of Abraham*, and as such *are heirs according to the promise*, and consequently are entitled to the great blessings and privileges of it." They were very unreasonable and unwise, in hearkening to those who at once endeavoured to deprive them of the truth and liberty of the gospel.

JAMIESON, FAUSSET, BROWN

superseded by Joshua, the type of Jesus, who leads the true Israel into their inheritance. The law leads us to Christ, and there its office ceases. **26. children**—*Greek,* "sons." **by**—*Greek,* "*through* faith." "Ye all" (Jews and Gentiles alike) are no longer *children* requiring a *tutor,* but SONS emancipated and walking at liberty. **27. baptized into Christ**—(Rom. 6:3). **have put on Christ**—Ye *did, in that very act* of being baptized into Christ, *put on,* or clothe yourselves with, Christ: so the *Greek* expresses. Christ is to you the *toga virilis* (the Roman garment of the full-grown man, assumed when ceasing to be a child) [BENGEL]. GATAKER defines a Christian, "One who has put on Christ." The argument is, By baptism ye have put on Christ; and therefore, He being the Son of God, ye become sons by adoption, by virtue of His Sonship by generation. This proves that baptism, *where it answers to its ideal,* is not a mere empty sign, but a means of spiritual transference from the state of legal condemnation to that of living union with Christ, and of sonship through Him in relation to God (Rom. 13:14). Christ alone can, by baptizing with His Spirit, make the inward grace correspond to the outward sign. But as He promises the blessing in the faithful use of the means, the Church has rightly presumed, in charity, that such is the case, nothing appearing to the contrary. **28.** There is in this sonship by faith in Christ, no class privileged above another, as the Jews under the law had been above the Gentiles (Rom. 10:12; I Cor. 12:13; Col. 3:11). **bond nor free**—Christ alike belongs to both by faith; whence he puts "bond" *before* "free." Cf. *Notes,* I Cor. 7:21, 22; Eph. 6:8. **neither male nor female**—rather, as *Greek,* "there is *not* male and female." There is no distinction into male and female. Difference of sex makes no difference in Christian privileges. But under the law the male sex had great privileges. Males alone had in their body circumcision, the sign of the covenant (contrast *baptism* applied to male and female alike); they alone were capable of being kings and priests, whereas all of either sex are now "kings and priests unto God" (Rev. 1:6); they had prior right to inheritances. In the resurrection the relation of the sexes shall cease (Luke 20:35). **one**—*Greek,* "one man"; masculine, not neuter, viz., "one new man" in Christ (Eph. 2:15). **29. and heirs**—The oldest MSS. omit "and." Christ is "Abraham's seed" (vs. 16): ye are "one in Christ" (vs. 28), and one with Christ, as having "put on Christ" (vs. 27); therefore YE are "Abraham's seed," which is tantamount to saying (whence the "and" is omitted), ye are "heirs according to the *promise*" (not "by the *law,*" vs. 18); for it was to Abraham's seed that the inheritance was promised (vs. 16). Thus he arrives at the same truth which he set out with (vs. 7). But one new "seed" of a righteous succession could be found. One single faultless grain of human nature was found by God Himself, the source of a new and imperishable seed: "the seed" (Ps. 22:30) who receive from Him a new nature and name (Gen. 3:15; Isa. 53:10, 11; John 12:24). In Him the lineal descent from David becomes extinct. He died without posterity. But He lives and shall reign on David's throne. No one has a legal claim to sit upon it but Himself, He being the only living direct representative (Ezek. 21:27). His spiritual seed derive their birth from the travail of His soul, being born again of His word, which is the incorruptible seed (John 1:12; Rom. 9:8; I Peter 1:23).

ADAM CLARKE

came wise unto salvation. It is worthy of remark that "the law" is used by Paul to signify, not only the law properly so called, but the whole of the Mosaic economy; so "the faith" is used by him to express, not merely the act of believing in Christ, but the whole of the gospel.

26. *For ye,* who have believed the gospel, *are all the children of God by faith in Christ Jesus.* But no man is a child of God by circumcision nor by any observance of the Mosaic law.

27. *As many of you as have been baptized into Christ.* All of you who have believed in Christ as the promised Messiah, and received baptism as a public proof that you had received Christ as your Lord and Saviour, *have put on Christ*—have received His Spirit, entered into His interests, and copied His manners. To *put on* or to "be clothed with" one is to assume the person and character of that one; and they who do so are bound to act his part, and to sustain the character which they have assumed. The profession of Christianity is an assumption of the character of Christ. He has left us an example that we should follow His steps; and we should, as Christians, have that mind in us which was in Him.

28. *There is neither Jew nor Greek. Greek* is put here for "heathen." Under the gospel all distinctions are done away, as either helping or hindering; all are equally welcome to Christ, and all have an equal need of Him. All persons of all sects and conditions and sexes who believe in Him become one family through Him. They are one body, of which He is the Head. *Neither male nor female.* With great reason the apostle introduces this. Between the privileges of men and women there was a great disparity among the Jews. A man might shave his head and rend his clothes in the time of mourning; a woman was not permitted to do so. A man might betroth his daughter; a woman had no such power. A man might sell his daughter; a woman could not. In many cases women were treated more like children than adults. Under the blessed spirit of Christianity, they have equal rights, equal privileges, and equal blessings; and, let me add, they are equally useful.

29. *And if ye be Christ's.* Or, as several good MSS. read, "If ye be one in Christ." If you have all received justification through His blood, and the mind that was in Him, *then are ye Abraham's seed;* you are that real, spiritual posterity of Abraham, that other seed, to whom the promises were made; and then *heirs according to the promise,* being fitted for the rest that remains for the people of God, that heavenly inheritance which was typified by the earthly Canaan.

CHAPTER 4 (Matthew Henry)

Verses 1–7

The apostle deals plainly with those who hearkened to the judaizing teachers.

I. He acquaints us with the state of the Old Testament church: it was like a child under age.

CHAPTER 4 (Jamieson, Fausset, Brown)

Vss. 1-31. THE SAME SUBJECT CONTINUED: ILLUSTRATION OF OUR SUBJECTION TO THE LAW ONLY TILL CHRIST CAME, FROM THE SUBJECTION OF AN HEIR TO HIS GUARDIAN TILL HE IS OF AGE. PETER'S GOOD WILL TO THE GALATIANS SHOULD LEAD THEM TO THE SAME GOOD WILL TO HIM AS THEY HAD AT FIRST SHOWN. THEIR DESIRE TO BE UNDER THE LAW SHOWN BY THE ALLEGORY OF ISAAC AND ISHMAEL TO BE INCONSISTENT WITH THEIR GOSPEL LIBERTY. **1-7.** The fact of God's sending His Son to redeem us who were under the law (vs. 4), and sending the Spirit of His Son into our hearts (vs. 6), confirms the conclusion (ch. 3:29) that we are "heirs according to the promise." **the heir**—(ch. 3:29). It is not, as in earthly inheritances, the death of the father, but our Father's sovereign will simply that makes us heirs. **child**—*Greek,* "one under age." **differeth nothing . . .**—i.e., has no more freedom than a slave (so the *Greek* for "servant" means). He is not at his own disposal. **lord of all**—by title and virtual ownership (cf. I Cor. 3:21, 22).

CHAPTER 4 (Adam Clarke)

1. *The heir, as long as he is a child.* Though he be appointed by his father's will heir of all his possessions, yet till he arrive at the legal age he is master of nothing, and does not differ from one of the common domestics.

MATTHEW HENRY

That was indeed a dispensation of grace, and yet it was comparatively a dispensation of darkness; for as the heir, in his minority, is *under tutors and governors till the time appointed of his father*, so it was with the Old Testament church. And as that was a dispensation of darkness, so of bondage too. The church then lay more under the character of *a servant*. The time appointed of the Father having come, we are under a dispensation of greater light and liberty.

II. He acquaints us with the much happier state under the gospel-dispensation, *v.* 4–7. *When the fulness of time had come he sent forth his Son*, &c.

He, in pursuance of the great design he had undertaken, submitted to be *made of a woman*—there is his incarnation; and to be *made under the law*—there is his subjection.

One great end of all this was *to redeem those that were under the law*. He was sent to redeem us, *that we might receive the adoption of sons*—that we might no longer be accounted as servants, but as sons grown up to maturity. Under the gospel, particular believers receive the adoption.

JAMIESON, FAUSSET, BROWN

tutors and governors—rather, "guardians (of the person) and stewards" (of the property.) Answering to "the law was our schoolmaster" or "tutor" (ch. 3: 24). **until the time appointed of the father**—in His eternal purposes (Eph. 1:9-11). The *Greek* is a legal term, expressing *a time defined* by law, or testamentary disposition. **3. we**—the Jews primarily, and inclusively the Gentiles also. For the "we" in vs. 5 plainly refers to *both* Jew and Gentile believers. The Jews in their bondage to the law of Moses, as the representative people of the world, include all mankind virtually amenable to God's law (Rom. 2: 14, 15; cf. ch. 3:13, 23, *Notes*). Even the Gentiles were under "bondage," and in a state of discipline suitable to nonage, till Christ came as the Emancipator. **were in bondage**—as "servants" (vs. 1). **under the elements**—or "rudiments"; rudimentary religion teaching of a non-Christian character: *the elementary lessons of outward things* (lit., "of the [outward] world"); such as the legal ordinances mentioned, vs. 10 (Col. 2:8, 20). Our childhood's lessons [CONYBEARE and HOWSON]. Lit., The *letters* of the alphabet (Heb. 5:12). **4. the fulness of the time**—viz., "the time appointed by the Father" (vs. 2). Cf. *Note,* Ephesians 1:10; Luke 1:57; Acts 2:1; Ezekiel 5:2. "The Church has its own ages" [BENGEL]. God does nothing prematurely, but, foreseeing the end from the beginning, waits till all is ripe for the execution of His purpose. Had Christ come directly after the fall, the enormity and deadly fruits of sin would not have been realized fully by man, so as to feel his desperate state and need of a Saviour. Sin was fully developed. Man's inability to save himself by obedience to the law, whether that of Moses, or that of conscience, was completely manifested; all the prophecies of various ages found their common center in *this* particular time; and Providence, by various arrangements in the social and political, as well as the moral world, had fully prepared the way for the coming Redeemer. God often permits physical evil long before he teaches the remedy. The smallpox had for long committed its ravages before inoculation, and then vaccination, was discovered. It was essential to the honor of God's law to permit evil long before He revealed the full remedy. Cf. "the set time" (Ps. 102:13). **was come**—*Greek*, "came." **sent forth**—*Greek, "sent forth out of* heaven *from* Himself" [ALFORD and BENGEL]. The same verb is used of the Father's sending forth the Spirit (vs. 6). So in Acts 7:12. Cf. with this verse, John 8:42; Isaiah 48:16. **his**—emphatical. *"His own* Son." Not *by adoption,* as we are (vs. 5); nor merely His Son by the anointing of the Spirit which God sends into the heart (vs. 6; John 1:18). **made of a woman**—"made" is used as in I Cor. 15:45, "The first man, Adam, *was made* a living soul," *Greek*, "made to be (*born*) of a woman." The expression implies a special interposition of God in His birth as man, viz., causing Him to be conceived by the Holy Ghost. So ESTIUS. **made under the law**—"made to be under the law." Not merely as GROTIUS and ALFORD explain, "Born subject to the law *as a Jew.*" But "made" by His Father's appointment, and His own free will, "subject to the law," to keep it all, ceremonial and moral, perfectly for us, as the Representative Man, and to suffer and exhaust the full penalty of our whole race's violation of it. This constitutes the significance of His circumcision, His being presented in the temple (Luke 2:21, 22, 27; cf. Matt. 5:17), and His baptism by John, when He said (Matt. 3:15), "Thus it becometh us to *fulfil all righteousness.*" **5. To**—*Greek, "That He might* redeem." **them . . . under the law**—primarily the Jews; but as these were the representative people of the world, *the Gentiles,* too, are included in the redemption (ch. 3:13). **receive**—The *Greek* implies the *suitableness* of the thing as long ago predestined by God. "Receive as something *destined* or *due*" (Luke 23:41; II John 8). Herein God makes of sons of men sons of God, inasmuch as God made of the Son of God the Son of man [ST. AUGUSTINE on Ps. 52]. **6. because ye are sons . . .**—The gift of the Spirit of prayer is the consequence of our adoption. The Gentile Galatians might think, as the Jews were under the law before their adoption, that so they, too, must first be under the law. Paul, by anticipation, meets this objection by saying, YE ARE sons, therefore ye need not be as children (vs. 1) under the tutorship of the law, as being already in the free state of "sons" of God by faith in Christ (ch. 3:26), no longer in your nonage (as "children," vs. 1). **the Spirit of his Son**—By faith ye are one with the Son, so that what is His is yours; His Sonship ensures your sonship; His Spirit ensures for you a share in the same. "If any man have not the Spirit of

ADAM CLARKE

2. *But is under tutors,* "guardians," *and governors,* those who have the charge of the family. These words are nearly similar; but we may consider the first as "executor," the last as the person who superintends the concerns of the family and estate till the heir become of age, such as we call "trustee." *Until the time appointed of the father.* The time mentioned in the father's will or testament.

3. *Even so we.* The whole Jewish people were in a state of nonage while under the law. *The elements of the world.* A mere Jewish phrase, "the principles of this world"; that is, the rudiments or principles of the Jewish religion. The apostle intimates that the law was not the science of salvation; it was only the elements or alphabet of it; and in the gospel this alphabet is composed into a most glorious system of divine knowledge. But as the alphabet is nothing of itself unless compounded into syllables, words, sentences, and discourses, so the law, taken by itself, gives no salvation. It contains indeed the outlines of the gospel, but it is the gospel alone that fills up these outlines.

4. *When the fulness of the time was come.* The time which God in His infinite wisdom counted best, in which all His counsels were "filled up"; the time which His Spirit, by the prophets, had specified; and the time to which He intended the Mosaic institutions should extend, and beyond which they should be of no avail.

God sent forth his Son, Him who came immediately from God himself, *made of a woman,* according to the promise, Gen. iii. 15; produced by the power of God in the womb of the Virgin Mary without any intervention of man. *Made under the law.* In subjection to it, that in Him all its designs might be fulfilled and by His death the whole might be abolished, the law dying when the Son of God expired upon the Cross.

5. *To redeem them.* To "pay down a price" for them, and thus "buy them off" from the necessity of observing circumcision, offering brute sacrifices, performing different ablutions, etc. *That we might receive the adoption of sons.* Which adoption we could not obtain by the law, for it is the gospel only that puts us among the children and gives us a place in the heavenly family.

6. *And because ye are sons.* By faith in Christ Jesus, being redeemed from both the bondage and the curse of the law. *God* the Father, called generally the First Person of the glorious Trinity, *hath sent forth the Spirit*—the Holy Ghost, the Second Person of that Trinity—*of his Son,* Jesus Christ, the Third Person of the Trinity,

MATTHEW HENRY

They have together therewith the Spirit of adoption, enabling them in prayer to eye God as a Father (*v.* 6): *Because you are sons, God hath sent forth the Spirit of his Son into your hearts, crying Abba, Father.* And hereupon (*v.* 7) the apostle concludes this argument: *Wherefore thou art no more a servant, but a son; and, if a son, then an heir of God through Christ;* we are no longer under the servitude of the law, but, upon our believing in Christ, become the sons of God, and, being the sons, we are also heirs of God.

1. The wonders of divine love and mercy towards us, particularly of God the Father, in sending his Son into the world to redeem and save us—of the Son of God, in suffering so much, for us—and of the Holy Spirit, in condescending to dwell in the hearts of believers for such gracious purposes.

2. The great and invaluable advantages which Christians enjoy under the gospel. We receive *the adoption of sons.* We who by nature are children of wrath and disobedience have become by grace children of love. We receive *the Spirit of adoption.* All who are received into the number partake of the nature of the children of God; for he will have all his children to resemble him. Those who have the nature of sons shall have the inheritance of sons.

Verses 8–11

I. He reminds them what they were before the gospel was preached to them. Then *they knew not God.* They were under the worst of slaveries, for *they did service to those which by nature were no gods,* and therefore were utterly unable to hear and help them. Those who are ignorant of the true God cannot but be inclined to false gods.

II. He calls upon them to consider the happy change made in them by the preaching of the gospel. *They had known God or rather were known of God;* this happy change in their state was not owing to themselves, but to him. All our acquaintance with God begins with him; we know him, because we are known of him.

III. The unreasonableness of their suffering themselves to be brought again into a state of bondage. *How turn you again,* &c., says he, *v.* 9. "How is it that you, who have been taught to worship God in the gospel way, should now be persuaded to comply with the ceremonial way of worship? They were more inexcusable than the Jews themselves, who might be supposed to have some fondness for that which had been of such long standing among them. Besides, what they suffered themselves to be brought into bondage to were but *weak and beggarly elements,* such things as had no power in them to cleanse the soul.

JAMIESON, FAUSSET, BROWN

Christ, he is none of His" (Rom. 8:9). Moreover, as the Spirit of God proceeds from God the Father, so the Spirit of the Son proceeds from the Son: so that the Holy Ghost, as the Creed says, "proceedeth from the Father and the Son." The Father was not *begotten:* the Son is *begotten* of the Father; the Holy Ghost *proceeding* from the Father and the Son. **crying**—Here the SPIRIT is regarded as the *agent* in praying, and the believer as *His organ.* In Romans 8:15, "The Spirit of adoption" is said to be that whereby WE cry, "Abba, Father"; but in Romans 8:26, "The SPIRIT ITSELF maketh intercession for us with groanings which cannot be uttered." The believers' prayer is His prayer: hence arises its acceptability with God. **Abba, Father**—The Hebrew says, "Abba" (a *Hebrew* term), the Greek, "Father" ("*Pater,*" a *Greek* term in the original), both united together in one Sonship and one cry of faith, "Abba, Father." So "Even so ('*Nai,*' *Greek*), Amen" (*Hebrew*), both meaning the same (Rev. 1: 7). Christ's own former cry is the believers' cry, "Abba, Father" (Mark 14:36). **7. Wherefore**—Conclusion inferred from vss. 4-6. **thou**—individualizing and applying the truth to each. Such an individual appropriation of this comforting truth God grants in answer to them who cry, "Abba, Father." **heir of God through Christ**—The oldest MSS. read, "an heir through God." This combines on behalf of man, the whole before-mentioned agency of THE TRINITY: the Father sent His Son and the Spirit; the Son has freed us from the law; the Spirit has completed our sonship. Thus the redeemed are heirs THROUGH the Triune GOD, not through the law, nor through fleshly descent [WINDISCHMANN in ALFORD]; (ch. 3:18 confirms this). **heir**—confirming ch. 3:29; cf. Romans 8:17. **8-11.** appeal to them not to turn back from their privileges as free sons, to legal bondage again. **then**—when ye were "servants" (vs. 7). **ye knew not God**—not opposed to Romans 1:21. The heathen *originally knew* God, as Romans 1:21 states, but did not choose to retain God in their knowledge, and so corrupted the original truth. They *might* still *have* known Him, in a measure, from His works, but as a matter of fact they knew Him not, so far as His eternity, His power as the Creator, and His holiness, are concerned. **are no gods**—i.e., have no existence, such as their worshippers attribute to them, in the nature of things, but only in the corrupt imaginations of their worshippers (*Notes,* I Cor. 8:4; 10:19, 20; II Chron. 13:9). Your "service" was a different bondage from that of the Jews, which was a true service. Yet theirs, like yours, was a burdensome yoke; how then is it ye wish to resume the yoke after that God has transferred both Jews and Gentiles to a free service? **9. known God or rather are known of God**—*They* did not first know and love God, but *God* first, in His electing love, knew and loved them as His, and therefore attracted them to the saving knowledge of Him (Matt. 7:23; I Cor. 8:3; II Tim. 2:19; cf. Exod. 33:12, 17; John 15:16; Phil. 3:12). God's great grace in this made their fall from it the more heinous. **how**—expressing indignant wonder at such a thing being possible, and even actually occurring (ch. 1:6). "How is it that ye turn back again?" **weak**—powerless to *justify:* in contrast to the justifying power of faith (ch. 3:24; cf. Heb. 7:18). **beggarly**—contrasted with the *riches* of the inheritance of believers in Christ (Eph. 1:18). The state of the "child" (vs. 1) is weak, as not having attained manhood; "beggarly," as not having attained the inheritance. **elements**—"rudiments." It is as if a schoolmaster should go back to learning the A, B, C's [BENGEL]. **again**—There are two *Greek* words in the original. "Ye desire again, *beginning afresh,* to be in bondage." Though the Galatians, as Gentiles, had never been under the Mosaic yoke, yet they had been under "the elements of the world" (vs. 3): the common designation for the Jewish and Gentile systems alike, in contrast to the Gospel (however superior the Jewish was to the Gentile). Both systems consisted in outward worship and cleaved to sensible forms. Both were in bondage to *the elements of sense,* as though these could give the justification and sanctification which the inner and spiritual power of God alone could bestow. **ye desire**—or "will." *Will-worship* is not acceptable to God (Col. 2:18, 23). **10.** To regard the observance of certain days as in itself meritorious as a work, is alien to the free spirit of Christianity. This is not incompatible with observing the Sabbath or the Christian Lord's day as obligatory, though *not as a work* (which was the Jewish and Gentile error in the observance of days), but as a holy mean appointed by the Lord for attaining the great end, holiness. The whole life alike belongs

ADAM CLARKE

crying, Abba, Father, from the fullest and most satisfactory evidence that God, the Father, Son, and Spirit, had become their portion.

7. *Thou art no more a servant.* You who have believed in Christ are no longer a "slave," either under the dominion of sin or under obligation to the Mosaic ritual; *but a son* of God, adopted into the heavenly family. *And if a son, then an heir.* Having a right to the inheritance because one of the family, for none can inherit but the children. But this heirship is the most extraordinary of all. It is not an heirship of any tangible possession, either in heaven or on earth; it is not to possess a part or even the whole of either. It is to possess Him who made all things; not God's works, but God himself; heirs *of God through Christ.*

8. *When ye knew not God.* Though it is evident from the complexion of the whole of this Epistle that the great body of the Christians in the churches of Galatia were converts from among the Jews or proselytes to Judaism, yet from this verse it appears that there were some who had been converted from heathenism, unless we suppose that the apostle here particularly addresses those who had been proselytes to Judaism and thence converted to Christianity, which appears to be most likely from the following verses.

9. *Now, after that ye have known God.* After having been brought to the knowledge of God as your Saviour. *Or rather are known of God.* Are approved of Him, having received the adoption of sons.

To the weak and beggarly elements. After receiving all this, will you turn again to the ineffectual rites and ceremonies of the Mosaic law—rites too weak to counteract your sinful habits, and too poor to purchase pardon and eternal life for you? If the Galatians were turning again to them, it is evident that they once had been addicted to them. And this they might have been, allowing that they had become converts from heathenism to Judaism and from Judaism to Christianity.

MATTHEW HENRY

Their weakness and folly were the more aggravated, in submitting to them, and in observing their various festivals, *days, and months, and times, and years.* It is possible for those who have made great professions of religion to be afterwards drawn into very great defections from the purity and simplicity of it. This the apostle lays a special stress upon, that after they had known God, or rather were known of him, they desired to be in bondage under the weak and beggarly elements of the law.

IV. He expresses his fears concerning them, *lest he had bestowed on them labour in vain.* He had been at a great deal of pains about them, but now they were rendering his labour among them fruitless, and with the thoughts of this he could not but be deeply affected.

Verses 12–16

I. How affectionately he addresses himself to them. He styles them brethren, though he knew their hearts were in a great measure alienated from him.

He would have them *to be as he was, for he was as they were, they had not injured him at all.* He had no quarrel with them upon his own account. Thus he endeavours to mollify their spirits towards him, that so they might receive the admonitions he was giving them. In reproving others we should take care to convince them that our reproofs do not proceed from any private pique but from a sincere regard to the honour of God and their truest welfare.

II. He magnifies their former affection. He puts them in mind of the difficulty under which he laboured when he came first among them: *I knew how, through infirmity of the flesh, I preached the gospel unto you at the first.*

When this *infirmity of the flesh* was, which in the following words he expresses by *his temptation that was in his flesh,* we can now have no certain knowledge of. It seems it made no impression on them to his disadvantage.

They did not despise him on the account of it, but on the contrary, *received him as an angel of God, even as Christ Jesus.*

III. He expostulates with them hereupon: *Where is then, the blessedness you spoke of?* "You once thought yourselves happy in receiving the gospel; have you now any reason to think otherwise?" Those who have left their first love would do well to consider, Where is now the blessedness they once spoke of?

He was a welcome messenger to them; yea, so great was their esteem of him, that *they could have plucked out their own eyes, and have given them to him.* How uncertain the respects of people are, how apt they are to change their minds, so that they are ready to pluck out the eyes of those for whom they would before have plucked out their own!

JAMIESON, FAUSSET, BROWN

to the Lord in the Gospel view, just as the whole world, and not the Jews only, belong to Him. But as in Paradise, so now one portion of time is needed wherein to draw off the soul more entirely from secular business to God (Col. 2:16). "Sabbaths, new moons, and set feasts" (I Chron. 23:31; II Chron. 31:3), answer to "days, months, times." "Months," however, may refer to the *first* and *seventh* months, which were sacred on account of the number of feasts in them. **times**—*Greek,* "seasons," viz., those of the three great feasts, the Passover, Pentecost, and Tabernacles. **years**—The sabbatical year was about the time of writing this Epistle, A.D. 48 [BENGEL]. **11. lest**—*Greek,* "lest *haply.*" My fear is not for my own sake, but for yours. **12. be as I am**—"As I have in my life among you cast off Jewish habits, so do ye; for I am become as ye are," viz., in the nonobservance of legal ordinances. "The fact of my laying them aside among Gentiles, shows that I regard them as *not at all contributing to justification* or *sanctification.* Do you regard them in the same light, and act accordingly." His observing the law among the Jews was not inconsistent with this, for he did so only in order to win them, without compromising principle. On the other hand, the Galatian Gentiles, by adopting legal ordinances, showed that they regarded them as needful for salvation. This Paul combats. **ye have not injured me at all**—viz., at the period when I first preached the Gospel among you, and when I made myself as you are, viz., living as a Gentile, not as a Jew. *You at that time did me no wrong;* "ye did not despise my temptation in the flesh" (vs. 14): nay, you "received me as an angel of God." Then in vs. 16, he asks, "Have I then, *since* that time, become your enemy by telling you the truth?" **13. how through infirmity**—rather, as *Greek,* "Ye know that *because* of an infirmity of *my* flesh I preached...." He implies that bodily sickness, having detained him among them, contrary to his original intentions, was the occasion of his preaching the Gospel to them. **at the first**—lit., "at the *former* time"; implying that at the time of writing he had been *twice* in Galatia. See my *Introduction;* also vs. 16, and ch. 5:21, *Notes.* His sickness was probably the same as recurred more violently afterward, "the thorn in the flesh" (II Cor. 12:7), which also was overruled to good (II Cor. 12:9, 10), as the "infirmity of the flesh" here. **14. my temptation**—The oldest MSS. read, "your temptation." My infirmity, which was, or might have been, a "temptation," or *trial, to you,* ye despised not, i.e., ye were not tempted by it to despise me and my message. Perhaps, however, it is better to punctuate and explain as LACHMANN, connecting it with vs. 13, "And (ye know) your temptation (i.e., the temptation to which ye were exposed through the infirmity) which was in my flesh. Ye despised not (through *natural* pride), nor rejected (through *spiritual* pride), but received me...." "Temptation does not mean here, as we now use the word, *tendency to an evil habit,* but BODILY TRIAL." **as an angel of God**—as a heaven-inspired and sent *messenger* from God: *angel* means messenger (Mal. 2:7). Cf. the phrase, II Samuel 19:27, a Hebrew and Oriental one for a person to be received with the highest respect (Zech. 12:8). An angel is free from the *flesh, infirmity,* and *temptation.* **as Christ**—being Christ's representative (Matt. 10:40). Christ is Lord of angels. **15. Where . . .**—*Of what value* was your *congratulation* (so the *Greek* for "blessedness" expresses) of yourselves, on account of your having among you me, the messenger of the Gospel, considering how entirely you have veered about since? Once you counted yourselves *blessed* in being favored with my ministry. **ye would have plucked out your own eyes**—one of the dearest members of the body—so highly did you value me: a proverbial phrase for the greatest selfsacrifice (Matt. 5:29). CONYBEARE and HOWSON think that this particular form of proverb was used with reference to a weakness in Paul's eyes, connected with a nervous frame, perhaps affected by the brightness of the vision described, Acts 22:11; II Corinthians 12:1-7. "You would have torn out your own eyes to supply the lack of mine." The divine power of Paul's words and works, contrasting with the feebleness of his person (II Cor. 10:10), powerfully at first impressed the Galatians, who had all the impulsiveness of the Keltic race from which they sprang. Subsequently they soon changed with the fickleness which is equally characteristic of Kelts. **16.** Translate, "Am I *then* become your enemy (an enemy in your eyes) *by telling* you the truth" (ch. 2:5, 14)? He plainly did not incur their enmity at his *first visit,* and the words here imply that he had

ADAM CLARKE

10. *Ye observe days.* You superstitiously regard the Sabbaths and particular days of your own appointment. *And months.* New moons. *Times*—festivals, such as those of Tabernacles, Dedication, Passover. *Years.* Annual atonements, sabbatical years, and jubilees.

11. *I am afraid of you.* I begin now to be seriously alarmed for you, and think you are so thoroughly perverted from the gospel of Christ that all my pains and labor in your conversion have been thrown away.

12. *Be as I am.* Thoroughly addicted to the Christian faith and worship, from the deepest conviction of its truth. *For I am as ye are.* I was formerly a Jew, and as zealously addicted to the rites and ceremonies of Judaism as you are, but I am saved from that means and unprofitable dependence. "Be therefore as I am now, who was once as you now are." *Ye have not injured me at all.* I do not thus earnestly entreat you to return to your Christian profession because your perversion has been any loss to me, nor because your conversion can be to me any gain. You have not injured me at all; you injure only yourselves.

13. *Ye know how through infirmity.* The apostle seems to say that he was much afflicted in body when he first preached the gospel to them. And is this any strange thing, that a minister so laborious as Paul was should be sometimes overdone and overcome by the severity of his labors? Surely not. This might have been only an occasional affliction while laboring in that part of Asia Minor, and not a continual and incurable infirmity, as some have too hastily conjectured.

14. *And my temptation which was in my flesh.* On this verse there are a great many various readings, as there are various opinions. Instead of *my temptation,* a number of MSS. and versions and several of the primitive fathers have "your temptation." The word which we translate *temptation* signifies "trial" of any kind. The verse therefore may be read, "You despised not the trial which was in my flesh"; or, "You despised not your trial, which was in my flesh"; i.e., what my flesh suffered on your account, the afflictions I passed through in consequence of my severe labors on your account. They received him *as an angel of God,* as a messenger from heaven, and *as Christ Jesus* himself. This appears to me to be the simple meaning of the apostle, and that he alludes to neither a bodily nor a mental infirmity which generally or periodically afflicted him, as some have imagined. Nor does he appear at all to speak of the same case as that mentioned in 2 Cor. xii. 7.

15. *Where is then the blessedness ye spake of? Ye spake of* should be in italics, there being no corresponding word in the Greek text. Perhaps there is not a sentence in the New Testament more variously translated than this. "What was then your blessedness!" Or, "How great was your happiness at that time!" Or, "What blessings did ye then pour on me!" It is worthy of remark that, instead of *what,* several MSS. and some of the fathers have *where;* and *was* is omitted by some. According to these authorities the text should be read thus: "Where then is your blessedness?" Having renounced the gospel, you have lost your "happiness." What have your false teachers given you to compensate the loss of communion with God, or that Spirit of adoption, that Spirit of Christ, by which you cried, "Abba, Father"! If, however, we understand the words as implying the benedictions they then heaped on the apostle, the sense will be sufficiently natural, and agree well with the concluding part of the verse; *for I bear you record, that, if . . . possible, ye would have plucked out your own eyes, and have given them to me.* You had then the strongest affection for me; you loved God, and you loved me for God's sake, and were ready to give me the most unequivocal proof of your love. Dearer than one's eyes, or to profess to give one's eyes for the sake of a person, appears to have been a proverbial expression, intimating the highest tokens of the strongest affection.

16. *Am I therefore become your enemy?*

MATTHEW HENRY

He again asks (*v.* 16), "*Am I become your enemy, because I tell you the truth?* How is it that I, who was heretofore your favourite, am now accounted your enemy? It is no uncommon thing for men to account those their enemies who are really their best friends; for so, undoubtedly, those are who tell them the truth. Ministers sometimes create enemies to themselves by the faithful discharge of their duty. Yet ministers must not forbear speaking the truth, for fear of offending others. If others have become their enemies, it is only for telling them the truth.

Verses 17, 18

He here gives them the character of those false teachers. He tells them they were designing men, who were aiming to set up themselves. "*They zealously affect you,*" says he; "and pretend a great deal of affection to you, *but not well*; for *they would exclude you, that you might affect them.* That which they are chiefly aiming at is to engage your affections to them." There may appear to be a great deal of zeal where yet there is but little truth and sincerity. The apostle gives us that excellent rule which we have, *v.* 18, *It is good to be zealously affected always in a good thing.* What our translation renders *in a good thing* some choose to render *to a good man*, and so consider the apostle as pointing to himself; *and not only when I am present with you.* It is a very good rule that zeal be exercised only upon that which is good; for zeal is then only good when it is in a good thing. It is good to be zealous always in a good thing; not for a time only, or now and then, like the heat of an ague-fit, but, like the natural heat of the body, constant. Happy would it be for the church of Christ if this rule were better observed among Christians!

Verses 19, 20

He here expresses his great affection to them. He was not like them—one thing when among them and another when absent from them. Nor was he like their false teachers, who pretended a great deal of affection to them, when at the same time they were only consulting their own interest. He calls them *his children*, as he justly might, yea, he styles them his *little children*, which may possibly have a respect to their present behaviour, whereby they showed themselves too much like little children. He expresses his concern for them. *He travailed in birth for them that Christ might be formed in them*, that they might become Christians indeed. From this we may note, 1. The very tender affection which faithful ministers bear towards those among whom they are employed; it is like that of the most affectionate parents to their little children. 2. That the chief thing they are longing for, on their account, is that Christ may be formed in them. How unreasonably must those people act who suffer themselves to be prevailed upon to desert or dislike such ministers! He adds (*v.* 20) that *he desired to be then present with them*, that thereupon he might find occasion to *change his voice* towards them; for at present *he stood in doubt of them.* He knew not well what to think of them. But he would be glad to find that matters were better with them than he feared, and that he might have occasion to commend them, instead of thus reproving and chiding them.

Verses 21–31

The apostle illustrates the difference between believers who rested in Christ only and those judaizers who trusted in the law, by a comparison taken from the story of Isaac and Ishmael. *Tell me*, says he, *you that desire to be under the law, do you not hear the law?*

He sets before them the history itself (*v.* 22, 23): *For it is written, Abraham had two sons*, &c. The one, Ishmael, *was by a bond-maid*, and the other, Isaac,

JAMIESON, FAUSSET, BROWN

since then, and *before* his now writing, incurred it: so that the occasion of his *telling* them the unwelcome truth, must have been at his second visit (Acts 18:23, see my *Introduction*). The fool and sinner hate a reprover. The righteous love faithful reproof (Ps. 141:5; Prov. 9:8). **17. They**—your flatterers: in contrast to Paul himself, who *tells* them *the truth.* **zealously**—zeal in proselytism was characteristic especially of the Jews, and so of Judaizers (ch. 1:14; Matt. 23:15; Rom. 10:2). **affect you**—i.e., court you (II Cor. 11:2. **not well**—not in a good way, or for a good end. Neither the *cause* of their zealous courting of you, nor the *manner,* is what it ought to be. **they would exclude you**—"They wish to shut you out" from the kingdom of God (i.e., they wish to persuade you that as uncircumcised Gentiles, you are shut out from it), "that ye *may zealously court them,*" i.e., become circumcised, as zealous followers of themselves. ALFORD explains it, that their wish was to shut out the Galatians from the general community, and attract them as a separate clique to their own party. So the English word "exclusive," is used. **18. good to be zealously affected**—rather, to correspond to "zealously court" in vs. 18, "to be zealously courted." I do not find fault with them for zealously courting you, nor with you for being *zealously courted:* provided it be "in a good cause" (translate so), "it is a good thing" (I Cor. 9:20-23). My reason for saying the "not well" (vs. 17: the *Greek* is the same as that for "good," and "in a good cause," in vs. 28), is that their *zealous courting of you* is not in a good cause. The older interpreters, however, support *English Version* (cf. ch. 1:14). **always**—Translate and arrange the words thus, "*At all times,* and not only when I am present with you." I do not desire that *I* exclusively should have the privilege of zealously courting you. Others may do so in my absence with my full approval, if only it be in a good cause, and if Christ be faithfully preached (Phil. 1: 15-18). **19. My little children**—(I Tim. 1:18; II Tim. 2:1; I John 2:1). My relation to you is not merely that of one *zealously courting* you (vss. 17, 18), but that of a *father* to his *children* (I Cor. 4: 15). **I travail in birth**—i.e., like a mother in pain till the birth of her child. **again**—a second time. The former time was when I was "present with you" (vs. 18; cf. *Note*, vs. 13). **Christ be formed in you**—that you may live nothing but Christ, and think nothing but Christ (ch. 2:20), and glory in nothing but Him, and His death, resurrection, and righteousness (Phil. 3:8-10; Col. 1:27). **20.** Translate as *Greek,* "I could wish." If circumstances permitted (which they do not), I would gladly be with you [M.STUART]. **now**—as I was twice already. Speaking face to face is so much more effective towards loving persuasion than writing (II John 12; III John 13, 14). **change my voice**—as a mother (vs. 19): adapting my tone of voice to what I saw in person your case might need. This is possible to one present, but not to one in writing [GROTIUS and ESTIUS]. **I stand in doubt of you**—rather, "I am perplexed about you," viz., how to deal with you, what kind of words to use, gentle or servere, to bring you back to the right path. **21. desire**—of your own accord madly courting that which must condemn and ruin you. **do ye not hear**—do ye not consider the mystic sense of Moses' words? [GROTIUS.] The law itself sends you away from itself to Christ [ESTIUS]. After having sufficiently maintained his point by argument, the apostle confirms and illustrates it by an inspired allegorical exposition of historical facts, containing in them general laws and types. Perhaps his reason for using allegory was to confute the Judaizers with their own weapons: subtle, mystical, allegorical interpretations, unauthorized by the Spirit, were their favorite arguments, as of the Rabbins in the synagogues. Cf. the Jerusalem Talmud, *Tractatu Succa, cap. Hechalil.* Paul meets them with an allegorical exposition, not the work of fancy, but sanctioned by the Holy Spirit. History, if properly understood. contains in its complicated phenomena, simple and *continually recurring divine laws.* The history of the elect people, like their legal ordinances, had, besides the literal, a typical meaning (cf. I Cor. 10:1-4; 15:45, 47; Rev. 11:8). Just as the extra-ordinarily-born Isaac, the gift of grace according to promise, supplanted, beyond all human calculations, the naturally-born Ishmael, so the new theocratic race, the spiritual seed of Abraham by promise, the Gentile, as well as Jewish believers, were about to take the place of the natural seed, who had imagined that to them exclusively belonged the kingdom of God. **22.** (Gen. 16:3-16; 21:2.) **Abraham**—whose sons ye wish to be (cf. Rom. 9:7-9). **a bond maid . . . a free woman**—rather, as *Greek,* 'the bond maid . . . *the* free woman.

ADAM CLARKE

How is it that you are so much altered towards me that you now treat me as an enemy, who formerly loved me with the most fervent affection? Is it *because I tell you the truth,* that very truth for which you at first so ardently loved me?

17. *They zealously affect you, but not well.* It is difficult for common readers to understand the meaning of these words; perhaps it would be better to translate: These false teachers "endeavor to conciliate your esteem, but not on honest or true principles." They work themselves into your good graces; they wish you to place all your affection upon themselves. *They would exclude you.* They wish to "shut you out" from the affection of your apostle, *that ye might affect them,* that you might love them alone, hear them alone, abide by their directions only, and totally abandon him who called you into the grace of the gospel of Christ. Some MSS. read "us" instead of *you*; they wish to shut us entirely out from among you, that you may receive and believe them alone. The sense is nearly the same but the former appears to be the more authentic reading.

18. *It is good to be zealously affected.* It is well to have a determined mind and an ardent heart in reference to things which are laudable and good. *Not only when I am present.* You were thus attached to me when I was among you, but now you have lost both your reverence and affection for me. Your false teachers pretended great concern for you, that you might put all your confidence in them. They have gained their end; they have estranged you from me, and got you to renounce the gospel, and have brought you again into your former bondage.

19. *My little children.* "My beloved children." As their conversion to God had been the fruit of much labor, prayers, and tears, so he felt them as his children and peculiarly dear to him because he had been the means of bringing them to the knowledge of the truth. Therefore he represents himself as suffering the same anxiety and distress which he endured at first when he preached the gospel to them, when their conversion to Christianity was a matter of great doubt and uncertainty. The metaphor which he uses needs no explanation. *Until Christ be formed in you.* Till you once more receive the Spirit and unction of Christ in your hearts, from which you are fallen by your rejection of the spirit of the gospel.

20. *I desire to be present with you.* I wish to accommodate my doctrine to your state; I know not whether you need stronger reprehension or to be dealt with more leniently. *I stand in doubt of you.* I have doubts concerning your state, the progress of error and conviction among you, which I cannot fully know without being among you. This appears to be the apostle's meaning, and tends much to soften and render palatable the severity of his reproofs.

21. *Ye that desire to be under the law.* You who desire to incorporate the Mosaic institutions with Christianity, and thus bring yourselves into bondage to circumcision and a great variety of oppressive rites. *Do ye not hear the law?* Do you not understand what is written in the Pentateuch relative to Abraham and his children? It is evident that the word *law* is used in two senses in this verse. It first means the Mosaic institutions; secondly, the Pentateuch, where the history is recorded to which the apostle refers.

22. *For it is written.* Viz., in Gen. xvi. 15 and xxii. 1, *that Abraham had two sons,* Ishmael and Isaac: *the one,* Ishmael, *by a bondmaid,* Hagar; *the other,* Isaac, *by a freewoman,* Sarah.

MATTHEW HENRY

by a free-woman; the former *was born after the flesh*, or by the ordinary course of nature, the other *was by promise*, when in the course of nature there was no reason to expect that Sarah should have a son.

He acquaints them with the meaning of this history (*v.* 24-27): *These things*, says he, *are an allegory*. These two, Agar and Sarah, *are the two covenants*.

The former, Agar, represented that which was given from mount Sinai, and *which gendereth to bondage. For this Agar is mount Sinai in Arabia and it answereth to Jerusalem which now is, and is in bondage with her children;* it justly represents the present state of the Jews, who adhering to that covenant, are still in bondage with their children.

But the other, Sarah, was intended to prefigure Jerusalem which is above, which is free both from the curse of the moral and the bondage of the ceremonial law, and *is the mother of us all*—a state into which all, both Jews and Gentiles, are admitted, upon their believing in Christ.

And to this greater freedom the apostle refers that of the prophet, Isa. liv. 1, where it is written, *Rejoice, thou barren that bearest not; break forth and cry, thou that travailest not: for the desolate hath many more children than she who hath a husband.*

He applies the history to the present case (*v.* 28): *Now we, brethren, as Isaac was, are the children of the promise.* We Christians, who have accepted Christ and look for justification and salvation by him alone, are entitled to the promised inheritance.

JAMIESON, FAUSSET, BROWN

23. after the flesh—born according to the usual course of nature: in contrast to Isaac, who was born "by virtue of *the* promise" (so the *Greek*), as the efficient cause of Sarah's becoming pregnant out of the course of nature (Rom. 4:19). Abraham was to lay aside all confidence in *the flesh* (after which Ishmael was born), and to live by faith alone in *the promise* (according to which Isaac was miraculously born, contrary to all calculations of flesh and blood). **24. are an allegory**—rather, "are allegorical," i.e., have *another besides the literal* meaning. **these are the two covenants**—"these [women] are (i.e., *mean;* omit 'the' with all the oldest MSS.) two covenants." As among the Jews the bondage of the mother determined that of the child, the children of the free covenant of promise, answering to Sarah, are free; the children of the legal covenant of bondage are not so. **one from**—i.e., *taking his* origin *from* Mount Sinai. Hence, it appears, he is treating of the moral law (ch. 3:19) chiefly (Heb. 12:18). Paul was familiar with the district of Sinai in Arabia (ch. 1:17), having gone thither after his conversion. At the gloomy scene of the giving of the Law, he learned to appreciate, by contrast, the grace of the Gospel, and so to cast off all his past legal dependencies. **which gendereth**—i.e., *bringing forth children* unto bondage. Cf. the phrase (Acts 3:25), "*children of the covenant* which God made . . . saying unto Abraham." **Agar** i.e., Hagar. **25.** Translate, "For this *word*, Hagar, is (imports) Mount Sinai in Arabia" (i.e., among the Arabians—*in the Arabian tongue*). So CHRYSOSTOM explains. HARAUT, the traveller, says that to this day the Arabians call Sinai, "Hadschar," i.e., *Hagar, meaning a rock* or *stone*. Hagar twice fled into the desert of Arabia (Gen. 16 and 21): from her the mountain and city took its name, and the people were called Hagarenes. Sinai, with its rugged rocks, far removed from the promised land, was well suited to represent the law which inspires with terror, and the spirit of bondage. **answereth**—lit., "stands in the same rank with"; "she corresponds to." **Jerusalem which now is**—i.e., the Jerusalem of the Jews, having only a present temporary existence, in contrast with the spiritual Jerusalem of the Gospel, which in germ, under the form of the *promise,* existed ages before, and shall be for ever in ages to come. **and**—The oldest MSS. read, "*For* she is in bondage." As Hagar was in bondage to her mistress, so Jerusalem that now is, is in bondage to the law, and also to the Romans: her civil state thus being in accordance with her spiritual state [BENGEL]. **26.** This verse stands instead of the sentence which we should expect, to correspond to vs. 24, "One from Mount Sinai," viz., *the other covenant* from the heavenly mount above, which is (answers in the allegory to) Sarah. **Jerusalem . . . above**—Hebrews 12:22, "the heavenly Jerusalem." "New Jerusalem, which cometh down out of heaven from my God" (Rev. 3:12; 21:2). Here "*the Messianic theocracy,* which before Christ's second appearing is *the Church,* and after it, Christ's kingdom of glory" [MEYER]. **free**—as Sarah was; opposed to "she is in bondage" (vs. 25). **all**—omitted in many of the oldest MSS., though supported by some. "Mother of us," viz., *believers* who are already members of the invisible Church, the heavenly Jerusalem, hereafter to be *manifested* (Heb. 12:22). **27.** (Isa. 54:1.) **thou barren**—Jerusalem above: the spiritual Church of the Gospel, the fruit of "the promise," answering to *Sarah,* who bore not "after the flesh": as contrasted with the law, answering to Hagar, who was fruitful in the ordinary course of nature. Isaiah speaks primarily of Israel's restoration after her longcontinued calamities; but his language is framed by the Holy Spirit so as to reach beyond this to the spiritual Zion: including not only the Jews, the natural descendants of Abraham and children of the law, but also *the Gentiles.* The spiritual Jerusalem is regarded as "barren" while the law trammeled Israel, for she then had no spiritual children of the Gentiles. **break forth**—into crying. **cry**—shout for joy. **many more**—Translate as *Greek,* "Many are the children of the desolate (the New Testament Church made up in the greater part from the Gentiles, *who once had not the promise,* and so was destitute of God as her husband), more than of her which hath an (*Greek,* 'THE') husband" (the Jewish Church having GOD for her *husband,* Isa. 54:5; Jer. 2:2). Numerous as were the children of the legal covenant, those of the Gospel covenant are more so. The force of the *Greek* article is, "Her who has THE husband of which the other is destitute." **28. we**—The oldest MSS. and versions are divided between "we" and "ye." "We" better accords with vs. 26, "mother of *us.*" **children of promise**—not children *after the flesh,* but through

ADAM CLARKE

23. *Was born after the flesh.* Ishmael was born according to the course of nature, his parents being both of a proper age, so that there was nothing uncommon or supernatural in his birth. This is the proper meaning of the apostle's *after* or "according to" *the flesh. By promise.* Both Abraham and Sarah had passed that age in which the procreation of children was possible on natural principles. The birth, therefore, of Isaac was supernatural; it was the effect of an especial promise of God, and it was only on the ground of that promise that it was either credible or possible.

24. *Which things are an allegory.* They are to be understood spiritually, more being intended in the account than meets the eye. *Allegory* signifies a "thing that is a representative of another," where the literal sense is the representative of a spiritual meaning. *For these are the two covenants.* These signify two different systems of religion: the one by Moses, the other by the Messiah. *The one from the mount Sinai.* On which the law was published, which was typified by Hagar, Abraham's bond maid. *Which gendereth to bondage.* For as the bond maid or slave could only gender, "bring forth her children," in a state of slavery, so all that are born and live under those Mosaic institutions are born and live in a state of bondage—a bondage to various rites and ceremonies; under the obligation to keep the whole law, yet from its severity and their frailness obliged to live in the habitual breach of it, and in consequence exposed to the curse which it pronounces.

25. *For this Agar is mount Sinai in Arabia.* This is the common reading; but it is read differently in some of the most respectable MSS., versions, and fathers—thus: "For this Sinai is a mountain of Arabia," the word *Agar* being omitted. *Answereth to Jerusalem.* Hagar, the bond maid, bringing forth children in a state of slavery, *answereth to Jerusalem which now is,* "points out" or "bears a similitude" to Jerusalem in her present state of subjection; which, *with her children,* her citizens, is not only *in bondage* to the Romans, but in a worse bondage to the law, to its oppressive ordinances, and to the heavy curse which it has pronounced against all those who do not keep them.

26. *But Jerusalem which is above.* The apostle still follows the Jewish allegory, showing not only how the story of Hagar and Sarah, Ishmael and Isaac, was allegorized, but pointing out also that even Jerusalem was the subject of allegory. *Is free, which is the mother of us all.* There is a spiritual Jerusalem, of which this is the type; and this Jerusalem, in which the souls of all the righteous are, is free from all bondage and sin. Or by this, probably, the kingdom of the Messiah was intended; and this certainly answers best to the apostle's meaning, as the subsequent verse shows. There is an earthly Jerusalem, but this earthly Jerusalem typifies a heavenly Jerusalem. The former, with all her citizens, is in bondage; the latter is a free city, and all her inhabitants are free also. And this Jerusalem is our *mother;* it signifies the Church of Christ, the metropolis of Christianity, or rather the state of liberty into which all true believers are brought. The word *panton, of . . . all,* is omitted by almost every MS. and version of antiquity and importance, and by the most eminent of the fathers who quote his place. It is undoubtedly spurious, and the text should be read thus: "But Jerusalem, which is above, is free, which is our mother."

27. *Rejoice, thou barren that bearest not.* This quotation is taken from Isa. liv. 1, and is certainly a promise which relates to the conversion of the Gentiles, as the following clause proves. *For the desolate,* the Gentile world, *hath many more children,* is a much larger and more numerous Church, *than she,* Jerusalem, the Jewish state, *which hath an husband,* has been so long in covenant with God, living under His continual protection and in possession of a great variety of spiritual advantages; and especially those offered to her by the gospel, which she has rejected, and which the Gentiles have accepted.

28. *Now we,* who believe in the Lord Jesus, *are the children of promise*—are the spiritual offspring of the Messiah, the Seed of Abraham,

MATTHEW HENRY

He tells them that *as then he that was born after the flesh persecuted him that was born after the Spirit*, they must expect it would be *so now*.

But, he desires them to consider what the scripture saith (Gen. xxi. 10), *Cast out the bond-woman and her son, for the son of the bond-woman shall not be heir with the son of the free-woman*. He concludes (*v.* 31), *So then, brethren, we are not children of the bond-woman, but of the free.*

CHAPTER 5

Verses 1–12

Since it appeared by what had been said that we can be justified only by faith in Jesus Christ, and that the law of Moses was no longer in force, he would have them to *stand fast in the liberty wherewith Christ hath made us free, and not to be again entangled with the yoke of bondage*. Under the gospel we are enfranchised, we are brought into a state of liberty. We owe this liberty to Jesus Christ. It is he who *has made us free*. It is therefore our duty to *stand fast in this liberty, and not to suffer ourselves to be again entangled in the yoke of bondage*.

I. Their submitting to circumcision, and depending on the works of the law for righteousness, were a forfeiture of all their advantages by Jesus Christ, *v.* 2–4.

1. With what solemnity the apostle declares this: *Behold, I Paul say unto you* (*v.* 2), and he repeats it (*v.* 3), *I testify unto you that if you be circumcised Christ shall profit you nothing*, &c. He looked upon it as a matter of the greatest consequence that they did not submit to it.

That this is his meaning appears from *v.* 4, where he expresses the same thing by their being *justified by the law*. *Christ would profit them nothing, that were debtors to do the whole law; Christ*

JAMIESON, FAUSSET, BROWN

the promise (vss. 23, 29, 31). "We *are*" so, and ought to wish to continue so. **29. persecuted**—Ishmael "mocked" Isaac, which contained in it the germ and spirit of persecution (Gen. 21:9). His mocking was probably directed against Isaac's piety and faith in God's promises. Being the older by natural birth, he haughtily prided himself above him that was born by promise: as Cain hated Abel's. piety. **him . . . born after the Spirit**—The language, though referring primarily to Isaac, born in a spiritual way (viz., by the promise or word of God, rendered by His Spirit efficient out of the course of nature, in making Sarah fruitful in old age), is so framed as especially to refer to believers justified by Gospel grace through faith, as opposed to carnal men, Judaizers, and legalists. **even so it is now**—(ch. 5:11; 6:12, 17; Acts 9:29; 13:45, 49, 50; 14:1, 2, 19; 17:5, 13; 18:5, 6). The Jews persecuted Paul, not for preaching Christianity in opposition to heathenism, but for preaching it as distinct from Judaism. Except in the two cases of Philippi and Ephesus (where the persons beginning the assault were pecuniarily interested in his expulsion), he was nowhere set upon by the Gentiles, unless they were first stirred up by the Jews. The coincidence between Paul's Epistles and Luke's history (the Acts) in this respect, is plainly undesigned, and so a proof of genuineness (see PALEY'S *Horæ Paulinæ*). **30.** Genesis 21:10, 12, where Sarah's words are, "shall not be heir with *my son, even with Isaac*." But what was there said literally, is here by inspiration expressed in its allegorical spiritual import, applying to the New Testament believer, who is antitypically "the son of the free woman." In John 8:35, 36, Jesus refers to this. **Cast out**—from the house and inheritance: literally, Ishmael; spiritually, the carnal and legalists. **shall not be heir**—The *Greek* is stronger, "*must not* be heir," or "inherit." **31. So then**—The oldest MSS. read, "Wherefore." This is the conclusion inferred from what precedes. In ch. 3:29 and 4:7, it was etstablished that we, New Testament believers, are "heirs." If, then, we are heirs, "we are not children of the bond woman (whose son, according to Scripture, was 'not to be heir,' vs. 30), but of the free woman" (whose son was, according to Scripture, to be heir). For we are not "cast out" as Ishmael, but accepted as sons and heirs.

CHAPTER 5

VSS. 1-26. PERORATION. EXHORTATION TO STAND FAST IN THE GOSPEL LIBERTY, JUST SET FORTH, AND NOT TO BE LED BY JUDAIZERS INTO CIRCUMCISION, OR LAW JUSTIFICATION: YET THOUGH FREE, TO SERVE ONE ANOTHER BY LOVE: TO WALK IN THE SPIRIT, BEARING THE FRUIT THEREOF, NOT IN THE WORKS OF THE FLESH. **1.** The oldest MSS. read, "in liberty (so ALFORD, MOBERLEY, HUMPHRY, and ELLICOTT. But as there is no *Greek* for 'in,' as there is in translating in I Cor. 16:13; Phil. 1:27; 4:1, I prefer 'It is FOR freedom that') Christ hath made us free (not *in*, or *for*, a state of bondage). Stand fast, therefore, and be not entangled again *in* a yoke of bondage" (viz., the law, ch. 4:24; Acts 15:10). On "again," see *Note*, ch. 4:9. **2. Behold**—i.e., Mark what I say. **I Paul**—Though you now think less of my authority, I nevertheless give my name and personal authority as enough by itself to refute all opposition of adversaries. **if ye be circumcised**—not as ALFORD, "If you will *go on being* circumcised." Rather, "If ye suffer yourselves to be circumcised," viz., under the notion of its being necessary to *justification* (vs. 4; Acts 15:1). Circumcision here is not regarded simply by itself (for, viewed as a mere *national* rite, it was practiced for conciliation's sake by Paul himself, Acts 16:3), but as the symbol of *Judaism* and *legalism in general*. If this be necessary, then the Gospel of grace is at an end. If the latter be the way of justification, then Judaism is in no way so. **Christ . . . profit . . . nothing**—(ch. 2:21). For righteousness of works and justification by faith cannot co-exist. "He who is circumcised [for justification] is so as fearing the law, and he who fears, disbelieves the power of grace, and he who disbelieves can profit nothing by that grace which he disbelieves [CHRYSOSTOM]. **3. For**—*Greek*, "Yea, more"; "Moreover." **I testify . . . to every man**—as well as "unto you" (vs. 2). **that is circumcised**—that submits to be circumcised. Such a one became a "proselyte of righteousness." **the whole law**—impossible for man to keep even in part, much less *wholly* (Jas. 2:10); yet none can be justified by the law, unless he keep it *wholly* (ch. 3:10). **4.** Lit., "Ye have become void from Christ," i.e., your connection with Christ has become void

ADAM CLARKE

in whom the promise stated that all the nations of the earth should be blessed.

29. *But as then he*, Ishmael, *that was born after the flesh*, whose birth had nothing supernatural in it but was according to the ordinary course of nature, *persecuted him*, Isaac, *that was born after the Spirit*—who had a supernatural birth, according to the promise, and through the efficacy of the Holy Spirit giving effect to that promise, "Sarah shall have a son," Gen. xvii. 16-21; xxi. 1. *Persecuted him;* the persecution here referred to is that mentioned in Gen. xxi. 9. It consisted in mocking his brother, Isaac. *Even so it is now*. So the Jews in every place persecute the Christian, and show thereby that they are rather of the posterity of Hagar than of Sarah.

30. *What saith the scripture?* (In Gen. xxi. 10.) *Cast out the bondwoman and her son.* And what does this imply in the present case? Why, that the present Jerusalem and her children shall be cast out of the favor of God, and *shall not be heir with the son of the freewoman*—shall not inherit the blessings promised to Abraham, because they believe not in the promised Seed.

31. *So then . . . we*, Jews and Gentiles, who believe on the Lord Jesus, *are not children of the bondwoman*, are not in subjection to the Jewish law, *but of the free;* and consequently are delivered from all its bondage, obligation, and curse.

CHAPTER 5

1. *Stand fast therefore in the liberty.* This is intimately connected with the preceding chapter, the apostle having said just before, "So then, brethren, we are not children of the bondwoman, but of the free," immediately adds, *Stand fast therefore in the liberty wherewith Christ hath made us free*. Hold fast your Christian profession; it brings spiritual liberty. On the contrary, Judaism brings spiritual bondage. The liberty mentioned by the apostle is freedom from Jewish rites and ceremonies, called properly here *the yoke of bondage;* and also liberty from the power and guilt of sin, which nothing but the grace of Christ can take away.

2. *If ye be circumcised.* By circumcision you take on you the whole obligation of the Jewish law, and consequently profess to seek salvation by means of its observances. Therefore Christ can profit you nothing; for by seeking justification by the works of the law you renounce justification by faith in Christ.

3. *He is a debtor to do the whole law.* Lays himself, by receiving circumcision, under the obligation to fulfill all its precepts and ordinances.

4. *Christ is become of no effect unto you.* It is vain for you to attempt to unite the two

MATTHEW HENRY

had become of no effect to them, they were fallen from grace. Thereby they renounced that way of justification which God had established. They became debtors to do the whole law, which required such an obedience as they were not capable of performing. Having thus revolted from Christ, and built their hopes upon the law, Christ would profit them nothing. He will not be the Saviour of any who will not own and rely upon him as their only Saviour.

II. To persuade them to steadfastness he sets before them his own example, and acquaints them what their hopes were; *through the Spirit they were waiting for the hope of righteousness by faith.* 1. What it is that Christians are waiting for: it is *the hope of righteousness*, by which we are chiefly to understand the happiness of the other world. It is the great object of their hope, which they are above everything else desiring and pursuing. It is the righteousness of Christ alone which has procured it for us, and on account of which we can expect to be brought to the possession of it. 2. How they hope to obtain this happiness, namely, by faith in our Lord Jesus Christ, not by the works of the law. 3. Whence it is that they are thus waiting for the hope of righteousness: it is *through the Spirit*. It is under his conduct, and by his assistance, that they are enabled to believe on Christ, and to look for the hope of righteousness through him.

III. He tells them (*v.* 6) that *in Christ Jesus neither circumcision availeth anything nor uncircumcision.* Christ, who is *the end of the law*, having come, now it was neither here nor there whether a man were circumcised or uncircumcised; he was neither the better for the one nor the worse for the other, nor would either the one or the other recommend him to God. Yet he informs them what would do so; *faith, which worketh by love.* Without it nothing else would stand them in any stead. Faith, where it is true, is a working grace: it works by love, love to God and love to our brethren; and faith, thus working by love, is all in all in our Christianity.

IV. To recover them from their backslidings he puts them in mind of their good beginnings.

1. *They did run well.* The life of a Christian is a race, wherein he must run, and hold on, if he would obtain the prize. It is not enough that we run in this race, but we must run well. Thus these Christians had done for awhile, but they were either turned out of the way or at least made to flag and falter in it.

2. He asks them, and calls upon them to ask themselves, *Who did hinder you?* He very well knew who they were, and what it was that hindered them; but he would have them to put the question to themselves. Many who set out fair in religion, and run well for awhile—are yet by some means or other hindered in their progress, or turned out of the way. It concerns those who have run well, but now begin either to turn out of the way or to tire in it, to enquire what it is that hinders them. Young converts must expect that Satan will be doing all he can to divert them from the course they are in. The apostle tells them that by hearkening to them they were kept from *obeying the truth.* The gospel which he had preached to them was the truth. It was necessary that they should obey it, that they should continue to govern their lives and hopes according to the directions of it. The truth is not only to be believed, but to be obeyed, to be received not only in the light of it, but in the love and power of it. Those do not rightly obey the truth, who do not steadfastly adhere to it.

V. He argues from the ill rise of that persuasion whereby they were drawn away (*v.* 8): *This persuasion,* says he, *cometh not of him that calleth you.* That is, either of God, or of the apostle himself. It could not come from God, for it was contrary to that way of justification and salvation which he had established; nor from Paul himself, for he had all along been an opposer and not a preacher of circumcision, he had never pressed the use of it upon Christians, much less imposed it upon them as necessary to salvation. He leaves them to judge whence it must arise; it could be owing to none but Satan and his instruments. The Galatians had every reason to reject it, and to continue steadfast in the truth which they had before embraced.

VI. The danger there was of the spreading of this infection, is a further argument which the apostle urges against their complying with false teachers. To convince them that there was more danger in it than they were aware of, he tells them (*v.* 9) that *a little leaven leaveneth the whole lump.* The whole lump of the Christian society may be infected by

JAMIESON, FAUSSET, BROWN

(vs. 2). Romans 7:2, "*Loosed* from the law," where the same *Greek* occurs as here. **whosoever of you are justified**—"are being justified," i.e., are *endeavoring* to be justified. **by the law**—*Greek,* "IN the law," as the element *in* which justification is to take place. **fallen from grace**—Ye no longer "*stand*" in grace (Rom. 5:2). Grace and legal righteousness cannot co-exist (Rom. 4:4, 5; 11:6). Christ, by circumcision (Luke 2:21), undertook to obey all the law, and fulfil all righteousness for us; any, therefore, that now seeks to fulfil the law for himself in any degree for justifying righteousness, severs himself from the grace which flows from Christ's fulfilment of it, and becomes "a debtor to do the whole law" (vs. 3). The decree of the Jerusalem council had said nothing so strong as this; it had merely decided that Gentile Christians were not bound to legal observances. But the Galatians, while not pretending to be so *bound,* imagined there was an efficacy in them to merit a higher degree of *perfection* (ch. 3:3). This accounts for Paul not referring to the decree at all. He took much higher ground. See PALEY'S *Horæ Paulinæ.* The natural mind loves outward fetters, and is apt to forge them for itself, to stand in lieu of holiness of heart. **5. For**—proof of the assertion, "fallen from grace," by contrasting with the case of *legalists,* the "hope" of *Christians.* **through the Spirit**—*Greek,* rather, "by the Spirit": in opposition to *by the flesh* (ch. 4:29), or fleshly ways of justification, as circumcision and legal ordinances. "We" is emphatical, and contrasted with "whosoever of you would be justified by the law" (vs. 4). **the hope of righteousness**—"We wait for the (realization of the) hope (which is the fruit) of the righteousness (i.e., justification which comes) by (lit., *from—out of*) faith," Rom. 5:1, 4, 5; 8:24, 25, "*Hope . . . we* with patience *wait for* it." This is a farther step than being "justified"; not only are we this, but "wait for the hope" which is connected with it, and is its full consummation. "Righteousness," in the sense of justification, is by the believer once for all already attained; but the consummation of it in future perfection above is the object of *hope* to be *waited for*: "the crown of righteousness laid up" (II Tim. 4:8): "the hope laid up for you in heaven" (Col. 1:5; I Pet. 1:3). **6. For**—confirming the truth that it is "by faith" (vs. 5). **in Jesus Christ**—*Greek,* "in Christ Jesus." In union with *Christ* (the ANOINTED Saviour), that is, *Jesus* of Nazareth. **nor uncircumcision**—This is levelled against those who, being not legalists, or Judaizers, think themselves Christians on this ground alone. **faith which worketh by love** *Greek,* "working. . . ." This corresponds to "a new creature" (ch. 6:15), as its definition. Thus in vss. 5, 6, we have the three, "faith," "hope," and "love." The *Greek* expresses, "Which effectually worketh"; which exhibits its *energy* by love (so I Thess. 2:13). *Love* is not joined with *faith* in justifying, but is the principle of the works which follow after justification by faith. Let not legalists, upholding circumcision, think that the essence of the law is set at naught by the doctrine of justification by faith only. Nay, "all the law is fulfilled in one word—love," which is the principle on which "faith worketh" (vs. 14). Let them, therefore, seek this "faith," which will enable them truly to fulfil the law. Again, let not those who pride themselves on uncircumcision think that, because the law does not justify, they are free to walk after "the flesh" (vs. 13). Let them, then, seek that "love" which is inseparable from true faith (Jas. 2:8, 12-22). Love is utterly opposed to the enmities which prevailed among the Galatians (vss. 15, 20). The Spirit (vs. 5) is a Spirit of "faith" and "love" (cf. Rom. 14:17; I Cor. 7:19). **7.** Translate, "Ye were running well" in the Gospel race (I Cor. 9:24-26; Phil. 3:13, 14). **who . . .**—none whom you ought to have listened to [BENGEL]: alluding to the Judaizers (cf. ch. 3:1). **hinder**—The *Greek* means, lit., "hinder by breaking up a road." **not obey the truth**—not submit yourselves to the true Gospel way of justification. **8. This persuasion**—*Greek, "The* persuasion," viz., to which you are yielding. There is a play on words in the original, the *Greek* for *persuasion* being akin to "*obey*" (vs. 7). This persuasion which ye have *obeyed.* **cometh not of**—i.e. "from". Does not emanate from Him, but from an enemy. **that calleth you**—(*V.* 13: ch. 1:6; Phil. 3:14; I Thess. 5:24). The calling is the rule of the whole race [BENGEL]. **9. A little leaven**—the *false teaching* of the Judaizers. A small portion of legalism, if it be mixed with the Gospel, corrupts its purity. To add legal ordinances and works in the least degree to justification by faith, is to undermine "the whole." So "leaven" is used of *false doctrine* (Matt. 16:12; cf. 13:33). In I Corinthians 5:6 it means the corrupt-

ADAM CLARKE

systems. You must have the law and no Christ or Christ and no law for your justification.

Ye are fallen from grace. From the gospel. They had been brought into the grace of the gospel, and now, by readopting the Mosaic ordinance, they had apostatized from the gospel as a system of religion, and had lost the grace communicated to their souls, by which they were preserved in a state of salvation. The peace and love of God, received by Jesus Christ, could not remain in the hearts of those who had rejected Christ. They had therefore in every sense of the word *fallen from grace,* and whether some of them ever rose again is more than we can tell.

5. *For we,* Christians, *through the Spirit,* through the operation of the Holy Ghost, under this spiritual dispensation of the gospel, *wait for the hope of righteousness*—expect that which is the object of our hope, on our being justified by faith in Christ. *Righteousness* may here, as in many other places of Paul's Epistles, mean "justification." And the hope of justification, or the hope excited and inspired by it, is the possession of eternal glory; for, says the apostle, Rom. v. 1-2, "Being justified by faith, we have peace with God . . . and rejoice in hope of the glory of God." As this glory is necessarily future, it is to be waited for. But this waiting, in a thorough Christian, is not only a blessed expectation, but also a continual anticipation of it; and therefore the apostle says we "receive out of it." This is no fanciful derivation; it exists in the experience of every genuine Christian. He is continually anticipating or receiving foretastes of that glory the fullness of which he expects after death. Thus Christians are receiving the end of their faith, the salvation of their souls, 1 Pet. i. 9.

6. *For in Jesus Christ.* By the dispensation of the gospel all legal observances as essential to salvation are done away; and uncircumcision, or the Gentile state, contributes as much to salvation as circumcision or the Jewish state. They are both equally ineffectual; and nothing now avails in the sight of God but that faith "which is made active [or energetic] by love." God acknowledges no faith as of the operation of His Spirit that is not active or obedient. But the principle of all obedience to God and beneficence to man is *love;* therefore faith cannot work unless it be associated with love.

7. *Ye did run well.* You once had the faith that worked by love—you were genuine, active, useful Christians. *Who did hinder?* Who prevented you from continuing to obey the truth? You could be turned aside only by your own consent. Paul here, as in 1 Cor. ix. 24, compares Christianity to a race.

8. *This persuasion,* of the necessity of your being circumcised and obeying the law of Moses, is *not of him that calleth you.* I never preached such a doctrine to you; I called you out of bondage to liberty, from a galling yoke to a cheerful service.

9. *A little leaven leaveneth the whole lump.* A proverbial expression (see 1 Cor. v. 6) very aptly applied to those who receive the smallest tincture of false doctrine relative to the things essential to salvation, which soon influences the whole conduct so that the man becomes totally perverted. They might have argued, "It is a small thing, and should not be made a subject

MATTHEW HENRY

one member of it, and therefore they were greatly concerned, to purge out the infection from among them. The doctrine which the false teachers were industrious to spread, and which some in these churches had been drawn into, was subversive of Christianity itself, and therefore considering the fatal tendency of it, he would not have them to be easy and unconcerned.

VII. He expresses the hopes he had concerning them (*v.* 10): *I have confidence in you, through the Lord, that you will be none otherwise minded.* He hoped that they might be brought to be of the same mind with him, and to own and abide by that truth and that liberty of the gospel which he had preached to them. We ought to hope the best even of those concerning whom we have cause to fear the worst. He lays the blame of it more upon others than themselves; for he adds, *But he that troubleth you shall bear his judgment, whosoever he be.* In reproving sin and error, we should always distinguish between the leaders and the led. Thus the apostle softens and alleviates the fault of these Christians, even while he is reproving them. But as for him or those that troubled them, he declares they *should bear their judgment.* He did not doubt but God would deal with them according to their deserts.

VIII. To dissuade these Christians from hearkening to their judaizing teachers, he represents them as men who had used very base methods to compass their designs: for they had misrepresented him. They had given out among them that Paul himself was a preacher of circumcision: for when he says (*v.* 11), *And I brethren, if I yet preach circumcision,* it plainly appears that they had reported him to have done so. Yet that he was a preacher of it he utterly denies. If he would have preached circumcision, he might have avoided persecution. If I yet preach circumcision, says he, *why do I yet suffer persecution*? If he had fallen in with them herein, instead of being exposed to their rage he might have been received into their favour. He was so far from preaching the doctrine he was charged with, that, rather than do so, he was willing to expose himself to the greatest hazards.

If he had yielded to the Jews herein, *then would the offence of the cross have ceased.* He rather chose to hazard his ease and credit, yea his very life itself, than thus to corrupt the truth and give up the liberty of the gospel.

He wishes that *they were even cut off*—not cut off from Christ and all hopes of salvation by him, but cut off by the censures of the church, which ought to witness against those teachers who thus corrupted the purity of the gospel.

Verses 13–26

The apostle comes to exhort these Christians to serious practical godliness.

I. They should not strive with one another, but love one another. He tells them (*v.* 13) that *they had been called unto liberty,* but yet he would have them be very careful that they did not *use this liberty as an occasion to the flesh.*

JAMIESON, FAUSSET, BROWN

ing influence of one bad *person;* so BENGEL understands it here to refer to the person (vss. 7, 8, 10) who misled them. Ecclesiastes 9:18, "One sinner destroyeth much good" (I Cor. 15:33). I prefer to refer it to false *doctrine,* answering to "persuasion" (vs. 8). **10.** *Greek,* "I (emphatical: "*I on my part*") have confidence in the Lord *with regard to* you (II Thess. 3:4), that ye will be none otherwise minded" (than what by this Epistle I desire you to be, Phil. 3:15). **but he that troubleth you**—(ch. 1:7; Acts 15:24; Josh. 7:25; I Kings 18:17, 18). Some one, probably, was prominent among the seducers, though the denunciation applies to them all (ch. 1:7; 4:17). **shall bear**—as a heavy burden. **his**—*his due and inevitable* judgment from God. Paul distinguishes the case of the seduced, who were misled through thoughtlessness, and who, now that they are set right by him, he confidently hopes, in God's goodness, will return to the right way, from that of the seducer who is doomed to judgment. **whosoever he be**—whether great (ch. 1:8) or small. **11.** Translate, "If I am still preaching (as I did before conversion) circumcision, why am I still persecuted?" The Judaizing troubler of the Galatians had said, "Paul himself preaches circumcision," as is shown by his having circumcised Timothy (Acts 16:3; cf. also Acts 20:6; 21:24). Paul replies by anticipation of their objection, As regards myself, the fact that I am still persecuted by the Jews shows plainly that I do *not* preach circumcision; for it is just because I preach Christ crucified, and not the Mosaic law, as the sole ground of justification, that they persecute me. If for conciliation he lived as a Jew among the Jews, it was in accordance with his principle enunciated (I Cor. 7:18, 20; 9:20). Circumcision, or uncircumcision, are things indifferent in themselves: their lawfulness or unlawfulness depends on the *animus* of him who uses them. The Gentile Galatians' animus in circumcision could only be their supposition that it influenced favorably their standing before God. Paul's living as a Gentile among Gentiles, plainly showed that, if he lived as a Jew among Jews, it was not that he thought it meritorious before God, but as a matter indifferent, wherein he might lawfully conform as a *Jew by birth* to those with whom he was, in order to put no needless stumbling block to the Gospel in the way of his countrymen. **then**—Presuming that I did so, "then," in that case, "the offense of (stumbling block, I Cor. 1:23 occasioned to the Jews by) the cross has become done away." Thus the Jews' accusation against Stephen was not that he preached Christ crucified, but that "he spake blasphemous words against this holy place and *the law.*" They would, in some measure, have borne the former, if he had mixed with it justification in part by circumcision and the law, and if he had, through the medium of Christianity, brought converts to Judaism. But if justification in any degree depended on legal ordinances, Christ's crucifixion in that degree was unnecessary, and could profit nothing (vss. 2, 4). Worldly Wiseman, of the town of Carnal Policy, turns Christian out of the narrow way of the Cross, to the house of Legality. But the way to it was up a mountain, which, as Christian advanced, threatened to fall on him and crush him, amidst flashes of lightning from the mountain (*Pilgrim's Progress*; Heb. 12:18-21). **12. they . . . which trouble you**—Translate, as the *Greek* is different from vs. 10, "they who are *unsettling* you." **were even cut off**—even as they desire your foreskin to be *cut off* and cast away by circumcision, so would that *they were even cut off* from your communion, being worthless as a castaway foreskin (ch. 1:7, 8; cf. Phil. 3:2). The fathers, JEROME, AMBROSE, AUGUSTINE, and CHRYSOSTOM, explain it, "Would that they would even cut themselves off," i.e., cut off not merely the foreskin, but the whole member: if *circumcision* be not enough for them, then let them have *excision* also; an outburst hardly suitable to the gravity of an apostle. But vss. 9, 10 plainly point to *excommunication* as the judgment threatened against the troublers: and danger of the bad "leaven" spreading, as the reason for it. **13.** The "ye" is emphatical, from its position in the *Greek,* "Ye brethren"; as opposed to those legalists "who trouble you." **unto liberty**—The *Greek* expresses, "on a footing of liberty." The *state* or *condition* in which ye have been called to salvation, is one of liberty. Gospel liberty consists in three things, freedom from the Mosaic yoke, from sin, and from slavish fear. **only . . .**—Translate, "Only turn not *your* liberty into an occasion for the flesh." Do not give the flesh the handle or pretext (Rom. 7:8, "occasion") for its indulgence which it eagerly seeks for; do not let it make Christian "liberty" its pretext for indulgence (vss. 16:17; I Pet. 2:16; II Pet. 2:19; Jude 4). **but**

ADAM CLARKE

of serious controversy, whether we be circumcised or not." Granted that in itself it is a small matter; but as every man who is circumcised "is a debtor to do the whole law," v. 3, then your circumcision leads necessarily to your total perversion; as the little portion of leaven, mixed with the batch, soon leavens the whole lump.

10. *I have confidence in you.* I now feel a persuasion from the Lord that I shall not be permitted to expostulate with you in vain. *That ye will be none otherwise minded*—that you will be aware of the danger to which you are exposed, that you will retreat in time, and recover the grace which you have lost. *But he that troubleth you.* The false teacher who sowed doubtful disputations among you, and thus has troubled the repose of the whole church, *shall bear his judgment,* shall meet with the punishment he deserves for having sown his tares among God's wheat.

11. *If I yet preach circumcision.* It is very likely that some of the false apostles, hearing of Paul's having circumcised Timothy, Acts xvi. 3, which must have been done about this time, reported him as being an advocate for circumcision, and by this means endeavored to sanction their own doctrine. To this the apostle replies: Were it so, that I am a friend to this measure, is it likely that I should suffer persecution from the Jews? But I am everywhere persecuted by them, and I am persecuted because I am known to be an enemy to circumcision.

Were I a friend to this doctrine, the *offence of the cross,* preaching salvation only through the sacrifice of Christ, would soon cease; because, to be consistent with myself, if I preached the necessity of circumcision I must soon cease to preach Christ crucified, and then the Jews would be no longer my enemies.

12. *I would they were even cut off which trouble you.* As the persons who were breeding all this confusion in the churches of Galatia were members of that church, the apostle appears to me to be simply expressing his desire that they might be *cut off* or "excommunicated" from the church.

13. *Ye have been called unto liberty.* A total freedom from all the burdensome rites and ceremonies of the Mosaic law. *Only use not that liberty for an occasion to the flesh.* By *flesh* here we may understand all the unrenewed desires and propensities of the mind, whatsoever is not under the influence and guidance of the Holy Spirit of God. Your liberty is from that which would oppress the spirit, not from that which would lay restraints on the flesh. The gospel proclaims liberty from the ceremonial law, but binds you still faster under the moral law. To be freed from the ceremonial law is the gospel liberty; to pretend freedom from the moral law is antinomianism.

MATTHEW HENRY

On the contrary, he would have them *by love to serve one another*. The liberty we enjoy as Christians is not a licentious liberty: though Christ has redeemed us from the curse of the law, yet he has not freed us from the obligation of it. Though we ought to stand fast in our Christian liberty, yet we should not insist upon it to the breach of Christian charity, but should always maintain such a temper towards each other as may dispose us by love to serve one another. Two considerations for this purpose: (1) *That all the law is fulfilled in one word, even in this, Thou shalt love thy neighbour as thyself, v.* 14. Love is the sum of the whole law. It will appear that we are the disciples of Christ indeed when we have love one to another (John xiii. 35); and, if it do not wholly extinguish those unhappy discords that are among Christians, yet at least the fatal consequences of them will be prevented. (2) The dangerous tendency of a contrary behaviour (*v.* 15): *But*, says he, if *you bite and devour one another, take heed that you be not consumed one of another*. Mutual strifes among brethren, if persisted in, are likely to prove a common ruin. Christian churches can only be ruined by their own hands; if Christians be as brute beasts, biting and devouring each other, what can be expected but that the God of love should deny his grace to them, and the Spirit of love should depart from them, and that the evil spirit should prevail?

II. They should all strive against sin; and happy would it be for the church if Christians would let all their quarrels be swallowed up of this, even a quarrel against sin. This is what we are chiefly concerned to fight against.

1. That there is in everyone a struggle between the flesh and the spirit (*v.* 17): *The flesh lusts against the spirit*. On the other hand, *the spirit* (the renewed part of us) strives *against the flesh*, hence it comes to pass *that we cannot do the things that we would*. Even as in a natural man there is something of this struggle (the convictions of his conscience and the corruption of his own heart strive with one another) so in a renewed man, there is a struggle between the old nature and the new nature, the remainders of sin and the beginnings of grace; and this Christians must expect as long as they continue in this world.

2. That it is our duty and interest in this struggle to side with the better part and with our graces against our lusts. He gives us this one general rule, to walk in the Spirit (*v.* 16): *This I say, then, Walk in the Spirit, and you shall not fulfil the lust of the flesh*. The duty here recommended to us is that we set ourselves to act under the guidance and influence of the blessed Spirit. We may depend upon it that, though we may not be freed from the stirrings of our corrupt nature, though it remain in us, yet it shall not obtain a dominion over us. The best antidote against the poison of sin is to walk in the Spirit.

So it would be a good evidence that they were Christians indeed; for, says the apostle (*v.* 18), *If you be led by the Spirit, you are not under the law*. If, in the prevailing bent and tenor of your lives, you be *led by the Spirit*, it will hence appear that you are not under the law, not under the condemning, though you are still under the commanding, power of it.

3. The apostle specifies the works of the flesh and the fruits of the Spirit, which must be cherished and brought forth (*v.* 19), &c. He begins with *the works of the flesh*, which, as they are many, so they are manifest. Some are sins against the seventh commandment, such as *adultery, fornication, uncleanness, lasciviousness.*

JAMIESON, FAUSSET, BROWN

by love serve one another—*Greek*, "Be servants (be in bondage) to one another." If ye must be *servants*, then *be servants to one another in love*. While free as to legalism, be *bound* by Love (the article in the *Greek* personifies love in the abstract) to serve one another (I Cor. 9:19). Here he hints at their unloving strifes springing out of lust of power."For the lust of power is the mother of heresies" [CHRYSOSTOM]. **14. all the law**—*Greek*, "the whole law," viz., the Mosaic law. *Love to God* is presupposed as the root from which *love to our neighbor* springs; and it is in this tense the latter *precept* (so "word" means here) is said to be the fulfilling of "*all* the law" (Lev. 19:18). Love is "the law of Christ" (ch. 6:2; Matt. 7:12; 22:39, 40; Rom. 13:9, 10). **is fulfilled**—Not as received text "is being fulfilled," but as the oldest MSS. read, "has been fulfilled"; and so "receives its full perfection," as rudimentary teachings are fulfilled by the more perfect doctrine. The law only united Israelites together; the Gospel unites all men, and that in relation to God [GROTIUS]. **15. bite**—*backbite* the character. **devour**—the substance by injuring, extortion, etc. (Hab. 1:13; Matt. 23:14; II Cor. 11:20). **consumed . . .**—Strength of soul, health of body, character, and resources, are all consumed by broils [BENGEL]. **16. This I say then**—Repeating in other words, and explaining the sentiment in vs. 13. "What I mean is this." **Walk in the Spirit**—*Greek*, "By (the rule of) the (Holy) Spirit." Cf. vss. 16-18, 22, 25; ch. 6:1-8, with Romans 7:22; 8:11. The best way to keep tares out of a bushel is to fill it with wheat. **the flesh**—the natural man, out of which flow the evils specified (vss. 19-21). The spirit and the flesh mutually exclude one another. It is promised, not that we should have no evil lusts, but that we should "not *fulfil*" them. If the spirit that is in us can be at ease under sin, it is not a spirit that comes from the Holy Spirit. The gentle dove trembles at the sight even of a hawk's feather. **17. For**—the reason why walking by the Spirit will exclude fulfilling the lusts of the flesh, viz., their mutual contrariety. **the Spirit**—not "lusteth," but "tendeth (or some such word is to be supplied) against the flesh." **so that ye cannot do the things that ye would**—The Spirit strives against the flesh and its evil influence; the flesh against the Spirit and His good influence, *so that neither the one nor the other can be fully carried out into action*. "But" (vs. 18) where "the Spirit" prevails, the issue of the struggle no longer continues doubtful (Rom. 7:15-20) [BENGEL]. The *Greek* is, "that ye may not do the things that ye would." "The flesh and Spirit are contrary one to the other," *so that* you must distinguish what proceeds from the Spirit, and what from the flesh; and *you must not fulfil what you desire according to the carnal self*, but what the Spirit within you desires [NEANDER]. But the antithesis of vs. 18 ("But . . ."), where the conflict is *decided*, shows, I think, that here vs. 17 contemplates the inability both for fully accomplishing the *good* we "would," owing to the opposition of the *flesh*, and for doing the *evil* our flesh would desire, owing to the opposition of *the Spirit* in the awakened man (such as the Galatians are assumed to be), until we yield ourselves wholly by the Spirit to "walk by the Spirit" (vss. 16, 18). **18.** "If ye *are* led (give yourselves up to be led) *by* (*Greek*) the Spirit, ye are not under the law." For ye are not working the works of the flesh (vss. 16, 19-21) which bring one "under the law" (Rom. 8:2, 14). The "Spirit makes free from the law of sin and death" (vs. 23). The law is made for a fleshly man, and for the works of the flesh (I Tim. 1:9), "not for a righteous man" (Rom. 6:14, 15). **19-23.** Confirming vs. 18, by showing the contrariety between the works of the flesh and the fruit of the Spirit. **manifest**—The hidden *fleshly* principle betrays itself palpably by its works, so that these are not hard to discover, and leave no doubt that they come not from the Spirit. **which are these**—*Greek*, "such as," for instance. **Adultery**—omitted in the oldest MSS. **lasciviousness**—rather, "wantonness" petulance, capricious insolence; it may display itself in "lasciviousness," but not necessarily or constantly so (Mark 7:21, 22. where it is not associated with fleshly lusts) [TRENCH]. "Works" (in the plural) are attributed to the "flesh," because they are divided, and often at variance with one another, and even when taken each one by itself, betray their fleshly origin. But the "*fruit* of the Spirit" (vs. 23) is singular, because, however manifold the results, they form one harmonious whole. The results of the flesh are not dignified by the name "fruit"; they are but "works" (Eph. 5:9, 11). He enumerates those fleshly *works* (committed against our neighbor, against God, and against ourselves) to which the Galatians were most prone (the Kelts have al-

ADAM CLARKE

By love serve one another. Having that "faith which worketh by love," serve each other to the uttermost of your power; serve each other, when necessary, as "slaves" serve their masters.

14. *For all the law*, which respects our duty to our fellows, *is fulfilled*, is comprehended, *in one word: Thou shalt love thy neighbour as thyself.*

15. *If ye bite and devour one another*. These churches seem to have been in a state of great distraction; there were continual altercations among them. They had fallen from the grace of the gospel; and as Christ no longer dwelt in their hearts by faith, pride, anger, ill will, and all unkind and uncharitable tempers took possession of their souls, and they were in consequence alternately destroying each other. Nothing is so destructive to the peace of man and to the peace of the soul as religious disputes; where they prevail, religion in general has little place.

16. *Walk in the Spirit*. Get back that Spirit of God which you have grieved and lost; take up that spiritual religion which you have abandoned. *Ye shall not fulfil the lust of the flesh*. If the Spirit of God dwell in and rule your heart, the whole carnal mind will be destroyed; and then, not only carnal ordinances will be abandoned, but also the works and propensities of the flesh.

17. *For the flesh lusteth against the Spirit*. God still continues to strive with you, notwithstanding your apostasy, showing you whence you have fallen and exciting you to return to Him; but your own obstinacy renders all ineffectual; and through the influence of these different principles you are kept in a state of self-opposition and self-distraction, *so that ye cannot do the things that ye would*. You are convinced of what is right, and you wish to do it; but having abandoned the gospel and the grace of Christ, the law and its ordinances which you have chosen in their place afford you no power to conquer your evil propensities. It was on this ground that the apostle exhorted them, v. 16, to "walk in the Spirit," that they might not "fulfil the lust of the flesh," as without the grace of God they could do nothing.

18. *But if ye be led of the Spirit*. If you receive again the gospel and the grace of Christ, and permit yourselves to be influenced by the Holy Spirit, whom you are now grieving, *ye are not under the law*, you will not feel those evil propensities which now disgrace and torment you; but they must prevail while you are not under the influence of the grace and Spirit of Christ.

19. *Now the works of the flesh are manifest*. By *flesh* we are to understand the evil and fallen state of the soul, no longer under the guidance of God's Spirit and right reason, but under the animal passions; and they are rendered even more irregular and turbulent by the influence of sin, so that man is in a worse state than the brute. And so all-commanding is this evil nature that it leads men into all kinds of crimes, among them the following, which *are manifest*—known to all, and most prevalent; and though these are most solemnly forbidden by your law, the observance of its ordinances gives no power to overcome them, and provides no pardon for the guilt and condemnation produced by them. *Adultery*. Illicit connection with a married person. This word is wanting in this place in the best MSS., versions, and fathers, the next term often comprehending both. *Fornication*. Illicit connection between single or unmarried persons, yet often signifying adultery also. *Uncleanness*. Whatever is opposite to purity; probably meaning here, as in Rom. i. 24; 2 Cor. xii. 21, unnatural practices; sodomy, bestiality. *Lasciviousness*. Whatever is contrary to chastity; all lewdness.

MATTHEW HENRY

Some are sins against the first and second commandments, as *idolatry* and *witchcraft*. Others are sins against our neighbour, such as *hatred, variance, emulations, wrath, strife, seditions, heresies, envyings*, and sometimes break out into *murders*, not only of the names and reputation, but even of the very lives of our fellow-creatures.

Others are sins against ourselves, such as *drunkenness and revellings*. Of these and *such like*, says he, *I tell you before, as I have also told you in times past*, that *those who do such things, shall not inherit the kingdom of God*. These are sins which will undoubtedly shut men out of heaven. He specifies the fruits of the Spirit, which as Christians we are concerned to bring forth, *v.* 22, 23. As sin is called *the work of the flesh*, because the flesh is the principle that moves men to it, so grace is said to be *the fruit of the Spirit*, because it wholly proceeds from the Spirit, as the fruit does from the root.

He particularly commends to us, *love* and *joy*, by which may be understood constant delight in God,—*peace*, with God, or a peaceableness towards others,—*long-suffering*,—*gentleness*,—a sweetness of temper, easy to be entreated when any have wronged us,—*goodness*, readiness to do good to all as we have opportunity,

JAMIESON, FAUSSET, BROWN

ways been prone to disputations and internal strifes): and those manifestations of the *fruit* of the Spirit most needed by them (vss. 13, 15). This passage shows that "the flesh" does not mean merely *sensuality*, as opposed to *spirituality*; for "divisions" in the catalogue here do not flow from sensuality. The identification of "the natural (*Greek, animal-souled*) man," with the "carnal" or *fleshly* man (I Cor. 2:14), shows that "the flesh" expresses *human nature as estranged from God*. TRENCH observes, as a proof of our fallen state, how much richer is every vocabulary in words for sins, than in those for graces. Paul enumerates *seventeen* "works of the flesh," only *nine* manifestations of "the fruit of the Spirit" (cf. Eph. 4:31). **20. witchcraft**—sorcery; prevalent in Asia (Acts 19:19; cf. Rev. 21). **hatred**—*Greek*, "hatreds." **variance**—*Greek*, "strife"; singular in the oldest MSS. **emulations**—in the oldest MSS. singular, "emulation," or rather, "jealousy"; for the sake of one's own advantage. "Envyings" (vs. 21) are even without advantage to the person himself [BENGEL]. **wrath**—*Greek*, plural, "passionate outbreaks" [ALFORD]. **strife**—rather as *Greek*, "factions," "cabals"; derived from a *Greek* root, meaning "a worker for hire": hence, *unworthy means for compassing ends, factious practices*. **seditions**—"dissensions," as to secular matters. **heresies**—as to sacred things (*Note*, I Cor. 11:19). Self-constituted *parties;* from a *Greek* root, to *choose*. A *schism* is a more recent split in a congregation from a difference of opinion. *Heresy* is a schism become inveterate [AUGUSTINE, *Con. Crescon. Don.*, 2, 7].

21. tell . . . before—viz., before the event. **I . . . told you in time past**—when I was with you. **you**—who, though maintaining justification by the law, are careless about keeping the law (Rom. 2:21-23). **not inherit . . . kingdom of God**—(I Cor. 6:9, 10; Eph. 5:5).

22. love—the leader of the band of graces (I Corinthians 13).

gentleness—*Greek*, "benignity," conciliatory to others; whereas "goodness," though ready to do good, has not such *suavity* of manner [JEROME]. ALFORD translates, "kindness."

ADAM CLARKE

20. *Idolatry*. Worshipping of idols; frequenting idol festivals; all the rites of Bacchus, Venus, etc., which were common among the Gentiles. *Witchcraft*. *Pharmaceia* from *pharmacon*, "a drug or poison"; because in all spells and enchantments, whether true or false, drugs were employed. *Hatred*. "Aversions" and "antipathies," when opposed to brotherly love and kindness. *Variance*. "Contentions," where the principle of hatred proceeds to open acts; hence contests, altercations, lawsuits, and disputes in general. *Emulations*. "Envies" or "emulations"; that is, strife to excel at the expense of another; lowering others to set up oneself; unholy zeal, fervently adopting a bad cause, or supporting a good one by cruel means. *Wrath*. Turbulent passions, disturbing the harmony of the mind, and producing domestic and civil broils and disquietudes. *Strife*. Disputations, janglings. *Seditions*. Divisions into separate factions; parties, whether in the church or state. *Heresies*. "Factions"; parties in the church separating from communion with each other, and setting up altar against altar. The word, which is harmless in itself, is here used in a bad sense.

21. *Envyings*. "Pain felt, and malignity conceived, at the sight of excellence or happiness," a passion the most base and the least curable of all that disgrace or degrade the fallen soul. *Murders*. Similarity of sound to the preceding seems to have suggested the word in this association; it is wanting in several MSS. Murder signifies the destruction of human life; and as he who hates his brother in his heart is ready to take away his life, so he is called a murderer. *Revellings*. Lascivious feastings, with obscene songs, music, etc. *And such like*. All that proceeds from the evil passions of a fallen spirit, besides those above specified; and all that the law of God specifies and condemns. *Of the which I tell you before*. When I first preached the gospel to you. *As I have also told you in time past*. When I paid my second visit to you, for the apostle did visit them twice. See Acts xvi. 6 and xviii. 23. *Shall not inherit*. They are not children of God, and therefore cannot inherit the Kingdom which belongs only to the children of the divine family.

22. *But the fruit of the Spirit*. Both "flesh," the sinful dispositions of the human heart, and spirit, the changed or purified state of the soul by the grace and Spirit of God, are represented by the apostle as trees, one yielding good, the other bad fruit; the productions of each being according to the nature of the tree, as the tree is according to the nature of the seed from which it sprang. The bad seed produced a bad tree, yielding all manner of bad fruit; the good seed produced a good tree, bringing forth fruits of the most excellent kind. The tree of the flesh, with all its bad fruits, we have already seen; the tree of the Spirit with its good fruits, we shall now see. *Love*. An intense desire to please God, and to do good to mankind; the very soul and spirit of all true religion; the fulfilling of the law, and what gives energy to faith itself. *Joy*. The exultation that arises from a sense of God's mercy communicated to the soul in the pardon of its iniquities, and the prospect of that eternal glory of which it has the foretaste in the pardon of sin. *Peace*. The calm, quiet, and order which take place in the justified soul instead of the doubts, fears, alarms, and dreadful forebodings which every true penitent more or less feels, and must feel till the assurance of pardon brings peace and satisfaction to the mind. *Longsuffering*. Long-mindedness, bearing with the frailties and provocations of others, from the consideration that God has borne long with ours and that, if He had not, we should have been speedily consumed; bearing up also through all the troubles and difficulties of life without murmuring or repining; submitting cheerfully to every dispensation of God's providence, and thus deriving benefit from every occurrence. *Gentleness*. Benignity, affability; a very rare grace, often wanting in many who have a considerable share of Christian excellence. A good education and polished manners, when brought under the influence of the grace of God, will bring out this grace with great effect. *Goodness*. The perpetual desire and sincere study, not only to abstain from every appearance of evil, but to do good to the bodies and souls of men to the utmost of our ability.

MATTHEW HENRY

—*faith*, in what we profess and promise to others,—*meekness*, not to be easily provoked, and, when we are so, to be soon pacified,—

and *temperance*. Concerning those in whom these fruits of the Spirit are found, the apostle says, *There is no law against them*. They are not under the law, but under grace; for these fruits of the Spirit, in whomsoever they are found, plainly show that such are *led by the Spirit*. So (*v.* 24) he informs us that this is the sincere care and endeavour of all real Christians: *And those that are Christ's have crucified the flesh with the affections and lusts*. They are now sincerely endeavouring to die unto sin, as he had died for it. They have not yet obtained a complete victory over it; they have still flesh as well as Spirit in them, and that has its affections and lusts, which continue to give them no little disturbance, but they are seeking the utter ruin and destruction of it. If we would approve ourselves to be Christ's, we must make it our constant care to crucify the flesh. Christ will never own those as his who yield themselves the servants of sin. It is not enough that we cease to do evil, but we must learn to do well. Our Christianity obliges us not only to oppose the works of the flesh, but to bring forth the fruits of the Spirit too. This must be our sincere care and endeavour as well as the other; and that it was the design of the apostle to represent both of these as our duty may be gathered from what follows (*v.* 25): *If we live in the Spirit, let us also walk in the Spirit*. He had before told us that the Spirit of Christ is a privilege bestowed on all the children of God, *ch.* iv. 6. Let us show it by behaviour agreeable hereunto; let us evidence our good principles by good practices. It must be by our *walking not after the flesh, but after the spirit*. We must set ourselves in good earnest both to mortify the deeds of the body, and to walk in newness of life.

4. The apostle concludes this chapter with a caution against pride and envy, *v.* 26. He here cautions them against being desirous of vainglory, because this would certainly lead them to provoke one another and to envy one another. Thus a foundation is laid for those quarrels and contentions which are inconsistent with that love which Christians ought to maintain towards each other. This therefore the apostle would have us by all means to watch against. (1) The glory which comes from men is vain-glory, which, instead of being desirous of, we should be dead to. (2) An undue regard to the applause of men is one great ground of the unhappy strifes and contentions that exist among Christians.

JAMIESON, FAUSSET, BROWN

faith—"faithfulness"; opposed to "heresies" [BENGEL]. ALFORD refers to I Corinthians 13:7, "Believeth all things": *faith* in the widest sense, toward God and man. "Trustfulness" [CONYBEARE and HOWSON].

23. temperance—The *Greek* root implies *self-restraint* as to one's desires and lusts. **against such**—not *persons*, but things, as in vs. 21. **no law**—confirming vs. 18, "Not under the law" (I Tim. 1:9, 10). The law itself commands love (vs. 14); so far is it from being "against such."

24. The oldest MSS. read, "They that are of Christ Jesus"; they that belong to Christ Jesus; being "led by (His) Spirit" (vs. 18). **have crucified the flesh**—They nailed it to the cross once for all when they became Christ's, on believing and being baptized (Rom. 6:3, 4): they keep it *now* in a state of crucifixion (Rom. 6:6): so that the Spirit can produce in them, comparatively uninterrupted by it, "the fruit of the Spirit" (vs. 22). "Man, by faith, is dead to the former standing-point of a sinful life, and rises to a new life (vs. 25) of communion with Christ (Col. 3:3). The act by which *they have crucified the flesh with its lust*, is already accomplished ideally in principle. But the practice, or outward conformation of the life, must harmonize with the tendency given to the inward life" (vs. 25) [NEANDER]. We are to be executioners, dealing cruelly with the body of sin, which has caused the acting of all cruelties on Christ's body. **with the affections**—Translate, "with its passions." Thus they are dead to the law's condemning power, which is only for the fleshly, and their lusts (vs. 23). **25. in . . . in**—rather, as *Greek*, "If we live (*Note*, vs. 24) BY the Spirit, let us also walk (vs. 16; ch. 6:16) BY the Spirit." Let our life in practice correspond to the ideal inner principle of our spiritual life, viz., our standing by faith as dead to, and severed from, sin, and the condemnation of the law. "Life by (or in) the Spirit" is not an occasional influence of the Spirit, but an abiding state, wherein we are continually alive, though sometimes sleeping and inactive. **26.** *Greek*, "Let us not BECOME." While not asserting that the Galatians are "*vainglorious*" now, he says they are liable to *become* so. **provoking one another**—an effect of "vaingloriousness" on the *stronger*: as "envying" is its effect on the *weaker*. A danger common both to the orthodox and Judaizing Galatians.

ADAM CLARKE

Faith. Here used for "fidelity"—punctuality in performing promises, conscientious carefulness in preserving what is committed to our trust, in restoring it to its proper owner, in transacting the business confided to us, neither betraying the secret of our friend nor disappointing the confidence of our employer.

23. *Meekness*. Mildness, indulgence toward the weak and erring, patient suffering of injuries without feeling a spirit of revenge, an even balance of all tempers and passions, the entire opposite to anger. *Temperance*. "Continence, self-government, or moderation," principally with regard to sensual or animal appetites. Moderation in eating, drinking, sleeping, etc. *Against such there is no law*. Those whose lives are adorned by the above virtues cannot be condemned by any law, for the whole purpose and design of the moral law of God is fulfilled in those who have the Spirit of God producing in their hearts and lives the preceding fruits.

24. *And they that are Christ's*, all genuine Christians, *have crucified the flesh*—are so far from obeying its dictates and acting under its influence that they have crucified their sensual appetites; they have nailed them to the cross of Christ, where they have expired with Him. Hence, says Paul, Rom. vi. 6, "our old man," the flesh, with its affections and lusts, "is crucified with him, that the body of sin might be destroyed, that henceforth we should not serve sin." By which we see that God has fully designed to save all who believe in Christ from all sin, whether outward or inward, with all the *affections*, irregular "passions," and *lusts*, disorderly "wishes" and "desires"—all that a man may feel contrary to love and purity, and all that he may desire contrary to moderation and that self-denial peculiar to the Christian character.

25. *If we live in the Spirit*, if we profess to believe a spiritual religion, *let us also walk in the Spirit*—let us show in our lives and conversation that the Spirit of God dwells in us.

26. *Let us not be desirous of vain glory*. "Let us not be vainglorious"—boasting of our attainments; vaunting ourselves to be superior to others; or seeking honor from those things which do not possess moral good, in birth, riches, or eloquence. *Provoking one another*. What this may refer to we cannot tell. Whether to the Judaizing teachers endeavoring to set themselves up beyond the apostle, and their attempts to lessen him in the people's eyes, that they might secure to themselves the public confidence and thus destroy Paul's influence in the Galatian churches, or whether to some other matter in the internal economy of the church, we know not. But the exhortation is necessary for every Christian, and for every Christian church. He who professes to seek the honor that comes from God should *not be desirous of vain glory*. He who desires to keep the unity of the Spirit in the bond of peace should not provoke another. He who knows that he never deserved any gift or blessing from God should not envy another those blessings which the divine goodness may have thought proper to bestow upon him.

MATTHEW HENRY — CHAPTER 6

Verses 1–10

I. We are here taught to deal tenderly with those who are overtaken in a fault, *v.* 1; *if a man be overtaken in a fault*, brought to sin by the surprise of temptation. It is one thing to overtake a fault by contrivance and deliberation, and another thing to be overtaken in a fault. Great tenderness should be used. *Those who are spiritual* must *restore such a one with the spirit of meekness*. 1. The duty we are directed to—to restore such. The original word signifies *to set in joint*, as a dislocated bone. We should endeavour to set them in joint again, comforting them in a sense of pardoning mercy, confirming our love to them. 2. The manner wherein this is to be done: *With the spirit of meekness;* not in wrath and passion, as those who triumph in a brother's falls. Many needful reproofs lose their efficacy by being given in wrath; but when they are managed with tenderness, and from sincere concern for the welfare of those to whom they are given, they are likely to make a due

JAMIESON, FAUSSET, BROWN — CHAPTER 6

Vss. 1-18. EXHORTATIONS CONTINUED; TO FORBEARANCE AND HUMILITY; LIBERALITY TO TEACHERS AND IN GENERAL. POSTSCRIPT AND BENEDICTION. **1. Brethren**—An expression of kindness to conciliate attention. Translate as *Greek*, "If a man *even* be overtaken" (i.e., caught in the very act [ALFORD and ELLICOTT]; BEFORE he expects: unexpectedly). BENGEL explains the "before" in the *Greek* compound verb, "If a man be overtaken in a fault *before ourselves*": If another has *really* been overtaken in a fault *the first;* for often he who is *first to find fault*, is the very one who has *first transgressed*. **a fault**—*Greek*, "a transgression," "a fall"; such as a falling back into legal bondage. Here he gives monition to those who have not so fallen, "the spiritual," to be not "vainglorious" (ch. 5:26), but forbearing to such (Rom. 15:1). **restore**—The *Greek* is used of a dislocated limb, reduced to its place. Such is the tenderness with which we should treat a fallen member of the Church in restoring

ADAM CLARKE — CHAPTER 6

1. *Brethren, if a man be overtaken*. If he be "surprised, seized on" without warning, "suddenly invaded, taken before he is aware"; all these meanings the word has in connections similar to this. *Ye which are spiritual*. You who still retain the grace of the gospel, and have wisdom and experience in divine things. *Restore such an one*. Bring the man "back into his place." It is a metaphor taken from a dislocated limb, brought back into its place by the hand of a skillful and tender surgeon. *In the spirit of meekness*. Use no severity nor haughty carriage towards him; as the man was suddenly overtaken, he is already deeply humbled and distressed, and needs much encouragement and lenient usage. There is a great difference between a man who being suddenly assailed falls into sin and the man who transgressed in consequence of having walked in the counsel of

MATTHEW HENRY

impression. 3. A very good reason why this should be done with meekness: *Considering thyself, lest thou also be tempted.* We ought to deal very tenderly with those who are overtaken in sin, it may some time or other be our own case. This will dispose us to do by others as we desire to be done by in such a case.

II. We are here directed *to bear one another's burdens, v.* 2. This may be considered either as referring to what goes before, and so may teach us to exercise forbearance and compassion towards one another, or a more general precept it directs us to sympathize with one another under the various trials and troubles that we may meet with. So we shall *fulfil the law of Christ.* This is to act agreeably to the law of his precept, which is the law of love, and it would also be agreeable to his pattern and example, which have the force of a law to us. Though as Christians we are freed from the law of Moses, yet we are under the law of Christ; and therefore, instead of laying unnecessary burdens upon others, it much more becomes us to fulfil the law of Christ by bearing one another's burdens. The apostle being aware how great a hindrance pride would be to the mutual condescension which he had been recommending (*v.* 3) takes care to caution us against this; he supposes it as a very possible thing for a man to think himself to be something—when in truth he is nothing. Such a one does but deceive himself; while he imposes upon others, by pretending to what he has not, he puts the greatest cheat upon himself. He is neither the freer from mistakes nor will he be the more secure against temptations for the good opinion he has of his own sufficiency, but rather the more liable to fall into them; for *he that thinks he stands has need to take heed lest he fall.* Self-conceit is but self-deceit. There is not a more dangerous cheat in the world than self-deceit.

III. We are advised everyone to prove his own work, *v.* 4. By our own work is chiefly meant our own actions or behaviour. These the apostle directs us to prove, that is, seriously to examine them by the rule of God's word. Instead of being forward to judge and censure others, it would much more become us to search and try our own ways; our business lies more at home than abroad, with ourselves than with other men. The best way to keep us from being proud of ourselves is to prove our ownselves: the better we are acquainted with our own hearts and ways, the less liable shall we be to despise and the more disposed to compassionate and help others.

1. This is the way to *have rejoicing in ourselves alone.* If we set ourselves in good earnest to *prove our own work,* this, he intimates, would be a much better ground of joy and satisfaction than to be able to rejoice *in another,* either in the good opinion which others may have of us, or by comparing ourselves with others. The joy that results thence is nothing to that which arises from trial of ourselves by the rule of God's word, and our being able thereupon to approve ourselves to him. Though we have nothing in ourselves to boast of, yet we may have the matter of rejoicing in ourselves. If our consciences can witness for us we may upon good ground rejoice therein. The true way to have *rejoicing in ourselves* is to be much in *proving our own works.* If we have the testimony of our consciences that we are accepted of God, we need not much concern ourselves about what others think or say of us.

2. The other argument which the apostle uses is that every man shall bear his own burden (*v.* 5). There is a day come when we must all give an account of ourselves to God; and he declares that then the judgment will proceed, and the sentence pass, according as our state and behaviour have really been in the sight of God. If we must certainly be called to an account hereafter, surely we ought to be often calling ourselves to an account here, to see whether or no we are such as God will own and approve then. If it were more our practice instead of bearing hard upon one another, we should be more ready to fulfil that law of Christ by which we must be judged in bearing one another's burdens.

IV. Christians are here exhorted to be free and liberal in maintaining their ministers (*v.* 6): *Let him that is taught in the word communicate to him that teacheth, in all good things.* As there are some to be taught, so there are others who are appointed to teach them. Reason itself directs us to put a difference between the teachers and the taught, and the scriptures sufficiently declare that it is the will of God we should do so. It is the word of God wherein ministers are to teach and instruct others. It is the word of God which is the only rule of faith and life. They are no further to be regarded than as they speak according to this rule. It is the duty of those who are taught in the word to support those who are appointed to teach

JAMIESON, FAUSSET, BROWN

him to a better state. **the spirit of meekness**—*the meekness* which is the gift *of the Holy Spirit* working in our spirit (ch. 5:22, 25). "Meekness" is that temper of spirit towards God whereby we accept His dealings without disputing; then, towards men, whereby we endure meekly their provocations, and do not withdraw ourselves from the burdens which their sins impose upon us [TRENCH]. **considering thyself**—Transition from the plural to the singular. When congregations are addressed collectively, each individual should take home the monition *to himself.* **thou also be tempted**—as is likely to happen to those who reprove others without meekness (cf. Matt. 7:2-5; II Tim. 2:25; Jas. 2:13). **2.** If ye, legalists, must "bear burdens," then instead of legal burdens (Matt. 23:4), "bear one another's burdens," lit., "weights." Distinguished by BENGEL from "burden," vs. 4 (a different *Greek* word, "load"): "weights" exceed the strength of those under them; "burden" is proportioned to the strength. **so fulfil**—or as other old MSS. read, "so ye will fulfil," *Greek,* "fill up," "thoroughly fulfil." **the law of Christ**—viz., "love" (ch. 5:14). Since ye desire "the law," then fulfil the law of Christ, which is not made up of various minute observances, but whose sole "burden" is "love" (John 13:34; 15:12); Romans 15:3 gives Christ as the example in the particular duty here. **3.** Self-conceit, the chief hindrance to forbearance and sympathy towards our fellow men, must be laid aside. **something**—possessed of some spiritual pre-eminence, so as to be exempt from the frailty of other men. **when he is nothing**—The *Greek* is subjective: "Being, if he would come to himself, and look on the real fact, nothing" [ALFORD] (vss. 2, 6; Rom. 12:3; I Cor. 8:2). **deceiveth himself**—lit., "he mentally deceives himself." Cf. James 1:26, "deceiveth his own heart."

4. his own work—not merely his own *opinion* of himself. **have rejoicing in himself alone**—Translate, "Have *his* (matter for) glorying in regard to himself alone, and not in regard to another" (viz., not in regard to his neighbor, by comparing himself with whom, he has fancied he has matter for boasting as that neighbor's superior). Not that really a man by looking to "himself alone" is likely to find cause for glorying in himself. Nay, in vs. 5, he speaks of a "burden" or *load,* not of matter for glorying, as what really belongs to each man. But he refers to *the idea those* whom he censures *had of themselves:* they *thought* they had cause for "glorying" in themselves, but it all arose from unjust self-conceited comparison of themselves with others, instead of looking at home. The only true glorying, if glorying it is to be called, is in the testimony of a good conscience, glorying in the cross of Christ. **5.** For (by this way, vs. 4, of proving himself, not depreciating his neighbor by comparison) each man shall bear his own "burden," or rather, "*load*" (viz., of sin and infirmity), the *Greek* being different from that in vs. 2. This verse does not contradict vs. 2. There he tells them to bear with others' "burdens" of infirmity in sympathy; here, that self-examination will make a man to feel he has enough to do with "his own load" of sin, without comparing himself boastfully with his neighbor. Cf. vs. 3. Instead of "thinking himself to be something," he shall feel the "load" of his own sin: and this will lead him to bear sympathetically with his neighbor's burden of infirmity. ÆSOP says a man carries two bags over his shoulder, the one with his own sins hanging behind, that with his neighbor's sins in front. **6.** From the mention of bearing one another's burdens, he passes to one way in which those burdens may be borne—by ministering out of their earthly goods to their spiritual teachers. The "but" in the *Greek,* beginning of this verse, expresses this: I said, Each shall bear his own burden; BUT I do not intend that he should not think of others, and especially of the wants of his ministers. **communicate unto him**—"impart a share unto his teacher": lit., *him that teacheth catechetically.* **in all good things**—in every kind of the good things *of this life,* according as the case may require (Rom. 15:27; I Cor. 9:11, 14).

ADAM CLARKE

the ungodly or stood in the way of sinners.

Considering thyself. Looking to thyself; as he fell through a moment of unwatchfulness, look about, that you are not surprised. As he fell, so may you. You are now warned at his expense; therefore keep a good lookout. *Lest thou also be tempted.* And having had this warning, you will have less to plead in extenuation of your offense.

2. *Bear ye one another's burdens.* Have sympathy; feel for each other; and consider the case of a distressed brother as your own. *And so fulfil the law of Christ.* That law or commandment, "Ye shall love one another"; or that, "Do unto all men as ye would they should do unto you." We should be as indulgent to the infirmities of others as we can be consistently with truth and righteousness. Our brother's infirmity may be his burden; and if we do not choose to help him to bear it, let us not reproach him because he is obliged to carry the load.

3. *If a man think himself to be something.* I.e., to be a proper Christian man. *When he is nothing;* being destitute of that charity which beareth, hopeth, and endureth all things. See 1 Cor. xiii. 1, etc. Those who suppose themselves to excel all others in piety, understanding, etc., while they are harsh, censorious, and overbearing, prove that they have not the charity that "thinketh no evil," and in the sight of God are only "as sounding brass" and "a tinkling cymbal." There are no people more censorious or uncharitable than those among some religious people who pretend to more light and a deeper communion with God. They are generally carried away with a sort of sublime, high-sounding phraseology which seems to argue a wonderfully deep acquaintance with divine things; stripped of this, many of them are like Samson without his hair.

4. *Prove his own work.* Let him examine himself and his conduct by the words and example of Christ, and if he find that they bear this touchstone, then he shall have *rejoicing in himself alone,* feeling that he resembles his Lord and Master, *and not in another*—not derive his consolation from comparing himself with another who may be weaker or less instructed than himself. The only rule for a Christian is the word of Christ; the only pattern for his imitation is the example of Christ. He should not compare himself with others; they are not his standard. Christ has left us an example that we should follow His steps.

5. *Every man shall bear his own burden.* All must answer for themselves, not for their neighbors. And every man must expect to be dealt with by the divine Judge, as his character and conduct have been. The greater offenses of another will not excuse your smaller crimes. Every man must give account of himself to God.

6. *Let him that is taught in the word,* he who receives instructions in Christianity by the public preaching of the Word. *Communicate unto him that teacheth,* contribute to the support of the man who has dedicated himself to the work of the ministry, and who gives up his time and his life to preach the gospel. It appears that some of the believers in Galatia could receive the Christian ministry without contributing to its support. This is both ungrateful and base. We do not expect that a common schoolmaster will give up his time to teach our children their alphabet without being paid for it; and can we suppose that it is just for any person to sit under the preaching of the gospel in order to grow wise unto salvation by it, and not contribute to the support of the spiritual teacher? It is unjust.

MATTHEW HENRY

them; for they are *to communicate to them in all good things*. It is but fit and equitable that, while they are *sowing to others spiritual things, they should reap their carnal things*.

V. A caution to take heed of mocking God, or of deceiving ourselves, by imagining that he can be imposed upon by mere professions (*v.* 7): *Be not deceived, God is not mocked*. Many are apt to excuse themselves from the work of religion, though at the same time they may make a show of it. Hereby they may possibly impose upon others, yet they do but deceive themselves if they think to impose upon God. As he cannot be deceived, so he will not be mocked. *Whatsoever a man soweth that shall he also reap*. Our present time is seed-time: in the other world there will be a great harvest. We shall reap then as we sow now. And he further informs us (*v.* 8) that, as there are two sorts of seedness, so accordingly will the reckoning be hereafter: *If we sow to the flesh, we shall of the flesh reap corruption*; a mean and short-lived satisfaction at present, and ruin and misery at the end of it. But, on the other hand, *those who sow to the Spirit*, may depend upon it that *of the Spirit they shall reap life everlasting*—they shall have the truest comfort in their present course, and an eternal life and happiness at the end of it. The God we have to do with will certainly deal with us hereafter, not according to our professions, but our practices.

VI. A further caution, *not to be weary in well doing*, *v.* 9. There is in all of us too great a proneness to this; we are very apt to flag and tire in duty. *In due season we shall reap, if we faint not*. There is a recompence of reward in reserve for all who sincerely employ themselves in well doing. Though our reward may be delayed, yet it will surely come.

VII. An exhortation to all Christians to do good in their places (*v.* 10): *As we have therefore an opportunity*, &c. It is not enough that we be good ourselves, but we must do good to others. 1. The objects of this duty are more generally all men. We are not to confine our charity and beneficence within too narrow bounds, but should be ready to extend it to all as far as we are capable. We are to have a special regard to the household of faith. Though others are not to be excluded, yet these are to be preferred. 2. The rule which we are to observe in doing good *as we have opportunity*. (1) We should be sure to do it while we have opportunity, or while our life lasts. We must not, as too many do, neglect it in our lifetime, and defer it till we come to die, under a pretence of doing something of this nature then: by leaving something behind us for the good of others, when we can no longer keep it ourselves. But we should take care to do good in our lifetime, yea, to make this the business of our lives. (2) We should be ready to improve every opportunity for it. Whenever God gives us an opportunity of being useful to others, he expects we should improve it, according to our capacity and ability. None who stand in need of us are to be wholly overlooked, yet there is a difference to be made between some and others.

Verses 11–18

The apostle seems as if he intended here to have put an end to the epistle. As a particular mark of his respect for them, he had written this large letter with his own hand, and had not made use of another as his amanuensis. But such is his affection to them that he cannot break off till he has once again given them the true character of those teachers.

I. False teachers were men who *desired to make a fair show in the flesh*, *v.* 12. They were very zealous for the externals of religion, though they had little or no regard to real piety, for, *neither do they themselves keep the law*. Frequently those have least of the substance of religion who are most solicitous to make a show of it. They constrained the Gentile Christians to be circumcised, *only lest they should suffer persecution for the cross of Christ*. They were willing to sleep in a whole skin, and to save their worldly cargo, and cared not though they made shipwreck of faith and a good conscience.

JAMIESON, FAUSSET, BROWN

God is not mocked—The *Greek* verb is, literally, to sneer with the nostrils drawn up in contempt. God does not suffer Himself to be imposed on by empty words: He will judge according to works, which are seeds sown for eternity of either joy or woe. Excuses for illiberality in God's cause (vs. 6) seem valid before men, but are not so before God (Ps. 50: 21). **soweth**—especially of his resources (II Cor. 9:6). **that**—*Greek*, "this"; this and nothing else. **reap**—at the harvest, the end of the world (Matt. 13: 39). **8.** Translate, "He that soweth *unto his own* flesh," with a view to fulfilling its desires. He does not say, "*His* spirit," as he does say, "His flesh." For in ourselves we are not spiritual, but carnal. The flesh is devoted to *selfishness*. **corruption**—i.e., destruction (Phil. 3:19). Cf. as to the deliverance of believers from "corruption" (Rom. 8:21). The use of the term "corruption" instead, implies that *destruction* is not an *arbitrary* punishment of fleshly-mindedness, but is its *natural* fruit; the corrupt flesh producing corruption, which is another word for destruction: corruption is the fault, and corruption the punishment (*Note*, I Cor. 3:17; II Pet. 2:12). Future life only expands the seed sown here. Men cannot mock God because they can deceive themselves. They who sow tares cannot reap wheat. They alone reap life eternal who sow to the Spirit (Ps. 126:6; Prov. 11:18; 22:8; Hos. 8: 7; 10:12; Luke 16:25; Rom. 8:11; Jas. 5:7). **9.** (II Thess. 3:13.) And when we do good, let us also persevere in it without fainting. **in due season**—in its own proper season, God's own time (I Tim. 6:15). **faint not**—lit., "be relaxed." Stronger than "be not weary." *Weary of well-doing* refers to the will; "faint not" to relaxation of the powers [BENGEL]. No one should faint, as in an earthly harvest sometimes happens. **10.** Translate, "*So then, according* as (i.e., in proportion as) we have *season* (i.e., opportunity), let us *work* (a distinct *Greek* verb from that for "do," in vs. 9) *that which is* (in each case) *good*." As thou art able, and while thou art able, and when thou art able (Eccles. 9:10). We have now the "season" for *sowing*, as also there will be hereafter the "due season" (vs. 9) for *reaping*. The whole life is, in one sense, the "seasonable opportunity" to us; and, in a narrower sense, there occur in it more especially convenient seasons. The latter are sometimes lost in looking for still more convenient seasons (Acts 24:25). We shall not always have the opportunity "we have" now. Satan is sharpened to the greater zeal in injuring us, by the shortness of his time (Rev. 12:12). Let us be sharpened to the greater zeal in well-doing by the shortness of ours. **them who are of the household**—Every right-minded man does well to the members of his own family (I Tim. 5:8); so believers are to do to those of the household of faith, i.e., those whom *faith* has made members of "the household of God" (Eph. 2:19); "the house of God" (I Tim. 3:15; I Pet. 4:17). **11.** Rather, "See *in how large letters* I have written." The *Greek* is translated "how great" in Hebrews 7:4, the only other passage where it occurs in the New Testament. Owing to his weakness of eyes (ch. 4:15) he wrote in large letters. So JEROME. All the oldest MSS. are written in uncial, i.e., capital letters, the *cursive*, or small letters, being of more recent date. Paul seems to have had a difficulty in writing, which led him to make the uncial letters larger than ordinary writers did. The mention of these is as a token by which they would know that he wrote the whole Epistle with his own hand; as he did also the pastoral Epistle, which this Epistle resembles in style. He usually dictated his Epistles to an amanuensis, excepting the concluding salutation, which he wrote himself (Rom. 16:22; I Cor. 16:21). This letter, he tells the Galatians, he writes with his own hand, no doubt in order that they may see what a regard he had for them, in contrast to the Judaizing teachers (vs. 12), who sought only their own ease. If *English Version* be retained, the words, "how large a letter" (lit., "in how large letters"), will not refer to the length of the Epistle *absolutely*, but that it was a large one for *him* to have written with his own hand. NEANDER supports *English Version*, as more appropriate to the earnestness of the apostle and the tone of the Epistle: "How *large*" will thus be put for "how *many*." **12.** Contrast between his zeal in their behalf, implied in vs. 11, and the zeal for self on the part of the Judaizers. **make a fair show**—(II Cor. 5:12). **in the flesh**—in outward things. **they**—it is "these" who. . . . **constrain you**—by example (vs. 13) and importuning. **only lest**—"only that they may not . . ." (cf. ch. 5:11). **suffer persecution**—They escaped in a great degree the Jews' bitterness against Christianity and the offense of the cross of Christ, by making the Mosaic law a

ADAM CLARKE

7. *Be not deceived.* Neither deceive yourselves nor permit yourselves to be deceived by others. He seems to refer to the Judaizing teachers. *God is not mocked.* You cannot deceive Him, and He will not permit you to mock Him with pretended instead of real services. *Whatsoever a man soweth.* Whatsoever kind of grain a man sows in his field, of that shall he reap; for no other species of grain can proceed from that which is sown.

8. *He that soweth to his flesh.* In like manner, he that *soweth to* the *flesh*, who indulges his sensual and animal appetites, shall have *corruption* as the crop: you cannot expect to lead a bad life and go to heaven at last. According as your present life is, so will be your eternal life; whether your sowing be to the flesh or to the Spirit, so will your eternal reaping be. To sow here means transacting the concerns of a man's natural life. To reap signifies his enjoyment or punishment in another world. Probably by *flesh* and *Spirit* the apostle means Judaism and Christianity. Circumcision of the flesh was the principal rite of the former; circumcision in the heart, by the Spirit, the chief rite of the latter. Hence the one may have been called *flesh;* the other, *Spirit.* He who rejects the gospel, and trusts only in the rites and ceremonies of the law for salvation, will reap endless disappointment and misery. He who trusts in Christ, and receives the gifts and graces of the Holy Spirit, shall reap life everlasting.

9. *Let us not be weary.* Well doing is easier in itself than ill doing; and the danger of growing weary in the former arises only from the opposition to good in our own nature, or the outward hindrances we may meet with from a gainsaying and persecuting world. *In due season we shall reap.* As a husbandman, in ploughing, sowing, and variously laboring in his fields, is supported by the hope of a plentiful harvest, which he cannot expect before the right and appointed time, so every follower of God may be persuaded that he shall not be permitted to pray, weep, deny himself, and live in a conformity to his Maker's will without reaping the fruit of it in eternal glory. And although no man obtains glory because he has prayed, yet none can expect glory who do not seek it in this way. This is sowing to the Spirit; and the Spirit and the grace are furnished by Christ Jesus, and by Him the kingdom of Heaven is opened to all believers; but only those who believe, love, and obey shall enter into it.

10. *As we have therefore opportunity.* While it is the time of sowing let us sow the good seed; and let our love be, as the love of Christ is, free, manifested to all. Let us help all who need help according to the uttermost of our power, but let the first objects of our regard be those *who are of the household of faith*—the members of the Church of Christ, who form one family, of which Jesus Christ is the Head. Those have the first claims on our attention; but all others have their claims also, and therefore we should *do good unto all.*

12. *A fair shew in the flesh.* The Jewish religion was general in the region of Galatia and was respectable. As it was then professed and practiced among the Jews, this religion had nothing very grievous to the old man; an unrenewed nature might go through all its observances with little pain or cross-bearing. On the other hand, Christianity could not be very popular; it was too strict. A Jew made a fair show there, according to his carnal system, and it was a temptation to a weak Christian to swerve into Judaism, that he might be exempted from persecution and be creditable among his countrymen.

MATTHEW HENRY

They were men who had no further zeal for the law than as it subserved their carnal designs; for they desired to have these Christians circumcised, *that they might glory in their flesh* (*v.* 13), that they might say they had gained them over to their side.

II. He acquaints us, on the other hand, with his own temper and behaviour.

1. His principal glory was in the cross of Christ: *God forbid that I should glory, save in the cross of our Lord Jesus Christ, v.* 14. This was what the Jews stumbled at and the Greeks accounted foolishness; and the judaizing teachers themselves were for mixing the observance of the law of Moses with faith in Christ, as necessary to salvation. But Paul was so far from being offended at the cross of Christ that he gloried in it, and rejected the thought of setting up anything in competition with it, with the utmost abhorrence. *God forbid,* &c. This was the ground of all his hope as a Christian, and whatever trials his firm adherence to it might bring upon him, he was ready not only to submit to them, but to rejoice in them. There is the greatest reason why we should glory in it, for to it we owe all our joys and hopes.

2. He was dead to the world. By Christ *the world was crucified to him, and he to the world.* He had got above both the smiles and the frowns of it, and had become as indifferent to it as one who is dying out of it. The more we contemplate the sufferings our dear Redeemer met with from the world the less likely shall we be to be in love with it.

3. He did not lay the stress of his religion on one side or the other of the contesting interests, but on sound Christianity, *v.* 15. What they laid so great a stress upon Paul made very little account of. He very well knew that *in Jesus Christ neither circumcision availed anything nor uncircumcision,* as to men's acceptance with God, *but a new creature.* Here he instructs us both wherein real religion does not and wherein it does consist. It does not consist in our being in this or the other denomination of Christians; but it consists in our being new creatures; in our being renewed in the spirit of our minds and having Christ formed in us. It is a change of mind and heart, whereby we are enabled to believe in the Lord Jesus and to live a life of devotedness to God. No outward professions, nor particular names, will ever be sufficient to recommend us to him. Were Christians duly concerned to experience this in themselves, and to promote it in others, if it did not make them lay aside their distinguishing names, yet it would at least take them off from laying so great a stress upon them as they too often do. *And as many as walk according to this rule peace be upon them, and mercy upon the Israel of God.* The blessings which he desires or which he gives them the hope and prospect of (for the words may be taken either as a prayer or a promise), are *peace and mercy.* A foundation is laid for these in that gracious change which is wrought in them. These, he declares, shall be the portion of *all the Israel of God,* all sincere Christians, whether Jews or Gentiles, all who are Israelites indeed. The Jews and judaizing teachers were for confining these blessings to such as were circumcised. Real Christians are such as walk by rule; not a rule of their own devising, but that which God himself has prescribed to them. Even those who walk according to this rule do yet stand in need of the mercy of God.

4. He had cheerfully suffered persecution for the sake of Christ and Christianity, *v.* 17. He had already suffered much in the cause of Christ, for *he bore in his body the marks of the Lord Jesus,* the scars of those wounds which he had sustained from persecuting enemies, for his steady adherence to him. With a becoming warmth and vehemence, suitable to his authority as an apostle and to the deep concern of mind he was under, he insists upon it that no man should henceforth trouble him, by opposing his doctrine or authority, or by any such reproaches as had been cast upon him. It may justly be presumed that men are fully persuaded of those truths in the defence of which they are willing to suffer. It is very unjust to charge those things upon others which are contrary not only to their profession, but their sufferings too.

III. The apostle concludes the epistle with his apostolical benediction, *v.* 18. He calls them his brethren, and takes his leave of them with this very affectionate prayer, that *the grace of our Lord Jesus Christ may be with their spirit.* This was a usual farewell wish of the apostle's. And herein he prays that they might enjoy the favour of Christ, all that grace which was needful to establish them in their Christian course, and to encourage and comfort them under all the trials of life and the prospect of death itself.

JAMIESON, FAUSSET, BROWN

necessary preliminary; in fact, making Christian converts into Jewish proselytes. **13.** Translate, "For not even do they who submit to circumcision, keep the law themselves (Rom. 2:17-23), but they wish you (emphatical) to be circumcised," etc. They arbitrarily selected circumcision out of the whole law, as though observing it would stand instead of their non-observance of the rest of the law. **that they may glory in your flesh**—viz., in the outward change (opposed to *an inward change wrought by the* SPIRIT) which they have effected in bringing you over to their own Jewish-Christian party. **14.** Translate, "But *as for me* (in opposition to those gloriers 'in your flesh,' vs. 13), God forbid that I . . . . **in the cross**—the atoning death on the cross. Cf. Philippians 3:3, 7, 8, as a specimen of his glorying. The "cross," the great object of shame to them, and to all carnal men, is the great object of glorying to me. For by it, the worst of deaths, Christ has destroyed all kinds of death [AUGUSTINE, *Tract* 36, on John, sec. 4]. We are to testify the power of Christ's death working in us, after the manner of crucifixion (ch. 5:24; Rom. 6.5, 6). **our**—He reminds the Galatians by this pronoun, that *they* had a share in the "Lord Jesus Christ" (the full name is used for greater solemnity), and therefore ought to glory in Christ's cross, as he did. **the world**—inseparably allied to the "flesh" (vs. 13). Legal and fleshly ordinances are merely outward, and "elements of the world" (ch. 4:3). **is**—rather, as *Greek,* "has been crucified to me" (ch. 2:20). He used "crucified" for *dead* (Col. 2:20, "dead with Christ"), to imply his oneness with Christ *crucified* (Phil. 3: 10): "the fellowship of His sufferings being made conformable unto His death." **15. availeth**—The oldest MSS. read, "is" (cf. ch. 5:6). Not only are they of no *avail,* but they *are nothing."* So far are they from being matter for "glorying," that they are "nothing." But Christ's cross is "all in all," as a subject for glorying, in "the new creature" (Eph. 2: 10, 15, 16). **new creature**—(II Cor. 5:17). A *transformation by the renewal of the mind* (Rom. 12:2).

16. as many—contrasting with the "as many," vs. 12. **rule**—lit., *a straight rule,* to detect crookedness; so a rule of life. **peace**—from God (Eph. 2:14-17; 6:23). **mercy**—(Rom. 15:9). **Israel of God**—not the Israel after the flesh, among whom those teachers wish to enrol you; but the spiritual seed of Abraham by faith (ch. 3:9, 29; Rom. 2:28, 29; Phil. 3:3).

17. let no man trouble me—by opposing my apostolic authority, seeing that it is stamped by a sure seal, viz., "I (in contrast to the Judaizing teachers who gloried in the flesh) bear" (as a high mark of honor from the King of kings). **the marks**—properly, marks branded on slaves to indicate their owners. So Paul's scars of wounds received for Christ's sake, indicate to whom he belongs, and in whose free and glorious service he is (II Cor. 11:23-25). The Judaizing teachers gloried in the circumcision mark in the flesh of *their followers;* Paul glories in the marks of suffering for Christ on *his own* body (cf. vs. 14; Phil. 3:10; Col. 1:24). **the Lord**—omitted in the oldest MSS.

18. Brethren—Place it, as *Greek, last* in the sentence, before the "Amen." After much rebuke and monition, he bids them farewell with the loving expression of *brotherhood* as his last parting word (*Note,* ch. 1:6). **be with your spirit**—which, I trust, will keep down the *flesh* (I Thess. 5:23; II Tim. 4:22; Philemon 25).

ADAM CLARKE

13. *Neither they themselves who are circumcised.* They received circumcision and professed Judaism, not from a desire to be conformed to the will of God, but Judaism was popular, and the more converts the false teachers could make, the more occasion of glorying they had; and they wished to get those Christian converts to receive circumcision, that they might glory in their flesh.

14. *But God forbid that I should glory.* Whatever others may do, or whatever they may exult or glory in, God forbid that I should "exult" except *in the cross of our Lord Jesus Christ;* in the grand doctrine that justification and salvation are only through Christ crucified, He having made an atonement for the sin of the world by His passion and death. And I glory also in the disgrace and persecution which I experience through my attachment to this crucified Christ.

By whom the world is crucified unto me. Jewish rites and Gentile vanities are equally insipid to me; I know them to be empty and worthless. If Jews and Gentiles despise me, I despise that in which they trust; through Jesus, all are *crucified unto me.*

15. *In Christ Jesus.* Under the dispensation of the gospel, of which He is Head and supreme, *neither circumcision,* nothing that the Jew can boast of, nothing that the Gentile can call excellent, *availeth any thing*—can in the least contribute to the salvation of the soul. *But a new creature.* "But a new creation"; not a *new creature* merely (for this might be restrained to any new power or faculty), but a total renewal of the whole man, of all the powers and passions of the soul; and as creation could not be effected but by the power of the Almighty, so this change cannot be effected but by the same energy.

16. *As many as walk according to this rule.* "This canon"; viz., what is laid down in the preceding verses, that redemption is through the sacrifice of Christ, that circumcision and uncircumcision are equally unavailable, and that none can be saved without being created anew. This is the grand canon or "rule" in Christianity. *Peace be on them.* Those who act from this conviction will have the *peace* and *mercy* of God; for it is in this way that *mercy* is communicated and *peace* obtained. *The Israel of God.* The true Christians, called here *the Israel of God,* to distinguish them from Israel according to the flesh.

17. *From henceforth let no man trouble me.* Put an end to your contentions among yourselves; return to the pure doctrine of the gospel; abandon those who are leading you astray; separate from the church those who corrupt and disturb it; and let me be grieved no longer with your defections from the truth. *I bear in my body the marks of the Lord Jesus.* The *stigmata,* of which the apostle speaks here, may be understood as implying the scars of the wounds which he had received in the work of the ministry; and that he had such scars we may well conceive when we know that he had been scourged, stoned, and maltreated in a variety of ways. The writer could show such scars himself, received in the same way. Or the apostle may allude to the *stigmata* or *marks* with which servants and slaves were often impressed, in order to ascertain whose property they were. You glory in your mark of circumcision; I glory in the marks which I bear in my body for the testimony of the Lord; I am an open, professed Christian, and have given full proof of my attachment to the cause of Christianity.

18. *The grace,* favor, benevolence, and continual influence of the Lord Jesus, *be with your spirit*—may it live in your heart, enlighten and change your souls, and be conspicuous in your life!

Unto the Galatians, written from Rome. This, or the major part of it, is wanting in the best and most ancient MSS.

THE EPISTLE TO THE EPHESIANS

I. Introduction (1:1, 2)
A. The message (1:1)
B. The salutation (1:2)

II. The Church—the heavenly calling (1:3-3:21)
A. Inclusive preliminary benediction (1:3)
B. Predestination—"before the foundation of the world" (1:4-23)
1. The predestined purpose (1:4-6)
2. The predestined method (1:7-14)
3. The parenthetical prayer (1:15-23)
B. Edification—"now . . . made nigh" (2:1-22)
1. The materials—individuals: the workmanship of God (2:1-10)
2. The building—the union of such individuals in one Church (2:11-22)
C. Vocation—"unto all generations for ever and ever" (3:1-21)
1. The personal parenthesis (3:2-13)
2. The great prayer (3:1, 14-19)
3. The great doxology (3:20, 21)

III. The Church—the earthly conduct (4:1-6:18)
A. Concerning the Church (4:1-16)
1. Basic unity (4:1-6)
2. Growth (4:7-12, 14-16)
3. Ultimate unity (4:13)
B. Concerning conduct (4:17-6:9)
1. Individual (4:17-5:21)
2. Family (5:22-6:4)
3. Household (6:5-9)
C. Concerning conflict (6:10-18)
1. "Put on the armor" (6:10-12)
2. "Take up the armor" (6:13)
3. "Stand" (6:14-18)

IV. Conclusion (6:19-24)
A. Personal conclusion (6:19-22)
B. Resultant final benediction (6:23, 24)

Some think that this epistle to the Ephesians was a circular letter sent to several churches. It is the only one of all Paul's epistles that has nothing in it peculiarly adapted to the case of that particular church; but it has much of common concernment to all Christians. It is an epistle that bears date out of a prison: and some have observed that what this apostle wrote when he was prisoner had the greatest relish and savor in it of the things of God. When his tribulations did abound, his consolations did much more abound. The apostle's design is to settle and establish the Ephesians in the truth, and further to acquaint them with the mystery of the gospel. In the former part he represents the great privilege of the Ephesians, who were now converted to Christianity and received into covenant with God (chs. 1-3). In the latter part he instructs them in the principal duties of religion.

CHAPTER 1

Verses 1, 2

1. The title St. Paul takes to himself—*Paul, an apostle of Jesus Christ,* &c. Such a one Paul was *by the will of God.* Every faithful minister of Christ may, with our apostle, reflect on it as an honour that he is what he is *by the will of God.* 2. The persons to whom this epistle is sent: *To the saints who are at Ephesus.* He calls them saints, for such they were in profession, and many of them were such. All Christians must be saints. He calls them *the faithful in Christ Jesus.* Those are not saints who are not faithful; *in Christ Jesus,* from whom they derive all their grace and spiritual strength. 3. The apostolical benediction: *Grace be to you,* &c. By *grace* we are to understand the free and undeserved love and favour of God, and those graces of the Spirit which proceed from it; by *peace* all other blessings, the fruits and product of the former. No peace without grace. No peace, nor grace, but *from God the Father, and from the Lord Jesus Christ.* These peculiar blessings proceed from God not as a Creator, but as a Father, and they come from our Lord Jesus Christ, who has a right to bestow them. The saints, and the faithful in Christ Jesus, had already received grace and peace. The best saints stand in need of fresh supplies of the graces of the Spirit: and therefore they should pray, each one for himself and all for one another, that such blessings may still abound unto them. The Spirit of God saw fit that his discourse of divine things in this chapter should be cast into prayers and praises. Prayer may preach; and praise may do so too.

Verses 3–14

He begins with thanksgivings and praise, and enlarges upon the exceedingly great and precious benefits which we enjoy by Jesus Christ.

I. He blesses God for *spiritual blessings, v.* 3, where he styles him *the God and Father of our Lord Jesus Christ.* All blessings come from God as the Father of our Lord Jesus Christ. *He hath blessed us with all spiritual blessings.* Spiritual blessings are the best blessings. He blesses us by bestowing such things upon us as make us really blessed. We cannot thus bless God in return; but by praising. Those whom God blesses with some he blesses with all spiritual blessings. It is not so with temporal blessings.

CHAPTER 1

VSS. 1-23. INSCRIPTION: ORIGIN OF THE CHURCH IN THE FATHER'S ETERNAL COUNSEL, AND THE SON'S BLOODSHEDDING: THE SEALING OF IT BY THE SPIRIT. THANKSGIVING AND PRAYER THAT THEY MAY FULLY KNOW GOD'S GRACIOUS POWER IN CHRIST TOWARDS THE SAINTS. **1. by**—rather, "*through* the will of God": called to the apostleship through that same "will" which originated the Church (vss. 5, 9, 11; cf. Gal. 1:4). **which are at Ephesus**—See *Introduction.* **to the saints . . . and to the faithful**—The same persons are referred to by both designations, as the *Greek* proves: "to those who are saints, and faithful in Christ Jesus." The *sanctification* by God is here put before man's *faith.* The twofold aspect of salvation is thus presented, God's grace in the first instance *sanctifying* us, (i.e., setting us apart in His eternal purposes as holy unto Himself); and our faith, by God's gift, laying hold of salvation (II Thess. 2:13; I Pet. 1:2). **2.** (Rom. 1:7; I Cor. 3; II Cor. 1:2; Galatians 1:3.) **3.** The doxologies in almost all the Epistles imply the real sense of grace experienced by the writers and their readers (I Pet. 1:3). From vs. 3 to vs. 14 sets forth summarily the Gospel of the grace of God: the FATHER'S work of love, vs. 3 (choosing us to *holiness,* vs. 4; to *sonship,* vs. 5; to *acceptance,* vs. 6): the SON'S, vs. 7 (*redemption,* vs. 7; *knowledge of the mystery of His will,* vs. 9; *an inheritance,* vs. 11); the HOLY SPIRIT'S, vs. 13 (*sealing,* vs. 13; giving an *earnest* of the inheritance, vs. 14). **the God and Father of . . . Christ**—and so the God and Father of us who are in Him (John 20:17). God is "the God" of the *man* Jesus, and "the Father" of the *Divine Word.* The *Greek* is, "*Blessed* us," not "hath blessed us"; referring to the past original counsel of God. As in creation (Gen. 1:22) so in redemption (Gen. 12: 3; Matt. 5:3-11; 25:34) God "blesses" His children; and that not in mere *words,* but in *acts.* **us**—all Christians. **blessings**—*Greek,* "blessing." "All," i.e., "*every possible* blessing for time and eternity, which *the Spirit* has to besow" (so "spiritual" means; not "spiritual," as the term is now used, as opposed to *bodily*). **in heavenly places**—a phrase five times found in this Epistle, and not elsewhere (vs. 20; ch. 2:6; 3:10; 6:12); *Greek,* "in *the* heavenly places." Christ's ascension is the means of intro-

CHAPTER 1

1. *To the saints which are at Ephesus.* By the term *saints* we are to understand those who in that place professed Christianity, and were members of the Christian Church. *Saint* properly signifies a "holy person," and such the gospel of Christ requires every man to be, and such every true believer is, in both heart and life; but *saint* appears to have been as ordinary a denomination of a believer in Christ in those primitive times as the term "Christian" is now. *The faithful in Christ Jesus.* The "believers"—the persons who received Christ as the promised Messiah and the Saviour of the world, and continued in the grace which they had received.

3. *Blessed be the God.* See the note on 2 Cor. i. 3, where the same form is used. *With all spiritual blessings.* With the pure doctrines of the gospel, and the abundant gifts and graces of the Holy Ghost, justifying, sanctifying, and building us up on our most holy faith. *In heavenly places.* "In heavenly things," such as those mentioned above; they were not yet in *heavenly places,* but they had abundance of heavenly things to prepare them for heavenly places. Some think the word should be understood as signifying *blessings* of the most exalted or excellent kind, such as are *spiritual* in opposition to those that are earthly, such as are eternal in opposition to those that are temporal; and all these in, through, and by Christ. We have already seen, on Gal. iv. 26, that the heavenly Jerusalem, or "Jerusalem which is from above," is used by the Jews to signify the days of the Messiah, and that state of grace and glory which should follow the Levitical worship and ceremonies; and it is possible that Paul may use "heavenly things," in this sense: "God hath blessed us with all spiritual blessings in heavenly things, or in this heavenly state," in which life and immortality are brought to light by the gospel. This is apparently the preferable sense.

MATTHEW HENRY

They are *spiritual blessings in heavenly places.* Or it may be read, *in heavenly things,* such as come from heaven, and are designed to prepare men for it. We should hence learn to mind spiritual and heavenly blessings as the best blessings with which we cannot be miserable, and without which we cannot but be so.

II. Particular spiritual blessings enlarged upon. 1. Election and predestination, *v.* 4, 5, 11. *Election,* or choice, respects that lump or mass of mankind from which they are separated.

Before the foundation of the world they were chosen in the counsel of God from all eternity. The alms which you give to beggars at your doors proceed from a sudden resolve; but the provision which a parent makes for his children is the result of many thoughts. He acts in pursuance of his eternal purpose in bestowing spiritual blessings upon his people. *He hath blessed us—according as he hath chosen us in him,* in Christ the great head of the election. One great end and design of this choice: *chosen—that we should be holy.* All who are chosen to happiness as the end are chosen to holiness as the means. *And without blame before him*—that their holiness might not be merely external and in outward appearance, but internal and real, such holiness as proceeds from love to God and to our fellow-creatures, this charity being the principle of all true holiness.

Predestination has respect to the blessings they are designed for; particularly *the adoption of children,* that in due time we should become his adopted children, and so have a right to all the privileges of children.

Here is also the rule and the fontal cause of God's election: it is *according to the good pleasure of his will* (*v.* 5), because it was his sovereign will.

2. The next is acceptance with God through Jesus Christ: *Wherein he hath made us accepted in the beloved, v.* 6. We cannot be thus accepted of God, but in and through Jesus Christ. He loves his people for the sake of the beloved.

JAMIESON, FAUSSET, BROWN

ducing us into the heavenly places, which by our sin were barred against us. Cf. the change made by Christ (Col. 1:20; ch. 1:20). While Christ in the flesh was in the form of a *servant,* God's people could not realize fully their heavenly privileges as *sons.* Now "our *citizenship* (*Greek*) is in heaven" (Phil. 3:20), where our High Priest is ever "blessing" us. Our "treasures" are there (Matt. 6:20, 21); our aims and affections (Col. 3: 1, 2); our hope (Col. 1: 5; Titus 2:13); our inheritance (I Pet. 1:4). The gift of the Spirit itself, the source of the "spiritual blessing," is by virtue of Jesus having ascended thither (ch. 4:8). **in Christ**—the center and source of all blessing to us. **4. hath chosen us**—*Greek,* "*chose* us out for Himself" (viz., *out of* the world, Gal. 1:4): referring to His original choice, spoken of as *past.* **in him**—The repetition of the idea, "in Christ" (vs. 3), implies the paramount importance of the truth that it is *in Him,* and by virtue of union to Him, the Second Adam, the Restorer ordained for us from everlasting, the Head of redeemed humanity, believers have all their blessings (ch. 3: 11). **before the foundation of the world**—This assumes the eternity of the Son of God (John 17:5, 24), as of the election of believers in Him (II Tim. 1:9; II Thess. 2:13). **that we should be holy**—positively (Deut. 14:2). **without blame**—negatively (ch. 5:27; I Thess. 3:13). **before him**—It is to Him the believer looks, walking as in His presence, before whom he looks to be accepted in the judgment (Col. 1:22; cf. Rev. 7:15). **in love**—joined by BENGEL and others with vs. 5, "in love having predestinated us . . . ." But *English Version* is better. The words qualify the whole clause, "that we should be holy . . . before Him." Love, lost to man by the fall, but restored by redemption, is the root and fruit and sum of all holiness (ch. 5:2; I Thess. 3:12, 13). **5. predestinated**—more special in respect to the *end* and precise *means,* than "chosen" or *elected.* We are "chosen" *out of the rest of the world;* "predestinated" *to all things that secure the inheritance* for us (vs. 11; Rom. 8:29). "*Foreordained.*" **by Jesus**—*Greek,* "*through* Jesus." **to himself**—the Father (Col. 1:20). ALFORD explains, "adoption . . . *into* Himself," i.e., so that we should be *partakers of the divine nature* (II Pet. 1:4). LACHMANN reads, "unto *Him.*" The context favors the explanation of CALVIN: God has regard *to Himself* and the glory of His grace (vss. 6, 12, 14) as His ultimate end. He had one only begotten Son, and He was pleased *for His own glory,* to choose out of a lost world many to become His adopted sons. Translate, "*unto* Himself."

the good pleasure of his will—So the *Greek* (Matt. 11:26; Luke 10:21). We cannot go beyond "the good pleasure of His will" in searching into the causes of our salvation, or of any of His works (vs. 9). (Job 33:13.) Why needest thou philosophize about an imaginary world of optimism? Thy concern is to take heed that thou be not bad. There was nothing in us which deserved His love (vss. 1, 9, 11) [BENGEL]. **6.** (Vss. 7, 17, 18.) The end aimed at (Ps. 50:23), i.e., that the glory of His grace may be praised by all His creatures, men and angels. **wherein**—Some of the oldest MSS. read, "*which.*" Then translate, "which He graciously bestowed on us." But *English Version* is supported by good MSS. and the oldest versions. **us accepted**—a kindred *Greek* word to "grace": *charitos, echaritosen:* translate, "graciously accepted"; "made us subjects of His grace"; "embraced us in the arms of His grace" (Rom. 3:24; 5: 15). **in the beloved**—pre-eminently so called (Matt. 3:17; 17:5; John 3:35; Col. 1:13). *Greek,* "Son of His love." It is only "IN HIS BELOVED" that He loves us (vs. 3; I John 4:9, 10).

ADAM CLARKE

4. *According as he hath chosen us in him.* As He has decreed from "the beginning of the world," and has kept in view from the commencement of the religious system of the Jews (which the phrase sometimes means) to bring us Gentiles to the knowledge of the glorious state of salvation by Christ Jesus. The Jews considered themselves an elect or chosen people, and wished to monopolize the whole of the divine love and beneficence. The apostle here shows that God had the Gentiles as much in the contemplation of His mercy and goodness as He had the Jews; and the blessings of the gospel, now so freely dispensed to them, were the proof that God had thus chosen them, and that His end in giving them the gospel was the same which He had in view by giving the law to the Jews, viz., that they might be holy and without blame before Him. And as His object was the same in respect to them both, they should consider that, as He loved them, so they should love one another. God having provided for each the same blessings, they should therefore be *holy*—fully separated from earth and sin, and consecrated to God; and *without blame*—having no spot nor imperfection, their inward holiness agreeing with their outward consecration. The words are a metaphor taken from the perfect and immaculate sacrifices which the law required the people to bring to the altar of God. But as *love* is the fulfilling of the law, and love the fountain whence their salvation flowed, therefore love must fill their hearts towards God and each other, and love must be the motive and end of all their words and works.

5. *Having predestinated us.* As the doctrine of eternal predestination has produced much controversy in the Christian world, it may be necessary to examine the meaning of the term, that those who do use it may employ it according to the sense it has in the oracles of God. The verb *proorizo,* from *pro,* "before," and *horizo,* "I define, finish, bound, or terminate," whence *horos,* "a boundary or limit," signifies to "define beforehand," and circumscribe by certain bounds or limits; and is originally a geographical term, but applied also to anything concluded, or determined, or demonstrated. Here the word is used to point out God's fixed purpose or predetermination to bestow on the Gentiles the blessing of the adoption of "sons" by Jesus Christ, which adoption had been before granted to the Jewish people; and without circumcision, or any other Mosaic rite, to admit the Gentiles to all the privileges of His Church and people. The apostle marks that all this was "foredetermined" by God, as He had foredetermined the bounds and precincts of the land which He gave them according to the promise made to their fathers; that the Jews had no reason to complain, for God had formed this purpose before He had given the law, or called them out of Egypt (for it was before the foundation of the world, v. 2); and that, therefore, the conduct of God in calling the Gentiles now—bringing them into His Church, and conferring on them the gifts and graces of the Holy Spirit—was in pursuance of His original design; and if He did not do so, His eternal purposes could not be fulfilled; and that, as the Jews were taken to be His peculiar people, not because they had any goodness or merit in themselves, so the Gentiles were called, not for any merit they had, but *according to the good pleasure of his will;* that is, according to His eternal benevolence, showing mercy and conferring privileges in this new creation, as He had done in the original creation.

6. *To the praise of the glory of his grace. The glory of his grace,* for "His glorious or illustrious grace," according to the Hebrew idiom. But the grace or mercy of God is peculiarly illustrated and glorified in the plan of redemption by Christ Jesus. By the giving of the law, God's justice and holiness were rendered most glorious; by the giving of the gospel, His grace and mercy are made equally conspicuous. *Wherein he hath made us accepted in the beloved.* This translation is not clear; "with which He has graciously favored us through the Beloved" is at once more literal and more intelligible. *In the beloved* must certainly mean "in Christ," who is termed God's beloved Son, Matt. iii. 17.

MATTHEW HENRY

3. Remission of sins, and redemption through the blood of Jesus, *v.* 7. No remission without redemption. The guilt and the stain of sin could be no otherwise removed than by the blood of Jesus. All our spiritual blessings flow down to us in that stream. It is according to the riches of God's grace. It was rich grace to provide such a surety as his own Son, when nothing of that nature could have entered into our thoughts, nor have been otherwise found out for us.

He has not only manifested riches of grace, but *has abounded towards us in all wisdom and prudence* (*v.* 8).

4. Another privilege is divine revelation—that God hath *made known to us the mystery of his will* (*v.* 9). This we owe to Christ, who came to declare his will to the children of men: *According to his good pleasure which he had purposed.* It is described (*v.* 13) *as the word of truth, and the gospel of our salvation.* O, how ought we to prize this glorious gospel and to bless God for it!

ALBERT BARNES:

10. "That in the dispensation." The word here rendered "dispensation" means properly "the management of household affairs." Then it means stewardship or administration; a dispensation or arrangement of things; a scheme or plan. The meaning here is that this plan was formed in order or "unto" this end, that in the full arrangement of times, or in the arrangements completing the filling up of the times, God might gather together in one all things. Tindal renders it, "to have it declared when the time was full come."

"The fulness of times." When the times were fully completed; when all the periods should have passed by which he had prescribed or judged necessary to the completion of the object. The period referred to here is that when all things shall be gathered together in the Redeemer at the winding up of human affairs, or the consummation of all things. The arrangement was made with reference to that, and embraced all things which conduced to that. The plan stretched from before "the foundation of the world" to the period when all times should be completed; and of course all the events occurring in that intermediate period were embraced in the plan.—*Popular Commentary*

JAMIESON, FAUSSET, BROWN

7. In whom—"the Beloved" (vs. 6; Rom. 3:24). **we have**—as a *present* possession. **redemption**—*Greek, "our* (lit., *'the')* redemption"; THE redemption which is the grand subject of all revelation, and especially of the New Testament (Rom. 3:24), viz., from the power, guilt, and penal consequences of sin (Matt. 1:21). If a man were unable to redeem himself from being a bond servant, his kinsman might redeem him (Lev. 25:48). Hence, antitypically the Son of God became the Son of man, that as our kinsman He might redeem us (Matt. 20:28). Another "redemption" follows, viz., that "of the purchased possession" hereafter (vs. 14). **through his blood**—(ch. 2:13)—as the instrument; the propitiation, i.e., the consideration (devised by His own love) for which He, who was justly angry (Isa. 12:1), becomes propitious to us; the expiation, the price paid to divine justice for our sin (Acts 20:28; Rom. 3:25; I Cor. 6:20; Col. 1:20; I Pet. 1:18, 19). **the forgiveness of sins**—*Greek,* "the remission of *our transgressions*": not merely "*pretermission,*" as the *Greek* (Rom. 3:25) ought to be translated. This "remission," being the explanation of "redemption," includes not only deliverance from sin's penalty, but from its pollution and enslaving power, negatively; and the reconciliation of an offended God, and a satisfaction unto a just God, positively. **riches of his grace**—(ch. 2:7)—"the exceeding riches of His grace." Cf. vs. 18, and ch. 3:16, "according to the riches of His glory": so that "grace" is His "glory." **8.** Rather, "which He made to abound towards us." **all wisdom and prudence**—"wisdom" in devising the plan of redeeming mankind; "prudence" in executing it by the means, and in making all the necessary arrangements of Providence for that purpose. Paul attributes to the Gospel of God's grace "all" possible "wisdom and prudence," in opposition to the boasts of wisdom and prudence which the unbelieving Jews and heathen philosophers and false apostles arrogated for their teachings. Christ crucified, though esteemed "foolishness" by the world, is "the wisdom of God" (I Cor. 1:18-30). Cf. ch. 3:10, "the *manifold* wisdom of God. **9.** "He hath abounded," or "made (grace) to abound toward us" (vs. 8), *in that He made known* to us, viz., experimentally, in our hearts. **the mystery**—God's purpose of redemption hidden heretofore in His counsels, but now revealed (ch. 6:19; Rom. 16:25; Col. 1:26, 27). This "mystery" is not like the heathen mysteries, which were imparted only to the initiated few. All Christians are the initiated. Only unbelievers are the uninitiated. **according to his good pleasure**—showing the cause why "He hath made known to us the mystery," viz., His own loving "good pleasure" toward us; also the *time* and *manner* of His doing so, are according to His good pleasure. **purposed**—(Vs. 11). **in himself**—God the Father. BENGEL takes it, "in *Him,*" i.e., *Christ,* as in vss. 3, 4. But the proper name, "in *Christ,*" vs. 10, immediately after, is inconsistent with His being here meant by the pronoun. **10.** Translate, "*Unto* the dispensation of the fulness of the times," i.e., "which He purposed in Himself" (vs. 9) *with a view to* the economy of (the gracious *administration belonging to*) the fulness of the times (*Greek,* "fit times," "seasons"). More comprehensive than "the fulness of the time" (Gal. 4:4). The whole of the Gospel *times* (plural) is meant, with the benefits to the Church *dispensed* in them severally and successively. Cf. "the ages to come" (ch. 2:7). "The ends of the ages" (*Greek,* I Cor. 10:11); "the times (same *Greek* as here, 'the seasons,' or 'fitly appointed times') of the Gentiles" (Luke 21:24); "the seasons which the Father hath put in His own power" (Acts 1:7); "the times of restitution of all things which God hath spoken by the prophets since the world began" (Acts 3:20, 21). The coming of Jesus at the first advent, "in the fulness of time," was *one* of these "times." The descent of the Holy Ghost, "when Pentecost was *fully come*" (Acts 2:1), was another. The testimony given by the apostles to Him "in due time" ("in its own seasons," *Greek*) (I Tim. 2:6) was another. The conversion of the Jews "when the *times* of the Gentiles are fulfilled," the second coming of Christ, the "restitution of all things," the millennial kingdom, the new heaven and earth, shall be severally instances of "the dispensation of the fulness of the times," i.e., "the dispensation of" the Gospel events and benefits belonging to their respective "times," when severally filled up or completed. God the Father, according to His own good pleasure and purpose, is the Dispenser both of the Gospel benefits and of their several fitting times (Acts 1:7). **gather together in one**—*Greek,* "sum up under one head"; "recapitulate." The "good pleasure which He purposed,"

ADAM CLARKE

7. *In whom we have redemption.* God has glorified His grace by giving us redemption by the blood of His Son, and this redemption consists in forgiving and delivering us from our sins; so then Christ's blood was the redemption price paid down for our salvation.

8. *Wherein he hath abounded.* That is, in the dispensation of mercy and goodness by Christ Jesus. *In all wisdom and prudence.* Giving us apostles the most complete instructions in heavenly things by the inspiration of His Spirit; and at the same time *prudence,* that we might know when and where to preach the gospel so that it might be effectual to the salvation of those who heard it. Nothing less than the Spirit of God could teach the apostles that *wisdom* by which they were to instruct a dark and sinful world; and nothing less than the same Spirit could inspire them with that *prudence* which was necessary to be exercised in every step of their life and ministry.

9. *Having made known unto us the mystery.* That the Gentiles should ever be received into the Church of God, and have all the privileges of the Jews, without being obliged to submit to circumcision and perform the rites and ceremonies of the Jewish law, was a *mystery*—a "hidden thing" which had never been published before; and now revealed only to the apostles. It was God's *will* that it should be so, but that will He kept hidden to the present time. A *mystery* signifies something hidden, but it ceases to be a mystery as soon as it is revealed. *Good pleasure.* "That benevolent design which He had purposed in himself," not being induced by any consideration from without.

10. *In the dispensation of the fulness of times.* The dispensation of the gospel, that plan by which God has provided salvation for a lost world; and according to which He intends to gather all believers, both Jews and Gentiles, into one Church under Jesus Christ, their Head and Governor. *The fulness of times*—By this phrase we are to understand either the gospel dispensation, which is the consummation of all preceding dispensations and the last that shall be afforded to man, or that advanced state of the world which God saw to be the most proper for the full manifestation of those benevolent purposes which He had formed in himself relative to the salvation of the world by Jesus Christ.

That he might gather together in one. The gathering together both Jews and Gentiles, who have believed in Christ, into one Church and

MATTHEW HENRY

5. Union in and with Christ is a great privilege. *He gathers together in one all things in Christ, v.* 10. All the lines of divine revelation meet in Christ; all religion centres in him. Jews and Gentiles were united to each other by being both united to Christ. *Things in heaven and things on earth* are gathered together in him; peace made between heaven and earth through him. The innumerable company of angels become one with the church through Christ: this God *purposed in himself.*

6. The eternal inheritance is the great blessing with which we are blessed in Christ: *In whom also we have obtained an inheritance, v.* 11. Heaven is the inheritance. *If children, then heirs.* All the blessings that we have in hand are but small if compared with the inheritance. What is laid out upon an heir in his minority is nothing to what is reserved for him when he comes to age.

It is *according to the purpose of him who worketh all things after the counsel of his own will* (*v.* 11). The last and great end is his own glory: *To the praise of the glory of his grace* (*v.* 6), *that we should be to the praise of his glory* (*v.* 12). The glory of God is his own end, and it should be ours in all that we do.

7. The seal and earnest of the Spirit. We are said to be *sealed with that Holy Spirit of promise, v.* 13. He makes us holy. He is the promised Spirit. By him believers are sealed and set apart for God.

The Spirit *is the earnest of our inheritance, v.* 14. The earnest is part of payment, and it secures the full sum. All his influences are heaven begun, glory in the seed and bud. His comforts are earnests of everlasting joys.

JAMIESON, FAUSSET, BROWN

was "to sum up all things (*Greek*, 'THE whole range of things') in Christ" (*Greek*, "the Christ," i.e., *His* Christ) [ALFORD]. God's purpose is to sum up the whole creation in Christ, the Head of angels, with whom He is linked by His invisible nature, and of men with whom He is linked by His humanity; of Jews and Gentiles; of the living and the dead (ch. 3:15); of animate and inanimate creation. Sin has disarranged the creature's relation of subordination to God. God means to gather up all together in Christ; or as Colossians 1:20 says, "By Him to reconcile all things unto Himself, whether things in earth or things in heaven." ALFORD well says, "The Church of which the apostle here mainly treats, is subordinated to Him in the highest degree of conscious and joyful union; those who are not His spiritually, in mere subjugation, yet consciously; the inferior tribes of creation unconsciously; but objectively, all are summed up in Him." **11. In whom**—by virtue of union to whom. **obtained an inheritance**—lit., "We were made to have an inheritance" [WAHL]. Cf. vs. 18, "*His* inheritance in the saints": as *His* inheritance is there said to be *in them*, so *theirs* is here said to be *in Him* (Acts 26:18). However, vs. 12, "That we should BE TO ... His glory" (not "that we should *have*"), favors the translation of BENGEL, ELLICOTT, and others, "We were *made* an inheritance." So the literal Israel (Deut. 4:20; 9:29; 32:9). "Also" does not mean "we also," nor as *English Version*, "in whom also"; but, besides His having "made known to us His will," we were also "made His inheritance," or "we have also obtained an inheritance." **predestinated**—(Vs. 5). The foreordination of Israel, as the elect nation, answers to that of the spiritual Israelites, believers, to an eternal inheritance, which is the thing meant here. The "we" here and in vs. 12, means *Jewish* believers (whence the reference to the election of Israel nationally arises), as contrasted with "you" (vs. 13) *Gentile* believers. **purpose**—repeated from "purposed" (vs. 9; ch. 3:11). The Church existed in the mind of God eternally, before it existed in creation. **counsel of his ... will**—vs. 5, "the good pleasure of His will." Not arbitrary caprice, but infinite wisdom ("counsel") joined with sovereign will. Cf. his address to the same Ephesians in Acts 20:27, "All the counsel of God" (Isa. 28:29). Alike in the natural and spiritual creations, God is not an agent constrained by necessity. "Wheresoever counsel is, there is election, or else it is vain; where a will, there must be freedom, or else it is weak" [PEARSON]. **12.** (*V.* 6, 14.) **who first trusted in Christ**—rather (we Jewish Christians), "who have before hoped in *the* Christ": who before the Christ came, looked forward to His coming, waiting for the consolation of Israel. Cf. Acts 26:6, 7, "I am judged for *the hope of the promise made of God unto our fathers: unto which our twelve tribes*, instantly serving God day and night, *hope to come.*" Acts 28:20, "*the hope of Israel*" [ALFORD]. Cf. vs. 18; ch. 2:12; 4:4. **13. In whom ye also**—Ye Gentiles. Supply as *English Version*, "trusted," from vs. 12; or "are." The priority of us Jews does not exclude you Gentiles from sharing in Christ (cf. Acts 13:46). **the word of truth**—the instrument of sanctification, and of the new birth (John 17:17; II Tim. 2:15; James. 1:18). Cf. Colossians 1:5, where also, as here, it is connected with "hope." Also ch. 4:21. **sealed**—as God's confirmed children, by the Holy Spirit as the seal (Acts 19:1-6; Rom. 8:16, 23; *Note*, II Cor. 1:22; I John 3:24). A seal impressed on a document gives undoubted validity to the contract in it (John 3:33; 6:27; cf. II Cor. 3:3). So the sense of "the love of God shed abroad in the heart by the Holy Ghost" (Rom. 5:5), and the sense of adoption given through the Spirit at regeneration (Rom. 8:15, 16), assure believers of God's good will to them. The Spirit, like a seal, impresses on the soul at regeneration the image of our Father. The "sealing" by the Holy Spirit is spoken of as *past* once for all. The witnessing to our hearts that we are the children of God, and heirs (vs. 11), is the Spirit's *present* testimony, the "earnest of the (coming) inheritance" (Rom. 8:16-18). **that Holy Spirit of promise**—rather, as the *Greek*, "The Spirit of promise, even the Holy Spirit": The *Spirit promised* both in the Old and New Testaments (Joel 2:28; Zech. 12:10; John 7:38, 39). "The word" *promised* the Holy Spirit. Those who "believed the word of truth" were sealed by the Spirit accordingly. **14. earnest**—the first instalment paid as a pledge that the rest will follow (Rom. 8:23; II Cor. 1:22). **until**—rather, "*Unto* the redemption ..."; joined thus, "ye were sealed (vs. 13) unto," i.e., *for the purpose of, and against*, the accomplishment of "the redemption," viz., not the *redemption* in its first stage,

ADAM CLARKE

flock. *All things . . . which are in heaven, and which are on earth.* This clause is variously understood. Some think by *things . . . in heaven* the Jewish state is meant; and by *things . . . on earth*, the Christian. The Jews had been long considered a divine or heavenly people. But there are others who imagine the *things . . . in heaven* mean the angelical hosts; and the *things . . . on earth*, believers of all nations, who shall all be joined together at last in one assembly to worship God throughout eternity. And some think that the *things . . . in heaven* mean the saints who died before Christ's advent, and who are not to be made perfect till the resurrection. And some think that, as the Hebrew phrase *shamayim vehaarets*, the "heavens and the earth," signifies all creatures, the words in the text are to be understood as signifying all mankind, without discrimination of peoples, kindreds, or tongues: Jews, Greeks, or barbarians—all that are saved of all nations (being saved in the same way, viz., by faith in Christ Jesus, without any distinction of nation or previous condition) and all gathered into one Church or assembly. I believe that the forming one Church out of both Jews and Gentiles is that to which the apostle refers. This agrees with what is said in chap. ii. 14-17.

11. *In whom*, Christ Jesus; *also we*—believing Jews; *have obtained an inheritance*—what was promised to Abraham and his spiritual seed, viz., the adoption of sons, and the kingdom of Heaven. *Being predestinated.* God having determined to bring both Jews and Gentiles to salvation, not by works nor by any human means or schemes, but by Jesus Christ; that salvation being defined and determined before in the divine mind, and the means by which it should be brought about all being according to His purpose, who consults not His creatures, but operates according to *the counsel of his own will*, that being ever wise, gracious, and good.

12. *That we.* Jews, now apostles and messengers of God, to whom the first offers of salvation were made, and who were the first that believed in Christ. *Should be to the praise of his glory.* By being the means of preaching Christ crucified to the Gentiles, and spreading the gospel throughout the world.

13. *In whom ye also trusted.* You Gentiles, having heard from us the *word*, the doctrine of the *truth*, which is *the gospel*, or glad tidings, *of your salvation*, have believed, as we Jews have done, and received similar blessings to those with which God has favored us. *In whom also*, Christ Jesus, *after that ye* had *believed*, viz., that He was the only Saviour, and that through His blood redemption might be obtained, *ye were sealed with that holy Spirit of promise.* It was customary among all nations, when a person purchased goods of any kind, to mark with his seal that which he had bought, in order that he might know it, and be able to claim it if mixed with the goods of others; to this custom the apostle may here allude. But it was also customary to set a seal upon what was dedicated to God, or what was to be offered to Him in sacrifice.

14. *Which is the earnest of our inheritance.* This Holy Spirit, sealing the soul with truth and righteousness, is the *earnest*, "foretaste," and "pledge" of the heavenly inheritance. And he who can produce this *earnest*—this witness of the Spirit—in the day of judgment shall have an abundant entrance into the holiest.

MATTHEW HENRY

He is said to be the earnest, *until the redemption of the purchased possession.* This earnest makes it as sure to the heirs as though they were already possessed of it; and it is purchased for them by the blood of Christ. The great end and design of God in bestowing all these spiritual privileges is *that we should be to the praise of his glory who first trusted in Christ.* Seniority in grace is a preferment: those who have for a longer time experienced the grace of Christ are under more special obligations to glorify God. This is the great design of God in all that he has done for us: it is *unto the praise of his glory, v.* 14.

Verses 15–23

Paul's earnest prayer to God in behalf of these Ephesians. He has laid up these spiritual blessings for us in the hands of his Son. He has appointed us to draw them out, and fetch them in, by prayer. We have no part nor lot in the matter, any further than we claim it by faith and prayer. Note, the good account he had of them, *of their faith in the Lord Jesus and love to all the saints, v.* 15. Those who love saints, as such, love all saints, how weak in grace, how mean in the world, how fretful and peevish soever, some of them may be. Another inducement to pray for them was because they had received the earnest of the inheritance. *Wherefore—I cease not to give thanks for you, making mention of you in my prayers, v.* 16. While he blessed God for giving them the Spirit, he ceases not to pray (*v.* 17), that he would give greater measures of the Spirit. The great thing he prays for is the illumination of their understandings, and that their knowledge might increase and abound; he means it of a practical and experimental knowledge. The graces and comforts of the Spirit are communicated to the soul by the enlightening of the understanding. Satan takes a contrary way: he gets possession by the senses and passions, Christ by the understanding.

I. Whence this knowledge must come; from *the God of our Lord Jesus Christ, v.* 17. The Lord *is a God of knowledge,* and there is no sound saving knowledge but what comes from him. He gives knowledge by giving the Spirit of knowledge; for the Spirit of God is the teacher of the saints, *the Spirit of wisdom and revelation.* We have the revelation of the Spirit in the word: but will that avail us, if we have not the wisdom of the Spirit in the heart? *In the knowledge of him.* This knowledge is first in the understanding. He prays that *the eyes of their understanding may be enlightened, v.* 18. Christians should not think it enough to have warm affections, but they should labour to have clear understandings; they should be ambitious of being knowing Christians, and judicious Christians.

II. What it is that he more particularly desires they should grow in the knowledge of. 1. *The hope of his calling, v.* 18. There is a hope in this calling; for those who deal with God deal upon trust. We ought to labour after, and pray earnestly for, a clearer insight into, and a fuller acquaintance with, the great objects of a Christian's hopes. 2. *The riches of the glory of his inheritance in the saints.* There is a present inheritance in the saints; for grace is glory begun, and holiness is happiness in the bud. There is a glory in this inheritance, and it is desirable to know this experimentally. It may be understood of the glorious inheritance in heaven, where God does, as it were, lay forth all his riches. Let us endeavour then, by reading, contemplation, and prayer, to know as much of heaven as we can, that we may be desiring and longing to be there. 3. *The exceeding greatness of God's power towards those who believe, v.* 19. It is a difficult thing to bring a soul to believe in Christ. It is nothing less than an almighty power that will work this in us.

JAMIESON, FAUSSET, BROWN

made by the blood of Christ, which secures our *title,* but, in its final completion, when the actual *possession* shall be ours, the full "redemption of the body" (Rom. 8:23), as well as of the soul, from every infirmity (ch. 4:30). The deliverance of the creature (the body, and the whole visible creation) from the bondage of corruption, and from the usurping prince of this world, into the glorious liberty of the children of God (Rom. 8:21-23; II Pet. 3:13). **of the purchased possession**—God's people *purchased* (acquired, *Greek*) as His *peculiar* (*Greek*) possession by the blood of Christ (Acts 20:28). We value highly that which we pay a high price for; so God, His Church (ch. 5:25, 26; I Pet. 1:18; 2:9; Mal. 3:17, *Margin,* "my *special* treasure"). **15. Wherefore**—because ye are in Christ and sealed by His Spirit (vss. 13, 14). **I also**—on my part, in return for God's so great benefits to *you.* **after I heard**—ever since I have heard. Not implying that he had only *heard* of their conversion: an erroneous argument used by some against the address of this Epistle to the Ephesians (*Note,* vs. 1); but referring to the report he had heard *since* he was with them, as to their Christian graces. So in the case of Philemon, his "*beloved fellow laborer*" (Philemon 1), he uses the same words (Philemon 4, 5). **your faith**—rather, as *Greek,* "the faith among you," i.e., which many (not all) of you have. **love unto all the saints**—of whatever name, simply because they are saints. A distinguishing characteristic of true Christianity (ch. 6:24). "*Faith* and *love* he often joins together. A wondrous pair" [CHRYSOSTOM]. *Hope* is added, vs. 18. **16.** (Col. 1:9.) **of you**—omitted in the oldest MSS. Then the translation may be as *English Version* still, or as ALFORD, "making mention of *them*" (your "faith and love"). **17. A** fit prayer for all Christians. **the God of our Lord Jesus**—appropriate title here; as in vss. 20-22 he treats of *God's* raising *Jesus* to be Head over all things to the Church. Jesus Himself called the Father "*My* God" (Matt. 27:46). **the Father of glory**—(Cf. Acts 7:2). The Father of that infinite glory which shines in the face of Christ, who is "the glory" (the true Shekinah); through whom also "the glory of the inheritance" (vs. 18) shall be ours (John 17:24; II Cor. 3:7 to 4:6). **the spirit of wisdom**—whose attribute is infinite wisdom and who works wisdom in believers (Isa. 11:2). **and revelation**—whose function it is to *reveal* to believers spiritual mysteries (John 16:14, 15; I Cor. 2:10). **in the knowledge**—rather, as *Greek* (see *Note,* I Cor. 13:12), "in the *full knowledge* of Him," viz., God. **18. understanding**—The oldest MSS., versions, and Fathers, read "heart." Cf. the contrary state of unbelieving, the *heart* being in fault (ch. 4:18; Matt. 13:15). Translate, "Having the eyes of your heart enlightened" (ch. 5:14; Matt. 4:16). The first effect of the Spirit moving in the new creation, as in the original physical creation (Gen. 1:3; II Cor. 4: 6). So THEOPHILUS to AUTOLYCUS, 1. 3, "the ears of the heart." Where spiritual *light* is, there is *life* (John 1:4). The heart is "the core of life" [HARLESS], and the fountain of the thoughts; whence "the heart" in Scripture includes the *mind,* as well as the inclination. Its "eye," or inward vision, both receives and contemplates the light (Matt. 6:22, 23). The eye is the symbol of intelligence (Ezek. 1:18). **the hope of his calling**—the hope appertaining to His having called you; or, to the calling wherewith He has called you. **and**—omitted in the oldest MSS. and versions. **riches of the glory . . .** —(Col. 1:27). **his inheritance in the saints**—The inheritance which he has in store in the case of the saints. I prefer explaining, "The inheritance which He has in his saints." (See *Note,* vs. 11; Deut. 32: 9.) **19. exceeding**—"surpassing." **power to us-ward who believe**—The whole of the working of His grace, which He is carrying on, and will carry on, in us who believe. By the term "saints" (vs. 18), believers are regarded as *absolutely perfected,* and so as being God's inheritance; in this verse, as in the course of *fighting* the good fight of faith. **according to**—in accordance with what might be expected from. **working**—*Greek,* "the energizing"; translate, "the effectual working" (ch. 3:7). The same superhuman power was needed and exerted to make us believe, as was needed and exerted to raise Christ from the dead (vs. 20). Cf. Philippians 3:10, "the power of His resurrection" (Col. 2:12; I Pet. 1:3-5). **of his mighty power**—*Greek,* "of the strength of His might."

ADAM CLARKE

The redemption of the purchased possession. That is, till the time when body and soul are redeemed from all their miseries and glorified in the kingdom of Heaven. *The redemption of the purchased possession.* All those who believe in Christ Jesus are considered as His peculiar people and property, and to them eternal glory is promised. The Spirit of promise, which is given them, is a pledge that they shall have a resurrection from the dead, and eternal blessedness; the *redemption,* or bringing to life of the body, cannot take place till the day of judgment, but the Holy Spirit promises this redemption, and is now in their hearts an *earnest* or "pledge" of this complete restoration at the great day, which will then be, in an especial manner, *unto the praise of his glory,* viz., of Christ, who has bought them by His blood.

15. *Faith in the Lord Jesus.* Cordial reception of the Christian religion, amply proved by their *love unto all the saints*—to all the Christians. Perhaps *love* here implies not only the kind affection so called but also all the fruits of love —benevolence and kind offices of every description.

16. *Cease not to give thanks.* The apostle intimates, so fully satisfied was he of the genuineness of their conversion, and of their steadiness since their conversion, that it was to him a continual cause of thanksgiving to God, who had brought them into that state of salvation; and of prayer, that they might be preserved blameless to the end. *Making mention of you.* While praying for the prosperity of the Christian cause generally, he was led, from his particular affection for them, to mention them by name before God.

17. *That the God of our Lord Jesus.* Jesus Christ, as Man and Mediator, has the *Father* for His God and Father; and it is in reference to this that He himself says: "I ascend unto my Father, and your Father; and to my God, and your God," John xx. 17. *The Father of glory.* The Author and Giver of that glory which you expect at the end of your Christian race. This may be a Hebraism for "glorious Father," but the former appears to be the best sense. *The spirit of wisdom and revelation.* I pray that God may give you His Holy Spirit, by whom His will is revealed to men, that He may teach and make you wise unto salvation, that you may continue to acknowledge Him, Christ Jesus, as your only Lord and Saviour.

18. *The eyes of your understanding being enlightened.* Instead of *of your understanding,* "of your heart," is the reading of several MSS. "The eyes of your heart" is undoubtedly the true reading. *The hope of his calling.* That you may clearly discern the glorious and important objects of your *hope,* to the enjoyment of which God has called or invited you. *The riches of the glory of his inheritance.* That you may understand what is the glorious abundance of the spiritual things to which you are entitled, in consequence of being made children of God; for if children, then heirs, heirs of that glorious inheritance which God has provided for the saints—for all genuine Christians, whether formerly Jews or Gentiles.

19. *The exceeding greatness of his power.* As the apostle is here speaking of the glorious state of believers after death, *the exceeding greatness of his power,* or that power which surpasses all difficulties, being itself omnipotent, is to be understood of that might which is to be exerted in raising the body at the last day; as it will require the same power or energy which He wrought in Christ, when He raised His body from the grave, to raise up the bodies of all mankind, the resurrection of the human nature of Christ being a proof of the resurrection of mankind in general. *According to the working of his mighty power.* "According to the energy of the power of His might." We may understand these words thus: "might" is the state or simple efficiency of this attribute in God; "power" is this might or efficiency in action; "energy" is the quantum of force, momentum, or velocity with which the power is applied. Though they appear to be synonymous terms they may be thus understood. Passive power is widely different from power in action; and power in action will be in its results ac-

MATTHEW HENRY

The apostle speaks as if he wanted words to express the *exceeding greatness of God's almighty power*, that power which God exerts towards his people, and by which *he raised Christ from the dead*, *v.* 20. That indeed was the great proof of the truth of the gospel to the world: but the transcript of that in ourselves is the great proof to us. Many understand the apostle here as speaking of that *exceeding greatness of power* which God will exert for raising believers to eternal life, even the same *mighty power which he wrought in Christ when he raised him*, &c. And how desirable a thing must it be to become at length acquainted with that power, by being raised thereby unto eternal life!

The apostle digresses a little to make mention of the Lord Jesus and his exaltation. He sits at the Father's *right hand in the heavenly places*, &c., *v.* 20, 21.

The Father *hath put all things under his feet* (*v.* 22). God GAVE *him to be head over all things.* It was a gift to Christ, and it was a gift to the church, to be provided with a head endued with so much power and authority. He gave him all power both in heaven and in earth. *The Father loves the Son, and hath given* ALL *things into his hands.* But that which completes the comfort of this is that he is the head over all things to the church.

The same power that supports the world supports the church; and we are sure he loves his church, for it *is his body* (*v.* 23), and he will care for it

It is *the fulness of him that filleth all in all.* Jesus Christ filleth all in all. Christ as Mediator would not be complete if he had not a church. How could he be a king if he had not a kingdom?

JAMIESON, FAUSSET, BROWN

20. in Christ—as our "first fruits" of the resurrection, and Head, in virtue of God's mighty working in whom His power to us-ward is made possible and actual [ALFORD]. **when he raised him**—"in that He raised Him." The raising of Christ is not only an earnest of our bodies being hereafter raised, but has a spiritual power in it involving (by virtue of our living union with Him, as members with the Head) the resurrection, spiritually of the believer's soul now, and, consequently, of his body hereafter (Rom. 6:8-11; 8:11). The Son, too, as God (though not as man), had a share in raising His own human body (John 2:19; 10:17, 18). Also the Holy Spirit (Rom. 1:4; I Pet. 3:18). **set him**—*Greek,* "made Him sit." The glorious spirits *stand* about the throne of God, but they do not *sit at God's right hand* (Heb. 1:13). **at his own right hand**—(Ps. 110:1). Where He remains till all His enemies have been put under His feet (I Cor. 15:24). Being appointed to "rule in the midst of His enemies" during their rebellion (Ps. 110:2), He shall resign His commission after their subjection [PEARSON] (Mark 16:19; Heb. 1:3; 10:12). **in the heavenly places**—(vs. 3). As Christ has a literal body, heaven is not merely a state, but a *place;* and where He is, there His people shall be (John 14:3). **21.** *Greek,* "Far (or high) above all (ch. 4:10) principality (or rule, I Cor. 15:24), and authority, and power (Matt. 28:18), and dominion (or lordship)." Cf. Philippians 2:9; Colossians 1:16; Hebrews 7:26; I Peter 3:22. Evil spirits (who are similarly divided into various ranks, ch. 6:12), as well as angels of light, and earthly potentates, are included (cf. Rom. 8:38). Jesus is "King of kings, and Lord of lords" (Rev. 19:16). The higher is His honor, the greater is that of His people, who are His members joined to Him, the Head. Some philosophizing teachers of the school of Simon Magus, in Western Asia Minor, had, according to IRENÆUS and EPIPHANIUS, taught their hearers these names of various ranks of angels. Paul shows that the truest wisdom is to know Christ as reigning above them all. **every name**—every being whatever. "Any other creature" (Rom. 8:39). **in this world**—*Greek,* "age," i.e., the present *order of things.* "Things present . . . things to come" (Rom. 8:38). **that . . . to come**—"Names which now we know not, but shall know hereafter in heaven. We know that the emperor goes before all, though we cannot enumerate all the satraps and ministers of his court; so we know that Christ is set above all, although we cannot *name* them all" [BENGEL]. **22. put . . . under**—*Greek,* "put in subjection under" (Ps. 8:6; I Cor. 15: 27). **gave . . . to the church**—for her special advantage. The *Greek* order is emphatic: "HIM He gave as Head over all things to the Church." Had it been anyone save HIM, her Head, it would not have been the boon it is to the Church. But as *He* is Head over all things who is also her Head (and she the body), all things are hers (I Cor. 3:21-23). He is OVER ("far above") all things; in contrast to the words, "TO *the Church,*" viz., *for her advantage.* The former are subject; the latter is joined with Him in His dominion over them. "Head" implies not only His dominion, but our union; therefore, while we look upon Him at the right hand of God, we see ourselves in heaven (Rev. 3:21). For the Head and body are not severed by anything intervening, else the body would cease to be the body, and the Head cease to be the Head [PEARSON from CHRYSOSTOM]. **23. his body**—His mystical and spiritual, not literal, body. Not, however, merely figurative, or metaphorical. He is really, though spiritually, the Church's Head. His life is her life. She shares His crucifixion and His consequent glory. He possesses everything, His fellowship with the Father, His fulness of the Spirit, and His glorified manhood, not merely for Himself, but *for her,* who has a membership of His body, of His flesh, and of His bones (ch. 5:30). **fulness**—"the filled-up receptacle" [EADIE]. The Church is *dwelt in and filled by Christ.* She is the receptacle, not of His inherent, but of His *communicated, plenitude* of gifts and graces. As His is the "fulness" (John 1: 16; Col. 1:19; 2:9) inherently, so she is His "fulness" by His impartation of it to her, in virtue of her union to Him (ch. 5:18; Col. 2:10). "The *full manifestation* of His being, because penetrated by His life" [CONYBEARE and HOWSON]. She is the continued revelation of His divine life in human form; *the fullest representative of His plenitude.* Not the angelic hierarchy, as false teachers taught (Col. 2:9, 10, 18), but Christ Himself is the "fulness of the God-head," and she represents Him. KOPPE translates less probably, "the whole universal multitude." **filleth all in all**—Christ as the Creator, Preserver, and Governor of the world, constituted

ADAM CLARKE

cording to the energy or momentum with which it is applied.

20. *Set him at his own right hand in the heavenly places.* Gave Him, as Mediator between God and man, the highest honors and dignities, Phil. ii. 9; in which state of exaltation He transacts all the affairs of His Church and rules the universe.

The *right hand* is the place of friendship, honor, confidence, and authority.

21. *Far above all principality.* Some think he has reference here to the different orders among good and evil angels; He is superior to all the former, and rules all the latter. Others think he refers to earthly governments; and as *principality,* the first word, signifies the most sovereign and extensive kind of dominion; and "lordship," the last word, signifies the lowest degree of authority; hence we are to understand that to our Lord, in His human nature, are subjected the highest, the intermediate, and the lowest orders of beings in the universe. It is certain that the apostle means that all created power, glory, and influence are under Christ; and hence it is added:

22. *And hath put all things under his feet.* All beings and things are subject to Him, whether they be thrones, dominions, principalities, or powers, Col. i. 16-18 and ii. 10; for He, God the Father, has given *him to be head*—chief, and supreme over all, *to the church,* the Church having no ruler but Jesus Christ. Others may be officers in His Church, but He alone is Head and supreme.

23. *Which is his body.* As he is "head over all things," he is Head to the Church; and this Church is considered as the body of which He is especially the Head; and from Him, as the Head, the Church receives light, life, and intelligence. And is *the fulness of him.* That in which He especially manifests His power, goodness, and truth; for though He fills all the world with His presence, yet He fills all the members of His mystical body with wisdom, goodness, truth, and holiness in an especial manner. Some understand the *fulness* here as signifying the "thing to be filled"; so the Christian Church is to be filled by Him, whose fullness fills all His members, with all spiritual gifts and graces. And this corresponds with what John says, chap. i. 16: "And of his fulness have all we received, and grace for grace." And with what is said in Col. ii. 9-10: "Ye are complete in him"; "And ye are in Him filled full"; i.e., with gifts and grace. How, in any other sense, the Church can be said to be the fullness of Him who fills all in all is difficult to say. However, as Jesus Christ is represented to be the Head, and the Church the body under that Head, the individuals being so many members in that body, and as it requires a body and members to make a head complete, so it requires a Church, or general assembly of believers, to make up the body of Christ. When therefore the Jews and Gentiles are brought into this Church, the body may be said to be complete; and thus Christ

MATTHEW HENRY

CHAPTER 2

Verses 1–3

Unregenerate souls are dead in trespasses and sins. All those who are in their sins, are dead in sins. Sin is the death of the soul. Wherever that prevails there is a privation of all spiritual life.

A state of sin is a state of conformity to this world, *v.* 2. *Wherein in time past you walked*; you lived and behaved yourselves in such a manner as the men of the world are used to do. We are by nature bond-slaves to sin and Satan. Those who walk according to the course of this world, walk *according to the prince of the power of the air*. Wicked men are slaves to Satan. The course and tenor of their lives are according to his suggestions; they are subject to him, and are led captive by him at his will, whereupon he is called the god of this world, and *the spirit that now worketh in the children of disobedience*. As the good Spirit works that which is good in obedient souls, so this evil spirit works that which is evil in wicked men; and he now works, not only heretofore.

Among whom also we all had our conversation in times past. We are by nature drudges to the flesh, and to our corrupt affections, *v.* 3, *fulfilling the desires of the flesh and of the mind*. We lived in the actual commission of all those sins to which corrupt nature inclined us. The carnal mind makes a man a perfect slave to his vicious appetite.—*The fulfilling of the wills of the flesh*, so the words may be rendered. We are *by nature the children of wrath, even as others*. One man is as much so as another by nature, not only by custom and imitation, but by reason of our natural inclinations and appetites. Our state and course are such as deserve wrath, and would end in eternal wrath, if divine grace did not interpose. What reason have sinners then to be looking out for that grace that will make them children of God and heirs of glory!

JAMIESON, FAUSSET, BROWN

by God (Col. 1:16-19), *fills all* the universe of things *with all* things. "Fills all creation with whatever it possesses" [ALFORD]. The *Greek* is, "filleth *for Himself*."

CHAPTER 2

Vss. 1-22. GOD'S LOVE AND GRACE IN QUICKENING US, ONCE DEAD, THROUGH CHRIST. HIS PURPOSE IN DOING SO: EXHORTATION BASED ON OUR PRIVILEGES AS BUILT TOGETHER, AN HOLY TEMPLE, IN CHRIST, THROUGH THE SPIRIT. **1. And you**—"You also," among those who have experienced His mighty power in enabling them to believe (vss. 19-23). *hath he quickened*—supplied from the *Greek* (vs. 5). **dead**—spiritually (Col. 2:13). A living corpse: without the gracious presence of God's Spirit in the soul, and so unable to think, will, or do aught that is holy. **in trespasses . . . sins**—*in* them, as the element in which the unbeliever is, and through which he is dead to the true life. Sin is the death of the soul. Isaiah 9:2; John 5:25, "dead" (spiritually), I Timothy 5:6. "Alienated from the *life* of God" (ch. 4:18). Translate, as *Greek*, "in *your* trespasses . . . ." "Trespass" in *Greek*, expresses a FALL OR LAPSE, such as the transgression of Adam whereby he fell. "Sin" (*Greek*, "*hamartia*") implies innate *corruption* and ALIENATION from God (lit., *erring of the mind from the rule of truth*), exhibited in *acts* of sin (*Greek*, "*hamartemata*"). BENGEL refers "trespasses" to the Jews who had the law, and yet revolted from it; "sins," to the Gentiles who know not God. **2. the course of this world**—the career (lit., "the age," cf. Gal. 1:4), or present system of *this* world (I Cor. 2:6, 12; 3:18, 19, as opposed to "the world to come"): alien from God, and lying in the wicked one (I John 5:19). "The age" (which is something more external and ethical) regulates "the world" (which is something more external). **the prince of the power of the air**—the unseen God who lies underneath guiding "the course of this world" (II Cor. 4:4); ranging through the *air* around us: cf. Mark 4:4, "fowls of the air" (*Greek*, "heaven") i.e., (vs. 15), "Satan" and his demons. Cf. ch. 6:12; John 12:31. Christ's ascension seems to have cast Satan out of heaven (Rev. 12:5, 9, 10, 12, 13), where he had been heretofore the accuser of the brethren (Job 1). No longer able to accuse *in heaven* those justified by Christ, the ascended Saviour (Rom. 8:33, 34), he assails them on earth with all trials and temptations; and "we live in an atmosphere poisonous and impregnated with deadly elements. But a mighty purification of the air will be effected by Christ's coming" [AUBERLEN], for Satan shall be bound (Rev. 12:12, 13, 15, 17; 20:2, 3). "The power" is here used collectively for the "powers of the air"; in apposition with which "powers" stand the "spirits," comprehended in the singular, "the spirit," taken also collectively: the aggregate of the "seducing spirits" (I Tim. 4:1) which "work now (*still;* not merely, as in your case, 'in time *past*') in the sons of disobedience" (a Hebraism: men who are not merely by accident disobedient, but who are essentially *sons of disobedience* itself: cf. Matt. 3:7), and of which Satan is here declared to be "the prince." The Greek does not allow "the spirit" to refer to *Satan*, "the prince" himself, but to "*the powers of the air*" of which he is prince. The powers of the air are the embodiment of that evil "spirit" which is the ruling principle of unbelievers, especially the heathen (Acts 26:18), as opposed to the spirit of the children of God (Luke 4:33). The potency of that "spirit" is shown in the "disobedience" of the former. Cf. Deuteronomy 32:20, "children in whom is no faith" (Isa. 30:9; 57:4). They disobey the Gospel both in faith and practice (II Thess. 1:8; II Cor. 2:12). **3. also we**—i.e., *we also*. Paul here joins himself in the same category with them, passing from the second person (vss. 1, 2) to the first person here. **all**—Jews and Gentiles. **our conversation**—"our way of life" (II Cor. 1:12; I Pet. 1:18). This expression implies an outwardly more *decorous* course, than the open "walk" in *gross sins* on the part of the majority of Ephesians in times past, the Gentile portion of whom may be specially referred to in vs. 2. Paul and his Jewish countrymen, though outwardly more seemly than the Gentiles (Acts 26:4, 5, 18), had been essentially like them in living to the unrenewed flesh, without the Spirit of God. **fulfilling**—*Greek*, "doing." **mind**—*Greek*, "our thoughts." Mental suggestions and purposes (independent of God), as distinguished from the blind impulses of "the flesh." **and were by nature**—He intentionally breaks off the construction, substituting "and we were" for "and being," to mark

ADAM CLARKE

has His visible fullness upon earth, and the Church may be said to be the fullness of Him.

CHAPTER 2

1. *And you hath he quickened*. This chapter should not have been separated from the preceding, with which it is most intimately connected. As Christ fills the whole body of Christian believers with His fullness (chap. i. 23), so had He dealt with the converted Ephesians, who before *were dead in trespasses and* dead in *sins*. Death is often used by all writers, and in all nations, to express a state of extreme misery. *Trespasses* may signify the slightest deviation from the line and rule of moral equity, as well as any flagrant offense; for these are equally transgressions, as long as the sacred line that separates between vice and virtue is passed over. *Sins* may probably mean here habitual transgression, sinning knowingly and daringly.

2. *Wherein in time past ye walked*. There is much force in these expressions. The Ephesians had not sinned casually, or now and then, but continually; they *walked* in trespasses and sins. And this was not a solitary case; all the nations of the earth acted in the same way. It was the *course of this world,* "according to the life," mode of living, or successive ages of this world. The word *aion*, the literal meaning of which is "constant duration," is often applied to things which have a complete course, as the Jewish dispensation, a particular government, and the "term of human life"; so, here, the whole of life is a tissue of sin, from the cradle to the grave; every human soul, unsaved by Jesus Christ, continues to transgress. *The prince of the power of the air.* As the former clause may have particular respect to the Jewish people, who are frequently denominated "this world," this latter clause may especially refer to the Gentiles, who were most manifestly under the power of the devil, as almost every object of their worship was a demon, to whom the worst of passions and practices were attributed, and whose conduct his votaries took care to copy. Satan is termed *prince of the power of the air,* because the air is supposed to be a region in which malicious spirits dwell, all of whom are under the direction and influence of Satan, their chief. *Children of disobedience.* Perhaps a Hebraism for "disobedient children"; but, taken as it stands here, it is a strong expression in which *disobedience* appears to be personified, and wicked men exhibited as her children; the *prince of the power of the air* being their father, while disobedience is their mother.

3. *Among whom also we all had our conversation.* We Jews, as well as you Gentiles, have lived in transgressions and sins; this was the "course of our life." The *lusts*—the evil, irregular, and corrupt affections of the heart, showed themselves in the perversion of the *mind* as well as in our general conduct. The *mind* was darkened by the lusts of the flesh, and both conjoined to produce acts of unrighteousness.

MATTHEW HENRY

Verses 4–10

The glorious change that was wrought in them by converting grace.

But God, who is rich in mercy, &c., *v.* 4. God himself is the author of this great and happy change. Love is his inclination to do us good considered simply as creatures: mercy respects us as apostate and as miserable creatures. That love of God is great love, and that mercy of his is rich mercy.

II. Wherein this change consists. 1. We who were dead are quickened (*v.* 5). Grace in the soul is a new life in the soul. As death seals up all the powers and faculties, so does a state of sin, as to anything that is good. Grace unlocks and opens all, and enlarges the soul. A regenerate sinner becomes a living soul, being born of God: *He hath quickened us together with Christ*. It is in him that we live: *Because I live, you shall live also*.

2. We who were buried are raised up, *v.* 6. When he raised Christ from the dead, he did in effect raise up all believers together with him, and when he placed him at his right hand in heavenly places, he advanced and glorified them in and with him.—*And made us sit together in heavenly places in Christ Jesus*. Sinners roll themselves in the dust; sanctified souls sit in heavenly places; the world is as nothing to them, compared with what it has been, and compared with what the other world is. They are exalted to reign with him; they sit upon the throne with Christ.

III. The great design of God in producing and effecting this change. 1. With respect to others: *That in the ages to come he might show*, &c. (*v.* 7), that he might give a proof of his great goodness and mercy, for the encouragement of sinners in future time. The goodness of God in saving sinners heretofore is a proper encouragement to others in after-time to hope in his grace and mercy. God having this in his design, poor sinners should take great encouragement from it.

By grace you are saved (*v.* 5), and *by grace are you saved through faith—it is the gift of God*, *v.* 8. Every converted sinner is a saved sinner. The grace that saves them is the free undeserved goodness and favour of God; and he saves them, not *by the works of the law*, but through faith in Christ Jesus. Both that faith and that salvation are the gift of God. God has ordered all so that the whole shall appear to be of grace.

JAMIESON, FAUSSET, BROWN

emphatically his and their *past* state by nature, as contrasted with their present state by grace. **children of wrath**—not merely "sons," as in the *Greek*, "sons of disobedience" (vs. 2), but "children" *by generation;* not merely *by adoption*, as "sons" might be. The *Greek* order more emphatically marks this innate corruption: "Those who in their (very) nature are children of wrath"; vs. 5, "grace" is opposed to "nature" here; and *salvation* (implied in vss. 5, 8, "saved") to "wrath." The phrase, "children of wrath," is a Hebraism, i.e., objects of God's wrath from childhood, in our natural state, as being born in the sin which God hates. So "son of death" (*Margin*, II Sam. 12:5); "son of perdition" (John 17:12; II Thess. 2:3). **as others**—*Greek*, "as the rest" of mankind are (I Thess. 4:13). **4. God, who is rich**—*Greek* "(as) *being* rich in mercy." **for**—i.e., "*because of* His great love." This was the *special* ground of God's saving us; as "rich in mercy" (cf. vs. 7; ch. 1:7; Rom. 2:4; 10:12) was the general ground. "*Mercy* takes away misery; *love* confers salvation" [BENGEL]. **5. dead in sins**—The best reading is in the *Greek*, "dead in *our* (lit., *'the'*) *trespasses*." **quickened**—"vivified" spiritually, and consequences hereafter, corporally. There must be a spiritual resurrection of the soul before there can be a comfortable resurrection of the body [PEARSON] (John 11:25, 26; Rom. 8:11). **together with Christ**—The Head being seated at God's right hand, the body also sits there with Him [CHRYSOSTOM]. We are already seated there IN Him ("in Christ Jesus," vs. 6), and hereafter shall be seated *by* Him; IN Him already as in our Head, which is the ground of our hope; *by* Him hereafter, as by the conferring cause, when hope shall be swallowed up in fruition [PEARSON]. What God wrought in Christ, He wrought (by the very fact) in all united to Christ, and one with Him. **by grace ye are saved**—*Greek*, "Ye are in a saved state." Not merely "ye are being saved," but ye "are passed from death unto life" (John 5:24). Salvation is to the Christian not a thing to be waited for hereafter, but already realized (I John 3:14). The parenthetic introduction of this clause here (cf. vs. 8) is a burst of Paul's feeling, and in order to make the Ephesians feel that *grace* from first to last is the sole source of salvation; hence, too, he says "ye," not "we." **6. raised us up together**—with Christ. The "raising up" presupposes previous quickening of Jesus in the tomb, and of us in the grave of our sins. **made us sit together**—with Christ, viz., in His ascension. Believers are bodily in heaven in point of right, and virtually so in spirit, and have each their own place assigned there, which in due time they shall take possession of (Phil. 3:20, 21). He does not say, "*on the right hand* of God"; a prerogative reserved to Christ peculiarly; though they shall share His throne (Rev. 3:21). **in Christ Jesus**—Our union with Him is the ground of our present spiritual, and future bodily, resurrection and ascension. "Christ Jesus" is the phrase mostly used in this Epistle, in which the *office* of the Christ, the Anointed Prophet, Priest and King, is the prominent thought; when the Person is prominent, "Jesus Christ" is the phrase used. **7.** *Greek*, "That He might show forth (middle reflexive voice; for His own glory, ch. 1:6, 12, 14) in the ages which are coming on," i.e., the blessed *ages* of the Gospel which supersede "the *age* (*Greek*, for 'course') of this world" (vs. 2), and the past "ages" from which the mystery was hidden (Col. 1:26, 27). These good ages, though beginning with the first preaching of the Gospel, *and thenceforth continually succeeding one another*, are not consummated till the Lord's coming again (cf. ch. 1:21; Heb. 6:5). The words, "coming on," do not exclude *the time then present*, but imply simply the ages *following* upon Christ's "raising them up together" spiritually (vs. 6). **kindness**—"benignity." **through Christ**—rather, as *Greek*, "in Christ"; the same expression as is so often repeated, to mark that all our blessings center "IN HIM." **8. For**—illustrating "the exceeding riches of His grace in kindness." Translate as in vs. 5, "Ye are in a saved state." **through faith**—the effect of the power of Christ's resurrection (ch. 1:19, 20; Phil. 3:10) whereby we are "raised together" with Him (vs. 6; Col. 2:12). Some of the oldest MSS. read, "through your (lit., *'the'*) faith." The instrument or mean of salvation on the part of the person saved; Christ alone is the *meritorious* agent. **and that**—viz., *the act of believing*, or "faith." "Of yourselves" stands in opposition to, "it is the gift of God" (Phil. 1:29). "That which I have said, 'through faith,' I do not wish to be understood so as if I excepted *faith* itself from *grace*" [ESTIUS]. "God justifies the believing man, not for the worthiness of his belief, but for the worthiness of Him in whom he believes" [HOOKER]. The

ADAM CLARKE

4. *But God, who is rich in mercy*. As they were corrupt in their nature, and sinful in their practice, they could possess no merit, nor have any claim upon God; and it required much mercy to remove so much misery and to pardon such transgressions. *His great love*. God's infinite love is the groundwork of our salvation; in reference to us that love assumes the form of mercy, and that mercy provides the Saviour, the Lord Jesus Christ. And therefore the apostle adds, v. 5: "By grace ye are saved"—it is by God's free mercy in Christ that you are brought into this state of salvation.

5. *Even when we were dead in sins*. Dead in our souls; dead towards God; dead in law; and exposed to death eternal. *Hath quickened us together with Christ*. God has given us as complete a resurrection from the death of sin to a life of righteousness as the body of Christ has had from the grave. And as this quickening, or making alive, was most gratuitous on God's part, the apostle, with great propriety, says: *By grace ye are saved*.

6. *And hath raised us up together . . . in Christ*. Or rather, "by Christ"; His resurrection being the proof that He had made the full atonement, and that we might be justified by His blood. Believing therefore the record which God gave of His Son, we received this atonement, and were raised from a death of sin to a life of righteousness; and now we sit in heavenly places—we have a right to the kingdom of God, anticipate this glory, and are indescribably happy in the possession of this salvation, and in our fellowship with Christ Jesus.

8. *For by grace are ye saved through faith*. As you are now brought into a state of salvation, your sins being all blotted out, and you made partakers of the Holy Spirit; and, having a hope full of immortality, you must not attribute this to any works or merit of yours; for when this gospel reached you, you were all found "dead in trespasses and sins." Therefore it was God's free mercy to you, manifested through Christ, in whom you were commanded to believe; and having believed by the power of the Holy Spirit, you received, and were sealed by, the Holy Spirit of promise; so that this salvation is in no sense *of yourselves*, but is the "free gift" of God and not of any kind of *works;* so that no man can *boast* as having wrought out his own salvation, or even contributed anything towards it. *By grace are ye saved through faith* in Christ. This is a true doctrine, and continues to be essential to the salvation of man to the end of the world. But whether are we to understand, faith or salvation, as being the *gift of God?* This question is answered by the Greek text: "By this grace ye are saved through faith; and this [*touto*, this salvation] not of you; it is the gift of God, not of works: so that no one can boast." "The relative *touto*, 'this,' which is in the neuter gender, cannot stand for *faith*, which is the feminine; but it has the whole sentence that goes before for its antecedent." But it may be asked: Is not faith the gift of God? Yes, as to the grace by which it is produced; but the grace or power to believe, and the act of believing, are two different things. Without the grace or power to believe no man ever did or can believe; but with that power the act of faith is a man's own.

MATTHEW HENRY

I. By whom, and in what manner, it was brought about. *Not of yourselves, v.* 8. *Not of works, lest any man should boast, v.* 9. These things are not brought to pass by anything done by us. There is no room for any man's boasting of his own abilities and power; or as though he had done anything that might deserve such immense favours from God.

With respect to the regenerated sinners themselves: *For we are his workmanship, created in Christ Jesus unto good works,* &c., *v.* 10. *We are his workmanship;* not only as men, but as saints. The new man is a new creature; and God is its Creator. *In Christ Jesus,* that is, on the account of what he has done and suffered. *Unto good works,* &c. Lest he should seem to discourage good works, he here observes that God, in his new creation, has designed us for good works: *Created unto good works; which God hath before ordained, that we should walk in them,* or glorify God by an exemplary conversation and by our perseverance in holiness.

Verses 11–13

The miserable condition of these Ephesians by nature. *Wherefore remember,* &c., *v.* 11. Converted sinners ought frequently to reflect upon the sinfulness and misery of the state they were in by nature. *Gentiles in the flesh,* that is, living in the corruption of their natures. *Who are called uncircumcision by that,* &c., "You were reproached and upbraided for it by the formal Jews." The misery of their case, *v.* 12. "*At that time* you were,"

1. "In a Christless condition without any saving relation to him." It must be a sad and deplorable thing for a soul to be without a Christ. Being without Christ, they were, 2. *Aliens from the commonwealth of Israel;* they did not belong to Christ's church. It is no small privilege to be placed in the church of Christ, and to share in the advantages peculiar to it.

3. *They are strangers from the covenants of promise*; the covenants of promise, because it is made up of promises. The Ephesians, in their gentilism, were strangers to this covenant, and all unregenerate sinners are strangers to it.

4. They had no hope. Those who are without Christ, and strangers from the covenant, can have no good hope.

They were in a state of estrangement from God: *Without God in the world.* The words are, *atheists in the world*; for, though they worshipped many gods, yet they were without the true God.

The happy change that was made in their state: *But now, in Christ Jesus, you who sometimes were far off,* &c. They were far off from Christ, and from God himself; and therefore from all good. "*But now in Christ Jesus,* &c., you are made

JAMIESON, FAUSSET, BROWN

initiation, as well as the increase, of faith, is from the Spirit of God, not only by an external proposal of the word, but by internal illumination in the soul [PEARSON]. Yet "faith" cometh by the means which man must avail himself of, viz., "hearing the word of God" (Rom. 10:17), and prayer (Luke 11: 13), though the blessing is wholly of God (I Cor. 3:6, 7). **9. Not of works**—This clause stands in contrast to "by grace," as is confirmed by Romans 4:4, 5; 11:6. **lest**—rather, as *Greek,* "that no man should boast" (Rom. 3:27; 4:2). **10. workmanship**—lit., "a thing of His making"; "handiwork." Here the spiritual creation, not the physical, is referred to (vss. 8, 9). **created**—having been created (ch. 4:24; Ps. 102:18; Isa. 43:21; II Cor. 5:5, 17). **unto good works**—"*for* good works." "Good works" cannot be performed until we are new "created unto" them. Paul never calls the works of the law "good works." We are not *saved by,* but *created unto,* good works. **before ordained**—*Greek,* "before made ready" (cf. John 5:36). God marks out for each in His purposes beforehand, the particular good works, and the time and way which He sees best. God both makes ready by His providence the opportunities for *the works,* and makes *us* ready for their performance (John 15:16; II Tim. 2:21). **that we should walk in them**—not "be saved" by them. Works do not justify, but the justified man works (Gal. 5:22-25). **11.** The *Greek* order in the oldest MSS. is, "That in time past (lit., *once*) ye ...." Such remembrance sharpens gratitude and strengthens faith (vs. 19) [BENGEL]. **Gentiles in the flesh**—i.e., Gentiles in respect to circumcision. **called Uncircumcision**—The Gentiles were called [in contempt], and *were,* the Uncircumcision; the Jews were called, but were not truly, the Circumcision [ELLICOTT]. **in the flesh made by hands**—as opposed to the true "circumcision of the heart in the Spirit, and not the letter" (Rom. 2:29), "made without the hands in putting off the body of the sins of the flesh by the circumcision of Christ" (Col. 2:11). **12. without Christ**—*Greek, "separate from* Christ"; having no part in Him; far from Him. A different *Greek* word (*aneu*) would be required to express, "Christ was not present with you" [TITTMANN]. **aliens**—*Greek,* "alienated from," not merely "separated from." The Israelites were cut off from the commonwealth of God, but it was as being self-righteous, indolent, and unworthy, not as *aliens* and *strangers* [CHRYSOSTOM]. The expression, "alienated from," takes it for granted that the Gentiles, before they had apostatized from the primitive truth, had been sharers in light and life (cf. ch. 4:18, 23). The hope of redemption through the Messiah, on their subsequent apostasy, was embodied into a definite "commonwealth" or *polity,* viz., that "of Israel," from which the Gentiles were alienated. Contrast vs. 13; ch. 3:6; 4:4, 5, with Psalm 147:20. **covenants of promise**—rather, "... of *the* promise," viz., "to thee and thy seed will I give this land" (Rom. 9:4; Gal. 3:16). The plural implies the several renewals of the covenant with Abraham, Isaac, and Jacob, and with the whole people at Sinai [ALFORD]. "The promise" is singular, to signify that the covenant, in reality, and substantially, is one and the same at all times, but only different in its accidents and external circumstances (cf. Heb. 1:1, "at sundry times and in divers manners"). **having no ... hope**—beyond this life (I Cor. 15:19). The CONJECTURES of heathen philosophers as to a future life were at best vague and utterly unsatisfactory. They had no divine "promise," and therefore no sure ground of "hope." Epicurus and Aristotle did not believe in it at all. The Platonists believed the soul passed through perpetual changes, now happy, and then again miserable; the Stoics, that it existed no longer than till the time of the general burning up of all things. **without God**—*Greek,* "atheists," i.e., they had not "God" in the sense we use the word, the Eternal Being who made and governs all things (cf. Acts 14:15, "Turn from these vanities unto *the living God* who made heaven, and earth, and the sea, and all things therein"), whereas the Jews had distinct ideas of God and immortality. Cf. also Galatians 4:8, "Ye knew not God ... ye did service unto them which are no gods" (I Thess. 4:5). So also pantheists are atheists, for an impersonal God is NO GOD, and an ideal immortality no immortality [THOLUCK]. **in the world**—in contrast to belonging to "the commonwealth of Israel." Having their portion and their all in this godless vain world (Ps. 17:14), from which Christ delivers His people (John 15:19; 17:14; Gal. 1:4). **13. now**—in contrast to "at that time" (vs. 12). **in Christ Jesus**—"Jesus" is here added, whereas the expression before (vs. 12) had been merely "Christ," to mark that they know Christ as the *personal* Saviour,

ADAM CLARKE

God never believes for any man any more than He repents for him; the penitent, through this grace enabling him, believes for himself. Nor does he believe necessarily or impulsively when he has that power; the power to believe may be present long before it is exercised, else why the solemn warnings with which we meet everywhere in the Word of God, and threatenings against those who do not believe? Is not this a proof that such persons have the power but do not use it?

10. *For we are his workmanship.* So far is this salvation from being our own work, or granted for our own works' sake, that we are ourselves not only the creatures of God, but our new creation was produced by His power; for we are *created in Christ Jesus unto good works.* He has saved us that we may show forth the virtues of Him who called us from darkness into His marvellous light. For though we are not saved for our good works, yet we are saved that we may perform good works, to the glory of God and the benefit of man. *Which God hath before ordained.* "For which God before prepared us, that we might walk in them." For being saved from sin, we are made partakers of the Spirit of holiness; and it is natural to that Spirit to lead to the practice of holiness; and he who is not holy in his life is not saved by the grace of Christ. The before ordaining, or rather preparing, must refer to the time when God began the new creation in their hearts; for from the first inspiration of God upon the soul it begins to love holiness, and obedience to the will of God is the very element in which a holy or regenerated soul lives.

11. *Wherefore remember.* That you may ever see and feel your obligations to live a pure and holy life, and be unfeignedly thankful to God for your salvation, remember that you were once heathens, in the flesh—without the pure doctrine, and under the influence of your corrupt nature; such as by the Jews (who gloried, in consequence of their *circumcision,* to be in covenant with God) were *called Uncircumcision;* i.e., persons out of the divine covenant, and having no right or title to any blessing of God.

12. *That at that time ye were without Christ.* Not only were not Christians, but had no knowledge of the Christ or Messiah, and no title to the blessings which were to proceed from Him. *Aliens from the commonwealth of Israel.* You were by your birth, idolatry, etc., alienated from the commonwealth of Israel—from the civil and religious privileges of the Jewish people. *Strangers from the covenants of promise.* Having no part in the promise of the covenant made with Abraham, whether considered as relating to his natural or spiritual seed.

Having no hope. Either of the pardon of sin or of the resurrection of the body, nor indeed of the immortality of the soul. Of all these things the Gentiles had no rational or well-grounded hope.

Without God in the world. They had gods many and lords many, but in no Gentile nation was the true God known: nor indeed had they any correct notion of the divine nature. He who has neither *God* nor *Christ* is in a most deplorable state; he has neither a God to worship nor a Christ to justify him. And this is the state of every man who is living without the grace and Spirit of Christ. All such, whatever they may profess, are no better than practical atheists.

13. *Ye who sometimes were far off.* To be *far off* and to be near are sayings much in use among the Jews. (1) Among them, to be near signifies to be in the approbation or favor of God, and to be *far off* signifies to be under His displeasure. A holy man, or a genuine penitent, might be said to be nigh to God, because such persons are in His favor. (2) Every person who offered a sacrifice to God was considered as

MATTHEW HENRY

nigh." They were brought home to God. God is a help at hand to his people; and this is *by the blood of Christ.* Every believing sinner owes his nearness to God, to the death and sacrifice of Christ.

Verses 14–22

The great privileges that converted Jews and Gentiles both receive from Christ. Those who were in a state of enmity are reconciled. Jesus Christ is our peace, *v.* 14. He made peace and came to reconcile, 1. Jews and Gentiles to each other. He *made both one.* He *broke down the middle wall of partition,* the ceremonial law, called *the partition-wall* by way of allusion to the partition in the temple, which separated the court of the Gentiles from that into which the Jews only had liberty to enter.

Thus *he abolished in his flesh the enmity, v.* 15. By his sufferings in the flesh, he took away the binding power of the ceremonial law, *the law of commandments contained in ordinances.* By taking these out of the way, he formed one church of believers, whether they had been Jews or Gentiles. Thus he made *in himself of twain one new man.* He framed both these parties into one new society, *so making peace.*

2. God and sinners, whether Jews or Gentiles. Christ came to slay that enmity, and to reconcile them both to God, *v.* 16.

Sin breeds a quarrel between God and men. Christ came to take up the quarrel, and to bring it to an end, and this *by the cross, having slain the enmity thereby.* The great advantages which both parties gain, *v.* 17. Christ came, partly in his own person, as to the Jews, who are here said to have been nigh, and partly in his apostles to the Gentiles, who are said to have been afar off. *And preached peace,* reconciliation with God.

JAMIESON, FAUSSET, BROWN

"Jesus." **sometimes**—*Greek,* "aforetime." **far off**—the Jewish description of the Gentiles. Far off from God and from the people of God (vs. 17; Isa. 57:19; Acts 2:39). **are**—*Greek,* "have been." **by**—*Greek,* "in." Thus "the blood of Christ" is made the seal of a covenant IN which their nearness to God consists. In ch. 1:7, where the blood is more directly spoken of as the *instrument,* it is "*through* His blood" [ALFORD]. **14. he**—*Greek,* "Himself" alone, pre-eminently, and none else. Emphatical. **our peace**—not merely "Peacemaker," but "Himself" the price of our (Jews' and Gentiles' alike) peace with God, and so the bond of union between "both" in God. He took both into Himself, and reconciled them, united, to God, by His assuming our nature and our penal and legal liabilities (vs. 15; Isa. 9:5, 6; 53:5; Mic. 5:5; Col. 1:20). His title, "Shiloh," means the same (Gen. 49:10). **the middle wall of partition**—*Greek,* ". . . of *the* partition" or "fence"; the *middle wall* which *parted* Jew and Gentile. There was a balustrade of stone which separated the court of the Gentiles from the holy place, which it was death for a Gentile to pass. But this, though incidentally alluded to, was but a symbol of the partition itself, viz., "the enmity" *between "both" and God* (vs. 15), the real cause of separation from God, and so the mediate cause of their separation from one another. Hence there was a twofold wall of partition, one the inner wall, severing the Jewish people from entrance to the holy part of the temple where the priests officiated, the other the outer wall, separating the Gentile proselytes from access to the court of the Jews (cf. Ezek. 44:7; Acts 21:28). Thus this twofold wall represented the Sinaitic law, which *both* severed all men, even the Jews, from access to God (through sin, which is the violation of the law), and also separated the Gentiles from the Jews. As the term "wall" implies the *strength* of the partition, so "fence" implies that it was easily removed by God when the due time came. **15.** Rather, make "enmity" an apposition to "the middle wall of partition"; "Hath broken down the middle wall of partition (not merely as *English Version, 'between us,'* but also *between all men and God*), to wit, the enmity (Rom. 8:7) by His flesh" (cf. vs. 16; Rom. 8:3). **the law of commandments** *contained* **in**—*Greek,* "the law of the commandments [consisting] in ordinances." This law was "the partition" or "fence," which embodied the expression of the "enmity" (the "wrath" of God against our sin, and our enmity to Him, vs. 3) (Rom. 4:15; 5:20; 7:10, 11; 8:7). Christ has in, or by, His crucified flesh, abolished it, so far as its condemning and enmity-creating power is concerned (Col. 2:14), substituting for it the law of love, which is the everlasting spirit of the law, and which flows from the realization in the soul of His love in His death for us. Translate what follows, "that He might make the two (Jews and Gentiles) into one new man." Not that He might merely reconcile the two to each other, but incorporate the two, reconciled in Him to God, into one new man; the old man to which both belonged, the enemy of God, having been slain in His flesh on the cross. Observe, too, ONE new man; we are all in God's sight but one in Christ, as we are but one in Adam [ALFORD]. **making peace**—primarily between all and God, secondarily between Jews and Gentiles; He being "our peace." This "peace-making" precedes its publication (vs. 17). **16.** Translate, "might altogether reconcile them both in one body (the Church, Col. 3:15) unto God through His cross." The *Greek* for "reconcile" (*apocatalaxe*), found only here and in Colossians 1:20, expresses not only a return to favor with one (*catallage*), but so to lay aside enmity that complete amity follows; to pass *from* enmity to *complete reconciliation* [TITTMANN]. **slain the enmity**—viz., that had been between man and God; and so that between Jew and Gentile which had resulted from it. By His being *slain,* He *slew* it (cf. Heb. 2:14). **thereby**—*Greek,* "therein"; "in" or "by the cross," i.e., His crucifixion (Col. 2:15). **17.** Translate, "He came and announced glad tidings of peace." "He came" of His own free love, and "announced peace" with His own mouth to the apostles (Luke 24:36; John 20:19, 21, 26); and by them to others, through His Spirit present in His Church (John 14:18). Acts 26:23 is strictly parallel; after His resurrection "He showed light to the people ('them that were nigh') and to the Gentiles" ("you that were afar off"), by His Spirit in His ministers (cf. I Pet. 3:19). **and to them**—The oldest MSS. insert "peace" again: "And peace to them." The repetition implies the joy with which both alike would dwell again and again upon the welcome word "peace." So Isaiah 57:19. **18.** Translate, "For it is through Him (John 14:6;

ADAM CLARKE

having access to Him by the blood of that sacrifice. Hence the priests, whose office it was to offer sacrifices, were considered as being nigh to God; and all who brought gifts to the altar were considered as approaching the Almighty. (3) Being *far off* signified the state of the Gentiles as contradistinguished from the Jews, who were *nigh.* You Gentiles, who were unacquainted with God, and were even without God in the world, are brought to an acquaintance with Him; and are now, through Christ Jesus, brought into the favor and fellowship of God.

14. *For he is our peace.* Jesus Christ has died for both Jews and Gentiles, and has become a "Peace Offering," to reconcile both to God and to each other. *Who hath made both one.* Formed one Church out of the believers of both people. *The middle wall of partition.* By abolishing the law of Jewish ordinances, He has removed that which kept the two parties not only in a state of separation but also at variance. This expression, *the middle wall,* can refer only to that most marked distinction which the Jewish laws and customs made between them and all other nations whatsoever.

15. *Having abolished in his flesh.* By His incarnation and death He not only made an atonement for sin, but He appointed the doctrine of reconciliation to God and of love to each other, to be preached in all nations. The *enmity* of which the apostle speaks was reciprocal among the Jews and Gentiles. The former detested the Gentiles and could hardly allow them the denomination of men; the latter had the Jews in contempt because of the peculiarity of their religious rites and ceremonies, which were different from those of all the other nations of the earth. *The law of commandments.* Contained in, or rather "concerning," *ordinances;* which law was made merely for the purpose of keeping the Jews a distinct people, and pointing out the Son of God till He should come. *To make in himself.* To make one Church out of both people, which should be considered the body of which Jesus Christ is the Head. Thus He makes *one new man*—one new Church; and thus He makes and establishes *peace.* I think the apostle still alludes to the "peace offering" among the Jews. They have a saying, *Sephra,* fol. 121: "Whosoever offers a peace offering sacrifice, brings peace to the world." Such a peace offering was the death of Christ, and by it peace is restored to the earth.

16. *That he might reconcile both unto God in one body.* That the Jews and Gentiles, believing on the Lord Jesus, might lay aside all their causes of contention and become one spiritual body, or society of men, influenced by the Spirit, and acting according to the precept of the gospel. *Having slain the enmity thereby.* Having by His death upon the Cross made reconciliation between God and man, and by His Spirit in their hearts removed the enmity of their fallen, sinful nature.

17. *And came and preached peace.* Proclaimed the readiness of God to forgive and save both Jews and Gentiles.

MATTHEW HENRY

Now the effect of this peace is the free access which both Jews and Gentiles have unto God (*v.* 18): *For through him we both have access.* The throne of grace is erected for us to come to, and liberty of approach to that throne is allowed us. Christ purchased for us leave to come to God, and the Spirit gives us a heart to come.

Now therefore you are no more strangers and foreigners, v. 19. They were now no longer *aliens from the commonwealth of Israel, but fellow-citizens with the saints, and of the household of God.* The church is compared to a city, and every converted sinner is free of it. It is also compared to a house, and every converted sinner is one of the family, a servant and a child in God's house.

In *v.* 20 the church is compared to a building. The apostles and prophets are *the foundation* of that building. *Jesus Christ himself being the chief corner-stone.*

CHARLES H. SPURGEON:

The religion of our Lord Jesus Christ contains in it nothing so wonderful as himself. It is a mass of marvels, but He is the miracle of it; the wonder of wonders is "the Wonderful" himself. If proof be asked of the truth which He proclaimed, we point men to Jesus Christ himself. His character is unique. We defy unbelievers to imagine another like Him. He is God and yet man, and we challenge them to compose a narrative in which the two apparently incongruous characters shall be so harmoniously blended—in which the human and divine shall be so marvelously apparent, without the one overshading the other. They question the authenticity of the four Gospels; will they try to write a fifth? Will they even attempt to add a few incidents to the life which shall be worthy of the sacred biography, and congruous with those facts which are already described? If it be all a forgery, will they be so good as to show us how it is done? Will they find a novelist who will write another biography of a man of any century they choose, of any nationality, or of any degree of experience, or any rank or station, and let us see if they can describe in that imaginary life a devotion, a self-sacrifice, a truthfulness, a completeness of character at all comparable to that of Jesus Christ himself? Can they invent another perfect character even if the divine element be left out? They must of necessity fail, for there is none like unto Jesus himself.

—The Treasury of the New Testament

Christ supports the building by his strength: *In whom all the building, fitly framed together,* &c., *v.* 21. All believers being united to Christ by faith, and among themselves by Christian charity, *grow unto a holy temple,* in which there is much communion between God and his people. The church is the place which God hath chosen to put his name there, and it becomes such a temple by grace and strength derived from himself—*in the Lord.*

In whom you also are built together, &c., *v.* 22. Every true believer is a living temple, is *a habitation of God through the Spirit.* God dwells in all believers now, an earnest of their dwelling together with him to eternity.

JAMIESON, FAUSSET, BROWN

Heb. 10:19) that we have *our* access (ch. 3:12; Rom. 5:2), both of us, in (i.e., united in, i.e., *by,* I Cor. 12: 13, *Greek*) one Spirit to the Father," viz., as our common Father, reconciled to both alike; whence flows the removal of all separation between Jew and Gentile. The *oneness* of "the Spirit," through which we both have our access, is necessarily followed by *oneness* of the body, the Church (vs. 16).

19. Now, therefore—rather, "So then" [ALFORD]. **foreigners**—rather, "sojourners"; opposed to "members of the household," as "strangers" is to "fellow citizens." Philippians 3:19, 20, "conversation," *Greek,* "citizenship." **but**—The oldest MSS. add, "are." **with the saints**—"the commonwealth of (spiritual) Israel" (vs. 12). **of God**—THE FATHER; as JESUS CHRIST appears in vs. 20, and THE SPIRIT in vs. 22. **20.** Translate as *Greek,* "Built up upon . . ." (participle; *having been built up upon;* omit, therefore, "and are"). Cf. I Corinthians 3:11, 12. The same image in ch. 3:18, recurs in his address to the Ephesian elders (Acts 20:32), and in his Epistle to Timothy at Ephesus (I Tim. 3:15; II Tim. 2:19), naturally suggested by the splendid architecture of Diana's temple; the glory of the Christian temple is eternal and real, not mere idolatrous gaud. The image of a building is appropriate also to the Jew-Christians; as the temple at Jerusalem was the stronghold of Judaism; as Diana's temple, of paganism. **foundation of the apostles . . .**—i.e., upon their ministry and living example (cf. Matt. 16:18). Christ Himself, the only true Foundation, was the grand subject of their ministry, and spring of their life. As one with Him and His fellow workers, they, too, in a secondary sense, are called "foundations" (Rev. 21:14). The "prophets" are joined with them closely; for the expression is here not "*foundations* of the apostles and *the* prophets," but "*foundations* of the apostles and *prophets.*" For the doctrine of both was essentially *one* (I Pet. 1:10, 11; Rev. 19:10). The apostles take the precedency (Luke 10:24). Thus he appropriately shows regard to the claims of the Jews and Gentiles: "the prophets" representing the old Jewish dispensation, "the apostles" the new. The "prophets" of the new also are included. BENGEL and ALFORD refer the meaning solely to these (ch. 3:5; 4:11). These passages imply, I think, that the New Testament prophets are not excluded; but the apostle's plain reference to Psalm 118:22, "the head stone of the corner," proves that the Old Testament prophets are a prominent thought. David is called a "prophet" in Acts 2:30. Cf. also Isaiah 28:16; another prophet present to the mind of Paul, which prophecy leans on the earlier one of Jacob (Gen. 49:24). The sense of the context, too, suits this: Ye were once aliens from the commonwealth *of Israel* (in the time of her *Old Testament prophets*), but now ye are members of the true Israel, built upon the foundation of her New Testament apostles and Old Testament prophets. Paul continually identifies his teaching with that of Israel's old prophets (Acts 26:22; 28:23). The costly foundation stones of the temple (I Kings 5:17) typified the same truth (cf. Jer. 51:26). The same stone is at once the cornerstone and the foundation stone on which the whole building rests. Paul supposes a stone or rock so large and so fashioned as to be both at once; supporting the whole as the foundation, and in part rising up at the extremities, so as to admit of the side walls meeting in it, and being united in it as the cornerstone [ZANCHIUS]. As the cornerstone, it is conspicuous, as was Christ (I Pet. 2:6), and coming in men's way may be stumbled over, as the Jews did at Christ (Matt. 21:42; I Pet. 2:7). **21. In whom**—as holding together the whole. **fitly framed**—so as exactly to fit together. **groweth**—"is growing" continually. Here an additional thought is added to the image; the Church has the *growth* of a living organism, not the mere *increase* of a building. Cf. I Peter 2:5; "*lively* stones . . . built up a spiritual house." Cf. ch. 4:16; Zechariah 6:12, "The *Branch* shall build the *temple* of the Lord," where similarly the growth of a branch, and the building of a temple, are joined. **holy**—as being the "habitation *of God*" (vs. 22). So "in the Lord" (Christ) answers to "through the Spirit" (vs. 22; cf. ch. 3:16, 17). "Christ is the inclusive Head of all the building, the element in which it has its being and now its growth" [ALFORD]. **22. are builded together**—Translate, "are being builded together." **through**—*Greek,* "*in* the Spirit." God, by His Spirit *in* believers, has them for His habitation (I Cor. 3:16, 17; 6:19; II Cor. 6:16).

ADAM CLARKE

18. *For through him,* Christ Jesus, *we both*—Jews and Gentiles—*have access by one Spirit,* through the influence of the Holy Ghost, *unto the Father*—God Almighty. This text is a plain proof of the Holy Trinity. No soul can have access to God but by Jesus Christ, and He introduces none but such as receive His Holy Spirit.

19. *Ye are no more strangers.* In this chapter the Church of God is compared to a city which has a variety of privileges, rights, etc., founded on regular charters and grants. The Gentiles, having believed in Christ, are all incorporated with the believing Jews in this holy city. Formerly, when any of them came to Jerusalem, being *strangers,* they had no rights whatever; nor could they, as mere heathens, settle among them. Again, if any of them, convinced of the errors of the Gentiles, acknowledged the God of Israel but did not receive circumcision, he might dwell in the land, but he had no right to the blessings of the covenant. Such might be called "sojourners"—persons who have no property in the land, and may only rent a house for the time being. *Fellowcitizens with the saints.* Called to the enjoyment of equal privileges with the Jews themselves, who, by profession, were a holy people; who were bound to be holy, and therefore are often called *saints,* or "holy persons," when both their hearts and conduct were far from being right in the sight of God. But the *saints* spoken of here are the converted or Christianized Jews. *Of the household of God.* The house of God is the "temple"; the Temple was a type of the Christian Church. This is now become God's house; all genuine believers are considered as being domestics of this house, the children and servants of God Almighty, having all equal rights, privileges, and advantages.

20. *And are built upon the foundation.* Following the same metaphor, comparing the Church of Christ to a city, and to the Temple, the believing Ephesians are represented as parts of that building; the living stones out of which it is principally formed, 1 Pet. ii. 4-5, having for *foundation*—the ground plan, specification, and principle on which it was builded—the doctrine taught by the *prophets* in the Old Testament and the *apostles* in the New; Jesus Christ being that *corner stone,* the chief angle or foundation Cornerstone, the connecting Medium by which both Jews and Gentiles were united in the same building.

21. *In whom.* By which foundation Cornerstone, Christ Jesus, *all the building,* composed of converted Jews and Gentiles, *fitly framed together,* "properly jointed and connected together," *groweth unto an holy temple*—is continually increasing as new converts from Judaism or heathenism flock into it. It is not a finished building, but will continue to increase and be more and more perfect till the day of judgment.

22. *In whom ye also are builded.* The apostle now applies the metaphor to the purpose for which he produced it, retaining however some of the figurative expressions. As the stones in a temple are all properly placed so as to form a complete house and be a habitation for the deity that is worshipped there, so you are all, both believing Jews and Gentiles, prepared by the doctrine of the prophets and apostles, under the influence of the Spirit of Christ, to become a habitation of God, a Church in which God shall be worthily worshipped, and in which He can continually dwell.

MATTHEW HENRY

CHAPTER 3

Verses 1–13

I. The tribulations and sufferings which he endured, *v.* 1. "*For this cause,*—for asserting that the great privileges of the gospel belong not only to the Jews, but to believing Gentiles also,—for this I am now a prisoner, but a *prisoner of Jesus Christ.*" Christ's servants, if they come to be prisoners, are his prisoners. Paul adhered to Christ, and Christ owned him, when he was in prison. *For you, Gentiles* the faithful ministers of Christ are to dispense his sacred truths whatever they themselves may suffer for doing so. He speaks again of his sufferings: *Wherefore I desire that you faint not at my tribulation for you, which is your glory*, *v.* 13. While he was in prison, he suffered much there; yet he would not have them discouraged nor dismayed at this. The apostle seems to have been more solicitous lest they should be discouraged and faint upon his tribulations than about what he himself endured. His sufferings, he says, were their glory. God not only sent his apostles to preach the gospel to them, but even to suffer for them.

II. The apostle informs them of God's appointing him to the office by a special revelation that he made unto him. 1. God appointed him to the office: *If you have heard of the dispensation of the grace of God, which is given me to you-ward*, *v.* 2.

Of the revelation of this truth he speaks, *v.* 3–5. The coalition of Jews and Gentiles in the gospel church was a mystery. It is called a mystery because the several circumstances of it were concealed and kept secret in God's own breast. And it is called the mystery of Christ because it was revealed by him, and because it relates so very much to him. Of this the apostle has given some hints *afore* in the preceding chapters. *Whereby, when you read;* or, as those words may be read, *unto which attending* (and it is not enough for us barely to read the scriptures, unless we attend to them) *you may understand my knowledge in the mystery of Christ. This mystery in other ages was not made known unto the sons of men, as it is now revealed unto his holy apostles and prophets by the Spirit* (*v.* 5). Who would have imagined that those who had been so long in the dark, and at so great a distance, would be enlightened with the marvellous light, and be made nigh? Let us learn hence not to despair of the worst, of the worst of persons, and the worst of nations. None so unworthy but God may please to confer great grace upon them.

2. God eminently qualified him for it, by a special revelation. (1) The mystery revealed is *that the Gentiles should be fellow-heirs, and of the same body, and partakers of his promise in Christ, by the gospel* (*v.* 6). And this *in Christ*, being united to Christ, *in whom all the promises are yea and amen; and by the gospel.* This was the great truth revealed to the apostles. He styles the gospel *the grace of God* because it is the gift of divine grace to sinful men; and it is also the great instrument in the hands of the Spirit by which God works grace in the souls of men. *Whereof I was made a minister*, &c., *v.* 7. He *was* MADE *a minister*—he did not make himself such—*according to the gift of the grace of God unto* him. God supplied and furnished him for his work *by the effectual working of his power*, in himself more especially, and also in great numbers of those to whom he preached. What God calls men to he fits them for, and does it with an almighty power.

JAMIESON, FAUSSET, BROWN

CHAPTER 3

VSS. 1-21. HIS APOSTOLIC OFFICE TO MAKE KNOWN THE MYSTERY OF CHRIST REVEALED BY THE SPIRIT: PRAYER THAT BY THE SAME SPIRIT THEY MAY COMPREHEND THE VAST LOVE OF CHRIST: DOXOLOGY ENDING THIS DIVISION OF THE EPISTLE. As the first chapter treated of THE FATHER's office; and the second, THE SON's, so this, that of THE SPIRIT. **1. of Jesus Christ**—*Greek*, "Christ Jesus." The *office* is the prominent thought in the latter arrangement; the *person*, in the former. He here marks the *Messiahship* of "Christ," maintained by him as the origin of his being a "prisoner," owing to the jealousy of the Jews being roused at his preaching it to *the Gentiles*. His very bonds were profitable to ("for" or "in behalf of you") Gentiles (vs. 13; II Tim. 2:10). He digresses at "For this cause," and does not complete the sentence which he had intended, until vs. 14, where he resumes the words, "For this cause," viz., because I know this your call of God as Gentiles (ch. 2:11-22), to be "fellow heirs" with the Jews (vs. 6), "I bow my knees to" the Father of our common Saviour (vss. 14, 15) to confirm you in the faith by His Spirit. "I Paul," expresses the agent employed by the Spirit to enlighten them, after he had been first enlightened himself by the same Spirit (vss. 3-5, 9). **2. If**—The *Greek* does not imply doubt: "Assuming (what I know to be the fact, viz.,) that ye have heard. . . ." "If, as I presume. . . ." The indicative in the *Greek* shows that no doubt is implied: "Seeing that doubtless. . . ." He by this phrase delicately reminds them of their having heard from himself, and probably from others subsequently, the fact. See *Introduction,* showing that these words do not disprove the address of this Epistle *to the Ephesians.* Cf. Acts 20:17-24. **the dispensation**—"The office of dispensing, as a steward, the grace of God which was (not 'is') given me to you-ward," viz., to dispense to you. **3. he made known**—The oldest MSS. read, "That by revelation *was* the mystery (viz., of the admission of the Gentiles, vs. 6; ch. 1:9) *made known* unto me (Gal. 1:12). **as I wrote afore**—viz., in this Epistle (ch. 1:9, 10), the words of which he partly repeats. **4. understand my knowledge**—"perceive my understanding" [ALFORD], or "intelligence." "When ye read," implies that, deep as are the mysteries of this Epistle, the way for all to understand them is to *read* it (II Tim. 3:15, 16). By *perceiving his understanding* of the mysteries, they, too, will be enabled to understand. **the mystery of Christ**—The "mystery" is Christ Himself, once hidden, but now revealed (Col. 1:27). **5. in other ages**—*Greek,* "generations." **not made known**—He does not say, "has not been *revealed.*" Making known by *revelation* is the source of making known by preaching [BENGEL]. The former was vouchsafed only to the prophets, in order that they might make known the truth so revealed to men in general. **unto the sons of men**—men in their state by birth, as contrasted with those illuminated "by the Spirit" (*Greek,* "IN the Spirit," cf. Rev. 1:10), Matt. 16:17. **as**—The mystery of the call of the Gentiles (of which Paul speaks here) was not unknown to the Old Testament prophets (Isa. 56:6, 7; 49:6). But they did not know it with the same explicit distinctness "AS" it has been now known (Acts 10:19, 20; 11:18-21). They probably did not know that the Gentiles were to be admitted without circumcision or that they were to be on a level with the Jews in partaking of the grace of God. The gift of "the Spirit" in its fulness was reserved for the New Testament that Christ might thereby be glorified. The epithet, "holy," marks the special consecration of the New Testament "prophets" (who are here meant) by the Spirit, compared with which even the Old Testament prophets were but "sons of men" (Ezek. 2:3, and elsewhere). **6.** Translate, "That the Gentiles *are* . . ." "and *fellow members* of the same body, and *fellow* partakers of *the* (so the oldest MSS. read, not 'His') promise, in Christ *Jesus* (added in the oldest MSS.), *through* the Gospel." It is "in Christ Jesus" that they are made "fellow heirs" in the inheritance of GOD: "of the same body" under the Head, CHRIST JESUS; and "fellow partakers of the promise" in the communion of THE HOLY SPIRIT (ch. 1:13; Heb. 6:4). The Trinity is thus alluded to, as often elsewhere in this Epistle (ch. 2:19, 20, 22). **7. Whereof**—"of which" Gospel. **according to**—in consequence of, and in accordance with, "the gift of the grace of God." **given**—"which (gift of grace) was given to me by (*Greek,* 'according to,' as in vs. 20; ch. 1:19: as the result of, and in proportion to) the effectual working (*Greek,* 'energy,' or 'in-working') of His power." **8. am**—Not merely *was* I in times past,

ADAM CLARKE

CHAPTER 3

1. *For this cause.* Because he maintained that the Gentiles were admitted to all the privileges of the Jews and all the blessings of the new covenant, without being obliged to submit to circumcision, the Jews persecuted him and caused him to be imprisoned, first at Caesarea, where he was obliged to appeal to the Roman emperor, in consequence of which he was sent prisoner to Rome. *The prisoner of Jesus Christ for you Gentiles.* For preaching the gospel to the Gentiles, and showing that they were not bound by the law of Moses, and yet were called to be fellow citizens with the saints; for this very cause the Jews persecuted him unto bonds, and conspired his death.

2. *If ye have heard of the dispensation.* The compound particle which is commonly translated "if indeed," in several places means "since indeed, seeing that," and should be translated so in this verse, and in several other places of the New Testament. "Seeing ye have heard of the dispensation of God, *which is given me to you-ward.*" By the *dispensation of the grace of God* we may understand either the apostolic office and gifts granted to Paul for the purpose of preaching the gospel among the Gentiles (see Rom. i. 5) or the knowledge which God gave him of that gracious and divine plan which He had formed for the conversion of the Gentiles.

3. *By revelation he made known unto me.* Instead of *he made known*, "was made known" is the reading of many MSS. It is doubtless the true reading. The apostle wishes the Ephesians to understand that it was not an opinion of his own, or a doctrine which he was taught by others, or which he had gathered from the ancient prophets; but one that came to him by immediate revelation from God, as he had informed them before *in few words*, referring to what he had said in chap. i. 9-12.

4. *Whereby, when ye read.* When you refer back to them. *Ye may understand my knowledge.* You may see what God has given me to know concerning what has been hitherto a *mystery*—the calling of the Gentiles and the breaking down the middle wall between them and the Jews, so as to make both one spiritual body, and on the same conditions.

5. *Which in other ages was not made known.* That the calling of the Gentiles was made known by the prophets in different ages of the Jewish church is exceedingly clear; but it certainly was not made known in that clear and precise manner in which it was now revealed by the Spirit unto the ministers of the New Testament. Nor was it made known unto them at all that the Gentiles should find salvation without coming under the yoke of the Mosaic law, and that the Jews themselves should be freed from that yoke of bondage; these were discoveries totally new, and now revealed for the first time by the Spirit of God.

6. *That the Gentiles should be fellowheirs.* This is the substance of that mystery which had been hidden from all ages, and which was now made known to the New Testament apostles and prophets, and more particularly to Paul. *His promise in Christ.* That the promise made to Abraham extended to the Gentiles, the apostle has largely proved in his Epistle to the Romans; and that it was to be fulfilled to them by and through Christ, he proves there also; and particularly in his Epistle to the Galatians—see Gal. iii. 14. And that these blessings were to be announced in the preaching of the gospel, and received on believing it, he everywhere declares, but more especially in this Epistle.

7. *Whereof I was made a minister.* A "deacon," a "servant" acting under and by the direction of the great Master, Jesus Christ; from whom, by an especial call and revelation, I received the apostolic gifts and office, and by the "energy," the "in-working of His power," this gospel which I preached was made effectual to the salvation of vast multitudes of Jews and Gentiles.

MATTHEW HENRY

III. How he was employed in this office with respect to the Gentiles, and to all men.

1. With respect to the Gentiles, he *preached* to them *the unsearchable riches of Christ, v.* 8. (1) How humbly he speaks of himself: *I am less than the least of all saints.* St. Paul, who was the chief of the apostles, calls himself *less than the least of all saints.* What can be less than the least? To speak himself as little as could be, he speaks himself less than could be. Where God gives grace to be humble, there he gives all other grace. While he magnifies his office, he debases himself.

(2) How highly he speaks of Jesus Christ: *The unsearchable riches of Christ.* There is a mighty treasury of mercy, grace, and love, laid up in Christ Jesus, and that both for Jews and Gentiles. And they are unsearchable riches, which we cannot find the bottom of. It was the apostle's business and employment to *preach* these *unsearchable riches of Christ among the Gentiles.* "*Unto me is this grace given;* this special favour God has granted to such an unworthy creature as I am." And it is an unspeakable favour to the Gentile world that to them *the unsearchable riches of Christ* are preached. Though many remain poor, and are not enriched with these riches, yet if we are not enriched with them, it is our own fault.

2. With respect to all men, *v.* 9. *To make all men see what is the fellowship of the mystery which from the beginning of the world hath been hid in God who created all things by Jesus Christ.* No wonder that he saves the Gentiles as well as the Jews; for he is the common Creator of them both.

JAMIESON, FAUSSET, BROWN

but I still am the least worthy of so high an office (cf. I Tim. 1:15, end). **least of all saints**—not merely "of all *apostles*" (I Cor. 15:9, 10). **is**—*Greek,* "has been given."

among—omitted in the oldest MSS. Translate, "to *announce* to the Gentiles *the glad tidings of* the unsearchable (Job 5:9) riches," viz., of Christ's *grace* (ch. 1:7; 2:7). Romans 11: 33, "unsearchable" as a mine inexhaustible, whose treasures can never be fully explored (vss. 18, 19).

9. to make all men see—*Greek,* "to enlighten all" (ch. 1:18; Ps. 18:28; Heb. 6:4). "All" (cf. Col. 1: 28). **fellowship**—The oldest MSS. read, "economy," or "dispensation" (cf. Col. 1:25, 26; and *Note,* ch. 1:10, above). "To make all see how it hath seemed good to God at this time to *dispense* (through me and others, His *stewards*) what heretofore was a mystery." ELLICOTT explains it, "the arrangement" or "regulation" of the mystery (the union of Jews and Gentiles in Christ) which was now to be humbly traced and acknowledged in the fact of its having secretly existed in the counsel of God, and now having been revealed to the heavenly powers by means of the Church. **from the beginning of the world**—*Greek,* "from (the beginning of) the ages." Cf. ch. 1:4; Romans 16:25; I Corinthians 2:7. The "ages" are the vast successive periods of time, marked by successive stages of creation and orders of beings. **in God**—"hidden in" His counsels (ch. 1:9).

created all things by Jesus Christ—God's creation of the world and all things therein is the foundation of the rest of the "economy," which is freely dispensed according to the universal power of God [BENGEL]. As God created "the whole range of things" (so the *Greek*), physical and spiritual alike, He must have an absolute right to adjust all things as He will. Hence, we may see His right to keep the mystery of world-wide salvation in Christ "hidden in Himself," till his own good time for revealing it. The oldest MSS. omit "by Jesus Christ." **10.** The design of God in giving Paul grace to proclaim to the Gentiles the mystery of salvation heretofore hidden. **now**—first: opposed to "hidden from the beginning of the world" (vs. 5). **unto the principalities and**—*Greek* adds "the"—**powers**—unto the various orders of *good* angels primarily, as these dwell "in the heavenly places" in the highest sense; "known" to their adoring joy (l Tim. 3:16; I Pet. 1:12). Secondarily, God's wisdom in redemption

ADAM CLARKE

8. *Less than the least of all saints.* As the design of the apostle was to magnify the grace of Christ in the salvation of the world, he uses every precaution to prevent the eyes of the people from being turned to anything but Christ crucified. And although he was obliged to speak of himself as the particular instrument which God had chosen to bring the Gentile world to the knowledge of the truth, yet he does it in such a manner as to show that the excellency of the power was of God and not of him. To lay himself as low as possible, consistently with his being in the number of divinely commissioned men, he calls himself *less than the least;* and is obliged to make a new word, by strangely forming a comparative degree, not from the positive, which would have been a regular grammatical procedure, but from the superlative. The adjective signifies "little," or *less,* and *least.* On the superlative of "little," Paul forms his comparative, *less than the least,* a word of which it would be vain to attempt a better translation than that given in our own version. It most strongly marks the unparalleled humility of the apostle; and the amazing condescension of God, in favoring him, who had been before a persecutor and blasphemer, with the knowledge of this glorious scheme of human redemption, and the power to preach it so successfully among the Gentiles. *The unsearchable riches of Christ.* The word from *a,* privative, and "to trace out," from *ichnos,* a "step," is exceedingly well-chosen here. It refers to the footsteps of God, the plans He had formed, the dispensations which He had published, and the innumerable providences which He had combined to prepare, mature, and bring to full effect and view His gracious designs in the salvation of a ruined world, by the incarnation, passion, death, and resurrection of His Son. There were in these schemes and providences such *riches*—such an abundance, such a variety, as could not be comprehended even by the naturally vast and, through the divine inspiration, unparalleledly capacious mind of the apostle.

9. *And to make all men see.* "And to illuminate all"; to give information to both Jews and Gentiles; to afford them a sufficiency of light, so that they might be able distinctly to discern the great objects exhibited in this gospel. *What is the fellowship of the mystery.* The word *koinonia,* which we properly translate *fellowship,* was used among the Greeks to signify their religious communities. Here it may intimate the association of Jews and Gentiles in one Church or body, and their agreement in that glorious mystery which was now so fully opened relative to the salvation of both. But instead of *koinonia,* "fellowship," *oikonomia,* "dispensation" or "economy," is the reading of most MSS. Some of the best printed editions of the Greek text have the same reading, and that in our common text has very little authority to support it. "Dispensation" or "economy" is far more congenial to the scope of the apostle's declaration in this place; he wished to show them the economy of that mystery of bringing Jews and Gentiles to salvation by faith in Christ Jesus which God from the beginning of the world had kept hidden in His own infinite mind, and did not think proper to reveal even when He projected the creation of the world, which had respect to the economy of human redemption. *Who created all things by Jesus Christ.* Some very judicious critics are of opinion that this does not refer to the material creation; and that we should understand the whole as referring to the formation of all God's dispensations of grace, mercy, and truth, which have been planned, managed, and executed by Christ, from the foundation of the world to the present time. But the words *by Jesus Christ* are wanting in several MSS. The text therefore should be read: "which from the beginning of the world had been hidden in God who created all things."

10. *That now unto the principalities and powers in heavenly places.* Who are these *principalities and powers?* Some think evil angels are intended, because they are thus denominated, chap. vi. 12. Others think good angels are meant; for as these heavenly beings are curious to investigate the wondrous economy of the gospel, though they are not its immediate objects (see 1 Pet. i. 12), it is quite consistent with the

MATTHEW HENRY

To the intent that now unto the principalities and powers in heavenly places might be known, by the church, the manifold wisdom of God, v. 10. *Of the manifold wisdom of God;* that is, of the great variety with which God wisely dispenses things, or of the many ways he takes in ordering his church, and especially in receiving the Gentiles into it.

And this is *according to the eternal purpose which he purposed in Christ Jesus our Lord*, v. 11.

The apostle, having mentioned our Lord Jesus Christ, subjoins concerning him, *In whom we have boldness and access with confidence by the faith of him* (v. 12). We have liberty to open our minds freely to God, as to a Father. We may come with humble boldness to hear from God, and we may expect to hear from him good words and comfortable.

Verses 14–21

Paul's affectionate prayer to God for his beloved Ephesians.—*For this cause.* This may be referred either to the immediately foregoing verse, *That you faint not*, &c., or, rather, the apostle is here resuming what he began at the first verse.

I. To whom he prays—to God, as *the Father of our Lord Jesus Christ.*

II. *I bow my knees.* When we draw nigh to God, we should reverence him in our hearts, and express our reverence in the most becoming behaviour.

JAMIESON, FAUSSET, BROWN

is made known to *evil* angels, who dwell "in heavenly places" in a lower sense, viz., the air (cf. ch. 2:2 with 6:12); "known" to their dismay (I Cor. 15: 24; Col. 2:15). **might be known**—Translate, "may be known."

by the church—"by means of," or "through the Church," which is the "theater" for the display of God's manifold wisdom (Luke 15:10; I Cor. 4:9): "a spectacle (*Greek*, 'theater') to angels." Hence, angels are but our "fellow servants" (Rev. 19:10). **manifold wisdom**—though essentially one, as Christ 10). **manifold wisdom**—though essentially one, as Christ is one, yet varying the economy in respect to places, times, and persons (Isa. 55:8, 9; Heb. 1:1). Cf. I Pet. 4:10, "stewards of the manifold grace of God." Man cannot understand aright its single acts till he can survey them as a connected whole (I Cor. 13:12). The call of the Church is no haphazard remedy, or afterthought, but part of the eternal scheme, which, amidst manifold varieties of dispensation, is one in its end.

11. which he purposed—*Greek,* "made." ELLICOTT translates, "wrought."

12. Translate, "*our* boldness and *our* access (ch. 2:18) *in* confidence *through our* faith *in* Him." ALFORD quotes as an instance, Romans 8:38, etc. "THE access" (*Greek*) implies the formal introduction into the presence of a monarch.

13. "I entreat you not to be dispirited." **for you**—in your behalf. **which is**—rather, "which *are* your glory," viz., inasmuch as showing that God loved you so much, as both to give His Son for you, and to permit His apostles to suffer "tribulations" for you [CHRYSOSTOM] in preaching the Gospel to the Gentiles. *Note*, vs. 1, "prisoner for you Gentiles." My tribulations are your spiritual "glory," as your faith is furthered thereby (I Cor. 4:10). **14. For this cause**—Resuming the thread of vs. 1, "For this cause." Because ye have such a standing in God's Church [ALFORD]. **bow my knees**—the proper attitude in humble prayer. Posture affects the mind, and is not therefore unimportant. See Paul's practice (Acts 20:36); and that of the Lord Himself on earth (Luke 22: 41). **unto the Father**—The oldest MSS. omit "of our Lord Jesus Christ." But *Vulgate* and some very old authorities retain them: vs. 15, "From whom," in either case, refers to "the Father" (*Patera*), as "family" (*patria*, akin in sound and etymology) plainly refers to Him. Still the foundation of all sonship is in Jesus Christ.

15. the whole family—ALFORD, MIDDLETON, and others translate,

ADAM CLARKE

goodness of God to give them that satisfaction which they require. And in this discovery of the gospel plan of salvation, which reconciles things in heaven and things on earth, both men and angels, these pure spirits are greatly interested, and their praises to the Divine Being rendered much more abundant. Others imagine the Jewish rulers and rabbins are intended, particularly those of them who were converted to Christianity, and who had now learned from the preaching of the gospel what, as Jews, they could never have known. *By the church.* That is, by the Christians, and by the wonderful things done in the Church; and by the apostles, who were its pastors. *The manifold wisdom of God.* "That multifarious and greatly diversified wisdom of God"; laying great and infinite plans, and accomplishing them by endless means, through the whole lapse of ages; making every occurrence subservient to the purposes of His infinite mercy and goodness. God's gracious design to save a lost world by Jesus Christ could not be defeated by any cunning skill or malice of man or devils. Whatever hindrances are thrown in the way, His wisdom and power can remove; and His infinite wisdom can never want ways or means to effect its gracious designs.

11. *According to the eternal purpose.* "According to the purpose concerning the periods." This seems to refer to the complete round of the Jewish system, and to that of the gospel. I have often observed that, though the proper grammatical meaning of the word is "everduring," or "endless duration," yet it is often applied to those systems, periods, and governments which have a complete duration, taking in the whole of them, from their commencement to their termination, leaving nothing of their duration unembraced. So, here, God purposed that the Jewish dispensation should commence at such a time and terminate at such a time; that the gospel dispensation should commence when the Jewish ended, and terminate only with life itself; and that the results of both should be endless. This is probably what is meant by the above phrase. *Which he purposed in Christ Jesus.* "Which He made or constituted in or for Christ Jesus." The manifestation of Christ and the glory which should follow were the grand objects which God kept in view in all His dispensations.

12. *In whom we have boldness.* "By whom we Gentiles have this liberty of speech," so that we may say anything by prayer and supplication, and this "introduction" into the divine presence by faith in Christ. It is only in His name we can pray to God, and it is only by Him that we can come to God; none can give us an "introduction" but Christ Jesus, and it is only for His sake that God will either hear or save us. It is on the ground of such scriptures as these that we conclude all our prayers in the name, and for the sake, of Jesus Christ, our Lord.

13. *I desire that ye faint not.* In those primitive times, when there was much persecution, people were in continual danger of falling away from the faith who were not well-grounded in it. This the apostle deprecates, and advances a strong reason why they should be firm.

14. *For this cause I bow my knees.* That you may not faint, but persevere, I frequently pray to God, who is our God and the Father of our Lord Jesus. Some very ancient and excellent MSS. and versions omit the words *of our Lord Jesus Christ.* And in them the passage reads: "I bow my knees unto the Father." Many parts of this prayer bear a strict resemblance to that offered up by Solomon when dedicating the Temple: "He . . . kneeled down upon his knees before all the congregation of Israel, and spread forth his hands towards heaven," 2 Chron. vi. 13. The apostle was now dedicating the Christian Church, that then was and that ever should be to God; and praying for those blessings which should ever rest on and distinguish it; and he kneels down after the example of Solomon, and invokes Him to whom the first Temple was dedicated, and who had made it a type of the gospel Church.

15. *Of whom the whole family.* Believers in the Lord Jesus Christ on earth, the spirits of

MATTHEW HENRY

The universal church has a dependence upon the Lord Jesus Christ: *Of whom the whole family in heaven and earth is named.* Understand it of the saints in heaven, who wear the crown of glory, and of saints on earth who are going on in the work of grace here. Both the one and the other make but one family; and from him they are *named* CHRISTIANS.

III. What the apostle asks of God for these his friends—spiritual blessings. 1. Spiritual strength for the work to which they were called. *That he would grant you, according to the riches of his grace, to be strengthened,* &c. And the apostle prays that this may be *according to the riches of his glory,* or according to his glorious riches, and this by his Spirit. Strength from the Spirit of God in the inner man is the best and most desirable strength.

2. The indwelling of Christ in their hearts, *v.* 17. Christ is an inhabitant in the soul of every good Christian. Where his Spirit dwells, there he dwells; and he dwells in the heart by faith. Faith opens the door of the soul, to receive Christ, faith admits him, and submits to him. By faith we are united to Christ. 3. The fixing of devout affections in the soul: *That you being rooted and grounded in love.* Many have some love to God and to his servants, but it is a flash, like the crackling of thorns under a pot, it makes a great noise, but is gone presently. We should earnestly desire that good affections may be fixed in us. Some understand it of their being settled and established in the sense of God's love to them. And how very desirable it is to have a settled fixed sense of the love of God and Christ to our souls, so as to be able to say with the apostle at all times, *He has loved me!* Now the best way to attain this is to be careful that we maintain a constant love to God in our souls.

JAMIESON, FAUSSET, BROWN

"every family": alluding to the several *families* in heaven and in earth supposed to exist (THEOPHYLACT, ŒCUMENIUS, in SUICER, 2. 633), the apostle thus being supposed to imply that God, in His relation of Father to us His adopted children, is the great prototype of the paternal relation wherever found. But the idea that "the holy angels are bound up in spiritual *families* or *compaternities,"* is nowhere else in Scripture referred to. And Acts 2:36, where the article is similarly omitted, and yet the translation is, *"All the* house of Israel," shows that in New Testament *Greek* the translation is justifiable, *"all the* family," or *"the whole* family": which accords with Scripture views, that angels and men, the saints militant and those with God, are one holy family joined under the one Father in Christ, the mediator between heaven and earth (ch. 1:10; Phil. 2:10). Hence angels are termed our "brethren" (Rev. 19:10), and "sons of God" by creation, as we are by adoption (Job 38:7). The Church is part of the grand family, or kingdom, which comprehends, besides men, the higher spiritual world, where the archetype, to the realization of which redeemed man is now tending, is already realized. This universal idea of the "kingdom" of God as one divine community, is presented to us in the Lord's Prayer. By sin men were estranged, not only from God, but from that higher spiritual world in which the kingdom of God is already realized. As Christ when He reconciled men to God, united them to one another in a divine community (joined to Himself, the one Head), breaking down the partition wall between Jew and Gentile (ch. 2:14), so also He joins them in communion with all those who have already attained that perfection in the kingdom of God, to which the Church on earth is aspiring (Col. 1:20) [NEANDER]. **is named**—derives its *origin* and its *name* as sons of God. To be named, and to be, are one with God. To bear God's name is to *belong to* God as *His own* peculiar people (Num. 6:27; Isa. 43:7; 44:5; Rom. 9:25, 26). **16. according to**—i.e. in abundance consonant to the riches of His glory; not "according to" the narrowness of our hearts. Colossians 1:11, "Strengthened with *all might according to His glorious power."* **by**—*Greek, "through"; "by means of* His Spirit." **in**—The *Greek* implies, "infused into."

the inner man—(ch. 4:22, 24; I Pet. 3:4)—"the hidden man of the heart." Not predicated of unbelievers, whose inward and outward man alike are carnal. But in believers, the "inner (new) man," their true self, stands in contrast to their old man, which is attached to them as a body of death daily being mortified, but not their true self.

17. That—So that. **dwell**—abidingly make His abode (John 14:23). Where the Spirit is there Christ is (John 14:16, 18). **by faith**—*Greek, "through* faith," which opens the door of the *heart* to Jesus (John 3:20). It is not enough that He be on the tongue, or flit through the brain: the heart is His proper seat [CALVIN]. "You being rooted and grounded in love" (cf. vs. 19), is in the *Greek* connected with this clause, not with the clause, "that ye may be able to comprehend." "Rooted" is an image from a *tree;* "grounded" (*Greek,* "founded," "having your foundations resting on"), from a *building* (cf. *Note,* ch. 2:20, 21; Col. 1:23; 2:7). Contrast Matthew 13:6, 21. "Love," the first fruit of the Spirit, flowing from Christ's love realized in the soul, was to be the basis on which should rest their further comprehension of all the vastness of Christ's love.

ADAM CLARKE

just men made perfect in a separate state, and all the holy angels in heaven make but one family, of which God is the Father and Head. Paul does not say, Of whom the "families," as if each order formed a distinct household; but he says *family,* because they are all one, and of One. And all this family *is named,* derives its origin and being, from God, as children derive their name from him who is the father of the family; holy persons in heaven and earth derive their being and their holiness from God, and therefore His name is called upon them.

16. *That he would grant you.* This prayer of the apostle is one of the most grand and sublime in the whole oracles of God. The riches of the grace of the gospel and the extent to which the soul of man may be saved here below are most emphatically pointed out here. Every word seems to have come immediately from heaven, laboring to convey ideas of infinite importance to mankind. No paraphrase can do it justice, and few commentators seem to have entered into its spirit, perhaps deterred by its unparalleled sublimity. *That he would grant you.* You can expect nothing from Him but as a free gift through Christ Jesus; let this be a ruling sentiment of your hearts when you pray to God. *According to the riches of his glory.* According to the measure of His own eternal fullness, God's infinite mercy and goodness being the measure according to which we are to be saved. In giving alms it is a maxim that everyone should act according to his ability. It would be a disgrace to a king or a nobleman to give no more than a tradesman or a peasant. God acts up to the dignity of His infinite perfections; He gives *according to the riches of his glory. To be strengthened with might.* You have many enemies, cunning and strong; many trials, too great for your natural strength; many temptations, which no human power is able successfully to resist; many duties to perform, which cannot be accomplished by the strength of man. Therefore you need divine strength; you must have might; and you must be strengthened everywhere, and every way fortified by that might, mightily and most effectually strengthened. *By his Spirit.* By the sovereign energy of the Holy Ghost. This Fountain of spiritual energy can alone supply the spiritual strength which is necessary for this spiritual work and conflict. *In the inner man.* In the soul. Every man is a compound being; he has a body and a soul. The outward man is that alone which is seen and considered by men; the inward man is that which stands particularly in reference to God and eternity. The outward man is strengthened by earthly food; the inward man, by spiritual and heavenly influences. The soul must be as truly fed and nourished by divine food as the body by natural food.

17. *That Christ may dwell in your hearts by faith.* In this as well as in many other passages, and particularly that in chap. ii. 21, the apostle compares the body or Church of true believers to a temple, which, like that of Solomon, is built to be a habitation of God through the Spirit. And as there could be no indwelling of God but by *Christ,* and no indwelling of Christ but by *faith,* he prays that they may have such faith in Christ as shall keep them in constant possession of His love and presence. This is what the apostle points out to the believing Ephesians, in praying that Christ might "intensely and constantly dwell in their hearts by faith." *That ye, being rooted and grounded in love.* Here is a double metaphor; one taken from agriculture, the other from architecture. As trees, they are to be *rooted . . . in love*—this is the soil in which their souls are to grow; into the infinite love of God their souls by faith are to strike their roots, and from this love derive all that nourishment which is essential for their full growth, till they have the mind in them that was in Jesus, or, as it is afterwards said, till they are "filled with all the fulness of God." As a building, their foundation is to be laid in this love. "God so loved the world, that he gave his only begotten Son." Here is the ground on which alone the soul, and all its hopes and expectations, can be safely founded. This is a foundation that cannot be shaken; and it is from this alone that the doctrine of redemption flows to man, and from this alone has the soul its form and comeliness.

MATTHEW HENRY

4. For their experimental acquaintance with the love of Jesus Christ. *That you may be able to comprehend with all saints*, &c. (*v.* 18, 19). Christians should not aim to comprehend above all saints; we should desire to comprehend *with all saints*, to have so much knowledge as the saints are allowed to have in this world. How magnificently the apostle speaks of the love of Christ. The dimensions of redeeming love are admirable: *The breadth, and length, and depth, and height*. By enumerating these dimensions, the apostle designs to signify the exceeding greatness of the love of Christ, the unsearchable riches of his love. We should desire to comprehend this love: it is the character of all the saints that they do so.

And to know the love of Christ which passeth knowledge, *v.* 19. If it passeth knowledge, how can we know it? We must pray and endeavour to know something, and should still covet to know more and more of it, though none can fully comprehend it: in its full extent it surpasses knowledge.

JAMIESON, FAUSSET, BROWN

18. **May be able**—even still further. *Greek*, "May be *fully* able." **breadth . . . length . . . depth . . . height**—viz., the full dimensions of the spiritual temple, answering to "the fulness of God" (vs. 19), to which the Church, according to its capacity, ought to correspond (cf. ch. 4:10, 13) as to "the fulness of *Christ*." The "breadth" implies Christ's world-wide love, embracing all men: the "length," its being extended through all ages (vs. 21); the "depth," its profound wisdom which no creature can fathom (Rom. 11:33); the "height," its being beyond the reach of any foe to deprive us of (ch. 4:8) [BENGEL]. I prefer to understand "the breadth," etc., to refer to *the whole of the vast mystery of free salvation in Christ for all, Gentile and Jew alike*, of which Paul had been speaking (vss. 3-9), and of which he now prays they may have a fuller comprehension. As subsidiary to this, and the most essential part of it, he adds, "and to know *the love of Christ*" (vs. 19). GROTIUS understands *depth* and *height* of God's goodness raising us from the lowest depression to the greatest height.

19. **passeth**—surpasseth, exceeds. The paradox "to know . . . which passeth knowledge," implies that when he says "know," he does not mean that we can *adequately* know; all we know is, that His love exceeds far our knowledge of it, and with even our fresh accessions of knowledge hereafter, will still exceed them. Even as God's power exceeds our thoughts (vs. 20).

ADAM CLARKE

In this, as its proper soil, it grows. *On* this, as its only foundation, it rests.

18. *May be able to comprehend with all saints.* These words are so exceedingly full of meaning that it is almost impossible to translate them. The first word, from *ex*, intensive, and *ischyo*, "to be strong," signifies that they might be "thoroughly able," by having been "strengthened with might," by God's power. The second word, from *kata*, intensive, and *lambano*, to "take, catch, or seize on," may be translated, "that you may fully catch, take in, and comprehend" this wonderful mystery of God. The mind must be rendered apt, and the soul invigorated, to take in and *comprehend* these mysteries. *What is the breadth, and length, and depth, and height.* Here the apostle still keeps up the metaphor, comparing the Church of God to a building; and as, in order to rear a proper building, a ground plan and specification must be previously made, according to which the building is to be constructed, the apostle refers to this. They were to be builded up a heavenly house, "an habitation of God through the Spirit"; and this must have its *breadth*, its *length*, its *height*, and its *depth*. But what can the apostle mean by the *breadth, length, depth*, and *height*, of the love of God? Imagination can scarcely frame any satisfactory answer to this question. It takes in the eternity of God. "God is *love*"; and in that, an infinity of *breadth, length, depth*, and *height* is included; or rather all *breadth, length, depth*, and *height* are lost in this immensity. It comprehends all that is above, all that is below, all that is past, and all that is to come. In reference to human beings, the love of God, in its *breadth*, is a girdle that encompasses the globe; its *length* reaches from the eternal purpose of the mission of Christ to the eternity of blessedness which is to be spent in His ineffable glories; its *depth* reaches to the lowest fallen of the sons of Adam, and to the deepest depravity of the human heart; and its *height*, to the infinite dignities of the throne of Christ. "He that overcometh will I give to sit down with Me upon My throne, as I have overcome and sat down with the Father upon His throne." Thus we see that the Father, the Son, and all true believers in Him are to be seated on the same throne! This is the *height* of the love of God, and the height to which that love raises the souls that believe in Christ Jesus!

19. *To know the love of Christ, which passeth knowledge.* It is only by the *love of Christ* that we can know the love of God. The love of God to man induced Him to give Christ for his redemption; Christ's love to man induced Him to give His life's blood for his salvation. The gift of Christ to man is the measure of God's love; the death of Christ for man is the measure of Christ's love. "God so loved the world." "Christ loved us, and gave himself for us." But how can *the love of Christ, which passeth knowledge*, be known? Many have labored to reconcile this seeming contradiction. If we take the verb in a sense in which it is frequently used in the New Testament, "to approve, acknowledge, or acknowledge with approbation," and *gnosis* to signify "comprehension," then the difficulty will be partly removed: "That you may acknowledge, approve, and publicly acknowledge that love of God which surpasseth knowledge." We can acknowledge and approve of that which surpasses our comprehension. We cannot comprehend God; yet we can know that He is; approve of, love, adore, and serve Him. In like manner, though we cannot comprehend the immensity of the love of Christ, yet we know that He has loved us, and washed us from our sins in His own blood; and we approve of, and acknowledge, Him as our only Lord and Saviour. In this sense we may be said to *know* the love of Christ that *passeth knowledge*. But it is more likely that the word *gnosis*, which we translate *knowledge*, signifies here science in general, and particularly that science of which the rabbins boasted, and that in which the Greeks greatly exulted. The former professed to have the key of knowledge, the secret of all divine mysteries; the latter considered their philosophers and their systems of philosophy superior to everything that had ever been known among men, and on this account reputed all other nations as barbarians. When the apostle

ALEXANDER MACLAREN:

We have no measure by which we can translate into the terms of our experience and so bring within the grasp of our minds what was the depth of the step which Christ took at the impulse of His love from the throne to the cross. We know not what He forewent; we know not, nor ever shall know, what depths of darkness and soul agony He passed through at the bidding of His all enduring love to us. Nor do we know the consequences of that great work of emptying himself of His glory. We have no means by which we can estimate the darkness and the depth of the misery from which we have been delivered, nor the height and the radiance of the glory to which we are to be lifted. And until we can tell and measure by our compasses both of these two extremes of possible human fate, till we have gone down into the deepest abyss of a bottomless pit of growing alienation and misery, and up above the highest reach of all unending progress into light and glory and God-likeness, we have not stretched our compasses wide enough to touch the two poles of this great sphere—the infinite love of Jesus Christ. So we bow before it, we know that we possess it with a knowledge more sure and certain, more deep and valid, than our knowledge of ought but ourselves; but yet it is beyond our grasp, and towers above us inaccessible in the altitude of its glory, and stretches deep beneath us in the profundity of its condescension.

And, in like manner, we may say that this known love passes knowledge, inasmuch as our experience of it can never exhaust it. We are like the settlers on some great island continent—as, for instance, on the Australian continent for many years after its first discovery—a thin fringe of population round the seaboard here and there, and all the bosom of the land untraversed and unknown. So after all experiences of and all blessed participation in the love of Jesus Christ which come to each of us by our faith, we have but skimmed the surface, but touched the edges, but received a drop of what, if it should come upon us in fullness of flood like a Niagara of love, would overwhelm our spirits.—*Expositions of Holy Scripture*

MATTHEW HENRY

5. He prays that they may *be filled with all the fulness of God.* It is a high expression: we should not dare to use it if we did not find it in the scriptures. Such a fulness as God is ready to bestow, who is willing to fill them all to the utmost of their capacity, and that with all those gifts and graces which he sees they need. Those who receive grace for grace from Christ's fulness may be said to be *filled with the fulness of God,* according to their capacity.

The apostle closes the chapter with a doxology, *v.* 20, 21. How he describes God, and how he ascribes glory to him. He describes him as a God that *is able to do exceedingly abundantly above all that we ask or think.* There is an inexhaustible fulness of grace and mercy in God, which the prayers of all the saints can never draw dry. We should encourage our faith by a consideration of his all-sufficiency and almighty power. *According to the power which worketh in us.* We have already had a proof of this power of God, in what he hath wrought in us and done for us. The power that still worketh for the saints is according to that power that hath wrought in them.

He ascribes glory to him. Unto him be glory in the church by Christ Jesus. The seat of God's praises is in the church. That little rent of praise which God receives from this world is from the church, every particular member of which, both Jew and Gentile, concurs in this work of praising God. The Mediator of these praises is Jesus Christ. All God's gifts come from him to us through the hand of Christ; and all our praises pass from us to him through the same hand. And God should and will be praised thus *throughout all ages, world without end. Amen.* So be it; and so it will certainly be.

JAMIESON, FAUSSET, BROWN

filled with—rather, as *Greek,* "filled even *unto* all the fulness of God" (this is the grand goal), i.e., filled, each according to your capacity, with the divine wisdom, knowledge, and love; *even as God is full,* and as Christ who dwells in your hearts, hath "all the fulness of the Godhead dwelling in Him bodily" (Col. 2:9).

20. unto him—contrasted with *ourselves* and *our needs.* Translate, "that is able above all things (what is above all things) to do exceeding abundantly above what we ask or (even) think": *thought* takes a wider range than *prayers.* The word, *above,* occurs thrice as often in Paul's writings, as in all the rest of the New Testament, showing the warm exuberance of Paul's spirit. **according to the power**—the indwelling Spirit (Rom. 8:26). He appeals to their and his experience.

21. Translate, "Unto Him be *the* glory (i.e., the whole glory of the gracious dispensation of salvation just spoken of) in the Church (as the theater for the manifestation of the glory, vs. 10) *in* Christ Jesus (as in Him all the glory centers, Zech. 6:13) to all the generations of eternal ages," lit., "of the age of the ages." Eternity is conceived as consisting of "ages" (these again consisting of "generations") endlessly succeeding one another.

ADAM CLARKE

prays that they may *know the love of Christ, which passeth knowledge,* he may refer to all the boasted knowledge of the Jewish doctors, and to all the greatly extolled science of the Greek philosophers. To know the love of Christ infinitely surpasses all other science. This gives a clear and satisfactory sense. *That ye might be filled with all the fulness of God.* Among all the great sayings in this prayer, this is the greatest. To be filled with God is a great thing; to be filled with the fullness of God is still greater; but to be *filled with all the fulness of God* utterly bewilders the sense and confounds the understanding. By the *fulness of God* we are to understand all those gifts and graces which He has promised to bestow on man, and which He dispenses to the Church. To be *filled with all the fulness of God* is to have the whole soul filled with meekness, gentleness, goodness, love, justice, holiness, mercy, and truth. And as what God fills neither sin nor Satan can fill, consequently it implies that the soul shall be emptied of sin, that sin shall neither have dominion over it nor a being in it.

20. *Now unto him.* Having finished his short but most wonderfully comprehensive and energetic prayer, the apostle brings in his doxology, giving praise to Him from whom all blessings come, and to whom all thanks are due. *That is able to do exceeding abundantly.* It is impossible to express the full meaning of these words. God is omnipotent; therefore He is able to do all things, and able to do "superabundantly above the greatest abundance." And who can doubt this who has any rational or scriptural views of His power or His love? *According to the power that worketh in us.* All that He can do and all that He has promised to do will be done *according* to what He has done, by that *power* of the Holy Ghost "which worketh strongly in us"—acts with "energy" in our hearts, expelling evil, purifying and refining the affections and desires, and implanting good.

21. *Unto him,* thus possessed of power and goodness, *be glory in the church*—be unceasing praises ascribed in all the assemblies of the people of God, wherever these glad tidings are preached, and wherever this glorious doctrine shall be credited. *By Christ Jesus.* Through whom, and for whom, all these miracles of mercy and power are wrought. *Throughout all ages.* "Through all succeeding generations"—while the race of human beings continues to exist on the face of the earth. *World without end.* "Throughout eternity"—in the coming world as well as in this. The song of praise, begun upon earth and protracted through all the generations of men, shall be continued in heaven by all that are redeemed from the earth, where eras, limits, and periods are no more forever. *Amen.* So be it! So let it be!

MATTHEW HENRY

CHAPTER 4

Verse 1

This is a general exhortation to walk as becomes our Christian profession. Paul was now a prisoner at Rome; and he was the *prisoner of the Lord.* He mentions this once and again, to show that he was not ashamed of his bonds. We have here the petition of a poor prisoner: "*I therefore, the prisoner of the Lord, beseech you,* &c. Considering what God has done for you I now come with an earnest request to you not to send me relief, nor to use your interest for the obtaining of my liberty, but, that you would approve yourselves good Christians: *That you walk worthily.*" We are called Christians; we must answer that name, and live like Christians. We are called to God's kingdom and glory; we must walk as becomes the heirs of them.

Verses 2–16

Exhortation to mutual love. Love is the law of Christ's kingdom, the lesson of his school, the livery of his family.

1. The means of unity: *Lowliness and meekness, longsuffering, and forbearing one another in love, v.* 2. By lowliness we are to understand humility opposed to pride, by *meekness,* that excellent disposition of soul which makes men unwilling to provoke others, and not easily to be provoked. *Long-suffering* implies a patient bearing of injuries, without seeking revenge.

JAMIESON, FAUSSET, BROWN

CHAPTER 4

Vss. 1-32. EXHORTATIONS TO CHRISTIAN DUTIES RESTING ON OUR CHRISTIAN PRIVILEGES, AS UNITED IN ONE BODY, THOUGH VARYING IN THE GRACES GIVEN TO THE SEVERAL MEMBERS, THAT WE MAY COME UNTO A PERFECT MAN IN CHRIST. **1.** Translate, according to the *Greek* order, "I beseech you, therefore (seeing that such is your calling of grace, chs. 1, 2, 3). I the prisoner in the Lord" (i.e., imprisoned in the Lord's cause). What the world counted ignominy, he counts the highest honor, and he glories in his bonds for Christ, more than a king in his diadem [THEODORET]. His bonds, too, are an argument which should enforce his exhortation. **vocation**—Translate, "calling" to accord, as the *Greek* does, with "called" (vs. 4; ch. 1:18; Rom. 8: 28, 30). Colossians 3:15 similarly grounds Christian duties on our Christian "calling." *The exhortations of this part of the Epistle are built on the conscious enjoyment of the privileges mentioned in the former part.* Cf. ch. 4:32, with ch. 1:7; 5:1, with 1:5; 4:30, with 1:13; 5:15, with 1:8.

2, 3. lowliness—In classic *Greek,* the meaning is *meanness of spirit:* the Gospel has elevated the word to express a Christian grace, viz., the esteeming of ourselves small, inasmuch as we are so; the thinking truly, and because truly, therefore lowlily, of ourselves [TRENCH]. **meekness**—that spirit in which we accept God's dealings with us without disputing and resisting; and also the accepting patiently of the

ADAM CLARKE

CHAPTER 4

1. *I therefore.* Therefore, because God has provided for you such an abundant salvation, and you have His testimonies among you, and have full liberty to use all the means of grace. *The prisoner of the Lord.* Who am deprived of my liberty for the Lord's sake. *Beseech you that ye walk.* You have your liberty, and may *walk;* I am deprived of mine, and cannot. This is a fine stroke, and wrought up into a strong argument. You who are at large can show forth the virtues of Him who called you into His marvellous light; I am in bondage, and can only exhort others by my writing, and show my submission to God by my patient suffering. *The vocation wherewith ye are called.* The "calling" is the free invitation they have had from God to receive the privileges of the gospel, and become His sons and daughters, without being obliged to observe Jewish rites and ceremonies. Their vocation, or calling, took in their Christian profession, with all the doctrines, precepts, privileges, duties, etc., of the Christian religion.

2. *With all lowliness.* It is by acting as the apostle here directs that a man walks worthy of this high vocation; *tapeinophrosyne* signifies "subjection" or "humility of mind." *Meekness.* The opposite to anger and irritability of disposition. *Longsuffering.* "Long-mindedness"—never permitting a trial or provocation to get

MATTHEW HENRY

Forbearing one another in love. The best Christians have need to make the best one of another, to provoke one another's graces and not their passions. We find much in ourselves which it is hard to forgive ourselves; and therefore we must not think it much if we find that in others which we think hard to forgive them, and yet we must forgive them. Now without these things unity cannot be preserved. The first step towards unity is humility. Pride and passion break the peace, and make all the mischief. Humility and meekness restore the peace. The more lowly-mindedness the more like-mindedness.

II The nature of that unity: it is *the unity of the Spirit, v.* 3. The seat of Christian unity is in the heart or spirit: it does not lie in one set of thoughts, nor in one form and mode of worship, but in one heart and one soul. This we should endeavour to keep. *Endeavouring* is a gospel word. We must do our utmost. If others will quarrel with us, we must take all possible care not to quarrel with them. *In the bond of peace.* Peace is a bond. Many slender twigs, bound together, become strong. The bond of peace is the strength of society. Not that it can be imagined that all good people, should be in everything just of the same length, and the same sentiments. As in a bundle of rods, they may be of different lengths and different strength; but, when they are tied together by one bond, they are stronger than any, even than the thickest and strongest was of itself.

III. The motives proper to promote this Christian unity and concord.

1. Consider how many unities there are. There should be one heart; for *there is one body, and one Spirit, v.* 4. Two hearts in one body would be monstrous. If there be but one body, all that belong to that body should have one heart. If we belong to Christ, we are all actuated by one and the same Spirit, and therefore should be one. *Even as you are called in one hope of your calling.* There is one Christ that they all hope in, and one heaven that they are all hoping for; and therefore they should be of one heart.

One Lord (*v.* 5), that is, Christ. *One faith,* that is, the gospel, or, it is the same grace of faith whereby all Christians are saved. *One baptism,* by by which we profess our faith.

One God and Father of all, v. 6. One God, who owns all the true members of the church for his children; and he *is above all, and through all,* by his providence upholding them: *and in you all,* in all believers, by his Spirit. If then there be so many *ones,* it is a pity but there should be one more—one heart, or one soul.

2. Consider the variety of gifts that Christ has bestowed among Christians: *But unto everyone of us is*

JAMIESON, FAUSSET, BROWN

injuries done us by men, out of the thought that they are permitted by God for the chastening and purifying of His people (II Sam. 16:11; cf. Gal. 6:1; II Tim. 2:25; Titus 3:2). It is only the *lowly,* humble heart that is also *meek* (Col. 3:12). As "lowliness and meekness" answer to "forbearing one another in love" (cf. "love," vss. 15, 16), so "long-suffering" answers to (vs. 4) "endeavoring (*Greek, 'earnestly'* or *'zealously giving diligence'*) to keep (maintain) the unity of the Spirit (the unity between men of different tempers, which flows from the presence of the Spirit, who is Himself 'one,' vs. 4) in (united in) the bond of peace" (the "bond" by which "peace" is maintained, viz., "love," Col. 3:14, 15 [BENGEL]; or, peace itself is the "bond" meant, uniting the members of the Church [ALFORD]). **4.** In the apostle's creed the article as to THE CHURCH properly follows that as to THE HOLY GHOST. To the Trinity naturally is annexed the Church, as the house to its tenant, to God His temple, the state to its founder [AUGUSTINE, *Enchir. ad Laurentium,* c. 15]. There is yet to be a Church, not merely potentially, but actually catholic or world-wide; then the Church and the world will be coextensive. Rome falls into inextricable error by setting up a mere man as a visible head, antedating that consummation which Christ, the true visible Head, at His appearing shall first realize. As the "SPIRIT" is mentioned here, so the "LORD" (Jesus), vs. 5, and "GOD the Father," vs. 6. Thus the Trinity is again set forth. **hope—here associated with** "the Spirit," which is the "earnest of our inheritance" (ch. 1:13, 14). As "faith" is mentioned, vs. 5, so "hope" here, and "love," vs. 2. The Holy Spirit, as the common higher principle of life (ch. 2:18, 22), gives to the Church its true unity. Outward uniformity is as yet unattainable; but beginning by having one mind, we shall hereafter end by having "one body." The true "body" of Christ (all believers of every age) is already "one," as joined to the one Head. But its unity is as yet not visible, even as the Head is not visible; but it shall appear when He shall appear (John 17:21-23; Col. 3:4). Meanwhile the rule is, "In essentials, unity; in doubtful questions, liberty; in all things, charity." There is more real unity where both go to heaven under different names than when with the same name one goes to heaven, the other to hell. Truth is the first thing: those who reach it, will at last reach unity, because truth is *one;* while those who seek unity as the first thing, may purchase it at the sacrifice of truth, and so of the soul itself. **of your calling**—the one "hope" *flowing from* our "calling," is the element "IN" which we are "called" to live. Instead of privileged classes, as the Jews under the law, a unity of dispensation was henceforth to be the common privilege of Jew and Gentile alike. Spirituality, universality, and unity, were *designed* to characterize the Church; and it shall be so at last (Isa. 2:2-4; 11:9, 13; Zeph. 3:9; Zech. 14:9). **5.** Similarly "faith" and "baptism" (the sacramental seal of faith) are connected Mark 16:16; Col. 2:12). Cf. I Corinthians 12:13, "Faith" is not here *that which we believe,* but the act of *believing,* the mean by which we apprehend the "one Lord." "Baptism" is specified, being the sacrament whereby we are *incorporated* into the "one body." Not the Lord's Supper, which is an act of matured communion on the part of those already incorporate, "a symbol of *union,* not of *unity*" [ELLICOTT]. In I Corinthians 10:17, where a breach of union was in question, it forms the rallying point [ALFORD]. There is not added, "One pope, one council, one form of government" [*Cautions for Times*]. The Church is one in *unity of faith* (vs. 5; Jude 3); *unity of origination* (ch. 2:19-21): *unity of sacraments* (vs. 5; I Cor. 10: 17; 12:13): *unity of "hope"* (vs. 4: Titus 1:2); *unity of charity* (vs. 3): *unity* (*not uniformity*) *of discipline and government:* for where there is no order, no ministry with Christ as the Head, there is no Church [PEARSON, *Creed,* Article 9]. **6. above**—"*over* all." The "one God over all" (in His sovereignty and by His grace) is the grand source and crowning apex of unity (ch. 2:19, end). **through all**—by means of Christ "who filleth all things" (vs. 10; ch. 2:20, 21), and is "a propitiation" for all men (I John 2:2). **in you all**—The oldest MSS. omit "you." Many of the oldest versions and Fathers and old MSS. read, "in *us* all." Whether the pronoun be read or not, it must be understood (either from the "ye," vs. 4, or from the "us," vs. 7); for other parts of Scripture prove that the Spirit is not "in all" men, but only in believers (Rom. 8:9, 14). God is "Father" both by generation (as Creator) and regeneration (ch. 2:10; Jas. 1:17, 18; I John 5:1). **7. But**—Though "one" in our common connection with "one Lord, one faith, etc., one God,"

ADAM CLARKE

to the end of your patience. *Forbearing one another.* "Sustaining one another"—helping to "support each" other in all the miseries and trials of life; or if the word be taken in the sense of "bearing with each other," it may mean that, through the love of God working in our hearts, we should bear with each other's infirmities, ignorance, etc., knowing how much others have been or are still obliged to bear with us.

3. *Endeavouring to keep the unity of the Spirit in the bond of peace.* There can be no doubt that the church at Ephesus was composed partly of converted Jews, as well as Gentiles. Now from the different manner in which they had been brought up, there might be frequent causes of altercation. Indeed the Jews, though converted, might be envious that the Gentiles were admitted to the same glorious privileges with themselves without being initiated into them by bearing the yoke and burden of the Mosaic law. The apostle guards them against this, and shows them that they should "intensely labor" (for so the word implies) to promote and preserve *peace* and *unity.* By the *unity of the Spirit* we are to understand, not only a spiritual unity, but also a unity of sentiments, desires, and affections, such as is worthy of and springs from the Spirit of God. By *the bond of peace* we are to understand a peace or union where the interests of all parties are concentrated, cemented, and sealed, the Spirit of God being the Seal upon this knot.

4. *There is one body.* Viz., of Christ, which is His Church. *One Spirit.* The Holy Ghost, who animates this body. *One hope.* Of everlasting glory, to which glory you have been called by the preaching of the gospel; through which you have become the body of Christ, instinct with the energy of the Holy Ghost.

5. *One Lord.* Jesus Christ, who is the Governor of this Church. *One faith.* One system of religion, proposing the same objects to the faith of all. *One baptism.* Administered in the name of the Holy Trinity; indicative of the influences, privileges, and effects of the Christian religion.

6. *One God.* The Fountain of all being, self-existent and eternal; *and Father of all,* both Jews and Gentiles, because He is the Father of the spirits of all flesh. *Who is above all.* "Who is over all"; as the King of Kings, and Lord of Lords. *And through all.* Pervading everything, being present with everything, providing for all creatures, and by His energy supporting all things. *And in you all.* By the energy of His Spirit enlightening, quickening, purifying, and comforting; in a word, making your hearts the temples of the Holy Ghost. Some think the mystery of the blessed Trinity is contained in this verse: God is "over all," as Father; *through all,* by the Logos or Word; and *in . . . all,* by the Holy Spirit.

7. *Unto every one of us is given grace.* Grace may here signify a particular office; as if the

MATTHEW HENRY

given grace according to the measure of the gift of Christ. Though the members of Christ's church agree in so many things, yet there are some things wherein they differ: but this should breed no difference of affection among them, since they are all derived from the same bountiful author. They had no reason to quarrel about them because all was given *according to the measure of the gift of Christ.* All the ministers, and all the members of Christ, owe all the gifts and graces that they are possessed of to him; and this is a good reason why we should love one another, *because to everyone of us is given grace.* All to whom Christ has given grace, and on whom he has bestowed his gifts *ought to love one another.* The apostle takes this occasion to specify some of the gifts. And that they were bestowed by Christ he makes appear by those words of David (Ps. lxviii. 18), *Wherefore he saith* (*v.* 8), *When he ascended up on high, he led captivity captive, and gave gifts unto men.* Let us set ourselves to think of the ascension of Jesus Christ: that our blessed Redeemer, having risen from the dead, is gone to heaven, where he sits at the right hand of the majesty on high. Christ, when he ascended into heaven, as a triumphant conqueror, *led captivity captive.* It is a phrase used in the Old Testament to signify a conquest over enemies, especially over such as formerly had led others captive. He conquered those who had conquered us; such as sin, the devil, and death. Indeed, he triumphed over these *on the cross;* but the triumph was completed at his ascension, when he became Lord over all. *And he gave gifts unto men:* in the psalm it is, *He received gifts for men.* He received for them, that he might give to them.

The apostle takes notice that he *descended first, v.* 9, *into the lower parts of the earth.* He descended to the earth in his incarnation.

He descended into the earth in his burial. *He that descended is the same also that ascended up far above all heavens* (*v.* 10) into the heaven of heavens *that he might fill all things,* all the members of his church, with gifts and graces.

The apostle next tells us what were Christ's gifts at his ascension: *He gave some apostles,* &c., *v.* 11. The great gift that Christ gave to the church at his ascension was that of the ministry of peace and reconciliation. The gift of the ministry is the fruit of Christ's ascension. The officers which Christ gave to his church were of two sorts—*extraordinary* ones:

JAMIESON, FAUSSET, BROWN

yet "each one of us" has assigned to him his own particular gift, to be used for the good of the whole: none is overlooked; none therefore can be dispensed with for the edifying of the Church (vs. 12). A motive to unity (vs. 3). Translate, "Unto *each* one of us was *the* grace (which was bestowed by Christ at His ascension, vs. 8) given according to . . . ." **the measure**—*the amount* "of the gift of Christ" (Rom. 12:3, 6). **8. Wherefore**—"For which reason," viz., in order to intimate that Christ, the Head of the Church, is the author of all these different gifts, and that giving of them is an act of His "grace" [ESTIUS]. **he saith**—God, whose word the Scripture is (Ps. 68:18). **When he ascended**—GOD is meant in the Psalm, represented by the ark, which was being brought up to Zion in triumph by David, after that "the Lord had given him rest round about from all his enemies" (II Sam. 6; 7:1; I Chron. 15). Paul quotes it of CHRIST ascending to heaven, who is therefore GOD. **captivity**—i.e., a band of captives. In the Psalm, the captive foes of David. In the antitypical meaning, the foes of Christ the Son of David, the devil, death, the curse, and sin (Col. 2:15; II Pet. 2:4), led as it were in triumphal procession as a sign of the destruction of the foe. **gave gifts unto men**—in the Psalm, "*received* gifts *for* men," *Hebrew,* "among men," i.e., "thou hast received gifts" *to distribute among* men. As a conqueror distributes in token of his triumph the spoils of foes as gifts among his people. The impartation of the gifts and graces of the Spirit depended on Christ's ascension (John 7:39; 14:12). Paul stops short in the middle of the verse, and does not quote "that the Lord God might dwell *among them."* This, it is true, is partly fulfilled in Christians being an "habitation of God through the Spirit" (ch. 2:22). But the Psalm (vs. 16) refers to "the Lord dwelling in Zion *for ever";* the ascension amidst attendant angels, having as its counterpart the second advent amidst "thousands of angels" (vs. 17), accompanied by the restoration of Israel (vs. 22), the destruction of God's enemies and the resurrection (vss. 20, 21, 23), the conversion of the kingdoms of the world to the Lord at Jerusalem (vss. 29-34). **9.** Paul reasons that (assuming Him to be God) His *ascent* implies a previous *descent;* and that the language of the Psalm can only refer to *Christ,* who first descended, then ascended. For God the Father does not ascend or descend. Yet the Psalm plainly refers to *God* (vss. 8, 17, 18). It must therefore be GOD THE SON (John 6:33, 62). As He declares (John 3:13), "No man hath ascended up to heaven, *but He that came down from heaven."* Others, though they did not previously descend, have ascended; but none save *Christ* can be referred to in the Psalm as having done so; for it is of *God* it speaks. **lower parts of the earth**—The antithesis or contrast to "far above all heavens," is the argument of ALFORD and others, to show that this phrase means more than simply the *earth,* viz., the regions *beneath* it, even as He ascended not merely to the visible heavens, but "far above" them. Moreover, His design "that He might fill *all* things" (vs. 10, *Greek,* "the whole universe of things") may imply the same.

Also the leading "captive" of the "captive band" ("captivity") of satanic powers, may imply that the warfare reached to *their habitation itself* (Ps. 63:9). Christ, as Lord of all, took possession first of the earth the unseen world beneath it (some conjecture that the region of the lost is in the central parts of our globe), then of heaven (Acts 2:27, 28). However, all we *surely* know is, that His soul at death descended to Hades, i.e., underwent the ordinary condition of departed spirits of men. The leading captive of satanic powers here, is not said to be at His descent, but *at His ascension;* so that no argument can be drawn from it for a descent to the abodes of Satan. Acts 2:27, 28, and Romans 10:7, favor the view of the reference being simply to His descent to *Hades.* So PEARSON *on Creed* (Phil. 2:10). **10. all heavens**—*Greek,* "all the heavens" (*Heb.* 7:26; 4:14), *Greek,* "passed *through* the heavens" to the throne of God itself. **might fill**—In *Greek,* the action is continued to the present time, both "*might*" and "may fill," viz., with His divine presence and Spirit, *not with His glorified body.* "Christ, as God, *is* present *everywhere;* as glorified man, He *can* be present *anywhere"* [ELLICOTT]. **11.** *Greek,* emphatical. "Himself" by His supreme power. "It is HE that gave. . ." **gave some, apostles**—Translate, ". . . some to be apostles, and some to be prophets. . . ." The men who filled the office, no less than the office itself, were a divine gift [EADIE]. Ministers did not give themselves. Cf. with the list here, I Corinthians 12:10, 28. As the apostles, prophets, and

ADAM CLARKE

apostle had said: Though we are all equal in the respects already mentioned, yet we have all different offices and situations to fill up in the Church and in the world; and we receive a free gift from Christ, according to the nature of the office, that we may be able to discharge it according to His own mind.

8. *Wherefore he saith.* The reference seems to be to Ps. lxviii. 18, which, however it may speak of the removal of the Tabernacle, appears to have been intended to point out the glorious ascension of Christ after His resurrection from the dead. *When he ascended up on high.* The whole of this verse, as it stands in the psalm, seems to refer to a military triumph. Take the following paraphrase: "Thou hast ascended on high"; the conqueror was placed in a very elevated chariot. "Thou hast led captivity captive"; the conquered kings and generals were usually bound behind the chariot of the conqueror, to grace the triumph. "Thou hast received gifts for [Paul, given gifts unto] men"; at such times the conqueror was wont to throw money among the crowd. Even to "the rebellious"; those who had fought against him now submit unto him, and share his munificence, for it is the property of a hero to be generous. "That the Lord God might dwell among them"; the conqueror being now come to fix his abode in the conquered provinces, and subdue the people to his laws.

9. *But that he also descended.* The meaning of the apostle appears to be this: The Person who *ascended* is the Messiah, and His ascension plainly intimates His descension; that is, His incarnation, humiliation, death, and resurrection.

10. *He that descended.* And He who descended so low is the same who has ascended so high. He came to "the lower parts of the earth"—the very deepest abasement; having emptied himself, taken upon Him the form of a servant, and humbled himself unto death, even the death of the Cross, now He is ascended *far above all heavens*—higher than all height; He has a name above every name. Here His descending into "the lower parts of the earth" is put in opposition to His ascending *far above all heavens.* His abasement was unparalleled; so also is His exaltation. *That he might fill all things.* That He might be the Fountain whence all blessings might flow, dispensing all good things to all His creatures, according to their several capacities and necessities; and, particularly, fill both converted Jews and Gentiles with all the gifts and graces of His Holy Spirit. Hence it follows:

11. *He gave some, apostles.* He established several offices in His Church; furnished these with the proper officers; and, to qualify them for their work, gave them the proper gifts. For a full illustration of this verse, the reader is requested to refer to the notes on 1 Cor. xii. 6-10 and 28-30.

MATTHEW HENRY

such were *apostles, prophets*, and *evangelists*. The apostles were chief. They having been the witnesses of his miracles and doctrine, he sent them forth to spread the gospel. The prophets seem to have been such as expounded the writings of the Old Testament. The evangelists were ordained persons whom the apostles took for their companions in travel. And then there are *ordinary* ministers, as *pastors* and *teachers*. Some take these two names to signify one office. Others think they design two distinct offices, and then pastors are such as are fixed at the head of particular churches; and they are frequently called bishops and elders: and the teachers were those whose work it was to instruct the people by way of exhortation. How rich is the church that has still such a variety of gifts! How kind is Christ to his church!

3. Christ's great end and design in giving gifts unto men. The gifts of Christ were intended for the good of his church. All are *for the perfecting of the saints* (*v.* 12); to bring into an orderly spiritual state those who had been dislocated and disjointed by sin, and then to advance them therein, that so each might contribute to the good of the whole.—*For the work of the ministry. For the edifying of the body of Christ;* that is, to build up the church, which is Christ's mystical body, by an increase of their graces, and an addition of new members. All are designed to prepare us for heaven: *Till we all come*, &c., *v.* 13. *Till they all come in the unity of the faith and of the knowledge of the Son of God*, not a bare speculative knowledge, but such as is attended with appropriation and affection.—*Unto a perfect man*, to our full growth of gifts and graces, free from those childish infirmities that we are subject to in the present world.—*Unto the measure of the stature of the fulness of Christ*, so as to be Christians of a full maturity in all the graces derived from Christ's fulness. We shall never come to the perfect man, till we come to the perfect world. God's children, as long as they are in this world, are growing. Now see God's design in his sacred institutions, and what effect they ought to have upon us.

(1) *We henceforth be no more children*, &c. (*v.* 14); no longer children in knowledge, weak in the faith, and inconstant in our judgments, easily yielding to every temptation, and being at everyone's beck. Children are easily imposed upon. We must take care of this, and of being *tossed to and fro*, like ships without ballast, *and carried about*, like clouds in the air, with such doctrines as have no truth nor solidity in them, and are therefore compared to wind. *By the sleight of men, and cunning craftiness, whereby they lie in wait to deceive*, as in an ambush, in order to circumvent the weak. The best method we can take to fortify ourselves against such is to study the sacred oracles, and to pray for the illumination and grace of the Spirit of Christ.

(2) We should *speak the truth in love* (*v.* 15). Love is an excellent thing; but we must be careful to preserve truth together with it. Truth is an excellent thing; yet it is requisite that we speak it in love, and not in contention. These two should go together—truth and peace. (3) We should *grow up into Christ in all things*. Into Christ, so as to be more deeply rooted in him. In all things; in knowledge, love, faith. We should grow up towards maturity, which is opposed to being children. The more we grow into an acquaintance with Christ, faith in him, love to him, dependence upon him, the more we shall flourish in every grace. (4) We should be helpful one to another, as members of the same body, *v.* 16. Here the apostle makes a comparison between the natural body and Christ's mystical body. As there must be communion of the members of the body among themselves, so there must be mutual love and unity among Christians, in order to their spiritual improvement and growth in grace. Particular Christians receive their gifts and graces from Christ for the sake and benefit of the whole body. *Unto the edifying of itself in love.* Mutual love among Christians is a great friend to spiritual growth: it is in love that the body edifies itself.

JAMIESON, FAUSSET, BROWN

evangelists were special and extraordinary ministers, so "pastors and teachers" are the ordinary stated ministers of a particular flock, including, probably, the bishops, presbyters, and deacons. Evangelists were itinerant preachers like our missionaries, as Philip the deacon (Acts 21:8); as contrasted with stationary "pastors and teachers" (II Tim. 4:5). The *evangelist* founded the Church; the *teacher* built it up in the faith already received. The "pastor" had the *outward rule* and *guidance* of the Church: the bishop. As to revelation, the "evangelist" testified infallibly of the past; the "prophet," infallibly of the future. The prophet derived all from the Spirit; the evangelist, in the special case of the Four, recorded matter of fact, cognizable to the senses, under the Spirit's guidance. No one form of Church polity as permanently *unalterable* is laid down in the New Testament though the apostolical order of bishops, or presbyters, and deacons, superintended by higher overseers (called bishops after the apostolic times), has the highest sanction of primitive usage.

12. For—*with a view to;* the ultimate aim. "Unto." **perfecting**—The *Greek* implies *correcting* in all that is deficient, *instructing* and completing in number and all parts. **for**—a different *Greek* word; the immediate object. Cf. Romans 15:2, "Let every one . . . please his neighbor *for* his good *unto* edification." **the ministry**—*Greek*, "ministration"; without the article. The office of the ministry is stated in this verse. The good aimed at in respect to the Church (vs. 13). The way of growth (vss. 14, 15, 16). **edifying**—i.e., *building up* as the temple of the Holy Ghost. **13. come in**—rather, "attain unto." ALFORD expresses the *Greek order,* "Until we arrive all of us at the unity. . . . **faith and . . . knowledge**—Full unity of *faith* is then found, when all alike thoroughly *know Christ,* the object of faith, and that in His highest dignity as "the Son of God" [DE WETTE] (ch. 3:17, 19; II Pet. 1:5). Not even Paul counted himself to have fully "attained" (Phil. 3:12-14). Amidst the variety of the gifts and the multitude of the Church's members, its "faith" is to be ONE: as contrasted with the state of "children carried about with EVERY WIND OF DOCTRINE" (vs. 14). **perfect man**—unto the "*full-grown* man" (I Cor. 2: 6; Phil. 3:15; Heb. 5:14); the *maturity* of an *adult;* contrasted with children (vs. 14). Not "perfect *men";* for the many members constitute but *one* Church joined to the one Christ. **stature . . .**—The standard of spiritual "stature" is "the fulness of Christ," i.e., which Christ has (ch. 1:23; 3:19; cf. Gal. 4:19); that the body should be worthy of the Head, the perfect Christ. **14.** Translate, "To the end that"; the aim of the bestowal of gifts stated negatively, as in vs. 13 it is stated positively. **tossed to and fro**—*inwardly,* even without wind; *like billows of the sea.* So the *Greek.* Cf. James 1:6. **carried about**—with every wind *from without.* **doctrine**—"teaching." The various *teachings* are the "winds" which keep them tossed on a sea of doubts (Heb. 13:9; cf. Matt. 11:7). **by**—*Greek,* "in"; expressing "the evil atmosphere *in* which the varying currents of doctrine exert their force" [ELLICOTT]. **sleight**—lit., "dice-playing." The player frames his throws of the dice so that the numbers may turn up which best suit his purpose. **of men**—contrasted with *Christ* (vs. 13). **and**—*Greek,* "in." **cunning craftiness, whereby they lie in wait to deceive**—Translate as *Greek,* "craftiness tending to the methodized system of deceit" ("the schemes of error") [ALFORD]. BENGEL takes "deceit," or "error," to stand for "the parent of error," Satan (cf. ch. 6:11); referring to his concealed mode of acting. **15. speaking the truth**—Translate, "holding the truth"; "following the truth"; opposed to "error" or "deceit" (vs. 14). **in love**—"Truth" is never to be sacrificed to so-called "charity"; yet it is to be maintained in charity. Truth in word and act, love in manner and spirit, are the Christian's rule (cf. vss. 21, 24). **grow up**—from the state of "children" to that of "full-grown men." There is growth only in the spiritually alive, not in the dead. **into him**—so as to be more and more incorporated with Him, and become one with Him. **the head**—(ch. 1:22). **16.** (Col. 2:19) **fitly joined together**—"being fitly framed together," as in ch. 2:21; all the parts being in their proper position, and in mutual relation. **compacted**—implying *firm consolidation.* **by that which every joint supplieth**—*Greek,* "by means of every joint of the supply"; joined with "maketh increase of the body," not with "compacted." "By every ministering (supplying) joint." The joints are the points of union where the supply passes to the different members, furnishing the body with the materials of its growth. **effectual working**—(ch. 1: 19; 3:7). According to the effectual *working of*

ADAM CLARKE

12. *For the perfecting of the saints.* For the complete instruction, purification, and union of all who have believed in Christ Jesus, both Jews and Gentiles. For the meaning of *perfecting,* see the note on 2 Cor. xiii. 9. *For the work of the ministry.* All these various officers, and the gifts and graces conferred upon them, were judged necessary, by the great Head of the Church, for its full instruction in the important doctrines of Christianity. *Edifying of the body. The body of Christ* is His Church, see chap. ii. 20, etc.; and its edification consists in its thorough instruction in divine things, and its being filled with faith and holiness.

13. *In the unity of the faith.* Jews and Gentiles being all converted according to the doctrines laid down in the faith—the Christian system. *The knowledge of the Son of God.* A true understanding of the mystery of the Incarnation: why God was manifest in the flesh, and why this was necessary in order to have human salvation. *Unto a perfect man.* One thoroughly instructed; the whole body of the Church being fully taught, justified, sanctified, and sealed. *Measure of the stature.* The full measure of knowledge, love, and holiness which the gospel of Christ requires.

14. *Be no more children. Children,* here, are opposed to the "perfect man" in the preceding verse; and the state of both is well explained by the apostle's allusions. The man is grown up strong and healthy, and has attained such a measure or height as qualifies him for the most respectable place in the ranks of his country. The child is ignorant, weak, and unsteady, tossed about in the nurse's arms, or whirled round in the giddy sports or mazes of youth; this seems to be the apostle's allusion. *By the sleight of men.* The words refer to the arts used by gamesters, who employ false dice that will always throw up one kind of number, which is that by which those who play with them cannot win. *Cunning craftiness.* It is difficult to give a literal translation of the original words: "By cunning, for the purpose of using the various means of deception." *Panourgia* signifies "craft" and "subtlety" in general, "cheating" and "imposition." *Methodia,* from which we have our term "method," signifies a "wile, a particular sleight, mode of tricking and deceiving." It is applied to the arts which the devil uses to deceive and destroy souls; see chap. vi. 11, called there the "wiles of the devil." From this it seems that various arts were used, by both the Greek sophists and the Judaizing teachers, to render the gospel of none effect or to adulterate and corrupt it.

15. *But speaking the truth in love.* The *truth* recommended by the apostle is the whole system of gospel doctrine; this they are to teach and preach, and this is opposed to the deceit mentioned above. This truth, as it is the doctrine of God's eternal love to mankind, must be preached in *love.* Scolding and abuse from the pulpit or press, in matters of religion, are truly monstrous. *Grow up into him.* This is a continuance of the metaphor taken from the members of a human body receiving nourishment equally and growing up, each in its due proportion to other parts and to the body in general. The truth of God should be so preached to all the members of the Church of God that they may all receive an increase of grace and life; so that each, in whatever state he may be, may get forward in the way of truth and holiness.

16. *From whom the whole body.* This verse is another proof of the wisdom and learning of the apostle. Not only the general ideas here are anatomical, but the whole phraseology is the same: the articulation of the bones, the composition and action of the muscles, the circulation of the fluids, carrying nourishment to every part and depositing some in every place, the energy of the system in keeping up all the functions, being particularly introduced, and the whole terminating in the general process of

MATTHEW HENRY

Verses 17–32

There follows an exhortation to Christian purity and holiness of heart and life, and that both more general (*v.* 17–24) and in several particular instances, *v.* 25–32. This is solemnly introduced: "*This I say therefore, and testify in the Lord.*"

I. The more general exhortation to purity and holiness of heart and life.

1. "*That you henceforth walk not as other Gentiles walk.*" Converted Gentiles must not live as unconverted Gentiles do. Though they live among them, they must not live like them.

(1) The wickedness of the Gentile world. [1] Their *understandings were darkened, v.* 18. They were void of all saving knowledge. They sat in darkness, and they loved it rather than light: and by their ignorance they were *alienated from the life of God.* They were estranged from a life of holiness.

Their wilful ignorance was the cause of their estrangement from this life of God. And what was the cause of their being thus ignorant? It was *because of the blindness* or the hardness *of their heart.* It was not because God did not make himself known to them by his works. They were ignorant because they would be so. Their ignorance proceeded from their obstinacy. [2] Their consciences were debauched and seared: *Who being past feeling, v.* 19. They had no sense of their sin, nor of the danger of their case.

They *gave themselves over unto lasciviousness.* They indulged themselves in their filthy lusts. They became the slaves and drudges of sin and the devil, *working all uncleanness with greediness.* When men's consciences are once seared, there are no bounds to their sins.

(2) These Christians must distinguish themselves from such Gentiles: *You have not so learned Christ, v.* 20. It may be read, *But you not so; you have learned Christ.* Those who have learned Christ are saved from the darkness which others lie under; and, as they know more, they are obliged to live in a better manner than others. Learn Christ! Is Christ a book, a lesson, a way, a trade? "*If so be that you have heard him* (*v.* 21), *and have been taught by him.*" Christ is the lesson; we must learn Christ: and Christ is the teacher; we are taught by him. *As the truth is in Jesus.* "You have been taught the real truth, as held forth by Christ himself, both in his doctrine and in his life." The truth of Christ then appears in its beauty and power, when it appears as in Jesus.

2. Another branch of the general exhortation follows. *That you put off, concerning the former conversation, the old man, &c., v.* 22–24. Here the apostle expresses himself in metaphors taken from garments. There must be sanctification, which con-

JAMIESON, FAUSSET, BROWN

grace in each member (or else, rather, "according to *each several member's working*"), proportioned to the measure of its need of supply. **every part**—*Greek,* "each one part"; each individual part. **maketh increase**—Translate, as the *Greek* is the same as vs. 15, "maketh (carrieth on) the *growth* of the body." **17. therefore**—resuming the exhortation which he had begun with, "I *therefore* beseech you that ye *walk* worthy. . . ." (vs. 1). **testify in the Lord**—in whom (as our element) we do all things pertaining to the ministry (I Thess. 4:1 [ALFORD]; Rom. 9:1). **henceforth . . . not**—*Greek,* "no longer"; resumed from vs. 14. **other**—*Greek,* "the *rest* of the Gentiles." **in the vanity . . .**—as their element: opposed to "in the Lord." "Vanity of mind" is the *waste* of the rational powers on worthless objects, of which idolatry is one of the more glaring instances. The root of it is departure from the knowledge of the true God (vss. 18, 19; Rom. 1:21; I Thess. 4:5). **18.** More lit., "Being darkened in their understanding," i.e., their *intelligence,* or *perceptions* (cf. ch. 5:8; Acts 26:18; I Thess. 5:4, 5). **alienated**—This and "darkened," imply that before the fall they (in the person of their first father) had been partakers of *life* and *light:* and that they had revolted from the primitive revelation (cf. ch. 2:12). **life of God**—that life whereby God lives in His own people: as He was the *life* and *light* in Adam before the irruption of death and darkness into human nature; and as He is the life in the regenerate (Gal. 2:20). "Spiritual life in believers is kindled from the life itself of God" [BENGEL]. **through**—rather as *Greek,* "*on account of* the ignorance," viz., of God. Wilful ignorance in the first instance, their fathers not "choosing to retain God in their knowledge." This is the beginning point of their misery (Acts 17:30; Rom. 1:21, 23, 28; I Pet. 1:14). **because of**—"on account of." **blindness**—*Greek,* "hardness," lit., the hardening of the skin so as not to be sensible of touch. Hence a soul's *callousness to feeling* (Mark 3:5). Where there is spiritual "life" ("the life of God") there is feeling; where there is not, there is "hardness." **19. past feeling**—senseless, shameless, hopeless; the ultimate result of a long process of "hardening," or habit of sin (vs. 18). "Being past hope," or despairing, is the reading of the *Vulgate;* though not so well supported as *English Version* reading, "past feeling," which includes the absence of hope (Jer. 2:25; 18:12). **given themselves over**—In Romans 1:24 it is, "*God* gave them up to uncleanness." Their giving *themselves* to it was punished in kind, *God* giving them up to it by withdrawing His preventing grace; their sin thus was made their punishment. They gave themselves up of their own accord to the slavery of their lust, to do all its pleasure, as captives who have ceased to strive with the foe. *God* gave them up to it, but not against their will; for *they* give themselves up to it [ZANCHIUS]. **lasciviousness**—"wantonness" [ALFORD]. So it is translated in Romans 13:13; II Peter 2:18. It does not necessarily include *lasciviousness;* but it means *intemperate,* reckless readiness for it, and for every self-indulgence. "The first beginnings of unchastity" [GROTIUS]. "Lawless insolence, and wanton caprice" [TRENCH]. **to work all uncleanness**—The *Greek* implies, "*with a deliberate view* to the working (as if it were their *work* or *business,* not a mere accidental fall into sin) of uncleanness *of every kind.*" **with greediness**—*Greek,* "in greediness." *Uncleanness* and *greediness* of gain often go hand in hand (ch. 5:3, 5; Col. 3:5); though "greediness" here includes *all kinds* of *self-seeking.* **20. learned Christ**—(Phil. 3:10). To know Christ Himself, is the great lesson of the Christian life: this the Ephesians began to learn at their conversion. "Christ," in reference to His *office,* is here specified as the object of learning. "Jesus," in the following verse, as the *person.* **21. If so be that**—not implying doubt; assuming what I have no reason to doubt, that . . . . **heard him**—The Him is emphatic: heard *Himself,* not merely heard *about* Him. **taught by him**—*Greek,* "taught IN HIM," i.e., being in vital union with Him (Rom. 16:7). **as the truth is . . .**—Translate in connection with "taught"; "And in Him have been taught, according as is truth in Jesus." There is no article in the *Greek.* "Truth" is therefore used in the most comprehensive sense, truth in its essence, and highest perfection, in Jesus; "if *according as* it is thus in Him, ye have been so taught in Him"; in contrast to "the *vanity* of mind of the Gentiles" (vs. 17; cf. John 1:14, 17; 18:37). Contrast John 8:44. **22. That ye**—following "Ye have been taught" (vs. 21). **concerning the former conversation**—"in respect to your former way of life." **the old man**—your old unconverted nature (Rom. 6:6). **is corrupt according to the deceitful**

ADAM CLARKE

nutrition, increasing the body, and supplying all the waste that had taken place in consequence of labor.

17. *Walk not as other Gentiles walk.* You are called to holiness by the gospel, The other Gentiles have no such calling; walk not as they walk. In this and the following two verses the apostle gives a most awful account of the conduct of the heathens who were without the knowledge of the true God. (1) They walked *in the vanity of their mind.* "In the foolishness of their mind"; want of genuine wisdom is that to which the apostle refers, and it was through this that the Gentiles became addicted to every species of idolatry; and they fondly imagined that they could obtain help from gods which were the work of their own hands!

18. (2) *Having the understanding darkened.* This is the second instance alleged by the apostle of the degradation of the Gentiles. Having no means of knowledge, the heart, naturally dark, became more and more so by means of habitual transgression, everything in the Gentile system having an immediate tendency to blind the eyes and darken the whole soul. (3) *Being alienated from the life of God.* The original design of God was to live in man; and the life of God in the soul of man was that by which God intended to make man happy, and without which true happiness was never found by any human spirit: from this *through the ignorance that is in them,* through the "substantial" or continually existing ignorance, their moral state became so wretched that they are represented as "abhorring" everything spiritual and pure, for this is the import of the word which we translate *alienated* in some of the best Greek writers. They abhorred everything that had a tendency to lay any restraint on their vicious passions and inclinations. (4) *Blindness of their heart.* Because of the "callousness" of their hearts. "Callous" signifies a thickening of the outward skin of any particular part, especially on the hands and feet, by repeated exercise or use, through which such parts are rendered insensible. This may be metaphorically applied to the conscience of a sinner, which is rendered stupid and insensible by repeated acts of iniquity.

19. (5) *Who being past feeling.* The verb signifies: (*a*) To throw off all sense of shame, and to be utterly devoid of pain, for committing unrighteous acts; (*b*) To be desperate, having neither hope nor desire to reformation; in a word, to be without remorse, and to be utterly regardless of conduct, character, or final blessedness. Several excellent MSS. and versions have "being without hope"; that is, persons who, from their manner of life in this world, could not possibly hope for blessedness in the world to come. (6) *Have given themselves over unto lasciviousness. Lasciviousness* is here personified; and the Gentiles in question are represented as having delivered themselves over to her jurisdiction. This is a true picture of the Gentile world. (7) *To work all uncleanness with greediness.* This is a complete finish of the most abandoned character. To do an unclean act is bad; to labor in it is worse; to labor in "all uncleanness" is worse still. But to do all this in every case to the utmost extent, "with a desire exceeding" time, place, opportunity, and strength, is worst of all, and leaves nothing more profligate or more abandoned to be described or imagined.

20. *But ye have not so learned Christ.* You have received the doctrines of Christianity, and therefore are taught differently; you have received the Spirit of Christ, and therefore are saved from such dispositions. Some would point and translate the original thus: "But you are not thus; you have learned Christ."

21. *If so be that ye have heard him.* "Seeing that, since indeed," you have heard us proclaim His eternal truth; we have delivered it to you as we received it from Jesus.

22. *That ye put off.* And this has been one especial part of our teaching, that you should abandon all these, and live a life totally opposite to what it was before. *Which is corrupt.* The whole of your former life was corrupt and

MATTHEW HENRY

sists of these two things: (1) The old man must be put off. The corrupt nature is called a man. It is the old man, as old Adam, from whom we derive it. It is bred in the bone, and we brought it into the world with us. It is said to be corrupt; for sin in the soul is the corruption of its faculties: and where it is not mortified, it grows daily worse and worse. *According to the deceitful lusts.* They promise men happiness, but render them more miserable. These therefore must be put off as an old garment that we should be ashamed to be seen in. These lusts prevailed in their *former conversation.* (2) The new man must be put on. It is not enough to shake off corrupt principles, but we must be actuated by gracious ones. "*Be renewed in the spirit of your mind* (*v.* 23),

And that you put on the new man," *v.* 24. By the new man is meant the new nature, the new creature. This new man *is created*, or produced out of confusion and emptiness, by God's almighty power. *After God:* The loss of God's image upon the soul was both the sinfulness and misery of man's fallen state; and that resemblance which it bears to God is the glory, and the happiness, of the new creature.

In righteousness towards men *and in holiness* towards God. *True holiness* in opposition to the ceremonial holiness of the Jews. We are said to put on this new man when we are endeavouring after this divine nature.

II. Those particular limbs of the old man that must be mortified, those filthy rags of the old nature that must be put off, and what are the peculiar ornaments of the new man. 1. Take heed of lying, and be ever careful to speak the truth (*v.* 25): "*Wherefore, putting away lying.*" Of this sin the heathen were very guilty, affirming that a profitable lie was better than a hurtful truth. That branch of the new man that must be put on in opposition to it is *speaking the truth* in all our converse with others. All who have grace make conscience of speaking the truth. *We are members one of another.* Truth is a debt we owe to one another; and, if we love one another, we shall not deceive one another. We belong to the same society or body, which falsehood or lying tends to dissolve; and therefore we should avoid it, and speak truth. Lying is a very great sin. 2. "Take heed of anger and ungoverned passions. *Be you angry, and sin not,*" *v.* 26. Here is an easy concession; for as such we should consider it. *Be you angry.* This we are apt enough to be, God knows: but we find it difficult enough to observe the restriction, *and sin not.* If we would be angry and not sin (says one), we must be angry at nothing but sin. One great and common sin in anger is to suffer it to burn into wrath, and then to let it rest.

Before night calm and quiet your spirits, be reconciled to the offender: *Let not the sun go down upon your wrath.* Though anger in itself is not sinful, yet there is the utmost danger of its becoming so if it be not carefully watched.

JAMIESON, FAUSSET, BROWN

lusts—rather, "which is being corrupted ('perisheth,' cf. Gal. 6:8, 'corruption,' i.e., *destruction*) according to (i.e., as might be expected from) the lusts of deceit." *Deceit* is personified; *lusts* are its servants and tools. In contrast to "the holiness of the truth," vs. 24, and "truth in Jesus," vs. 21; and answering to Gentile "vanity," vs. 17. Corruption and destruction are inseparably associated together. The man's old-nature-lusts are his own executioners, fitting him more and more for eternal corruption and death. **23. be renewed**—The *Greek* (*ananeousthai*) implies "the *continued* renewal in the *youth* of the new man." A different *Greek* word (*anakainousthai*) implies "renewal *from the old state.*" **in the spirit of your mind**—As there is no *Greek* for "in," which there is at vs. 17, "*in* the vanity of their mind," it is better to translate, "*By* the Spirit of your mind," i.e., by your new spiritual nature; the restored and divinely informed leading principle of the mind. The "spirit" of man in New Testament is only then used in its proper sense, as worthy of its place and governing functions, when it is one spirit with the Lord. The natural, or animal man, is described as "not having the Spirit" (Jude 19) [ALFORD]. Spirit is not in this sense attributed to the unregenerate (I Thess. 5:23). **24. put on the new man**—Opposed to "the old man," which is to be "put off" (vs. 22). The *Greek* here (*kainon*) is different from that for "re-*new*-ed" (vs. 23). Put on not merely a *renovated* nature, but a new, i.e., altogether *different* nature, a changed nature (cf. Col. 3:10, *Note*). **after God . . .**—Translate, "Which hath been created (once for all: so the *Greek* aorist means: in Christ, ch. 2:10; so that in each believer it has not to be created again, but to be put on) after (the image of) God" (Gen. 1:27; Col. 3:10; I Pet. 1:15), etc. God's image in which the first Adam was originally created, is restored, to us far more gloriously in the second Adam, the image of the invisible God (II Cor. 4:4; Col. 1:15; Heb. 1:3). **in righteousness**—"IN" it as the *element* of the renewed man. **true holiness**—rather, as the *Greek*, "holiness *of the truth*"; holiness flowing from sincere following of "the truth of God" (Rom. 1:25; 3:7; 15:8): opposed to "the lusts *of deceit*" (*Greek*, vs. 22); cf. also vs. 21, "truth is in Jesus." "Righteousness" is in relation to our fellow men, the second table of the law; "Holiness," in relation to God, the first table; the religious observance of offices of piety (cf. Luke 1:75). In the parallel (Col. 3:10) it is, "renewed in *knowledge* after the image . . . ." As at Colosse the danger was from false pretenders to *knowledge,* the true "knowledge" which flows from renewal of the heart is dwelt on; so at Ephesus, the danger being from the corrupt morals prevalent around, the renewal in "holiness," contrasted with the Gentile "uncleanness" (vs. 19), and "righteousness," in contrast to "greediness," is made prominent. **25. Wherefore**—From the general character of "the new man," there will necessarily result the particular features which he now details. **putting away**—*Greek,* "having put away" *once for all.* **lying**—"falsehood": the abstract. "Speak ye truth each one with his neighbor," is quoted, slightly changed, from Zechariah 8:16. For "to," Paul quotes it "with," to mark our inner connection *with* one another, as "members *one of another*" [STIER]. Not merely members *of one body.* Union to one another in Christ, not merely the external command, instinctively leads Christians to fulfil mutual duties. One member could not injure or deceive another, without injuring himself, as all have a mutual and common interest. **26. Be ye angry, and sin not**—So the LXX, Psalm 4:4. Should circumstances arise to call for anger on your part, let it be as Christ's "anger" (Mark 3:5), without sin. Our natural feelings are not wrong when directed to their legitimate object, and when not exceeding due bounds. As in the future literal, so in the present spiritual, resurrection, no essential constituent is annihilated, but all that is a perversion of the original design is removed. Thus indignation at dishonor done to God, and wrong to man, is justifiable anger. *Passion* is sinful (derived from "passio," *suffering:* implying that amidst seeming energy. a man is really *passive*, the slave of his anger, instead of ruling it). **let not the sun go down upon your wrath**—"wrath" is absolutely forbidden; "anger" not so, though, like poison sometimes used as medicine, it is to be used with extreme caution. The sense is not, Your *anger* shall not be imputed to you if you put it away before nightfall; but "let no *wrath* (i.e., as the *Greek*, personal 'irritation' or 'exasperation') mingle with your 'anger,' even though the latter be righteous" [TRENCH, *Synonyms*]. "Put it away *before sunset*" (when the Jewish day began), is proverbial

ADAM CLARKE

abominable; you lived in the pursuit of pleasure and happiness; you sought this in the gratification of the lusts of the flesh; and were ever deceived by these lusts, and disappointed in your expectations.

23. *And be renewed in the spirit of your mind.* Their old mode of living was to be abandoned; a new one to be assumed. The mind is to be renovated, and not only its general complexion, but the very spirit of it; all its faculties and powers must be thoroughly, completely, and universally renewed.

24. *Put on the new man.* Get a new nature; for in Christ Jesus, under the Christian dispensation, neither circumcision avails anything, nor uncircumcision, but a new creation. Therefore you must be renewed in the spirit of your mind. *Which after God is created in righteousness.* Here is certainly an allusion to the creation of man. Moses tells us, Gen. i. 27, that "God created man in his own image"; that is, God was the Model according to which he was formed in the spirit of his mind. Paul says here that they should *put on the new man, which after God is created in righteousness and true holiness*, or "in the holiness of truth." Both certainly refer to the same thing, and the one illustrates the other. From the apostle we learn what Moses meant by the "image of God"; it was "righteousness and the truth of holiness."

25. *Wherefore putting away lying.* All falsity, all prevarication, because this is opposite to the truth as it is in Jesus, v. 21, and to the holiness of truth, v. 24. *Speak every man truth with his neighbour.* Truth was but of small account among many of even the best heathens, for they taught that on many occasions a lie was to be preferred to the truth itself. *We are members one of another.* Consider yourselves as one body, of which Jesus Christ is the Head; and as a man's right hand would not deceive or wrong his left hand, so deal honestly with each other.

26. *Be ye angry, and sin not.* Here is the same as "If ye be angry, do not sin." We can never suppose that the apostle delivers this as a precept, if we take the words as they stand in our version. Perhaps the sense is, "Take heed that you be not angry, lest you sin"; for it would be very difficult, even for an apostle himself, to be angry and not sin. If we consider anger as simply implying displeasure, then there are a multitude of cases in which a man may be innocently—yea, laudably—angry; for he should be displeased with everything which is not for the glory of God and the good of mankind. But, in any other sense, I do not see how the words can be safely taken. *Let not the sun go down upon your wrath.* That is: If you do get angry with anyone, see that the fire be cast with the utmost speed out of your bosom. Do not go to sleep with any unkind or unbrotherly feeling; anger, continued in, may produce malice and revenge.

MATTHEW HENRY	JAMIESON, FAUSSET, BROWN	ADAM CLARKE

Neither give place to the devil, *v.* 27. Those who persevere in sinful anger and in wrath let the devil into their hearts. "*Neither give place to the* calumniator, or the false accuser" (so some read the words); "let your ears be deaf to whisperers, tale-bearers, and slanderers." 3. We are here warned against the sin of stealing, and advised to honest industry and to beneficence: *Let him that stole steal no more*, *v.* 28. But we must not only take heed of the sin, but conscientiously abound in the opposite duty: not only not steal, *but rather let him labour, working with his hands the thing that is good.* Idleness makes thieves. Men should therefore be diligent and industrious, not in any unlawful way, but in some honest calling: *Working the thing which is good.* Industry will keep people out of temptation of doing wrong. But there is another reason that they may be capable of doing some good. *That he may have to give to him that needeth.* They must labour not only that they may live themselves. Those who have but little for themselves, must cast their mite into the treasury. God must have his dues and the poor are his receivers.

4. We are here warned against corrupt communication; and directed to that which is useful and edifying, *v.* 29. Filthy and unclean words and discourse are poisonous and infectious, as putrid rotten meat. Christians should beware of all such discourse. We must not only put off corrupt communication, but *put on that which is good to the use of edifying.* Christians should endeavour to promote a useful conversation: *that it may minister grace unto the hearers.* It is the great duty of Christians to take care that they offend not with their lips, and that they improve discourse for the good of others.

And grieve not the Holy Spirit of God, *v.* 30. We must not do that which is contrary to his holy nature and his will; we must not refuse to hearken to his counsels, nor rebel against his government. Provoke not the blessed Spirit of God to withdraw his presence and his gracious influences from you! *By him we are sealed unto the day of redemption.* The body is to be redeemed from the power of the grave at the resurrection-day; then our full and complete happiness commences. All true believers are sealed to that day. God has distinguished them from others, and the Spirit of God is the seal. We should be undone should God take away his Holy Spirit from us.

5. Another caution against wrath and anger, with further advice to mutual love, *v.* 31, 32. By *bitterness*, *wrath*, and *anger*, are meant violent inward resentment against others: and, by *clamour*, intemperate speeches, by which bitterness, wrath, and anger, vent themselves. Christians should not be clamorous with their tongues. *Evil speaking* signifies all railing against such as we are angry with. *Malice*, that rooted anger which prompts men to design mischief to others. The contrary to all this follows: *Be you kind one to another.* This implies the principle of love in the heart, and the outward expression of it. *Tender-hearted;* that is, merciful, so as to be quickly moved to compassion and pity.

for put it away *at once* before *another day begin* (Deut. 24:15); *also* before you part with your brother for the night, perhaps never in this world to meet again. So JONA, "Let not night and anger against anyone sleep with you, but go and conciliate the other party, though he have been the first to commit the offense." Let not your "anger" at another's wickedness verge into hatred, or contempt, or revenge [VATABLUS]. **27. Neither give place**—i.e., *occasion*, or *scope*, to the devil, by continuing in "wrath." The keeping of anger through the darkness of night, is giving place to the devil, the prince of darkness (ch. 6:12). **28.** *Greek*, "Let him that *stealeth*." The imperfect or *past* tense is, however, mainly meant, though not to the exclusion of the present. "Let the stealing person steal no more." *Bandits* frequented the mountains near Ephesus. Such are meant by those called "thieves" in the New Testament. **but rather**—For it is not enough to cease from a sin, but the sinner must also enter on the path that is its very opposite [CHRYSOSTOM]. The thief, when repentant, should labor more than he would be called on to do, if he had never stolen. **let him labour**—Theft and idleness go together. **the thing which is good**—in contrast with theft, the thing which was evil in his past character. **with his hands**—in contrast with his former thievish use of his hands. **that he may have to give**—"that he may have *wherewith* to *impart*." He who has stolen should exercise liberality beyond the restitution of what he has taken. Christians in general should make not selfish gain their aim in honest industry, but the acquisition of the means of greater usefulness to their fellow men; and the being independent of the alms of others. So Paul himself (Acts 20:35; II Thess. 3:8) acted as he taught (I Thess. 4:11). **29. corrupt**—lit., "insipid," without "the salt of grace" (Col. 4:6), so *worthless* and then becoming *corrupt:* included in "foolish talking" (ch. 5:4). Its opposite is "that which is good to edifying." **communication**—language. **that which . . .**—*Greek*, "*whatever* is good." **use of edifying**—lit., "for edifying of the need," i.e., *for edifying where it is needed*. Seasonably edifying; according as the occasion and present needs of the hearers require, now censure, at another time consolation. Even words good in themselves must be introduced seasonably lest by our fault they prove injurious instead of useful. TRENCH explains, Not vague generalities, which would suit a thousand other cases equally well, and probably equally ill: our words should be as nails fastened in a sure place, words suiting the present time and the present person, being "for the edifying of the occasion" (Col. 4:6). **minister**—*Greek*, "give." The word spoken "gives grace to the hearers" when God uses it as *His* instrument for that purpose. **30. grieve not**—A condescension to human modes of thought most touching. Cf. "*vexed* His Holy Spirit" (Isa. 63:10; Ps. 78:40); "fretted me" (Ezek. 16:43: implying His tender love to us); and of hardened unbelievers, "resist the Holy Ghost" (Acts 7:51). This verse refers to *believers*, who grieve the Spirit by inconsistencies such as in the context are spoken of, corrupt or worthless conversation, etc. **whereby ye are sealed**—rather, "wherein (or 'IN whom') ye *were* sealed." As in ch. 1:13, believers are said to be sealed "*in*" *Christ,* so here" *in the Holy Spirit,*" who is one with Christ, and who reveals Christ in the soul: the *Greek* implies that the sealing was done already once for all. It is the *Father* "BY" whom believers, as well as the Son Himself, were sealed (John 6:27). The Spirit is represented as itself the *seal* (ch. 1:13, where see, for the image employed, the *Note*). Here the Spirit *is the element* IN *which* the believer is sealed, His gracious influences being the seal itself. **unto**—kept safely against the day of redemption, viz., of the *completion* of redemption in the deliverance of the body as well as the soul from all sin and sorrow (ch. 1:14; Luke 21:28; Rom. 8:23). **31. bitterness**—both of spirit and of speech: opposed to "kind." **wrath**—passion for a time: opposed to "tender-hearted." Whence BENGEL translates for "wrath," *harshness*. **anger**—lasting resentment: opposed to "forgiving one another." **clamour**—compared by CHRYSOSTOM to a horse carrying anger for its rider: "Bridle the horse, and you dismount its rider." "Bitterness" begets "wrath"; "wrath," "anger"; "anger," "clamor"; and "clamor," the more chronic "evil-speaking," slander, insinuations, and surmises of evil. "Malice" is the secret root of all: "fires fed within, and not appearing to bystanders from without, are the most formidable" [CHRYSOSTOM]. **32.** (Luke 7:42; Col. 3:12.) **even as**—God hath shown Himself "kind, tender-hearted, and forgiving to you"; it is but just that you in turn shall be so to your fellow men,

27. *Neither give place to the devil.* Your adversary will strive to influence your mind and irritate your spirit; watch and pray that he may not get any place in you, or ascendancy over you. As the word *diabolos* is sometimes used to signify a "calumniator, talebearer, whisperer, or backbiter," here it may have the same signification: Do not open your ear to the talebearer, to the slanderer, who comes to you with accusations against your brethren, or with surmisings and evil speakings.

28. *Let him that stole steal no more.* Stealing, overreaching, defrauding, purloining, etc., are consistent with no kind of religion that acknowledges the true God. If Christianity does not make men honest, it does nothing for them.

29. *Let no corrupt communication.* "A "useless, putrid, unsavory, and obscene word or conversation." *But that which is good to the use of edifying.* To be good for a thing is a Graecism, as well as an Anglicism, for to be "fit, proper, suitable." *That it may minister grace.* This may be understood thus: (1) Let your conversation be pure, wise, and holy, that it may be the means of conveying grace, or divine influences, to them that hear. (2) Let it be such as to be grateful or acceptable to the hearers. This is the meaning in some of the most correct Greek writers. Never wound modesty, truth, or religion with your discourse; endeavor to edify those with whom you converse; and, if possible, speak so as to please them.

30. *Grieve not the holy Spirit of God* by giving way to any wrong temper, unholy word, or unrighteous action. Even those who have already a measure of the light and life of God, both of which are not only brought in by the Holy Spirit, but maintained by His constant indwelling, may give way to sin, and so grieve this Holy Spirit that He shall withdraw both His light and presence; and in proportion as He withdraws, then hardness and darkness take place. What is still worse, a state of insensibility is the consequence; for the darkness prevents the fallen state from being seen, and the hardness prevents it from being felt. *Whereby ye are sealed.* The Holy Spirit in the soul of a believer is God's Seal, set on his heart to testify that he is God's property, and that he should be wholly employed in God's service.

31. *Let all bitterness.* It is astonishing that any who profess the Christian name should indulge bitterness of spirit. Those who are censorious, who are unmerciful to the failings of others, who have fixed a certain standard by which they measure all persons in all circumstances, and unchristianize everyone that does not come up to this standard, these have the *bitterness* against which the apostle speaks. *And wrath.* More properly "anger," which may be considered the commencement of the passion. *Anger.* More properly "wrath"—the passion carried to its highest pitch, accompanied with injurious words and outrageous acts, some of which are immediately specified. *And clamour.* Loud and obstreperous speaking, brawling, railing, boisterous talk, often the offspring of wrath; all of which are highly unbecoming the meek, loving, quiet, sedate mind of Christ and His followers. *And evil speaking.* "Blasphemy"; that is, "injurious speaking"—words which tend to hurt those of whom or against whom they are spoken. *With all malice.* "All malignity"; as anger produces wrath, and wrath clamor, so all together produce malice; that is, settled, sullen, fell wrath, which is always looking out for opportunities to revenge itself by the destruction of the object of its indignation.

32. *Be ye kind one to another.* Be kind and obliging to each other; study good breeding and gentleness of manners. A Christian cannot be a savage, and he need not be a boor. Never put any person to needless pain. *Tenderhearted.* "Compassionate."

MATTHEW HENRY

Forgiving one another. Occasions of difference will happen among Christ's disciples; and therefore they must be ready to forgive, therein resembling God himself, who *for Christ's sake hath forgiven them.* Those who are forgiven of God should be of a forgiving spirit, and should forgive even as God forgives. All these particulars that the apostle has insisted on belong to the second table. He who does not conscientiously discharge them can never fear nor love God in truth and in sincerity, whatever he may pretend to.

CHAPTER 5

Verses 1, 2

Exhortation to mutual love. "Because God, for Christ's sake, has forgiven you, therefore be you followers of God, or *imitators* of him"; for so the word signifies. This puts a great honour upon practical religion, that it is the imitating of God. We must be holy as God is holy, merciful as he is merciful, perfect as he is perfect. But there is no one attribute of God more recommended to our imitation than that of his goodness. Be you imitators of God, especially in his love. *As dear children,* as children (who are wont to be greatly beloved by their parents) usually resemble them in the features of their faces, and in the dispositions of their minds. Children are obliged to imitate their parents in what is good, especially when dearly beloved by them. The character that we bear of God's children obliges us to resemble him. And those only are God's dear children who imitate him. *And walk in love, v.* 2. It should be the principle from which we act; it should direct the ends at which we aim. *As Christ also hath loved us.* We are all joint sharers in that love and therefore should love one another, Christ having loved us all, *he hath given himself for us.*

An offering and a sacrifice to God; or an offering, even a sacrifice, *for a sweet-smelling savour.* As he offered himself with a design to be accepted of God, so God did accept, was pleased with, that sacrifice. His example should be prevailing with us, and we should carefully copy it.

Verses 3–20

Filthy lusts must be suppressed, in order to the supporting of holy love. *Walk in love,* and *shun fornication and all uncleanness.* Now these sins must be dreaded and detested in the highest degree: *Let it not be once named among you as becometh saints.* The apostle not only cautions against the gross acts of sin, but against what some may be apt to make light of, and think to be excusable.

Neither filthiness (*v.* 4), *nor foolish talking,* such vain discourse as betrays much folly and indiscretion, *nor jesting.* There is no doubt an innocent and inoffensive jesting, which we cannot suppose the apostle here forbids. But the context seems to restrain it to such pleasantry of discourse as is filthy and obscene.

They are not convenient. Indeed there is more than inconvenience, even a great deal of mischief, in them. Those things do not become Christians. Christians are allowed to be cheerful and pleasant; but they must be merry and wise.

JAMIESON, FAUSSET, BROWN

who have not erred against you in the degree that you have erred against God (Matt. 18:33). **God for Christ's sake**—rather as *Greek,* "God in Christ" (II Cor. 5:19). It is *in Christ* that God vouchsafes forgiveness to us. It cost God the death of His Son, as man, to forgive us. It costs us nothing to forgive our fellow man. **hath forgiven**—rather as *Greek,* "*forgave* you." God has, *once for all,* forgiven sin in Christ, as a *past historical fact.*

CHAPTER 5

Vss. 1-33. Exhortations to Love: and against Carnal Lusts and Communications. Circumspection in Walk: Redeeming the Time: Being Filled with the Spirit: Singing to the Lord with Thankfulness: The Wife's Duty to the Husband Rests on That of the Church to Christ. **1. therefore**—seeing that "God in Christ forgave you" (ch. 4:32). **followers**—*Greek,* "imitators" of God, in respect to "love" (vs. 2): God's essential character (I John 4: 16). **as dear children**—*Greek,* "as children *beloved*"; to which vs. 2 refers, "As Christ also *loved* us" (I John 4:19). "We are sons of men, when we do ill; sons of God, when we do well" [Augustine, Ps. 52]; (cf. Matt. 5:44, 45, 48). Sonship infers an absolute necessity of *imitation,* it being vain to assume the title of son without any similitude of the Father [Pearson]. **2. And**—in proof that you are so. **walk**—resuming ch. 4:1, "*walk* worthy of the vocation. . . ." **as Christ . . . loved us**—From the love of the Father he passes to the love of the Son, in whom God most endearingly manifests His love to us. **given himself for us**—*Greek,* "given Himself *up* (viz., to death, Gal. 2:20) for us," i.e., *in our behalf:* not here vicarious substitution, though that is *indirectly* implied, "in *our* stead." The offerer, and the offering that He offered, were one and the same (John 15:13; Rom. 5:8). **offering and a sacrifice**—"Offering" expresses *generally* His presenting Himself to the Father, as the Representative undertaking the cause of the whole of our lost race (Ps. 40:6-8), including His *life* of obedience; though not excluding His offering of His body for us (Heb. 10: 10). It is usually an *unbloody offering,* in the more limited sense. "Sacrifice" refers to His *death* for us exclusively. Christ is here, in reference to Psalm 40:6 (quoted again in Heb. 10:5), represented as the antitype of all the offerings of the law, whether the unbloody or bloody, eucharistical or propitiatory. **for a sweet-smelling savour**—*Greek,* "for an odor of a sweet smell," i.e., God is well pleased with the offering on the ground of its sweetness,and so is reconciled to us (ch. 1:6; Matt. 3:17; II Cor. 5:18, 19; Heb. 10:6-17). The ointment compounded of principal spices, poured upon Aaron's head, answers to the variety of the graces by which He was enabled to "offer Himself a sacrifice for a sweet-smelling savor." Another type, or prophecy by figure, was "the sweet savor" (*savor of rest, Margin*) which God smelled in Noah's sacrifice (Gen. 8:21). Again, as what Christ is, believers also are (I John 4:17), and ministers are: Paul says (II Cor. 2:17) "we are unto God a sweet savor of Christ." **3. once named**—*Greek,* "Let it not be even named" (vss. 4, 12). "Uncleanness" and "covetousness" are taken up again from ch. 4:19. The two are so closely allied that the *Greek* for "covetousness" (*pleonexia*) is used sometimes in Scripture, and often in the Greek Fathers, for sins of impurity. The common principle is the longing to fill one's desire with material objects of sense, outside of God. The expression, "not be even named," applies better to impurity, than to "covetousness." **4. filthiness**—obscenity in *act* or *gesture.* **foolish talking**—the *talk* of fools, which is folly and sin together. The *Greek* of it, and of "filthiness," occurs nowhere else in the New Testament. **nor**—rather, "or" (cf. vs. 3). **jesting**—*Greek,* "*eutrapelia*"; found nowhere else in the New Testament: implying strictly that *versatility* which turns about and adapts itself, without regard to principle, to the shifting circumstances of the moment, and to the varying moods of those with whom it may deal. Not scurrile buffoonery, but refined "persiflage" and "badinage," for which Ephesus was famed (Plautus, *Miles Gloriosus,* 3.1, 42-52), and which, so far from being censured, was and is thought by the world a pleasant accomplishment. In Colossians 3:8, "filthy communication" refers to the *foulness;* "foolish talking," to the *folly;* "jesting," to the *false refinement* [and *trifling witticism,* Tittmann] of discourse unseasoned with the salt of grace [Trench]. **not convenient**—"unseemly"; not

ADAM CLARKE

Forgiving one another. Should you receive any injury from a brother, or from any man, be as ready to forgive him, on his repentance and acknowledgment, as God was, for Christ's sake, to forgive you when you repented of your sins, and took refuge in His mercy.

CHAPTER 5

1. *Be ye therefore followers of God.* The beginning of this chapter is properly a continuation of the preceding, which should have ended with the second verse of this. The word which we translate *followers* signifies such as personate others, assuming it is from this Greek word that we have the word "mimic." Though this term is often used in a ludicrous sense, yet here it is to be understood in a very solemn and proper sense. Let your whole conduct be like that of your Lord; "imitate" Him in all your actions, words, spirit, and inclinations; imitate Him as children do their beloved parents, and remember that you stand in the relation of beloved children to Him.

2. *And walk in love.* Let every act of life be dictated by love to God and man. *As Christ also hath loved us.* Laying down your lives for your brethren if necessary; counting nothing too difficult to be done in order to promote their eternal salvation. *Hath given himself for us.* Christ has died in our stead, and become thereby a Sacrifice for our sins. *An offering.* An oblation, a eucharistic offering. It means any offering by which gratitude was expressed for temporal blessings received from the bounty of God. *A sacrifice.* A "sin offering, a victim for sin." These terms may be justly considered as including every kind of sacrifice, offering, and oblation made to God on any account; and both these terms are with propriety used here, because the apostle's design was to represent the sufficiency of the offering made by Christ for the sin of the world. *For a sweetsmelling savour.* The same as is expressed in Gen. viii. 21; Lev. i. 9; iii. 16: "a sweet savour unto the Lord"; i.e., an offering of His own prescription, and one with which He was well-pleased, and by accepting of which He showed that He accepted the person who offered it. The *sweetsmelling savour* refers to the burnt offerings, the fumes of which ascended from the fire in the act of burning; and as such odors are grateful to man, God represents himself as pleased with them when offered by an upright worshipper according to His own appointment.

3. *But fornication.* It is probable that the three terms used here by the apostle refer to different species of the same thing. The word *fornication* may imply not only fornication but adultery also, as it frequently does; *uncleanness* may refer to all abominable and unnatural lusts—sodomy, bestiality, etc.; and *covetousness,* to "excessive indulgence" in that which, moderately used, is lawful. As the covetous man never has enough of wealth, so the pleasure-taker and the libertine never have enough of the gratifications of sense, the appetite increasing in proportion to its indulgence. If, however, simple *covetousness,* i.e., the "love of gain," be here intended, it shows from the connection in which it stands (for it is linked with fornication and all uncleanness) how degrading it is to the soul of man and how abominable it is in the eye of God. In other places it is ranked with idolatry, for the man who has an inordinate love of gain makes money his god. *Let it not be once named.* Let no such things ever exist among you, for you are called to be saints.

4. *Neither filthiness.* Anything base or vile in words or acts. *Foolish talking.* Scurrility, buffoonery, ridicule, or what tends to expose another to contempt. *Nor jesting.* Artfully turned discourses or words; words that can be easily turned to other meanings; chaste words which, from their connection and the manner in which they are used, convey an obscene or offensive meaning. *Which are not convenient.* "They do not come up" to the proper standard; they are utterly improper in themselves, and highly unbecoming in those who profess Chris-

MATTHEW HENRY

But rather giving of thanks: that he may delight his mind, and make himself cheerful, by a grateful remembrance of God's goodness and mercy to him, and by blessing and praising him on account of these. A reflection on the grace and goodness of God to us, to excite our thankfulness to him, is proper to delight the Christian's mind, and to make him cheerful. If men abounded more in good and pious expressions, they would not be so apt to utter ill and unbecoming words.

I. To fortify us against the sins of uncleanness, &c., the apostle urges several arguments, and prescribes several remedies.

1. He urges several arguments, (1) Consider that these are sins which shut persons out of heaven: *For this you know,* &c., *v.* 5. There is spiritual idolatry in the love of this world. As the epicure makes a god of his belly, so the covetous man makes a god of his money. He serves mammon instead of God. Of these persons it is said that they *have no inheritance in the kingdom of Christ and of God.* In this kingdom the saints and servants of God have an inheritance. But those who allow themselves either in the lusts of the flesh or the love of the world, belong not to the kingdom of grace, nor shall they ever come to the kingdom of glory. Let us then be on our guard against those sins which would shut us out of heaven. (2) These sins bring the wrath of God upon those who are guilty of them: "*Let no man deceive you with vain words,*" &c., *v.* 6. Those who flatter themselves with hopes of impunity in sin do but put a cheat upon themselves. They are *vain words* indeed, *for because of these things cometh the wrath of God upon the children of disobedience.* Disobedience is the very malignity of sin. *The wrath of God comes upon* such, sometimes in this world, but more especially in the next. And dare we make light of that which will lay us under the wrath of God? *Be not you therefore partakers with them, v.* 7. "Do not partake with them in their sins, that you may not share in their punishment." (3) Consider what obligations Christians are under to live at another rate, *For you were sometimes darkness, but now,* &c., *v.* 8. The apostles call their former condition *darkness.* A state of sin is a state of darkness. Sinners, like men in the dark, are going they know not whither, and doing they know not what. *Now are you light in the Lord. Walk as children of light.* "Now, being such, live up to the obligation you are under by that knowledge and those advantages you enjoy".

2. Some remedies against them. (1) We must bring forth *the fruits of the Spirit, v.* 9. This is expected from the children of light, that they be also sanctified by the Spirit, and thereupon bring forth his fruit, which *is in all goodness and righteousness.* All religion is goodness and righteousness. With these must be *truth.*

—Proving what is acceptable unto the Lord (*v.* 10), searching diligently what God has revealed to be his will. We must not only dread and avoid that which is displeasing to God, but enquire and consider what will be acceptable to him.

(2) We must have no fellowship with sin nor sinners, *v.* 11. Sinful works are works of darkness. These works of darkness are *unfruitful works;* there is nothing got by them in the long run, whatever profit is pretended by sin, it will by no means balance the loss. We must therefore *have no fellowship* with these unfruitful works. If we share with others in their sin, we must expect to share with them in their plagues. Rather than have fellowship with them, we must *reprove them.* We must witness against the sins of others, and endeavour to convince them of their sinfulness in our words; but especially by the holiness of our lives. Reprove their sins by abounding in the contrary duties.

For it is a shame even to speak of those things, &c., *v.* 12; much more must it be a shame to have any fellowship with them. *The things which are done of them in secret.* A good man is ashamed to speak that which many wicked people are not ashamed to act.

JAMIESON, FAUSSET, BROWN

such "as become saints" (vs. 3). **rather giving of thanks**—a happy play on sounds in *Greek, eucharistia* contrasted with *eutrapelia;* refined "jesting" and subtle humor sometimes offend the tender feelings of grace; "giving of thanks" gives that real cheerfulness of spirit to believers which the worldly try to get from "jesting" (vs. 19, 20; Jas. 5:13). **5. this ye know**—The oldest MSS. read, "Of this ye are sure knowing"; or as ALFORD, "This ye know being aware." **covetous . . . idolater**—(Col. 3:5). The best reading may be translated, That is to say, lit., *which is* (in other words) *an idolater.* Paul himself had forsaken all for Christ (II Cor. 6:10; 11:27). Covetousness is worship of the creature instead of the Creator, the highest treason against the King of kings (I Sam. 15:3; Matt. 6:24; Phil. 3:19; I John 2:15). **hath**—The *present* implies the fixedness of the exclusion, grounded on the eternal verities of that kingdom [ALFORD]. **of Christ and of God**—rather, as one *Greek* article is applied to both, "of Christ and God," implying their perfect oneness, which is consistent only with the doctrine that Christ is God (cf. II Thess. 1:12; I Tim. 5:21; 6:13). **6. vain**—empty, unreal words, viz., palliations of "uncleanness," vss. 3, 4; Isaiah 5:20 (that it is natural to indulge in love), "covetousness" (that it is useful to society that men should pursue gain), and "jesting" (that it is witty and clever, and that God will not so severely punish for such things). **because of these things**—*uncleanness, covetousness,* etc. (vss. 3-5). **cometh**—present, not merely "shall come." Is as sure as if already come. **children**—rather, "*sons* of disobedience" (ch. 2:2, 3). The children of unbelief in doctrine (Deut. 32:20) are "children of disobedience" in *practice,* and these again are "children of wrath." **7.** Here fellowship with wicked workers is forbidden; in vs. 11, with their wicked works. **8. sometimes**—"once." The emphasis is on "were." Ye ought to have no fellowship with sin, which is darkness, for your state as darkness is now PAST. Stronger than "in darkness" (Rom. 2:19). **light**—not merely "enlightened"; but *light* enlightening others (vs. 13). **in**—in union with the Lord, who is THE LIGHT. **children of light**—not merely "of the light"; just as "children of disobedience" is used on the opposite side; those whose distinguishing characteristic is *light.* PLINY, a heathen writing to Trajan, bears unwilling testimony to the extraordinary purity of Christians' lives, contrasted with the people around them. **9. fruit of the Spirit**—taken by transcribers from Galatians 5:22. The true reading is that of the oldest MSS., "The fruit of THE LIGHT"; in contrast with "the unfruitful works of darkness" (vs. 11). This verse is parenthetic. Walk as children of light, i.e., in all good works and words, "FOR the fruit of the light is [borne] in [ALFORD; but BENGEL, 'consists in'] all goodness [opposed to 'malice,' ch. 4:31], righteousness [opposed to 'covetousness,' vs. 3] and truth" [opposed to "lying," ch. 4:25]. **10. Proving**—construed with "walk" (vs. 8; Rom. 12:1, 2). As we prove a coin by the eye and the ear, and by using it, so by accurate and continued study, and above all by *practice* and experimental trial, we may prove or test "what is acceptable unto the Lord." This is the office of "light," of which believers are "children," to manifest what each thing is, whether sightly or unsightly. **11. unfruitful works of darkness**—Sins are terminated in themselves, and therefore are called "works," not "fruits" (Gal. 5:19, 22). Their only fruit is that which is not in a true sense fruit (Deut. 32:32), viz., "death" (Rom. 6:21; Gal. 6:8). Plants cannot bear "fruit" in the absence of light. Sin is "darkness," and its parent is *the prince of darkness* (ch. 6:12). Graces, on the other hand, as flourishing in "the light," are reproductive, and abound in fruits; which, as harmoniously combining in *one* whole, are termed (in the singular) "the FRUIT of the Spirit" (vs. 9). **rather . . .**—Translate as *Greek,* "rather *even* reprove them" (cf. Matt. 5:14-16). Not only "have no fellowship, but *even* reprove them," viz., in words, and in your deeds, which, shining with "the light," virtually reprove all that is contrary to light (vs. 13; John 3:19-21). "Have no fellowship," does not imply that we can avoid all intercourse (I Cor. 5:10), but "avoid such fellowship as will defile yourselves"; just as light, though it touch filth, is not soiled by it; nay, as light *detects* it, so, "even *reprove* sin." **12.** The *Greek* order is, "For the things done in secret by them, it is a shame even to speak of." The "for" gives his reason for "not naming" (cf. vs. 3) in detail the works of darkness, whereas he describes definitely (vs. 9) "the fruit of the light" [BENGEL]. "Speak of," I think, is used here as "speaking of *without reproving,*" in contrast to "even reprove them." Thus the "for" expresses this, Reprove them, for

ADAM CLARKE

tianity. *But rather giving of thanks.* Prayer or praise is the most suitable language for man; and he who is of a trifling, light disposition is ill fitted for either.

5. *For this ye know.* You must be convinced of the dangerous and ruinous tendency of such a spirit and conduct, when you know that persons of this character can never inherit the kingdom of God.

6. *Let no man deceive you.* Suffer no man to persuade you that any of these things are innocent, or that they are unavoidable frailties of human nature. They are all sins and abominations in the sight of God; those who practice them are *children of disobedience;* and on account of such practices the *wrath of God,* divine punishment, must come upon them.

7. *Be not ye therefore partakers with them.* Do not act as your fellow citizens do; nor suffer their philosophy, *with vain words,* with "empty doctrines," to lead you astray from the path of truth.

8. *For ye were sometimes* ("formerly") *darkness.* While you lived in darkness, you lived in these crimes. *But now are ye light in the Lord.* When you were in heathenish *darkness* you served divers lusts and pleasures, but now you have the *light*—the wisdom and teaching which come from God; therefore *walk as children of the light*—let the world see that you are not slaves to the flesh, but free, willing, rational servants of the Most High.

9. *For the fruit of the Spirit.* Instead of *Spirit,* some MSS., together with several of the fathers, read "light," which is supposed by most critics to be the true reading, because there is no mention made of the Spirit in any part of the context. As light, v. 8, not only means the divine influence upon the soul, but also the gospel, with great propriety it may be said: The fruit of the light, i.e., of the gospel, *is in all goodness and righteousness and truth. Goodness,* in the principle and disposition; *righteousness,* the exercise of that goodness in the whole conduct of life; *truth,* the director of that principle, and its exercise, to the glorification of God and the good of mankind.

10. *Proving what is acceptable.* By walking in the light—under the influence of the divine Spirit, according to the dictates of the gospel—you shall be able to try and bring to full proof that by which God is best pleased. You shall be able to please Him well in all things.

11. *Have no fellowship.* Have no religious connection whatever with heathens or their worship. *Unfruitful works of darkness.* Probably alluding to the mysteries among the heathens, and the different lustrations and rites through which the initiated went in the caves and dark recesses where these mysteries were celebrated; all which he denominates *works of darkness,* because they were destitute of true wisdom; and *unfruitful works,* because they were of no use to mankind, the initiated being obliged, on pain of death, to keep secret what they had seen, heard, and done. *Rather reprove them.* Bear a "testimony" against them; "convince" them that they are wrong; "confute" them in their vain reasons; *reprove* them for their vices, which are flagrant, while pretending to superior illumination. All these meanings has the Greek word which we generally render "to convince" or "reprove."

12. *For it is a shame even to speak.* This no doubt refers to the Eleusinian and Bacchanalian mysteries, which were performed in the night and darkness, and were known to be so impure and abominable, especially the latter, that the Roman senate banished them both from Rome and Italy.

MATTHEW HENRY

But all things that are reproved are made manifest by the light, v. 13. By that instructive light which is diffused by the holiness of your lives and by your exemplary walk. *For whatsoever doth make manifest is light,* and accordingly it becomes those who are *children of light,* who are *light in the Lord,* to discover to others their sins, thus shining as lights in the world.

The apostle further urges this duty from the example of God or Christ: *Wherefore he saith,* &c. (*v.* 14). *Awake, thou that sleepest, and arise from the dead.*

They would break off their sins by repentance, and he encourages them to do their utmost that way, by that gracious promise, *And Christ shall give thee light.* When we are endeavouring to convince sinners, and to reform them from their sins, we are imitating God and Christ in that which is their great design throughout the gospel. (3) Another remedy against sin is circumspection, (*v.* 15): *Sce then,* &c. "If you arc to reprove others for their sins you must look well to yourselves, and to your own behaviour and conduct." We have here another preservative from the before-mentioned sins; it being impossible to maintain purity and holiness of heart and life without great circumspection and care. *Walk circumspectly,* exactly in the right way, in order to which we must be frequently consulting our rule. *Not as fools,* who walk at all adventures, and who through neglect, and want of care, fall into sin, and destroy themselves; *but as wise,* as persons taught of God. Circumspect walking is the effect of true wisdom, but the contrary is the effect of folly. *Redeeming the time* (*v.* 16), literally, *buying the opportunity.* It is a metaphor taken from merchants and traders who diligently observe and improve the seasons for merchandise and trade. Good Christians must be good husbands of their time. They should make the best use they can of the present seasons of grace. Our time is a talent given us by God for some good end, and it is misspent and lost when it is not employed according to his design. If we have lost our time heretofore, we must endeavour to redeem it by doubling our diligence for the future.

Because the days are evil. Those were times of persecution wherein the apostle wrote this: the Christians were in jeopardy every hour. When the days are evil we know not how soon they may be worse. People are very apt to complain of bad times; it were well if that would stir them up to redeem time.

"*Wherefore* (*v.* 17), *be you not unwise, but understanding what the will of the Lord is.*" Acquaintance with the will of God, and a care to comply with it, bespeak the best and truest wisdom.

JAMIESON, FAUSSET, BROWN

to *speak of* them *without reproving* them, is a shame (vs. 3). Thus "works of *darkness*" answers to "things done *in secret.*" **13. that are reproved**—rather, "when they are reproved," viz., by you (vs. 11). **whatsoever doth make manifest**—rather, "everything that is (i.e., suffers itself to be) made manifest (or 'shone upon,' viz., by your 'reproving,' vs. 11) is (thenceforth no longer 'darkness,' vs. 8, but) light." The devil and the wicked will not suffer themselves to be made manifest by the light, but love darkness, though *outwardly* the light shines round them. Therefore, "light" has no transforming effect on *them,* so that they do not become light (John 3:19, 20). But, says the apostle, you being now light yourselves (vs. 8), by bringing to light through reproof those who are in darkness, will convert them to light. Your consistent lives and faithful reproofs will be your "armor of light" (Rom. 13:12) in making an inroad on the kingdom of darkness. **14. Wherefore**—referring to the whole foregoing argument (vss. 8, 11, 13). Seeing that light (spiritual) dispels the pre-existing darkness, He (God) saith . . . (cf. the same phrase, ch. 4:8). **Awake**—The reading of all the oldest MSS. is "Up!" or, "Rouse thee!" a phrase used in stirring men to activity. The words are a paraphrase of Isaiah 60: 1, 2, not an exact quotation. The word "Christ," shows that in quoting the prophecy, he views it in the light thrown on it by its *Gospel fulfilment.* As Israel is called on to "awake" from its previous state of "darkness" and "death" (Isa. 59:10; 60:2), for that her Light is come; so the Church, and each individual is similarly called to awake. *Believers* are called on to "awake" out of *sleep; unbelievers,* to "arise" from the *dead* (cf. Matt. 25:5; Rom. 13: 11; I Thess. 5:6, with ch. 2:1). **Christ**—"the true light," "the Sun of righteousness." **give thee light**—rather, as *Greek,* "shall shine upon thee" (so enabling thee by being "made manifest" to become, and be, by the very fact, "light," vs. 13; then being so "enlightened," ch. 1:18, thou shalt be able, by "reproving," to enlighten others). **15. that**—rather as *Greek,* "See *how* ye walk. . . ." The double idea is compressed into one sentence: "See (take heed) *how* ye walk," and "See *that* ye walk circumspectly." The *manner,* as well as the *act* itself, is included. See *how* ye are walking, with a view to your *being* circumspect (lit., *accurate, exact*) in your walk. Cf. Colossians 4:5, "Walk in *wisdom* (answering to 'as wise' here) toward them that are without" (answering to "circumspectly," i.e., *correctly, in relation to the unbelievers around,* not giving occasion of stumbling to any, but edifying all by a consistent walk). **not as fools**—*Greek,* "not as unwise, but as wise." **16. Redeeming the time**—(Col. 4:5). *Greek,* "Buying up for yourselves the seasonable time" (whenever it occurs) of good to yourselves and to others. Buying *off from* the vanities of "them that are without" (Col. 4:5), and of the "unwise" (here in Ephesians), the opportune time afforded to you for the work of God. In a narrower sense, *special favorable seasons for good,* occasionally presenting themselves, are referred to, of which believers ought diligently to avail themselves. This constitutes true "wisdom" (vs. 15). In a larger sense, *the whole season from the time that one is spiritually awakened,* is to be "redeemed" from vanity for God (cf. II Cor. 6:2; I Pet. 4:2-4). "Redeem" implies the preciousness of the opportune season, a jewel to be bought at any price. WAHL explains, "Redeeming for yourselves (i.e., availing yourselves of) the opportunity (offered you of acting aright), and commanding the time as a master does his servant." TITTMANN, "Watch the time, and make it your own so as to control it; as merchants look out for opportunities, and accurately choose out the best goods; serve not the time, but command it, and it shall do what you approve." So PINDAL, *Pythia,* 4. 509, "The time followed him as his servant, and was not as a runaway slave." **because the days are evil**—The days of life in general are so exposed to evil, as to make it necessary to make the most of the seasonable opportunity so long as it lasts (ch. 6:13 Gen. 47:9; Ps. 49:5; Eccles. 11:2; 12:1; John 12:35). Besides, there are many *special* evil days (in persecution, sickness, etc.) when the Christian is laid by in silence; therefore he needs the more to improve the seasonable times afforded to him (Amos 5:13), which Paul perhaps alludes to. **17. Wherefore**—seeing that ye need to walk so circumspectly, choosing and using the right opportunity of good. **unwise**—a different *Greek* word from that in vs. 15. Translate, "foolish," or "senseless." **understanding**—not merely *knowing* as a matter of fact (Luke 12:47), but *knowing with understanding.* **the will of the Lord**—as to how each opportunity is to be used. The Lord's will, ulti-

ADAM CLARKE

14. *Wherefore he saith.* It is a matter of doubt and controversy whence this saying is derived. Some think it taken from Isa. xxvi. 19: "Thy dead men shall live, together with my dead body shall they arise. Awake and sing, ye that dwell in the dust." Others think that it is taken from Isa. lx. 1-3: "Arise, shine; for thy light is come." But it seems more natural to understand the words *he saith* as referring to the light, i.e., the gospel, mentioned in v. 13; and should be translated, "Wherefore it saith, Awake thou." That is, This is the general, the strong, commanding voice of the gospel in every part—Receive instruction; leave your sins, which are leading you to perdition; believe on the Lord Jesus Christ, and He will enlighten and save you.

15. *Walk circumspectly.* Our word "circumspect," from the Latin *circumspicio,* signifies to look round about on all hands; to be every way watchful, wary, and cautious, in order to avoid danger, discern enemies before they come too nigh, and secure a man's interest by every possible and lawful means. But the original word signifies "correctly, accurately, consistently, or perfectly." You who have received the truth, be careful of your conduct; walk by the rule which God has given you. Do this as well in little as in great matters. Exemplify your principles, which are holy and good, by a corresponding conduct; do not only profess, but live, the gospel. *Not as fools, but as wise.* The heathens affected to be called "wise men." The apostle here takes the term *sophos,* and applies it to the Christian; and, instead of it, gives the empty Gentile philosopher the title of *fool.*

16. *Redeeming the time.* Buying up those moments which others seem to throw away; steadily improving every present moment, that you may in some measure regain the time you have lost. Let time be your chief commodity; deal in that alone; buy it all up, and use every portion of it yourselves. Time is that on which eternity depends; in time you are to get a preparation for the kingdom of God. If you get not this in time, your ruin is inevitable; therefore buy up the time.

Because the days are evil. The present times are dangerous; they are full of trouble and temptations, and only the watchful and diligent have any reason to expect that they shall keep their garments unspotted.

17. *Wherefore be ye not unwise.* "Do not become madmen." Here is a most evident allusion to the orgies of Bacchus, in which his votaries acted like madmen: running about, tossing their heads from shoulder to shoulder, appearing to be in every sense completely frantic. *But understanding what the will of the Lord is.* It is the will of God that you should be sober, chaste, holy, and pure. Get a thorough understanding of this; acquaint yourselves with God's will, that you may know how to glorify Him.

MATTHEW HENRY

II. The apostle warns against some other particular sins, and urges some other duties. 1. He warns against the sin of drunkenness: *And be not drunk with wine, v.* 18. The apostle adds, *wherein is excess.* Drunkenness is a sin that seldom goes alone, but often involves men in other instances of guilt: it is a great hindrance to the spiritual life. 2. Instead of being filled with wine, he exhorts them to be *filled with the Spirit.* Those who are full of drink are not likely to be full of the Spirit. Men should labour for a plentiful measure of the graces of the Spirit, that would fill their souls with great joy, and courage, which things sensual men expect their wine should inspire them with. We ought not to be satisfied with a little of the Spirit, but to be filled with the Spirit. Now by this means we shall come to *understand what the will of the Lord is.*

The apostle exhorts, 3. To sing unto the Lord, *v.* 19. Drunkards are wont to sing obscene and profane songs. The joy of Christians should express itself in songs of praise to their God. In these they should *speak to themselves* in their assemblies. Though Christianity is an enemy to profane mirth, yet it encourages joy and gladness. God's people have reason to rejoice, and to sing for joy. They are to *sing and to make melody in their hearts;* not only with their voices, but with inward affection, and then it will be done to the Lord.

4. Thanksgiving is another duty, *v.* 20. We should be *always giving thanks*; and we should give thanks *for all things.* It is our duty in *everything to give thanks unto God and the Father.*

Verses 21–33

The discharge of relative duties. As a general foundation for these duties, he lays down that rule, *v.* 21. There is a mutual submission that Christians owe one to another. *In the fear of God,* for his sake, that hereby we may give proof that we truly fear him. Where there is this mutual submission, the duties of all relations will be the better performed.

I. The duty prescribed to wives is submission to their husbands in the Lord (*v.* 22).

The reason of this submission from wives: *For the husband is the head of the wife, v.* 23. God has given the man the pre-eminence and a right to direct and govern by creation. Generally, too, the man has (what he ought to have) a superiority in wisdom and knowledge. He is therefore the head, *even as Christ is the head of the church, and he is the Saviour of the body.* Christ's authority is exercised over the church for the saving of her from evil, and the supplying of her with everything good for her. In like manner should the husband be employed for the protection and comfort of his spouse.

JAMIESON, FAUSSET, BROWN

mately, is our "sanctification" (I Thess. 4:3); and that "in every thing," meantime, we should "give thanks" (I Thess. 5:18; cf. above, vs. 10). **18. excess**—*worthless,* ruinous, reckless prodigality. **wherein**—not in the wine itself when used aright (I Tim. 5: 23), but in the "excess" as to it. **but be filled with the Spirit**—The effect in inspiration was that the person was "filled" with an ecstatic exhilaration, like that caused by wine; hence the two are here connected (cf. Acts 2:13-18). Hence arose the abstinence from wine of many of the prophets, e.g., John Baptist, viz., in order to keep distinct before the world the ecstasy caused by the Spirit, from that caused by wine. So also in ordinary Christians the Spirit dwells not in the mind that seeks the disturbing influences of excitement, but in the well-balanced prayerful mind. Such a one expresses his joy, not in drunken or worldly songs, but in Christian hymns of thankfulness. **19.** (Col. 3:16.) **to yourselves**—"to one another." Hence soon arose the antiphonal or responsive chanting of which PLINY writes to Trajan: "They are wont on a fixed day to meet before daylight [to avoid persecution] and to recite a hymn *among themselves by turns,* to Christ, as if being God." The Spirit gives true eloquence; wine, a spurious eloquence. **psalms**—generally accompanied by an instrument. **hymns**—in direct praise to God (cf. Acts 16:25; I Cor. 14: 26; Jas. 5:13). **songs**—the general term for lyric pieces; "spiritual" is added to mark their being here restricted to sacred subjects, though not merely to direct praises of God, but also containing exhortations, prophecies, etc. Contrast the drunken "songs," Amos 8:10. **making melody**—*Greek,* "playing and singing with an instrument." **in your heart**—not merely with the tongue; but the serious feeling of the heart accompanying the singing of the lips (cf. I Cor. 14:15; Ps. 47:7). The contrast is between the heathen and the Christian practice, "Let your songs be not the drinking songs of heathen feasts, but psalms and hymns; and their accompaniment, *not the music of the lyre,* but *the melody of the heart*" [CONYBEARE and HOWSON]. **to the Lord**—See Pliny's letter quoted above: "To *Christ* as God." **20. thanks . . . for all things**—even for adversities; also for blessings, unknown as well as known (Col. 3:17; I Thess. 5:18). **unto God and the Father**—the Fountain of every blessing in Creation, Providence, Election, and Redemption. **Lord Jesus Christ**—by whom all things, even distresses, become ours (Rom. 8:35, 37; I Cor. 3:20-23). **21.** (Phil. 2:3; I Peter 5:5.) Here he passes from our relations to God, to those which concern our fellow men. **in the fear of God**—All the oldest MSS. and authorities read, "in the fear of CHRIST." The believer passes from under the bondage of the law as a letter, to be "the servant of *Christ*" (I Cor. 7: 22), which, through the instinct of love to Him, is really to be "the Lord's freeman"; for he is "under the law to *Christ*" (I Cor. 9:21; cf. John 8:36). Christ, not the Father (John 5:22), is to be our judge. Thus reverential fear of displeasing Him is the motive for discharging our relative duties as Christians (I Cor. 10:22; II Cor. 5:11; I Pet. 2:13). **22.** (Ch. 6:9.) The Church's relation to Christ in His everlasting purpose, is the foundation and archetype of the three greatest of earthly relations, that of husband and wife (vss. 22-33), parent and child (ch. 6:1-4), master and servant (ch. 6:4-9). The oldest MSS. omit "submit yourselves"; supplying it from vs. 21, "Ye wives (submitting yourselves) unto your own husbands." "Your own" is an argument for submissiveness on the part of the wives; it is not a stranger, but *your own* husbands whom you are called on to submit unto (cf. Gen. 3:16; I Cor. 7:2; 14:34; Col. 3:18 Titus 2:5; I Pet. 3:1-7). Those subject ought to submit themselves, of whatever kind their superiors are. "Submit" is the term used of *wives:* "obey," of *children* (ch. 6:1), as there is a greater equality between wives and husbands, than between children and parents. **as unto the Lord**—Submissiveness is rendered by the wife to the husband under the eye of Christ, and so is rendered to Christ Himself. The husband stands to the wife in the relation that the Lord does to the Church, and this is to be the ground of her submission: though that submission is inferior in kind and degree to that which she owes Christ (vs. 24). **23.** (I Cor. 11:3.) **even as**—*Greek,* "as also." **and he is**—The oldest MSS. read, "Himself (being) Saviour. . . ." omitting "and," and "is." In Christ's case, the Headship is united with, nay gained by, His having SAVED the body in the process of redemption; so that (Paul implies) I am not alleging Christ's Headship as one entirely identical with that other, for He has a claim to it, and office in it, peculiar to Himself [ALFORD]. The husband is not saviour of

ADAM CLARKE

18. *Be not drunk with wine, wherein is excess.* This is a further allusion to the Bacchanalian mysteries; in them his votaries got drunk, and ran into all manner of excesses. Plato, though he forbade drunkenness in general, yet allowed that the people should get drunk in the solemnities of that god who invented wine. The word which we translate *excess* means profligacy and debauchery of every kind; such as are the general concomitants of drunkenness, and especially among the votaries of Bacchus in Greece and Italy. *But be filled with the Spirit.* The heathen priests pretended to be filled with the influence of the god they worshipped, and it was in these circumstances that they gave out their oracles. The apostle exhorts the Ephesians not to resemble these, but, instead of being filled with wine, to be filled with the Spirit of God; in consequence of which, instead of those discoveries of the divine will to which in their drunken worship the votaries of Bacchus pretended, they should be wise indeed, and should understand what the will of the Lord is.

19. *Speaking to yourselves in psalms.* We can scarcely say what is the exact difference between these three expressions. *Psalms* may probably mean those of David. *Hymns.* Extemporaneous effusions in praise of God, uttered under the influence of the divine Spirit, or a sense of His especial goodness. *Songs.* "Odes"; premeditated and regular poetic compositions. But in whatever form they were composed, we learn that they were all *spiritual,* tending to magnify God and edify men. *Singing and making melody in your heart.* The heart always going with the lips. It is a shocking profanation of divine worship to draw nigh to God with the lips while the heart is far from Him. It is too often the case that in public worship men are carried off from the sense of the words by the sounds that are put to them. And how few choirs of singers are there in the universe whose hearts ever accompany them in what they call singing the praises of God!

20. *Giving thanks always.* God is continually loading you with His benefits. You deserve nothing of His kindness; therefore give Him thanks for His unmerited bounties. *God and the Father.* That is, God, who is your Father, and the Father of mercies. *In the name of our Lord Jesus.* He is the only Mediator, and through Him alone can you approach to God.

21. *Submitting yourselves one to another.* Let no man be so tenacious of his own will or his opinion in matters indifferent as to disturb the peace of the church; in all such matters give way to each other, and let love rule. *In the fear of God.* Instead of *in the fear of God.* "in the fear of Christ" is the reading of the best MSS.

22. *Wives, submit yourselves unto your own husbands.* As the *Lord,* viz., Christ, is the Head or Governor of the Church, and the Head of the man, so is the man the head or governor of the woman. The husband should not be a tyrant, and the wife should not be the governor.

As unto the Lord. The word "Church" seems to be necessarily understood here; that is, Act under the authority of your husbands, as the Church acts under the authority of Christ.

23. *For the husband is the head of the wife.* This is the reason which the apostle gives for his injunctions. *He is the saviour of the body.* As Christ exercises authority over the Church so as to save and protect it, so let the husband exercise authority over his wife by protecting, comforting, and providing her with every necessary and comfort of life, according to his power.

MATTHEW HENRY

Therefore as the church is subject unto Christ (*v.* 24), with cheerfulness, with fidelity, with humility, *so let the wives be to their own husbands in everything.*

II. The duty of husbands is to love their wives (*v.* 25); for without this they would abuse their superiority, it being a special and peculiar affection that is required in her behalf. The love of Christ to the church is proposed as an example of this, which love of his is a constant affection, and that notwithstanding the imperfections and failures that she is guilty of. The greatness of his love to the church appeared in his giving himself unto the death for it. The love which God requires from the husband in behalf of his wife will make amends for the subjection which he demands from her to her husband; and the prescribed subjection of the wife will be an abundant return for that love of the husband which God has made her due.

The reason why he gave himself for it: *That he might sanctify and cleanse it, with the washing of water by the word* (*v.* 26).

That he might present it to himself, a glorious church, not having spot, nor wrinkle, nor any such thing, holy and without blemish, free from the least remains of sin. The church in general, and particular believers, will not be without spot or wrinkle till they come to glory.

JAMIESON, FAUSSET, BROWN

the wife, in which particular Christ excels; hence, "But" (vs. 24) follows [BENGEL]. **24. Therefore**—Translate, as *Greek,* "But," or "Nevertheless," i.e., though there be the difference of headships mentioned in vs. 23, *nevertheless,* thus far they are one, viz., in the subjection or submission (the same *Greek* stands for "is *subject,*" as for "*submit,*" vss. 21, 22) of the Church to Christ, being the prototype of that of the wife to the husband. **their own**—not in most of the oldest MSS., and not needed by the argument. **in every thing**—appertaining to a husband's legitimate authority; "in the Lord" (Col. 3:18); everything not contrary to God. **25.** "Thou hast seen the measure of obedience; now hear also the measure of love. Do you wish your wife to obey you, as the Church is to obey Christ? Then have a solicitude for her as Christ had for the Church [vs. 23, 'Himself the Saviour of the body']; and if it be necessary to give thy life for her, or to be cut in ten thousand pieces, or to endure any other suffering whatever, do not refuse it; and if you suffer thus, not even so do you do what Christ has done; for you indeed do so being already united to her, but He did so for one that treated Him with aversion and hatred. As, therefore, He brought to His feet one that so treated Him, and that even wantonly spurned Him, by much tenderness of regard, not by threats, insults, and terror: so also do you act towards your wife, and though you see her disdainful and wantonly wayward, you will be able to bring her to your feet by much thoughtfulness for her, by love, by kindness. For no bound is more sovereign in binding than such bonds, especially in the case of husband and wife. For one may constrain a servant by fear, though not even he is so to be bound to you; for he may readily run away. But the companion of your life, the mother of your children, the basis of all your joy, you ought to bind to you, not by fear and threats, but by love and attachment" [CHRYSOSTOM]. **gave himself**—*Greek,* "gave Himself *up.*" **for it**—Translate, "for *her.*" The relation of the Church to Christ is the ground of Christianity's having raised woman to her due place in the social scale, from which she was, and is, excluded in heathen lands. **26. sanctify**—i.e., consecrate her to God. Cf. John 17:19, meaning, "I *devote* Myself as a *holy* sacrifice, that My disciples also may be devoted or consecrated as holy in (through) the truth" [NEANDER] (Heb. 2:11; 10:10, *Note;* 13:12). **and cleanse**—rather, as *Greek,* "cleansing," without the "and." **with the washing of water**—rather as *Greek,* "with," or "by the *laver* of *the* water," viz., *the* baptismal water. So it ought to be translated in Titus 3:5, the only other passage in the New Testament where it occurs. As the bride passed through a purifying bath before marriage, so the Church (cf. Rev. 21:2). He speaks of baptism according to its high *ideal* and *design,* as if the inward grace accompanied the outward rite; hence he asserts of outward baptism whatever is involved in a believing appropriation of the divine truths it symbolizes, and says that Christ, by baptism, has purified the Church [NEANDER] (I Pet. 3:21). **by the word**—*Greek,* "IN the word." To be joined with "cleansing it," or "her." The "word of faith" (Rom. 10:8, 9, 17), of which confession is made in baptism, and which carries the real cleansing (John 15:3; 17:17) and regenerating power (I Pet. 1:23; 3:21) [ALFORD]. So AUGUSTINE, *Tract* 80, in John, "Take away the word, and what is the water save water? Add the word to the element, and it becomes a sacrament, being itself as it were the visible word." The regenerating efficacy of baptism is conveyed in, and by, the divine word alone. **27. he**—The oldest MSS. and authorities read, "That He might *Himself* present unto Himself the Church glorious," viz., as a bride (II Cor. 11:2). *Holiness* and *glory* are inseparable. "Cleansing" is the necessary preliminary to both. *Holiness* is *glory* internal; *glory* is *holiness* shining forth outwardly. *The laver of* baptism is the vehicle, but *the word* is the nobler and true instrument of the *cleansing* [BENGEL]. It is Christ that prepares the Church with the necessary ornaments of grace, for presentation to Himself, as the Bridegroom at His coming again (Matt. 25:1, etc.; Rev. 19:7; 21:2). **not having spot**—(Song of Sol. 4:7). The visible Church now contains clean and unclean together, like Noah's ark; like the wedding room which contained some that had, and others that had not, the wedding garment (Matt. 22:10-14; cf. II Tim. 2:20); or as the good and bad fish are taken in the same net because it cannot discern the bad from the good, the fishermen being unable to know what kind of fish the nets have taken under the waves. Still the Church is termed "holy" in the creed, in reference to her ideal and ultimate destination. When the Bridegroom comes, the bride

ADAM CLARKE

24. *In every thing.* That is, every lawful thing; for it is not intimated that they should obey their husbands in anything criminal, or in anything detrimental to the interests of their souls. The husband may be profligate, and may wish his wife to become such also; he may be an enemy to true religion, and use his authority to prevent his wife from those means of grace which she finds salutary to her soul. In none of these things should she obey him.

25. *Husbands, love your wives.* Here is a grand rule according to which every husband is called to act: "Love your wife as Christ loved the Church." But how did Christ love the Church? He *gave himself for it*—He laid down His life for it. So then husbands should, if necessary, lay down their lives for their wives. And there is more implied in the words than mere protection and support; for, as Christ gave himself for the Church to save it, so husbands should by all means in their power labor to promote the salvation of their wives and their constant edification in righteousness. Thus we find that the authority of the man over the woman is founded on his love to her, and this love must be such as to lead him to risk his life for her. As the care of the family devolves on the wife, and the children must owe the chief direction of their minds and formation of their manners to the mother, she has need of all the assistance and support which her husband can give her; and if she performs her duty well, she deserves the utmost of his love and affection.

26. *That he might sanctify and cleanse it.* The Church is represented as the spouse of Christ, as the woman is the spouse of the man; and to prepare this Church for himself He washes, cleanses, and sanctifies it. There is certainly an allusion here to the ancient method of purifying women, who were appointed to be consorts to kings. Twelve months, it appears, were in some instances spent in this purification: "Six months with oil of myrrh, and six months with sweet odours, and with other things for the purifying of the women." See the case of Esther, chap. ii. 12; see also Ps. xlv. 13-14; Ezek. xvi. 7-14. *With the washing of water.* Baptism, accompanied by the purifying influences of the Holy Spirit.

By the word. The "doctrine" of Christ crucified, through which baptism is administered, sin cancelled, and the soul purified from all unrighteousness, the death of Christ giving efficacy to all.

27. *That he might present it to himself.* It was usual to bring the royal bride to the king in the most sumptuous apparel; and is there not here an allusion to Ps. xlv. 13-14: "The king's daughter is all glorious within: her clothing is of wrought gold. She shall be brought unto the king in raiment of needlework"? This presentation here spoken of by the apostle will take place on the last day. *A glorious church.* Every way splendid and honorable, because pure and holy. *Not having spot.* No "blemish" on the face, no spots upon the garment, the heart and life both holy. *Wrinkle.* No mark of decay. The word is commonly applied to wrinkles on the face, indicative of sickness or decrepitude. *Holy and without blemish.* In every sense holy, pure, and perfect. Now it was for this purpose that Christ gave himself for the Church; and for this purpose He continues the different ordinances which He has appointed; and particularly the preaching of the Word—the doctrine of reconciliation through faith in His blood. And it is in this life that all this purification is to take place; for none shall be presented at the day of judgment to Him who has not here been sanctified, cleansed, washed, made glorious, having neither spot, wrinkle, blemish, nor any such thing.

MATTHEW HENRY

Those, and those only, who are sanctified now, will be glorified hereafter.—*So ought men to love their wives as their own bodies, &c., v.* 28. The wife being made one with her husband this is an argument why he should love her with as ardent an affection as that with which he loves himself. *For no man ever yet hated his own flesh, v.* 29—*he nourishes and cherishes it: even as the Lord the church. For we are members of his body, of his flesh and of his bones, v.* 30.

ALBERT BARNES:

"Of his flesh, and of his bones." There is an allusion here evidently to the language which Adam used respecting Eve. "This is now bone of my bones, and flesh of my flesh" (Gen. 2:23). It is language which is employed to denote the closeness of the marriage relation and which Paul applies to the connection between Christ and his people. Of course, it cannot be understood literally. It is not true literally that our bones are a part of the bones of Christ, or our flesh of his flesh; nor should language ever be used that would imply a miraculous union. It is not a physical union, but a union of attachment, of feeling, of love. If we avoid the notion of a physical union, however, it is scarcely possible to use too strong language in describing the union of believers with the Lord Jesus. The Scriptures make use of language which is stronger than that employed to describe any other connection; and there is no union of affection so powerful as that which binds the Christian to the Savior. So strong is it that he is willing for it to forsake father, mother, and home; to leave his country and to abandon his possessions; to go to distant lands and dwell among barbarians to make the Redeemer known; or to go to the cross or the stake from simple love to the Savior. Account for it as men may, there has been manifested on earth nowhere else so strong an attachment as that which binds the Christian to the cross. It is stronger love than that which a man has for his own flesh and bones; for it makes him willing that his flesh should be consumed by fire, or his bones broken on the wheel rather than deny him. Can the infidel account for this strength of attachment on any other principle than that it has a divine origin?—*Popular Commentary*

For this cause (because they are one, as Christ and his church are one) *shall a man leave his father and mother.* This relation is to be preferred to all others, there being a nearer union between these two than between any others.

—*And they two shall be one flesh. This is a great mystery, v.* 32. Those words have also a hidden mystical sense in them, relating to the union between Christ and his church. *I speak concerning Christ and the church.*

JAMIESON, FAUSSET, BROWN

shall be presented to Him wholly without spot, the evil being cut off from the body for ever (Matt. 13: 47-50). Not that there are two churches, one with bad and good intermingled, another in which there are good alone; but one and the same Church in relation to different times, now with good and evil together, hereafter with good alone [PEARSON]. **28.** Translate, "So ought husbands *also* (thus the oldest MSS. read) to love their own (cf. *Note,* vs. 22) wives as their own bodies." "He that loveth his own wife . . ." (vs. 28). So there is the same love and the same union of body between Christ and the Church (vss. 30, 32). **29. For**—Supply, and we all love ourselves: "For no man. . . ." **his own flesh**—(*V.* 31, end). **nourisheth**—*Greek,* "nourisheth it up," viz., to maturity. "Nourisheth," refers to food and internal sustenance; "cherisheth," to clothing and external fostering. **even as**—Translate, "even as also." **the Lord**—The oldest MSS. read, "Christ." Exodus 21:10 prescribes three duties to the husband. The two former (food and raiment) are here alluded to in a spiritual sense, by "nourisheth and cherisheth"; the third "duty of marriage" is not added in consonance with the holy propriety of Scripture language: its antitype is, "know the Lord" (Hos. 2:19, 20) [BENGEL]. **30. For**—*Greek,* "Because" (I Cor. 6:15). Christ nourisheth and cherisheth the Church as being of one flesh with Him. Translate, "Because we are members of His body (His literal body), *being* OF His flesh and of His bones" [ALFORD] (Gen. 2:23, 24). The *Greek* expresses, "Being formed *out of,*" or "of the substance of His flesh." Adam's deep sleep, wherein Eve was formed from out of his opened side, is an emblem of Christ's death, which was the birth of the Spouse, the Church. John 12:24; 19:34, 35, to which verses 25, 26, 27 allude, as implying atonement by His *blood,* and sanctification by the "water," answering to that which flowed from His side (cf. also John 7:38, 39; I Cor. 6:11). As Adam gave Eve a new name, *Hebrew, Isha,* "woman," formed from his own rib, *Ish,* "man," signifying her formation from him, so Christ, Revelation 2:17; 3: 12. Genesis 2:21, 23, 24 puts the *bones* first because the reference there is to the *natural* structure. But Paul is referring to the *flesh of Christ.* It is not our bones and flesh, but *"we"* that are *spiritually* propagated (in our soul and spirit now, and in the body hereafter, regenerated) from the manhood of Christ which has flesh and bones. We are members of His glorified body (John 6:53). The two oldest existing MSS., and *Coptic* or *Memphitic version,* omit "of His flesh and of His bones"; the words may have crept into the text through the *Margin* from Genesis 2:23, LXX. However, IRENÆUS, 294, and the old *Latin* and *Vulgate versions,* with some good old MSS., have them. **31. For this cause**—The propagation of the Church from Christ, as that of Eve from Adam, is the foundation of the spiritual marriage. The natural marriage, wherein "a man leaves father and mother (the oldest MSS. omit 'his') and is joined unto his wife," is not the principal thing meant here, but *the spiritual marriage* represented by it, and on which it rests, whereby Christ left the Father's bosom to woo to Himself the Church out of a lost world: vs. 32 proves this: His earthly mother *as such,* also, He holds in secondary account as compared with His spiritual Bride (Luke 2:48, 49; 8:19-21; 11:27, 28). He shall again leave His Father's abode to consummate the union (Matt. 25:1-10; Rev. 19:7). **they two shall be one flesh**—So the Samaritan Pentateuch, LXX, etc., read (Gen. 2:24), instead of "they shall be one flesh." So Matthew 19:5. In natural marriage, husband and wife combine the elements of one perfect human being: the one being incomplete without the other. So Christ, as God-man, is pleased to make the Church, the body, a necessary adjunct to Himself, the Head. He is the archetype of the Church, from whom and according to whom, as the pattern, she is formed. He is her Head, as the husband is of the wife (Rom. 6:5; I Cor. 11:3; 15:45). Christ will never allow any power to sever Himself and His bride, indissolubly joined (Matt. 19:6; John 10:28, 29; 13:1). **32.** Rather, "This mystery is a great one." This *profound truth, beyond man's power of discovering, but now revealed,* viz., of the spiritual union of Christ and the Church, represented by the marriage union, is a great one, of deep import. See *Note,* vs. 30. So "mystery" is used of a divine truth not to be discovered save by revelation of God (Rom. 11:25; I Cor. 15:51). The *Vulgate* wrongly translates, "This is a great *sacrament,*" which is made the plea by the Romish Church (in spite of the blunder having been long ago exposed by their own commentators, CAJETAN and ESTIUS) for making marriage a *sacrament;* it is plain

ADAM CLARKE

28. *As their own bodies.* For the woman is, properly speaking, a part of the man; for God made man "male and female," and the woman was taken out of his side. Therefore is she flesh of his flesh and bone of his bone; and therefore he that loves his wife loves himself, for they two are one flesh. The apostle in all these verses refers to the creation and original state of the first human pair.

29. *No man ever yet hated his own flesh.* And this is a natural reason why he should love his wife, and nourish and cherish her.

30. *We are members of his body.* He has partaken of our nature as we have partaken of the nature of Adam. And as He is the Head of the Church and the Saviour of this body, so we, being members of the Church, are members of His mystical body. That is, we are united to Him by one Spirit in the closest intimacy, even similar to that which the members have with the body.

31. *Shall be joined unto his wife.* He shall be "glued" or "cemented" to her; and as a well-glued board will sooner break in the whole wood than in the glued joint, so death alone can part the husband and wife; and nothing but death should dissolve their affection.

32. *This is a great mystery.* "This mystery is great." By *mystery* we may understand a natural thing by which some spiritual matter is signified, which signification the Spirit of God alone can give. So the creation and union of Adam and Eve were intended, in the design of God, to point out the union of Christ and the Church, a union the most important that can be conceived; and therefore the apostle calls it *a great mystery.*

MATTHEW HENRY

A brief summary of the duty of husbands and wives, *v.* 33. "*Nevertheless let everyone of you in particular so love his wife even as himself. And the wife see that she reverence her husband.*" Reverence consists of love and esteem. That the wife thus reverence her husband is the will of God and the law of the relation.

CHAPTER 6

Verses 1–9

I. The duty of children to their parents: to obey their parents (*v.* 1). That obedience which God demands from their children includes an inward reverence, as well as the outward expressions and acts. Obey in the Lord. "Obey your parents, especially in those things which relate to the Lord. Your parents teach you good manners, and therein you must obey them. They teach you what is for your health, and in this you must obey them: but the chief things in which you are to do it are the things pertaining to the Lord." In these things especially they must see that they be obedient. *For this is right*, there is a natural equity in it, God has enjoined it. It is the order of nature that parents command and children obey. The apostle quotes the law of the fifth commandment. *Honour thy father and mother* (*v.* 2), *which is the first commandment with promise.* The promise is, *That it may be well with thee*, &c., *v.* 3.

Outward prosperity and long life are blessings promised to those who keep this commandment. Obedient children are often rewarded with outward prosperity. Not indeed that it is always so; but *ordinarily* obedience is thus rewarded. The gospel has its temporal promises, as well as spiritual ones. We are allowed to have respect to the promised reward. This may be considered as a motive and encouragement to our obedience.

II. The duty of parents: *And you fathers, v.* 4. 1. "*Do not provoke your children to wrath.* Your children are pieces of yourselves, and therefore ought to be governed with great tenderness and love. When you caution them, when you counsel them, when you reprove them, do it in such a manner as not to *provoke them to wrath*, endeavouring to convince their judgments and to work upon their reason." 2. "*Bring them up* well, *in the nurture and admonition of the Lord.* Give them a good education." It is the great duty of parents to be careful in the education of their children. Not only bring them up as men, but as Christians, in the admonition of the Lord. Let them have a religious education.

III. The duty of servants. This also is summed up in one word, *obedience.* These servants were generally slaves. Civil servitude is not inconsistent with Christian liberty. Those may be the Lord's freemen who are slaves to men. "*Your masters according to the flesh* (*v.* 5), who have the command of your bodies, but not of your souls and consciences." 1. That they obey *with fear and trembling.* They are to reverence those who are over them. 2. That they be sincere in their obedience: *In singleness of heart:* serving them with faithfulness. 3. They should have an eye to Jesus Christ in all the service that they perform to their masters (*v.* 5–7), *doing service as to the Lord, and not to men.* Service done to their earthly masters, with an eye to him, becomes acceptable service to him also. 4. They must not serve their masters *with eye-service* (*v.* 6)—that is, only when their master's eye is upon them. Their Master in heaven beholds them: and therefore they must not act as *men-pleasers.* A steady regard to the Lord Jesus Christ will make men faithful and sincere in every station of life.

JAMIESON, FAUSSET, BROWN

not marriage in general, but that of Christ and the Church, is what is pronounced to be a "great mystery," as the words following prove, "*I* [emphatic] say it in regard to Christ and to the Church" (so the *Greek* is best translated). "I, while I quote these words out of Scripture, use them in a higher sense" [CONYBEARE and HOWSON]. **33. Nevertheless** —not to pursue further the mystical meaning of marriage. Translate, as *Greek*, "Do ye also (as Christ does) severally each one so love. . . ." The words, "severally each one," refer to them in their *individual* capacity, contrasted with the previous *collective view* of the members of the Church as the bride of Christ.

CHAPTER 6

VSS. 1-24. MUTUAL DUTIES OF PARENTS AND CHILDREN: MASTERS AND SERVANTS: OUR LIFE A WARFARE: THE SPIRITUAL ARMOUR NEEDED AGAINST SPIRITUAL FOES. CONCLUSION. **1. obey**—stronger than the expression as to wives, "submitting," or "being subject" (ch. 5:21). *Obedience* is more unreasoning and implicit; *submission* is the willing *subjection* of an inferior in point of order to one who has a right to command. **in the Lord**—Both parents and children being Christians "in the Lord," expresses the *element* in which the obedience is to take place, and the *motive* to obedience. In Colossians 3:20, it is, "Children, obey your parents *in all things.*" This clause, "in the Lord," would suggest the due limitation of the obedience required (Acts 5:29; cf. on the other hand, the abuse, Mark 7:11-13). **right**—Even by *natural law* we should render obedience to them from whom we have derived life. **2.** Here the authority of *revealed law* is added to that of natural law. **which is . . . promise**—The "promise" is not made the *main* motive to obedience, but an incidental one. The main motive is, because it is God's will (Deut. 5:16, "Honor thy father and mother, *as the Lord thy God hath* COMMANDED *thee*"); and that it is so peculiarly, is shown by His accompanying it "*with a promise.*" **first** —in the decalogue with a *special* promise. The promise in the second commandment is a *general* one. Their duty is more expressly prescribed to children than to parents; for love descends rather than ascends [BENGEL]. This verse proves the law in the Old Testament is not abolished. **3. long on the earth**—In Exodus 20:12, "long upon *the land which the Lord thy God giveth thee,*" which Paul adapts to Gospel times, by taking away the local and limited reference peculiar to the Jews in Canaan. The godly are equally blessed in every land, as the Jews were in the land which God gave them. This promise is always fulfilled, either literally, or by the substitution of a higher blessing, viz., one spiritual and eternal (Job 5:26; Prov. 10:27). The substance and essence of the law are eternally in force: its accidents alone (applying to Israel of old) are abolished (Rom. 6:15). **4. fathers**—including *mothers;* the fathers are specified as being the fountains of domestic authority. Fathers are more prone to passion in relation to their children than mothers, whose fault is rather over-indulgence. **provoke not**—irritate not, by vexatious commands, unreasonable blame, and uncertain temper [ALFORD]. Colossians 3:21, "lest they be discouraged." **nurture**—*Greek*, "discipline," viz., *training* by chastening in *act* where needed (Job 5:17; Heb. 12:7). **admonition**—training by *words* (Deut. 6:7; Prov. 22:6, *Margin,* "catechise"), whether of encouragement, or remonstrance, or reproof, according as is required [TRENCH]. Contrast I Samuel 3:13, *Margin.* **of the Lord**—such as the Lord approves, and by His Spirit dictates. **5. Servants**—lit., "slaves." **masters according to the flesh**—in contrast to your true and heavenly Master (vs. 4). A consolatory hint that the mastership to which they were subject, was but for a time [CHRYSOSTOM]; and that their real liberty was still their own (I Cor. 7:22). **fear and trembling**—not slavish terror, but (I Cor. 2:3, *Note;* II Cor. 7:15) an anxious eagerness to do your duty, and a fear of displeasing, as great as is produced in the ordinary slave by "threatenings" (vs. 9). **singleness**—without double-mindedness, or "eyeservice" (vs. 6), which seeks to please outwardly, without the sincere desire to make the master's interest at all times the first consideration (I Chron. 29:17; Matt. 6:22, 23; Luke 11:34). "Simplicity." **6.** (Col. 3:22.) Seeking to please their masters only so long as these have their eyes on them: as Gehazi was a very different man in his master's presence from what he was in his absence (II Kings 5). **men-pleasers**—not Christ-pleasers (cf. Gal. 1:10; I Thess. 2:4). **doing the**

ADAM CLARKE

33. *Nevertheless.* "Moreover," or "therefore," on the consideration of God's design in the institution of marriage, *let every one of you . . . love his wife as himself,* because she is both naturally and by a divine ordinance a part of himself. *That she reverence her husband.* Let the wife ever consider the husband as her head; and this he is, not only by nature, but also by the ordinance of God. These are very important matters, and on them the apostle lays great stress.

CHAPTER 6

1. *Children, obey your parents.* This is a duty with which God will never dispense; He commands it, and one might think that gratitude, from a sense of the highest obligations, would most strongly enforce the command. *In the Lord.* This clause is wanting in several reputable MSS. and in some versions. *In the Lord* may mean on account of the commandment of the Lord, or as far as the parents' commands are according to the will and word of God. For surely no child is called to obey any parent if he give unreasonable or unscriptural commands.

4. *Fathers, provoke not your children to wrath.* Avoid all severity; this will hurt your own souls, and do them no good; on the contrary, if punished with severity or cruelty, they will be only hardened and made desperate in their sins. Cruel parents generally have bad children. He who corrects his children according to God and reason will feel every blow on his own heart more sensibly than his child feels it on his body. Parents are called to correct, not to punish, their children. Those who punish them do it from a principle of revenge; those who correct them do it from a principle of affectionate concern. *Bring them up.* Literally, "Nourish them in the discipline and instruction of the Lord." The mind is to be nourished with wholesome discipline and instruction, as the body is with proper food. "Discipline" may refer to all that knowledge which is proper for children, including elementary principles and rules for behavior. "Instruction" may imply whatever is necessary to form the mind; to touch, regulate, and purify the passions; and necessarily includes the whole of religion. Both these should be administered in the Lord—according to His will and Word, and in reference to His eternal glory.

5. *Servants, be obedient.* Though *doulos* frequently signifies a "slave" or "bondman," yet it often implies a servant in general, or anyone bound to another, either for a limited time or for life. Even a slave, if a Christian, was bound to serve him faithfully by whose money he was bought, howsoever illegal that traffic may be considered. *According to the flesh.* Your masters in secular things; for they have no authority over your religion nor over your souls. *With fear and trembling.* Because the law gives them a power to punish you for every act of disobedience. *In singleness of your heart.* Not merely through fear of punishment, but from a principle of uprightness, serving them as you would serve Christ.

6. *Not with eyeservice.* Not merely in their presence, when their eye is upon you, as unfaithful and hypocritical servants do, without consulting conscience in any part of their work.

MATTHEW HENRY

5. What they do they must do cheerfully: *Doing the will of God from the heart*, serving their masters as God wills they should. This is *doing it with goodwill* (*v.* 7). Service, performed with conscience, and from a regard to God, though it be to unrighteous masters, will be accounted by Christ as service done to himself.

6. Let faithful servants trust God for their wages, while they do their duty in his fear: *Knowing that whatsoever good thing* (*v.* 8)—*the same shall he receive of the Lord.* Though his master on earth should neglect or abuse him, instead of rewarding him, he shall certainly be rewarded by the Lord Christ, *whether he be bond or free.* Christ regards not these differences of men at present; nor will he in the great and final judgment.

IV. The duty of masters: *And you masters, do the same things unto them* (*v.* 9). Masters are under as strict obligations to discharge their duty to their servants as servants are to be obedient and dutiful to them. "*Forbearing threatening.* Be not tyrannical and imperious over them, *knowing that your Master also is in heaven*; you and they are but fellow-servants in respect of Christ. You are therefore to show favour to others, as ever you expect to find favour with him; and you will never be a match for him, though you may be too hard for your servants." *Neither is there respect of persons with him.* He will call masters and servants to an impartial account for their conduct one to another. If both masters and servants would consider their relation to God and the account they must shortly give to him, they would be more careful of their duty to each other.

Verses 10–18

Is not our life a warfare? It is so; for we struggle with the common calamities of human life. Is not our religion much more a warfare? It is so; for we struggle with the opposition of the powers of darkness. "*Finally, my brethren* (*v.* 10), it yet remains that you apply yourselves to your work and duty as Christian soldiers."

I. They must see that they be stout-hearted. *Be strong in the Lord*, &c. Those who have so many battles to fight, and who, in their way to heaven, must dispute every pass, with dint of sword, have need of a great deal of courage. *Be strong therefore.* Let a soldier be ever so well armed without, if he have not within a good heart, his armour will stand him in little stead. Spiritual strength and courage are very necessary for our spiritual warfare. We have no sufficient strength of our own. All our sufficiency is of God. In his strength we must go forth and go on. We must fetch in grace and help from heaven to enable us to do that which of ourselves we cannot do in our Christian work and warfare.

II. They must be well armed: "*Put on the whole armour of God* (*v.* 11). Get and exercise all the Christian graces, the whole armour, that no part be naked and exposed to the enemy." Those who would have true grace must aim at all grace, the whole armour. We have no armour of our own that will be armour of proof in a trying time. Nothing will stand us in stead but the armour of God. This armour is prepared for us, but we must put it on.

The Christian should be completely armed *that he may be able to stand against the wiles of the devil*—that he may be able to hold out, and to overcome.

1. What our danger is, and what need we have to put on this whole armour. *For we wrestle not against flesh and blood, &c., v.* 12. The combat is not against ordinary human enemies, not barely against men compounded of *flesh and blood.* (1) We have to do with an enemy who uses wiles and stratagems, as *v.* 11. He has a thousand ways of beguiling unstable souls.

JAMIESON, FAUSSET, BROWN

will of God—the unseen but ever present Master: the best guarantee for your serving faithfully your earthly master alike when present and when absent. **from the heart**—lit., *soul* (Ps. 111:1; Rom. 13:5). **7. good will**—expressing his feeling towards his master; as "doing the will of God from the heart" expresses the source of that feeling (Col. 3:23). "Good will" is stated by XENOPHON (*Economics*) to be the principal virtue of a slave towards his master: a real regard to his master's interest as if his own, a *good will* which not even a master's severity can extinguish. **8. any man doeth**—*Greek*, "any man shall have done," i.e., shall be found at the Lord's coming to have done. **the same**—in full payment, in heaven's currency. **shall . . . receive**—(II Cor. 5: 10; Col. 3:25; but all of grace, Luke 17:10). **bond or free**—(I Cor. 7:22; 12:13; Gal. 3:28; Col. 3:11). Christ does not regard such distinctions in His present dealings of grace, or in His future judgment. The slave that has acted faithfully for the Lord's sake to his master, though the latter may not repay his faithfulness, shall have the Lord for his Paymaster. So the freeman who has done good for the Lord's sake, though man may not pay him, has the Lord for his Debtor (Prov. 19:17). **9. the same things**—*Mutatis mutandis.* Show the same regard to God's will, and to your servants' well-being, in your relation to them, as they ought to have in their relation to you. Love regulates the duties both of servants and masters, as one and the same light attempers various colors. Equality of nature and faith is superior to distinctions of rank [BENGEL]. Christianity makes all men brothers: cf. Leviticus 25:42, 43; Deuteronomy 15:12; Jeremiah 34:14 as to how the Hebrews were bound to treat their brethren in service; much more ought Christians to act with love. **threatening**—*Greek, "the* threatening" which masters commonly use. "Masters" in the *Greek*, is not so strong a term as "despots": it implies *authority*, but not absolute *domination.* **your Master also**—The oldest MSS. read, "the Master both of them and you": "their Master and yours." This more forcibly brings out the equality of slaves and masters in the sight of God. SENECA, *Thyestes*, 607, says, "Whatever an inferior dreads from you, this a superior Master threatens yourselves with: every authority here is under a higher above." As you treat your servants, so will He treat you. **neither . . . respect of persons**—He will not, in judging, acquit thee because thou art a master, or condemn him because he is a servant (Acts 10:34; Rom. 2:11; Gal. 2:6; Col. 3:25; I Pet. 1:17). Derived from Deuteronomy 10:17; II Chronicles 19:7. **10. my brethren**—Some of the oldest MSS. omit these words. Some with *Vulgate* retain them. The phrase occurs nowhere else in the Epistle (see, however, vs. 23); if genuine, it is appropriate here in the close of the Epistle, where he is urging his fellow soldiers to the good fight in the Christian armor. Most of the oldest MSS. for "finally," read, "henceforward," or "from henceforth" (Gal. 6:17). **be strong**—*Greek*, "be strengthened." **in the power of his might**—*Christ's* might: as in ch. 1:19, it is *the Father's* might. **11. the whole armour**—the armor of light (Rom. 13:12); on the right hand and left (II Cor. 6:7). The panoply offensive and defensive. An image readily suggested by the Roman armory, Paul being now in Rome. Repeated emphatically, vs. 13. In Romans 13:14 it is, "Put ye on *the Lord Jesus Christ*"; in putting on Him, and the new man in Him, we put on "the whole armor of God." No opening at the head, the feet, the heart, the belly, the eye, the ear, or the tongue, is to be given to Satan. Believers have once for all overcome him; but on the ground of this fundamental victory gained over him, they are ever again to fight against and overcome him, even as they who once die with Christ have continually to mortify their members upon earth (Rom. 6:2-14; Col. 3:3, 5). **of God**—furnished by God; not our own, else it would not stand (Ps. 35:1-3). Spiritual, therefore, and mighty through God, not carnal (II Cor. 10:4). **wiles**—lit., "*schemes sought out*" for deceiving (cf. II Cor. 11:14). **the devil**—the ruling chief of the foes (vs. 12) organized into a kingdom of darkness (Matt. 12:26), opposed to the kingdom of light. **12.** *Greek*, "For our wrestling ('*the* wrestling' in which we are engaged) is not against flesh . . . ." Flesh and blood foes are Satan's mere tools, the real foe lurking behind them is Satan himself, with whom our conflict is. "Wrestling" implies that it is a hand-to-hand and foot-to-foot struggle for the mastery: to wrestle successfully with Satan, we must wrestle with GOD in irresistible prayer like Jacob (Gen. 32:24-29; Hos. 12:4). Translate, "*The* principalities . . . *the* powers" (ch. 1:21; *Note*, 3:10; Col. 1:16). The same

ADAM CLARKE

Doing the will of God. Seeing that you are in the state of servitude, it is the will of God that you should act conscientiously in it.

7. *With good will.* With "cheerfulness"; do not take up your service as a cross or bear it as a burden; but take it as coming in the order of God's providence and a thing that is pleasing to Him.

8. *Whatsoever good thing any man doeth.* Though your masters should fail to give you the due reward of your fidelity and labor, yet, as you have done your work as unto the Lord, He will take care to give you the proper recompense. *Whether he be bond.* A "slave," bought with money. *Or free.* A person who has hired himself of his own free accord.

9. *Ye masters, do the same things unto them.* Act in the same affectionate, conscientious manner towards your slaves and servants as they do towards you. *Forbearing threatening.* If they should transgress at any time, lean more to the side of mercy than justice; and when you are obliged to punish, let it be as light and as moderate as possible; and let revenge have no part in the chastisement, for that is of the devil, and not of God. The words *forbearing threatening* signify to mitigate, relax, or not exact threatening; that is, the threatened punishment.

Knowing that your Master also is in heaven. You are their masters; God is yours. As you deal with them, so God will deal with you; for do not suppose, because their condition on earth is inferior to yours, that God considers them to be less worthy of His regard than you are. This is not so, for there is no *respect of persons with Him.*

10. *Finally.* Having laid before you your great and high calling and all the doctrines and precepts of the gospel, it is necessary that I should show you the enemies that will oppose you, and the strength which is requisite to enable you to repel them. *Be strong in the Lord.* You must have strength, and strength of a spiritual kind, and such strength too as the Lord himself can furnish; and you must have this strength through an indwelling God, the power of His might working in you.

11. *Put on the whole armour of God.* The apostle considers every Christian as having a warfare to maintain against numerous, powerful, and subtle foes; and that therefore they would need much strength, much courage, complete armor, and skill to use it. The "panoply" which is mentioned here refers to the armor of the heavy troops among the Greeks; those who were to sustain the rudest attacks, who were to sap the foundations of walls, storm cities. Their ordinary armor was the shield, the helmet, the sword, and the greaves or brazen boots. To all these the apostle refers below.

The wiles of the devil. "The methods of the devil"; the different means, plans, schemes, and machinations which he uses to deceive, entrap, enslave, and ruin the souls of men.

12. *For we wrestle not against flesh and blood.* Our wrestling or contention is not with men like ourselves. *Flesh and blood* is a Hebraism for "men," or human beings. *Against principalities.* "Chief rulers"; beings of the first rank and order in their own kingdom. *Powers.* "Authorities," derived from and constituted by the above.

MATTHEW HENRY

(2) He is a powerful enemy: *Principalities*, and *powers*, and *rulers*. They are numerous, they are vigorous, and rule in those heathen nations which are yet in darkness. Satan's is a kingdom of darkness; whereas Christ's is a kingdom of light.

(3) They are spiritual enemies: *Spiritual wickedness in high places*, or wicked spirits, as some translate it. Our danger is the greater from our enemies because they are unseen, and assault us ere we are aware of them. These enemies are said to be *in high places*, or in heavenly places, so the word is. Our enemies strive to prevent our ascent to heaven. They assault us in the things that belong to our souls. We have need of faith in our Christian warfare, because we have spiritual enemies to grapple with, as well as of faith in our Christian work, because we have spiritual strength to fetch in.

2. What our duty is: to put on the whole armour of God, and then to stand our ground, and withstand our enemies.

(1) We must *withstand*, *v.* 13. We must not yield to the devil's allurements and assaults, but oppose them. If he stand up against us, we must stand against him. To stand against Satan is to strive against sin. *That you may be able to withstand in the evil day*, in the day of temptation, or of any sore affliction.

(2) We must stand our ground: *And, having done all, to stand*. Resist him, and he will flee. If we give back, he will get ground. Our present business is to withstand the assaults of the devil, and to stand it out; and then our warfare will be accomplished, and we shall be finally victorious.

(3) We must stand armed. Here is a Christian in complete armour: and the armour is divine: *Armour of God*. The apostle specifies the particulars of this armour, both offensive and defensive. The military girdle or belt, the breast-plate, the greaves (or soldier's shoes), the shield, the helmet, and the sword. It is observable that, among them all, there is none for the back; if we turn our back upon the enemy, we lie exposed. [1] Truth is our girdle, *v.* 14. This is the strength of our loins; and it girds on all other pieces of our armour, and therefore is first mentioned. I know no religion without sincerity. [2] Righteousness must be our breast-plate. The breast-plate secures the vitals, shelters the heart. The righteousness of Christ implanted in us is our breast-plate to fortify the heart against the attacks which Satan makes against us.

[3] Resolution must be as the greaves to our legs: *And their feet shod with the preparation of the gospel of peace*, *v.* 15. Shoes, or greaves of brass, were formerly part of the military armour to defend the feet against the gall-traps, and sharp sticks, which were wont to be laid to obstruct the marching of the enemy, those who fell upon them being unfit to march. *The preparation of the gospel of peace* signifies a resolved frame of heart which will enable us to walk with a steady pace in the way of religion.

JAMIESON, FAUSSET, BROWN

grades of powers are specified in the case of the demons here, as in that of angels there (cf. Romans 8:38; I Cor. 15:24; Col. 2:15). The Ephesians had practiced sorcery (Acts 19:19), so that he appropriately treats of evil spirits in addressing them. The more clearly any book of Scripture, as this, treats of the economy of the kingdom of light, the more clearly does it set forth the kingdom of darkness. Hence, nowhere does the satanic kingdom come more clearly into view than in the Gospels which treat of Christ, the true Light. **rulers of the darkness of this world**—*Greek*, "age" or "course of the world." But the oldest MSS. omit "of world." Translate, "Against the world rulers of this (present) darkness" (ch. 2:2; 5:8; Luke 22:53; Col. 1:13). On Satan and his demons being "world rulers," cf. John 12:31; 14:30; 16:11; Luke 4:6; II Cor. 4:4; I John 5:19, *Greek*, "lieth in the wicked one." Though they be "world rulers," they are not the ruler of the universe; and their usurped rule of the world is soon to cease, when He shall "come whose right it is" (Ezek. 21:27). Two cases prove Satan not to be a mere subjective fancy: (1) Christ's temptation; (2) the entrance of demons into the swine (for these are incapable of such fancies). Satan tries to parody, or imitate in a perverted way, God's working (II Cor. 11:13, 14). So when God became incarnate, Satan, by his demons, took forcible possession of human bodies. Thus the demoniacally possessed were not peculiarly wicked, but miserable, and so fit subjects for Jesus' pity. Paul makes no mention of demoniacal possession, so that in the time he wrote, it seems to have ceased; it probably was restricted to the period of the Lord's incarnation, and of the foundation of His Church. **spiritual wickedness**—rather as *Greek*, "*The* spiritual *hosts of* wickedness." As three of the clauses describe the *power*, so this fourth, the *wickedness* of our spiritual foes (Matt. 12:45). **in high places** —*Greek*, "heavenly places": in ch. 2:2, "the air," where see the *Note*. The alteration of expression to "in heavenly places," is in order to mark the higher range of their powers than ours, they having been, up to the ascension (Rev. 12:5, 9, 10), dwellers "in the heavenly places" (Job 1:7), and being now in the regions of the air which are called the heavens. Moreover, pride and presumption are the sins *in heavenly places* to which they tempt especially, being those by which they themselves fell from heavenly places (Isa. 14:12-15). But believers have naught to fear, being "blessed with all spiritual blessings in the heavenly places" (ch. 1:3). **13. take . . . of God**—not "make," God has done that: you have only to "take up" and put it on. The Ephesians were familiar with the idea of the gods giving armor to mythical heroes: thus Paul's allusion would be appropriate. **the evil day**—the day of Satan's special assaults (vss. 12, 16) in life and at the dying hour (cf. Rev. 3:10). We must have our armor always on, to be ready against the evil day which may come at any moment, the war being perpetual (Ps. 41:1, *Margin*). **done all**—rather, "accomplished all things," viz., necessary to the fight, and becoming a good soldier. **14. Stand**—The repetition in vss. 11, 14, shows that *standing*, i.e., *maintaining our ground*, not yielding or fleeing, is the grand aim of the Christian soldier. Translate as *Greek*, "Having girt about your loins with truth," i.e., with truthfulness, sincerity, a good conscience (II Cor. 1:12; I Tim. 1:5, 18; 3:9). Truth is the band that girds up and keeps together the flowing robes, so as that the Christian soldier may be unencumbered for action. So the Passover was eaten with the loins girt, and the shoes on the feet (Exod. 12:11; cf. Isa. 5:27; Luke 12:35). *Faithfulness* (LXX, "truth") is the girdle of Messiah (Isa. 11:5): so *truth* of His followers. **having on**—*Greek*, "having put on." **breastplate of righteousness**—Isaiah 59:17, similarly of Messiah. "Righteousness" is here joined with "truth," as in ch. 5:9: *righteousness* in works, *truth* in words [ESTIUS] (I John 3:7). Christ's righteousness inwrought in us by the Spirit. "Faith and love," i.e., faith working righteousness by love, are "the breastplate" in I Thess. 5:8. **15.** Translate, "Having shod your feet" (referring to the sandals, or to the military shoes then used). **the preparation**—rather, "the preparedness," or "readiness of," i.e., arising from the "Gospel" (Ps. 10:17). Preparedness to do and suffer all that God wills; readiness for march, as a Christian soldier.

ADAM CLARKE

Spiritual wickedness. "The spiritual things of wickedness" or "the spiritualities of wickedness"; highly refined and sublimed evil; disguised falsehood in the garb of truth; antinomianism in the guise of religion. The *spiritual wickedness* is supposed to be the angels which kept not their first estate; who fell from the heavenly places but are ever longing after and striving to regain them; and which have their station in the regions of the air.

13. *Wherefore*. Because you have such enemies to contend with, *take unto you*, assume, as provided and prepared for you, *the whole armour of God;* which armor if you put on and use, you shall be both invulnerable and immortal. The ancient heroes are fabled to have had armor sent to them by the gods. *That ye may be able to withstand*. That you may not only stand fast in the liberty wherewith Christ has made you free, but also discomfit all your spiritual foes; and continuing in your ranks, maintain your ground against them, never putting off your armor, but standing always ready, prepared to repel any new attack. *And having done all, to stand*. Rather, "And having conquered all, stand." This is a military phrase, and is repeatedly uesd in this sense by the best Greek writers. By *evil day* we may understand any time of trouble, affliction, and sore temptation.

14. *Stand therefore*. Prepare yourselves for combat, *having your loins girt about with truth*. He had told them before to take the whole armor of God, v. 13, and to put on this whole armor. Having got all the pieces of it together, and the defensive parts put on, they were then to gird them close to their bodies with the girdle; and instead of a fine ornamented belt, such as the ancient warriors used, they were to have *truth*. The gospel of Jesus Christ is the truth of God. *Truth* may be taken here for "sincerity"; for if a man be not conscious to himself that his heart is right before God, and that he makes no false pretenses to religion, in vain does he enter the spiritual lists. This alone can give him confidence. *The breastplate of righteousness*. The word *righteousness*, we have often had occasion to note, is a word of very extensive import. It signifies the principle of righteousness; it signifies the practice of righteousness, or living a holy life; it signifies God's method of justifying sinners; and it signifies justification itself. Here it may imply a consciousness of justification through the blood of the Cross; the principle of righteousness or true holiness implanted in the heart; and a holy life, a life regulated according to the testimonies of God. As the *breastplate* defends the heart and lungs, and all those vital functionaries that are contained in what is called the region of the thorax, so this righteousness, this life of God in the soul of man, defends everything on which the man's spiritual existence depends. While he possesses this principle and acts from it, his spiritual and eternal life is secure.

15. *Your feet shod*. The "greaves" were deemed of essential importance in the ancient armor; if the feet or legs are materially wounded, a man can neither stand to resist his foe, pursue him if vanquished, nor flee from him should he have the worst of the fight. That the apostle has obedience to the gospel in general in view, there can be no doubt. But he appears to have more than this, a readiness to publish the gospel; for "how beautiful upon the mountains are the feet of him that bringeth good tidings, that publisheth peace; that bringeth good tidings of good, that publisheth salvation; that saith unto Zion, Thy God reigneth!" (Isa. lii. 7; Rom. x. 15) *The preparation of the gospel*. The word which we translate *preparation* is variously understood. Some think it means a habitual readiness in walking in the way prescribed by the gospel; others, that firmness and solidity which the gospel gives to them who conscientiously believe its doctrines; others, those virtues and graces which in the first planting of Christianity were indispensably necessary to those who published it. Should we take the word *preparation* in its common acceptation, it may imply that, by a conscientious belief of the gospel, receiving the salvation provided by its Author, and walking in the way of obedience which is pointed out by it, the soul

MATTHEW HENRY

It is styled *the gospel of peace* because it brings all sorts of peace. This will certainly preserve you from many great temptations and persecutions, as did those shoes of brass the soldiers from those gall-traps.

[4] Faith must be our shield: *Above all, taking the shield of faith, v.* 16. This is more necessary than any of them. Faith is all in all to us in an hour of temptation. The breast-plate secures the vitals; but with the shield we turn every way. Faith is like a shield, a sort of universal defence. Our enemy the devil is here called *the wicked one.* He is wicked himself, and he endeavours to make us wicked. His temptations are called *fiery darts,* by way of allusion to the poisonous darts which were wont to inflame the parts which were wounded. Violent temptations, by which the soul is set on fire of hell, are the darts which Satan shoots at us. Faith is the shield with which we must quench these fiery darts, that they may not hit us, or at least that they may not hurt us.

[5] Salvation must be our helmet (*v.* 17); that is, *hope,* which has salvation for its object. He would tempt us to despair; but good hope keeps us trusting in God, and rejoicing in him.

[6] The word of God is the sword of the Spirit. It is called *the sword of the Spirit,* because he renders it efficacious and powerful. This, being hid in the heart, will preserve from sin.

[7] Prayer must buckle on all the other parts of our Christian armour, *v.* 18. We must join prayer with all these graces, and we must pray always. Not as though we were to do nothing else but pray, for there are other duties that are to be done in their place and season; but we should keep up constant times of prayer. We must pray upon all occasions. We must intermix ejaculatory prayers with other duties, and with common business. Though set and solemn prayer may sometimes be unseasonable, yet pious ejaculations *can* never be so.

JAMIESON, FAUSSET, BROWN

gospel of peace—(cf. Luke 1:79; Rom. 10: 15). The "peace" within forms a beautiful contrast to the raging of the outward conflict (Isa. 26:3; Phil. 4:7).

16. Above all—rather, "Over all"; so as to cover all that has been put on before. Three integuments are specified, the breastplate, girdle, and shoes; two defenses, the helmet and shield; and two offensive weapons, the sword and the spear (prayer). ALFORD translates, "Besides all," as the *Greek* is translated, Luke 3:20. But if it meant this, it would have come *last* in the list (cf. Col. 3: 14). **shield**—the large oblong oval door-like shield of the Romans, four feet long by two and a half feet broad; not the small round buckler. **ye shall be able**—not *merely* "ye may." The shield of faith will *certainly* intercept, and so "quench, all the fiery darts" (an image from the ancient fire-darts, formed of cane, with tow and combustibles ignited on the head of the shaft, so as to set fire to wood-work, tents, etc.) **of the wicked**—rather "of the EVIL ONE." Faith conquers him (I Pet. 5:9), and his darts of temptation to wrath, lust, revenge, despair, etc. It overcomes the world (I John 5:4), and so the prince of the world (I John 5:18).

17. take—a different *Greek* word from that in vss. 13, 16; translate, therefore, "receive," "accept," viz., the helmet offered by the Lord, viz., "salvation" appropriated, as I Thessalonians 5:8, "Helmet, the hope of salvation"; not an uncertain hope, but one that brings with it no shame of disappointment (Rom. 5:5). It is subjoined to the shield of faith, as being its inseparable accompaniment (cf. Rom. 5:1, 5). The head of the soldier was among the principal parts to be defended, as on it the deadliest strokes might fall, and it is the head that commands the whole body. The head is the seat of the *mind,* which, when it has laid hold of the sure Gospel "hope" of eternal life, will not receive false doctrine, or give way to Satan's temptations to *despair.* God, by this hope, "lifts up the head" (Ps. 3:3; Luke 21:28). **sword of the Spirit**—i.e., furnished by the Spirit, who inspired the writers of the word of God (II Pet. 1:21). Again the Trinity is implied: the Spirit here; and Christ in "salvation" and God the Father, vs. 13 (cf. Heb. 4:12; Rev. 1: 16; 2:12). The two-edged sword, cutting both ways (Ps. 45:3, 5), striking some with conviction and conversion, and others with condemnation (Isa. 11:4; Rev. 19:15), is in the *mouth* of Christ (Isa. 49:2), in the *hand* of His saints (Ps. 149:6). Christ's use of this sword in the temptation is our pattern as to how we are to wield it against Satan (Matt. 4:4, 7, 10). There is no armor specified for the back, but only for the front of the body; implying that we must never turn our back to the foe (Luke 9:62); our only safety is in resisting ceaselessly (Matt. 4:11; Jas. 4: 7). **18. always**—*Greek,* "in every season"; implying *opportunity* and *exigency* (Col. 4:2). Paul uses the very words of Jesus in Luke 21:36 (a Gospel which he quotes elsewhere, in undesigned consonance with the fact of Luke being his associate in travel (I Cor. 11:23, etc.; I Tim. 5:18). Cf. Luke 18:1; Romans 12:12; I Thessalonians 5:17. **with all**—i.e., every kind of. **prayer**—a sacred term for *prayer* in general.

ADAM CLARKE

is prepared for the kingdom of Heaven. The gospel is termed the *gospel of peace* because it establishes peace between God and man, and proclaims peace and goodwill to the universe. Contentions, strife, quarrels, and all wars being as alien from its nature and design as they are opposed to the nature of Him who is love and compassion to man.

16. *Above all,* "over all" the rest of the armor, *taking the shield of faith.* In the word *thureos* the apostle alludes to the great oblong shield, or *scutum,* which covers the whole body. And as *faith* is the grace by which all others are preserved and rendered active, so it is properly represented here under the notion of a *shield,* by which the whole body is covered and protected. Faith, in this place, must mean that evidence of things unseen which every genuine believer has, that God, for Christ's sake, has blotted out his sins, and by which he is enabled to call God his Father, and feel Him to be his Portion. It is such an appropriating faith as this which can quench any dart of the devil. *The fiery darts of the wicked. Belos,* "a dart," signifies any kind of missile weapon; everything that is projected to a distance by the hand, as a javelin or short spear; or by a bow, as an arrow; or a stone by a sling. *The fiery darts of the wicked,* or devil, are evil thoughts and strong injections, as they are termed, which in the unregenerate inflame the passions and excite the soul to acts of transgression. While the faith is strong in Christ it acts as a shield to quench these. He who walks so as to feel the witness of God's Spirit that he is His child has all evil thoughts in abhorrence; and though they pass through his mind, they never fix in his passions. They are caught on this shield, blunted, and extinguished.

17. *Take the helmet of salvation.* Or, as it is expressed, 1 Thess. v. 8, "And for an helmet, the hope of salvation." So the hope of conquering every adversary and surmounting every difficulty, through the blood of the Lamb, is as a helmet that protects the head; an impenetrable one, that the blow of the battle-axe cannot cleave. *The sword of the Spirit.* The *sword* of which Paul speaks is, as he explains it, *the word of God;* that is, the revelation which God has given of himself, or what we call the Holy Scriptures. This is called *the sword of the Spirit* because it comes from the Holy Spirit and receives its fulfilment in the soul through the operation of the Holy Spirit. An ability to quote this on proper occasions, and especially in times of temptation and trial, has a wonderful tendency to cut in pieces the snares of the adversary. In God's Word a genuine Christian may have unlimited confidence, and to every purpose to which it is applicable it may be brought with the greatest effect. The shield, faith, and the *sword . . . the word of God*—or faith in God's unchangeable Word—are the principal armor of the soul.

18. *Praying always.* The apostle does not put praying among the armor; had he done so he would have referred it, as he has done all the rest, to some of the Grecian armor; but as he does not do this, therefore we conclude that his account of the armor is ended, and that now, having equipped his spiritual soldier, he shows him the necessity of praying, that he may successfully resist those principalities, powers, the rulers of the darkness of this world, and the spiritual wickednesses in heavenly places, with whom he has to contend. The "panoply," or whole armor of God, consists in (1) the girdle, (2) the breastplate, (3) the greaves, (4) the shield, (5) the helmet, and (6) the sword. He who had these was completely armed. And as it was the custom of the Grecian armies, before they engaged, to offer prayers to the gods for their success, the apostle shows that these spiritual warriors must depend on the Captain of their salvation, and pray with all prayer, i.e., incessantly, being always in the spirit of prayer, so that they should be ever ready for public, private, mental, or ejaculatory prayer; always depending on Him who can alone save and who alone can destroy. When the apostle exhorts Christians to pray with all prayer, we may at once see that he neither means spiritual nor formal prayer, in exclusion of the other. *Praying* refers to the state of the spirit as well as to

MATTHEW HENRY

We must pray *with all prayer and supplications*, with all kinds of prayer. We must pray *in the Spirit*. We must do it by the grace of God's good Spirit. We must *watch thereunto*, endeavouring to keep our hearts in a praying frame, and taking all occasions for the duty. This we must do *with all perseverance*. We must continue in it as long as we live in the world. And we must pray *with supplication*, not for ourselves only, but *for all saints*. None are so much saints, and in so good a condition in this world, but they need our prayers, and they ought to have them.

Verses 19–24

I. He desires their prayers for him, *v.* 19. Having mentioned *supplication for all saints*, he puts himself into the number. We must pray for all saints, and particularly for God's faithful ministers. "*That utterance may be given unto me; and that I may open my mouth boldly. To make known the mystery of the gospel*." The whole gospel was a mystery, till made known by divine revelation. Paul had a great command of language; they called him Mercury, because he was the chief speaker (Acts xiv. 12), and yet he would have his friends ask of God the gift of utterance for him. He was a man of great courage, yet he would have them pray that God would give him boldness. He knew as well what to say as any man; yet he desires them to pray for him, that he may *speak as he ought to speak*. For the sake of the gospel he was *an ambassador in bonds*, *v.* 20. He was persecuted and imprisoned for preaching the gospel; though, notwithstanding, he continued in the embassy committed to him by Christ. The best ministers may receive advantage by the prayers of good Christians; and therefore should earnestly desire them.

II. He recommends Tychicus unto them, *v.* 21, 22. He sent him with this epistle, that he might acquaint them how he did, and what he did. It is desirable to good ministers both that their Christian friends should know their state and that they should be acquainted with the condition of their friends; for by this means they may the better help each other in their prayers.—*And that he might comfort their hearts*, by giving such an account of his sufferings, as might prevent their fainting at his tribulations and even minister matter of joy and thanksgiving unto them. Tychicus was *a beloved brother and faithful minister in the Lord*. He was very dear to Paul, which makes Paul's love to these Christian Ephesians the more observable, in that he should now part with so good and dear a friend for their sakes. But the faithful servants of Jesus Christ are wont to prefer the public good to their own personal interests.

III. He concludes with his good wishes and prayers for them, and not for them only, but for all the brethren, *v.* 23, 24. *Peace be to the brethren, and love with faith*; faith and love including all the rest. It is the continuance and increase of these that he desires for them, in whom they were already begun. *From God the Father*, &c. The closing benediction is more extensive than the former; for in this he prays for all true believers at Ephesus, and everywhere else. Our love to Christ is not acceptable, unless it be in sincerity: indeed there is no such thing as love to Christ, whatever men may pretend, where there is not sincerity. Grace, that is, the favour of God, and all good, the product of it, are and shall be with all those who thus love our Lord Jesus Christ. And it is, or ought to be, the prayer of every lover of Christ that it may be so with all his fellow-christians. *Amen*, so be it.

JAMIESON, FAUSSET, BROWN

supplication—a common term for a special kind of prayer [HARLESS], *an imploring request*. "Prayer" for obtaining blessings, "supplication" for averting evils which we fear [GROTIUS]. **in the Spirit**—to be joined with "praying." It is he *in us*, as the Spirit of adoption, who prays, and enables us to pray (Rom. 8:15, 26; Gal. 4:6; Jude 20). **watching**—not sleeping (ch. 5:14; Ps. 88:13; Matt. 26:41). So in the temple a perpetual watch was maintained (cf. Anna, Luke 2:37). **thereunto**—"watching unto" (with a view to) prayer and supplication. **with**—*Greek*, "in." *Persevering constancy* ("perseverance") *and* (i.e., exhibited in) *supplication* are to be the element in which our watchfulness is to be exercised. **for all saints**—as none is so perfect as not to need the intercessions of his fellow Christians. **19. for me**—a different *Greek* preposition from that in vs. 18; translate, therefore, "on my behalf." **that I may open my mouth boldly**—rather, "that there may be given to me 'utterance,' or 'speech' *in the opening of my mouth* (when I undertake to speak; a formula used in *set and solemn* speech, Job 3:1; Dan. 10:16), so as *with boldness to make known* . . . ." etc. Bold plainness of speech was the more needed, as the Gospel is a "mystery" undiscoverable by mere reason, and only known by revelation. Paul looked for utterance to be *given* him; he did not depend on his natural or acquired power. The shortest road to any heart is by way of heaven; pray to God to open the door and to open your mouth, so as to avail yourself of every opening (Jer. 1:7, 8; Ezek. 3:8, 9, 11; II Cor. 4:13). **20. For**—*Greek*, as in vs. 19, "*On behalf of* which." **an ambassador in bonds**—a paradox. Ambassadors were held inviolable by the law of nations, and could not, without outrage to every sacred right, be put in chains. Yet Christ's "ambassador is in *a chain!*" The *Greek* is singular. The Romans used to bind a prisoner to a soldier by *a single chain*, in a kind of free custody. So Acts 28:16, 20, "I am bound with this *chain*." The term, "bonds" (plural), on the other hand, is used when the prisoner's hands or feet were bound together (Acts 26:29); cf. Acts 12:6, where the plural marks the distinction. The singular is only used of the particular kind of custody described above; an undesigned coincidence [PALEY]. **21. that ye also**—as I have been discussing things relating to you, so that ye also may know about me (cf. Col. 4:7, 8). NEANDER takes it, "Ye also," as well as the Colossians (Col. 4:6). **my affairs**—*Greek*, "the things concerning me." **how I do**—how I fare. **Tychicus**—an Asiatic, and so a fit messenger bearing the respective Epistles to Ephesus and Colosse (Acts 20:4; II Tim. 4:12). **a . . .**—*Greek*, "*the* beloved brother"; the same epithet as in Colossians 4:7. **minister**—i.e., *servant*. **in the Lord**—in the Lord's work. **22. for the same purpose**—*Greek*, "for this very purpose." Colossians 4:8 is almost word for word the same as this verse. **our affairs**—*Greek*, "the things concerning us," viz., concerning myself. "Aristarchus, my fellow prisoner, and Marcus, sister's son to Barnabas" (Col. 4:10). **23. love with faith**—Faith is presupposed as theirs; he prays that love may accompany it (Gal. 5:6). **24.** Contrast the malediction on all who love Him not (I Cor. 16:22). **in sincerity**—*Greek*, "*in incorruption*," i.e., not as *English Version*, but "with an immortal (constant) love" [WAHL]. Cf. "that which is not corruptible" (I Pet. 3:4). Not a fleeting, earthly love, but a spiritual and eternal one [ALFORD]. Contrast Colossians 2:22, worldly things "which perish with the using." Cf. I Corinthians 9:25, "corruptible . . . *incorruptible* crown." "Purely," "holily" [ESTIUS], without the corruption of sin (*Note*, I Cor. 3:17; II Pet. 1:4; Jude 10). Where the Lord Jesus has a true believer, there I have a brother [BISHOP M'ILWAINE]. He who is good enough for Christ, is good enough for me [R. HALL]. The differences of opinion among real Christians are comparatively small, and show that they are not following one another like silly sheep, each trusting the one before him. Their agreement in the main, while showing their independence as witnesses by differing in non-essentials, can only be accounted for by their being all in the right direction (Acts 15:8, 9; I Cor. 1:2; 12:3).

ADAM CLARKE

the act. *With all prayer* refers to the different kinds of prayer that are performed in public, in the family, in the closet, in business, on the way, in the heart without a voice, and with the voice from the heart. All these are necessary to the genuine Christian, and he whose heart is right with God will be frequent in the whole. *And supplication*. There is a difference between *prayer* and *supplication*. Some think the former means prayer for the attainment of good; the latter, prayer for averting evil. Supplication however seems to mean prayer continued in, strong and incessant pleadings, till the evil is averted or the good communicated. There are two things that must be attended to in prayer: (1) That it be "in every time, season, or opportunity"; (2) That it should be "in or through the Spirit"—that the heart should be engaged in it, and that its infirmities should be helped by the Holy Ghost. *Watching thereunto*. Being always on your guard lest your enemies should surprise you. Watch, not only against evil, but also for opportunities to do good, and for opportunities to receive good. Without watchfulness, prayer and all the spiritual armor will be ineffectual. *With all perseverance*. Being always intent on your object, and never losing sight of your danger, or of your interest. The word implies "stretching out the neck" and "looking about" in order to discern an enemy at a distance. *For all saints*. For all Christians; for this was the character by which they were generally distinguished.

19. *And for me, that utterance may be given unto me*. Kypke has proved by many examples that *logon didonai* signifies permission and power to defend oneself in a court of justice; and this sense of the phrase is perfectly applicable to the case of Paul, who was "an ambassador in bonds" (v. 20), and expected to be called to a public hearing, in which he was not only to defend himself, but to prove the truth and excellency of the Christian religion.

20. *An ambassador in bonds*. An ambassador being the representative of his king, his person was in all civilized countries held sacred. Contrary to the rights of nations, this ambassador of the King of heaven was put in chains! He had, however, the opportunity of defending himself and of vindicating the honor of his Master.

21. *That ye also*. As well as other churches to whom I have communicated the dealings of both God and man to me. *May know my affairs*. May be acquainted with my situation and circumstances. *And how I do*. How I employ my time, and what fruit there is of my apostolical labors. *Tychicus, a beloved brother*. We learn, from Acts xx. 4, that Tychicus was of Asia, and that he was a useful companion of Paul. This same person, and with the same character and commendation, is mentioned in the Epistle to the Colossians, chap. iv. 7. He is mentioned also in Titus iii. 12 and in 2 Tim. iv. 12; from all these places it is evident that he was a person in whom the apostle had the highest confidence, and that he was a very eminent minister of Christ.

22. *Whom I have sent unto you for the same purpose*. Namely, that the Ephesians might know his affairs and those of the church at Rome; messengers of this kind frequently passed between the churches in those ancient times. *Comfort your hearts*. By showing you how powerfully he was upheld in all his tribulations, and how God turned his bonds to the furtherance of the gospel. This must have been great consolation to all the followers of God.

23. *Peace*. All prosperity, and continual union with God and among yourselves; *and love* to God and man, the principle of all obedience and union; *with faith*, continually increasing, and growing stronger and stronger, *from God the Father*, as the Fountain of all our mercies, *and the Lord Jesus Christ*, through whose sacrifice and mediation they all come.

24. *Grace be with all them*. May the divine "favor" and all the benedictions flowing from it be with all them who love our Lord Jesus Christ, who has so loved us as to give His life to redeem ours and to save us unto life eternal. *In sincerity*. In "incorruptibility." Those who show the genuineness of their love by walking before Him in holiness of life.

THE EPISTLE TO THE PHILIPPIANS

I. Introduction (1:1, 2)
A. The writers (1:1a)
B. The readers (1:1b)
C. The salutation (1:2)

II. Experience (1:3-26)
A. The joy of memory (1:3-11)
1. Its consciousness (1:3-7)
2. Its activity (1:8-11)
B. The joy of experience (1:12-18)
1. The value of bonds (1:12-14)
2. The preaching of Christ (1:15-18)
C. The joy of expectation (1:19-26)
1. Christ shall be magnified (1:19-24)
2. I shall abide (1:25, 26)

III. Exposition (1:27-4:1)
A. Manner of life worthy of Gospel (1:27-30)
1. Stand fast in one (1:27)
2. Nothing affrighted (1:28)
3. To suffer with Christ (1:29, 30)
B. The mind of Christ (2:1-18)
1. Its activity (2:1-4)
2. Its nature (2:5-11)
3. Its value (2:12-18)
C. Parenthesis—Timothy and Epaphroditus (2:19-30)
D. Joy in the Lord (3:1-4:1)
1. The peril (3:1-3)
2. The illustration (3:4-14)
3. The responsibility (3:15-4:1)

IV. Exhortation (4:2-20)
A. An illustration—Euodia and Syntyche (4:2, 3)
1. A difference to be healed (4:2)
2. Neglect to cease (4:3)
B. The treatment (4:4-9)
1. For differences (4:4-7)
2. For neglect (4:8, 9)
C. The confidence (4:10-20)
1. The revival (4:10-14)
2. The beginning (4:15-18)
3. The future (4:19, 20)

V. Conclusion (4:21-23)
A. The salutation of saints (4:21, 22)
B. The benediction (4:23)

Philippi was a chief city of the western part of Macedonia. This remarkable epistle was written when Paul was a prisoner at Rome. Paul seems to have had a very particular kindness for the church at Philippi, which he himself had been instrumental in planting; he had, upon that account, a particular fatherly, tender care of this. He looked upon them as his children, and, having "begotten them by the gospel," he was desirous by the same gospel to nourish and nurse them up.

I. He was called in an extraordinary manner to preach the gospel at Philippi. A vision appeared to Paul in the night: "There stood a man of Macedonia, and prayed him, saying, Come over into Macedonia, and help us." He saw God going before him.

II. At Philippi he suffered hard things; yet he had not the less kindness for the place. We must never love our friends the less for the ill treatment which our enemies give us.

III. The beginnings of that church were very small; yet that did not discourage him. If good be not done at first, it may be done afterward and the last works may be more abundant.

IV. It seems that this church at Philippi grew into a flourishing church, and particularly that the brethren were very kind to Paul. He acknowledges the receipt of a present they had sent him (4.18), and this when no other church communicated with him as concerning giving and receiving (4:15).

MATTHEW HENRY

CHAPTER 1

Verses 1, 2

I. The persons writing the epistle—*Paul and Timotheus, the servants of Jesus Christ.* The highest honour of the greatest apostle, and most eminent ministers, is to be the servants of Jesus Christ; not the masters of the churches, but the servants of Christ.

II. The persons to whom it is directed. 1. To *all the saints in Christ who are at Philippi.* He mentions the church before the ministers, because the ministers are for the church, not the churches for the ministers. They are not only the servants of Christ, but the servants of the church for his sake. It is directed to *all the saints,* one as well as another, even the meanest, the poorest, and those of the least gifts. Christ makes no difference; the rich and the poor meet together in him: *Saints in Christ Jesus.* Out of Christ the best saints will appear sinners, and unable to stand before God. 2. *With the bishops and deacons,* the bishops or elders, whose office it was to teach and rule, and the deacons, or overseers of the poor, who took care of the outward business of the house of God. These were all the offices which were then known in the church, and which were of divine appointment.

JAMIESON, FAUSSET, BROWN

CHAPTER 1

VSS. 1-30. INSCRIPTION. THANKSGIVING AND PRAYERS FOR THE FLOURISHING SPIRITUAL STATE OF THE PHILIPPIANS. HIS OWN STATE AT ROME, AND THE RESULT OF HIS IMPRISONMENT IN SPREADING THE GOSPEL. EXHORTATION TO CHRISTIAN CONSISTENCY.

1. Timotheus—mentioned as being well known to the Philippians (Acts 16:3, 10-12), and now present with Paul. Not that Timothy had any share in writing the Epistle; for Paul presently uses the first person singular, "I," not "we" (vs. 3). The mention of his name implies merely that Timothy joined in affectionate remembrances to them. **servants of Jesus Christ**—The oldest MSS. read the order, "Christ Jesus." Paul does not call himself "an apostle," as in the inscriptions of other Epistles; for the Philippians needed not to be reminded of his apostolic authority. He writes rather in a tone of affectionate familiarity. **all**—so vss. 4, 7, 8, 25; ch. 2:17, 26. It implies comprehensive affection which desired not to forget any one among them "all." **bishops**—synonymous with "presbyters" in the apostolical churches; as appears from the same persons being called "elders of the Church" at Ephesus (Acts 20:17), and "overseers" (Acts 20:28), *Greek,* "bishops." And Titus 1:5, cf. with vs. 7. This is the earliest letter of Paul where bishops and deacons are mentioned, and the only one where they are separately addressed in the salutation. This accords with the probable course of events, deduced alike from the letters and history. While the apostles were constantly visiting the churches in person or by messengers, regular pastors would be less needed; but when some were removed by various causes, provision for the permanent order of the churches would be needed. Hence the three pastoral letters, subsequent to this Epistle, give instruction as to the due appointment of bishops and deacons.

ADAM CLARKE

CHAPTER 1

1. *Paul and Timotheus.* That Timothy was at this time with the apostle in Rome we learn from chap. ii. 19, and also that he was very high in the apostle's estimation. He had also accompanied the apostle on his two voyages to Philippi (see Acts xvi and xx), and was therefore deservedly dear to the church in that city. It was on these accounts that Paul joined his name to his own, not because he was in any part the author of this Epistle, but he might have been the apostle's amanuensis, though the subscription to the Epistle gives this office to Epaphroditus. Neither in this Epistle nor in those to the Thessalonians and to Philemon does Paul call himself an apostle; the reason of which appears to be that in none of these places was his apostolical authority called in question. *Bishops and deacons.* The "overseers" of the Church of God, and those who ministered to the poor, and preached occasionally. There has been a great deal of paper wasted on the inquiry, "Who is meant by bishops here, as no place could have more than one bishop?" To which it has been answered: "Philippi was a metropolitan see, and might have several bishops." This is the extravagance of trifling. I believe no such officer is meant as we now term "bishop."

MATTHEW HENRY

III. The apostolical benediction: *Grace be unto you, and peace, from God our Father, and from the Lord Jesus Christ, v.* 2. This is the same, almost word for word, in all the epistles, we must not be shy of forms, though we are not to be tied down to them. *Grace and peace*—the free favour and goodwill of God, and all the blessed fruits and effects of it, and that *from God our Father, and from the Lord Jesus Christ.* No peace without grace. Inward peace springs from a sense of divine favour. No grace and peace but from God our Father, the fountain and original of all blessings. No grace and peace from God our Father, but in and through our Lord Jesus Christ.

Verses 3–6

The apostle proceeds to thanksgiving for the saints at Philippi.

I. Paul remembered them: he bore them much in his thoughts. *Upon every mention of you.* As he often thought of them, so he often spoke of them, and delighted to hear them spoken of. It is a pleasure to hear of the welfare of an absent friend.

II. He remembered them with joy. At Philippi he was maltreated; and yet he remembers Philippi with joy. So far was he from being ashamed of them, or loth to hear of the scene of his sufferings, that he remembered it with joy.

III. He remembered them in prayer: *Always in every prayer of mine for you all, v.* 4. The best remembrance of our friends is to remember them at the throne of grace. He had seasons of prayer for the church at Philippi. God gives us leave to be thus free with him, though, for our comfort, he knows whom we mean when we do not name them.

IV. He thanked God upon every joyful remembrance of them. Thanksgiving must have a part in every prayer. What we have the comfort of, God must have the glory of. He thanked God, as well as made requests with joy.

V. *I thank my God.* It encourages us in prayer, and enlarges the heart in praise, to see every mercy coming from the hand of God as our God.—*I thank my God upon every remembrance of you.* He gives thanks to God. 1. For the comfort he had in them: for *your fellowship in the gospel, from the first day until now, v.* 5. Gospel fellowship is a good fellowship. Those who sincerely receive the gospel have fellowship in it *from the very first day*: a new-born Christian, if he is true-born, is interested in all the promises of the gospel from the first day of his becoming such. —*Until now.* It is a great comfort to ministers when those who begin well hold on and persevere. 2. For the confidence he had concerning them (*v.* 6): *Being confident of this very thing,* &c. The confidence of Christians is the great comfort of Christians, and we may fetch matter of praise from our hopes as well as from our joys. Paul speaks with much confidence. *That he who has begun a good work in you will perform it unto the day of Jesus Christ.* A good work *among you*—he who hath planted Christianity in the world will preserve it as long as the world stands. But it is rather to be applied to particular persons, and then it speaks of the certain accomplishment of the work of grace wherever it is begun. (1) The work of grace is a good work. It makes us like God, and fits us for the enjoyment of God. (2) Wherever this good work is begun it is of God's beginning: *He has begun a good work in you.* We could not begin it ourselves, for we are by nature *dead in trespasses and sins*: and what can dead men do towards raising themselves to life? It is God who quickens those who are thus dead. (3) The work of grace is but begun in this life; it is not finished here. (4) If the same God who begins the good work did not undertake the carrying on and finishing of it, it would lie for ever unfinished. (5) We may be confident that God will finish the work of his own hands. (6) The work of grace will never be perfected *till the day of Jesus Christ.* When he shall come to judge the world, then this work will be complete.

Verses 7, 8

The ardent affection he had for them: *I have you in my heart, v.* 7. 1. Why he had them in his heart: *Inasmuch as both in my bonds, and in the defence and confirmation of the gospel, you are all partakers of my grace;* they were partakers of that grace of God which by him was communicated to them. This makes people dear to their ministers—their receiving benefit by their ministry. Or, "*You are partakers of my grace,* you have joined with me in doing and suffering." They were partakers of his affliction by sympathy and concern, and readiness to assist him. Those shall share in the reward, who bear their part of the burden. He loved them because they adhered to him in his bonds, and in the *defence and confirmation of the gospel*: they were as ready to appear in

JAMIESON, FAUSSET, BROWN

2. Grace ... peace—The very form of this salutation implies the union of Jew, Greek, and Roman. The Greek salutation was "joy" (*chairein*), akin to the *Greek* for "grace" (*charis*). The Roman was "health," the intermediate term between *grace* and *peace.* The Hebrew was "peace," including both temporal and spiritual prosperity. *Grace* must come first if we are to have true *peace.* **from ... from**—Omit the second "from": as in the *Greek,* "God our Father" and "the Lord Jesus Christ," are most closely connected.

3. Translate, "In all my remembrance of you."

4. making request—Translate, "making *my* request." **for you all**—The frequent repetition in this Epistle of "all" with "you," marks that Paul desires to declare his love for *all* alike, and will not recognize any divisions among them. **with joy**—the characteristic feature in this Epistle, as *love* is in that to the Ephesians (cf. vs. 18; ch. 2:2, 19, 28; 3:1; 4:1, 4). *Love* and *joy* are the two first fruits of the Spirit. *Joy* gives especial animation to prayers. It marked his high opinion of them, that there was almost everything in them to give him *joy,* and almost nothing to give him pain. **5.** Ground of his "thanking God" (vs. 3): "For your (continued) fellowship (i.e., real spiritual participation) in (lit., 'in regard to') the Gospel from the first day (of your becoming *partakers* in it) until now." Believers have the fellowship of the Son of God (I Cor. 1:9) and of the Father (I John 1:3) in the Gospel, by becoming partakers of "the fellowship of the Holy Ghost" (II Cor. 13:14), and exercise that fellowship by acts of communion, not only the communion of the Lord's Supper, but holy liberality to brethren and ministers (ch. 4:10, 15, "*communicated* ... concerning giving"; II Cor. 9:13; Gal. 6:6; Heb. 13:16, "To communicate forget not"). **6. confident**—This confidence nerves prayers and thanksgivings (vss. 3, 4). **this very thing**—*the very thing* which he prays for (vs. 4) is the matter of his believing confidence (Mark 11:24; I John 5:14, 15). Hence the result is sure. **he which hath begun**—God (ch. 2:13). **a good work**—Any work that God begins, He will surely finish (I Sam. 3:12). Not even men begin a work at random. Much more the fact of His beginning the work is a pledge of its completion (Isa. 26:12). So as to the particular work here meant, the *perfecting of their fellowship in the Gospel* (vs. 5; Ps. 37:24; 89:33; 138:8; John 10:28, 29; Rom. 8:29, 35-39; 11:1, 2; Heb. 6:17-19; Jas. 1:17; Jude 24). As God cast not off Israel for ever, though chastening them for a time, so He will not cast off the spiritual Israel (Deut. 33:3; Isa. 27:3, I Pet. 1:5). **perform it until**—"perfect it up to" [ALFORD, ELLICOTT, and others]. **the day of ... Christ**—(vs. 10). The Lord's coming, designed by God in every age of the Church to be regarded as near, is to be the goal set before believers' minds rather than their own death.

7. meet—*Greek,* "just." **to think this**—to have the prayerful confidence I expressed (vss. 4-6). **of you**—lit., "*in behalf of* you." Paul's confident prayer *in their behalf* was that God would perfect His own good work of grace in them. **because ...**—Punctuate and translate, "Because I have you in my heart (so vs. 8); otherwise the *Greek* and the words immediately following in the verse, favor MARGIN, '*Ye* have *me* in *your* heart ... being partakers of my grace' (both, in my bonds, and in *my* defense and confirmation of the Gospel), you (I say) all being fellow partakers of my grace." This last clause thus assigns the reason why he has them *in his heart* (i.e., cherished in his love, II Cor. 3:2; 7: 3), even in his bonds, and in his defense and con-

ADAM CLARKE

3. *Upon every remembrance.* As often as you recur to my mind, so often do I thank God for the great work wrought among you. Some think that the words should be translated, "for all your kind remembrance," referring to their kind attention to the apostle in supplying his wants.

4. *Always in every prayer.* I pray often for you, and have great pleasure in doing it, seeing what God has already wrought among you.

5. *For your fellowship in the gospel.* If we consider *koinonia* as implying spiritual *fellowship* or "communion," then it signifies, not only their attention to the gospel, their readiness to continue it, and perseverance in it, but also their unity and affection among themselves. Some understand the word as expressing their liberality to the apostle, and to the gospel in general; for the term may not only be applied to communion among themselves, but to communications to others. This sense, though followed by Chrysostom and Theophylact, does not appear to be the best; though we know it to be a fact that they were liberal in supplying the apostle's necessities, and, no doubt, in ministering to the support of others.

6. *Being confident.* There shall be nothing lacking on God's part to support you; and to make you wise, holy, and happy; and bring you at last to His kingdom and glory.

7. *It is meet for me to think this.* It is "just" that I should think so, because *I have you in my heart*—you live in my warmest love and most affectionate remembrance. *Inasmuch as both in my bonds.* Because you have set your hearts upon me in my bonds, sending Epaphroditus to minister to me in my necessities, chap. ii. 25, and contributing of your own substance to me, chap. iv. 14, sending once and again to me while I was in bonds for the defense of the faith, vv. 15-16; those things which, being "a sweet savour, a sacrifice well pleasing and acceptable to God," v. 18, confirm my hope concerning you; especially when I find you yet standing firm under the like afflictions, "having the same conflict which ye saw in me" (when

MATTHEW HENRY

their places for the defence of the gospel, as the apostle was in his. Fellow sufferers should be dear one to another. 2. The evidence of it: *It is meet for me to think this of you all, because I have you in my heart.* By this it appeared that he had them in his heart, because he had a good opinion of them. It is very proper to think the best of other people, and as well as we can of them. 3. An appeal to God concerning the truth of this (*v.* 8): *For God is my record how greatly I long after you all in the bowels of Jesus Christ.* Having them in his heart, he longed after them. He had *joy in them* (*v.* 4), because of the good he saw and heard of among them. He *longed after them all*, not only those among them who were witty and wealthy, but even the meanest and poorest; and he *longed greatly* after them. And this *in the bowels of Jesus Christ*, with that tender concern which Christ himself has and has shown to precious souls. Paul was herein a follower of Christ, and all good ministers should aim to be so. Shall not we pity and love those souls whom Christ had such a love and pity for? For this he appeals to God: *God is my record.* "Whether you know it or not, God, who knows the heart, knows it."

Verses 9–11

The prayers he put up for them. Paul often let his friends know what it was he begged of God for them, that they might know what to beg for themselves, and that they might be encouraged to hope they should receive from God the comforting grace which Paul asked of God for them. He prayed, 1. That they might be a loving people: *That your love might abound yet more and more.* Those who abound much in any grace have still need to abound more and more, because we are imperfect in our best attainments. 2. That they might be a knowing and judicious people: that love might abound *in knowledge and in all judgment.* It is not a blind love that will recommend us to God. Strong passions, without knowledge and a settled judgment, will not make us complete in the will of God, and sometimes do more hurt than good. 3. That they might be a discerning people. *That you may approve the things which are excellent* (*v.* 10); or, as it is in the margin, *Try the things which differ;* that we may approve the things which are excellent upon the trial of them, and discern their difference from other things. The truths and laws of Christ are excellent things. We only need to try them, to approve of them. 4. That they might be an honest upright-hearted people: *That you may be sincere.* Sincerity is our gospel perfection. When we are really what we appear to be, and mean honestly, then we are sincere. 5. That they might be an inoffensive people: that you may be *without offence until the day of Christ*; not apt to take offence; and very careful not to give offence to God or their brethren. And we must continue to the end *blameless*, that we may be presented so at the *day of Christ*. 6. That they might be a fruitful useful people (*v.* 11): *Being filled with the fruits of righteousness*, &c. From God is our fruit found, and therefore from him it must be asked. *Being filled* with them. Fear not being emptied by bringing forth the fruits of righteousness, for you will be filled with them. These fruits are *by Jesus Christ*, and they are *unto the glory and praise of God.* We must not aim at our own glory in our fruitfulness. It is much for the honour of God, when Christians not only are good, but do good, and *abound in good works.*

Verses 12–20

He was now a prisoner at Rome; this might be a stumbling-block to those who had received the gospel by his ministry. They might be shy of owning this doctrine, lest they should be involved in the same trouble themselves. Now to take off the offence of the cross, he expounds this dark and hard chapter of his sufferings.

I. He suffered by the sworn enemies of the gospel; but they should not be stumbled at this, for good was brought out of it, and it tended to the furtherance of the gospel (*v.* 12): *The things which happened unto me have fallen out rather unto the furtherance of the gospel.*

A strange chemistry of Providence this, to extract so great a good as the enlargement of the gospel out of so great an evil as the confinement of the apostle.

1. It alarmed those who were without (*v.* 13): *My bonds in Christ are manifest in all the palace and in all other places.* Paul's sufferings made him known at court, and this might lead some of them to enquire after the gospel for which he suffered, which they might otherwise have never heard of. When his bonds were manifest in the palace, they were manifest in all other places.

JAMIESON, FAUSSET, BROWN

firmation of the Gospel (such as he was constantly making in private, Acts 28:17-23; his self-defense and confirmation of the Gospel being necessarily conjoined, as the *Greek* implies; cf. vs. 17), viz., "inasmuch as ye are fellow partakers of my grace": inasmuch as ye share with me in "the fellowship of the Gospel" (vs. 5), and have manifested this, both by suffering as I do for the Gospel's sake (vss. 28-30), and by imparting to me of your substance (ch. 4:15). It is natural and right for me thus confidently to pray in your behalf. (ELLICOTT, and others translate, "To be thus minded for you all"), because of my having you in my warmest remembrances even in my bonds, since you are sharers with me in the Gospel grace. Bonds do not bind love. **8.** Confirmation of vs. 7. **record**—i.e., *witness.* **in the bowels of Jesus Christ**—"Christ Jesus" is the order in the oldest MSS. My *yearning love* (so the *Greek* implies) to you is not merely from natural affection, but from devotedness to Christ Jesus. "Not Paul, but Jesus Christ lives in Paul; wherefore Paul is not moved in the bowels [i.e., the tender love, Jer. 31:20] of Paul, but of Jesus Christ" [BENGEL]. All real spiritual love is but a portion of Christ's love which yearns in all who are united to Him [ALFORD]. **9.** The subject of his prayer for them (vs. 4). **your love**—to Christ, producing love not only to Paul, Christ's minister, as it did, but also to one another, which it did not altogether as much as it ought (ch. 2:2; 4:2). **knowledge**—of doctrinal and practical truth. **judgment**—rather, "perception"; "perceptive sense." Spiritual perceptiveness: spiritual sight, spiritual hearing, spiritual feeling, spiritual taste. Christianity is a vigorous plant, not the hotbed growth of enthusiasm. "Knowledge" and "perception" guard love from being ill-judged. **10.** Lit., "*With a view to* your *proving* (and so approving and embracing) *the things that excel*" (Rom. 2:18); not merely things not bad, but the things best among those that are good; the things of more advanced excellence. Ask as to things, not merely, Is there no harm, but is there any good, and which is the best? **sincere**—from a *Greek* root. *Examined in the sunlight and found pure.*

without offence—not stumbling; running the Christian race without falling through any stumbling block, i.e., temptation, in your way. **till**—rather, "unto," "against"; so that when the day of Christ comes, ye may be found pure and without offense. **11.** The oldest MSS. read the singular, "fruit." So Galatians 5:22 (see *Note*); regarding the works of righteousness, however manifold, as *one* harmonious whole, "the *fruit* of the Spirit" (Eph. 5:9); Jas. 3:18, "the fruit of righteousness" (Heb. 12:11); Rom. 6:22, "fruit unto holiness." **which are**—"which *is* by (*Greek, through*) Jesus Christ." Through His sending to us the Spirit from the Father. "We are wild and useless olive trees till we are graffed into Christ, who, by His living root, makes us fruit-bearing branches" [CALVIN]. **12. understand**—*Greek,* "know." The Philippians probably had feared that his imprisonment would hinder the spread of the Gospel; he therefore removes this fear. **the things which happened unto me**—*Greek,* "the things concerning me." **rather**—so far is my imprisonment from hindering the Gospel. Faith takes in a favorable light even what seems adverse [BENGEL] (vss. 19, 28; ch. 2:17). **13. my bonds in Christ**—rather as *Greek,* "So that my bonds *have become manifest in Christ,*" i.e., known, as endured in Christ's cause. **palace**—lit., "Prætorium," i.e., the barrack of the Prætorian guards attached to the palace of Nero, on the Palatine hill at Rome; not the general Prætorian camp outside of the city; for this was not connected with "Cæsar's household," which ch. 4:22 shows the Prætorium here meant was. The emperor was "Prætor," or Commander-in-Chief; naturally then the barrack of his bodyguard was called the Prætorium. Paul seems now not to have been at large in his own hired house, though chained to a soldier, as in Acts 28:16, 20, 30, 31, but in strict custody in the Prætorium; a change which probably took place on Tigellinus becoming Prætorian Prefect. See my *Introduction.* **in all other places**—so CHRYSOSTOM. Or else, "TO all the rest," i.e., "manifest to all the other" Prætorian soldiers stationed elsewhere, through the instrumentality of the Prætorian household guards who might for the time be attached to the emperor's palace, and who relieved one another in succession. Paul had been now upwards of two years a prisoner, so that there was time for his cause and the Gospel having become widely known at Rome.

ADAM CLARKE

I was among you, Acts xvi. 12, etc.), "and now hear to be in me," chap. i. 30.

8. *For God is my record.* I call God to witness that I have the strongest affection for you, and that I love you with that same kind of tender concern with which Christ loved the world when He gave himself for it; for I am even ready to "be offered upon the sacrifice and service of your faith," chap. ii. 17.

9. *This I pray.* This is the substance of all my prayers for you, *that your love* to God, to one another, and to all mankind, *may abound yet more and more;* that it may be like a river, perpetually fed with rain and fresh streams, so that it continues to swell and increase till it fills all its banks and floods the adjacent plains. *In knowledge.* Of God's nature, perfections, your own duty and interest, His work upon your souls, and His great designs in the gospel. *And in all judgment.* In all "spiritual or moral feeling"; that you may at once have the clearest perception and the fullest enjoyment of those things which concern your salvation.

10. *That ye may approve things that are excellent.* "To the end that you may put to proof the things that differ," or the things that are "more profitable." By the pure and abundant love which they received from God they would be able to try whatever differed from the teaching they had received, and from the experience they had in spiritual things. *That ye may be sincere.* The word which we translate "sincerity" is compounded of *eile,* the "splendor of the sun," and *krino,* "I judge"; a thing which may be examined in the clearest and strongest light without the possibility of detecting a single flaw or imperfection. Be so purified and refined in your souls, by the indwelling Spirit, that even the light of God shining into your hearts shall not be able to discover a fault that the love of God has not purged away. Our word sincerity is from the Latin *sinceritas,* which is compounded of *sine,* "without," and *cera,* "wax," and is a metaphor taken from clarified honey; for the pure or clarified honey is that which is *sine cera,* without wax, no part of the comb being left in it. Sincerity, taken in its full meaning, is a word of the most extensive import; and, when applied in reference to the state of the soul, is as strong as the word "perfection" itself. The soul that is sincere is the soul that is without sin. *Without offence.* Neither offending God nor your neighbor; being neither stumbled yourselves nor the cause of stumbling to others. *Till the day of Christ.* Till He comes to judge the world, or till the day in which you are called into the eternal world. According to this prayer a man, under the power and influence of the grace of God, may so love as never to offend his Maker, to the latest period of his life. Those who deny this must believe that the Spirit of God either cannot or will not do it, or that the blood of Christ cannot cleanse from all unrighteousness.

11. *Being filled with the fruits of righteousness.* By *righteousness* we may understand here the whole work of the Spirit of God in the soul of a believer; and by the *fruits* of righteousness, all holy tempers, holy words, and right actions. And with these they are to be *filled,* "filled up, filled full"; the whole soul and life occupied with them, ever doing something by which glory is brought to God, or good done to man. *By Jesus Christ.* That is, according to His doctrine, through the power of His grace, and by the agency of His Spirit. *Unto the glory and praise of God.* God being honored when the work of His grace thus appears to men in the fruits of righteousness; and God is praised by all the faithful when His work thus appears.

12. *That the things which happened unto me.* Paul was at this time a prisoner at Rome, and it appears probable that he had already been called to make a defense for himself, and to vindicate the doctrines of the gospel; and this he had been enabled to do in such a manner that the honor of the gospel had been greatly promoted by it.

13. *My bonds in Christ are manifest in all the palace.* In consequence of the public defense which he was obliged to make, his doctrines must be fully known in the court and throughout the whole city, as on his trial he would necessarily explain the whole. The *praetorium,* which we here translate *palace,* signifies the

MATTHEW HENRY

2. It emboldened those who were within. As his enemies were startled at his sufferings, so his friends were encouraged by them. *Many of the brethren in the Lord waxing confident by my bonds, v.* 14. When they saw Paul imprisoned for Christ, they were so far from being deterred from preaching Christ and praising his name, that it made them the more bold. If they should be hurried from the pulpit to the prison, they could be reconciled to it, because they would be there in such good company. Besides, the comfort which Paul had in his sufferings greatly encouraged them. They saw that those who served Christ served a good Master, who could both bear them up and bear them out. *Waxing confident by my bonds.* That which was intended by the enemy to discourage the preachers of the gospel was overruled for their encouragement. And *are much more bold to speak the word without fear*: they see the worst of it, and therefore are not afraid to venture.

II. He suffered from false friends as well as from enemies (*v.* 15, 16): *Some preach Christ even of envy and strife. The one preach Christ of contention, not sincerely.* There were those who envied Paul's reputation in the churches, and endeavoured to supplant and undermine him. *Supposing to add affliction to my bonds.* However, there were others who were animated by Paul's sufferings to preach Christ the more vigorously: *Some also of goodwill, and love.—Knowing that I am set for the defence of the gospel.* This made them the more bold to preach the word.

III. How easy he was in the midst of all: *Notwithstanding every way, whether in pretence or in truth, Christ is preached; and I therein do rejoice, yea, and I will rejoice, v.* 18. It is God's prerogative to judge of the principles men act upon; this is out of our line. Paul was so far from envying those who had liberty to preach the gospel that he rejoiced in the preaching of it even by those who do it in pretence, and not in truth.

1. It tended to the salvation of the souls of men: *I know that this shall turn to my salvation, v.* 19. God can bring good out of evil. What reward can those expect who preach Christ out *of strife, and envy, and contention*, and to add affliction to a faithful minister's bonds? who preach in pretence, and not in truth? And yet even this may turn to the salvation of others; and Paul's rejoicing in it turned to his salvation too. *Through your prayers, and the supply of the Spirit of Christ.* The prayers of the people may bring a supply of the Spirit to their ministers, to support them in suffering, as well as in preaching the gospel.

2. It would turn to the glory of Christ, *v.* 20. *According to my earnest expectation and hope, that in nothing I shall be ashamed*, &c.

JAMIESON, FAUSSET, BROWN

14. Translate as *Greek,* "And *that* (vs. 13) *most* of the brethren in the Lord . . . ." "In the Lord," distinguishes them from "brethren after the flesh," Jewish fellow countrymen. ELLICOTT translates, "*Trusting in the Lord.*" **by my bonds**—encouraged by my patience in bearing my bonds. **much more bold**—Translate as *Greek,* "are more abundantly bold." **15.** "Some indeed *are preaching* Christ even *for* envy, i.e., to carry out the *envy* which they felt towards Paul, on account of the success of the Gospel in the capital of the world, owing to his steadfastness in his imprisonment; they wished through envy to transfer the credit of its progress from him to themselves. Probably Judaizing teachers (Rom. 14; I Cor. 3:10-15; 9:1, etc.; II Cor. 11:1-4). **some also of**—rather for—**good will**—answering to "the brethren" (vs. 14); some being *well disposed* to him. **16, 17.** The oldest MSS. transpose these verses, and read, "*These* (last) *indeed out of* love (to Christ and me), knowing (the opposite of 'thinking' below) that I am set (i.e., appointed by God, I Thess. 3:3) for the defense of the Gospel (vs. 7, not on my own account). But the others *out of* contention (or rather, 'a factious spirit'; 'cabal'; a spirit of intrigue, using unscrupulous means to compass their end; *Note*, Gal. 5:20; 'self-seeking' [ALFORD]) *proclaim* (the *Greek* is not the same as that for 'preach,' but, '*announce*') Christ, not sincerely (answering to 'but of a spirit of intrigue,' or 'self-seeking'). Lit., 'not purely'; not with a pure intention; the Jewish leaven they tried to introduce was in order to *glorify themselves* (Gal. 6:12, 13; see, however, *Note*, vs. 18), thinking (but in vain) *to raise up* (so the oldest MSS. read) *tribulation* to my bonds." Their *thought* was, that taking the opportunity of my being laid aside, they would exalt themselves by their Judaizing preaching, and depreciate me and my preaching, and so cause me trouble of spirit in my bonds; they thought that I, like themselves, sought my own glory, and so would be mortified at their success over mine. But they are utterly mistaken; "I rejoice" at it (vs. 18), so far am I from being *troubled* at it. **18.** "What then?" What follows from this? Does this trouble me as they thought it would? "Notwithstanding" their unkind *thought* to me, and self-seeking intention, the cause I have at heart is furthered "every way" of preaching, "whether in pretense (with a by motive, vs. 16) or in truth (out of true 'love' to Christ, vs. 17), Christ is *proclaimed;* and therein I do rejoice, yea, and I will rejoice." From this it would seem that these self-seeking teachers in the main "proclaimed Christ," not "another Gospel," such as the Judaizers in Galatia taught (Gal. 1:6-8); though probably having some of the Jewish leaven (*Note,* vss. 15, 16, 17), their *chief* error was their selfseeking envious *motive,* not so much error of doctrine; had there been *vital* error, Paul would not have *rejoiced.* The *proclamation of* CHRIST, however done, roused attention, and so was sure to be of service. Paul could thus rejoice at the good result of their bad intentions (Ps. 76:10; Isa. 10:5, 7). **19. turn to my salvation**—"turn out *to* me *for* (or *unto*) salvation." This proclamation of Christ every way will turn out to *my spiritual good.* Christ, whose interests are my interests, being glorified thereby; and so the coming of His kingdom being furthered, which, when it does come, will bring completed "SALVATION" (Heb. 9:28) to me and all whose "earnest expectation" (vs. 20) is that Christ may be magnified in them. So far is their preaching from causing me, as they thought, *tribulation in my bonds* (vs. 16). Paul plainly quotes and applies to himself the very words of the LXX (Job 13:16), "This shall turn out to my salvation," which belong to all God's people of every age, in their tribulation (cf. Job 13:15). **through your prayer and the supply**—The *Greek* intimately joins the two nouns together, by having but one preposition and one article: "Through your prayer and (*the consequent*) supply of the Spirit of Jesus Christ" (obtained for me through your prayer). **20. According to my earnest expectation**—The *Greek* expresses, "expectation *with uplifted head* (Luke 21:28) *and outstretched neck.*" Romans 8:19 is the only other place in the New Testament that the word occurs. TITTMANN says, in both places it implies not mere *expectation*, but *the anxious desire of an anticipated prosperous issue in afflictive circumstances.* The subject of his earnest expectation which follows, answers to "my salvation" (vs. 19). **in nothing I shall be ashamed**—in nothing have reason to be ashamed of "my work for God, or His work in me" [ALFORD]. Or, "in nothing be *disappointed* in my *hope*, but that I may fully obtain it" [ESTIUS]. So "ashamed" is used in Romans 9:33. **all bold-**

ADAM CLARKE

court where causes were heard and judged by the *praetor* or civil magistrate; it sometimes signifies the "general's tent," and at others the "emperor's palace." It is supposed that it is used in this latter sense here. There were, no doubt, persons belonging to the emperor's household who would bring the news of so remarkable a case to the palace; for we find that there were Christians even in Caesar's household; chap. iv. 22.

14. *Waxing confident.* Finding the effect produced by the public defense which the apostle made, they were greatly encouraged, and the more boldly and openly proclaimed the doctrine of Christ crucified.

15. *Some indeed preach Christ even of envy and strife.* These must have been the Judaizing teachers, who insisted on the necessity of connecting the Mosaic rites with the Christian institutions; and probably denounced Paul to the Jews dwelling at Rome as not only an enemy to the law and the prophets, but also as a very imperfect Christian, because he declared strongly against the doctrine of circumcision; and no doubt endeavored to prejudice him with the heathen Romans. *Some also of good will.* Some, through mere benevolence to the apostle, both espoused his doctrine and vindicated his cause.

16. *Preach Christ of contention.* The Judaizing teachers, they also preach Christ; they acknowledge that Jesus is the Christ or promised Messiah, and preach Him as such. *Not sincerely.* "Not chastely," garbling the gospel; not speaking the whole truth, but just what served their purpose; and at the same time they denounced the apostle as an enemy to the divine institutions, because he spoke against circumcision.

17. *The other of love.* Through a sincere desire, not only to make known the way of salvation to the people, but also to vindicate and help the apostle, because they considered him as appointed by God to preach and defend the gospel. The sixteenth and seventeenth verses are transposed by several MSS.

18. *What then?* It is a matter of little importance to me how Christ is preached, provided He be preached. I rejoice that anything is known of Him; and am truly glad that the gospel is even made partially known, for this will lead to further inquiries and in the end be of service to the truth.

19. *This shall turn to my salvation.* That is: It will be the means of my temporal "safety"; of my "deliverance"; for so the word *soteria* is here to be understood. The Jews had denounced the apostle as an enemy to Caesar; but he knew that, when the nature of the gospel should be fully known, the Romans would see that he could be no enemy to Caesar who proclaimed a prince whose kingdom was not of this world. *Through your prayer.* Knowing them to be genuine followers of Christ, he was satisfied that their prayers would be very available in his behalf; and under God he places much dependence upon them. *The supply of the Spirit of Jesus Christ.* The word which we translate *supply* signifies also "furnishing whatever is necessary." The Spirit of God he expected to help all his infirmities and to furnish him with all the wisdom, prudence, strength of reason, and argument which might be necessary for him in the different trials he had to pass through with his persecutors, and the civil powers, at whose judgment seat he stood.

20. *Earnest expectation.* He had the most confident expectation that God would stand by him, so that he should be enabled, with the "utmost liberty of speech," to testify the gospel of the grace of God; and, should he have the liberty of doing so, he was utterly regardless what the issue might be relative to himself.

MATTHEW HENRY

The great desire of every true Christian is that Christ may be magnified and glorified. Those who truly desire that Christ may be magnified desire that he may be *magnified in their body.* They are willing to serve his designs with every member of their body, as well as faculty of their soul. *That in nothing I shall be ashamed, but that with all boldness Christ may be magnified.* The boldness of Christians is the honour of Christ. Those who make Christ's glory their desire may make it their expectation and hope. If it be truly aimed at, it shall certainly be attained. Those who desire that Christ may be magnified in their bodies have a holy indifference *whether it be by life or by death.* They refer it to him which way he will make them serviceable to his glory, whether by their living to his honour in working for him or dying to his honour in suffering for him.

Verses 21–26

We have here an account of the life and death of blessed Paul: his life was Christ, and his death was gain. It is the undoubted character of every good Christian that to him to live is Christ. The glory of Christ ought to be the end of our life. All those to whom to live is Christ to them to die *will be gain.* Death is a great loss to a carnal worldly man; but to a good Christian it is gain. It delivers him from all the evils of life, and brings him to the possession of the chief good. Some read the whole expression thus: *To me, living and dying, Christ is gain.* "I desire no more, neither while I live nor when I die, but to win Christ and be found in him."

I. *If I live in the flesh, this is the fruit of my labour* (*v.* 22), that is, Christ is. He reckoned his labour well bestowed, if he could be instrumental to advance the kingdom of Christ in the world. It is worth while for a good Christian and a good minister to live in the world as long as he can glorify God and do good to his church. *Yet what I shall choose I wot not; for I am in a strait betwixt two.* It was a blessed strait which Paul was in, not between two evil things, but between two good things. Paul was in a strait between two blessings—living to Christ, and being with him.

1. His inclination was for death. We have naturally an aversion to death, but he had an inclination to it (*v.* 23); *Having a desire to depart, and to be with Christ.* It is being with Christ which makes a departure desirable to a good man. If I cannot be with Christ without departing, I shall reckon it desirable on that account to depart. *Which is far better.* Those who know the value of Christ and heaven will readily acknowledge it far better to be in heaven than to be in this world, to be with Christ. If we come to be with Christ, farewell sin and temptation, farewell sorrow and death, for ever.

2. His judgment was rather to live awhile longer in this world, for the service of the church (*v.* 24): *Nevertheless to abide in the flesh is more needful for you.* Paul's strait was not between living in this world and living in heaven; between these two there is no comparison: but his strait was between serving Christ in this world and enjoying him in another. To advance the interest of Christ and his church, he chose rather to tarry here, where he met with oppositions and difficulties, and to deny himself for awhile the satisfaction of his reward.

II. *And, having this confidence, I know that I shall abide and continue with you all for your furtherance and joy of faith, v.* 25. What a great confidence Paul had in the divine Providence, that it would order all for the best to him. Whatsoever is best for the church, we may be sure God will do. What ministers are continued for: *For our furtherance and joy of faith,* our further advancement in holiness and comfort. What promotes our *faith and joy of faith* is very much for our furtherance in the way to heaven. The more faith the more joy, and the more faith and joy the more we are furthered in our Christian course.

III. *That your rejoicing may be more abundant in Jesus Christ for me, by my coming to you again, v.* 26. They rejoiced in the hope of seeing him, and enjoying his further labours among them. All our joys should terminate in Christ. Our joy in good ministers should be our joy *in Christ Jesus for them.*

Verses 27–30

I. He exhorts them to strictness of conversation (*v.* 27): *Only let your conversation be as becometh the gospel of Christ.* Let it be in all respects as those who belong to the kingdom of God among men. It is an ornament to our profession when our conversation is of a piece with it.—*That whether I come and see you, or else be absent, I may hear of your affairs.* Our religion must not be bound up in the hands of our ministers. Whether ministers come or no, Christ is always at hand. Let me hear of you *that*

JAMIESON, FAUSSET, BROWN

ness—"all" is opposed to "in nothing," as "boldness" is the opposite to "ashamed." **so now also**—when "my body" is "in bonds" (vs. 17). **Christ**—not Paul, "shall be magnified." **life, or by death**—Whatever be the issue, I cannot lose; I must be the gainer by the event. Paul was not omniscient; in the issue of things pertaining to themselves, the apostles underwent the same probation of faith and patience as we. **21. For**—in either event (vs. 20) I must be the gainer, "For to me . . . ." **to live is Christ**—whatever life, time, and strength, I have, is Christ's; Christ is the sole object for which I live (Gal. 2:20). **to die is gain**—not the act of dying, but as the *Greek* ("to have died") expresses, *the state after death.* Besides the glorification of Christ by my death, which is my primary object (vs. 20), the change of state caused by death, so far from being a matter of *shame* (vs. 20) or loss, as my enemies suppose, will be a positive "gain" to me. **22.** Rather as *Greek,* "But if to live in the flesh (if), this (I say, the continuance in life which I am undervaluing) be the fruit of my labor (i.e., be the condition in which the fruit of my ministerial labor is involved), *then* what I shall choose I know not" (I cannot determine with myself, if the choice were given me, both alternatives being great goods alike). So ALFORD and ELLICOTT. BENGEL takes it as *English Version,* which the *Greek* will bear by supposing an ellipsis, "If to live in the flesh (be my portion), this (continuing to live) is the fruit of my labor," i.e., this continuance in life will be the occasion of my bringing in "the fruit of labor," i.e., will be the occasion of "labors" which are their own "fruit" or reward; or, this my continuing "to live" will have this "fruit," viz., "labors" for Christ. GROTIUS explains "the fruit of labor" as an idiom for "worth-while"; If I live in the flesh, this is worth my while, for thus Christ's interest will be advanced, "For to me to live is Christ" (vs. 21; cf. ch. 2:30; Rom. 1:13). The second alternative, viz., dying, is taken up and handled, ch. 2:17, "If I be offered." **23. For**—The oldest MSS. read, "But." "I know not (vs. 22), BUT am in a strait (am perplexed) betwixt *the* two (viz., 'to live' and 'to die'), having *the* desire *for* departing (lit., *to loose* anchor, II Tim. 4:6) and being with Christ; FOR (so the oldest MSS.) it is by far better"; or as the *Greek,* more forcibly, "by far *the more preferable";* a double comparative. This refutes the notion of the soul being dormant during its separation from the body. It also shows that, while he regarded the Lord's advent as at all times near, yet that his death before it was a very possible contingency. The *partial* life eternal is in the interval between death and Christ's second advent; the *perfectional,* at that advent [BISHOP PEARSON]. *To depart* is better than to remain in the flesh; *to be with Christ is far, far better;* a New Testament hope (Heb. 12:24), [BENGEL]. **24. to abide**—to continue somewhat longer. **for you**—*Greek,* "on your account"; "for your sake." In order to be of service to *you,* I am willing to forego my entrance a little sooner into blessedness; heaven will not fail to be mine at last. **25.** Translate, "And being confident of this." **I know . . .**—by prophetical intimations of the Spirit. He did not yet know the issue, as far as *human appearances* were concerned (ch. 2:23). He doubtless returned from his first captivity to Philippi (Heb. 13:19; Philemon 22). **joy of faith**—*Greek,* "joy in your faith." **26.** Translate, "That your matter of glorying (or *rejoicing*) may abound in Christ Jesus in me (i.e., in my case; *in respect to me,* or *for me* who have been granted to your prayers, vs. 19) through my presence again among you." ALFORD makes the "matter of glorying," *the possession of the Gospel,* received from Paul, which would abound, be assured and increased, by his presence among them; thus, "in me," implies that Paul is the worker of the material of abounding in Christ Jesus. But "my *rejoicing* over you" (ch. 2:16), answers plainly to "your *rejoicing* in respect to me" here.

27. Only—Whatever happens as to my coming to you, or not, make this your one only care. By supposing this or that future contingency, many persuade themselves they will be such as they ought to be, but it is better always without evasion to perform present duties under present circumstances [BENGEL]. **let your conversation be**—(Cf. ch. 3:20.) The *Greek* implies, "Let your *walk as citizens* (viz., of the heavenly state; 'the city of the living God,' Heb. 12:22, 'the heavenly Jerusalem,' 'fellow citizens of the saints,' Eph. 2:19) be . . . ." **I . . . see . . . hear**—so vs. 30. "Hear," in order to include both alternatives, must include the meaning *know.*

ADAM CLARKE

21. *For to me to live is Christ.* "Whether I live or die, Christ is gain to me." While I live I am Christ's property and servant, and Christ is my Portion. If I die, if I be called to witness the truth at the expense of my life, this will be gain; I shall be saved from the remaining troubles and difficulties in life, and be put immediately in possession of my heavenly inheritance.

22. *But if I live in the flesh.* Should I be spared longer, I shall labor for Christ as I have done; and *this is the fruit of my labour,* that Christ shall be magnified by my longer life, v. 20. *Yet what I shall choose I wot not.* Had I the two conditions left to my own choice, whether to die now and go to glory or whether to live longer in persecutions and affliction (glorifying Christ by spreading the gospel), I could not tell which to prefer.

23. *For I am in a strait betwixt two.* Viz., the dying now and being immediately with God or living longer to preach and spread the gospel and thus glorify Christ among men. *Having a desire to depart, and to be with Christ.* It appears to be a metaphor taken from the commander of a vessel, in a foreign port, who feels a strong desire "to set sail," and get to his own country and family; but this desire is counterbalanced by a conviction that the general interests of the voyage may be best answered by his longer stay in the port where his vessel now rides.

24. *To abide in the flesh.* It would certainly be gain to myself to die, but it will be a gain to you if I live.

25. *Having this confidence, I know that I shall abide.* Convinced that it is necessary that I should live longer, for the spreading and defense of the gospel, I am persuaded that I shall now be liberated. This was in fact the case, for, after having been two years in bonds at Rome, he was released. *For your furtherance.* In the way of righteousness. *And joy of faith.* And happiness in that way.

26. *That your rejoicing may be more abundant.* Men rejoice more in recovering a thing that was lost than they do in a continual possession of what is of much greater value.

27. *Let your conversation be as it becometh the gospel.* The apostle considers the church at Philippi as a free or imperial city, which possesses great honors, dignities, and privileges; and he exhorts them to act "worthy of or suitably to" those honors and privileges. This is the idea that is expressed by the word, "act according to the nature of your political situation," the citizenship and privileges which you possess in consequence of your being free inhabitants of Christ's imperial city, the Church. The apostle resumes the same metaphor, chap. iii. 20: "For our citizenship is in heaven." *Whether I come and see you.* Leaving the matter still in doubt as to them, whether he should again visit them.

MATTHEW HENRY

you stand fast in one spirit, with one mind striving together for the faith of the gospel. It becomes those who profess the gospel to strive for it. There is much opposition, and there is need of striving. A man may sleep and go to hell; but he who will go to heaven must look about him and be diligent. The unity and unanimity of Christians become the gospel: *Strive together*, not strive one with another. One spirit and one mind become the gospel. Steadfastness becomes the gospel: *Stand fast in one spirit, with one mind.* It is a shame to religion when the professors of it are off and on, unfixed in their minds, and unstable as water. Those who would strive for the faith of the gospel must stand firm to it.

II. He exhorts them to courage and constancy in suffering: *And in nothing terrified by your adversaries, v.* 28. Whatever oppositions we meet with, we must not be frightened at them. Persecuting is an *evident token of perdition.* Those who oppose the gospel of Christ are marked out for ruin. But being persecuted is a token of salvation. Not that it is a certain mark; many hypocrites have suffered for their religion; but it is a good sign that we are in good earnest in religion, when we are enabled in a right manner to suffer for the cause of Christ.—*For to you it is given on the behalf of Christ not only to believe, but also to suffer for his name, v.* 29. To believe in him. Faith is God's gift on the behalf of Christ. To suffer for the sake of Christ is a valuable gift too. If we suffer reproach and loss for Christ, we are to reckon it a great gift, always provided we behave under our sufferings with the genuine temper of martyrs (*v.* 30): "*Having the same conflict which you saw in me, and now hear to be in me;* suffering in the same manner as you saw and now hear of me that I suffer." It is not simply the suffering, but the cause, and not only the cause, but the spirit, which makes the martyr.

JAMIESON, FAUSSET, BROWN

your affairs—your state. **in one spirit**—the fruit of partaking of the Holy Spirit (Eph. 4:3, 4). **with one mind**—rather as *Greek, "soul,"* the sphere of the affections; subordinate to the "Spirit," man's higher and heavenly nature. "There is sometimes natural antipathies among believers; but these are overcome, when there is not only unity of spirit, but also of *soul*" [BENGEL]. **striving together**—with united effort.

28. terrified—lit., said of horses or other animals startled or suddenly scared; so of sudden *consternation* in general. **which**—your not being terrified. **evident token of perdition**—if they would only perceive it (II Thess. 1:5). It attests this, that in contending hopelessly against you, they are only rushing on to their own perdition, not shaking your united faith and constancy. **to you of salvation**—The oldest MSS. read, "of *your* salvation"; not merely *your temporal safety.* **29. For**—rather, a proof that this is an evident token from God of your salvation, *"Because . . . ."* **it is given**—*Greek,* "it *has been* granted *as a favor,*" or "gift of grace." Faith is the gift of God (Eph. 2:8), not wrought in the soul by the will of man, but by the Holy Ghost (John 1:12, 13). **believe on him**—"To believe *Him,*" would merely mean to believe He speaks the truth. "To believe *on Him,*" is to believe in, and trust through, Him to obtain eternal salvation. *Suffering for Christ* is not only not a mark of God's anger, but *a gift of His grace.* **30. ye saw in me**—(Acts 16:12, 19, etc.; I Thess. 2:2). I am "in nothing terrified by mine adversaries" (vs. 29), so ought not ye. The words here, "ye saw . . . and . . . hear," answer to "I come and *see* you, or else . . . *hear*" (vs. 27).

ADAM CLARKE

In one spirit. Being all of one mind under the influence of the Holy Ghost. *Striving together.* "Wrestling together," not in contention with each other, but in union against the enemies of the gospel faith.

28. *In nothing terrified by your adversaries.* So it appears that the church at Philippi was then under persecution.

29. *Unto you it is given in the behalf of Christ.* "To you it is graciously given"; it is no small privilege that God has so far honored you as to permit you to suffer on Christ's account. It is only His most faithful servants that He thus honors. Be not therefore terrified by your enemies; they can do nothing to you which God will not turn to your eternal advantage.

30. *Having the same conflict.* When Paul preached the gospel at Philippi he was grievously persecuted, as we learn from Acts xvi. 19-40, being stripped, scourged, thrown into prison, even into the dungeon, and his feet made fast in the stocks. This was the *conflict* they had seen in him; and now they heard that he had been sent prisoner to Rome as an evildoer, and that he was at present in bonds, and shortly to be tried for his life before the Roman emperor, to whom he had been obliged to appeal.

MATTHEW HENRY — CHAPTER 2

Verses 1–11

Further exhortations to Christian duties.

I. The great gospel precept pressed upon us; to love one another. This he represents (*v.* 2) by being *like-minded, having the same love, being of one accord, of one mind.* Christians should be one in affection, whether they can be one in apprehension or no. *Having the same love.* Christian love ought to be mutual love. Love, and you shall be loved. *Being of one accord, and of one mind;* unanimously agreeing in the great things of God and keeping the *unity of the Spirit* in other differences.

1. The pathetic pressing of the duty. The inducements to brotherly love are these: (1) "If there is any *consolation in Christ.* Have you experienced consolation in Christ? Evidence that experience by loving one another." Do we expect consolation in Christ? If we would not be disappointed, we must love one another. (2) "*Comfort of love.* If there is any comfort in God's love to you, in your love to God, or in your brethren's love to us, be you like-minded." (3) "*Fellowship of the Spirit.* If there is such a thing as communion with God and Christ by the Spirit, such a thing as the communion of saints, be you like-minded." (4) "*Any bowels and mercies,* in God and Christ, towards you. If you expect the benefit of God's compassions to yourselves, be you compassionate one to another." (5) Another argument is the comfort it would be to him: *Fulfil you my joy.* It is the joy of ministers to see people like-minded and living in love. He had been instrumental in bringing them to the grace of Christ and the love of God. "Now," says he, "*fulfil the joy* of your poor minister, who preached the gospel to you."

2. Some means to promote it. (1) *Do nothing through strife and vain glory, v.* 3. Christ came to slay all enmities; therefore let there not be among Christians a spirit of opposition. Christ came to humble us, and therefore let there not be among us a spirit of pride. (2) We must *esteem others in lowliness of mind better than ourselves,* be severe upon our own faults and charitable in our judgment of others. We must esteem the good which is in others above that which is in ourselves; for we best know our own unworthiness and imperfections.

JAMIESON, FAUSSET, BROWN — CHAPTER 2

VSS. 1-30. CONTINUED EXHORTATION: TO UNITY: TO HUMILITY AFTER CHRIST'S EXAMPLE, WHOSE GLORY FOLLOWED HIS HUMILIATION: TO EARNESTNESS IN SEEKING PERFECTION, THAT THEY MAY BE HIS JOY IN THE DAY OF CHRIST: HIS JOYFUL READINESS TO BE OFFERED NOW BY DEATH, SO AS TO PROMOTE THEIR FAITH. HIS INTENTION TO SEND TIMOTHY: HIS SENDING EPAPHRODITUS MEANTIME. **1.** The "therefore" implies that he is here expanding on the exhortation (ch. 1:27), "In one Spirit, with one mind" (*soul*). He urges *four influencing motives* in this verse, to inculcate the four Christian duties corresponding respectively to them (vs. 2). "That ye be *like-minded,* having the same *love,* of *one accord,* of one mind"; (1) "If there be (with you) *any consolation in Christ,*" i.e., any *consolation of which Christ is the source,* leading you to wish *to console me* in my afflictions borne for Christ's sake, ye owe it to me to grant my request "that ye be like-minded" [CHRYSOSTOM and ESTIUS]: (2) 'If there be any comfort of (i.e., flowing from) love," the adjunct of "consolation in Christ"; (3) "If any fellowship of (communion together as Christians, flowing from joint participation in) the Spirit" (II Cor. 13:14). As *Pagans* meant literally those who were of one village, and *drank of one fountain,* how much greater is the union which conjoins those who drink of the same Spirit! (I Cor. 12:4, 13) [GROTIUS]: (4) "If any bowels (tender emotions) and mercies" (compassions), the adjuncts of "fellowship of the Spirit." The opposites of the two pairs, into which the four fall, are reprobated, vss. 3, 4. **2. Fulfil**—i.e., Make full. I have joy in you, *complete* it by that which is still wanting, viz., *unity* (ch. 1:9). **likeminded**—lit., "that ye be of the same mind"; more general than the following "of one mind." **having the same love**—equally disposed to love and be loved. **being of one accord**—lit., "with united *souls.*" This pairs with the following clause, thus, "With united souls, being of one mind"; as the former two also pair together, "That ye be like-minded, having the same love." **3.** *Let* **nothing** *be done*—The italicized words are not in the *Greek.* Perhaps the ellipsis had better be supplied from the *Greek* (vs. 2), *"Thinking* nothing in the way of strife" (or rather, "factious intrigue," "self-seeking," *Note,* ch. 1:16). It is the *thought* which characterizes the action as good or bad before God. **lowliness of mind**—The *direct* relation of this grace is to God alone; it is the sense of dependence of the creature on the Creator as such, and it places all created beings in this respect on a level. The man "lowly of mind" as to his spiritual life is independent of men, and free from all slavish feeling, while sensible of his continual dependence on God. Still it INDIRECTLY affects his behavior toward his fellow

ADAM CLARKE — CHAPTER 2

1. *If there be therefore any consolation.* The *if* does not express any doubt here, but on the contrary is to be considered as a strong affirmation; "as there is" consolation in Christ, as there is comfort of love. The word translated here *consolation* is in other places rendered "exhortation," and is by several critics understood so here; as if he had said: If exhorting you in the name of Christ has any influence with you. It is extremely difficult to give the force of these expressions; they contain a torrent of most affecting eloquence, the apostle pouring out his whole heart to a people whom with all his heart he loved, and who were worthy of the love even of an apostle. *If any comfort of love.* If the followers of Christ, by giving proofs of their ardent love to each other in cases of distress, alleviate the sufferings of the persecuted. *If any fellowship of the Spirit.* If there be an intimate relation established among all Christians, by their being made mutual partakers of the Holy Ghost. *If any bowels and mercies.* If you, as persons whom I have brought to God at the hazard of my life, feel sympathetic tenderness for me now in a further state of suffering.

2. *Fulfil ye my joy.* You ought to complete my joy, who have suffered so much to bring you into the possession of these blessings, by being *likeminded* with myself, *having the same love* to God. His cause, and me as I have to Him, His cause, and you.

3. *Let nothing be done through strife.* Never be opposed to each other; never act from separate interests. You are all brethren, and of one body; therefore let every member feel and labor for the welfare of the whole. *But in lowliness of mind.* Have always a humbling view of yourselves, and this will lead you to prefer others to yourselves; for, as you know your own secret defects, charity will lead you to suppose that your brethren are more holy and more devoted to God than you are; and they will think the same of you, their secret defects also being known only to themselves.

MATTHEW HENRY

(3) We must interest ourselves in the concerns of others, in Christian love and sympathy: *Look not every man on his own things, but every man also on the things of others, v.* 4. A selfish spirit is destructive of Christian love. We must love our neighbour as ourselves, and make his case our own.

II. A gospel pattern proposed is the example of our Lord Jesus Christ: *Let this mind be in you which was also in Christ Jesus, v.* 5. Christians must be of Christ's mind. We must bear a resemblance to his life, if we would have the benefit of his death. He was eminently humble, and this is what we are peculiarly to learn of him. If we were lowly-minded, we should be like-minded; and, if we were like Christ, we should be lowly-minded. Walk in the same spirit with the Lord Jesus, who humbled himself to sufferings and death for us.

1. Here are the two natures of Christ. His divine nature: *Who being in the form of God* (*v.* 6), partaking of the divine nature, as the eternal Son of God.

He thought it no robbery to be equal with God; did not think himself guilty of any invasion of what did not belong to him. It is the highest degree of robbery for any mere man or mere creature to pretend to be equal with God.

His human nature: He was *made in the likeness of men,* and *found in fashion as a man.* He was really and truly man. And he voluntarily assumed human nature; it was his own act. We cannot say that our participation of the human nature is so. Herein he *emptied himself,* to clothe himself with the rags of human nature.

Here are, 2. His two estates, of humiliation and exaltation. (1) His humiliation. The *form of a servant.* He was not only God's servant, but he came to minister to men, and was among them as one who serveth. One would think that the Lord Jesus, if he would be a man, should have been a prince. But quite the contrary: *He took upon him the form of a servant.* He was brought up meanly, probably working with his supposed father at his trade. His whole life was a life of humiliation.

JAMIESON, FAUSSET, BROWN

men; for, conscious of his entire dependence on God for all his abilities, even as they are dependent on God for theirs, he will not pride himself on his abilities, or exalt self in his conduct toward others (Eph. 4:2; Col. 3:12) [NEANDER]. **let each esteem**—Translate as *Greek,* "esteeming each other superior to *yourselves."* Instead of fixing your eyes on those points in which you excel, fix them on those in which your neighbor excels you: this is true "humility." **4.** The oldest MSS. read, "Not *looking each of you* (plural, *Greek*) on his own things (i.e., not *having regard* solely to them), but *each of you* on the things of others" also. Cf. vs. 21; also Paul's own example (ch. 1:24). **5.** The oldest MSS. read, "Have this mind in you. . . ." He does not put forward himself (see *Note,* vs. 4, and ch. 1:24) as an example, but Christ, THE ONE pre-eminently who sought not His own, but "humbled Himself" (vs. 8), first in taking on Him our nature, secondly, in humbling Himself further in that nature (Rom. 15: 3). **6.** Translate, "Who *subsisting* (or *existing,* viz., originally: the *Greek* is not the simple substantive verb, *to be*) in the form of God (the divine *essence* is not meant: but the *external self-manifesting characteristics of God,* the *form* shining forth from His glorious essence. The divine nature had infinite BEAUTY in itself, even without any creature contemplating that beauty: that beauty was 'the form of God'; as 'the *form* of a servant' (vs. 7), which is in contrasted opposition to it, takes for granted the *existence* of His human nature, so 'the form of God' takes for granted His divine nature [BENGEL], cf. John 5:37; 17:5; Col. 1:15, 'Who is the IMAGE of the invisible God' at a time *before* 'every creature,' II Corinthians 4:4, *esteemed* (the same *Greek* verb as in vs. 3) His being *on an equality* with God "no (act of) robbery" or *self-arrogation;* claiming to one's self what does not belong to him. ELLICOTT, WAHL, and others have translated, "*A thing* to be grasped at," which would require the *Greek* to be *harpagma,* whereas *harpagmos* means the *act* of seizing. So *harpagmos* means in the only other passage where it occurs, PLUTARCH, *De educatione puerorum,* 120. The same insuperable objection lies against ALFORD'S translation, "He regarded not as *self-enrichment* (i.e., an *opportunity for self-exaltation*) His equality with God." His argument is that the antithesis (vs. 7) requires it, "He used His equality with God as *an opportunity, not for self-exaltation,* but for self-abasement, or *emptying Himself.* But the antithesis is not between His *being on an equality with God,* and His *emptying Himself;* for He never emptied Himself of the fulness of His Godhead, or His "BEING *on an equality with God*"; but between His being "in the FORM (i.e., the outward glorious self-manifestation) of God," and His "taking on Him *the form of a servant,*" whereby He in a great measure emptied Himself of His precedent "form," or outward self-manifesting glory as God. Not "looking on His own things" (vs. 4), He, though existing in the form of God, He esteemed it no robbery to be on an equality with God, yet made Himself of no reputation. "Being on an equality with God," is not identical with "subsisting in the form of God"; the latter expresses the *external characteristics,* majesty, and beauty of the Deity, which "He emptied Himself of," to assume "the *form* of a servant"; the former, "HIS BEING," or NATURE, His already existing STATE OF EQUALITY with God, both the Father and the Son having the same ESSENCE. A glimpse of Him "in the form of God," previous to His incarnation, was given to Moses (Exod. 24:10, 11), Aaron, etc. **7. made himself of no reputation, and . . . and**—rather as the *Greek,* "*emptied* Himself, *taking* upon him the form of a servant, *being* made in the likeness of men." The two latter clauses (there being no conjunctions, "and—and," in the *Greek*) expresses *in what* Christ's "emptying of Himself" consists, viz., in "taking the form of a servant" (*Note,* Heb. 10:5; cf. Exod. 21:5, 6, and Ps. 40:6, proving that it was at the time when He assumed a *body,* He took "the form of a *servant*"), and in order to explain *how* He took "the form of a servant," there is added, by "being made in the likeness of men." His subjection to the law (Luke 2:21; Gal. 4:4) and to His parents (Luke 2:51), His low state as a carpenter, and carpenter's reputed son (Matt. 13:55; Mark 6: 3), His betrayal for the price of a bond-servant (Exod. 21:32), and slave-like death to relieve us from the slavery of sin and death, finally and chiefly, *His servant-like dependence as man on God,* while His divinity was not outwardly manifested (Isa. 49: 3, 7), are all marks of His "form as a servant." This proves: (1) He was in the form of a servant as soon as He was made man. (2) He was "in the form of God" *before* He was "in the form of a servant."

ADAM CLARKE

4. *Look not every man on his own things.* Do nothing through self-interest in the things of God nor arrogate to yourselves gifts, graces, and fruits which belong to others; you are all called to promote God's glory and the salvation of men.

5. *Let this mind be in you, which was also in Christ Jesus.* Christ labored to promote no separate interest; as man He studied to promote the glory of God and the welfare and salvation of the human race. See then that you have the same "disposition" that was in Jesus.

6. *Thought it not robbery to be equal with God.* The word which we translate *robbery* has been supposed to imply "a thing eagerly to be seized, coveted, or desired," and on this interpretation the passage has been translated: "Who, being in the form of God, did not think it a matter to be earnestly desired to appear equal to God; but made himself of no reputation." Though He was from eternity in the form of God—possessed of the same glory—yet He thought it right to veil this glory and not to appear with it among the children of men; and therefore He was made in the *likeness of men* and took upon Him the *form* or "appearance" of a *servant.* On this account I prefer this sense of the word before that given in our text, which does not agree so well with the other expressions in the context.

7. *But made himself of no reputation.* "He emptied himself"—did not appear in His glory, for He assumed the form of a servant, being made in the likeness of man.

MATTHEW HENRY

But the lowest step of his humiliation was his dying the death of the cross. *He became obedient to death, even the death of the cross.* He not only suffered, but was voluntarily obedient. There is an emphasis laid upon the manner of his dying, which had in it all the circumstances possible which are humbling: *Even the death of the cross,* a cursed, shameful death,—full of pain,—and the death of a malefactor and a slave, not of a freeman,—exposed as a public spectacle.

(2) His exaltation: *Wherefore God also hath highly exalted him.* Because he humbled himself, God exalted him; and he *highly exalted him.* He exalted his whole person, the human nature as well as the divine. His exaltation here is made to consist in honour and power. *He had a name above every name. Every knee must bow to him.*

The whole creation must be in subjection to him: *things in heaven, and things in earth, and things under the earth,* the inhabitants of heaven and earth, the living and the dead. *At the name of Jesus* all should pay a solemn homage.

Every tongue should confess that Jesus Christ is Lord. The kingdom of Christ reaches to heaven and earth, and to all the creatures in each, and to the dead as well as the living.—*To the glory of God the Father.* Whatever respect is paid to Christ redounds to the honour of the Father.

Verses 12, 13

He urges this from the consideration of their readiness always to obey the gospel: "*As you have always obeyed, not as in my presence only, but now much more in my absence,*" *v.* 12. They were not merely awed by the apostle's presence, but did it even *much more in his absence.*

I. He exhorts them to diligence and seriousness in the Christian course: *Work out your own salvation.* It concerns us above all things to secure the welfare of our souls: whatever becomes of other things, let us take care of our best interests. It is our own salvation. It is not for us to judge other people; we have enough to do to look to ourselves. We are required to *work out our salvation.* The word signifies *working thoroughly* and taking *true pains.* We must

JAMIESON, FAUSSET, BROWN

(3) He did as really subsist in the divine nature, as in the form of a servant, or in the nature of man. For He was as much "in the form of God" as "in the form of a servant"; and was so in the form of God as "to be on an equality with God"; He therefore could have been none other than God; for God saith, "To whom will ye liken Me and make Me equal?" (Isa. 46:5), [BISHOP PEARSON]. His *emptying Himself* presupposes His previous *plenitude of Godhead* (John 1:14; Col. 1:19; 2:9). He remained full of this; yet He bore Himself as if He were *empty.* **8. being found in fashion as a man**—*being already, by His "emptying Himself," in the form of a servant,* or likeness of man (Rom. 8:3), "He humbled Himself (still further by) *becoming* obedient *even* unto death (not as *English Version,* 'He humbled Himself *and became . . .'*; the *Greek* has no 'and,' and has the *participle,* not the verb), and that the death of the cross." "Fashion" expresses that He had the *outward guise, speech,* and *look.* In vs. 7, in the *Greek,* the emphasis is on *Himself* (which stands before the Greek verb), "He emptied *Himself," His divine self,* viewed in respect to what He had heretofore been; in vs. 8 the emphasis is on *"humbled"* (which stands before the *Greek* "Himself"); He not only "emptied Himself" of His previous "form of God," but submitted to *positive* HUMILIATION. He "became obedient," viz., to God, as His "servant" (Rom. 5:19; Heb. 5:8). Therefore "*God*" is said to "exalt" Him (vs. 9), even as it was God to whom He became voluntarily "obedient." "Even unto death" expresses the climax of His obedience (John 10:18). **9. Wherefore**—as the just consequence of His self-humiliation and obedience (Ps. 8:5, 6; 110:1, 7; Matt. 28:18; Luke 24:26; John 5:27; 10:17; Rom. 14:9; Eph. 1:20-22; Heb. 2:9). An intimation, that if we would hereafter be exalted, we too must, after His example. now humble ourselves (vss. 3, 5; ch. 3:21; I Pet. 5:5, 6). Christ emptied Christ; God exalted Christ as man to equality with God [BENGEL]. **highly exalted**—*Greek,* "*super-eminently* exalted" (Eph. 4:10). **given him**—*Greek,* "bestowed on Him." **a name**—along with the corresponding *reality,* glory and majesty. **which**—Translate, (viz.), "that which is above every name." The name "JESUS" (vs. 10), which is even now in glory His name of honor (Acts 9:5). "Above" not only men, but angels (Eph. 1:21). **10. at the name**—rather as *Greek,* "in the name." **bow**—rather, "bend," in token of worship. Referring to Isaiah 45:23; quoted also in Romans 14:11. To worship "in the name of Jesus," is to worship Jesus *Himself* (cf. vs. 11; Prov. 18:10), or *God in Christ* (John 16:23; Eph. 3:14). Cf. "Whosoever shall call upon *the name of the Lord* (i.e., whosoever shall call on *the Lord in His revealed character*) shall be saved" (Rom. 10:13; I Cor. 1:2); "all that call upon *the name of Jesus Christ our Lord*" (cf. II Tim. 2:22); "call on the Lord"; Acts 7:59, "calling upon . . . and saying, Lord Jesus" (Acts 9:14, 21; 22:16). **of things in heaven**—angels. They worship Him not only as God, but as the ascended *God-man,* "Jesus" (Eph. 1:21; Heb. 1:6; I Pet. 3:22). **in earth**—men; among whom He tabernacled for a time. **under the earth**—the dead; among whom He was numbered once (Rom. 14:9, 11; Eph. 4:9, 10; Rev. 5:13). The demons and the lost may be included *indirectly,* as even they give homage, though one of fear, not love, to Jesus (Mark 3:11; Luke 8:31; Jas. 2:19, see *Note,* vs. 11). **11. every tongue**—Cf. "every knee" (vs. 10). *In every way* He shall be acknowledged as Lord (no longer as "servant," vs. 7). As none can fully do so "but by the Holy Ghost" (I Cor. 12:3), the spirits of good men who are dead, must be the class *directly* meant, vs. 10, "under the earth." **to the glory of God the Father**—the grand end of Christ's mediatorial office and kingdom, which shall cease when this end shall have been fully realized (John 5:19-23, 30; 17:1, 4-7; I Cor. 15:24-28. **12. Wherefore**—Seeing that we have in Christ such a specimen of glory resulting from "*obedience*" (vs. 8) and humiliation, see that ye also be "obedient," and so "*your* salvation" shall follow your obedience. **as ye have . . . obeyed**—"*even as* ye have *been obedient.*" viz., to God, as Jesus was "obedient" unto God (*Note,* vs. 8). **not as . . .**—"not *as if*" it were a matter to be done "in my presence only, but now (as things are) much more (with more earnestness) (in my absence)" (because my help is withdrawn from you) [ALFORD]. **work out**—carry out to its full perfection. "Salvation" is "worked in" (vs. 13; Eph. 1:11) believers by the Spirit, who enables them through faith to be justified *once for all;* but it needs, as a progressive work, to be "worked *out*" by obedience, through the help of the same Spirit, unto perfection (II Pet. 1:5-8).

ADAM CLARKE

8. *And being found in fashion as a man.* This clause should be joined to the preceding, and thus translated: "Being made in the likeness of man, and was found in fashion as a man." *He humbled himself.* Laid himself as low as possible: (1) In emptying himself—laying aside the effulgence of His glory. (2) In being incarnate—taking upon Him the human form. (3) In becoming a Servant—assuming the lowest innocent character, that of being the Servant of all. (4) In condescending to die, to which He was not naturally liable, as having never sinned, and therefore had a right in His human nature to immortality, without passing under the empire of death. (5) In condescending, not only to death, but to the lowest and most ignominious kind of death, *the death of the cross,* the punishment of the meanest of slaves and worst of felons. What must sin have been in the sight of God when it required such abasement in Jesus Christ to make an atonement for it, and undo its influence and malignity!

9. *Wherefore God also hath highly exalted him.* He has *given him a name,* "the name," *which is above every name.* This makes it much more emphatic. According to Eph. i. 20-21, the Man Christ Jesus is exalted to the right hand of God, "far above all principality, and power, and might, and dominion, and every name that is named, not only in this world, but also in that which is to come." But if we refer to any particular epithet, then the name Jesus or "Saviour" must be that which is intended; as no being either in heaven or earth can possess this name as He who is the Redeemer of the world does.

10. *That at the name of Jesus every knee should bow.* That all human beings should consider themselves redeemed unto God by His blood. In a word, that all the spirits of just men made perfect, now in a state of blessedness; all human beings still in their state of probation on earth; and all that are in the shades below, who have, through their own fault, died without having received His salvation; should acknowledge Him.

11. *And that every tongue should confess.* That all those before mentioned should acknowledge that Jesus Christ is Lord, or "absolute Governor," and thus glorify God the Father, who has exalted this human nature to this state of ineffable glory, in virtue of its passion, death, resurrection, and the atonement which it has made, by which so many attributes of the divine nature have become illustrated, the divine law magnified and made honorable, and an eternal glory provided for man. Others by "things in heaven" understand the holy angels; by "things on earth," human beings generally; and by "things under the earth," fallen spirits of every description. Perhaps the three expressions are designed to comprehend all beings of all kinds, all creatures.

12. *As ye have always obeyed.* Continue to act on the same principles and from the same motives; having the same disposition which was in Christ; laboring so as to promote His glory.

MATTHEW HENRY

not only work at our salvation, by doing something now and then about it; but we must work out our salvation, by doing all that is to be done, and persevering therein to the end. We cannot attain salvation without the utmost care and diligence.

With fear and trembling, that is, with great care and circumspection. Fear is a great guard and preservative from evil.

"And because *it is God who worketh in you*, do you work out your salvation. Work, for he worketh." God is ready to concur with his grace, and assist our faithful endeavours. The operations of God's grace in us are so far from excusing, that they are intended to quicken our endeavours.

"And work out our salvation *with fear and trembling*, for *he worketh in you*. Work with *fear*, for he works of his *good pleasure*."—*To will and to do*. It is the grace of God which inclines the will to that which is good: and then enables us to perform it. *Of his good pleasure*. As we cannot act without God's grace, so we cannot pretend to deserve it.

Verses 14–18

The apostle exhorts them to adorn their Christian profession by a suitable temper and behaviour. 1. By a cheerful obedience to the commands of God (*v.* 14): "*Do all things without murmurings*. Mind your work, and do not quarrel with it." God's commands were given to be obeyed, not to be disputed. 2. By peaceableness and love one to another. "Do all things *without disputing*. The light of truth and the life of religion are often lost in the heats and mists of disputation."

3. By a blameless conversation towards all men (*v.* 15): "*That you may be blameless and harmless, the sons of God, without rebuke*." We should endeavour not only not to do hurt, but not to come under the just suspicion of it. The *sons of God*. The children of God should differ from the sons of men. *Without rebuke*. We should endeavour, not only to get to heaven, but to get thither without a blot. *In the midst of a crooked and perverse generation*. Where there is no true religion, little is to be expected but crookedness and perverseness; and the more crooked and perverse others are among whom we live, the more careful we should be to keep ourselves blameless and harmless. *Among whom you shine as lights in the world*. Good Christians are lights in the world. When God raises up a good man in any place, he sets up a light in that place. They must shine as well as be sincere.—*Holding forth the word of life*, *v.* 16. It is our duty not only to hold fast, but to hold forth the word of life; to hold it forth for the benefit of others, to hold it forth as the candlestick holds forth the candle.

"*That I may rejoice in the day of Christ;* not only rejoice in your steadfastness, but in your usefulness." He would have them think that *he had not run in vain, nor laboured in vain*. Running denotes vehemence and vigour; labour denotes constancy and close application. It is a great joy to ministers when they perceive that they have not *run in vain, nor laboured in vain*; and it will be their rejoicing in the day of Christ, when their converts will be their crown.

JAMIESON, FAUSSET, BROWN

your own—The emphasis is on this. Now that *I* am not present to further the work of your salvation, "work out *your own* salvation" yourselves the more carefully. Do not think this work cannot go on because I am absent; "for (vs. 13) it is God that worketh in you. . . ." In this case adopt a rule different from the former (vs. 4), but resting on the same principle of "lowliness of mind" (vs. 3), viz., "look each on *his own* things," instead of "disputings" with others (vs. 14). **salvation**—which is in "Jesus" (vs. 10), as His name (meaning God-Saviour) implies. **with fear and trembling**—the very feeling enjoined on "servants," as to what ought to accompany their "obedience" (Eph. 6:5). So here: See that, as "servants" to God, after the example of Christ, ye be so "with the fear and trembling" which becomes servants; not slavish fear, but *trembling anxiety not to fall short of the goal* (I Cor. 9:26, 27; Heb. 4:1, "Let us *fear*, lest a promise being left us of entering into His rest, any should come short of it"), *resulting from a sense of our human insufficiency, and from the consciousness that all depends on the power of God*, "who worketh both to will and to do" (Rom. 11:20). "Paul, though joyous, writes seriously" [J. J. WOLF]. **13. For**—encouragement to work: "For it is God who worketh in you," always present with you, though I be absent. It is not said, "Work out your own salvation, *though* it is God . . . ," but, "*because* it is God who. . . ." The *will*, and the power *to work*, being first instalments of His grace, encourage us to make full proof of, and carry out to the end, the "salvation" which He has first "worked," and is still "working *in*" us, enabling us to "work it *out*." "Our will does nothing thereunto without grace; but grace is inactive without our will" [ST. BERNARD]. Man is, in different senses, entirely active, and entirely passive: *God producing all, and we acting all*. **worketh**—rather as *Greek*, "worketh *effectually*." We cannot of ourselves embrace the Gospel of grace: "the will" (Ps. 110:3; II Cor. 3:5) comes solely of God's gift to whom He will (John 6:44, 65); so also the power "to do" (rather, "*to work effectually*," as the *Greek* is the same as that for "worketh in"), i.e., effectual perseverance to the end, is wholly of God's gift (ch. 1:6; Heb. 13:21). **of his good pleasure**—rather as *Greek*, "FOR His good pleasure"; *in order to carry out* His sovereign gracious purpose towards you (Eph. 1:5, 9). **14. murmurings**—*secret murmurings* and complaints against your fellow men arising from selfishness: opposed to the example of Jesus just mentioned (cf. the use of the word, John 7:12, 13; Acts 6:1; I Peter 4:9; Jude 16). **disputings**—The *Greek* is translated "doubting" in I Tim. 2:8. But here referring to profitless "disputings" with our fellow men, in relation to whom we are called on to be "blameless and harmless" (vs. 15): so the *Greek* is translated, Mark 9:33, 34. These disputings flow from "vainglory" reprobated (vs. 3); and abounded among the Aristotelian philosophers in Macedon, where Philippi was. **15. blameless and harmless**—without either the repute of mischief, or the inclination to do it [ALFORD]. **sons**—rather as *Greek*, "the children of God" (Rom. 8:14-16). Imitation of our heavenly Father is the instinctive guide to our duty as His children, more than any external law (Matt. 5:44, 45, 48). **without rebuke**—"without (giving handle for) *reproach*." The whole verse tacitly refers by contrast to Deuteronomy 32:5, "Their *spot* . . . not . . . of His *children* . . . a *perverse* and *crooked* generation" (cf. I Pet. 2:12). **ye shine**—lit., "appear" [TRENCH]. "Show yourselves" (cf. Matt. 5:14-16; Eph. 5:8-13). **as lights in the world**—The *Greek* expresses "as *luminaries* in the world," as the sun and moon, "the lights," or "great lights," in the *material* world or in the firmament. LXX uses the very same *Greek* word in the passage, Genesis 1:14, 16; cf. *Note*, Revelation 21:11. **16. Holding forth**—to them, and so *applying* it (the common meaning of the *Greek;* perhaps here including also the other meaning, "holding *fast*"). The image of *light-bearers* or *luminaries* is carried on from vs. 15. As the heavenly luminaries' *light* is closely connected with the *life* of animals, so ye hold forth the light of Christ's "word" (received from me) which is the "life" of the Gentiles (John 1:4; I John 1:1, 5-7). Christ is "the Light of the world" (John 8:12); believers are only "lightbearers" reflecting His light. **that I may rejoice in**—lit., "*with a view to* (your being) *a subject of rejoicing* to me *against* the day of Christ" (ch. 4:1; II Cor. 1:14; I Thess. 2:19). **that I have not run in vain**—that it was not in vain that I labored for your spiritual good. **17. Yea, and if**—rather as *Greek*, "Yea, if even"; implying that he regarded the contingency as not unlikely: He had assumed the *possibility* of his being found

ADAM CLARKE

Work out your own salvation. Go on, walking by the same rule and minding the same thing, till your salvation be completed.

With fear and trembling. Considering the difficulty of the work and the danger of miscarriage.

13. *To will and to do*. The power to will and the power to act must necessarily come from God, who is the Author of both soul and body, and of all their powers and energies; but the act of volition and the act of working come from the man. Because God works in them the power to will and the power to do, therefore the apostle exhorts them to work out their own salvation, most manifestly showing that the use of the powers of volition and action belongs to themselves. They cannot do God's work; they cannot produce in themselves a power to will and to do. And God will not do their work; He will not work out their salvation with fear and trembling.

14. *Do all things without murmurings*. "Without grumblings and altercations."

15. *That ye may be blameless*. In yourselves, and harmless to others. *The sons of God*. Showing by your holy conduct that you are partakers of the divine nature.

Without rebuke. Persons against whom no charge of transgression can justly be laid. *Among whom ye shine*. Be like the sun and moon; bless even the perverse and disobedient by your light and splendor.

16. *Holding forth the word of life*. An allusion, some think, to those towers which were built at the entrance of harbors, on which fires were kept during the night to direct ships into the port.

MATTHEW HENRY

The apostle not only ran and laboured for them with satisfaction, he was ready to suffer for their good (*v.* 17): *Yea, and if I be offered upon the sacrifice and service of your faith, I joy and rejoice with you all.* He could willingly be a sacrifice at their altars, to serve the faith of God's elect. Could Paul think it worth while to shed his blood for the service of the church, and shall we think it much to take a little pains?

He could rejoice to seal his doctrine with his blood (*v.* 18): *For the same cause also do you joy and rejoice with me.* It is the will of God that good Christians should be much in rejoicing; and those who are happy in good ministers have a great deal of reason to joy and rejoice with them.

Verses 19–30

I. He speaks of Timothy, whom he intended to send to the Philippians. *For I have no man like-minded, who will naturally care for your state.* Timothy was a non-such. None comparable to Timothy, a man of an excellent spirit and tender heart. *Who will naturally care for your state.* It is best with us when our duty becomes in a manner natural to us. *Naturally,* that is, sincerely, and not in pretence only. It is the duty of ministers to care for the state of their people and be concerned for their welfare. It is a rare thing to find one who does it naturally. *All seek their own, not the things which are Jesus Christ's, v.* 21. Did Paul say this in haste, as David said, *All men are liars?* He means the generality; *all,* either the most, or all in comparison of Timothy. Many prefer their own credit, ease, and safety, before truth, holiness, and duty, but Timothy was none of these.—*You know the proof of him, v.* 22. Timothy was a man who had been tried, and was faithful in all that befell him. All the churches with whom he had acquaintance knew the proof of him. He was a man as good as he seemed to be. *As a son with a father, he hath served with me in the gospel.* He was Paul's assistant in many places. Their ministrations together were with great respect on the one side and great tenderness and kindness on the other—an admirable example to elder and younger ministers united in the same service. *Him therefore I hope to send presently, as soon as I shall see how it will go with me, v.* 23. He was now a prisoner, and did not know what would be the issue. He hoped to come himself (*v.* 24): *But I trust in the Lord that I also myself shall come shortly.* Paul desired his liberty, not that he might take his pleasure, but that he might do good.—*I trust in the Lord.* He expresses his hope of seeing them, with a humble submission to the divine will.

II. Concerning Epaphroditus, whom he calls *his brother, and companion in labour, and fellow-soldier,*

JAMIESON, FAUSSET, BROWN

alive at Christ's coming (for in every age Christ designed Christians to stand in preparedness for His coming as at hand): he here puts a supposition which he regards as more likely, viz., his own death before Christ's coming. **I be offered**—rather as *Greek,* "I am poured out." "I am made a libation." Present, not future, as the danger is threatening him *now.* As in sacrifices libations of wine were "*poured* upon" the offerings, so he represents his Philippian converts, offered through faith (or else their *faith* itself), as the sacrifice, and *his blood as the libation* "poured upon" it (cf. Rom. 15:16; II Tim. 4:6). **service**—*Greek,* "priest's ministration"; carrying out the image of a sacrifice. **I joy**—for myself (ch. 1: 21, 23). His expectation of release from prison is much fainter, than in the Epistles to Ephesians, Colossians, and Philemon, written somewhat earlier from Rome. The appointment of Tigellinus to be Prætorian Prefect was probably the cause of this change. See *Introduction.* **rejoice with you all**—ALFORD translates, "I *congratulate* you all," viz. on the honor occurring to you by my blood being poured out on the sacrifice of your faith. If *they rejoiced* already (as *English Version* represents), what need of his urging them, "Do *ye also* joy." **18.** "Do ye also rejoice" at this honor to you, "and congratulate me" on my blessed "gain" (ch. 1:21). **19.** Vs. 22, "ye know the proof of him . . that . . . he hath served with me," implies that Timothy had been long with Paul at Philippi. Accordingly, in the history (Acts 16:1-4; 17:10, 14), we find them *setting out* together from Derbe in Lycaonia, and together again at Berea in Macedonia, near *the conclusion* of Paul's missionary journey: an *undesigned* coincidence between the Epistle and history, a mark of genuineness [PALEY]. From vss. 19-50, it appears Epaphroditus was to set out at once to allay the anxiety of the Philippians on his account, and at the same time bearing the Epistle; Timothy was to follow after the apostle's liberation was decided, when they could arrange their plans more definitely as to *where* Timothy should, on his return with tidings from Philippi, meet Paul, who was designing by a wider circuit, and slower progress, to reach that city. Paul's reason for sending Timothy so soon after having heard of the Philippians from Epaphroditus was that they were now suffering persecutions (ch. 1:28-30); and besides, Epaphroditus' delay through sickness on his journey to Rome from Philippi, made the tidings he brought to be of less recent date than Paul desired. Paul himself also hoped to visit them shortly. **But I trust**—Yet my death is by no means certain; yea, "I *hope* (*Greek*) in the Lord" (i.e., by the Lord's help). **unto you**—lit., "*for* you," i.e., to your satisfaction, not merely motion, *to you.* **I also**—that not only you "may be of good *courage*" (so *Greek*) on hearing of me (vs. 23), but "I also, when I know your state." **20.** His reason for sending Timothy above all others: I have none so "likeminded," lit., "like-*souled,*" with myself as is Timothy. Cf. Deuteronomy 13:6, "Thy friend which is as thine own *soul*" (Ps. 55:14). Paul's second self. **naturally**—*Greek,* "genuinely"; "with *sincere* solicitude." A case wherein the Spirit of God so changed man's nature, that to be *natural* was with him to be *spiritual:* the great point to be aimed at. **21.** Translate as *Greek,* "*They* all" (viz., who are now with me, ch. 1:14, 17; ch. 4:21: such Demas, then with him, proved to be, Col. 4:14; cf. II Tim. 4:10; Philemon 24). **seek their own**—opposed to Paul's precept (vs. 4; I Cor. 10:24, 33; 13:5). This is spoken, by comparison with Timothy; for ch. 1: 16, 17 implies that some of those with Paul at Rome were genuine Christians, though not so self-sacrificing as Timothy. Few come to the help of the Lord's cause, where ease, fame, and gain have to be sacrificed. Most help only when Christ's gain is compatible with their own (Judg. 5:17, 23). **22.** Rare praise (Neh. 7:2). **as a son with the father**—Translate, "as a *child* (*serveth*) *a father.*" **served with me**—When we might expect the sentence to run thus, "As a child *serveth a father,* so he *served me*"; he changes it to "served *with* me" in modesty; as Christians are not *servants* TO *one another,* but *servants of God* WITH *one another* (cf. ch. 3:17). **in the gospel**—*Greek,* "*unto,*" or "*for* the Gospel." **23. so soon as I shall see**—i.e., so soon *as I shall have known for certain.* **24. also myself**—as well as Timothy. **25. I supposed**—"I thought it necessary." **to send**—It was properly a *sending* Epaphroditus *back* (ch. 4:18). But as he had come intending to stay some time with Paul, the latter uses the word "send" (cf. vs. 30). **fellow soldier**—in the "good fight" of faith (ch. 1:27, 30; II Tim. 2:3; 4:7). **your messenger**—lit., "apostle." The "apostles" or "messengers *of the churches*" (Rom. 16:7; II Cor. 8:23), were distinct from the "apostles" specially com-

ADAM CLARKE

17. *Yea, and if I be offered upon the sacrifice and service.* The metaphor appears to be carried on. As it was customary for the weather-beaten mariner, when he had gained his port, to offer a sacrifice to God of some particular animal which he had vowed while in his state of danger, and this was considered to be a "religious service," the apostle, pursuing the idea, states himself to be willing to become the "libation" that was to be "poured upon the sacrifice."

18. *For the same cause also do ye joy.* Should I be thus offered, as I shall rejoice in it, do you also rejoice that I am counted worthy of this high honor.

19. *But I trust in the Lord Jesus.* He is Governor and Disposer of all events, being above all principality and power; and I humbly confide in His power and goodness that I shall be a little longer spared to visit you again, v. 24, and to be able to send Timothy shortly to you. *When I know your state.* By the correct information which I shall receive from Timothy.

20. *For I have no man likeminded.* He is "of the same soul"; a man after my own heart.

21. *For all seek their own.* This must relate to the persons who preached Christ "even of envy and strife," chap. i. 15.

22. *Ye know the proof of him, that, as a son with the father, he hath served with me.* The Philippians had full proof of the affectionate attachment of Timothy to Paul, for he had labored with him there, as we learn from Acts xvi. 1-3 and xvii. 14; and we find from what is said here that Timothy was not a servant to the apostle, but that he had served with him.

23. *How it will go with me.* The apostle was now in captivity; his trial appears to have been approaching, and of its issue he was doubtful, though he seems to have had a general persuasion that he should be spared (see v. 19 and v. 24).

MATTHEW HENRY

who ministered to my wants. He had an earnest desire to come to them, and Paul was willing he should.

1. Epaphroditus had been sick: *They had heard that he had been sick, v.* 26. And *indeed he was sick, nigh unto death, v.* 27. 2. The Philippians were exceedingly sorry to hear of his sickness. He was one for whom they had a particular respect and affection, and thought fit to choose out to send to the apostle. 3. It pleased God to recover and spare him: *But God had mercy on him, v.* 27. The apostle owns it is a great mercy to himself, as well as to Epaphroditus and others. He was sensibly touched with the thoughts of so great a loss: *Lest I should have sorrow upon sorrow.* "Lest, besides the sorrow of my own imprisonment, I should have the sorrow of his death." 4. Epaphroditus was willing to pay a visit to the Philippians, that he might be comforted with those who had sorrowed for him when he was sick: "*That when you see him again you may rejoice*" (*v.* 28). He gave himself the pleasure of comforting them by the sight of so dear a friend. "*Receive him therefore in the Lord with all gladness, and hold such in reputation:* account such men valuable, who are zealous and faithful, and let them be highly loved and regarded." It seems he had caught his illness in the work of God: *It was for the work of Christ that he was nigh to death, and to supply their lack of service to him.* The apostle reckons they ought to love him the more upon that account. What is given us in answer to prayer should be received with great thankfulness and joy.

JAMIESON, FAUSSET, BROWN

missioned *by Christ*, as the Twelve and Paul. **ministered to my wants**—by conveying the contributions from Phillippi. The *Greek leitourgon*, lit., implies *ministering in the ministerial office.* Probably Epaphroditus was a presbyter or else a deacon. **26. For**—reason for thinking it "necessary to send" "Epaphroditus. Translate as *Greek*, "*Inasmuch as* he *was longing* after you all." **full of heaviness**—The *Greek* expresses the being *worn out* and *overpowered with heavy grief.* **because that ye had heard that he had been sick**—rather, "that he *was* sick." He felt how exceedingly saddened you would be in hearing it; and he now is hastening to relieve your minds of the anxiety. **27.** Epaphroditus' sickness proves that the apostles had not ordinarily the *permanent* gift of miracles, any more than of inspiration: both were vouchsafed to them only for each particular occasion, as the Spirit thought fit. **lest I should have sorrow upon sorrow**—viz., the sorrow of losing him by death, in addition to the sorrow of my imprisonment. Here only occurs anything of a sorrowful tone in this Epistle, which generally is most joyous. **29. Receive him**—There seems to be something behind respecting him. If extreme affection had been the sole ground of his "heaviness," no such exhortation would have been needed [ALFORD]. **in reputation**—"in honor." **30. for the work of Christ**—viz., the bringing of a supply to me, the minister of Christ. He was probably in a delicate state of health in setting out from Philippi; but at all hazards he undertook this service of Chirstian love, which cost him a serious sickness. **not regarding his life**—Most of the oldest MSS. read, "hazarding. . . ." **to supply your lack of service**—Not that Paul would imply, they lacked the *will:* what they "lacked" was the "*opportunity*" by which to send their accustomed bounty (ch. 4:10). "That which ye would have done if you could [but which you could not through absence], he did for you; therefore receive him with all joy" [ALFORD].

ADAM CLARKE

27. *Lest I should have sorrow upon sorrow.* The sorrows of his death, added to the sorrow he endured on account of his sickness; or he may refer to his own state of affliction, being imprisoned and maltreated.

28. *The more carefully.* With the "more haste or dispatch"; because, having suffered so much on account of his apprehended death, they could not be too soon comforted by seeing him alive and restored.

29. *Receive him therefore in the Lord.* For the Lord's sake receive him, and as the Lord's servant.

30. *For the work of Christ.* Preaching the gospel, and ministering to the distressed. *He was nigh unto death.* Having labored far beyond his strength. *Not regarding his life.* Instead of *not regarding his life,* "risking his life" is the reading of some MSS.

MATTHEW HENRY

CHAPTER 3

It seems the church of the Philippians, though a faithful and flourishing church, was disturbed by the judaizing teachers.

I. He exhorts them to *rejoice in the Lord* (*v.* 1). The more we take of the comfort of our religion the more closely we shall cleave to it: the more we rejoice in Christ the more willing we shall be to suffer for him, and the less danger of being drawn away from him.

II. He cautions them to take heed of those false teachers: *To write the same thing to you to me indeed is not grievous, but for you it is safe.* Ministers must not think anything grievous to themselves which they have reason to believe is safe and edifying to the people. It is good for us often to hear the same truths. It is a wanton curiosity to desire always to hear some new thing. *Beware of dogs, v.* 2. *Dogs,* for their malice against the faithful professors of the gospel of Christ, barking at them and biting them.

They cried up good works in opposition to the faith of Christ; but Paul calls them evil workers: they boasted themselves to be of the circumcision; but he calls them the concision.

JAMIESON, FAUSSET, BROWN

CHAPTER 3

Vss. 1-21. WARNING AGAINST JUDAIZERS: HE HAS GREATER CAUSE THAN THEY TO TRUST IN LEGAL RIGHTEOUSNESS, BUT RENOUNCED IT FOR CHRIST'S RIGHTEOUSNESS, IN WHICH HE PRESSES AFTER PERFECTION: WARNING AGAINST CARNAL PERSONS: CONTRAST OF THE BELIEVER'S LIFE AND HOPE. **1. Finally**—rather, not with the notion of time, but making a transition to another general subject, "Furthermore" [BENGEL and WAHL] as in I Thessalonians 4:1. Lit., "As to what remains. . . ." It is often used at the conclusion of Epistles for "finally" (Eph. 6:10, II Thess. 3:1). But it is not restricted to this meaning, as ALFORD thinks, supposing that Paul used it here intending to close his Epistle, but was led by the mention of the Judaizers into a more lengthened dissertation. **the same things**—concerning "rejoicing," the prevailing feature in this Epistle (ch. 1:18, 25; 2:17; 4:4, where, cf. the "again I say," with "the same things" here). **In the Lord**—marks the true ground of joy, in contrast with "having confidence in the flesh," or in any outward sensible matter of boasting (vs. 3). **not grievous**—"not irksome." **for you it is safe**—Spiritual *joy* is the best safety against error (vs. 2; Neh. 8:10, end). **2. Beware**—*Greek,* "Have your eye on" so as to beware of. Contrast "mark," or "observe," viz., so as to follow vs. 17. **dogs**—*Greek,* "the dogs," viz., those impure persons "of whom I have told you often" (vs. 18, 19); "the abominable" (cf. Rev. 21:8, with 22:15; Matt. 7:6; Titus 1:15, 16): "dogs" in filthiness, unchastity, and snarling (Deut. 23:18; Ps. 59:6, 14, 15; II Pet. 2:22): especially "enemies of the cross of Christ" (vs. 18; Ps. 22:16, 20). The Jews regarded the Gentiles as "dogs" (Matt. 15:26); but by their own unbelief they have ceased to be the true Israel, and are become "dogs" (cf. Isa. 56:10, 11). **evil workers**—II Corinthians 11:13, "deceitful workers." Not simply "evildoers" are meant, but men who "worked," indeed, ostensibly for the Gospel, but worked for evil: "serving not our Lord, but their own belly" (vs. 19; cf. Rom. 16:18). Translate, "*The* evil *workmen,*" i.e., bad *teachers* (cf. II Tim. 2:15). **concision**—*Circumcision* had now lost its spiritual significance, and was now become to those who rested on it as any ground of justification, a senseless mutilation. Christians have the only true *circumcision,* viz., that of the heart; legalists have only "concision," i.e., *the cutting off of the flesh.* To make "cuttings in the flesh" was expressly prohibited by the law (Lev. 21:5): it was a Gentile-heathenish practice (I Kings 18:28); yet this, writes Paul indignantly, is what these *legalists* are virtually doing in violation of the law.

ADAM CLARKE

CHAPTER 3

1. *Rejoice in the Lord.* Be always happy, but let that happiness be such as you derive from the Lord. *For you it is safe.* It is much better to have these divine things committed to writing than confided to memory.

2. *Beware of dogs.* The Jews, who have here the same appellative which they formerly gave to the Gentiles.

Evil workers. Judaizing teachers, who endeavored to pervert the gospel.

The concision. The "cutting" or "excision"; not the "circumcision." The word is used by the apostle to degrade the pretensions which the Jews made to sanctity by the cutting in their flesh. Circumcision was an honorable thing, for it was a sign of the covenant; but as they now had rejected the new covenant, their circumcision was rendered uncircumcision, and is termed a "cutting," by way of degradation.

MATTHEW HENRY

III. He describes true Christians. *We are the circumcision, who worship God in the spirit, and rejoice in Christ Jesus, and have no confidence in the flesh.* Here are three characters: 1. They worshipped in the spirit, in opposition to the carnal ordinances of the Old Testament. Christianity teaches us to be inward with God in all the duties of religious worship. The work of religion is to no purpose any further than the heart is employed in it. 2. They *rejoice in Christ Jesus.* Now that the substance has come the shadows are done away, and we are to rejoice in Christ Jesus only. 3. They have no *confidence in the flesh,* in those carnal ordinances and outward performances. Our confidence, as well as our joy, is proper to him.

Verses 4–8

The apostle here proposes himself for an example of trusting in Christ only.

I. He shows what he had to boast of as a Jew and a Pharisee. *If any other man thinketh that he hath whereof to trust in the flesh, I more, v.* 4. He had as much to boast of as any Jew of them all. 1. His birth-right privileges. He was not a proselyte, but a native Israelite: *of the stock of Israel.* And he was *of the tribe of Benjamin. A Hebrew of the Hebrews,* an Israelite on both sides, and from one generation to another; none of his ancestors had matched with Gentiles. 2. He could boast of his relations to the covenant, for he was *circumcised the eighth day.* 3. For learning, he was a Pharisee, brought up at the feet of Gamaliel. He was a *Pharisee, the son of a Pharisee* (Acts xxiii. 6). 4. He had a blameless conversation: *Touching the righteousness which is of the law, blameless.* As to the mere letter of the law and outward observance of it, he could acquit himself from the breach of it and could not be accused by any. 5. He had been an active man for his religion. *Concerning zeal, persecuting the church.* He showed that he was in good earnest, though he had a zeal without knowledge. All this was stock sufficient to set up with for his justification.

II. How little account he made of these: *But what things were gain to me those have I counted loss for Christ* (*v.* 7). "I should have reckoned myself an unspeakable loser if, to adhere to them, I had lost Jesus Christ." The apostle did not persuade them to quit anything but what he had himself quitted.—*Yea doubtless, and I count all things but loss for the excellency of the knowledge of Christ Jesus my Lord, v.* 8. 1. He tells us what it was that he reached after: it was the knowledge of Christ Jesus his Lord, a believing experimental acquaintance with Christ as Lord; not a speculative, but a practical knowledge of him. And it is the excellency of knowledge. There is an abundant and transcendent excellency in the doctrine of Christ, above all the knowledge of nature, and improvements of human wisdom. 2. He shows how he had quitted his privileges as a Jew and a Pharisee: *Yea doubtless;* his expression rises with a holy triumph and elevation. *But indeed even also do I count all things but loss.* He had spoken before of *those things,* his Jewish privileges: here he speaks of *all things.* There he had said that he did count them but loss; but it might be asked, "Did he continue still in the same mind?" Now he speaks in the present tense: *Yea doubtless, I do count them but loss.* He tells us that he had himself practised according to this estimate of the case: *For whom I have suffered the loss of all things.* When he embarked in the bottom of the Christian religion, he ventured all in it, and suffered the loss of all for the privileges of a Christian. He not only counted them loss, but dung—*offals* thrown to dogs; they are not only less valuable than Christ, but in the highest degree contemptible, when they come in competition with him.

Verses 9–14

What he laid hold on: Christ and heaven.

I. The apostle had his heart upon Christ. 1. He desired to win Christ. *That I may win him;* as the runner wins the prize, as the sailor makes the port he is bound for. 2. That he *might be found in him* (*v.* 9). We are undone without a righteousness wherein to appear before God. There is a righteousness provided for us in Jesus Christ. "*Not having my own righteousness, which is of the law;* not thinking that my outward observances and good deeds are able to atone for my bad ones. The righteousness is that *which is through the faith of Christ,* not a legal, but evangelical righteousness: *The righteousness which is of God by faith,* ordained and appointed of God." Faith is the ordained means of saving benefit in all the purchase of his blood.

JAMIESON, FAUSSET, BROWN

3. "We are the (real) circumcision" (Rom. 2:25-29; Col. 2:11). **worship God in the Spirit**—The oldest MSS. read, "worship *by the Spirit of God*"; our religious *service* is rendered by the Spirit (John 4:23, 24). Legal worship was outward, and consisted in outward acts, restricted to certain times and places. Christian worship is *spiritual,* flowing from the inworkings of the Holy Spirit, not relating to certain isolated acts, but embracing the whole life (Rom. 12:1). In the former, men trusted in something human, whether descent from the theocratic nation, or the righteousness of the law, or mortification of "the flesh" ("Having confidence," or "glorying in the flesh") [NEANDER] (Rom. 1:9). **rejoice in Christ Jesus**—"make our *boast* in Christ Jesus," not in the law: the ground of their boasting. **have no confidence in the flesh**—but in the Spirit. **4.** "although *I* (emphatical) might have confidence *even* in the flesh." Lit., "I *having,*" but not using, "confidence in the flesh." **I more**—have more "whereof I might *have confidence* in the flesh." **5. In three particulars** he shows how he "might have confidence in the flesh" (vs. 4): (1) His pure Jewish blood. (2) His legal preciseness and high status as such. (3) His zeal for the law. The *Greek* is literally, "Being in circumcision an eighth-day person," i.e., not one circumcised in later life as a proselyte, but on the eighth day after birth, as the law directed in the case of Jew-born infants. **of the tribe of Benjamin** —son of Rachel, not of the maid servant [BENGEL]. **Hebrew of the Hebrews**—neither one or other parent being Gentile. The "Hebrew," wherever he dwelt, retained the *language* of his fathers. Thus Paul, though settled in Tarsus, a Greek city, calls himself a Hebrew. A "Grecian" or Hellenist, on the other hand, in the New Testament, is the term used for a *Greek-speaking* Jew [TRENCH]. **touching the law**—i.e., as to legal status and strictness. **a Pharisee**—"of the straitest sect" (Acts 26:5). **6. Concerning**—Translate as before and after, "*As touching* Zeal" (cf. Acts 22:3; 26:9). **blameless**—*Greek,* "*having become* blameless" as to *ceremonial* righteousness: having attained *in the eyes of man blameless* legal perfection. As to the holiness *before God,* which is the inner and truest spirit of the law, and which flows from "the righteousness of God by faith," he on the contrary declares (vss. 12-14) that he has *not* attained perfection. **7. gain**—rather as *Greek,* "gains"; including all possible advantages of outward status, which he had heretofore enjoyed. **I counted**—*Greek,* "I *have* counted for Christ's sake loss." He no longer uses the plural as in "gains"; for he counts them all but one great "loss" (Matt. 16:26; Luke 9:25). **8. Yea doubtless**—The oldest MSS. omit "doubtless" (*Greek, "ge"*): translate, "nay more." Not only "*have* I counted" *those* things just mentioned "loss for Christ's sake, but, moreover, I *even* DO count ALL things but loss. . . ." **for the excellency**—*Greek,* "On account of the surpassing excellency (the super-eminence above them all) of the knowledge of Christ Jesus." **my Lord**—believing and loving appropriation of Him (Ps. 63: 1; John 20:28). **for whom**—"on account of whom." **I have suffered the loss**—not merely I "*counted*" them "loss," but have actually lost them. **all things** —The *Greek* has the article, referring to the preceding "all things"; "I have suffered the loss of *them all.*" **dung**—*Greek,* "refuse (such as excrements, dregs, dross) *cast to the dogs,*" as the derivation expresses. A "loss" is of something having value; but "refuse" is thrown away as not worthy of being any more touched or looked at. **win**—Translate, to accord with the translation, vs. 7, "*gain* Christ." A man cannot make other things his "gain" or chief confidence, and at the same time "gain Christ." He who loses all things, and even himself, on account of Christ, gains Christ: Christ is His, and He is Christ's (Song of Sol. 2:16; 6:3; Luke 9:23, 24; I Cor. 3:23). **9. be found in him**—"be found" at His coming again, living spiritually "in Him" as the element of my life. Once *lost,* I have been "found," and I hope to be perfectly "found" by Him (Luke 15:8). **own righteousness . . . of the law**—(*V.* 6; Rom. 10:3, 5.) "Of," i.e., *from.* **righteousness . . . of God by faith**—*Greek,* "which is *from* God (resting) *upon* faith." Paul was transported from legal bondage into Christian freedom at once, and without any gradual transition. Hence, the bands of Pharisaism were loosed instantaneously; and opposition to Pharisaic Judaism took the place of opposition to the Gospel. Thus God's providence fitly prepared him for the work of overthrowing all idea of legal justification. "The righteousness of faith," in Paul's sense, is the righteousness or perfect holiness of Christ appropriated by faith, as the *objective* ground of confidence for the believer, and

ADAM CLARKE

3. *We are the circumcision.* We who have embraced the faith of Christ crucified are now entered into the new covenant, and according to that new covenant, *worship God in the Spirit,* "exulting," "making our boast of Christ Jesus," as our only Saviour, having *no confidence in the flesh*—in any outward rite or ceremony prescribed by the Jewish institutions.

4. *Though I might also have confidence.* If any of them have any cause to boast in outward rites and privileges, I have as much; yea, *more.*

5. *Circumcised the eighth day.* This was the time that the law required the males to be circumcised. *Of the stock of Israel.* Regularly descended from the patriarch Jacob. *Of the tribe of Benjamin.* The most favorite son of that patriarch; and a tribe that did not revolt with Jeroboam, 1 Kings xii. 21, nor pollute the worship of God by idolatry. *An Hebrew of the Hebrews.* Though born in a heathen country, Tarsus, yet both my parents were Hebrews; nor has there ever been any strange blood mixed with that of our family. *Touching the law, a Pharisee.* One that not only received the law and the prophets as coming from God, but belonged to that sect which, of all others, was most scrupulously attached to it.

6. *Concerning zeal.* As to my zeal for Pharisaism, I gave the fullest proof of it by persecuting the Church of Christ; and this is known to all my countrymen. *Touching the righteousness.* And as to that plan of "justification," which justification the Jews say is to be obtained by an observance of the law, I have done everything so conscientiously from my youth up that in this respect I am *blameless;* and may, with more confidence than most of them, expect that justification which the law appears to promise.

7. *But what things were gain.* The credit and respect which I had, as being zealously attached to the law and to the traditions of the elders, *I counted loss for Christ*—I saw that this could stand me in no stead, that all my acts of righteousness were nothing on which I could depend for salvation, and that Christ crucified could alone profit me.

8. *I count all things but loss.* Not only my Jewish privileges, but all others of every kind. *The excellency of the knowledge of Christ.* That superior light, information, and blessedness which come through the gospel of Jesus Christ. *I have suffered the loss of all things.* Some translate, "for whom I have thrown away all things"—I have made a voluntary choice of Christ, His cross, His poverty, and His reproach; and for these I have freely sacrificed all I had from the world, and all I could expect from it. *And do count them but dung.* The word means the vilest dross or "refuse" of anything, the worst excrement.

9. *And be found in him.* Be found a believer in Christ, *not having mine own righteousness*—not trusting in anything I have done or could do, in order to my salvation; relying on no scheme of justification, set up formerly either by myself or by others. *But that which is through the faith of Christ.* That justification which is received by faith through the atonement made by Christ. *The righteousness which is of God.* God's method of justifying sinners through faith in His Son.

MATTHEW HENRY

3. That he might know Christ (*v.* 10): *That I may know him, and the power of his resurrection, and the fellowship of his sufferings.* Knowing him here is believing in him: it is an experimental knowledge. The apostle was as ambitious of being sanctified as he was of being justified. 4. That he might be conformable unto him. We are then made conformable to his death when we die to sin, as Christ died for sin, when we are crucified with Christ, and the *world is crucified to us.*

II. The apostle had his heart upon heaven as his happiness: *If by any means I might attain to the resurrection of the dead, v.* 11.

1. The happiness of heaven is here called the resurrection of the dead. This the apostle had his eye upon; this he would attain. There will be a resurrection of the unjust, and our care must be to escape that: but the joyful and glorious resurrection of saints is called *the resurrection by eminence.* To the saints it will be indeed a resurrection, while the resurrection of the wicked is a rising from the grave, but a return to a second death.

2. This joyful resurrection the apostle pressed towards. He speaks as if they were in danger of missing it, and coming short of it. A holy fear of coming short is an excellent means of perseverance. Paul himself did not hope to attain it through his own merit, but through the merit of Jesus Christ.

(1) He looks upon himself to be in a state of imperfection and trial: *Not as though I had already attained, or were already perfect, v.* 12. The best men in the world will readily own their imperfection in the present state. If Paul had not attained to perfection, much less have we. *Brethren, I count not myself to have apprehended* (*v.* 13). Those who think they have grace enough give proof that they have little enough, or rather that they have none at all; because, wherever there is true grace, there is a desire of more grace.

(2) What the apostle's actings were under this conviction. "*I follow after* (*v.* 12), *I pursue* with vigour. *If that I may apprehend that for which also I am apprehended of Christ Jesus.*" It is not our laying hold of Christ first, but his laying hold of us, which is our happiness and salvation. Not our keeping hold of Christ, but his keeping hold of us, is our safety. *To apprehend that for which we are apprehended of Christ.* To apprehend that for which he apprehended us is to attain the perfection of our bliss. He adds further (*v.* 13): *This one thing I do, forgetting those things which are behind, and reaching forth to those things which are before.* Paul forgot the things which were behind, he was still for having more and more. So he *reached forth.*

(3) The apostle's aim. *I press towards the mark, for the prize of the high calling of God in Christ Jesus, v.* 14. The fitter we grow for heaven the faster we must press towards it. Heaven is the *prize of the high calling*; what we aim at in all we do, and what will reward all our pains. It is of God, from whom we are to expect it. But it is in Christ Jesus; through his hand it must come to us. There is no getting to heaven as our home but by Christ as our way.

JAMIESON, FAUSSET, BROWN

also as a new *subjective* principle of life. Hence it includes the essence of a new disposition, and may easily pass into the idea of sanctification, though the two ideas are originally distinct.

10. That I may know him—experimentally. The aim of the "righteousness" just mentioned. This verse resumes, and more fully explains, "the excellency of the knowledge of Christ" (vs. 8). To know HIM is more than merely to know a *doctrine* about Him. Believers are brought not only to redemption, but to the Redeemer Himself. **the power of his resurrection**—assuring believers of their justification (Rom. 4:25; I Cor. 15:17), and raising them up spiritually with Him, by virtue of their identification with Him in this, as in all the acts of His redeeming work for us (Rom. 6:4; Col. 2:12; 3:1). The power of the Divine Spirit, which raised Him from literal death, is the same which raises believers from spiritual death now (Eph. 1:19, 20), and shall raise their bodies from literal death hereafter (Rom. 8:11). **the fellowship of his sufferings**—by identification with Him in His sufferings and death, *by imputation;* also, in *actually* bearing the cross whatever is laid on us, after His example, and so "filling up that which is behind of the afflictions of Christ" (Col. 1:24); and in the *will* to bear aught for His sake (Matt. 10:38; 16:24; II Tim. 2:11). As He bore all our sufferings (Isa. 53:4), so we participate in His. **made conformable unto his death**—"conformed to the likeness of His death," viz., by continued sufferings for His sake, and mortifying of the carnal self (Rom. 8:29; I Cor. 15:31; II Cor. 4:10-12; Gal. 2:20). **11. If by any means**—not implying uncertainty of the issue, but the earnestness of the struggle of faith (I Cor. 9:26, 27), and the urgent need of jealous selfwatchfulness (I Cor. 10:12). **attain unto the resurrection of the dead**—The oldest MSS. read, "... the resurrection *from* (out of) the dead," viz., the first resurrection; that of believers at Christ's coming (I Cor. 15:23; I Thess. 4:15; Rev. 20:5, 6). The *Greek* word occurs nowhere else in the New Testament. "The power of Christ's resurrection" (Rom. 1:4), ensures the believer's attainment of the "resurrection from the (rest of the) dead" (cf. vss. 20, 21). Cf. "accounted worthy to *obtain the resurrection from the dead*" (Luke 20:35). "The resurrection of the just" (Luke 14:14). **12.** Translate, "Not *that* I...." (I do *not* wish to be understood as saying *that*....) **attained**—"obtained," viz., a perfect knowledge of Christ, and of the power of His death, and fellowship of His sufferings, and a conformity to His death. **either were already perfect**—"or *am* already *perfected,*" i.e., *crowned* with the garland of victory, my course *completed,* and *perfection absolutely reached.* The image is that of a *racecourse* throughout. See I Corinthians 9:24; Hebrews 12:23. See TRENCH, *Synonyms of New Testament.* **I follow after**—"I press on." **apprehend ... apprehended**—if *so be* that I may *lay hold on* that (viz., the *prize,* vs. 14) for which also *I was laid hold on* by Christ" (viz., at my conversion, Song of Sol. 1:4; I Cor. 13:12). **Jesus**—omitted in the oldest MSS. Paul was close to "apprehending" the prize (II Tim. 4:7, 8). Christ the Author, is also the Finisher of His people's "race." **13. I**—whatever others count as to themselves. He who counts himself perfect, must deceive himself by calling sin infirmity (I John 1:8); at the same time, each must *aim* at perfection, to be a Christian at all (Matt. 5:48). **forgetting those things ... behind**—*Looking back* is sure to end in *going back* (Luke 9:62): So Lot's wife (Luke 17:32). If in stemming a current we cease pulling the oar against it, we are carried back. God's word to us is as it was to Israel, "Speak unto the children of Israel that they go forward" (Exod. 14:15). The Bible is our landmark to show us whether we are progressing or retrograding. **reaching forth**—with hand and foot, like a runner in a race, and the body bent forward. The Christian is always humbled by the contrast between what he is and what he desires to be. The eye reaches before and draws on the hand, the hand reaches before and draws on the foot [BENGEL]. **unto**—towards (Heb. 6:1). **14. high calling**—lit., "the calling that is *above*" (Gal. 4:26; Col. 3:1): "the *heavenly* calling" (Heb. 3:1). "The prize" is "the crown of righteousness" (I Cor. 9:24; II Tim. 4:8). Revelation 2:10, "crown of life." I Peter 5:4, "a crown of glory that fadeth not away." "The high," or "heavenly calling," is not restricted, as ALFORD thinks, to Paul's own calling as an apostle by the summons of God from heaven; but *the common calling of all Christians to salvation in Christ,* which coming from heaven invites us to heaven, whither accordingly our minds ought to be uplifted. **15. therefore**—resuming vs.

ADAM CLARKE

10. *That I may know him.* To be the true and promised Messiah, and experience all that salvation which He has bought by His blood. *And the fellowship of his sufferings.* Christ died, not only as a Victim for sin, but as a Martyr to the truth. No creature can have *fellowship* with Him in His vicarious sufferings; as a martyr to the truth, Paul wished to imitate Him.

11. *The resurrection of the dead.* That is, the resurrection of those who, having died in the Lord, rise to glory and honor; and hence Paul uses a peculiar word which occurs nowhere else in the New Testament. The words, as they stand in the best MSS., are as follows: "to that resurrection which is of the dead."

12. *Not as though I had already attained.* For I have not yet received the prize; I am not glorified, for I have not finished my course; and I have a conflict still to maintain, and the issue will prove whether I should be crowned. From the beginning of the eleventh to the end of the seventeenth verse there is one continued allusion to the contests at the Olympic games; exercises with which, and their laws, the Philippians were well acquainted. *Either were already perfect.* "Nor am I yet perfect"; I am not yet crowned, in consequence of having suffered martyrdom. I am quite satisfied that the apostle here alludes to the Olympic games, and the word *teteleiomai* is the proof; spoken of those who have completed their race, reached the goal, and are honored with the prize. Paul therefore is not speaking here of any deficiency in his own grace or spiritual state; he does not mean by not being yet *perfect* that he had a body of sin and death cleaving to him, and was still polluted with indwelling *sin,* as some have imagined. He speaks of his not having terminated his course by martyrdom, which he knew would sooner or later be the case. *But I follow after.* "But I pursue." Several are gone before me in this glorious way, and have obtained the crown of martyrdom; I am hurrying after them. *That I may apprehend.* That I may receive those blessings to which I am called by Christ Jesus. There is still an allusion here to the stadium, and exercises there. The apostle considers Christ as the *brabeus,* or Judge in the games, who proclaimed the victor and distributed the prizes; and he represents himself as being introduced by this very *brabeus,* or Judge, into the contest; and this *brabeus* brought him in with the design to crown him, if he contended faithfully. To complete this faithful contention is what he has in view; that he may *apprehend,* or "lay hold" on, *that for which* he had been *apprehended,* or "taken by the hand," *by Christ,* who had converted, strengthened, and endowed him with apostolical powers, that he might fight the good fight of faith, and "lay hold" on eternal life.

13. *I count not myself to have apprehended.* Whatever gifts, graces, or honors I may have received from Jesus Christ, I consider everything as incomplete till I have finished my course, got this crown, and have my body raised and fashioned after His glorious body. *This one thing I do.* This is the concern, as it is the sole business, of my life. *Reaching forth.* The Greek word points out the strong exertions made in the race; every muscle and nerve is exerted, and he puts forth every particle of his strength in running. He was running for life, and running for his life.

14. *I press toward the mark.* "I pursue along the line"; this is a reference to the white lines that marked the ground in the stadium, from the starting place to the goal, on which the runners were obliged to keep their eyes fixed; for they who transgressed or went beyond this line did not run lawfully, and were not crowned, even though they got first to the goal. What is called *scopos,* "mark" or "scope," here is called *canon,* the "line," i.e., the marked line, v. 16. When it was said to Diogenes, the cynic, "Thou art now an old man, rest from thy labors"; to this he answered: "If I have run long in the race, will it become me to slacken my pace when I come near the end; should I not rather stretch forward?" *For the prize of the high calling of God.* The reward which God from above calls me, by Christ Jesus, to receive. The apostle still keeps in view his crown of martyrdom and his glorious resurrection.

MATTHEW HENRY

Verses 15, 16

This was the thing wherein all good Christians were agreed, to make Christ all in all, and set their hearts upon another world. This is that whereto we have all attained. Therefore let us walk by the same rule, and mind the same thing. Having made Christ our all, *to us to live must be Christ.*

Christians who differ in smaller matters should yet bear with one another, because they are agreed in the main matter: "*If in anything you be otherwise minded,* you must not judge one another, while you all meet now in Christ as your centre, and hope to meet shortly in heaven as your home.

God shall reveal even this unto you. Whatever it is wherein you differ, you must wait till God give you a better understanding. *As far as you have attained, you* must go together in the ways of God, and wait for further light in the minor things wherein you differ."

Verses 17–21

I. He warns them against following the examples of evil teachers (*v.* 18, 19): *Many walk, of whom I have told you often, and now tell you weeping, that they are the enemies of the cross of Christ.*

1. There are many called by Christ's name who are enemies to Christ's cross. Their walk is a surer evidence what they are than their profession. *I have told you often.* We so little heed the warnings given us that we have need to have them repeated. *I now tell you weeping.* What we say often we may say again, if we say it affectionately.

2. The characters of those who were the enemies of the cross of Christ. (1) Whose God is their belly. They minded nothing but their sensual appetites. The same observance which good people give to God epicures give to their appetites. (2) They glory in their shame. "They value themselves for what is their blemish and reproach." (3) They mind earthly things. Those who mind earthly things act directly contrary to the cross of Christ. They set their hearts and affections on earthly things. How absurd it would be for Christians to follow the example of such! To deter us all from so doing, he reads their doom. (4) Whose end is destruction. Their way seems pleasant, but death and hell are at the end of it. If we choose their way, we have reason to fear their end.

II. He proposes himself and his brethren for an example: *Brethren, be followers together of me, and mark those who walk as you have us for an example, v.* 17. He explains himself (*v.* 20) by their regard to Christ and heaven: *For our conversation is in heaven.* Good Christians, even while they are here on earth, have their conversation in heaven. This world is not our home, but that is. The life of a Christian is in heaven, where his home is, and where he hopes to be shortly. It is good having fellowship with those who have fellowship with Christ, and conversation with those whose conversation is in heaven.

1. We look for the Saviour from heaven (*v.* 20): *Whence also we look for the Saviour, the Lord Jesus Christ.* We expect his second coming thence.

JAMIESON, FAUSSET, BROWN

3. "As many of us then, as are perfect," i.e., *full grown* (no longer "babes") in the Christian life (vs. 3, "worshipping God in the Spirit, and having no confidence in the flesh"), I Corinthians 2:6, fully established in things of God. Here, by "perfect," he means one *fully fit for running* [BENGEL]; knowing and complying with the *laws* of the course (II Tim. 2:5). Though "perfect" in this sense, he was not yet "made perfect" (*Greek*) in the sense intended in vs. 12, viz., "crowned with *complete* victory," and having attained *absolute perfection.* **thus minded**–having the mind which he had described, vss. 7-14. **otherwise minded**–having too high an opinion of yourselves as to your attainment of Christian *perfection.* "He who thinks that he has attained everything, hath nothing" [CHRYSOSTOM]. Probably, too, he refers to those who were tempted to think to attain to *perfection* by the law (Gal. 3:3): who needed the warning (vs. 3), "Beware of the concision," though on account of their former piety, Paul hopes confidently (as in Gal. 5:10) that God will reveal the path of right-mindedness to them. Paul taught externally God "reveals" the truth internally by His Spirit (Matt. 11:25; 16: 17; I Cor. 3:6). **unto you**–who sincerely strive to do God's will (John 7:17; Eph. 1:17). **16.** The expectation of a new revelation is not to make you less careful in walking according to whatever degree of knowledge of divine things and perfection you have already attained. God makes further revelations to those who walk up to the revelations they already have (Hos. 6:3). **rule, let us mind the same thing**–omitted in the oldest MSS. Perhaps partly inserted from Galatians 6:16, and ch. 2:2. Translate then, "Whereunto we have attained, let us walk on (a military term, *march in order*) in the same" (the measure of knowledge already attained). **17. followers**–*Greek,* "imitators together." **of me**–as I am an *imitator of Christ* (I Cor. 11:1): Imitate me no farther than as I imitate Christ. Or as BENGEL "My fellow imitators of God" or "Christ"; "imitators of Christ together with me" (*Note,* ch. 2:22; Eph. 5:1). **mark**–for imitation. **which walk so as ye have us for an ensample**–In *English Version* of the former clause, the translation of this clause is, "those who are walking so as ye have an example in us." But in BENGEL's translation, "inasmuch as," or "since," instead of "as." **18. many walk**–in such a manner. Follow not evildoers, because they are "many" (Exod. 23:2). Their numbers are rather a presumption against their being Christ's "little flock" (Luke 12:32). **often**–There is need of constant warning. **weeping**–(Rom. 9:2). A hard tone in speaking of the inconsistencies of professors is the very opposite of Paul's spirit, and David's (Ps. 119: 136), and Jeremiah's (Jer. 13:17). The Lord and His apostles, at the same time, speak more strongly against empty professors (as the Pharisees), than against open scoffers. **enemies of the cross of Christ**–in their *practice,* not in doctrine (Gal. 6:14; Heb. 6:6; 10:29). **19. destruction**–everlasting at Christ's coming. Ch. 1:28, "perdition"; the opposite word is "Saviour" (vs. 20). **end**–fixed doom. **whose god is their belly**–(Rom. 16:18)–hereafter to be destroyed by God (I Cor. 6:13). In contrast to our "body" (vs. 21), which *our God,* the Lord Jesus, shall "fashion like unto His glorious body." Their belly is now pampered, our body now wasted; then the respective states of both shall be reversed. **glory is in their shame**–As "glory" is often used in the Old Testament for "God" (Ps. 106:20), so here it answers to "whose *God,*" in the parallel clause; and "shame" is the Old Testament term contemptuously given to an idol (Judg. 6:32, *Margin*). Hosea 4:7 seems to be referred to by Paul (cf. Rom. 1:32). There seems no allusion to circumcision, as no longer *glorious,* but a *shame* to them (vs. 2). The reference of the immediate context is to sensuality, and carnality in general. **mind earthly things**–(Rom. 8:5). In contrast to vs. 20; Col. 3:2. **20. our conversation**–rather, "our state" or "country"; *our citizenship: our life as citizens.* We are but *pilgrims* on earth; how *then* should we "mind earthly things?" (vs. 19; Heb. 11:9, 10, 13-16). Roman citizenship was then highly prized; how much more should the heavenly citizenship (Acts 22:28; cf. Luke 10:20)? **is**–*Greek,* "has its existence." **in heaven**–*Greek,* "in the heavens." **look for the Saviour, the Lord Jesus Christ**–"We wait for (so the same *Greek* is translated, Rom. 8:19) the Lord Jesus as (i.e., in the capacity of a) Saviour" (Heb. 9:28). That He is "the Lord," now exalted above every name, assures our expectation (ch. 2:9-11). Our High Priest is gone up into the Holy of Holies not made with hands, there to atone for us; and as the Israelites stood outside the tabernacle, expecting Aaron's

ADAM CLARKE

15. *As many as be perfect.* As many as are "thoroughly instructed" in divine things, who have cast off all dependence on the law and on every other system for salvation, and who discern God calling them from above by Christ Jesus. *Be thus minded;* be intensely in earnest for eternal life, nor ever halt till the race is finished. The word *teleioi, perfect,* is taken here in the same sense in which it is taken in 1 Cor. xiv. 20: "Be not *children* in understanding . . . but in understanding be ye *men," teleioi*—"thoroughly instructed, deeply experienced." 1 Cor. ii. 6: "We speak wisdom among them that are perfect," among those who are fully instructed, adults in Christian knowledge. Eph. iv. 13: "Till we all come . . . unto a perfect man"; *teleion,* to the state of adults in Christianity. Heb. v. 14: "But strong meat belongeth to them that are of full age"; *teleion,* "the perfect"—those who are thoroughly instructed and experienced in divine things. *Let us therefore,* says the apostle, *as many as be perfect,* as have entered fully into the spirit and design of the gospel, *be thus minded,* viz., Forget the things which are behind, and stretch forward along the mark for the prize. *If in any thing ye be otherwise minded.* If you have not yet entered into the full spirit and design of this gospel, if any of you have yet remaining any doubts relative to Jewish ordinances or their expediency in Christianity, *God shall reveal even this unto you;* for while you are sincere and upright, God will take care that you shall have full instruction in these divine things.

16. *Whereto we have already attained.* Let us not lose that part of the race which we have already run. *Let us walk by the same rule*—let us keep the white line continually in view. *Let us mind the same thing,* always considering the glorious prize which is held out by God through Christ Jesus to animate and encourage us.

17. *Brethren, be followers together of me.* In the things of Christ let me be your "line"; and my writing, preaching, and conduct, your "rule." *And mark them.* Still alluding to the "line" in the stadium; keep your eye steadily fixed on those *which walk,* "live," *as ye have us*—myself, Timothy, and Epaphroditus—*for an ensample.*

18. *For many walk.* The Judaizing teachers continue to preach, who wish to incorporate circumcision and other ordinances of the law with the gospel. *They are the enemies of the cross of Christ.* They rather attribute justification to the Levitical sacrifices than to the sacrificial death of Christ; and thus they are enemies to that Cross, and will not suffer persecution for its sake.

19. *Whose end is destruction.* This is the issue of their doctrine and of their conduct. They are here described by three characters: (1) Their *god is their belly*—they live not in any reference to eternity.

(2) Their *glory is in their shame*—they lay it down as a proof of their address that they can fare sumptuously every day in consequence of preaching a doctrine which flatters the passions of their hearers.

(3) They *mind earthly things*—their whole study and attention are taken up with earthly matters.

20. *Our conversation is in heaven.* "Our citizenship" or "civil rights."

MATTHEW HENRY

2. At the second coming of Christ we expect to be happy and glorified there. *Who shall change our vile bodies, that they may be fashioned like unto his glorious body, v.* 21. There is a glory reserved for the saints, which they will be instated in at the resurrection. The body is now at the best a *vile body, the body of our humiliation.* But it will be made a glorious body. *According to the working whereby he is able even to subdue all things unto himself.* It is matter of comfort to us that he can subdue all things to himself. And the resurrection will be wrought by this power. Let this confirm our faith of the resurrection, that we not only have the scriptures, which assure us it shall be, but we *know the power of God,* which can effect it. As Christ's resurrection was a glorious instance of the divine power, so will our resurrection be. And then all the enemies of the Redeemer's kingdom will be completely conquered.

CHAPTER 4

Verses 1-9

I. Steadfastness in our Christian profession, *v.* 1. Seeing our *conversation is in heaven,* and we look for the Saviour to come thence and fetch us thither, *therefore let us stand fast.* The believing prospect of eternal life should engage us to be constant, in our Christian course. *My brethren, dearly beloved and longed for, my joy and crown;* and again, *My dearly beloved.* Thus he expresses the pleasure he took in them to convey his exhortations to them with so much the greater advantage. Being brethren he loved them, and loved them dearly: *Dearly beloved;* and again, *My dearly beloved.* Brotherly love must always go along with the brotherly relation. He loved them and longed for them. He loved them and rejoiced in them. They were his joy. He loved them and gloried in them. They were his crown as well as his joy. *So stand fast in the Lord.* Being in Christ, they must stand fast in him, close and constant unto the end. Or, To *stand fast in the Lord* is to stand fast in his strength and by his grace; not trusting in ourselves.

II. He exhorts them to unanimity and mutual assistance (*v.* 2, 3): *I beseech Euodias and Syntyche that they be of the same mind in the Lord.* This is directed to some particular persons. Sometimes there is need of applying the general precepts of the gospel to particular persons and cases. Euodias and Syntyche, it seems, were at variance, either one with the other or with the church. "Desire them from me to be of the same mind in the Lord, to keep the peace and live in love, to be of the same mind with the rest of the church." Then he exhorts to mutual assistance (*v.* 3), and this exhortation he directs to particular persons: *I entreat thee also, true yoke-fellow.* Who this person was whom he calls true yoke-fellow is uncertain. He exhorts his yoke-fellow to *help the women who laboured with him.* Whoever was the yoke-fellow with the apostle must be a yoke-fellow too with his friends. It seems, there were women who laboured with Paul in the gospel. Women may be helpful to ministers in the work of the gospel. *Do thou help them.* Those who help others should be helped themselves when there is occasion.—*With Clement also, and other my fellow-labourers.* Paul had a kindness for all his fellow-labourers, *Whose names are in the book of life.* There is a book of life; there are names in that book and not characters and conditions only. We cannot search into that book, or know whose names are written there; but we may conclude that those who labour in the gospel have their names in the book of life.

III. *Rejoice in the Lord always, and again I say, Rejoice, v.* 4. All our joy must terminate in God; and our thoughts of God must be delightful thoughts. It is our duty and privilege to rejoice in God, and to rejoice in him always; at all times, in all conditions. There is enough in God to furnish us with matter of joy in the worst circumstance on earth. *Rejoice in the Lord always; and again I say, Rejoice.* If good men have not a continual feast, it is their own fault.

IV. We are here exhorted to gentleness, and good temper towards our brethren: "*Let your moderation be known to all men, v.* 5. In things indifferent do not run into extremes; judge charitably concerning one another." Some understand it of the patient bearing of afflictions, or the sober enjoyment of worldly good.

JAMIESON, FAUSSET, BROWN

return (cf. Luke 1:21), so must we look unto the heavens expecting Christ thence. **21.** *Greek,* "Who shall *transfigure* the body *of our humiliation* (viz., in which our humiliation has place, II Cor. 4:10; Eph. 2:19; II Tim. 2:12), that it may be *conformed* unto the body *of His glory* (viz., in which His glory is manifested), according to the *effectual working* whereby...." Not only shall He come as our "Saviour," but also as our *Glorifier.* **even**—not only to make *the body* like His own, but "to subdue *all things,*" even death itself, as well as Satan and sin. He gave a sample of the coming *transfiguration* on the mount (Matt. 17:1, etc.). Not a change of *identity,* but of *fashion* or *form* (Ps. 17:15; I Cor. 15:51). Our spiritual resurrection now is the pledge of our bodily resurrection to glory hereafter (vs. 20; Rom. 8:11). As Christ's glorified body was essentially identical with His body of humiliation; so our resurrection bodies as believers, since they shall be like His, shall be identical essentially with our present bodies, and yet "spiritual bodies" (I Cor. 15:42-44). Our "hope" is, that Christ, by His rising from the dead, hath obtained the power, and is become the pattern, of our resurrection (Mic. 2:13).

CHAPTER 4

Vss. 1-23. Exhortations: Thanks for the Supply from Philippi: Greeting; and Closing Benediction. **1.** "Wherefore"; since we have such a glorious hope (ch. 3:20, 21). **dearly beloved**—repeated again at the close of the verse, implying that his great love to them should be a motive to their obedience. **longed for**—"yearned after" in your absence (ch. 1:8). **crown**—in the day of the Lord (ch. 2:16; I Thess. 2:19). **so**—as I have admonished you. **stand fast**—(Ch. 1:27). **2.** Euodia and Syntyche were two women who seem to have been at variance; probably deaconesses of the church. He repeats, "I beseech," as if he would admonish each separately, and with the utmost impartiality. **in the Lord**—the true element of Christian union; for those "in the Lord" by faith to be at variance, is an utter inconsistency. **3. And**—*Greek,* "Yea." **true yoke-fellow**—yoked with me in the same Gospel yoke Matt. 11:29, 30; cf. I Tim. 5:17, 18). Either Timothy, Silas (Acts 15:40; 16:19, *at Philippi*), or the chief bishop of Philippi. Or else the *Greek, Sunzugus,* or *Synzygus,* is a proper name: "Who art truly, as thy name means, a *yoke-fellow.*" Certainly not *Paul's wife,* as I Corinthians 9:5 implies he had none. **help those women**—rather, as *Greek,* "help *them,*" viz., Euodia and Syntyche. "Cooperate with them" [Birks]; or as Alford, "Help in the work of their reconciliation." **which laboured with me**—"*inasmuch as* they labored with me." At Philippi, women were the first hearers of the Gospel, and Lydia the first convert. It is a coincidence which marks genuineness, that in this Epistle alone, special instructions are given to women who labored with Paul in the Gospel. In selecting the first teachers, those first converted would naturally be fixed on. Euodia and Syntyche were doubtless two of "the women who resorted to the riverside, where prayer was wont to be made" (Acts 16:13), and being early converted, would naturally take an active part in teaching other women called at a later period; of course not in public preaching, but in a less prominent sphere (I Tim. 2:11, 12). **Clement**—bishop of Rome shortly after the death of Peter and Paul. His Epistle from the Church of Rome to the Church of Corinth is extant. It makes no mention of the supremacy of the See of Peter. He was the most eminent of the apostolical fathers. Alford thinks that the Clement here was *a Philippian,* and not necessarily Clement, bishop of Rome. But Origen (*Comment,* John 1:29) identifies the Clement here with the bishop of Rome. **in the book of life**—the register-book of those whose "citizenship is in heaven" (Luke 10:20; Phil. 3:20). Anciently, free cities had a roll-book containing the names of all those having the right of citizenship (cf. Exod. 32:32; Ps. 69:28; Ezek. 13:9; Dan. 12:1; Rev. 20:12; 21:27). **4.** (Isa. 61:10.) **alway**—even amidst the afflictions now distressing you (ch. 1:28-30). **again**—as he had already said, "Rejoice" (ch. 3:1). Joy is the predominant feature of the Epistle. **I say**—*Greek,* rather, "I *will* say." **5. moderation**—from a *Greek* root, "to yield," whence *yieldingness* [Trench]; or from a root, "it is fitting," whence "*reasonableness of dealing*" [Alford], that considerateness for others, *not urging one's own rights to the uttermost,* but waiving a part, and thereby rectifying the injustices of justice. The archetype of this grace is God, who presses not the strictness of His law against us as we deserve (Ps.

ADAM CLARKE

21. *Who shall change our vile body.* Who will "refashion" or "alter the fashion and condition of," the body of our humiliation; this body that is dead—adjudged to death because of sin, and must be putrefied, dissolved, and decomposed. *That it may be fashioned like unto his glorious body.* "That it may bear a similar form to the body of His glory." That is: The bodies of true believers shall be raised up at the great day in the same likeness, immortality, and glory of the glorified humanity of Jesus Christ; and be so thoroughly changed as to be not only capable through their immortality of eternally existing, but also of the infinite spiritual enjoyments at the right hand of God. *According to the working.* "According to that energy, by which He can bring all things under subjection to himself."

CHAPTER 4

1. *Therefore, my . . . beloved.* Because you have this armor, and those enemies, and God for your support, see that you stand fast in Him. This verse most unquestionably belongs to the preceding chapter.

2. *I beseech Euodias, and beseech Syntyche.* These were two pious women, as it is generally supposed, who were deaconesses in the church at Philippi, and who in some points of doctrine and discipline had disagreed. He exhorts them to be of the same mind, that is, to compose their differences; and if they could not perfectly agree, to think and let think, and to avoid all public opposition, as their dissension would strengthen the hands of the common enemy and stumble those who were weak.

3. *Help those women which laboured with me.* Both in the Grecian and Asiatic countries women were kept much secluded, and it was not likely that even the apostles had much opportunity of conversing with them. It was therefore necessary that they should have some experienced Christian women with them who could have access to families and preach Jesus to the female part of them. The apostle tells us that certain women labored with him in the gospel, and were assistants to others also who had assisted him.

With Clement also. Supposed to be the same who was afterwards bishop of Rome, and who wrote an Epistle to the Corinthians, which is still extant.

Whose names are in the book of life. Who are genuine Christians; who are enlisted or enrolled in the armies of the Lord, and have received a title to eternal glory.

4. *Rejoice in the Lord alway.* Be continually happy; but this happiness you can find only *in the Lord.* Genuine happiness is spiritual; as it can come only from God, so it infallibly tends to Him.

5. *Let your moderation be known.* The word is of very extensive signification; it means the same as mildness, patience, yieldingness, gentleness, clemency, unwillingness to litigate or contend; but *moderation* is expressive enough as a general term.

MATTHEW HENRY

The Lord is at hand. "He will take vengeance on your enemies, and reward your patience."

V. A caution against disquieting perplexing care (*v.* 6): *Be careful for nothing.* Avoid anxious care and distracting thought in the wants and difficulties of life. It is the duty and interest of Christians to live without care. There is a care of diligence which is our duty, but there is a care of distrust which is our sin and folly.

VI. He recommends to us constant prayer: *In everything by prayer and supplication, with thanksgiving, let your requests be made known to God.* We must pray upon every particular emergency: *In everything by prayer.* When anything burdens our spirits, we must ease our minds by prayer; when our affairs are perplexed or distressed, we must seek direction and support. We must join thanksgiving with our prayers and supplications. We must not only seek supplies of good, but own receipts of mercy. Prayer is the offering up of our desires to God: *Let your requests be made known to God.* Not that God needs to be told either our wants or desires; but he will know them from us.

The effect of this will be the *peace of God keeping our hearts, v.* 7. The *peace of God which passeth all understanding* is a greater good than can be sufficiently valued or duly expressed.

This peace will *keep our hearts and minds through Christ Jesus*; it will keep us from sinning under our troubles, and from sinking under them.

VII. We are exhorted to get and keep a good name: *Whatsoever things are true and honest* (*v.* 8), a regard to truth and to becomingness in our behaviour. Whatsoever things are *just and pure*, without the impurity or mixture of sin. Whatsoever things are *lovely and of good report*, that will render us beloved, and make us well spoken of. *If there is any virtue, if there is any praise.*

The apostle would have the Christians learn anything which was good of their heathen neighbours: "*If there be any virtue, think of these things*—imitate them in what is truly excellent among them." We should not be ashamed to learn any good thing of bad men. Virtue has its praise, and will have. *Those things which you have learned, and received, and heard and seen in me, do.* Paul's

JAMIESON, FAUSSET, BROWN

130:3, 4); though having exacted the fullest payment for us from our Divine Surety. There are included in "moderation," *candor* and *kindliness. Joy in the Lord* raises us above rigorism towards others (vs. 5), and carefulness (vs. 6) as to one's own affairs. Sadness produces *morose harshness* towards others, and a troublesome spirit in ourselves. **Let . . . be known**—i.e., in your conduct to others, let nothing inconsistent with "moderation" be seen. Not a precept to make a *display* of moderation. Let this grace "be known" to men in *acts;* let "your requests be made to God" in word (vs. 6). **unto all men**—even to the "perverse" (ch. 2:15), that so ye may win them. Exercise "forbearance" even to your persecutors. None is so ungracious as not to be kindly to someone, from some motive or another, on some occasion; the believer is to be so "unto all men" at all times. **The Lord is at hand**—The Lord's coming again speedily is the grand motive to every Christian grace (Jas. 5:8,9). Harshness to others (the opposite of "moderation") would be taking into our own hands prematurely the prerogatives of judging, which belongs to the Lord alone (I Cor. 4:5); and so provoking God to judge us by the strict letter of the law (Jas. 2:12, 13). **6.** Translate, "Be anxious about nothing." Care and prayer are as mutually opposed as fire and water [BENGEL]. **by prayer and supplication**—*Greek,* "by *the* prayer and *the* supplication" appropriate to each case [ALFORD]. *Prayer* for blessings; and the general term. *Supplication,* to avert ills; a special term, *suppliant entreaty* (*Note,* Eph. 6:18). **thanksgiving**—for every event, prosperity and affliction alike (I Thess. 5:18; Jas. 5:13). The Philippians might remember Paul's example at Philippi when in the innermost prison (Acts 16:25). Thanksgiving gives effect to prayer (II Chron. 20: 21), and frees from *anxious carefulness* by making all God's dealings matter for *praise,* not merely for *resignation,* much less *murmuring.* "Peace" is the companion of "thanksgiving" (vs. 7; Col. 3:15). **let your requests be made known unto God**—with generous, filial, unreserved confidence; not keeping aught back, as too great, or else too small, to bring before God, though you might feel so as to your fellow men. So Jacob, when fearing Esau (Gen. 32:9-12); Hezekiah fearing Sennacherib (II Kings 19:14; Ps. 37:5). **7. And**—The inseparable consequence of thus laying everything before God in "prayer with thanksgiving." **peace**—the dispeller of "anxious care" (vs. 6). **of God**—coming from God, and resting in God (John 14:27; 16:33; Col. 3:15). **passeth**—*surpasseth,* or *exceedeth,* all man's notional powers of understanding its full blessedness (I Cor. 2:9, 10; Eph. 3:20; cf. Prov. 3:17). **shall keep**—rather, "shall *guard*"; shall keep as a well-garrisoned stronghold (Isa. 26:1, 3). The same *Greek* verb is used in I Peter 1:5. There shall be peace secure within, whatever outward troubles may besiege. **hearts and minds**—rather, "hearts (the *seat* of the thoughts) and *thoughts*" or purposes. **through**—rather as *Greek,* "*in* Christ Jesus." It is in Christ that we are "kept" or "guarded" secure. **8.** Summary of all his exhortations as to relative duties, whether as children or parents, husbands or wives, friends, neighbors, men in the intercourse of the world, etc. **true**—sincere, *in words.* **honest**—Old English for "seemly," viz., *in action;* lit., *grave, dignified.* **just**—towards *others.* **pure**—"chaste," in relation to *ourselves.* **lovely**—lovable (cf. Mark 10:21; Luke 7:4, 5). **of good report**—referring to the *absent* (ch. 1: 27); as "lovely" refers to what is lovable *face to face.* **if there be any virtue**—"whatever virtue there is" [ALFORD]. "Virtue," the standing word in heathen ethics, is found once only in Paul's Epistles, and once in Peter's (II Pet. 1:5); and this in uses different from those in heathen authors. It is a term rather earthly and human, as compared with the names of the spiritual graces which Christianity imparts; hence the rarity of its occurrence in the New Testament. Piety and true morality are inseparable. Piety is love with its face towards God; morality is love with its face towards man. Despise not anything that is good in itself; only let it keep its due place. **praise**—whatever is *praiseworthy;* not that Christians should make man's praise their aim (cf. John 12:43); but they should live so as to *deserve* men's praise. **think on**—have a continual regard to, so as to "do" these things (vs. 9) whenever the occasion arises. **9. both**—rather, "The things *also* which ye have learned . . . , these *practice*"; the things which besides recommending them in words, have been *also* recommended *by my example,* carry into practice. **heard**—though ye have not yet sufficiently "received" them. **seen**—though ye have not as yet

ADAM CLARKE

The Lord is at hand. A phrase something similar to the Maranatha of 1 Cor. xvi. 22. The Lord is Judge, and is at hand to punish.

6. *Be careful for nothing.* Be not anxiously solicitous. Do not give place to carking care, let what will occur; for anxiety cannot change the state or condition of anything from bad to good, but will infallibly injure your own souls. *By prayer and supplication.* God alone can help you; He is disposed to do it, but you must ask by prayer and supplication; without this He has not promised to help you. *By prayer*—solemn application to God from a sense of want. *Supplication*—continuance in earnest prayer. *With thanksgiving,* for innumerable favors already received; and for dangers, evils, and deaths turned aside.

7. *And the peace of God.* That harmonizing of all passions and appetites which is produced by the Holy Spirit, and arises from a sense of pardon and the favor of God.

Shall keep your hearts. Shall keep them as in a strong place or castle. *Your hearts*—the seat of all your affections and passions, *and minds*—your understanding, judgment, and conscience. *Through Christ Jesus;* by whom you were brought into this state of favor, through whom you are preserved in it, and in whom you possess it, for Christ keeps that heart in peace in which He dwells and rules.

8. *Finally, brethren.* The object of the apostle is to recommend holiness and righteousness to them in every point of view; and to show that the gospel of Christ requires all its professors to have the mind that was in Christ, and to walk as He himself also walked. *Whatsoever things are true.* All that is agreeable to unchangeable and eternal truth. *Whatsoever things are honest.* Whatever is "grave, decent, and venerable." Whatever becomes you as men, as citizens, and as Christians. *Whatsoever things are just.* Whatsoever is agreeable to justice and righteousness. All that you owe to God, to your neighbor, and to yourselves. *Whatsoever things are pure.* Whatsoever is "chaste." In reference to the state of the mind and to the acts of the body. *Whatsoever things are lovely.* Whatsoever is "amiable" on its own account and on account of its usefulness to others, whether in your conduct or conversation. *Whatsoever things are of good report.* Whatsoever things the public agree to acknowledge as useful and profitable to men; such as charitable institutions of every kind, in which genuine Christians should ever take the lead. *If there be any virtue.* If they be calculated to promote the general good of mankind, and are thus praiseworthy. *Think on these things.* Esteem them highly, recommend them heartily, and practice them fervently.

9. *Those things, which ye have . . . learned.* From my preaching and writing. *And received.* By faith, as a revelation from God. *And heard.*

MATTHEW HENRY

doctrine and life were of a piece. He could propose himself as well as his doctrine to their imitation. It gives a great force to what we say to others when we can appeal to what they have seen in us.

Verses 10–19

Grateful acknowledgment of the kindness of the Philippians.

He excuses their neglect of late. *Now at the last their care of him flourished again* (*v.* 10), like a tree in the spring, which seemed all the winter to be quite dead. He makes an excuse for them: *Wherein you were also careful, but you lacked opportunity.* They would have done it if a fair opportunity had offered.

Not that I speak in respect of want (*v.* 11); not in respect of any want he felt, nor of any want he feared. As to the former, he was content with the little he had, and that satisfied him; as to the latter, he depended upon the providence of God to provide for him from day to day, and that satisfied him. *For I have learned, in whatsoever state I am, therewith to be content.* That was the lesson he had as much need to learn as most men, considering the hardships and sufferings with which he was exercised.—*I know both how to be abased and I know how to abound, v.* 12. This is a special act of grace, to accommodate ourselves to every condition of life. To accommodate ourselves to an afflicted condition—to know how to be abased. To a prosperous condition—to know how to abound, how to be full, so as not to be proud, or secure. And this is as hard a lesson as the other; for the temptations of fulness and prosperity are not less than those of affliction and want. *I can do all things through Christ who strengthens me, v.* 13. We need his strength to teach us to be content in every condition. The apostle had seemed to boast of himself, and of his own strength: *I know how to be abased* (*v.* 12); but here he transfers all the praise to Christ. It is by his constant and renewed strength I am enabled to act in everything.

He commends their present liberality: *Notwithstanding, you have well done that you did communicate with my affliction, v.* 14. Here see Christian sympathy; not only to be concerned for our friends in their troubles, but to do what we can to help them. He rejoiced greatly in it (*v.* 10), because it was an evidence of their affection to him and the success of his ministry among them.

He takes occasion to acknowledge their former kindnesses to him, *v.* 15, 16. Paul had a grateful spirit. Wherever this epistle shall be read there shall this which they did to Paul be told for a memorial of them. Surely never was present so well repaid. *In the beginning of the gospel no church communicated with me as to giving and receiving but ye only, v.* 15, not only while he was with them, but when *he departed from Macedonia*; and this when no other church did so. They were the only church who were thus just and generous.

Even in Thessalonica you sent once and again to my necessity, v. 16. Just such things as he had need of; he did not desire superfluities nor dainties. *You sent once and again.* Many people make it an excuse for their charity that they have given once; why should the charge come upon them again? But the Philippians sent once and again.

"*Not because I desired a gift* (*v.* 17). I welcome your kindness because it adds to your account. *I desire fruit that may abound to your account. I have all, and abound, v.* 18. What can a man desire more than enough?" *I am full, having received from Epaphroditus the things which were sent by you.* A covetous worldling, if he has ever so much, would still have more; but a heavenly Christian, though he has little, has enough.

The apostle assures them that God did accept, and would recompense, their kindness to him. He did accept it: *It is an odour of a sweet smell, a sacrifice acceptable, well-pleasing to God.* A sacrifice of acknowledgment, and *well-pleasing to God.* It was more acceptable to God as it was the fruit of their grace than it was to Paul as it was the supply of his want.

JAMIESON, FAUSSET, BROWN

sufficiently "learned" them [BENGEL]. **and**—"and then," as the necessary result (vs. 7). Not only "the peace of God," but "the God of peace" Himself "shall be with you." **10. But**—transitional conjunction. But "now" to pass to another subject. **in the Lord**—He views everything with reference to Christ. **at the last**—"at last"; implying he was expecting their gift, not from a selfish view, but as a "fruit" of their faith, and to "abound" to their account (vss. 11, 17). Though long in coming, owing to Epaphroditus' sickness and other delays, he does not imply their gift was too late. **your care . . . hath flourished again**—*Greek,* "Ye have flourished again (*revived,* as trees sprouting forth *again* in spring) in your care *for* me." **wherein ye were also careful**—in respect to which (*revival,* viz., the sending of a supply to me) "ye were also (all along) careful, but ye lacked opportunity"; whether from want of means or want of a messenger. Your "lack of service" (ch. 2:30), was owing to your having "lacked opportunity." **11. I have learned**—The *I* in *Greek* is emphatical. I leave it to others if they will, to be discontented. *I,* for my part, have learned, by the teaching of the Holy Spirit, and the dealings of Providence (Heb. 5:8), to be content in every state. **content**—The *Greek,* literally expresses "independent of others, and having *sufficiency in one's self.*" But Christianity has raised the term above the haughty *self-sufficiency* of the heathen Stoic to the *contentment* of the Christian, whose *sufficiency* is not in *self,* but in *God* (II Cor. 3:5; I Tim. 6:6, 8; Heb. 13:5; cf. Jer. 2:36; 45:5). **12. abased**—in low circumstances (II Cor. 4:8; 6:9, 10). **everywhere**—rather [ALFORD], "in each, and in all things." **instructed**—in the secret. Lit., "initiated" in a secret teaching, which is a *mystery* unknown to the world. **13. I can do all things**—*Greek, "I have strength for all* things"; not merely "how to be abased and how to abound." After special instances he declares his *universal* power—how triumphantly, yet how humbly! [MEYER.] **through Christ which strengtheneth me**—The oldest MSS. omit "Christ"; then translate, "In *Him* who giveth me *power,*" i.e., by virtue of my living union and identification with Him, who is my strength (Gal. 2:20). Cf. I Timothy 1:12, whence probably, "Christ" was inserted here by transcribers. **14.** He here guards against their thinking from what he has just said, that he makes light of their bounty. **ye did communicate with my affliction**—i.e., ye made yourselves *sharers with* me in my present affliction, viz., by sympathy; of which sympathy your *contribution* is the proof. **15. Now**—"Moreover." Arrange as *Greek,* "Ye also know" (as well as I do myself). **in the beginning of the gospel**—dating from the *Philippian* Christian era; at the first preaching of the Gospel at Philippi. **when I departed from Macedonia**—(Acts 17:14). The Philippians had followed Paul with their bounty when he left Macedonia and came to Corinth. II Corinthians 11:8, 9 thus accords with the passage here, the dates assigned to the donation in both Epistles agreeing; viz., "in the *beginning* of the Gospel" here, and there, at the time of his *first* visit to Corinth [PALEY's *Horæ Paulinæ*]. However, the supply meant here is not that which he received at Corinth, but the supply sent to him when "in Thessalonica, once and again" (vs. 16), [ALFORD]. **as concerning giving and receiving**—In the account between us, "the giving" was all on your part; "the receiving" all on mine. **ye only**—We are not to wait for others in a good work, saying, "I will do so, when others do it." We must go forward, though *alone.* **16. even in Thessalonica**—"even" as early as when I had got no further than Thessalonica, ye sent me supplies for my necessities more than once. **17. a gift**—*Greek,* "*the* gift." Translate, "It is not that *I seek after the* gift, but *I do seek after the* fruit that *aboundeth* to your account"; what I do seek is your spiritual good, in the abounding of fruits of your faith which shall be put down to your account, against the day of reward (Heb. 6:10). **18. But**—Though "the gift" is not what I chiefly "seek after" (vs. 17), *yet* I am grateful for the gift, and hereby acknowledge it as ample for all my needs. Translate, "I have all" that I want, "and more than enough." Lit., as *English Version,* "I abound" over and above my needs. **I am full**—*Greek,* "I am filled full." **the odour of a sweet smell**—(*Note,* Eph. 5:2.) The figure is drawn from the sweet-smelling incense which was burnt along with the sacrifices; their gift being in faith was not so much to Paul, as *to God* (Matt. 25:40), before whom it "came up for a memorial" (Acts 10:4), sweet-smelling in God's presence (Gen. 8:21; Rev. 8:3, 4). **sacrifice acceptable**—(Heb. 13:16). **19. my**—Paul calls God

ADAM CLARKE

From my preaching, and that of those who labored with me; and heard from me in my private communications with you; and heard of me from other churches. *And seen in me.* While living and laboring among you. *Do.* Take them for the rule of your faith and practice. *And the God of peace.* He who is the Author of peace, the Lover of peace, and the Maintainer of peace; He who has made peace between heaven and earth, by the mission and sacrifice of His Son, shall be ever with you while you believe and act as here recommended.

10. *But I rejoiced in the Lord.* Every good comes from God, either immediately from His providence or from His grace; therefore the apostle thanks God for the kindness of the Philippians towards him; for it was God who gave them the power, and directed their hearts to use it. *Hath flourished again.* They had helped him before, chap. ii. 25; they had ceased for a time, and now they began again. This is evidently designed by the apostle, as the word implies, which is a metaphor taken from the reviviscence of flowers in spring which seemed dead in winter. For the time in which they were apparently remiss he makes a delicate apology: *Ye were . . . careful, but ye lacked opportunity;* or rather, "You had not ability; you wanted the means."

11. *Not that I speak in respect of want.* I am quite unconcerned in this respect, leaving the whole of my support, while bound for the testimony of Jesus, to the providence of God. *For I have learned.* How true is the proverb, "A contented mind is a continual feast"! What do we get by murmuring and complaining?

12. *I know . . . how to be abased.* I have passed through all these states; I know how to conduct myself in each, and how to extract good from all. And he had passed through these things, especially the hardships, so that he had learned the lesson "perfectly," as the word implies; he was thoroughly instructed, fully initiated into all the mysteries of poverty and want, and of the supporting hand of God in the whole.

13. *I can do all things.* It was not a habit which he had acquired by frequent exercise; it was a disposition which he had by grace; and he was enabled to do all by the power of an indwelling Christ. "Through Him who strengtheneth me" is the reading of some of the best MSS., versions, and fathers, the word *Christ* being omitted.

14. *Ye have well done.* Though I have learned all these important lessons, and am never miserable in want, yet you have done well in sending me relief in the time of affliction.

15. *In the beginning of the gospel.* When, having preached to you, I went forth into Macedonia, I received help from none of the churches which I had founded but from you alone.

16. *For even in Thessalonica.* While laboring to plant the church there, he was supported partly by working with his hands, 1 Thess. ii. 9; 2 Thess. iii. 7-9, and partly by the contributions sent him from Philippi.

17. *Not because I desire a gift.* I do not speak thus to incite you to send me a further gift; I speak this on the general subject because I wish you to bear such fruit as shall abound to your account in the day of the Lord.

18. *I have all.* You have now sent me so much by Epaphroditus that I abound in all the necessaries of life. *Having received . . . the things.* Probably a supply of clothes and such like necessaries, as well as of money. *An odour of a sweet smell.* Alluding to the sacrifices offered up under the law. With what you have done to me, His servant, God is well pleased.

MATTHEW HENRY

He would recompense it: *But my God shall supply all your wants according to his riches in glory by Christ Jesus, v.* 19. He does as it were draw a bill upon the exchequer in heaven, and leaves it to God. "You have supplied my needs, according to your poverty; and he shall supply yours, according to his riches." But still it is by Christ Jesus. Not of debt, but of grace.

Verses 20–23

1. Praises to God: *Now unto God and our Father be glory for ever and ever, Amen, v.* 20. God is to be considered by us as our Father. It is a title peculiar to the gospel dispensation. We should look upon God, under all our weaknesses and fears, not as a tyrant, but as a Father, who is disposed to pity us and help us. We must thankfully own the receipt of all from him, and give the praise of all to him. And our praise must be constant and perpetual; it must be *glory for ever and ever.*

2. Salutations to his friends at Philippi: *Salute every saint in Christ Jesus* (*v.* 21). Paul had a kind affection to all good Christians.

3. Salutations from those who were at Rome: "*The brethren who are with me salute you;* all the saints here. *Chiefly those who are of Cæsar's household;* the Christian converts who belonged to the emperor's court." There were saints in Cæsar's household. The gospel early obtained among some of the rich and great.

4. The apostolical benediction, as usual: "*The grace of our Lord Jesus Christ be with you all, Amen.*"

JAMIESON, FAUSSET, BROWN

here "my God," to imply that God would reward their bounty to HIS servant, by "fully supplying" (translate so, lit., *fill to the full*) their every "need" (II Cor. 9:8), even as they had "fully" supplied his "need" (vss. 16, 18). My Master will fully repay you; I cannot. The Philippians invested their bounty well since it got them such a glorious return. **according to his riches**—The measure of His supply to you will be the immeasurable "riches of His grace" (Eph. 1:7). **in glory**—These words belong to the whole sentence. "Glory" is the element IN which His rich grace operates; and it will be the element IN which He will "supply fully all your need." **by Christ Jesus**—by virtue of your being "IN" (so *Greek*, not "by") Christ Jesus, the Giver and Mediator of all spiritual blessings. **20. God and our Father**—Translate, "Unto *our God and Father.*" **be glory**—rather as the *Greek*, "be *the* glory." Not to us, but to Him be "*the* glory" alike of your gift, and of His gracious recompense to you. **21. Salute every saint**—*individually.* **greet**—salute you. **The brethren which are with me**—Perhaps Jewish believers are meant (Acts 28: 21). I think ch. 2:20 precludes our thinking of "closer friends," "colleagues in the ministry" [ALFORD]; he had only one close friend with him, viz., Timothy. **22. they that are of Cæsar's household**—the slaves and dependents of Nero who had been probably converted through Paul's teaching while he was a prisoner in the Prætorian barrack attached to the palace. Philippi was a Roman "colony," hence there might arise a tie between the citizens of the mother city and those of the colony; especially between those of both cities who were Christians, converted as many of them were by the same apostle, and under like circumstances, he having been imprisoned at Philippi, as he now is at Rome. **23.** (Gal. 6:18.) **be with you all. Amen**—The oldest MSS. read, "Be with your spirit," and omit "Amen."

ADAM CLARKE

19. *My God shall supply all your need.* As you have given to me in my distress, God will never suffer you to want without raising up help to you, as He raised you up for help to me.

21. *Salute every saint.* Remember to present my affectionate wishes to every Christian at Philippi. *The brethren which are with me.* Those who were fellow laborers with him, generally supposed to be Aristarchus, Mark, Justus, Epaphras, Luke, and Demas.

22. *All the saints.* All the Christians now at Rome. *They that are of Caesar's household.* Nero was at this time emperor of Rome. A more worthless, cruel, and diabolic wretch never disgraced the name or form of man; yet in "his family" there were Christians. But whether this relates to the members of the imperial family, or to guards, or courtiers, or to servants, we cannot tell. If even some of his slaves were converted to Christianity, it would be sufficiently marvellous.

23. *The grace of our Lord.* The word *our* is omitted by many MSS. and several versions, which simply read, "The grace of the Lord Jesus Christ."

THE EPISTLE TO THE COLOSSIANS

I. Introduction (1:1-8)
- *A. The salutation (1:1, 2)*
- *B. Thanksgiving (1:3-8)*
  1. Faith (1:3, 4)
  2. Hope (1:5, 6)
  3. Love (1:7, 8)

II. The glorious Christ and His Church provision (1:9-2:5)
- *A. Introductory (1:9-14)*
  1. The need indicated (1:9-12a)
  2. The provision (1:12b-14)
- *B. The glorious Christ (1:15-23)*
  1. The person (1:15-19)
  2. The purpose (1:20-23)
- *C. The glorious Church (1:24-2:3)*
  1. The mystery of the Church (1:24-26)
  2. The mystery of the Christian (1:27-29)
  3. The mystery of the Christ (2:1-3)
- *D. Conclusion—the reason for the statement (2:4, 5)*

III. The Church and her glorious Christ possession (2:6-4:6)
- *A. Introductory (2:6-10)*
  1. The central injunction (2:6, 7)
  2. The central warning (2:8)
  3. The central truth (2:9, 10)
- *B. The Church identified with Christ (2:11-3:4)*
  1. The argument (2:11-15)
  2. Interpolated application to Colossian perils (2:16-19)
  3. The appeal (2:20-3:4)
- *C. Christ identified with the Church (3:5-4:1)*
  1. The general responsibility (3:5-17)
  2. The particular applications (3:18-4:1)
- *D. Conclusion—conditions (4:2-6)*

IV. Conclusion (4:7-18)
- *A. Recommendation (4:7-9)*
- *B. Messages (4:10-14)*
- *C. Instructions (4:15-17)*
- *D. The last words (4:18)*

Colosse was a considerable city of Phrygia, and probably not far from Laodicea and Hierapolis; we find these mentioned together (4:13). It is now buried in ruins, and the memory of it chiefly preserved in this epistle. The design of the epistle is to warn them of the danger of the Jewish zealots. He professes a great satisfaction in their steadfastness and constancy. It was written while he was now a prisoner at Rome. He was not idle in his confinement, and the Word of God was not bound.

The epistle, like that to the Romans, was written to those he had never seen. The church planted at Colosse was not by Paul's ministry, but by the ministry of Epaphras, whom he delegated to preach the gospel among the Gentiles; and yet, there was a flourishing church in Colosse, and one which was eminent and famous among the churches. God is sometimes pleased to make use of the ministry of those who are of less note, and lower gifts, for doing great service to his church. God uses what hands he pleases, and is not tied to those of note. Though Paul had not the planting of this church, yet he did not therefore neglect it. The Colossians were as dear to him as the Philippians, or any others who were converted by his ministry.

MATTHEW HENRY

CHAPTER 1

Verses 1, 2

I. He calls himself an *apostle of Jesus Christ by the will of God.* He thought himself engaged to do his utmost, as an apostle, because he was made so by the will of God. He joins Timothy in commission with himself, and, though he elsewhere calls him his son, yet here he calls him his brother. He calls the Christians at Colosse *saints, and faithful brethren in Christ.* All good Christians are brethren one to another. Towards God they must be saints. And in both these, as saints to God and as brethren to one another, they must be faithful. Faithfulness runs through every character and relation of the Christian life, and is the crown and glory of them all.

II. *Grace be unto you, and peace, from God our Father, and the Lord Jesus Christ.* He wishes them *grace and peace,* the free favour of God and all the blessed fruits of it.

Verses 3–8

I. He gave thanks to God for them. In his prayers for them he gave thanks for them. Thanksgiving ought to be a part of every prayer. 1. Whom he gives thanks to: *To God, even the Father of our Lord Jesus Christ.* In our thanksgiving we must have an eye to God as God, and as the Father of our Lord Jesus Christ, in and through whom all good comes to us. 2. What he gives thanks to God for—for the graces of God in them. *Since we heard of your faith in Christ Jesus, and of the love you have to all the saints; for the hope which is laid up for you in heaven, v.* 4, 5. Faith, hope, and love, are the three principal graces in the Christian life. (1) He gives thanks for their faith in Christ Jesus, that they were brought to believe in him. (2) For their love. Besides the general love which is due to all men, there is a particular love owing to the saints. We must love all the saints, notwithstanding smaller points of difference, and many real weaknesses. (3) For their hope: *The hope which is laid up for you in heaven, v.* 5. What is laid out upon believers in this world is much; but what is laid up for them in heaven is much more. The more we fix our hopes on the recompence of reward in the other world, the more free shall we be of our earthly treasure upon all occasions of doing good.

JAMIESON, FAUSSET, BROWN

CHAPTER 1

Vss. 1-29. ADDRESS: INTRODUCTION: CONFIRMING EPAPHRAS' TEACHING: THE GLORIES OF CHRIST: THANKSGIVING AND PRAYER FOR THE COLOSSIANS: HIS OWN MINISTRY OF THE MYSTERY. **1. by the will of God**—*Greek,* "through . . ." (cf. *Note,* I Cor. 1:1). **Timothy**—(Cf. *Notes,* II Cor. 1:1; Phil. 1:1.) He was with Paul at the time of writing in Rome. He had been companion of Paul in his first tour through Phrygia, in which Colosse was. Hence the Colossians seem to have associated him with Paul in their affections, and the apostle joins him with himself in the address. Neither, probably, had *seen* the Colossian *Church* (cf. ch. 2:1); but had seen, during their tour through Phrygia, individual Colossians, as Epaphras, Philemon, Archippus, and Apphia (Philemon 2), who when converted brought the Gospel to their native city. **2. Colosse**—written in the oldest MSS., "Colasse." As "saints" implies union with God, so "the faithful brethren" union with Christian men [BENGEL]. **and the Lord Jesus Christ**—supported by some oldest MSS., omitted by others of equal antiquity. **3.** Thanksgiving for the "faith, hope, and love" of the Colossians. So in the twin Epistle sent at the same time and by the same bearer, Tychicus (Eph. 1:15, 16). **We**—I and Timothy. **and the Father**—So some of the oldest MSS. read. But others better omit the "and," which probably crept in from Ephesians 1:3. **praying always for you**—with thanksgiving (Phil. 4:6). See next verse. **4. Since we heard**—lit., "Having heard." The language implies that he had only heard of, and not *seen,* them (ch. 2:1). Cf. Romans 1:8, where like language is used of a Church which he had not at the time visited. **love . . . to all**—the absent, as well as those present [BENGEL]. **5. For**—to be joined with the words immediately preceding: "The love which ye have to all the saints *because* of (lit., *on account* of) the hope . . . ." The hope of eternal life will never be in us an inactive principle but will always produce "love." This passage is abused by Romanists, as if the hope of salvation depended upon works. A false argument. It does not follow that our hope is founded on our works because we are strongly stimulated to live well; since nothing is more effectual for this

ADAM CLARKE

CHAPTER 1

1. *Paul, an apostle of Jesus Christ by the will of God.* The word *apostle* signifies "one sent," an envoy or messenger. *And Timotheus.* Though Timothy is here joined in the salutation, yet he has never been understood as having any part in composing this Epistle. He has been considered as the amanuensis or scribe of the apostle.

4. *Since we heard of your faith.* This is very similar to Eph. i. 15. And it is certain that the apostle seems to have considered the church at Ephesus and that at Colossae to have been in nearly the same state, as the two Epistles are very similar in their doctrine and phraseology.

5. *For the hope which is laid up for you in heaven.* That eternal life, of both body and soul, which the apostle mentions, Titus i. 2: "In hope of eternal life, which God, that cannot lie, promised before the world began." The *hope* is here used for the object of hope; as every person that is born of God hopes for the resurrection of his body, and the glorification of both it and his soul in the realms of eternal blessed-

MATTHEW HENRY

II. He blesses God for the means of grace which they enjoyed: *Wherein you heard before in the word of the truth of the gospel.* The gospel is the word of truth, and what we may safely venture our immortal souls upon. He calls it *the grace of God in truth, v.* 6. It is a great mercy to hear this word of truth.

"*Which has come unto you, as it hath to all the world, and bringeth forth fruit, as it doth also in you,*" *v.* 6. All who hear the word of the gospel ought to bring forth the fruit of the gospel. Wherever the gospel comes, it will bring forth fruit to the honour and glory of God. We mistake, if we think to monopolise the comforts and benefits of the gospel to ourselves.

III. The minister by whom they believed (*v.* 7, 8): *As you also learned of Epaphras, our dear fellow-servant, who is for you a faithful minister of Christ.* He calls him his fellow-servant. They were fellow-labourers in the work of the Lord. He calls him his dear fellow-servant: it is an endearing consideration that they are engaged in the same service. He represents him as one who was a faithful minister of Christ to them. He does not say who is your minister; but *who is the minister of Christ for you.* It is by his authority and appointment.

He represents him as one who gave them a good word: *Who also declared unto us your love in the Spirit, v.* 8. He recommends him to their affection, from the good report he made of their sincere love, which was wrought in them by the Spirit. Faithful ministers are glad to be able to speak well of their people.

Verses 9–11

He heard that they were good, and he prayed that they might be better. *We do not cease to pray for you.* It may be he could hear of them but seldom, but he constantly prayed for them.

I. *Filled with the knowledge of his will, in all wisdom and spiritual understanding.* A mere empty notion of the greatest truths is insignificant. Our knowledge of the will of God must be always practical: we must know it, in order to do it. Our knowledge is then a blessing indeed when it is in wisdom, when we know how to apply our general knowledge to our particular occasions. Christians should endeavour to be filled with knowledge; not only to know the will of God, but to know more of it, and to *increase in the knowledge of God* (as it is *v.* 10).

JAMIESON, FAUSSET, BROWN

purpose than the sense of God's free grace [CALVIN]. **laid up**—a treasure *laid up* so as to be out of danger of being lost (II Tim. 4:8). *Faith, love,* and *hope* (vss. 4, 5), comprise the sum of Christianity. Cf. vs. 23, "the hope of the Gospel." **in heaven**—*Greek,* "in the heavens." **whereof ye heard before**—viz., at the time when it was preached to you. **in the word . . .**—That "hope" formed part of "the word of the truth of the Gospel" (cf. Eph. 1:13), i.e., part of the Gospel truth preached unto you. **6. Which is come unto you**—*Greek,* "Which is present among you," i.e., which has come to, and remains with, you. He speaks of the word as a living person *present* among them. **as it is in all the world**—*virtually,* as it was by this time preached in the leading parts of the then known world; *potentially,* as Christ's command was that the Gospel should be preached to all nations, and not be limited, as the law was, to the Jews (Matt. 13:38; 24:14; 28:19). However, the true reading, and that of the oldest MSS., is that which omits the following "and," thus (the "*it is*" of *English Version* is not in the original *Greek*): "As in all the world it is bringing forth fruit *and growing* (so the oldest MSS. read; *English Version* omits 'and growing,' without good authority), even as it doth in you also." Then what is asserted is not that the Gospel has been preached in all the world, but that it is *bearing fruits* of righteousness, and (like a tree *growing* at the same time that it is *bearing fruit*) *growing in numbers* of its converts in, or throughout, all the world. **heard of it**—rather, "heard *it.*" **and knew**—rather, "came to know"; became *fully* experimentally *acquainted* with. **the grace of God in truth**—i.e., in its truth, and with true knowledge [ALFORD]. **7. As ye also learned**—"Also" is omitted in the oldest MSS. The insertion implied that those inserting it thought that *Paul* had preached the Gospel to the Colossians as well as Epaphras, Whereas the omission in the oldest MSS. implies that *Epaphras alone* was the founder of the Church at Colosse. **of**—"*from* Epaphras." **dear**—*Greek,* "beloved." **fellow servant**—viz., of Christ. In Philemon 23 he calls him "my fellow prisoner." It is possible that Epaphras may have been apprehended for his zealous labors in Asia Minor; but more probable that Paul gave him the title, as his faithful companion in his imprisonment (cf. *Note,* ch. 4:10, as to MEYER's conjecture). **who is for you . . .**—Translate, "who is faithful in your behalf as a minister of Christ"; hinting that he is one not to be set aside for the new and erroneous teachers (ch. 2). Most of the oldest MSS. read, "for (or *in behalf of*) US." *Vulgate,* however, with one of the oldest MSS., supports *English Version.* **8. your love**—(vs. 4)—"to all the saints." **in the Spirit**—the sphere or element IN which alone true love is found; as distinguished from the state of those "in the flesh" (Rom. 8:9). Yet even they needed to be stirred up to greater love (ch. 3:12-14). Love IS the first and chief fruit of the Spirit (Gal. 5:22). **9. we also**—on our part. **heard it**—(vs. 4). **pray**—Here he states what in *particular* he prays for; as in vs. 3 he stated *generally* the fact of his praying for them. **to desire**—"to make request." **might be filled**—rather, "*may* be filled"; a verb often found in this Epistle (ch. 4:12, 17). **knowledge**—*Greek,* "*full and accurate* knowledge." Akin to the *Greek* for "knew" (*Note,* vs. 6). **of his will**—as to how ye ought to walk (Eph. 5:17); as well as chiefly that "mystery of His will, according to His good pleasure which He purposed in Himself; that in the fulness of times He might gather together in one all things in Christ" (Eph. 1:9, 10); God's "will," whereby He eternally purposed to reconcile to Himself, and save men by Christ, not by angels, as the false teachers in some degree taught (ch. 2:18) [ESTIUS]. There seems to have been a want of *knowledge* among the Colossians; notwithstanding their general excellencies; hence he so often dwells on this subject (vs. 28; ch. 2:2, 3; 3:10, 13; 4:5, 6). On the contrary he less extols wisdom to the Corinthians, who were puffed up with the conceit of knowledge. **wisdom**—often mentioned in this Epistle, as opposed to the (false) "philosophy" and "show of wisdom" (ch. 2:8, 23; cf. Eph. 1:8). **understanding**—sagacity to discern what on each occasion is suited to the place and the time; its seat is "the understanding" or intellect; *wisdom* is more general and has its seat in the whole compass of the faculties of the soul [BENGEL]. "Wouldst thou know that the matters in the word of Christ are real things? Then never read them for mere knowledge sake." [Quoted by GAUSSEN.] Knowledge is desirable only when seasoned by "spiritual understanding." **10.** *Greek,* "So as to walk"; so that ye may walk. True knowledge of God's will is inseparable from walking conformably to it.

ADAM CLARKE

ness. *In the word of the truth of the gospel.* In the "doctrine" of that gospel of your salvation which is the *truth* of God. Of this hope, by this doctrine, they had *heard before,* probably by persons who had heard and received the gospel either at Ephesus or some other place, in either Asia Minor or Greece, where the apostles had preached.

6. *And bringeth forth fruit.* Wherever the pure gospel of Christ is preached it is the *seed of the kingdom,* and must be fruitful in all those who receive it by faith, in simplicity of heart. After *bringeth forth fruit,* many MSS., together with many of the fathers, add "and increaseth." It had not only brought forth fruit, but was multiplying its own kind. This reading is very important, and is undoubtedly genuine.

7. *As ye also learned of Epaphras . . . who is for you.* That he was a Colossian is evident from chap. iv. 12: "Epaphras, who is one of you," and some think that he was the first who preached the gospel among this people, and hence called an apostle.

8. *Your love in the Spirit.* The heavenly flame in the heart of this minister communicated itself to those who heard him; it was "like priest, like people." They enjoyed a spiritual, energetic ministry, and they were a spiritual people; they had a loving spirit, and love through the Spirit of God, who dwelt in them.

CHARLES H. SPURGEON:

For the church that was at Colosse, Paul gave hearty thanks to God for many most important blessings, especially for their faith, their love, and their hope. It would be a very useful exercise to our hearts if we would often give thanks to God for the gifts and graces which we discover in our Christian brethren. I am afraid we are more inclined to spy out their faults, and to suppose that we deplore them, than we are to discern the work of the Holy Spirit in them, and from the bottom of our hearts to give thanks to God for them. Paul felt encouraged by what he saw in the Colossian believers to pray to God to enrich them yet further. It should be our desire that our best brethren should be better, and that those who are most like Jesus should be still more completely conformed to His image. We cannot more wisely show our love to our friends than by first acknowledging the grace which is in them, and then by praying that God may give them more. Paul, as with an eagle eye, surveyed the church at Colosse and noted that it was somewhat lacking in knowledge. The Colossians had fewer gifted brethren among them who could act as teachers, and, though this was no fault of theirs, it impoverished them in the matter of knowledge, and as Paul would not have them come behind in any desirable attainment, he therefore prayed for them that they might be filled with knowledge in all wisdom and spirtual undertanding.

—*The Treasury of the New Testament*

MATTHEW HENRY

II. **Good knowledge without a good life will not profit.** *That you may walk worthy of the Lord unto all pleasing* (*v.* 10). The agreeableness of our conversation to our religion is pleasing to God as well as to good men. *Being fruitful in every good work.* Good words will not do without good works. We must abound in good works, and in every good work. There must be a regular uniform regard to all the will of God. And the more fruitful we are in good works the more we shall *increase in the knowledge of God.*

III. *Strengthened with all might, according to his glorious power* (*v.* 11). Where there is spiritual life there is still need of spiritual strength. To be strengthened is to be furnished by the grace of God for every good work, and fortified by that grace against every evil one. In the praying for spiritual strength we are not straitened in the promises, and therefore should not be straitened in our own hopes and desires. He prayed that they might be strengthened with might: that they might be mightily strengthened. It is with all might. With all that might which we have occasion for, to enable us to discharge our duty or preserve our innocence, that grace which is sufficient for us in all the trials of life. It is *according to his glorious power.* The grace of God in the hearts of believers is the power of God; and there is a glory in this power. The communications of strength are not according to our weakness, but according to his power. *That you may be strengthened unto all patience and long-suffering with joyfulness.* He prays not only that they may be *supported* under their troubles, but *strengthened* for them. Strengthened *according to his glorious power.* 1. To all patience. Then we are strengthened to all patience—when we not only bear our troubles patiently, but receive them as gifts from God, and are thankful for them. 2. This is even unto long-suffering, not only to bear trouble awhile, but to bear it as long as God pleases to continue it. 3. It is with joyfulness, to rejoice in tribulation, to rejoice that we are counted worthy to suffer for his name, to have joy as well as patience in the troubles of life. This we could never do by any strength of our own, but as we are strengthened by the grace of God.

Verses 12–29

Here is a summary of the doctrine of the gospel concerning the great work of our redemption by Christ. It comes in here as the matter of a thanksgiving: *Giving thanks unto the Father, v.* 12.

I. The operations of the Spirit of grace. We must give thanks for them: *Giving thanks to the Father,* &c., *v.* 12, 13. Those in whom the work of grace is wrought must give thanks unto the Father. 1. "He hath *delivered us from the power of darkness, v.* 13. He hath saved us from the dominion of sin, which is darkness." 2. "He hath *translated us into the kingdom of his dear Son,* made us members of the church of Christ, which is a state of light and purity." The conversion of a sinner is the translation of a soul into the kingdom of Christ out of the kingdom of the devil. It is the kingdom of his dear Son. 3. "He hath *made us meet to partake of the inheritance of the saints in light, v.* 12." God gives *grace and glory.* (1) What that glory is. It is the *inheritance of the saints in light.* It is an inheritance, and belongs to them as children. And it is an inheritance of the saints. Those who are not saints on earth will never be saints in heaven. And it is an inheritance in light; by communion with God, who is light. (2) What this grace is. It is a meetness for the inheritance: "*He hath made us meet to be partakers.*" All who are designed for heaven hereafter are prepared for heaven now. Those who are sanctified and renewed go out of the world with their heaven about them. Those who have the inheritance of sons have the education of sons. This meetness for heaven is the earnest of the Spirit in our heart, which is part of payment, and assures the full payment.

II. The Redeemer. Glorious things are here said of him; for blessed Paul was full of Christ. He speaks of him distinctly as God, and as Mediator. 1. As God he speaks of him, *v.* 15–17. (1) He is the *image of the invisible God.* He is so the image of God as the son is the image of his father, who has a natural likeness to him.

JAMIESON, FAUSSET, BROWN

worthy of the Lord—(Eph. 4:1). **unto**—so as in every way to be well-pleasing to God. **pleasing**—lit., "*desire of pleasing.*" **being fruitful**—*Greek,* "bearing fruit." This is the first manifestation of their "walking worthy of the Lord." The second is, "increasing (growing) in the knowledge of God" (or as the oldest MSS. read, "growing BY the full knowledge of God"); thus, as the *Gospel word* (vs. 6) was said to "bring forth fruit," and to "grow" in all the world, even as it did in the Colossians, ever since the day they *knew* the grace of God, so here it is Paul's prayer that *they* might continue to "bring forth fruit," and "grow" more and more *by the full knowledge* of God, the more that "knowledge" (vs. 9) was imparted to them. The full knowledge of God is the real *instrument* of enlargement in soul and life of the believer [ALFORD]. The third manifestation of their walk is (vs. 11), "Being strengthened with all might . . . ." The fourth is (vs. 12), "Giving thanks unto the Father . . . ." **11.** *Greek,* "Being made mighty with (lit., *in*) all might." **according to his glorious power**—rather, "according to the power (the characteristic of 'His glory,' here appropriate to Paul's argument, Eph. 1:19; 6:10; as its exuberant 'riches,' in Eph. 3:16) of His glory." His power is inseparable from His glory (Rom. 6: 4). **unto all patience**—so as to attain to all *patient endurance;* persevering, enduring continuance in the faith, in spite of trials of persecutors, and seductions of false teachers. **long-suffering**—towards those whom one could repel. "Patience," or "endurance," is exercised in respect to those whom one cannot repel [CHRYSOSTOM]. **with joyfulness**—joyful endurance (Acts 16:25; Rom. 5:3, 11). **12.** *You* "giving thanks unto the Father." See *Note,* vs. 10; this clause is connected with "that *ye* may be filled' (vs. 9), and "that *ye* may walk" (vs. 10). The connection is not, "*We* do not cease to pray for you (vs. 9) giving thanks." **unto the Father**—of Jesus Christ, and so *our* Father by adoption (Gal. 3:26; 4:4, 5, 6). **which hath made us meet**—*Greek,* "who *made* us meet." Not "*is making* us meet" by progressive growth in holiness; but *once for all made* us meet. It is not *primarily* the *Spirit's* work that is meant here, as the text is often used; but the *Father's* work in putting us by adoption, once for all, in a new standing, viz., *that of children.* **to be partakers . . .**—*Greek,* "for the (or *our*) portion of the inheritance (Acts 20:32; 26:18; Eph. 1:11) of the saints in light." "Light" begins in the believer here, descending from "the Father of lights" by Jesus, "the true light," and is perfected in the kingdom of light, which includes knowledge, purity, love, and joy. It is contrasted here with the "darkness" of the unconverted state (vs. 13; cf. I Pet. 2:9). **13. from**—*Greek,* "*out of* the power," out of the sphere in which his power is exercised. **darkness**—blindness, hatred, misery [BENGEL]. **translated**—Those thus translated as to state, are also transformed as to character. Satan has an organized dominion with various orders of powers of evil (Eph. 2:2; 6:12). But the term "kingdom" is rarely applied to his usurped rule (Matt. 12:26); it is generally restricted to the kingdom of God. **his dear Son**—rather as *Greek,* "the Son of His love": the Son on whom His love rests (John 17:26; Eph. 1:6): contrasted with the "darkness" where all is hatred and hateful. **14.** (Eph. 1:7.) **redemption**—rather as *Greek, "our* redemption." **through his blood**—omitted in the oldest MSS.; probably inserted from Ephesians 1:7. **sins**—Translate as *Greek, "our* sins." The more general term: for which Ephesians 1:7, *Greek,* has, "our *transgressions,*" the more special term. **15.** They who have experienced in themselves "redemption" (vs. 14), know Christ in the glorious character here described, as above the highest angels to whom the false teachers (ch. 2:18) taught worship was to be paid. Paul describes Him: (1) in relation to God and creation (vss. 15-17); (2) in relation to the Church (vss. 18-20). As the former regards Him as the Creator (vss. 15, 16) and the Sustainer (vs. 17) of the natural world; so the latter, as the source and stay of the new moral creation. **image**—exact likeness and perfect Representative. Adam was made "in the image of God" (Gen. 1:27). But Christ, the second Adam, perfectly reflected visibly "the invisible God" (I Tim. 1:17), whose glories the first Adam only in part represented. "Image" (*eicon*) involves "likeness" (*homoiosis*); but "likeness" does not involve "image." "Image" always supposes a prototype, which it not merely resembles, but from which it is drawn: the exact counterpart, as the reflection of the sun in the water: the child the living image of the parent. "Likeness" implies mere *resemblance,* not the exact *counterpart* and *derivation* as "image" expresses; hence it is nowhere applied to

ADAM CLARKE

ALEXANDER MACLAREN:

The form of the word "strengthened" here would be more fully represented by "being strengthened," and suggests an unintermitted process of bestowal and reception of God's might rendered necessary by our continuous human weakness and by the tear and wear of life. As in the physical life there must be constant renewal because there is constant waste, and as every bodily action involves destruction of tissue so that living is a continual dying, so is it in the mental and still more in the spiritual life. Just as there must be a perpetual oxygenation of blood in the lungs, so there must be an uninterrupted renewal of spiritual strength for the highest life. It is demanded by the conditions of our human weakness. It is no less rendered necessary by the nature of the divine strength imparted, which is ever communicating itself, and like the ocean cannot but pour so much of its fullness as can be received into every creek and crack on its shore.

The Apostle not merely emphasizes the continuousness of this communicated strength, but its many-sided variety, by designating it "all power." In this whole context that word "all" seems to have a charm for him. Here the comprehensive completeness of the strength available for our many-sided weakness is marvelously revealed. There is "infinite riches in a narrow room." All power means every kind of power, be it bodily or mental, for all variety of circumstances.

—*Expositions of Holy Scripture*

---

12. *Giving thanks unto the Father.* Knowing that you have nothing but what you have received from His mere mercy, and that in point of merit you can never claim anything from Him. *Which hath made us meet.* Who has "qualified" us to be partakers. *Of the inheritance.* A plain allusion to the division of the Promised Land by lot among the different families of the twelve Israelitish tribes. *Of the saints in light. Light,* in the sacred writings, is used to express knowledge, felicity, purity, comfort, and joy of the most substantial kind; here it is put to point out the state of glory at the right hand of God.

13. *Delivered us from the power of darkness. Darkness* is here personified and is represented as having *power,* "authority, and sway," all Jews and Gentiles who had not embraced the gospel being under this authority and power. *Translated us into the kingdom.* He has thoroughly changed our state, brought us out of the dark region of vice and impiety, and placed us in the Kingdom under the government of *his dear Son,* "the Son of His love"; the Person whom, in His infinite love, He has given to make an atonement for the sin of the world.

14. *In whom we have redemption.* Who has paid down the redemption price, even His own blood, that our sins might be cancelled, and we made fit to be partakers of the inheritance among the saints in light. The clause *through his blood* is omitted by most MSS. and versions of weight and importance, and by most of the Greek fathers. It is likely that the reading here is not genuine. The same phrase is used Eph. i. 7, where there is no various reading in any of the MSS., versions, or fathers. *The forgiveness of sins.* "The taking away of sins"; all the power, guilt, and infection of sin.

15. *Who is the image of the invisible God.* The Counterpart of God Almighty; and if *the image of the invisible God,* consequently nothing that appeared in Him could be that image.

MATTHEW HENRY

(2) He is the *first-born of every creature. Born* or *begotten before all the creation,* which is the scripture-way of representing eternity. It signifies his dominion over all things, as the first-born in a family is heir and lord of all.

(3) He is so far from being himself a creature that he is the Creator: *For by him were all things created, which are in heaven and earth, visible and invisible, v.* 16.

He speaks here as if there were several orders of angels: *Whether thrones, or dominions, or principalities, or powers.*

All things are created by him and for him. He is the end, as well as the cause of all things.

(4) He *was before all things.* He had a being before the world was made, and therefore from all eternity. He not only had a being before he was born of the virgin, but he had a being before all time. (5) *By him all things consist.* The whole creation is kept together by the power of the Son of God, and made to consist in its proper frame.

2. What he is as Mediator, *v.* 18, 19. (1) He is the *head of the body the church*: not only a head of government and direction, but a head of vital influence, as the head in the natural body: for all grace and strength are derived from him.

JAMIESON, FAUSSET, BROWN

the Son, while "image" is here, cf. I Corinthians 11: 7 [TRENCH]. (John 1:18; 14:9; II Cor. 4:4; I Tim. 3:16; Heb. 1:3.) Even before His incarnation He was the image of the invisible God, as the Word (John 1:1-3) by whom God created the worlds, and by whom God appeared to the patriarchs. Thus His *essential* character as *always* "the image of God," (1) before the incarnation, (2) in the days of His flesh, and (3) now in His glorified state, is, I think, contemplated here by the verb "is." **first-born of every creature**—Hebrews 1:6, "the first-begotten": "begotten of His Father before all worlds" [NICENE *Creed*]. Priority and superlative dignity is implied (Ps. 89:27). *English Version* might seem to favor Arianism, as if Christ were a creature. Translate, "Begotten (lit., born) *before* every creature," as the context shows, which gives the reason why He is so designated. "For . . ." (vss. 16, 17) [TRENCH]. This expression is understood by ORIGEN (so far is the *Greek* from favoring Socinian or Arian views) as declaring *the Godhead* of Christ, and is used by Him as a phrase to mark that *Godhead,* in contrast with His *manhood* (B. 2., sec. *contra Celsus*). The *Greek* does not strictly admit ALFORD'S translation, "the first-born of all creation." **16. For**—*Greek,* "Because." This gives the proof that He is not included in the things created, but is the "first-begotten" before "every creature" (vs. 15), begotten as "the Son of God's love" (vs. 13), antecedently to all other emanations: "for" all these other emanations came from Him, and whatever was created, *was created by Him.* **by him**—rather as *Greek, "in* Him": as the conditional element, pre-existent and all-including: the creation of all things BY *Him* is expressed afterwards, and is a different fact from the present one, though implied in it [ALFORD]. God revealed Himself in the Son, the Word of the Father, *before all created existence* (vs. 15). **all things**—*Greek, "the* universe of things." That the *new creation* is not meant in this verse (as Socinians interpret), is plain; for *angels,* who are included in the catalogue, were not *new created* by Christ; and he does not speak of the new creation till vs. 18. The creation "of the things that are in the *heavens*" (so *Greek*) includes the creation of the *heavens themselves:* the former are rather named, since the inhabitants are more noble than their dwellings. Heaven and earth and all that is in them (I Chron. 29:11; Neh. 9:6; Rev. 10:6). **invisible**—the world of spirits. **thrones, or dominions** —*lordships:* the thrones are the greater of the two. **principalities, or powers**—rather, *"rules,* or *authorities":* the former are stronger than the latter (cf. *Note,* Eph. 1:21). The latter pair refer to offices *in respect to God's creatures:* "thrones and dominions" express exalted *relation to God,* they being the *chariots* on which He rides displaying His glory (Ps. 68:17). The existence of various orders of **angels** is established by **this passage. all things**—*Greek,* "the whole universe of things." **were**—rather, to distinguish the *Greek* aorist, which precedes from the perfect tense here, *"have been* created." In the former case the creation was viewed as *a past act at a point of time,* or as done once for all; here it is viewed, not merely as one historic act of creation in the past, but as the *permanent result now and eternally continuing.* **by him**—as the instrumental Agent (John 1:3). **for him** —as the grand *End* of creation; containing in Himself the reason why creation is at all, and why it is as it is [ALFORD]. He is the *final* cause as well as the *efficient* cause.

17. (John 8:58.) Translate as *Greek,* "And *He Himself* (the great HE) is (implying *divine essential being*) before all things," in *time,* as well as in dignity. Since He is before all things, He is *before even time,* i.e., *from eternity.* Cf. "the first-born of every creature" (vs. 15). **by him**—*Greek,* "IN Him" (as the conditional element of existence, vs. 16) [ALFORD]. **consist**—"subsist." Not only are called into being from nothing, but *are maintained in their present state.* The Son of God is the *Conserver,* as well as the *Creator* of all things [PEARSON]. BENGEL less probably explains, "All things in Him come together into one *system:* the universe found its completion in Him" (Isa. 41:4; Rev. 22:13). Cf. as to GOD, Romans 11:36: similar language; therefore *Christ* must be God. **18.** Revelation of Christ to the Church and the new creation, as the Originator of both. **he**—emphatical. Not angels in opposition to the false teachers' doctrine concerning angel-worship, and the power of Œons or (imaginary) spirit-emanations from God (ch. 2:10, 18). **head of the body, the church**—The Church is His body by virtue of His entering into communion corporeally with human nature

ADAM CLARKE

The first-born of every creature. I suppose this phrase to mean the same as that in Phil. ii. 9: "God . . . hath . . . given him a name which is above every name." He is a Man at the head of all the creation of God; nor can He with any propriety be considered as a creature, having himself created all things, and existed before anything was made. If it be said that God created Him first, and that He by a delegated power from God created all things, this is most flatly contradicted by the apostle's reasoning in the sixteenth and seventeenth verses. As the Jews term Jehovah "the firstborn of all the world" or "of all the creation," to signify His having created or produced all things, so Christ is here termed, and the words which follow in the sixteenth and seventeenth verses are the proof of this. The phraseology is Jewish; and as they apply it to the Supreme Being merely to denote His eternal preexistence, and to point Him out as the Cause of all things, it is most evident that Paul uses it in the same way, and illustrates his meaning in the following words, which would be absolutely absurd if we could suppose that by the former he intended to convey any idea of the inferiority of Jesus Christ.

16-17. *For by him were all things created.* Four things are here asserted: (1) That Jesus Christ is the Creator of the universe, of all things visible and invisible.

(2) That whatsoever was created was created for himself.

(3) That He was prior to all creation, to all beings, whether in the visible or invisible world. (4) That He is the Preserver and Governor of all things; for *by him all things consist.*

18. *He is the head of the body.* What the apostle has said in the preceding two verses refers to the divine nature of Jesus Christ. He now proceeds to speak of His human nature, and to show how highly that is exalted beyond all created things, and how, in that, He is Head of *the church*—the Author and Dispenser of

MATTHEW HENRY

(2) He is the *beginning, the first-born from the dead*, the principle of our resurrection. The first and only one who rose by his own power, and has given us evidence of our resurrection from the dead.

(3) He hath in *all things the pre-eminence*, preferred above angels and all the powers in heaven. Among men he should have the pre-eminence.

(4) All fulness dwells in him, and it pleased the Father it should do so (*v.* 19), not only a fulness of abundance for himself, but abundance for us.

III. The work of redemption.

1. Wherein it consists. (1) In the remission of sin: *In whom we have redemption, even the forgiveness of sins, v.* 14. If we are redeemed, we must be redeemed from sin; and this is by forgiveness. (2) In reconciliation to God. God by him *reconciled all things to himself, v.* 20. He is the Mediator of reconciliation, who procures peace as well as pardon for sinners, and will bring all holy creatures into one blessed society at last: *things in earth, or things in heaven.*

JAMIESON, FAUSSET, BROWN

[NEANDER], (Eph. 1:22). The same One who is the Head of all things and beings by creation, is also, by virtue of being "the first-born from the dead," and so "the first-fruits" of the new creation among men, the Head of the Church. **who is**—i.e., in that He is the Beginning [ALFORD]. **the beginning**—viz., of the new creation, as of the old (Prov. 8:22; John 1:1; cf. Rev. 1:8): the beginning of the Church of the first-born (Heb. 12: 23), as being Himself the "first-born from the dead" (Acts 26:23; I Cor. 15:20,23). Christ's primogeniture is threefold: (1) From eternity the "first-begotten" of the Father (vs. 15); (2) As the first-born of His mother (Matt. 1:25); (3) As the Head of the Church, mystically begotten of the Father, as it were to a new life, on the day of His resurrection, which is His "regeneration," even as His people's coming resurrection will be their "regeneration" (i.e., the resurrection which was begun in the soul, extended to the body and to the whole creation, Romans 8:21, 22) (Matt. 19:28; Acts 13:33; Rev. 1: 5). Sonship and resurrection are similarly connected (Luke 20:36; Rom. 1:4; 8:23; I John 3:2). Christ by rising from the dead is the efficient cause (I Cor. 15:22), as having obtained the power, and the exemplary cause, as being the pattern (Mic. 2: 13; Rom. 6:5; Phil. 3:21), of our resurrection: the resurrection of "the Head" involves consequentially that of the members. **that in all things**—He resumes the "all things" (vs. 20). **he might have the pre-eminence**—*Greek*, "He HIMSELF *may* (thus) become the One holding the first place," or, "take the precedency." Both ideas are included, priority in *time* and priority in *dignity:* now in the regenerated world, as before in the world of creation (vs. 15). "Begotten before every creature, or "first-born of every creature" (Ps. 89:27; John 3:13). **19.** *Greek*, "(God) was *well pleased* . . . ." **in him**—i.e., in the Son (Matt. 3:17). **all fulness**—rather as *Greek*, "all *the* fulness," viz., *of God*, whatever divine excellence is in God the Father (ch. 2:9; Eph. 3:19; cf. John 1:16; 3:34). The Gnostics used the term "fulness," for the assemblage of emanations, or angelic powers, coming from God. The Spirit presciently by Paul warns the Church, that the true "fulness" dwells in Christ alone. This assigns the reason why Christ takes precedence of every creature (vs. 15). For two reasons Christ is Lord of the Church: (1) Because the fulness of the divine attributes (vs. 19) dwells in Him, and so He has the *power* to govern the universe; (2) Because (vs. 20) what He has done for the Church gives Him the *right* to preside over it. **should . . . dwell**—as in a temple (John 2:21). *This indwelling of the Godhead in Christ* is the foundation of *the reconciliation* by Him [BENGEL]. Hence the "and" (vs. 20) connects as cause and effect the two things, *the Godhead in Christ*, and *the reconciliation by Christ.* **20.** The Greek order is, "And through Him (Christ) to reconcile again completely (see *Note*, Eph. 2:16) all things (*Greek*, 'the whole universe of things') unto Himself (unto God the Father, II Cor. 5:19), having made peace (God the Father having made peace) through the blood of His (Christ's) cross," i.e., shed by Christ *on* the cross: the price and pledge of our reconciliation with God. The Scripture phrase, "God reconciles man to Himself," implies that He takes away by the blood of Jesus the barrier which God's justice interposes against man's being in union with God (cf. *Note*, Rom. 5:10; II Cor. 5:18). So the LXX, I Samuel 29:4, "Wherewith should he reconcile himself unto his master," i.e., *reconcile his master* unto him by appeasing his wrath. So Matthew 5:23, 24. **by him**—"through Him" (the instrumental agent in the new creation, as in the original creation): emphatically repeated, to bring the person of Christ, as the Head of both creations alike, into prominence. **things in earth . . . in heaven**—Good angels, in one sense, do not need reconciliation to God; fallen angels are excluded from it (Jude 6). But probably redemption has effects on the world of spirits unknown to us. Of course, His reconciling *us*, and His reconciling *them*, must be by a different process, as He took not on Him the nature of angels, so as to offer a *propitiation* for them. But the effect of redemption on them, as He is *their* Head as well as *ours*, is that they are thereby *brought nearer God*, and so gain an increase of blessedness [ALFORD], and *larger views of the love and wisdom of God* (Eph. 3:10). All creation subsists in Christ, all creation is therefore affected by His propitiation: sinful creation is strictly "reconciled" from its enmity; sinless creation, comparatively distant from His unapproachable purity (Job 4:18; 15:15; 25:5), is lifted into nearer participation of Him, and in this wider sense is reconciled.

ADAM CLARKE

light, life, and salvation, to the Christian world; or in other words, that from Him, as the Man in whom the fulness of the Godhead bodily dwelt, all the mercy and salvation of the gospel system is to be received. *The beginning, the firstborn from the dead.* In 1 Cor. xv. 20, Christ is called "the firstfruits of them that slept"; and here, the chief and *firstborn from the dead;* He being the first that ever resumed the natural life, with the employment of all its functions, nevermore to enter the empire of death, after having died a natural death, and in such circumstances as precluded the possibility of deception. The *arche,* "chief, head, or first," answers in this verse to the *aparche,* or "firstfruits," 1 Cor. xv. 20. Jesus Christ is not only the first who rose from the dead to die no more, but He is the firstfruits of human beings, for as surely as the firstfruits were an indication and pledge of the harvest, so surely was the resurrection of Christ the proof that all mankind should have a resurrection from the dead.

That in all things he might have the preeminence. That He might be considered, in consequence of His mediatorial office, as possessing the first place in and being chief over all the creation of God. For is it to be wondered at that the human nature, with which the great Creator condescended to unite himself, should be set over all the works of His hands?

19. *For it pleased the Father that in him should all fulness dwell.* As the words *the Father* are not in the original text, some have translated the verse thus: "For in him it seemed right that all fulness should dwell"; that is, that the majesty, power, and goodness of God should be manifested in and by Christ Jesus, and thus by Him the Father reconciles all things to himself. The *fulness* must refer here to the divine nature dwelling in the Man Christ Jesus.

20. *And, having made peace through the blood of his cross.* Peace between God and man. *To reconcile all things unto himself.* The enmity was on the part of the creature; though God is angry with the wicked every day, yet He is never unwilling to be reconciled. But man, whose carnal mind is enmity to God, is naturally averse from this reconciliation; it requires, therefore, the *blood of his cross* to atone for the sin, and the influence of the Spirit to reconcile the transgressor to Him against whom he has offended!

Things in earth, or things in heaven. If the phrase be not a kind of collective phrase to signify "all the world" or "all mankind," the *things in heaven* may refer, according to some, to those persons who died under the Old Testament dispensation, and who could not have a title to glory but through the sacrificial death of Christ.

MATTHEW HENRY

The Gentiles, who were alienated, and *enemies in their minds by wicked works, yet now hath he reconciled, v.* 21. This *enmity is slain*, and we are now reconciled. The greatest enemies to God may be reconciled, if it be not their own fault.

2. How the redemption is procured: *it is through his blood* (*v.* 14); he has *made peace through the blood of his cross* (*v.* 20), and it is *in the body of his flesh through death, v.* 22. There was such a value in the blood of Christ that, on account of Christ's shedding it, God was willing to deal with men upon new terms, to pardon and accept to favour all who comply with them.

The duty of those who are interested in this redemption: *If you continue in the faith, grounded and settled, and be not moved away from the hope of the gospel which you have heard, v.* 23. We can expect the happy end of our faith only when we continue in the faith, and are so far grounded and settled in it as not to be moved from it.

IV. The preaching of this redemption.

1. To whom it was preached: *To every creature under heaven* (*v.* 23). The gospel excludes none who do not exclude themselves.

2. By whom it was preached: *Whereof I Paul am made a minister*. He looks upon it as the highest of his titles of honour to be a minister of the gospel of Jesus Christ.

JAMIESON, FAUSSET, BROWN

21. The Colossians are included in this general reconciliation (cf. Eph. 2:1, 12). **sometime**—"once." **alienated**—from God and salvation: objectively *banished from* God, through the barrier which God's justice interposed against your sin: subjectively *estranged* through the alienation of your own wills from God. The former is the prominent thought (cf. Rom. 5:10), as the second follows, "enemies in your mind." "Actual *alienation* makes habitual 'enemies'" [BENGEL]. **in your mind**—*Greek,* "in your understanding" or "thought" (Eph. 2:3; 4:18). **by wicked works**—rather as *Greek, "in your* wicked works" (wicked works were the element *in* which your *enmity* subsisted). **yet now**—*Notwithstanding* the former alienation, *now* that Christ has come, *God* hath *completely reconciled,* or restored to His friendship *again* (so the *Greek,* cf. *Note,* vs. 20). **22. In the body of his flesh**—the element in which His reconciling sufferings had place. Cf. vs. 24, "afflictions of Christ *in my flesh*" (I Pet. 2:24). Angels who have not a "body of flesh" are not in any way our reconciling mediators, as your false teachers assert, but He, the Lord of angels, who has taken our *flesh,* that *in* it He might atone for our fallen manhood. **through death**—rather as *Greek,* "through *His* death" (which could only take place in a body like ours, of flesh, Heb. 2:14). This implies He took on Him our true and entire manhood. *Flesh* is the sphere in which His human sufferings could have place (cf. vs. 24; Eph. 2:15). **to present you**—(Eph. 5:27). The end of His reconciling atonement by death. **holy**—positively; and in relation to God. **unblamable . . . unreprovable**—negatively. "Without blemish" (as the *former Greek* word is translated as to Jesus, our Head, I Pet. 1:19) *in one's self. Irreproachable* (the *Greek* for the *second* word, *one who gives no occasion for his being brought to a law court*) *is in relation to the world without. Sanctification,* as the fruit, is here treated of; *justification,* by Christ's reconciliation, as the tree, having preceded (Eph. 1:4; 5:26, 27; Titus 2:14). At the same time, our sanctification is regarded here as *perfect* in Christ, into whom we are grafted at regeneration or conversion, and who is "made of God unto us (perfect) sanctification" (I Cor. 1:30; I Pet. 1:2; Jude 1): not merely *progressive* sanctification, which is the *gradual development* of the sanctification which Christ is made to the believer from the first. **in his sight**—in God's sight, at Christ's appearing. **23. If**—"Assuming that . . .": not otherwise shall ye be so presented at His appearing (vs. 22). **grounded**—*Greek,* "founded," "fixed on the *foundation*" (cf. *Note,* Eph. 3:17; Luke 6:48, 49). **settled**—"steadfast." "Grounded" respects the *foundation* on which believers rest; "settled," *their own steadfastness* (I Pet. 5:10). I Corinthians 15:58 has the same *Greek.* **not moved away**—by the false teachers. **the hope of the gospel**—(Eph. 1:18). **which ye have heard . . . which was preached to every creature . . . whereof I . . . am . . . a minister**—Three arguments against their being "moved away from the Gospel": (1) Their having heard it; (2) The universality of the preaching of it; (3) Paul's ministry in it. For "to (*Greek,* 'in') every creature," the oldest MSS. read, "in *all creation.*" Cf. "in all the world," vs. 6; "all things . . . in earth," vs. 20 (Mark 16:15): thus he implies that the Gospel from which he urges them *not to be moved,* has this mark of truth, viz., the universality of its announcement, which accords with the command and prophecy of Christ Himself (Matt. 24:14). By "*was* preached," he means not merely "*is being preached,*" but *has been actually, as an accomplished fact, preached.* PLINY, not many years subsequently, in his famous letter to the Emperor Trajon (B. X., Ep. 97), writes, "Many of every age, rank, and sex, are being brought to trial. For the contagion of that superstition [Christianity] has spread over not only cities, but villages and the country." **whereof I Paul am**—rather as *Greek,* "*was made* a minister." Respect for me, the minister of this world-wide Gospel, should lead you not to be moved from it. Moreover (he implies), the Gospel which ye heard from Epapharas, your "minister" (vs. 7), is the same of which "I was made a minister" (vs. 25; Eph. 3:7): if you be moved from it, ye will desert the teaching of the recognized ministers of the Gospel for unauthorized false teachers. **24. Who**—The oldest MSS. omit "who"; then translate, "Now I rejoice." Some very old MSS., and the best of the Latin versions, and *Vulgate,* read as *English Version.* To enhance the glory of Christ as paramount to all, he mentions his own sufferings for the Church of Christ. "Now" stands in contrast to "I *was made,*" in the past time (vs. 23). **for you**—"on your be-

ADAM CLARKE

21. *And you, that were sometime alienated.* All men are *alienated* from God, and all are *enemies in* their *mind* to Him, and show it by their *wicked works;* but this is spoken particularly of the Gentiles. The word which we render to alienate, "to give to another, to estrange," expresses the state of the Gentiles. While the Jews were, at least by profession, dedicated to God, the Gentiles were *alienated,* that is, "given up to others"; they worshipped not the true God, but had gods many and lords many, to whom they dedicated themselves, their religious service, and their property. *Enemies in your mind.* They had the carnal mind, which is enmity against God; and this was expressed in their outward conduct by *wicked works.* The *mind* is taken here for all the soul, heart, affections, passions.

22. *In the body of his flesh.* By Christ's assumption of a human body, and dying for man, He has made an atonement for sin, through which men become reconciled to God and to each other. *To present you holy.* Having saved you from your sins. *Unblameable.* Having filled you with His Spirit, and written His law in your hearts, so that His love, shed abroad in your hearts, becomes the principle and motive to every action. *And unreproveable.* For, being filled with love, joy, peace, meekness, gentleness, and goodness, against these there is no law. *In his sight.* At the day of judgment. None can enjoy heaven who have not been reconciled to God here, and shown forth the fruits of that reconciliation in being made *holy and unblameable,* that, when they come to be judged, they may be found *unreproveable.*

23. *If ye continue in the faith.* This will be the case if you, who have already believed in Christ Jesus, continue in that faith, *grounded* in the knowledge and love of God, and *settled,* made firm and perseveringly steadfast, in that state of salvation. *And be not moved away.* Not permitting yourselves to be seduced by false teachers. *The hope of the gospel.* The resurrection of the body, and the glorification of it and the soul together, in the realms of blessedness. This is properly the gospel hope. *To every creature which is under heaven.* A Hebraism for the whole human race.

ALBERT BARNES:

23. "If ye continue in the faith." In the belief of the gospel and in holy living. If this were done, they would be presented unblamable before God; if not, they would not be. The meaning is that it will be impossible to be saved unless we continue to lead lives becoming the gospel. "Grounded." On a firm foundation (Eph. 3:17). "And settled." Firm—as a building that is founded on a rock (Matt. 7:25). "And be not moved away from the hope of the gospel." By the arts of philosophy and the allurements of sin.—*Popular Commentary*

MATTHEW HENRY

(3) What kind of preacher Paul was.

[1] He was a suffering preacher: *Who now rejoice in my sufferings for you, v.* 24. He suffered for preaching the gospel to them. And, while he suffered in so good a cause, he could rejoice in his sufferings. *And fill up that which is behind of the afflictions of Christ in my flesh.* The suffering of Paul and other good ministers made them conformable to Christ. They are said to fill up what was behind of the sufferings of Christ, as the wax fills up the vacuities of the seal, when it receives the impression of it. Or it may be meant of his suffering for Christ. He *filled that which was behind.* He was still filling up more and more what was behind, or remained of them to his share.

(1) Whence Paul had his ministry: it was *according to the dispensation of God which was given to him* (*v.* 25). He received it from God as a gift, and took it as a favour.

(2) For whose sake he had his ministry: *It is for you.* We are Christ's ministers for the good of his people, to *fulfil the word of God* (that is, fully to preach it).

3. The gospel which was preached. *Even the mystery which hath been hid from ages, and from generations, but is now made manifest to his saints, v.* 26, 27. The mystery of the gospel was long hidden.

This mystery now is made manifest to the saints. And what is this mystery? It is the riches of God's glory among the Gentiles. This mystery, thus made known, *is Christ in you, the hope of glory.* Christ is the hope of glory. The ground of our hope is Christ in the world. The evidence of our hope is Christ in the heart.

[2] He was a close preacher. *Whom we preach, warning every man, and teaching every man in all wisdom, v.* 28. When we warn people of what they do amiss, we must teach them to do better: warning and teaching must go together. Men must be warned and taught in all wisdom. We must choose the fittest seasons, and accommodate ourselves to the different capacities of those we have to do with.

JAMIESON, FAUSSET, BROWN

half," that ye may be confirmed in resting solely on Christ (to the exclusion of angel-worship) by the glorification of Christ in my sufferings (Eph. 3:1). **fill up that which is behind**—lit., "the deficiencies"—all that are lacking of the afflictions of Christ (cf. *Note,* II Cor. 1:5). Christ is "afflicted in all His people's afflictions" (Isa. 63:9). "The Church is His body in which He is, dwells, lives, and therefore also suffers" [VITRINGA]. Christ was destined to endure certain afflictions in this figurative body, as well as in His literal; these were "that which is behind of the afflictions of *Christ,*" which Paul "filled up." His own meritorious sufferings in expiation for sin were once for all completely filled up on the Cross. But His Church (His second Self) has her whole measure of afflictions fixed. The more Paul, a member, endured, the less remain for the rest of the Church to endure; the communion of saints thus giving them an interest in his sufferings. It is in reference to the Church's afflictions, which are "Christ's afflictions, that Paul here saith, "I fill up the deficiencies," or "what remain behind of the afflictions of Christ." She is afflicted to promote her growth in holiness, and her completeness in Christ. Not one suffering is lost (Ps. 56:8). All her members have thus a mutual interest in one another's sufferings (I Cor. 12:26). But Rome's inference hence, is utterly false that the Church has a stock treasury of the merits and satisfactions of Christ and His apostles, out of which she may dispense indulgences; the context has no reference to sufferings in *expiation of sin* and productive of *merit.* Believers should regard their sufferings less in relation to themselves as individuals, and more as parts of a grand whole, carrying out God's perfect plan. **25. am**—*Greek,* "*I was* made a minister": resuming vs. 23, "whereof I Paul was made a minister." **dispensation**—the *stewardship* committed to me to dispense in the house of God, the Church, to the whole family of believers, the goods of my Master (Luke 12:42; I Cor. 4:1, 2; 9:17; Eph. 3:2). **which is given**—*Greek,* "which *was* given." **for you**—with a view to you, Gentiles (vs. 27; Rom. 15:16). **to fulfil**—to bring it fully to all: the end of his stewardship: "fully preached" (Rom. 15:19). "The *fulness* of Christ (vs. 19), and of the times (Eph. 1:10) required him so to do" [BENGEL]. **26. the mystery**—(*Notes,* Eph. 1:9, 10; 3:5-9). The *mystery,* once hidden, now revealed, is redemption for the whole Gentile world, as well as for the Jews, "Christ in *you* (Gentiles) the hope of glory" (vs. 27). **from ages**—"from," according to ALFORD, refers to time, not "hidden from": from the time of the ages; still what is meant is that the mystery was hidden from *the beings living in those "ages."* The "ages" are the vast successive periods marked by successive orders of beings and stages of creation. *Greek,* "Æons," a word used by the Gnostics for angelic beings emanating from God. The Spirit by Paul presciently, in opposition to Gnostic error already beginning (ch. 2:18), teaches, that the mystery of redemption was hidden in God's purposes in Christ, alike from the *angelic beings* (cf. Eph. 3:10) of the pre-Adamic "ages," and from the subsequent *human* "generations." Translate as *Greek,* "*the* ages . . . *the* generations." **made manifest to his saints**—to His apostles and prophets primarily (Eph. 3:5), and through them to *all His saints.* **27. would**—rather as *Greek,* "*willed,*" or "*was pleased* to make known." He resolves all into God's *good pleasure* and *will,* that man should not glory save in God's grace. **what**—How full and inexhaustible! **the riches of the glory of this mystery**—He accumulates phrase on phrase to enhance the greatness of the blessing in Christ bestowed by God on the Gentiles. Cf. ch. 2:3, "all the *treasures*" of *wisdom;* Ephesians 3:8, "the unsearchable *riches* of *Christ*"; Ephesians 1:7, "*riches* of His *grace.*" "*The glory* of this mystery" must be the glory which this once hidden, and now revealed, truth makes you Gentiles partakers of, partly now, but mainly when Christ shall come (ch. 3:4; Rom. 5:2; 8:17, 18; Eph. 1:18). This sense is proved by the following: "Christ in you the hope of *the* (*so Greek*) *glory.*" The lower was the degradation of you Gentiles, the higher is the richness of the glory to which the mystery revealed now raises you. You were "without *Christ,* and having *no hope*" (Eph. 2:12). Now you have "*Christ* in you the *hope of the* glory" just mentioned. **28. preach**—rather as *Greek,* "announce" or "proclaim." **warning . . . teaching**—"Warning" is connected with *repentance,* refers to one's *conduct,* and is addressed primarily to the *heart.* "Teaching" is connected with *faith,* refers to *doctrines,* and is addressed primarily to the *intellect.* These are the two heads of evangelical teaching. **every . . . every man**—without distinc-

ADAM CLARKE

24. *Rejoice in my sufferings for you.* Paul always considers his persecutions, as far as the Jews were concerned in them, as arising from this simple circumstance—his asserting that God had chosen the Gentiles, and called them to enjoy the very same privileges with the Jews, and to constitute one Church with them. *That which is behind of the afflictions of Christ.* I have still some afflictions to pass through before my race of glory be finished, afflictions which fall on me on account of the gospel, such as Christ bore from the same persecuting people. It is worthy of remark that the apostle does not say the "passion" of Christ, but simply the "afflictions," such as are common to all good men who bear a testimony against the ways and fashions of a wicked world. In these the apostle had his share; in the passion of Christ he could have none. *His body's sake.* Believers, of both Jews and Gentiles, who form that one *body,* of which Christ is the Head.

25. *Whereof I am made a minister.* Having received especial commission from God to preach salvation to the Gentiles. *According to the dispensation.* According to the gospel "economy" of "institution," the scheme or plan of salvation by Christ crucified. *To fulfil the word of God.* The Greek may be translated, "fully to preach the doctrine of God."

26. *The mystery which hath been hid.* The mystery is this: that God had designed to grant the Gentiles the same privileges with the Jews, and make them His people who were not His people.

Made manifest to his saints. It is fully known to all who have embraced the doctrine of Christ crucified, to all Christians.

27. *The riches of the glory.* God manifests to these how abundantly glorious this gospel is among the Gentiles, and how effectual to the salvation of multitudes is this doctrine of Christ crucified.

MATTHEW HENRY

That which he aimed at was to *present every men perfect in Christ Jesus.* Ministers ought to aim at the improvement and salvation of every particular person who hears them.

He was a laborious preacher (*v.* 29): *Whereunto I also labour, striving according to his working, which worketh in me mightily.* As Paul laid out himself to do much good, so he had this favour, that the power of God wrought in him the more effectually.

JAMIESON, FAUSSET, BROWN

tion of Jew or Gentile, great or small (Rom. 10:12, 13). **in all wisdom**—with all the wisdom *in our method of teaching* that we possess: so ALFORD. But vs. 9, and ch. 3:16, favor ESTIUS' view, which refers it to the *wisdom communicated to those being taught:* keeping back nothing, but instructing all in the perfect knowledge of the mysteries of faith which is the true *wisdom* (cf. I Cor. 2:6, 7; 12:8; Eph. 1:17). **present**—(*Note,* vs. 22)—at Christ's coming. **every man**—Paul is zealous lest the false teachers should seduce *one single* soul of Christ's people at Colosse. So each individual among them should be zealous for himself and his neighbor. Even one soul is of incalculable value. **perfect in Christ**—who is the *element in living union with* whom alone each believer can find *perfection: perfectly instructed* (Eph. 4:13) in doctrine, and *full grown* or *matured* in faith and practice. "Jesus" is omitted in all the oldest MSS. **29. Whereunto**—viz., "to present every man perfect in Christ." **I also labour**—rather, "I labor also." I not only "proclaim" (*English Version,* "preach") Christ, but I *labor* also. **striving**—in "conflict" (ch. 2:1) of spirit (cf. Rom. 8:26). The same *Greek* word is used of Epaphras (ch. 4:12), "*laboring fervently* for you in prayers": lit., "agonizing," "striving as in the agony of a contest." So Jesus in Gethsemane when praying (Luke 22:44): so "strive" (the same *Greek* word, "agonize"), Luke 13:24. So Jacob "*wrestled*" in prayer (Gen. 32:24-29). Cf. "contention," *Greek,* "agony," or "striving earnestness," I Thessalonians 2:2. **according to his working**—Paul avows that he has power to "strive" in spirit for his converts, so far only as *Christ* works in him and by him (Eph. 3:20; Phil. 4:13). **mightily**—lit., "in power."

ADAM CLARKE

29. *Whereunto I also labour.* In order to accomplish this end, I labor with the utmost zeal and earnestness, and with all that strength with which God has most powerfully furnished me. Whoever considers the original words will find that no verbal translation can convey their sense. God worked "energetically" in Paul, and he "wrought energetically" with God; and all this was in reference to the salvation of mankind.

MATTHEW HENRY

CHAPTER 2

Verses 1–3

The apostle had never been at Colosse, and yet he had as tender a care of it as if it had been the only people of his charge (*v.* 1): *For I would that you knew what great conflict I have for you, and for those at Laodicea, and for as many as have not seen my face in the flesh.* Paul's care of the church was such as amounted to a conflict. He was in a sort of agony. We may keep up a communion by faith, hope, and holy love, even with those of whom we have no personal knowledge. Those we never saw in the flesh we may hope to meet in heaven.

I. What was it that the apostle desired for them? *That their hearts may be comforted, being knit together in love,* &c., *v.* 2. It was their spiritual welfare about which he was solicitous, that their *hearts may be comforted.* The prosperity of the soul is the best prosperity. A description of soul-prosperity.

1. When our knowledge grows to an understanding of the mystery of God, and of the Father, and of Christ. *To understand the mystery.* Not barely to speak of it by rote, but to enter into the meaning and design of it.

2. When our faith grows to a full assurance and bold acknowledgment of this mystery. To a full assurance, or a well-settled judgment. To a free acknowledgment, and we not only believe with the heart, but are ready to make confession with our mouth. This is called the *riches of the full assurance of understanding.* Great knowledge and strong faith make a soul rich.

3. *That their hearts might be comforted.* The soul prospers when it is filled with joy and peace.

4. *Being knit together in love.* The stronger our faith is, and the warmer our love, the greater will our comfort be.

JAMIESON, FAUSSET, BROWN

CHAPTER 2

VSS. 1-23. HIS STRIVINGS IN PRAYER FOR THEIR STEADFASTNESS IN CHRIST; FROM WHOM HE WARNS THEM NOT TO BE LED AWAY BY FALSE WISDOM. **1. For**—He explains in what respect he "labored *striving*" (ch. 1:29). Translate as *Greek,* "I *wish you to know how* great a conflict (the same *Greek* word as in ch. 1:29, "*agony* of a conflict" of fervent, anxious prayer; not conflict with the false teachers, which would have been impossible for him now in prison) I have for you." **them at Laodicea**—exposed to the same danger from false teachers as the Colossians (cf. ch. 4:16). This danger was probably the cause of his writing to Laodicea, as well as to Colosse. **not seen my face in the flesh**—including those in Hierapolis (ch. 4:13). Paul considered himself a "debtor" to all the Gentiles (Rom. 1:14). "His face" and presence would have been a "comfort" (vs. 2; Acts 20:38). Cf. ch. 1:4, 7, 8, in proof that he had not *seen,* but only *heard of* the Colossians. Hence he strives by earnest *conflict* with God in anxious prayer for them, to make up for the loss of his bodily presence among them. Though "absent in the *flesh,* I am with you in the *Spirit*" (vs. 5). **2.** Translate, "That their hearts *may* be comforted." Their hearts would be comforted by "knowing what conflict he had for" them, and how much he is interested for their welfare; and also by being released from doubts on learning from the apostle, that the doctrine which they had heard from Epaphras was true and certain. In writing to churches which he had instructed face to face, he enters into particular details concerning them, as a father directing his children. But to those among whom he had not been in person, he treats of the more general truths of salvation. **being**—Translate as *Greek* in oldest MSS., "They being knit together." **in love**—the bond and element of perfect *knitting together;* the antidote to the dividing schismatical effect of false doctrine. Love to God and to one another in Christ. **unto**—the object and end of their being "knit together." **all riches**—*Greek,* "all *the* riches of the full assurance (I Thess. 1:5; Heb. 6:11; 10:22) of *the* (Christian) understanding." The accumulation of phrases, not only "understanding," but "the full assurance of understanding"; not only this, but "the *riches* of . . ."; not only this, but "*all* the riches of . . ." implies how he desires to impress them with the momentous importance of the subject in hand. **to**—Translate "unto." **acknowledgment**—The *Greek* implies, "full and accurate knowledge." It is a distinct *Greek* word from "knowledge," vs. 3. ALFORD translates, "thorough . . . knowledge." *Acknowledgment* hardly is strong enough; they did in a measure *acknowledge* the truth; what they wanted was the *full and accurate knowledge* of it (cf. *Notes,* ch. 1:9, 10; Phil. 1:9). **of God, and of the Father and of**

ADAM CLARKE

CHAPTER 2

1. *What great conflict.* The word *agon,* which we here render *conflict,* is to be understood as implying earnest care and solicitude, accompanied, undoubtedly, with the most fervent application to the throne of grace in their behalf. The *agonizomenos* of the preceding verse gave the apostle occasion to use the word *agon* here. He "agonized" with God, and his "agony" was for them.

2. *That their hearts might be comforted.* That they might have continual happiness in God, having constant affiance in Him.

Being knit together in love. The word signifies being united, as the beams or the timbers of a building, by mortices and pins. The visible Church of Christ cannot be in union with God unless it have unity in itself, and without *love* this unity is impossible. *Unto all riches of the full assurance of understanding.* That is, that they might have the most indubitable certainty of the truth of Christianity, of their own salvation, and of the general design of God to admit the Gentiles into His Church. This is the grand mystery of God, which was now laid open by the preaching of the gospel.

MATTHEW HENRY

Having occasion to mention Christ (*v.* 2), he makes this remark to his honour (*v.* 3): *In whom are hidden all the treasures of wisdom and knowledge.* The treasures of wisdom are hidden not from us, but for us, in Christ. We must spend upon the stock which is laid up for us in him, and draw from the treasures which are hidden in him.

Verses 4-12

The apostle cautions the Colossians against deceivers (*v.* 4): *And this I say lest any man beguile you with enticing words;* and *v.* 8, *Lest any man spoil you.* Satan spoils souls by beguiling them. He deceives them, and by this means slays them. He could not ruin us if he did not cheat us; and he could not cheat us but by our own folly. Satan's agents beguile them with enticing words. How many are ruined by the flattery of those who lie in wait to deceive! "That which they aim at is to spoil you."

His concern for them is repeated (*v.* 5): *Though I am absent in the flesh, yet am I with you in the spirit, joying, and beholding your order, and the steadfastness of your faith in Christ.* We may be present in spirit with those from whom we are absent in body. Though he had never seen them he tells them he could easily think himself among them, and look with pleasure upon their good behaviour. The more steadfast our faith in Christ is, the better order there will be in our whole conversation.

I. A sovereign antidote against seducers (*v.* 6, 7): *As you have therefore received Christ Jesus the Lord, so walk you in him, rooted and built up,* &c. All Christians have, in profession at least, *received Jesus Christ the Lord,* consented to him, taken him for theirs in every relation and every capacity. The great concern of those who have received Christ is *to walk in him.* We must walk with him in our daily course and keep up our communion with him. The more closely we walk with Christ the more we are *rooted and established in the faith.* If we walk in him, we shall be rooted in him; and the more firmly we are rooted in him the more closely we shall walk in him: *Rooted and built up.—As you have been taught.* A good education has a good influence upon our establishment. We must be *established in the faith, as we have been taught, abounding therein.* And this with thanksgiving.

II. The fair warning given us of our danger: *Beware lest any man spoil you through philosophy and vain deceit, after the tradition of men, after the rudiments of the world, and not after Christ, v.* 8. There is a philosophy which is a noble exercise of our reasonable faculties. But there is a philosophy which is vain and deceitful.

JAMIESON, FAUSSET, BROWN

Christ—The oldest MSS. omit "and of the Father, and of"; then translate, "Of God (viz.), Christ." Two very old MSS. and *Vulgate* read, "Of God the Father of Christ." **3.** Translate in the *Greek* order, "In whom (not as ALFORD, 'in which' *mystery;* Christ is Himself the 'mystery' (vs. 2; I Tim. 3:16), and to Christ the relative refers) are all the treasures of wisdom and knowledge hidden." The "all" here, answers to "all" in vs. 2; as "treasures" answer to the "riches"; it is from the *treasures* that *the riches* (vs. 2) are derived. "Are" is the predicate of the sentence; all the treasures ARE in Him; *hidden* is predicated of the state or manner in which they are in Him. Like a mine of unknown and inexhaustible wealth, the *treasures* of wisdom are all in Him *hidden,* but not in order to remain so; they only need to be explored for you to attain "unto the riches" in them (vs. 2); but until you, Colossians, press after attaining *the full knowledge* (see *Note,* vs. 2) of them, they remain "hidden."

wisdom—general, and as to *experimental* and *practical* truth; whence comes "understanding" (vs. 2). **knowledge**—*special* and *intellectual,* in regard to *doctrinal* truth; whence comes "the full knowledge" (vs. 2). **4. And**—"Now." Cf. with "lest any man . . ." vss. 8, 16, 18. He refers to the blending of Judaism with Oriental philosophy, and the combination of this mixture with Christianity. **enticing words**—plausible as wearing the guise of *wisdom* and *humility* (vss. 18, 23). **5. For**—argument against their suffering themselves to be *beguiled,* drawn from a regard to his personal authority as though he were present. **joying and beholding**—beholding with joy. **order**—your *good order;* answering to "knit together" (vs. 2) as a well-organized body; the same *Greek* as that for "*knit together,*" is used of the body" of the Church "*compacted,*" in Ephesians 4:16. Cf. I Corinthians 14:33, 40. **steadfastness**—*Greek,* "*the firm* (or *solid*) *foundation.*" As "order" expresses the outward aspect of the Church; so "steadfastness" expresses the inner basis on which their Church rested. The *Greek* literally implies not an abstract quality, but the *thing* in the concrete; thus their "faith" here is *the solid thing* which constituted the *basis* of their Church. **6.** "As therefore ye received (once for all; the aorist tense; from Epaphras) Jesus *the* Christ *as your* Lord (cf. I Cor. 12:3; II Cor. 4:5; Phil. 3:8), so walk in Him." He says not merely, "Ye received" the doctrine of Christ, but "Jesus" Himself; this is the essence of faith (John 14:21, 23; Gal. 1:16). Ye have received once for all the Spirit of *life* in Christ; carry into practice that life in your *walk* (Gal. 5:25). This is the main scope of the Epistle. **7. Rooted**—(Eph. 3:17). **built up**—*Greek,* "*being* builded up." As "rooted" implies their *vitality;* so "builded up," massive *solidity.* As in the Song of Solomon, when one image is not sufficient to express the varied aspects of divine truth, another is employed to supply the idea required. Thus "walking," a third image (vs. 6), expresses the thought which "rooted" and "built," though each suggesting a thought peculiar to itself, could not express, viz., onward *motion.* "Rooted" is in the *past* tense, implying their first *conversion* and vital grafting "in Him." "Built up" is *present* (in the *Greek*), implying their progressive *increase* in religion by union with Him. Ephesians 2:20 refers to the *Church;* but the passage here to their *individual* progress in edification (Acts 20:32). **stablished**—confirmed. **as**—"even as." **abounding therein with thanksgiving**—advancing to fuller maturity (cf. vs. 2) in the faith, "with thanksgiving" to God as the gracious Author of this whole blessing. **8.** Translate, "Beware (lit., 'Look' well) lest there *shall be* (as I fear there is: the *Greek* indicative expresses this) any man (pointing to some known emissary of evil, Gal. 1:7) *leading you away as his spoil* (not merely gaining spoil out of you, but making *yourselves* his spoil) through (by means of) his philosophy," etc. The apostle does not condemn *all* philosophy, but "*the* philosophy" (so *Greek*) of the Judæic-oriental heretics at Colosse, which afterwards was developed into Gnosticism. You, who may have "the *riches* of *full* assurance" and "the *treasures* of wisdom," should not suffer yourselves to be led away as a *spoil* by *empty,* deceitful philosophy: "riches" are contrasted with spoil; "full" with "vain," or *empty* (vss. 2, 3, 9). **after**—"according to." **tradition of men**—opposed to, "the fulness of the Godhead." Applied to *Rabbinical traditions,* Mark 7:8. When men could not make revelation even *seem* to tell about deep mysteries which they were curious to pry into, they brought in human philosophy and pretended traditions to help it, as if one should bring a lamp to the sundial to find the hour [*Cautions for times,* p. 85]. The false teachers boasted of a higher wisdom in theory, trans-

ADAM CLARKE

And of the Father, and of Christ. These words are variously written in different MSS., versions, and fathers. This great variety of versions leaves the strongest presumption that the words in question are glosses which have crept into the text and are of no authority.

3. *In whom are hid.* Or rather "in which," referring to the "mystery" mentioned above. In this glorious scheme of Christianity *all the treasures*—the abundance and excellency—*of wisdom and knowledge* are contained.

4. *Lest any man should beguile you.* The word means to deceive by sophistry or subtle reasoning, in which all the conclusions appear to be fairly drawn from the premises, but the premises are either assumed without evidence or false in themselves; but this not being easily discovered, the unthinking or unwary are carried away by the conclusions which are drawn from these premises. And this result is clearly intimated by the term *enticing words,* "plausible conclusions or deductions" from this mode of reasoning. The apostle seems to allude to the Gentile philosophers, who were notorious for this kind of argumentation.

6. *As ye have therefore received Christ Jesus.* Many persons lay a certain stress on the words *as* and *so,* and make various fine heads of discourses from them; viz., *As* you received Christ in a spirit of humility, so walk in Him. This may be all proper in itself, but nothing of the kind was intended by the apostle. His meaning is simply this: Seeing you have embraced the doctrine of Christ, continue to hold it fast, and not permit yourselves to be turned aside by sophistical or Judaizing teachers.

7. *Rooted and built up in him.* It is not usual with the apostle to employ this double metaphor, taken partly from the growth of a tree and the increase of a building. They are to be *rooted;* as the good seed had been already sown, it is to take root, and the roots are to spread far, wide, and deep. They are to be "grounded"; as the foundation has already been laid, they are to build thereon. In the one case, they are to bear much fruit; in the other, they are to grow up to be "an habitation of God through the Spirit." See the notes on Eph. ii. 21-22 and iii. 17. *Abounding therein with thanksgiving.* No limitation is ever set to the operations of God on the soul or to the growth of the soul in the knowledge, love, and image of God. Those who are brought into such a state of salvation should abound in gratitude and loving obedience as they grow in grace.

8. *Beware lest any man spoil you.* The word signifies to "rob," or "spoil" of their goods, as if by violence or rapine. Their goods were the salvation they had received from Christ; and both the Gentile and Jewish teachers endeavored to deprive them of these, by perverting their minds and leading them off from the truths of Christianity. *Philosophy and vain deceit.* Or "the vain or empty deceit of philosophy"; such philosophizing as the Jewish and Gentile teachers used. As the term *philosophy* stood in high repute among the Gentiles, the Jews of this time affected it; and both Philo and Josephus use the word to express the whole of the Mosaic institutions.

MATTHEW HENRY

After the tradition of men, after the rudiments of the world. The Jews governed themselves by the traditions of their elders. The Gentiles mixed their maxims of philosophy with their Christian principles; and both alienated their minds from Christ. Those who pin their faith on other men's sleeves have turned away from following after Christ.

1. We have in Christ the substance of all the shadows of the ceremonial law. Had they then the Shechinah, or special presence of God? So have we now in Jesus Christ (*v.* 9): *For in him dwelleth all the fulness of the Godhead bodily.* It dwells in him bodily; not as the body is opposed to the spirit, but as the body is opposed to the shadow. The fulness of the Godhead dwells in Christ really, and not figuratively.

Again, The Jews thought themselves complete in the ceremonial law; but we are *complete in Christ, v.* 10. That was imperfect and defective. But all the defects of it are made up in the gospel of Christ. *Which is the head of all principality and power.* As the Old Testament priesthood had its perfection in Christ, so likewise had the kingdom of David. He is the Lord and head of all the powers in heaven and earth. Had they circumcision, which was the seal of the covenant? In Christ we are *circumcised with the circumcision made without hands* (*v.* 11). *It is made without hands;* not by the power of any creature, but by the power of the blessed Spirit of God.

2. We have communion with Christ in his whole undertaking (*v.* 12): *Buried with him in baptism, wherein also you have risen with him.* We are both buried and rise with him, and both are signified by our baptism.

JAMIESON, FAUSSET, BROWN

mitted by tradition among the initiated; in practice they enjoined asceticism, as though matter and the body were the sources of evil. Phrygia (in which was Colosse) had a propensity for the mystical and magical, which appeared in their worship of Cybele and subsequent Montanism [NEANDER]. **rudiments of the world**—(*Note,* Gal. 4:3). "The rudiments" or elementary lessons "of the (outward) world," such as legal ordinances; our Judaic childhood's lessons (vss. 11, 16, 20; Gal. 4:1-3). But NEANDER, "the *elements* of the world," in the sense, *what is earthly, carnal and outward,* not "the rudiments of religion," in Judaism and heathenism. **not after Christ**—Their boasted higher "philosophy" is but human tradition, and a cleaving to the carnal and worldly, and not to Christ. Though acknowledging Christ nominally, in spirit they by their doctrine deny Him. **9. For**—"Because." *Their* philosophy" (vs. 8) is not "after Christ," as all true philosophy is, everything which comes not from, and tends not to, Him, being a delusion; "For in Him (alone) dwelleth" *as in a temple. . . .* **the fulness**—(ch. 1:19; John 14:10). **of the Godhead**—The *Greek* (*theotes*) means the ESSENCE and NATURE *of the Godhead,* not merely the *divine perfections* and attributes of Divinity (*Greek,* "theiotes"). He, as man, was not merely God-like, but in the fullest sense, GOD. **bodily**—not merely as before His incarnation, but now "bodily in Him" as the incarnate word (John 1:14, 18). Believers, by union with Him, partake of His fulness of the divine nature (John 1: 16; *Note,* Eph. 3:19; II Pet. 1:4). **10. And**—And *therefore;* and so. Translate in the *Greek* order, "Ye are in Him (by virtue of union with Him) *filled full*" of all that you need (John 1:16). Believers receive of the divine unction which flows down from their Divine Head and High Priest (Ps. 133: 2). He is *full of* the "fulness" itself; we, *filled* from Him. Paul implies, Therefore ye Colossians need no supplementary sources of grace, such as the false teachers dream of. Christ is "the Head of all *rule* and *authority*" (so the *Greek*), Ephesians 1:10; He, therefore, alone, not these subject "authorities" also, is to be adored (vs. 18). **11.** Implying that they did not need, as the Judaizers taught, the outward rite of circumcision, since they had already the inward spiritual reality of it. **are**—rather, as the *Greek,* "Ye *were* (once for all) circumcised (spiritually, at your conversion and baptism, Rom. 2:28, 29; Phil. 3:3) with a (so the *Greek*) circumcision made without hands"; opposed to "the circumcision in the flesh *made by hands*" (Eph. 2:11). Christ's own body, by which the believer is sanctified, is said to be "not made with hands" (Mark 14:58; Heb. 9:11; cf. Dan. 2:45). **in putting off**—rather as *Greek,* "in your putting off"; as an old garment (Eph. 4:22); alluding to the putting off the foreskin in circumcision. **the body of the sins of the flesh**—The oldest MSS. read, "the body of the flesh," omitting "of the sins," i.e., "the body," of which the prominent feature is *fleshiness* (cf. Rom. 8:13, where "flesh" and "the body" mutually correspond). This fleshly body, in its sinful aspect, is put off in baptism (where baptism answers its ideal) as the seal of regeneration where received in repentance and faith. In circumcision the *foreskin* only was put off; in Christian regeneration "the *body* of the flesh" is spiritually put off, at least it is so in its ideal conception, however imperfectly believers *realize* that ideal. **by**—*Greek, "in."* This spiritual circumcision is realized in, or by, union with Christ, whose "circumcision," whereby He became responsible for us to keep the whole law, is imputed to believers for justification; and union with whom, in all His vicarious obedience, including HIS CIRCUMCISION, is the source of our sanctification. ALFORD makes it explanatory of the previous, "a circumcision made without hands," viz., "the circumcision brought about by your union with Christ." The former view seems to me better to accord with 12; ch. 3:1, 3, 4, which similarly makes the believer, by spiritual union with Christ, to have personal fellowship in the several states of Christ, viz., His death, resurrection, and appearing in glory.

12. Translate, "*Having been* buried with Him in *your* baptism." The past participle is here coincident in time with the preceding verb, "ye were (*Greek*) circumcised." Baptism is regarded as the burial of the old carnal life, to which the act of immersion symbolically corresponds; and in warm climates where *immersion* is safe, it is the mode most accordant with the significance of the ordinance; but the spirit of the ordinance is kept by affusion, where immersion would be inconvenient or dangerous; to insist on literal immersion in all cases would be mere legal ceremonialism (Rom. 6:3, 4). **are risen**—rather as *Greek,*

ADAM CLARKE

After the rudiments of the world. According to the doctrine of the Jewish teachers; or according to the Mosaic institutions, as explained and glossed by the scribes, Pharisees, and rabbins in general. *Not after Christ.* Not according to the simple doctrine of Christ, viz., He died for our offenses; believe on the Lord Jesus, and you shall be saved.

9. *For in him dwelleth all the fulness.* This is opposed to the vain or "empty" doctrine of the Gentile and Jewish philosophers: there is a *fulness* in Christ suited to the empty, destitute state of the human soul; but in the philosophy of the Jews and Gentiles nothing like this was found, nor indeed in the more refined and correct philosophy of the present day. No substitute has ever been found for the grace of the Lord Jesus. By the *Godhead* or "Deity" we are to understand the "state or being of the divine nature"; and by the *fulness* of that Deity, the infinite attributes essential to such a nature. *Bodily.* Signifies "truly, really"; in opposition to "typically, figuratively." There was a symbol of the Divine Presence in the Hebrew Tabernacle, and in the Jewish Temple. But in the body of Christ, the Deity, with all its plenitude of attributes, dwelt "really" and "substantially"; for so the word means.

10. *And ye are complete in him.* "And you are filled with Him." Our word *complete* quite destroys the connection subsisting in the apostle's ideas. The philosophy of the world was "empty," but there was a "fulness" in Christ. The Colossians were empty, spoiled and deprived of every good, while following the empty philosophy and groundless traditions of Jewish and Gentile teachers; but since they had received Christ Jesus they were "filled" with Him. This is the true meaning of the word, and by this the connection and assemblage of ideas in the apostle's mind are preserved. No fanciful "completeness in Christ" of a believer, while incomplete in himself, is either expressed or intended by Paul. It is too bad a doctrine to exist in the oracles of God.

11. *In whom also ye are circumcised.* All that was designed by circumcision, literally performed, is accomplished in them that believe through the Spirit and power of Christ. It is not a cutting off of a part of the flesh, but a *putting off the body of the sins of the flesh,* through the circumcision of Christ, He having undergone and performed this and all other rites necessary to qualify Him to be a Mediator between God and man. But by the circumcision of Christ, the operation of His grace and Spirit may be intended. The law required the circumcision of the flesh; the gospel of Christ required the circumcision of the heart. The words *of the sins* are omitted by several MSS.

12. *Buried with him in baptism.* Alluding to the immersions practiced in the case of adults, wherein the person appeared to be buried under the water, as Christ was buried in the heart of the earth. His rising again the third day, and their emerging from the water, was an emblem of the resurrection of the body; and, in them, of a total change of life.

MATTHEW HENRY

He is speaking of the *circumcision made without hands*; and says it is *through the faith of the operation of God*. God in baptism engages to be to us a God, and we become engaged to be his people, and by his grace to die to sin and to live to righteousness.

Verses 13–15

The privileges we Christians have above the Jews.

I. Christ's death is our life: *And you, being dead in your sins and the uncircumcision of your flesh, hath he quickened together with him, v.* 13. A state of sin is a state of spiritual death. Those who are in sin are dead in sin. As the death of the body is the corruption of it, so sin is the corruption of the soul. As a man who is dead is unable to help himself by any power of his own, so an habitual sinner is morally impotent. This is our state. Now through Christ we, who were dead in sins, are quickened. *Quickened together with him.* Christ's death was the death of our sins; Christ's resurrection is the quickening of our souls.

II. Through him we have the remission of sin: *Having forgiven you all trespasses.* The pardon of the crime is the life of the criminal.

III. Whatever was in force against us is taken out of the way. He has obtained for us a legal discharge from the *hand-writing of ordinances, which was against us* (*v.* 14). *Cursed is everyone who continues not in everything.* This was a hand-writing which was *against us, and contrary to us.*

When he was nailed to the cross, the curse was as it were nailed to the cross. It must be understood of the ceremonial law, the *hand-writing of ordinances.* The Lord Jesus *took it out of the way, nailed it to his cross*; disannulled the obligation of it. When the substance came, the shadows fled away.

IV. He has obtained a glorious victory for us over the powers of darkness: *And, having spoiled principalities and powers, he made a show of them openly, triumphing over them in it, v.* 15. As the curse of the law was against us, so the power of Satan was against us. Out of the hands of Satan the executioner he redeemed us by power and with a high hand. The devil and all the powers of hell were conquered and disarmed by the dying Redeemer. The Redeemer conquered by dying. See his crown of thorns turned into a crown of laurels.

JAMIESON, FAUSSET, BROWN

were raised with Him." **through the faith of . . .**—*by means of your* faith *in* the operation of God; so "faith of," for "faith *in*" (Eph. 3:12; Phil. 3:9). Faith in God's mighty operation in raising again Jesus, is saving faith (Rom. 4:24; 10:9); and it is wrought in the soul by His same "mighty working" whereby He "raised Jesus from the dead" (Eph. 1:19, 20). **13. you, being dead**—formerly (Eph. 2:1, 2); even as Christ was among the dead, before that God raised Him "from the dead" (vs. 12). **sins**—rather as *Greek* is translated at end of this verse, "trespasses," lit., "fallings aside" from God's ways; actual transgressions, as that of Adam. **uncircumcision of your flesh**—your not having put off the old fleshly nature, the carnal foreskin, or *original sin,* which now by spiritual circumcision, i.e., conversion and baptism, you have put off. **he quickened**—GOD "quickened together with Him" (CHRIST). Just as Christ's resurrection proved that He was delivered from the sin laid on Him, so our spiritual quickening proves that we have been forgiven our sins (I Pet. 3:22; 4:1, 2). **forgiven you**—So *Vulgate* and HILARY. But the oldest MSS. read, "us," passing from the particular persons, the Colossians, to the general Church (ch. 1:14; Eph. 1:7). **all trespasses**—*Greek,* "all *our* trespasses." **14. Blotting out**—*Greek,* "Having wiped out"; coincident in time with "having forgiven you" (vs. 13); hereby having *cancelled* the law's indictment against you. The law (including especially the *moral* law, wherein lay the chief difficulty in obeying) is abrogated to the believer, as far as it was a compulsory, accusing code, and as far as "righteousness" (justification) and "life" were sought for by it. It can only produce outward works, not inward obedience of the will, which in the believer flows from the Holy Spirit in Him (Rom. 3:21; 7:2, 4; Gal. 2:19). **the handwriting of ordinances**—rather, "IN ordinances" (*Note,* Eph. 2: 15); "the law of commandments contained in ordinances." "The handwriting" (alluding to the Decalogue, the representative of the law, *written by the hand* of God) is *the whole law,* the obligatory bond, under which all lay; the Jews primarily were under the bond, but they in this respect were the representative people of the world (Rom. 3:19); and in their inability to keep the law was involved the inability of the Gentiles also, in whose hearts "the work of the law was written" (Rom. 2:15); and as they did not keep this, they were condemned by it. **that was against us . . . contrary to us**—*Greek "adversary* to us"; so it is translated, Hebrews 10:27. "Not only was the law *against us* by its demands, but also *an adversary* to us by its accusations" [BENGEL]. TITTMANN explains the *Greek,* "having a *latent* contrariety to us"; not *open designed* hostility, but virtual unintentional opposition through *our* frailty; not through any opposition in *the law itself* to our good (Rom. 7:7-12, 14; I Cor. 15:56, Gal. 3:21; Heb. 10:3). The "WRITING" is part of "that which was contrary to us"; for "the *letter* killeth" (*Note,* II Cor. 3:6). **and took it**—*Greek,* and hath taken it out of the way" (so as to be no longer a hindrance to us), by "nailing it to *the* cross." Christ, by bearing the curse of the broken law, has redeemed us from its curse (Gal. 3:13). In His person nailed to the cross, the law itself was nailed to it. One ancient mode of cancelling bonds was by striking a nail through the writing: this seems at that time to have existed in Asia [GROTIUS]. The bond cancelled in the present case was the obligation lying against the Jews as representatives of the world, and attested by their *amen,* to keep the whole law under penalty of the curse (Deut. 27:26; Neh. 10:29). **15.** ALFORD, ELLICOTT, and others translate the *Greek* to accord with the translation of the same *Greek,* ch. 3:9, "Stripping off from Himself the principalities and the powers:" GOD put off from Himself *the angels,* i.e., their ministry, not employing them to be promulgators of the Gospel in the way that He had given the law by their "disposition" or ministry (Acts 7:53; Gal. 3:19; Heb. 2:2, 5): God manifested Himself without a veil in Jesus. "THE principalities and THE powers" refers back to vs. 10, Jesus, "the Head of all principality and power," and ch. 1: 16. In the sacrifice of Jesus on the cross, God subjected all the principalities, etc., to Jesus, declaring them to be powerless as to His work and His people (Eph. 1:21). Thus Paul's argument against those grafting on Christianity Jewish observances, along with angel worship, is, whatever part angels may be supposed to have had under the law, now at an end, God having put the legal dispensation itself away. But the objection is, that the context *seems* to refer to a triumph over *bad angels:* in II Corinthians 2: 14, however, Christ's *triumph* over those subjected to Him, is not a triumph for destruction, but for

ADAM CLARKE

The faith of the operation of God. They were quickened, changed, and saved by means of faith in Christ Jesus, which faith was produced by the operation or energy of God. Believing is the act of the soul; but the grace or power to believe comes from God himself.

14. *Blotting out the handwriting of ordinances.* By the handwriting of ordinances the apostle most evidently means the ceremonial law.

Blotting out the handwriting is probably an allusion to Num. v. 23, where the curses written in the book, in the case of the woman suspected of adultery, are directed to be blotted out with the bitter waters.

This was *against* them, for they were bound to fulfil it; and it was *contrary* to them, as condemning them for their neglect and transgression of it.

Nailing it to his cross. When Christ was nailed to the Cross, our obligation to fulfill these ordinances was done away.

15. *And having spoiled principalities and powers.* Here is an allusion to the treatment of enemies when conquered. They are "spoiled of their armor"; and they are "exhibited" with contumely and reproach to the populace, especially when the victor has the honor of a "triumph"; to the former of which there is an allusion in the words "making a public exhibition of them"; and to the latter in the words *triumphing over them.* And the *principalities and powers* refer to the emperors, kings, and generals taken in battle, and reserved to grace the victor's triumph. It is very likely that by the *principalities and powers* over whom Christ triumphed the apostle means the *nesioth* and *roshoth,* who were the rulers and chiefs in the Sanhedrin and synagogues, and who had great authority among the people, both in making constitutions and in explaining traditions. The propagation of Christianity in Judea quite destroyed their spiritual power and domination.

MATTHEW HENRY

He *spoiled them* and *made a show of them openly*. Never had the devil's kingdom such a mortal blow given to it as was given by the Lord Jesus. *Triumphing over them in it*; in His Cross and by His death.

Verses 16-23

I. A caution to take heed of judaizing teachers. *Let no man therefore judge you in meat nor in drink*, &c., *v.* 16. "Let no man impose those things upon you, for God has not imposed them."

These things *were shadows of things to come* (*v.* 17): they are now done away. *But the body is of Christ:* the body, of which they were shadows, has come. They had the shadows, we have the substance.

II. He cautions them to take heed of those who would introduce the worship of angels as the Gentile philosophers did: *Let no man beguile you of your reward, in a voluntary humility and worshipping of angels, v.* 18.

Though it has a show of humility, it is a voluntary, not a commanded humility; and therefore it is not acceptable, yea, it is not warrantable.

Besides, the notions upon which this practice was grounded were merely the inventions of men—the proud conceits of human reason: *Intruding into those things which he hath not seen, vainly puffed up by his fleshly mind.* Though there was a show of humility in the practice, there was a real pride in the principle. Pride is at the bottom of a great many errors and corruptions, and even of many evil practices, which have a great show and appearance of humility.

JAMIESON, FAUSSET, BROWN

their salvation, so that good angels *may* be referred to (ch. 1:20). But the *Greek* middle is susceptible of *English Version,* "having spoiled," or, lit. [TITTMANN], "having *completely* stripped," or "despoiled" *for Himself* (cf. Rom. 8:38; I Cor. 15:24; Eph. 6:2). *English Version* accords with Matt. 12:29; Luke 11:22; Hebrews 2:14. Translate as the *Greek,* "The *rules and authorities.*" **made a show of them openly**—at His ascension (*Notes,* Eph. 4:8; confirming *English Version* of this verse). **openly**—John 7:4; 11:54, support *English Version* against ALFORD'S translation, "in openness of speech." **in it**—viz., His cross, or crucifixion: so the Greek fathers translate. Many of the Latins, "In *Himself,*" or "in Him." Ephesians 2:16 favors *English Version,* "reconcile . . . by *the cross,* having slain the enmity thereby." If "in Him," i.e., Christ, be read, still the Cross will be the place and means of God's triumph in Christ over the principalities (Eph. 1:20; 2:5). **16. therefore**—because ye are complete in Christ, and God in Him has dispensed with all subordinate means as *essential* to acceptance with Him. **meat . . . drink**—*Greek,* "eating . . . .drinking" (Rom. 14:1-17). Pay no regard to any one who sits in judgment on you as to legal observances in respect to foods. **holyday**—*a feast* yearly. Cf. the three, I Chronicles 23:31. **new moon**—monthly. **the sabbath**—Omit "THE," which is not in the *Greek* (cf. *Note,* Gal. 4:10). "SABBATHS" (not "the sabbaths") of the day of atonement and feast of tabernacles have come to an end with the Jewish services to which they belonged (Lev. 23:32, 37-39). The weekly sabbath rests on a more permanent foundation, having been instituted in Paradise to commemorate the completion of creation in six days. Leviticus 23:38 expressly distinguished "the sabbath of the Lord" from the other sabbaths. **17. things to come**—the blessings of the Christian covenant, the substance of which Jewish ordinances were but the type. Cf. "ages to come," i.e., the Gospel dispensation (Eph. 2:7). Hebrews 2:5, "the world to come." **the body is of Christ**—The *real substance* (of the blessings typified by the law) belongs to Christ (Heb. 8:5; 10:1). **18. beguile**—Translate, "Defraud you of your prize," lit., "to adjudge a prize out of hostility away from him who deserves it" [TRENCH]. "To be umpire in a contest to the detriment of one." This *defrauding of their prize* the Colossians would suffer, by letting any self-constituted *arbitrator* or *judge* (i.e., false teacher) draw them away from Christ," the righteous Judge" and Awarder of the prize (II Tim. 4:8; Jas. 1:12; I Pet. 5:4), to angel-worship. **in a voluntary humility**—So "will worship" (vs. 23). Lit., "Delighting [WAHL] in humility"; *loving* (so the *Greek* is translated, Mark 12:38, "*love* to go in long clothing") to indulge himself *in a humility* of his own imposing: *a volunteer in humility* [DALLÆUS]. Not as ALFORD, "Let no one *of purpose* defraud you. . . ." Not as GROTIUS, "If he ever so much wish" (to defraud you). For the participle "wishing" or "delighting," is one of the series, and stands in the same category as "intruding," "puffed up," "not holding"; and the *self-pleasing* implied in it stands in happy contrast to the (mock) *humility* with which it seems to me, therefore, to be connected. His "humility," so called, is a *pleasing of self: thus* it stands in parallelism to "his fleshly mind" (its real name, though *he* styles it "humility"), as "wishing" or "delighting" does to "puffed up." The *Greek* for "humility" is lit., "lowliness of *mind,"* which forms a clearer parallel to "puffed up by his fleshly *mind.*" Under pretext of humility, as if they durst not come directly to God and Christ (like the modern Church of Rome), they invoked angels: as Judaizers, they justified this on the ground that the law was given by angels. This error continued long in Phrygia (where Colosse and Laodicea were), so that the Council of Laodicea (A.D. 360) expressly framed its 35th canon against the "*Angelici*" (as AUGUSTINE, *Hœreses,* 39, calls them) or "invokers of angels." **intruding into . . .things which he hath not seen**—So very old MSS. and *Vulgate* and ORIGEN read. But the oldest MSS. and LUCIFER omit "not"; then translate, "haughtily treading on ('standing on' [ALFORD]) the things which he hath seen." TREGELLES refers this to *fancied* visions of angels. But if Paul had meant a *fancied seeing,* he would have used some qualifying word, as, "which he *seemed to* see," not "which he *hath* seen." Plainly the things were *actually* seen by him, whether of demoniacal origination (I Sam. 28:11-20), or phenomena resulting from natural causation, mistaken by him as if supernatural. Paul, not stopping to discuss the nature of the things so seen, fixes on the radical error, the tendency of such a

ADAM CLARKE

In it. The words refer rather to Christ than to the Cross, if indeed they be genuine; of which there is much reason to doubt, as the versions and fathers differ so greatly in quoting them.

16. *Let no man therefore judge you in meat, or in drink.* The apostle speaks here in reference to some particulars of the "handwriting of ordinances," which had been taken away, viz., the distinction of meats and drinks, what was clean and what unclean, according to the law; and the necessity of observing certain holy days or festivals, such as the new moons and particular sabbaths, or those which should be observed with more than ordinary solemnity. All these had been taken *out of the way* and nailed to the Cross, and were no longer of moral obligation.

17. *Which are a shadow.* All these things were types, and must continue in force till the Christ, whom they represented, came; the apostle therefore says that the *body*—the substance or design of them, was *of Christ*—pointed Him out, and the excellent blessings which He has procured. The word *shadow* is often used to express anything "imperfect" or "unsubstantial"; while the term *body* was used in the opposite sense, and expressed anything "substantial, solid, and firm." The law was but the shadow or representation of good things to come; none should rest in it. All that it pointed out is to be sought and obtained in Christ.

18. *Let no man beguile you.* Let no man take the "prize" from you which the *brabeus,* or judge in the contests, has assigned you in consequence of your having obtained the victory. *In a voluntary humility and worshipping of angels.* The whole passage has been paraphrased thus: "Let no man spoil you of the prize adjudged to you, who delights in mortifying his body, and walking with the apparent modesty of an angel, affecting superior sanctity in order to gain disciples; intruding into things which he has not seen; and, notwithstanding his apparent humility, his mind is carnal, and he is puffed up with a sense of his superior knowledge and piety."

MATTHEW HENRY

Those who do so do *not hold the head, v.* 19. When men let go their hold of Christ, they catch at that which is next them and will stand them in no stead.—*From which all the body, by joints and bands, having nourishment ministered, and knit together, increaseth with the increase of God.* Jesus Christ is not only a head of government over the church, but a head of vital influence to it. The body of Christ is a growing body: *it increaseth with the increase of God,* with a large and abundant increase.

III. He takes occasion hence to warn them again: "*Wherefore, if you be dead with Christ from the rudiments of the world, why, as though living in the world, are you subject to ordinances?* (*v.* 20). Such observances as, *Touch not, taste not, handle not,*" *v.* 21, 22, *which all are to perish with the using,* having no other authority than the traditions and injunctions of men.

Which things have indeed a show of wisdom in will-worship and humility. They thought themselves wiser than their neighbours. There is nothing of true devotion in these things, for the gospel teaches us to worship God in spirit and truth and not by ritual observances, and through the mediation of Christ alone and not of any angels. Such things have only a show of wisdom, but are really folly. It is true wisdom to keep close to the appointments of the gospel, and an entire subjection to Christ, the only head of the church.

JAMIESON, FAUSSET, BROWN

one in all this to walk by SENSE (viz., what he *haughtily prides himself on having* SEEN), rather than by FAITH in the UNSEEN "Head" (vs. 19; cf. John 20: 29; II Cor. 5:7; Heb. 11:1). **puffed up**—implying that the previous so called "humility" (*Greek,* "lowliness of mind") was really a "puffing up." **fleshly mind**—*Greek,* "By the mind of his own flesh." The flesh, or sensuous principle, is the fountain head whence his mind draws its craving after religious objects of *sight,* instead of, in true *humility* as a member, "holding fast the (unseen) Head." **19.** Translate, "Not holding *fast* the Head." He who does not hold Christ solely and supremely above all others, does not hold Him at all [BENGEL]. The want of firm holding of Christ has set him loose to [pry into, and so] "tread haughtily on (pride himself on) things which he hath seen." Each must hold fast the Head for himself, not merely be attached to the other members, however high in the body [ALFORD]. **from which**—rather, "from whom." **the body**—i.e., all the members of the body (Eph. 4:16). **joints**—the points of union where the supply of nourishment passes to the different members, furnishing the body with the materials of growth. **bands**—the sinews and nerves which bind together limb and limb. Faith, love, and peace, are the spiritual bands. Cf. "knit together in love" (vs. 2; ch. 3:14; Eph. 4:3). **having nourishment ministered**—i.e., supplied to it continually. "Receiving ministration." **knit together**—The *Greek* is translated, "compacted," Ephesians 4:16: implying firm consolidation. **with the increase of God**—(Eph. 4: 16)—i.e., *wrought by* God, the Author and Sustainer of the believer's spiritual life, in union with Christ, the Head (I Cor. 3:6); and tending to the honor of God, being worthy of Him, its Author. **20. Wherefore**—The oldest MSS. omit "Wherefore." **if ye be dead**—*Greek,* "if ye died (so as to be freed) from..." (cf. Rom. 6:2; 7:2, 3; Gal. 2:19). **rudiments of the world**—(vs. 8). Carnal, outward, worldly, legal ordinances. **as though living**—as though you were not dead to the world like your crucified Lord, into whose death ye were buried (Gal. 6:14; I Pet. 4:1, 2). **are ye subject to ordinances**—Why do ye submit to be made subject to ordinances? Referring to vs. 14: you are again being made subject to "ordinances," the "handwriting" of which had been "blotted out" (vs. 14). **21.** Cf. vs. 16, "meat . . . drink." He gives instances of the "ordinances" (vs. 20) in the words of their imposers. There is an ascending climax of superstitious prohibitions. The first *Greek* word (*hapse*) is distinguished from the third (*thiges*), in that the former means *close contact* and *retention;* the latter, *momentary contact* (cf. I Cor. 7:1; John 20:17, *Greek,* "Hold me not"; cling not to me"). Translate, "*Handle* not, *neither* taste, *nor even touch.*" The three refer to meats. "*Handle* not" (a stronger term than "nor even *touch*"), "nor taste" with the *tongue,* "nor even touch," however slight the contact. **22. Which**—things, viz., the three things handled, touched, and tasted. **are to perish**—lit., "are constituted by their very nature) for perishing (or *destruction by corruption*) in (or *with*) their using up" (consumption). Therefore they cannot really and lastingly defile a man (Matt. 15:17; I Cor. 6:13). **after**—according to. Referring to vss. 20, 21. All these "ordinances" are according to human, not divine, injunction. **doctrines**—*Greek,* teachings." ALFORD translates, (doctrinal) "systems." **23. have**—*Greek,* "are having"; implying the *permanent* characteristic which these ordinances are supposed to have. **show of wisdom**—rather, "a *reputation* of wisdom" [ALFORD]. **will worship**—arbitrarily invented worship: *would-be worship,* devised by *man's own will,* not God's. So jealous is God of human will worship, that He struck Nadab and Abihu dead for burning strange incense (Lev. 10:1-3). So Uzziah was stricken with leprosy for usurping the office of priest (II Chron. 26:16-21). Cf. the will worship of Saul (I Sam. 13:8-14) for which he was doomed to lose his throne. **neglecting of the body**—*Greek,* "not sparing of the body." This asceticism seems to have rested on the Oriental theory that matter is the source of evil. This also looked plausible (cf. I Cor. 9:27). **not in any honour**—of the body. As "neglecting of the body" describes asceticism *positively;* so this clause, *negatively.* Not paying any of that "honor" which is due to the body as redeemed by such a price as the blood of Christ. We should not degrade, but have a just estimation of ourselves, not in ourselves, but in Christ (Acts 13:46; I Cor. 3:21; 6:15; 7:23; 12:23, 24; I Thess. 4:4). True self-denial regards the spirit, and not the forms of ascetical self-mortification in "meats which profit not those occupied therein" (Heb. 13:9), and is consistent with Christian self-respect, the "honor" which

ADAM CLARKE

It is very likely that the apostle here alludes to the Essenes, who were remarkably strict and devout, spent a principal part of their time in the contemplation of the Divine Being, abstained from all sensual gratifications, and affected to live the life of angels upon earth.

19. *And not holding the Head.* Not acknowledging Jesus Christ as the only Saviour of mankind, and the only *Head* or "chief" of the Christian Church, on whom every member of it depends, and from whom each derives both light and life. For a further explanation of these words see the notes on Eph. iv. 16, where the figures and phraseology are the same.

20. *If ye be dead with Christ.* See the notes on Rom. vi. 3, 5. *From the rudiments of the world.* You have renounced all hope of salvation from the observance of Jewish rites and ceremonies, which were only *rudiments,* "first elements" or the "alphabet," out of which the whole science of Christianity was composed. We have often seen that *the world* and "this world" signify the Jewish dispensation, or the rites, ceremonies, and services performed under it. *Why, as though living in the world.* Why, as if you were still under the same dispensation from which you have been already freed, are you subject to its ordinances, performing them as if expecting salvation from this performance?

21. *Touch not; taste not; handle not.* These are forms of expression very frequent among the Jews.

22. *Which all are to perish with the using.* These are not matters of eternal moment; the different kinds of meats were made for the body, and go with it into corruption. In like manner, all the rites and ceremonies of the Jewish religion now perish, having accomplished the end of their institution; namely, to lead us to Christ, that we might be justified by faith. *After the commandments and doctrines of men.* These words should follow the twentieth verse, of which they form a part; and it appears from them that the apostle is here speaking of the traditions of the elders, and the load of cumbrous ceremonies which they added to the significant rites prescribed by Moses.

23. *Which things have indeed a shew of wisdom.* All these prescriptions and rites have indeed the appearance of wisdom, and are recommended by plausible reasons; but they form a worship which God has not commanded, and enjoin macerations of the body, accompanied with a humiliation of spirit, that are neither profitable to the soul nor of any advantage to the body; so that the whole of their religion is worth nothing. What is here termed *will worship* signifies simply a mode of worship which a man chooses for himself, independently of the revelation which God has given.

MATTHEW HENRY

JAMIESON, FAUSSET, BROWN

belongs to the believer as dedicated to the Lord. Cf. "vainly," vs. 18. **to the satisfying of the flesh**—This expresses the *real* tendency of their human ordinances of bodily asceticism, voluntary humility, and will worship of angels. While seeming to *deny* self and the body, they really are *pampering* the flesh. Thus "satisfying of the *flesh*" answers to "puffed up by his *fleshly* mind" (vs. 18), so that "flesh" is used in its ethical sense, "the carnal nature" as opposed to the *spiritual;* not in the sense "body."

ADAM CLARKE

MATTHEW HENRY — CHAPTER 3

Verses 1–4

Though we are made free from the ceremonial law, it does not therefore follow that we may live as we list. We must walk the more closely with God. *If you then have risen with Christ, seek those things which are above.* We must mind the concerns of another world more than the concerns of this. *Christ sits at the right hand of God.* He who is our best friend has gone before to secure to us the heavenly happiness; and therefore we should seek what he has purchased at so vast an expense.

I. He explains this duty (*v.* 2): *Set your affections on things above, not on things on the earth.* Upon the wings of affection the heart soars upwards. *Things on earth* are here set in opposition to *things above.* Heaven and earth are contrary one to the other, and the prevalence of our affection to one will proportionably weaken our affection to the other.

II. He assigns three reasons for this, *v.* 3, 4.

1. We are dead to present things. And if we are dead to the earth, and have renounced it as our happiness, it is absurd for us to *set our affections* upon it, and *seek* it.

2. Our true life lies in the other world: *You are dead, and your life is hid with Christ in God, v.* 3. The new man has its livelihood thence. It is *hid with Christ*: not hid from us only, in point of secrecy, but hid for us, denoting security. This is our comfort, that our *life is hid with him*, and laid up safely with him.

3. At the second coming of Christ we hope for the perfection of our happiness. *When Christ, who is our life, shall appear, we shall also appear with him in glory, v.* 4. Christ is a believer's life. He is the principle and end of the Christian's life. Christ will appear again. He is now *hid*, but he will appear in *his own glory and his Father's glory.* We shall then appear with him in glory. It will be his glory to have his redeemed with him, and it will be their glory to come with him. Do we look for such a happiness, and should we not set our affections upon that world, and live above this? Our head is there, our home is there, our treasure is there, and we hope to be there for ever.

Verses 5–7

It is our duty to mortify our *members which are upon the earth*, and which naturally incline us to the things of the world.

JAMIESON, FAUSSET, BROWN — CHAPTER 3

Vss. 1-25. Exhortations to Heavenly Aims, as Opposed to Earthly, on the Ground of Union to the Risen Saviour; To Mortify and Put Off the Old Man, and to Put on the New; in Charity, Humility, Words of Edification, Thankfulness; Relative Duties. **1. If . . . then**—The connection with ch. 2:18, 23, is, he had condemned the "fleshly mind" and the "satiating to the full the flesh"; in contrast to this he now says, "If then ye have been once for all raised up (*Greek*, aorist) together with Christ" (viz., at your conversion and baptism, Rom. 6:4). **seek those things . . . above**—(Matt. 6:33; Phil. 3:20.) **sitteth**—rather, as *Greek*, "Where Christ is, sitting on the right of God" (Eph. 1:20). The Head being quickened, the members are also quickened with Him. Where the Head is, there the members must be. The contrast is between the believer's former state, alive to the world but dead to God, and his present state, dead to the world but alive to God; and between the earthly abode of the unbeliever and the heavenly abode of the believer (I Cor. 15:47, 48). We are already seated there *in* Him as our Head; and hereafter shall be seated *by* Him, as the Bestower of our bliss. **2.** Translate, "Set your *mind* on the things above, not on the things . . ." (ch. 2:20). Contrast "who *mind* earthly things" (Phil. 3:19). Whatever we make an idol of, will either be a cross to us if we be believers, or a curse to us if unbelievers. **3.** The *Greek* aorist implies, "For ye have died once for all" (ch. 2:12; Rom. 6:4-7). It is not said, Ye must die practically to the world in order to become dead with Christ; but the latter is assumed as *once for all* having taken place in the regeneration; what believers are told is, Develop this spiritual life in practice. "No one longs for eternal, incorruptible, and immortal life, unless he be wearied of this temporal, corruptible, and mortal life" [Augustine]. **your life . . . hid**—Psalm 83:3—like a seed buried in the earth; cf. "planted," Romans 6:5. Cf. Matthew 13:31 and 33, "like . . . leaven . . . *hid.*" As the glory of Christ now is hid from the world, so also the glory of believers' inner life, proceeding from communion with Him, is still hidden with Christ in God; but (vs. 4) when Christ, the Source of this life, shall manifest Himself in glory, then shall their hidden glory be manifest, and correspond in appearance to its original [Neander]. The Christian's secret communion with God will now at times make itself seen without his intending it (Matt. 5:14, 16); but his full manifestation is at Christ's manifestation (Matt. 13:43; Rom. 8:19-23). "It doth not yet appear (*Greek*, 'is not yet *manifested*') what we shall be" (I John 3:2; I Pet. 1:7). As yet Christians do not always recognize the "life" of one another, so *hidden* is it, and even at times doubt as to their own life, so weak is it, and so harassed with temptations (Ps. 51; Rom. 7). **in God**—to whom Christ has ascended. Our "life" is "laid up for" us *in God* (ch. 1:5), and is secured by the decree of Him who is invisible to the world (II Tim. 4:8). **4.** Translate, "When Christ shall *be manifested* who is our life (John 11:25; 14:6, 19), then shall ye also with Him *be manifested* in glory" (I Pet. 4:13). The *spiritual* life our souls have now in Him shall be extended to our *bodies* (Rom. 8:11). **then**—and not till then. Those err who think to find a perfect Church before then. The true Church is now militant. Rome errs in trying to set up a Church now regnant and triumphant. The true Church shall be visible as a perfect and reigning Church, when Christ shall be visibly manifested as her reigning Head. **5. Mortify**—*Greek*, "make a corpse of"; "make dead"; "put to death." **therefore**—(*Note*, vs. 3). Follow out to its necessary consequence the fact of your *having once for all* died with Christ spiritually at your regeneration, by daily "deadening your members," of which united "the body of the sins of the flesh" consists (cf. 2:11). "The members" to be mortified are the fleshly instruments of lust, in so far as the members

ADAM CLARKE — CHAPTER 3

1. *If ye then.* "Seeing then that you are risen with Christ"; this refers to what he had said, chap. ii. 12: "Buried with him in baptism, wherein also ye are risen with him." As therefore you have most cordially received the doctrine of Christ, and profess to be partakers of a spiritual religion that promises spiritual and eternal things, *seek those things,* and look to be prepared for the enjoyment of them.

2. *Set your affection on things above.* This is a very good general rule: "Be as much in earnest for heavenly and eternal things as you formerly were for those that are earthly and perishing."

CHARLES H. SPURGEON:

What are these "things above" which we should set our affection upon? I ask you now to lift your eyes above yon clouds, and this lower firmament is the residence of God. What see you there? First, there is *God himself.* Make Him the subject of your thoughts, your desires, your emotions, your love. "Delight thyself also in the Lord, and he will give thee the desires of thine heart." "My soul, wait thou only upon God, for my expectation is from him." Call Him "God my exceeding joy." Let nothing come between you and your heavenly Father. What is all the world if you have not God, and when you once have God, what matters if all the world be gone? God is all things, and when you can say, "God is mine," you are richer than Croesus. Oh, to say, "Whom have I in heaven but thee." Oh, to love God with all our heart, and with all our soul, and with all our mind, and with all our strength: that is what the law required; it is what the gospel enables us to render.

What see I next? I see *Jesus,* who is God, but yet is truly man. Need I press upon you, to set your love upon the Well-beloved? Has He not won your heart, and does He not hold it now as under a mighty spell? I know you love Him. Fix your mind on Him then. Often meditate upon His divine person, His perfect work, His mediatorial glory, His second coming, His glorious reign, His love for you, your own security in Him, your union with Him. Oh, let these sweet thoughts possess your breasts, fill your mouths, and influence your lives. Let the morning break with thoughts of Christ, and let your last thought at night be sweetened with His presence. Set your affection upon Him who has set His affection upon you.

—The Treasury of the New Testament

5. *Mortify therefore your members.* "Put them to death." The verb is used metaphorically to signify "to deprive a thing of its power, to destroy its strength." Use no member of your body to sin against God; keep all under dominion, and never permit the beast to run away with the man.

MATTHEW HENRY

I. The lusts of the flesh: *Fornication, uncleanness, inordinate affection, evil concupiscence*—which were so contrary to the Christian state and the heavenly hope.

II. The love of the world: *And covetousness, which is idolatry;* that is, an inordinate love of present good and outward enjoyments. Covetousness is spiritual idolatry: it is the giving of that love and regard to worldly wealth which are due to God only. Among all the instances of sin which good men are recorded in the scripture to have fallen into there is no instance of any good man charged with covetousness. How necessary it is to mortify sins, *v.* 6, 7. If we do not kill them, they will kill us: *For which things' sake the wrath of God cometh on the children of disobedience, v.* 6. See what we are all by nature more or less: we are *children of disobedience.* The wrath of God comes upon all the children of disobedience. Those who do not obey the precepts of the law incur the penalties of it. We should mortify these sins because they have lived in us: *In which you also walked some time, when you lived in them, v.* 7. The consideration that we have formerly lived in sin is a good argument why we should now forsake it. We have walked in by-paths, therefore let us walk in them no more. *When you lived among those who did such things* (so some understand it), then you walked in those evil practices. Let us keep out of the way of evil-doers.

Verses 8–11

We are to mortify inordinate passions (*v.* 8): *But now you also put off all these, anger, wrath, malice.* Anger and wrath are bad, but malice is worse; it is anger heightened and settled. So the product of them in the tongue; as *blasphemy*, which seems there to mean, not so much speaking ill of God as speaking ill of men,—*filthy communication*, all lewd and wanton discourse, which propagates the same defilements in the hearers. *Lie not one to another* (*v.* 9). Lying makes us like the devil (who is the *father of lies*). Seeing *you have put off the old man with his deeds, and have put on the new man, v.* 10. Those who have put off the old man have put it off with its deeds; and those who have put on the new man must put on all its deeds, *renewed in knowedge*, because an ignorant soul cannot be a good soul. Light is the first thing in the new creation, as it was in the first: *after the image of him who created him.* It was the honour of man in innocence that he was made after the image of God.

In the privilege of sanctification *there is neither Greek nor Jew, circumcision nor uncircumcision, Barbarian, Scythian, bond nor free, v.* 11. It is as much the duty of the one as of the other to be holy, and as much the privilege of the one as of the other to receive from God the grace to be so.

Christ is all in all. Christ is a Christian's all, all his hope and happiness.

JAMIESON, FAUSSET, BROWN

of the body are abused to such purposes. Habitually repress and do violence to corrupt desires of which the members are the instruments (cf. Rom. 6:19; 8:13; Gal. 5:24, 25). **upon the earth**—where they find their support [BENGEL] (cf. vs. 2, "things on earth"). See Ephesians 5:3, 4. **inordinate affection**—"lustful passion." **evil concupiscence**—more general than the last [ALFORD], the disorder of the *external* senses; "lustful passion," *lust within* [BENGEL]. **covetousness**—marked off by the *Greek* article as forming a whole genus by itself, distinct from the genus containing the various species just enumerated. It implies a self-idolizing, grasping spirit; far worse than another *Greek* term translated "the love of money" (I Tim. 6:10). **which is**—i.e., inasmuch as it is "idolatry." Cf. *Note*, Ephesians 4:19, on its connection with sins of impurity. *Self* and *mammon* are deified in the heart instead of God (Matt. 6:24; *Note*, Eph. 5:5). **6.** (*Note*, Eph. 5:6.) **7. sometime**—"once." **walked . . . when ye lived in them**—These sins were the very element in which ye "*lived*" (before ye became once for all dead with Christ to them); no wonder, then, that ye "*walked*" in them. Cf. on the opposite side, "*living* in the Spirit," having as its legitimate consequence, "*walking* in the Spirit" (Gal. 5:25). The *living* comes first in both cases, the *walking* follows. **8. But now**—that ye are no longer *living* in them. **ye also**—like other believers; answering to "ye also" (vs. 7) like other unbelievers formerly. **put off**—"Do ye also put away all these," viz., those just enumerated, and those which follow [ALFORD]. **anger, wrath**—(*Note*, Eph. 4:31). **blasphemy**—rather, "reviling," "evil-speaking," as it is translated in Ephesians 4:31. **filthy communication**—The context favors the translation, "*abusive language*," rather than impure conversation. "Foul language" best retains the ambiguity of the original. **9.** (Eph. 4:22, 25.) **put off**—*Greek*, "*wholly* put off"; utterly renounced [TITTMANN]. **the old man**—the unregenerate nature which ye had before conversion. **his deeds**—habits of acting. **10. the new man**—(*Note*, Eph. 4:23). Here (*neon*) the *Greek*, means "the *recently*-put-on nature"; that lately received at regeneration (see *Note*, Eph. 4:23, 24). **which is renewed**—*Greek*, "which is being renewed" (*anakainoumenou*); viz., its development into a perfectly renewed nature is continually progressing to completion. **in knowledge**—rather as the *Greek*, "unto perfect knowledge" (*Notes*, ch. 1:6, 9, 10). Perfect knowledge of God excludes all sin (John 17:3). **after the image of him that created him**—viz., of God that created the *new man* (Eph. 2:10; 4:24). The new creation is analogous to the first creation (II Cor. 4:6). As man was then made in the image of God naturally, so now spiritually. But the image of God formed in us by the Spirit of God, is as much more glorious than that borne by Adam, as the Second Man, the Lord from heaven, is more glorious than the first man. Genesis 1:26, "Let us make man in our *image*, after our *likeness*." The "image" is claimed for man, I Corinthians 11:7; the "likeness," James 3:9. **11. Where**—Translate, "Wherein," viz., in the sphere of the renewed man. **neither . . . nor . . . nor . . . nor**—Translate as *Greek*, "There is *no such thing* as Greek *and* Jew (the difference of privilege between those born of the natural seed of Abraham and those not, is abolished), circumcision *and* uncircumcision (the difference of legal standing between the circumcised and uncircumcised is done away, Gal. 6:15)—bondman, freeman." **The present Church** is one *called out of the flesh*, and the present *world-course* (Eph. 2:2), wherein such distinctions exist, to life in the Spirit, and to the future first resurrection: and this because Satan has such power now over the flesh and the world. **Scythian**—heretofore regarded as more barbarian than the barbarians. Though the relation of bond and free actually existed, yet in relation to Christ, all alike were free in one aspect, and servants of Christ in another (I Cor. 7:22; Gal. 3:28). **Christ is all**—Christ absorbs in Himself all distinctions, being to all alike, everything that they need for justification, sanctification, and glorification (I Cor. 1:30; 3:21-23; Gal. 2:20). **in all**—who believe and are renewed, without distinction of person; the sole distinction now is, how much each draws from Christ. The unity of the divine life shared in by all believers, counterbalances all differences, even as great as that between the polished "Greek" and the rude "Scythian." Christianity imparts to the most uncivilized the only spring of sound, social and moral culture. **12. the elect of God**—There is no "the" in the *Greek*, "God's elect" (cf. Rom. 8:3; I Thess. 1:4). The order of the words "elect, holy, beloved," answers to the order of the things. *Election* from eternity precedes *sanc-*

ADAM CLARKE

Inordinate affection. "Unnatural and degrading passion"; bestial lusts.

Covetousness, which is idolatry. For the covetous man makes his money his god.

7. *In the which ye also walked sometime.* When you were in your unconverted state, you served divers lusts and pleasures.

8. *But now ye also put off all these.* See on Eph. iv. 22. Being now converted, sin had no more dominion over them. *Anger, wrath.* They had not only lived in the evils mentioned in v. 5, but also in those enumerated here; and they had not only laid aside the former, but they had laid aside the latter also. *Blasphemy.* The word seems here to mean "injurious and calumnious speaking."

9. *Lie not one to another.* Do not deceive each other; speak the truth in all your dealings. *Ye have put off the old man.* See the notes on Rom. vi. 6, and particularly on Rom. xiii. 11-14. You have received a religion widely different from that you had before; act according to its principles.

10. *And have put on the new man.* See on Rom. xii. 1-2. *Is renewed in knowledge.* Ignorance was the grand characteristic of the heathen state; knowledge, of the Christian.

After the image of him that created him. The image in which man was made, and in which he must be "remade," "made anew," consists in knowledge, righteousness, and true holiness.

11. *Where there is neither Greek nor Jew.* In which new creation no inquiry is made what nation the persons belonged to or from what ancestry they had sprung, whether in Judea or Greece. *Circumcision nor uncircumcision.* Nor is their peculiar form of religion of any consideration, whether circumcised like the *Jews* or uncircumcised like the heathens. *Bond nor free.* Nor does the particular state or circumstances in which a man may be found either help him to or exclude him from the benefit of this religion, the slave having as good a title to salvation by grace as the freeman.

But Christ is all, and in all. All mankind are His creatures, all conditions are disposed and regulated by His providence, and all human beings are equally purchased by His blood. He alone is the Source whence all have proceeded, and to Him alone all must return. He is the Maker, Preserver, Saviour, and Judge of all men.

MATTHEW HENRY

Verses 12–17

Put on therefore bowels of mercy, v. 12. We must not only put off anger and wrath (as *v.* 8), but we must put on compassion and kindness.

I. *Put on, as the elect of God, holy and beloved.* Those who are the elect of God, are beloved, and ought to conduct themselves in everything as becomes them. What we must put on. 1. Compassion towards the miserable: *Bowels of mercy.* Those who owe so much to mercy ought to be merciful. 2. *Kindness.* The design of the gospel is not only to soften the minds of men, but to sweeten them, and to promote friendship among men as well as reconciliation with God. 3. *Humbleness of mind.* There must not only be a humble demeanour, but a humble mind. 4. *Meekness.* Prudently bridle our own anger, and patiently bear the anger of others. 5. *Long-suffering.* Many can bear a short provocation who are weary of bearing when it grows long. If God is long-suffering to us we should exercise long-suffering to others. 6. Mutual forbearance: *Forbearing one another.* We have all of us something which needs to be borne with. We need the same good turn from others which we are bound to show them. 7. *Forgiving one another, if any man have a quarrel against any.* Quarrels will sometimes happen, even among the elect of God, who are holy and beloved. But it is our duty to forgive one another in such cases. *Even as Christ forgave you, so also do you.* It is a branch of his example which we are obliged to follow, if we ourselves would be forgiven.

II. In order to all this, we are exhorted: 1. To clothe ourselves with love (*v.* 14): *Above all things put on charity.* He lays the foundation in faith, and the top-stone in charity, *which is the bond of perfectness.* Christian unity consists of unanimity and mutual love. 2. To submit ourselves to the government of the *peace of God* (*v.* 15): *Let the peace of God rule in your hearts,* prevail and govern there, or as an umpire decide all matters of difference among you.

—To which you are called in one body. Being united in one body, we are called to be at peace one with another. We must be thankful. The work of thanksgiving to God is such a sweet and pleasant work that it will help to make us sweet and pleasant towards all men. 3. To let the *word of Christ dwell in us richly, v.* 16. It must dwell in us, or *keep house,* not as a servant but as a master. It must dwell in us; that is, be always ready and at hand to us in everything. It must dwell in us richly: not only keep house in our hearts, but keep a good house. Many have the word of Christ dwelling in them, but it dwells in them but poorly. The soul prospers when the word of God *dwells in us richly.* And this in all wisdom. The word of Christ must dwell in us, not in all notion and speculation, to make us doctors, but in all wisdom, to make us good Christians. 4. To teach and admonish one another. We sharpen ourselves by quickening others. We must *admonish one another in psalms and hymns.* Religious poesy seems countenanced by these expressions and is capable of great edification. But, when we sing psalms, we make no melody unless we sing with grace in our hearts. And we are not only to quicken and encourage ourselves, but to *teach and admonish one another.*

JAMIESON, FAUSSET, BROWN

tification in time; the *sanctified,* feeling God's *love,* imitate it [BENGEL]. **bowels of mercies**—Some of the oldest MSS. read singular, "mercy." *Bowels* express the yearning compassion, which has its seat in the heart, and which we feel to act on our inward parts (Gen. 43:30; Jer. 31:20; Luke 1:78, *Margin*). **humbleness of mind**—True "lowliness of mind"; not the mock "humility" of the false teachers (ch. 2:23; Eph. 4:2, 32). **13. Forbearing**—as to present offenses. **forgiving**—as to past offenses. **quarrel**—rather as *Greek,* "cause of blame," "cause of complaint." **Christ**—who had so infinitely greater cause of complaint against us. The oldest MSS. and *Vulgate* read "the Lord." *English Version* is supported by one very old MS. and old versions. It seems to have crept in from Ephesians 4:32. **14. above**—rather "over," as in Ephesians 6:16. Charity, which is the crowning grace, covering the multitude of others' sins (I Pet. 4:8), must *overlie* all the other graces enumerated. **which is**—i.e., "*for it is*"; lit., "*which thing is.*" **bond of perfectness**—an upper garment which *completes* and keeps together the rest, which, without it, would be loose and disconnected. Seeming graces, where love is wanting, are mere hypocrisy. Justification by faith is assumed as already having taken place in those whom Paul addresses, vs. 12, "elect of God, holy . . . beloved," and ch. 2:12; so that there is no plea here for Rome's view of justification by works. Love and its works "*perfect,*" i.e., manifest the full maturity of faith developed (Matt. 5:44, 48). Love . . . be ye *perfect* . . . (Jas. 2:21, 22; I John 2:5). "If we love one another, God's love is *perfected* in us" (Rom. 13:8; I Cor. 13; I Tim. 1:5; I John 4:12). As to "bond," cf. ch. 2:2, "*knit together* in love" (Eph. 4:3), "keep the unity of the Spirit in the bond of peace." **15. peace of God**—The oldest MSS. and versions read, "The peace of CHRIST" (cf. Phil. 4:7). "The peace of GOD." Therefore Christ is God. Peace was His legacy to His disciples before He left them (John 14:27), "MY peace I give unto you." Peace is peculiarly His to give. Peace follows *love* (vs. 14; Eph. 4:2, 3). **rule**—lit., "sit as umpire"; the same *Greek* verb simple, as appears compounded (ch. 2:18). The false teacher, as a self-constituted *umpire,* defrauds you of your prize; but if the peace of Christ be your umpire ruling in your hearts, your reward is sure. "Let the peace of Christ act as umpire when anger, envy, and such passions arise; and restrain them." Let not those passions give the award, so that you should be swayed by them, but let Christ's peace be the decider of everything. **in your hearts**—Many wear a peaceful countenance and speak peace with the mouth, while war is *in their hearts* (Ps. 28:3; 55:21). **to the which**—i.e., with a view to which state of Christian peace (Isa. 26:3); I Cor. 7:15, "God hath called us to peace." **ye are called**—*Greek,* "ye were also called." The "also" implies that besides Paul's exhortation, they have *also* as a motive to "peace," their having been once for all called. **in one body**—(Eph. 4:4). The unity of the body is a strong argument for "peace" among the members. **be ye thankful**—for your "calling." Not to have "peace ruling in your hearts" would be inconsistent with the "calling in one body," and would be practical unthankfulness to God who called us (Eph. 5:4, 19, 20). **16.** The form which "thankfulness" (vs. 15) ought to take. **Let the word of Christ**—the Gospel *word* by which ye have been called. **richly**—(ch. 2:2; Rom. 15:14)—**in all wisdom**—ALFORD joins this clause with "teaching. . . ." not with "dwell in you," as *English Version,* for so we find in ch. 1:28, "teaching in all wisdom," and the two clauses will thus correspond, "In all wisdom teaching," and "in grace singing in your hearts" (so the *Greek* order). **and . . . and**—The oldest MSS. read "psalms, hymns, spiritual songs" (*Note,* Eph. 5:19). At the *Agapæ* or love-feasts, and in their family circles, they were to be so full of the Word of Christ *in the heart* that the mouth should give it utterance in hymns of instruction, admonition, and praise (cf. Deut. 6:7). TERTULLIAN, *Apology,* 39, records that at the love-feasts, after the water had been furnished for the hands and the lights had been lit, according as any had the power, whether by his remembrance of Scripture, or by his powers of composition, he used to be invited to sing praises to God for the common good. Paul contrasts (as in Eph. 5:18, 19) the songs of Christians at their social meetings, with the bacchanalian and licentious songs of heathen feasts. Singing usually formed part of the entertainment at Greek banquets (cf. Jas. 5:13). **with grace**—*Greek,* "IN grace," the element in which your singing is to be: "*the* grace" of the indwelling Holy Spirit. This clause expresses the seat and source of true psalmody, whether in private or public, viz., the *heart* as well as the voice; singing

ADAM CLARKE

12. *Bowels of mercies.* Be merciful, not in act merely, but in spirit and affection. In all cases of this kind let your heart dictate to your hand; be clothed with bowels of mercy—let your tenderest feelings come in contact with the miseries of the distressed as soon as ever they present themselves.

13. *Forbearing one another.* Avoid all occasions of irritating or provoking each other. *Forgiving one another.* If ye receive offense, be instantly ready to forgive on the first acknowledgment of the fault. *Even as Christ forgave you.* Who required no satisfaction and sought for nothing in you but the broken, contrite heart, and freely forgave you as soon as you returned to Him.

14. *And above all these things.* "Upon all, over all"; as the outer garment envelopes all the clothing, so let *charity* or "love" invest and encompass all the rest. *Which is the bond of perfectness.* Love to God and man is not only to cover all, but also to unite and consolidate the whole. It is therefore represented here under the notion of a girdle, by which all the rest of the clothing is bound close about the body. To love God with all the heart, soul, mind, and strength, and one's neighbor as oneself, is the perfection which the new covenant requires, and which the grace and Spirit of Christ work in every sincerely obedient, humble believer.

15. *And let the peace of God.* Instead of *God,* "Christ" is the reading of several MSS., with several of the fathers.

Rule in your hearts. Let the peace of Christ "judge, decide, and govern" in your hearts, as the *brabeus,* or judge, does in the Olympic contests. No heart is right with God where the peace of Christ does not rule, and the continual prevalence of the peace of Christ is the decisive proof that the heart is right with God.

In one body. You cannot have peace with God, in yourselves nor among each other, unless you continue in unity; and, as *one body,* continue in connection and dependence on Him who is your only Head; to this *ye are called.* It is a glorious state of salvation, and you should be forever *thankful* that you are thus privileged.

16. *Let the word of Christ dwell in you richly.* I believe the apostle means that the Colossians should be "well instructed in the doctrine of Christ"; that it should be their constant study; that it should be frequently preached, explained, and enforced among them; and that *all* the *wisdom* comprised in it should be well understood. Through bad pointing this verse is not very intelligible; the several members of it should be distinguished thus: "Let the doctrine of Christ dwell richly among you; teaching and admonishing each other in all wisdom; singing with grace in your hearts unto the Lord, in psalms, hymns, and spiritual songs." This arrangement the original will not only bear, but it absolutely requires it, and is not sense without it.

MATTHEW HENRY

5. That all must be done in the name of Christ (*v.* 17): *And whatsoever you do in word or deed, do all in the name of the Lord Jesus. Giving thanks to God and the Father by him.* Those who do all things in Christ's name will never want matter of thanksgiving to God, even the Father.

Verses 18–25

Exhortations to relative duties. We must never separate the privileges and duties of the gospel religion.

I. The duties of wives and husbands (*v.* 18): *Wives, submit yourselves unto your own husbands, as it is fit in the Lord.* Submission is the duty of wives. It is agreeable to the order of nature and the reason of things, as well as the appointment and will of God. It is submission to a husband, and to her own husband, who stands in the nearest relation, and is under strict engagements to proper duty too. And *this is fit in the Lord. Husbands must love their wives, and not be bitter against them, v.* 19. They must love them with tender and faithful affection, as Christ loved the church. And they must not be bitter against them, but be kind and obliging to them in all things.

II. The duties of children and parents: *Children, obey your parents in all things, for this is well-pleasing unto the Lord, v.* 20. They must be willing to do all their lawful commands, as those who have a natural right and are fitter to direct them than themselves. And this is *well-pleasing to God.* And parents must be tender, as well as children obedient (*v.* 21): "*Fathers, provoke not your children to anger, lest they be discouraged.* Let not your authority over them be exercised with rigour and severity, but with kindness and gentleness, lest you, by holding the reins too tight make them fly out with the greater fierceness."

III. Servants and masters: *Servants, obey your masters in all things according to the flesh, v.* 22. Servants must do the duty of the relation in which they stand in *all things*—not only when their master's eye is upon them. *In singleness of heart, fearing God.* The fear of God ruling in the heart will make people good in every relation. "And *whatsoever you do, do it heartily* (*v.* 23), with diligence, not idly and slothfully."—*As to the Lord, and not as to men.* It sanctifies a servant's work when it is done as unto God, and not merely as unto men. We are really doing our duty to God when we are faithful in our duty to men. A good and faithful servant is never the further from heaven for his being a servant: "*Knowing that of the Lord you shall receive the reward of the inheritance, for you serve the Lord Christ, v.* 24. Serving your masters according to the command of Christ, you serve Christ, and he will be your paymaster. Though you are now servants, you will receive the inheritance of sons." *He who does wrong will receive for the wrong which he has done, v.* 25. He will be sure to punish the unjust as well as reward the faithful servant: as well if masters wrong their servants.—*And there is no respect of persons with him.* The righteous Judge of the earth will be impartial, and carry it with an equal hand towards master and servant. How happy would the gospel religion make the world, if it everywhere prevailed; and how much would it influence every state of things and every relation of life!

CHAPTER 4

Verse 1

The apostle proceeds with the duty of masters to their servants. Justice is required of them: *Give unto your servants that which is just and equal* (*v.* 1), not only strict justice, but equity and kindness. "*Knowing that you also have a Master in heaven.* You who are masters of others have a Master yourself, and are accountable to one above you. Deal with your servants as you expect God should deal with you. You are both servants of the same Lord and are equally accountable to him at last."

Verses 2–4

This is the duty of everyone—to *continue in prayer. Watching in the same.* Christians should lay hold of all opportunities for prayer, and choose the fittest seasons, and keep their minds lively in the duty.—

JAMIESON, FAUSSET, BROWN

(cf. vs. 15, "peace . . . rule *in your hearts*"), the psalm of love and praise being in the heart before it finds vent by the lips, and even when it is not actually expressed by the voice, as in closet-worship. The *Greek* order forbids *English Version,* "with grace in your hearts"; rather, "singing in your hearts." **to the Lord**—The oldest MSS. read, "to God." **17.** Lit., "And everything whatsoever ye do . . . do all . . ."; this includes *words* as well as *deeds.* **in the name of the Lord Jesus**—*as disciples called by His name as His,* seeking His guidance and help, and desiring to act so as to gain His approval (Rom. 14:8; I Cor. 10:31; II Cor. 5:15; I Pet. 4:11). Cf. "in the Lord," vss. 18, and 11, "Christ is *all.*" **God and the Father**—The oldest MSS. omit "and," which seems to have crept in from Ephesians 5:20. **by him**—*Greek, "through* Him" as the channel of His grace to us, and of our thanksgiving to Him (John 14:6, end). **18. unto your own husbands**—The oldest MSS. omit "own," which crept in from Ephesians 5:22. **as it is fit in the Lord**—*Greek, "was* fit," implying that there was at Colosse some degree of failure in fulfilling this duty, "as it was your duty to have done as disciples of the Lord." **19.** (Eph. 5:22-33.) **be not bitter**—ill-tempered and provoking. Many who are polite abroad, are rude and bitter at home because they are not afraid to be so there. **20.** (Eph. 6:1.) **unto the Lord**—The oldest MSS. read, "IN the Lord," i.e., this is acceptable to God when it is done *in the Lord,* viz., from the principle of faith,and as disciples in union with the Lord. **21.** (Eph. 6:4.) It is a different *Greek* verb, therefore translate here, "*irritate* not." By perpetual fault-finding "children" are "discouraged" or "disheartened." A broken-down spirit is fatal to youth [BENGEL]. **22.** (Eph. 6:5, 6.) This is to fear God, when, though none sees us, we do no *evil:* but if we do evil, it is not God, but men, whom we fear. **singleness**—"*simplicity* of *heart.*" **fearing God**—The oldest MSS. read, "the Lord." **23. And**—omitted in the oldest MSS. (cf. Eph. 6:7, 8). Cf. the same principle in the case of all men, Hezekiah (II Chron. 31:21; Rom. 12:11). **do, do it**—two distinct *Greek* verbs, "Whatsoever ye *do, work at it*" (or *labor at* it). **heartily**—not from servile constraint, but with hearty good will. **24. the reward of the inheritance**—"Knowing that it is from the Lord (the ultimate source of reward), ye shall receive the compensation (or recompense, which will make ample amends for your having no earthly possession, as slaves now) consisting of the inheritance" (a term excluding the notion of meriting it by *works:* it is all of grace, Rom. 4:14; Gal. 3:18). **for ye serve**—The oldest MSS. omit "for," then translate as *Vulgate,* "Serve ye the Lord Christ;" cf. vs. 23, "To the Lord and not unto men" (I Cor. 7:22, 23). **25. But**—The oldest MSS. read, "for," which accords with "serve ye . . ." (vs. 24), the oldest reading: the *for* here gives a motive for obeying the precept. He addresses the slaves: Serve ye the Lord Christ, and leave your wrongs in His hands to put to rights: (translate), "For he that doeth wrong shall receive *back the wrong* which he hath done (by just retribution in kind), and there is no respect of persons" with the Great Judge in the day of the Lord. He favors the master no more than the slave (Rev. 6:15).

CHAPTER 4

VSS. 1-18. EXHORTATIONS CONTINUED. TO PRAYER: WISDOM IN RELATION TO THE UNCONVERTED: AS TO THE BEARERS OF THE EPISTLE, TYCHICUS AND ONESIMUS: CLOSING SALUTATIONS. **1. give**—*Greek* "render": lit., "afford." **equal**—i.e., as the slaves owe their duties to you, so you *equally* owe to them your duties as masters. Cf. "ye masters do the *same* things" (*Note,* Eph. 6:9). ALFORD translates, "fairness," "equity," which gives a large and liberal interpretation of justice in common matters (Philemon 16). **knowing**—(Ch. 3:24). **ye also**—as well as they.

2. Continue—*Greek,* "Continue perseveringly," "persevere" (Eph. 6:18), "watching *thereunto*"; here, "watch *in the same,*" or "*in it,*" i.e., in prayer: watching against the indolence as to prayer, and in prayer, of our corrupt wills.

ADAM CLARKE

17. *Whatsoever ye do in word or deed.* Let your words be right and your actions upright. *Do all in the name of the Lord Jesus.* Begin with Him and end with Him; invoke His name and pray for His direction and support in all that you do; and thus every work will be crowned with all requisite success. *Giving thanks to God.* Even praises, as well as prayers, must ascend to God through this Mediator.

18. *Wives, submit yourselves.* Having done with general directions, the apostle comes to particular duties, which are commonly called relative, because they belong only to persons in certain situations and are not incumbent on all. The directions here to wives, husbands, children, parents, servants, and masters are so exactly the same in substance with those in Eph. v. 22-33 and vi. 1-9 that there is no need to repeat what has been said on those passages; and to the notes there the reader is requested to refer. *As it is fit in the Lord.* God commands it, and it is both proper and decent.

19. *Be not bitter against them.* Wherever bitterness is, there love is wanting. And where love is wanting in the married life, there is hell upon earth.

20. *Children, obey your parents in all things.* That is, in the Lord, in everything that your parents command you which is not contrary to the will or word of God.

24. *The reward of the inheritance.* Here you have neither lands nor property; you are servants or slaves. Be not discouraged; you have an inheritance in store. Be faithful unto God and to your employers, and Christ will give you a heavenly inheritance.

CHAPTER 4

1. *Masters, give unto your servants.* This verse should have been added to the preceding, to which it properly belongs; and this chapter should have begun with v. 2. *That which is just and equal.* As they are "bondmen" or "slaves" of whom the apostle speaks, we may at once see with what propriety this exhortation is given. The condition of slaves among the Greeks and Romans was wretched in the extreme; they could appeal to no law, and they could neither expect justice nor equity. The apostle therefore informs the proprietors of these slaves that they should act towards them both according to justice and equity; for God, their Master, required this of them, and would at last call them to account for their conduct in this respect.

2. *Continue in prayer.* This was the apostle's general advice to all; without this neither wives, husbands, children, parents, servants, nor masters could fulfil the duties which God, in their respective stations, required of them. *Watch in the same.* Be always on your guard; and when you have got the requisite grace by praying, take care of it, and bring it into its proper action by watchfulness; by which you

MATTHEW HENRY

With thanksgiving. Thanksgiving must have a part in every prayer.—*Withal praying also for us, v.* 3. The people must pray particularly for their ministers, and bear them upon their hearts at all times at the throne of grace. As if he had said, "Do not forget us, whenever you pray for yourselves." *That God would open to us a door of utterance,* that is, either afford opportunity to preach the gospel, or else give me ability and courage. *And for me, that utterance may be given to me, that I may open my mouth boldly, to speak the mystery of Christ, for which I am also in bonds.* He would have them pray for him, that he might not be discouraged in his work, nor driven from it by his sufferings: *That I may make it manifest, as I ought to speak, v.* 4. He had been particular in telling them what he prayed for on their behalf, *ch.* i. Here he tells them particularly what he would have them pray for on his behalf. Paul knew as well as any man how to speak; and yet he begged their prayers for him, that he might be taught to speak.

Verses 5, 6

The apostle exhorts them further to a prudent conduct towards the heathen world, or those out of the Christian church among whom they lived (*v.* 5): *Walk in wisdom towards those who are without.* Be careful to get no hurt by them, and to do no hurt to them, or increase their prejudices against religion. Do them all the good you can, and by all the fittest means recommend religion to them.—*Redeeming the time;* either "improving every opportunity of doing them good," or else "walking with circumspection, to give them no advantage against you.

Let *your speech be always with grace v.* 6. Let all your discourse be as becomes Christians—savoury, discreet, seasonable." Though it be not always of grace, it must be always with grace. It must be in a Christian manner: *seasoned with salt.* Grace is the salt which seasons our discourse, makes it savoury, and keeps it from corrupting. *That you may know how to answer every man.* We have need of a great deal of wisdom and grace to give proper answers to every man, particularly in answering the questions and objections of adversaries against our religion, giving the reasons of our faith.

Verses 7–18

I. Concerning Tychicus, *v.* 7. By him this epistle was sent. He knew they would be glad to hear how it fared with him. The churches cannot but be concerned for good ministers and desirous to know their state. *A beloved brother and faithful minister.* Faithfulness in any one is truly lovely, and renders him worthy our affection and esteem. *And a fellow-servant in the Lord.* It adds much to the beauty and strength of the gospel ministry when ministers are thus loving one to another. *Whom I have sent unto you for the same purpose, that he might know your estate, and comfort your hearts, v.* 8. He was as willing to hear from them as they could be to hear from him. It is a great comfort to have the mutual concern of fellow-christians.

II. Concerning Onesimus (*v.* 9): *With Onesimus, a faithful and beloved brother, who is one of you.* This was he whom Paul had begotten in his bonds, Philem. 10. He was converted at Rome, whither he had fled from his master's service. Though he was a poor servant, and had been a bad man, yet, being now a convert, Paul calls him a *faithful and beloved brother.* The meanest circumstance of life, and greatest wickedness of former life, make no difference in the spiritual relation among sincere Christians.

III. *Aristarchus, a fellow-prisoner.* Those who join in services and sufferings should be thereby engaged to one another in holy love.

JAMIESON, FAUSSET, BROWN

with thanksgiving—for everything, whether joyful, or sorrowful, mercies temporal and spiritual, national, family, and individual (I Cor. 14:17; Phil. 4:6; I Thess. 5:18). **3. for us**—myself and Timothy (ch. 1:1). **a door of utterance**—Translate, "a door for the word." Not as in Ephesians 6:19, where power of "utterance" is his petition. Here it is an opportunity for *preaching the word,* which would be best afforded by his release from prison (I Cor. 16:9; II Cor. 2:12; Philemon 22; Rev. 3:8). **to speak**—so that we may speak. **the mystery of Christ**—(Ch. 1:27). **for which . . . also**—*on account of which I am* (not only "an ambassador," Eph. 6: 20, but) ALSO in *bonds.* **4.** ALFORD thinks that Paul asks their prayers for his release as if it were the *only* way by which he could "make it (the Gospel) manifest" as he ought. But while this is *included* in their subject of prayer, Philippians 1:12, 13, written somewhat later in his imprisonment, clearly shows that "a door for the word" could be opened, and was opened, for its *manifestation,* even while he remained imprisoned (cf. II Tim. 2:9). **5.** (*Notes,* Eph. 5:15, 16.) **in wisdom**—practical Christian prudence. **them . . . without**—Those not in the Christian brotherhood (I Cor. 5:12; I Thess. 4:12). The brethren, through love, will make allowances for an indiscreet act or word of a brother; the world will make none. Therefore be the more on your guard in your intercourse with the latter, lest you be a stumbling block to their conversion. **redeeming the time**—The *Greek* expresses, buying up for yourselves, and *buying off* from worldly vanities the *opportunity,* whenever it is afforded you, of good to yourselves and others. *"Forestall the opportunity,* i.e., to buy up an article out of the market, so as to make the largest profit from it" [CONYBEARE and HOWSON]. **6. with grace**—*Greek,* "IN grace" as its element (ch. 3:16; Eph. 4:29). Contrast the case of those "of the world" who "therefore *speak of the world*" (I John 4:5). Even the smallest leaf of the believer should be full of the sap of the Holy Spirit (Jer. 17:7, 8). His conversation should be cheerful without levity, serious without gloom. Cf. Luke 4:22; John 7:46, as to Jesus' speech. **seasoned with salt**—i.e., the *savor* of fresh and lively spiritual wisdom and earnestness, excluding all "corrupt communication," and also tasteless *insipidity* (Matt. 5:13; Mark 9:50; Eph. 4: 29). Cf. all the sacrifices *seasoned with salt* (Lev. 2:13). Not far from Colosse, in Phrygia, there was a salt lake, which gives to the image here the more appropriateness. **how ye ought to answer every man**—(I Pet. 3:15). **7. Tychicus**—(*Note,* Eph. 6:2). **who is a beloved brother**—rather, "the beloved brother"; the article "the" marks him as *well known to them.* **8. for the same purpose**—*Greek,* "for this very purpose." **that he might know your estate**—Translate, "that he may know your state": answering to vs. 7. So one very old MS. and *Vulgate* read. But the oldest MSS. and the old Latin versions, "that YE may know OUR state." However, the latter reading seems likely to have crept in from Ephesians 6:22. Paul was the more anxious to know the state of the Colossians, on account of the seductions to which they were exposed from false teachers; owing to which he had "great conflict for" them (ch. 2:1). **comfort your hearts**—distressed as ye are by my imprisonment, as well as by your own trials. **9. Onesimus**—the slave mentioned in the Epistle to Philemon 10, 16, "a brother beloved." **a faithful . . . brother**—rather, "the faithful brother," he being known to the Colossians as the slave of Philemon, their fellow townsman and fellow Christian. **one of you**—belonging to your city. **They shall make known unto you all things**—*Greek,* "all the things here." This substantial repetition of "all my state shall Tychicus declare unto you," strongly favors the reading of *English Version* in vs. 8, "that *he* might (may) know your state," as it is unlikely the same thing should be stated *thrice.* **10. Aristarchus**—a Macedonian of Thessalonica (Acts 27:2), who was dragged into the theater at Ephesus, during the tumult with Gaius, they being "Paul's companions in travel." He accompanied Paul to Asia (Acts 20:4), and subsequently (Acts 27:2) to Rome. He was now at Rome with Paul (cf. Philemon 23: 24). As he is here spoken of as Paul's "fellow prisoner," but in Philemon 24 as Paul's "fellow laborer"; and vice versa, Epaphras in Philemon 23, as his "fellow prisoner," but here (ch. 1:7) "fellow servant," MEYER in ALFORD, conjectures that Paul's friends voluntarily shared his imprisonment by turns, Aristarchus being his fellow prisoner when he wrote to the Colossians, Epaphras when he wrote to Philemon. The *Greek* for "fellow prisoner" is literally, *fellow captive,* an image from prisoners

ADAM CLARKE

will know when, and where, and how to apply it. *With thanksgiving.* Being always grateful to God, who has called you into such a state of salvation, and affords you such abundant means and opportunities to glorify Him.

3. *Praying also for us.* Let the success and spread of the gospel be ever dear to you; and neglect not to pray fervently to God that it may have free course, run, and be glorified. *A door of utterance.* The word *thyra,* which commonly signifies a *door,* or suchlike entrance into a house or passage through a wall, is often used metaphorically for an "entrance" to any business, "occasion" or "opportunity" to commence or perform any particular work. *The mystery of Christ.* The gospel, which had been hidden from all former times, and which revealed that purpose long hidden in the divine councils, that the Gentiles should be called to enjoy the same privileges with the Jews. *For which I am also in bonds.* He was suffering under Jewish malice, and for preaching this very mystery; for they could not bear to hear announced, as from heaven, that the Gentiles, whom they considered eternally shut out from any participation of the divine favor, should be made fellow heirs with them of the grace of life; much less could they bear to hear that they were about to be reprobated and the Gentiles elected in their place. It was for asserting these things that they persecuted Paul at Jerusalem, so that to save his life he was obliged to appeal to Caesar; and being taken to Rome, he was detained a prisoner till his case was fully heard; and he was a prisoner at Rome on this very account when he wrote this Epistle to the Colossians.

4. *That I may make it manifest.* It was a mystery, and he wished to make it *manifest*—to lay it open, and make all men see it.

5. *Walk in wisdom.* Act wisely and prudently in reference to them who are *without*—who yet continue unbelieving Gentiles or persecuting Jews.

6. *Let your speech be alway with grace, seasoned with salt.* Let all your conversation be such as may tend to exemplify and recommend Christianity; let it not only be holy, but wise, gracious, and intelligent. A harsh method of proposing or defending the doctrines of Christianity only serves to repel men from those doctrines, and from the way of salvation. *Salt,* from its use in preserving good from corruption, and rendering it both savory and wholesome, has always been made the emblem of wisdom. *How ye ought to answer every man.* That your discourse may be so judiciously managed that you may discern how to treat the prejudices and meet the objections of both Jews and Gentiles.

7. *All my state shall Tychicus.* See the note on Eph. vi. 21. Tychicus well knew the apostle's zeal and perseverance in preaching the gospel, his sufferings on that account, his success in converting both Jews and Gentiles, and the converts which were made in Caesar's household.

8. *That he might know your estate.* Instead of "that he may know your affairs," read "that you may know our affairs," which is probably the true reading. Tychicus was sent to them, not to know their affairs, but with Onesimus, to carry this Epistle and make the apostle's state known to them, and comfort their hearts by the good news which he brought. The next verse confirms this meaning.

9. *With Onesimus . . . who is one of you.* Onesimus was a native of some part of Phrygia, if not of Colossae itself; and being lately converted to the Christian faith by the instrumentality of the apostle, he would be able, on this account, to give them satisfactory information concerning the apostle's state, which would be doubly acceptable to them as he was their countryman. See the Epistle to Philemon.

10. *Aristarchus my fellow prisoner.* Concerning Aristarchus, see Acts xix. 29; xx. 4; and xxvii. 2 Aristarchus and Epaphras are mentioned as saluters in this Epistle, and in that to Philemon written at the same time.

MATTHEW HENRY

IV. *Marcus, sister's son to Barnabas,* who wrote the gospel which bears his name.

If he come unto you receive him. Paul had a quarrel with Barnabas upon the account of this Mark, yet Paul is not only reconciled to him himself, but recommends him to the respect of the churches. If men have been guilty of a fault, it must not be always remembered against them. We must forget as well as forgive.

V. Here is one who is called *Jesus,* which is the Greek name for the Hebrew *Joshua. Who is called Justus. These are my fellow-labourers unto the kingdom of God, who have been a comfort unto me.* One is his fellow-servant, another his fellow-prisoner, and all his fellow-workers.

VI. *Epaphras* (*v.* 12). He is *one of you; he salutes you. Always labouring fervently for you in prayers.* Epaphras has learned of Paul to be much in prayer for his friends. We must be earnest in prayer, not only for ourselves, but for others also. *That you may stand perfect and complete in all the will of God.* To stand perfect and complete in the will of God is what we should earnestly desire both for ourselves and others.

He had a great zeal for them: "*I bear him record.*" And his zeal extended to all about them: to *those who are in Laodicea and Hierapolis.*

VII. *Luke* is another here mentioned, whom he calls the *beloved physician.* This is he who wrote the Gospel and Acts, and was Paul's companion.

JAMIESON, FAUSSET, BROWN

taken in warfare, Christians being "fellow soldiers" (Phil. 2:25; Philemon 2), whose warfare is "the good fight of faith." **Mark**—John Mark (Acts 12: 12, 25); the Evangelist according to tradition. **sister's son**—rather, "cousin," or "kinsman to Barnabas"; the latter being the better known is introduced to designate Mark. The relationship naturally accounts for Barnabas' selection of Mark as his companion when otherwise qualified; and also for Mark's mother's house at Jerusalem being the place of resort of Christians there (Acts 12:12). The family belonged to *Cyprus* (Acts 4:36); this accounts for Barnabas' choice of Cyprus as the first station on their journey (Acts 13:4), and for Mark's accompanying them readily so far, it being the country of his family; and for Paul's rejecting him at the second journey for not having gone further than Perga, in Pamphylia, but having gone thence home to his mother at Jerusalem (Matt. 10:37) on the first journey (Acts 13:13). **touching whom**—viz., Mark. **ye received commandments**—possibly *before* the writing of this Epistle; or the "commandments" were *verbal* by Tychicus, and *accompanying this letter,* since the *past* tense was used by the ancients (where we use the present) in relation to the time which it would be when the letter was read by the Colossians. Thus (Philemon 19), "I have written," for "I write." The substance of them was, "If he come unto you, receive him." Paul's rejection of him on his second missionary journey, because he had turned back at Perga on the first journey (Acts 13:13; 15:37-39), had caused an alienation between himself and Barnabas. Christian love soon healed the breach; for here he implies his restored confidence in Mark, makes honorable allusion to Barnabas, and desires that those at Colosse who had regarded Mark in consequence of that past error with suspicion, should now "receive" him with kindness. Colosse is only about 110 miles from Perga, and less than 20 from the confines of Pisidia, through which province Paul and Barnabas preached on their return during the same journey. Hence, though Paul had not personally visited the Colossian Church, they knew of the past unfaithfulness of Mark; and needed this recommendation of him, after the temporary cloud on him, so as to receive him, now that he was about to visit them as an evangelist. Again, in Paul's last imprisonment, he, for the last time, speaks of Mark (II Tim. 4:11). **11. Justus**—i.e., *righteous;* a common name among the Jews; *Hebrew, tzadik* (Acts 1:23). **of the circumcision**—This implies that Epaphras, Luke, and Demas (vss. 12, 14) were *not* of the circumcision. This agrees with Luke's Gentile name (the same as Lucanus), and the Gentile aspect of his Gospel. **These only . . .**—viz., of the Jews. For the Jewish teachers were generally opposed to the apostle of the Gentiles (Phil. 1:15). Epaphras, etc., were also fellow laborers, but Gentiles. **unto**—i.e., in promoting the Gospel kingdom. **which have been**—*Greek,* "which have been *made,*" or "have become," i.e., *inasmuch as* they have become a comfort to me. The *Greek* implies *comfort* in forensic dangers; a different *Greek* word expresses comfort in domestic affliction [BENGEL]. **12. Christ**—The oldest MSS. add "Jesus." **labouring fervently**—As the *Greek,* is the same, translate, "striving earnestly" (*Note,* ch. 1: 29; 2:1), lit., *striving as in the agony of a contest.* **in prayers**—Translate as *Greek,* "in *his* prayers." **complete**—The oldest MSS. read, "fully assured." It is translated, "fully persuaded," Rom. 4:21; 14:5. In the expression "perfect," he refers to what he has already said, ch. 1:28; 2:2; 3:14. "Perfect" implies the attainment of the *full maturity* of a Christian. BENGEL joins "in all the will of God" with "stand." **13. a great zeal**—The oldest MSS. and *Vulgate* have "much *labor.*" **for you**—lest you should be seduced (ch. 2:4); a motive why you should be anxious for yourselves. **them that are in Laodicea . . . Hierapolis**—churches probably founded by Epaphras, as the Church in Colosse was. Laodicea, called from Laodice, queen of Antiochus II, on the river Lycus, was, according to the subscription to I Timothy, "the chiefest city of Phrygia Pacatiana." All the three cities were destroyed by an earthquake in A.D. 62 [TACITUS, *Annals,* 14. 27] Hierapolis was six Roman miles north of Laodicea. **14.** It is conjectured that Luke "the beloved physician" (the same as the Evangelist), may have first become connected with Paul in professionally attending on him in the sickness under which he labored in Phrygia and Galatia (in which latter place he was detained by sickness), in the early part of that journey wherein Luke first is found in his company (Acts 16:10; cf. *Note,* Gal. 4:13). Thus the allusion to his medical profession is appropriate in writing to

ADAM CLARKE

Marcus. See the account of this person, Acts xv. 39. Though there had been some difference between the apostle and this Mark, yet from this, and 2 Tim. iv. 11, we find that they were fully reconciled, and that Mark was very useful to Paul in the work of the ministry.

ALBERT BARNES:

"And Marcus, sister's son to Barnabas." John Mark, in relation to whom Paul and Barnabas had formerly disagreed so much as to cause a separation between Barnabas and Paul. The ground of the disagreement was that Barnabas wished to take him, probably on account of relationship, with them in their travels; Paul was unwilling to take him because he had, on one occasion, departed from them. They afterward became reconciled and Paul mentions Mark here with affection. He sent for him when he sent Tychicus to Ephesus, and it seems that he had come to him in obedience to his request (2 Tim. 4:11). Mark had probably become more decided, and Paul did not harbor unkind and unforgiving feelings toward anyone. "Touching whom ye received commandments." What these directions were and how they were communicated, whether verbally or by writing, is now unknown. It was, not improbably, on some occasion when Paul was with them. He refers to it here in order that they might know distinctly whom he meant. "If he come to you, receive him." In Philem. 24, Mark is mentioned as a "fellow laborer" of Paul. It would seem probable, therefore, that he was not a prisoner. Paul here intimates that he was about to leave Rome, and he enjoins it on the Colossians to receive him kindly. This injunction may have been necessary, as the Colossians may have been aware of the breach between him and Paul and may have been disposed to regard him with suspicion. Paul retained no malice and now commended in the warmest manner, one from whom he was formerly constrained to separate.
—*Popular Commentary*

11. *Jesus, which is called Justus. Jesus,* Joshua or Jehoshua, was his name among his countrymen the Jews; *Justus* was the name which he bore among the Greeks and Romans. *These only.* That is, only Aristarchus, Marcus, and Jesus Justus, who were formerly Jews or proselytes; for they were *of the circumcision,* and assisted the apostle in preaching the gospel.

12. *Epaphras, who is one of you.* A native of some part of Phrygia, and probably of Colossae itself. *A servant of Christ.* A minister of the gospel. *Labouring fervently for you.* "Agonizing"; very properly expressed by our translators, *labouring fervently. That ye may stand perfect and complete.* That you may stand firm, perfectly instructed, and fully persuaded of the truth of those doctrines which have been taught you as the revealed will of God: this I believe to be the meaning of the apostle. Instead of complete or "filled up," almost all the MSS. of the Alexandrian recension, which are considered the most authentic and correct, have "that ye may be fully persuaded."

13. *He hath a great zeal for you.* Instead of "much zeal," some MSS., versions, and fathers, read "much labor"; they are here nearly of the same meaning, though the latter appears to be the better and genuine reading. *Them that are in Laodicea, and them in Hierapolis.* These were both cities of Phrygia, between which Colossae was situated. The latter was called *Hierapolis,* or the "holy city," from the multitude of its temples. Apollo, Diana, Aesculapius, and Hygeia were all worshipped here, as appears by the coins of this city still extant.

14. *Luke, the beloved physician.* This is generally supposed to be the same with Luke the Evangelist.

MATTHEW HENRY

VIII. *Demas.* We read (2 Tim. iv. 10), *Demas hath forsaken me, having loved this present world.* Many who have made a great figure in profession, and gained a great name among Christians, have yet shamefully apostatized.

IX. The *brethren in Laodicea* living in the neighbourhood of Colosse: and Paul sends salutations to them, and orders that this epistle should be read in the church of the Laodiceans (*v.* 16). And some think Paul sent another epistle at this time to Laodicea: *And that you likewise read the epistle from Laodicea.* If so, that epistle is now lost.

X. *Nymphas* is mentioned (*v.* 15) as one who lived at Colosse, and had a church in his house.

XI. Concerning *Archippus.* They are bidden to admonish him to mind his work as a minister, to *take heed to it, and to fulfil it.* The ministry we have received is a great honour; for it is *received in the Lord,* and is by his appointment. The people may put their ministers in mind of their duty, and excite them to it: *Say to Archippus, Take heed to the ministry.*

XII. Concerning himself (*v.* 18): *The salutation of me Paul. Remember my bonds.* These words he wrote with his own hand. "*Grace be with you.* The favour of God, and all good, be with you, and be your portion."

JAMIESON, FAUSSET, BROWN

men of Phrygia. Luke ministered to Paul in his last imprisonment (II Tim. 4:11). **Demas**—included among his "fellow laborers" (Philemon 24), but afterwards a deserter from him through love of this world (II Tim. 4:10). He alone has here no honorable or descriptive epithet attached to his name. Perhaps, already, his real character was betraying itself. **15. Nymphas**—of Laodicea. **church . . . in his house**—So old MSS. and *Vulgate* read. The oldest read, "THEIR house"; and one MS., "HER house," which makes Nymphas a woman. **16. the epistle from Laodicea**—viz., the Epistle which I wrote to the Laodiceans, and which you will get *from* them on applying to them. Not the Epistle to the Ephesians. See INTRODUCTIONS to the Epistles to the Ephesians and Colossians. The Epistles from the apostles were publicly read in the church assemblies. IGNATIUS, ad *Ephesum* 12; POLYCARP, *ad Philippenses,* 3. 11, 12; CLEMENT, *ad Corinthios* 1. 47; I Thessalonians 5:27; Revelation 1:3, "Blessed is *he* that *readeth,* and *they that hear.*" Thus, they and the Gospels were put on a level with the Old Testament, which was similarly read (Deut. 31:11). The Holy Spirit inspired Paul to write, besides those extant, other Epistles which He saw necessary for *that* day, and for particular churches; and which were not so for the Church of all ages and places. It is possible that as the Epistle to the Colossians was to be read for the edification of other churches besides that of Colosse; so the Epistle to the Ephesians was to be read in various churches besides Ephesus, and that Laodicea was the last of such churches before Colosse, whence he might designate the Epistle to the Ephesians here as "the Epistle *from* Laodicea." But it is equally possible that the Epistle meant was one to the Laodiceans themselves. **17. say to Archippus**—*The Colossians* (not merely the clergy, but the laymen) are directed, "Speak *ye* to Archippus." This proves that Scripture belongs to the laity as well as the clergy; and that laymen may profitably admonish the clergy in particular cases when they do so in meekness. BENGEL suggests that Archippus was perhaps prevented from going to the Church assembly by weak health or age. The word, "fulfil," accords with his ministry being near its close (ch. 1:25; cf. Philemon 2). However, "fulfil" may mean, as in II Timothy 4:5, "*make full proof of* thy ministry." "Give all diligence to follow it out fully"; a monition perhaps needed by Archippus. **in the Lord**—The element in which every work of the Christian, and especially the Christian minister, is to be done (vs. 7; I Cor. 7:39; Phil. 4:2). **18.** Paul's autograph salutation (so I Cor. 16:21; II Thess. 3:17), attesting that the preceding letter, though written by an amanuensis, is from himself. **Remember my bonds**—Already in this chapter he had mentioned his "bonds" (vs. 3), and again vs. 10, an incentive why they should love and pray (vs. 3) for him; and still more, that they should, in reverential obedience to his monitions in this Epistle, shrink from the false teaching herein stigmatized, remembering what a conflict (ch. 2:1) he had in their behalf amidst his *bonds.* "When we read of his chains, we should not forget that they moved over the paper as he wrote; his [right] hand was chained to the [left hand of the] soldier who kept him" [ALFORD]. **Grace be with you**—*Greek,* "THE grace" which every Christian enjoys in some degree, and which flows from God in Christ by the Holy Ghost (Titus 3:15; Heb. 13:25)

ADAM CLARKE

15. *Salute . . . Nymphas, and the church which is in his house.* This person, and his whole family, which probably was very numerous, appear to have received the gospel; and it seems that, for their benefit and that of his neighbors, he had opened his house for the worship of God. In those primitive times there were no consecrated places, for it was supposed that the simple setting apart of any place for the worship of God was a sufficient consecration.

16. *Cause that it be read also in the church of the Laodiceans.* That is: Let a copy be taken and sent to them, that it may be read there also. This appears to have been a regular custom in the apostolic Church. *That ye likewise read the epistle from Laodicea.* Some suppose that this was an epistle sent from Laodicea to the apostle, which he now sent by Aristarchus to the Colossians, that they might peruse it. Others think that the Epistle to the Ephesians is the epistle in question, and that it was originally directed to them, and not to the Ephesians. But others, equally learned, think that there was an epistle, different from that to the Ephesians, sent by Paul to the Laodiceans, which is now lost.

17. *Say to Archippus.* Who this person was we cannot tell; there have been various conjectures concerning him. Some think he was bishop, or overseer of the church at Colossae, in the absence of Epaphras.

18. *The salutation by the hand of me Paul.* The preceding part of the Epistle was written by a scribe, from the mouth of the apostle; this, and what follows, was written by the hand of Paul himself. A similar distinction we find in 1 Cor. xvi. 21 and in 2 Thess. iii. 17; and this, it seems, was the means by which the apostle authenticated every Epistle which he sent to the different churches. *Remember my bonds.* See what proof you have of the truth of the gospel; I am in bonds on this account. I suffer patiently, yea, exult in the Lord Jesus, so perfectly am I upheld by the grace of the gospel. *Remember my bonds,* and take courage. How eloquent were these concluding words! *Amen.* This is omitted by the most ancient and correct MSS.

THE FIRST EPISTLE TO THE THESSALONIANS

I. Introduction (1:1-10)
A. Salutation (1:1)
B. General thanksgiving (1:2-10)
1. The reason of thanksgiving (1:2, 3)
a. "Work of faith" (1:2a)
b. "Labor of love" (1:2b)
c. "Patience of hope (1:2c, 3)
2. The demonstration of the reason (1:4-9a)
3. The reason of the demonstration (1:9b, 10)
a. "Ye turned" (1:9b)
b. "To serve" (1:9b)
c. "To wait" (1:10)

II. The work of faith "ye turned" (2:1-20)
A. The work of faith—"ye turned" (2:1-12)
1. Not vain (2:1)
2. The ministry producing (2:2-12)
B. The labor of love—"to serve" (2:13-16)
1. Reception of the Word (2:13)
2. Service and suffering (2:14-16)
C. The patience of hope—"to wait" (2:17-20)
1. The separation (2:17, 18)
2. The advent (2:19, 20)

III. The labor of love—"to serve" (3:1-4:12)
A. The labor of love—"to serve" (3:1-10)
1. The sending of Timothy (3:1-5)
2. The comforting report (3:6-8)
3. Thanksgiving and prayer (3:9-10)
B. The patience of hope—"to wait" (3:11-13)
1. Separation (3:11, 12)
2. The advent (3:13)
C. The work of faith—"ye turned" (4:1-12)
1. The consequent walk—personal (4:1-8)
2. Love of the brethren (4:9-10)
3. Toward them without (4:11, 12)

IV. The patience of hope—"to wait" (4:13-5:22)
A. The patience of hope—"to wait" (4:13-18)
1. The 'fallen asleep' at His coming (4:13-15)
2. The glorious program (4:16, 17)
3. The injunction to comfort (4:18)
B. The work of faith—"ye turned" (5:1-11)
1. The Day of the Lord (5:1-3)
2. "Ye brethren" (5:4-11)
C. The labor of love—"to serve" (5:12-22)
1. Submission to teachers (5:12, 13a)
2. Mutual relationships (5:13b-15)
3. General injunctions (5:16-22)

V. Conclusion (5:23-28)
A. The final desire of assurance (5:23-24)
B. Personal words (5:25-28)

Thessalonica was formerly the metropolis of Macedonia. The apostle Paul, being directed after an extraordinary manner to preach the gospel in Macedonia (Acts 16:9, 10), went from Troas to Samothracia, thence to Neapolis, and then to Philippi, where he had good success in his ministry, but met with hard usage, being cast into prison with Silas, from which being wonderfully delivered, they comforted the brethren there and departed. Passing through Amphipolis and Apollonia, they came to Thessalonica, where the apostle planted a church. But a tumult being raised in the city, Paul and Silas, for their safety, were sent away by night unto Berea. Afterward Paul was conducted to Athens, leaving Silas and Timothy behind him. When they came, Timothy was sent to Thessalonica to inquire after their welfare and to establish them in the faith (1 Thess. 3:2), and was sent again, together with Silas, to visit the churches in Macedonia. So that Paul, being left at Athens alone (1 Thess. 3:1), departed thence to Corinth, where he continued a year and a half, and then he wrote this epistle to the church of Christ at Thessalonica, which, though it is placed after the other epistles of this apostle, is supposed to be first in time of all Paul's epistles.

MATTHEW HENRY

CHAPTER 1

Verse 1

I. The inscription. The persons from whom this epistle came. Paul was the writer of this epistle. He joins Silvanus (or Silas) and Timotheus with himself.

The persons to whom this epistle is written, the church of the Thessalonians, the converted Jews and Gentiles. This church is said to *be in God the Father and in the Lord Jesus Christ.* The Gentiles among them were turned to God from idols, and the Jews among them believed Jesus to be the promised Messias. All of them were devoted and dedicated to God the Father and the Lord Jesus Christ.

JAMIESON, FAUSSET, BROWN

CHAPTER 1

Vss. 1-10. Address: Salutation: His Prayerful Thanksgiving for their Faith, Hope, and Love. Their First Reception of the Gospel, and their Good Influence on all Around. **1. Paul**—He does not add "an apostle," because in their case, as in that of the Philippians (*Note,* Philippians 1:1), his apostolic authority needs not any substantiation. He writes familiarly as to faithful friends, not but that his apostleship was recognized among them (ch. 2:6). On the other hand, in writing to the Galatians, among whom some had called in question his apostleship, he strongly asserts it in the superscription. An undesigned propriety in the Epistles, evincing genuineness. **Silvanus**—a "chief man among the brethren" (Acts 15:22), and a "prophet" (vs. 32), and one of the deputies who carried the decree of the Jerusalem council to Antioch. His age and position cause him to be placed before "Timothy," then a youth (Acts 16:1; I Timothy 4:12). Silvanus (the Gentile expanded form of "Silas") is called in I Pet. 5:12, "a faithful brother" (cf. II Cor. 1:19). They both aided in planting the Thessalonian Church, and are therefore included in the address. This, the first of Paul's Epistles, as being written before various evils crept into the churches, is without the censures found in other Epistles. So realizing was their Christian faith, that they were able hourly to look for the Lord Jesus. **unto the church**—not merely as in the Epistles to Romans, Ephesians, Colossians, Philippians, "to the saints," or "the faithful at Thessalonica." **in**—implying *vital union.* **God the Father**—This marks that they were no longer *heathen.* **the Lord Jesus Christ**—This marks that they were not *Jews,* but Christians. **Grace be unto you, and peace**—that ye may have in

ADAM CLARKE

CHAPTER 1

1. *Paul, and Silvanus, and Timotheus.* Though Paul himself dictated this letter, yet he joins the names of Silas and Timothy, because they had been with him at Thessalonica, and were well-known there.

And Silvanus. This was certainly the same as Silas, who was Paul's companion in all his journeys through Asia Minor and Greece; see Acts xv. 22; xvi. 19; xvii. 4, 10. The apostle took him and Timothy with him into Macedonia, and they continued at Berea when the apostle went from thence to Athens; from this place Paul sent for them to come to him speedily, and though it is not said that they came while he was at Athens, yet it is most probable that they did; after which, having sent them to Thessalonica, he proceeded to Corinth, where they afterwards rejoined him, and from whence he wrote this Epistle.

MATTHEW HENRY

II. The salutation. *Grace be with you, and peace from God our Father and the Lord Jesus Christ.* The free grace or favour of God is the spring of all the peace and prosperity we can enjoy. As all good comes from God, so no good can be hoped for by sinners but from God in Christ. And the best good may be expected from God as our Father for the sake of Christ.

Verses 2–5

I. The apostle begins with thanksgiving to God. Being about to mention the things that were matter of joy to him, and highly praiseworthy in them, he chooses to do this by way of thanksgiving to God. Even when we do not actually give thanks to God by our words, we should have a grateful sense of God's goodness upon our minds.

II. He joined prayer with his praise or thanksgiving. When we give thanks for any benefit we receive we should join prayer. As there is much that we ought to be thankful for, so there is much occasion of constant prayer for further supplies of good.

III. The particulars for which he was so thankful to God.

1. The saving benefits bestowed on them. (1) Their faith and their work of faith. Their faith was a true and living faith, because a working faith. Wherever there is a true faith, it will work. (2) Their love and the labour of love. Love will show itself by labour. (3) Their hope and the patience of hope. Wherever there is a well-grounded hope of eternal life, it will appear by the exercise of patience.

2. The apostle not only mentions these three cardinal graces, faith, hope, and love, but also takes notice of the sincerity of them: being in the *sight of God even our Father.* Then is the work of faith, or labour of love, or patience of hope, sincere, when it is done as under the eye of God.

He mentions the fountain whence these graces flow, God's electing love: *Knowing, brethren beloved, your election of God, v.* 4. Thus he runs up these streams to the fountain, and that was God's eternal election. He calls them, *brethren beloved.* It is a good reason why we should *love one another,* because we are all beloved of God. The election of God is of his own good pleasure and mere grace, not for the sake of any merit in those who are chosen. The election of God may be known by the fruits thereof.

3. Another ground of the apostle's thanksgiving is the success of his ministry among them. He was thankful on his own account as well as theirs, that he had not laboured in vain. Their ready entertainment of the gospel he preached to them was an evidence of their being elected and beloved of God. The gospel came to them also not in word only, but in power. It did not merely tickle the ear and please the fancy, but it affected their hearts: a divine power went along with it. By this we may know our election, if we not only speak of the things of God by rote as parrots, but feel the influence of these things in our hearts. It came in the Holy Ghost. Unless the Spirit of God accompany the word of God it will be to us but as a dead letter; and the letter killeth, it is the Spirit that giveth life. The gospel came to them in much assurance. They were fully convinced of the truth of it. They were willing to leave all for Christ, and to venture their souls upon the verity of the gospel revelation. The Thessalonians thus knew what manner of men the apostle and his fellow-labourers were among them, and what they did for their sake.

Verses 6–10

The evidence of the apostle's success among the Thessalonians.

I. They were careful to imitate the good examples of the apostles and ministers of Christ, *v.* 6. The Thessalonians showed a conscientious care to be followers of them. Herein they became also followers of the Lord, who is the perfect example we must strive to imitate.

JAMIESON, FAUSSET, BROWN

God that *favor* and *peace* which men withhold [ANSELM]. This is the salutation in all the Epistles of Paul, except the three pastoral ones, which have "grace, mercy, and peace." Some of the oldest MSS. support, others omit the clause following, "from God our Father and the Lord Jesus Christ." It may have crept in from I Corinthians 1:3; II Corinthians 1:2. **2.** (Rom. 1:9; II Tim. 1:3.) The structure of the sentences in this and the following verses, each successive sentence repeating with greater fulness the preceding, characteristically marks Paul's abounding love and thankfulness in respect to his converts, as if he were seeking by words heaped on words to convey some idea of his exuberant feelings towards them. **We**—I, Silvanus, and Timotheus. Romans 1:9 supports ALFORD in translating, "making mention of you in our prayers without ceasing" (vs. 3). Thus, "without ceasing," in the second clause, answers in parallelism to "always," in the first. **3. work of fatih**—*the working reality of your faith;* its alacrity in *receiving* the truth, and in *evincing* itself by its fruits. Not an otiose assent; but a *realizing, working faith;* not "in word only," but in *one* continuous chain of "work" (singular, not plural, *works*), vss. 5-10; James 2:22. So "the work of faith" in I Thessalonians 1:11 implies its *perfect development* (cf. Jas. 1:4). The other governing substantives similarly mark respectively the characteristic manifestation of the grace which follows each in the genitive. *Faith, love,* and *hope,* are the three great Christian graces (ch. 5:8; I Cor. 13:13). **labour of love**—The *Greek* implies *toil,* or *troublesome labor,* which we are stimulated by love to bear (ch. 2:9); Rev. 2:2). For instances of self-denying *labors of love,* see Acts 20:35; Romans 16:12. Not here *ministerial* labors. Those who shun trouble for others, *love* little (cf. Heb. 6:10). **patience**—Translate, "*endurance* of hope"; the *persevering endurance* of trials which flows from "hope." Romans 15:4 shows that "patience" also nourishes "hope." **hope in our Lord Jesus**—lit., "hope *of* our Lord Jesus," viz., of His coming (vs. 10): a hope that looked forward beyond all present things for the manifestation of Christ. **in the sight of God**—Your "faith, hope, and love" were not merely such as would pass for genuine *before men,* but "in the sight of God," the Searcher of hearts [GOMARUS]. Things are really what they are before God. BENGEL takes this clause with "remembering." Whenever we *pray,* we *remember before God* your faith, hope, and love. But its separation from "remembering" in the order, and its connection with "your . . . faith . . ." make me to prefer the former view. **and . . .**—The *Greek* implies, "in the sight of *Him who is* [at once] God and our Father." **4. Knowing**—Forasmuch as we know. **your election of God**—The *Greek* is rather, "beloved by God"; so Romans 1:7; II Thessalonians 2:13. "Your election" means that *God has elected you* as individual believers to eternal life (Rom. 11:5, 7; Col. 3:12; II Thess. 2:13). **5. our gospel**—viz., the Gospel which we preached. **came**—*Greek,* "was made," viz., by God, its Author and Sender. God's having made our preaching among you to be attended with such "power," is the proof that you are "elect of God" (vs. 4). **in power**—in the efficacy of the Holy Spirit clothing us with power (see end of verse; Acts 1:8; 4:33; 6:5, 8) in preaching the Gospel, and making it in you the power of God unto salvation (Rom. 1:16). As "power" produces *faith;* so "the Holy Ghost," *love;* and "much assurance" (Col. 2:2, *full persuasion*), *hope* (Heb. 6:11), resting on faith (Heb. 10:22). So *faith, love,* and *hope* (vs. 3). **as ye know**—answering to the "knowing," i.e., *as* WE *know* (vs. 4) your character as *the elect of God,* so YE *know* ours as *preachers.* **for your sake**—The purpose herein indicated is not so much that of the apostles, as that of *God.* "You know what *God enabled us to be . . . how mighty in preaching the word* . . . for your sakes . . . thereby proving that He had *chosen* (vs. 4) you for His own" [ALFORD]. I think, from ch. 2:10-12, that, in "what manner of men we were among you," besides the *power in preaching,* there is included also Paul's and his fellow missionaries' whole *conduct* which confirmed their preaching; and in this sense, the "for your sake" will mean "in order to win you." This, though not the sole, yet would be a strong, motive to holy circumspection, viz., so as to win those without (Col. 4:5; cf. I Cor. 9:19-23). **6. And ye**—answering to "*For our* Gospel," vs. 5. **followers**—*Greek,* "imitators." The Thessalonians in their turn became "ensamples" (vs. 7) for others to *imitate.* **of the Lord**—who was the apostle of the Father, and taught the word, which He brought from heaven, under adversities [BENGEL]. This was the point in which they imitated Him and His apos-

ADAM CLARKE

3. *Your work of faith.* This verse contains a very high character of the believers at Thessalonica. They had *faith,* not speculative and indolent, but true, sound, and operative; their faith worked. They had *love,* not that gazed at and became enamored of the perfections of God, but such a love as labored with faith to fulfill the whole will of God. Faith worked; but love, because it can do more, did more, and therefore labored—worked energetically, to promote the glory of God and the salvation of men. They had *hope;* not an idle, cold, heartless expectation of future good, from which they felt no excitement, and for which they could give no reason, but such a hope as produced a satisfying expectation of a future life and state of blessedness, the reality of which faith had descried, and love anticipated.

4. *Knowing . . . your election of God.* Being assured, from the doctrine which I have delivered to you, and which God has confirmed by various miracles, and gifts of the Holy Spirit, that He has chosen and called the Gentiles to the same privileges to which He chose and called the Jews; and that, as they have rejected the offers of the gospel, God has now elected the Gentiles in their stead. This is the election which the Thessalonians knew; and of which the apostle treats at large in his Epistle to the Romans, and also in his Epistles to the Galatians and Ephesians. No irrespective, unconditional, eternal, and personal election to everlasting glory is meant by the apostle.

5. *For our gospel.* That is, the glad tidings of salvation by Jesus Christ and of your being elected to enjoy all the privileges to which the Jews were called, without being obliged to submit to circumcision or to fulfill the rites and ceremonies of the Mosaic law. *Came not unto you in word only.* It was not by simple teaching or mere reasoning that the doctrines which we preached recommended themselves to you. We did not insist on your using this or the other religious institution; we insisted on a change of heart and life, and we held out the energy which was able to effect it. *And in the Holy Ghost.* By His influence upon your hearts, in changing and renewing them; and by the testimony which you received from Him, that you were accepted through the Beloved, and become the adopted children of God. *And in much assurance.* The Holy Spirit who was given you left no doubt on your mind, with respect to either the general truth of the doctrine or the safety of your own state. *What manner of men we were.* How we preached, and how we lived, our doctrines and our practices ever corresponding. And *for your sake* we sustained difficulties, endured hardships, and were incessant in our labors.

6. *Ye became followers of us.* You became "imitators."

MATTHEW HENRY

The Thessalonians acted thus, notwithstanding their affliction. They were willing to share in the sufferings that attended the embracing of Christianity. Perhaps this made the word more precious, being dear-bought. *With joy in the Holy Ghost,* who, when our afflictions abound, makes our consolations much more to abound.

II. They were themselves examples to all about them, *v.* 7, 8.

1. Their example was very effectual to make good impressions upon many others. They were *stamps,* or instruments to make impression with. They had themselves received good impressions, and they made good impressions. Christians should be so good as by their example to influence others.

2. It was very extensive, and reached beyond the confines of Thessalonica, even to the believers of all Macedonia, and further in Achaia.

3. It was very famous. The word of the Lord was famous and well known, in the regions round about that city, and *in every place;* so that, from the good success of the gospel among them, many others were encouraged to entertain it, and to be willing, when called, to suffer for it. The readiness of their faith was famed abroad. These Thessalonians embraced the gospel as soon as it was preached to them. The effects of their faith were famous. They quitted their idolatry. They gave themselves up to God, to the living and true God.

They set themselves to wait for the Son of God from heaven, *v.* 10. And this is one of the peculiarities of our holy religion, to wait for Christ's second coming, as those who believe he will come and hope he will come to our joy.

JAMIESON, FAUSSET, BROWN

tles, *joyful* witness for *the word in much affliction:* the second proof of their *election of God* (vs. 4); vs. 5 is the first (see *Note,* vs. 5). **received the word in much affliction**–(ch. 2:14; 3:2-5; Acts 17:5-10). **joy of**–i.e., *wrought* by "the Holy Ghost." "The oil of gladness" wherewith the Son of God was "anointed above His fellows" (Ps. 45:7), is the same oil with which He, by the Spirit, anoints His fellows too (Isa. 61:1, 3; Rom. 14:17; I John 2:20, 27). **7. ensamples**–So some of the oldest MSS. read. Others, "ensample" (singular), the whole Church being regarded as *one.* The *Macedonian* Church of Philippi was the only one in Europe converted before the Thessalonians. Therefore he means their past conduct is an ensample to all believers now; of whom he specifies those "in Macedonia" because he had been there since the conversion of the Thessalonians, and had left Silvanus and Timotheus there; and those in "Achaia," because he was now at Corinth in Achaia. **8. from you sounded . . . the word of the Lord**–not that they actually became missionaries: but they, by the *report* which spread abroad of their "faith" (cf. Rom. 1:8), and by Christian merchants of Thessalonica who travelled in various directions, bearing "the word of the Lord" with them, were *virtually* missionaries, recommending the Gospel to all within reach of their influence by word and by example (vs. 7). In "sounded," the image is that of a trumpet filling with its clear-sounding echo all the surrounding places. **to Godward**–no longer directed to idols. **so that we need not to speak any thing**–to them in praise of your faith; "for (vs. 9) they themselves" (the people in Macedonia, Achaia, and in every place) know it already. **9.** Strictly there should follow, "For they themselves show of you . . ."; but, instead, he substitutes that which was the instrumental cause of the Thessalonians' conversion and faith, "for they themselves show of US what manner of entering in we had *unto you";* cf. vs. 5, which corresponds to this former clause, as vs. 6 corresponds to the latter clause. "And how ye turned from idols to serve the living . . . God. . . ." Instead of *our* having "to speak any thing" to them (in Macedonia and Achaia) in your praise (vs. 8), **"they *themselves* (have the** start of us in speaking of you, and) *announce concerning* (so the *Greek* of 'show of' means) us, what manner of (how effectual an) entrance we had unto you" (vs. 5; ch. 2:1). **the living and true God**–as opposed to the *dead* and *false* gods from which they had "turned." In the *English Version* reading, Acts 17:4, "of *the devout Greeks* a great multitude," no mention is made, as here, of the conversion of *idolatrous* Gentiles at Thessalonica; but the reading of some of the oldest MSS. and *Vulgate* singularly coincides with the statement here: "Of the devout AND of Greeks (viz., *idolaters*) a great multitude"; so in vs. 17, "the devout persons," i.e., Gentile proselytes to Judaism, form a separate class. PALEY and LACHMANN, by distinct lines of argument, support the "AND." **10.** This verse distinguishes them from the *Jews,* as vs. 9 from the *idolatrous* Gentiles. To wait for the Lord's coming is a sure characteristic of a true believer, and was prominent amidst the graces of the Thessalonians (I Cor. 1:7, 8). His *coming* is seldom called his *return* (John 14:3); because the two advents are regarded as different phases of the same coming; and the second coming shall have features altogether new connected with it, so that it will not be a mere repetition of the first, or a mere coming *back again.* **his Son . . . raised from the dead**–the grand proof of His divine *Sonship* (Rom. 1:4). **delivered**–rather as *Greek,* "who *delivereth us."* Christ has once for all *redeemed* us; He is *our Deliverer* ALWAYS. **wrath to come**–(ch. 5:9; Col. 3:6).

ADAM CLARKE

Having received the word in much affliction. That they received the doctrine of the gospel in the midst of much persecution we may learn from the history in general, and from Acts xvii. 5-6. *With joy of the Holy Ghost.* The consolations which they received in consequence of believing in Christ more than counterbalanced all the afflictions which they suffered from their persecutors.

7. *Ye were ensamples.* "Types," models, or patterns; according to which all the churches in Macedonia and Achaia formed both their creed and their conduct.

8. *From you sounded out.* As Thessalonica was very conveniently situated for traffic, many merchants from thence traded through Macedonia, Achaia, and different parts of Greece. By these, the fame of the Thessalonians having received the doctrine of the gospel was doubtless carried far and wide.

9. *How ye turned to God from idols.* This could not be spoken either of the Jews or of the devout persons, but of the heathen Greeks; and of such it appears that the majority of the church was formed. The *true God*—in opposition to the whole system of idolatry, which was false in the objects of its adoration, false in its pretensions, false in its promises, and false in all its prospects.

10. *And to wait for his Son from heaven.* To expect a future state of glory, and resurrection of the body, according to the gospel doctrine, after the example of Jesus Christ, who was raised from the dead and ascended unto heaven, ever to appear in the presence of God for us.

Delivered us from the wrath to come. From all the punishment due to us for our sins, and from the destruction which is about to come on the unbelieving and impenitent Jews.

CHAPTER 2

MATTHEW HENRY

Verses 1–6

He could appeal to the Thessalonians how faithfully he, and Silas, and Timotheus, had discharged their office: *You yourselves, brethren, know our entrance in unto you. His preaching was not in vain,* or, as some read it, *was not vain.* It was not fruitless or in vain (according to our translation), or, as others think, it was not vain and empty. The subject-matter of the apostle's preaching was sound and solid truth. He had no worldly design in his preaching, which he puts them in mind to have been,

JAMIESON, FAUSSET, BROWN

VSS. 1-20. HIS MANNER OF PREACHING, AND THEIRS OF RECEIVING, THE GOSPEL; HIS DESIRE TO HAVE REVISITED THEM FRUSTRATED BY SATAN. **1. For**–confirming ch. 1:9. He discusses the manner of his fellow missionaries' preaching among them (ch. 1:5, and former part of vs. 9) from vs. 1 to vs. 12; and the Thessalonians' reception of the word (cf. ch. 1:6, 7, and latter part of vs. 9) from vss. 13 to 16. **yourselves**–Not only do strangers report it, but *you* know it to be true [ALFORD] "yourselves." **not in vain**–*Greek,* "not vain," i.e., it was full of "power" (ch. 1:5). The *Greek* for "was," expresses rather "hath been and is," implying the *permanent* and continuing character of his preaching. **2. even after that we had suffered before**–at Philippi (Acts 16): a circumstance which would have deterred mere natural, unspiritual men from further

ADAM CLARKE

1. *Our entrance in unto you.* His first coming to preach the gospel was particularly owned of the Lord, many of them having been converted under his ministry.

MATTHEW HENRY

I. With courage and resolution: *We were bold in our God to speak unto you the gospel of God, v.* 2. The apostle was inspired with a holy boldness, nor was he discouraged at the afflictions he met with. He had met with ill usage at Philippi, as these Thessalonians well know. There it was that he and Silas were put in the stocks; yet no sooner were they set at liberty than they went to Thessalonica, and preached the gospel with as much boldness as ever. Suffering in a good cause should rather sharpen than blunt the edge of holy resolution. Those who preached it preached it *with contention,* which denoted either the apostles' striving in their preaching or their striving against the opposition they met with. Paul was neither daunted in his work, nor driven from it.

II. With great simplicity and godly sincerity: *Our exhortation was not of deceit, nor of uncleanness, nor in guile, v.* 3. This, no doubt, was matter of the greatest comfort to the apostle—the consciousness of his own incerity; and was one reason of his success. The gospel he preached was without deceit, it was true and faithful. Nor was it of uncleanness. His gospel was pure and holy, and, as the matter of the apostle's exhortation was thus true and pure, the manner of his speaking was without guile. The apostle not only asserts his sincerity, but subjoins the reasons and evidences thereof.

1. They were stewards, *put in trust* with the gospel. The gospel which Paul preached was not his own, but the gospel of God. Ministers have a great favour shown them, and honour put upon them, and trust committed to them.

2. Their design was to please God and not men. If sincerity be wanting, all that we do cannot please God. The gospel of Christ is not accommodated to the vain fancies and lusts of men, but, on the contrary, it was designed for the mortifying of their corrupt affections, that they might be brought under the power of faith.

3. They acted as in the sight of him who *tries our hearts.* He is well acquainted with all our aims and designs, as well as our actions. And it is from this God who trieth our hearts that we must receive our reward. The evidences of the apostles' sincerity: (1) He avoided flattery: *Neither at any time used we flattering words, as you know, v.* 5. He and his fellow-labourers preached Christ and him crucified, and did not aim to gain an interest in men's affections for themselves, nor did he flatter men in their sins. He did not flatter them with vain hopes. (2) He avoided covetousness. He did not make the ministry *a cloak,* or a covering, for *covetousness, as God was witness, v.* 5. His design was not to enrich himself by preaching the gospel: so far from this, he did not stipulate with them for bread. (3) He avoided ambition and vain-glory: *Nor of men sought we glory, neither of you nor yet of others, v.* 6. They expected neither people's purses nor their caps.

Verses 7–12

I. He mentions the gentleness of their behaviour: *We were gentle among you, v.* 7. He showed the kindness and care of a nurse that cherishes her children. This is the way to win people, rather than to rule with rigour.

As a nursing mother bears with frowardness in a child, and condescends to mean offices for its good, cherishing it in her bosom, so in like manner should the ministers of Christ behave towards their people. This gentleness the apostle expressed several ways. 1. By the most affectionate desire of their welfare: *Being affectionately desirous of you, v.* 8. It was their spiritual and eternal welfare that he was earnestly desirous of. 2. By great readiness to do them good, willingly imparting to them, *not the gospel of God only, but also our own souls, v.* 8. He was willing to spend and be spent in the service of men's souls.

JAMIESON, FAUSSET, BROWN

preaching. **shamefully entreated**—ignominiously scourged (Acts 16:22, 23). **bold**—(Acts 4:29; Eph. 6:20). **in our God**—The ground of our boldness in speaking was the realization of God as "OUR God." **with much contention**—i.e., lit., as of *competitors in a contest:* striving earnestness (Col. 1:29; 2:1). But here *outward* conflict with persecutors, rather than *inward* and mental, was what the missionaries had to endure (Acts 17:5, 6; Phil. 1:30). **3. For**—The ground of his "boldness" (vs. 2), his freedom from all "deceit, uncleanness, and guile"; *guile,* before God, *deceit* (*Greek,* "imposture"), towards men (cf. II Cor. 1:12; 2:17 Eph. 4:14); *uncleanness,* in relation to one's self (impure motives of carnal self-gratification in gain, vs. 5), or lust; such as actuated false teachers of the Gentiles (Phil. 1:16; II Pet. 2: 10, 14; Jude 8; Rev. 2:14, 15). So Simon Magus and Cerinthus taught [ESTIUS]. **exhortation**—The *Greek* means "consolation" as well as "exhortation." The same Gospel which exhorts comforts. **Its first lesson to each** is that of peace in believing amidst outward and inward sorrows. It comforts them that mourn (cf. vs. 11; Isa. 61:2, 3; II Cor. 1:3, 4). **of**—*springing from—having its source in*—deceit, etc. **4. as**—according as; even as. **allowed**—*Greek,* "We have been approved on trial," "deemed fit." This word corresponds to "God which *trieth* our hearts" below. This approval as to sincerity depends solely on the grace and mercy of God (Acts 9:15; I Cor. 7:25; II Cor. 3:5; I Tim. 1:11, 12). **not as pleasing**—not as persons who seek to please men; characteristic of false teachers (Gal. 1:10). **5. used we flattering words**—lit., "become (i.e., have we been found) in (the use of) language of flattery"; the resource of those who try to "please men." **as ye know**—"Ye know" as to whether I *flattered* you; as to "covetousness," GOD, the Judge of the heart, alone can be "my witness." **cloak of**—i.e., any specious guise under which I might cloak "covetousness." **6.** Lit., "Nor of men (have we been found, vs. 5) seeking glory." The "of" here represents a different *Greek* word from "of" in the clause "*of* you . . .*of* others." ALFORD makes the former (*Greek, ex*) express the *abstract ground* of the glory; the latter (*apo*) the *concrete object* from which it was to come. The former means "originating from"; the latter means "on the part of." Many teach heretical novelties, though not for fain, yet for "glory." Paul and his associates were free even from this motive [GROTIUS], (John 5:44). **we might have been burdensome**—i.e., by claiming maintenance (vs. 9; II Cor. 11:9; 12:16; II Thess. 3:8). As, however, "glory" precedes, as well as "covetousness," the reference cannot be *restricted* to the latter, though I think it is not *excluded.* Translate, "when we might have borne heavily upon you," by pressing you *with the weight* of *selfglorifying authority,* and *with the burden* of our *sustenance.* **as the apostles**—i.e., as being apostles. **7. we were**—*Greek,* "we were *made*" by God's grace. **gentle**—*Greek,* "*mild* in bearing with the faults of others" [TITTMANN]; one, too, who is gentle (though firm) in reproving the erroneous opinions of others (II Tim. 2:24). Some of the oldest MSS. read, "we became *little children*" (cf. Matt. 18:3, 4). Others support the *English Version* reading, which forms a better antithesis to vss. 6, 7, and harmonizes better with what follows; for he would hardly, in the same sentence, compare himself both to the "infants" or "little children," and to "a nurse," or rather, "suckling mother." *Gentleness* is the fitting characteristic of *a nurse.* **among you**—*Greek,* "in the midst of you," i.e., in our intercourse with you being *as one of yourselves.* **nurse**—a suckling mother. **her**—*Greek,* "*her own* children" (cf. vs. 11). So Galatians 4:19. **8. So**—to be joined to "we were willing"; "*As* a nurse cherisheth . . .,*so* we were willing . . ." [ALFORD]. But BENGEL, "So," i.e., *seeing that we have such affection for you.* **being affectionately destrous**—The oldest reading in the *Greek* implies, lit., *to connect one's self with another;* to be closely *attached* to another. **willing**—The *Greek* is stronger, "we were *well content*"; "we would *gladly* have imparted. . . ." "even our own *lives*" (so the *Greek* for "souls" ought to be translated); as we showed in the sufferings we endured in giving you the Gospel (Acts 17). As a nursing mother is ready to impart not only her milk to them, but her life for them, so we not only imparted gladly the spiritual milk of the word to you, but risked our own lives for your spiritual nourishment, imitating Him who laid down His life for His friends, the greatest proof of love (John 15:13). **ye were**—*Greek,* "ye were become," as having become our spiritual children. **dear**—*Greek,* "dearly beloved." **9. labour and travail**—The *Greek* for "labor" means *hardship in bearing;* that for "travail," *hardship in doing;* the former,

ADAM CLARKE

2. *Shamefully entreated . . . at Philippi.* There Paul and Silas had been beaten with many stripes, shut up in the inner prison, and their feet made fast in the stocks. See Acts xvi. 23 ff. *With much contention.* The words not only signify "with intense labor and earnestness," but may here mean "exposed to the greatest danger," "at the peril of our lives."

3. *Our exhortation.* The word has a very extensive meaning; it signifies not only "exhortation" but also "encouragement, consolation," and the like. *Not of deceit.* We did not endeavor to allure you with false pretenses; we did not deceive you, nor were we deceived ourselves. *Nor of uncleanness.* Such as the teachings of the Gentile philosophers were; their supreme gods were celebrated for their adulteries, fornication, uncleannesses, thefts, barbarities, and profligacies of the most odious kind. Our gospel was pure; came from the pure and holy God; was accompanied with the influences of the Holy Spirit, and produced purity both in the hearts and in the lives of all that received it. *Nor in guile.* We had no false pretenses, and were influenced by no sinister motives.

4. *But as we were allowed of God.* "As we were accounted worthy" to be put in trust, as God put confidence in us and sent us on His most especial message to mankind, *even so we speak,* keeping the dignity of our high calling continually in view; and acting as in the sight of God, we speak not to please or flatter men, but to please that God who searches the heart.

5. *Flattering words.* Though we proclaimed the gospel or glad tidings, yet we showed that without holiness none should see the Lord. *Ye know.* That while we preached the whole gospel we never gave any countenance to sin. *Nor a cloke of covetousness.* We did not seek temporal emolument; nor did we preach the gospel for a cloak to our covetousness. *God is witness* that we did not; we sought you, not yours.

6. *Nor of men sought we glory.* As we preached not for worldly gain, so we preached not for popular applause; we had what we sought for—the approbation of God and the testimony of a good conscience. *When we might have been burdensome.* They had a right to their maintenance while they devoted themselves wholly to the work of the gospel for the sake of the people's souls.

7. *But we were gentle among you.* Far from assuming the authority which we had, we acted towards you as a tender nurse or parent does to a delicate child. We fed, counselled, cherished, and bore with you; we taught you to walk, preserved you from stumbling, and led you in a right path.

8. *Being affectionately desirous of you.* We had such intense love for you that we were not only willing and forward to preach the unsearchable riches of Christ to you, but also to give our "own lives" for your sake, *because ye were dear,* "because you were beloved by us." The words used here by the apostle are expressive of the strongest affection and attachment.

9. *Ye remember, brethren, our labour and travail.* From this it appears that Paul spent much more time at Thessalonica than is general-

MATTHEW HENRY

3. By bodily labour that his ministry might not be burdensome to them: *You remember our labour and travail; for, labouring night and day,* &c., *v.* 9. To the labour of the ministry he added that of his calling, as a tent-maker, that he might get his own bread. He spent part of the night, as well as the day, in this work; that he might have an opportunity to do good to the souls of men in the day time.

4. By the holiness of their conversation, concerning which he appeals not only to them, but to God also (*v.* 10): *You are witnesses, and God also.* They were observers of their outward conversation in public before men, and God was witness not only of their behaviour in secret, but of the inward principles from which they acted.

II. He mentions their faithful discharge of the work of the ministry, *v.* 11, 12. Paul and his fellow-labourers were not only good Christians, but faithful ministers. Paul exhorted the Thessalonians, and he comforted them also, *and charged every one* of them by personal addresses: this is intended by the similitude of a father's charging his children. He was their spiritual father; and, as he cherished them like a nursing mother, so he charged them as a father, with a father's affection rather than a father's authority. That *they would walk worthy of God, who hath called them to his kingdom and glory, v.* 12. **1. What is our great gospel privilege—that God has called us to his kingdom and glory. 2. What is our great gospel duty —that we walk worthy of God.**

Verses 13–16

I. The success of his ministry among these Thessalonians (*v.* 13).

1. The manner of their receiving the word of God: *When you received the word of God, which you heard of us, you received it, not as the word of men, but* (*as it is in truth*) *the word of God.* The word of the gospel is preached by men like ourselves, men of like passions and infirmities with others. However, it is in truth the word of God. Such was the word the apostles preached by divine inspiration, and such is that which is left upon record, and such is that word which in our days is preached. Those are greatly to blame who give out their own fancies or injunctions for the word of God. Those are also to blame who, in hearing the word, look no further than to the ministry of men, or the words of men. We should receive the word of God as the word of God. The words of men are frail and perishing, like themselves, and sometimes false, foolish, and fickle: but God's word is holy, wise, just, and faithful, and abides for ever.

2. The wonderful operation of this word they received: *It effectually worketh in those that believe, v.* 13. Such as have this inward testimony of the truth of the scriptures have the best evidence of their divine original, though this is not sufficient to convince others who are strangers thereto.

II. The good effects which his successful preaching had,

1. Upon himself and fellow-labourers. It was a constant cause of thankfulness: *For this cause thank we God without ceasing, v.* 13. He never could be sufficiently thankful that God had counted him faithful, and made his ministrations successful.

JAMIESON, FAUSSET, BROWN

toil with the utmost solicitude; the latter, the being wearied with fatigue [GROTIUS]. ZANCHIUS refers the former to *spiritual* (see ch. 3:5), the latter to *manual* labor. I would translate, "weariness (so the *Greek* is translated, II Cor. 11:27) and travail" (hard labor, *toil*). **for**—omitted in the oldest MSS. **labouring**—*Greek,* "working," viz., at tent-making (Acts 18:3). **night and day**—The Jews reckoned the day from sunset to sunset, so that "night" is put before "day" (cf. Acts 20:31). Their labors with their hands for a scanty livelihood had to be engaged in not only by day, but by night also, in the intervals between spiritual labors. **because we would not be chargeable**—*Greek, "with a view to* not *burdening* any of you" (II Cor. 11:9, 10). **preached unto you**—*Greek,* "unto and among you." Though but "three Sabbaths" are mentioned, Acts 17:2, these refer merely to the time of his preaching *to the Jews in the synagogue.* When rejected by them as a body, after having converted a few Jews, he turned to the Gentiles; of these (whom he preached to in a place distinct from the synagogue) "a great multitude believed" (Acts 17:4, where the oldest MSS. read, "of the devout [proselytes] AND Greeks a great multitude"); then after he had, by labors continued *among the Gentiles* for some time, gathered in many converts, the Jews, provoked by his success, assaulted Jason's house, and drove him away. His receiving "once and again" supplies from Philippi, implies a longer stay at Thessalonica than three weeks (Phil. 4:16). **10. Ye are witnesses** —as to our outward conduct. **God**—as to our inner motives. **holily**—towards God. **justly**—towards men. **unblamably**—in relation to ourselves. **behaved ourselves**—*Greek,* "were made to be," viz., by God. **among you that believe**—rather, "*before* (i.e., in the eyes of) you that believe"; whatever we may have seemed in the eyes of the unbelieving. As vs. 9 refers to their outward occupation in the world; so vs. 10, to their character among believers. **11. exhorted and comforted**—*Exhortation* leads one to do a thing willingly; *consolation,* to do it joyfully [BENGEL], (ch. 5:14). Even in the former term, "exhorted," the *Greek* includes the additional idea of *comforting* and *advocating* one's cause: "encouragingly exhorted." Appropriate in this case, as the Thessalonians were in sorrow, both through persecutions, and also through deaths of friends (ch. 4: 13). **charged**—"conjured solemnly," lit., "testifying"; *appealing solemnly* to you before God. **every one of you**—in private (Acts 20:20), as well as publicly. The minister, if he would be useful, must not deal merely in generalities, but must individualize and particularize. **as a father**—with mild gravity. The *Greek* is, "*his own* children." **12. worthy of God**—"worthy *of the Lord*" (Col. 1:10); "worthily *of the saints*" (Rom. 16:2, *Greek*): "*. . . of the Gospel*" (Phil. 1:27) "*. . . . of the vocation* wherewith ye are called" (Eph. 4:1). Inconsistency would cause God's name to be "blasphemed among the Gentiles" (Rom. 2:24). The *Greek* article is emphatical, "Worthy of THE God who is calling you." **hath called**—So one of the oldest MSS. and *Vulgate.* Other oldest MSS., "Who *calleth* us." **his kingdom** —to be set up at the Lord's coming. **glory**—that ye may share His glory (John 17:22; Col. 3:4). **13. For this cause**—Seeing ye have had such teachers (vss. 10, 11, 12) [BENGEL], "we also (as well as 'all that believe' in Macedonia and Achaia) thank God without ceasing ('always' . . . 'in our prayers,' ch. 1: 2), that when ye received the word of God which ye heard from us (lit., 'God's word of hearing from us,' Rom. 10:16, 17), ye accepted it not as the word of men, but, even as it is truly, the word of God." ALFORD omits the "as" of *English Version.* But the "as" is required by the clause, "even as it is truly." "Ye accepted it, not (*as*) the word of men (which it might have been *supposed* to be), but (as) the word of God, *even as it really is.*" The *Greek* for the first "received," implies simply the hearing of it; the *Greek* of the second is "accepted," or "welcomed" it. The proper object of faith, it hence appears, is *the word of God,* at first oral, then for security against error, written (John 20:30, 31; Rom. 15:4; Gal. 4:30). Also, that faith is *the work of divine grace,* is implied by Paul's *thanksgiving.* **effectually worketh also in you that believe**—"Also," besides your accepting it with your hearts, it evidences itself in your lives. It shows its *energy* in its practical effects on you; for instance, working in you patient endurance in trial (vs. 14; cf. Gal. 3:5; 5:6). **14. followers**—*Greek,* "imitators." Divine *working* is most of all seen and felt in affliction. **in Judea**—The churches of Judea were naturally the patterns to other churches, as having been the first founded, and that on the very scene of Christ's own ministry. Reference to them is specially appro-

ADAM CLARKE

ly supposed; for the expressions in this verse denote a long continuance of a constantly exercised ministry, interrupted only by manual labor for their own support; *labouring night and day, because we would not be chargeable unto . . . you.* Probably Paul and his companions worked with their hands by day, and spent a considerable part of the night, or evenings, in preaching Christ to the people.

10. *Ye are witnesses, and God also, how holily.* I.e., in reference to God; how *justly* in reference to men; and *unblameably* in reference to our spirit and conduct, as ministers of Christ, *we behaved ourselves among you.* What a consciousness of his own integrity must Paul have had to use the expressions that are here!

11. *How we exhorted.* What pastoral care is marked here! They *exhorted*—were continually teaching and instructing the objects of their charge. *And comforted.* They found many under trials and temptations, and those they encouraged. *And charged.* Continued to "witness" to the people that all the threatenings and promises of God were true; that He required faith, love, and obedience; that He could not behold sin with allowance; that Jesus died to save them from their sins; and that, without holiness, none should see God. And all these things they did, not in a general way only, but they spoke to *every* man; none was left unnoticed, unadmonished, uncomforted. The spirit in which they performed all these branches of the pastoral care was that which was most likely to insure success; as a *father* treats *his children,* so they treated every member of the church.

12. *That ye would walk worthy of God.* That they should, in every respect, act up to their high calling, that it would not be a reproach to the God of holiness to acknowledge them as His sons and daughters. *His kingdom and glory.* His Church here, for that is the kingdom of God among men; and His *glory* hereafter, for that is the state to which the dispensations of grace in His Church lead. The words, however, may signify His "glorious kingdom."

13. *Ye received the word of God.* You received the "doctrine" of God, not as anything fabricated by man, but as coming immediately from God himself, we being only His messengers to declare what He had previously revealed to us. And you have had the fullest proof that you have not believed in vain; for that doctrine, under the power and influence of the Holy Ghost, has "worked most powerfully" in you, filling you with light, life, and holiness.

MATTHEW HENRY

2. Upon them. The word wrought effectually in them. In constancy and patience under sufferings: *You became followers of the churches of God, and have suffered like things as they have done* (*v.* 14). The cross is the Christian's mark. It is a good effect of the gospel when we are enabled to suffer for its sake. The sufferings of the churches of God, which *in Judæa were in Christ Jesus*. Those in Judæa first heard the gospel, and they first suffered for it: for the Jews were the most bitter enemies Christianity had. Bitter zeal and fiery persecution will set countrymen at variance. They were the ringleaders of persecution in all places; so in particular it was at Thessalonica.

Upon this occasion, the apostle gives a character of the unbelieving Jews (*v.* 15). They *killed the Lord Jesus*. They killed *their own prophets*. They hated the apostles, and did them all the mischief they could. No marvel, if they killed the Lord Jesus, that they persecuted his followers. They *pleased not God*. They had quite lost all sense of religion. They were *contrary to all men*. Their persecuting spirit was a perverse spirit. *Forbidding the apostles to speak to the Gentiles, that they might be saved*. They were envious against the Gentiles, and angry that they should be admitted to share in the means of salvation. Thus did the Jews fill up their sins. For the sake of these things *wrath has come upon them to the uttermost*; wrath was determined against them, and would soon overtake them. It was not many years after this that Jerusalem was destroyed, and the Jewish nation cut off by the Romans.

Verses 17–20

The apostle apologizes for his absence: *We, brethren, were taken from you*, *v.* 17. He was unwillingly sent away by night to Berea. Though he was absent in body, yet he was present in heart. Even his bodily absence was but for a short time. This world is not a place where we are always, or long, to be together. It is in heaven that holy souls shall meet, and never part more. He earnestly desired and endeavoured to see them again: *We endeavoured more abundantly to see your face with great desire*, *v.* 17. But men of business are not masters of their own time. Paul did his endeavour, and he could do no more, *v.* 18.

Satan hindered his return (*v.* 18). Satan is a constant enemy to the work of God, and does all he can to obstruct it.

He assures them of his affection and high esteem for them. They were his *hope, and joy, and crown of rejoicing*; *his glory*

JAMIESON, FAUSSET, BROWN

priate here, as the Thessalonians, with Paul and Silas, had experienced from Jews in their city persecutions (Acts 17:5-9) similar to those which "the churches in Judea" experienced from Jews in that country. **in Christ Jesus**—not merely "in God"; for the synagogues of the Jews (one of which the Thessalonians were familiar with, Acts 17:1) were also *in God*. But the Christian churches alone were not only *in God*, as the Jews in contrast to the Thessalonian idolaters were, but also *in Christ*, which the Jews were not. **of your own countrymen**—including primarily the Jews settled at Thessalonica, from whom the persecution originated, and also the Gentiles there, instigated by the Jews; thus, "fellow countrymen" (the *Greek* term, according to HERODIAN, implies, not the *enduring* relation of fellow citizenship, but sameness of country *for the time being*), including naturalized Jews and native Thessalonians, stand in contrast to the pure "Jews" in Judea (Matt. 10:36). It is an undesigned coincidence, that Paul at this time was suffering persecutions of the Jews at Corinth, whence he writes (Acts 18:5, 6, 12); naturally his letter would the more vividly dwell on Jewish bitterness against Christians. **15. the Lord Jesus**—rather as *Greek*, "Jesus THE LORD." This enhances the glaring enormity of their sin, that in killing Jesus they killed the LORD (cf. Acts 3:14, 15). **their own**—omitted in the oldest MSS. **prophets**—(Matt. 21:33-41; 23:31-37; Luke 13:33). **persecuted us**—rather as *Greek* (see *Margin*), "By persecution drove us out" (Luke 11:49). **please not God**—i.e., they do not *make it their aim to* please God. **16. Forbidding**—*Greek*, "Hindering us from speaking. . . ." **to fill up their sins alway**—Tending thus "to the filling up (the full measure of, Gen. 15:16; Dan. 8:23; Matt. 23:32) their sins at all times," i.e., *now as at all former times*. Their hindrance of the Gospel preaching to the Gentiles was the last measure added to their continually accumulating iniquity, which made them fully ripe for vengeance. **for**—Greek, "but." "But," they shall proceed no further, for (II Tim. 3:8) "the"divine "wrath *has* (so the *Greek*) come upon (overtaken unexpectedly; the past tense expressing the speedy certainty of the divinely destined stroke) them to the uttermost"; not merely partial wrath, but wrath to its full extent, "even to the finishing stroke" [EDMUNDS]. The past tense implies that the fullest visitation of wrath was already begun. Already in A.D. 48, a tumult had occurred at the Passover in Jerusalem, when about 30,000 (according to some) were slain; a foretaste of the whole vengeance which speedily followed (Luke 19:43, 44; 21:24). **17. But we**—resumed from vs. 13; in contrast to *the Jews*, vss. 15, 16. **taken**—rather as *Greek*, "severed (violently, Acts 17:7-10) from you," as parents bereft of their children. So "I will not leave you comfortless," *Greek*, "orphanized" (John 14:18). **for a short time**—lit., "for the space of an hour." "When we had been severed from you but a very short time (perhaps alluding to the suddenness of his unexpected departure), we the more abundantly (the shorter was our separation; for the desire of meeting again is the more vivid, the more recent has been the parting) endeavored..." (Cf. II Tim. 1:4.) He does not hereby, as many explain, anticipate a short separation from them, which would be a false anticipation; for he did not soon revisit them. The *Greek* past participle also forbids their view. **18. Wherefore**—The oldest MSS. read, "Because," or "Inasmuch as." **we would**—*Greek*, "*we wished* to come"; we intended to come. **even I Paul**—My fellow missionaries as well as myself wished to come; I can answer for *myself* that I intended it more than once. His slightly distinguishing himself here from his fellow missionaries, whom throughout this Epistle he associates with himself in the plural, accords with the fact that Silvanus and Timothy stayed at Berea when Paul went on to Athens; where subsequently Timothy joined him, and was thence sent *by Paul alone* to Thessalonica (ch. 3:1). **Satan hindered us**—On a different occasion "the Holy Ghost, the Spirit *of Jesus*" (so the oldest MSS. read), Acts 16:6, 7, forbad or hindered them in a missionary design; here it is *Satan*, acting perhaps by wicked men, some of whom had already driven him out of Thessalonica (Acts 17:13, 14; cf. John 13:27), or else by some more direct "messenger of Satan—a thorn in the flesh" (II Cor. 12:7; cf. 11:14).

The *Greek* for "hindered" is lit., "to cut a trench between one's self and an advancing foe, to prevent his progress"; so Satan opposing the progress of the missionaries. **19. For**—giving the reason for his earnest desire to see them. **Are not even ye in the presence of . . . Christ**—"Christ" is

ADAM CLARKE

CHARLES H. SPURGEON:

I only call your attention to the fact that the apostle says, "Ye, brethren, became followers of the churches of God which in Judea are in Christ Jesus." Here are people converted in Judea, and they are of strongly Jewish type; quite another set of people over at Thessalonica become converted to Christ, and though they are thoroughly of the Greek type, they are very like the converts in Judea. They know nothing about the law of Moses, they have been heathens, worshiping idols; and yet, when they are converted, the strange thing is that they are exceedingly like those Jews over yonder, to whom idolatry was an abomination. Greek believers are like Hebrew believers. They have never spoken to one another, and nobody has been there to tell them the peculiarities of Christians, and yet a family likeness is distinctly visible. Were you never startled with this, that if, in the preaching of the gospel today, we were to bring to the Lord Jesus a person of high rank, and another of the very lowest extraction, they have the same experience, and upon the greatest of subjects they talk in the same way? "Oh, but," you say," they pick up certain phrases." No, no! They differ in speech: the likeness is in heart and character. I frequently meet with converts who have not attended this place of worship more than six times, but they have been converted, and when they come to tell the story of their inner life you would suppose that they had been born and bred among us, and had learned all our ways; for, though they do not use the phrases which we use, yet they say the same things. The fact is, we are all alike lost and ruined, and we are born again in the same way, and we find the Savior in the same way, and we rejoice in Him when we do find Him after much the same fashion, and express ourselves very much after the same style. Believers differ in many things, and yet they are alike in the main things. There are no two exactly alike in all the family of God, and yet the likeness to the Elder Brother is to be seen more or less in each one.

—*The Treasury of the New Testament*

17. *Being taken from you for a short time*. Through the persecution raised by the Jews, see Acts xvii, he was obliged to leave Thessalonica, and yield to a storm that it would have been useless for him to withstand. *Being taken from you . . . in presence, not in heart*. The apostle had compared himself to a parent or nurse, vv. 7 and 11; and the people he considered as his most beloved children. Here he represents himself as feeling what an affectionate father must feel when "torn from his children"; for this is the import of the word "bereft of children," which we tamely translate *being taken from you*. *Endeavoured the more abundantly*. His separation from them did not destroy his parental feelings, and the manner in which he was obliged to leave them increased his desire to visit them as soon as possible.

18. *Even I Paul*. He had already sent Timothy and Silas to them; but he himself was anxious to see them, and had purposed this *once and again;*

but Satan hindered; i.e., some "adversary," as the word means, whether the devil himself or some of his children.

19. *For what is our hope?* I can have no prospects from earth; I have forsaken all for the gospel. Why then should I continually labor

MATTHEW HENRY

and joy. Those that sow and those that reap shall rejoice together, *in the presence of our Lord Jesus Christ at his coming*. Though he should never be able to come to them, yet our Lord Jesus Christ will come.

CHAPTER 3

Verses 1–5

An account of his sending Timothy to the Thessalonians. Paul was content, for their good, *to be left alone at Athens*.

I. The character he gives of Timothy (*v.* 2): *We sent Timotheus, our brother*. Elsewhere he calls him his son; here he calls him brother. He calls him also a minister of God. He calls him also his fellow-labourer in the gospel of Christ. Ministers should strengthen one another's hands, not strive and contend one with another (which will hinder their work), but strive together to carry on the great work they are engaged in.

II. The end why Paul sent Timothy: *To establish you and to comfort you concerning your faith*, *v.* 2. He was desirous that they might be confirmed and comforted. The more we are comforted, the more we shall be confirmed. The apostle's design was to establish and comfort the Thessalonians concerning their faith,—concerning the object of their faith,—concerning the recompence of faith.

III. The motive, a godly fear lest they should be moved from the faith of Christ, *v.* 3.

1. He apprehended there was danger, and feared the consequence.

(1) There was danger by reason of *affliction* and persecution for the sake of the gospel, *v.* 3. Those who made profession of the gospel were persecuted, and without doubt these Thessalonians themselves were afflicted. The apostle was afraid lest by any means the tempter had tempted him, *v.* 5. The devil is a subtle and unwearied tempter. He has often been successful in his attacks upon persons under afflictions.

(2) The consequence the apostle feared was lest his labour should be in vain. It is the devil's design to hinder the good fruit and effect of the preaching of the gospel. If he cannot hinder ministers from labouring he will, if he be able, hinder them of the success of their labours.

2. The apostle tells them what care he took in sending Timothy, (1) To put them in mind of what he had told them before concerning suffering tribulation (*v.* 4), he says (*v.* 3), *We are appointed thereunto*. Their troubles and persecutions did not come merely from the malice of the enemies of religion, but by the *appointment of God*. Being fore-warned, they should be fore-armed. Besides, it might prove a confirmation of their faith, when they perceived that it only happened to them as was predicted before. (2) To know their faith, whether they remained steadfast. If their faith did not fail, they would be able to stand their ground against the tempter and all his temptations.

JAMIESON, FAUSSET, BROWN

omitted in the oldest MSS. Are not even ye (viz., among others; the "even" or "also," implies that not *they alone* will be his crown) our hope, joy, and crown of rejoicing before Jesus, when He shall come (II Cor. 1:14; Phil. 2:16; 4:1)? The "hope" here meant is his hope (in a lower sense), that these his converts might be found in Christ at His advent (ch. 3:13). Paul's *chief* "hope" was JESUS CHRIST (I Tim. 1:1). **20.** Emphatical repetition with increased force. Who but ye and our other converts are our *hope*, etc., *hereafter*, at Christ's coming? For it is *ye who* ARE now *our glory and joy*.

CHAPTER 3

VSS. 1-13. PROOF OF HIS DESIRE AFTER THEM IN HIS HAVING SENT TIMOTHY: HIS JOY AT THE TIDINGS BROUGHT BACK CONCERNING THEIR FAITH AND CHARITY: PRAYERS FOR THEM. **1. Wherefore**—because of our earnest love to you (ch. 2:17-20). **forbear**—"endure" the suspense. The *Greek* is lit. applied to a watertight vessel. When we could no longer contain ourselves in our yearning desire for you. **left at Athens alone** This implies that he sent Timothy *from Athens*, whither the latter had followed him. It was an act of self-denial for their sakes that Paul deprived himself of the presence of Timothy at Athens, which would have been so cheering to him in the midst of philosophic cavillers; but from love to the Thessalonians, he is well content to be left all "alone" in the great city. **2. minister of God and our fellow labourer**—Some oldest MSS. read, "fellow workman with God"; others, "minister of God." The former is probably genuine, as copyists probably altered it to the latter to avoid the bold phrase, which, however, is sanctioned by I Corinthians 3:9; II Corinthians 6:1. *English Version* reading is not well supported, and is plainly compounded out of the two other readings. Paul calls Timothy "our *brother*" here; but in I Corinthians 4:17, "my *son*." He speaks thus highly of one so lately ordained, both to impress the Thessalonians with a high respect for the delegate sent to them, and to encourage Timothy, who seems to have been of a timid character (I Tim. 4:12; 5:23). "Gospel ministers do the work of God *with* Him, *for* Him, and *under* Him" [EDMUNDS]. **establish**—*Greek*, "confirm." In II Thessalonians 3:3, GOD is said to stablish": He is the true establisher: ministers are His "instruments." **concerning**—*Greek*, "in behalf of," i.e., *for the furtherance* of your faith. The *Greek* for "comfort" includes also the idea, "exhort." The Thessalonians in their trials needed both (vs. 3; cf. Acts 14: 22). **3. moved**—"shaken," "disturbed." The *Greek* is lit. said of dogs *wagging* the tail in fawning on one. Therefore TITTMANN explains it, "That no man should, amidst his calamities, be *allured* by the *flattering* hope of a more pleasant life to abandon his duty." So ELSNER and BENGEL, "cajoled out of his faith." In afflictions, relatives and opponents combine with the ease-loving heart itself in flatteries, which it needs strong faith to overcome. **yourselves know**—We always candidly told you so (vs. 4; Acts 14:22). None but a religion from God would have held out such a trying prospect to those who should embrace it, and yet succeed in winning converts. **we**—Christians. **appointed thereunto**—by God's counsel (ch. 5:9). **4. that we should suffer**—*Greek*, "that we are about (we are sure) to suffer" according to the *appointment* of God (vs. 3). **even as**—"*even* (exactly) as it *both* came to pass *and* ye know"; ye know *both* that it came to pass, *and* that we foretold it (cf. John 13:19). The correspondence of the event to the prediction powerfully confirms faith: "Forewarned, forearmed" [EDMUNDS]. The repetition of "ye know," so frequently, is designed as an argument, that being forewarned of coming affliction, they should be less readily "moved" by it. **5. For this cause**—Because I know of your "tribulation" having actually begun (vs. 4). **when I**—*Greek*, "when I *also* (as well as Timothy, who, Paul delicately implies, was equally anxious respecting them, cf. "we," vs. 1), could no longer contain myself" (*endure* the suspense). **I sent**—Paul was the actual sender; hence the "I" here: Paul, Silas, and Timothy himself had agreed on the mission already, before Paul went to Athens: hence the "we," (vs. 1 *Note*). **to know**—to learn the state of your faith, whether it stood the trial (Col. 4:8). **lest . . . have tempted . . . and . . . be**—The indicative is used in the former sentence, the subjunctive in the latter. Translate therefore, "To know . . . *whether haply* the tempter *have* tempted you (the indicative implying that he supposed such *was* the case), and

ADAM CLARKE

at the risk of my life, preaching the gospel? Is it not to get your souls saved that you may be *my crown of rejoicing* in the day of Christ?

20. *For ye are our glory and joy*. You are the seal of our apostleship; your conversion and steadiness are a full proof that God has sent us.

CHAPTER 3

1. *Wherefore when we could no longer*. The apostle was anxious to hear of their state, and as he could obatin no information without sending a messenger express, he therefore sent Timothy from Athens, choosing rather to be left alone than to continue any longer in uncertainty relative to their state.

2. *Timotheus, our brother*. It appears that Timothy was but a youth when converted to God; he had now however been some years in the work of God. Paul therefore calls him his *brother;* elsewhere he calls him his "own son," 1 Tim. i. 2; and his "dearly beloved son," 2 Tim. i. 2; because he was brought to the knowledge of the true God and to salvation by Christ through the apostle's instrumentality. *Minister of God*. Employed by God to preach the gospel; this was God's work, and He had appointed Timothy to do it, and to do it at this time in conjunction with Paul; and therefore he calls him his *fellowlabourer*.

3. *That no man should be moved*. That is, caused to apostatize from Christianity.

We are appointed thereunto. "We are exposed to this; we lie open to such." They are unavoidable in the present state of things.

4. *That we should suffer tribulation*. I prepared you for it, because I knew that it was according to their nature for wicked men to persecute the followers of God.

5. *For this cause*. Knowing that you would be persecuted, and knowing that your apostasy was possible, *I sent to know your faith*—whether you continued steadfast in the truth.

MATTHEW HENRY

Verses 6–10

Paul's great satisfaction upon the return of Timothy with good tidings.

I. The good report Timothy made concerning them, *v.* 6. *Concerning their faith,* that they were not shaken in mind, nor turned aside. *Their love* also continued; their love to the gospel, and the ministers of the gospel. They *desired greatly to see them again,* and there was no love lost for the apostle was as desirous to see them.

II. The great comfort the apostle had in this good report (*v.* 7, 8): *Therefore, brethren, we were comforted in all our affliction and distress.* The apostle thought this good news of them was sufficient to balance all the troubles he met with. This put new life and spirit into the apostle. Thus he was not only comforted, but greatly rejoiced also: *Now we live, if you stand fast in the Lord, v.* 8. It would have been a killing thing if the professors of religion had been unsteady, whereas nothing was more encouraging than their constancy.

III. The effects of this were thankfulness and prayer to God on their behalf. 1. How thankful the apostle was, *v.* 9. When we are most cheerful we should be most thankful. Paul speaks as if he could not tell how to express his thankfulness to God, or his joy and rejoicing for their sakes. His heart was enlarged with love to them and with thanksgiving to God.

2. He prayed for them night and day (*v.* 10), in the midst of the business of the day or slumber of the night lifting up his heart to God in prayer. He prayed exceedingly. When we are most thankful we should always give ourselves to prayer. There was something still lacking in their faith; Paul desired that this might be perfected, and to see their face in order thereunto. The best of men have something wanting in their faith, if not as to the matter of it, yet as to the clearness and certainty of their faith.

Verses 11–13

He desired to be instrumental in the further benefit of the Thessalonians; and the only way to be so while at a distance was by prayer for them, together with his writing or sending to them.

I. Whom he prays to, namely, God and Christ. Prayer is not only to be offered in the name of Christ, but offered up to Christ himself, as our Lord and our Saviour.

II. What he prays for.

1. He prays that their way might be directed to them, *v.* 11. The taking of a journey to this or that place, one would think, is a thing depending on a man's own will, and lies in his own power. But the apostle knew that God our Father directs and orders his children whither they shall go and what they shall do. Let us acknowledge God in all our ways, and he will direct our paths.

2. He prays for the prosperity of the Thessalonians. (1) That they might increase and abound in love (*v.* 12), in love to one another and in love to all men. Love is of God, and is the fulfilling of the gospel as well as of the law. Timothy brought good tidings of their faith, yet something was lacking therein; and of their charity, yet the apostle prays that this might increase and abound. We are beholden to God not only for the stock put into our hands at first, but for the improvement of it also. And to our prayer we must add endeavour. The apostle again mentions his abounding love, towards them. The more we are beloved, the more affectionate we should be.

(2) That they might be established unblameable in holiness, *v.* 13. *To the end that he* (the Lord) *may establish your hearts.* Holiness is required of all those who would go to heaven, and therein we must be unblameable. Our desire should be to have our hearts established in holiness before God, and that we may be unblameable before God, even the Father, now, and be presented blameless when the Lord Jesus shall come with all his saints.

JAMIESON, FAUSSET, BROWN

lest (in that case) our labor *may prove to be* in vain" (cf. Gal. 4:11). Our labor in preaching would in that case be vain, so far as *ye* are concerned, but not as concerns *us* in so far as *we* have sincerely labored (Isa. 49:4; I Cor. 3:8). **6.** Join "now" with "come"; "But Timotheus having *just now come* from you unto us" [ALFORD]. Thus it appears (cf. Acts 18:5) Paul is writing from Corinth. **your faith and charity**—(ch. 1:3; cf. II Thess. 1:3, whence it seems their faith subsequently increased still more). *Faith* was the solid foundation: *charity* the cement which held together the superstructure of their practice on that foundation. In that *charity* was included their "good (kindly) remembrance" of their teachers. **desiring greatly**—*Greek,* "having a yearning desire for." **we also**—The desires of loving friends for one another's presence are reciprocal. **7. over you**—in respect to you. **in**—in the midst of: notwithstanding "all our distress (*Greek,* 'necessity') and affliction," viz., external trials at Corinth, whence Paul writes (cf. vs. 6, with Acts 18:5-10). **8. now**—as the case is; seeing ye stand fast. **we live**—we flourish. It *revives us* in our affliction to hear of your steadfastness (Ps. 22:26; II John 3:4). **if**—implying that the vivid joy which the missionaries "now" feel, *will continue* if the Thessalonians continue steadfast. They still needed exhortation, vs. 10; therefore he subjoins the conditional clause, "if ye . . . (Phil. 4:1). **9. what . . .**—*what sufficient* thanks? **render . . . again**—in return for His goodness (Ps. 116:12). **for you**—"concerning you." **for all the joy**—on account of all the joy. It was "comfort," vs. 7, now it is more, viz., *joy.* **for your sakes**—on your account. **before our God**—It is a joy which will bear God's searching eye: a joy as in the presence of God, not selfseeking, but disinterested, sincere, and spiritual (cf. ch. 2:20; John 15:11). **10. Night and day**—(*Note,* ch. 2:9). Night is the season for the saint's holiest meditations and prayers (II Tim. 1:3). **praying**—connected with, "we joy"; we joy while we pray; or else as ALFORD, *What thanks can we render to God while we pray?* The *Greek* implies a *beseeching* request. **exceedingly**—lit., **"more than exceeding abundantly"** (cf. Eph. 3:20). **that which is lacking**—Even the Thessalonians had points in which they needed improvement [BENGEL], (Luke 17:5). Their doctrinal views as to the nearness of Christ's coming, and as to the state of those who had fallen asleep, and their practice in some points, needed correction (ch. 4:1-9). Paul's method was to begin by commending what was praiseworthy, and then to correct what was amiss; a good pattern to all admonishers of others. **11.** Translate, "*May* God Himself, *even* our Father (there being but one article in the *Greek,* requires this translation, 'He who is at once God and our Father'), direct. . . . "The "Himself" stands in contrast with "we" (ch. 2:18); *we* desired to come but could not through Satan's hindrance; but if God *Himself* direct our way (as we pray), none can hinder Him (II Thess. 2:16, 17). It is a remarkable proof of *the unity of the Father and Son,* that in the *Greek* here, and in II Thessalonians 2:16, 17, the verb is *singular,* implying that the subject, the Father and Son, are but *one in essential Being,* not in mere unity of will. Almost all the chapters in both Epistles to the Thessalonians are sealed, each with its own prayer (ch. 5:23; II Thess. 1:11; 2:16; 3:5, 16) [BENGEL]. Paul does not think the prosperous issue of a journey an unfit subject for prayer (Rom. 1:10; 15:32) [EDMUNDS]. His prayer, though the answer was deferred, in about five years afterwards was fulfilled in his return to Macedonia. **12.** The "you" in the *Greek* is emphatically put *first;* "But" (so the *Greek* for "and") what concerns "YOU," whether we come or not, "may the Lord make you to increase and abound in love. . . ." The *Greek* for "increase" has a more *positive* force; that for "abound" a more *comparative* force, "make you *full* (supplying "that which is lacking," vs. 10) and even abound." "The Lord" may here be the Holy Spirit; so the Three Persons of the Trinity will be appealed to (cf. vs. 13), as in II Thessalonians 3:5. So the Holy Ghost is called "the Lord" (II Cor. 3:17). "Love" is the fruit of the Spirit (Gal. 5:22), and His office is "to stablish in holiness" (vs. 13; I Pet. 1:2). **13. your hearts**—which are naturally the spring and seat of unholiness. **before God, even our Father**—rather, "before Him who is at once God and our Father." Before not merely men, but Him who will not be deceived by the mere show of holiness, i.e., may your holiness be such as will stand His searching scrutiny. **coming**—*Greek,* "presence," or "arrival." **with all his saints**—including both the holy angels and the holy elect of men (ch. 4:14; Dan. 7:10; Zech. 14:5; Matt. 25:31; II Thess. 1:7). The saints are "His" Acts 9:13).

ADAM CLARKE

6. *When Timotheus came.* We have already seen that he and Silas stayed behind at Thessalonica, when Paul was obliged to leave it, for the persecution seems to have been principally directed against him. When Paul came to Athens, he sent pressingly to Timothy and Silas to come to him with all speed to that city. We are not informed that they did come, but it is most likely that they did, and that Paul sent Timothy back to Thessalonica to comfort and build up these new converts. After Paul had sent away Timothy, it is likely he went himself straight to Corinth, and there Timothy soon after met him with the good news of the steadiness of the Thessalonian church. *Your faith and charity.* The good tidings which Timothy brought from Thessalonica consisted of three particulars: (1) Their *faith;* they continued steadfast in their belief of the gospel. (2) Their *charity;* they loved one another, and lived in unity and harmony. (3) They were affectionately attached to the apostle; they had *good remembrance* of him, and desired earnestly to see him.

8. *For now we live.* Your steadfastness in the faith gives me new life and comfort; I now feel that I live to some purpose, as my labor in the Lord is not in vain.

10. *Night and day praying exceedingly.* Supplicating God at all times; mingling this with all my prayers; "abounding and superabounding in my entreaties to God" to permit me to revisit you. How strong was his affection for this church! *Might perfect that which is lacking.* That I might have the opportunity of giving you the fullest instructions in the doctrine of Christ, so that the great outlines of truth which you already know may be filled up, that you may be perfectly fitted to every good word and work.

11. *Now God himself and our Father.* That is, God, who is our Father, who has adopted us into the heavenly family, and called us His sons and daughters. *Direct our way.* As he was employed in God's work he dared not consult his own inclinations; he looked for continual directions from God, where, when, and how to do his Master's work.

12. *Make you to increase and abound in love.* They had already love to each other, so as to unite them in one Christian body; and he prays that they may have an increase and an abundance of it, that they might feel the same love to each other which he felt for them all.

13. *To the end he may establish your hearts.* Without love to God and man there can be no establishment in the religion of Christ. It is love that produces both solidity and continuance. *At the coming of our Lord.* God is coming to judge the world. But who in that great day shall give up his accounts with joy? That person only whose heart is established in holiness *before God;* i.e., so as to bear the eye and strict scrutiny of his Judge.

MATTHEW HENRY | JAMIESON, FAUSSET, BROWN | ADAM CLARKE

We must have "holiness" if we are to be numbered with His holy ones or "saints." On "unblamable," cf. Revelation 14:5. This verse (cf. vs. 12) shows that "love" is the spring of true "holiness" (Matt. 5:44-48; Rom. 13:10; Col. 3:14). God is He who really "stablishes"; Timothy and other ministers are but instruments (vs. 2) in "stablishing."

MATTHEW HENRY

CHAPTER 4

Verses 1–8

I. An exhortation to *abound more and more* in that which is good, *v.* 1, 2.

1. The manner in which the exhortation is given—very affectionately. The apostle entreats them as brethren; he exhorts them very earnestly: *We beseech and exhort you.*

2. The matter of his exhortation—that they would abound more and more in holy walking. The apostle would have them further to excel others. Those who most excel others fall short of perfection. We must not only persevere to the end, but we should grow better.

3. The arguments with which the apostle enforces his exhortation. They had been informed of their duty. They had received or been taught, *how they ought to walk.* The design of the gospel is to teach men not only what they should believe, but also how they ought to live. The apostle taught them how to walk, not how to talk. To talk well without living well will never bring us to heaven. The apostle taught and exhorted them in the name of the Lord Jesus Christ. Herein they would please God. We should not be men-pleasers, but should walk so as to please God. The rule according to which they ought to walk and act—*the commandments they had given them by the Lord Jesus Christ.* Though they had great authority from Christ, yet that was to teach men what Christ had commanded, not to give forth commandments of their own. The Thessalonians knew what commandments he gave them, that they were no other than what he had received from the Lord Jesus.

II. A caution against uncleanness.

1. *That you should abstain from fornication* (*v.* 3), by which we are to understand all uncleanness whatsoever. All that is contrary to chastity in heart, speech, and behaviour, is contrary to the command of God and contrary to that holiness which the gospel requires.

2. This branch of sanctification in particular is the will of God, *v.* 3. Not only does God require holiness in the heart, but also purity in our bodies. This will be greatly for our honour: so much is plainly implied, *v.* 4. The body is here called the vessel of the soul, which dwells therein, and it must be kept pure from defiling lusts. What can be more dishonourable than for a rational soul to be enslaved by bodily affections and brutal appetites? To indulge the lust of concupiscence is to live and act like heathens. *Even as the Gentiles who know not God, v.* 5. Christians should not walk as unconverted Gentiles. The sin of uncleanness, especially adultery, is a great piece of injustice that God will be the avenger of; so we may understand those words, *That no man go beyond or defraud his brother* (*v.* 6) *in any matter.* Some understand these words as a further warning and caution against injustice and oppression, which are certainly contrary to the gospel. But the meaning may rather be to show the injustice and wrong that are done by the sin of uncleanness. And, as this sin is of such a heinous nature, so it follows that God will be the avenger of it.

The sin of uncleanness is contrary to the design of our Christian calling: *For God hath called us not unto uncleanness, but unto holiness, v.* 7.

The contempt therefore of God's law and gospel is the contempt of God himself: *He that despises, despises God, not man* only.

JAMIESON, FAUSSET, BROWN

CHAPTER 4

Vss. 1-18. EXHORTATIONS TO CHASTITY; BROTHERLY LOVE; QUIET INDUSTRY; ABSTINENCE FROM UNDUE SORROW FOR DEPARTED FRIENDS, FOR AT CHRIST'S COMING ALL HIS SAINTS SHALL BE GLORIFIED. **1. Furthermore**—*Greek,* "As to what remains." Generally used towards the close of his Epistles (Eph. 6:10; Phil. 4:8). **then**—with a view to the *love* and *holiness* (ch. 3:12, 13) which we have just prayed for in your behalf, we now give you exhortation. **beseech**—"ask" as if it were a personal favor. **by . . .**—rather as *Greek,* "IN the Lord Jesus"; in communion with the Lord Jesus, as Christian ministers dealing with Christian people [EDMUNDS]. **as ye . . . received**—when we were with you (ch. 2:13). **how**—*Greek,* the "how," i.e., *the manner.* **walk and . . . please God**—i.e., *"and so* please God," viz., by your walk; in contrast to the Jews who "please not God" (ch. 2:15). **The oldest** MSS. add a clause here, "even as also ye do walk" (cf. ch. 4:10; 5:11). These words, which he was able to say of them with truth, conciliate a favorable hearing for the precepts which follow. Also the expression, "abound *more and more,"* implies that there had gone before a recognition of their already in some measure *walking so.* **2. by the Lord Jesus**—by His authority and direction, not by our own. He uses the strong term, "commandments," in writing to this Church not long founded, knowing that they would take it in a right spirit, and feeling it desirable that they should understand he spake with divine authority. He seldom uses the term in writing subsequently, when his authority was established, to other churches. I Corinthians 7:10; 11:17; and I Timothy 1:5 (vs. 18, where the subject accounts for the strong expression) are the exceptions. "The Lord" marks His paramount authortiy, requiring implicit obedience. **3. For**—enforcing the assertion that his "commandments" were "by (the authority of) the Lord Jesus" (vs. 2). Since "this is the will of God," let it be your will also. **fornication**—not regarded as a sin at all among the heathen, and so needing the more to be denounced (Acts 15:20). **4. know**—by moral self-control. **how to possess his vessel**—rather as *Greek,* "how to *acquire* (get for himself) *his own* vessel," i.e., that each should have *his own wife* so as to avoid fornication (vs. 3; I Cor. 7:2). The emphatical position of "his own" in the *Greek,* and the use of "vessel" for *wife,* in I Pet. 3:7, and in common Jewish phraseology, and the correct translation "acquire," all justify this rendering. **in sanctification**—(Rom. 6:19; I Cor. 6:15, 18). Thus, "his own" stands in opposition to dishonoring his brother by lusting after *his* wife (vs. 6). **honour**—(Heb. 13:4) contrasted with *"dishonor* their own bodies" (Rom. 1:24). **5. in the lust**—*Greek,* "passion"; which implies that such a one is unconsciously the *passive* slave of lust. **which know not God**—and so know no better. Ignorance of true religion is the parent of unchastity (Eph. 4:18, 19). A people's morals are like the objects of their worship (Deut. 7:26; Ps. 115:8; Rom. 1:23, 24). **6. go beyond**—transgress the bounds of rectitude in respect to his brother. **defraud**—"overreach" [ALFORD]; "take advantage of" [EDMUNDS]. **in any matter**—rather as *Greek,* "in *the* matter"; a decorous expression for the matter now in question; the conjugal honor of his neighbor as a husband, vs. 4; vs. 7 also confirms this view; the word "brother" enhances the enormity of the crime. It is your *brother* whom you wrong (cf. Prov. 6:27-33). **the Lord**—the coming Judge (II Thess. 1:7, 8). **avenger**—the Righter. **of all such**—*Greek,* "concerning all *these things";* in all such cases of wrongs against a neighbor's conjugal honor. **testified**—*Greek,* "*constantly* testified [ALFORD]. **7. unto**—*Greek,* "for the purpose of." **unto**—rather as *Greek,* "in"; marking that "holiness" is the element in which our calling has place; in a sphere of holiness. *Saint* is another name for Christian. **8. despiseth . . .**—*Greek,* "setteth at naught" such engagements imposed on him in his calling, vs. 7; in relation to his "brother," vs. 6. He who doth so, "sets at naught not man (as for instance his brother), but God" (Ps. 51:4). Or, as the *Greek* verb (Luke 10:16; John 12:48) is used of *despising* or *rejecting* God's min-

ADAM CLARKE

CHAPTER 4

1. *We beseech you, brethren, and exhort.* We give you proper instructions in heavenly things, and request you to attend to our advice. The apostle used the most pressing entreaties; for he had a strong and affectionate desire that this church should excel in all righteousness and true holiness. *Please God . . . more and more.* God sets no bounds to the communications of His grace and Spirit to them that are faithful. And as there are no bounds to the graces, so there should be none to the exercise of those graces.

2. *Ye know what commandments we gave you.* This refers to his instructions while he was among them.

3. *This is the will of God, even your sanctification.* God has called you to holiness; He requires that you should be holy, for without holiness none can see the Lord. *That ye should abstain from fornication.* The word includes all sorts of uncleanness.

4. *How to possess his vessel.* Let every man use his wife for the purpose alone for which God created her and instituted marriage. The word answers to the Hebrew *keli,* which, though it signifies *vessel* in general, has several other meanings. The rabbins frequently express "wife" by it; and to me it appears very probable that the apostle uses it in that sense here. Peter calls the wife the "weaker vessel," 1 Pet. iii. 7. Others think that the body is meant, which is the vessel in which the soul dwells. In this sense Paul uses it in 2 Cor. iv. 7: "We have this treasure in earthen vessels"; and in this sense it is used by both Greek and Roman authors.

6. *That no man go beyond and defraud his brother.* That no man should by any means endeavor to corrupt the wife of another, or to alienate her affections or fidelity from her husband.

7. *God hath not called us unto uncleanness.* He is the Creator of male and female, and the Institutor of marriage, and He has called men and women to this state; but the end of this and all the other callings of God to man is *holiness,* not *uncleanness.* And they who use the marriage state as he directs will find it conducive to their holiness and perfection.

8. *He therefore that despiseth.* He who will not receive these teachings, and is led either to undervalue or despise them, despises not us but God, from whom we have received our commission and by whose Spirit we give these directions.

MATTHEW HENRY

God hath given Christians his Spirit. The Holy Ghost is given unto us to arm us against these sins.

Verses 9–12

I. Of brotherly love. This he exhorts them to increase in yet more and more. They were remarkable in the exercise of it, which made it less needful that he should write to them about it, *v.* 9. Thus by his good opinion of them he insinuated himself into their affections, and so made way for his exhortation to them.

1. What it is that the apostle commends in them. It was not so much their own virtue as God's grace. God had taught them this good lesson: *You yourselves are taught of God to love one another, v.* 9. Whoever does that which is good is taught of God to do it. All who are savingly taught of God are taught this lesson, to love one another. This is the livery of Christ's family. The Thessalonians gave good evidence of their being taught of God by *their love to the brethren in all Macedonia, v.* 10. Their love was extensive. And a true Christian's is so to all the saints.

2. The exhortation itself is to increase more and more in brotherly love, *v.* 10. They must be exhorted to pray for more, and labour for more. There are none on this side heaven who love in perfection.

II. Of quietness and industry in their callings. *Study to be quiet, v.* 11. It is the most desirable thing to have a calm and quiet temper, and to be of a peaceable and quiet behaviour. Satan is very busy to disquiet us; and we have that in our own hearts that disposes us to be disquiet; therefore let us study to be quiet. *Do your own business.* Those who are busy-bodies, meddling in other men's matters, generally have but little quiet in their own minds and cause great disturbances among their neighbours; at least they seldom mind the other exhortation, to be diligent in their own calling, *to work with their own hands.* Christianity does not discharge us from the work of our particular callings, but teaches us to be diligent therein. Thus we shall walk honestly, or decently and creditably, towards those that are without, *v.* 12. This will be to act as becomes the gospel, and will gain a good report from those that are strangers, yea, enemies to it. We shall live comfortably, and have lack of nothing, *v.* 12. Such as are diligent in their own business live comfortably and have lack of nothing. They earn their own bread, and have the greatest pleasure in so doing.

Verses 13–18

The apostle comforts the Thessalonians who mourned for the death of their relations and friends that died in the Lord. His design is to dissuade them from excessive grief. *All* grief for the death of friends is far from being unlawful; we may weep for our own loss, though it may be their gain. Yet we must not be immoderate in our sorrows.

I. This looks as if we had no hope, *v.* 13. It is to act too much like the Gentiles, who had no hope of a better life after this. This hope is more than enough to balance all our griefs.

II. This is an effect of ignorance concerning those who are dead, *v.* 13. There are some things which we cannot but be ignorant of concerning those that are asleep. Yet there are some things concerning those especially who die in the Lord that we need not to be ignorant of. They will be sufficient to allay our sorrow concerning them.

JAMIESON, FAUSSET, BROWN

ister, it may mean here, "He who despiseth" or "rejecteth" these our ministerial precepts. **who hath also given unto us**—So some oldest MSS. read, but most oldest MSS. read, "Who (without 'also') *giveth* (present) unto *you*" (not "us"). **his Spirit**—*Greek,* "His own Spirit, the Holy (One)"; thus emphatically marking "holiness" (vs. 7) as the end for which the *Holy* (One) is being given. "Unto you," in the *Greek,* implies that the Spirit is being given *unto, into* (put *into* your hearts), *and among* you (cf. ch. 2:9; Eph. 4:30). "Giveth" implies that sanctification is not merely a work once for all accomplished in the past, but a *present progressive* work. So the Church of England Catechism, "*sanctifieth* (present) all the elect people of God." "His own" implies that as He gives you that which is essentially identical with Himself, He expects you should become like Himself (I Pet. 1:16; II Pet. 1:4). **9. brotherly love . . .**—referring here to acts of brotherly kindness in relieving distressed brethren. Some oldest MSS. support *English Version* reading, "YE have"; others, and those the weightiest, read, "WE have." *We* need not write, as *ye yourselves* are taught, and that by *God;* viz., in the heart by the Holy Spirit (John 6:45; Heb. 8:11; I John 2:20, 27). **to love**—*Greek,* "with a view to," or "to the end of your loving one another." Divine teachings have their confluence in love [BENGEL]. **10. And indeed**—*Greek,* "For even." **11. study to be quiet**—*Greek,* "*make it your ambition* to be quiet, and to do *your own business.*" In direct contrast to the world's *ambition,* which is, "to make a great stir," and "to be busybodies" (II Thess. 3:11, 12). **work with your own hands**—The Thessalonian converts were, it thus seems, chiefly of the *working* classes. Their expectation of the immediate coming of Christ led some enthusiasts among them to neglect their daily work and be dependent on the bounty of others. See end of vs. 12. The expectation was right in so far as that the Church should be always looking for Him; but they were wrong in making it a ground for neglecting their daily work. The evil, as it subsequently became worse, is more strongly reproved in II Thessalonians 3:6-12. **12. honestly**—in the Old English sense, "becomingly," as becomes your Christian profession; not bringing discredit on it in the eyes of the outer world, as if Christianity led to sloth and poverty (Rom. 13:13; I Pet. 2:12). **them . . . without**—outside the Christian Church (Mark 4:11). **have lack of nothing**—not have to beg from others for the supply of your wants (cf. Eph. 4:28). So far from needing to beg from others, we ought to work and get the means of supplying the need of others. Freedom from pecuniary embarrassment is to be desired by the Christian on account of the liberty which it bestows. **13.** The leading topic of Paul's preaching at Thessalonica having been the coming *kingdom* (Acts 17:7), some perverted it into a cause for fear in respect to friends lately deceased, as if these would be excluded from the glory which those found alive alone should share. This error Paul here corrects (cf. ch. 5:10). **I would not**—All the oldest MSS. and versions have "*we* would not." **My** fellow labourers (Silas and Timothy) and myself desire that ye should not be ignorant. **them which are asleep**—The oldest MSS. read *present tense,* "them which are *sleeping*"; the same as "the dead in Christ" (vs. 16), to whose bodies (Dan. 12:2, not their *souls;* Eccl. 12:7; II Cor. 5:8) death is a calm and holy sleep, from which the resurrection shall waken them to glory. The word "cemetery" means *a sleeping-place.* Observe, the glory and chief hope of the Church are not to be realized at death, but at the Lord's coming; one is not to anticipate the other, but all are to be glorified together at Christ's coming (Col. 3:4; Heb. 11:40). **ye sorrow not, even as others**—*Greek,* "the rest"; all the rest of the world besides Christians. Not all natural *mourning* for dead friends is forbidden: for the Lord Jesus and Paul sinlessly gave way to it (John 11:31, 33, 35; Phil. 2:27); but sorrow as though there were "no hope," which indeed the heathen had not (Eph. 2:12): the Christian *hope* here meant is that of *the resurrection.* Psalm 16:9, 11; 17:15; 73:24; Proverbs 14:32, show that the Old Testament Church, though not having the hope *so bright* (Isa. 38:18, 19), yet *had* this hope. Contrast CATULLUS, 5. 4, "When once our brief day has set, we must sleep one everlasting night." The sepulchral inscriptions of heathen Thessalonica express the hopeless view taken as to those once dead: as ÆSCHYLUS writes, "Of one once dead there is no resurrection." Whatever glimpses some heathen philosophers, had of the existence of the soul after death, they had none whatever of the body (Acts 17:18, 20, 32). **14. For if**—confirmation of his statement, vs. 13, that the removal of *ignorance* as to the sleeping be-

ADAM CLARKE

Hath also given unto us his holy Spirit. Instead of *unto us,* "unto you" is the reading of a great many MSS. This seems to be the better reading.

9. *Touching brotherly love.* They were remarkable for this; and though the apostle appears to have had this as a topic on which he intended to write to them, yet from the account which he received of their prosperous state by Timothy, he finds that it is unnecessary to spend any time in inculcating a doctrine which they fully understood and practiced.

10. *Ye do it toward all the brethren.* You not only love one another at Thessalonica, but you love all the brethren in Macedonia; you consider them all as children of the same Father.

11. *That ye study to be quiet.* Though in general the church at Thessalonica was pure and exemplary, yet there seem to have been some idle, tattling people among them, who disturbed the peace of others. To these the apostle gives those directions which the whole Church of God should enforce wherever such troublesome and dangerous people are found; viz., that they should *study to be quiet,* "to hold their peace," as their religious cant will never promote true religion; that they should *do* their *own business,* and let that of others alone; and that they should *work with* their *own hands,* and not be a burden to the Church of God. An idle person, though able to discourse like an angel or pray like an apostle, cannot be a Christian; all such are hypocrites and deceivers. The true members of the Church of Christ walk, work, and labor.

12. *That ye may walk honestly.* "Becomingly, decently, respectably"; as is consistent with the purity, holiness, gravity, and usefulness of your Christian calling. *Them that are without.* The unconverted Gentiles and Jews. *That ye may have lack of nothing.* That you may be able to get your bread by honest labor, which God will ever bless, and be chargeable to no man. He that is dependent on another is necessarily in bondage; and he who is able to get his own bread by the sweat of his brow should not be under obligation even to a king.

13. *I would not have you to be ignorant.* Instead of *have,* "wish," is the reading of many MSS. and many of the Greek fathers. This is undoubtedly the true reading: "Brethren, I would not wish you to be ignorant." This was probably one of the points which were lacking in their faith, that he wished to go to Thessalonica to instruct them in. *Them which are asleep.* That is, those who are dead. It is supposed that the apostle had heard that the Thessalonians continued to lament over their dead, as the heathens did in general who had no hope of the resurrection of the body, and that they had been puzzled concerning the doctrine of the resurrection.

MATTHEW HENRY

1. They sleep in Jesus. They are asleep, *v.* 13. They have retired out of this troublesome world, to rest from all their labours and sorrows, and they sleep in Jesus, *v.* 14. They are not lost, nor are they losers, but great gainers by death, and their removal out of this world is into a better.

2. They shall be raised up from the dead, and awakened out of their sleep, for *God will bring them with him, v.* 14. They then are with God, and are better where they are than when they were here; and when God comes he will bring them with him. The doctrine of the resurrection and the second coming of Christ is a great antidote against the fear of death and inordinate sorrow for the death of our Christian friends; and this doctrine we have a full assurance of, because we *believe that Jesus died and rose again, v.* 14.

3. Their state and condition shall be glorious and happy at the second coming of Christ. This the apostle informs the Thessalonians of *by the word of the Lord* (*v.* 15).

The Lord Jesus will come down from heaven in all the pomp and power of the upper world (*v.* 16): *The Lord himself shall descend from heaven with a shout.*

He will descend from heaven into this our air, *v.* 17. The appearance will be with pomp and power, *with a shout*—with *the voice of the archangel.* The glorious appearance of this great Redeemer and Judge will be proclaimed and ushered in by the *trump of God.* The dead shall be raised: *The dead in Christ shall rise first* (*v.* 16). Those who shall then *be found alive shall not prevent those that are asleep, v.* 15. Those that shall be found alive will then be changed.

They shall *be caught up together with them in the clouds, to meet the Lord in the air, v.* 17. Those who are raised, and thus changed, shall meet together in the clouds, and there meet with their Lord. Here is the bliss of the saints at that day: they shall *be ever with the Lord, v.* 17. The principal happiness of heaven is this, *to be with the Lord,* to see him, live with him, and enjoy him, for ever.

JAMIESON, FAUSSET, BROWN

lievers would remove undue grief respecting them. See vs. 13, "hope." Hence it appears our *hope* rests on our *faith* ("if we believe"). "As surely as we all believe that Christ died and rose again (the very doctrine specified as taught at Thessalonica, Acts 17:3), *so also* will God bring *those laid to sleep by Jesus* with Him" (Jesus. So the order and balance of the members of the *Greek* sentence require us to translate). Believers are laid in sleep by Jesus, and so will be brought back from sleep with Jesus in His train when He comes. The disembodied souls are not here spoken of; the reference is to the sleeping *bodies.* **15. by the word of the Lord**—*Greek,* "in," i.e., *in virtue* of a direct revelation from the Lord to me. So I Kings 20:35. This is the "mystery," a truth once hidden, now revealed, which Paul shows (I Cor. 15:51, 52). **prevent**—i.e., "anticipate." So far were the early Christians from regarding their departed brethren as *anticipating* them in entering glory, that they needed to be assured that those who remain to the coming of the Lord "will not anticipate them that are asleep." The "we" means *whichever of us* are alive and remain unto the coming of the Lord. The Spirit designed that believers in each successive age should live in continued expectation of the Lord's coming, not knowing but that *they* should be among those found alive at His coming (Matt. 24:42). It is a sad fall from this blessed hope, that *death* is looked for by most men, rather than the coming of our Lord. Each successive generation in its time and place represents the generation which shall actually survive till His coming (Matt. 25:13; Rom. 13:11; I Cor. 15:51; Jas. 5:9; I Pet. 4:5, 6). The Spirit subsequently revealed by Paul that which is not inconsistent with the expectation here taught of the Lord's coming at any time; viz., that His coming would not be until there should be a "falling away first" (II Thess. 2:2, 3); but as symptoms of this soon appeared, none could say but that still this precursory event might be realized, and so the Lord come in his day. **16. himself**—in all the Majesty of His presence in person, not by deputy. **descend**—even as He ascended (Acts 1:11). **with**—*Greek,* "in," implying one concomitant circumstance attending His appearing. **shout**—*Greek,* "signal shout," "war shout." Jesus is represented as a victorious King, giving the word of command to the hosts of heaven in His train for the last onslaught, at His final triumph over sin, death, and Satan (Rev. 19:11-21). **the voice of . . . archangel**—distinct from the "signal shout." Michael is perhaps meant (Jude 9; Rev. 12:7), to whom especially is committed the guardianship of the people of God (Dan. 10:13). **trump of God**—the trumpet blast which usually accompanies God's manifestation in glory (Exod. 19:16; Ps. 47:5); here the last of the three accompaniments of His appearing: as the trumpet was used to convene God's people to their solemn convocations (Num. 10:2, 10; 31:6), so here to summon God's elect together, preparatory to their glorification with Christ (Ps. 50:1-5; Matt. 24:31; I Cor. 15:52). **shall rise first**—previously to the living being "caught up." The "first" here has no reference to the *first* resurrection, as contrasted with that of "the rest of the dead." That reference occurs elsewhere (Matt. 13:41, 42, 50; John 5:29; I Cor. 15: 23, 24; Rev. 20:5, 6); it simply stands in opposition to "then," vs. 17. FIRST, "the *dead* in Christ" shall rise, THEN the *living* shall be caught up. The Lord's people alone are spoken of here. **17. we which are alive . . . shall be caught up**—after having been "changed in a moment" (I Cor. 15:51, 52). Again he says, "we," recommending thus the expression to Christians of all ages, each generation bequeathing to the succeeding one a continually increasing obligation to look for the coming of the Lord. [EDMUNDS]. **together with them**—all together: the raised dead, and changed living, forming one joint body. **in the clouds**—*Greek,* "in clouds." The same honor is conferred on them as on their Lord. As He was taken in a cloud at His ascension (Acts 1:9), so at His return with clouds (Rev. 1:7), they shall be caught up in clouds. The clouds are His and their triumphal chariot (Ps. 104:3; Dan. 7:13). ELLICOTT explains the *Greek,* "robed round by upbearing clouds" (*Aids to Faith*). **in the air**—rather, "*into* the air"; caught up *into* the region just above the earth, where the *meeting* (cf. Matt. 25:1, 6) shall take place between them ascending, and their Lord descending towards the earth. Not that the air is to be the place of their *lasting abode* with Him. **and so shall we ever be with the Lord**—no more parting, and no more going out (Rev. 3:12). His point being established, that the dead in Christ shall be on terms of equal advantage with those found alive at Christ's coming, he leaves undefined here

ADAM CLARKE

14. *For if we believe that Jesus died and rose again.* "Seeing that we believe"; knowing that the resurrection of Christ is as fully authenticated as His detah. *Even so them.* It necessarily follows that they who *sleep*—die, in Him—in the faith of the gospel, *will God bring with him*—He will raise them up as Jesus was raised from the dead, in the same manner, i.e., by His own eternal power and energy; and He will bring them *with him*—with Christ, for He is the Head of the Church, which is His body.

15. *This we say unto you by the word of the Lord.* This I have, by express revelation, from the Lord. What he now delivers he gives as coming immediately from the Spirit of God. *We which are alive and remain.* By the pronoun *we* the apostle does not intend himself and the Thessalonians to whom he was then writing; he is speaking of the genuine Christians which shall be found on earth when Christ comes to judgment. From not considering the manner in which the apostle uses this word, some have been led to suppose that he imagined that the day of judgment would take place in that generation, and while he and the then believers at Thessalonica were in life. *Shall not prevent them which are asleep.* Those who shall be found living in that day, though they shall not pass through death, but be suddenly changed, shall not go to glory before them that are dead, for "the dead in Christ shall rise first"—they shall be raised, their bodies made glorious, and be caught up to meet the Lord, before the others shall be changed. And this appears to be the meaning of the apostle's words which we translate *shall not prevent;* for although this word *prevent,* from *prae* and *venio,* literally signifies to "go before," yet we use it now in the sense of "to hinder or obstruct."

16. *The Lord himself.* That is, Jesus Christ. *Shall descend from heaven.* Shall descend in like manner as He was seen by His disciples to ascend; i.e., in His human form, but now infinitely more glorious. *With a shout.* Or "order," and probably in these words: "Arise, ye dead, and come to judgment"; which order shall be repeated by the archangel, who shall accompany it with the sound of the trump of God, whose great and terrible blasts, like those on Mount Sinai, sounding louder and louder, shall shake both the heavens and the earth!

CHARLES H. SPURGEON:

In due time the last trump shall sound and Christ shall come, but the saints shall be with Him. The infinite providence has so arranged that Christ shall not come without His people, for "them also that sleep in Jesus shall God bring with him." The saints shall be with Him in the advent as they are now. Our souls shall hear the shout of victory and join in it; the voice of the archangel shall be actually heard by all His redeemed, and the trump of God shall be sounded in the hearing of every one of His beloved, for we shall be with Jesus all through that glorious transaction. Whatever the glory and splendor of the second advent, we shall be with Jesus in it. I am not going to give you glimpses of the revealed future, or offer any suggestion as to the sublime history which is yet to be written, but most certainly there is to be a last general judgment, and then we shall be with Christ, assessors with Him at that day. Being ourselves first acquitted, we shall take our seat upon the judgment bench with Him. What saith the Holy Ghost by the apostle—"Do ye not know that we shall judge angels?" The fallen angels, to their shame, shall in part receive the verdict of their condemnation from the lips of men, and thus vengeance shall be taken upon them for all the mischief they have done to the sons of men. Oh, think of it: amidst the terror of the tremendous day you shall be at ease, resting in the love of God, and beholding the glory of Christ, and "so shall you ever be with the Lord."

—The Treasury of the New Testament

MATTHEW HENRY

This should comfort the saints upon the death of their friends. We and they with all the saints shall meet our Lord, and be with him for ever, no more to be separated either from him or from one another for ever. And the apostle would have us *comfort one another with these words, v.* 18.

CHAPTER 5

Verses 1–5

I. The apostle tells the Thessalonians it was needless or useless to enquire about the particular time of Christ's coming: *Of the times and seasons you need not that I write unto you, v.* 1. There is a certain time appointed for his coming; but he had no revelation given him; nor should they or we enquire into this secret. There are times and seasons for us to do our work in: these it is our duty and interest to know and observe; but the time and season when we must give up our account we know not. There are many things which our vain curiosity desires to know which there is no necessity at all of our knowing, nor would our knowledge of them do us good.

II. He tells them that the coming of Christ would be a great surprise to most men, *v.* 2. *As a thief in the night.* As the thief usually cometh in the dead time of the night, when he is least expected, such a *surprise* will the day of the Lord be.

III. He tells them how terrible Christ's coming would be to the ungodly, *v.* 3. It will be to their destruction in that day of the Lord. It will be sudden. It will overtake them in the midst of their carnal security and jollity, when they say in their hearts, *Peace and safety,* and think not of it,—*as travail cometh upon a woman with child,* at the set time indeed, but not perhaps just then expected. It will be unavoidable destruction too: *They shall not escape.*

IV. He tells them how comfortable this day will be to the righteous, *v.* 4, 5. Their character and privilege. They are the children of the light, &c. This was the happy condition of the Thessalonians as it is of all true Christians. They were not in a state of sin and ignorance as the heathen world. They were the *children of the day,* for the day-star had risen upon them. They were no longer under the darkness of heathenism, but under the gospel, which brings life and immortality to light. Their great advantage on this account: that *that day should not overtake them as a thief, v.* 4. They had fair warning, and might hope to stand with comfort and confidence before the Son of man, as a friend in the day, not as a thief in the night.

Verses 6–10

Exhortations to several needful duties.

I. To watchfulness and sobriety, *v.* 6. These duties are distinct, yet they mutually befriend one another. We shall not keep sober, unless we be upon our guard, and, unless we keep sober, we shall not long watch. 1. Then *let us not sleep as do others, but let us watch;* we must not be secure and careless, nor indulge spiritual sloth and idleness. The generality of men are too careless of their duty and regardless of their spiritual enemies. Either they do not consider the things of another world at all, because they are asleep; or they do not consider them aright, because they dream. But let us watch, and act like men that are awake, and that stand upon their guard. 2. Let us also *be sober.* Let us keep our natural desires and appetites after the things of this world within due bounds. Watchfulness and sobriety are most suitable to the Christian's character and privilege, as being *children of the day;* because *those that sleep, sleep in the night, and those that are drunken are drunken in the night, v.* 7. They were not sensible of their danger, therefore they *slept;* they were not sensible of their duty, therefore they were drunk: but it ill becomes Christians to do thus.

II. To be well armed as well as watchful. Our spiritual enemies are many, and mighty, and malicious. We have need to arm ourselves against their attempts, and this spiritual armour consists of the three great graces of Christians, faith, love, and hope, *v.* 8. 1. We must live by faith, and this will keep us watchful and sober. Faith will be our best defence against the assaults of our enemies. 2. We must get a heart inflamed with love. True and fervent love to God, and

JAMIESON, FAUSSET, BROWN

the other events foretold elsewhere (as not being necessary to his discussion), Christ's reign on earth with His saints (I Cor. 6:2, 3), the final judgment and glorification of His saints in the new heaven and earth. **18. comfort one another**–in your mourning for the dead (vs. 13).

CHAPTER 5

Vss. 1-28. The Suddenness of Christ's Coming a Motive for Watchfulness: Various Precepts: Prayer for Their Being Found Blameless, Body, Soul, and Spirit, at Christ's Coming: Conclusion. **1. times**–the general and indefinite term for chronological periods. **seasons**–the *opportune times* (Dan. 7:12; Acts 1:7). *Time* denotes quantity; *season,* quality. *Seasons* are parts of *times.* **ye have no need**–those who watch do not need to be told *when* the hour will come, for they are always ready [Bengel]. **cometh**–present: expressing its *speedy* and awful *certainty.* **2. as a thief in the night**–The apostles in this image follow the parable of their Lord, expressing how the Lord's coming shall take men by surprise (Matt. 24:43; II Pet. 3:10). "The *night* is wherever there is quiet unconcern" [Bengel]. "At midnight" (perhaps figurative: to some parts of the earth it will be *literal* night), Matthew 25:6. The thief not only gives no notice of his approach but takes all precaution to prevent the household knowing of it. So the Lord (Rev. 16:15). *Signs* will precede the coming, to confirm the patient hope of the watchful believer; but the coming itself shall be sudden at last (Matt. 24-32-36; Luke 21:25-32, 35).

3. they–the men of the world. Verses 5, 6; ch. 4:13, "others," all the rest of the world save Christians. **Peace**–(Judg. 18:7, 9, 27, 28; Jer. 6:14; Ezek. 13:10). **then**–*at the very moment* when they least expect it. Cf. the case of Belshazzar, Daniel 5:1-5, 6, 9, 26-28; Herod, Acts 12:21-23. **sudden**–"unawares" (Luke 21:34). **as travail**–"As *the* labor pang" comes in an instant on the woman when otherwise engaged (Ps. 48:6; Isa. 13:8). **shall not escape**–*Greek,* "shall not at all escape." Another awful feature of their ruin: there shall be then no possibility of shunning it however they desire it (Amos 9:2, 3; Rev. 6:15, 16). **4. not in darkness**–not in darkness of understanding (i.e., spiritual ignorance) or of the moral nature (i.e., a state of sin), Ephesians 4:18. **that**–*Greek,* "in order that"; with God results are all purposed. **that day**–*Greek,* "the day"; the *day* of the Lord (Heb. 10:25, "*the* day"), in contrast to "darkness." **overtake**–unexpectedly (cf. John 12:35). **as a thief**–The two oldest MSS. read, "as (the daylight overtakes) *thieves*" (Job 24:17). Old MSS. and *Vulgate* read as *English Version.* **5.** The oldest MSS. read, "For ye are all...." Ye have no reason for fear, or for being taken by surprise, by the coming of the day of the Lord: "*For* ye are all sons (so the *Greek*) of light and sons of day"; a *Hebrew* idiom, implying that as *sons* resemble their fathers, so you are *in character* light (intellectually and morally illuminated in a spiritual point of view), Luke 16:8; John 12:36. **are not of**–i.e., *belong not to* night nor darkness. The change of person from "ye" to "we" implics this: *Ye* are sons of light because ye are Christians; and *we,* Christians, are not of night nor darkness. **6. others**–*Greek,* "the rest" of the world: the unconverted (ch. 4:13). "Sleep" here is worldly apathy to spiritual things (Rom. 13:11; Eph. 5:14); in vs. 7, ordinary *sleep;* in vs. 10, death. **watch**–for Christ's coming; lit., "be wakeful." The same *Greek* occurs in I Corinthians 15:34; II Timothy 2:26. **be sober**–refraining from carnal indulgence, mental or sensual (I Pet. 5:8). **7.** This verse is to be taken in the literal sense. Night is the time when sleepers sleep, and drinking men are drunk. To sleep by day would imply great indolence; to be drunken by day, great shamelessness. Now, in a spiritual sense, "we Christians profess to be day people, not night people; therefore our work ought to be day work, not night work; our conduct such as will bear the eye of day, and such has no need of the veil of night" [Edmunds], (vs. 8). **8.** *Faith, hope,* and *love,* are the three pre-eminent graces (ch. 1:3; I Cor. 13:13). We must not only be awake and sober, but also *armed;* not only watchful, but also guarded. The armor here is only *defensive;* in Ephesians 6:13-17, also *offensive.* Here, therefore, the reference is to the Christian means of being *guarded* against being surprised by the day of the Lord as a thief in the night. The *helmet* and *breastplate* defend the two vital parts, the head and

ADAM CLARKE

CHAPTER 5

1-2. *But of the times and the seasons.* It is natural to suppose, after what he had said in the conclusion of the preceding chapter concerning the coming of Christ, the raising of the dead, and rendering those immortal who should then be found alive without obliging them to pass through the empire of death, that the Thessalonians would feel an innocent curiosity to know, as the disciples did concerning the destruction of Jerusalem, when those things should take place, and what should be the signs of those times, and of the coming of the Son of Man. And it is remarkable that the apostle answers here to these anticipated questions as our Lord did, in the above case, to the direct question of His disciples; and he seems to refer in these words, *Of the times and the seasons . . . ye have no need that I write unto you. For yourselves know . . . that the day of the Lord . . . cometh as a thief in the night,* to what our Lord said, Matt. xxiv. 44; xxv. 13; and the apostle takes it for granted that they were acquainted with our Lord's prediction on the subject. It is very likely therefore that the apostle, like our Lord, couples these two grand events—the destruction of Jerusalem and the final judgment. And it appears most probable that it is of the former event chiefly that he speaks here, as it was certainly of the latter that he treated in the conclusion of the preceding chapter. In the notes on Acts i. 6-7, it has already been shown that the *times* or *seasons* refer to the destruction of the Jewish commonwealth, and we may fairly presume that they have the same meaning in this place.

3. *For when they shall say, Peace and safety.* This points out, very particularly, the state of the Jewish people when the Romans came against them; and so fully persuaded were they that God would not deliver the city and Temple to their enemies that they refused every overture that was made to them. *Sudden destruction.* In the storming of their city, the burning of their Temple, and the massacre of several hundreds of thousands of themselves; the rest being sold for slaves, and the whole of them dispersed over the face of the earth. *As travail upon a woman.* This figure is perfectly consistent with what the apostle had said before, viz., that the times and seasons were not known, though the thing itself was expected, our Lord having predicted it in the most positive manner. So a woman with child knows that, if she is spared, she will have a bearing time; but the week, the day, the hour, she cannot tell.

4. *But ye, brethren, are not in darkness.* Probably Paul refers to a notion that was very prevalent among the Jews. The words in Midrash Tehillim, on Ps. ix. 8, are the following: "When the holy blessed God shall judge the Gentiles, it shall be in the night season, in which they shall be asleep in their transgressions; but when he shall judge the Israelites, it shall be in the day time, when they are occupied in the study of the law." This maxim the apostle appears to have in view in vv. 4-8.

5. *Ye are all the children of light.* You are children of God, and enjoy both His light and life.

6. *Let us not sleep, as do others.* Let us who are of the day—who believe the gospel and belong to Christ—not give way to a careless, unconcerned state of mind, like to the Gentiles and sinners in general, who are stupefied and blinded by sin. *Let us watch.* Be always on the alert; *and be sober,* making a moderate use of all things.

7. *For they that sleep.* Sleepers and drunkards seek the night season; so the careless and the profligate persons indulge their evil propensities and avoid all means of instruction; they prefer their ignorance to the word of God's grace and to the light of life.

8. *Putting on the breastplate.* We are not

MATTHEW HENRY

the things of God, will keep us watchful and sober. 3. We must make salvation our hope. This good hope of eternal life, will be as a helmet to defend the head, and hinder our being intoxicated with the pleasures of sin, which are but for a season. The apostle shows what grounds Christians have to hope for this salvation. He says nothing of their meriting it. No, the doctrine of our merits is altogether unscriptural and antiscriptural.

But our hopes are to be grounded, (1) Upon God's appointment: because *God hath not appointed us to wrath, but to obtain salvation, v.* 9. If we would trace our salvation to the first cause, that is God's appointment.

On this we build unshaken hope, especially when we consider, (2) Christ's merit and grace, and that salvation is by our Lord Jesus Christ who died for us. Our salvation therefore is owing to, and our hopes of it are grounded on, Christ's atonement as well as God's appointment. *That whether we wake or sleep we should live together with Christ,* live in union and in glory with him for ever. Christ died for us, that, living and dying, we might be his; that we might live to him while we are here, and live with him when we go hence.

Verses 11–15

Several duties.

I. Towards those who were nearly related one to another. Such should comfort themselves, or exhort one another, and edify one another, *v.* 11. They must comfort or exhort themselves and one another. We should not only be careful about our own comfort and welfare, but of others also. They must edify one another. We should communicate our knowledge and experiences one to another. We should join in prayer and praise one with another. We should set a good example one before another. This the Thessalonians did (*which also you do*). Those who do that which is good have need of further exhortations to excite them to do more good, as well as continue in doing what they do.

II. Towards their ministers, *v.* 12, 13.

1. How the ministers of the gospel are described by the work of their office. Ministers must labour among their people, labour with diligence, and unto weariness (so the word in the original imports). They are called labourers, and should not be loiterers. Ministers are to rule their people also. They must rule, not with rigour, but with love. They must rule as spiritual guides, by setting a good example to the flock. They are over the people in the Lord, and must rule the people by Christ's laws. They must also admonish the people. They must instruct them to do well, and should reprove when they do ill.

2. What the duty of the people is towards their ministers. The people must know them. As the shepherd should know his flock, so the sheep must know their shepherd. They must esteem their ministers highly in love; and this for their work's sake, because their business is to promote the honour of Christ and the welfare of men's souls. Faithful ministers ought to be so far from being lightly esteemed because of their work that they should be highly esteemed on account of it.

III. Touching the duty Christians owe to one another. *To be at peace among themselves, v.* 13. The people should be at peace among themselves, doing all they can to hinder any differences from rising or continuing among them, and using all proper means to preserve peace and harmony.

To warn the unruly, v. 14. There will be in all societies some who walk disorderly. Such should be reproved and told plainly of the injury they do their own souls, and the hurt they may do to others. *To comfort the feeble-minded, v.* 14, the timorous and faint-hearted, or such as are dejected and of a sorrowful spirit. Such should be encouraged; we should not despise them, but comfort them; and who knows what good a kind and comfortable word may do them?

JAMIESON, FAUSSET, BROWN

the heart respectively. "With head and heart right, the whole man is right" [EDMUNDS]. The head needs to be kept from error, the heart from sin. For "the breastplate of righteousness," Ephesians 6:14, we have here "the breastplate of faith and love"; for the righteousness which is imputed to man for justification, is "faith working by love" (Rom. 4:3, 22-24; Gal. 5:6). "Faith," as the motive *within,* and "love," exhibited in *outward* acts, constitute the perfection of *righteousness.* In Ephesians 6:17 the helmet is "salvation"; here, "the *hope* of salvation." In one aspect "salvation" is a present possession (John 3:36; 5:24; I John 5:13); in another, it is a matter of "hope" (Rom. 8:24, 25). Our Head primarily wore the "breastplate of righteousness" and "helmet of salvation," that we might, by union with Him, receive both. **9. For**—assigning the ground of our "hopes" (vs. 8). **appointed us**—Translate, "set" (Acts 13:47), in His everlasting purpose of love (ch. 3:3; II Tim. 1:9). Contrast Romans 9:22; Jude 4. **to**—i.e., *unto* wrath. **to obtain**—*Greek,* "to the acquisition of salvation"; said, according to BENGEL, of one saved out of a general wreck, when all things else have been lost: so of the elect saved out of the multitude of the lost (II Thess. 2:13, 14). The fact of God's "appointment" of His grace "through Jesus Christ" (Eph. 1:5), takes away the notion of our being able to "acquire" salvation *of ourselves.* Christ "acquired" (so the *Greek* for 'purchased') the Church (and its salvation) with His own blood" (Acts 20:28); each member is said to be appointed by God to the "acquiring of salvation." In the primary sense, God does the work; in the secondary sense, man does it. **10. died for us**—*Greek,* "in our behalf." **whether we wake or sleep**—whether we be found at Christ's coming awake, i.e., alive, or asleep, i.e., in our graves. **together**—*all* of us *together;* the living not preceding the dead in their glorification "with Him" at His coming (ch. 4:13). **11. comfort yourselves**—*Greek,* "one another." Here he reverts to the same consolatory strain as in ch. 4:18. **edify one another**—rather as *Greek,* "edify (ye) the one the other"; "edify," lit., "build up," viz., in faith, hope, and love, by discoursing together on such edifying topics as the Lord's coming, and the glory of the saints (Mal. 3:16). **12. beseech**—"Exhort" is the expression in vs. 14; here, "we beseech you," as if it were a personal favor (Paul making the cause of the Thessalonian presbyters, as it were, his own). **know**—to have a regard and respect for. Recognize their office, and treat them accordingly (cf. I Cor. 16:18) with reverence and with liberality in supplying their needs (I Tim. 5:17). The Thessalonian Church having been newly planted, the ministers were necessarily novices (I Tim. 3:6), which may have been in part the cause of the people's treating them with less respect. Paul's practice seems to have been to ordain elders in every Church soon after its establishment (Acts 14:23). **them which labour . . . are over . . . admonish you**—not three classes of ministers, but one, as there is but one article common to the three in the *Greek.* "Labor" expresses their laborious life; "are over you," their pre-eminence as presidents or superintendents ("bishops," i.e., *overseers,* Phil. 1:1, "them that have rule over you," lit., *leaders,* Heb. 13:17; "pastors," lit., *shepherds,* Eph. 4:11); "admonish you," one of their leading functions; the *Greek* is "put in mind," implying not arbitrary authority, but gentle, though faithful, admonition (II Tim. 2:14, 24, 25; I Pet. 5:3). **in the Lord**—Their presidency over you is *in divine things;* not in worldly affairs, but in things appertaining to the Lord. **13. very highly**—*Greek,* "exceeding abundantly." **for their work's sake**—The high nature of their work alone, the furtherance of your salvation and of the kingdom of Christ, should be a sufficient motive to claim your reverential love. At the same time, the word "work," teaches ministers that, while claiming the reverence due to their office, it is not a sinecure, but a "work"; cf. "*labor*" (even to *weariness:* so the *Greek*), vs. 12. **be at peace among yourselves**—The "and" is not in the original. Let there not only be peace between ministers and their flocks, but also no party rivalries among yourselves, one contending in behalf of some one favorite minister, another in behalf of another (Mark 9:50; I Cor. 1:12; 4:6). **14. brethren**—This exhortation to "warm (*Greek,* 'admonish,' as in vs. 12) the unruly (those 'disorderly' persons, II Thessalonians 3:6, 11, who would not work, and yet expected to be maintained, lit., said of soldiers who will *not* remain *in their ranks,* cf. ch. 4:11; also those insubordinate as to Church discipline, in relation to those 'over' the Church, vs. 12), comfort the feeble-minded" (the *faint-hearted,* who are ready to sink "without hope" in afflictions, ch. 4:13, and

ADAM CLARKE

only called to work, but we are called also to fight; and that we may not be surprised, we must watch; and that we may be in a condition to defend ourselves, we must be sober; and that we may be enabled to conquer, we must be armed: and what the *breastplate* and *helmet* are to a soldier's heart and head, such are faith, love, and hope to us. *Faith* enables us to endure, "as seeing him who is invisible"; *love* excites us to diligence and activity, and makes us bear our troubles and difficulties pleasantly; *hope* helps us to anticipate the great end, the glory that shall be revealed, and which we know we shall in due time obtain if we faint not.

9. *For God hath not appointed us to wrath.* So then it appears that some were *appointed . . . to wrath,* "to punishment"; on this subject there can be no dispute. But who are they? When did this appointment take place? And for what cause? It is very obvious that in the preceding verses the apostle refers simply to the destruction of the Jewish polity and to the terrible judgments which were about to fall on the Jews as a nation; therefore they are the people who were appointed to wrath; and they were thus appointed, not from eternity, nor from any indefinite or remote time, but from that time in which they utterly rejected the offers of salvation made to them by Jesus Christ and His apostles. The privileges of their election were still continued to them even after they had crucified the Lord of glory; for when He gave commandment to His disciples to go into all the world and preach the gospel to every creature, He bade them begin at Jerusalem. When the Jews were rejected and appointed to wrath, then the Gentiles were elected and appointed to *obtain salvation* by our Lord Jesus Christ, whose gospel they gladly received and continue to prize.

10. *Who died for us.* His death was an atoning sacrifice for the Gentiles as well as for the Jews. *Whether we wake or sleep.* Whether we "live" or "die," whether we are in this state or in the other world, we shall live together with Him—shall enjoy His life and the consolations of His Spirit while here, and shall be glorified together with Him in the eternal world.

11. *Comfort . . . one another.* Rest assured that in all times and circumstances it shall be well with the righteous; let every man lay this to heart; and with this consideration *comfort* and *edify* each other in all trials and difficulties.

12. *Know them.* Act kindly toward them; "acknowledge" them as the messengers of Christ, and treat them with tenderness and respect. This is a frequent meaning of the word. *Them which labour among you.* The words have appeared to some as expressing those who had labored among them; but as it is the participle of the present tense, there is no need to consider it in this light. Both it and the word "superintendents" refer to persons then actually employed in the work of God.

13. *Esteem them very highly in love.* Christian ministers who preach the whole truth and labor in the word and doctrine are entitled to more than respect; the apostle commands them to be esteemed, "abundantly, and super-abundantly." And this is to be done *in love;* and as men delight to serve those whom they love, it necessarily follows that they should provide for them, and see that they want neither the necessaries nor conveniences of life.

14. *Warn them that are unruly.* The whole phraseology of this verse is military; I shall consider the import of each term. Those who are "out of their ranks," and are neither in a disposition nor situation to perform the work and duty of a soldier; those who will not do the work prescribed, and who will meddle with what is not commanded. *Comfort the feeble-minded.* Those of "little souls"; the "faint-hearted"; those who, on the eve of a battle, are

MATTHEW HENRY

To support the weak, *v.* 15. Some are not well able to perform their work, nor bear up under their burdens; we should therefore help their infirmities, and lift at one end of the burden, and so help to bear it. *To be patient towards all men*, *v.* 14. We must bear and forbear. And this duty must be exercised towards all men, good and bad, high and low. We must endeavour to make the best we can of everything, and think the best we can of everybody. *Not to render evil for evil to any man*, *v.* 15. We must by all means forbear to avenge ourselves. It becomes us to forgive, as those that are, and that hope to be, forgiven of God. *Ever to follow that which is good*, *v.* 15. We must study to do what is pleasing to God. Whatever men do to us, we must do good to others, both among ourselves and then, *as we have opportunity, unto all men.*

Verses 16–22

Here we have divers short exhortations. The duties are of great importance, and we may observe how they are connected together. 1. *Rejoice evermore*, *v.* 16. If we do rejoice in God we may do that evermore. A religious life is a pleasant life, it is a life of constant joy. 2. *Pray without ceasing*, *v.* 17. The way to rejoice evermore is to pray without ceasing. We should rejoice more if we prayed more. The meaning is not that men should do nothing but pray, but that nothing else we do should hinder prayer in its proper season. Prayer will help forward and not hinder all other lawful business, and every good work. 3. *In everything give thanks*, *v.* 18. If we pray without ceasing, we shall not want matter for thanksgiving *in everything*. We should be thankful in every condition, even in adversity as well as prosperity. It is never so bad with us but it might be worse. We never can have any reason to complain of God, and have always much reason to praise and give thanks. This is the *will of God in Christ Jesus concerning us, that we give thanks.* He allows us to rejoice evermore, and appoints us in everything to give thanks. 4. *Quench not the Spirit* (*v.* 19). Christians are said to *be baptized with the Holy Ghost and with fire.* We must be careful not to quench this holy fire. As fire is put out by withdrawing fuel, so we quench the Spirit if we do not stir up our spirits. And as fire is quenched by pouring water, or putting a great quantity of dirt upon it, so we must be careful not to quench the Holy Spirit by indulging carnal lusts and affections, or minding only earthly things.

5. *Despise not prophesyings* (*v.* 20). By *prophesyings* here we are to understand the preaching of the word. We must not despise preaching, though it be plain, and though we be told no more than what we knew before. It is useful, and many times needful, to have our affections and resolutions excited, to those things that we knew before to be our interest and our duty.

6. *Prove all things, but hold fast that which is good*, *v.* 21. We must not take things upon trust from the preacher. We must search the scriptures, whether what they say be true or not. But we must not be always trying, always unsettled; no, at length we must be settled, and hold fast that which is good. Proving all things must be in order to holding fast that which is good. 7. *Abstain from all appearance of evil*, *v.* 22. Corrupt affections indulged in the heart, and evil practices allowed of in the life, will greatly tend to promote fatal errors in the mind; whereas purity of heart, and integrity of life, will dispose men to receive the truth in the love of it. He who is not shy of the appearances of sin will not long abstain from the actual commission of sin.

Verses 23–29

I. Paul's prayer for them, *v.* 23. 1. To whom the apostle prays, *The very God of peace.* By their peaceableness and unity those things would best be obtained which he prays for. 2. The things he prays for are their sanctification, that *God would sanctify them wholly*;

JAMIESON, FAUSSET, BROWN

temptations), applies to all clergy and laity alike, though primarily the duty of the clergy (who are meant in vs. 12). **support**—lit., "lay fast hold on so as to support." **the weak**—spiritually. Paul practiced what he preached (I Cor. 9:22). **be patient toward all men**—There is no believer who needs not the exercise of patience "toward" him; there is none to whom a believer ought not to show it; many show it more to strangers than to their own families, more to the great than to the humble; but we ought to show it "toward *all men*" [BENGEL]. Cf. "the long-suffering of our Lord" (II Cor. 10:1; II Pet. 3:15). **15.** (Rom. 12:17; I Pet. 3:9.) **unto any man**—whether unto a Christian, or a heathen, however great the provocation. **follow**—as a matter of earnest pursuit. **16, 17.** In order to "rejoice evermore," we must "pray without ceasing." He who is wont to thank God for all things as happening for the best, will have continuous joy [THEOPHYLACT]. Ephesians 6:18; Philippians 4:4, 6, "Rejoice *in the Lord* . . . by prayer and supplication with thanksgiving"; Romans 14:17, *"in the Holy Ghost"; Romans 12:12, "in hope"; Acts 5:41, "in being counted worthy to suffer shame for Christ's name"; James 1:2, in falling "into divers temptations."* The *Greek* is, "Pray *without intermission*"; without allowing prayerless gaps to intervene between the times of prayer. **18. In every thing**—even what *seems* adverse: for nothing is *really* so (cf. Rom. 8:28; Eph. 5:20). See Christ's example (Matt. 15:36; 26:27; Luke 10:21; John 11:41). **this**—That ye should "rejoice evermore, pray without ceasing, (and) in every thing give thanks," "is the will of God in Christ Jesus (as the Mediator and Revealer of that will, observed by those who are *in Christ* by faith, cf. Phil. 3:14) concerning you." *God's will* is the believer's law. LACHMANN rightly reads commas at the end of the three precepts (vss. 16, 17, 18), making "this" refer to all three. **19. Quench not**—the Spirit being a holy *fire:* "where the Spirit is, He burns" [BENGEL] (Matt. 3:11; Acts 2:3;7:51). Do not throw cold water on those who, under extraordinary inspiration of the Spirit, stand up to speak with tongues, or reveal mysteries, or pray in the congregation. The enthusiastic exhibitions of some (perhaps as to the nearness of Christ's coming, exaggerating Paul's statement, II Thess. 2:2, By *spirit*), led others (probably the presiding ministers, who had not always been treated with due respect by enthusiastic novices, vs. 12), from dread of enthusiasm, to discourage the free utterances of those really inspired, in the Church assembly. On the other hand, the caution (vs. 21) was needed, not to receive "all" pretended revelations as divine, without "proving" them. **20. prophesyings**—whether exercised in inspired teaching, or in predicting the future. "Despised" by some as beneath "tongues," which seemed most miraculous; therefore declared by Paul to be a greater gift than tongues, though the latter were more showy (I Cor. 14:5). **21, 22.** Some of the oldest MSS. insert "But." You ought indeed not to "quench" the manifestations of "the Spirit," nor "despise prophesyings"; "but," at the same time, do not take "all" as genuine which professes to be so; "prove (test) all" such manifestations. The means of testing them existed in the Church, in those who had the "discerning of spirits" (I Cor. 12:10; 14:29; I John 4:1). Another sure test, which we also have, is, to try the professed revelation whether it accords with Scripture, as the noble Bereans did (Isa. 8:20; Acts 17:11; Gal. 1:8, 9).

hold fast that which is good—Join this clause with the next clause (vs. 22), not merely with the sentence preceding. As the result of your "proving all things," and especially all *prophesyings*, "*hold fast* (Luke 8:15; I Cor. 11:2; Heb. 2:1) the good, and *hold yourselves aloof from* every appearance of evil" ("*every evil species*" [BENGEL and WAHL]). Do not accept even a professedly spirit-inspired communication, if it be at variance with the truth taught you (II Thess. 2:2) "Hold yourselves aloof from every evil appearance" or "form." **23. the very God**—rather as the *Greek*, "the God of peace *Himself*"; who can do for you by His own power what *I* cannot do by all my monitions, nor *you* by all your efforts (Rom. 16:20; Heb. 13:20), viz., keep you from all evil, and give you all that is good. **sanctify you**—for *holiness* is the necessary condition of "peace" (Phil. 4:6-9). **wholly**—*Greek*, (so that you should be) "perfect in every respect" [TITTMANN]. **and**—i.e., "*and* so (omit 'I pray God'; not in the *Greek*) may your . . . spirit and soul and body be preserved. . . ." **whole**—A different *Greek* word from "wholly." Translate, "entire"; with none of the integral parts wanting [TITTMANN]. It refers to man in his normal integrity, as originally

ADAM CLARKE

dispirited, because of the number of the enemy and their own feeble and unprovided state. *Support the weak.* "Shore up, prop" them that are weak; strengthen those wings and companies that are likely to be most exposed, that they be not overpowered and broken in the day of battle. *Be patient toward all.* The disorderly, *the feebleminded,* and *the weak* will exercise your patience and try your temper. If the troops be irregular, and cannot in every respect be reduced to proper order and discipline, let not the officers lose their temper nor courage; let them do the best they can. God will be with them, and a victory will give confidence to their troops.

15. *See that none render evil for evil.* Every temper contrary to love is contrary to Christianity. A peevish, fretful, vindictive man may be a child of Satan; he certainly is not a child of God. *Follow that which is good.* That by which you may profit your brethren and your neighbors of every description, whether Jews or Gentiles.

16. *Rejoice evermore.* Be always happy; the religion of Christ was intended to remove misery. He that has God for his Portion may constantly exult.

17. *Pray without ceasing.* You are dependent on God for every good; without Him you can do nothing. Feel that dependence at all times, and you will always be in the spirit of prayer; and those who feel this spirit will, as frequently as possible, be found in the exercise of prayer.

18. *In every thing give thanks.* For this reason, that all things work together for good to them that love God; therefore every occurrence may be a subject of gratitude and thankfulness. While you live to God, prosperity and adversity will be equally helpful to you. *For this is the will of God.* That you should be always happy; that you should ever be in the spirit of prayer; and that you should profit by every occurrence in life, and be continually grateful and obedient—for gratitude and obedience are inseparably connected.

19. *Quench not the Spirit.* The Holy Spirit is represented as a fire, because it is His province to enlighten and quicken the soul; and to purge, purify, and refine it. This Spirit is represented as being quenched when any act is done, word spoken, or temper indulged contrary to its dictates. It is the Spirit of love, and therefore anger, malice, revenge, or any unkind or unholy temper will quench it so that it will withdraw its influences; and then the heart is left in a state of hardness and darkness. It has been observed that fire may be quenched as well by heaping earth on it as by throwing water on it; and so the love of the world will as effectually grieve and quench the Spirit as any ordinary act of transgression.

20. *Despise not prophesyings.* Do not suppose that you have no need of continual instruction; without it you cannot preserve the Christian life nor go on to perfection.

21. *Prove all things.* Whatever you hear in these "prophesyings" or preachings, examine by the words of Christ, and by the doctrines which, from time to time, we have delivered unto you in our preaching and writings. Try the spirits, the different teachers, by the Word of God. *Hold fast that which is good.* Whatever in these prophesyings has a tendency to increase your faith, love, holiness, and usefulness, that receive and hold fast.

22. *Abstain from all appearance of evil.* Sin not, and avoid even the *appearance* of it. Do not drive your morality so near the bounds of evil as to lead even weak persons to believe that you actually touch, taste, or handle it. Let not the "form" of it appear with or among you, much less the substance.

23. *And the very God of peace.* That same God who is the Author of peace, the Giver of peace, and who has sent for the redemption of the world the Prince of Peace—may that very God *sanctify you wholly;* leave no more evil in your hearts than His precepts tolerate evil in your conduct. The word *wholly* means precisely the same as our phrase "to all intents and purposes." May He sanctify you to the end and to the uttermost. *Your whole spirit and soul and body.* Some think that the apostle

MATTHEW HENRY

and their preservation, that they might be *preserved blameless.* All those who are sanctified in Christ Jesus shall be preserved to the coming of our Lord Jesus Christ. We should pray to God to perfect his work, and *preserve us blameless,* till at length we are *presented faultless before the throne of his glory with exceeding joy.*

II. His comfortable assurance that God would hear his prayer: *Faithful is he who calleth you, who will also do it, v.* 24. The faithfulness of God was their security that they should persevere to the end. God would do what he desired; he would accomplish all the good pleasure of his goodness towards them. Our fidelity to God depends upon his faithfulness to us.

III. His request of their prayers: *Brethren, pray for us, v.* 25. Brethren should thus express brotherly love. The more people pray for their ministers the more good ministers may have from God, and the more benefit people may receive by their ministry.

IV. His salutation: *Greet all the brethren with a holy kiss, v.* 26. Thus the apostle sends a friendly salutation from himself, and Silvanus, and Timotheus, and would have them salute each other in their names; and thus he would have them signify their mutual love and affection to one another.

V. His solemn charge for the reading of this epistle, *v.* 27. This is not only an exhortation, but an adjuration by the Lord. And this epistle was to be read to all the holy brethen. In order to this, these holy oracles should not be kept concealed in an unknown tongue, but translated into the vulgar languages. The scriptures should be read in the public assemblies of Christians also.

VI. The apostolical benediction that is usual in other epistles: *The grace of our Lord Jesus Christ be with you. Amen, v.* 28. We need no more to make us happy than to know that grace which our Lord Jesus Christ has manifested. This is an ever-flowing and overflowing fountain of grace to supply all our wants.

JAMIESON, FAUSSET, BROWN

designed; an ideal which shall be attained by the glorified believer. All three, spirit, soul, and body, each in its due place, constitute man "entire." The "spirit" links man with the higher intelligences of heaven, and is that highest part of man which is receptive of the quickening Holy Spirit (I Cor. 15: 47). In the unspiritual, the spirit is so sunk under the lower animal *soul* (which it ought to keep under) that such are termed "animal" (*English Version,* "sensual," having merely the *body* of organized matter, and the *soul* the immaterial animating essence), having *not the Spirit* (cf. I Cor. 2:14; *Notes,* 15:44; 46-48; John 3:6). The unbeliever shall rise with an *animal* (soul-animated) *body,* but not like the believer with a *spiritual* (spirit-endued) body like Christ's (Rom. 8:11). **blameless unto**–rather as *Greek,* "blamelessly (so as to be in a blameless state) at the coming of Christ." In *Hebrew,* "peace" and "wholly" (perfect in every respect) are kindred terms; so that the prayer shows what the title "God of peace" implies. BENGEL takes "wholly" as *collectively,* all the Thessalonians without exception, so that no one should fail. And "whole" (entire), *individually,* each one of them entire, with "spirit, soul, and body." The mention of the preservation of the *body* accords with the subject (ch. 4:16). TRENCH better regards "wholly" as meaning, "having perfectly attained the moral *end,*" viz., to be a full-grown man in Christ. "Whole," *complete,* with no grace which ought to be wanting in a Christian. **24. Faithful**–to His covenant promises (John 10:27-29; I Cor. 1:9; 10:23; Phil. 1:6). **he that calleth you**–God, the caller of His people, will cause His calling not to fall short of its designed end. **do it**–preserve and present you blameless at the coming of Christ (vs. 23; Rom. 8:30; I Pet. 5:10). You must not look at the foes before and behind, on the right hand and on the left, but to God's faithfulness to His promises, God's zeal for His honor, and God's love for those whom He calls. **25.** Some oldest MSS. read, "Pray ye *also* for (lit., *concerning*) us"; make us and our work the subject of your prayers, even as *we* have been just praying for you (vs. 23). Others omit the "also." The clergy need much the prayers of their flocks. Paul makes the same request in the Epistles to Romans, Ephesians, Philippians, Colossians, Philemon, and in II Corinthians; not so in the Epistles to Timothy and Titus, whose intercessions, as his spiritual sons, he was already sure of; nor in the Epistles, I Corinthians and Galatians, as these Epistles abound in rebuke. **26.** Hence it appears this Epistle was first handed to the elders, who communicated it to "the brethren." **holy kiss**–pure and chaste. "A kiss of charity" (I Pet. 5:14). A token of Christian fellowship in those days (cf. Luke 7:45; Acts 20:37), as it is a common mode of salutation in many countries. The custom hence arose in the early Church of passing the kiss through the congregation at the holy communion (JUSTIN MARTYR, *Apology,* 1. 65; *Apostolic Constitutions,* 2. 57), the men kissing the men, and the women the women, in the Lord. So in the Syrian Church each takes his neighbor's right hand and gives the salutation, "Peace." **27. I charge**–*Greek,* "I adjure you." **read unto all**–viz., publicly in the congregation at a particular time. The *Greek* aorist implies a single act done at a particular time. The earnestness of his adjuration implies how solemnly important he felt this divinely inspired message to be. Also, as this was the FIRST of the Epistles of the New Testament, he makes this the occasion of a solemn charge, that so its being publicly read should be a sample of what should be done in the case of the others, just as the Pentateuch and the Prophets were publicly read under the Old Testament, and are still read in the synagogue. Cf. the same injunction as to the public reading of the Apocalypse, the LAST of the New Testament canon (Rev. 1:3). The "all" includes women and children, and especially those who could not read it themselves (Deut. 31:12; Josh. 8:33-35). What Paul commands with an adjuration, Rome forbids under a curse [BENGEL]. Though these Epistles had difficulties, the laity were all to hear them read (I Pet. 4:11; II Pet. 3:10; even the very young, II Tim. 1:5; 3:15). "Holy" is omitted before "brethren" in most of the oldest MSS., though some of them support it. **28.** (*Note,* II Cor. 13:14.) Paul ends as he began (ch. 1:1), with "grace." The oldest MSS. omit "Amen," which probably was the response of the Church after the public reading of the Epistle.

ADAM CLARKE

alludes to the Pythagorean and Platonic doctrine, which was acknowledged among the Thessalonians. I should rather believe that he refers simply to the fact that the creature called man is a compound being, consisting: (1) Of a *body,* an organized system, formed by the creative energy of God out of the dust of the earth; (2) Of a *soul,* which is the seat of the different affections and passions, such as love, hatred, anger, with sensations, appetites, and propensities of different kinds; (3) Of *spirit,* the immortal principle, the source of life to the body and soul; and which alone possesses the faculty of intelligence, understanding, thinking, and reasoning, and produces the faculty of speech wherever it resides, if accident have not impaired the organs of speech. The apostle prays that this compound being, in all its parts, powers, and faculties, which he terms their *whole,* comprehending all parts, everything that constitutes man and manhood, may be sanctified and preserved *blameless* till the coming of Christ. Thus we learn that the sanctification is not to take place in, at, or after death.

24. *Faithful is he that calleth you.* In a great variety of places in His Word, God has promised to sanctify His followers, and His faithfulness binds Him to fulfill His promises; therefore He will do it. He who can believe will find this thing also possible to him.

25. *Pray for us.* Even apostles, while acting under an extraordinary mission, and enjoying the inspiration of the Holy Ghost, felt the necessity of the prayers of the faithful.

27. *I charge you by the Lord that this epistle be read.* There must have been some particular reason for this solemn charge. He certainly had some cause to suspect that the Epistle would be suppressed in some way or other, and that the whole church would not be permitted to hear it; or he may refer to the smaller churches contiguous to Thessalonica, or the churches in Macedonia in general, whom he wished to hear it, as well as those to whom it was more immediately directed. There is no doubt that the apostles designed that their epistles should be copied and sent to all the churches in the vicinity of that to which they were directed. Had this not been the case, a great number of churches would have known scarcely anything of the New Testament. As every Jewish synagogue had a copy of the law and the prophets, so every Christian church had a copy of the Gospels and the Epistles, which were daily, or at least every Sabbath, read for the instruction of the people. This the apostle deemed so necessary that he adjured them by the Lord to read this Epistle to all the brethren; i.e., to all the Christians in that district.

28. *The grace of our Lord Jesus.* As the Epistle began, so it ends; for the grace of Christ must be at the beginning and end of every work, in order to complete it and bring it to good effect. *Amen.* This is wanting in some MSS. It was probably not written by Paul.

THE SECOND EPISTLE TO THE THESSALONIANS

I. Introduction (1:1-5)
A. Salutation (1:1, 2)
B. Thanksgiving (1:3-5)

II. Consolation—the second advent and their tribulation (1:6-12)
A. The revelation of the Lord Jesus (1:6-10)
1. The central fact—twofold aspect (1:6-9)
a. Rest to the saints (1:6, 7)
b. Vengeance to the evil (1:8, 9)
2. The union of the saints with Him—the medium of manifestations (1:10)
B. The prayer (1:11, 12)
1. Its immediate desires (1:11)
2. Its ultimate desire (1:12)

III. Instruction—the second advent as to its order (2:1-12)
A. The coming and the day (2:1-5)
1. The distinction (2:1)
2. The signs of the coming of the day (2:2-5)
a. A falling away (2:2, 3)
b. Manifestation of man of sin (2:4, 5)
B. Lawlessness and the Lord Jesus (2:6-12)
1. The two forces (2:6, 7)
a. Mystery of lawlessness (2:6)
b. One that restraineth (2:7)
2. The two revealings (2:8-12)
a. The lawless one (2:8-10)
b. The Lord Jesus (2:11, 12)

IV. Exhortation—the second advent and their present duty (2:13-3:15)
A. Chosen stand (2:13-17)
1. Chosen to salvation (2:13, 14)
2. Stand fast in the Truth (2:15-17)
B. Pray—do (3:1-5)
1. "Pray for us" (3:1, 2)
2. Declaration of his confidence in them (3:3-5)
C. Work (3:6-15)
1. The apostolic example—some neglecting their calling (3:6-11)
2. No work, no food—the mistaken one to be admonished as a brother (3:12-15)

V. Conclusion (3:16-18)
A. Benediction (3:16)
1. The need (3:16a)
2. The Lord (3:16b)
B. Salutation (3:17)
C. The benediction (3:18)

This second epistle was written soon after the former, and seems to have been designed to prevent a mistake concerning the second coming of Christ, as if it were near at hand. The apostle informs them that there were many intermediate counsels yet to be fulfilled before that day of the Lord should come, though, because it is sure, he had spoken of it as near.

MATTHEW HENRY

CHAPTER 1

Verses 1–4

I. The introduction (*v.* 1, 2), in the same words as in the former epistle. This church of the Thessalonians was built, as all true churches are; *in God our Father and the Lord Jesus Christ.*

II. The apostle's expression of the high esteem he had for them.

1. How his esteem of them is expressed. (1) He glorified God on their behalf, *v.* 3. It is our duty to be thankful to God for all the good that is found in us or others: and it not only is an act of kindness to our fellow-christians, but our duty, to thank God on their behalf. (2) He also *glories in them before the churches of God, v.* 4. The apostle never flattered his friends, but he took pleasure in speaking well of them, to the glory of God.

2. For what he esteemed them and thanked God. In his former epistle (*ch.* i. 3) he gave thanks for their faith, love, and patience; here he gives thanks for the increase of all those graces. Where there is the truth of grace there will be increase of it. And where there is the increase of grace God must have all the glory of it. We are as much indebted to him for the improvement of grace, as we are for the very beginning of it. We may be tempted to think that though when we were bad we could not make ourselves good, yet when we are good we can easily make ourselves better. Their faith grew exceedingly, *v.* 3. The growth of their faith appeared by the works of faith; and, where faith grows, all other graces grow proportionably. Their charity abounded (*v.* 3). Where faith grows love will abound.

JAMIESON, FAUSSET, BROWN

CHAPTER 1

VSS. 1-12. ADDRESS AND SALUTATION: INTRODUCTION: THANKSGIVING FOR THEIR GROWTH IN FAITH AND LOVE, AND FOR THEIR PATIENCE IN PERSECUTIONS, WHICH ARE A TOKEN FOR GOOD EVERLASTING TO THEM, AND FOR PERDITION TO THEIR ADVERSARIES AT CHRIST'S COMING: PRAYER FOR THEIR PERFECTION. **1. in God our Father**—still more endearing than the address, I Thessalonians 1:1 "in God THE Father." **2. from God our Father**—So some oldest MSS. read. Others omit "our." **3. We are bound**—*Greek,* "We owe it as a debt" (ch. 2:13). They had prayed for the Thessalonians (I Thess. 3:12) that they might "increase and abound in love"; their prayer having been heard, it is a small but a bounden return for them to make, to thank God for it. Thus, Paul and his fellow missionaries practice what they preach (I Thess. 5:18). In I Thessalonians 1:3, their thanksgiving was for the Thessalonians' faith, love, and patience"; here, for their *exceeding growth* in *faith,* and for their *charity abounding.* **We are bound**—expresses the duty of thanksgiving from its subjective side as an inward conviction. "As it is meet," from the *objective* side as something answering to the state of circumstances [ALFORD]. Observe the exact correspondence of the prayer (I Thess. 3:12, "The Lord make you to *abound* in love") and the answer, "The love of every one of you all toward each other aboundeth" (cf. I Thess. 4:10). **meet**—right. **4. glory in you**—make our boast of you, lit., "in your case." "Ourselves" implies that not merely did they hear others speaking of the Thessalonians' faith, but they, the missionaries *themselves,* boasted of it. Cf. I Thessalonians 1:8, wherein the apostle said, their faith was so well known in various places, that he and his fellow missionaries had no need to speak of it; but here he says, so abounding is their love, combined with faith and patience, that he and his fellow missionaries *themselves,* make it a matter of glorying in the various churches elsewhere (he was now at Corinth in Achaia, and boasted there of the faith of the Macedonian

ADAM CLARKE

CHAPTER 1

1. *Paul, and Silvanus.* See the notes on 1 Thess. i. 1. This Epistle was written a short time after the former; and as Silas and Timothy were still at Corinth, the apostle joins their names with his own, as in the former case.

3. *Your faith groweth exceedingly.* The word signifies "to grow luxuriantly," as a good and healthy tree planted in a good soil; and if a fruit tree bearing an abundance of fruit to compensate the labor of the husbandman.

4. *We ourselves glory in you in the churches of God.* We hold you up as an example of what the grace of God can produce when communicated to honest and faithful hearts.

MATTHEW HENRY

Their patience as well as faith increased in all their persecutions and tribulations. And patience has then its perfect work when it extends itself to all trials. They endured all these by faith, and endured them with patience, not with an insensibility under them, but with patience arising from Christian principles.

Verses 5–10

I. The present happiness and advantage of their sufferings, *v.* 5. They were improved by their sufferings, were *counted worthy of the kingdom of God.* Religion, if it is worth anything, is worth everything, and those either have no religion at all, or know not how to value it, that cannot find in their hearts to suffer for it.

II. The future recompence that shall be given to persecutors and persecuted.

1. In this future recompence there will be, (1) A punishment inflicted on persecutors, *v.* 6. And there is nothing that more infallibly marks a man for eternal ruin than a spirit of persecution. God will render a recompence, and will trouble those that trouble his people. (2) A reward for those that are persecuted, *v.* 7. There is a rest that remains for the people of God, a rest from sin and sorrow. The future rest will abundantly recompence all their present troubles. There is enough in heaven to countervail all that we may lose or suffer for the name of Christ in this world.

2. Concerning this future recompence.

(1) The certainty of it: *It is a righteous thing with God* (*v.* 6). God's suffering people will lose nothing by their sufferings, and their enemies will gain nothing.

(2) When this righteous recompence shall be made, *v.* 7. The Lord Jesus will in that day appear from heaven. He will be revealed with his mighty angels (*v.* 7).

He will come in flaming fire, *v.* 8. A refining fire, to purify the saints. A consuming fire to the wicked. The effects of this appearance will be terrible to some and joyful to others.

First, They will be terrible to some. Those that sinned against the principles of natural religion, and rebelled against the light of nature (*v.* 8). Those that rebel against the light of revelation.

To such persons the revelation of our Lord Jesus Christ will be terrible, because of their doom, *v.* 9. They will then be punished. They did sin's work, and must receive sin's wages. Their punishment will be no less than destruction. This destruction shall come from the *presence of the Lord.* It shall come from the *glory of his power.*

JAMIESON, FAUSSET, BROWN

churches, II Cor. 10:15-17; 8:1, at the same time giving the glory to the Lord), not only looking forward to glorying thereat at Christ's coming (I Thess. 2:19), but doing so even now. **patience**—in I Thessalonians 1:3, "patience *of hope.*" Here *hope* is tacitly implied as the ground of their patience; vss. 5, 7 state the object of their hope, viz., the kingdom for which they suffer. **tribulations**—lit., "pressures." The Jews were the instigators of the populace and of the magistrates against Christians (Acts 17:6, 8). **which ye endure**—*Greek*, "are (now) enduring." **5. Which**—Your *enduring* these tribulations is a "token of the righteous judgment of God," manifested in your being enabled to endure them, and in your adversaries thereby filling up the measure of their guilt. The judgment is even now begun, but its consummation will be at the Lord's coming. David (Ps. 73:1-14) and Jeremiah (12:1-4) were perplexed at the wicked prospering and the godly suffering. But Paul, by the light of the New Testament, makes this fact a matter of consolation. It is a *proof* (so the *Greek*)of the future judgment, which will set to rights the anomalies of the present state, by rewarding the now suffering saint, and by punishing the persecutor. **that ye may be counted worthy**—expressing the purpose of God's "righteous judgment" as regards you. **for which**—*Greek*, "*in behalf of* which ye are also suffering" (cf. Acts 5:41; 9:16; Phil. 1:29). "Worthy" implies that, though men are justified by faith, they shall be judged "according to their works" (Rev. 20:12; cf. I Thess. 2:12; I Pet. 1:6, 7; Rev. 20:4). The "also" implies the connection between *the suffering for the kingdom* and *being counted worthy* of it. Cf. Romans 8:17, 18. **6. seeing it is a righteous thing**—This justifies the assertion above of there being a "*righteous* judgment" (vs. 5), viz., "seeing that it is (lit., '*if at least*,' '*if at all events it is*') a *righteous* thing with (i.e., in the estimation of) God" (which, as we all feel, it certainly is). Our own innate feeling of what is just, in this confirms what is revealed. **recompense**—requite *in kind*, viz., *tribulation* to them that trouble you (*affliction* to those that *afflict* you); and to you who are *troubled, rest from trouble.* **7. rest**—governed by "to recompense" (vs. 6). The *Greek* is lit., "relaxation"; loosening of the *tension* which had preceded; *relaxing* of the strings of endurance now so tightly drawn. The *Greek* word for "rest," Matthew 11:28, is distinct, viz., *cessation* from labor. Also, Hebrews 4:9, "A keeping of sabbath." **with us**—viz., Paul, Silas, and Timothy, the writers, who are troubled like yourselves. **when**—at the time when . . .; not sooner, not later. **with his mighty angels**—rather as the *Greek*, "with the angels of His might," or "power," i.e., the angels who are the ministers by whom He makes His might to be recognized (Matt. 13:41, 52). It is not *their* might, but HIS might, which is the prominent thought **8. In flaming fire**—*Greek*, "In flame of fire"; or, as other oldest MSS. read, *in fire of flame.* This *flame of fire* accompanied His manifestation in the bush (Exod. 3:2); also His giving of the law at Sinai (Exod. 19:18). Also it shall accompany His revelation at His advent (Dan. 7:9, 10), symbolizing His own bright glory and His consuming vengeance against His foes (Heb. 10:27; 12:29; II Pet. 3:7, 10). **taking**—lit., "*giving*" them, as their portion, "vengeance." **know not God**—the Gentiles primarily (Ps. 79:6; Gal. 4:8; I Thess. 4:5); not of course those *involuntarily* not knowing God, but those *wilfully* not knowing Him, as Pharaoh, who might have known God if he would, but who boasted "I know not the Lord" (Exod. 5:2); and as the heathen persecutors who might have known God by the preaching of those whom they persecuted. Secondarily, all who "profess to know God but in works deny Him" (Titus 1:16). **obey not the gospel**—primarily the unbelieving Jews (Rom. 10:3, 16); secondarily, all who obey not the truth (Rom. 2:8). **Christ**—omitted by some of the oldest MSS., and retained by others. **9. Who**—*Greek*, "persons who . . . ." **destruction from the presence of the Lord**—driven *far from* His presence [ALFORD]. The sentence *emanating from Him* in person, sitting as Judge [BENGEL], and *driving them far from* Him (Matt. 25:41; Rev. 6:16; 12:14; cf. I Pet. 3:12; Isa. 2:10, 19). "The presence of the Lord" is the source whence the sentence goes forth; "the glory of His power" is the instrument whereby the sentence is carried into execution [EDMUNDS]. But ALFORD better interprets the latter clause (see vs. 10), driven "from the manifestation of His power *in the glorification of His saints.*" *Cast out from the presence of the Lord* is the idea at the root of eternal death, the law of evil left to its unrestricted working, without one counteracting influence of the presence

ADAM CLARKE

For your patience and faith. From Acts xvii. 5, 13 and from 1 Thess. ii. 14, we learn that the people of Thessalonica had suffered much persecution from both the Jews and their own countrymen; but being thoroughly convinced of the truth of the gospel, and feeling it to be the power of God unto salvation, no persecution could turn them aside from it. And having suffered for the truth, it was precious to them. Persecution never essentially injured the genuine Church of God.

5. *A manifest token of the righteous judgment of God.* The persecutions and tribulations which you endure are a manifest proof that God has judged righteously in calling you Gentiles into His Church. The words, however, may be understood in another sense, and will form this maxim: "The sufferings of the just, and the triumphs of the wicked, in this life, are a sure proof that there will be a future judgment, in which the wicked shall be punished and the righteous rewarded." This maxim is not only true in itself, but it is most likely that this is the apostle's meaning.

6. *Seeing it is a righteous thing.* Though God neither rewards nor punishes in this life in a general way, yet He often gives proofs of His displeasure, especially against those who persecute His followers. They therefore who have given you tribulation shall have tribulation in recompense.

7. *And to you who are troubled rest with us.* And while they have *tribulation*, you shall have that eternal *rest* which remains for the people of God. *When the Lord Jesus shall be revealed.* But this fullness of *tribulation* to them and *rest* to you shall not take place till the Lord Jesus comes to judge the world. *With his mighty angels.* The coming of God to judge the world is scarcely ever spoken of in the sacred writings without mentioning the holy angels, who are to accompany Him and to form His court or retinue. See Deut. xxxiii. 2; Matt. xxv. 31; xvi. 27; xxvi. 64; Mark viii. 38.

8. *In flaming fire*, in thunder and lightning, *taking vengeance*, inflicting just punishment, *on them that know not God*—the heathen who do not worship the true God, and will not acknowledge Him, but worship idols; and on them *that obey not the gospel*—the Jews, particularly who have rejected the gospel and persecuted Christ and His messengers; and all nominal Christians who, though they believe the gospel as a revelation from God, yet do not obey it as a rule of life.

9. *Who shall be punished.* What this *everlasting destruction* consists in we cannot tell. It is not annihilation, for their being continues; and as the destruction is *everlasting*, it is an eternal continuance and presence of substantial evil and absence of all good; for a part of this punishment consists in being banished *from the presence of the Lord*, excluded from His approbation forever. *The glory of his power.* Never to see the face of God throughout eternity is a heart-rending, soul-appalling thought; and to be banished from the *glory of his power*, that power the glory of which is peculiarly manifested in saving the lost and glorifying the faithful, is what cannot be reflected on without confusion and dismay.

MATTHEW HENRY

Secondly, It will be a joyful day to some, even to the saints. Christ Jesus will be glorified and admired by his saints. Christ will be glorified and admired in them. His grace and power will be magnified in the salvation of his saints. How will they be wondered at in this great and glorious day; or, rather, how will Christ be admired!

Verses 11, 12

His earnest and constant prayer for them: *Wherefore also we pray,* &c.

I. What the apostle prayed for, *v.* 11. 1. That God would begin his good work of grace in them; so we may understand this expression: *That our God would count you* (or, as it might be read, *make you*) *worthy of this calling.* We are called to God's kingdom and glory. Now, if this be our calling, our great concern should be to be worthy of it. We should pray that he would make us worthy. 2. That God would carry on the good work that is begun. The good pleasure of God denotes his gracious purposes towards his people. Now, there are various and manifold purposes of grace and goodwill in God towards his people; and the apostle prays that all of them may be fulfilled towards these Thessalonians. In particular, the apostle prays that God would fulfil in them the *work of faith with power.*

II. Why the apostle prayed for these things (*v.* 12). Our good works should so shine before men that others may glorify God, that Christ may be glorified in and by us, and then we shall be glorified in and with him.

JAMIESON, FAUSSET, BROWN

of God, who is the source of all light and holiness (Isa. 66:24; Mark 9:44). **10.** "When He shall have come." **glorified in his saints**—as the element and mirror IN which His glory shall shine brightly (John 17:10). **admired in all them that believe**—*Greek,* "them that *believed.*" Once they *believed,* now they *see:* they had taken His word on trust. Now His word is made good and they need faith no longer. With *wonder* all celestial intelligences (Eph. 3:10) shall see and *admire* the Redeemer on account of the excellencies which He has wrought in them. **because . . .**—Supply for the sense, among whom (viz., those who shall be found to have believed) *you,* too, shall be; "because our testimony unto (so the *Greek* for 'among') you was believed" (and was not rejected as by those "who obey not the Gospel," vs. 8). The early preaching of the Gospel was not abstract discussions, but a *testimony* to facts and truths experimentally known (Luke 24:48; Acts 1:8). **11. Wherefore**—*Greek,* "With a view to which," viz., His glorification in you as His saints. **also**—We not only anticipate the coming glorification of our Lord *in His saints, but we also pray concerning* (so the *Greek*) YOU. **our God**—whom we serve. **count you worthy**—The prominent position of the "YOU" in the *Greek* makes it the emphatic word of the sentence. May *you* be found among the saints whom God shall count worthy of their calling (Eph. 4:1)! There is no dignity in us independent of God's calling of us (II Tim. 1:9). *The calling* here is not merely the first actual call, but the whole of God's electing act, originating in His "purpose of grace given us in Christ before the world began," and having its consummation in glory. **the good pleasure of . . .**—on the part of God [BENGEL]. **faith**—on your part. **with power**—Greek, "in power," i.e., "*powerfully fulfil* in you" (Col. 1:11). **12. the name of our Lord Jesus**—Our Lord Jesus *in His manifested personality* as the God-man. **in you, and ye in him**—reciprocal glorification; cf. Isaiah 28:5, "*The Lord of hosts* shall be . . . a crown of glory and . . . a diadem of beauty unto . . . . His people," with Isaiah 62:3, "*Thou* (Zion) shalt be a crown of glory in the hand of the Lord, and a royal diadem . . ." (John 21:10; Gal. 1:24; I Pet. 4:14). The believer's graces redound to Christ's glory, and His glory, as their Head, reflects glory on them as the members. **the grace of our God and the Lord Jesus Christ**—There is but one *Greek* article to both, implying the inseparable unity of God and the Lord Jesus.

ADAM CLARKE

10. *When he shall come to be glorified in his saints.* As the grace of God is peculiarly glorified in saving sinners and making them into saints, this gracious power will be particularly manifested in the great day when countless millions will appear before that throne who have come out of great tribulation, and have washed their robes and made them white in the blood of the Lamb. *And to be admired.* "To be wondered at among" and on the account of *all them that believe.* Instead of *them that believe,* "them that have believed" is the reading of many MSS. and most of the Greek fathers. This reading is undoubtedly genuine. *Because our testimony among you was believed in that day.* The members of this sentence seem to have been strangely transposed. I believe it should be read thus: "In that day, when He shall come to be glorified in His saints, and admired among all them that have believed; for our testimony was believed among you." The Thessalonians had credited what the apostles had said and written, not only concerning Jesus Christ in general, but concerning the day of judgment in particular.

11. *We pray . . . that our God would count you worthy.* It is our earnest prayer that God would "make you worthy," afford those continual supplies of grace by His Holy Spirit without which you cannot adorn your holy vocation.

12. *That the name of our Lord.* This is the great end of your Christian calling, that Jesus, who has died for you, may have His passion and death magnified in your life and happiness; that you may show forth the virtues of Him who called you from darkness into His marvellous light. *And ye in him.* That His glorious excellence may be seen upon you; that you may be adorned with the graces of His Spirit, as He is glorified by your salvation from all sin. *According to the grace.* That your salvation may be such as God requires, and such as is worthy of His grace to communicate. God saves as becomes God to save, and thus the dignity of His nature is seen in the excellence and glory of His work.

MATTHEW HENRY

CHAPTER 2

Verses 1–3

Some among the Thessalonians had mistaken the apostle's meaning about the coming of Christ, by thinking that it was near at hand. The apostle is careful to rectify this mistake. If errors and mistakes arise among Christians, we should take the first opportunity to rectify them, and good men will be especially careful to suppress errors that may arise from a mistake of their words and actions. We have a subtle adversary, who will sometimes promote errors even by means of the words of scripture.

I. How very earnest this apostle was, *v.* 1. He entreats them as brethren who might have charged them as a father charges his children. And this is the best way to deal with men when we would preserve or recover them from errors, to deal gently and affectionately with them.

1. It is most certain that the Lord Jesus Christ will come to judge the world. Whatever mistakes may arise about the time of his coming, his coming itself is certain.

2. At the second coming of Christ all the saints will be gathered together to him. It will be the completing of the happiness of his saints. There will then be a general meeting of all the saints, and none but saints; all the Old Testament saints, and all the New Testament saints. They shall be gathered *together to Christ.* He will be the great centre of their unity. To be with him for ever, and altogether happy in his presence to all eternity.

II. The Thessalonians should not be deceived about the time of Christ's coming, and so *be shaken in mind, or be troubled.* Errors in the mind tend greatly to weaken our faith, and such as are weak in faith and of troubled minds are oftentimes apt to be deceived.

JAMIESON, FAUSSET, BROWN

CHAPTER 2

Vss. 1-17. CORRECTION OF THEIR ERROR AS TO CHRIST'S IMMEDIATE COMING. THE APOSTASY THAT MUST PRECEDE IT. EXHORTATION TO STEADFASTNESS, INTRODUCED WITH THANKSGIVING FOR THEIR ELECTION BY GOD. **1. Now**—rather, "But"; marking the transition from his prayers *for* them to entreaties *to* them. **we beseech you**—or "entreat you." He uses affectionate entreaty, rather than stern reproof, to win them over to the right view. **by**—rather, "with respect to"; as the *Greek* for "of" (II Cor. 1:8). **our gathering together unto him**—the consummating or final gathering together of the saints to Him at His coming, as announced, Matthew 24:31; I Thessalonians 4:17. The *Greek* noun is nowhere else found except in Hebrews 10:25, said of *the assembling together* of believers for *congregational* worship. Our instinctive fears of the judgment are dispelled by the thought of being gathered together UNTO HIM ("even as the hen gathereth her chickens under her wings"), which ensures our safety. **2. soon**—on trifling grounds, without due consideration. **shaken**—lit., "tossed" as ships tossed by an agitated sea. Cf. for the same image, Ephesians 4:14. **in mind**—rather as the *Greek,* "*from* your mind," i.e., from your mental steadfastness on the subject. **troubled**—This verb applies to *emotional* agitation; as "shaken" to *intellectual.* **by spirit**—by a *person professing* to have the *spirit* of prophecy (I Cor. 12:8-10, I John 4:1-3). The Thessalonians had been warned (I Thess. 5:20, 21) to "prove" such professed prophesyings, and to "hold fast (only) that which is good." **by word**—*of mouth* (cf. vss. 5, 15); some word or saying alleged to be that of Paul, orally communicated. If oral tradition was liable to such perversion in the apostolic age (cf. a similar instance, John 21:23), how much more in our age! **by letter as from us**—purporting to be from us, whereas it is a forgery. Hence he gives a test by which to know his genuine letters (ch. 3:17). **day of Christ**—The oldest MSS. read, "day of *the Lord.*" **is at hand**—rather, "is

ADAM CLARKE

CHAPTER 2

1. *We beseech you, brethren, by the coming of our Lord.* It is evident that the Thessalonians, incited by deceived or false teachers, had taken a wrong meaning out of the words of the First Epistle, chap. iv. 15 ff., concerning the day of judgment, and were led then to conclude that that day was at hand; and this had produced great confusion in the church. To correct this mistake the apostle sent them this second letter, in which he shows that this day must be necessarily distant, because a great work is to be done previously to its appearing. Of the day of general judgment he had spoken before, and said that it should "come as a thief in the night," i.e., when not expected; but he did not attempt to fix the time, nor did he insinuate that it was either near at hand or far off. Now, however, he shows that it must necessarily be far off, because of the great transactions which must take place before it can come.

2. *Be not soon shaken in mind.* "From the mind"; i.e., that they should retain the persuasion they had of the truths which he had before delivered to them; that they should still hold the same opinions, and hold fast the doctrines which they had been taught. *Neither by spirit.* Any pretended revelation. *Nor by word.* Anything which any person may profess to have heard the apostle speak. *Nor by letter.* Either the former one which he had sent, some passages of which have been misconceived and misconstrued, or by any other letter, *as from us*—pretending to have been written by us, the apostles, containing predictions of this kind. There is a diversity of opinion among critics concerning this last clause, some supposing that

MATTHEW HENRY

The apostle would not have them be deceived, *v.* 3. There are many who lie in wait to deceive, and they have many ways of deceiving; we have reason therefore to stand upon our guard. The apostle cautions them not to be deceived about the near approach of Christ's coming, as if it was to have been in the apostle's days. He gives them warning. He would not have their faith weakened. They ought not to waver in their minds as to this great thing, which is the faith and hope of all the saints. False doctrines are like the winds, that toss the water to and fro, and they are apt to unsettle the minds of men, who are sometimes as unstable as water. He would not have their comforts lessened with false alarms. In itself it should be matter of the believer's hope and joy. We should always watch and pray, but must not be discouraged nor uncomfortable at the thought of Christ's coming.

Verses 3–12

The apostle confutes the error against which he had cautioned them. There are several events previous to the second coming of Christ.

I. A general apostasy, *v.* 3. The apostle speaks of some very great apostasy such as should give occasion to the revelation or rise of that *man of sin.* This, he says (*v.* 5), he had told them of when he was with them. No sooner was Christianity planted and rooted in the world than there began to be a defection in the Christian church. It was so in the Old Testament church, and therefore it was no strange thing that after the planting of Christianity there should come a falling away.

II. A revelation of that man of sin (*v.* 3). The apostle afterwards speaks of the revelation of that wicked one (*v.* 8): here he seems to speak of his rise. He is called the man of sin, and he is the son of perdition, because he himself is devoted to certain destruction, and is the instrument of destroying many others.

The characters here given, *v.* 4. The antichrist is some usurper of God's authority who claims divine honours.

JAMIESON, FAUSSET, BROWN

immediately imminent," lit., "is *present*"; "is *instantly* coming." Christ and His apostles always taught that the day of the Lord's coming *is at hand;* and it is not likely that Paul would imply anything contrary here; what he denies is, that it is so *immediately imminent, instant,* or *present,* as to justify the neglect of everyday worldly duties. CHRYSOSTOM, and after him ALFORD, translates, "is [already] present" (cf. II Tim. 2:18), a kindred error. But in II Timothy 3:1, the same *Greek* verb is translated "come." WAHL supports this view. The *Greek* is usually used of actual presence; but is quite susceptible of the translation, "is all but present." **3. by any means**—*Greek,* "in any manner." Christ, in Matthew 24:4, gives the same warning in connection with the same event. He had indicated three ways (vs. 2) in which they might be deceived (cf. other ways, vs. 9, and Matthew 24:5, 24). **a falling away**—rather as the *Greek,* "*the* falling away," or "apostasy," viz., *the* one of which "I told you" before (vs. 5), "when I was yet with you," and of which the Lord gave some intimation (Matt. 24:10-12; John 5:43). **that man of sin be revealed**—The *Greek* order is, "And there have been revealed the man of sin." As Christ was first in *mystery,* and afterwards *revealed* (I Tim. 3:16), so Antichrist (the term used I John 2:18; 4:3) is first in mystery, and afterwards shall be developed and revealed (vss. 7-9). As righteousness found its embodiment in Christ, "the Lord our righteousness," so "sin" shall have its embodiment in "the man of sin." *The hindering* power meanwhile restrains its manifestation; when that shall be removed, then this manifestation shall take place. **the son of perdition**—a title applied besides to Judas (the traitor, John 17:12), and to none else. **Anti**christ (the second "beast" coming up out of the earth; therefore he shall at first be "like a lamb, while he speaks as a dragon" (Rev. 13:11); "coming in peaceably and by flatteries," "working deceitfully," but "his heart shall be against the holy covenant" (Dan. 11:21, 23, 28, 30). Seeds of "the falling away" soon appear (I Tim. 4:1-3), but the full development and concentration of these anti-Christian elements in one person are still to appear. **4.** Daniel 11:36, 37 is here referred to. The words used there as to Antiochus Epiphanes, Paul implies, shall even be more applicable to the man of sin, who is the New Testament actual Antichrist, as Antiochus was the Old Testament typical Antichrist. The previous world kingdoms had each one extraordinary person as its representative head and embodiment (thus Babylon had Nebuchadnezzar, Dan. 2:38, end; Medo-Persia had Cyrus; Greece had Alexander, and Antiochus Epiphanes, the forerunner of Antichrist); so the fourth and last world kingdom, under which we now live, shall have one final head, the concentrated embodiment of all the *sin* and *lawless iniquity* which have been in pagan and papal Rome. Rome's final phase will probably be an unholy alliance between idolatrous superstition and godless infidelity. **Who opposeth and exalteth himself**—There is but one *Greek* article to both participles, implying that the reason why he *opposeth himself* is in order that he may *exalt himself above ....* ALFORD takes the former clause absolutely, "He that withstands (CHRIST)," i.e., Antichrist (I John 2: 18). Antichrist shall exalt himself above *every* object of worship, whether on earth as the Cæsar, or in heaven as God. The various prefigurations of Antichrist, Mohammed, Rome, Napoleon, and modern infidel secularism, contain only *some,* not *all,* his characteristics. It is the union of all in some one person that shall form the full Antichrist, as the union in one Person, Jesus, of all the types and prophecies constituted the full Christ [OLSHAUSEN]. **in the temple of God... that he is God**—"He will reign a time, times, and half a time" (Dan. 7:25), i.e., three and a half years, and will sit *in the temple at Jerusalem;* then the Lord shall come from heaven and cast him into the lake of fire and shall bring to the saints the times of their reigning, the seventh day of hallowed rest, and give to Abraham the promised inheritance" [IRENÆUS, *Adversus Hæreses,* 30. 4]. **showing himself**—with blasphemous and arrogant DISPLAY (cf. a type, Acts 12:21-23). "Lucifer" (a title of Messiah, assumed by Antichrist, Rev. 22: 16); "I will exalt my throne above the stars of God." "I will sit upon the *mount of the congregation* (i.e., God's place of meeting His people of old, the temple), *in the sides of the north* (Ps. 48:2); I will be like the Most High." Revelation 11:1, 2, "The temple of God... the holy city" (viz., Jerusalem, Matt. 4:5), cf. Psalm 68:18, 29, referring to a period since Christ's ascension, therefore not yet fulfilled

ADAM CLARKE

it refers simply to the First Epistle, others supposing that a forged epistle is intended. I have joined the two senses. The word "to be shaken" signifies to be agitated as a ship at sea in a storm, and strongly marks the confusion and distress which the Thessalonians had felt in their false apprehension of this coming of Christ.

3. *Except there come a falling away first.* We have the original word in our word "apostasy"; and by this term we understand a dereliction of the essential principles of religious truth—either a total abandonment of Christianity itself or such a corruption of its doctrines as renders the whole system completely inefficient to salvation. *That man of sin.* The same as the Hebrew expresses by *ish aven* and *ish beliyaal;* the perverse, obstinate, and iniquitous man. *The son of perdition.* "The son of destruction"; the same epithet that is given to Judas Iscariot, John xvii. 12.

The *son of perdition* and the *man of sin* or, as some excellent MSS. and versions, with several of the fathers, read, "the lawless man," must mean the same person or thing. It is also remarkable that the wicked Jews are styled by Isaiah, chap. i. 4, "children of perdition," persons who destroy themselves and destroy others.

4. *Who opposeth and exalteth.* He "stands against" and exalts himself above all divine authority and above every object of adoration and every institution relative to divine worship, himself being the source whence must originate all the doctrines of religion and all its rites and ceremonies; so that sitting in the temple of God—having the highest place and authority in the Christian Church, he acts as God—taking upon himself God's titles and attributes, and arrogating to himself the authority that belongs to the Most High. The words *as God* are wanting in many MSS. and the chief of the Greek fathers. There is indeed no evidence of their being authentic, and the text reads much better without them.

MATTHEW HENRY

His rise is mentioned, *v.* 6, 7. There was something that hindered, or *let, until it was taken away.*

ALBERT BARNES:

"That he might be revealed in his time." The man of sin. The meaning is, that there was then a restraint operating which would prevent the development of this antichristian power until the proper time; that is, till the state of the world should be such that in the divine arrangements it would be proper to permit it. It was not to be permitted until the gospel should be extensively preached, and had had an opportunity of showing its fair effects on the nations; until it had become so planted and established that even the rise of this antichristian power could not effectually uproot it. Had the "man of sin" been permitted to rise at once, the consequence might have been that the new religion would have been crushed, so that it could never have revived again. There was then a providential arrangement by which this growth of wickedness should be checked and restrained until the new religion should take deep root in the earth, and its perpetuity should be secured. Then the great trial was to be permitted under the "man of sin."—*Popular Commentary*

This mystery of iniquity was gradually to arrive at its height. The apostle calls it a *mystery of iniquity.* This mystery of iniquity did *already work.* While the apostles were yet living *the enemy came and sowed tares.*

The fall or ruin of the antichristian state is declared, *v.* 8. The head of this antichristian kingdom is called *that wicked one.* The revelation or discovery of this to the world would be the sure presage of his ruin. The apostle assures the Thessalonians that the Lord would destroy him. The power of antichrist in due time will be totally and finally destroyed, and this will be by the brightness of Christ's coming.

JAMIESON, FAUSSET, BROWN

(Isa. 2:1-3; Ezek., chs. 40-44; Zech. 14:16-20; Mal. 3:1). **5. Remember . . .**—confuting those who represent Paul as having labored under error as to Christ's immediate coming when writing his first Epistle, and as now correcting that error. **I told you**—more than once, lit., "I was telling," or "used to tell." **6. now ye know**—by my having told you. The power must have been one "known" to the Thessalonians. **what withholdeth**—that which *holds* him *back;* "keeps him in check": the power that has restrained the man of sin from his full and final development, is *the moral and conservative influence of political states* [OLSHAUSEN]: *the fabric of human polity* as a *coercive* power; as "he who now letteth" refers to *those who rule that polity* by which the great upbursting of godlessness is kept down [ALFORD]. The "what withholdeth" refers to the *general hindrance;* "he who now letteth," to *the person in whom that hindrance is summed up.* **that he might be**—*Greek,* "in order that": ye know that which keeps him back, in God's purposes, from being sooner manifested, "*in order that* he *may* be revealed in *his own* time" (i.e., the time appointed by God to him as his proper time for being manifested), not sooner (cf. Dan. 11:35). The removal of the withholding power will be when the civil polity, derived from the Roman empire, which is to be, in its last form, divided into ten kingdoms (Rev. 17:3, 11-13), shall, with its leading representative head for the time being ("he who now letteth," *Greek,* "withholdeth," as in vs. 6), yield to the prevalent godless "lawlessness" with "the lawless one" as its embodiment. **the mystery of iniquity**—the counterwork to "the mystery of godliness" (I Tim. 3:16). Anti-Christianity *latently* working, as distinguished from its final *open* manifestation. "Mystery" in Scripture means, not what remains always a secret, but that which is for a while hidden, but in due time manifested (cf. Eph. 3:4, 5). "Iniquity," *Greek, lawlessness;* defiant rejection of God's *law* (cf. *Note,* Zech. 5:9, 10). *"Wickedness"* (translated by the LXX by the same *Greek,* meaning "lawlessness," which Paul employs here), embodied there as a woman, answers to "the mystery of iniquity," here embodied finally in "the man of sin" **already**—(II John 9:10; Col. 2:18-23; I Tim. 4:1)—cf. "even now already" (I John 2:18; 4:3) as distinguished from "in his own time" of being revealed *hereafter.* Antiquity, it appears from hence, is not a justification for unscriptural usages or dogmas, since these were "already," even in Paul's time, beginning to spring up: the written word is the only sure test. "Judaism infecting Christianity is the fuel; the mystery of iniquity is the spark." "It is one and the same impurity diffusing itself over many ages" [BENGEL]. **only he who now letteth** *will let*—The italicized words are not in the *Greek.* Therefore, translate rather, "only (i.e., the continuance of *the* MYSTERY *of iniquity-working* will be *only*) until he who now *withholdeth* (the same *Greek* as in vs. 6) be taken out of the way." "Only (*waiting,* Heb. 10:13) until he . . . ." Then it will work no longer in *mystery,* but in open manifestation. **8.** Translate, "the lawless one"; the embodiment of all the godless "lawlessness" which has been working in "mystery" for ages (vs. 7): "the man of sin" (vs. 3). **whom the Lord**—Some of the oldest MSS. read, "the Lord *Jesus.*" How awful that He whose very name means *God-Saviour,* should appear as the Destroyer; but the *salvation* of the Church requires the destruction of her foe. As the reign of Israel in Canaan was ushered in by judgments on the nations for *apostasy* (for the Canaanites were originally worshippers of the true God: thus Melchisedek, king of Salem, was the "priest of the most high God," Gen. 14:18: Ammon and Moab came from righteous Lot), so the Son of David's reign in Zion and over the whole earth, is to be ushered in by judgments on the apostate Christian world. **consume . . . and . . . destroy**—So Daniel 7:26, "consume and destroy"; Daniel 11:45. He shall "consume" him by His mere breath (Isa 11:4; 30:33): the sentence of judgment being the sharp sword that goeth out of His mouth (Rev. 19: 15, 21). Antichrist's manifestation and destruction are declared in the same breath; at his greatest height he is nearest his fall, like Herod his type (Isa. 1:24-27; Acts 12:20-23). **with the brightness of his coming**—*Greek,* "the *manifestation* (or *appearance*) of His *presence":* the first outburst of His advent—the first gleam of His presence—is enough to *abolish* utterly all traces of Antichrist, as darkness disappears before the dawning day. Next, his adherents are "slain with the sword out of His mouth" (Rev. 19:21).

ADAM CLARKE

5. *I told you these things.* In several parts of this description of the man of sin, the apostle alludes to a conversation which had taken place between him and the members of this church when he was at Thessalonica; and this one circumstance will account for much of the obscurity that is in these verses. Besides, the apostle appears to speak with great caution, and does not at all wish to publish what he had communicated to them; the hints which he drops were sufficient to call the whole to their remembrance.

6. *And now ye know what withholdeth.* I told you this among other things; I informed you what it was that prevented this man of sin, this son of perdition, from revealing himself fully.

7. *For the mystery of iniquity doth already work.* There is a system of corrupt doctrine which will lead to the general apostasy, already in existence, but it is a *mystery.* It is as yet hidden; it dare not show itself, because of that which "hindereth" or "withholdeth."

But when that which now "restraineth" shall be taken out of the way, then shall that wicked one be revealed—it will then be manifest who he is and what he is.

8. *Whom the Lord shall consume.* He shall "blast" him so that he shall "wither" and "die away"; and this shall be done by *the spirit of his mouth*—the words of eternal life, the true doctrine of the gospel of Jesus; this shall be the instrument used to destroy this man of sin. Therefore it is evident his death will not be a sudden but a gradual one; because it is by the preaching of the truth that he is to be exposed, overthrown, and finally destroyed. *The brightness of his coming.* This may refer to that full manifestation of the truth which had been obscured and kept under by the exaltation of this man of sin.

MATTHEW HENRY

The apostle further describes the rule of this man of sin. A divine power is pretended for the support of this kingdom, but it is only after the working of Satan.

The apostle calls it *all deceiveableness of unrighteousness*, *v.* 10. Many are the subtle artifices the man of sin has used. His willing subjects, *v.* 10.

Had they loved the truth, they would have persevered in it, and been preserved by it; but no wonder if they easily parted with what they never had any love to.

The *sin and ruin of the subjects* of antichrist's kingdom declared, *v.* 11, 12. An erroneous mind and vicious life often go together and help forward one another. He will punish men for their unbelief, and for their dislike of the truth and love to sin and wickedness. He sometimes withdraws his grace from such sinners as are here mentioned; he gives them up to their own hearts' lusts, and leaves them to themselves, and then sin will follow of course.

Verses 13–15

I. The consolation the Thessalonians might take, *v.* 13, 14. The apostle reckoned himself bound in duty to be thankful to God on this account. And there was good reason, because they were beloved by the Lord.

1. The stability of the election of grace, *v.* 13. God had chosen them from the beginning. He had loved them with an everlasting love. (1) The eternal date of it—it is from the beginning. (2) The end to which they were chosen—salvation, complete and eternal salvation. (3) The means in order to obtaining this end—*sanctification of the spirit and belief of the truth.* We are not elected of God because we were holy, but that we might be holy. Being chosen of God, we must not live as we list. Faith and holiness must be joined together, as well as holiness and happiness.

JAMIESON, FAUSSET, BROWN

9. whose coming—The same *Greek* as was used for *the* Lord's coming (vs. 8) or personal "presence." **is**—in its essential character. **after**—*according to* the working ("energy") of Satan, as opposed to the *energy* or *working* of the Holy Spirit in the Church (*Note*, Eph. 1:19). As Christ is related to God, so is Antichrist to Satan, his visible embodiment and manifestation: Satan works through him. Revelation 13:2, "The dragon gave him (the beast) his power . . . seat . . . great authority." **lying wonders**—lit., "wonders" or "prodigies of falsehood." His "power, signs, and wonders," all have *falsehood* for their base, essence, and aim (John 8:44), [ALFORD]. **10. deceivableness**—rather as *Greek,* "deceit of (to promote) unrighteousness" (vs. 12). **in**—The oldest MSS. and versions omit "in." Translate. "*unto* them that *are perishing*" (II Cor. 2:15, 16; 4:3): the victims of him whose very name describes his *perishing* nature, "the son of perdition"; in contrast to *you* whom (vs. 13) "God hath from the beginning chosen to *salvation* through *sanctification* of the Spirit and belief of the truth." **because**—lit., "in requital for"; in just retribution for their having no *love* for the truth which was within their reach (on account of its putting a check on their bad passions), and for their having "pleasure in unrighteousness" (vs. 12; Rom. 1:18); they are *lost* because they loved not, but rejected, the truth which would have *saved* them. **received not**—*Greek,* "welcomed not"; admitted it not cordially. **love of the truth**—not merely love of *truth,* but love of THE *truth* (and of Jesus who is *the Truth,* in opposition to Satan's "lie," vss. 9, 11; John 8:42-44), **can** *save* (Eph. 4:21). We are required not merely to assent to, but to *love* the truth (Ps. 119:97). The Jews rejected Him who came in His divine Father's name; they will receive Antichrist coming in *his own* name (John 5:43). Their pleasant sin shall prove their terrible scourge. **11. for this cause**—because "they received not the love of the truth." The best safeguard against error is "the love of the truth." **shall send**—*Greek,* "sends," or "is sending"; the "delusion" is already beginning. God judicially sends hardness of heart on those who have rejected the truth, and gives them up in righteous judgment to Satan's delusions (Isa. 6:9, 10; Rom. 1:24-26, 28). They first cast off the love of the truth, then God gives them up to Satan's delusions, then they settle down into "believing the lie": an awful climax (I Kings 22:22, 23; Ezek. 14:9; Job 12: 16; Matt. 24:5, 11; I Tim. 4:1). **strong delusion**—*Greek,* "the powerful working of error," answering to the energizing "working of Satan" (vs. 9); the same expression as is applied to the Holy Ghost's operation in believers: "powerful" or "effectual (energizing) working" (Eph. 1:19). **believe a lie**—rather, "*the* lie" which Antichrist tells them, appealing to his miracles as proofs of it . . . . (vs. 9). **12. they all . . . damned**—rather as *Greek,* "that *all* . . . ." He here states the general proposition which applies specially to Antichrist's adherents. Not all in the Church of Rome, or other anti-Christian systems, shall be damned, but only "all who believed not the truth" *when offered to them,* "but had pleasure in unrighteousness" (Rom. 1:32; 2:8). Love of *unrighteousness* being the great obstacle to *believing the truth.* **13. But**—In delightful contrast to the damnation of the lost (vs. 12) stands the "salvation" of Paul's converts. **are bound**—in duty (ch. 1:3). **thanks . . . to God**—not to ourselves, your ministers, nor to you, our converts. **beloved of the Lord**—Jesus (Rom. 8:37; Gal. 2:20; Eph. 5:2, 25). Elsewhere *God the Father* is said to love us (vs. 16; John 3:16; Eph. 2:4; Col. 3:12). Therefore Jesus and the Father are one. **from the beginning**—"before the foundation of the world" (Eph. 1:4; cf. I Cor. 2:7; II Tim. 1:9); in contrast to those that shall "worship the beast, whose names are not written in the book of life of the Lamb slain from the foundation of the world" (Rev. 13:8). Some of the oldest MSS. read as *English Version,* but other oldest MSS. and *Vulgate* read, "as *first fruits.*" The Thessalonians were among the first converts in Europe (cf. Rom. 16:5; I Cor. 16:15). In a more general sense, it occurs in James 1:18; Revelation 14:4; so I understand it here including the more restricted sense. **chosen you**—The *Greek,* is not the ordinary word for "elected," implying His eternal *selection;* but *taken for Himself,* implying His having *adopted* them in His eternal purpose. It is found in the LXX (Deut. 7:7; 10:15). **through**—rather as *Greek,* "*in* sanctification" as the element in which *the choice to salvation* had place (cf. I Pet. 1. 2), standing in contrast to the "unrighteousness," the element in which Antichrist's followers are given over by God to *damnation* (vs. 12). **of the Spirit**—wrought by the Spirit who sanctifies all the elect

ADAM CLARKE

9. *Whose coming is after the working of Satan.* The operation of God's Spirit sends His messengers; the operation of Satan's spirit sends his emissaries. The one comes *after* or "according to the energy" or inward powerful *working of* God; the other comes according to the energy or inward working of Satan. *With all power.* All kinds of miracles, like the Egyptian magicians. *And signs and lying wonders.* The word *lying* may be applied to the whole of these; they were *lying* miracles, *lying* signs, and *lying* wonders; only appearances of what was real, and done to give credit to his presumption and imposture. Whereas God sent His messengers with real miracles, real signs, and real wonders; such Satan cannot produce.

10. *And with all deceivableness of unrighteousness.* With every art that cunning can invent and unrighteousness suggest, in order to delude and deceive. *In them that perish.* "Among them that are destroyed";

and they are destroyed and perish because they would not receive *the love of the truth, that they might be saved.* So they perish because they obstinately refuse to be saved, and receive a lie in preference to the truth.

11. *God shall send them strong delusion. For this* very *cause,* that they would not receive the love of the truth, "but had pleasure in unrighteousness," therefore God permits *strong delusion* to occupy their minds; so that they *believe a lie* rather than the truth, prefer false apostles and their erroneous doctrines to the pure truths of the gospel, brought to them by the well-accredited messengers of God; being ever ready to receive any false Messiah, while they systematically and virulently reject the true One.

12. *That they all might be damned.* "So that they may all be condemned who believed not the truth" when it was proclaimed to them; but took *pleasure in unrighteousness,* preferring that to the way of holiness. Their condemnation was the effect of their refusal to believe the truth, and they refused to believe it because they loved their sins.

13-14. *God hath from the beginning chosen you to salvation.* In your calling God has shown the purpose that He had formed from the beginning, to call the Gentiles to the same privileges with the Jews, not through circumcision and the observance of the Mosaic law, but by faith in Christ Jesus; but this simple way of salvation referred to the same end—holiness, without which no man, whether Jew or Gentile, can see the Lord.

MATTHEW HENRY

2. The efficacy of the gospel call, *v.* 14. They were called thereunto by the gospel. It is a call to honour and happiness, even the *glory of our Lord Jesus Christ*. Such shall be with Christ, to behold his glory, and they shall be glorified with Christ and partake of his glory.

II. He does not say, "You are chosen to salvation, and therefore you may be careless and secure"; but *therefore stand fast*. The Thessalonians are exhorted to steadfastness in their Christian profession.

Verses 16, 17

The apostle's earnest prayer for them.

I. To whom he prays: *Our Lord Jesus Christ himself, and God, even our Father*. We may and should direct our prayers, not only to God the Father, but also *to our Lord Jesus Christ himself*.

II. From what he takes encouragement—from the consideration of what God had already done for him and them (*v.* 16). The love of God is the spring and fountain of all the good we have or hope for. From this fountain all our consolation flows. And the consolation of the saints is an everlasting consolation. The comforts of the saints are not dying things. Their consolation is founded on the hope of eternal life. The free grace and mercy of God are what they hope for, and what their hopes are founded on.

III. What it is that he asks of God for them, *v.* 17. He prayed that they might have more abundant consolation, and he prayed that they might be established. Comfort is a means of establishment; for the more pleasure we take in the ways of God, the more likely we shall be to persevere therein. Our establishment in the ways of God is a likely means in order to comfort. If we are halting and faltering in our duty, no wonder if we are strangers to the pleasures and joys of religion. We must be established in every good word and work. Christ must be honoured by our good works and good words.

CHAPTER 3

Verses 1–5

1. The apostle desires the prayers of his friends, *v.* 1. He always remembered them in his prayers, and would not have them forget him and his fellow-labourers. This is one way by which the communion of saints is kept up, not only by their praying together but by their praying for one another when they are absent one from another. What they are desired to pray for: 1. For the success of the gospel ministry, *v.* 1. He desired that the word of the Lord might run (so it is in the original), that it might get ground, and not only go forward, but go apace. We should pray that the gospel may have free course to the hearts and the consciences of men, that it may be glorified in the conversion of sinners. God will glorify the gospel, and so will glorify his own name. 2. For the safety of gospel ministers. He asks their prayers, not for preferment, but for preservation, *v.* 2. Those who are enemies to the preaching of the gospel are unreasonable and wicked men. There is the greatest absurdity in the world, as well as impiety. Godly and faithful ministers are as the standard-bearers,

JAMIESON, FAUSSET, BROWN

people of God, first by eternally consecrating them to perfect holiness in Christ, once for all, next by progressively imparting it. **belief of the truth**—contrasted with "believed not the truth" (vs. 12). **14. you**—The oldest MSS. read, "us." **by our gospel**—"*through*" the Gospel which we preach. **to . . . glory**—In vs. 13 it was "salvation," i.e., deliverance from all evil, of body and soul (I Thess. 5:9); here it is positive good, even "glory," and that "the glory of our Lord Jesus" Himself, which believers are privileged to share with Him (John 17:22, 24; Rom. 8:17, 29; II Tim. 2:10). **15. Therefore**—God's sovereign choice of believers, so far from being a ground for inaction on their part, is the strongest incentive to action and perseverance in it. Cf. the argument, Philippians 2:12, 13, "Work out *your own* salvation, FOR it is God which worketh in you . . . ." We cannot fully explain this in *theory;* but to the sincere and humble, the *practical* acting on the principle is plain. "Privilege first, duty afterwards" [EDMUNDS]. **stand fast**—so as not to be "shaken or troubled" (vs. 2). **hold**—so as not to let go. Adding nothing, subtracting nothing [BENGEL]. The Thessalonians had not held fast his oral instructions but had suffered themselves to be imposed upon by pretended spirit-revelations, and words and letters pretending to be from Paul (vs. 2), to the effect that "the day of the Lord was instantly imminent." **traditions**—truths *delivered* and *transmitted* orally, or in writing (ch. 3:6; I Cor. 11:2; *Greek,* "traditions"). The *Greek* verb from which the noun comes, is used by Paul in I Corinthians 11:23; 15:3.

Oral inspiration was necessary in their case, until the canon of the written Word should be complete; they proved their possession of inspiration by miracles wrought in support of the new revelation, which revelation, moreover, accorded with the existing Old Testament revelation; an additional test needed besides miracles (cf. Deut. 13: 1-6; Acts 17:11). When the canon was complete, the infallibility of the living men was transferred to the written Word, now the sole unerring guide, interpreted by the Holy Spirit. Little else has come down to us by the most *ancient* and *universal* tradition save this, the all-sufficiency of Scripture for salvation. Therefore, by tradition, we are constrained to cast off all tradition not contained in, or not provable by, Scripture.

our epistle—as distinguished from a "letter AS from us," vs. 2, viz., that purports to be from us, but is not. He refers to his first Epistle to the Thessalonians. **16, 17. himself**—by His own might, as contrasted with our feebleness; ensuring the efficacy of our prayer. Here *our Lord Jesus* stands first; in I Thessalonians 3:11. "God our Father." **which . . . loved us**—in the work of our redemption. Referring both to *our Lord Jesus* (Rom. 8:37; Gal. 2: 20) and *God our Father* (John 3:16). **everlasting consolation**—not transitory, as worldly consolations in trials (Rom. 8:38, 39). This for all time present, and then "good hope" for the future [ALFORD]. **through grace**—rather as *Greek* "IN grace"; to be joined to "hath given." Grace is the element *in* which the gift was made. **Comfort your hearts**—unsettled as you have been through those who announced the immediate coming of the Lord. **good word and work**—The oldest MSS. invert the order, "work and word." *Establishment* in these were what the young converts at Thessalonica needed, not fanatical teaching (cf. I Cor. 15:58).

CHAPTER 3

Vss. 1-18. HE ASKS THEIR PRAYERS: HIS CONFIDENCE IN THEM: PRAYER FOR THEM: CHARGES AGAINST DISORDERLY IDLE CONDUCT; HIS OWN EXAMPLE: CONCLUDING PRAYER AND SALUTATION. **1. Finally**—lit., "As to what remains." **may have free course**—lit., "may run"; spread rapidly without a drag on the wheels of its course. That the new-creating word may "run" as "swiftly" as the creative word at the first (Ps. 147:15). The opposite is the word of God being "bound" (II Tim. 2:9). **glorified**—by sinners accepting it (Acts 13:48; Gal. 1:23, 24). Contrast "evil spoken of" (I Pet. 4:14). **as it is with you**—(I Thess. 1:6; 4:10; 5:11). **2. that we . . . be delivered from unreasonable . . . men**—lit., men *out of place, inept,* unseemly: *out of the way bad:* more than ordinarily bad. An undesigned coincidence with Acts 18:5-9. Paul was now at Corinth, where the JEWS "opposed themselves" to his preaching: in answer to his prayers and those of his converts at Thessalonica and elsewhere, "the Lord, in vision," assured him of exemption from "the hurt," and of success in bringing in "much

ADAM CLARKE

15. *Therefore, brethren, stand fast.* Their obtaining eternal glory depended on their faithfulness to the grace of God; for this calling did not necessarily and irresistibly lead to faith; nor their faith to the sanctification of the spirit; nor their sanctification of the spirit to the glory of our Lord Jesus. Had they not attended to the calling, they could not have believed; had they not believed, they could not have been sanctified; had they not been sanctified they could not have been glorified. All these things depended on each other; they were stages of the great journey; and at any of these stages they might have halted, and never finished their Christian race.

Hold the traditions which ye have been taught. The word which we render "tradition" signifies anything "delivered" in the way of teaching; and here most obviously means the doctrines delivered by the apostle to the Thessalonians, whether in his preaching, private conversation, or by these Epistles; and particularly the First Epistle, as the apostle here states.

16. *Now our Lord Jesus.* As all your grace came from God through Christ, so the power that is necessary to strengthen and confirm you unto the end must come in the same way. *Everlasting consolation.* The glad tidings of the gospel and the comfort which you have received through believing, a gift which God had in His original purpose in reference to the Gentiles, a purpose which has respected all times and places and which shall continue to the conclusion of time; for the gospel is everlasting, and shall not be superseded by any other dispensation. *And good hope through grace.* The *hope* of the gospel was the resurrection of the body, and the final glorification of it and the soul throughout eternity. This was the good hope which the Thessalonians had, not a hope that they should be pardoned or sanctified. Pardon and holiness they enjoyed; therefore they were no objects of hope. But the resurrection of the body and eternal glory were necessarily future; these they had in expectation; these they hoped for; and through the *grace* which they had already received they had a *good hope,* a well-grounded expectation, of the glorious state.

17. *Comfort your hearts.* Keep your souls ever under the influence of His Holy Spirit; *and stablish you*—confirm and strengthen you in your belief in every *good word* or doctrine which we have delivered unto you, and in the practice of every *good work* recommended and enjoined by the doctrines of the gospel.

CHAPTER 3

1. *Finally, brethren.* The words do not mean *finally,* but "furthermore," "to come to a conclusion," "what remains is this," "I shall only add"—any of these phrases expresses the sense of the original. *Pray for us.* God, in the order of His grace and providence, has made even the success of His gospel dependent in a certain measure on the prayers of His followers. Why He should do so we cannot tell, but that He has done so we know; and they are not a little criminal who neglect to make fervent supplications for the prosperity of the cause of God. *May have free course.* They were to pray that "the doctrine of the Lord" "might run," an allusion to the races in the Olympic games; that, as it had already got into the stadium or race-course, and had started fairly, so it might "run on," get to the goal, and *be glorified;* i.e., gain the crown appointed for him that should get first to the end of the course.

2. *Unreasonable and wicked men.* The word

MATTHEW HENRY

who are most struck at. Many do not believe the gospel; no wonder if such are restless in their endeavours to oppose the gospel, and disgrace the ministers of the word; and too many have not common faith or honesty; there is no confidence that we can safely put in them, and we should pray to be delivered from those who have no conscience nor honour.

II. He encourages them to trust in God.

1. What the good is which we may expect from the grace of God—establishment, and preservation from evil. We stand no longer than God holds us up. We have as much need of the grace of God for our perseverance to the end as for the beginning of the good work.

2. What encouragement we have to depend upon the grace of God. He is faithful to his promises. When once the promise is made, performance is sure and certain. He is a faithful God and a faithful friend. Let it be our care to be true and faithful in our promises, and to the relations we stand in to this faithful God.

3. A further ground of hope that God would do this for them, *v.* 4. The apostle had this confidence in them, and this was founded upon his confidence in God; for there is otherwise no confidence in man.

III. He makes a short prayer for them, *v.* 5, that their hearts may be brought into the love of God. This is not only most reasonable in order to our happiness, but is our happiness itself. We can never attain to this unless God by his grace direct our hearts aright, for our love is apt to go astray after other things. We must wait for Christ, which supposes our faith in him, that we believe he came once in flesh and will come again in glory. We *have need of patience*, patience for Christ's sake and after Christ's example.

Verses 6–15

Commands and directions to some who were faulty, correcting some things that were amiss among them. The best society of Christians may have some faulty persons among them. Perfection is not to be found on this side heaven: but evil manners beget good laws.

I. That which was amiss among the Thessalonians.

1. There were some who *walked disorderly, not after the tradition they received* from the apostle, *v.* 6.

II. The good laws which were occasioned by these evil manners.

1. Whose laws they are: they are commands of the apostles of our Lord, that is, the commands of our Lord himself, *v.* 6, 12. The authority of Christ should awe our minds to obedience, and his grace and goodness should allure us.

2. What the good laws and rules are.

(1) His commands and directions to the whole church. [1] Their behaviour towards the disorderly persons (*v.* 6). Note that man is charged with not obeying the word of God. We must have sufficient proof of his fault before we proceed further. Admonish him in a friendly manner; we must put him in mind of his sin, and of his duty. If he will not hear do not keep company with him, that ye may not learn his evil ways; for he who follows vain persons is in danger of becoming like them. Another reason is for the shaming, and so the reforming, of those that offend. Love therefore to the persons of our offending brethren should be the motive of our withdrawing from them; and even those who are under the censures of the church must not be accounted as enemies (*v.* 15). [2] Their general conduct ought to be according to the good example the apostle had given them, *v.* 7. The particular good example the apostle mentions was their diligence: "*We behaved not ourselves disorderly among you* (*v.* 7), we did not spend our time idly." They took pains in their ministry and in getting their own living, *v.* 8. Those who preach the gospel may of right expect to live by the gospel. This is a just debt that people owe to their ministers, and the apostle had power or authority to have demanded this (*v.* 9); but he waived his right from affection to them, and that he might be an example for them to follow (*v.* 9).

JAMIESON, FAUSSET, BROWN

people." On the unreasonable, out-of-the-way perversity of the Jews, as known to the Thessalonians, see I Thessalonians 2:15, 16. **have not faith**—or as *Greek,* "the faith" of the Christian: the only antidote to what is "unreasonable and wicked." The Thessalonians, from their ready acceptance of the Gospel (I Thess. 1:5, 6), might think "all" would similarly receive it; but the Jews were far from having such a readiness to believe the truth. **3. faithful**—alluding to "faith" (vs. 2): though many will not believe, the Lord (other very old MSS. read "God") is still to be believed in as faithful to His promises (I Thess. 5:24; II Tim. 2:13). *Faith* on the part of man answers to faithfulness on the part of God. **stablish you**—as he had prayed (ch. 2:17). Though it was on himself that wicked men were making their onset, he turns away from asking the Thessalonians' prayers for HIS deliverance (vs. 2: so unselfish was he, even in religion), to express his assurance of THEIR establishment in the faith, and preservation from evil.

4. we have confidence in the Lord—as "faithful" (vs. 3). Have confidence in no man when left to himself [BENGEL]. **that ye both do**—Some of the oldest MSS. insert a clause, "that ye both have done" before, "and are doing, and will do." He means the *majority* by "ye," not *all* of them (cf. vs. 11; ch. 1:3; I Thess. 3:6). **5.** If "the Lord" be here the Holy Ghost (II Cor. 3:17), the three Persons of the Trinity will occur in this verse. **love of God**—love to God. **patient waiting for Christ**—rather as *Greek,* "the patience (endurance) of Christ," viz., which Christ showed [ALFORD] (ch. 2:4; I Thess. 1:3). ESTIUS, however, supports *English Version* (cf. Rev. 1:9; 3:10). At all events, this grace, "patience," or *persevering endurance,* is connected with the "hope" (I Thess. 1:3, 10) of *Christ's coming.* In ALFORD'S translation we may compare Hebrews 12: 1, 2, "Run with *patience* (*endurance*) . . . looking to JESUS . . . who, for the joy that was before Him, *endured* the cross"; so WE are to endure, as looking for the hope to be realized at His coming (Heb. 10: 36, 37). **6. we command you**—Hereby he puts to a particular test their obedience in general to his *commands,* which obedience he had recognized in vs. 4. **withdraw**—lit., "to furl the sails"; as we say, *to steer clear of* (cf. vs. 14). Some had given up labor as though the Lord's day was immediately coming. He had enjoined mild censure of such in I Thessalonians 5:14, "*Warn* . . . the unruly"; but now that the mischief had become more confirmed, he enjoins stricter discipline, viz., withdrawal from their company (cf. I Cor.. 5:11; II John 10:11): not a formal sentence of excommunication, such as was subsequently passed on more heinous offenders (as in I Cor. 5:5; I Tim. 1:20). He says "brother," i.e., professing Christian; for in the case of unprofessing heathen, believers needed not be so strict (I Cor. 5: 10-13). **the tradition**—the oral instruction which he had given to them when present (vs. 10), and subsequently committed to writing (I Thess. 4:11, 12). **which he received of us**—Some oldest MSS. read, "*ye* received"; others, "*they* received." The *English Version* reading has no very old authority. **7. how ye ought to follow us**—how ye ought to live so as *to "imitate* (so the *Greek* for 'follow') *us*" (cf. *Note,* I Cor. 11:1; I Thess. 1:6). **8. eat any man's bread**—*Greek,* "eat bread *from* any man," i.e., live at anyone's expense. Contrast vs. 12, "*eat* THEIR OWN bread." **wrought**—(Acts 20: 34). In both Epistles they state they maintained themselves by labor; but in this second Epistle they do so in order to offer themselves herein as an example to the idle; whereas, in the first, their object in doing so is to vindicate themselves from all imputation of mercenary motives in preaching the Gospel (I Thess. 2:5, 9) [EDMUNDS]. They preached gratuitously though they might have claimed maintenance from their converts. **labour and travail**—"toil and hardship" (*Note,* I Thess. 2:9). **night and day**—scarcely allowing time for repose. **chargeable**—*Greek,* "a burden," or "burdensome." The Philippians did not regard it as a *burden* to contribute to his support (Phil. 4:15, 16), sending to him while he was in this very Thessalonica (Acts 16:15, 34, 40). Many Thessalonians, doubtless, would have felt it a privilege to contribute, but as he saw some idlers among them who would have made a pretext of his example to justify themselves, he waived his right. His reason for the same course at Corinth was to mark how different were his aims from those of the false teachers who sought their own lucre (II Cor. 11:9, 12, 13). It is at the very time and place of writing these Epistles that Paul is expressly said to have *wrought at tent-making* with Aquila (Acts 18: 3); an undesigned coincidence. **9.** (I Cor. 9:4-6, etc.; Gal. 6:6.) **10. For even**—Translate, "For *also.*"

ADAM CLARKE

which we translate *unreasonable* signifies rather "disorderly, unmanageable"; persons "out of their place"—under no discipline, regardless of law and restraint, and ever acting agreeably to the disorderly and unreasonable impulse of their own minds. *For all men have not faith.* The word is, without doubt, to be taken here for "fidelity" or "trustworthiness," and not for *faith;* and this is agreeable to the meaning given to it in the very next verse: "But the Lord is faithful."

3. *From evil.* May be translated, "from the evil one." They had disorderly men, wicked men, and the evil one or the devil to contend with; God alone could support and give them the victory. He had promised to do it, and He might ever be confided in as being invariably *faithful.*

4. *And we have confidence.* We have no doubt of God's kindness towards you; He loves you, and will support you; and we can confide in you that you are now acting as we have desired you, and will continue so to do.

5. *The Lord direct your hearts into the love of God.* "Give a proper direction" to all its passions, and keep them in order, regularity, and purity. The patience of *Christ.* Such patience, under all your sufferings and persecutions, as Christ manifested under His. He bore meekly the contradiction of sinners against himself; and when He was reviled, He reviled not again.

6. *That ye withdraw yourselves.* Have no fellowship with those who will not submit to proper discipline; who do not keep their place; such as are "out of their rank," and act according to their own wills and caprices; and particularly such as are idle and busybodies. These he had ordered, 1 Thess. iv. 11-12, that they should study to be quiet, mind their own business, and work with their hands; but it appears that they had paid no attention to this order, and now he desires the church to exclude such from their communion. *And not after the tradition.* This evidently refers to the orders contained in the First Epistle; and that First Epistle was the *tradition* which they had received from him.

7. *We behaved not ourselves disorderly.* "We did not go out of our rank"—we kept our place, and discharged all its duties.

8. *Neither did we eat any man's bread for nought.* We paid for what we bought, and worked with our hands that we might have money to buy what was necessary.

Labour and travail night and day. We were incessantly employed, either in preaching the gospel, visiting from house to house, or working at our calling. As it is very evident that the church at Thessalonica was very pious, and most affectionately attached to the apostle, they must have been very poor, seeing he was obliged to work hard to gain himself the necessaries of life.

9. *Not because we have not power.* We have the power, the "right," to be maintained by those in whose behalf we labor. "The labourer is worthy of his hire" is a maxim universally acknowledged and respected; and "they which preach the gospel should live of the gospel." The apostle did not claim his privilege, but labored for his own support, that he might be an example to those whom he found otherwise disposed, and that he might spare the poor.

MATTHEW HENRY

(2) He commands those that lived idle lives to reform, *v.* 10. The labourer is worthy of his meat; but what is the loiterer worthy of? None should live like useless drones in the world.

There were among them some *idle persons and busy-bodies, v.* 11. It does not appear that they were gluttons or drunkards, but idle, and therefore disorderly people. It is not enough for any to say they do no hurt; for it is required of all persons that they do good. It is probable that these persons had a notion concerning the near approach of the coming of Christ, which served them for a pretence to leave off the work of their calling, and live in idleness. Industry in our particular callings as men is a duty required of us by our general calling as Christians. There were busy-bodies among them. The same persons who were idle were busy-bodies also. Most commonly those persons who have no business of their own to do, or who neglect it, busy themselves in other men's matters. If we are idle, the devil will soon find us something to do. The mind of man is a busy thing; if it be not employed in doing good, it will be doing evil.

It was not the mere humour of the apostle, it was the command of our Lord Jesus Christ, that *with quietness we work, and eat our own bread, v.* 12. Men ought some way or other to earn their own living, otherwise they do not eat their own bread. We must study to be quiet, and do our own business. This is an excellent but rare composition, to be of an active yet quiet spirit, active in our own business and yet quiet as to other people's.

(3) He exhorts *those that did well, not* to be *weary in well-doing* (*v.* 13). You must never give over, nor tire in your work. It will be time enough to rest when you come to heaven.

Verses 16–18

The apostle's benediction and prayers for these Thessalonians.

I. That God would give them peace. Peace is the blessing pronounced or desired. This peace is desired for them always. Peace by all means: for peace is often difficult, as it is always desirable. If we have any peace that is desirable, God must give it.

II. That the presence of God might be with them. We need nothing more to make us safe and happy, nor can we desire anything better for ourselves and our friends. It is the presence of God that makes heaven to be heaven, and this will make this earth to be like heaven.

III. That the *grace of our Lord Jesus Christ might be with them.* It is through the grace of our Lord Jesus Christ that we may comfortably hope to have peace with God and enjoy the presence of God. It is this grace that is all in all to make us happy.

JAMIESON, FAUSSET, BROWN

We not only set you the example, but gave a positive "command." **commanded**—*Greek* imperfect, "We were commanding"; we kept charge of you. **would not work**—*Greek, "is unwilling* to work." BENGEL makes this to be the argument: not that such a one is to have his food withdrawn from him by others; but he proves from the necessity of *eating* the necessity of *working;* using this pleasantry, Let him who will not work *show himself an angel,* i.e., do without food as the angels do (but since he cannot do without food, then he ought to be not unwilling to work). It seems to me simpler to take it as a punishment of the idle. Paul often quotes good adages current among the people, stamping them with inspired approval. In the *Hebrew, Bereshith Rabba,* the same saying is found; and in the book *Zeror,* "He who will not work before the sabbath, must not eat on the sabbath." **11. busy bodies**—In the *Greek* the similarity of sound marks the antithesis, "Doing none of their own business, yet overdoing in the business of others." Busy about everyone's business but their own. "Nature abhors a vacuum"; so if not doing one's own business, one is apt to meddle with his neighbor's business. Idleness is the parent of busybodies (I Tim. 5:13). Contrast I Thessalonians 4:11. **12. by**—The oldest MSS. read, "IN **the** Lord Jesus." So the *Greek,* I Thessalonians 4:1, implying the sphere wherein such conduct is appropriate and consistent. "We exhort you thus, as *ministers* IN *Christ,* exhorting our people IN Christ." **with quietness**—quiet industry; laying aside restless, bustling, intermeddling officiousness (vs. 11). **their own**—bread earned by themselves, not another's bread (vs. 8). **13. be not weary**—The oldest MSS. read, "Be not cowardly in"; do not be wanting in strenuousness in doing well. EDMUNDS explains it: Do not *culpably* neglect to do well, viz., with patient industry do your duty in your several callings. In contrast to the "disorderly, not-working busybodies" (vs. 11; cf. Gal. 6:9). **14. note that man**—mark him in your own mind as one to be avoided (vs. 6). **that he may be ashamed**—*Greek,* "made to turn and look into himself, and so be put to shame." Feeling himself shunned by godly brethren, he may become ashamed of his course. **15. admonish him as a brother**—not yet excommunicated (cf. Lev. 19:17). Do not shun him in contemptuous silence, but tell him why he is so avoided (Matt. 18:15; I Thess. 5:14). **16. Lord of peace**—Jesus Christ. The same title is given to Him as to the Father, **"the** GOD of peace" (Rom. 15:33; 16:20; II Cor. 13:11). An appropriate title in the prayer here, where the harmony of the Christian community was liable to interruption from the "disorderly." The *Greek* article requires the translation, "Give you *the* peace" which it is "His to give." "Peace" outward and inward, here and hereafter (Rom. 14:17). **always**—unbroken, not changing with outward circumstances. **by all means**—*Greek,* "in every way." Most of the oldest MSS. read, "in every *place*"; thus he prays for their peace *in all times* ("always") *and places.* **Lord be with you all**—May He bless you not only with *peace,* but also with His *presence* (Matt. 28:20). Even the disorderly brethren (cf. vs. 15, "a brother") are included in this prayer. **17.** The Epistle was written by an amanuensis (perhaps Silas or Timothy), and only the closing salutation written by Paul's "own hand" (cf. Rom. 16:22; I Cor. 16:21; Col. 4:18). Wherever Paul does not subjoin this autograph salutation, we may presume he wrote the whole Epistle himself (Gal. 6:11). **which**—*which* autograph salutation. **the token**—to distinguish genuine Epistles from spurious ones put forth in my name (ch. 2:2). **in every epistle**—Some think he signed his name to every Epistle with his own hand; but as there is no trace of this in any MSS. of *all* the Epistles, it is more likely that he alludes to *his writing with his own hand in closing every Epistle,* even in those Epistles (Romans, II Corinthians, Ephesians, Philippians, I Thessalonians) wherein he does not specify his having done so. **so I write**—so I sign my name: this is a specimen of my *handwriting,* by which to distinguish my geniune letters from forgeries. **18.** He closes every Epistle by praying for GRACE to those whom he addresses. **Amen**—omitted in the oldest MSS. It was doubtless the response of the congregation after hearing the Epistle read publicly; hence it crept into copies.

The Subscription is spurious, as the Epistle was written not "from Athens," but from *Corinth.*

ADAM CLARKE

10. *If any would not work, neither should he eat.* This is a just maxim, and universal nature inculcates it to man. If man will work, he may eat; if he do not work, he neither can eat nor should he eat. The maxim is founded on these words of the Lord: "In the sweat of thy face shalt thou eat bread." Industry is crowned with God's blessing; idleness is loaded with His curse.

11. *For we hear that there are some.* It is very likely that Paul kept up some sort of correspondence with the Thessalonian church; for he had heard everything that concerned their state, and it was from this information that he wrote his Second Epistle. *Disorderly.* "Out of their rank"—not keeping their own place. *Working not at all.* Either lounging at home or becoming religious gossips; "doing nothing." *Busybodies.* Doing everything they should not do—impertinent meddlers with other people's business; prying into other people's circumstances and domestic affairs; magnifying or minifying, mistaking or underrating everything; newsmongers and telltales; an abominable race, the curse of every neighborhood where they live, and a pest to religious society.

12. *With quietness they work.* "With silence"; leaving their talebearing and officious intermeddling. Less noise and more work! *Eat their own bread.* Their *own* bread because earned by their own honest industry. What a degrading thing to live on the bounty or mercy of another while a man is able to acquire his own livelihood!

13. *Be not weary in well doing.* While you stretch out no hand of relief to the indolent and lazy, do not forget the real poor—the genuine representatives of an impoverished Christ; and rather relieve a hundred undeserving objects than pass by one who is a real object of charity.

14. *If any man obey not.* They had disobeyed his word in the First Epistle, and the church still continued to bear with them; now he tells the church, if they still continue to disregard what is said to them, and particularly his word by this Second Epistle, they are to mark them as being totally incorrigible and have no fellowship with them. Some construe the words, "Give me information of that man by a letter"—let me hear of his continued obstinacy, and send me his name. The words of the original will bear either construction, that in the text or that given above.

15. *Count him not as an enemy.* Consider him still more an enemy to himself than to you; and *admonish him as a brother,* though you have ceased to hold religious communion with him. His soul is still of infinite value; labor to get it saved.

16. *The Lord of peace.* Jesus Christ, who is called "our peace," Eph. ii. 14; and "The Prince of Peace," Isa. ix. 6. May He *give you peace,* for He is the Fountain and Dispenser of it. *The Lord be with you all.* This is agreeable to the promise of our Lord: "Lo, I am with you alway, even unto the end of the world," Matt. xxviii. 20. May the Lord, who has promised to be always with His true disciples, be with you!

17. *The salutation of Paul with mine own hand.* It is very likely that Paul employed an amanuensis generally, either to write what he dictated or to make a fair copy of what he wrote. In either case the apostle always subscribed it, and wrote the salutation and benediction with his own hand; and this was what authenticated all his Epistles. A measure of this kind would be very necessary is forged epistles were carried about in those times.

18. *The grace.* The favor, blessing, and influence of our Lord Jesus Christ. *Be with you all*—be your constant companion. May you ever feel His presence, and enjoy His benediction!

THE FIRST EPISTLE TO TIMOTHY

I. Introduction (1:1, 2)
A. Paul's introduction of himself—a declaration of authority (1:1)
B. Paul's greeting to Timothy—a revelation of tenderness (1:2)

II. Timothy's charge—the Church (1:3-3:16)
A. The Church and man—her Gospel (1:3-20)
1. The Gospel (1:3-11)
2. Experimental illustration (1:12-17)
3. Timothy charged and warned (1:18-20)
B. The Church and God—her intercession (2:1-15)
1. Common prayer (2:1-7)
2. The worshippers (2:8-15)
C. The Church herself—her officers and office (3:1-16)
1. Her officers (3:1-13)
a. The bishop (3:1-7)
b. Deacons (3:8-13)
2. Her office (3:14-16)
a. The depository of truth (3:14, 15)
b. The truth deposited (3:16)

III. Charge to Timothy—the ministry (4:1-6:16)
A. His duty toward the truth (4:1-16)
1. The perils of spurious pietism (4:1-3)
2. The breadth of true Godliness to be declared by Timothy as corrective (4:4-9)
3. The strength in which he is to do this (4:10-16)
B. His duty toward his flock (5:1-6:2)
1. Men (5:1)
2. Women (5:2)
3. Widows (5:3-16)
4. Bishops (5:17-22)
5. Personal parenthesis (5:23-25)
6. Servants (6:1, 2)
C. His duty toward himself (6:3-16)
1. The manner and method of the false teachers (6:3-10)
2. Timothy's duty by contrast (6:11-16)

IV. Conclusion (6:17-21)
A. Postscript (6:17-19)
B. Summing up (6:20, 21a)
C. Benediction (6:21b)

Hitherto Paul's epistles were directed to churches; now follow some to particular persons: two to Timothy, one to Titus, and another to Philemon. Timothy and Titus were evangelists. Their commission and work was much the same with that of the apostles, and accordingly they were itinerants, as we find Timothy was. Timothy was first converted by Paul, and therefore he calls him his "own son in the faith."

The scope of these two epistles is to direct Timothy how to discharge his duty as an evangelist at Ephesus, where he now was.

MATTHEW HENRY

CHAPTER 1

Verses 1–4

I. The inscription of the epistle. His credentials were unquestionable. He had a commandment, not only from God our Saviour, but from Jesus Christ. Jesus Christ is a Christian's hope: all our hope of eternal life is built upon him. He calls Timothy his own son, because he had been an instrument of his conversion, and because he had been a son that served him. Timothy had not been wanting in the duty of a son to Paul, and Paul was not wanting in the care and tenderness of a father to him.

II. The benediction. In all the epistles to the churches the apostolical benediction is *grace and peace*; in these two epistles to Timothy and that to Titus it is *grace, mercy, and peace.* Ministers need more mercy than others. If Timothy needed the increase and continuance of it, how much more do we ministers.

III. Paul tells Timothy what was the end of his appointing him to this office. His business was to take care to fix both the ministers and the people of that church, that they do not add to the Christian doctrine, that they do not alter it, but cleave to it as it was delivered to them.

JAMIESON, FAUSSET, BROWN

CHAPTER 1

VSS. 1-20. ADDRESS: PAUL'S DESIGN IN HAVING LEFT TIMOTHY AT EPHESUS, VIZ., TO CHECK FALSE TEACHERS; TRUE USE OF THE LAW; HARMONIZING WITH THE GOSPEL; GOD'S GRACE IN CALLING PAUL, ONCE A BLASPHEMER, TO EXPERIENCE AND TO PREACH IT; CHARGES TO TIMOTHY. **1. by the commandment of God**—the authoritative *injunction,* as well as the commission, of God. In the earlier Epistles the phrase is, "by the *will* of God." Here it is expressed in a manner implying that a necessity was laid on him to act as an apostle, not that it was merely at his option. The same expression occurs in the doxology, probably written long after the Epistle itself [ALFORD] (Rom. 16:26). **God our Saviour**—The Father (ch. 2:3; 4:10; Luke 1:47; II Tim. 1:9; Titus 1:3; 2:10; 3:4; Jude 25). It was a Jewish expression in devotion, drawn from the Old Testament (cf. Ps. 106:21). **our hope**—(Col. 1:27; Titus 1:2; 2:13). **2. my own son**—lit., "a *genuine* son" (cf. Acts 16:1; I Cor. 4:14-17). See *Introduction.* **mercy**—added here, in addressing Timothy, to the ordinary salutation, "Grace unto you (Rom. 1:7; I Cor. 1:3,etc.), and peace." In Galatians 6: 16, "peace and *mercy*" occur. "Mercy" is grace of a more tender kind, exercised towards the *miserable,* the experience of which in one's own case especially fits for the Gospel MINISTRY. Cf. as to Paul himself (vss. 14, 16; I Cor. 7:25; II Cor. 4:1; Heb. 2:17) [BENGEL]. He did not use "mercy" as to the churches, because "mercy" in all its fulness already existed towards them; but in the case of an individual minister, fresh measures of it were continually needed. "Grace" has reference to the *sins* of men; "mercy" to their *misery.* God extends His *grace* to men as they are guilty; His *mercy* to them as they are miserable [TRENCH]. **Jesus Christ**—The oldest MSS. read the order, "Christ Jesus." In the Pastoral Epistles "Christ" is often put before "Jesus," to give prominence to the fact that the *Messianic* promises of the Old Testament, well known to Timothy (II Tim. 3: 15), were fulfilled in Jesus. **I besought thee to remain**—He meant to have added, "*so* I still beseech thee," but does not complete the sentence until he does so *virtually,* not formally, at vs. 18. **at Ephesus**—Paul, in Acts 20:25, declared to the Ephesian elders, "I *know* that ye all shall see my face no more." If, then, as the balance of arguments seems to favor, this Epistle was written

ADAM CLARKE

CHAPTER 1

1. *Paul an apostle . . . by the commandment of God.* We have already seen that the term *apostle* literally signifies a person sent from one to another, without implying any particular dignity in the person or importance in the message. But it is differently used in the New Testament, being applied to those who were sent expressly from God Almighty with the message of salvation to mankind. It is therefore the highest character any human being can have; and the message is the most important which even God himself can send to His intelligent creatures. It was by the express command of God that Paul went to the Gentiles preaching the doctrine of salvation by faith in Christ Jesus. *Jesus Christ . . . our hope.* Without Jesus, the world was hopeless; the expectation of being saved can come to mankind only by His gospel. He is called *our hope,* as He is called our Life, our Peace, our Righteousness, because from Him hope, life, peace, righteousness, and all other blessings proceed.

2. *My own son in the faith.* Brought to salvation through Christ by my ministry alone. Probably the apostle speaks here according to this Jewish maxim: "He who teaches the law to his nighbor's son is considered by the Scripture as if he had begotten him." *In the faith.* The word *faith* is taken here for the whole of the Christian religion, faith in Christ being its essential characteristic. *Grace, mercy, and peace. Grace,* the favor and approbation of God. *Mercy,* springing from that grace, pardoning, purifying, and supporting. *Peace,* the consequence of this manifested mercy, peace of conscience, and peace with God; producing internal happiness, quietness, and assurance.

3. *I besought thee.* The apostle had seen that a bad seed had been sown in the church; and, as he was obliged to go then into Macedonia, he wished Timothy, on whose prudence, piety, and soundness in the faith he could depend, to stay behind and prevent the spreading of a doctrine that would have been pernicious to the people's souls. I have already supposed that this Epistle was written after Paul had been delivered from his first im-

MATTHEW HENRY

In the times of the apostles there were attempts made to corrupt Christianity, otherwise this charge to Timothy might have been spared. He must not only see to it that he did not preach any other doctrine, but he must charge others that they preach it pure and uncorrupt.

F. B. MEYER:

A charge against vain talking. The relation of Paul to Timothy is an example of one of those beautiful friendships between an older and a younger man, in which each is the complement of the other (1 Cor. 4:17; Phil. 2:22). Timothy was a lad of fifteen when converted at Lystra, and was probably about thirty-five years of age when this epistle was addressed to him. He was enthusiastic and devoted, but at times showed signs of timidity, and the apostle watched over him with tender interest.

In this chapter the young minister is warned against the Gnostic heresy, i.e., the heresy of the "knowing-ones," who pretended to give revelations about angels and their ministry and to bridge the gulf between man and God by a whole series of mysterious imaginary beings. Their teaching led from spiritual pride to sensuality, for they accounted the body as inherently evil. All this was contrary to "sound" or "healthy" doctrine. That word is peculiar to the pastoral epistles (1 Tim. 6:3; 2 Tim. 1:13; 4:3; Titus 1:9; 2:1). It suggests a certain test of the various teachers who cross our paths. The question always is, Do these words of theirs promote the health of the soul, and above all "love out of a pure heart and a good conscience"?—*Bible Commentary*

They will be the corrupting and ruining of religion among you, for *they minister questions rather than edifying.* That which gives occasion for doubtful disputes pulls down the church rather than builds it up. Godly edifying is the end ministers should aim at in all their discourses. Godly edifying must be in faith. It is by faith that we come to God at first, and it must be in the same way, and by the same principle of faith, that we must be edified. Ministers should avoid what will occasion disputes. Even disputes about great and necessary truths eat out the vitals of religion, which consist in practice and obedience as well as in faith.

Verses 5–11

Here the apostle shows the use of the law, and the glory of the gospel.

I. The end and uses of the law: it is intended to promote love.

1. The main scope and drift of the divine law are to engage us to the love of God and one another. Surely the gospel, which obliges us to love our enemies, to do good to those who hate us (Matt. v. 44), does not design to supersede a commandment the end whereof is love? Those therefore who boasted of their knowledge of the law, but used it only as a colour for the disturbance that they gave to the preaching of the gospel, defeated that which was the very end of the commandment, and that is love, love *out of a pure heart.*

JAMIESON, FAUSSET, BROWN

subsequently to Paul's first imprisonment, the apparent discrepancy between his prophecy and the event may be reconciled by considering that the terms of the former were not that *he* should never visit *Ephesus* again (which this verse implies he did), but that *they all* should "see his face no more." I cannot think with BIRKS, that this verse is compatible with his theory, that Paul did not actually visit Ephesus, though in its immediate neighborhood (cf. ch. 3:14; 4:13). The corresponding conjunction to "as" is not given, the sentence not being completed till it is virtually so at vs. 18. **I besought**—a mild word, instead of authoritative command, to Timothy, as a fellow helper. **some**—The indefinite pronoun is *slightly* contemptuous as to them (Gal. 2:12; Jude 4), [ELLICOTT]. **teach no other doctrine**—than what I have taught (Gal. 1:6-9). His prophetic bodings some years before (Acts 20:29, 30) were now being realized (cf. ch. 6:3). **4. fables**—legends about the origin and propagation of angels, such as the false teachers taught at Colosse (Col. 2:18-23). "Jewish fables" (Titus 1:14). "Profane, and old wives' fables" (ch. 4:7; II Tim. 4:4). **genealogies**—not merely such civil genealogies as were common among the Jews, whereby they traced their descent from the patriarchs, to which Paul would not object, and which he would not as here class with "fables," but Gnostic genealogies of spirits and aeons, as they called them, "Lists of Gnostic emanations" [ALFORD]. So TERTULLIAN, *Adversus Valentinianos*, c. 3, and IRENÆUS, *Præf.* The Judaizers here alluded to, while maintaining the perpetual obligation of the Mosaic law, joined with it a theosophic ascetic tendency, pretending to see in it mysteries deeper than others could see. The *seeds, not the fullgrown* Gnosticism of the post-apostolic age, then existed. This formed the transition stage between Judaism and Gnosticism. "Endless" refers to the tedious unprofitableness of their lengthy genealogies (cf. Titus 3:9). Paul opposes to their "aeons," the "King of *the aeons* (so the *Greek*, vs. 17), whom be glory throughout the aeons of aeons." The *word* "aeons" was probably not used in the technical sense of the latter Gnostics as yet; but "the only wise God" (vs. 17), by anticipation, confutes the subsequently adopted notions in the Gnostics' own phraseology.

questions—of mere speculation (Acts 25:20), not practical; generating merely curious discussions. "Questions and strifes of words" (ch. 6:4): "to no profit" (II Tim. 2:14); "gendering strifes" (II Tim. 2:23). "Vain jangling" (vss. 6, 7) of would-be "teachers of the law."

godly edifying—The oldest MSS. read, "*the dispensation* of God," the Gospel dispensation of God towards man (I Cor. 9:17), "which is (has its element) in faith." CONYBEARE translates, "The exercising of *the stewardship* of God" (I Cor. 9:17). He infers that the false teachers in Ephesus were presbyters, which accords with the prophecy, Acts 20:30. However, the oldest Latin versions, and IRENÆUS and HILARY, support *English Version* reading. Cf. vs. 5, "faith unfeigned."

5. But—in contrast to the doctrine of the false teachers. **the end**—the aim. **the commandment**—*Greek*, "of the charge" which you ought to urge on your flock. Referring to the same *Greek* word as in vss. 3, 18; here, however, in a larger sense, as including *the Gospel "dispensation* of God" (*Notes*, vs. 4 and vs. 11). which was the sum and substance of the "charge" committed to Timothy wherewith he should "charge" his flock. **charity**—LOVE; the sum and end of the law and of the Gospel alike, and that wherein the Gospel is the fulfilment of the spirit of the law in its every essential jot and tittle (Rom. 13:10). The foundation is *faith* (vs. 4), the "end" is *love* (vs. 14; Titus 3:15). **out of**—springing as from a fountain. **pure heart**—a heart purified by faith (Acts 15:9; II Tim. 2:22; Titus 1:15). **good**

ADAM CLARKE

prisonment at Rome. When therefore the apostle came from Rome into Asia, he no doubt visited Ephesus, where ten years before he had planted a Christian church; and as he had not time to tarry then, he left Timothy to correct abuses. *That thou mightest charge some.* He does not name any person. The Judaizing teachers are generally supposed to be those intended; and the term *some,* "certain persons," which he uses, is expressive of high disapprobation, and at the same time of delicacy. They were not apostles nor apostolic men; but they were undoubtedly members of the church at Ephesus, and might yet be reclaimed.

4. *Neither give heed to fables.* Idle fancies; things of no moment; doctrines and opinions unauthenticated; silly legends, of which no people ever possessed a greater stock than the Jews. *Endless genealogies.* I suppose the apostle to mean those genealogies which were "uncertain"—that never could be made out, in either the ascending or the descending line; and, principally, such as referred to the great promise of the Messiah, and to the priesthood. The Jews had scrupulously preserved their genealogical tables till the advent of Christ; and the Evangelists had recourse to them and appealed to them in reference to our Lord's descent from the house of David; Matthew taking this genealogy in the descending, Luke in the ascending, line. All was then certain; but we are told that Herod destroyed the public registers. He, being an Idumean, was jealous of the noble origin of the Jews; and that none might be able to reproach him with his descent, he ordered the genealogical tables, which were kept among the archives in the Temple, to be burnt. From this time the Jews could refer to their genealogies only from memory, or from those imperfect tables which had been preserved in private hands; and to make out any regular line from these must have been endless and uncertain. It is probably to this that the apostle refers; I mean the endless and useless labor which the attempts to make out these genealogies must produce, the authentic tables being destroyed. Some learned men suppose that the apostle alludes here to the Aeons among the Gnostics and Valentinians, of whom there were endless numbers to make up what was called their *pleroma.* But it is certain that these heresies had not arrived to any formidable head in the apostle's time; and it has long been a doubt with me whether they even existed at that time. I think it the most simple way, and most likely to be the intention of the apostle, to refer all to the Jewish genealogies, which he calls "Jewish fables," Titus i. 14. *Which minister questions.* They are the foundation of endless altercations and disputes; for, being uncertain and not consecutive, every person had a right to call them in question; as we may naturally suppose, from the state in which the genealogical tables of the Jews then were, that many chasms must be supplied in different lines and consequently much must be done by conjecture. *Rather than godly edifying.* Such discussions as these had no tendency to promote piety. Many, no doubt, employed much of that time in inquiring who were their ancestors, which they should have spent in obtaining that grace by which, being born from above, they might have become the sons and daughters of God Almighty. Instead of *godly edifying,* "the economy or dispensation of God" is the reading of almost every MS. in which this part of the Epistle is extant, and of almost all the versions, and the chief of the Greek fathers. Of the genuineness of this reading scarcely a doubt can be formed.

5. *Now the end of the commandment is charity.* These genealogical questions lead to strife and debate; and the dispensation of God leads to "love" to both God and man, through faith in Christ. These genealogical questions leave the heart under the influence of all its vile tempers and evil propensities; *faith* in Jesus purifies the heart. The *end,* aim, and design of God in giving this dispensation to the world is that men may have an *unfeigned faith,* such as lays hold on Christ crucified, and produces a *good conscience* from a sense of the pardon received, and leads on to purity of heart; love to God and man being the grand issue of the grace of Christ here below, and this fully preparing the soul for eternal glory. He

MATTHEW HENRY

Our hearts must be cleansed from all sinful love; our love must arise *out of a good conscience*; a real belief of the truth of the word of God, here called a *faith unfeigned*. It is love without dissimulation: the faith that works by it must be of the like nature, genuine and sincere.

When persons swerve from the great law of charity they will turn aside to vain jangling; when a man misses his end it is no wonder that every step he takes is out of the way.

Jangling, especially in religion, is vain, and yet many people's religion consists of little else but vain jangling.

2. The use of the law (*v.* 8). The Jews used it unlawfully. They set it up for justification, and so used it unlawfully. Call it back to its right use and take away the abuses, for the law is still very useful as a rule of life. It is good to teach us what is sin and what is duty. It is the grace of God that changes men's hearts; but the terrors of the law may be of use to tie their hands and restrain their tongues. The law is not made primarily for the righteous, but for sinners of all sorts, whether in a greater or less measure, *v.* 9, 10.

ALBERT BARNES:

"The law is not made for a righteous man." There has been great variety in the interpretation of this passage. Some suppose that the law here refers to the ceremonial laws of Moses; others, to the denunciatory part of the law; and others, that it means that the chief purpose of the law was to restrain the wicked. It seems clear, however, that the apostle does not refer merely to the ceremonial law, for he specifies that which condemns the unholy and profane. It was not the ceremonial law which condemned these things, but the moral law. It cannot be supposed, moreover, that the apostle meant to say that the law was not binding on a righteous man, or that he was under no obligation to obey it—for he everywhere teaches that the moral law is obligatory on all nankind. To suppose also that a righteous man is released from the obligation to obey the law, that is, to do right, is absurdity. Nor does he seem to mean that the law was not given for the purpose of justifying a righteous man—for this was originally one of its designs. Had man always obeyed it, he would have been justified by it.

The meaning seems to be that the purpose of the law was not to fetter and perplex those who were righteous and who aimed to please God. It was not intended to produce a spirit of servitude and bondage. As the Jews interpreted it, it did this, and this interpretation appears to have been adopted by the teachers at Ephesus, to whom Paul refers. The whole tendency of their teaching was to bring the soul into a state of bondage and to make religion a condition of servitude. Paul teaches that religion was a condition of freedom and that the main purpose of the law was not to fetter the minds of the righteous by numberless observances and minute regulations, but that it was to restrain the wicked from sin. This is the case with all law. No good man feels himself fettered and manacled by wholesome laws, nor does he feel that the purpose of law is to reduce him to a state of servitude. It is only the wicked who have this feeling—and in this sense the law is made for a man who intends to do wrong.

—Popular Commentary

JAMIESON, FAUSSET, BROWN

conscience—a conscience cleared from guilt by the effect of sound faith in Christ (vs. 19; ch. 3:9; II Tim. 1:3; I Pet. 3:21). Contrast I Timothy 4:2; Titus 1:15; cf. Acts 23:1. John uses "heart," where Paul would use "conscience." In Paul the understanding is the seat of *conscience;* the *heart* is the seat of *love* [BENGEL]. A good conscience is joined with sound faith; a bad conscience with unsoundness in the faith (cf. Heb. 9:14). **faith unfeigned**—not a hypocritical, dead, and unfruitful faith, but faith working by love (Gal. 5:6). The false teachers drew men off from such a loving, working, real faith, to profitless, speculative "questions" (vs. 4) and jangling (vs. 6). **6. From which**—viz., from a pure heart, good conscience, and faith unfeigned, the well-spring of love. **having swerved**—lit., "having missed the mark (the 'end') to be aimed at." It is translated, "erred," ch. 6:21; II Tim. 2:18. Instead of aiming at and attaining the graces above named, they "have turned aside (ch. 5:15; II Tim. 4:4; Heb. 12:13) unto vain jangling"; lit., "vain talk," about the law and genealogies of angels (vs. 7; Titus 3:9; 1:10); I Timothy 6:20, "vain babblings and oppositions." It is the greatest vanity when divine things are not truthfully discussed (Rom. 1: 21) [BENGEL]. **7.** Sample of their "vain talk" (vs. 6). **Desiring**—They are *would-be* teachers, not really so. **the law**—the Jewish law (Titus 1:14; 3:9). The Judaizers here meant seem to be distinct from those impugned in the Epistles to the Galatians and Romans, who made the works of the law necessary to justification in opposition to Gospel grace. The Judaizers here meant corrupted the law with "fables," which they pretended to found on it, subversive of morals as well as of truth. Their error was not in maintaining the *obligation* of the law, but in *abusing* it by fabulous and immoral interpretations of, and additions to, it. **neither what they say, nor whereof**—neither understanding *their own assertions,* nor the *object* itself about which they make them. They understand as little about the one as the other [ALFORD]. **8. But**—"*Now* we know" (Rom. 3:19; 7:14). **law is good**—in full agreement with God's holiness and goodness. **if a man**—primarily, *a teacher;* then, every Christian. **use it lawfully**—in its lawful place in the Gospel economy, viz., not as a means of a "righteous man" attaining higher perfection than could be attained by the Gospel alone (ch. 4:8; Titus 1:14), which was the perverted use to which the false teachers put it, but as a means of awakening the sense of sin in the ungodly (vss. 9, 10; cf. Rom. 7:7-12; Gal. 3:21). **9. law is not made for a righteous man**—not for one standing by faith in the righteousness of Christ put on him for justification,and imparted inwardly by the Spirit for sanctification. "One not forensically amenable to the law" [ALFORD]. For *sanctification,* the law gives no inward power to fulfil it; but ALFORD goes too far in speaking of the righteous man as "not morally needing the law." Doubtless, in proportion as he is inwardly led by the Spirit, the justified man needs not the law, which is only an outward rule (Rom. 6:14; Gal. 5:18, 23). But as the justified man often does not give himself up wholly to the inward leading of the Spirit, he *morally* needs the outward *law* to show him his sin and God's requirements. The reason why the ten commandments have no power to condemn the Christian, is not that they have no *authority* over him, but because Christ has fulfilled them as our surety (Rom. 10:4). **disobedient**—*Greek,* "not subject"; insubordinate; it is translated "unruly," Titus 1:6, 10; "lawless and disobedient" refer to opposers of the *law,* for whom it is "enacted" (so the *Greek, for* "is made"). **ungodly and . . . sinners**—*Greek,* he who does *not reverence* God, and he who *openly sins* against Him; the opposers of *God,* from the law comes. **unholy and profane**—those inwardly *impure,* and those deserving exclusion from the outward participation in services of the sanctuary; sinners against the third and fourth commandments. **murderers**—or, as the *Greek* may mean, '*smiters*' of fathers and . . . mothers; sinners against the fifth commandment. **manslayers**—sinners against the sixth commandment. **10. whoremongers . . .**—sinners against the seventh commandment. **men-stealers**—i.e., slave dealers. The most heinous offense against the eighth commandment. No stealing of a man's goods can equal in atrocity the stealing of a man's liberty. Slavery is not directly assailed in the New Testament; to have done so would have been to revolutionize violently the existing order of things. But Christianity teaches principles sure to undermine, and at last overthrow it, wherever Christianity has had its natural development (Matt. 7: 12). **liars . . . perjured**—offenders against the ninth commandment. **if there be any other thing . . .**—

ADAM CLARKE

whose soul is filled with love to God and man has a *pure heart,* a *good conscience,* and *faith unfeigned.* "A faith not hypocritical." The apostle appears to allude to the Judaizing teachers, who pretended faith in the gospel merely that they might have the greater opportunity to bring back to the Mosaic system those who had embraced the doctrine of Christ crucified. This is evident from the following verse.

6. *From which some having swerved. From which some,* though they have pretended to aim at the "scope," or "mark," have missed that mark. This is the import of the original word. *Turned aside unto vain jangling.* The original term signifies "empty or vain talking"; discourses that turn to no profit; a great many words and little sense.

7. *Teachers of the law.* To be esteemed or celebrated as rabbins; to be reputed cunning in solving knotty questions and enigmas, which answered no end to true religion. *Understanding neither what they say.* This is evident from almost all the Jewish comments which yet remain. Things are asserted which are either false or dubious; words, the import of which they did not understand, were brought to illustrate them.

8. *But we know that the law is good.* The law as given by God is both *good* in itself and has a good tendency. This is similar to what the apostle had asserted, Rom. vii. 12-16: "The law is holy, and the commandment holy, and just, and good." *If a man use it lawfully.* That is, interpret it according to its own spirit and design, and use it for the purpose for which God has given it.

9. *The law is not made for a righteous man.* There is a moral law as well as a ceremonial law. As the object of the latter is to lead us to Christ, the object of the former is to restrain crimes, and inflict punishment on those that commit them. It was, therefore, not made for the *righteous* as a restrainer of crimes and an inflicter of punishments; for the righteous avoid sin, and by living to the glory of God expose not themselves to its censures. This seems to be the mind of the apostle; he does not say that the law was not *made for a righteous man,* but it does not "lie against a righteous man," because he does not transgress it: but it "lies against" the wicked. The word "lies" refers to the custom of writing laws on boards and hanging them up in public places within reach of every man, that they might be read by all; thus all would see against whom the law lay. *The lawless.* Those who will not be bound by a law, and acknowledge none, therefore have no rule of moral conduct. *Disobedient.* Those who acknowledge no authority; from *a,* negative, and *hypotasso,* "to subject." *For the ungodly.* The "irreligious"—those who do not worship God or have no true worship; from *a,* negative, and *sebo,* "to worship." *For unholy.* Persons "totally polluted"—unclean within and unclean without; from *a,* negative, and *hosios,* "holy." *And profane.* Such who are so unholy and abominable as not to be fit to attend any public worship. *Murderers of fathers.* The murderer of a father or a mother, notwithstanding the deep fall of man and the general profligacy of the world, has been so rare and is a crime so totally opposite to nature that few civilized nations have found it necessary to make laws against it. Yet such monsters, like the most awful and infrequent *portents,* have sometimes terrified the world with their appearance. But I think the original may mean simply "beating or striking a father or mother." *Manslayers.* "Murderers" simply, all who take away the life of a human being contrary to law.

10. *For whoremongers.* Adulterers, fornicators, and prostitutes of all sorts. *Menstealers.* "Slave dealers"; whether those who carry on the traffic in human flesh and blood or those who steal a person in order to sell him into bondage; or those who buy such stolen men or women, no matter of what color or what country. *For liars.* They who speak for truth what they know to be false; and even they who tell the truth in such a way as to lead others to draw a contrary meaning from it. *For perjured persons.* Such as do or leave undone anything contrary to an oath or moral engagement, whether that engagement be made by what is

MATTHEW HENRY

II. He shows the glory and grace of the gospel. The glorious gospel, for so it is: much of the glory of God appears in the works of creation and providence, but much more in the gospel, where it shines in the face of Jesus Christ. Paul reckoned it a great honour put upon him, and a great favour done him, that this glorious gospel was committed to his trust.

Verses 12-17

I. Thanks to Jesus Christ for putting him into the ministry. It is Christ's work to put men into the ministry. Ministers cannot make ministers, much less can persons make themselves ministers; for it is Christ's work. Those whom he puts into the ministry he fits for it; whom he calls he qualifies. Christ gives not only ability, but fidelity, to those whom he puts into the ministry. Christ's ministers are trusty servants. A call to the ministry is a great favour.

II. He gives an account of his conversion.

1. What he was before his conversion. Frequently those who are designed for great and eminent services are left to themselves before their conversion. The greatness of sin is no bar to our acceptance with God, nor to our being employed for him, if it be truly repented of. True penitents will not be backward to own their former condition. This good apostle often confessed what his former life had been.

2. The great favour of God to him.

(1) Because he did it ignorantly and in unbelief, he obtained mercy. What we do ignorantly is a less crime than what we do knowingly; yet a sin of ignorance is a sin. Ignorance in some cases will extenuate a crime, though it does not take it away. Unbelief is at the bottom of what sinners do ignorantly. For these reasons Paul obtained mercy.

JAMIESON, FAUSSET, BROWN

answering to the tenth commandment in its widest aspect. He does not particularly specify it because his object is to bring out the *grosser* forms of transgression; whereas the tenth is deeply spiritual, so much so indeed, that it was by it that the sense of sin, in its subtlest form of "lust," Paul tells us (Rom. 7:7), was brought home to his own conscience. Thus, Paul argues, these *would-be teachers of the law,* while boasting of a higher perfection through it, really bring themselves down from the Gospel elevation to the level of the grossly "lawless," for whom, not for Gospel believers, the law was designed. **sound**—*healthy,* spiritually *wholesome* (ch. 6:3; II Tim. 1:13; Titus 1:13; 2:2), as opposed to *sickly, morbid* (as the *Greek* of "doting" means, ch. 6:4), and "canker" (II Tim. 2:17). "The doctrine," or "teaching, which is according to godliness" (ch. 6:3). **11. According to the glorious gospel**—The *Christian's freedom from the law as a sanctifier, as well as a justifier,* implied in the previous, vss. 9, 10, is what this vs. 11 is connected with. This exemption of the righteous from the law, and assignment of it to the lawless as its true object, is "according to the Gospel *of the glory* (so the *Greek,* cf. *Note,* II Cor. 4:4) of the blessed God." The Gospel manifests God's glory (Eph. 1:17; 3:16) in accounting "righteous" the believer, through the righteousness of Christ, without "the law" (vs. 9); and in imparting that righteousness whereby he loathes all those sins against which (vss. 9, 10) the law is directed. The term, "blessed," indicates at once *immortality* and *supreme happiness.* The supremely blessed One is He from whom all blessedness flows. This term, as applied to GOD, occurs only here and in ch. 6:15: appropriate in speaking here of the Gospel blessedness, in contrast to the *curse* on those under the law (vs. 9; Gal. 3:10). **committed to my trust**—Translate as in the *Greek* order, which brings into prominent emphasis *Paul,* "committed in trust to me"; in contrast to the kind of law-teaching which *they* (who had no Gospel commission), the false teachers, *assumed to themselves* (vs. 8; Titus 1:3). **12.** The honor done him in having the Gospel ministry committed to him suggests the digression to what he once was, no better (vs. 13) than those lawless ones described above (vss. 9, 10), when the grace of our Lord (vs. 14) visited him. **and**—omitted in most (not all) of the oldest MSS. **I thank**—*Greek,* "I have (i.e., feel) gratitude." **enabled me**—the same *Greek* verb as in Acts 9:22, "Saul increased the more in strength." An undesigned coincidence between Paul and Luke, his companion. *Enabled* me, viz., for the ministry. "It is not in my own strength that I bring this doctrine to men, but as strengthened and nerved by Him who saved me" [THEODORET]. Man is by nature "without strength" (Rom. 5:6). True conversion and calling confer power [BENGEL]. **for that**—the main ground of his "thanking Christ." **he counted me faithful**—He foreordered and foresaw that I would be faithful to the trust committed to me. Paul's *thanking* God for this shows that the merit of his faithfulness was due solely to God's grace, not to his own natural strength (I Cor. 7:25). *Faithfulness* is the quality required in a steward (I Cor. 4:2). **putting me into**—rather as in I Thessalonians 5:9, "appointing me (in His sovereign purposes of grace) unto the ministry" (Acts 20:24). **13. Who was before**—*Greek,* "Formerly being a blasphemer." *"Notwithstanding that I was* before a blasphemer . . ." (Acts 26:9, 11). **persecutor**—Gal. 1:13). **injurious**—*Greek,* "insulter"; one who acts injuriously from arrogant contempt of others. Translate, Romans 1:30, "despiteful." One who added insult to injury. BENGEL translates, "a despiser." **I obtained mercy**—God's mercy, and Paul's want of it, stand in sharp contrast [ELLICOTT]; *Greek,* "I was made the object of mercy." The sense of mercy was perpetual in the mind of the apostle (cf. *Note,* vs. 2). Those who have felt mercy can best have mercy on those out of the way (Heb. 5:2, 3). **because I did it ignorantly**—*Ignorance* does not in itself deserve pardon; but it is a less culpable cause of unbelief than pride and wilful hardening of one's self against the truth (John 9:41; Acts 26:9). Hence it is Christ's plea of intercession for His murderers (Luke 23:34); and it is made by the apostles a mitigating circumstance in the Jews' sin, and one giving a hope of a door of repentance (Acts 3:17; Rom. 10:2).

14. And—*Greek,* "But." Not only so (was *mercy* shown me), but. . . **the grace**—by which "I obtained mercy" (vs. 13). **was exceeding abundant**—*Greek,* "superabounded." Where sin abounded, grace did much more abound" (Rom. 5:20). **with faith**—*accompanied with* faith, the opposite of "unbelief" (vs. 13). **love**—in contrast to "a blasphemer,

ADAM CLARKE

called swearing or by an affirmation or promise of any kind. *And if there be any other thing.* Every species of vice and immorality, all must be necessarily included that is contrary to *sound doctrine*—to the immutable moral law of God, as well as to the pure precepts of Christianity where that law is incorporated, explained, and rendered, if possible, more and more binding.

11. *According to the glorious gospel.* The "sound doctrine" mentioned above, which is here called "the gospel of the glory of the blessed or happy God"—a dispensation which exhibits the glory of all His attributes; and by saving man in such a way as is consistent with the glory of all the divine perfections, while it brings peace and goodwill among men, brings glory to God in the highest.

12. *I thank Christ.* I feel myself under infinite obligation to Christ, who hath "strengthened me," and put *me into the ministry,* the "deaconship," the "service" of mankind, by preaching the gospel, for that he *counted me*—He knew that I would be—*faithful* to the charge that was delivered to me.

13. *A blasphemer.* Speaking impiously and unjustly of Jesus, His doctrine, His ways, and His followers. *And a persecutor.* Endeavoring to the uttermost of his power to exterminate all who called on the name of the Lord Jesus. *And injurious.* As full of insolence as I was of malevolence; and yet all the while thinking I did God service, while sacrificing men and women to my own prejudices and intolerance.

14. *The grace of our Lord was exceeding abundant.* The original is very emphatic, "that grace of our Lord hath superabounded"—it manifested itself in a way of extraordinary mercy. *With faith and love.* Not only pardoning such offenses, but leading me to the full experimental knowledge of Christianity, of that

MATTHEW HENRY

(2) The abundant grace of Jesus Christ, *v.* 14, that grace of Christ which appears in his glorious gospel (*v.* 15). Here we have the sum of the whole gospel, *that Jesus Christ came into the world.* It is good news, worthy of all acceptation; and yet not too good to be true, for it is a faithful saying. Paul was a sinner of the first rank; so he acknowledges himself to have been. Persecutors are some of the worst of sinners: such a one Paul had been. He that elsewhere calls himself the *least of all saints* (Eph. iii. 8) here calls himself the chief of sinners. The chief of sinners may become the chief of saints. This is a faithful saying which may be depended on.

(3) The mercy which Paul found with God.

[1] For the encouragement of others to repent and believe (*v.* 16). It was an instance of the long-suffering of Christ that he would bear so much with one who had been so very provoking; and it was designed for a pattern to all others, that the greatest sinners might not despair of mercy with God.

[2] He mentions it to the glory of God. He could not go on with his letter without inserting a thankful acknowledgement of God's goodness to him. Those who are sensible of their obligations to the mercy and grace of God will have their hearts enlarged in his praise. When we have found God good we must not forget to pronounce him great; and his kind thoughts of us must not at all abate our high thoughts of him, but rather increase them. God's gracious dealings with us should fill us with admiration of his glorious attributes. "*To him be glory for ever and ever.*"

JAMIESON, FAUSSET, BROWN

persecutor, and injurious." **which is in Christ**—as its element and home [ALFORD]: here as its source whence it flows to us. **15. faithful**—worthy of credit, because "God" who says it "is faithful" to His word (I Cor. 1:9; I Thess. 5:24; II Thess. 3:3; Rev. 21:5; 22:6). This seems to have become an axiomatic *saying* among Christians the phrase, "faithful saying," is peculiar to the Pastoral Epistles (ch. 2:11; 4:9; Titus 3:8). Translate as *Greek,* "Faithful is the saying." **all**—all possible; full; to be received by all, and with all the faculties of the soul, mind, and heart. Paul, unlike the false teachers (vs. 7), *understands what he is saying, and whereof he affirms;* and by his simplicity of style and subject, setting forth the grand fundamental truth of salvation through Christ, confutes the false teachers' abstruse and unpractical speculations (I Cor. 1:18-28; Titus 2:1). **acceptation**—*reception* (as of a boon) into the heart, as well as the understanding, with all gladness; this is faith acting on the Gospel offer, and welcoming and appropriating it (Acts 2:41). **Christ**—as promised. **Jesus**—as manifested [BENGEL]. **came into the world**—which was full of sin (John 1:29; Rom. 5:12; I John 2:2). This implies His pre-existence. John 1:9, *Greek,* "the true Light that, *coming into the world,* lighteth every man." **to save sinners**—even notable sinners like Saul of Tarsus. His instance was without a rival since the ascension, in point of the greatness of the sin and the greatness of the mercy: that the consenter to Stephen, the proto-martyr's death, should be the successor of the same! **I am**—not merely, "I *was* chief" (I Cor. 15:9; Eph. 3:8; cf. Luke 18:13). To each believer his own sins must always appear, as long as he lives, greater than those of others, which he never can know as he can know his own. **chief**—the same *Greek* as in vs. 16, "first," which alludes to this 15th verse, Translate in both verses, "foremost." Well might he infer where there was mercy for *him,* there is mercy for all who will come to Christ (Matt. 18:11; Luke 19:10). **16. Howbeit**—*Greek,* "But"; contrasting his own conscious sinfulness with God's gracious visitation of him in mercy. **for this cause**—for this very purpose. **that in me**—in my case. **first**—"foremost." As I was "foremost" (*Greek* for *chief,* vs. 15) in sin, so God has made me the "foremost" sample of *mercy.* **show**—to His own glory (the middle *Greek,* voice), Ephesians 2:7. **all long-suffering**—*Greek,* "the whole (of His) long-suffering," viz., in bearing so long with me while I was a persecutor. **a pattern**—a sample (I Cor. 10:6, 11) to assure the greatest sinners of the certainty that they shall not be rejected in coming to Christ, since even Saul found mercy. So David made his own case of pardon, notwithstanding the greatness of his sin, a sample to encourage other sinners to seek pardon (Ps. 32:5, 6). The *Greek* for "pattern" is sometimes used for a "sketch" or outline—the filling up to take place in each man's own case. **believe on him**—Belief rests ON Him as the only foundation on which faith relies. **to life everlasting**—the ultimate aim which faith always keeps in view (Titus 1:2). **17.** A suitable conclusion to the beautifully simple enunciation of the Gospel, of which his own history is a living sample or pattern. It is from the experimental sense of grace that the doxology flows [BENGEL]. **the King, eternal**—lit., "King of the (eternal) ages." The LXX translates Exodus 15:18, "The Lord shall reign *for ages and beyond them.*" Psalm 145:13, *Margin,* "Thy kingdom is an everlasting kingdom," lit., "a kingdom of all ages." The "life everlasting" (vs. 16) suggested here "the King *eternal,*" or *everlasting.* It answers also to "for ever and ever" at the close, lit., "to the ages of the ages" (the countless succession of ages made up of ages). **immortal**—The oldest MSS. read, "incorruptible." *Vulgate,* however, and one very old MS. read as *English Version* (Rom. 1:23). **invisible**—(ch. 6:16; Exod. 33:20; John 1:18; Col. 1:15; Heb. 11:27). **the only wise God**—The oldest MSS. omit "wise," which probably crept in from Romans 16:27, where it is more appropriate to the context than here (cf. Jude 25). "The only Potentate" (ch. 6:15; Ps. 86:10; John 5:44). **for ever...**—See *Note,* above. The thought of eternity (terrible as it is to unbelievers) is delightful to those assured of grace (vs. 16) [BENGEL]. **18.** He resumes the subject begun at vs. 3. The conclusion (apodosis) to the foregoing, "*as I besought thee . . . charge*" (vs. 3), is here given, if not formally, at least substantially. **This charge**—viz., "that thou in them (so the *Greek*) mightest war," i.e., fulfil thy high calling, not only as a Christian, but as a *minister* officially, one function of which is, to "*charge* some that they teach no other doctrine" (vs. 3). **I commit**—as a sacred deposit (ch. 6:20; II Tim. 2:2) to be laid before thy hearers.

ADAM CLARKE

faith and *love* which are essential to it, and giving me authority to proclaim it to mankind.

15-16. *Christ Jesus came into the world to save sinners.* This is one of the most glorious truths in the Book of God, the most important that ever reached the human ear or can be entertained by the heart of man. This *saying* or "doctrine" he calls, first, a *faithful* or "true" saying. It is a doctrine that may be "credited" without the slightest doubt or hesitation. God himself has spoken it; and the death of Christ and the mission of the Holy Ghost, sealing pardon on the souls of all who believe, have confirmed and established the truth. Secondly, it is *worthy of all acceptation;* as all need it, it is worthy of being received by all.

Of whom I am chief. Confounding Paul the apostle, in the fullness of his faith and love, with Saul of Tarsus, in his ignorance, unbelief, and persecuting rage, we are in the habit of saying: "This is a hyperbolical expression, arguing the height of the apostle's modesty and humility; and must not be taken according to the letter." I take it not in this light; I take it not with abatement; it is strictly and literally true. Take into consideration the whole of the apostle's conduct previously to his conversion, and was there a greater sinner converted to God from the Incarnation to his own time? Not one; he **was the *chief;* and keeping his blasphemy, persecution, and contumely in view, he asserts:** Of all that the Lord Jesus came into the world to save, and of all that He had saved to that time, *I am chief.* He could with propriety say, "I am the first"; the "first" who, from a blasphemer, persecutor (and might we not add "murderer"? see the part he took in the martyrdom of Stephen), became a preacher of that gospel which I had persecuted. And hence, keeping this idea strictly in view, he immediately adds (v. 16): *Howbeit for this cause I obtained mercy, that in me first Jesus Christ might shew forth all longsuffering, for a pattern to them which should hereafter believe on him to life everlasting.*

17. *Now unto the King eternal.* This burst of thanksgiving and gratitude to God naturally arose from the subject then under his pen and eye. God has most wondrously manifested His mercy, in this beginning of the gospel, by saving me, and making me a pattern to all them that shall hereafter believe on Christ. He is "the king of eternities": the eternity that was before time was, and the eternity that shall be when time is no more. *Immortal.* "Incorruptible"—not liable to decay or corruption; a simple, uncompounded essence, incapable therefore of decomposition, and consequently permanent and eternal. *Invisible.* One who fills all things, works everywhere, and yet is *invisible* to angels and men; the perfect reverse of false gods and idols, who are confined to one spot, work nowhere, and, being stocks and stones, are seen by everybody. *The only wise God.* The word *wise* is omitted by some MSS. Some of the Greek fathers quote it sometimes and omit it at others; which shows that it was an unsettled reading, probably borrowed from Rom. xvi. 27. Without it the reading is very strong and appropriate: "To the only God," nothing visible or invisible being worthy of adoration but himself. *Be honour,* all the respect and reverence that can be paid by intelligent beings, ascribing to Him at the same time all the *glory*—excellences, and perfections, which can be possessed by an intelligent, unoriginated, independent, and eternal Being; and this *for ever and ever*—through eternity.

18. *This charge.* It was a *charge* that the Judaizing teachers should not teach differently from that doctrine which the apostle had delivered to him.

MATTHEW HENRY

Verses 18–20

The charge he gives to Timothy to proceed in his work with resolution, *v.* 18. It seems, there had been prophecies before concerning Timothy. This encouraged Paul to commit this charge to him.

The ministry is a good warfare against sin and Satan. Ministers must war this good warfare diligently and courageously. The prophecies which went before concerning Timothy are a motive to stir him up to a vigorous discharge of his duty; so the good hopes that others have entertained concerning us should excite us to our duty. *Holding faith and a good conscience, v.* 19.

Those that put away a good conscience will soon make shipwreck of faith; we must look to the one as well as the other.

As for those who had made shipwreck of the faith, he specifies two, *Hymenæus and Alexander*, who had made a profession of the Christian religion.

Paul had delivered them to Satan, had declared them to belong to the kingdom of Satan *that they might learn not to blaspheme*. God can, if he please, work by contraries: *Hymenæus and Alexander* are delivered to Satan, that they may learn not to blaspheme, when one would rather think they would learn of Satan to blaspheme the more. Let us hold faith and a good conscience, for if we once let go our hold of these we do not know where we shall stop.

JAMIESON, FAUSSET, BROWN

according to—in pursuance of; in consonance with. **the prophecies which went before on thee**—the intimations given by prophets respecting thee at thy ordination, ch. 4:14 (as, probably, by Silas, a companion of Paul, and "a prophet," Acts 15:32). Such prophetical intimation, as well as the good report given of Timothy by the brethren (Acts 16:2), may have induced Paul to take him as his companion. Cf. similar prophecies as to others: Acts 13:1-3, in connection with laying on of hands; 11:28; 21:10, 11; cf. I Corinthians 12:10; 14:1; Ephesians 4:11. In Acts 20:28, it is expressly said that *"the Holy Ghost* had made them [the Ephesian presbyters] overseers." CLEMENT OF ROME, *Epistola ad Corinthios*, states it was the custom of the apostles "to make trial by the Spirit," i.e., by the "power of discerning," in order to determine who were to be overseers and deacons in the several churches planted. So CLEMENT OF ALEXANDRIA says as to the churches near Ephesus, that the overseers were marked out for ordination by a revelation of the Holy Ghost to St. John. **by them**—*Greek*, "in them"; arrayed as it were in them; armed with them. **warfare**—not the mere "fight" (ch. 6:12; II Tim. 4:7), but the *whole campaign;* the military service. Translate as *Greek*, not *"a,"* but *"the* good warfare." **19. Holding**—Keeping hold of "faith" and "good conscience" (vs. 5); not "putting the latter away" as "some." *Faith* is like a very precious liquor; *a good conscience* is the clean, pure glass that contains it [BENGEL]. The loss of *good conscience* entails the *shipwreck of faith*. Consciousness of sin [unrepented of and forgiven] kills the germ of faith in man [WIESINGER]. **which**—*Greek* singular, viz., "good conscience," not "faith" also; however, the result of *putting away* good conscience is, one *loses* faith also. **put away**—a wilful act. They thrust it from them as a troublesome monitor. It reluctantly withdraws, extruded by force, when its owner is tired of its importunity, and is resolved to retain his sin at the cost of losing it. One cannot be on friendly terms with it and with sin at one and the same time. **made shipwreck**—"with respect to THE faith." *Faith* is the vessel in which they had professedly embarked, of which "good conscience" is the anchor. The ancient Church often used this image, comparing the course of faith to navigation. The *Greek* does not imply that one having once had *faith* makes shipwreck of it, but that they who put away good conscience "make shipwreck with respect to THE faith." **20. Hymeneus**—There is no difficulty in supposing him to be the Hymeneus of II Timothy 2:17. Though "delivered over to Satan" (the lord of all outside the Church, Acts 26:18, and the executor of wrath, when judicially allowed by God, on the disobedient, I Cor. 5:5; II Cor. 12:7), he probably was restored to the Church subsequently, and again troubled it. Paul, as an apostle, though distant at Rome pronounced the sentence to be executed at Ephesus, involving, probably, the excommunication of the offenders (Matt. 18:17, 18). The sentence operated not only spiritually, but also physically, sickness, or some such visitation of God, falling on the person excommunicated, in order to bring him to repentance and salvation. Alexander here is probably "the coppersmith" who did Paul "much evil" when the latter visited Ephesus. The "delivering him to Satan" was probably the consequence of his *withstanding* the apostle (II Tim. 4:14, 15); as the same sentence on Hymeneus was the consequence of his "saying that the resurrection is past already" (II Tim. 2:18; his putting away *good conscience*, naturally producing *shipwreck concerning* FAITH, vs. 19. If one's religion better not his morals, his moral deficiencies will corrupt his religion. The rain which falls pure from heaven will not continue pure if it be received in an unclean vessel [ARCHBISHOP WHATELY]). It is possible that he is the Alexander, *then* a Jew, put forward by the Jews, doubtless against Paul, at the riot in Ephesus (Acts 19:33). **that they may**—not "might"; implying that the effect still continues—the sentence is as yet unremoved. **learn**—*Greek*, "be disciplined," viz., by *chastisement* and suffering. **blaspheme**—the name of God and Christ, by doings and teachings unworthy of their Christian profession (Rom. 2:23, 24; Jas. 2:7). Though the apostles had the power of excommunication, accompanied with bodily inflictions, miraculously sent (II Cor. 10:8), it does not follow that fallible ministers now have any power, save that of excluding from church fellowship notorious bad livers.

ADAM CLARKE

According to the prophecies. This may refer to some predictions by inspired men relative to what Timothy should be, and he wishes him to act in all things conformably to those predictions. It was predicted that he should have this high and noble calling; but his behavior in that calling was a matter of contingency, as it respected the use he might make of the grace of his calling.

The apostle therefore exhorts him to *war a good warfare*. Some think that "the foregoing prophecies" refer to revelations which the apostle himself had received concerning Timothy; while others think that the word is to be understood of advices, directions, and exhortations which the apostle had previously delivered to him. This is a very sober and good sense of the passage. *War a good warfare.* The trials and afflictions of the followers of God are often represented as a *warfare* or "campaign."

19. *Holding faith.* All the truths of the Christian religion, firmly believing them, and fervently proclaiming them to others. *And a good conscience.* So holding the truth as to live according to its dictates, that a *good conscience* may be ever preserved. *Which some having put away.* Having "thrust away"; as a foolhardy soldier might his shield and his breastplate or a mad sailor his pilot, helm, and compass. *Concerning faith.* The great truths of the Christian religion.

Have made shipwreck. Being without the faith, that only infallible system of truth; and a good conscience, that skillful pilot, that steady and commanding helm, that faithful and invariable loadstone; having been driven to and fro by every wind of doctrine, and getting among shoals, quicksands, and rocks, have been shipwrecked and engulfed.

20. *Of whom is Hymenaeus and Alexander.* Who had the faith but thrust it away; who had a good conscience through believing, but made shipwreck of it. Hence we find that all this was not only possible, but did actually take place, though some have endeavored to maintain the contrary; who, confounding eternity with a state of probation, have supposed that if a man once enter into the grace of God in this life he must necessarily continue in it to all eternity. Thousands of texts and thousands of facts refute this doctrine. *Delivered unto Satan.* For the destruction of the flesh, that the spirit might be saved in the day of the Lord Jesus. See what is noted on 1 Cor. v. 5; what this sort of punishment was no man now living knows. There is nothing of the kind referred to in the Jewish writings. It seems to have been something done by mere apostolical authority, under the direction of the Spirit of God. *Hymenaeus,* it appears, denied the resurrection, see 2 Tim. ii. 17-18; but whether this *Alexander* be the same with "Alexander the coppersmith," 2 Tim. iv. 14, or the Alexander in Acts xix. 33, cannot be determined. Probably he was the same with the "coppersmith." Whether they were brought back to the acknowledgment of the truth does not appear. From what is said in the Second Epistle the case seems extremely doubtful. Let him who most assuredly standeth take heed lest he fall.

MATTHEW HENRY

CHAPTER 2

Verses 1–8

I. A charge given to Christians to pray for all men in general, and particularly for all in authority. Paul does not send him any prescribed form of prayer. Paul thought it enough to give them general heads; they, having the scripture to direct them in prayer and the Spirit of prayer poured out upon them, needed not any further directions. The disciples of Christ must be praying people. There must be prayers for ourselves in the first place; this is implied here. We must also pray *for all men.* See how far the Christian religion was from being a sect, when it taught men this diffusive charity, to pray for all men.

Pray for kings (*v.* 2); though the kings at this time were heathens, yet they must pray for them. *For kings, and all that are in authority.* We must give thanks for them, pray for their welfare and for the welfare of their kingdoms, that in the peace thereof we may have peace. He does not say, "that we may get preferments under them, grow rich, and be in honour and power under them"; no, the summit of the ambition of a good Christian is to lead a quiet and peaceable life. We cannot expect to be kept quiet and peaceable unless we keep in all godliness and honesty. Here we have our duty as Christians summed up in two words: godliness, that is, the right worshipping of God; and honesty, that is, a good conduct towards all men. These two must go together. Christians are to be men much given to prayer. In our prayers we are to have a generous concern for others as well as for ourselves; we are to pray for all men, and to give thanks for all men. Kings themselves, and those who are in authority, are to be prayed for. They want our prayers, for they have many difficulties to encounter, many snares to which their exalted stations expose them.

II. He shows God's love to mankind in general, *v.* 4.

1. God bears a goodwill to all mankind. There is one God (*v.* 5), and one only. This one *God will have all men to be saved, and to come to the knowledge of the truth.* It concerns us to get the knowledge of the truth, because that is the way to be saved.

2. There is one Mediator, and that Mediator gave himself a ransom for all. As the mercy of God extends itself to all his works, so the mediation of Christ extends to all the children of men, so that they are not now under the law as a covenant of works, but as a rule of life. They are under grace. We deserved to have died. Christ died for us. He put himself into the office of Mediator between God and man. A mediator supposes a controversy. Sin had made a quarrel between us and God. Jesus Christ is a Mediator who undertakes to make peace, to bring God and man together.

JAMIESON, FAUSSET, BROWN

CHAPTER 2

Vss. 1-15. PUBLIC WORSHIP. DIRECTION AS TO INTERCESSIONS FOR ALL MEN, SINCE CHRIST IS A RANSOM FOR ALL. THE DUTIES OF MEN AND WOMEN RESPECTIVELY IN RESPECT TO PUBLIC PRAYER. WOMAN'S SUBJECTION; HER SPHERE OF DUTY. **1. therefore**—taking up again the general subject of the Epistle in continuation (II Tim. 2:1). "What I have therefore to say to thee by way of a *charge* (ch. 1:3, 18), is . . . ." **that, first of all . . . be made**—ALFORD takes it, "I *exhort first of all to make.*" "First of all," doubtless, is to be connected with "I exhort"; what I *begin with* (for special reasons), is . . . . As the destruction of Jerusalem drew near, the Jews (including those at Ephesus) were seized with the dream of freedom from every yoke; and so virtually "blasphemed" (cf. ch. 1:20) God's name by "speaking evil of dignities" (ch. 6:1; II Pet. 2:10; Jude 8). Hence Paul, in opposition, gives prominence to the injunction that prayer be made for *all* men, especially for *magistrates* and *kings* (Titus 3:1-3) [OLSHAUSEN]. Some professing Christians looked down on all not Christians, as doomed to perdition; but Paul says *all men* are to be prayed for, as Christ died for all (vss. 4-6). **supplications**—a term implying the suppliant's *sense of need,* and of *his own insufficiency.* **prayers**—implying devotion. **intercessions**—properly *the coming near to God* with childlike confidence, generally *in behalf of another.* The accumulation of terms implies prayer in its every form and aspect, according to all the relations implied in it. **2. For kings**—an effectual confutation of the adversaries who accused the Christians of disaffection to the ruling powers (Acts 17:7; Rom. 13:1-7). **all . . . in authority**—lit., " . . . in eminence"; in stations of eminence. The "quiet" of Christians was often more dependent on subordinate rulers, than on the supreme king; hence, "*all* . . . in authority" are to be prayed for. **that we may lead**—that we may be blessed with such good government as to lead . . .; or rather, as *Greek,* "to *pass*" or "spend." The prayers of Christians for the government bring down from heaven peace and order in a state. **quiet**—not troubled *from without.* **peaceable**—"tranquil"; not troubled *from within* [OLSHAUSEN]. "He is *peaceable* (*Greek*) who makes no disturbance; he is *quiet* (*Greek*) who is himself free from disturbance" [TITTMANN]. **in all godliness**—"in all (possible . . . requisite) *piety*" [ALFORD]. A distinct *Greek* word, vs. 10, expresses "godliness." **honesty** *Greek,* "gravity" (Titus 2:2, 7), "decorum," or propriety of conduct. As "piety" is in relation to *God,* "gravity" is propriety of behavior among men. **3. this**—praying for all men. **in the sight of God**—not merely *before men,* as if it were their favor that we sought (II Cor. 8:21). **our Saviour**—a title appropriate to the matter in hand. He who is "our Saviour" *is willing that all should be saved* (vs. 4; Rom. 5:18); therefore we should meet the will of God in behalf of others, by praying for the salvation of all men. More would be converted if we would pray more. He has actually saved *us* who believe, being "*our* Saviour." He is willing that all should be saved, even those who do not as yet believe, if they will believe (cf. ch. 4:10; Titus 2:11). **4.** "Imitate God." Since He wishes that all should be saved, do you also wish it; and if you wish it, pray for it. For prayer is the instrument of effecting such things [CHRYSOSTOM]. Our prayers ought to include *all, as* God's grace included *all.* **to come**—They are not forced. **unto the knowledge**—*Greek,* "the *full* knowledge" or "recognition" (*Note,* I Cor. 13:12; Phil. 1:9). **the truth**—the saving truth as it is in, and by, Jesus (John 17:3, 17). **5. For there is one God**—God's *unity* in essence and purpose is a proof of His comprehending all His human children alike (created in His image) in His offer of grace (cf. the same argument from His unity, Rom. 3:30; Gal. 3:20); therefore all are to be prayed for. Verse 4 is proved from vs. 5; vs. 1, from vs. 4. The *one God* is common to all (Isa. 45:22; Acts 17:26). The one Mediator is mediator between God and all men potentially (Rom. 3:29; Eph. 4. 5, 6; Heb. 8:6; 9:15; 12:24). They who have not this one God by one Mediator, have none: lit., a "go-between." The Greek order is not "*and* one mediator," but "one mediator *also* between . . . . While God will have all men to be saved by knowing God and the Mediator, there is a legitimate, holy order in the exercise of that will wherewith men ought to receive it. All mankind constitute, as it were, ONE MAN before God [BENGEL]. **the man**—rather "man," absolutely and generically: not a mere *individual man:* the Second Head of humanity, rep-

ADAM CLARKE

CHAPTER 2

1. *I exhort therefore, that, first of all.* Prayer for the pardon of sin and for obtaining necessary supplies of grace and continual protection from God, with gratitude and thanksgiving for mercies already received, are duties which our sinful and dependent state renders absolutely necessary; and which should be chief in our view, and *first of all* performed. It is difficult to know the precise difference between the four words used here by the apostle. They are sometimes distinguished thus: *Supplications.* Prayers for averting evils of every kind. *Prayers.* Prayers for obtaining the good things, spiritual and temporal, which ourselves need. *Intercessions.* Prayers in behalf of others. *Giving of thanks.* Praises to God, as the Parent of all good, for all the blessings which we and others have received. It is probable that the apostle gives directions here for public worship, and that the words may be thus paraphrased: "Now I exhort first of all that in the public assemblies deprecations of evils, and supplications for such good things as are necessary, and intercessions for their conversion, and thanksgiving for mercies be offered in behalf of all men—for heathens as well as for Christians, and for enemies as well as for friends."

2. *For kings.* As it is a positive maxim of Christianity to pray for all secular governors, so it has ever been the practice of Christians. *That we may lead a quiet and peaceable life.* We thus pray for the government that the public peace may be preserved. Good rulers have power to do much good; we pray that their authority may be ever preserved and well-directed. Bad rulers have power to do much evil; we pray that they may be prevented from thus using their power.

4. *Who will have all men to be saved.* Because He wills the salvation of all men, therefore He wills that all men should be prayed for. In the face of such a declaration, how can any Christian soul suppose that God ever unconditionally and eternally reprobated any man?

5. *One mediator.* The word *mediator* signifies literally a "middle person," one whose office it is to reconcile two parties at enmity; and hence Suidas explains it by "a peacemaker."

MATTHEW HENRY

He is a ransom that *was to be testified in due time*. This doctrine of Christ's mediation Paul was entrusted to preach to every creature. He was commissioned particularly to preach to the Gentiles, faithfully and truly. God has a goodwill to the salvation of all; so that it is not so much the want of a will in God to save them as it is a want of will in themselves to be saved in God's way. Those who are saved must come to the knowledge of the truth.

Without knowledge the heart cannot be good; if we do not know the truth, we cannot be ruled by it. Paul was ordained a minister, to declare this to the Gentiles, that Christ is the one Mediator between God and men, who gave himself a ransom for all. Ministers must preach the truth; they are, like our apostle, to preach in faith and verity, and they must also be faithful and trusty.

III. A direction how to pray, *v*. 8. Men must pray everywhere: no place is amiss for prayer, no place more acceptable to God than another. *Lifting up holy hands*, or pure hands, pure from the pollution of sin.

We must pray in charity: *Without wrath*, or malice, or anger at any person. We must pray in faith *without doubting*, or as some read it, *without disputing*.

JAMIESON, FAUSSET, BROWN

resenting and embodying in Himself *the whole human race and nature*. There is no "the" in the *Greek*. This epithet is thus the strongest corroboration of his argument, viz., that Christ's mediation affects the whole race, since there is but the one Mediator, designed as the Representative Man for all men alike (cf. Rom. 5:15; I Cor. 8:6; II Cor. 5:19; Col. 2:14). His being "man" was necessary to His being a Mediator, sympathizing with us through experimental knowledge of our nature (Isa. 50:4; Heb. 2:14; 4:15). **gave himself**—(Titus 2:14). Not only *the Father* gave Him for us (John 3:16); but *the Son* gave Himself (Phil. 2:5-8). **ransom**—properly of a captive slave. Man was the captive slave of Satan, sold under sin. He was unable to ransom himself, because absolute obedience is due to God, and therefore no act of ours can satisfy for the least offense. Leviticus 25:48 allowed one sold captive to be redeemed by one of his brethren. The Son of God, therefore, became man in order that, being made like unto us in all things, sin only excepted, as our elder brother He should redeem us (Matt. 20:28; Eph. 1:7; I Pet. 1:18, 19). The *Greek* implies not merely *ransom*, but a *substituted* or *equivalent ransom:* the *Greek* preposition, *"anti,"* implying reciprocity and vicarious substitution. **for all**—*Greek,* "in behalf of all": not merely for a privileged few; cf. vs. 1: the argument for *praying in behalf of all* is given here. **to be testified**—*Greek,* "the testimony (that which was to be testified of, I John 5:8-11) in its own due times," or *seasons,* i.e., in the times appointed by God for its being testified of (ch. 6:15; Titus 1:3). The oneness of the Mediator, involving the universality of redemption [which faith, however, alone appropriates], was the great subject of Christian testimony [ALFORD] (I Cor. 1:6; 2:1; II Thess. 1:10). **7. Whereunto**—For the giving of which testimony. **I am ordained**—lit., "I was set": the same *Greek,* as "puttting me . . ." (ch. 1:12). **preacher**—lit., "herald" (I Cor. 1:21; 9:27; 15:11; II Tim. 1:11; Titus 1:3). He recurs to himself, as in ch. 1:16, in *himself* a living *pattern* or announcement of the Gospel, so here "a herald and teacher of (it to) the Gentiles" (Gal. 2:9; Eph. 3:1-12; Col. 1:23). The universality of his commission is an appropriate assertion here, where he is arguing to prove that prayers are to be made "for *all* men" (vs. 1). **I speak the truth . . . and lie not**—a strong asseveration of his universal commission, characteristic of the ardor of the apostle, exposed to frequent conflict (Rom. 11:1; II Cor. 11:13). **in faith and verity**—rather, "in *the* faith and *the* truth." The sphere in which his ministry was appointed to be exercised was *the faith* and *the truth* (vs. 4): *the Gospel truth,* the subject matter of *the faith* [WIESINGER]. **8. I will**—The *active* wish, or desire, is meant. **that men**—rather as *Greek,* "that *the* men," as distinguished from "the women," to whom he has something different to say from what he said to the men (vss. 9-12; I Cor. 11:14, 15; 14:34, 35). The *emphasis,* however, is not on this, but on the precept of *praying,* resumed from vs. 1. **everywhere**—*Greek,* "in every place," viz., of public prayer. Fulfilling Malachi 1:11, *"In every place* . . . from the rising of the sun even unto the going down of the same . . . incense shall be offered unto My name"; and Jesus' words, Matthew 18:20; John 4:21, 23. **lifting up holy hands**—The early Christians turned up their palms towards heaven, as those craving help do. So also Solomon (I Kings 8:22; Ps. 141:2). The Jews washed their hands before prayer (Ps. 26:6). Paul figuratively (cf. Job 17:9; Jas. 4:8) uses language alluding to this custom here: so Isaiah 1:15, 16. The *Greek* for "holy" means hands *which have committed no impiety,* and *observed every sacred duty.* This (or at least the contrite desire to be so) is a needful qualification for effectual prayer (Ps. 24:3, 4). **without wrath**—*putting* it *away* (Matt. 5:23, 24; 6:15). **doubting**—rather, "disputing," as the *Greek* is translated in Philippians 2:14. Such things *hinder prayer* (Luke 9:46; Rom. 14:1; I Pet. 3:7). BENGEL supports *English Version* (cf. an instance, II Kings 7:2; Matt. 14:31; Mark 11:22-24; Jas. 1:6). **9, 10.** The context requires that we understand these directions as to women, in relation to their deportment *in public worship,* though the rules will hold good on *other* occasions *also.* **in modest apparel**—"in seemly guise" [ELLICOTT]. The adjective means properly, *orderly, decorous,* becoming; the noun in secular writings means *conduct, bearing.* But here "apparel." Women are apt to love fine dress; and at Ephesus the riches of some (ch. 6:17) would lead them to dress luxuriously. The *Greek* in Titus 2:3 is a more general term meaning "deportment." **shamefacedness**—TRENCH spells this word according

ADAM CLARKE

6. *Who gave himself a ransom.* The word *lytron* signifies a ransom paid for the redemption of a captive; and *antilytron,* the word used here, and applied to the death of Christ, signifies that ransom which consists in the exchange of one person for another, or the redemption of life by life. *To be testified in due time.* The original words are not very clear and have been understood variously. The most authentic copies of the printed Vulgate have simply, "Thus rendering testimony at the appointed time." And this was rendered literally by our first translator: "Whos witnessinge is confermyd in his timis." This appears to be the apostle's meaning: Christ gave himself a Ransom for all. This, in the times which seemed best to the divine wisdom, was to be testified to every nation, and people, and tongue.

7. *I am ordained a preacher.* "I am set apart, appointed." The word does not imply any imposition of hands by either bishop or presbytery. *A teacher of the Gentiles.* Being specially commissioned to preach the gospel, not to the Jews, but to the "nations" of the world. *In faith and verity.* "Faithfully" and "truly"; preaching the truth, the whole truth, and nothing but the truth; and this fervently, affectionately, and perseveringly.

8. *I will therefore.* Seeing the apostle had his authority from Christ, and spoke nothing but what he received from Him, his *I will* is equal to "I command." *That men pray.* That is, for the blessings promised in this testimony of God. For although God has provided them, yet He will not give them to such as will not pray. *Every where.* "In every place." This may refer to a Jewish superstition. They thought at first that no prayer could be acceptable that was not offered at the Temple at Jerusalem; afterward this was extended to the Holy Land. But when they became dispersed among the nations, they built oratories or places of prayer, principally by rivers and by the seaside; and in these they were obliged to allow that public prayer might be legally offered, but nowhere else. In opposition to this the apostle, by the authority of Christ, commands men to pray *every where;* that all places belong to God's dominions; and, as He fills every place, in every place He may be worshipped and glorified. *Lifting up holy hands.* It was a common custom, not only among the Jews, but also among the heathens, to "lift up" or spread out their arms and hands in prayer. It is properly the action of entreaty and request, and seems to be an effort to embrace the assistance requested. But the apostle probably alludes to the Jewish custom of laying their hands on the head of the animal which they brought for a sin offering, confessing their sins, and then giving up the life of the animal as an expiation for the sins thus confessed. And this very notion is conveyed in the original term. This shows us how Christians should pray. They should come to the altar; set God before their eyes; humble themselves for their sins; bring as a sacrifice the Lamb of God; lay their hands on this Sacrifice; and by faith offer it to God in their souls' behalf, expecting salvation through His meritorious death alone. *Without wrath.* Having no vindictive feeling against any person, harboring no unforgiving spirit, while they are imploring pardon for their own offenses. The *holy hands* refer to the Jewish custom of washing their hands before prayer; this was done to signify that they had put away all sin, and purposed to live a holy life. *And doubting.* "Reasonings, dialogues."

9. *In like manner also.* That is, he wills or commands what follows, as he had commanded what went before. *With shamefacedness* or "modesty." This would lead them to avoid everything unbecoming in the mode or fashion of their dress.

MATTHEW HENRY

Verses 9–15

I. Women who profess the Christian religion should be modest, sober, silent, and submissive. They must be very modest in their apparel (you may read the vanity of a person's mind in the gaiety and gaudiness of his habit), because they have better ornaments with which they should *adorn themselves*. Good works are the best ornament. Those that profess godliness should, in their dress, as well as other things, act as becomes their profession. Women must learn the principles of their religion, learn Christ, learn the scriptures. They must be silent, submissive, and not usurp authority.

II. The extensiveness of the rules of Christianity; they reach not only to men, but to women. Women are to profess godliness as well as men, and, to their honour be it spoken, many of them were eminent professors of Christianity in the days of the apostles, as the book of Acts will inform us. The best ornaments for professors of godliness are good works. Women must be learners, and are not allowed to be public teachers in the church; the woman must not usurp authority over the man, but is to be in silence. But, notwithstanding this prohibition, good women ought to teach their children at home the principles of religion. Timothy from a child had known the holy scriptures; and who should teach him but his mother and grandmother? Two very good reasons given for the man's authority over the woman, and her subjection to the man, *v.* 13, 14. Here is much for her support and encouragement, *v.* 15. Though in sorrow, yet she shall bring forth, and be a living mother of living children.

Adam was first formed, then Eve out of him. And as she was last in the creation, so she was first in the transgression.

A word of comfort (*v.* 15) that those who continue in sobriety shall be *saved in child-bearing*, or *with* child-bearing. The sentence which they are under for sin shall be no bar to their acceptance with Christ.

ALBERT BARNES:

15. "Notwithstanding she shall be saved." The promise in this verse is designed to alleviate the apparent severity of the remarks just made about the condition of woman, and of the allusion to the painful facts of her early history. What the apostle had just said would carry the mind back to the period in which woman introduced sin into the world, and, by an obvious and easy association, to the sentence which had been passed on her in consequence of her trangression, and to the burden of sorrows which she was doomed to bear. By the remark in this verse, however, Paul shows that it was not his intention to overwhelm her with anguish. He did not design to harrow up her feelings by an unkind allusion to a melancholy fact in her history. It was necessary for him to state, and for her to know, that her place was secondary and subordinate, and he wished this truth ever to be kept in memory among Christians. It was not unkind or improper also to state the reasons for this opinion, and to show that her own history had demonstrated that she was not designed for headship. But she was not to be regarded as degraded and abandoned. She was not to be overwhelmed. There were consolations in her case. There was a special divine interposition which she might look for, evincing tender care on the part of God in those deep sorrows which had come upon her in consequence of her transgression; and instead of being crushed and brokenhearted, she should remember that the everlasting arms of God would sustain her in her condition of sorrow and pain. Paul, then, would speak to her the language of consolation, and while he would have her occupy her proper place, he would have her feel that God was her Friend.

— Popular Commentary

JAMIESON, FAUSSET, BROWN

to its true derivation, "shamefastness" (that which is made fast by an honorable shame); as "steadfastness" (cf. vss. 11, 12). **sobriety**—"self-restraint" [ALFORD]. Habitual inner self-government [TRENCH]. I prefer ELLICOTT's translation, "sober-mindedness": the well-balanced state of mind arising from habitual self-restraint. **with**—*Greek,* "in.' **braided hair**—lit., "plaits," i.e., plaited hair: probably with the "gold and pearls" intertwined (I Pet. 3:3). Such gaud is characteristic of the spiritual harlot (Rev. 17:4). **10. professing**—*Greek,* "promising": engaging to follow. **with good works**—The *Greek* preposition is not the same as in vs. 9; "by means of"; "*through* good works." Their adorning is to be effected *by means of* good works: not that they are to be clothed *in,* or *with,* them (Eph. 2:10). **11. learn**—not "teach" (vs. 12; I Cor. 14:34). She should not even put questions in the public assembly (I Cor. 14:35). **with all subjection**—not "usurping authority" (vs. 12). She might teach, but not in public (Acts 18:26). Paul probably wrote this Epistle from Corinth, where the precept (I Cor. 14:34) was in force. **12. usurp authority**—"to lord it over the man" [ALFORD], lit., "to be an autocrat." **13. For**—reason of the precept; the original order of creation. **Adam... first**—before Eve, who was created *for him* (I Cor. 11:8, 9). **14. Adam was not deceived**—as Eve was *deceived* by the serpent; but was *persuaded* by his wife. Genesis 3:17, "hearkened unto... voice of ... wife." But in Genesis 3:13, Eve says, "The *serpent beguiled* me." Being more easily deceived, she more easily deceives [BENGEL], (II Cor. 11:3). Last in being, she was first in sin—indeed, she alone was *deceived*. The subtle serpent knew that she was "the weaker vessel." He therefore tempted her, not Adam. She yielded to the temptations of sense and the *deceits of Satan;* he, to *conjugal* love. **being deceived**—The oldest MSS. read the compound *Greek* verb for the simple, "Having been *seduced by deceit*": implying how *completely* Satan *succeeded in deceiving* her. **was in the transgression**—*Greek,* "*came to be* in the transgression": became involved in the existing state of transgression, lit., "the going beyond a command"; breach of a positive precept (Rom. 4:15). **15. be saved in child-bearing** *Greek,* "in (lit., *through*) (*her* lit., *the*) child-bearing." *Through,* or *by,* is often so used to express not *the means of* her salvation, but *the circumstances* AMIDST *which* it has place. Thus I Corinthians 3:15, "He... shall be saved: yet so as by (lit., *through,* i.e., amidst) fire": in spite of the fiery ordeal which he has necessarily to pass *through,* he shall be saved. So here, "*In spite of* the trial of child-bearing which she passes *through* (as her portion of the curse, Gen. 3:16, 'in sorrow shalt thou *bring forth children*'), she shall be saved." Moreover, I think it is *implied* indirectly that the very curse will be turned into a condition favorable to her salvation, by her faithfully performing her part in doing and suffering what God has assigned to her, viz., *child-bearing* and home duties, *her* sphere, as distinguished from public teaching, which is not hers, but *man's* (vss. 11, 12). In this home sphere, not ordinarily in one of active duty for advancing the kingdom of God, which contradicts the position assigned to her by God, she will be saved on the same terms as all others, viz., by living faith.

"She shall be saved ([though] with child-bearing)," i.e., though suffering her part of the primeval curse in childbearing; just as a man shall be saved, though having to bear his part, viz., the sweat of the brow. **if they...**—"if *the women* (plural, taken out of "the woman," vs. 14, which is put for *the whole sex*) continue," or more lit., "shall (be found at the judgment to) have continued." **faith and charity**—the essential way to salvation (ch. 1:5). *Faith* is in relation to God. *Charity,* to our fellow man. *Sobriety,* to one's self. **sobriety**—"sober-mindedness" (*Note,* vs. 9, as contrasted with the unseemly forwardness reproved in vs. 11). Mental receptivity and activity in family life were recognized in Christianity as the destiny of woman. One reason alleged here by Paul, is the greater danger of self-deception in the weaker sex, and the spread of errors arising from it, especially in a class of addresses in which sober reflectiveness is least in exercise [NEANDER]. The case (Acts 21:9) was doubtless in private, not in public.

ADAM CLARKE

With *sobriety.* Moderation would lead them to avoid all unnecessary expense. They might follow the custom or costume of the country as to the dress itself, for nothing was ever more becoming than the Grecian; but they must not imitate the extravagance of those who through impurity or littleness of mind decked themselves merely to attract the eye of admiration or set in lying action the tongue of flattery.

10. *But (which becometh).* That is, good works are the only ornaments with which women professing Christianity should seek to be adorned.

11. *Let the woman learn in silence.* That is generally supposed to be a prohibition of women's preaching. I have already said what I judge necessary on this subject in the notes on 1 Cor. xi. 5, etc., and xiv. 34-35, to which places I beg leave to refer the reader.

12. *Nor to usurp authority.* A woman should attempt nothing, either in public or in private, that belongs to man as his peculiar function. This was prohibited by the Roman laws.

13. *For Adam was first formed, then Eve.* And by this very act God designed that he should have the preeminence. God fitted man by the robust construction of his body to live a public life, to contend with difficulties, and to be capable of great exertions. The structure of woman's body plainly proves that she was never designed for those exertions required in public life.

14. *Adam was not deceived.* It does not appear that Satan attempted the man; the woman said: "The serpent beguiled me, and I did eat." Adam received the fruit from the hand of his wife; he knew he was transgressing; he was not deceived. However, she led the way, and in consequence of this she was subjected to the domination of her husband: "Thy desire shall be to thy husband, and he shall rule over thee," Gen. iii. 16.

15. *She shall be saved in childbearing.* "She shall be saved through childbearing"—she shall be saved by means, or through the instrumentality, of childbearing or of bringing forth a child. There are innumerable instances of women dying in childbed who have lived in faith and charity and holiness, with sobriety; and equally numerous instances of worthless women, slaves to different kinds of vices, who have not only been saved in childbearing, but have passed through their travail with comparatively little pain. Hence that is not the sense in which we should understand the apostle. Yet it must be a matter of great consolation and support to all pious women laboring of child to consider that by the holy Virgin's childbearing salvation is provided for them and the whole human race; and that, whether they die or live, though their own childbearing can contribute nothing to their salvation, yet He who was born of a woman has purchased them and the whole human race by His blood.

If they continue. "If they live"; for so it signifies in other passages, particularly Phil. i. 25.

MATTHEW HENRY

CHAPTER 3

Verses 1–7

Timothy, we suppose, was an evangelist who was left at Ephesus. They were very loth to part with Paul, especially because he told them they should *see his face no more* (Acts xx. 38), and therefore Paul left Timothy with them.

I. The ministry is a work. The office of a scripture-bishop is an office of divine appointment, and not of human invention. This office of a Christian bishop is a work which requires diligence and application. Ministers should always look more to their work than to the honour and advantage of their office. It is a good work, a work of the greatest importance. The ministry is conversant about no lower concerns than the life and happiness of immortal souls. There ought to be an earnest desire of the office in those who would be put into it.

II. The workman must be duly qualified. 1. A minister must be blameless, he must not lie under any scandal. 2. He must be the husband of one wife.

3. He must be vigilant and watchful against Satan. 4. He must be sober, temperate, moderate in all his actions, and in the use of all creature-comforts. 5. He must be of good behaviour, and not light, vain, and frothy. 6. He must be given to hospitality.

7. Apt to teach, both able and willing to communicate to others the knowledge which God has given him. 8. No drunkard. 9. No striker; one who is not quarrelsome, but does everything with mildness, love, and gentleness.

JAMIESON, FAUSSET, BROWN

CHAPTER 3

VSS. 1-16. RULES AS TO BISHOPS (OVERSEERS) AND DEACONS. THE CHURCH, AND THE GOSPEL MYSTERY NOW REVEALED TO IT, ARE THE END OF ALL SUCH RULES. **1.** Translate as *Greek*, "Faithful is the saying." A needful preface to what follows: for the office of a bishop or overseer in Paul's day, attended as it was with hardship and often persecution, would not seem to the world generally a desirable and "good work." **desire**—lit., "stretch one's self forward to grasp"; "aim at": a distinct *Greek* verb from that for "desireth." What one does voluntarily is more esteemed than what he does when asked (I Cor. 16:15). This is utterly distinct from ambitious desires after office in the Church. (Jas. 3:1). **biship**—overseer: as yet identical with "presbyter" (Acts 20:17, 28; Titus 1:5-7). **good work**—lit., "honorable work." Not the honor associated with it, but the *work*, is the prominent thought (Acts 15:38; Phil. 2:30; cf. II Tim. 4:5). He who aims at the office must remember the high qualifications needed for the due discharge of its functions. **2.** The existence of Church organization and presbyters at Ephesus is presupposed (ch. 5:17, 19). The institution of Church widows (ch. 5) accords with this. The directions here to Timothy, the president or apostolic delegate, are as to filling up *vacancies* among the bishops and deacons, or *adding* to their number. New churches in the neighborhood also would require presbyters and deacons. Episcopacy was adopted in apostolic times as the most expedient form of government, being most nearly in accordance with Jewish institutions, and so offering the less obstruction through Jewish prejudices to the progress of Christianity. The synagogue was governed by presbyters, "elders" (Acts 4:8; 24:1), called also *bishops* or *overseers*. Three among them presided as "rulers of the synagogue," answering to "bishops" in the modern sense [LIGHTFOOT, *Horæ*.], and one among them took the lead. AMBROSE (in *Amularius de Officiis*, 2. 13, as also BINGHAM, *Ecclesiastical Antiquities*, 2. 11) says, "They who are now called bishops were originally called apostles. But those who ruled the Church after the death of the apostles had not the testimony of miracles, and were in many respects inferior. Therefore they thought it not decent to assume to themselves the name of apostles; but dividing the names, they left to presbyters the name of the *presbytery*, and they themselves were called *bishops*." *"Presbyter"* refers to the *rank;* "bishop," to the *office* or function. Timothy (though not having the name) exercised the power at Ephesus then, which bishops in the modern sense more recently exercised. **blameless**—"unexceptionable"; giving no *just* handle for blame. **husband of one wife**—confuting the celibacy of Rome's priesthood. Though the Jews practiced polygamy, yet as he is writing as to a Gentile Church, and as polygamy was never allowed among even laymen in the Church, the ancient interpretation that the prohibition here is against polygamy in a candidate bishop is not correct. It must, therefore, mean that, though laymen might lawfully marry again, candidates for the episcopate or presbytery were better to have been married only *once*. As in ch. 5:9, "wife of one man," implies a woman married but once; so "husband of one wife" here must mean the same. The feeling which prevailed among the Gentiles, as well as the Jews (cf. as to Anna, Luke 2:36, 37), against a second marriage would, on the ground of expediency and conciliation in matters indifferent and not involving compromise of principle, account for Paul's prohibition here in the case of one in so prominent a sphere as a bishop or a deacon. Hence the stress that is laid in the context on *the repute* in which the candidate for orders is held among those over whom he is to preside (Titus 1: 16).

vigilant—lit., "sober"; ever on the watch, as sober men alone can be; keenly alive, so as to foresee what ought to be done (I Thess. 5:6-8). **sober**—sober-minded. **of good behaviour**—*Greek*, "orderly." *"Sober"* refers to the inward mind; *"orderly,"* to the *outward* behavior, tone, look, gait, dress. The new man bears somewhat of a sacred festival character, incompatible with all confusion, disorder, excess, violence, laxity, assumption, harshness, and meanness (Phil. 4:8) [BENGEL]. **apt to teach**—(II Tim. 2:24). **3. Not given to wine**—The *Greek* includes *besides* this, not indulging in *the brawling, violent conduct towards others,* which proceeds from being given to wine. The opposite of "patient" or (*Greek*) "forbearing," reasonable to others (*Note*, Phil. 4:5). **no striker**—with either hand or tongue: not as some teachers pretending a holy zeal

ADAM CLARKE

CHAPTER 3

1. *This is a true saying.* "This is a true doctrine." These words are joined to the last verse of the preceding chapter by several of the Greek fathers, and by them referred to the doctrine there stated. *The office of a bishop.* The "episcopacy, overseership, or superintendency." The word *oregetai*, which we translate *desire*, signifies "earnest, eager, passionate desire," and *epithymei*, which we translate *desire*, also signifies "earnestly to desire or covet." *A good work.* A work it then was—heavy, incessant, and painful. There were no unpreaching prelates in those days, and should be none now.

2. *A bishop then must be blameless.* Our term *bishop* comes from the Anglo-Saxon, which is mere corruption of the Greek *episcopos*, and the Latin *episcopus*. The former, being compounded of *epi*, "over," and *skeptomai*, to "look or inspect," signifies one who has the inspection or oversight of a place, persons, or business; what we commonly term a "superintendent." Let us consider the qualifications of a Christian bishop. *First*: This Christian bishop must be blameless; a person against whom no evil can be proved. The word is a metaphor, taken from the case of an expert and skillful pugilist, who so defends every part of his body that it is impossible for his antagonist to give one hit. So this Christian bishop is one that has so conducted himself as to put it out of the reach of any person to prove that he is either unsound in a single article of the Christian faith or deficient in the fulfillment of any duty incumbent on a Christian. *Second*: He must be *the husband of one wife.* He should be a married man, but he should be no polygamist; and have only *one wife*, i.e., one at a time. It does not mean that, if he has been married and his wife die, he should never marry another. *Third*: He must be *vigilant;* "watchful." *Fourth*: He must be *sober;* "prudent," or, according to the etymology of the word, "a man of a sound mind." *Fifth*: He must be *of good behaviour;* "orderly, decent, grave, and correct" in the whole of his appearance, carriage, and conduct. The preceding term refers to the mind; this latter, to the external manners. *Sixth*: He must be *given to hospitality;* literally, a "lover of strangers"; one who is ready to receive into his house and relieve every necessitous stranger. *Hospitality* in those primitive times was a great and necessary virtue; then there were few inns or places of public entertainment; to those who were noted for benevolence the necessitous stranger had recourse. A Christian bishop, professing love to God and all mankind, preaching a religion one-half of the morality of which was included in "Thou shalt love thy neighbour as thyself," would naturally be sought to by those who were in distress and destitute of friends. *Seventh*: He should be *apt to teach;* one "capable of teaching"; not only wise himself, but ready to communicate his wisdom to others. One whose delight is to instruct the ignorant and those who are out of the way. He must be a preacher; an able, zealous, fervent, and assiduous preacher.

3. An *eighth* article in his character is, he must *not* be *given to wine.* This word not only signifies one who is inordinately attached to wine, a winebibber or tippler, but also one who is imperious, abusive, insolent, whether through wine or otherwise. *Ninth*: He must be *no striker;* not "quarrelsome"; not ready to strike a person who may displease him; no persecutor of those who may differ from him; not prone, as one wittily said,

To prove his doctrine orthodox
By apostolic blows and knocks.

MATTHEW HENRY

10. One who is not greedy of filthy lucre, who is dead to the wealth of this world, lives above it. 11. He must be patient, and not a brawler, of a mild disposition. As not a striker with his hands, so not a brawler with his tongue. 12. Not covetous. Covetousness is bad in any, but it is worst in a minister. 13. He must be one who keeps his family in good order. The families of ministers ought to be examples of good to all other families.—*With all gravity*. The best way to keep inferiors in subjection, is to be grave with them. Not having his children in subjection with all austerity, but with all gravity.

14. He must not be a novice, who knows no more of religion than the surface of it, for such a one is apt to be lifted up with pride: the more ignorant men are the more proud they are.

We should take heed of pride, because it is a sin that turned angels into devils.

15. He must be of good reputation among his neighbours.

III. What great reason we have to cry out, as Paul does, *Who is sufficient for these things?* (2 Cor. ii. 16). What holy watchfulness is necessary in this work! Have not the most faithful and concientious ministers just reason to complain against themselves? How far short do the best come of what they should be and what they should do! Yet let those bless God, and be thankful, whom the Lord has enabled, and counted faithful. He will fit us for our work and reward our faithfulness with a crown of glory.

Verses 8–13

The character of deacons. They must be *grave*. Gravity becomes all Christians, but especially those who are in office in the church.

Not doubled-tongued; a double tongue comes from a double heart; flatterers and slanderers are double-tongued.

Not given to much wine; for this opens the door to many temptations. *Not greedy of filthy lucre;* this would especially be bad in the deacons, who were entrusted with the church's money, *v.* 9.

JAMIESON, FAUSSET, BROWN

(II Cor. 11:20), answering to "not a brawler" or fighter (cf. I Kings 22:24; Neh. 13:25; Isa. 58:4; Acts 23:2; II Tim. 2:24, 25). **not covetous**—*Greek,* "not a lover of money," whether he have much or little (Titus 1:7). **4. ruleth**—*Greek,* "presiding over." **his own house**—children and servants, as contrasted with "the church" (house) of God (vss. 5, 15) which he may be called on to preside over. **having his children**—rather as *Greek,* "having children (who are) in subjection" (Titus 1:6). **gravity** propriety: *reverent* modesty on the part of the children [ALFORD]. The fact that *he has children* who are *in subjection to him in all gravity,* is the recommendation in his favor as one likely to rule well the Church. **5. For**—*Greek,* "But." **the church**—rather, "*a* church" or congregation. How shall he who cannot perform the lesser function, perform the greater and more difficult? **6. not a novice**—one just converted. This proves the Church of Ephesus was established now for some time. The absence of this rule in the Epistle to Titus, accords with the recent planting of the Church at Crete. *Greek, neophyte,* lit., "a young plant"; luxuriantly verdant (Rom. 6:5; 11:-17; I Cor. 3:6). The young convert has not yet been disciplined and matured by afflictions and temptations. Contrast Acts 21:16, "an old disciple." **lifted up with pride**—*Greek,* lit., "wrapt in smoke," so that, inflated with self-conceit and exaggerated ideas of his own importance, he cannot see himself or others in the true light (ch. 6: 4; II Tim. 3:4). **condemnation of the devil**—into the same condemnation as Satan fell into (vs. 7; II Tim. 2:26). Pride was the cause of Satan's condemnation (Job 38:15; Isa. 14:12-15; John 12:31; 16:11; II Pet. 2:4; Jude 6). It cannot mean condemnation or accusation *on the part of the devil.* The devil may bring a *reproach* on men (vs. 7), but he cannot bring them into *condemnation,* for he does not judge, but is judged [BENGEL]. **7. a good report**—*Greek,* "testimony." So Paul was influenced by the good report given of Timothy to choose him as his companion (Acts 16:2). **of them which are without**—from the as yet unconverted Gentiles around (I Cor. 5:12; Col. 4:5; I Thess. 4:12), that they may be the more readily won to the Gospel (I Pet. 2:12), and that the name of Christ may be glorified. Not even the former life of a bishop should be open to reproach [BENGEL]. **reproach and the snare of the devil**—*reproach* of men (ch. 5:14) proving the occasion of his falling into *the snare of the devil* (ch. 6:9; Matt. 22:15; II Tim. 2:26). The *reproach* continually surrounding him for former sins might lead him into *the snare* of becoming as bad as his reputation. Despair of recovering *reputation* might, in a weak moment, lead some into recklessness of living (Jer. 18:12). The reason why only moral qualities of a general kind are specified is, he presupposes in candidates for a bishopric the special gifts of the Spirit (ch. 4:14) and true faith, which he desires to be evidenced outwardly; also he requires qualifications *in a bishop* not so indispensable in others. **8.** The *deacons* were chosen by the voice of the people. CYPRIAN (*Epistle* 2. 5) says that good bishops never departed from the old custom of consulting the people. The deacons answer to the chazzan of the synagogue: the attendant *ministers,* or subordinate coadjutors of the presbyter (as Timothy himself was to Paul, ch. 4:6; Philemon 13; and John Mark, Acts 13:5). Their duty was to read the Scriptures in the Church, to instruct the catechumens in Christian truths, to assist the presbyters at the sacraments, to receive oblations, and to preach and instruct. As the chazzan covered and uncovered the ark in the synagogue, containing the law, so the deacon in the ancient Church put the covering on the communion table. (See CHRYSOSTOM, 19, *Homily* on Acts; THEOPHYLACT on Luke 19; and BALSAMAN on *Canon* 22, *Council of Laodicea.*) The appointing of "the seven" in Acts 6 is perhaps not meant to describe the *first* appointment of the deacous of the Church. At least the chazzan previously suggested the similar order of deacons. **double-tongued**—lit., "of double-speech"; saying one thing to this person, and another to that person [THEODORET]. The extensive personal intercourse that deacons would have with the members of the Church might prove a temptation to such a fault. Others explain it, "Saying one thing, thinking another" (Prov. 20:19; Gal. 2:13). I prefer the former. **not greedy of filthy lucre**—All gain is filthy (lit., "base") which is set before a man as a by-end in his work for God [ALFORD] (I Pet. 5:2). The deacon's office of collecting and distributing alms would render this a necessary qualification. **9. the mystery of the faith**—*holding the faith,* which to the natural man remains *a mystery,* but which has been revealed by the Spirit to them

ADAM CLARKE

Tenth: He must *not* be *greedy of filthy lucre,* "not desirous of base gain," not using base and unjustifiable methods to raise and increase his revenues, not trading or trafficking; for what would be honorable in a secular character would be base and dishonorable in a bishop. Though such a trait should never appear in the character of a Christian prelate, yet there is much reason to suspect that the words above are not authentic. They are omitted in many MSS. and by most of the Greek fathers. Griesbach has left it out of the text, in which it does not appear that it ever had a legitimate place. The word *covetous,* which we have below, expresses all the meaning of this. *Eleventh:* He must be *patient;* "meek, gentle"; the opposite to "a quarrelsome person," which it immediately follows when the spurious word is removed. *Twelfth*: He must *not* be *a brawler;* not "contentious or litigious," but quiet and peaceable. *Thirteenth:* He must *not* be *covetous;* "not a lover of money"; not desiring the office for the sake of its emoluments.

4. The *fourteenth* qualification of a Christian bishop is that he ***ruleth well his own house,*** one who "properly presides over and governs his own family." One who has the command of his own house, not by sternness, severity, and tyranny, but with all *gravity.*

5. *For if a man know not.* Method is a matter of great importance in all the affairs of life. It is a true saying, "He that does little with his head must do much with his hands"; and even then the business is not half done for want of method. He who has a disorderly family has no government of that family; he probably has none because he has no method, no plan, of presiding.

6. *Fifteenth*: It is required that he be *not a novice.* Not a "young plant," not "recently ingrafted," that is, one not newly converted to the faith. One who has been of considerable standing in the Christian church, if he have the preceding qualifications, may be safely trusted with the government of that church. It is impossible that one who is not long and deeply experienced in the ways of God can guide others in the way of life. Hence presbyters or elders were generally appointed to have the oversight of the rest, and hence presbyter and bishop seem to have been two names for the same office; yet all presbyters or elders certainly were not bishops, because all presbyters had not the qualifications marked above. But the apostle gives another reason: *Lest being lifted up with pride he fall into the condemnation of the devil.* It is natural for man to think himself of more importance than his fellows when they are entrusted to his government. The apostle's term "puffed up, inflated," is a metaphor taken from a bladder when filled with air or wind. From these words of the apostle we are led to infer that *pride* or "self-conceit" was the cause of the devil's downfall.

7. The *sixteenth* requisite is that he should *have a good report of them which are without;* that he should be one who had not been previously a profligate, or scandalous in his life. Such a person, when converted, may be a worthy private member of religious society; but I believe God rarely calls such to the work of the ministry, and never to the episcopate. *Them which are without* are the Jews, Gentiles, and the unconverted of all kinds. *Lest he fall into reproach.* For his former scandalous life. *And the snare of the devil.* Snares and temptations such as he fell in and fell by before. This is called *the snare of the devil;* for as he well knows the constitution of such persons and what is most likely to prevail, he infers that what was effectual before to their transgressing may be so still; therefore on all suitable occasions he tempts them to their old sins.

8. *Likewise must the deacons.* The term deacon simply signifies a "regular or stated servant." As nearly the same qualifications were required in the *deacons* as in the bishops, the reader may consult what is said on the preceding verses. *Grave.* Of a sedate and dignified carriage and conduct. *Not doubletongued.* Speaking one thing to one person and another thing to another on the same subject. This is hypocrisy and deceit. This word might also be translated "liars." *Not given to much wine.*

MATTHEW HENRY

If we keep a pure conscience, this will preserve in our souls the mystery of faith, *v.* 10. The soundness of their judgments, their zeal for Christ, and the blamelessness of their conversation, must be proved.

Their wives likewise must have a good character (*v.* 11). All who are related to ministers must double their care to walk as becomes the gospel of Christ, lest the ministry be blamed.

As he said before of the bishops or ministers, so here of the deacons, they must be *the husband of one wife;* they must *rule their children and their own houses well:* the families of deacons should be examples to other families.

The reason why the deacons must be thus qualified (*v.* 13). In the primitive church there were but two orders of ministers or officers, *bishops* and *deacons.* The design of the deacon's office was to mind the temporal concerns of the church, such as the salaries of the ministers and providing for the poor. Integrity and uprightness in an inferior office are the way to be preferred to a higher station in the church: *They purchase to themselves a good degree.* This will also give a man great boldness in the faith, whereas a want of integrity and uprightness will make a man timorous.

Verses 14–16

He hoped shortly to come to him, to give him further directions and assistance in his work, and he therefore wrote the more briefly to him.

But he wrote *lest he should tarry long, that* Timothy *might know how to behave himself in the house of God.*

I. Ministers ought to behave themselves well: their office binds them to their good behaviour, for any behaviour will not do in this case. The church is the house of God, he dwells there.

JAMIESON, FAUSSET, BROWN

(Rom. 16:25; I Cor. 2:7-10), *in a pure conscience* (ch. 1:5, 19). ("Pure," i.e., in which nothing base or foreign is intermixed [TITTMANN]). **10.** "And moreover . . ." [ALFORD]. **be proved**—not by a period of probation, but by a searching inquiry, conducted by Timothy, the ordaining president (ch. 5:22), whether they be "blameless"; then when found so, "let them act as deacons." **blameless**—*Greek,* "unexceptionable"; as the result of public investigation unaccused [TITTMANN]. **11. their wives**—rather, "the women," i.e., *the deaconesses.* For there is no reason that special rules should be laid down as to the wives of the deacons, and not also as to the wives of the bishops or overseers. Moreover, if the wives of the deacons were meant, there seems no reason for the omission of "their" (not in the *Greek*). Also the *Greek* for "even so" (the same as for "likewise," vs. 8, and "in like manner," ch. 2:9), denotes a transition to another class of persons. Further, there were doubtless deaconesses at Ephesus, such as Phœbe was at Cenchrea (Rom. 16:1, "servant," *Greek,* "deaconess"), yet no mention is made of them in this Epistle if not here; whereas, supposing them to be meant here, ch. 3 embraces in due proportion all the persons in the service of the Church. Naturally after specifying the qualifications of the deacon, Paul passes to those of the kindred office, the deaconess. "Grave" occurs in the case of both. "Not slanderers" here, answers to "not double-tongued" in the deacons; so "not false accusers" (Titus 2:3). "Sober" here answers to "not given to much wine," in the case of the deacons (vs. 8). Thus it appears he requires the same qualifications in female deacons as in deacons, only with such modifications as the difference of sex suggested. PLINY, in his celebrated letter to Trajan, *calls* them "female ministers." **faithful in all things**—of life as well as faith. Trustworthy in respect to the alms committed to them and their other functions, answering to "not greedy of filthy lucre," vs. 8, in the case of the deacons. **12. husbands of one wife**—(*Note,* vs. 2). **ruling their children**—There is no article in the *Greek,* "ruling children"; implying that he regarded the *having children to rule* as a qualification (vs. 4; Titus 1:6). **their own houses**—as distinguished from "the Church of God" (*Note,* vs. 5). In the case of the deacons, as in that of the bishops, he mentions the first condition of receiving office, rather than the special qualifications for its discharge.

13. purchase to themselves a good degree—lit., "are *acquiring* . . . a . . . *step.*" Therefore, what those who have faithfully discharged the diaconate acquire for themselves is "a good standing-place" [ALFORD] (a well-grounded *hope* of salvation) against the day of judgment, ch. 6:19; I Cor. 3:13, 14 (the figurative meaning of "degree" or "step," being *the degree of worth* which one has obtained in the eye of God [WIESINGER]); and boldness (resting on that *standing-place*), as well for preaching and admonishing others now (Eph. 6:19; a firm standing forth for the truth against error), as also especially in relation to God their coming Judge, before whom they may be boldly confident (Acts 24:16; I John 2:28; 3:21; 4:17; Heb. 4:16). **in the faith**—rather as *Greek,* "in faith," i.e., boldness resting on their own faith. **which is in Christ Jesus**—resting *in* Christ Jesus. **14. write I . . . hoping**—i.e., "though I hope to come unto thee shortly" (ch. 4:13). As his hope was not very confident (vs. 15), he provides for Timothy's lengthened superintendence by giving him the preceding rules to guide him. He now proceeds to give more general instructions to him as an evangelist, having a "gift" committed to him (ch. 4:14). **shortly**—*Greek,* "sooner,' viz., than is presupposed in the preceding directions given to him.

15. But if I tarry long—before coming to thee. **that**—i.e., I *write* (vs. 14) "that thou mayest know. . . ." **behave thyself**—in directing the Church at Ephesus (ch. 4:11). **the house of God**—the Church (Heb. 3:2, 5, 6; 10:21; I Pet. 4:17; I Cor. 3:16, "the temple of God"; Eph. 2:22). **which is**—i.e., inasmuch as it is. **the church**—"the congregation." The fact that the sphere of thy functions is "the congregation of the living God" (who is the ever living Master of the house, II Tim. 2:19, 20, 21), is the strongest motive to faithfulness in this *behavior as president* of a department of the house." *The living God* forms a striking contrast to the lifeless idol, Diana of Ephesus (I Thess. 1:9). He is the fountain of "truth," and the foundation of our "trust" (ch. 4:10). Labor directed to a particular Church is service to the one great house of God, of which each particular Church is a part, and each Christian a lively stone (I Pet. 2:5). **the pillar and ground of the truth**—

ADAM CLARKE

Neither a drunkard, tippler, nor what is called a "jovial companion." All this would be inconsistent with gravity.

10. *Let these also first be proved.* Let them not be young converts or persons lately brought to the knowledge of the truth. This is the same in spirit with what is required of the bishops, v. 6. *Being found blameless.* Being irreproachable; persons against whom no evil can be proved. The same as in v. 2, though a different word is used.

11. *Even so must their wives be grave.* I believe the apostle does not mean here the *wives* of either the bishops or the deacons in particular, but the Christian "women" in general. The original is simply: "Let the women likewise be grave." Whatever is spoken here becomes women in general; but if the apostle had those termed "deaconesses" in his eye, which is quite possible, the words are peculiarly suitable to them.

Not slanderers. Literally "not devils." See on v. 7. This may be properly enough translated *slanderers,* for all these are of their father, the devil, and his lusts they will do. *Faithful in all things.* The deaconesses had much to do among the poor, and especially among poor women, in dispensing the bounty of the church. They were not only faithfully to expend all they had got, and for the purpose for which they got it, but they must do this with impartiality, showing no respect of persons.

12. *Let the deacons be the husbands of one wife.* This is the same that is required of the bishops. See on vv. 2, 4-5.

13. *That have used the office of a deacon well.* They who, having been tried or proved, v. 10, have shown by their steadiness, activity, and zeal that they might be raised to a higher office are here said to have purchased *to themselves a good degree,* for instead of having to administer to the bodily wants of the poor, the faithful deacons were raised to minister in holy things; and instead of ministering the bread that perisheth, they were raised to the presbyterate or episcopate, to minister the bread of life to immortal souls. And hence the apostle adds:

And great boldness in the faith; "great liberty of speech"; i.e., in teaching the doctrines of Christianity, and in expounding the Scriptures, and preaching.

14. *These things write I.* That is, I write only these things, because I hope *to come unto thee shortly.*

15. *But if I tarry long.* That is, notwithstanding I hope to come to you shortly, and therefore do not feel the necessity of writing at large; yet, lest I should be delayed, I write what I judge necessary to direct your conduct in the Church of God. *The house of God.* This is spoken in allusion to the ancient Tabernacle, which was God's house, and in which the symbol of the Divine Majesty dwelt. So the Christian Church is God's house, and every believer is a habitation of God through the Spirit. *The church of the living God.* The assembly in which God lives and works; each member of which is a living stone, all of whom, properly united among themselves, grow up unto a holy temple in the Lord. *The pillar and ground of the truth.* To what, or to whom, does *the pillar and ground of the truth* refer? (1) Some say to Timothy, who is called the pillar,

MATTHEW HENRY

II. It is the great support of the church that it is the church of the living *God.*

1. It is *the pillar and ground of truth.* (1) The church itself is the pillar and ground of truth. The church holds forth the scripture and the doctrine of Christ, as the pillar to which a proclamation is affixed holds forth the proclamation. (2) Others understand it of Timothy. He as an evangelist, he and other faithful ministers, are the pillars and ground of truth; it is their business to maintain the truths of Christ in the church. Let us be diligent and impartial in our own enquiries after truth; let us buy the truth at any rate, and not think much of any pains to discover it. Let us be careful to keep and preserve it. Let us take care to publish it.

2. But what is the truth which the churches and ministers are the pillars and grounds of? He tells us (*v.* 16).

(1) Christianity is a mystery that could not have been found out by reason or the light of nature, because it is above reason, though not contrary thereto. It is a mystery of godliness, and herein it exceeds all the mysteries of the Gentiles.

(2) It is Christ. [1] He is God manifest in the flesh.

[2] He is *justified in the Spirit.* Whereas he was reproached as a sinner, and put to death as a malefactor, being raised again, he was justified in the Spirit.

[3] He was *seen of angels.* Angels ministered to him, for he is the Lord of angels. [4] He is *preached unto the Gentiles.* This is a great part of the mystery of godliness, that Christ was offered to the Gentiles a Redeemer and Saviour.

JAMIESON, FAUSSET, BROWN

evidently predicated of *the Church,* not of "the mystery of godliness" (an interpretation not started till the 16th century; so BENGEL); for after two weighty predicates, "pillar and ground," and these substantives, the third, a much weaker one, and that an adjective, "confessedly," or "without controversy great," would not come. "Pillar" is so used metaphorically of the three apostles on whom principally the Jewish Christian Church depended (Gal. 2:9; cf. Rev. 3:12). The Church is "the pillar of the truth," as the continued existence (historically) of the truth rests on it; for it supports and preserves the word of truth. He who is of the truth belongs by the very fact to the Church. Christ is the alone ground of the truth in the highest sense (I Cor. 3: 11). The apostles are foundations in a secondary sense (Eph. 2:20; Rev. 21:14). The Church rests on the truth as it is in Christ; not the truth on the Church. But the truth *as it is in itself* is to be distinguished from the truth *as it is acknowledged in the world.* In the former sense it needs no *pillar,* but supports itself; in the latter sense, it needs the Church as its pillar, i.e., its supporter and preserver [BAUMGARTEN]. The importance of Timothy's commission is set forth by reminding him of the excellence of "the house" in which he serves; and this in opposition to the coming heresies which Paul presciently forewarns him of immediately after (ch. 4: 1). **16. And**—following up vs. 15: The pillar of the truth is the Church in which thou art required to minister; "AND (that thou mayest know how grand is that *truth* which the Church so upholds) confessedly (so the *Greek* for 'without controversy') great is the mystery of godliness: (viz.) HE WHO (so the oldest MSS. and versions read for 'God') was manifested in (the) flesh (He who) was justified in the Spirit. . . . There is set before us the whole dignity of Christ's person. If He were not essentially superhuman (Titus 2:13), how could the apostle emphatically declare that He was *manifested in* (the) *flesh*? [TREGELLES, *Printed text, Greek New Testament.*] (John 1:14; Phil. 2:7; I John 1:2; 4:2.) Christ, in all His aspects, is Himself "the mystery of godliness." He who before was hidden "with God" was made *manifest* (John 1:1, 14; Rom. 16:25, 26; Col. 1:26; II Tim. 1:10; Titus 2:11; 3:4; I John 3:5, 8). "Confessedly," i.e., by the universal confession of the members of "the Church," which is in this respect the "pillar" or upholder "of *the truth.*" **the mystery**—the divine scheme embodied in CHRIST (Col. 1:27), once hidden from, but now revealed to, us who believe. **of godliness**—rather, "piety"; a different *Greek,* expresses godliness (ch. 2:10). In opposition to the *ungodliness* or *impiety* inseparable from error (*departure from the faith:* "doctrines of devils," "profane fables," ch. 4:1, 7; cf. ch. 6:3). To the victims of such error, the "mystery of piety" (i.e., Christ Himself) remains a *mystery unrevealed* (ch. 4:2). **justified**—i.e., approved to be righteous [ALFORD]. Christ, while "in the flesh," seemed to be just such a one as men in the flesh, and in fact bore their *sins;* but by having died to sin, and having risen again, He gained for Himself and His people *justifying righteousness* (Isa. 50:8; John 16:10; Acts 22:14; Rom. 4:25; 6:7, 10; Heb. 9:28; I Pet. 3:18; 4:1; I John 2:1) [BENGEL]; or rather, as the antithesis to "was manifest in the flesh" requires, He was justified in the Spirit *at the same time* that He was manifest in the flesh, i.e., He was vindicated as divine "in His Spirit," i.e., in *His higher nature;* in contrast to "in the flesh," *His visible human nature.* This contrasted opposition requires "in the Spirit" to be thus explained: not "by the Spirit," as ALFORD explains it. So Romans 1:3, 4, "Made of the seed of David according to the flesh, and *declared to be the Son of God with power,* according to the Spirit of holiness, by the resurrection from the dead." So "justified" is used to mean *vindicated in one's true character* (Matt. 11:19; Luke 7:35; Rom. 3:4). **seen of angels**—answering to "preached unto the Gentiles" (or rather "among *the nations*"; including the Jews), on the other hand (Matt. 28:19; Rom. 16:25, 26). "Angels saw the Son of God with us, not having seen Him before" [CHRYSOSTOM]: "not even they had seen His divine nature, which is not visible to any creature, but they saw Him incarnate" [THEODORET](Eph. 3:8, 10; I Pet. 1:12; cf. Col. 1:16, 20). What angels came to know by *seeing,* the nations learned by *preaching.* He is a new message to the one class as well as to the other; in the wondrous union in His person of things most opposite, viz., heaven and earth, lies "the mystery" [WIESINGER]. If the *English Version,* "Gentiles," be retained, the antithesis will be between the *angels* who are so *near* the Son of God, the Lord of angels, and *the Gentiles*

ADAM CLARKE

because left there to support and defend the truth of God against false doctrines and false teachers; and is so called for the same reason that Peter, James, and John are said to be "pillars," i.e., supporters of the truth of God, Gal. ii. 9. (2) Others suppose that *the pillar and ground of the truth* is spoken of God, and that "who is" should be supplied as referring immediately to *God,* just before. (3) Others think that the words should be understood of *the church of the living God.* That is: The full revelation of God's truth is in the Christian Church.

16. *And without controversy.* "And confessedly, by general consent," it is a thing which no man can or ought to dispute; any phrase of this kind expresses the meaning of the original.

God was manifest in the flesh. Instead of *God,* several MSS., versions, and fathers have "who" or "which." And this is generally referred to the word *mystery; "Great is the mystery of godliness,* which was *manifest in the flesh."*

Justified in the Spirit. By the miracles which were wrought by the apostle in and through the name of Jesus, as well as by His resurrection from the dead, through the energy of the Holy Ghost, by which He was proved to be the Son of God with power. Christ was justified from all the calumnies of the Jews, who crucified Him as an impostor.

Seen of angels. By *angeloi* here, some understand not those celestial or infernal beings commonly called *angels,* but apostles and other persons who became "messengers," to carry far and wide and attest the truth of His resurrection from the dead. If, however, we take the word *seen,* in its Jewish acceptation, for "made known," we may here retain the term *angels* in its common acceptation. For it is certain that previously to our Lord's ascension to heaven these holy beings could have little knowledge of the necessity, reasons, and economy of human salvation; nor of the nature of Christ as God and man. Peter informs us that the "angels desire to look into" these things, 1 Pet. i. 12. And Paul says the same thing, Eph. iii. 9-10. *Preached unto the Gentiles.* This was one grand part of the mystery which had been hidden in God, that the Gentiles should be made fellow heirs with the Jews and be admitted into the kingdom of God.

MATTHEW HENRY

[5] He was *believed on in the world.* Who would have thought that the world, which lay in wickedness, would believe in the Son of God, would take him to be their Saviour who was himself crucified at Jerusalem? [6] He was *received up into glory.* It is not only his ascension that is meant, but his sitting at the right hand of God, where he ever lives. He who was manifest in flesh was God, really and truly God. This makes it to be a mystery. Godliness is a mystery in all its parts and branches. It being a great mystery, we should rather humbly adore it, than curiously pry into it.

Verses 1–5

A prophecy of the apostasy of the latter times.

I. The prophecies concerning antichrist, as well as the prophecies concerning Christ, came from the Spirit. *Some shall depart from the faith,* an apostasy from the faith. Some, not all; for in the worst of times God will have a remnant.

1. One of the great instances of the apostasy, giving heed to doctrines of demons, or concerning demons.

2. The instruments of promoting and propagating this apostasy and delusion. It will be done by hypocrisy of those that speak lies, *v.* 2, who have *their consciences seared with a red-hot iron,* who are perfectly lost to the very first principles of virtue and moral honesty.

Another part of their character is that they forbid to marry, and that they command *to abstain from meats,* and place religion in such abstinence at certain times and seasons.

3. The apostasy of the latter times should not surprise us, because it was expressly foretold by the Spirit. The Spirit speaks expressly, but the oracles of the heathen were always doubtful and uncertain. In such general apostasies all are not carried away, but only some. Men must be hardened, and their consciences seared, before they can depart from the faith, and draw in others to side with them.

JAMIESON, FAUSSET, BROWN

who were so utterly "afar off" (Eph. 2:17). **believed on in the world**—which lieth in wickedness (I John 2:15; 5:19). Opposed to "glory" (John 3:16, 17). This followed upon His being "preached" (Rom. 10:14). **received up into glory**—*Greek,* "in glory." However, *English Version* may be retained thus, "Received up (*so as now to be*) *in* glory," i.e., *into glory* (Mark 16:19; Luke 24:51; Acts 1:11). His reception in heaven answers to His reception on earth by being "believed on."

CHAPTER 4

Vss. 1-16. Prediction of a Coming Departure from the Faith: Timothy's Duty as to It: General Directions to Him. The "mystery of iniquity" here alluded to, and already working (II Thess. 2:7), stands opposed to the "mystery of godliness" just mentioned (I Timothy 3:16). **1. Now**—*Greek,* "But." In contrast to the "mystery of godliness." **the Spirit**—speaking by the prophets in the Church (whose prophecies rested on those of the Old Testament, Dan. 7:25; 8:23, etc.; 11:30, as also on those of Jesus in the New Testament, Matt. 24:11-24), and also by Paul himself, II Thessalonians 2:3 (with whom accord II Pet. 3:3; I John 2:18; Jude 18). **expressly**—"in plain words." This shows that he refers to prophecies of the Spirit then lying before him. **in the latter times**—in the times *following upon the times in which he is now writing.* Not some remote future, but times *immediately subsequent,* the beginnings of the apostasy being already discernible (Acts 20:29): these are the forerunners of "the *last* days" (II Tim. 3:1). **depart from the faith**—The apostasy was to be within the Church, the faithful one becoming the harlot. **giving heed**—(ch. 1:4; Titus 1:14). **seducing spirits**—working in the heretical teachers. I John 4:2, 3, 6, "the spirit of error," opposed to "the spirit of truth," "the Spirit" which "speaketh" in the true prophets against them. **doctrines of devils**—lit., "teachings of (i.e. suggested by) demons." James 3:15, "wisdom . . . devilish"; II Corinthians 11:15, "Satan's ministers." **2.** Rather translate, "Through (lit., '*in*'; the element *in* which the apostasy has place) the hypocrisy of lying speakers"; this expresses the means *through* which "some shall (be led to) depart from the faith," viz., the feigned sanctity of the seducers (cf. "deceivers," Titus 1:10). **having their conscience seared**—*Greek,* "having *their own* conscience . . ., i.e., not only "speaking lies" *to others,* but also having *their own* conscience seared. Professing to lead others to holiness, *their* own conscience is all the while defiled. Bad consciences always have recourse to hypocrisy. As *faith* and a *good conscience* are joined (ch. 1:5); so *hypocrisy* (i.e., *unbelief,* Matt. 24:5, 51; cf. Luke 12:46) and a *bad conscience* here. Theodoret explains like *English Version,* "seared," as implying their extreme *insensibility;* the effect of cauterizing being to deaden sensation. The *Greek,* however, primarily means "branded" with the consciousness of crimes committed against their better knowledge and conscience, like so many scars burnt in by a branding-iron. Cf. Titus 1:15; 3:11, "condemned of himself." **3.** Sensuality leads to false spiritualism. Their own inward impurity is reflected in their eyes in the world without them, and hence their asceticism (Titus 1:14, 15) [Wiesinger]. By a spurious spiritualism (II Tim. 2:18), which made moral perfection consist in abstinence from outward things, they pretended to attain to a higher perfection. Austerity gained for them a show of sanctity while preaching false doctrine (Col. 2:23). Eusebius (*Ecclesiastical History,* 4. 29) quotes from Irenæus (1. 28) a statement that Saturninus, Marcion, and the Encratites preached abstinence from marriage and animal meats. Paul prophetically warns against such notions, the seeds of which already were being sown (ch. 6:20; II Tim. 2:17, 18). **to be received**—*Greek,* "to be partaken of." **of them**—lit., (created and designed) "*for* them," Though *all* (even the unbelieving, Ps. 104:14; Matt. 5:45) are partakers in these foods created by God, "they which believe" alone fulfil God's design in creation *by partaking of them with thanksgiving;* as opposed to those who *abstain* from them, or in partaking of them, do not do so *with thanksgiving.* The unbelieving have not the designed use of such foods by reason of their "conscience being defiled" (Titus 1:15). The children of God alone "inherit the earth"; for obedience is the necessary qualification (as it was in the original grant of the earth to Adam), which they

ADAM CLARKE

Believed on in the world. Was received by mankind as the promised Messiah, the Anointed of God, and the only Saviour of fallen man. *Received up into glory.* Even that human nature which He took of the Virgin Mary was not only raised from the grave but taken up into glory. His reception into glory is of the utmost consequence to the Christian faith; as, in consequence, Jesus Christ in His human nature ever appears before the throne as our Sacrifice and as our Mediator.

CHAPTER 4

1. *Now the Spirit speaketh expressly.* "Manifestly, openly." It is very likely that the apostle refers here to a prophecy then furnished by the Holy Ghost, and probably immediately after he had written the words in the preceding verses; and as this prophecy contains things nowhere else spoken of in the sacred writings and of the utmost moment to the Christian Church, we cannot hear or read them with too much reverence or respect.

In the latter times. This does not necessarily imply the last ages of the world, but any times consequent to those in which the Church then lived. *Depart from the faith.* They will "apostatize" from the faith, i.e., from Christianity; renouncing the whole system in effect, by bringing in doctrines which render its essential truths null and void, or denying and renouncing such doctrines as are essential to Christianity as a system of salvation. A man may hold all the truths of Christianity, and yet render them of none effect by holding other doctrines which counteract their influence; or he may apostatize by denying some essential doctrine, though he bring in nothing heterodox. *Giving heed to seducing spirits.* Pretenders to inspiration and false teachers of every kind belong to this class. *And doctrines of devils.* "Demons."

2. *Speaking lies in hypocrisy.* Persons pretending, not only to divine inspiration, but also to extraordinary degrees of holiness, self-denial, mortification, in order to accredit the *lies* and false doctrines which they taught. *Having their conscience seared with a hot iron.* They bear the marks of their hypocrisy as evidently and as indelibly in their conscience in the sight of God as those who have been cauterized for their crimes do in their bodies in the sight of men. It was customary in ancient times to mark those with a *hot iron* who had been guilty of great crimes, such as sacrilege.

3. *Forbidding to marry.* These hypocritical priests pretending that a single life was much more favorable to devotion and to the perfection of the Christian life. This sentiment was held by the Essenes, a religious sect among the Jews; and we know that it is a favorite opinion among the Romanists, who oblige all their clergy to live a single life by a vow of continency. *To abstain from meats.* Both among the heathens, Jews, and Romanists, certain *meats* were prohibited; some always, others at particular times. This the apostle informs us was directly contrary to the original design of God, and says that those who *know the truth* know this.

MATTHEW HENRY

II. The apostle takes occasion to lay down the doctrine of the Christian liberty,—that, whereas under the law there was a distinction of meats between clean and unclean, all this is now taken away. We are to look upon our food as that which God has created; we have it from him, and therefore must use it for him. We must not refuse the gifts of God's bounty, nor be scrupulous in making differences where God has made none; but receive them, and be thankful, *v.* 4. God's good creatures are then good, and doubly sweet to us, when they are received with thanksgiving, *v.* 5. It is a desirable thing to have a sanctified use of our creature-comforts. Now they are sanctified to us: By the word of God. By prayer, which blesses our meat to us. Every creature is God's, for he made all. Every creature of God is good. The blessing of God makes every creature nourishing to us, and therefore nothing ought to be refused. We ought therefore to sanctify the creatures we receive by prayer.

Verses 6–16

The apostles reckoned it a main part of their work to put their hearers in remembrance; for we are apt to forget, and slow to learn and remember, the things of God. The best way for ministers to grow in knowledge and faith is to put the brethren in remembrance; while we teach others, we teach ourselves.

I. Godliness is here pressed upon him and others, *v,* 7, 8. Those who would be godly must exercise themselves unto godliness; it requires a constant exercise. What will it avail us to mortify the body if we do not mortify sin? There is a great deal to be got by godliness. The promises made to godly people relate to the life that now is, but especially they relate to the life that is to come. If godly people have but little of the good things of the life that now is, yet it shall be made up to them in the good things of the life that is to come. It is not enough that we refuse profane and old wives' fables, but we must exercise ourselves to godliness.

II. The encouragement which we have to proceed in the ways of godliness (*v.* 8). Will the profit balance the loss?

JAMIESON, FAUSSET, BROWN

alone possess. **and know the truth**—explanatory and defining who are "they which believe." Translate as *Greek,* "and have *full* knowledge of the truth" (*Note,* Phil. 1:9). Thus he contradicts the assumption of superior *knowledge* and higher moral perfection, put forward by the heretics, on the ground of their abstinence from marriage and meats. "The *truth*" stands in opposition to their "*lies*" (vs. 2). **4, 5.** Translate as *Greek,* "Because" (expressing a reason resting on an *objective fact;* or, as here, a Scripture quotation)—"For" (a reason resting on something *subjective* in *the writer's mind*). **every creature . . . good**—(Gen. 1:31; Rom. 14:14, 20). A refutation by anticipation of the Gnostic opposition to creation: the seeds of which were now lurking latently in the Church. Judaism (Acts 10: 11-16; I Cor. 10:25, 26) was the starting-point of the error as to meats: Oriental Gnosis added new elements. The old Gnostic heresy is now almost extinct; but its remains in the celibacy of Rome's priesthood, and in its fasts from animal meats, enjoined under the penalty of mortal sin, remain. **if . . . with thanksgiving**—Meats, though pure in themselves, become impure by being received with an unthankful mind (Rom. 14:6; Titus 1:15). **5. sanctified**—"hallowed"; set apart as holy for the use of believing men: separated from "the creature," which is under *the bondage of vanity and corruption* (Romans 8:19, etc.). **word of God and prayer**—i.e., "by means of *intercessory* prayer" (so the *Greek*)—i.e., *consecratory* prayer in behalf of "the creature" or food—that prayer mainly consisting of "the word of God." **6. If thou put . . . in remembrance**—rather as *Greek,* "If thou *suggest* to (bring under the notice of) the brethren. . . ." **these things**—viz., the truths stated in vss. 4, 5, in opposition to the errors foretold, vss. 1-3. **minister**—"servant." **nourished up**—The *Greek* is *present,* not *past:* "*continually being* nourished in" (II Tim. 1:5; 3:14, 15). **the words of faith**—rather, ". . . of *the* faith" (cf. vs. 12). **good doctrine**—"the good *teaching.*" Explanatory of "the faith," in opposition to the "teachings of demons" (*English Version,* "doctrines of devils," vs. 1) which Timothy was to counteract. Cf. "sound doctrine" (ch. 1:10; 6:3; Titus 1:9; 2:1). **whereunto thou hast attained**—"the *course* of which thou hast *followed*"; hast *followed along* by tracing its course and accompanying it [ALFORD]. Thou hast begun to follow up [BENGEL]. The same *Greek* occurs, "thou hast fully known" (II Tim. 3: 10), "having had perfect understanding" (Luke 1: 3). It is an undesigned coincidence that the *Greek* verb is used only by Paul and *Paul's companion,* Luke. **7. refuse**—reject, avoid, *have nothing to do with* (II Tim. 2:23; Titus 3:10.) **old wives' fables**—anile myths (ch. 1:4, 9; Titus 1:14). They are "profane," because leading away from "godliness" or "piety" (ch. 1:4-7; 6:20; II Tim. 2:16; Titus 1:1, 2). **exercise thyself**—lit., "exercise thyself" as one undergoing training in a gymnasium. Let thy self-discipline be not in ascetical exercises as the false teachers (vss. 3, 8; cf. II Tim. 2:22, 23; Heb. 5:14; 12:11), but with a view to godliness or "piety" (ch. 6:11, 12). **8. profiteth little**—*Greek,* "profiteth to (but) a small extent." Paul does not deny that fasting and abstinence from conjugal intercourse for a time, with a view to reaching the inward man through the outward, do profit somewhat, Acts 13: 3; I Corinthians 7:5, 7; 9:26, 27 (though in its degenerate form, asceticism, dwelling solely on what is outward, vs. 3, is not only not profitable but injurious). Timothy seems to have had a leaning to such outward self-discipline (cf. ch. 5:23). Paul, therefore, while not disapproving of this in its due proportion and place, shows the vast superiority of *godliness* or *piety,* as being *profitable* not merely "to a small extent," but unto *all* things; for, having its seat within, it extends thence to the whole outward life of a man.
having promise . . .—Translate as *Greek,* "Having promise of life, that which now is, and that which is to come." "Life" in its truest and best sense now and hereafter (II Tim. 1:1). Length of life now so far as it is really good for the believer; life in its truest enjoyments and employments now, and life blessed and eternal hereafter (Matt. 6:33; Mark 10:29, 30). "Now in this time" (Ps. 84:11; 112: Rom. 8:28; I Cor. 3:21, 22, "*all* things are yours . . . the world, life . . . things present, things to come"). Christianity, which seems to aim only at our happiness hereafter, effectually promotes it here (ch. 6:6; II Pet. 1:3). Cf. Solomon's prayer and the answer (I Kings 3:7-13). **9.** (Ch. 1:15.) This verse (*Greek*), "faithful is the saying . . ." confirms the assertion as to the "promise" attached to "godliness," vs. 8, and forms a prefatory introduction to vs. 10, which is joined to vs. 9 by "For." So II

ADAM CLARKE

4. *For every creature of God is good.* That is, every creature which God has made for man's nourishment is good for that purpose, and to be thankfully received whenever necessary for the support of human life; and *nothing* of that sort is at any time *to be refused,* "rejected or despised."

5. *For it is sanctified by the word of God.* "By the command of God"; probably referring to Gen. i. 29: "And God said . . . I have given you every herb . . . and every tree . . . to you it shall be for meat"; and to chap. ix. 3: "Every moving thing that liveth shall be meat for you; even as the green herb have I given you all things"; i.e., I have given you every animal that is proper for food, as I have given you every herb and fruit proper for nourishment. Therefore all this was sanctified, "set apart," and appropriated to this use by this command. And when man is about to use it, he is to sanctify or set it apart to that use by *prayer* to God.

6. *If thou put the brethren in remembrance of these things.* Show the church that even now there is danger of this apostasy; put them on their guard against it, for the forewarned are half armed. *Nourished up in the words of faith.* By acting as I command you, you will show that you are a good minister of Jesus Christ, and that you have been nourished from your youth up in the doctrines of faith. The apostle seems to allude here to Timothy's Christian education. *Whereunto thou hast attained.* Which you have "thoroughly understood."

7. *But refuse profane and old wives' fables.* This seems to refer particularly to the Jews, whose Talmudical writings are stuffed with the most ridiculous and profane fables that ever disgraced the human intellect. It may with equal propriety be applied to the legends of the Romish church. *Exercise thyself rather unto godliness.* To understand this expression it is necessary to know that the apostle alludes here to the gymnastic exercises among the Greeks, which were intended as a preparation for their contests at the public games.

8. *For bodily exercise profiteth little.* Those gymnastic exercises, so highly esteemed among the Greeks, are but little worth; they are but of short duration; they refer only to this life, and to the applause of men. But godliness has the promise of this life and the life to come; it is profitable for all things, and for both time and eternity. *But godliness is profitable unto all things.* By *godliness* we are to understand everything that the Christian religion either promises or prescribes: the life of God in the soul of man and the glory of God as the object and end of that life. *Having promise of the life that now is.* The man that fears, loves, and serves God has God's blessing all through life. His religion saves him from all those excesses in both action and passion which sap the foundations of life and render existence itself often a burden. The peace and love of God in the heart produce a serenity and calm which cause the lamp of life to burn clear, strong, and permanent.

MATTHEW HENRY

Here is another of Paul's faithful sayings, worthy of all acceptation—that all our labours and losses in the service of God will be abundantly recompenced, so that though we lose for Christ we shall not lose by him, *v.* 10.

1. Toil and trouble are to be expected by us in this world, not only as men, but as saints.

2. Those who labour and suffer reproach in the service of God may depend upon the living God that they shall not lose by it. Let this encourage them. He is *the Saviour of all men.* Now, if he be thus the Saviour of all men, we may hence infer that much more he will be the rewarder of those who seek and serve him. The salvation he has in store for those that believe is sufficient to recompence them for all their services and sufferings. The life of a Christian is a life of labour and suffering: *We labour and suffer.* The best we can expect to suffer in the present life is reproach for our well-doing, for our work of faith and labour of love.

III. An exhortation to Timothy,

1. To *command and teach these things* that he had now been teaching him.

2. To conduct himself with that gravity and prudence which might gain him respect, notwithstanding his youth. Men's youth will not be despised if they do not by youthful vanities and follies make themselves despicable; and this men may do who are old, who may therefore thank themselves if they be despised.

3. To confirm his doctrine by a good example. Those who teach by their doctrine must teach by their life, else they pull down with one hand what they build up with the other.

4. He charges him to study hard, *v.* 13. Though Timothy had extraordinary gifts, yet he must use ordinary means. Or it may be meant of the public reading of the scriptures; he must *read and exhort.* He must teach them both what to do and what to believe. The best way for ministers to avoid being despised is to teach and practise the things that are given them in charge. Those ministers that are the best accomplished for their work must yet mind their studies, and they must mind also their work.

5. He charges him to beware of negligence, *v.* 14. The gifts of God will wither if they be neglected.

JAMIESON, FAUSSET, BROWN

Timothy 2:11. Godly men seem to suffer loss as to this life: Paul hereby refutes the notion [BENGEL]. "God is the *Saviour* specially of those that believe" (vs. 10), both as to "the life that now is," and also as to "the life which is to come" (vs. 8). **10. therefore**—*Greek,* "with a view to this." *The reason why* "we both ('both' is omitted in the oldest MSS.) labor (endure hardship) and suffer reproach (some oldest MSS. read 'strive') is *because* we have rested, and do rest our hope, on the living (and therefore, *life-giving,* vs. 8) God." **Saviour**—even in this life (vs. 8). **specially of those that believe**—Their "labor and reproach" are not inconsistent with their having from the living God, their Saviour, even the present life (Mark 10:30, "a hundred fold now in this time . . . with persecutions"), much more the life to come. If God is in a sense "Saviour" of unbelievers (ch. 2:4, i.e., is *willing* to be so *everlastingly,* and *is temporally here* their *Preserver* and *Benefactor*), much more of believers. He is the Saviour of all men *potentially* (ch. 1:15); of believers alone *effectually.* **11.** These truths, to the exclusion of those useless and even injurious teachings (vss. 1-8), while weighing well thyself, charge also upon others.

12. Let no man despise thy youth—Act so as to be respected in spite of thy youth (I Cor. 16:11; Titus 2:15); cf. "youthful" as to Timothy (II Tim. 2:22). He was but a mere youth when he joined Paul (Acts 16:1-3). Eleven years had elapsed since then to the time subsequent to Paul's first imprisonment. He was, therefore, still young; especially in comparison with Paul, whose place he was filling; also in relation to elderly presbyters whom he should "entreat as a father" (ch. 5:1), and generally in respect to his duties in rebuking, exhorting, and ordaining (ch. 3:1), which ordinarily accord best with an elderly person (ch. 5:19). **be thou an example**—*Greek, "become a pattern"* (Titus 2:7); the true way of making men not to despise (slight, or disregard) thy youth. **in word**—in all that thou sayest in public and private. **conversation**—i.e., "behavior" the Old English sense of the word. **in charity . . . faith**—the two cardinal principles of the Christian (Gal. 5:6). The oldest MSS. omit, "in spirit."

in purity—simplicity of holy motive followed out in consistency of holy action [ALFORD] (ch. 5:22; II Cor. 6:6; Jas. 3:17; 4:8; I Pet. 1:22). **13. Till I come**—when Timothy's commission would be superseded for the time by the presence of the apostle himself (ch. 1:3; 3:14). **reading**—especially in the public congregation. The practice of reading Scripture was transferred from the Jewish synagogue to the Christian Church (Luke 4:16-20; Acts 13:15; 15:21; II Cor. 3:14). The New Testament Gospel and Epistles being recognized as inspired by those who had the gift of *discerning spirits,* were from the first, according as they were written, read along with the Old Testament in the Church (I Thess. 5:21, 27; Col. 4:16), [JUSTIN MARTYR, *Apology,* 1. 67]. I think that while *public reading* is the prominent thought, the Spirit intended also to teach that Scripture reading in private should be "the fountain of all wisdom from which pastors ought to draw whatever they bring before their flock" [ALFORD]. **exhortation**—addressed to the feelings and will with a view to the regulation of the conduct. **doctrine**—*Greek* (ministerial), "teaching" or *instruction.* Addressed to the understanding, so as to impart knowledge (ch. 6:2; Rom. 12:7, 8). Whether in public or private, *exhortation* and *instruction* should be based on *Scripture reading.* **14. Neglect not the gift**—by letting it lie unused. In II Timothy 1:6 the gift is represented as a *spark* of the Spirit lying within him, and sure to smoulder by neglect, the *stirring up* or keeping in lively exercise of which depends on the will of him on whom it is bestowed (Matt. 25:18, 25, 27, 28). The *charism* or spiritual gift, is that of the Spirit which qualified him for "the work of an evangelist" (Eph. 4:11; II Tim. 4:5), or perhaps *the gift of discerning spirits,* specially needed in his function of ordaining, as overseer [BISHOP HINDS].

ADAM CLARKE

10. *For therefore we both labour.* This verse was necessary to explain what he had before said; and here he shows that his meaning was not that the followers of God should enjoy worldly prosperity and exemption from natural evils; for it is because we exercise ourselves to godliness that we have both labor and reproach, and we have these because we trust in the living God. But still we have mental happiness, and all that is necessary for our passage through life; for in the midst of persecutions and afflictions we have the peace of God that passeth knowledge, and have all our crosses and sufferings so sanctified to us that we consider them in the number of our blessings. *Who is the Saviour of all men.* Who has provided salvation for the whole human race, and has freely offered it to them in His Word and by His Spirit. *Specially of those that believe.* What God intends for all He actually gives to them that believe in Christ.

11. *These things command and teach.* Let it be the sum and substance of your preaching that true religion is profitable for both worlds, that vice destroys both body and soul, that Christ tasted death for every man, and that He saves to the uttermost all them that believe in His name.

12. *Let no man despise thy youth.* Act with all the gravity and decorum which become your situation in the Church. As you are in the place of an elder, act as an elder. *Be thou an example of the believers.* It is natural for the flock to follow the shepherd; if he go wrong, they will go wrong also. *In word.* "In doctrine"; teach nothing but the truth of God, because nothing but that will save souls. *In conversation.* In the whole of your "conduct" in every department which you fill in all your domestic as well as public relations. *In charity.* "In love" to God and man; show that this is the principle and motive of all your conduct. *In spirit.* In the "manner" and "disposition" in which you do all things. These words are wanting in some MSS. They have in all probability been added by a later hand. *In faith.* This word is probably taken here for "fidelity," a sense which it often bears in the New Testament. It cannot mean doctrine, for that has been referred to before. Be faithful to your trust, to your flock, to your domestics, to the public, to your God. "Fidelity" consists in honestly keeping, preserving, and delivering up when required, whatever is intrusted to our care; as also in improving whatever is delivered in trust for that purpose. Lose nothing that God gives, and improve every gift that He bestows. *In purity.* "Chastity" of body and mind; a direction peculiarly necessary for a young minister, who has more temptations to break its rules than perhaps any other person. "Converse sparingly with women, and especially with young women," was the advice of a very holy and experienced minister of Christ.

13. *Give attendance to reading.* Timothy could easily comprehend the apostle's meaning, but at present this is not so easy. What books does the apostle mean? The books of the Old Testament were probably what he intended; these testified of Jesus, and by these he could either convince or confound the Jews. But was the reading of these to be public or private? Probably both. It was customary to read the law and the prophets in the synagogue, and doubtless in the assemblies of the Christians, after which there was generally an exhortation founded upon the subject of the prophecy. Hence the apostle says: *Give attendance to reading, to exhortation, to doctrine.* Timothy was therefore to be diligent in reading the sacred writings at home, that he might be the better qualified to read and expound them in the public assemblies to the Christians and to others who came to these public meetings.

14. *Neglect not the gift that is in thee.* The word here must refer to the "gifts" and "graces" of the divine Spirit, which Timothy received when set apart to the work of an evangelist by the imposition of Paul's hands, 2 Tim. i. 6, and by that of the presbytery or eldership. For it most evidently appears from this verse and that above quoted that he received this double imposition, not probably at different times, but on one and the same occasion. These very gifts and graces might be improved; and we

MATTHEW HENRY

Here see the scripture-way of ordination: it was by the laying on of hands, and the laying on of the hands of the presbytery. The office of the ministry is a gift, it is the gift of Christ, and this was a very kind gift to his church. Ministers ought not to neglect the gift bestowed upon them, whether the office of the ministry or the qualifications for that office.

6. Having this work committed to him, he must *give himself wholly* to it, and make it appear that he improved in knowledge. Ministers are to be much in meditation. They are to meditate on the great trust committed to them. Ministers must be wholly in these things. By this means their profiting will appear in all things.

7. He presses it upon him to be very cautious. This will be the way to *save thyself, and those that hear thee*. "Save thyself in the first place, so shalt thou be instrumental to save those that hear thee." The best way to answer both these ends is to take heed to ourselves.

JAMIESON, FAUSSET, BROWN

given thee—by God (I Cor. 12:4, 6). **by prophecy**—i.e., by the Holy Spirit, at his general ordination, or else consecration, to the special see of Ephesus, speaking through the prophets God's will to give him the graces needed to qualify him for his work (ch. 1:18; Acts 13:1-3). **with . . . laying on of . . . hands**—So in Joshua's case (Num. 27:18-20; Deut. 34:9). The gift was connected with the symbolical act of laying on hands. But the *Greek* "with" implies that the *presbyter's* laying on hands was the mere *accompaniment* of the conferring of the gift. "By" (II Tim. 1:6) implies that *Paul's* laying on his hands was the actual *instrument* of its being conferred. **of the presbytery**—In II Timothy 1:6 the apostle mentions only *his own* laying on of hands. But there his aim is to remind Timothy specially of the part he himself took in imparting to him the gift. Here he mentions the fact, quite consistent with the other, that the neighboring presbyters took part in the ordination or consecration, he, however, taking the foremost part. **15. Meditate**—*Greek*, "*Meditate* CAREFULLY *upon*" (Ps. 1:2; 119:15; cf. "Isaac," Gen. 24:63). **these things**—(vss. 12-14). As food would not nourish without digestion, which assimilates the food to the substance of the body, so spiritual food, in order to benefit us, needs to be appropriated by prayerful meditation. **give thyself wholly to**—lit., "BE *in* these things"; let them engross thee wholly; be wholly absorbed in them. *Entire selfdedication*, as in other pursuits, so especially in religion, is the secret of proficiency. There are changes as to all other studies, fashionable today, out of fashion tomorrow; this study alone is never obsolete, and when made the all-engrossing aim sanctifies all other studies. The exercise of the ministry threatens the spirit of the ministry, unless it be sustained within. The minister must be first his own scholar before he can be another's teacher. **profiting**—*Greek*, "progress" towards perfection in the Christian life, and especially towards the fullest realization of the ideal of a Christian minister (vs. 12). **may appear to all**—not for thy glory, but for the winning of souls (Matt. 5:16). **16. Take heed**—Give heed (Acts 3:5). **thyself, and . . . doctrine**—"and unto thy teaching." The two requisites of a good pastor: His teaching will be of no avail unless his own life accord with it; and his own purity of life is not enough unless he be diligent in teaching [CALVIN]. This verse is a summary of vs. 12. **continue in them**—(II Tim. 3:14). **in doing this**—not "*by* doing this," as though he could save himself by works. **thou shalt . . . save thyself, and them . . .**—(Ezek. 33:9; Jas. 5:20). In performing faithfully his duty to others, the minister is promoting his own salvation. Indeed he cannot "give heed unto the teaching" of others, unless he be at the same time "giving heed unto himself."

ADAM CLARKE

have reason to believe if not improved would be withdrawn by the great Head of the Church. *Given thee by prophecy.* It has already been conjectured that there had been some remarkable prediction relative to the future destiny and usefulness of Timothy. And probably it was in consequence of this that he was set apart to the office of evangelist and bishop in the church at Ephesus.

15. *Meditate upon these things.* Revolve them frequently in your mind; consider deeply their nature and importance; get them deeply fastened in your heart, and let all your conduct flow from this inward feeling and conviction. *Give thyself wholly to them.* "Be thou in these things." Occupy yourself wholly with them; make them not only your chief but your sole concern. You are called to save your own soul and the souls of them that hear you, and God has given you the divine gifts for this and no other purpose. To this let all your reading and study be directed; this is your great business, and you must perform it as the servant and steward of the Lord.

That thy profiting may appear to all. By being made a universal blessing, convincing and converting sinners, and building up the Church of God on its most holy faith.

16. *Take heed unto thyself.* See that the life of God remains and the work of God prospers in your own soul. *Take heed . . . unto the doctrine*, that the matter be pure and orthodox; that you teach nothing for truth but what God has revealed. *Continue in them.* I.e., in taking heed to yourself and to your doctrine, for this must be your continual study.

MATTHEW HENRY

CHAPTER 5

Verses 1, 2

Ministers are reprovers by office; it is a part, though the least pleasing part, of their office. Be very tender in rebuking elders. Respect must be had to the dignity of their years and place. The younger must be rebuked as brethren, with love and tenderness. There is need of a great deal of meekness in reproving those who deserve reproof.

The elder women must be reproved, as mothers. The younger women must be reproved, but reproved as *sisters, with all purity*.

Verses 3-16

The general rule is to *honour widows that are widows indeed*, to maintain them, to relieve them with respect and tenderness.

II. The church should not be charged with the maintenance of those widows who had relations of their own that were able to maintain them (*v.* 4).

JAMIESON, FAUSSET, BROWN

CHAPTER 5

Vss. 1-25. GENERAL DIRECTIONS AS TO HOW TIMOTHY SHOULD DEAL WITH DIFFERENT CLASSES IN THE CHURCH. **1. an elder**—*in age;* probably not an elder *in the ministry;* these latter are not mentioned till vs. 17, "the elders that rule." Cf. Acts 2:17, "your old men," lit., "elders." Contrasted with "the younger men." As Timothy was admonished so to conduct himself as to give no man reason to *despise* his *youth* (ch. 4:12); so here he is told to bear in mind his youth, and to behave with the modesty which becomes a young man in relation to his elders. **Rebuke not**—lit., "Strike not hard upon"; *Rebuke not sharply:* a different word from "rebuke" in II Timothy 4:2. **entreat**—exhort. **as brethren**—and therefore equals; not lording it over them (I Pet. 5:1-3). **2. with all purity**—respectful treatment of the other sex will promote "purity." **3. Honour**—by setting on the church roll, as fit objects of charitable sustenance (vss. 9, 17, 18; Acts 6:1). So "honor" is used for *support* with necessaries (Matt. 15:4, 6; Acts 28:10). **widows indeed**—(vs. 16). Those really desolate; not like those (vs. 4) having children or relations answerable for their support, nor like those (in vs. 6) "who live in pleasure"; but such as, from their earthly desolation as to friends, are most likely to trust wholly in God, persevere in continual prayers, and carry out the religious duties assigned to Church widows (vs. 5). Care for widows was transferred from the Jewish economy to the Christian (Deut. 14:29; 16:11; 24:17, 19). **4. if any widow . . .**—not "a widow indeed," as having children who ought to support her. **nephews**—rather, as *Greek*, "descendants,"

ADAM CLARKE

CHAPTER 5

1. *Rebuke not an elder.* That is, an elderly person; for the word is here taken in its natural sense, and signifies one advanced in years. At v. 17 it is taken in what may be termed its ecclesiastical meaning and signifies an officer in the church, what we commonly call a "presbyter" or "bishop"; for sometimes these terms were confounded. There are but few cases in which it at all becomes a young man to reprove an old man, and especially one who is a father in the church. If such a one does wrong or gets out of the way, he should be entreated as a father, with great caution and respect. *The younger men as brethren.* Showing humility, and arrogating nothing to yourself on account of your office. Feel for them as you ought to feel for your own brethren.

2. *The elder women as mothers.* Treating them with the respect due to their age. *With all purity.* With all chastity.

3. *Honour widows that are widows indeed.* One meaning of the word to *honour* is to "support, sustain," Matt. xv. 4-5; and here it is most obviously to be taken in this sense. Provide for those widows especially which are *widows indeed*—persons truly destitute, being aged and helpless, and having neither children nor friends to take care of them, and who behave as becomes their destitute state.

4. *But if any widow have children or nephews.* This shows that "widows indeed" are those that have neither children nor nephews,

MATTHEW HENRY

So *v.* 16. The respect of children to their parents, with their care of them, is fitly called piety. Children can never sufficiently requite their parents for the care they have taken of them, but they must endeavour to do it.

I. She is to be reckoned a widow indeed, who, being *desolate, trusteth in God, v.* 5, 6. Those who trust in God must *continue in prayer.*

But she is not a widow indeed *that lives in pleasure* (*v.* 6). A jovial widow is not a widow indeed. *She that lives in pleasure is dead while she lives,* is no living member of the church, but as a carcase in it, or a mortified member. They are in the world to no purpose, buried alive as to the great ends of living.

He speaks of this again (*v.* 8). If they spend that upon their lusts which should maintain their families, they have denied the faith (*v.* 16).

III. Directions concerning the characters of the widows that were to receive the church's charity. Particular care ought to be taken to relieve those who, when they had wherewithal, were ready to every good work. Those who would find mercy when they are in distress must show mercy when they are in prosperity.

JAMIESON, FAUSSET, BROWN

or "grandchildren" [HESYCHIUS]. "Nephews" in old English meant "grandchildren" [HOOKER, *Ecclesiastical Polity,* 5. 20]. **let them**–the children and descendants. **learn first**–ere it falls to the Church to support them. **to show piety at home**–filial piety towards their widowed mother or grandmother, by giving her sustenance. Lit., ". . . towards *their own house.*" "Piety is applied to the reverential discharge of filial duties; as the parental relation is the earthly representation of God our heavenly Father's relation to us. *"Their own"* stands in opposition to *the Church,* in relation to which the widow is comparatively a stranger. She has a claim on *her own* children, prior to her claim on the Church; let them fulfil this prior claim which she has on them, by sustaining her and not burden ing the Church. **parents**–*Greek,* (living) "progenitors," i.e., their mother or grandmother, as the case may be. "Let them learn," implies that abuses of this kind had crept into the Church, widows claiming Church support though they had children or grandchildren able to support them. **good and**–The oldest MSS. omit. The words are probably inserted by a transcriber from ch. 2:3. **5. widow indeed, and desolate**–contrasted with her who has children or grandchildren to support her (vs. 4). **trusteth in God**–perfect tense in *Greek,* "hath rested, and doth rest her hope in God." This vs. 5 *adds another* qualification in a widow for Church maintenance, besides her being" desolate" or destitute of children to support her.

in supplications and prayers–*Greek,* "in *her* supplications and prayers"; the former signifies *asking under a sense of need,* the latter, *prayer* (*Notes,* ch. 2:1; Phil. 4:6). **night and day**–another coincidence with Luke (Luke 18:7, "cry day and night"); contrast Satan's accusations "day and night" (Rev. 12:10). **6. she that liveth in pleasure**–the opposite of such a widow as is described in vs. 5, and therefore one utterly undeserving of Church charity. The *Greek* expresses *wanton prodigality* and excess [TITTMANN]. The root expresses *weaving* at a fast rate, and so lavish excess (*Note,* Jas. 5:5). **dead while she liveth**–dead in the Spirit while alive in the flesh (Matt. 8:22; Eph. 5: 14). **7. these things**–just now spoken (vss. 5, 6). **that they may be blameless**–viz., the widows supported by the Church. **8. But**–reverting to vs. 4, "If any (a general proposition; therefore including in its application *the widow's children* or *grandchildren*) provide not for his own (relations in general), and especially for those of his own house (in particular), he hath (practically) denied the faith." Faith without love and its works is dead; "for the subiect matter of faith is not mere opinion, but the grace and truth of God, to which he that believes gives up his spirit, as he that loves gives up his heart" [MACK]. If in any case a duty of love is plain, it is in relation to one's own relatives; to fail in so plain an obligation is a plain proof of want of love, and therefore of want of faith. "Faith does not set aside natural duties, but strengthens them" [BENGEL]. **worse than an infidel**–because even an infidel (or unbeliever) is taught by nature to provide for his own relatives, and generally recognizes the duty; the Christian who does not so, is worse (Matt. 5:46, 47). He has less excuse with his greater light than the infidel who may break the laws of nature. **9.** Translate, "As a widow (i.e., of the ecclesiastical order of *widowhood;* a kind of *female presbytery*), let none be enrolled (in the catalogue) who is less than sixty years old." These were not *deaconesses,* who were chosen at a younger age (forty was the age fixed at the Council of Chalcedon), and who had virgins (in a later age called *widows*) as well as widows among them, but a band of widows set apart, though not yet formally and finally, to the service of God and the Church. Traces of such a class appear in Acts 9:41. Dorcas herself was such a one. As it was expedient (*Note,* ch. 3:2; Titus 1:6) that the presbyter or bishop should have been but once married, so also in her case. **wife of one man**–in order not to throw a stumbling block in the way of Jews and heathen, who regarded with disfavor second marriages (*Note,* ch. 3:2; Titus 1:6). This is the force of "blameless," giving no offense, even in matters indifferent. **10. for good works**–Greek, "IN *honourable* (excellent) works"; the sphere or element *in* which the good report of her had place (Titus 2:7). This answers to ch. 3:7, as to the bishop or presbyter, "He must have a good report of them which are without." **if**–if, in addition to being "well reported of," she . . . . **she . . . brought up children**–either her own (ch. 3:4, 12), or those of others, which is one of the "good works"; a qualification adapting her for ministry to

ADAM CLARKE

i.e., no relatives that either will or can help them, or no near relative alive. *Let them learn first to shew piety at home.* Let these children and nephews provide for their aged or helpless parents or relatives, and not burden the church with them while they are able to support them.

And to requite their parents. Let them learn to give benefit for benefit. Your parents supported and nourished you when you were young and helpless; you ought therefore to support them when they are old and destitute. This is called showing piety; and there is doubtless allusion to the fifth commandment; "Honour thy father and thy mother"—provide for them in their old age and afflictions; God commands this.

5. *And desolate.* "Left entirely alone"—having neither children nor relatives to take care of her. *Trusteth in God.* Finding she has no other helper, she continues in prayer and supplication, that she may derive that from God which, in the course of His providence, He has deprived her of among men.

6. *But she that liveth in pleasure.* "She that liveth delicately"—voluptuously indulging herself with dainties; it does not indicate grossly criminal pleasures, but simply means one who indulges herself in good eating and drinking, pampering her body at the expense of her mind. The word is used in reference to what we term petted and spoiled children. *Is dead while she liveth.* No purpose of life is answered by the existence of such a person. Seneca, in Epist. 60, says of pleasure-takers and those who live a voluptuous life: "We rank such persons with brutes, not with men; and some of them not even with brutes, but with dead carcasses. They anticipate their own death."

8. *But if any provide not for his own.* His own people or relatives. *Those of his own house.* That is, his own family, or a poor widow or relative that lives under his roof. *Hath denied the faith.* The Christian religion, which strongly inculcates love and benevolence to all mankind.

Is worse than an infidel. For what are called the dictates of nature lead men to feel for and provide for their own families. Heathen writers are full of maxims of this kind, Tacitus says: "Nature dictates that to every one his own children and relatives should be most dear." And Cicero, in *Epist. ad Caption.*: "Every man should take care of his own family.

9. *Taken into the number.* Let her not be taken into the list of those for which the church must provide. But some think that the apostle means the list of those who were deaconesses in the church, and that no widow was to be admitted into that rank who did not answer to the following character. *Under threescore years.* As it might be supposed that, previously to this age, they might be able to do something towards their own support. *Having been the wife of one man.* Having lived in conjugal fidelity with her husband, or having had but one husband at a time; or, according to others, having never been but once married. But the former is the opinion of some of the most eminent of the Greek fathers, and appears to be that most consistent with the scope of the place and with truth.

10. *Well reported of for good works.* Numbers being able to "bear testimony," as the word implies, that she has not only avoided all sin but that she has walked according to the testimony of God. *Brought up children.* It was customary among the Gentiles to expose their children, when so poor that they were not able to provide for them. Pious and humane people took these up and fed, clothed, and educated them. The words *brought up* may refer to the

MATTHEW HENRY

IV. Take heed of admitting into the number those who are likely to be no credit to them (*v.* 11): *The younger widows refuse;* they will be weary of living by rule, as they must do; so they *will marry, and cast off their first faith.*

ALBERT BARNES:

"Because they have cast off their first faith." This does not mean that they would lose all their religion or wholly fall away, but that this would show that they had not the strong faith, the deadness to the world, the simple dependence on God (v. 5), and the desire which they had to be weaned from worldly cares and influences, which they once had. When they became widows, all their earthly hopes seemed to be blasted. They were then dead to the world and felt their sole dependence on God. But if, under the influence of these strong emotions, they were admitted to the "class of widows" in the church, there was no certainty that they would continue in this state of mind. Time would do much to modify their grief. There would be a reviving love of the world, and under the influence of this they would be disposed to enter again into the marriage relation, and thus show that they had not the strong and simple faith which they had when the blow which made them widows fell heavily upon them.
—*Popular Commentary*

The apostle here advises the younger widows to marry (*v.* 14). It is seldom that those who are idle are idle only; they learn to make mischief among neighbours, and sow discord among brethren. If housekeepers do not mind their business, but are tattlers, they give occasion to the adversaries of Christianity to reproach the Christian name. In the primitive church there was care taken of poor widows, and the churches of Christ in these days should follow so good an example.

Great care is to be taken that those share in the public bounty who most want it and best deserve it. The credit of religion, and the reputation of Christian churches, are very much concerned in the character and behaviour of those that receive alms of the church. Christianity obliges its professors to relieve their indigent friends.

Rich people should be ashamed to burden the church with their poor relations.

JAMIESON, FAUSSET, BROWN

orphan children, and to mothers of families. **lodged strangers**—ch. 3:2, "given to hospitality" (Titus 1:8); in the case of *presbyters.* **washed . . . saints' feet**—after the example of the Lord (John 13: 14); a specimen of the universal spirit of humbly "by love serving one another," which actuated the early Christians. **relieved the afflicted**—whether by pecuniary or other relief. **followed . . . good**—(I Thess. 5:15; cf. instances in Matt. 25:35, 36). **11. younger**—than sixty years old (vs. 9). **refuse**—to take on the roll of presbyteress widows. **wax wanton**—lit., "over-strong" (II Chron. 26:16). **against Christ**—rebelling against Christ, their proper Bridegroom [JEROME]. **they will**—*Greek,* "they wish"; their *desire* is to marry again. **12. Having** —Bringing on themselves, and so *having* to bear as a burden (Gal. 5:10) *judgment* from God (cf. ch. 3:6), weighing like a load on them. **cast off their first faith**—viz., pledged to Christ and the service of the Church. There could be no hardship at the age of sixty or upwards in not marrying again (end of vs. 9), for the sake of serving better the cause of Christ as presbyteresses; though, to ordinary widows, no barrier existed against re-marriage (I Cor. 7:39). This is altogether distinct from Rome's unnatural vows of celibacy in the case of young marriageable women. The widow-presbyteresses, moreover, engaged to remain single, not as though single life were holier than married life (according to Rome's teaching), but because the interests of Christ's cause made it desirable (*Note,* ch. 3:2). They had pledged "their first faith" to Christ as presbyteress widows; they now wish to transfer their faith to a husband (cf. I Cor. 7:32, 34). **13. withal**—"at the same time, moreover." **learn**—usually in a good sense. But these women's "learning" is *idleness, trifling,* and *busybodies' tattle.* **wandering**—*Greek,* "going about." **from house to house**—of the members of the Church (II Tim. 3:6). "They carry the affairs of this house to that, and of that to this; they tell the affairs of all to all" [THEOPHYLACT]. **tattlers**—lit., "*trifling* talkers." In III John 10, translated "prating." **busybodies**—mischievously *busy;* inconsiderately *curious* (II Thess. 3:11). Acts 19:19, "curious," the same *Greek. Curiosity* usually springs from idleness, which is itself the mother of *garrulity* [CALVIN]. **speaking**—not merely "*saying.*" The *subject matter,* as well as the *form,* is involved in the *Greek* word [ALFORD]. **which they ought not**—(Titus 1: 11). **14. younger women**—rather, as ellipsis ought to be supplied, "the younger *widows,*" viz., younger widows in general, as distinguished from *the older widows taken on the roll of presbyteresses* (vs. 9). The "therefore" means *seeing that young widows are exposed to such temptations,* "I will," or "desire . . ." (vss. 11-13). The precept here that they should marry again is not inconsistent with I Corinthians 7:40; for the circumstances of the two cases were distinct (cf. I Cor. 7:26). Here remarriage is recommended as an antidote to *sexual passion, idleness,* and the other evils noted in vss. 11-13. Of course, where there was no tendency to these evils, marriage again would not be so requisite; Paul speaks of what is generally desirable, and supposing there should be danger of such evils, as was likely. "He does not impose *a law,* but points out *a remedy,* to younger widows" [CHRYSOSTOM]. **bear children**—(ch. 2:15)—thus gaining one of the qualifications (vs. 10) for being afterwards a presbyteress widow, should Providence so ordain it. **guide**—*Greek,* "*rule* the house" in the woman's due place; not *usurping authority* over the man (ch. 2: 12). **give none occasion**—lit., "starting-point": handle of reproach through the loose conduct of nominal Christians. **the adversary**—of Christianity, Jew or Gentile. Philippians 1:28; Titus 2:8, "He that is of the contrary part." Not *Satan,* who is introduced in a different relation (vs. 15.) **to speak reproachfully**—lit., "for the sake of reproach" (ch. 3:7; 6:1; Titus 2:5, 10). If the *handle* were given, *the adversary* would use it *for the sake of reproach.* The adversary is eager to exaggerate the faults of a few, and to lay the blame on the whole Church and its doctrines [BENGEL]. **15. For**—*For* in the case of some this result has already ensued; "Some (widows) are already turned aside after Satan," the seducer (not by falling away from the faith in general, but) by such errors as are stigmatized in vss. 11-13, sexual passion, idleness, etc., and so have *given occasion of reproach* (vs. 14). "Satan finds some mischief still for the idle hands to do." **16. If any . . . have widows**—of his family, however related to him.

ADAM CLARKE

children of others, who were educated in the Christian faith by pious Christian women. *Lodged strangers.* If she have been given to hospitality, freely contributing to the necessitous, when she had it in her power. *Washed the saints' feet.* This was an office of humanity shown to all strangers and travellers in the Eastern countries, who, either walking barefoot, or having only a sort of sole to defend the foot, needed washing when they came to their journey's end. Pious women generally did this act of kindness. *Relieved the afflicted.* Visited and ministered to the sick. *Diligently followed every good work.* In a word, if she have been altogether a Christian, living according to the precepts of the gospel, and doing the Lord's work with all her heart, soul, and strength. From the character given here of the "widow indeed," it may be doubted whether "widow" was not in some cases the name of an office, which name it might have from being ordinarily filled by widows. It can hardly be supposed that any widow, unless she had considerable property, could have done the things enumerated in this verse, some of which would occasion no small expense. The "widow indeed" may mean a person who was to be employed in some office in the church; and Timothy is enjoined not to take any into that office unless she had been before remarkable for piety and humanity.

11. *But the younger widows refuse.* Do not admit those into this office who are under sixty years of age. Probably those who were received into such a list promised to abide in their widowhood. But as young or comparatively young women might have both occasion and temptations to remarry and so break their engagement to Christ, they should not be admitted. Not that the apostle condemns their remarrying as a crime in itself, but because it was contrary to their engagement. *Wax wanton.* A metaphor taken from a pampered horse, from whose mouth the rein has been removed, so that there is nothing to check or confine him.

12. *Having damnation.* In the sense in which we use this word I am satisfied the apostle never intended it. It is likely that he refers here to some promise or engagement which they made when taken on the list already mentioned, and now they have the guilt of having violated that promise; this is the "condemnation" of which the apostle speaks. *They have cast off their first faith.* By pledging their fidelity to a husband they have cast off their fidelity to Christ, as a married life and their previous engagement are incompatible.

13. *And withal they learn to be idle.* They do not love work, and they will not work. *Wandering about from house to house.* Gadding, gossiping; never contented with home; always visiting. *And not only idle.* If it went no further, this would be intolerable; but they are *tattlers*—talebearers; whisperers; light, trifling persons; all noise and no work. *Busybodies.* Persons who meddle with the concerns of others, who mind everyone's business but their own. *Speaking things which they ought not.* Lies, slanders, calumnies; backbiting their neighbors, and everywhere sowing the seed of dissension.

14. *I will therefore that the younger women marry.* As the preceding discourse has been about the younger widows, and this is an inference from it, it is most evident that by the *younger women* the apostle means the young widows. These he considers unfit for the office of the female diaconate, and therefore wills them to marry, educate children, and give themselves wholly up to domestic affairs. Here the apostle, so far from forbidding second marriages, positively enjoins or at least recommends them. *The adversary.* Any person, whether Jew or Gentile, who might be watching for an occasion to reproach, through the misconduct of its professors, the cause of Christianity.

15. *For some are already turned aside.* Some of these young widows, for he appears to be still treating of them, are turned aside to idolatry, to follow Satan instead of Christ. Slight deviations from a right line may lead at last to an infinite distance from Christ.

16. *If any man or woman that believeth.* If any Christian man or woman have poor *widows,*

MATTHEW HENRY

There should be prudence in the choice of the objects of charity, that it may not be thrown away upon those who are not properly so, that there may be the more for those who are real objects of charity.

Verses 17-25

I. Concerning the supporting of ministers. Care must be taken that they be honourably maintained (*v.* 17). They had not, in the primitive church, one to preach to them and another to rule them, but ruling and teaching were performed by the same persons. The work of ministers consists principally in two things: ruling well and labouring in the word and doctrine. Those who were not idle, but laborious in this work, were worthy of double honour.

Thou shalt not muzzle the ox that treads out the corn. Does God take care for oxen, and will he not take care of his own servants? The ox only treads out the corn of which they make the bread that perishes; but ministers break the bread of life which endures for ever. Those who would have ministers starved, or not comfortably provided for, God will require it of them another day.

II. Concerning the accusation of ministers (*v.* 19). There must be an accusation; it must not be a flying uncertain report. This accusation is not to be received unless supported by two or three credible witnesses; and the accusation must be received before them, that is, the accused must have the accusers face to face.

Great care should be taken that the thing alleged against him be well proved, "but (*v.* 20) *those that sin rebuke before all*; that the plaster may be as wide as the wound, and that those who are in danger of sinning by the example of their fall may take warning by the rebuke given them for it, *that others also may fear*." Public rebuke is designed for the good of others as well as for the good of the party rebuked.

Concerning Timothy himself. A charge to him to be careful of his office, *v.* 21. He charges him to guard against partiality. Ministers must give an account to God and the Lord Jesus Christ, and woe to them if they have been partial in their ministrations.

JAMIESON, FAUSSET, BROWN

let them—rather as *Greek,* "let him," or "her"; "let such a one" (vs. 10). **be charged**—lit., "be *burdened*" with their support. **widows indeed**—really helpless and friendless (vss. 3, 4). **17.** The transition from the widow presbyteresses (vs. 9) to the presbyters here, is natural. **rule well**—lit., "preside well," with wisdom, ability, and loving faithfulness, over the flock assigned to them. **be counted worthy of double honour**—i.e., the honor which is expressed by gifts (vss. 3, 18) and otherwise. If a presbyter as such, in virtue of his office, is already worthy of honor, he who *rules well* is *doubly so* [WIESINGER] (I Cor. 9:14; Gal. 6:6; I Thess. 5:12). Not literally that a presbyter who rules well should get *double the salary* of one who does not rule well [ALFORD], or of a presbyteress widow, or of the deacons [CHRYSOSTOM]. "Double" is used for *large* in general (Rev. 18:6). **specially they who labour in the word and doctrine**—*Greek,* "teaching"; preaching of the word, and instruction, catechetical or otherwise. This implies that of the *ruling presbyters* there were two kinds, those who *labored in the word and teaching,* and those who did not. Lay presbyters, so called merely because of their *age,* have no place here; for both classes mentioned here alike are *ruling* presbyters. A college of presbyters is implied as existing in each large congregation. As in ch. 3 their qualifications are spoken of, so here the acknowledgments due to them for their services. **18. the scripture**—(Deut. 25:4; quoted before in I Cor. 9:9). **the ox that treadeth out**—*Greek, "An* ox *while treading."* **The labourer is worthy of his reward**—or "hire"; quoted from Luke 10:7, whereas Matthew 10:10 has "his meat," or "food." If Paul extends the phrase, "Scripture saith," to this second clause, as well as to the first, he will be hereby recognizing the Gospel of Luke, his own helper (whence appears the undesigned appositeness of the quotation), as inspired *Scripture.* This I think the correct view. The Gospel according to Luke was probably in circulation then about eight or nine years. However, it is possible "Scripture saith" applies only to the passage quoted from Deuteronomy 25:4; and then his quotation will be that of a common proverb, quoted also by the Lord, which commends itself to the approval of all, and is approved by the Lord and His apostle. **19. Against an elder**—a presbyter of the Church. **receive not**—"entertain not" [ALFORD]. **but before two or three witnesses**—A *judicial conviction* was not permitted in Deuteronomy 17:6; 19:15, except on the testimony of at least two or three witnesses (cf. Matt. 18:16; John 8:17; II Cor. 13:1; I John 5:6, 7). But Timothy's *entertaining an accusation* against anyone is a different case, where the object was not judicially to punish, but to admonish: here he might *ordinarily* entertain it *without the need of two or three witnesses;* but not in the case of an elder, since the more earnest an elder was to *convince gainsayers* (Titus 1:9), the more exposed would he be to vexatious and false accusations. How important then was it that Timothy should not, without strong testimony, entertain a charge against presbyters, who should, in order to be efficient, be "blameless" (ch. 3:2; Titus 1:6).
20. Them that sin—whether presbyters or laymen. **rebuke before all**—publicly before the Church (Matt. 18:15-17; I Cor. 5:9-13; Eph. 5:11). Not until this "rebuke" was disregarded was the offender to be excommunicated. **others . . . fear**—that other members of the Church may have a wholesome fear of offending (Deut. 13:11; Acts 5: 11). **21. I charge thee**—rather as *Greek,* "I *adjure* thee"; so it ought to be translated (II Tim. 4:1). **before**—"*in the presence of* God." **Lord**—omitted in the oldest MSS. *God the Father, and Christ the Son,* will testify against thee, if thou disregardest my injunction. He vividly sets before Timothy *the last judgment,* in which God shall be revealed, and Christ seen face to face with His angels [BENGEL]. **elect angels**—an epithet of reverence. The objects of divine electing love (I Pet. 2:6). Not only "*elect*" [according to the everlasting purpose of God] in contradistinction to *the reprobate* angels (II Pet. 2:4), but also to mark the excellence of the angels in general [as God's chosen ministers, "holy angels," "angels of light"], and so to give more solemnity to their testimony [CALVIN] as witnesses to Paul's adjuration. Angels take part by action and sympathy in the affairs of the earth (Luke 15: 10; I Cor. 4:9). **these things**—the injunctions, vss. 19, 20. **without preferring one before another**—rather as *Greek, "prejudice"*; "judging before" hearing all the facts of a case. There ought to be judgment, but not prejudging. Cf. "suddenly," vs. 22, also vs. 24. **partiality**—*in favor of* a man, as "prej-

ADAM CLARKE

which are their relatives, let them relieve them —provide them with the necessaries of life, and not burden the church with their maintenance, that the funds may be spared for the support of those widows who were employed in its service, teaching children, visiting the sick.

17. *Let the elders that rule well.* Elder is probably here the name of an ecclesiastical officer, similar to what we now term "presbyter." *Double honour.* Almost every critic of note allows that *time* (Greek) here signifies "reward, stipend, wages." Let him have a double or a larger salary who rules well. And why? Because in the discharge of his office he must be at expense, in proportion to his diligence, in visiting and relieving the sick, in lodging and providing for strangers; in a word, in his being given to hospitality, which was required of every bishop or presbyter. *Especially they who labour in the word and doctrine.* Those who not only preach publicly, but instruct privately, catechize. Some think this refers to distinct ecclesiastical orders; but these technical distinctions were, in my opinion, a work of later times.

18. *The scripture saith, Thou shalt not muzzle the ox.* This is a manifest proof that by "honour" in the preceding verse the apostle means "salary" or "wages": "Let the elders that rule well be accounted worthy of double honour," a larger salary than any of the official widows mentioned before, for "the labourerer is worthy of his hire." The maintenance of every man in the church should be in proportion to his own labor, and the necessities of his family.

19. *Against an elder.* Be very cautious of receiving reports against those whose business it is to preach to others and correct their vices. Do not consider an elder as guilty of any alleged crime unless it be proved by two or three witnesses. This the law of Moses required in respect to all.

20. *Them that sin rebuke before all.* That is, before the members of the church; which was the custom of the Jews in their synagogues. *That others also may fear.* This is the grand object of church censures, to reclaim the transgressors and to give warning to others.

21. *I charge thee before God.* The apostle would have Timothy to consider that all he did should be done as in the sight of God, the Father of the spirits of all flesh; in the sight of Christ, the Saviour of sinners, who purchased the Church with His own blood; and in the sight of the most holy, approved, and eminent angels, whose office it was to minister to the heirs of salvation. The word *elect,* applied to the angels here, is supposed to distinguish those who stood when others fell from their first estate. *Without preferring one before another.* "Without prejudice." Promote no man's cause; make not up your mind on any case till you have weighed both sides and heard both parties, with their respective witnesses, and then act impartially, as the matter may appear to be proved. Do not treat any man, in religious matters, according to the rank he holds in life, or according to any personal attachment you may have for him. Every man should be dealt with in the church as he will be dealt with at the judgment seat of Christ.

MATTHEW HENRY

III. Concerning the ordination of ministers (*v.* 22), it seems to be meant of the ordaining of men to the office of the ministry. Some understand it of absolution: "Be not too hasty in laying hands on any." Those who are rash will make themselves partakers in other men's sins.

To take care of his health Paul advises nim to use wine for the helping of his stomach and the recruiting of his nature. It is the will of God that people should take all due care of their bodies, to use them so that they may be most fit and helpful to us in the service of God. Wine should be used as a help, and not a hindrance, to our work and usefulness.

IV. Concerning absolution, to which *v.* 24, 25, seem to refer. Some men's sins are so plain and obvious that there is no dispute concerning the bringing of them under the censures of the church.—*Others they follow after;* their wickedness does not presently appear, nor till after a due search has been made concerning it. So also, as to the evidences of repentance. There are secret, and there are open sins. Some are humbled and brought to repentance while it is quite otherwise with others. The incorrigible cannot be hid.

JAMIESON, FAUSSET, BROWN

udice" is bias *against* a man. Some of the oldest MSS. read, "in the way of *summoning* (brethren) *before a* (heathen) *judge.*" But *Vulgate* and other good authorities favor the more probable reading in *English Version.* **22. Lay hands**—i.e., ordain (ch. 4:14; II Tim. 1:6; Titus 1:5). The connection is with vs. 19. The way to guard against scandals occurring in the case of presbyters is, be cautious as to the character of the candidate before ordaining him; this will apply to other Church officers so ordained, as well as to presbyters. **suddenly**—hastily: vss. 24, 25 show that waiting for a time is salutary. **neither be partaker of other men's sins**—by negligence in ordaining ungodly candidates, and so becoming in some degree responsible for their sins. Or, there is the same transition from the *elders* to *all in general* who may sin, as in vss. 19, 20. Be not a partaker in other men's sins by not "rebuking them that sin before all," as well as those that are candidates for the presbytery, as also all "that sin." **keep thyself pure**—"thyself" is emphatic. "Keep THYSELF" *clear* of participation in OTHER men's sin by not failing to *rebuke them that sin* (vs. 20). Thus the transition is easy to vs. 23, which is concerning Timothy *personally;* cf. also vs. 24. **23. no longer**—as a habit. This injunction to drink wine occasionally is a modification of the preceding "keep thyself pure." The presbyter and deacon were enjoined to be "not given to wine" (ch. 3:3, 8). Timothy seems to have had a tendency to undue ascetical strictness on this point (cf. *Note,* ch. 4:8; cf. the Nazarene vow, Num. 6:1-4; John Baptist, Luke 1:15; Rom. 14). Paul therefore modifies the preceding words, "keep thyself pure," virtually saying, "Not that I mean to enjoin that kind of purity which consists in asceticism, nay, *be no longer a water-drinker,*" i.e., no longer drink *only* water, but *use a little wine,* as much as is needed for thy health. So ELLICOTT and WIESINGER. ALFORD thus: Timothy was of a feeble frame (*Note,* I Cor. 16:10, 11), and prone to timidity in his duties as overseer where vigorous action was needed; hence Paul exhorts him to take all proper means to raise his bodily condition above these infirmities. God hereby commands believers to use all due means for preserving health, and condemns by anticipation the human traditions which among various sects have denied the use of wine to the faithful. **24.** Two kinds of sins are specified: those *palpably manifest* (so the *Greek* for "open *beforehand*" ought to be translated; so in Heb. 7:14, it is translated "evident"; lit., "*before*" *the eyes,* i.e., notorious), further explained as "going before to judgment"; and those which follow after the men ("some men they, i.e., their sins, follow after"), viz., not going beforehand, loudly accusing, but hidden till they come to the judgment: so vs. 25, *the good works* are of two classes. those *palpably manifest* (translate so, instead of "manifest beforehand") and "those that are otherwise," i.e., not *palpably manifest.* Both alike "cannot be hid"; the former class in the case of bad and good are *manifest* already; the latter class in the case of both are not manifest now, but shall be so at *the final judgment.* **going before to judgment**—as heralds; crying sins which accuse their perpetrator. The connection seems to me this: He had enjoined Timothy, vs. 20, "Rebuke *them that sin* before all": and in vs. 22, "Neither be partaker of other men's sins," by ordaining ungodly men; having then by a digression at the clause, "keep thyself pure," guarded against an ascetical error of Timothy in fancying purity consisted in asceticism, and having exhorted him to use wine for strengthening him in his work, he returns to the subject of his being vigorous as an overseer in *rebuking sin,* whether in presbyters or people, and in avoiding participation in men's sins by ordaining ungodly candidates. He says, therefore, there are two classes of *sins,* as there are two classes of *good works:* those palpably *manifest,* and those not so; the former are those on which thou shouldest act decidedly at once when called on, whether to rebuke in general, or to ordain ministers in particular; as to the latter, the final *judgment* alone can decide; however hidden now they "cannot be hid" then. This could only be said of *the final judgment* (I Cor. 4:5; therefore, ALFORD's reference of this verse to *Timothy's judgment* in choosing elders must be wrong); all judgments before then are fallible. Thus he implies that Timothy can only be responsible if he connive at *manifest,* or evident sins; not that those *that are otherwise* shall escape judgment at last: just as in the case of *good works,* he can only be responsible for taking into account in his judgments those which are patent to all, not those secret good works which nevertheless will not remain hidden at the final judgment.

ADAM CLARKE

22. *Lay hands suddenly on no man.* Do not hastily appoint any person to the sacred ministry; let the person be well proved before he receives the imposition of hands.

Neither be partaker of other men's sins. It is a sin for any improper person to thrust himself into the sacred office; and he partakes of that sin who introduces, helps him forward, or sanctions him in it. *Keep thyself pure.* From this and every other evil.

23. *Drink no longer water, but use a little wine.* The priests under the Mosaic law, while performing sacred rites, were forbidden to drink wine: "Do not drink wine nor strong drink, thou, nor thy sons with thee, when ye go into the tabernacle of the congregation, lest ye die: it shall be a statute for ever throughout your generations," Lev. x. 9; Ezek. xliv. 21. From Athenaeus we learn that the Greeks often mingled their wine with water; sometimes one part of wine to two of water, three parts of water to one of wine, and at other times three parts of water to two of wine. "And among the Romans, no servant, nor free woman, nor youths of quality, drank any wine till they were thirty years of age." And it was a maxim among all that continued water-drinking injured the stomach.

24. *Some men's sins are open beforehand.* In appointing men to sacred offices in the church, among the candidates Timothy would find: (1) Some of whom he knew nothing, but only that they professed Christianity; let such be tried before they are appointed. (2) Some of whose faith and piety he had the fullest knowledge, and whose usefulness in the church was well-known. (3) Some whose lives were not at all or but partially reformed, who were still unchanged in their hearts and unholy in their lives. The sins of these latter were known to all; they go *before to judgment,* "to condemnation." The sins of others might be found out *after,* or in consequence of, this investigation; and those that were otherwise could not be long hid from his knowledge or the knowledge of the church. On all these accounts the exhortation is necessary: "Lay hands suddenly on no man."

25. *Likewise also the good works of some.* Though those who are very holy and very useful in the church cannot be unknown, yet there are others not less holy who need to be brought forward, who do much good in private and their character and good works are not fully known till after diligent inquiry.

MATTHEW HENRY

CHAPTER 6

Verses 1–5

I. Here is the duty of servants. They are yoked to work, not to be idle. They must respect their masters, they must count them worthy of all that honour which was fit for them to receive. If servants that embraced the Christian religion should grow disobedient to their masters, the doctrine of Christ would be reflected on for their sakes. If the professors of religion misbehave themselves, *the name of God and his doctrine* are in danger of being blasphemed. And this is a good reason why we should all conduct ourselves well. Or suppose the master were a Christian, and a believer, and the servant a believer too? They must think themselves the more obliged to serve them because the faith and love that bespeak men Christians oblige them to do good. Believing masters and servants are brethren, and partakers of the benefit.

II. Paul here warns Timothy to withdraw from those who corrupted the doctrine of Christ. *If any man teach otherwise* (*v.* 3–5). We are not required to consent to any words as wholesome words except the words of our Lord Jesus Christ. But he that does not consent to the words of Christ *is proud* (*v.* 4), knowing nothing. Commonly those are most proud who know least. Those who fall off from the plain practical doctrines of Christianity fall in with controversies. When men are not content with the words of the Lord Jesus Christ, but will frame notions of their own and impose them, they sow the seeds of all mischief in the church (*v.* 5); disputes that are all subtlety, and no solidity. Men of corrupt minds are *destitute of the truth.* The words of our Lord Jesus Christ are wholesome words, they are the fittest to prevent or heal the church's wounds, as well as to heal a wounded conscience. When men leave the wholesome words of our Lord Jesus Christ, they will never agree in other words, either of their own or other men's invention, but will perpetually wrangle and quarrel about them. Such persons as are given to perverse disputings appear to be men of corrupt minds, and destitute of the truth; especially such as act in this manner for the sake of gain, which is all their godliness. Christians will withdraw themselves from such.

JAMIESON, FAUSSET, BROWN

CHAPTER 6

VSS. 1-21. EXHORTATIONS AS TO DISTINCTIONS OF CIVIL RANK; THE DUTY OF SLAVES, IN OPPOSITION TO THE FALSE TEACHINGS OF GAIN-SEEKERS; TIMOTHY'S PURSUIT IS TO BE GODLINESS, WHICH IS AN EVERLASTING POSSESSION: SOLEMN ADJURATION TO DO SO AGAINST CHRIST'S COMING; CHARGE TO BE GIVEN TO THE RICH. CONCLUDING EXHORTATION. **1. servants**—to be taken as predicated thus, "Let as many as are under the yoke (as) slaves" (Tit. 2:9). The exhortation is natural as there was a danger of Christian slaves inwardly feeling above their heathen masters. **their own masters**—The phrase "their own," is an argument for submissiveness; it is not *strangers,* but *their own masters* whom they are required to respect. **all honour**—*all* possible and fitting *honor;* not merely outward subjection, but that inward *honor* from which will flow spontaneously right outward conduct (*Note,* Eph. 5:22). **that the name of God**—by which Christians are called. **blasphemed**—Heathen masters would say, What kind of a God must be the God of the Christians, when such are the fruits of His worship (Rom. 2:24; Titus 2:5, 10)? **2. And**—rather, "But." The opposition is between those Christian slaves *under the yoke* of heathen, and *those that have believing masters* (he does not use the phrase "under the yoke" in the latter case, for service under believers is not a *yoke*). Connect the following words thus, "Let them (the slaves) not, because they (the masters) are brethren (and so *equals,* masters and slaves alike being Christians), despise them" (the masters). **but rather . . .**—"but all the more (so much the more: with the greater good will) do them service because they (the masters) are faithful (i.e., believers) and beloved who receive (in the mutual *interchange* of relative duties between master and servant; so the *Greek*) the benefit" (*English Version* violates *Greek* grammer). This latter clause is parallel to, "because they are brethren"; which proves that "they" refers to the *masters,* not the *servants,* as TITTMANN takes it, explaining the verb in the common sense (Luke 1:54; Acts 20:35), "who *sedulously labor for* their (masters') benefit." The very term "benefit" delicately implies service done with the right *motive,* Christian "good will" (Eph. 6:7). If the common sense of the *Greek* verb be urged, the sense must be, "Because they (the masters) are faithful and beloved who *are sedulously intent on the benefiting*" of their servants. But PORPHYRY (*de abstin.* 1. 46) justifies the sense of the *Greek* verb given above, which also better accords with the context; for otherwise, the article "*the,*" will have nothing in the preceding words to explain it, whereas in my explanation above "*the* benefit" will be that of the slaves' *service.* **These things teach**—(ch. 4:11; Titus 2:15). **3. teach otherwise**—than I desire thee to "teach" (vs. 2). The *Greek* indicative implies, he puts not a merely supposed case, but one actually existing, ch. 1:3, "*Every one* who *teaches* otherwise," i.e., who teaches *heterodoxy.* consent not—*Greek,* "accede not to." **wholesome**—"sound" (ch. 1:10): opposed to the false teachers' words, *unsound* through profitless science and immorality. **words of our Lord Jesus Christ**—Paul's inspired words are not merely his own, but are also *Christ's* words. **4. He is proud**—lit., "wrapt in smoke"; filled with the fumes of self-conceit (ch. 3:6) while "knowing nothing," viz., of the doctrine which is according to godliness (vs. 3), though arrogating pre-eminent knowledge (ch. 1:7). **doting about**—lit., "*sick* about"; the opposite of "*wholesome*" (vs. 3). *Truth* is not the center *about* which his investigations move, but mere *word-strifes.* **questions**—of controversy. **strifes of words**—rather than about *realities* (II Tim. 2:14). These stand with them instead of "godliness" and "wholesome words" (vs. 3; ch. 1:4; Titus 3:9). **evil surmisings**—as to those who are of a different party from themselves. **5. Perverse disputings**—useless disputings. The oldest MSS. read, "lasting contests" [WIESINGER]; "incessant collisions" [ALFORD]. "Strifes of words" had already been mentioned so that he would not be likely to repeat the same idea (as in the *English Version* reading) again. **corrupt minds**—*Greek,* "of men corrupted (depraved) in mind." The inmost source of the evil is in the perverted mind (vs. 4; II Tim. 3:8; Titus 1:15). **destitute of the truth**—(Titus 1:14). They had had the truth, but through want of moral integrity and of love of the truth, they were misled by a pretended deeper gnosis (knowledge) and higher ascetical holiness, of which they made a trade [WIESINGER]. **supposing . . .**—The *Greek* requires, "supposing (regarding the matter in this point of view) that piety (so translated for 'godliness') is a means of gain"

ADAM CLARKE

CHAPTER 6

1. *Let as many servants as are under the yoke.* The word here means slaves converted to the Christian faith; and the *yoke* is the state to understand the heathen masters of those Christianized slaves. Even these, in such circumstances and under such domination, are commanded to treat their masters with *all honour* and respect, *that the name of God,* by which they were called, and the *doctrine* of God, Christianity, which they had professed, might *not be blasphemed*—might not be evilly spoken of in consequence of their improper conduct. Civil rights are never abolished by any communications from God's Spirit. The civil state in which a man was before his conversion is not altered by that conversion, nor does the grace of God absolve him from any claims which either the state or his neighbor may have on him.

2. *And they that have believing masters.* Who have been lately converted as well as themselves. *Let them not despise them.* Supposing themselves to be their equals because they are their brethren in Christ. *But rather do them service.* Obey them the more cheerfully *because they are faithful and beloved; faithful* to God's grace, *beloved* by Him and His true followers. *Partakers of the benefit.* "Joint partakers of the benefit." This is generally understood as referring to the master's participation in the services of his slaves. "Because those who are partakers of the benefit of your services are faithful and beloved"; or it may apply to the servants who are partakers of many benefits from their Christian masters. Others think that *benefit* here refers to the grace of the gospel, the common salvation of believing masters and slaves.

3. *If any man teach otherwise.* It appears that there were teachers of a different kind in the church, a sort of religious levellers, who preached that the converted servant had as much right to the master's service as the master had to his. *And consent not to wholesome words.* "Healing doctrines"—doctrines which give nourishment and health to the soul, which is the true character of all the doctrines taught by our Lord Jesus Christ; doctrines which are *according to godliness*—securing as amply the honor and glory of God as they do the peace, happiness, and final salvation of man. All this may refer to the general tenor of the gospel; and not to anything said, or supposed to have been said, by our Lord relative to the condition of slaves. With political questions or questions relative to private rights, our Lord scarcely ever meddled. He taught all men to love one another; to respect each other's rights; to submit to each other; to show all fidelity; to be obedient, humble, and meek; and to know that His kingdom was not of this world.

4. *He is proud.* He is "blown up" or "inflated" with a vain opinion of his own knowledge; whereas his knowledge is foolishness, for he knows nothing. *Doting about questions.* He is "sick, distempered," about these questions relative to the Mosaic law and the traditions of the elders; for it is most evident that the apostle has the Judaizing teachers in view, who were ever, in questions of theology, straining out a gnat and swallowing a camel. *Strifes of words. Logomachies;* verbal contentions; splitting hairs. *Whereof cometh envy, strife.* How little good have religious disputes ever done to mankind or to the cause of truth! Most controversialists have succeeded in getting their own tempers soured and in irritating their opponents.

5. *Perverse disputings of men of corrupt minds.* Disputations that cannot be settled because their partisans will not listen to the truth; and they will not listen to the truth because their minds are corrupt. Both under the law and under the gospel the true religion was: Thou shalt love the Lord thy God with all thy heart, soul, mind, and strength; and thy neighbor as thyself. Where therefore the love of God and man does not prevail, there there is no religion. *Supposing that gain is godliness.* Professing religion only for the sake of secular profit, defending their own cause for the emoluments it produced, and having no respect to another world.

MATTHEW HENRY

Verses 6–12

I. The excellency of contentment and the evil of covetousness.

1. The excellency of contentment, *v.* 6–8. Though Christianity is the worst trade, it is the best calling in the world. Those that make a trade of it, merely to serve their turn for this world, will find it a sorry trade; but those that mind it as their calling, and make a business of it, will find it a gainful calling.

(1) The truth he lays down is that *godliness with contentment is great gain.* Godliness is itself great gain, and, wherever there is true godliness, there will be contentment. Christian contentment is great gain. He that is godly is sure to be happy in another world; and if withal he do by contentment accommodate himself to his condition in this world he has enough. It is not like the little gain of worldlings, who are so fond of a little worldly advantage. Godliness is ever accompanied with contentment. All truly godly people have learned with Paul, in whatever state they are, to be therewith content.

(2) The reason he gives for it, *v.* 7. We can challenge nothing as a debt that is due to us, for we came naked into the world. Whatever we have had since, we are obliged to the providence of God for it. We cannot be poorer than when we came into this world, and yet then we were provided for; therefore let us trust in God for the remaining part of our pilgrimage. We shall carry nothing with us out of this world. Why should we not be content with a little, because, how much soever we have, we must leave it behind us?

(3) Hence he infers, *v.* 8. If God give us the necessary supports of life, we ought to be content therewith. What will worldlings do when death shall strip them of their happiness and portion, and they must take an everlasting farewell of all these things, on which they have so much doted? The necessaries of life are the bounds of a true Christian's desire. A few comforts of this life, will serve him, and these he may hope to enjoy.

2. The evil of covetousness *v.* 9. It is not said, those that are rich, but those that will be rich, that place their happiness in worldly wealth. When the devil sees which way their lusts carry them, he will soon bait his hook accordingly.

(1) Some will be rich; they are resolved upon it. Such will not be safe nor innocent. Worldly lusts are foolish and hurtful, for they drown men in destruction and perdition.

(2) The apostle affirms that *the love of money is the root of all evil, v.* 10. People may have money, and yet not love it; but, if they love it inordinately, it will push them on to all evil.

Covetous persons will quit the faith, if that be the way to get money. Those that depart from God do but treasure up sorrows for themselves.

II. Hence he takes occasion to caution Timothy. He addresses himself to him as *a man of God.* Ministers are men of God, and ought to conduct themselves accordingly. He charges Timothy to take heed of the love of money. It ill becomes men of God to set their hearts upon the things of this world; men of God should be taken up with the things of God. To arm him against the love of the world, he directs him to follow that which is good. It is not enough that men of God flee these things, but they must follow after what is directly contrary thereto. What excellent persons men of God are who follow after righteousness! They are the excellent of the earth, they should be approved of men.

JAMIESON, FAUSSET, BROWN

(i.e., a way of advancing one's worldly interests: a different *Greek* form, *poriswa,* expresses *the thing gained, gain*); not "that gain is godliness," as *English Version.* **from such withdraw thyself**—omitted in the oldest MSS. The connection with vs. 6 favors the omission of these words, which interrupt the connection. **6. But**—Though they err in this, there is a sense in which "piety is" not merely gain, but "*great* means of gain": not the *gaining* which they **pursue, and which makes men to be** *discontented* **with their present possessions, and to use religion** as "a cloak of covetousness" (I Thess. 2:5) and *means of earthly gain,* but *the present and eternal gain* which *piety,* whose accompaniment is *contentment,* secures to the soul. **7. For**—confirming the reasonableness of "contentment." **and it is certain**—*Vulgate* and other old versions support this reading. The oldest MSS., however, omit "and it is certain"; then the translation will be, "We brought nothing into the world (to teach us to remember) that neither can we carry anything out" (Job 1:21; Eccles. 5:15). Therefore, we should have no gain-seeking anxiety, the breeder of discontent (Matt. 6:25). **8. And**—*Greek,* "But." In contrast to the greedy gain-seekers (vs. 5). **having**—so long as we have food. (The *Greek* expresses "food sufficient in each case for our continually recurring wants" [ALFORD]). It is implied that we, as believers, shall *have* this (Isa. 23:16). **raiment**—*Greek,* "covering"; according to some including a *roof to cover us,* i.e., a dwelling, as well as clothing. **let us be therewith content**—lit., "we shall be sufficiently provided"; "we shall be sufficed" [ALFORD]. **9. will be rich**—have more than "*food* and raiment." *Greek,* "*wish* to be rich"; not merely *are willing,* but are resolved, and earnestly *desire* to have riches at any cost (Prov. 28:20, 22). This *wishing* (not the riches themselves) is fatal to "contentment" (vs. 6). Rich men are not told to cast away their riches, but not to "trust" in them, and to "do good" with them (vss. 17, 18; Ps. 62:10). **fall into temptation**—not merely "are exposed to temptation," but actually "*fall into*" it. The *falling into* it is what we are to pray against, "Lead us not into temptation" (Jas. 1:14); such a one is already in a sinful state, even before any overt act of sin. The *Greek for* "temptation" and "gain" contains a play on sounds—*porasmus, peirasmus.* **snare**—a further step downwards (ch. 3:7). He falls into "the snare of the devil." **foolish**—irrational. **hurtful**—to those who fall into the snare. Cf. Ephesians 4:22, "deceitful lusts" which deceive to one's deadly hurt. **lusts**—With the one evil lust ("*wish* to be rich") many others join themselves: the one is the "root of *all* evils" (vs. 10). **which**—*Greek,* "whatever (lusts)." **drown**—an awful descending climax from "fall into"; this is the last step in the terrible descent (Jas. 1:15); translated "sink," Luke 5:7. **destruction . . . perdition**—*destruction* in general (temporal or eternal), and *perdition* in particular, viz., that of body and soul in hell. **10. the love of money**—not the money itself, but the *love* of it—the *wishing to be rich* (vs. 9)—"is *a* root (ELLICOTT and MIDDLETON: not as *English Version,* "*the* root") of all *evils.*" (So the *Greek* plural.) **The wealthiest may be rich** not in a bad sense; the poorest may covet to be so (Ps. 62:10). *Love of money* is not the sole root of evils, but it is a leading "root of bitterness" (Heb. 12:15), for "it destroys faith, the root of all that is good" [BENGEL]; its offshoots are "temptation, a snare, lusts, destruction, perdition." **coveted after**—lusted after. **erred from**—lit., "have been made to err from the faith" (ch. 1:19; 4:1). **pierced**—(Luke 2:35). **with . . . sorrows**—"pains": "thorns" of the parable (Matt. 13:22) which choke the word of "faith." "The prosperity of fools destroys them" (Prov. 1:32). BENGEL and WIESINGER make them the gnawings of conscience, producing remorse for wealth badly acquired; the harbingers of the future "perdition" (vs. 9). **11. But thou**—in contrast to the "some" (vs. 10). **man of God**—who hast God as thy true riches (Gen. 15:1; Ps. 16:5; Lam. 3:24). Applying primarily to Timothy as a minister (cf. II Pet. 1:21), just as the term was used of Moses (Deut. 33:1), Samuel (I Sam. 9:6), Elijah, and Elisha; but, as the exhortation is as to duties *incumbent also on all Christians,* the term applies secondarily to him (so II Tim. 3:17) as a Christian man *born of God* (Jas. 1:18; I John 5:1), no longer a *man of the world* raised above earthly things; therefore, God's property, not his own, bought with a price, and so having parted with all right in himself: Christ's work is to be *his* great work: he is to be Christ's living representative. **flee these things**—viz., "the love of money" with its evil results (vs. 9, 10). **follow after righteousness**—(II Tim. 2:22). **godliness**—"piety." *Righteousness* is

ADAM CLARKE

From such withdraw thyself. Have no religious fellowship with such people. But this clause is wanting in some MSS. It is probably spurious.

6. *But godliness with contentment is great gain.* The word *godliness* here and in several other places of this Epistle signifies the true religion, Christianity; and the word *contentment* signifies a "competency," a "sufficiency"; that measure or portion of secular things which is necessary for the support of life, while the great work of regeneration is carrying on in the soul. So if a man have the life of God in his soul, and just a sufficiency of food and raiment to preserve and not burden life, he has what God calls *great gain,* an abundant portion.

7. *We brought nothing into this world.* There are some sayings in Seneca which are almost verbatim with this of Paul: "No man is born rich; everyone that comes into the world is commanded to be content with food and raiment."

8. *Having food and raiment let us be therewith content.* Let us consider this a "competency." The word which we translate *raiment* signifies "covering" in general; and here means house or lodging, as well as clothing.

9. *But they that will be rich.* The words are emphatic, and refer to persons who are "determined" to get riches.

And into many foolish and hurtful lusts. The whole conduct of such a person is a tissue of folly; scraping, gathering, and heaping up riches, and scarcely affording to take the necessaries of life out of them for himself. These lusts or desires are not only *foolish,* but they are *hurtful.* The mind is debased and narrowed by them; benevolent and generous feelings become extinct; charity perishes; and selfishness, the last and lowest principle in mental degradation, absorbs the soul. For these *foolish and hurtful lusts . . . drown men in destruction and perdition*—the soul is destroyed by them here and brought through them into a state of perdition hereafter.

10. *The love of money is the root of all evil.* Perhaps it would be better to translate "of all these evils"; i.e., the evils enumerated above; for it cannot be true that the love of money is the root of *all evil.* It certainly was not the root whence the transgression of Adam sprang, but it is the root whence all the evils mentioned in the preceding verse spring. This text has been often very incautiously quoted; for how often do we hear, "The Scripture says, Money is the root of all evil"! No, the Scripture says no such thing. Money is the root of no evil, nor is it an evil of any kind; but the love of it is the root of all the evils mentioned here. *While some coveted after.* "Insatiably desiring." *Have erred from the faith.* Have "totally erred"—have made a most fatal and ruinous departure from the religion of Christ. *And pierced themselves through with many sorrows.* The word signifies to be "transfixed in every part"; and is an allusion to one of those "snares" mentioned in v. 9, where a hole is dug in the earth and filled full of sharp stakes, and being slightly covered over with turf, is not perceived; and whatever steps on it falls in and is pierced through and through with these sharp stakes, the "many torments" mentioned by the apostle.

11. *But thou, O man of God.* You who have taken God for your Portion, and are seeking a city that has foundations, *flee these things.* Escape for your life. Even you are not out of the reach of the love of money. *Follow after righteousness*—justice and uprightness in all your dealings with men. *Godliness*—a thorough conformity to the image of God and the mind of Christ.

MATTHEW HENRY

He exhorts him to do the part of a soldier. Those who will get to heaven must fight their way thither. It is a good fight, it is a good cause, and it will have a good issue. It is the fight of faith. Eternal life is the crown proposed to us. This we must lay hold on, as those that are afraid of coming short of it and losing it. Lay hold, and take heed of losing your hold.

He reminds him of the confession that he himself had made, *v.* 12. The obligation of that was still upon him, and he must live up to that.

Verses 13–21

I. He gives him a solemn charge. He charges him as he will answer it at the great day to that God whose eyes are upon us all, who sees what we are and what we do. This should quicken us to the service of God that we serve a God who quickens all things. He charges him before Christ Jesus. Christ died not only as a sacrifice, but as a martyr; and he witnessed a good confession when he was arraigned before Pilate. That good confession of his before Pilate, *My kingdom is not of this world,* should be effectual to draw off all his followers from the love of this world.

He reminds him of Christ's second coming. The Lord Jesus Christ will appear, and it will be a glorious appearing. Ministers should have an eye to this appearing of the Lord Jesus Christ, and, till his appearing, they are to keep this commandment without spot, unrebukable. The appearing of Christ is certain, but it is not for us to know the time and season of it. Let this suffice us, that in time he will show it.

1. Concerning Christ and God the Father the apostle here speaks great things. God is the only Potentate; the powers of earthly princes are all derived from him. He is the blessed and the only Potentate, infinitely happy. He only has immortality. He dwells in inaccessible light. No man can get to heaven but those whom he is pleased to bring thither, and admit into his kingdom. He is invisible. It is impossible that mortal eyes should bear the brightness of the divine glory. No man can see God and live.

2. He concludes with a doxology. What an evil is sin when committed against such a God! What are we then, that the blessed God, the King of kings and Lord of lords, should seek after us? Blessed are those who are admitted to dwell with this great and blessed Potentate.

JAMIESON, FAUSSET, BROWN

more in relation to our fellow man; *piety* ("godliness") to God; *faith* is the root of both (*Note,* Titus 2:12). **love**—by which "faith worketh." **patience**—*enduring perseverance* amidst trials. **meekness**—The oldest MSS. read, "meek-spiritedness," viz., towards the opponents of the Gospel. **12. Fight the good fight**—BIRKS thinks this Epistle was written from Corinth, where contests in the national games recurred at stated seasons, which will account for the allusion here as in I Corinthians 9:24-26. Contrast "strifes of words" (vs. 4). Cf. ch. 1:18; II Tim. 4:7. The "good profession" is connected with the "good fight" (Ps. 60:4). **lay hold on eternal life**—the crown, or garland, the prize of victory, laid hold of by the winner in the *good fight* (II Tim. 4: 7, 8; Phil. 3:12-14). *"Fight* (lit., 'strive') with such striving earnestness as to *lay hold on* the prize, *eternal life."* **also**—not in the oldest MSS. **professed a good profession**—*Greek,* "didst confess THE good *confession,"* viz., *the Christian* confession (as the *Greek* word is the same in this verse as that for "confession" in vs. 13, probably the *profession* here is the confession *that Christ's kingdom is the kingdom of the truth,* John 18:36, 37), at thy being set apart to thy ministerial function (whether in general, or as overseer at Ephesus): the same occasion as is referred to in ch. 1:18; 4:14; II Tim. 1: 4. **before many witnesses**—who would testify against thee if thou shouldest fall away [BENGEL]. **13. quickeneth all things**—i.e., "maketh alive." But the oldest MSS. read, "preserveth alive"; as the same *Greek* means in Acts 7:19; cf. Nehemiah 9:6. He urges Timothy to faithfulness here by the present manifestation of God's power in preserving all things, as in vs. 14, by the future manifestation of God's power at the appearing of Christ. The assurance that "eternal life," vs. 12, will be the result of "fighting the good fight," rests on the fulness and power of Him who is the God of all life, present and to come. **witnessed**—It was the Lord's part to *witness,* Timothy's part to *confess* (or "profess," vs. 12) *"the* good confession" [BENGEL]. *The* confession was His testimony that He was King, and His kingdom that of *the truth* (vs. 15; *Note,* vs. 12; Matt. 27:11). Christ, in attesting, or bearing witness to this truth, attested the truth of the whole of Christianity. Timothy's *profession,* or *confession,* included therefore the whole of the Christian truth. **14. keep this commandment**—*Greek,* "the commandment," i.e., the Gospel rule of life (ch. 1:5; John 13:34; II Pet. 2:21; 3:2). **without spot, unrebukeable**—agreeing with "thou." Keep the commandment and so be without spot . . . . "Pure" (ch. 5:22; Eph. 5:27; Jas. 1:27; II Pet. 3:14). **until the appearing of . . . Christ**—*His coming in person* (II Thess. 2:8; Titus 2:13). Believers then used in their practice to set before themselves the day of Christ as near at hand; we, the hour of death [BENGEL]. The fact has in all ages of the Church been certain, the time as uncertain to Paul, as it is to us; hence, vs. 15, he says, "in HIS times": the Church's true attitude is that of continual expectation of her Lord's return (I Cor. 1:8; Phil. 1:6, 10). **15. in his times**—*Greek, "His own* [fitting] times" (Acts 1:7). The plural implies successive stages in the manifestation of the kingdom of God, each having its own appropriate time, the regulating principle and knowledge of which rests with the Father (ch. 2: 6; II Tim. 1:9; Titus 1:3; Heb. 1:1). **he shall show**—"display": an expression appropriate in reference to His "APPEARING," which is stronger than His "coming," and implies its *visibility;* "manifest": *make visible* (cf. Acts 3:20): "He" is *the Father* (vs. 16). **blessed**—in Himself: so about to be the source of *blessing* to His people at Christ appearing, whence flows their "blessed hope" (ch. 1:11; Titus 2:13). **only**—(John 17:3; Rom. 16:27; Rev. 15:4). **King of kings**—elsewhere applied also to Jesus (Rev. 1:5; 17:14; 19:16). **16. Who only hath immortality**—in His own essence, not merely at the will of another, as all other immortal beings [JUSTIN MARTYR, *Quœst ad Orthod.,* 61]. **dwelling in the light which no man can approach unto**—After *life* comes mention of *light,* as in John 1:4. That *light* is *unapproachable* to creatures, except in so far as they are admitted by Him, and as He goes forth to them [BENGEL]. It is *unapproachable* on account of its exceeding brightness [THEOPHYLACT]. If one cannot gaze steadfastly at the sun, which is but a small part of creation, by reason of its exceeding heat and power, how much less can mortal man gaze at the inexpressible glory of God [THEOPHYLACT, *ad Autolycus*] (Ps. 104:2; I John 1:5). **no man hath seen**—(Exod. 23:20; John 1:18; Col. 1:15; Heb. 11:27; I John 4:12). Perhaps even in the perfect state no creature shall fully see God. Still the

ADAM CLARKE

Faith in Jesus, and in all that He has spoken; and "fidelity" to the talents you have received and the office with which you are entrusted. *Love* to God and all mankind. *Patience* in all trials and afflictions. *Meekness.* Bearing up with an even mind under all adversities and contradictions.

12. *Fight the good fight of faith.* "Agonize the good agony." You have a contest to sustain in which your honor, your life, your soul, are at stake. *Lay hold on eternal life.* All this is in allusion to the exercises in the public Grecian games. Fight, conquer, and seize upon the prize; carry off the crown of eternal life! *Whereunto thou art also called.* The allusion to the public games is still carried on. You have been called into this palaestra; you have been accepted as one proper to enter the lists with any antagonists that may offer; "in the presence of many witnesses" you have taken the necessary engagements upon yourself, and submitted to be governed by the laws of the stadium; many eyes are upon you, to see whether you will fight manfully and be faithful.

13. *I give thee charge.* This is similar to that in v. 21 of the preceding chapter.

A good confession. The confession made by Christ before Pontius Pilate is that He was Messiah, the King, but that His kingdom was not of this world; and that hereafter He should be seen coming in the clouds of heaven to judge the quick and dead. See John xviii. 36-37 and Mark xiv. 61-62.

14. *That thou keep this commandment without spot.* Two things are mentioned here: (1) That the *commandment* itself, the whole doctrine of Christ, should be kept entire. (2) That his life should be agreeable to that doctrine. Keep it *without spot*—let there be no blot on the sacred Book; add nothing to it; take nothing from it; change nothing in it. Deliver down to your successors the truth as you have had it from God himself. *Unrebukeable.* Let there be nothing in your conduct or spirit contrary to this truth. Keep the truth, and the truth will keep you. *Until the appearing of our Lord.* Hand it down pure and let your conduct be a comment on it, that it may continue in the world and in the Church till the coming of Christ.

15. *Which in his times he shall shew.* Jesus will appear in the most proper time, the time which the infinite God in His wisdom has appointed for the second coming of His Son. *The blessed and only Potentate. Potentate* is applied to secular governors; but none of these can be styled "the happy and only One"; *the King of kings,* or "the King over all kings"; and "the Lord over all lords or rulers." These are titles which could not be given to any mortals. This is made more specific by the verse following.

16. *Who only hath immortality.* All beings that are not eternal must be mutable; but there can be only one eternal Being, that is, God; and He only can have *immortality. Dwelling in the light which no man can approach unto.* All this is said by the apostle in three words: "inhabiting unapproachable light." Such is the excessive glory of God that neither angel nor man can approach it. *Whom no man hath seen, nor can see.* Moses himself could only see the symbol of the Divine Presence, but the face of God no man could ever see. Because He is infinite and eternal, therefore He is incomprehensible; and if incomprehensible to the mind, consequently invisible to the eye. *To whom,* as the Author of being and the Dispenser of all good, be ascribed *honour and power*—the sole authority of all-pervading, all-superintending, all-preserving, and everlasting might.

MATTHEW HENRY

IV. The apostle adds a lesson for rich people, *v.* 17–19.

1. Timothy must charge those that are rich to beware of the temptations, and improve the opportunities of their prosperous estate. He must caution them to take heed of pride. He must caution them against vain confidence in their wealth. Nothing is more uncertain than the wealth of this world; many have had much of it one day and been stripped of all the next.

Those who are rich must see God giving them their riches, and giving them to enjoy them richly; for many have riches, but enjoy them poorly, not having a heart to use them.

He must charge them to do good with what they have. Those are truly rich who are rich in good works. He must charge them to think of another world, and prepare for that which is to come by works of charity.

2. Ministers must not be afraid of the rich. They must caution them against pride, and vain confidence in their riches. A lesson for ministers in the charge given to Timothy: *Keep that which is committed to thy trust.* Every minister is a trustee. The truths of God, the ordinances of God, keep these. Keep close to the written word, for that is committed to our trust.

Some who have been very proud of their learning, their *science, which is falsely so called,* have by that been drawn away from the faith of Christ, which is a good reason why we should keep to the plain word of the gospel. *O Timothy, keep that which is committed to thy trust!* as if he had said, "I cannot conclude without charging thee again; whatever thou doest, be sure to keep this trust, for it is too great a trust to be betrayed." That science which opposes the truth of the gospel is falsely so called. Those who are for advancing reason above faith are in danger of leaving faith.

V. Our apostle concludes with a solemn prayer and benediction. Grace is an earnest, yea, a beginning, of glory; for, wherever God gives grace, he will give glory. Grace be with you all. Amen.

JAMIESON, FAUSSET, BROWN

saints shall, in some sense, have the blessedness of *seeing* Him, which is denied to mere *man* (Matt. 5:8; I Cor. 13:12; I John 3:2; Rev. 22:4). **rich in this world**—constrasted with the riches of the future kingdom to be the portion of believers at Christ's "appearing," vs. 14. **high-minded**—often the character of the rich (see Rom. 12:16). **trust**—*Greek,* "to have their trust resting." **in . . . in**—rather, "upon . . . upon," as the oldest MSS. **uncertain riches**—rather as *Greek,* "the *uncertainty of* riches." They who rest their trust on riches, rest trust on *uncertainty* itself (Prov. 23:5). Now they belong to one person, now to another, and that which has many masters is possessed by none [THEODORET]. **living God**—The best MSS. and versions omit "living." He who trusts in riches transfers to them the duty he owes to God [CALVIN]. **who giveth**—*Greek,* "affordeth." **all things richly**—temporal and eternal, for the body and for the soul. In order to be truly rich, seek to be blessed of, and in, God (Prov. 10:22; II Pet. 1:3). **to enjoy**—*Greek,* "for enjoyment." Not that the heart may cleave to them as its idol and *trust* (ch. 4:3). *Enjoyment* consists in giving, not in holding fast. Nonemployment should be far removed, as from man, so from his resources (Jas. 5:2, 3) [BENGEL]. **18. do good**—like God Himself (Ps. 119:68; Acts 14:17) and Christ (Acts 10:38). TITTMANN translates, "to do," or "act well"; as the *Greek* for "to be beneficent" is a distinct word, *agathopoiein.* **rich in good works**—so "rich in faith," which produces good works (Jas. 2:5). Contrasted with "rich in this world," vs. 17. Lit., it is "rich in honorable (right) works." *Greek, kalois, ergois,* are works good or *right* in themselves: *agathois,* good to another. **ready to distribute**—free givers [ALFORD]; the heart not cleaving to possessions, but ready to impart to others. **willing to communicate**—ready *contributors* [ALFORD]: liberal in admitting others to share our goods in *common with* ourselves (Gal. 6:6; Heb. 13:16). **19. Laying up in store**—"therefrom (i.e., by this means [ALFORD]; but BENGEL makes the *Greek apo* mean laying apart *against a future time*), laying up for themselves as a treasure" [ALFORD] (Matt. 6:19, 20). This is a treasure which we act wisely in *laying up in store,* whereas the wisest thing we can do with earthly treasures is "to distribute" them and give others a share of them (vs. 18). **good foundation**—(*Note,* ch. 3:13; Luke 6:48; I Cor. 3:11). The sure reversion of the future heavenly inheritance: earthly riches *scattered* in faith lay up in store a sure *increase* of heavenly riches. We gather by scattering (Prov. 11:24; 13:7; Luke 16:9). **that . . . eternal life**—The oldest MSS. and versions read, "*that which is really* life," its joys being solid and enduring (Ps. 16:11).

O Timothy—a personal appeal, marking at once his affection for Timothy, and his prescience of the coming heresies. **keep**—from spiritual thieves, and from enemies who will, while men sleep, sow tares amidst the good seed sown by the Son of man. **that which is committed to thy trust**—*Greek,* "the deposit" (ch. 1:18; II Tim. 1:12, 14; 2:2). *The true* or *sound doctrine* to be taught, as opposed to *the science falsely so called,* which leads to *error concerning the faith* (vs. 21). "It is not thine: it is another's property with which thou hast been entrusted: Diminish it not at all" [CHRYSOSTOM] **avoiding**—"turning away from" (cf. II Tim. 3:4). Even as they have "turned away from the truth" (ch. 1:6; 5:15; II Tim. 4:4). **profane**—(ch. 4:7; II Tim. 2:16). **vain**—*Greek,* "empty": mere "strifes of words," vs. 4, producing no moral fruit. **oppositions**—dialectic antithesis of the false teachers [ALFORD]. WIESINGER, not so probably, "oppositions to the sound doctrine." I think it likely germs existed already of the heresy of dualistic oppositions, viz., between the good and evil principle, afterwards fully developed in Gnosticism. Contrast Paul's just antithesis (ch. 3:16; 6:5, 6; II Tim. 2:15-23). **science falsely so called**—where there is not faith, there is not knowledge [CHRYSOSTOM]. There was true "knowledge," a special gift of the Spirit, which was abused by some (I Cor. 8:1; 12:8; 14:6). **21. Which some professing**—viz., professing these *oppositions of science falsely so called.* **erred**—(*Note,* ch. 1:6; 2:11—lit., "missed the mark" (II Tim. 3:7, 8). True sagacity is inseparable from faith. **Grace**—*Greek,* "*the* grace," viz., of God, for which we Christians look, and in which we stand [ALFORD]. **be with thee**—He restricts the salutation to Timothy, as the Epistle was not to be read in public [BENGEL]. But the oldest MSS. read, "be with you"; and the "thee" may be a transcriber's alteration to harmonize with II Timothy 4:22; Titus 3:15. **Amen**—omitted in the oldest MSS.

ADAM CLARKE

17. *Charge them that are rich.* He had before, in vv. 9-10, given them a very awful lesson concerning their obtaining riches; and now he gives them one equally so concerning their use of them. *That they be not highminded.* That they do not value themselves on account of their wealth, for this adds nothing to mind or moral worth. *Nor trust in uncertain riches.* The uncertainty of riches; things which are never at a stay, are ever changing, and seldom continue long with one proprietor. Therefore, as well as on many other accounts, they are not to be trusted in; they cannot give happiness, because they are not fixed and permanent; neither can they meet the wishes of an immortal spirit. *But in the living God,* who is the unchangeable Fountain of perfection. *Who giveth us richly all things to enjoy.* Who not only has all good, but dispenses it liberally for the supply of the wants of all His creatures; and He does not give merely what is necessary, but He gives what tends to render life comfortable. The comforts of life come from God, as well as the necessaries. He not only gives us a bare subsistence, but He gives us enjoyments.

18. *That they do good.* That they relieve the wants of their fellow creatures, according to the abundance which God has given them—the highest luxury a human being can enjoy on this side of the grave. *Rich in good works.* That their good works may be as abundant as their riches. *Ready to distribute.* That they give nothing through partiality or favor, but be guided in their distribution by the necessities of the objects presented to them; and that they confine not their charity at home, but scatter it abroad. *Willing to communicate.* Bringing every poor person into a state of fellowship with themselves.

19. *Laying up in store for themselves a good foundation.* Paul seems to have borrowed this form of speech from Tobit. See chap. iv. 8-9: "If thou hast abundance, give alms accordingly: if thou hast but a little, be not afraid to give according to that little: for thou treasurest up a good reward for thyself against the day of necessity."

20. *O Timothy, keep that which is committed to thy trust.* This is another repetition of the apostolic charge. (See chap. i. 5, 18-19; iv. 6-7, 14-16; v. 21; vi. 13.) Carefully preserve that doctrine which I have delivered to you. Nothing can be more solemn and affectionate than this charge. *Avoiding profane and vain babblings.* See on chap. i. 4 and iv. 7.

21. *Which some professing.* Which inspired knowledge some pretending to, have set up Levitical rites in opposition to the great Christian Sacrifice, and consequently *have erred concerning the faith*—have completely mistaken the whole design of the gospel. *Grace be with thee.* May the favor and influence of God be with you, and preserve you from these and all other errors! *Amen.* This word, as in former cases, is wanting in the most ancient MSS. In a majority of cases it appears to have been added by different transcribers nearly in the same way in which we add the word *Finis,* simply to indicate the end of the work.

THE SECOND EPISTLE TO TIMOTHY

I. Introduction (1:1-5)
A. Personal introduction (1:1)
B. Greeting to Timothy (1:2)
C. Thanksgiving (1:3-5)

II. Personal responsibility (1:6-2:13)
A. Gifts (1:6-18)
1. The injunction (1:6-8)
2. The incentives (1:9-18)
B. Grace (2:1-13)
1. The injunctions (2:1-6)
2. The incentives (2:7-13)

III. Church responsibility (2:14-3:13)
A. Present perils and duties (2:14-26)
1. The workman and the destroyers (2:14-19)
2. The Lord's servant (2:20-26)
B. The coming troubles (3:1-13)
1. Description (3:1-9)
2. Paul's experience (3:10-13)

IV. Truth responsibility (3:14-4:5)
A. The Scriptures and their value (3:14-17)
1. "Abide" (3:14)
2. The value of the writings (3:15, 16)
3. The purpose of abiding (3:17)
B. The final charge (4:1-5)
1. His work (4:1-4)
2. His character (4:5)

V. Conclusion (4:6-22)
A. Paul's final attitudes (4:6-18)
1. As to his ministry (4:6-8)
2. As to his associates (4:9-13)
3. As to his enemies (4:14-18)
B. The last salutation (4:19-22)

This second epistle Paul wrote to Timothy from Rome when he was a prisoner there and in danger of his life; "I am now ready to be offered, and the time of my departure is at hand" (4:6). He had been brought before the emperor Nero, which he calls "his first answer, when no man stood with him, but all men forsook him" (4:16). And interpreters agree that this was the last epistle he wrote. Where Timothy now was is not certain.

MATTHEW HENRY

CHAPTER 1

Verses 1–5

I. The inscription of the epistle. The gospel is the promise of life in Christ Jesus; life is the end, and Christ the way. Paul was an apostle of Jesus Christ by the will of God; his commission to be an apostle was not by the will of man. God called him to be an apostle. We have the promise of life. This, as well as all other promises, is in and through Jesus Christ. The grace, mercy, and peace, which Timothy wanted, comes from God the Father and Christ Jesus our Lord. The best want these blessings, and they are the best we can ask for our dearly-beloved friends.

II. Paul's thanksgiving to God for Timothy's faith and holiness. Paul was much in prayer, he prayed night and day. Prayer was his constant business, and he never forgot his friends in his prayers, as we often do. It was a comfort to him that he was of the seed of those that served God; as likewise that he had served him with a pure conscience. Timothy was sorry to part with Paul, he wept at parting, and therefore Paul desired to see him again, because he had perceived by that what a true affection he had for him.

JAMIESON, FAUSSET, BROWN

CHAPTER 1

Vss. 1-18. Address: Thankful Expression of Love and Desire to See Him: Remembrance of His Faith and That of His Mother and Grandmother. Exhortation to Stir Up the Gift of God in Him, and Not Shrink from Affliction, Enforced by the Consideration of the Freeness of God's Grace in Our Gospel Calling, and by the Apostle's Example. The Defection of Many: The Steadfastness of Onesiphorus. **1.** This Epistle is the last testament and swanlike death-song of Paul [Bengel]. **according to the promise of life . . . in Christ**—Paul's *apostleship* is *in order to carry into effect* this promise. Cf. "according to the faith . . . in hope of eternal life . . . promise . . ." (Titus 1:1, 2). This "promise of life in Christ" (cf. vs. 10; ch. 2:8) was needed to nerve Timothy to fortitude amidst trials, and to boldness in undertaking the journey to Rome, which would be attended with much risk (vs. 8). **2. my dearly beloved son**—In I Timothy 1:2, and Titus 1:4, written at an earlier period than this Epistle, the expression used is in the *Greek*, "my *genuine* son." **I thank**—*Greek*, "I *feel gratitude* to God." **whom I serve from my forefathers**—*whom I serve* (Rom. 1:9) *as did my forefathers*. He does not mean to put on the same footing the Jewish and Christian service of God; but simply to assert his own conscientious service of God as he had received it from his *progenitors* (not Abraham, Isaac, etc., whom he calls "the fathers," not "progenitors" as the *Greek* is here; Rom. 9:5). The memory of those who had gone before to whom he is about to be gathered, is now, on the eve of death, pleasant to him; hence also, he calls to mind the faith of the mother and grandmother of Timothy; as he walks in the faith of his forefathers (Acts 23:1; 24:14; 26:6, 7; 28:20), so Timothy should persevere firmly in the faith of his parent and grandparent. **I have remembrance of thee**—"*how* unceasing I *make my mention* concerning thee" (cf. Philemon 4). The cause of Paul's feeling thankful is, not that he remembers Timothy unceasingly in his prayers, but for what Timothy is in faith (vs. 5) and graces; cf. Romans 1:8, 9, from which supply the elliptical sentence thus, "I thank God [for thee, for God is my witness] whom I serve . . . that (or *how*) without ceasing I have remembrance (or *make mention*) of thee . . . ." **night and day**—(*Note*, I Tim. 5:5). **4. desiring**—*Greek*, "with *yearning* as for one much *missed*." **mindful of thy tears**—not only at our parting (Acts 20:37), but also often when under pious feelings. **that I may be filled with joy**—to be joined with "desiring to see thee" (Rom. 1:11, 12; 15:32). **5. When I call to remembrance . . .**—This

ADAM CLARKE

CHAPTER 1

1. *Paul an apostle.* Paul at once shows his office, the authority on which he held it, and the end for which it was given him. He was an *apostle*—an extraordinary ambassador from heaven. He had his apostleship by the *will of God*—according to the counsel and design of God's infinite wisdom and goodness. And he was appointed that he might proclaim that eternal *life* which God had in view for mankind by the incarnation of His Son, Jesus Christ, and which was the end of all the promises He had made to men and the commandments He had delivered to all His prophets since the world began.

3. *Whom I serve from my forefathers.* Being born a Jew, I was carefully educated in the knowledge of the true God and the proper manner of worshipping Him. *With pure conscience.* Ever aiming to please Him, even in the time when through ignorance I persecuted the Church.

Without ceasing I have remembrance of thee. The apostle thanks God that he has constant remembrance of Timothy in his prayers. It is a very rare thing now in the Christian Church that a man particularly thanks God that he is enabled to pray for others.

4. *Being mindful of thy tears.* Whether the apostle refers to the affecting parting with the Ephesian church, mentioned in Acts xx. 37, or to the deep impressions made on Timothy's heart when he instructed him in the doctrine of Christ crucified, or to some interview between themselves, it is not certainly known. The mention of this by the apostle is no small proof of his most affectionate regard for Timothy, whom he appears to have loved as a father loves his only son.

MATTHEW HENRY

He thanks God that Timothy kept up the religion of his ancestors, *v.* 5. It is a comfortable thing when children imitate the faith and holiness of their godly parents, and tread in their steps. The faith that dwells in real believers is unfeigned; it is a faith that will stand the trial, and it dwells in them as a living principle. It was the matter of Paul's thanksgiving that Timothy inherited the faith of his mother Eunice and his grandmother Lois.

Verses 6–14

Exhortation and excitation of Timothy to his duty (*v.* 6). The best men need remembrancers.

I. Stir up the gift that is in them as fire under the embers.

Use gifts, and have gifts. He must take all opportunities to use these gifts, for that is the best way of increasing them.

The great hindrance of usefulness in the increase of our gifts is slavish fear. Paul therefore warns Timothy against this, *v.* 7. God hath delivered us from the spirit of fear, and hath given us the spirit *of power, and of love, and of a sound mind.* The spirit of power, or of courage and resolution; the spirit of love to God which will set us above the fear of man, and the spirit of a sound mind, or quietness of mind, for we are oftentimes discouraged in our work by the creatures of our own imagination, which a sober, thinking mind would obviate.

II. He exhorts him to count upon afflictions, and get ready for them. Be not thou ashamed of the gospel.

JAMIESON, FAUSSET, BROWN

increased his "desire to see" Timothy. The oldest MSS. read, "When I *called* to remembrance"; implying that some recent incident (perhaps the contrasted cowardice of the hypocrite Demas, who forsook him) had reminded him of the sincerity of Timothy's faith. **faith that is in thee**—ALFORD translates, "that *was* in thee." He remembers Timothy's faith in the *past* as a fact; its *present* existence in him is only matter of his confident *persuasion* or hope. **which**—*Greek,* "such as." **dwelt**—"made its dwelling" or abode (John 14:23). The past tense implies they were now dead. **first**—before it dwelt in thee. She was the furthest back of the progenitors of Timothy whom Paul knew. **mother Eunice**—a believing Jewess; but his father was a Greek, i.e., a heathen (Acts 16:1). **persuaded that**—*it dwells, or it shall dwell* "in thee also." The mention of the faith of his mother and grandmother is designed as an incentive to stir up his faith. **6. Wherefore**—*Greek,* "For which cause," **viz.**, because thou hast inherited, didst once possess, and I trust ["am persuaded"] still dost possess, such unfeigned faith [ALFORD]. **stir up**—lit., "rekindle," "revive the spark of"; the opposite of "quench" or *extinguish* (I Thess. 5:19). Paul does not doubt the existence of real faith in Timothy, but he desires it to be put into active exercise. Timothy seems to have become somewhat remiss from being so long without Paul (ch. 2:22). **gift of God**—the spiritual grace received for his ministerial office, either at his original ordination, or at his consecration to the particular office of superintending the Ephesian Church (*Note,* I Tim. 4:14), imparting *fearlessness, power, love, and a sound mind* (vs. 7). **by the putting on of my hands**—In I Timothy 4:14, it is "*with* [not *by*] the laying on of the hands *of the presbytery*." The apostle was chief in the ordination, and to him "BY" is applied. The presbytery were his assistants; so "with," implying merely *accompaniment,* is said of them. Paul was the instrument in Timothy's ordination and reception of the grace then conferred; the presbyters were the concurrent participants in the act of ordination; so the *Greek, dia* and *meta.* So in ordinations by a bishop in our days, he does the *principal* act; they join in laying on hands *with* him. **7. For . . .**—implying that Timothy needed the exhortation "to stir up the gift of God in him," being constitutionally *timid:* "For God *did not give* us (so the *Greek,* viz., at our ordination or consecration) the spirit of *fear.*" The spirit which He gave us, was not the spirit of timidity (lit., "cowardice," which is weakness), but of "power" (exhibited in a fearless "testimony" for Christ, vs. 8). "Power is the invariable accompaniment of the gift of *the Holy Ghost.* Luke 24:49; Acts 1:8; cf. 6:6, "full of faith and of the *Holy Ghost,*" with vs. 8," full of faith and *power.*" Fear is the result of "the spirit of bondage" (Rom. 8:15). Fear *within* exaggerates the causes of fear *without.* "The spirit of power" is the spirit of man dwelt in by the Spirit of God imparting *power;* this power "casteth out fear" from ourselves, and stimulates us to try to cast it out of others (I John 4:18). **love**—which moves the believer while "speaking the truth" with *power,* when giving his testimony for Christ (vs. 8), at the same time to do so "in love" (Eph. 4:15). **a sound mind**—The *Greek,* is rather, "the bringing of men to a sound mind" [WAHL]. BENGEL supports *English Version,* "a sound mind," or "sober-mindedness"; a duty to which a young man like Timothy especially needed to be exhorted (ch. 2:22; I Tim. 4:12; Titus 2:4, 6). So Paul urges him, in ch. 2:4, to give up worldly entanglements, which as *thorns* (Luke 8:14) choke the word. These three gifts are preferable to any miraculous powers whatever. **8. therefore**—seeing that God hath given us such a spirit, not that of *fear.* **Be not thou . . . ashamed**—I agree with ELLICOTT, in opposition to ALFORD, that the *Greek* subjunctive here, with the negative, implies action *completed at one time,* not *continued action,* which the present imperative would express; thus implying that Timothy had *not* decidedly *yet* evinced such feeling of *shame;* though I think, Paul, amidst the desertion of others who once promised fair, and from being aware of Timothy's constitutional *timidity* (*Note,* vs. 7), felt it necessary to stir him up and guard him against the possibility of unchristian dereliction of duty as to bold confession of Christ. *Shame* (vs. 8) is the companion of *fear* (vs. 7); if fear be overcome, false shame flees [BENGEL]. Paul himself (vs. 12), and Onesiphorus (vs. 16), were instances of fearless profession removing false shame. He presents in contrast sad instances of fear and shame (vs. 15). **of the testimony of our Lord**—*of the testimony* which thou art bound to give in the cause *of our Lord;* he says "our," to connect Timothy and him-

ADAM CLARKE

5. *The unfeigned faith that is in thee.* Timothy had given the fullest proof of the sincerity of his conversion and of the purity of his faith. *Which dwelt first in thy grandmother Lois.* In Acts xvi. 1, we are informed that Paul "came . . . to Derbe and Lystra: and, behold, a certain disciple was there, named Timotheus, the son of a certain woman, which was a Jewess, and believed; but his father was a Greek." Paul, in mentioning the grandmother, mother, and son, passes by the father in silence; which intimates that either the father remained in his unconverted state or was now dead. Lois, the grandmother, appears to have been the first convert to Christianity; she instructed her daughter, Eunice, and both brought up Timothy in the Christian faith.

6. *Stir up the gift of God, which is in thee.* The *gift* which Timothy had received was the Holy Spirit; and through Him, a particular power to preach and defend the truth. This *gift* is represented here under the notion of a fire, which if it be not frequently stirred up and fresh fuel added to it will go out. This is the precise idea which the apostle had in his mind; hence the term which signifies to "stir up the fire; to add fresh fuel to it." *By the putting on of my hands.* See on 1 Tim. iv. 14.

7. *God hath not given us the spirit of fear.* Here is an allusion to the giving of the law on Mount Sinai. This was communicated with such terrible majesty as to engender fear in all the Israelites; even Moses, on the occasion, "did exceedingly fear and tremble." The gospel was ushered in, in a much milder manner; everything was placed on a level with the human intellect and within reach of every human spirit. Nothing was terrific, nothing forbidding; but all was inviting. The very spirit and genius of it was a spirit of power, of love, and of a sound mind. *But of power,* to work miracles, to confound enemies, to support us in trials, and enable us to do that which is lawful and right in His sight. *And of love,* which enables us to hear, believe, hope, and endure all things; and is the incentive to all obedience. *Of a sound mind,* of "self-possession," according to some. But a sound mind implies much more; it means a clear understanding, a sound judgment, a rectified will, holy passions, heavenly tempers; in a word, the whole soul harmonized in all its powers and faculties, and completely regulated and influenced so as to think, speak, and act aright in all things.

8. *Be not . . . ashamed of the testimony.* The testimony of Christ is the gospel in general, which proclaims Christ crucified and redemption through His blood.

MATTHEW HENRY

1. We must not be ashamed of those who are suffering for the gospel of Christ. Timothy must not be ashamed of good old Paul, though he was now in bonds. The gospel is the testimony of our Lord; in and by this he bears testimony of himself to us, and by professing our adherence to it we bear testimony of him and for him. Paul was the Lord's prisoner. For his sake he was bound with a chain. If we are ashamed of either now, Christ will be ashamed of us hereafter. "Expect afflictions for the gospel's sake, be willing to take thy lot with the suffering saints in this world. *Be partaker of the afflictions of the gospel.*"

2. He takes notice what great things God has done for us by the gospel, *v.* 9, 10.

(1) The nature of that gospel and the glorious designs of it. The gospel aims at our salvation: and we must not think much to suffer for that which we hope to be saved by. It is designed for our sanctification. All who shall be saved hereafter are sanctified now. Wherever the call of the gospel is an effectual call, it is found to be a holy call.

The origin of it is the free grace and eternal purpose of God in Christ Jesus. If we had merited it, it had been hard to suffer for it; but our salvation by it is of free grace, and therefore we must not think much to suffer for it. *In Christ Jesus*, for all the gifts that come from God to sinful man come in and through Christ Jesus. The gospel is the manifestation of this purpose and grace.

Did Jesus Christ suffer for it, and shall we think much to suffer for it? By the gospel of Christ death is abolished. Death once an enemy has become a friend; it is the gate by which we pass out of a troublesome, sinful world, into a world of perfect peace and purity. Death does not triumph over those who believe the gospel, but they triumph over it.

He has *brought life and immortality to light by the gospel.* He has brought it to light, not only set it before us, but offered it to us, by the gospel.

(2) Consider the example of blessed Paul, *v.* 11, 12. He was appointed to preach the gospel, and particularly appointed to teach the Gentiles.

He thought it a cause worth suffering for, and why should not Timothy think so too? No man needs to be afraid nor ashamed to suffer for the cause of the gospel. Good men often suffer many things for the best cause in the world. They need not be ashamed, the cause will bear them out. Those who trust in Christ know whom they have trusted.

JAMIESON, FAUSSET, BROWN

self together in the testimony which both should give for their common Lord. *The testimony which Christ gave before Pilate* (I Tim. 6:12, 13), is an incentive to the believer that he should, after His Lord's example, *witness a good testimony* or *confession.* **nor of me his prisoner**—The cause of God's servants is the cause of God Himself (Eph. 4:1). Timothy might easily be tempted to be ashamed of one in prison, especially as not only worldly shame, but great risk, attended any recognition of Paul the prisoner. **be thou partaker** —*with me.* **of the gospel**—rather, as *Greek*, "*for* the Gospel," i.e., suffered *for the Gospel* (ch. 2:3-5; Philemon 13). **according to the power of God**—exhibited in having *saved* and *called* us (vs. 9). God who has done the greater act of power (i.e., saved us), will surely do the less (carry us safe through *afflictions* borne *for the Gospel*). "Think not that thou hast to bear these afflictions by thine own power; nay, it is by the power of God. It was a greater exercise of power than His making the heaven, His persuading the world to embrace salvation" [CHRYSOSTOM]. **9. Who . . . called us**—viz., God the Father (Gal. 1:6). The having "saved us" in His eternal purpose of "grace, given us in Christ before the world began," precedes his actual "calling" of us in due time with a call made effective to us by the Holy Spirit; therefore, "saved us" comes before "called us" (Rom. 8:28-30). **holy calling**—the actual call *to* a life of *holiness.* Hebrews 3:1, "heavenly calling" [TITTMANN, *Synonyms*]; whereas we were *sinners* and *enemies* (Eph. 1:18; 4:1). The call comes wholly *from* God and claims us wholly *for* God. "Holy" implies the *separation* of believers from the rest of the world unto God. **not according to**—not having regard to our works in His election and calling of grace (Rom. 9:11; Eph. 2:8, 9). **his own purpose**—The origination of salvation was of *His own purpose*, flowing from His own goodness, not for works of ours coming first, but wholly because of His own gratuitous, electing love [THEODORET and CALVIN]. **grace . . . given us** —in His everlasting purpose, regarded as the same as when actually accomplished in due time. **in Christ**—believers being regarded by God as IN HIM, with whom the Father makes the covenant of salvation (Eph. 1:4; 3:11). **before the world began**—*Greek*, "before the times (periods) of ages"; the enduring ages of which no end is contemplated (I Cor. 2:7; Eph. 3:11). **10. But . . . now . . . manifest** —in contrast to its concealment heretofore in the eternal purpose of God "before the world began" (vs. 9; Col. 1:16; Titus 1:2, 3). **appearing**—the visible manifestation in the flesh. **abolished death** —*Greek*, "taken away *the power* from death" [TITTMANN]. The *Greek* article before "death" implies that Christ abolished death, not only in some particular instance, but in its very essence, being, and idea, as well as in all its aspects and consequences (John 11:26; Rom. 8:2, 38; I Cor. 15:26, 55; Heb. 2:14). The carrying out of the abolition of death into full effect is to be at the resurrection (Rev. 20: 14). The death of the body meanwhile is but temporary, and is made no account of by Christ and the apostles. **brought . . . to light**—making visible by the Gospel what was before hidden in God's purpose. **life**—of the Spirit, acting first on the soul here, about to act on the body also at the resurrection. **immortality**—*Greek*, "incorruptibility" of the new life, not merely of the risen body [ALFORD], (Rom. 8:11). **through**—*by means of the Gospel*, which *brings to light the life and immortality* purposed by God from eternity, but manifested now first to man by Christ, who in His own resurrection has given the pledge of His people's final triumph over death through Him **11. Whereunto**—For the publication of which Gospel. **I am appointed**—*Greek*, "I was appointed." **preacher**—*Greek*, "herald." **teacher of the Gentiles**—(I Tim. 2:7). He brings forward his own example in this verse and vs. 12, as a pattern for Timothy, as a *public* "preacher," an "apostle," or *missionary* from place to place, and a "teacher" *in private* instructing His flock with patient perseverance. **12. For the which cause**—For the Gospel cause of which I was appointed a preacher (vss. 10, 11). **I also suffer**—besides my *active* work as a missionary. ELLICOTT translates, "I suffer even these things"; the sufferings attendant on my being a prisoner (vss. 8, 15). **I am not ashamed**—neither be thou (vs. 8). **for**—Confidence as to the future drives away shame [BENGEL]. **I know**—though the world knows Him not (John 10:14; 17:25). **whom** —I know what a *faithful*, promisekeeping God He is (ch. 2:13). It is not, I know *how* I have believed, but, I know WHOM I have believed; a feeble faith may clasp a strong Saviour. **believed**—rather,

ADAM CLARKE

Nor of me his prisoner. When our friends are in power and credit, we can readily acknowledge them, and take opportunities to show that we have such and such connections; but when the person falls into disgrace or discredit, though we cannot pretend not to know him, yet we take care not to acknowledge him. This induced Cicero, in relation to friendships, to give for a maxim, "A true friend is known in adverse circumstances"; and from this we have borrowed our proverb, "A friend in need is a friend indeed." *Be thou partaker of the afflictions of the gospel.* No parent could love a child better than Paul loved Timothy; and, behold! he who could wish him nothing but what was great, honorable, and good wishes him to be a *partaker of the afflictions of the gospel!* Because to suffer for Christ was the highest glory to which any human being in this state could arrive. The royal way to the crown of glory is by the cross of Christ. *According to the power of God.* While you have no more affliction than you have grace to sustain you, you can have no cause to complain. And God will take care that, if a faithful discharge of your duty shall expose you to afflictions, His power manifested in you shall be in proportion to your necessities. His load cannot be oppressive who is strengthened to bear it by the power of God.

9. *Who hath saved us.* From sin; the spirit of bondage, and all tormenting fear. This is the design of the gospel. *And called us with an holy calling.* Invited us to holiness and comfort here and to eternal glory hereafter. *Not according to our works.* We have not deserved any part of the good we have received, and can never merit one moment of the exceeding great and eternal weight of glory which is promised.

Before the world began. Before the Mosaic dispensation took place, God purposed the salvation of the Gentiles by Christ Jesus; and the Mosaic dispensation was intended only as the introducer of the gospel.

10. *But is now made manifest.* This purpose of God to save the Gentiles as well as the Jews, and call them to the same state of salvation by Jesus Christ, was, previously to the manifestation of Christ, generally hidden; and what was revealed of it was only through the means of types and ceremonies. *Who hath abolished death.* Who has "counterworked death." By death here we are not to understand merely natural death, but that corruption and decomposition which take place in consequence of it, and which would be naturally endless but for the work and energy of Christ. *Brought life and immortality to light.* The literal translation of the original is, "He hath illustrated life and incorruption by the gospel." Jesus Christ died and lay under the empire of death. He arose again from the dead and thus "illustrated" the doctrine of the resurrection. He took the same human body up into heaven, in the sight of His disciples, and ever appears in the presence of God for us; and thus has "illustrated" the doctrine of "incorruption."

11. *Whereunto I am appointed a preacher.* "A herald." *And an apostle.* Sent immediately from God to man. *A teacher.* One whose business it is to instruct men, and particularly the Gentiles, to whom he was especially sent; to proclaim the doctrines of eternal life, the resurrection and final incorruptibility of the human body; and, in a word, the salvation of both the body and soul of man by Christ Jesus.

12. *I am not ashamed.* Though I suffer for the gospel, I am not ashamed of the gospel; nor am I confounded in my expectation, His grace being at all times sufficient for me. *For I know whom I have believed.* I am well-acquainted with the goodness, mercy, and power of Christ, and know that I cannot confide in Him in vain.

MATTHEW HENRY

What must we commit to Christ? The salvation of our souls, and their preservation to the heavenly kingdom; and what we so commit to him he will keep. There is a day coming when we must give an account of our souls: now, if by an active obedient faith we commit it to Jesus Christ, we may be sure he is able to keep it.

III. He exhorts him to *hold fast the form of sound words, v.* 13. Adhere to it in opposition to all heresies and false doctrine. But how must it be held fast? Faith and love must go together; it is not enough to believe the sound words, but we must love them, believe their truth and love their goodness. It must be faith and love fastening upon Jesus Christ. *Of hearing words,* so it may read; there is a healing virtue in the word of God. To the same purport is *v.* 14. That good thing was the form of sound words, the Christian doctrine, which was committed to Timothy in his baptism, and in his ordination. The Christian doctrine is a trust committed to us. It is a good thing, of unspeakable value in itself, and which will be of unspeakable advantage to us. It is committed to us to be preserved pure and entire, and to be transmitted to those who shall come after us. Even those who are ever so well taught cannot keep what they have learned, any more than they could at first learn it, without the assistance of the Holy Spirit. We must not think to keep it by our own strength, but keep it by the Holy Ghost. The assistance and indwelling of the Holy Ghost do not exclude men's endeavours, but they very well consist together.

Verses 15–18

I. He mentions the apostasy of many from the doctrine of Christ, *v.* 15. He does not say that they had turned away from the doctrine of Christ, but they had turned away from him.

II. He mentions the constancy of Onesiphorus, *v.* 16. He often refreshed him and he was not ashamed of his chains. When Onesiphorus was at Rome he took care to seek Paul out, *v.* 17. A good man will seek opportunities of doing good. At Ephesus he had ministered to him, and been very kind to him. How Paul returns his kindness, *v.* 16–18. He repays him with his prayers.

III. He prays for Onesiphorus himself, as well as for his house: *That he may find mercy in that day,* in the day of death and of judgment. We need desire no more to make us happy than to find mercy of the Lord in that day. If you would have mercy then, you must seek for it now of the Lord. The best thing we can ask, either for ourselves or our friends, is that the Lord will grant to them that they may find mercy of the Lord in that day.

JAMIESON, FAUSSET, BROWN

"trusted"; carrying out the metaphor of a depositor depositing his pledge with one whom he *trusts.* **am persuaded**—(Rom. 8:38). **he is able**—in spite of so many foes around me. **that which I have committed unto him**—*Greek,* "my deposit"; the body, soul, and spirit, which I have deposited in God's safe keeping (I Thess. 5:23; I Pet. 4:19). So Christ Himself in dying (Luke 23:46). "God deposits with us His word; we deposit with God our spirit" [GROTIUS]. There is one deposit [His revelation] committed by God to us, which we ought to keep (vss. 13, 14) and transmit to others (ch. 2:2); there is another committed by God to us, which we should commit to His keeping, viz., ourselves and our heavenly portion. **that day**—the day of His appearing (vs. 18; ch. 4:8). **13. Hold fast the form**—rather as *Greek, "Have* (i.e., keep) a *pattern* of sound (*Greek,* 'healthy') words which thou hast heard from me, in faith and love." "Keep" suits the reference to a *deposit* in the context. The secondary position of the verb in the *Greek* forbids our taking it so strongly as *English Version,* "Hold fast." The *Greek* for "form" is translated "pattern" in I Timothy 1:16, the only other passage where it occurs. Have such a *pattern* drawn from my *sound* words, in opposition to the *unsound* doctrines so current at Ephesus, *vividly impressed* (WAHL translates it "delineation"; the verb implies "to make *a lively and lasting impress*") on thy mind. **in faith and love**—the element IN which my sound words had place, and in which thou art *to have the vivid impression* of them as thy *inwardly delineated pattern,* moulding conformably thy outward profession. So nearly BENGEL explains, I Timothy 3:9. **14.** Translate as *Greek,* "That goodly deposit keep through the Holy Ghost," viz., "the sound words which I have committed to thee" (vs. 13; ch. 2:2). **in us**—in all believers, not merely in you and me. The indwelling Spirit enables us to keep from the robbers of the soul the deposit of His word committed to us by God. **15. all they which are in Asia**—Proconsular Asia; "all who are there *now, when they were in Rome* (not "*be*" or *are,* but) turned from me" then; were "ashamed of my chain," in contrast to ONESIPHORUS; did not stand with me but forsook me (ch. 4:16). It is possible that the occasion of their turning from him was at his apprehension in Nicopolis, whither they had escorted him on his way to Rome, but from which they turned back to Asia. A hint to Timothy, now in Asia, not to be like them, but to imitate rather ONESIPHORUS, and to come to him (ch. 4:21). **Phygellus and Hermogenes**—specified perhaps, as being persons from whom such pusillanimous conduct could least be expected; or, as being well known to Timothy, and spoken of before in conversations between him and Paul, when the latter was in Asia Minor. **16. The Lord give mercy**—even as ONESIPHORUS had abounded in works of *mercy.* **the house of Onesiphorus**—He himself was then absent from Ephesus, which accounts for the form of expression (ch. 4:19). His *household* would hardly retain his name after the master was dead, as BENGEL supposes him to have been. Nowhere has Paul prayers for the dead, which is fatal to the theory, favored by ALFORD also, that he was dead. God blesses not only the righteous man himself, but all his household. **my chain**—Paul in the second, as in his first imprisonment, was bound by a chain to the soldier who guarded him. **17. found me**—in the crowded metropolis. So in turn "may he *find* mercy of the Lord in that day" when the whole universe shall be assembled. **18. grant unto him**—as well as "unto his house" (vs. 16). **the Lord**—who rewards a kindness done to His disciples as if done to Himself (Matt. 25:45). **of**—*from* the Lord; "the Lord" is emphatically put instead of "from Himself," for solemnity and emphasis (II Thess. 3: 5). **in how many things**—"how many acts of ministry he rendered." **unto me**—omitted in the oldest MSS., so that the "ministered" may include services rendered *to others* as well as to Paul. **very well**—rather as *Greek,* "Thou knowest better" (than I can tell thee, seeing that thou art more of a regular resident at Ephesus).

ADAM CLARKE

That which I have committed unto him. This is variously understood. Some think he means his life, which he had put, as it were, into the hands of Christ in order that he might receive it again in the resurrection, at the great day. Others think he means his faithful Creator, knowing that, although wicked men might be permitted to take away his life, yet they could not destroy his soul nor disturb its peace. Others think that he is speaking of the gospel, which he knows will be carefully preserved by the great Head of the Church. For though he shall be soon called to seal the truth with his blood, yet he knows that God will take care that the same truth shall be proclaimed to the world by others whom God shall raise up for that very purpose.

13. *Hold fast the form.* The word signifies the "sketch, plan, or outline" of a building, picture, etc.; and here refers to the plan of salvation which the apostle had taught Timothy.

In faith and love. Faith credits the divine doctrines. *Love* reduces them all to practice. *Faith* lays hold on Jesus Christ, and obtains that *love* by which every precept is cheerfully and effectually obeyed.

14. *That good thing.* The everlasting gospel. *Keep by the Holy Ghost,* for without a continual spiritual energy man can do nothing.

15. *All they which are in Asia.* It seems as if the apostle must refer to the Asiatic Christians which were then at Rome or had been lately there. Finding the apostle in disgrace and thinking it dangerous to own him or his cause, they neither visited him nor confessed Christianity. He cannot be speaking of any general defection of the Asiatic churches, but of those Asiatics who had professed a particular friendship for him. *Phygellus and Hermogenes.* These were two of the persons of whom he complains; but who they were or what office they held or whether they were anything but private Christians who had for a time ministered to Paul in prison and, when they found the state determined to destroy him, ceased to acknowledge him, we cannot tell.

16. *The Lord give mercy. Onesiphorus* had acknowledged him, and continued to do so; he and his *house,* or "family," ministered to him in prison, and were not ashamed of their imprisoned pastor nor of the cause for which he was in disgrace and suffering. As he showed mercy to the apostle, the apostle prays the Lord to show mercy to him.

17. *When he was in Rome.* Onesiphorus was no doubt an Asiatic who had frequent business at Rome; and when he came sought out the apostle, who, it is supposed, had been confined in some close and private prison, so that it was with great difficulty he could find him out. This man had entertained the apostle when he was at Ephesus, and now he sought him out at Rome. Pure love feels no loads. Here was a true friend, one "that sticketh closer than a brother."

18. *The Lord grant . . . that he may find mercy of the Lord.* Some think that this is a prayer to God the Father to communicate grace to him, that he might find mercy in the great day at the hand of Jesus Christ, the Judge. It is probably only a Hebraism for "God grant that he may here be so saved by divine grace that in the great day he may receive the mercy of the Lord Jesus Christ unto eternal life." See a similar form of expression, Gen. ix. 16; xix. 24; Exod. xxiv. 1-2.

MATTHEW HENRY — CHAPTER 2

Verses 1–7

Paul encourages Timothy to constancy and perseverance in his work, *v.* 1. Those who have work to do for God must strengthen themselves for it. Where there is the truth of grace there must be a labouring after the strength of grace. We have need to grow stronger and stronger in that which is good.

JAMIESON, FAUSSET, BROWN — CHAPTER 2

VSS. 1-26. EXHORTATIONS; TO FAITHFULNESS AS A GOOD SOLDIER OF CHRIST; ERRORS TO BE SHUNNED; THE LORD'S SURE FOUNDATION; THE RIGHT SPIRIT FOR A SERVANT OF CHRIST. **1. Thou therefore**—following my example (ch. 1:8, 12), and that of ONESIPHORUS (ch. 1:16-18), and shunning that of those who forsook me (ch. 1:15). **my son**—*Children*

ADAM CLARKE — CHAPTER 2

MATTHEW HENRY

Or it may be understood in opposition to our being strong in our own strength: "Be strong, not confiding in thy own sufficiency, but in the grace that is in Jesus Christ." There is grace enough in him for all of us. We must be strong in this grace; not in ourselves, or in the grace we have already received, but in the grace that is in him.

I. Timothy must count upon sufferings, even unto blood, and therefore he must train up others to succeed him in the ministry of the gospel, *v.* 2. He must lodge the gospel as a trust in their hands, and so commit to them the things which he had heard. Two things he must have an eye to in ordaining ministers: Their fidelity or integrity, and also their ministerial ability. They must not only be knowing themselves, but be apt to teach.

II. He must *endure hardness* (*v.* 3). All Christians, but especially ministers, *are soldiers of Jesus Christ.* The soldiers of Jesus Christ must approve themselves good soldiers, faithful to their captain, resolute in his cause. Those who would approve themselves good soldiers of Jesus Christ must endure hardness; we must count upon it in this world, and bear it patiently when it comes.

III He must not entangle himself in the affairs of this world, *v* 4. If we have given up ourselves to be Christ's soldiers, we must sit loose to this world; and though we must employ ourselves in the affairs of this life while we are here (we have something to do here), we must not entangle ourselves with those affairs. The great care of a soldier should be to please his general; so the great care of a Christian should be to please Christ.

IV. He must see to it that in carrying on the spiritual warfare he went by rule, that he observed the laws of war (*v.* 5). In doing that which is good we must take care that we do it in a right manner, that our good may not be evil spoken of. Those who do so shall be crowned at last.

V. He must be willing to wait for a recompence (*v.* 6). If we would be partakers of the fruits, we must labour. We must do the will of God, before we receive the promises.

The apostle further commends what he had said to the attention of Timothy. Timothy must be reminded to use his considering faculties about the things of God. Consideration is as necessary to a good conversation as to a sound conversion. He prays for him: *The Lord give thee understanding in all things.* The most intelligent man needs more and more of this gift. If he who gave the revelation in the word does not give the understanding in the heart, we are nothing.

Verses 8–13

I. To encourage Timothy in suffering, the apostle puts him in mind of the resurrection of Christ (*v.* 8). The consideration of it should make us faithful to our Christian profession. The incarnation and resurrection of Jesus Christ, heartily believed and rightly considered, will support a Christian under all sufferings in the present life.

II. Another thing to encourage him in suffering was that he had Paul for an example.

1. How the apostle suffered (*v.* 9). We must not think it strange if those who do well fare ill in this world, and if the best of men meet with the worst of treatment; but this was his comfort *that the word of God was not bound.* Persecuting powers cannot hinder the operation of the word of God upon men's hearts and consciences; that cannot be bound by any human force. This might encourage Timothy not to be afraid of bonds for the testimony of Jesus.

2. Why he suffered cheerfully, *v.* 10. Next to the salvation of our own souls we should be willing to do and suffer any thing to promote the salvation of the souls of others.

JAMIESON, FAUSSET, BROWN

ought to imitate their father. **be strong**—lit., "be invested with *power.*" Have power, and show thyself to have it; implying an abiding state of power. **in the grace**—the *element* IN which the believer's strength has place. Cf. ch. 1:7, "God hath given us the spirit of *power.*" **2. among**—*Greek,* "through," i.e., with the attestation (lit., "intervention") of many witnesses, viz., the presbyters and others present at his ordination or consecration (I Tim. 4:14; 6:12). **commit**—in trust, as a *deposit* (ch. 1:14). **faithful**—the quality most needed by those having a trust committed to them. **who**—*Greek,* "(persons) *such as* shall be competent to teach (them to) others also." Thus the way is prepared for inculcating the duty of faithful endurance (vss. 3-13). Thou shouldest consider as a motive to endurance, that thou hast not only to keep the deposit for thyself, but to transmit it unimpaired to others, who in their turn shall fulfil the same office. **3. Thou therefore endure hardness**—The oldest MSS. have no "*Thou therefore,*" and read, "Endure hardship *with*" (me). "Take thy share in suffering" [CONYBEARE and HOWSON]. **4.** "No one while serving as a soldier." **the affairs . . .**—"the businesses of life" [ALFORD]; mercantile, or other than military. **him who hath chosen him**—the general who at the first enlisted him as a soldier. Paul himself worked at tent-making (Acts 18:3). Therefore what is prohibited here is, not all other save religious occupation, but the becoming *entangled,* or over-engrossed therewith. **5. And**—"Moreover." **strive for masteries**—"strive in the games" [ALFORD]; viz., the great national games of Greece. **yet is he not crowned, except**—even though he gain the victory. **strive lawfully**—observing all the conditions of both the contest (keeping within the bounds of the course and stript of his clothes) and the preparation for it, viz., as to selfdenying diet, anointing, exercise, self-restraint, chastity, decorum, etc. (I Cor. 9:24-27). **6. must be first partaker**—The right of *first partaking of the fruits* belongs to him *who is laboring;* do not thou, therefore, relax thy labors, as thou wouldest be foremost in partaking of the reward. CONYBEARE explains "first," *before the idler.* **7.** Consider the force of the illustrations I have given from the soldier, the contender in the games, and the husbandmen, as *applying to thyself in thy ministry.* **and the Lord give thee . . .**—The oldest MSS. read, "*for* the Lord *will give* thee understanding." Thou canst understand my meaning so as personally to apply it to thyself; for the Lord will give thee understanding when thou seekest it from Him "in all things." Not intellectual perception, but personal appropriation of the truths metaphorically expressed, was what he needed to be given him by the Lord. **8.** Rather as *Greek,* "Remember Jesus Christ, raised from the dead." Remember Christ risen, so as to follow Him. As He was raised after death, so if thou wouldest share His risen "life," thou must now share His "death" (vs. 11). The *Greek* perfect passive participle, implies a *permanent character* acquired by Jesus as *the risen* Saviour, and *our permanent interest in Him as such.* Christ's resurrection is put prominently forward as being the truth now assailed (vs. 18), and the one best calculated to stimulate Timothy to steadfastness in sharing Paul's sufferings for the Gospel's sake (*Note,* vs. 3). **of the seed of David**—The one and only genealogy (as contrasted with the "endless genealogies," (I Tim. 1: 4) worth thinking of, for it proves Jesus to be the Messiah. **my gospel**—that which I always taught. **9. Wherein**—in proclaiming which Gospel. **suffer trouble**—lit., "evil." I am a sufferer of evil as though I were a doer of evil. **bonds**—(ch. 1:16). **word . . . not bound**—Though my person is bound, my tongue and my pen are not (ch. 4:17; Acts 28: 31). Or he alludes not merely to *his own* proclamation of the Gospel, though in chains, but to the freedom of its circulation *by others,* even though his power of circulating it is now prescribed (Phil. 1: 18). He also hints to Timothy that he being free ought to be the more earnest in the service of it. **10. Therefore**—Because of the anxiety I feel that the Gospel should be extended; that anxiety being implied in vs. 9. **endure**—not merely "I passively *suffer,*" but "I actively and perseveringly *endure,*" and "am ready to endure patiently all things." **the elect's sakes**—for the sake of the Church: all the members of Christ's spiritual body (Col. 1:24). **they . . . also**—as well as myself: both God's elect not yet converted and those already so. **salvation . . . glory**—not only *salvation* from wrath, but *glory* in *reigning* with Him eternally (vs. 12). *Glory* is the full expansion of *salvation* (Acts 2:47; Rom. 8: 21-24, 30; Heb. 9:28). So *grace* and *glory* (Ps. 84:

ADAM CLARKE

1. *Be strong in the grace.* Though the genuine import of the word *grace* is "favor," yet it often implies an active principle communicated from God; light directing how to act, and power enabling to act according to the light.

2. *The things that thou hast heard of me.* Those doctrines which I have preached the most publicly and which many persons can attest. But he seems to refer here to the doctrines delivered to him when, in the presence of many witnesses, he laid his hands upon him; see 1 Tim. vi. 12. Then the apostle gave him the proper form of sound words which he was to teach; and now he tells him to commit those truths to faithful men in the same way that they were committed to him, that the truth might be preserved in the Church, and holy men appointed successively to preach it.

3. *Endure hardness.* He considers a Christian minister under the notion of a soldier, not so much for his continual conflicts with the world, the devil, and the flesh, for these are in a certain sense common to all Christians, but for the hardships and difficulties to which he must be exposed who faithfully preaches the gospel of Christ.

4. *No man that warreth entangleth.* It is well remarked by Grotius, on this passage, that the legionary soldiers among the Romans were not permitted to engage in husbandry, merchandise, mechanical employments, or anything that might be inconsistent with their calling. He who will preach the gospel thoroughly, and wishes to give full proof of his ministry, had need to have no other work. He should be wholly in this thing, that his profiting may appear unto all.

5. *If a man also strive for masteries.* "If a man contend in the public games"—the Olympic or Isthmian games among the Greeks. *Is he not crowned,* though he may have conquered, *except he strive lawfully,* unless he enter according to the rules of the athletae, and act as these direct.

6. *The husbandman that laboureth.* That is: The *husbandman* must *first* till his ground before he can expect a crop; and he must till it according to the proper rules of agriculture, else he cannot have a crop.

7. *Consider what I say.* Apply my metaphors and similitudes in a proper manner. *And the Lord give thee understanding.* But instead of "may He give," several MSS., besides versions and fathers, have "He will give." Consider properly, and God will give you a proper understanding of all things that concern your own peace and the peace and prosperity of His Church. Think as well as read.

8. *Remember that Jesus Christ.* The apostle seems to say: Whatever tribulations or deaths may befall us, let us remember that Jesus Christ, who was slain by the Jews, rose again from the dead, and His resurrection is the proof and pledge of ours. *According to my gospel.* The false teaching of Hymenaeus and Philetus stated that the resurrection was past already. Paul preached the resurrection from the dead, and founded his doctrine on the resurrection and promise of Christ. This was his gospel; the other was of a different nature.

10. *For the elect's sakes.* For the sake of the Gentiles, elected by God's goodness to enjoy every privilege formerly possessed by the Jews, and, in addition to these, all the blessings of the gospel: the salvation of Christ here, and eternal glory hereafter.

MATTHEW HENRY

III. Another thing with which he encourages Timothy is the prospect of a future state.

1. Those who faithfully adhere to Christ, whatever it cost them, will certainly have the advantage of it in another world, *v.* 11. If we be dead to this world we shall go to live with him in a better world, to be for ever with him. *Those who suffer for Christ* on earth shall reign with Christ in heaven, *v.* 12.

2. It is at our peril if we prove unfaithful to him. That man must needs be for ever miserable whom Christ disowns at last. This will certainly be the issue, whether we believe it or no (*v.* 13). If we be faithful to Christ, he will certainly be faithful to us. If we be false to him, he will be faithful to his threatenings This is a faithful saying, and may be depended on and ought to be believed.

Verses 14–18

He comes in the next place to direct him in his work.

I. He must make it his business to edify those who were under his charge. This is the work of ministers; not to tell people that which they never knew before, but to put them in mind of that which they do know, *charging them that they strive not about words.* If people did but consider of what little use most of the controversies in religion are, they would not be so zealous in their strifes of words. People are very prone to strive about words, and such strifes never answer any other ends than to shake some and subvert others. *Study to show thyself approved unto God, v.* 15, *a workman that need not be ashamed.* Workmen that are unskilful, or unfaithful, or lazy, have need to be ashamed; but those who mind their business, and keep to their work, are workmen that need not be ashamed. And what is their work? Not to invent a new gospel, but rightly to divide the gospel that is committed to their trust.

II. He must take heed of that which would be a hindrance to him in his work, *v.* 16. He must take heed of error: *Shun profane and vain babblings.* When once men became fond of those *they will increase unto more ungodliness.* The way of error is down-hill. The infecting of one often proves the infecting of many, or the infecting of the same person with one error often proves the infecting of him with many errors. The apostle mentions some who had lately advanced erroneous doctrines: *Hymeneus and Philetus.*

JAMIESON, FAUSSET, BROWN

12). **11.** *Greek,* "Faithful is the saying." **For**—"For" the fact is so that, "if we be dead with Him (the *Greek* aorist tense implies *a state once for all entered into in past times* at the moment of regeneration, Rom. 6:3, 4, 8; Col. 2:12), we shall also live with Him." The symmetrical form of "the saying," vss. 11-13, and the rhythmical balance of the parallel clauses, makes it likely, they formed part of a Church hymn (*Note,* I Tim. 3:16), or accepted formula, perhaps first uttered by some of the Christian "prophets" in the public assembly (I Cor. 14:26). The phrase "faithful is the saying," which seems to have been the usual formula (cf. I Tim. 1:15; 3:1; 4:9; Titus 3:8) in such cases, favors this. **12. suffer**—rather, as the *Greek* is the same as in vs. 10, "If we endure (with Him)," (Rom. 8:17). **reign with him**—The peculiar privilege of the elect Church now suffering with Christ, then to reign with Him (*Note,* I Cor. 6:2). *Reigning* is something more than mere *salvation* (Rom. 5:17; Rev. 3:21; 5:10; 20:4, 5). **deny**—*with the mouth.* As "believe" *with the heart follows,* vs. 12. Cf. the opposite, "confess with thy mouth" and "believe in thine heart" (Rom. 10:9, 10). **he also will deny us**—(Matt. 10:33). **13. believe not**—"If we are unbelievers (lit., 'unfaithful'), He remains *faithful*" (Deut. 7:9, 10). The oldest MSS. read, *"For* He cannot (it is an *impossibility* that He should) deny Himself." *He* cannot be unfaithful to His word that He will deny those who deny Him, though *we* be not faithful to our profession of faith in Him (Rom. 3:3). Three things are impossible to God, to die, to lie, and to be deceived [AUGUSTINE, *Symbolism ad Catechumenos,* 1. 1], (Heb. 6:18). This impossibility is not one of infirmity, but of infinite power and majesty. Also, indirectly, comfort is suggested to believers, that He is faithful to His promises to them; at the same time that apostates are shaken out of their self-deceiving fancy, that because they change, Christ similarly may change. A warning to Timothy to be steadfast in the faith. **14. them**—those over whom thou dost preside (Titus 3:1). **charging**—*Greek,* "testifying continually": "adjuring them." **before the Lord**—(I Tim. 5:21). **that they strive not about words**—rather, "strive with words": "not to have a (mere) *war of words*" (vss. 23, 24; I Tim. 6:4) where the most vital matters are at stake (vss. 17, 18; Acts 18:15). The oldest MSS. put a stop at "charging them before the Lord" (which clause is thus connected with "put them in remembrance") and read the imperative, "Strive not thou in words . . . ." **to no profit**—not qualifying "words"; but *Greek* neuter, in apposition with "strive in words," "(a thing tending) to no profit," lit., "profitable for nothing"; the opposite of "meet for the master's use" (vs. 21). **to the subverting**—sure to subvert (overturn) the hearers: the opposite of "edifying" (building up) (II Cor. 13:10). **15. Study**—*Greek,* "Be earnest," or "diligent." **to show**—*Greek,* "present," as in Romans 12:1. **thyself**—as distinguished from those whom Timothy was to charge (vs. 14). **approved**—tested by trial: opposed to "reprobate" (Titus 1:16). **workman**—alluding to Matthew 20:1 etc. **not to be ashamed**—by his work not being "approved" (Phil. 1:20). Contrast "deceitful workers" (II Cor. 11: 13). **rightly dividing**—"rightly handling" [*Vulgate*]; "rightly administering" [ALFORD]; lit., cutting "straight" or "right": the metaphor being from a father or a steward (I Cor. 4:1) *cutting* and *distributing* bread among his children [VITRINGA and CALVIN], (Luke 12:42). LXX, Proverbs 3:6 and 11:5, use it of "making one's way": so BENGEL here takes Paul to mean that Timothy may *make ready a straight way for* "the word of truth," and may himself walk straight forward according to this line, turning neither to the right nor to the left, "teaching no other doctrine" (I Tim. 1:3). The same image of a *way* appears in the *Greek* for "increase" (*Note,* vs. 16). The opposite to "rightly handling," or "dispensing," is, II Corinthians 2:17, "corrupt the word of God." **truth**—*Greek, "the* truth" (cf. vs. 18). **16. shun**—lit., "stand above," separate from, and superior to. **vain**—opposed to "the truth" (vs. 15). **babblings**—with loud voice: opposed to the temperate "word" (Titus 3:9). **increase**—*Greek,* advance"; lit., "strike forward": an image from pioneers *cutting* away all obstacles *before* an advancing army. They pretend *progress;* the only kind of *progress* they make is to a greater pitch of impiety. **more ungodliness**—*Greek,* "a greater degree of impiety." **17. will eat**—lit., "will have pasture." The consuming progress of mortification is the image. They pretend to give rich spiritual *pasture* to their disciples: the only *pasture* is that of a spiritual cancer feeding on their vitals. **canker**— a "cancer" or "gangrene." **Hymeneus**—

ADAM CLARKE

11. *If we be dead with him.* That is: As surely as Christ rose again from the dead, so surely shall we rise again, and if we die for Him, we shall surely live again with Him. This, says the apostle, is "a true doctrine."

13. *If we believe not.* Should we deny the faith and apostatize, He is the same, as true to His threatenings as to His promises; *he cannot deny,* act contrary to, *himself.*

14. *That they strive not about words.* Words, not things, have been a most fruitful source of contention in the Christian world; and among religious people, the principal cause of animosity has arisen from the different manner of apprehending the same term, while in essence both meant the same thing. All preachers and divines should be very careful, in both speaking and writing, to explain the terms they use, and never employ them in any sense but that in which they have explained them. *The subverting of the hearers.* This is the general tendency of all polemical divinity and controversial preaching, when angry passions are called in to support the doctrines of the gospel.

15. *Study to shew thyself approved unto God.* Endeavor so to cultivate and improve your heart and mind that you may not be a reproach to Him from whom you profess to receive your commission. *Rightly dividing the word of truth.* The word signifies (1) simply to "cut straight," (2) to "walk in the right way." Therefore, by *rightly dividing the word of truth* we are to understand his continuing in the true doctrine and teaching that to every person.

16. *Shun profane and vain babblings.* This is the character he gives of the preaching of the false teachers. Whatever was not agreeable to the doctrine of truth was, in the sight of God, "empty and profane babbling"; engendering nothing but *ungodliness,* and daily increasing in that.

17. *Their word will eat as doth a canker.* "As a gangrene"; i.e., as a mortification in the flesh, where the circulation is entirely stopped and putrefaction takes place, which continues to corrupt all the circumjacent flesh, spreading more and more till death takes place, unless stopped by a timely and judicious application of medicine. Such is the influence of false doctrine; it fixes its mortal seed in the soul, which continues to corrupt and assimilate everything to itself till, if not prevented by a timely application of the word of life, under the direction of the heavenly Physician, it terminates in the bitter pains of an eternal death. To such a gangrene the apostle compares the corrupt doctrines of Hymenaeus and Philetus.

MATTHEW HENRY

They did not deny the resurrection, but they put a corrupt interpretation upon that true doctrine, saying that the resurrection was past already. By this they *overthrew the faith of some.* Whatever takes away the doctrine of a future state overthrows the faith of Christians. Error is very productive and on that account the more dangerous. When men err concerning the truth, they always endeavour to have some plausible pretence for it.

Verses 19–21

I. The unbelief of men cannot make the promise of God of no effect. The prophets and apostles, that is, the doctrines of the Old and New Testament, are still firm; and they have a seal with two mottoes upon it, one on the one side, and the other on the other, as is usual in a broad seal.

One expresses our comfort—that *the Lord knows those that are his.* He will never lose them. Another declares our duty—that everyone who names the name of Christ must depart from iniquity. We must depart from iniquity, else he will not own us.

II. Though there are some whose faith is overthrown, yet there are others who keep their integrity, and hold it fast (*v.* 20). There are some professors of religion that are like the vessels of wood and earth, they are vessels of dishonour. But at the same time all are not vessels of dishonour. When we are discouraged by the badness of some, we must encourage ourselves by the goodness of others. Now we should see to it that we be vessels of honour: sanctified for our Master's use. Every vessel must be fit for its Master's use; everyone in the church whom God approves must be devoted to his Master's service and meet for his use.

Verses 22–26

I. Paul here exhorts Timothy to beware of *youthful lusts, v.* 22. The lusts of the flesh are youthful lusts, which young people must carefully watch against. He prescribes an excellent remedy against youthful lusts. Youthful lusts are very dangerous, for they war against the soul. The exciting of our graces will be the extinguishing of our corruptions; the more we follow that which is good the faster and the further we shall flee from that which is evil. Our prayers to God and Christ are not acceptable except they come out of a pure heart.

II. He cautions him against contention, and (*v.* 23) cautions him against *foolish and unlearned questions,*

JAMIESON, FAUSSET, BROWN

(*Note,* I Tim. 1:20). After his excommunication he seems to have been re-admitted into the Church and again to have troubled it. **18. erred**—*Greek,* "missed the aim" (*Note,* I Tim. 6:21). **is past already**—has already taken place. The beginnings of the subsequent Gnostic heresy already existed. They "wrested" (II Pet. 3:16) Paul's own words (Rom. 6:4; Eph. 2:6 Col. 2:12) "to their own destruction," as though the resurrection was merely the spiritual raising of souls from the death of sin. **overthrow**—trying to subvert "the foundation" on which alone faith can rest secure (vs. 19; cf. Titus 1:11). **19. Nevertheless**—Notwithstanding the subversion of *their* faith, "the firm foundation of *God* standeth" fast (so the *Greek* ought to be translated). The "foundation" here is "the Church" [ALFORD], "the ground" or basement support "of the truth" (I Tim. 3:15), Christ Himself being the ultimate "foundation" (I Cor. 3:11). In the steadfast standing of *the Church* there is involved the steadfast certainty of the *doctrine* in question (vs. 18). **having**—seeing that it has [ELLICOTT]. **seal**—"inscription": indicating *ownership* and *destination;* inscriptions were often engraven on a "foundation" stone (Rev. 21:14) [ALFORD]. This will agree with the view that "the foundation" is *the Church* (Eph. 2:20). If it be taken God's *immovable faithfulness,* the "seal" will be regarded as attached to His covenant promise, with the inscription or legend, on one side of its round surface, "The Lord knoweth (it is 'knew' in LXX, Num. 16:5, to which Paul here alludes, altering it for his purpose by the Spirit) them that are His"; on the observe side, "Let every one that nameth (as *his* Lord, Ps. 20:7, or preacheth in His name, Jer. 20:9) Christ. . . ." **depart**—*Greek,* "stand aloof." **from iniquity**—(Isa. 52:11). In both clauses there may be an allusion to Num. 16:5, 26, LXX. God's part and man's part are marked out. God chooseth and knoweth His elect; our part is to believe, and by the Spirit depart from all iniquity, an unequivocal proof of our being the Lord's (cf. Deut. 29:29; Luke 13: 23-27). **20. in a great house**—i.e., the visible professing Christian Church (I Tim. 3: 15). Paul is speaking, not of those without, but of the [visible] family of God [CALVIN]. So the parable of the sweep net (Matt. 13:47-49) gathering together of every kind, good and bad: as the good and bad cannot be distinguished while under the waves, but only when brought to shore, so believers and unbelievers continue in the same Church, until the judgment makes the everlasting distinction. "The ark of Noah is a type of the Church; as in the former there were together the leopard and the kid, the wolf and the lamb; so in the latter, the righteous and sinners, vessels of gold and silver, with vessels of wood and earth" [JEROME, *contra Luciferianos,* 302] (cf. Matt. 20:16). **vessels of gold . . . silver**—precious and able to endure fire. **of wood and earth**—worthless, fragile, and soon burnt (II Cor. 3:12-15; 15:47). **some . . . some**—the former . . . the latter. **to dishonour**—(Prov. 16:4; Rom. 9:17-23). **21. If a man . . . purge himself from these**—The *Greek* expresses "If one (e.g., thou, Timothy) purify himself (so as to separate) *from among these*" (*vessels* unto dishonor). **sanctified**—set apart as wholly consecrated to the Lord. **and meet**—Some oldest MSS. omit "and." **the master's**—the Lord's. Paul himself was such a vessel: once one among those of earth, but afterwards he became by grace one of gold. **prepared unto every good work**—(Ch. 3:17; Titus 3:1). Contrast Titus 1:16. **22. Flee**—There are many lusts from which our greatest safety is in *flight* (Gen. 39:12). Avoid occasions of sin. From the abstemious character of Timothy (I Tim. 5:23) it is likely that not animal indulgences, but the impetuosity, rash self-confidence, hastiness, strife, and vainglory of young men (I John 2:14-16), are what *he* is here warned against: though the Spirit probably intended the warning to include *both* in its application to the Church *in general.* **also**—*Greek,* "But"; in contrast to "every good work," vs. 21. **youthful**—Timothy was a youth (I Tim. 4:12). **righteousness**—the opposite of "iniquity," i.e., unrighteousness (vs. 19; cf. I Tim. 6:11). **peace, with . . .**—rather put no comma, "*peace with them* that call on the Lord out of a pure heart" (I Tim. 1:5; Eph. 6:5; Col. 3:22). We are to *love* all men, but it is not possible to be at *peace* with all men, for this needs community of purpose and opinion; they alone who call on the Lord sincerely [as contrasted with the false teachers who had only the form of godliness, ch. 3:5, 8; Titus 1:15, 16] have this community [THEODORET]. (Rom. 12:18). **23.** (Titus 3: 9.) **unlearned**—*Greek,* "undisciplined"; not tending to promote the discipline of faith and morals (Prov.

ADAM CLARKE

18. *Who concerning the truth have erred.* They had the truth, but *erred* or "wandered from it," saying *the resurrection* was already *past,* and thus denying the resurrection of the body and, by consequence, future rewards and punishments.

19. *The foundation of God standeth sure.* The word signifies literally a *foundation,* and especially the foundation of a building; and metaphorically, the building itself, and often a noble mansion or palace. In this place the apostle compares the religion of Christ to a great or noble mansion. See v. 20. And as this religion is founded on the authority and power of the Almighty, it necessarily must stand sure and be permanent. This house has an "inscription" on it, for so *seal* is frequently understood; and this is evidently an allusion to the ancient temples. Above the door of the temple of Delphi there was the Greek word, "Thou art," on which Plutarch has written an express treatise. And we know that there was an inscription on the mitre of the high priest among the Jews, viz., "Holiness to the Lord"; Exod. xxviii. 36; xxxix. 30.

But some suppose here a "contract" or "covenant" by which two parties are bound to fulfill certain conditions and duties, the obligation to which each takes on him by sealing the instrument with his seal. The twofold inscription, i.e., one on the seal of each party, may be here alluded to; that on God's seal is, *"The Lord* approveth of *them that are his."* That on the seal of His followers is, *"Let every one that nameth the name of* the Lord (every Christian) *depart from iniquity."* "Lord," instead of *Christ,* is the reading of almost all the MSS. of importance, and the principal versions. *The Lord knoweth.* I.e., Approves, watches over, and provides for, them that are His true followers. To this His followers most cheerfully subscribe, and say: "Let every one that nameth this Lord avoid every appearance of evil."

20. *But in a great house.* Here the apostle carries on the allusion introduced in the preceding verse. As the "foundation of God" refers to God's building, i.e., the whole system of Christianity, so here the *great house* is to be understood of the same; and the different kinds of vessels mean the different teachers, as well as the different kinds of members. In this sacred house at Ephesus there were *vessels of gold and of silver*—eminent, holy, sincere, and useful teachers and members; and also *vessels of wood and of earth*—false and heretical teachers, such as Hymenaeus and Philetus, and their followers.

21. *If a man therefore purge himself from these.* He that takes heed to his ways and to his doctrines, and walks with God, will separate himself, not only from all false doctrine, but from all wicked men, and thus be sanctified and proper to be employed by the Master in every good word and work. The apostle has not made the application of these different similes, and it is very difficult to tell what he means.

22. *Flee also youthful lusts.* Not only all irregular and sensual desires, but pride, ambition, and, above all, the lust of power, to which most men will sacrifice all other propensities, their ease, pleasure, health, etc. This is the most bewitching passion in the human heart. Both in church and state it is ruinous, but particularly so in the former. Timothy was now between thirty and forty years of age, the very age in which ambition and the love of power most generally prevail. Carnal pleasures are the sins of youth; ambition and the love of power, the sins of middle age; covetousness and carking cares, the crimes of old age. *Follow righteousness.* Flee from sin, pursue goodness. *Righteousness*—whatever is just, holy, and innocent. *Faith*—fidelity to both God and man, improving that grace by which your soul may be saved, and faithfully discharging the duties of your office. *Charity*—love to God and man. *Peace* among all the members of the church, and as far as possible with all men.

23. *Foolish and unlearned questions.* See the notes on 1 Tim. i. 4; iv. 7; and Titus iii. 9.

MATTHEW HENRY

strifes of words. Those who advanced them thought themselves wise and learned; but Paul calls them foolish and unlearned. They breed debates and quarrels among Christians. Religion consists more in believing and practising what God requires than in subtle disputes.—*The servant of the Lord must not strive, v.* 24. The servant of the Lord must be *gentle to all men.—Apt to teach.* Those are unapt to teach who are apt to strive. *In meekness instructing* (*v.* 25) not only those who subject themselves, but those who oppose themselves. This is the way to convey truth in its light and power, and to overcome evil with good. That which ministers must have in their eyes, in instructing those who oppose themselves, is their recovery. Repentance is God's gift. It is a gift with a *peradventure* in the case of those who oppose themselves. The same God who gives us the discovery of the truth does by his grace bring us to the acknowledging of it, otherwise our hearts would continue in rebellion against it. And thus sinners recover themselves out of the snare of the devil.

The misery of sinners, *v.* 26. They are slaves to the worst of task-masters. They are taken in a snare, and in the worst snare, because it is the devil's. The happiness of those who repent: they recover themselves out of this snare. Those who before were led captive by the devil at his will come to be led into the glorious liberty of the children of God.

JAMIESON, FAUSSET, BROWN

5:23). "Uninstructive"; in contrast with "instructing" (vs. 25), and "wise unto salvation" (ch. 3:15). **avoid**—"decline." **24. not strive**—"The servant of the Lord" must imitate his master in not *striving contentiously,* though uncompromising in earnestly contending for the faith (Jude 3; Matt. 12:19). **gentle unto all men**—"patient" (*Greek,* "patient in bearing wrongs") in respect to adversaries. He is to be *gentle* so that he may occasion no evils; *patient* so that he may endure evils. **apt to teach**—implying not only solid teaching and ease in teaching, but patience and assiduity in it [BENGEL]. **25. instructing**—*Greek,* "disciplining," *instructing with correction,* which those who deal in *"uninstructive"* or "undisciplined questions" need (*Notes,* vs. 23; I Tim. 1:20). **those that oppose themselves**—*Greek,* "oppositely affected"; those of a different opinion. **if... peradventure**—*Greek,* "if at any time." **repentance**—which they need as antecedent to *the full knowledge* (so the *Greek* for *"acknowledgment"*) *of the truth* (I Tim. 2:4), their minds being corrupted (ch. 3:8), and their lives immoral. The cause of the spiritual ignorance which prompts such "questions" is moral, having its seat in the *will,* not in the intellect (John 7:17). Therefore repentance is their first need. That, not man, but God alone can "give" (Acts 5:31). **26. recover themselves**—*Greek,* "awake to soberness," viz., from the spiritual intoxication whereby they have fallen into the snare of the devil. **the snare**—(Eph. 6:11, "the wiles of the devil"; I Tim. 3:7; 6:9). **taken captive by him at his will**—*so as to follow the will of* "THAT" (the *Greek* emphatically marks Satan thus) foe.

ADAM CLARKE

24. *The servant of the Lord must not strive.* See on 1 Tim. iii. 2-3.

25. *Those that oppose.* This seems to refer to those who opposed the apostle's authority, and hence the propriety of the allusion to the rebellion of Korah and his company. *If God peradventure.* He was to use every means which he had reason to believe God might bless; and the apostle intimates that, bad as they were, they were not out of the reach of God's mercy.

CHAPTER 3 (MATTHEW HENRY)

Verses 1–9

Timothy must not think it strange if there were in the church bad men; for the net of the gospel was to enclose both good fish and bad, Matt. xiii. 47, 48. Even in gold ore there will be dross, and a great deal of chaff among the wheat when it lies on the floor.

I. In the *last days* (*v.* 1), in gospel times, there would *come perilous times,* not so much on account of persecution from without as on account of corruptions within. Two traitors within the garrison may do more hurt to it than two thousand besiegers without. Perilous times shall come, for men shall be wicked. Sin makes the time perilous.

II. Paul tells Timothy what shall be the marks and signs whereby these times may be known, *v.* 2, &c. Self-love will make the times perilous. Instead of Christian charity, which takes care for the good of others, they will mind themselves only. Covetousness. When men are lovers of themselves, no good can be expected from them, as good may be expected from those who love God. When every man is for what he can get and for keeping what he has, this makes men dangerous to one another. Pride and vain-glory. When men are *boasters and blasphemers.* When men do not fear God they will not regard man. When children are disobedient to their parents. What wickedness will those stick at who will be abusive to their own parents and rebel against them? Unthankfulness and unholiness make the times perilous. What is the reason that men are unholy and without the fear of God, but that they are unthankful for the mercies of God? When they are *without natural affection,* and *truce-breakers, v.* 3. When children are disobedient to their parents (*v.* 2) and when parents are without natural affection to their children, *v.* 3. And those who will not be bound by natural affection, no marvel that they will not be bound by the most solemn leagues and covenants. *They are truce-breakers.* When men are *false accusers* one of another—*devils* one to another. When men have no government of themselves and their own appetites: they are *incontinent,* they are *fierce.* When that which is good and ought to be honoured is generally despised.

When men are generally treacherous, wilful, and haughty (*v.* 4). When men are puffed up, behaving scornfully to all about them, then the times are perilous. When men are generally *lovers of pleasure more than lovers of God.* That is a carnal mind, and is full of enmity against him, which prefers anything before him, especially such a sordid thing as carnal pleasure is. When they *have the form of godliness* (*v.* 5). A form of godliness is a very different thing from the power of it; men may have the one and be wholly destitute of the other.

CHAPTER 3 (JAMIESON, FAUSSET, BROWN)

VSS. 1-17. COMING EVIL DAYS: SIGNS OF EVIL ALREADY: CONTRAST IN THE DOCTRINE AND LIFE OF PAUL, WHICH TIMOTHY SHOULD FOLLOW IN ACCORDANCE WITH HIS EARLY TRAINING IN SCRIPTURE. **1. also**—*Greek,* "but." **last days**—preceding Christ's second coming (II Pet. 3:3; Jude 18). "The *latter* times," I Timothy 4:1, refer to a period not so remote as "the *last* days," viz., the long days of papal and Greek anti-Christianity. **perilous**—lit., *"difficult* times," in which it is difficult to know what is to be done: "grievous times." **shall come**—*Greek,* "shall be imminent"; "shall come unexpectedly" [BENGEL]. **2. men**—in the professing Church. Cf. the catalogue, Romans 1:29, etc., where much the same sins are attributed to heathen men; it shall be a relapse into virtual heathendom, with all its beastike propensities, whence the symbol of it is "a beast" (Rev. 13:1, 11, 12, etc.; 17:3, 8, 11). **covetous**—Translate, "money-loving," a distinct *Greek* word from that for "covetous" (*Note,* Col. 3:5). The cognate *Greek* substantive (I Tim. 6:10) is so translated, "the *love of money* is a (*Greek,* not "the") root of all evil." **boasters**—empty boasters [ALFORD]; boasting of having what they have not. **proud**—overweening: lit., *showing* themselves *above* their fellows. **blasphemous**—rather, "evil-speakers," revilers. **disobedient to parents**—The character of the times is even to be gathered especially from the manners of the young [BENGEL]. **unthankful**—The obligation to *gratitude* is next to that of *obedience to parents.* **unholy**—irreligious [ALFORD]; inobservant of the offices of piety. **3. trucebreakers**—rather as the *Greek* is translated in Romans 1:31, "implacable." **false accusers**—slanderers (I Tim. 3:11; Titus 2:3). **incontinent, fierce**—at once both soft and hard: incontinently indulging themselves, and inhuman to others. **despisers ...** —"no lovers of good" [ALFORD]; the opposite of "a lover of good" (Titus 1:8).

4. heady—precipitate in action and in passion. **high-minded**—lit., "puffed up" with pride, as with smoke blinding them. **lovers of pleasure ... God**—Love of pleasure destroys the love and sense of God.

5. form—outward semblance. **godliness**—piety. **denying**—rather as *Greek,* "*having* denied," i.e., renounced. **the power**—the living, regenerating, sanctifying influence of it.

CHAPTER 3 (ADAM CLARKE)

1. *In the last days.* This often means the days of the Messiah, and is sometimes extended in its signification to the destruction of Jerusalem, as this was properly the last days of the Jewish state. But the phrase may mean any future time, whether near or distant.

2. *Lovers of their own selves.* "Selfish," studious of their own interest, and regardless of the welfare of all mankind. *Covetous.* "Lovers of money," because of the influence which riches can procure. *Boasters.* Vainglorious: self-assuming; valuing themselves beyond all others. *Proud.* Airy, light, trifling persons; those who love to make a show—who are all outside. *Blasphemers.* Those who speak impiously of God and sacred things, and injuriously of men. *Disobedient to parents.* Headstrong children, whom their parents cannot persuade. *Unthankful.* Persons without grace, or gracefulness; who think they have a right to the services of all men, yet feel no obligation, and consequently no gratitude. *Unholy.* Without piety; having no heart reverence for God.

3. *Without natural affection.* Without that affection which parents bear to their young, and which the young bear to their parents. *Trucebreakers.* The word means those who are bound by no promise, held by no engagement, obliged by no oath; persons who readily promise anything because they never intend to perform. *False accusers.* "Devils"; but properly enough rendered *false accusers,* for this is a principal work of the devil. Slanderers; striving ever to ruin the characters of others. *Incontinent.* Those who are slaves to uncleanness. *Fierce.* Wild, impetuous, whatever is contrary to pliability and gentleness. *Despisers of those that are good.* "Not lovers of good men." Here is a remarkable advantage of the Greek over the English tongue, one word of the former expressing five or six of the latter. Those who do not love the good must be radically bad themselves.

4. *Traitors.* Those who deliver up to an enemy the person who has put his life in their hands. *Heady.* Headstrong, precipitate, rash, inconsiderate. *Highminded.* The frivolously aspiring; those who are full of themselves and empty of all good. *Lovers of pleasures more than lovers of God.* Pleasure, sensual gratification, is their god, and this they love and serve; God they do not.

5. *Having a form of godliness.* The original word signifies a "draught, sketch, or summary," and will apply well to those who have all their religion in their creed, confession of faith, catechism, bodies of divinity, while destitute of

MATTHEW HENRY

III. Paul warns Timothy to take heed of certain seducers. He shows how industrious they were to make proselytes (*v.* 6). They crept into houses, to insinuate themselves into the good opinion of people, and so to draw them over to their party. And see what sort of people those were that they gained; they were such as were weak, and such as were wicked. A foolish head and a filthy heart make persons an easy prey to seducers.

He shows how far they were from coming to the knowledge of the truth, though they pretended to be *ever learning*, *v.* 7.

He foretells the certain stop that should be put to their progress (*v.* 8, 9). Those heretics *resisted the truth* and were men *of corrupt minds, reprobate concerning the faith, but they shall proceed no further.* Though the spirit of error may be let loose for a time, God has it in a chain. *Their folly shall be manifest,* it shall appear that they are impostors, and every man shall abandon them.

Verses 10–17

I. The apostle sets before him his own example (*v.* 10). Christ's apostles had no enemies but those who did not know them, or did not know them fully; those who knew them best loved and honoured them the most. Paul kept back nothing from his hearers, but declared to them the whole counsel of God, so that if it were not their own fault they might fully know it. He had fully known his conversation. His manner of life was of a piece with his doctrine, and did not contradict it. Those cannot expect to profit the people at all that preach well and live ill. Timothy fully knew what was the great thing that Paul had in view: "Thou hast known *my purpose*, what I drive at." Timothy fully knew Paul's good character. He knew that he had suffered ill for doing well (*v.* 11), (he mentions those only which happened to him while Timothy was with him, *at Antioch, at Iconium, at Lystra*). He knew what care God had taken of him. As he never failed his cause, so his God never failed him. Thou hast fully known my *afflictions*. When we *fully* know the afflictions, not only how they suffer, but how they are supported and comforted under their sufferings, then, instead of being discouraged, we shall be animated by them, especially considering that we are told before that we must count upon such things (*v.* 12). Those who will live godly must expect it; especially those who will live godly *in Christ Jesus*, especially when they are resolute in it. The apostle's life was very exemplary for three things: for his *doctrine*, for his *life*, and for his *persecutions and sufferings*. His life was a life of great usefulness, yet it was a life of great sufferings. The apostle mentions the Lord's delivering him out of them all, for Timothy's and our encouragement under sufferings.

JAMIESON, FAUSSET, BROWN

turn away—implying that some of such characters, forerunners of the last days, were already in the Church. **6. of this sort**—*Greek,* "of these," such as were described (vs. 5). **creep into**—stealthily. **laden with sins**—(Isa. 1:4)—applying to the "silly women" whose consciences are burdened with sins, and so are a ready prey to the false teachers who promise ease of conscience if they will follow them. A bad conscience leads easily to shipwreck of faith (I Tim. 1:19). **divers lusts**—not only animal lusts, but passion for change in doctrine and manner of teaching; the running after fashionable men and fashionable tenets, drawing them in the most opposite directions [ALFORD]. **7. Ever learning**—some new point, for mere curiosity, to the disparagement of what they seemed to know before. **the knowledge**—*Greek,* "the *perfect* knowledge"; the only safeguard against further novelties. Gnosticism laid hold especially of the female sex [IRENÆUS, 1. 13. 3.]: so Roman Jesuitism. **8. Now**—*Greek,* "But"; it is no wonder there should be now such opponents to the truth, for their prototypes existed in ancient times [ALFORD]. **Jannes . . . Jambres**—traditional names of the Egyptian magicians who resisted Moses (Exod. 7:11, 22), derived from "the unwritten teaching of the Jews" [THEODORET]. In a point so immaterial as the names, where Scripture had not recorded them, Paul takes the names which general opinion had assigned the magicians. EUSEBIUS, *Præparatio Evangelica,* quotes from NUMENIUS, "Jannes and Jambres were *sacred scribes* (a lower order of priests in Egypt) skilled in magic." HILLER interprets Jannes from the Abyssinian language *a trickster,* and Jambres *a juggler* (Acts 13:8). **resist**—"withstand," as before. They did so by trying to rival Moses' miracles. So the false teachers shall exhibit lying wonders in the last days (Matt. 24:24; II Thess. 2:9; Rev. 13:14, 15). **reprobate**—*incapable of testing* the truth (Rom. 1:28) [BENGEL]. ALFORD takes passively, "not abiding the test"; rejected on being tested (Jer. 6:30). **9. they shall proceed no further**—Though *for a time* (ch. 2:16) "they shall *advance* or *proceed* (*English Version,* 'increase') unto more ungodliness," yet there is a *final* limit beyond which they shall not be able to "proceed further" (Job 38:11; Rev. 11:7, 11). They themselves shall "wax worse and worse" (vs. 13), but they shall at last be for ever prevented from seducing others. "Often malice proceeds deeper down, when it cannot extend itself" [BENGEL]. **their folly**—lit., "dementation": *wise* though they think themselves. **shall be manifest**—*Greek,* "shall be brought forth from concealment into open day" [BENGEL], (I Cor. 4:5). **as theirs . . . was**—as that of those magicians was, when not only could they no longer try to rival Moses in sending boils, but the boils fell upon themselves: so as to the lice (Exod. 8:18; 9:11). **10. fully known**—lit., "fully followed up" and traced; viz., with a view to following me as thy pattern, so far as I follow Christ; the same *Greek* as in Luke 1:3, "*having had perfect understanding of* all things." **doctrine**—"teaching." **manner of life**—"conduct," "behavior." **purpose**—The *Greek* is elsewhere usually used of *God's* "purpose." But here, as in Acts 11:23, of Paul's determined "purpose of heart in cleaving unto the Lord." My *set aim,* or *resolution,* in my apostolic function, and in every action is, not my selfish gain, but the glory of God in Christ. **long-suffering**—towards my adversaries, and the false teachers; towards brethren in bearing their infirmities; towards the unconverted, and the lapsed when penitent (ch. 4:2; II Cor. 6:6; Gal. 5:22; Eph. 4:2; Col. 3:12). **charity**—*love* to all men. **patience**—"endurance"; *patient continuance* in well-doing amidst adversities (vs. 11; Rom. 2:7). **11. afflictions**—"sufferings." **which**—*Greek,* "such as." **in Antioch**—of Pisidia (Acts 13:14, 50, 51). **Iconium**—(Acts 14: 1-5). **Lystra**—(Acts 14:6, 19). **what**—How grievous. **out of . . . all . . . Lord delivered me**—(ch. 4: 17; Ps. 34:17; II Cor. 1:10). An encouragement to Timothy not to fear persecutions. **12. Yea, and**—an additional consideration for Timothy: if he *wishes to live godly in Christ,* he must make up his mind to encounter persecution. **that will . . .**—*Greek,* "all whose *will is to* live . . ." So far should persecution be from being a stumbling block to Timothy, he should consider it a mark of the pious. So the same *Greek* is used of the same thing, Luke 14:28, 33, "intending (*Greek, wishing*) to build a tower . . . counteth the cost." **live godly in Christ**—(Gal. 2:20; Phil. 1:21). There is no godliness (*Greek,* "piously") or *piety* out of Christ. The world easily puts up with the mask of a religion which depends on itself, but the piety which derives its vigor directly from Christ is as odious to modern Christians as it was to the ancient Jews [BENGEL].

ADAM CLARKE

the life of God in their souls; and are not only destitute of this life, but deny that such life or power is here to be experienced or known. They have religion in their creed, but none in their hearts. *From such turn away*—not only do not imitate them, but have no kind of fellowship with them; they are a dangerous people, and but seldom suspected, because their outside is fair.

6. *For of this sort are they.* He here refers to false teachers and their insinuating manners, practicing upon weak women, who, seeing in them such a semblance of piety, entertain them with great eagerness, and at last become partakers with them in their impurities.

7. *Ever learning,* from their false teachers, *and never able to come to the knowledge of the truth,* because that teaching never leads to the truth.

8. *Now as Jannes and Jambres withstood Moses.* This refers to the history of the Egyptian magicians, given in Exodus vii. *Men of corrupt minds.* It appears as if the apostle were referring still to some Judaizing teachers who were perverting the church with their doctrines, and loudly calling in question the authority and doctrine of the apostle. *Reprobate concerning the faith.* "Undiscerning" or "untried"; they are base metal, unstamped; and should not pass current, because not standard. This metaphor is frequent in the sacred writings.

9. *But they shall proceed no further.* Such teaching and teachers shall never be able ultimately to prevail against the truth; for "the foundation of God standeth sure." *Their folly shall be manifest.* As the Scriptures, which are the only rule of morals and doctrine, shall ever be preserved; so, sooner or later, all false doctrines shall be tried by them, and the folly of men setting up their wisdom against the wisdom of God must become manifest to all.

10. *Thou hast fully known my doctrine.* And having long had the opportunity of knowing me, the *doctrine* I preached, my "conduct" founded on these doctrines, the "object" I have in view by my preaching, my "fidelity" to God and to my trust, my *longsuffering* with those who walked disorderly, my "love" to them and to the world in general, and my *patience* in all my adversities, you are capable of judging between me and the false teachers, and can easily discern the difference between their doctrines, conduct, motives, temper, spirit, and mine.

11. *Persecutions, afflictions, which came unto me at Antioch.* The *Antioch* mentioned here was Antioch in Pisidia, to which place Paul and Barnabas came in their first apostolic progress, and where Paul delivered that memorable discourse which is preserved in the thirteenth chapter of Acts, vv. 16-43. In this city, it is said, "the Jews stirred up the devout and honourable women, and the chief men of the city, and raised persecution against Paul and Barnabas, and expelled them out of their coasts. But they shook off the dust of their feet against them, and came to Iconium," Acts xiii. 50-51. Here "there was an assault made both of the Gentiles, and also of the Jews with their rulers, to treat them despitefully, and to stone them . . . and [they] fled unto Lystra and Derbe . . . And there came thither certain Jews . . . who persuaded the people, and, having stoned Paul, drew him out of the city, supposing he had been dead." The historian informs us that his life was miraculously restored, and that he departed thence and came to Derbe, and afterwards returned to Lystra, Iconium, and Antioch, where they had lately been so grievously persecuted. See Acts xiv. 5-6, 19-21. These are the persecutions to which the apostle alludes; and we find that he mentions them here precisely in the same order in which, according to the relation of Luke, they occurred.

12. *All that will live godly.* So opposite to the spirit and practice of the world is the whole of Christianity that he who gives himself entirely up to God, making the Holy Scriptures the rule of his words and actions, will be more or less reviled and persecuted.

MATTHEW HENRY

II. He warns Timothy of the fatal end of seducers, *v.* 13. As good men, by the grace of God, grow better and better, so bad men, through the subtlety of Satan and the power of their own corruptions, grow worse and worse.

III. He directs him particularly to what he had learned out of the holy scriptures (*v.* 14, 15). It is not enough to learn that which is good, but we must continue in it, and persevere in it unto the end. If Timothy would adhere to the truth as he had been taught it, this would arm him against the snares and insinuations of seducers.

1. It is a great happiness to know the certainty of the things wherein we have been instructed. Consider of *whom thou hast learned them*; not of evil men and seducers, but good men, who had themselves experienced the power of the truths they taught thee. "Knowing especially the firm foundation upon which thou hast built (*v.* 15): *That from a child thou hast known the holy scriptures.*"

2. Those who would acquaint themselves with the things of God, must know the holy scriptures.

3. It is a great happiness to know the holy scriptures from our childhood. The age of children is the learning age; and those who would get true learning must get it out of the scriptures.

4. They must not lie by us neglected, and seldom or never looked into.

(1) What is the excellency of the scripture (*v.* 16). The prophets and apostles did not speak from themselves, but what they received of the Lord that they delivered unto us.

(2) What use it will be of to us. *It is able to make us wise to salvation.* Those are wise indeed who are wise to salvation. *"Through faith."* The scriptures will make us wise to salvation, if they be mixed with faith. For, if we do not believe their truth and goodness, they will do us no good.

It is *profitable* to us for all the purposes of the Christian life. It instructs us in that which is true, reproves us for that which is amiss, directs us in that which is good.

That the man of God may be perfect, *v.* 17. That which furnishes a man of God in this world is the scripture. By it we are *thoroughly furnished for every good work.* Scripture has various uses, and answers divers ends and purposes. Scripture is a perfect rule of faith and practice. If we consult the scripture which was given by inspiration of God, and follow its directions, we shall be made men of God, *perfect and thoroughly furnished to every good work.* O that we may love our Bibles more, and keep closer to them than ever!

JAMIESON, FAUSSET, BROWN

shall suffer persecution—and will not decline it (Gal. 5:11). **13.** Reason why persecutions must be expected, and these becoming worse and worse as the end approaches. The breach between light and darkness, so far from being healed, shall be widened [ALFORD]. **evil men**—in contrast to the "godly" (vs. 12). **seducers**—lit., "conjurors." Magical arts prevailed at Ephesus (Acts 19:19), and had been renounced by many Ephesians on embracing Christianity: but now when Paul was writing to Ephesus, symptoms of a return to *conjuring* tricks appeared: an undesigned coincidence [BURTON]. Probably *sorcery* will characterize the final apostasy (Rev. 13:15; 18:23; 22:15). **wax worse**—lit., "advance in the direction of worse" (*Note*, vs. 9). Not contradictory to that verse: there the *diffusion* of the evil was spoken of; here its *intensity* [ALFORD]. **deceiving, and being deceived**—He who has once begun to deceive others, is the less easily able to recover himself from error, and the more easily embraces in turn the errors of others [BENGEL]. **14. But . . . thou**—Whatever they may do. Resuming the thread begun at vs. 10. **learned**—from me and thy mother and grandmother (ch. 1: 5; 2:2). **assured of**—from Scripture (vs. 15). **of whom**—plural, not singular, in the oldest MSS., "from what teachers." Not only from me, but from Lois and Eunice. **15. from a child**—lit., "from an infant." The tender age of the first dawn of reason is that wherein the most lasting impressions of faith may be made. **holy scriptures**—The Old Testament taught by his *Jewish* mother. An undesigned coincidence with ch. 1:5; Acts 16:1-3. **able**—in themselves: though through men's own fault they often do not *in fact* make men savingly alive. **wise unto salvation**—i.e., *wise* unto the attainment of salvation. Contrast "folly" (vs. 9). *Wise* also in extending it to others. **through faith**—as the *instrument* of this wisdom. Each *knows* divine things only as far as *his own experience* in himself extends. He who has not faith, has not *wisdom* or *salvation.* **which is in**—i.e., rests on Christ Jesus. **16. All scripture**—*Greek,* "Every Scripture," i.e., Scripture in its every part. However, *English Version* is sustained, though the *Greek* article be wanting, by the technical use of the term "Scripture" being so well known as not to need the article (cf. *Greek,* Eph. 3:15; 2:21). The *Greek* is never used of *writings* in general, but only of the sacred Scriptures. The *Greek,* "God-inspired," is found nowhere else. Most of the New Testament books were written when Paul wrote this his latest Epistle: so he includes in the clause "All Scripture is God-inspired," not only the *Old Testament,* in which alone Timothy was taught when a child (vs. 15), but the New Testament books according as they were recognized in the churches which had men gifted with "discerning of spirits," and so able to distinguish really inspired utterances, persons, and so their writings from spurious. Paul means, "All Scripture is God-inspired *and therefore* useful"; because *we* see no utility in any words or portion of it, it does not follow it is not God-inspired. It is *useful,* because *God-inspired,* not *God-inspired,* because useful. **doctrine**—*Greek,* "teaching," i.e., *teaching the ignorant dogmatic* truths which they cannot otherwise know. He so uses the Old Testament, Romans 1:17. **reproof**—"refutation," *convicting the erring* of their error. Including *polemical* divinity. As an example of this use of the Old Testament, cf. Gal. 3:6, 13, 16. "Doctrine and reproof" comprehend the *speculative* parts of divinity. Next follow the *practical:* Scripture is profitable for: (1) *correction* (*Greek,* "setting one right"; cf. an example, I Cor. 10:1-10) and *instruction* (*Greek,* "disciplining," as a father does his child, *Note,* ch. 2:25; Eph. 6:4; Heb. 12:5, 11, or "training" by instruction, warning, example, kindnesses, promises, and chastisements; cf. an example, I Cor. 5:13). Thus the whole science of theology is complete in Scripture. Since Paul is speaking of Scripture in general and in the notion of it, the only *general* reason why, in order to *perfecting* the godly (vs. 17), it should extend to *every department* of revealed truth, must be that it was intended to be the *complete and sufficient rule* in all things touching perfection. See Article VI, *Common Prayer Book.* **in**—*Greek,* "instruction *which is in* righteousness," as contrasted with the "instruction" in worldly rudiments (Col. 2:20, 22). **17. man of God**—(*Note,* I Tim. 6:11). **perfect, throughly furnished**—*Greek,* "thoroughly perfected," and so "perfect." The man of God is perfectly accoutred out of Scripture for his work, whether he be a minister (cf. ch. 4:2 with ch. 3:16) or a spiritual layman. No oral tradition is needed to be added.

ADAM CLARKE

13. *Evil men and seducers shall wax worse.* They will yet get on for a season, deceiving themselves and deceiving others; but by and by "their folly shall be manifest unto all," v. 9. The word which we render *seducers* signifies "jugglers, pretenders to magical arts"; probably persons dealing in false miracles, with whom the Church in all ages has been not a little disgraced.

14. *But continue thou.* No man, however well-instructed in the things of God or grounded in divine grace, is out of the reach of temptation, apostasy, and final ruin; hence the necessity of watching unto prayer, depending upon God, continuing in the faith, and persevering unto the end.

15. *From a child thou hast known the holy scriptures.* The early religious education of Timothy already has been sufficiently noticed; see chap. i. 5. Paul introduces this circumstance again here for the confirmation of Timothy's faith. *Able to make thee wise unto salvation.* The apostle is here evidently speaking of the Jewish Scriptures and he tells us that they are able to make us *wise unto salvation* provided we have faith in Jesus Christ. This is the simple use of the Old Testament. No soul of man can be made wise unto salvation by it but as he refers all to Christ Jesus.

16. *All scripture is given by inspiration of God.* This sentence is not well-translated; the original should be rendered: "Every writing divinely inspired is profitable for doctrine." The apostle is here, beyond all controversy, speaking of the writings of the Old Testament, which, because they came by divine inspiration, he terms "the holy scriptures," v. 15; and it is of them alone that this passage is to be understood; and although all the New Testament came by as direct an inspiration as the Old, yet, as it was not collected at that time, nor indeed complete, the apostle could have no reference to it.

The doctrine of the inspiration of the sacred writings has been a subject of much discussion, and even controversy, among Christians. There are two principal opinions on the subject: (1) That every thought and word were inspired by God, and that the writer did nothing but merely write as the Spirit dictated. (2) That God gave the whole matter, leaving the inspired writers to their own language, and hence the great variety of style and different modes of expression. Is *profitable for doctrine.* To teach the will of God, and to point out Jesus Christ till He should come. *For reproof.* To "convince" men of the truth; and to confound those who should deny it. *For correction.* For "restoring things" to their proper uses and places, correcting false notions and mistaken views. *Instruction in righteousness.* For communicating all initiatory religious knowledge; for schooling mankind. All this is perfectly true of the Jewish Scriptures; and let faith in Christ Jesus be added, see v. 15, and then all that is spoken in the following verse will be literally accomplished.

17. *That the man of God.* The preacher of righteousness, the minister of the gospel, the person who derives his commission from God, and always appears as His herald and servant. *May be perfect.* It properly signifies an "integer" or "whole number" in arithmetic, to which nothing needs to be added to make it complete. *Throughly furnished.* Not only "complete" in himself as to his integrity, religious knowledge, faith in Jesus, and love to God and man, but that he should have all those qualifications which are necessary to complete the character and insure the success of a preacher of the gospel. Timothy was to teach, reprove, correct, and instruct others; and was to be to them a pattern of good works.

MATTHEW HENRY

CHAPTER 4

Verses 1–8

I. How awfully this charge is introduced (*v.* 1). The best of men have need to be awed into the discharge of their duty. The eye of God and Jesus Christ was upon him: *I charge thee before God and the Lord Jesus Christ.* He charges him as he will answer it at the great day, reminding him of the judgment to come. He will appear; he will come the second time, and it will be a glorious appearance. Then his kingdom shall appear in its glory: *At his appearing and kingdom;* for he will then appear in his kingdom.

II. What is the matter of the charge, *v.* 2–5.

1. To *preach the word.* This is ministers' business. It is not their own notions and fancies that they are to preach, but the pure plain word of God.

2. To urge what he preached: "*Be instant in season and out of season, reprove, rebuke, exhort;* do this work with all fervency of spirit. *In season,* when some special opportunity offers itself of speaking to them with advantage. *Out of season,* because thou dost not know but the Spirit of God may fasten upon them."

3. He must tell people of their faults. Endeavour, by dealing plainly with them, to bring them to repentance.

4. He must direct, encourage, and quicken those who began well. "*Exhort them with all longsuffering and doctrine.*" He must do it very patiently. While God shows to them all longsuffering, let ministers exhort with all longsuffering. He must do it rationally, not with passion, but *with doctrine.* Teach them the truth as it is in Jesus, and this will be a means both to reclaim them from evil and to bring them to good.

5. He must *watch in all things.* "Watch to thy work; watch against the temptations of Satan; watch over the souls of those who are committed to thy charge."

6. He must count upon afflictions and endure them. "Inure thyself to hardships."

7. He must remember his office, and discharge its duties. The office of the evangelist was, as the apostles' deputy, to water the churches that they planted. This was Timothy's work.

8. He must fulfil his ministry: *Make full proof of it.* Perform all the parts of his office with diligence and care. The best way to make full proof of our ministry is to fulfil it, to fill it up in all its parts with proper work.

III. The reasons to enforce the charge.

1. Because errors and heresies were likely to creep into the church (*v.* 3, 4). "Improve the present time when they will endure it." They will grow weary of the old plain gospel of Christ, and then they will be greedy of fables. False teachers were not of God's sending; but they chose them to please their itching ears. People do so when they will not endure sound doctrine; that preaching which is searching, plain, and to the purpose. There is a wide difference between the word of God and the word of such teachers; the one is sound doctrine, the word of truth, the other is only fables.

2. Because Paul for his part had almost done his work, *v.* 6.

(1) "Therefore there will be the more occasion for thee." The fewer hands there are to work the more industrious those hands must be that are at work.

(2) "I have done the work of my day and generation; do thou in like manner do the work of thy day and generation."

(3) The comfort and cheerfulness of Paul, in the prospect of his approaching departure, might encourage Timothy. "I can look back upon my warfare with a great deal of satisfaction; and therefore be not afraid of the difficulties thou must meet with. The crown of life is as sure to thee as if it were already upon thy head." Here the apostle looks forward, upon his death approaching, and he looks upon it now as near at hand: I am *already poured out.* Observe,

[1] With what pleasure he speaks of dying. He calls it his departure, or his release. Death to a good man is his release from the imprisonment of this world and his departure to the enjoyments of another world; he does not cease to be, but is only removed from one world to another.

[2] With what pleasure he looks back upon the life he had lived (*v.* 7). He did not fear death, because he had the testimony of his conscience that by the grace of God he had in some measure answered the ends of living. He had fought a good fight. His life was a course, and he had now finished it; as his warfare was accomplished, so his race was run. "*I have kept the faith.*" We must fight this good fight; we must fight it out, and finish our course.

JAMIESON, FAUSSET, BROWN

CHAPTER 4

VSS. 1-22. SOLEMN CHARGE TO TIMOTHY TO DO HIS DUTY ZEALOUSLY, FOR TIMES OF APOSTASY ARE AT HAND, AND THE APOSTLE IS NEAR HIS TRIUMPHANT END: REQUESTS HIM TO COME AND BRING MARK WITH HIM TO ROME, AS LUKE ALONE IS WITH HIM, THE OTHERS HAVING GONE: **1. charge**–*Greek,* "adjure." **therefore**–omitted in the oldest MSS. **the Lord Jesus Christ**–The oldest MSS. read simply, "Christ Jesus." **shall judge**–His *commission* from God is mentioned, Acts 10:42; his resolution to do so, I Peter 4:5; the execution of his commission, here. **at his appearing**–The oldest MSS. read, "and" for "at"; then translate, "(I charge thee *before God* . . .) and *by* His appearing." **and his kingdom**–to be set at His appearing, when we hope to reign with Him. His kingdom is real now, but not visible. It shall then be both real *and visible* (Luke 22:18, 30; Rev. 1:7 11:15; 19:6). *Now* he reigns *in the midst of His enemies* expecting till they shall be overthrown (Ps. 110:2; Heb. 10:13). *Then* He shall reign with His adversaries prostrate. **2. Preach** lit., "proclaim as a herald." The term for the discourses in the synagogue was *daraschoth;* the corresponding *Greek* term (implying dialectial style, dialogue, and discussion, Acts 17:2, 18; 18:4, 19) is applied in Acts to *discourses* in the Christian Church.
be instant–i.e., urgent, earnest, in the whole work of the ministry. **in season, out of season**–i.e., at all seasons; whether they regard your speaking as seasonable or unseasonable. **reprove**–"convict," "confute." **with . . .**–*Greek,* "IN (the *element in* which the exhortation ought to have place) all long-suffering (ch. 2:24, 25; 3:10) and *teaching*"; cf. ch. 2:24, "apt to teach." The *Greek* for "doctrine" here is *didache,* but in ch. 3:16 *didascalia.* "*Didascalia*" is what one receives; *didache* is what is communicated [TITTMANN]. **3. they**–professing Christians. **sound doctrine**–*Greek,* "the sound (*Note,* I Tim. 1:10) doctrine" (*didascalias*) or "teaching," viz., of the Gospel. Presently follows the concrete, teachers." **after their own lusts**–Instead of regarding the will of God they dislike being interrupted in their lusts by true teachers. **heap**–one on another: an indiscriminate mass of false teachers. Variety delights itching ears. "He who despises sound teaching, leaves sound teachers; they seek instructors like themselves" [BENGEL]. It is the corruption of the people in the first instance, that creates priestcraft (Exod. 32:1).
to themselves–such as will suit their depraved tastes; *populus vult decipi, et decipiatur*–"the people wish to be deceived, so let them be deceived." "Like priest, like people" (I Kings 12:31; Hos. 4:9).
itching–like to hear teachers who give them mere pleasure (Acts 17:19-21), and do not offend by truths grating to their ears. They, as it were, tickle with pleasure the levity of the multitude [CICERO], who come as to a theater to hear what will delight their ears, not to learn [SENECA, Ep. 10. 8] what will do them good. "Itch in the ear is as bad in any other part of the body, and perhaps worse" [SOUTH].
4. The ear brooks not what is opposed to the man's lusts. **turned**–*Greek,* "turned aside" (I Tim. 1:6). It is a righteous retribution, that when men *turn away* from the truth, they should be *turned to* fables (Jer. 2:19). **fables**–(I Tim. 1:4). **5.** I am no longer here to withstand these things; be thou a worthy successor of me, no longer depending on me for counsel, but thine own master, and swimming without the corks [CALVIN]; follow my steps, inherit their result, and the honor of their end [ALFORD].
watch thou–lit., "with the wakefulness of one *sober.*" **in all things**–on all occasions and under all circumstances (Titus 2:7). **endure affliction**–suffer hardships [ALFORD]. **evangelist**–a missionary bishop preacher, and teacher. **make full proof of**–fulfil in all its requirements, leaving nothing undone (Acts 12:25; Rom. 15:19; Col. 4:17). **6.** *Greek,* "For I am already being offered"; lit., as a *libation;* appropriate to the shedding of *his blood.* Every sacrifice began with an initiatory libation on the victim's head (*Note,* cf. Phil. 2:17). A motive to stimulate Timothy to faithfulness–the departure and final blessedness of Paul; it is the end that crowns the work [BENGEL]. As the time of his departure was indicated to Peter, so to Paul (II Pet. 1:14). **my departure**–lit., "loosing anchor" (*Note,* Phil. 1:23). *Dissolution.* **7.** "I have striven the good strife"; the *Greek* is not restricted to a *fight,* but includes any competitive *contest,* e.g., that of the racecourse (I Tim. 6:12 [ALFORD]; I Cor. 9:24, etc.; Heb. 12:1, 2). **kept the faith**–the Christian faith committed to me as a believer and an apostle (cf. ch. 1:14; Rev. 2:10; 3:10).

ADAM CLARKE

CHAPTER 4

1. *I charge thee therefore before God.* Whose herald you are; and before *the Lord Jesus Christ,* whose salvation you are to proclaim, and who is coming to *judge* the world—all that shall be found then "alive," and all that have died from the foundation of the world.

2. *Preach the word.* "Proclaim the doctrine," the doctrine of Christ crucified for the sins of the whole world; the doctrine that the Gentiles are invited to be fellow heirs with the Jews, and that for Jews and Gentiles there is no salvation but by faith in Christ. *Be instant in season, out of season.* Be urgent whether the times be prosperous or adverse, whenever there is an opportunity; and when there is none, strive to make one. *Reprove.* "Confute" the false teacher. *Rebuke.* Reprove "cuttingly and severely" those who will not abandon their sins. *Exhort.* "Comfort the feebleminded," the diffident and the tempted. *With all longsuffering.* In reference to each and all of these cases. *And doctrine.* The different modes of teaching suited to each.

3. *For the time will come.* There is a time coming to the Church when men will not hear the practical truths of the gospel, when they will prefer speculative opinions, which either do no good to the soul or corrupt and destroy it, to that wholesome doctrine of "Deny thyself, take up thy cross, and follow Me," which Jesus Christ has left in His Church. *But after their own lusts.* For these they will follow, and hate those preachers and that doctrine by which they are opposed. *Shall they heap to themselves teachers.* They will add one teacher to another, run and gad about after all, to find out those who insist not on the necessity of bearing the cross, of being crucified to the world, and of having the mind that was in Jesus. *Having itching ears.* Endless curiosity, an insatiable desire of variety; and they get their ears tickled with the language and accent of the person, abandoning the good and faithful preacher for the fine speaker.

4. *And they shall turn away their ears from the truth.* The truth strips them of their vices, sacrifices their idols, darts its lightnings against their easily besetting sins, and absolutely requires a conformity to a crucified Christ; therefore they turn their ears away from it. *And shall be turned unto fables.* Believe any kind of stuff and nonsense; for as one has justly observed, "Those who reject the truth are abandoned by the just judgment of God to credit the most degrading nonsense."

5. *But watch thou in all things.* It is possible to be overtaken in a fault, to neglect one's duty, and to lose one's soul. Watching unto prayer prevents all these evils. *Endure afflictions.* Let no sufferings affright you; nor let the dread of them either cause you to abandon the truth or relax in your zeal for the salvation of men. *Do the work of an evangelist.* That is: Preach Christ crucified for the sins of the whole world; for this, and this alone, is doing the work of an evangelist, or preacher of the glad tidings of peace and salvation by Christ.

6. *For I am now ready to be offered.* "I am already poured out as a libation." See the note on Phil. ii. 17. He considers himself as on the eve of being sacrificed, and looks upon his blood as the libation which was poured on the sacrificial offering. He could not have spoken thus positively had not the sentence of death already been passed upon him.

7. *I have fought a good fight.* Every reader will perceive that the apostle, as was his very frequent custom, alludes to the contests at the Grecian games: "I have wrestled that good wrestling"—I have struggled hard, and have overcome, in a most honorable cause. *I have finished my course.* I have started for the prize, and have come up to the goal, outstripping all my competitors, and have gained this prize also. *I have kept the faith.* As the laws of these games must be most diligently observed and kept (for though a man overcome, yet is he not crowned except he strive lawfully), so I have kept the rules of the spiritual combat and race; and thus, having contended lawfully and conquered in each exercise, I have a right to expect the prize.

MATTHEW HENRY

Towards the end of our days to be able to speak in this manner, what comfort, unspeakable comfort, will it afford!

[3] With what pleasure he looks forward to the life he was to live hereafter (*v.* 8). Let this encourage Timothy to endure hardness as a good soldier of Jesus Christ that there is a crown of life before us. It is called *a crown of righteousness*, because our holiness and righteousness will there be perfected, and will be our crown.

And yet this crown of righteousness was not peculiar to Paul, as if it belonged only to apostles and martyrs, but *to all those also that love his appearing*. It is the character of all the saints that they love the appearing of Jesus Christ: they love his second appearing at the great day; love it, and long for it. This crown, which believers shall wear, is laid up for them; they have it not at present, for here they are but heirs; they have it not in possession, and yet it is sure.

Verses 9–15

1. He bids him hasten to him (*v.* 9). Paul wanted Timothy's company and help; and the reason he gives is because several had left him (*v.* 10): *Demas hath forsaken me, having loved this present world.* Love to this present world is often the cause of apostasy from the truths and ways of Jesus Christ. *Crescens* had gone one way and *Titus* another way.

Luke ever remained with Paul (*v.* 11, 12). 2. He speaks respectfully concerning *Mark*. This Mark was he about whom Paul and Barnabas had contended, Acts xv. 39. Paul would not take him with him to the work, because he had once flinched and drawn back: but now, says he, *Take Mark, and bring him with thee.* By this it appears that Paul was now reconciled to Mark. We must not disclaim for ever making use of those that are profitable and useful, though they may have done amiss.

3. Paul orders Timothy as he came through Troas to bring with him thence those things which he had left behind him there (*v.* 13), the cloak he had left there, which Paul had the more occasion for in a cold prison.

JAMIESON, FAUSSET, BROWN

8. a crown—rather as *Greek*, "*the* crown." The "henceforth" marks the decisive moment; he looks to his state in a threefold aspect: (1) The past "I have fought"; (2) The immediate present; "there is laid up for me". (3) The future "the Lord will give in that day" [BENGEL]. **crown**—a crown, or garland, used to be bestowed at the Greek national games on the successful competitor in wrestling, running, etc. (cf. I Pet. 5:4; Rev. 2:10). **of righteousness**—The reward is *in recognition of righteousness* wrought in Paul by God's Spirit; the crown is prepared for the righteous; but it is a crown *which consists in righteousness. Righteousness will be its own reward* (Rev. 22:11). **give**—*Greek*, "shall award" in righteous requital as "Judge" (Acts 17:31; II Cor. 5:10; II Thess. 1:6, 7). **in that day**—not until His appearing (ch. 1:12). The partakers of the first resurrection may receive a *crown* also *at the last day*, and obtain in that general assembly of all men, a *new* award of praise. The favorable sentence passed on the "brethren" of the Judge, who sit with Him on His throne, is in Matthew 25:40, taken for granted as *already* awarded, when that affecting those who benefited them is being passed [BENGEL]. **me**—individual appropriation. *Greek*, "not only to me." **them that love**—*Greek*, "have loved, and do love"; *habitual* love and desire for Christ's appearing, which presupposes *faith* (cf. Heb. 9:28). Cf. the sad contrast, vs. 10, "having *loved* this present world." **9.** (vs. 21; ch. 1:4, 8.) Timothy is asked to come to be a comfort to Paul, and also to be strengthened by Paul, for carrying on the Gospel work after Paul's decease. **10. Demas**—once a "fellow laborer" of Paul, along with Mark and Luke (Col. 4:14; Philemon 24). His motive for forsaking Paul seems to have been love of worldly ease, safety, and comforts at home, and disinclination to brave danger with Paul (Matt. 13:20, 21, 22). CHRYSOSTOM implies that Thessalonica was his home. **Galatia**—One oldest MS. supports the reading "Gaul." But most oldest MSS., etc., "Galatia." **Titus**—He must have therefore left Crete after "setting in order" the affairs of the churches there (Titus 1:5). **Dalmatia**—part of the Roman province of Illyricum on the coast of the Adriatic. Paul had written to him (Titus 3:12) to come to him in the winter to Nicopolis (in Epirus), intending in the spring to preach the Gospel in the adjoining province of Dalmatia. Titus seems to have gone thither to carry out the apostle's intention, the execution of which was interrupted by his arrest. Whether he went of his own accord, as is likely, or was sent by Paul, which the expression "is departed" hardly accords with, cannot be positively decided. Paul here speaks only of his personal attendants having forsaken him; he had still friends among the Roman Christians who visited him (ch. 4:21), though they had been afraid to stand by him at his trial (vs. 16). **11. Take**—*Greek*, "take up" on thy journey (Acts 20:13, 14). John Mark was probably in, or near, Colosse, as in the Epistle to the Colossians (Col. 4:10), written two years before this, **he** is mentioned as about to visit them. Timothy was now absent from Ephesus and somewhere in the interior of Asia Minor; hence he would be sure to fall in with Mark on his journey. **he is profitable to me for the ministry**—Mark had been under a cloud for having forsaken Paul at a critical moment in his missionary tour with Barnabas (Acts 15:37-40; 13:5, 13). Timothy had subsequently occupied the same post in relation to Paul as Mark once held. Hence Paul, appropriately here, wipes out the past censure by high praise of Mark and guards against Timothy's making self-complacent comparisons between himself and Mark, as though he were superior to the latter (cf. Philemon 24). Demas apostatizes. Mark returns to the right way, and is no longer unprofitable, but is profitable for the Gospel ministry (Philemon 11). **12. And**—*Greek*, "But." Thou art to come to me, *but* Tychicus I have sent to Ephesus to supply thy place (if thou so willest it) in presiding over the Church there in thy absence (cf. Titus 3:12). It is possible Tychicus was the bearer of this Epistle, though the omission of "to thee" is rather against this view. **13. cloak . . . I left**—probably obliged to leave it in a hurried departure from Troas. **Carpus**—a faithful friend to have been entrusted with so precious deposits. The mention of his "cloak," so far from being unworthy of inspiration, is one of those graphic touches which sheds a flood of light on the last scene of Paul's life, on the confines of two worlds; in this wanting a cloak to cover him from the winter cold, in that covered with the righteousness of saints, "clothed upon with his house from heaven" [GAUSSEN]. So the inner vesture and outer garment of

ADAM CLARKE

8. *Henceforth there is laid up for me a crown.* This I can claim as my due; but the crown I expect is not one of fading leaves, but *a crown of righteousness;* the reward which God, in His kindness, has promised to them who are faithful to the grace He has bestowed upon them.

The Lord, the righteous judge. He alludes here to the *brabeus*, or umpire in the Grecian games, whose office it was to declare the victor and to give the crown. *At that day.* The day of judgment; the morning of the resurrection from the dead.

Unto all them also that love his appearing. All who live in expectation of the coming of Christ, who anticipate it with joyfulness.

9. *Do thy diligence to come shortly unto me.* He appears to have wished Timothy to be present at his death, that he might have his faith confirmed by seeing how a Christian could die; and as he had but a short time to live, he begs Timothy to hasten his visit, and particularly so as he had scarcely now any companions.

10. *Demas hath forsaken me.* This is another proof of the posteriority of this Epistle; for Demas was with the apostle in his first imprisonment, and joins in the salutations, see Col. iv. 14, which were written when Paul was a prisoner at Rome for the first time. *Crescens to Galatia.* Whether the departure of Crescens was similar to that of Demas, as intimated above, or whether he went on an evangelical embassy, we know not. Charity would hope the latter; for we can hardly suppose that Titus, who is here said to have departed to Dalmatia, had abandoned his Cretan churches, his apostolical office, and especially his aged father and friend, now about to seal the truth with his blood! It is probable that both these persons had gone on sacred missions, and perhaps had been gone some time before the apostle was brought into such imminent danger.

11. *Only Luke is with me.* This was Luke the Evangelist, and writer of the Acts of the Apostles, who was always much attached to Paul, and it is supposed continued with him even to his martyrdom. *Take Mark, and bring him with thee.* This was John Mark, who, after having wavered a little at first, became a steady, zealous, and useful man. *For he is profitable to me for the ministry.* "For service"; that is, he would be very useful to the apostle, to minister to him in his present close confinement.

12. *Tychicus have I sent to Ephesus.* For this person see Acts xx. 4; Eph. vi. 21; Col. iv. 7. It is rather strange that the apostle should say, I have sent Tychicus to Ephesus, if Timothy was at Ephesus at this time; but it is probable that Tychicus had been sent to Ephesus some time before this, and therefore the apostle might say, though writing now to Ephesus, *Tychicus have I sent.*

13. *The cloke that I left at Troas.* By several translated "bag"; and it is most likely that it was something of this kind, in which he might carry his clothes, books, and traveling necessaries.

MATTHEW HENRY

He would have his books with him. Whereas he had exhorted Timothy to give attendance to reading, so he did himself.

4. He mentions *Alexander*, and the mischief that he had done him, *v.* 14, 15. Paul foretells that God would reckon with him. The Lord *will reward him according to his works.* Some who were once Paul's hearers and admirers did not give him reason to remember them with much pleasure; for one forsook him, and another did him much evil. At the same time he mentions some with pleasure; the badness of some did not make him forget the goodness of others.

Verses 16–22

I. He gives Timothy an account of his own present circumstances.

1. He had lately been called to appear before the emperor (*v.* 16).

The Christians at Rome were forward to go and meet him (Acts xxviii); but when it came to the pinch, and they would be in danger of suffering with him, then they all forsook him. Paul had his trials in his friends' forsaking him in a time of danger as well as in the opposition made by enemies: all forsook him. God might lay it to their charge, but Paul endeavours to prevent it by his earnest prayers.

2. When he had nobody to keep him in countenance, God made his face to shine. Paul knew how to preach at the bar as well as in the pulpit. *And that all the Gentiles might hear;* the emperor himself and the great men who would never have heard Paul preach if he had not been brought before them. *And I was delivered out of the mouth of the lion.*

And the Lord shall deliver me from every evil work. See how Paul improved his experiences. "*And shall preserve me to his heavenly kingdom.*" If the Lord stand by us, he will strengthen us, and his presence will more than supply everyone's absence. Former deliverances should encourage future hopes. We ought to give God the glory of all past, present, and future deliverances: *To whom be glory for ever and ever. Amen.*

II. He sends salutations, *v.* 19.

JAMIESON, FAUSSET, BROWN

Jesus, Paul's master, are suggestive of most instructive thought (John 19). **books**—He was anxious respecting these that he might transmit them to the faithful, so that they might have the teaching of his writings when he should be gone. **especially the parchments**—containing perhaps some of his inspired Epistles themselves. **14. Alexander the coppersmith**—or "smith" in general. Perhaps the same as the Alexander (I Tim. 1:20, *Note*) at Ephesus. Excommunicated then he subsequently was restored, and now vented his personal malice because of his excommunication in accusing Paul before the Roman judges, whether of incendiarism or of introducing a new religion. See my *Introduction.* He may have been the Alexander put forward by the Jews in the tumult at Ephesus (Acts 19: 33, 34). **reward**—The oldest MSS. read, "*shall* reward," or "requite him." Personal revenge certainly did not influence the apostle (vs. 16, end). **15. our words**—the arguments of us Christians for our common faith. Believers have a common cause. **16. At my first answer**—i.e., "defense" in court, at my first public examination. Timothy knew nothing of this, it is plain, till Paul now informs him. But during his *former* imprisonment at Rome, Timothy was with him (Phil. 1:1, 7). This must have been, therefore, a *second* imprisonment. He must have been set free before the persecution in A.D. 64, when the Christians were accused of causing the conflagration in Rome; for, had he been a prisoner then, he certainly would not have been spared. The tradition [EUSEBIUS, 2. 25] that he was finally *beheaded,* accords with his not having been put to death in the persecution, A.D. 64, when *burning to death* was the mode by which the Christians were executed, but subsequently to it. His "first" trial in his second imprisonment seems to have been on the charge of complicity in the conflagration; his absence from Rome may have been the ground of his acquittal on that charge; his final condemnation was probably on the charge of introducing a new and unlawful religion into Rome. **stood with me**—*Greek,* "came forward with me" [ALFORD] as a friend and advocate. **may** [it] **not be laid to their charge**—The position of "their," in the *Greek,* is emphatic. "May it not be laid to THEIR charge," for they were intimidated; *their* drawing back from me was not from bad disposition so much as from fear; it is sure to be laid to the charge of those who intimidated them. Still Paul, like Stephen, would doubtless have offered the same prayer for his persecutors themselves (Acts 7:60). **17. the Lord**—the more because *men* deserted me. **stood with me**—stronger than "came forward with me" (*Greek,* vs. 16). **strengthened**—*Greek,* "*put strength in* me." **by me**—"through me"; through my means. One single occasion is often of the greatest moment. **the preaching**—"the Gospel proclamation." **might be fully known**—might be fully made (*Note,* vs. 5). **that all the Gentiles**—present at my trial, "might hear" the Gospel proclaimed then. Rome was the capital of the Gentile world, so that a proclamation of the truth to the Romans was likely to go forth to the rest of the Gentile world. **I was delivered out of the mouth of the lion**—viz., Satan, the roaring, devouring lion (Luke 22:31; I Pet. 5:8). I was prevented falling into his snare (ch. 2:26; Ps. 22: 21; II Pet. 2:9); vs. 18 agrees with this interpretation, "The Lord shall *deliver* me *from every evil* work," viz., both from evil and the evil one, as the *Greek* of the Lord's Prayer expresses it. It was not deliverance from Nero (who was called *the lion*) which he rejoiced in, for he did not fear *death* (vss. 6-8), but deliverance from the temptation, through fear, to deny His Lord: so ALFORD. **18. And the Lord shall . . .**—Hope draws its conclusions from the past to the future [BENGEL]. **will preserve me**—lit., "will save" (Ps. 22:21), "will bring me safe to." Jesus is the Lord and the Deliverer (Phil. 3:20; I Thess. 1:10: He saves from evil; He gives good things. **heavenly kingdom**—*Greek,* "His kingdom which is a heavenly one." **to whom . . .**—*Greek,* "to whom be *the* glory unto the ages of ages." The very *hope* produces a doxology: how much greater will be the doxology which the actual *enjoyment* shall produce! [BENGEL]. **19. Prisca and Aquila**—(Acts 18:2, 3; Rom. 16:3, 4; I Cor. 16:19, written from Ephesus, where therefore Aquila and Priscilla must then have been). **household of Onesiphorus**—If he were dead at the time, the "household" would not have been called "the household *of Onesiphorus.*" He was probably *absent* (*Note,* ch. 1:16). **20.** In order to depict his desertion, he informs Timothy that Erastus, one of his usual companions (Acts 19:22, possibly the same Erastus as in Rom. 16:23, though how he could leave his official duties for missionary journeys is not clear), stayed behind

ADAM CLARKE

What the *books* were we cannot tell; it is most likely they were his own writings. And as to the *parchments,* they were probably the Jewish Scriptures and a copy of the Septuagint. These he must have had at hand at all times.

14. *Alexander the coppersmith.* We are not to understand this of any tradesman, but of some rabbin; for it was not unusual for the Jews to apply the name of some trade as an epithet to their rabbins and literary men. He is in all probability the very same mentioned in Acts xix. 33, where see the note; and it is not unlikely that he may have been the same whom the apostle was obliged to excommunicate, 1 Tim. i. 20. *The Lord reward him.* But instead of *apodoe,* which has here the power of a solemn imprecation, *apodosei,* "He will reward," is the reading of the very best MSS., several of the versions, and some of the chief Greek fathers. This makes the sentence declaratory: "The Lord will reward him according to his works." This reading is most like the spirit and temper of this heavenly man.

15. *Of whom be thou ware also.* It seems that this rabbin travelled about from place to place for the purpose of opposing the gospel, the Jews putting him forward, as it is said, Acts xix. 33. *He hath greatly withstood our words.* Has been a constant opposer of the Christian doctrines.

16. *At my first answer.* "At my first apology"; this word properly signifies a "defense" or "vindication." This is the meaning of what we call the "apologies" of the primitive fathers; they were vindications or defenses of Christianity. It is generally allowed that when Paul had been taken this second time by the Romans he was examined immediately and required to account for his conduct; and that, so odious was Christianity through the tyranny of Nero, he could procure no person to plead for him. Nero, who had himself set fire to Rome, charged it on the Christians, and they were in consequence persecuted in the most cruel manner. He caused them to be wrapped up in pitched clothes, and then, chaining them to a stake, he ordered them to be set on fire to give light in the streets after night. *I pray God that it may not be laid to their charge.* How much more simple, elegant, and expressive are the apostle's own words: "Let it not be placed to their account!" Let them not have to reckon for it with the supreme Judge at the great day!

17. *The Lord stood with me.* When all human help failed, God, in a more remarkable manner, interposed; and thus the excellency plainly appeared to be of God, and not of man. *That by me the preaching might be fully known.* When called on to make his defense, he took occasion to preach the gospel, and to show that the great God of heaven and earth had designed to illuminate the Gentile world with the rays of His light and glory. This must have endeared him to some, while others might consider him an opposer of their gods and be the more incensed against him. *I was delivered out of the mouth of the lion.* I escaped the imminent danger at that time. Probably he was seized in a tumultuous manner and expected to be torn to pieces. The words "to be rescued from *the mouth* or jaws *of the lion*" are a proverbial form of speech for deliverance from the most imminent danger.

18. *And the Lord shall deliver me from every evil work.* None of the evil designs formed against me to make me unfaithful or unsteady, to cause me to save my life at the expense of faith and a good conscience, shall succeed; my life may go, but He will preserve me *unto his heavenly kingdom.*

19. *Salute Prisca and Aquila.* Several MSS., versions, and fathers have Priscilla instead of Prisca: they are probably the same as those mentioned in Acts xviii. 18, 26. *The household of Onesiphorus.* See chap. i. 16. Onesiphorus was probably dead at this time; his "family" still remained at Ephesus.

20. *Erastus abode at Corinth.* He was treasurer of that city, as we learn from Rom. xvi. 23. The apostle had sent him and Timothy on a mission to Macedonia, Acts xix. 22, whence it is probable he returned to Corinth and there

MATTHEW HENRY

He mentions his leaving *Trophimus sick at Miletum* (*v.* 20).

III. He hastens Timothy to *come to him before winter* (*v.* 21).

IV. He sends commendations to him from *Eubulus, Pudens, Linus, Claudia,* and all the *brethren.*

V. He concludes with a prayer, that the *Lord Jesus would be with his spirit.* We need no more to make us happy than to have the Lord Jesus Christ with our spirits. And it is the best prayer we can put up for our friends. *Grace be with you. Amen.* And if grace be with us here to convert and change us, to make us holy, to keep us humble, and to enable us to persevere to the end, glory will crown us hereafter.

JAMIESON, FAUSSET, BROWN

at Corinth, his native place, or usual residence, of which city he was "chamberlain," or city steward and treasurer (Rom. 16:23); and Trophimus he left behind at Miletus sick. (See on his former history, Acts 20:4; 21:29.) This verse is irreconcilable with the imprisonment from which he writes being the *first:* for he did not pass by Corinth or Miletus on his way to Rome when about to be imprisoned for the first time. As Miletus was near Ephesus, there is a presumption that Timothy was *not* at Ephesus when Paul wrote, or he would not need to inform Timothy of Trophimus lying sick in his immediate neighborhood. However, Trophimus may not have been still at Miletus at the time when Paul wrote, though he had left him there on his way to Rome. Prisca and Aquila were most likely to be at *Ephesus* (vs. 19), and he desires Timothy to *salute them:* so also Onesiphorus' household (ch. 1:18). Paul had not the power of healing at will (Acts 19:12), but as the Lord allowed him. **21. before winter**—when a voyage, according to ancient usages of navigation, would be out of the question: also, Paul would need his "cloak" against the winter (vs. 13). **Pudens . . . Claudia**—afterwards husband and wife (according to MARTIAL IV, 13; XI, 54), he a Roman knight, she a Briton, surnamed *Rufina.* TACITUS, *Agricola,* 14, mentions that territories in southeast Britain were given to a British king; Cogidunus, in reward for his fidelity to Rome, A.D. 52, while Claudius was emperor. In 1772 a marble was dug up at Chichester, mentioning Cogidunus with the surname Claudius, added from his patron, the emperor's name; and *Pudens* in connection with Cogidunus, doubtless his father-in-law. His daughter would be Claudia, who seems to have been sent to Rome for education, as a pledge of the father's fidelity. Here she was under the protection of Pomponia, wife of Aulus Plautius, conqueror of Britain. Pomponia was accused of *foreign superstitions,* A.D. 57 [TACITUS, *Annals,* 3. 32], probably *Christianity.* She probably was the instrument of converting Claudia, who took the name *Rufina* from her, that being a cognomen of the Pomponian gens (cf. Rom. 16:13, *Rufus,* a Christian). Pudens in Martial and in the Chichester inscription, appears as a *pagan;* but perhaps he or his friends concealed his Christianity through fear. Tradition represents *Timothy,* a son of Pudens, as taking part in converting the Britons. **Linus**—put third; therefore not at this time yet, as he was afterwards, *bishop.* His name being here inserted between Pudens and Claudia, implies the two were not yet married. "Eubulus" is identified by some with Aristobulus, who, with his converts, is said to have been among the first evangelists of Britain. Paul himself, says CLEMENT, "visited *the farthest west* [perhaps Britain, certainly *Spain*], and was martyred under the rulers at Rome," who were Nero's vicegerents in his absence from the city. **22. Grace be with you**—plural in oldest MSS., "with YOU," i.e., thee and the members of the Ephesian and neighboring churches.

ADAM CLARKE

became finally settled. *Trophimus have I left at Miletum sick.* Even the apostles could not work miracles when they pleased; that power was but rarely given, and that for very special purposes. Trophimus was an Ephesian. See Acts xx. 4. Miletus was a maritime town of Ionia, not far from Ephesus; but there was another Miletus, in Crete, which some learned men think to be intended here. It appears that Paul went from Macedonia to Corinth, where he left Erastus; from Corinth he proceeded to Troas, where he lodged with Carpus; from Troas he went to Ephesus, where he visited Timothy; from Ephesus he went to Miletus, where he left Trophimus sick; and having embarked at Miletus, he went by sea to Rome. It is most likely, therefore, that the Miletus of Ionia is the place intended.

21. *Come before winter.* (1) Because the apostle's time was short and uncertain. (2) Because sailing in those seas was very dangerous in winter. Whether Timothy saw the apostle before he was martyred is not known. *Eubulus.* This person is nowhere else mentioned in the New Testament. *Pudens.* Of this person we have traditions and legends, but nothing certain. The Catholics make him bishop of Rome.

Linus. He also is made, by the same persons, bishop of Rome; but there is no sufficient ground for these pretensions. *Claudia.* Supposed to be the wife of Pudens. Some think she was a British lady converted by Paul, and that she was the first that brought the gospel to Britain. *All the brethren.* All the Christians, of whom there were many at Rome; though of Paul's companions in travel only Luke remained there.

22. *The Lord Jesus Christ be with thy spirit.* This is a prayer addressed to Christ by one of the most eminent of His apostles; another proof of the untruth of the assertion that prayer is never offered to Christ in the New Testament. He prays that Christ may be with his spirit, enlightening, strengthening, and confirming it to the end. *Grace be with you.* These words show that the Epistle was addressed to the whole church, and that it is not to be considered of a private nature.

THE EPISTLE TO TITUS

I. Introduction (1:1-5)
A. Personal introduction—divine authority (1:1-3)
B. Address to Titus (1:4, 5)

II. Church government (1:6-16)
A. The office
1. Elders
2. Bishops (compare 5 and 7)

B. The functions
1. God's steward (1:7)
2. The teacher (1:9)

C. The character (1:6-9)
1. Blameless in family (1:6)
2. Blameless personally (1:7, 8)
3. Blameless in doctrine (1:9)

D. Parenthesis—local reason for the instruction (1:10-16)

III. Church behavior (2:1-15)
A. The precepts (2:1-10)
1. Aged men (2:1, 2)
2. Aged women (2:3)
3. Young women (2:4, 5)
4. Young men (2:6-8)
5. Servants (2:9, 10)

B. The power (2:11-15)
1. The two epiphanies (2:11-13)
2. The gift and its purpose (2:14, 15)

IV. Church and state (3:1-11)
A. The Church's duty (3:1, 2)
B. The Church's impulse (3:3-7)
C. The method of realization (3:8-11)

V. Conclusion (3:12-15)
A. Personal (3:12)
B. Zenas and Apollos (3:13)
C. Postscript (3:14)
D. Valuation and Benediction (3:15)

This epistle of Paul to Titus is much of the same nature with those to Timothy. We read much of this Titus. He was a Greek (Gal. 2:3). Paul called him "his son" (Titus 1:4), "his brother" (2 Cor. 2:13), "his partner and fellow helper" (2 Cor. 8:23). He went up with the apostles to the church at Jerusalem (Gal. 2:1), was much conversant at Corinth, for which church he had "an earnest care" (2 Cor. 8:16). Paul's second epistle to them was sent by his hand (2 Cor. 8:16-18, 23; 9:2-4; 12:18). He was with the apostle at Rome, and thence went into Dalmatia (2 Tim. 4:10), after which no more occurs of him in the Scriptures. In Crete the gospel had got some footing; and here were Paul and Titus in one of their travels; but the apostle could not himself tarry long at this place. He therefore left Titus some time there, to carry on the work which had been begun, wherein, probably, meeting with more difficulty than ordinary, Paul wrote this epistle to him; and yet, perhaps not so much for his own sake as for the people's, that the endeavors of Titus might be more significant and effectual among them.

MATTHEW HENRY

CHAPTER 1

Verses 1–4

I. The writer. *Paul,* a Gentile name taken by the apostle of the Gentiles, Acts xiii. 9, 46, 47. Ministers will accommodate even smaller matters, so that there may be any furthering of acceptance in their work. *A servant of God, and an apostle of Jesus Christ.* The highest officers in the church are but servants. (Much divinity and devotion are comprehended in the inscriptions of the epistles.)

According to the faith of God's elect. Their doctrine agreed with the faith of all the elect. Faith is the first principle of sanctification.

The gospel is truth; the great, sure, and saving truth. Divine faith rests not on fallible reasonings and profitable opinions, but on the truth itself, *which is after godliness.* All gospel truth is after godliness; it is truth not only to be known, but acknowledged; it must be held forth in word and practice.

To bring to this knowledge and faith, and to the acknowledging of the truth which is after godliness, is the great end of the gospel ministry, *v.* 2. This is the further intent of the gospel, to beget hope as well as faith. The faith and godliness of Christians lead to eternal life, and give hope of it; for *God, that cannot lie, hath promised it.* Here is the stability and antiquity of the promise of eternal life to the saints. God, who cannot lie, hath promised before the world began.

JAMIESON, FAUSSET, BROWN

CHAPTER 1

VSS. 1-16. ADDRESS: FOR WHAT END TITUS WAS LEFT IN CRETE. QUALIFICATIONS FOR ELDERS: GAINSAYERS IN CRETE NEEDING REPROOF. **1. servant of God**—not found elsewhere in the same connection. In Romans 1:1 it is "servant of Jesus Christ" (Gal. 1:10; Phil. 1:1; cf. Acts 16:17; Rev. 1:1; 15:3). In Romans 1:1, there follows, "called to be an *apostle,*" which corresponds to the general designation of the office first, "*servant of* GOD," here, followed by the special description, "*apostle* of *Jesus Christ.*" The full expression of his apostolic office answers, in both Epistles, to the design, and is a comprehensive index to the contents. The *peculiar* form here would never have proceeded from a forger. **according to the faith**—rather, "for," "with a view to subserve the faith"; this is the object of my apostleship (cf. vss. 4, 9; Rom. 1:5). **the elect**—for whose sake we ought to endure all things (II Tim. 2:10). This election has its ground, not in anything belonging to those thus distinguished, but in the purpose and will of God from everlasting (II Tim. 1:9; Rom. 8:30-33; cf. Luke 18:7; Eph. 1:4; Col. 3:12). Acts 13:48 shows that all faith on the part of the elect, rests on the divine foreordination: they do not become *elect* by their faith, but receive *faith,* and so become believers, because they are *elect.* **and the acknowledging of the truth**—"and (for promoting) the *full knowledge* of the truth," i.e., the Christian truth (Eph. 1:13). **after godliness**—i.e., which belongs to *piety:* opposed to the knowledge which has not for its object the truth, but error, doctrinal and practical (vss. 11, 16; I Tim. 6:3); or even which has for its object mere earthly truth, not growth in the divine life. "Godliness," or "piety," is a term peculiar to the Pastoral Epistles: a fact explained by the apostle having in them to combat doctrine tending to "ungodliness" (II Tim. 2:16; cf. ch. 2:11, 12). **2. In hope of eternal life**—connected with the whole preceding sentence. That whereon rests my aim as an apostle to promote *the elect's faith and full knowledge of the truth,* is, "the hope of eternal life" (ch. 2:13; 3:7; Acts 23:6; 24:15; 28:20). **that cannot lie**—(Rom. 3:4; 11:29; Heb. 6:18). **promised before the world began**—a contracted expression for "*purposed* before the world began (lit., before the ages of time), and *promised* actually in time," the promise springing from the eternal purpose; as in II Timothy 1:9, the *gift* of

ADAM CLARKE

CHAPTER 1

1. *Paul, a servant of God.* In several places of his other Epistles, Paul styles himself the "servant of Jesus Christ," but this is the only place where he calls himself the *servant of God.*

The faith of God's elect. The Christians. *The acknowledging of the truth.* For the propagation of that truth, or system of doctrines, which is calculated to promote godliness, or a holy and useful life.

2. *In hope of eternal life.* In expectation of a state of being and well-being which should last through eternity, when time should be no more. *Which God, that cannot lie, promised.* We have often seen that the phrase "the foundation of the world" means the Jewish economy; and "before the foundation of the world," the times antecedent to the giving of the law. This is evidently the meaning here. See 2 Tim. i. 9-11.

MATTHEW HENRY

No wonder if the contempt of it be punished severely, since he has not only promised it of old, *but* (*v.* 3) *has in due times manifested his word through preaching.* That which some called *foolishness of preaching* has been thus honoured. *Which is committed unto me.* The ministry is a trust; none taketh this honour, but he who is thereunto appointed; and whoso is appointed and called must preach the word. *According to the commandment of God our Saviour.* Let none rest therefore in men's calling, without God's.

II. The person written to, *Titus,* a Gentile Greek, yet called both to the faith and ministry. The grace of God is free and powerful. What worthiness or preparation was there in one of heathen stock and education? *My own* (or *my genuine*) *son,* not by natural generation, but by supernatural regeneration. "*After the common faith,* that faith which is common to all the regenerate, and which thou hast in truth, and expressest in the life."

III. The salutation and prayer, wishing all blessings to him. The blessings wished: *Grace, mercy, and peace.* Grace is the fountain of all blessings. Mercy, and peace, and all good, spring out of this. Get into God's favour, and all must be well; for, the persons from whom blessings are wished: *From God the Father,* the fountain of all good. Every blessing, every comfort, comes to us from God, as a Father. *And the Lord Jesus Christ our Saviour.* All is from the Father by the Son.

Verse 5

I. More generally. Titus was to go on in settling what the apostle himself had not time for, in his short stay there. 1. The apostle's great diligence in the gospel; when he had set things on foot in one place, he hastened away to another. 2. His faithfulness and prudence. He neglected not the places that he went from; but left some to cultivate the young plantation. 3. His humility; he disdained not to be helped in his work, and that by such as were not of so great gifts as himself. 4. Titus, though inferior to an apostle, was yet above the ordinary fixed pastors or bishops, who were to tend particular churches as their peculiar stated charge; but Titus was in a higher sphere, to ordain such ordinary pastors where wanting, and settle things in their first state and form, and then to pass to other places. Here at Crete Titus was but occasionally, and for a short time; Paul willed him to despatch the business he was left for, and come to him at Nicopolis, where he purposed to winter; after this he was sent to Corinth, was with the apostle at Rome, and was sent thence into Dalmatia, which is the last we read of him in scripture.

II. In special: *To ordain elders in every city.* These presbyters or elders were to have the ordinary and stated care and charge of the churches. Presbyters here therefore are gospel ministers, to dispense Christ's ordinances, and to *feed the church of God.* A church without a fixed and standing ministry in it is imperfect and wanting. Where a fit number of believers is, presbyters or elders must be set; their continuance in churches is as necessary as their first appointment, for *perfecting the saints, and edifying the body of Christ.*

Verses 6–16

The apostle here gives Titus directions about ordination.

I. Of those whom he should ordain.

1. Their qualifications respecting their life.

(1) More general: *If any be blameless;* not absolutely without fault, so none are; nor altogether unblamed, this is rare and difficult; for Christ himself and his apostles were blamed. But he must be one who lies not under an ill character.

(2) More particularly.

[1] There is his relative character. In his own person, he must be of conjugal chastity. And, as to his children, *having faithful children,* obedient and good, brought up in the true Christian faith, and living according to it, at least as far as the endeavours of the parents can avail. *Not accused of riot, nor unruly.* The most innocent may be falsely so charged; they must look to it therefore that there be no colour for such censure. Children so faithful and obedient, will be a good sign of faithfulness and diligence in the parent. From his faithfulness in the less, there may be encouragement to commit to him the greater, the rule of the church of God. The ground of this qualification is shown from the nature of his office (*v.* 7). Being such bishops and overseers of the flock, who were to be examples to them, and God's stewards to take care of the affairs of his house, there is great reason that they should be blameless.

[2] The more absolute ones are expressed, *First,* Negatively. *Not self-willed.* The prohibition is of large extent, excluding self-opinion,—self-love, making self the centre of all,—also self-confidence and self-

JAMIESON, FAUSSET, BROWN

grace was the result of the eternal purpose "before the world began." **3. in due times**—*Greek,* "in *its own seasons,*" the seasons appropriate to it, and fixed by God for it (Acts 1:7). **manifested**—implying that the "promise," vs. 2, had lain hidden in His eternal purpose heretofore (cf. Col. 1:26; II Tim. 1:9, 10). **his word**—equivalent to "eternal life" (vs. 2; John 5:24; 6:63; 17:3, 17). **through preaching**—*Greek,* "*in* preaching," or rather as ALFORD (*Note,* cf. II Tim. 4:17), "in the (Gospel) *proclamation* (the thing preached, the Gospel) with which I was entrusted." **according to**—in pursuance of (cf. I Tim. 1:1). **of God our Saviour**—rather as *Greek,* "of *our Saviour God.*" *God* is predicated of *our Saviour* (cf. Jude 25; Luke 1:47). Also Psalm 24:5; Isaiah 12:2; 45:15, 21, LXX. Applied to Jesus, vs. 4; ch. 2:13; 3:6; II Timothy 1:10. **4. Titus, mine own son** *Greek,* "my *genuine* child" (I Tim. 1:2), i.e., converted by my instrumentality (I Cor. 4:17; Philemon 10). **after the common faith**—a genuine son in respect to (in virtue of) the faith *common* to all the people of God, comprising in a common brotherhood Gentiles as well as Jews, therefore embracing Titus a Gentile (II Pet. 1:1; Jude 3). **Grace, mercy, and peace**—"mercy" is omitted in some of the oldest MSS. But one of the best and oldest MSS. supports it (*Notes,* cf. I Tim. 1:2; II Tim. 1:2). There are many similarities of phrase in the Pastoral Epistles. **the Lord Jesus Christ**—The oldest MSS. read only "Christ Jesus." **our Saviour**—found thus added to "Christ" only in Paul's *Pastoral Epistles,* and in II Pet. 1:1, 11; 2:20; 3:18. **5. I left thee**—"I left thee *behind*" [ALFORD] when I left the island: *not* implying *permanence* of commission (cf. I Tim. 1:3). **in Crete**—now Candia. **set in order**—rather as *Greek,* "that thou mightest *follow up* (the work begun by me), setting right the things that are wanting," which I was unable to complete by reason of the shortness of my stay in Crete. Christianity, doubtless, had long existed in Crete: there were some Cretans among those who heard Peter's preaching on Pentecost (Acts 2:11). The number of Jews in Crete was large (vs. 10), and it is likely that those scattered in the persecution of Stephen (Acts 11:19) preached to them, as they did to the Jews of Cyprus,etc. Paul also was there on his voyage to Rome (Acts 27:7-12). By all these instrumentalities the Gospel was sure to reach Crete. But until Paul's later visit, after his first imprisonment at Rome, the Cretan Christians were without Church organization. This Paul began, and had commissioned (before leaving Crete) Titus to go on with, and now reminds him of that commission. **ordain**—rather, "appoint," "constitute." **in every city**—"from city to city." **as I . . . appointed thee**—i.e., as I directed thee; prescribing as well the *act* of constituting elders, as also the *manner* of doing so, which latter includes the qualifications required in a presbyter presently stated. Those called "elders" here are called "bishops" in vs. 7. *Elder* is the term of *dignity* in relation to the college of presbyters; *bishop* points to the *duties* of his office in relation to the flock. From the unsound state of the Cretan Christians described here, we see the danger of the want of Church government. The appointment of presbyters was designed to check idle *talk* and speculation, by setting forth the "faithful word." **6.** (*Notes,* cf. I Tim. 3:2-4.) The thing dwelt on here as the requisite in a bishop, is a good reputation among those over whom he is to be set. The immorality of the Cretan professors rendered this a necessary requisite in one who was to be a *reprover:* and their unsoundness in doctrine also made needful great steadfastness in the faith (vss. 9, 13). **having faithful children**—i.e., *believing* children. He who could not bring his children to faith, how shall he bring others? [BENGEL.] ALFORD explains, "established in the faith." **not accused**—not merely not riotous, but "not (even) accused of riot" ("profligacy" [ALFORD]; "dissolute life" [WAHL]). **unruly**—*insubordinate;* opposed to "in subjection" (I Tim. 3:4). **7. For . . . must**—The emphasis is on "must." The reason why I said "blameless," is the very idea of a "bishop" (an overseer of the flock; he here substitutes for "presbyter" the term which expresses his *duties*) involves the *necessity* for such blamelessness, if he is to have influence over the flock. **steward of God**—The greater the master is, the greater the virtues required in His servant [BENGEL], (I Tim. 3:15); the Church is God's house, over which the minister is set as a steward (Heb. 3:2-6; I Pet. 4:10, 17). Note: ministers are not merely *Church* officers, but God's stewards; Church government is of divine appointment. **not self-willed**—lit., "self-pleasing"; unaccommodating to others; *harsh,* the opposite of "a lover of hospitality" (vs. 6); so Nabal (I Sam. 25); self-loving and imperious; such

ADAM CLARKE

3. *But hath in due times.* "In its own times." See 1 Tim. ii. 6; Gal. iv. 4; Eph. i. 10; ii. 7. God caused the gospel to be published in that time in which it could be published with the greatest effect. It is impossible that God should prematurely hasten or causelessly delay the accomplishment of any of His works. Jesus was manifested precisely at the time in which that manifestation could best promote the glory of God and the salvation of man. *Manifested his word.* "His doctrine"—the doctrine of eternal life, by the incarnation, passion, death, and resurrection of Jesus Christ. *Which is committed unto me.* That is, to preach it among the Gentiles. *According to the commandment of God our Saviour.* This evidently refers to the commission which he had received from Christ. See Acts ix. 15; xxvi. 16, etc. This is the commandment, and according to it he became the apostle of the Gentiles. *God our Saviour.* As the commission was given by Jesus Christ alone, the person whom he terms here *God our Saviour* must be Jesus Christ only; and this is another proof that Paul believed Jesus Christ to be God. This "eternal life" God had "promised" in a comparatively obscure way before the foundation of the world, the Jewish dispensation; but now under the gospel He had "made it manifest"—produced it with all its brightness, illustrations, and proofs.

4. *To Titus, mine own son.* Him whom I have been the instrument of converting to the Christian faith and in whom, in this respect, I have the same right as any man can have in his own begotten son.

5. *For this cause left I thee in Crete.* That Paul had been in Crete, though nowhere else intimated, is clear from this passage. That he could not have made such an important visit and evangelized an island of the first consequence without its being mentioned by his historian Luke, had it happened during the period embraced in the Acts of the Apostles, must be evident. That the journey therefore must have been performed after the time in which Luke ends his history, that is, after Paul's first imprisonment at Rome, seems almost certain. *Set in order the things that are wanting.* It appears from this that the apostle did not spend much time in Crete, and that he was obliged to leave it before he had got the church properly organized. The supplying of this defect, he tells Titus, he had confided to him as one whose spiritual views coincided entirely with his own. *Ordain elders in every city.* That thou mightest "appoint" *elders*—persons well-instructed in divine things, who should be able to instruct others, and observe and enforce the discipline of the church. It appears that those who are called *elders* in this place are the same as those termed "bishops" in v. 7. We have many proofs that bishops and elders were of the same order in the apostolic Church, though afterwards they became distinct. *In every city.* This seems to intimate that the apostle had gone over the whole of the "hundred cities" for which this island was celebrated. Indeed it is not likely that he would leave one in which he had not preached Christ crucified.

6. *If any be blameless.* See the notes on 1 Tim. iii. 2. *Having faithful children.* Whose family is converted to God. It would have been absurd to employ a man to govern the church whose children were not in subjection to himself; for it is an apostolic maxim that he who cannot rule his own house cannot rule the church of God, 1 Tim. iii. 5.

7. *Not selfwilled.* Not one who is determined to have his own way in everything, setting up his own judgment to that of all others.

MATTHEW HENRY

pleasing, set on one's own will and way. A great honour it is to a minister to be ready to ask and to take advice, to be ready to defer to the mind and will of others, becoming all things to all men, that they may gain some. *Not soon angry.* How unfit are those to govern a church who cannot govern themselves. *Not given to wine.* Moderate use of this, as of the other good creatures of God, is not unlawful. But excess therein is shameful in all, especially in a minister. *Not given to filthy lucre;* not entering into the ministry with base worldly views. Nothing is more unbecoming a minister, who is to direct his own and others' eyes to another world, than to be too intent upon this. *Secondly,* Positively: he must be (*v.* 8) *a lover of hospitality.* Such a spirit and practice, according to ability and occasion, are very becoming such as should be examples of good works. *A lover of good men,* or of *good things;* ministers should be exemplary in both. *Sober,* or *prudent;* a needful grace in a minister both for his ministerial and personal carriage and management. *Just* in things belonging to civil life. *Holy* in what concerns religion. *Temperate;* it comes from a word that signifies *strength,* and denotes one who has power over his appetite and affections.

2. As to doctrine,

(1) Here is his duty: *Holding fast the faithful word, as he has been taught*—holding it fast in his own belief and profession, and in teaching others. Ministers must hold fast, and hold forth, the faithful word in their teaching and life.

(2) Here is the end: *That he may be able, by sound doctrine, both to exhort, and to convince the gainsayers.* How should he do this if he himself were uncertain or unsteady, not holding fast that *faithful word and sound doctrine.*

II. Whom he should reject or avoid. The reasons he takes both from bad teachers and hearers among them, *v.* 10, to the end.

1. From bad teachers. (1) Those false teachers are described. They were *unruly,* headstrong and ambitious of power, refractory and untractable. *And vain talkers and deceivers,* falling into errors and mistakes, and fond of them, and studious and industrious to draw others into the same. Many such there were, *especially those of the circumcision,* who yet were for mingling Judaism and Christianity together, and so making a corrupt medley. (2) Here is the apostle's direction how to deal with them (*v.* 11): *Their mouths must be stopped* by confutation and conviction. (3) The reasons are given for this. From the pernicious effects of their errors. Their base end in what they do: serving a worldly interest under pretence of religion.

2. In reference to their people or hearers, who are described from ancient testimony given of them.

(1) Here is the witness (*v.* 12): One of the Cretans, likely to know and unlikely to slander them. *A prophet of their own;* so their poets were accounted.

(2) Here is the matter of his testimony: *The Cretans are always liars, evil beasts, slow bellies.* Even to a proverb, they were infamous for falsehood and lying; to play the *Cretan,* or to lie, is the same; and they were compared to evil beasts for their sly hurtfulness and savage nature, and called slow bellies for their laziness and sensuality, more inclined to eat than to work.

(3) Here is the verification of this by the apostle himself: *v.* 13. The apostle saw too much ground for that character.

(4) He instructs Titus how to deal with them. When Paul wrote to Timothy he bade him instruct with meekness; but now, when he writes to Titus, he bids him rebuke them sharply. Timothy had a more polite people to deal with, and therefore he must rebuke them with meekness; and Titus had to do with those who were more rough and uncultivated. Their corruptions were many and gross, and therefore should be dealt with accordingly. There must in reproving be a distinguishing between sins and sins; some are more gross and heinous in their nature: and between sinners and sinners; some are of a more tender and tractable temper, apter to be wrought on by gentleness; others are more hardy and stubborn, and need more cutting language.

(5) Here is the end of it noted (*v.* 14), that they may show themselves truly and effectually changed. The sharpest reproofs must aim at the good of the reproved, to reclaim and reform the erroneous and the guilty. Soundness in the faith is most desirable and necessary. This is the soul's health and vigour. A special means to soundness in the faith is to turn away the ear from fables and the fancies of men. Fancies and devices of men in the worship of God are contrary to truth and piety.

(6) He gives the reasons of this. To good Christians that are sound in the faith and thereby purified *all*

JAMIESON, FAUSSET, BROWN

a spirit would incapacitate him for *leading* a willing flock, instead of *driving.*

not given to wine—(*Notes,* I Tim. 3:3, 8). **not given to filthy lucre**—not making the Gospel a means of gain (I Tim. 3:3, 8). In opposition to those "teaching for filthy lucre's sake" (vs. 11; I Tim. 6:5; I Pet. 5:2).

8. lover of hospitality—needed especially in those days (Rom. 12:13; I Tim. 3:2; Heb. 13:2; I Pet. 4:9; III John 5). Christians travelling from one place to another were received and forwarded on their journey by their brethren. **lover of good men**—*Greek,* "a lover of (all that is) good," men or things (Phil. 4:8, 9). **sober** towards *one's self;* "discreet"; self-restrained" [ALFORD], (*Note,* I Tim. 2:9). **just**—towards *men.* **holy**—towards *God* (*Note,* I Thess. 2:10). **temperate**—"One having his passions, tongue, hand and eyes, at command" [CHRYSOSTOM]; "continent." **9. Holding fast**—Holding firmly to (cf. Matt. 6:24; Luke 16:13). **the faithful**—true and trustworthy (I Tim. 1:15). **word as he has been taught**—lit., "the word (which is) according to the teaching" which he has received (cf. I Tim. 4:6, end; II Timothy 3: 14). **by**—*Translate* as *Greek,* "to exhort *in* doctrine (*instruction*) which is sound"; *sound doctrine* or *instruction* is the element IN which his *exhorting* is to have place. On "sound" (peculiar to the Pastoral Epistles), see I Timothy 1:10; 6:3. **convince**—rather, "reprove" [ALFORD], (vs. 13). **10. unruly**—"insubordinate." **and**—omitted in the oldest MSS. "There are many unruly persons, vain talkers, and deceivers"; "unruly" being predicated of both *vain talkers* and deceivers. **vain talkers**—opposed to "holding fast the faithful word" (vs. 9). "Vain jangling" (I Tim. 1:6); "foolish questions, unprofitable and vain" (ch. 3:9). The source of the evil was corrupted Judaism (vs. 14). Many Jews were then living in Crete, according to JOSEPHUS; so the Jewish leaven remained in some of them after conversion. **deceivers**—lit., "deceivers of the minds of others" (*Greek,* Gal. 6:3). **11. mouths... stopped**—lit., "muzzled," "bridled" as an unruly beast (cf. Ps. 32:9). **who**—*Greek,* "(seeing that they are) such men as"; or "inasmuch as they" [ELLICOTT]. **subvert ... houses**—"overthrowing" their "faith" (II Tim. 2: 18). "They are the devil's levers by which he subverts the houses of God" [THEOPHYLACT]. **for filthy lucre**—(I Tim. 3:3, 8; 6:5). **12. One**—Epimenides of Phæstus, or Gnossus, in Crete, about 600 B.C. He was sent for to purify Athens from its pollution occasioned by Cylon. He was regarded as a diviner and *prophet.* The words here are taken probably from his treatise "*concerning oracles.*" Paul also quotes from two other heathen writers, ARATUS (Acts 17:28) and MENANDER (I Cor. 15:33), but he does not honor them so far as even to mention their names. **of themselves... their own**—which enhances his authority as a witness. "To Cretanize" was proverbial for *to lie;* as "to Corinthianize" was for *to be dissolute.* **alway liars**—not merely *at times,* as every natural man is. Contrast vs. 2, "God that *cannot lie.*" They love "fables" (vs. 14); even the heathen poets laughed at their lying assertion that they had in their country the sepulchre of Jupiter. **evil beasts**—rude, savage, cunning, greedy. Crete was *a country without wild beasts.* Epimenides' sarcasm was that its human inhabitants supplied the place of wild beasts. **slow bellies**—indolent through pampering their bellies. *They themselves* are called "bellies," for that is the member for which they live (Rom. 16:18; Phil. 3: 19). **13. This witness**—"This testimony (though coming from a Cretan) is true." **sharply**—Gentleness would not reclaim so perverse offenders. **that they**—that *those seduced* by the false teachers may be brought back to *soundness* in the faith. Their malady is strifes about words and questions (ch. 3: 9; I Tim. 6:4). **14. Jewish fables**—(*Notes,* I Tim. 1:4; 4:7; II Tim. 4:4). These formed the transition stage to subsequent Gnosticism; as yet the error was but profitless, and not tending to godliness, rather than openly opposed to the faith. **commandments of men**—as to *ascetic* abstinence (vs. 15; Mark 7:7-9; Col. 2:16, 20-23; I Tim. 4:3). **that turn from the truth**—whose characteristic is that they turn away from the truth (II Tim. 4:4).

ADAM CLARKE

Not soon angry. Not a choleric man; one who is irritable, who is apt to be inflamed on every opposition; one who has not proper command over his own temper.

8. *A lover of hospitality.* "A lover of strangers." See the note on 1 Tim. iii. 2. *A lover of good men.* "A lover of goodness" or of good things in general. *Sober.* Prudent in all his conduct. Just in all his dealings. Holy in his heart. *Temperate*—self-denying and abstemious in his food and raiment; not too nice on points of honor, nor magisterially rigid in the exercise of his ecclesiastical functions.

9. *Holding fast the faithful word.* Conscientiously retaining, and zealously maintaining, the true Christian doctrine, "according to the instructions," or according to the institutions, form of sound doctrine, or confession of faith, which I have delivered to you. *That he may be able by sound doctrine.* If the doctrine be not sound, vain is the profession of it, and vain its influence. *To exhort* them to hold the faith, that they may persevere. *And to convince.* Refute the objections, confound the sophistry, and convert the gainsayers; and thus defend the truth.

10. *There are many unruly.* Persons who will not receive the sound doctrine nor come under wholesome discipline. *Vain talkers.* Empty boasters of knowledge, rights, and particular privileges; all noise, empty parade, and no work. *Deceivers* of the souls of men by their specious pretensions. *They of the circumcision.* The Judaizing teachers, who maintained the necessity of circumcision and of observing the rites and ceremonies of the Mosaic law in order to the perfecting of the gospel.

11. *Whose mouths must be stopped.* Unmask them at once; exhibit them to the people; make manifest their ignorance and hypocrisy, and let them be confounded before the people whom they are endeavoring to seduce. *Subvert whole houses.* Turn whole Christian families from the faith.

12. *One of themselves, even a prophet of their own.* This was Epimenides, who was born at Gnossus, in Crete. He died about 538 years before the Christian era. When Paul calls him a *prophet of their own,* he only intimates that he was, by the Cretans, reputed a prophet. And according to Plutarch, the Cretans paid him divine honors after his death. *The Cretians are alway liars.* The words quoted here by the apostle are, according to Jerome, Socrates, Nicephorus, and others, taken from a work of Epimenides, now no longer extant, entitled *Concerning Oracles.* The words form a hexameter verse: "The Cretans are always liars; destructive wild beasts; sluggish gluttons." That the Cretans were reputed to be egregious liars several of the ancients declare, insomuch that "to act like a Cretan" signifies "to lie." The other Greeks reputed them liars because they said that among them was the sepulchre of Jupiter, who was the highest object of the Greek and Roman worship. *Evil beasts.* Ferocious and destructive in their manners. *Slow bellies.* Addicted to voluptuousness, idleness, and gluttony; sluggish or hoggish men.

13. *This witness is true.* What Epimenides said of them nearly six hundred years before continued still to be true. *Rebuke them sharply.* "Cuttingly, severely"; show no indulgence to persons guilty of such crimes. *That they may be sound in the faith.* That they may receive the incorrupt doctrine, and illustrate it by a holy and useful life.

14. *Not giving heed to Jewish fables.* See on 1 Tim. i. 4 and iv. 7. *Commandments of men.* The injunctions of the scribes and Pharisees which they added to the law of God. *That turn from the truth.* For such persons made the Word of God of none effect by their traditions. Sometimes the verb signifies to be "averse from, slight, or despise." So here the persons in question despised the truth and taught others to do the same.

MATTHEW HENRY

things are pure, but to those that are defiled and unbelieving nothing is pure. They suck poison out of that from which others draw sweetness; their mind and conscience, being defiled, a taint is communicated to all they do.

There are many who profess to know God, and yet in their lives deny and reject him; their practice is a contradiction to their profession. The apostle, instructing Titus to rebuke sharply, does himself rebuke sharply; he gives them very hard words, yet doubtless no harder than their case warranted, and their need required. *Being abominable,* deserving that God and good men should turn away their eyes from them as nauseous and offensive. *And disobedient.* They might do divers things; but it was not the obedience of faith. *To every good work reprobate,* without skill or judgment to do anything aright. See the miserable condition of hypocrites. Let us not be so ready to fix this charge on others as careful that it agree not to ourselves.

JAMIESON, FAUSSET, BROWN

15. all things—external, "are pure" in themselves; the distinction of *pure* and *impure* is not in the things, but in the disposition of him who uses them; in opposition to "the commandments of men" (vs. 14), which forbade certain things as if impure intrinsically. "To the pure" inwardly, i.e., those purified in heart by *faith* (Acts 15:9; Rom. 14:20; I Tim. 4:3), all outward things are pure; all are open to their use. Sin alone touches and defiles the soul (Matt. 23:26; Luke 11:41). **nothing pure**—either within or without (Rom. 14:23). **mind**—their mental sense and intelligence. **conscience**—their moral consciousness of the conformity or discrepancy between their motives and acts on the one hand, and God's law on the other. A conscience and a mind defiled are represented as the source of the errors opposed in the Pastoral Epistles (I Tim. 1:19; 3:9; 6:5). **16. They profess**—i.e., *make a profession* acknowledging God. He does not deny their theoretical knowledge of God, but that they *practically* know Him. **deny him**—the opposite of the previous "profess" or "confess" Him (I Tim. 5:8; II Tim. 2:12; 3:5). **abominable**—themselves, though laying so much stress on the contracting of abomination from outward things (cf. Lev. 11:10-13; Rom. 2:22). **disobedient**—to God (ch. 3:3; Eph. 2:2; 5:6). **reprobate**—rejected as worthless *when tested* (*Notes,* Rom. 1:28; I Cor. 9:27; II Tim. 3:8).

ADAM CLARKE

15. *Unto the pure all things are pure.* This appears to have been spoken in reference to the Jewish distinctions of clean and unclean meats. To the genuine Christian every kind of meat proper for human nourishment is pure, is lawful and may be used without scruple. This our Lord had long before decided. See on Luke xi. 39-41. *But unto them that are defiled,* in their consciences, and *unbelieving,* "unfaithful," *is nothing pure.* Their *mind* is contaminated with impure and unholy images and ideas, and their *conscience is defiled* with the guilt of sins already committed against God.

16. *They profess that they know God.* He still speaks concerning the unbelieving Jews, the seducing teachers, and those who had been seduced by their bad doctrine. None were so full of pretensions to the knowledge of the true God as the Jews. *But in works they deny him.* Their profession and practice were at continual variance. Full of a pretended faith, while utterly destitute of those *works* by which a genuine faith is accredited and proved. *Being abominable.* This word sometimes refers to unnatural lusts. *And disobedient.* "Unpersuadable, unbelieving." *Unto every good work reprobate.* "Adulterate"; like a bad coin, deficient in both the weight and the goodness of the metal, and without the proper sterling stamp.

MATTHEW HENRY — CHAPTER 2

Verses 1–10

Here he exhorts him,

I. Generally, to a faithful discharge of his own office. His ordaining others to preach would not excuse himself from preaching, nor might he take care of ministers and elders only, but he must instruct private Christians also in their duty. The true doctrines of the gospel are *sound doctrines,* they are in themselves good and holy, and make the believers so.

II. Specially and particularly, he instructs him to apply this sound doctrine to several sorts of persons, from *v.* 2–10. Ministers must be particular as well as practical in their preaching; they must teach men their duty, and must teach all and each his duty.

1. To the aged men. Old disciples of Christ must conduct themselves in everything agreeably to the Christian doctrine. *That the aged men be sober;* they must keep measure in things, both for health and for fitness, for counsel and example to the younger. *Grave:* levity is unbecoming in any, but especially in the aged. *Temperate. Sound in the faith,* sincere and steadfast. Those who are full of years should be full of grace and goodness, the inner man renewing more and more as the outer decays. *In charity,* or love; this is fitly joined with *faith,* which works by, and must be seen in, love. It must be sincere love, without dissimulation: love of God for himself, and of men for God's sake. And *in patience.* Aged persons are apt to be peevish and therefore need to be on their guard against such infirmities. Faith, love, and patience, are three main Christian graces, and soundness in these is much of gospel perfection.

2. To the aged women. These also must be instructed and warned. Those virtues before mentioned (*sobriety, gravity, temperance, soundness in the faith, charity, and patience*) recommended to aged men, are not proper to them only, but applicable to both sexes. There is not one way of salvation for one sex or sort, and another for another; but both must learn and practise the same things; the virtues and duties are common. *That the aged women likewise be in behaviour as becometh holiness;* or as beseems and is proper for holy persons, such as they profess to be. Whatsoever things are beseeming or unbeseeming holiness form a measure and rule of conduct to be looked to. *Not false accusers*—slandering and backbiting their neighbours, a great and too common fault; not only loving to speak, but to speak ill, of people, and to separate very friends. *Not given to much wine.* This is unseemly and evil in any, but especially in this sex and age, and was too much to be found among the Greeks of that time and place. *Teachers of good things.* Not public preachers, that is forbidden, but otherwise teach they may and should, by example and good life. Those whose actions and behaviour become holiness are thereby teachers of good things; and, besides this, they may and should also teach by doctrinal instruction at home, and in a private way. Their business is, and they may be called on to it, to be teachers of good things.

3. There are lessons for young women also, whom the aged women must teach. For teaching such things

JAMIESON, FAUSSET, BROWN — CHAPTER 2

VSS. 1-15. DIRECTIONS TO TITUS: HOW TO EXHORT VARIOUS CLASSES OF BELIEVERS: THE GRACE OF GOD IN CHRIST OUR GRAND INCENTIVE TO LIVE GODLY. **1. But . . . thou**—in contrast to the reprobate seducers stigmatized in ch. 1:11, 15, 16. "He deals more in exhortations, because those intent on useless questions needed chiefly to be recalled to the study of a holy, moral life; for nothing so effectually allays men's wandering curiosity, as the being brought to recognize those duties in which they ought to exercise themselves" [CALVIN]. **speak**—without restraint: contrast ch. 1:11, "mouths . . . stopped." **doctrine**—"instruction" or "teaching." **2. sober**—Translated "vigilant," as *sober* men alone can be (I Tim. 3:2). But "sober" here answers to "not given to wine," vs. 3; ch. 1:7. **grave**—"dignified"; behaving with *reverent propriety.* **temperate**—"self-restrained"; "discreet" [ALFORD], (ch. 1:8; I Tim. 2:9). **faith . . . charity** [love] . . . **patience**—combined in I Timothy 6:11. "Faith, *hope,* charity" (I Cor. 13:13). "Patience," *Greek,* "enduring perseverance," is the attendant on, and is supported by, "hope" (I Cor. 13:7; I Thess. 1:3). It is the grace which especially becomes *old men,* being the fruit of ripened experience derived from trials overcome (Rom. 5:3).

3. behaviour—"deportment." **as becometh holiness**—"as becometh women consecrated to God" [WAHL]: being by our Christian calling priestesses unto God (Eph. 5:3; I Tim. 2:10). "Observant of sacred decorum" [BENGEL]. **not false accusers**—not slanderers: a besetting sin of some elderly women. **given to much wine**—the besetting sin of the Cretans (ch. 1:12). Lit., "enslaved to much wine." Addiction to wine is *slavery* (Rom. 6:16; II Pet. 2:19). **teachers**—in private: not in public (I Cor. 14:34; I Tim. 2:11, 12); influencing for good the younger women by precept and example.

ADAM CLARKE — CHAPTER 2

1. *But speak thou the things.* This is a conclusion drawn from the preceding chapter. The Judaizing teachers not only taught a false doctrine, but they led an unholy life. Titus was to act directly opposite; he must teach a sacred doctrine and the things which become it; he must proclaim the truth and illustrate that truth. The people must not only be well-instructed, but they must be holy in their lives. Principle and practice must go hand in hand.

2. *That the aged men be sober.* It is very likely that the word *aged* is to be taken here in its literal sense; that it refers to advanced years and not to any office in the Church; the whole context seems to require this sense.

3. *The aged women likewise.* I believe elderly women are meant and not deaconesses. *That they be in behaviour.* That they be in their dress, gait, and general deportment such as their holy calling requires; that they be not like the world but like the Church, decent throughout, and adorned with holiness within. *Not false accusers.* "Not devils"; we have had the same expression applied in the same way, 1 Tim. iii. 11. *Not given to much wine.* Not enslaved by much wine, not habitual drunkards or tipplers; habit is a species of slavery. Both among the Greeks and Romans old women were generally reputed to be fond of much wine.

MATTHEW HENRY

aged women have often better access than the men, even than ministers have. *To be sober and discreet*, contrary to the vanity and rashness which younger years are subject to. *Discreet* and *chaste* stand well together; many expose themselves to fatal temptations by that which at first might be but indiscretion. *Chaste*, and *keepers at home*, are well joined too. Not but there are occasions of going abroad; but a gadding temper for merriment and company sake is the opposite evil intended. *Good*, generally, in opposition to all vice; and specially kind, helpful, and charitable. It may also have a more particular sense; one of a meek and yet cheerful spirit and temper, not sullen nor bitter. *To love their husbands, and to be obedient to them:* and where there is true love this will be no difficult command. God would have a resemblance of Christ's authority over the church held forth in the husband's over the wife. Christ is the head of the church, to protect and save it, to supply it with all good, and secure it from evil; and so is the husband over the wife, to keep her from injuries, and to provide comfortably for her. It is not then a slavish subjection that is required; but a loving subordination. *And to love their children*, not with a natural affection only, but a spiritual; not a fond foolish love, neglecting due reproof and correction where necessary, but a regular Christian love, forming their life and manners aright, taking care of their souls as well as of their bodies. *That the word of God may not be blasphemed.* "What are these the better for this their new religion?" would the infidels be ready to say. "Judge what a God he is by these his servants; and what his word, and doctrine, and religion, are by these his followers."

4. Here is the duty of young men. They are apt to be eager and hot, therefore they must be earnestly exhorted to be considerate, not rash; humble and mild, not haughty and proud; for there are more young people ruined by pride than by any other sin.

5. With these instructions to Titus the apostle inserts some directions to himself. For his conversation, *v.* 7. Without this, he would pull down with one hand what he built with the other. Good doctrine and good life must go together. *In all things;* some read, *above all things.* Above all things, example, especially that of the teacher himself, is needful; hereby both light and influence are more likely to go together. Ministers must be examples to the flock, and the people followers of them, as they are of Christ. For his teaching and doctrine, as well as for his life, *v.* 7, 8. In their preaching, therefore, the display of human learning or oratory, is not to be affected; but sound speech must be used, which cannot be *condemned*; scripture-language in expressing scripture-truths. This is sound speech, that cannot be condemned. Thus be an example *in word*; and *in conversation*, the life corresponding with the doctrine. The reason both for the strictness of the minister's life and the gravity and soundness of his preaching. Adversaries would be seeking occasion to reflect, and would do so could they find anything amiss in doctrine or life. Faithful ministers will have enemies watching, such as will endeavour to find or pick holes in their teaching or behaviour; the more need therefore for them to look to themselves.

6. The directions respecting servants. Servants must know and do their duty to their earthly masters, but with an eye to their heavenly one.

(1) The duties themselves are these:

[1] *v.* 9: Obedience the prime duty, that by which they are characterized. Their will must be subject to their master's will, and their time and labour at their master's disposal and command. If he be a master, the duties of a servant are to be paid to him as such.

[2] *To please them well in all things.* We are not to understand it either of obeying or pleasing them, without any limitation; but always with a reserve of God's right. If his command and the earthly master's come in competition, we are instructed to obey God rather than man. And not only must the will of God be the measure of the servant's obedience, but the reason of it also. All must be done with a respect to him, in virtue of his authority, and for pleasing him primarily and chiefly.

[3] *Not answering again.* When conscious of a fault, to palliate or stand in justification of it doubles it. Yet this not answering again excludes not turning away wrath with a soft answer, when season and circumstances admit. Good and wise masters will be ready to hear and do right.

[4] *Not purloining, but showing all good fidelity.* This is another great essential of good servants, to be *honest*. They must be just and true, and do for their masters as they would or should for themselves. Be it so that the master is hard and strait, scarcely making sufficient provision for servants; yet

JAMIESON, FAUSSET, BROWN

4. to be sober—*Greek*, "self-restrained," "discreet"; the same *Greek* as in vs. 2, "temperate." (But see *Note* vs. 2; cf. *Note*, II Tim. 1:7.) ALFORD therefore translates, "That they school [admonish in their duty] the young women to be lovers of their husbands . . ." (the foundation of all domestic happiness). It was judicious that Titus, a young man, should admonish the young women, not directly, but through the older women. **5. keepers at home**—as "guardians of the house," as the *Greek* expresses. The oldest MSS. read, "*Workers* at home": active in household duties (Prov. 7:11; I Tim. 5:13). **good**—kind, *beneficent* (Matt. 20:15; Rom. 5:7; I Pet. 2:18). Not churlish and niggardly, but thrifty as housewives. **obedient**—rather "submissive," as the *Greek* is translated; (see *Notes*, Eph. 5:21, 22, 24). **their own**—marking the duty of subjection which they owe them, as being *their own* husbands (Eph. 5:22; Col. 3:18).

blasphemed—"evil spoken of." That no reproach may be cast on the Gospel, through the inconsistencies of its professors (vs. 8, 10; Rom. 2:24; I Tim. 5:14; 6:1). "Unless we are virtuous, blasphemy will come through us to the faith" [THEOPHYLACT]. **6. Young**—*Greek*, "The younger men." **sober-minded**—self-restrained [ALFORD]. "Nothing is so hard at this age as to overcome pleasures and follies" [CHRYSOSTOM].

7. In—*with respect to* all things. **thyself a pattern**—though but a young man thyself. All teaching is useless unless the teacher's example confirm his word. **in doctrine**—*in* thy ministerial *teaching* (showing) *uncorruptness*, i.e., *untainted purity* of motive on thy part (cf. II Cor. 11:3), so as to be "a pattern" to all. As "gravity," etc., refers to Titus himself, so "uncorruptness"; though, doubtless, uncorruptness of *the doctrine* will be sure to follow as a consequence of the Christian minister being of simple, uncorrupt integrity himself. **gravity**—dignified seriousness in setting forth the truth. **sincerity**—omitted in the oldest MSS. **8. speech**—discourse in public and private ministrations. **he that is of the contrary part**—**the adversary** (ch. 1:9; II Tim. 2:25), whether he be heathen or Jew. **may be ashamed**—put to confusion by the power of truth and innocence (cf. vss. 5, 10; I Tim. 5:14; 6:1). **no evil thing**—*in our acts*, or *demeanor*. **of you**—So one of the oldest MSS. Other very old MSS. read, "of us," Christians.

9. servants—"slaves." **to please them well**—"to give satisfaction" [ALFORD]. *To be complaisant in everything;* to have that zealous desire to gain the master's goodwill which will anticipate the master's wish and do even more than is required. The reason for the frequent recurrence of injunctions to slaves to *subjection* (Eph. 6:5, etc.; Col. 3:22; I Tim. 6:1, etc.; I Pet. 2:18) was, that in no rank was there more danger of the doctrine of the *spiritual* equality and freedom of Christians being misunderstood than in that of slaves. It was natural for the slave who had become a Christian, to forget his place and put himself on a *social* level with his master. Hence the charge for each to abide in the sphere in which he was when converted (I Cor. 7:20-24). **not answering again**—*in contradiction* to the master: so the *Greek*, "not contradicting" [WAHL]. **10. Not purloining**—*Greek*, "Not *appropriating*" what does not belong to one. It means "keeping back" dishonestly or deceitfully (Acts 5:2, 3). **showing**—manifesting in acts. **all good**—really good; not so in mere appearance (Eph. 6:5, 6; Col. 3:22-24). "The heathen do not judge of the Christian's doctrines from the doctrine, but from his actions and life" [CHRYSOSTOM]. Men will write, fight, and even die for their religion; but how few *live* for it! Translate, "That they may adorn the doctrine of our Saviour God," i.e., God the Father, the originating author of salvation (cf. *Note*, I Tim. 1:1). God deigns to have His Gospel-doctrine adorned even by slaves, who are regarded by the world as no better

ADAM CLARKE

4. *That they may teach the young women to be sober.* That it was natural for the young to imitate the old will be readily allowed; it was therefore necessary that the old should be an example of godly living to the young. Jerome, taking it for granted that drunkenness and impurity are closely connected, asks this serious question: "How can an elderly woman teach young women chastity when, if the young woman should imitate the drunkenness of the matron, it would be impossible for her to be chaste?" *To love their husbands.* The duties recommended in this and the following verses are so plain as to need no comment, and so absolutely necessary to the character of a wife that no one deserves the same who does not live in the practice of them.

5. *Keepers at home.* A woman who spends much time in visiting must neglect her family. Instead of "keepers of the house," or *keepers at home*, some MSS. have "workers at home"; not only staying in the house and keeping the house, but working in the house. *That the word of God be not blasphemed.* The enemies of the gospel are quick-eyed to spy out imperfections in its professors; and if they find women professing Christianity living an irregular life, they will not fail to decry the Christian doctrine on this account.

6. *Young men likewise exhort to be sober minded.* Reformation should begin with the old; they have the authority, and they should give the example. The young of both sexes must also give an account of themselves to God; sober-mindedness in young men is a rare qualification.

7. *In all things shewing thyself a pattern.* As the apostle had given directions relative to the conduct of old men, v. 2; of old women, v. 3; of young women, v. 4; and of young men, v. 6, the words which we translate *in all things* should be rather considered in reference to the above persons and the behavior required in them: "showing thyself a pattern of good works to all these persons"—being in sobriety, gravity, temperance what thou requirest others to be. *In doctrine shewing uncorruptness.* Mixing nothing with the truth; taking nothing from it; adding nothing to it; and exhibiting it in all its connection, energy, and fullness.

8. *Sound speech. Sound* or "healing doctrine." Human nature is in a state of disease, and the doctrine of the gospel is calculated to remove the disease and restore all to perfect health and soundness. *He that is of the contrary part.* Whether this may refer to the Judaizing teachers in general or to someone who might, by his false doctrine, have been disturbing the peace of the churches in Crete, we cannot tell. *Having no evil thing to say of you.* Against a person who is sound in his doctrine and holy in his life, no evil can be justly alleged. He who reports evil of such a person must be confounded when brought to the test. Instead of *of you*, "of us" is the reading of numerous MSS. and several of the primitive fathers. This reading makes a better sense and is undoubtedly genuine.

9. *Exhort servants to be obedient.* The apostle refers to those who were "slaves" and the property of their masters; even these are exhorted to be obedient "to their own despots." *Please them well in all things.* They were to endeavor to do this in all things, though they could not hope to succeed in everything. *Not answering again.* "Not contradicting or gainsaying." This is no part of a servant's duty; a servant is hired to do his master's work, and this his master has a right to appoint.

10. *Not purloining.* Neither "giving away, privately selling," nor in any way wasting the master's goods. The word signifies not only stealing but embezzling another's property, keeping back a part of the price of any commodity sold on the master's account. In Acts v. 2 we translate it "to keep back part of the price," the crime of which Ananias and Sapphira were guilty. It has been remarked that among the heathens this species of fraud was very frequent.

MATTHEW HENRY

they must not be their own carvers, nor go about by theft to right themselves. He must not only not steal nor waste, but must improve his master's goods, and promote his prosperity to his utmost. He that increased not his master's talent is accused of unfaithfulness, though he had not embezzled nor lost it.

(2) The consideration with which Titus was to enforce them: *That they may adorn the doctrine of God our Saviour in all things.* If they be careful to do their duty, it will redound to the glory of God and the credit of religion. The unbelieving masters would think the better of that despised way when they found that those of their servants who were Christians were better than their other servants. True religion is an honour to the professors of it; and they should see that they do not any dishonour to it.

Verses 11–14

The grounds upon which all the foregoing directions are urged.

I. From the nature and design of the gospel. Let all sorts do their respective duties, for this is the very aim and business of Christianity, to instruct persons, to a right frame and conduct.

1. They are put under the dispensation of *the grace of God.* Now grace is obliging and constraining to goodness. Without this effect, grace is received in vain.

2. This gospel grace *brings salvation.* Hence it is called *the word of life*; it brings to faith, and so to life.

3. *It hath appeared.* The old dispensation was comparatively dark and shadowy; this is a clear and shining light.

4. It hath appeared *to all men.* Gospel grace is open to all, and all are invited to come and partake of the benefit of it. The doctrine of grace and salvation by the gospel is for all ranks and conditions of men (slaves and servants, as well as masters).

5. This gospel revelation is to *teach.* It directs what to shun and what to follow, what to avoid and what to do. The gospel is not for speculation only or chiefly, but for practice and right ordering of life.

(1) *Denying ungodliness and worldly lusts.* "Put away ungodliness and irreligion, all unbelief of the divine Being, not loving, nor fearing, nor trusting in him, nor obeying him as we should. *And worldly lusts,* all corrupt and vicious desires and affections that prevail in worldly men." An earthly sensual conversation suits not a heavenly calling.

(2) *To live soberly, righteously, and godly,* &c. Religion is not made up of negatives only; there must be doing good as well as eschewing evil. We should live soberly with respect to ourselves, keeping the limits of moderation and temperance; and righteously towards all men, rendering to all their due, and injuring none, but rather doing good to others. Selfishness is a sort of unrighteousness; it robs others of that share in us which is their due. Live righteously therefore as well as soberly. And godly towards God. Regard to him indeed should run through all.

(3) *Looking for that blessed hope, and the glorious appearing of the great God and our Saviour Jesus Christ.* Hope is put for the thing hoped for, heaven and the felicities thereof, called emphatically *that hope,* because it is the great thing we look for; and a *blessed hope,* because, when attained, we shall be completely happy for ever. This denotes both the time of the accomplishing of our hope and the sureness and greatness of it. *The great God and our Saviour* (or *even our Saviour*) *Jesus Christ.* Christ then is the *great God,* not figuratively, but properly and absolutely, *the true God.* In his second coming he will reward his servants, and bring them to glory with him. [1] There is a common and blessed hope for all true Christians in the other world. By hope is meant the thing hoped for, Christ himself, who is called *our hope,* and blessedness in and through him, hence fitly termed here *that blessed hope.* [2] The design of the gospel is to stir up all to a good life by this blessed hope. *Denying ungodliness and worldly lusts, live soberly, righteously, and godly, in this present world, looking for the blessed hope;* not as mercenaries, but as dutiful and thankful Christians. [3] At the glorious appearing of Christ will the blessed hope of Christians be attained. The glory of the great God and our Saviour will then break out as the sun. The work and design of the gospel are to raise the heart to wait for this second appearing of Christ. Let us then look to this hope. [4] The comfort and joy of Christians are that their Saviour is the great God, and will gloriously manifest himself.

II. From the end of Christ's death, *v.* 14. To bring us to holiness and happiness was the end of Christ's death, as well as the scope of his doctrine.

1. The purchaser of salvation—Jesus Christ, *that great God and our Saviour,* who saves not simply as

JAMIESON, FAUSSET, BROWN

than beasts of burden. "Though the service be rendered to an earthly master, the honor redounds to God, as the servant's goodwill flows from the fear of God" [THEOPHYLACT]. Even slaves, low as is their status, should not think the influence of their example a matter of no consequence to religion: how much more those in a high position. His love in being "our Saviour" is the strongest ground for our adorning His doctrine by our lives. This is the force of "For" in vs. 11. **11. the grace of God**—God's *gratuitous favor* in the scheme of redemption. **hath appeared**—*Greek,* "hath been *made to appear,*" or "*shine* forth" (Isa. 9:2; Luke 1:79). "hath been *manifested*" (ch. 3:4), after having been long hidden in the loving counsels of God (Col. 1:26; II Tim. 1:9, 10). The image is illustrated in Acts 27:20. The grace of God hath now been embodied in Jesus, the *brightness* of the Father's glory," *manifested* as the "Sun of righteousness," "the Word made flesh." The Gospel dispensation is hence termed "the day" (I Thess. 5:5, 8; there is a double "appearing," that of "grace" here, that of "glory," vs. 13; cf. Rom. 13:12). Connect it not as *English Version,* but, "The grace . . . that *bringeth salvation to all men* hath appeared," or "been manifested" (I Tim. 2:4; 4:10). Hence God is called "our *Saviour*" (vs. 10). The very name *Jesus* means the same. **to all**—of whom he enumerated the different classes (vss. 2-9): even to servants; to us Gentiles, once aliens from God. Hence arises our obligation to all men (ch. 3:2). **12. Teaching**—*Greek,* "disciplining us." Grace exercises *discipline,* and is imparted in connection with disciplining chastisements (I Cor. 11:32; Heb. 12:6, 7). The education which the Christian receives from "the grace" of God is a discipline often trying to flesh and blood: just as children need disciplining. The *discipline* which it exercises *teaches* us to *deny ungodliness and worldly lusts, and to live soberly, righteously, and godly, in this present world* (*Greek,* "age," or course of things) where such self-discipline is needed, seeing that its spirit is opposed to God (ch. 1:12, 16; I Cor. 1:20; 3:18, 19): in the coming world we may gratify every desire without need of self-discipline, because all desires there will be conformable to the will of God. **that**—*Greek,* "in order that"; the end of the "disciplining" is "*in order that* . . . we may live soberly. . . ." This point is lost by the translation, "*teaching* us." **denying . . . lusts**—(Luke 9:23). The *Greek* aorist expresses "denying *once for all.*" We deny them when we withhold our consent from them, when we refuse the delight which they suggest, and the act to which they solicit us, nay, tear them up by the roots out of our soul and mind [ST. BERNARD, *Serm.* 11]. **worldly lusts**—The *Greek* article expresses, "*the* lusts of the world," "*all* worldly lusts" [ALFORD], (Gal. 5:16; Eph. 2:3; I John 2:15-17; 5:19). The *world* (*cosmos*) will not come to an end when this present *age* (*aeon*) or course of things shall end. **live soberly, righteously, and godly**—the *positive* side of the Christian character; as "denying . . . lusts" was the *negative.* "Soberly," i.e., *with self-restraint,* in relation to *one's self;* "righteously" or *justly,* in relation to our *neighbor;* "godly" or *piously,* in relation to *God* (not merely *amiably* and *justly,* but something higher, *godly,* with love and reverence toward God). These three comprise our "disciplining" in *faith* and *love,* from which he passes to *hope* (vs. 13). **13.** (Phil. 3:20, 21). **Looking for**—with constant *expectation* (so the *Greek*) and with joy (Rom. 8:19). This will prove the antidote to worldly lusts, and the stimulus to "live in this present world" conformably to this *expectation.* The *Greek* is translated, "waiting for," in Luke 2:25. **that**—*Greek,* "the." **blessed**—bringing blessedness (Rom. 4:7, 8). **hope**—i.e., object of hope (Rom. 8:24; Gal. 5:5; Col. 1:5). **the glorious appearing—the great God and our Saviour Jesus**—There is but one *Greek* article to "God" and "Saviour," which shows that both are predicated of one and the same Being. "Of Him who is at once the great God and our Saviour." Also (2) "appearing" (*epiphaneia*) is never by Paul predicated of God the Father (John 1:18; I Tim. 6:16), or even of "His glory" (as ALFORD explains it): it is *invariably* applied to CHRIST'S coming, to which (at His first advent, cf. II Tim. 1:10) the kindred verb "appeared" (*epephanee*), vs. 11, refers (I Tim. 6:14; II Tim. 4:1, 8). Also (3) in the context (vs. 14) there is no reference to the Father, but to Christ alone; and here there is no occasion for reference to *the Father* in the exigencies of the context. Also (4) the expression "great God," as applied to Christ, is in accordance with the context, which refers to *the glory of His appearing;* just as "the true God" is predicated of Christ, I John 5:20.

ADAM CLARKE

11. *The grace of God that bringeth salvation hath appeared to all men.* Literally translated, the words stand thus: "For the grace of God, that which saves, hath shone forth upon all men." Or, as it is expressed in the margin of our Authorized Version: "The grace of God, that bringeth salvation to all men, hath appeared." As God's *grace* signifies "God's favor," any benefit received from Him may be termed God's *grace.* Now it cannot be said, except in a very refined and spiritual sense, that this gospel had then *appeared to all men;* but it may be well said that "it bringeth salvation to all men"; this is its design. There is a beauty and energy in the word "hath shined out" that is rarely noted; it seems to be a metaphor taken from the sun. As by his rising in the east and "shining out" he enlightens successively the whole world, so the Lord Jesus, who is called "the Sun of righteousness," Mal. iv. 2, arises on the whole human race "with healing in his wings." And as the light and heat of the sun are denied to no nation nor individual, so the grace of the Lord Jesus also shines out upon all; and God designs that all mankind shall be as equally benefited by it in reference to their souls as they are in respect to their bodies by the sun that shines in the firmament of heaven.

12. *Teaching us that, denying.* Instructing us as children are instructed. *Denying ungodliness.* All things contrary to God. *Worldly lusts.* Such desires, affections, and appetites as men are governed by who have their portion in this life and live without God in the world. *We should live soberly.* Having every temper, appetite, and desire under the government of reason, and reason itself under the government of the Spirit of God. *Righteously.* Rendering to every man his due; injuring no person in his body, mind, reputation, or property; doing unto all as we would they should do to us. *And godly.* Just the reverse of what is implied in "ungodliness." *In this present world.* Not supposing that anything will be purified in the world to come that is not cleansed in this. The three words above evidently include our duty to God, to our neighbor, and to ourselves. (1) We are to live *soberly* in respect to ourselves, (2) *righteously* in respect to our neighbor, and (3) *godly,* or piously, in respect to our Maker.

13. *Looking for that blessed hope.* Expecting the grand object of our hope, eternal life. This is what the gospel teaches us to expect, and what the grace of God prepares the human heart for. This is called a *blessed* hope; those who have it are "happy" in the sure prospect of that glory which shall be revealed. *The glorious appearing.* This clause, literally translated, is as follows: "And the appearing of the glory of the great God, even our Saviour Jesus Christ." Some think that the *blessed hope* and *glorious appearing* mean the same thing, but I do not think so. The *blessed hope* refers simply to eternal glorification in general; *the glorious appearing,* to the resurrection of the body. For when Christ appears He will change this vile body, and make it "like unto his glorious body, according to the working whereby he is able even to subdue all things unto himself." See Phil. iii. 20-21.

MATTHEW HENRY

God, much less as man alone; but as God-man. Man, that he might obey, and suffer, and die, for man; and God, that he might support the manhood.

2. The price of our redemption: *He gave himself.* The Father gave him, but he gave himself too; and, in the freeness and voluntariness, as well as the greatness of the offering, lay the acceptableness and merit of it. The human nature was the offering, and the divine the altar, sanctifying the gift.

3. The persons for whom He died. He gave himself *for us,* not only for our good, but in our stead. *He loved us, and gave himself for us;* what can we do less than love and give up ourselves to him?

4. The ends of his giving himself for us, (1) *That he might redeem us from all iniquity.* This is fitted to the first lesson, *denying ungodliness and worldly lusts.* Christ gave himself to redeem us from these, therefore put them away. To love and live in sin is to trample under foot redeeming blood. But how could the short sufferings of Christ redeem us from all iniquity? Through the infinite dignity of his person. He who was God suffered, though not as God. *The great God and our Saviour gave himself for us;* this accounts for it. Happy end and fruit of Christ's death, redemption from all iniquity! Christ died for this: and, (2) *To purify to himself a peculiar people.* This enforces the second lesson: *To live soberly, righteously, and godly, in this present world.* Christ died to purify as well as to pardon—to heal the nature, as well as to free from guilt and condemnation. Thus does he make *to himself a peculiar people,* by purifying them. Thus are they distinguished from the world that lies in wickedness. Redemption from sin and sanctification of the nature go together, and both made a peculiar people unto God. And (3) *Zealous of good works.* This peculiar people must be seen to be so by doing good, and having a zeal therein.

Verse 15

A summary direction to Titus in which we have the matter and manner of ministers' teaching.

I. The matter of ministers' teaching: *These things,* namely, those before mentioned: the truths and duties of the gospel, of avoiding sin, and living soberly, righteously, and godly, in this present world.

II. The manner; by doctrine, and exhortation, and reproof with all authority. The great and necessary truths and duties of the gospel, especially, these *speak and exhort, press with much earnestness.* Ministers must not be cold and lifeless in delivering heavenly doctrine and precepts, as if they were indifferent things; but they must urge them with earnestness. *And rebuke;* convince and reprove such as contradict or gainsay, or neglect and do not receive the truth as they should. *Rebuke with all authority,* as coming in the name of God. Ministers are reprovers in the gate.

III. "*Let no man despise thee. Speak and exhort these things,* press them upon all, with boldness and faithfulness reprove sin, and carefully look to thyself and thy own conduct, and then none will despise thee."

JAMIESON, FAUSSET, BROWN

14. gave himself—"The forcible 'Himself, His whole self, the greatest gift ever given,' must not be overlooked." **for us**—*Greek,* "in our behalf."

redeem us—*deliver us from bondage by paying the price* of His precious *blood.* An appropriate image in addressing bond servants (vss. 9, 10). **from all iniquity**—the essence of sin, viz., "transgression of the law": in bondage to which we were till then. The aim of His redemption was to redeem us, not merely from the penalty, but from the being of all iniquity. Thus he reverts to the "teaching" in righteousness, or *disciplining* effect of the grace of God that bringeth salvation (vss. 11, 12). **peculiar**—*peculiarly His own,* as Israel was of old. **zealous**—in doing and promoting "good works."

15. with all authority—Translate, "authoritativeness" (cf. "sharply," ch. 1: 13). **Let no man despise thee**—Speak with such vigor as to command respect (I Tim. 4:12). Warn them with such authority that no one may *think himself above* (so the *Greek* lit.) the need of admonition [TITTMANN, *Synonyms of New Testament*].

ADAM CLARKE

14. *Who gave himself for us.* Who gave His own life as a "ransom price" to redeem ours. This is evidently what is meant, as the (Greek) words imply. Jesus gave His life for the world, and thus has purchased men unto himself; and having purchased the slaves from their thraldom, He is represented as stripping them of their sordid vestments, cleansing and purifying them unto himself, that they may become His own servants. Thus redeemed, they now become His willing servants and are *zealous of good works*—affectionately attached to that noble employment which is assigned to them by that Master whom it is an inexpressible honor to serve.

15. *These things speak.* That is, "teach." *And exhort.* Repeat them again and again, and urge them on their attention and consciences.

And rebuke. Demonstrate the importance, utility, and necessity of them; and show them that God requires their obedience. *With all authority.* With all that authority with which your office invests you, and which you have received from God. *Let no man despise thee.* That is, act so that no person shall have any cause to despise you, either for your work or the manner and spirit in which you perform it.

MATTHEW HENRY

CHAPTER 3

Verses 1-8

The apostle had directed Titus in reference to the particular duties of several sorts of persons; now he bids him exhort to what concerned them more in common.

I. The duties themselves. 1. *Put them in mind to be subject to principalities and powers, to obey magistrates,* that is, all civil rulers. That they be subject to them and obey them in things lawful and honest. The Christian religion was misrepresented by its adversaries as prejudicial to the rights of princes and civil powers, and tending to faction and sedition, and to rebellion against lawful authority. Christians must be reminded to show themselves examples rather of all due subjection and obedience to the government that is over them. 2. *To be ready to every good work.* The precept regards doing good of every kind and on every occasion that may offer, whether respecting God, ourselves, or our neighbour. Mere harmlessness, or good words and good meanings only, are not enough without good works. "Not only take, but seek, occasion for doing good. Put all in mind of this." And, 3. *To speak evil of no man.* If no good can be spoken, rather than speak evil unnecessarily, say nothing.4. *To be no brawlers; no fighters,* either with hand or tongue. Contention and strife arise from men's lusts, which must be curbed, not indulged; and Christian's need to be reminded of these things. 5. *But gentle, equitable and just,* not taking words or actions in the worst sense; and for peace sometimes yielding somewhat

JAMIESON, FAUSSET, BROWN

CHAPTER 3

Vss. 1-15. WHAT TITUS IS TO TEACH CONCERNING CHRISTIANS' BEHAVIOR TOWARDS THE WORLD: HOW HE IS TO TREAT HERETICS: WHEN AND WHERE HE IS TO MEET PAUL. SALUTATION. CONCLUSION. **1. Put them in mind**—as they are in danger of forgetting their duty, though knowing it. The opposition of Christianity to heathenism, and the natural disposition to rebellion of the Jews under the Roman empire (of whom many lived in Crete), might lead many to forget practically what was a recognized Christian principle in theory, submission to the powers that be. Diodorus Siculus mentions the tendency of the Cretans to riotous insubordination. **to be subject**—"willingly" (so the *Greek*). **principalities . . . powers**—*Greek,* magistracies . . . authorities.'. **to obey**—the *commands* of "magistrates"; not necessarily implying *spontaneous* obedience. *Willing* obedience is implied in "ready to every good work." Cf. Romans 13:3, as showing that obedience to the magistracy would tend to good works, since the magistrate's aim *generally* is to favor the good and punish the bad. Contrast "disobedient" (vs. 3). **2. To speak evil of no man**—especially, not of "dignities" and magistrates. **no brawlers**—"not quarrelsome," not attacking others. **gentle**—towards those who attack us. Yielding, considerate, not urging one's rights to the uttermost, but forbearing and kindly (*Note,* Phil. 4: 5). Very different from the *innate greediness* and spirit of aggression towards others which characterized the Cretans. **showing**—in acts. **all**—all pos-

ADAM CLARKE

CHAPTER 3

1. *Put them in mind to be subject to principalities.* By *principalities* we are to understand the Roman emperors, or the supreme civil powers in any place. By *powers* we are to understand the deputies of the emperors, such as proconsuls and all such as are in authority under the supreme civil powers in any place. This doctrine of obedience to the civil powers was highly necessary for the Cretans, who were reputed a people exceedingly jealous of their civil privileges, and ready to run into a state of insurrection when they suspected any attempt on the part of their rulers to infringe their liberties.

2. *To speak evil of no man.* To "blaspheme" no person, to reproach none, to speak nothing to any man's injury.

MATTHEW HENRY

of strict right. 6. *Showing all meekness to all men.* Not only have meekness in our hearts, but show it in our speech and conduct. *All meekness*—meekness in all instances and occasions, not towards friends only, but *to all men.* Meekness of spirit and demeanour renders religion amiable; it is a commanded imitation of Christ, and brings its own reward with it.

II. He adds the reasons.

1. From their own past condition. *We ourselves also were sometimes,* (1) *Foolish;* without true spiritual understanding, ignorant of heavenly things. Those should be most disposed to bear with others' follies who may remember many of their own. And, (2) *Disobedient;* heady and unpersuadable, resisting the word. Well are these set together, *foolish* and *disobedient.* For what folly like this, to disobey God and his laws, natural or revealed? (3) *Deceived,* or wandering, out of the ways of truth and holiness. Man in this his degenerate state is of straying nature. He is weak, and ready to be imposed upon by the wiles of Satan, and of men lying in wait to seduce and mislead. (4) *Serving divers lusts and pleasures.* Carnal people think they enjoy their pleasures; the word calls it servitude and vassalage. It is the misery of the servants of sin that they have many masters, one lust hurrying them one way, and another another. The lusts that tempt them promise them liberty, but in yielding they become the servants of corruption. (5) *Living in malice.* Malice desires hurt to another and rejoices in it. (6) *And envy,* which grudges and repines at another's good. Both are roots of bitterness, whence many evils spring. These were some of the sins in which we lived in our natural state. (7) *Hateful.* (8) *And hating one another.* It is the misery of sinners that they hate one another, as it is the duty and happiness of saints to love one another. The consideration of its having been thus with us should dispose us to be more meek and tenderhearted, towards those who are such.

2. From their present state. "We are delivered out of that our miserable condition by no merit nor strength of our own." The apostle again opens the causes of our salvation, *v.* 4–7.

(1) The prime author of our salvation—God the Father, therefore termed here *God our Saviour.* All things belonging to the new creation, and recovery of fallen man to life and happiness, are of God the Father. The Father begins, the Son manages, and the Holy Spirit works and perfects all.

(2) The spring and rise of it—the divine *philanthropy,* or *kindness and love of God to man.* By grace we are saved from first to last. This is the ground and motive. The occasion is in man, his misery and wretchedness. Sin bringing that misery, wrath might have issued out rather than compassion; but God would pity and save rather than destroy. He delights in mercy.

(3) Here is the means—the shining out of this love and grace of God in the gospel, *after it appeared.* The appearing of love and grace has, through the Spirit, great virtue to change and turn to God.

(4) False grounds are here removed: *Not by works of righteousness which we have done, but according to his mercy, he saved us.* Works must be in the saved but not among the causes of his salvation; they are the way to the kingdom, not the meriting price of it. Faith and all saving graces are God's free gift and his work; the beginning, increase, and perfection of them in glory, all are from him.

(5) The formal cause of salvation, regeneration or spiritual renewing, as it is here called. A new prevailing principle of grace and holiness is wrought, which makes the man a new man, having new thoughts, desires, and affections. *He saved us.* What is so begun, as sure to be perfected in time, is expressed as if it already were so. We must be initially saved now, by regeneration, if on good ground we would expect complete salvation in heaven. The change then will be but in degree, not in kind. Grace is glory begun, as glory is but grace in its perfection.

(6) The outward sign and seal thereof in baptism, called therefore *the washing of regeneration.* The work itself is inward and spiritual; but it is outwardly signified and sealed in this ordinance. Baptism saves figuratively and sacramentally, where it is rightly used. Slight not this outward sign and seal, yet rest not in the outward washing. The covenant sealed in baptism binds to duties, as well as conveys benefits and privileges; if the former be not minded, in vain are the latter expected.

(7) The principal efficient, the *renewing of the Holy Ghost.* In the economy of our salvation, the applying and effecting part is especially attributed to the Holy Spirit. We are said to be born of the Spirit, to be quickened and sanctified by the Spirit, to be led and guided, strengthened and helped, by the Spirit. Earn-

JAMIESON, FAUSSET, BROWN

sible. **meekness**—(*Note,* II Cor. 10:1)—the opposite of passionate severity. **unto all men**—The duty of Christian conduct towards *all men* is the proper consequence of the universality of God's grace to all men, so often set forth in the pastoral Epistles.

3.
For—Our own past sins should lead us to be lenient towards those of others. "Despise none, for such wast thou also." As the penitent thief said to his fellow thief, "Dost thou not fear God . . . seeing that thou art in the same condemnation." **we**—Christians. **were**—Contrast vs. 4, "But when," i.e., *now:* a favorite contrast in Paul's writing, that between our *past* state by nature, and our *present* state of deliverance from it by grace. As God treated us, we ought to treat our neighbor. **sometimes**—once. **foolish**—wanting right reason in our course of living. Irrational. The exact picture of human life without grace. Grace is the sole remedy for foolishness. **disobedient**—to God. **deceived**—led astray. The same *Greek,* "out of the way" (Heb. 5:2). **serving**—*Greek,* "in *bondage to,*" serving as *slaves.*" **divers**—The cloyed appetite craves constant variety. **pleasures**—of the flesh. **malice**—malignity. **hateful . . . hating**—correlatives. Provoking the hatred of others by their detestable character and conduct, and in turn hating them. **4.** To show how little reason the Cretan Christians had to be proud of themselves, and despise others not Christians (*Notes,* vss. 2, 3). It is to the "kindness and love of God," not to their own merits, that they owe salvation. **kindness**—*Greek,* "goodness," "benignity," which manifests His *grace.* **love . . . toward man**—teaching us to have such "love (benevolence) toward *man*" (*Greek,* "philanthropy"), "showing all meekness unto all *men*" (vs. 2), even as God had "*toward man*" (ch. 2:11); opposed to the "hateful and hating" characteristics of unrenewed men, whose wretchedness moved God's *benevolent kindness.* **of God our Saviour**—*Greek,* "of our Saviour God," viz., the Father (ch. 1:3), who "saved us" (vs. 5) "through Jesus Christ our Saviour" (vs. 6). **appeared**—*Greek,* "was made to appear"; was manifested. **5. Not by**—*Greek,* "Out of"; "not as a result springing *from* works. . . ." **of righteousness**—*Greek,* "*in* righteousness," i.e., wrought *in a state of righteousness;* as "deeds . . . wrought *in* God." There was an utter absence in us of the element ("righteousness") in which alone righteous works could be done, and so necessarily an absence of the works. "We neither did works of righteousness, nor were saved in consequence of them; but His goodness did the whole" [THEOPHYLACT]. **we**—emphatically opposed to "His." **mercy**—the prompting cause of our salvation individually: "*In pursuance of* His mercy." His *kindness* and *love to man* were manifested in redemption once for all wrought by Him for mankind *generally;* His *mercy* is the prompting cause for our *individual* realization of it. *Faith* is presupposed as the instrument of our being "saved"; our being so, then, is spoken of as an *accomplished fact. Faith* is not mentioned, but only *God*'s part. as Paul's object here is not to describe man's new state, but the saving agency of *God* in bringing about that state, *independent of all merit on the man's part* (*Note,* vs. 4). **by**—*Greek,* "through"; by means of. **the washing**—rather, "the laver," i.e., the baptismal font. **or regeneration**—*designed* to be the visible instrument of regeneration.

Adult candidates for baptism are presupposed to have had repentance and faith (for Paul often assumes in faith and charity that those addressed are what they profess to be, though in fact some of them were not so, I Cor. 6:11), in which case baptism would be the visible "laver or regeneration" to them, "faith being thereby *confirmed,* and grace *increased,* by virtue of prayer to God" (Church of England, Article 27). "Regeneration" occurs only once more in New Testament, Matthew 19:28, i.e., *the new brith of the heaven and earth* at Christ's second coming to renew all material things, the human body included, when the creature, now travailing in labor-throes to the birth, shall be delivered from the bondage of corruption into the glorious liberty of the children of God. Regeneration, which now begins in the believer's soul, shall then be extended to his body, and thence to all creation. **and renewing**—not "*the laver* ('washing') of renewing," but "and BY the renewing . . ." following "saved us." To make "renewing of the Holy Ghost" follow "the laver" would destroy the balance of the clauses of the sentence, and would make baptism the seal, not only of *regeneration,* but also of the

ADAM CLARKE

3. *For we ourselves.* All of us, whether Jews or Gentiles, were before our conversion to Christ foolish, disobedient, and deceived. There is no doubt that the apostle felt he could include himself in the above list previously to his conversion. The manner in which he persecuted the Christians, to whose charge he could not lay one moral evil, is sufficient proof that, though he walked according to the letter of the law, as to its ordinances and ceremonies, blameless, yet his heart was in a state of great estrangement from God, from justice, holiness, mercy, and compassion. *Foolish.* "Without understanding" —ignorant of God, His nature, His providence, and His grace. *Disobedient.* "Unpersuaded, unbelieving, obstinate, and disobedient." *Deceived.* "Erring"—wandering from the right way in consequence of our ignorance, not knowing the right way; and in consequence of our unbelief and obstinacy, not choosing to know it. It is a true saying, "There are none so blind as those who will not see." Such persons are proof against conviction; they will not be convinced by either God or man. *Serving divers lusts and pleasures.* Not served or gratified by our lusts and pleasures, but living, as their "slaves"; a life of misery and wretchedness. *Divers lusts.* Strong and irregular appetites of every kind. *Pleasures*—"Sensual pleasures." Persons intent only on the gratification of sense, living like the brutes, having no rational or spiritual object worthy the pursuit of an immortal being. *Living in malice and envy.* "Spending our lives in wickedness and envy"—not bearing to see the prosperity of others because we feel ourselves continually wretched. *Hateful.* "Abominable"; "hateful as hell." The word comes from Styx, the infernal river by which the gods were wont to swear; and he who (according to the mythology of the heathens) violated this oath was expelled from the assembly of the gods and was deprived of his nectar and ambrosia for a year; hence the river was hateful to them beyond all things.

4. *But after that the kindness.* The "essential goodness" of the divine nature; that which is the spring whence all kindness, mercy, and beneficence proceed. *Love . . . toward man*—"Philanthropy." Philanthropy is a character which God gives here to himself; while human nature exists, this must be a character of the divine nature. Where love is it will be active and will show itself. So the philanthropy of God *appeared;* it "shone out" in the incarnation of Jesus Christ and in His giving His life for the life of the world.

5. *Not by works of righteousness.* Those who were foolish, disobedient, and deceived, serving divers lusts and pleasures, could not possibly have *works of righteousness* to plead; therefore, if saved at all, they must be saved by *mercy.*

By the washing of regeneration. Undoubtedly the apostle here means baptism, the rite by which persons were admitted into the Church, and the visible sign of the cleansing, purifying influences of the Holy Spirit, which the apostle immediately subjoins. Baptism is only a sign, and therefore should never be separated from the thing signified; but it is a rite commanded by God himself, and therefore the thing signified should never be expected without it.

By the *renewing of the Holy Ghost* we are to understand, not only the profession of being bound to live a new life, but the grace that renews the heart and enables us thus to live; so the renewing influences are here intended. Baptism changes nothing; the grace signified by it cleanses and purifies.

MATTHEW HENRY

estly therefore is he to be sought, and greatly to be heeded by us, that we quench not his holy motions. As we act towards him, so may we expect he will to us; if we slight, and resist, and oppose his workings, he will slacken them; if we continue to vex him, he will retire.

(8) The manner of God's communicating this Spirit in the gifts and graces of it; not with a scanty and niggardly hand, but most freely and plentifully: *Which he shed on us abundantly*. More of the Spirit in its gifts and graces is poured out under the gospel than was under the law. A measure of the Spirit the church has had in all ages, but more since the coming of Christ, than before. There was then great abundance of common gifts of illumination, outward calling and profession, and general faith, and of more special gifts of sanctification too, such as faith, and hope, and love.

(9) The procuring cause of all, namely, Christ: *Through Jesus Christ our Saviour*. All come through him, and through him as a Saviour. Let us praise God for him above all; let us go to the Father by him. Have we grace? Let us thank him with the Father and Spirit for it, and grow and increase therein more and more.

(10) The ends why we are brought into this new spiritual condition, justification, and heirship, and hope of eternal life: *That being justified by his grace, we should be made heirs according to the hope of eternal life*. Justification is the free remission of a sinner, and accepting him as righteous through the righteousness of Christ received by faith. This God does freely as to us, yet through the intervention of Christ's sacrifice and righteousness, laid hold on by faith. It is by grace, as the spring and rise, though *through the redemption that is in Christ*, and by faith applying that redemption. Inherent righteousness we must have, and the fruits of it in works of obedience; as fruits of our justification, and evidences of our interest in Christ and qualification for life and happiness, and the very beginning and part of it; but the procuring of all this is by Christ, that, *being justified by his grace, we should be made heirs*. Our justification is *by the grace of God*, and our justification by that grace is necessary in order to our being made *heirs of eternal life*. Eternal life is set before us in the promise.

III. When he has opened the grace of God towards us, he immediately presses the necessity of good works; for we must not expect the benefit of God's mercy: unless we make conscience of our duty (*v.* 8). It must be an operative working faith. They must make it their care *to maintain good works*, not to do them occasionally only. *These things are good and profitable unto men;* these *good works*, say some, or *the teaching of these things*, rather than idle questions, as follows.

Verses 9–15

What Titus should avoid in teaching; how he should deal with a heretic; with some other directions.

I. He tells Titus what, in teaching, he should shun, *v.* 9. Idle and foolish enquiries must be shunned.—*And genealogies.* Some lawful and useful enquiries might be made into these things, to see the fulfilling of the scriptures in some cases, and especially in the descent of Christ the Messiah; but all that served to pomp only, and to feed vanity, in boasting of a long pedigree, these Titus must withstand as foolish and vain.—*And contentions, and strivings about the law.* There were those who were for the Mosaic rites and ceremonies, and would have them continued in the church. Titus must give no countenance to these, but avoid and oppose them; *for they are unprofitable and vain:* this is to be referred to all those *foolish questions and genealogies*, as well as those *strivings about the law.* They are so far from instructing and building up in godliness, that they are hindrances of it rather. Ministers must not only teach things good and useful, but shun and oppose the contrary; nor should people have itching ears, but love and embrace sound doctrine.

II. But because there will be *heresies* and *heretics* in the church, the apostle next directs Titus how to deal with such, *v.* 10. "Admonish him once and again, that, if possible he may be brought back, and thou mayest gain thy brother; but, if this will not reduce him, cast him out of the communion. Those who will not be reclaimed by admonitions, but are obstinate in their sins and errors, *are subverted and self-condemned.* How great an evil real heresy is. Such a one is *subverted* or perverted—a metaphor from a building so ruined as to render it difficult if not impossible to repair and raise it up again. Real heretics have seldom been recovered to the true faith: not so much defect of judgment, as perverseness of the will, being in the case. Pains and patience must

JAMIESON, FAUSSET, BROWN

subsequent process of *progressive* sanctification ("renewing of the Holy Ghost"). *Regeneration* is a thing once for all done; *renewing* is a process daily proceeding. As "the washing," or "laver," is connected with *"regeneration,"* so the "renewing of the Holy Ghost" is connected with "shed on us abundantly" (vs. 6). **6. Which**—the Holy Ghost. **he shed**—*Greek,* "poured out"; not only on the Church in general at Pentecost, but also "on us" individually. This *pouring out* of the Spirit comprehends the grace received before, in, and subsequently to, baptism. **abundantly**—*Greek,* "richly" (Col. 3:16).

through Jesus Christ—the channel and Mediator of the gift of the Holy Ghost. **our Saviour**—immediately; as the Father is mediately "our Saviour." The Father is the author of our salvation and saves us by Jesus Christ.

7. That . . .—the purpose which He aimed at in having "saved us" (vs. 5), viz., "That being (having been) justified (*accounted righteous* through faith at our 'regeneration,' and *made righteous* by the daily 'renewing of the Holy Ghost') by His grace (as opposed to *works,* vs. 5) we should be made heirs." **his grace**—*Greek,* "the grace of *the former,"* i.e., *God* (vs. 4; Rom. 5:15). **heirs**—(Gal. 3:29). **according to the hope of eternal life**—Ch. 1:2, and also the position of the *Greek* words, confirm *English Version,* i.e., *agreeably to* the hope of eternal life; the eternal inheritance fully satisfying the hope. BENGEL and ELLICOTT explain it, "*heirs of eternal life,* in the way of hope," i.e., not yet in actual possession. Such a *blessed hope,* which once was not possessed, will lead a Christian to practice holiness and meekness toward others, the lesson especially needed by the Cretans. **8.** *Greek,* "faithful is the saying." A formula peculiar to the Pastoral Epistles. Here "the saying" is the statement (vss. 4-7) as to the gratuitousness of God's gift of salvation. Answering to the "Amen." **these things . . .**—*Greek* "*concerning* these things (the truths dwelt on, vss. 4-7; not as *English Version,* what follow), I will that thou affirm (*insist*) *strongly* and *persistently, in order that* they who have *believed God* (the *Greek* for 'believed *in* God' is different, John 14:1. 'They who have learnt to credit God' in what He saith) may be careful ('solicitously sedulous'; *diligence is necessary*) *to* maintain (lit., 'to set before themselves so as to sustain') good works." No longer applying their *care* to "unprofitable" and unpractical speculations (vs. 9). **these things**—These results of doctrine ("good works" are "good and profitable unto men," whereas no such practical results flow from "foolish questions." So GROTIUS and WIESINGER. But ALFORD, to avoid the tautology, "these (good works) are good unto men," explains, "these *truths*" (vss. 4-7). **9. avoid**—stand aloof from. Same *Greek,* as in *Note,* II Timothy 2:16. **foolish**—*Greek,* "insipid"; producing no moral fruit. "Vain talkers." **genealogies**—akin to the "fables" (see *Note,* I Tim. 1:4). Not so much direct heresy as yet is here referred to, as profitless discussions about genealogies of aeons, etc., which ultimately led to Gnosticism. Synagogue discourses were termed *daraschoth,* i.e., discussions. Cf. "*disputer* of this world (*Greek,* 'dispensation')." **strivings about the law**—about the authority of the "commandments of men," which they sought to confirm by the law (ch. 1:14; *Note,* I Tim. 1:7), and about the mystical meaning of the various parts of the law in connection with the "genealogies." **10. heretic**—*Greek* "heresy," originally meant a *division* resulting from individual self-will; the individual doing and teaching what he *chose,* independent of the teaching and practice of the Church. In course of time it came to mean definitely "heresy" in the modern sense; and in the later Epistles it has almost assumed this meaning. The heretics of Crete, when Titus was there, were in doctrine followers of their own self-willed "questions" reprobated in vs. 9, and immoral in practice. **reject**—decline, avoid; not formal excommunication, but, "have nothing more to do with him," either in admonition or intercourse. **11. is . . . subverted**—"is become perverse." **condemned of himself**—He cannot say, no one told him better; continuing the same after frequent admonition, he is self-condemned. "He sinneth" wilfully against knowledge.

ADAM CLARKE

6. *Which he shed on us abundantly.* "Which He poured out on us," as the water was poured out on them in baptism, to which there is here a manifest allusion. But as this was sometimes only sprinkled on the person, the heavenly gift was "poured out," not in drops, but "richly," in "great abundance."

Through Jesus Christ. Baptism is nothing in itself, and there had been no outpouring of the Holy Spirit had there been no saving and atoning Christ. Through Him alone all good comes to the souls of men.

7. *That being justified by his grace.* Being freed from sin; for the term "justification" is to be taken here as implying the whole work of the grace of Christ on the heart in order to its preparation for eternal glory. *Should be made heirs.* The gospel not only gave them the hope of an endless state of glory for their souls, but also of the resurrection and final glorification of their bodies, and they who were children of God were to be made *heirs* of His glory.

8. *This is a faithful saying.* "This is the true doctrine," the doctrine that cannot fail. *And these things I will.* "And I will, or desire, you to maintain earnestly what concerns these points." The things to which the apostle refers are those of which he had just been writing. *These things are good and profitable.* They are good in themselves, and calculated to promote the well-being of men.

9. *Avoid foolish questions, and geneaologies.* In these the Jews particularly delighted; they abounded in the most frivolous questions; and, as they had little piety themselves, they were solicitous to show that they had descended from godly ancestors. *Contentions, and strivings about the law.* Of legal contentions and different and conflicting decisions about the meaning of particular rites and ceremonies, the Talmud is full.

10. *A man that is an heretick.* Generally defined, one that is obstinately attached to an opinion contrary to the peace and comfort of society, and will submit to neither Scripture nor reason. Here it means a person who maintains Judaism in opposition to Christianity, or who insists on the necessity of circumcision in order to be saved. This is obviously the meaning of the word *heretick* in the only place in which it occurs in the sacred writings. *After the first and second admonition reject.* Labor to convince him of his error; but if he will not receive instruction, if he have shut his heart against conviction, then—"shun him."

11. *Is subverted.* "Is turned out of the way" in which he may be saved, and consequently *sinneth*—enters into that way that leads to destruction. *Being condemned of himself.* This refers to the Judaizing teacher who maintained his party and opinions for filthy lucre's sake. He was conscious of his own insincerity; and that he proclaimed not his system from a conscientious love of truth, but from a desire to get his livelihood.

MATTHEW HENRY

be used about those that err most grievously. They must be admonished, instructed, and warned. Upon continued obstinacy the church is obliged, to preserve its own purity, by severing such a corrupt member; which discipline may by God's blessing become effectual to reform the offender.

III. The apostle subjoins some further directions, *v.* 12, 13.

1. Titus should hold himself ready to come to Paul at *Nicopolis*, as soon as *Artemas* or *Tychicus* should be sent to Crete, to supply his place. Of Artemas we read little, but Tychicus is mentioned on many occasions with respect. Paul calls him *a beloved brother, and faithful minister, and fellow-servant in the Lord*: one fit therefore for the service intimated.

2. The other personal charge to Titus is that he would bring two of his friends on their journey diligently, and see them furnished, so that nothing should be wanting to them. *Zenas* is styled *the lawyer*. *Apollos* was an eminent and faithful minister. Accompanying such persons part of their way, and accommodating them for their work and journeys, was a pious and needful service.

Let Christians learn to *maintain good works, that they be not unfruitful*. Christianity is not a fruitless profession. It is not enough that they be harmless, but they must be profitable, doing good, as well as eschewing evil.—"*Let ours* set up and maintain some honest labour and employment, to provide for themselves and their families, that they be not unprofitable burdens on the earth"; so some understand it. Let them not think that Christianity gives them a writ of ease. *To maintain good works for necessary uses;* not living like drones on the labours of others, but themselves fruitful to the common benefit.

IV. The apostle concludes with salutations and benedictions, *v.* 15. Great comfort and encouragement it is to have the heart and prayers of other Christians with and for us. *Grace be with you all. Amen.* This is the apostle's wish and prayer. Grace is the chief thing to be wished and begged for, with respect to ourselves or others; it is, summarily, all good. *Amen* shuts up the prayer, expressing desire and hope, that so it may, and so it shall be.

JAMIESON, FAUSSET, BROWN

12. When I shall send—have sent—**Artemas or Tychicus**—to supply thy place in Crete. Artemas is said to have been subsequently bishop of Lystra. Tychicus was sent twice by Paul from Rome to Lesser Asia in his first imprisonment (which shows how well qualified he was to become Titus' successor in Crete); Ephesians 6:21; and in his second, II Timothy 4:12. Tradition makes him subsequently bishop of Chalcedon, in Bithynia. **Nicopolis**—"the city of victory," called so from the battle of Actium, in Epirus. This Epistle was probably written from Corinth in the autumn. Paul purposed a journey through Œtolia and Acarnania, into Epirus, and there "to winter."

13. Bring . . . on their journey—Enable them to proceed forward by supplying necessaries for their journey. **Zenas**—the contracted form of Zenodorus. **lawyer**—a Jewish "scribe," who, when converted, still retained the title from his former occupation. A *civil* lawyer. **Apollos**—with Zenas, probably the bearers of this Epistle. In I Cor. 16:12, Apollos is mentioned as purposing to visit Corinth; his now being at Corinth (on the theory of Paul being at Corinth when he wrote) accords with this purpose. Crete would be on his way either to Palestine or his native place, Alexandria. Paul and Apollos thus appear in beautiful harmony in that very city where their names had been formerly the watchword of unchristian party work. It was to avoid this party rivalry that Apollos formerly was unwilling to visit Corinth though Paul desired him. HIPPOLYTUS mentions Zenas as one of the Seventy, and afterwards bishop of Diospolis. **14. And . . . also**—*Greek,* "But . . . also." Not only *thou,* but let others also of "our" fellow believers (or "whom we have gained over at Crete") with thee. **for necessary uses**—*to supply the necessary wants* of Christian missionaries and brethren, according as they stand in need in their journeys for the Lord's cause. Cf. ch. 1:8, "a lover of hospitality." **15. Greet**—"*Salute* them that love us in the faith." All at Crete had not this *love* rooted in *faith,* the true bond of fellowship. A salutation peculiar to this Epistle, such as no forger would have used. **Grace**—*Greek,* "*The* grace," viz., *of God.* **with you all**—not that the Epistle is addressed to *all* the Cretan Christians, but Titus would naturally impart it to his flock.

ADAM CLARKE

12. *When I shall send Artemas unto thee, or Tychicus.* These were either deacons or presbyters which the apostle intended to send to Crete to supply the place of Titus. Who Artemas was we know not; he is not mentioned in any other place in the New Testament. Tychicus was a native of Asia, as we learn from Acts xx. 4. *For I have determined there to winter.* Hence the apostle was at liberty, seeing his spending the winter at this or at any other practicable place depended on his own determination. It was probably now pretty late in the autumn, and the apostle was now drawing near to Nicopolis; for he certainly was not yet arrived, else he would not have said, *I have determined there to winter.*

13. *Bring Zenas the lawyer.* This person is mentioned only in this place; whether he was a Jewish, Roman, or Greek lawyer we cannot tell. *And Apollos.* Of this person we have some valuable particulars in Acts xviii. 24; 1 Cor. i. 12; iii. 5-6; and iv. 6. Either Paul had left these at Crete when he visited that island or he had heard that in their evangelical itinerancy they were about to pass through it. *On their journey diligently.* Afford them the means to defray their expenses. The churches through which these evangelists passed bore their expenses from one to the other. See 3 John, v. 6.

14. *And let ours also learn to maintain good works.* There is something very remarkable in this expression. The words which we translate *to maintain good works* occur also in v. 8: and some think they mean "to provide for our own, and the necessities of others, by working at some honest occupation"; and that this was necessary to be taught to the Cretans, *let ours also learn,* who were naturally and practically "idle gluttons." *For necessary uses.* That they may be able at all times to help the Church of God, and those that are in want. *That they be not unfruitful.* As they must be if they indulge themselves in their idle, slothful disposition.

15. *All that are with me.* He means his companions in the ministry. *Salute thee.* Wish thee well, and desire to be affectionately remembered to thee. *Greet them that love us in the faith.* All that love us for Christ's sake, and all that are genuine Christians.

THE EPISTLE TO PHILEMON

I. Introduction (1-3)
- *A. To Philemon (1)*
- *B. Also the Church (2, 3)*

II. The approach (4-7)
- *A. Thanksgiving for Philemon's love (4, 5)*
- *B. Thanksgiving for Philemon's faith (6, 7)*

III. The argument (8-16)
- *A. Paul introduces his subject by introducing himself (8, 9)*
- *B. Paul strengthens his argument by reference to Onesimus (10-16)*

IV. The appeal (17-21)
- *A. Direct—"receive him as myself" (17)*
- *B. I owe you (18, 19a)*
- *C. You owe me (19b)*
- *D. Confidence (20, 21)*

V. Conclusion (22-25)
- *A. "Prepare me a lodging" (22)*
- *B. Salutation (23, 24)*
- *C. Benediction (25)*

Philemon, one of note and probably a minister in the church of Colosse, a city of Phrygia, had a servant named Onesimus, who, having stolen his goods, ran away from him, and came to Rome, where Paul was then a prisoner for the gospel, and was, by the blessing of God, converted by him, after which he ministered awhile to the apostle in bonds. Understanding him to be another man's servant, Paul would not, without his consent, detain him, but sends him back with this letter-commendatory, wherein he earnestly sues for his pardon and kind reception. There is no reason to doubt but Paul prevailed with Philemon to forgive and receive Onesimus.

MATTHEW HENRY

CHAPTER 1

Verses 1–7

I. In the first two verses of the preface we have the persons from and to whom it is written,

1. The persons writing: Paul, the principal, who calls himself *a prisoner of Jesus Christ.* This was proper to move Philemon upon the request made to him by such a one, especially when strengthened too with the concurrence of Timothy. What could be denied to two such petitioners?

2. The persons written to are *Philemon and Apphia,* and with them Archippus, and the church in Philemon's house. Philemon, the master of Onesimus, was the principal; a good man he was, and probably a minister, and on both accounts dearly beloved by Paul. With Philemon Apphia is joined, probably his yoke-fellow. She was a party offended and injured by Onesimus, and therefore proper to be taken notice of in a letter for reconciliation and forgiveness. These are the principal parties written to. The less principal are, *Archippus, and the church in Philemon's house.* Archippus was a minister in the church of Colosse, Philemon's friend. Paul might think him one whom Philemon would advise with, and who might be capable of furthering the good work of peace-making and forgiveness. *And to the church in thy house,* his whole family, in which the worship of God was kept up. Families which generally may be most pious and orderly may yet have one or other in them impious and wicked. This was the aggravation of Onesimus's sin, that it was where he might have learned better.

II. The apostle's salutation of those named by him (*v.* 3). He wishes for them the best things; not gold, nor silver, nor any earthly good, but *grace and peace from God in Christ. Grace,* the spring and fountain of all blessings; *and peace,* all good, as the fruit and effect of that grace. *From God our Father and the Lord Jesus Christ.* From the Father, who is our Father in Christ; and from Christ, his favour and goodwill as God, and the fruits of it through him as Mediator. The favour of God and peace with him, as in itself it is the best and most desirable good, so is it the cause of all other, and what puts sweetness into every mercy and can make happy even in the want of all earthly things.

III. He expresses the singular affection he had for him, by thanksgiving and prayer to God in his behalf, and the great joy for the many good things he knew and heard to be in him, *v.* 4–7.

1. The object of Paul's praises and prayers for Philemon, *v.* 4. It is the privilege of good men that in their praises and prayers they come to God as their God: *I thank my God,* said Paul. Our prayers and praises should be offered up to God, not for ourselves only, but for others also. In this lies no little part of the communion of saints. Paul, in his private thanksgivings and prayers, was often particular in remembering his friends. This is a means of exercising love, and obtaining good for others.

2. The circumstance: *Always making mention of thee.* So must we remember Christian friends much and often, as their case may need.

JAMIESON, FAUSSET, BROWN

CHAPTER 1

Vs. 1-25. ADDRESS. THANKSGIVING FOR PHILEMON'S LOVE AND FAITH. INTERCESSION FOR ONESIMUS. CONCLUDING REQUEST AND SALUTATIONS. This Epistle affords a specimen of the highest wisdom as to the manner in which Christians ought to manage social affairs on more exalted principles. **1. prisoner of Jesus Christ**—one whom Christ's cause has made a prisoner (cf. "in the bonds of the Gospel," (vs. 13). He does not call himself, as in other Epistles, "Paul an apostle," as he is writing familiarly, not authoritatively. **our . . . fellow labourer**—in building up the Church at Colosse, while we were at Ephesus. See my *Introduction* to Colossians. **2. Apphia**—the Latin "Appia"; either the wife or some close relative of Philemon. She and Archippus, if they had not belonged to his family, would not have been included with Philemon in the address of a letter on a domestic matter. **Archippus**—a minister of the Colossian Church (Col. 4: 17). **fellow soldier**—(II Tim. 2:3).

church in thy house—In the absence of a regular church building, the houses of particular saints were used for that purpose. Observe Paul's tact in associating with Philemon those associated by kindred or Christian brotherhood with his *house,* and not going beyond it.

4. always—joined by ALFORD with, "I thank my God."

ADAM CLARKE

CHAPTER 1

1. *Paul, a prisoner of Jesus Christ.* It has already been noted, in the preface, that Paul was a prisoner at Rome when he wrote this Epistle and those to the Colossians and Philippians. But some think that the term *prisoner* does not sufficiently point out the apostle's state, and that the original word should be translated "bound with a chain." This is certainly its meaning; and it shows us in some measure his circumstances—one arm was bound with a chain to the arm of the soldier to whose custody he had been delivered. *Unto Philemon our dearly beloved.* There is a peculiarity in the use of proper names in this Epistle which is not found in any other part of Paul's writings. The names to which we refer are Philemon, Apphia, Archippus, and Onesimus. "Affectionate" or "beloved"; this led the apostle to say: *Unto Philemon our dearly beloved.*

2. *Apphia.* Appha is the affectionate address of a brother or sister; or the diminutive of a brother and sister, used to express kindness and affection. *Archippus.* The "ruler" or "master of the horse." Heroes of old were, among both the Greeks and the Trojans, celebrated for their skill in managing and taming the horse and employing him in war; this frequently occurs in Homer. The import of the name of Archippus might suggest this idea to the apostle's mind, and lead him to say: *Archippus our fellowsoldier. Onesimus.* "Useful" or "profitable." The import of this name led the apostle to play upon the word thus: "I beseech thee for my son Onesimus . . . which in time past was to thee unprofitable, but now profitable to thee and to me." *To the church in thy house.* The congregation of Christians frequently assembling in Philemon's house; for at this time the Christians had neither temples, churches, nor chapels. It is very probable that Apphia was the wife of Philemon; and Archippus, their son, the pastor of the church at Philemon's house.

4. *I thank my God.* For all the good He has bestowed upon you, *making mention of thee always in my prayers,* that you may hold fast all that you have, and get all that you need further.

MATTHEW HENRY

3. The matter both of his praises and prayers, in reference to Philemon.

(1) Of his praises. He thanks God for the love which he heard Philemon had towards the Lord Jesus. For his faith in Christ also. Love to Christ, and faith in him, are prime Christian graces, for which there is great ground of praise to God. He praises God likewise for Philemon's love to all the saints. These two must go together. Different sentiments and ways in what is not essential will not make a difference of affection as to the truth. Mere external differences are nothing here. Paul calls a poor converted slave *his bowels*. We must love, as God does, all saints. *Hearing of thy love and faith, which thou hast towards the Lord Jesus, and towards all saints.* Love to saints, if it be sincere, will be catholic and universal love towards all saints; faith and love, though in the heart they are hidden things, are known by the effects of them.

(2) The apostle joins prayer with his praises, that the fruits of Philemon's faith and love might be more and more conspicuous, that the communication of them might constrain others to the acknowledgment of all the good things that were in him and in his house towards Christ Jesus.

4. He adds a reason, both of his prayer and his praises (*v.* 7). The good thou hast done and still doest is abundant matter of joy and comfort to me and others, who therefore desire you may continue and abound in such good fruits more and more.

Verses 8–25

I. The main business of the epistle, which was to plead with Philemon on behalf of Onesimus. Many arguments Paul urges for this purpose, *v.* 8–21. The

1st Argument is taken from what was before noted: "Seeing so much good is reported of thee and found in thee, especially thy love to all saints, now let me see it on a fresh and further occasion." A disposition to do good, together with past instances and expressions of it, is a good handle to take hold of for pressing to more.

2nd Argument is from the authority of him that was now making this request to him, *v.* 8. This was a matter within the compass of the apostle's power to require, though he would not in this instance act up to it.

3rd Argument. He chooses to entreat it of him (*v.* 9). He argues from love rather than authority, which doubtless must carry engaging influence with it.

4th Argument. Being such a one as Paul the aged, and now also a prisoner of Jesus Christ. Years bespeak respect. The request of an aged apostle, and now suffering for Christ and his gospel, should be tenderly considered.

5th Argument. From the spiritual relation now between Onesimus and himself, *v.* 10. *My son, whom I have begotten in my bonds;* he was dear to him, and he hoped would be so to Philemon, under this consideration. Prison mercies are sweet.

JAMIESON, FAUSSET, BROWN

5. **Hearing**—the ground of his thanksgiving. It is a delicate mark of authenticity, that he says "hearing" as to churches and persons whom he had not seen or *then* visited. Now Colosse, Philemon's place of residence, he had never yet seen. Yet vs. 19 here implies that Philemon was his convert. Philemon, doubtless, was converted at Ephesus, or in some other place where he met Paul. **love and faith**—The theological order is first *faith* then *love,* the fruit of faith. But he purposely puts Philemon's *love* in the first place, as it is to an act of love that he is exhorting him. **toward . . . toward**—different *Greek,* words: "towards" . . . "unto." *Towards* implies simply direction; *unto,* to the advantage of. **6. That . . .**—The aim of my thanksgiving and prayers for thee is, *in order that the. . . .* **the communication of thy faith** —*the imparting of it and its fruits* (viz., acts of love and beneficence: as Heb. 13:16, "to communicate," i.e., to impart a share) *to others;* or, *the liberality to others flowing from thy faith* (so the *Greek* is translated, "liberal distribution," II Cor. 9:13). **effectual by**—*Greek,* "in"; the element *in* which his liberality had place, i.e., may be *proved by acts in. . . .* **acknowledging**—*Greek,* "the thorough knowledge," i.e., the experimental or practical *recognition.* **of every good thing which is in you**—The oldest MSS. read, "which is in US," i.e., the practical recognition of every grace which is in us *Christians,* in so far as we realize the Christian character. In short, that thy faith may by acts be proved to be "a faith which worketh by love." **in Christ Jesus**—rather as *Greek, "unto* Christ Jesus," i.e., to the glory of Christ Jesus. Two of the oldest MSS. omit "Jesus." This verse answers to vs. 5, "thy love and faith toward all saints"; Paul never ceases to mention him in his prayers, *in order that* his faith may still further show its power in his relation to others, by exhibiting every grace which is in Christians to the glory of Christ. Thus he paves the way for the request in behalf of Onesimus. **7. For**—a reason for the prayer, vss. 4-6. **we have**—*Greek,* "we had." **joy and consolation**—joined in II Corinthians 7:4. **saints are refreshed by thee**—His house was open to them. **brother**—put last, to conciliate his favorable attention to the request which follows. **8. Wherefore**—Because of my love to thee, I prefer to *"beseech,"* rather than "enjoin," or *authoritatively command.* **I might . . . enjoin**—in virtue of the obligation to *obedience* which Philemon lay under to Paul, as having been converted through his instrumentality. **in Christ**—the element in which his boldness has place.

9. for love's sake—mine to thee, and [what ought to be] thine to Onesimus. Or, that Christian love of which thou showest so bright an example (vs. 7). **being such an one**—Explain, *Being such a one* as thou knowest me to be, viz., *Paul* (the founder of so many churches, and an apostle of Christ, and thy father in the faith)*the aged* (a circumstance calculated to secure thy respect for anything I request), *and now also a prisoner of Jesus Christ* (the strongest claim I have on thy regard: if for no other reason, at least in consideration of this, through commiseration gratify me).

10. I beseech thee—emphatically repeated from vs. 9. In the *Greek,* the name "Onesimus" is skilfully put last, he puts first a favorable description of him before he mentions the name that had fallen into so bad repute with Philemon. "I beseech thee for my son, whom I have begotten in my bonds, Onesimus." Scripture does not sanction slavery, but at the same time does not begin a political crusade against it. It sets forth *principles of love* to our fellow men which were sure (as they have done) in due time to undermine and overthrow it, without violently convulsing the then existing political fabric, by stirring up slaves against their masters.

ADAM CLARKE

6. *That the communication of thy faith.* The words the "fellowship" or *communication of thy faith* may be understood as referring to the work of love towards the saints—the poor Christians—which his faith in Christ enabled him to perform, faith being taken here for its effects. Indeed the word *koinonia* itself is not unfrequently used to denote "liberality, almsgiving"; and this is very properly remarked by Theophylact here: "He terms almsgiving the communication of faith, because it is the fruit of much faith." Instead of *in you,* "in us" is the reading of all the best MSS., as well as of several versions and fathers.

7. *For we have great joy.* This verse does not read harmoniously. The Greek authorizes the following arrangement: "For we have great joy and consolation in your love, O brother, because the bowels of the saints are refreshed by you." The apostle speaks here of the works of charity in which Philemon abounded towards poor Christians.

8. *Wherefore, though I might be much bold.* It would be better to read: "Wherefore, although I have much authority through Christ to command you to do what is proper, yet, on account of my love to you, I entreat you." There is certainly something very melting and persuasive in this and every part of the Epistle. Yet in my opinion the character of Paul prevails in it throughout. The warm, affectionate, authoritative teacher is interceding with an absent friend for a beloved convert. He urges his suit with an earnestness befitting, perhaps, not so much the occasion as the ardor and sensibility of his own mind. Here also, as everywhere, he shows himself conscious of the weight and dignity of his mission. Nor does he suffer Philemon, for a moment, to forget it: *I might be much bold in Christ to enjoin thee that which is convenient.* He is careful also to recall, though obliquely, to Philemon's memory the sacred obligation under which he had laid him by bringing him to the knowledge of Christ: "I do not say to thee how thou owest unto me even thine own self besides." Without laying aside, therefore, the apostolic character, our author softens the imperative style of his address by mixing with it every sentiment and consideration that could move the heart of the correspondent. Aged, and in prison, he is content to supplicate and entreat. Onesimus was rendered dear to him by his conversation and his services; the child of his affliction, and ministering unto him "in the bonds of the gospel." This ought to recommend him, whatever had been his fault, to Philemon's forgiveness: "Receive him as myself," as my own bowels. Everything, however, should be voluntary. Paul was determined that Philemon's compliance should flow from his own bounty: "Without thy mind would I do nothing; that thy benefit should not be as it were of necessity, but willingly"; trusting, nevertheless, to his gratitude and attachment for the performance of all that he requested, and for more: "Having confidence in thy obedience I wrote unto thee, knowing that thou wilt also do more than I say."

9. *Paul the aged.* If we allow Paul to have been about twenty-five years of age at the utmost, in the year 31, when he was assisting at the martyrdom of Stephen, Acts vii. 58; as this Epistle was written about A.D. 62, he could not have been at this time more than about fifty-six years old. This could not constitute him an aged man in our sense of the term; yet when the whole length of his life is taken in, being martyred about four years after this, he may not improperly be considered an aged or elderly man, though it is generally allowed that his martyrdom took place in A.D. 66. But the word signifies not only an "old man," but also an "ambassador," because old or elderly men were chosen to fulfill such an office because of their experience and solidity; hence some have thought that we should translate here, "Paul the ambassador." This would agree very well with the scope and even the design of the place.

10. *I beseech thee for my son Onesimus.* It is evident from this that Onesimus was converted by Paul while he was a prisoner at Rome, and perhaps not long before he wrote this Epistle.

MATTHEW HENRY

6*th Argument* is from Philemon's own interest, *v.* 11. Unsanctified persons are unprofitable persons. Grace makes good for somewhat: "*In time past unprofitable but now profitable*, as he has since his conversion been here to me, ministering to me in my confinement." There seems an allusion to the name Onesimus, which signifies *profitable*. Now he will answer to his name. How tenderly does Paul here speak, when he is pleading with Philemon not to make severe reflections on his servant's misconduct, but to forgive. What happy changes conversion makes—of evil good! of unprofitable useful!

7*th Argument*. He urges Philemon from the strong affection that he had to Onesimus, *v.* 12. Even good men may sometimes need great earnestness and entreaty to forgive those who have injured and offended them.

8*th Argument* is from the apostle's denying himself in sending back Onesimus, *v.* 13, 14. Paul was now in prison, and wanted a friend or servant to assist him, for which he found Onesimus fit and ready, and therefore would have detained him to minister to him. Yet he would not take this liberty, though his circumstances needed it: *I have sent him back* to thee, that any good office of thine to me might not be *of necessity, but willingly*. He might indeed have presumed on Philemon's willingness; but, notwithstanding his need, he would deny himself rather than take that way.

9*th Argument*. Such a change was now wrought in Onesimus that Philemon needed not fear his ever running from him, or injuring him any more, *v.* 15. Charity would so hope and judge, yea, so it would be. How tenderly still the sins of penitents are spoken of; he calls it a *departure for a season* instead of giving it the term that it deserved. True penitents will not return to folly. Observe the goodness, and power of God, that he should be led into the way of salvation who had fled from it, and find means made effectual at Rome who had been hardened under them at Colosse.

10*th Argument* is taken from the capacity under which Onesimus now would return, and must be received by Philemon (*v.* 16). There is a spiritual brotherhood between all true believers, however distinguished in civil and outward respects; they are all children of the same heavenly Father. Christianity does not annul nor confound the respective civil duties, but strengthens the obligation to them. Religious servants are more than mere ordinary servants; they have grace in their hearts, and have found grace in God's sight, and so will in the sight of religious masters. "*A brother beloved, specially to me, but how much more to thee, both in the flesh and in the Lord*. He is God's servant and thine too; here are more ties than he is under to me."

11*th Argument*. From the communion of saints, *v.* 17. Own and treat him as thou wouldst me, with a like ready and true, though perhaps not equal, affection.

12*th Argument*. A promise of satisfaction to Philemon, *v.* 18, 19.

(1) A confession of Onesimus's debt to Philemon. True penitents will be ingenuous in owning their faults, and especially is this to be done in cases of injury to others.

(2) Paul here engages for satisfaction. The communion of saints does not destroy distinction of property: Onesimus is yet Philemon's servant still, and indebted to him for wrongs that he had done. Suretiship is not in all cases unlawful, but in some is a good and merciful undertaking. Hereby he expresses his real and great affection for Onesimus, and his full belief of the sincerity of his conversion.

(3) The reason of things between him and Philemon: "*Albeit, I do not say to thee how thou owest unto me even thy own self besides.*" The apostle glances at the benefits he had conferred on Philemon. I have been the instrument of all that spiritual good to thee; and what thy obligation to me on this account is I leave to thee to consider.

13*th Argument* is from the joy and comfort the apostle hereby would have on Philemon's own account, as well as on Onesimus's, *v.* 20. Philemon was Paul's son in the faith, yet he entreats him as a brother: Onesimus a poor slave, yet he solicits for

JAMIESON, FAUSSET, BROWN

11. Which . . . was . . . unprofitable—belying his name Onesimus, which means "profitable." Not only was he "unprofitable," but positively injurious, having "wronged" his master. Paul uses a mild expression. **now profitable**—Without godliness a man has no station. *Profitable* in spiritual, as well as in *temporal* things. **12. mine own bowels**—as dear to me as my own heart [ALFORD]. Cf. vs. 17, "as myself." The object of my most intense affection as that of a parent for a child.

13. I—emphatical. I for my part. Since *I* had such implicit trust in him as to desire to keep him with me for his services, *thou* mayest. **I would have retained**—different *Greek* from the "would," vs. 14, "I could have *wished*," "I was *minded*" here; but "I was not *willing*," vs. 14. **in thy stead**—that he might supply in your place all the services to me which you, if you were here, would render in virtue of the love you bear to me (vs. 19). **bonds of the gospel**—my bonds endured for the Gospel's sake (vs. 9). **14. without thy mind**—i.e., consent. **should not be as**—"should not appear as a matter of necessity, but of free will." Had Paul kept Onesimus, however willing to gratify Paul Philemon might be, he would have no opportunity given him of showing he was so, his leave not having been asked.

15. perhaps—speaking in human fashion, yet as one believing that God's Providence probably (for we cannot dogmatically define the hidden purposes of God in providence) overruled the past evil to ultimately greater good to him. This thought would soften Philemon's indignation at Onesimus' past offense. So Joseph in Genesis 45:5. **departed**—lit., "was parted from thee"; a softening term for "ran away," to mitigate Philemon's wrath. **receive him**—*Greek*, "have him for thyself in full possession" (*Note*, Phil. 4:18). The same *Greek* as in Matthew 6:2. **for ever**—in this life and in that to come (cf. Exod. 21:6). Onesimus' time of absence, however long, was but a short "hour" (so *Greek*) compared with the everlasting devotion henceforth binding him to his master. **16.** No longer as a mere servant or slave (though still he is that), but above a servant, so that thou shalt derive from him not merely the services of a slave, but higher benefits: a *servant* "in the flesh," he is a *brother* "in the Lord." **beloved, specially to me**—who am his spiritual father, and who have experienced his faithful attentions. Lest Philemon should dislike Onesimus being called "brother," Paul first recognizes him as a brother, being the spiritual son of the same God. **much more unto thee**—to whom he stands in so much nearer and more lasting relation. **17. a partner**—in the Christian fellowship of faith, hope, and love. **receive him as myself**—resuming "receive him that is mine own bowels."

18. *Greek,* "But it (thou art not inclined to 'receive him' because) he hath wronged thee"; a milder term than "robbed thee." Onesimus seems to have confessed some such act to Paul. **put that on mine account**—I am ready to make good the loss to thee if required. The latter parts of vss. 19, 21, imply that he did not expect Philemon would probably demand it. **19. with mine own hand**—not employing an amanuensis, as in other Epistles: a special compliment to Philemon which he ought to show his appreciation of by granting Paul's request. Contrast Colossians 4:18, which shows that the Epistle to the Colossian Church, accompanying this Epistle, had only its closing "salutation" written by Paul's own hand. **albeit . . .**—lit., "that I may not say . . . not to say. . . ." **thou owest . . . even thine own self**—not merely thy possessions. For to my instrumentality thou owest thy salvation. So the debt which "he oweth thee" being transferred upon me (I making myself responsible for it) is cancelled. **20. let me**—"me" is emphatic: "Let *me* have profit (so *Greek* 'for joy,' *onaimen*, referring to the name *Onesimus*, 'profitable') from *thee*, as *thou* shouldst have had from Onesimus"; for "thou owest thine

ADAM CLARKE

11. *Was to thee unprofitable*. Alluding to the meaning of Onesimus' name, as has been already noted, though the apostle uses a different Greek word to express the same idea.

12. *Whom I have sent again*. The Christian religion never cancels any civil relations; a slave, on being converted and becoming a free man of Christ, has no right to claim on that ground emancipation from the service of his master. Justice therefore required Paul to send Onesimus back to his master, and conscience obliged Onesimus to agree in the propriety of the measure; but love to the servant induced the apostle to write this conciliating letter to the master.

13. *That in thy stead he might have ministered unto me*. As Philemon was one of Paul's converts, he thereby became his spiritual father and had a right to his services when in need. This was a strong argument, to induce Philemon not only to forgive his servant, but to send him back to the apostle, that he might minister to him in his master's stead.

14. *That thy benefit should not be as it were of necessity*. If the apostle had kept Onesimus in his service and written to Philemon to forgive him and permit him to stay, to this it is probable he would have agreed. But the benefit thus conceded might have lost much of its real worth by the consideration that, had he been at Colossae, Philemon would not have sent him to Rome; but, being there and in the apostle's service, he could not with propriety order him home. Thus the benefit to the apostle would have appeared to have been of necessity. The apostle therefore, by sending him back again, gave Philemon the opportunity to do all as if self-moved to it. This is a very delicate touch.

15. *He therefore departed for a season*. This is another most delicate stroke. He departed your slave, your unfaithful slave; he departed "for a short time." But so has the mercy of God operated in his behalf, and the providence of God in thine, that he now returns, not an unfaithful slave, in whom you could repose no confidence, but as a *brother*, a beloved brother in the Lord, to be in the same heavenly family with you forever.

16. *Not now as a servant*. Do not receive him merely as your slave, nor treat him according to that condition; but as *a brother*—as a genuine Christian, and particularly dear to me. *Both in the flesh and in the Lord*. There is no reason to believe that Onesimus was of the kindred of Philemon; and we must take the term *flesh* here as referring to the right which Philemon had in him. He was a part of his property and of his family; as a slave, this was his condition. But he now stood in a twofold relation to Philemon: (1) According to the *flesh*, as above explained, he was one of his family. (2) *In the Lord*, he was now also a member of the heavenly family, and of the church at Philemon's house.

17. *If thou count me therefore a partner*. If you do consider me as a friend, if I still have the place of a friend in your affection, *receive him as myself;* for, as I love him as my own soul, in receiving him you receive me.

18. *If he hath wronged thee, or oweth thee ought*. Had the apostle been assured that Onesimus had robbed his master, he certainly would not have spoken in this hypothetical way. He only puts a possible case: If he have wronged you, or owes you anything, place all to my account; I will discharge all he owes you.

19. *I Paul have written it with mine own hand*. It is likely that the whole of the letter was written by Paul himself, which was not his usual custom. See on 2 Thess. iii. 17. But by thus speaking he bound Phileomon to do what he requested, as an act of common civility, if he could not feel a higher motive from what he had already urged. *Albeit I do not say to thee how thou owest unto me*. I ask you to do this thing to oblige me, though I will not say how much you owe me; *even thine own self*, as having been the means of your conversion.

20. *Yea, brother*. It is even so that you are thus indebted to me. *Let me have joy of thee*, in forgiving Onesimus and receiving him into your favor. In the words which we should translate, "Let me have profit of thee," there is

MATTHEW HENRY

him as if he were seeking some great thing for himself. Christians should do the things that may rejoice the hearts of one another. From the world they expect trouble; and where may they look for comfort and joy but in one another? It is not any selfish respect I am actuated by, but what is pleasing to Christ.

14*th Argument*. This lies in the good hope and opinion which he expresses of Philemon, *v.* 21. Good thoughts and expectations of us more strongly move and engage us to do the things expected from us. Good persons will be ready for good works, and not narrow and pinching, but abundant in them.

II. The conclusion.

1. He signifies his good hope of deliverance, through their prayers, and that shortly he might see them, desiring Philemon to make provision for him, *v.* 22.

(1) *Prepare me also a lodging*. He wills Philemon to do it, intending to be his guest. Who would not show the utmost of affectionate regards to such a one?

(2) *For I trust that through your prayers I shall be given unto you.* He did not know how God might deal with him, but the benefit of prayer he had often found, and hoped he should again, for deliverance, and liberty to come to them. Trust must be with the use of means, prayer especially; this hath unlocked heaven and opened prison-doors. The least may in this way be helpful to the greatest. Though prayer obtains, yet it does not merit the things obtained: they are God's gift, and Christ's purchase. *I trust that through your prayers I shall be freely bestowed on you.* In praying for faithful ministers, people in effect pray for themselves: "*I trust I shall be given unto you*, for your service, and comfort."

2. He sends salutations from one who was his fellow-prisoner, and four more who were his fellow-labourers, *v.* 23, 24. *Epaphras, my fellow-prisoner in Christ Jesus.* He was of Colosse, and so countryman and fellow-citizen with Philemon, who, being at Rome, perhaps accompanying Paul, was confined in the same prison, and for the same cause. *My fellow-prisoner in Christ Jesus* is mentioned as his glory and the apostle's comfort. So God sometimes lightens the sufferings of his servants by the communion of saints, the sweet fellowship they have one with another in their bonds. Never more enjoyment of God have they found than when suffering together for God.—*Marcus, Aristarchus, Demas, Lucas, my fellow-labourers.* The mention of these seems in a manner to interest them in the business of the letter. How ill would it look by denial of the request of it to slight so many worthy names as most of these, at least, were! *Marcus*, cousin of Barnabas, and son of Mary, who was so hospitable to the saints at Jerusalem. Though some failing seems to have been in him when Paul and he parted, yet in conjunction with Barnabas he went on with his work, and here Paul and he, we perceive, were reconciled. *Aristarchus* is mentioned with Marcus (Col. iv. 10), and called there by Paul his fellow-prisoner. Next is *Demas*: no mark of disgrace lay on him here, but he is joined with others who were faithful. *Lucas* is the last, that *beloved physician* and evangelist, who came to Rome, companion with Paul.

3. Here is the apostle's closing prayer and benediction, *v.* 25. What is wished and prayed for: *Grace*, the free favour and love of God; with this the apostle begins and ends. From whom: *Our Lord Jesus Christ*. All grace to us is from Christ; he purchased, and he bestows it. To whom: *Your spirit*, not of Philemon only, but of all who were named in the inscription. All the house saluted are here joined in the closing benediction, the more to quicken all to further the end of the epistle.

Amen is added, not only for strong and affectionate summing up the prayer and wish, *so let it be*; but as an expression of faith that it will be heard, *so shall it be*. The grace of Christ with their spirits, Philemon's especially, would sweeten and mollify them, and dispose to forgive others as God for Christ's sake hath forgiven us.

JAMIESON, FAUSSET, BROWN

own self to me." **in the Lord**—not in worldly gain, but in thine increase in the graces of the Lord's Spirit [ALFORD]. **my bowels**—my heart. Gratify my feelings by granting this request. **in the Lord**—The oldest MSS. read, "*in Christ,*" the element or sphere in which this act of Christian love naturally ought to have place. **21. Having confidence in thy obedience**—to my apostolic authority, if I were to "enjoin" it (vs. 8), which I do not, preferring to beseech thee for it as a favor (vs. 9). **thou wilt also do more**—towards Onesimus: hinting at his possible manumission by Philemon, *besides* being kindly received.

22. This prospect of Paul's visiting Colosse would tend to secure a kindly reception for Onesimus, as Paul would know in person how he had been treated. **your . . . you**—referring to Philemon, Apphia, Archippus, and the Church in Philemon's house. The same expectation is expressed by him, Philippians 2:23, 24, written in the same imprisonment.

23.
The same persons send salutations in the accompanying Epistle, except that "Jesus Justus" is not mentioned here. **Epaphras, my fellow prisoner**—He had been sent by the Colossian Church to inquire after, and minister to, Paul, and possibly was cast into *prison* by the Roman authorities on suspicion. However, he is not mentioned as a *prisoner* in Colossians 4:12, so that "fellow prisoner" here may mean merely one who was a faithful companion to Paul in his imprisonment, and by his society put himself in the position of a prisoner.

So also "Aristarchus, my fellow prisoner," Colossians 4:10, may mean. BENSON conjectures the meaning to be that on some *former* occasion these two were Paul's "fellow prisoners," *not at the time.*

25. be with your spirit—(Gal. 6:18; II Timothy 4:22).

ADAM CLARKE

an evident play on the name of Onesimus. See on vv. 2 and 11. *Refresh my bowels.* Gratify the earnest longing of my soul in this. I ask neither your money nor goods; I ask what will enrich, not impoverish, you to give.

21. *Having confidence in thy obedience.* I know that it will please you thus to oblige your friend; and I know that you will do more than I request, because you feel the affection of a son to your spiritual father. Some think that the apostle hints to Philemon that he should manumit Onesimus.

22. *But withal prepare me also a lodging.* Does not the apostle mention this as conferring an obligation on Philemon? I will begin to repay you by taking up my abode at your house as soon as I shall be freed from prison. But some think he wished Philemon to hire him a house, that he might have a lodging of his own when he returned to Colossae. *For I trust that through your prayers.* It is very likely that this Epistle was written a short time before the liberation of the apostle from his first imprisonment at Rome (see Acts xxviii. 30 and Phil. ii. 24), and that he had that liberation now in full prospect.

23. *Epaphras, my fellowprisoner.* Epaphras was a Colossian, as we learn from Col. iv. 12: "Epaphras, who is one of you." But there is no account there of his being in prison, though the not mentioning of it does not necessarily imply that he was not. Some time or other he had suffered imprisonment for the truth of the gospel, and on that account Paul might, in a general way, call him his fellow prisoner.

24. *Marcus, Aristarchus.* These were all acquaintances of Philemon, and probably Colossians, and may be all considered as joining here with Paul in his request for Onesimus. *Aristarchus* was probably the same with him mentioned in Acts xix. 29; xx. 4; xxvii. 2. See Col. iv. 10. *Demas.* Is supposed to be the same who continued in his attachment to Paul till his last imprisonment at Rome; after which he left him for what is supposed to have been the love of the world, 2 Tim. iv. 10. *Lucas.* Is supposed to be Luke the Evangelist, and author of the Acts of the Apostles.

25. *The grace of our Lord Jesus Christ be with your spirit.* By using the plural *your* the apostle in effect directs or addresses the Epistle, not only to Philemon, but to all the church at his house. *Amen.* Is wanting as usual in the best MSS.

THE EPISTLE TO THE HEBREWS

I. Introduction (1:1-2a)
- *A. Unargued truth*
  - 1. God
  - 2. God speaks
- *B. The two economies*
  - 1. "Of old time"
  - 2. "At the end of these days"

II. The argument—foundations of faith (1:2b-10:37)
- *A. Superiority of the speech of the Son (1:2b-7:28)*
  - 1. Superior to angels—Genesis (1:2b-2:18)
    Exhortation and warning (2:1-4)
  - 2. Superiority to leaders—Exodus, Joshua (3:1-4:13)
    - a. Moses (3:1-6)
      Exhortation and warning (3:7-4:7)
    - b. Joshua (4:8-10)
      Exhortation and warning (4:11-13)
  - 3. Superior to Priesthood—Leviticus (4:14-7:28)
    - a. Aaronic (4:14-5:10)
      Exhortation and warning (5:11-6:12)
    - b. Levitic (6:13-7:28)
- *B. Superiority of consequent relationships (8:1-10:37)*
  - 1. The better covenant (8:1-13)
  - 2. The better worship (9:1-10:18)
  - 3. The better fellowship (10:19-25)
    Exhortation and warning (10:26-37)

III. The appeal—fruitfulness of faith (10:38-12:29)
- *A. The witnesses (10:38-12:3)*
  - 1. The old economy—a cloud of witnesses (10:38-11:40)
  - 2. The new economy—the one witness (12:1-3)
- *B. The great appeal (12:4-29)*
  - 1. The perils (12:4-17)
    - a. Failure to respond to chastening (12:4-13)
    - b. Falling short of the grace of God (12:14-17)
  - 2. The encouragement (12:18-24)
    - a. The old—terror and majesty (12:18-21)
    - b. The new—tenderness and mercy (12:22-24)
  - 3. The appeal (12:25-29)
    - a. "See that ye refuse not . . . for" (12:25-27)
    - b. "Let us have grace . . . for" (12:28, 29)

IV. Conclusion (13:1-25)
- *A. Closing injunctions (13:1-17)*
  - 1. Conduct of faith (13:1-6)
  - 2. Anchorage of faith (13:7-9)
  - 3. Worship of faith (13:10-15)
  - 4. Fellowship of faith (13:16, 17)
- *B. Personal conclusion (13:18-25)*

Concerning this epistle we must inquire: (1) Into the divine authority of it, for this has been questioned by some. The divine original of it shines forth with such strong and unclouded rays that he who runs may read it as an eminent part of the canon of Scripture. Its general reception in the church of God in all ages—these are the evidences of its divine authority. (2) As to its author. Of this we are not so certain; it does not bear the name of any in the front if it, as the rest of the epistles do, and there has been some dispute among the learned to whom they should ascribe it. But it is generally assigned to the apostle Paul. In the primitive times it was generally ascribed to him. (3) As to its scope and design. It is very evident that it was clearly to inform the minds, and strongly to confirm the judgment, of the Hebrews in the transcendent excellency of the gospel above the law. The design of this epistle was to press the believing Hebrews to a constant adherence to the Christian faith, and perseverance in it, notwithstanding all the sufferings they might meet with in so doing. It must be acknowledged that there are many things in this epistle hard to be understood, but the sweetness we shall find therein will make us abundant amends for all the pains we take to understand it.

MATTHEW HENRY

CHAPTER 1

Verses 1–3

The apostle begins with a general declaration of the excellency of the gospel dispensation above that of the law.

I. The way wherein God communicated himself and his will to men under the Old Testament. The persons by whom God delivered his mind under the Old Testament; they were *the prophets*, that is, persons chosen of God, and qualified by him, for that office of revealing the will of God to men. The persons to whom God spoke by the prophets: *To the fathers*, to all the Old Testament saints. The order in which God spoke to men in those past times: he spoke to his ancient people *at sundry times and in divers manners. By several parts*, as the word signifies, which may refer either to the several ages of the Old Testament dispensation; or to the several gradual openings of his mind concerning the Redeemer. *In divers manners*, according to the different ways in which God thought fit to communicate his mind to his prophets.

JAMIESON, FAUSSET, BROWN

CHAPTER 1

VSS. 1-14. THE HIGHEST OF ALL REVELATIONS IS GIVEN US NOW IN THE SON OF GOD, WHO IS GREATER THAN THE ANGELS, AND WHO, HAVING COMPLETED REDEMPTION, SITS ENTHRONED AT GOD'S RIGHT HAND. The writer, though not inscribing his name, was well known to those addressed (ch. 13:19).

1. at sundry times—*Greek,* "in many portions." All was not revealed to each one prophet; but one received one portion of revelation, and another another. To Noah the quarter of the world to which Messiah should belong was revealed; to Abraham, the nation; to Jacob, the tribe; to David and Isaiah, the family; to Micah, the town of nativity; to Daniel, the exact time; to Malachi, the coming of His forerunner, and His second advent; through Jonah, His burial and resurrection; through Isaiah and Hosea, His resurrection. Each only knew in part; but when that which was perfect came in Messiah, that which was in part was done away (I Cor. 13: 12). **in divers manners**—e.g., internal suggestions, audible voices, the Urim and Thummim, dreams, and visions. "In one way He was seen by Abraham, in another by Moses, in another by Elias, and in another by Micah; Isaiah, Daniel, and Ezekiel, beheld different forms" [THEODORET] (cf. Num. 12: 6-8). The Old Testament revelations were fragmentary in substance, and manifold in form; the very *multitude* of prophets shows that they prophesied only *in part*. In Christ, the revelation of God is full, not in shifting hues of separated color, but Himself the pure light, uniting in His one person the whole spectrum (vs. 3). **spake**—the expression usual for a Jew to employ in addressing Jews. So Matthew, a Jew writing especially for Jews, quotes Scripture, not by the formula, "It is written," but "said. . . ." **in time past**—From Malachi, the last of the Old Testament prophets, for four hundred

ADAM CLARKE

CHAPTER 1

1. *God, who at sundry times and in divers manners.* We can scarcely conceive anything more dignified than the opening of this Epistle. The sentiments are exceedingly elevated; and the language, harmony itself. The infinite God is at once produced to view, not in any of those attributes which are essential to the divine nature, but in the manifestations of His love to the world, by giving a revelation of His will relative to the salvation of mankind, and thus preparing the way, through a long train of years, for the introduction of that most glorious Being, His own Son. This Son, in the fullness of time, was manifested in the flesh that He might complete all vision and prophecy, supply all that was wanting to perfect the great scheme of revelation for the instruction of the world, and then die to put away sin by the sacrifice of himself. The description which he gives of this glorious personage is elevated beyond all comparison. In short, this first chapter, which may be considered the introduction to the whole Epistle, is, for importance of subject, dignity of expression, harmony and energy of language, compression and yet distinctness of ideas, equal, if not superior, to any other part of the New Testament. *Sundry times. Polymeros,* from *polys,* "many," and *meros,* "a part"; giving portions of revelation at different times. *Divers manners. Polytropos,* from *polys,* "many," and *tropos,* "a manner, turn, or form of speech." The words are rather intended to point out the imperfect state of divine revelation under the Old Testament; it was not complete, nor can it without the New be considered a sufficiently ample discovery of the divine will. Under the Old Testament, revelations were made at various times, by various persons, in various laws

MATTHEW HENRY

II. God's method of communicating his mind and will under the New Testament dispensation, these last days as they are called. Now we must expect no new revelation, but only more of the Spirit of Christ to help us better to understand what is already revealed. It is the final, the finishing revelation. It is a revelation which God has made by his Son, the most excellent messenger that was ever sent into the world.

1. The glory of his office. God hath appointed him to be heir of all things. By him God made the worlds, both visible and invisible, the heavens and the earth. By him he made the old creation, by him he makes the new creature, and by him he rules and governs both. He upholds all things by the word of his power. The weight of the whole creation is laid upon Christ: he supports the whole and all the parts.

2. Hence the apostle passes to the glory of the person of Christ, *v.* 3. He is the only-begotten Son of God, and as such he must have the same nature. The person of the Son is the glory of the Father, shining forth with a truly divine splendour. Jesus Christ in his person is God manifest in the flesh. The person of the Son is the true image and character of the person of the Father. In beholding the power, wisdom, and goodness, of the Lord Jesus Christ, we behold the power, wisdom, and goodness, of the Father. This is the glory of the person of Christ; the fulness of the Godhead dwells in him.

3. From the glory of the person of Christ he proceeds to mention the glory of his grace. The sufferings of Christ had this great honour in them, to be a full satisfaction for the sins of his people: *By himself he purged away our sins*; he has made atonement for sin. Himself, the glory of his person and nature, gave to his sufferings such merit as was a sufficient reparation of honour to God, who had suffered injury and affront by the sins of men.

4. From the glory of his sufferings we are at length led to consider the glory of his exaltation. Having assumed our nature, and suffered in it on earth, he has taken it up with him to heaven.

Now it was by no less a person than this that God in these last days spoke to men. The dispensations of the gospel must therefore exceed, very far exceed, the dispensation of the law.

JAMIESON, FAUSSET, BROWN

years, there had arisen no prophet, in order that the Son might be the more an object of expectation [BENGEL]. As God (the Father) is introduced as having *spoken* here; so God the Son, ch. 2:3; God the Holy Ghost, ch. 3:7. **the fathers**—the Jewish fathers. The Jews of former days (I Cor. 10:1). **by**—*Greek,* "in." A mortal king speaks *by* his ambassador, not (as the King of kings) *in* his ambassador. The Son is the last and highest manifestation of God (Matt. 21:34, 37); not merely a measure, as in the prophets, but the fulness of the Spirit of God dwelling in Him bodily (John 1:16; 3:34; Col. 2:9). Thus he answers the Jewish objection drawn from their prophets. Jesus is the end of all prophecy (Rev. 19:10), and of the law of Moses (John 1:17; 5:46). **2. in these last days**—In the oldest MSS. the *Greek* is, "At the last part of these days." The Rabbins divided the whole of time into "this age," or "world," and "the age to come" (ch. 2:5; 6:5). The days of Messiah were the transition period or "last part of these days" (in contrast to "in times past"), the close of the existing dispensation, and beginning of the final dispensation of which Christ's second coming shall be the crowning consummation. **by** ***his*** **Son**—*Greek,* "IN (His) Son" (John 14:10). The true "Prophet" of God. "His majesty is set forth: (1) *Absolutely* by the very name 'Son,' and by three glorious predicates, 'whom He hath appointed,' 'by whom He made the worlds,' 'who sat down on the right hand of the Majesty on high;' thus His course is described from the beginning of all things till he reached the goal (vss. 2, 3). (2) *Relatively,* in comparison with the angels, vs. 4; the *confirmation* of this follows, and the very name 'Son' is proved at vs. 5; the 'heirship,' vss. 6-9; the 'making the worlds,' vss. 10-12; the 'sitting at the right hand' of God, vss. 13, 14." His being made *heir* follows His *sonship,* and preceded His *making the worlds* (Prov. 8:22, 23; Eph. 3:11). As *the first begotten,* He is heir of the universe (vs. 6), which He made instrumentally, ch. 11:3, where "by the Word of God" answers to "by whom" (the Son of God) here (John 1:3). Christ was "appointed" (in God's eternal counsel) to creation as an office; and the universe so created was assigned to Him as a kingdom. He is "heir of all things" by right of creation, and especially by right of redemption. The promise to Abraham that he should be heir of the world had its fulfilment, and will have it still more fully, in Christ (Rom. 4:13; Gal. 3:16; 4:7). **worlds**—the inferior and the superior worlds (Col. 1:16). Lit., "ages" with all things and persons belonging to them; the universe, including all space and ages of time, and all material and spiritual existences. The *Greek* implies, He not only appointed His Son heir of all things before creation, but *He also* (better than "also He") made by Him the worlds. **3. Who being**—by pre-existent and essential being. **brightness of his glory**—*Greek,* the *effulgence* of His glory. "Light of (from) light" [NICENE *Creed*]. "Who is so senseless as to doubt concerning the eternal being of the Son? For when has one seen light without effulgence?" [ATHANASIUS *against* ARIUS, *Orat.* 2]. "The sun is never seen without effulgence, nor the Father without the Son" [THEOPHYLACT]. It is *because* He is the brightness, etc., and *because* He upholds, etc., that He *sat down on the right hand,* etc. It was a return to His divine glory (John 6:62; 17:5; cf. *Wisd.* 7:25, 26, where similar things are said of wisdom). **express image**—"impress." But veiled in the flesh.

of his person—*Greek,* "of His substantial essence"; *hypostasis.* **upholding all things**—*Greek, "the* universe." Cf. Colossians 1:15, 17, 20, which enumerates the three facts in the same order as here. **by the word**—Therefore the Son of God is a Person; for He has the word [BENGEL]. *His* word is *God's* word (ch. 11:3). **of his power**—"The word" is the utterance which comes from His (the Son's) power, and gives expression to it. **by himself**—omitted in the oldest MSS. **purged**—*Greek, "made purification* of . . . sins," viz., in His atonement, which graciously covers the guilt of sin. "Our" is omitted in the oldest MSS. Sin was the great *uncleanness* in God's sight, of which He has effected the purgation by His sacrifice [ALFORD]. Our nature, as guilt-laden, could not, without our great High Priest's blood of atonement sprinkling the heavenly mercy seat, come into immediate contact with God. **sat down on the right hand of the Majesty on high**—fulfilling Psalm 110:1. This sitting of the Son at God's right hand was by the act of the Father (ch. 8:1; Eph. 1:20); it is never used of His pre-existing state coequal with the Father, but always of His exalted state as Son of man after His sufferings, and as Mediator for man in the presence of God (Rom. 8:34): a relation towards

ADAM CLARKE

and forms of teaching, with various degrees of clearness, under various shadows, types, and figures, and with various modes of revelation, such as by angels, visions, dreams, mental impressions. See Num. xii. 6, 8. But under the New Testament all is done simply by one Person, i.e., Jesus, who has fulfilled the prophets and completed prophecy. One great object of the apostle is to put the simplicity of the Christian system in opposition to the complex nature of the Mosaic economy; and also to show that what the law could not do because it was weak through the flesh, Jesus has accomplished by the merit of His death and the energy of His Spirit.

2. *Last days.* The gospel dispensation, called the *last days* and the "last time" because not to be followed by any other dispensation or the conclusion of the Jewish church and state now at their termination. *By his Son.* It is very remarkable that the pronoun *his* is not found in the text; nor is it found in any MS. or version. We should not therefore supply the pronoun as our translators have done; but simply read "by a son" or "in a son." The apostle begins with the lowest state in which Christ has appeared: (1) His being a Son, born of a woman, and made under the law. He then ascends (2) to His being an *heir,* and an *heir of all things.* (3) He then describes Him as the Creator of all *worlds.* (4) As the "brightness" of the divine glory. (5) As "the express image of his person," or "character of the divine substance." (6) As sustaining the immense fabric of the universe, and this "by the word of his power." (7) As having made an atonement for the sin of the world, which was the most stupendous of all His works. (8) As being on the right hand of God, infinitely exalted above all created beings, and the Object of adoration to all the angelic host. (9) As having an eternal throne, neither His person nor His dignity ever changing or decaying. (10) As continuing to exercise dominion when the earth and the heavens are no more!

3. *The brightness of his glory.* The resplendent outbeaming of the essential glory of God. *The express image of his person.* "The character or impression of His hypostasis or substance." It is supposed that these words expound the former, *image* expounding *brightness,* and *person* "substance," *glory.* The hypostasis of God is that which is essential to Him as God; and the "character" or *image* is that by which all the likeness of the original becomes manifest, and is a perfect facsimile of the whole. It is a metaphor taken from sealing, the die or seal leaving the full impression of its every part on the wax to which it is applied. *Upholding all things by the word of his power.* This is an astonishing description of the infinitely energetic and all-pervading power of God. He spoke, and all things were created; He speaks, and all things are sustained. The Jewish writers frequently express the perfection of the divine nature by the phrases, "He bears all things, both above and below"; "He carries all His creatures"; "He bears his world"; "He bears all worlds by His power." The Hebrews, to whom this Epistle was written, would, from this and other circumstances, fully understand that the apostle believed Jesus Christ to be truly and properly God.

The right hand of the Majesty on high. As it were associated with the supreme Majesty, in glory everlasting, and in the government of all things in time and in eternity; for the *right hand* is the place of the greatest eminence, I Kings ii. 19.

MATTHEW HENRY

Verses 4–14

The apostle now proceeds to show that he is much superior not only to the prophets, but to the angels themselves. Both in nature and office Christ is vastly superior to the angels themselves.

I. The superior nature of Christ is proved from his superior name.

II. The superiority of the name and nature of Christ above the angels is declared in the holy scriptures, and is to be deduced thence. Now here are several passages of scripture cited, in which those things are said of Christ that were never said of the angels.

1. It was said of Christ, *Thou art my Son, this day have I begotten thee* (Ps. ii. 7). Now this was never said concerning the angels, and therefore by inheritance he has a more excellent nature and name than they.

2. It is said concerning Christ, but never concerning the angels, *I will be to him a Father, and he shall be to me a Son.*

W. E. VINE:

PROTOTOKOS, firstborn (from *protos,* first, and *tikto,* to beget), is used of Christ as born of the Virgin Mary (Luke 2:7); further, in His relationship to the Father, expressing His priority to, and preeminence over, creation, not in the sense of being the first to be born. It is used occasionally of superiority of position in the O.T.

The five passages in the N.T. relating to Christ may be set forth chronologically thus: (a) Col. 1:15, where His eternal relationship with the Father is in view, and the clause means both that He was the Firstborn before all creation and that He himself produced creation; (b) Col. 1:18 and Rev. 1:5, in reference to His resurrection; (c) Rom. 8:29, His position in relationship to the Church; (d) Heb. 1:6, R.V., His Second Advent (the R.V. "when he again bringeth in," puts "again" in the right place, the contrast to His First Advent, at His birth, being implied). —*Vine's Expository Dictionary*

3. It is said of Christ, *When God bringeth his First-begotten into the world, let all the angels of God worship him.* The proof of this is taken out of Ps. xcvii 7, *Worship him, all you gods,* "All you that are superior to men, own yourselves to be inferior to Christ in nature and power."

JAMIESON, FAUSSET, BROWN

God and us about to come to an end when its object has been accomplished (I Cor. 15:28). **4. Being made . . . better**—by His exaltation by the Father (vss. 3, 13): in contrast to His being "made lower than the angels" (ch. 2:9). "Better," i.e., *superior* to. As "being" (vs. 3) expresses His essential being so "being made" (ch. 7:26) marks what He became in His assumed manhood (Phil. 2:6-9). Paul shows that His humbled form (at which the Jews might stumble) is no objection to His divine Messiahship. **by inheritance obtained**—He always had the *thing* itself, viz., *Sonship;* but *He* "obtained by inheritance," according to the promise of the Father, *the name* "Son," whereby He is made known to men and angels. He is "the Son of God" is a sense far exalted above that in which angels are called "sons of God" (Job 1:6; 38:7). "The fulness of the glory of the peculiar name 'the Son of God,' is unattainable by human speech or thought. All appellations are but fragments of its glory—beams united in it as in a central sun. Revelation 19:12. *A name that no man knew but He Himself."* **5. For**—substantiating His having "obtained a more excellent name than the angels." **unto which**—A frequent argument in this Epistle is derived from *the silence of Scripture* (vs. 13; ch. 2:16; 7:3, 14) [BENGEL]. **this day have I begotten thee**—(Ps. 2:7). Fulfilled at the resurrection of Jesus, whereby the Father "declared," i.e., made manifest His divine Sonship, heretofore veiled by His humiliation (Acts 13:33; Rom. 1:4). Christ has a fourfold right to the title "Son of God"; (1) By *generation,* as begotten of God; (2) By *commission,* as sent by God; (3) By *resurrection,* as "the first-begotten of the dead" (cf. Luke 20:36; Rom. 1:4; Rev. 1:5); (4) By *actual possession,* as heir of all [BISHOP PEARSON]. The Psalm here quoted applied primarily in a less full sense to Solomon, of whom God promised by Nathan to David, "I will be his father and he shall be my son." But as the whole theocracy was of Messianic import, the triumph of David over Hadadezer and neighboring kings (II Sam. 8; Psalm 2:2, 3, 9-12) is a type of God's ultimately subduing all enemies under His Son, whom He sets (*Hebrew,* "anointed," Ps. 2:6) on His "holy hill of Zion," as King of the Jews and of the whole earth, the antitype to Solomon, son of David. The "I" in *Greek* is emphatic; *I* the Everlasting Father have begotten Thee this day, i.e., on this day, the day of Thy being manifested as My Son, "the first-*begotten* of the dead" (Col. 1:18; Rev. 1:5), when Thou hast ransomed and opened heaven to Thy people. He had been always Son, but now first was manifested as such in His once humbled, now exalted manhood united to His Godhead. ALFORD refers "this day" to the *eternal* generation of the Son: the day in which the Son was begotten by the Father is an everlasting *today:* there never was a yesterday or past time to Him, nor a tomorrow or future time: "Nothing there is to come, and nothing past, but an eternal NOW doth ever last" (Prov. 30:4; John 10:30, 38; 16:28; 17:8). The communication of the divine essence in its fulness, involves eternal generation; for the divine essence has no beginning. But the context refers to a definite point of time, viz., that of His having entered on the *inheritance* (vs. 4). The "bringing the firstbegotten into the world" (vs. 6), is not subsequent, as ALFORD thinks, to vs. 5, but anterior to it (cf. Acts 2:30-35). **6. And**—*Greek,* "But." Not only this proves His superiority, BUT a more decisive proof is Psalm 97:7, which shows that not only at His resurrection, but also in prospect of His being *brought into the world* (cf. ch. 9:11; 10:5) as man, in His incarnation, nativity (Luke 2:9-14), temptation (Matt. 4:10, 11), resurrection (Matt. 28:2), and future second advent in glory, angels were designed by God to be subject to Him. Cf. I Tim. 3:16, "seen of angels"; God manifesting Messiah as one to be gazed at with adoring love by heavenly intelligences (Eph. 3:10; II Thess. 1:9, 10; I Pet. 3:22). The fullest realization of His Lordship shall be at His second coming (Ps. 97:7; I Cor. 15:24, 25; Phil. 2:9). "Worship Him all ye gods" ("gods," i.e., *exalted beings,* as *angels*), refers to *God;* but it was universally admitted among the Hebrews that God would dwell, in a peculiar sense, in Messiah (so as to be in the Talmud phrase, "capable of being pointed to with the finger"); and so what was said of God was true of, and to be fulfilled in, Messiah. KIMCHI says that Psalms 93-101 contain in them the mystery of Messiah. God ruled the theocracy in and through Him. **the world**—subject to Christ (ch. 2:5). As "the first-begotten" He has the rights of *primogeniture* (Rom. 8:29); Col. 1:15, 16, 18). In Deuteronomy 32:43, the LXX has, "Let all the angels of God worship Him," words not now found in the

ADAM CLARKE

4. *So much better than the angels.* Another argument in favor of the divinity of our Lord. The Jews had the highest opinion of the transcendent excellence of angels; they even associate them with God in the creation of the world, and suppose them to be of the privy council of the Most High; and thus they understand Gen. i. 26: "Let us make man in our image, after our likeness"; "And the Lord said to the ministering angels that stood before Him, and who were created the second day, Let us make man." *By inheritance obtained.* The verb signifies generally to "participate, possess, obtain, or acquire." It is not by *inheritance* that Christ possesses a more excellent name than angels, but as God. He has it naturally and essentially; and, as God manifested in the flesh, He has it in consequence of His humiliation, sufferings, and meritorious death. See Phil. ii. 9.

5. *Thou art my Son, this day have I begotten thee.* These words are quoted from Ps. ii. 7, a psalm that seems to refer only to the Messiah; and they are quoted by Paul, Acts xiii. 33, as referring to the resurrection of Christ. And this application of them is confirmed by the same apostle, Rom. i. 4, as by His resurrection from the dead he was "declared," manifestly proved, "to be the Son of God with power." By His resurrection His innocence was demonstrated, as God could not work a miracle to raise a wicked man from the dead. The words *This day have I begotten thee* must refer either to His incarnation, when He was miraculously conceived in the womb of the Virgin by the power of the Holy Spirit, or to His resurrection from the dead, when God by this sovereign display of His almighty energy declared Him to be His Son. This most important use of this saying has passed unnoticed by almost every Christian writer which I have seen, and yet it lies here at the foundation of all the apostle's proofs. If Jesus was not thus the Son of God, the whole Christian system is vain and baseless; but His *resurrection* demonstrates Him to have been the Son of God. *He shall be to me a Son.* This place, which is quoted from 2 Sam. vii. 14, shows us that the Seed which God promised to David, and who was to sit upon his throne, and whose throne should be established forever, was not Solomon, but Jesus Christ; and indeed He quotes the words so as to intimate that they were so understood by the Jews.

6. *And again, when he bringeth in the first-begotten.* This is not a correct translation of the Greek. "But when He bringeth again, or the second time, the Firstborn into the habitable world." This most manifestly refers to His resurrection, which might be properly considered a second incarnation; for as the human soul, as well as the fullness of the Godhead bodily, dwelt in the man Christ Jesus on and during His incarnation, so when He expired upon the Cross both the Godhead and the human spirit left His dead body; and as on His resurrection these were reunited to His revivified manhood, therefore with the strictest propriety does the apostle say that the Resurrection was a second bringing of Him into the world.

I have translated *oikoumene* the "habitable world," and this is its proper meaning; and thus it is distinguished from *cosmos,* which signifies the "globe," independently of its inhabitants, though it often expresses both the inhabited and uninhabited parts. Our Lord's first coming into the world is expressed by this latter word, chap. x. 5: "Wherefore when he cometh into the world" (*cosmos*), and this simply refers to His being incarnated, that He might be capable of suffering and dying for man. But the word is changed on this second coming, I mean His resurrection, and then *oikoumene* is used. And why? Because He was now to dwell with man; to send His gospel everywhere to all the inhabitants of the earth. *Let all the angels of God worship him.* The apostle recurs here to his former assertion, that Jesus is higher than the angels, v. 4. To worship any creature is idolatry. Jesus Christ can be no creature, else the angels who worship Him must be guilty of idolatry, and God the Author of that idolatry, who commanded those angels to worship Christ. There has been some difficulty in ascertaining the place from which the apostle quotes these words;

MATTHEW HENRY

4. God has said concerning Christ, *Thy throne, O God, is for ever and ever*, &c., *v.* 8–12. But of the angels he has only said that *he hath made them spirits, and his ministers a flame of fire*, *v.* 7.

(1) What does God say here of the angels? *He maketh his angels spirits, and his ministers a flame of fire*. The office of the angels: they are God's ministers, or *servants, to do his pleasure*. He endows them with light and zeal, readiness and resolution to do his pleasure: they are no more than what God has made them to be.

(2) How much greater things are said of Christ by the Father. Here two passages of scripture are quoted.

[1] One of these is out of Ps. xlv. 5, 7, where God declares of Christ, *First*, His true and real divinity, *Thy throne, O God*. And, if God the Father declares him to be so, he must be really and truly so. *Secondly*, God declares his dignity and dominion, as having a throne, a kingdom, and a sceptre of that kingdom. *Thirdly*, God declares the eternal duration of the dominion and dignity of Christ: *Thy throne, O God, is for ever and ever*. This distinguishes Christ's throne from all earthly thrones, which are tottering, and will at length tumble down; but the throne of Christ shall be as the days of heaven. *Fourthly*, God declares of Christ the perfect equity of his administration, *v.* 8. He came righteously to the sceptre, and he uses it in perfect righteousness, *v.* 9. Christ came to fulfil all righteousness. He came to finish transgression, and to make an end of sin as a hateful as well as hurtful thing. *Fifthly*, God declares of Christ how he was qualified for the office of Mediator, and how he was installed and confirmed in it (*v.* 9). Christ has the name Messiah from his being anointed. This anointing of Christ was *with the oil of gladness*, that joy which was set before him as the reward of his service and sufferings, that crown of glory and gladness which he should wear for ever after the suffering of death. This anointing of Christ was above the anointing of his fellows. All God's other anointed ones had only the Spirit in a certain measure; Christ had the Spirit above measure, without any limitation.

[2] The other passage of scripture is taken out of Ps. cii. 25–27, and is recited in *v.* 10–12, where the omnipotence of the Lord Jesus Christ is declared as it appears both in creating the world and in changing it. In creating the world (*v.* 10). His right, as God with the Father, was absolute, resulting from his creating power. This power he had before the beginning of the world, and he exerted it in giving a beginning and being to the world. He not only founded the earth, but the heavens too are the work of his hands, the hosts of heaven, the angels themselves; and therefore he must needs be infinitely superior to them.

In changing the world that he has made. *a* This world is mutable, all created nature is so; this world has passed through many changes, and shall pass through more (*v.* 11, 12).

JAMIESON, FAUSSET, BROWN

Hebrew. This passage of the LXX may have been in Paul's mind as to the *form*, but the *substance* is taken from Psalm 97:7. The type David, in the Psalm 89:27 (quoted in vs. 5), is called "God's *first-born*, higher than the *kings* of the earth"; so the antitypical first-begotten, the son of David, is to be worshipped by all inferior *lords*, such as *angels* ("gods," Ps. 97:7); for He is "King of kings and Lord of lords" (Rev. 19:16). In the *Greek*, "again" is transposed; but this does not oblige us, as ALFORD thinks, to translate, "when He *again shall have introduced...*" viz., at Christ's second coming; for there is no previous mention of a *first* bringing in; and "again" is often used in quotations, not to be joined with the verb, but parenthetically ("that I may again quote Scripture"). *English Version* is correct (cf. Matt. 5:33; *Greek*, John 12:39). **7. of**—The *Greek* is rather, "In reference TO the angels." **spirits**—or "winds": Who employeth His angels as the winds, His ministers as the lightnings; or, He maketh His angelic ministers the directing powers of winds and flames, when these latter are required to perform His will. "Commissions them to assume the agency or form of flames for His purposes" [ALFORD]. *English Version*, "maketh His angels *spirits,*" means, He maketh them of a subtle, incorporeal nature, swift as the wind. So Psalm 18:10, "a *cherub* . . . the wings of the *wind*." Verse 14, "ministering *spirits,*" favors *English Version* here. As "spirits" implies the windlike velocity and subtle nature of the *cherubim*, so "flame of fire" expresses the burning devotion and intense all-consuming zeal of the adoring *seraphim* (meaning "burning"), Isaiah 6:1. **8. O God**—the *Greek* has the article to mark emphasis (Ps. 45:6, 7). **for ever . . . righteousness**—*Everlasting duration* and *righteousness* go together (Ps. 45:2; 89:14). **a sceptre of righteousness**—lit., "a rod of rectitude," or "straightforwardness." The oldest MSS. prefix "and" (cf. Esther 4:11). **9. iniquity**—"unrighteousness." Some oldest MSS. read, "lawlessness." **therefore**—because God loves righteousness and hates iniquity. **God . . . thy God**—JEROME, AUGUSTINE, and others translate Psalm 45:7, "O God, Thy God, hath anointed thee," whereby Christ is addressed as God. This is probably the true translation of the *Hebrew* there, and also of the *Greek* of Hebrews here; for it is likely the Son is addressed, "O God," as in vs. 8. The *anointing* here meant is not that at His baptism, when He solemnly entered on His ministry for us; but that with the "oil of gladness," or "exulting joy" (which denotes a *triumph*, and follows as the consequence of His manifested *love of righteousness* and *hatred of iniquity*), wherewith, after His triumphant completion of His work, He has been anointed by the Father above His fellows (not only above us, His fellow men, the adopted members of God's family. whom "He is not ashamed to call His brethren," but above the angels, fellow partakers in part with Him, though infinitely His inferiors, in the glories, holiness, and joys of heaven; "sons of God," and angel "messengers," though subordinate to the divine Angel—"Messenger of the covenant"). Thus He is antitype to Solomon, "chosen of all David's many sons to sit upon the throne of the kingdom of the Lord over Israel," even as His father David was chosen before all the house of his father's sons. The image is drawn from the custom of anointing guests at feasts (Ps. 23:5); or rather of anointing kings: not until His ascension did He assume *the kingdom* as Son of man. A fuller accomplishment is yet to be, when He shall be VISIBLY the anointed King over the whole earth (set by the Father) on His holy hill of Zion, Psalm 2:6, 8.
10. And—In another passage (Ps. 102:25-27) He says. **in the beginning**—*English Version*, Psalm 102:25, "of old": *Hebrew*, "before," "aforetime." LXX, "in the beginning" (as in Gen. 1:1) answers by contrast to *the end* implied in "They shall perish. . . ." The *Greek* order here (not in the LXX) is, "Thou in the beginning, O Lord," which throws the "Lord" into emphasis. "Christ is preached even in passages where many might contend that the Father was principally intended" [BENGEL]. **laid the foundation of**—"*firmly* founded" is included in the idea of the *Greek*. **heavens**—plural: not merely one, but manifold, and including various orders of heavenly intelligences (Eph. 4:10). **works of thine hands**—the heavens, as a woven veil or curtain spread out. **11. They**—The earth and the heavens in their present state and form "shall perish" (ch. 12:26, 27; II Pet. 3:13). "Perish" does not mean *annihilation;* just as it did not mean so in the case of "the world that being overflowed with water, *perished*" under Noah (II Pet. 3:6). The covenant of the possession of the earth was renewed

ADAM CLARKE

some suppose Ps. xcvii. 7: "Worship him, all ye gods"; which the Septuagint translates thus: "Worship him, all ye his angels." But it is not clear that the Messiah is intended in this psalm, nor are the words precisely those used here by the apostle. Our marginal references send us with great propriety to the Septuagint version of Deut. xxxii. 43, where the passage is found verbatim; but there is nothing answering to the words in the present Hebrew text. In Romans iii there is a large quotation from Psalms xiv, where there are six whole verses in the apostle's quotation which are not found in the present Hebrew text, but are preserved in the Septuagint! How strange it is that this venerable and important version, so often quoted by our Lord and all His apostles, should be so generally neglected, and so little known!

7. *Who maketh his angels spirits.* They are so far from being superior to Christ that they are not called God's sons in any peculiar sense, but His "servants," as tempests and lightenings are. It is very likely that the apostle refers here to the opinions of the Jews relative to the angels. In *Pirkey R. Elieser*, c. 4, it is said: "The angels which were created the second day, when they minister before God, become fire."

8. *Thy throne, O God, is for ever and ever.* If this be said of the Son of God, i.e., Jesus Christ, then Jesus Christ must be God; and indeed the design of the apostle is to prove this. The words here quoted are taken from Ps. xlv. 6-7, which the most intelligent rabbins refer to the Messiah. *A sceptre of righteousness.* The sceptre, which was a sort of staff or instrument of various forms, was the ensign of government, and is here used for government itself. This the ancient Jewish writers understand also of the Messiah.

9. *Thou hast loved righteousness.* This is the characteristic of a just governor: he abhors and suppresses iniquity; he countenances and supports righteousness and truth. *Therefore God, even thy God.* The original may be thus translated: "Therefore, O God, Thy God hath anointed Thee." The form of speech is nearly the same with that in the preceding verse. *With the oil of gladness.* We have often had occasion to remark that, anciently, kings, priests, and prophets were consecrated to their several offices by anointing; and that this signified the gifts and influences of the divine Spirit. Christ signifies "The Anointed One," the same as the Hebrew Messias, and He is here said to be anointed with the oil of gladness above His fellows. None was ever constituted prophet, priest, and king but himself. Thus He is infinitely exalted "beyond His fellows"—all that had ever borne the regal, prophetic, or sacerdotal offices. *Gladness* is used to express the festivities which took place on the inauguration of kings.

10. *And, Thou, Lord.* This is an address to the Son as the Creator, see v. 2; for this is implied in laying the foundation of the earth. The heavens, which are the work of His hands, point out His infinite wisdom and skill.

11. *They shall perish.* Permanently fixed as they seem to be, a time shall come when they shall be dissolved, and afterward new heavens and a new earth be formed, in which righteousness alone shall dwell. See 2 Pet. iii. 10-13.

MATTHEW HENRY

Not only men and beasts and trees grow old, but this world itself grows old, and is hastening to its dissolution; it changes like a garment, has lost much of its beauty and strength. It bears the symptoms of a dying world. But then its dissolution will not be its utter destruction, but its change. Christ will fold up this world as a garment not to be abused any longer. Sin has made a great change in the world for the worse, and Christ will make a great change in it for the better. *b* Christ is immutable. Thus the Father testifies of him, *Thou remainest, thy years shall not fail.* Christ is the same in himself, and the same to his people in all the changes of time. Christ is immutable and immortal: his years shall not fail. Christ lives to take care of us while we live, and of ours when we are gone.

III. The superiority of Christ to the angels appears in this that God never said to the angels what he has said to Christ, *v.* 13, 14.

1. What has God said to Christ? He has said, "*Sit thou at my right hand, till I make thy enemies thy footstool*, Ps. cx. 1. Christ Jesus has his enemies, enemies even among men. Let us not think it strange then if we have our enemies. Christ never did anything to make men his enemies; he has done a great deal to make them all his friends and his Father's friends, and yet he has his enemies. All the enemies of Christ shall be made his footstool. God the Father has undertaken for this, and, though it be not done presently, it shall certainly be done. Christ shall go on to rule and reign till this be done; he shall not leave any of his great designs unfinished. And it becomes his people to go on in their duty, till he make them conquerors over all their spiritual enemies.

2. What has God said to the angels? *They are ministering spirits, sent forth to minister for those who shall be the heirs of salvation.* (1) What the angels are as to their nature: they are spirits. (2) What the angels are as to their office: they are ministering spirits. They are the ministers of divine Providence. The angels are sent forth for this end—to minister to those who shall be the heirs of salvation. The description given of the saints—they are *heirs of salvation*; at present they are under age, heirs, not inheritors. They are heirs because they are children of God. The dignity and privilege of the saints—the angels are sent forth to minister for them. Bless God for the ministration of angels.

JAMIESON, FAUSSET, BROWN

with Noah and his seed on the renovated earth. So it shall be after the perishing by fire (II Pet. 3:12, 13). **remainest**—*through* (so the *Greek*) all changes. **as . . . a garment**—(Isa. 51:6). **12. vesture**—*Greek,* "an enwrapping cloak." **fold them up**—So the LXX, Psalm 102:26; but the *Hebrew,* "*change* them." The Spirit, by Paul, treats the *Hebrew* of the Old Testament, with independence of handling, presenting the divine truth in various aspects; sometimes as here sanctioning the LXX (cf. Isa. 34:4; Rev. 6:14); sometimes the *Hebrew;* sometimes varying from both. **changed**—as one lays aside a garment to put on another. **thou art the same**—(Isa. 46:4; Mal. 3:6). The same in nature, therefore in covenant faithfulness to Thy people. **shall not fail**—*Hebrew,* "shall not end." Israel, in the Babylonian captivity, in Psalm 102, casts her hopes of deliverance on Messiah, the unchanging covenant God of Israel. **13.** Quotation from Psalm 110:1. The image is taken from the custom of conquerors putting the feet on the necks of the conquered (Josh. 10:24, 25).

14. ministering spirits—referring to vs. 7, "spirits . . . ministers." They are incorporeal *spirits,* as God is, but *ministering* to Him as inferiors. **sent forth**—present participle: "being sent forth "*continually,* as their regular service in all ages. **to minister**—*Greek,* "unto (i.e., 'for') ministry." **for them**—*Greek,* "*on account of* the." Angels are sent forth on *ministrations to God and Christ,* not primarily to men, though *for the good* of "those who are about to inherit salvation" (so the *Greek*): the elect, who believe, or shall believe, for whom all things, angels included, work together for good (Rom. 8:28). Angels' ministrations are not properly rendered to men, since the latter have no power of commanding them, though their ministrations to God are often directed to the good of men. So the superiority of the Son of God to angels is shown. They "all," how ever various their ranks, "minister"; He is ministered to. They "*stand*" (Luke 1:19) before God, or are "*sent* forth" to execute the divine commands on behalf of them whom He pleases to save; He "*sits* on the right hand of the Majesty on high" (vss. 3, 13). He rules; they serve.

ADAM CLARKE

Shall wax old as doth a garment. As a garment by long using becomes unfit to be longer used, so shall all visible things; they shall wear old, and wear out, and hence the necessity of their being renewed. It is remarkable that our word "world" is a contraction of "wear old," a term by which our ancestors expressed the sentiment contained in this verse. That the word was thus compounded and that it had this sense in our language may be proved from the most competent and indisputable witnesses. It was formerly written "weorold."

12. *And they shall be changed.* Not destroyed ultimately or annihilated. They shall be changed and renewed. *But thou art the same.* These words can be said of no being but God; all others are changeable or perishable, because temporal; only that which is eternal can continue essentially and, speaking after the manner of men, formally the same. *Thy years shall not fail.* There is in the divine duration no circle to be run, no space to be measured, no time to be reckoned. All is eternity—infinite—and onward.

13. *But to which of the angels?* We have already seen, from the opinions and concessions of the Jews, that if Jesus Christ could be proved to be greater than the angels, it would necessarily follow that He was God: and this the apostle does most amply prove by these various quotations from their own Scriptures; for he shows that while He is the supreme and absolute Sovereign, they are no more than His messengers and servants.

14. *Are they not all ministering spirits?* That is, "They are *all ministering spirits*"; for the Hebrews often express the strongest affirmative by an interrogation.

MATTHEW HENRY — CHAPTER 2

Verses 1–4

He now comes to apply this doctrine both by way of exhortation and argument.

I. By way of exhortation, *v.* 1. It is the great concern of everyone under the gospel to give the most earnest heed to all gospel discoveries and directions. We must embrace them in our hearts and affections, retain them in our memories, and finally regulate our words and actions according to them.

II. He adds strong motives to enforce the exhortation.

1. From the great loss we shall sustain if we do not take this earnest heed to the things which we have heard: *We shall let them slip.* Our minds and memories are like a leaky vessel, they do not without much care retain what is poured into them. Those meet with an inconceivable loss who let gospel truths slip out of their minds. All is lost, if the gospel be lost. If we do not well attend, we shall not long retain the word of God; inattentive hearers will soon be forgetful hearers.

2. Another argument is taken from the dreadful punishment we shall incur if we do not do this duty, *v.* 2, 3. (1) How the law is described: it was the *word spoken by angels, and declared to be steadfast.* It is like the promise, *yea and amen*; it is truth and faithfulness, and it will abide and have its force whether men obey it or no; *for every transgression and disobedience will receive a just recompence of reward.* If men trifle with the law of God, the law will not trifle with them. Punishments are as just, and as much due to sin as rewards are to obedience. (2) How the gospel is described. It is salvation, a great salvation, so great that none can fully express, no, nor yet conceive, how great it is. It shows how we may be saved from so great sin and so great misery, and be restored to so great holiness and so great happiness. (3) How sinning against the gospel is described: it is declared to be a *neglect of this great salvation*; it is a contempt put upon the saving grace of God in Christ, making light of it, not caring for it. Let us all take heed that we be not found among those wicked wretched sinners who neglect the grace of the gospel. (4) How the misery of such sinners is described: it is declared to be unavoidable (*v.* 3): *How*

JAMIESON, FAUSSET, BROWN — CHAPTER 2

Vss. 1-18. Danger of Neglecting So Great Salvation, First Spoken by Christ; to Whom, Not to Angels, the New Dispensation Was Subjected; though He Was for a Time Humbled below the Angels: This Humiliation Took Place by Divine Necessity for Our Salvation. **1. Therefore**—Because Christ the Mediator of the new covenant is so far (ch. 1) above all angels, the mediators of the old covenant. **the more earnest**—*Greek,* "the more abundantly." **heard**—spoken by God (ch. 1:1); and by the Lord (vs. 3). **let them slip**—lit., "flow past them" (ch. 4:1). **2.** (Cf. vs. 3.) Argument a fortiori. **spoken by angels**—the Mosaic law spoken by the ministration of angels (Deut. 33:2; Ps. **68:17**; Acts 7:53; Gal. 3:19). When it is said, Exodus 20:1, "God spake," it is meant He spake by angels as His mouthpiece, or at least angels repeating in unison with His voice the words of the Decalogue; whereas the Gospel was first spoken by the Lord alone. **was steadfast**—*Greek,* "*was made* steadfast," or "confirmed": was enforced by penalties on those violating it. **transgression**—by doing evil; lit., *overstepping* its bounds: a positive violation of it. **disobedience**—by neglecting to do good: a negative violation of it. **recompense**—(Deut. 32:35). **3. we**—who have received the message of salvation so clearly delivered to us (cf. ch. 12:25). **so great salvation**—embodied in Jesus, whose very name means "salvation," including not only deliverance from foes and from death, and the grant of temporal blessings (which the law promised to the obedient), but also grace of the Spirit, forgiveness of sins, and the promise of heaven, glory, and eternal life (vs. 10). **which**—"*inasmuch as it is a* salvation *which* began. . . ." **spoken by the Lord**—as the instrument of proclaiming it. Not as the law, spoken by the instrumentality of angels (vs. 2). Both law and Gospel came from God; the difference here referred to lay in *the instrumentality* by which each respectively was promulgated (cf. vs. 5). Angels recognize Him as "the Lord" (Matt. 28:6; Luke 2:11). **confirmed unto us**—not by penalties, as the law was *confirmed,* but by spiritual gifts (vs. 4). **by them that heard** *him*—(Cf. Luke 1: 2).

ADAM CLARKE — CHAPTER 2

1. *Therefore.* Because God has spoken to us by His Son, and because that Son is so great and glorious a Personage, and because the subject which is addressed to us is of such infinite importance to our welfare. *We ought to give the more earnest heed.* We should hear the doctrine of Christ with care, candor, and deep concern. *Lest at any time we should let them slip.* "Lest at any time we should leak out." Superficial hearers lose the benefit of the word preached as the unseasoned vessel does its fluid; nor can anyone hear to the saving of his soul unless he give "most earnest heed."

2. *If the word spoken by angels.* The law (according to some), which was delivered by the mediation of angels, God frequently employing these to communicate His will to men. See Acts vii. 53 and Gal. iii. 19. But the apostle probably means those particular messages which God sent by angels, as in the case of Lot, Gen. xix, and suchlike. *Was stedfast.* Was so confirmed by the divine authority and so strict that it would not tolerate any offense, but inflicted punishment on *every* act of *transgression,* every case in which the bounds laid down by the law were "passed over," and every act of *disobedience* in respect to the duties enjoined. *Received a just recompence.* That kind and degree of punishment which the law prescribed for those who broke it.

3. *How shall we escape?* If they who had fewer privileges than we have, to whom God spoke in divers manners by angels and prophets, fell under the displeasure of their Maker and were often punished with a sore destruction, *how shall we escape* wrath to the uttermost if we neglect the salvation provided for us and proclaimed to us by the Son of God? Those who *neglect* it are not only they who oppose or persecute it, but they who pay no regard to it. *Which at the first began to be spoken.* Though John the Baptist went before our Lord to prepare His way, yet he could not be properly said to preach

MATTHEW HENRY

shall we escape? The despoilers of this salvation are condemned already, under arrest and in the hands of justice already. There is no escaping out of this condemned state, but by accepting the great salvation discovered in the gospel; as for those who neglect it, the wrath of God is upon them, and it abides upon them. There is no door of mercy left open for them; there will be no more sacrifice for sin.

3. Another argument to enforce the exhortation is taken from the person by whom the gospel began to be spoken (*v.* 3): that is, the Lord Jesus Christ. Now surely it may be expected that all will reverence this Lord, and take heed to a gospel that began to be spoken by one who spoke so as never *man spoke.*

4. Another argument is taken from the character of those who were witnesses to Christ and the gospel (*v.* 3, 4). (1) The promulgation of the gospel was continued and confirmed by the evangelists and apostles, who were eye and ear-witnesses of what Jesus Christ began both to do and to teach, Acts i. 1. These witnesses could have no worldly end to serve hereby. They exposed themselves by their testimony to the loss of all that was dear to them in this life, and many of them sealed it with their blood. (2) *God himself bore witness* to those who were witnesses for Christ. He bore them witness *by signs, and wonders, and divers miracles, and gifts of the Holy Ghost, according to his will.* It was the will of God that we should have sure footing for our faith, and a strong foundation for our hope in receiving the gospel. As at the giving forth of the law there were signs and wonders, so he witnesses to the gospel by more and greater miracles, as to a more excellent and abiding dispensation.

Verses 5–9

For to the angels hath he not put in subjection the world to come, whereof we speak.

I. Here the apostle lays down a negative proposition, including a positive one—That the state of the gospel-church, which is here called *the world to come,* is *not subjected to the angels.* This new world is committed to Christ, and put in absolute subjection to him only. His angels were too weak for such a charge.

II. A scripture-account of that blessed Jesus. It is taken from Ps. viii. 4–6. These words are to be considered both as applicable to mankind in general, and as applied here to the Lord Jesus Christ.

1. As applicable to mankind in general, an affectionate thankful expostulation with the great God concerning his kindness to the sons of men. (1) In remembering them, or being mindful of them. God is always mindful of us, let us never be forgetful of him. (2) In visiting them. He comes to see us, how it is with us; and by his visitation our spirit is preserved. (3) In making man the head of all the creatures in this lower world. (4) In crowning him with glory and honour, the honour of having noble powers and faculties. (5) In giving him dominion over the inferior creatures.

JAMIESON, FAUSSET, BROWN

4. them—rather, "God also [as well as Christ, vs. 3] bearing witness to *it*" . . . "joining in attestation of it." **signs and wonders**—performed by Christ and His apostles. "Signs" and miracles, or other facts regarded as *proofs* of a divine mission; "wonders" are miracles viewed as prodigies, causing *astonishment* (Acts 2:22, 33); "powers" are miracles viewed as evidences of superhuman *power.* **divers miracles**—*Greek,* "varied (miraculous) *powers*" (II Cor. 12:12) granted to the apostles after the ascension. **gifts . . .**—*Greek,* "distributions." The gift of the Holy Spirit was given to Christ without measure (John 3:34), but to us it is distributed in various measures and operations (Rom. 12:3, 6, etc.; I Cor. 12:4-11). **according to his own will**—God's free and sovereign will, assigning one gift of the Spirit to one, another to another (Acts 5:32; Eph. 1:5). **5. For**—confirming the assertion, vss. 2, 3, that the new covenant was spoken by One higher than the mediators of the old covenant, viz., angels. Translate in the *Greek* order, to bring out the proper emphasis, "Not the angels hath He. . . . **the world to come**—implying, He *has* subjected to angels *the existing world,* the Old Testament dispensation (then still partly existing as to its framework), vs. 2, the political kingdom of the earth (Dan. 4:13; 10:13, 20, 21; 12:1), and the natural elements (Rev. 9:11; 16:4), and even individuals (Matt. 18:10). "The world to come" is the new dispensation brought in by Christ, beginning in grace here, to be completed in glory hereafter. It is called "to come," or "about to be," as at the time of its being subjected to Christ by the divine decree, it was as yet a thing of the future, and is still so to us, in respect to its full consummation. In respect to the *subjecting* of all things to Christ in fulfilment of Psalm 8, the realization is still "to come." Regarded from the Old Testament standpoint, which looks prophetically forward to the New Testament (and the Jewish priesthood and Old Testament ritual were in force then when Paul wrote, and continued till their forcible abrogation by the destruction of Jerusalem), it is "the world to come"; Paul, as addressing Jews, appropriately calls it so, according to their conventional way of viewing it. We, like them, still pray, "Thy kingdom come"; for its *manifestation* in glory is yet future. "This world" is used in contrast to express the present fallen condition of the world (Eph. 2:2). Believers belong not to this present world-course, but by faith rise in spirit to "the world to come," making it a present, though internal, reality. **6. But**—It is not to angels the Gospel kingdom is subject, BUT. . . . **one. . . testified**—the usual way of quoting Scripture to readers familiar with it. Psalm 8:5-7 praises Jehovah for exalting MAN, so as to subject all the works of God on earth to him: this dignity having been lost by the first Adam, is realized only in Christ the Son of **man, the Representative Man** and Head of our redeemed race. Thus Paul proves that it is to MAN, not to *angels,* that God has subjected the "world to come." In vss. 6-8, MAN is spoken of *in general* ("him . . . him . . . his"); then at vs. 9, first JESUS is introduced as fulfilling, as man, all the conditions of the prophecy, and passing through death Himself; and so consequently bringing us men, His "brethren," to "glory and honor." **What . . .**—How insignificant in himself, yet how exalted by God's grace! (Cf. Ps. 144:3). The *Hebrew, Enosh* and *Ben-Adam,* express "man" and "Son of man" in his weakness: "Son of man" is here used of *any* and *every child of man:* unlike, seemingly, the lord of creation, such as he was originally (Gen. 1 and 2), and such as he is designed to be (Ps. 8), and such as he actually is by title and shall hereafter more fully be in the person of, and in union with, Jesus, pre-eminently the Son of man (vs. 9). **art mindful**—as of one absent. **visitest**—*lookest after* him, as one present. **7. a little**—not as BENGEL, "a little *time.*" **than the angels**—*Hebrew,* "than God," *Elohim,* i.e., the abstract qualities of God, such as *angels* possess in an inferior form; viz., heavenly, spiritual, incorporeal natures. Man, in his original creation, was set next beneath them. So the man Jesus, though Lord of angels, when He emptied Himself of the externals of His Divinity (*Note,* Phil. 2:6, 7), was in His human nature "a little lower than the angels"; though this is not the primary reference here, but *man* in general. **crownedst him with glory and honour**—as the appointed kingly vicegerent of God over this earth (Gen. 1 and 2). **and didst set him over the works of thy hands**—omitted in some of the oldest MSS.; but read by others and by oldest versions: so Psalm 8:6, "Thou madest him to have dominion over the works of thy hands." **8.** (I Cor. 15:27.) **For in that**—i.e., "For in that" *God saith in the* 8*th Psalm,* "He put *the* all

ADAM CLARKE

the gospel; and even Christ's preaching was only a beginning of the great proclamation. It was His own Spirit in the apostles and evangelists, the men who heard Him preach, that opened the whole mystery of the kingdom of Heaven.

4. *God also bearing them witness.* He did not leave the confirmation of these great truths to the testimony of men; He bore His own testimony to them by *signs, wonders,* various *miracles,* and "distributions *of the Holy Ghost.*" And all these were proved to come from himself; for no man could do those miracles at his own pleasure, but the power to work them was given according to God's *own will;* or rather, God himself wrought them, in order to accredit the ministry of His servants.

5. *The world to come.* That *the world to come* meant the "days of the Messiah" among the Jews is most evident, and has been often pointed out in the course of these notes.

6. *But one in a certain place.* This *one* is David; and the *certain place,* Ps. viii. 4-6. But why does the apostle use this indeterminate mode of quotation? Because it was common thus to express the testimony of any of the inspired writers. So Philo. Thus even the heathens were accustomed to quote high authorities; so Plato. The mode of quotation therefore implies, not ignorance, but reverence. *What is man?* This quotation is verbatim from the Septuagint; the Greek is not so emphatic as the Hebrew: "What is miserable man, that thou rememberest him? and the son of Adam, that thou visitest him?"

7. *Thou madest him a little lower than the angels.* If this be spoken of man as he came out of the hands of his Maker, it places him at the head of all God's works; for literally translated it is: "Thou hast made him less than God." And this is proved by his being made in the image and likeness of God, which is spoken of no other creature either in heaven or on earth. If we take the words as referring to Jesus Christ, then they must be understood as pointing out the time of His humiliation, as in v. 9; and the *little lower* in both verses must mean "for a short time" or "a little while." And indeed the whole of the passage suits Him better than it does any of the children of men; for it is only under the feet of Jesus that all things are put in subjection, and it was in consequence of His humiliation that He had "a name . . . above every name: that at the name of Jesus every knee should bow, of things in heaven, and things in earth, and things under the earth," Phil. ii. 9-11. *Thou crownedst him with glory and honour.* This was strictly true of Adam in his state of innocence, for he was set over all things in this lower world; "all sheep and oxen . . . the beasts of the field; the fowl of the air, and the fish of the sea, and whatsoever passeth through the paths of the seas," Ps. viii. 7-8. So far all this perfectly applies to Adam; but it is evident the apostle takes *all* in a much higher sense, that of universal dominion; and hence he says, He "left nothing that is not put under him." These verses, collated with the above passage from the Epistle to the Philippians, mutually illustrate each other. And the crowning Christ with glory and honor must refer to His exaltation after His resurrection, in which, as the victorious Messiah, He had all power given to Him in heaven and earth. And although we do not yet see all things put under Him, for evil men and evil spirits are only under the subjection of control, yet we look forward to that time when the whole world shall be bowed to His sway, and when the stone cut out of the mountain without hands shall become great and fill the whole earth.

MATTHEW HENRY

2. As applied to the Lord Jesus Christ, *v.* 8, 9. The moving cause of all the kindness God shows to men is the grace of God. The fruits of this free grace of God is that God crowned the human nature of Christ with glory and honour, in his being perfectly holy; that by his sufferings he might make satisfaction, tasting death for every man. As a reward of his humiliation in suffering death, he was crowned with glory and honour.

Verses 10–13

The apostle here proceeds to remove the scandal of the cross.

I. It became God that Christ should suffer, *v.* 10.

1. God is described as the final end and first cause of all things, and as such it became him to secure his own glory in all that he did.

2. He is declared to have acted up to this glorious character in the work of redemption.

(1) In the choice of the end; and that was to bring many sons to glory. We must be the sons of God both by adoption and regeneration, before we can be brought to the glory of heaven. Though the sons of God are but a few in one place and at one time, yet when they shall be all brought together it will appear that they are many.

(2) In the choice of the means. In finding out such a person as should be the captain of our salvation. In making this captain of our salvation perfect through sufferings. He perfected the work of our redemption by shedding his blood. He found his way to the crown by the cross, and so must his people too.

II. How much they should be benefited by the cross and sufferings of Christ. Hereby they are brought into a near union with Christ, and into a very endearing relation.

1. Into a near union (*v.* 11). Christ, who is the

JAMIESON, FAUSSET, BROWN

things (so the *Greek, the* all things just mentioned) in subjection under him (man), He left nothing. . . . As no limitation occurs in the sacred writing, the "all things" must include heavenly, as well as earthly things (cf. I Cor. 3:21, 22). **But now**—As things now are, we see not yet *the* all things put under man. **9. But**—We see not *man* as yet exercising lordship over all things, "*but rather,* Him who was made a little lower than the angels (cf. Luke 22:43), we behold (*by faith:* a different *Greek* verb from that for 'we *see,*' vs. 8, which expresses the impression which our eyes *passively* receive from objects around us; whereas, 'we behold,' or 'look at,' implies the *direction* and *intention* of one *deliberately* regarding something which he tries to see: so ch. 3:19; 10:25, *Greek*), viz., Jesus, on account of His suffering of death, crowned. . . ." He is already crowned, though unseen by us, save by faith; hereafter all things shall be subjected to Him visibly and fully. The ground of His exaltation is "on account of His having suffered death" (vs. 10; Phil. 2:8, 9). **that he by the grace of God**—(Titus 2:11; 3:4). The reading of ORIGEN, "That He *without God*" (*laying aside His Divinity;* or, for every being *save God;* or perhaps alluding to His having been temporarily "forsaken," as the Sin-bearer, by the Father on the cross), is not supported by the MSS. The "that . . ." is connected with "crowned with glory . . ." thus: His exaltation after sufferings is the *perfecting* or consummation of His work (vs. 10) for us: without it His death would have been ineffectual; with it, and from it, flows the result *that His tasting of death is available for* (in behalf of, for the good of) *every man.* He is crowned as the Head in heaven of our common humanity, presenting His blood as the all-prevailing plea for us. This coronation above makes His death applicable for *every* individual *man* (observe the singular; not merely "for all men"), ch. 4:14; 9:24; I John 2:2. "Taste death," implies His personal experimental undergoing of death: death of the body, and death (spiritually) of the soul, in His being forsaken of the Father. **10. For**—giving a reason why "the grace of God" required that Jesus "should taste death." **it became him**—The whole plan was [not only not derogatory to, but] highly *becoming* God, though unbelief considers it a *disgrace* [BENGEL]. An answer to the Jews, and Hebrew Christians, whosoever, through impatience at the delay in the promised advent of Christ's glory, were in danger of apostasy, stumbling at Christ *crucified.* The Jerusalem Christians especially were liable to this danger. This scheme of redemption was altogether such a one as harmonizes with the love, justice, and wisdom of God. **for whom**—God the Father (Rom. 11:36; I Cor. 8:6; Rev. 4:11). In Colossians 1:16 the same is said of Christ. **all things**—*Greek,* "*the* universe of things," "*the* all things." He uses for "God," the periphrasis, "Him for whom . . . by whom are all things," to mark the becomingness of Christ's suffering as the way to His being "perfected" as "Captain of our salvation," seeing that His is the way that pleased Him whose will and whose glory are *the end* of all things, and by whose *operation* all things exist. **in bringing**—The *Greek* is past, "having brought as He did," viz., *in His electing purpose* (cf. "ye *are* sons," viz., in His purpose, Gal. 4:6; Eph. 1:4), a purpose which is accomplished in Jesus being "perfected through sufferings." **many**—(Matt. 20:28)." The Church" (vs. 12), "the general assembly" (ch. 12:23). **sons**—no longer *children* as under the Old Testament law, but *sons* by adoption. **unto glory**—to share Christ's "glory" (vs. 9; cf. 7; John 17:10, 22, 24; Rom. 8:21). Sonship, holiness (vs. 11), and glory, are inseparably joined. "Suffering," "salvation," and "glory," in Paul's writings, often go together (II Tim. 2:10). *Salvation* presupposes *destruction,* deliverance from which for us required Christ's "sufferings." **to make . . . perfect**—"to consummate"; to bring to consummated glory through sufferings, as the appointed avenue to it. "He who suffers for another, not only benefits him, but becomes himself the brighter and more perfect" [CHRYSOSTOM]. Bringing to the end of troubles, and to the *goal* full of glory: a metaphor from the contests in the public games. **captain of . . .**—lit., *Prince-leader:* as Joshua, not Moses, led the people into the Holy Land, so will our Joshua, or Jesus, lead us into the heavenly inheritance (Acts 13:39). The same *Greek* is in ch. 12:2, "*Author* of our faith." Acts 3:15, "*Prince* of life" (5:31). Preceding others by His example, as well as the originator of our salvation. **11. he that sanctifieth**—Christ who once for all consecrates His people to God (Jude 1, bringing them nigh to Him as the consequence) and everlasting glory, by having

ADAM CLARKE

9. ***Should taste death for every man.*** **It was a custom in ancient times to take off criminals by making them drink a cup of poison. Socrates was adjudged to drink a cup of the juice of hemlock by order of the Athenian magistrates. The reference in the text seems to point out the whole human race as being accused, tried, found guilty, and condemned, each having his own poisoned cup to drink; and Jesus, the wonderful Jesus, takes the cup out of the hand of each, and cheerfully and with alacrity drinks off the dregs! Thus having drunk every man's poisoned cup, He tasted that death which they must have endured had not their cup been drunk by Another. Is not this the cup to which He refers, Matt. xxvi. 39: "O my Father, if it be possible, let this cup pass from me"? But without His drinking it, the salvation of the world would have been impossible; and therefore He cheerfully drank it in the place of every human soul and thus made atonement for the sin of the whole world; and this He did by the grace, mercy, or infinite goodness of God.**

10. ***For it became him.*** **It was suitable to the divine wisdom, the requisitions of justice, and the economy of grace to offer Jesus as a Sacrifice, in order to bring** ***many sons*** **and daughters to** ***glory. For whom . . . and by whom.*** **God is the Cause of all things, and He is the Object or End of them.**

Perfect through sufferings. **Without suffering He could not have died, and without dying He could not have made an atonement for sin. The sacrifice must be "consummated," in order that He might be qualified to be the** ***captain*** **or Author of the salvation of men, and lead all those who become children of God, through faith in Him, into eternal glory. I believe this to be the sense of the passage; and it appears to be an answer to the grand objection of the Jews: "The Messiah is never to be conquered, or die; but will be victorious, and endure forever."**

11. ***For both he that sanctifieth.*** **The word does not merely signify one who sanctifies or makes holy, but one who makes atonement or reconciliation to God; and answers to the He-**

MATTHEW HENRY

agent in this work of sanctification, and Christians, are all of one. They are all of one heavenly Father. They are of one earthly father, Adam. Christ and believers have the same human nature. They are of one spirit, the same mind is in them that was in Christ.

2. Into an endearing relation.

(1) He declares what this relation is: he is not ashamed to call them *brethren.* Christ and believers are brethren in what is heavenly as well as in what is earthly. He will never be ashamed of any who are not ashamed of him, and who take care not to be a shame and reproach to him and to themselves.

(2) He illustrates this from three texts of scripture.

[1] The first is out of Ps. xxii. 22. Christ should have a church or *congregation* in the world, a company of volunteers, freely willing to follow him. These should not only be brethren to one another, but to Christ himself. He would declare his Father's name to them.

[2] The second scripture is quoted from Ps. xviii. 2. His brethren must suffer and trust too.

[3] The third scripture is taken from Isa. viii. 18. Christ's children were given him of the Father. And they are given to Christ at their conversion. Christ receives them, rejoices in them, takes them up to heaven, and there presents them to his Father.

Verses 14-18

The reasons and designs of the incarnation of Christ are declared.

1. For no higher nor lower nature than man's that had sinned could so suffer for the sin of man as to satisfy the justice of God, and raise man up to a state of hope.

JAMIESON, FAUSSET, BROWN

consecrated Himself for them in His being made "perfect (as their expiatory sacrifice) through sufferings" (vs. 10; ch. 10:10, 14, 29; John 17:17, 19). **they who are sanctified**—*Greek,* "they that are being sanctified" (cf. the use of "sanctified," I Cor. 7:14). **of one**—Father, God: not in the sense wherein He is Father of *all* beings, as angels; for these are excluded by the argument (vs. 16); but as He is Father of His *spiritual human* sons, Christ the Head and elder Brother, and His believing people, the members of the body and family. Thus, this and the following verses are meant to justify his having said, "many *sons*" (vs. 10). **he is not ashamed**—though being the Son *of God,* since they have now by adoption obtained a like dignity, so that His majesty is not compromised by brotherhood with them (cf. ch. 11:16). It is a striking feature in Christianity that it unites such amazing contrasts as "our brother and our God" [THOLUCK]. "God makes of sons of men sons of God, because God hath made of the Son of God the Son of man" [ST. AUGUSTINE on Psalm 2]. **12.** (Psalm 22:22). Messiah declares the name of the Father, not known fully as Christ's Father, and therefore *their* Father, till after His crucifixion (John 20:17), among His brethren ("the Church," i.e., the congregation), that they in turn may praise Him (Ps. 22:23). At vs. 22, the 22d Psalm, which begins with Christ's cry, "My God, my God, why hast thou forsaken me?" and details minutely His sorrows, passes from Christ's sufferings to His triumph, prefigured by the same in the experience of David. **will I sing**—as leader of the choir (Ps. 8:2). **13. I will put my trust in him**—from the LXX, Isaiah 8:17, which immediately precedes the next quotation, "Behold, I and the children. . . ." The only objection is the following words, "and again," usually introduce a *new* quotation, whereas these two are parts of one and the same passage. However, this objection is not valid, as the two clauses express distinct ideas; "I will put my trust in Him" expresses His *filial* confidence in God as His Father, to whom He flees from His sufferings, and is not disappointed; which His believing brethren imitate, *trusting* solely in the Father through Christ, and not in their own merits. **Behold I and the children . . .**—(Isa. 8:18). "Sons" (vs. 10), "brethren" (vs. 12), and "children," imply His right and property in them from everlasting. He speaks of them as "children" of God, though not yet in being, yet considered as such in His *purpose,* and presents them before God the Father, who has given Him them, to be glorified with Himself. Isaiah (meaning "salvation of Jehovah") typically represented Messiah, who is at once Father and Son, Isaiah and Immanuel (Isa. 9:6). He expresses his resolve to rely, he and his children, not like Ahaz and the Jews on the Assyrian king, against the confederacy of Pekah of Israel, and Rezin of Syria, but on Jehovah; and then foretells the deliverance of Judah by God, in language which finds its antitypical full realization only in the far greater deliverance wrought by Messiah. Christ, the antitypical Prophet, similarly, instead of the human confidences of His age, Himself, and with Him GOD THE FATHER'S *children* (who are therefore *His* children, and so antitypical to *Isaiah's* children, though here regarded as His "brethren," cf. Isaiah 9:6; "Father" and "His *seed,*" 53:10) led by Him, trust wholly in God for salvation.

14. He who has thus been shown to be the "Captain (*Greek,* 'Leader') of salvation" to the "many sons," by *trusting* and *suffering* like them, must therefore become *man* like them, in order that His death may be efficacious for them [ALFORD]. **the children**—before mentioned (vs. 13); those existing in His eternal purpose, though not in actual being. **are partakers of**—lit., "have [in His purpose] been partakers" all in common. **flesh and blood**—*Greek* oldest MSS. have "blood and flesh." The inner and more important element, the *blood,* as the more immediate vehicle of the soul, stands before the more palpable element, the flesh; also, with reference to *Christ's blood-shedding* with a view to which He entered into community with our *corporeal* life. "The life of the *flesh* is in the *blood;* it is the blood that maketh an atonement for the soul" (Lev. 17:11, 14). **also**—*Greek,* "in a *somewhat* similar manner"; not *altogether* in a like manner. For He, unlike them, was conceived and born not in sin (ch. 4:15). But mainly "in like manner"; not in mere *semblance* of a body, as the Docetæ heretics taught. **took part of**—participated in. The forfeited inheritance (according to Jewish law) was ransomed by the nearest of kin; so Jesus became our nearest of kin by His assumed humanity, in order to be our Redeemer. **that through**

ADAM CLARKE

brew *caphar,* "to expiate." See Exod. xxix. 33-36. He that sanctifies is He that makes atonement and they who are sanctified are they who receive that atonement and, being reconciled unto God, become His children by adoption, through grace. In this sense our Lord uses the word, John xvii. 19: "For their sakes I sanctify myself"; on their account I consecrate myself to be a sacrifice. This is the sense in which this word is used generally through this Epistle. *Are all of one.* What this *one* means has given rise to various conjectures. Father, family, blood, seed, race, nature have all been substituted. Nature seems to be that intended (see v. 14), and the conclusion of this verse confirms it. Both the Sanctifier and the sanctified, both Christ and His followers, are all of the same nature; for as the children were partakers of flesh and blood, i.e., of human nature, He partook of the same, and thus He was qualified to become a Sacrifice for man. *He is not ashamed to call them brethren.* Though, as to His Godhead, He is infinitely raised above men and angels, yet as He has become incarnate, notwithstanding His dignity, He blushes not to acknowledge all His true followers as His brethren.

12. *I will declare thy name.* See Ps. xxii. 22. The apostle certainly quotes this psalm as referring to Jesus Christ, and these words as spoken by Christ unto the Father, in reference to His incarnation; as if He had said: "When I shall be incarnated, I will declare Thy perfections to mankind; and among My disciples I will give glory to Thee for Thy mercy to the children of men." See the fulfillment of this, John i. 18: "No man hath seen God at any time; the only begotten Son, which is in the bosom of the Father, he hath declared him." Nor were the perfections of God ever properly known or declared till the manifestation of Christ.

13. *I will put my trust in him.* It is not clear to what express place of Scripture the apostle refers. Words to this effect frequently occur; but the place most probably is Ps. xviii. 2, several parts of which psalm seem to belong to the Messiah. *Behold I and the children which God hath given me.* This is taken from Isa. viii. 18. The apostle does not intend to say that the portions which he has quoted have any particular reference, taken by themselves, to the subject in question. They are only catchwords of whole paragraphs, which, taken together, are full to the point; because they are prophecies of the Messiah, and are fulfilled in Him. This is evident from the last quotation: "Behold, I and the children whom the Lord hath given me are for signs and for wonders in Israel." Jesus and His disciples wrought a multitude of the most stupendous signs and wonders in Israel. The expression also may include all genuine Christians; they are for signs and wonders throughout the earth. And as to the eighteenth psalm, the principal part of it seems to refer to Christ's sufferings; but the miracles which were wrought at His crucifixion, the destruction of the Jewish state and polity, the calling of the Gentiles, and the establishment of the Christian Church appear also to be intended.

14. *The children are partakers of flesh and blood.* Since those children of God who have fallen and are to be redeemed are human beings, in order to be qualified to redeem them by suffering and dying in their stead, *He also himself likewise took part of the same*—He became incarnate. By *the children* here we are to understand, not only the disciples and all genuine Christians, as in v. 13, but also the whole human race, all Jews and all Gentiles.

MATTHEW HENRY

2. He became man that he might die. The legal sacrifices and offerings God could not accept as a propitiation. A body was prepared for Christ.
3. The devil was the first sinner, and the first tempter to sin, and sin was the procuring cause of death. He draws men into sin, the ways whereof are death. In these respects he may be said to have had the power of death. But now Christ has so far destroyed him who had the power of death that he can keep none under the power of spiritual death; nor can he draw any into sin.

4. That he might deliver his own people from the slavish fear of death to which they are often subject, Christ became man, and died, to deliver them from perplexities of soul, by letting them know that death is not only a conquered enemy, but a reconciled friend. Death is not now in the hand of Satan, but in the hand of Christ.

The incarnation of Christ is asserted (*v.* 16). He took our nature into union with his divine nature, and became really and truly man. He did not lay hold of angels, but he laid hold of the seed of Abraham. The nature of angels could not be an atoning sacrifice for the sin of man. He took upon him the human nature from one descended from the loins of Abraham, that the same nature that had sinned might suffer. Now there is hope and help for the chief of sinners in and through Christ.

ALEXANDER MACLAREN:

Now, if the likeness here be the possession of true manhood, then my text is mere tautology, and it would simply be saying, "He became a man, wherefore it behooved him to become a man." The same conclusion is to be deduced from the last words of our chapter, where the fact of His suffering and being tempted are stated as His preparation to help and as His qualification as a merciful and faithful High Priest. That is to say, the "all things" of which our Lord became partaker like us His brethren are here the whole mass—in all its variety of pressure and diversity of nauseousness and bitterness—the whole mass of human sorrow which has ever made men's hearts bleed and men's eyes weep. Christ, in His single manhood, says the writer, gathered unto himself every form of pain, of misery, of weariness, of burden, which can weigh upon and wear out a human spirit; and no single ingredient that ever made any man's cup distasteful was left out, in that dreadful draught which He emptied to the dregs ere He passed the chalice to our lips, saying, "Drink ye all of it."

This is the great lesson and blessed thought of our text that no suffering soul, no harassed heart, no lonely life, has ever been able to say, "Ah! I have to bear this by myself, for Jesus Christ never knew anything like this." All the pain and sorrow of adverse circumstances that try some of us, He knows who had "not where to lay his head"; who was a poor man all His days, to whom the women had to minister of their charity, and who depended upon others for His sustenance in life. The sorrows that belong to a physical frame overwrought and crushed by excessive toil; the sorrows of weakness, of sickness, the pains of death—He understands them all.

—*Expositions of Holy Scripture*

JAMIESON, FAUSSET, BROWN

death—which He could not have undergone as God but only by becoming man. Not by Almighty power but *"by His death"* (so the *Greek*) He overcame death. **destroy**—lit., "render powerless"; deprive of all power to hurt His people. "That thou mighest still the enemy and avenger" (Psalm 8:2). The same *Greek* verb is used in II Timothy 1:10, "abolished death." **power**—Satan is "strong" (Matt. 12: 29). **of death**—implying that *death* itself is a *power* which, though originally foreign to human nature, now reigns over it (Rom. 5:12; 6:9). The power which death has Satan wields. The author of sin is the author of its consequences. Cf. "power of the enemy" (Luke 10:19). Satan has acquired over man (by God's law, Gen. 2:17; Rom. 6:23) the power of death by man's sin, death being the executioner of sin, and man being Satan's *"lawful* captive." **15. fear of death**—even before they had experienced its actual *power*. **all their lifetime**—Such a life can hardly be called life. **subject to bondage**—lit., "subjects *of* bondage"; not merely *liable to* it, but *enthralled in* it (cf. Rom. 8:15; Gal. 5:1). Contrast with this *bondage,* the *glory* of the "sons" (vs. 10). **"Bondage"** is defined by Aristotle, "The living not as one chooses"; "liberty," "the living as one chooses." Christ by delivering us from the curse of God against our sin, has taken from death all that made it formidable. Death, viewed apart from Christ, can only fill with horror, if the sinner dares to think. **16. For verily**—*Greek, "For as we all know"*; "For as you will doubtless grant." Paul probably alludes to Isaiah 41:8 Jeremiah 31:32, LXX, from which all *Jews* would know well that the prophets had led them to expect. **took not on him . . .**—rather, "It is not angels that He *is helping* (the present implies *duration*); but it is the seed of Abraham that He is *helping."* The verb is lit., *to help by taking one by the hand,* as in ch. 8:9, "When I took them by the hand. . . ." Thus it answers to "succor," vs. 18, and "deliver," vs. 15. "Not angels," who have no flesh and blood, but "the children," who have "flesh and blood," He takes hold of to help by "Himself taking part of the same" (vs. 14). **seed of Abraham**—He views Christ's redemption (in compliment to the Hebrews whom he is addressing, and as enough for his present purpose) with reference to Abraham's seed, *the Jewish nation,* primarily; not that he excludes the Gentiles (vs. 9, "for every man"), who, when believers, are the seed of Abraham spiritually (cf. vs. 12; Ps. 22:22, 25, 27), but direct reference to them (such as is in Rom. 4:11, 12, 16; Gal. 3:7, 14, 28, 29) would be out of place in his present argument. **17. Wherefore**—*Greek,* "Whence." Found in *Paul's* speech, Acts 26:19. **in all things**—which are incidental to manhood, the being born, nourished, growing up, suffering. *Sin* is not, in the original constitution of man, a necessary attendant of manhood, so He had no sin. **it behooved him**—by moral necessity, considering what the justice and love of God required of Him as Mediator (cf. ch. 5:3), the office which He had voluntarily undertaken in order to "help" man (vs. 16). **his brethren**—(vs. 11)—"the seed of Abraham" (vs. 16), and so also the spiritual seed, His elect out of all mankind. **be . . .**—rather as *Greek,* "that He might *become* High Priest"; He was *called* so, when He was "made perfect by the things which He suffered" (vs. 10; ch. 5:8-10). He was actually *made* so, when He entered within the veil, from which last flows His ever continuing intercession as Priest for us. The death, as man, must first be, in order that the bringing in of the blood into the heavenly Holy Place might follow, in which consisted the expiation as High Priest. **merciful**—to "the *people"* deserving wrath by "sins." *Mercy* is a prime requisite in a priest, since his office is to help the wretched and raise the fallen: such *mercy* is most likely to be found in one who has a fellowfeeling with the afflicted, having been so once Himself (ch. 4:15); not that the Son of God needed to be taught by suffering to be merciful, but that in order to save us He needed to take our manhood with all its sorrows, thereby qualifying Himself, by experimental suffering with us, to be our sympathizing High Priest, and assuring us of His entire fellow-feeling with us in every sorrow. So in the main CALVIN remarks here. **faithful**—true to God (ch. 3:5, 6) and to man (ch. 10:23) in the mediatorial office which He has undertaken. **high priest**—which Moses was not, though "faithful" (ch. 2). Nowhere, except in Psalm 110, Zechariah 6:13, and in this Epistle, is Christ expressly called a *priest.* In this Epistle alone His priesthood is professedly discussed; whence it is evident how necessary is this book of

ADAM CLARKE

That through death. That by the merit of His own death, making atonement for sin, and procuring the almighty energy of the Holy Spirit, He might "counterwork" or "render useless and ineffectual" all the operations of him who had the *power* or "influence" to bring death into the world; so that *death,* which was intended by him who was a murderer from the beginning to be the final ruin of mankind, becomes the instrument of their exaltation and endless glory; and thus the death brought in by Satan is counterworked and rendered ineffectual by the death of Christ. *Him that had the power of death.* This is spoken in conformity to an opinion prevalent among the Jews that there was a certain fallen angel who was called the "angel of death."

15. *And deliver them who through fear of death.* It is very likely that the apostle has the Gentiles here principally in view. As they had no revelation and no certainty of immortality, they were continually in bondage to the fear of death.

16. *For verily he took not on him the nature of angels.* "Moreover, He doth not at all take hold of angels; but of the seed of Abraham He taketh hold." This is the marginal reading and is greatly to be preferred to that in the text. Jesus Christ, intending not to redeem angels but to redeem man, did not assume the angelic nature but was made man, coming directly by *the seed* or "posterity" *of Abraham,* with whom the original covenant was made, that in his seed all the nations of the earth should be blessed; and it is on this account that the apostle mentioned *the seed of Abraham,* and not the seed of Adam. The word itself signifies not only to "take hold of" but to "help, succor, save from sinking." The rebel angels, who sinned and fell from God, were permitted to "fall downe, alle downe," as one of our old writers expresses it, till they fell into perdition. Man sinned and fell, and was falling "downe, alle downe," but Jesus laid hold on him and prevented him from falling into endless perdition.

17. *Wherefore in all things.* Because He thus laid hold on man in order to redeem him, it was necessary that He should in all things become like to man, that He might suffer in his stead, and make an atonement in His nature.

That he might be a merciful and faithful high priest. "That He might be merciful"—that He might be affected with a feeling of our infirmities, that, partaking of our nature with all its innocent infirmities and afflictions, He might know how to compassionate poor, afflicted, suffering man. And that He might be a "faithful high priest in those things which relate to God," whose justice requires the punishment of the transgressors, or a suitable expiation to be made for the sins of the people—"to make propitiation or atonement for sins by sacrifice."

MATTHEW HENRY

5. He must be faithful to God and merciful to men. In things pertaining to God, to his justice, and to his honour—to make reconciliation for the sins of the people.

In things pertaining to his people, to their support and comfort, *v.* 18. Christ's passion: *He suffered being tempted;* and his temptations were not the least part of his sufferings. Christ's compassion: *He is able to succour those that are tempted.* He knows how to deal with tempted sorrowful souls, because he has been himself sick of the same disease, not of sin, but of temptation and trouble of soul. The best of Christians are subject to many temptations. Temptations bring our souls into such distress and danger that they need support and succour.

JAMIESON, FAUSSET, BROWN

the New Testament. In Psalm 110, and Zechariah 6:13, there is added mention of the *kingdom* of Christ, which elsewhere is spoken of without the *priesthood,* and that frequently. On the cross, whereon as Priest He offered the sacrifice, He had the title "King" inscribed over Him [BENGEL]. **to make reconciliation for the sins**—rather as *Greek,* "to propitiate (in respect to) the sins"; "to expiate the sins." Strictly divine *justice* is "propitiated"; but God's *love* is as much from everlasting as His justice; therefore, lest Christ's sacrifice, or its typical forerunners, the legal sacrifices, should be thought to be antecedent to God's grace and love, neither are said in the Old or New Testament to have *propitiated God;* otherwise Christ's sacrifices might have been thought to have first induced God to love and pity man, instead of (as the fact really is) His love having *originated* Christ's sacrifice, whereby divine justice and divine love are harmonized. The sinner is brought by that sacrifice into God's favor, which by sin he had forfeited; hence his right prayer is, "God *be propitiated* (so the *Greek*) to me who am a sinner" (Luke 18:13). Sins bring death and "the fear of death" (vs. 15). He had no sin Himself, and "made reconciliation for the iniquity" of all others (Dan. 9:24). **of the people**—"the seed of Abraham" (vs. 16); the literal Israel first, and then (in the design of God), through Israel, the believing Gentiles, the spiritual Israel (I Pet. 2:10). **18. For**—explanation of how His being *made like His brethren in all things* has made Him *a merciful and faithful High Priest* for us (vs. 17). **in that**—rather as *Greek,* "wherein He suffered Himself; having been tempted, He is able to succor them *that are being tempted*" in the same temptation; and as "He was tempted (tried and afflicted) in *all* points," He is able (by the power of *sympathy*) to succor us in all possible temptations and trials incidental to man (ch. 4:16; 5:2).

ADAM CLARKE

18. *For in that he himself hath suffered.* The maxim on which this verse is founded is the following: A state of suffering disposes persons to be compassionate, and those who endure most afflictions are they who feel most for others. The apostle argues that, among other causes, it was necessary that Jesus Christ should partake of human nature, exposed to trials, persecutions, and various sufferings, that He might the better feel for and be led to succor those who are afflicted and sorely tried. Were the rest of the Scripture silent on this subject, this verse might be an ample support for every tempted soul.

MATTHEW HENRY — CHAPTER 3

Verses 1–6

The application of the doctrine concerning the priesthood of our Lord Jesus Christ.

I. The apostle exhorts Christians to have this high priest much in their thoughts.

1. The honourable compellation used towards those to whom he wrote: *Holy brethren, partakers of the heavenly calling.* Brethren, not only my brethren, but the brethren of Christ, and in him brethren to all the saints. Holy brethren; holy not only in profession and title, but in principle and practice, in heart and life. *Partakers of the heavenly calling*—partakers of the means of grace, and of the Spirit of grace, that came from heaven; that calling which brings down heaven into the souls of men.

2. The titles he gives to Christ, whom he would have them consider, (1) As the apostle of our profession, the great revealer of that faith which we profess to hold and of that hope which we profess to have. (2) Not only the apostle, but the high priest, too, of our profession, upon whose satisfaction and intercession we profess to depend for pardon of sin, and acceptance with God. (3) As Christ, the Messiah. (4) As Jesus, our Saviour, our healer.

II. The duty we owe to him who bears all these high and honourable titles. Look unto Jesus, the author and finisher of your faith. Even those that are holy brethren, and partakers of the heavenly calling, have need to stir up one another to think more of Christ than they do; the best of his people think too seldom and too slightly of him.

III. Several arguments to enforce this duty of considering Christ the apostle and high priest of our profession.

1. The first is taken from his fidelity, *v.* 2. He was faithful to him that appointed him, as Moses was in all his house. Moses was faithful in the discharge of his office to the Jewish church in the Old Testament, and so is Christ under the New; this was a proper argument to urge upon the Jews.

JAMIESON, FAUSSET, BROWN — CHAPTER 3

Vss. 1-19. THE SON OF GOD GREATER THAN MOSES, WHEREFORE UNBELIEF TOWARDS HIM WILL INCUR A HEAVIER PUNISHMENT THAN BEFELL UNBELIEVING ISRAEL IN THE WILDERNESS. **1. Wherefore**—*Greek,* "Whence," i.e., seeing we have such a sympathizing Helper you ought to "consider attentively," "contemplate"; fix your eyes and mind on Him with a view to profiting by the contemplation (ch. 12:2). The *Greek* word is often used by Luke, Paul's companion (Luke 12:24, 27). **brethren**—in Christ, the common bond of union. **partakers**—"of the Holy Ghost." **heavenly calling**—coming to us from heaven, and leading us to heaven whence it comes. Philippians 3:14, "the high calling"; *Greek* "the calling *above,*" i.e., *heavenly.* **the Apostle and High Priest of our profession**—There is but one *Greek* article to both nouns, "Him who is at once Apostle and High Priest"—*Apostle,* as Ambassador (a higher designation than "angel"-*messenger*) sent by the Father (John 20:21), pleading the cause of *God with us; High Priest,* as pleading *our* cause *with God.* Both His Apostleship and High Priesthood are comprehended in the one title, *Mediator* [BENGEL]. Though the title "Apostle" is nowhere else applied to Christ, it is appropriate here in addressing Hebrews, who used the term of the delegates sent by the high priest to collect the temple tribute from Jews resident in foreign countries, even as Christ was Delegate of the Father to this world far off from Him (Matt. 21:37). Hence as what applies to Him, applies also to His people, the Twelve are designated His apostles, even as He is the Father's (John 20:21). So Jesus, "the Apostle of our profession," is *delegated* to intercede for the Church before the Father. The words "of our profession," mark that it is not of the legal ritual, but of our Christian faith, that He is the High Priest. Paul compares Him as an *Apostle* to Moses; as High Priest to Aaron. He alone holds both offices combined, and in a more eminent degree than either, which those two brothers held apart. **profession**—"confession," corresponds to God having *spoken* to us by His Son, sent as Apostle and High Priest. What God proclaims we confess. **2.** He first notes the feature of *resemblance* between Moses and Christ, in order to conciliate the Hebrew Christians whom He addressed, and who still entertained a very high opinion of Moses; he afterwards brings forward Christ's superiority to Moses. **Who was faithful**—The *Greek* implies also that He still is faithful, viz., as our mediating High Priest, faithful to the trust God has assigned Him (ch. 2:17). So Moses *in*

ADAM CLARKE — CHAPTER 3

1. *Holy brethren.* Persons "consecrated to God," as the word literally implies, and called, in consequence, to be holy in heart, holy in life, and useful in the world. The Israelites are often called a "holy people, saints," because consecrated to God, and because they were bound by their profession to be holy; and yet these appellations are given to them in numberless instances where they were very unholy. The not attending to this circumstance, and the not discerning between actual positive holiness and the call to it as the consecration of the persons, has led many commentators and preachers into destructive mistakes. A man may be a Christian in profession and not such in heart; and those who pretend that, although they are unholy in themselves, they are reputed holy in Christ, because His righteousness is imputed to them, most awfully deceive their own souls. *Heavenly calling.* The Israelites had an earthly calling; they were called out of Egypt to go into the Promised Land. Christians have a heavenly calling; they are invited to leave the bondage of sin and go to the kingdom of God. *Apostle and High Priest of our profession.* Among the Jews the high priest was considered to be also the apostle of God, and it is in conformity to this notion that the apostle speaks. And he exhorts the Hebrews to *consider* Jesus Christ to be both their *High Priest* and *Apostle,* and to expect these offices to be henceforth fulfilled by Him, and by Him alone. This was the fullest intimation that the Mosaic economy was at an end and the priesthood changed. By *our profession,* or "that confession of ours," the apostle undoubtedly means the Christian religion. Moses was the apostle under the old testament, and Aaron the priest. When Moses was removed, the prophets succeeded him; and the sons of Aaron were the priests after the death of their father. This system is now annulled; and Jesus is the Prophet who declares the Father's will, and He is the Priest who ministers in the things pertaining to God.

2. *Who was faithful to him.* In Num. xii. 7, God gives this testimony to Moses: "My servant Moses . . . is faithful in all mine house"; and to this testimony the apostle alludes. *House* means not only the place where a family dwells, but also the family itself. The whole congregation of Israel was the house or family of God; and Moses was His steward, and was faithful in the

MATTHEW HENRY

2. The superior glory and excellence of Christ above Moses (*v.* 3-6). (1) Christ was a maker of the house, Moses but a member in it. Christ, who is God, drew the ground-plan of the church, provided the materials, and disposed them to receive the form; he has compacted and united this his house, and crowned all with his own presence, which is the true glory of this house of God.

(2) Christ was the master of this house, as well as the maker, *v.* 5, 6. Moses was only a faithful servant.

Christ, as the eternal Son of God, is the rightful owner and sovereign ruler of the church. Christ is worthy of more glory than Moses, and of greater regard and consideration.

Now follows a comfortable accommodation of it to himself and all true believers. *Whose house we are.*

A characteristic description of those persons who constitute this house: "*If we hold fast the confidence, and the rejoicing of the hope, firmly to the end.*" There must not only be a setting out well in the ways of Christ, but a steadfastness and perseverance therein unto the end.

JAMIESON, FAUSSET, BROWN

God's *house* (Num. 12:7). **appointed him**—"*made* Him" HIGH PRIEST; to be supplied from the preceding context. *Greek*, "made"; so in ch. 5:5; I Samuel 12:6, *Margin;* Acts 2:36; so the *Greek* fathers. Not as ALFORD, with AMBROSE and the Latins, "*created* Him," i.e., as man, in His incarnation. The likeness of Moses to Messiah was foretold by Moses himself (Deut. 18:15). Other prophets only *explained Moses,* who was in this respect superior to them; but Christ was *like Moses,* yet superior. **3. For**—assigning the reason why they should "consider" attentively "Christ" (vs. 1), highly as they regard Moses who resembled Him in *faithfulness* (vs. 2). **was**—*Greek,* "has been." **counted worthy of more glory**—by God, when He exalted Him to His own right hand. The Hebrew Christians admitted the fact (ch. 1:13). **builded the house**—*Greek,* "inasmuch as He hath more honor than the house, who *prepared* it," or "*established* it" [ALFORD]. The *Greek* verb is used purposely instead of "builded," in order to mark that the building meant is not a literal, but a spiritual house: the Church both of the Old Testament and New Testament; and that the building of such a house includes all the *preparations* of providence and grace needed to furnish it with "living stones" and fitting "servants." Thus, as Christ the Founder and Establisher (in Old Testament as well as the New Testament) is greater than the house so established, including the servants, He is greater also than Moses, who was but a "servant." Moses, as a servant, is a portion of the house, and less than the house; Christ, as the Instrumental Creator of all things, must be God, and so greater than the house of which Moses was but a part. *Glory* is the result of *honor*. **4.** Someone must be the establisher of every house; Moses was not the establisher of the house, but a portion of it (but He who established all things, *and therefore* the spiritual house in question, is God). Christ, as being instrumentally the Establisher of all things, must be the Establisher of the house, and so greater than Moses.

5. faithful in all his house—i.e., in all GOD'S house (vs. 4). **servant**—not here the *Greek* for "slave," but "a ministering attendant"; marking the high office of Moses towards God, though inferior to Christ, a kind of *steward*. **for a testimony . . .**—in order that he might in his typical institutions give "testimony" to Israel "of the things" of the Gospel "which were to be spoken afterwards" by Christ (ch. 8:5; 9:8, 23; 10:1).

6. But Christ—was and is faithful (vs. 2). **as a son over his own house**—rather, "over *His* (GOD'S, vs. 4) house"; and therefore, as *the inference* from His being one with God, *over His own house.* So ch. 10:21, "having an High Priest over the house *of God.*" Christ enters His Father's house as the Master [OVER it], but Moses as a servant [IN it, vss. 2, 5] [CHRYSOSTOM]. An ambassador in the absence of the king is very distinguished—in the presence of the king he falls back into the multitude [BENGEL].

whose house are we—Paul and his Hebrew readers. One old MS., with *Vulgate* and LUCIFER, reads, "*which* house"; but the weightiest MSS. support *English Version* reading.

the rejoicing—rather, "the matter of rejoicing." **of the hope**—"of *our* hope." Since all our good things lie in hopes, we ought so to hold fast our hopes as already to rejoice, as though our hopes were realized [CHRYSOSTOM]. **firm unto the end**—omitted in LUCIFER and AMBROSE, and in one oldest MS., but supported by most oldest MSS.

ADAM CLARKE

discharge of his office. Jesus Christ has His house—the whole great family of mankind, for all of whom He offered His sacrificial blood to God; and the Christian Church, which is especially His own household, is composed of His own children and servants, among and in whom He lives and constantly resides. He has been *faithful* to the trust reposed in Him as the Apostle of God; He has faithfully proclaimed the will of the Most High.

3. *For this man was counted.* The pronoun should have been translated "this person," and this would have referred immediately to Jesus Christ, v. 1. *More glory than Moses.* We have already seen that the apostle's design is to prove that Jesus Christ is higher than the angels, higher than Moses, and higher than Aaron. That He is higher than the angels has been already proved; that He is higher than Moses he is now proving. *He who hath builded the house.* There can be no doubt that a man who builds a house for his own accommodation is more honorable than the house itself; but the *house* here intended is the Church of God. This Church, here called a *house* or "family," is built by Christ; He must therefore be greater than Moses, who was only a member and officer in that Church.

4. *For every house is builded by some man.* The literal sense is plain enough: "Every structure plainly implies an architect, and an end for which it was formed. The architect may be employed by him for whose use the house is intended; but the efficient cause of the erection is that which is here to be regarded." The word *house* here is still taken in a metaphorical sense as above; it signifies "family" or Church. Now the general meaning of the words, taken in this sense, is: "Every family has an author, and a head or governor. Man may found families, civil and religious communities, and be the head of these; but God alone is the Head, Author, and Governor of all the families of the earth; He is the Governor of the universe."

5. *As a servant.* The fidelity of Moses was the fidelity of a *servant;* he was not the framer of that Church or house; He was employed, under God, to arrange and order it; he was steward to the Builder and Owner. *For a testimony of those things.* Every ordinance under the law was typical; everything bore a *testimony* to the things which were to be spoken after; i.e., to Jesus Christ, His suffering, death, and the glory which should follow; and to His gospel in all its parts. The faithfulness of Moses consisted in his scrupulous attention to every ordinance of God, his framing everything according to the pattern showed him by the Lord, and his referring all to that Christ of whom he spoke as the Prophet who should come after him.

6. *But Christ as a son over his own house.* Moses was faithful as a servant *in* the house; Jesus was faithful as the firstborn Son *over* the house of which He is the Heir and Governor. Here then is the conclusion of the argument in reference to Christ's superiority over Moses. Moses did not found the house or family; Christ did. Moses was but in the house, or one of the family; Christ was over the house as its Ruler. Moses was but servant in the house; Christ was the Son and Heir. Moses was in the house of another; Christ, in His own house. *Whose house are we.* We Christians are His Church and "family"; He is our Father, Governor, and Head. *If we hold fast the confidence.* We are now His Church, and shall continue to be such and be acknowledged by Him *if* we maintain our Christian profession, "that liberty of access to God," which we now have, and the *rejoicing of the hope,* i.e., of eternal life, which we shall receive at the resurrection of the dead. The word which is here translated *confidence,* and which signifies "freedom of speech, liberty of access," seems to be used here to distinguish an important Christian privilege. Under the old testament no man was permitted to approach to God; even the very mountain on which God published His laws must not be touched by man nor beast; and only the high priest was permitted to enter the holy of holies, and that only once a year, on the great Day of Atonement; and even then he must have the blood of the victim to propitiate the divine justice. Under the Christian dispensation the way to the holiest is now laid

MATTHEW HENRY

Verses 7-19

Here the apostle proceeds in pressing upon them serious counsels and cautions; and he recites a passage out of Ps. xcv. 7, &c.

I. What he counsels them to do—to give a speedy and present attention to the call of Christ. "Hear his voice; apply it to yourselves and set about it this very day, for to-morrow it may be too late."

II. What he cautions them against—hardening their hearts, turning the deaf ear to the calls and counsels of Christ. The hardening of our hearts is the spring of all our other sins.

III. Whose example he warns them by—that of the Israelites their fathers in the wilderness: *As in the provocation and day of temptation;* this refers to Exod. xvii. 2-7. Days of temptation are often days of provocation. The sins of others should be a warning to us. Our fathers' sins and punishments should be remembered by us, to deter us from following their evil examples. The sin they were guilty of: they distrusted God, murmured against Moses, and would not attend to the voice of God. The aggravations of their sin: they sinned when they saw his works—works of wonder wrought for their deliverance out of Egypt, and their support and supply in the wilderness. They continued thus to sin against God for forty years. The source and spring of such aggravated sins. They erred in their hearts; and these heart-errors produced many other errors in their lips and lives. They did not know God's ways, though he had walked before them. They did not observe either his providences or his ordinances.

The just resentment God had at their sins, and yet the great patience he exercised towards them (*v.* 10). All sin does not only anger and affront God, but it grieves him. If they by their sins continue to grieve the Spirit of God, their sins shall be made grievous to their own spirits, either in a way of judgment or mercy.

God swore in his wrath that they should not enter into his rest. Sin, long continued in, will kindle the divine wrath. His wrath will make their condition a restless condition; there is no resting under the wrath of God.

IV. What use the apostle makes of their awful example, *v.* 12, 13, &c.

1. He gives the Hebrews a proper caution; the word is, *Take heed—look to it.* "Look about you; be upon your guard against enemies both within and without." The ruin of others should be a warning to us to take heed of the rock they split upon.

2. He enlarges upon the matter of the admonition: *Take heed, brethren, lest there be in any of you an evil heart of unbelief in departing from the living God.* A heart of unbelief is an evil heart. An evil heart of unbelief is at the bottom of all our sinful departures from God; if once we allow ourselves to distrust God, we may soon desert him.

JAMIESON, FAUSSET, BROWN

7-11.—Exhortation from Psalm 95, not through unbelief to lose participation in the spiritual house. **Wherefore**—Seeing that we are the house of God if we hold fast our confidence . . . (vs. 6). Jesus is "faithful," be not ye unfaithful (vss. 2, 12). The sentence beginning with "wherefore," interrupted by the parenthesis confirming the argument from Psalm 95, is completed at vs. 12, "Take heed . . . ." **Holy Ghost saith**—by the inspired Psalmist; so that the words of the latter are the words of God Himself. **Today**—at length; in David's day, as contrasted with the days of Moses in the wilderness, and the whole time since then, during which they had been rebellious against God's voice; as for instance, in the wilderness (vs. 8). The Psalm, each fresh time when used in public worship, by "today," will mean the particular day when it was, or is, used. **hear**—obediently. **his voice**—of grace. **8. Harden not your hearts**—This phrase here only is used of *man's* own act; usually of *God's* act (Rom. 9:18). When man is spoken of as the agent in hardening, the phrase usually is, "harden his neck," or "back" (Neh. 9:17). **provocation . . . temptation**—Massah-meribah, translated in *Margin* "tentation . . . chiding," or "strife" (Exod. 17:1-7). Both names seem to refer to that one event, the murmuring of the people against the Lord at Rephidim for want of water. The first offense especially ought to be guarded against, and is the most severely reproved, as it is apt to produce many more. Numbers 20: 1-13 and Deuteronomy 33:8 mention a second similar occasion in the wilderness of Sin, near Kadesh, also called Meribah. **in the day**—*Greek,* "according to the day of." **9. When**—rather, "Where," viz., in the wilderness. **your fathers**—The authority of the *ancients* is not conclusive [BENGEL]. **tempted me, proved me**—The oldest MSS. read, "tempted (Me) in the way of testing," i.e., *putting* (*Me*) *to the proof* whether I was able and willing to relieve them, not believing that I am so. **saw my works forty years**—They saw, without being led thereby to repentance, My works of power partly in affording miraculous help, partly in executing vengeance, forty years. The "forty years" joined in the *Hebrew* and LXX, and below, vs. 17, with "I was grieved," is here joined with "they saw." Both are true; for, during the same forty years that they were tempting God by unbelief, notwithstanding their seeing God's miraculous works, God was being grieved. **10. grieved**—displeased. Cf. "walk contrary," Leviticus 26:24, 28. **that generation**—"*that*" implies alienation and estrangement. But the oldest MSS. read, "this." **said**—"*grieved,*" or "displeased," at their first offense. Subsequently when they hardened their heart in unbelief still more, He *sware* in His *wrath* (vs. 11); an ascending gradation (cf. vss. 17, 18). **and they have not known**—*Greek,* "But these very persons . . . ." They perceived I was displeased with them, yet they, the same persons, did not a whit the more wish to know my ways [BENGEL]; cf. "but they," Psalm 106: 43. **not known my ways**—not known practically and believingly the ways in which I would have had them go, so as to reach My rest (Exod. 18:20). **11. So**—lit., "as." **I sware**—BENGEL remarks the oath of God preceded the forty years. **not**—lit., "If they shall enter . . . (God do so to me and more also)," II Sam. 3:35. The *Greek* is the same, Mark 8:12. **my rest**—Canaan, primarily, their rest after wandering in the wilderness: still, even when in it, they never *fully* enjoyed rest; whence it followed that the threat extended farther than the exclusion of the unbelieving from the literal land of rest, and that the rest promised to the believing in its full blessedness was, and is, yet future: Psalm 25:13; 37: 9, 11, 22, 29, and Christ's own beatitude (Matt. 5:5) all accord with this, vs. 9. **12. Take heed**—to be joined with "wherefore," vs. 7. **lest there be**—*Greek* (indicative), "lest there *shall* be"; lest there be, as I fear there is; implying that it is not merely a *possible* contingency, but that there is ground for thinking *it will be so.* **in any**—"in any one of you." Not merely ought all in general be on their guard, but they ought to be so concerned for the safety of *each one* member, as not to suffer any one to perish through their negligence [CALVIN]. **heart**—The *heart* is not to be trusted. Cf. vs. 10, "They do always err in their heart." **unbelief**—*faithlessness.* Christ is *faithful;* therefore, saith Paul to the Hebrews, we ought not to be *faithless* as our fathers were under Moses. **departing**—apostatizing. The opposite of "come unto" Him (ch. 4:16). God punishes such apostates in kind. He departs from them—the worst of woes. **the living God**—real: the distinctive characteristic of the God of Israel, not like the lifeless gods of the heathen; therefore One

ADAM CLARKE

open; and we have "liberty of access," even to the holiest, by the blood of Jesus. Having such access unto God, by such a Mediator, we may obtain all that grace which is necessary to fit us for eternal glory; and having the witness of His Spirit in our heart, we have a well-grounded hope of endless felicity and exult in the enjoyment of that hope. But *if* we retain not the grace, we shall not inherit the glory.

7. *Wherefore (as the Holy Ghost saith, To day.* These words are quoted from Ps. xcv. 7; and as they were written by David, and attributed here to the Holy Ghost, it proves that David wrote by the inspiration of God's Holy Spirit. As these words were originally a warning to the Israelites not to provoke God, lest they should be excluded from that rest which He had promised them, the apostle uses them here to persuade the Christians in Palestine to hold fast their religious privileges and the grace they had received, lest they should come short of that state of future glory which Christ had prepared for them. The words strongly imply, as indeed does the whole Epistle, the possibility of falling from the grace of God and perishing everlastingly; and without this supposition these words and all suchlike, which make more than two-thirds of the whole of divine revelation, would have neither sense nor meaning. Why should God entreat man to receive His mercy if He have rendered this impossible? Why should He exhort a believer to persevere if it be impossible for him to fall away?

8. *Harden not your hearts.* Which you will infallibly do if you will not hear His voice. *Provocation.* The "exasperation" or "bitter provocation."

9. *When your fathers tempted me.* It would be better to translate "where" than *when,* as the Vulgate has done in its *ubi;* and this translation has been followed by Wycliffe, Coverdale, Tyndale, and our first translators in general.

10. *Wherefore I was grieved.* God represents himself as the Father of this great Jewish family, for whose comfort and support He had made every necessary provision, and to whom He had given every proof of tenderness and fatherly affection; and because they disobeyed Him, and walked in that way in which they could not but be miserable, therefore He represents himself as grieved and exceedingly displeased with them.

11. *So I sware in my wrath.* God's grief at their continued disobedience became *wrath* at their final impenitence, and therefore He excluded them from the promised rest.

12. *Take heed, brethren, lest there be in any of you.* Take warning by those disobedient Israelites; they were brought out of the house of bondage, and had the fullest promise of a land of prosperity and rest. By their disobedience they came short of it, and fell in the wilderness. You have been brought from the bondage of sin, and have a most gracious promise of an everlasting inheritance among the saints in light. Through unbelief and disobedience they lost their rest; through the same you may lose yours. *An evil heart of unbelief* will lead away *from the living God.*

MATTHEW HENRY

3. That which would be a remedy against this evil heart of unbelief, *v.* 13. Since tomorrow is none of ours, we must make the best improvement of today. There is a great deal of deceitfulness in sin; it promises much, but performs nothing. The deceitfulness of sin is of a hardening nature. Every act of sin confirms the habit.

4. He conforts those who not only set out well, but hold on well, and hold out to the end (*v.* 14). The saints' privilege: they are made partakers of Christ, in all that he is, in all that he has done, or can do. The condition on which they hold that privilege, their perseverance. Not but they shall persevere, being kept by the mighty power of God through faith to salvation, but to be pressed thus to it is one means by which Christ helps his people to persevere. The same spirit with which Christians set out in the ways of God they should maintain to the end. There are a great many who in the beginning show a great deal of courage and confidence, but do not hold them fast to the end.

5. The apostle resumes what he had quoted before, *v.* 15, 16, &c. The apostle tells them that though some who had heard the voice of God did provoke him, yet all did not so. God will have a remnant that shall be obedient to his voice.

6. The apostle puts some queries upon what had been before mentioned (*v.* 17–19). God is grieved only with those of his people who sin against him, and continue in sin. Unbelief (with rebellion which is the consequent of it) is the great damning sin of the world. This sin shuts up the heart of God, and shuts up the gate of heaven, against them.

JAMIESON, FAUSSET, BROWN

whose threats are awful realities. To apostatize from Christ is to apostatize from the living God (ch. 2:3). **13. one another**–*Greek,* "yourselves"; let each exhort himself and his neighbor. **daily**–*Greek,* "on each day," or "day by day." **while it is called Today**–while the "today" lasts (the day of grace, Luke 4:21, before the coming of the day of glory and judgment at Christ's coming, ch. 10:25, 37). Tomorrow is the day when idle men work, and fools repent. Tomorrow is Satan's today; he cares not what good resolutions you form, if only you fix them for tomorrow. **lest . . . of you**–The "you" is emphatic, as distinguished from "your fathers" (vs. 9). "That from among you no one (so the *Greek* order is in some of the oldest MSS.) be hardened" (vs. 8). **deceitfulness**–causing you to "err in your heart." **sin**–unbelief. **14. For . . .**–enforcing the warning, vs. 12. **partakers of Christ**–(Cf. vss. 1, 6). So "partakers of the Holy Ghost" (ch. 6:4). **hold**–*Greek,* "hold fast." **the beginning of our confidence**–i.e., the confidence (lit., *substantial, solid confidence*) of faith which we have begun (ch. 6:11; 12:2). A Christian so long as he is not *made perfect,* considers himself as a *beginner* [BENGEL]. **unto the end**–unto the coming of Christ (ch. 12:2). **15. While it is said**–connected with vs. 13, "exhort one another . . . while it is said, Today": vs. 14, "for we are made partakers . . . ," being a parenthesis. "It entirely depends on yourselves that the invitation of the 95th Psalm be not a mere invitation, but also an actual enjoyment." ALFORD translates, "Since (i.e., for) it is said . . . ," regarding vs. 15 as a proof that we must "hold . . . confidence . . . unto the end," in order to be "partakers of Christ." **16. For some**–rather interrogatively, "For WHO was it that, when they had heard (referring to 'if ye will *hear,*' vs. 15), did provoke (God)?" The "For" implies, Ye need to take heed against unbelief: *for,* was it not because of unbelief that all our fathers were excluded (Ezek. 2:3)? "Some," and "not all," would be a faint way of putting his argument, when his object is to show the *universality* of the evil. Not merely *some,* but *all* the Israelites, for the solitary exceptions, Joshua and Caleb, are hardly to be taken into account in so general a statement. So vss. 17, 18, are interrogative: (1) the beginning of the provocation, soon after the departure from Egypt, is marked in vs. 16; (2) the forty years of it in the wilderness, vs. 17; (3) the denial of entrance into the land of rest, vs. 18. *Note,* cf. I Corinthians 10:5, "with the majority of them God was displeased." **howbeit**–"Nay (why need I put the question?), was it not all that came out of Egypt?" (Exod. 17:1, 2). **by Moses**–by the instrumentality of Moses as their leader. **17. But**–Translate, "Moreover," as it is not in contrast to vs. 16, but carrying out the same thought. **corpses**–lit., "limbs," implying that their bodies fell limb from limb. **18. to them that believed not**–rather as *Greek,* "to them that *disobeyed.*" *Practical* unbelief (Deut. 1:26). **19. they could not enter**–though desiring it.

ADAM CLARKE

13. *But exhort one another daily.* This supposes a state of close church fellowship, without which they could not have had access to each other. *While it is called To day.* Use time while you have it, for by and by there will be no more present time. All will be future; all will be eternity. *Daily* signifies time continued; *to day,* all present time.

14. *For we are made partakers of Christ.* Having believed in Christ as the promised Messiah and embraced the whole Christian system, they were consequently made partakers of all its benefits in this life, and entitled to the fulfillment of all its exceeding great and precious promises relative to the glories of the eternal world. The former they actually possessed; the latter they could have only in case of their perseverance. Therefore the apostle says, *If we hold the beginning of our confidence stedfast unto the end,* i.e., of life. For our participation of glory depends on our continuing steadfast in the faith, to the end of our Christian race. The word *hypostasis,* which we here translate *confidence,* signifies properly a "basis" or "foundation"; that on which something else is builded, and by which it is supported. Their faith in Christ Jesus was this *hypostasis* or "foundation"; on that all their peace, comfort, and salvation was builded. If this were not held fast to the end, Christ in His saving influences could not be held fast; and no Christ, no heaven.

16. *For some, when they had heard, did provoke.* There is a various reading here, which consists merely in the different placing of an accent, and yet gives the whole passage a different turn—*tines,* if read with the accent on the epsilon. *Tines* is the plural indefinite, and signifies *some,* as in our translation; if read with the accent on the iota, it has an interrogative meaning; and, according to this, the whole clause, "But who were those hearers who did bitterly provoke? Were they not all they who came out of the land of Egypt by Moses?" Or the whole clause may be read with one interrogation: "But who were those hearers that did bitterly provoke, but all those who came out of Egypt by Moses?" It is more likely that this is the true reading, as all that follows to the end of the eighteenth verse is a series of interrogations.

17. *Whose carcasses fell.* "Whose members fell," the members of the body.

18. *To whom sware he.* God never acts by any kind of caprice; whenever He pours out His judgments, there are the most positive reasons to vindicate His conduct.

19. *So we see that they could not enter in.* It was no decree of God that prevented them; it was no want of necessary strength to enable them; it was through no deficiency of divine counsel to instruct them. All these they had in abundance; but they chose to sin, and *would* not believe. Unbelief produced disobedience, and disobedience produced hardness of heart and blindness of mind; and all these drew down the judgments of God, and wrath came upon them to the uttermost.

MATTHEW HENRY

CHAPTER 4

Verses 1–10

I. Our privileges by Christ under the gospel are not only as great, but greater than those enjoyed under the Mosaic law. We have a promise left us of entering into his rest. This promise of spiritual rest is a promise left us by the Lord Jesus Christ in his last will and testament, as a precious legacy. Our business is to see to it that we be the legatees, and so have the prospect and earnest of perfect and everlasting rest in heaven.

Those who enjoy the gospel should maintain a holy fear and jealousy over themselves, *v.* 1. Those who might have attained salvation by faith may fall short by unbelief. It is a dreadful thing so much as to seem to fall short of the gospel salvation. It is much more dreadful really to fall short. Maintain a holy and religious fear lest we should fall short. Presumption is the high road to ruin.

II. We have as great advantages as they (*v.* 2); the same gospel for substance was preached under both Testaments. We have the gospel as well as they, and in greater purity and perspicuity than they had.

JAMIESON, FAUSSET, BROWN

CHAPTER 4

Vss. 1-16. THE PROMISE OF GOD'S REST IS FULLY REALIZED THROUGH CHRIST: LET US STRIVE TO OBTAIN IT BY HIM, OUR SYMPATHIZING HIGH PRIEST. **1. Let us . . . fear**–not with slavish terror, but godly "fear and trembling" (Phil. 2:12). Since so many have fallen, we have cause to fear (ch. 3:17-19). **being left us**–still *remaining* to us after the others have, by neglect, lost it. **his rest**–God's heavenly rest, of which Canaan is the type. "Today" still continues, during which there is the danger of failing to reach the *rest.* "Today," rightly used, terminates in the *rest* which, when once obtained, is never lost (Rev. 3:12). A foretaste of the rest is given in the inward rest which the believer's soul has in Christ. **should seem to come short of it**–*Greek,* "to *have* come short of it"; *should be found,* when the great trial of all shall take place [ALFORD], to have fallen short of attaining the promise. The word "seem" is a mitigating mode of expression, though not lessening the reality. BENGEL and OWEN take it, Lest there should be any *semblance* or appearance of falling short. **2. gospel preached . . . unto them**–in type: the earthly Canaan, wherein they failed to realize perfect rest, suggesting to them

ADAM CLARKE

CHAPTER 4

1. *Let us therefore fear.* Seeing the Israelites lost the rest of Canaan through obstinacy and unbelief, let us be afraid lest we come short of the heavenly rest through the same cause. *Should seem to come short of it.* "Lest any of us should actually come short of it"; i.e., miss it. *Come short.* The verb is applied here metaphorically; it is an allusion, of which there are many in this Epistle, to the races in the Grecian games.

2. *For unto us was the gospel preached.* "For we also have received good tidings as well as they." They had a gracious promise of entering into an earthly rest; we have a gracious promise of entering into a heavenly rest. God gave them every requisite advantage; He has done the same to us. Moses and the elders spoke the word of God plainly and forcibly to them; Christ and His apostles have done the same to us. They might have persevered; so may we. They disbelieved, disobeyed and fell; and so may we. *But the word preached did not profit them.* "But the word of hearing did not profit them." The word and promise to which the apostle most prob-

MATTHEW HENRY

III. The reason why so few of the ancient Jews profited by that dispensation of the gospel was their want of faith, *v.* 2. The word is preached to us that we may profit by it; it is a price put into our hands to get wisdom. There have been in all ages a great many unprofitable hearers. Those who are not gainers by hearing are great losers. That which is at the bottom of all our unprofitableness is our unbelief. If the hearers have not faith in their souls to mix with the word, they will be never the better for it. This faith must mingle with every word, and be in act and exercise while we are hearing.

V. The apostle confirms the happiness of all those who truly believe the gospel.

1. By asserting so positively the truth of it, from the experience of himself and others: "*We who have believed, do enter into rest,*" *v.* 3.

2. He illustrates and confirms it. (1) From God's finishing his work of creation, and so entering into his rest (*v.* 3, 4). He will cause those who believe to finish their work, and then to enjoy their rest.

JAMIESON, FAUSSET, BROWN

that they should look beyond to the heavenly land of rest, to which *faith* is the avenue, and from which *unbelief* excludes, as it did from the earthly Canaan. **the word preached**—lit., "the word of hearing": *the word heard by them.* **not being mixed with faith in them that heard**—So the *Syriac* and the *Old Latin Versions,* older than any of our MSS., and LUCIFER, read, "As the world did not unite with the hearers in faith." The word heard being the food which, as the bread of life, must pass into flesh and blood through man's appropriating it to himself in faith. Hearing alone is of as little value as undigested food in a bad stomach [THOLUCK]. The whole of oldest *extant* MS. authority supports a different reading, "unmingled as *they* were (*Greek* accusative agreeing with 'them') in faith with its hearers," i.e., with its *believing, obedient* hearers, as Caleb and Joshua. So "hear" is used for "obey" in the context, vs. 7, "Today, if ye will hear His voice." The disobedient, instead of being blended in "the same body," separated themselves as Korah: a tacit reproof to like separatists from the Christian assembling together (ch. 10:25; Jude 19).

3. For—justifying his assertion of the need of "faith," vs. 2. **we which have believed**—we who at Christ's coming shall be found to have believed. **do enter**—i.e., are to enter: so two of the oldest MSS. and LUCIFER and the old Latin. Two other oldest MSS. read, "Let us enter." **into rest**—*Greek,* "into *the* rest" which is promised in the 95th Psalm. **as he said**—God's saying that *unbelief* excludes from entrance implies that *belief* gains an entrance into the rest. What, however, Paul mainly here dwells on in the quotation is that the promised "*rest*" has not *yet* been entered into. At vs. 11 he again, as in ch. 3:12-19 already, takes up *faith* as the indispensable qualification for entering it. **although . . .**—Although God had finished His works of creation and entered on *His* rest from creation long before Moses' time, yet under that leader of Israel another rest was promised, which most fell short of through unbelief; and although the rest in Canaan was subsequently attained under Joshua, yet long after, in David's days, God, in the 95th Psalm, still speaks of *the rest of God* as not yet attained. THEREFORE, there must be meant a rest *still future,* viz., that which "remaineth for the people of God" in heaven, vss. 3-9, when they shall rest from their works, as God did from His, vs. 10. The argument is to show that by "My rest," God means a future rest, not *for Himself,* but *for us.* **finished**—*Greek,* "brought into existence," "made." **4. he spake**—God (Gen. 2:2). **God did rest the seventh day**—a rest not ending with the seventh day, but beginning then and still continuing, into which believers shall hereafter enter. God's rest is not a rest necessitated by fatigue, nor consisting in idleness, but is that upholding and governing of which creation was the beginning [ALFORD]. Hence Moses records the end of each of the first six days, but not of the seventh. **from all his works**—*Hebrew,* Genesis 2:2, "from all His *work.*" God's "work" was *one,* comprehending, however, many "*works.*" **5. in this place**—In this passage of the Psalm again, it is implied that the rest was even then still future. **6. it remaineth**—still to be realized. **some must enter**—The denial of entrance to unbelievers is a virtual promise of entrance to those that believe. God wishes not His rest to be empty, but furnished with guests (Luke 14:23). **they to whom it was first preached entered not**—lit., "they who first (in the time of Moses) had the Gospel preached to them," viz., in type, as *Note,* vs. 2. **unbelief**—*Greek,* rather "disobedience" (*Note,* ch. 3:18).

7. Again—*Anew* the promise recurs. Translate as the *Greek* order is, "He limited a certain day, 'Today.'" Here Paul

ADAM CLARKE

ably refers is that in Deut. i. 20-21. "Ye are come unto the mountain of the Amorites, which the Lord our God doth give unto us. Behold, the Lord thy God hath set the land before thee: go up and possess it, as the Lord God of thy fathers hath said unto thee; fear not." But instead of attending to the word of the Lord by Moses, the whole congregation murmured against him and Aaron, and "said one to another, Let us make a captain, and let us return into Egypt," Num. xiv. 2, 4. *Not being mixed with faith in them that heard.* The word *mixed* is peculiarly expressive; it is a metaphor taken from the nutrition of the human body by mixing the aliment taken into the stomach with the saliva and gastric juice, in consequence of which it is concocted, digested, reduced into chyle, which, absorbed by the lacteal vessels and thrown into the blood, becomes the means of increasing and supporting the body, all the solids and fluids being thus generated; so that on this process, properly performed, depend (under God) strength, health, and life itself. Should the most nutritive aliment be received into the stomach, if not *mixed* with the above juices, it would be rather the means of death than of life; or, in the word of the apostle, it would *not profit* because not thus *mixed. Faith* in the word preached, in reference to that God who sent it, is the grand means of its becoming the power of God to the salvation of the soul.

3. *For we which have believed do enter into rest.* The great spiritual blessings, the forerunners of eternal glory, which were all typified by that earthly rest or felicity promised to the ancient Israelites, we Christians do, by believing in Christ Jesus, actually possess. We have peace of conscience and joy in the Holy Ghost, are saved from the guilt and power of sin, and thus enjoy an inward rest. But this is a rest differing from the seventh day's rest, or Sabbath, which was the original type of Canaan, the blessings of the gospel, and eternal glory; seeing God said, concerning the unbelieving Israelites in the wilderness, *I have sworn in my wrath* that they shall not *enter into my rest,* notwithstanding *the works* of creation *were finished,* and the seventh day's rest was instituted *from the foundation of the world;* consequently the Israelites had entered into that rest before the oath was sworn. *From the foundation of the world.* The foundation of the world means the completion of the work of creation in six days.

4. *For he spake in a certain place.* This *certain place* or "somewhere" is probably Gen. ii. 2; and refers to the completion of the work of creation, and the setting apart the seventh day as a day of rest for man, and a type of everlasting felicity.

5. *And in this place again.* In the ninety-fifth psalm, already quoted, v. 3. This was a second rest which the Lord promised to the believing, obedient seed of Abraham; and as it was spoken of in the days of David, when the Jews actually possessed this long promised Canaan, therefore it is evident that that was not the rest which God intended, as the next verse shows.

6. *It remaineth that some must enter therein.* Why our translators put in the word *must* here I cannot even conjecture. I hope it was not to serve a system, as some have since used it: "Some *must* go to heaven, for so is the doctrine of the decree; and there *must* be certain persons infallibly brought thither as a reward to Christ for His sufferings; and in this the will of man and free agency can have no part." Now supposing that even all this was true, yet it does not exist either positively or by implication in the text. The words literally translated are as follows: "Seeing then it remaineth for some to enter into it"; or, "Whereas therefore it remaineth that some enter into it, and they to whom it was first preached (they to whom the promise was given; they who first received the good tidings; i.e., the Israelites, to whom was given the promise of entering into the rest of Canaan) did not enter in because of their unbelief"; and the promise still continued to be repeated even in the days of David; therefore some other rest must be intended.

7. *He limiteth a certain day.* The term *day* signifies not only time in general, but also present time, and a particular space. *Day* here

MATTHEW HENRY

(2) From God's continuing the observance of the sabbath. There is a more spiritual sabbath remaining for the people of God than that into which Joshua led the Jews (*v.* 6–9). Believers shall enter into their rest, *v.* 10.

VI. The apostle confirms the misery of those who do not believe; they shall never enter into this spiritual rest, either of grace here or glory hereafter. It remains only for the people of God; others by their sin abandon themselves to eternal restlessness.

Verses 11-16

I. A serious exhortation, *v.* 11. The end proposed—rest in Christ on earth, with Christ in heaven. The way to this end prescribed—labour, diligent labour; this is the only way to rest; those who will not work now shall not rest hereafter. Let us therefore labour, let us all call upon one another to this diligence. Now is our working time, our rest remains.

II. Powerful motives to make the advice effectual.

1. *Lest any man fall after the same example of unbelief.* To have seen so many fall before us will be a great aggravation of our sin, if we will not take warning by them.

2. The great help we may have from the word of God that we may obtain this rest, *v.* 12.

JAMIESON, FAUSSET, BROWN

interrupts the quotation by, "In (the Psalm of) David saying after so long a time" (after 500 years' possession of Canaan), and resumes it by, "as it *has been* said *before* (so the *Greek* oldest MS., *before,* viz., ch. 3:7, 15), Today if ye hear His voice . . ." [ALFORD]. **8.** Answer to the objection which might be made to his reasoning, viz., that those brought into Canaan by Joshua (so "Jesus" here means, as in Acts 7:45) did enter the *rest* of God. If the rest of God meant Canaan, God would not after their entrance into that land, have spoken (or speak [ALFORD]) of another (future) day of entering the rest. **9. therefore**—because God "speaks of another day" (*Note,* vs. 8). **remaineth**—still to be realized hereafter by the "some (who) must enter therein" (vs. 6), i.e., "the people of God," the true Israel who shall enter into *God's rest* ("My rest," vs. 3). God's rest was a Sabbatism; so also will ours be. **a rest**—*Greek,* "Sabbatism." In time there are many Sabbaths, but then there shall be the enjoyment and keeping of a Sabbath rest: one perfect and eternal. The "rest" in vs. 8 is *Greek catapausis; Hebrew, Noah;* rest from weariness, as the ark rested on Ararat after its tossings to and fro; and as Israel, under Joshua, enjoyed at last rest from war in Canaan. But the "rest" in this vs. 9 is the nobler and more exalted (*Hebrew*) *"Sabbath" rest;* lit., "cessation": rest from *work when finished* (vs. 4), as God rested (Rev. 16:17). The two ideas of "rest" combined, give the perfect view of the heavenly Sabbath. Rest from weariness, sorrow, and sin; and rest in the completion of God's new creation (Rev. 21:5). **10. For**—justifying and explaining the word "rest," or "Sabbatism," just used (*Note,* vs. 9). **he that is entered**—whosoever once enters. **his rest**—*God's* rest: the rest prepared *by God* for His people [ESTIUS]. Rather, *His* rest: the *man's* rest: that assigned to him by God as *his.* The *Greek* is the same as that for "his own" immediately after. **hath ceased**—The *Greek* aorist is used of indefinite time, "*is wont to* cease," or rather, "rest": *rests.* The past tense implies at the same time the *certainty* of it, as also that in this life a kind of foretaste in Christ is already given [GROTIUS] (Jer. 6:16; Matt. 11:28, 29). Our highest happiness shall, according to this verse, consist in our being united in one with God, and moulded into conformity with Him as our archetype [CALVIN]. **from his own works**—even from those that were good and suitable to the time of doing work. Labor was followed by rest even in Paradise (Gen. 2: 3, 15). The work and subsequent rest of God are the archetype to which we should be conformed. The argument is: He who once enters rest, rests from labors; but God's people have not yet rested from them, therefore they have not yet entered the rest, and so it must be still future. ALFORD translates, "He that entered into his (or else God's, but rather 'his'; Isa. 11:10, 'His rest': 'the joy *of the Lord,*' Matt. 25:21,23) rest (viz., *Jesus,* our Forerunner, vs. 14; ch. 6:20, 'The Son of God that *is passed through the heavens*': in contrast to Joshua the type, who did *not bring* God's people *into* the heavenly rest), he *himself* (*emphatical*) rested from his works (vs. 4), as God (did) from *His own*" (so the *Greek,* "works") **11. Let us . . . therefore**—Seeing such a promise is before us, which we may, like them, fall short of through unbelief. **labour**—*Greek,* "strive diligently." **that rest**—which is still future and so glorious. Or, in ALFORD's translation of vs. 10, "That rest into which *Christ* has entered before" (vs. 14; ch. 6:20). **fall**—with the soul, not merely the body, as the rebel Israelites fell (ch. 3:17). **after the same example**—ALFORD translates, "fall *into* the same example." The less prominent place of the "fall" in the *Greek* favors this. The sense is, "lest any fall into such *disobedience* (so the *Greek* for 'unbelief' means) as they gave a sample of" [GROTIUS]. The Jews say, "The parents are a sign (warning) to their sons." **12. For**—Such *diligent striving* (vs. 11) is incumbent on us(FOR we have to do with a God whose "word" whereby we shall be judged, is heart-searching, and whose eyes are all-seeing (vs. 13). The qualities here attributed to *the word of God,* and the whole context, show that it is regarded in its JUDICIAL power, whereby it doomed the disobedient Israelites to exclusion from Canaan, and shall exclude unbelieving so-called Christians from the heavenly rest. The written Word of God is not the prominent thought here, though the passage is often quoted as if it were. Still the word of God (the same as that preached, vs. 2), used here in the broadest sense, but with special reference to its *judicial* power, INCLUDES the Word of God, the sword of the Spirit with double edge, one edge for convicting and converting some (vs. 2), and the other for condemning

ADAM CLARKE

seems to have the same meaning as "rest" in some other parts of this verse. The day or time of rest relative to the ancient Jews being over and past, and a long time having elapsed between God's displeasure shown to the disobedient Jews in the wilderness and the days of David, and the true rest not having been enjoyed, God in His mercy has instituted another day—has given another dispensation of mercy and goodness by Christ Jesus; and now it may be said, as formerly, *To day, if ye will hear his voice, harden not your hearts.* God speaks now as He spoke before; His voice is in the gospel as it was in the law. Believe, love, obey, and you shall enter into this rest.

8. *For if Jesus had given them rest.* It is truly surprising that our translators should have rendered the text *Jesus,* and not "Joshua," who is most clearly intended. They must have known that the *Yehoshua* of the Hebrew, which we write "Joshua," is everywhere rendered *Jesus* by the Septuagint; and it is their reading which the apostle follows. It is "Joshua" in Coverdale's Testament, 1535; in Tindal's 1548; several modern translators, Wesley, Macknight, Wakefield, etc., read "Joshua," as does our own in the margin. What a pity it had not been in the text, as all the smaller Bibles have no marginal readings and many simple people are bewildered with the expression! The apostle shows that, although Joshua did bring the children of Israel into the Promised Land, yet this could not be the intended rest, because long after this time the Holy Spirit, by David, speaks of this rest. The apostle therefore concludes,

9. *There remaineth therefore a rest to the people of God.* It was not (1) the rest of the Sabbath; it was not (2) the rest in the Promised Land, for the Psalmist wrote long after the days of Joshua. Therefore there is another rest, a state of blessedness, for the people of God; and this is the gospel, the blessings it procures and communicates, and the eternal glory which it prepares for, and has promised to, genuine believers.

There are two words in this chapter which we indifferently translate *rest, katapausis* and *sabbatismos,* the first signifying a "cessation from labour," so that the weary body is rested and refreshed; the second meaning, not only a rest from labor, but a "religious rest"—a rest of a sacred kind, of which both soul and body partake. This is true whether we understand the rest as referring to gospel blessings, or to eternal felicity, or to both.

10. *For he that is entered into his rest.* The man who has believed in Christ Jesus has entered into His rest, the state of happiness which He has provided and which is the forerunner of eternal glory. *Hath ceased from his own works.* No longer depends on the observance of Mosaic rites and ceremonies for his justification and final happiness. He rests from all these works of the law as fully as God has rested from His works of creation. Those who restrain the word *rest* to the signification of eternal glory say that ceasing from our own works relates to the sufferings, tribulations, afflictions of this life, as in Rev. xiv. 13. I understand it as including both.

11. *Let us labour therefore.* The word implies every exertion of body and mind which can be made in reference to the subject. *Lest any man fall.* Lest he fall off from the grace of God, from the gospel and its blessings, and perish everlastingly. This is the meaning of the apostle, who never supposed that a man might not make final shipwreck of faith and of a good conscience as long as he was in a state of probation.

12. *For the word of God is quick, and powerful.* Commentators are greatly divided concerning the meaning of the phrase *the word of God;* some supposing the whole of divine revelation to be intended; others, the doctrine of the gospel faithfully preached; others, the mind of God or the divine intellect; and others, the Lord Jesus Christ, who is thus denominated in John i and Rev. xix. 13, the only places in which He is thus incontestably characterized in the New Testament. Mr. Wesley's note on this verse is expressed with his usual precision and accuracy: *"For the word of God*—preached, v. 2, and armed with threatenings, v. 3, *is living and*

MATTHEW HENRY

It is *quick;* it is very lively and active, in seizing the conscience of the sinner, in cutting him to the heart, and in comforting him and binding up the wounds of the soul. It is *powerful.* It convinces powerfully, converts powerfully, and comforts powerfully. It is powerful to batter down Satan's kingdom, and to set up the kingdom of Christ upon the ruins thereof. It is *sharper than any two-edged sword.*

It will enter where no other sword can, and make a more critical dissection: it *pierces to the dividing asunder of the soul and the spirit,* the soul and its habitual prevailing temper; it makes a soul that has been a long time of a proud spirit to be humble, of a perverse spirit to be meek and obedient. This sword divides between *the joints and the marrow.* This sword can make men willing to undergo the sharpest operation for the mortifying of sin.

It is *a discerner of the thoughts and intents of the heart.* The word will turn the inside of a sinner out, and let him see all that is in his heart.

3. The perfections of the Lord Jesus Christ.

(1) His person, particularly his omniscience, *v.* 13. None of the creatures can be concealed from Christ; and there are none of the motions and workings of our heads and hearts but what are open and manifest to him. This omniscience of Christ should engage us to persevere in faith and obedience.

(2) His office, and this particular office of our high priest.

[1] What kind of high priest Christ is (*v.* 14). *First,* A great high priest. The greatness of our high priest is set forth by his having passed into the heavens. Christ executed one part of his priesthood on earth, in dying for us; the other he executes in heaven, by pleading the cause of his people. The greatness of Christ is set forth by his name, *Jesus*—a physician and a Saviour, able to save to the uttermost all who come to God by him.

Secondly, He is not only a great, but a gracious high priest, merciful, compassionate, and sympathizing with his people, *v.* 15. He is touched with the feeling of our infirmities, not only that he might be able to satisfy for us, but to sympathize with us.

JAMIESON, FAUSSET, BROWN

and destroying the unbelieving (vs. 14). **quick**—*Greek,* "living"; having living power, as "the rod of the mouth and the breath of the lips" of "the living God." **powerful**—*Greek,* "energetic"; not only *living,* but *energetically efficacious.* **sharper**—"more cutting." **two-edged**—sharpened at both edge and back. Cf. "sword of the Spirit . . . word of God" (Eph. 6:17). Its *double* power seems to be implied by its being "two-edged." "It judges all that is in the heart, for there it passes through, at once *punishing* [unbelievers] and searching" [both believers and unbelievers] [CHRYSOSTOM]. **piercing**—*Greek,* "coming through." **even to the dividing asunder of soul and spirit**—i.e., reaching through even to the separation of the animal *soul,* the lower part of man's incorporeal nature, the seat of animal desires, which he has in common with the brutes; cf. the same *Greek,* I Corinthians 2:14, "the natural [animalsouled] man" (Jude 19), from the spirit (the higher part of man, receptive of the Spirit of God, and allying him to heavenly beings). **and of the joints and marrow**—rather, (*reaching even* TO) "*both* the joints (so as to divide them) and marrow." Christ "knows what is in man" (John 2: 25): so His word reaches as far as to the most intimate and accurate knowledge of man's most hidden parts, feelings, and thoughts, dividing, i.e., *distinguishing* what is *spiritual* from what is *carnal* and *animal* in him, the *spirit* from the *soul:* so Proverbs 20:27. As the knife of the Levitical priest reached to dividing parts, closely united as the *joints* of the limbs, and penetrated to the innermost parts, as the *marrows* (the *Greek* is *plural*); so the word of God divides the closely joined parts of man's immaterial being, soul and spirit, and penetrates to the innermost parts of the spirit. **discerner of the thoughts**—*Greek,* "capable of judging the purposes." **intents**—rather, "conceptions" [CRELLIUS]; "ideas" [ALFORD]. As the *Greek* for "thoughts" refers to the *mind* and *feelings,* so that for "intents," or rather "mental conceptions," refers to the *intellect.* **13. creature**—visible or invisible. **in his sight**—in *God's* sight (vs. 12). "God's wisdom, simply manifold, and uniformly multiform, with incomprehensible comprehension, comprehends all things incomprehensible." **opened**—lit., "thrown on the back so as to have the neck laid bare," as a victim with neck exposed for sacrifice. The *Greek* perfect tense implies that this is our *continuous* state in relation to God. "Show, O man, *shame* and *fear* towards thy God, for no veil, no twisting, bending, coloring, or disguise, can cover *unbelief*" (*Greek,* "disobedience," vs. 11). Let us, therefore, earnestly labor to enter the rest lest any fall through practical unbelief (vs. 11). **14. having, therefore . . .**—resuming ch. 2:17. **great**—as being "the Son of God, higher than the heavens" (ch. 7:26): the archetype and antitype of the legal high priest. **passed into the heavens**—rather, "passed *through* the heavens," viz., those which come between us and God, the aerial heaven, and that above the latter containing the heavenly bodies, the sun, moon, etc. These heavens were the veil which our High Priest *passed through* into the heaven of heavens, the immediate presence of God, just as the Levitical high priest passed through the veil into the Holy of Holies. Neither Moses, nor even Joshua, could bring us into this rest, but Jesus, as our Forerunner, already spiritually, and hereafter in actual presence, body, soul, and spirit, brings His people into the heavenly rest. **Jesus**—the antitypical Joshua (vs. 8). **hold fast**—the opposite of "let slip" (ch. 2:1); and "fall away" (ch. 6: 6). As the *genitive* follows, the lit., sense is, "Let us *take hold* of our profession," i.e., of the faith and hope which are subjects of our profession and confession. The accusative follows when the sense is "hold fast" [TITTMANN]. **15. For**—the motive to "holding our profession" (vs. 14), viz., the sympathy and help we may expect from our High Priest. Though "great" (vs. 14), He is not above caring for us; nay, as being in all points one with us as to manhood, sin only excepted, He sympathizes with us in every temptation. Though exalted to the highest heavens, He has changed His place, not His nature and office in relation to us, His condition, but not His affection. Cf. Matthew 26:38, "watch with me": showing His desire in the days of His flesh for *the sympathy of those whom He loved:* so He now gives His suffering people *His sympathy.* Cf. Aaron, the type, bearing the names of the twelve tribes in the breastplate of judgment on his heart, when he entered into the holy place, for a memorial before the Lord continually (Exod. 28:29). **cannot be touched with the feeling of**—*Greek,* "cannot sympathize with our infirmities": our *weaknesses,* physical and moral (not sin, but

ADAM CLARKE

powerful—attended with the power of the living God, and conveying either life or death to the hearers; *sharper than any twoedged sword*—penetrating the heart more than this does the body; *piercing* quite through, and laying open, *the soul and spirit, joints and marrow*—the inmost recesses of the mind, which the apostle beautifully and strongly expresses by this heap of figurative words; *and is a discerner, not only of the thoughts,* but also of the *intentions.*" The law, the Word of God in general, is repeatedly compared to *a twoedged sword* among the Jewish writers. *Is a discerner of the thoughts.* "Is a critic of the propensities and suggestions of the heart." How many have felt this property of God's Word where it has been faithfully preached! How often has it happened that a man has seen the whole of his own character and some of the most private transactions of his life held up as it were to public view by the preacher, and yet the parties absolutely unknown to each other! Some, thus exhibited, have even supposed that their neighbors must have privately informed the preacher of their character and conduct; but it was the Word of God which, by the direction and energy of the divine Spirit, thus searched them out, was a critical Examiner of the propensities and suggestions of their hearts, and had pursued them through all their public haunts and private ways. Every genuine minister of the gospel has witnessed such effects as these under his ministry in repeated instances.

13. *Neither is there any creature that is not manifest.* God, from this word comes and by whom it has all its efficacy, is infinitely wise. And so infinite is He in His knowledge, and so omnipresent is He, that the whole creation is constantly exposed to His view; nor is there a creature of the affections, mind, or imagination that is not constantly under His eye. *But all things are naked and opened.* The verb *opened* signifies to have the "neck bent back" so as to expose the face to full view, that every feature might be seen; and this was often done with criminals, in order that they might be the better recognized and ascertained. *With whom we have to do.* "To whom we must give an account." He is our Judge, and is well-qualified to be so, as all our hearts and actions are *naked* and *opened* to him.

14. *Seeing then that we have a great high priest.* It is contended, and very properly, that the particle which we translate *seeing,* as if what followed was an immediate inference from what the apostle had been speaking, should be translated "now"; for the apostle, though he had before mentioned Christ as the "High Priest of our profession," chap. iii. 1, and as the High Priest who made "reconciliation for the sins of the people," chap. ii. 17, does not attempt to prove this in any of the preceding chapters, but now enters upon that point, and discusses it at great length to the end of chap. x.

After all, it is possible that this may be a resumption of the discourse from chap. iii. 6, the rest of that chapter and the preceding thirteen verses of this being considered as a parenthesis. These parts left out, the discourse runs on with perfect connection. It is very likely that the words here are spoken to meet an objection of those Jews who wished the Christians of Palestine to apostatize: "You have no Tabernacle—no Temple—no high priest—no sacrifice for sin. Without these there can be no religion; return therefore to us, who have the perfect Temple service appointed by God." To these he answers: *"We have a . . . high priest, that is passed into the heavens, Jesus the Son of God;* therefore *let us hold fast our profession.* Three things the apostle professes to prove in this Epistle: (1) That Christ is greater than the *angels.* (2) That He is greater than *Moses.* (3) That He is greater than *Aaron* and all *high priests.* The former two arguments, with their applications and illustrations, he has already dispatched; and now he enters on the third. See the preface to this Epistle.

15. *For we have not an high priest.* To the objection, "Your High Priest, if entered into the heavens, can have no participation with you, and no sympathy for you, because out of the reach of human feelings and infirmities," he answers: "We have not a high priest who can-

MATTHEW HENRY

Thirdly, He is a sinless high priest: *He was in all things tempted as we are, yet without sin.* We seldom meet with temptations but they give us some shock. We are apt to give back, though we do not yield; but our great high priest came off clear in his encounter with the devil.

[2] How we should demean ourselves towards him. Let us hold fast our profession of faith in him, *v.* 14. Let us never deny him, never be ashamed of him before men. Christians must not only set out well, but they must hold out. We should encourage ourselves to come boldly to the throne of grace, *v.* 16. There is a throne of grace set up. God might have set up a tribunal of strict justice, but he has chosen to set up a throne of grace. There grace reigns, and acts with sovereign freedom, power, and bounty. It is our duty to be often found before this throne of grace. It is good for us to be there. Our business at the throne of grace should be that we *may obtain mercy and find grace to help in time of need.* Mercy and grace are the things we want, mercy to pardon all our sins and grace to purify our souls. In all our approaches to this throne of grace for mercy, we should come with a humble freedom and boldness; we should ask in faith, nothing doubting. We are indeed to come with reverence and godly fear; not as if we were dragged before the tribunal of justice, but kindly invited to the mercy-seat, where grace reigns, and loves to exert and exalt itself towards us. The office of Christ, as being our high priest, and such a high priest, should be the ground of our confidence in all our approaches to the throne of grace.

JAMIESON, FAUSSET, BROWN

liability to its assaults). He, though sinless, can sympathize with us sinners; His understanding more acutely perceived the forms of temptation than we who are weak can; His will repelled them as instantaneously as the fire does the drop of water cast into it. He, therefore, experimentally knew what power was needed to overcome temptations. He is capable of sympathizing, for He was at the same time tempted without sin, and yet truly tempted [BENGEL]. In Him alone we have an example suited to men of every character and under all circumstances. In sympathy He adapts himself to each, as if He had not merely taken on Him man's nature in general, but also the peculiar nature of that single individual. **but**—"nay, rather, He was (one) tempted" [ALFORD]. **like as we are** —*Greek,* "according to (our) similitude." **without sin**—*Greek, choris,* "*separate* from sin" (ch. 7:26). If the *Greek aneu* had been used, *sin* would have been regarded as the object absent from Christ the subject; but *choris* here implies that Christ, the *subject,* is regarded as separated from sin the object [TITTMANN]. Thus, throughout His temptations in their origin, process, and result, sin had nothing in Him; He was apart and separate from it [ALFORD]. **16. come**—rather as *Greek,* "approach," "draw near." **boldly**—*Greek,* "with confidence," or "freedom of speech" (Eph. 6:19). **the throne of grace**—God's throne is become to us a *throne of grace* through the mediation of our High Priest at God's right hand (ch. 8:1; 12:2). Pleading our High Priest Jesus' meritorious death, we shall always find God on a *throne of grace.* Contrast Job's complaint (Job 23:3-8) and Elihu's "IF . . ." (Job 33:23-28). **obtain**—rather, "receive." **mercy**—"Compassion," by its derivation (lit., fellow feeling from *community of suffering*), corresponds to the character of our High Priest "touched with the feeling of our infirmities" (vs. 15). **find grace**—corresponding to "throne *of grace.*" *Mercy* especially refers to the remission and removal of sins; *grace,* to the saving bestowal of spiritual gifts [ESTIUS]. Cf. Come unto Me . . . and I will *give* you rest (the rest *received* on first believing); take My yoke on you . . . and ye shall *find* rest (the continuing rest and peace *found* in daily submitting to Christ's easy yoke; the former answers to "*receive* mercy" here; the latter, to "*find* grace," Matt. 11:28, 29). **in time of need**—*Greek,* "seasonably." Before we are overwhelmed by the temptation; when we most need it, in temptations and persecutions; such as is suitable to the time, persons, and end designed (Ps. 104:27). A supply of grace is in store for believers against all exigencies; but they are only supplied with it according as the need arises. Cf. "in due time," Romans 5. 6. Not, as ALFORD explains, "help in time," i.e., *today,* while it is yet open to us; the accepted time (II Cor. 6:2). **help**—Cf. ch. 2:18, "He is able to *succor* them that are tempted."

ADAM CLARKE

not sympathize with our weakness." Though He be the Son of God and equal in His divine nature with God, yet, having partaken of human nature, and having submitted to all its trials and distresses, and being *in all points tempted like as we are . . . without* feeling or consenting to *sin,* He is able to succor them that are tempted. See chap. ii. 18. The words might be translated "in all points according to the likeness," i.e., as far as His human nature could bear affinity to ours. For though He had a perfect human body and human soul, yet that body was perfectly tempered; it was free from all morbid action, and consequently from all irregular movements. His mind, or human soul, being free from all sin, being every way perfect, could feel no irregular temper, nothing that was inconsistent with infinite purity.

16. *Let us therefore come boldly unto the throne of grace.* The allusion to the high priest and his office on the Day of Atonement is here kept up. The approach mentioned here is to the propitiatory or mercy seat. This was the covering of the ark of the testimony or covenant, at each end of which was a cherub, and between them the *shechinah,* or symbol of the divine majesty, which appeared to, and conversed with, the high priest. The throne of grace in heaven answers to this propitiatory, but to this *all* may approach who feel their need of salvation; and they may approach with freedom, confidence, liberty of speech, in opposition to the fear and trembling of the Jewish high priest. Here nothing is to be feared, provided the heart be right with God, truly sincere, and trusing alone in the sacrificial Blood. *That we may obtain mercy.* "That we may take mercy"—that we may receive the pardon of all our sins; there is mercy for the taking. *And find grace. Mercy* refers to the pardon of sin, and being brought into the favor of God. *Grace* is that by which the soul is supported after it has received this mercy, and by which it is purified from all unrighteousness, and upheld in all trials and difficulties, and enabled to prove faithful unto death. *To help in time of need.* "For a seasonable support"; that is, support when necessary, and as necessary, and in due proportion to the necessity. The word is properly rendered "assistance, help, or support"; but it is an assistance in consequence of the earnest cry of the person in distress, for the word signifies "to run at the cry."

MATTHEW HENRY

CHAPTER 5

Verses 1-9

An account of the nature of the priestly office in general.

I. Of what kind of beings the high priest must be. He must be taken from among men; he must be a man, one of ourselves. This implies that God would not admit sinful man to come to him immediately and alone; that God was pleased to take one from among men, by whom they might approach God in hope.

II. For whom every high priest is ordained: *For men in things pertaining to God*, for the glory of God and the good of men.

III. For what purpose every high priest was ordained: *That he might offer both gifts and sacrifices for sin.*

1. That he might offer gifts or free-will offerings, as an acknowledgment that our all is of him and from him. All we bring to God must be free and not forced; it must be a gift.

2. That he might offer sacrifices for sin. Christ is constituted a high priest for both these ends. Our good deeds must be presented by Christ, and our evil deeds must be expiated by the sacrifice of himself.

IV. How this high priest must be qualified, *v.* 2.

1. He must be one that can have compassion *on the ignorant*. He must be one who can find in his heart to pity them, one that is willing to instruct those that are dull of understanding.

JAMIESON, FAUSSET, BROWN

CHAPTER 5

VSS. 1-14. CHRIST'S HIGH PRIESTHOOD; NEEDED QUALIFICATIONS; MUST BE A MAN; MUST NOT HAVE ASSUMED THE DIGNITY HIMSELF, BUT HAVE BEEN APPOINTED BY GOD; THEIR LOW SPIRITUAL PERCEPTIONS A BAR TO PAUL'S SAYING ALL HE MIGHT ON CHRIST'S MELCHISEDEC-LIKE PRIESTHOOD. **1. For**—substantiating ch. 4:15. **every**—i.e., every legitimate high priest; for instance, the Levitical, as he is addressing Hebrews, among whom the Levitical priesthood was established as the legitimate one. Whatever, reasons Paul, is excellent in the Levitical priests, is also in Christ, and besides excellencies which are not in the Levitical priests. **taken from among men**—not from among angels, who could not have a fellow feeling with us men. This qualification Christ has, as being, like the Levitical priest, *a man* (ch. 2:14, 16). Being "*from* men," He can be "*for* (i.e., in behalf of, for the good of) men." **ordained**—*Greek,* "constituted," "appointed." **both gifts**—to be joined with "for sins," as "sacrifices" is (the "both . . . and" requires this); therefore not the *Hebrew, mincha,* unbloody offerings, but animal whole burnt offerings, *spontaneously given.* "Sacrifices" are the animal sacrifices *due according to the legal ordinance* [ESTIUS]. **2. Who can**—*Greek,* "being able"; *not pleasing himself* (Rom. 15:3). **have compassion**—*Greek,* "estimate mildly," "feel leniently," or "moderately towards"; "to make allowance for"; not showing stern rigor save to the obstinate (ch. 10:28). **ignorant**—sins not committed in resistance of light and knowledge, but as Paul's past sin (I Tim. 1:13). No sacrifice was appointed for wilful sin com-

ADAM CLARKE

CHAPTER 5

1. *For every high priest taken from among men.* This seems to refer to Lev. xxi. 10, where it is intimated that the high priest shall be taken from his brethren; i.e., he shall be of the tribe of Levi, and of the family of Aaron. *Is ordained for men.* Is appointed to preside over the divine worship in those things which relate to man's salvation. *That he may offer both gifts and sacrifices for sins.* God ever appeared to all His followers in two points of view: (1) as the Author and Dispenser of all temporal good; (2) as their Lawgiver and Judge. In reference to this twofold view of the Divine Being, His worship was composed of two different parts: (1) "offerings" or *gifts;* (2) *sacrifices.* As the Creator and Dispenser of all good, He had "offerings" by which His bounty and providence were acknowledged. As the Lawgiver and Judge, against whose injunctions offences had been committed, He had *sacrifices* offered to Him to make atonement for sin. The *gifts* mentioned here by the apostle included every kind of eucharistical offering. The *sacrifices* included victims of every sort, or animals whose lives were to be offered in sacrifice and their blood poured out before God as an atonement for sins.

2. *Who can have compassion on the ignorant.* The word signifies not merely to *have compassion* but to "acts with moderation" and to "bear with each in proportion" to his ignorance, weakness, and untoward circumstances, all taken

MATTHEW HENRY

On those that are out of the way. He must be one who has tenderness enough to lead them back from the by-paths of error, sin, and misery, into the right away: this will require great patience and compassion, even the compassion of a God.

2. He must also be compassed with infirmity; and so be able from himself to sympathize with us. Thus Christ was qualified.

V. How the high priest was to be called of God. (*v.* 4). The office of the priesthood was a very great honour. Those only can expect his presence and blessing on them and their administrations, that are called of God; others may expect a blast instead of a blessing.

VI. How this is brought home and applied to Christ, *v.* 5. Though Christ reckoned it his glory to be made a high priest, yet he would not assume that glory to himself. He did not run without being sent; and, if he did not, surely others should be afraid to do it.

VII. The apostle prefers Christ before Aaron. In the manner of his call, in which God said unto him, *Thou art my Son, this day have I begotten thee.* Now God never said thus to Aaron. Another expression that God used in the call of Christ, *v.* 6. God the Father appointed him a priest of a higher order than that of Aaron. The priesthood of Aaron was to be but temporary; the priesthood of Christ was to be perpetual. In the holiness of his person. Other priests were to offer up sacrifices, as for the *sins of others, so for themselves, v.* 3. But Christ needed not to offer for sins for himself.

VIII. Christ's discharge of this his office, and the consequences of that discharge, *v.* 7–9.

1. The discharge of his office of the priesthood (*v.* 7). He took to him flesh; he became a mortal man. Christ, in the days of his flesh, subjected himself to death; he was a tempted, bleeding, dying Jesus! God the Father was able to save him from death. What would have become of us if God had saved Christ from dying? It was in kindness to us that the Father would not suffer that bitter cup to pass away from him; for then we must have drunk the dregs of it. Christ, in the days of his flesh, offered up prayers and supplications to his Father. A great many instances we have of Christ's praying. This refers to his prayer in his agony, and to that before his agony.

The prayers and supplications that Christ offered up were joined with strong cries and tears, herein setting us an example. How many dry prayers, how few wet ones, do we offer up to God!

JAMIESON, FAUSSET, BROWN

mitted with a high hand; for such were to be punished with death; all other sins, viz., ignorances and errors, were confessed and expiated with sacrifices by the high priest. **out of the way**—not deliberately and altogether wilfully erring, but deluded through the fraud of Satan and their own carnal frailty and thoughtlessness. **infirmity**—moral weakness which is sinful, and makes men capable of sin, and so requires to be expiated by sacrifices. This kind of "infirmity" Christ had not; He had the "infirmity" of body whereby He was capable of suffering and death. **3. by reason hereof**—"on account of this" infirmity. **he ought . . . also for himself, to offer for sins**—the Levitical priest ought; in this our High Priest is superior to the Levitical. The second "for" is a different *Greek* term from the first; "*in behalf of* the people . . . , *on account* of sins." **4. no man**—of any other family but Aaron's, according to the Mosaic law, can take to himself the office of high priest. This verse is quoted by some to prove the need of an apostolic succession of ordination in the Christian ministry; but the reference here is to the *priesthood,* not the Christian *ministry.* The analogy in our Christian dispensation would warn ministers, seeing that God has separated them from the congregation of His people to bring them near Himself, and to do the service of His house, and to minister (as He separated the Levites, Korah with his company), that content with this, they should beware of assuming the sacrificial priesthood also, which belongs to Christ alone. The sin of Korah was, not content with the ministry as a Levite, he took the sacerdotal priesthood also. No Christian minister, as such, is ever called *Hiereus,* i.e., sacrificing priest. All Christians, without distinction, whether ministers or people, have a metaphorical, not a literal, priesthood. The sacrifices which they offer are spiritual, not literal, their bodies and the fruit of their lips, praises continually (ch. 13:15). Christ alone had a proper and true sacrifice to offer. The law sacrifices were typical, not metaphorical, as the Christian's, nor proper and true, as Christ's. In Roman times the Mosaic restriction of the priesthood to Aaron's family was violated. **5. glorified not himself**—did not assume the glory of the priestly office of Himself without the call of God (John 8:54). **but he that said**—i.e., the Father glorified Him or appointed Him to the priesthood. This appointment was involved in, and was the result of, the *Sonship* of Christ, which qualified Him for it. None but the divine Son could have fulfilled such an office (ch. 10:5-9). The connection of *Sonship* and *priesthood* is typified in the *Hebrew* title for *priests* being given to David's *sons* (II Sam. 8:18). Christ did not constitute *Himself* the Son of God, but was from everlasting the only-begotten *of the Father.* On His Sonship depended His glorification, and His being called of God (vs. 10), as Priest. **6.** He is here called simply "Priest"; in vs. 5, "High Priest." He is a *Priest* absolutely, because He stands alone in that character without an equal. He is "High Priest" in respect of the Aaronic type, and also in respect to us, whom He has made *priests* by throwing open to us access to God [BENGEL]. "The *order* of Melchisedec" is explained in ch. 7:15, "the *similitude* of Melchisedec." The priesthood is similarly combined with His kingly office in Zechariah 6:13. Melchisedec was at once man, priest, and king. Paul's selecting as the type of Christ one not of the stock of Abraham, on which the Jews prided themselves, is an intimation of Messianic universalism. **7. in the days of his flesh**—(ch. 2:14; 10:20). Verses 7-10 state summarily the subject about to be handled more fully in chs. 7 and 8. **when he had offered**—rather, "*in that* He *offered.*" His crying and tears were part of the experimental lesson of obedience which He submitted to learn from the Father (when God was qualifying Him for the high priesthood). "Who" is to be construed with "learned obedience" (or rather as *Greek,* "*His* obedience"; *the* obedience which we all know about). This all shows that "Christ glorified not Himself to be made an High Priest" (vs. 5), but was appointed thereto by the Father. **prayers and supplications**—*Greek,* "*both* prayers and supplications." In Gethsemane, where He prayed *thrice,* and on the cross, where He cried, My God, my God . . . , probably repeating inwardly *all* the 22d Psalm. "Prayers" refer to the mind: "supplications" also to the body [viz., the suppliant attitude] (Matt. 26:39) [BENGEL]. **with strong crying and tears**—The "tears" are an additional fact here communicated to us by the inspired apostle, not recorded in the Gospels, though implied. Matthew 26:37, "sorrowful and very heavy." Mark 14:33; Luke 22:44, "in an agony

ADAM CLARKE

into consideration with the offenses he has committed; in a word, to pity, feel for, and excuse as far as possible; and when the provocation is at the highest, to moderate one's passion towards the culprit, and be ready to pardon; and when punishment must be administered, to do it in the gentlest manner. The reason given why the high priest should be slow to punish and prone to forgive is that he himself is also "compassed with weakness"; "weakness lies all around him."

3. *And by reason hereof.* As he is also a transgressor of the commands of God, and unable to observe the law in its spirituality, he must offer sacrifices for sin, not only for the people, but for himself also; this must teach him to have a fellow feeling for others.

4. *This honour.* "The office," which is one meaning of the word in the best Greek writers. It is here an honorable office, because the man is the high priest of God, and is appointed by God himself to that office. *But he that is called of God, as was Aaron.* God himself appointed the tribe and family out of which the high priest was to be taken, and Aaron and his sons were expressly chosen by God to fill the office of the high priesthood.

5. *Christ glorified not himself.* The man Jesus Christ was also appointed by God to this most awful yet glorious office of being the High Priest of the whole human race. *Thou art my Son.* See on chap. i. 5.

6. *He saith also in another place.* That is, in Ps. cx. 4, a psalm of extraordinary importance, containing a very striking prediction of the birth, preaching, suffering, death, and conquests of the Messiah. For the mode of quotation here, see the note on chap. ii. 6. *Thou art a priest for ever.* As long as the sun and moon endure, Jesus will continue to be High Priest to all the successive generations of men, as He was the Lamb slain from the foundation of the world. If He be *a priest for ever,* there can be no succession of priests. *After the order of Melchisedec.* Who this person was must still remain a secret. We know nothing more of him than is written in Gen. xiv. 18, etc.

7. *Who in the days of his flesh.* The time of His incarnation, during which He took all the infirmities of human nature upon Him, and was afflicted in His body and human soul just as other men are, irregular and sinful passions excepted. The Redeemer of the world appears here as simply man; but He is the Representative of the whole human race. He must make expiation for sin by suffering, and He can suffer only as men. Suffering was as necessary as death; for man, because he has sinned, must suffer, and because he has broken the law, should die. Jesus took upon himself the nature of man, subject to all the trials and distresses of human nature. Though He was the Son of God, conceived and born without sin, or anything that could render Him liable to suffering or death, yet to constitute Him a complete Saviour, He must submit to whatever the law required; and therefore He is stated to have "learned . . . obedience by the things which he suffered," v. 8, that is, subjection to all the requisitions of the law; "and being made perfect," that is, having finished the whole by dying, He by these means became the "author of eternal salvation unto all them that obey him," v. 9; to them who, according to His own command, repent and believe the gospel, and under the influence of His Spirit walk in holiness of life. *Prayers and supplications.* There may be an allusion here to the manner in which the Jews speak of prayer. "There are three degrees of prayer, each surpassing the other in silence; crying, with a loud voice; but tears surpass all" (*Synops. Sohar,* p. 33). The apostle shows that Christ made every species of prayer, and those especially by which they allowed a man must be successful with his Maker.

The word *hiketerias,* which we translate *supplications,* exists in no other part of the New Testament. *Hiketes* signifies a supplicant: "He who, in the most humble and servile manner, entreats and begs anything from another."

MATTHEW HENRY

Christ was heard in that he feared. He was answered by present supports in his agonies, and in being carried well through death, and delivered from it by a glorious resurrection. He was carried through death; and there is no real deliverance from death but to be carried well through it. We may have many recoveries from sickness, but we are never saved from death till we are carried well through it.

2. The consequences of this discharge of his office, *v.* 8, 9, &c.

(1) By these his sufferings *he learned obedience, though he was a Son, v.* 8. Let none then who are the children of God by adoption expect an absolute freedom from suffering. Though he never was disobedient, yet he never performed such an act of obedience as when he became obedient to death, even to the death of the cross. We should learn by all our afflictions a humble obedience to the will of God.

(2) Hereby he has become the author of eternal salvation to men. This salvation is actually bestowed on none but those who obey Christ. We must hearken to his word, and obey him. He is exalted to be a prince to rule us, as well as a Saviour to deliver us; and he will be a Saviour to none but to those to whom he is a prince. But to those who obey him, he will be the author—the grand cause of their salvation.

Verses 10–14

I. He had many things which he could say to them concerning this mysterious person called Melchisedec, whose priesthood was eternal. There are great mysteries in the person and offices of the Redeemer; Christianity is the great mystery of godliness.

II. The reason why he did not say all those things concerning Christ, our Melchisedec, that he had to say: *You are dull of hearing.* Dull hearers make the preaching of the gospel a difficult thing, and even many who have some faith are but dull hearers.

III. It was not a mere natural infirmity, but it was a sinful infirmity, *v.* 12.

1. They might have been so well instructed in the doctrine of the gospel as to have been teachers of others.

2. *You have need that one should teach you again,* &c. In the oracles of God there are some first principles, plain to be understood and necessary to be learned. There are also deep and sublime mysteries.

JAMIESON, FAUSSET, BROWN

He prayed more earnestly . . . His sweat . . . great drops of blood falling down to the ground." Psalm 22:1 ("roaring . . . cry"), 2, 19, 21, 24; 69:3, 10, "I *wept.*" **able to save him from death**—Mark 14:36, "All things are *possible* unto Thee" (John 12:27). His cry showed His entire participation of man's infirmity: His reference of His wish to the will of God, His sinless faith and obedience. **heard in that he feared**—There is no intimation in Psalm 22, or the Gospels that Christ prayed to be saved from the mere act of dying. What He feared was the hiding of the Father's countenance. His holy filial love must rightly have shrunk from this strange and bitterest of trials without the imputation of impatience. To have been passively content at the approach of such a cloud would have been, not faith, but sin. The cup of death He prayed to be freed from was, not corporal, but spiritual death, i.e., the (temporary) separation of His human soul from the light of God's countenance. His prayer was "heard" in His Father's strengthening Him so as to hold fast His unwavering faith under the trial (*My* God, *my* God, was still His filial cry under it. still claiming God as His, though God hid His face), and soon removing it in answer to His cry during the darkness on the cross, "My God, my God . . . ." But see below a further explanation of how He was heard. The *Greek* lit., is, "Was heard *from His fear,*" i.e., so as to be saved from His fear. Cf. Psalm 22:21, which well accords with this, "Save me *from* the lion's mouth (His prayer): thou hast heard me *from* the horns of the unicorns." Or what better accords with the strict meaning of the *Greek* noun, "*in consequence of His* REVERENTIAL FEAR," i.e., in that He *shrank from* the horrors of separation from the bright presence of the Father, yet was *reverentially cautious* by no thought or word of impatience to give way to a shadow of distrust or want of perfect filial love. In the same sense ch. 12:28 uses the noun, and ch. 11:7 the verb. **8.** Though He WAS (so it ought to be translated: a positive admitted fact: not a mere supposition as *were* would imply) God's divine Son (whence, even in His agony, He so lovingly and often cried, *Father,* Matt. 26:39), yet He learned *His* (so the *Greek*) obedience, not from His Sonship, but from His sufferings. As the Son, He was always obedient to the Father's will; but *the* special obedience needed to qualify Him as our High Priest, He learned experimentally in practical suffering. Cf. Philippians 2:6-8, "*equal with God,* but . . . took upon Him the form of a *servant,* and became *obedient* unto death . . . ." He was *obedient* already before His passion, but He stooped to a still more humiliating and trying form of *obedience* then. The *Greek* adage is, *Pathemata mathemata,* "sufferings, disciplinings." *Praying* and *obeying,* as in Christ's case, ought to go hand in hand. **9. made perfect**—completed, brought to His goal of learning and suffering through death (ch. 2:10) [ALFORD], viz., at His glorious resurrection and ascension. **author**—*Greek,* "cause." **eternal salvation**—obtained for us in the *short* "days of Jesus' flesh" (vs. 7; cf. vs. 6, "for ever," Isa. 45: 17). **unto all . . . that obey him**—As Christ *obeyed* the Father, so must we *obey* Him by faith. **10.** *Greek,* rather, "*Addressed* by God (by the appellation) High Priest." Being formally recognized by God as High Priest at the time of His being "made perfect" (vs. 9). He was High Priest already *in the purpose of God* before His passion; but after it, when perfected, He was formally addressed so. **11.** Here he digresses to complain of the low spiritual attainments of the Palestinian Christians and to warn them of the danger of falling from light once enjoyed; at the same time encouraging them by God's faithfulness to persevere. At ch. 6:20 he resumes the comparison of Christ to Melchisedec. **hard to be uttered**—rather as *Greek,* "hard *of interpretation* to speak." Hard for me to state intelligibly to you owing to your dulness about spiritual things. Hence, instead of *saying many things,* he writes in comparatively *few words* (ch. 13:22). In the "we," Paul, as usual, includes Timothy with himself in addressing them. **ye are**—*Greek,* "ye have *become* dull" (the *Greek,* by derivation, means *hard to move*): this implies that *once,* when first "enlightened," they were earnest and zealous, but had *become* dull. **12. for the time**—considering the long time that you have been Christians. Therefore this Epistle was not one of those written early. **which be the first principles**—*Greek,* "the *rudiments of the beginning* of." A Pauline phrase (*Notes,* Gal. 4:3, 9). Ye need not only to be taught *the first elements,* but also "*which* they be." **oracles of God**—viz., of the Old Testament:

ADAM CLARKE

To save him from death. I have already observed that Jesus Christ was the Representative of the human race; and have made some observations on the peculiarity of His sufferings, following the common acceptation of the words in the text, which things are true, howsoever the text may be interpreted. But here we may consider the pronoun *him* as implying the collective body of mankind. So he made *supplications with strong crying and tears unto him that was able to save* them *from death;* for I consider "them," of chap. ii. 15, the same or implying the same thing as *him* in this verse; and, thus understood, all the difficulty vanishes away. On this interpretation I shall give a paraphrase of the whole verse: "Jesus Christ, in the days of His flesh (for He was incarnated that He might redeem the seed of Abraham, the fallen race of man), and in His expiatory sufferings, when representing the whole human race, offered up prayers and supplications with strong crying and tears to Him who was able to save them from death. The intercession was prevalent, the passion and sacrifice were accepted, the sting of death was extracted, and Satan was dethroned."

9. *And being made perfect.* "And having finished all"—having died and risen again. Signifies to have "obtained the goal"; to have ended one's labor, and enjoyed the fruits of it. So when Christ had finished His course of tremendous sufferings and consummated the whole by His death and resurrection, He became the Cause *of eternal salvation unto all them that obey him.* He was consecrated both High Priest and Sacrifice by His offering upon the Cross. He "tasted death for every man"; but He is the *author* and "cause of eternal salvation only to them who *obey him.* It is not merely believers, but obedient believers, who shall be finally saved. Therefore this text is an absolute, unimpeachable evidence that it is not the imputed obedience of Christ that saves any man.

10. *Called of God an high priest.* Being "constituted, hailed, and acknowledged" to be a High Priest.

11. *Of whom we have many things to say.* The words which we translate *of whom* are variously applied: (1) To Melchisedec; (2) To Christ, (3) To the endless priesthood. It is likely that the words are to be understood as meaning Jesus, or that endless priesthood of which he was a little before speaking, and which is a subject that carnal Christians cannot easily comprehend. *Hard to be uttered.* "Difficult to be interpreted," because Melchisedec was a typical person. Or if it refer to the priesthood of Christ, that is still more difficult to be explained, as it implies not only His being constituted a Priest after this typical order, but His paying down the ransom for the sins of the whole world. *Dull of hearing.* Your souls do not keep pace with the doctrines and exhortations delivered to you. Signifies a person who walks heavily and makes little speed.

12. *For when for the time.* They had heard the gospel for many years, and had professed to be Christians for a long time; on these accounts they might reasonably have been expected to be well-instructed in divine things, so as to be able to instruct others. *Which be the first principles.* "Certain first principles or elements." The literal translation of the passage is this: "You have need that one teach you a second time certain elements of the doctrines of Christ, or oracles of God"; i.e., the notices which the prophets gave concerning the priesthood of Jesus Christ, such as are found in Psalms cx and in Isaiah liii. By the *oracles of God* the writings of the Old Testament are undoubtedly meant. *And are*

MATTHEW HENRY

IV. There are in the church babes and persons of full age (*v.* 12–14), and there are in the gospel milk and strong meat.

Those that are babes, unskilful in the word of righteousness, must be fed with milk. Christ despises not his babes; he has provided suitable food for them.

There is strong meat for those that are of full age, *v.* 14. The deeper mysteries of religion belong to those that are of a higher class in the school of Christ. Every true Christian stands in need of nourishment. The word of God is food and nourishment to the life of grace.

There are spiritual senses as well as those that are natural. The soul has its sensations as well as the body; these are much depraved and lost by sin, but they are recovered by grace. It is by use and exercise that these senses are improved, made more quick and strong to taste the sweetness of what is good and true, and the bitterness of what is false and evil.

JAMIESON, FAUSSET, BROWN

instead of seeing Christ as the end of the Old Testament Scripture, they were relapsing towards Judaism, so as not only not to be capable of understanding the typical reference to Christ of such an Old Testament personage as Melchisedec, but even much more elementary references. **are become**—through indolence. **milk . . . not . . . strong meat**—"Milk" refers to such fundamental first principles as he enumerates in ch. 6:1, 2. The *solid meat,* or *food,* is not absolutely necessary for preserving life, but is so for acquiring greater strength. Especially in the case of the Hebrews, who were much given to allegorical interpretations of their law, which they so much venerated, the application of the Old Testament types, to Christ and His High Priesthood, was calculated much to strengthen them in the Christian faith [LIMBORCH].

13. useth—*Greek,* "partaketh," i.e., taketh as *his portion.* Even strong men partake of milk, but do not make milk their chief, much less their sole, diet. **the word of righteousness**—the Gospel wherein "the righteousness of God is revealed from faith to faith" (Rom. 1:17), and which is called "the ministration of righteousness" (II Cor. 3:9). This includes the doctrine of *justification* and sanctification: the first *principles,* as well as the *perfection, of the doctrine of Christ:* the nature of the offices and person of Christ as the true Melchisedec, i.e., "King of *righteousness*" (cf. Matt. 3:15). **14. strong meat**—"solid food." **them . . . of full age**—lit., "perfect": akin to "perfection" (ch. 6:1).

by reason of use—*Greek,* "habit." **senses**—organs of sense. **exercised**—similarly connected with "righteousness" in ch. 12:11. **to discern both good and evil**—as a child no longer an infant (Isa. 7:16): so able to distinguish between sound and unsound doctrine. The mere child puts into its mouth things hurtful and things nutritious, without discrimination: but not so the adult. Paul again alludes to their tendency not to discriminate, but to be carried about by strange doctrines, in ch. 13:9.

ADAM CLARKE

become such. The words seem to intimate that they had once been better instructed, and had now forgotten that teaching; and this was occasioned by their being "dull of hearing." Either they had not continued to hear or they had heard so carelessly that they were not profited by what they heard. They had probably totally omitted the preaching of the gospel and consequently forgotten all they had learned. Indeed it was to reclaim those Hebrews from backsliding and preserve them from total apostasy that this Epistle was written. *Such as have need of milk. Milk* is a metaphor by which many authors, both sacred and profane, express the first principles of religion and science. On the contrary, those who had well learned all the first principles of religion and science and knew how to apply them were considered as adults who were capable of receiving "solid food"; i.e., the more difficult and sublime doctrines. The rabbins abound with this figure; it occurs frequently in Philo, and in the Greek ethic writers also. But all these are to derive their nourishment or spiritual instruction from *the oracles of God.* The word oracle is used by the best Greek writers to signify a "divine speech, or answer of a deity to a question proposed."

13. *For every one that useth milk.* It is very likely that the apostle, by using this term, refers to the doctrines of the law, which were only the rudiments of religion and were intended to lead us to Christ, that we might be justified by faith. *The word of righteousness.* "The doctrine of justification." I believe this to be the apostle's meaning. He that uses *milk,* rests in the ceremonies and observances of the law, *is unskilful in* "the doctrine of justification"; for this requires faith in the sacrificial death of the promised Messiah.

14. *But strong meat.* The high and sublime doctrines of Christianity: the atonement, justification by faith, the gift of the Holy Ghost, the fullness of Christ dwelling in the souls of men, the resurrection of the body, the glorification of both body and soul in the realms of blessedness, and an endless union with Christ in the throne of His glory. This is the "strong food" which the genuine Christian understands, receives, digests, and by which he grows. *By reason of use.* Who, by constant hearing, believing, praying, and obedience, *use* all the graces of God's Spirit; and in the faithful use of them find every one improved, so that they daily grow in grace and in the knowledge of Jesus Christ, our Lord. *Have their senses exercised.* The word signifies the different organs of sense through which we gain the sensations called seeing, hearing, tasting, smelling, and feeling. There is something in the soul that answers to all these senses in the body. In the adult Christian these senses are said to be *exercised,* a metaphor taken from the athletes or contenders in the Grecian games, who were wont to employ all their powers, skill, and agility in mock fights, running, wrestling, that they might be the better prepared for the actual contests when they took place.

MATTHEW HENRY — CHAPTER 6

Verses 1–8

In order to their growth, Christians must leave the principles of the doctrine of Christ. They must not lose them, they must not despise them, they must not forget them. But they must not rest in them, they must not be always laying the foundation, they must go on, and build upon it. Though some of them were but weak, yet others of them had gained more strength; and they must be provided for suitably. He hoped they would be growing and so be able to digest stronger meat.

I. Several foundation-principles, which must be well laid at first, and then built upon.

1. Repentance from dead works. Take care that you return not to sin again, for then you must have the foundation to lay again. Repentance for and from dead works is a foundation-principle, which must not be laid again, though we must renew our repentance daily.

JAMIESON, FAUSSET, BROWN — CHAPTER 6

VSS. 1-14. WARNING AGAINST RETROGRADING, WHICH SOON LEADS TO APOSTASY; ENCOURAGEMENT TO STEADFASTNESS FROM GOD'S FAITHFULNESS TO HIS WORD AND OATH. **1. Therefore**—Wherefore: seeing that ye ought not now to be still "babes" (ch. 5:11-14). **leaving**—getting further forward than the elementary "principles." "As in building a house one must never leave the foundation: yet to be always laboring in 'laying the foundation' would be ridiculous" [CALVIN]. **the principles of the doctrine**—*Greek,* "the word *of* the beginning," i.e., the discussion of the "first principles of Christianity (ch. 5:12). **let us go on**—*Greek,* "let us be borne forward," or "bear ourselves forward"; implying active exertion: press on. Paul, in teaching, here classifies himself with the Hebrew readers, or (as they ought to be) learners, and says, Let us together press forward. **perfection**—the matured knowledge of those who are "of full age" (ch. 5:14) in Christian attainments. **foundation of**—i.e., *consisting in* "repentance." **repentance from dead works**—viz., not springing from the *vital* principle of faith and love toward God, and so counted, like their

ADAM CLARKE — CHAPTER 6

1. *Therefore.* Because you have been so indolent, slow of heart, and still have so many advantages *Leaving the principles of the doctrine of Christ.* Ceasing to continue in the state of babes, who must be fed with milk—with the lowest doctrines of the gospel, when you should be capable of understanding the highest. *Let us go on unto perfection.* Let us never rest till we are adult Christians—till we are saved from all sin, and are filled with the Spirit and power of Christ. The original is very emphatic: "Let us be carried on to this perfection." God is ever ready by the power of His Spirit to carry us forward to every degree of light, life, and love necessary to prepare us for an eternal weight of glory. Many make a violent outcry against the doctrine of *perfection,* i.e., against the heart being cleansed from all sin in this life and filled with love to God and man, because they judge it to be impossible! Is it too much to say of these that they know neither the Scripture nor the power of God? Surely the Scripture promises

MATTHEW HENRY

2. Faith towards God. Repentance from dead works, and faith towards God, are connected, and always go together; they are inseparable twins, the one cannot live without the other.

3. The doctrine of baptisms. This ordinance of baptism is a foundation to be rightly laid, and daily remembered, but not repeated.

4. Laying on of hands, on persons passing solemnly from their initiated state by baptism to the confirmed state. Or by this may be meant ordination of persons to the ministerial office. This is to be done but once.

5. The resurrection of the dead.

6. Eternal judgment.

These are the great foundation-principles, and from these they must never depart.

II. The apostle declares his readiness to assist the Hebrews in building themselves up on these foundations, *v.* 3. That resolution is right which is not only made in the sincerity of our hearts, but in a humble dependence upon God. Ministers should not only teach people what to do, but go before them, and along with them, in the way of duty.

III. Spiritual growth is the surest way to prevent apostasy from the faith.

1. He shows how far persons may go in religion, and, after all, fall away, and perish for ever, *v.* 4, 5. (1) They may be *enlightened.* It is rather to be understood of notional knowledge and common illumination, of which persons may have a great deal, and yet come short of heaven.

(2) They may *taste of the heavenly gift* like persons in the market, who taste of what they will not come up to the price of, and so but take a taste, and leave it.

(3) They may be *made partakers of the Holy Ghost,* of his extraordinary and miraculous gifts. Such gifts in the apostolic age were sometimes bestowed upon those who had no true saving grace.

(4) They may *taste of the good word of God*; they may hear the word with pleasure, and talk well of it, and yet never have it dwelling richly in them.

JAMIESON, FAUSSET, BROWN

doer, *dead* before God. This *repentance from dead works* is therefore paired with "faith toward God." The three pairs of truths enumerated are designedly such as JEWISH believers might in some degree have known from the Old Testament, but had been taught more clearly when they became Christians. This accounts for the omission of *distinct* specification of some essential first principle of Christian truth. Hence, too, he mentions "faith toward *God,*" and not *explicitly* faith toward *Christ* (though of course included). Repentance and faith were the first principles taught under the Gospel. **2. the doctrine of baptisms**—paired with "laying on of hands," as the latter followed on Christian baptism, and answers to the rite of *confirmation* in Episcopal churches. Jewish believers passed, by an easy transition, from Jewish *baptismal purifications* (ch. 9:10, "washings"), baptism of proselytes, and John's baptism, and legal imposition of hands, to their Christian analogues, *baptism,* and the subsequent *laying on of hands,* accompanied by the gift of the Holy Ghost (cf. vs. 4). *Greek, baptismoi,* plural, including *Jewish* and *Christian baptisms,* are to be distinguished from *baptisma,* singular, *restricted* to Christian baptism. The six particulars here specified had been, as it were, *the Christian Catechism* of the Old Testament; and such Jews who had begun to recognize Jesus as the Christ immediately on the new light being shed on these fandamental particulars, were accounted as having the elementary *principles* of the doctrine of Christ [BENGEL]. The first and most obvious elementary instruction of Jews would be the *teaching* them the typical significance of their own ceremonial law in its Christian fulfilment [ALFORD]. **resurrection . . .**—held already by the Jews from the Old Testament: confirmed with clearer light in Christian *teaching* or "doctrine." **eternal judgment**—judgment fraught with eternal consequences either of joy or of woe. **3. will we do**—So some of the oldest MSS. read; but others, "Let us do." "This," i.e., "Go on unto perfection." **if God permit**—For even in the case of good resolutions, we cannot carry them into effect, save through God "working in us both to will and to do of His good pleasure" (Phil. 2:13). The "for" in vs. 4 refers to this: I say, if God permit, *for* there are cases where God does not permit, e.g., "it is impossible," etc. Without God's blessing, the cultivation of the ground does not succeed (vs. 7). **4.** We must "go on toward perfection"; for if we *fall away,* after having received enlightenment, it will be *impossible to renew* us *again to repentance.* **for those**—"in the case of those." **once enlightened**—once for all illuminated by the word of God taught in connection with "baptism" (to which, in vs. 2, as once for all done," once enlightened" here answers); cf. Ephesians 5:26. This passage probably originated the application of the term "illumination" to baptism in subsequent times. *Illumination,* however, was not supposed to be the inseparable accompaniment of *baptism:* thus CHRYSOSTOM says, "Heretics have *baptism,* not *illumination:* they are baptized in body, but not enlightened in soul: as Simon Magus was baptized, but not illuminated." That "enlightened" here means *knowledge of the word of truth,* appears from comparing the same *Greek* word "illuminated," ch. 10:32, with 26, where "knowledge of the truth" answers to it. **tasted of the heavenly gift**—tasted *for themselves.* As "enlightened" refers to the sense of *sight:* so here *taste* follows. "The heavenly gift"; *Christ* given by the Father and revealed by the enlightening word preached and written: as conferring peace in the remission of sins; and as the Bestower of the gift of the Holy Spirit (Acts 8:19, 20),**made partakers of the Holy Ghost**—specified as distinct from, though so inseparably connected with, "enlightened," and "tasted of the heavenly gift," Christ, as answering to "laying on of hands" after baptism, which was then generally accompanied with the impartation of *the Holy Ghost* in miraculous *gifts.* **5. tasted the good word of God**—distinct from "tasted OF (genetive) the heavenly gift"; we do not yet enjoy *all* the fulness of Christ, but only have a taste OF Him, the heavenly gift now; but believers may taste the *whole* word (accusative) of God already, viz., God's "good word" *of promise.* The Old Testament promise of Canaan to Israel typified "the good word of God's" promise of the heavenly rest (ch. 4). Therefore, there immediately follows the clause, "the powers of the world to come." As "enlightening" and "tasting of the heavenly gift," Christ, the Bread of Life, answers to FAITH: so "made partakers of the Holy Ghost," to CHARITY, which is the first fruit of the Spirit: and "tasted the good word of *God,* and the powers of the world to come," to HOPE. Thus the triad of privileges an-

ADAM CLARKE

the thing, and the power of God can carry us on to the possession of it. *Laying again the foundation of repentance.* The phrase *dead works* occurs but once more in the sacred writings, and that is in chap. ix. 14 of this Epistle; and in both places it seems to signify "such works as deserve death"—works of those who were dead in sins, and dead by sentence of the law, because they had by these works broken the law. Repentance may be properly called the *foundation* of the work of God in the soul of man, because by it we forsake sin and turn to God to find mercy. *Faith toward God* is also a *foundation,* or fundamental principle, without which it is impossible to please God, and without which we cannot be saved. By repentance we feel the need of God's mercy; by faith we find that mercy.

2. *Of the doctrine of baptisms.* I am inclined to think that all the terms in this verse, as well as those in the former, belong to the Levitical law and are to be explained on that ground. *Baptisms,* or immersions of the body in water, sprinklings, and washings, were frequent as religious rites among the Hebrews, and were all emblematical of that purity which a holy God requires in His worshippers, and without which they cannot be happy here nor glorified in heaven. *Laying on of hands* was also frequent, especially in sacrifices. The person bringing the victim laid his hands on its head, confessed his sins over it, and then gave it to the priest to be offered to God, that it might make atonement for his transgressions. This also had respect to Jesus Christ, that Lamb of God who takes away the sins of the world. The doctrines also of the *resurrection of the dead* and of *eternal judgment* were both Jewish, but were only partially revealed and then referred to the gospel. Daniel has taught both, chap. xii. 2: "And many of them that sleep in the dust of the earth shall awake, some to everlasting life, and some to shame and everlasting contempt."

3. *And this will we do.* God being my Helper, I will teach you all the sublime truths of the gospel, and show you how all its excellences were typified by the law, and particularly by its sacrificial system.

4. *For it is impossible for those who were once enlightened.* Before I proceed to explain the different terms in these verses, it is necessary to give my opinion of their design and meaning: (1) I do not consider them as having any reference to any person professing Christianity. (2) They do not belong, nor are they applicable, to backsliders of any kind. (3) They belong to apostates from Christianity; to such as reject the whole Christian system, and its Author, the Lord Jesus. (4) And to those of them only who join with the blaspheming Jews, call Christ an impostor, and vindicate His murderers in having crucified Him as a malefactor; and thus they render their salvation impossible, by willfully and maliciously rejecting the Lord that bought them. No man believing in the Lord Jesus as the great Sacrifice for sin, and acknowledging Christianity as a divine revelation, is here intended, though he may have unfortunately backslidden from any degree of the salvation of God. *Once enlightened.* Thoroughly instructed in the nature and design of the Christian religion, having received the knowledge of the truth, chap. x. 32; and being convinced of sin, righteousness, and judgment; and led to Jesus, the Saviour of sinners. *Tasted of the heavenly gift.* Having received the knowledge of salvation by the remission of sins, through the Dayspring which from on high had visited them; such having received Christ, the *heavenly gift* of God's infinite love, John iii. 16. *Partakers of the Holy Ghost.* The Spirit himself witnessing with their spirits that they were the children of God, and thus assuring them of God's mercy towards them, and of the efficacy of the atonement through which they had received such blessings.

5. *And have tasted the good word of God.* Have had this proof of the excellence of the promise of God in sending the gospel, the gospel being itself the good word of a good God, the reading and preaching of which they find sweet to the taste of their souls. Genuine believers have an appetite for the Word of God; they taste it, and then their relish for it is the more

MATTHEW HENRY

(5) They may have *tasted of the powers of the world to come.* These lengths hypocrites may go, and, after all, turn apostates.

ALBERT BARNES:

It may be remarked respecting the various expressions used here (vv. 4, 5): (1) That they are such as properly denote a renewed state. They obviously describe the condition of a Christian. If they are not, it would be difficult to find any language which would be properly descriptive of the character of a sincere Christian. I regard the description here, therefore, as that which is clearly designed to denote the state of those who were born again, and who were the true children of God; and it seems plain to me that no other interpretation would have ever been thought of, if this view had not seemed to conflict with the doctrine of the "perseverance of the saints." (2) There is a regular gradation here from the first elements of piety in the soul to its highest developments; and, whether the apostle so designed it or not, the language describes the successive steps by which a true Christian advances to the highest stage of Christian experience. The mind is (a) enlightened; then (b) tastes the gifts of heaven, or has some experience of it; then (c) it is made to partake of the influences of the Holy Ghost; then (d) there is experience of the excellence and loveliness of the Word of God; and (e) finally there is a participation of the full "powers" of the new dispensation; of the extraordinary energy which God puts forth in the gospel to sanctify and save the soul.
—*Popular Commentary*

2. The dreadful case of such as fall away. The greatness of the sin of apostasy. It is *crucifying the Son of God afresh, and putting him to open shame.* They declare that they approve of what the Jews did in crucifying Christ, and that they would be glad to do the same thing again, and would have him to be a public shame and reproach. The great misery of apostates. It is impossible to renew them again unto repentance. God can renew them to repentance, but he seldom does it; and with men themselves it is impossible.

Their misery is exemplified by a proper similitude, *v.* 8. To give this the greater force, here is observed the difference that there is between the good ground and the bad. A description of the good ground: It *drinketh in the rain that cometh often upon it.* Believers do not only taste of the word of God, but they drink it in; and this good ground bringeth forth fruit. And this fruit-field or garden receives the blessing.

JAMIESON, FAUSSET, BROWN

swers to the Trinity, the Father, Son, and Spirit, in their respective works toward us. "The world to come," is the Christian dispensation, viewed especially in its *future glories,* though already begun in grace here. The *world to come* thus stands in contrast to *course of this world,* altogether disorganized because God is not its spring of action and end. By faith, Christians make the world to come a present reality, though but a foretaste of the perfect future. The powers of this new spiritual world, partly exhibited in outward miracles at that time, and then, as now, especially consisting in the Spirit's inward quickening influences are the earnest of the coming inheritance above, and lead the believer who gives himself up to the Spirit to seek to live as the angels, to sit with Christ in heavenly places, to set the affections on things above, and not on things on earth, and to look for Christ's coming and the full manifestation of the world to come. This "world to come," in its future aspect, thus corresponds to "resurrection of the dead and eternal life" (vs. 2), the *first* Christian principles which the Hebrew believers had been taught, by the Christian light being thrown back on their Old Testament for their instruction (*Note,* vss. 1, 2). "The world to come," which, as to its "powers," exists already in the redeemed, will pass into a fully realized fact at Christ's coming (Col. 3:4). **6. If**—*Greek, And* (yet) *have* fallen away"; cf. a less extreme falling or declension, Galatians 5:4, "Ye are fallen from grace." Here an entire and wilful apostasy is meant; the Hebrews had not yet so fallen away; but he warns them that such would be the final result of retrogression, if, instead of "going on to perfection," they should need to learn again the first principles of Christianity (vs. 1). **to renew them again**—They have been "once" (vs. 4) already *renewed,* or made anew, and now they need to be *"renewed"* over "again." **crucify to themselves the Son of God**—*"are crucifiying* to themselves" Christ, instead of, like Paul, *crucifying the world unto them by the cross of Christ* (Gal. 6:14). So in ch. 10:29, "trodden under foot the Son of God, and counted the blood of the covenant, wherewith . . . sanctified, an unholy thing." "The Son of God," marking His dignity, shows the greatness of their offense. **put him to an open shame**—lit., "make a public example of" Him, as if He were a malefactor suspended on a tree. What the carnal Israel did outwardly, those who fall away from light do inwardly, they virtually crucify again the Son of God; "they tear him out of the recesses of their hearts where He had fixed His abode and exhibit Him to the open scoffs of the world as something powerless and common" [BLEEK in ALFORD]. The Montanists and Novatians used this passage to justify the lasting exclusion from the Church of those who had once lapsed. The Catholic Church always opposed this view, and readmitted the lapsed on their repentance, but did not rebaptize them.

"He who is led into the whole (?) compass of Christian experiences, may yet cease to abide in them; he who abides not in them, was, at the very time when he had those objective experiences, not *subjectively* true to them; otherwise there would have been fulfilled in him, 'Whosoever hath, to him shall be given, and he shall have more abundance' (Matt. 13:12), so that he would have abided in them and not have fallen away" [THOLUCK]. Such a one was never truly a Spirit-led disciple of Christ (Rom. 8:14-17). The sin against the Holy Ghost, though somewhat similar, is not identical with this sin; for *that* sin may be committed by those *outside* the Church (as in Matt. 12:24, 31, 32); this, only by those *inside.* **7. the earth**—rather as *Greek* (no article), "land." **which drinketh in**—*Greek,* "which *has* drunk in"; not merely receiving it on the surface. Answering to those who have enjoyed the privilege of Christian experiences, being in some sense renewed by the Holy Ghost; true alike of those who persevere and those who "fall away." **the rain that cometh oft upon it**—not merely falling *over* it, or *towards* it, but falling and resting *upon* it so as to *cover* it (the *Greek* genitive, not the accusative). The "oft" implies, on God's part, the riches of His abounding grace ("coming" spontaneously, and often); and, on the apostate's part, the wilful perversity whereby he has done continual despite to the oft-repeated motions of the Spirit. Cf. "How *often.*" Matthew 23:37. The rain of heaven falls both on the elect and the apostates. **bringeth forth**—as the *natural* result of *"having drunk in* the rain." See above. **herbs**—provender. **meet**—fit. Such as the master of the soil wishes. The opposite of "rejected," vs. 8. **by whom**—rather as *Greek,* "for (i.e., on account of) whom," viz., the lords of the soil; not the laborers, as *English Version,* viz., God

ADAM CLARKE

abundantly increased. *The powers of the world to come.* These words are understood two ways: (1) They may refer to the stupendous miracles wrought in confirmation of the gospel, the gospel dispensation being "the world to come" in the Jewish phraseology, as we have often seen; and that *dynamis* is often taken for a "mighty work" or "miracle" is plain from various parts of the Gospels. The prophets had declared that the Messiah, when He came, should work many miracles, and should be as mighty in word and deed as was Moses; see Deut. xviii. 15-19. And they particularly specify the giving sight to the blind, hearing to the deaf, strength to the lame, and speech to the dumb, Isa. xxxv. 5-6. All these miracles Jesus Christ did in the sight of this very people; and thus they had the highest evidence they could have that Jesus was this promised Messiah, and could have no pretense to doubt His mission or apostatize from the Christian faith which they had received. (2) The words have been supposed to apply to those communications and foretastes of eternal blessedness, or of the joys of the world to come, which they who are justified through the Blood of the covenant, and walk faithfully with their God, experience; and to this sense the word *have tasted* is thought more properly to apply. But "to taste," signifies "to experience or have full proof" of a thing. Thus, to "taste of death," Matt. xvi. 28, is "to die." It seems, therefore, that the first opinion is the best founded.

6. *If they shall fall away.* "And having fallen away." I can express my own mind on this translation nearly in the words of Dr. Macknight: "The participles *who were enlightened, have tasted,* and *were made partakers,* being aorists, are properly rendered by our translators in the past time; wherefore *parapesontas,* being an aorist, ought likewise to have been translated in the past time, 'HAVE *fallen away.'* Nevertheless, our translators, following Beza, who without any authority from ancient MSS. has inserted in his version the word *'if,'* have rendered this clause, IF *they fall away,* that this text might not appear to contradict the doctrine of the perseverance of the saints. But as no translator should take upon him to add to or alter the Scriptures, for the sake of any favourite doctrine, I have translated *parapesontas* in the past time, *'have fallen away,'* according to the true import of the word, as standing in connection with the other aorists in the preceding verses." *To renew them again unto repentance.* As *repentance* is the first step that a sinner must take in order to return to God, and as sorrow for sin must be useless in itself unless there be a proper sacrificial offering, these having rejected the only available sacrifice, their repentance for sin, had they any, would be nugatory, and their salvation impossible on this simple account; and this is the very reason which the apostle immediately subjoins. *Seeing they crucify to themselves the Son of God.* They reject Him on the ground that He was an impostor, and justly put to death. And thus they are said to crucify Him to themselves—to do that in their present apostasy which the Jews did; and they show thereby that, had they been present when He was crucified, they would have joined with His murderers. *And put him to an open shame.* "And have made Him a public example"; or, "crucifying unto themselves and making the Son of God a public example." That is, they show openly that they judge Jesus Christ to have been worthy of the death which He suffered, and was justly made a public example by being crucified. This shows that it is final apostasy, by the total rejection of the gospel and blasphemy of the Saviour of men, that the apostle has in view. See the note on v. 4.

7. *For the earth which drinketh in the rain.* As much as if he had said: In giving up such apostates as utterly incurable, we act as men do in cultivating their fields; for as the ground, which drinketh in the rain by which the providence of God waters it, brings forth fruit to compensate the toil of the tiller, and continues to be cultivated, God granting His blessing to the labors of the husbandman; so,

MATTHEW HENRY

Here is the different case of the bad ground: It *bears briers and thorns*; it is not only barren of good fruit, but fruitful in that which is bad, briers and thorns. Such ground is rejected. And that is not all, but such ground *is nigh unto cursing*; so far is it from receiving the blessing. Its end is to be burned. This is the sad end to which apostasy leads, and therefore Christians should go on and grow in grace, lest, if they do not go forward, they should go backward.

Verses 9–20

The apostle proceeds to apply himself to their hopes.

I. He declares the good hope he had concerning them, *v.* 9. There are things that accompany salvation, things that are never separated from salvation. Ministers must sometimes speak by way of caution to those of whose salvation they have good hopes. And those who have in themselves good hopes should yet consider seriously how fatal a disappointment it would be if they should fall short. Thus they are to work out their salvation with fear and trembling.

II. Encouragements to them to go on. God had wrought a principle of holy love and charity in them, *v.* 10. Good works and labour proceeding from love to God are commendable; and what is done to any in the name of God shall not go unrewarded.

JAMIESON, FAUSSET, BROWN

and His Christ (I Cor. 3:9). The heart of man is the earth; man is the dresser; herbs are brought forth meet, not for the dresser, by whom, but for God, the owner of the soil, *for* whom it is dressed. The plural is general, *the owners whoever they may be;* here *God*. **receiveth**—"partaketh of." **blessing**—fruitfulness. Contrast God's curse causing unfruitfulness (Gen. 3:17, 18); also spiritually (Jer. 17:5-8). **from God**—Man's use of means is vain unless God bless (I Cor. 3:6, 7). **8. that which**—rather as *Greek* (no article), "But *if it* (the 'land' vs. 7) *bear";* not so favorable a word as "bringeth forth," vs. 7, said of the good soil. **briers**—*Greek,* "thistles." **rejected**—after having been *tested;* so the *Greek* implies. *Reprobate . . . rejected* by the Lord. **nigh unto cursing**—on the verge of being given up to its own barrenness by the just curse of God. This "nigh" softens the severity of the previous "It is impossible . . ." (vss. 4, 6). The ground is not yet actually *cursed*. **whose**—"of which (*land*) the end is unto burning," viz., with the consuming fire of the last judgment; as the land of Sodom was given to "brimstone, salt, and *burning*" (Deut. 29: 23); so as to the ungodly (Matt. 3:10, 12; 7:19; 13: 30; John 15:6; II Pet. 3:10). Jerusalem, which had so resisted the grace of Christ, was then nigh unto cursing, and in a few years was burned. Cf. Matthew 22:7, "*burned* up their city" an earnest of a like fate to all wilful abusers of God's grace (ch. 10:26, 27).

9. beloved—appositely here introduced; LOVE to you prompts me in the strong warnings I have just given, not that I entertain unfavorable thoughts of you; nay, I anticipate *better things* of you; *Greek "the* things which *are* better"; that ye are not *thorn-bearing,* or *nigh unto cursing,* and doomed *unto burning,* but heirs of *salvation* in accordance with God's faithfulness (ch. 6:10). **we are persuaded**—on good grounds; the result of proof. Cf. Romans 15:14, "I myself am persuaded of you, my brethren, that ye are full of *goodness.*" A confirmation of the Pauline authorship of this Epistle. **things that accompany**—*Greek,* "things that hold by," i.e., are close unto "salvation." Things that are linked unto salvation (cf. vs. 19). In opposition to "nigh unto cursing." **though**—*Greek,* "if even we thus speak." "For it is better to make you afraid with words, that ye may not suffer in fact." **10. not unrighteous**—not *unfaithful* to His own gracious promise. Not that we have any inherent *right to claim* reward; for (1) a *servant* has no merit, as he only does that which is his bounden duty; (2) our best performances bear no proportion to what we leave undone; (3) all strength comes from God; but God has *promised of His own grace* to reward the good works of His people (already accepted through faith in Christ); it is His *promise,* not our merits, which would make it *unrighteous* were He not to reward His people's works. God will be no man's debtor. **your work**—your whole Christian life of active obedience. **labour of love**—The oldest MSS. omit "labor of," which probably crept in from I Thess. 1:3. As "love" occurs here, so "hope," vs. 11, "faith," vs. 12; as in I Corinthians 13:13: the *Pauline* triad. By their *love* he sharpens their *hope* and *faith.* **ye have showed**—(Cf. ch. 10:32-34). **toward his name**—Your acts *of love to* the saints were done for His name's sake. The distressed condition of the Palestinian Christians appears from the collection for them. Though receiving bounty from other churches, and therefore not able to minister much by *pecuniary* help, yet those somewhat better off could minister to the greatest sufferers in their Church in various other ways (cf. II Tim. 1:18). Paul, as elsewhere, gives them the utmost credit for their graces, while delicately hinting the need of perseverance, a lack of which had probably somewhat begun to show itself. **11. And**—*Greek,* "But." **desire**—*Greek,* "*earnestly* desire." The language of fatherly affection, rather than command. **every one of you**—

ADAM CLARKE

8. *That which beareth thorns and briers is rejected.* That is: The land which, notwithstanding the most careful cultivation, receiving also in due times the early and latter rain, produces nothing but thorns and briers, or noxious weeds of different kinds, is rejected, is given up as unimprovable; its briers, thorns, and brushwood burnt down; and then left to be pastured on by the beasts of the field. This seems to be the custom in husbandry to which the apostle alludes. *Is nigh unto cursing.* It is acknowledged, on almost all hands, that this Epistle was written before the destruction of Jerusalem by the Romans. This verse is in my opinion a proof of it, and here I suppose the apostle refers to that approaching destruction; and perhaps he has this all along in view, but speaks of it covertly, that he might not give offense.

There is a good sense in which all these things may be applied to the Jews at large, who were favored by our Lord's ministry and miracles. They were "enlightened" by His preaching; "tasted" of the benefits of the "heavenly gift"—the Christian religion established among them; saw many of their children and relatives "made partakers of the Holy Ghost"; "tasted the good word of God," by the fulfillment of the promise made to Abraham; and saw the almighty power of God exerted, in working a great variety of miracles. Yet after being convinced that never man spake as this Man, and that none could do those miracles which He did except God were with him; after having followed Him in thousands for three years while He preached to them the gospel of the kingdom of God; they "fell away" from all this, crucified Him who, even in His sufferings as well as His resurrection, was demonstrated by miracles to be the Son of God; and then to vindicate their unparalleled wickedness, endeavored to make Him a public example by reproaches and blasphemies. Therefore their state, which had received much moral cultivation from Moses, the prophets, Christ and His apostles; and now bore nothing but the most vicious fruits—pride, unbelief, hardness of heart, contempt of God's Word and ordinances, blasphemy, and rebellion—was *rejected,* reprobated, of God; was *nigh unto cursing*—about to be cast off from the divine protection; and their city and Temple were shortly to be burnt up by the Roman armies.

9. *But, beloved.* Here he softens what he had before said. Having given them the most solemn warning against apostasy, he now encourages them to persevere, commends the good that is in them, and excites them to watchfulness and activity. *Better things of you.* Than that you shall resemble that unfruitful ground that can be improved by no tillage, and is thrown into waste, and is fit only for the beasts of the forests to roam in. *Things that accompany salvation.* "Things that are suitable to a state of salvation"; you give proofs still that you have not, whatever others have done, departed from the living God. Several of your brethren have already apostatized, and the whole nation is in a state of rebellion against God; and in consequence of their final rejection of Christ and His gospel are about to be finally rejected by God. They must meet with destruction; they have the things that are suitable to, and indicative of, a state of reprobation; the wrath of God will come upon them to the uttermost; but while they meet with destruction, you shall meet with salvation.

10. *God is not unrighteous.* God is bound to men only by His own promise. This promise He is not obliged to make; but, when once made, His righteousness or justice requires Him to keep it. Therefore whatever He has promised He will certainly perform. The word *labour,* prefixed to *love,* is wanting in almost every MS. and version of importance. *Ministered to the saints.* Have contributed to the support and comfort of the poor Christians who were suffering persecution in Judea. As they had thus ministered, and were still ministering, they gave full proof that they had a common cause with the others; and this was one of the things that proved them to be in a state of salvation.

11. *We desire.* We "earnestly wish" that each person among you may continue to "manifest, exhibit to full view," the same diligence. There

MATTHEW HENRY

Those who expect a gracious reward for the labour of love must continue in it as long as they have ability and opportunity. Those who persevere in a diligent discharge of their duty shall attain to the full assurance of hope in the end. Full assurance is a higher degree of hope; they differ not in nature, but only in degree. Full assurance is attainable by great diligence and perseverance to the end.

III. Caution and counsel how to attain this full assurance of hope to the end. They should not be slothful. They must not love their ease, nor lose their opportunities. They should follow the good examples of those who had gone before, *v.* 12. There are some who from assurance have gone to inherit the promises. The way by which they came to the inheritance was that of faith and patience. We must follow them in the way of faith and patience.

IV. The assured truth of the promises of God, *v.* 13, *to the end.*

1. They are all confirmed by the oath of God. Those whom he has blessed indeed he will go on to bless. *He swore by himself.* No greater security can be given or desired. It was made good to him after he had patiently endured. There is always an interval, and sometimes a long one, between the promise and the performance. That interval is a trying time to believers.

Those who patiently endure shall assuredly obtain the blessedness promised, as sure as Abraham did, *v.* 16. This is the nature and design of an oath, in which men swear by the greater, by the Lord himself. Now, if God would condescend to take an oath to his people, he will surely remember the nature and design of it.

2. The promises of God are all founded in his eternal counsel; and this counsel of his is an immutable counsel. God never needs to change his counsels.

3. The promises of God may safely be depended upon.

(1) Who they are to whom God has given such full security of happiness. They are the heirs of the promise. They are such as have fled for refuge to the hope set before them. Here is a refuge for all sinners who shall have the heart to flee to it.

(2) What God's design towards them is—that they might have strong consolation. God is concerned for the consolation of believers. The consolations of God are strong enough to support his people under their strongest trials. The comforts of this world are too weak, but the consolations of the Lord are neither few nor small.

JAMIESON, FAUSSET, BROWN

implying that *all* in the Palestinian churches had not shown the same diligence as some of those whom he praises in vs. 10. "He cares alike for great and small, and overlooks none." "Every one of them," even those dilligent in acts of LOVE (vs. 10), needed to be stimulated to *persevere* in the same diligence with a view to the full assurance of HOPE unto the end. They needed, besides love, patient perseverance, resting on *hope* and *faith* (ch. 10:36; 13:7). Cf. "the full assurance of faith," ch. 10:22: Romans 4:21; I Thessalonians 1:5. **unto the end**—the coming of Christ.

12. be not—*Greek,* "*become* not." In ch. 5:11, he said, "Ye have become dull (*Greek, slothful*) *of hearing*"; here he warns them not to become "slothful" *absolutely,* viz., also in mind and deed. He will not become slothful who keeps always *the end* in view; *hope* is the means of ensuring this. **followers**—*Greek,* "imitators"; so in Ephesians 5:1, *Greek;* I Corinthians 11:1. **patience**—*Greek,* "*long-suffering* endurance." There is the *long-suffering patience,* or *endurance* of *love,* I Corinthians 13:4, and that of *faith,* vs. 15. **them who . . . inherit the promises**—*Greek,* ". . . who *are inheriting* . . ."; to whom the promises are their inheritance. Not that they *have* actually entered on the *perfect* inheritance, which ch. 11:13, 39, 40 explicitly denies; though doubtless the dead in Christ have, in the disembodied soul, a foretaste of it; but "them (enumerated in ch. 11) who in every age have been, are, or shall be, *inheritors* of the promises"; of whom Abraham is an illustrious example (vs. 13). **13. For**—confirming the reasonableness of resting on "the promises" as infallibly sure, resting as they do on God's oath, by the instance of Abraham. "He now gives consolation, by *the oath of God's grace,* to those whom, in chs. 3 and 4, he had warned by the *oath* of God's 'wrath.' The oath of wrath did not primarily extend its force beyond the wilderness; but the oath of grace is in force for ever" [BENGEL]. **14 multiplying . . . multiply**—Hebraism for *superabundantly multiply.* **thee**—The increase of Abraham's *seed* is virtually an increase of *himself.* The argument here refers to Abraham *himself* as an example; therefore Paul quotes Genesis 22:17, "thee," instead of "thy seed." **15. so**—thus relying on the promise. **16. for confirmation**—not to be joined, as *English Version,* to "an oath"; but to "an end" [ALFORD]. I prefer, "The oath is to them, in respect to confirmation (of one's solemn promise or covenant; as here, *God's*), an end of all *contradiction*" (so the *Greek* is translated, ch. 12:3), or "gainsaying." This passage shows: (1) an oath is sanctioned even in the Christian dispensation as lawful; (2) that the limits to its use are, that it only be employed where it can *put an end to contradiction in disputes,* and *for confirmation* of a solemn promise. **17. Wherein**—i.e., *Which being the case* among men, God, in accommodation to their manner of confirming covenants, superadded to His sure *word* His *oath:* the "TWO immutable things" (vs. 18). **willing . . . counsel**—*Greek,* "willing . . . *will*"; words akin. Expressing the utmost benignity [BENGEL]. **more abundantly**—than had He not sworn. His word would have been amply enough; but, to make assurance doubly sure, He "interposed with an oath" (so the *Greek*). Lit., *He acted as Mediator,* coming between Himself and us; as if He were less, while He swears, than Himself by whom He swears [for the less among men usually swear by the greater]. Dost thou not yet believe, thou that hearest the promise? [BENGEL]. **heirs of promise**—not only Abraham's literal, but also his spiritual, seed (Gal. 3:29). **18, immutable**—Translate, as in vs. 17, "unchangeable." **impossible . . . to lie**—"*ever* to lie"; this is the force of the *Greek* aorist [ALFORD]. His not being able to deny Himself is a proof, not of weakness, but of strength incomparable. **consolation**—under doubts and fears, and so "encouragement," lit., "exhortation." **fled for refuge**—as if from a shipwreck; or, as one fleeing to one of the six cities of refuge. Kadesh, i.e., *holy,* implies the holiness of Jesus, our Refuge. Shechem, i.e., *shoulder,* the government is upon his shoulder (Isa. 9:6). Hebron, i.e., *fellowship,* believers are called into the fellowship of Christ. Bezer, i.e., *a fortress,* Christ is so to all who trust in Him. Ramoth, i.e., *high,* for Him hath God exalted with His right hand (Acts 5:31). Golan, i.e., *joy,* for in Him all the saints are justified and shall glory. **lay hold upon the hope**—i.e.,the object of our hope, as upon a preservative from sinking. **set before us**—as a prize for which we strive; a new image, viz., the race-course (ch. 12:1, 2).

ADAM CLARKE

might be reason to suspect that some, through fear of man, might not wish the good they did to be seen, lest they also should suffer persecution. *To the full assurance of hope.* The person who has this *full assurance of hope* is he who not only knows and feels that his sins are forgiven through Christ Jesus, but also that his heart is purified from all unrighteousness, that the whole body of sin and death is destroyed, and that he is fully made a partaker of the divine nature. As without holiness—complete, entire holiness—no man can see God, so without this none can scripturally or rationally hope for eternal glory, it being a contradiction to profess to have the full assurance of hope to enjoy a state and place for which the soul is conscious it is not prepared.

12. *That ye be not slothful.* This shows how the full assurance of hope is to be regulated and maintained. They must be diligent; slothfulness will deprive them of both hope and faith. That "faith which worketh by love" will maintain hope in its full and due exercise. *Followers of them.* "That you be imitators of them who are inheriting the promises." And they inherited these promises by faith in Him who is invisible, and who, they knew, could not lie; and they patiently endured, through difficulties and adversities of every kind, and persevered unto death.

13. *When God made promise to Abraham.* The promise referred to is that made to Abraham when he had offered his son Isaac on the altar, Gen. xxii. 16-18: "By myself have I sworn, saith the Lord, for because thou hast done this thing, and hast not withheld thy son, thine only son: that in blessing I will bless thee, and in multiplying I will multiply thy seed as the stars of the heaven, and as the sand which is upon the sea shore; and thy seed shall possess the gate of his enemies; and in thy seed shall all the nations of the earth be blessed." *He sware by himself.* He pledged His eternal power and Godhead for the fulfillment of the promise; there was no being superior to himself to whom He could make appeal, or by whom He could be bound.

14. *Saying, Surely blessing I will bless thee.* I will continue to bless you. *Multiplying I will multiply thee.* I will continue to increase your posterity. In the most literal manner God continues to fulfill this promise; genuine Christians are Abraham's seed, and God is increasing their number daily.

15. *He obtained the promise.* Isaac was supernaturally born; and in his birth God began to fulfill the promise. While he lived, he saw a provision made for the multiplication of his seed; and, having continued steadfast in the faith, he received the end of all the promises in the enjoyment of an eternal glory. And the inference from this is: If we believe and prove faithful unto death, we shall also inherit the promises.

16. *Men verily swear by the greater.* One who has greater authority.

17. *The heirs of promise.* All the believing posterity of Abraham, and the nations of the earth or Gentiles in general. *The immutability of his counsel.* His unchangeable purpose, to call the Gentiles to salvation by Jesus Christ; to justify every penitent by faith; to accept faith in Christ for justification in place of personal righteousness; and finally to bring every persevering believer, whether Jew or Gentile, to eternal glory.

18. *That by two immutable things.* The promise and oath of God: the promise pledged His faithfulness and justice; the oath, all the infinite perfections of His Godhead, for He sware by himself. *We might have a strong consolation.* There appears to be an allusion here to the cities of refuge and to the persons who fled to them for safety. As the person who killed his neighbor unawares was sure if he gained the city of refuge he should be safe, and had strong consolation in the hope that he should reach it, this hope animated him in his race to the city. He ran, he fled, knowing that, though in danger the most imminent of losing his life, yet as he was now acting according to an ordinance of God, he was certain of safety provided he got to the place.

MATTHEW HENRY

(3) What use the people of God should make of their hope and comfort, *v.* 19. We are in this world as a ship at sea, in danger of being cast away. Heaven is the harbour to which we sail. We have need of an anchor to keep us sure and steady. Gospel hope is our anchor. It is sure and steadfast. It is sure in its own nature; it is not a flattering hope made out of the spider's web, but it is a true work of God. It is steadfast as to its object; it is an anchor that has taken good hold. It does not seek to fasten in the sands, but enters within the veil, and fixes there upon Christ; he is the anchor-hold of the believer's hope.

W. E. VINE:

PRODROMOS, forerunner, an adjective signifying running forward, going in advance, is used as a noun, of those who were sent before to take observations, acting as scouts, especially in military matters; or of one sent before a king to see that the way was prepared (Isa. 40:3); (cf. Luke 9:52; and, of John the Baptist, Matt. 11:10). In the N.T. it is said of Christ in Heb. 6:20, as going in advance of His followers who are to be where He is, when He comes to receive them to himself.

—Vine's Expository Dictionary

JAMIESON, FAUSSET, BROWN

19. *Hope* is found represented on coins by an *anchor.* **sure and steadfast**—*sure* in respect to *us: steadfast,* or "firm" [ALFORD], in *itself.* Not such an *anchor* as will not keep the vessel from tossing, or an anchor unsound or too light [THEOPHYLACT]. **which entereth into that**—i.e., the place—**within the veil**—two images beautifully combined: I. The *soul* is *the ship;* the *world* the *sea:* the *bliss beyond* the world, *the distant coast;* the *hope* resting on faith, the *anchor* which prevents the vessel being tossed to and fro; the *encouraging consolation* through the *promise* and *oath* of God, the cable connecting the ship and anchor. II. The world is the fore-court; heaven, the Holy of Holies; Christ, the High Priest going before us, so as to enable us, after Him, and through Him, to enter within the veil. ESTIUS explains, As the anchor does not stay in the waters, but enters the ground hidden beneath the waters, and fastens itself in it, so hope, our anchor of the soul, is not satisfied with merely coming to the vestibule, i.e., is not content with merely earthly and visible goods, but penetrates even to those which are within the veil, viz., to the Holy of Holies, where it lays hold on God Himself, and heavenly goods, and fastens on them. **veil**—*Greek, catapetasma;* the *second* veil which shut in the Holiest Place. The outer veil was called by a distinct *Greek* term, *calumma:* "the second (i.e., the inner) veil." **20.** The absence of the *Greek* article requires ALFORD's translation, "Where, AS forerunner for us (i.e., in our behalf), entered Jesus" [*and is now:* this last clause is implied in the "where" of the *Greek,* which implies being IN a place: "whither" is understood to "entered," taken out of "where"; whither *Jesus entered,* and *where* He is now]. The "for us" implies that it was not for Himself. as God, He needed to enter there, but as our High Priest, representing and introducing us, His followers, opening the way to us, by His intercession with the Father, as the Aaronic high priest entered the Holiest Place once a year to make propitiation for the people. The first fruits of our nature are ascended, and so the rest is sanctified. Christ's ascension is our promotion: and whither the glory of the Head has preceded, thither the hope of the body, too, is called. We ought to keep festal day, since Christ has taken up and set in the heavens the first fruit of our lump, that is, the human flesh [CHRYSOSTOM]. As John Baptist was Christ's forerunner on earth, so Christ is ours in heaven.

ADAM CLARKE

19. *Which hope we have as an anchor.* The apostle here changes the allusion; he represents the state of the followers of God in this lower world as resembling that of a vessel striving to perform her voyage through a troublesome, tempestuous, dangerous sea. At last she gets near the port; but the tempest continues; the water is shallow, broken, and dangerous, and she cannot get in. In order to prevent her being driven to sea again, she heaves out her sheet anchor, which she has been able to get within the pierhead by means of her boat, though she could not herself get in. Then, swinging at the length of her cable, she rides out the storm in confidence, knowing that her anchor is sound, the ground good in which it is fastened, and the cable strong. The comparison of *hope* to an *anchor* is frequent among the ancient heathen writers, who supposed it to be as necessary to the support of a man in adversity as the anchor is to the safety of the ship when about to be driven on a lee shore by a storm.

20. *Whither the forerunner.* The word *prodromos* does not merely signify one that goes or runs before another, but also one who shows the way, he who first does a particular thing. So in the Septuagint, Isa. xxviii. 4, *prodromos sykou* signifies the "first fruits of the fig tree." To this meaning of the word Pliny refers, *Hist. Nat.*, xvi, c. 26: "The fig tree produces some figs which are ripe before the rest, and these are called by the Athenians *prodromos,* forerunner." The word is interpreted in the same way by Hesychius; it occurs in no other part of the New Testament, but may be found in Ecclus. xii. 8 and in Isa. xxviii. 4, quoted above from the Septuagint. From this we may at once perceive the meaning of the phrase: Jesus is the "Firstfruits" of human nature that has entered into the heavenly Kingdom. And He is entered *for us,* as the Firstfruits of all who have found redemption in His blood. *After the order of Melchisedec.* After a long digression the apostle resumes his explanation of Ps. cx. 4, which he had produced, chap. v. 6, 10, in order to prove the permanency of the high priesthood of Christ.

CHAPTER 7 (MATTHEW HENRY)

Verses 1–10

Here the apostle sets before them some of the strong meat he had spoken of before.

I. The great question that first offers itself is, Who was this Melchisedec? All the account we have of him in the Old Testament is in Gen. xiv. 18, &c., and in Ps. cx. 4. We are much in the dark about him.

1. The opinions concerning him that are best worthy our consideration are these three: (1) The rabbin, and most of the Jewish writers, think he was Shem the son of Noah. (2) Many Christian writers have thought him to be Jesus Christ himself. (3) The most general opinion is that he was a Canaanite king, who reigned in Salem.

2. How Christ is represented thereby, *v.* 1–3. (1) Melchisedec was a king, and so is the Lord Jesus. (2) He was *king of righteousness*: his name signifies *the righteous king.* Jesus Christ is a rightful and a righteous king. (3) He was king of Salem, that is, king of peace; first king of righteousness, and after that king of peace. So is our Lord Jesus. (4) He was *priest of the most high God.* So is the Lord Jesus. (5) The scripture has chosen to set him forth as an extraordinary person, without giving us his genealogy, that he might be a fitter type of Christ, whose priesthood is without descent, but is personal and perpetual. (6) He *met Abraham returning from the slaughter of the kings, and blessed him.* He gave as a king, and blessed as a priest. Thus our Lord Jesus meets his people, refreshes them, renews their strength, and blesses them. (7) *Abraham gave him a tenth part of all* (*v.* 2). And thus are we obliged to make all possible returns of love and gratitude to the Lord Jesus for all the favours we receive from him.

CHAPTER 7 (JAMIESON, FAUSSET, BROWN)

VSS. 1-28. CHRIST'S HIGH PRIESTHOOD AFTER THE ORDER OF MELCHISEDEC SUPERIOR TO AARON'S. **1. this Melchisedec**—(ch. 6:20; Ps. 110:4). The verb does not come till vs. 3, "abideth." **king . . . priest**—Christ unites these offices in their highest sense, and so restores the patriarchal union of these offices. **Salem**—Jerusalem, i.e., *seeing peace;* others make Salem distinct, and to be that mentioned (Gen. 33: 18; John 3:23). **the most high God**—called also "Possessor of heaven and earth" (Gen. 14:19, 22). This title of God, "the Most High," handed down by tradition from the primitive revelation, appears in the Phœnician god "Elion," i.e., *Most High.* **who met Abraham**—in company with the king of Sodom (Gen. 14:17, 18). **slaughter**—perhaps *defeat,* as ALFORD translates. So Genesis 14:17 (cf. 15) may be translated. Arioch, king of Ellasar, lived and reigned after the disaster [BENGEL]. However, if Chedorlaomer and Amraphel and Tidal were slain, though Arioch survived, "*slaughter* of the kings" would be correct. **blessed him**—As priest he first blessed Abraham on God's part; next he blessed God on Abraham's part: a reciprocal blessing. **2. gave**—*Greek,* "apportioned"; assigned as his portion. **tenth . . . of all**—viz., the booty taken. The tithes given are closely associated with the priesthood: the mediating priest received them as a pledge of the giver's whole property being God's; and as he conveyed God's gifts to man (vs. 1, "blessed him"), so also man's gifts to God. **first being**—Paul begins the mystical explanation of the historical fact (allegorical explanations being familiar to JEWS), by mentioning the significancy of the name. **righteousness**—not merely righteous: so Christ. *Hebrew Malchi* means *king: Tzedek, righteousness.* **King of Salem**—not only his own name, but that of the city which he ruled, had a typical significance, viz., *peace.* **Christ is the true *Prince* of *peace.*** The *peace* which He brings is the fruit of *righteousness.* **3. Without father . . .**—explained by "without genealogy" (so the *Greek* is for "with-

CHAPTER 7 (ADAM CLARKE)

1. *For this Melchisedec, king of Salem.* The name Melchisedec is thus expounded in *Bereshith Rabba,* "The Justifier of those who dwell in him." *Salem* is generally understood to be Jerusalem; but some think that it was that city of Shechem mentioned in Josh. xx. 7. Jerome was of this opinion.

2. *Gave a tenth part of all.* It was an ancient custom among all the nations of the earth to consecrate a part or tenth of the spoils taken in war to the objects of their worship.

3. *Without father, without mother.* The object of the apostle in thus producing the example

MATTHEW HENRY

(8) This Melchisedec was *made like unto the Son of God, and abideth a priest continually.* He bore the image of God in his piety and authority, and stands upon record as an immortal high priest.

TODAY'S DICTIONARY OF THE BIBLE:

Melchizedek—king of righteousness—the king of Salem. All we know of him is recorded in Gen. 14:18-20. He is subsequently mentioned only once in the Old Testament, in Ps. 110:4. The typical significance of his history is set forth in detail in Hebrews 7. The apostle there points out the superiority of his priesthood to that of Aaron in these several respects: (1) Even Abraham paid him tithes; (2) he blessed Abraham; (3) he is the type of a Priest who lives forever; (4) Levi, yet unborn, paid him tithes in the person of Abraham; (5) the permanence of his priesthood in Christ implied the abrogation of the Levitical system; (6) he was made priest not without an oath; and (7) his priesthood can neither be transmitted nor interrupted by death: "This man, because he continueth ever, hath an unchangeable priesthood."

His appearance in Scripture as the king of a city called Salem = peace and having a name meaning "king of righteousness" has made him the perfect object of speculation. A fragment of a document from cave eleven at Qumran gives evidence of the Jewish speculation about Melchizedek. It sees him as a divinely appointed judge in the court of heaven. Another Jewish tradition saw him as Shem, the son of Noah. Melchizedek was a Canaanite prince, a worshiper of the true God, and in his brief history and character an instructive type of our Lord, the great High Priest (Heb. 5:6, 7; 6:20).

II. Let us now consider how great this Melchisedec was, and how far his priesthood was above that of the order of Aaron (*v.* 4, 5, &c.). The greatness of this man and his priesthood appears from Abraham's paying the tenth of the spoils unto him;

It appears also it was Melchisedec's blessing of Abraham, *v.* 6, 7. Abraham's great dignity and felicity—was that he had the promises. That man is rich and happy indeed who has an estate in bills and bonds under God's own hand and seal.

JAMIESON, FAUSSET, BROWN

out descent"); cf. vs. 6, i.e., his genealogy is *not known,* whereas a Levitical priest could not dispense with the proof of his descent. **having neither beginning of days nor end of life**—viz., history not having recorded his beginning nor end, as it has the beginning and end of Aaron. The *Greek* idiom expressed by "without father. . ." one whose parentage was humble or *unknown.* **"Days" mean his time** of discharging his *function.* So the eternity spoken of in Psalm 110:4 is that of the *priestly office* chiefly. **made like**—It is not said that he was absolutely "like." *Made like,* viz., in the particulars here specified. Nothing is said in Genesis of the end of his priesthood, or of his having had in his priesthood either predecessor or successor, which, in a typical point of view, represents Christ's eternal priesthood, without beginning or end. Aaron's *end* is recorded; Melchisedec's not: typically significant. "The Son of God" is not said to be made like unto Melchisedec, but Melchisedec to be "made like the Son of God." When ALFORD denies that Melchisedec was made like the Son of God *in respect of his priesthood,* on the ground that Melchisedec was *prior in time* to our Lord, he forgets that Christ's eternal priesthood was an archetypal reality *in God's purpose from everlasting,* to which Melchisedec's priesthood was "made like" in due time. The Son of God is the more ancient, and is the archetype: cf. ch. 8:5, where the heavenly things are represented as the *primary archetype of the Levitical ordinances.* The epithets, "without father, . . ." beginning of days, "nor end," "abideth continually," belong to Melchisedec only *in respect to his priesthood,* and in *so far as he is the type of the Son of God,* and are strictly true of Him alone. **Melchisedec was, in his priesthood, "made like" Christ,** as far as the imperfect type could represent the lineaments of the perfect archetype. "The portrait of a living man can be seen on the canvas, yet the man is very different from his picture." There is nothing in the account, Genesis 14, to mark Melchisedec as a superhuman being: he is classed with the other kings in the chapter as a living historic personage: not as ORIGEN thought, an angel; nor as the Jews thought, Shem, son of Noah; nor as CALMET, Enoch; nor as the Melchisedekites, that he was the Holy Ghost; nor as others, the Divine Word.

4. consider—not merely *see,* but *weigh with attentive contemplation,* the fact. **even**—"to whom (as his superior) Abraham *even* paid tithe (went so far as to pay tithe) of (consisting of, lit., 'from') *the best of the spoils*" (lit., "the top of the heap"; whether of corn, the first fruits of which, taken from the top, used to be consecrated to God; or of spoils, from the top of which the general used to take some portion for consecration to God, or for his own use). He paid "tithes of ALL," and those tithes were taken out of the topmast and best portion of the whole spoils. **the patriarch**—in the *Greek* emphatically standing at the end of the whole sentence: And this payer of **tithe being no less a** personage than "the patriarch," the first forefather and head of our Jewish race and nation See *Note,* vs. 3, on Melchisedec's superiority as specially consecrated *king-priest,* above the other *patriarch-priests.* **5. sons of Levi**—viz., those alone who belonged to the family of Aaron, to whom the priesthood was restricted. Tithes originally paid to the whole tribe of Levi, became at length attached to the priesthood. **according to the law**—sanctioned by Jehovah (ch. 9:19). **of their brethren**—with whom, in point of natural descent, they are on a level. **though . . .**—Though thus on a level by common descent from Abraham, they yet pay tithe to the Levites, whose brethren they are. Now the Levites are subordinate to the priests; and these again to Abraham, their common progenitor; and Abraham to Melchisedec. "How great" (vs. 4) then, must this Melchisedec be in respect to his priesthood, as compared with the Levitical, though the latter received tithes! and now unspeakably great must "the Son of God" be, to whom, as the sacerdotal archetype (in God's purpose), Melchisedec was made like! **6. he whose descent is not counted from them**—not from "the sons of Levi," as those "who receive the priesthood." This verse explains "without descent" (*Greek,* "genealogy" in both verses, vs. 3). He who needs not, as the Levitical priests, to be able to trace his genealogy back to Levi. **received**—*Greek,* "*hath* received tithes." **blessed**—*Greek,* "*hath* blessed." The perfect tense implies that the significance of the fact endures to the present time. **him that had**—"the possessor of the promises," Abraham's peculiar distinction and designation. Paul exalts Abraham in order still more to exalt Melchisedec. When Christ is the subject, the singular "promise" is used. "The prom-

ADAM CLARKE

of Melchisedec was to show: (1) That Jesus was the Person prophesied of in the 110th psalm, which psalm the Jews uniformly understood as predicting the Messiah. (2) To answer the objections of the Jews against the legitimacy of the priesthood of Christ, taken from the stock from which He proceeded. The objection is this: If the Messiah is to be a true Priest, He must come from a legitimate stock, as all the priests under the law have regularly done; otherwise we cannot acknowledge Him to be a Priest. But Jesus of Nazareth has not proceeded from such a stock; therefore we cannot acknowledge Him for a Priest, the Antitype of Aaron. To this objection the apostle answers that it was not necessary for the priest to come from a particular stock, for Melchisedec was a priest of the most high God, and yet was not of the stock of either Abraham or Aaron, but a Canaanite. He who could not support his pretensions by just genealogical evidences was said by the Jews to be *without father.* In this way both Christ and Melchisedec were *without father* and *without mother;* i.e., were not descended from the original Jewish sacerdotal stock. Yet Melchisedec, who was a Canaanite, was a priest of the most high God. The old Syriac has given the true meaning by translating thus: **"Whose father** and mother are not inscribed among the genealogies." The Arabic is nearly the same: "He had neither father nor mother; the genealogy not being reckoned." The Aethiopic: "He had neither father nor mother upon earth, nor is his genealogy known." *Made like unto the Son of God.* Melchisedec was without father and mother, *having neither beginning of days, nor end of life.* His genealogy is not recorded; when he was born and when he died are unknown. His priesthood, therefore, may be considered as perpetual. In these respects he was like to Jesus Christ, who, as to His Godhead, had neither father nor mother, beginning of time, nor end of days; and has an everlasting priesthood.

4. *Consider how great this man was.* There is something exceedingly mysterious in the person and character of this king of Salem, and to find out the whole is impossible. He seems to have been a sort of universal priest, having none superior to him in all that region; and confessedly superior even to Abraham himself, the father of the faithful and the source of the Jewish race.

5. *They that are of the sons of Levi.* The priests who are of the posterity of the Levites, and receive the priesthood in virtue of their descent from Aaron, have authority from the law of God to receive tithes from the people. *According to the law.* That is, the Levites received a tenth from the people. The priests received a tenth of this tenth from the Levites, who are here called their brethren, because they were of the same tribe and employed in the same sacred work. The apostle is proceeding to show that Melchisedec was greater even than Abraham, the head of the fathers, for to him Abraham gave tithes; and as the Levites were the posterity of Abraham, they are represented here as paying tithes to Melchisedec through him. Yet Melchisedec was not of this family, and therefore must be considered as having a more honorable priesthood than even Aaron himself; for he took the tenth from Abraham, not for his maintenance, for he was a king, but in virtue of his office as universal high priest of all that region.

6. *Blessed him that had the promises.* This is a continuation of the same argument, namely, to show the superiority of Melchisedec, and in consequence to prove the superiority of the priesthood of Christ beyond that of Aaron. As in the seed of Abraham all the nations of the earth were to be blessed, Abraham received a sacerdotal blessing from Melchisedec, who was

MATTHEW HENRY

Melchisedec's greater honour—was his privilege to bless Abraham; and it is an incontested maxim *that the less is blessed of the greater, v.* 7.

it is well observed that Levi paid tithes to Melchisedec in Abraham, *v.* 9. Levi paid tithes to Melchisedec, as to a greater and higher priest than himself.

Verses 11–28

The necessity there was of raising up another priest, after the order of Melchisedec and not after the order of Aaron, *v.* 11, 12, &c.

I. It is asserted that perfection could not come by the Levitical priesthood and the law.

II. Therefore another priest must be raised up, after the order of Melchisedec, by whom perfection might come.

JAMIESON, FAUSSET, BROWN

ises" in the plural, refer to God's promise of greatness to himself and his seed, and of the possession of Canaan, twice repeated before the blessing of Melchisedec. As the priests, though above the people (vs. 7) whom it was their duty to "bless," were yet subordinate to Abraham; and as Abraham was subordinate to Melchisedec, who blessed him, Melchisedec must be much above the Levitical priests. **7.** The principle that the blesser is superior to him whom he blesses, holds good only in a blessing given with divine authority; not merely a prayerful wish, but one that is divinely efficient in working its purport, as that of the patriarchs on their children: so Christ's blessing, Luke 24:51; Acts 3: 26. **8.** Second point of superiority: Melchisedec's is an *enduring,* the Levitical a *transitory,* priesthood. As the law was a *parenthesis* between Abraham's dispensation of promise of grace, and its enduring fulfilment at Christ's coming (Rom. 5:20,*Greek,* "The law entered as something adscititious and by the way"): so the Levitical priesthood was parenthetical and temporary, between Melchisedec's typically enduring priesthood, and its antitypical realization in our ever continuing High Priest, Christ. **here**–in the *Levitical* priesthood. **there**–in the priesthood *after the order of Melchisedec.* In order to bring out the typical parallel more strongly, Paul substitutes, "He of whom it is witnessed that he liveth," for the more untypical, "He *who is made like to Him* that liveth." Melchisedec "liveth" merely in his *official* capacity, his priesthood being continued in Christ. Christ, on the other hand, is, in *His own person,* "ever living after the power of an endless life" (vss. 16, 25). Melchisedec's death not being recorded, is expressed by the positive term "liveth," for the sake of bringing into prominence the antitype, Christ, of whom alone it is strictly and perfectly true, "that He liveth." **9. as I may so say** –to preclude what he is about to say being taken in the mere literal sense; *I may say* that, *virtually,* Levi, in the person of his father Abraham, acknowledged Melchisedec's superiority, and paid tithes to him. **who receiveth tithes**–(Cf. vs. 5). **in Abraham**–*Greek,* "by means of (by the hand of) Abraham"; through Abraham. "Paid tithes," lit., "hath been tithed," i.e., been taken tithes of. **10. in the loins of his father**–i.e., *forefather* Abraham. *Christ* did not, in this sense, pay tithes in Abraham, for He never was in the loins of an earthly father [ALFORD]. Though, in respect to His mother, He was "of the fruit of (David's, and so of) Abraham's loins," yet, being supernaturally, without human father, conceived, as He is above the natural law of birth, so is he above the law of tithes. Only those born in the natural way, and so in sin, being under the curse, needed to pay tithe to the priest, that he might make propitiation for their sin. Not so Christ, who derived only His flesh, not also the taint of the flesh, from Abraham. BENGEL remarks, The blessings which Abraham had *before* meeting Melchisedec were the *general* promises, and the special one of a *natural seed,* and so of Levi; but the promises under which *Christ* was comprehended, and the faith for which Abraham was so commended, followed *after* Abraham's meeting Melchisedec, and being *blessed by him:* to which fact. Genesis 15:1, "*After* these things," calls our attention. This explains why Christ, the supernatural seed, is not included as paying tithes through Abraham to Melchisedec. **11. perfection**–absolute: "the bringing of man to his highest state, viz., that of salvation and sanctification." **under it**–The reading in the oldest MSS. is, "*Upon* it (i.e., on the ground of it as the basis, the priest having to administer the law, Malachi 2:7: it being presupposed) the people (ch. 9:19, '*all* the people') have received the law" (the *Greek* is *perfect,* not aorist; implying the people were still observing the law). **what further need**–(ch. 8:7). For God does nothing needless. **another** –rather as *Greek,* "that a *different* priest (one of a different order) should arise" (*anew,* vs. 15). **not be called**–*Greek,* "not be *said* (*to be*) after the order of Aaron," i.e., that, when spoken of in the Psalm 110:4, "He is not said to be (as we should expect, if the Aaronic priesthood was perfect) after the order of Aaron."

ADAM CLARKE

the representative of the Messiah, the promised Seed, to show that it was through Him, as the High Priest of the human race, that this blessing was to be derived on all mankind.

7. *The less is blessed of the better.* That the superior blesses the inferior is a general proposition. But Abraham was blessed of Melchisedec; therefore Melchisedec was greater than Abraham.

8. *Here men that die receive tithes.* The apostle is speaking of the ecclesiastical constitution of the Jews, which was standing at the time this Epistle was written. Under the Jewish dispensation, though the priests were successively removed by death, yet they were as duly replaced by others appointed from the same family, and the payment of tithes was never interrupted. But as there is no account of Melchisedec ceasing to be a priest or of his dying, he is represented as still living, the better to point him out as a type of Christ, and to show his priesthood to be more excellent than that which was according to the law, as an unchanging priesthood must be more excellent than that which was continually changing. *But there he receiveth them.* The *here* in the first clause of this verse refers to Mosaical institutions, as then existing; the *there* in this clause refers to the place in Genesis (chap. xiv. 20) where it is related that Abraham gave tithes to Melchisedec, who is still considered as being alive or without a successor, because there is no account of his death nor of any termination of his priesthood.

9. *And as I may so say.* "And so to speak a word." This form of speech, which is very frequent among the purest Greek writers, is generally used to soften some harsh expression, or to limit the meaning when the proposition might otherwise appear to be too general. It answers fully to our "so to speak—as one would say—I had almost said—in a certain sense." *Payed tithes in Abraham.* The Levites, who were descendants of Abraham, paid tithes to Melchisedec "through" Abraham, their progenitor and representative.

10. *For he was yet in the loins of his father.* That is, Levi was seminally included in Abraham, his forefather.

11. *If therefore perfection were by the Levitical priesthood.* The word *teleiosis* signifies the "completing" or "finishing" of anything, so as to leave nothing imperfect and nothing wanting. Applied here to the Levitical priesthood, it signifies the accomplishment of that for which a priesthood is established, viz., giving the Deity an acceptable service, enlightening and instructing the people, pardoning all offenses, purging the conscience from guilt, purifying the soul and preparing it for heaven, and regulating the conduct of the people according to the precepts of the moral law. This perfection never came, and never could come, by the Levitical law; it was the shadow of good things to come, but was not the substance. It represented a perfect system, but was imperfect in itself. *For under it the people received the law.* That is, as most interpret this place, under the priesthood, because on the priesthood the whole Mosaical law and the Jewish economy depended. But it is much better to understand "on account of it," instead of *under it;* for it is a positive fact that the law was given before any priesthood was established, for Aaron and his sons were not called nor separated to this office till Moses came down the second time from the mount with the tables renewed, after that he had broken them, Exod. xl. 12-14. But it was in reference to the great sacrificial system that the law was given, and on that law the priesthood was established; for why was a priesthood necessary but because that law was broken and must be fulfilled? *That another priest should rise.* The law was given that the offense might abound and sin appear exceeding sinful, and to show the absolute necessity of the sacrifice and mediation of the great Messiah. But it was neither perfect in itself, nor could it confer perfection, nor did it contain the original priesthood. Melchisedec had a priesthood more than four hundred years before the law was given; and David prophesied, Ps. cx. 4, that another priest should arise after the order of Melchisedec, nearly five hundred years after the law was given. The law therefore did not contain the original priest-

MATTHEW HENRY

III. It is asserted that the priesthood being changed there must of necessity be a change of the law.

IV. It is not only asserted, but proved, that the priesthood and law are changed, *v.* 13, 14. A dispensation is now set up, by which true believers may be made perfect.

1. There is a change in the tribe of which the priesthood comes, *v.* 14. This change of the family shows a real change of the law of priesthood.

2. There is a change in the form and order of making the priests. The law by which Christ was constituted a priest, after the order of Melchisedec, was the power of an endless life. This gives the preference infinitely to Christ and the gospel. The high priest of our profession holds his office by that innate power of endless life which he has in himself, to communicate eternal life to all those who duly rely upon his sacrifice and intercession.

3. There is a change in the efficacy of the priesthood, *v.* 18, 19. The Levitical priesthood brought nothing to perfection. But the priesthood of Christ brings along with it a better hope; it shows us the true foundation of all the hope we have towards God for pardon and salvation. By this hope we are encouraged to draw nigh unto God, to live a life of communion with him.

JAMIESON, FAUSSET, BROWN

12. For—the reason why Paul presses the words "after the order of Melchisedec" in Psalm 110:4, viz., because these presuppose a change or transference of the priesthood, and this carries with it a change also of the law (which is inseparably bound up with the priesthood, both stand and fall together, vs. 11). This is his answer to those who might object, What need was there of a new covenant? **13.** Confirming the truth that *a change is made of the law* (vs. 12), by another fact showing the distinctness of the new priesthood from the Aaronic. **these things**—(Ps. 110:4). **pertaineth**—*Greek,* "hath partaken of" (the perfect tense implies the *continuance* still of His manhood). **another**—"a *different* tribe" from that of Levi. **14. evident**—lit., "manifest before the eyes" as a thing indisputable; a proof that whatever difficulties may now appear, *then* Jesus Christ's genealogy labored under none. **our Lord**—the only place where this now common title occurs without "Jesus," or "Christ," except II Peter 3:15. **sprang**—as a plant, and a branch. **Judah**—Genesis 49:10; Luke 1:27, 39 (Hebron of Judah, where LIGHTFOOT thinks Jesus was conceived); 2:4, 5; Rev. 5:5. **of which tribe ... priesthood**—"*in respect to* which tribe Moses spake nothing concerning priests" (so the oldest MSS. read, nothing to imply that priests were to be taken from it). **15.** Another proof that the law, or economy, is changed, viz., forasmuch as Christ is appointed Priest, "not according to the law of a carnal (i.e., a mere *outward*) commandment," but "according to the power of an *indissoluble* (so the *Greek*) life." The 110th Psalm appoints Him "for ever" (vs. 17). The Levitical law required a *definite carnal* descent. In contrast stands "the power"; Christ's spiritual, inward, living power of overcoming death. Not agreeably to a *statute* is Christ appointed, but according to an inward *living power.* **it**—the change of the law or economy, the statement (vss. 12, 18). **far more**—*Greek,* "more abundantly." **for that**—"seeing that," lit., "if"; so Romans 5:10. **after the similitude of Melchisedec**—answering to "after the order of Melchisedec" (ch. 5:10). The "order" cannot mean a *series of priests,* for Melchisedec neither received his priesthood from, nor transmitted it to, any other mere man; it must mean "answering to the *office* of Melchisedec." Christ's priesthood is similar to Melchisedec's in that it is "for ever" (vss. 16, 17). **another**—rather as *Greek,* "a different." **16. carnal ... endless**—mutually contrasted. As "form" and "power" are opposed, II Timothy 3:5; so here "the law" and "power," cf. Romans 8:3, "The law was *weak* through the flesh"; and vs. 18, "weakness." "The law" is here not the law in general, but the *statute* as to the priesthood. "Carnal," as being only *outward and temporary,* is contrasted with "endless," or, as *Greek,* "indissoluble." Commandments is contrasted with "life." The *law* can give a *commandment,* but it cannot give *life* (vs. 19). But our High Priest's inherent "power," now in heaven, has in Him "life for ever"; ch. 9:14, "through the *eternal Spirit";* ch. 7:25, "able" ... "ever liveth" (John 5:26). It is in the power of His resurrection life, not of His earthly life, that Christ officiates as a Priest. **17. For**—proving His *life* to be "endless" or indissoluble (vs. 16). The emphasis is on "for ever." The oldest MSS. read, "*He is testified of,* that Thou art.... **18. there is**—*Greek,* "there takes place," according to Psalm 110:4. **disannuling**—a repealing. **of the commandment**—ordaining the Levitical priesthood. And, as the Levitical priesthood and the law are inseparably joined, since the former is repealed, the latter is so also (*Note,* vs. 11). **going before**—the legal ordinance introducing and giving place to the Christian, the antitypical and permanent end of the former. **weakness and unprofitableness**—The opposite of "power" (vs. 16). **19. For ...**—justifying his calling the law *weak* and *unprofitable* (vs. 18). The law could not bring men to true justification or sanctification before God, which is the "perfection" that we all need in order to be accepted of Him, and which we have in Christ. **nothing**—not merely "no one," but "nothing." The law brought nothing to its perfected end; everything in it was introductory to its antitype in the Christian economy, which realizes the perfection contemplated; cf. "unprofitableness," vs. 18. **did**—rather connect with vs. 18, thus, "There takes place (by virtue of Ps. 110:4) a repealing of the commandment (on the one hand), but (on the other) *a* bringing in *afterwards* (the *Greek* expresses that there is a bringing in of something *over and above* the law; a *superinducing,* or *accession of something new,* viz., something better than the good things which the pre-existing law promised [WAHL]) of a better hope," not one weak and unprofitable, but, as elsewhere the Christian

ADAM CLARKE

hood; this existed typically in Melchisedec, and really in Jesus Christ.

12. *The priesthood being changed.* That is, the order of Aaron being now abrogated to make way for that which had preceded it, the order of Melchisedec. *There is made of necessity a change also of the law.* The very essence of the Levitical law consisting in its sacrificial offerings; and as these could not confer perfection, could not reconcile God to man, purify the unholy heart, nor open the kingdom of Heaven to the souls of men, consequently it must be abolished, according to the order of God himself.

13. *For he of whom these things are spoken.* That is, Jesus, the Messiah, spoken of in Ps. cx. 4, who came, not from the tribe of Levi, but from the tribe of Judah, of which tribe no priest ever ministered at a Jewish altar, nor could minister according to the law.

14. *For it is evident.* As the apostle speaks here with so much confidence, it follows that our Lord's descent from the tribe of Judah was incontrovertible. The genealogical tables, in both Matthew and Luke, establish this point.

15. *And it is yet far more evident.* "And besides, it is more abundantly, strikingly manifest." It is very difficult to translate these words, but the apostle's meaning is plain, viz., that God designed the Levitical priesthood to be changed, because of the oath in Ps. cx, where, addressing the Messiah, he says: "Thou art a priest for ever after the order [or similitude] of Melchisedek," who was not only a priest, but also a king. None of the Levitical priests sustained this double office; but they both, with that of prophet, appear and were exercised in the person of our Lord, who is the Priest to which the apostle alludes.

16. *Who is made.* Appointed to this high office by God himself, not succeeding one that was disabled or dead. This is probably all that the apostle intends by the words *carnal commandment,* for *carnal* does not always mean sinful or corrupt, but feeble, frail, or what may be said of or concerning man in his present dying condition. *But after the power of an endless life.* Not dying, or ceasing through weakness to be a priest, but properly immortal himself, and having the power to confer life and immortality on others.

17. *For he testifieth.* That is, either the Scripture, in the place so often quoted, or God by that Scripture. *Thou art a priest for ever.* This is the proof that He was not appointed according to the carnal commandment, but according to the power of an endless life, because He is a Priest *for ever;* i.e., One that never dies and is never disabled from performing the important functions of His office.

18. *For there is verily a disannulling.* There is a total abrogation "of the former law" relative to the Levitical priesthood. See v. 19. *For the weakness.* It had no energy; it communicated none; it had no Spirit to minister; it required perfect obedience, but furnished no assistance to those who were under it. *And unprofitableness.* No man was benefited by the mere observance of its precepts. It pardoned no sin, changed no heart, reformed no life; it found men dead in trespasses and sins, and it consigned them to eternal death. It was therefore weak in itself and unprofitable to men.

19. *For the law made nothing perfect.* It completed nothing; it was only the outline of a great plan, the shadow of a glorious substance; see on v. 11. It neither pardoned sin or purified the heart, nor gave strength to obey the moral precepts. *Nothing* is put here for "no person." *But the bringing in of a better hope.* The original is very emphatic, the "superintroduction" or the "after introduction"; and this seems to be put in opposition to the "the preceding commandment," or former Levitical law, of v. 18. This went before to prepare the way of the Lord, to show the exceeding sinfulness of sin and the strict justice of God. The *better hope,* which referred not to earthly but to spiritual good, not to temporal but eternal felicity, founded on the priesthood and atonement of Christ, was afterwards introduced for the purpose of doing what the law could not do, and giving privileges and advantages which the law would not afford. One

MATTHEW HENRY

4. There is a change in God's way of acting in this priesthood. Christ was made a priest with the oath of God, *v.* 21.

5. There is a change in the dispensation of that covenant. The gospel dispensation is more full, free, and efficacious, than that of the law. He, as surety, has united the divine and human nature together in his own person, and therein given assurance of reconciliation; and he has, as surety, united God and man together in the bond of the everlasting covenant.

6. There is a remarkable change in the number of the priests. In that of Aaron there was a multitude of priests; but in this of Christ there is but one and the same. *They were not suffered to continue by reason of death.*

Our high priest continues for ever, and his priesthood is *an unchangeable one.* There can be no vacancy in this priesthood, no hour nor moment in which the people are without a priest to negotiate their spiritual concerns in heaven.

This ever-living high priest is able to save to the utmost all who come to God by him, *v.* 25.

JAMIESON, FAUSSET, BROWN

dispensation is called, "everlasting," "true," "the second," "more excellent," "different," "living," "new," "to come," "perfect." Cf. ch. 8:6, bringing us *near to God,* now in spirit, hereafter both in spirit and in body. **we draw nigh unto God**—the sure token of "perfection." *Weakness* is the opposite of this filial confidence of access. The access through the legal sacrifices was only symbolical and through the medium of a priest; that through Christ is immediate, perfect, and spiritual. **20.** Another proof of the superiority of Christ's Melchisedec-like priesthood; the oath of God gave a solemn weight to it which was not in the law-priesthood, which was not so confirmed. **he was made priest**—rather supply from vs. 22, which completes the sentence begun in this verse, vs. 21 being a parenthesis, "inasmuch as not without an oath *He was made surety of the testament* (for . . .), of so much better a testament hath Jesus been made the surety." **21.** Translate in the *Greek* order, "For they indeed (the existing legal priests) without the (solemn) *promise on* oath (so the *Greek* [TITTMANN]) are made priests." **by him**—God. **unto him**—the Lord, the Son of God (Ps. 110:1). **not repent**—never change His purpose. **after the order of Melchisedec**—omitted in some oldest MSS., contained in others. **22. surety**—ensuring in His own person the certainty of the covenant to us. This He did by becoming responsible for our guilt, by sealing the covenant with His blood, and by being openly acknowledged as our triumphant Saviour by the Father, who raised Him from the dead. Thus He is at once God's surety for man, and man's surety for God, and so Mediator between God and man (ch. 8:6). **better**—ch. 8:6; 13:20, "everlasting." **testament**—sometimes translated, "covenant." The *Greek* term implies that it is *appointed* by God, and comprises the relations and bearings partly of a *covenant,* partly of a *testament:* (1) the appointment made without the concurrence of a second party, of somewhat concerning that second party; a last will or testament, so in ch. 9:16, 17; (2) a mutual agreement in which both parties consent. **23.** Another proof of superiority; the Levitical priests were many, as death caused the need of continually new ones being appointed in succession. Christ dies not, and so hath a priesthood which passes not from one to another. **were**—*Greek,* "are made." **many**—one after another; opposed to His "*unchangeable* (that does not pass from one to another) priesthood" (vs. 24). **not suffered to continue**—*Greek,* "*hindered* from *permanently* continuing," *viz., in the priesthood.* **24. he**—emphatic; *Greek,* "Himself." So in Psalm 110:4, "THOU art a *priest*"; singular, not *priests,* "many." **continueth**—*Greek,* simple verb, not the compound as in vs. 23. "Remaineth," viz., *in life.* **unchangeable**—*Greek,* "hath His priesthood unchangeable"; *not passing from one to another, intransmissible.* Therefore no earthly so-called apostolic succession of priests are His vicegerents. The Jewish priests had *successors* in office, because "they could not continue by reason of death." But this Man, because He liveth ever, hath no successor in office, not even Peter (I Pet. 5:1). **25. Wherefore**—*Greek,* "Whence"; inasmuch as "He remaineth *for ever.*" **also**—as a natural consequence flowing from the last, at the same time *a new and higher* thing [ALFORD]. **save**—His very name JESUS (vs. 22) meaning *Saviour* —**to the uttermost**—altogether, perfectly, so that nothing should be wanting afterwards for ever [TITTMANN]. It means "in any wise," "utterly," in Luke 13:11. **come unto God**—by faith. **by him**—*through Him* as their mediating Priest, instead of through the Levitical priests. **seeing he ever liveth** —resuming "He continueth ever," vs. 24; therefore "He is able to the uttermost"; He is not, like the Levitical priest, prevented by *death,* for "He ever liveth" (vs. 23). **to make intercession**—There was but the *one offering* on earth once for all. But the *intercession* for us in the heavens (vs. 26) is ever continuing, whence the result follows, that we can never be separated from the love of God in Christ. He *intercedes* only for those who come unto God through Him, not for the unbelieving world (John 17:9). As samples of His intercession, cf. the *prophetical* descriptions in the Old Testament. "By an humble omnipotency (for it was by His *humiliation* that He obtained *all power*), or omnipotent humility, appearing in the presence, and presenting His postulations at the throne of God [BISHOP PEARSON]. He was not only the offering, but the priest who offered it. Therefore, He has become not only a sacrifice, but an intercessor; His intercession being founded on His voluntary offering of Himself without spot to God. We are not only then in virtue of His sacrifice forgiven, but in virtue of the intercession admitted to favor and grace

ADAM CLARKE

of these privileges immediately follows: *By the which we draw nigh unto God.* This is a sacerdotal phrase. The high priest alone could approach to the Divine Presence in the holy of holies; but not without the blood of the sacrifice, and that only once in the year. But through Christ, as our High Priest, all believers in Him have an entrance to the holiest by His blood, and through Him perform acceptable service to God. The *better hope* means, in this place, Jesus Christ, who is the Author and Object of the hope of eternal life, which all His genuine followers possess.

21. *Those priests,* the Levitical, *were made without an oath,* to show that the whole system was changeable and might be abolished. *But this,* the everlasting priesthood of Christ, *with an oath,* to show that the gospel dispensation should never change and never be abolished. *By him,* God the Father, *that said unto him,* the promised Messiah, Ps. cx. 4, *The Lord sware,* to show the immutability of His counsel, *and will not repent,* can never change His mind nor purpose, *Thou art a priest for ever*—as long as time shall run and the generations of men be continued on earth. Till the necessity of the mediatorial Kingdom be superseded by the fixed state of eternity, till this Kingdom be delivered up unto the Father, and God shall be All in All, shall this priesthood of Christ endure.

22. *By so much,* this solemn, unchangeable oath of God, *was Jesus made a surety,* a "Mediator," One who brings the two parties together, witnesses the contract, and offers the covenant sacrifice on the occasion. *A better testament.* "A better covenant"; thus contradistinguished from the Mosaic, which was the old covenant; and this is called the new and better covenant, because God has in it promised other blessings, to other people, on other conditions, than the old covenant did. The new covenant is better than the old in the following particulars: (1) God promised to the Jewish nation certain secular blessings, peculiar to that nation, on condition of their keeping the law of Moses; but under the new covenant He promises pardon of sin, and final salvation to all mankind, on condition of believing on Jesus Christ and walking in His testimonies. (2) The Jewish priests, fallible, dying men, were mediators of the old covenant by means of their sacrifices, which could not take away sin, nor render the comers thereunto perfect. But Jesus Christ, who liveth forever, who is infinite in wisdom and power, by the sacrifice of himself has established this new covenant, and by the shedding of His blood has opened the kingdom of Heaven to all believers.

23. *And they truly were many priests.* Under the Mosaic law it was necessary there should be a succession of priests because, being mortal, they were not suffered to continue always by reason of death.

24. *But this.* "But He," that is, Christ, *because he continueth ever,* is eternal, *hath an unchangeable priesthood,* "a priesthood that passeth not away" from Him. He lives forever, and He lives a Priest forever.

25. *Wherefore.* Because He is an everlasting Priest and has offered the only available sacrifice, *he is able . . . to save* from the power, guilt, nature, and punishment of sin. *To the uttermost,* to all intents, degrees, purposes; and always, and in and through all times, places, and circumstances; for all this is implied in the original word. But "in and through all times" seems to be the particular meaning here, because of what follows, *he ever liveth to make intercession for them;* this depends on the perpetuity of His priesthood and the continuance of His mediatorial office. But none can be saved by His grace that do not *come unto God by [through] him;* i.e., imploring mercy through Him as their Sacrifice and Atonement. The phrase "to make intercession" for a person has a considerable latitude of meaning. It signifies: (1) To come to or meet a person on any cause whatever. (2) To intercede, pray for, or entreat in the behalf of, another. (3) To defend or vindicate a person. (4) To commend. (5) To furnish any kind of assistance or help.

MATTHEW HENRY

7. There is a remarkable difference in the moral qualifications of the priests. He is *such a high priest as became us, holy, harmless, and undefiled,* &c., *v.* 26–28. Our case, as sinners, needed a high priest to make satisfaction and intercession for us. No priest could be suitable or sufficient for our reconciliation to God but one who was perfectly righteous. The Lord Jesus was exactly such a high priest as we wanted, for he has a personal holiness, absolutely perfect. He is holy. No sin dwells in him, though it does in the best of Christians. He is harmless, never did the least wrong to God or man. He is undefiled, though he took upon him the guilt of our sins, yet he never involved himself in the fact and fault of them. He is separate from sinners. Though he took a true human nature, yet the miraculous way in which it was conceived set him upon a separate footing from all the rest of mankind.

He is made higher than the heavens, for he is exalted at the right hand of God, to perfect the design of his priesthood.

The validity and prevalency of Christ's priesthood in *v.* 27 are placed in the impartiality and disinterestedness of it. He needed not to offer up for himself: it was a disinterested mediation; he mediated for that mercy for others which he did not need for himself.

JAMIESON, FAUSSET, BROWN

[ARCHBISHOP MAGEE]. **26. such**—as is above described. The oldest MSS. read, "also." "For to US (as *sinners;* emphatical) there was also becoming (besides the other excellencies of our High Priest) such an High Priest." **holy**—"pious" (a distinct *Greek* word from that for *holy,* which latter implies *consecration*) towards *God;* perfectly answering God's will in reverent piety (Ps. 16:10). **harmless**—lit., "free from evil" and guile, in relation to *Himself.* **undefiled**—not defiled by stain contracted from others, in relation to *men.* Temptation, to which He was exposed, left no trace of evil in Him. **separate**—rather, "*separated* from sinners," viz., in His heavenly state as our High Priest above, after He had been *parted from the earth,* as the Levitical high priest was separated from the people in the sanctuary (whence he was not to go out), Lev. 21:12. Though justifying through faith the ungodly, He hath no contact with them *as such.* He is lifted above our sinful community, being "made higher than the heavens," at the same time that He makes believers *as such* (not as sinners), "to sit together (with Him) in heavenly places" (Eph. 2:6). Just as Moses *on the mount* was separated from and above the people, and alone with God. This proves Jesus is GOD. "Though innumerable lies have been forged against the venerable Jesus, none dared to charge Him with any intemperance" [ORIGEN]. **made**—Jesus WAS higher before (John 17:5), and as the *God*-MAN was *made* so by the Father after His humiliation (cf. ch. 1:4). **higher than the heavens**—for "He passed *through* [so the *Greek*] the heavens" (ch. 4:14). **27. daily**—"day by day." The priests *daily* offered sacrifices (ch. 9:6; 10:11; Exod. 29:38-42). The high priests took part in these daily-offered sacrifices only on festival days; but as they represented the whole priesthood, the daily offerings are here attributed to them; their exclusive function was to offer the atonement "once every year" (ch. 9:7), and "year by year continually" (ch. 10:1). The "daily" strictly belongs to *Christ,* not to the high priests, "who needeth not daily, as those high priests (*year by year,* and their subordinate priests daily), to offer. . . ." **offer up**—The *Greek* term is peculiarly used of *sacrifices for sin.* The high priest's double offering on the day of atonement, the bullock for himself, and the goat for the people's sins, had its counterpart in the TWO lambs offered daily by the ordinary priests. **this he did**—not "died first for His own sins and then the people's," but *for the people's only.* The negation is twofold: He needeth not to offer (1) daily; nor (2) to offer for His own sins also; for He offered Himself a spotless sacrifice (vs. 26; ch. 4:15). The sinless alone could offer for the sinful. **once**—rather as *Greek,* "once for all." The sufficiency of the *one* sacrifice to atone for *all* sins *for ever,* resulted from its absolute spotlessness. **28. For**—reason for the difference stated in vs. 27, between His one sacrifice and their oft repeated sacrifices, viz., because of His entire freedom from the sinful *infirmity* to which they are subject. *He needed not, as they, to offer* FOR HIS OWN SIN; and being now exempt from death and "perfected for evermore," *He needs not to* REPEAT *His sacrifice.* **the word**—"the word" confirmed by "the oath." **which**—which *oath* was after the law, viz., in Psalm 110:4, abrogating the preceding law-priesthood. **the Son**—contrasted with "men." **consecrated**—*Greek,* "made perfect" once for all, as in ch. 2:10; 5:9, *Notes.* Opposed to "having infirmity." *Consecrated as a perfected priest* by His perfected sacrifice, and consequent anointing and exaltation to the right hand of the Father.

ADAM CLARKE

26. *Such an high priest became us.* Such a High Priest was in every respect suitable to us, every way qualified to accomplish the end for which He came into the world. There is probably here an allusion to the qualifications of the Jewish high priest: (1) He was required to be *holy,* answering to the Hebrew *chasid,* "merciful." Holiness was his calling; and, as he was the representative of his brethren, he was required to be merciful and compassionate. (2) He was to be *harmless,* "without evil"—holy without and holy within; injuring none, but rather living for the benefit of others. (3) He was *undefiled,* answering to the Hebrew "without blemish"—having no bodily imperfection. Nothing low, mean, base, or unbecoming in his conduct. (4) He was *separate from sinners.* By his office he was separated from all men and worldly occupations, and entirely devoted to the service of God. (5) Higher than the heavens. There may be some reference here to the exceeding dignity of the high priesthood; it was the highest office that could be sustained by man, the high priest himself being the immediate representative of God. But these things suit our Lord in a sense in which they cannot be applied to the high priest of the Jews. (1) He was *holy,* infinitely so; and "merciful." Witness His shedding His blood for the sins of mankind. (2) *Harmless*—perfectly without sin in His humanity as well as His divinity. (3) *Undefiled*—contracted no sinful infirmity in consequence of His dwelling among men. (4) *Separate from sinners*—absolutely unblameable in the whole of His conduct, so that He could challenge the most inveterate of His enemies with, "Which of you convicteth me of sin?" (5) *Higher than the heavens*—more exalted than all the angels of God, than all created beings, whether thrones, dominions, principalities, or powers, because all these were created by Him and for Him, and derive their continued subsistence from His infinite energy.

27. *Who needeth not daily.* Though the high priest offered the great atonement only once in the year, yet in the Jewish services there was a daily acknowledgement of sin, and a daily sacrifice offered by the priests, at whose head was the high priest, for their own sins and the sins of the people. The Jews held that a priest who neglected his own expiatory sacrifice would be smitten with death. *For this he did once.* For himself He offered no sacrifice; and the apostle gives the reason—he needed none, because he was "holy, harmless, undefiled, separate from sinners"; and for the people He offered himself once for all, when He expired upon the Cross.

28. *For the law maketh men high priests.* The Jewish priests have need of these repeated offerings and sacrifices because they are fallible, sinful men. *But the word of the oath* (still referring to Ps. cx. 4), *which was since the law.* For David, who mentions this, lived nearly five hundred years after the giving of the law; and consequently that oath, constituting another priesthood, abrogates the law. And by this the *Son . . . is consecrated,* "is perfected," *for evermore.* Being a High Priest without blemish, immaculately holy, every way perfect, immortal, and eternal, He is a Priest "to eternity."

MATTHEW HENRY

CHAPTER 8

Verses 1–5

I. A summary recital of what had been said before concerning the excellency of Christ's priesthood, *v.* 1, 2. What we have in Christ; we have a high priest, and such a high priest as no other people ever had; all others were but types and shadows of this high priest. Where he now resides: *He sits on the right hand of the throne of the Majesty on high.* This is the reward of his humiliation.

JAMIESON, FAUSSET, BROWN

CHAPTER 8

VSS. 1-13. CHRIST, THE HIGH PRIEST IN THE TRUE SANCTUARY, SUPERSEDING THE LEVITICAL PRIESTHOOD; THE NEW RENDERS OBSOLETE THE OLD COVENANT. **1. the sum**—rather, "the principal point"; for the participle is present, not *past,* which would be required if the meaning were "the sum." "The chief point in (or, 'in the case'; so the *Greek,* ch. 9:10, 15, 17) the things which we are speaking," lit., "which are being spoken." **such**—so transcendently pre-eminent, viz., in this **respect, that** "He is set on the right hand of. . . ." **Infinitely** above all other priests in this one grand respect, He exercises His priesthood IN HEAVEN, not in the *earthly* "holiest place" (ch. 10:12). The Levitical high priests, even when they entered the Holiest Place once a year, only STOOD for a *brief space before the symbol* of God's throne; but Jesus SITS *on the throne* of the Divine Majesty in the heaven itself, and this *for ever* (ch. 10:11, 12).

ADAM CLARKE

CHAPTER 8

1. *Of the things which we have spoken this is the sum.* The word which we translate *sum* signifies the "chief," the "principal," or "head." *Who is set on the right hand of the throne.* This is what the apostle states to be the chief or most important point of all that he had yet discussed. His sitting down at the right hand of the throne of God, proves: (1) That He is higher than all the high priests that ever existed. (2) That the sacrifice which He offered for the sins of the world was sufficient and effectual, and as such accepted by God. (3) That He has all power in the heavens and in the earth, and is able to save and defend to the uttermost all that come to God through Him. (4) That He did not, like the Jewish high priest, depart out of the holy of holies after having offered the atonement; but abides there at the throne of God as a continual Priest, in the

MATTHEW HENRY

What is that sanctuary of which he is a minister, *v.* 2. There was an outer part, in which was the altar where they were to offer their sacrifices, which typified Christ dying; and there was an interior part within the veil, which typified Christ interceding for the people in heaven. Having finished the work of satisfaction in the true tabernacle of his own body, he is now a minister of the sanctuary, the holy of holies, the true tabernacle in heaven. He is not only in heaven enjoying great dominion and dignity, but as the high priest of his church.

II. The apostle sets before the Hebrews what it was that belonged to that office, *v.* 3, 4. It necessarily belongs to the priesthood of Christ that he should have somewhat to offer; and he had himself to offer, as the great atoning sacrifice.

Christ must now execute his priesthood in heaven; having finished the work of sacrificing here, he must go into heaven, to present his righteousness and to make intercession there. *If Christ were on earth, he would not be a priest* (*v.* 4), that is, not according to the Levitical law. If he had still continued on earth, he could not have been a perfect priest; and an imperfect one he could not be.

Verses 6–13

The apostle illustrates and confirms the superior excellency of the priesthood of Christ. His ministry is more excellent, by how much he is the Mediator of a better covenant.

What is here said of the New Testament dispensation.

1. That it is a better covenant (*v.* 6). It is without fault, well ordered in all things. It requires nothing but what it promises grace to perform. All is put into a good and safe hand.

2. That it is established upon better promises. This covenant contains in it promises of assistance and acceptance in duty, promises of progress and perseverance in grace and holiness, of bliss and glory in heaven.

JAMIESON, FAUSSET, BROWN

2. minister—The *Greek* term implies *priestly ministry* in the temple. **the sanctuary**—*Greek,* "the holy places"; the Holy of Holies. Here the heavenly sanctuary is meant. **the true**—the archetypal and antitypical, as contrasted with the typical and symbolical (ch. 9:24). *Greek alethinos* (used here) is opposed to that which does not fulfil its idea, as for instance, *a type; alethes,* to that which is untrue and unreal, as *a lie.* The measure of *alethes* is reality; that of *alethinos,* ideality. In *alethes* the idea corresponds to the thing; in *alethinos,* the thing to the idea [KALMIS in ALFORD]. **tabernacle**—(ch. 9:11). *His body.* Through His glorified body as the tabernacle, Christ passes into the heavenly "Holy of Holies," the immediate immaterial presence of God, where He intercedes for us. This tabernacle in which God dwells, is where God in Christ meets us who are "members of His body, of His flesh, and of His bones." This tabernacle answers to the heavenly Jerusalem, where God's *visible* presence is to be manifested to His perfected saints and angels, who are united in Christ the Head; in contradistinction to His personal *invisible* presence in the Holy of Holies unapproachable save to Christ. John 1:14, "Word . . . dwelt among us," *Greek,* "tabernacled." **pitched**—*Greek,* "fixed" firmly. **not man**—as Moses (vs. 5). **3. For**—assigning his reason for calling him "minister of the sanctuary" (vs. 2). **somewhat**—He does not offer again His *once for all* completed sacrifice. But as the high priest did *not* enter the Holy Place *without blood,* so Christ has entered the heavenly Holy Place *with His own blood.* That "blood of sprinkling" is in heaven. And is thence made effectual to sprinkle believers as the end of their election (I Pet. 1:2). The term "consecrate" as a priest, is lit., to *fill the hand,* implying that an offering is given into the hands of the priest, which it is his duty to present to God. If a man be a priest, he must have some gift in his hands to offer. Therefore, Christ, as a priest, has His blood as His oblation to offer before God. **4.** Implying that Christ's priestly office is exercised in heaven, not in earth; in the power of His resurrection life, not of His earthly life. **For**—The oldest MSS. read, "accordingly then." **if . . .**—"if He were on earth, He would *not even* (so the *Greek*) be a priest" (cf. ch. 7:13, 14); therefore, certainly, He could not exercise the high priestly function in the earthly Holy of Holies. **seeing that . . .**—"since there are" already, and exist now (the temple service not yet being set aside, as it was on the destruction of Jerusalem), "those (the oldest MSS. omit 'priests') who offer *the* (appointed) gifts according to (the) law." *Therefore, His sacerdotal "ministry" must be "in the heavens," not on earth* (vs. 1). "If His priesthood terminated on the earth, He would not even be a priest at all" [BENGEL].

5. Who—viz., the priests. **serve unto the example**—not "*after* the example," as BENGEL explains. But as in ch. 13:10, "serve the tabernacle," i.e., do it service: so "serve (the tabernacle which is but) *the outline* and shadow." The *Greek* for "example" is here taken for the *sketch, copy,* or *suggestive representation* of the heavenly sanctuary, which is the antitypical reality and primary archetype. "The mount" answers to *heaven,* ch. 12:22. **admonished**—The *Greek* especially applies to *divine responses* and *commands.* **to make**—"perfectly": so the *Greek.* **See**—Take heed, accurately observing the pattern, that so thou mayest make . . . . **saith he**—God. **the pattern**—an accurate representation, presented in vision to Moses, of the heavenly real sanctuary. Thus the earthly tabernacle was copy of a copy; but the latter accurately representing the grand archetypical original in heaven (Exod. 25:40). **6. now**—not *time;* but "as it is." **more excellent ministry**—than any earthly ministry. **by how much**—in proportion as. **mediator**—coming between us and God, to carry into effect God's covenant with us. "The messenger (angel) of the covenant." **which**—*Greek,* "one which" [ALFORD]: *inasmuch as being one which.* **established**—*Greek,* "enacted as a law." So Romans 3:27, "law of faith"; and 8:2; 9:31, apply "law" to the Gospel covenant. It is implied hereby, the Gospel is founded on the law, in the spirit and essence of the latter. **upon**—resting upon. **better promises**—enumerated vss. 10, 11. The Old Testament promises were mainly of earthly, the New Testament promises, of heavenly blessings: the exact fulfilment of the earthly promises was a pledge of the fulfilment of the heavenly. Cf. Jeremiah 7:21, 22, which shows that God's original design in the old covenant ritual system was, that it should be

ADAM CLARKE

permanent act of offering His crucified body unto God in behalf of all the succeeding generations of mankind.

2. *A minister of the sanctuary.* "A public minister of the holy things" or places. The word means a person who officiated for the public, a public officer, in whom, and his work, all the people had a common right; hence our word "liturgy," the public work of prayer and praise, designed for the people at large. Properly speaking, the Jewish priest was the servant of the public; he transacted the business of the people with God. Jesus Christ is also the same kind of public officer; both as Priest and Mediator, He transacts the business of the whole human race with God. He performs the "holy things" or acts in the *true tabernacle,* heaven, of which the Jewish Tabernacle was the type. The Tabernacle was the place among the Jews where God, by the symbol of His presence, dwelt. This could only typify heaven, where God in His essential glory dwells; and hence heaven is called here the *true tabernacle* to distinguish it from the type. *Which the Lord pitched.* The Jewish Tabernacle was man's work, though made by God's direction; the heavens, this *true tabernacle,* the work of God alone. The Tabernacle was also a type of the human nature of Christ, John i. 14: "And the Word was made flesh, and dwelt among us" (and "tabernacled" among us). For, as the Divine Presence dwelt in the Tabernacle, so the fullness of the Godhead, bodily, dwelt in the Man Christ Jesus. And this human body was the peculiar work of God, as it came not in the way of natural generation.

3. *Every high priest is ordained.* "Is set apart," for this especial work. *Gifts and sacrifices.* Eucharistic "offerings," and *sacrifices* for sin. By the former, God's government of the universe and His benevolence to His creatures in providing for their support were acknowledged. By the latter, the destructive and ruinous nature of sin and the necessity of an atonement were confessed. *Wherefore it is of necessity.* If Christ be a High Priest, and it be essential to the office of a high priest to offer atoning sacrifices to God, Jesus must offer such. Now it is manifest that, as he is the Public Minister, officiating in the true tabernacle as High Priest, He must make an atonement; and His being at the right hand of the throne shows that He has offered and continues to offer such an atonement.

4. *For if he were on earth.* As the Jewish Temple was standing when this Epistle was written, the whole Temple service continued to be performed by the legal priests, descendants of Aaron, of the tribe of Levi. Therefore if Christ had been then on earth, He could not have performed the office of a priest, being of the tribe of Judah, to which tribe the office of the priesthood did not appertain. *There are priests that offer gifts.* This is an additional proof that this Epistle was written before the destruction of Jerusalem.

5. *Who serve.* Who perform divine worship. *Unto the example and shadow.* "With the representation and shadow." The whole Levitical service was a representation and shadow of heavenly things; it appears, therefore, absurd to say that the priests served *unto an example* or "representation" *of heavenly things;* they served rather unto the substance of those things, with appropriate representations and shadows. *As Moses was admonished.* As Moses was divinely warned or admonished of God. *According to the pattern.* According to the "type," plan, or form. It is very likely that God gave a regular plan and specification of the Tabernacle and all its parts to Moses, and that from this divine plan the whole was constructed. See on Exod. xxv. 40.

6. *Now hath he obtained a more excellent ministry.* His office of priesthood is more excellent than the Levitical because the covenant is better, and established on better promises. The old covenant referred to earthly things; the new covenant, to heavenly. The old covenant had promises of secular good; the new covenant, of spiritual and eternal blessings. As far as Christianity is preferable to Judaism, as far as Christ is preferable to Moses, as far as spiritual blessings are preferable to earthly blessings, and as far as the enjoyment of God throughout eternity is preferable to the communication of earthly

MATTHEW HENRY

3. It is a new covenant. This will always be a new covenant, in which all who truly take hold of it shall be always found preserved by the power of God.

That this covenant was not found faultless (*v.* 7, 8). It was perfect in its kind, and fitted to answer its end, but very imperfect in comparison of the gospel.

What is here said of the old covenant. That it was made with the fathers of the Jewish nation at Mount Sinai (*v.* 9).

That it was not sure or steadfast, *v.* 9. God will regard those who remain in his covenant, but will reject those who cast away his yoke from them.

4. The articles of this covenant are sealed between God and his people by baptism and the Lord's supper. (1) God articles with his people, *v.* 10. He once wrote his laws to them, now he will write his laws in them. Their souls shall be a table and transcript of the law of God.

(2) He articles with them to take them into a near and very honourable relation to himself. He will be to them a God. Nothing more can be said in a thousand volumes than is comprehended in these few words: *I will be a God to them.* They shall be to him a people, to love, honour, observe, and obey him in all things. This those must do and will do who have God for their God; this they shall do, for God will enable them to do it. It is God himself who first founds the relation, and then fills it up with grace suitable and sufficient, and helps them in their measure to fill it up with love and duty.

(3) He articles with them that they shall grow more and more acquainted with their God (*v.* 11). There shall not be so much need of one neighbour teaching another the knowledge of God. This private instruction shall not be so necessary under the New Testament as it was under the Old. There shall be a mighty increase and spreading of Christian knowledge in persons of all sorts, of each sex, and of all ages. O that this promise might be fulfilled in our days!

JAMIESON, FAUSSET, BROWN

pædagogical, as a schoolmaster leading and preparing men for Christ. **7.** Same reasoning as in ch. 7:11. **faultless**—perfect in all its parts, so as *not to be found fault with* as wanting anything which ought to be there: answering all the purposes of a law. The law in its *morality* was *blameless, Greek-amomos;* but *in saving us* it was defective, and so not *faultless, Greek-amemptos.* **should no place have been sought**—as it has to be now; and as it is sought in the prophecy (vss. 8-11). The old covenant would have anticipated all man's wants, so as to give no occasion for *seeking* something more perfectly adequate. Cf. on the phrase "place . . . sought," ch. 12:17. **8. finding fault with them**—the people of the old covenant, who were not made "faultless" by it (vs. 7); and whose *disregard* of God's covenant made Him to *"regard* them *not"* (vs. 9). The law is **not** *in itself* **blamed,** but *the people* who had not observed it. **he saith** —(Jer. 31:31-34; cf. Ezek. 11:19; 36:25-27).

Behold, the days come—the frequent formula introducing a Messianic prophecy. **make**—*Greek,* "perfect"; "consummate." A suitable expression as to the new covenant, which perfected what the old could not (cf. end of vs. 9, with end of vs. 10). **Israel . . . Judah**—Therefore, the ten tribes, as well as Judah, share in the new covenant. As both shared the exile, so both shall share the literal and spiritual restoration. **9. Not according to . . .**—very different from, and far superior to, the old covenant, which only "worked wrath" (Rom. 4:15) through man's "not regarding" it. The new covenant enables us to obey by the Spirit's inward impulse producing love because of the forgiveness of our sins. **made with**—rather as *Greek,* "made to": the Israelites being only recipients, not co-agents [ALFORD] *with* God. **I took them by the hand**—as a father takes his child by the hand to support and guide his steps. "There are three periods: (1) that of the promise; (2) that of the pædagogical instruction; (3) that of fulfilment" [BENGEL]. The second, that of the pædagogical pupilage, began at the exodus from Egypt. **I regarded them not**—*English Version,* Jeremiah 31:32, translates, "Although *I was an husband unto* them." Paul's translation here is supported by LXX, *Syriac,* and GESENIUS, and accords with the kindred *Arabic.* The Hebrews *regarded not* God, so God, in righteous retribution, *regarded* them *not.* On "continued not in my covenant," SCHELLING observes: The law was in fact the mere *ideal* of a religious constitution: in *practice,* the Jews were throughout, before the captivity, more or less polytheists, except in the time of David, and the first years of Solomon [the type of Messiah's reign]. Even after the return from Babylon, idolatry was succeeded by what was not much better, formalism and hypocrisy (Matt. 12:43). The law was (1) a typical picture, tracing out the features of the glorious Gospel to be revealed; (2) it had a delegated virtue from the Gospel, which ceased, therefore, when the Gospel came. **10. make with**—*Greek,* "make *unto.*" **Israel**—comprising the before disunited (vs. 8) ten tribes' kingdom, and that of Judah. They are united in the spiritual Israel, the elect Church, now: they shall be so in the literal restored kingdom of Israel to come. **I will put**—lit., "(I) giving." This is the first of the "better promises" (vs. 6). **mind**—their intelligent faculty. **in . . .**—rather, "ON their hearts." Not on tables of stone as the law (II Cor. 3:3). **write**—*Greek,* "inscribe." **I will be to them a God . . .**—fulfilled first in the outward kingdom of God. Next, in the inward Gospel kingdom. Thirdly, in the kingdom at once outward and inward, the spiritual being manifested outwardly (Rev. 21:3). Cf. a similar progression as to the priesthood (1) Exodus 19:6; (2) I Peter 2:5; (3) Isaiah 61:6; Revelation 1:6. This progressive advance of the significance of the Old Testament institutions, etc., says THOLUCK, shows the *transparency* and prophetic character which runs throughout the whole. **11.** Second of the "better promises" (vs. 6). **they shall not**—"they shall not have to teach" [ALFORD]. **his neighbour**—So *Vulgate* reads; but the—oldest MSS. have "his (fellow) *citizen.*" **brother**—a closer and more endearing relation than *fellow citizen.* **from the least to the greatest**—*Greek,* "from the little one to the great one." Zechariah 12:8, "He that is feeble among them shall be as David." Under the old covenant, the priest's lips were to keep knowledge, and at his mouth the people were to seek the law: under the new covenant, the Holy Spirit teaches every believer. Not that the mutual teaching of brethren is excluded while the covenant is being promulgated; but when once the Holy Spirit shall have fully taught all the remission of their sins and

ADAM CLARKE

good during time, so far does the new covenant exceed the old.

7. *If that first . . . had been faultless.* This is nearly the same argument with that in chap. vii. 11. The simple meaning is: If the first covenant had made a provision for and actually conferred pardon and purity, and given a title to eternal life, then there could have been no need for a second. But the first covenant did not give these things; therefore a second was necessary.

8. *For finding fault with them.* The meaning is evidently this: God, in order to show that the first covenant was inefficient, saith to *them,* the Israelites, *Behold, the days come . . . when I will make a new covenant."* He found fault with the covenant, and addressed the people concerning His purpose of giving another covenant, that should be such as the necessities of mankind required. As this place refers to Jer. xxxi. 31-34, the words *finding fault with them* may refer to the Jewish people, of whom the Lord complains that they had broken His covenant though He was a Husband to them. *With the house of Israel and with the house of Judah.* That is, with all the descendants of the twelve sons of Jacob. This is thought to be a promise of the conversion of all the Jews to Christianity, both of the lost tribes and of those who are known to exist in Asiatic and European countries.

9. *Not according to the covenant.* The new covenant is of a widely different nature to that of the old; it was only temporal and earthly in itself, though it pointed out spiritual and eternal things. The new covenant is totally different from this, as we have already seen; and such a covenant, or system of religion, the Jews should have been prepared to expect, as the Prophet Jeremiah had in the above place so clearly foretold it. *And I regarded them not.* "And I neglected them or despised them"; but the words in the Hebrew text of the prophet we translate, "although I was an husband unto them." Let it be observed: (1) That the apostle quotes from the Septuagint. (2) The Hebrew words will bear a translation much nearer to the Septuagint and the apostle than our translation intimates. The words might be literally rendered, "And I was Lord over them," or, "I lorded or ruled over them"; i.e., I chastised them for their transgressions and punished them for their iniquities; "I took no further care of them," and gave them up into the hands of their enemies, and so they were carried away into captivity. This pretty nearly reconciles the Hebrew and the Greek, as it shows the act of God in reference to them is nearly the same when the proper meaning of the Hebrew and Greek words is considered.

10. *This is the covenant.* This is the nature of that glorious system of religion which I shall publish among them *after those days,* i.e., in the times of the gospel. *I will put my laws into their mind.* I will influence them with the principles of law, truth, holiness; and their understandings shall be fully enlightened to comprehend them. *And write them in their hearts.* All their affections, passions, and appetites shall be purified and filled with holiness and love to God and man; so that they shall willingly obey, and feel that love is the fulfilling of the law. Instead of being written on tables of stone, they shall be written on the fleshly tables of their hearts. *I will be to them a God.* These are the two grand conditions by which the parties in this covenant or agreement are bound: (1) "I will be your God." (2) "Ye shall be my people." To be God's people implies that they should give God their whole hearts, serve Him with all their might and strength, and have no other object of worship or dependence but himself. Any of these conditions broken, the covenant is rendered null and void, and the other party absolved from his engagement.

11. *They shall not teach every man his neighbour.* The prophecy here indicates that there should be, under the gospel dispensation, a should be, under the gospel dispensation, a profusion of divine light; and this we find to be the case by the plentiful diffusion of the sacred writings, and by an abundant gospel ministry. And these blessings are not confined to temples or palaces, but are found in every corner of the land;

MATTHEW HENRY

(4) God articles with them about the pardon of their sins (*v.* 12). The freeness of this pardon. It does not result from merit in man, but from mercy in God. The fulness of this pardon; it extends to all kinds of sin. The fixedness of this pardon. It is so final and so fixed that God will remember their sins no more; he will not recall his pardon. It is the effect of that mercy that is from everlasting, and the earnest of that mercy that shall be to everlasting. Therefore we have great reason to rejoice that the former dispensation is antiquated and has vanished away.

That it is decayed, grown old, and vanisheth away, *v.* 13. It is antiquated, of no more use in gospel times than candles are when the sun has risen.

CHAPTER 9

Verses 1–7

I. The apostle gives an account of the tabernacle. It was divided into two parts, called a first and a second tabernacle, an inner and an outer part. We are also told what was placed in each part of the tabernacle.

1. In the outer part. (1) The candlestick; doubtless not an empty and unlighted one, but where the lamps were always burning. And there was need of it, for there were no windows in the sanctuary. Their light was only candle-light, in comparison of the fulness of light which Christ, the Sun of righteousness, would bring along with him. (2) The table and the show-bread set upon it. This table was set directly opposite to the candlestick. We must not come in the dark to his table, but by light from Christ must discern the Lord's body. He is the bread of life; in our Father's house there is bread enough and to spare; we may have fresh supplies from Christ, especially every Lord's day.

JAMIESON, FAUSSET, BROWN

inward sanctification, then there shall be no further need of man teaching his fellow man. Cf. I Thessalonians 4:9; 5:1, an earnest of that perfect state to come. On the way to that perfect state every man should teach his neighbor. "The teaching is not hard and forced, because grace renders all teachable; for it is not the ministry of the letter, but of the spirit (II Cor. 3:6). The believer's firmness does not depend on the *authority* of human teachers. God Himself teaches" [BENGEL]. The New Testament is shorter than the Old Testament, because, instead of the *details* of an outward letter law, it gives the all-embracing *principles* of the spiritual law written on the conscience, leading one to spontaneous instinctive obedience in outward details. None save the Lord can teach effectually, "know the Lord." **12. For . . .**—the *third* of "the better promises" (vs. 6). The *forgiveness of sins* is, and will be, the root of this new state of inward grace and knowledge of the Lord. Sin being abolished, sinners obtain grace. **I will be merciful** *Greek,* "propitious"; the *Hebrew, salach,* is always used of God only in relation to men. **and their iniquities**—not found in *Vulgate, Syriac, Coptic,* and one oldest *Greek* MS.; but most oldest MSS. have the words (cf. ch. 10:17). **remember no more**—Contrast the law, ch. 10:3. **13. he**—God. **made . . . old**—"hath (at the time of speaking the prophecy) antiquated the first covenant." From the time of God's mention of a NEW covenant (since God's words are all realities) the first covenant might be regarded as ever dwindling away, until its complete abolition on the actual introduction of the Gospel. Both covenants cannot exist side by side. **Mark** how verbal inspiration is proved in Paul's argument turning wholly on the one word "NEW" (covenant), occurring but once in the Old Testament. **that which decayeth**—*Greek,* "that which is being antiquated," viz., at the time when Jeremiah spake. For in Paul's time, according to his view, the new had absolutely set aside the old covenant. The *Greek* for (*Kaine*) *New* (Testament) implies that it is *of a different kind* and *supersedes the old:* not merely *recent* (*Greek, nea*). Cf. Hosea 3:4, 5.

Vss. 1-28. INFERIORITY OF THE OLD TO THE NEW COVENANT IN THE MEANS OF ACCESS TO GOD: THE BLOOD OF BULLS AND GOATS OF NO REAL AVAIL: THE BLOOD OF CHRIST ALL-SUFFICIENT TO PURGE AWAY SIN, WHENCE FLOWS OUR HOPE OF HIS APPEARING AGAIN FOR OUR PERFECT SALVATION. **1. Then verily**—*Greek,* "Accordingly then." Resuming the subject from ch. 8:5. In accordance with the command given to Moses, "the first covenant had . . . ." **had**—not "has," for as a *covenant* it no longer existed, though its rites were observed till the destruction of Jerusalem. **ordinances**—of divine right and institution. **service**—worship. **a worldly sanctuary**—*Greek,* "its (lit., *the*) sanctuary worldly," mundane; consisting of the elements of the visible world. Contrasted with *the heavenly sanctuary*. Cf. vss. 11, 12, "not of this building," vs. 24. Material, outward, perishing (however precious its materials were), and also defective religiously. In vss. 2-5, "*the worldly sanctuary*" is discussed; in vs. 6, etc., the "ordinances of worship." The outer tabernacle the Jews believed, signified *this world;* the Holy of Holies, *heaven*. JOSEPHUS calls the outer, divided into two parts, "a secular and common place," answering to "the earth and sea"; and the inner holiest place, the third part, appropriated to God and not accessible to men. **2.** Defining "the worldly tabernacle." **a tabernacle**—"the tabernacle." **made**—built and furnished. **the first**—the anterior tabernacle.

candlestick . . . table—typifying *light* and *life* (Exod. 25:31-39). The candlestick consisted of a shaft and six branches of gold, seven in all, the bowls made like almonds, with a knop and a flower in one branch. It was carried in Vespasian's triumph, and the figure is to be seen on Titus' arch at Rome. The *table* of shittim wood, covered with gold, was for the shewbread (Exod. 25:23-30). **shew-bread**—lit., "the setting forth of the loaves," i.e., the loaves set forth: "the show of the bread" [ALFORD]. In the outer holy place: so the Eucharist continues until our entrance into the heavenly Holy of Holies (I Cor. 11:26). **which . . .**—"which (tabernacle) is called the holy place," as distinguished from "the Holy of Holies."

ADAM CLARKE

so that, literally, all the people, *from the least to the greatest,* know and acknowledge the only true God, and Jesus Christ, whom He has sent. Almost every man, at least in this land, has a Bible, and can read it; and there is not a family that has not the opportunity of hearing the gospel preached, explained, and enforced. Some have thought that *from the least to the greatest* is intended to signify the order in which God proceeds with a work of grace; He generally begins with the poor, and through these the great and the high often hear the gospel of Christ.

12. *I will be merciful to their unrighteousness.* In order to be their God, as mentioned under the preceding verse, it is requisite that their iniquity should be pardoned; this is provided for by the immolation of Jesus Christ as the covenant Sacrifice. All spiritual evil against the nature and law of God is represented here under the following terms: (1) *Unrighteousness,* "injustice" or "wrong." This is against God, his neighbor, and himself. (2) Sin, deviation from the divine law; "missing the mark." (3) Iniquity, "lawlessness"; not having, knowing, or acknowledging a law; having no law written in their hearts, and restrained by none in the conduct of their lives.

13. *He hath made the first old.* That is, He has considered it as "antiquated," and as being no longer of any force. *That which decayeth and waxeth old.* Here is an allusion to the ancient laws which either had perished from the tables on which they were written through old age, or were fallen into disuse, or were abrogated. *Is ready to vanish away.* "Is about to be abolished." The word is used to express the abolition of the law. The apostle therefore intimates that the old covenant was just about to be abolished; but he expresses himself cautiously and tenderly, that he might not give unnecessary offense.

CHAPTER 9

1. *The first covenant had also ordinances.* Our translators have introduced the word *covenant,* the whole context showing that *covenant* is that to which the apostle refers, as that was the subject in the preceding chapter and this is a continuation of the same discourse. *Ordinances.* Rites and ceremonies. *A worldly sanctuary.* It is supposed that the term worldly here is opposed to the term "heavenly," chap. viii. 5, and that the whole should be referred to the secular nature of the Tabernacle service. But I think there is nothing plainer than that the apostle is speaking here in praise of this sublimely emblematic service, and hence he proceeds to enumerate the various things contained in the first Tabernacle, which added vastly to its splendor and importance; such as the table of the shewbread, the golden candlestick, the golden censer, the ark of the covenant overlaid round about with gold, in which was the golden pot that had the manna, Aaron's rod that budded, and the two tables which God had written with His own finger.

2. *For there was a tabernacle made; the first, wherein.* The sense is here very obscure and the construction involved: leaving out all punctuation, which is the case with all the very ancient MSS., the verse I suppose an indifferent person, who understood the language, would without hesitation render, "For there was the first Tabernacle constructed, in which were the candlestick," etc. And this Tabernacle or dwelling may be called the first dwelling place which God had among men, to distinguish it from the second dwelling place, the Temple built by Solomon; for *tabernacle* here is to be considered in its general sense, as implying a dwelling. To have a proper understanding of what the apostle relates here, we should endeavor to take a concise view of the Tabernacle erected by Moses in the wilderness. In the holy place, as the apostle observes, there were: (1) the golden *candlestick* of seven branches, (2) the golden altar, or altar of incense, (3) the altar or *table* of the *shewbread;* where the twelve loaves, representing the twelve tribes, were laid before the Lord. *Which is called the sanctuary.* "This is called holy." This clause may apply to any

MATTHEW HENRY

2. We have an account of what was in the inner part of the sanctuary, which was within the second veil, and is called *the holiest of all.* Now in this part were, (1) The golden censer, which was to hold the incense, or the golden altar set up to burn the incense upon.

(2) The ark of the covenant overlaid round about with pure gold, *v.* 4. Now here we are told both what was in this ark and what was over it. [1] What was in it. *First, The golden pot that had manna.* This was a memorial of God's miraculously feeding his people in the wilderness, that they might never forget such signal favour, nor distrust God for the time to come.

Secondly, Aaron's rod that budded. This was that rod of God with which Moses and Aaron wrought such wonders; and this was a type of Christ, by whom God has wrought wonders for his people. *Thirdly, The tables of the covenant,* in which the moral law was written, signifying the regard God has to the preservation of his holy law, and the care we all ought to have that we keep the law of God. [2] What was over the ark (*v.* 5). The mercy-seat, which was the covering of the ark. It was of pure gold, as long and as broad as the ark in which the tables of the law were laid. It was an eminent type of Christ, and of his perfect righteousness, ever adequate to the dimensions of the law of God, and covering all our transgressions. *The cherubim of glory* shadowing the mercy-seat, represented the holy angels of God.

II. The apostle proceeds to speak of the duties and services performed in those places, *v.* 6.

1. The ordinary priests went always into the first tabernacle, to accomplish the service of God. None but priests were to enter into the first part of the tabernacle. The ordinary priests were only to enter into the first part of the tabernacle, it would have been fatal presumption in them to have gone into the holiest of all.

2. Into the second, the interior part, went the high priest alone, *v.* 7. None but the high priest must go into the holiest; so none but Christ could enter into heaven by his own right, and by his own merits. The high priest must not enter without blood. None of us can enter either into God's gracious presence here or his glorious presence hereafter, but by the blood of Jesus. The high priest offered up that blood for himself and his own errors first, and then for the errors of the people, *v.* 7. Christ is a more excellent person and high priest than any under the law, for he has no errors of his own to offer for. Ministers, when in the name of Christ they intercede for others, must first apply the blood of Christ to themselves for their pardon. When the legal high priest had offered for himself, he must not stop there, but must also offer for the errors of the people. Our high priest forgets not to offer for his people; he pleads the merit of his sufferings for the benefit of his people on earth.

Verses 8–14

The apostle undertakes to deliver to us the mind and meaning of the Holy Ghost in all the ordinances of the tabernacle.

I. The way into the holiest of all was not yet made manifest, *v.* 8. There was not that free access to God then that there is now; God has now opened a wider door.

JAMIESON, FAUSSET, BROWN

3. And—*Greek,* "But." **after**—behind: within. **second veil**—There were two veils or curtains, one before the Holy of Holies (*catapetasma*), here alluded to, the other before the tabernacle door (*calumma*). **called**—as opposed to "the true." **4. golden censer**—The *Greek,* must not be translated "altar of incense," for *it* was not in "the holiest" place "after the second veil," but in "the holy place"; but as in II Chronicles 26:19, and Ezekiel 8:11, "censer": so *Vulgate* and *Syriac.* This GOLDEN censer was only used on the day of atonement (other kinds of censers on other days), and is therefore associated with *the holiest place,* as being taken into it on that anniversary by the high priest. The expression "which had," does not mean that the golden censer was deposited there, for in that case the high priest would have had to go in and bring it out before burning incense in it; but that the golden censer was one of the articles *belonging to,* and used for, the yearly service in the holiest place. **ark**—of shittim wood, i.e., acacia. Not in the second temple, but in its stead was a stone basement (called "the stone of foundation"), three fingers high. **pot**—"golden," added in the LXX, and sanctioned by Paul. **manna**—an omer, each man's daily portion. In I Kings 8:9; II Chronicles 5:10, it is said there was nothing in the ark of Solomon's temple save the two stone tables of the law put in by Moses. But the expression that there was nothing THEN therein save the two tables, leaves the inference to be drawn that formerly there were the other things mentioned by the Rabbis and by Paul here, the pot of manna (the memorial of God's providential care of Israel) and the rod of Aaron, the memorial of the lawful priesthood (Num. 17:3, 5, 7, 10). **tables of the covenant**—(Deut. 9:9; 10:2). **5. over it**—over "the ark of the covenant." **cherubim**—representing the ruling powers by which God acts in the moral and natural world.

Hence sometimes they answer to the ministering angels; but mostly to the elect redeemed, by whom God shall hereafter rule the world and set forth His manifold wisdom: redeemed humanity, combining in, and with itself, the highest forms of subordinate creaturely life; not angels. They stand on the mercy seat, and *on that ground* become the habitation of God, from which His glory is to shine upon the world. **glory**—The cherubim were *bearers* of the divine *glory,* whence, perhaps, they derive their name. The Shekinah, or cloud of *glory,* in which Jehovah appeared between the cherubim over the mercy seat, the lid of the ark, is doubtless the reference.

mercy seat—*Greek,* "the propitiatory": the golden cover of the ark, on which was sprinkled the blood of the propitiatory sacrifice on the day of atonement; the footstool of Jehovah, the meeting-place of Him and His people. **we cannot**—conveniently: besides what met the eye in the sanctuary, there were spiritual realities symbolized which it would take too long to discuss in detail, our chief subject at present being the *priesthood* and the *sacrifices.* "Which" refers not merely to the cherubim, but to *all* the contents of the sanctuary enumerated in vss. 2-5. **6.** The use made of the sanctuary so furnished by the high priest on the anniversary of atonement. **ordained**—arranged. **always**—twice at the least every day, for the morning and evening care of the lamps, and offering of incense (Exod. 30:7, 8). **went**—*Greek,* "enter": present tense. **7. once every year**—the tenth day of the seventh month. He entered within the veil *on that day* twice at least. Thus "once" means here *on the one occasion only.* The two, or possibly more, entrances on that one day were regarded as parts of the one whole. **not without blood**—(ch. 8:3). **offered**—*Greek,* "offers." **errors**—*Greek,* "ignorances": "inadvertent errors." They might have known, as the law was clearly promulged, and they were bound to study it; so that their *ignorance* was culpable (cf. Acts 3:17; Eph. 4:18; I Pet. 1:14). Though one's ignorance may mitigate one's punishment (Luke 12:48), it does not wholly exempt from punishment. **8. The Holy Ghost**—Moses himself did not comprehend the typical meaning (I Pet. 1:11, 12). **signifying**—by the typical exclusion of all from the holiest, save the high priest once a year. **the holiest of all**—heaven, the antitype. **the first tabernacle**—the anterior tabernacle, representative of the whole Levitical system. *While it* (the first tabernacle, and that which represents the Levitical system) *as yet "has a standing"* (so the *Greek,* i.e., "has continuance": "lasts"), *the way to heaven* (the antitypical "holiest place") *is not yet made manifest* (cf. ch. 10:19, 20). The Old Testament econ-

ADAM CLARKE

of the nouns in this verse, in the nominative case, which are all of the feminine gender; and the adjective "holy" may be considered here as the nominative singular feminine. The word *tabernacle* may be the proper antecedent.

3. *And after the second veil.* The first veil, of which the apostle has not yet spoken, was at the entrance of the holy place, and separated the temple from the court, and prevented the people, and even the Levites, from seeing what was in the holy place. The second veil, of which the apostle speaks here, separated the holy place from the holy of holies. *The tabernacle which is called the Holiest of all.* That is, that part of the Tabernacle which is called the holy of holies.

4. *Which had the golden censer.* The apostle says that the *golden censer* was in the holy of holies, but this is nowhere mentioned by Moses. But he tells us that the high priest went in, once every year, with the golden censer to burn incense; and Calmet thinks this censer was left there all the year, and that its place was supplied by a new one, brought in by the priest the year following. Others think it was left just within the veil, so that the priest by putting his hand under the curtain could take it out and prepare it for his next entrance into the holiest. *The ark of the covenant.* This was a sort of chest overlaid with plates of gold, in which the two tables of the law, Aaron's rod, the pot of manna, etc., were deposited. Its top, or lid, was the propitiatory or mercy seat.

5. *And over it the cherubims of glory.* Cherubim is the plural of cherub, and it is absurd to add our plural termination (*s*) to the plural termination of the Hebrew. The *glory* here signifies the Shechinah or symbol of the Divine Presence. *Shadowing the mercyseat.* One at each end of the ark, with their faces turned toward each other, but looking down on the cover or proptiatory, here called the *mercyseat. Of which we cannot now speak particularly.* What these point out or signify is thus explained by Cyril: "Although Christ be but one, yet he is understood by us under a variety of forms. He is the *Tabernacle,* on account of the human body in which he dwelt. He is the *Table,* because he is our Bread of life. He is the *Ark* which has the law of God enclosed within, because he is the Word of the Father. He is the *Candlestick,* because he is our spiritual light. He is the *Altar of Incense,* because he is the sweet-smelling odour of sanctification. He is the *Altar of Burnt Offering,* because he is the victim, by death on the Cross, for the sins of the whole world."

6. *When these things were thus ordained.* When the Tabernacle was made, and its furniture placed in it, according to the divine direction. *The priests went always into the first tabernacle.* That is, into the first part of the Tabernacle, or holy place, into which he went every day twice, *accomplishing the service,* which included his burning the incense at the morning and evening sacrifice, dressing the lamps, and sprinkling the blood of the sin offerings before the veil, Lev. iv. 6.

7. *But into the second.* That is, the holy of holies, or second part of the Tabernacle, *The high priest alone once every year;* that is, on one day in the year only, which was the day on which the general atonement was made. The high priest could enter into this place only on one day in the year, but on that day he might enter several times. See Leviticus xvi. *Not without blood.* The day prescribed by the law for this great solemnity was the tenth of the month Tisri, in which the high priest brought in the incense or perfumes, which he placed on the golden censer. He brought also the blood of the bullock, and sprinkled some portion of it seven times before the ark and the veil which separated the holy place from the holy of holies. See Lev. xvi. 14. He then came out, and taking some of the blood of the goat which had been sacrificed, he sprinkled it between the veil and the ark of the covenant, v. 15. *Which he offered for himself, and for the errors of the people.* For transgressions of which they were not conscious.

8. *The Holy Ghost this signifying.* These services were divinely appointed, and by each of them the Holy Spirit of God is supposed to

MATTHEW HENRY

II. The first tabernacle was only a figure for the time then present, *v.* 9.

III. None of the gifts and sacrifices there offered could make the offerers perfect as pertaining to conscience (*v.* 9); they could not deliver conscience from a dread of the wrath of God. He might thereby be saved from temporal punishments, but he could not be saved by them from sin.

IV. The Old Testament institutions were but imposed upon them until the time of reformation, *v.* 10. These were never designed for a perpetuity, but only till the better things provided for them were actually bestowed upon them. We have far greater advantages under the gospel than they had under the law; and either we must be better or we shall be worse.

V. As he writes to those who believed that Jesus was the Christ, so he very justly infers that he is infinitely above all legal high priests (*v.* 11, 12).

1. *Christ is a high priest of good things to come.* The Old Testament set forth in shadows what was to come; the New Testament is the accomplishment of the Old. All the good things yet to come, when the promises shall be accomplished; all these depend upon Christ and his priesthood, and shall be fulfilled; all the good things to come in the heavenly state, which will perfect both the Testaments; as the state of glory will perfect the state of grace.

JAMIESON, FAUSSET, BROWN

omy is represented by the holy place, the New Testament economy by the Holy of Holies. Redemption, by Christ, has opened the Holy of Holies (access to heaven by *faith* now, ch. 4:16; 7:19, 25; 10:19, 22; by *sight* hereafter, Isa. 33:24; Rev. 11:19; 21:2, 3) to all mankind. The *Greek* for "not yet" (*me po*) refers to the mind of the Spirit: the Spirit intimating that men should *not think* the way was yet opened [TITTMANN]. The *Greek* negative, *ou po,* would deny the *fact* objectively; *me po* denies the thing subjectively. **9. Which**—"The which," viz., anterior tabernacle: *"as being that which* was" [ALFORD]. **figure**—*Greek,* "parable": *a parabolic setting forth of the character of the Old Testament.* **for**—*"in reference to the existing time." The time of the temple worship* really belonged to the Old Testament, but *continued still in Paul's time and that of his Hebrew readers.* "The time of reformation" (vs. 10) stands in contrast to this, "the existing time"; though, in reality, "the time of reformation," the New Testament time, was now *present* and existing. So "the age *to come,*" is the phrase applied to the Gospel, because it was *present only to believers,* and its fulness even to them is still *to come.* Cf. vs. 11, "good things to come." **in which**—*tabernacle,* not *time,* according to the reading of the oldest MSS. Or translate, "according to which" *parabolic representation,* or *figure.* **were**—*Greek,* "are." **gifts**—unbloody oblations. **could not**—*Greek,* "cannot": are not able. **him that did the service**—any worshipper. The *Greek* is *latreuein, serve* God, which is all men's duty; not *leitourgein,* to serve in a *ministerial office.* **make . . . perfect**—perfectly remove the sense of guilt, and sanctify inwardly through love. **as pertaining to the conscience**—"in respect to the (moral-religious) consciousness." They can only reach as far as the outward flesh (cf. "*carnal* ordinances," vss. 10, 13, 14). **10.** *Which*—sacrifices. *stood*—consisted in [ALFORD]; or, *have attached to them* only things which appertain to the use of foods, etc. The rites of meats, etc., go *side by side with* the sacrifices [THOLUCK and WAHL]; cf. Colossians 2:16. **drinks**—(Lev. 10:9; 11:4). Usage subsequently to the law added many observances as to meats and drinks. **washings**—(Exod. 29:4). **and carnal ordinances**—One oldest MS., *Syriac* and *Coptic,* omit "and." "Carnal ordinances" stand in apposition to "sacrifices" (vs. 9). *Carnal* (outward, affecting only the *flesh*) is opposed to *spiritual.* Contrast "flesh" with "conscience" (vss. 13, 14). **imposed**—as a burden (Acts 15:10, 28) continually pressing heavy. **until the time of reformation**—*Greek,* "the *season* of *rectification,*" when the reality should supersede the type (ch. 8:8-12). Cf. "better," vs. 23. **11. But**—in contrast to "*could not* make . . . perfect" (vs. 9). **Christ**—The Messiah, of whom all the prophets foretold; not "Jesus" here. From whom the "reformation" (vs. 10), or *rectification,* emanates, which frees from the yoke of carnal ordinances, and which is being realized gradually now, and shall be perfectly in the consummation of "the age (world) to come." "Christ . . . High Priest," exactly answers to Leviticus 4:5, "the priest that is anointed." **being come an . . .**—rather, "having come forward (cf. ch. 10:7, a different *Greek* word, picturesquely presenting Him before us) *as* High Priest." The Levitical priests must therefore retire. Just as on the day of atonement, no work was done, no sacrifice was offered, or priest was allowed to be in the tabernacle while the high priest went into the holiest place to make atonement (Lev. 16:17, 29). So not our righteousness, nor any other priest's sacrifice, but Christ alone atones; and as the high priest before offering incense had on common garments of a priest, but after it wore his holy garments of "glory and beauty" (Exod. 28) in entering the holiest, so Christ entered the heavenly holiest in His glorified body. **good things to come**—*Greek,* "*the* good things to come," ch. 10:1; "better promises," (ch. 8:6; the "eternal inheritance," vs. 15; I Peter 1:4; the "things hoped for," ch. 11:1. **by a . . . tabernacle**—joined with "He entered." Translate, "*Through the . . . tabernacle*" (of which we know) [ALFORD]. As the Jewish high priest passed *through* the anterior tabernacle into the holiest place, so Christ passed through *heaven* into the inner abode of the unseen and unapproachable God. Thus, "the tabernacle" here is the *heavens through* which He passed (*Note,* ch. 4:14). But "the tabernacle" is also *the glorified body of Christ* (*Note,* ch. 8:2), "not of this building" (not of the mere natural "*creation,* but of the spiritual and heavenly, *the new creation*"), the Head of the mystical body, the Church. *Through* this glorified body He passes into the

ADAM CLARKE

speak. *The way into the holiest.* That full access to God was not the common privilege of the people while the Mosaic economy subsisted. That the apostle means that it is only by Christ that any man and every man can approach God is evident from chap. x. 19-22. I have already observed that the apostle appears to use the word *tabernacle* in the general sense of a dwelling place and therefore applies it to the Temple, which was reputed the house or dwelling place of God, as well as the ancient Tabernacle. Therefore what he speaks here concerning the *first tabernacle* may be understood as applying with propriety to the then Jewish Temple, as well as to the ancient Tabernacle, which, even with all their sacrifices and ceremonies, could not make the way of holiness plain nor the way to God's favor possible.

9. *Which,* Tabernacle and its services, *was a figure,* a dark enigmatical representation, *for the time then present*—for that age and dispensation, and for all those who lived under it. *In which,* "during which," time or dispensation *were offered both gifts and sacrifices,* eucharistic offerings and victims for sin, *that could not make him that did the service,* whether the priest who made the offering or the person who brought it in the behalf of his soul, *perfect, as pertaining to the conscience*—could not take away guilt from the mind nor purify the conscience from dead works. The whole was a *figure,* or dark representation, of a spiritual and more glorious system; and although a sinner who made these offerings and sacrifices according to the law might be considered as having done his duty, and thus he would be exempted from many ecclesiastical and legal disabilities and punishments, yet his *conscience* would ever tell him that the guilt of sin was still remaining. The words *in which,* referred in the above paraphrase to *the time,* are read by several versions as referrring to the Tabernacle, and this is the reading which our translators appear to have followed.

10. *In meats and drinks, and divers washings.* He had already mentioned eucharistic and sacrificial offerings, and nothing properly remained but the different kinds of clean and unclean animals which were used, or forbidden to be used, as articles of food; together with the different kinds of drinks, *washings,* "baptisms," immersions, sprinklings, and washings of the body and the clothes, and *carnal ordinances,* or things which had respect merely to the body and could have no moral influence upon the soul, unless considered in reference to that of which they were the similitudes or figures. *Carnal ordinances.* Rites and ceremonies pertaining merely to the body. *Imposed on them until the time of reformation.* These rites and ceremonies were enacted, by divine authority, as proper representations of the gospel system, which should reform and rectify all things. *The time of reformation,* "the time of rectifying," signifies the gospel dispensation, under which everything is set straight; everything referred to its proper purpose and end; the ceremonial law fulfilled and abrogated; the moral law exhibited and more strictly enjoined (see our Lord's sermon upon the mount); and the spiritual nature of God's worship taught, and grace promised to purify the heart. So that, through the power of the eternal Spirit, all that was wrong in the soul is "rectified"; the affections, passions, and appetites purified; the understanding enlightened; the judgment corrected; the will refined; in a word, all things made new.

11. *But Christ being come an high priest of good things.* I think this and the succeeding verses not happily translated; indeed, the division of them has led to a wrong translation. Therefore they must be taken together thus: "But the Christ, the High Priest of those good things (or services) which were to come, through a greater and more perfect tabernacle, not made with hands, that is, not of the same workmanship, entered once for all into the sanctuary; having obtained eternal redemption for us, not by the blood of goats and calves, but by His own blood. For if the blood of goats, and bulls, and calves, and a heifer's ashes, sprinkled on the unclean, sanctifieth to the cleansing of the flesh, how much more shall the blood of Christ, who, through the eternal Spirit, offered himself

MATTHEW HENRY

2. Christ is a high priest *by a greater and more perfect tabernacle* (*v.* 11), his own body, or rather human nature, conceived by the Holy Ghost overshadowing the blessed virgin. This was a new fabric, a new order of building.

3. Christ, our high priest, has entered into heaven, not as their high priest entered into the holiest, with the blood of bulls and of goats, but by his own blood.

4. Our high priest entered into heaven *once for all*, and has obtained eternal redemption.

5. The Holy Ghost showed what was the efficacy of the blood of the Old Testament sacrifices. The efficacy of the blood of the legal sacrifices extended to the purifying of the flesh (*v.* 13): from ceremonial uncleanness.

The far greater efficacy of the blood of Christ (*v.* 14). What it was that gave such efficacy to the blood of Christ. It was his offering himself to God. It was Christ's offering up himself to God through the eternal Spirit.

It was Christ's offering himself to God without spot, without any sinful stain. What the efficacy of Christ's blood is. It is sufficient to purge the conscience from dead works, it reaches to the very soul and conscience. It is sufficient to enable us to serve the living God by sanctifying and renewing the soul through the gracious influences of the Holy Spirit.

JAMIESON, FAUSSET, BROWN

heavenly holiest place (vs. 24), the immaterial, unapproachable presence of God, where He intercedes for us. *His glorified body*, as the meeting-place of God and all Christ's redeemed, and the angels, answers to *the heavens* through which He passed, and passes. His *body* is opposed to the *tabernacle*, as His blood to the blood of goats, etc. **greater**—as contrasted with the small dimensions of the earthly anterior tabernacle. **more perfect**—effective in giving pardon, peace, sanctification, and access to closest communion with God (cf. vs. 9, ch. 10:1). **not made with hands**—but by the Lord Himself (ch. 8:2). **12. Neither**—"Nor yet." **by**—"through"; as the means of His approach. **goats . . . calves**—not a bullock, such as the Levitical high priest offered for himself, and a goat for the people, on the day of atonement (Lev. 16:6, 15), *year by year*, whence the plural is used, *goats . . . calves*. **by**—"through," as the means of His entrance; the key unlocking the heavenly Holy of Holies to Him. The *Greek* is forcible, "through THE blood of His own" (cf. vs. 23). **once**—"once for all." **having obtained**—having *thereby* obtained; lit., "found for Himself," as a thing of insuperable difficulty to all save Divine Omnipotence, self-devoting zeal, and love, to find. The access of Christ to the Father was arduous (ch. 5:7). None before had trodden the path. **eternal**—The entrance of our Redeemer, *once for all*, into the heavenly holiest place, secures *eternal* redemption to us; whereas the Jewish high priest's entrance was repeated year by year, and the effect temporary and partial, "On redemption," cf. Matt. 20:28; Eph. 1:7; Col. 1:14; I Tim. 2:5, Titus 2:14; I Pet. 1:19. **13. if**—as we know is the case; so the *Greek* indicative means. Argument from the less to the greater. If the blood of mere brutes could purify in any, however small a degree, how much more shall inward purification, and complete and eternal salvation, be wrought by the blood of Christ, in whom dwelt all the fulness of the Godhead? **ashes of an heifer**—(Num. 19:16-18). The type is full of comfort for us. The water of separation, made of the ashes of the red heifer, was the provision for removing ceremonial defilement whenever incurred *by contact with the dead*. **the unclean**—*Greek*, "those defiled" on any particular occasion. **purifying**—*Greek*, "purity." **the flesh**—Their effect in themselves extended no further. Ceremonial sacrifices released from *temporal penalties* and *ceremonial disqualifications;* Christ's sacrifice releases from *everlasting penalties* (vs. 12), and *moral impurities on the conscience* disqualifying from access to God (vs. 14). The purification of the *flesh* (the mere outward man) was by "sprinkling"; the *washing* followed by inseparable connection (Num. 19: 19). So *justification* is followed by *renewing*. **14. offered himself**—The voluntary nature of the offering gives it especial efficacy. He "through the eternal Spirit," i.e., His divine Spirit (Rom. 1:4, in contrast to His "flesh," vs. 3; *His Godhead*, I Tim. 3:16; I Pet. 3:18), "His inner personality" [ALFORD], which gave a free consent to the act, offered Himself. The animals offered had no *spirit* or will to consent in the act of sacrifice; they were offered *according to the law;* they had a life neither enduring, nor of any intrinsic efficacy. But He from eternity, with *His divine and everlasting Spirit*, concurred with the Father's will of redemption by Him. His offering began on the altar of the cross, and was completed in His entering the holiest place with His blood. The *eternity* and infinitude of His divine Spirit (cf. ch. 7:16) gives *eternal* ("*eternal* redemption," vs. 12, also cf. vs. 15) and infinite merit to His offering, so that not even the infinite justice of God has any exception to take against it. It was "through His most burning love, flowing from His eternal Spirit," that He offered Himself [ŒCOLAMPADIUS]. **without spot**—The animal victims had to be without *outward* blemish; Christ on the cross was a victim *inwardly* and *essentially* stainless (I Pet. 1:19). **purge**—purify from fear, guilt, alienation from Him, and selfishness, the source of *dead works* (vss. 22, 23). **your**—The oldest MSS. read "our." *Vulgate*, however, supports *English Version* reading. **conscience**—moral religious *consciousness*. **dead works**—All works done in the natural state, which is a state of sin, are *dead;* for they come not from living faith in, and love to, "the *living* God" (ch. 11:6). As contact with a dead body defiled ceremonially (cf. the allusion, "ashes of an heifer," vs. 13), so dead works defile the inner consciousness spiritually. **to serve**—*so as to* serve. The ceremonially unclean could not *serve God* in the outward communion of His people; so the unrenewed cannot serve God in spiritual communion. **living God**—therefore requiring

ADAM CLARKE

without spot to God, cleanse your consciences from dead works, in order to worship (or that you may worship) the living God?"

In the above translation I have added, in v. 13, "of goats," on the authority of several MSS. *High priest of good things.* Or "services," *to come.* He is the High Priest of Christianity. *A greater and more perfect tabernacle.* This appears to mean our Lord's human nature. That, in which dwelt all the fullness of the Godhead bodily, was fitly typified by the Tabernacle and Temple, in both of which the majesty of God dwelt. *Not made with hands.* Though our Lord's body was a perfect human body, yet it did not come in the way of natural generation; His miraculous conception will sufficiently justify the expressions used here by the apostle.

12. *But by his own blood.* Here the redemption of man is attributed to the blood of Christ; and this Blood is stated to be shed in a sacrificial way, precisely as the blood of bulls, goats, and calves was shed under the law. *Once.* "Once for all," in opposition to the annual entering of the high priest into the holiest with the blood of the annual victim. *The holy place*, or "sanctuary," signifies heaven, into which Jesus entered with His own blood, as the high priest entered into the holy of holies with the blood of the victims which he had sacrificed. *Eternal redemption.* A redemption price which should stand good forever, when once offered; and an endless redemption from sin, in reference to the pardon of which, and reconciliation to God, there needs no other sacrifice. It is eternal in its merit and efficacy.

13. *Sanctifieth to the purifying of the flesh.* Answers the end proposed by the law; namely, to remove legal disabilities and punishments, having the body and its interests particularly in view, though adumbrating or typifying the soul and its concerns.

14. *Who through the eternal Spirit.* This expression is understood two ways: (1) Of the Holy Ghost himself. As Christ's miraculous conception was by the Holy Spirit, and He wrought all His miracles by the Spirit of God, so His death or final offering was made through or by the eternal Spirit; and by that Spirit He was raised from the dead, I Pet. iii. 18. (2) Of the eternal Logos or Deity which dwelt in the Man Christ Jesus, through the energy of which the offering of His humanity became an infinitely meritorious victim; therefore the deity of Christ is here intended. But we cannot well consider one of these distinct from the other. It is probable that the Holy Ghost, not the Logos, is what the apostle had more immediately in view. But still we must say that the Holy Spirit, with the eternal Logos and the almighty Father, equally concurred in offering up the sacrifice of the human nature of Christ in order to make atonement for the sin of the world. *Purge your conscience.* "Purify your conscience." The term "purify" should be everywhere, both in the translation of the Scriptures and in preaching the gospel, preferred to the word *purge*, which at present is scarcely ever used in the sense in which our translators have employed it. *Dead works.* Sin in general, or acts to which the penalty of death is annexed by the law.

MATTHEW HENRY

Verses 15–22

I. The gospel is here considered as a testament. A covenant is an agreement between two or more parties about things that are in their own power; this agreement takes effect at such time and in such manner as therein declared. A testament is a voluntary act and deed of a single person, bestowing legacies on such legatees as are described by the testator, and which can only take effect upon his death. Christ is the Mediator of a New Testament (*v.* 15), to redeem persons from their transgressions committed against the law or first testament; to qualify all those that are effectually called to receive the promise of an eternal inheritance.

II. To make this New Testament effectual, it was necessary that Christ should die. This he proves by two arguments: 1. From the general nature of every will or testamentary disposition, *v.* 16. No estate, no right, is conveyed by will, till the testator's death has made it effectual.

2. From the particular method that was taken by Moses in the ratification of the first testament, which was not done without blood, *v.* 18, 19, &c. God accepted the blood of bulls and goats; and by these means the covenant of grace was ratified under the former dispensation.

Moses spoke every precept to all the people, according to the law, *v.* 19.

JAMIESON, FAUSSET, BROWN

living spiritual service (John 4:24). **15. for this cause**–Because of the all-cleansing power of His blood, this fits Him to be Mediator (ch. 8:6, ensuring to both parties, God and us, the ratification) of the new covenant, which secures both forgiveness for the sins not covered by the former imperfect covenant or testament, and also an eternal inheritance to the called. **by means of death**–rather, as *Greek*, "death having taken place." **redemption of . . . transgressions . . . under . . . first testament**–the transgressions of *all men* from Adam to Christ, first against the primitive revelation, then against the revelations to the patriarchs, then against the law given to Israel, the representative people of the world. The "first testament" thus includes the whole period from Adam to Christ, and not merely that of the covenant with Israel, which was a concentrated representation of *the covenant made with* (or *the first testament* given to) *mankind by sacrifice*, down from the fall to redemption. Before the *inheritance by the New Testament* (for here the idea of the "INHERITANCE," following as the result of Christ's "death," being introduced, requires the *Greek* to be translated "testament," as it was before *covenant*) could come in, there must be *redemption* of (i.e., deliverance from the penalties incurred by) the *transgressions* committed *under the first testament*, for the propitiatory sacrifices under the first testament reached only as far as removing outward ceremonial defilement. But in order to obtain the inheritance which is a reality, there must be a real propitiation, since God could not enter into covenant relation with us so long as past sins were unexpiated; Romans 3:24, 25, "a propitiation . . . His righteousness for the remission of sins that are past." **might**–*Greek, "may* receive," which previously they could not (ch. 11:39, 40). **the promise**–to Abraham. **16.** A general axiomatic truth; it is "*a* testament"; not *the testament*. The testator must die before his *testament* takes effect (vs. 17). This is a common meaning of the *Greek* noun *diathece*. So in Luke 22:29, "I appoint (by testamentary disposition; the cognate *Greek* verb *diatithemai*) unto you a kingdom, as my Father hath appointed unto me." The need of death before the testamentary appointment takes effect, holds good in Christ's relation as MAN to us; of course not in *God's* relation to Christ. **be**–lit., be borne": "be involved in the case"; *be inferred;* or else, "be brought forward in court," so as to give effect to the will. Plainly, the death is supposed to be *past* (aorist, "made"); and the fact of the death is *brought* (*Greek*) before court to give effect to the will. These requisites of a will, or testament, concur here: (1) a testator; (2) heirs; (3) goods; (4) the death of the testator; (5) the fact of the death *brought forward* in court. In Matthew 26:28 two other requisites appear: *witnesses,* the disciples; and *a seal,* the sacrament of the Lord's Supper, the sign of His *blood* wherewith the testament is primarily sealed. It is true the *heir* is ordinarily the *successor* of him who dies and so ceases to have the possession. But in this case Christ comes to life again, and is Himself (including all that He hath), in the power of His now endless life, His people's inheritance; in *His* being Heir (ch. 1:2), *they* are heirs. **17. after**–lit., "over," as we say "*upon* the death of the testators"; not as THOLUCK, "on the condition that slain sacrifices be there," which the *Greek* hardly sanctions. **otherwise**–"seeing that it is never availing" [ALFORD]. BENGEL and LACHMANN read with an interrogation, "Since, is it ever in force (surely not) while the testator liveth?" **18. Whereupon**–rather, "Whence." **dedicated**–"inaugurated." The Old Testament strictly and formally began on that day of inauguration. "Where the *disposition,* or *arrangement,* is ratified by the blood of another, viz., of animals, which cannot make a *covenant,* much less make a *testament,* it is not strictly a *testament,* where it is ratified by the death of him that makes the arrangement, it is strictly, *Greek diathece, Hebrewberith,* taken in a wider sense, a *testament*" [BENGEL]; thus, in vs. 18, referring to the old dispensation, we may translate, "the first (*covenant*)": or better, retain "the first (*testament*)," not that the old dispensation, *regarded by itself,* is a *testament,* but it is so when regarded as the *typical representative of the new,* which is strictly a *Testament.* **19. For**–confirming the general truth, vs. 16. **spoken . . . according to the law**–strictly adhering to every direction of "the law of commandments contained in ordinances" (Eph. 2:15). Cf. Exodus 24:3, "Moses told the people *all the words of the Lord, and all the judgments;* and *all the people* answered with one voice . . . ." **the blood of calves**–*Greek,* "the calves," viz., those sacrificed

ADAM CLARKE

15. *And for this cause.* Some translate "on account of this" (Blood). Perhaps it means no more than a mere inference, such as "therefore" or "wherefore." *He is the mediator of the new testament.* There was no proper reason why our translators should render *diatheke* by *testament* here, when in almost every other case they render it "covenant," which is its proper ecclesiastical meaning, as answering to the Hebrew *berith.* Very few persons are satisfied with the translation of the following verses to the twentieth, particularly the sixteenth and seventeenth; at all events the word "covenant" must be retained. *He,* Jesus Christ, *is the mediator;* the *mediator* was the person who witnessed the contract made between the two contracting parties, slew the victim, and sprinkled each with its blood. *Of the new testament.* The "new contract" betwixt God and the whole human race, by Christ Jesus, the Mediator, distinguished here from the old covenant between God and the Israelites, in which Moses was the mediator. *That by means of death.* His own death upon the Cross. *For the redemption of the transgressions.* To make atonement for the transgressions which were committed under the old covenant, which the blood of bulls and calves could not do; so the death of Jesus had respect to all the time antecedent to it, as well as to all the time afterward till the conclusion of the world. *They which are called,* the Gentiles, *might receive the promise*—might, by being brought into a covenant with God, have an equal right with the Jews, not merely to an inheritance such as the Promised Land, but to an *eternal inheritance,* and consequently infinitely superior to that of the Jews.

16. *For where a testament is.* A learned and judicious friend furnishes me with the following translation of this and the seventeenth verse: "For where there is a covenant, it is necessary that the death of the appointed victim should be exhibited, because a covenant is confirmed over dead victims, since it is not at all valid while the appointed victim is alive." Mr. Wakefield has translated the passage in nearly the same way: "For where a covenant is, there must be necessarily introduced the death of that which establisheth the covenant; because a covenant is confirmed over dead things, and is of no force at all whilst that which establisheth the covenant is alive." This is undoubtedly the meaning of this passage; and we should endeavor to forget that *testament* and *testator* were ever introduced, as they totally change the apostle's meaning.

18. *Whereupon.* "Wherefore," as a victim was required for the ratification of every covenant, the first covenant made between God and the Hebrews, by the mediation of Moses, *was* not *dedicated,* "renewed" or solemnized, *without blood*—without the death of a victim and the aspersion of its blood.

19. ***When Moses had spoken every precept.*** **The place to which the apostle alludes is Exod. xxiv. 4-8.**

MATTHEW HENRY

Then he took the blood of calves and of goats, with water, and scarlet wool, and hyssop, and applied this blood by sprinkling it. With these Moses sprinkled, (1) The book of the law and covenant. (2) The people. The blood of Christ will be no advantage to us if it be not applied to us.

Moses at the same time used these words, *This is the blood of the testament which God hath enjoined unto you.*

(3) The tabernacle and all the utensils of it. All the sacrifices offered up and services performed there were accepted only through the blood of Christ.

Verses 23-29

I. The necessity of purifying the patterns of the things in heaven, *v.* 23. The sanctuary of God on earth is a pattern of heaven, and communion with God in his sanctuary is to his people a heaven upon earth.

JAMIESON, FAUSSET, BROWN

by the "young men" whom he sent to do so (Exod. 24:5). **with water**—prescribed, though not in Exodus 24, yet in other purifications; e.g., of the leper, and the water of separation which contained the ashes of the red heifer. **scarlet wool, and hyssop**—ordinarily used for purification. *Scarlet* or *crimson,* resembling blood: it was thought to be a peculiarly deep, fast dye, whence it typified sin (*Note,* Isa. 1:18). So Jesus wore a scarlet robe, the emblem of the deep-dyed sins He bore *on* Him, though He had none *in* Him. Wool was used as imbibing and retaining water; the hyssop, as a bushy, tufty plant (wrapt round with the scarlet wool), was used for sprinkling it. The wool was also a symbol of purity (Isa. 1:18). The *Hyssopus officinalis* grows on walls, with small lancet-formed woolly leaves, an inch long, with blue and white flowers, and a knotty stalk about a foot high. **sprinkled . . . the book**—viz., out of which he had read "every precept": the book of the testament or covenant. This sprinkling of the book is not mentioned in Exodus 24. Hence BENGEL translates, "And (having taken) the book itself (so Exod. 24:7), he both sprinkled all the people, and (vs. 21) moreover sprinkled the tabernacle." But the *Greek* supports *English Version.* Paul, by inspiration, supplies the particular specified here, not in Exodus 24:7. The sprinkling of the *roll* (so the *Greek* for "book") of the covenant, or testament, as well as of the people, implies that neither can *the law* be fulfilled, nor the people be purged from their sins, save by the sprinkling of the blood of Christ (I Pet. 1:2). **20.** Exodus 24:8, "*Behold* the blood of the covenant, which *the Lord* has made with you concerning all these words." The change is here made to accord with Christ's inauguration of the new testament, or covenant, as recorded in Luke 22:20, "This cup (is) the new Testament in My blood, which is shed for you": the only Gospel in which the "is" has to be supplied. Luke was *Paul's* companion, which accounts for the correspondence, as here too "is" has to be supplied. **testament**—(*Note,* vss. 16, 17). The *Greek diathece* means both "testament" and "covenant": the term "covenant" better suits the old dispensation, though the idea *testament* is included, for the old was one in its typical relation to the new dispensation, to which the term "testament" is better suited. Christ has sealed the testament with His *blood,* of which the Lord's Supper is the sacramental sign. **enjoined unto you**—*commissioned* me to ratify *in relation to you.* In the old dispensation the condition to be fulfilled on the people's part is implied in the words, Exodus 24:8, "(Lord made with you) *concerning all these words.*" **21.** *Greek,* "*And,* moreover, *in like manner.*" The *sprinkling of the tabernacle with blood* is added by inspiration here to the account in Exodus 30:25-30; 40:9, 10, which mentions only Moses' anointing the tabernacle and its vessels. In Leviticus 8:10, 15, 30, the sprinkling of blood upon Aaron and his garments, and upon his sons, and upon the altar, is mentioned as well as the anointing, so that we might naturally infer, as JOSEPHUS has distinctly stated, that the tabernacle and its vessels were sprinkled with blood as well as being anointed: Leviticus 16. 16, 20, 33, virtually sanctions this inference. The tabernacle and its contents needed purification (II Chron. 29:21). **22. almost**—to be joined with "all things," viz., *almost all things* under the old dispensation. The exceptions to *all things being purified by blood* are, Exodus 19:10; Leviticus 15:5, etc., 16:26, 28; 22:6; Numbers 31:22-24. **without**—*Greek,* "apart from." **shedding of blood**—*shed* in the slaughter of the victim, and poured out at the altar subsequently. The *pouring out of the blood on the altar* is the main part of the sacrifice (Lev. 17:11), and it could not have place apart from the previous *shedding of* the blood in the slaying. Paul has, perhaps, in mind here, Luke 22:20, "This cup is the new testament in my blood, which is shed for you." **is**—*Greek,* "takes place": comes to pass. **remission**—of sins: a favorite expression of Luke, Paul's companion. Properly used of remitting a debt (Matt. 6:12; 18:27, 32); our sins are debts. On the truth here, cf. Leviticus 5:11-13, an exception because of poverty, confirming the general rule. **23. patterns**—"the suggestive representations"; the typical copies (*Note,* ch. 8:5). **things in the heavens**—the heavenly tabernacle and the things therein. **purified with these**—with the blood of bulls and goats. **heavenly things themselves**—the archetypes. Man's sin had introduced an element of disorder into the relations of God and His holy angels in respect to man. The *purification* removes this element of disorder and changes God's

ADAM CLARKE

And sprinkled both the book. The sprinkling of the *book* is not mentioned in the place to which the apostle refers, nor did it in fact take place. The words "and the book itself" should be referred to "having taken," and not to "he sprinkled." The verse should therefore be read thus: "For after every commandment of the law had been recited by Moses to all the people, he took the blood of the calves, and of the goats, with water and scarlet wool, and the book itself, and sprinkled all the people." The rite was performed thus: Having received the blood of the calves and goats into basins, and mingled it with water to prevent it from coagulating, he then took a bunch of *hyssop,* and having bound it together with thread made of *scarlet wool,* he dipped this in the basin, and sprinkled the blood and water upon the people who were nearest to him, and who might be considered on this occasion the representatives of all the rest.

20. *This is the blood of the testament* (covenant). Our Lord refers to the conduct of Moses here, and partly quotes his words in the institution of the Eucharist: "This is my blood of the new testament [covenant], which is shed for many for the remission of sins," Matt. xxvi. 28. And by thus using the words and applying them, He shows that His sacrificial blood was intended by the blood shed and sprinkled on this occasion, and that by it alone the remission of sins is obtained.

21. *He sprinkled with blood . . . all the vessels of the ministry.* To intimate that everything used by sinful man is polluted, and that nothing can be acceptable in the sight of a holy God that has not in effect the sprinkling of the atoning Blood.

22. *And almost all things are by the law purged with blood.* The apostle says *almost,* because in some cases certain vessels were purified by water, some by fire, Num. xxxi. 23, and some with the ashes of the red heifer, Num. xix. 2-10, but it was always understood that everything was at first consecrated by the blood of the victim. *And without shedding of blood is no remission.* The apostle shows fully here what is one of his great objects in the whole of this Epistle, viz., that there is no salvation but through the sacrificial death of Christ, and to prefigure this the law itself would not grant any remission of sin without the blood of a victim. This is a maxim even among the Jews themselves, "There is no expiation but by blood." **Every sinner has forfeited his life by** his transgressions, and the law of God requires his death; the blood of the victim, which is its life, is shed as a substitute for the life of the sinner. By these victims the sacrifice of Christ was typified. He gave His life for the life of the world; human life for human life, but a life infinitely dignified by its union with God.

23. *The patterns of things in the heavens.* That is, the Tabernacle and all its utensils, services, etc., must be purified by *these,* viz.,

MATTHEW HENRY

II. The things themselves are better than the patterns, and must therefore be consecrated with better sacrifices. These heavenly things are the privileges of the gospel state, begun in grace, perfected in glory. Now it is very evident that the sacrifice of Christ is infinitely better than those of the law, 1. From the places in which the sacrifices were offered. Those under the law were the holy places made with hands, *v.* 24. Christ's sacrifice was by himself carried up into heaven, for he appears in the presence of God for us.

2. From the sacrifices themselves, *v.* 26. Those under the law were the lives and blood of other creatures. The sacrifice of Christ was the oblation of himself; he offered his own blood, and it was of infinite value. 3. From the frequent repetition of the legal sacrifices. This showed the imperfection of that law; but it is the perfection of Christ's sacrifice, that being once offered, it was sufficient to all the ends of it. *But now once in the end of the world hath he appeared, to put away sin by the sacrifice of himself.*

4. From the inefficacy of the legal sacrifices, and the efficacy of Christ's sacrifice. The legal sacrifices could not of themselves put away sin. Jesus Christ by one sacrifice has made an end of sin.

III. The apostle illustrates the argument from the appointment of God concerning men (*v.* 27, 28).

JAMIESON, FAUSSET, BROWN

wrath against man in heaven (designed to be the place of God's revealing His grace to men and angels) into a smile of reconciliation. Cf. "peace in heaven" (Luke 19:38). "The uncreated heaven of God, though in itself untroubled light, yet needed a purification in so far as the light of love was obscured by the fire of wrath against sinful man" [DELITZSCH *in* ALFORD]. **sacrifices**—The plural is used in expressing the general proposition, though strictly referring to the *one* sacrifice of Christ once for all. Paul implies that His one sacrifice, by its matchless excellency, is equivalent to the Levitical many sacrifices. It, though but one, is manifold in its effects and applicability to many. **24.** Resumption more fully of the thought, "He entered in once into the holy place," vs. 12. He has in vss. 13, 14, expanded the words "by his own blood," vs. 12; and in vss. 15-23, he has enlarged on "an High Priest of good things to come." **not . . . into . . . holy places made with hands**—as was the Holy of Holies in the earthly tabernacle (*Note,* vs. 11). **figures**—copies "of the true" holiest place, heaven, the original archetype (ch. 8:5). **into heaven itself**—the immediate presence of the invisible God beyond all the created heavens, *through* which latter Jesus passed (*Note,* ch. 4:14; I Tim. 6:16). **now**—ever since His ascension in the present economy (cf. vs. 26). **to appear**—TO PRESENT HIMSELF; *Greek,* "to be made to appear." Mere man may have a vision through a medium, or veil, as Moses had (Exod. 33:18, 20-23). Christ alone beholds the Father without a veil, and is His perfect image. Through seeing HIM only can we see the Father. **in the presence of God**—*Greek, "to the face* of God." The saints shall hereafter see God's face in Christ (Rev. 22:4): the earnest of which is now given (II Cor. 3:18). Aaron, the Levitical high priest *for* the people, stood *before the ark* and only saw the *cloud,* the symbol of God's glory (Exod. 28:30). **for us**—in our behalf as our Advocate and Intercessor (ch. 7:25; Rom. 8:34; I John 2:1). **25.** As in vs. 24, Paul said, it was not into the typical, but the true sanctuary, that Christ is entered; so now he says, that His sacrifice needs not, as the Levitical sacrifices did, to be repeated. Construe, "*Nor yet* did He enter for this purpose *that He may offer Himself often,*" i.e., *present Himself in the presence of God,* as the high priest does (Paul uses the *present tense,* as the legal service was then existing), year by year, on the day of atonement, entering the Holy of Holies. **with**—lit., "in." **blood of others**—*not his own,* as Christ did. **26. then**—in that case. **must . . . have suffered**—rather as *Greek,* "It would have been necessary for Him often to suffer." **since the foundation of the world**—The continued sins of men, from their first creation, would entail a continual suffering on earth, and consequent oblation of His blood in the heavenly holiest place, *since the foundation of the world,* if the one oblation "in the fulness of time" were not sufficient. **now**—as the case is. **once**—for all; without need of renewal. **end of the world**—*Greek,* "at the consummation of the ages"; the winding up of all the previous ages from the foundation of the world; to be followed by a new age (ch. 1:1, 2). The last age, beyond which no further age is to be expected before Christ's speedy second coming, which is the complement of the first coming; lit., "the ends of the ages"; Matthew 28:20 is lit., "the consummation of *the age,*" or *world* (singular; not as here, plural, *ages*). Cf. "the fulness of times," Ephesians 1:10. **appeared**—*Greek,* "been manifested" on earth (I Tim. 3:16; I Pet. 1:20). **away**—abolish; doing away sin's power as well by delivering men from its guilt and penalty, so that it should be powerless to condemn men, as also from its yoke, so that they shall at last sin no more. **sin**—singular number; all the sins of men of every age are regarded as *one mass* laid on Christ. He hath not only atoned for all *actual sins,* but destroyed *sin itself*. John 1:29, "Behold the Lamb of God that taketh away the *sin* (not merely *the sins:* singular, not plural) of the world." **by the sacrifice of himself**—*Greek,* "by (through) *His own* sacrifice"; not by "blood *of others*" (vs. 25). ALFORD loses this contrast in translating, "by His sacrifice." **27. as**—inasmuch as. **it is appointed**—*Greek,* "it is *laid up* (as our appointed lot)," Colossians 1:5. The word "appointed" (so *Hebrew seth* means) in the case of man, answers to "anointed" in the case of Jesus; therefore "the Christ," i.e., *the anointed,* is the title here given designedly. He is the representative man; and there is a strict correspondence between the history of *man* and that of *the Son of man.* The two most solemn facts of

ADAM CLARKE

the blood of calves and goats, and the sprinkling of the blood and water with the bunch of hysop bound about with scarlet wool. These are called *patterns,* "exemplars," earthly things, which were the representatives of *heavenly things.* Purification implies, not only cleansing from defilement, but also dedication or consecration. All the utensils employed in the Tabernacle service were thus *purified* though incapable of any moral pollution. *But the heavenly things themselves.* Some think this means heaven itself, which, by receiving the sacrificed body of Christ, which appears in the presence of God for us, may be said to be *purified,* i.e., "set apart," for the reception of the souls of those who have found redemption in His blood. Others think the body of Christ is intended, which is the tabernacle in which His divinity dwelt; and that this might be said to be purified by its own sacrifice, as He is said, John xvii. 19, to sanctify himself; that is, to "consecrate" himself unto God as a Sin Offering for the redemption of man. Others suppose the Church is intended, which He is to present to the Father without entrance to the holy of holies must be made by the sprinkling of the blood of the sacrifice, and as that holy of holies represented heaven, the apostle's meaning seems to be that there was and could be no entrance to the holiest but through His blood. And therefore, when by "a more perfect tabernacle," vv. 11-12, He passed into the heavens, not with the blood of bulls and goats, but by His own blood, He thus purified or laid open the entrance to the holiest, by a more valuable sacrifice than those required to open the entrance of the holy of holies. *It was . . . necessary,* therefore, for God had appointed it so, that the Tabernacle and its parts, which were *patterns of things in the heavens,* should be "consecrated" and entered with such sacrifices as have already been mentioned. But the heaven of heavens into which Jesus entered, and whither He will bring all His faithful followers, must be propitiated, consecrated, and entered by the infinitely better sacrifice of His own body and blood. That this is the meaning appears from the following verse.

24. *Christ is not entered into the holy places made with hands.* He is not gone into the holy of holies of the Tabernacle or Temple, as the Jewish high priest does once in the year with the blood of the victim, to sprinkle it before the mercy seat there; but *into heaven itself,* which He has thus opened to all believers, having made the propitiatory offering by which both He and those whom He represents are entitled to enter and enjoy eternal blessedness.

25. *Nor yet that he should offer himself often.* The sacrifice of Christ is not like that of the Jewish high priest. His must be offered every year; Christ has offered himself once for all.

26. *For then must he often have suffered.* In **the counsel of God, Christ was considered the** "Lamb slain from the foundation of the world," Rev. xiii. 8, so that all believers before His advent were equally interested in His sacrificial death with those who have lived since His coming. *The end of the world.* The conclusion of the Jewish dispensation, the Christian dispensation being that which shall continue till the end of time.

To put away sin. "To abolish the sin offerings"; i.e., to put an end to the Mosaic economy by His one offering of himself. Some think that the expression should be applied to the putting away the guilt, power, and being of sin from the souls of believers.

27. *As it is appointed.* It is "laid before" them by the divine decree: "Dust thou art, and unto dust shalt thou return." *Unto men* generally, during the course of the present world.

MATTHEW HENRY

1. The appointment of God concerning men contains in it two things. They must once die. This is matter of comfort to the godly, that they shall die well and die but once; but it is matter of terror to the wicked, who die in their sin. After death they shall come to judgment. This is the unalterable decree of God concerning men—they must die, and they must be judged.

2. The appointment of God concerning Christ. He must be once offered to bear the sins of many. He was not offered for any sin of his own; he was wounded for our transgressions.

Christ shall appear the second time without sin, to the salvation of those who look for him. He appeared in the form of sinful flesh; but his second appearance will be without any such charge upon him. This will be to the salvation of all who look for him; he will then perfect their holiness, their happiness.

JAMIESON, FAUSSET, BROWN

our being are here connected with the two most gracious truths of our dispensation, our death and judgment answering in parallelism to Christ's first coming to die for us, and His second coming to consummate our salvation. **once**–and no more. **after this the judgment**–viz., at Christ's appearing, to which, in vs. 28, "judgment" in this verse is parallel. Not, "after this comes the heavenly glory." The intermediate state is a state of joyous, or else agonizing and fearful, *expectation* of "judgment"; after the judgment comes the full and final state of joy, or else woe. **28. Christ**–*Greek,* "THE Christ"; the representative MAN; representing all men, as the first Adam did. **once offered**–not "often," vs. 25; just as "men," of whom He is the representative Head, are appointed by God *once* to die. **to bear the sins**–referring to Isaiah 53:12, "He bare the sins of many," viz., *on Himself;* so "bear" means, Leviticus 24:15; Numbers 5:31; 14:34. The *Greek* is lit. "to bear up" (I Pet. 2:24). "Our sins were laid on Him. When, therefore, He was lifted up on the cross, He bare up our sins along with Him" [BENGEL]. **many**–not opposed to *all,* but to *few.* He, *the One,* was offered for *many;* and that *once for all* (cf. Matt. 20:28). **look for him**–*with waiting expectation even unto the end* (so the *Greek*). It is translated "wait for" in Romans 8:19, 23; I Cor. 1:7, which see. **appear**–rather, as *Greek,* "be seen." No longer in the alien "form of a servant," but in His own proper glory. **without sin**–apart from, separate from, sin. Not bearing the sin of many *on* Him as at His first coming (even then there was no sin *in* Him). That sin has been at His first coming once for all taken away, so as to need no repetition of His sin offering of Himself (vs. 26). At His second coming He shall have no more to do with sin. **unto salvation**–to bring in completed salvation; redeeming then the body which is as yet subject to the bondage of corruption. Hence, in Philippians 3:20 he says, "we look for THE SAVIOUR."

ADAM CLARKE

28. *So Christ was once offered.* He shall die no more; He has borne away the sins of many, and what He has done once shall stand good forever.

Yet He will appear a second time *without sin,* "without a sin offering"; that He has already made.

Unto salvation. To deliver the bodies of believers from the empire of death, to reunite them to their purified souls, and bring both into His eternal glory. This is salvation, and the very highest of which the human being is capable.

MATTHEW HENRY

CHAPTER 10

Verses 1–6

Here the apostle sets himself to lay low the Levitical dispensation.

I. The law had but a shadow, of good things to come. These good things were to come, not clearly discovered. The Jews then had but the shadow of the good things of Christ; we under the gospel have the substance.

II. The law was not the very image of the good things to come, but was only a shadow. The law was a very rough draught of the great design of divine grace, and therefore not to be so much doted on.

III. The legal sacrifices, being offered year by year, could never make the comers thereunto perfect, *v.* 1, 2. Under the gospel, the atonement is perfect, and the sinner, once pardoned, is ever pardoned as to his state, and only needs to renew his repentance and faith.

JAMIESON, FAUSSET, BROWN

CHAPTER 10

VSS. 1-39. CONCLUSION OF THE FOREGOING ARGUMENT. THE YEARLY RECURRING LAW SACRIFICES CANNOT PERFECT THE WORSHIPPER, BUT CHRIST'S ONCE-FOR-ALL OFFERING CAN. **1.** Previously the *oneness* of Christ's offering was shown; now is shown its perfection as contrasted with the law sacrifices. **having**–inasmuch as it has but "the shadow, not the very image," i.e., not the exact likeness, reality, and full revelation, such as the Gospel has. The "image" here means the *archetype* (cf. ch. 9:24), the original, solid image [BENGEL] realizing to us those heavenly verities, of which the law furnished but *a shadowy outline* before. **good things to come**–(ch. 9:11)–belonging to "the world (age) to come." *Good things* in part made present by faith to the believer, and to be fully realized hereafter in actual and perfect enjoyment.

never–at any time (vs. 11). **with those sacrifices**–rather, "with *the same* sacrifices. **year by year**–This clause in the *Greek* refers to the whole sentence, not merely to the words "which they the priests offered" (*Greek,* "offer"). Thus the sense is, not as *English Version,* but, *the law year by year, by the repetition of the same sacrifices, testifies its inability to perfect the worshippers;* viz., on the YEARLY *day of atonement.* The "*daily*" sacrifices are referred to, vs. 11. **continually**–*Greek,* "continuously," implying that they offer a toilsome and ineffectual "*continuous*" *round* of the "same" atonement-sacrifices *recurring* "year by year." **comers thereunto**–those so *coming unto* God, viz., the worshippers (the whole people) coming to God in the person of their representative, the high priest. **perfect**–fully meet man's needs as to justification and sanctification (*Note,* ch. 9:9). **2. For**–if the law could, by its sacrifices, have perfected the worshippers. **they**–the sacrifices. **once purged**–IF they were *once for all cleansed* (ch. 7:27). **conscience**–"*consciousness* of sin" (ch. 9:9). **3. But**–so far from *those sacrifices ceasing to be offered* (vs. 2). **in . . .**–in the fact of their being offered, and in the course of their being offered on the day of atonement. Contrast vs. 17. **a remembrance**–a recalling to mind by the high priest's confession, on the day of atonement, of the sins both of each past year and of all former years, proving that the expiatory sacrifices of former years were not felt by men's consciences to have fully atoned for former sins; in fact, the expiation and remission

ADAM CLARKE

CHAPTER 10

1. *The law having a shadow of good things to come.* (1) *A shadow* signifies, literally the shade cast from a body of any kind. (2) It signifies, technically, a sketch, rude plan, or imperfect draught of a building, landscape, man, beast, etc. (3) It signifies, metaphorically, any faint adumbration, symbolical expression, imperfect or obscure image of a thing; and is opposed to "body," or the thing intended to be thereby defined. *And not the very image. Image* signifies: (1) a simple representation, (2) the form or particular fashion of a thing, (3) the model according to which anything is formed, (4) the perfect image of a thing as opposed to a faint representation. The law, with all its ceremonies and sacrifices, was only a *shadow* of spiritual and eternal good. The gospel is the *image* or thing itself, as including every spiritual and eternal good. *Can never . . . make the comers thereunto perfect.* Cannot remove guilt from the conscience or impurity from the heart.

2. *Would they not have ceased to be offered?* Had they made an effectual reconciliation for the sins of the world, and contained in their once offering a plenitude of permanent merit, they would have ceased to be offered.

MATTHEW HENRY

IV. As the legal sacrifices did not of themselves take away sin, so it was impossible they should, *v.* 4. The atoning sacrifice must be one capable of consenting, and must voluntarily substitute himself in the sinner's stead: Christ did so.

V. There was a time fixed and foretold by the great God, and that time had now come, when these legal sacrifices would be no longer accepted by him nor useful to men. This time of the repeal of the Levitical laws was foretold by David (Ps. xl. 6, 7).

ALBERT BARNES:

"But a body hast thou prepared me." This is one of the passages which has caused a difficulty in understanding this quotation from the Psalm. The difficulty is that it differs from the Hebrew and that the apostle builds an argument upon it, though it thus differs. It is not unusual, indeed, in the New Testament to make use of the language of the Septuagint even where it varies somewhat from the Hebrew; and where no argument is based on such a passage, there can be no difficulty in such a usage, since it is not uncommon to make use of the language of others to express our own thoughts. But the apostle does not appear to have made such a use of the passage here, but to have applied it in the way of argument.

The argument, indeed, does not rest wholly, perhaps not principally, on the fact that a "body had been prepared" for the Messiah; but still, that a body had been thus prepared was evidently in the view of the apostle an important consideration, and this is the passage on which the proof of this is based. The Hebrew (Ps. 40:6) is, "Mine ears hast thou opened," or, as it is in the margin, "digged." The idea there is that the ear had been, as it were, excavated, or dug out, so as to be made to hear distinctly; that is, certain truths had been clearly revealed to the speaker; or perhaps it may mean that he had been made "readily and attentively obedient" (Stuart). Compare with Isa. 50:5, "The Lord God hath opened my ear, and I was not rebellious." In the Psalm, the proper connection would seem to be that the speaker had been made obedient, or had been so led that he was disposed to do the will of God. This was expressed by the fact that the ear had been opened so as to be quick to hear, since an indisposition to obey is often expressed by the fact that the ears are "stopped." The Hebrew in the Psalm the Septuagint translates, "A body hast thou prepared me," and this rendering has been adopted by the apostle. Various ways have been restored to for explaining the fact that the translators of the Septuagint rendered it in this manner, none of which are entirely free from difficulty.—*Popular Commentary*

Verses 7–18

He recommends Christ to them as the true high priest, the true atoning sacrifice. This he illustrates,

I. From the purpose and promise of God concerning Christ, which are frequently recorded in the volume of the book of God, *v.* 7.

II. From what God had done in preparing a body for Christ (that is, a human nature), that he might be qualified to be our Redeemer and Advocate.

III. From the readiness and willingness that Christ discovered to engage in this work, when no other sacrifice would be accepted, *v.* 7–9. Christ voluntarily came into it: "*Lo, I come! I delight to do thy will, O God!*" This should endear Christ and our Bibles to us, that in Christ we have the fulfilling of the scriptures.

JAMIESON, FAUSSET, BROWN

were only legal and typical (vss. 4, 11). The Gospel remission, on the contrary, is so complete, that sins are "remembered no more" (vs. 17) by God. It is unbelief to "forget" this once-for-all purgation, and to fear on account of "former sins" (II Pet. 1:9). The believer, once for all *bathed,* needs only to "wash" his hands and "feet" of soils, according as he daily contracts them, in Christ's blood (John 13:10). **4. For . . .**—reason why, necessarily, there is a continually recurring "remembrance of sins" in the legal sacrifices (vs. 3). ***Typically,* "the blood** of bulls," etc., sacrificed, had power; but it was only in virtue of the power of the one real antitypical sacrifice of Christ; they had no power *in themselves;* **take away**—"take *off.*" The *Greek,* vs. 11, is stronger, explaining the weaker word here, "take away *utterly.*" The blood of beasts could not take away the sin of *man.* A MAN must do that (*Notes,* ch. 9:12-14). **5.** Christ's voluntary self-offering, in contrast to those inefficient sacrifices, is shown to fulfil perfectly "the will of God" as to our redemption, by completely atoning "for (our) sins." **Wherefore**—seeing that a nobler than animal sacrifices was needed to "take away sins." **when he cometh**—*Greek,* "coming." But the time of "coming" is *present;* not "when He had come," but "when *coming* into the world"; so, in order to accord with ALFORD's view, "the world" must mean His PUBLIC ministry: when coming, or about to come, into *public.* **a body hast thou prepared me**—*Greek,* "Thou didst *fit* for Me a body." "In Thy counsels *Thou didst determine to make for Me a body,* to be given up to death as a sacrificial victim" [WAHL]. In the *Hebrew,* Psalm 40:6, it is "mine ears hast thou opened," or "dug." Perhaps this alludes to the custom of *boring the ear of a slave who volunteers to remain under his master when he might be free.* Christ's assuming a human *body,* in obedience to the Father's will, in order to die the death of a slave (ch. 2:14), was virtually the same act of voluntary submission to service as that of a slave suffering his ear to be bored by his master. His *willing obedience to the Father's will* is what is dwelt on as giving especial virtue to His sacrifice (vss. 7, 9, 10). The *preparing,* or *fitting of a body* for Him, is not with a view to His mere incarnation, but to His expiatory *sacrifice* (vs. 10), as the *contrast* to "sacrifice and offering" requires; cf. also Rom. 7:4; Eph. 2:16; Col. 1:22. More probably "opened mine ears" means *opened mine inward ear,* so as to be attentively obedient to what God wills me to do, viz., to assume the body He has prepared for me for my sacrifice, so Job, *Margin,* 33:16; 36:10 (doubtless the boring of a slave's *ear* was the symbol of *such willing obedience*); Isaiah 50:5, "The Lord God hath opened mine ear," i.e., made me *obediently* attentive as a slave to his master. Others somewhat similarly explain, "Mine ears hast thou digged," or "*fashioned,*" not with allusion to Exodus 21:6, but to the true office of the ear—a willing, submissive attention to the voice of God (Isa. 50:4, 5). The forming of the ear implies the preparation of the body, i.e., the incarnation; this secondary idea, really in the *Hebrew,* though less prominent, is the one which Paul uses for his argument. In either explanation the idea of Christ taking on Him the form, and becoming *obedient as a servant,* is implied. As He assumed a body in which to make His self-sacrifice, so ought we *present* our *bodies a living sacrifice* (Rom. 12:1). **6. burnt offerings**—*Greek,* "*whole* burnt offerings." **thou hast had no pleasure**—as if these could in themselves atone for sin: God had pleasure in (*Greek,* "approved," or "was *well pleased* with") them, in so far as they were an act of obedience to His positive command under the Old Testament, but not as having an intrinsic efficacy such as Christ's sacrifice had. Contrast Matthew 3:17. **7. I come**—rather, "I am come" (*Note,* vs. 5). "Here we have the creed, as it were, of Jesus: "*I am come* to fulfil the law, Matthew 5:17; to preach, Mark 1:38; to call sinners to repentance, Luke 5:32; to send a sword and to set men at variance, Matthew 10:34, 35; I came down from heaven to do the will of Him that sent me, John 6:38, 39 (so here, Psalm 40:7, 8); I am sent to the lost sheep of the house of Israel, Matthew 15:24; I am come into this world for judgment, John 9:39; I am come that they might have life, and might have it more abundantly, John 10:10; to save what had been lost, Matthew 18:11; to seek and to save that which was lost, Luke 19:10; cf. I Timothy 1:15; to save men's lives, Luke 9:56; to send fire on the earth, Luke 12:49; to minister, Matthew 20:28; as "the Light," John 12:46; to bear witness unto the truth, John 18:37.' **in the volume . . .**—lit., "the roll": the parchment MS. be-

ADAM CLARKE

4. *For it is not possible.* Common sense must have taught them that shedding the blood of bulls and goats could never satisfy divine justice nor take away guilt from the conscience; and God intended that they should understand the matter so; and this the following quotation from the Psalmist sufficiently proves.

5. *When he* (the Messiah) *cometh into the world,* was about to be incarnated, *he saith* to God the Father, *Sacrifice and offering thou wouldest not*—It was never Thy will and design that the sacrifices under Thy own law should be considered as making atonement for sin; they were only designed to point out My incarnation and consequent sacrificial death. And therefore *a body hast thou prepared me,* by a miraculous conception in the womb of a virgin, according to Thy word, "The seed of the woman shall bruise the head of the serpent." *A body hast thou prepared me.* The quotation in this and the following two verses is taken from Ps. xl. 6-8, as they stand now in the Septuagint, with scarcely any variety of reading; but although the general meaning is the same, they are widely different in verbal expression in the Hebrew. David's words we translate, "Mine ears hast thou opened"; but they might be more properly rendered, "My ears hast Thou bored"; that is, Thou hast made me Thy servant forever, to dwell in Thine own house; for the allusion is evidently to the custom mentioned in Exod. xxi. 2, etc.: "If thou buy an Hebrew servant, six years he shall serve: and in the seventh he shall go out free . . . but if the servant shall plainly [positively] say, I love my master . . . I will not go out free: then his master shall bring him to . . . the door post; and . . . shall bore his ear through with an aul; and he shall serve him for ever." But how is it possible that the Septuagint and the apostle should take a meaning so totally different from the sense of the Hebrew? Dr. Kennicott supposes that the Septuagint and apostle express the meaning of the words as they stood in the copy from which the Greek translation was made, and that the present Hebrew text is corrupted. It is remarkable that all the offerings and sacrifices which were considered to be of an atoning or cleansing nature, offered under the law, are here enumerated by the Psalmist and the apostle, to show that none of them nor all of them could take away sin, and that the grand sacrifice of Christ was that alone which could do it. Four kinds are here specified, by both the Psalmist and the apostle, viz., sacrifice, offering, burnt offering, sin offering. Of all these we may say, with the apostle, it was impossible that the blood of bulls and goats should take away sin.

6. *Thou hast had no pleasure.* Thou couldst never be pleased with the victims under the law; Thou couldst never consider them as atonements for sin, as they could never satisfy Thy justice nor make Thy law honorable.

7. *In the volume of the book.* "In the roll of the book." Anciently, books were written on

MATTHEW HENRY

IV. From the errand and design upon which Christ came. Christ came to do the will of God in two instances. 1. In taking away the first priesthood, which God had no pleasure in. 2. In establishing the second, his own priesthood and the everlasting gospel. This is the great design upon which the heart of God was set from all eternity. And it is not more agreeable to the will of God than it is advantageous to the souls of men.

From the place to which our Lord Jesus is now exalted, *v.* 12, 13. 1. To what honour Christ is exalted—to the right hand of God, the seat of power, the giving hand; the receiving hand; the working hand; this is the highest post of honour. 2. How Christ came to this honour—as a reward due to his sufferings. He will never quit it, nor cease to employ it for his people's good. This is his rest for ever. He has further expectations, which shall not be disappointed. One would think such a person as Christ could have no enemies except in hell; but it is certain that he has enemies on earth. Let not Christians then wonder that they have enemies. But Christ's enemies shall be made his footstool; this he is expecting. When his enemies shall be subdued, their enemies shall be subdued also.

JAMIESON, FAUSSET, BROWN

ing wrapped around a cylinder headed with knobs. Here, the Scripture "volume" meant is the 40th Psalm. "By this very passage 'written of Me,' I undertake to do Thy will [viz., that I should die for the sins of the world, in order that all who believe may be saved, not by animal sacrifices, vs. 6, but by My death]." This is the written contract of Messiah (cf. Neh. 9:38), whereby He engaged to be our surety. So complete is the inspiration of all that is written, so great the authority of the Psalms, that what David says is really what Christ then and there said. **8. he**—Christ. **Sacrifice . . .**—The oldest MSS. read, "*Sacrifices* and *offerings*" (plural). This verse combines the two clauses previously quoted distinctly, vss. 5, 6, in contrast to the sacrifice of Christ with which God was well pleased. **9. Then said he**—"At that time (viz., when speaking by David's mouth in the 40th Psalm) He hath said." The rejection of the legal sacrifices involves, as its concomitant, the voluntary offer of Jesus to make the self-sacrifice with which God is well pleased (for, indeed, it was God's own "will" that He *came to do* in offering it: so that *this* sacrifice could not but be well pleasing to God). **I come**—"I am come." **taketh away**—"sets aside the first," viz., "the legal system of sacrifices" which God wills not. **the second**—"the will of God" (vss. 7, 9) that Christ should redeem us by His self-sacrifice. **10. By**—*Greek*, "In." So "in," and "through," occur in the same sentence, I Pet. 1:22, "Ye have purified your souls *in* obeying the truth *through* the Spirit." Also, I Peter 1:5, in the *Greek*. The "*in* (fulfilment of) which will" (cf. the use of *in*, Ephesians 1:6, "wherein [in which grace] He hath made us accepted in the Beloved"), expresses the *originating* cause; "THROUGH the offering . . . of Christ," the *instrumental* or *mediatory* cause. The whole work of redemption flows from "the will" of God the Father, as the First Cause, who decreed redemption from before the foundation of the world. The "will" here (*boulema*) is His *absolute sovereign will*. His "good will" (*eudokia*) is a particular aspect of it. **are sanctified**—once for all, and as our *permanent state* (so the *Greek*). It is the finished work of Christ in having sanctified us (i.e., having translated us from a state of unholy alienation into a state of *consecration* to God, having "no more conscience of sin," vs. 2) once for all and permanently, not the process of gradual sanctification, which is here referred to. **the body**—"prepared" for Him by the Father (vs. 5). As the atonement, or reconciliation, is by the blood of Christ (Lev. 17. 11), so our *sanctification* (consecration to God, holiness and eternal bliss) is by the *body* of Christ (Col. 1:22). **once for all**—(ch. 7:27; 9:12, 26, 28; 10:12, 14). **11. And**—a new point of contrast; the frequent repetition of the sacrifices. **priest**—The oldest MSS. read, "high priest." Though he did not in person stand "daily" offering sacrifices, he did so by the subordinate priests of whom, as well as of all Israel, he was the representative head. So "daily" is applied to the high priests (ch. 7:27). **standeth**—the attitude of one ministering; in contrast to "*sat down* on the right hand of God," vs. 12, said of Christ; the posture of one being ministered to as a king. **which**—*Greek*, "the which," i.e., of such a kind as. **take away**—utterly; lit., "strip off all round." Legal sacrifices might, *in part*, produce the sense of forgiveness, yet scarcely even that (*Note*, vs. 4); but *entirely* to strip off one's guilt they never could. **12. this man**—emphatic (ch. 3:3). **for ever**—joined in *English Version* with "offered one sacrifice"; offered one sacrifice, the efficacy of which endures for ever; lit., "continuously," (cf. vs. 14). "The offering of Christ, once for all made, will continue the one and only oblation for ever; no other will supersede it" [BENGEL]. **13. expecting**—"waiting." *Awaiting* the execution of His Father's will, that all His foes should be subjected to Him. The Son *waits* till the Father shall "send Him forth to triumph over all His foes." He is now *sitting* at rest (vs. 12), invisibly reigning, and having His foes virtually, by right of His death, subject to Him. His present *sitting* on the unseen throne is a necessary preliminary to His coming forth to subject His foes openly. He shall then come forth to a visibly manifested kingdom and conquest over His foes. Thus He fulfils Psalm 110:1. This agrees with I Corinthians 15:23-28. **be made his footstool**—lit., "be placed (rendered) footstool of His feet." **his enemies**—Satan and Death, whose strength consists in "sin"; this being taken away (vs. 12), the power of the foes is taken away, and their destruction necessarily follows. **14. For**—The sacrifice being "for ever" in its efficacy (vs. 12) needs no renewal.

ADAM CLARKE

skins and rolled up. Among the Romans these were called *volumina*, from *volvo*, "I roll"; and Pentateuch, in the Jewish synagogues, is still written in this way. There are two wooden rollers; on one they roll on, on the other they roll off, as they proceed in reading. The *book* mentioned here must be the Pentateuch, or five books of Moses, for in David's time no other part of divine revelation had been committed to writing. This whole *book* speaks about Christ and His accomplishing the *will* of God. *To do thy will.* God willed not the sacrifices under the law, but He willed that a human victim of infinite merit should be offered for the redemption of mankind. That there might be such a victim, a "body" was prepared for the eternal Logos and in that body He came to do the will of God, that is, to suffer and die for the sins of the world.

9. *He taketh away the first.* The offerings, sacrifices, burnt offerings, and sacrifices for sin which were prescribed by the *law*. *That he may establish the second.* The offering of the body of Jesus once for all.

10. *By the which will we are sanctified.* Closing in with this so solemnly declared will of God that there is no name given under heaven among men by which we can be saved but Jesus the Christ, we believe in Him, find redemption in His blood, and are sanctified unto God through the sacrificial offering of His body.

11. *Every priest standeth.* The office of the Jewish priest is here compared with the office of our High Priest. The Jewish priest stands daily at the altar, like a servant ministering, repeating the same sacrifices; our High Priest offered himself once for all, and sat down at the right hand of God, as the only begotten Son and Heir of all things, v. 12. This continual offering argued the imperfection of the sacrifices. Our Lord's once offering proves His was complete.

13. *Till his enemies be made his footstool.* Till all that oppose His high priesthood and sacrificial offering shall be defeated, routed, and confounded; and acknowledge in their punishment the supremacy of His power as universal and eternal King, who refused to receive Him as their atoning and sanctifying Priest.

MATTHEW HENRY

V. From the perfect efficacy of the priesthood of Christ (*v.* 14). This is what the Levitical priesthood could never do; and, if we indeed are aiming at a perfect state, we must receive the Lord Jesus as the only high priest that can bring us to that state.

The apostle recommends Christ from the witness the Holy Ghost has given in the scriptures concerning him (*v.* 15): *Whereof the Holy Ghost is a witness.* The passage is cited from Jer. xxxi. 31. God promises that he will pour out his Spirit upon his people; he will put his laws in their hearts, and write them in their minds, *v.* 16.

Their sins and iniquities he will remember no more (*v.* 17), which will alone show the sufficiency of Christ's satisfaction, that it needs not be repeated, *v.* 18. This was much more than the Levitical priesthood and sacrifices could effect.

Verses 19-39

I. Here the apostle sets forth the dignities of the gospel state. The privileges are, 1. Boldness to enter into the holiest. They have access to God till they are prepared to enter into his glorious presence in heaven. 2. A high priest over the house of God, even this blessed Jesus. God is willing to dwell with men on earth, and to have them dwell with him in heaven; but fallen man cannot dwell with God without a high priest.

II. The way and means by which Christians enjoy such privileges—*by the blood of Jesus.* The apostle enters further into the particulars of it, *v.* 20. 1. It is the only way. 2. It is a new way. It is a way that will always be effectual. 3. It is a living way. This way we may come to God, and live. It is by a living Saviour who, though he was dead is alive; and it is a way that gives life and lively hope to those who enter into it. 4. It is a way that Christ has consecrated for us through the veil, that is, his flesh. Our way to heaven is by a crucified Saviour; his death is to us the way of life.

III. The duties binding upon them on account of these privileges, *v.* 22, 23, &c.

1. They must draw near to God, and that in a right manner. They must draw near in conformity to God, and communion with him, still endeavouring to get nearer and nearer, till they come to dwell in his presence. (1) With a true heart. God is the searcher of hearts, and he requires truth in the inward parts. (2) In full assurance of faith. We should lay aside all sinful distrust. Without faith it is impossible to please God. (3) Having our hearts sprinkled from an evil conscience. They may be cleansed from guilt, and whatever evils the consciences of men are subject to by reason of sin.

JAMIESON, FAUSSET, BROWN

them that are sanctified—rather as *Greek,* "them that *are being* sanctified." The sanctification (consecration to God) of the elect (I Pet. 1:2) believers is perfect in Christ once for all (*Note,* vs. 10). (Contrast the law, ch. 7:19; 9:9; 10:1.) The development of that sanctification is progressive. **15.** The *Greek,* has "moreover," or "now." **is a witness**—of the truth which I am setting forth. The Father's witness is given ch. 5:10. The Son's, ch. 10:5. Now is added that of the Holy Spirit, called accordingly "the Spirit of grace," vs. 29. The testimony of all Three leads to the same conclusion (vs. 18). **for after that he had said . . .**—The conclusion to the sentence is in vs. 17, "*After* He had said before, This is the covenant that I will make with them (*with the house of Israel,* ch. 8:10; here extended to the spiritual Israel) . . . , saith the Lord; I will put (lit., "giving," referring to the *giving* of the law; not now as then, *giving into the hands,* but *giving*) My laws into their hearts ("mind," ch. 8:10) and in their minds ("hearts," ch. 8:10); I will *inscribe* (so the *Greek*) them (here He omits the addition quoted in ch. 8:10, 11, *I will be to them a God . . . , and they shall not teach every man his neighbor . . .*), and (i.e., *after He had said the foregoing,* HE THEN ADDS) their sins . . . will I remember no more." **18. where remission of these is**—as there is under the Gospel covenant (vs. 17). "Here ends the finale (ch. 10:1-18) of the great tripartite arrangement (ch. 7:1-25; 7:26 to 9:12; 9:13 to 10:18) of the middle portion of the Epistle. **19.** Here begins the third and last division of the Epistle; *our duty now while waiting for the Lord's second advent.* Resumption and expansion of the exhortation (ch. 4:14-16; cf. vss. 22, 23 here) wherewith he closed the first part of the Epistle, preparatory to his great doctrinal argument, beginning at ch. 7:1. **boldness**—"free confidence," grounded on the consciousness that our sins have been forgiven. **to enter**—lit., "as regards the entering." **by**—*Greek,* "in"; it is *in* the blood of Jesus that our boldness to enter is grounded. Cf. Ephesians 3:12, "*In* whom we have boldness and access with confidence." It is His having once for all entered as our Forerunner (ch. 6:20) and High Priest (vs. 21), making atonement for us with His blood, which is continually there (ch. 12:24) before God, that gives us confident access. **20. which . . .**—The antecedent in the *Greek* is "the entering"; not as *English Version,* "way." Translate, "which (entering) He has consecrated (not as though it were already existing, but *has been the first to open,* INAUGURATED *as a new thing: Note,* ch. 9:18, where the *Greek* is the same) for us (as) a new (*Greek,* 'recent'; recently opened, Rom. 16:25, 26) and living way" (not like the lifeless way through the law offering of the blood of *dead* victims, but real, *vital,* and of perpetual efficacy, because the *living* and *life-giving* Saviour is that *way.* It is a *living hope* that we have, producing not *dead,* but *living,* works). Christ, the first fruits of our nature, has ascended, and the rest is sanctified thereby. "Christ's ascension is our promotion; and whither the glory of the Head hath preceded, thither the hope of the body, too, is called" [LEO]. **the veil**—As the *veil* had to be passed *through* in order to enter the holiest place, so the weak, human suffering *flesh* (ch. 5:7) of Christ's humanity (which veiled His God head) had to be passed through by Him in entering the heavenly holiest place for us; in putting off His *rent flesh,* the temple veil, its type, was simultaneously rent from top to bottom (Matt. 27:51). Not His *body,* but His weak suffering *flesh,* was the veil; His body was the temple (John 2:19). **21. high priest**—As a different *Greek* term (*archiereus*) is used always elsewhere in this Epistle for "high priest," translate as *Greek* here, "A *Great* Priest"; one who is at once King and "Priest on His throne" (Zech. 6:13); a royal Priest, and a priestly King. **house of God**—the spiritual house, the *Church,* made up of believers, whose home is *heaven,* where Jesus now is (ch. 12:22, 23). Thus, by "the house of God," over which Jesus is, *heaven* is included in meaning, as well as the *Church,* whose home it is. **22.** (Ch. 4:16; 7:19.) **with a true heart**—without hypocrisy; "in truth, and with a perfect heart"; a heart thoroughly imbued with "the truth" (vs. 26). **full assurance**—(ch. 6:11)—with no doubt as to our acceptance when coming to God by the blood of Christ. As "*faith*" occurs here, so "*hope,*" and "*love,*" vss. 23, 24. **sprinkled from**—i.e., sprinkled *so as to be cleansed* from. **evil conscience**—a consciousness of guilt unatoned for, and uncleansed away (vs. 2; ch. 9:9). Both the *hearts* and the *bodies* are cleansed. The legal purifications were with blood of animal victims and

ADAM CLARKE

14. *For by one offering.* His death upon the Cross. *He hath perfected for ever.* He has procured remission of sins and holiness; for it is well observed here, and in several parts of this Epistle, that "to make perfect" is the same as "to procure remission of sins." *Them that are sanctified.* Them that have received the sprinkling of the Blood of this offering. These, therefore, receiving redemption through that blood, have no need of any other offering; as this was a complete atonement, purification, and title to eternal glory.

15. *The Holy Ghost also is a witness to us.* The words are quoted from Jer. xxxi. 33-34, and here we are assured that Jeremiah spoke by the inspiration of the Spirit of God. *Had . . . said before.* See chap. viii. 10, 12.

18. *Now where remission of these is.* In any case, where sin is once pardoned, there is no further need of a sin offering; but every believer on Christ has his sin blotted out, and therefore needs no other offering for that sin.

19. *Having therefore, brethren, boldness.* The apostle, having now finished the doctrinal part of his Epistle and fully shown the superiority of Christ to all men and angels, and the superiority of His priesthood to that of Aaron and his successors, the absolute inefficacy of the Jewish sacrifices to make atonement for sin, and the absolute efficacy of that of Christ to make reconciliation of man to God, proceeds now to show what influence these doctrines should have on the hearts and lives of those who believe in His merits and death. *Boldness to enter.* "Liberty, full access to the entrance of the holy place." This is an allusion to the case of the high priest going into the holy of holies. He went with fear and trembling, because, if he had neglected the smallest item prescribed by the law, he could expect nothing but death. Genuine believers can come even to the throne of God with confidence, as they carry into the divine presence the infinitely meritorious Blood of the great atonement.

20. *By a new and living way.* It is a *new* way; no human being had ever before entered into the heaven of heavens. Jesus in human nature was the first, and thus He has opened the way to heaven to mankind, His own resurrection and ascension to glory being the proof and pledge of ours. *Through the veil.* As the high priest lifted up or drew aside the veil that separated the holy from the most holy place, in order that he might have access to the Divine Majesty; and as the veil of the Temple was rent from the top to the bottom at the crucifixion of Christ, to show that the way to the holiest was then laid open; so we must approach the throne through the mediation of Christ, and through His sacrificial death. Here the veil—His humanity—is rent, and the kingdom of Heaven opened to all believers.

21. *An high priest over the house of God. The house* or family *of God* is the Christian Church, or all true believers in the Lord Jesus. Over this Church, house, or family Christ is the High Priest—in their behalf He offers His own blood, and their prayers and praises.

22. *Let us draw near.* Let us come with the blood of our Sacrifice to the throne of God; the expression is sacrificial. *With a true heart.* Deeply convinced of our need of help, and truly in earnest to obtain it. *In full assurance of faith.* Being fully persuaded that God will accept us for the sake of His Son, and that the sacrificial death of Christ gives us full authority to expect every blessing we need. *Having our hearts sprinkled.* Not our bodies, as was the case among the Hebrews, when they had contracted any pollution, for they were to be sprinkled with the water of separation (see Num. xix 2-10); but our *hearts,* sprinkled by the cleansing efficacy of the blood of Christ, without which we cannot draw nigh to God. *From an evil conscience.* Having that deep sense of guilt which our conscience felt taken all away, and the peace and love of God shed

MATTHEW HENRY

(4) Our bodies washed with pure water, that is, with the water of baptism, or with the sanctifying virtue of the Holy Spirit, cleansing from the filthiness of the flesh as well as of the spirit.

2. The apostle exhorts believers to hold fast the profession of their faith, *v.* 23. (1) The duty itself—to hold fast the profession of our faith. Our spiritual enemies will do what they can to wrest our faith, and hope, out of our hands, but we must hold fast. (2) The manner in which we must do this—without wavering. Those who begin to waver are in danger of falling away. (3) The motive or reason enforcing this duty: *He is faithful that hath promised.* There is no fickleness with him, and there should be none with us. We must depend more upon his promises to us than upon our promises to him.

IV. We have the means prescribed for promoting our fidelity and perseverance, *v.* 24, 25, &c. 1. We should *consider one another, to provoke to love and to good works.* Christians ought to have a tender consideration and concern for one another. A good example given to others is the best and most effectual provocation to love and good works.

2. *Not to forsake the assembling of ourselves together, v* 25. Even in those times there were some who forsook these assemblies. The communion of saints is a great help and privilege, and a good means of steadiness and perseverance.

3. To exhort one another, to watch over one another, and be jealous of ourselves and one another with a godly jealousy. This, would be the best friendship.

4. We should observe the approaching of times of trial. Christians ought to observe the signs of the times, such as God has foretold. There is a trying day coming on us all, the day of our death, and we should observe all the signs of its approaching, and improve them to greater watchfulness and diligence in duty.

V. The apostle proceeds to enforce his exhortations (*v.* 26, 27, &c.).

1. From the description he gives of the sin of apostasy. It is *sinning wilfully after we have received the knowledge of the truth.* The sin here mentioned is a total and final apostasy, when men reject Christ, the only Saviour, and renounce the gospel, the only way of salvation, and the words of eternal life, after they have professed the Christian religion.

JAMIESON, FAUSSET, BROWN

with water, and could only cleanse the *flesh* (ch. 9: 13, 21). Christ's blood purifies the *heart* and conscience. The Aaronic priest, in entering the holy place, washed with *water* (ch. 9:19) in the brazen laver. Believers, as priests to God, are once for all washed in BODY (as distinguished from "hearts") at baptism. As we have an immaterial, and a material nature, the cleansing of both is expressed by "hearts" and "body," the inner and the outer man; so the whole man, material and immaterial. The baptism of the body, however, is not the mere putting away of material filth, nor an act operating by intrinsic efficacy, but the sacramental seal, applied to the outer man, of a spiritual washing (I Pet. 3: 21). "Body" (not merely "flesh," the *carnal* part, as II Cor. 7:1) includes the *whole* material man, which needs cleansing, as being redeemed, as well as the soul. The body, once polluted with sin, is washed, so as to be fitted like Christ's holy body, and by His body, to be spiritually a pure and living offering. On the "pure water," the symbol of consecration and sanctification, cf. John 19:34; I Corinthians 6:11; I John 5:6; Ezekiel 36:25. The perfects "having . . . hearts *sprinkled* . . . body (the *Greek* is singular) *washed,*" imply a continuing state produced by a once-for-all accomplished act, viz., our justification by faith through Christ's blood, and consecration to God, sealed sacramentally by the baptism of our body. **23.** Ch. 3:6, 14; 4:14. **profession**—*Greek,* "confession." **our faith**—rather as *Greek,* "our hope"; which is indeed *faith* exercised as to the future inheritance. *Hope* rests on faith, and at the same time quickens *faith,* and is the ground of our bold *confession* (I Pet. 3:15). *Hope* is similarly (vs. 22) connected with *purification* (I John 3:3). **without wavering**—without declension (ch. 3:14), "steadfast unto the end." **he**—God is faithful to His promises (ch. 6:17, 18; 11:11; 12:26, 28; I Cor. 1:9; 10:13; I Thess. 5:24; II Thess. 3:3; see also Christ's promise, John 12:26); but man is too often unfaithful to his duties. **24.** Here, as elsewhere, *hope* and *love* follow *faith;* the Pauline triad of Christian graces. **consider**—with the mind attentively fixed on "one another" (*Note,* ch. 3:1), contemplating with continual consideration the characters and wants of our brethren, so as to render mutual help and counsel. Cf. "consider," Psalm 41:1, and ch. 12:15, "(All) looking diligently lest *any* fail of the grace of God." **to provoke**—*Greek, "with a view to provoking* unto love," instead of provoking to hatred, as is too often the case. **25. assembling of ourselves together**—The *Greek, episunagoge,* is only found here and II Thessalonians 2:1 (the gathering together of the elect to Christ at His coming, Matt. 24:31). The assembling or gathering of ourselves for Christian communion in private and public, is an earnest of our being gathered together to Him at His appearing. Union is strength; continual assemblings together beget and foster *love,* and give good opportunities for "provoking to good works," by "exhorting one another" (ch. 3:13). IGNATIUS says, "When ye frequently, and in numbers meet together, the powers of Satan are overthrown, and his mischief is neutralized by your likemindedness in the faith." To neglect such assemblings together might end in apostasy at last. He avoids the *Greek* term *sunagoge,* as suggesting the Jewish *synagogue* meetings (cf. Rev. 2:9). **as the manner of some is**—"manner," i.e., habit, custom. This gentle expression proves he is not here as yet speaking of *apostasy.* **the day approaching**—This, the shortest designation of the day of the Lord's coming, occurs elsewhere only in I Corinthians 3:13; a confirmation of the Pauline authorship of this Epistle. The Church being *in all ages* kept uncertain how soon Christ is coming, *the day* is, and has been, in each age, practically always near; whence, believers have been called on always to be watching for it as nigh at hand. The Hebrews were now living close upon one of those great types and foretastes of it, the destruction of Jerusalem (Matt. 24), "the bloody and fiery dawn of the great day; that day is the day of days, the ending day of all days, the settling day of all days, the day of the promotion of time into eternity, the day which, for the Church, breaks through and breaks off the night of the present world" [DELITZSCH in ALFORD]. **26.** Cf. on this and following verses, ch. 6:4, etc. There the warning was that if there be not diligence in progressing, a falling off will take place, and apostasy may ensue: here it is, that if there be lukewarmness in Christian communion, apostasy may ensue. **if we sin**—*Greek* present participle: if we be found *sinning,* i.e., not isolated acts, but a *state* of sin [ALFORD]. A violation not only of the *law,* but of the whole economy of the New Testament (vss. 28, 29).

ADAM CLARKE

abroad in our hearts by the Holy Ghost given unto us. *Our bodies washed with pure water.* The high priest, before he entered into the inner tabernacle or put on his holy garments, was to wash his flesh in water, Lev. xvi. 4, and the Levites were to be cleansed the same way, Num. viii. 7. The apostle probably alludes to this in what he says here, though it appears that he refers principally to baptisms, the washing by which was an emblem of the purification of the soul by the grace and Spirit of Christ. But it is most likely that it is to the Jewish baptisms, and not the Christian, that the apostle alludes.

23. *Let us hold fast the profession.* The word implies that general consent that was among Christians on all the important articles of their faith and practice; particularly their acknowledgment of the truth of the gospel, and of Jesus Christ as the only Victim for sin and the only Saviour from it. If the word "washed" above refer to Christian baptism in the case of adults, then the profession is that which the baptized then made of their faith in the gospel, and of their determination to live and die in that faith. The various readings on this clause are many in the MSS. But among all these, the confession or "profession of hope" is undoubtedly the genuine reading. Now among the primitive Christians the hope which they professed was the resurrection of the body and everlasting life. The apostle exhorts them to *hold fast* this "confession" *without wavering*—never to doubt the declarations made to them by their Redeemer, but having the "full assurance of faith" that their hearts were sprinkled from an evil conscience, that they had found redemption in the blood of the Lamb, they might expect to be glorified with their living Head in the kingdom of their Father. *He is faithful that promised.* The eternal life, which is the object of your hope, is promised to you by Him who cannot lie. As He then is *faithful* who has given you this promise, hold fast the profession of your hope.

24. *And let us consider one another.* Let us "diligently and attentively consider" each other's trials, difficulties, and weaknesses; feel for each other, and "excite" each other to an increase of *love* to God and man; and, as the proof of it, to be fruitful in *good works.* The words "to the provocation" are often taken in a good sense, and signify "excitement, stirring up" to do anything laudable, useful, honorable, or necessary.

25. *Not forsaking the assembling of ourselves.* Whether this means public or private worship is hard to say; but as the word is but once more used in the New Testament, (2 Thess. ii. 1) and there means the "gathering together" of redeemed of the Lord at the day of judgment, it is as likely that it means here private religious meetings for the purpose of mutual exhortation; and this sense appears the more natural here because it is evident that the Church was now in a state of persecution, and therefore their meetings were most probably held in private. For fear of persecution it seems as if some had deserted these meetings, "as the custom of certain persons is." They had given up these strengthening and instructive means, and the others were in danger of following their example. *The day.* "That day"—the time in which God would come and pour out His judgments on the Jewish nation. We may also apply it to the day of death and the day of judgment. Both of these are approaching to every human being. He who wishes to be found ready will carefully use every means of grace, and particularly the communion of saints, if there be even but two or three in the place where he lives, who statedly meet together in the name of Christ. Those who relinquish Christian communion are in a backsliding state; those who backslide are in danger of apostasy. To prevent this latter, the apostle speaks the awful words following.

26. *For if we sin wilfully.* If we deliberately, for fear of persecution or from any other motive, renounce the profession of the gospel and the Author of that gospel, after having *received the knowledge of the truth* so as to be convinced that Jesus is the promised Messiah, and that He had sprinkled our hearts from an evil conscience—for such *there remaineth no . . . sacrifice for sins.* For as the Jewish sacrifices are abolished, as appears by the declaration of God

MATTHEW HENRY

2. From the dreadful doom of such apostates. (1) There remains no more sacrifice for such sins, no other Christ to come to save such sinners. Those under the gospel who will not accept of Christ, that they may be saved by him, have no other refuge left them. (2) There remains for them only a certain fearful looking for of judgment, *v.* 27. God gives some notorious sinners, while on earth, a fearful foreboding in their own consciences, with a despair of ever being able either to endure or escape it.

3. From the methods of divine justice with those who despised Moses's law. These, when convicted by two or three witnesses, were put to death; they died without mercy.

Hence the apostle infers the heavy doom that will fall upon those that apostatize from Christ. They have *trodden under foot the Son of God.* What punishment can be too great for such men?

They have *counted the blood of the covenant, wherewith he was sanctified, an unholy thing.* Men who have seemed before to have the blood of Christ in high esteem may come to account it an unholy thing.

Those have done despite unto the Spirit of grace. They have grieved, resisted, yea, done despite to him, which is the highest act of wickedness, and makes the case of the sinner desperate, refusing to have the gospel salvation applied to him.

4. From the description we have of the nature of God's vindictive justice, *v.* 30. The terrors of the Lord are known both by revelation and reason. The other quotation is from Deut. xxxii. 36, *The Lord will judge his people;* he will search and try his visible church, and will punish the sinners in Zion with the greatest severity. Now those who know him who hath said, *Vengeance belongeth to me, I will recompense,* must needs conclude, as the apostle does (*v.* 31). Those who know the joy that results from the favour of God can thereby judge of the power and dread of his vindictive wrath.

JAMIESON, FAUSSET, BROWN

wilfully—presumptuously, *Greek* "willingly." After receiving "full knowledge (so the *Greek,* cf. I Tim. 2:4) of the truth," by having been "enlightened," and by having "tasted" a certain measure even of grace of "the Holy Ghost" (the Spirit of truth, John 14:17; and "the Spirit of grace," vs. 29): to *fall away* (as "sin" here means, ch. 3:12, 17; cf. ch. 6:6) and apostatize (ch. 3:12) to Judaism or infidelity, is not a sin of *ignorance,* or error (*"out of the way,"* the result) of infirmity, but a *deliberate sinning* against the Spirit (vs. 29; ch. 5:2): *such* sinning, where a consciousness of Gospel obligations not only was, but *is* present: a sinning presumptuously and preseveringly against Christ's redemption *for* us, and the Spirit of grace *in* us. "He only who stands high can fall low. A lively reference in the soul to what is good is necessary in order to be thoroughly wicked; hence, man can be more reprobate than the beasts, and the apostate angels than apostate man" [THOLUCK]. **remaineth no more sacrifice**—For there is but ONE Sacrifice that can atone for sin; they, after having fully known that sacrifice, deliberately reject it. **27. a certain**—an extraordinary and indescribable. The indefiniteness, as of something *peculiar of its kind,* makes the description the more terrible (cf. *Greek,* Jas. 1:18). **looking for**—"expectation": a later sense of the *Greek.* ALFORD strangely translates, as the *Greek* usually means elsewhere, "reception." The transition is easy from "giving a reception to" something or someone, to "looking for." Contrast the "expecting" (the very same *Greek* as here), vs. 13, which refutes ALFORD. **fiery indignation**—lit., "zeal of fire." Fire is personified: glow or ardor of fire, i.e., of Him who is "a consuming fire." **devour**—continually. **28.** Cf. ch. 2:2, 3; 12:25. **despised**—"set at naught" [ALFORD]: utterly and heinously violated, not merely some minor detail, but *the whole law and covenant;* e.g., by idolatry (Deut. 17:2-7). So here *apostasy* answers to such an utter violation of the old covenant. **died**—*Greek,* "dies": the normal punishment of such transgression, then still in force. **without mercy**—lit., "mercies": removal out of the pale of mitigation, or a respite of his doom. **under**—on the evidence of. **29. sorer**—*Greek,* "worse," viz., "punishment" (lit., "vengeance") than any mere temporal punishment of the body. **suppose ye**—an appeal to the Hebrews' reason and conscience. **thought worthy**—by God at the judgment. **trodden under foot the Son of God**—by "wilful" apostasy. So he treads under foot God Himself who "glorified His *Son* as an high priest" (ch. 5:5; 6:6). **an unholy thing**—lit., "common," as opposed to "sanctified." No better than the blood of a common man, thus involving the consequence that Christ, in claiming to be God, was guilty of blasphemy, and so deserved to die! **wherewith he was sanctified**—for Christ died even for him. "Sanctified," in the fullest sense, belongs only to the saved elect. But in some sense it belongs also to those who have gone a far way in Christian experience, and yet fall away at last. The higher such a one's past Christian experiences, the deeper his fall. **done despite unto**—by repelling in *fact:* as "blasphemy" is despite in *words* (Mark 3:29). "Of the Jews who became Christians and relapsed to Judaism, we find from the history of URIEL ACOSTA, that they required a blasphemy against Christ. 'They applied to Him epithets used against Molech the adulterous branch,'" etc. [THOLUCK]. **the Spirit of grace**—the Spirit that confers grace. "He who does not accept the benefit, insults Him who confers it. He hath made thee a son: wilt thou become a slave? He has come to take up His abode with thee; but thou art introducing evil into thyself" [CHRYSOSTOM]. "It is the curse of evil eternally to propagate evil: so, for him who profanes the Christ *without him,* and blasphemes the Christ *within him,* there is subjectively no renewal of a change of mind (ch. 6:6), and objectively no new *sacrifice for sins*" (ch. 10:26) [THOLUCK]. **30. him**—God, who enters no empty threats. **Vengeance belongeth unto me**—*Greek,* "To Me belongeth vengeance": exactly according with *Paul's* quotation, Romans 12:19, of the same text. **Lord shall judge his people**—in grace, or else anger, according as each deserves: here, "judge," so as to punish the reprobate apostate; there, "judge," so as to interpose in behalf of, and save His people (Deut. 32. 36). **31. fearful . . . to fall into the hands . . .**—It is good like David *to fall into the hands of God,* rather than man, when one does so with filial *faith* in his father's love, though God *chastises* him. "It is fearful" to fall into His hands as a reprobate and presumptuous sinner doomed to His just vengeance as Judge (vs. 27). **living God**—therefore able to

ADAM CLARKE

himself in the fortieth psalm, and Jesus being now the only Sacrifice which God will accept, those who reject Him have none other; therefore their case must be utterly without remedy. This is the meaning of the apostle, and the case is that of a deliberate apostate—one who has utterly rejected Jesus Christ and His atonement, and renounced the whole gospel system. It has nothing to do with backsliders in our common use of that term. A man may be overtaken in a fault, or he may deliberately go into sin, and yet neither renounce the gospel nor deny the Lord that bought him. His case is dreary and dangerous, but it is not hopeless; no case is hopeless but that of the deliberate apostate, who rejects the whole gospel system, after having been saved by grace or convinced of the truth of the gospel. To him there remaineth no more sacrifice for sin; for there was but the one, Jesus, and this he has utterly rejected.

27. *A certain fearful looking for of judgment.* From this it is evident that God will pardon no man without a sacrifice for sin. *And fiery indignation.* A "zeal," or fervor of fire"; something similar to the fire that came down from heaven and destroyed Korah and his company, Num. xvi. 35.

28. *He that despised Moses' law.* He that rejected it, "threw it aside," and denied its divine authority by presumptuous sinning, *died without mercy*—without any extenuation or mitigation of punishment, Num. xv. 30. *Under two or three witnesses.* That is, when convicted by the testimony of two or three respectable witnesses. See Deut. xvii. 6.

29. *Of how much sorer punishment?* Such offenses were trifling in comparison of this, and in justice the punishment should be proportioned to the offense. *Trodden under foot the Son of God.* Treated Him with the utmost contempt and blasphemy. *The blood of the covenant . . . an unholy thing. The blood of the covenant* means here the sacrificial death of Christ, by which the new covenant between God and man was ratified, sealed, and confirmed. And counting this *unholy,* or "common," intimates that they expected nothing from it in a sacrificial or atoning way. How near to those persons, and how near to their destruction do they come in the present day who reject the atoning Blood and say "that they expect no more benefit from the blood of Christ than they do from that of a cow or a sheep"! Is not this precisely the crime of which the apostle speaks here, and to which he tells us God would show no mercy? *Despite unto the Spirit of grace.* Hath "insulted" the Spirit of grace. The apostle means the Holy Spirit, whose gifts were bestowed in the first age on believers for the confirmation of the gospel. See chap. vi. 4-6. Wherefore if one apostatized in the first age, after having been witness to these miraculous gifts, much more after having possessed them himself, he must, like the scribes and Pharisees, have ascribed them to evil spirits, than which a greater indignity could not be done to the Spirit of God.

30. *Vengeance belongeth unto me.* This is the saying of God, Deut. xxxii. 35, in reference to the idolatrous Gentiles, who were the enemies of His people; and is here with propriety applied to the above apostates, who, being enemies to God's ordinances and Christ's ministry and merits, must also be enemies to Christ's people. *The Lord shall judge his people.* That is, He shall execute judgment *for* them; for this is evidently the sense in which the word is used in the place from which the apostle quotes, Deut. xxxii. 36: "For the Lord shall judge his people, and repent himself for his servants, when he seeth that their power is gone." So God will avenge and vindicate the cause of Christianity by destroying its enemies, as He did in the case of the Jewish people, whom He destroyed from being a nation.

31. *It is a fearful thing to fall into the hands of the living God.* To fall into the hands of God is to fall under His displeasure. How dreadful to have the displeasure of an eternal, almighty Being to rest on the soul forever!

MATTHEW HENRY

5. He presses them to perseverance by putting them in mind of their former sufferings for Christ. When they had suffered: *In former days, after* they were *illuminated.* A natural state is a dark state, and those who continue in that state meet with no disturbance from Satan and the world; but a state of grace is a state of light, and therefore the powers of darkness will violently oppose it. What they suffered: they *endured a great fight of afflictions.* They were afflicted in themselves. In their own persons. In their names and reputations (*v.* 33), by many reproaches. Christians ought to value their reputation, because the reputation of religion is concerned: this makes reproach a great affliction. They were afflicted in the afflictions of their brethren. The Christian spirit is a sympathizing spirit, not a selfish spirit, but a compassionate spirit. Christians are one body, the children of that God who is afflicted in all the afflictions of his people. If one member of the body suffers, all the rest suffer with it.

The apostle takes particular notice how they had sympathized with him (*v.* 34). How they had suffered. They took their sufferings patiently, and not only so, but joyfully received it from God, that they should be thought worthy to suffer reproach for the name of Christ. What it was that enabled them thus to bear up under their sufferings. They knew in themselves that they had in heaven a better and a more enduring substance. The happiness of the saints in heaven is substance. All things here are but shadows. It is a better substance than any thing they can have or lose here. It will out-live time and run parallel with eternity. In heaven they shall have everything better. Christians should know this in themselves. The assured knowledge of this will help them to endure any fight of afflictions they may be encountered with in this world.

6. He presses them to persevere (*v.* 35). He exhorts them not to cast away their confidence, but to hold fast that profession for which they had suffered so much. The reward of their holy confidence would be very great. It carries a present reward in it, in holy peace and joy, and it shall have a great recompence of reward hereafter.

He shows them how necessary a grace the grace of patience is in our present state (*v.* 36). They must first do the will of God before they receive the promise; and, after they have done the will of God, they have need of patience to wait for the time when the promise shall be fulfilled. We must be God's waiting servants when we can be no longer his working servants.

To help their patience, he assures them of the near approach of Christ's coming (*v.* 37). There is an appointed time and beyond that time he will not tarry.

7. He presses them to perseverance, by telling them that this will be their happiness, whereas apostasy is the reproach, and will be the ruin, of all who are guilty of it (*v.* 38, 39). It is the honourable character of just men that in times of the greatest affliction they can live by faith. Faith puts life and vigour into them. They can trust God, and live upon him. As their faith maintains their spiritual life now, it shall be crowned with eternal life hereafter.

JAMIESON, FAUSSET, BROWN

punish for ever (Matt. 10:28). **32.** As previously he has warned them by the awful end of apostates, so here he stirs them up by the remembrance of their own former faith, patience, and self-sacrificing love. So Revelation 2:3, 4. **call to remembrance**—habitually: so the present tense means. **illuminated**—"enlightened": come to "the knowledge of the truth" (vs. 26) in connection with baptism (*Note,* ch. 6:4). In spiritual baptism, Christ, who is "the Light," is put on. "On the one hand, we are not to sever the sign and the grace signified where the sacrifice truly answers its designs; on the other, the glass is not to be mistaken for the liquor, nor the sheath for the sword" [BENGEL]. **fight of**—i.e., *consisting of* afflictions. **33.** The persecutions here referred to seem to have been endured by the Hebrew Christians at their first conversion, not only in Palestine, but also in Rome and elsewhere, the Jews in every city inciting the populace and the Roman authorities against Christians. **gazing-stock**—as in a *theater* (so the *Greek*): often used as the place of punishment in the presence of the assembled multitudes. Acts 19:29; I Corinthians 4:9, "Made a *theatrical* spectacle to the world." **ye became**—of your own accord: attesting your Christian sympathy with your suffering brethren. **companions of**—sharers in affliction with. **34. ye had compassion on me in my bonds**—The oldest MSS. and versions omit "me," and read, "Ye both sympathized with *those in bonds* (answering to the last clause of vs. 33; cf. ch. 13:3, 23; 6:10), and accepted (so the *Greek* is translated in ch. 11:35) with joy (Jas. 1:2; *joy* in tribulations, as exercising faith and other graces, Rom. 5:3; and the pledge of the coming glory, Matt. 5:12) the plundering of your (own) goods" (answering to the first clause of vs. 33). **in yourselves**—The oldest MSS. omit "in": translate, "knowing that ye have *for* (or *to*) *yourselves.*" **better**—a heavenly (ch. 11:16). **enduring**—not liable to *spoiling.* **substance**—possession: peculiarly our own, if we will not *cast away* our birthright. **35-37.** Consequent exhortation to confidence and endurance, as Christ is soon coming. **Cast not away**—implying that they now have "confidence," and that it will not withdraw of itself, unless they "cast it away" wilfully (cf. ch. 3:14). **which**—*Greek,* "the which": inasmuch as being such as. **hath**—present tense: it is as certain as if you had it in your hand (vs. 37). It hath in reversion. **recompense of reward**—of grace not of debt: a reward of a kind which no mercenary selfseeker would seek: holiness will be its own reward; self-devoting unselfishness for Christ's sake will be its own rich recompense (*Note,* ch. 2:2; 11:26). **36. patience**—*Greek,* "waiting endurance," or "enduring perseverance": the kindred *Greek* verb in the LXX, Habakkuk 2:3, is translated, "*wait for it*" (cf. Jas. 5:7). **after ye have done the will of God**—"that whereas ye have done the will of God" hitherto (vss. 32-35), ye may now show also *patient, persevering endurance,* and so "receive the promise," i.e., the promised reward: eternal life and bliss commensurate with our work of faith and love (ch. 6:10-12). We must not only *do,* but also *suffer* (I Pet. 4:19). God first uses the *active* talents of His servants; then polishes the other side of the stone, making the *passive* graces shine, *patience, meekness,* etc. It may be also translated, "That ye may do the will of God, and receive . . ." [ALFORD]: "patience" itself is a further and a persevering doing of "God's will"; otherwise it would be profitless and no real grace (Matt. 7:21). We should look, not merely for individual bliss now and at death, but for the great and general consummation of bliss of all saints, both in body and soul. **37, 38.** Encouragement to patient endurance by consideration of the shortness of the time till Christ shall come, and God's rejection of him that draws back, taken from Habakkuk 2:3, 4. **a little while—(John 16:16). he that shall come**—lit., "the Comer." In Habakkuk, it is *the vision* that is said to be about to come. *Christ,* being the grand and ultimate subject of all prophetical vision, is here made by Paul, under inspiration, the subject of the Spirit's prophecy by Habakkuk, in its final and exhaustive fulfilment. **38. just**—The oldest MSS. and *Vulgate* read, "*my* just man." God is the speaker: "He who is just in My sight." BENGEL translates, "The just shall live by *my faith*": answering to the *Hebrew,* Habakkuk 2:4; lit., "the just shall live by the faith *of Him,*" viz., *Christ,* the final subject of "the vision," who "will not lie," i.e., disappoint. Here not merely the first beginning, as in Galatians 3:11, but the *continuance,* of the spiritual life of the justified man is referred to, as opposed to declension and apostasy. As the justified man receives his first spiritual life by faith, so it is *by faith* that he *shall*

ADAM CLARKE

32. *But call to remembrance.* It appears from this, and indeed from some parts of the gospel history, that the first believers in Judea were greatly persecuted. Our Lord's crucifixion, Stephen's martyrdom, the persecution that arose after the death of Stephen, Acts viii. 1, Herod's persecution, Acts xii. 1, in which James was killed, and the various persecutions of Paul, sufficiently show that this disposition was predominant among that bad people. *A great fight of afflictions.* "A great combat or contention of sufferings." Here we have an allusion to the combats at the Grecian games or to exhibitions of gladiators at the public spectacles.

33. *Ye were made a gazingstock.* You were exhibited as wild beasts and other shows at the theaters. *Companions of them that were so used.* It appears, from I Thess. ii. 14-15, that the churches of God in Judea were greatly persecuted, and that they behaved with courage and constancy in their persecutions. When any victim of persecuting rage was marked out, the rest were prompt to take his part and acknowledge themselves believers in the same doctrine for which he suffered.

34. *Ye had compassion of me in my bonds.* "You suffered with me; you sympathized with me," when bound for the testimony of Jesus. This probably refers to the sympathy they showed towards him and the help they afforded him during his long imprisonment in Caesarea and Jerusalem.

Took joyfully the spoiling of your goods. They were deprived of their inheritances, turned out of their houses, and plundered of their goods; "they wandered about in sheepskins and goatskins; being destitute, afflicted, tormented." To suffer such persecution patiently was great; to endure it without a murmur was greater; to rejoice in it was greatest of all. But how could they do all this? The next clause informs us. *Knowing in yourselves.* They had the fullest evidence that they were the children of God, the Spirit itself bearing this witness to their spirits; "and if children then heirs; heirs of God, and joint-heirs with Christ." They knew that heaven was their portion, and that to it they had a sure right and indefeasible title by Christ Jesus. This accounts, and this alone can account, for their taking joyfully the spoiling of their goods.

35. *Cast not away therefore your confidence.* "Your liberty of access" to God; your title and right to approach His throne; your birthright as His sons and daughters; and the clear evidence you have of His favor, which, if you be not steady and faithful, you must lose. "Do not throw it away." There is a reference here to cowardly soldiers who throw away their shields and run away from the battle.
Great recompence of reward. No less than God's continual approbation, the peace that passeth all understanding ruling the heart here, and the glories of heaven as an eternal portion. Conscientiously keep the shield, and all these shall be yours. This will be your *reward.*

36. *Ye have need of patience.* Having so great a fight of sufferings to pass through, and they of so long continuance. God furnishes the grace; you must exercise it. *Patience* and "perseverance" are nearly the same. *Have done the will of God.* By keeping the faith and patiently suffering for it.

37. *For yet a little while.* "For yet a very little time." In a very short space of time the Messiah will come, and execute judgment upon your rebellious country. This is determined, because they have filled up the measure of their iniquity, and their destruction slumbereth not. The apostle seems to refer to Hab. ii. 3-4, and accommodates the words to his own purpose.

38. *Now the just shall live by faith.* "But the just by faith," i.e., he who is justified by faith, *shall live*—shall be preserved when this overflowing scourge shall come. *But if any man draw back.* "But if he draw back"; he, the man who is justified by faith; for it is of him, and none other, that the text speaks. The insertion of the words *any man,* if done to serve the purpose of a particular creed, is a wicked perversion of the words of God. They were evidently intended to turn away the relative

MATTHEW HENRY

Apostasy is the mark of those in whom God takes no pleasure; and it is a cause of God's severe displeasure and anger.

The apostle concludes with declaring his good hope concerning himself and these Hebrews (*v.* 39). Professors may go a great way, and after all draw back; and this drawing back from God is drawing on to perdition: the further we depart from God the nearer we approach to ruin. Those who have been kept faithful in great trials for the time past have reason to hope that the same grace will be sufficient to help them still to live by faith. If we live by faith, and die in faith, our souls will be safe for ever.

JAMIESON, FAUSSET, BROWN

continue to *live* (Luke 4:4). The *faith* meant here is that fully developed living trust in the unseen (ch. 11:1) Saviour, which can keep men steadfast amidst persecutions and temptations (vss. 34-36). **but**—*Greek*, "and." **if** *any man* **draw back**—So the *Greek* admits: though it might also be translated, as ALFORD approves, "if *he* (the just man) draw back." Even so, it would not disprove the final perseverance of saints. For "the just man" in this latter clause would mean one seemingly, and in part really, though not savingly, "just" or *justified:* as in Ezekiel 18:24, 26. In the *Hebrew,* this latter half of the verse stands first, and is, "Behold, his soul which is lifted up, is not upright in him." Habakkuk states the *cause* of drawing back: *a soul lifted up,* and in self-inflated unbelief setting itself up against God. Paul, by the Spirit, states the *effect*, it *draws back*. Also, what in Habakkuk is, "His soul is not upright in him," is in Paul, "My soul shall have no pleasure in him." Habakkuk states the *cause,* Paul the effect: He who is not right in his own soul, does not stand right with God; God has no pleasure in him. BENGEL translates Habakkuk, "His soul is not upright in *respect to him,"* viz., Christ, the subject of "the vision," i.e., *Christ has no pleasure in him* (cf. ch. 12:25). Every flower in spring is not a fruit in autumn. **39.** A Pauline elegant turning-off from denunciatory warnings to charitable hopes of his readers (Rom. 8:12). **saving of the soul**—lit., "acquisition (or *obtaining*) of the soul." The kindred *Greek* verb is applied to Christ's *acquiring* the Church as the *purchase* of His blood (Acts 20:28). If we *acquire* or *obtain* our soul's salvation, it is through **Him** who has obtained it for us by His blood-shedding. "The unbelieving man *loses his soul:* for not being God's, neither is he his own [cf. Matt. 16:26 with Luke 9:25]: faith saves the soul by linking it to God" [DELITZSCH *in* ALFORD].

ADAM CLARKE

from the antecedent, in order to save the doctrine of final and unconditional perseverance, which doctrine this text destroys. *My soul shall have no pleasure in him.* My very heart shall be opposed to him who makes shipwreck of faith and a good conscience. The word *hypostellein* signifies not only to *draw back,* but to "slink away and hide through fear." In this sense it is used by the very best Greek writers, as well as by Josephus and Philo.

39. *But we are not of them who draw back.* "We are not the cowards, but the courageous." I have no doubt of this being the meaning of the apostle, and the form of speech requires such a translation; it occurs more than once in the New Testament. We are not cowards who slink away, and notwithstanding meet destruction; but we are faithful, and have our souls saved alive.. The words signify the "preservation of the life." He intimates that, notwithstanding the persecution was hot, yet they should escape with their lives. It is very remarkable, and I have more than once called the reader's attention to it, that not one Christian life was lost in the siege and destruction of Jerusalem. Every Jew perished, or was taken captive; all those who had apostatized and slunk away from Christianity perished with them; all the genuine Christians escaped with their lives. This very important information, which casts light on many passages in the New Testament, and manifests the grace and providence of God in a very conspicuous way, is given by Eusebius: "When the whole congregation of the Church in Jerusalem, according to an oracle given by revelation to the approved persons among them before the war, were commanded to depart from the city, and inhabit a certain city which they call Pella, beyond Jordan, to which, when all those who believed in Christ had removed from Jerusalem, and when the saints had totally abandoned the royal city which is the metropolis of the Jews; then the Divine vengeance seized them who had dealt so wickedly with Christ and his apostles, and utterly destroyed that wicked and abominable generation."

MATTHEW HENRY — CHAPTER 11

Verses 1–3

I. A definition of the grace of faith in two parts. It *is the substance of things hoped for*. Faith and hope go together; and the same things that are the object of our hope are the object of our faith. It is a firm persuasion and expectation that God will perform all that he has promised to us in Christ. Believers in the exercise of faith *are filled with joy unspeakable and full of glory.*

It is *the evidence of things not seen.* Faith demonstrates to the eye of the mind the reality of those things that cannot be discerned by the eye of the body. It is designed to serve the believer instead of sight, and to be to the soul all that the senses are to the body.

JAMIESON, FAUSSET, BROWN — CHAPTER 11

VSS. 1-40. DEFINITION OF THE FAITH JUST SPOKEN OF (ch. 10:39): EXAMPLES FROM THE OLD COVENANT FOR OUR PERSEVERANCE IN FAITH. **1.** *Description* of the great things which *faith* (in its widest sense: not here restricted to *faith* in the Gospel sense) does for us. Not a full *definition* of faith in its whole nature, but a description of its great characteristics in relation to the subject of Paul's exhortation here, viz., to perseverance. **substance . . .**—It substantiates promises of God which we hope for, as future in fulfilment, making them present realities to us. However, the *Greek* is translated in ch. 3:14, "confidence"; and it also here mav mean "sure confidence." By *faith* alone we are sure of eternal things that they ARE: but by *hope* we are confident that WE SHALL HAVE them. All hope presupposes faith (Rom. 8:25). **evidence**—"demonstration": convincing proof to the believer: the soul thereby seeing what the eye cannot see. **things not seen**—the whole invisible and spiritual world; not things future and things pleasant, as the "things hoped for," but also the past and present, and those the reverse of pleasant. "Eternal life is promised to us, but it is when we are dead: we are told of a blessed resurrection, but meanwhile we moulder in the dust; we are declared to be justified, and sin dwells in us; we hear that we are blessed, meantime we are overwhelmed in endless miseries: we are promised abundance of all goods, but we still endure hunger and thirst; God declares He will immediately come to our help, but He seems deaf to our cries. What should we do if we had not faith and hope to lean on, and if our mind did not emerge amidst the darkness above the world by the shining of the Word and Spirit of God?" [CALVIN]. Faith is an assent unto truths credible upon the testimony of God [not on the *reasonableness* of the thing revealed, though by this we may judge as to whether it be what it professes, a genuine revelation], delivered unto us in the writings of the apostles and prophets. Thus Christ's ascension is the cause, and His absence the crown, of our faith: because He ascended, we the more believe, and because we believe in Him who hath ascended, our faith is the more accepted [BISHOP PEARSON]. Faith believes what it sees not;

ADAM CLARKE — CHAPTER 11

1. *Faith is the substance of things hoped for.* "Faith is the subsistence of things hoped for," "the demonstration of things not seen." The word *hypostasis,* which we translate **substance** signifies "subsistence," that which becomes a foundation for another thing to stand on. And *elenchos (evidence)* signifies such a "conviction" as it produced in the mind by the "demonstration" of a problem, after which demonstration no doubt can remain, because we see from it that the thing is, that it cannot but be, and that it cannot be otherwise than as it is and is proved to be. Such is the faith by which the soul is justified; or rather, such are the effects of justifying faith. *Elenchos* is defined by logicians, "A demonstration of the certainty of a thing by sure arguments and indubitable reasons." Aristotle uses it for a mathematical demonstration, and properly defines it thus: "Elenchos, or Demonstration, is that which cannot be otherwise, but is so as we assert."

Things hoped for are the peace and approbation of God, and those blessings by which the soul is prepared for the kingdom of Heaven. A penitent hopes for the pardon of his sins and the favor of his God; faith in Christ puts him in possession of this pardon, and thus the thing that was hoped for is enjoyed by faith. In an extended sense the *things hoped for* are the resurrection of the body, the new heavens and the new earth, the introduction of believers into the heavenly country, and the possession of eternal glory. The things unseen, as distinguished from the things hoped for, are, in an extended sense, the creation of the world from nothing, the destruction of the world by the deluge, the miraculous conception of Christ, His resurrection from the dead, His ascension to glory, His mediation at the right hand of God, His government of the universe, etc., all which we as firmly believe on the testimony of God's Word as if we had seen them. But this faith has particular respect to the being, good-

MATTHEW HENRY

II. An account of the honour it reflects upon all those who have lived in the exercise of it (*v.* 2). True faith is an old grace, and has the best plea to antiquity: it is not a new invention, a modern fancy. The eldest and best men that ever were in the world were believers. They were an honour to their faith, and their faith was an honour to them. It put them upon doing *the things that were of good report.*

III. We have here one of the first articles of faith, the creation of the *worlds by the word of God,* not out of pre-existent matter, but out of nothing, *v.* 3. The grace of faith has a retrospect as well as prospect; it looks not only forward to the end of the world, but back to the beginning of the world. Now what does faith give us to understand concerning *the worlds.* 1. *That these worlds were* not eternal, nor did they produce themselves, but they were made by another. 2. That the maker of the worlds is God. 3. That God made the world by his word and by his active will. 4. That the world was thus framed out of nothing. These things we understand by faith.

Verses 4–31

The apostle now proceeds to set before us some illustrious examples of it in the Old Testament times, and these may be divided into two classes: 1. Those whose names are mentioned, and the particular actings of whose faith are specified. 2. Those whose names are barely mentioned, and an account given in general of the exploits of their faith.

I. The leading instance and example of faith here recorded is that of Abel. It begins with Abel, one who lived by faith, and died for it, and therefore a fit pattern for the Hebrews to imitate.

1. *He offered up a more acceptable sacrifice than Cain.* After the fall, God opened a new way for the children of men to return to him in religious worship. After the fall, God must be worshipped by sacrifices. Cain was the elder brother, but Abel has the preference. It is not seniority of birth, but grace, that makes men truly honourable. Abel brought a sacrifice of atonement, *brought of the firstlings of the flock.* Cain brought only a sacrifice of acknowledgment, a mere thank-offering, *the fruit of the ground.*

2. What Abel gained by his faith. In this place we are told that he obtained by his faith some special advantages: *Witness that he was righteous.* God gave witness to the righteousness of his person, by testifying his acceptance of his gifts. *By it he, being dead, yet speaketh.* He had the honour to leave behind him an instructive speaking case; and what does it speak to us? That fallen man has leave to go in to worship God, with hope of acceptance. That God will not suffer the injuries done to his people to remain unpunished, nor their sufferings unrewarded.

JAMIESON, FAUSSET, BROWN

for if thou seest there is no faith; the Lord has gone away so as not to be seen: He is hidden that He may be believed; the yearning desire by faith after Him who is unseen is the preparation of a heavenly mansion for us; when He shall be seen it shall be given to us as the reward of faith [AUGUSTINE]. As Revelation deals with spiritual and invisible things exclusively, faith is the faculty needed by us, since it is the evidence of things not seen. By faith we venture our eternal interests on the bare word of God, and this is altogether reasonable. **2. For**—So high a description of faith is not undeserved; for . . . [ALFORD]. **by it**—*Greek,* "in it": in respect to . . . in the matter of," it, "or, as *Greek* more emphatically, "this." **the elders**—as though still living and giving their powerful testimony to the reasonableness and excellence of faith (ch. 12:1). "The elders," as "the fathers," is a title of honor given on the ground of their bright faith and practice. **obtained a good report**—*Greek,* "were testified of," viz., favorably (cf. ch. 7:8). It is a phrase of Luke, Paul's companion. Not only men, but God, gave testimony to their faith (vss. 4, 5, 39). Thus they being testified of themselves have become "witnesses" to all others (ch. 12:1). **3. we understand**—We perceive with our spiritual intelligence the fact of the world's creation by God, though we see neither Him nor the act of creation as described in Genesis 1. The natural world could not, without revelation, teach us this truth, though it confirms the truth when apprehended by faith (Rom. 1:20). Adam is passed over in silence here as to his faith, perhaps as being the first who fell and brought sin on us all; though it does not follow that he did not repent and believe the promise. **worlds**—lit., "ages"; all that exists in time and space, visible and invisible, present and eternal. **framed**—"fitly formed and consolidated"; including the creation of the single parts and the harmonious organization of the whole, and the continual providence which maintains the whole throughout all ages. **by the word of God**—not here, the *personal* word (*Greek, logos.* John 1:1) but *the spoken word* (*Greek, rhema*); though by the instrumentality of the personal word (ch. 1:2). **not made . . .**—Translate as *Greek,* "so that not out of things which appear hath that which is seen been made"; not as in the case of all things which we see reproduced from previously existing and visible materials, as, for instance, the plant from the seed, the animal from the parent, etc., has the visible world sprung into being from apparent materials. So also it is implied in the first clause of the verse that the invisible spiritual worlds were framed not from previously existing materials. We were not spectators of creation; it is by faith we perceive it. **4. more excellent sacrifice**—because offered in *faith.* Now *faith* must have some *revelation of God* on which it fastens. The revelation in this case was doubtless God's command to sacrifice *animals* ("the firstlings of the flock") in token of the forfeiture of men's life by sin, and as a type of the promised bruiser of the serpent's head (Gen. 3:15), the one coming sacrifice; this command is implied in God's having made coats of skin for Adam and Eve (Gen. 3:21): for these skins must have been taken from animals slain *in sacrifice;* inasmuch as it was not for *food* they were slain, animal food not being permitted till after the flood; nor for mere *clothing,* as, were it so, clothes might have been made of the fleeces without the needless cruelty of killing the animal; but a coat of skin put on Adam from a sacrificed animal typified the covering or atonement (the *Hebrew* for *atone* means to *cover*) resulting from Christ's sacrifice. The sacrifice seems to have been a holocaust, and the sign of the divine acceptance of it was probably the consumption of it by fire from heaven (Gen. 15:17). Hence, "to accept" a burnt sacrifice is in *Hebrew* "to turn it to ashes" (*Margin,* Ps. 20:3). A flame seems to have issued from the Shekinah, or flaming cherubim, east of Eden ("the presence of the Lord," Gen. 4:16), where the first sacrifices were offered. Cain, in unbelieving self-righteousness, presented merely a *thank offering,* not like Abel feeling his need of the propitiatory sacrifice appointed on account of sin. God "had respect (first) unto Abel, and (then) to his offering" (Gen. 4:4). Faith causes the believer's person to be accepted, and then his offering. Even an animal sacrifice, though of God's appointment, would not have been accepted, had it not been offered in faith. **he obtained witness**—*God* by fire attesting His acceptance of him as "righteous by faith." **his gifts**—the common term for *sacrifices,* implying that they must be freely *given.* **by it**—by faith exhibited in his animal sacrifice. **dead, yet speaketh**—His *blood crying from the ground to God,* shows how precious,

ADAM CLARKE

ness, providence, grace, and mercy of God, as the subsequent verses sufficiently show.

2. *For by it the elders obtained a good report.* By the *elders* are meant "ancestors, forefathers," such as the patriarchs and prophets, several of whom he afterwards particularly names and produces some fact from the history of their lives. It is very remarkable that among the whole there is not one word concerning poor Adam and his wife, though both Abraham and Sarah are mentioned. There was no good report concerning them; not a word of their repentance, faith, or holiness. The word which we translate *obtained a good report* literally signifies "were witnessed of"; and thus leads us naturally to God, who by His Word, as the succeeding parts of the chapter show, bore testimony to the faith and holiness of His servants. The apostle does not mention one of whom an account is not given in the Old Testament. This therefore is God's witness or testimony concerning them.

3. *Through faith we understand.* By *worlds* we are to understand the material fabric of the universe: and as the word is used in the plural number, it may comprehend, not only the earth and visible heavens, but the whole planetary system; the different worlds which, in our system at least, revolve round the sun. The apostle states that these things were not made out of a preexistent matter.

4. *By faith Abel offered unto God a more excellent sacrifice.* "More sacrifice"; as if he had said: Abel, by faith, made more than one offering; and hence it is said, God testified of his gifts. The plain state of the case seems to have been this: Cain and Abel both brought offerings to the altar of God, probably the altar erected for the family worship. As Cain was a husbandman, he brought a eucharistic offering, of the fruits of the ground, by which he acknowledged the being and providence of God. Abel, being a shepherd or a feeder of cattle, brought, not only the eucharistic offering, but also of the produce of his flock as a sin offering to God, by which he acknowledged his own sinfulnsss, God's justice and mercy, as well as His being and providence. Cain, not at all apprehensive of the demerit of sin or God's holiness, contented himself with the thank offering. This God could not, consistently with His holiness and justice, receive with complacency; the other, as referring to Him who was the Lamb slain from the foundation of the world, God could receive, and did particularly testify His approbation. Now by this faith, thus exercised, in reference to an atonement, he, Abel, though "dead, yet speaketh"; i.e., preacheth to mankind the necessity of an atonement, and that God will accept no sacrifice unless connected with this.

MATTHEW HENRY

II. The faith of Enoch, *v.* 5.

1. What is here reported of him. (1) *He walked with God.* (2) *He was translated, that he should not see death,* nor any part of him be found upon earth. (3) *Before his translation he had this testimony, that he pleased God.* He had the evidence of it in his own conscience, and the Spirit of God witnessed with his spirit.

2. What is here said of his faith, *v.* 6. We cannot please God without such a faith as helps us to walk with God, an active faith. God is again to be found of us through Christ. God has prescribed means and ways wherein he may be found.

Those who would find God must *seek him diligently*; and when once they have found him, they will never repent the pains they have spent in seeking after him.

III. The faith of Noah, *v.* 7.

1. The ground of Noah's faith—a warning he had received from God of things as yet not seen. God usually warns sinners before he strikes, and, where his warnings are slighted, the blow will fall the heavier.

2. The actings of Noah's faith, and the influence it had both upon his mind and practice. He was *moved with fear.* Faith first influences our affections, then our actions; and faith works upon those affections that are suitable to the matter revealed. If it be some good thing, faith stirs up love and desire; if some evil thing, faith stirs up fear. His faith influenced his practice. His fear moved him to prepare an ark. His faith set him to work in earnest.

3. The rewards of Noah's faith. (1) Hereby himself and his house were saved, when a whole world of sinners were perishing about them. (2) Hereby he judged and condemned the world; his holy fear condemned their vain confidence; his faith condemned their unbelief; his obedience condemned their contempt. Good examples will either convert sinners or condemn them. This is the best way the people of God can take to condemn the wicked; not by harsh and censorious language, but by a holy exemplary conversation. (3) Hereby *he became an heir of the righteousness which is by faith.* He was possessed of a true justifying righteousness; he was *heir to it.*

IV. The faith of Abraham, the friend of God, and father of the faithful, in whom the Hebrews boasted. The apostle enlarges more upon the heroic achievements of Abraham's faith than of that of any other of the patriarchs; and in the midst of his account of the faith of Abraham he inserts the story of Sarah's faith.

1. The ground of Abraham's faith, the call and promise of God, *v.* 8. (1) This call was the call of God. This was an effectual call, by which he was converted from the idolatry of his father's house, Gen. xii. 1. The grace of God is absolutely free, in taking some of the worst of men. God must come to us before we come to him. This calls us not only to leave sin, but sinful company. (2) The promise of God. God promised Abraham that the place he was called to he should afterwards receive for an inheritance. God calls his people to an inheritance. This inheritance is not immediately possessed by them, but the promise is sure.

2. The exercise of Abraham's faith. *He went out, not knowing whither he went.* He put himself into the hand of God, to send him whithersoever he pleased. All that are effectually called resign up their own will and wisdom to the will and wisdom of God. Though they know not always their way, yet they know their guide. *He sojourned in the land of promise as in a strange country.* This was an exercise of his faith. Abraham lived in Canaan as a sojourner only. He dwelt in tabernacles with Isaac and Jacob, heirs

JAMIESON, FAUSSET, BROWN

because of his "faith," he was still in God's sight, even when dead. So he becomes a witness to us of the blessed effects of faith. **5.** *Faith* was the ground of his *pleasing God;* and his *pleasing God* was the ground of his *translation.* **translated**—(Gen. 5:22, 24). Implying a *sudden* removal (the same *Greek* as in Galatians 1:6) from mortality without death to immortality: such a CHANGE as shall pass over the living at Christ's coming (I Cor. 15:51, 52). **had this testimony**—viz., of Scripture; the *Greek* perfect implies that this testimony continues still: "he *has* been testified of." **pleased God**—The Scripture testimony virtually expresses that he *pleased God,* viz., "Enoch walked with God." LXX translates the *Hebrew* for "walked with God," Genesis 6:9, *pleased God.* **6. without**—*Greek,* "*apart from* faith": if one be destitute of faith (cf. Rom. 14:23). **to please**—Translate, as ALFORD does, the *Greek* aorist, "It is impossible to please God *at all*" (Rom. 8:8). Natural amiabilities and "works done before the grace of Christ are not pleasant to God, forasmuch as they spring not of faith in Jesus Christ; yea, rather, for that they are not done as God hath willed them to be done, we doubt not but they have the nature of sin" [Article XIII, *Book of Common Prayer*]. Works not rooted in God are splendid sins [AUGUSTINE]. **he that cometh to God**—as a worshipper (ch. 7:19). **must believe**—*once for all: Greek* aorist. **that God is**—IS: is the true self-existing Jehovah (as contrasted with all so-called gods, not gods, Gal. 4:8), the source of all being, though he sees Him not (vs. 1) as being "invisible" (vs. 27). So Enoch; this passage implies that he had not been favored with *visible* appearances of God, yet he *believed* in God's *being,* and in God's *moral government,* as the Rewarder of His diligent worshippers, in opposition to antediluvian skepticism. Also Moses was not so favored before he left Egypt the first time (vs. 27); still he believed. **and . . . is**—a different *Greek* verb from the former "is." Translate, "is eventually"; *proves to be;* lit., "becomes." **rewarder**—renderer of reward [ALFORD]. So God proved to be to Enoch. The reward is *God Himself* diligently "sought" and "walked with" in partial communion here, and to be fully enjoyed hereafter. Cf. Genesis 15:1, "I am thy exceeding great reward." **of them**—and them only. **diligently seek**—*Greek,* "seek out" God. Cf. "seek *early,*" Proverbs 8:17. Not only "ask" and "seek," but "knock," Matthew 7:7; cf. ch. 11:12; Luke 13:24, "Strive" as in an agony of contest. **7. warned of God**—The same **Greek,** ch. 8:5, "admonished of God." **moved with fear**—not mere slavish fear, but as in *Note,* ch. 5:7; *Greek,* "reverential fear": opposed to the world's sneering disbelief of the revelation, and self-deceiving security. Join "by faith" with "prepared an ark" (I Pet. 3:20). **by the which**—faith. **condemned the world**—For since he believed and was saved, so might they have believed and been saved, so that their condemnation by God is by his case shown to be just. **righteousness which is by faith**—*Greek,* "according to faith." A Pauline thought. Noah is first called "righteous" in Genesis 6:9. Christ calls Abel so, Matthew 23:35. Cf. as to Noah's righteousness, Ezekiel 14:14, 20; II Peter 2:5, "a preacher of righteousness." Paul here makes *faith* the principle and ground of his righteousness. **heir**—the consequence of sonship which flows from faith. **8.** From the antediluvian saints he passes to the patriarchs of Israel, to whom "the promises" belonged. **called**—by God (Gen. 12:1). The oldest MSS. and *Vulgate* read, "He that was called Abraham," his name being changed from Abram to Abraham, on the occasion of God's making with him and his seed a covenant sealed by circumcision, many years after his call out of Ur. "By faith, he who was (afterwards) called Abraham (*father of nations,* Gen. 17:5, in order to become which was the design of God's bringing him out of Ur) obeyed (the command of God: to be understood in this reading), *so as to go out. . . .*" **which he should after receive**—He had not fully received even this promise when he went out, for it was not *explicitly* given him till he had reached Canaan (Gen. 12:1, 6, 7). When the promise of the land was given him the Canaanite was still in the land, and himself a stranger; it is in the new heaven and new earth that he shall receive his personal inheritance promised him; so believers sojourn on earth as strangers, while the ungodly and Satan lord it over the earth; but at Christ's coming that same earth which was the scene of the believer's conflict shall be the inheritance of Christ and His saints. **9. sojourned**—as a "stranger and pilgrim." **in**—*Greek,* "into," i.e., he went *into* it and sojourned there. **as in a strange country**—a country *not belonging to him,* but to others (so the *Greek*), Acts 7:5, 6. **dwel-**

ADAM CLARKE

5. ***By faith Enoch was translated.*** **It is said, in Gen. v. 24, that Enoch walked with God, and "he was not; for God took him." Here the apostle explains what God's taking him means, by saying that he *was translated that he should not see death;* from which we learn that he did not die, and that God took him to a state of blessedness without obliging him to pass through death. See his history explained at large in the above place, in Gen. v. 22-24.**

6. ***He that cometh to God.*** **The man who professes that it is his duty to worship God must, if he act rationally, do it on the conviction that there is such a Being, infinite, eternal, unoriginated, and self-existent; the Cause of all other being; on whom all being depends; and by whose energy, bounty, and providence all other beings exist, live, and are supplied with the means of continued existence and life. He must believe also that He rewards *them that diligently seek him;* that He is not indifferent about His own worship; that He requires adoration and religious service from men; and that He blesses and especially protects and saves those who in simplicity and uprightness of heart seek and serve Him. This requires faith, such a faith as is mentioned above; a faith by which we can *please* God; and now that we have an abundant revelation, a faith according to that revelation; a faith in God through Christ, the great Sin Offering, without which a man can no more please Him or be accepted of Him than Cain was.**

7. ***By faith Noah.*** **See the whole of this history, Gen. vi. 13. *Warned of God.* As we know from the history in Genesis that God did "warn" Noah, we see from this the real import of the verb as used in various parts of the New Testament; it signifies "to utter oracles, to give divine warning." *Moved with fear.* "Influenced by religious fear or reverence towards God." This is mentioned to show that he acted not from a fear of losing his life, but from the fear of God, and hence that fear is here properly attributed to faith. *He condemned the world.* He credited God; they did not. He walked in the way God had commanded; they did not. He repeatedly admonished them, I Pet. iii. 20; they regarded it not. This aggravated their crimes, while it exalted his faith and righteousness. *Became heir of the righteousness.* He became entitled to that justification which is by faith, and his temporal deliverance was a pledge of the salvation of his soul.**

8. ***Abraham, when he was called.*** **See on Gen. xii. 1-4. *Not knowing whither he went.* Therefore his obedience was the fullest proof of his faith in God, and his faith was an implicit faith. He obeyed, and went out from his own country, having no prospect of any good or success but what his implicit faith led him to expect from God, as the "rewarder of them that diligently seek him." In all the preceding cases, and in all that follow, the apostle keeps this maxim fully in view.**

9. ***By faith he sojourned in the land of promise.*** **It is remarkable that Abraham did not acquire any right in Canaan except that of a burying place; nor did he build any house in**

MATTHEW HENRY

with him of the same promise. The promise is made to believers and their children, and it is pleasant to see parents and children sojourning together in this world as heirs of the heavenly inheritance.

3. The supports of Abraham's faith (*v.* 10). It is a city that hath foundations, even the immutable purposes and almighty power of God. The due regard that Abraham had to this heavenly city: he looked for it. He waited for it, and in the mean time he conversed in it by faith. It was a support to him under all the trials of his sojourning state.

V. The faith of Sarah.

1. The difficulties of Sarah's faith. The prevalency of unbelief for a time: she laughed at the promise, as impossible to be made good. The great improbability of the thing promised, that she should be the mother of a child.

2. The actings of her faith. Her unbelief is pardoned and forgotten, but her faith prevailed and is recorded, *v.* 11.

3. The rewards of her faith. *She received strength to conceive seed.* He can make the barren soul fruitful, as well as the barren womb. *She was delivered of a child,* a child of the promise. From them, by this son, sprang a numerous progeny of illustrious persons, *as the stars of the sky* (*v.* 12).

VI. The faith of the other patriarchs, *v.* 13.

1. The trial of their faith. They had not received the promises. One imperfection of the present state of the saints on earth is that their happiness lies more in promise than in actual enjoyment and possession.

2. The actings of their faith. Though they had not received the promises, yet,

(1) They saw them afar off. Faith has a clear and a strong eye, and can see promised mercies at a great distance.

(2) They were persuaded of them, that they were true and should be fulfilled.

(3) They embraced them. Faith has a long arm, and can lay hold of blessings at a great distance.

(4) They *confessed that they were strangers and pilgrims on earth.* They are strangers as saints, whose home is heaven; they are pilgrims as they are travelling towards their home.

(5) Hereby they declared plainly that they sought another country (*v.* 14), heaven.

(6) They gave full proof of their sincerity. They were not mindful of that country whence they came, *v.* 15. Those that are once savingly called out of a sinful state have no mind to return into it again; they now know better things. They did not take the opportunity that offered itself for their return. But they steadfastly adhered to God. We must show the truth of our faith and profession by a steady adherence to him. Their sincerity appeared not only in not returning to their former country, but in desiring a better country, that is, a heavenly. All true believers desire this better country. The stronger faith is the more fervent those desires will be.

(7) They died in the faith of those promises, *v.* 13. That faith held out to the last.

JAMIESON, FAUSSET, BROWN

ling in tabernacles—*tents:* as *strangers* and *sojourners* do: moving from place to place, as having no fixed possession of their own. In contrast to the abiding "city" (vs. 10). **with**—Their kind of dwelling being the same is a proof that their faith was the same. They all alike were content to wait for their good things hereafter (Luke 16:25). Jacob was fifteen years old at the death of Abraham. **heirs with him of the same promise**—Isaac did not inherit it from Abraham, nor Jacob from Isaac, but they all inherited it from God directly as "fellow heirs." **10. looked for**—*Greek,* "he was expecting"; waiting for with eager expectation (Rom. 8:19). **a city**—*Greek, "the* city," already alluded to. Worldly Enoch, son of the murderer Cain, was the first to build his *city* here: the godly patriarchs waited for their city hereafter (vs. 16; ch. 12:22; 13:14). **foundations**—*Greek, "the* foundations" which the *tents* had not, nor even men's present cities have. **whose builder and maker**—*Greek, "designer* [Eph. 1:4, 11] and master-builder," or *executor of the design.* The city is worthy of its Framer and Builder (cf. vs. 16; ch. 8:2). Cf. "found," *Note,* ch. 12. **11. also Sara herself**—though being the weaker vessel, and though at first she doubted. **was delivered of a child**—omitted in the oldest MSS.: then translate, "and that when she was past age" (Rom. 4:19). **she judged him faithful who had promised**—after she had ceased to doubt, being instructed by the angel that it was no jest, but a matter in serious earnest. **12. as good as dead**—lit., "deadened"; no longer having, as in youth, energetic vital powers. **stars ... sand**—(Gen. 22:17). **13-16.** Summary of the characteristic excellencies of the patriarchs' faith. **died in faith**—died as *believers,* waiting for, not actually *seeing* as yet their good things promised to them. They were true to this principle of *faith* even unto, and especially in, their dying hour (cf. vs. 20). **These all**—beginning with "Abraham" (vs. 8), to whom *the promises were made* (Gal. 3:16), and who is alluded to in the end of vs. 13 and in vs. 15 [BENGEL and ALFORD]. But the "ALL" can hardly but include Abel, Enoch, and Noah. Now as these did not receive the promise of entering literal Canaan, *some other promise made in the first ages,* and often repeated, must be that meant, viz., the promise of a coming Redeemer made to Adam, viz., "the seed of the woman shall bruise the serpent's head." Thus the promises cannot have been merely temporal, for Abel and Enoch mentioned here received no temporal promise [ARCHBISHOP MAGEE]. This promise of eternal redemption is the inner essence of the promises made to Abraham (Gal. 3:16). **not having received**—It was this that constituted their "faith." If they had "received" THE THING PROMISED (so "the promises" here mean: the plural is used because of the *frequent renewal* of the promise to the patriarchs: verse 17 says he *did* receive the *promises,* but not *the thing promised*), it would have been *sight,* not *faith.* **seen them afar off**—(John 8:56). Christ, as the Word, was preached to the Old Testament believers, and so became the seed of life to their souls, as He is to ours. **and were persuaded of them**—The oldest MSS. omit this clause. **embraced them**—as though they were not "afar off," but within reach, so as to draw them to themselves and clasp them in their embrace. **confessed ... were strangers**—so Abraham to the children of Heth (Gen. 23:4); and Jacob to Pharaoh (Gen. 47:9; Ps. 119:19). Worldly men hold fast the world; believers sit loose to it. *Citizens of the world* do not confess themselves "strangers on the earth." **pilgrims**—*Greek,* "temporary (lit., by the way) sojourners." **on the earth**—contrasted with "an heavenly" (vs. 16): "our *citizenship* is in heaven" (*Greek:* ch. 10:34; Ps. 119:54; Phil. 3: 20). "Whosoever professes that he has a Father in heaven, confesses himself a stranger on earth; hence there is in the heart an ardent longing, like that of a child living among strangers, in want and grief, far from his fatherland" [LUTHER]. "Like ships in seas while *in, above* the world." **14. For**—proof that "faith" (vs. 13) was their actuating principle. **declare plainly**—make it plainly evident. **seek**—*Greek,* "seek *after*"; implying the direction towards which their desires ever tend. **a country**—rather as *Greek,* "a fatherland." In confessing themselves *strangers* here, they evidently imply that they regard not this as their home or fatherland, but seek after another and a better. **15.** As Abraham, had he desired to leave his pilgrim life in Canaan, and resume his former fixed habitation in Ur, among the carnal and worldly, had in his long life ample opportunities to have done so; and so spiritually, as to all believers who came out from the world to become God's people, they might, if they had been

ADAM CLARKE

it. His faith showed him that it was only a type and pledge of a better country, and he kept that better country continually in view. He, *with Isaac and Jacob,* who were *heirs . . . of the same promise,* were contented to dwell in tents, without any fixed habitation.

10. *For he looked for a city which hath foundations.* He knew that earth could afford no permanent residence for an immortal mind, and he looked for that heavenly building of which God is the Architect and Owner. *Whose builder and maker is God.* The word *technites* signifies an "architect," one who plans, calculates, and constructs a building. The word *demiourgos* signifies the "governor of a people," one who forms them by institutions and laws, the framer of a political constitution. God is here represented the Maker or Father of all the heavenly inhabitants, and the Planner of their citizenship in that heavenly country.

11. *Through faith also Sara.* Her history, as far as the event here is concerned, may be seen in Gen. xvii. 19 and xxi. 2. Sarah at first treated the divine message with ridicule, judging it to be absolutely impossible, not knowing then that it was from God; and this her age and circumstances justified, for, humanly speaking, such an event was impossible. But when she knew that it was God who said this, it does not appear that she doubted anymore, but implicitly believed that what God had promised He was able to perform.

12. *Him as good as dead.* According to nature, long past the time of the procreation of children. The birth of Isaac, the circumstances of the father and mother considered, was entirely supernatural; and the people who proceeded from this birth were a supernatural people, and were and are most strikingly singular through every period of their history to the present day.

13. *These all died in faith.* That is, Abraham, Sarah, Isaac, and Jacob continued to believe, to the end of their lives, that God would fulfill this promise; but they neither saw the numerous seed nor did they get the promised rest in Canaan.

Strangers and pilgrims. Strangers, persons who are out of their own country, who are in a foreign land. *Pilgrims,* sojourners only for a time, not intending to take up their abode in that place nor to get naturalized in that country. How many use these expressions, professing to be *strangers and pilgrims* here below, and yet the whole of their conduct, spirit, and attachments show that they are perfectly at home!

14. *Declare plainly that they seek a country.* A man's *country* is that in which he has constitutional rights and privileges; no stranger or sojourner has any such rights in the country where he sojourns. These, by declaring that they felt themselves strangers and sojourners, professed their faith in a heavenly country and state, and looked beyond the grave for a place of happiness.

15. *If they had been mindful of that country.* They considered their right to the promises of God as dependent on their utter renunciation of Chaldea, and it was this that induced Abraham to cause his steward Eliezer to swear that he would not carry his son Isaac to Chaldea; see Gen. xxiv. 5-8. There idolatry reigned; and God had called them to be the patriarchs and progenitors of a people among whom the knowledge of the true God, and the worship required by Him, should be established and preserved.

MATTHEW HENRY

3. The gracious reward of their faith, *v.* 16. He is called their God. He calls himself so; he gives them leave to call him so. God is not ashamed to be called *their God*: such is his love to them. Let them take care that they be not a shame and reproach to their God, and so provoke him to be ashamed of them. As the proof of this, God has prepared for them a city, a happiness suitable to the relation into which he has taken them. If God neither could nor would give his people anything better than this world affords, he would be ashamed to be called their God.

VII. Now after the apostle has given this account of the faith of others, with Abraham, he returns to him again, and gives us an instance of the greatest trial and act of faith that stands upon record. This was his offering up Isaac, *v.* 17.

1. The trial of Abraham's faith. God had before this tempted or tried the faith of Abraham. But this trial was greater than all; he was commanded to offer up his son Isaac. "Take thy son, thy only son by Sarah, Isaac thy laughter, the child of thy joy and delight; take him away to the land of Moriah; do not only leave him there, but offer him for a burnt-offering." Some things that very much added to the greatness of this trial. He was put upon it after he had received the promises (*v.* 18). In being called to offer up his Isaac, he seemed to be called to cut off his own family, to cancel the promises of God. This Isaac was his only-begotten son by his wife Sarah, the only one he was to have by her, and the only one that was to be the child and heir of the promise. Besides his most tender affection to this his son, all his expectations were bound up in him, and, if he perished, must perish with him. To have this son offered up as a sacrifice, and that by his own hand; it was a trial that would have overset the firmest and the strongest mind.

2. The actings of Abraham's faith in so great a trial: he obeyed. He went as far in it as to the very critical moment, and would have gone through with it if God had not prevented him.

3. The supports of his faith, *v.* 19. He knew that God was able to raise him from the dead, and he believed that God would do so. God is able to raise the dead, to raise dead bodies, and to raise dead souls.

4. The reward of his faith in this great trial (*v.* 19). He received his son. He had parted with him to God, and God gave him back again. He received him from the dead, for he gave him up for dead.

VIII. The faith of Isaac, *v.* 20.

1. The actings of his faith: He *blessed Jacob and Esau concerning things to come.* Both Jacob and Esau were blessed as Isaac's children. Jacob had the precedency and the principal blessing. If one has his portion in this world, and the other in the better world, it is God who makes the difference; for even the comforts of this life are more and better than any of the children of men deserve.

2. The difficulties Isaac's faith struggled with. He seemed to have forgotten how God had determined the matter at the birth of these his sons, Gen. xxv. 23. When he came to pronounce the blessing, *he trembled very exceedingly* (Gen. xxvii. 33); and he charged Jacob that he had subtly taken away Esau's blessing. But, notwithstanding all this, Isaac's faith recovered itself, and he ratified the blessing: *I have blessed him, yea, and he shall be blessed.* Now, the faith of Isaac thus prevailing over his unbelief, it has pleased the God of Isaac to pass by the weakness of his faith, to commend the sincerity of it.

IX. The faith of Jacob (*v.* 21). There were a great many instances of the faith of Jacob; his life was a life of faith.

1. The actings of his faith.

(1) *He blessed both the sons of Joseph*, Ephraim and Manasseh. He made them both heads of different tribes, as if they had been his own immediate sons. As Isaac did before, so now Jacob prefers the younger, Ephraim; though Joseph had placed them so that the right hand of his father should be laid on Manasseh, the elder.

JAMIESON, FAUSSET, BROWN

so minded, have easily gone back. **16.** Proving the truth that the old fathers did not, as some assert, "look only for transitory promises" (Article VII, *Book of Common Prayer*). **now**—as the case is. **is not ashamed**—*Greek,* "IS not ashamed of them." Not merely once did God call himself *their God,* but He is NOW not ashamed to have Himself called so, they being *alive* and abiding with Him where He is. Not only is He *not ashamed,* but glories in the name and relation to His people. The "wherefore" does not mean that God's *good pleasure* is the meritorious, but the *gracious,* consequence of their obedience (that obedience being the result of His Spirit's work in them in the first instance). He first so "called" Himself, then they so called Him. **for**—proof of His being "*their* God," viz., "He hath prepared (in His eternal counsels, Matt. 20:23, 25:34, and by the progressive acts of redemption, John 14:2) for them a city," the city in which He Himself reigns, so that their yearning *desires* shall not be disappointed (vss. 14,16). **a city**—on its garniture by God (cf. Rev. 21:10-27). **17. offered up**—lit., "hath offered up," as if the work and its praise were yet enduring [ALFORD]. As far as His intention was concerned, he did sacrifice Isaac; and in actual fact "he offered him," as far as the presentation of him on the altar as an offering to God is concerned. **tried**—*Greek,* "tempted," as in Genesis 22:1. *Put to the proof* of his faith. Not that God "tempts" *to sin,* but God "tempts" in the sense of *proving* or *trying* (Jas. 1:13-15). **and**—and so. **he that had received**—rather as *Greek,* "accepted," i.e., *welcomed* and embraced by faith, not merely "had the promises," as in ch. 7:6. This added to the difficulty in the way of his faith, that it was in Isaac's posterity the promises were to be fulfilled; how then could they be fulfilled if Isaac were sacrificed? **offered up**—rather as *Greek,* "was offering up"; he was in the act of offering. **his only-begotten son**—Cf. Genesis 22:2, "Take now thy son, thine only son." EUSEBIUS, *Præparatio Evangelica,* 1. 10, and 4. 16, has preserved a fragment of a *Greek* translation of Sanchoniatho, which mentions a mystical sacrifice of the Phœnicians, wherein a prince in royal robes was the offerer, and his only son was to be the victim: this evidently was a tradition derived from Abraham's offering, and handed down through Esau or Edom, Isaac's son. Isaac was Abraham's "only-begotten son" in respect of Sarah and the promises: he sent away his other sons, by other wives (Gen. 25:6). Abraham is a type of the Father not sparing His only-begotten Son to fulfil the divine purpose of love. God nowhere in the Mosaic law allowed human sacrifices, though He claimed the firstborn of Israel as His. **18. Of whom**—rather as *Greek* "He (*Abraham,* not Isaac) TO whom it was said" [ALFORD]. BENGEL supports *English Version.* So ch. 1:7 uses the same *Greek* preposition, "unto," for "in respect to," or "of." This verse gives a dіfinition of the "only-begotten Son" (vs. 17). **in Isaac shall thy seed be called**—(Gen. 21:12). The posterity of Isaac alone shall be accounted as the seed of Abraham, which is the heir of the promises (Rom. 9:7). **19.** Faith answered the objections which reason brought against God's command to Abraham to offer Isaac, by suggesting that what God had promised He both could and would perform, however impossible the performance might seem (Rom. 4:20, 21). **able to raise** *him*—rather, in general, "able to raise from the dead." **he received him**—"received him back" [ALFORD]. **in a figure**—*Greek,* "in a parable." ALFORD explains, "Received him back, risen from that death which he had undergone in, under, *the figure of the ram.*"

It was then that Abraham saw Christ's day (John 8:56): accounting God was able to raise even from the dead: from which state of the dead he received him back *as a type of the resurrection in Christ.* **20.** Jacob is put before Esau, as heir of the chief, viz., the *spiritual* blessing. **concerning things to come**—*Greek,* "*even* concerning things to come": not only concerning things present. Isaac, *by faith,* assigned to his sons things future, as if they were present. **21. both the sons**—*Greek,* "*each* of the sons" (Gen. 47:29, 48:8-20). He knew not Joseph's sons, and could not distinguish them by sight, yet *he did distinguish them by faith,* transposing his hands intentionally, so as to lay his right hand on the younger, Ephraim, whose posterity was to be greater than that of Manasseh: he also adopted these grandchildren as his own sons, after having transferred the right of primogeniture to Joseph (Gen. 48:22). **and worshipped . . .**—This did not take place in immediate connection with the foregoing, but before it, when Jacob made Joseph swear that he would bury him with his fathers in

ADAM CLARKE

16. *But now they desire a better.* They all expected spiritual blessings and a heavenly inheritance. They sought God as their Portion, and in such a way and on such principles that He is not *ashamed to be called their God;* and He shows His affection for them by preparing *for them a city,* to wit, heaven, as themselves would seek no city on earth, which is certainly what the apostle has here in view. And from this it is evident that the patriarchs had a proper notion of the immortality of the soul and expected a place of residence widely different from Canaan.

17. *Abraham, when he was tried.* See the history of this whole transaction explained at large in the notes on Gen. xxii. 1-9. *Offered up his only begotten.* Abraham did, in effect, offer up Isaac; he built an altar, bound his son, laid him upon the altar, had ready the incense, took the knife, and would immediately have slain him had he not been prevented by the same authority by which the sacrifice was enjoined. Isaac is here called *his only begotten,* as he was the only son he had by his legitimate wife, who was heir to his property, and heir of the promises of God. The man who proved faithful in such a trial deserved to have his faith and obedience recorded throughout the world.

19. *To raise him up, even from the dead.* Abraham "staggered not at the promise . . . through unbelief; but was strong in faith, giving glory to God." The resurrection of the dead must have been a doctrine of the patriarchs; they expected a heavenly inheritance. They saw they died as did other men, and they must have known that they could not enjoy it but in consequence of a resurrection from the dead. *He received him in a figure. Parabole* sometimes means a "daring exploit, a jeoparding of the life." I think it should be so understood here, as pointing out the very imminent danger he was in of losing his life. The clause may therefore be thus translated: "Accounting that God was able to raise him up from the dead, from whence he had received him, he being in the most imminent danger of losing his life." It is not therefore the natural deadness of Abraham and Sarah to which the apostle alludes, but the death to which Isaac on this occasion was exposed, and which he escaped by the immediate interference of God.

20. *By faith Isaac blessed Jacob and Esau.* He believed that God would fulfill His promise to his posterity, and God gave him to see what would befall them in their future generations. The apostle does not seem to intimate that one should be an object of the divine hatred and the other of divine love in reference to their eternal states.

21. *Blessed both the sons of Joseph.* That is, Ephraim and Manasseh. See the account in Gen. xlviii. 5, etc. *Worshipped, leaning upon the top of his staff.* This subject is particularly considered in the note on Gen. xlvii. 31. It appears that at the time Joseph visited his father

MATTHEW HENRY

(2) *He worshipped, leaning on his staff;* he praised God for what he had done for him, and for the prospect he had of approaching blessedness. He was not able to support himself, so far as to sit up in his bed without a staff, and yet he would not make this an excuse for neglecting the worshipping of God; he would do it as well as he could with his body, as well as with his spirit.

2. When Jacob thus acted his faith: when he was dying. He lived by faith, and he died by faith and in faith.

X. The faith of Joseph, *v.* 22.

1. What he did by his faith. He made mention by faith of the departing of the children of Israel, that the time should come when they should be delivered out of Egypt. Though he should not live to see their deliverance, yet he could die in the faith of it. He gave commandment concerning his bones, that they should preserve them unburied in Egypt. Though he had lived and died in Egypt, yet he did not live and die an Egyptian, but an Israelite. He preferred a significant burial in Canaan before a magnificent one in Egypt.

2. When the faith of Joseph acted after this manner: when he was dying. God often gives his people living comforts in dying moments.

XI. The faith of the parents of Moses. 1. The acting of their faith: they hid this their son three months. Moses was persecuted betimes, and forced to be concealed; in this he was a type of Christ, who was persecuted almost as soon as he was born, and his parents were obliged to flee with him into Egypt for his preservation. 2. The reasons of their thus acting. No doubt, natural affection could not but move them; but there was something further. They *saw he was a proper child.* There appeared in him something uncommon; the beauty of the Lord sat upon him. Sometimes, not always, the countenance is the index of the mind. 3. The prevalency of their faith over their fear. They were not afraid of the king's commandment. They believed that God would preserve his people, and that the time was coming when it would be worth while for an Israelite to live. Some must hazard their own lives to preserve their children, and they were resolved to do it. Faith is a great preservative against the sinful slavish fear of men.

XII. The faith of Moses himself (*v.* 24, 25, &c.).

1. An instance of his faith in conquering the world. (1) He *refused to be called the son of Pharaoh's daughter,* whose foundling he was, and her fondling too. How glorious was the triumph of his faith. He *refused to be called the son of Pharaoh's daughter* lest he should undervalue the truer honour of being a son of Abraham, the father of the faithful; lest it should look like renouncing his religion as well as his relation to Israel; and no doubt both these he must have done if he had accepted this honour.

(2) He was willing to take his lot with the people of God here, though it was a suffering lot, that he might have his portion with them hereafter (*v.* 25). Herein he acted rationally as well as religiously. The pleasures of sin must end in speedy repentance or in speedy ruin. The pleasures of this world, and especially those of a court, are too often the pleasures of sin. A true believer will despise them. Suffering is to be chosen rather than sin, there being more evil in the least sin than there can be in the greatest suffering.

(3) See how Moses weighed matters: in one scale he put the worst of religion—*the reproaches of Christ,* in the other scale the best of the world—*the treasures of Egypt* (*v.* 26). The worst of religion weighed down the best of the world. The reproaches of the church of God are *the reproaches of Christ.* God's people are, and always have been, a reproached people. Christ accounts himself reproached in their reproaches and, while he thus interests himself in their reproaches, they become riches. Faith discerns this, and acts accordingly.

2. The circumstance of time is taken notice of, when Moses by his faith gained this victory (*v.* 24); not only in years of discretion, but of experience, to the age of forty years. He made this choice when he had grown ripe for judgment and enjoyment, able to know what he did and why he did it. It was not the act of a child, but it proceeded from mature deliberation. It is an excellent thing for persons to despise the world when they are most capable of relishing and enjoying it.

3. What it was that supported and strengthened the faith of Moses: *He had respect unto the recompence of reward.* Believers may and ought to have respect to this recompence of reward. It will prove a land-mark to direct their course, a load-stone to draw their hearts, and a cordial to refresh them.

JAMIESON, FAUSSET, BROWN

Canaan, not in Egypt. The assurance that Joseph would do so filled him with pious gratitude to God, which he expressed by raising himself on his bed to an attitude of *worship.* His faith, as Joseph's (vs. 22), consisted in his so confidentially anticipating the fulfilment of God's promise of Canaan to his descendants, as to desire to be buried there as his proper possession. **leaning upon the top of his staff**—Genesis 47:31, *Hebrew* and *English Version,* "upon the bed's head." LXX translates as Paul here. JEROME justly reprobates the notion of modern Rome, that Jacob *worshipped the top of Joseph's staff,* having on it an image of Joseph's power, to which Jacob bowed in recognition of the future sovereignty of his son's tribe, the father bowing to the son! The *Hebrew,* as translated in *English Version,* sets it aside: *the bed* is alluded to afterwards (Gen. 48:2; 49:33), and it is likely that Jacob turned himself in his *bed* so as to have his face toward the pillow, Isaiah 38:2 (there were no *bedsteads* in the East). Paul by adopting the LXX version, brings out, under the Spirit, *an additional fact,* viz., that the aged patriarch used *his own* (not Joseph's) *staff* to lean on in worshipping on his bed. The *staff,* too, was the *emblem of his pilgrim state* here on his way to his heavenly city (vss. 13, 14), wherein God had so wonderfully supported him. Genesis 32:10, "With my *staff* I passed over Jordan, and now I am become . . ." (cf. Exod. 12:11; Mark 6:8). In I Kings 1:47, the same thing is said of David's "bowing on his bed," an act of adoring thanksgiving to God for God's favor to his son before death. He omits the more leading blessing of the twelve sons of Jacob; because "he plucks only the flowers which stand by his way, and leaves the whole meadow full to his readers" [DELITZSCH *in* ALFORD]. **22. when he died**—"when dying." **the departing**—"the exodus" (Gen. 50:24, 25). Joseph's eminent position in Egypt did not make him regard it as his home: in faith he looked to God's promise of Canaan being fulfilled and desired that his bones should rest there: testifying thus: (1) that he had no doubt of his posterity obtaining the promised land: and (2) that he believed in the resurrection of the body, and the enjoyment in it of the heavenly Canaan. His wish was fulfilled (Josh. 24:32; Acts 4:16). **23. parents**—So the LXX has the plural, viz., Amram and Jochebed (Num. 26:59); but in Exod. 2:2, the mother alone is mentioned; but doubtless Amram sanctioned all she did, and secrecy being their object, he did not appear prominent in what was done. **a proper child**—*Greek,* "a comely child." Acts 7:20, "exceeding fair," *Greek,* "fair to God." The "faith" of his parents in saving the child must have had some divine revelation to rest on (probably at the time of his birth), which marked their "exceeding fair" babe as one whom God designed to do a great work by. His *beauty* was probably "the sign" appointed by God to assure their faith. **the king's commandment**—to slay all the males (Exod. 1:22). **24.** So far from *faith* being opposed to *Moses,* he was an eminent example of it [BENGEL]. **refused**—in believing self-denial, when he might possibly have succeeded at last to the throne of Egypt. Thermutis, Pharaoh's daughter, according to the tradition which Paul under the Spirit sanctions, adopted him, as JOSEPHUS says, with the consent of the king. Josephus states that when a child, he threw on the ground the diadem put on him in jest, a presage of his subsequent formal rejection of Thermutis' adoption of him. Faith made him to prefer the adoption of the King of kings, unseen, and so to choose (vss. 25, 26) things, the very last which flesh and blood relish. **25.** He balanced the best of the world with the worst of religion, and decidedly chose the latter. "Choosing" implies a deliberate resolution, not a hasty impulse. He was forty years old, a time when the judgment is matured. **for a season**—If the world has "pleasure" (*Greek,* "enjoyment") to offer, it is but "for a season." If religion bring with it "affliction," it too is but for a season; whereas its "pleasures are for evermore." **26. Esteeming**—Inasmuch as he esteemed. **the reproach of Christ**—i.e., the reproach which falls on the Church, and which Christ regards as His own reproach, He being the Head, and the Church (both of the Old and New Testament) His body. Israel typified Christ; Israel's sufferings were Christ's sufferings (cf. II Cor. 1:5; Col. 1:24). As uncircumcision was Egypt's *reproach,* so circumcision was the badge of Israel's expectation of Christ, which Moses especially cherished, and which the Gentiles reproached Israel on account of. Christ's people's reproach will ere long be their great glory. **had respect unto . . .**—*Greek, "turning his eyes away from* other considerations, *he fixed them on* the

ADAM CLARKE

he was very weak and generally confined to his couch, having at hand his staff; either that with which he usually supported his feeble body or that which was the ensign of his office as patriarch or chief of a very numerous family. The ancient chiefs in all countries had this staff or sceptre continually at hand. It is said, Gen. xlviii. 2, that when Joseph came to see his father, Jacob, who was then in his last sickness, "Israel strengthened himself, and sat upon the bed, with his feet on the floor, he supported himself with his staff. When Joseph sware to him that he should be carried up from Egypt, he "bowed himself upon the bed's head," still supporting himself with his staff, which probably with this last act he laid aside, "gathered up his feet," and reclined wholly on his couch. It was therefore indifferent to say that he worshipped or bowed himself on his staff or on his bed's head. But as *shachah* signifies not only to "bow," but also to "worship," because acts of adoration were performed by bowing and prostration; and as *mittah,* a "bed," by the change of the vowel points becomes *matteh,* a "staff," hence the Septuagint have translated the passage, "And Israel bowed or worshipped on the head of his staff." This reading the apostle follows here.

22. *Joseph, when he died.* "When he was dying."

23. *By faith Moses.* See the notes on Exod. ii. 2 and Acts vii. 20. We know that Moses was brought up at the Egyptian court, and there was considered to be the son of Pharaoh's daughter, and probably might have succeeded to the throne of Egypt. But finding that God had visited His people and given them a promise of spiritual and eternal blessings, he chose rather to take the lot of this people, i.e., God as his Portion forever, than to "enjoy the pleasures of sin," which, however gratifying to the animal senses, could only be "temporary."

26. *The reproach of Christ.* The *Christ* or Messiah had been revealed to Moses; of Him he prophesied, Deut. xviii. 15; and the *reproach* which God's people had, in consequence of their decided opposition to idolatry, may be termed *the reproach of Christ,* for they refused to become one people with the Egyptians, because the promise of the rest was made to them, and in this rest Christ and His salvation were included. But, although it does not appear these things were known to the Hebrews at large, yet it is evident that there were sufficient intimations given to Moses concerning the great Deliverer (of whom himself was a type) that determined his conduct in the above respect, as he fully understood that he must renounce his interest in the promises and in the life eternal to which they led, if he did not obey the divine call in the present instance. Many have been stumbled by the word *Christ* here, because they cannot see how Moses should have any knowledge of Him. It may be said that it was just as easy for God Almighty to reveal Christ to Moses as it was for Him to reveal Him to Isaiah, or to the shepherds, or to John Baptist; or to manifest Him in the flesh. After all, there is much reason to believe that by *Christ* the apostle means the whole body of the Israelitish or Hebrew people; for as the word signifies "the anointed," and anointing was a consecration to God, all the Hebrew people were considered thus anointed or consecrated; and it is worthy of remark that *Christos* is used in this very sense by the Septuagint, I Sam. ii. 35; Ps. cv. 15; and Hab. iii. 13, where the word is necessarily restrained to this meaning. *He had respect unto the recompence.* He "looked attentively" to it; his eyes were "constantly directed" to it. This is the import of the original word, and the whole conduct of Moses was an illustration of it.

MATTHEW HENRY

4. We have another instance of the faith of Moses, *v.* 27. (1) The product of his faith: *He forsook Egypt.* Twice Moses forsook Egypt: As a supposed criminal, when the king's wrath was incensed against him for killing the Egyptian. As a commander after God had employed him to humble Pharaoh and make him willing to let Israel go. (2) The prevalency of his faith. It raised him above the fear of the king's wrath. Those who forsook Egypt must expect the wrath of men; but they need not fear it. (3) The principle upon which his faith acted in these his motions: *He endured, as seeing him that was invisible.* By faith we may see this invisible God. We may be fully assured of his existence, and of his gracious and powerful presence with us. Such a sight of God will enable believers to endure to the end.

5. We have yet another instance of the faith of Moses, *v.* 28. The passover was one of the most solemn institutions of the Old Testament, and a very significant type of Christ. To entitle them to this distinguishing favour, a lamb must be slain; the blood of it must be sprinkled with a bunch of hyssop upon the lintel of the door, and on the two side-posts. Christ is that Lamb, he is our Passover, he was sacrificed for us. His blood must be sprinkled; it must be applied to those who have the saving benefit of it. It is not owing to our inherent righteousness that we are saved from the wrath of God, but to the blood of Christ and his imputed righteousness. Wherever this blood is applied, the soul receives Christ by faith, and lives upon him. All our spiritual privileges on earth should quicken us to set out early, and get forward, in our way to heaven.

XIII. The Israelites passing through the Red Sea under the conduct of Moses their leader, *v.* 29.

1. The safe passage of the Israelites through the Red Sea, when there was no other way to escape from Pharaoh and his host. Israel's danger was very great. Their deliverance was very glorious. The grace of faith will help us through all the dangers we meet with in our way to heaven.

2. The destruction of the Egyptians. Their rashness was great, and their ruin was grievous. When God judges, he will overcome; and it is plain that the destruction of sinners is of themselves.

XIV. The Israelites, under Joshua their leader, before the walls of Jericho. The story we have Joshua vi. 5, &c. The means prescribed of God to bring down the walls of Jericho. Here was a great trial of their faith. The method prescribed seemed very improbable to answer such an end. But this was the way God commanded them to take, and he loves to do great things by small and contemptible means, that his own arm may be made bare. The powerful success of the prescribed means. The walls of Jericho fell before them. God can in his own time cause all the powerful opposition that is made to his interest to fall down, and the grace of faith is mighty through God for the pulling down of strongholds. When he has some great thing to do for them, he raises up great and strong faith in them.

XV. The faith of Rahab, *v.* 31.

1. Who this Rahab was. She was a Canaanite, a *stranger to the commonwealth of Israel*, and had but little help for faith, and yet she was a believer. She was a harlot, and lived in a way of sin. Christ has saved the chief of sinners. *Where sin has abounded, grace has superabounded.*

2. What she did by her faith: *She received the spies in peace.* She not only bade them welcome, but she concealed them from their enemies, and she made a noble confession of her faith. True faith will show itself in good works, especially towards the people of God.

3. What she gained by her faith. She escaped perishing with those that believed not. It was an utter destruction that befell that city: man and beast were cut off. The signal preservation of Rahab.

Verses 32–40

The apostle now concludes his narrative with a more summary account of another set of believers. He prefaces this part of the narrative with an elegant expostulation: *What shall I say more? Time would fail me.* We should be pleased to think how great the number of believers was under the Old Testament, and how strong their faith.

I. The apostle mentions,

1. Gideon. He was an eminent instrument raised up of God to deliver his people from the oppression of the Midianites. God put the whole army of the Midianites to confusion and ruin.

2. Barak. He obtained a great victory by his faith over all the host of Sisera.

3. Samson. If Samson had not had a strong faith as well as a strong arm, he had never performed such exploits. True faith is acknowledged and accepted, even when mingled with many failings. The believer's

JAMIESON, FAUSSET, BROWN

(eternal) recompense" (vss. 39, 40). **27. not fearing the wrath of the king**—But in Exodus 2:14 it is said, "Moses feared, and fled from the face of Pharaoh." He was *afraid,* and fled from the danger where no duty called him to stay (to have stayed without call of duty would have been to tempt Providence, and *to sacrifice his hope of being Israel's future deliverer according to the divine intimations;* his great aim, *Note,* vs. 23). He *did not fear the king* so as to neglect his duty and not return when God called him. It was *in spite of the king's prohibition he left Egypt,* not fearing the consequences which were likely to overtake him if he should be caught, after having, in defiance of the king, left Egypt. If he had stayed and resumed his position as adopted son of Pharaoh's daughter, his slaughter of the Egyptian would doubtless have been connived at; but his resolution to take his portion with oppressed Israel, which he could not have done had he stayed, was the motive of his flight, and constituted the "faith" of this act, according to the express statement here. The exodus of Moses with Israel cannot be meant here, for it was made, not in defiance, but by the desire, of the king. Besides, the chronological order would be broken thus, the next particular specified here, viz., the institution of the *Passover,* having taken place *before the exodus.* Besides, it is Moses' *personal* history and faith which are here described. The faith of the people ("THEY passed") is not introduced till vs. 29. **endured**—steadfast in faith amidst trials. He had fled, *not* so much from *fear of Pharaoh,* as from a revulsion of feeling in finding God's people insensible to their high destiny, and from disappointment at not having been able to inspire them with those hopes for which he had sacrificed all his earthly prospects. This accounts for his strange reluctance and despondency when commissioned by God to go and arouse the people (Exod. 3:15; 4:1, 10-12). **seeing him . . . invisible**—as though he had not to do with men, but only with God, ever before his eyes by faith, though *invisible* to the bodily eye (Rom. 1:20; I Tim. 1:17; 6:16). Hence he feared not the wrath of *visible* man; the characteristic of *faith* (vs. 1; Luke 12: 4, 5). **28. kept**—*Greek, "hath* kept," the Passover being, in Paul's day, still observed. His *faith* here was his belief in the invisible God's promise that the destroying angel should *pass over,* and not *touch* the inmates of the blood-sprinkled houses (Exod. 12:23). "He acquiesced in the bare word of God where the thing itself was not apparent" [CALVIN]. **the first-born**—*Greek* neuter; *both of man and beast.* **29. they**—Moses and Israel. **Red Sea**—called so from its red seaweed, or rather from Edom (meaning "red"), whose country adjoined it. **which . . . assaying to do**—*Greek,* "of which (Red Sea) the Egyptians having made experiment." *Rashness* and *presumption* mistaken by many for *faith;* with similar rash presumption many rush into eternity. The same thing when done by the believer, and when done by the unbeliever, is not the same thing [BENGEL]. What was *faith* in Israel, was *presumption* in the Egyptians. **were drowned**—*Greek,* "were swallowed up," or "engulfed." They sank in the sands as much as in the waves of the Red Sea. Cf. Exodus 15:12, "the *earth* swallowed them." **30.** The soundings of trumpets, though one were to sound for ten thousand years, cannot throw down walls, but *faith* can do all things [CHRYSOSTOM]. **seven days**—whereas sieges often lasted for years. **31.** Rahab showed her "faith" in her confession, Joshua 2:9, 11, "I know that Jehovah hath given you the land; Jehovah your God, is God in heaven above, and in earth beneath." **the harlot**—Her former life adds to the marvel of her repentance, faith, and preservation (Matt. 21:31-32). **believed not**—*Greek,* "were disobedient," viz., to the will of God manifested by the miracles wrought in behalf of Israel (Josh. 2:8-11). **received**—in her house (Josh. 2:1, 4, 6). **with peace**—peaceably; so that they had nothing to fear in her house. Thus Paul, quoting the same examples (vss. 17, 31) for the power of *faith,* as James (2:21, 25; see my *Notes* there) does for justification by *works* evidentially, shows that in maintaining justification by faith alone, he means not a dead faith, but "faith which *worketh* by love" (Gal. 5:6). **32. the time**—suitable for the length of an Epistle. He accumulates collectively some out of many examples of faith. **Gedeon**—put before Barak, not chronologically, but as being more celebrated. Just as Samson for the same reason is put before Jephthae. The mention of Jephthae as an example of "faith," makes it unlikely he sacrificed the *life* of his daughter for a rash vow. David, the warrior king and prophet, forms the transition from warrior chiefs to the "prophets," of whom "Samuel" is mentioned as the

ADAM CLARKE

27. *He forsook Egypt.* He believed that God would fulfill the promise He had made, and he cheerfully changed an earthly for a heavenly portion. *Not fearing the wrath of the king.* The apostle speaks here of the departure of Moses with the Israelites, not of his flight to Midian, Exod. ii. 14-15; for he was then in great fear. But when he went to Pharaoh with God's authority, to demand the dismission of the Hebrews, he was without fear, and acted in the most noble and dignified manner; he then feared nothing but God.

As seeing him who is invisible. He continued to act as one who had the Judge of his heart and conduct always before his eyes. By calling the Divine Being the *invisible,* the apostle distinguishes Him from the gods of Egypt, who were visible, corporeal, gross, and worthless. The Israelites were worshippers of the true God, and this worship was not tolerated in Egypt.

28. *He kept the passover.* God told him that He would destroy the firstborn of the Egyptians, but would spare all those whose doors were sprinkled with the blood of the paschal lamb. Moses believed this, kept the Passover, and sprinkled the blood. See the notes on Exodus xii.

29. *By faith they passed through the Red sea.* See the notes on Exod. xiv. 22. The Egyptians thought they could walk through the sea as well as the Israelites; they tried, and were drowned, while the former passed in perfect safety. The one walked by faith, the other by sight; one perished, the other was saved.

30. *The walls of Jericho fell down.* This is particularly explained Josh. vi. 1, etc. God had promised that the walls of Jericho should fall down if they compassed them about seven days. They believed, did as they were commanded, and the promise was fulfilled.

31. *The harlot Rahab perished not.* See this account in Josh. ii. 1, 9, 11 and vi. 23, where it is rendered exceedingly probable that the word *zonah* in Hebrew and *porne* in Greek, which we translate *harlot,* should be rendered "innkeeper," as there is no proper evidence that the person in question was such a woman as our translation represents her. As to her having been a harlot before and converted afterwards, it is a figment of an idle fancy. She was afterwards married to Salmon, a Jewish prince; see Matt. i. 5. *Received the spies with peace.* "Giving them a kind welcome, good fare, and protection."

32. *Time would fail me.* A very usual mode of expression with the best Greek writers, when they wish to intimate that much important intelligence remains to be communicated on the subject already in hand, which must be omitted because of other points which have not yet been handled. *Gedeon.* Who by faith in God, with 300 men, destroyed a countless multitude of Midianites and Amalekites, and delivered Israel from oppression and slavery, Judges vi—viii. *Barak.* Who overthrew Jabin, king of Canaan, and delivered Israel from servitude, Judges iv. *Samson.* Who was appointed by God to deliver Israel from the oppressive yoke of the Philistines; and by extraordinary assistance discomfited them on various occasions, Judges xiii—xvi. *Jephthae.* Who, under the same guidance, defeated the Ammonites, and delivered Israel, Judges xi—xii. *David.* King of Israel, whose whole life was a life of faith and dependence on God. *Samuel.* The last of the Israelitish judges, to whom succeeded a race of kings, of whom Saul and David were the first two, and were both anointed by this most eminent man.

MATTHEW HENRY

faith endures to the end, and, in dying, gives him victory over death and all his deadly enemies; his greatest conquest he gains by dying.

4. Jephthah. As various and new enemies rise up against the people of God, various and new deliverers are raised up for them. The grace of God often finds out, and fastens upon, the most undeserving and ill-deserving persons, to do great things for them and by them. Jephthah was the son of a harlot. Faith will not only put men upon making their vows to God, but paying their vows after the mercy received; yea, though they have vowed to their own great grief, as in the case of Jephthah and his daughter.

5. David that great man after God's own heart. Few ever met with greater trials, and few ever discovered a more lively faith. The same faith made him a very successful and victorious prince, and, after a long life of virtue and honour (though not without some foul stains of sin), he died in faith, and he has left behind him such excellent memoirs of the trials and acts of faith in the book of Psalms as will ever be of great esteem and use.

6. Samuel, raised up to be a most eminent prophet of the Lord to Israel, as well as a ruler over them. God revealed himself to Samuel when he was but a child, and continued to do so till his death.

7. To Samuel he adds, *and of the prophets*, who were employed of God sometimes to denounce judgment, sometimes to promise mercy, always to reprove sin; sometimes to foretell remarkable events; and chiefly to give notice of the Messiah. A true faith was very requisite for the right discharge of such an office as this.

II. What things were done by their faith.

1. *By faith they subdued kingdoms, v.* 33. The interests and powers of kings and kingdoms are often set up in opposition to God and his people. God can easily subdue all those kings and kingdoms that set themselves to oppose him.

2. They *wrought righteousness*. They believed God, and it was imputed to them for righteousness. It is a greater happiness to work righteousness than to work miracles.

3. They *obtained promises*. It is by faith that we are prepared to wait for the promises, and in due time to receive them.

4. They *stopped the mouths of lions*. Faith engages the power of God for his people, whenever it shall be for his glory, to overcome brute beasts and brutish men.

5. They *quenched the violence of the fire, v.* 34. So did the three children, or rather mighty champions, Dan. iii. 17-27. Never was the grace of faith more severely tried, never more nobly exerted, nor ever more gloriously rewarded, than theirs was.

6. They *escaped the edge of the sword*. The swords of men are held in the hand of God. Faith takes hold of that hand of God which has hold of the swords of men; and God had often suffered himself to be prevailed upon by the faith of his people.

7. *Out of weakness they were made strong*. It is the same grace of faith that from spiritual weakness helps men to recover and renew their strength.

8. They *grew valiant in fight*. True faith gives truest courage and patience, as it discerns the strength of God, and thereby the weakness of all his enemies. And they were not only valiant, but successful. God, as a reward and encouragement of their faith, *put to flight the armies of the aliens*; God made them flee and fall before his faithful servants.

9. *Women received their dead raised to life again, v.* 35. Many of the weaker sex have been strong in faith. God has sometimes yielded so far to the tender affections of sorrowful women as to restore their dead children to life again.

III. The apostle tells us what these believers endured by faith. They *were tortured, not accepting deliverance, v.* 35. They bore the torture, and would not accept of deliverance. That which animated them thus to suffer was the hope they had of *obtaining a better resurrection*. They endured *trials of cruel mockings and scourgings, and bonds and imprisonment, v.* 36. They were persecuted in their reputation by *mockings*, which are cruel to an ingenuous mind; in their persons by *scourging*, the punishment of slaves; in their liberty by *bonds and imprisonment*. They were put to death in the most cruel manner. Their enemies clothed death in all the array of cruelty and terror, and yet they boldly met it and endured it. Those who escaped death were used so ill that death might seem more eligible than such a life. Their enemies spared them, only to prolong their misery, *v.* 37, 38.

JAMIESON, FAUSSET, BROWN

first. **33. subdued kingdoms**—as David did (II Sam. 8:1, etc.); so also Gideon subdued Midian (Judg. 7). **wrought righteousness**—as Samuel did (I Sam. 8:9; 12:3-23 15:33); and David (II Sam. 8:15). **obtained promises**—as "the prophets" (vs. 32) did; for through them the promises were given (cf. Dan. 9:21) [BENGEL]. Rather, "obtained *the fulfilment* of promises," which had been previously the object of their *faith* (Josh. 21:45; I Kings 8:56). Indeed, Gideon, Barak, etc., also *obtained* the things which God promised. Not "*the* promises," which are still future (vss. 13, 39). **stopped the mouths of lions** —Note the words, "because he *believed* in his God." Also Samson (Judg. 14:6), David (I Sam. 17:34-37), Benaiah (II Sam. 23:20). **34. Quenched the violence of fire**—(Dan. 3:27). Not merely "quenched the fire," but "quenched the power (so the *Greek*) of the fire." Daniel 3 and 6 record the last miracles of the Old Testament. So the martyrs of the Reformation, though not escaping *the fire*, were delivered from its having *power* really or lastingly to hurt them. **escaped . . . sword**—So Jephthah (Judg. 12: 3); and so David escaped Saul's sword (I Sam. 18: 11; 19:10, 12); Elijah (I Kings 19:1, etc.; II Kings 6: 14). **out of weakness . . . made strong**—Samson (Judg. 16:28; 15:19). Hezekiah (Isa. 37 and 38). Milton says of the martyrs, "They shook the powers of darkness with the irresistible power of weakness." **valiant in fight**—Barak (Judg. 4:14, 15). And the Maccabees, the sons of Matthias, Judas, Jonathan, and Simon, who delivered the Jews from their cruel oppressor, Antiochus of Syria. **armies**—lit., "camps" referring to Judges 7:21. But the reference may be to the Maccabees having put to flight the Syrians and other foes. **35. Women received their dead raised**—as the widow of Zarephath (I Kings 17:17-24). The Shunammite (II Kings 4:17-35). The two oldest MSS. read. "They received women of aliens by raising their dead." I Kings 17:24 shows that the raising of the widow's son by Elijah led her to the faith, so that he thus *took* her into fellowship, an *alien* though she was. Christ, in Luke 4:26, makes especial mention of the fact that Elijah was sent to an alien from Israel, a woman of Sarepta. Thus Paul may quote this as an instance of Elijah's faith, that at God's command he went to a Gentile city of Sidonia (contrary to Jewish prejudices), and there, as the fruit of faith, not only raised her dead son, but *received* her as a convert into the family of God, as *Vulgate* reads. Still, *English Version* may be the right reading. **and**—*Greek*, "but"; in contrast to those raised again to life. **tortured**—"broken on the wheel." Eleazar (II Maccabees 6: 18, end; 19:20, 30). The sufferer was stretched on an instrument like a drumhead and scourged to death. **not accepting deliverance**—when offered to them. So the seven brothers, II Maccabees 7:9, 11, 14, 29, 36; and Eleazar, II Maccabees 6:21, 28, 30, "Though I might have been delivered from death, I endure these severe pains, being beaten." **a better resurrection**—than that of the women's children "raised to life again"; or, than the resurrection which their foes could give them by delivering them from death (Dan. 12:2; Luke 20:35; Phil. 3: 11). The fourth of the brethren (referring to Dan. 12:2) said to King Antiochus, "To be put to death by men, is to be chosen to look onward for the hopes which are of God, to be raised up again by Him; but for thee there is no resurrection to life." The writer of II Maccabees *expressly disclaims inspiration,* which prevents our mistaking Paul's allusion here to it as if it sanctioned the Apocrypha as inspired. In quoting Daniel, he quotes a book *claiming inspiration,* and so tacitly sanctions that claim. **36. others**—of a *different* class of confessors for the truth (the *Greek* is different from that for "others," vs. 35, *alloi, heteroi*). **trial**—testing their *faith*. **imprisonment**—as Hanani (II Chron. 16:10), imprisoned by Asa. Micaiah, the son of Imlah, by Ahab (I Kings 22:26, 27). **37. stoned**—as Zechariah, son of Jehoiada (II Chron. 24:20-22; Matt. 23:35). **sawn asunder**—as Isaiah was said to have been by Manasseh; but see my *Introduction* to Isaiah. **tempted**—*by their foes,* in the midst of their tortures, to renounce their faith; the most bitter aggravation of them. Or else, *by those of their own household,* as Job was [ESTIUS]; or by the fiery darts of Satan, as Jesus was in His last trials [GLASSIUS]. Probably it included all three; they were *tempted* in every possible way, by friends and foes, by human and satanic agents, by caresses and afflictions, by words and deeds, to forsake God, but in vain, through the power of faith. **sword**—lit., "they died in the murder of the sword." In vs. 34 the contrary is given as an effect of *faith,* "they escaped the edge of the sword." Both alike are marvellous effects of faith. In both accomplishes great things

ADAM CLARKE

33. *Who through faith subdued kingdoms.* As *Joshua,* who subdued the seven Canaanitish nations; and *David,* who subdued the Moabites, Syrians, Ammonites, and Edomites, 2 Samuel viii; etc. *Wrought righteousness.* Did a great variety of works indicative of that faith in God without which it is impossible to do anything that is good. *Obtained promises.* This is supposed to refer to Joshua and Caleb, who through their faith in God obtained the Promised Land, while all the rest of the Israelites were excluded; to Phineas also, who for his act of zealous faith in slaying Zimri and Cosbi got the promise of an everlasting priesthood; and to David, who for his faith and obedience obtained the kingdom of Israel, and had the promise that from his seed the Messiah should spring. *Stopped the mouths of lions.* Daniel, who, though cast into a den of lions for his fidelity to God, was preserved among them unhurt and finally came to great honor.

34. *Quenched the violence of fire.* As in the case of the three faithful Hebrews—Shadrach, Meshach, and Abed-nego—who for their steady attachment to God's worship were cast into a fiery furnace, in which they were preserved and from which they escaped unhurt, Daniel iii. *Escaped the edge of the sword.* Moses, who escaped the sword of Pharaoh, Exod. xviii. 4; Elijah, that of Jezebel; and David, that of Saul; and many others. *Out of weakness were made strong.* Were miraculously restored from sickness, which seemed to threaten their life; as Hezekiah, Isa. xxxviii. 21. *Waxed valiant in fight.* Like Gideon, who overthrew the camp of the Midianites, and Jonathan, that of the Philistines, in such a way as must have proved that God was with them.

35. *Women received their dead.* As did the widow of Zarephath, I Kings xvii. 21, and the Shunammite, 2 Kings iv. 34. *Others were tortured.* This word signifies to "beat violently."

36. *Had trial of cruel mockings and scourgings.* We do not know the cases to which the apostle refers. The *mockings* here can never mean such as those of Ishmael against Isaac or the youths of Bethel against Elisha. It is more probable that it refers to public exhibitions of the people of God at idol feasts and the like; and Samson's case before Dagon, when the Philistines had put out his eyes, is quite in point. As to *scourgings,* this was a common way of punishing minor culprits; and even those who were to be punished capitally were first scourged. See the case of our Lord. *Bonds and imprisonment.* Joseph was cast into prison; Jeremiah was cast into a dungeon full of mire, chap. xxxvii. 16 and xxxviii. 6; and the Prophet Micaiah was imprisoned by Ahab, I Kings xxii. 27.

37. *They were stoned.* As Zechariah, the son of Barachiah or Jehoida, was, between the altar and the Temple; see the account in 2 Chron. xxiv. 21. And as Naboth the Jezreelite, who, on refusing to give up his father's inheritance to a covetous king, because it had respect to the promise of God, was falsely accused and stoned to death, 1 Kings xxi. 1-14. *They were sawn asunder.* There is a tradition that the Prophet Isaiah was thus martyred. In *Yevomoth,* fol. 49, 2, it is thus written: "Manasseh slew Isaiah; for he commanded that he should be slain with a wooden saw. They then brought the saw, and cut him in two; and when the saw reached his mouth, his soul fled forth." *Were tempted. Epeirasthesan.* I believe this word has vexed the critics more than any other in the New Testament. How being *tempted* can be ranked among the heavy sufferings of the primitive martyrs and confessors is not easy to discern, because to be tempted is the common lot of every godly man. This difficulty has induced learned men to mend the text by conjecture. Alberti thinks the original reading was *epeirasthesan,* "they were strangled." Many more differences have been proposed by learned men, all bearing a very near resemblance to the words now found in the Greek text. *Were slain with the sword.* As in the case of the eighty-five priests slain by Doeg, see 1 Sam. xxii. 18; and the prophets, of whose slaughter by the sword Elijah complains, 1 Kings xix. 10. Probably the word means being "beheaded," which was formerly done with a *sword* and not with an axe,

MATTHEW HENRY

Such sufferings as these they endured then for their faith; and such they endured through the power of the grace of faith: and which shall we most admire, the wickedness of human nature, or the excellency of divine grace, that is able to bear up the faithful under such cruelties, and to carry them safely through all?

IV. What they obtained by their faith. 1. A most honourable commendation from God—that *the world was not worthy* of such men; the world did not deserve such blessings. The righteous are not worthy to live in the world, and God declares the world is not worthy of them.

2. They *obtained a good report* (*v.* 39) of all good men, add the truth itself. 3. They had a title to the promises, though they received not the great things promised. They had shadows, but had not seen the substance; and yet, under this imperfect dispensation, they discovered this precious faith. This the apostle insists upon to render their faith more illustrious.

He tells the Hebrews that God had *provided some better things for* them (*v.* 40), and therefore they might be assured that he expected at least as good things from them. Their faith should be much more perfect than the faith of the Old Testament saints; for their state and dispensation were more perfect than the former.

JAMIESON, FAUSSET, BROWN

and suffers great things, without counting it suffering [CHRYSOSTOM]. Urijah was so slain by Jehoiakim (Jer. 26:23); and *the prophets* in Israel (I Kings 19:10).

in sheepskins—as Elijah (I Kings 19:13, LXX). They were *white;* as the "goatskins" were *black* (cf. Zech. 13:4). **tormented**—*Greek,* "in evil state." **38. Of whom the world was not worthy**—So far from their being unworthy of living in the world, as their exile in deserts, etc., might seem to imply, "the world was not worthy of them." The world, in shutting them out, shut out from itself a source of blessing; such as Joseph proved to Potiphar (Gen. 39:5), and Jacob to Laban (Gen. 30:27). In condemning them, the world condemned itself. **caves**—lit., "chinks." Palestine, from its hilly character, abounds in *fissures* and caves, affording shelter to the persecuted, as the fifty hid by Obadiah (I Kings 18:4, 13) and Elijah (I Kings 19:8, 13); and Mattathias and his sons (I Maccabees 2:28, 29); and Judas Maccabeus (II Maccabees 5:27). **39. having obtained a good report**—*Greek,* "being borne witness of." *Though* they were so, yet "they received not the promise," i.e., the *final completion* of "salvation" *promised* at Christ's coming again (ch. 9:28); "the eternal inheritance" (ch. 9:15). Abraham did *obtain* the very thing *promised* (ch. 6:15) *in part,* viz., blessedness *in soul* after death, by virtue of faith in Christ about to come. The *full* blessedness of body and soul shall not be till the full number of the elect shall be accomplished, and all together, no one preceding the other, shall enter on the full glory and bliss. Moreover, in another point of view, "It is probable that some accumulation of blessedness was added to holy souls, when Christ came and fulfilled all things even as at His burial many rose from the dead, who doubtless ascended to heaven with Him" [FLACIUS *in* BENGEL] (cf. *Note,* Eph. 4:8). The *perfecting* of believers in title, and in respect to conscience, took place once for all, at the death of Christ, by virtue of His being made by death *perfect* as Saviour. Their *perfecting in soul* at, and ever after Christ's death, took place, and takes place at their death. But the universal and final perfecting will not take place till Christ's coming. **40. provided**—with divine forethought from eternity (cf. Gen. 22:8, 14). **some better thing for us**—(ch. 7:19) —than they had here. It is not *we* who are perfected *with them,* but rather *they with us.* They *waited* for His coming; we enjoy Him as having come (ch. 1:1; 2:3). Christ's death, the means of *perfecting* what the Jewish *law could not perfect,* was reserved for our time. Cf. ch. 12:2, "*perfecter* (*Greek*) of our faith." Now that Christ is come, they in soul share our blessedness, being "the spirits of the just made perfect" (ch. 12:23); so ALFORD; however, see *Note* there. Ch. 9:12 shows that the blood of Christ, brought into the heavenly holy place by Him, first opened an entrance into heaven (cf. John 3:13). Still, the fathers were in blessedness by faith in the Saviour to come, at death (ch. 6:15; Luke 16:22).

ADAM CLARKE

and in the East is done by the sword to the present day. *They wandered about in sheepskins.* "Sheepskins dressed with the wool on." This was probably the sort of mantle that Elijah wore, and which was afterwards used by Elisha; for the Septuagint, in 2 Kings ii. 8, 13, expressly say: "And Elijah took his sheepskin" (mantle); "And he [Elisha] took the sheepskin of Elijah which had fallen from off him." It is likely that the prophets themselves wore such garments, and that the false prophets imitated them in this, in order that they might gain the greater credit. "And it shall come to pass in that day, that the prophets shall be ashamed every one of his vision . . . neither shall they wear a rough garment to deceive," Zech. xiii. 4; "a hairy skin," Septuagint, probably the *goatskins* mentioned above. In general, this was an upper garment; but in the cases to which the apostle alludes, the *sheepskins and goatskins* seem to have been the only covering. *Being destitute.* "In want" of all the comforts and conveniences of life, and often of its necessaries. *Afflicted.* In consequence of enduring such privations. *Tormented.* "Maltreated, harassed," variously persecuted by those to whom they brought the message of salvation.

38. *Of whom the world was not worthy.* Yet they were obliged to wander by day in *deserts* and *mountains,* driven from the society of men, and often obliged to hide by night *in dens and caves of the earth* to conceal themselves from the brutal rage of men. Perhaps he refers here principally to the case of Elijah and the hundred prophets hidden in caves by Obadiah and fed with bread and water. See 1 Kings xviii. 4. David was often obliged thus to hide himself from Saul, 1 Sam. xxiv. 3, etc.

39. *Having obtained a good report* (having been witnessed to; see v. 2) *through faith.* It was faith in God which supported all those eminent men who, in different parts of the world and in different ages, were persecuted for righteousness' sake. *Received not the promise.* They all heard of the promises made to Abraham of a Messiah, for this was a constant tradition; but they died without having seen this Anointed of the Lord. This must be the promise without receiving of which the apostle says they died.

40. *God having provided some better thing for us.* This is the dispensation of the gospel, with all the privileges and advantages it confers. *That they without us should not be made perfect.* Believers before the Flood, after the Flood, under the law, and since the law, make but one Church. The gospel dispensation is the last, and the Church cannot be considered as "complete," *perfect,* till the believers under all dispensations are gathered together. As the gospel is the last dispensation, the preceding believers cannot be consummated even in glory till the gospel Church arrive in the heaven of heavens.

MATTHEW HENRY

CHAPTER 12

Verses 1–3

The great duty which the apostle urges upon the Hebrews. The duty consists of two parts.

I. Preparatory: *Lay aside every weight, and the sin,* &c. *Every weight,* that is, all inordinate affection and concern for the body, and the present life and world. *The sin that doth so easily beset us;* the sin that has the greatest advantage against us, by the circumstances we are in, our constitution, our company.

JAMIESON, FAUSSET, BROWN

CHAPTER 12

VSS. 1-29. EXHORTATION TO FOLLOW THE WITNESSES OF FAITH JUST MENTIONED: NOT TO FAINT IN TRIALS: TO REMOVE ALL BITTER ROOTS OF SIN: FOR WE ARE UNDER, NOT A LAW OF TERROR, BUT THE GOSPEL OF GRACE, TO DESPISE WHICH WILL BRING THE HEAVIER PENALTIES, IN PROPORTION TO OUR GREATER PRIVILEGES. **1. we also**—as well as those recounted in vs. 11. **are compassed about**—*Greek,* "have so great a cloud (a numberless multitude *above* us, like a cloud, 'holy and pellucid,' [CLEMENS ALEXANDRINUS]) of witnesses surrounding us." The image is from a "race," an image common even in Palestine from the time of the Græco-Macedonian empire, which introduced such Greek usages as national games. The "witnesses" answer to the spectators pressing round to see the competitors in their contest for the prize (Phil. 3:14). Those "witnessed of" (*Greek,* ch. 11: 5, 39) become in their turn "witnesses" in a twofold way: (1) attesting by their own case the faithfulness of God to His people [ALFORD] (ch. 6:12), some of them *martyrs* in the modern sense; (2) witnessing our struggle of faith; however, this second sense of "witnesses," though agreeing with the *image* here if it is to be pressed, is not *positively,* unequivocally, and *directly* sustained by Scripture. It gives vividness to the image; as the crowd of spectators gave additional spirit to the combatants, so the *cloud of witnesses* who have themselves been in the same

ADAM CLARKE

CHAPTER 12

1. *Wherefore.* This is an inference drawn from the examples produced in the preceding chapter, and on this account both should be read in connection. *Compassed about.* Here is another allusion to the Olympic games. The agonistae, or contenders, were often greatly animated by the consideration that the eyes of the principal men of their country were fixed upon them; and by this they were induced to make the most extraordinary exertions. *Cloud of witnesses.* Both the Greeks and Latins frequently use the term *cloud* to express a great number of persons or things. *Let us lay aside every weight.* As those who ran in the Olympic races would throw aside everything that might impede them in their course, so Christians, professing to go to heaven, must throw aside everything that might hinder them in their Christian race. Whatever weighs down our hearts or affections to earth and sense is to be carefully avoided; for no man with the love of the world in his heart can ever reach the kingdom of Heaven. *The sin which doth so easily beset.* "The well-circumstanced sin"; that which has everything in its favor, time, and place, and opportunity; the heart and the object; and a sin in which all these things frequently occur, and consequently the transgression is frequently committed; the sin that stands well, or is favor-

MATTHEW HENRY

II. Perfective: *Run with patience the race that is set before us.*

1. Christians have a race to run.

2. This race is set before them; it is marked out unto them, both by the word of God and the examples of the faithful servants of God, that cloud of witnesses with which they are compassed about.

3. This race must be run with patience and perseverance. Faith and patience are the conquering graces, and therefore must be always cultivated.

4. Christians have a greater example to encourage them than any who have been mentioned before, *v.* 2.

(1) What our Lord Jesus is to his people: he is *the author and finisher of* their *faith*, not only the object, but the author. He is the great leader and precedent of our faith. He is *the finisher of our faith*. He is the finisher of grace, and of the work of faith with power in the souls of his people; and he is the judge and the rewarder of their faith.

(2) What trials Christ met with in his race and course. He *endured the contradiction of sinners against himself* (*v.* 3), yet he endured their evil manners with great patience. He endured all. He *endured the cross*—all those sufferings that he met with in the world; for he took up his cross betimes, and was at length nailed to it. Yet all this he endured with invincible patience and resolution. He *despised the shame*. All the reproaches that were cast upon him, both in his life and at his death, he despised.

(3) What it was that supported the human soul of Christ, *the joy that was set before him.* He rejoiced to see that by his sufferings he should make satisfaction to the injured justice of God, that he should make peace between God and man, that he should open a way of salvation.

(4) The reward of his suffering: he *has sat down at the right hand of the throne of God. He ever lives to make intercession for* his people.

(5) What is our duty. We must look unto him; we must set him continually before us as our example. We must consider him, meditate much upon him. We shall find that as his sufferings far exceeded ours, so his patience far excels ours.

(6) The advantage we shall reap by thus doing: it will be a means to prevent our weariness and fainting (*v.* 3). There is a proneness in the best to grow weary and to faint under their trials and afflictions. The best way to prevent this is to look unto Jesus. Faith and meditation will fetch in fresh supplies of strength, comfort, and courage.

Verses 4–17

I. The gentle and moderate measure of their sufferings, *v.* 4. He owns that they had suffered much; they had been striving to an agony against sin. He puts them in mind that they might have suffered more; for they had *not yet resisted unto blood.* Our Lord Jesus does not call his people out to the hardest trials at first, but wisely trains them up by less sufferings to be prepared for greater. The gentleness of Christ in accommodating their trials to their strength. They should not magnify their afflictions, but should take notice of the mercy that is mixed with them.

JAMIESON, FAUSSET, BROWN

contest, ought to increase our earnestness, testifying, as they do, to God's faithfulness. **weight**—As corporeal unwieldiness was, through a disciplinary diet, laid aside by candidates for the prize in racing; so carnal and worldly lusts, and all, whether from without or within, that would impede the heavenly runner, are the spiritual *weight* to be laid aside. "Encumbrance," *all superfluous weight;* the lust of the flesh, the lust of the eye, and the pride of life, and even harmless and otherwise useful things which would positively retard us (Mark 10:50, the blind man *casting away his garment* to come to Jesus; 9: 42-48; cf. Eph. 4:22; Col. 3:9, 10). **the sin which doth so easily beset us**—*Greek,* "sin which easily stands around us"; so LUTHER, "which always so clings to us"; "sinful propensity always surrounding us, ever present and ready" [WAHL]. It is not primarily "*the sin,*" etc., but *sin* in general, with, however, special reference to "apostasy," against which he had already warned them, as one to which they might *gradually* be seduced; the besetting sin of the Hebrews, UNBELIEF. **with patience**—*Greek,* "in persevering endurance" (ch. 10:36). On "run" cf. I Corinthians 9:24, 25. **2. Looking unto**—lit.. "Looking from afar" (*Note,* ch. 11:26); fixing the eyes upon Jesus seated on the throne of God.

author—"Prince-leader." The same *Greek* is translated, "Captain (of salvation)," ch. 2:10; "Prince (of life)," Acts 3:15. Going before us as the Originator of our faith, and the Leader whose matchless example we are to follow always. In this He is distinguished from all those examples of faith in ch. 11. (Cf. I Cor. 11:1.) On His "faith" cf. ch. 2:13; 3:2. Believers have ever looked to Him (ch. 11:26; 13:8). **finisher**—*Greek,* "Perfecter," referring to ch. 11:40. **of our faith**—rather as *Greek,* "of *the* faith," including both His faith (as exhibited in what follows) and our faith. He fulfilled the ideal of faith Himself, and so, both as a vicarious offering and an example, He is the object of our faith.

for the joy ... set before him—viz., of presently after *sitting down at the right hand of the throne of God;* including besides His own personal joy, the joy of sitting there as a Prince and Saviour, to give repentance and remission of sins. The coming joy disarmed of its sting the present pain. **cross ... shame**—the great stumbling block to the Hebrews. "Despised," i.e., disregarded.

3. For—justifying his exhortation, "Looking unto Jesus." **consider**—by way of comparison with yourselves, so the *Greek.* **contradiction**—unbelief, and every kind of opposition (Acts 28:19). **sinners**—*Sin* assails us. Not *sin,* but *sinners,* contradicted Christ [BENGEL].

be wearied and faint—*Greek,* "lest ye weary fainting." Cf. Isaiah 49:4, 5, as a specimen of Jesus not being *wearied out* by the *contradiction* and strange unbelief of those among whom He *labored,* preaching as never man did, and exhibiting miracles wrought by His inherent power, as none else could do. **4. not yet resisted unto blood**—image from *pugilism,* as he previously had the image of a *race,* both being taken from the great national Greek games. Ye have suffered the loss of *goods,* and *been a gazing-stock by reproaches and afflictions;* ye have not shed your *blood* (*Note,* ch. 18:7). "The athlete who hath seen his own *blood,* and who, though cast down by his opponent, does not let his spirits be cast down, who as often as he hath fallen hath risen the more determined, goes down to the encounter with great hope" [SENECA]. **against sin**—*Sin* is personified as an adversary; sin, whether within you, leading you to *spare* your blood, or in our adversaries, leading them to *shed* it, if they cannot through your faithfulness even unto blood, induce you to apostatize.

ADAM CLARKE

ably situated, ever surrounding the person and soliciting his acquiescence. What we term the "easily besetting sin" is the sin of our constitution, the sin of our trade, that in which our worldly honor, secular profit, and sensual gratification are most frequently felt and consulted. Some understand it of original sin, as that by which we are inveloped in body, soul, and spirit. Whatever it may be, the word gives us to understand that it is what meets us at every turn; that it is always presenting itself to us; that as a pair of compasses describe a circle by the revolution of one leg while the other is at rest in the center, so this, springing from that point of corruption within, called the "carnal mind," surrounds us in every place; we are bounded by it, and often hemmed in on every side. *Let us run with patience the race.* "Let us start, run on, and continue running" till we get to the goal. This figure is a favorite among the Greek writers.

2. *Looking unto Jesus.* "Looking *off* and *on,* or *from* and *to*"; looking off or from the world and all secular concerns to Jesus and all the spiritual and heavenly things connected with Him. This is still an allusion to the Grecian games. Those who ran were to keep their eyes fixed on the mark of the prize; they must keep the goal in view. The exhortation implies (1) That they should place all their hope and confidence in Christ, as their sole Helper in this race of faith; (2) That they should consider Him their Leader in this contest and imitate His example. *The author and finisher of our faith. Archegos,* translated here *author,* signifies in general captain or leader, or the first inventor of a thing; see chap. ii. 10. But the reference here seems to be to the *brabeus,* or judge in the games, whose business it was to admit the contenders and to give the prize to the conqueror. Jesus is here represented as this Officer; every Christian is a contender in this race of life, and for eternal life. The heavenly course is begun under Jesus, and under Him it is completed. He is the *finisher* by awarding the prize to them that are faithful unto death. Thus He is the *author* or the Judge under whom and by whose permission and direction, according to the rules of the heavenly race, they are permitted to enter the lists and commence the race; and He is the *finisher,* the "Perfecter," by awarding and giving the prize which consummates the combatants at the end of the race. *Who for the joy that was set before him.* The joy of fulfilling the will of the Father, Ps. xl. 6, etc., in tasting death for every man; and having endured the Cross and despised the shame of this ignominious death, He is set down at the right hand of God, ever appearing in the presence of God for us, and continuing His exhibition of himself as our Sacrifice, and His intercession as our Mediator.

3. *For consider him.* "Attentively observe" and "analyze" every part of His conduct, enter into His spirit, examine His motives and object, and remember that, as He acted, you are called to act; He will furnish you with the same Spirit, and will support you with the same strength. He bore a continual opposition of sinners against himself, but He conquered by meekness, patience, and perseverance; He has left you an example that you should follow His steps. If you trust in Him, you shall receive strength. Therefore, howsoever great your opposition may be, you shall not be weary; if you confide in and attentively look to Him, you shall have continual courage to go on, and never *faint* in your minds. Here is a continued allusion to the contenders in the Grecian games, who, when exhausted in bodily strength and courage, yielded the palm to their opponents, and were said "to be weary or exhausted"; "to be dissolved, disheartened, or to have lost all bravery and courage."

4. *Ye have not yet resisted unto blood.* Many of those already mentioned were martyrs for the truth; they persevered unto death, and lost their lives in bearing testimony to the truth. Though you have had opposition and persecution, yet you have not been called, in bearing your testimony against sin and sinners, to seal the truth with your blood. *Striving against sin.* An allusion to boxing at the Grecian games. In the former passages the apostle principally refers to the footraces.

MATTHEW HENRY

II. He argues from the nature of those sufferings. They are divine chastisements; their heavenly Father has his hand in all; of this he has given them due notice, and they should not forget it, *v.* 5.

1. Those afflictions which may be truly persecution as far as men are concerned in them are fatherly rebukes and chastisements as far as God is concerned in them. Men persecute them because they are religious; God chastises them because they are not more so.

2. God has directed his people how they ought to behave themselves under all their afflictions. They must not despise the chastening of the Lord. Those who make light of affliction make light of God and make light of sin. They must not faint when they are rebuked.

3. Afflictions, though they may be the fruits of God's displeasure, are yet proofs of his paternal love to his people and care for them (*v.* 6, 7). The best of God's children have their faults and follies, which need to be corrected. He will correct sin in his own children; they are of his family. In this he acts as becomes a father; no wise and good father will wink at faults in his own children as he would in others.

To be suffered to go on in sin without a rebuke is a sad sign of alienation from God; such are bastards, not sons. They are the spurious offspring of another father, not of God, *v.* 7, 8.

4. Those that are impatient under the discipline of their heavenly father behave worse towards him than they would do towards earthly parents, *v.* 9, 10. It is the duty of children to give the reverence of submission to their correction when they have been disobedient. He recommends humble and submissive behaviour towards our heavenly Father, when under his correction. (1) Our earthly fathers are but *the fathers of our flesh*, but God is *the Father of our spirits*. Our fathers on earth were instrumental in the production of our bodies, which are but flesh. We must owe much more to him who is the Father of our spirits. (2) Our earthly parents *chastened us for their own pleasure*. Sometimes they did it to gratify their passion rather than to reform our manners. This is a weakness the fathers of our flesh are subject to. It should be *for our profit*. God loves his children so that he would have them to be as like himself as can be, and for this end he chastises them when they need it. (3) The fathers of our flesh corrected us for *a few days*, in our state of childhood, and when we came to maturity we loved and honoured them the more for it. Our whole life here is a state of childhood; when we come to a state of perfection we shall be fully reconciled to all the measures of God's discipline over us now.

(4) God's correction is no condemnation. He does it to prevent the death and destruction of their souls, that they may live to God, and be like God, and be for ever with him.

JAMIESON, FAUSSET, BROWN

5. forgotten—"utterly," so the *Greek.* Cf. vss. 15-17, in which he implies how utterly *some* of them had forgotten God's word. His *exhortation* ought to have more effect on you than the cheers and exhortations of the spectators have on the competitors striving in the games. **which**—*Greek,* "the which," of which the following is a specimen [ALFORD]. **speaketh unto you**—as in *a dialogue* or *discourse,* so the *Greek,* implying God's loving condescension (cf. Isa. 1:18). **despise not**—lit., "Do not *hold of little account.*" Betraying a *contumacious spirit of unbelief* (ch. 3:12), as "faint" implies a broken-down, weak, and *desponding spirit.* "Chastening" is to be borne with "subjection" (vs. 9); "rebuke" (more severe than *chastening*) is to be borne with *endurance* (vs. 7). "Some in adversity kick against God's will, others despond; neither is to be done by the Christian, who is peculiarly the child of God. To him such adverse things occur only by the decree of God, and that designed in kindness, viz., to remove the defilements adhering to the believer, and to exercise his patience" [GROTIUS]. **6.** (Rev. 3:19.) **and**—*Greek,* "yea and," "and moreover"; bringing out an additional circumstance. **scourgeth**—which draws forth "blood" (vs. 4). **receiveth**—accepts. Takes to Himself as a son "in whom He *delighteth*" (Prov. 3:12). **7.** In vss. 7, 8 the need of "chastening" or "discipline" is inculcated; in vs. 9, the duty of those to whom it is administered. **If**—The oldest MSS. read, "With a view to chastening (i.e., since God's chastisement is with a view to your chastening, i.e., disciplinary amelioration) endure patiently"; so *Vulgate.* ALFORD translates it as indicative, not so well, "It is for chastisement that *ye are enduring.*" **dealeth with you**—"beareth Himself toward you" in the very act of chastening. **what son is he**—"What son is there" even in ordinary life? Much more God as to His sons (Isa. 48:10; Acts 14:22). The most eminent of God's saints were the most afflicted. God leads them by a way they know not (Isa. 42:16). We too much look at each trial by itself, instead of taking it in connection with the whole plan of our salvation, as if a traveller were to complain of the steepness and roughness of one turn in the path, without considering that it led him into green pastures, on the direct road to the city of habitation. The New Testament alone uses the *Greek* term for education (*paideia*), to express "discipline" or *correction,* as of a *child* by a wise father. **8. if ye be without**—excluded from participation in chastisement, and wishing to be so. **all**—all *sons:* all the worthies enumerated in ch. 11: all the *witnesses* (vs. 1). **are**—*Greek,* "have been made." **then are ye bastards**—of whom their fathers take no care whether they are educated or not; whereas every rightminded father is concerned for the moral well-being of his legitimate son. "Since then not to be chastised is a mark of bastardy, we ought [not to refuse, but] rejoice in chastisement, as a mark of our genuine sonship" [CHRYSOSTOM]. **9. fathers . . . which corrected us**—rather as *Greek,* "We had the fathers of our flesh as correctors." **subjection**—See the punishment of insubordination, Deuteronomy 21:18. **Father of spirits**—contrasted with "the fathers of our flesh." "Generation by men is carnal, by God is spiritual" [BENGEL]. As "Father of spirits," He is both the Originator, and the Providential and Gracious Sustainer, at once of animal and spiritual life. Cf. "and LIVE," viz., spiritually; also vs. 10, "that we might be partakers of HIS holiness" (II Pet. 1:4). God is a spirit Himself, and the Creator of spirits like Himself, in contrast to men who are flesh, and the progenitors of flesh (John 3:6). Jesus our pattern "learned obedience" experimentally by suffering (ch. 5:8). **and live**—and so, thereby live spiritually and eternally. **10.** Showing wherein the chastisement of our heavenly Father is preferable to that of earthly fathers. **for a few days**—i.e., *with a view to* our well-being in *the few days* of our earthly life: so the *Greek.* **after their own pleasure**—*Greek,* "according to what seemed fit to themselves." Their rule of chastening is what may seem fit to their own often erring judgment, temper, or caprice. The two defects of human education are: (1) the prevalence in it of a view to the interests of our *short* earthly term of *days;* (2) the absence in parents of the unerring wisdom of our heavenly Father. "They err much at one time in severity, at another in indulgence [I Sam. 3:13; Eph. 6:4], and do not so much chasten as THINK they chasten" [BENGEL]. **that we might be partakers of his holiness**—becoming holy as He is holy (John 15:2). To become *holy* like God is tantamount to being educated for passing *eternity* with God (vs. 14; II Pet. 1:4). So this "partaking of God's holiness" stands in contrast to the "few days"

ADAM CLARKE

5. *And ye have forgotten.* Or "Have you forgotten the exhortation?" This quotation is made from Prov. iii. 11-12, and shows that the address there, which at first sight appears to be from Solomon to his son or from some fatherly man to a person in affliction, is properly from God himself to any person in persecution, affliction, or distress. *Despise not thou the chastening.* "Do not neglect the correction of the Lord." That man neglects correction and profits not by it who does not see the hand of God in it or, in other words, does not fear the rod and Him who hath appointed it, and consequently does not humble himself under the mighty hand of God, deplore his sin, deprecate divine judgment, and pray for mercy. *Nor faint.* Do not be discouraged nor despair, for the reasons immediately alleged.

6. *For whom the Lord loveth he chasteneth.* Here is the reason why we should neither neglect correction nor faint under it. It is a proof of the fatherly love of God Almighty, and shows His most gracious designs towards us, from which we may be fully convinced that the affliction will prove the means of good to our souls if we make a proper use of it. *And scourgeth every son whom he receiveth.* This is a quotation from the Septuagint of Prov. iii. 12, of which place our version is: "Even as a father the son in whom he delighteth." But howsoever near this may appear to be the Hebrew, it bears scarcely any affinity to the apostle's words. The translation therefore of the Septuagint and apostle is perfectly consonant to the Hebrew text, and our version of Prov. iii. 12 is wrong.

7. *If ye endure chastening.* If you submit to His authority, humble yourselves under His hand, and pray for His blessing, you will find that He deals with you as beloved children, correcting you that He may make you partakers of His holiness. *God dealeth with you as with sons.* He acknowledges by this that you belong to the family, and that He, as your Father, has you under proper discipline. It is a maxim among the Jewish rabbins that "the love which is not conjoined with reproof is not genuine."

8. *Then are ye bastards.* This proceeds on the general fact that bastards are neglected in their manners and education; the fathers of such, feeling little affection for, or obligation to regard, their spurious issue. But *all* that are legitimate children *are partakers of chastisement* or "discipline"; for the original word does not imply stripes and punishments, but the whole "discipline" of a child, both at home and at school.

9. *We have had fathers of our flesh.* The fathers of our flesh, i.e., our natural parents, were correctors; and we reverenced them, notwithstanding their corrections often arose from whim or caprice. But *shall we not rather be in subjection to the Father of spirits;* to Him from whom we have received both body and soul; who is our Creator, Preserver, and Supporter; to whom both we and our parents owe our life and our blessings; and who corrects us only for our profit, that we may *live* and be "partakers of his holiness"? The apostle in asking, *Shall we not much rather be in subjection unto the Father of spirits, and live?* alludes to the punishment of the stubborn and rebellious son, Deut. xxi. 18-21: "If a man have a stubborn and rebellious son, which will not obey the voice of his father, or the voice of his mother, and that, when they have chastened him, will not hearken unto them: then shall his father and his mother lay hold on him, and bring him out unto the elders of his city . . . and they shall say . . . This our son is stubborn and rebellious, he will not obey our voice . . . And all the man of his city shall stone him with stones, that he die."

10. *For . . . a few days.* The chastisement of our earthly parents lasted only a short time; that of our Heavenly Father also will be but a short time, if we submit. And as our parents ceased to correct when we learned obedience, so will our Heavenly Father when the end for which He sent the chastisement is accomplished. God delights not in the rod; judgment is His strange work.

MATTHEW HENRY

5. The children of God ought not to judge of his dealings with them by present sense, but by reason, and faith, and experience, *v.* 11.

(1) The judgment of sense. Afflictions are not grateful to the sense, but grievous.

(2) The judgment of faith. Affliction produces peace, by producing more righteousness; for the fruit of righteousness is peace. Their great concern is that the chastening they are under may be endured by them with patience, and improved to a greater degree of holiness.

[1] That their affliction may be endured with patience, *v.* 12. A burden of affliction is apt to make the Christian's hands hang down, and his knees grow feeble, to dispirit him and discourage him; but this he must strive against; that he may the better run his spiritual race. Faith, and patience, and holy courage and resolution, will make him walk more steadily. He must encourage and not dispirit others. There are many that are in the way to heaven who yet walk but weakly and lamely in it. Such are apt to discourage one another; but it is their duty to help one another forward in the way to heaven.

[2] That their affliction may be improved to a greater degree of holiness, *v.* 14. Faith and patience will enable them to follow peace and holiness too. Sufferings are apt to sour the spirit and sharpen the passions; but the children of God must follow peace with all men. Peace and holiness are connected together. This true Christian peaceableness is never found separate from holiness. *Without holiness no man shall see the Lord.*

6. Where afflictions and sufferings for the sake of Christ are not considered by men as the chastisement of their heavenly Father, they will be a dangerous temptation to apostasy (*v.* 15, 16).

(1) A serious caveat against apostasy.

[1] The nature of apostasy. It is *failing of the grace of God,* coming short of a principle of true grace in the soul, and so coming short of the love and favour of God here and hereafter. The consequences of apostasy: where persons fail of having the true grace of God, a root of bitterness will spring up, corruption will prevail and break forth. It produces to themselves corrupt principles. It also produces bitter fruits to others.

JAMIESON, FAUSSET, BROWN

of this life, with a view to which earthly fathers generally educate their sons. **11. joyous . . . grievous**—*Greek,* "matter of joy . . . matter of grief." The objection that chastening is grievous is here anticipated and answered. It only seems so to those being chastened, whose judgments are confused by the present pain. Its ultimate *fruit* amply compensates for any temporary pain. The real object of the fathers in chastening is not that they find pleasure in the children's pain. Gratified wishes, our Father knows, would often be our real curses. **fruit of righteousness**—*righteousness* (in practice, springing from faith) is the *fruit* which chastening, the tree yields (Phil. 1:11). "Peaceable" (cf. Isa. 32:17): in contrast to the ordeal of conflict by which it has been won. "Fruit of righteousness to be enjoyed in peace after the conflict" [THOLUCK]. As the olive garland, the emblem of *peace* as well as *victory,* was put on the victor's brow in the games. **exercised thereby**—as athletes exercised in training for a contest. *Chastisement* is the *exercise* to give experience, and make the spiritual combatant irresistibly victorious (Rom. 5:3).

12. He addresses them as runners in a race, and pugilists, and warriors [CHRYSOSTOM]. The "wherefore" is resumed from vs. 1. **lift up**—In Isaiah 35:3, from which Paul here quotes, it is, "*Strengthen* ye the weak hands." The *hand* is the symbol of one's strength. ALFORD translates, "Put straight again the relaxed hands." *English Version* expresses the sense well. **feeble**—lit., "paralyzed"; a word used only by Luke, *Paul's* companion, in the New Testament. Lift up not only *your own* hands and knees, but also those *of your brethren* (cf. vs. 15; Isa. 35:4). **13.** Quoted from Proverbs 4:26, LXX, "Make straight paths for thy feet." **straight**—i.e., leading by a straight road to joy and grace (vss. 1, 2, 15). Cease to "halt" between Judaism and Christianity [BENGEL]. **paths**—lit., "wheel tracks." Let your walk be so firm and so unanimous in the right direction that a plain track and "highway" may be thereby established for those who accompany and follow you, to perceive and walk in (Isa. 35:8) [ALFORD]. **that which is lame**—those "weak in the faith" (Rom. 14:1), having still Judaizing prejudices. **be turned out of the way**—(Prov. 4:27)—and, so missing the way, lose the prize of "the race" (vs. 1). **rather he healed**—Proper exercise of itself contributes to health; the habit of walking straight onward in the right way tends to *healing.* **14. follow peace with all men**—with the brethren especially (Rom. 14:19), that so the "lame" among them be not "turned out of the way" (vs. 13), and that no one of them "fail of the grace of God" (vs. 15). **holiness**—a distinct *Greek* word from God's "holiness" (vs. 10). Translate here "sanctification." His is absolute *holiness:* our part is to put on His holiness, becoming "holy as He is holy," by *sanctification.* While "following peace with all men," we are not so to seek to please them, as to make God's will and our sanctification a secondary object; this latter must be our first aim. (Gal. 1:10). **without which**—*Greek,* "apart from which." **no man shall see the Lord**—no man *as a son;* in heavenly glory (Rev. 22:3, 4). In the East, none but the greatest favorites are admitted to the honor of seeing the king (cf. II Sam. 14:24). The Lord being pure and holy, none but the pure and holy shall see Him (Matt. 5:8). Without holiness in them, they could not enjoy Him who is holiness itself (Zech. 14:20). The connection of *purity* with *seeing the Lord,* appears in I John 3:2, 3; Ephesians 5:5. Contrast vs. 16 (cf. I Thess. 4:3). In Matthew 24:30; Revelation 1:7, it is said that all shall see the Lord; but, that shall be as a *Judge,* not as their lasting portion and God, which is meant here. The *Greek* verb does not denote the mere action of seeing, but the seer's state of mind to which the object is presented: so in Matthew 5:8 they shall *truly comprehend* God [TITTMANN]. None but the holy could *appreciate* the holy God, none else therefore shall abide in His presence. **15. lest any . . . fall**—*Greek,* "lest any (viz., through sloth in running) *failing,*" or "*falling short of* the grace of God . . . *trouble you.*" The image is taken from a company of travellers, one of whom lags behind, and so never reaches the end of the long and laborious journey [CHRYSOSTOM]. **root of bitterness**—not merely a "*bitter* root," which might possibly bring forth sweet fruits; this, a root whose *essence* is "*bitterness,*" never could. Paul here refers to Deuteronomy 29:18, "Lest there should be among you a root that beareth gall and wormwood" (cf. Acts 8:23). *Root of bitterness* comprehends every *person* (cf. vs. 16) and every *principle* of doctrine or practice so radically corrupt as to spread corruption all around. The only safety is in rooting out such

ADAM CLARKE

11. *No chastening for the present seemeth to be joyous.* Neither correction, wholesome restraint, domestic regulations, nor gymnastic discipline are pleasant to them that are thus exercised; but it is by these means that obedient children, scholars, and great men are made. And it is by God's discipline that Christians are made. He who does not bear the yoke of Christ is good for nothing to others, and never gains rest to his own soul. *The peaceable fruit of righteousness.* I.e., The joyous, prosperous fruits; those fruits by which we gain much, and through which we are made happy. *Exercised thereby.* "To the trained." There is still an allusion to the Grecian games, and in the word before us to those "gymnastic exercises" by which the candidates for the prizes were trained to the different kinds of exercises in which they were to contend when the games were publicly opened.

12. *Wherefore lift up the hands.* The apostle refers to Isa. xxxv. 3. The words are an address to persons almost worn out with sickness and fatigue, whose *hands* hang down, whose *knees* shake, and who are totally discouraged. These are exhorted to exert themselves, and take courage, with the assurance that they shall infallibly conquer if they persevere.

13. *Make straight paths for your feet.* That is, Take the straight path that is before you; do not go in crooked or rough ways, where are stones, briers, and thorns, by which you will be inevitably lamed, and so totally prevented from proceeding in the way; whereas if you go in the even, proper path, though you have been wounded by getting into a wrong way, that which was wounded will *be healed* by moderate, equal exercise, all impediments being removed. The application of all this to a correct, holy deportment in religious life is both natural and easy.

14. *Follow peace with all men.* Cultivate, as far as you possibly can, a good understanding, with both Jews and Gentiles. "Pursue peace" with the same care, attention, and diligence as beasts do their game; follow it through all places; trace it through all winding circumstances; and have it with all men, if you can with a safe conscience. *And holiness.* That state of continual "sanctification," that life of purity and detachment from the world and all its lusts, without which detachment and sanctity *no man shall see the Lord*—shall never enjoy His presence in the world of blessedness. "To see God," in the Hebrew phrase, is to "enjoy Him"; and without holiness of heart and life this is impossible. No soul can be fit for heaven that has not suitable dispositions for the place.

15. *Looking diligently.* "Looking about, over, and upon"; being constantly on your guard. *Lest any man fail of the grace of God.* "Lest any person should come behind, or fall off from, this grace or gift of God"; this state of salvation, viz., the gospel system or Christianity, for this is most evidently the meaning of the apostle. It is not the falling from a work of grace in their own souls, but from the gospel, to apostatize from which they had now many temptations; and to guard them against this, the whole Epistle was written. *Lest any root of bitterness springing up.* A root of bitterness signifies a "poisonous plant." The Hebrews call every species of poison a "bitter," and with considerable propriety, as most plants are poisonous in proportion to the quantum of the bitter principle they possess. The *root of bitterness* is here used metaphorically for a bad man, or a man holding unsound doctrines, and endeavoring to spread them in the church. *Trouble you.* This alludes to the effects of poison taken into the body. The blood itself (the principle, under God, of life) becomes putrescent; and probably

MATTHEW HENRY

Many are defiled, tainted with those bad principles, and drawn into defiling practices.

[2] The apostle backs the caution with an awful example, that of Esau. Esau's sin. He profanely despised and sold the birthright, and all the advantages attending it. So do apostates.

Esau's punishment. His conscience was convinced of his sin and folly, when it was too late. He now saw that the blessing he had made so light of was worth the having. He was rejected of God: *He found no place of repentance.* Esau, in his great wickedness, had made the bargain, and God, in his righteous judgment, ratified and confirmed it.

(2) Apostasy from Christ is the fruit of preferring the gratification of the flesh to the blessing of God. Sinners will not always have such mean thoughts of the divine blessing and inheritance as now they have. When the day of grace is over they will find no place for repentance. Christians should never give up their hope of their Father's blessings by deserting their holy religion, to avoid suffering.

Verses 18–29

I. He shows how much the gospel church differs from the Jewish church, and how much it excels, *v.* 18–21. 1. It was a gross sensible state. Mount Sinai was a *mount that might be touched* (*v.* 18), a gross palpable place; so was the dispensation. The state of the gospel church on Mount Zion is more spiritual.

JAMIESON, FAUSSET, BROWN

a root of bitterness. **many**—rather, "*the* many," i.e., the whole congregation. So long as it is hidden under the earth it cannot be remedied, but when it "springs up," it must be dealt with boldly. Still remember the caution (Matt. 13:26-30) as to rooting out *persons.* No such danger can arise in rooting out bad *principles.* **16. fornicator**—(ch. 13:4; I Cor. 10:8). **or profane**—*Fornication* is nearly akin to gluttony, Esau's sin. He *profanely* cast away his spiritual privilege for the gratification of his palate. Genesis 25:34 graphically portrays him. An example well fitted to strike needful horror into the Hebrews, whosoever of them, like Esau, were only sons of Isaac according to the flesh [BENGEL]. **for one morsel**—The smallness of the inducement only aggravates the guilt of casting away eternity for such a trifle, so far is it from being a claim for mercy (cf. Gen. 3:6). *One* single act has often the greatest power either for good or for evil. So in the cases of Reuben and Saul, for evil (Gen. 49:4; I Chron. 5:1; I Sam. 13:12-14); and, on the other hand, for good, Abraham and Phinehas (Gen. 12:1, etc.; 15:5, 6; Num. 25:6-15). **his birthright**—*Greek,* "his own (so the oldest MSS. read, intensifying the suicidal folly and sin of the act) rights of primogeniture," involving the high spiritual privilege of being ancestor of the promised seed, and heir of the promises in Him. The Hebrews whom Paul addressed, had, as Christians, the spiritual rights of primogeniture (cf. vs. 23): he intimates that they must exercise holy selfcontrol, if they wish not, like Esau, to forfeit them. **17. afterwards**—*Greek,* "*even* afterward." He despised his birthright, accordingly *also* he was despised and rejected when he wished to have the blessing. As in the believer's case, so in the unbeliever's, there is an "afterwards" coming, when the believer shall look on his past griefs, and the unbeliever on his past joys, in a very different light from that in which they were respectively viewed at the time. Cf. "Nevertheless afterward . . ." vs. 11, with the "afterward" here. **when he would**—when he *wished* to have. "He that will not when he may, when he will, shall have nay" (Prov. 1:24-30; Luke 13:34, 35; 19:42). **he was rejected**—not as to every blessing, but only that which would have followed the primogeniture. **he found no place of repentance**—The *cause* is here put for the *effect,* "repentance" for the object which Esau aimed at in his so-called *repentance,* viz., *the change of his father's determination* to give the chief blessing to Jacob. Had he *sought* real *repentance with tears* he would have *found* it (Matt. 7:7). But he did not find it because this was not what he sought. What proves his *tears* were not those of one seeking true repentance is, immediately after he was foiled in his desire, he resolved to murder Jacob! He shed tears, not for his sin, but for his suffering the penalty of his sin. His were tears of vain regret and remorse, not of repentance. **For**—The fact that we are not under the law, but under a higher, and that the last dispensation, the Gospel, with its glorious privileges, is the reason why especially the Hebrew Christians should "look diligently . . ." (vss. 15, 16). **are not come**—*Greek,* "have not come near to." Alluding to Deuteronomy 4:11, "Ye *came near* and stood under the mountain; and the mountain burned with fire . . . with darkness, clouds, and thick darkness." "In your *coming near unto God,* it has not been to. . . ." **the mount**—The oldest MSS. and *Vulgate* omit "the mount." But still, "the mount" must be supplied from vs. 22. **that might be touched**—palpable and material. Not that any save Moses was allowed to touch it (Exod. 19:12, 13). The Hebrews drew near to the material Mount Sinai with material bodies; we, to the spiritual mount in the spirit. The "darkness" was that formed by the clouds hanging round the mount; the "tempest" accompanied the thunder. **19. trumpet**—to rouse attention, and herald God's approach (Exod. 19:16). **entreated that the word should not be spoken**—lit., "that speech should not be added to them"; not that they refused to hear the word of God, but they wished that God should not Himself speak, but employ Moses as His mediating spokesman. "The voice of words" was the Decalogue, spoken by God Himself, a voice issuing forth, without *any* form being seen: after which "He *added* no more" (Deut. 5:22). **20. that which was commanded**—"the interdict" [TITTMANN]. A *stern interdictory mandate* is meant. **And**—rather, "Even if a beast (much more a man) touch. . . ." **or thrust through with a dart**—omitted in the oldest MSS. The *full* interdict in Exodus 19:12, 13 is abbreviated here; the beast alone, being put for "whether man or beast"; the *stoning,* which applies to the *human* offender, alone being specified, the beast's punishment, viz., the being *thrust through with a dart,*

ADAM CLARKE

to this the intelligent apostle alludes when he says, *and thereby many be defiled,* "corrupted or contaminated."

16. *Lest there be any fornicator.* Any licentious person who would turn the gospel of the grace of God into lasciviousness. *Or profane person, as Esau.* It is not intimated that Esau was a *fornicator;* and the disjunctive *or* separates the *profane person* from the *fornicator.* And Esau is here termed *profane* because he so far disregarded the spiritual advantages connected with his rights of primogeniture that he alienated the whole for a single mess of pottage. See the note on Gen. xxv. 34. The word which we translate *profane* was applied to those who were not initiated into the sacred mysteries or who were despisers of sacred things, and consequently were to be denied admittance to the Temple and were not permitted to assist at holy rites. Indeed, among the Greeks it signified any thing or person which was "not consecrated to the gods." The Latin *profanus,* from which we have our word, is compounded of *procul a fano,* "far from the temple," properly an "irreligious man." *Sold his birthright.* The firstborn, in patriarchal times: (1) Had a right to the priesthood, Exod. xxii. 29; (2) And a double portion of all the father's possessions, Deut. xxi. 17; (3) And was lord over his brethren, Gen. xxvii. 29, 37; xlix. 3; (4) And in the family of Abraham the firstborn was the very source whence the Messiah, as the Redeemer of the world, and the Church of God were to spring. In short, the rights of primogeniture were among the most noble, honorable, and spiritual in the ancient world.

17. *When he would have inherited the blessing.* When he wished to have the lordship over the whole family conveyed to him, and sought it earnestly with tears, he found no place for a "change" in his father's mind and counsel, who now perceived that it was the will of God that Jacob should be made lord of all. *Repentance.* Here *metanoia* is not to be taken in a theological sense, as implying contrition for sin, but merely "change of mind or purpose"; nor does the word refer here to Esau at all, but to his father, whom Esau could not, with all his tears and entreaties, persuade to reverse what he had done. "I have blessed him," said he, "yea, and he must be blessed"; I cannot reverse it now. Nothing spoken here by the apostle, nor in the history in Genesis to which he refers, concerns the eternal state of either of the two brothers. The use made of the transaction by the apostle is of great importance: Take heed lest, by apostatizing from the gospel, you forfeit all right and title to the heavenly birthright, and never again be able to retrieve it; because they who reject the gospel reject the only means of salvation.

18-21. *For ye are not come unto the mount that might be touched.* I believe the words should be translated "to a palpable or material mountain"; for that it was not a mountain that on this occasion *might be touched,* the history, Exod. xix. 12-13, shows; and the apostle himself, in v. 20, confirms. It is called here a palpable or material mount to distinguish it from that spiritual "mount Sion," of which the apostle is speaking.

The apostle's design is to show that the dispensation of the law engendered terror; that it was most awful and exclusive; that it belonged only to the Jewish people; and that, even to them, it was so terrible that they *could not endure that which was commanded,* and entreated that God would not communicate with them in His own person, but by the ministry of Moses.

MATTHEW HENRY

2. It was a dark dispensation. Upon that mount there were blackness and darkness. The gospel state is clear and bright. 3. It was a dreadful and terrible dispensation; the Jews could not bear the terror of it, *v.* 19. Yea, Moses himself said, *I exceedingly fear and quake.* The gospel state is mild, and kind, suited to our weak frame. 4. It was a limited dispensation; all might not approach to that mount. Under the gospel we have all access with boldness to God. This was the state of the Jewish church, fitted to set forth the strict and tremendous justice of God.

II. He shows how much the gospel church represents the church triumphant in heaven. The gospel church is called *Mount Zion, the heavenly Jerusalem.* In coming to Mount Zion, believers come into heavenly places, and into a heavenly society.

1. Into heavenly places. (1) *Unto the city of the living God.* God has taken up his gracious residence in the gospel church, which on that account is an emblem of heaven. (2) To *the heavenly Jerusalem,* as free denizens there.

2. To a heavenly society. (1) *To an innumerable company of angels.* Those who by faith are joined to the gospel church are joined to the angels, and shall at length be like them. (2) *To the general assembly and church of the first-born, that are written in heaven,* to the universal church, however dispersed. By faith we come to them, have communion with them in the same blessed hope, and walk in the same way of holiness. Here will be the general assembly of the first-born, the saints of former and earlier times. The names of these are written in heaven: they have a name in God's house, and are enrolled in the Lamb's book of life, as citizens are enrolled in the livery-books.

(3) *To God the Judge of all,* that great God who will judge both Jew and Gentile according to the law they are under.

(4) *To the spirits of just men made perfect;* to the best sort of men, the righteous, to the best part of just men, their spirits, and to these in their best state, made perfect.

JAMIESON, FAUSSET, BROWN

being left to be understood. **21. the sight**—the *vision* of God's majesty. **quake**—*Greek,* "I am in trembling"; "fear" affected his *mind;* "trembling," his body. Moses is not recorded in Exodus to have used these words. But Paul, by inspiration, supplies (cf. Acts 20:35; II Tim. 3:8) this detail. We read in Deuteronomy 9:19, LXX, of similar words used by Moses after breaking the two tables, through fear of God's anger at the people's sin in making the golden calves. He doubtless similarly "feared" in hearing the ten commandments spoken by the voice of Jehovah. **22. are come**—*Greek,* "have come near unto" (cf. Deut. 4:11). Not merely, ye *shall* come, but, *ye have already come.* **Mount Sion**—antitypical Sion, the heavenly Jerusalem, of which the spiritual invisible Church (of which the first foundation was laid in literal Zion, John 12:15; I Pet. 2:6) is now the earnest; and of which the restored literal Jerusalem hereafter shall be the earthly representative, to be succeeded by the everlasting and "new Jerusalem, coming down from God out of heaven" (Rev. 21:2-27; cf. ch. 11:10). **22, 23. to an innumerable company of angels, to the general assembly and church**—The *city* of God having been mentioned, the mention of its citizens follows. Believers being like the angels (Job 1:6; 38: 7), "sons of God," are so their "equals" (Luke 20: 36); and, being reconciled through Christ, are adopted into God's great and blessed family. For the full completion of this we pray (Matt. 6:10). *English Version* arrangement is opposed: (1) by "and" always beginning each new member of the whole sentence; (2) "general assembly and Church," form a kind of tautology; (3) "general assembly," or rather, "*festal* full assembly," "the jubilant full company" (such as were the Olympic games, celebrated with joyous singing, dancing, etc.), applies better to the *angels* above, ever hymning God's praises, than to the Church, of which a considerable part is now militant on earth. Translate therefore, "to myriads (ten thousands, cf. Deut. 33:2; Ps. 68: 17; Dan. 7:10; Jude 14; namely), the full festal assembly of angels, and the Church of the firstborn." Angels and saints together constitute the *ten thousands.* Cf. "*all* angels, *all nations*" Matthew 25: 31, 32. Messiah is pre-eminently "the First-born," or "First-begotten" (ch. 1:6), and all believers become so by adoption. Cf. the type, Leviticus 3: 12, 45, 50; I Peter 1:18. As the kingly and priestly succession was in the first-born, and as Israel was God's "first-born" (Exod. 4:22; cf. 13:2), and a "kingdom of priests" to God (Exod. 19:6), so believers (Rev. 1:6). **written in heaven**—enrolled as citizens there. *All* those who at the coming of "God the Judge of all" (which clause therefore naturally follows), shall be found "written in heaven," i.e., *in the Lamb's book of life.* Though still fighting the good fight on earth, still, in respect to your destiny, and present life of *faith* which substantiates things hoped for, ye *are* already members of the heavenly citizenship. "We are one citizenship with angels; to which it is said in the psalm, *Glorious things are spoken of thee, thou city of God*" [AUGUSTINE]. I think ALFORD wrong in *restricting* "the Church of the first-born written in heaven," to those militant on earth; it is rather, *all* those who *at the Judge's coming* shall be found written in heaven (the true patent of heavenly nobility; contrast "written in the earth," Jer. 17:13, and Esau's profane sale of his birthright, vs. 16); these all, from the beginning to the end of the world, forming *one* Church to which every believer is already come. The *first-born* of Israel were "written" in a roll (Num. 3:40). **the spirits of just men made perfect**—at the resurrection, when the "JUDGE" shall appear, and believers' bliss shall be consummated by the union of the glorified *body* with the *spirit;* the great hope of the New Testament (Rom. 8:20-23; I Thess. 4:16). The place of this clause *after* "the JUDGE OF ALL," is my objection to BENGEL and ALFORD'S explanation, the souls of the just *in their separate state perfected.* Cf. (*Note*) ch. 11:39, 40, to which he refers here, and which I think confirms my view; those heretofore *spirits,* but now to be perfected by being clothed upon with the body. Still the phrase, "*spirits* of just men made perfect," not merely "just men made perfect," may favor the reference to the happy spirits in their separate state. The *Greek* is not "the *perfected spirits,*" but "the spirits of *the perfected just.*" In no other passage are *the just* said to be *perfected* before the resurrection, and the completion of the full number of the elect (Rev. 6:11); I think, therefore, "spirits of the just," may here be used to express *the just whose predominant element in their perfected state shall be spirit.* So *spirit* and *spirits* are used of *a man* or *men in the body, under the influence of the spirit,* the opposite of *flesh*

ADAM CLARKE

And even to Moses, who held the highest intimacy with Jehovah, the revealed glories, the burning fire, the blackness, the darkness, the tempest, the loud-sounding trumpet, and the voice of words were so terrible that he said, "I exceedingly fear and tremble." These were the things which were exhibited on that material mountain; but the gospel dispensation is one grand, copious, and interesting display of the infinite love of God. It is all encouragement; breathes nothing but mercy; is not an exclusive system; embraces the whole human race; has Jesus, the sinner's Friend, for its Mediator; is ratified by His blood; and is suited, most gloriously suited, to all the wants and wishes of every soul of man.

22. *But ye are come unto mount Sion.* In order to enter fully into the apostle's meaning we must observe: (1) That the Church, which is called here *the city of the living God, the heavenly Jerusalem,* and *mount Sion,* is represented under the notion of a city. (2) That the great assembly of believers in Christ is here opposed to the congregation of the Israelites assembled at Mount Sinai. (3) That the *innumerable company of angels* is here opposed to those angels by whom the law was ushered in, Acts vii. 53; Gal. iii. 19. (4) That the gospel "firstborn," whose names are "written in heaven," are here opposed to the enrolled firstborn among the Israelites, Exod. xxiv. 5; xix. 22. (5) That the "mediator of the new covenant," the Lord Jesus, is here opposed to Moses, the mediator of the old. (6) And that "the blood of sprinkling," of Christ, our High Priest, refers to the act of Moses, Exod. xxiv. 8: "And Moses took the blood, and sprinkled it on the people, and said, Behold the blood of the covenant, which the Lord hath made with you concerning all these words." *The heavenly Jerusalem.* This phrase means the Church of the New Testament. *To an innumerable company of angels.* "To myriads, tens of thousands, of angels." These are represented as the attendants upon God when He manifests himself in any external manner to mankind. When He gave the law at Mount Sinai, it is intimated that myriads of these holy beings attended Him. "The chariots of God are twenty thousand, even thousands of angels: the Lord is among them, as in Sinai, in the holy place," Ps. lxviii. 17. And when He shall come to judge the world, He will be attended with a similar company. "Thousand thousands ministered unto him, and ten thousand times ten thousand stood before him," Dan. vii. 10. In both these cases, as in several others, these seem to be, speaking after the manner of men, the bodyguard of the Almighty.

23. *To the general assembly.* This word is joined to the preceding by some of the best MSS., and is quoted in connection by several of the fathers: "Ye are come . . . to the general assembly of innumerable angels"; and this is probably the true connection. *The firstborn.* Those who first received the gospel of Christ, and who are elsewhere termed the "firstfruits." This is spoken in allusion to the firstborn among the Israelites, who were all considered as the Lord's property, and were dedicated to Him. The Jews gave the title "firstborn" to those who were very eminent or excellent, what we would term the head or top of his kin. The *church of the firstborn* is the assembly of the most excellent. *Which are written in heaven.* Who are enrolled as citizens of the New Jerusalem, and are entitled to all the rights, privileges, and immunities of the Church here and of heaven above. This is spoken in allusion to the custom of enrolling or writing on tables, etc., the names of all the citizens of a particular city; and all those thus registered were considered as having a right to live there, and to enjoy all its privileges. *God the Judge of all.* The supreme God is ever present in this general assembly. To Him they are all gathered; by Him they are admitted to all those rights, etc.; under His inspection they continue to act; and it is He alone who erases from the register those who act unworthily of their citizenship. *Judge* here is to be taken in the Jewish use of the term, i.e., one who exercises sovereign rule and authority. *The spirits of just men made perfect.* We cannot understand these terms without the assistance of Jewish phraseology. The Jews divide mankind into three classes: (1) the just perfect,

MATTHEW HENRY

(5) *To Jesus the Mediator of the new covenant, and to the blood of sprinkling, that speaketh better things than that of Abel.* This is none of the least of the many encouragements there are to perseverance. [1] The gospel covenant is a new covenant, distinct from the covenant of works. [2] Christ is the Mediator of this new covenant. [3] This covenant is ratified by the blood of Christ sprinkled upon our consciences. This blood of Christ pacifies God and purifies the consciences of men.

[4] This is speaking blood, and it speaks better things than that of Abel. It speaks to God in behalf of sinners; it pleads not for vengeance, but for mercy. It speaks to sinners, in the name of God. It speaks pardon to their sins, peace to their souls.

III. The apostle closes the chapter by improving the argument in a manner suitable to the weight of it (*v.* 25, &c.). Then he spoke on earth, now he speaks from heaven.

1. When God speaks to men in the most excellent manner he justly expects from them the most strict attention. He now speaks from a higher and more glorious throne—heaven. He speaks now more powerfully and effectually. Then indeed his voice shook the earth, but now he hath shaken not only the earth, but the heavens. It is by the gospel from heaven that God shook to pieces the Jewish nation, and introduced a new state of the church.

2. When God speaks to men in the most excellent manner, the guilt of those who refuse him is the greater, *v.* 25.

JAMIESON, FAUSSET, BROWN

(John 3:6). The resurrection bodies of the saints shall be *bodies* in which the *spirit* shall altogether preponderate over the *animal soul* (*Note,* I Cor. 15:44). **24. new**—not the usual term (*kaine*) applied to the Christian covenant (ch. 9:15), which would mean *new* as *different from,* and superseding the *old;* but *Greek, nea,* recent, lately established, having the *freshness* of *youth,* as opposed to age. The mention of Jesus, *the Perfecter* of our faith (vs. 2), and Himself perfected through sufferings and death, in His resurrection and ascension (ch. 2:10; 5:9), is naturally suggested by the mention of "the just *made perfect*" at their resurrection (cf. ch. 7: 22). Paul uses "Jesus," dwelling here on Him as the Person realized as our loving friend, not merely in His *official* character as the *Christ.* **and to the blood of sprinkling**—here enumerated as distinct from "Jesus." BENGEL reasonably argues as follows: His blood was entirely "poured out" of His body by the various ways in which it was shed, His bloody sweat, the crown of thorns, the scourging, the nails, and after death the spear, just as the blood was entirely poured out and extravasated from the animal sacrifices of the law. It was *incorruptible* (I Pet. 1:18, 19). No Scripture states it was again put into the Lord's body. At His ascension, as our great High Priest, He entered the heavenly holiest place "BY His own blood" (not *after* shedding His blood, nor *with* the blood in His body, but), carrying it separately from his body (cf. the type, ch. 9:7, 12, 25; 13:11). Paul does not say, by the efficacy of His blood, but, "by *His own proper* blood" (ch. 9:12); not MATERIAL blood, but "the blood of Him who, through the eternal Spirit, offered Himself without spot unto God" (ch. 9:14). So in ch. 10:29, *the Son of God* and *the blood of the covenant wherewith* (the professor) *was sanctified,* are mentioned separately. Also in ch. 13:12, 20; also cf. ch. 10:19, with 21. So in the Lord's Supper (I Cor. 10:16; 11:24-26), *the body* and *blood* are separately represented. The blood itself, therefore, continues still in heaven before God, the perpetual ransom-price of "the eternal covenant" (ch. 13:20). Once for all Christ sprinkled the blood peculiarly for us at His ascension (ch. 9:12). **speaketh better things than that of Abel**—viz., than the sprinkling (the best MSS. read the article *masculine,* which refers to "sprinkling," not to "blood," which last is neuter) of blood by Abel in his sacrifice spake. This comparison between two *things of the same kind* (viz., Christ's sacrifice, and Abel's sacrifice) is more natural, than between two things different in kind and in results (viz., Christ's sacrifice, and Abel's own blood [ALFORD], which was not a sacrifice at all); cf. ch. 11:4; Genesis 4:4. This accords with the whole tenor of the Epistle, and of this passage in particular (vss. 18-22), which is to show the superiority of Christ's sacrifice and the new covenant, to the Old Testament sacrifices (of which Abel's is the first recorded; it, moreover, was testified to by God as acceptable to Him above Cain's), cf. ch. 9 and 10. The word "better" implies superiority to something that is good: but Abel's *own* blood was not at all good for the purpose for which Christ's blood was efficacious; nay, it cried for vengeance. **25. refuse not**—through unbelief. **him that speaketh**—God in Christ. As the *blood of sprinkling* is represented as *speaking* to God for us, vs. 24; so here God is represented as speaking to us (ch. 1:1, 2). His word now is the prelude of the last "shaking" of all things (vs. 27). The same word which is heard in the Gospel *from heaven,* will shake heaven and earth (vs. 26). **who refused him**—*Greek,* "refusing as they did." Their seemingly submissive entreaty that the word should not be spoken to them by God any more (vs. 19), covered over refractory hearts, as their subsequent deeds showed (ch. 3:16). **that spake**—*revealing with oracular warnings His divine will:* so the *Greek.* **if we turn away**—*Greek,* "we who turn away." The word implies greater refractoriness than "refused," or "declined." **him that speaketh from heaven**—God, by His Son in the Gospel, speaking from His heavenly throne. Hence, in Christ's preaching frequent mention is made of "the kingdom *of the heavens*" (*Greek,* Matt. 3:2). **26. then shook**—when He gave the law on Sinai. **now**—under the Gospel. **promised**—The announcement of His coming to break up the present order of things, is to the ungodly a terror, to the godly a promise, the fulfilment of which they look for with joyful hope. **Yet once more**—Cf. my *Notes,* Haggai 2:6, 21, 22, both of which passages are condensed into **one** here. The shaking began at the first coming of Messiah; it will be completed at His second coming, prodigies in the world of nature accompanying

ADAM CLARKE

(2) the wicked perfect, (3) those between. The "just perfect" are those (1) who have conquered all brutal appetites and gross passions, (2) who have stood in the time of strong temptation, (3) who give alms with a sincere heart, (4) who worship the true God only, (5) who are not invidious, (6) from whom God has taken evil concupiscence, and given the good principle. In several parts of this Epistle *teleios,* "the just man," signifies one who has a full knowledge of the Christian system, who is justified and saved by Christ Jesus; and the *teteleiomenoi* used here are the adult Christians, who are opposed to the babes in knowledge and grace. See chap. v. 12-14; viii. 11; and Gal. iv. 1-3. *The spirits of just men made perfect,* or the "righteous perfect," are the full-grown Christians; those who are justified by the blood and sanctified by the Spirit of Christ. Being come to such implies that spiritual union which the disciples of Christ have with each other, and which they possess how far soever separate. For they are all joined in one Spirit, Eph. ii. 18; they are "in the unity of the Spirit," Eph. iv. 3-4; "and of one soul," Acts iv. 32. This is a unity which was never possessed even by the Jews themselves in their best state; it is peculiar to real Christianity.

24. *And to Jesus the mediator of the new covenant.* The old covenant and its mediator, Moses, are passed away. See chap. viii. 13. The new covenant, i.e., the gospel, is now in force, and will be to the end of the world; and Jesus, the Son of God, the brightness of the Father's glory, the Maker and Preserver of all things, the Saviour and the Judge of all men, is its Mediator. *To the blood of sprinkling.* This is an allusion, as was before observed, to the sprinkling of the blood of the covenant sacrifice upon the people when that covenant was made upon Mount Sinai; to the sprinkling of the blood of the sin offerings before the mercy seat; and probably to the sprinkling of the blood of the paschal lamb on their houses, to prevent their destruction by the destroying angel. But all these sprinklings were partial and inefficacious, and had no meaning but as they referred to the Blood of sprinkling under the new covenant. *Better things than that of Abel.* God accepted Abel's sacrifice, and was well-pleased with it; for Abel was a righteous man, and offered his sacrifice by faith in the great promise. But the blood of Christ's sacrifice was infinitely more precious than the blood of Abel's sacrifice, as Jesus is infinitely greater than Abel; and the blood of Christ avails for the sins of the whole world, whereas the blood of Abel's sacrifice could avail only for himself.

25. *See,* "take heed," *that ye refuse not him,* the Lord Jesus, the Mediator of the new covenant, who now *speaketh from heaven,* by His gospel, to the Jews and to the Gentiles, having in His incarnation come down from God. *Him that spake on earth.* Moses, who spoke on the part of God to the Hebrews, every transgression of whose word "received a just recompence of reward," none being permitted to escape punishment. Consequently, if you turn away from Christ, who speaks to you from heaven, you may expect a much sorer punishment, the offense against God being so much the more heinous as the privileges slighted are more important and glorious.

26. *Whose voice then shook the earth.* Namely, at the giving of the law on Mount Sinai; and from this it seems that it was the voice of Jesus that then shook the earth, and that it was He who came down on the mount.

MATTHEW HENRY

CHARLES H. SPURGEON:

We must, in approaching God, remember what we have received of Him; and is it not wonderful that it should be written, "We receiving a kingdom"? What a gift to receive! This is a divine gift; we have received, not a pauper's pension, but a kingdom—"a kingdom which cannot be moved." The old dispensation or kingdom has passed away; its ceremonial laws are abrogated; its very spirit is superseded by a higher spirit, and we have entered upon another kingdom in which the ruling principle is not law but love. We are not under the yoke of Moses, but we are the subjects of King Jesus, whose yoke is easy and whose burden is light. The kingdom of Jesus will never end while time shall last, for He is the King Eternal and Immortal; neither will His laws be changed, nor shall His subjects die. Till that day when He shall deliver up the kingdom unto God, even the Father: and God shall be all in all, Jesus must reign; and even when the earthly mediatorial reign is consummated, the kingdom of God, the kingdom of heaven, shall be continued unto us and we shall still be members and citizens of it. We have received an eternal kingdom, and for this we ought to be eternally grateful. The shadows have vanished, but the substance abides: we have risen out of the types of Judaism into His kingdom by whom grace and truth have come unto us. This gospel state abideth; above the wreck of all things it remains, and the gates of hell shall not prevail against it. Ours is the kingdom of Jesus Christ, in which the gospel is the law, believers are the privileged subjects, and grace and glory are the revenue—a kingdom daily growing in brightness, a kingdom which shall consummate its glory in the eternal world when Christ shall have put all enemies under His feet, and His people shall reign with Him forever and ever.

—*The Treasury of the New Testament*

It was by the sound of the gospel trumpet that a new kingdom was erected for God in the world, which can never be so shaken as to be removed. This was a change made once for all. The apostle justly concludes, (1) How necessary it is for us to obtain *grace from God, to serve him acceptably.* We lose all our labour in religion if we be not accepted of God.

(2) We cannot worship God acceptably, unless we worship him with *godly reverence and fear.* As faith, so holy fear, is necessary to acceptable worship. (3) It is only the grace of God that enables us to worship God in a right manner. (4) God is the same just and righteous God under the gospel that he appeared to be under the law. He is in himself a consuming fire; that is, a God of strict justice.

JAMIESON, FAUSSET, BROWN

the overthrow of all kingdoms that oppose Messiah. The *Hebrew* is lit., "it is yet one little," i.e., a single brief space till the series of movements begins ending in the advent of Messiah. Not merely the earth, as at the establishment of the Sinaitic covenant, but heaven also is to be shaken. The two advents of Messiah are regarded as one, the complete shaking belonging to the second advent, of which the presage was given in the shakings at the first advent: the convulsions connected with the overthrow of Jerusalem shadowing forth those about to be at the overthrow of all the God-opposed kingdoms by the coming Messiah. **27. this** *word,* **Yet once more**—So Paul, by the Spirit, sanctions the LXX rendering of Haggai 2:6, giving an additional feature to the prophecy in the *Hebrew,* as rendered in *English Version,* not merely that it shall be *in a little while,* but that it is to be "*once* more" as the final act. The stress of his argument is on the "ONCE." *Once for all; once and for ever.* "In saying 'once more,' the Spirit implies that something has already passed, and something else shall be which is to remain, and is no more to be changed to something else; for the *once* is exclusive, i.e., *not many times*" [ESTIUS]. **those things that are shaken**—the heaven and the earth. As the shaking is to be *total,* so shall the removal be, making way for the better things that are unremovable. Cf. the Jewish economy (the type of the whole present order of things) giving way to the new and abiding covenant: the forerunner of the everlasting state of bliss. **as of things . . . made**—viz., of this present *visible creation:* cf. II Corinthians 5:1; and ch. 9:11, "made with hands . . . of this creation," i.e., things so *made* at creation that they would not remain of themselves, but be removed. The new abiding heaven and earth are also *made* by God, but they are of a higher nature than the material creation, being made to partake of the divine nature of Him who is *not made:* so in this relation, as one with the uncreated God, they are regarded as not of the same class as the *things made.* The things *made* in the former sense do *not remain;* the things of the new heaven and earth, like the uncreated God, "shall REMAIN before God" (Isa. 66:22). The Spirit, the seed of the new and heavenly being, not only of the believer's soul, but also of the future body, is an *uncreated* and immortal principle. **28. receiving**—as we do, in prospect and sure hope, also in the possession of the Spirit the first fruits. This is our privilege as Christians. **let us have grace**—"let us have thankfulness" [ALFORD after CHRYSOSTOM]. But (1) this translation is according to classical Greek, not Paul's phraseology for "to be thankful." (2) "To God" would have been in that case added. (3) "Whereby we may serve God," suits the *English Version* "grace" (i.e. Gospel grace, the work of the Spirit, producing faith exhibited in *serving God*), but does not suit "thankfulness." **acceptably**—*Greek,* "wellpleasingly." **reverence and godly fear**—The oldest MSS. read, "reverent caution and fear." *Reverent caution* (same *Greek* as in ch. 5:7; see *Note* there) lest we should offend God, who is of purer eyes than to behold iniquity. *Fear* lest we should bring destruction on ourselves. **29.** *Greek,* "For even": "for also"; introducing an *additional* solemn incentive to diligence. Quoted from Deuteronomy 4:24. **our God**—in whom we *hope,* is also to be *feared.* He is love; yet there is another side of His character; God has *wrath* against sin (ch. 10: 27, 31).

ADAM CLARKE

Not the earth only, but also heaven. Probably referring to the approaching destruction of Jerusalem and the total abolition of the political and ecclesiastical constitution of the Jews, the one being signified by the *earth,* the other by *heaven;* for the Jewish state and worship are frequently thus termed in the prophetic writings. And this seems to be the apostle's meaning, as he evidently refers to Hag. ii. 6, where this event is predicted. It may also remotely refer to the final dissolution of all things.

27. *The removing of those things that are shaken.* The whole of the Jewish polity, which had been in a shaken state from the time that Judea had fallen under the power of the Romans. *As of things that are made.* That is, subjects intended to last only for a time. God never designed that the Jewish religion should become general, nor be permanent. *Those things which cannot be shaken.* The whole gospel system, which cannot be moved by the power of man. *May remain.* Be permanent, God designing that this shall be the last dispensation of His grace and mercy, and that it shall continue till the earth and the heavens are no more.

28. *We receiving a kingdom.* The gospel dispensation, frequently termed the "kingdom of God" and the "kingdom of heaven," because in it God reigns among men, and He reigns in the hearts of them that believe; and His kingdom is righteousness, peace, and joy in the Holy Ghost. *Which cannot be moved.* Which never can fail, because it is the last dispensation. *Let us have grace.* "Let us have, keep, or hold fast, the benefit or gift," that is, the heavenly Kingdom which God has given us. This is the meaning of the word, 2 Cor. viii. 4, and is so rendered by our translators; and it is only by this heavenly gift of the gospel that we can serve God acceptably, for He can be pleased with no service that is not performed according to the gospel of His Son. If we prefer the common meaning of the word *grace,* it comes to the same thing. Without the *grace,* the especial succor and influence of Christ, we cannot *serve,* "pay religious worship to," *God;* for He receives no burnt offering that is not kindled by fire from His own altar. *Acceptably.* In such a way as to "please" Him well. And the offering with which He is well pleased, He will graciously accept; and if He accept our service, His Spirit will testify in our conscience that our ways please Him. When Abel sacrifices, God is well-pleased; where Cain offers, there is no approbation. *Reverence.* With "modesty." *Godly fear.* "Religious fear." We have "boldness to enter into the holiest by the blood of Jesus," but let that boldness be ever tempered with "modesty" and "religious fear"; for we should never forget that we have sinned, and that God "is a consuming fire."

29. *For our God is a consuming fire.* The apostle quotes Deut. iv. 24, and by doing so he teaches us this great truth, that sin under the gospel is as abominable in God's sight as it was under the law; and that the man who does not labor to serve God with the principle and in the way already prescribed will find that fire to consume him which would otherwise have consumed his sin.

MATTHEW HENRY

CHAPTER 13

Verses 1–17

The apostle calls the believing Hebrews to the performance of many excellent duties.

I. To brotherly love (*v.* 1). The spirit of Christianity is a spirit of love. Faith works by love. The true religion is the strongest bond of friendship. This brotherly love was in danger of being lost, and that in a time of persecution, when it would be most necessary. Christians should always love and live as brethren, and the more they grow in devout affection to God their heavenly Father, the more they will grow in love to one another for his sake.

II. To hospitality, *v.* 2. We must add to brotherly kindness, charity. The duty required—*to entertain strangers.* Seeing they are without any certain dwelling place, we should allow them room in our hearts and in our houses, as we have opportunity and ability.

JAMIESON, FAUSSET, BROWN

CHAPTER 13

VSS. 1-25. EXHORTATION TO VARIOUS GRACES, ESPECIALLY CONSTANCY IN FAITH, FOLLOWING JESUS AMIDST REPROACHES. CONCLUSION, WITH PIECES OF INTELLIGENCE AND SALUTATIONS. **1. brotherly love**—a distinct special manifestation of "charity" or "love" (II Pet. 1:7). The Church of Jerusalem, to which in part this Epistle was addressed, was distinguished by this grace, we know from Acts (cf. ch. 6:10; 10:32-34; 12:12, 13). **continue**—*Charity* will itself *continue.* See that it *continue with you.* **2.** Two manifestations of "brotherly love," *hospitality* and *care for those in bonds.* **Be not forgetful**—implying it was a duty which they all recognized, but which they might forget to act on (vss. 3, 7, 16). The enemies of Christianity themselves have noticed the practice of this virtue among Christians [JULIAN, *Ep.* 49]. **entertained angels unawares**—Abraham and Lot did so (Gen. 18:2; 19:1). To obviate the natural distrust felt of strangers, Paul says, an unknown guest

ADAM CLARKE

CHAPTER 13

1. *Let brotherly love continue.* Feel for, comfort, and support each other; and remember that he who professes to love God should love his brother also. They had this brotherly love among them; they should take care to retain it. As God is remarkable for His "philanthropy," or love to man, so should they be for *philadelphia,* or love to each other. See the note on Titus iii. 4.

2. *To entertain strangers.* In those early times, when there were scarcely any public inns or houses of entertainment, it was an office of charity and mercy to receive, lodge, and entertain travellers; and this is what the apostle particularly recommends. *Entertained angels.* Abraham and Lot are the persons particularly referred to. Their history, the angels whom they

MATTHEW HENRY

The motive: *Thereby some have entertained angels unawares.* God has often bestowed honours and favours upon his hospitable servants, beyond all their thoughts, *unawares.*

III. To Christian sympathy, *v.* 3.

1. The duty. Those that are themselves at liberty must sympathise with those that are in bonds and adversity, as if they were bound with them in the same chain.

2. The reason of the duty: *As being yourselves in the body;* not only in the body natural, but in the same mystical body. It would be unnatural in Christians not to bear each other's burdens.

IV. To purity and chastity, *v.* 4. A recommendation of God's ordinance of marriage, that it *is honourable in all.* It is *honourable* and happy, when persons come together pure and chaste, and preserve the marriage bed undefiled.

A dreadful but just censure of impurity and lewdness: *Whoremongers and adulterers God will judge.* He will call such sins by their proper names, not by the names of love and gallantry, but of whoredom and adultery. He will bring them into judgment. He will convict them, condemn them.

V. To Christian contentment, *v.* 5, 6. The sin that is contrary to his grace and duty—*covetousness.* We must take care not only to keep this sin down, but to root it out of our souls. The duty that is contrary to covetousness—being satisfied and pleased *with such things as we have.* What God gives us from day to day we must be content with. We must bring our minds to our present condition. Those who cannot do it would not be contented though God should raise their condition to their minds, for the mind would rise with the condition. Paul, though abased and empty, had *learned in* every *state,* in any *state, therewith to be content.* What reason Christians have to be contented with their lot, *v.* 5, 6. This promise contains the sum and substance of all the promises.

From this comprehensive promise they may assure themselves of help from God, *v.* 6. Men can do nothing against God, and God can make all that men do against his people to turn to their good.

VI. To the duty Christians owe to their ministers, and that both to those that are dead and to those that are yet alive.

1. To those that are dead, *v.* 7.

(1) The description given of them. They were such as had the rule over them, and had spoken to them the word of God.

(2) The duties owing to them. "*Remember them. Follow* their *faith;* labour after the grace of faith by which they lived and died so well. *Consider the end of their conversation!*"

JAMIESON, FAUSSET, BROWN

may be better than he looks: he may be unexpectedly found to be as much a *messenger* of God for good, as the angels (whose name means *messenger*) are; nay more, if a Christian, he represents Christ Himself. There is a play on the same *Greek* word, *Be not forgetful* and *unaware;* let *not* the duty of hospitality to strangers *escape* you; for, by entertaining strangers, it has *escaped* the entertainers that they were entertaining angels. Not unconscious and forgetful of the duty, they have unconsciously brought on themselves the blessing. **3. Remember**—in prayers and acts of kindness. **bound with them**—by virtue of the unity of the members in the body under one Head, Christ (I Cor. 12:26). **suffer adversity**—*Greek,* "are in evil state." **being yourselves also in the body**—and so liable to the adversities incident to the natural body, which ought to dispose you the more to sympathize with them, not knowing how soon your own turn of suffering may come. "One experiences adversity almost his whole life, as Jacob; another in youth, as Joseph; another in manhood, as Job; another in old age" [BENGEL]. **4. is . . .**—Translate, "Let marriage *be treated as* honorable": as vs. 5 also is an exhortation. **in all**—"in the case of all men": "among all." "To avoid fornication let EVERY MAN have his own wife" (I Cor. 7:2). Judaism and Gnosticism combined were soon about to throw discredit on marriage. The venerable Paphnutius, in the Council of Nice, quoted this verse for the justification of the married state. If one does not himself marry, he should not prevent others from doing so. Others, especially Romanists, translate, "in all *things,*" as in vs. 18. But the warning being against lasciviousness, the contrast to "*whoremongers* and *adulterers*" in the parallel clause, requires the "in all" in this clause to refer to *persons.* **the bed undefiled**—Translate, as *Greek* requires "undefiled" to be a *predicate,* not an epithet, "And let the bed *be* undefiled." **God will judge**—Most whoremongers escape the notice of human tribunals; but God takes particular cognizance of those whom man does not punish. Gay immoralities will then be regarded in a very different light from what they are now. **5. conversation**—"manner of life." The love of filthy lust and the love of filthy lucre follow one another as closely akin, both alienating the heart from the Creator to the creature. **such things as ye have**—lit., "present things" (Phil. 4:11). **I will never leave thee, nor forsake thee**—A promise tantamount to this was given to Jacob (Gen. 28:15), to Israel (Deut. 31:6, 8), to Joshua (Josh. 1:5), to Solomon (I Chron. 28:20). It is therefore like a divine adage. What was said to them, extends also to us. He will neither withdraw His *presence* ("never leave thee") nor His *help* ("nor forsake thee") [BENGEL].

6. may—rather as *Greek,* expressing confidence actually realized, "So that we boldly (confidently) *say*" (Ps. 56:4. 11; 118:6). Punctuate as both the *Hebrew* and the *Greek* require, "And (so) I will not fear: what (then) shall man do unto me?" **7. Remember**—so as to imitate: not to *invoke* in prayer, as Rome teaches. **have the rule**—rather, "who have *had* the rule over you": your spiritual leaders. **who**—*Greek,* "the which": such persons as. **have spoken unto you**—"spake" (so the *Greek* aorist means) during their lifetime. This Epistle was among those written later, when many of the heads of the Jerusalem Church had passed away. **whose faith**—even unto death: probably death by martyrdom, as in the case of the instances of *faith* in ch. 11:35. Stephen, James the brother of our Lord and bishop of Jerusalem, as well as James the brother of John (Acts 12:2), in the Palestinian Church, which Paul addresses, suffered martyrdom. **considering**—*Greek,* "looking up to," "diligently contemplating all over," as an artist would a model. **the end**—the termination, at death. The *Greek,* is used of *decease* (Luke 9:31; II Pet. 1:15). **of their conversation**—"manner of life": "religious walk" (Gal. 1:13; Eph. 4:22; I Tim. 4:12; Jas. 3:13). *Considering* how they manifested the soundness of their faith by their holy *walk,* which they maintained even to *the end of that walk* (their death by martyrdom).

ADAM CLARKE

entertained, not knowing them to be such, and the good they derived from exercising their hospitality on these occasions, are well-known; and have been particularly referred to in the notes on Gen. xviii. 3; xix. 2.

3. *Remember them that are in bonds.* He appears to refer to those Christians who were suffering imprisonment for the testimony of Jesus. *As bound with them.* Feel for them as you would wish others to feel for you were you in their circumstances, knowing that, being in the body, you are liable to the same evils, and may be called to suffer in the same way for the same cause.

4. *Marriage is honourable in all.* Let this state be highly esteemed as one of God's own instituting, and as highly calculated to produce the best interests of mankind. This may have been said against the opinions of the Essenes, who held marriage in little repute, and abstained from it themselves as a state of comparative imperfection. At the same time it shows the absurdity of the popish tenet that marriage in the clergy is both dishonorable and sinful; which is, in fact, in opposition to the apostle, who says *marriage is honourable in all;* and to the institution of God, which evidently designed that every male and female should be united in this holy bond; and to nature, which in every part of the habitable world has produced men and women in due proportion to each other. *The bed undefiled.* Every man cleaving to his own wife, and every wife cleaving to her own husband, because *God will judge,* i.e., punish, all "fornicators and adulterers."

5. *Let your conversation.* That is, the whole tenor of your conduct, the "manner of your life," or rather the disposition of your hearts in reference to all your secular transactions; for in this sense the original is used by the best Greek writers. *Be without covetousness.* Desire nothing more than what God has given you; and especially covet nothing which the Divine Providence has given to another man, for this is the very spirit of robbery. *Content with such things as ye have.* "Being satisfied with present things." The covetous man is ever running out into futurity with insatiable desires after secular good; and, if this disposition be not checked, it increases as the subject of it increases in years. Covetousness is the vice of old age. *I will never leave thee, nor forsake thee.* These words were, in sum, spoken to Joshua, chap. i. 5: "As I was with Moses, so will I be with thee: I will not fail thee, nor forsake thee." They were spoken also by David to Solomon, 1 Chron. xxviii. 20: "David said to Solomon his son, Be strong and of good courage, and do it: fear not, nor be dismayed: for the Lord God, even my God, will be with thee; he will not fail thee, nor forsake thee." The apostle, in referring to the same promises, feels authorized to strengthen the expressions, as the Christian dispensation affords more consolation and confidence in matters of this kind than the old covenant did.

6. *So that we may boldly say.* We, in such circumstances, while cleaving to the Lord, may confidently apply to ourselves what God spoke to Joshua and to Solomon; and what He spoke to David, *The Lord is my helper, and I will not fear what man shall do.* God is omnipotent; man's power is limited; howsoever strong he may be, he can do nothing against the Almighty.

7. *Remember them which have the rule over you.* This clause should be translated, "Remember your guides who have spoken unto you the doctrine of God." Theodoret's note on this verse is very judicious: "He intends the saints who were dead, Stephen the first martyr, James the brother of John, and James called the Just. And there were many others who were taken off by the Jewish rage. 'Consider these (said he), and, observing their example, imitate their faith.'" *Considering the end of their conversation.* "The issue of whose course of life most carefully consider." They lived to get good and do good; they were faithful to their God and His cause; they suffered persecution, and for the testimony of Jesus died a violent death. God never left them; no, He never forsook them; so that they were happy in their afflictions and glorious in their death.

MATTHEW HENRY

Now this duty of following the same true faith in which they had been instructed the apostle enlarges much upon by referring to the immutability and eternity of the Lord Jesus Christ. The great head of the church ever lives, and is ever the same; and they should be steadfast and immovable, in imitation of Christ. Furthermore he describes erroneous doctrines which they must avoid.

[1] They were divers and various (*v.* 9), different from what they had received and inconsistent with themselves.

[2] They were strange doctrines.

[3] They were of an unsettling, distracting nature. They were quite contrary to that grace of God which fixes and establishes the heart.

[4] They were about external, little, perishing things, such as *meats and drinks*, &c.

[5] They were unprofitable. They did not make them more holy, nor more humble, nor more thankful, nor more heavenly.

[6] They would exclude those who embraced them from the privileges of the Christian altar (*v.* 10): *We have an altar.* The Christian church has its altar. Not a material altar, but a personal one, and that is Christ; he is both our altar, and our sacrifice. This altar furnishes out a feast for true believers. The Lord's supper is the feast of the gospel passover. Those who adhere to the tabernacle or the Levitical dispensation, or return to it again, exclude themselves from the privileges of this altar. This part of the argument he first proves and then improves.

a. This servile adherence to the Jewish state is a bar to the privileges of the gospel altar. The gospel feast is the fruit of the sacrifice, which those have no right to who do not acknowledge the sacrifice itself.

ALBERT BARNES:

13. "Let us go forth therefore unto him without the camp." As if we were going forth with him when he was led away to be crucified. He was put to death as a malefactor. He was the object of contempt and scorn. He was held up to derision and was taunted and reviled on his way to the place of death, and even on the cross. To have been identified with him then; to follow him; to sympathize with him; to be regarded as his friend, would have subjected one to similar shame and reproach. The meaning here is that we should be willing to regard ourselves as identified with the Lord Jesus and to bear the same shame and reproaches which he did. When he was led away amidst scoffing and reviling to be put to death, would we, if we had been there, have been willing to be regarded as his followers and to have gone out with him as his avowed disciples and friends? Alas, how many are there who profess to love him when religion subjects them to no reproach, who would have shrunk from following him to Calvary!—*Popular Commentary*

JAMIESON, FAUSSET, BROWN

8. This verse is not, as some read it, in apposition with "the end of their conversation" (vs. 7), but forms the transition. "Jesus Christ, yesterday and to-day (is) the same, and (shall be the same) unto the ages" (i.e., unto all ages). The *Jesus Christ* (the full name being given, to mark with affectionate solemnity both His *person* and His *office*) who supported your spiritual *rulers* through life even unto their *end* "yesterday" (in times past), being at once "the Author and the Finisher of their faith" (ch. 12:2), remains still the same Jesus Christ "to-day," ready to help you also, if like them you walk by "faith" in Him. Cf. "this same Jesus," Acts 1:11. He who *yesterday* (proverbial for the past time) suffered and died, is *today* in glory (Rev. 1:18). **9. about**—rather, as oldest MSS. read, "carried *aside*"; viz., cf. Eph. 4:14. **divers**—differing from the one faith in the one and the same Jesus Christ, as taught by them who had the rule over you (vs. 7). **strange**—foreign to the truth. **doctrines**—"teachings." **established with grace; not with meats**—not with observances of Jewish distinctions between clean and unclean meats, to which ascetic Judaizers added in Christian times the rejection of some meats, and the use of others: noticed also by *Paul* in I Corinthians 8:8, 13; 6:13. Romans 14:17, an exact parallel to this verse: these are some of the "divers and strange doctrines" of the previous sentence. Christ's body offered once for all for us, is our true spiritual "meat" to "eat" (vs. 10), "the stay and the staff of bread" (Isa. 3:1), the mean of all "grace." **which have not profited**—*Greek,* "in which they who walked were not profited"; viz., in respect to justification, perfect cleansing of the conscience, and sanctification. Cf. on "walked," Acts 21:21; viz., with superstitious scrupulosity, as though the worship of God in itself consisted in such legal observances. **10. an altar**—the cross of Christ, whereon His body was offered. The Lord's table represents this altar, the cross; as the bread and wine represent the sacrifice offered on it. Our meat, which we by faith spiritually eat, is the flesh of Christ, in contrast to the typical ceremonial meats. The two cannot be combined (Gal. 5:2). That not a literal eating of the sacrifice of Christ is meant in the Lord's Supper, but a spiritual is meant, appears from comparing vs. 9 with vs. 10, "with GRACE, NOT with MEATS." **11, 12.** For just as "the bodies of those beasts whose blood is brought into the sanctuary by . . . are burned without the camp," so "Jesus also that . . . suffered without the gate" of ceremonial Judaism, of which His crucifixion outside the gate of Jerusalem is a type. **for**—reason why they who serve the tabernacle, are excluded from share in Christ; because His sacrifice is not like one of those sacrifices in which they had a share but answers to one which was "wholly burned" outside (the *Greek* is "burnt completely," "consumed by burning"), and which consequently they could not eat of. Leviticus 6:30, gives the general rule, "No sin offering whereof any of the blood is brought into the tabernacle of the congregation to reconcile withal in the holy place, shall be eaten; it shall be burnt in the fire." The sin offerings are twofold: the *outward,* whose blood was sprinkled on the outward altar, and of whose bodies the priests might eat; and the *inward,* the reverse. **the sanctuary**—here *the Holy of Holies,* into which the blood of the sin offering was brought on the day of atonement. **without the camp**—in which were the tabernacle and Levitical priests and legal worshippers, during Israel's journey through the wilderness; replaced afterwards by Jerusalem (containing the temple), outside of whose walls Jesus was crucified. **12. Wherefore Jesus**—In order that the Antitype might fulfil the type. **sanctify**—Though not brought into the temple "sanctuary" (vs. 11) His blood has been brought into the heavenly sanctuary, and "sanctifies the people" (ch. 2:11, 17), by cleansing them from sin, and consecrating them to God. **his own**—not blood of animals. **without the gate**—of Jerusalem; as if unworthy of the society of the covenant people. The fiery ordeal of His *suffering* on the cross, answers to the *burning* of the victims; thereby His mere fleshly life was completely destroyed, as their bodies were; the second part of His offering was His carrying His blood into the heavenly holiest before God at His ascension, that it should be a perpetual atonement for the world's sin. **13. therefore**—This "therefore" breathes the deliberate fortitude of believers [BENGEL]. **without the camp**—"outside the legal polity" [THEODORET] of Judaism (cf. vs. 11) "Faith considers Jerusalem itself as a *camp,* not a *city* [BENGEL]. He contrasts with the Jews, who serve an earthly sanctuary, the Christians to whom

ADAM CLARKE

8. *Jesus Christ the same yesterday.* In all past times there was no way to the holiest but through the blood of Jesus, either actually shed or significantly typified. *To day*—He is the Lamb newly slain, and continues to appear in the presence of God for us. *For ever*—to the conclusion of time, He will be "the way, the truth, and the life," none coming to the Father but through Him; and throughout eternity it will appear that all glorified human spirits owe their salvation to His infinite merit.

9. *Be not carried about.* "Be not whirled about." But almost every MS. of importance has "be not carried away," which is undoubtedly the true reading, and signifies here, "Do not apostatize," permit not yourselves to be carried off from Christ and His doctrine. *Divers and strange doctrines.* "Variegated doctrines"; those that blended the law and the gospel, and brought in the Levitical sacrifices and institutions in order to perfect the Christian system. Remember the old covenant is abolished; the new alone is in force. *Strange doctrines,* "foreign" doctrines, such as have no apostolical authority to recommend them. *That the heart be established with grace.* It is well to have the heart, the mind, and conscience fully satisfied with the truth and efficacy of the "gospel"; for so the word *charis* should be understood here, which is put in opposition to *bromasin, meats,* signifying here the Levitical institutions, and especially its sacrifices, these being emphatically termed *meats* because the offerers were permitted to feast upon them after the blood had been poured out before the Lord. See Lev. vii. 15; Deut. xii. 6-7. *Which have not profited them.* Because they neither took away guilt, cleansed the heart, nor gave power over sin.

10. *We have an altar.* The altar is here put for the sacrifice on the altar; the Christian *altar* is the Christian Sacrifice, which is Christ Jesus, with all the benefits of His passion and death. To these privileges they had no right who continued to offer the Levitical sacrifices and to trust in them for remission of sins.

11. *For the bodies of those beasts.* Though in making covenants, and in some victims offered according to the law, the flesh of the sacrifice was eaten by the offerers, yet the flesh of the sin offering might no man eat. When the blood was sprinkled before the holy place to make an atonement for their souls, the skins, flesh, entrails, etc., were carried without the camp, and there entirely consumed by fire; and this entire consumption, according to the opinion of some, was intended to show that sin was not pardoned by such offerings. For as eating the other sacrifices intimated they were made partakers of the benefits procured by those sacrifices, so not being permitted to eat of the sin offering proved that they had no benefit from it, and that they must look to the Christ, whose sacrifice is pointed out, that they might receive that real pardon of sin which the shedding of His blood could alone procure. While therefore they continued offering those sacrifices and refused to acknowledge the Christ, they had no right to any of the blessings procured by Him, and it is evident they could have no benefit from their own.

12. *That he might sanctify the people.* That He might consecrate them to God and make an atonement for their sins, He *suffered without the gate* at Jerusalem, as the sin offering was consumed "without the camp" when the Tabernacle abode in the wilderness. Perhaps all this was typical of the abolition of the Jewish sacrifices and the termination of the whole Levitical system of worship. He left the city, denounced its final destruction, and abandoned it to its fate; and *suffered without the gate* to bring the Gentiles to God.

MATTHEW HENRY

b. To improve this argument (*v.* 13–15): *Let us go forth therefore unto him without the camp.* Let us be willing to *bear his reproach.* We must submit to it; and we have the more reason because we must necessarily go forth in a little time by death; for *here we have no continuing city.* We should go forth now by faith, and seek in Christ the rest and settlement which this world cannot afford us, *v.* 14.

Let us make a right use of this altar. Let us bring our sacrifices to this altar, *v.* 15, 16. 1. The sacrifice of praise to God, which we should offer up to God continually. In this are included all adoration and prayer, as well as thanksgiving; this is *the fruit of our lips.*

2. The sacrifice of alms-deeds, and Christian charity, *v.* 16, not contending ourselves to offer the sacrifice of our lips, mere words, but the sacrifice of good deeds.

2. To their living ministers (*v.* 17). The duty—to obey them, and submit themselves to them. Christians must submit to be instructed by their ministers, and not think themselves too wise, too good, or too great, to learn from them; and they must obey them. The motives to this duty. (1) They have the rule over the people; their office is truly authoritative.

(2) They watch for the souls of the people. They are to watch against everything that may be hurtful. They are to watch for all opportunities of helping the souls of men forward in the way to heaven. (3) They must give an account how they have discharged their duty. They would be glad to give a good account. If they can then give in an account of their own fidelity and success, it will be a joyful day to them. If they give up their account with grief, it will be the people's loss as well as theirs.

Verses 18–25

I. The apostle recommends himself, and his fellow-sufferers, to the prayers of the Hebrew believers (*v.* 18).

1. This is one part of the duty which people owe

JAMIESON, FAUSSET, BROWN

the altar in heaven stands open, while it is closed against the Jews. As Jesus suffered without the gate, so spiritually must those who desire to belong to Him, withdraw from the earthly Jerusalem and its sanctuary, as from this world in general. There is a reference to Exodus 33:7, when the tabernacle was moved *without the camp,* which had become polluted by the people's idolatry of the golden calves; so that "every one who sought the Lord went out unto *the tabernacle of the congregation* (as Moses called the tabernacle outside the camp), which was without the camp"; a lively type of what the Hebrews should do, viz., come out of the carnal worship of the earthly Jerusalem to worship God in Christ in spirit, and of what we all ought to do, viz., come out from all carnalism, worldly formalism, and mere sensuous worship, and know Jesus in His spiritual power apart from worldliness, seeing that "we have no continuing city" (vs. 14). **bearing**—as Simon of Cyrene did. **his reproach**—the reproach which He bare, and which all His people bear with Him. **14. here**—on earth. Those Hebrews who clung to the earthly sanctuary are representatives of all who cling to this earth. The earthly Jerusalem proved to be no "abiding city," having been destroyed shortly after this Epistle was written, and with it fell the Jewish civil and religious polity; a type of the whole of our present earthly order of things soon to perish. **one to come**—(ch. 2:5; 11:10, 14, 16; 12:22; Phil. 3:20). **15.** As the "altar" was mentioned in vs. 10, so the "sacrifices" here (cf. I Pet. 2:5, viz., *praise* and *doing good,* vs. 16). Cf. Psalm 119:108: Rom. 12:1. **By him**—as the Mediator of our prayers and praises (John 14:13, 14); not by Jewish observances (Ps. 50:14, 23; 69:30, 31; 107:22; 116:17). It was an old saying of the rabbis, "At a future time all sacrifices shall cease, but praises shall not cease." **praise**—for salvation. **continually**—not merely at fixed seasons, as those on which the legal sacrifices were offered, but throughout all our lives. **fruit of** *our* **lips**—(Isa. 57:19; Hos. 14:2). **giving thanks**—*Greek,* "confessing." BENGEL remarks that the Hebrew, *todah,* is beautifully emphatic. It literally means "acknowledgment" or "confession." In praising a creature, we may easily exceed the truth; but in praising God we have only to go on *confessing* what He really is to us. Hence it is impossible to exceed the truth, and here is *genuine* praise. **16. But**—But the sacrifice of praise with the lips (vs. 15) is not enough; there must be also *doing good* (beneficence) and communicating (i.e., imparting a share of your means, Gal. 6:6) to the needy. **with such**—and not mere ritualistic sacrifices. **17. Obey them that have the rule over you**—(Cf. vss. 7, 24). This threefold mention of the *rulers* is peculiar to this Epistle. In other Epistles Paul includes the *rulers* in his exhortations. But here the address is limited to the *general body of the Church,* in contrast to the *rulers* to whom they are charged to yield reverent submission. Now this is just what might be expected when the apostle of the Gentiles was writing to the Palestine Christians, among whom James and the eleven apostles had exercised a more immediate authority. It was important he should not seem to set himself in opposition to their guides, but rather strengthen their hands; he claims no authority directly or indirectly over these rulers themselves [BIRKS]. **they**—on their part; so the *Greek.* As they do their part, so do you yours. So Paul exhorts, I Thessalonians 5:12, 13. **watch**—"are vigilant" (*Greek*). **for**—*Greek,* "in behalf of." **must give account**—The strongest stimulus to *watchfulness* (Mark 13:34-37). CHRYSOSTOM was deeply struck with these words, as he tells us (*De Sacerdotio,* B. 6), "The fear of this threat continually agitates my soul." **do it**—"watch for your soul's eternal salvation." It is a perilous responsibility for a man to have to give account for others' deeds, who is not sufficient for his own [ESTIUS, from AQUINAS]. **with joy**—at your obedience; anticipating, too, that you shall be their "joy" in the day of giving account (Phil. 4:1). **not with grief**—at your disobedience; apprehending also that in the day of account you may be among the lost, instead of being their crown of rejoicing. **that**—*Grief* in your pastors is *unprofitable for you,* for it weakens their spiritual power; nay, more, "the *groans* (so the *Greek* for 'grief') of other creatures are heard; how much more of pastors!" [BENGEL]. So God will be provoked to avenge on you their "groaning" (*Greek*). If they must render God an account of their negligence, so must you for your ingratitude to them [GROTIUS]. **18. Pray for us**—Paul usually requests the Church's intercessions for him in closing his Epistles, just as he begins with assuring them of his having them at

ADAM CLARKE

13. *Let us go forth therefore unto him.* Let us leave this city and system, devoted to destruction, and take refuge in Jesus alone, *bearing his reproach*—being willing to be accounted the refuse of all things, and the worst of men, for His sake who bore the contradiction of sinners against himself and was put to death as a malefactor.

14. *For here have we no continuing city.* Here is an elegant and forcible allusion to the approaching destruction of Jerusalem. The Jerusalem that was below was about to be burned with fire and erased to the ground; the Jerusalem that was from above was that alone which could be considered to be "permanent."

15. *By him therefore let us offer the sacrifice of praise.* He has now fulfilled all vision and prophecy, has offered the last bloody sacrifice which God will ever accept; and as He is the Gift of God's love to the world, let us through Him offer the sacrifice of praise to God continually, this being the substitute for all the Levitical sacrifices. The Jews allowed that in the time of the Messiah all sacrifices, except the sacrifice of praise, should cease. To this maxim the apostle appears to allude; and understood in this way, his words are much more forcible. "Rabbi Phineas, Rabbi Levi, and Rabbi Jochanan, from the authority of Rabbi Menachem of Galilee, said, 'In the time of the Messiah all sacrifice shall cease except the sacrifice of praise.'" This was in effect quoting the authority of one of their own maxims, that now was the time of the Messiah, that Jesus was that Messiah, that the Jewish sacrificial system was now abolished, and that no sacrifice would now be accepted of God except the sacrifice of praise for the gift of His Son. *That is, the fruit of our lips.* This expression is probably borrowed from Hos. xiv. 2, in the version of the Septuagint, which in the Hebrew text is "the heifers of our lips." This may refer primarily to the sacrifices, heifers, calves, etc., which they had vowed to God; so that the "calves of their lips" were the sacrifices which they had promised. But how could the Septuagint translate "calves" by *fruit*? Very easily, if they had in their copy *peri,* the *mem* being omitted; and thus the word would be literally *fruit,* and not "calves."

16. *But to do good and to communicate.* These are continual sacrifices which God requires, and which will spring from a sense of God's love in Christ Jesus. Praise to God "for his unspeakable gift," and acts of kindness to men for God's sake. No reliance, even on the infinitely meritorious sacrifice of Christ, can be acceptable in the sight of God if a man have not love and charity towards his neighbor. Praise, prayer, and thanksgiving to God, with works of charity and mercy to man, are the sacrifices which every genuine follower of Christ must offer: and they are the proofs that a man belongs to Christ; and he who does not bear these fruits gives full evidence, whatever his creed may be, that he is no Christian.

17. *Obey them that have the rule over you.* "Obey your leaders." He is not fit to rule who is not capable of guiding. See on v. 7 in the former verse the apostle exhorts them to remember those who had been their leaders and to imitate their faith; in this he exhorts them to obey the leaders they now had, and to submit to their authority in all matters of doctrine and discipline, on the ground that they watched for their souls, and should have to give an account of their conduct to God. If this conduct were improper, they must give in their report before the great tribunal with *grief,* but it must be given; if holy and pure, they would give it in with *joy.*

18. *Pray for us.* Even the success of apostles depended, in a certain way, on the prayers of the Church. Few Christian congregations feel, as they ought, that it is their bounden duty to pray for the success of the gospel, both among themselves and in the world. The Church is weak, dark, poor, and imperfect because it prays little.

MATTHEW HENRY

to their ministers. Ministers need the prayers of the people; and the more earnestly the people pray for their ministers the more benefit they may expect to reap from their ministry.

2. There are good reasons why people should pray for their ministers.

(1) *We trust we have a good conscience*, &c., *v.* 18. Many of the Jews had a bad opinion of Paul. He here modestly asserts his own integrity. *We trust!* he might have said, *We know;* but he chose to speak in a humble style. "We trust we have a good conscience *in all things*. We would act honestly and sincerely in all things." A good conscience has a respect to all God's commands and all our duty. Those who have this good conscience, yet need the prayers of others.

(2) Another reason why he desires their prayers, *v.* 19, intimating that, now he was absent from them, he had a great desire and real intention to come again to them,—and that the best way to facilitate his return to them, was to make it a matter of their prayer.

II. He offers up his prayers to God for them: *Now the God of peace*, &c., *v.* 20. The title given to God—*the God of peace*, who has found out a way for peace and reconciliation between himself and sinners.

The great work ascribed to him: *He hath brought again from the dead our Lord Jesus*, &c. That divine power by which he was raised is able to do everything for us that we stand in need of. The titles given to Christ—our Lord Jesus, our sovereign, our Saviour, and the great shepherd of the sheep. They are the flock of his pasture, and his care and concern are for them.

The way and method in which God is reconciled, and Christ raised from the dead: *Through the blood of the everlasting covenant*. This blood is the sanction and seal of an everlasting covenant between God and his people.

The mercy prayed for, *v.* 21. The perfection of the saints in every good work is the great thing desired by them and for them. The way in which God makes his people perfect; it is by working in them always what is pleasing in his sight. To this every one should say, *Amen.*

JAMIESON, FAUSSET, BROWN

heart in his prayers (but in this Epistle not till vss. 20, 21), Romans 15:30. "Us," includes both himself and his companions; he passes to himself alone, vs. 19. **we trust we have a good conscience**—in spite of your former jealousies, and the charges of my Jewish enemies at Jerusalem, which have been the occasion of my imprisonment at Rome. In refutation of the Jews' aspersions, he asserts in the same language as here his own *conscientiousness* before God and man, Acts 23:1-3; 24:16, 20, 21 (wherein he virtually implies that his reply to Ananias was not sinful impatience; for, indeed, it was a prophecy which he was inspired at the moment to utter, and which was fulfilled soon after). **we trust** *Greek,* "we are persuaded," in the oldest MSS. Good conscience produces confidence, where the Holy Spirit rules the conscience (Rom. 9:1). **honestly**—"in a *good* way." The same *Greek* word as "*good* conscience." *Lit.,* "rightly," "becomingly." **19. the rather**—*Greek, "I the more abundantly* beseech you." **to do this**—to pray for me. **that I may be restored to you**—(Philemon 22). It is here first in the letter he mentions himself, in a way so unobtrusive, as not to prejudice his Hebrew readers against him, which would have been the result had he commenced this as his other Epistles, with authoritatively announcing his name and apostolic commission. **20.** Concluding prayer. **God of peace**—So Paul, Romans 15:33; 16:20; II Corinthians 13:11; Philippians 4:9; I Thessalonians 5: 23; II Thessalonians 3:16. The Judaizing of the Hebrews was calculated to sow seeds of discord among them, of disobedience to their pastors (vs. 17), and of alienation towards Paul. *The God of peace* by giving unity of true doctrine, will unite them in mutual love. **brought again from the dead** —*Greek,* "brought up . . .": God brought the Shepherd; the Shepherd shall bring the flock. Here only in the Epistle he mentions the resurrection. He would not conclude without mentioning the connecting link between the two truths mainly discussed; the *one perfect sacrifice* and the *continual priestly intercession*—the depth of His humiliation and the height of His glory—the "altar" of the cross and the ascension to the heavenly Holy of Holies. **Lord Jesus**—the title marking His *person* and His *Lordship* over us. But vs. 21, "through Jesus *Christ*." His *office*, as the *Anointed* of the Spirit, making Him the medium of communicating the Spirit to us, the holy unction flowing down from the Head on the members (cf. Acts 2:36). **great**—(Ch. 4. 14.) **shepherd of the sheep**—A title familiar to his Hebrew readers, from their Old Testament (Isa. 63:11; LXX): primarily *Moses,* antitypically *Christ:* already compared together, ch. 3:2-7. The transition is natural from their earthly pastors (vs. 17), to the Chief Pastor, as in I Peter 5:1-4. Cf. Ezekiel 34:23 and Jesus' own words, John 10:2, 11, 14. **through the blood**—*Greek,* "in," *in virtue of* the blood (ch. 2:9); it was because of His bloody death for us, that the Father raised and crowned Him with glory. The "blood" was the seal of the everlasting covenant entered into between the Father and Son; *in virtue of the Son's blood,* first Christ was raised, then Christ's people shall be so (Zech. 9:11, seemingly referred to here; Acts 20:28). **everlasting**—The *everlastingness* of the *covenant* necessitated the resurrection. This clause, "the blood of the everlasting covenant," is a summary retrospect of the Epistle (cf. ch. 9:12).

21. Make you perfect—properly said of healing a rent; *join you together in perfect harmony* [BENGEL]. **to do his will, working in you**—(Ch. 10:36) —rather as *Greek, "doing* in you." Whatever good we *do,* God *does* in us. **well-pleasing in his sight**—(Isa. 53:10; Eph. 5:10).

through Jesus Christ—"God *doing* (working) in you that . . . *through Jesus Christ*" (Phil. 1:11). **to whom**—to Christ. He closes as he began (ch. 1), with giving glory to Christ.

ADAM CLARKE

We trust we have a good conscience. We are persuaded that we have a conscience that not only acquits us of all fraud and sinister design, but assures us that in simplicity and godly sincerity we have labored to promote the welfare of you and of all mankind. *To live honestly.* "Willing in all things to conduct ourselves well" —to behave with decency and propriety.

19. *The rather to do this.* That is, pray for us, that, being enabled to complete the work which God has given us here to do, we may be the sooner enabled to visit you. It is evident from this that the people to whom this Epistle was written knew well who was the author of it, nor does there appear in any place any design in the writer to conceal his name; how the Epistle came to lack a name it is impossible to say.

20. *Now the God of peace.* We have often seen that *peace* among the Hebrews signifies "prosperity" of every kind. *The God of peace* is the same as the God of all blessedness, who has at His disposal all temporal and eternal good; who loves mankind, and has provided them a complete salvation. *Brought again from the dead our Lord.* As our Lord's sacrificial death is considered as an atonement offered to the divine justice, God's acceptance of it as an atonement is signified by His raising the human nature of Christ from the dead; and hence this raising of Christ is, with the utmost propriety, attributed to God the Father, as this proves His acceptance of the sacrificial offering. *That great shepherd of the sheep.* This is a title of our blessed Lord, given to Him by the prophets; so Isa. xl. 11; "He shall feed his flock like a shepherd: he shall gather the lambs with his arm, and carry them in his bosom, and shall gently lead those that are with young"; and Ezek. xxxiv. 23; "I will set up one shepherd over them, and he shall feed them, even my servant David [i.e., the beloved, viz., Jesus]; he shall feed them, and he shall be their shepherd"; and Zech. xiii. 7; "Awake, O sword, against my shepherd . . . smite the shepherd, and the sheep shall be scattered." In all these places the term *shepherd* is allowed to belong to our blessed Lord; and He appropriates it to himself, John x. 11, by calling himself "the good shepherd" who lays down "his life for the sheep." *Through the blood of the everlasing covenant.* Some understand this in the following way, that "God brought back our Lord from the dead on account of His having shed His blood to procure the everlasting covenant." Others, that "the Lord Jesus became the great Shepherd and Saviour of the sheep by shedding His blood to procure and ratify the everlasting covenant." The sense, however, will appear much plainer if we connect this with the following verse: "Now the God of peace, that brought again from the dead our Lord Jesus, that great shepherd of the sheep, make you, through the blood of the everlasting coveant, perfect in every good work to do his will." The Christian system is termed the *everlasting covenant,* to distinguish it from the temporary covenant made with the Israelites at Mount Sinai, and to show that it is the last dispensation of grace to the world and shall endure to the end of time.

21. *Make you perfect.* "Put you completely in joint." See the note on 2 Cor. xiii. 9. From the following terms we see what the apostle meant by the perfection for which he prays. They were to do the will of God in every good work, from God *working* in them *that which is well-pleasing in his sight.* (1) This necessarily implies a complete change in the whole soul, that God may be well-pleased with whatsoever He sees in it; and this supposes its being cleansed from all sin, for God's sight cannot be pleased with anything that is unholy. (2) This complete inward purity is to produce an outward conformity to God's will, so they were to be made *perfect in every good work.* (3) The perfection within and the perfection without were to be produced by "the blood of the everlasting covenant"; for although "God is love," yet it is not consistent with His justice or holiness to communicate any good to mankind but through His Son, and through Him as having died for the offenses of the human race. *To whom be glory for ever.* As God does all in, by, and through Christ Jesus, to Him be the honor of His own work ascribed through time and eternity.

MATTHEW HENRY

IV. He closes with salutations, and a solemn, though short benediction (*v.* 22).

III. He was pleased with the hopes of not only seeing Timothy, but seeing the Hebrews with him, *v.* 23.

1. The salutation. From himself to them all, ministers and people. From the Christians in Italy to them.

2. The solemn, though short benediction (*v.* 25).

JAMIESON, FAUSSET, BROWN

22. suffer the word—The Hebrews not being the section of the Church assigned to Paul (but the Gentiles), he uses gentle entreaty, rather than authoritative command. **few words**—compared with what might be said on so important a subject. *Few,* in an Epistle which is more of a *treatise* than an Epistle (cf. I Pet. 5:12). On the seeming inconsistency with Galatians 6:11, cf. *Note* there. **23. our brother Timothy**—So Paul, I Corinthians 4:17; II Corinthians 1:1; Colossians 1:1; I Thessalonians 3:2. **is set at liberty**—from prison. So Aristarchus was imprisoned with Paul. BIRKS translates, "dismissed," "sent away," viz., on a mission to Greece, as Paul promised (Phil. 2:19). However, *some* kind of previous detention is implied before his being *let go* to Philippi. Paul, though now at large, was still *in Italy,* whence he sends the salutations of Italian Christians (vs. 24), waiting for Timothy to join him, so as to start for Jerusalem: we know from I Timothy 1:3, he and Timothy were together at Ephesus after his departing from Italy eastward. He probably left Timothy there and went to Philippi as he had promised. Paul implies that if Timothy shall not *come shortly,* he will start on his journey to the Hebrews at once.

24. all—The Scriptures are intended for *all,* young and old, not merely for ministers. Cf. the different classes addressed, "wives," Ephesians 5:22; little children, I John 2:18; "all," I Peter 3:8; 5:5. He says here "all," for the Hebrews whom he addresses were not all in one place, though the Jerusalem Hebrews are chiefly addressed. **They of Italy**—not merely the brethren at Rome, but of other places in Italy.

25. *Paul's* characteristic salutation in every one of his other thirteen Epistles, as he says himself, I Corinthians 16:21, 23; Colossians 4:18; II Thessalonians 3:17. It is found in no Epistle written by any other apostle in Paul's lifetime. It is used in Revelation 22:21, written subsequently, and in CLEMENT OF ROME. Being known to be his badge, it is not used by others in his lifetime. The *Greek* here is, "*The* grace (viz., of our Lord Jesus Christ) be with you all."

ADAM CLARKE

22. *Suffer the word of exhortation.* Bear the word or doctrine of this exhortation. This seems to be an epithet of this whole Epistle; and as the apostle had in it shown the insufficiency of the Levitical system to atone for sin and save the soul, and had proved that it was the design of God that it should be abolished, and had proved also that it was now abolished by the coming of Christ, whom he had shown to be a greater Priest than Aaron, higher than all the angels, the only Son of God as to His human nature, and the Creator, Governor, and Judge of all, and that their city was shortly to be destroyed, he might suppose that they would feel prejudiced against him, and thus lose the benefit of his kind intentions toward them. Therefore he entreats them to bear the exhortation which, notwithstanding the great extent of the subject, he had included in a short compass. *I have written a letter unto you in few words.* Perhaps it would be better to translate, "I have written to you briefly."

23. *Know ye that our brother Timothy.* The word *our,* which is supplied by our translators, is very probably genuine, as it is found in several MSS. and in the Syriac, the Coptic, Armenian, Slavonic, and Vulgate. *Is set at liberty.* "Is sent away," for there is no evidence that Timothy had been imprisoned. It is probable that the apostle refers here to his being sent into Macedonia, Phil. ii. 19-24, in order that he might bring the apostle an account of the affairs of the church in that country. In none of Paul's Epistles, written during his confinement in Rome, does he give any intimation of Timothy's imprisonment, although it appears from Phil. i. 1; Col. i. 1; and Philemon 1 that he was with Paul during the greatest part of the time. *With whom, if he come shortly, I will see you.* Therefore Paul himself, or the writer of this Epistle, was now at liberty, as he had the disposal of his person and time in his own power. Some suppose that Timothy did actually visit Paul about this time, and that both together visited the churches in Judea.

24. *Salute all them that have the rule over you.* "Salute all your leaders" or "guides." See on vv. 7 and 17. *And all the saints.* All the Christians, for this is the general meaning of the term in most parts of Paul's writings. But a Christian was then a saint, i.e., by profession a holy person; and most of the primitive Christians were actually such. But in process of time the term was applied to all that bore the Christian name, as "elect, holy people, sanctified" were to the nation of the Jews when both their piety and morality were at a very low ebb. *They of Italy salute you.* Therefore it is most likely that the writer of this Epistle was then in some part of Italy, from which he had not as yet removed after his being released from prison. By *they of Italy* probably the apostle means the Jews there who had embraced the Christian faith. These salutations show what a brotherly feeling existed in every part of the Christian Church; even those who had not seen each other yet loved one another, and felt deeply interested for each other's welfare.

25. *Grace be with you all.* May the divine favor ever rest upon you and among you; and may you receive, from that source of all good, whatsoever is calculated to make you wise, holy, useful, and happy! And may you be enabled to persevere in the truth to the end of your lives!

THE EPISTLE OF JAMES

I. Introduction (1:1)
A. No details of human relationship, only that to Christ and God
B. Addressed to Jewish Christians scattered abroad

II. Faith as a principle of victory in temptation (1:2-27)
A. Temptation (1:2-15)
1. As adversity of circumstances (1:2-12)
2. As allurement to sin (1:13-15)

B. The principle of victory—faith's hold on the Word (1:16-25)
1. The admission—every good and perfect gift from God (1:16, 17)
2. The test—those born of the Word must realize the ideal (1:18)
3. The responsibilities (1:19-25)
   a. The Word received (1:19-21)
   b. The Word obeyed (1:22-25)

C. The contrast (1:26, 27)
1. "Seemeth to be religious" (1:26)
2. "Pure religion" (1:27)

III. Faith as a principle of action toward men (2:1-26)
A. The failure (2:1-11)
1. Judge not (2:1-4)
2. "Ye despise the poor"—"theirs is the Kingdom" (2:5-7)
3. The positive statement—"if ye fulfill . . ." (2:8-11)

B. The correction (2:12-25)
1. Injunction to act as those to be judged by the law of liberty (2:12, 13)
2. The profitlessness of creed without conduct (2:14-20)
3. The illustrations (2:21-25)

C. The principle—the central vein of the Epistle (2:26)

IV. Faith as a principle of wisdom in speech (3:1-18)
A. A warning to public teachers (3:1)
B. The tongue (3:2-12)
1. Its power for evil (3:2-6)
2. Its untameable nature (3:7-8)
3. Its inconsistency (3:9-12)

C. The effect of faith (3:13-18)
1. The power of silence (3:13-16)
2. Wisdom from above—the true source of speech (3:17, 18)

V. Faith as a principle of purity in character (4:1-17)
A. The failure (4:1-5)
1. Wars and fightings
2. Arising from lust
3. Issuing in evil
4. Daring to lay tribute on prayer

B. The correction (4:6-10)
1. The gift (4:6)
2. The responsibility (4:7-10)

C. The principle (4:11-17)
1. Toward man (4:11, 12)
2. Toward God (4:13-16)
3. Summary (4:17)

VI. Conclusion (5:1-20)
A. Address to the oppressors (5:1-6)
B. Address to the oppressed (5:7-12)
C. Final words (5:13-20)

The writer of this epistle was not James the son of Zebedee, for he was put to death by Herod (Acts 12). It is called a general epistle, because (as some think) it is not directed to any particular person or church, but is more like a circular letter. The time when this epistle was written is uncertain. The design of it is to reprove Christians for their great degeneracy both in faith and manners. It was also a special intention of the author of this epistle to awaken the Jewish nation to a sense of the greatness and nearness of those judgments which were coming upon them; and to support all true Christians in the way of their duty, under the calamities and persecutions they might meet with.

MATTHEW HENRY

CHAPTER 1

Verse 1

The inscription of this epistle.

I. The character by which our author desires to be known: *James, a servant of God, and of the Lord Jesus Christ.* Though James is called by the evangelist *the brother of our Lord*, yet it was his glory to serve Christ in the spirit, rather than to boast of his being akin according to the flesh. Hence let us learn to prize this title above all others in the world—*the servants of God and of Christ.* We cannot acceptably serve the Father, unless we are also servants of the Son.

II. *The twelve tribes which are scattered abroad.* They were dispersed in mercy. They were scattered in several countries for the diffusing of the light of divine revelation. They began now to be scattered in wrath. Even good people among them shared in the common calamity. These Jews of the dispersion were those who had embraced the Christian faith. It is often the lot even of God's own tribes to be scattered abroad. While God's tribes are scattered abroad, he will send to look after them. Here is an apostle writing to the scattered; an epistle from God to them. We should not despond and think ourselves rejected, under outward calamities, God remembers and sends comfort to his scattered people.

III. James here shows the respect he had even for the dispersed: *greeting.* It was the desire of this apostle's heart that those who were scattered might

JAMIESON, FAUSSET, BROWN

CHAPTER 1

VSS. 1-27. INSCRIPTION: EXHORTATION ON HEARING, SPEAKING, AND WRATH. The last subject is discussed in ch. 3:13 to 4:17. **1. James**—an apostle of the circumcision, with Peter and John, James in Jerusalem, Palestine, and Syria; Peter in Babylon and the East; John in Ephesus and Asia Minor. Peter addresses the dispersed *Jews of Pontus, Galatia, and Cappadocia;* James, the *Israelites of the twelve tribes scattered abroad.* **servant of God**—not that he was not an *apostle;* for Paul, an apostle, also calls himself so; but as addressing the Israelites generally, including even indirectly the unbelieving, he in humility omits the title "apostle"; so Paul in writing to the Hebrews; similarly Jude, an apostle, in his General Epistle. **Jesus Christ**—not mentioned again save in ch. 2:1; not at all in his speeches (Acts 15:14, 15, and 21:20, 21), lest his introducing the name of Jesus oftener should seem to arise from vanity, as being "the Lord's brother" [BENGEL]. His teaching being practical, rather than doctrinal, required less frequent mention of Christ's name. **scattered abroad**—lit., "which are in the dispersion." The dispersion of the Israelites, and their connection with Jerusalem as a center of religion, was a divinely ordered means of propagating Christianity. The pilgrim troops of the law became caravans of the Gospel [WORDSWORTH]. **greeting**—found in no other Christian letter, but in James and the Jerusalem Synod's Epistle to the Gentile churches; an un-

ADAM CLARKE

CHAPTER 1

1. *James, a servant of God.* He neither calls himself an apostle nor does he say that he was the brother of Christ or bishop of Jerusalem. *To the twelve tribes which are scattered abroad.* To the Jews, whether converted to Christianity or not, who lived out of Judea and sojourned among the Gentiles for the purpose of trade or commerce. *Greeting.* "Health"; a mere expression of benevolence, a wish for their prosperity; a common form of salutation; see Acts xv. 23; xxiii. 26.

MATTHEW HENRY

be comforted.

Verses 2–12

I. The suffering state of Christians in this world is represented. It is implied that troubles and afflictions may be the lot of the best Christians. Such as have a title to the greatest joy may yet endure very grievous afflictions. The trials of a good man are such as he does not create to himself, nor sinfully pull upon himself; but they are such as he is said to fall into.

II. The graces and duties of a state of trial and affliction.

1. One Christian grace to be exercised is joy, *v.* 2. We must not sink into a sad and disconsolate frame of mind, which would make us faint under our trials. Philosophy may instruct men to be calm under their troubles; but Christianity teaches them to be joyful. Our trials will brighten our graces now and our crown at last. There is the more reason for joy in afflictions if we consider the other graces that are promoted by them.

2. Faith, *v.* 3; and then in *v.* 6. There must be a sound believing of the great truths of Christianity, and a resolute cleaving to them, in times of trial.

3. There must be patience: *The trial of faith worketh patience.* The trying of one grace produces another. To exercise Christian patience aright, we must let it work. Stoical apathy and Christian patience are very different: by the one men become, in some measure, insensible of their afflictions; but by the other they become triumphant in and over them. Let us give it leave to work, and it will work wonders in a time of trouble. We must let it have its perfect work. When we bear all that God appoints, and as long as he appoints, and when we not only bear troubles, but rejoice in them, then patience hath its perfect work. When the work of patience is complete, then the Christian is entire, and nothing will be wanting.

4. Prayer. What we ought more especially to pray for—wisdom. We should not pray so much for the removal of an affliction as for wisdom to make a right use of it. To be wise in trying times is a special gift of God. In what way this is to be obtained—upon our asking for it. Let the foolish become beggars at the throne of grace, and they are in a fair way to be wise. We have the greatest encouragement to do this: *he giveth to all men liberally, and upbraideth not. It shall be given, v.* 5. He to whom we are sent, has it to give: and he is of a giving disposition. Nor is there any fear of his favours being limited to some for *he gives to all men.* If you should say you want a great deal of wisdom, a small portion will not serve your turn, he *gives liberally;* and lest you should be afraid of being put to shame for your folly, he *upbraideth not.* Ask when you will, and as often as you will, you will meet with no upbraidings. The promise is: *It shall be given him.*

There is one thing necessary to be observed in our asking, *v.* 6. There must be *no wavering,* no staggering at the promise of God through unbelief.

5. Sincerity of intention, and a steadiness of mind, constitute another duty required under affliction: *He that wavereth is like a wave of the sea, driven with the wind, and tossed.* To be sometimes lifted up by faith, and then thrown down again by distrust—this is very fitly compared to a wave of the sea, that rises and falls, swells and sinks, just as the wind tosses it higher or lower, that way or this.

The success of prayer is spoiled hereby, *v.* 7. Such a distrustful shifting, unsettled person is not likely to value a favour from God as he should do, and therefore cannot expect to receive it. A wavering faith and spirit has a bad influence upon our conversations, *v.* 8. There will be great unsteadiness in all our conversation and actions. He that is unstable as water shall not excel.

JAMIESON, FAUSSET, BROWN

designed coincidence and mark or genuineness. In the original Greek (*chairein*) for "greeting," there is a connection with the "joy" to which they are exhorted amidst their existing distresses from poverty and consequent oppression. Cf. Romans 15:26, which alludes to their poverty. **2. My brethren**—a phrase often found in James, marking community of nation and of faith. **all joy**—cause for the highest joy [GROTIUS]. Nothing but joy [PISCATOR]. Count *all* "divers temptations" to be *each* matter of *joy* [BENGEL]. **fall into**—unexpectedly, so as to be *encompassed by* them (so the original *Greek*). **temptations**—not in the limited sense of allurements to sin, but *trials* or distresses of any kind which test and purify the Christian character. Cf. "tempt," i.e., try, Genesis 22:1. Some of those to whom James writes were "sick," or otherwise "afflicted" (ch. 5:13). Every possible trial to the child of God is a masterpiece of strategy of the Captain of his salvation for his good. **3. the trying**—the *testing* or *proving* of your faith, viz., by "divers temptations." Cf. Romans 5:3, "*tribulation*" worketh patience, and patience *experience* (in the original *dokime,* akin to *dokimion,* "trying," here; there it is *experience:* here the "trying" or *testing,* whence experience flows). **patience**—The original implies more; *persevering endurance* and *continuance* (cf. Luke 8:15). **4.** Let endurance have a perfect *work* (taken out of the previous "*worketh* patience" or endurance), i.e., have its *full effect,* by showing the most perfect degree of endurance, viz., "joy in bearing the cross" [MENOCHIUS], and enduring to the end (Matt. 10:22), [CALVIN]. **ye may be perfect**—fully developed in all the attributes of a Christian character. For this there is required "joy" [BENGEL], as part of the "perfect work" of probation. The work of God in a man *is* the man. If God's teachings by patience have had a perfect work in you, *you* are perfect [ALFORD]. **entire**—that which has all *its parts complete, wanting no integral part;* I Thessalonians 5:23, "your whole (lit., 'entire') spirit, soul, and body"; as "perfect" implies *without a blemish in its parts.* **5.** *English Version* omits "But," which the *Greek* has, and which is important. "But (as this *perfect entireness wanting nothing* is no easy attainment) if any. . . ." **lack**—rather, as the Greek word is repeated after James's manner, from vs. 4, "*wanting* nothing," translate, "If any of you *want* wisdom," viz., the wisdom whereby ye may "count it all joy when ye fall into divers temptations," and "let patience have her perfect work." This "wisdom" is shown in its effects in detail, ch. 3:7. The highest wisdom, which governs patience alike in poverty and riches, is described in vss. 9, 10. **ask**—(Ch. 4:2). **liberally**—So the *Greek* is rendered by *English Version.* It is rendered *with simplicity,* Romans 12:8. God gives without adding aught which may take off from the graciousness of the gift [ALFORD]. God requires the same "simplicity" in His children ("eye . . . single," Matt. 6:22, lit., "simple"). **upbraideth not**—an illustration of God's giving *simply.* He gives to the humble suppliant without upbraiding him with his past sin and ingratitude, or his future abuse of God's goodness. The Jews pray, "Let me not have need of the gifts of men, whose gifts are few, but their upbraidings manifold; but give me out of Thy large and full hand." **6. ask in faith**—i.e., the persuasion that God can and will give. James begins and ends with *faith.* In the middle of the Epistle he removes the hindrances to faith and shows its true character [BENGEL]. **wavering**—between belief and unbelief. Cf. the case of the Israelites, who seemed to partly believe in God's power, but leaned more to unbelief by "limiting" it. On the other hand, cf. Acts 10:20; Romans 4:20 ("*staggered not . . .* through unbelief," lit., as here, "*wavered not*"); I Timothy 2:8. **like a wave of the sea**—Isaiah 57:20; Ephesians 4:14, where the same *Greek* word occurs for "tossed to and fro," as is here translated, "driven with the wind" **driven with the wind**—from without. **tossed**—from within, by its own instability [BENGEL]. At one time cast on the shore of faith and hope, at another rolled back into the abyss of unbelief; at one time raised to the height of worldly pride, at another tossed in the sands of despair and affliction [WIESINGER]. **7. For**—resumed from "For" in vs. 6. **that man**—such a wavering self-deceiver. **think**—Real *faith* is something more than a mere *thinking* or *surmise.* **anything**—viz., of the things that he prays for: he does receive many things from God, food, raiment, etc., but these are the general gifts of His providence: of the things specially granted in answer to prayer, the waverer shall not receive "anything," much less wisdom. **8. double-minded**—lit., "double-souled," the one soul directed towards God, the other to something else. The *Greek* favors ALFORD'S

ADAM CLARKE

2. *Count it all joy.* The word which we translate *temptations* signifies affliction, persecution, or trial of any kind; and in this sense it is used here, not intending diabolic suggestion, or what is generally understood by the word *temptations.*

3. *The trying of your faith.* Trials put religion, and all the graces of which it is composed, to proof. The man that stands in such trials gives proof that his religion is sound, and the evidence afforded to his own mind induces him to take courage, bear patiently, and persevere.

4. *Let patience have her perfect work.* That is, continue faithful, and your patience will be crowned with its full reward; for in this sense is *ergon,* which we translate *work,* to be understood. The *perfect work* is the "full reward." *That ye may be perfect and entire.* "Fully instructed" in every part of the doctrine of God and in His whole will concerning you. Having all your parts, members, and portions; that you may have every grace which constitutes the mind that was in Christ, so that your knowledge and holiness may be complete, and bear a proper proportion to each other. These expressions in their present application are by some thought to be borrowed from the Grecian games. The man was *perfect* who in any of the athletic exercises had got the victory; he was *entire,* having everything complete, who had the victory in each of the five exercises. Of this use in the last term I do not recollect an example, and therefore think the expressions are borrowed from the sacrifices under the law. A victim was *perfect* that was perfectly sound, having no disease; it was *entire* if it had all its members, having nothing deficient.

5. *If any of you lack wisdom.* Wisdom signifies, in general, knowledge of the best end and the best means of attaining it; but in Scripture it signifies the same as true religion, the thorough practical knowledge of God, of oneself, and of a Saviour. *Let him ask of God.* Because God is the only Teacher of this wisdom. *That giveth to all men liberally.* Who has all good, and gives all necessary good to everyone that asks fervently. He who does not ask thus does not feel his need of divine teaching. The ancient Greek maxim appears at first view strange, but it is literally true: "The knowledge of ignorance is the beginning of knowledge."

6. *Let him ask in faith.* Believing that God is, that He has all good, and that He is ever ready to impart to His creatures whatever they need. *Nothing wavering.* "Not judging otherwise"; having no doubt concerning the truth of these grand and fundamental principles, never supposing that God will permit him to ask in vain, when he asks sincerely and fervently. *Is like a wave of the sea.* The man who is not thoroughly persuaded that if he ask of God he shall receive resembles *a wave of the sea;* he is in a state of continual agitation; *driven with the wind and tossed;* now rising by hope, then sinking by despair.

7. *Let not that man think.* The man whose mind is divided, who is not properly persuaded either of his own wants or God's sufficiency. Such persons may pray, but having no faith, they can get no answer.

8. *A double minded man.* The "man of two souls," who has one for earth and another for heaven; who wishes to secure both worlds; he

MATTHEW HENRY

III. Both poor and rich are directed on what grounds to build their joy and comfort, *v.* 9–11. Those of low degree are to be looked upon as brethren. Good Christians may be rich in the world, *v.* 10. Grace and wealth are not wholly inconsistent. Both these are allowed to rejoice. No condition of life puts us out of a capacity of rejoicing in God. All who are brought low, and made lowly by grace, may rejoice in the prospect of their exaltation at the last in heaven. What reason rich people have to be humble: *As the flower of the grass he shall pass away.* He, and his wealth with him, *v.* 11. *For the sun has no sooner risen with a burning heat than it withereth the grass.* As a flower fades before the heat of the scorching sun, *so shall the rich man fade away in his ways.* For this reason let him that is rich rejoice, not so much in the providence of God, that makes him rich, as in the grace of God, that makes and keeps him humble.

IV. A blessing is pronounced on those who endure their exercises and trials, *v.* 12. It is not the man who suffers only that is blessed, but he who endures. Afflictions cannot make us miserable. A blessing may arise from them. Sufferings and temptations are the way to eternal blessedness: *When he is tried, he shall receive the crown of life, when he is approved,* when his graces are found to be true and of the highest worth (so metals are tried as to their excellency by the fire). The tried Christian shall be a crowned one: and the crown he shall wear will be a crown of life. We only bear the cross for a while, but we shall wear the crown to eternity. This blessedness is a promised thing to the righteous sufferer. It is therefore what we may most surely depend upon. Our enduring temptations must be from a principle of love to God and to our Lord Jesus Christ: *The Lord hath promised to those that love him.* The crown of life is promised to all those who have the love of God reigning in their hearts.

Verses 13–18

I. God is not the author of any man's sin. Some professors might fall in the hour of temptation. The blame of their misconduct must lie entirely upon themselves. There is nothing in the nature of God that they can lay the blame upon. There is nothing in the providential dispensations of God that the blame of any man's sin can be laid upon (*v.* 13). As God cannot be tempted with evil himself, so neither can he be a tempter of others. It is very bad to sin; but it is much worse, when we have done amiss, to charge it upon God, and say it was owing to him. Afflictions are designed to draw out our graces, but not our corruptions.

II. Where the true cause of evil lies, and where the blame ought to be laid (*v.* 14). The true original of evil and temptation is in our own hearts. The combustible matter is in us, though the flame may be blown up by some outward causes. The method of sin in its proceeding. First it draws away, then entices. The heart is carried from that which is good, and enticed to cleave to that which is evil, estranged from the life of God, and then by degrees fixed in a course of sin. The word here rendered *drawn away* signifies a being forcibly haled or compelled. The word translated *enticed* signifies being wheedled and beguiled. The force and power of sin could never prevail, were it not for its cunning and guile.

JAMIESON, FAUSSET, BROWN

translation, "He (the waverer, vs. 6) *is* a man double-minded, unstable . . ."; or better, BEZA's. The words in this vs. 8 are in apposition with "that man," vs. 7; thus the "us," which is not in the original, will not need to be supplied, "A man double-minded, unstable in all his ways!" The word for "double-minded" is found here and in ch. 4:8, for the first time in Greek literature. It is not a *hypocrite* that is meant, but a *fickle,* "wavering" man, as the context shows. It is opposed to *the single eye* (Matt. 6:22). **9, 10.** Translate, "*But* let the brother . . .," i.e., the best remedy against *double-mindedness* is that Christian *simplicity* of spirit whereby the "brother," low in outward circumstances, may "rejoice" (answering to vs. 2) "in that he is exalted," viz., by being accounted a son and heir of God, his very sufferings being a pledge of his coming glory and crown (vs. 12), and the rich may rejoice "in that he is made low," by being stripped of his goods for Christ's sake [MENOCHIUS]; or in that he is made, by sanctified trials, lowly in spirit, which is true matter for rejoicing [GOMARUS]. The design of the Epistle is to reduce all things to an equable footing (ch. 2:1; 5:13). The "low," rather than the "rich," is here called "the brother" [BENGEL]. **11.** Taken from Isaiah 40:6-8. **heat**—rather, "the hot wind" from the (east or) south, which scorches vegetation (Luke 12:55). The "burning heat" of the sun is not at its *rising,* but rather at noon; whereas the scorching *Kadim* wind is often at sunrise (Jonah 4:8) [MIDDLETON, *Greek Article*]. Matthew 20:12 uses the *Greek* word for "heat." Isaiah 40:7, "*bloweth* upon it," seems to answer to "the hot *wind*" here. **grace of the fashion**—i.e., of the external appearance. **in his ways**—referring to the burdensome extent of the rich man's devices [BENGEL]. Cf. "his ways," i.e., his course of life, vs. 8. **12. Blessed**—Cf. the beatitudes in the Sermon on the Mount (Matt. 5:4, 10, 11). **endureth temptation**—not the "falling into divers temptations" (vs. 2) is the matter for "joy," but the *enduring* of temptation "unto the end." Cf. Job 5:17. **when he is tried**—lit., "when he has become tested" or "approved," when he has passed through the "trying" (vs. 3), his "faith" having finally gained the victory. **the crown**—not in allusion to the crown or garland given to winners in the games; for this, though a natural allusion for Paul in writing to the heathen, among whom such games existed, would be less appropriate for James in addressing the Jewish Christians, who regarded Gentile usages with aversion. **of life**—"life" constitutes the crown, lit., *the* life, the only true life, the highest and eternal life. The crown implies a *kingdom* (Ps. 21:3). **the Lord**—not found in the best MSS. and versions. The believer's heart fills up the omission, without the name needing to be mentioned. The "faithful One who promised" (Heb. 10:23). **to them that love him**—In II Timothy 4:8, "the crown of righteousness to them that love His appearing." Love produces patient *endurance:* none attest their love more than they who suffer for Him. **13. when . . . tempted**—tried by *solicitation to evil.* Heretofore the "temptation" meant was that of *probation by afflictions.* Let no one fancy that God lays upon him an inevitable necessity of sinning. God does not send trials on you in order to make you worse, but to make you better (vss. 16, 17). Therefore do not sink under the pressure of evils (I Cor. 10:13). **of God**—by agency proceeding *from* God. The *Greek* is not "tempted *by,*" but, "from," implying indirect agency. **cannot be tempted with evil . . .**—"Neither do any of our sins tempt God to entice us to worse things, nor does He tempt any *of His own accord*" (lit., "of Himself"; cf. the antithesis, vs. 18, "*Of His own will* He begat us" to holiness, so far is He from tempting us *of His own will*) [BENGEL]. God is said in Genesis 22:1 to have "tempted Abraham"; but there the *tempting* meant is that of *trying* or *proving,* not that of seducement.

14. Every man, when tempted, is so through being drawn away of (again here, as in vs. 13, the *Greek* for "of" expresses the actual *source,* rather than the agent of temptation) his own lust. The cause of sin is in ourselves. Even Satan's suggestions do not endanger us before they are made *our own.* Each one has *his own peculiar* (so the *Greek*) lust, arising from his own temperament and habit. Lust flows from the original birth-sin in man, inherited from Adam. **drawn away**—the *beginning* step in temptation: drawn away from truth and virtue. **enticed**—lit., "taken with a bait," as fish are. The *further progress:* the man *allowing himself* (as the *Greek* middle voice implies) *to be enticed* to evil [BENGEL]. "Lust" is here personified as the harlot that allures the man. **15.** The guilty union is committed by the will embracing the tempt-

ADAM CLARKE

will not give up earth, and he is loath to let heaven go. This was a usual term among the Jews to express the man who attempted to worship God and yet retained the love of the creature. Perhaps James refers to those Jews who were endeavoring to incorporate the law with the gospel, who were divided in their minds and affections, not willing to give up the Levitical rites and yet unwilling to renounce the gospel. Such persons could make no progress in divine things.

9. *Let the brother of low degree.* The poor, destitute Christian may "glory" in the cross of Christ, and the blessed hope laid up for him in heaven; for, being a child of God, he is an heir of God and a joint heir with Christ.

10. *But the rich, in that he is made low.* "In his humiliation"—in his being brought to the foot of the Cross to receive, as a poor and miserable sinner, redemption through the Blood of the Cross; and especially let him rejoice in this, because all outward glory is only as the flower of the field and, like that, will wither and perish.

11. *For the sun is no sooner risen.* All human things are transitory; rise and fall, or increase and decay, belong to all the productions of the earth, and to all its inhabitants.

12. *Blessed is the man that endureth temptation.* Every man is in this life in a state of temptation or trial, and in this state he is a candidate for another and a better world; he that stands in his trial *shall receive the crown of life, which the Lord hath promised to them that love him.* There may be an allusion here to the contests in the Grecian games. He is crowned who conquers, and none else.

13. *Let no man say.* Lest the former sentiment should be misapplied, as the word temptation has two grand meanings—solicitation to sin, and trial from providential situation or circumstances—James, taking up the word in the former sense, after having used it in the latter, says: *Let no man say, when he is tempted* [*solicited to sin*], *I am tempted of God; for God cannot be tempted with evil, neither tempteth he* [*thus*] *any man.*"

14. *But every man is tempted,* successfully solicited to sin, *when he is drawn away of his own lust*—when, giving way to the evil propensity of his own heart, he does that to which he is solicited by the enemy of his soul. Among the rabbins we find some fine sayings on this subject. "Evil concupiscence is, at the beginning, like the thread of a spider's web: afterwards it is like a cart rope" (*Sanhedrim,* fol. 99). In the words *drawn away of his own lust, and enticed,* there is a double metaphor: the first referring to the dragging a fish out of the water by a hook which it had swallowed, because concealed by a bait; the second, to the enticements of impure women, who draw away the unwary into their snares and involve them in their ruin.

MATTHEW HENRY

The success of corruption in the heart (*v.* 15). Sin being allowed to excite desires in us, it will soon ripen those desires into consent, and then it is said to have *conceived.* The final issue of sin: *Sin, when it is finished, bringeth forth death.* There is death upon the soul, and death comes upon the body.

III. We are taught yet further that *God is the Father and fountain of all good, v.* 16, 17. We should take particular care not to err in our conceptions of God: "*Do not err, my beloved brethren, do not wander.*" God is not, cannot be, the author of anything that is evil; but must be acknowledged as the cause and spring of everything that is good, *v.* 17. God is unchangeable, and our changes and shadows are not from any mutability or shadowy alterations in him, but from ourselves. The Father of lights, *with whom there is no variableness, neither shadow of turning.* Every good gift is from him. He gives the light of reason. He gives also the light of learning. The light of divine revelation is more immediately from above. So that we have nothing good but what we receive from God.

Our regeneration, and all the holy happy consequences of it, must be ascribed to him (*v.* 18). A true Christian is a creature begotten anew. It is of God's own will; not by our skill or power; but purely from the goodwill and grace of God. The means whereby this is effected, *the word of truth,* that is, the gospel. This gospel is indeed a word of truth, or else it could never produce such real, such lasting, such great and noble effects. The end and design of God's giving renewing grace, *That we should be a kind of first-fruits of his creatures.* Christ is the first-fruits of Christians, Christians are the first-fruits of creatures.

Verses 19–27

We are required,

I. To restrain the workings of passion. This we shall learn if we are indeed begotten again by the word of truth, *v.* 19. Be ready to hear and consider what God's word teaches. This may be applied to the afflictions and temptations spoken of in the beginning of the chapter. Instead of censuring God under our trials, let us open our ears and hearts to hear what he will say to us. This may be understood as referring to the disputes and differences that Christians were running into among themselves. We should be swift to hear reason and truth on all sides, and be slow to speak: and, when we do speak, there should be nothing of wrath. If men would govern their tongues, they must govern their passions. If we would be slow to speak, we must be slow to wrath.

JAMIESON, FAUSSET, BROWN

ress. "Lust," the harlot, then, "brings forth sin," viz., of that kind to which the temptation inclines. Then *the particular sin* (so the *Greek* implies), "when it is completed, brings forth death," with which it was all along pregnant [ALFORD]. This "death" stands in striking contrast to the "crown of *life*" (vs. 12) which "patience" or *endurance* ends in, when it has its "perfect work" (vs. 4). He who will fight Satan with Satan's own weapons, must not wonder if he finds himself overmatched. Nip sin in the bud of lust. **16.** Do not err in attributing to God temptation to evil; nay (as he proceeds to show), "every good," all that is good on earth, comes from God. **17. gift . . . gift**—not the same words in *Greek:* the first, *the act of giving,* or the gift in its *initiatory* stage; the second, *the thing given, the boon, when perfected.* As the "good gift" stands in contrast to "sin" in its initiatory stage (vs. 15), so the "perfect boon" is in contrast to "sin when it is finished," bringing forth *death* (II Pet. 1:3). **from above**—(Cf. ch. 3:15). **Father of lights**—Creator *of the lights in heaven* (cf. Job. 38:28 [ALFORD]; Gen. 4:20, 21; Heb. 12:9). This accords with the reference to the changes in the light of the heavenly bodies alluded to in the end of the verse. Also, Father of the spiritual lights in the kingdom of grace and glory [BENGEL]. These were typified by the supernatural lights on the breastplate of the high priest, the Urim. As "God is light, and in Him is no darkness at all" (I John 1:5), He cannot in any way be the Author of sin (vs. 13), which is darkness (John 3:19). **no variableness . . . shadow of turning**—(Mal. 3:6). None of the alternations of light and shadow which the physical "lights" undergo, and which even the spiritual lights are liable to, as compared with God. "Shadow of turning," lit., the dark "shadow-mark" cast *from* one of the heavenly bodies, arising from its "turning" or revolution, e.g., when the moon is eclipsed by the shadow of the earth, and the sun by the body of the moon. BENGEL makes a climax, "no variation—not even the shadow of a turning"; the former denoting a change in the *understanding;* the latter, in the *will.* **18.** (John 1:13.) The believer's regeneration is the highest example of nothing but good proceeding from God. **Of his own will**—Of his own good pleasure (which shows that it is God's essential nature to do good, not evil), not induced by any external cause. **begat he us**—spiritually: a once-for-all accomplished act (I Pet. 1:3, 23). In contrast to "lust when it hath conceived, *bringeth forth* sin, and sin . . . *death*" (vs. 15). *Life* follows naturally in connection with *light* (vs. 17). **word of truth**—the Gospel. The objective mean, as *faith* is the appropriating mean of regeneration by the Holy Spirit as the efficient agent. **a kind of first fruits**—Christ is, in respect to the resurrection, "the first fruits" (I Cor. 15:20, 23): believers, in respect to regeneration, are, *as it were,* first fruits (image from the consecration of the first-born of man, cattle, and fruits to God; familiar to the Jews addressed), i.e., they are the first of God's regenerated creatures, and the pledge of the ultimate regeneration of the creation, Romans 8:19, 23, where also the Spirit, the divine agent of the believer's regeneration, is termed "the first fruits," i.e., the earnest that the regeneration now begun in the soul, shall at last extend to the body too, and to the lower parts of creation. Of all God's visible creatures, believers are the noblest part, and like the legal "first-fruits," sanctify the rest; for this reason they are much tried now. **19. Wherefore**—as your evil is of yourselves, but your good from God. However, the oldest MSS. and versions read thus: "YE KNOW IT (so Eph. 5:5; Heb. 12:17), my beloved brethren; BUT (consequently) let every man be swift to hear," i.e., docile in receiving "the word of truth" (vss. 18, 21). The true method of hearing is treated in vss. 21-27, and ch. 2. **slow to speak**—(Prov. 10:19; 17:27, 28; Eccles. 5:2). A good way of escaping one kind of temptation arising from ourselves (vs. 13). Slow to speak authoritatively as a master or teacher of others (cf. ch. 3:1): a common Jewish fault: slow also to speak such hasty things of God, as in vs. 13. Two ears are given to us, the rabbis observe, but only one tongue: the ears are open and exposed, whereas the tongue is walled in behind the teeth. **slow to wrath**—(ch. 3:13, 14; 4:5). Slow in becoming heated by debate: another Jewish fault (Rom. 2:8), to which much *speaking* tends. TITTMANN thinks not so much "wrath" is meant, as an *indignant* feeling of *fretfulness* under the calamities to which the whole of human life is exposed; this accords with the "divers temptations" in vs. 2. Hastiness of temper hinders hearing God's word; so Naaman, II Kings 5:11; Luke 4:28. **20.** Man's angry zeal in debating, as if jealous for the honor of God's righteousness,

ADAM CLARKE

15. *When lust hath conceived.* When the evil propensity works unchecked, *it bringeth forth sin*—the evil act between the parties is perpetrated. *And sin, when it is finished.* When this breach of the law of God and of innocence has been a sufficient time completed, it *bringeth forth death*—the spurious offspring is the fruit of the criminal connection, and the evidence of that *death* or "punishment" due to the transgressors. Sin is a small matter in its commencement; but by indulgence it grows great, and multiplies itself beyond all calculation. To use the rabbinical metaphor lately adduced, it is, in the commencement, "like the thread of a spider's web"—almost imperceptible through its extreme fineness, and as easily broken; afterwards it becomes like a cart rope. It has, by being indulged, produced strong desire and delight; next, consent. Then time, place, and opportunity serving, that which was conceived in the mind and finished in the purpose is consummated by act.

16. *Do not err.* By supposing that God is the author of sin or that He impels any man to commit it.

17. *Every good gift and every perfect gift is from above.* Whatever is good is from God; whatever is evil is from man himself. As from the sun all light comes, so from God all good comes. *With whom is no variableness.* The sun, the fountain of light to the whole of our system, may be obscured by clouds; or the different bodies which revolve round him, and particularly the earth, may from time to time suffer a diminution of his light by the intervention of other bodies eclipsing his splendor, and his apparent *shadow of turning;* when for instance, in our winter, he has declined to the southern tropic, so that our days are greatly shortened, and we suffer in consequence a great diminution of both light and heat. But there is nothing of this kind with God; He is never affected by the changes and chances to which mortal things are exposed.

18. *Of his own will begat he us.* God's will here is opposed to the lust of man, v. 15; His truth, the means of human salvation, to the sinful means referred to in the above verse; and the new creatures, to the sin conceived and brought forth, as above. As the will of God is essentially good, all its productions must be good also; as it is infinitely pure, all its productions must be holy. The *word* or doctrine of *truth,* what Paul calls "the word of the truth of the gospel," Col. i. 5, is the means which God uses to convert souls. *A kind of firstfruits.* By *creatures* we are here to understand the Gentiles, and by *firstfruits* the Jews, to whom the gospel was first sent; and those of them that believed were the firstfruits of that astonishing harvest which God has since reaped over the whole Gentile world.

19. *Swift to hear.* "Talk little and work much," is a rabbinical adage (*Pirkey Aboth,* cap. i. 15). "The righteous speak little, and do much; the wicked speak much, and do nothing" (*Bava Metzia,* fol. 87).

Slow to wrath. Those who are hasty in speech are generally of a peevish or angry disposition. A person who is careful to consider what he says is not likely to be soon angry.

MATTHEW HENRY

II. A very good reason is given for suppressing anger, *v.* 20. The worst thing we can bring to a religious controversy is anger. *Wrath* is a human thing, and the wrath of man stands opposed to the righteousness of God. Those who pretend to serve the cause of God hereby show that they are acquainted neither with God nor his cause.

III. We are called upon to suppress other corrupt affections, as well as rash anger, *v.* 21. Hereby we are taught, as Christians, to watch against, and lay aside, all the disorders of a corrupt heart, which would prejudice it against the word and ways of God. There is abundance of that which is evil in us, to be watched against; there is *superfluity of naughtiness.* It is not enough to restrain evil affections, but *they must be cast from us, or laid apart.* This must extend not only to outward sins, but to all sin of thought and affection as well as speech and practice; *all filthiness.*

IV. Concerning hearing the word of God.

1. We are required to prepare ourselves for it (*v.* 21).

2. How to hear it: *Receive with meekness the engrafted word, which is able to save your souls.* In hearing the word of God, we are to receive it; receive it as the stock does the graft; so that the fruit which is produced may be, not according to the nature of the sour stock, but according to the nature of the gospel which is engrafted into our souls. We must therefore yield ourselves to the word of God, with most submissive tempers: this is to *receive it with meekness.* Being willing to hear of our faults, and taking it not only patiently, but thankfully. In all our hearing we should aim at the salvation of our souls. It is the design of the word of God to make us wise to salvation.

3. What is to be done after hearing (*v.* 22). Hearing is in order to doing; the most attentive and the most frequent hearing of the word of God will not avail us, unless we be also doers of it. It is not enough to remember what we hear. Bare hearers are self-deceivers. Self-deceit will be found the worst deceit at last.

4. What is the proper use of the word of God, *v.* 23–24. The use we are to make of God's word may be learnt from its being compared to a glass, in which a man may *behold his natural face.* As a looking-glass shows us the spots and defilements upon our faces, so the word of God shows us our sins. It shows us what is amiss, that it may be amended. When we attend to *the word of God,* so as to see ourselves, our true state and condition, and dress ourselves anew by the glass of God's word, this is to make a proper use of it. We have here an account of those who do not use this glass of the word as they ought, *v.* 24.

In vain do we hear God's word, and look into the gospel glass, if we go away, and forget our spots, and forget our remedy. This is the case of those who do not hear the word as they ought. Those also are described who hear aright, and who use the glass of God's word as they should do (*v.* 25). The gospel is a law of liberty, or *of liberation.* The ceremonial law was a yoke of bondage; the gospel of Christ is a law of liberty. It is a perfect law.

In hearing the word, we look into this perfect law. Then only do we look into the law of liberty as we should when we *continue therein.* Those who thus do, and *continue in the law and word of God,* are, and *shall be, blessed in their deed.* This blessedness does not lie in knowing, but in doing the will of God. It is not talking, but walking, that will bring us to heaven.

JAMIESON, FAUSSET, BROWN

is far from working that which is really righteousness in God's sight. True "righteousness is sown in peace," not in wrath (ch. 3:18). The oldest and the received reading is "worketh," **produceth not.** best reading means "worketh," i.e., *practiceth* not: **21. lay apart**—"once for all" (so the *Greek*): as a filthy garment. Cf. Joshua's filthy garments, Zechariah 3:3, 5; Revelation 7:14. "Filthiness" is cleansed away by hearing the word (John 15:3). **superfluity of naughtiness**—*excess* (for instance, the *intemperate* spirit implied in "wrath," vss. 19, 20), which arises from *malice* (our natural, *evil disposition* towards one another). I Peter 2:1 has the very same words in the *Greek.* So "malice" is the translation, Ephesians 4:31; Colossians 3:8. *"Faulty* excess" [BENGEL] is not strong enough. Superfluous excess in *speaking* is also reprobated as "coming of *evil"* (the *Greek* is akin to the word for "naughtiness" here) in the Sermon on the Mount (Matt. 5:37), with which James' Epistle is so connected. **with meekness**—*in mildness* towards one another [ALFORD], the opposite to "wrath" (vs. 20): answering to "as new-born babes" (I Pet. 2:2). *Meekness,* I think, includes also a childlike, *docile, humble,* as well as an uncontentious, spirit (Ps. 25: 9; 45:4; Isa. 66:2; Matt. 5:5; 11:28-30; 18:3, 4; contrast Rom. 2:8). On "receive," applied to ground receiving seed, cf. Mark 4:20. Contrast Acts 17:11; I Thessalonians 1:6 with II Thessalonians 2:10. **engrafted word**—the Gospel *word,* whose proper attribute is to be *engrafted* by the Holy Spirit, so as to be livingly incorporated with the believer, as the fruitful shoot is with the wild natural stock on which it is engrafted. The law came to man only from without, and admonished him of his duty. The Gospel is *engrafted* inwardly, and so fulfils the ultimate design of the law (Deut. 6:6 11:18; Ps. 119: 11). ALFORD translates, "The *implanted* word," referring to the parable of the sower (Matt. 13). I prefer *English Version.* **able to save**—a strong incentive to correct our dulness in hearing the word: that word which we hear so carelessly, is able (instrumentally) to save us [CALVIN]. **souls**—your true selves, for the "body" is now liable to sickness and death: but the soul being now saved, both soul and body at last shall be so (ch. 5:15, 20). **22.** Qualification of the precept, "Be swift to *hear*": "Be ye doers . . . not hearers only"; not merely "*Do* the word," but "*Be* doers" systematically and continually, as if this was your regular business. James here again refers to the Sermon on the Mount (Matt. 7:21-29). **deceiving your own selves**—by the logical fallacy (the *Greek* implies this) that the mere hearing is all that is needed. **23. For**—the logical self-deceit (vs. 22) illustrated. **not a doer**—more lit., "a notdoer" [ALFORD]. The true disciple, say the rabbis, learns in order that he may do, not in order that he may merely know or teach. **his natural face**—lit., "the countenance of his birth": the face he was born with. As a man may behold his *natural face* in a mirror, so the hearer may perceive his *moral* visage in God's Word. This faithful portraiture of man's soul in Scripture, is the strongest proof of the truth of the latter. In it, too, we see mirrored God's glory, as well as our natural vileness. **24. beholdeth**—more lit., "he *contemplated* himself and hath *gone* his way," i.e., no sooner has he contemplated his image than he is gone his way (vs. 11). "Contemplate" answers to hearing the word: "goeth his way," to relaxing the attention after hearing—letting the mind go elsewhere, and the interest of the thing heard pass away: then *forgetfulness* follows [ALFORD] (cf. Ezek. 33:31). "Contemplate" here, and in vs. 23, implies that, though cursory, yet some knowledge of one's self, at least for the time, is imparted in hearing the word (I Cor. 14:24). **and . . . and**—The repetition expresses hastiness joined with levity [BENGEL]. **forgetteth what manner of man he was**—in the mirror. Forgetfulness is no excuse (vs. 25; II Pet. 1:9). **25. looketh into**—lit., "stoopeth down to take a close look into." Peers into: stronger than "beholdeth," or "contemplated," vs. 24. A blessed curiosity if it be efficacious in bearing fruit [BENGEL]. **perfect law of liberty**—the Gospel rule of life, perfect and perfecting (as shown in the Sermon on the Mount, Matt. 5:48), and making us truly walk at liberty (Ps. 119:32, *Church of England Prayer Book Version*). Christians are to aim at a higher standard of holiness than was generally understood under the law. The *principle* of love takes the place of the letter of the law, so that by the Spirit they are free from the yoke of sin, and free to obey by spontaneous instinct (ch. 2:8, 10, 12; John 8:31-36; 15:14, 15; cf. I Cor. 7:22; Gal. 5:1, 13; I Pet. 2:16). The law is thus *not made void,* but *fulfilled.* **continueth therein**—contrasted with "goeth his way," vs. 24:

ADAM CLARKE

21. *All filthiness.* This word signifies any impurity that cleaves to the body; but applied to the mind, it implies all impure and unholy affections, such as those spoken of in v. 15, which pollute the soul. In this sense it is used by the best Greek writers. *Superfluity of naughtiness.* The "overflowing of wickedness."

The engrafted word. That doctrine which has already been planted among you, which has brought forth fruit in all them that have meekly and humbly received it, and is as powerful to save your souls as the souls of those who have already believed. When those who were Jews, and who had been originally planted by God as altogether a right vine, received the faith of the gospel, it is represented as being engrafted on that right stock, the pure knowledge of the true God and His holy moral law. This indeed was a good stock on which to implant Christianity.

22. *But be ye doers of the word.* They had heard this doctrine; they had believed it; but they had put it to no practical use. *Deceiving your own selves.* Imposing on your own selves by sophistical arguments; this is the meaning of the words. They had reasoned themselves into a state of carnal security, and the object of James is to awake them out of their sleep.

23. *Beholding his natural face in a glass.* This metaphor is very simple, but very expressive. A man wishes to see his own face, and how, in its natural state, it appears; for this purpose he looks into a mirror, by which his real face, with all its blemishes and imperfections, is exhibited. He is affected with his own appearance; he sees deformities that might be remedied; spots, superfluities, and impurities that might be removed. While he continues to look into the mirror he is affected, and wishes himself different to what he appears, and forms purposes of doing what he can to render his countenance agreeable. On going away he soon forgets "what manner of person he was." The doctrines of God, faithfully preached, are such a mirror; he who hears cannot help discovering his own character and being affected with his own deformity. He sorrows and purposes amendment; but when the preaching is over, the mirror is removed, and not being careful to examine the records of his salvation, the "perfect law of liberty," v. 25, or not continuing to look therein, he soon forgets "what manner of man he was."

25. *But whoso looketh into the perfect law.* The word which we translate *looketh into* is very emphatic and signifies that deep and attentive consideration given to a thing or subject which a man cannot bring up to his eyes, and therefore must "bend his back and neck, stooping down," that he may see it to the greater advantage. The *law of liberty* must mean the gospel. It is a *law,* for it imposes obligations from God and prescribes a rule of life; and it punishes transgressors and rewards the obedient. It is, nevertheless, a law that gives *liberty* from the guilt, power, dominion, and influence of sin; and it is *perfect,* providing a fullness of salvation for the soul: and it may be called *perfect* here in opposition to the law, which was a system of types and representations of which the gospel is the sum and substance. *And continueth.* Takes time to see and examine the state of his soul, the grace of his God, the extent of his duty, and the height of the promised glory. The metaphor here is taken from those females who spend much time at their glass, in order that they may decorate themselves to the greatest advantage, and not leave one hair, or the smallest ornament, out of its place.

MATTHEW HENRY

V. How we may distinguish between a vain religion and that which is pure and approved of God.

1. What is a vain religion: *If any man among you seemeth to be religious, and bridleth not his tongue, but deceives his own heart, this man's religion is vain.* In a vain religion there is much of show. When men are more concerned to seem religious than really to be so, it is a sign that their religion is but vain. In a vain religion there is much censuring of others. When we hear people ready to speak of the faults of others, that they themselves may seem the wiser and better, this is a sign that they have but a vain religion. The man who has a detracting tongue cannot have a truly humble gracious heart. There is no strength nor power in that religion which will not enable a man to bridle his tongue. In a vain religion a man deceives his own heart. When once religion comes to be a vain thing, how great is the vanity!

2. Wherein true religion consists, *v.* 27. It is the glory of religion to be pure and undefiled. A holy life and a charitable heart show a true religion.

That religion is pure and undefiled which is so before God and the Father. True religion teaches us to do everything as in the presence of God.

Compassion and charity to the poor and distressed form a very great and necessary part of true religion: *Visiting the fatherless and widow in their affliction.* By them we are to understand all who are proper objects of charity, all who are in affliction. If the sum of religion be drawn up in two articles this is one—to be charitable and relieve the afflicted. An unspotted life must accompany an unfeigned love and charity: *To keep himself unspotted from the world.* The world is apt to spot and blemish the soul, and it is hard to live in it, and have to do with it, and not be defiled; but this must be our constant endeavour. Herein consists pure and undefiled religion.

JAMIESON, FAUSSET, BROWN

continues both *looking into* the mirror of God's word, and doing its precepts. **doer of the work**—rather, "a doer of work" [ALFORD], an actual worker. **blessed in his deed**—rather, "in his *doing*"; in the very doing there is blessedness (Ps. 19:11). **26, 27.** An example of *doing work*. **religious . . religion**—The *Greek* expresses the *external service* or exercise *of religion*, "godliness" being the internal soul of it. "If any man *think himself to be* (so the *Greek*) religious, i.e., *observant of the offices of religion*, let him know these consist not so much in outward observances, as in such acts of mercy and humble piety (Mic. 6:7, 8) as *visiting the fatherless*, etc., and *keeping one's self unspotted from the world*" (Matt. 23:23). James does not mean that these *offices* are the great essentials, or sum total of religion; but that, whereas the law service was merely ceremonial, the very *services* of the Gospel consist in acts of mercy and holiness, and it has light for its *garment*, its very *robe* being righteousness [TRENCH]. The *Greek* word is only found in Acts 26:5, "after the straitest sect of our *religion* I lived a Pharisee." Colossians 2:18, "*worshipping* of angels." **bridleth not . . . tongue**—Discretion in speech is better than fluency of speech (cf. ch. 3:2, 3). Cf. Psalm 39:1. God alone can enable us to do so. James, in treating of the law, naturally notices this sin. For they who are free from grosser sins, and even bear the outward show of sanctity, will often exalt themselves by detracting others under the pretense of zeal, while their real motive is love of evil-speaking [CALVIN]. **heart**—It and the tongue act and react on one another. **27. Pure . . . and undefiled**—"Pure" is that love which has in it *no foreign admixture*, as self-deceit and hypocrisy. "Undefiled" is the means of its being "pure" [TITTMANN]. "Pure" expresses the *positive*, "undefiled" the *negative* side of religious service; just as *visiting the fatherless and widow* is the active, *keeping himself unspotted from the world*, the passive side of religious duty. This is the nobler shape that our religious exercises take, instead of the ceremonial offices of the law. **before God and the Father**—lit., "before Him who is (our) God and Father." God is so called to imply that if we would be like our Father, it is not by fasting, etc., for He does none of these things, but in being "merciful as our Father is merciful" [CHRYSOSTOM]. **visit**—in sympathy and kind offices to alleviate their distresses. **the fatherless**—whose "Father' is God (Ps. 68:5); peculiarly helpless. **and**—not in the *Greek*; so close is the connection between active works of mercy to others, and the maintenance of personal unworldliness of spirit, word, and deed; no copula therefore is needed. Religion in its rise interests us about *ourselves*; in its progress, about our *fellow creatures*; in its highest stage, about the honor of God. **keep himself**—with jealous watchfulness, at the same time praying and depending on God as alone able to keep us (John 17:15; Jude 24).

ADAM CLARKE

He being not a forgetful hearer. This seems to be a reference to Deut. iv. 9: "Only take heed to thyself, and keep thy soul diligently, lest thou forget the things which thine eyes have seen, and lest they depart from thy heart all the days of thy life." "He who studies and forgets is like to a woman who brings forth children, and immediately buries them" (*Aboth R. Nathan*, cap. 23). *Shall be blessed in his deed.* In *Pirkey Aboth*, cap. v. 14, it is said: "There are four kinds of men who visit the synagogues: (1) He who enters but does not work; (2) He who works but does not enter; (3) He who enters and works; (4) He who neither enters nor works. The first two are indifferent characters; the third is the righteous man; the fourth is wholly evil." As the path of duty is the way of safety, so it is the way of happiness; he who obeys God from a loving heart and pure conscience will infallibly find continual blessedness.

27. *Pure religion and undefiled.* James's definition rather refers to the effects of *pure religion* than to its nature. The "life of God in the soul of man," producing love to God and man, will show itself in the acts which James mentions here. It is *pure* in the principle, for it is divine truth and divine love. It is *undefiled* in all its operations. It can produce nothing unholy, because it ever acts in the sight of God; and it can produce no ungentle word nor unkind act, because it comes from the *Father.* The words *pure* and *undefiled* are supposed to have reference to a diamond or precious stone, whose perfection consists in its being free from flaws. True religion is the ornament of the soul; and its effects, the ornament of the life. *To visit the fatherless and widows in their affliction.* Works of charity and mercy are the proper fruits of religion, and none are more especially the objects of charity and mercy than the orphans and widows. False religion may perform acts of mercy and charity: but its motives not being pure, and its principle being defiled, the flesh, self, and hypocrisy spot the man, and spot his acts. True religion does not merely give something for the relief of the distressed, but it visits them, it takes the oversight of them, it takes them under its care.

MATTHEW HENRY

CHAPTER 2

Verses 1–7

He shows how much mischief there is in the sin of *respect of persons.*

I. A caution against this sin laid down in general, *v.* 1. The character of Christians fully implied: they are such as have the faith of our Lord Jesus Christ. They have it as a trust; they have it as a treasure. How honourably James speaks of Jesus Christ; he calls him *the Lord of glory.* Christ's being the Lord of glory should teach us not to respect Christians for anything so much as their conformity to Christ. We should not show respect to men, so as to cloud or lessen the glory of our glorious Lord. This is certainly a very heinous sin.

JAMIESON, FAUSSET, BROWN

CHAPTER 2

VSS. 1-26. THE SIN OF RESPECT OF PERSONS: DEAD, UNWORKING FAITH SAVES NO MAN. **1-13.** James illustrates "the perfect law of liberty" (ch. 1:25) in one particular instance of a sin against it, concluding with a reference again to that law (vss. 12, 13). **1. brethren**—The equality of all Christians as "brethren," forms the groundwork of the admonition. **the faith of . . . Christ**—i.e., the Christian faith. James grounds Christian practice on Christian faith. *the Lord* **of glory**—So I Corinthians 2:8. As all believers, alike rich and poor, derive all their glory from their union with Him, "the Lord of glory," not from external advantages of worldly fortune, the sin in question is peculiarly inconsistent with His "faith." **with respect of persons**—lit., "*in respectings* of persons"; *in* the practice of partial preferences of persons in various ways and on various occasions. **2. assembly**—lit., "synagogue"; this, the latest honorable use, and the only *Christian* use of the term in the New Testament, occurs in James's Epistle, the apostle who maintained to the latest possible moment the bonds between the Jewish synagogue and the Christian Church. Soon the continued resistance of the truth by the Jews led Christians to leave the term to them exclusively (Rev. 3:9). The "synagogue" implies a mere *assembly* or congregation not necessarily united by any common tie. "Church," a people bound together by mutual ties and laws, though often it may happen that the members are not assembled [TRENCH and VITRINGA]. Partly from James' Hebrew tendencies, partly from the Jewish Christian churches retaining most of the Jewish

ADAM CLARKE

CHAPTER 2

1. *My brethren, have not.* This verse should be read interrogatively: "My brethren, do you not make profession of the faith or religion of our glorious Lord Jesus Christ with acceptance of persons?" That is, preferring the rich to the poor merely because of their riches, and not on account of any moral excellence, personal piety, or public usefulness. *Faith* is put here for religion; and *of glory* should, according to some critics, be construed with it as the Syriac and Coptic have done. Some connect it with *our Lord Jesus Christ*—"the religion of our glorious Lord Jesus Christ." Others translate thus, "the faith of the glory of our Lord Jesus." There are many various readings in the MSS. and versions on this verse; the meaning is clear enough, though the connection be rather obscure.

2. *If there come unto your assembly.* "Into the synagogue." It appears from this that the apostle is addressing Jews who frequented their synagogues. Our word *assembly* does not express the original; and we cannot suppose that these synagogues were at this time occupied with Christian worship, but that the Christian Jews continued to frequent them for the purpose of hearing the law and the prophets read, as they had formerly done, previously to their conversion to the Christian faith.

MATTHEW HENRY

II. We have this sin described and cautioned against, by an example of it (*v.* 2, 3). You act partially, and determine wrong, merely because the one makes a better appearance than the other. God has his remnant among all sorts of people, among those that wear soft and gay clothing, and among those that wear, poor and vile raiment. In matters of religion, rich and poor stand upon a level; no man's riches set him in the least nearer to God, nor does any man's poverty set him at a distance from God. All undue honouring of worldly greatness and riches should especially be watched against in Christian societies. If a poor man be a good man, we must not value him a whit the less for his poverty; and, if a rich man be a bad man, we must not value him any whit the more for his riches. There is many a humble, heavenly, good Christian, who is clothed meanly; but neither should he nor his Christianity be thought the worse of on this account.

III. We have the greatness of this sin set forth, *v.* 4, 5. *Are you not then partial in yourselves?* According to the strict rendering of the original, the question is, "*Have you not made a difference?* And, in that difference, do you not judge by a false rule, and go upon false measures?" This respect of persons is owing to the evil and injustice of the thoughts. "*You have become judges of evil thoughts;* you are judges according to those unjust estimations and corrupt opinions which you have formed to yourselves. You secretly prefer outward pomp before inward grace, and the things that are seen before those which are not seen." The deformity of sin is never truly and fully discerned till the evil of our thoughts be disclosed. This respect of persons is a heinous sin, because it is to show ourselves most directly contrary to God (*v.* 5–6). God has made those heirs of a kingdom whom you make of no reputation. Many of the poor of this world are the chosen of God. Their being God's chosen does not prevent their being poor; their being poor does not at all prejudice the evidences of their being chosen. God designed to recommend his holy religion, not by the external advantages of gaiety and pomp, but by its intrinsic worth; and therefore chose the poor of this world. Many poor of the world are rich in faith; thus the poorest may become rich. It is expected from those who have wealth that they be rich in good works; but it is expected from the poor in the world that they be rich in faith. Believing Christians are heirs of a kingdom, though they may be very poor as to present possessions. Where any are rich in faith, there will be also divine love. We read of the crown promised to those that love God, in the former chapter (*v.* 12); we here find there is a kingdom too. And, as the crown is a crown of life, so the kingdom will be an everlasting kingdom. After such considerations as these, the charge is cutting indeed, *v.* 6.

Respecting persons on account of their riches or outward figure, is shown to be a very great sin, because of the mischiefs which are owing to worldly wealth and greatness, *v.* 7. This will make your sin appear exceedingly sinful and foolish, in setting up that which tends to pull you down, and to dishonour that worthy name by which you are called.

Verses 8–13

How the matter may be mended.

I. The law that is to guide us, *v.* 8. As the scripture teaches us to love all our neighbours, be they rich or poor, as ourselves, so, in our having a steady regard to this rule, *we shall do well.* The rule for Christians to walk by is settled in the scriptures. The scripture gives us this as a law, to love our neighbour as ourselves. This law is a royal law, it comes from the King of kings. Its own worth and dignity deserve it should be thus honoured. A pretence of observing this royal law, when it is interpreted with partiality, will not excuse men in any unjust proceedings.

JAMIESON, FAUSSET, BROWN

forms, this term "synagogue" is used here instead of the Christian term "Church" (*ecclesia,* derived from a root, "called out," implying the union of its members in spiritual bonds, independent of space, and called out into separation from the world); an undesigned coincidence and mark of truth. **2, 3.** "If there chance to have come" [ALFORD]. **goodly apparel . . . gay clothing**—As the *Greek,* is the same in both, translate both alike, "gay," or "splendid clothing." **have respect to him . . .**—though ye know not who he is, when perhaps he may be a heathen. It was the office of the deacons to direct to a seat the members of the congregation [CLEMENT, *Constitut.* 2. 57, 58]. **unto him**—not in the best MSS. Thus "thou" becomes more demonstratively emphatic. **there**—at a distance from where the good seats are. **here**—near the speaker. **under my footstool**—not literally so; but on the ground, down by my footstool. The poor man must either *stand,* or if he sits, *sit* in a degrading position. The speaker has a footstool as well as a good seat. **4. Are ye not . . . partial**—lit., "Have ye not made distinctions or "differences" (so as to prefer one to another)? So in Jude 22. **in yourselves**—in your minds, i.e., according to your carnal inclination [GROTIUS]. **are become judges of evil thoughts**—The *Greek* words for "judges" and for "partial," are akin in sound and meaning. A similar translation ought therefore to be given to both. Thus, either for "judges . . ." translate, "*distinguishers* of (i.e., *according to* your) evil thoughts"; or, do ye not *partially judge between* men, and are become *evilly-thinking judges* (Mark 7:21)? The "evil thoughts" are in the judges themselves; as in Luke 18:6, the *Greek,* "judge of injustice," is translated, "unjust judge." **5. Hearken**—James *brings to trial* the self-constituted "judges" (vs. 4). **poor of this world**—The best MSS. read, "those poor *in respect to the* world." In contrast to "the rich in this world" (I Tim. 6:17). Not of course *all* the poor; but the poor, *as a class,* furnish more believers than the rich as a class. The rich, if a believer, renounces riches as his portion; the poor, if an unbeliever, neglects that which is the peculiar advantage of poverty (Matt. 5:3; I Cor. 1:26, 27, 28). **rich in faith**—*Their* riches consist *in faith.* Luke 12:21, "rich toward God." I Timothy 6:18, "rich in good works" (Rev. 2:9; cf. II Cor. 8:9). Christ's poverty is the source of the believer's riches. **kingdom . . . promised**—(Luke 12:32; I Cor. 2:9; II Tim. 4:8). **6.** The world's judgment of the poor contrasted with God's. **ye**—Christians, from whom better things might have been expected; there is no marvel that men of the world do so. **despised**—lit., "dishonored." To dishonor the poor is to dishonor those whom God honors, and so to invert the order of God [CALVIN]. **rich**—as a class. **oppress**—lit., "abuse their power against" you. **draw you**—Translate, "is it not *they* (those very persons whom ye partially prefer, vss. 1-4) that *drag* you" (viz., with violence) [ALFORD]. **before . . . judgment seats**—instituting persecutions for religion, as well as oppressive lawsuits, against you. **7.** "Is it not they that blaspheme . . . ?" as in vs. 6 [ALFORD]. Rich heathen must here chiefly be meant; for none others would directly blaspheme the name of Christ. Only *indirectly* rich Christians can be meant, who, by their inconsistency, *caused* His name *to be blasphemed;* so Ezekiel 36:21, 22; Romans 2:24. Besides, there were few rich Jewish Christians at Jerusalem (Rom. 15:26). They who dishonor God's name by wilful and habitual sin, "take (or *bear*) the Lord's name in vain" (cf. Prov. 30:9, with Exod. 20:7). **that worthy name**—which is "good before the Lord's saints" (Ps. 52:9; 54:6); which ye pray may be "hallowed" (Matt. 6:9), and "by which ye are called," lit., "which was invoked" (or, "called upon) by you" (cf. Gen. 48:16; Isa. 4:1, *Margin;* Acts 15:17), so that at your baptism "*into* the name" (so the *Greek,* Matt. 28:19) of Christ, ye became Christ's people (I Cor. 3:23). **8.** I think the translation is, "If *in very deed* (or *indeed on the one hand*) ye fulfil the royal law . . . , ye do well, but if (on the other hand) ye respect persons, ye practice sin." The Jewish Christians boasted of, and rested in, the "law" (Acts 15:1; 21:18-24; Rom. 2:17; Gal. 2:12). To this the "indeed" alludes. "(Ye rest in the law): If *indeed* (then) ye fulfil it, ye do well; but if . . ." **royal**—the law that is king of all laws, being the sum and essence of the ten commandments. The great King, God, is love; His law is the royal law of love, and that law, like Himself, reigns supreme. He "is no respecter of persons"; therefore to respect persons is at variance with Him and His royal law, which is at once a law of love and of liberty (vs. 12). The law is the "whole"; "the (particular) Scripture" (Lev. 19:18) quoted is

ADAM CLARKE

With a gold ring, in goodly apparel. The ring on the finger and the splendid garb were proofs of the man's opulence; and his ring and his coat, not his worth, moral good qualities, or the righteousness of his cause, procured him the respect of which James speaks. *There come in also a poor man.* In ancient times petty courts of judicature were held in the synagogues; and it is probable that the case here adduced was one of a judicial kind, where, of the two parties, one was rich and the other poor; and the master or ruler of the synagogue, or he who presided in this court, paid particular deference to the rich man and neglected the poor man; though, as plaintiff and defendant, they were equal in the eye of justice, and should have been considered so by an impartial judge.

3. *Sit here under my footstool.* Thus evidently prejudging the cause, and giving the poor man to see that he was to expect no impartial administration of justice in his cause.

4. *Are ye not then partial?* "Do you not make a distinction," though the case has not been heard and the law has not decided? *Judges of evil thoughts.* "Judges of evil reasonings"; that is, "judges who reason wickedly"; who in effect say in your hearts, We will espouse the cause of the rich, because they can befriend us; we will neglect that of the poor, because they cannot help us, nor have they power to hurt us.

5. *Hath not God chosen the poor of this world?* This seems to refer to Matt. xi. 5: "And the poor have the gospel preached to them." These believed on the Lord Jesus and found His salvation; while the rich despised, neglected, and persecuted Him.

6. *Do not rich men oppress you?* The administration of justice was at this time in a miserable state of corruption among the Jews; but a Christian was one who was to expect no justice anywhere but from his God. The words "exceedingly oppress" and "drag you to courts of justice" show how grievously oppressed and maltreated the Christians were by their countrymen the Jews, who made law a pretext to afflict their bodies and spoil them of their property.

7. *Blaspheme that worthy name.* They took every occasion to asperse the Christian name and the Christian faith.

8. *The royal law.* This epithet, of all the New Testament writers, is peculiar to James; but it is frequent among the Greek writers in the sense in which it appears James uses it. *Royal* is used to signify anything that is of general concern, is suitable to all, and necessary for all, as brotherly love is. This commandment, *Thou shalt love thy neighbour as thyself,* is a *royal law,* not only because it is ordained of God, and proceeds from His kingly authority over men, but because it is so useful, suitable, and necessary to the present state of man.

MATTHEW HENRY

II. This general law is to be considered together with a particular law, *v.* 9. The very royal law itself, rightly explained, would serve to convict them, because it teaches them to put themselves as much in the places of the poor as in those of the rich.

III. The extent of the law, and how far obedience must be paid to it. They must fulfil the royal law, have a regard to one part as well as another, *v.* 10. Do you plead for your respect to the rich, because you are to love your neighbour as yourselves? Well then show also an equitable and due regard to the poor, because you are to love your neighbour as yourself: or else your offending in one point will spoil your pretence of observing that law at all.

This is further illustrated by putting a case different from that before mentioned (*v.* 11). One, perhaps, is very severe in the case of adultery; but less ready to condemn murder: another has a prodigious dread of murder, but has more easy thoughts of adultery; whereas one who looks at the authority of the Lawgiver, will see the same reason for condemning the one as the other. If we offend in one point, we contemn the authority of him who gave the whole law, and so far are guilty of all.

IV. James directs Christians to govern and conduct themselves by the law of Christ, *v.* 12. The gospel is called a law. It prescribes duty, as well as administers comfort; and Christ is a king to rule us as well as a prophet to teach us, and a priest to sacrifice and intercede for us. It is a *law of liberty*, the service of God, according to the gospel, is perfect freedom. We must all be judged by this law of liberty. It concerns us therefore so to speak and act now as becomes those who must shortly be judged by this law of liberty; that we be of a gospel temper, and that our conversation be a gospel conversation. The consideration of our being judged by the gospel should engage us more especially to be merciful in our regards to the poor (*v.* 13). Such as show no mercy now shall find no mercy in the great day. There will be such as shall become instances of the triumph of mercy, in whom mercy rejoices against judgment.

Verses 14-26

The apostle shows the error of those who rested in a bare profession of the Christian faith, as if that would save them. A man is justified, not by faith only, but by works.

I. Upon this arises a very great question, namely, how to reconcile Paul and James. Paul, in his epistles to the Romans and Galatians, seems to assert the directly contrary thing, *that we are justified by faith only, and not by the works of the law.* It may be sufficient only to observe these few things following: When Paul says that *a man is justified by faith, without the deeds of the law* (Rom. iii. 28), he plainly speaks of another sort of work than James does, but not of another sort of faith. Paul speaks of works wrought in obedience to the law of Moses, and before men's embracing the faith of the gospel. James speaks of works done in obedience to the gospel. Both are concerned to magnify the faith of the gospel, as that which alone could save us and justify us. Paul had to do with those who depended on the merit of their works in the sight of God. James had to do with those who cried up faith, but would not allow works to be used even as evidences. Those who cry up the gospel so as to set aside the law, and those who cry up the law so as to set aside the gospel, are both in the wrong. The justification of which Paul speaks is different from that spoken of by James; the one speaks of our persons being justified before God, the other speaks of our faith being justified before men: "*Show me thy faith by thy works,*" says James. Paul speaks of justification in the sight of God.

II. Let us see what is more particularly to be learnt from this excellent passage of James.

1. Faith without works will not profit, and cannot save us. *What doth it profit, my brethren, if a man say he hath faith, and have not works? Can faith save him?* Faith which does not save will not really profit us. All things should be accounted profitable

JAMIESON, FAUSSET, BROWN

a part. To break a part is to break the whole (vs. 10). **ye do well**—being "blessed in your deed" ("doing," *Margin*) as a doer, not a forgetful hearer of the law (ch. 1:25). **9.** *Respect of persons* violates the command to *love all alike* "as thyself." **ye commit sin**—lit., "ye work sin," Matthew 7:23, to which the reference here is probably, as in ch. 1:22. Your *works* are sin, whatever boast of the law ye make in words (*Note,* vs. 8). **convinced**—*Old English* for "convicted." **as transgressors**—not merely of this or that particular command, but of the whole absolutely. **10.** The best MSS. read, "Whosoever *shall have kept* the whole law, and yet *shall have offended* (lit., 'stumbled'; not so strong as 'fall,' Rom. 11:11) in one (point; here, the *respecting of persons*), is (hereby) become guilty of all." The law is one seamless garment which is rent if you but rend a part; or a musical harmony which is spoiled if there be one discordant note [TIRINUS]; or a golden chain whose completeness is broken if you break one link [GATAKER]. You thus break *the whole law,* though not the whole of the law, because you offend against *love,* which is the fulfilling of the law. If any part of a man be leprous, the whole man is judged to be a leper. God requires perfect, not partial, obedience. We are not to choose out parts of the law to keep, which suit our whim, while we neglect others. **11.** He is One who gave the whole law; therefore, they who violate His will in one point, violate it all [BENGEL]. The law and its Author alike have a complete unity. **adultery . . . kill**—selected as being the most glaring cases of violation of duty towards one's neighbor. **12.** Summing up of the previous reasonings. **speak**—referring back to ch. 1:19, 26; the fuller discussion of the topic is given ch. 3. **judged by the law of liberty**—(ch. 1:25)—i.e., the Gospel law of love, which is not a law of external constraint, but of internal, *free,* instinctive inclination. The law of liberty, through God's mercy, frees us from the curse of the law, that henceforth we should be free to love and obey willingly. If we will not in turn practice the law of love to our neighbor, that law of grace condemns us still more heavily than the old law, which spake nothing but wrath to him who offended in the least particular (vs. 13). Cf. Matthew 18:32-35; John 12:48; Revelation 6:16, "Wrath of the (merciful) Lamb." **13.** The converse of, "Blessed are the merciful, for they shall obtain mercy" (Matt. 5:7). Translate, "*The* judgment (which is coming on all of us) shall be without mercy to him who hath showed no mercy." It shall be such toward every one as every one shall have been [BENGEL]. "Mercy" here corresponds to "love," vs. 8. **mercy rejoiceth against judgment**—Mercy, so far from fearing judgment in the case of its followers, actually *glorifieth against* it, knowing that it cannot condemn them. Not that *their* mercy is the ground of their acquittal, but the mercy of God in Christ towards them, producing mercy on their part towards their fellow men, makes them to *triumph over judgment,* which all in themselves otherwise deserve. **14.** James here, passing from the particular case of "mercy" or "love" violated by "respect of persons," notwithstanding profession of the "faith of our Lord Jesus" (vs. 1), combats the Jewish tendency (transplanted into their Christianity) to substitute a lifeless, inoperative acquaintance with the letter of the law, for change of heart to practical holiness, as if justification could be thereby attained (Rom. 2:3, 13, 23). It seems hardly likely but that James had seen Paul's Epistles, considering that he uses the same phrases and examples (cf. vss. 21, 23, 25, with Rom. 4:3; Heb. 11:17, 31; and vss. 14, 24, with Rom. 3:28; Gal. 2:16). Whether James individually designed it or not, the Holy Spirit by him combats not Paul, but those who abuse Paul's doctrine. The teaching of both alike is inspired, and is therefore to be received without wresting of words; but each has a different class to deal with; Paul, self-justiciaries; James, Antinomian advocates of a mere notional faith. Paul urged as strongly as James the need of works as evidences of faith, especially in the later Epistles, when many were abusing the doctrine of faith (Titus 2:14; 3:8). "Believing and doing are blood relatives" [RUTHERFORD]. **What doth it profit**—lit., "What is the profit?" **though a man say**—James' expression is not, "If a mon have faith," but "if a man *say* he hath faith"; referring to a mere *profession* of faith, such as was usually made at baptism. Simon Magus so "*believed* and was baptized," and yet had "neither part nor lot in this matter," for his "heart," as his words and works evinced, was not right in the sight of God. ALFORD wrongly denies that "say" is emphatic. The illustration, vs. 16, proves it is: "If one of you *say*"

ADAM CLARKE

9. *But if ye have respect to persons,* in judgment or in any other way; *ye commit sin* against God and against your brethren, *and are convinced,* "convicted," by *the law;* by this royal law, "Thou shalt love thy neighbour as thyself"; *as transgressors,* having shown this sinful acceptance of persons which has led you to refuse justice to the poor man and uphold the rich in his oppressive conduct.

10. *For whosoever shall keep the whole law.* This is a rabbinical form of speech. In the tract *Shabbath,* fol. 70, where they dispute concerning the thirty-nine works commanded by Moses, Rabbi Yochanan says: "But if a man do the whole, with the omission of one, he is guilty of the whole, and of every one."

11. *For he that said.* That is, the Authority that gave one commandment gave also the rest; and he who breaks one resists this Authority; so that the breach of any one commandment may be justly considered a breach of the whole law.

12. *So speak ye, and so do.* Have respect to every commandment of God, for this the *law of liberty,* the gospel of Jesus Christ, particularly requires; and this is the law by which all mankind who have had the opportunity of knowing it shall be judged. But all along James particularly refers to the precept, "Thou shalt love thy neighbour as thyself."

13. *For he shall have judgment.* He who shows no mercy to man, or in other words, he who does not exercise himself in works of charity and mercy to his needy fellow creatures, shall receive no mercy at the hand of God; for He has said, "Blessed are the merciful: for they shall obtain mercy." *Mercy rejoiceth against judgment.* These words are variously understood. (1) *Mercy,* the merciful man, the abstract for the concrete, exults over judgment; that is, he is not afraid of it, having acted according to the law of liberty, "Thou shalt love thy neighbour as thyself." (2) You shall be exalted by mercy above judgment. (3) For He (God) exalts mercy above judgment. (4) A merciful man rejoices rather in opportunities of showing mercy than in acting according to strict justice. (5) In the great day, though justice might condemn every man according to the rigor of the law, yet God will cause mercy to triumph over justice in bringing those into His glory who, for His sake, had fed the hungry, clothed the naked, ministered to the sick, and visited the prisoners. See what our Lord says, Matt. xxv. 31-46. In the MSS. and versions there is a considerable variety of readings on this verse, and some of the senses given above are derived from those readings. The spirit of the saying may be found in another scripture, "I will have mercy, and not sacrifice"—I prefer works of charity and mercy to everything else, and especially to all acts of worship.

14. *What doth it profit . . . though a man say he hath faith?* We now come to a part of this Epistle which has appeared to some eminent men to contradict other portions of the divine records. In short, it has been thought that James teaches the doctrine of justification by the merit of good works, while Paul asserts this to be insufficient, and that man is justified by faith. Luther, supposing that James did actually teach the doctrine of justification by works, which his good sense showed him to be absolutely insufficient for salvation, was led to condemn the Epistle in toto, as a production unauthenticated by the Holy Spirit, and consequently worthy of no regard; he therefore termed it "a chaffy epistle," an "epistle of straw," fit only to be burned. Learned men have spent much time in striving to reconcile these two writers, and to show that Paul and James perfectly accord: one teaching the pure doctrine, the other guarding men against the abuse of it. Mr. Wesley sums the whole up in the following words, with his usual accuracy and precision: "From chap. i. 22 the apostle has been enforcing Christian practice. He now applies to those who neglect this under the pretense of faith. Paul had taught that a man is justified by faith without the works of the law. This some already began to wrest to their own destruction. Wherefore James, purposely repeating, vv. 21, 23, 25, the same phrases, testimonies, and examples which Paul had used, Rom. iv. 3; Heb. xi. 17,

MATTHEW HENRY

or unprofitable to us as they tend to forward or hinder the salvation of our souls. For a man to have faith, and to say he has faith, are two different things. Men may boast of that to others, and be conceited of that in themselves, of which they are really destitute.

2. As love or charity is an operative principle, so is faith. By trying how it looks for a person to pretend he is very charitable who yet never does any works of charity, you may judge what sense there is in pretending to have faith without the fruits of it, *v.* 15-17. What will such a charity as this, that consists in bare words, avail either you or the poor? You might as well pretend that your love and charity will stand the test without acts of mercy as think that a profession of faith will bear you out before God without works of piety and obedience, *v.* 17. We are too apt to rest in a bare profession of faith, and to think that this will save us. Mock-faith is as hateful as mock-charity, and both show a heart dead to all real godliness.

3. Compare a faith boasting of itself without works and a faith evidenced by works, by looking on both together, to try how this comparison will work upon our minds, *v.* 18. "Thou makest a profession, and sayest thou hast faith; I make no such boasts, but leave my works to speak for me." This is the evidence by which the scriptures all along teach men to judge both of themselves and others. And this is the evidence according to which Christ will proceed at the day of judgment.

4. Look upon a faith of bare speculation and knowledge as the faith of devils, *v.* 19. That instance of faith which the apostle here chooses to mention is the first principle of all religion. But to rest here, and take up a good opinion of thy state towards God, merely on account of thy believing in him, this will render thee miserable: *The devils also believe, and tremble.* If thou contentest thyself with a bare assent to articles of faith, and some speculations upon them, thus far the devils go. They tremble, not out of reverence, but hatred and opposition to that one God on whom they believe.

5. He who boasts of faith without works is to be looked upon at present as a foolish condemned person, *v.* 20. Faith without works is said to be *dead,* not only as void of all those operations which are the proofs of spiritual life, but as unavailable to eternal life.

6. A justifying faith cannot be without works, from two examples.

(1) The first instance is that of Abraham (*v.* 21). By what Abraham did, it appeared that he truly believed.

JAMIESON, FAUSSET, BROWN

to a naked brother, "Be ye warmed, notwithstanding ye give not those things needful." The inoperative *profession* of sympathy answering to the inoperative *profession* of faith. **can faith save him**—rather, "can such a faith (lit., "the faith") save him?"—*the* faith you pretend to: the empty name of boasted faith, contrasted with true fruit-producing faith. So that which self-deceivers claim is called "wisdom," though not true wisdom, ch. 3:15. The "him" also in the *Greek* is emphatic; the particular man who professes faith without having the works which evidence its vitality. **15.** The *Greek* is, *"But* if . . .": the "But" taking up the argument against such a one as "said he had faith, and yet had not works," which are its fruits. **a brother . . .**—a *fellow Christian,* to whom we are specially bound to give help, independent of our general obligation to help all our fellow creatures. **be**—The *Greek* implies, *"be found,* on your access to them." **16.** The habit of receiving passively sentimental impressions from sights of woe without carrying them out into active habits only hardens the heart. **one of you**—James brings home the case to his hearers individually. **Depart in peace**—as if all their wants were satisfied by the mere words addressed to them. The same words in the mouth of Christ, whose faith they said they had, were accompanied by efficient deeds of love. **be . . . warmed**—with clothing, instead of being as heretofore "naked" (vs. 15; Job 31:20). **filled**—instead of being "destitute of food" (Matt. 15:37). **what doth it profit**—concluding with the same question as at the beginning, vs. 14. **faith . . . being alone**—ALFORD joins "is dead *in itself."* So BENGEL, "If the works which living faith produces have no existence, it is a proof that faith itself (lit., "in respect to itself) has no existence; i.e., that what one boasts of as faith, is *dead."* "Faith" is said to be "dead *in itself,"* because when it has works it is *alive,* and it is discerned to be so, not in respect to its works, but in respect to *itself. English Version,* if retained, must not be understood to mean that faith can exist "alone" (i.e., severed from works), but thus: Even so *presumed* faith, if it have not works, is dead, being by itself "alone," i.e., severed from works of charity; just as the body would be "dead" if alone, i.e., severed from the spirit (vs. 26). So ESTIUS. **18.** *"But* some *one will* say": so the *Greek.* **show me thy faith without thy works**—if thou canst; but thou canst not SHOW, i.e., *manifest* or *evidence* thy alleged (vs. 14, "say") faith without works. "Show" does not mean here to *prove* to me, but *exhibit* to me. Faith is unseen save by God. To *show* faith to man, works in some form or other are needed: we are justified judicially by God (Rom. 8:33); meritoriously, by Christ (Isa. 53:11); mediately, by faith (Rom. 5:1); evidentially, by works. The question here is not as to the *ground* on which believers are justified, but about the *demonstration* of their faith: so in the case of Abraham.

The tree *shows* its life by its fruits, but it was alive before either fruits or even leaves appeared. **19. Thou**—emphatic. Thou self-deceiving claimant to faith without works. **that there is one God**—rather, "that God is one": God's *existence,* however, is also asserted. The fundamental article of the creed of Jews and Christians alike, and the point of faith on which especially the former boasted themselves, as distinguishing them from the Gentiles, and hence adduced by James here. **thou doest well**—so far good. But unless thy faith goes farther than an assent to this truth, "the evil spirits (lit., 'demons': 'devil' is the term restricted to *Satan,* their head) believe" so far in common with thee, "and (so far from being saved by such a faith) shudder" (so the *Greek*), Matt. 8:29; Luke 4:34; II Pet. 2:4; Jude 6; Rev. 20:10. Their faith only adds to their torment at the thought of having to meet Him who is to consign them to their just doom: so thine (Heb. 10:26, 27, it is not the faith of love, but of fear, that hath torment, I John 4: 18). **20. wilt thou know**—"Vain" men are not *willing* to know, since they have no wish to *do* the will of God. James beseeches such a one to lay aside his perverse *unwillingness* to know what is palpable to all who are willing to do. **vain**—who deceivest thyself with a delusive hope, resting on an unreal faith. **without works**—The *Greek,* implies *separate from the* works [ALFORD] which ought to flow from it if it were real. **is dead**—Some of the best MSS. read, "is idle," i.e., unavailing to effect what you hope, viz., to save you. **21. Abraham . . . justified by works**—*evidentially,* and *before men* (see *Note,* vs. 18). In vs. 23, James, like Paul, recognizes the Scripture truth, that it was his *faith* that was counted to Abraham for right-

ADAM CLARKE

31, refutes, not the doctrine of Paul, but the error of those who abused it. There is therefore no contradiction between the apostles; they both delivered the truth of God, but in a different manner, as having to do with different kinds of men. This verse is a summary of what follows: 'What profiteth it?' is enlarged on, vv. 15-17; *though a man say,* vv. 18-19; *can* that *faith save him?* v. 20. It is not *though he have faith,* but *though he say, I have faith.* Here therefore true, living faith is meant. But in other parts of the argument the apostle speaks of a dead, imaginary faith. He does not therefore teach that true faith *can,* but that it *cannot,* subsist without works. Nor does he oppose *faith* to *works,* but that empty name of faith to real faith working by love. *Can* that *faith* which is without works *save him?* No more than it can profit his neighbor."

15. *If a brother or sister be naked.* That is, ill-clothed; for *naked* has this meaning in several parts of the New Testament, signifying bad clothing, or the want of some particular article of dress. See Matt. xxv. 36, 38, 43-44 and John xxi. 7.

16. *Be ye warmed and filled.* Your saying so to them while you give them nothing will profit them just as much as your professed faith, without those works which are the genuine fruits of true faith, will profit you in the day when God comes to sit in judgment upon your soul.

17. *If it hath not works, is dead.* The faith that does not produce works of charity and mercy is without the living principle which animates all true faith; that is, love to God and love to man.

18. *Shew me thy faith without thy works.* Your pretending to have faith while you have no works of charity or mercy is utterly vain. For as *faith,* which is a principle in the mind, cannot be discerned but by the effects—that is, good works—he who has no good works has, presumptively, no faith. *I will shew thee my faith by my works.* My works of charity and mercy will show that I have faith; and that it is the living tree, whose root is love to God and man, and whose fruit is the good works here contended for.

19. *Thou believest that there is one God.* This is the faith in which these persons put their hope of pleasing God and of obtaining eternal life. Believing in the being and unity of God distinguished them from all the nations of the world; and having been circumcised, and thus brought into the covenant, they thought themselves secure of salvation. The insufficiency of this James immediately shows. *The devils also believe, and tremble.* It is well to believe there is one only true God; this truth universal nature proclaims. Even the devils believe it; but far from justifying or saving them, it leaves them in their damned state, and every act of it only increases their torment. "They shudder with horror"; they *believe, and tremble,* are increasingly tormented; but they can neither love nor obey.

20. *But wilt thou know?* Are you willing to be instructed in the nature of true saving faith? Then attend to the following examples.

21. *Was not Abraham our father?* Did not the conduct of Abraham, in offering up his son Isaac on the altar, sufficiently prove that he believed in God, and that it was his faith in

MATTHEW HENRY

The faith of Abraham was a working faith (*v.* 22). Abraham believed God, *and it was imputed unto him for righteousness, v.* 23. And thus he became the *friend of God.*

You see then (*v.* 24) how that *by works a man is justified, and not by faith only;* not by believing without obeying, but by having such a faith as is productive of good works. Those who would have Abraham's blessings must be careful to copy after his faith: to boast of being Abraham's seed will not avail any. Those works which evidence true faith must be such as God himself commands, and not the mere fruits of our own imagination and devising. The actings of faith make it grow perfect, as the truth of faith makes it act. Such an acting faith will make others, as well as Abraham, friends of God.

(2) The second example is Rahab, *v.* 25. The former instance was of one renowned for his faith all his life long. This is of one noted for sin. The strongest faith will not do, nor the meanest be allowed to go without works. That which proved her faith sincere was, that, to the hazard of her life, she *received the messengers, and sent them out another way.* Where great sins are pardoned, there must be great acts of self-denial. Her former acquaintance must be discarded, her former course of life entirely abandoned, and she must give signal proof and evidence of this.

7. The apostle draws this conclusion, *As the body without the spirit is dead, so faith without works is dead also, v.* 26. The best works, without faith, are dead; they want their root and principle. It is by faith that anything we do is really good. The most plausible profession of faith, without works, is dead: as the root is dead when it produces nothing green, nothing of fruit. Faith is the root, good works are the fruits, and we must see to it that we have both. We must not think that either, without the other, will justify and save us.

CHAPTER 3

Verses 1–12

The foregoing chapter shows how unprofitable and dead faith is without works. Such a faith is, however, apt to make men conceited in their tempers and their talk. The best need to be cautioned against a dictating, censorious use of their tongues. We are therefore taught,

I. Not to use our tongues so as to lord it over others, *v.* 1. We must not affect to speak and act as those who are continually assuming the chair, we must not prescribe to one another, so as to make our own sentiments a standard by which to try all others. "Therefore be not many *masters* (or *teachers*, as some read it); but rather speak with the humility and spirit of learners." Those who thus set up for judges and censurers *shall receive the greater condemnation.* Our judging others will but make our own judgment the more strict and severe, Matt. vii. 1, 2. Another reason is because we are all sinners, *v.* 2. Were we to think more of our own mistakes

JAMIESON, FAUSSET, BROWN

eousness in his justification before God. **when he had offered**—rather, "when he offered" [ALFORD], i.e., brought as an offering at the altar; not implying that he actually offered him. **22.** Or, "thou seest." **how**—rather, "that." In the two clauses which follow, emphasize "faith" in the former, and "works" in the latter, to see the sense [BENGEL]. **faith wrought with his works**—for it was *by faith* he offered his son. Lit., "was working (at the time) with his works." **by works was faith made perfect**—not was *vivified,* but attained its *fully consummated development,* and is *shown to be real.* So "my strength is *made perfect* in weakness," i.e., *exerts itself most perfectly,* shows how great it is [CAMERON]: so I John 4:17; Hebrews 2:10; 5:9. **scripture was fulfilled**—Genesis 15:6, quoted by Paul, as realized in Abraham's justification by *faith;* but by James, as realized subsequently in Abraham's *work* of offering Isaac, which, he says, *justified* him. Plainly, then, James must mean by *works* the same thing as Paul means by *faith,* only that he speaks of faith at its manifested development, whereas Paul speaks of it in its germ. Abraham's offering of Isaac was not a mere act of obedience, but an act of faith. **called the Friend of God**—He was not so *called* in his lifetime, though he *was* so even then from the time of his justification; but he was *called* so, being recognized as such by all on the ground of his works of faith. "He was the *friend* (in an active sense), the *lover of God,* in reference to his works; and (in a passive sense) *loved by God* in reference to his justification by works. Both senses are united in John 15:14, 15" [BENGEL]. **24. justified and, not by faith only**—i.e., by "faith without (*separated* from: *severed from*) works," its proper fruits (*Note,* vs. 20). Faith to justify must, from the first, include obedience in germ (to be developed subsequently), though the former alone is the ground of justification. The scion must be grafted on the stock that it may live; it must bring forth fruit to prove that it does live. **25.** It is clear from the nature of Rahab's act, that it is not quoted to prove justification by works as such. She *believed* assuredly what her other countrymen disbelieved, and this in the face of every improbability that an unwarlike few would conquer well-armed numbers. In this belief she hid the spies at the risk of her life. Hence, Hebrews 11:31 names this as an example of *faith,* rather than of obedience. "By *faith* the *harlot* Rahab perished not with them that *believed* not." If an instance of obedience were wanting, Paul and James would hardly have quoted a woman of previously bad character, rather than the many moral and pious patriarchs. But as an example of free grace justifying men through an *operative,* as opposed to a mere verbal *faith,* none could be more suitable than a saved "harlot." **messengers**—spies. **had received . . . had sent**—rather, "received . . . thrust them forth" (in haste and fear), [ALFORD]. **another way**—from that whereby they entered her house, viz., through the window of her house on the wall, and thence to the mountain. **26.** Faith is a spiritual thing: works are material. Hence we might expect *faith* to answer to the *spirit, works* to the *body.* But James reverses this. He therefore does not mean that faith in all cases answers to the body; but the FORM *of faith* without *the working reality* answers to the *body* without the *animating spirit.* It does not follow that *living faith* derives its life from works, as the body derives its life from the animating spirit.

CHAPTER 3

VSS. 1-18. DANGER OF EAGERNESS TO TEACH, AND OF AN UNBRIDLED TONGUE: TRUE WISDOM SHOWN BY UNCONTENTIOUS MEEKNESS. **1. be not**—lit., "become not": taking the office too hastily, and of your own accord. **many**—The office is a noble one; but few are fit for it. Few govern the tongue well (vs. 2), and only such as can govern it are fit for the office; therefore, "teachers" ought not to be many. **masters**—rather, "teachers." The Jews were especially prone to this presumption. The idea that faith (so called) without works (ch. 2) was all that is required, prompted "many" to set up as "teachers," as has been the case in all ages of the Church. At first all were allowed to teach in turns. Even their inspired gifts did not prevent liability to abuse, as James here implies: much more is this so when self-constituted teachers have no such miraculous gifts. **knowing**—as all might know. **we . . . greater condemnation**—James in a humble, conciliatory spirit, includes himself: if *we* teachers abuse the office, we shall

ADAM CLARKE

Him that led him to this extraordinary act of obedience?

22. *Seest thou how faith wrought?* Here is a proof that faith cannot exist without being active in works of righteousness. His faith in God would have been of no avail to him had it not been manifested by works. For *by works,* by his obedience to the commands of God, his *faith* was *made perfect.* It dictated obedience; he obeyed; and thus faith "had its consummation." Even true faith will soon die if its possessor does not live in the spirit of obedience.

23. *The scripture was fulfilled.* He *believed God.* This faith was never inactive; it was accounted to *him for righteousness;* and, being justified by thus believing, his life of obedience showed that he had not received the grace of God in vain. *The Friend of God.* The highest character ever given to man.

24. *Ye see then how.* It is evident from this example that Abraham's faith was not merely believing that there is a God, but a principle that led him to credit God's promises relative to the future Redeemer and to implore God's mercy; this he received and was justified by faith. His faith now began to work by love, and therefore he was found ever obedient to the will of his Maker. He brought forth the fruits of righteousness; and his works *justified*—proved the genuineness of his faith. Obedience to God is essentially requisite to maintain faith. Faith lives, under God, by works; and works have their being and excellence from faith. Neither can subsist without the other, and this is the point which James labors to prove, in order to convince the antinomians of his time that their faith was a delusion, and that the hopes built on it must needs perish.

25. *Rahab the harlot.* See the notes on Josh. ii. 1 ff. and Heb. xi. 31 ff. Rahab had the approbation due to genuine faith, which she actually possessed, and gave the fullest proof that she did so by her conduct. As justification signifies, not only the pardon of sin, but receiving the divine approbation, James seems to use the word in this latter sense. God approved of them because of their obedience to His will, and He approves of no man who is not obedient.

26. *For as the body without the spirit is dead.* There can be no more a genuine faith without good works than there can be a living human body without a soul.

CHAPTER 3

1. *Be not many masters.* Do not affect the "teacher's" office, for many wish to be teachers who have more need to learn. There were many teachers or rabbins among the Jews, each affecting to have the truth and to draw disciples after him. We find a caution against such persons, and of the same nature with that of James, in *Pirkey Aboth.* c. i. 10: "Love labour, and hate the rabbin's office." This caution is still necessary; there are multitudes whom God has never called and never can call, because He has never qualified them for the work, who earnestly wish to get into the priest's office. Their case is awful; they *shall receive the greater condemnation* than common sinners. They have not only sinned in thrusting themselves into that office to which God has never called them, but through their insufficiency the flocks over whom they have assumed the mastery perish for lack of knowledge, and their blood will God require at the watchman's hand.

MATTHEW HENRY

and offences, we should be less apt to judge other people. Self-justifiers are commonly self-deceivers. Their magisterial deportment, and censorious tongues, may prove worse than any faults they condemn in others.

II. To govern our tongue so as to prove ourselves perfect and upright men, and such as have an entire government over ourselves. But, on the other hand, *if a man seemeth to be religious and bridleth not his tongue, that man's religion is vain.* Further, he that offends not in word will not only prove himself a sincere Christian, but a very much advanced Christian. For the wisdom and grace which enable him to rule his tongue will enable him also to rule all his actions.

JAMIESON, FAUSSET, BROWN

receive greater condemnation than those who are mere hearers (cf. Luke 12:42-46). CALVIN, like *English Version,* translates, "masters" i.e., self-constituted *censors* and reprovers of others. Ch. 4:12 accords with this view. **2. all**—The *Greek* implies "all without exception": even the apostles. **offend not**—lit., "stumbleth not": is void of offence or *slip* in word: in which respect one is especially tried who sets up to be a "teacher."

ADAM CLARKE

2. *In many things we offend all.* "We all stumble or trip." Some have produced these words as a proof that "no man can live without sinning against God; for James himself, a holy apostle, speaking of himself, all the apostles, and the whole Church of Christ, says, *In many things we offend all.*" This is a very bad and dangerous doctrine; and pushed to its consequences, would greatly affect the credibility of the whole gospel system. *Offend not in word, the same is a perfect man.* To understand this properly we must refer to the caution James gives in the preceding verse: "Be not many masters" (or teachers)—do not affect that for which you are not qualified. But, says he, *if any man offend not,* "trip not in doctrine," teaching the truth, the whole truth, and nothing but the truth, *the same is* "a man fully instructed" in divine things. How often the term *logos,* which we render *word,* is used to express "doctrine," and the doctrine of the gospel, we have seen in many parts of the preceding comment. And how often the word *teleios,* which we translate *perfect,* is used to signify an "adult Christian," one "thoroughly instructed" in the doctrines of the gospel, may be seen in various parts of Paul's writings. See, among others, 1 Cor. ii. 6; xiv. 20; Eph. iv. 13; Phil. iii. 15; Col. iv. 12; Heb. v. 14. The man, therefore, who advanced no false doctrine and gave no imperfect view of any of the great truths of Christianity, that man proved himself thereby to be "thoroughly instructed" in divine things; to be no novice, and consequently, among the many teachers, to be a perfect master and worthy of the sacred vocation. *Able also to bridle the whole body.* Grotius, by *body,* believed that the Church of Christ was intended; and this the view we have taken of the preceding clauses renders very probable. But some think the passions and appetites are intended; yet these persons understand "not offending in word" as referring simply to well-guarded speech. Now how a man's cautiousness in what he says can be a proof that he has every passion and appetite under control, I cannot see. Indeed, I have seen so many examples of a contrary kind that I can have no doubt of the impropriety of this exposition.

A. B. SIMPSON:

An unbridled tongue is a sure sign of an unsanctified, undisciplined, and perhaps unsaved soul. It is a sign of whether or not he is under the government of his conscience, his will and the Holy Spirit. This is a most heart-searching test. Let us take it home. Can we stand it? It was a foolish and hasty word that lost Moses the Land of Promise. He would have taken it back if he could have, but it was phonographed. It had gone upon the record and it had to stand, and for that one little speech Moses lost the hope of a lifetime.

When Isaiah was called to his ministry, it was his lips that were first sanctified. The live coal was applied to these members, and the word spoken, "Lo, this hath touched thy lips; and thine iniquity is taken away, and thy sin is purged" (Isa. 6:7). His tongue had to be purified before God could use him.

On the day of Pentecost, it was cloven tongues, tongues of fire that came, tongues possessed by the Holy Ghost. If you have received the baptism of the Spirit, your tongue has received the first touch. You will never talk as you used to talk, you will never have the same unlicensed freedom, but your language will be under the control of a watchful spirit.

We find even in common life, that if a man has sense enough to hold this peace, "though a fool, he will be counted wise." Quiet, self-contained people are often taken for more than they really are, while many a man and woman of beautiful qualities wreck their whole lives by an uncontrolled tongue. If it settles our influence and character here, then how much more in the sight of Him who has said, "By thy words thou shalt be justified, and by thy words thou shalt be condemned" (Matt. 12:37).—*Christ in the Bible*

MATTHEW HENRY

This we have illustrated by two comparisons: 1. The governing and guiding of all the motions of a horse, by the bit which is put into his mouth, *v.* 3. There is a great deal of brutish fierceness and wantonness in us. This shows itself very much by the tongue, so that this must be bridled. As an unruly and ungovernable horse runs away with his rider, or throws him, so an unruly tongue will serve those who have no command over it. 2. The governing of a ship by the right management of the helm, *v.* 4, 5. As the helm is a very small part of the ship, so is the tongue a very small part of the body: but the right governing of the helm will steer and turn the ship, and a right management of the tongue is, in a great measure, the government of the whole man. Things of small bulk may yet be of vast use. We should learn to make the due management of our tongues more our study, because, though they are little members, they are capable of doing a great deal of good or a great deal of hurt.

III. To dread an unruly tongue as one of the greatest and most pernicious evils, *v.* 5, 6. There is such an abundance of sin in the tongue that it may be called *a world of iniquity. So is the tongue among the members that it defileth the whole body.* The whole body is often drawn into sin and guilt by the tongue. *It setteth on fire the course of nature.* The affairs of mankind and of societies are often thrown into confusion, and all is on a flame, by the tongues of men. *And it is set on fire of hell.* Hell has more to do in promoting the fire of the tongue than men are generally aware of. When it is set on fire of hell, as in all undue heats it is, there it is mischievous, producing rage and hatred, and those things which serve the purposes of the devil.

JAMIESON, FAUSSET, BROWN

3. Behold—The best authorities read, "but if," i.e., *Now whensoever* (in the case) of horses (such is the emphatic position of "horses" in the *Greek*) we put *the* bits (so lit., "the customary bits") into their mouths that they may obey us, we turn about *also* their whole body. This is to illustrate how *man* turns about his whole body with the little tongue. "The same applies to the pen, which is the substitute for the tongue among the absent" [BENGEL]. **4.** Not only animals, but *even ships.* **the governor listeth**—lit., "the impulse of the steersman pleaseth." The feeling which moves the tongue corresponds with this. **5. boasteth great things**—There is *great* moment in what the careless think "little" things [BENGEL]. Cf. "a world," "the course of nature," "hell," vs. 6, which illustrate how the little tongue's great words produce great mischief. **how great a matter a little fire kindleth**—The best MSS. read, "*how little* a fire kindleth how great a . . . ." ALFORD, for "matter," translates, "forest." But GROTIUS translates as *English Version,* "material for burning": a pile of fuel.

6. Translate, "The tongue, that world of iniquity, is a fire." As man's little world is an image of the greater world, the universe, so the tongue is an image of the former [BENGEL]. **so**—omitted in the oldest authorities. **is**—lit., "is constituted." "The tongue is (constituted), among the members, the one which defileth . . ." (viz., as fire defiles with its smoke). **course of nature**—"the orb (cycle) of creation." **setteth on fire . . . is set on fire**—habitually and continually. While a man inflames others, he passes out of his own power, being consumed in the flame himself. **of hell**—i.e., of the devil. *Greek,* "Gehenna"; found here only and in Matthew 5:22. James has much in common with the Sermon on the Mount (Prov. 16:27).

ADAM CLARKE

3. *Behold, we put bits in the horses' mouths.* In order to show the necessity of regulating the tongue, to which James was led by his exhortation to them who wished to thrust themselves into the teacher's office, supposing, because they had the gift of a ready flow of speech, that therefore they might commence teachers of divine things, he proceeds to show that the tongue must be bridled as the horse and governed as the ships; because, though it is small, it is capable of ruling the whole man, and of irritating and offending others.

5. *Boasteth great things.* That is, can do great things, whether of a good or evil kind. He seems to refer here to the powerful and all-commanding eloquence of the Greek orators. They could carry the great mob whithersoever they wished; calm them to peaceableness and submission, or excite them to furious sedition. *Behold, how great a matter!* See what a flame of discord and insubordination one man, merely by his persuasive tongue, may kindle among the common people.

6. *The tongue is a fire.* It is often the instrument of producing the most desperate contentions and insurrections. *A world of iniquity.* This is an unusual form of speech, but the meaning is plain enough; *world* signifies here a mass, a great collection, an abundance. We use the term in the same sense—a "world of troubles," a "world of toil." *Setteth on fire the course of nature.* "And setteth on fire the wheel of life." I question much whether this verse be in general well understood. There are three different interpretations of it: (1) James does not intend to express the whole circle of human affairs, so much affected by the tongue of man; but rather the penal wheel of the Greeks, and not unknown to the Jews, on which they were accustomed to extend criminals to induce them to confess or to punish them for crimes; under which wheels, fire was often placed to add to their torments. (2) But is it not possible that by the "wheel of life" James may have the circulation of the blood in view? Angry or irritating

MATTHEW HENRY

IV. We are next taught how very difficult a thing it is to govern the tongue, *v.* 7, 8. Fierce creatures have not been subdued nor tamed by miracle only. What is here spoken of is something commonly done; not only hath been tamed, but is tamed of mankind. Yet the tongue is worse than these, and cannot be tamed by the power and art which serves to tame these things. The apostle does not intend to represent it as a thing impossible, but as a thing extremely difficult, which therefore will require great watchfulness, and pains, and prayer.

And sometimes all is too little; *for it is an unruly evil, full of deadly poison.* The tongue is apt to break through all bounds and rules, and to spit out its poison on one occasion or other, notwithstanding the utmost care.

V. We are taught to think of the use we make of our tongues in religion and in the service of God, *v.* 9, 10. How absurd it is that those who use their tongues in prayer and praise should ever use them in cursing, slandering, and the like! That tongue which addresses with reverence the divine Being cannot, without the greatest inconsistency, turn upon fellow-creatures with reviling brawling language.

These things ought not so to be; and, if such considerations were always at hand, surely they would not be. Further, to fix this thought, the apostle shows that contrary effects from the same causes are monstrous, and not to be found in nature, and therefore cannot be consistent with grace, *v.* 11, 12. True religion will not admit of contradictions; and a truly religious man can never allow of them either in his words or his actions.

Verses 13–18

The difference between men's pretending to be wise and their being really so, and between the wisdom which is from beneath and that which is from above.

I. We have some account of true wisdom, *v.* 13. A wise man will not value himself merely upon knowing things, if he has not wisdom to make a right application of that knowledge. These two things must be put together to make up the account of true wisdom. A good conversation. If we are wiser than others, this should be evidenced by the goodness of our conversation, not by the roughness or vanity of it. True wisdom may be known by its works. The conversation here does not refer only to words, but to the whole of men's practice; therefore it is said, Let him show out of a good conversation his works. Not he who thinks well, or he who talks well, is allowed to be wise, if he do not live and act well. True wisdom may be known by the meekness of the spirit and temper. It is a great instance of wisdom prudently to bridle our own anger, and patiently to bear the anger of others. When we are mild and calm, we are best able to hear reason, and best able to speak it. Wisdom produces meekness, and meekness increases wisdom.

JAMIESON, FAUSSET, BROWN

7. every kind—rather, "every nature" (i.e., natural disposition and characteristic power). **of beasts**—i.e., quadrupeds of every disposition; as distinguished from the three other classes of creation, "birds, creeping things (the *Greek* includes not merely 'serpents,' as *English Version*), and things in the sea." **is tamed, and hath been**—is continually being tamed, and hath been so long ago. **of mankind**—rather, "by the nature of man": man's characteristic power taming that of the inferior animals. The dative in the *Greek* may imply, "Hath suffered itself to be brought into tame subjection TO the nature of men." So it shall be in the millennial world; even now man, by gentle firmness, may tame the inferior animal, and even elevate its nature. **8. no man**—lit., "no one of men": neither can a man control his neighbor's, nor even his own tongue. Hence the truth of vs. 2 appears. **unruly evil**—The *Greek,* implies that it is at once *restless* and *incapable of restraint.* Nay, though nature has hedged it in with a double barrier of the lips and teeth, it bursts from its barriers to assail and ruin men [ESTIUS]. **deadly**—lit., "death-bearing." **9. God**—The oldest authorities read, "Lord." "Him who is Lord and Father." The uncommonness of the application of "Lord" to the Father, doubtless caused the change in modern texts to "God" (ch. 1:27). But as Messiah is called "Father," Isaiah 9:6, so God the Father is called by the Son's title, "Lord": showing the unity of the Godhead. "Father" implies His *paternal* love; "Lord," His dominion. **men, which**—not "men *who";* for what is meant is not particular men, but men *generically* [ALFORD]. **are made after . . . similitude of God**—Though in a great measure man has lost the *likeness* of God in which he was originally made, yet enough of it still remains to show what once it was, and what in regenerated and restored man it shall be. We ought to reverence this remnant and earnest of what man shall be in ourselves and in others. "Absalom has fallen from his father's favor, but the people still recognize him to be the king's son" [BENGEL]. Man resembles in humanity the Son of man, "the express image of His person" (Heb. 1:3), cf. Genesis 1:26; I John 4:20. In the passage, Genesis 1:26, "image" and "likeness" are distinct: "image," according to the Alexandrians, was something *in* which men were created, being common to all, and continuing to man after the fall, while the "likeness" was something *toward* which man was created, to strive after and attain it: the former marks man's physical and intellectual, the latter his moral pre-eminence. **10.** The tongue, says ÆSOP, is at once the best and the worst of things. So in a fable, a man with the same breath blows hot and cold. "Life and death are in the power of the tongue" (cf. Ps. 62:4). **brethren**—an appeal to their consciences by their *brotherhood* in Christ. **ought not so to be**—a mild appeal, leaving it to themselves to understand that such conduct deserves the most severe reprobation. **11. fountain**—an image of the *heart:* as the *aperture* (so the *Greek* for "place" is lit.) of the fountain is an image of man's *mouth.* The image here is appropriate to the scene of the Epistle, Palestine, wherein salt and bitter springs are found. Though "sweet" springs are sometimes found near, yet "sweet and bitter" (water) do not flow "at the same place" (*aperture*). Grace can make the same mouth that "sent forth the bitter" once, send forth the sweet for the time to come: as the wood (typical of Christ's cross) changed Marah's bitter water into sweet. **12.** Transition from the mouth to the heart. **Can the fig tree . . .**—implying that it is an *impossibility:* as before in vs. 10 he had said it "*ought* not so to be." James does not, as Matthew (7:16, 17), make the question, "Do men gather figs of *thistles?*" His argument is, No tree "can" bring forth *fruit inconsistent with its nature,* as e.g., the fig tree, olive berries: so if a man speaks bitterly, and afterwards speaks good words, the latter must be so only seemingly, and in hypocrisy, they *cannot* be real. **so can no fountain . . . salt . . . and fresh**—The oldest authorities read, "Neither can a salt (water spring) yield fresh." So the mouth that emits cursing, cannot really emit also blessing. **13. Who**—(Cf. Ps. 34:12, 13). All wish to appear "wise": few are so. **show**—"by works," and not merely by profession, referring to ch. 2:18. **out of a good conversation his works**—by *general* "good conduct" manifested in *particular* "works." "Wisdom" and "knowledge," without these being "shown," are as dead as faith would be without works [ALFORD]. **with meekness of wisdom**—with the meekness inseparable from true "wisdom."

ADAM CLARKE

language has an astonishing influence on the circulation of the blood: the heart beats high and frequently; the blood is hurried through the arteries to the veins, through the veins to the heart, and through the heart to the arteries again, and so on; an extraordinary degree of heat is at the same time engendered; the eyes become more prominent in their sockets; the capillary vessels suffused with blood; the face flushed; and, in short, the whole wheel of nature is set on fire of hell. (3) It is true, however, that the rabbins use the term "the wheel of generations" to mark the successive generations of men, and it is possible that James might refer to this; as if he had said: "The tongue has been the instrument of confusion and misery through all the ages of the world." But the other interpretations are more likely.

7. *Every kind of beasts.* That is, every "species" of wild beasts *is tamed,* i.e., brought under man's power and dominion.

8. *But the tongue can no man tame.* No cunning, persuasion, or influence has ever been able to silence it. *It is an unruly evil.* "An evil that cannot be restrained"; it cannot be brought under any kind of government; it breaks all bounds. *Full of deadly poison.* He refers here to the tongues of serpents, supposed to be the means of conveying their poison into wounds made by their teeth. Throughout the whole of this poetic and highly declamatory description James must have the tongue of the slanderer, calumniator, backbiter, whisperer, and talebearer particularly in view. Vipers and rattlesnakes are not more dangerous to life than these are to the peace and reputation of men.

9. *Therewith bless we God.* The tongue is capable of rehearsing the praises and setting forth the glories of the eternal King; what a pity that it should ever be employed in a contrary work! It can proclaim and vindicate the truth of God, and publish the gospel of peace and goodwill among men; what a pity that it should ever be employed in falsehoods, calumny, or in the cause of infidelity! *And therewith curse we men.* In the true Satanic spirit, many pray to God the Father to destroy those who are objects of their displeasure! These are the common swearers, whose mouths are generally full of direful imprecations against those with thom they are offended.

10. *Out of the same mouth.* This saying is something like that of Prov. xviii. 21: "Death and life are in the power of the tongue."

11. *Doth a fountain send forth . . . sweet water and bitter?* In many things nature is a sure guide to man; but no such inconsistency is found in the natural world as this blessing and cursing in man. No fountain, at the same opening, sends forth sweet water and bitter; no fig tree can bear olive berries; no vine can bear figs; nor can the sea produce salt water and fresh from the same place. These are all contradictions, and indeed impossibilities, in nature. And it is depraved man alone that can act the monstrous part already referred to.

12. *So can no fountain both yield salt water and fresh.* For the reading of the common text, which is, "So no fountain can produce salt water and sweet," there are various other readings in the MSS. and versions. The true reading appears to be, "Neither can salt water produce sweet," or, "Neither can the sea produce fresh water"; and this is a new comparison, and not an inference from that in v. 11. There are therefore four distinct comparisons here: (1) A fountain cannot produce sweet water and bitter. (2) A fig tree cannot produce olive berries. (3) A vine cannot produce figs. (4) Salt water cannot be made sweet. That is, according to the ordinary operations of nature, these things are impossible.

13. *Who is a wise man?* One truly religious; who, although he can neither bridle nor tame other men's tongues, can restrain his own. *And endued with knowledge.* And qualified to teach others. *Let him shew.* Let him by a holy life and chaste conversation show, through meekness and gentleness, joined to his divine information, that he is a Christian indeed; his works and his spirit proving that God is in him of a truth; and that, from the fullness of a holy heart, his feet walk, his hands work, and his tongue

MATTHEW HENRY

II. We have the glorying taken away of those who are of a contrary character, *v.* 14–16. Envying and strife are opposed to the meekness of wisdom. The heart is the seat of both; but envy and wisdom cannot dwell together in the same heart. The order of things here laid down. Envying is first and excites strife; strife, vain-glorying and lying; and then (*v.* 16) hereupon ensue confusion and every evil work. One sin begets another, and it cannot be imagined how much mischief is produced: *there* is every evil work. Whence such wisdom cometh, *v.* 15. It springs from earthly principles. It is sensual, indulging the flesh. It is devilish. And therefore those who are lifted up with such wisdom as this must fall into the condemnation of the devil.

III. We have the lovely picture of that wisdom which is from above more fully drawn, *v.* 17, 18. True wisdom is God's gift. It comes from above. It is pure, without mixture of maxims or aims that would debase it: studious of holiness both in heart and life. The wisdom that is from above is peaceable. Those who are truly wise do what they can to preserve peace, that it may not be broken; and to make peace, that where it is lost it may be restored. Heavenly wisdom makes men peaceable. It is gentle, not being rude and overbearing in conversation, nor harsh and cruel in temper. Heavenly wisdom is *easy to be entreated,* it is very *persuadable,* either to what is good or from what is evil. There is an easiness that is weak and faulty; but it is not a blameable easiness to yield ourselves to the persuasions of God's word, and to all just requests of our fellow-creatures. Heavenly wisdom is full of mercy and good fruits, both to relieve those who want and to forgive those who offend. Heavenly wisdom is without partiality. The margin reads it, *without wrangling.* The wisest men are least apt to be censurers. That wisdom which is from above is without hypocrisy. It has no disguises nor deceits. It is sincere and open, steady and uniform, and consistent with itself.

True wisdom will go on to sow the fruits of righteousness in peace, and thus, to make peace in the world, *v.* 18. And that which is sown in peace will produce a harvest of joys.

JAMIESON, FAUSSET, BROWN

14. if ye have—*as is the case* (this is implied in the *Greek* indicative). **bitter**—Ephesians 4:31, "bitterness." **envying**—rather, "emulation," or lit., "zeal": kindly, generous emulation, or zeal, is not condemned, but that which is "bitter" [BENGEL]. **strife**—rather, "rivalry." **in your hearts**—from which flow your words and deeds, as from a fountain. **glory not, and lie not against the truth**—To *boast of your wisdom* is virtually a lying against the truth (the gospel), while your lives belie your glorying. Vs. 15; ch. 1:18, "The word of truth." Romans 2:17.23, speaks similarly of the same contentious Jewish Christians. **15. This wisdom**—in which ye "glory," as if ye were "wise" (vss. 13, 14). **descendeth not from above**—lit., "is not one descending . . .": "from the Father of lights" (true illumination and wisdom), ch. 1:17; through "the Spirit of truth," John 15:26. **earthly**—opposed to *heavenly.* Distinct from "earthy," I Corinthians 15:47. *Earthly* is what is IN the earth; *earthy,* what is of the earth. **sensual**—lit., "animal-like": the wisdom of the "natural" (the same *Greek*) man, not born again of God; "not having the Spirit" (Jude 19). **devilish**—in its origin (from "hell," vs. 6; not from God, the Giver of true wisdom, ch. 1: 5), and also in its character, which accords with its origin. Earthly, sensual, and devilish, answer to the three spiritual foes of man, the world, the flesh, and the devil. **16. envying**—So *English Version* translates the *Greek,* which usually means "zeal"; "*emulation,*" in Romans 13:13. "The envious man stands in his own light. He thinks his candle cannot shine in the presence of another's sun. He aims directly at men, obliquely at God, who makes men to differ." **strife**—rivalry [ALFORD]. **confusion**—lit., "tumultuous anarchy": both in society (translated "commotions," Luke 21:9; "tumults," II Cor. 6:5), and in the individual mind; in contrast to the "peaceable" composure of true "wisdom," vs. 17. James does not honor such effects of this earthly wisdom with the name "fruit," as he does in the case of the wisdom from above. Vs. 18; cf. Galatians 5:19-22, "*works* of the flesh . . . *fruit* of the Spirit." **17. first pure**—lit., "chaste," "sanctified"; pure from all that is "earthly, sensual (animal), devilish" (vs. 15). This is put, "*first of all,*" before "peaceable" because there is an unholy peace with the world which makes no distinction between clean and unclean. Cf. "undefiled" and "unspotted from the world," ch. 1:27; 4:4, 8, "purify . . . hearts"; I Peter 1:22, "*purified* . . . souls" (the same *Greek*). **gentle** "forbearing"; making allowances for others; lenient towards neighbors, as to the DUTIES they owe us. **easy to be entreated**—lit., "easily persuaded," tractable; not harsh as to a neighbor's FAULTS. **full of mercy**—as to a neighbor's MISERIES. **good fruits**—contrasted with "every evil work," vs. 16. **without partiality**—recurring to the warning against partial "respect to persons," ch. 2:1, 4, 9. ALFORD translates as the *Greek* is translated, ch. 1:6, "wavering," "*without doubting.*" But thus there would be an epithet referring to *one's self* inserted amidst those referring to one's conduct towards others. *English Version* is therefore better. **without hypocrisy**—Not as ALFORD explains from ch. 1:22, 26, "Without deceiving yourselves" with the name without the reality of religion. For it must refer, like the rest of the six epithets, to our relations to others; our peaceableness and mercy towards others must be "without dissimulation." **18.** "The peaceable fruit of righteousness." He says "righteousness"; because it is itself the true wisdom. As in the case of the earthly wisdom, after the characteristic description came its *results;* so in this verse, in the case of the heavenly wisdom. There the results were present; here, future. **fruit . . . sown**—Cf. Psalm 97: 11; Isaiah 61:3, "trees of righteousness." Anticipatory, i.e., the seed whose "fruit," viz., "righteousness," shall be ultimately reaped, is now "sown in peace." "Righteousness," now in germ, when fully developed as "fruit" shall be itself the everlasting *reward* of the righteous. As "sowing in peace" (cf. "*sown in* dishonor," I Cor. 15:43) produces the "fruit of righteousness," so conversely "the work" and "effect of righteousness" is "peace." **of them that make peace**—"by (implying also that it is *for* them, and *to* their good) them that work peace." They, and they alone, are "blessed." "Peacemakers," not merely they who reconcile others, but who *work peace.* "Cultivate peace" [ESTIUS]. Those truly wise towards God, while peaceable and tolerant towards their neighbors, yet make it their chief concern to sow righteousness, not cloaking men's sins, but reproving them with such peaceable moderation as to be the physicians, rather than the executioners, of sinners [CALVIN].

ADAM CLARKE

speaks. We may learn from this that genuine wisdom is ever accompanied with meekness and gentleness. Those proud, overbearing, and disdainful men who pass for great scholars and eminent critics may have learning, but they have not wisdom.

14. *If ye have bitter envying and strive.* If you are under the influence of an unkind, fierce, and contemptuous spirit, even while attempting or pretending to defend true religion, "do not boast" of either your exertions or success in silencing an adversary. You have no religion, and no true wisdom; and to profess either is to *lie . . . against the truth.*

15. *This wisdom descendeth not from above.* God is not the author of it, because it is bitter—not meek. *Is earthly.* Having this life only in view.

Sensual. "Animal"—having for its object the gratification of the passions and animal propensities. *Devilish.* "Demoniacal"—inspired by demons.

16. *For where envying and strife is.* "Zeal," fiery, inflammatory passion, and "contention," altercations about the different points of the law, of no use for edification; such as those mentioned in Titus iii. 9.

17. *The wisdom that is from above.* The pure religion of the Lord Jesus, bought by His blood and infused by His Spirit. See the rabbinical meaning of this phrase at the end of this chapter. *Is first pure.* "Chaste, holy, and clean." *Peaceable.* Living in peace with others, and promoting peace among men. *Gentle.* "Meek, modest, of an equal mind," taking everything in good part, and putting the best construction upon all the actions of others. *Easy to be intreated.* Not stubborn nor obstinate; of a yielding disposition in all indifferent things. *Full of mercy.* Ready to pass by a transgression, and to grant forgiveness to those who offend, and performing every possible act of kindness. *Good fruits.* Each temper and disposition producing fruits suited to and descriptive of its nature. *Without partiality.* "Without making a difference"—rendering to every man his due; and being never swayed by self-interest, worldly honor, or the fear of man. *Without hypocrisy.* Without pretending to be what it is not; acting always in its own character; never working under a mask.

18. *And the fruit of righteousness is sown.* The whole is the principle of righteousness in the soul, and all the above virtues are the fruits of that righteousness. *Is sown in peace.* When the peace of God rules the heart, all these virtues and graces grow and flourish abundantly. *Of them that make peace.* The peacemakers are continually recommending this wisdom to others, and their own conduct is represented as a sowing of heavenly seed, which brings forth divine fruit. Some render this verse, which is confessedly obscure, thus: "And the peaceable fruits of righteousness are sown for the practicers of peace. He who labors to live peaceably shall have peace for his reward."

Almost the whole of the preceding chapter is founded on maxims highly accredited in the rabbinical writings, and without a reference to those writings it would have been impossible, in some cases, to have understood James's meaning. There is one phrase, the rabbinical meaning and use of which I have reserved for this place, viz. "The wisdom that is from above." This they seem to understand to be a peculiar inspiration of the Almighty, or a teaching communicated immediately by the angels of God. In *Sohar Yalcut Rubeni,* fol. 19, Rabbi Chiya said: "The wisdom from above was in Adam more than in the supreme angels, and he knew all things." In *Sohar Chadash,* fol. 35, it is said concerning Enoch, "That the angels were sent from heaven, and taught him the *wisdom that is from above.*" It is another word for the life of God in the soul of man, or true religion; it is the teaching of God in the human heart.

MATTHEW HENRY

CHAPTER 4

Verses 1–10

This chapter speaks of a lust after worldly things as that which carried their divisions to a shameful height.

I. The apostle here reproves the Jewish Christians for their wars, and for their lusts as the cause of them, *v.* 1. The origin of their wars and fightings was not (as they pretended) a true zeal for their country, and for the honour of God, their prevailing lusts were the cause of all. What is shrouded under a specious pretence of zeal for God and religion often comes from men's pride. They make a war within as well as fightings without. From lust of power and dominion, lust of pleasure, or lust of riches, arise all the broils and contentions that are in the world. It is therefore the right method for the cure of contention to lay the axe to the root, and mortify those lusts that war in the members.

It should kill these lusts to think of their disappointment, *v.* 2. Inordinate desires are either totally disappointed, or they are not to be appeased and satisfied by obtaining the things desired. Worldly and fleshly lusts are the distemper which will not allow of contentment or satisfaction in the mind.

Sinful desires and affections generally exclude prayer: "*You fight and war, yet you have not, because you ask not.* You do not consult God in your undertakings, and you do not commit your way to him, but follow your own corrupt views and inclinations: therefore you meet with continual disappointments. Your lusts spoil your prayers," *v.* 3. Pride, vanity, luxury, and sensuality, are what you would serve by your successes, and by your very prayers. You disgrace devotion and dishonour God by such gross and base ends; and therefore your prayers are rejected. They ask God to give them success in their callings or undertakings; not that they may glorify their heavenly Father and do good with what they have, but that they may *consume it upon their lusts.* When we speed not in our prayers it is *because we ask amiss;* either we do not ask for right ends or not in a right manner. When our prayers are rather the language of our lusts than of our graces, they will return empty.

II. We have fair warning to avoid all criminal friendships with this world, *v.* 4. There is this brand put upon worldly-mindedness—that it is enmity to God. A man may have a competent portion of the good things of this life, and yet may keep himself in the love of God, but it is constructive treason and rebellion against God to set the world upon his throne in our hearts. *Whosoever therefore is the friend of the world is the enemy of God.* Hence arise wars and fightings, even from this adulterous idolatrous love of the world.

What peace can there be among men, so long as there is enmity towards God? (*v.* 5). Natural corruption principally shows itself by envying, and there is a continual propensity to this. Now this way of the world, affecting pomp and pleasure, and falling into strifes and quarrels for the sake of these things, is the certain consequence of being friends to the world. Christians, to avoid contentions, must avoid the friendship of the world. If we belong to God, he gives more grace than to live and act as the generality of the world do. The grace of God will correct and cure the spirit that naturally dwells in us; where he giveth grace, he giveth another spirit than that of the world.

JAMIESON, FAUSSET, BROWN

CHAPTER 4

VSS. 1-17. AGAINST FIGHTINGS AND THEIR SOURCE; WORLDLY LUSTS; UNCHARITABLE JUDGMENTS, AND PRESUMPTUOUS RECKONING ON THE FUTURE. **1. whence**—The cause of quarrels is often sought in external circumstances, whereas internal lusts are the true origin. **wars . . .**—contrasted with the "peace" of heavenly wisdom. "Fightings" are the active carrying on of "wars." The best authorities have a second "whence" before "fightings." Tumults marked the era before the destruction of Jerusalem when James wrote. He indirectly alludes to these. The members are the first seat of war; thence it passes to conflict between man and man, nation and nation. **come they not . . .**—an appeal to their consciences. **lusts**—lit., "pleasures," i.e., the lusts which prompt you to "desire" (*Note,* vs. 2) *pleasures;* whence you seek self at the cost of your neighbor, and hence flow "fightings." **that war**—"campaign, as an army of soldiers encamped within" [ALFORD] the soul; tumultuously war against the interests of your fellow men, while lusting to advance self. But while warring thus against others they (without his knowledge) war against the soul of the man himself, and against the Spirit; therefore they must be "mortified" by the Christian. **2. Ye lust**—A different *Greek* word from that in vs. 1. "Ye desire"; lit., "ye set your *mind* (or heart) *on*" an object. **have not**—The lust of desire does not ensure the actual possession. Hence "ye kill" (not as *Margin,* without any old authority, "envy") to ensure possession. Not probably in the case of professing Christians of that day in a literal sense, but "kill and envy" (as the *Greek* for "desire to have" should be translated), i.e., harass and oppress through envy [DRUSIUS]. Cf. Zechariah 11:5, "slay"; *through envy, hate,* and desire to get out of your way, and so are "murderers" in God's eyes [ESTIUS]. If literal murder [ALFORD] were meant, I do not think it would occur so early in the series; nor had Christians then as yet reached so open criminality. In the Spirit's application of the passage to all ages, literal *killing* is included, flowing from the desire to possess so David and Ahab. There is a climax: "Ye desire," the individual lust for an object; "ye kill and envy," the feeling and action of individuals against individuals; "ye fight and war," the action of many against many. **ye have not, because ye ask not**—God promises to those who pray, not to those who fight. The petition of the lustful, murderous, and contentious is not recognized by God as *prayer.* If ye prayed, there would be no "wars and fightings." Thus this last clause is an answer to the question, vs. 1, "Whence come wars and fightings?" **3.** Some of them are supposed to say in objection, But we do "ask" (pray); cf. vs. 2. James replies, It is not enough to ask for good things, but we must ask with a good spirit and intention. "Ye ask amiss, that ye may consume *it* (your object of prayer) upon (lit., "in") your lusts" (lit., "pleasures"); not that ye may have the things you need for the service of God. Contrast ch. 1:5 with Matthew 6:31, 32. If ye prayed aright, all your proper wants would be supplied; the improper cravings which produce "wars and fightings" would then cease. Even believers' prayers are often best answered when their desires are most opposed. **4.** The oldest MSS. omit "adulterers and," and read simply, "Ye adulteresses." God is the rightful husband; the men of the world are regarded collectively as one *adulteress,* and individually as *adulteresses.* **the world**—in so far as the men of it and their motives and acts are aliens to God, e.g., its selfish "lusts" (vs. 3), and covetous and ambitious "wars and fightings" (vs. 1). **enmity**—not merely "inimical"; a state of enmity, and that enmity itself. Cf. I John 2:15, "love . . . the world . . . the love of the Father." **whosoever . . . will be**—The *Greek* is emphatic, "shall *be resolved* to be." Whether he succeed or not, if his *wish* be to be the friend of the world, he *renders himself, becomes* (so the *Greek* for "is") by the very fact, "the enemy of God." Contrast "Abraham the friend of God." **5. in vain**—No word of Scripture can be so. The quotation here, as in Ephesians 5:14, seems to be not so much from a particular passage as one gathered by James under inspiration from the general tenor of such passages in both the Old and New Testaments, as Numbers 14:29; Proverbs 21:20; Galatians 5:17. **spirit that dwelleth in us**—Other MSS. read, "that God hath made to dwell in us" (viz., at Pentecost). If so translated, "Does the (Holy) Spirit that God hath placed in us lust to (towards) envy" (viz., as ye do in your worldly "wars and fightings")? Certainly not; ye are therefore walking in the flesh, not in the Spirit, while ye thus *lust towards,* i.e.,

ADAM CLARKE

CHAPTER 4

1. *From whence come wars and fightings?* About the time in which James wrote we find, according to the accounts given by Josephus, that the Jews, under pretense of defending their religion, and procuring that liberty to which they believed themselves entitled, made various insurrections in Judea against the Romans, which occasioned much bloodshed and misery to their nation. The factions also into which the Jews were split had violent contentions among themselves, in which they massacred and plundered each other. In the provinces, likewise, the Jews became very turbulent; particularly in Alexandria and different other parts of Egypt, of Syria, and other places, where they made war against the heathens, killing many, and being massacred in their turn. These are probably the *wars* and *fightings* to which James alludes. *Come they not hence, even of your lusts?* This was the principle from which these Jewish contentions and predatory wars proceeded, and the principle from which all the wars that have afflicted and desolated the world have proceeded.

2. *Ye lust, and have not.* You are ever covetous, and ever poor. *Ye kill, and desire to have.* You are constantly engaged in insurrections and predatory wars, and never gain any advantage. *Ye have not, because ye ask not.* You get no especial blessing from God, as your fathers did, because you do not pray. Worldly good is your god; you leave no stone unturned in order to get it; and as you ask nothing from God but to consume it upon your evil desires and propensities, your prayers are not heard.

3. *Ye ask, and receive not.* Some think that this refers to their prayers for the conversion of the heathen; and on the pretense that they were not converted thus, they thought it lawful to extirpate them and possess their goods. *Ye ask amiss.* "Ye ask evilly, wickedly." You have not the proper dispositions of prayer, and you have an improper object. You ask for worldly prosperity, that you may employ it in riotous living. This is properly the meaning of the original, "That ye may expend it upon your pleasures." The rabbins have many good observations on asking amiss or asking improperly, and give examples of different kinds of this sort of prayer; the phrase is Jewish, and would naturally occur to James in writing on this subject.

4. *Ye adulterers and adulteresses.* The Jews, because of their covenant with God, are represented as being espoused to Him; and hence their idolatry and their iniquity in general are represented under the notion of adultery. And although they had not since the Babylonish captivity been guilty of idolatry, according to the letter, yet what is intended by idolatry—having their hearts estranged from God, and seeking their portion in this life and out of God—is that of which the Jews were then notoriously guilty. *Whosoever therefore will be a friend of the world.* How strange it is that people professing Christianity can suppose that with a worldly spirit, worldly companions, and their lives governed by worldly maxims, they can be in the favor of God, or ever get to the kingdom of Heaven! When the world gets into the Church, the Church becomes a painted sepulchre, its spiritual vitality being extinct.

5. *Do ye think that the scripture saith in vain?* This verse is exceedingly obscure. We cannot tell what scripture James refers to; many have been produced by learned men as that which he had particularly in view. Some think Gen. vi. 5: "Every imagination of the thoughts of his heart was only evil continually." Gen. viii. 21: "The imagination of man's heart is evil from his youth." Num. xi. 29: "Moses said unto him, Enviest thou for my sake?" and Prov. xxi. 10: "The soul of the wicked desireth evil." None of these scriptures, nor any others, contain the precise words in this verse; and therefore James may probably refer, not to any particular portion, but to the spirit and design of the Scripture in those various places where it speaks against envying, covetousness, worldly associations. Perhaps the word in this and the two succeeding verses may be well paraphrased thus: "Do you think that concerning these things the Scripture speaks falsely, or that the Holy

MATTHEW HENRY

III. The difference God makes between pride and humility, *v.* 6. This is represented as the language of scripture in the Old Testament. 1. The disgrace cast upon the proud: God resists them. The proud resists God. Let proud spirits hear this and tremble—*God resists them.* He will certainly fill with shame the faces of such as have filled their hearts with pride. 2. The honour and help God gives to the humble. Grace, as opposed to disgrace, is honour; this God gives to the humble. Wherever God gives true grace, he will give more. He will especially give more grace to the humble, because they see their need of it, will pray for it and be thankful for it; and such shall have it.

IV. We are taught to submit ourselves entirely to God, *v.* 7. Christians should forsake the friendship of the world, and should by grace learn to glory in their submissions to God We are subjects, and as such must be submissive; not only through fear, but through love. Now, as this subjection and submission to God are what the devil most industriously strives to hinder, so we ought with great care and steadiness to resist his suggestions. "*Resist him and he will flee from you.*" If we basely yield to temptations, the devil will continually follow us; but if we stand it out against him, he will be gone from us. Resolution shuts and bolts the door against temptation.

V. We are directed how to act towards God, *v.* 8-10. 1. *Draw nigh to God.* The heart that has rebelled must be brought to the foot of God; the spirit that was estranged from a life of communion with God must become acquainted with him. 2. *Cleanse your hands.* He who comes unto God must have clean hands. The hands must be cleansed or it will be in vain for us to draw nigh to God. 3. The hearts of the double-minded must be purified. To *purify the heart* is to be sincere.

4. *Be afflicted, and mourn, and weep.* 'What afflictions God sends take them as he would have you, and be duly sensible of them. Times of contention and division are times to mourn in, and the sins that occasion wars and fightings should be mourned for. *Let your laughter be turned to mourning and your joy to heaviness.*" This may be taken either as a prediction of sorrow or a prescription of seriousness. They are directed, before things come to the worst, to lay aside their vain mirth and their sensual pleasures, that they might indulge godly sorrow and penitential tears. 5. "*Humble yourselves in the sight of the Lord.* Let there be a thorough humiliation in bewailing everything that is evil; let there be great humility in doing that which is good."

VI. We have great encouragement to act thus towards God (*v.* 8-10). Those that draw nigh to God in a way of duty shall find God drawing nigh to them in a way of mercy. If there be not a close communion between God and us, it is our fault, and not his. *He shall lift up the humble.* If we be truly penitent and humble under the marks of God's displeasure, we shall in a little time know the advantages of his favour; he will lift us up out of trouble, or he will lift us up in our spirits and comfort us under trouble. The highest honour in heaven will be the reward of the greatest humility on earth.

Verses 11-17

I. We are cautioned against the sin of evil-speaking, *v.* 11. We must not speak evil things of others, though they be true, unless there be some necessary occasion for it; much less must we report evil things when they are false. Our lips must be guided by the law of kindness, as well as truth and justice. 1. Because you are brethren. It is required of us that we be tender of the good name of our brethren; where we cannot speak well, we had better say nothing than speak evil.

JAMIESON, FAUSSET, BROWN

with envy against one another. The friendship of the world tends to breed *envy;* the Spirit produces very different fruit. ALFORD attributes the epithet "with envy," in the unwarrantable sense of *jealously,* to the Holy Spirit: "The Spirit *jealously desires* us for His own." In *English Version* the sense is, "the (natural) spirit that hath its dwelling in us lusts with (lit., "to," or "towards") envy." Ye lust, and because ye have not what ye lust after (vss. 1, 2), ye envy your neighbor who has, and so the *spirit of envy* leads you on to "fight." James also here refers to ch. 3:14, 16. **6. But**—"Nay, rather." **he**—God. **giveth more grace**—ever increasing grace; the farther ye depart from "envy" [BENGEL]. **he saith**—The same God who causes His spirit to dwell in believers (vs. 5), by the Spirit also speaks in Scripture. The quotation here is probably from Proverbs 3:34; as probably Proverbs 21:10 was generally referred to in vs. 5. In *Hebrew* it is "scorneth the scorners," viz., those who think "Scripture speaketh in vain." **resisteth**—lit., "setteth Himself in array against"; even as they, like Pharaoh, set themselves against Him. God repays sinners in their own coin. "Pride" is the mother of "envy" (vs. 5); it is peculiarly satanic, for by it Satan fell. **the proud**—The *Greek* means in derivation one who *shows himself above* his fellows, and so lifts himself against God. **the humble**—the unenvious, uncovetous, and unambitious as to the world. Contrast vs. 4. **7. Submit to . . . God**—so ye shall be among "the humble," vs. 6; also vs. 10; I Peter 5:6. **Resist . . . devil**—Under his banner *pride* and *envy* are enlisted in the world; resist his temptations to these. Faith, humble prayers, and heavenly wisdom, are the weapons of resistance. The language is taken from warfare. "Submit" as a good soldier puts himself in complete subjection to his captain. "Resist," stand bravely against. **he will flee**—Translate, "he *shall* flee." For it is a promise of God, not a mere assurance from man to man [ALFORD]. He shall flee worsted as he did from Christ. **8. Draw nigh to God**—So "cleave unto Him," Deuteronomy 30:20, viz., by prayerfully (vss. 2, 3) "resisting Satan," who would oppose our access to God. **he will draw nigh**—propitious. **Cleanse . . . hands**—the outward instruments of action. None but the cleanhanded can ascend into the hill of the Lord (justified through Christ, who alone was perfectly so, and as such "ascended" thither). **purify . . . hearts**—lit., "make chaste" of your spiritual *adultery* (vs. 4, i.e., worldliness) "your hearts": the inward source of all impurity. **double-minded**—divided between God and the world. The "double-minded" is at fault in *heart;* the *sinner* in his *hands* likewise.

9. Be afflicted . . .—lit., "Endure misery," i.e., mourn over your wretchedness through sin. *Repent with deep sorrow* instead of your present laughter. A blessed *mourning.* Contrast Isaiah 22:12, 13; Luke 6:25. James does not add here, as in ch. 5:1, "howl," where he foretells the *doom of the impenitent* at the coming destruction of Jerusalem. **heaviness**—lit., "falling of the countenance," casting down of the eyes.

10. in the sight of the Lord—as continually in the presence of Him who alone is worthy to be exalted: recognizing His presence in all your ways, the truest incentive to *humility.* The tree, to grow upwards, must strike its roots deep downwards; so man, to be exalted, must have his mind deep-rooted in humility. In I Peter 5:6, it is, Humble yourselves under the mighty hand of God, viz., in His dealings of Providence: a distinct thought from that here. **lift you up**—in part in this world, fully in the world to come.

11. Having mentioned sins of the tongue (ch. 3), he shows here that *evil-speaking* flows from the same spirit of exalting self at the expense of one's neighbor as caused the "fightings" reprobated in this chapter (vs. 1). **Speak not evil**—lit., "Speak not

ADAM CLARKE

Spirit, who dwells in us, can excite us to envy others instead of being contented with the state in which the providence of God has placed us? Nay, far otherwise; for He gives us more grace to enable us to bear the ills of life, and to lie in deep humility at His feet, knowing that His Holy Spirit has said, Prov. iii. 34: 'God resisteth the proud, but giveth grace to the humble.' Seeing these things are so, submit yourselves to God; resist the devil, who would tempt you to envy, and he will flee from you; draw nigh to God, and He will draw nigh to you." I must leave this sense as the best I can give, without asserting that I have hit the true meaning.

6. *But he giveth more grace.* "A greater benefit" than all the goods that the world can bestow; for He gives genuine happiness, and this the world cannot confer. May this be James's meaning? *God resisteth the proud.* "Sets himself in battle array" against him. *Giveth grace unto the humble.* The sure way to please God is to submit to the dispensations of His grace and providence; and when a man acknowledges Him in all his ways, He will direct all his steps. The covetous man grasps at the shadow and loses the substance.

7. *Submit . . . to God.* Continue to bow to all His decisions and to all His dispensations. *Resist the devil.* He cannot conquer you if you continue to resist. Strong as he is, God never permits him to conquer the man who continues to resist him; he cannot force the human will.

8. *Draw nigh to God.* Approach Him, in the name of Jesus, by faith and prayer, and *he will draw nigh to you*—He will meet you at your coming. When a soul sets out to seek God, God sets out to meet that soul; so that while we are drawing near to Him, He is drawing near to us. *Cleanse your hands, ye sinners.* This I think to be the beginning of a new address, and to different persons, and should have formed the commencement of a new verse. Let your whole conduct be changed. "Cease to do evil; learn to do well." Washing or cleansing the hands was a token of innocence and purity. *Purify your hearts.* Separate yourselves from the world, and consecrate yourselves to God; this is the true notion of sanctification. We have often seen that to sanctify signifies to separate a thing or person from profane or common use, and consecrate it or him to God. The person or thing thus consecrated or separated is considered to be "holy" and to be God's property. There are therefore two things implied in a man's sanctification: (1) That he separates himself from evil ways and evil companions, and devotes himself to God; (2) That God separates guilt from his conscience and sin from his soul, and thus makes him internally and externally "holy."

9. *Be afflicted, and mourn.* Without true and deep repentance you cannot expect the mercy of God. *Let your laughter be turned to mourning.* It appears most evidently that many of those to whom James addressed this Epistle had lived very irregular and dissolute lives. He had already spoken of their lust and pleasures, and he had called them adulterers and adulteresses; and perhaps they were so in the grossest sense of the words. He speaks here of their *laughter* and their *joy;* and all the terms taken together show that a dissolute life is intended.

10. *Humble yourselves in the sight of the Lord.* In v. 7 they were exhorted to submit to God; here they are exhorted to humble themselves in His sight. Submission to God's authority will precede humiliation of soul, and genuine repentance is performed as in the sight of God; for when a sinner is truly awakened to a sense of his guilt and danger, he seems to see, whithersoever he turns, the face of a justly incensed God turned against him. *He shall lift you up.* Mourners and penitents lay on the ground and rolled themselves in the dust. When comforted and pardoned, they arose from the earth, shook themselves from the dust, and clothed themselves in their better garments. God promises to raise these from the dust, when sufficiently humbled.

11. *Speak not evil one of another.* Perhaps this exhortation refers to evil speaking, slander, and backbiting in general, the writer having no particular persons in view. It may, however, refer to the contentions among the different

MATTHEW HENRY

2. Because this is to judge the law. He who quarrels with his brother, and condemns him for the sake of anything not determined in the word of God, does thereby reflect on that word of God, as if it were not a perfect rule. Let us take heed of judging the law, for the law of the Lord is perfect; if men break the law, leave that to judge them; if they do not break it, let us not judge them. Those who are most ready to set up for judges of the law generally fail most in their obedience to it. 3. Because God, the Lawgiver, has reserved the power of passing the final sentence on men wholly to himself, *v.* 12. God is the supreme Lawgiver, who only can give law to the conscience, and who alone is to be absolutely obeyed. His right to enact laws is incontestable, because he has such a power to enforce them. He *is able to save, and to destroy*. He has power fully to reward the observance of his laws, and to punish all disobedience. Here he cautions against being many judges. Let us not prescribe to our brethren. It is sufficient that we have the law of God, which is a rule to us all; and therefore we should not set up other rules.

II. We are cautioned against a presumptuous confidence of the continuance of our lives, *v.* 13, 14. Reflect a little on this way of thinking and talking; call yourselves to account for it. There were some who said of old, as too many say still, *We will go to such a city, and do this or that*, while all serious regards to the disposals of Providence were neglected. 1. How apt worldly men are to leave God out of their schemes. 2. How much of worldly happiness lies in the promises men make to themselves beforehand. Their heads are full of fine visions, as to what they shall do in some future time. 3. How vain a thing it is to look for anything good in futurity, without the concurrence of Providence. *We will go to such a city* (say they). Something might possibly stop their way, or call them elsewhere. Many who have set out on a journey have gone to their long home, and never reached their journey's end. But, suppose they should reach the city they designed, how did they know they should continue there? Something might happen to shorten their stay They could not be certain that they should buy and sell there. Suppose they should go to that city, and continue there a year, yet they might not get gain; getting of gain in this world is at best but an uncertain thing. The frailty, shortness, and uncertainty of life, ought to check the presumptuous confidence of such projectors for futurity, *v.* 14. God hath wisely left us in the dark concerning future events. We *know not what shall be on the morrow*; we may know what we intend to do and to be, but a thousand things may happen to prevent us. We are not sure of life itself, since it is but as a *vapour. It appears but for a little time, and then vanisheth away*.

III. We are taught to keep up a constant sense of our dependence on the will of God, *v.* 15. The apostle now directs them how to be and do better: "You ought to say it in your hearts at all times, that if the Lord will give leave, you have such and such designs to accomplish." *With the leave and blessing of God* was used by the Greeks in the beginning of every undertaking. *If the Lord will, we shall live*. We must remember that our times are not in our own hands, but at the disposal of God, and therefore must be submissive to him. *If the Lord will, we shall do this or that*. All our actions and designs are under the control of Heaven. Therefore both our counsels for action and our conduct in action should be entirely referred to God.

IV. We are directed to avoid vain boasting, *v.* 16. They promised themselves life and prosperity, and great things in the world, without any just regard to God; and then they boasted of these things. *Such rejoicing is evil;* it is foolish and it is hurtful. If we rejoice in God that our times are in his hand, that all events are at his disposal, and that he is our God, this rejoicing is good. But, if we rejoice in our own vain confidences and presumptuous boasts, this is evil.

V. We are taught to act up to our own convictions, that we never go contrary to our own knowledge (*v.* 17). It is aggravated sin; it is sinning with a witness; and it is to have the worst witness against a man that can be, when he sins against his own conscience. Omissions are sins which will come into judgment, as well as commissions. He that does not the good he knows should be done, as well as he who does the evil he knows should not be done, will be condemned.

JAMIESON, FAUSSET, BROWN

against" one another. **brethren**—implying the inconsistency of such depreciatory speaking of one another in *brethren*. **speaketh evil of the law**—for the law in commanding, "Love thy neighbor as thyself" (ch. 2:8), virtually condemns evil-speaking and judging [ESTIUS]. Those who superciliously condemn the acts and words of others which do not please themselves, thus aiming at the reputation of sanctity, put their own moroseness in the place of the law, and claim to themselves a power of censuring above the law of God, condemning what the law permits [CALVIN]. Such a one acts as though the law could not perform its own office of *judging*, but he must fly upon the office [BENGEL]. This is the last mention of the law in the New Testament. ALFORD rightly takes the "law" to be the old moral law applied in its comprehensive spiritual fulness by Christ: "the law of liberty." **if thou judge the law, thou art not a doer . . . but a judge**—Setting aside the Christian *brotherhood* as all alike called to be *doers* of the law, in subjection to it, such a one arrogates the office of a *judge*. **12. There is one lawgiver**—The best authorities read in addition," "and judge." Translate, "There is One (alone) who is (at once) Lawgiver and Judge, (namely) He who is able to save and destroy." Implying, God alone is Lawgiver and therefore Judge, since it is He alone who can execute His judgments; our inability in this respect shows our presumption in trying to act as judges, as though we were God. **who art thou . . .** —The order in the *Greek* is emphatic, "But (inserted in oldest MSS.) thou, who art thou that . . .?" How rashly arrogant in judging thy fellows, and wresting from God the office which belongs to Him over thee and THEM alike! **another**—The oldest authorities read, "thy neighbor."

13. Go to now—"Come now"; said to excite attention. **ye that say**—*boasting* of the morrow. **Today or tomorrow**—as if ye had the free choice of either day as a certainty. Others read, "Today *and* tomorrow." **such a city**—lit., "this the city" (viz., the one present to the mind of the speaker). *This city here*. **continue . . . a year**—rather, "spend one year." Their language implies that when this one year is out, they purpose similarly settling plans for to come [BENGEL]. **buy and sell**—Their plans for the future are all worldly. **14. what**—lit., "of what nature" is your life? i.e., how evanescent it is. **It is even**—Some oldest authorities read, "For ye are." BENGEL, with other old authorities, reads, "For it shall be, the future referring to the "morrow" (vss. 13-15). The former expresses, "Ye yourselves are transitory"; so everything of yours, even your life, must partake of the same transitoriness. Received text has no old authority. **and then vanisheth away**—"afterwards vanishing as it came"; lit., "afterwards (as it appeared), *so vanishing*" [ALFORD]. **15.** Lit., "instead of your saying . . ." This refers to "ye that say" (vs. 13). **we shall live**—The best MSS. read, "We shall *both* live *and* do. . . ." The boasters spoke as if *life, action*, and the particular kind of action were in their power, whereas all three depend entirely on the will of the Lord. **16. now**—as it is. **rejoice in . . . boastings**—"ye boast in arrogant presumptions," viz., vain confident fancies that the future is certain to you (vs. 13). **rejoicing**—boasting [BENGEL]. **17.** The general principle illustrated by the particular example just discussed is here stated: knowledge without practice is imputed to a man as great and presumptuous sin. James reverts to the principle with which he started. Nothing more injures the soul than wasted impressions. Feelings exhaust themselves and evaporate, if not embodied in practice. As we will not act except we feel, so if we will not act out our feelings, we shall soon cease to feel.

ADAM CLARKE

factions then prevailing among this wretched people, or to their calumnies against those of their brethren who had embraced the Christian faith. *He that speaketh evil of his brother*. It was an avowed and very general maxim among the rabbins that "no one could speak evil of his brother without denying God, and becoming an atheist." *Speaketh evil of the law*. The law condemns all evil speaking and detraction. He who is guilty of these, and allows himself in these vices, in effect judges and condemns the law; i.e., he considers it unworthy to be kept, and that it is no sin to break it. *Thou art not a doer of the law, but a judge*. You reject the law of God, and set up your own mischievous conduct as a rule of life; or, by allowing this evil speaking and detraction, intimate that the law that condemns them is improper, imperfect, or unjust.

12. *There is one lawgiver*. "And judge" is added here by about thirty MSS. On this evidence Griesbach has received it into the text. The man who breaks the law, and teaches others so to do, thus in effect sets himself up as a *lawgiver* and judge. But there is only one such "lawgiver and judge"—God Almighty, who is *able to save* all those who obey Him, and *able . . . to destroy* all those who trample underfoot His testimonies. *Who art thou that judgest another?* Who are you who dare to usurp the office and prerogative of the supreme Judge? But what is that law of which James speaks? and who is this *lawgiver* and "judge"? Most critics think that the law mentioned here is the same as that which he elsewhere calls "the royal law" and "the law of liberty," thereby meaning the gospel; and that Christ is the Person who is called the Lawgiver and Judge. This, however, is not clear to me. I believe James means the Jewish law; and by the *lawgiver* and "judge," God Almighty, as acknowledged by the Jewish people. I find, or think I find, from the closest examination of this Epistle, but few references to Jesus Christ or His gospel. His Jewish creed, forms, and maxims, this writer keeps constantly in view; and it is proper he should, considering the persons to whom he wrote. Some of them were doubtless Christians; some of them, certainly no Christians; and some of them, half Christians and half Jews. The two latter descriptions are those most frequently addressed.

13. *Go to now*. "Come now," the same in meaning as the Hebrew "come," Gen. xi. 3-4, 7. "Come, and hear what I have to say, *ye that say," To day or to morrow we will go*. This presumption on a precarious life is here well reproved. *And continue there a year, and buy and sell*. This was the custom of those ancient times; they traded from city to city, carrying their goods on the backs of camels.

14. *Whereas ye know not*. This verse should be read in a parenthesis. It is not only impious, but grossly absurd, to speak thus concerning futurity when you know not what a day may bring forth. *It is even a vapour*. "It is a smoke," always fleeting, uncertain, evanescent. This is a frequent metaphor with the Hebrews. See Ps. cii. 11; "My days are like a shadow"; Job viii. 9; "Our days upon earth are a shadow"; 1 Chron. xxix. 15; "Our days on the earth are as a shadow, and there is none abiding."

16. *But now ye rejoice in your boastings*. You glory in your proud and self-sufficient conduct, exulting that you are free from the trammels of superstition, and that you can live independently of God Almighty. "All such boasting is wicked."

17. *To him that knoweth to do good*. As if he had said: After this warning none of you can plead ignorance; if therefore any of you shall be found to act their ungodly part, not acknowledging the divine providence, the uncertainty of life, and the necessity of standing every moment prepared to meet God—as you will have the greater sin, you will infallibly get the greater punishment. This may be applied to all who know better than they act. He who does not the Master's will because he does not know it will be beaten with few stripes; but he who knows it and does not do it shall be beaten with many; Luke xii. 47-48. James may have the Christians in view who were converted from Judaism to Christianity.

MATTHEW HENRY

CHAPTER 5

Verses 1–11

The apostle is here addressing first sinners and then saints.

I. The address to sinners; and here we find James seconding what his great Master had said: *Woe unto you that are rich; for you have received your consolation*, Luke vi. 24. The poor among the Jews received the gospel, and many of them believed; but the generality of the rich rejected Christianity, and persecuted those who believed on Christ.

1. He foretells the judgments of God that should come upon them, *v.* 1–3. They should have miseries come upon them, misery that should arise from the very things in which they placed their happiness. *Go to now, you rich men.* Rich men are apt to say to themselves (and others are ready to say to them), *Eat, drink, and be merry;* but God says, *Weep and howl.* Those who live like beasts are called to howl like such. "Corruption, decay, rust, and ruin, will come upon all your goodly things (*v.* 2). Those things which you now inordinately affect will be of no worth, of no use to you," *v.* 3. They think to heap up treasure for their latter days, but, alas! they are only heaping up treasures that will prove at last to be only treasures of wrath.

2. What those sins are which should bring such miseries. Covetousness is laid to the charge of this people. God gives us our worldly possessions that we may honour him and do good with them; but if, instead of this, we sinfully hoard them up, this is a very heinous crime, and will be witnessed against by the very rust and corruption of the treasure thus heaped together.

Another sin is oppression, *v.* 4. Those who have wealth in their hands get power into their hands, and then they are tempted to abuse that power to oppress such as are under them. They made as hard bargains with the poor as they could, and even after that would not make good their bargains as they should have done.

Another sin is sensuality and voluptuousness, *v.* 5. God does not forbid us to use pleasure; but to live in them as if we lived for nothing else is a very provoking sin. Luxury makes people wanton. Wantonness and luxury are commonly the effects of great plenty and abundance. "*You have nourished your hearts as in a day of slaughter:* you live as if it were every day a day of sacrifices, a festival." Some may say, "What harm is there in good cheer, provided people do not spend above what they have?" What! Is it no harm for people to make gods of their bellies, and to give all to these, instead of abounding in acts of charity and piety? Pride, and idleness, and fulness of bread, mean the same thing with living in pleasure, and being wanton, and nourishing the heart as in a day of slaughter. Another sin is persecution, *v.* 6. This fills up the measure of their iniquity. When such do suffer, and yield without resistance to the unjust sentence of oppressors, this is marked by God, to the honour of the sufferers and the infamy of their persecutors.

JAMIESON, FAUSSET, BROWN

CHAPTER 5

VSS. 1-20. WOES COMING ON THE WICKED RICH: BELIEVERS SHOULD BE PATIENT UNTO THE LORD'S COMING: VARIOUS EXHORTATIONS. **1. Go to now**—Come now. A phrase to call solemn attention. **ye rich**—who have neglected the true enjoyment of riches, which consists in doing good. James intends this address to rich Jewish unbelievers, not so much for themselves, as for the saints, that they may bear with patience the violence of the rich (vs. 7), knowing that God will speedily avenge them on their oppressors [BENGEL]. **miseries that shall come**—lit., "that are coming upon you" unexpectedly and swiftly, viz., at the coming of the Lord (vs. 7); primarily, at the destruction of Jerusalem; finally, at His visible coming to judge the world. **2. corrupted**—*about to be destroyed* through God's curse on your oppression, whereby your riches are accumulated (vs. 4). CALVIN thinks the sense is, Your riches perish without being of any use either to others or even to yourselves, for instance, your garments which are moth-eaten in your chests. **garments . . . moth-eaten**—referring to Matthew 6: 19, 20. **3. is cankered**—"rusted through" [ALFORD]. **rust . . . witness against you**—in the day of judgment; viz., that your riches were of no profit to any, lying unemployed and so contracting rust. **shall eat your flesh**—The rust which once ate your riches, shall then gnaw your conscience, accompanied with punishment which shall prey upon your bodies for ever. **as . . . fire**—not with the slow process of *rusting*, but with the swiftness of consuming *fire*. **for the last days**—Ye have heaped together, not treasures as ye suppose (cf. Luke 12: 19), but wrath against the last days, viz., the coming judgment of the Lord. ALFORD translates more lit., "*In* these last days (before the coming judgment) ye laid up (worldly) treasure" to no profit, instead of repenting and seeking salvation (see *Note*, vs. 5). **4. Behold**—calling attention to their coming doom as no vain threat. **labourers**—lit., "workmen." **of you kept back**—So *English Version* rightly. Not as ALFORD, "crieth out *from* you." The "keeping back of the hire" was, *on the part OF* the rich, virtually an act of "*fraud*," because the poor laborers were not immediately paid. The phrase is therefore not, "kept back *by* you," but "*of* you"; the latter implying *virtual*, rather than overt, fraud. James refers to Deuteronomy 24:14, 15, "At this day . . . give his *hire*, neither shall the sun go down upon it, lest he CRY against thee unto the Lord, and it be sin unto thee." Many sins "cry" to heaven for vengeance which men tacitly take no account of, as unchastity and injustice [BENGEL]. Sins peculiarly offensive to God are said to "cry" to Him. The rich ought to have given freely to the poor; their not doing so was sin. A still greater sin was their not paying their debts. Their greatest sin was not paying them to the poor, whose wages is their all. **cries of them**—a double cry; both that of the hire abstractly, and that of the laborers hired. **the Lord of sabaoth**—here only in the New Testament. In Romans 9:29 it is a quotation. It is suited to the Jewish tone of the Epistle. It reminds the rich who think the poor have no protector, that the Lord of the whole hosts in heaven and earth is the guardian and avenger of the latter. He is identical with the "coming Lord" Jesus (vs. 7). **5.** Translate, "Ye have luxuriated . . . and wantoned." The former expresses *luxurious effeminacy;* the latter, *wantonness* and *prodigality*. Their luxury was at the expense of the defrauded poor (vs. 4). **on the earth**—The same earth which has been the scene of your wantonness, shall be the scene of the judgment coming on you: instead of earthly delights ye shall have punishments. **nourished . . . hearts**—i.e., glutted your bodies like beasts to the full extent of your hearts' desire; ye live to eat, not eat to live. **as in a day of slaughter**—The oldest authorities omit "as." Ye are like beasts which eat to their hearts' content *on* the very day of their approaching slaughter, unconscious it is near. The phrase answers to "the last days," vs. 3, which favors ALFORD's translation there, "in," not "for." **6. Ye have condemned . . . the just**—The *Greek* aorist expresses, "Ye are *accustomed* to condemn . . . the just." Their condemnation of Christ, "the Just," is foremost in James' mind. But all the innocent blood shed, and to be shed, is included, the Holy Spirit comprehending James himself, called "the Just," who was slain in a tumult. This gives a peculiar appropriateness to the expression in this verse, the same "as the righteous (*just*) man" (vs. 16). The justice or righteousness of Jesus and His people is what peculiarly provoked the ungodly great men of

ADAM CLARKE

CHAPTER 5

1. *Go to now.* See on chap. iv. 13. *Weep and howl for your miseries.* James seems to refer here, in the spirit of prophecy, to the destruction that was coming upon the Jews, not only in Judea, but in all the provinces where they sojourned.

2. *Your riches are corrupted.* Are "putrefied." The term *riches* is to be taken here, not for gold, silver, or precious stones (for these could not putrefy), but for the produce of the fields and flocks, the different stores of grain, wine, and oil, which they had laid up in their granaries, and the various changes of raiment which they had amassed in their wardrobes.

3. *Your gold and silver is cankered.* Instead of helping the poor, and thus honoring God with your substance, you have, through the principle of covetousness, kept all to yourselves. *The rust of them shall be a witness against you.* Your putrefied stores, your moth-eaten garments, and your tarnished coin are so many proofs that it was not for want of property that you assisted not the poor, but through a principle of avarice; loving money, not for the sake of what it could procure, but for its own sake, which is the genuine principle of the miser. This was the very character given to this people by our Lord himself; He called them "lovers of money." *Shall eat your flesh as it were fire.* This is a very bold and sublime figure. He represents the rust of their coin as becoming a canker that should produce gangrenes in their flesh, till it should be eaten away from their bones. By the *last days* we are not to understand the day of judgment, but the last days of the Jewish commonwealth, which were not long distant from the date of this Epistle.

4. *The hire of the labourers.* The law, Lev. xix. 13, had ordered: "The wages of him that is hired shall not abide with thee all night until the morning," every day's labor being paid for as soon as ended. This is more clearly stated in another law, Deut. xxiv. 15: "At his day thou shalt give him his hire, neither shall the sun go down upon it . . . lest he cry against thee unto the Lord, and it be sin unto thee." And that God particularly resented this defrauding of the hireling we see from Mal. iii. 5: "I will come near to you in judgment; and I will be a swift witness against . . . those who oppress the hireling in his wages." And on these laws and threatenings is built what we read in *Synopsis Sohar*, p. 100, n. 45: "When a poor man does any work in a house, the vapour proceeding from him, through the severity of his work, ascends toward heaven. Woe to his employer if he delay to pay him his wages." To this James seems particularly to allude when he says: *"The cries of them which have reaped are entered into the ears of the Lord of* hosts." *The Lord of sabaoth.* James often conceives in Hebrew though he writes in Greek. It is well-known that *Yehovah tsebaoth*, "Lord of hosts," or "Lord of armies," is a frequent appellation of God in the Old Testament; and signifies His uncontrollable power and the infinitely numerous means He has for governing the world, and defending His followers, and punishing the wicked.

5. *Ye have lived in pleasure.* "You have lived luxuriously"; feeding yourselves without fear, pampering the flesh. *And been wanton.* "You have lived lasciviously." You have indulged all your sinful and sensual appetites to the uttermost. *Ye have nourished your hearts.* "You have fattened your hearts," and have rendered them incapable of feeling, *as in a day of slaughter*, "a day of sacrifice," where many victims are offered at once and where the people feast upon the sacrifices: many no doubt turning, on that occasion, a holy ordinance into a riotous festival.

6. *Ye have condemned and killed the just; and he doth not resist you.* Several by "the just one" understand Jesus Christ, who is so called, Acts iii. 14; vii. 52; xxii. 14. But the structure of the sentence and the connection in which it stands seem to require that we should consider this as applying to the just or righteous in general, who were persecuted and murdered by those oppressive rich men; and their death was the consequence of their drag-

MATTHEW HENRY

II. An address to saints. From what has been said concerning wicked and oppressing rich men, occasion is given to administer comfort to God's afflicted people.

1. Attend to your duty. (1) "*Be patient* though God should not appear for you immediately. Wait for him." When we have done our work, we have need of patience to stay for our reward. This Christian patience is not a mere yielding to necessity, as the moral patience taught by some philosophers was, but it is a humble acquiescence in the wisdom and will of God. *Be patient to the coming of the Lord.* And because this is a lesson Christians must learn, though ever so hard or difficult to them, it is repeated in *v.* 8.

(2) "*Establish your hearts*—let your faith be firm, your practice of what is good constant and continued, and your resolutions for God and heaven fixed, in spite of all sufferings or temptations." (3) *Grudge not one against another; Groan* not one against another. Do not make yourselves uneasy and make one another uneasy by groaning to and grieving one another. Those who are in the midst of common enemies, and in any suffering circumstances, should be more especially careful not to groan against one another, otherwise judgments will come upon them as well as others.

2. Consider what encouragement here is for Christians to be patient. "Look to the example of the husbandman. When you sow your corn in the ground, you wait many months for the former and latter rain, and are willing to stay till harvest for the fruit of your labour. Consider him that waits for a crop of corn; and will not you wait for a crown of glory? If you should be called to wait a little longer than the husbandman does, is it not something proportionably greater and infinitely more worth your waiting for? Think how short your waiting time may possibly be (*v.* 8–9). Do not be impatient, do not quarrel with one another; the great Judge is at hand: as near as one who is just knocking at the door." *Grudge not, lest you be condemned.* Fretfulness and discontent expose us to the just judgment of God, and we bring more calamities upon ourselves by our groans and grudgings against one another, than we are aware of. We are encouraged to be patient by the example of the prophets (*v.* 10). When we think that the best men have had the hardest usage in this world, we should hereby be reconciled to affliction. Those who were the greatest examples of suffering affliction were also the best and greatest examples of patience. *We count those happy who endure* (*v.* 11).

Job also is proposed as an example, *v.* 11. Under all he could bless God and what came to him in the end?

God accomplished those things for him which plainly prove that *the Lord is very pitiful, and of tender mercy.* The tender mercy of God is such that he will make his people an abundant amends for all their sufferings and afflictions. Let us serve our God, and endure our trials, as those who believe the end will crown all.

JAMIESON, FAUSSET, BROWN

the world. **he doth not resist you**—The very patience of the Just one is abused by the wicked as an incentive to boldness in violent persecution, as if they may do as they please with impunity. God doth "resist the proud" (ch. 4:6); but Jesus as man, "as a sheep is dumb before the shearers, so He opened not His mouth": so His people are meek under persecution. The day will come when God will resist (lit., "set Himself in array against") His foes and theirs. **7. Be patient therefore**—as judgment is so near (vss. 1, 3), ye may well afford to be "patient" after the example of the *unresisting Just one* (vs. 6). **brethren**—contrasted with the "rich" oppressors, vss. 1-6. **unto the coming of the Lord**—Christ, when the trial of your patience shall cease. **husbandman waiteth for**—i.e., patiently bears toils and delays through hope of the harvest at last. Its "preciousness" (cf. Ps. 126:6, "precious seed") will more than compensate for all the past. Cf. the same image, Galatians 6:3, 9. **hath long patience for it**—"over it," *in respect to* it. **until he receive**—"until *it* receive" [ALFORD]. Even if *English Version* be retained, the receiving of the early and latter rains is not to be understood as the object of his hope, but *the harvest* for which those rains are the necessary preliminary. The early rain fell at sowing time, about November or December; the latter rain, about March or April, to mature the grain for harvest. The latter rain that shall precede the coming spiritual harvest, will probably be another Pentecost-like effusion of the Holy Ghost. **8. coming . . . draweth nigh**—The *Greek* expresses present time and a settled state. I Peter 4:7, "is at hand." We are to live in a continued state of expectancy of the Lord's coming, as an event *always* nigh. Nothing can more "stablish the heart" amidst present troubles than the realized expectation of His speedy coming. **9. Grudge not**—rather "Murmur not"; "grumble not." The *Greek* is lit., "groan": a half-suppressed murmer of impatience and harsh judgment, not uttered aloud or freely. Having exhorted them to patience in bearing wrongs from the wicked, he now exhorts them to a forbearing spirit as to the offenses given by brethren. Christians, who bear the former patiently, sometimes are impatient at the latter, though much less grievous. **lest . . . condemned**—The best MS. authorities read, "judged." James refers to Matthew 7:1, "Judge not lest ye be *judged.*" To "murmur against one another" is virtually to *judge,* and so to become liable to be *judged.* **judge . . . before the door**—referring to Matthew 24:33. The *Greek* is the same in both passages, and so ought to be translated here as there, "doors," plural. The phrase means "near at hand" (Gen. 4:7, which in the oldest interpretations [the Targums of Jonathan and Jerusalem] is explained, "thy sin is reserved *unto the judgment of the world to come.*" Cf. "the everlasting doors" (Ps. 24:7, whence He shall come forth). The Lord's coming to destroy Jerusalem is primarily referred to; and ultimately, His coming again visibly to judgment. **10. the prophets**—who were especially persecuted, and therefore were especially "blessed." **example of suffering affliction**—rather, simply, "of affliction," lit., "evil treatment." **11. count them happy**—(Matt. 5:10). **which endure**—The oldest authorities read, "which have endured," which suits the sense better than *English Version:* "Those who in past days, like the prophets and Job, have endured trials." Such, not those who "have lived in pleasure and been wanton on the earth" (vs. 5), are "happy." **patience**—rather, "endurance," answering to "endure": the *Greek* words similarly corresponding. Distinct from the *Greek* word for "patience," vs. 10. The same word ought to be translated, "endurance," ch. 1:3. He here reverts to the subject which he began with. **Job**—This passage shows the history of him is concerning a real, not an imaginary person; otherwise his case could not be quoted as an example at all. Though he showed much of impatience, yet he always returned to this, that he committed himself wholly to God, and at last showed a perfect spirit of enduring submission. **and have seen**—(with the eyes of your mind). ALFORD translates from the old and genuine reading, "see also . . . ." The old reading is, however, capable of being translated as *English Version.* **the end of the Lord**—the end which the Lord gave. If Job had much to "endure," remember also Job's happy "end." Hence, learn, though much tried, to "endure to the end." **that**—ALFORD and others translate, "inasmuch as," "for." **pitiful . . . of tender mercy**—The former refers to the *feeling;* the latter, to the *act.* His *pity* is shown in not laying on the *patient endurer* more trials than he is able to bear; His *mercy,* in

ADAM CLARKE

ging them before the judgment seats, chap. ii. 6, where, having no influence, and none to plead their cause, they were unjustly condemned and executed. *And he doth not resist you.* In the word *he doth not resist* the idea is included of defense in a court of justice. These poor righteous people had none to plead their cause; and if they had it would have been useless, as their oppressors had all power and all influence, and those who sat on these judgment seats were lost to all sense of justice and right. Some think that *he doth not resist you* should be referred to God; as if he had said, God permits you to go on in this way at present, but He will shortly awake to judgment, and destroy you as enemies of truth and righteousness.

7. *Be patient therefore.* Because God is coming to execute judgment on this wicked people, therefore be patient till He comes. He seems here to refer to the coming of the Lord to execute judgment on the Jewish nation, which shortly afterwards took place. *The husbandman waiteth.* The seed of your deliverance is already sown, and by and by the harvest of your salvation will take place. God's counsels will ripen in due time. *The early and latter rain.* The rain of seedtime and the rain of ripening before harvest. The first fell in Judea about the beginning of November, after the seed was sown; and the second, toward the end of April, when the ears were filling, and this prepared for a full harvest. Without these two rains the earth would have been unfruitful. These God had promised: "I will give you the rain of your land in his due season, the first rain and the latter rain, that thou mayest gather in thy corn, and thy wine, and thine oil," Deut. xi. 14.

8. *Be ye also patient.* Wait for God's deliverance, as you wait for His bounty in providence. *Stablish your hearts.* Take courage; do not sink under your trials. *The coming of the Lord draweth nigh.* "Is at hand." He is already on His way to destroy this wicked people, to raze their city and Temple, and to destroy their polity forever; and this judgment will soon take place.

9. *Grudge not.* "Groan not"; grumble not; do not murmur through impatience; and let not any ill treatment which you receive induce you to vent your feelings in imprecations against your oppressors. Leave all this in the hands of God. *Lest ye be condemned.* By giving way to a spirit of this kind you will get under the condemnation of the wicked. *The judge standeth before the door.* His eye is upon everything that is wrong in you and every wrong that is done to you, and He is now entering into judgment with your oppressors.

10. *Take . . . the prophets.* The prophets who had spoken to their forefathers by the authority of God were persecuted by the very people to whom they delivered the divine message; but they suffered affliction and persecution with patience, commending their cause to Him who judgeth righteously; therefore, imitate their example.

11. *We count them happy which endure.* According to that saying of our blessed Lord, "Blessed are ye, when men shall revile you, and persecute you . . . for so persecuted they the prophets which were before you," Matt. v. 11, etc. *Ye have heard of the patience of Job.* Stripped of all his worldly possessions, deprived at a stroke of all his children, tortured in body with sore disease, tempted by the devil, harassed by his wife, and calumniated by his friends, he nevertheless held fast his integrity, resigned himself to the divine dispensations, and charged not God foolishly. *And have seen the end of the Lord.* The issue to which God brought all his afflictions and trials, giving him children, increasing his property, lengthening out his life, and multiplying to him every kind of spiritual and secular good. This was God's end with respect to him; but the devil's end was to drive him to despair, and to cause him to blaspheme his Maker. This mention of Job shows him to have been a real person, for a fictitious person would not have been produced as an example of any virtue so highly important as that of patience and perseverance. *The end of the Lord* is a Hebraism for the "issue" to which God brings any thing or business. *The Lord is very pitiful,*

MATTHEW HENRY

Verses 12–20

I. The sin of swearing is cautioned against, *v.* 12. Some have translated the words, *before all things*; they should not, in common conversation, *before everything they say*, put an oath. All customary needless swearing is all along in scripture condemned, as a very grievous sin. Profane swearing was very customary among the Jews. Some of the looser sort of those who were called Christians might be guilty also of this.

1. *Above all things, swear not;* but how many are there who mind this the least of all things, and who make light of nothing so much as common profane swearing! It strikes most directly at the honour of God and most expressly throws contempt upon his name and authority. This sin has, of all sins, the least temptation to it. It is with most difficulty left off when once men are accustomed to it, therefore it should above all things he watched against. *"Above all things swear not."* But "all this is so far from forbidding necessary oaths that it is but to conform them, by preserving the due reverence of them." The Jews thought if they did but omit the great oath they were safe. But they grew so profane as to swear by the creature, as if it were God. On the other hand, those who swear commonly and profanely by the name of God do hereby put him upon the level with every common thing.

2. *But let your yea be yea, and your nay nay; lest you fall into condemnation.* Be sure to stand to your word, and be true to it, so as to give no occasion for your being suspected of falsehood. It is being suspected of falsehood that leads men to swearing.

II. As Christians we are taught to suit ourselves to the dispensations of Providence (*v.* 13). Our condition in this world is various; and our wisdom is to submit to its being so, and to behave as becomes us both in prosperity and under affliction. Afflictions should put us upon prayer, and prosperity should make us abound in praise. 1. In a day of affliction nothing is more seasonable than prayer. Times of affliction should be praying times. God sends afflictions, that we may be engaged to seek him early; and that those who at other times have neglected him may be brought to enquire after him. Afflictions naturally draw out complaints; and to whom should we complain but to God in prayer? It is necessary to exercise faith and hope under afflictions; and prayer is the appointed means both for obtaining and increasing these graces in us. 2. In a day of mirth and prosperity singing psalms is very proper and seasonable. This we are sure of, that the singing of psalms is a gospel ordinance, and that our joy should be holy joy, consecrated to God. Holy mirth becomes families and retirements, as well as public assemblies.

III. We have particular directions given as to sick persons, *v.* 14, 15. It lies upon sick people as a duty to send for ministers, and to desire their assistance and their prayers. It is the duty of ministers to pray over the sick, when thus desired and called for. The *sick were to be anointed with oil in the name of the Lord.* When miracles ceased, this institution ceased also. Some have thought that it should not be wholly laid aside in any age, but that where there are extraordinary measures of faith in the person anointing, and in those who are anointed, an extraordinary blessing may attend the observance of this direction for the sick. There is one thing carefully to be observed here, that the saving of the sick is not ascribed to the *anointing with oil*, but to prayer, *v.* 15. Prayer over the sick must proceed from, and be accompanied with, a lively faith. There must be faith both in the person praying and in the person prayed for. *And, if he have committed sins, they shall be forgiven him.* The great thing therefore we should beg of God for ourselves and others in the time of sickness is the pardon of sin. Sin is both the root of sickness and the sting of it. If sin be pardoned, either affliction shall be removed in mercy or we shall see there is mercy in the continuance of it.

IV. Christians are directed to *confess their faults one to another*, *v.* 16. The confession here required is that of Christians to one another. Where persons have injured one another. Where persons have tempted one another to sin, or have consented in the same evil actions. So far as confession is necessary to our reconciliation with such as are at variance with us, or for reparation of wrongs done to any, making our own spirits quiet and easy, so far we should be ready to confess our faults. And sometimes also it may be of good use to Christians to disclose their peculiar weaknesses and infirmities to one another. Those who make confession of their faults one to another should thereupon pray with and for one another.

JAMIESON, FAUSSET, BROWN

His giving a happy "end" to the trials [BENGEL]. **12. But above all**—as swearing is utterly alien to the Christian meek "endurance" just recommended. **swear not**—through impatience, to which trials may tempt you (vss. 10, 11). In contrast to this stands the proper use of the tongue, vs. 13. James here refers to Matthew 5:34, etc. **let your yea be yea**—Do not use oaths in your everyday conversation, but let a simple affirmative or denial be deemed enough to establish your word. **condemnation**—lit., "judgment," viz., of "the Judge" who "standeth before the doors" (vs. 9). **13. afflicted**—referring to the "suffering affliction" (vs. 10). **let him pray**—not "swear" in rash impatience. **merry**—joyous in mind. **sing psalms**—of praise. Paul and Silas sang psalms even in affliction. **14. let him call for the elders**—not some *one* of the elders, as Roman Catholics interpret it, to justify their usage in *extreme unction*. The prayers of the elders over the sick would be much the same as though the whole Church which they represent should pray [BENGEL]. **anointing him with oil**—The usage which Christ committed to His apostles was afterwards continued with laying on of hands, as a token of the highest faculty of medicine in the Church, just as we find in I Corinthians 6:2 the Church's highest judicial function. Now that the miraculous gift of healing has been withdrawn for the most part, to use the sign where the reality is wanting would be unmeaning superstition. Cf. other apostolic usages now discontinued rightly, I Corinthians 11:4-15; 16:20. "Let them use oil who can by their prayers obtain recovery for the sick: let those who cannot do this, abstain from using the empty sign" [WHITAKER]. Romish extreme unction is administered to those *whose life is despaired of*, to heal the *soul,* whereas James' unction was to heal the body. CARDINAL CAJETAN (*Commentary*) admits that James cannot refer to extreme unction. Oil in the East, and especially among the Jews (see the Talmud, *Jerusalem* and *Babylon*), was much used as a curative agent. It was also a sign of the divine grace. Hence it was an appropriate sign in performing miraculous cures. **in the name of the Lord**—by whom alone the miracle was performed: men were but the instruments. **15. prayer**—He does not say *the oil* shall save: it is but the symbol. **save**—plainly not as Rome says, "save" *the soul*, but *heal* "the sick": as the words, "the Lord shall raise him up," prove. So the same *Greek* is translated, "made (thee) whole," Matthew 9:21, 22. **and if . . . sins**—for not all who are sick are so because of some special sins. Here a case is supposed of one visited with sickness for special sins. **have committed**—lit., "*be* in a state of *having committed* sins, i.e., be under the consequences of sins committed. **they**—rather, "it": *his having committed sins* shall be forgiven him. The connection of sin and sickness is implied in Isaiah 33:24; Matthew 9:2-5; John 5:14. The absolution of the sick, retained in the Church of England, refers to the sins which the sick man confesses (vs. 16) and repents of, whereby outward scandal has been given to the Church and the cause of religion; not to sins in their relation to God, the only Judge. **16.** The oldest authorities read, "Confess, THEREFORE . . . ." Not only in the particular case of sickness, but universally confess. **faults**—your *falls* and *offenses,* in relation to one another. The word is not the same as *sins*. Matthew 5:23, 24; Luke 17:4, illustrate the precept here. **one to another**—not to the priest, as Rome insists. The Church of England *recommends* in certain cases. Rome *compels* confession in all cases. Confession is desirable in the case of (1) *wrong* done to a neighbor; (2) when under a troubled conscience we ask *counsel* of a godly minister or friend as to how we may obtain God's forgiveness and strength to sin no more, or when we desire their intercessory prayers for us ("Pray for one another"): "Confession may be made to anyone who can pray" [BENGEL]; (3) *open* confession of sin before the Church and the world, in token of penitence. Not *auricular* confession. **that ye may be healed**—of your bodily sicknesses. Also that, if your sickness be the punishment of sin, the latter being forgiven on intercessory prayer, "ye may be healed" of the former. Also, that ye may be healed spiritually. **effectual**—intense and fervent, not "wavering" (ch. 1:6), [BEZA]. "When *energized*" by the Spirit, as those were who performed miracles [HAMMOND]. This suits the collocation of the Greek words and the sense well. A righteous man's prayer is always heard generally, but his particular request for the *healing* of another was then likely to be granted when he was one *possessing a special charism of the Spirit.* ALFORD translates, "Availeth much *in its working*." The

ADAM CLARKE

and of tender mercy. Very pitiful might be rendered "of much sympathy."

12. *Above all things . . . swear not.* What relation this exhortation can have to the subject in question, I confess I cannot see. It may not have been designed to stand in any connection, but to be a separate piece of advice, as in the several cases which immediately follow. That the Jews were notoriously guilty of common swearing is allowed on all hands; and that swearing by heaven, earth, Jerusalem, the Temple, the altar, different parts of the body, was not considered by them as binding oaths has been sufficiently proved. Rabbi Akiba taught that "a man might swear with his lips, and annul it in his heart; and then the oath was not binding." See the notes on Matt. v. 33. *Let your yea be yea.* Do not pretend to say *yea* with your lips, and annul it in your heart; let the *yea* or the *nay* which you express be bona fide such. Do not imagine that any mental reservation can cancel any such expressions of obligation in the sight of God. *Lest ye fall into condemnation.* "Lest you fall under judgment."

13. *Is any among you afflicted? let him pray.* The Jews taught that the meaning of the ordinance, Lev. xiii. 45, which required the leper to cry, "Unclean! unclean!" was "that thus making known his calamity, the people might be led to offer up prayers to God in his behalf." They taught also that when any sickness or affliction entered a family they should go to the wise men and implore their prayers.

14. *Is any sick among you? let him call for the elders.* This was also a Jewish maxim. Rabbi Simeon, in *Sepher Hachaiyim*, said: "What should a man do who goes to visit the sick? *Ans.* He who studies to restore the health of the body should first lay the foundation in the health of the soul. The wise men have said, No healing is equal to that which comes from the word of God and prayer. Rabbi Phineas, the son of Chamma, hath said, 'When sickness or disease enters into a man's family, let him apply to a wise man, who will implore mercy in his behalf.'"

15. *And the prayer of faith shall save the sick.* That is, God will often make these the means of a sick man's recovery; but there often are cases where faith and prayer are both ineffectual, because God sees it will be prejudicial to the patient's salvation to be restored; and therefore all faith and prayer on such occasions should be exerted on this ground: "If it be most for Thy glory, and the eternal good of this man's soul, let him be restored; if otherwise, Lord, pardon, purify him, and take him to Thy glory." *And if he have committed sins.* So as to have occasioned his present malady, *they shall be forgiven him;* for being the cause of the affliction, it is natural to conclude that, if the effect be to cease, the cause must be removed. We find that in the miraculous restoration to health under the powerful hand of Christ, the sin of the party is generally said to be forgiven, and this also before the miracle was wrought on the body. Hence there was a maxim among the Jews, and it seems to be founded in common sense and reason, that God never restores a man miraculously to health till He has pardoned his sins; because it would be incongruous for God to exert His miraculous power in saving a body the soul of which was in a state of condemnation to eternal death because of the crimes it had committed against its Maker and Judge.

16. *Confess your faults one to another.* This is a good general direction to Christians who endeavor to maintain among themselves the communion of saints. This social confession tends much to humble the soul and to make it watchful. *The effectual fervent prayer.* The words signify "energetic supplication," or such a prayer as is suggested to the soul and wrought in it by a divine energy. When God designs to do some particular work in His Church, He pours out on His followers the spirit of grace and supplication; and this He does sometimes when He is about to do some especial work for an individual. When such a power of prayer is granted, faith should be immediately called into exercise, that the blessing may be given; the spirit of prayer is the proof that the power of God is present to heal. Long prayers give no particular evidence of divine inspiration. The

MATTHEW HENRY

V. The great advantage and efficacy of prayer are declared and proved, *v.* 17, 18. He who prays must be a righteous man. The prayer itself must be a fervent, in-wrought, well-wrought prayer. Such prayer avails much. It is of great advantage to ourselves, it may be very beneficial to our friends, and we are assured of its being acceptable to God. Elijah was *a man of like passions with us.* He was a zealous good man and a very great man, but he had his infirmities. In prayer we must not look to the merit of man, but to the grace of God. He prayed earnestly, or, as it is in the original, *in prayer he prayed.* It is not enough to say a prayer, but we must pray in prayer. Elijah *prayed that it might not rain*; and God heard him, so that *it rained not on the earth for the space of three years and six months. Again he prayed, and the heaven gave rain,* &c. This is recorded for encouragement even to ordinary Christians to be instant and earnest in prayer. Where there may not be so much of miracle in God's answering our prayers, yet there may be as much of grace.

VI. The epistle concludes with an exhortation to do all we can to promote the conversion and salvation of others, *v.* 19, 20. "If any err, and one convert him, let him be who he will that does so good an office for another, he is therein an instrument of saving a soul from death." Be they ever so great, you must not be afraid to show them their error; and, be they ever so weak and little, you must not disdain to make them wiser and better. If they err from the truth, whether it be in opinion or practice, you must endeavour to bring them again to the rule. Errors in judgment and in life generally go together. If we are instrumental in the conversion of any, *we* are said to convert them, though this be the work of God. And, if we can do no more towards the conversion of sinners, yet we may do this—pray for the grace and Spirit of God to convert and change them. He that is said to *err from the truth* in *v.* 19 is described as *erring in his way* in *v.* 20 and we cannot be said to convert any merely by altering their opinions, unless we can bring them to correct and amend their ways. This is conversion. He who thus converteth a sinner from the error of his ways *shall save a soul from death.* By such conversion of heart and life, a *multitude of sins shall be hid.* Though our sins are many, even a multitude, yet they may be hid or pardoned. Let people contrive to cover their sin as they will, there is no way effectually to hide it but by forsaking it. Some make the sense of this text to be, that conversion shall *prevent* a multitude of sins; and it is a truth beyond dispute that many sins are prevented in the party converted, many also may be prevented in others that he may have an influence upon.

JAMIESON, FAUSSET, BROWN

"righteous" is one himself careful to avoid "faults," and showing his faith by works (ch. 2:24). **17. Elias . . . like passions as we**—therefore it cannot be said that he was so raised above us as to afford no example applicable to common mortals like ourselves. **prayed earnestly**—lit., "prayed with prayer": Hebraism for *prayed intensely*. Cf. Luke 22:15, "With desire I have desired," i.e., earnestly desired. ALFORD is wrong in saying, Elias' prayer that it might not rain "is not even hinted at in the Old Testament history." In I Kings 17:1 it is plainly implied, "As the Lord God of Israel liveth, *before whom I stand,* there shall not be dew nor rain these years, but *according to my word.*" His prophecy of the fact was according to a divine intimation given to him in answer to prayer. In jealousy for God's honor (I Kings 19:10), and being of one mind with God in his abhorrence of apostasy, he prayed that the national idolatry should be punished with a national judgment, drought; and on Israel's profession of repentance he prayed for the removal of the visitation, as is implied in I Kings 18:39-42: cf. Luke 4:25. **three years . . .**—Cf. I Kings 18:1, "The third year," viz., from Elijah's going to Zarephath; the prophecy (vs. 1) was probably about five or six months previously. **18. prayed . . . and**—i.e., "and so." Mark the connection between the prayer and its accomplishment. **her fruit**—her usual and due fruit, heretofore withheld on account of sin. Three and a half years is the time also that the two witnesses prophesy who "have power to shut and open heaven that it rain not." **19.** The blessing of reclaiming an erring sinner by the mutual consent and intercessory prayer just recommended. **do err**—more lit., "be led astray." **the truth**—the Gospel doctrine and precepts. **one**—lit., "any"; as "*any*" before. *Everyone* ought to seek the salvation of *everyone* [BENGEL]. **20. Let him**—the converted—**know**—for his comfort, and the encouragement of others to do likewise. **shall save**—future. The salvation of the one so converted shall be manifested hereafter. **shall hide a multitude of sins**—not his own, but the sins of the converted. The *Greek* verb in the middle voice requires this. Proverbs 10:12 refers to charity "covering" the sins of others *before men;* James to one's effecting by the conversion of another that that other's sins be covered *before God,* viz., with Christ's atonement. He effects this by making the convert partaker in the Christian covenant for the remission of all sins. Though this hiding of sins was included in the previous "shall save," James expresses it to mark in detail the greatness of the blessing conferred on the penitent through the converter's instrumentality, and to incite others to the same good deed.

ADAM CLARKE

following was a maxim among the ancient Jews, "The prayers of the righteous are short." This is exemplified in almost every instance in the Old Testament.

17. *Elias was a man subject to like passions.* This was Elijah, and a consistency between the names of the same persons as expressed in the Old and the New Testaments should be kept up. The word *homoiopathes* signifies of "the same constitution," a human being just as ourselves are. *And he prayed earnestly.* "He prayed with prayer"; a Hebraism for "He prayed fervently." *That it might not rain.* See this history, 1 Kings xvii. 1 ff. *And it rained not on the earth.* "On that land," viz., the land of Judea; for this drought did not extend elsewhere. *Three years and six months.* This is the term mentioned by our Lord, Luke iv. 25; but this is not specified in the original history. In 1 Kings xviii. 1 it is said, "In the third year" "the word of the Lord came to Elijah," that is, concerning the rain; but this third year is to be computed from the time of his going to live at Zarephath, which happened many days after the drought began, as is plain from this, that he remained at the brook Cherith till it was dried up, and then went to Zarephath, in the country of Zidon; 1 Kings xvii. 7-9. Therefore the *three years and six months* must be computed from his announcing the drought, at which time that judgment commenced.

18. *And he prayed again.* This second prayer is not mentioned in the history in express words. But as in 1 Kings xviii. 42, it is said, "He cast himself down upon the earth, and put his face between his knees," that was probably the time of the second praying, namely, that rain might come, as this was the proper posture of prayer.

19. *Err from the truth*—stray away from the gospel of Christ; *and one convert him*—reclaim him from his error and bring him back to the fold of Christ.

20. *Let him know.* Let him duly consider, for his encouragement, that he who is the instrument of converting a sinner shall save a soul from eternal death, and a body from ruin, *and shall hide a multitude of sins;* for in being the means of his conversion we bring him back to God, who, in His infinite mercy, hides or blots out the numerous sins which he had committed during the time of his backsliding. It is not the man's sins who is the means of his conversion, but the sins of the backslider, which are here said to be hidden.

THE FIRST EPISTLE OF PETER

I. Introduction (1:1, 2)
A. The apostle and his elect readers (1:1)
B. Explanation of "elect" (1:2)

II. Established for testing in confidence (1:3-2:3)
A. The life of faith (1:3-5)
1. The beginning—"begat us again" (1:3)
2. The issue—"An inheritance" (1:4)
3. The assurance—"... are guarded" (1:5)

B. The proving of faith (1:6-12)
1. The value of proof (1:6, 7)
2. The principle of believing (1:8, 9)
3. The testimony of the past (1:10-12)

C. The practice of faith (1:13-2:3)
1. Personal (1:13-21)
2. Relative (1:22-2:3)

III. Established for testing in conduct (2:4-3:9)
A. The life of holiness (2:4-10)
1. Composition—Living Stone and living stones (2:4-6)
2. Quality—the preciousness of the Living Stone (2:7, 8)
3. Vocation—exhibiting the excellencies (2:9, 10)

B. The practice of holiness (2:11-3:9)
1. General instructions—personal (2:11, 12)
2. National relationships (2:13-17)
3. Household relationships (2:18-25)
4. Home relationships (3:1-7)
5. General instructions—corporate (3:8, 9)

IV. Established for testing in character (3:10-5:7)
A. The life of victory (3:10-22)
1. Principle: "If ye should suffer" (3:10-17)
2. Pattern: "Christ also suffered" (3:18-22)

B. The process of victory (4:1-5:7)
1. The equipment: "arm yourselves with the same mind" (4:1-11)
2. The principle: "partakers of Christ's sufferings" (4:12-19)
3. Responsibilities (5:1-7)

V. Established for testing in conflict (5:8-11)
A. The life of conflict (5:8, 9a)
1. The adversary (5:8)
2. The attitude (5:8, 9a)

B. The fellowship of conflict—"the God of all grace" (5:9b)
C. The strength of conflict (5:10, 11)

VI. Conclusion (5:12-14)

Two epistles we have enrolled in the sacred canon of the Scripture written by Peter. When our Savior called his apostles and gave them their commission, he nominated Peter first in the list; and by his behavior toward Peter, he seems to have distinguished him as a special favorite among the twelve. Many instances of our Lord's affection to him, both during his life and after his resurrection, are upon record. Peter himself modestly styles himself an "apostle of Jesus Christ"; and, when he writes to the presbyters of the church, he humbly places himself in the same rank with them: "The elders who are among you I exhort, who am also an elder" (5:1).

The design of this first epistle is (1) to explain more fully the doctrines of Christianity to these newly converted Jews; (2) to direct and persuade them to a holy conversation; (3) to prepare them for sufferings. This seems to be his principal intention, for he has something to this purport in every chapter.

MATTHEW HENRY

CHAPTER 1

Verses 1, 2

I. The author of it, described, 1. By his name—*Peter*. Jesus Christ gave him the surname of *Peter*, which signifies *a rock*, as a commendation of his faith. 2. By his office—*an apostle of Jesus Christ*. It signifies the highest office in the Christian church. Peter, (1) Asserts his own character as an apostle. To pretend to what we have not is hypocrisy; and to deny what we have is ingratitude. (2) He mentions his apostolical function as his warrant and call to write this epistle to these people.

II. The persons to whom this epistle was addressed are described,

1. By their external condition—*Strangers dispersed throughout Pontus, Galatia,* &c. At present their circumstances were poor and afflicted. The best of God's servants may, through the hardships of times, be dispersed about, and forced to leave their native countries. The value of good people ought not to be estimated by their present external condition.

JAMIESON, FAUSSET, BROWN

CHAPTER 1

VSS. 1-25. ADDRESS TO THE ELECTED OF THE GODHEAD: THANKSGIVING FOR THE LIVING HOPE TO WHICH WE ARE BEGOTTEN, PRODUCING JOY AMIDST SUFFERINGS: THIS SALVATION AN OBJECT OF DEEPEST INTEREST TO PROPHETS AND TO ANGELS: ITS COSTLY PRICE A MOTIVE TO HOLINESS AND LOVE, AS WE ARE BORN AGAIN OF THE EVER-ABIDING WORD OF GOD. **1. Peter**—*Greek* form of Cephas, *man of rock.* **an apostle of Jesus Christ**—"He who preaches otherwise than as a messenger of Christ, is not to be heard; if he preach as such, then it is all one as if thou didst hear Christ speaking in thy presence" [LUTHER]. **to the strangers scattered**—lit., "sojourners *of the dispersion*"; only in John 7:35 and James 1:1, in New Testament, and LXX, Psalm 147:2, "the outcasts of Israel"; the designation peculiarly given to *the Jews* in their dispersed state throughout the world ever since the Babylonian captivity. These he, as the apostle of the circumcision, primarily addresses, but not in the limited temporal sense only; he regards their temporal condition as a shadow of their spiritual calling to be *strangers* and pilgrims on earth, looking for the heavenly Jerusalem as their home. So the *Gentile* Christians, as the spiritual Israel, are included secondarily, as having the same high calling. He (ch. 1:14; 2:10; 4:3) plainly refers to Christian *Gentiles* (cf. vs. 17; ch. 2:11). Christians, if they rightly consider their calling, must never settle themselves here, but feel themselves *travellers.* The *order* of the provinces is that in which they would be viewed by one writing from the east from *Babylon* (ch. 5:13); from northeast southwards to Galatia, southeast to Cappadocia, then Asia, and back to Bithynia, west of Pontus. Contrast the order, Acts 2:9. He now was ministering to those same peoples as he preached to on Pentecost: "Parthians, Medes, Elamites, dwellers in Mesopotamia and Judea," i.e., the Jews now subject to the Parthians, whose capital was *Babylon,* where he labored in person; "dwellers in Cappadocia, Pontus, Asia, Phrygia, Bithynia," the Asiatic dispersion derived from Babylon, whom he ministers to by letter. **2.**

ADAM CLARKE

CHAPTER 1

1. *Peter, an apostle.* Simon Peter, called also Cephas. He was a fisherman, son of Jonah, brother of Andrew, and born at Bethsaida; and one of the first disciples of our Lord. *The strangers scattered throughout.* Jews first, who had believed the gospel in the different countries here specified; and converted Gentiles also. Though the word *strangers* may refer to all truly religious people, yet the inscription may have a special reference to those who were driven by persecution to seek refuge in those heathen provinces to which the influence of their persecuting brethren did not extend.

Pontus. An ancient kingdom of Asia Minor, originally a part of Cappadocia. *Galatia.* The ancient name of a province of Asia Minor. *Cappadocia.* An ancient kingdom of Asia, comprehending all the country lying between Mount Taurus and the Euxine Sea. *Asia.* That province of Asia Minor of which Ephesus was the capital. It appears that it is in this sense that it is used here by Peter, because Pontus, Galatia, and Bithynia, are comprised in the provinces of Asia Minor. *Bithynia.* An ancient kingdom of Asia, formerly called Mysia.

MATTHEW HENRY

2. They are described by their spiritual condition. (1) *Elect according to the foreknowledge of God the Father.* Election is either to an office, or it is to the enjoyment of special privileges, or it is to eternal salvation. This is the election here spoken of. [1] This election is said to be *according to the foreknowledge of God.* Foreknowledge may be taken in two ways: *First,* For mere prescience, foresight, or understanding, that such a thing will be, before it comes to pass. Thus a mathematician certainly foreknows that at such a time there will be an eclipse. But such a prescience is not the cause why anything is so or so. *Secondly,* Foreknowledge sometimes signifies counsel, appointment, and approbation. The death of Christ was not only foreseen, but foreordained, as *v.* 20. Take it thus here; so the sense is, *elect according to the counsel, ordination, and free grace of God.* [2] It is added, according to the foreknowledge of *God the Father.* In the affair of man's redemption, election is ascribed to the Father, as reconciliation is to the Son and sanctification to the Holy Ghost.

(2) They were elect *through sanctification of the Spirit, unto obedience, and sprinkling of the blood of Jesus Christ.* Every elect person must be sanctified by the Spirit, and justified by the blood of Jesus. By sanctification here understand living to God in all the duties of a Christian life, which is here summed up in one word, *obedience.* By *the Spirit* is meant the Holy Ghost, the author of sanctification. *Unto obedience.* This word denotes the end of sanctification, which is, to bring rebellious sinners to obedience again, *You have purified your souls in obeying the truth through the Spirit, v.* 22.

(3) They were elected also to the *sprinkling of the blood of Jesus.* Here is a manifest allusion to the typical sprinklings of blood under the law. The blood of Christ, the grand and all-sufficient sacrifice, was not only shed, but must be sprinkled and communicated to every one of these elect Christians. All that are chosen to eternal life as the end are chosen to obedience as the way. Unless a person be sanctified by the Spirit, and sprinkled with the blood of Jesus, there will be no true obedience in the life.

III. The salutation follows. The blessings desired for them are *grace and peace. Grace*—the free favour of God, with all its proper effects. *Peace.* All sorts of peace may be here intended: peace with God, with the feeling of it in our own consciences. The request or prayer, in relation to these blessings—that they may be multiplied. He wishes them the continuation, the increase, and the perfection of them. The best blessings we can desire for ourselves, or one for another, are grace and peace, with the multiplication of them. Peace cannot be enjoyed where there is no true grace; first grace, then peace. Peace without grace is mere stupidity; but grace may be true where there is for a time no actual peace. Christ was once in an agony. The increase of grace and peace, as well as the first gift of them, is from God.

Verses 3–5

I. A thanksgiving to God.

1. The duty performed, which is blessing God.

2. The object of this blessing described by his relation to Jesus Christ: *The God and Father of our Lord Jesus Christ.* Here are three names of one person, denoting his threefold office. He is *Lord,* a universal king. *Jesus,* a priest or Saviour. *Christ,* a prophet.

3. The reasons that oblige us to this duty of blessing God, which are comprised in *his abundant mercy.* He *hath begotten us again,* and this deserves our thanksgiving to God, especially if we consider the fruit it produces in us, which is that excellent grace of hope, a lively hope, a living, durable hope, as that hope must needs be that has such a solid foundation as *the resurrection of Jesus Christ from the dead.* A good Christian's condition is never so bad but he has great reason still to bless God. In our prayers and praises we should address God as *the Father of our Lord Jesus Christ*; it is only through him that we and our services are accepted. The best of men owe their best blessings to the abundant mercy of God. All the evil in the world is from man's sin, but all the good in it is from *God's mercy.* We subsist entirely upon divine mercy. Regeneration produces a lively hope of eternal life. Those who are begotten to a new and spiritual life are begotten to a new and spiritual hope. The hope of a Christian has this excellency, it is a living hope. The hope of eternal life in a true Christian is a hope that keeps him alive, quickens him, supports him, and conducts him to heaven. The delusive hopes of the unregenerate are vain and perishing; the hypocrite and his hope expire and die both together. *The resurrection of Jesus Christ from the dead* is the ground or foundation of a Christ-

JAMIESON, FAUSSET, BROWN

foreknowledge—*foreordaining* love (vs. 20), inseparable from God's *foreknowledge,* the origin *from* which, and pattern *according to* which, election takes place. Acts 2:23, and Romans 11:2, prove "foreknowledge" to be *foreordination.* God's *foreknowledge* is not the perception of any ground of action out of Himself; still in it liberty is comprehended, and all absolute constraint debarred [ANSELM *in* STEIGER]. For so the Son of God was "foreknown" (so the *Greek* for "foreordained," vs. 20) to be the sacrificial Lamb, not against, or without His will, but His will rested in the will of the Father; this includes self-conscious action; nay, even cheerful acquiescense. The *Hebrew* and *Greek* "know" include *approval* and *acknowledging* as one's own. The *Hebrew* marks the oneness of *loving* and *choosing,* by having one word for both, *bachar* (LXX, *Greek, hairetizo*). Peter descends from the eternal "election" of God through the *new birth,* to the believer's "sanctification," that from this he might again raise them through the consideration of their *new birth* to a "living hope" of the heavenly "inheritance" [HEIDEGGER]. The divine three are introduced in their respective functions in redemption. **through**—*Greek,* "in"; the element in which we are elected. The "election" of God realized and manifested itself "IN" their sanctification. Believers are "sanctified through the offering of Christ once for all" (Heb. 10:10). "Thou must believe and know that thou art holy; not, however, through thine own piety, but through the blood of Christ" [LUTHER]. This is the true sanctification of the Spirit, to obey the Gospel, to trust in Christ [BULLINGER]. **sanctification**—the Spirit's setting apart of the saint as consecrated to God. The execution of God's *choice* (Gal. 1:4). God the Father gives us salvation by gratuitous election; the Son earns it by His blood-shedding; the Holy Spirit applies the merit of the Son to the soul by the Gospel word [CALVIN]. Cf. Numbers 6:24-26, the Old Testament triple blessing. **unto obedience**—the result or *end aimed at* by God as respects us, the *obedience* which consists in faith, and that which flows from faith; "obeying the truth through the Spirit" (vs. 22). Romans 1:5, "obedience to the faith," and obedience the fruit of faith. **sprinkling . . .**—not in justification through the atonement once for all, which is expressed in the previous clauses, but (as the order proves) *the daily being sprinkled by Christ's blood, and so cleansed from all sin,* which is the privilege of one already justified and "walking in the light." **Grace**—the source of "peace." **be multiplied**—still further than already. Daniel 4:1, "Ye have now peace and grace, but still not in perfection; therefore, ye must go on increasing until the old Adam be dead" [LUTHER]. **3.** He begins, like Paul, in opening his Epistles with giving thanks to God for the greatness of the salvation; herein he looks forward (1) into the future (vss. 3-9); (2) backward into the past (vss. 10-12) [ALFORD]. **Blessed**—A distinct *Greek* word (*eulogetos,* "Blessed BE") is used of God, from that used of man (*eulogemenos,* "Blessed IS"). **Father**—This whole Epistle accords with the Lord's prayer; "Father," ch. 1:3, 14, 17, 23; 2:2; "Our," ch. 1:4, end; "In heaven," ch. 1:4; "Hallowed be Thy name," ch. 1:15, 16; 3:15; "Thy kingdom come," ch. 2:9; "Thy will be done," ch. 2:15; 3:17; 4:2, 19; "daily bread," ch. 5:7; "forgiveness of sins," ch. 4:8, 1; "temptation," ch. 4:12; "deliverance," ch. 4:18 [BENGEL]; cf. ch. 3:7 and 4:7, for allusions to *prayer. Barak, Hebrew* "bless," is lit. "kneel." God, as the original source of blessing, must be blessed through all His works. **abundant**—*Greek,* "much," "full." That God's "mercy" should reach *us,* guilty and enemies, proves its fulness. "Mercy" met our *misery;* "grace," our *guilt.* **begotten us again**—of the *Spirit* by the *word* (vs. 23); whereas we were children of wrath naturally, and *dead* in sins. **unto**—so that we have. **lively**—*Greek,* "living." It has life in itself, gives life, and looks for life as its object [DE WETTE]. *Living* is a favorite expression of Peter (vs. 23; ch. 2:4, 5). He delights in contemplating *life* overcoming death in the believer. *Faith* and *love* follow *hope* (vss. 8, 21, 22). "(Unto) a lively hope" is further explained by "(To) an inheritance incorruptible . . . fadeth not away," and "(unto) salvation . . . ready to be revealed in the last time." I prefer with BENGEL and STEIGER to join as in *Greek,* "Unto a hope *living* (possessing life and vitality) *through* the resurrection of Jesus Christ." Faith, the subjective means of the spiritual resurrection of the soul, is wrought by the same power whereby Christ was raised from the dead. Baptism is an objective means (ch. 3:21). Its moral fruit is a new life. The connection of our sonship with the resurrection

ADAM CLARKE

2. *Elect according to the foreknowledge of God.* If the apostle had directed his letter to persons elected to eternal life, no one, as Drs. Lardner and Macknight properly argue, could have received such a letter, because no one could have been sure of his election in this way till he had arrived in heaven. But the persons to whom the apostle wrote were all, with propriety, said to be *elect according to the foreknowledge of God;* because, agreeably to the original purpose of God, discovered in the prophetical writings, Jews and Gentiles, indiscriminately, were called to be the visible Church, and entitled to all the privileges of the people of God, on their believing the gospel.

Through sanctification of the Spirit—through the renewing and purifying influences of His Spirit on their souls, *unto obedience*—to engage and enable them to yield themselves up to all holy obedience, the foundation of all which is the *sprinkling of the blood of Jesus Christ*—the atoning blood of Jesus Christ which was typified by the sprinkling of the blood of sacrifices under the law, in allusion to which it is called the "blood of sprinkling."

3. *Blessed be the God and Father.* "Blessed be God even the Father" or "Blessed be God, the Father of our Lord Jesus Christ." *Begotten us again unto a lively hope.* I think the apostle has a reference here to his own case, and that of his fellow apostles, at the time that Christ was taken by the Jews and put to death. Previously to this time they had strong confidence that He was the Messiah, and that it was He who should redeem Israel; but when they found that He actually expired upon the Cross, and was buried, they appear to have lost all hope of the great things which before they had in prospect. This is feelingly expressed by the two disciples whom our Lord, after His resurrection, overtook on the road going to Emmaus; see Luke xxiv. 13-24. And the hope that with them died with their Master, and seemed to be buried in His grave, was restored by the certainty of His resurrection. The expressions, however, may include more particulars than what are above specified; as none can inherit eternal life except those who are children in the heavenly family, and none are children but those who are born again, then Peter may be considered as laying here the foundation of the hope of eternal life in the regeneration of the soul.

MATTHEW HENRY

ian's hope. There being an inseparable union between Christ and his flock, they rise by virtue of his resurrection as a head.

II. The apostle goes on to describe that life under the notion of *an inheritance.* He tells them they were new-born to a new inheritance, infinitely better than what they had lost. They are put in mind of a noble inheritance reserved in heaven for them.

1. Heaven is the undoubted inheritance of all the children of God. God giveth his gifts unto all, but the inheritance to none but his children. This inheritance is not our purchase, but our Father's gift; not wages that we merit, but the effect of grace.

2. The incomparable excellencies of this inheritance. It is incorruptible, in which respect it is like its Maker. All corruption is a change from better to worse, but heaven is without change and without end; the house is eternal in the heavens. This inheritance is undefiled. Sin and misery have no place there. It fadeth not away, but always retains its vigour and beauty.

"*Reserved in heaven for you.*" It is certain, a reversion in another world, safely kept and preserved till we come to the possession of it. The persons for whom it is reserved are described by their character: everyone that is *begotten again to a lively hope.*

III. The apostle supposes some doubt or uneasiness whether they might not possibly fall short by the way. He answers that they should be kept and preserved from all such destructive temptations as would prevent their safe arrival at eternal life. The heirs of heaven shall certainly be conducted safely to the possession of it. The blessing here promised is preservation: You *are kept*; the author of it is *God*; the means in us made use of for that end are our own *faith* and care; the end to which we are preserved is *salvation*; and the time when we shall see the safe end and issue of all is *the last time.* Their being kept implies both danger and deliverance; they may be attacked, but shall not be overcome. The preservation of the regenerate to eternal life is the effect of God's power. Preservation by God's power does not supersede man's endeavour and care for his own salvation. Faith is a sovereign preservative of the soul through a state of grace unto a state of glory. This salvation is *ready to be revealed in the last time.* It is now prepared and reserved in heaven for them. Though it be made ready now, yet it is in a great measure hidden and unrevealed at present, even to the heirs of salvation themselves. It shall be fully and completely *revealed in the last time. Life and immortality are now brought to light by the gospel,* but this life will be revealed more gloriously at death, when the soul shall be admitted into the presence of Christ, and behold his glory.

Verses 6-9

The first word, *wherein,* refers to the apostle's foregoing discourse about the excellency of their present state, and their grand expectations for the future, *v.* 6.

I. Several things in mitigation of their sorrows. Every sound Christian has always something wherein he may greatly rejoice. The chief joy of a good Christian arises from things spiritual and heavenly. His joy arises from his treasure, which consists of matters of great value, and the title to them is sure. The best Christians may yet be in great heaviness through manifold temptations. All sorts of adversities are temptations, or trials. These seldom go singly, but are manifold, and come from different quarters, the effect of all which is great heaviness. The afflictions and sorrows of good people are but for a season. The shortness of any affliction does much abate the heaviness of it. Great heaviness is often necessary to a Christian's good: *If need be, you are in heaviness.* God does not afflict his people willingly, but acts with judgment, in proportion to our needs. These troubles, that lie heavy, never come upon us but when we have need, and never stay any longer than needs must.

II. He expresses the end of their afflictions and the ground of their joy under them, *v.* 7. The afflictions of serious Christians are designed for the trial of their faith. God's design in afflicting his people is their probation, not their destruction. This trial is made upon faith principally, because the trial of this

JAMIESON, FAUSSET, BROWN

appears also in Luke 20:36; Acts 13:33. **4. To an inheritance**—the object of our "hope" (vs. 3), which is therefore not a *dead,* but a "*living*" hope. The inheritance is the believer's already by title, being actually assigned to him; the entrance on its possession is future, and hoped for as a certainty. Being "begotten again" as a "son," he is an "heir," as earthly fathers *beget* children who shall *inherit* their goods. The *inheritance* is "salvation" (vss. 5, 9); "the grace to be brought at the revelation of Christ" (vs. 13); "a crown of glory that fadeth not away." **incorruptible**—not having within the germs of death. Negations of the imperfections which meet us on every side here are the chief means of conveying to our minds a conception of the heavenly things which "have not entered into the heart of man," and which we have not faculties now capable of fully knowing. **undefiled**—not stained as earthly goods by sin, either in the acquiring, or in the using of them; unsusceptible of any stain. **that fadeth not away**—Contrast vs. 24. Even the most delicate part of the heavenly inheritance, its bloom, continues *unfading.* "In *substance* incorruptible; in *purity* undefiled; in *beauty* unfading" [ALFORD]. **reserved**—*kept up* (Col. 1:5, "*laid up* for you in heaven," II Tim. 4:8); *Greek* perfect, expressing a *fixed and abiding state,* "which has been and is reserved." **in heaven**—*Greek,* "in the heavens," where it can neither be destroyed nor plundered. It does not follow that, because it is *now* laid up in *heaven,* it shall not *hereafter* be on *earth* also. **for you**—It is secure not only in itself from all misfortune, but also from all alienation, so that no other can receive it in your stead. He had said US (vs. 3; he now turns his address to the elect in order to encourage and exhort them. **5. kept**—*Greek,* "who are being guarded." He answers the objection, Of what use is it that salvation is "reserved" for us in heaven, as in a calm secure haven, when we are tossed in the world as on a troubled sea in the midst of a thousand wrecks? [CALVIN]. As the inheritance is "kept" (vs. 4) safely for the far distant "heirs," so must they be "guarded" in their persons so as to be sure of reaching it. Neither shall it be wanting to them, nor they to it. "We are *guarded in the world* as our inheritance is *kept in heaven.*" This defines the "you" of vs. 4. **by**—*Greek,* "in." The believer lives spiritually *in* God, and in virtue of His power, and God lives in him. "In" marks that the cause is inherent in the means, working organically through them with living influence, so that the means, in so far as the cause works organically through them, exist also in the cause. The power of God which guards the believer is no external force working upon him from without with mechanical necessity, but the spiritual power of God in which he lives, and with whose Spirit he is clothed. **unto salvation**—the final end of the new birth. "Salvation," not merely accomplished for us in title by Christ, and made over to us on our believing, but *actually manifested, and finally completed.* **ready to be revealed**—When Christ shall be revealed, it shall be revealed. The preparations for it are being made now, and began when Christ came: "All things are now *ready";* the salvation is already accomplished, and only waits the Lord's time to be manifested: He "is ready to judge." **last time**—the last day, closing the day of grace; the day of judgment, of redemption, of the restitution of all things, and of perdition of the ungodly. **6. Wherein**—in which prospect of final salvation. **greatly rejoice**—"exult with joy": "are exuberantly glad." *Salvation* is realized by faith (vs. 9) as a thing so actually present as to cause exulting joy in spite of existing afflictions. **for a season**—*Greek,* "for a little time." **if need be**—"if it be God's will that it should be so" [ALFORD], for not all believers are afflicted. One need not invite or lay a cross on himself, but only "take up" the cross which God imposes ("his cross"). **ye are in heaviness**—*Greek,* "ye were grieved." The "grieved" is regarded as *past,* the "exculting joy" present. Because the realized joy of the coming salvation makes the *present grief* seem as a thing of the *past.* At the first shock of affliction ye *were grieved,* but now *by anticipation ye rejoice,* regarding the present grief as past. **through**—*Greek,* "IN": the element in which the grief has place. **manifold**—many and of various kinds (ch. 4:12, 13). **temptations**—"trials" testing your faith. **7.** Aim of the "temptations." **trial**—testing, proving. That your *faith so proved* "may be found (aorist; *once for all,* as the result of its being proved on the judgment-day) unto (eventuating in) praise . . ." viz., the praise to be bestowed by the Judge. **than that of gold**—rather "than gold."

ADAM CLARKE

4. *To an inheritance.* Called an *inheritance* because it belongs to the children of God.

Incorruptible. It has no principles of dissolution or decay in it. *Undefiled.* Nothing impure can enter it. *Fadeth not away.* "It cannot wither"; it is always in bloom—a metaphor taken from those flowers that never lose their hue nor their fragrance. *Reserved in heaven.* Such a place as that described above is not to be expected on earth.

5. *Who are kept.* Who are "defended as in a fortress or castle." There is a remarkable correspondence between the two verbs used in this sentence. The verb *tereo* signifies to "keep, watch, guard"; and *phroureo* signifies to "keep as under a military guard." The true disciples of Christ are under the continual watchful care of God, and the inheritance is "guarded" for them.

By the power of God. By the mighty and miracle-working power of God. But this *power of God* is interested in the behalf of the soul by *faith.* To believe is our work; the exertion of the almighty power is of God.

Ready to be revealed. Or rather, "prepared to be revealed." The inheritance is prepared for you; but its glories will not be revealed till the *last time*—till you have done with life and passed through your probation, having held fast faith and a good conscience. Some by *salvation* understand the deliverance of the Christians from the sackage of Jerusalem, the end of the Jewish polity being called the *last time;* others suppose it to refer to the day of judgment, and the glorification of the body and soul in heaven.

6. *Wherein ye greatly rejoice.* Some refer *wherein* to the "salvation" mentioned above; others, to the "last time" in v. 5; others think that it applies to the being kept by the power of God through faith; and others, that it refers to all the preceding advantages and privileges. It was in the present salvation of God that they rejoiced or gloried, though not without having an eye to the great recompense of reward. *Though now for a season.* "A little while yet"—during your pilgrimage here below, which is but a point when compared with eternity. *If need be.* "If it be necessary"—if your situation and circumstances be such that you are exposed to trials and persecutions which you cannot avoid, unless God were to work a miracle for your deliverance, which would not be for your ultimate good, as He purposes to turn all your trials and difficulties to your advantage. Those to whom Peter wrote rejoiced greatly, "danced for joy," while they were "grieved" with "various trials."

7. *That the trial of your faith, being much more precious than of gold.* As by the action of fire gold is separated from all alloy and heterogeneous mixtures, and is proved to be gold by its enduring the action of the fire without losing anything of its nature, weight,

MATTHEW HENRY

is, in effect, the trial of all that is good in us. Christ prays for this apostle, *that his faith might not fail;* if that be supported, all the rest will stand firm. A tried faith is much more precious than tried gold. Here is a double comparison of faith and gold. Gold is the most valuable and durable of all the metals; so is faith among the Christian virtues; it lasts till it brings the soul to heaven. The trial of faith is much more precious than the trial of gold. Gold does not increase and multiply by trial in the fire, it rather grows less; but *faith* is established and multiplied by the afflictions that it meets with. *Gold* must perish at last—*gold that perisheth;* but *faith* never will. The trial of faith will be found to praise, and honour and glory. If a tried faith be found to praise, honour, and glory, let this recommend faith to you, as much more precious than gold, though it be assaulted and tried by afflictions. Jesus Christ will appear again in glory. The trial will soon be over, but the glory, honour, and praise will last to eternity.

III. He particularly commends the faith of these primitive Christians.

1. The excellency of its object, the unseen Jesus, *v.* 8. It is one thing to believe God, or Christ (so the devils believe), and another thing to believe in him.

2. Two notable productions or effects of their faith, *love* and *joy*, and this joy so great as to be above description.

(1) Sense converses with things sensible and present; reason is a higher guide, but faith ascends further still. It is *the evidence of things not seen.*

(2) True faith is never alone, but produces a strong love to Jesus Christ. True Christians have a sincere love to Jesus, because they believe in him.

(3) Where there are true faith and love to Christ there is *joy unspeakable and full of glory.* It cannot be described by words; the best discovery is by an experimental taste of it; it is *full of glory*, full of heaven. There is much of heaven and the future glory in the present joys of improved Christians; their faith removes the causes of sorrow, and affords the best reasons for joy. Well might these primitive Christians rejoice with joy unspeakable, since they were every day *receiving the end of their faith, the salvation of their souls, v.* 4. The blessing they were receiving: *The salvation of their souls*, which salvation is here called *the end of their faith*, the end wherein faith terminates. The salvation of the soul was the prize these Christians sought for, the end they aimed at, which came nearer and more within their reach every day. Every faithful Christian is daily receiving the salvation of his soul. These believers had the beginnings of heaven in the possession of holiness and a heavenly mind. They were on the losing side in the world, but the apostle puts them in mind of what they were receiving; if they lost an inferior good, they were all the while receiving the salvation of their souls. The glory of God and our own felicity are so connected that if we regularly seek the one we must attain the other.

Verses 10–12

The apostle goes on to show them what warrant he had for what he had delivered. He produces the authority of the prophets to convince them that the doctrine of salvation by faith in Jesus Christ was no new doctrine.

I. Who made this diligent search—*the prophets*, who were persons inspired by God.

II. The object of their search, which was *salvation*, and *the grace of God which should come unto you.* They foresaw glorious times of light, grace, and comfort, which made the prophets and righteous men desire to see and hear the things which came to pass in the days of the gospel.

III. The manner of their enquiry: they *enquired and searched diligently.* The words are strong and emphatic, alluding to miners, who dig to the bottom, and break through not only the earth, but the rock, to come to the ore; so these holy prophets had an earnest desire to know, and were proportionably diligent in their enquiries. Their being inspired did not make their industrious search needless. The doctrine of man's salvation by Jesus Christ has been the study and admiration of the greatest and wisest of men. Those who would be acquainted with this great salvation, and the grace that shines therein, must enquire and search diligently into it.

IV. The particular matters which the ancient prophets chiefly searched into, *v.* 11. Jesus Christ was the main subject of their studies.

1. His humiliation and death, and the glorious consequences of it. This enquiry would lead them into a view of the whole gospel.

2. Undoubtedly these holy prophets earnestly desired to see the days of the Son of man; and therefore their minds were set upon the time of its accom-

JAMIESON, FAUSSET, BROWN

though—"which perisheth, YET is tried with fire." If gold, though perishing (vs. 18), is yet tried with fire in order to remove dross and test its genuineness, how much more does your faith, which shall never perish, need to pass through a fiery trial to remove whatever is defective, and to test its genuineness and full value? **glory**—"Honor" is not so strong as "glory." As "praise" is in *words, so* "honor" is in deeds: *honorary reward.* **appearing**—*Translate* as in vs. 13, "revelation." At Christ's revelation shall take place also the revelation of the sons of God (Rom. 8:19, "manifestation," *Greek*, "revelation"; I John 3:2, *Greek*, "manifested . . . manifested," for "appear . . . appear"). **8. not having seen, ye love**—though in other cases it is *knowledge* of the person that produces *love* to him. They are more "blessed that have not seen and yet have believed," than they who believed because they have seen. On Peter's own love to Jesus, cf. John 21:15-17. Though the apostles had seen Him, they now ceased to know Him merely after the flesh. **in whom**—connected with "believing": the result of which is "ye rejoice" (*Greek*, "exult"). **now**—*in the present state*, as contrasted with the *future* state when believers "shall see His face." **unspeakable**—(I Cor. 2:9.) **full of glory**—*Greek*, "glorified." A joy now already *encompassed with glory.* The "glory" is partly in present possession, through the presence of Christ, "the Lord of glory," in the soul; partly in assured anticipation. "The Christian's *joy* is bound up with *love* to Jesus: its ground is *faith;* it is not therefore either self-seeking or self-sufficient" [STEIGER]. **9. Receiving**—in sure anticipation; "the end of your faith," i.e., its crowning consummation, finally completed "salvation" (Peter here confirms Paul's teaching as to *justification by faith*): also receiving *now* the title to it and the first fruits of it. In the next verse (vs. 10) the "salvation" is represented as *already present*, whereas "the prophets" had it not as yet present. It must, therefore, in this verse, refer to the present: *Deliverance now from a state of wrath:* believers even now "receive salvation," though its full "revelation" is future. **of . . . souls**—The immortal *soul* was what was lost, so "salvation" primarily concerns the soul; the *body* shall share in redemption hereafter; the *soul* of the believer is saved already: an additional proof that "receiving . . . salvation" is here a thing present. **10.** The magnitude of this "salvation" is proved by the earnestness with which "prophets" and even "angels" searched into it. Even from the beginning of the world this salvation has been testified to by the Holy Spirit. **prophets**—Though there is no *Greek* article, yet *English Version* is right, "*the* prophets" generally (including all the Old Testament *inspired* authors), as "*the* angels" similarly refer to them in general. **inquired**—perseveringly: so the *Greek*. Much more is manifested to us than by diligent inquiry and search the prophets attained. Still it is not said, they searched *after* it, but "*concerning*" (so the *Greek* for "of") it. They were already certain of the redemption being about to come. They did not like us fully *see*, but they *desired* to see the one and the same Christ whom we fully see in spirit. "As Simeon was anxiously desiring previously, and tranquil in peace only when he had seen Christ, so all the Old Testament saints saw Christ only hidden, and as it were absent—absent not in power and grace, but inasmuch as He was not yet manifested in the flesh" [CALVIN]. The prophets, as *private individuals*, had to reflect on the hidden and far-reaching sense of their own prophecies; because their words, *as prophets, in their public function*, were not so much their own as the Spirit's, speaking by and in them: thus Caiaphas. A striking testimony to verbal inspiration; the *words* which the inspired authors wrote are God's words expressing the mind of the Spirit, which the writers themselves searched into, to fathom the deep and precious meaning, even as the believing readers did. "Searched" implies that they had determinate marks to go by in their search. **the grace that should come unto you**—viz., the grace of the New Testament: an earnest of **"the grace" of** perfected "salvation" "to be brought at the (second) revelation of Christ." Old Testament believers also possessed the grace of God; they were children of God, but it was as children in their nonage, so as to be like servants; whereas we enjoy the full privileges of adult sons. **11. what**—*Greek*, "*In reference to* what, or what manner of time." *What* expresses the *time* absolutely: what was to be the era of Messiah's coming; "*what manner of time*"; what events and features should characterize the time of His coming. The "or" implies that some of the prophets, if they could not as individuals

ADAM CLARKE

color, or any other property, so genuine faith is proved by adversities, especially such as the primitive Christians were obliged to pass through.

8. *Whom having not seen, ye love.* Those to whom the apostle wrote had never seen Christ in the flesh; and yet, such is the realizing nature of faith, they loved Him as strongly as any of His disciples could to whom He was personally known.

Ye rejoice with joy unspeakable. You have unutterable happiness through believing; and you have the fullest, clearest, strongest evidence of eternal glory.

9. *Receiving the end of your faith.* You are put in possession of the salvation of your souls, which was the thing presented to your faith when you were called by the gospel of Christ. The word *end* is often used so as to imply the "issue" or "reward" of any labor or action. *Salvation of your souls.* The object of the Jewish expectations in their Messiah was the salvation or deliverance of their bodies from a foreign yoke; but the true Messiah came to save the soul from the yoke of the devil and sin. This glorious salvation these believers had already received.

10. *Of which salvation the prophets have enquired.* The incarnation and suffering of Jesus Christ and the redemption procured by Him for mankind were made known, in a general way, by the prophets; but they themselves did not know the time when these things were to take place, nor the people among and by whom He was to suffer. They therefore "inquired accurately or earnestly," and *searched diligently.*

11. *The glory that should follow.* Not only the glory of His resurrection, ascension, exaltation, and the effusion of His Spirit; but that grand manifestation of God's infinite love to the world in causing the gospel of His Son to be everywhere preached, and the glorious moral

MATTHEW HENRY

plishment, so far as the Spirit of Christ, which was in them, had signified anything towards that purpose. The nature of the times was also under their strict consideration. From the example of Christ Jesus learn to expect a time of services and sufferings before you are received to glory. It was so with him, and *the disciple is not above his Lord.*

V. The success with which their enquiries were crowned. God gave them a satisfactory revelation to quiet and comfort their minds. They were informed that these things should not come to pass in their time: *Not unto themselves, but to us;* and we must report them, under the infallible direction of the Holy Ghost, to all the world. *Which things the angels,* &c.

You have here three sorts of enquirers: 1. *The prophets,* who *searched diligently* into it. 2. The apostles, who consulted all the prophecies, and were witnesses of the accomplishment of them, and so reported what they knew to others in the preaching of the gospel. 3. The angels, who most attentively pry into these matters. A diligent endeavour after the knowledge of Christ will certainly be answered with good success. The holiest and best of men sometimes have their lawful and pious requests denied. God is pleased to answer our necessities rather than our requests. It is the practice of a Christian to be useful to others rather than to himself. The prophets ministered to others, not unto themselves. The revelations of God to his church are all perfectly consistent; the doctrine of the prophets and that of the apostles exactly agree, as coming from the same Spirit of God. The gospel is the ministration of the Spirit; the success of it depends upon his operation and blessing. The mysteries of the gospel are so glorious that the blessed angels earnestly desire to look into them.

Verses 13–23

I. He exhorts them to sobriety and holiness.

1. *Wherefore gird up the loins of your mind,* &c., *v.* 13. Let the loins or strength and vigour of your minds be exerted in your duty; disengage yourselves from all that would hinder you, and go on resolutely in your obedience.

Be sober, be vigilant against all your spiritual dangers and enemies, and be temperate and modest in the whole of your behaviour. Be sober-minded also in opinion, as well as in practice. The main work of a Christian lies in the right management of his heart and mind. The best Christians have need to be exhorted to sobriety. A Christian's work is not over as soon as he has got into a state of grace; he must still hope and strive for more grace. We must hope perfectly, and yet gird up our loins, and address ourselves vigorously to the work we have to do, encouraging ourselves from the grace of Jesus Christ.

2. *As obedient children,* &c., *v.* 14. An argument to press them to holiness from the consideration of what they now are, children of obedience, and what they were when they lived in lust and ignorance.

JAMIESON, FAUSSET, BROWN

discover the exact *time,* searched into its characteristic features and events. The *Greek* for "time" is *the season,* the epoch, the fit time in God's purposes. **Spirit of Christ . . . in them**—(Acts 16:7, in oldest MSS., "the Spirit of Jesus"; Rev. 19:10.) So JUSTIN MARTYR says, "Jesus was He who appeared and communed with Moses, Abraham, and the other patriarchs." CLEMENS ALEXANDRINUS calls Him "the Prophet of prophets, and Lord of all the prophetical spirit." **did signify**—"did give intimation." **of**—*Greek,* "the sufferers (appointed) *unto* Christ," or *foretold in regard to Christ.* "Christ" *the anointed* Mediator whose *sufferings* are the price of our "salvation" (vss. 9, 10), and who is the channel of "the grace that should come unto you." **the glory**—*Greek,* "glories," viz., of His resurrection, of His ascension, of His judgment and coming kingdom, the necessary consequence of the sufferings. **that should follow**—*Greek,* "after these (sufferings)," ch. 3:18-22; 5: 1. **12.** Not only was the future revealed to them, but this also, that these revelations of the future were given them not for themselves, but for our good in Gospel times. This, so far from disheartening, only quickened them in unselfishly testifying in the Spirit for the partial good of their own generation (only of believers), and for the full benefit of posterity. **us**—The oldest MSS. read "you," as in vs. 10. This verse implies that *we,* Christians, may understand the prophecies by the Spirit's aid in their most important part, viz., so far as they have been already fulfilled. **with the Holy Ghost sent down**—on Pentecost. The oldest MSS. omit *Greek* preposition *en,* i.e., "in"; then translate, "by." The Evangelists speaking by the Holy Spirit were infallible witnesses. "The Spirit of Christ" was in the prophets also (vs. 11), but not manifestly, as in the case of the Christian Church and its first preachers, "SENT down from heaven." **things**—"the things now reported unto you" by the evangelistic preachers "Christ's sufferings and the glory that should follow" (vss. 11, 12). **angels**—still higher than "the prophets" (vs. 10). Angels do not any more than ourselves possess an INTUITIVE knowledge of redemption. "To look into" in *Greek* is lit., "to bend over so as to look deeply into and see to the bottom of a thing." See *Note* on same word, James 1:25. As the cherubim stood bending over the mercy seat, the emblem of redemption, in the holiest place, so the angels intently gaze upon and desire to fathom the depths of "the great mystery of godliness, God manifest in the flesh, justified in the Spirit, *seen of angels."* Their "ministry to the heirs of salvation" naturally disposes them to wish to penetrate this mystery as reflecting such glory on the love, justice, wisdom, and power of their and our God and Lord. They can know it only through its manifestation in the Church, as they personally have not the direct share in it that we have. **13. Wherefore**—Seeing that the prophets ministered unto you in these high Gospel privileges which they did not themselves fully share in, though "searching" into them, and seeing that even angels "desire to look into" them, how earnest you ought to be and watchful in respect to them! **gird up . . . loins**—referring to Christ's own words, Luke 12:35; an image taken from the way in which the Israelites ate the passover with the loose outer robe girded up about the waist with a girdle, as ready for a journey. Workmen, pilgrims, runners, wrestlers, and warriors (all of whom are types of the Christians), so gird themselves up, both to shorten the garment so as not to impede motion, and to gird up the body itself so as to be braced for action. The believer is to have his mind (mental powers) collected and always ready for Christ's coming. "Gather in the strength of your spirit" [HENSLER]. *Sobriety,* i.e., spiritual *self-restraint,* lest one be overcome by the allurements of the world and of sense, and patient *hopeful* waiting for Christ's revelation, are the true ways of "girding up the loins of the mind." **to the end**—rather, "perfectly," so that there may be nothing deficient in your hope, no *casting away of your confidence.* **14.** From *sobriety of spirit* and *endurance of hope* he passes to *obedience, holiness,* and *reverential fear.* **As**—marking their present actual character as "born again" (vss. 3, 22). **obedient**—*Greek,* "children of obedience": children to whom *obedience* is their characteristic and ruling nature, as a child is of the same nature as the mother and father. Contrast Ephesians 5:6, "the children of disobedience." Cf. vs. 17, "obeying the Father" whose "children" ye are. Having the obedience of *faith* (cf. vs. 22) and so of *practice* (cf. vss. 16, 18). "Faith is the highest obedience,

ADAM CLARKE

changes which should take place in the world under that preaching, and the final glorification of all them who had here received the report and continued faithful unto death.

12. ***Unto whom it was revealed.*** **We may presume that in a great variety of cases the prophets did not understand the meaning of their own predictions. They had a general view of God's designs; but of particular circumstances connected with those great events they seem to have known nothing, God reserving the explanation of all particulars to the time of the issue of such prophecies. If all succeeding interpreters of the prophecies had been contented with the same information relative to the predictions still unaccomplished, we should have had fewer books and more wisdom.**

Angels desire to look into. **"To stoop down to"; the posture of those who are earnestly intent on finding out a thing, especially a writing difficult to be read. They bring it to the light, place it so that the rays may fall on it as collectively as possible, and then stoop down in order to examine all the parts, that they may be able to make out the whole. We learn from the above that it was "the Spirit of Christ" in the Jewish prophets that prophesied of Christ; it was that Spirit which revealed Him; and it is the same Spirit which takes of the things of Christ and shows them unto us.**

13. ***Gird up the loins of your mind.*** **The allusion here is to the long robes of the Asiatics, which, when they were about to perform any active service, they tucked in their girdles.**

Hope to the end for the grace. **Continue to expect all that God has promised, and particularly that utmost salvation, that glorification of body and soul, which you shall obtain at the revelation of Christ, when He shall come to judge the world.**

MATTHEW HENRY

The children of God ought to prove themselves to be such by their obedience to God. The best of God's children have had their times of lust and ignorance. Persons, when converted, differ exceedingly from what they were formerly.

3. *But as he who hath called you, &c., v.* 15, 16. It is required in strong terms, and enforced by three reasons, taken from the grace of God in calling us,—from his command, *it is written,*—and from his example.

Be you holy, for I am holy. It is a great favour to be called effectually by divine grace into the possession of all the blessings of the new covenant; and great favours are strong obligations; they enable as well as oblige to be holy. Complete holiness is the desire and duty of every Christian. It must, for the extent of it, be universal. We must *be holy,* and be so *in all manner of conversation,* towards all people, friends and enemies; in all our intercourse and business still we must be holy. For the pattern of it, we must *be holy, as God is holy*: we must imitate him, though we can never equal him. The consideration of the holiness of God should oblige us to the highest degree of holiness we can attain unto.

4. *If you call on the Father, &c., v.* 17. The whole time of our sojourning here is to be passed in the fear of God. Holy confidence in God as a Father, and an awful fear of him as a Judge, are very consistent.

The judgment of God will be without respect of persons: *According to every man's work.* God will not respect persons from personal considerations, but judge them according to their work.

5. He adds (*v.* 18) a second argument. Herein he puts them in mind, (1) That they were redeemed by a ransom paid to the Father. (2) What the price paid for their redemption was.

(3) From what they were redeemed. (They knew this, and cannot pretend ignorance.) The consideration of our redemption ought to be a constant and powerful inducement to holiness, and the fear of God. God expects that a Christian should live answerably to what he knows. Neither silver nor gold, nor any of the corruptible things of this world, can redeem so much as one soul. They are corruptible, and therefore cannot redeem an incorruptible and immortal soul.

JAMIESON, FAUSSET, BROWN

because discharged to the highest command" [LUTHER]. **fashioning**—The outward *fashion* (*Greek, schema*) is fleeting, and merely on the surface. The "form," or *conformation* in the New Testament, is something deeper and more perfect and essential. **the former lusts in**—which were characteristic of your state of ignorance of God: true of both Jews and Gentiles. The sanctification is first described negatively (vs. 14, "not fashioning yourselves . . ."; the putting off the old man, even in the outward *fashion,* as well as in the inward *conformation*), then positively (vs. 15, putting on the new man, cf. Eph. 4:22, 24). **15.** Lit., "But (rather) after the pattern of Him who hath called you (whose characteristic is that He is) holy, be (*Greek,* 'become') ye yourselves also holy." God is our grand model. God's *calling* is a frequently urged motive in Peter's Epistles. Every one that begets, begets an offspring resembling himself [EPIPHANIUS]. "Let the acts of the offspring indicate similarity to the Father" [AUGUSTINE]. **conversation**—deportment, course of life: one's way of going about, as distinguished from one's internal nature, to which it must outwardly correspond. Christians are already holy unto God by consecration; they must be so also in their *outward walk and behavior in all respects.* The outward must correspond to the inward man. **16.** *Scripture* is the true source of all authority in questions of doctrine and practice. **Be ye . . . for I am**—It is I with whom ye have to do. Ye are mine. Therefore abstain from Gentile pollutions. We are too prone to have respect unto men [CALVIN]. As I am the fountain of holiness, being holy in My *essence,* be ye therefore zealous to be *partakers* of holiness, that ye may be as I also am [DIDYMUS]. God is essentially holy: the creature is holy in so far as it is sanctified by God. God, in giving the command, is willing to give also the power to obey it, viz., through the sanctifying of the Spirit (vs. 2). **17. if**—i.e., "*seeing that* ye call on," for all the regenerate pray as *children* of God, "Our *Father* who art in heaven." **the Father**—rather, "Call upon *as Father* Him who without acceptance of persons (Acts 10:34; Rom. 2:11; Jas. 2:1, not accepting the Jew above the Gentile, II Chron. 19:7; Luke 20:21; properly said of a judge not biassed in judgment by respect of persons) judgeth . . . ." The Father judgeth by His Son, His Representative, exercising His delegated authority (John 5:22). This marks the harmonious and complete unity of the Trinity. **work**—Each man's *work* is *one* complete whole, whether good or bad. The particular works of each are manifestations of the general character of his lifework, whether it was of faith and love whereby alone we can please God and escape condemnation. **pass**—*Greek,* "conduct yourselves during." **sojourning**—The outward state of the Jews in their *dispersion* is an emblem of the *sojourner-like* state of all believers in this world, away from our true Fatherland. **fear**—reverential, not slavish. He who is your Father, is also your Judge—a thought which may well inspire reverential fear. **18.** Another motive to reverential, vigilant *fear* (vs. 17) of displeasing God, the consideration of the costly price of our redemption from sin. Observe, it is *we* who are bought by the blood of Christ, not heaven. The blood of Christ is not in Scripture said to buy heaven for us: heaven is the "inheritance" (vs. 4) given to us as sons, by the promise of God. **corruptible**—Cf. vs. 7, "gold that perisheth," 23. **silver and gold**—*Greek,* "or." Cf. Peter's own words, Acts 3:6: an undesigned coincidence. **redeemed**—Gold and silver being liable to corruption themselves, can free no one from spiritual and bodily death; they are therefore of too little value. Contrast vs. 19, Christ's "*precious* blood." The Israelites were ransomed with half a shekel each, which went towards purchasing the *lamb* for the daily sacrifice (Exod. 30:12-16; cf. Num. 3:44-51). But the Lamb who redeems the spiritual Israelites does so "without money or price." Devoted by sin to the justice of God, the Church of the first-born is redeemed from sin and the curse with Christ's precious blood (Matt. 20:28; I Tim. 2:6; Titus 2:14; Rev. 5:9). In all these passages there is the idea of *substitution,* the giving of one for another by way of a ransom or equivalent. **vain**—self-deceiving, unreal, and unprofitable: promising good which it does not perform. Cf. as to the Gentiles, Acts 14:15; Romans 1:21; Ephesians 4:17; as to human philosophers, I Corinthians 3:20; as to the disobedient Jews, Jeremiah 4:14. **conversation**—course of life. To know what our sin is we must know what it cost. **received by tradition from your fathers**—The Jews' traditions.

ADAM CLARKE

14. ***Not fashioning yourselves.*** **As the offices of certain persons are known by the garb they wear, so are transgressors.**

15. ***But as he which hath called you.*** **Here Christianity has an infinite advantage over heathenism. God is holy, and He calls upon all who believe in Him to imitate His holiness; and the reason why they should be holy is that God, who has called them,** ***is holy,*** **v. 15.**

17. ***Who without respect of persons.*** **God is said to be "no respecter of persons" for this reason among many others, that, being infinitely righteous, He must be infinitely impartial. He cannot prefer one to another, because He has nothing to hope or fear from any of His creatures. God's judgment will be according to** ***every man's work,*** **and a man's work or "conduct" will be according to the moral state of his mind. No favoritism can prevail in the day of judgment; nothing will pass there but holiness of heart and life.**

18. ***Ye were not redeemed with corruptible things.*** **To "redeem" signifies to procure life for a captive or liberty for a slave by paying a price, and the precious blood of Christ is here stated to be the price at which the souls of both Jews and Gentiles were redeemed.**

Vain conversation. **Empty, foolish, and unprofitable conduct.**

MATTHEW HENRY

The blood of Jesus Christ is the only price of man's redemption. The design of Christ in shedding his most precious blood was to redeem us, not only from eternal misery hereafter, but from a vain conversation in this world. Not only the open wickedness, but the vanity and unprofitableness of our conversation are highly dangerous. A man's conversation may plead antiquity, custom, and tradition, in its defence, and yet after all be a most vain conversation. Antiquity is no certain rule of verity.

6. Some things relating both to the Redeemer and the redeemed, *v.* 20, 21.

(1) The Redeemer is further described as one, [1] That was *fore-ordained before the foundation of the world.* It imports an act of the will, a resolution that the thing shall be.

[2] That was *manifested in these last days for them.* He was manifested to be that Redeemer whom God had fore-ordained. "This was done in these last times of the New Testament and of the gospel. You have the comfort of the manifestation and appearance of Christ, if you believe on him."

[3] That was raised from the dead by the Father, who gave him glory, proclaimed him to all the world to be his Son by his resurrection from the dead, and glorified him with that glory which he had with God before the world was.

(2) The redeemed are also described here by their faith and hope, the cause of which is Jesus Christ: "*You do by him believe in God.*"

(3) The decree of God to send Christ to be a Mediator was from everlasting. God had purposes of special favour towards his people long before he made any manifestations of such grace to them. Great is the happiness of the last times in comparison with what the former ages of the world enjoyed. Our gratitude and services should be suitable to such favours.

II. He exhorts them to brotherly love.

1. He supposes that the gospel had already produced at least an *unfeigned love of the brethren, v.* 22. It is not to be doubted but that every sincere Christian purifies his soul. The apostle takes this for granted: *Seeing you have,* &c. The word of God is the great instrument of a sinner's purification. Many hear the truth, but are never purified by it, because they will not submit to it nor obey it. The Spirit of God is the great agent in the purification of man's soul. The Spirit excites our endeavours, and makes them successful. The aid of the Spirit does not supersede our own industry; these people purified their own souls, but it was through the Spirit. The souls of Christians must be purified before they can so much as love one another unfeignedly. There is no charity but out of a pure heart.

JAMIESON, FAUSSET, BROWN

19. precious—of inestimable value. The *Greek* order is, "With precious blood, as of a lamb without blemish (*in itself*) and without spot (*contracted by contact with others*), [even the blood] of Christ." Though very man, He remained pure *in Himself* ("without blemish"), and uninfected by any impression of sin *from without* ("without spot"), which would have unfitted Him for being our atoning Redeemer: so the passover lamb, and every sacrificial victim; so too, the Church, the Bride, by her union with Him. **20.** God's eternal foreordination of Christ's redeeming sacrifice, and completion of it *in these last times for us,* are an additional obligation on us to our maintaining a holy walk, considering how great things have been thus done for us. Peter's language in the history corresponds with this here: an undesigned coincidence and mark of genuineness. Redemption was no afterthought, or remedy of an unforeseen evil, devised at the time of its arising. God's *foreordaining* of the Redeemer refutes the slander that, on the Christian theory, there is a period of 4000 years of nothing but an incensed God. God *chose us in Christ before the foundation of the world.* **manifest**—in His incarnation in the fulness of the time. He existed from eternity before He was *manifested.* **in these last times**—I Corinthians 10:11, "the ends of the world." This last dispensation, made up of "times" marked by great changes, but still retaining a general unity, stretches from Christ's ascension to His coming to judgment. **21. by him**—Cf. "the *faith* which is *by Him,*" Acts 3:16. *Through* Christ: His Spirit, obtained for us in His resurrection and ascension, enabling us to believe. This verse excludes all who do not "by Him believe in God," and includes all of every age and clime that do. Lit., "*are believers* in God." *To believe* IN (*Greek, eis*) *God* expresses an *internal* trust: "by believing to love God, going INTO Him, and cleaving to Him, incorporated into His members. By this faith the ungodly is justified, so that *thenceforth* faith itself begins to work by love" [P. LOMBARD]. To *believe* ON (*Greek, epi,* or dative case) *God* expresses the confidence, which grounds itself *on* God, reposing ON Him. **that raised him**—The raising of Jesus by God is the special ground of our "believing": (1) because by it God declared openly His acceptance of Him as our righteous substitute; (2) because by it and His glorification He received power, viz., the Holy Spirit, to impart to His elect "faith": the same power enabling us to believe as raised Him from the dead. **that your faith and hope might be in God**—the object and effect of *God's raising Christ.* He states what was the actual result and fact, not an exhortation, except *indirectly.* Your *faith* flows from His *resurrection;* your *hope* from God's having "given Him glory" (cf. vs. 11, "glories"). Remember God's having raised and glorified Jesus as the anchor of your faith and hope in God, and so keep alive these graces. Apart from Christ we could have only feared, not *believed* and *hoped* in God. Cf. vss. 3, 7-9, 13, on *hope* in connection with *faith; love* is introduced in vs. 22. **22. purified ... in obeying the truth**—*Greek,* "in *your* (or *the*) obedience of (i.e., *to*) the truth" (the Gospel way of salvation), i.e., in the fact of your *believing. Faith* purifies the heart as giving it the only pure motive, love to God (Acts 15:9; Rom. 1:5, "*obedience* to the faith"). **through the Spirit**—omitted in the oldest MSS. The Holy Spirit is the purifier by bestowing the obedience of faith (vs. 2; I Cor. 12:3). **unto**—with a view to: the proper result of the *purifying* of your hearts by faith. "For what end must we lead a chaste life? That we may thereby be saved? No: but for this, that we may serve our neighbor" [LUTHER]. **unfeigned**—ch. 2:1, 2, "laying aside ... *hypocrisies* ... sincere." **love of the brethren**—i.e., of Christians. Love to the brethren is the evidence of our regeneration and justification by faith. **love one another**—When the *purifying by faith into love of the brethren* has formed the *habit,* then the *act* follows, so that the "love" is at once *habit* and *act.* **with a pure heart**—The oldest MSS. read, **"(love) from the heart." fervently**—*Greek,* "intensely": with all the powers *on the stretch* (ch. 4:8). "Instantly" (Acts 26:7). **23.** Christian brotherhood flows from our new birth of an imperishable seed, the abiding word of God. This is the consideration urged here to lead us to exercise *brotherly love.* As natural relationship gives rise to natural affection, so spiritual relationship gives rise to spiritual, and therefore abiding love, even as the *seed* from which it springs is abiding, not transitory as earthly things. **of ... of ... by**—"The word of God" is not the material of the spiritual new birth, but its mean or medium. By

ADAM CLARKE

19. *The precious blood of Christ.* "The valuable Blood"; how valuable neither is nor could be stated. *As of a lamb.* Such as was required for a sin offering to God; the Lamb of God that takes away the sin of the world. *Without blemish* in himself *and without spot* from the world, being perfectly pure in His soul and righteous in His life.

20. *Who verily was foreordained.* "Foreknown"; appointed in the divine purpose to be sent into the world, because infinitely approved by the divine justice. *Before the foundation of the world.* Before the law was given, or any sacrifice prescribed by it. Its whole sacrificial system was appointed in reference to this foreappointed Lamb, and consequently from Him derived all its significance and virtue. The phrase *foundation of the world* occurs often in the New Testament, and is supposed by some learned men and good critics to signify the commencement of the Jewish state. Perhaps it may have this meaning in Matt. xiii. 35; Luke xi. 50; Eph. i. 4; Heb. iv. 3; and ix. 26. But if we take it here in its common signification, the creation of universal nature, then it shows that God, foreseeing the fall and ruin of man, appointed the remedy that was to cure the disease. *Last times.* The gospel dispensation, called the *last times,* as we have often seen, because never to be succeeded by any other.

21. *Who by him do believe in God.* This is supposed to refer to the Gentiles, who never knew the true God till they heard the preaching of the gospel.

Gave him glory. Raised Him to His right hand. *That your faith* in the fulfillment of all His promises, and *hope* of eternal glory, *might be in God,* who is unchangeable in His counsels and infinite in His mercies.

22. *Seeing ye have purified your souls*—having purified your souls, *in obeying the truth*—by believing in Christ Jesus, *through* the influence and teaching of *the Spirit,* and giving full proof of it by *unfeigned love* to the *brethren,* you *love one another,* or "you will love each other," *with a pure heart fervently,* "intensely or continually"; the full proof that their brotherly love was *unfeigned*—"without hypocrisy."

MATTHEW HENRY

2. He further presses upon Christians the duty of loving one another with a pure heart fervently from the consideration of their spiritual relation. All Christians are born again. They are brought into a new and a near relation to one another, they become brethren by their new birth. This new and second birth is much more desirable and excellent than the first. By the one we become the children of men, by the other the sons and daughters of the Most High. Brethren by nature are bound to love one another; but the obligation is double where there is a spiritual relation.

Verses 24, 25

He now sets before us the vanity of the natural man. Nothing can make him a solid substantial being, but the being born again of the incorruptible seed, the word of God; and this word is daily set before you in the preaching of the gospel. Man, in his utmost flourish and glory, is still a withering, fading, dying creature. His wit, beauty, strength, vigour, wealth, honour—these are but as the flower of grass, which soon withers and dies away.

The only way to render this perishing creature solid and incorruptible is for him to entertain and receive the word of God; for this will preserve him to everlasting life, and abide with him for ever.

JAMIESON, FAUSSET, BROWN

means of the *word* the man receives the incorruptible *seed of the Holy Spirit,* and so becomes one "born again": John 3:3-5, "born *of water and the Spirit*": as there is but one *Greek* article to the two nouns, *the* close connection of the sign and the grace, or new birth signified is implied. The *word* is the remote and anterior instrument; *baptism,* the proximate and sacramental instrument. The word is the instrument in relation to the individual; baptism, in relation to the Church as a society (Jas. 1:18). We are born again *of the Spirit,* yet not without the use of means, but by the word of God. The word is not the begetting principle itself, but only that by which it works: the vehicle of the mysterious germinating power [ALFORD]. **which liveth and abideth for ever**—It is because the Spirit of God accompanies it that the word carries in it the germ of life. They who are so born again *live and abide for ever,* in contrast to those who sow to the flesh. **24.** Scripture proof that the word of God lives for ever, in contrast to man's natural frailty. If ye were born again of flesh, corruptible seed, ye must also perish again as the grass; but now that from which you have derived life remains eternally, and so also will render you eternal. **flesh**—man in his mere earthly nature. **as**—omitted in some of the oldest MSS. **of man**—The oldest MSS. read, "of it" (i.e., of the flesh). "The glory" is the wisdom, strength, riches, learning, honor, beauty, art, virtue, and righteousness of the NATURAL man (expressed by "flesh"), which all are transitory (John 3:6), not OF MAN (as *English Version* reads) absolutely, for the glory of *man, in his true ideal* realized in the believer, is eternal. **withereth**—*Greek,* aorist: lit., "withered," i.e., is withered as a thing of the past. So also the *Greek* for "falleth" is "*fell* away," i.e., is fallen away: it no sooner is than it is gone. **thereof**—omitted in the best MSS. and versions. "The grass" is the *flesh:* "the flower" its *glory.* **25.** (Ps. 119:89.) **this is the word . . . preached unto you**—That is eternal which is born of incorruptible seed (vs. 24): but ye have received the incorruptible seed, the word (vs. 25); therefore ye are born for eternity, and so are bound now to live for eternity (vss. 22, 23). Ye have not far to look for the word; it is among you, even the joyful Gospel message which we preach.

ADAM CLARKE

23. *Being born again.* For being born of Abraham's seed will not avail to the entering of the kingdom of Heaven. *Not of corruptible seed.* By no human generation or earthly means; *but of incorruptible*—a divine and heavenly principle which is not liable to decay, nor to be affected by the changes and chances to which all sublunary things are exposed. *By the word of God.* "By the doctrine of the living God, which remaineth forever."

25. *But the word of the Lord.* The doctrine delivered by God concerning Christ endureth forever. *And this is the word.* "What is spoken," by the gospel preached unto you.

MATTHEW HENRY

CHAPTER 2

Verses 1–3

I. Lay aside or put off what is evil.

1. The sins to be put off, or thrown aside. *Malice.* Malice is settled overgrown anger, retained till it inflames a man to design mischief. *Guile,* or deceit in words. *Hypocrisies.* The word being plural comprehends all sorts of hypocrisies. *Envies;* which is a grieving at the good and welfare of another. *Evil speaking,* speaking against another, or defaming him.

2. The best Christians have need to be cautioned and warned against the worst sins. They are but sanctified in part, and are still liable to temptations. Our best services towards God will neither please him nor profit us if we be not conscientious in our duties to men. One sin, not laid aside, will hinder our spiritual profit and everlasting welfare.

II. The apostle, like a wise physician, goes on to direct to wholesome food, that they may grow thereby. The duty exhorted to is a strong and constant desire for the *word of God.* This milk of the word must be *sincere,* not adulterated by the mixtures of men: *As new-born babes.* A new life requires suitable food. Infants desire common milk, and their desires towards it are fervent and frequent.

JAMIESON, FAUSSET, BROWN

CHAPTER 2

1. laying aside—once for all: so the *Greek* aorist expresses as a garment *put off.* The exhortation applies to Christians alone, for in none else is the new nature existing which, as "the inward man" (Eph. 3:16) can cast off the old as an outward thing, so that the Christian, through the continual renewal of his inward man, can also exhibit himself externally as a new man. "Malice," etc., are utterly inconsistent with the "love of the brethren," unto which ye have "purified your souls" (ch. 1:22). The vices here are those which offend against the BROTHERLY LOVE inculcated above. Each succeeding one springs out of that which immediately precedes, so as to form a *genealogy* of the sins against love. Out of *malice* springs *guile;* out of *guile, hypocrises* (pretending to be what we are not, and not showing what we really are; the opposite of "love unfeigned," and "without dissimulation"); out of *hypocrisies, envies* of those to whom we think ourselves obliged to play the hypocrite; out of *envies, evil-speaking,* malicious, envious detraction of others. **2. newborn babes**—altogether without "guile" (vs. 1). As long as we are here we are "babes," in a specially tender relation to God (Isa. 40:11). The childlike spirit is indispensable if we would enter heaven. "Milk" is here not elementary truths in contradistinction to more advanced Christian truths, as in I Corinthians 3:2; Hebrews 5:12, 13; but in contrast to "guile, hypocrisies . . ." (vs. 1); the simplicity of *Christian doctrine in general* to the childlike spirit. The same "word of grace" which is the instrument in regeneration, is the instrument also of *building up.* "The mother of the child is also its natural nurse" [STEIGER]. The babe, instead of chemically analyzing, instinctively desires and feeds on the milk; so our part is not self-sufficient rationalizing and questioning, but simply receiving the truth in the love of it (Matt. 11: 25). **desire**—*Greek,* "have a yearning desire for," or "longing after," a natural impulse to the regenerate, "for as no one needs to teach newborn babes what food to take, knowing instinctively that a table is provided for them in their mother's breast," so the believer of himself thirsts after the word of God (Ps. 119). Cf. Tatius' language as to

ADAM CLARKE

CHAPTER 2

1. *Wherefore laying aside.* This is in close connection with the preceding chapter, from which it should not have been separated; and the subject is continued to the end of the tenth verse.

Laying aside all malice. See the notes on Eph. iv. 22-31. These tempers and dispositions must have been common among the Jews, as they are frequently spoken against. Christianity can never admit of such; they show the mind, not of Christ, but of the old murderer.

2. *As newborn babes.* In the preceding chapter, v. 23, the apostle states that they had been "born again"; and as the newborn infant desires that aliment which nature has provided for it, so they, being born again, born from above, should as earnestly require that heavenly nourishment which is suited to their new nature.

MATTHEW HENRY

Such must Christians' desires be for the word of God: that they may grow thereby. Strong desires and affections to the word of God are a sure evidence of a person's being born again. Growth and improvement in wisdom and grace are the desire of every Christian. The word of God, does not leave a man as it finds him.

III. He adds an argument from their own experience, *v.* 3. The apostle does not express a doubt, but affirms that these good Christians had tasted the goodness of God. Our Lord Jesus Christ is very gracious to his people; he has in him a fulness of grace. The graciousness of our Redeemer is best discovered by an experimental taste of it. We cannot taste at a distance, as we may see, and hear, and smell. To taste the graciousness of Christ experimentally supposes our being united to him by faith. The best of God's servants have in this life but a taste of the grace of Christ.

Verses 4–12

I. A description of Jesus Christ as a living stone.

1. He is called a stone, to denote his invincible strength and everlasting duration, and to teach his servants that he is the foundation on which they are built. He is the living stone, having eternal life in himself. The reputation and respect he has with God and man are very different. He is disallowed of men, but chosen of God, and gracious. *To whom coming*; by faith, whereby we are united to him at first, and draw nigh to him afterwards. Jesus Christ is the very foundation-stone of all our hopes and happiness. However Christ may be disallowed by an ungrateful world, yet he is chosen of God, and precious in his account. Those who expect mercy from this gracious Redeemer must come to him, which is our act, though done by God's grace—a real endeavour, not a fruitless wish.

2. The apostle goes on to speak of the superstructure, the materials built upon him, *v.* 6. The apostle is recommending the Christian church and constitution to these dispersed Jews. The Christian church is a much nobler fabric than the Jewish temple; it is a living temple. Christ, the foundation, is a living stone. Christians are lively stones, and they are a holy priesthood. They offer spiritual sacrifices, acceptable to God by Jesus Christ. All sincere Christians have in them a principle of spiritual life communicated to them from Christ; not dead in trespasses and sins, but alive to God. The church of God is a spiritual house. This house is daily built up, every part of it improving, and the whole supplied in every age by the addition of new particular members. All good Christians are a holy priesthood. This holy priesthood must and will offer up spiritual sacrifices to God. The most spiritual sacrifices of the best men are not acceptable to God, but through Jesus Christ; therefore bring all your oblations to him, and by him present them to God.

II. He confirms what he had asserted of Christ being a *living stone*, &c., from Isa. xxviii. 16. In their quotations they kept rather to the sense than the words of scripture. The true sense of scripture may be justly and fully expressed in other than scripture-words, but in the weighty matters of religion we must depend entirely upon scripture-proof. The word of God is the only rule God hath given us.

JAMIESON, FAUSSET, BROWN

Achilles. **sincere**—*Greek,* "guileless." Cf. vs. 1, "laying aside *guile.*" IRENÆUS says of heretics, They mix chalk with the milk. The article, "the," implies that besides *the well-known pure milk, the* Gospel, there is no other pure, unadulterated doctrine; it alone can make us *guileless* (vs. 1). **of the word**—Not as ALFORD, "spiritual," nor "reasonable," as *English Version* in Romans 12:1. The *Greek logos* in Scripture is not used of the *reason,* or *mind,* but of the WORD; the preceding context requires that "the word" should be meant here; the adjective *logikos follows* the meaning of the noun *logos,* "word." **grow**—The oldest MSS. and versions read, "grow *unto salvation.*" Being BORN *again unto salvation,* we are also to *grow unto salvation.* The end to which growth leads is perfected *salvation.* **thereby**—*Greek,* "*in it*"; fed *on it; in its strength* (Acts 11:14). "The word is to be desired with appetite as the cause of life, to be swallowed in the hearing, to be chewed as cud is by rumination with the understanding, and to be digested by faith" [TERTULLIAN]. **3.** Peter alludes to Psalm 34:8. The first *tastes* of God's goodness are afterwards followed by fuller and happier experiences. A taste whets the appetite [BENGEL]. **gracious**—*Greek,* "good," benignant, kind; as God is revealed to us in Christ, "the Lord" (vs. 4), we who are born again ought so to be *good* and *kind* to the brethren (ch. 1:22). "Whosoever has not tasted the word to him it is not sweet it has not reached the heart; but to them who have experienced it, who with the heart believe, 'Christ has been sent *for me* and is become *my own;* my miseries are His, and His *life* mine,' it tastes sweet" [LUTHER]. **4. coming**—*drawing near* (same *Greek* as here, Hebrews 10:22) by faith continually; present tense: not having come once for all at conversion. **stone**—*Peter* (i.e., *a stone,* named so by Christ) desires that all similarly should be *living stones* BUILT ON CHRIST, THE TRUE FOUNDATION-STONE; cf. his speech in Acts 4:11.

He herein confirms Paul's teaching. Omit the *as unto* of *English Version.* Christ is positively termed the "living stone"; *living,* as having life in Himself from the beginning, and as raised from the dead to live evermore (Rev. 1:18) after His rejection by men, and so the source of life to us. Like no earthly *rock,* He lives and gives life. Cf. I Corinthians 10:4, and the type, Exodus 17:6; Numbers 20:11. **disallowed**—rejected, reprobated; referred to also by Christ Himself: also by Paul; cf. the kindred prophecies, Isaiah 8:14; Luke 2:34. **chosen of God**—lit., "*with* (or *in the presence and judgment of*) God elect," or, "chosen out" (vs. 6). Many are alienated from the Gospel, because it is not everywhere in favor, but is on the contrary rejected by most men. Peter answers that, though rejected by men, Christ is peculiarly the *stone* of salvation honored by God, first so designated by Jacob in his deathbed prophecy. **5. Ye also, as lively stones**—partaking of the name and life which is in "THE LIVING STONE" (vs. 4; I Cor. 3:11). Many names which belong to Christ in the singular are assigned to Christians in the plural. He is "THE SON," "High Priest," "King," "Lamb"; they, "sons," "priests," "kings," "sheep," "lambs." So the Shulamite called from Solomon [BENGEL]. **are built up**—*Greek,* "are being built up," as in Ephesians 2:22. Not as ALFORD, "Be ye built up." Peter grounds his exhortations, vs. 2, 11, etc., on their conscious sense of their high privileges as *living stones in the course of being built up into a spiritual house* (i.e., the habitation of the Spirit"). **priesthood**—Christians are both the spiritual *temple* and the *priests* of the temple. There are two *Greek* words for "temple"; *hieron* (*the sacred place*), the whole building, including the courts wherein the sacrifice *was killed*; and *naos* (*the dwelling,* viz., of God), the inner shrine wherein God peculiarly manifested Himself, and where, in the holiest place, the *blood* of the slain sacrifice was presented before Him. All believers alike, and not merely ministers, are now the dwelling of God (and are called the *naos, Greek,* not the *hieron*) and priests unto God (Rev. 1:6). The minister is not, like the Jewish priest (*Greek, hiercus*), admitted nearer to God than the people, but merely for order's sake leads the spiritual services of the people. The Spirit never, in New Testament, gives the name *hiereus,* or *sacerdotal* priest, to ministers of the Gospel. **holy**—consecrated to God. **spiritual sacrifices**—not the literal one of the mass, as the Romish self-styled disciples of Peter teach. Cf. Isaiah 56:7, which cf. with "*acceptable* to God" here; Psalm 4:5; 50:14; 51:17, 19; Hosea 14:2; Philippians 4:18. "Among spiritual sacrifices the first place belongs to the general oblation of ourselves. For never can we offer anything to God until we have offered ourselves (II

ADAM CLARKE

And this the apostle calls the *sincere milk of the word*, or, as some translate, "the rational unadulterated milk"; i.e., the pure doctrines of the gospel, as delivered in the Epistles and Gospels, and as preached by the apostles and their successors.

That ye may grow thereby. "Unto salvation" is added here by about forty MSS. The reading is undoubtedly genuine, and is very important. It shows why they were regenerated, and why they were to desire the unadulterated doctrines of the gospel, viz., that they might "grow up unto salvation."

3. *If so be ye have tasted.* "Seeing ye have tasted." *That the Lord is gracious.* This seems to refer to Ps. xxxiv. 8: "O taste and see that the Lord is good."

4. *To whom coming, as unto a living stone.* This is a reference to Isa. xxviii. 16: "Behold, I lay in Zion for a foundation a stone, a tried stone, a precious corner stone, a sure foundation." Jesus Christ is, in both the prophet and apostle, represented as the Foundation on which the Christian Church is built, and on which it must continue to rest; and the stone or foundation is called here *living,* to intimate that He is the Source of life to all His followers, and that it is in union with Him that they live. *Disallowed indeed of men.* That is, rejected by the Jews. This is a plain reference to the prophecy, Ps. cxviii. 22: "The stone which the builders refused is become the head stone of the corner." *Chosen of God.* To be the Saviour of the world and the Founder of the Church, and the Foundation on which it rests. *Precious.* "Honorable." Howsoever despised and rejected by men, Jesus, as the Sacrifice for a lost world, is infinitely honorable in the sight of God.

5. *Ye also, as lively stones.* "Living stones"; each being instinct with the principle of life, which proceeds from Him who is the Foundation, called above "a living stone." The metaphor in this and the following verse is as bold as it is singular; and commentators and critics have found it difficult to hit on any principle of explanation. The Church of Christ is represented under the figure of a *house,* or rather "household"; and as a household must have a place of residence, hence, by a metonymy, the house itself, or material building, is put for the household or family which occupies it. This point will receive the fullest illustration if we have recourse to the Hebrew. *Beith* signifies both a "house" and a "family"; *ben,* a son; *bath,* a daughter; and *eben,* a stone. Of all these nouns, *banah,* "he built," is, I believe, the common root. Now as *beith,* "a house," is built of *abanim,* "stones," hence *banah,* "he built," is a proper radix for both "stones" and "building"; and as *beith,* "a family or household" (Ps. lxviii. 6), is constituted or made up of *banim,* "sons," and *banoth,* "daughters," hence the same root, *banah,* "he built," is common to all; for sons and daughters build up or constitute a family, as stones do a building. Here then is the ground of the metaphor: The spiritual house is the holy or Christian family or household; this family or household is composed of the sons and daughters of God Almighty; and hence the propriety of "living stones," because this is the living house or spiritual family. And as all the stones, sons and daughters, that constitute the spiritual building are made partakers of the life of Christ, consequently they may with great propriety be called "living stones," that is, sons and daughters of God, who live by Christ Jesus, because He

MATTHEW HENRY

The accounts that God hath given us in scripture concerning his Son Jesus Christ are what require our strictest attention. *Behold, I lay,* &c. The constituting of Christ Jesus head of the church is an eminent work of God: *I lay in Zion.* Jesus Christ is the chief corner-stone that God hath laid in his spiritual building. The corner-stone stays inseparably with the building, supports it, unites it, and adorns it. So does Christ by his holy church, his spiritual house.

III. He deduces an important inference, *v.* 7. "You who believe will be so far from being ashamed of him that you will boast of him and glory in him for ever." The disobedient will go on to disallow Jesus Christ; but God is resolved that he shall be, in despite of all opposition, the head of the corner. The apostle draws an inference from the prophet's testimony. The prophet did not expressly say so, but yet he said that from which the consequence was unavoidable. The business of a faithful minister is to apply general truths to the particular condition and state of his hearers. The apostle quotes a passage (*v.* 6) out of the prophet, and applies it severally to good and bad. This requires wisdom, courage, and fidelity; but it is very profitable to the hearers. Disobedient people have no true faith. These may have some right notions, but no solid faith. Those that ought to be builders of the church of Christ are often the worst enemies that Christ has in the world. God will carry on his own work notwithstanding the falseness of pretended friends and the opposition of his worst enemies.

IV. The apostle adds a further description, still preserving the metaphor of a stone, *v.* 8. The words are taken from Isa. viii. 13, 14.

1. The builders, the chief-priests, refused him, and the people followed their leaders; and so Christ became to them *a stone of stumbling, and a rock of offence.* All those that are disobedient take offence at the word of God. They are offended with Christ himself, with his doctrine and the purity of his precepts. The same blessed Jesus who is the author of salvation to some is to others the occasion of their sin and destruction. Those who reject him as a Saviour will split upon him as a Rock.

2. Those who received him were highly privileged, *v.* 9. The Jews were exceedingly tender of their ancient privileges.

(1) The apostle answers, that if they did not submit they were ruined (*v.* 7, 8), but that if they did submit they should lose no real advantage, but continue still *a chosen generation, a royal priesthood,* &c. All true Christians *are a chosen generation*; they all make one family, a sort and species of people distinct from the common world. All the true servants of Christ are a royal priesthood, separated from sin and sinners, consecrated to God, and offering to God spiritual services and oblations, acceptable to God through Jesus Christ.

JAMIESON, FAUSSET, BROWN

Cor. 8:5] in sacrifice to Him. **by Jesus Christ**—as our mediating High Priest before God. Connect these words with "offer up." Christ is both *precious* Himself and makes us *accepted* [BENGEL]. As the temple, so also the priesthood, is built on Christ (vss. 4, 5) [BEZA]. Imperfect as are our services, we are not with unbelieving timidity, which is close akin to refined self-righteousness, to doubt their acceptance THROUGH CHRIST. After extolling the dignity of Christians he goes back to CHRIST as the sole source of it. **6. Wherefore also**—The oldest MSS. read, "Because that." The statement above is so "*because* it is contained in Scripture." **Behold**—calling attention to the glorious announcement of His eternal counsel.

elect—so also believers (vs. 9, "chosen," *Greek,* "*elect* generation"). **precious**—in *Hebrew,* Isaiah 28:16, "a cornerstone of preciousness." See all my *Note* there. So in vs. 7, Christ is said to be, to believers, "precious," *Greek,* "preciousness." **confounded**—same *Greek* as in Romans 9:33 (Peter here as elsewhere confirming Paul's teaching. See *Introduction,* also Rom. 10: 11,) "ashamed." In Isaiah 28:16, "make haste," i.e., flee in sudden panic, covered with the *shame* of confounded hopes. **7.** Application of the Scripture just quoted first to the believer, then to the unbeliever. On the opposite effects of the same Gospel on different classes, cf. John 9:39; II Corinthians 2: 15, 16. **precious**—*Greek,* "THE preciousness" (vs. 6). To you believers belongs *the preciousness* of Christ just mentioned. **disobedient**—to the faith, and so disobedient in practice. **the stone which . . . head of . . . corner**—(Ps. 118:22). Those who rejected the STONE were all the while in spite of themselves unconsciously contributing to its becoming Head of the corner. The same magnet has two poles, the one repulsive, the other attractive; so the Gospel has opposite effects on believers and unbelievers respectively. **8. stone of stumbling . . .**—quoted from Isaiah 8:14. Not merely they *stumbled,* in that their prejudices were offended; but their stumbling implies the *judicial punishment* of their reception of Messiah; they hurt themselves in stumbling over the cornerstone, as "stumble" means in Jeremiah 13:16; Daniel 11:19. **at the word**—rather join "being disobedient to the word"; so ch. 3:1; 4:17. **whereunto**—to penal *stumbling*; to the judicial punishment of their unbelief. See above. **also**—an additional thought; God's ordination; not that God ordains or *appoints* them to *sin,* but they are given up to "the fruit of *their own* ways" according to the eternal counsel of God. The moral ordering of the world is altogether of God. God appoints the ungodly to be *given up unto* sin, and a *reprobate mind,* and its necessary penalty. "Were appointed," *Greek,* "set," answers to "*I lay,*" *Greek,* "set," vs. 6. God, in the active, is said to *appoint* Christ and the elect [directly]. Unbelievers, in the passive, are said to be *appointed* [God acting less directly in the appointment of the sinner's awful course] [BENGEL]. God ordains the wicked to punishment, not to crime [J. CAPPEL]. "Appointed" or "set" (not here "FOREordained") refers, not to the eternal counsel so directly, as to the penal justice of God. Through the same Christ whom sinners rejected, they shall be rejected; unlike believers, they are by God *appointed unto wrath* as FITTED for it. The lost shall lay all the blame of their ruin on their own sinful perversity, not on God's decree; the saved shall ascribe all the merit of their salvation to God's electing love and grace.

9. Contrast in the privileges and destinies of believers. Cf. the similar contrast with the preceding context. **chosen**—"elect" of God, even as Christ your Lord is. **generation**—implying the unity of spiritual origin and kindred of believers as a class distinct from the world. **royal**—kingly. Believers, like Christ, the antitypical Melchisedec, are at once *kings* and *priests.* Israel, in a spiritual sense, was designed to be the same among the nations of the earth. The full realization on earth of this, both to the literal and the spiritual Israel, is as yet future.

ADAM CLARKE

lives in them. Now, following the metaphor, these various living stones become one grand temple, in which God is worshipped, and in which He manifests himself as He did in the Temple of old. Every stone, son and daughter, being a spiritual sacrificer or priest, they all offer up praise and thanksgiving to God through Christ; and such sacrifices, being offered up in the name and through the merit of His Son, are all acceptable in His sight.

6. *Behold, I lay in Sion.* This intimates that the foundation of the Christian Church should be laid at Jerusalem; and there it was laid, for there Christ suffered, and there the preaching of the gospel commenced. *A chief corner stone.* This is the same as the foundation stone; and it is called here the *chief corner stone* because it is laid in the foundation, at an angle of the building where its two sides form the groundwork of a side and end wall. And this might probably be designed to show that, in Jesus, both Jews and Gentiles were to be united. *Elect, precious.* "Chosen" and "honorable." *Shall not be confounded.* These words are quoted from Isa. xxviii. 16; but rather more from the Septuagint than from the Hebrew text. The latter we translate, "He that believeth shall not make haste"—he who comes to God, through Christ, for salvation, shall never be confounded; he need not "haste" to flee away, for no enemy shall ever be able to annoy him.

7. *Unto you therefore which believe.* You, both Jews and Gentiles. *He is precious.* "The honor is to you who believe"; i.e., the honor of being in this building, and of having your souls saved through the blood of the Lamb, and becoming sons and daughters of God Almighty. *Them which be disobedient.* The Jews who continue to reject the gospel; that very Person whom they reject is *head of the corner*—is Lord over all, and has all power in the heavens and the earth.

8. *A stone of stumbling.* Because in Him all Jews and Gentiles who believe are united, and because the latter were admitted into the Church and called by the gospel to enjoy the same privileges which the Jews, as the peculiar people of God, had enjoyed for two thousand years before, therefore they rejected the Christian religion; they would have no partakers with themselves in the salvation of God. This was the true cause why the Jews rejected the gospel; and they rejected Christ because He did not come as a secular prince. In the one case He was a *stone of stumbling*—He was poor, and affected no worldly pomp; in the other He was a *rock of offence,* for His gospel called the Gentiles to be a peculiar people whom the Jews believed to be everlastingly reprobated and utterly incapable of any spiritual good. *Whereunto also they were appointed.* Some good critics read the verse thus, carrying on the sense from the preceding: "Also a stone of stumbling, and a rock of offense: The disobedient stumble against the word, to which verily they were appointed." Peter refers to Isa. viii. 14-15: "And he shall be for a sanctuary; but for a stone of stumbling and for a rock of offence to both the houses of Israel, for a gin and for a snare to the inhabitants of Jerusalem. And many among them shall stumble, and fall, and be broken." The *disobedient,* therefore, being appointed to stumble against the Word, or being prophesied of as persons that should stumble, necessarily means, from the connection in which it stands and from the passage in the prophet, that their stumbling, falling, and being broken is the consequence of their disobedience or unbelief; but there is no intimation that they were *appointed* or "decreed" to disobey, that they might stumble and fall and be broken. They stumbled and fell through their obstinate unbelief; and thus their stumbling and falling, as well as their unbelief, were of themselves. In consequence of this they were *appointed* to be broken; this was God's work of judgment.

9. *Ye are a chosen generation.* The titles formerly given to the whole Jewish church. The Israelites were a *chosen* or "elected race," to be a special people unto the Lord their God, "above all people that are upon the face of the earth," Deut. vii. 6. They were also *a royal priesthood,* or what Moses calls "a kingdom of

MATTHEW HENRY

All Christians, wheresoever they be, compose one holy nation. It is the honour of the servants of Christ that they are God's peculiar people.

These dignities and virtues of Christians are not natural to them; for their first state is a state of horrid darkness, but they are effectually called out of darkness that they should show forth the virtues and praises of him who hath called them.

(2) The apostle advises them to compare their former and their present state. Time was when they were not a people, nor had they obtained mercy, but now they are taken in again to be the people of God, and have obtained mercy.

V. He warns them to beware of fleshly lusts, *v.* 11. Knowing the difficulty, and yet the importance of the duty, he uses his utmost interest in them: *Dearly beloved, I beseech you.* The duty is to abstain from fleshly lusts. These Christians ought to avoid, considering, 1. The respect they have with God: They are *dearly beloved.* 2. Their condition in the world: *They are strangers and pilgrims,* and should not impede their passage by giving in to the lusts of the country through which they pass.

3. The grand mischief that sin does to man is this, it *wars against the soul.* Of all sorts of sin, none are more injurious to the soul than *fleshly lusts.*

VI. He exhorts them further to an honest conversation. They lived among the Gentiles who were inveterate enemies to them, and constantly spoke evil of them *as of evil-doers.* "A good conversation may not only stop their mouths, but may possibly be a means to bring them to glorify God, and turn to you, when they shall see you excel all others in good works. Vindicate yourselves by good works, this is the way to convince them. When the gospel shall come among them, and take effect, a good conversation will encourage them in their conversion, but an evil one will obstruct it."

JAMIESON, FAUSSET, BROWN

holy nation—antitypical to Israel. **peculiar people**—lit., "a people *for an acquisition,*" i.e., whom God chose to be *peculiarly His:* Acts 20: 28, "purchased," lit., "acquired." God's "*peculiar treasure*" above others. **show forth**—*publish abroad.* **praises**—*Greek,* "virtues," "excellencies": His glory, *mercy* (vs. 10), *goodness* (*Greek,* vs. 3; Num. 14:17, 18; Isa. 63:7). The same term is applied to believers, II Pet. 1:5. **of him who hath called you**—(II Pet. 1:3). **out of darkness**—of heathen and even Jewish ignorance, sin, and misery, and so out of the dominion of the prince of darkness. **marvellous**—Peter still has in mind Ps. 118:23. **light**—It is called "His," i.e., God's. Only the (spiritual) *light* is created by God, not *darkness.* In Isaiah 45:7, it is physical darkness and evil, not moral, that God is said to *create,* the punishment of sin, not sin itself. Peter, with characteristic boldness, brands as *darkness* what all the world calls *light;* reason, without the Holy Spirit, in spite of its vaunted power, is spiritual darkness. "It cannot apprehend what faith is: there it is stark blind; it gropes as one that is without eyesight, stumbling from one thing to another, and knows not what it does" [LUTHER]. **10.** Adapted from Hosea 1:9, 10; 2:23. Peter plainly confirms Paul, who quotes the passage as implying the call of the Gentiles to become spiritually that which Israel had been literally, "the people of God." Primarily, the prophecy refers to literal Israel, hereafter to be fully that which in their best days they were only partially, God's people. **not obtained mercy**—lit., "who were men not compassionated." Implying that it was God's pure *mercy,* not their merits, which made the blessed change in their state; a thought which ought to kindle their lively *gratitude,* to be shown with their life, as well as their lips. **11.** As heretofore he exhorted them to walk worthily of their calling, in contradistinction to their own former walk, so now he exhorts them to glorify God before unbelievers. **Dearly beloved**—He gains their attention to his exhortation by assuring them of his love. **strangers and pilgrims**—(ch. 1:17). *Sojourners,* lit., settlers having a *house* in a city without being *citizens* in respect to the rights of citizenship; a picture of the Christian's position on earth; *and pilgrims,* staying for a time in a foreign land. FLACIUS thus analyzes the exhortation: (1) Purify your souls (a) as *strangers* on earth who must not allow yourselves to be kept back by earthly lusts, and (b) because these lusts war against the soul's salvation. (2) Walk piously among unbelievers (a) so that they may cease to calumniate Christians, and (b) may themselves be converted to Christ. **fleshly lusts**—enumerated in Galatians 5:19, etc. Not only the gross appetites which we have in common with the brutes, but all the thoughts of the unrenewed mind. **which**—*Greek,* "*the* which," i.e., inasmuch as being such as "war," etc. Not only do they impede, but they assail [BENGEL]. **the soul**—i.e., against the regenerated soul; such as were those now addressed. The regenerated soul is besieged by sinful lusts. Like Samson in the lap of Delilah, the believer, the moment that he gives way to fleshly lusts, has the locks of his strength shorn, and ceases to maintain that spiritual separation from the world and the flesh of which the Nazarite vow was the type. **12. conversation**—"behavior"; "conduct."

honest—honorable, becoming, proper (ch. 3:16). Contrast "vain conversation," ch. 1:18. A good walk does not make us pious, but we must first be pious and believe before we attempt to lead a good course. Faith first receives from God, then love gives to our neighbor [LUTHER]. **whereas they speak against you**—*now* (vs. 15), that they may, nevertheless, at some time or other *hereafter* glorify God. The *Greek* may be rendered, "*Wherein* they speak against you . . . , that (*herein*) they may, by your good works, which *on a closer inspection they shall behold,* glorify God." **evildoers**—Because as Christians they could not conform to heathenish customs, they were accused of disobedience to all legal authority; in order to rebut this charge, they are told to *submit to every ordinance of man* (not sinful in itself). **by**—owing to. **they shall behold**—*Greek,* "they shall be *eyewitnesses of*"; "shall behold *on close inspection*"; as opposed to their "ignorance" (vs. 15) of the true character of Christians and Christianity, by judging on mere hearsay. The same *Greek* verb occurs in a similar sense in ch. 3:2. **glorify**—forming a high estimate of the God whom Christians worship, from the exemplary conduct of Christians themselves. We must do good, not with a view to *our own* glory, but to the glory *of God.* **the day of visitation**—of God's grace; when God shall *visit* them *in mercy.* **13. every ordinance of man**—"every human institution" [AL-

ADAM CLARKE

priests," Exod. xix. 6. They were *an holy nation,* Exod. xix. 6; for they were separated from all the people of the earth, that they might worship the one only true God, and abstain from the abominations that were in the heathen world. They were also a *peculiar people,* a "purchased people"; a "private property," belonging to God Almighty, Deut. vii. 6. But they were called to this state of salvation *out of darkness,* idolatry, superstition, and ungodliness, *into his marvellous light,* the gospel dispensation, which, in reference to the discoveries it had made of God, His nature, will, and gracious promises towards mankind, differed as much from the preceding dispensation of the Jews as the light of the meridian sun from the faint twinkling of a star. And they had these privileges that they might *shew forth the praises of him who* had thus *called* them; "the virtues," those perfections of the wisdom, justice, truth, and goodness of God, that shone most illustriously in the Christian dispensation. These they were to exhibit in a holy and useful life, being transformed into the image of God, and walking as Christ himself walked.

10. *Which in time past were not a people.* This is a quotation from Hos. i. 9-10 and ii. 23, where the calling of the Gentiles by the preaching of the gospel is foretold. From this it is evident that the people to whom the apostle now addresses himself had been Gentiles.

11. *Which war against the soul.* Which are "marshalled and drawn up in battle array," to fight against the soul; either to slay it or to bring it into captivity. This is the object and operation of every earthly and sensual desire. How little do those who indulge them think of the ruin which they produce!

12. *Having your conversation honest.* Living in such a manner among the Gentiles, in whose country you sojourn, as becomes the gospel which you profess.

In the day of visitation. I believe this refers to the time when God should come to execute judgment on the disobedient Jews in the destruction of their civil polity and the subversion of their Temple and city. That *the day of visitation* means a time in which punishment should be inflicted is plain from Isa. x. 3: "And what will ye do in the day of visitation, and in the desolation which shall come from far?"

MATTHEW HENRY

Verses 13-25

A Christian conversation must be honest.

I. The case of subjects. Christians were not only reputed innovators in religion, but disturbers of the state; it was highly necessary, therefore, that the apostle should settle the rules of obedience to the civil magistrate.

1. The duty required is submission.

2. The persons or objects to whom this submission is due are described. More generally: *Every ordinance of man.* Magistracy is certainly of divine right; and this is a general rule, binding in all nations, let the established form of government be what it will. Particularly: *To the king, as supreme, or unto governors,* who *are sent by him,* commissioned by him to govern.

3. The reasons to enforce this duty are,

(1) *For the Lord's sake,* who has ordained magistracy for the good of mankind.

(2) From the end and use of the magistrate's office, which are, to punish evil-doers and to praise and encourage all those that do well. True religion is the best support of civil government. The best way the magistrate can take to discharge his own duty, and to amend the world, is to punish well and reward well.

(3) Christians should submit to the civil magistrate, *v.* 15. *The will of God is,* to a good man, the strongest reason for any duty. A Christian must endeavour, in all relations, to behave himself so as to put to silence the unreasonable reproaches of the most ignorant and foolish men.

(4) The spiritual nature of Christian liberty. The apostle tells the Christians that they were free, but from what? Not from duty or obedience to God's law, which requires subjection to the civil magistrate. They were free spiritually, but must still remember they were *the servants of God.* All the servants of Christ are free men. The servants of Jesus Christ ought to be very careful not to abuse their Christian liberty.

4. The apostle concludes with four admirable precepts: (1) *Honour all men.* A due respect is to be given to all men; the poor are not to be despised; the wicked must be honoured, not for their wickedness, but for any other qualities.

(2) *Love the brotherhood.* All Christians are a fraternity. They should therefore love one another with an especial affection. (3) *Fear God* with the highest reverence. If this be wanting, none of the other three duties can be performed as they ought. (4) *Honour the king.*

II. The case of servants. They imagined that their Christian liberty set them free from their unbelieving and cruel masters; *Servants, be subject, v.* 18.

JAMIESON, FAUSSET, BROWN

FORD], lit., "every human *creation.*" For though of divine appointment, yet in the mode of nomination and in the exercise of their authority, earthly governors are but human institutions, being *of men,* and *in relation to men.* The apostle speaks as one raised above all human things. But lest they should think themselves so ennobled by faith as to be raised above subordination to human authorities, he tells them to *submit themselves for the sake of Christ,* who desires you to be subject, and who once was subject to earthly rulers Himself, though having all things subject to Him, and whose honor is at stake in you as His earthly representatives. Cf. Romans 13:5, "Be subject for conscience' sake." **king**—The Roman emperor was "supreme" in the Roman provinces to which this Epistle was addressed. The Jewish zealots refused obedience. The distinction between "the king as supreme" and "governors sent by him" implies that "if the king command one thing, and the subordinate magistrate another, we ought rather to obey the superior" [AUGUSTINE *in* GROTIUS]. Scripture prescribes nothing upon the form of government, but simply subjects Christians to that everywhere subsisting, without entering into the question of the *right* of the rulers (thus the Roman emperors had by force seized supreme authority, and Rome had, by unjustifiable means, made herself mistress of Asia), because the *de facto* governors have not been made by chance, but by the providence of God. **14. governors**—subordinate to the emperor, "sent," or delegated by Cæsar to preside over the provinces. **for the punishment**—No tyranny ever has been so unprincipled as that some appearance of equity was not maintained in it; however corrupt a government be, God never suffers it to be so much so as not to be better than anarchy [CALVIN]. Although bad kings often oppress the good, yet that is scarcely ever done by public authority (and it is of what is done by public authority that Peter speaks), save under the mask of right. Tyranny harasses many, but anarchy overwhelms the whole state [HORNEIUS]. The only justifiable exception is in cases where obedience to the earthly king plainly involves disobedience to the express command of the King of kings. **praise of them that do well**—Every government recognizes the excellence of truly Christian subjects. Thus PLINY, in his letter to the Emperor Trajan, acknowledges, "I have found in them nothing else save a perverse and extravagant superstition." The recognition in the long run mitigates persecution (ch. 3:13). **15.** Ground of his directing them to *submit themselves* (vs. 13). **put to silence**—lit., "to muzzle," "to stop the mouth." **ignorance**—spiritual not having "the knowledge of God," and therefore ignorant of the children of God, and misconstruing their acts; influenced by mere appearances, and ever ready to open their mouths, rather than their eyes and ears. Their *ignorance* should move the believer's pity, not his anger. **As free**—as the Lord's freemen," connected with vs. 15, *doing well as* being *free.* "Well-doing" (vs. 15) is the natural fruit of being *freemen* of Christ, made free by "the truth" from the bondage of sin. Duty is enforced on us to guard against licentiousness, but the *way* in which it is to be fulfilled, is by love and the holy instincts of Christian liberty. We are given *principles,* not *details.* **not using**—*Greek,* "not *as having* your liberty for a veil (cloak) of *badness,* but as the servants of God," and therefore bound to *submit to every ordinance of man* (vs. 13) which is of God's appointment. **17. Honour all men**—*according to whatever honor is due in each case.* Equals have a respect due to them. Christ has dignified our humanity by assuming it; therefore we should not dishonor, but be considerate to and honor our common humanity, even in the very humblest. The first "honor" is in the *Greek aorist* imperative, implying, "*In every case render promptly* every man's due" [ALFORD]. The second is in the *present,* implying, *Habitually and continually* honor the king. Thus the first is the general precept; the three following are its three great divisions. **Love**—present: *Habitually love* with the special and congenial affection that you ought to feel to brethren, besides the general *love* to all men. **Fear God . . . the king**—The king is to be *honored;* but God alone, in the highest sense, *feared.* **18. Servants**—*Greek,* "household servants": not here the *Greek* for "slaves." Probably including *freedmen* still remaining in their master's house. **be subject**—*Greek,* "being subject": the participle expresses a particular instance of the general exhortation to good conduct, vss. 11, 12, of which the first particular precept is given vs. 13, "Submit yourselves to every ordinance of man for the Lord's sake." The general exhortation is taken up again in vs. 16; and so

ADAM CLARKE

13. *Submit yourselves to every ordinance of man.* In every settled state, and under every form of political government, where the laws are not in opposition to the laws of God, it may be very soundly and rationally said: "Genuine Christians have nothing to do with the laws but to obey them." The words literally signify, not *every ordinance of man,* but "every human creature"; it is better to understand the words thus, "All the constituted authorities." The meaning of Peter appears to be this: The Jews thought it unlawful to obey any ruler that was not of their own stock; the apostle tells them they should obey the civil magistrate, let him be of what stock he may, whether a Jew or a Gentile, and let him exercise the government in whatsoever form. This is the general proposition: and then he instances "emperors" and their "deputies"; and, far from its being unlawful for them to obey a heathen magistrate, they were to do it *for the Lord's sake,* "on account of the Lord," whose will it was and who commanded it.

14. *Or unto governors.* By "king, as supreme" the Roman emperor is meant; and by *governors* are meant leaders, governors, presidents, proconsuls, and other chief magistrates, sent by him into the provinces dependent on the Roman Empire. *For the punishment of evildoers.* This was the object of their mission; they were to punish delinquents, and encourage and protect the virtuous.

15. *For so is the will of God.* God, as their supreme Governor, shows them that it is His will that they should act uprightly and obediently at all times, and thus confound *the ignorance of foolish men,* who were ready enough to assert that their religion made them bad subjects. The word which we translate *put to silence* signifies to "muzzle," i.e., stop their mouths, leave them nothing to say.

16. *As free.* The Jews pretended that they were a free people, and owed allegiance to God alone; hence they were continually rebelling against the Roman government, to which God had subjected them because of their rebellion against Him. Thus they used their liberty *for a cloke of maliciousness*—for a pretext of rebellion, and by it endeavored to vindicate their seditious and rebellious conduct. *But as the servants of God.* These were free from sin and Satan, but they were the *servants of God*—"bound" to obey Him; and as He had made it their duty to obey the civil magistrate, they served God by submitting "to every ordinance of man for the Lord's sake."

17. *Honour all men.* That is, give honor to whom honor is due, Rom. xiii. 7.

Love the brotherhood. All true Christians, who form one great family of which God is the Head. *Fear God,* who gives you these commandments, lest He punish you for disobedience. *Honour the king.* Pay that respect to the "emperor" which his high authority requires, knowing that civil power is of God.

18. *Servants, be subject.* See the notes on Eph. vi. 5; Col. iii. 22; and Titus ii. 9.

MATTHEW HENRY

1. He orders them to *be subject*, and that *not only to the good and gentle*, but even to the crooked and perverse. The sinful misconduct of one relation does not justify the sinful behaviour of the other; the servant is bound to do his duty, though the master be sinfully froward and perverse. Good people are meek and gentle to their servants and inferiors.

2. He condescends to reason with them about it. (1) If they were patient under their hardships, while they suffered unjustly, this would be acceptable to God, *v.* 19, 20. There is no condition so mean but a man may glorify God in it; the meanest servant may do so. The most conscientious persons are very often the greatest sufferers. *For conscience towards God, they suffer wrongfully; they do well, and suffer for it;* but sufferers of this sort are praiseworthy, they do honour to God and they are accepted of him. Deserved sufferings must be endured with patience. (2) More reasons to encourage Christian servants to patience under unjust sufferings, *v.* 21. From their Christian calling. From the example of Christ. Good Christians are a sort of people called to be sufferers, and therefore they must expect it; they are bound to deny themselves, and take up the cross. Jesus Christ *suffered for* you, or *for us*, in our stead and for our good, *v.* 24.

The sufferings of Christ should quiet us under the most unjust and cruel sufferings we meet with in the world. Shall not we sinners submit to the light afflictions of this life, which work for us unspeakable advantages afterwards?

3. The example of Christ's subjection and patience is here explained: *Christ suffered*, (1) Wrongfully, *v.* 22. His words, as well as his actions, were all sincere, just, and right. (2) Patiently, *v.* 23. Provocations to sin can never justify the commission of it. The reasons for sin can never be so great, but we have always stronger reasons to avoid it.

4. Lest any should think that Christ's death was designed merely for an example of patience under sufferings, the apostle here adds a more glorious design and effect of it: *Who his own self.* The person suffering—Jesus Christ: *His own self—in his own body.* The expression *his own self* is emphatic to distinguish him from the Levitical priests (who offered the blood of others). The sufferings he underwent were *stripes and the death of the cross*—servile and ignominious punishments! The reason of his sufferings: He *bore our sins.* Christ, in his sufferings, stood charged with our sins. He bore the punishment of them. As the scape-goat did typically bear the sins of the people on his head, and then carried them quite away, so the Lamb of God does first bear our sins in his own body, and thereby take away the sins of the world.

JAMIESON, FAUSSET, BROWN

the participle vs. 18, "being subject," is joined to the hortatory imperatives going before, viz., "abstain," "submit yourselves." "honor all men." **with**—*Greek, "in."* **all**—all possible: under all circumstances, such as are presently detailed. **fear**—the awe of one subject: God, however, is the ultimate object of the "fear": *fear* "for the Lord's sake" (vs. 13), not merely slavish fear of masters. **good**—kind. **gentle**—indulgent towards errors: considerate: yielding, not exacting all which justice might demand. **froward**—perverse: harsh. Those bound to obey must not make the disposition and behavior of the superior the measure of the fulfilment of their obligations. **19.** Reason for subjection even to froward masters. **thankworthy**—(Luke 6:33). A course out of the common, and especially *praiseworthy* in the eyes of God: not as Rome interprets, earning merit, and so a work of supererogation (cf. vs. 20). **for conscience toward God**—lit., "consciousness of God": from a conscientious regard to God, more than to men. **endure**—*Greek*, "patiently bear up under": as a superimposed burden [ALFORD]. **grief**—*Greek*, "griefs." **20. what**—*Greek*, "what kind of." **glory**—what peculiar *merit.* **buffeted**—the punishment of slaves, and suddenly inflicted [BENGEL]. **this is**—Some oldest MSS. read, "for." Then the translation is, "But if when . . . ye take it patiently (it is a glory), *for* this is. . . . **acceptable**—*Greek*, "thankworthy," as in vs. 19. **21.** Christ's example a proof that patient endurance under undeserved sufferings is acceptable with God. **hereunto**—to the patient endurance of unmerited suffering (ch. 3:9). Christ is an example to servants, even as He was once in "the form of a servant." **called**—with a heavenly calling, though slaves. **for us**—*His dying for us* is the highest exemplification of "doing well" (vs. 20). Ye must patiently suffer, being innocent, as Christ also innocently suffered (not for Himself, but *for us*). The oldest MSS. for "us . . . us," read, "you . . . for you." Christ's sufferings, while they are for an example, were also primarily sufferings *"for us,"* a consideration which imposes an everlasting obligation on us to please Him. **leaving**—*behind:* so the *Greek:* on His departure to the Father, to His glory. **an example**—*Greek*, "a copy," lit., "a writing copy" set by masters for their pupils. Christ's precepts and sermons were the *transcript* of His life. Peter *graphically* sets before servants those features especially suited to their case. **follow**—*close upon:* so the *Greek.* **his steps**—*footsteps*, viz., of His *patience* combined with *innocence.* **22.** Illustrating Christ's *well-doing* (vs. 20) though suffering. **did**—*Greek* aorist. Never in a single instance did" [ALFORD]. Quoted from Isaiah 53:9, end, LXX. **neither**—nor yet: not even [ALFORD]. Sinlessness as to the *mouth* is a mark of *perfection. Guile* is a common fault of servants. "If any boast of his innocency, Christ surely did not suffer as an evildoer" [CALVIN], yet He took it patiently (vs. 20). On Christ's sinlessness, cf. II Corinthians 5:21; Hebrews 7:26. **23.** Servants are apt to "answer again" (Titus 2:9). *Threats* of divine judgment against oppressors are often used by those who have no other arms, as for instance, slaves. Christ, who as Lord could have threatened with truth, never did so. **committed** *himself*—or *His cause*, as man in His suffering. Cf. the type, Jeremiah 11:20. In this Peter seems to have before his mind Isaiah 53:8. Cf. Romans 12:19, on our corresponding duty. Leave your case in His hands, not desiring to make Him executioner of your revenge, but rather praying for enemies. God's *righteous judgment* gives tranquillity and consolation to the oppressed. **24. his own self**—there being *none other* but *Himself* who could have done it. His *voluntary* undertaking of the work of redemption is implied. The *Greek* puts in antithetical juxtaposition, OUR, and His OWN SELF, to mark the idea of *His substitution for us.* His "well-doing" in His sufferings is set forth here as an example to servants and to us all (vs. 20). **bare**—to sacrifice: *carried and offered up:* a sacrificial term. Isaiah 53:11, 12, "He *bare* the sin of many": where the *idea of bearing on Himself* is the prominent one; here the *offering in sacrifice* is combined with that idea. So the same *Greek* means in ch. 2:5. **our sins**—In *offering* or *presenting in sacrifice* (as the *Greek* for "bare" implies) His body, Christ offered in it the *guilt* of our sins upon the cross, as upon the altar of God, that it might be expiated in Him, and so taken away from us. Cf. Isaiah 53:10, "Thou shalt make His soul an offering for sin."

on the tree—the cross, the proper place for One on whom the *curse* was laid: this curse stuck to Him until it was legally (through His death as the guilt-bearer) destroyed in His body; thus the handwriting of the bond against us is can-

ADAM CLARKE

With all fear. With all submission and reverence. *The froward.* The crooked, perverse, unreasonable, morose, and austere.

19. *For this is thankworthy.* If, in a conscientious discharge of your duty, you suffer evil, this is in the sight of God thankworthy, pleasing, and proper.

20. *For what glory is it?* It appears from this that the poor Christians, and especially those who had been converted to Christianity while in a state of slavery, were often grievously abused; they were *buffeted* because they were Christians, and because they would not join with their masters in idolatrous worship.

21. *Hereunto were ye called.* You were called to a state of suffering when you were called to be Christians; for the world cannot endure the yoke of Christ, and they that will live godly in Christ must suffer persecution; they will meet with it in one form or other. *Christ also suffered for us.* And left us the example of His meekness and gentleness; for when He was reviled, He reviled not again. You cannot expect to fare better than your Master; imitate His example, and His Spirit shall comfort and sustain you. Many MSS. and most of the versions, instead of *Christ also suffered for us, leaving us,* read, "suffered for you, leaving you." This reading, which I think is genuine, is noticed in the margin.

22. *Who did no sin.* He suffered, but not on account of any evil He had either done or said. It is very likely that the apostle mentions *guile*, because those who do wrong generally strive to screen themselves by prevarication and lies. These words appear to be a quotation from Isa. liii. 9.

23. *But committed himself.* Though He could have inflicted any kind of punishment on His persecutors, yet to give us, in this respect also, an example that we should follow His steps, He committed His cause to Him who is the righteous Judge. To avoid evil tempers and the uneasiness and danger of avenging ourselves, it is a great advantage in all such cases to be able to refer our cause to God, and to be assured that the Judge of all the earth will do right.

24. *Bare our sins in his own body.* Bore the punishment due to our sins. In no other sense could Christ bear them. To say that they were so imputed to Him as if they had been His own, and that the Father beheld Him as blackened with imputed sin, is monstrous, if not blasphemous.

MATTHEW HENRY

The fruits of Christ's sufferings. Our sanctification. Our justification. *By his stripes we are healed.*

5. The difference between their former and present condition, *v.* 25. (1) Man's sin: he goes astray; it is his own act. (2) His misery: he goes astray from the shepherd, and from the flock.

(3) The recovery of these by conversion. This return is to Christ, who is the true careful shepherd, that loves his sheep, who is the most vigilant pastor, and bishop, or overseer of souls.

JAMIESON, FAUSSET, BROWN

celled by His death. **that we being dead to sins**—the effect of His death to "sin" in the aggregate, and to all particular "sins," viz., that we should be as entirely *delivered from* them, as a slave that is *dead* is delivered from service *to* his master. This is our spiritual *standing* through faith by virtue of Christ's death: our actual mortification of particular *sins* is in proportion to the degree of our effectually being made conformable to His death. "That we should *die to the sins* whose collected guilt Christ carried away in His death, and SO LIVE TO THE RIGHTEOUSNESS (cf. Isa. 53:11. 'My *righteous* servant shall *justify* many'), the gracious relation to God which He has brought in" [STEIGER]. **by whose stripes** [*Greek,* "stripe"] **ye were healed**—a paradox, yet true. "Ye servants (cf. 'buffeted,' 'the tree,' vss. 20, 24) often bear *the strife;* but it is not more than your Lord Himself bore; learn from Him patience in wrongful sufferings. **25.** (Isa. 53:6.) **For**—Assigning their natural need of *healing* (vs. 24). **now**—Now that the atonement for all has been made, the foundation is laid for *individual conversion:* so "*ye are returned,*" or "*have become converted* to. . . ."

Shepherd and Bishop—The designation of the *pastors* and *elders* of the Church belongs in its fullest sense to the great Head of the Church, "the good Shepherd." As the "*bishop*" *oversees* (as the *Greek* term means), so "the *eyes of the Lord are over* the righteous" (ch. 3:12). He gives us His spirit and feeds and guides us by His word. "Shepherd," *Hebrew, Parnas,* is often applied to *kings,* and enters into the composition of names, as *Pharna*bazus.

ADAM CLARKE

That we, being dead to sins. "That we, being freed from sin"—delivered out of its power, and from under its tyranny. *Should live unto righteousness.* That *righteousness* should be our master now, as sin was before. *By whose stripes ye were healed.* The apostle refers here to Isa. liii. 4-6; and he still keeps the case of these persecuted servants in view, and encourages them to suffer patiently by the example of Christ, who was buffeted and scourged, and who bore all this that the deep and inveterate wounds, inflicted on their souls by sin, *might be healed.*

25. *For ye were as sheep going astray.* Formerly you were not in a better moral condition than your oppressors; you were like stray sheep, in the wilderness of ignorance and sin, till Christ, the true and merciful Shepherd, called you back from your wanderings by sending you the gospel of His grace. *Bishop of your souls.* Unless we consider the word *Bishop* as a corruption of the word *episcopos,* and that this literally signifies an "overseer," an "inspector," or "one that has the oversight," it can convey to us no meaning of the original. Jesus Christ is the "Overseer of souls"; He has them continually under His eye; He knows their wants, wishes, dangers, and provides for them. As their *Shepherd,* He leads them to the best pastures, defends them from their enemies, and guides them by His eye. Jesus is the good Shepherd that laid down His life for His sheep. All human souls are inexpressibly dear to Him, as they are the purchase of His blood. He is still supreme *Bishop* or "Overseer" in His Church.

MATTHEW HENRY

CHAPTER 3

Verses 1–7

I. Lest the Christian matrons should imagine that their conversion to Christ exempted them from subjection to their pagan or Jewish husbands, the apostle here tells them,

1. In what the duty of wives consists.

(1) In *subjection,* which obliging conduct would be the most likely way to win those unbelieving husbands who had rejected the word, or who attended to no other evidence of the truth of it than what they saw in the exemplary *conversation of their wives.* A cheerful *subjection,* and a loving, reverential respect, are duties which Christian women owe their husbands, whether they be good or bad. There is nothing more powerful, next to the word of God, to win people, than a good conversation.

(2) In *fear,* or reverence to their husbands.

(3) In a *chaste conversation.* Evil men are strict observers of the conversation of the professors of religion. *A chaste conversation* is an excellent means to win them to the faith of the gospel.

(4) In preferring the ornaments of the mind to those of the body, *v.* 3. Here are three sorts of ornaments forbidden: *plaiting of hair,* which was commonly used in those times by lewd women; *wearing of gold; putting on of apparel* with too much nicety and costliness in it. Religious people should take care that all their external behaviour be answerable to their profession. The outward adorning of the body is very often sensual and excessive. The attire of a harlot can never become a chaste Christian matron.

JAMIESON, FAUSSET, BROWN

CHAPTER 3

VSS. 1-22. RELATIVE DUTIES OF HUSBANDS AND WIVES: EXHORTATIONS TO LOVE AND FORBEARANCE: RIGHT CONDUCT UNDER PERSECUTIONS FOR RIGHTEOUSNESS' SAKE, AFTER CHRIST'S EXAMPLE, WHOSE DEATH RESULTED IN QUICKENING TO US THROUGH HIS BEING QUICKENED AGAIN, OF WHICH BAPTISM IS THE SACRAMENTAL SEAL. **1. Likewise**—*Greek,* "In like manner," as "servants" in their sphere; cf. the reason of the woman's subjection, I Corinthians 11:8-10; I Timothy 2:11-14. **your own**—enforcing the obligation: it is not strangers ye are required to *be subject to.* Every time that obedience is enjoined upon women to their husbands, the *Greek, idios,* "one's own peculiarly," is used, while the wives of men are designated only by *heauton,* "of themselves." **that, if**—*Greek,* "that even if." *Even if* you have a husband that obeys not the word (i.e., is an unbeliever). **without the word**—*independently of hearing the word preached,* the usual way of *faith* coming. But BENGEL, "without word," i.e., *without direct* Gospel *discourse* of the wives, "they *may* (lit., in oldest MSS., shall, which marks the almost objective *certainty* of the result) be won" indirectly. "Unspoken acting is more powerful than unperformed speaking" [ŒCUMENIUS]. "A soul converted is *gained* to itself, to the pastor, wife, or husband, who sought it, and to Jesus Christ; added to His treasury who thought not His own precious blood too dear to lay out for this gain" [LEIGHTON]. "The discreet wife would choose first of all to persuade her husband to share with her in the things which lead to blessedness; but if this be impossible, let her then alone diligently press after virtue, in all things obeying him so as to do nothing at any time against his will, except in such things as are essential to virtue and salvation" [CLEMENS ALEXANDRINUS]. **2. behold**—on narrowly looking into it, lit., "having closely observed." **chaste**—pure, spotless, free from all impurity. **fear**—*reverential,* towards your husbands. Scrupulously pure, as opposed to the noisy, ambitious character of worldly women. **3.** Lit., "To whom let there belong [viz., as their peculiar ornament] not the outward adornment [usual in the sex which first, by the fall, brought in the need of covering, *Note,* ch. 5:5] of . . ." **plaiting**—artificial braiding, in order to attract admiration. **wearing**—lit., "putting round," viz., the head, as a diadem—the arm, as a bracelet—the finger, as rings. **apparel**—showy and costly. "Have the blush of modesty on thy face instead of paint, and moral worth and discretion instead of gold and emeralds" [MELISSA]. **4. But**—"Rather." The "outward adornment" of jewelry, etc., is forbidden, in so far as woman loves such things, not in so far as she uses them from a sense of propriety, and does not *abuse* them. Singularity mostly comes

ADAM CLARKE

CHAPTER 3

1. *Ye wives, be in subjection.* Consider that your husband is, by God's appointment, the head and ruler of the house. Do not, therefore, attempt to usurp his government; for even though he *obey not the word,* is "not a believer in the Christian doctrine," his rule is not thereby impaired. For Christianity never alters civil relations; and your affectionate, obedient conduct will be the most likely means of convincing him of the truth of the doctrine which you have received. *Without the word.* That your holy conduct may be the means of begetting in them a reverence for Christianity, the preaching of which they will not hear. See the notes on 1 Cor. xiv. 34.

2. *Chaste conversation coupled with fear.* While they see that you join modesty, chastity, and the purest manners, to the fear of God. Or perhaps *fear* is taken, as in Eph. v. 33, for the "reverence" due to the husband.

3. *Whose adorning.* See the note on Heb. ix. 1, where the word *cosmos,* "world" or "ornament," is defined. *Plaiting the hair, and of wearing of gold.* Plaiting the hair, and variously folding it about the head, was the most ancient and most simple mode of disposing of this chief ornament of the female head. Thin plates of gold were often mixed with the hair, to make it appear more ornamental by the reflection of light. Small golden buckles were also used in different parts; and among the Roman ladies, pearls and precious stones of different colors. But it is evident, from many remaining monuments, that in numerous cases the *hair* differently plaited and curled was the only ornament of the head. Often a simple pin, sometimes of ivory, pointed with gold, seemed to connect the plaits. In monuments of antiquity the heads of the married and single women may be known, the former by the hair being parted from the forehead over the middle of the top of the head, the latter by being quite close, or being plaited and curled all in a general mass. There is a remarkable passage in Plutarch very like that in the text: "An ornament, as Crates said, is that which becomes her best. This is neither gold, nor pearls, nor scarlet; but those things which are an evident proof of gravity, regularity, and modesty." The wife of Phocion, a celebrated Athenian general, receiving a visit from a lady who was elegantly adorned with gold and jewels, and her hair with pearls, took occasion to call the attention of her guest to the elegance and costliness of her dress, remarking at the same time, "My ornament is my husband, now for

MATTHEW HENRY

He directs Christian wives to put on much more excellent and beautiful ornaments, *v.* 4. *First*, The part to be adorned: *The hidden man of the heart.* Take care to adorn and beautify your souls rather than your bodies.

Secondly, The ornament prescribed. It must be something *not corruptible.* The ornaments of the body perish in the using; but the grace of God, the longer we wear it, the brighter and better it is. The finest ornament of Christian women is *a meek and quiet spirit.* If the husband be harsh, and averse to religion, there is no way so likely to win him as a prudent meek behaviour. A true Christian's chief care lies in the right ordering and commanding of his own spirit. Where the hypocrite's work ends, there the true Christian's work begins. The endowments of the inner man are the chief ornaments of a Christian; but especially a composed, calm, and quiet spirit, renders either man or woman beautiful and lovely.

2. The apostle enforces them by the example, (1) Of the holy women of old, who trusted in God, *v.* 5. "The duties imposed upon you are not new, but what have ever been practised by the greatest and best women in the world."

(2) Of Sara, who obeyed her husband, and followed him. "*Whose daughters you are* if you imitate her in faith and good works." The subjection of wives to their husbands is a duty which has been practised universally by holy women in all ages. Christians ought to do their duty to one another, not out of fear, nor from force, but from a willing mind, and in obedience to the command of God.

II. The husband's duty to the wife.

1. The particulars are: *Cohabitation. Dwelling with the wife according to knowledge*, as wise and sober men, who know the word of God and their own duty. *Giving honour to the wife*—giving due respect to her, and placing a due trust and confidence in her.

2. The reasons are, Because she is *the weaker vessel.* The wife is, in other and higher respects, equal to her husband; they are *heirs together of the grace of life*, and therefore should live peaceable one with another, and, if they do not, their prayers one with another and one for another will be hindered.

Verses 8–15

I. How Christians and friends should treat one another. Christians should endeavour to be all of one mind in the great points of faith, in real affection, and in Christian practice. Though Christians cannot be exactly of the same mind, yet they should have compassion one for another, and love as brethren. Christianity requires pity to the distressed, and civility to all.

JAMIESON, FAUSSET, BROWN

from pride and throws needless hindrances to religion in the way of others. Under costly attire there may be a humble mind. "Great is he who uses his earthenware as if it were plate; not less great is he who uses his silver as if it were earthenware" [SENECA *in* ALFORD]. **hidden**—*inner* man, which the Christian instinctively *hides* from public view. **of the heart**—*consisting in the heart* regenerated and adorned by the Spirit. This "inner man of the heart" is the subject of the verb "be," vs. 3, *Greek:* "Of whom let the inner man be," viz., the distinction or adornment. **in that**—consisting or standing *in that* as its element. **not corruptible**—not transitory, nor tainted with corruption, as all earthly adornments. **meek and quiet**—*meek*, not creating disturbances: *quiet*, bearing with tranquillity the disturbances caused by others. *Meek* in affections and feelings; *quiet* in words, countenance, and actions [BENGEL]. **in the sight of God**—who looks to inward, not merely outward things. **of great price**—The results of redemption should correspond to its costly price (ch. 1:19). **5. after this manner**—with the *ornament of a meek and quiet spirit* (cf. the portrait of the godly wife, Prov. 31:10-31). **trusted**—*Greek*, "hoped." "Holy" is explained by "hoped in (so as to be *united to, Greek*) God." Hope in God is the spring of true holiness [BENGEL]. **in subjection**—Their ornament consisted in their subordination. Vanity was forbidden (vs. 3) as being contrary to female *subjection.*

6. Sara—an example of *faith.* **calling him lord**—(Gen. 18:12). **ye are**—*Greek*, "ye have become": "children" of Abraham and Sara by *faith*, whereas ye were Gentile aliens from the covenant.

afraid with any amazement—*Greek*, "fluttering alarm," "consternation." *Act well, and be not thrown into sudden panic*, as weak females are apt to be, by any opposition from without. BENGEL *translates*, "Not afraid OF *any fluttering terror* coming from without" (vss. 13-16). So LXX, Proverbs 3:25 uses the same *Greek* word, which Peter probably refers to. Anger assails men; *fear*, women. You need fear no man in doing what is right: not thrown into fluttering agitation by any sudden outbreak of temper on the part of your unbelieving husbands, while you *do well.* **7. dwell**—*Greek*, "dwelling": connected with the verb, ch. 2:17, "Honor all." **knowledge**—Christian knowledge: appreciating the due relation of the sexes in the design of God, and acting with tenderness and forbearance accordingly: *wisely: with wise consideration. them* . . . **giving honour to the wife**—translate and punctuate the *Greek* rather, "dwelling according to knowledge with the female (*Greek adjective*, qualifying 'vessel'; not as *English Version*, a noun) as with the weaker vessel (*Note*, I Thess. 4:4). Both husband and wife are vessels in God's hand, and of God's making, to fulfil His gracious purposes. Both weak, the woman the *weaker.* The sense of his own weakness, and that she, like himself, is God's *vessel* and fabric, ought to lead him to act with tender and wise consideration towards her who is the *weaker fabric*), giving (lit., '*assigning*,' '*apportioning*') honor as being also (besides being man and wife) heirs together . . ."; or, as the Vatican MS. reads, "as to those who are also (besides being your wives) fellow heirs." (The reason why the man should *give honor* to the woman is, because *God gives honor to both* as fellow heirs; cf. the same argument, vs. 9.) He does not take into account the case of an *unbelieving* wife, as she might yet believe. **grace of life**—God's *gracious* gift of *life* (ch. 1:4, 13). **that your prayers be not hindered**—by dissensions, which prevent *united* prayer, on which depends the blessing. **8.** *General* summary of relative duty, after having detailed *particular* duties from ch. 2:18. **of one mind**—as to the faith. **having compassion one of another**—*Greek*, "sympathizing" in the joy and sorrow of others. **love as brethren**—*Greek*, "loving the brethren." **pitiful**—towards the afflicted. **courteous**—genuine Christian politeness; not the tinsel of the world's politeness; stamped with *unfeigned love* on one side, and *humility* on the other. But the oldest MSS. read, "humble-minded." It is slightly different from "humble," in that it marks a *conscious effort* to be truly *humble.*

ADAM CLARKE

the twentieth year general of the Athenians."

4. *The hidden man of the heart.* This phrase is of the same import with that of Paul, Rom. vii. 22, the "inner man"; that is, the soul, with the whole system of affections and passions. Every part of the Scripture treats man as a compound being: the "body" is the outward or visible man; the "soul," the inward, hidden, or invisible man. *A meek and quiet spirit.* That is, a mind that will not give provocation to others, nor receive irritation by the provocation of others. Meekness will prevent the first; "quietness" will guard against the last. *Great price.* All the ornaments placed on the head and body of the most illustrious female are, in the sight of God, of no worth; but a "meek and silent spirit" are, in His sight, invaluable.

5. *For after this manner.* Simplicity reigned in primitive times; natural ornaments alone were then in use. Trade and commerce brought in luxuries; and luxury brought pride, and all the excessive nonsense of dress. *Being in subjection unto their own husbands.* It will rarely be found that women who are fond of dress and extravagant in it have any subjection to their husbands but what comes from mere necessity. Indeed, their dress, which they intend as an attractive to the eyes of others, is a sufficient proof that they have neither love nor respect for their own husbands.

6. *Even as Sara obeyed.* Almost the same words are in *Rab. Tanchum, fol.* 9, 3: "The wife of Abraham reverenced him, and called him lord, as it is written, Gen. xviii. 12: 'And my lord is old.'" The words of the apostle imply that she acknowledged his superiority, and her own subjection to him, in the order of God. *Whose daughters ye are.* As Abraham is represented the father of all his male believing descendants, so Sara is represented as the mother of all her believing female posterity. *As long as ye do well.* For you cannot maintain your relationship to her longer than you believe, and you cannot believe longer than you continue to obey. *And are not afraid with any amazement.* It is difficult to extract any sense out of this clause. The original is not very easy: "And not fearing with any terror." If you do well, and act conscientiously your part as faithful wives, you will at no time live under the distressing apprehension of being found out, or terrified at every appearance of the discovery of infidelities or improper conduct.

7. *Dwell with them according to knowledge.* Give your wives, by no species of unkind carriage, any excuse for delinquency. How can a man expect his wife to be faithful to him if he be unfaithful to her? *Giving honour unto the wife.* Using your superior strength and experience in her behalf, and thus honoring her by becoming her protector and support. But the word *honour* signifies "maintenance" as well as "respect"—maintain, provide for the wife. *As unto the weaker vessel.* Being more delicately, and consequently more slenderly, constructed. Roughness and strength go hand in hand; so likewise do beauty and frailty. The female has what the man wants—beauty and delicacy. The male has what the female wants—courage and strength. The one is as good in its place as the other; and by these things God has made an equality between the man and the woman, so that there is properly very little superiority on either side. *Being heirs together.* Both the man and woman being equally called to eternal glory; and as prayer is one great means of obtaining a meetness for it, it is necessary that they should live together in such a manner as to prevent all family contentions, that they may not be prevented, by disputes or misunderstandings, from uniting daily in this most important duty—family and social prayer.

8. *Be ye all of one mind.* Unity, both in the family and in the Church, being essentially necessary to peace and salvation. See on Rom. xii. 16 and xv. 5. *Having compassion.* "Being sympathetic"; feeling for each other; bearing each other's burdens. *Love as brethren.* "Be lovers of the brethren." *Pitiful.* "Tenderhearted." *Courteous.* Be "friendly-minded," is the reading of more than twenty MSS. and some of the fathers. This is probably the true reading.

MATTHEW HENRY

II. He instructs us how to behave towards enemies. 1. "When they rail at you, do you bless them; when they give you evil words, do you give them good ones; for Christ has called you to bless those that curse you, and has settled a blessing on you as your everlasting inheritance." The laws of Christ oblige us to return blessing for railing (Matt. v. 44). We must pity, pray for, and love those who rail at us. A Christian's calling, as it invests him with glorious privileges, so it obliges him to difficult duties.

2. An excellent prescription for a comfortable happy life in this quarrelsome ill-natured world (*v.* 10): it is quoted from Ps. xxxiv. 12–14. It is lawful to consider temporal advantages as motives and encouragements to religion. The practice of religion, particularly the right government of the tongue, is the best way to make this life comfortable and prosperous; a sincere, inoffensive, discreet tongue, is a singular means to pass us peaceably and comfortably through the world. It is the duty of Christians not only to embrace peace when it is offered, but to seek and pursue it when it is denied.

3. Christians need not fear that such patient inoffensive behaviour will invite the cruelty of their enemies (*v.* 12). *His ears are open to their prayers. But the face of the Lord is against those that do evil.* He is more an enemy to wicked persecutors than men are. God hath a special care and paternal affection towards all his righteous people. God doth always hear the prayers of the faithful.

4. This patient humble behaviour of Christians is further urged. This will be the best and surest way to prevent suffering, *v.* 13. "Ordinarily, there will be but few so diabolical and impious as to harm those who live so innocently and usefully as you do."

But if you suffer for righteousness' sake (*v.* 14), it will be your glory and your happiness. "You need not be afraid of anything they can do to strike you with terror, neither be much troubled nor concerned about the rage or force of your enemies." To follow always that which is good is the best course we can take to keep out of harm's way. To suffer for righteousness' sake is the honour and happiness of a Christian. Christians have no reason to be afraid of the threats or rage of any of their enemies.

Instead of terrifying yourselves with the fear of men, be sure to *sanctify the Lord God in your hearts* (*v.* 15).

"When this principle is laid deeply into your hearts, the next thing, as to men, is to be always ready *to give an answer to every man that asketh a reason of your hope.* The hope and faith of a Christian are defensible against all the world. Every Christian is bound to answer for the hope that is in him. Christians should have a reason ready for their Christianity, that it may appear they are not actuated either by folly or fancy. These confessions of our faith ought to be made *with meekness and fear.*

JAMIESON, FAUSSET, BROWN

9. evil—in deed. **railing**—in word. **blessing**—your revilers; participle, not a noun after "rendering." **knowing that**—The oldest MSS. read merely, "because." **are**—*Greek, "were* called." **inherit a blessing**—not only passive, but also active; receiving spiritual blessing from God by faith, and in your turn blessing others from love [GERHARD *in* ALFORD]. "It is not in order to inherit a blessing that we must bless, but because our portion is blessing." No *railing* can injure you (vs. 13). Imitate God who *blesses* you. The first fruits of His *blessing* for eternity are enjoyed by the righteous even now (vs. 10) [BENGEL]. **10. will love**—*Greek,* "wishes to love." He who *loves life* (present and eternal), and *desires to continue to do so,* not involving himself in troubles which will make this life a burden, and cause him to forfeit eternal life. Peter confirms his exhortation, vs. 9, by Psalm 34:12-16. **refrain**—curb, lit., "cause to cease"; implying that our natural inclination and custom is to speak evil. "Men commonly think that they would be exposed to the wantonness of their enemies if they did not strenuously vindicate their rights. But the Spirit promises a life of blessedness to none but those who are gentle and patient of evils" [CALVIN]. **evil . . . guile**—First he warns against sins of the *tongue,* evil-speaking, and deceitful, double-tongued speaking; next, against *acts* of injury to one's neighbor. **11.** In oldest MSS., *Greek,* "*Moreover* (besides his *words,* in *acts*), let him." **eschew**—"turn from." **ensue**—*pursue* as a thing hard to attain, and that flees from one in this troublesome world. **12.** Ground of the promised present and eternal life of blessedness to the meek (vs. 10). The Lord's *eyes* are ever over them for good. **ears . . . unto their prayers**—(I John 5:14, 15). **face . . . against**—The *eyes* imply *favorable* regard; the *face* of the Lord *upon* (not as *English Version,* "against") them that do evil, implies that He narrowly observes them, so as not to let them really and lastingly hurt His people (cf. vs. 13). **13. who . . . will harm you**—This fearless confidence in God's protection from harm, Christ, the Head, in His sufferings realized; so His members. **if ye be**—*Greek,* "if ye have *become.*" **followers**—The oldest MSS. read "emulous," "zealous of" (Titus 2:14). **good**—The contrast in *Greek* is, "Who will do you *evil,* if ye be zealous of *good?*" **14. But and if**—"But *if even.*" "The promises of *this* life extend only so far as it is expedient for us that they should be fulfilled" [CALVIN]. So he proceeds to state the exceptions to the promise (vs. 10), and how the truly wise will behave in such exceptional cases. "If ye should *suffer*"; if it should so happen; "suffer," a milder word than *harm.* **for righteousness**—"not the suffering, but the cause for which one suffers, makes the martyr" [AUGUSTINE]. **happy**—Not even can *suffering* take away your *blessedness,* but rather promotes it. **and**—*Greek,* "but." Do not impair your blessing (vs. 9) by *fearing* man's *terror* in your times of adversity. Lit., "Be not terrified with their terror," i.e., with that which they try to strike into you, and which strikes themselves when in adversity. This verse and v. 15 is quoted from Isaiah 8:12, 13. God alone is to be feared; he that fears God has none else to fear. **neither be troubled**—the threat of the law, Leviticus 26:36; Deuteronomy 28: 65, 66; in contrast to which the Gospel gives the believer a heart assured of God's favor, and therefore unruffled, amidst all adversities. Not only be not *afraid,* but be not even *agitated.* **15. sanctify**—*hallow; honor as holy,* enshrining Him *in your hearts.* So in the Lord's Prayer, Matthew 6:9. God's holiness is thus glorified in our hearts as the dwelling-place of His Spirit. **the Lord God**—The oldest MSS. read "Christ." Translate, "Sanctify *Christ as Lord.*" **and**—*Greek,* "but," or "moreover." *Besides* this inward sanctification of God *in the heart, be also ready always to give* . . . . **answer**—an apologetic answer defending your faith. **to every man that asketh you**—The last words limit the universality of the "always"; not to a railer, but to everyone among the heathen who inquires honestly. **a reason**—a reasonable account. This refutes Rome's dogma, "I believe it, because the Church believes it." Credulity is believing without evidence; faith is believing on evidence. There is no repose for reason itself but in faith. This verse does not impose an obligation to bring forward a learned proof and logical defense of revelation. But as believers deny themselves, crucify the world, and brave persecution, they must be buoyed up by some strong "hope"; men of the world, having no such hope themselves, are moved by curiosity to *ask* the secret of this hope; the believer must be *ready* to give an *experimental account* "how this hope arose in him, what it contains, and on what it

ADAM CLARKE

9. *Not rendering evil for evil.* Purposing, saying, doing nothing but good; and invariably returning good for evil. *Ye are thereunto called.* This is your calling, your business in life—to do good, and to do good for evil, and to implore God's blessing even on your worst enemies.

10-11. *For he that will love life.* This is a quotation from Ps. xxxiv. 12-16, as it stands in the Septuagint; only the aorist of the imperative is changed from the second into the third person. He who wishes to live long and prosperously must act as he is here directed. (1) He must refrain from evil speaking, lying, and slandering. (2) He must avoid flattery and fair speeches, which cover hypocritical or wicked intentions. (3) He must "avoid" *evil,* keep "going away" from evil. (4) He must *do good;* he must walk in the way of righteousness. (5) He must live peaceably with all men; *seek peace* where it has been lost; and "pursue it" where it seems to be flying away. He who lives thus must live happy in himself.

12. *The eyes of the Lord are over the righteous.* That is, he is continually under God's notice and His care; God continually watches for him and watches over him, and he is under His constant protection. *And his ears are open unto their prayers.* The original is very emphatic: "The eyes of the Lord are upon the righteous, and His ears to their prayers." The righteous man ever attracts the divine notice, and wherever he is, there is the ear of God; for, as every righteous man is a man of prayer, wherever he prays, there is the ear of God, into which the prayer, as soon as formed, enters. *But the face of the Lord.* Far from His eye being upon them, or His ear open to their requests (for prayer they have none), His *face,* His "approbation," His providence and blessing, are turned away from them.

13. *Who is he that will harm you?* Is it possible that a man can be wretched who has God for his Friend? *If ye be followers.* "If you are imitators of the good One," i.e., of God. "The good One" is one of God's prime epithets, see Matt. xix. 17; and Satan is distinguished by the reverse, "the evil one," Matt. xxiii. 19. Instead of *followers,* or rather "imitators," "zealous" of what is good is the reading of numerous MSS., with some of the fathers. This is a very probable reading.

14. *But and if ye suffer.* God may permit you to be tried and persecuted for righteousness' sake, but this cannot essentially harm you; He will press even this into your service and make it work for your good. *Happy are ye.* This seems to refer to Matt. v. 10, "Blessed or happy are you when men persecute you." *Be not afraid of their terror.* "Fear not their fear"; see Isa. viii. 12. Sometimes fear is put for the object of a man's religious worship; see Gen. xxxi. 42; Prov. i. 26; and the place in Isaiah just quoted. The exhortation may mean, "Fear not their gods," they can do you no hurt; and supposing that they curse you by them, yet be not troubled. "He who fears God need have no other fear."

15. *But sanctify the Lord God in your hearts.* To sanctify God may signify to offer Him the praises due to His grace; but as to *sanctify* literally signifies to "make holy," it is impossible that God should be thus sanctified. We have often already seen that *hagiazo* signifies to separate from earth, that is, from any common use or purpose, that the thing or person thus separated may be devoted to a sacred use. Perhaps we should understand Peter's words thus: Entertain just notions of God; of His nature, power, will, justice, goodness, and truth. Thus *sanctify the Lord God in your hearts,* and you will ever be *ready . . . to give . . . a reason of the hope that is in you* to every serious and candid inquirer after truth. Most religious systems and creeds are incapable of rational explanation, because founded on some misconception of the divine nature. Instead of *God,* some MSS. have "Christ." "Sanctify Christ in your hearts" as Lord. The word *apologia,* which we translate *answer,* signifies a "defense"; from this we have our word "apology," which did not originally signify an excuse for an act but a defense of that act. The defenses of Christianity by the primitive fathers are called "apologies." *With meekness and fear.* Several

MATTHEW HENRY

Verses 16, 17

The confession of a Christian's faith cannot credibly be supported but by *a good conscience* and a *good conversation.* Conscience is good when it is kept clear from guilt. *A good conversation in Christ* is a holy life. "Look well to your conscience, and to your conversation; and then, though men falsely accuse you as evil-doers, you will bring them to shame. Be not discouraged, for it is better for you, though worse for your enemies, that you suffer for well-doing than for evil-doing." The most conscientious persons cannot escape the censures and slanders of evil men. Christ and his apostles were so used. False accusation generally turns to the accuser's shame. As well-doing sometimes exposes a good man to suffering, so evil-doing will not exempt an evil man from it. If the sufferings of good people for well-doing be so severe, what will the sufferings of wicked people be for evil-doing?

Verses 18–20

I. The example of Christ is proposed as an argument for patience. Jesus Christ himself was not exempted from sufferings in this life. The reason of Christ's suffering was the sins of men: *Christ suffered for sins.* In the case of our Lord's suffering, it was the just that suffered for the unjust. He that knew no sin suffered instead of those that knew no righteousness. The merit and perfection of Christ's sacrifice. The legal sacrifices were repeated but the sacrifice of Christ, once suffered, purgeth away sin. The blessed design of our Lord's sufferings was to bring us to God. The issue of Christ's suffering. He was put to death in his human nature, but he was quickened and raised again by the Spirit. If Christ was not exempted from sufferings, why should Christians expect it? If he, though perfectly just,. why should not we, who are all criminals? If he once suffered, and then entered into glory, shall not we be patient under trouble?

JAMIESON, FAUSSET, BROWN

rests" [STEIGER]. **with**—The oldest MSS. read, "*but* with." Be ready, *but* with "meekness." Not pertly and arrogantly. **meekness**—(vs. 4.) The most effective way; not self-sufficient impetuosity. **fear**—due respect towards man, and reverence towards God, remembering His cause does not need man's hot temper to uphold it. **16. Having a good conscience**—the secret spring of *readiness to give account* of our *hope.* So *hope* and *good conscience* go together in Acts 24:15, 16. Profession without practice has no weight. But those who *have a good conscience* can afford to give an account of their hope "with meekness." **whereas**—(ch. 2:12). **they speak evil of you, as of evildoers**—One oldest MS. reads, "ye are spoken against," omitting the rest. **falsely accuse**—"calumniate"; the *Greek* expresses malice shown in deeds as well as in words. It is translated, "despitefully use," Matthew 5:44; Luke 6:28. **conversation**—life, conduct. **in Christ**—who is the very element of your life as Christians. **"In Christ" defines "good." It is your good walk *as Christians,* not as citizens, that calls forth malice** (ch. 4:4, 5, 14). **17. better**—One may object, I would not bear it so ill if I had deserved it. Peter replies, it is *better* that you did not deserve it, in order that doing well and yet being spoken against, you may prove yourself a true Christian [GERHARD]. **if the will of God be so**—rather as the optative is in the oldest MSS., "if the will of God should will it so." Those who honor God's will as their highest law (ch. 2:15) have the comfort to know that suffering is God's appointment (ch. 4:19). So Christ Himself; our inclination does not wish it. **18.** Confirmation of vs. 17, by the glorious results of Christ's suffering innocently. **For**—"Because." That is "better," vs. 17, means of which we are rendered more like to Christ in death and in life; for His death brought the best issue to Himself and to us [BENGEL]. **Christ**—the Anointed *Holy* One of God; the *Holy* suffered for *sins,* the *Just* for the *unjust.* **also**—as well as yourselves (vs. 17). Cf. ch. 2:21; there His suffering was brought forward as an example to us; here, as a proof of the blessedness of suffering for well-doing. **once**—for all; never again to suffer. It is "better" for us also once to suffer with Christ, than for ever without Christ [BENGEL]. **for sins**—as though He had Himself committed them. He exposed Himself to death by His "confession," even as we are called on to "give an answer to him that asketh a reason of our hope." **that he might bring us to God**—together with Himself in His ascension to the right hand of God (vs. 22). He brings us, "the unjust," justified together with Him into heaven. So the result of Christ's death is His *drawing men to Him;* spiritually now, in our having *access into the Holiest,* opened by Christ's ascension; literally hereafter. **put to death**—the means of His *bringing us to God.* **in the flesh**—i.e., *in respect to* the life of *flesh* and blood. **quickened by the Spirit**—The oldest MSS. omit the *Greek* article. Translate with the preposition "in," as the antithesis to the previous "*in* the flesh" requires, "IN spirit," i.e., in respect to His Spirit. "Put to death" in the former *mode of life*; "quickened" in the other. Not that His Spirit ever died and was *quickened,* or made alive again, but whereas He had lived after the manner of mortal men in the flesh, He *began to live a spiritual* "resurrection" (vs. 21) *life,* whereby He has the power to bring us to God. Two ways of explaining vss. 18, 19, are open to us: (1) "Quickened in Spirit," i.e., *immediately* on His release from the "flesh," the energy of His undying spirit-life was "quickened" by God the Father, into new modes of action, viz., "in the Spirit He *went* down (as subsequently He *went* up to heaven, vs. 22, the same *Greek* verb) and heralded [not *salvation,* as ALFORD, contrary to Scripture, which everywhere represents man's state, whether saved or lost, after death irreversible. Nor is any mention made of the *conversion* of the spirits in prison. See *Note,* vs. 20. Nor is the phrase here 'preached *the Gospel*' (*evangelizo*), but 'heralded' (*ekeruxe*) or 'preached'; but simply *made the announcement* of His finished work; so the same *Greek* in Mark 1:45, 'publish,' confirming Enoch and Noah's testimony, and thereby declaring the virtual condemnation of their unbelief, and the salvation of Noah and believers; a sample of the similar opposite effects of the same work on *all* unbelievers, and believers, respectively; also a consolation to those whom Peter addresses, in their sufferings at the hands of unbelievers; specially selected for the sake of 'baptism,' its 'antitype' (vs. 21), which, as a seal, marks believers as separated from the rest of the doomed world] to the spirits (His *Spirit* speaking to the *spirits*) in prison (in Hades or Sheol, awaiting the judgment, II Pet. 2:4), which were of old disobedient when. . . ." (2) The strong-

ADAM CLARKE

excellent MSS. add the word "but" here, and it improves the sense considerably: "Be ready always to give an answer to every man that asketh you a reason of the hope that is in you, but with meekness and fear." Do not permit your readiness to answer, nor the confidence you have in the goodness of your cause, lead you to answer pertly or superciliously to any person. Defend the truth with all possible gentleness and fear, lest while you are doing it you should forget His presence whose cause you support, or say anything unbecoming the dignity and holiness of the religion which you have espoused, or inconsistent with that heavenly temper which the Spirit of your indwelling Lord must infallibly produce.

16. *Having a good conscience.* The testimony of God in your own soul "that in simplicity and godly sincerity" you have your "conversation in the world." *Whereas they speak evil of you.* See the same sentiment in chap. ii. 11, and the note there.

17. *For it is better.* See on chap. ii. 19-20.

18. *Christ also hath once suffered.* See the notes on Rom. v. 6; Heb. ix. 28. *Put to death in the flesh.* In His human nature.

But quickened by the Spirit. That very dead body revived by the power of His divinity.

MATTHEW HENRY

A. B. SIMPSON:

This is His ministry in the interval between His death and resurrection of which Peter is almost the exclusive witness. It is true the Apostle Paul alludes to it when he speaks of Him who "also descended first into the lower parts of the earth." Peter, however, tells us definitely that during the interval after His death, He was quickened in the spirit, and in this state "he went and preached unto the spirits in prison." There is little room to question the literal reference of this passage to the disembodied spirits of those who had lived in the days of Noah, and who were now in prison in the realm of the dead, the region called Hades in the Scriptures.

That Christ visited this region is certain and that He gave some message there is also plain. That it was a message of salvation to these imprisoned spirits there is no reason to believe, and there is no hint of it anywhere in the Scriptures. The word translated "preached" here is not the word usually employed for the preaching of the Gospel, but it literally means to herald, to give a proclamation. It is not difficult for us to surmise what He might have proclaimed in the realms of the dead. These souls had heard the Gospel for a hundred and twenty years in the days of Noah, and rejected it with scorn while God's Spirit strove with them. Now they are informed by the authority of the Son of God that the message which they rejected and ridiculed is true, and has been at last fulfilled.

At the same time how natural it would be for Him to proclaim to the other spirits in Hades that had died in faith and waited for His coming, that at last the great redemption was complete, that sin was canceled, that death was conquered, and that He was about to open their prison doors and lead their captivity captive, and take them up with Him to heaven, to which He was about to ascend and open its portals henceforth to all believers. When He did ascend to heaven, we know He took with Him these captive spirits; and since that time the souls of believers, like Stephen, no longer pass into Hades to wait for their reward but pass immediately into glory and are with Jesus Christ himself in heaven, awaiting the resurrection of their bodies and their full inheritance and reward at His Second Coming.—*Christ in the Bible*

II. The apostle passes from the example of Christ to that of the old world. They had now an offer of mercy; those that accepted of it should be saved, but those who rejected Christ should be as certainly destroyed as ever the disobedient in the times of Noah were. 1. The preacher—Christ Jesus. *He went and preached*, by his Spirit striving with them. 2. The hearers. He properly calls them spirits now *in prison*; not that they were *in prison when Christ preached to them.*

3. The sin of these people: They were *disobedient*. This their sin is aggravated from the patience and *long-suffering of God*.

JAMIESON, FAUSSET, BROWN

est point in favor of (I) is the position of "sometime," i.e., *of old*, connected with "disobedient"; whereas if the *preaching* or announcing were a thing long past, we should expect "sometime," or *of old*, to be joined to "went and preached." But this transposition may express that *their disobedience preceded His preaching.* The *Greek* participle expresses the reason of His *preaching*, *"inasmuch as* they were sometime disobedient" (cf. ch. 4:6). Also "went" seems to mean a *personal* going, as in vs. 22, not merely *in spirit*. But see the answer below. The objections are "quickened" must refer to Christ's *body* (cf. vs. 21, end), for as His *Spirit* never ceased to live, it cannot be said to be "quickened." Cf. John 5:21; Romans 8:11, and other passages, where "quicken" is used of the *bodily* resurrection. Also, not His *Spirit*, but His *soul*, went to Hades. His Spirit was commended by Him at death to His Father, and was thereupon "in Paradise." The theory—(1) would thus require that His descent to the spirits in prison should be *after* His resurrection! Cf. Ephesians 4:9, 10, which makes the *descent* precede the *ascent*. Also Scripture elsewhere is silent about such a heralding, though possibly Christ's death had immediate effects on the state of both the godly and the ungodly in Hades: the souls of the godly heretofore in comparative confinement, perhaps then having been, as some Fathers thought, translated to God's immediate and heavenly presence; but this cannot be *proved* from Scripture. Cf. however, John 3:13; Colossians 1:18. *Prison* is always used in a *bad* sense in Scripture. "Paradise" and "Abraham's bosom," the abode of good spirits in Old Testament times, are separated by a wide gulf from Hell or Hades, and cannot be called "prison." Cf. II Corinthians 12:2, 4, where "paradise" and the "third heaven" correspond. Also, why should the antediluvian unbelievers in particular be selected as the objects of His preaching in Hades? Therefore explain: "Quickened in spirit, in which (as distinguished from *in person*; the words "in which," i.e., *in spirit*, expressly obviating the objection that "went" implies a *personal going*) He went (in the person of Noah, "a preacher of righteousness," II Pet. 2:5: ALFORD's own *Note*, Eph. 2:17, is the best reply to his argument from "went" that a *local* going to Hades *in person* is meant. As "He CAME and preached peace" *by His Spirit* in the apostles and ministers after His death and ascension: so before His incarnation He preached in Spirit through Noah to the antediluvians, John 14: 18, 28; Acts 26:23. "Christ should show," lit., "*announce* light to the Gentiles") and preached unto the spirits in prison, i.e., the antediluvians, whose bodies indeed seemed free, but their spirits were in prison, shut up in the earth as one great condemned cell (exactly parallel to Isa. 24: 22, 23 "upon the earth . . . they shall be gathered together as *prisoners* are gathered in the pit, and shall be shut up *in the prison* . . ." [just as the fallen angels are judicially regarded as "in chains of darkness," though for a time now at large on the earth, I Pet. 2:4], where vs. 18 has a plain allusion to the flood, "the *windows from on high* are open," cf. Gen. 7:11); from this prison the only way of escape was that preached by Christ in Noah. Christ, who in our times came in the flesh, in the days of Noah preached *in Spirit* by Noah to the spirits then in prison (Isa. 61:1, end, "the Spirit of the Lord God hath sent me to *proclaim* the opening of the *prison* to them that are bound"). So in ch. 1:11, "the Spirit of Christ" is said to have testified in the prophets. As Christ suffered even to death by enemies, and was afterwards quickened in virtue of His "Spirit" (or divine nature, Rom. 1:3, 4; I Cor. 15:45), which henceforth acted in its full energy, the first result of which was the raising of His body (vs. 21, end) from the prison of the grave and His soul from Hades; so the same Spirit of Christ enabled Noah, amidst reproach and trials, to preach to the disobedient spirits fast bound in wrath. That Spirit in you can enable you also to suffer patiently now, looking for the resurrection deliverance. **20. once**—not in the oldest MSS. **when . . . the long-suffering of God waited in the days of Noah**—Oldest MSS. *Greek*, *"was continuing to* wait *on"* (if haply men in the 120 years of grace would repent until the *end* of His waiting came in their death by the flood. This refutes ALFORD's idea of a second day of grace having been given in Hades. Noah's days are selected, as the ark and the destroying flood answer respectively to "baptism" and the coming destruction of unbelievers by fire. **while the ark was a-preparing**—(Heb. 11:7). A long period of God's "long-suffering and waiting," as Noah had few to help him, which rendered the world's unbelief the more inexcusable. **wherein**—lit., "(by having entered) *into* which." **eight**—seven (the

ADAM CLARKE

A. T. ROBERTSON:

Luther admits that he does not know what Peter means. Bigg has no doubt that the event recorded took place between Christ's death and his resurrection and holds that Peter is alluding to Christ's *Descensus ad Inferos* in Acts 2:27 (with which he compares Matt. 27:52 f.; Luke 23:34; Eph. 4:9). With this Windisch agrees. But Wohlenberg holds that Peter means that Christ in his preexistent state preached to those who rejected the preaching of Noah who are now in prison. Augustine held that Christ was in Noah when he preached. Bigg argues strongly that Christ during the time between his death and resurrection preached to those who once heard Noah (but are now in prison) and offered them another chance and not mere condemnation. If so, why did Jesus confine his preaching to this one group? So the theories run on about this passage.
—*Word Pictures in the New Testament*

19. *By which.* Spirit, His own divine energy and authority. *He went and preached.* By the ministry of Noah, 120 years. *Unto the spirits in prison.* The inhabitants of the antediluvian world, who, having been "disobedient" and convicted of the most flagrant transgressions against God, were sentenced by His just law to destruction. But their punishment was delayed to see if they would repent; and "the longsuffering of God waited" 120 years, which were granted to them for this purpose; during which time, as criminals tried and convicted, they are represented as being *in prison*—detained under the arrest of divine justice, which waited either for their repentance or the expiration of the respite, that the punishment pronounced might be inflicted. This I have long believed to be the sense of this difficult passage, and no other that I have seen is so consistent with the whole scope of the place. That the Spirit of God did strive with, convict, and reprove the antediluvians, is evident from Gen. vi. 3: "My spirit shall not always strive with man, for that he also is flesh: yet his days shall be an hundred and twenty years." And it was by this Spirit that Noah became a "preacher of righteousness," and condemned that ungodly world, Heb. xi. 7, who would not believe till wrath, divine punishment, came upon them to the uttermost. The word *spirits* is supposed to render this view of the subject improbable, because this must mean disembodied spirits; but this certainly does not follow, for "the spirits of just men made perfect," Heb. xii. 23, certainly means righteous men, and men still in the Church militant; and the "Father of spirits," Heb. xii. 9, means men still in the body; and "the God of the spirits of all flesh," Num. xvi. 22 and xxvii. 16, means men not in a disembodied state. There is no ground to believe that the text speaks of Christ's going to hell to preach the gospel to the damned, or of His going to some feigned place where the souls of the patriarchs were detained, to whom He preached, and whom He delivered from that place and took with Him to paradise.

20. *When once the longsuffering of God waited.* In *Pirkey Aboth*, cap. v. 2, we have these words: "There were ten generations from Adam to Noah, that the long-suffering of God might appear; for each of these generations provoked him to anger, and went on in their iniquity, till at last the deluge came."

MATTHEW HENRY

4. The event of all: Their bodies were drowned. Noah and his family, who believed and were obedient, *were saved in the ark.* Though the patience of God wait long upon sinners, yet it will expire at last; it is beneath the majesty of the great God always to wait upon man in vain. The way of the most is neither the best, the wisest, nor the safest way to follow: better to follow the eight in the ark.

Verses 21, 22

Noah's salvation in the ark upon the water prefigured the salvation of all good Christians by baptism.

I. What he means by saving baptism; not the outward ceremony of washing with water, but it is that baptism wherein there is a faithful answer of a resolved good conscience.

II. The efficacy of baptism to salvation depends not upon the work done, but upon the resurrection of Christ. The sacrament of baptism, rightly received, is a means and a pledge of salvation. *Baptism now saveth us.*

The external participation of baptism will save no man without an answerable good conscience and conversation. There must be the answer of a good conscience towards God.

III. The apostle proceeds to speak of his ascension, and sitting at the right hand of the Father, *v.* 22. If the advancement of Christ was so glorious after his deep humiliation, let not his followers despair, but expect that after these short distresses they shall be advanced to transcendent joy and glory. Upon his ascension into heaven, Christ is enthroned at the right hand of the Father. Angels, authorities, and powers, are all made subject to Christ Jesus.

JAMIESON, FAUSSET, BROWN

sacred number) with ungodly Ham. **few**—so now. **souls**—As this term is here used of *living* persons, why should not "spirits" also? Noah preached to their ears, but Christ *in spirit,* to their *spirits,* or spiritual natures. **saved by water**—The same water which drowned the unbelieving, buoyed up the ark in which the eight were saved. Not as some translate, "were brought safe *through* the water." However, the sense of the preposition may be as in I Corinthians 3:15, "they were safely preserved through the water," though having to be *in the water.* **21. whereunto**—The oldest MSS. read, "which": lit., "which (viz., *water,* in general; being) the antitype (of the water of the flood) is now saving (the salvation being not yet fully realized by us, cf. I Corinthians 10:1, 2, 5; Jude 5; *puts into a state of salvation*) us also (two oldest MSS. read *'you'* for 'us': *You also,* as well as Noah and his party), to wit, baptism." Water saved Noah not of itself, but by sustaining the ark built in *faith* resting on God's word: it was to him the sign and mean of a kind of *regeneration* of the earth. The antitypical water, viz., baptism, saves you also not of itself, nor the mere material water, but the spiritual thing conjoined with it, repentance and faith, of which it is the sign and seal, as Peter proceeds to explain. Cf. the union of the sign and thing signified, John 3:5; Ephesians 5:26; Titus 3:5; Hebrews 10:22; cf. I John 5:6. **not the . . .**—"flesh" bears the emphasis. "Not the putting away of the filth of *the flesh*" (as is done by a mere water baptism, unaccompanied with the Spirit's baptism, cf. Eph. 2: 11), but of the soul. It is the ark (Christ and His Spirit-filled Church), not the water, which is the instrument of salvation: the water only flowed round the ark; so not the mere water baptism, but the water when accompanied with the Spirit. **answer**—*Greek,* "interrogation"; referring to the *questions* asked of candidates for baptism; eliciting a confession of faith "toward God" and a renunciation of Satan [AUGUSTINE, *ad Catechumenos,* B. 4., c. 1; CYPRIAN, *Ep.* 7., *ad Rogatian*], which, when flowing from "a good conscience," assure one of being "saved." Lit., "a good conscience's interrogation (including the satisfactory *answer*) toward God." **by the resurrection of Jesus**—joined with "saves you": In so far as baptism applies to us the power of Christ's resurrection. As Christ's death unto sin is the source of the believer's death unto, and so deliverance from, sin's penalty and power; so His resurrection life is the source of the believer's new spiritual life. **22.** (Ps. 110:1; Rom. 8:34, 38; I Cor. 15: 24; Eph. 1:21; 3:10; Col. 1:16; 2:10-15.) The fruit of His patience in His voluntary endured and undeserved sufferings: a pattern to us, vss. 17, 18. **gone**—(Luke 24:51). Proving against rationalists an actual material ascension. Lit., "is on the right hand of God, *having gone* into heaven." The oldest MSS. of the *Vulgate* and the *Latin* Fathers, add what expresses the benefit to us of Christ's sitting on God's right hand, "Who is on the right hand of God, *having swallowed up death that we may become heirs of everlasting life*"; involving for us A STATE OF LIFE, saved, glorious, and eternal. The GREEK MSS., however, reject the words. Cf. with this verse Peter's speeches, Acts 2:32-35; 3:21, 26; 10: 40, 42.

ADAM CLARKE

Were saved by water. While the ark was a preparing, only Noah's family believed; these amounted to *eight persons.* And only these were saved from the deluge on the water; all the rest perished in the water.

21. *The like figure whereunto.* There are many difficulties in this verse, but the simple meaning of the place may be easily apprehended. Noah believed in God, walked uprightly before Him, and found grace in His sight; he obeyed Him in building the ark, and God made it the means of his salvation from the waters of the deluge. *Baptism* implies a consecration and dedication of the soul and body to God, the Father, Son, and Holy Spirit. He who is faithful to his baptismal covenant, taking God through Christ, by the eternal Spirit, for his Portion, is saved here from his sins; and through the resurrection of Christ from the dead has the well-grounded hope of eternal glory. This is all plain; but was it the deluge itself, or the ark, or the being saved by that ark from the deluge, that was the antetype of which Peter speaks? Noah and his family were "saved by water"; i.e., it was the instrument of their being saved through the good providence of God. So the water of *baptism,* typifying the regenerating influence of the Holy Spirit, is the means of salvation to all those who receive this Holy Spirit in His quickening, cleansing efficacy. Now as the waters of the Flood could not have saved Noah and his family had they not made use of the ark, so the water of baptism saves no man but as it is the means of his getting his heart purified by the Holy Spirit, and typifying to him that purification.

22. *Who is gone into heaven.* Having given the fullest proof of His resurrection from the dead, and of His having accomplished the end for which He came into the world. *On the right hand of God.* In the place of the highest dignity, honor, and influence. *Angels and authorities and powers.* That is, all creatures and beings, both in the heavens and in the earth, are put under subjection to Jesus Christ.

CHAPTER 4

MATTHEW HENRY

Verses 1-3

I. How the exhortation is expressed. *Christ had suffered* for us in the flesh, or in his human nature. *"Arm* and fortify *yourselves likewise with the same mind.* As Christ suffered in his human nature, do you make your corrupt nature suffer, by putting to death the body of sin by self-denial and mortification. *Cease from sin."* Some of the strongest and best arguments against all sorts of sin are taken from the sufferings of Christ. All sympathy and tenderness for Christ as a sufferer are lost if you do not put away sin. The beginning of all true mortification lies in the mind, not in penances and hardships upon the body.

II. How it is further explained, *v.* 2. Negatively, a Christian ought *no longer to live the rest of his time in the flesh,* but, positively, he ought to conform himself to the revealed will of the holy God. The lusts of men are the springs of all their wickedness. Let occasional temptations be what they will, they

JAMIESON, FAUSSET, BROWN

VSS. 1-19. LIKE THE RISEN CHRIST, BELIEVERS HENCEFORTH OUGHT TO HAVE NO MORE TO DO WITH SIN. *As the end is near, cultivate self-restraint, watchful prayerfulness, charity, hospitality, scriptural speech, ministering to one another according to your several gifts to the glory of God: Rejoicing patience under suffering.* **1. for us**—supported by some oldest MSS. and versions, omitted by others. **in the flesh**—in His mortal body of humiliation. **arm**—(Eph. 6:11, 13). **the same mind**—of suffering with patient willingness what God *wills* you to suffer. **he that hath suffered**—for instance, Christ first, and in His person the believer: a general proposition. **hath ceased**—lit., "has been made to cease," *has obtained* by the very fact of His having suffered once for all, *a cessation from sin,* which had heretofore lain on Him (Rom. 6:6-11, especially, vs. 7). The Christian is by faith one with Christ: as then Christ by death is judicially freed from sin; so the Christian who has in the person of Christ died, has no more to do with it judicially, and ought to have no more to do with it actually. "The flesh" is the sphere in which sin has place. **2. That he . . .**—"That he (the believer, who has once for all obtained cessation from sin by suffering, in the person of Christ, viz., in virtue of his union with the crucified Christ) should

ADAM CLARKE

1. *As Christ hath suffered.* He is your proper Pattern; have the same disposition He had; the same forgiving spirit, with meekness, gentleness, and complete self-possession. *He that hath suffered in the flesh hath ceased from sin.* The man who suffers generally reflects on his ways, is humbled, fears approaching death, loathes himself because of his past iniquities, and ceases from them.

2. *That he no longer should live . . . in the flesh*—Governed by the base principle of giving up his faith to save his life; *to the lusts of men*—according to the will of his idolatrous per-

MATTHEW HENRY

could not prevail, were it not for men's own corrupttions. True conversion makes a marvellous change in the heart and life of everyone who partakes of it. It alters the mind and conversation of everyone who has experienced it.

III. How it is enforced (*v.* 3). "It is but just that as you have hitherto all the former part of your life served sin and Satan, so you should now serve the living God." When a man is truly converted, it is very grievous to him to think how the time past of his life has been spent. While the will of man is unsanctified and corrupt, he walks continually in wicked ways, and he makes a bad condition daily worse and worse. One sin, allowed, draws on another. Here are six named. (1) *Lasciviousness*, expressed in looks, gesture, or behaviour. (2) *Lusts*, acts of lewdness. (3) *Excess of wine.* (4) *Revellings*, too frequent, too full, or too expensive. (5) *Banquetings*, by which is meant gluttony. (6) *Abominable* idolatry; the idol-worship of the Gentiles. It is a Christian's duty not only to abstain from what is grossly wicked, but also from those things that are generally the occasions of sin.

Verses 4–6

I. Here you have the visible change wrought in those who were represented as having been in the former part of their life very wicked. The conduct of their wicked acquaintance towards them. 1. *They think it strange* that their old friends should not run with as much violence as they used to do *to the same excess of riot.* 2. *They speak evil of them.* Those that are once really converted will not return to their former course of life. Neither persuasion nor reproach will prevail with them to be or to do as they were wont to do. The temper and behaviour of true Christians seem very strange to ungodly men. The ungodly cannot comprehend. The best actions of religious people cannot escape the censures and slanders of those who are irreligious. They will speak evil of good people, though they themselves reap the fruits of their charity, piety, and goodness.

II. For the comfort of the servants of God, it is here added,

1. That all wicked people shall *give an account* to him who is ready to judge. The malignant world shall in a little time give an account to the great God of all their evil speeches against his people.

2. That *for this cause was the gospel preached also to those that are dead, v.* 6. The mortifying of our sins and living to God are the expected effects of the gospel preached to us. God will certainly reckon with all those who have had the gospel preached to them, but without these good effects produced by it. It is no matter how we are judged according to men in the flesh, if we do but live according to God in the Spirit.

Verses 7–11

We have here an awful position and an inference drawn from it. The position is that the *end of all things is at hand.* Consequently, the time of their persecution is but very short. Your own life and that of your enemies will soon come to their utmost period. Nay, the world itself will not continue very long. The inference from this comprises a series of exhortations.

1. To sobriety and watchfulness, *v.* 7. Do not suffer yourselves to be caught with your former sins and temptations, *v.* 3. *And watch unto prayer.* Take care that you be frequent in prayers, lest this end come upon you unawares. Those who would pray to purpose must *watch unto prayer.*

2. To charity, *v.* 8. Christians ought to love one another. This mutual affection must not be cold, but fervent, that is, sincere, strong, and lasting. This sort of earnest affection is recommended *above all things*, which shows the importance of it. One excellent effect of it is that it will *cover a multitude of sins. Have charity among yourselves.* There is a special relation between all sincere Christians, and a particular amiableness and good in them, which require special affection. It is not enough for Christians not to bear malice, nor to have common respect for one another, they must intensely and fervently love each other. It is the property of true charity *to cover a multitude of sins.* It inclines people to forgive and forget offences against themselves, to cover the sins of others, rather than aggravate them and spread them abroad. It prepares for mercy at the hand of God, who hath promised to forgive those that forgive others.

JAMIESON, FAUSSET, BROWN

no longer live the rest of his time in the flesh to the lusts of men, but to the will of God" as his rule. *"Rest of his time in the flesh"* (the *Greek* has the preposition "in" here, not in vs. 1 as to Christ) proves that the reference is here not to Christ, but to the believer, whose remaining time for glorifying God is short (vs. 3). "Live" in the truest sense, for heretofore he was *dead.* Not as ALFORD, *"Arm yourselves . . .* with a view no longer to live the rest of *your* time." **3. may suffice**—*Greek,* "is sufficient." Peter takes the lowest ground: for not even the past time ought to have been wasted in lust; but since you cannot recall it, at least lay out the future to better account. **us**—omitted in oldest MSS. **wrought**—*Greek,* "wrought out." **Gentiles**—heathen: which many of you were. **when . . .**—"walking as ye have done [ALFORD] in *lasciviousness*"; the *Greek* means *petulant, immodest, wantonness,* unbridled conduct: not so much filthy lust. **excess of wine**—"wine-bibbings" [ALFORD]. **abominable**—"nefarious," "lawless idolatries," violating God's most sacred law; not that *all* Peter's readers (*Note,* ch. 1:1) *walked* in these, but many, viz., the Gentile portion of them. **4. Wherein**—In respect to which abandonment of your former *walk* (vs. 3). **run not with them**—eagerly, in troops [BENGEL]. **excess**—lit., "profusion"; a sink: stagnant water remaining after an inundation. **riot**—profligacy. **speaking evil**—charging you with pride, singularity, hypocrisy, and secret crimes (vs. 14; II Pet. 2:2). However, there is no "of you" in the *Greek*, but simply "blaspheming." It seems to me always to be used, either directly or indirectly, in the sense of *impious reviling against God, Christ, or the Holy Spirit,* and the Christian religion, not merely against men as such; *Greek,* vs. 14, below. **5. They who now call you to account falsely, shall have to give account themselves for this very evil-speaking (Jude 15), and be condemned justly.** **ready**—very speedily (vs. 7; II Pet. 3:10). Christ's coming is to the believer always near. **6. For**—giving the reason for vs. 5, "judge the *dead.*" **gospel preached also to . . . dead**—as well as to them now living, and to them that shall be found alive at the coming of the Judge. "Dead" must be taken in the same literal sense as in vs. 5, which refutes the explanation "dead" *in sins.* Moreover, the absence of the *Greek* article does not necessarily restrict the sense of "dead" to particular dead persons, for there is no *Greek* article in vs. 5 also, where "the dead" is universal in meaning. The sense seems to be, Peter, as representing the true attitude of the Church in every age, expecting Christ at any moment, says, The Judge is ready to judge the quick and dead—*the dead,* I say, *for* they, too, in their lifetime, have had the Gospel preached to them, that so they might be judged at last in the same way as those living now (and those who shall be so when Christ shall come), viz.., "men in the flesh," and that they might, having escaped condemnation by embracing the Gospel so preached, live unto God in the spirit (though death has passed over their flesh), Luke 20:38, thus being made like Christ in death and in life (*Note,* ch. 3:18). **7.** Resuming the idea in vs. 5. **the end of all things**—and therefore also of the wantonness (vss. 3, 4) of the wicked, and of the sufferings of the righteous [BENGEL]. The nearness meant is not that of mere *time,* but that *before the Lord;* as he explains to guard against misapprehension, and defends God from the charge of procrastination: We live in the last dispensation, not like the Jews under the Old Testament. The Lord will come as a thief; He is "ready" (vs. 5) to judge the world at any moment; it is only God's long-suffering and His will that the Gospel should be preached as a witness to all nations, that induces Him to lengthen out the time which is with Him still as nothing. **sober**—"self-restrained." The opposite duties to the sins in vs. 3 are here inculcated. Thus "sober" is the opposite of "lasciviousness" (vs. 3). **watch**—*Greek,* "be soberly vigilant"; not intoxicated with worldly cares and pleasures. Temperance promotes *wakefulness* or watchfulness, and both promote prayer. Drink makes drowsy, and drowsiness prevents prayer. **prayer**—*Greek,* "prayers"; the end for which we should exercise vigilance. **8. above all things**—not that "charity" or *love* is placed above "prayer," but because *love* is the animating spirit, without which all other duties are dead. Translate as *Greek,* "Having your mutual (lit., 'towards yourselves') charity intense." He presupposes its existence among them; he urges them to make it more fervent. **charity shall cover the multitude . . .**—The oldest MSS. have "covereth." Quoted from Proverbs 10: 12; cf. 17:9. "Covereth" so as not harshly to condemn or expose faults; but forbearingly to bear the other's burdens, forgiving and forgetting past of-

ADAM CLARKE

secutors; *but to the will of God*—which will of God is that he should retain the truth and live according to its dictates, though he should suffer for it.

3. *The time past of our life.* This is a complete epitome of the Gentile or heathen state, and a proof that those had been Gentiles to whom the apostle wrote. They *walked in lasciviousness,* every species of lewdness and impurity; *lusts,* strong irregular appetites and desires of all kinds; *excess of wine,* "inflamed with wine"; *revellings,* lascivious feastings, with drunken songs; *banquetings,* "wine feasts, drinking matches"; *abominable idolatries,* that is, the abominations practiced at their idol feasts, where they not only worshipped the idol, but did it with the most impure, obscene, and abominable rites. This was the general state of the Gentile world, and with this monstrous wickedness Christianity had everywhere to struggle.

4. *They think it strange.* They wonder and are astonished at you, that you can renounce these gratifications of the flesh for a spiritual something, the good of which they cannot see. *Excess of riot.* "Flood of profligacy"; bearing down all rule, order, and restraints before it. *Speaking evil of.* Literally, "blaspheming"; i.e., speaking impiously against God, and calumniously of *you.*

5. *To judge the quick and the dead.* They shall give account of these irregularities to Him who is prepared to judge both the Jews and the Gentiles. The Gentiles, previously to the preaching of the gospel among them, were reckoned to be "dead in trespasses and sins," Eph. ii. 1-5; under the sentence of death, because they had sinned. The Jews had at least, by their religious profession, a name to live; and by that profession were bound to live to God.

6. *Was the gospel preached also to them that are dead.* But if the apostle had the same fact in view which he mentions in chap. iii. 19-20, then the antediluvians are the persons intended. *For this cause*—that Christ is prepared "to judge the quick and the dead," and to dispense righteous judgment in consequence of having afforded them every necessary advantage; *was the gospel preached* by Noah *also to them that are dead*—the antediluvian world, then dead in trespasses and sins, and condemned to death by the righteous judgment of God. But in His great compassion He afforded them a respite, that though they were condemned as *men in the flesh* (Gen. vi. 3), yet, hearing this gospel by Noah, they might believe, *and live according to God in the spirit*—live a blessed life in eternity according to the mercy of God, who sent His Spirit to strive with them.

7. *But the end of all things is at hand.* I think that here also Peter keeps the history of the deluge before his eyes, finding a parallel to the state of the Jews in his own time in that of the antediluvians in the days of Noah. In Gen. vi. 13, God said unto Noah, "The end of all flesh is come before me." This was spoken at a time when God had decreed the destruction of the world by a flood. Peter says, *The end of all things is at hand;* and this he spoke when God had determined to destroy the Jewish people and their polity by one of the most signal judgments that ever fell upon any nation or people. The end of the Temple, the end of the Levitical priesthood, the end of the whole Jewish economy, was then at hand. *Be . . . sober, and watch unto prayer. Be . . . sober*—make a prudent and moderate use of all you possess; and *watch* against all occasions of sin; and pray for the supporting hand of God to be upon you for good, that you may escape the destruction that is coming upon the Jews, and that you may be saved from among them when the scourge comes.

8. *Have fervent charity.* "Intense love; for love shall cover a multitude of sins." A loving disposition leads us to pass by the faults of others, to forgive offenses against ourselves, and to excuse and lessen, as far as is consistent with truth, the transgressions of men. It does not mean that our love to others will induce God to pardon our offenses.

MATTHEW HENRY

3. To hospitality, *v.* 9. The proper objects of Christian hospitality are one another. The manner of performing this duty is this: it must be done in an easy, kind, handsome manner, *without grudging* or grumbling at the expense or trouble. Christians ought not only to be charitable, but hospitable, one to another.

4. To the improvement of talents, *v.* 11.

(1) Whatever gift, whatever power, of doing good is given to us, we should minister with the same *one to another.* In receiving and using the manifold gifts of God we must look upon ourselves as stewards only.

(2) The apostle exemplifies his direction about gifts in two particulars—speaking and ministering. *If any man speak* or teach, he must do it *as the oracles of God.* What Christians in private, or ministers in public, teach and speak must be the pure word and oracles of God. *If any man minister let him do it as of the ability which God giveth. That God in all things* may be glorified, *through Jesus Christ,* to whom *be praise and dominion for ever and ever. Amen. First,* It is the duty of Christians in private, as well as ministers in public, to speak to one another of the things of God. *Secondly,* It highly concerns all preachers of the gospel to keep close to the word of God, and to treat that word as becomes the oracles of God. *Thirdly,* Whatever we are called to do for the honour of God and the good of others we should do it with all our might. *Fourthly,* In all the duties and services of life we should aim at the glory of God; all other views must be subservient to this. *Fifthly, God in all things must be glorified through Jesus Christ,* who is the only way to the Father.

Verses 12–19

The frequent repetition of comfort to Christians, considered as sufferers, in every chapter of this epistle, shows that the greatest danger these new converts were in arose from the persecutions to which their embracing Christianity exposed them. The apostle comes here to direct them in the necessary duty of patience under sufferings.

I. The apostle's kind manner of address: they were his *beloved, v.* 9.

II. His advice to them, relating to their sufferings.

1. They should not think them strange, nor be surprised at them.

(1) Though they be sharp and fiery, yet they are designed only to try, not to ruin them. They ought rather to rejoice under their sufferings, because theirs may properly be called Christ's sufferings. He suffers in them, and feels in our infirmities; and, if we be partakers of his sufferings, we shall also be made *partakers of his glory.* The apostle owns these poor afflicted Christians, and calls them his beloved. True Christians never look more amiable one to another than in their adversities. There is no reason for Christians to wonder at the unkindnesses and persecutions of the world, because they are forewarned of them. Christ himself endured them. Christians ought not only to be patient, but to rejoice, in their sharpest sorest sufferings for Christ. Those who rejoice in their sufferings for Christ shall eternally triumph and rejoice with him in glory.

(2) The apostle descends to a lower degree of persecution, *v.* 14. They would be reviled, evil-spoken of, and slandered for the name or sake of Christ. In such case he asserts, *Happy are you.* "You have the Spirit of God with you and the Spirit of God is also the Spirit of glory. This glorious Spirit *resteth upon you.* By your patience and fortitude in suffering *he is on your part glorified*; but by the contempt and reproaches cast upon you *the Spirit itself* is evil-spoken of and blasphemed." The happiness of good people not only consists with, but even flows from, their afflictions: *Happy are you.* That man who hath the Spirit of God resting upon him cannot be miserable, let his afflictions be ever so great. When good people are vilified *for the name of Christ* his Holy Spirit is glorified in them.

JAMIESON, FAUSSET, BROWN

fenses. Perhaps the *additional* idea is included, By prayer for them, *love tries to have them covered by God;* and so being the instrument of converting the sinner from his error, "covereth a (not 'the,' as *English Version*) multitude of sins"; but the former idea from Proverbs is the *prominent* one. **9.** (Rom. 12:13; Heb. 13:2.) Not the spurious hospitality which passes current in the world, but the entertaining of those *needing* it, especially those exiled for the faith, as the representatives of Christ, and all hospitality to whomsoever exercised from genuine Christian love. **without grudging**–*Greek,* "murmuring." "He that giveth, let him do it with simplicity," i.e. open-hearted sincerity; with cordiality. Not secretly speaking against the person whom we entertain, or upbraiding him with the favor we have conferred in him. **10. every**–"even as *each* man hath received," in whatever degree, and of whatever kind. The Spirit's *gifts* (lit., "gift *of grace,*" i.e., *gratuitously* bestowed) are the common property of the Christian community, each Christian being but a steward for the edifying of the whole, not receiving the gift merely for his own use. **minister the same**–not discontentedly envying or disparaging *the gift of another.* **one to another**–*Greek* as in vs. 8, "towards yourselves"; implying that all form but one body, and in seeking the good of other members they are promoting the good of *themselves.* **stewards**–referring to Matthew 25:15, etc.; Luke 19:13-26. **11. If any . . . speak**–viz., as a prophet, or divinely taught *teacher* in the Church assembly. **the . . .**–The *Greek* has no article: "as oracles of God." This may be due to *Greek:* "God," having no article, it being a principle when a governed noun omits the *Greek* article that the governing noun should omit it, too. In Acts 7:38 also, the *Greek* article is wanting; thus *English Version,* "as *the* oracles of God," viz., *the Old Testament,* would be right, and the precept be similar to Romans 12:6, "prophesy according to *the analogy of the faith.*" But the context suits better thus, "Let him speak as (becomes one speaking) *oracles* OF GOD." His divinely inspired words are *not his own,* but *God's,* and as a *steward* (4:10) having them committed to him, he ought so to speak them. Jesus was the pattern in this respect (Matt. 7:29; John 12:49; 14:10; cf. Paul, II Cor. 2:17). Note, the very same term as is applied in the only other passages where it occurs (Acts 7:38; Rom. 3:2; Heb. 5:12), to the *Old Testament* inspired writings, is here predicated of the inspired *words* (the substance of which was afterwards committed to *writing*) of the *New Testament* prophets. **minister**–in *acts;* the other sphere of spiritual activity besides *speaking.* **as of**–"out of" the store of his "strength" (*Greek, physical* power in relation to outward service, rather than moral and intellectual "ability"; so in Mark 12:30). **giveth**–*Greek,* "supplieth"; originally said of a *choragus,* who *supplied* the chorus with all necessaries for performing their several parts. **that God in all things may be glorified**–the final end of all a Christian's acts. **through Jesus Christ**–the mediator through whom all our blessings come down to us, and also through whom all our praises ascend to God. Through Christ alone can God be glorified in us and our sayings and doings. **to whom**–Christ. **be**–*Greek,* "is." **for ever and ever**–*Greek,* "unto the ages of the ages." **12. strange**–they might *think it strange* that God should allow His chosen children to be sore tried. **fiery trial**–like the fire by which metals are tested and their dross removed. The *Greek* adds, "in your case." **which is to try you**–*Greek,* "which is taking place for a trial to you." Instead of its "*happening* to you" as some strange and untoward *chance,* it "is taking place" with the gracious *design* of trying you; God has a wise design in it–a consolatory reflection. **13. inasmuch as**–The oldest MSS. read, "in proportion as"; "in as far as" ye by suffering are partakers of Christ's sufferings, i.e., by faith enter into realizing fellowship with them; willingly for His sake suffering as He suffered. **with exceeding joy**–*Greek,* "*exulting* joy"; now ye *rejoice* amidst sufferings; then ye shall EXULT, for ever free from sufferings (ch. 1:6, 8). If we will not bear suffering for Christ now, we must bear eternal sufferings hereafter. **14. for**–*Greek,* "IN the name of Christ," viz., *as Christians* (vs. 16; ch. 3:14, above); "*in My name,* because *ye belong to Christ.*" The emphasis lies on this: vs. 15, "as a murderer, thief," etc., stands in contrast. Let your suffering be on account of Christ, not on account of evil-doing (ch. 2:20). **reproached**–*Reproach* affects noble minds more than loss of goods, or even bodily sufferings. **the spirit . . . upon you**–the same Spirit as rested on Christ (Luke 4:18). "The Spirit of glory" is *His* Spirit, for He is the "Lord *of glory*" (Jas. 2:1). Be-

ADAM CLARKE

9. *Use hospitality.* Be ever ready to divide your bread with the hungry, and to succor the stranger. *Without grudging.* "Without grumblings." Do nothing merely because it is commanded, but do it from love to God and man; then it will be without grumbling.

10. *Hath received the gift.* "A gift"; any blessing of providence or grace. I cannot think that the word means here the Holy Ghost, or any of His supernatural gifts or influences; it may include those, but it signifies anything given by the mere mercy and bounty of God. But perhaps in this place it may signify some or any office in the Church; and this sense, indeed, the connection seems to require. *Stewards of the manifold grace.* Whatever gifts or endowments any man may possess, they are, properly speaking, not his own; they are the Lord's property, and to be employed in His work, and to promote His glory.

11. *If any man speak.* In order to explain or enforce God's Word, and edify his neighbor, let him do it as those did to whom the living oracles were committed; they spoke as they were inspired by the Holy Ghost.

Of the ability which God giveth. Perhaps the ministering here may refer to the care of the poor, and the *ability* is the means which God may have placed in their hands; and they are to minister this as coming immediately from God, and lead the minds of the poor to consider Him as their Benefactor, that He in all things may be glorified through Christ Jesus.

12. *Think it not strange concerning the fiery trial.* "The burning." The metaphor is old, but noble; it represents the Christians at Pontus as having fire cast upon them for the trying of their faith, as gold is tried by fire, chap. i. 7, to which the apostle alludes.

14. *If ye be reproached for the name of Christ.* To be reproached for the *name of Christ* is to be reproached for being a Christian. This is the highest honor to which any man can arrive in this world, and therefore the apostle says to such, *Happy are ye.*

MATTHEW HENRY

2. They should take care they did not suffer justly, as evil-doers, *v.* 15. Their enemies charged them with these and other foul crimes: therefore the apostle thought these cautions necessary. *If any man suffer* for the cause of Christianity, and with a patient Christian spirit, he ought not to account it a shame, and ought to glorify God who hath thus dignified him, *v.* 16. But there is very little comfort in sufferings when we bring them upon ourselves by our own sin and folly. It is not the suffering, but the cause, that makes the martyr.

3. Their trials were now at hand, *v.* 17, 18.

(1) The time had come when *judgment must begin at the house of God.* This renders all the foregoing exhortations to patience necessary for you. These judgments will but *begin* with you that are God's house. "Your troubles will be but light and short, in comparison of what shall befall the wicked world. *What shall the end be of those who obey not the gospel of God?*" The best of God's servants have so much amiss in them as renders it fit and necessary that God should sometimes correct and punish them. *Judgment* begins at the house of God. Those who are the family of God have their worst things in this life. Their worst condition is tolerable, and will soon be over. The apostle distinguishes the disobedient from the house of God. *What shall the end be of those that obey not the gospel?*

(2) He intimates the irremediable doom of the wicked, *v.* 18. The grievous sufferings of good people in this world are sad presages of much heavier judgments coming upon impenitent sinners. It is as much as the righteous can do to be saved. Let the absolute necessity of salvation balance the difficulty of it. Your difficulties are greatest at first; God offers his grace and help.

4. When called to suffer, *according to the will of God,* they should look chiefly to the safety of their souls, *committing them to God,* who will undertake the charge, for he is their Creator, *v.* 19. All the sufferings that befall good people come upon them *according to the will of God.* It is the duty of Christians to look more to the keeping of their souls than to the preserving of their bodies. Good people have great encouragement to commit their souls to God, because he is their Creator, and faithful in all his promises.

JAMIESON, FAUSSET, BROWN

lievers may well overcome the "*reproach*" (cf. Heb. 11:26), seeing that "the Spirit of *glory*" rests upon them, as upon Him. It cannot prevent the happiness of the righteous, if they are reproached for Christ, because they retain before God their *glory* entire, as having the Spirit, with whom *glory* is inseparably joined [CALVIN]. **and of God**–*Greek,* "and *the* (Spirit) of God"; implying that *the Spirit of glory* (which is Christ's Spirit) is at the same time also *the Spirit of God.* **on their part he is evil spoken of, but on your part he is glorified**–omitted in the two oldest *Greek* MSS. and *Syriac* and *Coptic versions,* but supported by one very old MS., *Vulgate, Sahidic, Cyprian,* etc. "Evil spoken of," lit., "blasphemed"; not merely do they "*speak against you,*" as in ch. 3:16, but *blasphemously mock Christ* and Christianity itself. **15. But**–*Greek,* "For." "Reproached *in the name of Christ*" I say (vs. 14), "FOR *let none* . . . ." **as . . . *as* . . . *as* . . . as**–the *as* twice in italics is not in the *Greek.* The second *Greek,* "as," distinguishes the class "busybody in other men's matters," from the previous class of delinquents. **16. a Christian**–the name given in contempt first at Antioch, Acts 11:26; 26:28; the only three places where the term occurs. At first believers had no distinctive name, but were called among themselves "brethren," Acts 6:3; "disciples," Acts 6:1; "those of the way," Acts 9:2; "saints," Romans 1:7; by the Jews (who denied that Jesus was the CHRIST, and so would never originate the name *Christian*), in contempt, "Nazarenes." At Antioch, where first *idolatrous* Gentiles (Cornelius, Acts 10, was not an idolater, but a proselyte) were converted, and wide missionary work began, they could be no longer looked on as a *Jewish sect,* and so *the Gentiles* designated them by the new name "Christians." **let him not be ashamed**–though the world is ashamed of shame. To suffer for one's own faults is no honor (vs. 15; ch. 2:20),–for Christ, is no *shame* (vs. 14; ch. 3:13). **but let him glorify God**–not merely glory in persecution; Peter might have said as the contrast, "but let him esteem it an honor to himself"; but the honor is to be given *to God,* who counts him worthy of such an honor, involving exemption from the coming judgments on the ungodly. **on this behalf**–The oldest MSS. and *Vulgate* read, "in this *name,*" i.e., in respect of suffering for such a name. **17.** Another ground of consolation to Christians. All must pass under the judgment of God; God's own household first, their chastisement being here, for which they should glorify Him as a proof of their membership in His family, and a pledge of their escape from the end of those whom the last judgment shall find disobedient to the Gospel. **the time**–*Greek,* "season," "fit time." **judgment must begin at the house of God**–the Church of living believers. Peter has in mind Ezekiel 9:6; cf. Amos 3:2; Jeremiah 25:29.

if . . . at us, what shall the end be of them . . .–If even the godly have chastening judgments now, how much more shall the ungodly be doomed to damnatory judgments at last. **gospel of God**–the very God who is to judge them. **18. scarcely**–Cf. "so as by fire," I Corinthians 3:15; having to pass through trying chastisements, as David did for his sin. "The righteous" man has always more or less of trial, but the issue is certain, and the entrance into the kingdom *abundant* at last. The "scarcely" marks the severity of the ordeal, and the unlikelihood (in a mere human point of view) of the righteous sustaining it; but the righteousness of Christ and God's everlasting covenant make it all sure. **ungodly**–having no regard for God; negative description. **sinner**–loving sin; positive; the same man is at once God-forgetting and sin-loving. **appear**–in judgment. **19.** General conclusion from vss. 17, 18. Seeing that the godly know that their sufferings are *by God's will,* to chasten them that they may not perish with the world, they have good reason to trust God cheerfully amidst sufferings, persevering *in well-doing.* **let them**–*Greek,* "let them *also,*" "let *even* them," as well as those not suffering. Not only under ordinary circumstances, but *also* in time of *suffering, let* believers *commit.* . . . (Cf. *Note,* ch. 3:14.) **according to the will of God**–(*Note,* ch. 3:17). God's will that the believer should suffer (vs. 17), is for his good. One oldest MS. and *Vulgate* read, "in *well-doings*"*;* contrast ill-doings, vs. 15. Our committing of ourselves to God is to be, not in indolent and passive quietism, but accompanied with active *well-doings.* **faithful**–to His covenant promises. **Creator**–who is therefore also our Almighty Preserver. He, not we, must *keep* our souls.

ADAM CLARKE

On their part he is evil spoken of. "By them He is blasphemed, by you He is honored."

15. *But let none of you suffer . . . as a busybody in other men's matters.* "The inspector of another"; meddling with other people's concerns, and forgetting their own.

16. *Yet if any man suffer as a Christian.* If he be persecuted because he has embraced the Christian faith, *let him not be ashamed; but let him* rather *glorify God* on this very account. Christ suffered by the Jews because He was holy; Christians suffer because they resemble Him. The word *Christian* is used only here and in Acts xi. 26; xxvi. 28.

17. *Judgment must begin at the house of God.* Our Lord had predicted that, previously to the destruction of Jerusalem, His own followers would have to endure various calamities; see Matt. xxiv. 9, 21-22; Mark xiii. 12-13; John xvi. 2 ff. Here His true disciples are called *the house* or "family" *of God.* That the converted Jews suffered much from their own brethren needs little proof. But probably the word which we here translate *judgment* may mean no more than affliction and distress; for it was a Jewish maxim that, when God was about to pour down some general judgment, He began with afflicting His own people in order to correct and amend them, that they might be prepared for the overflowing scourge. *And if it first begin at us*—Jews who have repented and believed on the Son of God; *what shall the end be of them*—the Jews who continue impenitent, and *obey not the gospel of God?*

18. *And if the righteous scarcely be saved?* If it shall be with extreme difficulty that the Christians shall escape from Jerusalem when the Roman armies shall come against it with the full commission to destroy it, *where shall the ungodly and the sinner appear?* Where shall the proud, Pharisaic boaster in his own outside holiness, and the profligate transgressor of the laws of God, "show themselves," as having escaped the divine vengeance? It is rather strange, but it is a fact, that this verse is the Septuagint translation of Prov. xi. 31: "Behold, the righteous shall be recompensed in the earth: much more the wicked and the sinner." For this the Septuagint and Peter have, *If the righteous scarcely be saved, where shall the ungodly and the sinner appear?*

19. *Suffer according to the will of God.* A man suffers according to the will of God who suffers for righteousness' sake; and who, being reviled, reviles not again. *Commit the keeping of their souls.* Place their lives confidently in His hand who, being their *Creator,* will also be their Preserver, and keep that safely which is committed to His trust. God is here represented as *faithful,* because He will always fulfill His promises, and withhold no good thing from them that walk uprightly.

MATTHEW HENRY

CHAPTER 5

Verses 1–4

I. The persons to whom this exhortation is given—elders by office, rather than by age, ministers of those churches to whom he wrote this epistle.

II. He tells them he was their fellow-elder, and so puts nothing upon them but what he was ready to perform himself.

He was also *a witness of the sufferings of Christ.* He was also *a partaker of the glory* that shall be completely enjoyed at the second coming of Jesus Christ. It was the peculiar honour of Peter, and a few more, to be the witnesses of Christ's sufferings; but it is the privilege of all true Christians to be partakers of the glory that shall be revealed.

III. The pastor's duty described. 1. *To feed the flock,* by preaching to them the sincere word of God.

2. The pastors of the church must *take the oversight thereof.* 3. They must be *examples to the flock,* and practice the holiness which they preach and recommend to their people. These duties must be performed, *not by constraint,* but from a willing mind that takes pleasure in the work: *not for filthy lucre, but of a ready mind,* regarding the flock more than the fleece; *neither as being lords over God's heritage,* tyrannizing over them. These poor, dispersed, suffering Christians were the flock of God. The rest of the world is a brutal herd. These are an orderly flock, redeemed to God by the great Shepherd. They are also dignified with the title of God's *heritage,* chosen out of the common multitude for his own people. They are God's people, and should be treated with love, meekness, and tenderness, for the sake of him to whom they belong.

IV. In opposition to that filthy lucre the apostle sets before them the crown of glory designed by the great shepherd for all his faithful ministers. Jesus Christ is *the chief shepherd* of the whole flock and heritage of God. He is also the chief shepherd over all inferior shepherds. This chief shepherd will appear, to judge all ministers and undershepherds. Those that are found to have done their duty shall receive from the grand shepherd *a crown of glory that fadeth not away.*

Verses 5–7

The apostle comes now to instruct the flock.

I. He exhorts those that are younger and inferior to *submit themselves to the elder.*

As to one another, the rule is that they should all *be subject one to another,* so far as to receive the reproofs and counsels one of another. He advises them to *be clothed with humility.*

JAMIESON, FAUSSET, BROWN

CHAPTER 5

Vss. 1-14. Exhortations to Elders, Juniors, and All in General. Parting Prayer. Conclusion. **1. elders**—alike in office and age (vs 5). **I . . . also an elder**—To put one's self on a level with those whom we exhort, gives weight to one's exhortations (cf. II John 1). Peter, in true humility for the Gospel's sake, does not put forward his *apostleship* here, wherein he *presided over the elders.* In the apostleship the apostles have no successors, for "the signs of an apostle" have not been transmitted. The presidents over the presbyters and deacons, by whatever name designated, *angel, bishop,* or *moderator,* etc., though *of the same* ORDER *as the presbyters,* yet have virtually succeeded to a superintendency of the Church analogous to that exercised by the apostles (this superintendency and priority existed from the earliest times after the apostles [Tertullian]); just as the Jewish synagogue (the model which the Church followed) was governed by a council of presbyters, presided over by one of themselves, "the chief ruler of the synagogue." (Cf. Vitringa, *Synagogue,* Part II, chs. 3 and 7.) **witness**—an *eyewitness* of Christ's sufferings, and so qualified to exhort you to believing patience in *suffering for well-doing* after His example (ch. 4:19; 2:20). This explains the "therefore" inserted in the oldest MSS., "I therefore exhort," resuming exhortation from ch. 4:19. His higher dignity as an *apostle* is herein delicately implied, as *eyewitnessing* was a necessary qualification for apostleship: cf. Peter's own speeches, Acts 1:21, 22; 2:32; 10:39. **also**—implying the righteous recompense corresponding to the sufferings. **partaker of the glory**—according to Christ's promise; an earnest of which was given in the transfiguration. **2. Feed**—*Greek,* "Tend as a shepherd," by discipline and doctrine. Lead, feed, heed: by prayer, exhortation, government, and example. The dignity is marked by the term *"elder"*; the *duties* of the office, to *tend* or *oversee,* by *"bishop."* Peter has in mind Christ's injunction to him, "Feed (*tend*) My sheep . . . Feed (*pasture*) My lambs" (John 21:16). He invites the elders to share with him the same duty (cf. Acts 20:28). The flock is Christ's. **which is among you**—While having a concern for *all* the Church, your special duty is to feed that portion of it "which is among you." **oversight**—*Greek,* "bishopric," or duty of bishops, i.e., overseer. **not by constraint**—Necessity is laid upon them, but willingness prevents it being felt, both in undertaking and in fulfilling the duty [Bengel]. **willingly**—One oldest MS., *Vulgate, Syriac,* and *Coptic,* add, "as God would have it to be done" (Rom. 8:27). **not for filthy lucre**—(Isa. 56:11; Titus 1:7). **of a ready mind**—promptly and heartily, without selfish motive of gain-seeking, as the Israelites gave their services *willing-heartedly* to the sanctuary. **3. being lords**—*Greek,* "lording it": implying pride and oppression. "Not that we have dominion over your faith." *God's* **heritage**—*Greek,* "the inheritances," i.e., the *portions* of the Church committed severally to your pastoral charge [Bengel]. It is explained by "the flock" in the next clause. **being**—*Greek,* "becoming." **ensamples**—the most effective recommendation of precept (I Tim. 4:12). Titus 2:7, "patterns." So Jesus. "A monstrosity it is to see the highest rank joined with the meanest mind, the first seat with the lowest life, a grandiloquent tongue with a lazy life, much talking with no fruit" [Bernard]. **4. And**—"And so": as the result of "being ensamples" (vs. 3). **chief Shepherd**—the title peculiarly Christ's own, not Peter's or the pope's. **when . . . shall appear**—*Greek,* "be manifested" (Col. 3:4). Faith serves the Lord while still unseen. **crown**—*Greek, stephanos,* a garland of *victory,* the prize in the Grecian games, woven of ivy, parsley, myrtle, olive, or oak. **glory**—*Greek, "the glory,"* viz., *to be* then *revealed* (vs. 1; ch. 4:13). **that fadeth not away**—*Greek,* "amaranthine" (cf. ch. 1:4). **5. ye younger**—The *deacons* were originally the younger men, the *presbyters* older; but subsequently as presbyter expressed the *office* of Church ruler or teacher, so *Greek neoteros* means not (as lit.) *young men* in age, but *subordinate ministers* and servants of the Church. So Christ uses the term "younger." For He explains it by "he that doth serve," lit., "he that ministereth as a deacon"; just as He explains "the greatness" by "he that is chief," lit., "he that *ruleth,*" the very word applied to the *bishops* or *presbyters.* **Yea**—to sum up all my exhortations in one. **be subject**—omitted in the oldest MSS. and Versions, but Tischendorf quotes the *Vatican* MS. for it. Then translate, "Gird (ch. 1:13; 4:1) fast on humility (lowliness of mind) to

ADAM CLARKE

CHAPTER 5

1. *The elders which are among you.* In this place the term *elders* or presbyters is the name of an office. They were as pastors or shepherds of the flock of God, the Christian people among whom they lived. They were the same as bishops, 1 Tim. v. 17. *Who am also an elder.* "A fellow elder"; one on a level with yourselves.

A witness of the sufferings of Christ. He was with Christ in the garden; he was with Him when He was apprehended; and he was with Him in the high priest's hall.

A partaker of the glory. He had the promise from his Lord and Master that he should be with Him in heaven, to behold His glory, John xvii. 21, 24.

2. *Feed the flock.* Do not fleece the flock. *Taking the oversight.* Discharging the office of bishops or superintendents. This is another proof that bishop and presbyter were the same order in the apostolic times, though afterwards they were made distinct. *Not by constraint.* The office was laborious and dangerous, especially in these times of persecution; it is no wonder then that even those who were best qualified for the office should strive to excuse themselves. *Not for filthy lucre.* Could the office of a bishop, in those early days and in the time of persecution, be a lucrative office? Does not the Spirit of God lead the apostle to speak these things rather for posterity than for that time? But of a ready mind. Doing all for Christ's sake, and through love to immortal souls.

3. *Neither as being lords over God's heritage.* This is the voice of Peter in his catholic Epistle to the catholic Church! According to him there are to be no *lords over God's heritage.* The bishops and presbyters who are appointed by the Head of the Church are to feed the flock, to guide and to defend it, not to fleece and waste it; and they are to look for their reward in another world, and in the approbation of God in their consciences. And in humility, self-abasement, self-renunciation, and heavenly-mindedness they are to be *ensamples,* "types," to the flock.

4. *When the chief Shepherd.* That is, the Lord Jesus Christ, whose is the flock, and who provides the pasture, and from whom, if you are legally called to the most awful work of preaching the gospel, you have received your commission. When he *shall appear* to judge the world in righteousness, you who have fed His flock, who have taken the superintendency of it, "not by constraint," nor for filthy lucre's sake, not as lords over the heritage, but with a ready mind, employing body, soul, spirit, time, and talents in endeavoring to pluck sinners as brands from eternal burnings, and build up the Church of Christ on its most holy faith—*ye shall receive a crown of glory that fadeth not away,* an eternal nearness and intimacy with the ineffably glorious God.

5. *Likewise, ye younger.* Probably means here "inferiors," or those not in sacred offices; and may be understood as referring to the people at large who are called to obey them that have the rule over them in the Lord. *Be subject one to another.* Strive all to serve each other; let the pastors strive to serve the people, and the people the pastors; and let there be no contention, but who shall do most to oblige and profit all the rest. *Be clothed with humility.* To be *clothed* with a thing or person is a Greek

MATTHEW HENRY

"If you be disobedient and proud, God will set himself to oppose you; for *he resisteth the proud*, when he *giveth grace to the humble*." Humility is the great preserver of peace and order in all Christian societies, consequently pride is the great disturber of them. There is a mutual opposition between God and the proud. Where God giveth grace to be humble, he will give more grace and humility. Hence the apostle adds: "Since God resisteth the proud, but giveth grace to the humble, therefore humble yourselves, not only one to another, but to the great God. His hand is almighty, and can easily pull you down if you be proud, or exalt you if you be humble." Humbling ourselves to God under his hand is the next way to deliverance and exaltation.

II. The apostle rightly supposes that what he had foretold of greater hardships yet coming might excite in them abundance of care. Foreseeing this anxious care would be a heavy burden, and a sore temptation, he gives them the best advice. His advice is to *cast all their care*, or *all care of themselves, upon God.* Trust in him with a firm, composed mind, *for he careth for you.* He is willing to release you of your care, and take the care of you upon himself. The best of Christians are apt to labour under the burden of anxious and excessive care. The cares even of good people are very burdensome, and too often very sinful. The best remedy against immoderate care is to *cast our care upon God.* A firm belief of the rectitude of the divine will calms the spirit of man.

Verses 8, 9

I. He shows them their danger from an enemy whom he describes,

1. By his characters and names. He is an adversary: "*That adversary of yours.*" *The devil, the grand accuser of all the brethren.* He is *a roaring lion*, the fierce and greedy pursuer of souls.

2. By his business: *He walks about, seeking whom he may devour;* his whole design is to devour and destroy souls.

II. Hence he infers that it is their duty to *be sober*, to *be vigilant*, to be watchful and diligent to prevent his designs and save their souls. To resist him *steadfast in the faith*. It was the faith of these people that Satan aimed at. This strong trial and temptation they must resist, by being steadfast in the faith.

III. The like afflictions befell their brethren in all parts of the world, all the people of God were their fellow-soldiers in this warfare. The devil is the grand persecutor, as well as *the deceiver and accuser*, of the *brethren.* Sobriety and watchfulness are necessary virtues at all times, but especially in times of suffering and persecution. If your faith give way, you are gone. The consideration of what others suffer is proper to encourage us to bear our own share in any affliction: *The same afflictions are accomplished in your brethren.*

Verses 10-14

We come now to the conclusion of this epistle.

I. The apostle begins with a most weighty prayer, which he addresses to God as *the God of all grace.*

1. What he prays for on their account. *After they had suffered awhile* that God would perfect his work in them. Those who are called to be heirs of eternal life through Jesus Christ must, nevertheless, suffer in this world, but their sufferings will be but for a little while. Therefore he is earnestly to be sought unto by continual prayer, and dependence upon his promises.

JAMIESON, FAUSSET, BROWN

one another." The verb is lit., "tie on with a fast *knot*" [WAHL]. Or, "*gird on* humility as *the slave dress* (*encomboma*)": as the Lord girded Himself with a towel to perform a servile office of humility and love, washing His disciples' feet, a scene in which Peter had played an important part, so that he would naturally have it before his mind. **God resisteth the proud**—Quoted, as James 4:6, from Proverbs 3:34. Peter had James before his mind, and gives his Epistle inspired sanction. Cf. vs. 9 with James 4:7, lit., "arrayeth Himself against." Other sins flee from God: pride alone opposeth itself to God; therefore, God also in turn *opposes Himself to* the proud [GERHARD in ALFORD]. Humility is the vessel of all graces [AUGUSTINE]. **6. under the mighty hand**—afflicting you (ch. 3:15): "accept" His chastisements, and turn to Him that smiteth you. He depresses the proud and exalts the humble. **in due time**—Wait humbly and patiently for His own fit time. One oldest MS. and *Vulgate* read, "In the season of visitation," viz., His visitation in mercy. **7. Casting**—*once for all:* so the *Greek* aorist. **care**—"anxiety." The advantage flowing from *humbling ourselves under God's hand* (vs. 6) is confident reliance on His goodness. Exemption from care goes along with humble submission to God. **careth for you**—lit., "*respecting* you." Care is a burden which faith casts off the man on his God. Cf. Psalm 22:10; 37:5; 55:22, to which Peter alludes; Luke 12:22, 37; Philippians 4:6. **careth**—not so strong a *Greek* word as the previous *Greek* "anxiety". **8.** Peter has in mind Christ's warning to himself to *watch* against *Satan*, from forgetting which he fell. **Be sober... vigilant**—"Care," i.e., *anxiety*, will intoxicate the soul; therefore be sober, i.e., self-restrained. Yet, lest this freedom from *care* should lead any to false security, he adds, "Be vigilant" against "your adversary." Let this be your "care." God provides, therefore do not be anxious. The devil seeks, therefore watch [BENGEL]. **because**—omitted in the oldest MSS. The broken and disjointed sentences are more fervid and forcible. LUCIFER of Cagliari reads as *English Version.* **adversary**—lit., "opponent in a court of justice" (Zech. 3:1). "Satan" means *opponent.* "Devil," *accuser* or slanderer (Rev. 12:10). "The enemy" (Matt. 13:39). "A murderer from the beginning" (John 8:44). He counteracts the Gospel and its agents. "The tempter." **roaring lion**—implying his violent and insatiable thirst for prey as a hungry lion. Through man's sin he got God's justice on his side against us; but Christ, our Advocate, by fulfilling all the demands of justice for us, has made our redemption altogether consistent with justice. **walketh about**—(Job 1:7; 2:2). So the children of the wicked one *cannot rest.* **devour**—entangle in worldly "care" (vs. 7) and other snares, so as finally to destroy. Cf. Revelation 12:15, 16. **9.** (Luke 4:13; Eph. 6:11-17; Jas. 4:7.) **steadfast**—Cf. established in the truth," II Pet. 1:12. Satan's power exists only in respect to the unbelieving; the faithful he cannot hurt (I John 5:18). Faith gives strength to prayer, the great instrument against the foe (Jas. 1:6, etc.). **knowing...**—"encouragement not to faint in afflictions": your brethren suffer the same; nothing beyond the common lot of Christians befalls you (I Cor. 10:13). It is a sign of God's favor rather than displeasure, that Satan is allowed to harass you, as he did Job. Your fellow Christians have the same battle of faith and prayer against Satan. **are**—*are being accomplished* according to the appointment of God. **in the world**—lying in the wicked one, and therefore necessarily the scene of "tribulation" (John 16:33). **10.** Comforting assurance that God will finally "perfect" His work of "grace" in them, after they have undergone the necessary previous suffering. **But**—Only do you watch and resist the foe: God will perform the rest [BENGEL]. **of all grace**—(Cf. ch. 4:10). The God to whom as its source all grace is to be referred; who in grace completes what in grace He began. He from the first "called YOU (so the oldest MSS. read for 'us') unto (with a view to) glory." He will not let His purpose fall short of completion. If He does so in punishing, much more in grace. The three are fitly conjoined: the *call*, the *glory* to which we are called, and the way (*suffering*); the fourth is the ground of the calling, viz., *the grace of God in Christ.* **by**—*Greek*, "in." Christ is He *in virtue of* whom, and *in union with* whom, believers are called to glory. The opposite is "in the world" (vs. 9; John 16:33). **after that ye have suffered**—Join to "called you": *suffering*, as a necessary preliminary to *glory*, was contemplated in God's *calling.* **a while**—short and inconsiderable, as compared with the *glory.* **perfect...**—

ADAM CLARKE

mode of speech for being that thing or person with which a man is said to be clothed. Be truly humble, and let your outward garb and conduct be a proof of the humility of your hearts.

6. *Humble yourselves.* Those who submit patiently to the dispensations of God's providence, He lifts up; those who lift themselves up, God thrusts down.

7. *Casting all your care.* Your "anxiety," your "distracting care." *Upon him; for he careth for you.* "For He concerns himself with the things that interest you." This is a plain reference to Ps. lv. 22: "Cast thy burden upon the Lord, and he shall sustain thee." He will bear both you and your burden.

8. *Be sober.* Avoid drunkenness of your senses, and drunkenness in your souls; be not overcharged with the concerns of the world. *Be vigilant.* Awake, and keep awake; be always "watchful"; never be off your guard. Your enemies are alert; they are never off theirs. *Your adversary the devil.* This is the reason why you should be sober and vigilant; you have an ever active, implacable, subtle enemy to contend with. He *walketh about*—he has access to you everywhere; he knows your feelings and your propensities, and informs himself of all your circumstances. Only God can know more and do more than he; therefore your care must be cast upon God. *As a roaring lion.* Satan tempts under three forms: (1) The subtle serpent; to beguile our senses, pervert our judgment, and enchant our imagination. (2) As an angel of light; to deceive us with false views of spiritual things. (3) As a roaring lion; to bear us down, and destroy us by violent opposition, persecution, and death. Thus he was acting towards the followers of God at Pontus, etc., who were now suffering a grievous persecution. *Walketh about.* Traversing the earth; a plain reference to Job ii. 2. *Seeking whom he may devour.* "Whom he may gulp down." There is a beauty in this verse, and a striking apposition between the first and last words, which I think have not been noticed: Be *sober*, from *ne*, "not," and *piein*, "to drink"—"do not drink, do not swallow down"; and the word from *kata*, "down," and *piein*, "to drink." If you swallow strong drink down, the devil will swallow you down.

9. *Whom resist.* Stand against him. *The same afflictions are accomplished in your brethren.* It is the lot of all the disciples of Christ to suffer persecution. The "brotherhood," the Christian Church, everywhere is exposed to the assaults of men and devils. You are persecuted by the heathen among whom you live, and from among whom you are gathered into the fold of Christ; but even those who profess the same faith with you, and who are resident among the Jews (for so I think *in the world* is here to be understood), are also persecuted, both heathens and Jews being equally opposed to the pure and holy doctrines of the gospel. Any man who has read the Greek Testament with any attention must have observed a vast number of places in which the word *cosmos*, which we translate *world*, means the Jewish people and the Jewish state, and nothing else.

10. *But the God of all grace.* The Fountain of infinite compassion, mercy, and goodness. *Who hath called us.* By the preaching of the gospel. *After that ye have suffered a while.* "Having suffered a little time"; that is, while you are enduring these persecutions, God will cause all to work together for your good. *Make you perfect.* All these words are read in the

MATTHEW HENRY

2. His doxology, *v.* 11.

III. He recommends *Silvanus,* the person by whom he sent them this brief epistle. The prejudices that some of these Jews might have against Silvanus, as a minister of the Gentiles, would soon wear off when they were once convinced that he was a faithful brother.

II. He recapitulates the design of his writing this epistle to them (*v.* 12). The doctrine of salvation, which he had explained and they had embraced, was the true account of the grace of God, foretold by the prophets and published by Jesus Christ.

As they had embraced the gospel, they would continue steadfast in it. A firm persuasion that we are in the true way to heaven will be the best motive to stand fast, and persevere therein.

IV. He closes with salutations and a solemn benediction. In this salutation he particularly joins Mark the evangelist, who was then with him, and who was his son in a spiritual sense.

All the churches of Jesus Christ ought to have a most affectionate concern one for another; they should love and pray for one another. He exhorts them to fervent love and charity one towards another, and to express this by giving *the kiss of peace* (*v.* 14), and so concludes with a benediction, which he confines to those *that are in Christ Jesus.* The blessing he pronounces upon them is *peace,* by which he means all necessary good.

JAMIESON, FAUSSET, BROWN

The *Greek* has, "shall HIMSELF perfect you": though you are called on to *watch* and *resist* the foe, God *Himself* must really do all in and through you. The same God who begins must *Himself* complete the work. The *Greek* for "stablish" (so as to be "steadfast in the faith," vs. 9) is the same as "strengthen," Luke 22:32. **11. To him**—emphatic. To Him and Him alone: not to ourselves. Cf. "Himself," *Note,* vs. 10. **glory and**—omitted in the oldest MSS. and versions. **dominion**—*Greek, "the* might" shown in so "perfecting," you, vs. 10. **12. Silvanus**—*Silas,* the companion of Paul and Timothy: a suitable messenger by whom to confirm, as Peter here does, *Paul's* doctrine of "the true grace of God" in the same churches (cf. II Pet. 3:16). **as I suppose**—Join "faithful unto you [STEIGER], as I suppose." Silvanus may have stood in a close relation to the churches in Asia, perhaps having taken the oversight of them after Paul's departure, and had afterwards gone to Peter, by whom he is now sent back to them with this Epistle. "By Silvanus, that faithful brother, as *expect,* I have written to you" [BIRKS]. **briefly**—*Greek,* "in few (words)," as compared with the importance of the subject (Heb. 13:22). **exhorting**—not so much formally *teaching doctrines,* which could not be done in so "few words." **testifying**—bearing my testimony *in confirmation* (so the *Greek* compound verb implies) of that truth which ye have already heard from Paul and Silas (I John 2:27). **that this**—of which I have just written, and of which Paul before testified to you (whose testimony, now that he was no longer in those regions, was called in question probably by some; cf. II Peter 3:15, 16). II Peter 1:12, "the present truth," viz., the grace formerly promised by the prophets, and *now* manifested to you. "Grace" is the keynote of Paul's doctrine which Peter now confirms (Eph. 2:5, 8). Their sufferings for the Gospel made them to need some attestation and confirmation of the truth, that they should not fall back from it. **wherein ye stand**—The oldest MSS. read imperatively, *"Stand ye."* Lit., *"into* which (having been already admitted, ch. 1:8, 21; 2:7, 8, 9) stand (therein)." **Babylon**—The Chaldean Babylon on the Euphrates. How unlikely that in a *friendly salutation* the enigmatical title of Rome given in *prophecy* (John, Rev. 17:5), should be used! Babylon was the center from which the Asiatic *dispersion* whom Peter addresses was derived. PHILO (*Legat. ad Caium,* sec. 36) and JOSEPHUS (*Antiquities,* 15. 2. 2; 23. 12) inform us that Babylon contained a great many Jews in the apostolic age (whereas those at Rome were comparatively few, about 8000 (JOSEPHUS 17. 11); so it would naturally be visited by the apostle of the circumcision. It was the headquarters of those whom he had so successfully addressed on Pentecost, Acts 2:9, Jewish "Parthians . . . dwellers in Mesopotamia" (the Parthians were then masters of Mesopotamian Babylon); these he ministered to *in person.* His other hearers, the Jewish "dwellers in Cappadocia, Pontus, Asia, Phrygia, Pamphylia," he now ministers to by letter. ERASMUS explains, "Mark *who is in the place of a son* to me": cf. Acts 12:12, implying Peter's connection with Mark; whence the mention of him in connection with *the Church* at Babylon, in which he labored under Peter before he went to Alexandria is not unnatural. PAPIAS reports from the presbyter John (B. 3.39), that Mark was interpreter of Peter, recording in his Gospel the facts related to him by Peter. Silvanus or Silas had been substituted for John Mark, as Paul's companion, because of Mark's temporary unfaithfulness. But now Mark restored is associated with Silvanus, Paul's companion, in Peter's esteem, as Mark was already reinstated in Paul's esteem. That Mark had a spiritual connection with the Asiatic churches which Peter addresses, and so naturally salutes them, appears from II Timothy 4:11; Colossians 4:10. **14. kiss of charity**—Romans 16:16, "an *holy* kiss": the token of love to God and the brethren. *Love* and *holiness* are inseparable. Cf. the instance, Acts 20:37. **Peace**—Peter's closing salutation; as Paul's is, "Grace be with you," though he accompanies it with "peace be to the brethren." "Peace" (flowing from *salvation*) was Christ's own salutation after the resurrection, and from Him Peter derives it. **be with you all that are in Christ**—The oldest MSS. omit "Jesus."

ADAM CLARKE

future tense by the best MSS. and versions. "He will make you perfect"—put you in "complete joint" as the timbers of a building. *Stablish.* Make you "firm" in every part. *Strengthen.* Cramp and bind every part so that there shall be no danger of warping, splitting, or falling. *Settle.* Cause all to rest so evenly and firmly upon the best and surest foundation that you may grow together to a holy temple in the Lord. In a word, that you may be "complete" in all the mind that was in Christ; "supported" in all your trials and difficulties; "strengthened" to resist and overcome all your enemies; and after all abide, firmly "founded," in the truth of grace. All these phrases are architectural; and the apostle has again in view the fine image which he produced in chap. ii. 5.

11. *To him*—the God of all grace; *be glory*—all honor and praise be ascribed; and *dominion*—the government of heaven, earth, and hell; *for ever*—through time; *and ever*—through eternity. *Amen*—so be it, so let it be, and so it shall be.

12. *By Silvanus, a faithful brother unto you, as I suppose.* To say the least of this translation, it is extremely obscure, and not put together with that elegance which is usual to our translators. I see no reason why the clause may not be thus translated: "I have written to you, as I consider, briefly, by Silvanus, the faithful brother." On all hands it is allowed that this Silvanus was the same as Silas, Paul's faithful companion in travel, mentioned in Acts xv. 40; xvi. 19; and if he were the same, Peter could never say *as I suppose* to his faith and piety: but he might well say this to the shortness of his Epistle, notwithstanding the many and important subjects which it embraced. *Exhorting.* Calling upon you to be faithful, humble, and steady. *And testifying.* "Earnestly witnessing" that it *is the true grace*—the genuine gospel of Jesus Christ, "in which *ye stand,"* and in which you should persevere to the end.

13. *Elected together with you.* "Fellow elect," or "elected jointly" with you.

And so doth Marcus my son. This is supposed to be the same person who is mentioned in Acts xii. 12, and who is known by the name of John Mark; he is the same who wrote the Gospel that goes under his name. He is called here Peter's son, i.e., according to the faith, Peter probably having been the means of his conversion. This is very likely, as Peter seems to have been intimate at his mother's house. See the account in Acts xii. 6-17.

14. *Greet ye one another with a kiss of charity.* See the notes on Rom. xvi. 16 and on 1 Cor. xvi. 20. In the above places the kiss is called "a holy kiss"; here, "a kiss of love"; i.e., as a mark of their love to each other, in order that misunderstandings might be prevented. *Peace be with you all.* May all "prosperity," spiritual and temporal, be with all *that are in Christ Jesus*—that are truly converted to Him, and live in His Spirit obedient to His will. *Amen.* Is wanting, as usual, in some of the principal MSS. and versions.

THE SECOND EPISTLE OF PETER

I. Introduction (1:1, 2)
A. The writer and the readers (1:1)
1. Simon Peter
2. Servant, apostle
3. "The like precious faith" (Luke 22:32)
B. His desire—"knowledge" (1:2)

II. The principles of preservation (1:3-21)
A. The principles stated (1:3-11)
1. Provision (1:3, 4)
2. Responsibility (1:5-11)
a. Diligent development (1:5-9)
b. The more diligence (1:10, 11)
B. The principles defended (1:12-21)
1. Determination in view of his Exodus (1:12-15)
2. The vision of the Holy Mount (1:16-21)
a. The vision—power and coming (1:16a)
b. The proofs (1:16b-21)

III. The perils (2:1-3:9)
A. Threatening the power—false teaching (2:1-22)
1. The peril declared (2:1-3a)
2. Judgment announced (2:3b-9)
3. The peril unmasked (2:10-22)
B. Threatening the coming—false living (3:1-9)
1. The peril declared (3:1-4)
2. The answer (3:5-9)

IV. Conclusion (3:10-18)
A. The coming (3:10-13)
B. The power (3:14-16)
C. Final (3:17, 18)

The design of this second epistle is the same with that of the former, as is evident from the first verse of the third chapter, whence observe that, in the things of God, we have need of "precept upon precept, and line upon line," and all little enough to keep them in remembrance; and yet these are the things which should be most faithfully recorded and frequently remembered by us.

MATTHEW HENRY

CHAPTER 1

Verses 1–4

I. We have here a description of the person who wrote the epistle, by the name of *Simon*, as well as *Peter*, and by the title of *servant*, as well as that of *apostle*. He here styles himself *a servant* (as well as an apostle) *of Jesus Christ*. How great an honour is it to be the servants of this Master! This is what we cannot, without sin, be ashamed of.

II. We have an account of the people to whom the epistle is written. They are described as *having obtained precious faith in our Lord Jesus Christ*. True saving faith is a precious grace. True faith is very excellent and of very great use and advantage to those who have it. *The just lives by faith*. Faith is alike precious in the private Christian and in the apostle; it produces the same precious effects in the one and in the other. Faith, in whomsoever it exists, takes hold of the same *precious* Saviour, and applies the same precious promises. This precious faith is obtained of God. Faith is the gift of God. The preciousness of faith, as well as our obtaining it, is through the righteousness of Christ.

III. We have the apostolical benediction.

1. An account of the way and means whereby *grace and peace are multiplied*—it is *through the knowledge of God and Jesus Christ*.

2. What we have already received should encourage us to ask for more. All things that have any relation to, and influence upon, the true spiritual life, the life and power of godliness, are from Jesus Christ.

JAMIESON, FAUSSET, BROWN

CHAPTER 1

VSS. 1-21. ADDRESS: EXHORTATION TO ALL GRACES, AS GOD HAS GIVEN US, IN THE KNOWLEDGE OF CHRIST, ALL THINGS PERTAINING TO LIFE: CONFIRMED BY THE TESTIMONY OF APOSTLES, AND ALSO PROPHETS, TO THE POWER AND COMING OF CHRIST. **1. Simon**—the *Greek* form: in oldest MSS., "Symeon" (*Hebrew*, i.e., "hearing"), as in Acts 15: 14. His mention of his original name accords with the design of this Second Epistle, which is to warn against the coming false teachers, by setting forth the true "knowledge" of Christ on the testimony of the *original apostolic eyewitnesses* like himself. This was not required in the First Epistle. **servant**—"slave": so Paul, Romans 1:1. **to them . . .**—He addresses a wider range of readers (*all* believers) than in the First Epistle, ch. 1, but means to include *especially* those addressed in the First Epistle, as ch. 3:1 proves. **obtained**—by grace. Applied by *Peter* to the receiving of the apostleship, lit., "by allotment": as the *Greek* is, Luke 1:9; John 19:24. They did not acquire it for themselves; the divine election is as independent of man's control, as the lot which is cast forth. **like precious**—"equally precious" to all: to those who believe, though not having seen Christ, as well as to Peter and those who have seen Him. **with us**—apostles and eyewitnesses (vs. 18). Though putting forward his *apostleship* to enforce his exhortation, he with true humility puts himself, as to "the faith," on a level with all other believers. The degree of faith varies in different believers; but *in respect to its objects*, present justification, sanctification, and future glorification, it is common alike to all. **Christ** is to all believers "made of God wisdom, righteousness, sanctification, and redemption." **through**—*Greek*, "in." Translate, as the one article to both nouns requires, "the righteousness of *Him who is* (at once) *our God and* (our) Saviour."
2. Grace . . . peace—(I Pet. 1:2). **through**—*Greek*, "in": the sphere IN which alone *grace* and *peace* can be multiplied. **knowledge**—*Greek*, "*full* knowledge." **of God, and of Jesus our Lord**—The *Father* is here meant by "God," but the *Son* in vs. 1: marking how entirely *one* the Father and Son are (John 14:7-11). The *Vulgate* omits "of God and"; but oldest MSS. support the words. Still the prominent object of Peter's exhortation is "the knowledge *of Jesus our Lord*" (a phrase only in Rom. 4: 24), and, only secondarily, of the Father through Him (vs. 8; ch. 2:20; 3:18). **3. According as . . .**—Seeing that [ALFORD]. "*As* He hath given us ALL things (needful) for life and godliness, (so) do you give us ALL diligence. . . ." The oil and flame are given wholly of grace by God, and "taken" by believers: their part henceforth is to "trim their lamps" (cf. vss. 3, 4 with 5, etc.). **life and godliness** Spiritual *life* must exist first before there can be true

ADAM CLARKE

CHAPTER 1

1. *Simon Peter*. "Symeon" is the reading of almost all the versions, and of all the most important MSS. And this is the more remarkable, as the surname of Peter occurs upwards of seventy times in the New Testament, and is invariably read *Simon*, except here, and in Acts xv. 14, where James gives him the name of "Symeon." *A servant*. Employed in his Master's work. *And an apostle*. Commissioned immediately by Jesus Christ himself to preach to the Gentiles, and to write these Epistles for the edification of the Church.

Precious faith. "Valuable faith"; faith worth a great price, and faith which cost a great price. *With us*. God having given to you, believing Gentiles, the same faith and salvation which He had given to us, believing Jews. *Through the righteousness of God*. Through His method of bringing a lost world, both Jews and Gentiles, to salvation by Jesus Christ; through His gracious impartiality, providing for Gentiles as well as Jews. *Of God and our Saviour Jesus Christ*. This is not a proper translation of the original, which is literally, "Of our God and Saviour Jesus Christ"; and this reading, which is indicated in the margin, should have been received into the text; and it is an absolute proof that Peter calls Jesus Christ "God," even in the properest sense of the word, with the article prefixed.

2. *Grace*—God's favor; *peace*—the effects of that favor in the communication of spiritual and temporal blessings. *Through the knowledge of God*. "By the acknowledging of God, and of Jesus our Lord."

3. *As his divine power*. His power, which no power can resist, because it is *divine*—that which properly belongs to the infinite Godhead. *Hath given unto us*. "Hath endowed us with the gifts," or hath "gifted us." By *life and godliness* we may understand: (1) a godly life; or (2) eternal life as the end, and godliness the way to it; or (3) what was essentially necessary for the present life, and what was requisite for the life to come.

MATTHEW HENRY

Knowledge of God, and faith in him, are the channel whereby all spiritual supports and comforts are conveyed to us; but then we must own and acknowledge God as the author of our effectual calling, for so he is here described: *Him that hath called us to glory and virtue*. The design of God in calling or converting men is to bring them to *glory and virtue*. It is the glory of God's power to convert sinners.

The apostle goes on to encourage their faith and hope in looking for an increase of grace and peace. (1) The good things which the promises make over are exceedingly great. Pardon of sin is one of the blessings here intended. To pardon sins that are numerous and heinous is a wonderful thing. (2) The promised blessings of the gospel are very precious. The great promise of the New Testament is the *Holy Ghost*. (3) Those who receive the promises of the gospel *partake of the divine nature*. Their hearts are set for God and his service. (4) Those in whom the Spirit works the divine nature are freed from the bondage of corruption. The dominion that sin has in the men of the world is through lust; their desires are to it, and therefore it rules over them. The dominion that sin has over us is according to the delight we have in it.

Verses 5–11

Having already obtained precious faith, and been made partakers of the divine nature is a very good beginning, but it is not to be rested in, as if we were already perfect. He exhorts them to press forward for the obtaining of more grace. Those who will make any progress in religion must be very industrious in their endeavours. Without *giving all diligence*, there is no gaining any ground in the work of holiness.

I. The believer's way is marked out step by step. 1. He must get *virtue*, by which some understand *justice*; and then the *knowledge, temperance, and patience* that follow. By *virtue* here we may understand *strength* and *courage*, without which the believer cannot stand up for good works. A cowardly Christian must expect that Christ will be ashamed of him another day. We have need of virtue while we live, and it will be of excellent use when we come to die. 2. The believer must add *knowledge* to his virtue, prudence to his courage. Christian prudence regards the persons we have to do with and the place and company we are in. 3. We must add *temperance to our knowledge*. We must be moderate in desiring and using the good things of natural life; an inordinate desire after these is inconsistent with an earnest desire after God and Christ. 4. Add to temperance *patience*, which must *have its perfect work*. We are born to trouble, and must through many tribulations enter into the kingdom of heaven. Our sufferings are less than our sins deserve. 5. To patience we must add *godliness*. When Christians bear afflictions patiently, they get an experimental *knowledge of the loving-kindness of their heavenly Father*, and hereby they are brought to the child-like fear and reverential love wherein true godliness consists. 6. We must add *brotherly-kindness*, a tender affection to all our fellow-christians, who are children of the same Father, and therefore are to be loved, as those who are peculiarly near and dear to us. 7. *Charity*, or a love of goodwill to all mankind. God has made of one blood all nations, and all the children of men are partakers of the same human nature, are all capable of the same mercies, and liable to the same afflictions. Thus must all believers in Christ evidence that they are the children of God, who is good to all.

JAMIESON, FAUSSET, BROWN

godliness. Knowledge of God experimentally is the first step to *life* (John 17:3). The child must have vital breath first, and then cry to, and walk in the ways of, his father. It is not by *godliness* that we obtain *life*, but by *life, godlines*. To *life* stands opposed *corruption;* to *godliness, lust* (vs. 4). **called us**—vs. 10—"calling" (I Pet. 2:9). **to glory and virtue**—rather, "*through* (His) glory." Thus *English Version* reads as one oldest MS. But other oldest MSS. and *Vulgate* read, "*By His own* (peculiar) glory and virtue"; being the explanation of "His divine power"; *glory* and *moral excellency* (the same attribute is given to God in I Peter 2:9, "praises," lit., "virtues" characterize God's "power." "Virtue," the standing word in heathen ethics, is found only once in Paul (Phil. 4:8), and in Peter in a distinct sense from its classic usage; it (in the heathen sense) is a term too low and earthly for expressing the gifts of the Spirit [TRENCH, *Synonyms*]. **4. Whereby . . .**—By His *glory* and *virtue:* His *glory* making the "promises" to be *exceeding great;* His *virtue* making them "precious" [BENGEL]. *Precious promises* are the object of *precious faith*. **given**—The *promises* themselves are a *gift:* for God's *promises* are as sure as if they were fulfilled. **by these**—*promises*. They are the object of faith, and even now have a sanctifying effect on the believer, assimilating him to God. Still more so, when they shall be *fulfilled*. **might . . .**—*Greek,* "that ye MAY become partakers of the divine nature," even now in part; hereafter perfectly; I John 3:2, "We shall be like Him." **the divine nature**—not God's essence, but His *holiness*, including His "glory" and "virtue," vs. 3; the opposite to "corruption through lust." Sanctification is the imparting to us of *God Himself* by the Holy Spirit in the soul. We by faith partake also of the material nature of Jesus (Eph. 5:30). The "divine *power*" enables us to be partakers of "the divine *nature*." **escaped the corruption**—which involves in, and with itself, *destruction* at last of soul and body; on "escaped" as from a condemned cell, cf. ch. 2:18-20; Genesis 19:17; Colossians 1:13. **through**—*Greek,* "in." "The corruption in the world" has its seat, not so much in the surrounding elements, as in the "lust" or concupiscence of men's hearts. **5. And beside this**—rather, "And for this very reason," viz., "seeing that His divine power hath given unto us all things that pertain to life and godliness" (vs. 3). **giving**—lit., "introducing," side by side with God's *gift*, on your part "diligence." Cf. an instance, vs. 10; ch. 3:14; II Corinthians 7:11. **all**—all possible. **add**—lit., "minister additionally," or, abundantly (cf. *Greek*, II Cor. 9:10); said properly of the one who *supplied* all the equipments of a chorus. So accordingly, "there will be *ministered abundantly* unto you an entrance into the everlasting kingdom of our Saviour" (vs. 11). **to**—*Greek,* "in"; *in* the possession of *your faith, minister virtue*. Their *faith* (answering to "knowledge of Him," vs. 3) is presupposed as the gift of God (vs. 3; Eph. 2:8), and is not required to be *ministered* by *us; in* its exercise, *virtue* is to be, moreover, ministered. Each grace being assumed, becomes the stepping-stone to the succeeding grace: and the latter in turn qualifies and completes the former. *Faith* leads the band; *love* brings up the rear [BENGEL]. The fruits of *faith* specified are *seven*, the perfect number. **virtue**—moral excellency; manly, strenuous energy, answering to the *virtue* (energetic excellency) of God. **and to**—*Greek,* "in"; "and in (the exercise of) your virtue knowledge," viz., practical discrimination of good and evil; intelligent appreciation of what is the will of God in each detail of practice. **6.** *Greek,* "And in your knowledge self-control." In the exercise of Christian *knowledge* or discernment of God's will, let there be the practical fruit of *self-control* as to one's lusts and passions. Incontinence weakens the mind; continence, or self-control, removes weakness and imparts strength [BENGEL]. "And in your self-control patient endurance" amidst sufferings, so much dwelt on in the First Epistle, chs. 2, 3 and 4. "And in your patient endurance godliness"; it is not to be mere stoical endurance, but united to [and flowing from] *God-trusting* [ALFORD]. **7.** "And in your godliness brotherly kindness"; not suffering your godliness to be moroseness, nor a sullen solitary habit of life, but kind, generous, and courteous [ALFORD]. Your natural affection and *brotherly kindness* are to be sanctified by *godliness*. "And in your brotherly kindness love," viz., to *all* men, even to enemies, in thought, word, and deed. From *brotherly kindness* we are to go forward to *love*. Cf. I Thessalonians 3:12, "Love one toward another (brotherly kindness), and toward all men" (charity). So *charity* completes the choir of graces in Colossians 3:14. In a retrograde order, he who has *love* will exercise *brotherly kind-*

ADAM CLARKE

That hath called us to glory and virtue. To *virtue* or "courage" as the means; and *glory*—the kingdom of Heaven, as the end. This is the way in which these words are commonly understood, and this sense is plain enough, but the construction is harsh. Others have translated "by His glorious benignity," and read the whole verse thus: "God by His own power hath bestowed on us everything necessary for a happy life and godliness, having called us to the knowledge of himself, by His own infinite goodness." It is certain that the word which we translate *virtue* or "courage," is used, 1 Pet. ii. 9, to express the perfection of the divine nature. But there is a various reading here which is of considerable importance, and which, from the authorities by which it is supported, appears to be genuine: Through the knowledge of Him who hath called us "by His own glory and power," or "by His own glorious power."

4. *Whereby are given unto us.* By His own glorious power He hath "freely given unto us exceeding great and invaluable promises." Peter intimates to these Gentiles that God had given unto them exceeding great promises; indeed all that He had given to the Jews, the mere settlement in the Promised Land excepted; and this also He had given in all its spiritual meaning and force. And besides these "superlatively great" promises, which distinguished the Mosaic dispensation, He had given them the "valuable" promises, those which came through the great price: enrollment with the Church of God, redemption in and through the Blood of the Cross, the continual indwelling influence of the Holy Ghost, the resurrection of the body, and eternal rest at the right hand of God. *That by these ye might be partakers.* The object of all God's promises and dispensations was to bring fallen man back to the image of God, which he had lost. This, indeed, is the sum and substance of the religion of Christ. We have partaken of an earthly, sensual, and devilish nature; the design of God by Christ is to remove this, and to make us *partakers of the divine nature;* and save us from all the *corruption* in principle and fact which *is in the world;* the source of which is *lust*—irregular, unreasonable, inordinate, and impure desire. *Lust* is the source whence springs all the corruption which is in the world. Lust conceives and brings forth sin; sin is finished or brought into act, and then brings forth death. This destructive principle is to be rooted out, and love to God and man is to be implanted in its place. This is every Christian's privilege. God has promised to purify our hearts by faith; and that as sin hath reigned unto death, even so shall grace reign through righteousness unto eternal life; that here we are to be delivered out of the hands of all our enemies, and have even "the thoughts of our hearts so cleansed by the inspiration of God's Holy Spirit that we shall perfectly love Him, and worthily magnify His holy name."

5. *And beside this.* Notwithstanding what God hath done for you, in order that you may not receive the grace of God in vain. *Giving all diligence.* "Furnishing all earnestness" and activity. The original is very emphatic. *Add to your faith.* "Lead up hand in hand." *Virtue.* "Courage" or "fortitude," to enable you to profess the faith before men in these times of persecution. *Knowledge.* True wisdom, by which your faith will be increased, and your courage directed.

6. *Temperance.* A proper and limited use of all earthly enjoyments, keeping every sense under proper restraints, and never permitting the animal part to subjugate the rational. *Patience.* Bearing all trials and difficulties with an even mind, enduring in all, and persevering through all. *Godliness.* Piety towards God; a deep, reverential, religious fear.

7. *Brotherly kindness.* "Love of the brotherhood"—the strongest attachment to Christ's flock. *Charity.* "Love" to the whole human race, even to your persecutors. True religion is neither selfish nor insulated; where the love of God is, bigotry cannot exist. Narrow, selfish people, and people of a party, who scarcely have any hope of the salvation of those who do not believe as they believe and who do not follow with them, have scarcely any religion, though

MATTHEW HENRY

II. All the forementioned graces must be had. The advantages that redound to all who successfully labour so as to get these things to *be and abound in them, v.* 8–11.

1. More generally, *v.* 8. The being and abounding of all Christian graces in us will make us neither inactive nor unfruitful, it will make us very zealous and lively, and eminently fruitful in the works of righteousness. These will bring much glory to God, by bringing forth much fruit among men, being *fruitful in knowledge, or the acknowledging of our Lord Jesus Christ*. This is the necessary consequence of adding one grace to another; for, where all Christian graces are in the heart, they improve and strengthen one another. Wherever grace abounds there will be an abounding in good works. How desirable it is to be in such a case the apostle evidences, *v.* 9. He who has not the forementioned graces *is blind*, that is, as to spiritual and heavenly things. *He cannot see far off.* This present evil world he can see, and dotes upon, but has no discerning at all of the world to come. How wretched is their condition who are thus blind as to the awfully great things of the other world. But this is not all the misery of those who do not *add to their faith virtue, knowledge*, &c. They are as unable to look backward as forward, their memories are slippery and unable to retain what is past. Often call to mind, and seriously meditate on, your solemn engagement to be the Lord's, to lay aside *all filthiness of flesh and spirit.*

2. Two particular advantages: stability in grace, and a triumphant entrance into glory. *Giving diligence to make our calling and election sure.* It requires a great deal of diligence and labour to make sure our calling and election; there must be a very close examination of ourselves.

"But, how great soever the labour is, do not think much of it, for great is the advantage you gain by it. By this you will be kept from falling." When many fall into errors, they shall be preserved sound in the faith, and stand perfect and complete in all the will of God. Those who are *growing in grace*, and *abounding in the work of the Lord*, shall have an *abundant entrance into the joy of their Lord*, and they shall *reign with him for ever and ever.*

Verses 12–15

I. Peter *will not be negligent*, but will be exemplarily diligent, and that in the work of a remembrancer. We need to be put in mind of what we already know to prevent our forgetting it, and to improve our knowledge, and reduce all to practice. We must be established in the belief of the truth, that we may not be shaken by every wind of doctrine, and especially in that which is the present truth, the truth more peculiarly necessary for us to know in our day. If the people need teaching and exhortation while they are in the body, it is very meet and just that ministers should, as long as they are in this tabernacle, instruct and exhort them, and bring those truths to their remembrance that they have formerly heard.

JAMIESON, FAUSSET, BROWN

ness; he who has *brotherly kindness* will feel *godliness* needful; the *godly* will mix nothing stoical with his *patience;* to the patient, *temperance* is easy; the temperate weighs things well, and so has *knowledge;* knowledge guards against sudden impulse carrying away its *virtue* [BENGEL]. **8. be**—*Greek,* "subsist" i.e., supposing these things to have an actual *subsistence* in you; "be" would express the mere matter-of-fact *being* (Acts 16:20). **abound**—*more than in others;* so the *Greek.* **make**—"render," "constitute you," habitually, by the very fact of possessing these graces. **barren**—"inactive," and, as a field lying fallow and *unworked* (*Greek*), so *barren* and *useless.* **unfruitful in**—rather, ". . . . *in respect to,*" "The *full knowledge* (*Greek*) of Christ" is the goal towards which all these graces tend. As their *subsisting* in us constitutes us *not barren* or idle, so their *abounding* in us constitutes us *not unfruitful* in respect to it. It is through *doing* His will, and so becoming like Him, that we grow in *knowing* Him (John 7:17). **9. But**—*Greek,* "For." Confirming the need of these graces (vss. 5-8) by the fatal consequences of the want of them. **he that lacketh**—*Greek,* "he to whom these are not present." **blind**—as to the spiritual realities of the unseen world. **and cannot see afar off**—explanatory of "blind." He *closes his eyes* (*Greek*) as unable to see distant objects (viz., heavenly things), and fixes his gaze on present and earthly things which alone he can see. Perhaps a degree of *wilfulness* in the blindness is implied in the *Greek,* "closing the eyes," which constitutes its culpability; hating and rebelling against the light shining around him. **forgotten**—*Greek,* "contracted forgetfulness," wilful and culpable obliviousness. **that he was purged**—The continually present sense of one's sins having been once for all forgiven, is the strongest stimulus to every grace (Ps. 130:4). **10. Wherefore**—seeking the blessed consequence of having, and the evil effects of not having, these graces (vss. 8, 9). **the rather**—the more earnestly. **brethren**—marking that it is affection for them which constrains him so earnestly to urge them. Nowhere else does he so address them, which makes his calling them so here the more emphatical. **give diligence**—The *Greek* aorist implies *one lifelong effect* [ALFORD]. **to make**—*Greek* middle voice; to make *so far as it depends on you;* to do *your part* towards making. "To make" absolutely and finally is God's part, and would be in the active. **your calling and election sure**—by "*ministering additionally in your faith virtue, and in your virtue knowledge . . .*" God must work all these graces in us, yet not so that we should be mere *machines,* but *willing instruments* in His hands in making His election of us "secure." The *ensuring* of our *election* is spoken of not in respect to God, whose counsel is steadfast and everlasting, but in respect to *our part.* There is no uncertainty on His part, but on ours the only security is our *faith* in His promise and the fruits of the Spirit (vss. 5-7, 11).

fall—*Greek,* "stumble" and fall finally (Rom. 11:11). Metaphor from one *stumbling* in a race (I Cor. 9:24). **11. an entrance**—rather as *Greek, "the* entrance" which ye look for. **ministered**—the same verb as in vs. 5. *Minister* in your faith virtue and the other graces, so shall there be *ministered to you* the entrance into that heaven where these graces shine most brightly. The reward of grace hereafter shall correspond to the work of grace here. **abundantly**—*Greek,* "richly." It answers to "abound," vs. 8. If these graces *abound* in you, you shall have your entrance into heaven not merely "scarcely" (as he had said, I Pet. 4:18), nor "so as by fire," like one escaping with life after having lost all his goods, but in triumph without "stumbling and falling." **12. Wherefore**—as these graces are so necessary to your abundant entrance into Christ's kingdom (vss. 10, 11). **I will not be negligent**—The oldest MSS. read, "*I will be about* always to put you in remembrance" (an accumulated future: I will regard you as always needing to be reminded): cf. "I will endeavor," vs. 15. "I will be sure always to remind you" [ALFORD]. "Always"; implying the reason why he writes the second Epistle so soon after the first. He feels *there is likely* to be more and more need of admonition on account of the increasing corruption (ch. 2:1, 2). **in the present truth**—*the Gospel truth now present with you:* formerly promised to Old Testament believers as *about to be, now* in the New Testament *actually present* with, and in, believers, so that they are "established" in it as a "present" reality. Its importance renders frequent monitions never superfluous: cf. Paul's similar apology, Romans 15:14, 15. **13. Yea**—*Greek,* "But"; though "you know" the truth (vs. 12). **this tabernacle**—soon to be taken down (II Cor. 5:1): I there-

ADAM CLARKE

in their own apprehension none is so truly orthodox or religious as themselves.

8. *For if these things be in you, and abound.* If you possess all these graces, and they increase and abound in your souls, *they* will *make,* show, you to be neither "idle" nor unfruitful, "in the acknowledgment of our Lord Jesus Christ." The common translation is here very unhappy. *Barren* and *unfruitful* certainly convey the same ideas; but "idle" or "inactive," which is the proper sense, takes away this tautology and restores the sense. The graces already mentioned by the apostle are in themselves active principles; he who was possessed of them, and had them abounding in him, could not be "inactive"; and he who is not inactive in the way of life must be fruitful.

9. *But he that lacketh these things.* He, whether Jew or Gentile, who professes to have faith in God, and has not added to that faith "fortitude, knowledge, temperance, patience, godliness, bortherly kindness, and universal love," is *blind*—his understanding is darkened; *and cannot see afar off,* "shutting his eyes against the light, winking," not able to look truth in the face, nor to behold that God whom he once knew was reconciled to him: and thus it appears he is willfully blind; *and hath forgotten that he was purged from his old sins*—has at last, through his non-improvement of the grace which he received from God, lost the evidence of things not seen.

10. *Wherefore.* Seeing the danger of apostasy and the fearful end of them who obey not the gospel, *give* all *diligence,* "hasten," be deeply careful, labor with the most intense purpose of soul. *To make your calling.* From deep Gentile darkness into the marvellous light of the gospel. *And election.* Your being chosen, in consequence of obeying the heavenly calling, to be the people and Church of God. *Sure.* "Firm, solid." For your calling to believe the gospel, and your election to be members of the Church of Christ, will be ultimately unprofitable to you unless you hold fast what you have received by adding to your faith virtue, knowledge, temperance. *For if ye do these things*—if you are careful and diligent to work out your own salvation, through the grace which you have already received from God. *Ye shall never fall*—"You shall at no time stumble or fall"; as the Jews have done, and lost their election, Rom. xi. 11, where the same word is used. We find, therefore, that they who do not these things shall fall; and thus we see that there is nothing absolute and unconditional in their election.

11. *For so an entrance shall be ministered.* If you give diligence, and do not fall, an abundant, free, honorable, and triumphant *entrance shall be ministered unto you . . . into the everlasting kingdom.* There seems to be here an allusion to the triumphs granted by the Romans to their generals who had distinguished themselves by putting an end to a war or doing some signal military service to the state. "You shall have a triumph, in consequence of having conquered your foes, and led captivity captive."

12. *Wherefore I will not be negligent.* He had already written one Epistle; this is the second.

13. *As long as I am in this tabernacle.* By *tabernacle* we are to understand his body.

MATTHEW HENRY

II. The apostle tells us (*v.* 14) what makes him earnest in this matter. The body is but the tabernacle of the soul. This tabernacle must be put off. We are not to continue long in this earthly house. The nearness of death makes the apostle diligent in the business of life.

He must soon be removed from those to whom he wrote; and his ambition being that they should remember the doctrine he had delivered to them, after he himself was taken away from them, he commits his exhortation to writing.

Verses 16–18

These things are not idle tales, or a vain thing, but of undoubted truth and vast concern. The gospel is not a *cunningly devised fable.* The apostle's preaching was a making of these things known. 1. The preaching of the gospel is a making known the power of Christ. 2. The coming of Christ also is made known by the preaching of the gospel. This coming of Christ the gospel is very plain and circumstantial in setting forth; but there is a second coming, which it likewise mentions. He will come to judge the world in righteousness by the everlasting gospel. During our blessed Saviour's abode here on earth he sometimes manifested himself to be God, and particularly to our apostle and the two sons of Zebedee, who *were eye-witnesses of his divine majesty, when he was transfigured before them.* Besides the visible glory there was an audible voice from heaven. What a gracious declaration was made: *This is my beloved Son, in whom I am well pleased*—the best voice that ever came from heaven to earth; God is well pleased with Christ. *He received honour and glory from God the Father.* This is the person whom God delights to honour. This voice is from heaven, called here *the excellent glory.* This voice was heard, and that so as to be understood, by Peter, James, and John. They not only heard a sound, but they understood the sense. God opens the ears and understandings of his people to receive what they are concerned to know. Blessed are those who not only hear, but understand, who believe the truth, and feel the power of the voice from heaven.

Verses 19–21

In these words the apostle lays down another argument to prove the truth and reality of the gospel. For this is foretold by the prophets of the Old Testament, who spoke and wrote according to the direction of the Spirit of God.

I. The description that is given of the scriptures of the Old Testament: they are called *a more sure word of prophecy.* It is a prophetical declaration of the power and coming of our Saviour. But the New Testament is a history of that whereof the Old Testament is a prophecy. Read the Old Testament as a prophecy of Christ, and with diligence and thankfulness use the New as the best exposition of the Old. How firm and sure should our faith be, who have such a firm and sure word to rest upon! All the

JAMIESON, FAUSSET, BROWN

fore need *to make the most of my short time* for the good of Christ's Church. The zeal of Satan against it, the more intense *as his time is short,* ought to stimulate Christians on the same ground. **by**—*Greek,* "in" (cf. ch. 3:1). **14. shortly I must put off**—*Greek,* "the putting off (as a garment) of my tabernacle is speedy": implying a *soon approaching,* and also a *sudden* death (as a violent death is). Christ's words, John 21:18, 19, "When thou art old . . .," were the ground of his "knowing," now that he was old, that his foretold martyrdom was near. Cf. as to Paul, II Timothy 4:6. Though a violent death, he calls it a "departure" (*Greek* for "decease," vs. 15), cf. Acts 7:60. **15. endeavour**—"use my diligence": the same *Greek* word as in vs. 10: this is the field in which my *diligence* has scope. Peter thus fulfils Christ's charge, "Feed My sheep." **decease**—"departure." The very word (exodus) used in the Transfiguration, Moses and Elias conversing about Christ's *decease* (*found nowhere else in the New Testament,* but Heb. 11:22, "the *departing* of Israel" out of Egypt, to which the saints' deliverance from the present bondage of corruption answers). "Tabernacle" is another term found here as well as there (Luke 9:31, 33): an undesigned coincidence confirming Peter's authorship of this Epistle. **that ye may be able**—by the help of this written Epistle; and perhaps also of Mark's Gospel, which Peter superintended. **always**—*Greek,* "on each occasion": as often as occasion may require. **to have . . . in remembrance**—*Greek,* "to exercise remembrance of." Not merely "to remember," as sometimes we do, things we care not about; but "have them in (earnest) remembrance," as momentous and precious truths. **16. For**—reason why he is so earnest that the remembrance of these things should be continued after his death. **followed**—out in detail. **cunningly devised**—*Greek,* "devised by (*man's*) *wisdom*"; as distinguished from what *the Holy Ghost* teaches (cf. I Cor. 3:13). But cf. also ch. 2:3, "feigned words." **fables**—as the heathen mythologies, and the subsequent Gnostic "fables and genealogies," of which the germs already existed in the junction of Judaism with Oriental philosophy in Asia Minor. A precautionary protest of the Spirit against the rationalistic theory of the Gospel history being *myth.* **when we made known unto you**—not that Peter himself had *personally* taught the churches in Pontus, Galatia, etc., but he was one of the apostles whose testimony was borne to them, and to *the Church in general,* to whom this Epistle is addressed (ch. 1:1, *including,* but not *restricted, as* I *Peter,* to the churches in Pontus, etc.). **power**—the opposite of "fables"; cf. the contrast of "word" and "power," I Corinthians 4:20. A specimen of His *power* was given at the Transfiguration also of His "*coming*" again, and its attendant glory. The *Greek* for "coming" is always used of His *second* advent. A refutation of the scoffers (ch. 3:4): I, James and John, saw with our own eyes a mysterious sample of His coming glory. **were**—*Greek,* "were made." **eyewitnesses**—As initiated spectators of mysteries (so the *Greek*), we were admitted into His innermost secrets, viz., at the Transfiguration. **his**—emphatical (cf. *Greek*): "THAT great ONE'S *majesty.*" **17. received . . . honour**—in the *voice* that spake to Him. **glory**—in the *light* which shone around Him. **came** *Greek,* "was borne": the same phrase occurs only in I Peter 1:13; one of several instances showing that the argument against the authenticity of this Second Epistle, from its dissimilarity of style as compared with I Peter, is not well founded. **such a voice**—as he proceeds to describe. **from the excellent glory**—rather as *Greek,* "by (i.e. uttered by) the magnificent glory" (i.e., by *God:* as His glorious manifested presence is often called by the Hebrews "the Glory," cf. "His Excellency," Deut. 33:26; Ps. 21:5). **in whom**—*Greek,* "*in regard to* whom" (accusative); but Matthew 17:5, "in whom" (dative) centers and rests My good pleasure. Peter also omits, as not required by his purpose, "hear Him," showing his independence in his inspired testimony. **I am**—*Greek* aorist, past time, "My good pleasure *rested* from eternity. **18. which came**—rather as *Greek,* "we heard borne from heaven." **holy mount**—as the Transfiguration mount came to be regarded, on account of the manifestation of Christ's divine glory there. **we**—emphatical: we, James and John, as well as myself. **We**—all believers. **a more sure**—rather as *Greek,* "we have *the* word of prophecy more sure" (confirmed). Previously we knew its *sureness* by faith, but, through that visible specimen of its hereafter entire fulfilment, assurance is made *doubly sure.* Prophecy assures us that Christ's *sufferings,* now past, are to be followed by Christ's *glory,* still future: the Transfiguration gives us a pledge to make our faith still stronger, that "the

ADAM CLARKE

14. *Knowing that shortly I must put off.* Peter plainly refers to the conversation between our Lord and himself related in John xxi. 18-19. And it is likely that he had now a particular intimation that he was *shortly* to seal the truth with his blood. But as our Lord told him that his death would take place when he should be old, being aged now he might on this ground fairly suppose that his departure was at hand.

15. *Moreover, I will endeavour.* And is not this endeavor seen in these two Epistles? By leaving these among them, even after his decease they had *these things always in remembrance. After my decease.* "After my going out," i.e., of his tabernacle.

16. *Cunningly devised fables.* I think from the apostle's using *eyewitnesses,* or rather "beholders," in the end of the verse, it is probable that he means those *cunningly devised fables* among the heathens, concerning the appearance of their gods on earth in human form. And to gain the greater credit to these fables, the priests and statesmen instituted what they called the "mysteries" of the gods, in which the fabulous appearance of the gods was represented in mystic shows. But one particular show none but the fully initiated were permitted to behold; hence they were entitled "beholders." This show was probably some resplendent image of the god, imitating life, which, by its glory, dazzled the eyes of the beholders, while their ears were ravished by hymns sung in its praise; to this it was natural enough for Peter to allude when speaking about the transfiguration of Christ. Here the indescribably resplendent majesty of the great God was manifested, as far as it could be, in conjunction with that human body in which the fullness of the Divinity dwelt. "And we," says the apostle, "were beholders of His own majesty." Here was no trick, no feigned show; we saw Him in His glory whom thousands saw before and afterwards; and we have made known to you the *power and coming,* the appearance and presence, of our Lord Jesus; and we call you to feel the exceeding greatness of this power in your conversion, and the glory of this appearance in His revelation by the power of His Spirit to your souls. These things we have witnessed, and these things you have experienced; and therefore we can confidently say that neither you nor we have followed cunningly devised fables, but that blessed gospel which is the power of God to the salvation of everyone that believes.

17. *For he received . . . honour and glory.* In His transfiguration our Lord received from the Father *honour* in the voice or declaration which said, "This is My Son, the beloved One, in whom I have delighted." And He received *glory* when, penetrated with and involved in that excellent glory, "the fashion of his countenance was altered," for His face did shine as the sun, "and his raiment was white and glistering," exceeding white like snow.

18. *And this voice . . . we heard.* That is, himself, James, and John heard it, and saw this glory; for these only were the "beholders" on the holy mount. It is worthy of remark that our blessed Lord, who came to give a new law to mankind, appeared on this *holy mount* with splendor and great glory, as God did when He came on the *holy mount,* Sinai, to give the old law to Moses. And when the voice came from the excellent glory, "This is My Son, the beloved One, in whom I have delighted; hear Him," the authority of the old law was taken away.

19. *We have also a more sure word of prophecy.* "We have the prophetic doctrine more firm or more confirmed"; for in this sense the word is used in several places in the New Testament. See 1 Cor. i. 6: "Even as the testimony of Christ was confirmed in [among] you"; 2 Cor. i. 21; Col. ii. 7; Heb. ii. 3; vi. 16. This is the literal sense of the passage in question, and this sense removes that ambiguity from the text

MATTHEW HENRY

prophecies of the Old Testament are more sure and certain to us who have the history of the accomplishment of them.

II. The encouragement the apostle gives us to search the scriptures. *We do well if we take heed to them;* apply our minds to understand the sense, and our hearts to believe the truth, of this sure word. If we thus apply ourselves to the word of God, we certainly do well in all respects, what is pleasing to God and profitable to ourselves. They must use the scripture as a light which God hath sent into the world, to dispel that darkness which is upon the face of the whole earth. They must acknowledge their own darkness. Every man in the world is naturally without that knowledge which is necessary in order to attain eternal life. If ever men are made wise to salvation, it is by the shining of the word of God into their hearts. Natural notions of God are not sufficient for fallen man. When the light of the scripture is darted into the dark understanding by the Holy Spirit of God, then the *spiritual day dawns and the day-star arises in that soul.* This enlightening of a dark benighted mind is like the day-break that spreads and diffuses itself through the whole soul, till it makes perfect day. It is a growing knowledge. All who do truth come to this light, while evil-doers keep at a distance from it.

III. The apostle lays down one thing as previously necessary, and that is the knowing that all prophecy is of divine origin. No scripture prophecy is of private interpretation, but the revelation of the mind of God. This was the difference between the prophets of the Lord and the false prophets. The prophets of the Lord did not speak nor do anything of their own mind. The prophets and penmen of the scripture spoke and wrote what was the mind of God. Every private man ought to search it, and come to understand the sense and meaning thereof. This important truth of the divine origin of the scriptures is to be known and owned by all who will give heed to the sure word of prophecy. As a man not barely believes, but knows assuredly that that very person is his particular friend in whom he sees all the distinguishing marks and characters of his friend, so the Christian knows that book to be the word of God in which he sees all the proper marks and characters of a divinely inspired book. The divinity of the scriptures must be known and acknowledged in the first place, before men can give good heed to them.

IV. The apostle (*v.* 21) tells us how the Old Testament came to be compiled. 1. They were holy men of God who were employed about that book which we receive as the word of God. All the penmen of the scriptures were holy men of God. 2. *These holy men were moved by the Holy Ghost.* The Holy Ghost is the supreme agent, the holy men are but instruments. The Holy Ghost inspired and dictated to them what they were to deliver of the mind of God. He effectually engaged them to speak (and write) what he had put into their mouths. Mix faith therefore with what you find in the scriptures; esteem and reverence your Bible as a book written by holy men, inspired, influenced, and assisted by the Holy Ghost.

JAMIESON, FAUSSET, BROWN

day" of His glory will "dawn" ere long. He does not mean to say that "the word of prophecy," or Scripture, is surer than *the voice of God* heard at the Transfiguration, as *English Version;* for this is plainly not the fact. The fulfilment of *prophecy* so far in Christ's history makes us the *surer* of what is yet to be fulfilled, His consummated glory. **whereunto**–to which word of prophecy, primarily the Old Testament in Peter's *day;* but now also in our day the New Testament, which, though brighter than the Old Testament (cf. I John 2:8, end), is but a *lamp* even still as compared with the brightness of the eternal day (cf. ch. 3:2). Oral teachings and traditions of ministers are to be tested by the written word (Acts 17:11). **dark**–The *Greek* implies *squalid,* having neither water nor light: such spiritually is the world without, and the smaller world (microcosm) within, the heart in its natural state. Cf. the "*dry* places" Luke 11:24 (viz., unwatered by the Spirit), through which the unclean spirit goeth. **dawn**–bursting *through* the darkness. **day star**–*Greek,* the morning star," as Revelation 22:16. The Lord Jesus. **in your hearts**–Christ's *arising in the heart* by His Spirit giving full assurance, creates spiritually full day in the heart, the means to which is prayerfully *giving heed to the word.* This is associated with the coming of *the day of the Lord,* as being the earnest of it. **20.** "Forasmuch as ye know this" (I Pet. 1:18). **first**–the *foremost* consideration in studying the word of prophecy. Laying it down as a *first principle* never to be lost sight of. **is**–*Greek,* not the simple verb, *to be,* but *to begin to be,* "proves to be," "becometh." No prophecy is found to be the result of "private (the mere individual writer's uninspired) *interpretation*" (*solution*), and so *origination.* The *Greek* noun *epilusis,* does not mean in itself *origination;* but that which the sacred writer could not always fully *interpret,* though being the speaker or writer (as I Pet. 1:10-12 implies), was plainly not of his own, but of God's *disclosure, origination,* and *inspiration,* as Peter proceeds to add, "But holy men . . . spake (and afterwards *wrote*) . . . moved by the Holy Ghost": a reason why ye should "give" all "heed" to it. The parallelism to vs. 16 shows that "*private interpretation,*" contrasted with "moved by the Holy Ghost," here answers to "fables *devised by* (*human*) *wisdom,*" contrasted with "we were eyewitnesses of *His majesty,*" as attested by the "voice from God." The words of the prophetical (and so of all) Scripture writers were not mere words *of the individuals,* and therefore to be *interpreted by them,* but of "the Holy Ghost" by whom they were "moved." "Private" is explained, vs. 21, "by the will of man" (viz., the individual writer). In a secondary sense the text teaches also, as the word is the *Holy Spirit's,* it cannot be *interpreted* by its *readers* (any more than by its *writers* by their mere *private* human powers, but by the teaching of *the Holy Ghost* (John 16:14). "He who is the author of Scripture is its supreme interpreter" [GERHARD]. ALFORD translates, "springs not out of human interpretation," i.e., is not a prognostication made by a man *knowing what he means* when he utters it, but . . . (John 11:49-52). Rightly: except that the verb is rather, *doth become,* or *prove to be.* It not being of private interpretation, you must "*give heed*" to it, looking for the *Spirit's* illumination "in your hearts" (cf. *Notes,* vs. 19). **21. came not in old time**–rather, "was never at any time borne" (to us). **by the will of man**–alone. Jeremiah 23:26, "prophets of the deceit *of their own heart.*" Cf. ch. 3:5, "willingly." **holy**–One oldest MS. has, "*men* FROM *God*": the emissaries from God. "Holy," if read, will mean because they had the Holy Spirit. **moved**–*Greek,* "borne" (along) as by a mighty wind: Acts 2:2, "*rushing* (the same *Greek*) wind": rapt out of themselves: still not in fanatical excitement (I Cor. 14:32). The *Hebrew nabi,* "prophet," meant an *announcer* or interpreter of God: he, as *God's spokesman, interpreted* not his own "private" will or thought, but God's "Man *of the Spirit*" (*Margin,* Hos. 9:7). "Thou testifiedst by Thy Spirit in Thy prophets." "Seer," on the other hand, refers to the *mode of receiving* the communications from God, rather than to the *utterance* of them to others. "Spake" implies that, both in its original oral announcement, and now even when in writing, it has been always, and is, *the living voice* of God *speaking* to us through His inspired servants. *Greek,* "borne (along)" forms a beautiful antithesis to "was borne." They were passive, rather than active instruments. The *Old Testament* prophets primarily, but including also *all* the inspired penmen, whether of the New or Old Testament (ch. 3:2).

ADAM CLARKE

which has given rise to so many different interpretations. Taken according to the common translation, it seems to say that *prophecy* is a surer evidence of divine revelation than miracles; and so it has been understood. The meaning of the apostle appears to be this: The voice from heaven and the miraculous transfiguration of His person have confirmed the prophetic doctrine concerning Him.

And to this doctrine, thus confirmed, you do well to take heed; for it is that light that shines in the dark place, in the Gentile world, as well as among the Jews; and this you must continue to do till the day of His second, last, and most glorious appearing to judge the world comes; and the *day star*—*phosphoros,* "this light-bringer"—*arise in your hearts*—manifest himself to your eternal consolation. The word *phosphoros* generally signified the planet Venus, when she is the morning star; and thus she is called in most European nations.

20. *Knowing this first.* Considering this as a first principle, *that no prophecy of the scripture,* whether that referred to above or any other, *is of any private interpretation*—proceeds from the prophet's own knowledge or invention. The word signifies also "impetus, impulse"; and probably this is the best sense here: not by the mere private impulse of his own mind.

21. *For the prophecy came not in old time.* That is, in any former time, *by the will of man,* by a man's own searching, conjecture, or calculation; *but holy men of God,* persons separated from the world and devoted to God's service, *spake . . . moved by the Holy Ghost.* So far were they from inventing these prophetic declarations concerning Christ or any future event that they were "carried away," out of themselves and out of the whole region, as it were, of human knowledge and conjecture, by the Holy Ghost, who, without their knowing anything of the matter, dictated to them what to speak and what to write.

MATTHEW HENRY

CHAPTER 2

Verses 1–3

I. In all ages of the church the devil sends some to deceive, false prophets in the Old Testament, and seducing teachers in the New.

Their business is to bring in destructive errors, *even damnable heresies*. Those who introduce destructive heresies *deny the Lord that bought them*.

Those who bring in errors destructive to others bring swift (and therefore sure) *destruction upon themselves*. Self destroyers are soon destroyed.

II. The consequence with respect to others. Corrupt leaders seldom fail of many to follow them. Men drink in iniquity like water, and are pleased to live in error. The spreading of error will bring up an evil report on the way of truth; the way of salvation by Jesus Christ.

III. The method seducers take to draw disciples after them: they use *feigned words*; they flatter, and by good words and fair speeches deceive the hearts of the simple. All this is through covetousness, with design to get more wealth, or credit, or commendation, by increasing the number of their followers.

Verses 3–6

How successful and prosperous soever false teachers may be, yet their *judgment lingereth not*. Such unbelievers are condemned already. Examples of the righteous judgment of God.

I. The angels who sinned. No excellency will exempt a sinner from punishment. God did not spare them. By how much the more excellent the offender, by so much the more severe the punishment. Sin debases and degrades the persons who commit it. The angels of heaven are divested of all their glory upon their disobedience. Sin is the work of darkness, and darkness is the wages of sin. Those who will not walk according to the light and direction of God's law shall be deprived of the light of God's countenance.

II. He spared not the old world. If the sin be universal, the punishment shall likewise extend to all.

JAMIESON, FAUSSET, BROWN

CHAPTER 2

VSS. 1-22. FALSE TEACHERS TO ARISE: THEIR BAD PRACTICES AND SURE DESTRUCTION, FROM WHICH THE GODLY SHALL BE DELIVERED, AS LOT WAS. **1. But**—in contrast to the prophets "moved by the Holy Ghost" (ch. 1:21). **also**—as well as the true prophets (ch. 1:19-21). Paul had already testified the entrance of false prophets into the same churches. **among the people**—Israel: he is writing to believing *Israelites* primarily (*Note,* I Pet. 1:1). Such a "false prophet" was Balaam (vs. 15). **there shall be**—Already symptoms of the evil were appearing (vss. 9-22; Jude 4-13). **false teachers**—teachers of falsehood. In contrast to the true teachers, whom he exhorts his readers to give heed to (ch. 3:2). **who**—*such as* (lit., "the which") shall. **privily**—not at first openly and directly, but *by the way,* bringing in error *by the side* of the true doctrine (so the *Greek*): Rome objects, Protestants cannot point out the exact date of the beginnings of the false doctrines superadded to the original truth; we answer, Peter foretells us it would be so, that the first introduction of them would be stealthy and unobserved (Jude 4). **damnable**—lit., "of destruction"; entailing destruction (Phil. 3:19) on all who follow them. **heresies**—*selfchosen* doctrines, not emanating from God (cf. "will worship," Col. 2:23). **even**—going *even* to such a length as to *deny* both in teaching and practice. *Peter* knew, by bitter repentance, what a fearful thing it is to *deny* the Lord (Luke 22:61, 62). **denying**—Him whom, above all others, they ought to *confess.* **Lord**—"Master and Owner" (*Greek*), cf. Jude 4, *Greek.* Whom the true doctrine teaches to be their OWNER *by* right of purchase. Lit., "denying Him who bought them (that He should be thereby), their Master." **bought them**—Even the ungodly were bought by His "precious blood." It shall be their bitterest self-reproach in hell, that, as far as Christ's redemption was concerned, they might have been saved. The denial of His *propitiatory* sacrifice is included in the meaning (cf. I John 4:3). **bring upon themselves**—cf. "God *bringing in* the flood *upon* the world," vs. 5. Man brings upon himself the vengeance which God brings upon him. **swift**—swiftly descending: as the Lord's coming shall be swift and sudden. As the ground swallowed up Korah and Dathan, and "they went down *quick* into the pit." Cf. Jude 11, which is akin to this passage. **2. follow**—out: so the *Greek.* **pernicious ways**—The oldest MSS. and *Vulgate* read, "licentiousness" (Jude 4). False doctrine and immoral practice generally go together (vss. 18, 19). **by reason of whom**—"on account of whom," viz., the followers of the false teachers. **the way of truth shall be evil spoken of**—"blasphemed" by those without, who shall lay on Christianity itself the blame of its professors' evil practice. Contrast I Peter 2:12. **3. through . . .**—*Greek,* "IN covetousness" as their element (vs. 14, end). Contrast II Corinthians 11:20; 12:17. **of a long time**—in God's eternal purpose. "*Before of old* ordained to condemnation" (Jude 4). **lingereth not**—though sinners think it lingers; "is not idle." **damnation**—*Greek,* "destruction" (*Note,* vs. 1). Personified. **slumbereth not**—though sinners *slumber.* **4. if**—The apodosis or consequent member of the sentence is not expressed, but is virtually contained in vs. 9. If God in past time has punished the ungodly and saved His people, He will be sure to do so also in our days (cf. end of vs. 3). **angels**—the highest of intelligent creatures (cf. with this verse, Jude 6), yet not spared when they sinned. **hell**—*Greek,* "Tartarus": nowhere else in New Testament or LXX: equivalent to the usual *Greek, Gehenna.* Not inconsistent with I Peter 5:8; for though their final doom is *hell,* yet for a time they are permitted to roam beyond it in "the darkness of this world." Slaves of *Tartarus* (called "the abyss," or "deep," Luke 8:31; "the bottomless pit," Revelation 9:11) may also come upon earth. Step by step they are given to Tartarus, until at last they shall be wholly bound to it. **delivered**—as the judge delivers the condemned prisoner to the officers (Rev. 20:2). **into chains**—(Jude 6). The oldest MSS. read, "dens," as ALFORD translates: the *Greek,* however, may, in Hellenistic *Greek,* mean "chains," as Jude expresses it. They are "reserved" unto hell's "mist of darkness" as their final "judgment" or doom, and meanwhile their exclusion from the light of heaven is begun. So the ungodly were considered as virtually "in prison," though at large on the earth, from the moment that God's sentence went forth, though not executed till 120 years after. **5. eighth**—i.e., Noah, and seven others. Contrasted with the densely peopled "world of the ungodly."

ADAM CLARKE

CHAPTER 2

1. *But there were false prophets.* There were not only holy men of God among the Jews, who prophesied by divine inspiration, but there were also false prophets, whose prophecies were from their own imagination, and perverted many. *As there shall be false teachers among you.* At a very early period of the Christian Church many heresies sprang up. *Damnable heresies.* "Heresies of destruction"; such as, if followed, would lead a man to perdition. And these they will "bring in privately"—cunningly, without making much noise, and as covertly as possible. It would be better to translate "destructive heresies" than *damnable.*

2. *Many shall follow.* "Will follow," because determined to gratify their sinful propensities. *Pernicious ways.* "Their destructions"; i.e., the "heresies of destruction," or "destructive opinions," mentioned above. But instead of "destructions," "lasciviousnesses or uncleannesses" is the reading of upwards of sixty MSS., most of which are among the most ancient, correct, and authentic. The word "lasciviousnesses" is undoubtedly the true reading, and this points out what the nature of the heresies was. It was a sort of antinomianism; they pampered and indulged the lusts of the flesh. *By reason of whom.* These were persons who professed Christianity; and because they were called Christians, and followed such abominable practices, *the way of truth,* the Christian religion, was "blasphemed." Had they called themselves by any name but that of Christ, His religion would not have suffered.

3. *And through covetousness,* that they might get money to spend upon their lusts, *with feigned words,* with "counterfeit tales, false narrations" of pretended facts, "lying miracles, fabulous legends." *Whose judgment now of a long time.* From the beginning God has condemned sin and inflicted suitable punishments on transgressors; and has promised in His Word, from the earliest ages, to pour out His indignation on the wicked. The punishment, therefore, so long ago predicted shall fall on these impure and incorrigible sinners; and the "condemnation" which is denounced against them *slumbereth not*—it is alert; it is on its way; it is hurrying on, and must soon overtake them.

4. *For if God spared not the angels.* The angels were originally placed in a state of probation, some having fallen and some having stood proves this. How long that probation was to last to them, and what was the particular test of their fidelity, we know not; nor indeed do we know what was their sin, nor when nor how they fell. Jude says, They "kept not their first estate, but left their own habitation"; which seems to indicate that they got discontented with their lot and aspired to higher honors, or perhaps to celestial domination. *But cast them down to hell, and delivered them into chains of darkness.* "But with chains of darkness confining them in Tartarus, delivered them over to be kept to judgment"; or, "Sinking them into Tartarus, delivered them over into custody for punishment, to chains of darkness." *Chains of darkness* is a highly poetic expression. Darkness binds them on all hands; and so dense and strong is this darkness that it cannot be broken through; they cannot deliver themselves nor be delivered by others. As the word "Tartarus" is found nowhere else in the New Testament, nor does it appear in the Septuagint, we must have recourse to the Greek writers for its meaning. The ancient Greeks appear to have received, by tradition, an account of the punishment of the "fallen angels," and of bad men after death; and their poets did, in conformity I presume with that account, make Tartarus the place where the giants who rebelled against Jupiter, and the souls of the wicked, were confined.

5. *Spared not the old world.* The apostle's argument is this: If God spared not the rebellious angels, nor the sinful antediluvians, nor the cities of Sodom and Gomorrah, He will not spare those wicked teachers who corrupt the pure doctrines of Christianity. *Saved Noah, the eighth.* Some think that the words should be translated, "Noah, the eighth preacher of righteousness"; but it seems most evident, from

MATTHEW HENRY

But if there be but a few righteous, they shall be preserved. God does not destroy the good with the bad. In wrath he remembers mercy. The procuring cause of destruction: *it was a world of ungodly men.* Ungodliness puts men out of the divine protection, and exposes them to utter destruction.

III. Sodom and Gomorrah. He destroys the *old world by water,* and Sodom by fire. He who keeps fire and water from hurting his people can make either to destroy his enemies; therefore they are never safe. Those who are sinners exceedingly before the Lord must expect the most dreadful vengeance. The punishment of sinners in former ages is designed for the example of those who come after. Men who live ungodly must see what they are to expect if they go on still in a course of impiety.

Verses 7–9

When God sends destruction on the ungodly, he commands deliverance for the righteous. This we have an instance of in his preserving Lot. 1. The character given of Lot; he is called *a just man.* He does not follow the multitude to do evil, but in a city of injustice he walks uprightly. 2. The impression the sins of others made upon this righteous man. In bad company we cannot escape either guilt or grief. 3. The duration and continuance of this good man's grief and vexation: it was *from day to day.* Being accustomed to hear and see their wickedness did not reconcile him to it. (1) *The Lord knows those that are his.* He has set apart him who is godly for himself; and, if there is but one in five cities, he knows him. (2) The wisdom of God is never at a loss about ways and means to deliver his people. They are often utterly at a loss; but he can find a way of escape. (3) The deliverance of the godly is the work of God, both his wisdom to contrive the way and his power to work out the deliverance *out of temptation.* (4) The unjust has no share in the salvation God works out for the righteous. The wicked are *reserved to the day of judgment.*

Verses 10–22

The apostle's design being to warn us of seducers, he now returns to discourse more particularly of them.

I. *These walk after the flesh.* They, in their lives, act directly contrary to God's righteous precepts, and comply with the demands of corrupt nature. Evil opinions are often accompanied with evil practices; and those who are for propagating error are for improving in wickedness. They go on in their sinful course, and increase unto more ungodliness. They also pour contempt on those whom God has set in authority over them and requires them to honour.

II. This he aggravates, by setting forth the very different conduct of more excellent creatures, even the *angels.* They *are greater in power and might,* and that even than those who are clothed with authority and power among the sons of men. *Angels bring* their *accusations* of sinful creatures *before the Lord.* It is before the Lord, who is the Judge, and will be the avenger, of all impiety and injustice. Good angels mingle no bitter revilings nor base reproaches with any of the accusations they bring. Let us imitate the angels. If we complain of wicked men, let it be to God, and that not with rage and reviling, but with compassion, that may evidence that we belong to him who is meek and merciful.

III. The apostle proceeds (*v.* 12) to show how like they are to the most inferior. Men, under the power of sin, are so far from observing divine revelation that they do not exercise reason. Brute-creatures follow the instinct of their sensitive appetite, and sinful man follows the inclination of his carnal mind.

These persons shall be utterly destroyed in their own corruption. Whatever they meet with is the just *reward of their unrighteousness.*

JAMIESON, FAUSSET, BROWN

preacher—not only "righteous" himself (cf. vs. 8), but also "a preacher of righteousness": adduced by Peter against the *licentiousness* of the false teachers (vs. 2) who have no prospect before them but destruction, even as it overtook the ungodly world in Noah's days. **6. with . . .**—"TO overthrow" [ALFORD]. **ensample**—"of (the fate that should befall) those who in after time should live ungodly." Cf. Jude 7, "set forth for an example." **7. just**—righteous. **filthy conversation**—lit., "behavior in licentiousness" (Gen. 19:5). **the wicked**—*Greek,* "lawless": who set at defiance the *laws* of nature, as well as man and God. The Lord reminds us of Lot's faithfulness, but not of his sin in the cave: so in Rahab's case. **8. vexed**—*Greek,* "tormented." **9. knoweth how**—He is at no loss for means, even when men see no escape. **out of**—not actually *from.* **temptations**—trials. **to be punished**—*Greek,* "being punished": as the fallen angels (vs. 4), actually under sentence, and awaiting its final execution. Sin is already its own penalty; hell will be its full development. **10. chiefly**—They *especially* will be punished (Jude 8). **after**—following after. **lust of uncleanness**—*defilement:* "hankering after polluting and unlawful use of the flesh" [ALFORD]. **government**—*Greek,* "lordship," "dominion" (Jude 8). **Presumptuous**—*Greek,* "Darers." *Self-will* begets *presumption.* Presumptuously daring. **are not afraid**—though they are so insignificant in *might; Greek,* "tremble not" (Jude 8, end). **speak evil of**—*Greek,* "blaspheme." **dignities**—*Greek,* "glories." **11. which are**—though they are. **greater**—than these blasphemers. Jude instances *Michael.* **railing accusation**—*Greek,* "blaspheming judgment" (Jude 9). **against them**—against "dignities," as for instance, the fallen angels: once exalted, and still retaining traces of their former power and glory. **before the Lord**—In the presence of the Lord, *the Judge,* in reverence, they abstain from judgment [BENGEL]. Judgment belongs to God, not the angels. How great is the dignity of the saints who, as Christ's assessors, shall hereafter judge angels! Meanwhile, *railing judgments,* though spoken with truth, *against dignities,* as being uttered irreverently, are of the nature of "blasphemies" (*Greek:* I Cor. 4:4, 5). If superior angels dare not, as being in the presence of God, the Judge, speak evil even of the bad angels, how awful the presumption of those who speak evil blasphemously of good "dignities." II Samuel 16: 7, 8, Shimei; Numbers 16:2, 3, Korah, etc., referred to also in Jude 11; Numbers 12:8, "Were ye (Aaron and Miriam) *not afraid to speak evil* of My servant Moses?" The angels who sinned still retain the indelible impress of majesty. Satan is still "a strong man": "prince of this world"; and under him are "principalities, powers, rulers of the darkness of this world." We are to avoid irreverence in regard to them, not on their account, but on account of God. A warning to those who use Satan's name irreverently and in blasphemy. "When the ungodly curseth Satan, he curseth his own soul." **12.** (Jude 10:19). **But**—In contrast to the "angels," vs. 11. **brute**—*Greek,* "irrational." In contrast to *angels* that "excel in strength." **beasts**—*Greek,* "animals" (cf. Ps. 49:20). **natural**—transposed in the oldest MSS., "born natural," i.e., born naturally so: being *in their very nature* (i.e., naturally) as such (irrational animals), born to be taken and destroyed (*Greek,* "unto capture and destruction," or *corruption, Note,* Gal. 6:8; cf. end of this verse, "shall perish," lit., "shall be corrupted," in their own *corruption.* Jude 10, *"naturally . . . corrupt* themselves," and so *destroy* themselves; for one and the same *Greek* word expresses *corruption,* the seed, and *destruction,* the developed fruit). **speak evil of**—*Greek, "in the case of* things which they understand not." Cf. the same presumption, the parent of subsequent Gnostic error, producing an opposite, though kindred, error, "the worshipping of good angels": Colossians 2:18, *"intruding into those things which he hath not seen."* **13. receive**—"shall carry *off* as their due." **reward of**—i.e., *for* their "unrighteousness" [ALFORD]. Perhaps it is implied, *unrighteousness* shall be its own *reward* or punishment. "Wages of unrighteousness" (vs. 15) has a different sense, viz., *the earthly gain to be gotten by* "unrighteousness." **in the daytime**—Translate as *Greek,* "counting the luxury which is in the daytime (not restricted to *night,* as ordinary revelling. Or as *Vulgate* and CALVIN, 'the luxury which is *but for a day"*: so Hebrews 11:25, "the pleasures of sin *for a season"*; and 12:16, Esau) to be pleasure," i.e., to be their chief good and highest enjoyment. **Spots**—*in themselves.* **blemishes**—disgraces: bringing *blame* (so the *Greek*) *on the Church and on Christianity* itself. **sporting them-**

ADAM CLARKE

1 Pet. iii. 20, that eight persons are here meant, which were the whole that were saved in the ark, viz., Shem, Ham, Japheth, and their three wives, six; Noah's wife, seven; and Noah himself, the eighth. The form of expression, *Noah, the eighth,* i.e., Noah and seven more, is most common in the Greek language. *World of the ungodly.* A whole race without God—without any pure worship or rational religion.

7. *Vexed with the filthy conversation.* "Being exceedingly pained with the unclean conduct of those lawless persons." What this was, see in the history, Genesis xix.

8. *That righteous man dwelling among them.* Lot, after his departure from Abraham, lived at Sodom a space of about twenty years. The word "tormented" is not less emphatic than the word "grievously pained" in the preceding verse, and shows what this man must have felt in dwelling so long among a people so abandoned.

9. *The Lord knoweth how to deliver the godly.* The preservation and deliverance of Lot gave the apostle occasion to remark that God knew as well to save as to destroy; and that His goodness led Him as forcibly to save righteous Lot as His justice did to destroy the rebellious in the instances already adduced.

10. *But chiefly them that walk.* That is, God will in the most signal manner punish them that walk after the flesh—addict themselves to sodomitical practices, and the "lust of pollution," probably alluding to those most abominable practices where men abuse themselves and abuse one another. *Despise government.* They brave the power and authority of the civil magistrate, practicing their abominations so as to keep out of the reach of the letter of the law. And they *speak evil of dignities*—they blaspheme civil government; they abhor the restraints laid upon men by the laws, and would wish all governments destroyed that they might live as they list. *Presumptuous are they.* They are bold and daring, headstrong, regardless of fear. *Selfwilled.* Self-sufficient; presuming on themselves; following their own opinions, which no authority can induce them to relinquish. *Are not afraid to speak evil of dignities.* They are lawless and disobedient, spurn all human authority, and speak contemptuously of all legal and civil jurisdiction.

11. *Whereas angels.* This is a difficult verse, but the meaning seems to be this: The holy angels, who are represented as bringing an account of the actions of the fallen angels before the Lord in judgment, simply state the facts without exaggeration, and without permitting anything of a bitter, reviling, or railing spirit to enter into their accusations. See Zech. iii. 1 and Jude 9, to the former of which Peter evidently alludes.

12. *But these, as natural brute beasts.* "As those natural animals void of reason," following only the gross instinct of nature, being governed by neither reason nor religion. *Made to be taken and destroyed.* Intended to be taken with nets and gins and then destroyed, because of their fierce and destructive nature. So these false teachers and insurgents must be treated; first incarcerated, and then brought to judgment, that they may have the reward of their doings. And thus, by "blaspheming what they do not understand," they at last perish in their own corruption; i.e., their corrupt doctrines and vicious practices.

13. *They that count it pleasure to riot in the day time.* Most sinners, in order to practice their abominable pleasures, seek the secrecy of the night; but these, bidding defiance to all decorum, decency, and shame, take the open day, and thus proclaim their impurities to the sun. *Spots . . . and blemishes.* They are a disgrace to the Christian name. *Sporting themselves.* Forming opinions which give license

MATTHEW HENRY

Such sinners as sport themselves in mischief deceive themselves and disgrace all they belong to, for by one sort of sins they prepare themselves for another; so that their *eyes are full of adultery*, their wanton looks show their own impure lusts and are directed to kindle the like in others; and this is what they *cannot cease* from. Those who are themselves incessant in sin are very often successful in drawing others into the same excess of riot. Those who are in the greatest danger of being led away into error and impiety, are the *unstable*. Those whose hearts are not established with grace are easily turned into the way of sin. These are not only riotous and lascivious, but *covetous* also; they pant after riches, and the desire of their souls is to the wealth of this world. If men abandon themselves to all sorts of lusts, we cannot wonder that the apostle should call them *cursed children*.

IV. The apostle (*v.* 15, 16) proves that they are *cursed children*. They *have forsaken the right way*. They have gone into a wrong way: they have erred and strayed from the way of life. This he makes out by showing it to be *the way of Balaam, the son of Bosor*. The love of riches and honour turned Balaam out of the way of his duty, although he knew that the way he took displeased the Lord.

Hardened sinners sometimes meet with rebukes for their iniquity. God stops them in their way. If rebuking a sinner for his iniquity would have made a man return to his duty, surely the rebuke of Balaam must have produced this effect. *The dumb ass* is enabled to speak, and she exposes *the madness* of his conduct and opposes his going on in this evil way, and yet all in vain.

V. The apostle proceeds (*v.* 17) to a further description of seducing teachers.

1. As *wells*, or fountains, *without water*. The word of truth is the water of life, but these deceivers are set upon spreading and promoting error, and therefore are set forth as empty, because there is no truth in them

2. As *clouds carried with a tempest*. These are clouds which yield no rain, for they are driven with the wind, but not of the Spirit, but the stormy tempest of their own ambition. Clouds obstruct the light of the sun, and darken the air, and, seeing these men are for promoting darkness in this world, it is very just that the mist of darkness should be their portion in the next. They allure those they deal with. It is *with great swelling words of vanity* which have a great sound but little sense. They work upon *the corrupt affections* and *carnal fleshly lusts of men*. By application and industry men attain a skilfulness and dexterity in promoting error. They are as artful and as successful as the fisher, who makes angling his daily employment. Persons who have for a while adhered to the truth, and kept clear of errors, may be so far deceived as to fall into those errors they had for a while *clean escaped*. To prevent these men's gaining proselytes, he tells us that they are the servants of corruption; their own lusts have gotten a complete victory over them, and they are actually in bondage to them.

This consideration should prevent our being led away by these seducers; and to this he adds another (*v.* 20). It is a real detriment to those who have clean escaped from those who live in error, for hereby their latter end is made worse than their beginning.

JAMIESON, FAUSSET, BROWN

selves—*Greek*, "luxuriating." **with**—*Greek*, "in." **deceivings**—or else passively, "deceits": *luxuries gotten by deceit*. Cf. Matthew 13:22, "Deceitfulness of riches"; Ephesians 4:22, "Deceitful lusts." While deceiving others, they are deceived themselves. Cf. with *English Version*, Philippians 3:19, "Whose glory is in their shame." **14. full of adultery**—lit., "full of an adulteress," as though they carried about adulteresses always dwelling in their eyes: the eye being the avenue of lust [HORNEIUS]. BENGEL makes the *adulteress* who fills their eyes, to be "alluring desire." **that cannot cease**—"that cannot *be made to cease* from sin." **beguiling**—"laying baits for." **unstable**—not firmly established in faith and piety. **heart**—not only the *eyes*, which are the channel, but the *heart*, the fountain head of lust. Job 31:7, "Mine *heart* walked after mine *eyes*." **covetous practices**—The oldest MSS. read singular, "covetousness." **cursed children**—rather as *Greek*, "children of curse," i.e., devoted to the curse. *Cursing* and *covetousness*, as in Balaam's case, often go together: the curse he designed for Israel fell on Israel's foes and on himself. True believers *bless*, and curse not, and *so are blessed*. **15. have**—Some of the seducers are spoken of as *already come*, others as *yet to come*. **following**—out: so the *Greek*. **the way**—(Num. 22:23, 32; Isa. 56:11). **son of Bosor**—the same as *Beor* (Num. 22: 5). This word was adopted, perhaps, because the kindred word *Basar* means *flesh;* and Balaam is justly termed *son of carnality*, as covetous, and the enticer of Israel to lust. **loved the wages of unrighteousness**—and therefore wished (in order to gain them from Balak) to curse Israel whom God had blessed, and at last gave the hellish counsel that the only way to bring God's curse on Israel was to entice them to *fleshly lust* and *idolatry*, which often go together. **16. was rebuked**—*Greek*, "had a rebuke," or *conviction;* an *exposure* of his specious wickedness on his being *tested* (the root verb of the *Greek* noun means to "convict on testing"). **his**—*Greek*, "his own": his own beast convicted him of *his own* iniquity. **ass**—lit., "beast of burden"; the ass was the ordinary animal used in riding in Palestine. **dumb**—*Greek*, "voiceless-speaking *in* man's *voice*"; marking the marvellous nature of the miracle. **forbade**—lit., "hindered." It was not the *words* of the ass (for it merely deprecated his beating it), but *the miraculous fact of its speaking at all*, which *withstood* Balaam's perversity in desiring to go after God had forbidden him in the first instance. Thus indirectly the ass, and directly the angel, *rebuked* his worse than asinine obstinacy; the ass *turned aside* at the sight of the angel, but Balaam, after God had plainly said, Thou shalt not go, persevered in wishing to go for gain; thus the ass, *in act, forbade* his madness. How awful a contrast—a *dumb beast* forbidding an *inspired prophet!* **17.** (Jude 12, 13.) **wells**—"clouds" in Jude; both *promising* (cf. vs. 19) water, but yielding none; so their "great swelling words" are found on trial to be but "vanity" (vs. 18). **clouds**—The oldest MSS. and versions read, "mists," *dark*, and not transparent and bright as "clouds" often are, whence the latter term is applied sometimes to the saints; fit emblem of the children of darkness. "Clouds" is a transcriber's correction from Jude 12, where it is appropriate, "clouds . . . without water" (promising what they do not perform); but not here, "mists driven along by a tempest." **mist**—*blackness;* "the *chilling horror* accompanying *darkness*" [BENGEL]. **18. allure**—*Greek*, "lay baits for." **through**—*Greek*, "in"; the *lusts of the flesh* being the element IN which they lay their baits. **much wantonness**—*Greek*, "by licentiousness"; the bait which they lay. **clean escaped**—*Greek*, "really escaped." But the oldest MSS. and *Vulgate* read, "scarcely," or "for but a little time"; scarcely have they escaped from them who live in error (the ungodly world), when they are allured by these seducers into sin again (vs. 20). **19. promise . . . liberty**—(Christian) —These promises are instances of their "great swelling words" (vs. 18). The *liberty* which they propose is such as fears not Satan, nor loathes the flesh. Pauline language, adopted by Peter here, and I Peter 2:16, *Note;* (cf. ch. 3:15; Rom. 6:16-22; 8:15, 21; Gal. 5:1, 13; cf. John 8:34). **corruption**—*Note*, vs. 12, "destroyed . . . perish . . . corruption." **of whom**—"by whatever . . . by the same . . . ." **20. after they**—*the seducers* "themselves" *have escaped* (vs. 19: *Note*, Heb. 6:46). **pollutions**—which bring "corruption" (vs. 19).

ADAM CLARKE

to sin and then acting on those opinions, and thus rioting in their own deceits. *While they feast with you*. It appears they held a kind of communion with the Church, and attended sacred festivals, which they desecrated with their own unhallowed opinions and conduct.

14. *Having eyes full of adultery*. "Of an adulteress"; being ever bent on the gratification of their sensual desires, so that they are represented as having an adulteress constantly before their eyes, and that their eyes can take in no other object but her. *Cannot cease from sin*. "Which cease not from sin"; they might cease from sin, but they do not; they love and practice it. *Beguiling unstable souls*. The metaphor is taken from adulterers seducing unwary, inexperienced, and light, trifling women; so do those false teachers seduce those who are not established in righteousness. *Exercised with covetous practices*. The metaphor is taken from the *agonistae* in the Grecian games, who exercised themselves in those feats, such as wrestling, boxing, running, in which they proposed to contend in the public games. These persons had their hearts schooled in nefarious practices; they had exercised themselves till they were perfectly expert in all the arts of seduction, overreaching, and every kind of fraud. *Cursed children*. Such not only live under God's curse here, but they are heirs to it hereafter.

15. *Which have forsaken the right way*. As Balaam did, who, although God showed him the right way, took one contrary to it, preferring the reward offered him by Balak to the approbation and blessing of God. *The way of Balaam* is the counsel of Balaam. He counselled the Moabites to give their most beautiful young women to the Israelitish youth, that they might be enticed by them to commit idolatry. See the notes on Num. xxii. 5 ff. and xxiii. 1 ff.

16. *The dumb ass speaking with man's voice*. See the note on Num. xxii. 28.

17. *These are wells without water*. Persons who by their profession should furnish the water of life to souls athirst for salvation, but they have not this water. *Clouds that are carried with a tempest*. In a time of great drought, to see clouds beginning to cover the face of the heavens raises the expectation of rain; but to see these "carried off" by a sudden *tempest* is a dreary disappointment. These false teachers were equally as unprofitable as the empty well, or the light, dissipated cloud. *To whom the mist of darkness is reserved*. That is, an eternal separation from the presence of God and the glory of His power. They shall be thrust into "outer darkness," Matt. viii. 12. Instead of *clouds*, "and mists" is the reading in a number of MSS. and in several of the fathers.

18. *They speak great swelling words of vanity*. The word signifies things of great magnitude, grand, superb, sublime; it sometimes signifies "inflated, bombastic." *Those that were clean escaped*. Those who, through hearing the doctrines of the gospel, had been converted were perverted by those false teachers.

19. *While they promise them liberty*. Either to live in the highest degrees of spiritual good or a freedom from the Roman yoke; or from the yoke of the law, or what they might term needless restraints. Their own conduct showed the falsity of their system, for they were slaves to every disgraceful lust. *For of whom a man is overcome*. This is an allusion to the ancient custom of selling for slaves those whom they had conquered and captivated in war.

20. *The pollutions of the world*. Sin in general, and particularly superstition, idolatry, and lasciviousness. These are called *miasmata*, things that "infect, pollute, and defile." The word was anciently used, and is in use at the present day, to express those noxious particles of effluvia proceeding from persons infected with contagious and dangerous diseases; or from dead and corrupt bodies, stagnant and putrid waters, marshes, etc., by which the sound and healthy may be infected and destroyed. The world is here represented as one large, putrid marsh, or corrupt body, sending off its destructive *miasmata* everywhere and in every direction, so that none can escape its contagion, and none can be healed of the great epidemic disease of sin, but by the mighty power and skill of God.

MATTHEW HENRY

Some men are, for a time, *kept from the pollutions of the world, by the knowledge of Christ.* A religious education has restrained many whom the grace of God has not renewed, but we must receive the love of the truth, and hide God's word in our heart, or it will not sanctify and save us. When men are once entangled, they are easily overcome. If men who have once *escaped are again entangled, the latter end is worse with them than the beginning.*

VI. A state of apostasy is worse than a state of ignorance; for it is a *condemning of the way of righteousness,* after they have had some knowledge of it. The misery of such deserters of Christ and his gospel is more intolerable than that of other offenders. God is more highly provoked by those who by their conduct despise the gospel, and pour contempt upon his grace. No wonder it should be so when they have licked up their own vomit again, returning to the same impieties that they had once cast off, and wallowing in that filthiness from which they appeared once to be really cleansed.

CHAPTER 3

Verses 1, 2

The better to recommend the matter, he tells them that what he would have them to remember are, *The words spoken by the holy prophets,* who were divinely inspired. *The commandments of the apostles of the Lord and Saviour.* What God has spoken by the prophets of the Old Testament, and Christ has commanded by the apostles of the New, cannot but demand and deserve to be frequently remembered. It is by these things the pure minds of Christians are to be stirred up.

Verses 3–7

There will be *scoffers,* men who will *make a mock of sin,* and of salvation from it. God's way of saving sinners by Jesus Christ is what men will scoff at, and that *in the last days,* under the gospel. The spirituality and simplicity of New Testament worship are directly contrary to the carnal mind of man. This is mentioned as a thing well known to all Christians.

I. What sort of persons they are: they *walk after their own lusts,* they follow the devices and desires of their own hearts. They live as they list, and they speak as they list. As they will walk in their own way, and talk their own language, so will they also think their own thoughts, and form principles which are altogether their own.

II. They will scoffingly say, *Where is the promise of his coming?* (*v.* 4). Without this, all the other articles of the Christian faith will signify very little; this is that which fills up and gives the finishing stroke to all the rest. Till our Lord shall have come, they will not themselves believe that he will come; nay, they will laugh at the very mention of his second coming. The believer not only desires that he may come, but, having a promise that he will come, he is also firmly and fully persuaded that he will come: on the other hand, these seducers, because they wish he never may, therefore do all that in them lies to cheat themselves and others into a persuasion that he never will come. They will laugh at that very promise: *Where is the promise,* say they, *of his coming?*

III. While they laugh they will pretend to argue too, *v.* 4. This is a subtle, though not a solid way of reasoning; it is apt to make impressions upon weak minds, and especially upon wicked hearts. Those are all dead to whom *the promise was made,* and it was never made good in their time, and there is no likelihood that it ever will be in any time; why should we trouble ourselves about it? To this very day *all things continue as they were,* without any change, even *from the beginning of the creation.* What he never has done they would conclude he never can do or never will.

IV. The apostle puts us in remembrance of a change already past, which was the drowning of the world in the days of Noah. *This they willingly are ignorant of* (*v.* 5), they choose to pass it over in silence. It is hard to persuade men to believe what they are not willing to find true. They do not know because they do not care to know. But let not sinners think that such ignorance as this will be admitted as an excuse for whatever sin it may betray them into.

JAMIESON, FAUSSET, BROWN

through—*Greek,* "in." **knowledge**—*Greek,* "full and accurate knowledge." **the Lord and Saviour Jesus Christ**—solemnly expressing in full the great and gracious One from whom they fall. **latter end is worse . . . than the beginning**—Peter remembers Christ's words. "Worse" stands opposed to "better" (vs. 21). **21. the way of righteousness**—"the way of truth" (vs. 2). Christian doctrine, and "the knowledge of the Lord and Saviour." **turn**—back again; so the *Greek.* **from the holy commandment** —the Gospel which enjoins *holiness;* in opposition to their *corruption.* "Holy," not that it makes holy, but because it ought to be **kept** *inviolate* [TITTMANN]. **delivered**—once for all; admitting no turning back. **22. But**—You need not wonder at the event; for *dogs* **and** *swine* they were before, and dogs and swine they will continue. They "scarcely" (vs. 18) have escaped from their filthy folly, when they again are entangled in it. Then they seduce others who have in like manner "for a little time escaped from them that live in error" (vs. 18). Peter often quoted Proverbs in his First Epistle (1: 7; 2:17; 4:8, 18); another proof that both Epistles come from the same writer.

CHAPTER 3

Vss. 1-18. SURENESS OF CHRIST'S COMING, AND ITS ACCOMPANIMENTS, DECLARED IN OPPOSITION TO SCOFFERS ABOUT TO ARISE. GOD'S LONG-SUFFERING A MOTIVE TO REPENTANCE, AS PAUL'S EPISTLES SET FORTH; CONCLUDING EXHORTATION TO GROWTH IN THE KNOWLEDGE OF CHRIST. **1. now**—"This now a second Epistle I write." Therefore he had lately written the former Epistle. The seven Catholic Epistles were written by James, John, and Jude, shortly before their deaths; previously, while having the prospect of being still for some time alive, they felt it less necessary to write [BENGEL]. **unto you**—The Second Epistle, though more general in its address, yet *included* especially the same persons as the First Epistle was particularly addressed to. **pure**—lit., "pure when examined by sunlight"; "sincere." *Adulterated with no error.* Opposite to "having the understanding *darkened.*" ALFORD explains, The mind, will, and affection, in relation to the outer world, being turned to God [the *Sun* of the soul], and not obscured by fleshly and selfish regards. **by way of**—*Greek,* "in," *in putting you in remembrance* (ch. 1:12, 13). Ye already *know* (vs. 3); it is only needed that I *remind* you (Jude 5). **2. prophets**—of the Old Testament. **of us**—The oldest MSS. and *Vulgate* read, "And of the commandment of the Lord and Saviour (declared) by YOUR apostles" (so "apostle *of the Gentiles,*" Rom. 11:13)—the apostles *who live among you in the present time,* in contrast to the *Old Testament* "prophets." **3. Knowing this first**—from the word of the apostles. **shall come**—Their very *scoffing* shall confirm the truth of the prediction. **scoffers** —The oldest MSS. and *Vulgate* add, "(scoffers) *in* (i.e., with) *scoffing.*" As Revelation 14:2, "harping with harps." **walking after their own lusts**— (ch. 2:10; Jude 16, 18). Their own pleasure is their sole law, unrestrained by reverence for God. **4.** (Cf. Ps. 10:11; 73:11.) Presumptuous skepticism and lawless lust, setting nature and its so-called laws above the God of nature and revelation, and arguing from the past continuity of nature's phenomena that there can be no future interruption to them, was the sin of the antediluvians, and shall be that of the scoffers in the last days. **Where**—implying that it ought to have taken place before this, if ever it was to take place, but that it never will. **the promise**—which you, believers, are so continually looking for the fulfilment of (vs. 13). What becomes of the promise which you talk so much of? **his**—*Christ's;* the subject of prophecy from the earliest days. **the fathers**—to whom *the promise* was made, and who rested all their hopes on it. **all things**—in the *natural world;* skeptics look not beyond this. **as they were**—*continue as they do;* as we see them to continue. From the time of the promise of Christ's coming as Saviour and King being given to the fathers, down to the present time, all things continue, and have continued, *as they now are,* from "the beginning of creation." **5.** Refutation of their scoffing from Scripture history. **willingly**—wilfully; they do not *wish* to know. Their ignorance is voluntary. **they . . . are ignorant of**—in contrast to vs. 8, "Be not ignorant of this." Lit., in both verses, "This escapes THEIR notice (sagacious philosophers though they think themselves)"; "let this not escape YOUR notice." They obstinately shut their eyes to the Scripture record of the creation

ADAM CLARKE

Now it is by *the knowledge of the Lord and Saviour Jesus Christ,* as says Peter, that we escape the destructive influence of these contagious *miasmata.* But if, after having been healed, and *escaped* the death to which we were exposed, we get *again entangled,* "enfolded, enveloped" with them, then *the latter end* will be *worse . . . than the beginning,* forasmuch as we shall have sinned against more light.

21. *For it had been better for them not to have known.* For the reasons assigned above; because they have sinned against more mercy, are capable of more sin, and are liable to greater punishment. *The holy commandment.* The whole religion of Christ is contained in this one commandment, "Thou shalt love the Lord thy God with all thy heart, with all thy soul, with all thy mind, and with all thy strength; and thy neighbor as thyself."

22. *According to the true proverb.* This seems to be a reference to Prov. xxvi. 11: "As a dog returneth to his vomit, so a fool returneth to [repeateth] his folly."

CHAPTER 3

1. *This second epistle.* In order to guard them against the seductions of false teachers, he calls to their remembrance the doctrine of the ancient prophets, and the commands or instructions of the apostles, all founded on the same basis.

3. *There shall come . . . scoffers.* Persons who shall endeavor to turn all religion into ridicule, as this is the most likely way to depreciate truth in the sight of the giddy multitude. The scoffers, having no solid argument to produce against revelation, affect to laugh at it, and get superficial thinkers to laugh with them. *Walking after their own lusts.* Here is the true source of all infidelity. The gospel of Jesus is pure and holy, and requires a holy heart and holy life. They wish to follow their own *lusts,* and consequently cannot brook the restraints of the gospel; therefore they labor to prove that it is not true. There is a remarkable addition here in almost every MS. and version of note: "There shall come in the last days, in mockery, scoffers walking after their own lusts." This is the reading of a number of MSS. and several of the fathers. They come "in mockery"; this is their spirit and temper. They have no desire to find out truth; they take up the Bible merely with the design of turning it into ridicule. *The last days* probably refer to the conclusion of the Jewish polity, which was then at hand.

5. *For this they willingly are ignorant of.* They shut their eyes against the light and refuse all evidence; what does not answer their purpose they will not know.

MATTHEW HENRY

1. The apostle's account of the destruction which has once already come upon the world (*v.* 5, 6). At the time of the universal deluge, the case is strangely altered; the waters which God had divided before, now does he, in anger, throw together again in a heap. All this was done by the word of God; it was by his powerful word that the world was made at first. *By the word of the Lord the heavens were of old and the earth standing out of the water and in the water.*

The after-confusion and ruin of the world, as well as the utter destruction of its inhabitants, were also by the same word. This was the change which God had before brought upon the world, and which these scoffers had overlooked.

2. What the apostle says of the destructive change which is yet to come upon it, *v.* 7. Here we have an awful account of the final dissolution of the world. The judgment here spoken of is yet to come, and will surely come, though we know not when. That the world has once been destroyed by a universal deluge renders it the more credible that it may be again ruined by a universal conflagration. Let therefore the scoffers, who laugh at the coming of our Lord to judgment, at least consider that it *may be. The heavens and the earth which now are, are kept in store.* They are *reserved unto fire.* The day of judgment is the day of *the perdition of ungodly men.* Those who now scoff at a future judgment shall find it a day of vengeance. "Give diligence therefore to be found in Christ, that that may be a time of refreshment and day of redemption to you."

Verse 8

We may clearly discern the tenderness and affection wherewith he speaks to them, calling them *beloved*; he had a compassionate concern and a love of goodwill for the ungodly wretches who refused to believe divine revelation, but he has a peculiar respect for the true believers.

I. The truth which the apostle asserts—*that with the Lord one day is as a thousand years, and a thousand years are as one day.* All things past, present, and future, are ever before him.

II. The importance of this truth: This is the *one thing* the apostle would not have us ignorant of. This is a truth that belongs to our peace, and therefore he endeavours that it may not be hidden from our eyes; as it is in the original, *Let not this one thing be hidden from you.* Yet how hard is it to conceive of eternity!

Verses 9, 10

We are here told that *the Lord is not slack*—he does not delay beyond the appointed time; he will keep to the time appointed in coming to judge the world. Good men are apt to think God stays beyond the appointed time, that is, the time which they have set, but they set one time and God sets another.

I. What men count slackness is truly *longsuffering*, and that *to us-ward*; it is giving more time to his own people that they may bring glory to God, and improve in a meetness for heaven; for God is not willing that any of these should perish, but that all of them should come to repentance. God has no delight in the death of sinners. His goodness and forbearance do in their own nature call to repentance all those to whom they are exercised; and, if men continue impenitent when God gives them space to repent, he will deal more severely with them.

II. *The day of the Lord will come as a thief in the night, v.* 10. 1. The certainty of the day of the Lord. The day has not yet come, it assuredly will come. God has *appointed a day* and he will keep his appointment. 2. The suddenness of this day: It *will come as a thief in the night*, at a time when men are sleeping and secure. The time which men think to be the most improper and unlikely, and when therefore they are most secure, will be the time of the Lord's coming.

JAMIESON, FAUSSET, BROWN

and the deluge; the latter is the very parallel to the coming judgment by fire, which Jesus mentions, as Peter doubtless remembered. **by the word of God**—not by a fortuitous concurrence of atoms [ALFORD]. **of old**—*Greek*, "from of old"; from the first beginning of all things. A confutation of their objection, "all things continue as they were FROM THE BEGINNING OF CREATION." Before the flood, the same objection to the possibility of the flood might have been urged with the same plausibility: The heavens (sky) and earth have been FROM OF OLD, how unlikely then that they should not *continue* so! But, replies Peter, the flood came in spite of their reasonings; so will the conflagration of the earth come in spite of the "scoffers" of the last days, changing the whole order of things (the present "world," or as *Greek* means, "order"), and introducing the new heavens and earth (vs. 13). **earth standing out of**—*Greek*, "consisting of," i.e., "formed out of the water." The waters under the firmament were at creation gathered together into one place, and the dry land emerged *out of*, and above, them. **in . . .**—rather, "*by means of* the water," as a great instrument (along with *fire*) in the changes wrought on the earth's surface to prepare it for man. Held together BY the water. The earth arose *out of* the water *by the efficacy of the water* itself [TITTMANN]. **6. Whereby**—*Greek*, "By which" (plural). *By means of which* heavens and earth (in respect to the WATERS which flowed together *from both*) *the then world perished* (i.e., in respect to its *occupants*, men and animals, and its then existing *order:* not *was annihilated*); for in the flood "the fountains of the great deep were broken up" from *the earth* (1) below, and "the windows of *heaven*" (2) above "were opened." The earth was deluged by that water *out of* which it had originally risen. **7.** (Cf. Job 28:5, end.) **which are now**—"the postdiluvian visible world." In contrast to "that *then was*," vs. 6. **the same**—Other oldest MSS. read, "His" (God's). **kept in store**—*Greek*, "treasured up." **reserved**—"kept." It is only God's constantly watchful providence which holds together the present state of things till His time for ending it. **8. be not ignorant**—as those scoffers are (vs. 5). Besides the refutation of them (vss. 5-7) drawn from the history of the deluge, here he adds another (addressed more to believers than to the mockers): God's delay in fulfilling His promise is not, like men's delays, owing to inability or fickleness in keeping His word, but through "long-suffering." **this one thing**—as the consideration *of chief importance* (Luke 10:42). **one day . . . thousand years**—Psalm 90:4: Moses there says, Thy *eternity*, knowing no distinction between a *thousand* years and a *day*, is the refuge of us creatures of a day. **thousand years as one day**—No delay which occurs is long to God: as to a man of countless riches, a thousand dollars are as a single penny. God's æonologe (*eternal-ages* measurer) differs wholly from man's horologe (*hour*-glass). His gnomon (dial-pointer) shows all the hours at once in the greatest activity and in perfect repose. To Him the hours pass away, neither more slowly, nor more quickly, than befits His economy. There is nothing to make Him need either to hasten or delay the end. The words, "with the Lord" (Ps. 90:4, "In Thy sight"), silence all man's objections on the ground of his incapability of understanding this [BENGEL]. **9. slack**—slow, tardy, *late;* exceeding the due time, as though that time were already come. Hebrews 10:37, "will not *tarry.*" **his promise**—which the scoffers cavil at. Verse 4, "Where is the promise?" It shall be surely fulfilled "according to His promise" (vs. 13). **some**—the "scoffers." **count**—His promise to be the result of "slackness" (tardiness). **long-suffering**—waiting until the full number of those appointed to "salvation" (vs. 15) shall be completed. **to us-ward**—The oldest MSS., *Vulgate, Syriac,* etc. read, "towards YOU." **any**—not desiring that any, yea, even that the scoffers, should perish, which would be the result if He did not give space for repentance. **come**—*go and be received to* repentance: the *Greek* implies there is *room* for their being *received* to repentance (cf. *Greek*, Mark 2:2; John 8:37). **10.** The certainty, suddenness, and concomitant effects, of the coming of the day of the Lord. **will**—emphatical. But (in spite of the mockers, and notwithstanding the delay) *come and be present* the day of the Lord SHALL. **as a thief**—Peter remembers and repeats his Lord's image (Luke 12:39, 41) used in the conversation in which he took a part; so also Paul (I Thess. 5:2) and John (Rev. 3:3; 16: 15). **the heavens**—which the scoffers say shall "continue" as they are (vs. 4; Matt. 24:35; Rev. 21: 1). **with a great noise**—with a rushing noise, like

ADAM CLARKE

By the word of God the heavens were of old. Moses: "In the beginning God created the heaven and the earth. And the earth was without form, and void; and darkness was upon the face of the deep." Now these heavens and earth which God made in the beginning, and which He says were at first formless and empty, and which He calls "the deep," are in the very next verse called "waters"; from which it is evident that Moses teaches that the earth was made out of some fluid substance, to which the name of "water" is properly given. The *earth*, which was originally formed *out of the water*, "subsists by water."

7. *But the heavens and the earth, which are now.* The present earth and its atmosphere, which are liable to the same destruction, because the same means still exist (for there is still water enough to drown the earth, and there is iniquity enough to induce God to destroy it and its inhabitants), are nevertheless *kept in store*, "treasured up," kept in God's storehouse, to be destroyed, not by water, but by *fire* at *the day of judgment.*

8. *Be not ignorant.* Though they are willfully ignorant, neglect not the means of instruction.

One day is with the Lord as a thousand years. That is: All time is as nothing before Him, because in the presence as in the nature of God all is eternity; therefore nothing is long, nothing short, before Him. The words of the apostle seem to be a quotation from Ps. xc. 4.

9. *But is longsuffering.* It is not slackness that induced God to prolong the respite of ungodly men, but His long-suffering, His unwillingness that any should perish; and therefore He spared them, that they might have additional offers of grace and be led to repentance. As God is *not willing that any should perish*, and as He is willing *that all should come to repentance*, consequently He has never devised nor decreed the damnation of any man, nor has He rendered it impossible for any soul to be saved.

10. *The day of the Lord will come.* See Matt. xxiv. 43, to which the apostle seems to allude.

MATTHEW HENRY

3. The solemnity of this coming. *The heavens shall pass away with a great noise. The elements shall melt with fervent heat. The earth also, and all the works that are therein, shall be burnt up.* All must pass through the fire, which shall be a consuming fire to all that sin has brought into the world, though it may be but a refining fire to the works of God's hand.

What a difference there will be between the first coming of Christ and the second! May we be so wise as to prepare for it, that it may not be a day of vengeance and destruction unto us.

Verses 11–18

The apostle, having instructed them in the doctrine of Christ's second coming,

I. Takes occasion thence to exhort them to purity and godliness in their whole conversation. *Seeing all these things must be dissolved, how holy should we be.* Inasmuch as this dissolution is in order to their being restored to their primitive beauty and excellency, how pure and holy should we be, in order to our being fit for the *new heaven and new earth, wherein dwelleth righteousness!* Those things which we now see must in a little while pass away, and be no more as they now are: let us look therefore at what shall abide and continue. This *looking for the day of God* is one of the directions the apostle gives us, in order to our being eminently *holy and godly in all manner of conversation.*

The coming of the day of God is what every Christian must hope for and earnestly expect. Though it cannot but affright the ungodly to see the visible heavens and the elements melting, yet the believer can rejoice in hope of more glorious heavens after these have been refined by that dreadful fire which shall burn up all the dross of this visible creation. 1. What true Christians look for: *new heavens and a new earth.* In these new heavens and earth only righteousness shall dwell. 2. What is the ground and foundation of this expectation and hope—*the promise of God.* To look for anything which God has not promised is presumption; but if our expectations are according to the promise, we cannot meet with a disappointment.

II. In *v.* 14 he resumes his exhortation from the consideration that they shall be again renewed. It nearly concerns you to see in what state you will be when the Judge of all the world shall come to pass sentence upon men, therefore get ready to *appear before the judgment-seat of Christ.*

1. "That you be *found of him in peace,* in a state of peace and reconciliation with God through Christ. Those whose sins are pardoned and their peace made with God are the only safe and happy people; therefore follow after peace." Peace with God through our Lord Jesus Christ. Peace in our own consciences. Peace with men.

2. That you be *found of Christ without spot, and blameless. Follow after holiness* as well as peace. We must be pressing towards spotless purity, absolute perfection. Christians must be *perfecting holiness.* It is only the diligent Christian who will be the happy Christian in the day of the Lord. He will certainly reward us if we be diligent in the work he has allotted us; now, that you may be diligent, *account the long-suffering of our Lord to be salvation.* "Does your Lord delay his coming? It is so much space to repent that men may have time to prepare for eternity." Our apostle quotes St. Paul as directing men to make the same good use of the divine forbearance. What an honourable mention does this apostle of the circumcision make of that very man who had openly, *before all, reproved him.* He calls him *brother,* not only that he is a fellow-christian, but a fellow-apostle. Though many seducing teachers denied Paul's apostleship, yet Peter owns him to be an apostle. He calls him *beloved.* He mentions Paul as one who had an uncommon measure of wisdom given unto him. How desirable is it that those who preach the same gospel should treat one another according to the pattern Peter here sets them! (1) The excellent wisdom that was in Paul is said to be *given* him. The understanding and knowledge that qualify men to preach the gospel are the gift of God.

JAMIESON, FAUSSET, BROWN

that of a *whizzing* arrow, or the crash of a devouring flame. **elements**—*the component materials of the world* [WAHL]. However, as "the works" in the earth are mentioned separately from "the earth," so it is likely by "elements," mentioned after "the heavens," are meant "the works therein," viz., *the sun, moon, and stars* (as THEOPHILUS OF ANTIOCH, p. 22, 148, 228; and JUSTIN MARTYR, *Apology,* 2. 44, use the word "elements"): these, as at creation, so in the destruction of the world, are mentioned [BENGEL]. But as "elements" is not so used in Scripture *Greek,* perhaps it refers to *the component materials* of "the heavens," including *the heavenly bodies;* it clearly belongs to the former clause, "the heavens," not to the following, "the earth . . ." **melt**—be dissolved, as in vs. 11. **the works . . . therein**—of nature and of art. **11.** Your duty, seeing that this is so, is to be ever eagerly expecting the day of God. **then**—Some oldest MSS. substitute "thus" for "then": a happy refutation of the "thus" of the scoffers, vs. 4 (*English Version,* "AS they were," *Greek,* "thus"). **shall be**—*Greek, "are being* (in God's appointment, soon to be fulfilled) dissolved"; the present tense implying *the certainty* as though it were actually present. **what manner of men . . .**—exclamatory. How watchful, prayerful, zealous! **to be**—not the mere *Greek* substantive verb of existence (*einai*), but (*huparchein*) denoting a *state* or *condition* in which one is supposed to be [TITTMANN]. What holy men ye ought to be found to be, when the event comes! This is "the holy commandment" mentioned in vs. 2. **conversation . . . godliness**—*Greek,* plural: *behaviors* (towards men), *godlinesses* (or *pieties* towards God) in their *manifold* modes of manifestation. **12. hasting unto**—*with the utmost eargerness desiring* [WAHL], praying for, and contemplating, the coming Saviour as at hand. The *Greek may* mean "hastening (i.e., *urging onward* [ALFORD] the day of God"; not that God's eternal appointment of the time is changeable, but God appoints *us* as instruments of accomplishing those events which must be first before the day of God can come. By praying for His coming, furthering the preaching of the Gospel for a witness to all nations, and bringing in those whom "the long-suffering of God" waits to save, we *hasten the coming of the day of God.* The *Greek* verb is always in New Testament used as neuter (as *English Version* here), not active; but the LXX uses it *actively. Christ* says, "Surely I come quickly. Amen." *Our* part is to *speed forward* this consummation by praying, "Even so, come, Lord Jesus." **the coming**—*Greek, "presence"* of a *person:* usually, of the Saviour. **the day of God**—God has given many myriads of days to *men:* one shall be the great "day of God" Himself. **wherein**—rather as *Greek,* "on account of (or *owing to*) which" day. **heavens**—the upper and lower regions of the sky. **melt**—Our igneous rocks show that they were once in a liquid state. **13. Nevertheless**—"But": in contrast to the destructive effects of the day of God stand its constructive effects. As the flood was the baptism of the earth, eventuating in a renovated earth, partially delivered from "the curse," so the baptism with fire shall purify the earth so as to be the renovated abode of regenerated man, wholly freed from the curse. **his promise**—(Isa. 65:17; 66:22). The "we" is not emphatical as in *English Version.* **new heavens**—new atmospheric heavens surrounding the renovated earth. **righteousness**—*dwelleth* in that coming world as its essential feature, all pollutions having been removed. **14. that ye . . . be found of him**—"in His sight" [ALFORD], at His coming; plainly implying a *personal* coming. **without spot**—at the coming marriage feast of the Lamb, in contrast to ch. 2:13, "Spots they are and blemishes while they feast," not having on the King's pure wedding garment. **blameless**—(I Cor. 1:8; Phil. 1:10; I Thess. 3:13; 5:23). **in peace**—in all its aspects, towards God, your own consciences, and your fellow men, and as its consequence eternal *blessedness:* "the God of peace" will effect this for you. **15. account . . . the long-suffering . . . is salvation**—is designed for the salvation of those yet to be gathered into the Church: whereas those scoffers "count it (to be the result of) slackness" on the Lord's part (vs. 9). **our beloved brother Paul**—a beautiful instance of love and humility. Peter praises the very Epistles which contain his condemnation. **according to the wisdom given unto him**—adopting Paul's own language, I Corinthians 3:10, "*According to the* grace of God which is *given unto* me as a *wise* masterbuilder." Supernatural and inspired wisdom "GIVEN" him, not acquired in human schools of learning. **hath written**—*Greek* aorist, "wrote," as a thing wholly *past:* Paul was by this time either

ADAM CLARKE

11. *All these things shall be dissolved.* They will all be "separated," all "decomposed," but none of them destroyed. And as they are the original matter out of which God formed the terraqueous globe, consequently they may enter again into the composition of a new system; and therefore the apostle says, v. 13: "We . . . look for new heavens and a new earth"—the others being decomposed, a new system is to be formed out of their materials. *What manner of persons ought ye to be?* Some put the note of interrogation at the end of this clause, and join the remaining part with the twelfth verse, thus: "Seeing then that all these things shall be dissolved, what manner of persons ought ye to be? By holy conversation and godliness, expecting and earnestly desiring the coming of the day of God," etc.

12. The word which we translate *hasting unto* should be rendered "earnestly desiring" or "wishing for," which is a frequent meaning of the word in the best Greek writers.

13. *We, according to his promise, look for new heavens.* The promise to which it is supposed the apostle alludes is found Isa. lxv. 17: "Behold, I create new heavens and a new earth: and the former shall not be remembered, nor come into mind"; and chap. lxvi. 22: "For as the new heavens and the new earth, which I will make, shall remain before me, saith the Lord, so shall your seed." Now although these may be interpreted of the glory of the gospel dispensation, yet, if Peter refer to them, they must have a more extended meaning.

14. *Seeing that ye look for such things.* As you profess that such a state of things shall take place and have the expectation of enjoying the blessedness of it, *be diligent* in the use of every means and influence of grace, *that ye may be found of him*—the Lord Jesus, the Judge of quick and dead; *without spot*—any contagion of sin in your souls; *and blameless*—being not only holy and innocent, but useful in your lives.

15. *And account that the longsuffering of our Lord.* Conclude that God's long-suffering with the world is a proof that He designs men to be saved. *According to the wisdom given unto him.* That is, according to the measure of the divine inspiration by which he was qualified for the divine work and by which he was so capable of entering into the deep things of God.

MATTHEW HENRY

(2) The apostle imparts to men according as he had received from God. He endeavours to lead others as far as he himself was led into the knowledge of the mysteries of the gospel.

But the apostle Peter proceeds to tell us that in those things which are to be met with in Paul's epistles there are some things hard to be understood. Some are not easy to be understood because of their own obscurity, others cannot be so easily understood because of their excellency and sublimity, and others are with difficulty taken in because of the weakness of men's minds.

And here the unlearned and unstable make wretched work; for they wrest and torture the scriptures. Those who are not well instructed and well established in the truth are in great danger of perverting the word of God. Where there is a divine power to establish as well as to instruct men in divine truth, persons are effectually secured from falling into errors. How great a blessing this is we learn by observing what is the pernicious consequence of the errors that ignorant and unstable men fall into—even their own destruction.

III. The apostle gives them a word of caution, *v.* 17, 18.

1. The knowledge we have of these things should make us very watchful, inasmuch as there is a twofold danger, *v.* 17. (1) We are in great danger *of* being seduced, and turned away from the truth. Many who have the scriptures and read them do not understand what they read; and too many of those who have a right understanding are not established in the belief of the truth, and all these are liable to fall into error. (2) We are in great danger *by* being seduced. If men corrupt the word of God, it tends to their own utter ruin. When men wrest the word of God, *they fall into the error of the wicked.* If we imbibe their opinions, we shall too soon imitate their practices. Those who are led away by error *fall from their own steadfastness.* They are wholly unhinged and unsettled, and know not where to rest.

2. The apostle directs us what to do, *v.* 18. We must *grow in grace.* By how much the stronger grace is in us, by so much the more steadfast shall we be in the truth. We must grow *in the knowledge of our Lord Jesus Christ.* Such a knowledge of Christ as conforms us more to him, and endears him more to us, must needs preserve us from falling off in times of general apostasy. *To him be glory both now and for ever. Amen.*

JAMIESON, FAUSSET, BROWN

dead, or had ceased to minister to them. **to you**—*Galatians,* Ephesians, *Colossians,* the same region as Peter addresses. Cf. "in peace," vs. 14, a practical exhibition of which Peter now gives in showing how perfectly agreeing Paul (who wrote the Epistle to the *Galatians*) and he are, notwithstanding the event recorded (Gal. 2:11-14). Colossians 4 refers to *Christ's second coming.* The Epistle to the Hebrews, too (addressed not only to the Palestinian, but also secondarily to the Hebrew Christians everywhere), may be referred to, as Peter primarily (though not exclusively) addresses in both Epistles the *Hebrew* Christians of the dispersion (*Note,* I Pet. 1:1). Hebrews 9:27, 28; 10:25, 37, "speak of these things" (vs. 16) which Peter has been handling, viz., the coming of the day of the Lord, delayed through His "long-suffering," yet near and sudden. **16. also in all his epistles**—Romans 2:4 is very similar to vs. 15, beginning. The Pauline Epistles were by this time become the *common* property of all the churches. The "all" seems to imply they were now completed. The subject of the Lord's coming is handled in I Thessalonians 4: 13; 5:11; cf. vs. 10 with I Thessalonians 5:2. Still Peter distinguishes Paul's Epistle, or Epistles, "TO YOU," from "*all* his (*other*) Epistles," showing that certain definite churches, or particular classes of believers, are meant by "you." **in which**—*Epistles.* The oldest MSS. read the feminine relative (*hais*); not as Received Text (*hois*), "in which *things.*" **some things hard to be understood**—viz., in reference to Christ's coming, e.g., the statements as to the man of sin and the apostasy, before Christ's coming. "Paul seemed thereby to delay Christ's coming to a longer period than the other apostles, whence some doubted altogether His coming" [BENGEL]. Though there be some things hard to be understood, there are enough besides, plain, easy, and sufficient for perfecting the man of God. "There is scarce anything drawn from the obscure places, but the same in other places may be found most plain" [AUGUSTINE]. It is our own prejudice, foolish expectations, and carnal fancies, that make Scripture difficult [JEREMY TAYLOR]. **unlearned**—Not those wanting *human* learning are meant, but those *lacking the learning imparted by the Spirit.* The humanly *learned* have been often most deficient in spiritual learning, and have originated many heresies. Cf. II Timothy 2:23, a different *Greek* word, "unlearned," lit., "untutored." When religion is studied as a science, nothing is more abstruse; when studied in order to know our duty and practice it, nothing is easier. **unstable**—not yet established in what they have learned; shaken by every seeming difficulty; who, in perplexing texts, instead of waiting until God by His Spirit makes them plain in comparing them with other Scriptures, hastily adopt distorted views. **wrest**—strain and twist (properly with a *hand screw*) what is straight in itself (e.g., II Tim. 2:18). **other scriptures**—Paul's Epistles were, therefore, by this time, recognized in the Church, as "Scripture": a term never applied in any of the fifty places where it occurs, save to the Old and New Testament sacred writings. Men in each Church having miraculous *discernment of spirits* would have prevented any uninspired writing from being put on a par with the Old Testament word of God; the apostles' lives also were providentially prolonged, Paul's and Peter's at least to thirty-four years after Christ's resurrection, John's to thirty years later, so that fraud in the canon is out of question. The three first Gospels and Acts are included in "the other Scriptures," and perhaps all the New Testament books, save John and Revelation, written later. **unto their own destruction**—not through Paul's fault (ch. 2:1). **17. Ye**—warned by the case of those "unlearned and unstable" persons (vs. 16). **knowing . . . before**—the event. **led away with**—the very term, as Peter remembers, used by Paul of Barnabas' being "carried," *Greek,* "led away with" Peter and the other Jews in their hypocrisy. **wicked**—"lawless," as in ch. 2:7. **fall from**—(*grace,* Gal. 5:4: the true source of) "steadfastness" or *stability* in contrast with the "unstable" (vs. 16): "established" (ch. 1:12): all kindred *Greek* terms. Cf. Jude 20, 21. **18. grow**—Not only do not "fall from" (vs. 17), but *grow onward:* the true secret of not going backward. Ephesians 4:15, "Grow up into Him, the Head, Christ." **grace and . . . knowledge of . . . Christ**—"the grace and knowledge of Christ" [ALFORD rightly]: *the grace* of which *Christ* is the author, and *the knowledge* of which *Christ* is the object. **for ever**—*Greek,* "to the day of eternity": the day that has no end: "the day of the Lord," beginning with the Lord's coming.

ADAM CLARKE

It is worthy of remark that Paul's Epistles are ranked among the "scriptures"; a term applied to those writings which are divinely inspired, and to those only.

16. *As also in all his epistles, speaking in them of these things.* For example, he has spoken of Christ's coming to judgment, 1 Thess. iii. 13; iv. 14-18; 2 Thess. i. 7-10; Titus ii. 13. And of the resurrection of the dead, 1 Cor. xv. 22; Phil. iii. 20-21. And of the burning of the earth, 2 Thess. i. 8. And of the heavenly country, 2 Cor. v. 1-10. And of the introduction of the righteous into that country, 1 Thess. iv. 17; Heb. iv. 9; xii. 14, 18, 24. And of the judgment of all mankind by Christ, Rom. xiv. 10.

ALBERT BARNES:

"Which they that are unlearned." The evil here is that which arises in cases where those without competent knowledge undertake to become expounders of the Word of God. It is not said that it is not proper for them to attempt to become instructed by the aid of the sacred writings; but the danger is, that without proper views of interpretation, of language, and of ancient customs, they might be in danger of perverting and abusing certain portions of the writings of Paul. Intelligence among the people is everywhere in the Bible presumed to be proper in understanding the sacred Scriptures; and ignorance may produce the same effects in interpreting the Bible which it will produce in interpreting other writings. Every good thing is liable to abuse; but the proper way to remove this danger is not to keep the people in ignorance or to appoint someone to be an infallible interpreter; it is to remove the ignorance itself by enlightening the people and rendering them better qualified to understand the sacred oracles.

"And unstable." Who have no settled principles and views. The evil here is that which arises where those undertake to interpret the Bible who have no established principles. They regard nothing as settled. They have no landmarks set up to guide their inquiries. They have no stability in their character, and of course nothing can be regarded as settled in their methods of interpreting the Bible. They are under the control of feeling and emotion, and are liable to embrace one opinion today and another directly opposite tomorrow. But the way to prevent this evil is not by attempting to give to a community an authoritative interpretation of the Bible; it is to diffuse abroad just principles, that men may obtain from the Bible an intelligent view of what it means.

—Popular Commentary

17. *Seeing ye know these things before.* Seeing that by prophets and apostles you have been thus forewarned, *beware,* "keep watch, be on your guard"; cleave to God and the word of His grace, lest you be *led away* from the truth delivered by the prophets and apostles, *by the error of the wicked,* "of the lawless"—those who wrest the Scriptures to make them countenance their lusts and lawless practices. *Fall from your own stedfastness.* From that faith in Christ which has put you in possession of that grace which establishes the heart.

18. *But grow in grace.* Increase in the image and favor of God. *To him,* the Lord Jesus, *be glory*—all honor and excellency attributed *both now,* in this present state, *and for ever,* "to the day of eternity"—that in which death, and misery, and trial, and darkness, and change, and time itself are to the righteous forever at an end. It is eternity; and this eternity is one unalterable, interminable, unclouded, and unchangeable day!

THE FIRST EPISTLE OF JOHN

The continued tradition of the church attests that this epistle came from John the apostle. There is scarcely a critic or competent judge of diction, or style of argument and spirit, who will not adjudge this epistle to the writer of the gospel of John.

The epistle is styled *general*, as being not inscribed to any particular church; it is, as a circular letter, sent to divers churches in order to confirm them in their steadfast adherence to the Lord Christ, against seducers; and to instigate them to adorn that doctrine by love to God and man, and particularly to each other.

MATTHEW HENRY

CHAPTER 1

Verses 1–4

I. An account of the Mediator's person. 1. *As the Word of life, v.* 1. He is not a mere vocal word, but a vital one: *the Word of life.* 2. *As eternal life,* He was from eternity. He is the eternal Word of the eternal living Father. 3. *As life manifested* (*v.* 2), manifested in the flesh. Kindness indeed, that eternal life should come to visit mortals, and to procure eternal life for them, and then confer it on them!

II. The evidences that the apostle and his brethren had of the Mediator's presence in this world. *The life, the word of life, the eternal life,* as such, could not be seen and felt; but the life manifested might be, and was so. 1. To their ears, *v.* 1, 3. The life assumed a mouth and tongue, that he might utter words of life. The divine word would employ the ear, and the ear should be devoted to the word of life. 2. To their eyes, *v.* 1–3. The Word would become visible, would not only be heard, but seen *with our eyes*—with all the use and exercise that we could make of our eyes. His apostles must be eye-witnesses as well as ear-witnesses of him. 3. To their internal sense, to the eyes of their mind: for so (possibly) may the next clause be interpreted: *Which we have looked upon.* The word is not applied to the immediate object of the eye, but to that which was rationally collected from what they saw. The senses are to be the informers of the mind. 4. To their hands and sense of feeling: *And our hands have handled of the Word of life.* The invisible life and Word was no despiser of the testimony of sense. Sense is a means that God has appointed for our information. Our Lord took care to satisfy all the senses of his apostles, that they might be the more authentic witnesses of him to the world. The apostles could not be deceived in such long and various exercise of their sense. Sense must minister to reason and judgment; and reason and judgment must minister to the reception of the Lord Jesus Christ and his gospel.

III. The apostles publish these assurances for our satisfaction, *v.* 2, 3. It became the apostles to open to the disciples the evidence by which they were led. It concerned the disciples to be well assured of the truth of the institution they had embraced. They should see the evidences of their holy religion.

IV. The reason of the apostle's asserting this summary of sacred faith.

1. That the believers of it may be advanced to the same happiness with them (with the apostles themselves), *v.* 3. It is communion with heaven, and in blessings that come thence and tend thither. There is a communion (or common participation of privilege and dignity) belonging to all saints, from the highest apostle to the lowest believer. What it is and where

JAMIESON, FAUSSET, BROWN

CHAPTER 1

VSS. 1-10. THE WRITER'S AUTHORITY AS AN EYEWITNESS TO THE GOSPEL FACTS, HAVING SEEN, HEARD, AND HANDLED HIM WHO WAS FROM THE BEGINNING: HIS OBJECT IN WRITING:HIS MESSAGE. IF WE WOULD HAVE FELLOWSHIP WITH HIM, WE MUST WALK IN LIGHT, AS HE IS LIGHT. **1.** Instead of a formal, John adopts a virtual address (cf. vs. 4). To wish *joy* to the reader was the ancient customary address. The sentence begun in vs. 1 is broken off by the parenthetic vs. 2, and is resumed at vs. 3 with the repetition of some words from vs. 1. **That which was**—not "began to be," but *was* essentially (*Greek, een,* not *egeneto*) before He was *manifested* (vs. 2); answering to "Him that is *from the beginning*" (ch. 2:13); so John's Gospel, 1:1, "In the beginning was the Word." Proverbs 8:23, "I was set up from everlasting, *from the beginning,* or ever the earth was." **we**—apostles. **heard . . . seen . . . looked upon . . . handled**—a series rising in gradation. *Seeing* is a more convincing proof than *hearing* of; *handling,* than even *seeing.* "*Have* heard . . . *have* seen" (perfects), as a possession *still abiding* with us; but in *Greek* (not as *English Version* "have," but simply) "looked upon" (not perfect, as of a *continuing* thing, but aorist, *past* time) while Christ the incarnate Word was still with us. **hands . . . handled**—Thomas and the other disciples on distinct occasions after the resurrection. John himself had leaned on Jesus' breast at the last supper. Contrast the wisest of the heathen *feeling after* (the same *Greek* as here; *groping after* WITH THE HANDS) *if haply they might find God.* This proves against Socinians he is here speaking of the *personal incarnate Word,* not of Christ's *teaching* from the beginning of His official life. **of**—"concerning"; following "heard." "Heard" is the verb most applying to the purpose of the Epistle, viz. the truth which John had *heard concerning the Word of life,* i.e., (Christ) *the Word* who is *the life.* "Heard," viz., from Christ Himself, including all Christ's teachings about Himself. **the life**—Jesus, "the Word of life." **was manifested**—who had previously been "with the Father." **show**—Translate as in vs. 3, "declare" (cf. vs. 5). *Declare* is the general term; *write* is the particular (vs. 4). **that eternal life**—*Greek,* "the life which is eternal." As the Epistle begins, so it ends with "eternal life," which we shall ever enjoy with, and in, Him who is "the life eternal." **which**—*Greek,* "the which," the before-mentioned (vs. 1) life *which* was with the Father "from the beginning" (cf. John 1:1). This proves the distinctness of the First and Second Persons in the one Godhead. **3. That which we have seen and heard**—resumed from vs. 1, wherein the sentence, being interrupted by vs. 2, parenthesis, was left incomplete. **declare we unto you**—Oldest MSS. add *also; unto you also* who have not *seen* or *heard* Him. **that ye also may have fellowship with us**—that *ye also* who have not seen, *may* have the *fellowship* with us which we who have seen enjoy; what that fellowship consists in he proceeds to state, "Our fellowship is with the Father and with His Son." Faith realizes what we have not seen as spiritually visible; not till by faith we too have seen, do we

ADAM CLARKE

CHAPTER 1

1. *That which was from the beginning.* That glorious Personage, Jesus Christ the Lord, who was from eternity; Him, being manifested in the flesh, we have heard proclaim the doctrine of eternal life; with our own eyes have we seen Him, not transiently, for we have looked upon Him frequently; *and our hands have handled*—frequently touched—His person; and we have had every proof of the identity and reality of this glorious Being that our senses of hearing, seeing, and feeling could possibly require.

2. *For the life was manifested.* The Lord Jesus, who is the Creator of all things and the Fountain of life, was manifested in the flesh, *and we have seen* Him, and in consequence bear witness to Him as the Fountain and Author of eternal life. For He who was from eternity with the Father *was manifested unto us,* His apostles, and to the whole of the Jewish nation, and preached that doctrine of *eternal life* which I have before delivered to the world in my gospel, and which I now further confirm by this Epistle.

3. *That which we have seen and heard.* We deliver nothing by hearsay, nothing by tradition, nothing from conjecture; we have had the fullest certainty of all that we write and preach. *That ye also may have fellowship with us.* That you may be preserved from all false doctrine, and have a real "participation" with us, apostles of the grace, peace, love, and life of God.

MATTHEW HENRY

it is: *And truly our fellowship* (or communion) *is with the Father and his Son Jesus Christ.* See to what the gospel revelation tends—to advance us far above sin and earth and to carry us to blessed communion with the Father and the Son. See for what end the eternal life was made flesh—that he might advance us to eternal life in communion with the Father and himself.

2. That believers may be enlarged and advanced in holy joy, *v.* 4. The mystery of the Christian religion is for the joy of mortals. Those live beneath the use and end of the Christian revelation who are not filled with spiritual joy. Were they confirmed in their holy faith, how would they rejoice!

Verses 5–7

I. Here is the message from the Lord Jesus (*v.* 5). The apostles are the messengers of the Lord Jesus; it is their honour to bring his messages to the world. He that put on human nature will honour earthen vessels. It was the ambition of the apostles faithfully to deliver the messages they had received. The present one is this—*That God is light, and in him is no darkness at all.* He is all that beauty and perfection that can be represented to us by light. There is no defect or imperfection, *v.* 5. It is meet that to this dark world the great God should be represented as pure and perfect light. What more could be included in one word than in this, *God is light, and in him is no darkness at all*?

II. There is a just conclusion to be drawn from this message. 1. For the conviction of such professors as have no true fellowship with God: *If we say we have fellowship with him, and walk in darkness, we lie, and do not the truth. To walk in darkness* is to live and act according to such ignorance, and erroneous practice, as are contrary to our holy religion. They may profess to have communion with God; and yet their lives may be irreligious, immoral, and impure. To such the apostle would not fear to give the lie: *They lie, and do not the truth.* Their practice gives their profession and pretences the lie, and demonstrates the folly and falsehood of them. 2. For the conviction and consequent satisfaction of those that are near to God: *But, if we walk in the light, we have fellowship one with another, and the blood of Jesus Christ his Son cleanseth us from all sin.* Those that so walk show that they know God. *Then we have fellowship one with another*, they with us and we with them, and both with God. *The blood of Jesus Christ his Son cleanseth us from all sin.* His blood procures for us those sacred influences by which sin is to be subdued more and more, till it is quite abolished.

Verses 8–10

I. The apostle, having supposed that even those of this heavenly communion have yet their sin, proceeds here to justify that supposition, *v.* 8. We must beware of deceiving ourselves in denying or excusing our sins. The Christian religion is the religion of sinners.

JAMIESON, FAUSSET, BROWN

know all the excellency of the true Solomon. He Himself is ours; He in us and we in Him. We are "partakers of the divine nature." We know God only by having fellowship with Him; He may thus be *known*, but not *comprehended*. The repetition of "with" before the "Son," distinguishes the *persons*, while the *fellowship* or *communion* with both *Father* and *Son*, implies their unity. **4. these things**—and none other, viz., this whole Epistle. **write we unto you**—Some oldest MSS. omit "unto you," and emphasize "we." Thus the antithesis is between "we" (apostles and eye-witnesses) and "your." *We* write thus that *your joy* may be full. Other oldest MSS. and versions read "OUR joy," viz., *that our joy may be filled full by* bringing you also into fellowship with the Father and Son. **5.** First division of the body of the Epistle (cf. *Introduction*). **declare**—*Greek*, "announce"; report in turn; a different *Greek* word from vs. 3. As the Son announced the message heard from the Father as His apostle, so the Son's apostles announce what they have heard from the Son. John nowhere uses the term "Gospel"; but the *witness* or *testimony*, *the word, the truth*, and here the *message*. **God is light**—What light is in the natural world, that God, the source of even material light, is in the spiritual, the fountain of wisdom, purity, beauty, joy, and glory. As all material life and growth depends on *light*, so all spiritual life and growth depends on GOD. As God here, so Christ, in ch. 2:8, is called "the true light." **no darkness at all**—strong negation; *Greek*, "No, not even one speck of darkness"; no ignorance, error, untruthfulness, sin, or death. John heard this from Christ, not only in express words, but in His acted words, viz., His is whole manifestation in the flesh as "the brightness of the Father's *glory*." Christ Himself was the embodiment of "the message," representing fully in all His sayings, doings, and sufferings, Him who is LIGHT. **6. say**—profess. **have fellowship with him**—(vs. 3). The essence of the Christian life. **walk**—in inward and outward action, whithersoever we turn ourselves [BENGEL]. **in darkness**—*Greek*, "in *the* darkness"; opposed to "the light" (cf. ch. 2:8, 11). **lie**—(ch. 2:4). **do not**—in *practice*, whatever we *say*. **the truth**—(Eph. (4: 21; John 3:21). **7.** Cf. Ephesians 5:8, 11-14. "WE WALK"; "God IS (*essentially* in His very nature as 'the light,' vs. 5) in the light." WALKING *in the light*, the element in which God Himself IS, constitutes the test of fellowship with Him. Christ, like us, *walked* in the light (ch. 2:6). ALFORD notices, Walking in the light as He is in the light, is no mere imitation of God, *but an identity in the essential element* of our daily walk with the essential element of God's eternal being. **we have fellowship one with another**—and of course *with God* (to be understood from vs. 6). Without having fellowship with God there can be no true and Christian fellowship one with another (cf. vs. 3). **and**—as the result of "walking in the light, as He is in the light." **the blood of Jesus . . . cleanseth us from all sin**—daily contracted through the sinful weakness of the flesh, and the power of Satan and the world. He is speaking not of justification through His blood once for all, but of the *present sanctification* ("cleanseth" is *present*) which the believer, *walking in the light* and having *fellowship with God and the saints*, enjoys as His privilege. Cf. John 13:10, *Greek*, "He that has been *bathed*, needeth not save to *wash* his feet, but is clean every whit." Cf. vs. 9, "*cleanse* us from all unrighteousness," a further step besides "*forgiving* us our sins." Christ's blood is the cleansing mean, whereby gradually, being already justified and in fellowship with God, we become *clean* from all sin which would mar our fellowship with God. Faith applies the cleansing, purifying blood. Some oldest MSS. omit "Christ"; others retain it. **8.** *The confession of sins* is a necessary consequence of "walking in the light" (vs. 7). **that we have no sin**—"HAVE," not "have *had*," must refer not to the past sinful life while unconverted, but to the *present* state wherein believers *have sin* even still. Observe, "sin" is in the singular; "(confess our) *sins*" (vs. 9) in the plural. *Sin* refers to the *corruption of the old man* still present in us, and the *stain* created by the actual *sins* flowing from that old nature in us. To confess our need of cleansing from *present* sin is essential to "walking in the light"; so far is the presence of some sin incompatible with our *in the main* "walking in light." But the believer hates, confesses, and longs to be delivered from all sin, which is *darkness*. "They who defend their sins, will see in the great day whether their sins can defend them." **deceive ourselves**—We cannot deceive God; we only make ourselves to err from the right path. **the truth**—(ch. 2:4). True

ADAM CLARKE

4. *That your joy may be full.* You have already tasted that the Lord is good; but I am now going to show you the height of your Christian calling, that your happiness may be complete, being thoroughly cleansed from all sin, and filled with the fullness of God.

5. *This then is the message.* This is the grand principle on which all depends, *which we have heard* from *him.*

God is light—the Source of wisdom, knowledge, holiness, and happiness; and *in him is no darkness at all*—no ignorance, no imperfection, no sinfulness, no misery.

6. *If we say that we have fellowship.* Having *fellowship*, "communion," with God necessarily implies a partaking of the divine nature. Now if a man profess to have such communion, and *walk in darkness*—live an irreligious and sinful life—he lies in the profession which he makes, and does *not the truth*—does not walk according to the directions of the gospel.

7. *But if we walk in the light.* If, having received the principle of holiness from Him, we live a holy and righteous life, deriving continual light, power, and life from Him, then *we have fellowship one with another;* that is, *we* have communion with God, and God condescends to hold communion with us.

The blood of Jesus Christ. The meritorious efficacy of His passion and death has purged our consciences from dead works, and *cleanseth us*, "continues to cleanse us," i.e., to keep clean what it has made clean. And being cleansed from all sin is what every believer should look for, what he has a right to expect, and what he must have in this life in order to be prepared to meet his God. Christ is not a partial Saviour; He saves to the uttermost, and He cleanses from all sin.

8. *If we say that we have no sin.* This is tantamount to v. 10: "If we say that we have not sinned." "All have sinned, and come short of the glory of God"; and therefore every man needs a Saviour, such as Christ is. It is very likely that the heretics, against whose evil doctrines the apostle writes, denied that they had any sin or needed any Saviour. Indeed the Gnostics even denied that Christ suffered; the Aeon, or Divine Being that dwelt in the man Christ Jesus, according to them, left Him when He was taken by the Jews; and He being but a common man, His sufferings and death had neither merit nor efficacy. *We deceive ourselves.* By supposing that we have no guilt, no sinfulness, and consequently have no need of the blood of Christ as an atoning sacrifice. *The truth is not in us.* We have no knowledge of the gospel of Jesus, the whole of which is founded on this most awful truth—all have sinned, all are guilty, all are unholy; and none can redeem himself. Hence it was necessary that Jesus Christ should become incarnated and suffer and die to bring men to God.

MATTHEW HENRY

II. The way to the continued pardon of the believer's sin. 1. His duty in order thereto, *v.* 9. Penitent confession and acknowledgment of sin are the means of his deliverance from his guilt. 2. His encouragement thereto. This is the righteousness, and clemency of God, to whom he makes such confession, *v.* 9. God is faithful to his word, wherein he has promised forgiveness to penitent believing confessors. He is clement and gracious also, and so will forgive, to the contrite confessor, all his sins and cleanse him from the guilt of all unrighteousness.

The Christian life is a life of continued repentance, of continual faith in, thankfulness for, and love to the Redeemer, *v.* 10. The denial of our sin not only deceives ourselves, it challenges his veracity. God has given his testimony to the continued sinfulness of the world, by providing a sacrifice for sin, that will be needed in all ages, and to the continued sinfulness of believers themselves by requiring them continually to confess their sins.

CHAPTER 2

Verses 1, 2

He gives them both dissuasion and support.

1. Dissuasion. He would leave no room for sin, *v.* 1. The design of this letter is to dissuade and drive them from sin. See the familiar affectionate compellation with which he introduces his admonition. Certainly the gospel most prevailed where such ministerial love most abounded.

II. The believer's support and relief in case of sin, *v.* 1. Believers themselves have yet their sins. There are some who, though they really sin, yet, in comparison with others, are said *not to sin.*

And this must be the support and refuge of believers: *We have an Advocate.* Here is an advocate in heaven and with the Father. The Judge with whom our advocate pleads is the Father. He who was our Judge in the legal court (the court of the violated law) is our Father in the gospel court, the court of heaven and of grace. His throne or tribunal is the mercy-seat. Our advocate is recommended to us upon these considerations: 1. By his person and personal names. *It is Jesus Christ the Son of the Father,* one anointed by the Father for the whole work of salvation, and consequently for that of the intercessor.

JAMIESON, FAUSSET, BROWN

faith. "The truth respecting God's holiness and our sinfulness, which is the very first spark of light in us, has no place in us" [ALFORD]. **9. confess**—with the lips, speaking from a contrite heart; involving also confession to our fellow men of offenses committed against them. **he**—God. **faithful**—to His own promises; "true" to His word. **just**—Not merely the mercy, but the *justice* or *righteousness* of God is set forth in the redemption of the penitent believer in Christ. God's promises of mercy, to which He is *faithful,* are in accordance with His *justice.* **to**—*Greek,* "in order that." His forgiving *us our sins and cleansing us from* . . . is in furtherance of the *ends* of His eternal *faithfulness* and *justice.* **forgive**—remitting the *guilt.* **cleanse**—purify from all filthiness, so that henceforth we more and more become free from the presence of sin through the Spirit of sanctification (cf. Heb. 9:14; and above, *Note,* vs. 7). **unrighteousness**—offensive to Him who "is just" or *righteous;* called "sin," vs. 7, because "sin is the transgression of the law," and the law is the expression of God's *righteousness,* so that *sin* is *unrighteousness.*

10. Parallel to vs. 8. **we have not sinned**—referring to the commission of actual *sins,* even after regeneration and conversion; whereas in vs. 8, "we have no sin," refers to the present GUILT remaining (until cleansed) from the *actual sins* committed, and to the SIN of our corrupt old nature still adhering to us. The perfect "have . . . sinned" brings down the commission of sins to the present time, not merely sins committed *before,* but *since, conversion.* **we make him a liar**—a gradation; vs. 6, "we lie"; vs. 8, "we deceive ourselves"; worst of all, "we make Him a liar," by denying His word that all men are sinners (cf. ch. 5:10). **his word is not in us**—"His word," which is "the truth" (vs. 8), accuses us truly; by denying it we drive it from our hearts (cf. John 5:38). Our rejection of "His word" in respect to our being sinners, implies as the consequence our rejection of His word and will revealed in the law and Gospel *as a whole;* for these throughout rest on the fact that *we have sinned,* and *have sin.*

CHAPTER 2

VSS. 1-29. THE ADVOCACY OF CHRIST IS OUR ANTIDOTE TO SIN WHILE WALKING IN THE LIGHT; FOR TO KNOW GOD, WE MUST KEEP HIS COMMANDMENTS AND LOVE THE BRETHREN, AND NOT LOVE THE WORLD, NOR GIVE HEED TO ANTICHRISTS, AGAINST WHOM OUR SAFETY IS THROUGH THE INWARD ANOINTING OF GOD TO ABIDE IN GOD: SO AT CHRIST'S COMING WE SHALL NOT BE ASHAMED. **1.** (Ch. 5:18). **My little children**—The diminutive expresses the tender affection of an aged pastor and spiritual father. *My own dear children,* i.e., sons and daughters (*Note,* vs. 12). **these things**—(ch. 1:6-10). My purpose in writing what I have just written is not that you should abuse them as giving a license to sin but, on the contrary, "in order that ye may not sin at all" (the *Greek* aorist implying the absence not only of the habit, but of *single acts* of sin [ALFORD]). **And . . .**—connected with the former; *Furthermore,* "if any man sin," let him, while loathing and condemning it, not fear to go at once to God, the Judge, confessing it, for "we have an Advocate with Him." He is speaking of a BELIEVER'S *occasional* sins of infirmity through Satan's fraud and malice. The use of "we" immediately afterwards implies that *we all* are *liable* to this, though not necessarily constrained to sin. **we have an advocate**—Advocacy is God's family blessing; other blessings He grants to good and bad alike, but justification, sanctification, continued intercession, and peace, He grants to His children alone. **advocate**—*Greek,* "paraclete," the same term as is applied to the Holy Ghost, as the "other Comforter"; showing the unity of the Second and Third Persons of the Trinity. Christ is the Intercessor *for us* above; and, in His absence, here below the Holy Ghost is the other Intercessor *in us.* Christ's *advocacy* is inseparable from the Holy Spirit's *comfort* and working in us, as the spirit of intercessory prayer. **righteous**—As our "advocate,"

ADAM CLARKE

9. *If we confess our sins.* If, from a deep sense of our guilt, impurity, and helplessness, we humble ourselves before God, acknowledging our iniquity, His holiness, and our own utter helplessness, and implore mercy for His sake who has died for us. *He is faithful,* because to such He has promised mercy, Ps. xxxii. 5; Prov. xxviii. 13; *and just,* for Christ has died for us, and thus made an atonement to the divine justice; so that God can now be just, and yet the Justifier of him who believes in Jesus. *And to cleanse us from all unrigheousness.* Not only to forgive the sin, but to purify the heart. Observe, (1) Sin exists in the soul after two modes or forms: (*a*) In *guilt,* which requires forgiveness or pardon; (*b*) In *pollution,* which requires cleansing. (2) *Guilt,* to be forgiven, must be confessed; and *pollution,* to be cleansed, must be also confessed. In order to find mercy, a man must know and feel himself to be a sinner, that he may fervently apply to God for pardon; in order to get a clean heart, a man must know and feel its depravity, acknowledge and deplore it before God, in order to be fully sanctified. (3) Few are pardoned, because they do not feel and confess their sins; and few are sanctified or cleansed from all sin, because they do not feel and confess their own sore, and the plague of their hearts. (4) As the blood of Jesus Christ, the merit of His passion and death, applied by faith, purges the conscience from all dead works, so the same cleanses the heart from all unrighteousness. (5) As all unrighteousness is sin, so he that is cleansed from all unrighteousness is cleansed from all sin. To attempt to evade this, and plead for the continuance of sin in the heart through life, is ungrateful, wicked, and even blasphemous; for as he who says he has not sinned, v. 10, makes God a liar, who has declared the contrary through every part of His revelation; so he that says the blood of Christ either cannot or will not cleanse us from all sin in this life gives also the lie to his Maker, who has declared the contrary, and thus shows that the word, the doctrine of God, is not in him. Reader, it is the birthright of every child of God to be cleansed from all sin, to keep himself unspotted from the world, and so to live as nevermore to offend his Maker. All things are possible to him that believes, because all things are possible to the infinitely meritorious blood and energetic Spirit of the Lord Jesus.

CHAPTER 2

1. *My little children.* "My beloved children"; the address of an affectionate father to children whom he tenderly loves. The term also refers to the apostle's authority as their spiritual father, and their obligation to obey as his spiritual children. *That ye sin not.* This is the language of the whole Scripture; of every dispensation, ordinance, institution, doctrine, and word of God.

And if any man sin. If, through ignorance, inexperience, the violence of temptation, unwatchfulness, you have fallen into sin and grieve the Spirit of God, do not continue in the sin nor under the guilt; do not despair of being again restored to the favor of God. Your case, it is true, is deeply deplorable, but not desperate; there is still hope, for—*we have an advocate with the Father.* We still have Him before the throne who died for our offenses and rose again for our justification; and there He makes intercession for us.

MATTHEW HENRY

2. By his qualification for the office. *It is Jesus Christ the righteous.* The clients are guilty; their innocence and legal righteousness cannot be pleaded. It is the advocate's own righteousness that he must plead for the criminals. He has been righteous to the death, righteous for them. Upon this score he pleads, that the clients' sins may not be imputed to them. 3. By the plea he has to make, the ground and basis of his advocacy, *v.* 2. He is the propitiatory sacrifice. The Mediator of intercession, the Advocate for us, is the Mediator of redemption, the propitiation for our sins. It is his propitiation that he pleads. *He ever lives to make intercession for those that come to God through him.*

4. By the extent of his plea. It is not confined to one nation, *v.* 2; not only for the past, or us present believers, but for the sins of all who shall hereafter come to God through him. The extent and intent of the Mediator's death reach to all tribes, nations, and countries.

Verses 3–6

Here now succeeds the trial or test of our light and of our love.

I. The trial of our light, *v.* 3. Divine light and knowledge are the beauty and improvement of the mind. Young Christians are apt to magnify their new light and applaud their own knowledge; and old ones are apt to suspect the sufficiency and fulness of their knowledge. Here is the evidence of the soundness of our knowledge, if it constrain us to *keep God's commandments.*

A careful conscientious obedience to his commands shows that the apprehension and knowledge of these things are graciously impressed upon the soul; and therefore it must follow in the reverse that *he that saith, I know him, and keepeth not his commandments, is a liar, and the truth is not in him, v.* 4. A disobedient life is the confutation and shame of pretended religious knowledge.

II. The trial of our love, *v.* 5. To keep the word of God, or of Christ, is sacredly to attend thereto in all the conduct and motion of life; in him that does so is the love of God perfected. The phrase denotes here our love to God; so *v.* 15, so *ch.* iii. 17. We know that we belong to him, and that we are united to him by that Spirit which assists us to this obedience; and if we acknowledge our relation to him, and our union with him, it must have this continued enforcement upon us: *He that saith he abideth in him ought himself to walk even as he walked, v.* 6. Those who profess to be on his side, and to abide with him, must walk with him, walk after his pattern and example.

Verses 7–11

The precept of fraternal love is recommended,

I. As an old one, *v.* 7. The precept of love must be as old as human nature. And so it is the *old commandment.*

JAMIESON, FAUSSET, BROWN

Christ is not a mere suppliant petitioner. He pleads for us on the ground of *justice,* or *righteousness,* as well as mercy. Though He can say nothing good *of* us, He can say much *for* us. It is His *righteousness,* or obedience to the law, and endurance of its full penalty for us, on which He grounds His claim for our acquittal. The sense therefore is, "in that He is *righteous*"; in contrast to our *sin* ("if any man *sin*"). **2. And he**—*Greek,* "And *Himself.*" He is our all-prevailing Advocate, because He is *Himself* "the propitiation"; *abstract,* as in I Corinthians 1:30: He is to us *all that is needed for propitiation* "in behalf of our sins"; *the propitiatory sacrifice,* provided by the Father's love, removing the estrangement, and appeasing the righteous wrath, on God's part, against the sinner. "There is no incongruity that a father should be *offended* with that son whom he loveth, and at that time offended with him when he *loveth* him" [BISHOP PEARSON]. The only other place in the New Testament where *Greek* "propitiation" occurs, is ch. 4:10; it answers in LXX to *Hebrew caphar,* to *effect an atonement* or *reconciliation* with God; and in Ezekiel 44:29, to the *sin offering.* In Romans 3:25, *Greek,* it is "propitiatory," i.e., the mercy seat, or lid of the ark whereon God, represented by the Shekinah glory above it, met His people, represented by the high priest who sprinkled the blood of the sacrifice on it. **and**—*Greek,* "yet." **ours**—believers: not *Jews,* in contrast to Gentiles; for he is not writing to Jews (ch. 5:21). **also for the sins of the whole world**—Christ's *advocacy* is limited to *believers* (vs. 1; ch. 1:7): His *propitiation* extends as widely as *sin* extends: *Note,* II Peter 2:1, "denying the Lord that *bought them.*" "The *whole* world" cannot be restricted to the *believing* portion of the world (cf. ch. 4:14; and "the whole world," (ch. 5:19). "Thou, too, art part of the world, so that thine heart cannot deceive itself and think, The Lord died for Peter and Paul, but not for me" [LUTHER]. **3. hereby**—*Greek,* "in this." "It is *herein,* and herein only, that we know (present) that we have knowledge of (perfect, once-for-all obtained and continuing *knowledge of) Him*" (vss. 4, 13, 14). Tokens whereby to discern grace are frequently given in this Epistle. The Gnostics, by the Spirit's prescient forewarning, are refuted, who boasted of *knowledge,* but set aside *obedience.* "Know Him," viz., as "the righteous" (vss. 1, 29); our "Advocate and Intercessor." **keep**—John's favorite word, instead of "do," lit., "watch", "guard," and "keep safe" as a precious thing; observing so as to keep. So Christ Himself. Not faultless conformity, but hearty acceptance of, and willing subjection to, God's whole revealed will, is meant. **commandments**—*injunctions* of faith, love, and obedience. John never uses "the law" to express the rule of Christian obedience: he uses it as the Mosaic law. **4. I know**—*Greek,* "I *have knowledge of* (perfect) Him." Cf. with this verse ch. 1:8. **5.** Not merely repeating the proposition, vs. 3, or asserting the merely opposite alternative to vs. 4, but expanding the "know Him" of vs. 3, into "in Him, verily (not as a matter of vain boasting) is the love of (i.e. towards) God perfected," and "we are in Him." *Love* here answers to *knowledge* in vs. 3. In proportion as we love God, in that same proportion we *know* Him, and vice versa, until our *love and knowledge* shall attain their full maturity of perfection. **5. his word**—*His word* is one (*Note,* ch. 1:5), and comprises His "*commandments,*" which are many (vs. 3). **hereby**—in our progressing towards this ideal of perfected love and obedience. There is a gradation: vs. 3, "*know* Him"; vs. 5, "we *are* in Him"; vs. 6, "*abideth* in Him"; respectively, *knowledge, fellowship, abiding constancy* [BENGEL]. **6. abideth**—implying a condition lasting, without intermission, and without end. **He that saith . . . ought**—so that his deeds may be consistent with his words. **even as he**—Believers readily supply the name, their hearts being full of Him (cf. John 20:15). "Even as He walked" when on earth, especially in respect to *love.* John delights in referring to Christ as the model man, with the words, "Even as He. . . ." "It is not Christ's walking on the sea, but His ordinary walk, that we are called on to imitate" [LUTHER]. **7. Brethren**—The oldest MSS. and versions read instead, "Beloved," appropriate to the subject here, *love.* **no new commandment**—viz., *love,* the main principle of walking *as Christ walked* (vs. 6), and that commandment, of which one exemplification is presently given, vss. 9, 10, *the love of brethren.* **ye had from the beginning**—from the time that ye first heard the Gospel word preached. **8. a new commandment**—It was "old," in that *Christians* as such had heard it *from the first;* but "new" (*Greek, kaine,* not *nea: new and different* from the *old* legal precept)

ADAM CLARKE

He is the *righteous;* He who suffered, "the just for the unjust, that he might bring us to God." Do not therefore despair, but have immediate recourse to God through Him.

2. *And he is the propitiation,* the "atoning sacrifice," *for our sins.* This is the proper sense of the word as used in the Septuagint, where it often occurs; and is the translation of *asham,* an "oblation for sin," Amos viii. 14; *chattath,* a "sacrifice for sin," Ezek. xliv. 27; *kippur,* an "atonement," Nom. v. 8. The word is used only here and in chap. iv. 10.

And not for ours only. It is not for us apostles that He has died, nor exclusively for the Jewish people, but for *the whole world,* Gentiles as well as Jews, all the descendants of Adam. The apostle does not say that He died for any select part of the inhabitants of the earth, but for all mankind, and the attempt to limit this is a violent outrage against God and His Word. For the meaning of the word which we here translate "advocate" see the note on John xiv. 16.

3. *And hereby we do know that we know him.* If we keep the commandments of God, loving Him with all our hearts, and our neighbors as ourselves, we have the fullest proof that we have the true saving knowledge of God and His Christ. The Gnostics pretended to much knowledge, but their knowledge left them in possession of all their bad passions and unholy habits; they therefore gave no proof that they had known either God or His Son, Jesus; nor is any man properly acquainted with God who is still under the power of his sins.

4. *He that saith, I know him.* This is a severe blow against those false teachers, and against all pretenders to religious knowledge, who live under the power of their sins; and against all antinomians, and false boasters in the righteousness of Christ as a covering for their personal unholiness. They are all liars, and no *truth* of God is in them.

5. *But whoso keepeth his word.* Conscientiously observes His doctrine, the spirit and letter of the religion of Christ. *Is the love of God perfected.* The design of God's love in sending Jesus Christ into the world to die for the sin of man "is accomplished" in that man who receives the doctrine and applies for the salvation provided for him. *That we are in him.* That we have entered into His spirit and views, received His salvation, have been enabled to walk in the light, and have communion with Him by the Holy Spirit.

6. *Abideth in him.* He who not only professes to have known Christ, but also that he has communion with Him and abides in His favor, should prove the truth of his profession by walking as Christ walked; living a life of devotion and obedience to God, and of benevolence and beneficence to his neighbor. Thus Christ walked; and He has left us an example that we should follow His steps. To "be in Christ," v. 5, is to be converted to the Christian faith, and to have received the remission of sins. To "abide in Christ," v. 6, is to continue in that state of salvation, growing in grace, and in the knowledge of our Lord Jesus Christ.

7. *Brethren, I write no new commandment.* There seems a contradiction between this and the next verse. But the apostle appears to speak, not so much of any difference in the essence of the precept itself, as in reference to the degrees of light and grace belonging to the Mosaic and Christian dispensations. It was ever the command of God that man should receive His light, walk by that light, and love Him and one another. But this commandment was renewed by Christ with much latitude and spirituality of meaning; and also with much additional light to see its extent, and grace to observe it. It may therefore be called the "old commandment," which was "from the beginning"; and also a "new commandment" revealed afresh and illustrated by Christ. Instead of *brethren,* a number of MSS., along with several of the fathers, have "beloved." This is without doubt the true reading.

MATTHEW HENRY

II. As a new one: "*Again, a new commandment I write unto you, which thing is true in him*, and it is true *in you*; this law is in some measure written upon your hearts; you are taught of God to love one another, and that *because the darkness is past*, your deplorable ignorance of God and of Christ is now past, *and the true light now shineth*" (*v*. 8). We should see that that grace which was true in Christ be true also in us. The more our darkness is past, and gospel light shines unto us, the deeper should our subjection be to the commandments of our Lord, whether considered as old or new.

Another trial of our Christian light; before, it was to be approved by obedience to God; here by Christian love. 1. He who wants such love in vain pretends his light, *v*. 9. These cannot be swayed by the sense of the love of Christ to their brethren, and therefore remain in their dark state. 2. He who is governed by such love approves his light to be good and genuine, *v*. 10. He sees how meet it is that we should love those whom Christ hath loved; *there is no occasion of stumbling in him* (*v*. 10). Christian love teaches us highly to value our brother's soul, and to dread everything that will be injurious to his innocence and peace. 3. Hatred is a sign of spiritual darkness, *v*. 11. He then who is possessed with malignity towards a Christian brother must needs be destitute of spiritual light; consequently *he walks in darkness, and he knows not whither he goes, because darkness hath blinded his eyes*, *v*. 11. It is the Lord Jesus that is the great Master of love: it is his school that is the school of love. His disciples are the disciples of love, and his family must be the family of love.

Verses 12–17

I. All Christians are not of the same standing and stature; there are babes in Christ, there are grown men, and old disciples. There are precepts and a correspondent obedience common to them all, as particularly mutual love and contempt of the world.

1. The lowest in the Christian school, *v*. 12. There are novices in religion, babes in Christ. He addresses *the children* in Christianity, (1) *Because their sins were forgiven them for his name's sake*, *v*. 12. The youngest sincere disciple is pardoned. Sins are forgiven either for God's name's sake, or *for Christ's name's sake*, and those that are forgiven of God are strongly obliged to relinquish this world. (2) Because of their knowledge of God, *v*. 13. We say, It is a wise child that knows his father. These children cannot but know theirs. Those that know the Father may well be withdrawn from the love of this world.

2. To those of the highest station, to the seniors in Christianity (*v*. 13, 14). The apostle immediately passes from the bottom to the top of the school. Those that are of longest standing in Christ's school have need of further advice and instruction. None are too old to learn. He writes to them upon the account of their knowledge, *v*. 13, 14. Those who know him that was from the beginning may well be induced thereby to relinquish this world.

JAMIESON, FAUSSET, BROWN

in that it was first *clearly* promulgated with Christianity; though the inner *spirit* of the law was *love* even to enemies, yet it was enveloped in some bitter precepts which caused it to be temporarily almost unrecognized, till the Gospel came. Christianity first put *love to brethren* on the *new* and highest MOTIVE, instinctive love to Him who first loved us, constraining us to love all, even enemies, thereby walking in the steps of Him who loved us when enemies. So Jesus calls it "new," John 13:34, 35, "Love one another *as I have loved you*" (the new motive); 15:12. **which thing is true in him and in you**—"*In Christ* all things are always true, and were so from the beginning; but *in Christ and in us* conjointly *the commandment* [the love of brethren] *is then true* when we acknowledge the truth which is *in Him*, and have the same flourishing *in us*" [BENGEL]. **darkness is past**—rather, as in ch. 2:17, "is passing away." It shall not be wholly "past" until "the Sun of righteousness" shall arise *visibly;* "the light is now shining" *already*, though but partially until the day bursts forth. **9-11.** There is no mean between *light and darkness, love* and *hatred, life* and *death, God* and the *world:* wherever spiritual *life* is, however weak, there *darkness* and *death* no longer reign, and *love* supplants *hatred;* and Luke 9:50 holds good: wherever *life* is not, *there death, darkness,* the *flesh*, the *world, and hatred,* however glossed over and hidden from man's observation, prevail; and Luke 11: 23 holds good. "Where love is not, there hatred is; for the heart cannot remain a void" [BENGEL]. **in the light**—as his proper element. **his brother**—his neighbor, and especially those of the Christian brotherhood. The very title "brother" is a reason why love should be exercised. **even until now**—notwithstanding that "the true light already has begun to shine" (vs. 8). **10.** Abiding in *love* is *abiding* in *the light;* for the Gospel light not only illumines the understanding, but warms the heart into love. **none occasion of stumbling**—In contrast to, "He that hateth his brother is in darkness, and walketh in darkness, and knoweth not whither he goeth, because that darkness hath blinded his eyes." "In him who loves there is neither blindness nor *occasion of stumbling* [to himself]: in him who does not love, there is both *blindness* and occasion of stumbling. **11. is in darkness . . . walketh**—"is" marks his continuing STATE: he has never come out of "the (so *Greek*) darkness; "walketh" marks his OUTWARD WALK and acts. **whither**—*Greek*, "where"; including not only the destination *to which,* but the way *whereby*. **hath blinded**—rather as *Greek* aorist, "blinded" of old. Darkness not only surrounds, but blinds him, and that a blindness of long standing. **12. little children**—*Greek*, "little *sons*," or "dear sons and daughters"; not the same *Greek* as in vs. 13, "little *children*," "infants" (in age and standing). He calls ALL to whom he writes, "little *sons*" (ch. 2:1, *Greek;* 2:28; 3:18; 4:4; 5:21); but only in vss. 13 and 18 he uses the term "little children," or "infants." Our Lord, whose Spirit John so deeply drank into, used to His disciples (John 13:33) the term "little sons," or *dear sons and daughters;* but in John 21:5, "little children." **are forgiven**—"have been, and are forgiven you": ALL God's *sons and daughters* alike enjoy this privilege. **13, 14.** All three classes are first addressed in the present. "I write"; then in the past (aorist) tense, "I wrote" (not "I have written"; moreover, in the oldest MSS. and versions, in the end of vs. 13, it is past, "I wrote," not as *English Version,* "I write"). Two classes, "fathers" and "young men," are addressed with the same words each time (except that the address to the *young men* has an addition expressing the source and means of their victory); but the "little sons" and "little children" are differently addressed. **have known**—and do know: so the *Greek* perfect means. The "I wrote" refers not to a former Epistle, but to this Epistle. It was an idiom to put the *past* tense, regarding the time from the *reader's* point of view; when he should receive the Epistle the writing would be *past*. When he uses "I write," he speaks from *his own* point of view. **him** *that is* **from the beginning**—Christ: "that which was from the beginning." **overcome**—The *fathers*, appropriately to their age, are characterized by *knowledge*. The *young men,* appropriately to theirs, by *activity in conflict*. The *fathers,* too, have *conquered;* but now their active service is past, and they and *the children* alike are characterized by *knowing* (the *fathers* know *Christ*, "Him that was from the beginning"; *the children* know the Father). The first thing that the *little children* realize is that God is their *Father;* answering in the parallel clause to "little sons . . . your sins are forgiven you for His name's sake," the universal first privilege of

ADAM CLARKE

8. *Which thing is true in him and in you.* It is true that Christ loved the world so well as to lay down His life for it; and it was true in them, in all His faithful followers at that time, who were ready to lay down their lives for the testimony of Jesus. *The darkness is past.* The total thick darkness of the heathen world and the comparative darkness of the Mosaic dispensation are now passing away, and the pure and superior light of Christianity is now diffusing its beams everywhere. He does not say that the darkness was all gone by, but "is passing away"; he does not say that the fullness of the light had appeared, but it "is now shining," and will shine more and more to the perfect day; for the darkness passes away in proportion as the light shines and increases.

9. *He that saith he is in the light.* He that professes to be a convert to Christianity, even in the lowest degree. *And hateth his brother*—not only does not love him, but wills and does him evil, as the Jews did the Gentiles. *Is in darkness*—has received no saving knowledge of the truth.

10. *He that loveth his brother.* That is, his neighbor, his fellow creature, whether Jew or Gentile, so as to bear him continual goodwill, and to be ready to do him every kind office. *Abideth in the light*—not only gives proof that he has received Christ Jesus the Lord, but that he walks in Him, that he retains the grace of his justification, and grows therein. *And there is none occasion of stumbling in him.* "And there is no stumbling block in him"; he neither gives nor receives offense. Love prevents him from giving any to his neighbor; and love prevents him from receiving any from his neighbor, because it leads him to put the best construction on everything.

11. *But he that hateth his brother is in darkness.* He is still in his heathen or unconverted state. *And walketh in darkness,* his conduct being a proof of that state. *And knoweth not whither he goeth*—having no proper knowledge of God or eternal things; and cannot tell whether he is going to heaven or hell, *because that darkness hath blinded his eyes*—darkened his whole soul, mind, and heart.

12. *I write unto you, little children.* "Beloved children" (see on v. 1), those who were probably the apostle's own converts, and members of the church over which he presided. But it may be applied to young converts in general; therefore he says of them that their sins were forgiven them for His name's sake; i.e., on account of Jesus, the Saviour.

13. *I write unto you, fathers.* By *fathers* it is very likely that the apostle means persons who had embraced Christianity on its first promulgation in Judea and in the Lesser Asia, some of whom had probably seen Christ in the flesh; for this appears to be what is meant by *Ye have known him . . . from the beginning.* But *him that is from the beginning* may mean Jesus Christ in the eternity of His nature; see John i. 1-2. *I write unto you, young man.* These were confirmed disciples of Christ; persons who were well-grounded in the truth, had been thoroughly exercised in the Christian warfare, were no longer agitated by doubts and fears, but had arrived at the abiding testimony of the Spirit of God in their consciences; hence they are said to have *overcome the wicked one,* v. 14. They were persons in the prime of life, and in the zenith of their faith and love. *I write unto you, little children.* A very different term from that used in the twelfth verse, which means "beloved children," as we have already seen. This is another class, and their state is differently described: *Ye have known the Father.*

MATTHEW HENRY

3. To the middle age of Christians, *v.* 13, 14. There are the adults in Christ Jesus. The apostle applies to them, (1) Upon the account of their martial exploits. Dexterous soldiers they are in the camp of Christ, *v.* 13. Those that are well taught in Christ's school can handle their arms and vanquish the evil one; and those that can vanquish him may be called to vanquish the world too.

(2) Upon the account of their strength, discovered in this their achievement, *v.* 14. Young men are wont to glory in their strength. It will be their glory, and it will try their strength, to overcome the devil. The same strength must be exerted in overcoming the world as is employed in overcoming the devil. (3) Because of their acquaintance with the word of God, *v.* 14. Those in whom the word of God dwells are well furnished for the conquest of the world.

II. A caution fundamental to vital practical religion, *v.* 15. Be crucified to the world. Their love should be reserved for God; throw it not away upon the world. The reasons of this dissuasion and caution.

1. The inconsistency of this love with the love of God, *v.* 15. The heart of man is narrow, and cannot contain both loves.
2. The prohibition of worldly love or lust; it is not ordained of God, *v.* 16. This love or lust is not appointed of God but it intrudes itself from the world. The things of the world are distinguished into three classes, according to the three predominant inclinations of depraved nature, (1) There is *the lust of the flesh.* This lust is usually called *luxury.* (2) There is *the lust of the eyes.* This is the lust of covetousness.

(3) There is *the pride of life.* This is ambition. The objects of these appetites must be abandoned and renounced, *v.* 16. The Father disallows them. The lust or appetite to these things must be mortified and subdued.

JAMIESON, FAUSSET, BROWN

all those really-dear *sons* of God. Thus this latter clause includes *all*, whereas the former clause refers to those more especially who are in the *first* stage of spiritual life, "little children." Of course, these can only know *the Father* as theirs through *the Son* (Matt. 11:27). **14. young men . . . strong** —*made* so *out of* natural *weakness*, hence enabled to *overcome* "the strong man armed" through Him that is "stronger." Faith is the victory that overcomes the world. This term "overcome" is peculiarly John's, adopted from his loved Lord. It occurs sixteen times in the Apocalypse, six times in the First Epistle, only thrice in the rest of the New Testament. In order to overcome the world on the ground, and in the strength, of the blood of the Saviour, we must be willing, like Christ, to part with whatever of the world belongs to us: **and . . .**—the secret of the young men's *strength:* the Gospel *word*, clothed with living power by the Spirit who *abideth* permanently in them; this is "the sword of the Spirit" wielded in prayerful waiting on God. Contrast the mere physical strength of young men, Isaiah 40:30, 31. *Oral teaching* prepared these youths for the profitable use of *the word* when *written.* "Antichrist cannot endanger you (vs. 18), nor Satan tear from you *the word of God.*" **the wicked one**—who, as "prince of this world," enthrals "the world" (vss. 15-17; ch. 5:19, *Greek*, "the wicked one"), especially the young. Christ came to destroy this "prince of the world". Believers achieve the first grand conquest over him when they pass from darkness to light, but afterwards they need to maintain a continual *keeping* of themselves from his assaults, looking to God by whom alone they are *kept* safe. **15. Love not the world**—that *lieth in the wicked one* (ch. 5:19), whom ye young men *have overcome.* Having once for all, through *faith, overcome the world* (ch. 4:4; 5:4), carry forward the conquest by not loving it. "The world" here means "man, and man's world" [ALFORD], in his and its state as *fallen from God.* "God loved [with the love of *compassion*] the world," and we should feel the same kind of love for the fallen world; but we are *not* to *love* the world with *congeniality* and *sympathy* in its alienation from God; we cannot have this latter kind of love for the God-estranged world, and yet have also "the love of the Father in" us. **neither**—*Greek*, "nor yet." A man might deny in general that he *loved the world,* while keenly following some one of THE THINGS IN IT: its riches, honors, or pleasures; this clause prevents him escaping from conviction. **any man**—therefore the warning, though primarily addressed to the young, applies to *all.* **love of**—i.e., *towards* "the Father." The two, God and the (sinful) world, are so opposed, that both cannot be congenially loved at once. **16. all that is in the world**—can be classed under one or other of the three; the world contains these and no more. **lust of the flesh**—i.e., the lust which has its seat and source in our lower animal nature. Satan tried this temptation the first on Christ: Luke 4:3, "Command this stone that it be made *bread.*" Youth is especially liable to fleshly lusts. **lust of the eyes**—the avenue through which outward things of the world, riches, pomp, and beauty, inflame us. Satan tried this temptation on Christ when he showed Him the kingdoms of the world in a moment. By the lust of the eyes David (II Sam. 11:2) and Achan fell (Josh. 7:21). Cf. David's prayer, Psalm 119:37; Job's resolve, Psalm 31:1 Matthew 5:28. The only good of worldly riches to the possessor is the beholding them with the *eyes.* Cf. Luke 14:18, "I must go and SEE it." **pride of life** —lit., "arrogant assumption": vainglorious display. *Pride* was Satan's sin whereby he fell and forms the link between the two foes of man, the *world* (answering to "the lust of the eyes") and the *devil* (as "the lust of the flesh" is the third foe). Satan tried this temptation on Christ in setting Him on the temple pinnacle that, in spiritual *pride* and *presumption,* on the ground of His Father's care, He should cast Himself down. The same three foes appear in the three classes of soil on which the divine seed falls: the wayside hearers, the *devil;* the thorns, *the world;* the rocky undersoil, *the flesh.* The world's awful *antitrinity,* the "lust of the flesh, the lust of the eyes, and the pride of life," similarly is presented in Satan's temptation of Eve: "When she saw that the tree was good for *food,* pleasant to the *eyes,* and a tree to be desired to make one *wise*" (one manifestation of "the pride of life," the desire to know above what God has revealed, Col. 2:8, the pride of unsanctified knowledge). **of**—does not spring *from* "the Father" (used in relation to the preceding "little children," vs. 12, or "little sons"). He who is born *of* God alone turns *to* God; he who is of the world turns to the world; the sources of

ADAM CLARKE

14. *The word of God abideth in you.* You have not only thoroughly known and digested the divine doctrine, but your hearts are molded into it.

15. *Love not the world.* The Holy Spirit saw it necessary to caution these against the love of the world, the inordinate desire of earthly things. Covetousness is the predominant vice of old age: Ye "fathers," *love not the world.* The things which are in the world, its profits, pleasures, and honors, have the strongest allurements for youth; therefore, you "young men, little children, and babes," love not *the things* of this world. *The love of the Father is not in him.* The love of God and the love of earthly things are incompatible.

16. *For all that is in the world.* All that it can boast of, all that it can promise, is only sensual, transient gratification, and even this promise it cannot fulfill; so that its warmest votaries can complain loudest of their disappointment.

Is not of the Father. Nothing of these inordinate attachments either comes from or leads to God. They are of this world; here they begin, flourish, and end. They deprave the mind, divert it from divine pursuits, and render it utterly incapable of spiritual enjoyments.

MATTHEW HENRY

3. The vain and vanishing state of earthly things, *v.* 17. The things of the world are fading and dying apace.

4. The immortality of the lover of God, *v.* 17. The object of his love in opposition to *the world* that *passeth away,* abideth for ever. Love shall never fail; and he himself is an heir of immortality and endless life.

Verses 18, 19

I. The end is coming, *v.* 18. It is meet that the disciples should be warned of the haste and end of time.

II. The sign of this last time (*v.* 18), that many oppose the kingdom of Christ. It should be no great offence nor prejudice to the disciples that there are such antichrists: 1. One great one has been foretold, *v.* 18. *Even now there are many antichrists,* the mystery of iniquity already worketh. 2. They were foretold also as the sign of this last time, *v.* 18.

III. Some account of these seducers or antichrists: "*They went out from us* (*v.* 19), from our company and communion." The purest churches may have their apostates. "*For, if they had been of us, they would have continued with us* (*v.* 19); had the sacred truth been rooted in their hearts it would have held them with us." Those that apostatize from religion sufficiently indicate that, before, they were hypocrites in religion. *But* this was done (or *they went out*) *that they might be made manifest that they were not all of us, v.* 19. Some of the hypocritical must be manifested here, and that for their own shame and benefit too, in their reduction to the truth.

Verses 20-27

Here, I. The apostle encourages the disciples in this hour of seducers. *But you have an unction from the Holy One, and you know all* things. 1. The blessing wherewith they were enriched: *You have an unction.* True Christians are anointed ones, their name intimates as much. They are anointed by the Spirit of grace. 2. From whom this blessing comes—*from the Holy One.* The Lord Christ disposes of the graces of the divine Spirit, and he anoints the disciples to make them like himself.

3. The effect of this unction: "*And* thereby *you know all things* (*v.* 20), all these things concerning Christ and his religion."

JAMIESON, FAUSSET, BROWN

love to God and love to the world, are irreconcilably distinct. **17. the world**—with all who are of the world worldly. **passeth away**—*Greek,* "is passing away" even now. **the lust thereof**—in its threefold manifestation (vs. 16). **he that doeth the will of God**—not his own *fleshly* will, or the will of the *world,* but that of God (vss. 3, 6), especially in respect to *love.* **abideth for ever**—"even as God also abideth for ever" (with whom the godly is one; cf. Ps. 55:19, "God, even He that abideth of old"): a true *comment,* which CYPRIAN and LUCIFER have added to the *text* without support of *Greek* MSS. In contrast to the three *passing* lusts of the world, the doer of God's will has three *abiding* goods, "riches, honor, and life" (Prov. 22:4). **18. Little children**—same *Greek* as vs. 13; children *in age.* After the *fathers* and *young men* were gone, "the last time" with its "many Antichrists" was about to come suddenly on *the children.* "In this *last hour* we all even still live" [BENGEL]. Each successive age has had in it some of the signs of "the last time" which precedes Christ's coming, in order to keep the Church in continual waiting for the Lord. The connection with vss. 15-17 is: There are coming those seducers who are of the world (ch. 4:5), and would tempt you to go out from us (vs. 19) and deny Christ (vs. 22). **as ye have heard**—from the apostles, preachers of the Gospel (e.g., II Thess. 2: 3-10; and in the region of Ephesus, Acts 20:29, 30). **shall come**—*Greek,* "cometh," viz., out of his own place. *Antichrist* is interpreted in two ways: a false Christ (Matt. 24:5, 24), lit., "*instead* of Christ"; or an *adversary* of Christ, lit., "*against* Christ." As John never uses *pseudo-Christ,* or "false Christ," for *Antichrist,* it is plain he means an *adversary of Christ,* claiming to himself what belongs to Christ, and wishing to substitute himself for Christ as the supreme object of worship.

are there—*Greek,* "there have begun to be"; there have arisen. These "many Antichrists" answer to "the spirit of lawlessness (*Greek*) doth already work." The Antichristian principle appeared then, as now, in evil men and evil teachings and writings; but still "THE Antichrist" means a hostile *person,* even as "THE Christ" is a personal Saviour. **19. out from us**—from our Christian communion. Not necessarily a formal secession or *going out:* thus Rome has spiritually *gone out,* though formally still of the Christian Church. **not of us**—by spiritual fellowship (ch. 1:3). **they would... have continued**—implying the indefectibility of grace in the elect. "Where God's call is effectual, there will be sure perseverance" [CALVIN]. Still, it is no fatal necessity, but a "voluntary necessity" [DIDYMUS], which causes men to remain, or else go from the body of Christ.

that they were not all of us—This translation would imply *that some of the Antichrists are of us*! Translate, therefore, "that all (who are for a time among us) are not of us." Cf. I Corinthians 11:19, "There must be heresies among you, that they which are approved may be made manifest among you." For "were" some of the oldest MSS. read "are." Such occasions test who are, and who are not, the Lord's people. **20. But**—*Greek,* "And." He here states the means which they as believers have wherewith to withstand. *Antichrists* (vs. 18), viz., the *chrism* (so the *Greek:* a play upon similar sounds), or "anointing unguent," viz., the Holy Spirit (more plainly mentioned further on, as in John's style, ch. 3:24; 4:13; 5:6), which *they* ("ye" is emphatical in contrast to those apostates, vs. 19) have "from the Holy One, *Christ* (John 1:33; 3:34; 15:26; 16:14): "the righteous" (vs. 1), "pure" (ch. 3:3), "the Holy One" (Acts 3:14) "of God"; Mark 1:24. Those anointed of God in *Christ* alone can resist those anointed with the spirit of Satan, *Antichrists,* who would sever them from the Father and from the Son. Believers have the anointing Spirit from *the Father* also, as well as from the Son; even as the Son is anointed therewith by the Father. Hence the Spirit is the token that we are in the Father and in the Son; without it a man is none of Christ's. The material unguent of costliest ingredients, poured on the head of priests and kings, typified this spiritual unguent, derived from Christ, the Head, to us, His members. We can have no share in Him as *Jesus,* except we become truly *Christians,* and so be in Him as *Christ,* anointed with that unction from the Holy One. The Spirit poured on Christ, the Head, is by Him diffused through all the members. "It appears that we all are the body of *Christ,* because we all are anointed: and we all in Him are both *Christ's* and *Christ,* because in some measure the whole *Christ* is Head and body." **and**—therefore. **ye know all things**—needful for acting aright

ADAM CLARKE

17. *The world passeth away.* All these things are continually fading and perishing, and the very state in which they are possessed is changing perpetually. *And the lust thereof.* The men of this world, their vain pursuits, and delusive pleasures are passing away in their successive generations, and their very memory perishes. *But he that doeth the will of God*—that seeks the pleasure, profit, and honor that comes from above—shall abide *for ever,* always happy through time and eternity, because God, the unchangeable Source of felicity, is his Portion.

18. *Little children, it is the last time.* This is the last dispensation of grace and mercy to mankind.

Antichrist shall come. Who is this antichrist? Any person, thing, doctrine, system of religion, polity, which is opposed to Christ, and to the spirit and spread of His gospel, is antichrist. *Many antichrists.* Many false prophets, false Messiahs, heretics, and corrupters of the truth. *Whereby we know that it is the last time.* That time which our Lord has predicted, and of which He has warned us.

19. *They went out from us.* These heretics had belonged to our Christian assemblies; they professed Christianity, and do so still. They are not Christians; we abhor their conduct and their creed. We never sent them to teach. *They were not of us.* For a considerable time before they left our assemblies they gave proofs that they had departed from the faith; *for if they had been of us,* if they had been apostles, and continued in the firm belief of the Christian doctrines, they would not have departed from us to form a sect of themselves. *That they were not all of us.* These false teachers probably drew many sincere souls away with them; and to this it is probable the apostle alludes when he says, *They were not all of us.* Some were; others were not.

20. *But ye have an unction.* The word *chrisma* signifies, not an *unction,* but an "ointment," the very thing itself by which anointing is effected; and so it was properly rendered in our former translations. Probably this is an allusion to the holy anointing oil of the law, and to Ps. xlv. 7: "God . . . . hath anointed thee with the oil of gladness"; He hath given Thee the plenitude of the Spirit, which none of "thy fellows," none of the prophets, ever received in such abundance. By this it is evident that not only the gifts of the Spirit, but the Holy Spirit himself, is intended. As oil was used among the Asiatics for the inauguration of persons into important offices, and this oil was acknowledged to be an emblem of the gifts and graces of the Holy Spirit, without which the duties of those offices could not be discharged; so it is put here for the Spirit himself, who presided in the Church, and from whom all gifts and graces flowed. The *chrism* or "ointment" here mentioned is also an allusion to the holy anointing ointment prescribed by God himself, Exod. xxx. 23-25, which was composed of fine myrrh, sweet cinnamon, sweet calamus, cassia lignea, and olive oil. This was an emblem of the gifts and graces of the divine Spirit. *Ye know all things.* Every truth of God necessary to your salvation and the salvation of man in general, and have no need of that knowledge of which the Gnostics boast.

But although the above is the sense in which this verse is generally understood, yet there is reason to doubt its accuracy. The adjective

MATTHEW HENRY

II. The mind and meaning with which he wrote to them. 1. By way of negation; not as suspecting their knowledge, *v.* 21. It is good to surmise well concerning our Christian brethren. A just confidence in religious persons may both encourage and contribute to their fidelity. 2. By way of assertion, *But because you know it* (you know *the truth in Jesus*), *and that no lie is of the truth.* Those who know the truth in any respect are thereby prepared to discern what is inconsistent therewith. No lie belongs to religion, either natural or revealed. *No lie is of the truth;* frauds and impostures then are very unfit means to support and propagate the truth.

III. The apostle further arraigns these seducers. 1. They are *liars*: *Who is a liar, but ye that denieth that Jesus is the Christ?* There is no truth so sacred and fully attested but some or other will contradict or deny it. 2. They are direct enemies to God as well as to the Lord Christ, *v.* 22. He that opposes Christ denies the witness and testimony of the father. The apostle may well infer, *Whosoever denies the Son the same has not the Father. But he that acknowledgeth the Son has the Father also*, *v.* 23.

IV. The apostle advises the disciples to continue in the old doctrines at first communicated to them, *v.* 24. Truth is older than error. The truth concerning Christ, that was at first delivered to the saints, is not to be exchanged for novelties. The Christian truth may plead antiquity, and be recommended thereby.

1. The sacred advantage they will receive by adhering to the primitive truth and faith. (1) They will continue thereby in holy union with God and Christ, *v.* 24. It is the truth of Christ abiding in us that is the means of severing us from sin and uniting us to the Son of God. (2) They will thereby secure the promise of eternal life, *v.* 25. Great is the promise that God makes to his faithful adherents. It is *eternal life*, which none but God can give.

2. The design of the apostle's writing to them. This letter is to fortify them against the deceivers of the age (*v.* 26), and therefore, if you continue not in what *you have heard from the beginning*, my writing and service will be in vain.

3. The instructive blessing they had received from heaven, *v.* 27. True Christians have an inward confirmation of the divine truth they have imbibed. This sacred chrism is commended on these accounts: (1) It is durable and lasting, *v.* 27. Divine illumination must be something continued. Temptations, snares, and seductions, arise. The anointing must abide. (2) It is better than human instruction, *v.* 27. You were instructed by us before you were anointed; but now our teaching is nothing in comparison to that. (3) It is a sure evidence of truth, *v.* 27. The Holy Spirit must needs be *the Spirit of truth.* The Spirit of truth will not lie; and he teacheth all things. (4) It will preserve those in whom it abides against seducers and their seduction, *v.* 27. It teaches you to abide in Christ; and, as it teaches you, it secures you.

Verses 28, 29

And now, little children, abide in him, v. 28. He would persuade by love, and prevail by endearment as well as by reason. Those that are anointed by the Lord Jesus are highly obliged to abide with him. This duty of perseverance and constancy is strongly urged: 1. From the consideration of his return at the great day of account, *v.* 28. It is here taken for granted that the Lord Jesus will come again. This was part of that truth they had heard from the beginning. Those who have continued with him throughout all their temptations shall have confidence, and joy, in the sight of him. On the contrary, those that have deserted him *shall be ashamed before him.* The apostle includes himself in the number. "Let not us be ashamed of you," as well as, "you will not be ashamed of yourselves."

JAMIESON, FAUSSET, BROWN

against Antichrist's seductions, and for Christian life and godliness. In the same measure as one hath *the Spirit*, in that measure (no more and no less) he knows all these things. **21. because ye know it, and that . . .**—Ye not *only know* what is the truth (concerning the Son and the Father, vs. 13), but also are able to detect a lie as a thing opposed to the truth. For right (a straight line) is the index of itself and of what is crooked [ESTIUS]. The *Greek* is susceptible of ALFORD's translation, "Because ye know it, and *because* no lie is of the truth" (lit., "every lie is excluded from being of the truth"). I therefore wrote (in this Epistle) to point out what the lie is, and who the liars are. **22. a liar**—*Greek*, "Who is the liar?" viz., guilty of *the* lie just mentioned (vs. 21). **that Jesus is the Christ**—the grand central truth. **He is Antichrist**—*Greek, "the* Antichrist"; not however here *personal*, but in the abstract; the ideal of Antichrist is "he that denieth the Father and the Son." To deny the latter is virtually to deny the former. Again, the truth as to the Son must be held in its integrity; to deny that Jesus is the Christ, or that He is the Son of God, or that He came in the flesh, invalidates the whole (Matt. 11:27). **23.** *Greek*, "Every one who denieth the Son, hath not the Father either" (ch. 4:2, 3): "inasmuch as God hath given Himself to us wholly to be enjoyed in Christ" [CALVIN]. **he**—*that acknowledgeth the Son hath the Father also*—These words ought not to be in italics, as though they were not in the original: for the oldest *Greek* MSS. have them. **hath**—viz., in his abiding possession as his "portion"; by living personal "fellowship." **acknowledgeth**—by open confession of Christ. **24. Let that**—truth respecting the Father and the Son, regarded as a seed not merely dropped in, but having taken root (ch. 3:9). **ye**—in the *Greek* standing emphatically at the beginning of the sentence. YE, therefore, *acknowledge the Son, and* so shall ye *have the Father also* (vs. 23). **from the beginning**—from the time of your first hearing the Gospel. **remain**—Translate as before, "abide." **ye also**—in your turn, as distinguished from "that which ye have heard," the seed *abiding in you.* Cf. vs. 27, "the anointing *abideth in you* . . . ye shall *abide in Him."* Having taken into us the living seed of the truth concerning the Father and the Son, we become transformed into the likeness of Him whose seed we have taken into us. **25. this is the promise**—*Eternal life* shall be the permanent consummation of thus *abiding in the Son and in the Father* (vs. 24). **he**—*Greek*, "Himself," Christ, "the Son" (cf. ch. 1:1). **promised**—(John 3:15, 36; 6:40, 47, 57; 17:2, 3). **26. These things**—(vss. 18-25). **have I written**—resumed from vs. 21 and vs. 14. **seduce you**—i.e., are trying to seduce or lead you into error. **27. But**—*Greek*, "And you (contrasting the believing readers with the *seducers;* the words "and you" stand prominent, the construction of the sentence following being altered, and no verb agreeing with 'and you' until 'need not') . . . the anointing . . ." (resumed from vs. 20). **received of him**—(John 1: 16). So we "are unto God a sweet savor of Christ." **abideth in you**—He tacitly thus admonishes them to say, when tempted by seducers, "The anointing abideth in us; we do not need a teacher [for we have the Holy Spirit as our teacher, Jer. 31:34; John 6:45; 16:13]; it teaches us the truth; in that teaching we will abide" [BENGEL]. **and**—and therefore. God is sufficient for them who are taught of Him; they are independent of all others, though, of course, not declining the Christian counsel of faithful ministers. "Mutual communication is not set aside, but approved of, in the case of those who are partakers of the anointing in one body" [BENGEL]. **the same anointing**—which ye once for all received, and which now still abides in you. **of**—"concerning." **all things**—essential to salvation; the point under discussion. Not that the believer is made infallible, for no believer here receives the Spirit in all its fulness, but only the measure needful for keeping him from soul-destroying error. So the Church, though having the Spirit in her, is not infallible (for many fallible members can never make an infallible whole), but is kept from ever wholly losing the saving truth. **no lie**—as Antichristian teaching. **ye shall abide in him**—(vs. 24, end)—even as "the anointing abideth in you." The oldest MSS. read the imperative, "*abide* in Him." **28. little children**—*Greek*, "little sons," as in vs. 12; believers of every stage and age. **abide in him**—Christ. John repeats his monition with a loving appellation, as a father addressing dear children. **when**—lit., "if"; the uncertainty is not as to the fact, but *the time.* **appear**—*Greek*, "be manifested." **we**—both writer and readers. **ashamed before him**—lit., "*from* Him"; shrink back *from Him* ashamed.

ADAM CLARKE

panta, which we translate *all things,* is most probably in the accusative case singular, having "man," or some such substantive, understood. The verse therefore should be translated: "You have an ointment from the Holy One, and you know or discern every man." This interpretation appears to be confirmed by v. 26, "those who are deceiving or misleading you"; and in the same sense should v. 27 be understood: "But as the same anointing teacheth you," not "of all things," but "of all men." It is plain from the whole tenor of the Epistle that John is guarding the Christians against seducers and deceivers, who were even then disturbing and striving to corrupt the Church.

21. *I have not written.* It is not because you are ignorant of these things that I write to you, *but because* you *know* them, and can by these judge of the doctrines of those false teachers, and clearly perceive that they are liars; for they contradict the truth which you have already received.

22. *Who is a liar but he that denieth that Jesus is the Christ?* Here we see some of the false doctrines which were then propagated in the world. There were certain persons who, while they acknowledged Jesus to be a divine teacher, denied Him to be the *Christ,* i.e., the Messiah. *He is antichrist, that denieth the Father and the Son.* He is antichrist who denies the supernatural and miraculous birth of Jesus Christ, who denies Jesus to be the Son of God, and who denies God to be the Father of the Lord Jesus; thus he denies the Father and the Son. The Jews in general, and the Gnostics in particular, denied the miraculous conception of Jesus; with both He was accounted no more than a common man, the son of Joseph and Mary. But the Gnostics held that a divine person, aeon, or angelic being, dwelt in him; but all things else relative to His miraculous generation and divinity they rejected. These were antichrists, who denied Jesus to be the Christ.

23. *Whosoever denieth the Son.* He who denies Jesus to be the Son of God, and consequently the Christ or Messiah, *he hath not the Father*—he can have no birth from above; he cannot be enrolled among the children of God, because none can be a child of God but by faith in Christ Jesus.

24. *Let that therefore abide in you.* Continue in the doctrines concerning the incarnation, passion, death, resurrection, ascension, and intercession of the Lord Jesus, which you have heard preached from the beginning by us, His apostles. *Ye also shall continue in the Son, and in the Father.* You who are preachers shall not only be acknowledged as ministers of the Church of Christ, but be genuine children of God, by faith in the Son of His love; and you all, thus continuing, shall have fellowship with the Father and with the Son.

25. *This is the promise.* God has promised eternal life to all who believe on Christ Jesus. So they who receive His doctrine, and continue in communion with the Father and the Son, shall have this *eternal life.*

26. *These things have I written.* Either meaning the whole Epistle or what is contained in the preceding verses, from the beginning of the eighteenth to the end of the twenty-fifth. *Them that seduce you.* That is, the "deceivers" that were among them, and who were laboring to pervert the followers of Christ.

27. *But the anointing which ye have received.* That "ointment," the gifts of the Holy Spirit, mentioned in v. 20. *Ye need not that any man teach you.* John does not say that those who had once received the teaching of the divine Spirit had no further need of the ministry of the gospel. No, but he says they had no need of such teaching as their false teachers proposed to them; nor of any other teaching that was different from that anointing, i.e., the teaching of the Spirit of God. No man, howsoever holy, wise, or pure, can ever be in such a state as to have no need of the gospel ministry; they who think so give the highest proof that they have never yet learned of Christ or His Spirit. *And is truth.* Because it is the Spirit of truth, John xvi. 13.

28. *And now, little children,* "beloved children," *abide in him*—in Christ Jesus. Let His

MATTHEW HENRY

2. From the consideration of the dignity of those who still adhere to Christ, *v.* 29. He that doeth righteousness may here be justly enough assumed as another name for him that abideth in Christ. Such a one must needs *be born of him.* He is renewed by the Spirit of Christ, after the image of Christ. He that is constant to the practice of religion in trying times gives good evidence that he is born from above, from the Lord Christ.

CHAPTER 3

Verses 1-3

The apostle,

I. Breaks forth into the admiration of that grace that is the spring of such a wonderful vouchsafement: *Behold what manner of love the Father hath bestowed upon us, that we should be called the sons of God!* It is wonderful condescending love of the eternal Father, that such as we should be made and called his sons. Strange, that the holy God is not ashamed to be called our Father, and to call us his sons!

II. Infers the honour of believers above the cognizance of the world, *v.* 1. Little does the world perceive the happiness of the genuine followers of Christ. Little does the world think that these poor, humble, contemned ones are the favourites of heaven, and will be inhabitants there ere long. Their Lord was here unknown as well as they, *v.* 1. Let the followers of Christ be content with hard fare here, since they are in a land of strangers, among those who little know them, and their Lord was so treated before them.

III. Exalts these persevering disciples in the prospect of the certain revelation of their state and dignity. 1. Their present honourable relation is asserted, *v.* 2. We have the nature of sons by regeneration. 2. The glory pertaining to the sonship and adoption is reserved for another world. The sons of God must walk by faith, and live by hope.

3. The time of the revelation of the sons of God is determined: *But we know that when he shall appear we shall be like him.* The sons of God will be known and be made manifest by their likeness to their head.

JAMIESON, FAUSSET, BROWN

Contrast "boldness in the day of judgment," ch. 4: 17; cf. ch. 3:21; 5:14. In the Apocalypse (written, therefore, BENGEL thinks, subsequently), Christ's coming is represented as put off to a greater distance. **29.** *The heading of the second division of the Epistle:* "God is righteous; therefore, every one that doeth righteousness is born of Him." Love is the grand feature and principle of "righteousness" selected for discussion, ch. 2:29 to 3:3. **If ye know . . . ye know**—distinct *Greek* verbs: "if ye *are aware* (are in possession of the knowledge) . . . ye *discern* or apprehend also that. . . ." Ye are already aware that *God* ("He" includes both "the Father," *of* whom the believer *is born* [end of this verse, and ch. 3:1], and "the Son," vss. 1, 23) *is righteous,* ye must necessarily, thereby, perceive also the consequence of that truth, viz., "that everyone that doeth righteousness (and he alone; lit., *the* righteousness such as the righteous God approves) is born of Him." The righteous produceth the righteous. We are never said to be *born* again *of Christ,* but of *God,* with whom Christ is one.

CHAPTER 3

VSS. 1-24. DISTINGUISHING MARKS OF THE CHILDREN OF GOD AND THE CHILDREN OF THE DEVIL. BROTHERLY LOVE THE ESSENCE OF TRUE RIGHTEOUSNESS. **1. Behold**—calling attention, as to some wonderful exhibition, little as the world sees to admire. This verse is connected with the previous ch. 2:29, thus: All our *doing* of *righteousness* is a mere sign that God, of His matchless love, has adopted us as children; it does not save us, but is a proof that we are saved of His grace. **what manner of**—of what surpassing excellence, how gracious on His part, how precious to us. **love . . . bestowed**—He does not say that God hath given us some gift, but *love itself* and the fountain of all honors, the heart itself, and that not for our works or efforts, but of His grace [LUTHER]. **that**—"what manner of love"; resulting in, proved by, our being. . . . The immediate *effect aimed at* in the bestowal of this love is, "*that* we should be called children of God." **should be called**—should have received the privilege of such a glorious *title* (though seeming so imaginary to the world), along with the glorious *reality.* With God *to call* is to *make really to be.* Who so great as God? What nearer relationship than that of *sons?* The oldest MSS. add, "And we ARE so" really. **therefore**—"on this account," because "we are (really) so." **us**—the children, like the Father. **it knew him not**—viz., the Father. "If they who regard not God, hold thee in any account, feel alarmed about thy state" [BENGEL]. Contrast ch. 5:1. The world's whole course is one great act of non-recognition of God. **2. Beloved**—by the Father, and therefore by me. **now**—in contrast to "not yet." We *now* already are really sons, though not recognized as such by the world, and (as the consequence) we look for the visible manifestation of our sonship, which *not yet* has taken place. **doth not yet appear**—*Greek,* "it hath not yet ('at any time'), *Greek* aorist) been visibly manifested what we shall be"—what further glory we shall attain by virtue of this our sonship. The "what" suggests a something inconceivably glorious. **but**—omitted in the oldest MSS. Its insertion in *English Version* gives a wrong antithesis. It is not, "*We do not yet know manifestly* what . . ., but we know. . . ." *Believers have* some degree of the manifestation already, though the *world has not.* The connection is, The manifestation *to the world* of what we shall be, has not yet taken place; *we know* (in general; as a matter of *well-assured knowledge;* so the *Greek*) that when (lit., "if"; expressing no doubt as to the fact, but only as to the time; also implying the coming preliminary fact, on which the consequence follows, Mal. 1:6; John 14:3) He (not "it," viz., that which is not yet manifested [ALFORD]) shall be manifested (vs. 5; ch. 2:28), we shall be like Him (Christ; all sons have a substantial resemblance to their father, and Christ, whom we shall be like, is "the express image of the Father's person," so that in resembling Christ, we shall resemble the Father). We *wait for the manifestation* (lit., the "apocalypse"; the same term as is applied to Christ's own manifestation) *of the sons of God.* After our natural birth, the new birth into the life of grace is needed, which is to be followed by the new birth into the life of glory; the two latter alike are termed "the regeneration" (Matt. 19:28). The resurrection of our bodies is a kind of coming out of the womb of the earth, and being born into another life. Our first temptation was that we should be like God in knowl-

ADAM CLARKE

word and Spirit continually abide in you, and have communion with the Father and the Son. *That, when he shall appear,* to judge the world, *we may have confidence,* "freedom of speech, liberty of access, boldness," from a conviction that our cause is good, and that we have had proper ground for exultation; *and not be ashamed,* confounded, when it appears that those who were brought to Christ Jesus have apostatized.

29. *If ye know that he is righteous,* that God is a holy God, *ye know* also, *that every one who doeth righteousness,* who lives a holy life, following the commandments of God, *is born of him,* "begotten of Him"—is made a partaker of the divine nature, without which he could neither have a holy heart nor live a holy life. This verse properly belongs to the following chapter and should not be separated from it. The subject is the same, and does not stand in any strict relation to that with which the twenty-eighth verse concludes.

CHAPTER 3

1. *Behold, what manner of love.* Whole volumes might be written upon this and the following two verses without exhausting the extraordinary subject contained in them, viz., the love of God to man. *What manner of love.* "What great love," as to both quantity and quality, for these ideas are included in the original term. The length, the breadth, the depth, the height, he does not attempt to describe. *The Father hath bestowed.* For we had neither claim nor merit that we should be called, that is, "constituted" or "made," *the sons of God,* who were before children of the wicked one. After "that we might be called," "and we are" is added by several MSS. *Therefore the world*—the Jews, and all who know not God, and are seeking their portion in this life. *Knoweth us not*—do not "acknowledge, respect, love, or approve" of us. In this sense the word is here to be understood. We have often seen that this is a frequent use of the term "know," in both Hebrew and Greek, in the Old Testament and also in the New. *Because it knew him not.* The Jews did not "acknowledge" Jesus; they "approved" neither of Him, His doctrine, nor His manner of life.

2. *Now are we the sons of God.* He speaks of those who are begotten of God and who work righteousness. *And it doth not yet appear what we shall be.* "It is not yet manifest"; though we know that we are the children of God, we do not know that state of glorious excellence to which, as such, we shall be raised.

When he shall appear. "When He shall be manifested"; i.e., when He comes the second time, and shall be manifested in His glorified human nature to judge the world. *We shall be like him,* for our vile bodies shall be made like unto His glorious body; *we shall see him as he is,* in all the glory and majesty of both the divine and human nature. See Phil. iii. 21; and John xvii. 24: "Father, I will that they also, whom thou hast given me, be with me where I am; that they may behold my glory."

MATTHEW HENRY

4. Their likeness to him is argued from the sight they shall have of him: *We shall be like him, for we shall see him as he is.* All shall see him, but not as *he is,* to those in heaven. The wicked shall see him in his frowns; but these shall see him in the smiles and beauty of his face. Their likeness shall enable them to see him as the blessed do in heaven.

IV. Urges to the prosecution of holiness, *v.* 3. The sons of God know that their Lord is holy and pure. Those then who hope to live with him must study the utmost purity, their hope of heaven will dictate and constrain them so to do. It is a contradiction to such hope to indulge sin and impurity. As we are sanctified by faith, we must be sanctified by hope. That we may be saved by hope we must be purified by hope.

Verses 4–10

Multiplied arguments against sin, and all communion with the works of darkness.

I. From the nature of sin. It is a contrariety to the divine law, *v.* 4. Commission of sin now is the rejection of the divine law, and this is the rejection of the divine authority, and consequently of God himself.

II. From the errand of the Lord Jesus in this world, which was to remove sin, *v.* 5. He takes sin away, that he may conform us to himself, *and in him is no sin.* Those that expect communion with Christ above should study communion with him here in the utmost purity.

III. From the opposition between sin and a real union with the Lord Christ, *v.* 6. He that abideth in Christ continues not in the practice of sin. Those that abide in Christ abide in their covenant with him. They abide in the potent light and knowledge of him; and therefore it may be concluded *that he that sinneth hath not seen him, neither known him.* Practical renunciation of sin is the great evidence of saving knowledge of the Lord Christ.

IV. From the connection between the practice of righteousness and a state of righteousness. The practice of sin and a justified state are inconsistent: "*Little children, let no man deceive you. He that doeth righteousness is righteous.*" It may appear that

JAMIESON, FAUSSET, BROWN

edge, and by that we fell; but being raised by Christ, we become truly like Him, by knowing Him as we are known, and by seeing Him as He is [PEARSON, *Creed*]. As the first immortality which Adam lost was to be able not to die, so the last shall be not to be able to die. As man's first free choice or will was to be able not to sin, so our last shall be not to be able to sin [AUGUSTINE, *Civit. Dei*, B. 22, c. 30]. The devil fell by aspiring to God's *power;* man, by aspiring to his *knowledge;* but aspiring after God's *goodness,* we shall ever grow in His likeness. The transition from *God* the Father to "He," "Him," referring to Christ (who alone is ever said in Scripture to be *manifested;* not the Father, John 1:18), implies the entire unity of the Father and the Son. **for . . .** —Continual beholding generates likeness (II Cor. 3: 18); as the face of the moon being always turned towards the sun, reflects its light and glory. **see him**—not in His innermost Godhead, but as manifested in Christ. None but the pure can see the infinitely Pure One. In all these passages the *Greek* is the same verb *opsomai;* not denoting the action of seeing, but the state of him to whose eye or mind the object is presented; hence the *Greek* verb is always in the middle or reflexive voice, to *perceive* and *inwardly appreciate* [TITTMANN]. Our spiritual bodies will appreciate and recognize spiritual beings hereafter, as our natural bodies now do natural objects. **3. this hope**—of being hereafter "like Him." *Faith* and *love,* as well as *hope,* occur in vss. 11, 23. **in**—rather, "(resting) *upon* Him"; grounded on His promises. **purifieth himself**—by Christ's Spirit in him (John 15:5, end). "Thou purifiest thyself, not of thyself, but of Him who comes that He may dwell in thee" [AUGUSTINE]. One's justification through faith is presupposed. **as he is pure**—unsullied with any uncleanness. The Second Person, by whom both the Law and Gospel were given. **4.** Sin is incompatible with birth from God (vss. 1-3). John often sets forth the same truth *negatively,* which he had before set forth *positively.* He had shown, birth from God involves self-purification; he now shows where sin, i.e., the want of self-purification, is, there is no birth from God. **Whosoever**—*Greek,* "Every one who." **committeth sin**—in contrast to vs. 3, "Every man that hath this hope in Him purifieth himself"; and vs. 7, "He that doeth righteousness." **transgresseth . . . the law**—*Greek,* "committeth transgression of law." God's law of purity; and so shows he has no such hope of being hereafter pure as God is pure, and, therefore, that he is not born of God. **for**—*Greek,* "and." **sin is . . . transgression of . . . law**—definition of *sin* in general. The *Greek* having the article to both, implies that they are convertible terms. The *Greek* "sin" (*hamartia*) is lit., "a missing of the mark." God's will being that mark to be ever aimed at. "By the law is the knowledge of sin." The crookedness of a line is shown by being brought into juxtaposition with a straight ruler. **5.** Additional proof of the incompatibility of sin and sonship; the very object of Christ's manifestation in the flesh was *to take away* (by one act, and entirely, aorist) all sins, as the scapegoat did typically. **and**—another proof of the same. **in him is no sin**—not "was," but "is," as in vs. 7, "He *is* righteous," and vs. 3, "He *is* pure." Therefore we are to be so. **6.** He reasons from Christ's own entire separation from sin, that those in him must also be separate from it. **abideth in him**—as the branch in the vine, by vital union living by His life. **sinneth not**—In so far as he abides in Christ, so far is he free from all sin. The ideal of the Christian. The life of sin and the life of God mutually exclude one another, just as darkness and light. In matter of fact, believers do fall into sins (ch. 1:8-10; 2:1, 2); but all such sins are alien from the life of God, and need Christ's cleansing blood, without application to which the life of God could not be maintained. He sinneth not so long as he abideth in Christ. **whosoever sinneth hath not seen him**—*Greek* perfect, "has not seen, and does not see Him." Again the *ideal* of Christian intuition and knowledge is presented (Matt. 7:23). All sin as such is at variance with the notion of one regenerated. Not that "whosoever is betrayed into sins has never seen nor known God"; but *in so far* as sin exists, *in that degree* the spiritual intuition and knowledge of God do not exist in him. **neither** —"not even." To *see* spiritually is a further step than *to know;* for by *knowing* we come to *seeing* by vivid realization and experimentally. **7, 8.** The same truth stated, with the addition that he who sins is, so far as he sins, "of the devil." **let no man deceive you**—as Antinomians try to mislead men. **righteousness**—*Greek,* "*the* righteousness," viz., of Christ or God. **he that doeth . . . is righteous**—Not his *doing* makes him *righteous,* but his *being right-*

ADAM CLARKE

3. *And every man that hath this hope in him.* All who have the hope of seeing Christ as He is; that is, of enjoying Him in His own glory. *Purifieth himself*—abstains from all evil, and keeps himself from all that is in the world, viz., the lusts of the flesh, of the eye, and the pride of life. God having purified his heart, it is his business to keep himself "in the love of God, looking for the mercy of our Lord Jesus Christ unto eternal life." The apostle does not here speak of any man purifying his own heart, because this is impossible; but of his persevering in the state of purity into which the Lord has brought him. The words, however, may be understood of a man's anxiously using all the means that lead to purity; and imploring God for the sanctifying Spirit, to "cleanse the thoughts of his heart by its inspiration, that he may perfectly love Him, and worthily magnify His name." *As he is pure.* Till he is as completely saved from his sins as Christ was free from sin. Many tell us that "this never can be done, for no man can be saved from sin in this life." Will these persons permit us to ask, How much sin may we be saved from in this life? Something must be ascertained on this subject: (1) That the soul may have some determinate object in view; (2) That it may not lose its time, or employ its faith and energy, in praying for what is impossible to be attained. Now, as "he was manifested to take away our sins," v. 5, to "destroy the works of the devil," v. 8; and as his blood cleanseth from all sin and unrighteousness, chap. i. 7, 9; is it not evident that God means that believers in Christ shall be saved from all sin? For if His blood cleanses from all sin, if He destroys the works of the devil (and sin is the work of the devil), and if he who "is born of God doth not commit sin," v. 9, then he must be cleansed from all sin; and while he continues in that state he lives without sinning against God; for the "seed [of God] remaineth in him: and he cannot sin, because he is born [or begotten] of God," v. 9. How strangely warped and blinded by prejudice and system must men be who, in the face of such evidence as this, will still dare to maintain that no man can be saved from his sin in this life; but must daily commit sin, in thought, word, and deed, as the Westminster divines have asserted! That is, every man is laid under the fatal necessity of sinning as many ways against God as the devil does through his natural wickedness and malice; for even the devil himself can have no other way of sinning against God except by thought, word, and deed. And yet, according to these, and others of the same creed, "even the most regenerate sin thus against God as long as they live." Could not the grace that saved them partially save them perfectly? Could not that power of God that saved them from habitual sin save them from occasional or accidental sin? Shall we suppose that sin, how potent soever it may be, is as potent as the Spirit and grace of Christ?

4. *Sin is the transgression of the law.* The spirit of the law as well as of the gospel is that "we should love God with all our powers, and our neighbor as ourselves." All disobedience is contrary to love; therefore *sin is the transgression of the law,* whether the act refers immediately to God or to our neighbor.

5. *And ye know that he was manifested to take away our sins.* He came into the world to destroy the power, pardon and guilt, and cleanse from the pollution of sin. *In him is no sin.* And therefore He is properly qualified to be the atoning Sacrifice for the sins of men.

6. *Whosoever abideth in him.* By faith, love, and obedience. *Sinneth not.* Because his heart if purified by faith. *Hath not seen him.* It is no unusual thing with this apostle, both in his Gospel and in his Epistles, to put occasionally the past for the present, and the present for the past tense. It is very likely that here he puts, after the manner of the Hebrew, the preterite for the present: He who sins against God "doth not see Him, neither doth he know Him."

7. *Let no man deceive you.* By asserting either that "you cannot be saved from sin in this life" or "that sin will do you no harm and cannot alter your state, if you are adopted into the family of God; for sin cannot annul this

MATTHEW HENRY

righteousness may in several places of scripture be justly rendered *religion*, as Matt. v. 10, *Blessed are those that are persecuted for righteousness' sake*, that is, for religion's sake. To do righteousness then is to practise religion. The practice of religion cannot subsist without a principle of integrity and conscience.

V. From the relation between the sinner and the devil, and thereupon from the design of the Lord Christ. 1. From the relation between the sinner and the devil. *To commit sin* is here to live under the power and dominion of it; and he who does so *is of the devil.*

2. From the design and office of the Lord Christ against the devil, *v.* 8. He came into our world that he might conquer him. Sin will he loosen and dissolve more and more, till he has quite destroyed it. Let not us serve or indulge what the Son of God came to destroy.

VI. From the connection between regeneration and the relinquishment of sin: *Whosoever is born of God doth not commit sin.* To be born of God is to be inwardly renewed, and restored to a holy rectitude of nature by the power of the Spirit of God. *Such a one committeth not sin, his seed remaineth in him.* Renewing grace is an abiding principle. Religion is not an art, an acquired dexterity and skill, but a new nature. And thereupon the consequence is the regenerate person *cannot sin.* He cannot continue in the course and practice of sin. And the reason is *because he is born of God.* There is that light in his mind which shows him the evil and malignity of sin. There is that bias upon his heart which disposes him to loathe and hate sin. There is the spiritual disposition, that breaks the force and fulness of the sinful acts. It is not reckoned the person's sin, in the gospel account, where the bent and frame of the mind and spirit are against it. The unregenerate person is morally unable for what is religiously good. The regenerate person is happily disabled for sin.

VII. From the discrimination between the children of God and the children of the devil. They have their distinct characters, *v.* 10. Now the seed of the serpent is known: 1. By neglect of religion: *Whosoever doeth not righteously is not of God*, but, on the contrary, of the devil. 2. By hatred of fellow-christians, *v.* 10.

Verses 11–13

I. He recommends fraternal Christian love, *v.* 11. We should love the Lord Jesus, and value his love, and consequently love all the objects of it.

II. He dissuades from what is contrary thereto and that by the example of Cain. He was as the first-born of the serpent's seed; was of *the wicked one.* He imitated and resembled the first wicked one, the devil. His ill-will had no restraint; it proceeded so far as to accomplish murder, *v.* 12. Sin, indulged, knows no bound. He was vexed with the superiority of Abel's service, and envied him the favour and acceptance he had with God. And for these he martyred his brother, *v.* 12. Ill-will will teach us to hate and revenge what we should admire and imitate.

III. He infers that it is no wonder that good men are so served now, *v.* 13. The serpentine nature still continues in the world. Wonder not then that the serpentine world hates and hisses at you.

Verses 14–19

The beloved apostle can scarcely touch upon the mention of sacred love, but he must enlarge upon the enforcement of it.

I. It is a mark of our transition into a state of life, *v.* 14. We may know it by the evidences of our faith in Christ, of which this love to our brethren is one. This love,

JAMIESON, FAUSSET, BROWN

eous (justified by the righteousness of God in Christ, Rom. 10:3-10) makes him to do *righteousness:* an inversion common in familiar language, logical in reality, though not in form, as in Luke 7:47; John 8:47. Works do not justify, but the justified man works. **8. He that committeth sin is of the devil**—in contrast to "He that doeth righteousness," vs. 7. He is *a son of the devil* (vs. 10; John 8:44). John does not, however, say, "born of the devil." as he does "born of God," for "the devil begets none, nor does he create any; but whoever imitates the devil becomes a child of the devil by imitating him, not by proper birth" [AUGUSTINE, *Tract*, 4. 10]. From the devil there is not generation, but corruption [BENGEL]. **sinneth from the beginning**—from the time that any began to sin [ALFORD]; from the time that he became what he is, the devil. He seems to have kept his first estate only a very short time after his creation [BENGEL]. *Since the fall of man* [at the beginning *of our world*] *the devil is* (*ever*) *sinning* (this is the force of "sinneth"; he has sinned from the beginning, is the cause of all sins, and still goes on sinning; present). As the author of sin, and prince of this world, he has never ceased to seduce man to sin [LUECKE]. **destroy**—break up and do away with; bruising and crushing the serpent's head. **works of the devil**—sin, and all its awful consequences. John argues, Christians cannot do that which Christ came to destroy. **9. Whosoever is born of God**—lit., "Everyone that is begotten of God." **doth not commit sin**—His higher nature, as one born or begotten of God, doth not sin. *To be begotten of God* and *to sin*, are states mutually excluding one another. In so far as one sins, he makes it doubtful whether he be *born of God.* **his seed**—the living word of God, made by the Holy Spirit the seed in us of a new life and the continual mean of sanctification. **remaineth**—abideth in him (*Note*, cf. vs. 6; John 5:38). This does not contradict ch. 1:8, 9; the regenerate show the utter incompatibility of *sin* with *regeneration*, by cleansing away every sin into which they may be betrayed by the old nature, at once in the blood of Christ. **cannot sin, because he is born of God**—"because it is *of God* that *he is born*" (so the *Greek* order, as compared with the order of the same words in the beginning of the verse); not "because he *was* born of God" (the *Greek* is perfect, which is *present* in meaning, not aorist); it is not said, Because a man was once for all born of God he never afterwards can sin; but, Because he is born of God, the seed abiding now in Him, he cannot sin; so long as it energetically abides, sin can have no place. Cf. Genesis 39:9, Joseph, "How CAN I do this great wickedness and sin against God?" The principle within me is at utter variance with it. The regenerate life is incompatible with sin, and gives the believer a hatred for sin in every shape, and an unceasing desire to resist it. **10. children of the devil**—(*Note*, vs. 8; Acts 13:10). There is no middle class between the children of God and the children of the devil. **doeth not righteousness**—Contrast ch. 2:29. **he that loveth not his brother**—(ch. 4:8)—a particular instance of that *love* which is the sum and fulfilment of all righteousness, and the token (not loud professions, or even seemingly good works) that distinguishes God's children from the devil's. **11. the message**—"announcement," as of something good; not a mere *command*, as the law. The Gospel *message* of Him who loved us, announced by His servants, is, that we *love the brethren;* not here all mankind, but those who are our brethren in Christ, children of the same family of God, of whom we have been born anew. **12.** *who*—not in the *Greek.* **of that wicked one**—Translate, "*evil* one," to accord with "Because his own works were *evil.*" Cf. vs. 8, "of the devil," in contrast to "of God," vs. 10. **slew he him? Because his own works were evil, and his brother's righteous**—through envy and hatred of his brother's piety, owing to which God accepted Abel's, but rejected Cain's offering. Enmity from the first existed between the seed of the woman and the seed of the serpent. **13. Marvel not**—The marvel would be if the world loved you. **the world**—of whom Cain is the representative (vs. 12). **hate you**—as Cain hated even his own brother, and that to the extent of murdering him. The world feels its bad works tacitly reproved by your good works. **14. We**—emphatical; hated though we be by the world, *we* know what the world knows not. **know**—as an assured fact. **passed**—*changed our state.* Colossians 1:13, "from the power of darkness . . . translated into the kingdom of His dear Son." **from death unto life**—lit., "*out of the* death (which enthrals the unregenerate) *into the* life" (of the regenerate). A palpable coincidence of language and

ADAM CLARKE

adoption." Hear God, you deceivers! *He that doeth righteousness is righteous*, according to his state, nature, and the extent of his moral powers, *Even as he is righteous.* Allowing for the disparity that must necessarily exist between that which is bounded and that which is without limits. As God, in the infinitude of His nature, is righteous, so they, being filled with Him, are in their limited nature righteous.

8. *He that committeth sin is of the devil.* Hear this, you who cannot bear the thought of that doctrine that states believers are to be saved from all sin in this life! *He that committeth sin is* a child *of the devil*, and shows that he has still the nature of the devil in him; *for the devil sinneth from the beginning*—he was the father of sin, brought sin into the world, and maintains sin in the world by living in the hearts of his own children, and thus leading them to transgression; and persuading others that they cannot be saved from their sins in this life, that he may secure a continual residence in their hearts. He knows that if he has a place there throughout life, he will probably have it at death; and, if so, throughout eternity. *For this purpose.* For "this very end," with this very design, was Jesus manifested in the flesh, *that he might destroy*, "that He might loose," the bonds of sin, and dissolve the power, influence, and connection of sin.

9. *Whosoever is born of God*, "begotten" of God, *doth not commit sin.* "That is," say some, "as he used to do; he does not sin habitually as he formerly did." This is bringing the influence and privileges of the heavenly birth very low indeed. We have the most indubitable evidence that many of the heathen philosophers had acquired, by mental discipline and cultivation, an entire ascendency over all their wonted vicious habits.

10. *In this the children of God are manifest.* Here is a fearful text. Who is a child of the devil? He that commits sin. Who is a child of God? He that works righteousness. By this text we shall stand or fall before God, whatever our particular creed may say to the contrary. *Neither he that loveth not his brother.* No man is of God who is not ready on all emergencies to do any act of kindness for the comfort, relief, and support of any human being. For, as God made of one blood all the nations of men to dwell upon the face of the whole earth, so all are of one family; and consequently all are brethren, and should love as brethren.

11. *For this is the message.* See chap. i. 5. *From the beginning* God has taught men that they should *love one another.*

12. *Not as Cain.* Men should not act to each other as Cain did to his brother, Abel. He murdered him because he was better than himself. But who was Cain? "He was of the devil."

13. *Marvel not . . . if the world hate you.* Expect no better treatment from unconverted Jews and Gentiles than Abel received from his wicked and cruel brother.

14. *We know that we have passed from death unto life. Death* and *life* are represented here as two distinct territories, states, or kingdoms, to either of which the inhabitants of either may be removed. This is implied in the term denoting "change of place," and "I go." It is the same figure which Paul uses, Col. i. 13: "Who hath delivered us from the power of darkness,

MATTHEW HENRY

1. Supposes a general love to mankind. Mankind are to be loved: (1) As the excellent work of God, made by him, and made in wonderful resemblance of him. (2) As being beloved in Christ. A world so beloved of God should accordingly be loved by us. This love will include all due love to enemies themselves.

2. It includes a peculiar love to the Christian society. They are not so much loved for their own sakes as for the sake of God and Christ, who have loved them. This is the issue of faith in Christ, of our passage from death to life.

II. The hatred of our brethren is a sign of our deadly state, *v.* 14. This the apostle argues, *v.* 15. Hatred of the person is a hatred of life and welfare, and naturally tends to desire the extinction of it. Now he who by the disposition of his heart is a murderer *cannot have eternal life abiding in him.*

III. The example of God and Christ should inflame our hearts with this holy love, *v.* 16. The great God has given his Son to the death for us. Surely we should love those whom God hath loved, and so loved.

IV. The apostle proceeds to show us what should be the effect of this our Christian love. 1. It must be so fervent as to make us willing to suffer even to death for the safety and salvation of the dear brethren, *v.* 16. How mortified should the Christian be to this life, and how well assured of a better!

2. It must be compassionate, liberal, and communicative to the necessities of the brethren, *v.* 17. Those who have this world's good must love a good God more, and their good brethren more, and be ready to distribute it for their sakes. This love to the brethren is love to God in them; and where there is none of this love to them there is no true love to God at all.

There may be other fruits of this love, *v.* 18. Compliments and flatteries become not Christians; but the sincere expressions of sacred affection, and the services or labours of love, do.

V. This love will evince our sincerity in religion, and give us hope towards God, *v.* 19. It is a great happiness to be assured of our integrity in religion. The way to secure our inward peace, is to abound in love and in the works of love.

JAMIESON, FAUSSET, BROWN

thought, the beloved disciple adopting his Lord's words. **because we love the brethren**—the ground, not of our *passing over out of death into life,* but of our *knowing* that we have so. *Love,* on our part, is the *evidence* of our justification and regeneration, not the *cause* of them. **He that loveth not**—Most of the oldest MSS. omit "his brother," which makes the statement more general. **abideth**—still. **in death**—"in *the* (spiritual) death" (ending in eternal death) which is the state of all by nature. His want of *love* evidences that no saving change has passed over him. **15. hateth**—equivalent to "loveth not" (vs. 14); there is no medium between the two. "Love and hatred, like light and darkness, life and death, necessarily replace, as well as necessarily exclude, one another" [ALFORD]. **is a murderer**—because indulging in that passion, which, if followed out to its natural consequences, would make him one. "Whereas, vs. 16 desires us to lay down our lives for the brethren; *duels* require one (awful to say!) to risk *his own* life, rather than not deprive *another* of life" [BENGEL]. God regards the inward disposition as tantamount to the outward act which would flow from it. Whomsoever one hates, one wishes to be dead. **hath**—Such a one still "abideth in death." It is not his *future* state, but his *present,* which is referred to. He who hates (i.e., loveth not) his brother (vs. 14), cannot in this his present state have eternal life abiding in him. **16.** What true *love to the brethren* is, illustrated by the love of Christ to us. **Hereby**—*Greek,* "Herein." **the love** *of God*—The words "of God" are not in the original. Translate, "We arrive at the knowledge of love"; we apprehend what true love is. **he**—Christ. **and we**—on our part, if absolutely needed for the glory of God, the good of the Church, or the salvation of a brother. **lives**—Christ alone laid down His one *life* for us all; we ought to lay down our *lives* severally for the lives of the brethren; if not actually, at least virtually, by giving our time, care, labors, prayers, substance: *"Non nobis, sed omnibus."* Our life ought not to be dearer to us than God's own Son was to Him. The apostles and martyrs acted on this principle. **17. this world's good**—lit., "livelihood" or substance. If we ought to lay down our *lives* for the brethren (vs. 16), how much more ought we not to withhold our *substance*? **seeth**—not merely *casually,* but deliberately *contemplates* as a spectator; *Greek,* "beholds." **shutteth up his bowels** *of compassion*—which had been momentarily opened by the *spectacle* of his brother's need. The "bowels" mean the *heart,* the seat of compassion. **how**—*How* is it possible that "the love of (i.e. *to*) God dwelleth (*Greek,* 'abideth') in him?" Our superfluities should yield to the necessities; our comforts, and even our necessaries in some measure, should yield to the extreme wants of our brethren. "Faith gives Christ to me; love flowing from faith gives me to my neighbor." **18.** When the venerable John could no longer walk to the meetings of the Church but was borne thither by his disciples, he always uttered the same address to the Church; he reminded them of that one commandment which he had received from Christ Himself, as comprising all the rest, and forming the distinction of the new covenant, "My little children, love one another." When the brethren present, wearied of hearing the same thing so often, asked why he always repeated the same thing, he replied, "Because it is the commandment of the Lord, and if this one thing be attained, it is enough" [JEROME]. **in word**—*Greek,* "*with* word . . . *with* tongue, but *in* deed and truth." **19. hereby**—*Greek,* "herein"; in our *loving in deed and in truth* (vs. 18). **we know**—The oldest MSS. have "we shall know," viz., if we fulfil the command (vs. 18). **of the truth**—that we are real disciples of, and belonging to, *the truth,* as it is in Jesus: begotten of God with the word of truth. Having herein *the truth* radically, we shall be sure not to love merely *in word and tongue.* (vs. 18). **assure**—lit., "persuade," viz., so as to cease to condemn us; satisfy the questionings and doubts of our consciences as to whether we be accepted *before* God or not (cf. Matt. 28:14; Acts 12:20, *"having made* Blastus their friend," lit., "persuaded"). The "heart," as the seat of the feelings, is our inward *judge;* the *conscience,* as the witness, acts either as our justifying advocate, or our condemning accuser, before God even now. John 8:9, has "conscience," but the passage is omitted in most old MSS. John nowhere else uses the term "conscience." Peter and Paul alone use it. **before him**—as in the sight of Him, the omniscient Searcher of *hearts. Assurance* is designed to be the ordinary experience and privilege of the believer. **20.** LUTHER and BENGEL take this verse as consoling the believer whom his *heart condemns;* and who,

ADAM CLARKE

and hath translated us into the kingdom" of the Son of His love. *We know,* says the apostle, *that* "we are passed over from the territory of death to the kingdom of life," *because we love the brethren,* which those who continue in the old kingdom—under the old covenant—can never do; for *he that loveth not his brother abideth in death.* He has never changed his original residence. He is still an unconverted, unrenewed sinner.

15. *Whosoever hateth his brother is a murderer.* He has the same principle in him which was in Cain, and it may lead to the same consequences. *No murderer hath eternal life.* Eternal life springs from an indwelling God, and God cannot dwell in the heart where hatred and malice dwell. This text has been quoted to prove that no murderer can be saved. This is not said in the text; and there have been many instances of persons who have been guilty of murder having had deep and genuine repentance, and who doubtless found mercy from His hands who prayed for His murderers, "Father, forgive them; for they know not what they do."

16. *Hereby perceive we the love of God.* This sixteenth verse of this third chapter of John's First Epistle is, in the main, an exact counterpart of the sixteenth verse of the third chapter of John's Gospel: "God so loved the world, that he gave his only begotten Son." Here the apostle says, We *perceive,* "we have known," *the love of God, because he laid down his life for us. Of God* is not in the text, but it is preserved in one MS. and in two or three of the versions; but though this does not establish its authenticity, yet *of God* is necessarily understood or "of Christ."

17. *But whoso hath this world's good.* Here is a test of this love; if we do not divide our bread with the hungry, we certainly would not lay down our lives for Him. Whatever love we may pretend to mankind, if we are not charitable and benevolent, we give the lie to our profession. *This world's good.* "The life of this world," i.e., the means of life. *How dwelleth the love of God in him?* That is, it cannot possibly dwell in such a person. Hardheartedness and God's love never meet together; much less can they be associated.

18. *My little children,* "my beloved children," *let us not love in word*—in merely allowing the general doctrine of love to God and man to be just and right. *Neither in tongue*—in making professions of love, and of a charitable and humane disposition, and resting there. *But in deed*—by humane and merciful acts. *And in truth*—feeling the disposition of which we speak.

19. *Hereby we know that we are of the truth,* that we have the true religion of the Lord Jesus, *and shall assure our hearts,* be persuaded in our consciences that we have the truth as it is in Jesus, as no man can impose upon himself by imagining he loves when he does not. He may make empty professions to others, but if he loves either God or man, he knows it because he feels it. And love unfelt is not love; it is "word" or "tongue." This the apostle lays down as a test of a man's Christianity, and it is the strongest and most infallible test that can be given.

MATTHEW HENRY

Verses 20–22

The apostle proceeds here,

I. To establish the court of conscience, *v.* 20. Our heart here is our self-reflecting judicial power, whereby we can take cognizance of ourselves, and accordingly pass a judgment upon our state towards God; and so it is the same with conscience. Conscience is God's viceregent, calls the court in his name, and acts for him. If conscience condemn us, God does so too. God is a greater witness than our conscience, and knoweth more against us than it does: *he knoweth all things.*

If conscience acquit us, God does so too (*v.* 21). Then have we assurance that he accepts us now, and will acquit us in the great day of account. Let conscience therefore be heard, be well-informed, and diligently attended to.

II. To indicate the privilege of those who have a good conscience towards God. They have interest in heaven; their suits are heard there, *v.* 22. Obedient souls are prepared for blessings, and they have promise of audience.

Verses 23–24

I. What his commandments are, *v.* 23. To discern what he is, according to his name, the Son of God, and the anointed Saviour of the world. To approve him in judgment and conscience. To consent to him as our Redeemer. To trust to him for the full discharge of his saving office. This faith is a needful requisite to those who would be prevalent petitioners with God, because it is by the Son that we must come to the Father. That we *love one another, as he gave us commandment, v.* 23. As goodwill to men was proclaimed from heaven, so goodwill to men must be carried in the hearts of those who go to God and heaven.

II. The blessedness of obedience to these commands. The obedient enjoy communion with God, *v.* 24. We dwell in God and God dwells in us. The trial of his divine inhabitation (*v.* 24), is by the frame of soul that he hath conferred upon us.

JAMIESON, FAUSSET, BROWN

therefore, like Peter, appeals from conscience to Him who is *greater than conscience.* "Lord, Thou *knowest all things:* thou knowest that I love Thee." Peter's conscience, though condemning him of his sin in denying the Lord, assured him of his *love;* but fearing the possibility, owing to his past fall, of deceiving himself, he appeals to the all-knowing God: so Paul, I Corinthians 4:3, 4. So if we be believers, even *if our heart condemns us of sin in general,* yet having the one sign of sonship, *love,* we may still *assure our hearts* (some oldest MSS, read *heart,* vs. 19, as well as vs. 20), as knowing *that God is greater than our heart, and knoweth all things.* Our hypocrisy in *loving by word and tongue,* not in *deed and truth,* does not escape even our conscience, though weak and knowing but little, how much less God who knows all things! Still the consolatory view may be the right one. For the *Greek* for "we shall *assure* our hearts" (see *Note,* vs. 19), is *gain over, persuade* so as to be stilled, implying that there was a previous state of *self-condemnation by the heart* (vs. 20), which, however, is *got over* by the consolatory thought, "God is greater than my heart" which condemns me, and "knows all things" (*Greek ginoskei, "knows,"* not *kataginoskei, "condemns"*), and therefore knows my *love* and desire to serve Him, and knows my *frame* so as to pity my weakness of faith. This *gaining over* the heart to peace is not so advanced a stage as the *having* CONFIDENCE *towards God* which flows from a *heart condemning us not.* The first "because" thus applies to the two alternate cases, vss. 20, 21 (giving the ground of saying, that *having love we shall gain over,* or *assure our minds before Him,* vs. 19); the second "because" applies to the first alternate alone, viz., "if our heart condemn us." When he reaches the second alternate, vs. 21, he states it independently of the former "because" which had connected it with vs. 19, inasmuch as CONFIDENCE *toward God* is a farther stage than *persuading our hearts,* though always preceded by it. **21. Beloved**—There is no "But" contrasting the two cases, vss. 20, 21, because "Beloved" sufficiently marks the transition to the case of the brethren walking in the full confidence of *love* (vs. 18). The two results of our being able to "assure our hearts before Him" (vs. 19), and of "our heart condemning us not" (of insincerity as to *the truth* in general, and as to LOVE in particular) are, (1) confidence toward God; (2) a sure answer to our prayers. John does not mean that all whose hearts do not condemn them, are therefore safe before God; for some have their conscience seared, others are ignorant of the truth, and it is not only *sincerity,* but *sincerity in the truth* which can save men. Christians are those meant here: knowing Christ's precepts and testing themselves by them. **22. we receive**—as a matter of fact, according to His promise. Believers, as such, ask only what is in accordance with God's will; or if they ask what God wills not, they bow their will to God's will, and so God grants them either their request, or something better than it. **because we keep his commandments**—Cf. Psalm 66:18; 34:15; 145:18, 19. Not as though our merits earned a hearing for our prayers, but when we are believers in Christ, all our works of faith being the fruit of *His* Spirit in us, are "pleasing in God's sight"; and our prayers being the voice of the same Spirit of God in us, naturally and necessarily are answered by Him. **23.** Summing up of God's commandments under the Gospel dispensation in one commandment. **this is his commandment**—singular: for *faith* and *love* are not *separate* commandments, but are indissolubly united. We cannot truly *love* one another without *faith* in Christ, nor can we truly believe in Him without love. **believe**—*once for all; Greek* aorist. **on the name of his Son**—on all that is revealed in the Gospel concerning Him, and on Himself in respect to His person, offices, and atoning work. **as he**—as *Jesus* gave us commandment. **24. dwelleth in him**—The believer dwelleth in Christ. **and he in him**—Christ in the believer. Reciprocity. "Thus he returns to the great keynote of the Epistle, *abide in Him,* with which the former part concluded" (ch. 2:28). **hereby**—"herein we (believers) know that He abideth in us, viz., from (the presence in us of) the Spirit which He hath given us." Thus he prepares, by the mention of the true Spirit, for the transition to the false "spirit," ch. 4:1-6; after which he returns again to the subject of *love.*

ADAM CLARKE

20. ***If our heart condemn us.*** **If we be conscious that our love is feigned, we shall feel inwardly condemned in professing to have what we have not. And** ***if our heart condemn us, God is greater than our heart,*** **for He knows every hypocritical winding and turning of the soul. He searches the heart, and tries the reins, and sees all the deceitfulness and desperate wickedness of the heart which we cannot see.**

21. ***If our heart condemn us not***—**if we be conscious to ourselves of our own sincerity, that we practice not deceit, and use no mask; then** ***have we confidence toward God***—**we can appeal to Him for our sincerity, and we can come with boldness to the throne of grace, to "obtain mercy, and find grace to help in time of need." And therefore says the apostle,**

22. ***Whatsoever we ask,*** **in such a spirit,** ***we receive of him;*** **for He delights to bless the humble, upright, and sincere soul.** ***Because we keep his commandments.*** **Viz., by loving Him and loving our neighbor. These are the great commandments of both the old covenant and the new. And whoever is filled with this love to God and man will** ***do those things that are pleasing*** **to Him, for love is the very soul and principle of obedience. The word "heart" is used in the preceding verses for conscience, and so the Greek fathers interpret it; but this is not an unfrequent meaning of the word in the sacred writings.**

23. ***That we should believe on the name of his Son.*** **We are commanded to believe on Christ; and being through Him redeemed from the guilt of sin, restored to the divine favor, and made partakers of the Holy Ghost, we are enabled to** ***love one another, as he gave us commandment;*** **for without a renewal of the heart, love to God and man is impossible, and this renewal comes by Christ Jesus.**

24. ***Dwelleth in him,*** **i.e., in God;** ***and he,*** **God,** ***in him,*** **the believer.** ***And hereby we know.*** **We know** ***by the Spirit which he hath given us*** **that we dwell in God, and God in us.**

MATTHEW HENRY

CHAPTER 4

Verses 1–3

I. He calls the disciples to caution and scrutiny about the spirits that had now risen. 1. To caution: "*Beloved, believe not every spirit;* follow not every pretender to the Spirit of God." There had been real communications from the divine Spirit and therefore others pretended thereto. 2. To scrutiny, to examination of the claims that are laid to the Spirit, *v.* 1. To the disciples is allowed a judgment of discretion. A reason is given for this trial, *v.* 1. It should not seem strange to us that false teachers set themselves up in the church: it was so in the apostles' times.

II. He gives a test whereby the disciples may try these pretending spirits. They were to be tried by their doctrine, *v.* 2. He who confesses and preaches Christ, does it by the Spirit of God. The sum of revealed religion is comprehended in the doctrine concerning Christ, his person and office. We see then the aggravation of a systematic opposition to him and it, *v.* 3. The anti-christian spirit began betimes, even in the apostles' days. But we have been forewarned that such opposition would arise, and the more we see the word of Christ fulfilled the more confirmed we should be in the truth of it.

Verses 4–6

The apostle encourages the disciples against this seducing antichristian spirit. He assures them of a more divine principle in them, *v.* 4, 6. *We are born of God.* He gives them hope of victory, *v.* 4. "There is a strong preserver within you, *v.* 4. The Spirit of God dwells in you, and that Spirit is more mighty than men or devils." The Spirit of God hath framed your mind for God and heaven; *but they are of the world, and therefore speak they of the world.* This worldly design procures them proselytes, *v.* 5. They are followed by such as themselves: the world will love its own, and its own will love it. "*He that knoweth God heareth us.* He who knows the purity and holiness of God, the love and grace of God, must know that he is with us; and he who knows this will attend to us, and abide with us. *He that is not of God heareth not us.* Thus you have a distinction between us and others," *v.* 6.

Verses 7–13

The Spirit of truth is known by love, *v.* 7. The apostle would unite them in his love, that he might unite them in love to each other.

JAMIESON, FAUSSET, BROWN

CHAPTER 4

VSS. 1-21. TESTS OF FALSE PROPHETS. LOVE, THE TEST OF BIRTH FROM GOD, AND THE NECESSARY FRUIT OF KNOWING HIS GREAT LOVE IN CHRIST TO US. **1. Beloved**—the affectionate address wherewith he calls their attention, as to an important subject. **every spirit**—which presents itself in the person of a prophet. The Spirit of truth, and the spirit of error, speak by men's spirits as their organs. There is but one Spirit of truth, and one spirit of Antichrist. **try**—by the tests (vss. 2, 3). All believers are to do so: not merely ecclesiastics. Even an angel's message should be tested by the word of God: much more men's teachings, however holy the teachers may seem. **because . . .**—the reason why we must "try," or *test* the spirits. **many false prophets**—not "prophets" in the sense "foretellers," but organs of the spirit that inspires them, *teaching* accordingly either truth or error: "many Antichrists." **are gone out**—as if from God. **into the world**—said alike of good and bad prophets (II John 7). The world is easily seduced (vss. 4, 5). **2. Hereby**—"Herein." **know . . . the Spirit of God**—whether he be, or not, in those teachers professing to be moved by Him. **Every spirit**—i.e., *Every teacher* claiming inspiration by the HOLY SPIRIT. **confesseth**—The truth is taken for granted as established. Man is required to *confess* it, i.e., in his teaching to profess it openly. **Jesus Christ is come in the flesh**—a twofold truth confessed, that *Jesus* is the *Christ,* and that *He is come* (the *Greek* perfect implies not a mere past historical fact, as the aorist would, but also the *present continuance* of the fact and its blessed effects) *in the flesh* ("clothed with flesh": not with a mere *seeming* humanity, as the Docetæ afterwards taught: He therefore was, previously, something far above flesh). His *flesh* implies His *death* for us, for only by assuming flesh could He die (for as God He could not), Hebrews 2:9, 10, 14, 16; and His death implies His LOVE for us (John 15:13). To deny the reality of *His flesh* is to deny His love, and so cast away the root which produces all true love on the believer's part (vss. 9-11, 19). Rome, by the doctrine of the immaculate conception of the Virgin Mary, denies Christ's proper humanity. **3. confesseth not that Jesus Christ is come in the flesh**—IRENÆUS (3. 8), LUCIFER, ORIGEN, on Matthew 25:14, and *Vulgate* read, "Every spirit which *destroys* (*sets aside,* or *does away with*) Jesus (Christ)." CYPRIAN and POLYCARP support *English Version* text. The oldest extant MSS., which are, however, centuries after POLYCARP, read, "Every spirit that confesseth not (i.e., refuses to confess) Jesus" (in His person, and all His offices and divinity), omitting "is come in the flesh." **ye have heard**—from your Christian teachers. **already is it in the world**—in the person of *the false prophets* (vss. 1). **4. Ye**—emphatical: YE who confess Jesus: in contrast to "them," the false teachers. **overcome them**—(ch. 5:4, 5)—instead of being "overcome and brought into (spiritual) bondage" by them (II Pet. 2:19). John 10:8, 5, "the sheep did *not hear them*": "a stranger will they not follow, but will flee from him: for they know not the voice of strangers." **he that is in you**—*God,* of whom ye are. **he that is in the world**—the spirit of Antichrist, the devil, "the prince of this world." **5. of the world**—They derive their spirit and teaching from the world, "unregenerate human nature, ruled over and possessed by Satan, the prince of this world" [ALFORD]. **speak they of the world**—They draw the matter of their conversation from the life, opinions, and feelings of the world. **the world heareth them**—(John 15:18, 19). *The world loves its own.* **6. We**—*true teachers* of Christ: in contrast to *them.* **are of God**—and therefore *speak of God:* in contrast to "speak they of the world," vs. 5. **knoweth God**—as his Father, being a child "*of God*" (ch. 2:13, 14). **heareth us**—Cf. John 18:37, "Every one that is of the truth, heareth My voice." **Hereby**—(vss. 2-6)—by their confessing, or not confessing, Jesus; by the kind of reception given them respectively by those who know God, and by those who are of the world and not of God. **spirit of truth**—*the Spirit* which comes from God and teaches *truth.* **spirit of error**—*the spirit* which comes from Satan and seduces into *error.* **7.** Resumption of the main theme (ch. 2:29). *Love,* the sum of *righteousness,* is the test of our being *born of God.* Love flows from a sense of God's love to us: cf. vs. 9 with ch. 3:16, which vs. 9 resumes; and vs. 13 with ch. 3:24, which similarly vs. 13 resumes. At the same time, vss. 7-21 is connected with the immediately preceding context, vs. 2 setting forth *Christ's incarnation, the great proof of God's love* (vs. 10). **Beloved**—an address

ADAM CLARKE

CHAPTER 4

1. *Beloved, believe not every spirit.* Do not be forward to believe every teacher to be a man sent of God. As in those early times every teacher professed to be inspired by the Spirit of God, because all the prophets had come thus accredited, the term *spirit* was used to express the man who pretended to be and teach under the Spirit's influence. See 1 Cor. xii. 1-12; 1 Tim. iv. 1. *Try the spirits.* Put these teachers to the proof. Try them by that testimony which is known to have come from the Spirit of God, the word of revelation already given. *Many false prophets.* Teachers not inspired by the Spirit of God.

2. *Hereby know ye the Spirit of God.* We know that the man who teaches that Jesus Christ is the promised Messiah, and that he *is come in the flesh, is of God*—is inspired by the divine Spirit; for no man can call Jesus Lord but by the Holy Ghost.

3. *Every spirit,* every teacher, *that confesseth not* Jesus *is not of God*—has not been inspired by God. The words *is come in the flesh* are wanting in several MSS. Griesbach has left them out of the text. *Ye have heard that it should come.* See 2 Thess. ii. 7. *Even now already is it in the world.* Is working powerfully among both Jews and Gentiles.

4. *Ye are of God.* You are under the influence of the divine Spirit. *And have overcome them*—your testimony, proceeding from the Spirit of Christ, has invalidated theirs, which has proceeded from the influence of Satan; for *greater is* the Holy Spirit which *is in you, than* the spirit which *is in the world.*

5. *They are of the world.* They have no spiritual views; they have no spirituality of mind; they seek the present world and its enjoyments. Their conversation is worldly, and worldly men hear them in preference to all others.

6. *We are of God.* We apostles have the Spirit of God, and speak and teach by that Spirit. *He that knoweth God,* who has a truly spiritual discernment, *heareth us,* acknowledges that our doctrine is from God; that it is spiritual, and leads from earth to heaven.

MATTHEW HENRY

I. The high and heavenly descent of love: *For love is of God, v.* 7. The Spirit of God is the Spirit of love. Love comes down from heaven.

II. Love argues a true apprehension of the divine nature, *v.* 7, 8. What attribute of the divine Majesty so clearly shines in all the world as his communicative goodness, which is love. *He that loveth not knoweth not God.* Knowledge of God dwells not in such a soul; *for God is love* (*v.* 8). Love is natural and essential to the divine Majesty: *God is love.* He hath loved us, such as we are (*v.* 9). Strange that God should love impure dust and ashes! He has loved us at such an incomparable value as he has given for us, *v.* 9. Mystery and miracle of divine love that such a Son should be sent into our world for us! God loved us first, *v.* 10. He loved us, when we had no love for him, when we lay in our guilt. He gave us his Son for such service and such an end. For such service, *to be the propitiation for our sins.* For such an end (*v.* 9), that we might live with God, and live in eternal glory and blessedness with him. O what love is here!

III. Divine love to the brethren should constrain ours, *v.* 11. This should be an invincible argument. Shall we refuse to love those whom the eternal God hath loved? We should be admirers of his love, and lovers of his love, and consequently lovers of those whom he loves.

IV. The Christian love is an assurance of the divine inhabitation, *v.* 12. The sacred lovers of the brethren are the temples of God; the divine Majesty has a peculiar residence there.

V. Herein the divine love attains accomplishment in us, *v.* 12. God's love is not perfected in him, but in and with us. Faith is perfected by its works, and love perfected by its operations. When the divine love has wrought us to the love of God, and thereupon to the love of the brethren, for his sake, it is therein perfected. How ambitious should we be of this love, when God reckons his own love to us perfected thereby, *v.* 13. One would think that to speak of God dwelling in us, and we in him, were to use words too high for mortals, had not God gone before us therein. What it fully is must be left to the revelation of the blessed world. But this mutual inhabitation we know, says the apostle, *because he hath given us of his Spirit.*

Verses 14–16

I. The fundamental article of the Christian religion, *v.* 14. 1. The Lord Jesus's relation to God; he is Son to the Father. 2. His relation and office towards us—*the Saviour of the world.* 3. The ground on which he became so: *The Father sent the Son.* 4. The apostle's assurance of this—he and his brethren had seen it; they had seen the Son of God in his human nature. 5. The apostle's attestation of this: "*We have seen and do testify.*"

II. The excellent privilege attending the due acknowledgment of this truth, *v.* 15. He who thus confesses Christ, and God in him, is possessed by the Spirit of God.

III. God's love is thus seen and exerted in Christ Jesus, *v.* 16. The Christian revelation is the revelation of the divine love; the articles of our revealed faith are but so many articles relating to the divine love. The history of the Lord Christ is the history of God's love to us.

1. *God is love;* he is essential boundless love; he has incomprehensible love for us of this world, which he has demonstrated in the mission of his beloved Son. What will he not do then when he designs to demonstrate his love, that he himself is love? In such a dispensation as that of giving an eternal Son for us and to us, he will commend his love to us indeed. Then may it well be inscribed upon the whole creation of God, *God is love.*

2. *He that dwelleth in love dwelleth in God, and God in him.* He that dwells in sacred love has *the love of God shed abroad upon his heart,* and will ere long go to dwell with God for ever.

Verses 17–21

He recommends it in both the branches of it, both as love to God, and love to our brother.

I. As love to God. 1. It will give us peace and satisfaction of spirit in the day when it will be most needed, *v.* 17. There must be a day of universal judgment. Happy they who shall have boldness before the Judge at that day, who shall be able to lift up their heads, and to look him in the face, as knowing he is their friend. So may do the lovers of God. And we have this boldness towards Christ because of our

JAMIESON, FAUSSET, BROWN

appropriate to his subject, "love." **love**—*All love* is *from God* as its fountain: especially that embodiment of love, God manifest in the flesh. The *Father* also is *love* (vs. 8). The *Holy Ghost* sheds *love* as its first *fruit* abroad in the heart. **knoweth God**—spiritually, experimentally, and habitually. **8. knoweth not**—*Greek* aorist: not only *knoweth* not now, but never *knew, has not once for all known* God. **God is love**—There is no *Greek* article to *love,* but to *God;* therefore we cannot translate, *Love is God.* God is fundamentally and essentially LOVE: not merely *is loving,* for then John's argument would not stand; for the conclusion from the premises then would be this, *This man is not loving: God is loving; therefore he knoweth not* God IN SO FAR AS GOD IS LOVING; still he might know Him in His *other* attributes. But when we take *love* as God's essence, the argument is sound: *This man doth not love, and therefore knows not love: God is essentially love, therefore he knows not God.* **9. toward us**—*Greek,* "in our case." **sent**—*Greek*, "*hath* sent." **into the world**—a proof against Socinians, that the Son existed before He was "sent into the world." Otherwise, too, He could not have been our *life* (vs. 9), our "*propitiation*" (vs. 10), or our "Saviour" (vs. 14). It is the grand *proof* of God's love, His having sent *His only-begotten Son, that we might live through Him,* who is *the Life,* and who has redeemed our forfeited life; and it is also the grand *motive* to our mutual love. **10. Herein is love**—*love* in the abstract: *love,* in its highest ideal, is herein. The love was all on God's side, none on ours. **not that we loved God**—though so altogether worthy of love. **he loved us**—though so altogether unworthy of love. The *Greek* aorist expresses, Not that we *did* any act of love *at any time* to God, but that He *did* the act of love to us in sending Christ. **11.** God's love to us is the grand motive for our love to one another (ch. 3:16). **if**—as we all admit as a fact. **we . . . also**—as being *born of God,* and therefore resembling our Father who is love. In proportion as we appreciate God's love to us, we love Him and also *the brethren,* the children (by regeneration) of the same God, the representatives of the unseen God. **12.** *God,* whom *no man hath seen at any time,* hath appointed His children as the *visible* recipients of our outward kindness which flows from love to Himself, "whom *not* having *seen,* we love," cf. *Notes,* vss. 11, 19, 20. Thus vs. 12 explains why, instead (in vs. 11) of saying, "If God so loved us, we ought also to love *God,*" he said, "We ought also to love *one another.*" **If we love one another, God dwelleth in us**—for God is love; and it must have been from Him dwelling in us that we drew the real love we bear to the brethren (vss. 8, 16). John discusses this in vss. 13-16. **his love**—rather, "the love of (i.e., to) Him" (ch. 2:5), evinced by our love to His representatives, our brethren. **is perfected in us**—John discusses this in vss. 17-19. Cf. ch. 2:5, "is perfected," i.e., attains its proper maturity. **13. Hereby**—"Herein." The token vouchsafed to us of God's dwelling (*Greek,* "abide") in us, though we see Him not, is this, that He hath given us "of His Spirit" (ch. 3:24). Where the Spirit of God is, there God is. ONE Spirit dwells in the Church: each believer receives a measure "of" that Spirit in the proportion God thinks fit. *Love* is His first fruit (Gal. 5:22). In Jesus alone the Spirit dwelt without measure (John 3:34). **14. And we**—primarily, *we apostles,* Christ's appointed eyewitnesses to testify to the facts concerning Him. The internal evidence of the indwelling Spirit (vs. 13) is corroborated by the external evidence of the eyewitnesses to the fact of the Father having "sent His Son to be the Saviour of the world." **seen**—*Greek,* "contemplated," "attentively beheld" (*Note,* ch. 1:1). **sent**—*Greek,* "*hath* sent": not an entirely past fact (aorist), but one of which the effects continue (perfect). **15. shall confess**—once for all: so the *Greek* aorist means. **that Jesus is the Son of God**—and therefore "the Saviour of the world" (vs. 14). **16. And we**—*John and his readers* (not as vs. 14, *the apostles* only). **known and believed**—True *faith,* according to John, is a faith of *knowledge* and experience: true *knowledge* is a knowledge of *faith* [LUECKE]. **to us**—*Greek,* "in our case" (*Note,* vs. 9). **dwelleth**—*Greek,* "abideth." Cf. with this verse, vs. 7. **17, 18.** (Cf. ch. 3:19-21.) **our love**—rather as the *Greek,* "LOVE (in the abstract, the principle of love [ALFORD]) is made perfect (in its relations) *with us.*" Love dwelling in us advances to its consummation "*with us*" i.e., as it is concerned *with us:* so *Greek.* Luke 1:58, "showed mercy upon (lit., 'with') her": II John 2, the truth "shall be *with us* for ever." **boldness**—"confidence": the same *Greek* as ch. 3:21, to which this passage is

ADAM CLARKE

7. *Beloved, let us love one another.* And ever be ready to promote each other's welfare, both spiritual and temporal. *For love is of God.* And ever acts like Him; He loves man, and daily loads him with His benefits. He that loveth most has most of God in him; and he that loveth God and his neighbor, as before described and commanded, *is born of God,* "is begotten of God"—is a true child of his Heavenly Father.

8. *He that loveth not,* as already described, *knoweth not God,* has no experimental knowledge of Him. *God is love.* How can a decree of absolute, unconditional reprobation of the greater part or any part of the human race stand in the presence of such a text as this? It has been well observed that, although God is holy, just, righteous, He is never called "holiness, justice," in the abstract, as He is here called *love.* This seems to be the essence of the divine nature, and all other attributes to be only modifications of this.

9. *In this was manifested the love of God.* The mission of Jesus Christ was the fullest proof that God could give, or that man could receive, of His infinite love to the world. *That we might live through him.* The whole world was sentenced to death because of sin, and every individual was dead in trespasses and sins; and Jesus came to die in the stead of the world, and to quicken every believer, that all might live to Him who died for them and rose again. This is another strong allusion to John iii. 16.

10. *Not that we loved God,* and that He was thereby induced to give His Son *to be a propitiation for our sins.*

11. *If God so loved us*—without any reason or consideration on our part, and without any desert in us. *We ought also,* in like manner, *to love one another.*

12. *No man hath seen God at any time.* We may feel Him, though we cannot see Him; and if we love one another, He *dwelleth in us, and his love is perfected in us*—it has then its full accomplishment, having molded us according to its own nature.

14. *And we have seen* Jesus Christ manifested in the flesh; see chap. i. 1. *And do testify*—bear witness, in consequence of having the fullest conviction—*that the Father sent the Son to be the Saviour of the world.* We have had the fullest proof of this from His doctrine and miracles, which we heard and saw during the whole time that He sojourned among men.

15. *Whosoever shall confess.* Much stress is laid on this confession, because the false teachers denied the reality of the Incarnation; but this confession implied also such a belief in Christ as put them in possession of His pardoning mercy and indwelling Spirit.

16. *God is love.* See on v. 8. *He that dwelleth in love*—he who is full of love to God and man is full of God, for *God is love.*

17. *Herein is our love made perfect.* By God dwelling in us and we in Him, having cast out all the carnal mind that was "enmity" against himself, and filled the whole heart with the spirit of love and purity. *May have boldness in the day of judgment.* "Freedom of speech," and "liberty of access," seeing in the person of our Judge Him who has died for us, regenerated

MATTHEW HENRY

conformity to him, *v.* 17. Love hath conformed us to him.

2. It prevents servile fear (*v.* 18); so far as love prevails, fear ceases. We must here distinguish between the fear of God and being afraid of him. The fear of God is often mentioned and commanded as the substance of religion. Such fear is consistent with love, yea, with perfect love. But then there is a being afraid of God, which arises from a sense of guilt; and so fear here may be rendered *dread*: *There is no dread in love.* Love puts off dread, and puts on joy in him; and, as love grows, joy grows too; so that *perfect love casteth out fear* or dread. They well know that God loves them, and they thereupon triumph in his love. *Because fear hath torment* (*v.* 18)—fear is known to be a disquieting passion, but perfect love casteth out torment, for it teaches the mind a perfect acquiescence in the beloved, and therefore *perfect love casteth out fear. He that feareth is not made perfect in love,* it is a sign that our love is far from being perfect. 3. We cannot but love so good a God, who loved us when we were both unloving and unlovely. The divine love stamped love upon our souls.

II. As love to our brother in Christ; such love is urged on these accounts: 1. As consonant to our Christian profession. In the profession of Christianity we profess to love God as the root of religion (*v.* 20). That such a one loves not God the apostle proves, *v.* 20. The eye is wont to affect the heart; things unseen less catch the mind, and thereby the heart. The member of Christ has much of God visible in him. How then shall the hater of a visible image of God pretend to love the invisible God himself? 2. As suitable to the express law of God, *v.* 21. We must love God originally and supremely, and others in him. It cannot but be a natural suitable obligation *that he who loves God should love his brother also.*

CHAPTER 5

Verses 1–5

I. Our Christian brethren are nearly related to God; they are his children, *v.* 1. Here the Christian brother is, 1. Described by his faith; he that *believeth that Jesus is the Christ* accordingly yields himself up to his care and direction. 2. Dignified by his descent, *v.* 1. All believers, though by nature sinners, are spiritually descended from God, and accordingly are to be beloved, *v.* 1. It seems but natural that he who loves the Father should love the children also.

II. The apostle shows, 1. How we may discern the truth of our love to the regenerate. The ground of it must be our love to God, *v.* 2. Our love to them appears to be sound and genuine when we love them because they are God's children, and so in them God himself is loved.

JAMIESON, FAUSSET, BROWN

parallel. The opposite of "fear," vs. 18. *Herein* is our love perfected, viz., *in God dwelling in us, and our dwelling in God* (vs. 16), involving as its *result* "that we can have confidence (or *boldness*) **in** the day of judgment" (so terrible to all other men, Acts 24:25; Rom. 2:16). **because . . .**—The ground of our "confidence" is, "*because* even as He (Christ) is, we also are in this world" (and He will not, in that day, condemn those who are *like Himself*), i.e., we are *righteous* as He is righteous, especially in respect to that which is the sum of righteousness, *love* (ch. 3:14). Christ IS righteous, and *love* itself, in heaven: so are we, His members, who are still "in this world." Our oneness with Him even *now* in His exalted position above (Eph. 2:6), so that all that belongs to Him of righteousness, etc., belongs to us also by perfect imputation and progressive impartation, is the ground of our *love* being *perfected so that we can have confidence in the day of judgment.* We are *in,* not *of,* this world. **18.** *Fear* has no place in *love. Bold confidence* (vs. 17), based on *love,* cannot coexist with *fear. Love,* which, when *perfected,* gives *bold confidence, casts out fear* (cf. Heb. 2:14, 15). The design of Christ's propitiatory death was to *deliver* from this *bondage* of *fear.* **but**—"nay" [ALFORD]. **fear hath torment**—*Greek,* "punishment." Fear is always revolving in the mind the punishment deserved [ESTIUS]. Fear, by anticipating punishment [through consciousness of deserving it], has it even now, i.e., the foretaste of it. *Perfect love* is incompatible with such a self-punishing *fear. Godly fear* of offending God is quite distinct from slavish fear of consciously deserved punishment. The latter *fear* is natural to us all until *love casts it out.* "Men's states vary: one is without fear and love; another, with fear without love; another, with fear and love; another, without fear with love" [BENGEL]. **19. him**—omitted in the oldest MSS. Translate, *We* (emphatical: WE on our part) love (in general: love alike *Him,* and *the brethren,* and *our fellow men*), because He (emphatical: answering to "we"; *because it was He who*) first loved us in sending His Son (*Greek* aorist of a definite act at a point of time). He was the first to love us: this thought ought to create in us *love casting out fear* (vs. 18). **20. loveth not . . . brother whom he hath seen, how can he love God whom he hath not seen**—It is easier for us, influenced as we are here by sense, to direct love towards one within the range of our senses than towards One unseen, appreciable only by faith. Thus, by faith in Christ, we learn to love both the true God, and the true man, and so to love the brethren as bearing His image. **hath seen**—and continually sees. **21.** Besides the argument (vs. 20) from the common feeling of men, he here adds a stronger one from God's express *commandment* (Matt. 22:39). He who loves, will do what the object of his love wishes. **he who loveth God**—he who wishes to be regarded by God as loving Him.

CHAPTER 5

VSS. 1-21. WHO ARE THE BRETHREN ESPECIALLY TO BE LOVED (ch. 4:21); OBEDIENCE, THE TEST OF LOVE, EASY THROUGH FAITH, WHICH OVERCOMES THE WORLD. LAST PORTION OF THE EPISTLE. THE SPIRIT'S WITNESS TO THE BELIEVER'S SPIRITUAL LIFE. TRUTHS REPEATED AT THE CLOSE: FAREWELL WARNING. **1. Whosoever**—*Greek,* "Everyone that." He could not be our "Jesus" (God-Saviour) unless He were "the Christ"; for He could not reveal the way of salvation, except He were a *prophet:* He could not work out that salvation, except He were a *priest:* He could not confer that salvation upon us, except He were a *king:* He could not be *prophet, priest,* and *king,* except He were the Christ [PEARSON *on the Creed*]. **born**—Translate, "begotten," as in the latter part of the verse, the *Greek* being the same. Christ IS the "only-begotten Son" by *generation;* we become begotten sons of God by *regeneration* and adoption. **every one that loveth him that begat**—sincerely, not in mere profession (ch. 4:20). **loveth him also that is begotten of him**—viz., "his brethren" (ch. 4:21). **2. By**—*Greek,* "In." As our *love to the brethren* is the sign and test of our *love to God,* so (John here says) our *love to God* (tested by our "keeping his commandments") is, conversely, the ground and only true basis of *love to our brother.* **we know**—John means here, not the *outward* criteria of genuine brotherly love, but the *inward spiritual* criteria of it, *consciousness of love to God* manifested in a hearty keeping of His commandments. When we have this inwardly and outwardly con-

ADAM CLARKE

our hearts, and who himself fills them.

As he is—pure, holy, and loving. *So are we in this world,* being saved from our sins, and made like to himself in righteousness and true holiness. No man can contemplate the day of judgment with any comfort or satisfaction but on this ground, that the blood of Christ hath cleansed him from all sin; and that he is kept by the power of God, through faith, unto salvation. This will give him boldness in the day of judgment.

18. *There is no fear in love.* The man who feels that he loves God with all his heart can never dread Him as his Judge. As he is now made a partaker of His Spirit, and carries a sense of the divine approbation in his conscience, he has nothing of that *fear* that produces "terror" or brings *torment.* The *perfect love,* that fullness of love which he has received, *casteth out fear,* removes all terror relative to this day of judgment, for it is of this that the apostle particularly speaks. *He that feareth*—he who is still uncertain concerning his interest in Christ. *Is not made perfect in love*—has not yet received the abiding witness of the Spirit that he is begotten of God; nor that fullness of love to God and man which excludes the "enmity" of the "carnal mind," and which it is his privilege to receive. We are not to suppose that the love of God casts out every kind of fear from the soul; it casts out only that which has *torment.*

20. *If a man say, I love God, and hateth his brother.* This, as well as many other parts of this Epistle, seems levelled against the Jews who pretended much love to God while they hated the Gentiles.

21. *This commandment have we.* The love of God and the love of man can never be separated He who loves God will love his brother; he who loves his brother gives this proof that he loves God.

CHAPTER 5

1. *Whosoever believeth.* "He that believeth that Jesus is the Messiah," and confides in Him for the remission of sins, "is begotten of God"; and they who are pardoned and begotten of God love Him in return for His love, and love all those who are His children.

2. *By this we know that we love the children of God.* Our love of God's followers is a proof that we love God. Our love to God is the cause why we love His children, and our keeping the *commandments* of God is the proof that we love Him.

MATTHEW HENRY

2. How we may learn the truth of our love to God, *v.* 2. Then we truly love God: *For this is the love of God, that we keep his commandments;* and the keeping of his commandments requires a spirit delighting therein, *v.* 3. His commandments are thereby made easy and pleasant to us.

3. What is the result of regeneration, *v.* 4. He that is born of God is born *for God*, and consequently for another world. He can repel and conquer this, *v.* 4. Faith is the cause of victory. In and by faith we cleave to Christ in opposition to the world. It receives and derives strength from the object of it, the Son of God, for conquering the world.

III. It is the real Christian that is the true conqueror of the world, *v.* 5. He who believes that Jesus is the Son of God believes therein that Jesus came from God to be the Saviour of the world. And he who so believes must needs by this faith overcome the world. He sees it must be a great part of the Saviour's work, and of his own salvation, to be redeemed and rescued from this malignant world. He perceives that the Lord Jesus conquered the world, not for himself only, but for his followers. He is possessed with a spirit and disposition that cannot be satisfied with this world, that looks beyond it. It is the Christian revelation that is the great means of conquering the world, and gaining another that is blessed and eternal. The Saviour designs not this world for the inheritance and portion of his saved company. It is the real Christian that is the proper hero, who vanquishes the world. Who in all the world but the believer on Jesus Christ can thus overcome the world?

Verses 6–9

The faith of the Christian believer had need to be well founded, and it is so; Christ brings his credentials along with him.

I. In the way and manner by which he came: *This is he that came by water and blood* (*v.* 6).

1. We are inwardly and outwardly defiled. Inwardly, by the pollution of sin in our nature. For our cleansing from this we need spiritual water. We are defiled outwardly by the guilt of sin upon our persons. From this we must be purged by atoning blood.

2. Both these ways of cleansing were represented in the old ceremonial institutions of God. Persons and things must be purified by water and blood.

3. Upon the death of Jesus Christ, his side being pierced with a soldier's spear, out of the wound there immediately issued water and blood. This the beloved apostle saw. Now this water and blood are comprehensive of all that is necessary to our salvation. By the water our souls are washed and purified. By the blood God is glorified, his law is honoured. By the blood we are justified, reconciled, and presented righteous to God. The water and the blood then comprehend all things that can be requisite to our salvation.

II. In the witness that attends him, *v.* 6. The apostle adds the commendation of this witness. He is the Spirit of God, and cannot lie. He is indeed the Spirit of truth. And that the Spirit is truth, and a witness worthy of all acceptation, appears in that he is a heavenly witness. But here,

JAMIESON, FAUSSET, BROWN

firmed *love to God*, we can *know* assuredly that we truly *love the children of God*. "*Love to one's brother* is prior, according to the order of nature (*Note*, ch. 4:20); *love to God* is so, according to the order of grace (ch. 5:2). **3. this is**—the *love* of God consists in this. **not grievous**—as so many think them. It is "the way of the transgressor" that "is hard." What makes them to the regenerate "not grievous," is *faith* which "overcometh the world" (vs. 4): in proportion as faith is strong, the grievousness of God's commandments to the rebellious flesh is overcome. The reason why believers feel any degree of irksomeness in God's commandments is, they do not realize fully by faith the privileges of their spiritual life. **4. For**—(*Note*, vs. 3). The reason why "His commandments are not grievous." Though there is a conflict in keeping them, the issue for the whole body of the regenerate is victory over every opposing influence; meanwhile there is a present *joy* to each believer in keeping them which makes them "not grievous." **whatsoever**—*Greek*, "*all* that is begotten of God." **overcometh**—habitually. **the world**—all that is opposed to keeping the commandments of God, or draws us off from God, in this world, including our corrupt *flesh*, on which the world's blandishments or threats act, as also including Satan, *the prince of this world*. **this is the victory that overcometh**—*Greek* aorist: "... that *hath* (already) *overcome* the world": the *victory* (where *faith* is) hereby is implied as having been *already obtained* (ch. 2:13; 4:4). **5. Who**—"Who" *else* "but he that believeth that Jesus is the Son of God—"the Christ" (vs. 1)? Confirming, by a triumphant question defying all contradiction, as an undeniable fact, vs. 4, that *the victory* which overcomes the world is *faith*. For it is by *believing* that we are made one with *Jesus the Son of God*, so that we partake of *His victory over the world*, and have dwelling in us One greater than he who is in the world (ch. 4:4). "Survey the whole world, and show me even one of whom it can be affirmed with truth that he overcomes the world, who is not a Christian, and endowed with this faith" [EPISCOPIUS *in* ALFORD]. **6. This**—the Person mentioned in vs. 5. This *Jesus*. **he that came by water and blood**—"by water," when His ministry was inaugurated by baptism in the Jordan, and He received the Father's testimony to His Messiahship and divine *Sonship*. Cf. vs. 5, "believeth that Jesus is the *Son of God*," with John 1:33, 34, "The Spirit ... remaining on Him ... I saw and bare record that this is *the Son of God*"; and vs. 8, below, "there are three that bear *witness* in earth, the Spirit, and the water, and the blood." Corresponding to this is *the baptism of water and the Spirit* which He has instituted as a standing seal and mean of initiatory incorporation with Him. **and blood**—He came by "the blood of His cross" (so "by" is used, Heb. 9:12: "by," i.e., *with*, "His own blood He entered in once into the holy place"): a fact *seen* and so solemnly *witnessed to* by John. "These two past facts in the Lord's life are this abiding *testimony* to us, by virtue of the permanent application to us of their cleansing and atoning power." **Jesus Christ**—not a mere appellation, but a solemn assertion of the Lord's Person and Messiahship. **not by ...**—*Greek*, "not IN *the* water only, but IN *the* water and IN (so oldest MSS. add) *the* blood." As "*by*" implies the mean *through*, or *with*, which He came: so "*in*," the element *in* which He came. "The" implies that *the water* and *the blood* were sacred and well-known symbols. John Baptist came only baptizing with water, and therefore was not the *Messiah*. Jesus came first to undergo Himself the double baptism of water and blood, and then to baptize us with the Spirit-cleansing, of which *water* is the sacramental seal, and with His atoning *blood*, the efficacy of which, once for all shed, is perpetual in the Church; and therefore is *the Messiah*. It was His shed *blood* which first gave *water baptism* its spiritual significancy. We are baptized *into His death:* the grand point of union between us and Him, and, through Him, between us and God. **it is the Spirit ...**—*The Holy Spirit* is an additional witness (cf. vs. 7), besides the *water* and the *blood*, to Jesus' *Sonship* and *Messiahship*. The Spirit attested these truths at Jesus' baptism by descending on Him, and throughout His ministry by enabling Him to speak and do what man never before or since has spoken or done; and "it is the Spirit that beareth witness" of Christ, now permanently in the Church: both in the inspired New Testament Scriptures, and in the hearts of believers, and in the spiritual reception of baptism and the Lord's Supper. **because the Spirit is truth**—It is His essential *truth* which gives His witness such

ADAM CLARKE

3. *For this is the love of God.* This the love of God necessarily produces. It is vain to pretend love to God while we live in opposition to His will. *His commandments,* to love Him with all our hearts, and our neighbor as ourselves, *are not grievous,* are not burdensome; for no man is burdened with the duties which his own love imposes. The old proverb explains the meaning of the apostle's words, "Love feels no loads."

4. *Whatsoever is born of God.* "Whatsoever [the neuter for the masculine] is begotten of God overcometh the world."

6. *This is he that came by water and blood.* Jesus was attested to be the Son of God and promised Messiah by *water,* i.e., His baptism, when the Spirit of God came down from heaven upon Him, and the voice from heaven said, "This is my beloved Son, in whom I am well pleased."

Jesus Christ came also by *blood.* He shed His blood for the sins of the world, and this was in accordance with all that the Jewish prophets had written concerning Him.

Here the apostle says that the Spirit witnesses this; that He came *not by water only*—being baptized, and baptizing men in His own name that they might be His followers and disciples; but by *blood* also—by His sacrificial death, without which the world could not be saved, and He could have had no disciples.

MATTHEW HENRY

1. We are stopped in our course by the contest there is about the genuineness of *v.* 7. It is alleged that many old Greek manuscripts have it not. We shall not here enter into the controversy. It can scarcely be supposed that, when the apostle is representing the Christian's faith in overcoming the world, and the foundation it relies upon in adhering to Jesus Christ, he should omit the supreme testimony that attended him (*v.* 9). Upon our present reading here is a noble enumeration of the several witnesses and testimonies supporting the truth of the Lord Jesus.

2. The apostle, having told us that the Spirit that bears witness to Christ is truth, shows us that he is so, by assuring us that he is in heaven, *v.* 7.

(1) Here is a trinity of heavenly witnesses, such as have testified and vouched to the world the authority of the Lord Jesus in his claims. The first that occurs in order is *the Father*; he set his seal to the commission of the Lord Christ all the while he was here. The second witness is the Word, a mysterious name. He must bear witness to the human nature, or to the man Christ Jesus. The third witness is the Holy Ghost. True and faithful must he be to whom the Spirit of holiness sets his seal. These are witnesses in heaven; and they bear record from heaven; and they are one.

(2) To these there is opposed, though with them joined, a trinity of witnesses on earth, *v.* 8. Of these witnesses the first is the *spirit*. The regeneration or renovation of souls is a testimony to the Saviour. It is a testimony on earth, because it continues with the church here. To this Spirit belong not only the regeneration and conversion of the church, but its progressive sanctification, victory over the world. The second is the *water*. This was before considered as a means of salvation, now as a testimony to the Saviour himself, and intimates his purity and purifying power. And so it seems to comprehend the testimony of John's baptism, who bore witness of him and to the purity of his own doctrine, by which souls are purified and washed. The baptism that he has appointed for the initiation of his disciples. The third witness is the blood; this he shed, and this was our ransom. This testifies for Jesus Christ; in that it demonstrated unspeakable love to us; and none will deceive those whom they entirely love. In that it lays obligation on his disciples to suffer and die for him. This shows that neither he nor his kingdom is of this world. These are signified and sealed in the institution of his own supper. Such are the witnesses on earth. These three witnesses *agree in one*, in one and the same thing among themselves.

III. The apostle concludes, *v.* 9. *Here is the* witness whereby God hath testified of his Son. He has by himself proclaimed him to the world. The authority and acceptableness of his testimony. It is truth itself, of highest authority and most unquestionable infallibility. The application of the rule to the present case. *God, that cannot lie*, hath given sufficient assurance to the world that Jesus Christ is his Son, the Son of his love, to reconcile the world unto himself; he testified therefore the truth and divine origin of the Christian religion, and that it is the sure appointed way of bringing us to God.

Verses 10–13

I. The privilege and stability of the real Christian, *v.* 10. He hath not only the outward evidence that others have, but he hath in his own heart a testimony for Jesus Christ. He can allege what Christ and the truth of Christ have done for his soul and what he has seen and found in him. Christ is formed in him, and he is growing up to the fulness and perfection, or perfect image of Christ, in heaven.

II. The aggravation of the unbeliever's sin, the sin of unbelief, *v.* 10. He must believe that God did not send his Son into the world, or that Jesus Christ was not the Son of God.

III. The matter of all this divine testimony concerning Jesus Christ, *v.* 11. This is the sum of the gospel. 1. *God hath given to us eternal life*. He has designed it for us. He has made it over to us. 2. *This life is in the Son*. He is eternal life to us.

JAMIESON, FAUSSET, BROWN

infallible authority. **7. three**—Two or three witnesses were required by law to constitute adequate testimony. The only *Greek* MSS. *in any form* which support the words, "in heaven, the Father, the Word, and the Holy Ghost, and these three are one; and there are three that bear witness in earth," are the *Montfortianus* of Dublin, copied evidently from the *modern* Latin Vulgate; the *Ravianus*, copied from the *Complutensian Polyglot;* a MS. at Naples, with the words added in the margin by a recent hand; *Ottobonianus*, 298, of the fifteenth century, the *Greek* of which is a mere translation of the accompanying Latin. All the old versions omit the words. The oldest MSS. of the *Vulgate* omit them: the earliest *Vulgate* MS. which has them being *Wizanburgensis*, 99, of the eighth century. A scholium quoted in *Matthæi*, shows that the words did not arise from fraud; for in the words in all *Greek* MSS., "there are *three* that bear record," as the Scholiast notices, the word "three" is *masculine*, because the three things (*the Spirit, the water*, and *the blood*) are SYMBOLS OF THE TRINITY. To this Cyprian, 196, also refers, "Of the *Father, Son* and *Holy Spirit*, it is written, '*And these* three are one (a unity)." There must be some mystical truth implied in using *"three"* (*Greek*) in the *masculine*, though the antecedents, "Spirit, water, and blood," are *neuter*. That THE TRINITY was the truth meant is a natural inference: the triad specified pointing to a still Higher Trinity; as is plain also from vs. 9, "the witness of GOD," referring to the *Trinity* alluded to in the Spirit, water, and blood. It was therefore first written as a *marginal* comment to complete the sense of the *text*, and then, as early at least as the eighth century, was introduced into the text of the *Latin Vulgate*. The testimony, however, could only be borne *on earth* to men, not in *heaven*. The marginal comment, therefore, that inserted "in heaven," was inappropriate. It is *on earth* that the context evidently requires the witness of the three, *the Spirit, the water*, and *the blood*, to be borne: mystically setting forth the divine *triune* witnesses, the Father, the Spirit, and the Son. **8. agree in one**—"tend unto one result"; their agreeing testimony to Jesus' Sonship and Messiahship they give by the sacramental grace in the *water* of baptism, received by the penitent believer, by the atoning efficacy of His *blood*, and by the internal witness of His *Spirit* (vs. 10): answering to the testimony given to *Jesus*' Sonship and Messiahship by His baptism, His crucifixion, and the Spirit's manifestations in Him (*Note*, vs. 6). **9. If . . .**—We do *accept* (and rightly so) the witness of veracious men, fallible though they be; much more ought we to accept *the* infallible witness of God (the Father). "The testimony of the Father is, as it were, the basis of the testimony of the Word and of the Holy Spirit; just as the testimony of *the Spirit* is, as it were, the basis of the testimony of *the water* and the *blood*" [BENGEL]. **for**—This principle applies in the present case, FOR . . . **which**—in the oldest MSS., "*because* He hath given testimony concerning His Son." What that testimony is we find above in vss. 1, 5, "Jesus is the Christ, the Son of God"; and below in vss. 10, 11. **10. hath the witness**—of God, by His *Spirit* (vs. 8). **in himself**—God's Spirit dwelling in him and *witnessing* that "Jesus is the Lord," "the Christ," and "the Son of God" (vss. 1, 5). The witness of the Spirit *in* the believer *himself* to his own sonship is not here expressed, but follows as a consequence of believing the witness of God to Jesus' divine Sonship. **believeth not God**—credits not His *witness*. **made him a liar**—a consequence which many who virtually, or even avowedly, do not believe, may well startle back from as fearful blasphemy and presumption (ch. 1:10). **believeth not the record**—*Greek*, "believeth not IN the record, or *witness*." Refusal to *credit* God's testimony ("believeth not God") is involved in refusal *to believe* IN (to rest one's trust in) Jesus Christ, the object of God's *record* or *testimony*. "Divine *faith* is an assent unto something as credible upon the testimony of God. This is the highest kind of *faith;* because the object hath the highest credibility, because grounded upon the testimony of God, which is infallible" [PEARSON *on Creed*]. "The authority on which we believe is divine; the doctrine which we follow is divine" [LEO]. **gave**—*Greek*, "hath testified, and now testifies." **of**—concerning. **11. hath given**—*Greek*, aorist: "gave" once for all. Not only *"promised"* it. **life is in his Son**—essentially (John 1:4; 11:25; 14:6); bodily (Col. 2:9); operatively (II Tim. 1:10) [LANGE *in* ALFORD]. It is in the second Adam, the Son of God, that this *life* is secured to us, which, if left to depend on us, we

ADAM CLARKE

7. *There are three that bear record in heaven.* It is likely that this verse is not genuine. It is wanting in every MS., one excepted.

A. T. ROBERTSON:

7. "For there are three who bear witness" (*hoti treis eisin hoi marturountes*). At this point the Latin Vulgate gives the words in the Textus Receptus, found in no Greek ms save two late cursives (162 in the Vatican Library of the fifteenth century, 34 of the sixteenth century in Trinity College, Dublin). Jerome did not have it. Cyprian applies the language of the Trinity and Priscillian has it. Erasmus did not have it in his first edition, but rashly offered to insert it if a single Greek ms had it and 34 was produced with the insertion, as if made to order. The spurious addition is: "in heaven, the Father, the Word, and the Holy Ghost: and these three are one. And there are three that bear witness in earth." The last clause belongs to verse 8. The fact and the doctrine of the Trinity do not depend on this spurious addition. Some Latin scribe caught up Cyprian's exegesis and wrote it on the margin of his text, and so it got into the Vulgate and finally into the Textus Receptus by the stupidity of Erasmus.

—*Word Pictures in the New Testament*

8. *The spirit, and the water, and the blood.* This verse is supposed to mean "the Spirit—in the word confirmed by miracles; the *water*—in baptism, wherein we are dedicated to the Son (with the Father and the Holy Spirit), typifying His spotless purity, and the inward purifying of our nature; *and the blood*—represented in the Lord's Supper, and applied to the consciences of believers: and all these harmoniously agree in the same testimony, that Jesus Christ is the divine, the complete, the only Saviour of the world" (Mr. Wesley's notes).

9. *If we receive the witness of men.* Which all are obliged to do, and which is deemed a sufficient testimony to truth in numberless cases. *The witness of God is greater*—He can neither be deceived nor deceive.

10. *He that believeth on the Son of God.* This is God's witness to a truth, the most important and interesting to mankind. God has witnessed that whosoever believeth on His Son shall be saved and have everlasting life; and shall have the witness of it in himself, the Spirit bearing witness with his spirit that he is a child of God. To know his sin forgiven, to have the testimony of this in the heart from the Holy Spirit himself, is the privilege of every true believer in Christ.

11. *This is the record.* The great truth to which the Spirit, the water, and the Blood bear testimony. *God hath given to us eternal life*—a right to endless glory, and a meetness for it. *And this life is in his Son;* it comes by and through Him.

MATTHEW HENRY

It must follow, (1) He that is united to the Son is united to life (*v.* 12). (2) He who refuses the Son, who is life itself, and the way to it refuses life.

IV. The end of the apostle's preaching this to believers. 1. For their satisfaction and comfort: These believers have eternal life. These believers may come to know that they have eternal life, and should be encouraged, and comforted, in the prospect of it

2. For their confirmation and progress in their holy faith (*v.* 13). Believers must persevere, or they do nothing.

Verses 14–17

I. A privilege belonging to faith in Christ, audience in prayer: *v.* 14. The Lord Christ emboldens us to come to God in all circumstances. Through him our petitions are accepted of God. The matter of our prayer must be agreeable to the declared will of God. We may have confidence that the prayer of faith shall be heard in heaven.

II. The advantage accruing to us by such privilege, *v.* 15. To know that his petitions are heard or accepted is as good as to know that they are answered.

III. Direction in prayer in reference to the sins of others, *v.* 16. 1. We ought to pray for others as well as for ourselves. 2. There is a great distinction in the heinousness and guilt of sin (*v.* 16), and (*v.* 17). (1) *There is a sin unto death.* There is a sin unto death in opposition to such sin as is here said *not to be unto death.* There is, therefore, (2) *A sin not unto death.* The gospel does not positively and peremptorily threaten death to the more visible sins of the members of Christ but only some gospel-chastisement. There is room left for divine wisdom or goodness, or even gospel severity, to determine how far the chastisement or the scourge shall proceed. There are sins which are unto death spiritual and evangelical, that is, are inconsistent with spiritual life in the soul and with an evangelical right to life above, such as total impenitence and unbelief.

IV. The direction for prayer according to the different sorts of sin. The prayer is supposed to be for life: *He shall ask, and he shall give them life.* Life is to be asked of God. He is the God of life; he gives it when and to whom he pleases. In the case of a brother's sin, which is not unto death, we may in faith and hope pray for him. But, in case of the sin unto death we have no allowance to pray. Perhaps the apostle's expression, *I do not say, He shall pray for it,* may intend no more than, "I have no promise for you in that case." The removal of evangelical penalties, or the prevention of death, can be prayed for only conditionally or provisionally. We cannot pray that the sins of the impenitent and unbelieving should, while they are such, be forgiven them. But we may pray for their repentance, for their being enriched with faith in Christ, and thereupon for all other saving mercies. The apostle seems to argue that there is sin that is not unto death (*v.* 17); for, were all unrighteousness unto death, then we were all peremptorily bound over to death, and, since it is not so, there must be sin that is not to death. Though there is no venial sin there is pardoned sin.

JAMIESON, FAUSSET, BROWN

should lose, like the first Adam. **12. the Son . . . life**—*Greek,* "THE life." BENGEL remarks, The verse has two clauses: in the former the Son is mentioned without the addition "of God," for believers know *the Son:* in the second clause the addition "of God" is made, that unbelievers may know thereby what a serious thing it is not to have Him. In the former clause "has" bears the emphasis; in the second, *life.* To *have the Son* is to be able to say as the bride, "I am my Beloved's, and *my Beloved is mine.*" *Faith* is the mean whereby the regenerate HAVE Christ as a *present* possession, and in having Him *have life* in its germ and reality now, and shall have life in its fully developed manifestation hereafter.

13. These things—This Epistle. He, towards the close of his Gospel (John 20:30, 31), wrote similarly, stating his purpose in having written. In ch. 1:4 he states the object of his writing this Epistle to be, "that your joy may be full." To "*know that we have eternal life*" is the sure way to "joy in God." **13.** The oldest MSS. and versions read, "These things have I written unto you [omitting *that believe on the name of the Son of God*] that ye may know that ye have eternal life (cf. vs. 11), THOSE (of you I mean) WHO believe (not as *English Version* reads, *and that ye may believe*) on the name of the Son of God." *English Version,* in the latter clause, will mean, "that ye may *continue to* believe . . ." (cf. vs. 12). **14. the confidence**—*boldness*" (ch. 4:17) in prayer, which results from *knowing that we have eternal life* (vs. 13; ch. 3:19, 22). **according to his will**—which is the believer's will, and which is therefore no restraint to his prayers. In so far as God's will is not our will, we are not abiding in faith, and our prayers are not accepted. ALFORD well says, If we *knew* God's will thoroughly, and *submitted* to it heartily, it would be impossible for us to ask anything for the spirit or for the body which He should not perform; it is this ideal state which the apostle has in view. It is the *Spirit* who teaches us inwardly, and Himself in us asks according to the will of God. **15. hear**—*Greek,* "that He *heareth* us." **we have the petitions that we desired of him**—*We have,* as present possessions, everything *whatsoever we desired* (*asked*) *from Him.* Not one of our *past* prayers offered in faith, *according to His will,* is lost. Like Hannah, we can rejoice over them as granted even before the event; and can recognize the event when it comes to pass, as not from chance, but obtained by our past prayers. Cf. also Jehoshaphat's believing confidence in the issue of his prayers, so much so that he appointed singers to praise the Lord beforehand. **16. If any . . . see**—on any particular occasion; *Greek* aorist. **his brother**—a fellow Christian. **sin a sin**—in the act of sinning, and continuing in the sin: present. **not unto death**—provided that it is *not unto death.* **he shall give**—The *asker* shall be the means, by his intercessory prayer, of *God giving* life to the sinning brother. Kindly reproof ought to accompany his intercessions. *Life* was in process of being forfeited by the sinning brother when the believer's intercession obtained its restoration. **for them**—resuming the proviso put forth in the beginning of the verse. "Provided that the sin is not unto death." "Shali give life," I say, *to,* i.e., obtain life "*for* (in the case of) them that sin not unto death." **I do not say that he shall pray for it**—The *Greek* for "pray" means a REQUEST as of one on an equality, or at least on terms of familiarity, with him from whom the favor is sought. "The Christian intercessor for his brethren, John declares, shall not assume the authority which would be implied in making request for a sinner who has sinned the sin unto death (I Sam. 15:35; 16:1; Mark 3:29), that it might be forgiven him" [TRENCH, *Synonyms of New Testament*]. **17.** "Every unrighteousness (even that of believers, cf. ch. 1:9; 3:4. Every coming short of *right*) is sin"; (but) not every sin is the sin unto death. **and there is a sin not unto death**—in the case of which, therefore, believers may intercede. *Death* and *life* stand in correlative opposition (vss. 11-13). *The sin unto death* must be one tending "towards" (so the *Greek*), and so resulting in, *death.* ALFORD makes it to be an appreciable ACT of sin, viz., *the denying Jesus to be the Christ, the Son of God* (in contrast to confess this truth, vss. 1, 5), ch. 2:19, 22; 4:2, 3; 5:10. Such wilful deniers of Christ are not to be received into one's house, or wished "God speed." Still, I think with BENGEL, not merely the *act,* but also the *state* of apostasy accompanying the *act,* is included—a "state of soul in which faith, love, and hope, in short, the new life, is extinguished. The chief commandment is *faith* and *love.* Therefore, the

ADAM CLARKE

12. *He that hath the Son hath life.* As the eternal life is given "in" the Son of God, it follows that it cannot be enjoyed without Him. No man can have it without having Christ; therefore *he that hath the Son hath life, and he that hath not the Son of God hath not life.*

13. *That ye may know that ye have eternal life.* It is not a blind reliance for, but an actual enjoyment of, salvation; Christ living, working, and reigning in the heart. *And that ye may believe.* That is, "continue to believe"; for Christ dwells in the heart only by faith, and faith lives only by love, and love continues only by obedience; he who believes loves, and he who loves obeys.

14. *This is the confidence,* the "liberty of access and speech," *that, if we ask any thing according to his will,* that is, which He has promised in His Word. All that God has promised we are justified in expecting; and what He has promised and we expect, we should pray for. Prayer is the language of the children of God.

15. *And if we know that he hear us.* Seeing we are satisfied that He hears the prayer of faith, requesting the things which himself has promised, *we know,* consequently, *that we have the petitions*—the answer to the *petitions—that we desired of him.* For He cannot deny himself; and we may consider them as sure as if we had them; and we shall have them as soon as we plead for and need them.

16. *A sin which is not unto death.* This is an extremely difficult passage, and has been variously interpreted. What is the *sin not unto death,* for which we should ask, and life shall be given to him that commits it? And what is the *sin unto death,* for which we should not pray? *The sin unto death* means a case of transgression, particularly of grievous backsliding from the life and power of godliness, which God determines to punish with temporal death, while at the same time He extends mercy to the penitent soul. The disobedient prophet, 1 Kings xiii. 1-32, is, on this interpretation, a case in point. Many others occur in the history of the Church, and of every religious community. The *sin not unto death* is any sin which God does not choose thus to punish. This view of the subject is that taken by the late Rev. J. Wesley, in a sermon entitled "A Call to Backsliders." I do not think the passage has anything to do with what is termed "the sin against the Holy Ghost." See the note on Matt. xii. 31-32.

17. *All unrighteousness is sin.* Every act contrary to justice is sin—is a transgression of the law which condemns all injustice.

MATTHEW HENRY

Verses 18–21

I. A recapitulation of the privileges of sound Christian believers. 1. They are secured against sin (*v.* 18); secured against that sin which is unto death. The new nature, and the inhabitation of the divine Spirit thereby, prevent the admission of such unpardonable sin.

2. They are fortified against the devil's destructive attempts (*v.* 18). It seems not to be barely a narration of the duty of the regenerate; but an indication of their power.

3. They are on God's side in opposition to the world, *v.* 19. Mankind are divided into two great parties, that which belongs to God and that which belongs to wickedness. The Christian believers belong to God. They are of God, and from him, and to him, and for him. On the contrary, *the whole world*, the rest, being by far the major part, *lieth in wickedness.* May the God of the Christian world continually demolish the devil's dominion, and translate souls into *the kingdom of his dear Son!*

4. They are enlightened in the knowledge of the true eternal God, *v.* 20. The Son of God has come into our world, and we have seen him, and know him. He has revealed unto us the true God, and he has opened our minds too to understand that revelation; and we are assured that it is the true God that he hath discovered to us. It is a great happiness to know the true God, to know him in Christ; it is eternal life. 5. They have a happy union with God and his Son, *v.* 20. The Son leads us to the Father, and we are in both, in the love and favour of both. In union with either, much more with both, we are united to *the true God and eternal life.*

II. The apostle's concluding monition, *v.* 21. Since you know the true God, and are in him, let your light and love guard you. Flee from the false gods of the heathen world. The God whom you have known is he who redeemed you by his Son, who has pardoned your sins, and given you eternal life. Cleave to him in faith, and love, and constant obedience. To this living and true God be glory and dominion for ever and ever *Amen.*

JAMIESON, FAUSSET, BROWN

chief sin is that by which faith and love are destroyed. In the former case is *life;* in the latter, death. As long as it is not evident (*Note,* 'see,' vs. 16) that it is a sin unto death, it is lawful to pray. But when it is deliberate rejection of grace, and the man puts from him life thereby, how can others procure for him life?" **18.** (Ch. 3:9.) **We know**—Thrice repeated emphatically, to enforce the three truths which the words preface, as matters of the brethren's joint experimental knowledge. This vs. 18 warns against abusing vss. 16: 17, as warranting carnal security. **whosoever**—*Greek,* "every one who." Not only advanced believers, but *every one* who is born again, "sinneth not." **he that is begotten**—*Greek* aorist, "has been (once for all in *past* time) begotten of God"; in the beginning of the verse it is perfect. "Is begotten," or "born," as a *continuing* state. **keepeth himself**—The *Vulgate* translates, "The having been begotten of God keepeth HIM" (so one of the oldest MSS. reads): so ALFORD. Lit., "He having been begotten of God (nominative pendent), *it* (the divine generation implied in the nominative) keepeth him." So ch. 3:9, "His seed remaineth in him." Still, in *English Version* reading, God's working by His Spirit inwardly, and man's working under the power of that Spirit as a responsible agent, is what often occurs elsewhere. That *God* must *keep* us, if we are to *keep ourselves* from evil, is certain. Cf. John 17:15 especially with this verse. **that wicked one toucheth him not**—so as to hurt him. In so far as he realizes his regeneration-life, the prince of this world *hath nothing in him* to fasten his deadly temptations on, as in Christ's own case. His divine regeneration has severed once for all his connection with the prince of this world. **19. world lieth in wickedness**—rather, "lieth in *the wicked one,*" as the *Greek* is translated in vs. 18; ch. 2:13, 14; cf. ch. 4:4; John 17:14, 15. The world *lieth* in the power of, and abiding in, the wicked one, as the resting-place and lord of his slaves; cf. "abideth in death," ch. 3:14; contrast vs. 20, "we are in Him that is true." While the believer has been delivered out of his power, the whole world *lieth* helpless and motionless still in it, just as it was; including the wise, great, respectable, and all who are not by vital union in Christ. **20.** Summary of our Christian privileges. **is come**—*is present, having come.* "HE IS HERE—all is full of Him—His incarnation, work, and abiding presence, is to us a living fact" [ALFORD]. **given us an understanding**—Christ's office is to give the inner spiritual understanding to discern the things of God. **that we may know**—Some oldest MSS. read, "(so) that *we know.*" **him that is true**—God, as opposed to every kind of *idol* or false god (vs. 21). Jesus, by virtue of His oneness with God, is also "He that is true" (Rev. 3:7). *even*—"we are in the true" God, *by virtue of being* "in His Son Jesus Christ." **This is the true God**—"*This* Jesus Christ (the last-named Person) is the true God" (identifying Him thus with the Father in His attribute, "the only true God," John 17:3, primarily attributed to the Father). **and eternal life**—predicated of the Son of God; ALFORD wrongly says, He was *the life,* but not *eternal life.* The Father is indeed *eternal life* as its source, but the Son also is that *eternal life manifested,* as the very passage (ch. 1:2) which ALFORD quotes, proves against him. Cf. also vss. 11, 13. Plainly it is as the *Mediator of* ETERNAL LIFE *to us* that Christ is here contemplated. The *Greek* is, "The true God and eternal life is this" Jesus Christ, i.e., In believing in Him we believe in the true God, and have eternal life. The Son is called "He that is TRUE," Revelation 3:7, as here. This naturally prepares the way for warning against *false* gods (vs. 21). Jesus Christ is the only "express image of God's person" which is sanctioned, the only true visible manifestation of God. All other representations of God are forbidden as *idols.* Thus the Epistle closes as it began (ch. 1:1, 2). **21.** Affectionate parting caution. **from idols**—Christians were then everywhere surrounded by *idolaters,* with whom it was impossible to avoid intercourse. Hence the need of being on their guard against any even indirect compromise or act of communion with idolatry. Some at Pergamos, in the region whence John wrote, fell into the snare of eating things sacrificed to idols. The moment we cease to abide "in Him that is true (by abiding) in Jesus Christ," we become part of "the world that lieth in the wicked one," given up to *spiritual,* if not in all places *literal, idolatry* (Eph. 5:5; Col. 3:5).

ADAM CLARKE

18. *Whosoever is born of God sinneth not.* This is spoken of adult Christians; they are cleansed from all unrighteousness, consequently from all sin, chap. i. 7-9.

Keepeth himself. That is, in the love of God, Jude 21, by building up himself on his most holy faith, and praying in the Holy Ghost;

and that wicked one, the devil, *toucheth him not,* finds nothing of his own nature in him on which he can work.

19. *The whole world lieth in wickedness.* "Lieth in the wicked one."

20. *We know that the Son of God is come.* in the flesh, and has made His soul an offering for sin; *and hath given us an understanding,* a more eminent degree of light than we ever enjoyed before.

21. *Little children.* "Beloved children"; he concludes with the same affectionate feeling with which he commenced. *Keep yourselves from idols.* That is a man's *idol* or god from which he seeks his happiness. That is a man's idol which prevents him from seeking and finding his all in God.

THE SECOND EPISTLE OF JOHN

I. Introduction (1-4)
A. Addresses and key word: truth (1, 2)
B. Salutation (3)
C. The apostle's joy (4)

II. Love—the commandment (5)

III. Love and light (6)
A. Love defined
B. Light defined

IV. Light and life (7-11)
A. A warning (7)
B. Injunction (8)
C. A test (9)
D. A requirement (10, 11)

V. Conclusion—the farewell (12, 13)

Here we find a canonical epistle inscribed, principally, not only to a single person, but to one also of the gentler sex. And why not to one of that sex? In gospel redemption, privilege, and dignity, "there is neither male nor female"; they are both one "in Christ Jesus." No wonder, then, that a heroine in the Christian religion should be dignified also by an apostolic epistle.

MATTHEW HENRY

CHAPTER 1

Verses 1–4

I. The saluter, not expressed by name, but by a chosen character: *The elder.* The expression, and style, and love, intimate that the penman was the same with that of the foregoing epistle. Possibly the oldest apostle now living. He was now old in holy service and experience, had seen and tasted much of heaven, and was much nearer than when at first he believed.

II. The saluted: *To the elect lady and her children.* A lady, a person of eminent quality. It is well that the gospel has got among such. It is a pity but lords and ladies should be acquainted with the Lord Christ and his religion. *The elect lady;* not only a choice one, but one chosen of God. *And her children;* probably the lady was a widow. We see that children may well be taken notice of in Christian letters, and they should know it too; it may avail to their encouragement. The respect paid them, 1. By the apostle himself: *Whom I love in the truth,* whom I sincerely and heartily love. He who was the beloved disciple had learnt the art or exercise of love. 2. By all her Christian acquaintance: *And not I only, but also all those that have known the truth.* Truth demands acknowledgment, and those who see the evidences of pure religion should confess and attest them. The ground of this love and respect was their regard to the truth: *For the truth's sake which dwelleth in us, and shall be with us for ever.* Those who love truth and piety in themselves should love it in others too. Religion should still dwell within us, in our minds and hearts, in our faith and love.

III. The salutation, which is indeed an apostolical benediction, *v.* 3. Sacred love pours out blessings upon this honourable Christian family; to those who have shall more be given.

1. From whom these blessings are craved, (1) *From God the Father.* He is the fountain of blessedness. (2) *From the Lord Jesus Christ.* He is also author and communicator of these heavenly blessings, *the Son of the Father.*

2. What the apostle craves, (1) *Grace*—divine favour and goodwill. (2) *Mercy*—free pardon and forgiveness; those who are already rich in grace have need of continual forgiveness. (3) *Peace*—tranquillity of spirit and serenity of conscience. And these are desired *in truth and love.* These blessings will continually preserve true faith and love *in the elect lady and her children.*

IV. The congratulation upon the prospect of the exemplary behaviour of other children of this excellent lady, *v.* 4. Possibly the lady's sons travelled abroad, and in their travels might come to Ephesus, where the apostle is supposed to have now resided, and might there happily converse with him. Let young travellers learn to carry their religion along with them, and not either leave it at home or learn the ill customs of the countries where they come. It is pleasant to see children treading in good parent's steps. How great a joy must it be to her ladyship to hear so good an account of them from so good a judge! We see here also the rule of true walking: *the commandment of the Father.* Then is our walk true, our converse right, when it is managed by the word of God.

Verses 5, 6

I. The apostle's request. Whether out of deference to her ladyship, or apostolical meekness, or both, he condescends to beseech: *And now I beseech thee,*

JAMIESON, FAUSSET, BROWN

CHAPTER 1

Vss. 1-13. Address: Greeting: Thanksgiving for the Elect Lady's Faithfulness in the Truth: Enjoins Love: Warns against Deceivers, lest We Lose Our Reward: Conclusion. **1. The elder**—In a familiar letter John gives himself a less authoritative designation than "apostle"; so I Peter 5. **1. lady**—Bengel takes the *Greek* as a proper name *Kyria,* answering to the *Hebrew* "Martha." Being a person of influence, "deceivers" (vs. 7) were insinuating themselves into her family to seduce her and her children from the faith [Tirinus], whence John felt it necessary to write a warning to her.
A particular *Church,* probably that at Babylon, was intended. "Church" is derived from *Greek Kuriake,* akin to *Kuria,* or *Kyria* here; the latter word among the Romans and Athenians means the same as *ecclesia,* the term appropriated to designate the *Church assembly.* **love in the truth**—Christian *love* rests on the Christian *truth* (vs. 3, end). Not merely "I love *in truth,*" but "I love in the truth." **all**—All Christians form one fellowship, rejoicing in the spiritual prosperity of one another. "The communion of love is as wide as the communion of faith" [Alford]. **2. For the truth's sake**—joined with "I love," vs. 1. "They who love *in* the truth, also love *on account of* the truth." **dwelleth in us, and shall be with us for ever**—in consonance with Christ's promise. **3. Grace be with you**—One of the oldest MSS. and several versions have "us" for *you.* The *Greek* is lit., "Grace *shall be* with us," i.e., with both *you and me.* A prayer, however, is implied besides a confident affirmation. **grace . . . mercy . . . peace**—"*Grace*" covers the sins of men; "mercy," their miseries. *Grace* must first do away with man's guilt before his misery can be relieved by *mercy.* Therefore *grace* stands before *mercy. Peace* is the result of both, and therefore stands third in order. Casting all our care on the Lord, with thanksgiving, maintains this peace. **the Lord**—The oldest MSS. and most of the oldest versions omit "the Lord." John never elsewhere uses this title in his Epistles, but "the Son of God." **in truth and love**—The element or sphere in which alone *grace, mercy,* and *peace,* have place. He mentions *truth* in vs. 4; *love,* in vs. 5. Paul uses faith and *love;* for *faith* and *truth* are close akin. **4. I found**—probably in one of his missionary tours of superintendence. See *Introduction,* at the end, and vs. 12; III John 10:14. **of thy children**—some. **in truth**—i.e., in *the* Gospel truth. **as**—even as. "The Father's commandment" is the standard of "the truth." **5. I beseech**—rather (cf. *Note,* I John 5:16), "I request thee," implying some degree of *authority.* **not . . . new commandment**—It was *old* in that Christians heard it from the first in the Gospel preaching; *new,* in that the Gospel rested love on the new principle of filial imitation of God who first loved us, and gave Jesus to die for *us;* and also, in that *love* is now set forth with greater clearness than in the Old Testament dispensation. Love performs both tables of the law, and is the end of the law and the Gospel alike (cf. *Note,* I John 2:7, 8). **that we**—implying that he already had love, and urging her to join him in the same Christian grace. This verse seems to me to decide that a *Church,* not an *individual lady,* is meant. For a man to urge a wo-

ADAM CLARKE

CHAPTER 1

1. *The elder.* John the apostle, who was now a very old man, generally supposed to be about ninety, and therefore he uses the term presbyter or *elder,* not as the name of an office, but as designating his advanced age. He is allowed to have been the oldest of all the apostles, and to have been the only one who died a natural death. *The elect lady.* As *kuria* may be the feminine of *kurios,* "lord," therefore it may signify *lady;* and so several, both ancients and moderns, have understood it. But others have considered it the proper name of a woman, Kyria; and that this is a very ancient opinion is evident from the Peshito Syriac, which uses it as a proper name, as does also the Arabic. Some have thought that Eclecta was the name of this matron, from the word which we translate *elect,* and which here signifies the same as "excellent, eminent, honorable," or the like. Others think that a particular church is intended, which some suppose to be the church at Jerusalem, and that the "elect sister," v. 13, means the church at Ephesus; but these are conjectures which appear to me to have no good ground. I am satisfied that no metaphor is here intended; that the Epistle was sent to some eminent Christian matron, not far from Ephesus, who was probably deaconess of the church, who, it is likely, had a church at her house, or at whose house the apostles and travelling evangelists frequently preached, and were entertained. *Whom I love in the truth.* Whom I love as the Christian religion requires us to love one another. *And not I only.* She was well-known in the churches; many had witnessed or heard of her fidelity, and partook of her hospitality.

2. *For the truth's sake.* On account of the gospel. *And shall be with us.* For God will preserve not only the Christian religion but its truth, all its essential doctrines, *for ever.*

3. *Grace be with you.* This is addressed to her, her household, and probably that part of the church which was more immediately under her care. *The Son of the Father.* The apostle still keeps in view the miraculous conception of Christ, a thing which the Gnostics absolutely denied, a doctrine which is at the groundwork of our salvation.

4. *That I found of thy children walking in truth.* I have already supposed this Christian matron to be mother of a family, probably a widow, for no mention is made of her husband; and that she was also a deaconess in the church, and one in whose house the travelling evangelists preached, and where they were entertained. The *children* mentioned here may either be her own children or those members of the church which were under her care, or some of both. The apostle was glad to find, probably by an epistle sent from herself to him or from the information of some of the itinerant evangelists, that the work of God was prospering in the place where she lived, and also in her own household. He does not say that all were walking in the truth, but "some" of her children.

MATTHEW HENRY

lady. Love will avail where authority will not; and we may often see that the more authority is urged the more it is slighted.

II. The thing requested—growth in love. Those that are eminent in any Christian virtue have yet room to grow therein.

1. This love is recommended: From the obligation thereto—*the commandment.* From the antiquity of the obligation, *v.* 5. This commandment must everywhere attend Christianity, that the disciples of it must love one another.

2. Then this love is illustrated, *v.* 5. This is the evidence of our sincere, mutual, Christian love—that we walk after God's commands. Universal obedience is the proof of the sincerity of Christian virtues. This is a fundamental duty in the gospel-charter (*v.* 6), that is, walk in this love.

Verses 7–9

I. The ill news communicated to the lady, *For many deceivers have entered into the world.* Your stability is likely to be tried. 1. The description of the deceiver and his deceit (*v.* 7); he brings some error or other concerning the person of the Lord Jesus. Strange that after such evidence any should deny that the Lord Jesus is the Son of God and Saviour of the world! 2. The aggravation of the case (*v.* 7); he deludes souls and undermines the kingdom of the Lord Christ.

II. The counsel given hereupon, *v.* 8. Two things they must beware of, for some begin well, but at last lose all their pains. 1. Professors should take care not to lose what they have gained. Sad it is that fair and splendid attainments in the school of Christ should all be lost at last. 2. That they lose not their reward, none of it. *That we receive a full reward.* The way to attain the full reward is to abide true to Christ, and constant in religion to the end.

III. The reason of the apostle's counsel. 1. The danger and evil of departure from gospel light. It is in reality a departure from God himself: *Whosoever transgresseth and abideth not in the doctrine of Christ, hath not God.* Those who revolt thence, in so doing revolt from God. 2. The advantage and happiness of firm adherence to Christian truth. *He that abideth in the doctrine of Christ, he hath both the Father and the Son.* We must retain that holy doctrine in faith and love, as we hope or desire to arrive at blessed communion with the Father and the Son.

Verses 10, 11

I. The apostle gives direction concerning the treatment of such: *If there come any unto you, and bring not this doctrine, receive him not into your house. Neither bid him God speed.* Bad work should not be consecrated or recommended to the divine benediction. God will be no patron of falsehood and sin. The propagation of fatal error we must not dare to countenance.

II. The reason of such direction: *For he that biddeth him God speed is partaker of his evil deeds.* Favour and affection partake of the sin. We may be sharers in the iniquities of others.

Verses 12, 13

The apostle concludes this letter, for some things are better spoken than written. The use of pen and ink may be a mercy and a pleasure; but a personal interview may be more so.

The children of thy elect sister greet thee. Grace was abundant towards this family; here are two elect sisters, and probably their elect children. May there be many such gracious ladies rejoicing in their gracious descendants and other relations! *Amen.*

JAMIESON, FAUSSET, BROWN

man ("THEE"; not *thee and thy children*) that he and she should *love one another*, is hardly like an apostolic precept, however pure may be the love enjoined; but all is clear if "the lady" represent a *Church.* **6.** "Love is the fulfilling of the law," and the fulfilling of the law is the sure test of love. **This is the commandment**—*Greek,* "The commandment is this," viz., *love,* in which all God's other commandments are summed up. **7.** As *love* and *truth* go hand in hand (vss. 3, 4), he feels it needful to give warning against teachers of untruth. **For**—giving the reason why he dwelt on *truth* and on *love,* which manifests itself in keeping God's commandments (vs. 6). **many**—(I John 2:18; 4:1). **are entered**—The oldest MSS. read, "have *gone forth,*" viz., from us. **confess not . . . Jesus . . . in the flesh**—the token of Antichrist. **is come**—*Greek,* "coming." He who denies Christ's *coming* in the flesh, denies the *possibility* of the incarnation; he who denies that he *has come,* denies its *actuality.* **This is a . . .**—*Greek,* "This (such a one as has been just described) is *the* deceiver and *the* Antichrist." The *many* who in a degree fulfil the character, are forerunners of the final personal Antichrist, who shall concentrate in himself all the features of previous Antichristian systems. **8. Look to yourselves**—amidst the widespread prevalence of deception so many being led astray. So Christ's warning, Matthew 24:4, 5, 24. **we lose not . . . we receive**—The oldest MSS. and versions read, "That YE lose not, but that YE receive." **which we have wrought**—So one oldest MS. reads. Other very old MSS., versions, and Fathers, read, "which YE have wrought." The *we* being seemingly the more difficult reading is less likely to have been a transcriber's alteration. Look that ye lose not the believing state of "truth and love," which WE (as God's workmen, II Cor. 6:1; II Tim. 2:15) were the instruments of working in you. **a full reward**—of grace not of debt. *Fully* consummated glory. If "which YE have wrought" be read with very old authorities, the reward meant is that of their "work (of faith) and labor of love." There are degrees of heavenly reward proportioned to the degrees of capability of receiving heavenly blessedness. Each vessel of glory hanging on Jesus shall be fully happy. **9.** The *loss* (vs. 8) meant is here explained: the *not having God,* which results from *abiding not in the doctrine of Christ.* **transgresseth**—The oldest MSS. and versions read, "Every one who *takes the lead*"; lit., "goes," or "leads on before"; cf. John 10:4, "He goeth before them" (not the same *Greek*). Cf. III John 9, "Loveth to have the *pre-eminence.*" **hath not God**—(I John 2:23; 5:15). The second "of Christ" is omitted in the oldest MSS., but is understood in the sense. **He**—emphatical: *He and He alone.* **10. If there come any**—as a teacher or brother. The *Greek* is indicative, not subjunctive; implying that such persons *do actually come,* and *are sure to come;* when any comes, as there will. True love is combined with hearty renunciation and separation from all that is false, whether persons or doctrines. **receive him not . . . neither bid him God speed**—This is not said of those who were always aliens from the Church, but of those who wish to be esteemed brethren, and subvert the true doctrine [GROTIUS]. The greeting salutation forbidden in the case of such a one is that *usual among Christian brethren* in those days, not a mere formality, but a token of *Christian brotherhood.* **11.** By wishing a false brother or teacher "God (or *good*) speed," you imply that he is capable as such of good speed and *joy* (the lit. meaning of the *Greek*), and that you wish him it while opposing Christ; so you identify yourself with "his evil deeds." The *Greek* of "partaker" is "having communion with." We cannot have communion with saints and with Antichrist at the same time. Here we see John's naturally fiery zeal directed to a right end.

12. I would not write—A heart full of love pours itself out more freely face to face, than by letter. **paper**—made of Egyptian papyrus. Pens were then reeds split. **ink**—made of soot and water, thickened with gum. Parchment was used for the permanent MSS. in which the Epistles were preserved. Writing *tablets* were used merely for temporary purposes, as our slates. **face to face**—lit., "mouth to mouth." **full**—*Greek,* "filled full." Your joy will be complete in hearing from me in person the joyful Gospel truths which I now defer communicating till I see you. On other occasions his writing the glad truths was for the same purpose. **13.** ALFORD confesses that the non-mention of the "lady" herself here seems rather to favor the hypothesis that a *Church* is meant.

ADAM CLARKE

5. *That which we had from the beginning.* The commandment to *love one another* was what they had heard from the first publication of Christianity, and what he wishes this excellent woman to inculcate on all those under her care. The mode of address here shows that it was a person, not a church, to which the apostle wrote.

6. *And this is love.* That is, our love is shown and proved by our walking according to the commandments of God; for love is the principle of obedience.

7. *For many deceivers.* Of these he had spoken before, see 1 John iv. 1 ff. And these appear to have been Gnostics, for they denied that Jesus was *come in the flesh.* And this doctrine, so essential to salvation, none could deny but a deceiver and an antichrist. Instead of *are entered into,* many excellent MSS. and versions have "are gone out." The sense is nearly the same.

8. *Look to yourselves.* Be on your guard against these seducers; watch, pray, love God and each other, and walk in newness of life. *That we lose not those things which we have wrought.* That we apostles, who have been the means of your conversion, may not be deprived of you as our crown of rejoicing in the day of the Lord Jesus. Instead of the first person plural, *we lose,* many MSS., versions, and fathers read the whole clause in the second person plural, "ye lose": "Take heed to yourselves, that ye lose not the things which ye have wrought, but that ye receive a full reward." This reading is more consistent and likely, and is supported by at least as good evidence as the other.

9. *Whosoever transgresseth*—he who "passes over" the sacred enclosure, or "goes beyond" the prescribed limits. *And abideth not in the doctrine*—does not remain within these holy limits, but indulges himself either in excesses of action or passion. *Hath not God* for his Father, nor the love of God in his heart. *Hath both the Father and the Son.* He who abideth in the doctrine of Christ, his body is a temple of the Holy Trinity, and he has communion with the Father as his Father, and with the Son as his Saviour and Redeemer.

10. *If there come any unto you,* under the character of an apostle or evangelist, to preach in your house. *And bring not this doctrine,* that Jesus is come in the flesh, and has died for the redemption of the world; *Receive him not into your house.* Give him no entertainment as an evangelical teacher. Let him not preach under your roof. *Neither bid him God speed.* "And do not say, Health to him"—do not salute him with "Peace be to you!" The words mean, according to the Eastern use of them, "Have no religious connection with him, nor act towards him so as to induce others to believe you acknowledge him as a brother."

11. *Is partaker of his evil deeds.* He that acts towards him as if he considered him a Christian brother, and sound in the faith, puts it in his power to deceive others, by thus apparently accrediting his ministry.

12. *Having many things to write.* That is, I have many things that I might write to you, but I think it best not to commit them to paper, because I hope to visit you shortly, and speak fully of those matters, which will be a means of increasing the comfort of both you and your family, as well as my own. There is more comfort in mutual interviews among friends than in epistolary correspondence.

13. *The children of thy elect sister.* Probably her own sister, who lived at Ephesus and, being acquainted with the apostle's writing, desired to be thus remembered to her. *Elect,* in both this and the first verse, signifies "excellent, eminent, or honorable." *Amen* is wanting in the most ancient MSS. and in most of the versions.

THE THIRD EPISTLE OF JOHN

I. Introduction (1-4)
A. The address (1)
B. The prayer (2)
C. The apostle's joy (3, 4)

II. Gaius: love practiced (5-8)
A. Gaius' hospitality (5, 6a)
B. Injunction to continue (6b)
C. The reason (7, 8)

III. Diotrephes (9, 10)
A. The reason of Diotrephes' disobedience (9)
B. The warning (10a)
C. The expression of Diotrephes' pride (10b)

IV. Demetrius: love, light, life (11, 12)
A. The injunction (11a)
B. Central statement (11b)
C. The example of Demetrius (12)

V. Conclusion (13, 14)
A. Anticipation of meeting (13)
B. A message of peace (14)

The apostle sends this encouraging epistle to his friend Gaius, in which also he complains of the quite opposite spirit of a certain minister, and confirms the good report concerning another.

MATTHEW HENRY

CHAPTER 1

Verses 1, 2

I. The sacred penman who writes and sends the letter; not here indeed notified by his name: *The elder*. Some have questioned whether this were John the apostle or no; but his style and spirit seem to shine in the epistle. Gaius could not question from whom the letter came.

II. The person saluted and honoured by the letter. He is notified, 1. By his name,—*Gaius*. We read of several of that name, particularly of one whom the apostle Paul baptized at Corinth. 2. By the kind expressions of the apostle to him: *The well-beloved*, and *whom I love in the truth*. Love expressed is wont to kindle love. To love our friends for the truth's sake is true love, gospel love.

III. The salutation or greeting. 1. The apostle's good opinion of his friend, that his *soul prospered*, the greatest blessing on this side heaven. 2. His good wish for his friend that his body may *prosper and be in health* as well as his soul. Grace will improve health, health will employ grace.

Verses 3–8

I. The good report that the apostle had received concerning this friend of his (*v*. 3–6). 1. The testimony concerning Gaius—the truth that was in him, and this evinced by his charity. Faith should work by love. 2. The witnesses—brethren that came from Gaius testified. A good report is due from those who have received good. 3. The auditory before which the report and testimony were given—*before the church*. This seems to be the church at which the apostle now resided. They could not but testify what they found and felt.

II. The report the apostle himself gives of him, *v*. 5. He was hospitable, good to the brethren, even to strangers. All who were of the household of faith were welcome to him. He was conscientious in what he did: "*Thou dosest faithfully whatsoever thou doest;* thou doest it as a faithful servant, and from the Lord Christ mayest thou expect the reward."

III. The apostle's joy therein, *v*. 3. The best evidence of our having the truth is our *walking in the truth*.

IV. Concerning further treatment of the brethren that were with him. It seems to have been customary in those days of love to attend travelling ministers and Christians, at least some part of their road. It is a kindness to a stranger to be guided in his way, and a pleasure to travellers to meet with suitable company: this is a work that may be done *after a godly sort*.

V. The reasons of this directed conduct: *Because that for his name's sake these brethren went forth, taking nothing of the Gentiles*. They went forth to preach the gospel; possibly they might be sent out by this apostle himself: they went forth to convert the Gentiles; they went forth for God and his name's sake; they went forth also to carry a free gospel about with them: *Taking nothing of the Gentiles*. There are those who are not called to preach the gospel themselves who may yet contribute to the progress of it. The gospel should be made without charge to those to whom it is first preached.

JAMIESON, FAUSSET, BROWN

CHAPTER 1

VSS. 1-14. ADDRESS: WISH FOR GAIUS' PROSPERITY: JOY AT HIS WALKING IN THE TRUTH. HIS HOSPITALITY TO THE BRETHREN AND STRANGERS THE FRUIT OF LOVE. DIOTREPHES' OPPOSITION AND AMBITION. PRAISE OF DEMETRIUS. CONCLUSION. **1.** I—emphatical: *I* personally, for my part. On Gaius or Caius, see *Introduction* before Second Epistle. **love in the truth**—(II John 1). "Beloved" is repeated often in this Epistle, indicating strong affection (vss. 1, 2, 5, 11). **2. above all things**—*Greek*, "*concerning* all things": so ALFORD: *in all respects*. But WAHL justifies *English Version* (cf. I Pet. 4:8). Of course, since his *soul's prosperity* is presupposed, "above all things" does not imply that John wishes Gaius' bodily health above that of his soul, but as the *first* object to be desired *next after spiritual health*. I know you are prospering in the concerns of your soul. I wish you similar prosperity in your body. Perhaps John had heard from the brethren (vs. 3) that Gaius was in bad health, and was tried in other ways (vs. 10), to which the wish, vs. 2, refers. **prosper**—in general. **be in health**—in particular. **3. testified of the truth that is in thee**—*Greek*, "of (or *to*) thy truth": thy share of that truth in which thou walkest [ALFORD]. **even as thou**—in contrast to Diotrephes (vs. 9). **4. my children**—members of the Church: confirming the view that the "elect lady" is a Church. **5. faithfully**—an act becoming a faithful man. **whatsoever thou doest**—a distinct *Greek* word from the former "doest": translate, "workest": whatsoever work, or labor of love, thou dost perform. So Matthew 26: 10, "She hath wrought a good *work* upon me." **and to strangers**—The oldest MSS., "and that (i.e., and those brethren) strangers." The fact of the brethren whom thou didst entertain being "strangers," enhances the love manifested in the act. **6. borne witness of thy charity before the church**—to stimulate others by the good example. The brethren so entertained by Gaius were missionary evangelists (vs. 7); and, probably, in the course of narrating their missionary labors for the edification of the Church where John then was, incidentally mentioned the loving hospitality shown them by Gaius. **bring forward on their journey**—"if thou (*continue to*) forward on their journey" by giving them provisions for the way. **after a godly sort**—*Greek*, "in a manner worthy of God," whose ambassadors they are, and whose servant thou art. He who honors God's missionary servants (vs. 7), honors God. **7. his name's sake**—Christ's. **went forth**—as missionaries. **taking nothing**—refusing to *receive* aught by way of pay, or maintenance, though justly entitled to it, as Paul at Corinth and at Thessalonica. **Gentiles**—the Christians just gathered out by their labors from among the heathen. As Gaius himself was a *Gentile* convert, "the Gentiles" here must mean *the converts just made from the heathen*, the Gentiles to whom they had *gone forth*. It would have been inexpedient to have taken aught (the *Greek meden* implies, not that they *got* nothing, though they had desired it, but that it was of *their own choice* they *took nothing*) from the infant churches among the heathen:

ADAM CLARKE

CHAPTER 1

1. *The elder*. See on the first verse of the preceding Epistle. *The wellbeloved Gaius*. *Gaius* is the Greek mode of writing the Roman name Caius, and thus it should be rendered in European languages. Several persons of the name of Gaius occur in the New Testament. In the Epistle to the Romans, chap. xvi. 23, Paul mentions a Gaius who lived at Corinth, whom he calls his "host," and the host "of the whole church." In 1 Cor. i. 14, Paul mentions a Gaius who lived at Corinth, whom he had baptized; but this is probably the same with the above. In Acts xix. 29, mention is made of a Gaius who was a native of Macedonia, who accompanied Paul, and spent some time with him at Ephesus. In Acts xx. 4 we meet a Gaius of Derbe, who was likewise a fellow traveller of Paul. Now whether this Gaius was one of the persons just mentioned or whether he was different from them all is difficult to determine, because Gaius was a very common name. Yet if we may judge from the similarity of character it is not improbable that he was the Gaius who lived at Corinth, and who is styled by Paul the "host . . . of the whole church"; for hospitality to his Christian brethren was the leading feature in the character of this Gaius to whom John wrote, and it is on this very account that he is commended by the apostle.

2. *I wish above all things*. Above all things I pray *that thou mayest prosper and be in health*.

3. *When the brethren came*. Probably the same of whom he speaks in the fifth and following verses, and who appear to have been itinerant evangelists. *The truth that is in thee*. The soundness of your faith and the depth of your religion.

4. *To hear that my children*. From this it has been inferred that Gaius was one of John's converts, and consequently not the Corinthian Gaius, who was converted, most probably, by Paul. But the apostle might use the term *children* here as implying those who were immediately under his pastoral care, and being an old man, he had a right to use such terms in addressing his juniors in both age and grace.

6. *Which have borne witness of thy charity*. Of your love and benevolence. *Before the church*. The believers at Ephesus, for to this church the apostle seems to refer. *Whom if thou bring forward*. If you continue to assist such, as you have done, *thou shalt do well*. *After a godly sort*. "Worthy of God"; and in such a way as He can approve.

7. *For his name's sake they went forth*. For the sake of preaching the gospel of the grace of God, and making known Jesus to the heathen. *Taking nothing of the Gentiles*. Receiving no emolument for their labor, but in every respect showing themselves to be truly disinterested. Sometimes, and on some special occasions, this

MATTHEW HENRY

We ought therefore to receive such, that we may be fellow-helpers to the truth. Those who cannot themselves proclaim it may yet help and countenance those who do.

Verses 9–11

I. Here is a very different example and character.

1. His name—a Gentile name: *Diotrephes,* attended with an unchristian spirit.

2. His temper and spirit—full of pride and ambition: *He loves to have the pre-eminence.*

3. His contempt of the apostle's authority, and letter, and friends. Of his authority: *The deeds which he doeth prating against us with malicious words.* Malice and ill-will in the heart will be apt to vent themselves by the lips. Of his letter (*v.* 9). To an ambitious aspiring spirit apostolical authority or epistle signifies but little. Of his friends, the brethren he recommended, *v.* 10. There might be some differences or different customs between the Jewish and Gentile Christians. Many are cast out of the church who should be received there with satisfaction and welcome.

4. The apostle's menace of this proud domineerer (*v.* 10). This seems to intimate apostolical authority.

II. Here is counsel upon that different character, *v.* 11. Caution and counsel are not needless to those who are good already. To this caution and counsel a reason is respectively subjoined. To the counsel: *Follow that which is good;* for *he that doeth good is of God.* To the caution: *Follow not that which is evil,* for *he that doeth evil hath not seen God.* Evil-workers vainly pretend or boast an acquaintance with God.

Verses 12–14

I. The character of another person, one *Demetrius,* not much known otherwise. But here his name will live. His commendation was, 1. General: *Demetrius has a good report of all men.* Few are well spoken of by all. But universal integrity and goodness are the way to (and sometimes obtain) universal applause. 2. Deserved and well founded, *v.* 12. 3. Confirmed by the apostle's and his friends' testimony: *Yea, and we also bear record; And you know that our record is true.* It is good to be well known, or known for good.

II. The conclusion of the epistle. The referring of some things to personal interview, *v.* 13, 14. Many things may be more proper for immediate communication than for letter. Good Christians may well be glad to see one another. The benediction: *Peace be to you.* The public salutation sent to Gaius: *Our friends salute thee.* The apostle's particular salutation of the Christians in Gaius's church or vicinity: *Greet the friends by name.* Those may well salute and greet one another on earth who hope to live together in heaven.

JAMIESON, FAUSSET, BROWN

the case was different in receiving hospitality from Gaius. **8. We**—in contradistinction to "the Gentiles" or "heathen" referred to, vs. 7. **therefore**—as they take nothing from the Gentiles or heathen. **receive**—The oldest MSS. read, "take up." As they *take* nothing from the Gentiles, we ought to *take* them *up* so as to support them. **fellow helpers**—with them. **to the truth**—i.e., *to promote* the truth. **9. I wrote**—The oldest MSS. add "something": *a communication,* probably, on the subject of *receiving the brethren* with brotherly love (vss. 8, 10). That Epistle was not designed by the Spirit for the universal Church, or else it would have been preserved. **unto the church**—of which Gaius is a member. **loveth . . . pre-eminence**—through ambition. Evidently occupying a high place in the Church where Gaius was (vs. 10). **among them**—*over* the members of the Church. **receiveth us not**—virtually, viz., by not *receiving* with love the brethren whom we recommended to be received (vss. 8, 10; cf. Matt. 10:40). **10. if I come**—(*V.* 14). **I will remember**—lit., "I will bring to mind" before all by stigmatizing and punishing. **prating**—with mere silly tattle. **neither doth he . . . receive the brethren**—with hospitality. "The brethren" are the missionaries on their journey. **forbiddeth them that would**—receive them. **casteth them**—those that would receive the brethren, by excommunication from the Church, which his influence, as a leading man (vs. 9) in it, enabled him to do. NEANDER thinks that the missionaries were JEWS by birth, whence it is said in their praise they *took nothing from* THE GENTILES: in contrast to other Jewish missionaries who abused ministers' right of maintenance elsewhere, as Paul tells us, II Corinthians 11:22; Philippians 3:2, 5, 19. Now in the Gentile churches there existed an ultra-Pauline party of anti-Jewish tendency, the forerunners of Marcion: Diotrephes possibly stood at the head of this party, which fact, as well as this domineering spirit, may account for his hostility to the missionaries, and to the apostle John, who had, by the power of love, tried to harmonize the various elements in the Asiatic churches. At a later period, Marcion, we know, attached himself to Paul alone, and paid no deference to the authority of John. **11. follow not that which is evil**—as manifested in Diotrephes (vss. 9, 10). **but . . . good**—as manifested in Demetrius (vs. 12). **is of God**—is born of God, who is good. **hath not seen God**—spiritually, not literally. **12. of all men**—who have had opportunity of knowing his character. **of the truth itself**—The Gospel standard of *truth* bears witness to him that he walks conformably to it, in acts of real love, hospitality to the brethren (in contrast to Diotrephes), etc. Cf. John 3:21 "He that doeth truth cometh to the light, that his deeds may be made manifest that they are wrought in God." **we also**—besides the testimony of "all men," and "of the truth itself." **ye know**—The oldest MSS. read, "thou knowest." **13. I will not**—rather as *Greek,* "I *wish* not . . . to write" more. **14. face to face**—*Greek,* "mouth to mouth." **Peace**—peace inward of conscience, peace fraternal of friendship, peace supernal of glory [LYRA]. **friends**—a title seldom used in the New Testament, as it is absorbed in the higher titles of "brother, brethren." Still Christ recognizes the relation of *friend* also, based on the highest grounds, obedience to Him from love, and entailing the highest privileges, admission to the intimacy of the holy and glorious God, and sympathizing Saviour; so Christians have "friends" in Christ. Here in a friendly letter, mention of "friends" appropriately occurs. **by name**—not less than if their names were written [BENGEL].

ADAM CLARKE

may be necessary; but "The labourer is worthy of his hire" is the maxim of the Author of Christianity. And those congregations of Christians are ever found to prize the gospel most, and profit most by it, who bear all expenses incident to it.

9. *I wrote unto the church,* the church where Gaius was. *But Diotrephes, who loveth to have the preeminence,* "who loves the presidency, or chief place" in the church. He was doubtless an officer in the church, at least a deacon, probably a bishop; and being one, he magnified himself in his office; he loved such eminence, and behaved himself haughtily in it. *Receiveth us not.* Does not acknowledge the apostolical authority.

10. *If I come, I will remember.* I will show him the authority which, as an apostle of Jesus Christ, I possess. *Prating against us.* Diotrephes might have been a converted Jew who was unwilling that the Gentiles should be received into the church; or a Judaizing Christian who wished to incorporate the law with the gospel, and calumniated the apostles who taught otherwise. This haughty and unfeeling man would give no countenance to the converted Gentiles; so far from it that he would not receive any of them himself, forbade others to do it, and excommunicated those who had been received into the church by the apostles.

11. *Follow not that which is evil.* "Do not imitate that wicked man," i.e., the conduct of Diotrephes; be merciful, loving, and kind.

12. *Demetrius hath good report.* Perhaps another member of the church where Gaius was; or he might have been one of those whom the apostle recommends to Gaius; or possibly the bearer of this letter from John to Gaius.

13. *I had many things to write.* That is, I have many things that I might write; but having the hope of seeing you shortly, I will not commit them to paper. *Ink* and *pen* are here mentioned, paper and ink in the preceding Epistle.

14. *Peace be to thee.* May you possess every requisite good, of both a spiritual and a temporal kind. *Our friends salute thee.* Desire to be affectionately remembered to you. *Greet the friends by name*—remember me to all those with whom I am acquainted, as if I had specified them by name.

THE EPISTLE OF JUDE

I. Introduction (1-3)
A. The writer and the readers (1)
B. Salutation (2)
C. The writing—change of purpose declared (3)

II. The danger (4-16)
A. Described (4-11)
1. Its nature (4)
2. Its peril (5-7)
3. Its arrogance (8-10)
4. Its doom (11)

B. Denounced (12-16)
1. Figurative denunciation (12, 13)
2. Enoch's prophecy applied to them (14, 15)
3. Final description (16)

III. The duty (17-23)
A. Recognition of the danger (17-19)
1. Declared by the apostles (17, 18)
2. Distinguished by two things (19)

B. The personal duty (20-23)
1. Central cause—"keep yourselves" (21)
2. How this is to be done (20, 21)
3. Duty towards others (22, 23)

IV. Conclusion (24, 25)
A. "Him that is able to guard you from stumbling" —continuity
B. "To set you before the presence of His glory" —consummation
C. "To Him be glory"

This epistle is styled (as are some few others) *general* because it is not immediately directed to any particular person, family, or church, but to the whole society of Christians. The general scope of it is much the same with that of the second chapter of the second epistle of Peter. It is designed to warn us against seducers, to inspire us with warm love to, and a hearty concern for, truth and that in the closest conjunction with holiness, of which charity is a most essential character.

MATTHEW HENRY

CHAPTER 1

Verses 1, 2

I. We have an account of the penman of this epistle, *Jude*, or *Judas*. He was name-sake to one of his ancestors, the patriarch-son of Jacob. This was a name of worth, eminency, and honour; yet, 1. He had a wicked name-sake. There was one Judas who was the betrayer of his and our Lord. The same names may be common to the best and worst persons. It may be instructive to be called after the names of eminently good men, but there can be no inference drawn thence as to what we shall prove, though we may conclude what sort of persons our good parents hoped we should be. But, 2. Our Judas was quite another man. He was a faithful servant of Jesus Christ, the other was his betrayer and murderer. Our apostle here calls himself a servant of Jesus Christ, esteeming that a most honourable title. He might have claimed kindred to Christ according to the flesh, but he waives this, and rather glories in being his servant. It is a great honour to the meanest sincere minister (and it holds proportionably as to every upright Christian) that he is *the servant of Christ Jesus*. The apostles were servants before they were apostles, and they were but servants still. *And brother of James*, to wit, of him whom the ancients style *the first bishop of Jerusalem*. Of this James our Jude was brother, whether in the strictest or a larger acceptation I determine not.

II. To whom this epistle is directed; to all those *who are sanctified by God the Father, and preserved in Jesus Christ, and called*. The apostle may speak of their being *called to be Christians*. Christians are the called, called out of the world,—called from sin to Christ. Sanctified: *Sanctified by God the Father*. All who are effectually called are sanctified. Our sanctification is not our own work. Our corruption and pollution are of ourselves; but our sanctification and renovation are of God and his grace. The called and sanctified are *preserved in Christ Jesus*. Where he begins he will perfect; though we are fickle, he is constant.

III. We have the apostolical benediction: *Mercy to you*, &c. The *mercy* of God is the spring and fountain of all the good we have or hope for. Next to mercy is *peace*, which we have from the sense of having obtained mercy. As from mercy springs peace, so from peace springs *love*, his love to us, our love to him, and our brotherly love to one another. These the apostle prays may be multiplied, that Christians may not be content with scraps and narrow scantlings of them.

Verses 3–7

I. The design of the apostle in writing this epistle: to establish them in the Christian faith, and a practice and conversation truly conformable thereunto, and in an open and bold profession thereof. 1. The gospel salvation is a common salvation, in a most sincere offer and tender of it to all mankind. None

JAMIESON, FAUSSET, BROWN

CHAPTER 1

Vss. 1-25. ADDRESS: GREETING: HIS OBJECT IN WRITING: WARNING AGAINST SUDUCERS IN DOCTRINE AND PRACTICE FROM GOD'S VENGENANCE ON APOSTATES, ISRAEL, THE FALLEN ANGELS, SODOM AND GOMORRAH. DESCRIPTION OF THESE BAD MEN, IN CONTRAST TO MICHAEL: LIKE CAIN, BALAAM, AND CORE: ENOCH'S PROPHECY AS TO THEM: THE APOSTLES' FOREWARNING: CONCLUDING EXHORTATION AS TO PRESERVING THEIR OWN FAITH, AND TRYING TO SAVE OTHERS: DOXOLOGY. **1. servant of Jesus Christ**—as His minister and apostle. **brother of James**—who was more widely known as bishop of Jerusalem and "brother of the Lord" (i.e., either *cousin*, or stepbrother, being son of Joseph by a former marriage; for ancient traditions universally agree that Mary, Jesus' mother, continued perpetually a virgin). Jude therefore calls himself modestly "brother of James." **to them . . . sanctified by God the Father**—The oldest MSS. and versions, ORIGEN, LUCIFER, and others read, "beloved" for *sanctified*. If *English Version* be read, cf. Colossians 1:12; I Peter 1:2. The *Greek* is not "by," but "in." God the Father's *love* is the element IN which they are "beloved." Thus the conclusion, vs. 21, corresponds, "Keep yourselves *in* the love of God." Cf. "beloved of the Lord" II Thessalonians 2:13. **preserved in Jesus Christ**—"kept." Translate not "in," but as *Greek*, "FOR Jesus Christ." "Kept *continually* (so the *Greek perfect* participle means) by God the Father for Jesus Christ," against the day of His coming. Jude, beforehand, mentions the source and guarantee for the final accomplishment of believers' salvation; lest they should be disheartened by the dreadful evils which he proceeds to announce [BENGEL]. **and called**—predicated of "them that are beloved in God the Father, and preserved in Jesus Christ: who are called." God's effectual *calling* in the exercise of His divine prerogative, guarantees their eternal safety. **2. Mercy**—in a time of wretchedness. Therefore *mercy* stands first; the mercy of *Christ* (vs. 21). **peace**—in the *Holy Ghost* (vs. 20). **love**—of *God* (vs. 21). The three answer to the divine Trinity. **be multiplied**—in you and towards you. **3.** Design of the Epistle (cf. vss 20, 21). **all diligence**—(II Pet. 1:5). As the minister is to give *all diligence* to admonish, so the people should, in accordance with his admonition, give *all diligence* to have all Christian graces, and to make their calling sure. **the common salvation**—wrought by Christ. Cf. *Note*, "obtained LIKE precious faith," II Pet. 1:1. This *community of faith*, and of the object of faith, *salvation*, forms the ground of mutual exhortation by appeals to common hopes and fears. **it was needful for me**—rather, "I felt it necessary to write (now *at once;* so the *Greek* aorist means; the *present* infinitive 'to write,' which precedes, expresses merely the general fact of writing) exhorting you." The reason why he felt it necessary "to

ADAM CLARKE

CHAPTER 1

1. *Jude, the servant of Jesus Christ*. Probably Jude the apostle, who was surnamed Thaddaeus and Lebbaeus, was son to Alphaeus, and brother to James the less, Joses, and Simon. *Brother of James*. Supposed to be James the less, bishop of Jerusalem, mentioned here because he was an eminent person in the Church. *To them that are sanctified by God*. Instead of "to the sanctified," several MSS., with several of the fathers, have "to them that are beloved." Jude writes to all believers everywhere, and not to any particular church; hence this Epistle has been called a general Epistle.

2. *Mercy unto you*. For even the best have no merit, and must receive every blessing and grace in the way of *mercy*. *Peace* with God and your consciences, *love* to both God and man, *be multiplied*, be unboundedly increased.

3. *When I gave all diligence*. This phrase is a Grecism for being "exceedingly intent" upon a subject, taking it up seriously with determination to bring it to good effect. The meaning of the apostle seems to be this: "Beloved brethren, when I saw it necessary to write to you concerning the common salvation, my mind being deeply affected with the dangers to which the Church is exposed from the false teachers that are gone out into the world, I found it extremely necessary to write and exhort you to hold fast the truth which you had received, and strenuously to contend for that only faith which, by our Lord and His apostles, has been delivered to the Christians." *The common salvation*. The Christian religion and the salvation which it brings. This is called *common* because it belongs equally to Jews and Gentiles.

MATTHEW HENRY

are excluded from the benefit of these gracious offers and invitations, but those who exclude themselves. It is made to all believers; it is made to the weak as well as to the strong. Here let us abide; here we are safe; if we stir a step further, we are in danger of being either entangled or seduced. The apostles and evangelists all wrote to us of this common salvation. They have fully declared to us all that is necessary *for every one to believe and do*, in order to obtain a personal interest in the common salvation. The apostle (though inspired) gave all diligence to write of the common salvation. Those who speak of sacred things ought always to speak of them with the greatest reverence, care, and diligence. Those who have received the doctrine of this common salvation must contend earnestly for it. *Earnestly*, not *furiously*. But how? As the apostles did; by suffering patiently and courageously for it.

II. The occasion the apostle had to write to this purport. As evil manners give rise to good laws, so dangerous errors often give just occasion to the proper defence of important truths. 1. Ungodly men are the great enemies of the faith of Christ and the peace of the church. Those who deny or corrupt the one, and disturb the other, are here expressly styled *ungodly men*. Ungodly men raise scruples, start questions, cause divisions, widen breaches. Nothing cuts us off from the church but that which cuts us off from Christ; namely, reigning infidelity and ungodliness. Those are ungodly men who live *without God in the world*, who have no regard to God and conscience.

2. Those are *the worst of ungodly men who turn the grace of God into lasciviousness*, who take encouragement to sin more boldly because the grace of God has abounded, and still abounds, so wonderfully. 3. Those who turn the grace of God into lasciviousness do in effect *deny the Lord God, and our Lord Jesus Christ*; they deny both natural and revealed religion. They strike at the foundation of natural religion, for they *deny the only Lord God*; and they overturn all the frame of revealed religion, for they deny *the Lord Jesus Christ*. These stand or fall together, and they mutually yield light and force to each other. Never two tallies answered more exactly to each other than these do. 4. Those who turn the grace of God into lasciviousness are ordained unto condemnation. Those who thus sin must needs die of their wounds, of their disease. 5. We ought to contend earnestly for the faith, in opposition to those who would corrupt or deprave it, such as have *crept in unawares*. The more busy and crafty the instruments and agents of Satan are, to rob us of the truth, the more solicitous should we be to hold it fast.

III. The fair warning which the apostle, in Christ's name, gives to those who, having professed his holy religion, do afterwards prove false to it, *v.* 5–7. *I will put you in remembrance*. What we already know we still need to be put in remembrance of. Preaching is not designed to teach us something new in every sermon; but *to put us in remembrance*, to call to mind things forgotten. *Though you know these things*, yet you still need to *know them better*.

1. The destruction of the unbelieving Israelites in the wilderness, *v.* 5. They had miracles in abundance: they were their daily bread; yet even they perished in unbelief. We have greater advantages than they had; let their error be our awful warning.

2. We are here put in remembrance of the fall of the angels, *v.* 6. There were a great number of the angels who *left their own habitation*. They quitted their post, and rebelled against God. But God did not spare them. Those who would not be servants to their Maker were made captives to his justice, and are *reserved in everlasting chains under darkness*. Hear and fear, O sinful mortals of mankind!

JAMIESON, FAUSSET, BROWN

write *with exhortation,*" he states, vs. 4, "For there are certain men crept in. . . ." Having intended to write generally of *the common salvation,* he found it necessary from the existing evils in the Church, to write specially that they should *contend for the faith against* those evils. **earnestly contend**—Cf. Philippians 1:27, "striving together for the faith of the Gospel." **once . . .**—*Greek, "once for all* delivered. . . ." No other faith or revelation is to supersede it. A strong argument for resisting heretical innovators (vs. 4). Believers, like Nehemiah's workmen, with one hand "build themselves up in their most holy faith"; with the other they" contend earnestly for the faith" against its foes. **the saints**—all Christians, *holy* (i.e., consecrated to God) by their calling, and in God's design. **4. certain men**—implying disparagement. **crept in unawares**—stealthily and unlawfully. *Note,* II Peter 2:1, "*privily* shall bring in damnable heresies." **before . . . ordained**—*Greek,* "forewritten," viz., in Peter's prophecy vss. 17, 18; and in Paul's before that, I Tim. 4:1; II Tim. 3:1; and by implication in the judgments which overtook the apostate angels. The disobedient Israelites, Sodom and Gomorrah, Balaam and Core, and which are *written* "for an example" (vs. 7, and vss. 5, 6, 11). God's eternal character as the Punisher of sin, as set forth in Scripture "of old," is the ground on which such apostate characters are ordained to condemnation. **to this condemnation**—Jude graphically puts their judgment as it were present before the eyes, "THIS." Enoch's prophecy comprises the "ungodly men" of the last days before Christ's coming to judgment, as well as their forerunners, the "ungodly men" before the flood, the type of the last judgment (Matt. 24:37-39; II Pet. 3:3-7). The disposition and the doom of both correspond. **the grace of our God**—A phrase for the Gospel especially sweet to believers who appropriate God in Christ as "*our* God," and so rendering the more odious the vile perversity of those who turn the Gospel state of grace and liberty into a ground of licentiousness, as if their exemption from the law gave them a license to *sin.* **denying the only Lord**—The oldest MSS., versions, and Fathers omit "God," which follows in *English Version.* Translate as the *Greek,* "the only Master"; here used of *Jesus Christ,* who is at once *Master* and "Lord" (a different *Greek* word). So II Peter 2:1, *Note.* By virtue of Christ's perfect oneness with the Father, He, as well as the Father, is termed "the ONLY" God and "MASTER." *Greek,* "Master," implies God's *absolute ownership* to dispose of His creatures as He likes. **5.** (Heb. 3:16; 4:13). **therefore**—Other oldest MSS. and *Vulgate* read, "But"; in contrast to the ungodly vs. 4. **though ye once**—rather, "once for all." Translate, "I wish to remind you, *as* knowing ALL (viz., *that I am referring to;* so the oldest MSS., versions, and Fathers) *once for all.*" *As* already they know all the facts once for all, he needs only to "remind" them. **the Lord**—The oldest MSS. and versions read, "Jesus." So "Christ" is said to have accompanied the Israelites in the wilderness; so perfectly is Jesus one with the God of the Israelite theocracy. **saved**—brought safely, and into a state of safety and salvation. **afterward**—*Greek,* "secondly"; in the next instance "destroyed them that believed not," as contrasted with His *in the first instance* having *saved* them. **6.** (II Pet. 2:4.) **kept not their first estate**—*Vulgate* translates, "their own *principality,*" which the fact of angels being elsewhere called "principalities," favors: "their own" implies that, instead of being content with the *dignity* once for all assigned to them under the Son of God, they aspired higher. **left**—on their own accord. **their own**—*Greek,* "their proper." **habitation**—heaven, all bright and glorious, as opposed to the "*darkness*" to which they now are doomed. Their ambitious designs seem to have had a peculiar connection with this earth, of which Satan before his fall may have been God's vicegerent, whence arises his subsequent connection with it as first the Tempter, then "the prince of this world." **reserved**—As the *Greek* is the same, and there is an evident reference to *their* having "*kept not* their first estate," translate, "He hath kept." Probably what is meant is, He hath kept them *in His purpose;* that is their sure doom; moreover, as yet, Satan and his demons roam at large on the earth. An earnest of their doom is their having been cast out of heaven, being already restricted to "the darkness of this present world," the "air" that surrounds the earth, their peculiar element now. They lurk in places of gloom and death, looking forward with agonizing fear to their final torment in the bottomless pit. He means not literal chains and darkness, but figurative in this present world where, with restricted powers and liberties,

ADAM CLARKE

4. *For there are certain men crept in unawares.* They had got into the Church under specious pretenses; and, when in, began to sow their bad seed. *Before of old ordained.* Such as were long ago "proscribed, and condemned in the most public manner"; this is the import of the word in this place, and there are many examples of this use of it in the Greek writers.

To this condemnation. To a similar punishment to that immediately about to be mentioned. In the sacred writings all such persons, false doctrines, and impure practices have been most openly proscribed and condemned; and the apostle immediately produces several examples, viz., the disobedient Israelites, the unfaithful angels, and the impure inhabitants of Sodom and Gomorrah. *Turning the grace of our God into lasciviousness.* Making the grace and mercy of God a covering for crimes, intimating that men might sin safely who believe the gospel, because in that gospel grace abounds. *The only Lord God, and our Lord Jesus Christ. God* is omitted by more than sixteen MSS. and by many of the fathers. It is very likely that it was originally inserted as a gloss, to ascertain to whom the title of "the only Sovereign," belonged; and thus make two persons where only one seems to be intended. The passage I believe belongs solely to Jesus Christ, and may be read thus: "Denying the only sovereign Ruler, even our Lord Jesus Christ."

5. *I will therefore put you in remembrance.* That is, how such persons were proscribed, and condemned to bear the punishment due to such crimes. *Though ye once knew this.* The word here translated *once* has greatly puzzled many interpreters. It has two meanings in the sacred writings, and indeed in the Greek writers also. It signifies (1) "once, one time"; (2) "altogether, entirely, perfectly." This appears to be the sense of the word in Heb. vi. 4: "those who were fully enlightened." Heb. x. 2: "thoroughly cleansed." Jude is to be understood as saying, "I will therefore put you in remembrance, though you are thoroughly instructed in this." *Saved the people.* Delivered them from the Egyptian bondage. *Afterward destroyed them.* Because they neither believed His word nor were obedient to His commands. This is the first example of what was mentioned in v. 4.

6. *The angels which kept not their first estate.* "Their own principality." The words may be understood of their having invaded the office or dignity of some others, or of their having by some means forfeited their own. This is spoken of those generally termed the "fallen angels"; but from what they fell, or from what cause or for what crime, we know not. They are produced as the second example. *But left their own habitation.* This seems to intimate that they had invaded the office and prerogatives of others, and attempted to seize on their place of residence and felicity. *He hath reserved in everlasting chains.* That is, in a state of confinement from which they cannot escape. *Under darkness.* Alluding probably to those dungeons or dark cells in prisons where the most flagitious culprits were confined. *The judgment of the great day.* The final judgment, when both angels and men shall receive their eternal doom.

MATTHEW HENRY

3. The apostle here calls to our remembrance the destruction of Sodom and Gomorrah, *v.* 7. Their ruin is a particular warning to all people to take heed of, and fly *from, fleshly lusts that war against the soul.* God is the same holy, just, pure Being now as then; and can the beastly pleasures of a moment make amends for your suffering the vengeance of eternal fire?

Verses 8–15

A charge against deceivers who were now seducing the disciples of Christ. He calls them *filthy dreamers*, forasmuch as delusion is a dream, and the beginning of, and inlet to, all manner of filthiness. *These filthy dreamers* dream themselves into a fool's paradise on earth, and into a real hell at last.

I. The character of these deceivers is described.

1. They *defile the flesh.* The flesh or body is the immediate seat, and often the irritating occasion, of many horrid pollutions; yet these, though done in and against the body, do greatly defile and grievously maim and wound the soul.

2. They *despise dominion, and speak evil of dignities.* Such evil-speakers despise the dominion of conscience, make a jest of it, and would banish it out of the world; and as for the word of God, the rule of conscience, they despise it. Religion and its serious professors have been always and everywhere evil spoken of.

The apostle brings in *Michael the archangel,* &c., *v.* 9. Interpreters are at a loss what is here meant by *the body of Moses.*

He durst not bring, &c. Not that he was afraid of the devil, but he believed God would be offended if, in such a dispute, he went that way to work. A memorandum to all disputants, never to bring railing accusations into their disputes. Truth needs no supports from falsehood or scurrility. *The Lord rebuke thee.* He would not stand disputing with the devil. Divine rebukes are harder to be borne than careless sinners now think for.

3. *They speak evil of the things which they know not,* &c., *v.* 10. If they had known them, they would have spoken well of them, for nothing but good and excellent can be truly said of religion. Men are most apt to speak evil of those persons and things that they know least of. On the other hand, retirement screens some even from just censure. *But what they know naturally,* &c. The apostle likens such to *brute beasts,* though they often think and boast themselves if not as the wisest, yet at least as the wittiest part of mankind. *In those things they corrupt themselves.* The fault, whatever it is, lies in their depraved wills.

4. In *v.* 11 the apostle represents them as followers *of Cain,* and in *v.* 12, 13, as atheistical and profane people,—as greedy and covetous, who, so they could but gain present worldly advantages, cared not what came next—who, like Core, ran into attempts in which they must assuredly perish, as he did.

JAMIESON, FAUSSET, BROWN

shut out from heaven, they, like condemned prisoners, await their doom. **7. Even as**—ALFORD translates, "I wish to remind you (vs. 5) *that.*" **Sodom . . .**—(II Pet. 2:6). **giving themselves over to fornication**—following fornication *extraordinarily,* i.e., *out of the* order of nature. On "in like manner *to them*" (*Greek*), cf. *Note,* vs. 6. Cf. on spiritual fornication, "go a *whoring from thee,*" Psalm 73: 27. **going after strange flesh**—departing from the course of nature, and going after that which is unnatural. In later times the most enlightened heathen nations indulged in the sin of Sodom without compunction or shame. **are set forth**—before our eyes. **suffering**—undergoing *to this present time;* alluding to the marks of volcanic fire about the Dead Sea. **the vengeance**—*Greek,* "righteous retribution." **eternal fire**—The lasting marks of the fire that consumed the cities irreparably, is a type of the eternal fire to which the inhabitants have been consigned. BENGEL translates as the *Greek* will admit, "*Suffering* (*the*) *punishment* (which they endure) as an example or *sample of eternal fire* (viz., that which shall consume the wicked)." **8. also**—rather, "In like manner nevertheless" (notwithstanding these warning examples) [ALFORD]. **these . . . dreamers**—The *Greek* has not "*filthy*" of *English Version.* The clause, "these men dreaming" (i.e., in their dreams), belongs to all the verbs, "defile," "despise," and "speak evil." All sinners are spiritually asleep, and their carnal activity is as it were a *dream* (I Thess. 5:6, 7). Their *speaking evil of dignities* is because they are *dreaming,* and *know not what they are speaking evil of* (vs. 10). **defile the flesh**—(*V.* 7). **dominion**—"lordship." **dignities**—lit., "glories." Earthly and heavenly *dignities.* **9. Michael, the archangel**—Nowhere in Scripture is the plural used, "archangels"; but only ONE, "archangel." The only other passage in the New Testament where it occurs, is I Thessalonians 4:16, where Christ is distinguished from the archangel, with whose voice He shall descend to raise the dead; they therefore err who confound Christ with Michael. The name means, *Who is like God*? In Daniel 10:13 he is called "One (*Margin, the first*) of the chief princes." He is the champion angel of Israel. In Revelation 12:7 the conflict between Michael and Satan is again alluded to. **about the body of Moses**—his literal body. Satan, as having the power of death, opposed the raising of it again, on the ground of Moses' sin at Meribah, and his murder of the Egyptian. That Moses' body was raised, appears from his presence with Elijah and Jesus (who were in the body) at the Transfiguration: the sample and earnest of the coming resurrection-kingdom, to be ushered in by Michael's standing up for God's people. **durst not**—from reverence for Satan's former *dignity* (vs. 8). **railing accusation**—*Greek,* "judgment of blasphemy," or *evil-speaking.* Peter said, Angels do not, in order to avenge themselves, rail at dignities, though ungodly, when they have to contend with them: Jude says that the archangel Michael himself did not rail even at the time when he fought with the devil, the prince of evil spirits—not from fear of him, but from reverence of God, whose delegated power in this world Satan once had, and even in some degree still has. From the word "disputed," or *debated in controversy,* it is plain it was a judicial contest. **10.** (II Peter 2:12.) **those things which**—*Greek,* "all things *whatsoever* they *understand not,*" viz., the things of the spiritual world. **but what . . . naturally**—Connect thus, "*Whatever* (so the *Greek*) things naturally (by natural, blind instinct), as the unreasoning (so the *Greek*) animals, they know. . . ." The *Greek* for the former "know" implies deeper knowledge; the latter "know," the mere perception of the "animal senses and faculties." **11. Woe**—*Note,* II Peter 2: 14, "*cursed* children." **Cain**—the murderer: the root of whose sin was hatred and envy of the godly, as it is the sin of these seducers. **ran greedily**—lit., "have been poured forth" like a torrent that has burst its banks. Reckless of what it costs, the loss of God's favor and heaven, on they rush after gain like Balaam. **perished in the gainsaying of Core**—(Cf. *Note,* vs. 12). When we read of Korah perishing by gainsaying, we read virtually also of these perishing in like manner through the same: for the same seed bears the same harvest. **12. spots**—So II Peter 2:13, *Greek, spiloi;* but here the *Greek* is *spilades,* which elsewhere, in secular writers, means *rocks,* viz., on which the Christian *love feasts* were in danger of being shipwrecked. The oldest MS. prefixes the article emphatically, "THE rocks." The reference to "clouds . . . winds . . . waves of the sea," accords with this image of *rocks. Vulgate* seems to have been misled by the similar sounding word to translate, as *English Version,* "spots"; cf. however,

ADAM CLARKE

7. *Even as Sodom and Gomorrha.* What their sin and punishment were may be seen in Genesis xix, and the notes there. This is the third example to illustrate what is laid down in v. 4.

Are set forth for an example. Both of what God will do to such transgressors and of the position laid down in v. 4, viz., that God has in the most open and positive manner declared that such and such sinners shall meet with the punishment due to their crimes. *Suffering the vengeance of eternal fire.* Subjected to such a punishment as an endless fire can inflict.

8. *Likewise also these filthy dreamers.* He means to say that these false teachers and their followers were as unbelieving and disobedient as the Israelites in the wilderness, as rebellious against the authority of God as the fallen angels, and as impure and unholy as the Sodomites; and that consequently they must expect similar punishment. *Despise dominion.* They "set all government at nought"—they will come under no restraints; they despise all law, and wish to live as they list. *Speak evil of dignities.* "They blaspheme or speak injuriously of supreme authority."

9. *Yet Michael the archangel.* Let it be observed that the word *archangel* is never found in the plural number in the sacred writings. There can be properly only one archangel, one chief or head of all the angelic host. Nor is the word "devil," as applied to the great enemy of mankind, ever found in the plural; there can be but one monarch of all fallen spirits. Michael is this archangel, and head of all the angelic orders; the devil, great dragon, or Satan, is head of all the diabolic orders. When these two hosts are opposed to each other they are said to act under these two chiefs, as leaders. Hence in Rev. xii. 7, it is said: "Michael and his angels fought against the dragon . . . and his angels." *Disputed about the body of Moses.* What this means I cannot tell, or from what source Jude drew it, unless from some tradition among his countrymen. *Durst not bring against him a railing accusation.* It was a Jewish maxim, as may be seen in *Synopsis Sohar,* page 92, note 6: "It is not lawful for man to prefer ignominious reproaches, even against wicked spirits."

10. *Speak evil of those things which they know not.* They do not understand the origin and utility of civil government; they revile that which ever protects their own persons and their property. *But what they know naturally.* They are destitute of reflection; their minds are uncultivated; they follow mere natural instinct, and are slaves to their animal propensities. *As brute beasts.* Like the irrational animals; but, in the indulgence of their animal propensities, *they corrupt themselves,* beyond the example of the brute beasts.

11. *They have gone in the way of Cain.* They are haters of their brethren, and they that are such are murderers; and by their false doctrine they corrupt and destroy the souls of the people. *The error of Balaam.* For the sake of gain they corrupt the Word of God and refine away its meaning and let it down so as to suit the passions of the profligate. *Gainsaying of Core.* See the account of the rebellion of Korah, Dathan, and Abiram, and their company, in Numbers xxii. It appears that these persons opposed the authority of the apostles of our Lord, as Korah and his associates did that of Moses and Aaron; and Jude predicts them a similar punishment.

12. *Spots in your feasts of charity.* It appears that these persons, unholy and impure as they were, still continued to have outward fellow-

MATTHEW HENRY

These are spots in your feasts of charity, or *love-feasts.* Yet how common in all Christian societies here on earth, the very best not excepted, are such blemishes!

When they feast with you, they feed themselves without fear. Arrant gluttons, no doubt, they were; such as minded only the gratifying of their appetites. In common eating and drinking a holy fear is necessary, much more in feasting.

Clouds they are without water, which promise rain in time of drought, but perform nothing of what they promise. Such is the case of formal professors. *Carried about of winds*, easily driven about as the wind happens to set; such are empty, ungrounded professors, an easy prey to every seducer. How happy would our world be if men either knew more or practically knew how little they know! *Trees whose fruit withereth*, &c. Trees they are, for they are planted in the Lord's vineyard, yet fruitless ones. *Twice dead.* One would think to be once dead were enough. They had been once dead in their natural state; but they seemed to recover, and to be brought to life again, when they took upon them the profession of the Christian religion. But now they are dead again by the evident proofs they have given of their hypocrisy: whatever they seemed, they had nothing truly vital in them.—*Plucked up by the roots*, as we commonly serve dead trees, from which we expect no more fruit. *Raging waves of the sea*, full of talk and turbulency, *foaming out their own shame*, creating much uneasiness to men of calmer tempers, which yet will in the end turn to their own greater shame and just reproach. Raging waves are a terror to sailing passengers; but, when they have got to port, the waves are forgotten, their noise and terror are for ever ended. *Wandering stars.* A very lively emblem of false teachers, who are sometimes here and sometimes there, so that one knows not where nor how to fix them.

II. The doom of this wicked people is declared. False teachers are to expect the worst of punishments in this and a future world. If this will not make both ministers and people cautious, I know not what will.

Of the prophecy of Enoch (*v.* 14, 15) we have no mention made in any other part or place of scripture.

The Lord cometh with his holy myriads, including both angels and the spirits of just men made perfect. What a glorious time will that be, when Christ shall *come with ten thousand of these!* He *cometh, To execute judgment upon* the wicked; *to convince* them. They shall have no excuse or apology to make that they either can or dare then stand by.

I cannot pass *v.* 15 without taking notice how often, and how emphatically, the word *ungodly* is repeated in it, no fewer than four times: ungodly men, ungodly sinners, ungodly deeds, ungodly committed. Godly or ungodly signifies little with men nowadays, unless it be to scoff at and deride even the very expressions; but it is not so in the language of the Holy Ghost. Hard speeches of one another, especially if ill-grounded, will most certainly come into account at *the judgment of the great day.*

JAMIESON, FAUSSET, BROWN

vs. 23, which favors *English Version*, if the *Greek* will bear it. Two oldest MSS., by the transcriber's effort to make Jude say the same as Peter, read here "deceivings" for "love feasts," but the weightiest MS. and authorities support *English Version* reading. The love feast accompanied the Lord's Supper (I Cor. 11, end). Korah the Levite, not satisfied with his *ministry*, aspired to the *sacrificing priesthood* also: so ministers in the Lord's Supper have sought to make it a *sacrifice*, and themselves the *sacrificing* priests, usurping the function of our only Christian sacerdotal *Priest*, Christ Jesus. Let them beware of Korahs doom! **feeding themselves**—*Greek*, "pasturing (tending) themselves." What they look to is the pampering of *themselves*, not the feeding of the flock. **without fear**—Join these words not as *English Version*, but with "feast." Sacred feasts especially ought to be celebrated *with fear*. Feasting is not faulty in itself [BENGEL], but it needs to be accompanied with *fear* of forgetting God, as Job in the case of his sons' feasts. **clouds**—from which one would expect refreshing rains. II Peter 2:17, "wells without water." Professors without practice. **carried about**—The oldest MSS. have "carried aside," i.e., out of the right course (cf. Eph. 4:14). **trees whose fruit withereth**—rather, "trees of the late (or *waning*) autumn," viz., when there are no longer leaves or fruits on the trees [BENGEL]. **without fruit**—having no good fruit of knowledge and practice; sometimes used of what is positively *bad*. **twice dead**—First when they cast their leaves in autumn, and seem during winter *dead*, but revive again in spring; secondly, when they are "plucked up by the roots." So these apostates, once dead in unbelief, and then by profession and baptism raised from the death of sin to the life of righteousness, but now having become *dead again* by apostasy, and so *hopelessly dead*. There is a climax. Not only *without leaves*, like *trees in late autumn*, but *without fruit:* not only so, but dead twice; and to crown all, "plucked up by the roots." **13. Raging**—wild. Jude has in mind Isaiah 57:29. **shame**—plural in *Greek*, "shames" (cf. Phil. 3:19). **wandering stars**—instead of moving on in a regular orbit, as lights to the world, bursting forth on the world like erratic comets, or rather, meteors of fire, with a strange glare, and then doomed to fall back again into the blackness of gloom. **14.** See *Introduction* on the source whence Jude derived this prophecy of Enoch. The Holy Spirit, by Jude, has sealed the truth of this much of the matter contained in the book of Enoch, though probably that book, as well as Jude, derived it from tradition (cf. *Note*, vs. 9). There are reasons given by some for thinking the book of Enoch copied from Jude rather than vice versa. It is striking how, from the first, prophecy hastened towards its consummation. The earliest prophecies of the Redeemer dwell on His second coming in glory, rather than His first coming in lowliness (cf. Gen. 3:15 with Rom. 16:20). Enoch, in his translation without death, illustrated that truth which he all his life preached to the unbelieving world, the certainty of the Lord's coming, and the resurrection of the dead, as the only effectual antidote to their skepticism and self-wise confidence in nature's permanence. **And Enoch**—*Greek*, "Moreover, also Enoch. . . ." **seventh from Adam**—*Seven* is the sacred number. In Enoch, freedom from death and the sacred number are combined: for every seventh object is most highly valued. Jude thus shows the antiquity of the prophecies. Cf. "of old," *Note*, vs. 4. There were only *five* fathers between Enoch and Adam. The *seventh* from Adam prophesied the things which shall close the *seventh age* of the world [BENGEL]. **of these**—in relation to these. The reference of his prophecies was not to the antediluvians alone, but to *all* the ungodly (vs. 15). His prophecy applied primarily indeed to the flood, but ultimately to the final judgment. **cometh**—lit., "came." Phophecy regards the future as certain as if it were *past.* **saints**—Holy angels (cf. Deut. 33:2; Dan. 7:10 Zech. 14:5; Matt. 25:31; Heb. 12:22). **15.** This verse and the beginning of Enoch's prophecy is composed in Hebrew poetic parallelism, the oldest specimen extant. Some think Lamech's speech, which is also in poetic parallelism, was composed in mockery of Enoch's prophecy: as Enoch foretold Jehovah's coming to judgment, so Lamech presumes on impunity in polygamy and murder (just as Cain the murderer seemed to escape with impunity). **convince**—convict. **hard speeches**—such as are noticed in vss. 8, 10, 16; Malachi 3:13, 14; contrast 16:17. **ungodly sinners**—not merely *sinners*, but proud *despisers of God: impious.* **against him**—They who speak against God's children are regarded by God as speaking *against Himself.* **16. murmurers**—in secret: *mut-*

ADAM CLARKE

ship with the Church! The *feasts of charity*, the "love feasts," of which the apostle speaks, were in use in the primitive Church till the middle of the fourth century, when, by the Council of Laodicea, they were prohibited to be held in the churches; and, having been abused, fell into disuse. In later days they have been revived, in all the purity and simplicity of the primitive institution, among the Moravians and the people called Methodists. *Feeding themselves without fear.* Eating, not to suffice nature, but to pamper appetite. It seems the provision was abundant, and they ate to gluttony and riot. It was this which brought the love feasts into disrepute in the Church, and was the means of their being at last wholly laid aside.

Clouds . . . without water. The doctrine of God is compared to the rain, Deut. xxxii. 2, and *clouds* are the instruments by which the rain is distilled upon the earth. In arid or parched countries the very appearance of a cloud is delightful, because it is a token of refreshing showers; but when sudden winds arise and disperse these clouds, the hope of the husbandman and shepherd is cut off. These false teachers are represented as *clouds;* they have the form and office of the teachers of righteousness, and from such appearances pure doctrine may be naturally expected. But these are *clouds . . . without water*—they distill no refreshing showers, because they have none; they are *carried* away and *about* by their passions, as those light, fleecy clouds are carried by the winds. *Trees whose fruit withereth.* "Galled or diseased trees." They have the appearance of ministers of the gospel, but they have no fruit. *Twice dead.* First, naturally and practically dead in sin, from which they had been revived by the preaching and grace of the gospel. Secondly, dead by backsliding or apostasy from the true faith, by which they lost the grace they had before received; and now likely to continue in that death because *plucked up* from *the roots*, their roots of faith and love being no longer fixed in Christ Jesus.

13. *Raging waves of the sea, foaming out their own shame.* The same metaphor as in Isa. lvii. 20: "The wicked are like the troubled sea, when it cannot rest, whose waters cast up mire and dirt." *Wandering stars.* These are uncertain, anomalous meteors, wills-o'-the-wisp. *The blackness of darkness.* They are such as are going headlong into that outer darkness where there are wailing, and weeping, and gnashing of teeth.

14. *Enoch also, the seventh from Adam.* He was the *seventh* patriarch, and is distinguished thus from Enoch, son of Cain, who was but the third from Adam; this appears plainly from the genealogy, 1 Chron. i. 1. Of the *Book of Enoch*, from which this prophecy is thought to have been taken, much has been said; but as the work is apocryphal, and of no authority, I shall not burden my page with extracts. Perhaps the word *prophesied* means no more than "preached, spoke, made declarations," concerning these things and persons; for doubtless he reproved the ungodliness of his own times. *Ten thousands of his saints.* This seems to be taken from Dan. vii. 10.

15. *To execute judgment.* This was originally spoken to the antediluvians, and the coming of the Lord to destroy that world was the thing spoken of in this prophecy or declaration.

MATTHEW HENRY

Verses 15–25

Here, I. The apostle enlarges further on the character of these evil men and seducers, *v.* 16. A murmuring complaining temper lays men under a very bad character; such are very weak at least, and for the most part very wicked. They are angry at everything that happens, and never pleased with their own state and condition in the world, as not thinking it good enough for them. Their will, their appetite, their fancy, are their only rule.

II. He proceeds to caution and exhort those to whom he is writing, *v.* 17–23.

1. He calls them to remember how they had been forewarned, *v.* 17. The accomplishment of it is a confirmation of their faith, instead of being in the least an occasion of shaking and unsettling them therein. Those who would persuade must make it evident that they sincerely love those whom they would persuade. Bitter words and hard usage never did nor ever will convince, much less persuade anybody. We must not think it strange, but comfort ourselves with this, that in the midst of all this confusion Christ will maintain his church, and make good his promise. The more religion is ridiculed and persecuted the faster hold we should take and keep of it; being forewarned, we should show that we are fore-armed; under such trials we should stand firm.

2. He guards them against seducers by a further description of their odious character, &c., *v.* 19.

Sensual men have not the Spirit, that is, of God and Christ, the Spirit of holiness. The worse others are the better should we endeavour to be; the more busy Satan, the more tenacious should we be of sound doctrine and a good conversation.

3. He exhorts them to persevering constancy in truth and holiness.

(1) *Building up yourselves in your most holy faith, v.* 20. Having laid our foundation well in a sound faith, we must build upon it; and we should take care with what materials we carry on our building. Right principles will stand the test even of the fiery trial.

(2) *Praying in the Holy Ghost.* Prayer is the nurse of faith. Our prayers are then most likely to prevail when we *pray in the Holy Ghost,* under his guidance and influence.

(3) *Keep yourselves in the love of God, v.* 21. Keep yourselves in the way of God, if you would continue in his love.

JAMIESON, FAUSSET, BROWN

tering murmurs against God's ordinances and ministers in Church and state. Cf. vs. 8, "speak evil of dignities"; 15, "hard speeches"; against the Lord. **complainers**—never satisfied with their lot (Num. 11:1; cf. the penalty, Deut. 28:47, 48). **walking after their own lusts**—(vs. 18). The secret of their *murmuring* and *complaining* is the restless insatiability of their desires. **great swelling words**—(II Pet. 2:18). **men's persons**—their mere outward appearance and rank. **because of advantage**—for the sake of what they may gain from them. While they *talk great swelling words,* they are really mean and fawning towards those of wealth and rank. **17. But; beloved . . . ye**—in contrast to those reprobates, vs. 20, again. **remember**—implying that his readers had been contemporaries of the apostles. For Peter uses the very same formula in reminding the contemporaries of himself and the other apostles. **spoken before**—spoken already before now. **the apostles**—Peter (*Notes,* II Pet. 3:2, 3), and Paul before Peter (Acts 20:29; I Tim. 4:1; II Tim. 3:1). Jude does not exclude himself from the number of *the apostles* here, for in vs. 18, immediately after, he says, "they told YOU," not *us* (rather as *Greek,* "used to tell you" implying that Jude's readers were contemporaries of the apostles, who *used to tell* them). **18. mockers**—In the parallel, II Peter 3:3, the same *Greek* is translated, "scoffers." The word is found nowhere else in the New Testament. How ALFORD can deny that II Peter 3:2, 3 is referred to (at least in part), I cannot imagine, seeing that Jude quotes the very words of *Peter* as the words which *the apostles* used to speak to his (Jude's) readers. **walk after their own ungodly lusts**—lit., "after (according to) their own lusts *of ungodliness.*" **19. These be they**—showing that their characters are such as Peter and Paul had foretold. **separate themselves**—from Church communion in its vital, spiritual reality: for outwardly they took part in Church ordinances (vs. 12). Some oldest MSS. omit "themselves": then understand it, "separate," cast out members of the Church by excommunication (Isa. 65:5; 66:5; Luke 6:22; John 9:34; cf. "casteth them out of the Church," III John 10). Many, however, understand "themselves," which indeed is read in some of the oldest MSS. as *English Version* has it. Arrogant setting up of themselves, as having greater sanctity and a wisdom and peculiar doctrine, distinct from others, is implied. **sensual**—lit., "animal-souled": as opposed to the *spiritual,* or "having the Spirit." It is translated, "the *natural* man," I Corinthians 2:14. In the threefold division of man's being, *body, soul, and spirit,* the due state in God's design is, that "the spirit," which is the recipient of the Holy Spirit uniting man to God, should be first, and should rule the soul, which stands intermediate between *the body* and *spirit;* but in the *animal,* or *natural* man, the spirit is sunk into subserviency to the animal soul, which is earthly in its motives and aims. The "carnal" sink somewhat lower, for in these *the flesh,* the lowest element and corrupt side of man's bodily nature, reigns paramount. **having not the Spirit**—In the animal and natural man *the spirit,* his higher part, which ought to be the receiver of the Holy Spirit, is not so; and therefore, his spirit not being in its normal state, he is said *not to have the spirit* (cf. John 3:5, 6). In the completion of redemption the parts of redeemed man shall be placed in their due relation: whereas in the ungodly, *the soul* severed from *the spirit* shall have for ever animal life without union to God and heaven—a living death. **20.** Resuming vs. 17. **building up yourselves**—the opposite to the "separate themselves" (vs. 19): as "in the Holy Ghost" is opposed to "having not the Spirit." **on**—as *on* a foundation. *Building on* THE FAITH is equivalent to building on *Christ,* the object of faith. **praying in the Holy Ghost**—(Rom. 8:26; Eph. 6:18). The Holy Spirit teaches *what we* are to pray for, and *how.* None can pray aright save by being *in the Spirit,* i.e., in the element of His influence. CHRYSOSTOM states that, among the charisms bestowed at the beginning of the New Testament dispensation, was *the gift of prayer,* bestowed on someone who prayed in the name of the rest, and taught others to pray. Moreover, their prayers so conceived and often used, were received and preserved among Christians, and out of them forms of prayer were framed. Such is the origin of liturgies [HAMMOND]. **21.** In vss. 20, 21, Jude combines the Father, the Son, and the Holy Ghost: and *faith, hope,* and *love.* **Keep yourselves**—not in your own strength, but "in the love of God," i.e., *God's love to you* and all His believing children, the only guarantee for their being *kept* safe. Man's need of watching is implied; at the same time he cannot *keep* himself, unless God in His love keep him.

ADAM CLARKE

16. *Having men's* p e r s o n s *in admiration.* **Timeservers and flatterers.** *Because of advantage.* **"For the sake of lucre." All the flatterers of the rich are of this kind; and especially those who profess to be ministers of the gospel and who, for the sake of a more advantageous living, will soothe the rich even in their sins.**

17. *Remember ye the words.* **Instead of following those teachers and their corrupt doctine, remember what Christ and His apostles have said, for they foretold the coming of such false teachers and impostors.**

19. *Who separate themselves.* **From the true Church, which they leave from an affectation of superior wisdom.**

Sensual. **"Animal"—living as brute beasts, guided simply by their own lusts and passions.**

For they have *not the Spirit* **—they are not spiritually minded, and have no Holy Ghost, no inspiration from God.**

20. *Building up yourselves.* **Having the** *most holy faith*—**the gospel of our Lord Jesus, and the writings of His apostles—for your foundation.**

Praying in the Holy Ghost. **Holding fast the divine influence which you have received, and under that influence making prayer and supplication to God. The prayer that is not sent up through the influence of the Holy Ghost is never likely to reach heaven.**

21. *Keep yourselves in the love of God.* **By "building up yourselves on your most holy faith," and "praying in the Holy Ghost"; for without this we shall soon lose the love of God.**

MATTHEW HENRY

(4) *Looking for the mercy*, &c. Eternal life is to be looked for only through *mercy*; mercy is our only plea, not merit. Through the mercy of *our Lord Jesus Christ* as Redeemer; all who come to heaven must come thither through our Lord Jesus Christ. A lively faith of the blessed hope will help us to mortify our cursed lusts.

4. He directs them how to behave towards erring brethren, *v.* 22, 23. We ought to do all we can to rescue others out of the snare of the devil. We are not only our own keepers, but every man ought to be, as much as in him lies, his *brother's keeper*. This must be done with *compassion, making a difference*. We must distinguish between the weak and the wilful. *Of some* we *must have compassion*, treat them with all tenderness, not be needlessly harsh and severe in our censures of them. If God has forgiven them, why should not we? We infinitely more need his forgiveness than they do ours. *Others save with fear*, urging upon them *the terrors of the Lord*: "Endeavour to frighten them out of their sins. Fear lest you frustrate your own good intentions, do not harden, instead of reclaiming." We are often apt to over-do, when we are sure we mean honestly, and think we are right in the main.

"Hating even the garment spotted with the flesh, keeping yourselves at the utmost distance from what is or appears evil."

III. The apostle concludes this epistle with a solemn ascription of glory to the great God, *v.* 24, 25. God is able, and he is as willing as able, *to keep us from falling and to present us faultless before the presence of his glory;* not as those who never have been faulty, but as those whose faults shall not be imputed.—*Before the presence of his glory*. The glory of the Lord will shortly be present. This is now the object of our faith, but hereafter it will be the object of our sense; whom we now believe in, him we shall shortly see. When believers shall be presented faultless it will be with exceeding joy. Where there is no sin there will be no sorrow; where there is the perfection of holiness, there will be the perfection of joy. Surely, the God who can and will do all this is worthy to have *glory, majesty, dominion, and power*, ascribed to him, *both now and for ever! Amen.*

JAMIESON, FAUSSET, BROWN

looking for—in hope. **the mercy of our Lord Jesus Christ**—to be fully manifested at His coming. *Mercy* is usually attributed to the Father: here to the Son; so entirely one are they. **22, 23.** None but those who "keep themselves" are likely to "save" others. **have compassion**—So one oldest MS. reads. But two oldest MSS., *Vulgate*, etc., read, "convict"; "reprove to their conviction"; "confute, so as to convince." **making a difference**—The oldest MSS. and versions read the accusative for the nominative, "when separating themselves" [WAHL], referring to vs. 19; or "when contending with you," as the *Greek* is translated, vs. 9. **23. save with fear**—The oldest MSS. do not read "with fear" in this position: but after "snatching them out of the fire" (with which, cf. Amos 4:11; I Cor. 3:15; Zech. 3:2, said of a most narrow escape), they add the following words, forming a THIRD class, "and others compassionate with (IN) fear." Three kinds of patients require three kinds of medical treatment. Ministers and Christians are said to "save" those whom they are made the instruments of saving; the *Greek* for "save" is present, therefore meaning "try to save." Jude already (vs. 9) had reference to the same passage (Zech. 3:1-3). The three classes are: (1) those who *contend with you* (accusative in oldest MSS.), whom you should *convict;* (2) those who are as brands already in *the fire*, of which hell-fire is the consummation: these you should *try to save by snatching them out;* (3) those who are objects of *compassion*, whom accordingly you should *compassionate* (and help if occasion should offer), but at the same time not let pity degenerate into connivance at their error. Your compassion is to be accompanied "with fear" of being at all defiled by them. **hating**—Even *hatred* has its legitimate field of exercise. Sin is the only thing which God hates: so ought we. **even the garment**—a proverbial phrase: avoiding the most remote contact with sin, and hating that which borders on it. As *garments* of the apostles wrought miracles of good in healing, so the very *garment* of sinners metaphorically, i.e., anything brought into contact with their pollution, is to be avoided. Cf. as to lepers and other persons defiled, Leviticus 13: 52-57; 15:4-17: the garments were held polluted; and anyone touching them was excluded, until purified, from religious and civil communion with the sanctified people of Israel. Christians who received at baptism the white garment in token of purity, are not to defile it by any approach to what is defiled. **24, 25.** Concluding doxology. **Now**—*Greek*, "But." **you**—ALFORD, on inferior authority, reads, "them." *You* is in contradistinction to those *ungodly men* mentioned above. **keep . . . from falling**—rather, "guard . . . (so as to be) *without falling*," or *stumbling*. **faultless**—*Greek*, "blameless." **before the presence of his glory**—i.e., *before Himself*, when He shall be revealed in *glory*. **with exceeding joy**—lit., "with exultation" as of those who *leap* for joy. **To the only . . . God our Saviour**—The oldest MSS. add, "through Jesus Christ our Lord." The transcribers, fancying that "Saviour" applied to Christ alone, omitted the words. The sense is, To the only God (the Father) who is our Saviour through (i.e., by the mediation of) Jesus Christ our Lord. **dominion**—*Greek*, "might." **power**—*authority: legitimate power*. The oldest MSS. and *Vulgate*, after "power," have "before all the age," i.e., before all time as to the *past;* "*and* now," as to the present; "and to all the ages," i.e., *for ever*, as to the time to come.

ADAM CLARKE

22. ***And of some have compassion, making a difference.*** **The general meaning of this exhortation is supposed to be, "You are not to deal alike with all those who have been seduced by false teachers; you are to make a difference between those who have been led away by weakness and imprudence and those who, in the pride and arrogance of their hearts and their unwillingness to submit to wholesome discipline, have separated themselves from the Church and become its inveterate enemies."**

24. ***Now unto him that is able to keep you from falling.*** **Who alone can preserve you from the contagion of sin, and preserve you from falling into any kind of error that might be prejudicial to the interests of your souls; and thus to** ***present you faultless. Before the presence of his glory,*** **where nothing can stand that does not resemble himself;** ***with exceeding*** **great** ***joy*** **in finding youselves eternally out of the reach of the possibility of falling, and for having now arrived at an eternity of happiness.**

25. ***To the only wise God.*** **Who alone can teach, who alone has declared the truth; that truth in which you now stand.** ***Our Saviour.*** **Who has by His blood washed us from our sins, and made us kings and priests unto God the Father.** ***Be glory.*** **Be ascribed all light, excellence, and splendor.** ***Majesty.*** **All power, authority, and preeminence.** ***Dominion.*** **All rule and government in the world and in the Church, in earth and in heaven.** ***And power.*** **All energy and operation to everything that is wise, great, good, holy, and excellent.** ***Both now.*** **In the present state of life and things.** ***And ever.*** **To the end of all states, places, dispensations, and worlds; and to a state which knows no termination, being that eternity in which this glory, majesty, dominion, and power ineffably and incomprehensibly dwell.**

After ***to the only wise God our Saviour,*** **many excellent MSS., etc., add "by Jesus Christ our Lord"; and after** ***dominion and power*** **they add "before all time"; and both these readings Griesbach has received into the text. The text therefore may be read thus: "To the only wise God our Saviour, by Christ Jesus our Lord, be glory and majesty, dominion and power, before all time; and now, and through all futurity. Amen."**

THE BOOK OF THE REVELATION

I. Opening (1:1-8)
A. Prologue (1:1-3)
1. The book—its nature, origin, method (1:1, 2)
2. The benediction (1:3)
B. Introduction (1:4-8)
1. The mutual benediction (1:4-6)
2. Central truths (1:7, 8)

II. Jesus Christ Himself (1:9-20)
A. The occasion (1:9-11)
B. The vision (1:12-16)
C. The voice (1:17, 18)
D. The commission (19, 20)

III. Jesus Christ and the Church (2:1-3:22)
A. Ephesus—apostolic (2:1-7)
B. Smyrna—persecution (2:8-11)
C. Pergamum—patronage (2:12-17)
D. Thyatira—corruption (2:18-29)
E. Sardis—reformation (3:1-6)
F. Philadelphia—evangelization (3:7-13)
G. Laodicea—apostasy (3:14-22)

IV. Jesus Christ and the Kingdom (4:1-22:5)
A. Millennial preparation (4:1-18:24)
1. The heavenly order (4:1-11)
2. The earthly administration (5:1-14)
3. The procedure (6:1-18:24)
a. Seals (6:1-8:5)
b. Trumpets (8:6-9:21, 11:15-19)
c. Parenthesis (10:1-11:14) (12:1-14:20)
d. Plagues (15:1-16:21)
e. Fall of Babylon (17:1-18:24)
B. The millennium (19:1-20:6)
1. The inauguration (19:1-20:3)
2. The reign (20:4-6)
C. Millennial issues (20:7-22:5)
1. "After the thousand years" (20:7-10)
2. The great assize (20:11-15)
3. The Kingdom of the Son (21:1-22:5)

V. Epilogue (22:6-21)
A. Final words of Jesus (22:6-19)
B. Final words of John (22:20, 21)

It ought to be no prejudice to the credit and authority of this book that it has been rejected by men of corrupt minds. The church of God has generally received it, and found good counsel and great comfort in it. Christ himself prophesied of the destruction of Jerusalem; and, about the time in which that was accomplished, he entrusted the apostle John with this book of revelation for the support of the faith of his people and the direction of their hope.

MATTHEW HENRY

CHAPTER 1

Verses 1, 2

I. It is *the revelation of Jesus Christ.* As the prophet of the church, he has made known to us the things that shall be hereafter. It is a revelation *which God gave unto Christ.* Our Lord Jesus is the great trustee of divine revelation; it is to him that we owe the knowledge we have of what we are to expect from God and what he expects from us. This revelation Christ *sent and signified by his angel.* Christ employed an angel to communicate it to the churches. The angels are God's messengers. The angels *signified it to the apostle John.* John was the apostle chosen for this service. Some think he was the only one surviving, the rest having sealed their testimony with their blood. John was to deliver this revelation to the church, to all his servants. They have all a right to the oracles of God.

II. The subject-matter of this revelation, the things that must shortly come to pass. We have in this revelation a general idea of the methods of divine providence. These events were such as should come to pass not only *surely,* but *shortly.*

III. Here is an attestation of the prophecy, *v.* 2. He was one who bore record of the word of God in general, and of the testimony of Jesus in particular, and of all things that he saw; he was an eye-witness, and he concealed nothing that he saw. As he added nothing to it, so he kept back no part of the counsels of God.

JAMIESON, FAUSSET, BROWN

CHAPTER 1

VSS. 1-20. TITLE: SOURCE AND OBJECT OF THIS REVELATION: BLESSING ON THE READER AND KEEPER OF IT, AS THE TIME IS NEAR: INSCRIPTION TO THE SEVEN CHURCHES: APOSTOLIC GREETING: KEYNOTE, "BEHOLD HE COMETH" (cf. at the close, ch. 22:20, "Surely I come quickly"): INTRODUCTORY VISION OF THE SON OF MAN IN GLORY, AMIDST THE SEVEN CANDLESTICKS, WITH SEVEN STARS IN HIS RIGHT HAND. **1. Revelation**—an apocalypse or *unveiling* of those things which had been veiled. A *manifesto* of the kingdom of Christ. **of Jesus Christ**—coming *from* Him. Jesus Christ, not John the writer, is the Author of the Apocalypse. Christ taught many things before His departure; but those which were unsuitable for announcement at that time He brought together into the Apocalypse [BENGEL]. **which God gave unto him**—The Father reveals Himself and His will in, and by, His Son. **to show**—The word recurs in ch. 22:6: so entirely have the parts of Revelation reference to one another.
his servants—not merely to "His servant John," but to *all* His servants (cf. ch. 22:3). **shortly**—*Greek,* "speedily"; lit., "in," or "with speed." Cf. "the time is at hand," vs. 3; ch. 22:6, "shortly"; 7, "Behold, I come *quickly.*" Not that the things prophesied were according to man's computation near; but this word "shortly" implies a corrective of our estimate of worldly events and periods. Though a "thousand years" (ch. 20 at least are included, the time is declared to be *at hand.* Luke 18:8, "speedily." The Israelite Church hastened eagerly to the predicted end, which premature eagerness prophecy restrains (cf. Dan. 9). **he sent**—Jesus Christ sent. **by his angel**—joined with "sent." The angel does not come forward to "signify" things to John until ch. 17:1; 19:9, 10. Previous to that John receives information from others. Jesus Christ opens the Revelation, vss. 10, 11; ch. 4:1; in ch. 6:1 one of the four living creatures acts as his informant; in ch. 7:13, one of the elders; in ch. 10:8, 9, the Lord and His angel who stood on the sea and earth. Only at the end (ch. 17:1) does the one angel stand by Him (cf. Dan. 8:16; 9:21; Zech. 1:19). **2. bare record of**—"testified the word of God" in this book. Where we would say "*testifies,*" the ancients in epistolary communications use the past tense. The word of God constitutes his testimony; vs. 3, "the words of this prophecy." **the testimony of Jesus**—"the Spirit of prophecy" (ch. 19:10). **and of all**

ADAM CLARKE

CHAPTER 1

1. *The Revelation of Jesus Christ.* The word from which we have our word Apocalypse signifies literally a "revelation, or discovery of what was concealed or hidden." It is here said that this revelation, or discovery of hidden things, was given by *God* to Jesus Christ, that Christ gave it to His angel, that this angel showed it to *John,* and that John sent it to the churches.

Things which must shortly come to pass. On the mode of interpretation devised by Wetstein, this is plain; for if the book were written before the destruction of Jerusalem, and the prophecies in it relate to that destruction, and the civil wars among the Romans, which lasted but three or four years, then it might be said the Revelation is of things which *must shortly come to pass.* But if we consider the book as referring to the state of the Church in all ages, the words here and those in v. 3 must be understood of the commencement of the events predicted; as if he had said: In a short time the train of these visions will be put in motion.

2. *Who bare record of the word of God.* Is there a reference here to the first chapter of John's Gospel, "In the beginning was the Word, and the Word was with God"? Of this *Word,* John did bear record. Or does the writer mean the fidelity with which he noted and related the word—doctrines or prophecies—which

MATTHEW HENRY

Verses 3–8

We have here an apostolic benediction on those who should give a due regard to this divine revelation.

I. More generally, to all who either read or hear the words of the prophecy. It is a blessed privilege to enjoy the oracles of God. It is a blessed thing to study the scriptures. It is a privilege not only to read the scriptures ourselves, but to hear them read by others. It is not sufficient to our blessedness that we read and hear the scriptures, but we must keep the things that are written.

II. The apostolic benediction is pronounced more especially and particularly to the seven Asian churches, *v.* 4. These seven churches are named in *v.* 11, and distinct messages sent to each of them.

1. What the blessing is. *Grace*, that is, the goodwill of God towards us and his good work in us; and *peace*, that is, the sweet evidence and assurance of this grace.

2. Whence this blessing is to come. In the name of God, of the whole Trinity. (1) The Father is first named: God the Father, *who is, and who was, and who is to come*, eternal, unchangeable.

(2) The Holy Spirit, called *the seven spirits*, the infinite perfect Spirit of God, in whom there is a diversity of gifts and operations. He is before the throne; for, as God made, so he governs, all things by his Spirit.

(3) The Lord Jesus Christ. Observe the particular account we have here of Christ, *v.* 5. *The faithful witness;* upon his testimony we may safely depend, for he is a faithful witness, cannot be deceived and cannot deceive us.

The first-begotten or first-born from the dead. The prince of the kings of the earth; by him their power is limited; by him their counsels are over-ruled, and to him they are accountable.

JAMIESON, FAUSSET, BROWN

things that . . .—The oldest MSS. omit "and." Translate, "whatsoever things he saw," in apposition with "the word of God and the testimony of Jesus Christ." **3. he that readeth, and they that hear**—viz., the *public reader* in Church assemblies, and *his hearers*. In the first instance, he by whom John sent the book from Patmos to the seven churches, read it publicly: a usage most scriptural and profitable. A special *blessing* attends him who *reads* or *hears* the apocalyptic "prophecy" with a view to *keeping* the things therein (as there is but one article to "they that hear and keep those things," not two classes, but only one is meant: "they who not only hear, but also keep those things," Rom. 2:13); even though he find not the key to its interpretation, he finds a stimulus to faith, hope, and patient waiting for Christ. Note, the term "prophecy" has relation to the human medium or *prophet* inspired, here John: "Revelation" to the Divine Being who reveals His will, here Jesus Christ. God gave the revelation to Jesus: He by His angel revealed it to John, who was to make it known to the Church. **4. John**—the apostle. For none but he (supposing the writer an honest man) would thus sign himself nakedly without addition. As sole survivor and representative of the apostles and eyewitnesses of the Lord, he needed no designation save his name, to be recognized by his readers. **seven churches**—not that there were not more churches in that region, but the number *seven* is fixed on as representing *totality*. These *seven* represent the universal Church of all times and places. See TRENCH'S (*Epistles to Seven Churches*) interesting Note, ch. 1:20, on the number *seven*. It is the *covenant number*, the sign of God's covenant relation to mankind, and especially to the Church.
Asia—Proconsular, governed by a Roman proconsul: consisting of Phrygia, Mysia, Caria, and Lydia: the kingdom which Attalus III had bequeathed to Rome. **Grace . . . peace**—Paul's apostolical greeting. In his Pastoral Epistles he inserts "mercy" in addition: so II John 3. **him which is . . . was . . . is to come**—a periphrasis for the incommunicable name JEHOVAH, the self-existing One, unchangeable. In *Greek* the indeclinability of the designation here implies His unchangeableness. Perhaps the reason why "He which is to come" is used, instead of "He that shall be," is because the grand theme of Revelation is the Lord's *coming* (vs. 7). Still it is THE FATHER as distinguished from "Jesus Christ" (vs. 5) who is here meant. But so one are the Father and Son that the designation, "which is to come," more immediately applicable to Christ, is used here of the Father. **the seven Spirits which are before his throne**—The oldest MSS. omit "are." **before**—lit., "in the presence of." The Holy Spirit in His sevenfold (i.e., perfect, complete, and universal) energy. Corresponding to "the *seven* churches." One in His own essence, manifold in His gracious influences. The *seven* eyes resting on the stone laid by Jehovah (ch. 5:6). Four is the number of the creature world (cf. the fourtold cherubim); *seven* the number of God's revelation in the world. **5. the faithful witness**—of the truth concerning Himself and His mission as Prophet, Priest, and King Saviour. "He was *the faithful witness,* because all things that He heard of the Father He faithfully made known to His disciples. Also, because He taught the way of God in truth, and cared not for man, nor regarded the persons of men. Also, because the truth which He taught in words He confirmed by miracles. Also, because the testimony to Himself on the part of the Father He denied not even in death. Lastly, because He will give true testimony of the works of good and bad at the day of judgment" [RICHARD OF ST. VICTOR *in* TRENCH]. The nominative in *Greek* standing in apposition to the genitive, "Jesus Christ," gives majestic prominence to "the faithful witness." **the first-begotten of the dead**—(Col. 1:18). Lazarus rose to die again. Christ rose to die no more. The image is not as if the grave was the womb of His resurrection-birth [ALFORD]; but as Acts 13:33; Romans 1:4, treat Christ's *resurrection* as the epoch and event which fulfilled the Scripture, Psalm 2:7, "This day (at the resurrection) have I *begotten* Thee." It was then that His divine Sonship as the Godman was manifested and openly attested by the Father.

the prince—or Ruler. The kingship of the world which the tempter offered to Jesus on condition of doing homage to him, and so shunning the cross, He has obtained by the cross. "The kings of the earth" conspired against the Lord's Anointed (Ps. 2:2): these He shall break in pieces (Ps. 2:9). Those who are wise in time and kiss the Son shall *bring their glory* unto Him at His manifestation as King of kings, after He has

ADAM CLARKE

he received at this time by revelation from God? This seems more consistent with the latter part of the verse.

3. *Blessed is he that readeth.* This is to be understood of the happiness or security of the persons who, reading and hearing the prophecies of those things which were to come to pass shortly, took proper measures to escape from the impending evils. *The time is at hand.* Either in which they shall be all fulfilled or begin to be fulfilled. See the note on v. 1. These three verses contain the introduction; now the dedication to the seven churches commences.

4. *John to the seven churches.* The apostle begins this much in the manner of the Jewish prophets. They often name themselves in the messages which they receive from God to deliver to the people. The *Asia* here mentioned was what is called Proconsular Asia; the *seven churches* were those of Ephesus, Smyrna, Pergamos, Thyatira, Sardis, Philadelphia, and Laodicea. These seven were those which lay nearest to the apostle, and were more particularly under his care; though the message was sent to the churches in general, and perhaps it concerns the whole Christian world. But the number *seven* may be used here as the number of perfection. *Grace be unto you.* This form of apostolical benediction we have often seen in the preceding Epistles. *From him which is, and which was, and which is to come.* This phraseology is purely Jewish, and probably taken from the Tetragrammaton, *Yehovah;* which is supposed to include in itself all time, past, present, and future. In *Chasad Shimuel*, Rab. Samuel ben David asks: "Why are we commanded to use three hours of prayer? Answer: These hours point out the holy blessed God; he who was, who is, and who shall be. The morning prayer points out him who was before the foundation of the world; the noonday prayer points out him who is; and the evening prayer points out him who is to come." This phraseology is exceedingly appropriate, and strongly expresses the eternity of God; for we have no other idea of time than as past, or now existing, or yet to exist. That which was is the eternity before time; that which is, is time itself; and that which is to come is the eternity which shall be when time is no more. *The seven Spirits which are before his throne.* The ancient Jews, who represented the throne of God as the throne of an Eastern monarch, supposed that there were seven ministering angels before this throne, as there were seven ministers attendant on the throne of a Persian monarch. We have an ample proof of this, *Tobit* xii. 15: "I am Raphael, one of the seven holy angels which present the prayers of the saints, and which go in and out before the glory of the Holy One." And in *Jonathan ben Uzziel's* Targum, on Gen. xi. 7: "God said to the seven angels which stand before him." That seven angels are here meant, and not the Holy Spirit, is most evident from the place, the number, and the tradition. Those who imagine the Holy Ghost to be intended suppose the number seven is used to denote His manifold gifts and graces. That these seven spirits are angels, see chap. iii. 1; iv. 5; and particularly v. 6, where they are called "the seven Spirits of God sent forth into all the earth."

5. *The faithful witness.* The true Teacher, whose testimony is infallible, and whose sayings must all come to pass. *The first begotten of the dead.* See the note on Col. i. 18.

The prince of the kings. The "Chief" or "Head" of all earthly potentates.

MATTHEW HENRY

The great friend of his church and people. He has loved them. *First, He has washed them from their sins in his own blood.* Sins leave a stain upon the soul. Nothing can fetch out this stain but the blood of Christ; and, rather than it should not be washed out, Christ was willing to shed his own blood. *Secondly,* He has *made them kings and priests to God and his Father.* Having justified and sanctified them, he makes them kings to his Father. As kings, they overcome the world. He hath made them priests, given them access to God.

For these high honours and favours they are bound to ascribe to him dominion and glory for ever.

He will be the Judge of the world, *v.* 7. This book, the Revelation, begins and ends with a prediction of the second coming of the Lord Jesus Christ. John speaks as if he saw that day: "*Behold, he cometh,* as sure as if you beheld him with your eyes. *He cometh with clouds,* which are his chariot and pavilion. *Every eye shall see him,* the eye of his people, the eye of his enemies, every eye, yours and mine." He shall come, to the terror of those who have pierced him and have not repented and of all who have wounded and crucified him afresh by their apostasy from him, and to the astonishment of the pagan world.

This account of Christ is ratified and confirmed by himself, *v.* 8. He is the beginning and the end; all things are from him and for him; he is the Almighty; he is the same eternal and unchangeable one.

JAMIESON, FAUSSET, BROWN

destroyed His foes. **Unto him that loved us**—The oldest MSS. read the present, "... *loveth* us." It is His evercontinuing character, *He loveth us,* and ever shall love us. His love rests evermore on His people. **washed us**—The two oldest MSS. read, "freed (*loosed* as from a bond) us": so ANDREAS and PRIMASIUS. One very old MS., *Vulgate,* and *Coptic* read as *English Version,* perhaps drawn from ch. 7:4. "loosed us in (virtue of) His blood," being the *harder* reading to understand, is less likely to have come from the transcribers. The reference is thus to *Greek, lutron,* the ransom paid for our release (Matt. 20:28). **6. And hath**—rather as *Greek,* "And (He) hath." **made us kings**—The oldest MSS. read, "a kingdom." One oldest MS. reads the dative, "for us." Another reads "us," accusative: so *Vulgate, Syriac, Coptic,* and *Andreas.* This seems preferable, "He made us (to be) a kingdom." So Exodus 19:6, "a kingdom of priests"; I Peter 2:9, "a royal priesthood." The saints shall constitute peculiarly a *kingdom* of God, and shall themselves be *kings* (ch. 5:10). They shall share His King-Priest throne in the millennial kingdom. The emphasis thus falls more on the *kingdom* than on *priests:* whereas in *English Version* reading it is equally distributed between both. This book lays prominent stress on the saints' *kingdom.* **priests**—who have preeminently the privilege of near access to the king. David's sons were priests (*Hebrew*), II Samuel 8:18. The distinction of *priests* and people, nearer and more remote from God, shall cease; all shall have nearest access to Him. All persons and things shall be holy to the Lord. **God and his Father**—There is but one article to both in the *Greek,* therefore it means, "Unto Him who is at once God and His Father." **glory and dominion**—*Greek,* "*the* glory and *the might.*" The fuller threefold doxology occurs, ch. 4:9, 11; fourfold, ch. 5:13; Jude 25; sevenfold, ch.7:12 ; I Chronicles 29:11. Doxology occupies the prominent place above, which prayer does below. **for ever and ever**—*Greek,* "unto the ages." **7. with clouds**—*Greek,* "*the* clouds," viz., of heaven. "A cloud received Him out of their sight" at His ascension (Acts 1:9). His ascension corresponds to the manner of His coming again (Acts 1:11). Clouds are the symbols of *wrath* to sinners. **every eye**—His coming shall therefore be a personal, visible appearing. **shall see**—It is because they do not now *see* Him, they will not believe. Contrast John 20:29. **they** *also*—they *in particular;* "whosoever." Primarily, at His pre-millennial advent *the Jews,* who shall "look upon Him whom they have pierced," and mourn *in repentance,* and say, "Blessed is He that cometh in the name of the Lord." Secondarily, and here *chiefly,* at the general judgment all the ungodly, not only those who actually pierced Him, but those who did so by their sins, shall look with trembling upon Him. John is the only one of the Evangelists who records the *piercing* of Christ's side. This allusion identifies him as the author of the Apocalypse. **all kindreds ... shall wail**—all the unconverted at the general judgment; and especially at His pre-millennial advent, the Antichristian confederacy (Zech. 12:3-6, 9; 14:1-4; Matt. 24:30). *Greek,* "all the *tribes* of the *land,*" or "the earth." See the limitation to "all," ch. 13:8. Even the godly while rejoicing in His love shall feel penitential sorrow at their sins, which shall all be manifested at the general judgment. **because of**—*Greek,* "*at,*" or "*in regard to* Him." **Even so, Amen**—Gods seal of His own word; to which corresponds the believer's prayer, ch. 22:20. The "even so" is *Greek;* "Amen" is *Hebrew.* To both Gentiles and Jews His promises and threats are unchangeable. **8.** *Greek,* "I am *the* Alpha and *the* Omega." The first and last letters of the alphabet. God in Christ comprises all that goes between, as well as the first and last. **the beginning and the ending**—omitted in the oldest MSS., though found in *Vulgate* and *Coptic.* Transcribers probably inserted the clause from ch. 21:6. In Christ, Genesis, the Alpha of the Old Testament, and Revelation, the Omega of the New Testament, meet together: the last book presenting to us man and God reconciled in Paradise, as the first book presented man at the beginning innocent and in God's favor in Paradise. Accomplishing *finally* what I *begin.* **the Lord**—The oldest MSS. read "the Lord God." **Almighty**—*Hebrew, Shaddai,* and *Jehovah Sabaoth,* i.e., of hosts; commanding all the hosts or powers in heaven and earth, so able to overcome all His Church's foes. It occurs often in Revelation, but nowhere else in the New Testament save II Corinthians 6:18, a quotation from Isaiah. **9. I John**—So "I Daniel" (Dan. 7:28; 9:2; 10:2). One of the many features of resem-

ADAM CLARKE

Unto him that loved us. This should begin a new verse, as it is the commencement of a new subject. Our salvation is attributed to the love of God, who gave His Son; and to the love of Christ, who died for us. See John iii. 16. *Washed us from our sins.* The redemption of the soul, with the remission of sins and purification from unrighteousness, is here, as in all the New Testament, attributed to the blood of Christ shed on the Cross for man.

6. *Kings and priests.* See on 1 Pet. ii. 5, 9. But instead of *kings and priests* the most reputable MSS., versions, and fathers have "a kingdom and priests"; i.e., a Kingdom of priests, or a royal priesthood. The regal and sacerdotal dignities are the two highest that can possibly exist among men; and these two are here mentioned to show the glorious prerogatives and state of the children of God.

To him be glory. That is, to Christ; for it is of Him that the prophet speaks, and of none other. *For ever and ever.* "To ages of ages"; or rather, through all indefinite periods; through all times, and through eternity. *Amen.* A word of affirmation and approbation; so it shall be, and so it ought to be.

7. *Behold, he cometh with clouds.* This relates to His coming to execute judgment on the enemies of His religion.

And all kindreds of the earth. "All the tribes of the land." By this the Jewish people are most evidently intended, and therefore the whole verse may be understood as predicting the destruction of the Jews, and is a presumptive proof that the Apocalypse was written before the final overthrow of the Jewish state. *Even so, Amen.* "Yea, Amen." It is true, so be it.

8. *I am Alpha and Omega.* I am from eternity to eternity. This mode of speech is borrowed from the Jews, who express the whole compass of things by *aleph* and *tau,* the first and last letters of the Hebrew alphabet; but as John was writing in Greek, he accommodates the whole to the Greek alphabet, of which *alpha* and *omega* are the first and last letters. With the rabbins "from aleph to tau" expressed the whole of matter, "from the beginning to the end." *The beginning and the ending.* This clause is wanting in almost every MS. and version of importance. It appears to have been added first as an explanatory note, and in process of time crept into the text.

MATTHEW HENRY

Verses 9–20

I. The person who was favoured with this vision. His present state and condition. A persecuted man, banished, and perhaps imprisoned, for his adherence to Christ. He was their *brother*, though an apostle. He was their companion in tribulation: the persecuted servants of God did not suffer alone. He was their companion in patience, not only a sharer with them in suffering circumstances, but in suffering graces. By this account he acknowledges his engagements to sympathize with them, and to endeavour to give them counsel and comfort. The place where he was when he was favoured with this vision: he was in *the isle Patmos*. Under this confinement it was the apostle's comfort that he did not suffer as an evil-doer, but that it was for the testimony of Jesus. This was a cause worth suffering for; and the Spirit of glory and of God rested upon this persecuted apostle.

The day and time in which he had this vision: it was *the Lord's day. He was in the Spirit.* He was not only in a rapture when he received the vision, but before he received it. God usually prepares the souls of his people for uncommon manifestations of himself, by the quickening influences of his good Spirit.

II. What he heard. An alarm was given as with the sound of a trumpet, and then *he heard a voice*, the voice of Christ, *the first and the last*, commanding the apostle to commit to writing the things that were now to be revealed to him, and to send it immediately *to the seven Asian churches.*

III. An account of what he saw. *He turned to see the voice*, and then a wonderful scene of vision opened itself to him.

1. He saw a representation of the church under the emblem of *seven golden candlesticks.* The churches are compared to candlesticks, because they hold forth the light of the gospel to advantage.

JAMIESON, FAUSSET, BROWN

blance between the Old Testament and the New Testament apocalyptic seers. No other Scripture writer uses the phrase. **also**—as well as being an apostle. The oldest MSS. omit "also." In his Gospel and Epistles he makes no mention of his *name,* though describing himself as "the disciple whom Jesus loved." Here, with similar humility, though naming himself, he does not mention his apostleship. **companion**—*Greek,* "fellow partaker in the tribulation." Tribulation is the necessary precursor of the kingdom," therefore "the" is prefixed. **patience**—Translate, "endurance." "Persevering, enduring continuance" (Acts 14:22); "the queen of the graces (virtues)" [CHRYSOSTOM]. **of . . .**—The oldest MSS. read "IN Jesus," or "Jesus Christ." It is IN Him that believers have the right to the *kingdom,* and the spiritual strength to enable them to *endure patiently* for it. **was**—*Greek,* "came to be." **in . . . Patmos**—now Patmo or Palmosa. See *Introduction* on this island, and John's exile to it under Domitian, from which he was released under Nerva. Restricted to a small spot on earth, he is permitted to penetrate the wide realms of heaven and its secrets. Thus John drank of Christ's cup, and was baptized with His baptism (Matt. 20:22). **for**—*Greek,* "for the sake of," "on account of"; so, "*because of* the word of God and . . . testimony." Two oldest MSS. omit the second "for"; thus "the Word of God" and "testimony of Jesus" are the more closely joined. Two oldest MSS. omit "Christ." The Apocalypse has been always appreciated most by the Church in adversity. Thus the Asiatic Church from the flourishing times of Constantine less estimated it. The African Church being more exposed to the cross always made much of it [BENGEL]. **10. I was**—*Greek,* "I came to be"; "I became," **in the Spirit**—in a state of ecstasy; the outer world being shut out, and the inner and higher life or spirit being taken full possession of by God's Spirit, so that an immediate connection with the invisible world is established. While the *prophet* "speaks" in the Spirit, the apocalyptic seer *is in* the Spirit in his whole person. The spirit only (that which connects us with God and the invisible world) is active, or rather recipient, in the apocalyptic state. With Christ this being "in the Spirit" was not the exception, but His continual state. **on the Lord's day**—Though forcibly detained from Church communion with the brethren in the sanctuary on the Lord's day, the weekly commemoration of the resurrection, John was holding spiritual communion with them. This is the earliest mention of *the term,* "the Lord's day." But the consecration of the day to worship, almsgiving, and the Lord's Supper, is implied in Acts 20:7; I Corinthians 16:2; cf. John 20:19-26. The name corresponds to "the Lord's Supper," I Corinthians 11:20. **great voice**—summoning solemn attention; *Greek* order, "I heard a voice behind me great (loud) as (that) of a trumpet." The trumpet summoned to religious feasts, and accompanies God's revelations of Himself. **11. I am Alpha and Omega, the first and the last; and**—The oldest MSS, omit all this clause. **write in a book** —To this *book,* having such an origin, and to the other books of Holy Scripture, who is there that gives the weight which their importance demands, preferring them to the *many books* of the world? [BENGEL.] **seven churches**—As there were many other churches in Proconsular Asia (e.g., Miletus, Magnesia, Tralles), besides the seven specified, doubtless the number *seven* is fixed upon because of its mystical signification, expressing *totality* and *universality.* The words, "which are in Asia" are rejected by the oldest MSS., A, B, C, CYPRIAN, *Vulgate,* and *Syriac; Coptic* alone supports them of old authorities. These seven are representative churches; and, as a complex whole, ideally complete, embody the chief spiritual characteristics of the Church, whether as faithful or unfaithful, in all ages. The churches selected are not taken at random, but have a many-sided completeness.

12. see the voice—i.e., *ascertain* whence the *voice* came; to *see* who was it from whom the *voice* proceeded. **that**—*Greek,* "of what kind it was *which.*" The voice is that of God the Father, as at Christ's baptism and transfiguration, so here in presenting Christ as our High Priest. **spake**—The oldest MSS., versions, and Fathers read, "was speaking." **being**—"having turned." **seven . . . candlesticks**—"lamp-stands" [KELLY]. The stand holding the lamp. In Exodus 25:31, 32, the seven are united in ONE candlestick or lamp-stand, i.e., six arms and a central shaft; so Zechariah 4:2, 11. Here the seven are *separate* candlesticks, typifying, as that *one,* the entire Church, but now no longer as the Jewish Church (represented by the *one* sevenfold

ADAM CLARKE

9. *Your brother.* A Christian, begotten of God, and incorporated in the heavenly family. *Companion in tribulation.* Suffering under the persecution in which you also suffer. *In the kingdom.* For we are a Kingdom of priests unto God. *And patience of Jesus.* Meekly bearing all indignities, privations, and sufferings for the sake and after the example of our Lord and Master.

The isle that is called Patmos. This island lies in the Aegean Sea. It has derived all its celebrity from being the place to which John was banished by one of the Roman emperors; whether Domitian, Claudius, or Nero is not agreed on, but it was most probably the latter. The whole island is about thirty miles in circumference. *For the testimony of Jesus Christ.* For preaching Christianity and converting heathens to the Lord Jesus.

10. *I was in the Spirit.* That is, I received the Spirit of prophecy, and was under its influence when the first vision was exhibited. *The Lord's day.* The first day of the week, observed as the Christian Sabbath, because on it Jesus Christ rose from the dead; therefore it was called *the Lord's day,* and has taken place of the Jewish Sabbath throughout the Christian world. *And heard behind me a great voice.* This voice came unexpectedly and suddenly. He felt himself under the divine afflatus, but did not know what scenes were to be represented. *As of a trumpet.* This was calculated to call in every wandering thought, to fix his attention, and solemnize his whole frame. Thus God prepared Moses to receive the law. See Exod. xix. 16, 19.

11. *I am Alpha and Omega, the first and the last: and.* This whole clause is wanting in many MSS. Griesbach has left it out of the text. *Saying . . . What thou seest, write in a book.* Carefully note down everything that is represented to you. John had the visions from heaven, but he described them in his own language and manner. *Send it unto the seven churches.* The names of which immediately follow. *In Asia.* This is wanting in the principal MSS. and versions. *Ephesus.* This was a city of Ionia, in Asia Minor, situated at the mouth of the river Cayster, on the shore of the Aegean Sea, about fifty miles south of Smyrna. *Smyrna,* now called also Ismir, is the largest and richest city of Asia Minor. It is situated about one hundred and eighty-three miles west by south of Constantinople, on the shore of the Aegean Sea. *Pergamos.* A town of Mysia, situated on the river Caicus. It was anciently famous for its library, which contained, according to Plutarch, two hundred thousand volumes. It was here that the *membranae Pergameniae,* Pergamenian skins, were invented; from which we derive our word "parchment." *Thyatira.* A city of Natolia, in Asia Minor, seated on the river Hermus, in a plain eighteen miles broad, and is about fifty miles from Pergamos. *Sardis.* Now called Sardo and Sart, a town of Asia, in Natolia, about forty miles east from Smyrna. *Philadelphia.* A city of Natolia, seated at the foot of mount Tmolus, by the river Cogamus. It is about forty miles east-southeast of Smyrna. *Laodicea.* A town of Phrygia, on the river Lycus. It was built by Antiochus Theos, and named after his consort Laodice.

12. *And I turned.* For he had heard the voice behind him. *To see the voice;* i.e., the person from whom the voice came. *Seven golden candlesticks.* "Seven golden lamps." These seven lamps represented the seven churches, in which the light of God was continually shining and the love of God continually burning. And they are here represented as *golden,* to show how precious they were in the sight of God. This is a reference to the Temple at Jerusalem, where

MATTHEW HENRY

J. A. SEISS:

"And his feet like unto fine brass, as if they burned in a furnace." Here we have the feet with which he is to tread down the wicked; and the description corresponds with the rest of the picture. Christ is all-glorious, even to his feet. They are like glowing brass—like brass in the fire heated unto whiteness. The glory of this metal, in such a state, is almost insufferable to the human gaze. It presents an image of pureness which is terrible. And it is upon these feet of dreadful holiness that our Lord walks among the churches, and shall tread down all abominations, and crush Antichrist and Satan and all who unhappily set aside his authority and his claims.

"And his voice as the sound of many waters." Consider that the day is approaching when "all that are in the graves shall hear the voice of the Son of man, and they that hear shall live." This majesty and power of voice is elsewhere more especially referred to the dreadfulness of Christ toward his faithless servants and enemies. His word came to Jeremiah, saying, "Say unto them, The Lord shall roar from on high, and utter his voice from his holy habitation; he shall mightily roar upon his habitation; he shall give a shout, as they that tread the grapes, against all the inhabitants of the earth. A noise shall come even to the ends of the earth, for the Lord hath a controversy with the nations; he will plead with all flesh; he will give them that are wicked to the sword, saith the Lord."

"And he had in his right hand seven stars." "The seven stars are the angels [ministers] of the seven churches," and, as such, they are distinct from the candlesticks. Christ walks among the candlesticks, but he holds these ministers in his right hand. The democratic idea of church organization, which makes all power proceed from the members, and makes the ministerial position nothing more than what inheres in every Christian, is thus scattered to the winds. Ministers partake directly of Christ's authority, and are responsible directly to him, and are upheld by his right hand, beyond the power of men or angels to displace them. What a lesson for ministers, as to the holiness of their office, the solemnity of their responsibilities, the necessity of unswerving fidelity, and the exercise of every confidence in their sacred functions. They are in Christ's hand. If they are unfaithful none can deliver them out of that hand; but if true to their position, none can touch them or quench their light. They shall shine as the stars forever and ever. What a lesson for the people as to the authority of those ministrations which they are so prone to despise.

"And out of his mouth went a sharp, two-edged sword." The sword is the symbol of magistracy and judgment. But this is not a *hand*-sword, but a *word*-sword. It accords exactly with what Christ himself has said, "He that rejecteth me, and receiveth not my words, hath one that judgeth him: the word that I have spoken, the same shall judge him in the last day." Even now the word of Christ is all the while absolving, or binding under condemnation, everyone to whom it is preached. A certain judicial process inheres in every faithful presentation of the Gospel. It is good news—glad tidings; but there is a sword in it; a sword of double edge; and that a sword of judgment.

—The Apocalypse

JAMIESON, FAUSSET, BROWN

candlestick) restricted to one outward unity and one place; the several churches are mutually independent as to external ceremonies and government (provided all things are done to edification, and schisms or needless separations are avoided), yet one in the unity of the Spirit and the Headship of Christ. The candlestick is not light, but the bearer of light, holding it forth to give light around. **13.** His glorified form as man could be recognized by John, who had seen it at the Transfiguration. **in the midst**—implying Christ's continual presence and ceaseless activity *in the midst* of His people *on earth*. In ch. 4, when He appears *in heaven*, His insignia undergo a corresponding change yet even there the rainbow reminds us of His everlasting covenant with them. **seven**—omitted in two of the oldest MSS., but supported by one. **Son of man**—The form which John had seen enduring the agony of Gethsemane, and the shame and anguish of Calvary, he now sees glorified. His glory (as *Son of man*, not merely *Son of God*) is the result of His humiliation as *Son of man*. **down to the foot**—a mark of high rank. The garment and girdle seem to be emblems of His *priesthood*. Cf. Exodus 28:2, 4, 31; LXX. Aaron's robe and girdle were "for glory and beauty," and combined the insignia of royalty and priesthood, the characteristics of Christ's antitypical priesthood "after the order of Melchisedec." His being *in the midst of the candlesticks* (only seen in the *temple*), shows that it is as a *king-priest* He is so attired. This priesthood He has exercised ever since His ascension; and, therefore He here wears its emblems. As Aaron wore these insignia when He came forth from the sanctuary to bless the people (Lev. 16:4, 23, 24, the *chetoneth*, or holy linen coat), so when Christ shall come again, He shall appear in the similar attire of "beauty and glory" (*Margin*, Isa. 4:2). **14.** *Greek*, "But," or "And." **like wool**—*Greek*, "like *white* wool." The *color* is the point of comparison; signifying *purity* and glory. (So in Isa. 1:18.) Not *age*, for hoary hairs are the sign of decay. **eyes . . . as . . . flame**—all-searching and penetrating like fire: at the same time, also, implying *consuming* indignation against sin, especially at His coming "in flaming fire, taking vengeance" on all the ungodly, which is confirmed as the meaning here, by Revelation 19: 11, 12. **15. fine brass**—*Greek, chalcolibanus*, derived by some from two *Greek* words, "brass" and "frankincense"; derived by BOCHART from *Greek, chalcos*, brass, and *Hebrew, libbeen*, to whiten; hence, "brass," which in the furnace has reached a *white* heat. Thus it answers to "burnished (flashing, or glowing) brass," Ezekiel 1:7; Revelation 10: 1, "His feet as pillars *of fire*." Translate, "*Glowing* brass, as if they had been made fiery (red-hot) in a furnace." The feet of the priests were bare in ministering in the sanctuary. So our great High Priest here. **voice as . . . many waters**—Ezekiel 43: 2; in Daniel 10:6, it is "like the voice of a *multitude*." As the Bridegroom's voice, so the bride's, ch. 14:2; 19:6; Ezekiel 1:24, the cherubim, or redeemed creation. His voice, however, is here regarded in its terribleness to His foes. Contrast Song of Solomon 2:8; 5:2, with which cf. ch. 3:20. **16. he had**—*Greek*, "having." John takes up the description from time to time, irrespective of the construction, *with separate strokes of the pencil* [ALFORD]. **in . . . right hand seven stars**—(vs. 20; ch. 2:1; 3:1). He holds them as a star-studded "crown of glory," or "royal diadem," in His hand: so Isaiah 62:3. He is their Possessor and Upholder. **out of . . . mouth went**—*Greek*, "going forth"; not wielded in the hand. His WORD is omnipotent in executing His will in punishing sinners. It is the sword of His Spirit. Reproof and punishment, rather than its converting winning power, is the prominent point. Still, as He encourages the churches, as well as threatens, the former quality of the Word is not excluded. Its *two* edges (back and front) may allude to its double efficacy, condemning some, converting others. **sword**—*Greek, romphaia*, the Thracian long and heavy broadsword: six times in Revelation, once only elsewhere in New Testament, viz., Luke 2:35. **sun . . . in his strength**—in unclouded power. So shall the righteous shine, reflecting the image of the Sun of righteousness. TRENCH notices that this description, sublime as a purely mental conception, would be intolerable if we were to give it an outward form. With the Greeks, æsthecial taste was the first consideration, to which all others must give way. With the Hebrews, truth and the full representation ideally of the religious reality were the paramount consideration, that representation being designed not to be outwardly embodied, but to remain a purely mental conception. This exalting of the essence above the

ADAM CLARKE

there was a candlestick or chandelier of seven branches; or rather six branches—three springing out on either side, and one in the centre. See Exod. xxxvii. 17-23. This reference to the Temple seems to intimate that the Temple of Jerusalem was a type of the whole Christian Church.

13. *Like unto the Son of man.* This seems a reference to Dan. vii. 13. This was our blessed Lord himself, v. 18. *Clothed with a garment down to the foot.* This is a description of the high priest, in his sacerdotal robes. Jesus is still our High Priest, even in heaven. He is still discharging the sacerdotal functions before the throne of God. *Golden girdle.* The emblem of both regal and sacerdotal dignity.

14. *His head and his hairs were white like wool.* This was not only an emblem of His antiquity, but it was the evidence of His glory; for the whiteness or splendor of His head and hair doubtless proceeded from the rays of light and glory which encircled His head, and darted from it in all directions. *His eyes were as a flame of fire.* To denote His omniscience, and the all-penetrating nature of the divine knowledge.

15. *His feet like unto fine brass.* An emblem of His stability and permanence, brass being considered the most durable of all metallic substances or compounds. The original word means the famous metal which, according to Suidas, was "a kind of amber, more precious than gold." It seems to have been a composition of gold, silver, and brass, and the same with the Corinthian brass, so highly famed and valued. It may however mean no more than copper melted with *lapis calaminaris*, which converts it into brass; and the flame that proceeds from the metal during this operation is one of the most intensely and unsufferably vivid that can be imagined. I have often seen several furnaces employed in this operation, and the flames bursting up through the earth (for these furnaces are underground) always called to remembrance this description given by John: *His feet of fine brass, as if they burned in a furnace. His voice as the sound of many waters.* The same description we find in Ezek. xliii. 2: "The glory of the God of Israel came from the way of the east: and his voice was like a noise of many waters; and the earth shined with his glory."

16. *In his right hand seven stars.* The *stars* are afterwards interpreted as representing the seven angels, messengers, or bishops of the seven churches. Their being in the right hand of Christ shows that they are under His special care and most powerful protection. *Out of his mouth went a sharp twoedged sword.* The *sharp twoedged sword* may represent the Word of God in general, according to that saying of the apostle, Heb. iv. 12: "The word of God is quick, and powerful, and sharper than any twoedged sword, piercing even to the dividing asunder of soul and spirit." And "the word of God" is termed "the sword of the Spirit," Eph. vi. 17. *And his countenance was as the sun shineth in his strength.* His face was like the disk of the sun in the brightest summer's day, when there were no clouds to abate the splendor of his rays. A similar form of expression is found in Judges v. 31: "Let them that love him be as the sun when he goeth forth in his might."

MATTHEW HENRY

2. He saw a representation of the Lord Jesus Christ in the midst of the golden candlesticks.

(1) The glorious form in which Christ appeared.

(2) The impression this appearance of Christ made upon the apostle John (*v.* 17). He was overpowered with the greatness of the lustre and glory in which Christ appeared, though he had been so familiar with him before.

(3) The condescending goodness of the Lord Jesus to his disciple, *v.* 17. He raised him up; he put strength into him, he spoke kind words to him. Words of comfort and encouragement: *Fear not.* Words of instruction, telling him particularly who he was that thus appeared to him. He acquaints him, *First,* With his divine nature: *The first and the last. Secondly,* With his former sufferings: *I was dead. Thirdly,* With his resurrection and life: "*I live, and am alive for evermore,* have conquered death, and am partaker of an endless life."

Fourthly, With his office and authority: *I have the keys of hell and of death,* a sovereign dominion in and over the invisible world.

Fifthly, With his will and pleasure: *Write the things which thou hast seen, and the things which are, and which shall be hereafter.*

Sixthly, With the meaning of the seven stars, and of the seven candlesticks.

JAMIESON, FAUSSET, BROWN

form marks their deeper religious earnestness. **17.** So fallen is man that God's manifestation of His glorious presence overwhelms him. **laid his right hand upon me**—So the same Lord Jesus did at the Transfiguration to the three prostrate disciples, of whom John was one, saying, Be not afraid. The "touch" of His hand, as of old, imparted strength. **unto me**—omitted in the oldest MSS. **the first . . . the last**—(Isa. 41:4; 44:6; 48:12). From eternity, and enduring to eternity: "the First by creation, the Last by retribution: the First, because before Me there was no God formed; the Last, because after Me there shall be no other: the First, because from Me are all things; the Last, because to Me all things return" [RICHARD OF ST. VICTOR]. **18.** Translate as *Greek,* "And THE LIVING ONE": connected with last sentence, vs. 17. **and was**—*Greek,* "and (yet) I *became.*" **alive for evermore**—*Greek,* "living unto the ages of ages": not merely "*I live,*" but I have life, and am the source of it to My people. "To Him belongs *absolute* being, as contrasted with the *relative* being of the creature; others may *share,* He only *hath* immortality: *being in essence, not by mere participation, immortal* [THEODORET in TRENCH]. One oldest MS., with *English Version,* reads "Amen." Two others, and most of the oldest versions and Fathers, omit it. His having passed through death as one of us, and now living in the infinite plenitude of life, reassures His people, since through Him death is the gate of resurrection to eternal life. **have . . . keys of hell**—*Greek,* "Hades"; *Hebrew,* "Sheol." "Hell" in the sense, the *place of torment,* answers to a different *Greek* word, viz., *Gehenna.* I can release from *the unseen world of spirits* and from DEATH whom I *will.* The oldest MSS. read by transposition, "Death and Hades," or Hell." It is death (which came in by sin, robbing man of his immortal birthright, Rom. 5:12) that peoples Hades, and therefore should stand first in order. *Keys* are emblems of authority, opening and shutting at will "the gates of Hades" (Ps. 9:13, 14; Isa. 38:10; Matt. 16:18). **19.** The oldest MSS. read, "Write *therefore*" (inasmuch as I, "the First and Last," have the keys of death, and vouchsafe to thee this vision for the comfort and warning of the Church). **things which are**—"the things which thou hast seen" are those narrated in this chapter (cf. vs. 11). "The things which are" imply the present state of things in the churches when John was writing, as represented in chs. 2 and 3. "The things which shall be hereafter," the things symbolically represented concerning the future history of chs. 4-22. **20. in**—*Greek,* "*upon* My right hand." **the mystery . . . candlesticks**—in apposition to, and explaining, "the things which thou hast seen," governed by "Write." *Mystery* signifies the hidden truth, veiled under this symbol, and now revealed; its correlative is *revelation. Stars* symbolize lordship (Num. 24:17; cf. Dan. 12:3, of faithful teachers; ch. 8:10; 12:4; Jude 13). **angels**—not as ALFORD, from ORIGEN *Homily* 13 on Luke, and 20 on Numbers, the guardian angels of the churches, just as individuals have their guardian angels. For how could heavenly angels be charged with the delinquencies laid here to the charge of these angels? Then, if a human angel be meant (as the Old Testament analogy favors, Hag. 1:13, "the Lord's Messenger in the Lord's message"; Mal. 2:7; 3:1), *the bishop,* or superintendent pastor, must be the angel. For whereas there were many presbyters in each of the larger churches (as e.g., Ephesus, Smyrna, etc.), there was but *one* angel, whom, moreover, the Chief Shepherd and Bishop of souls holds responsible for the spiritual state of the Church under him.

ADAM CLARKE

17. *I fell at his feet as dead.* The appearance of the glory of the Lord had the same effect upon Ezekiel, chap. i. 28; and the appearance of Gabriel had the same effect on Daniel, chap. vii. 17. The terrible splendor of such majesty was more than the apostle could bear, and he fell down deprived of his senses, but was soon enabled to behold the vision by a communication of strength from our Lord's *right hand.*

18. *I am he that liveth, and was dead.* I am Jesus, the Saviour, who, though the Fountain of life, have died for mankind; and being raised from the dead I shall die no more, the great sacrifice being consummated.

And have the keys of death and the grave, so that I can destroy the living and raise the dead. The key here signifies the power and authority over life, *death,* and the grave. This is also a rabbinical form of speech. We should understand *hades* here, not as *hell,* nor the place of separate spirits, but merely as the "grave"; and the key we find to be merely the emblem of power and authority. Christ can both save and destroy, can kill and make alive. Death is still under His dominion, and He can recall the dead whensoever He pleases. He is "the resurrection, and the life."

20. *The mystery.* That is, the allegorical explanation of the *seven stars* is the seven *angels* or ministers of the churches; and the allegorical meaning of the "seven golden lamps" is the *seven churches* themselves.

CHAPTER 2

MATTHEW HENRY — CHAPTER 2

JAMIESON, FAUSSET, BROWN — CHAPTER 2

Vss. 1-29. EPISTLES TO EPHESUS, SMYRNA, PERGAMOS, THYATIRA. Each of the seven epistles in this chapter and ch. 3, commences with, "I know thy works." Each contains a promise from Christ, "To him that overcometh." Each ends with, "He that hath an ear, let him hear what the Spirit saith unto the churches." The title of our Lord in each case accords with the nature of the address, and is mainly taken from the imagery of the vision, ch. 1. Each address has a threat or a promise, and most of the addresses have both. Their order seems to be ecclesiastical, civil, and geographical: **Ephesus first,** as being the Asiatic metropolis (termed "the light of Asia," and "first city of Asia"), the nearest to Patmos, where John received the epistle to the seven churches, and also as being that Church with which John was especially connected; then the churches on the west coast of Asia; then those in the interior. Smyrna and Philadelphia alone receive unmixed

ADAM CLARKE — CHAPTER 2

I must here advise my readers: (1) That I do not perceive any metaphorical or allegorical meaning in the epistles to these churches. (2) I consider the churches as real; and that their spiritual state is here really and literally pointed out; and that they have no reference to the state of the Church of Christ in all ages of the world, as has been imagined; and that the notion of what has been termed the Ephesian state, the Smyrnian state, the Pergamenian state, the Thyatirian state, etc., is unfounded, absurd, and dangerous; and such expositions should not be entertained by any who wish to arrive at a sober and rational knowledge of the Holy Scriptures. (3) I consider the angel of the church as signifying the messenger, the pastor, sent by Christ and His apostles to teach and edify that church. (4) I consider what is spoken to this angel as spoken to the whole church; and that

MATTHEW HENRY

Verses 1–7

I. The inscription. 1. *To the church of Ephesus.* 2. From whom this epistle to Ephesus was sent. *He that holds the stars in his right hand.* The ministers of Christ are under his special care and protection. The ministers of the gospel are in his hand. He supports them, or else they would soon be falling stars; and all the good they do is done by his hand with them. *He walks in the midst of the golden candlesticks.* This intimates his relation to his churches. Though Christ is in heaven, he walks in the midst of his churches on earth.

II. The contents of the epistle.

1. The commendation Christ gave this church, which he brings in by declaring that he knows their works, and therefore both his commendation and reprehension are to be strictly regarded; for he does not in either speak at a venture: he knows what he says. Now the church of Ephesus is commended, (1) For their diligence in duty, *v.* 2–3. (2) For their patience in suffering, *v.* 2. It is not enough that we be diligent, but we must be patient—no Christian can be without it. There must be bearing patience, and there must be waiting patience, that they may receive the promise, *v.* 3. (3) For their zeal against what was evil, *v.* 2. We must show all meekness to men, yet we must show a just zeal against their sins. True zeal proceeds with discretion; none should be cast off till they be tried.

2. The rebuke given to this church, *v.* 4. Those that have much good in them may have something much amiss in them. *Thou hast left thy first love;* not left and forsaken the object of it, but lost the fervent degree of it that at first appeared. The first affections of men towards Christ are usually lively and warm. These lively affections will abate and cool if great care be not taken.

3. The advice and counsel given them from Christ. Those that have lost their first love *must remember whence they have fallen*; they must compare their present with their former state, and consider how much better it was with them then than now. They must repent. They must return and do their first works. They must as it were begin again. They must endeavour to revive and recover their first zeal.

4. This good advice is enforced and urged, (1) By a severe threatening, if it should be neglected. If the presence of Christ's grace and Spirit be slighted, we may expect the presence of his displeasure.

JAMIESON, FAUSSET, BROWN

praise. Sardis and Laodicea receive almost solely censure. In Ephesus, Pergamos, and Thyatira, there are some things to praise, others to condemn, the latter element preponderating in one case (Ephesus), the former in the two others (Pergamos and Thyatira). Thus the main characteristics of the different states of different churches, in all times and places, are portrayed, and they are suitably encouraged or warned. **1. Ephesus**—famed for the temple of Diana, one of the seven wonders of the world. For three years Paul labored there. He subsequently ordained Timothy superintending overseer or bishop there: probably his charge was but of a temporary nature. John, towards the close of his life, took it as the center from which he superintended the province. **holdeth**—*Greek,* "holdeth fast," as in vs. 25; ch. 3:11; cf. John 10:28, 29. The title of Christ here as "holding fast the seven stars (from ch. 1:16: only that, for *having* is substituted *holding fast* in His grasp), and walking in the midst of the seven candlesticks," accords with the beginning of His address to the *seven* churches representing the universal Church. *Walking* expresses His unwearied activity in the Church, guarding her from internal and external evils, as the high priest moved to and fro in the sanctuary. **2. I know thy works**—expressing His omniscience. Not merely "thy professions, desires, good resolutions" (ch. 14:13, end). **thy labour**—Two oldest MSS. omit "thy"; one supports it. The *Greek* means "labor *unto weariness.*" **patience**—persevering *endurance.* **bear**—*evil men* are a *burden* which the Ephesian Church regarded as intolerable. We are to *"bear* (the same *Greek,* Gal. 6:2) one another's burdens" in the case of *weak* brethren; but not to bear *false brethren.* **tried**—by experiment; not the *Greek* for "test," as I John 4:1. The apostolical churches had the miraculous gift of *discerning spirits.* Cf. Acts 20:28-30, wherein Paul presciently warned the *Ephesian* elders of the coming false teachers, as also in writing to Timothy at Ephesus. TERTULLIAN, *De baptism,* 17, and JEROME, *in Catal. Vir. Illustr. in Lucca* 7, record of John, that when a writing, professing to be a canonical history of the acts of Paul, had been composed by a presbyter of Ephesus, John convicted the author and condemned the work. So on one occasion he would not remain under the same roof with Cerinthus the heretic. **say they are apostles**—probably Judaizers. IGNATIUS, *Ad Ephesum* 6, says subsequently, "Onesimus praises exceedingly your good discipline that no heresy dwells among you"; and 9, "Ye did not permit those having evil doctrine to sow their seed among you, but closed your ears." **3. borne . . . patience**—The oldest MSS. transpose these words. Then translate as *Greek,* "persevering endurance . . . borne." "Thou hast borne" My reproach, but "thou canst not bear the evil" (vs. 2). A beautiful antithesis. **and . . . hast laboured, and hast not fainted**—The two oldest MSS. and oldest versions read, "and . . . hast not labored," omitting "and hast fainted." The difficulty which transcribers by *English Version* reading tried to obviate, was the seeming contradiction, "I know thy *labor* . . . and thou hast *not labored.*" But what is meant is, "Thou hast not been *wearied out* with labor." **4. somewhat . . . because**—Translate, "I have against thee (this) *that* . . ." It is not a mere "somewhat"; it is everything. How characteristic of our gracious Lord, that He puts foremost all He can find to approve, and only after this notes the shortcomings! **left thy first love**—to Christ. Cf. I Timothy 5:12, "cast off their first faith." See the Ephesians' first *love,* Ephesians 1:15. This epistle was written under Domitian, when thirty years had elapsed since Paul had written his Epistle to them. Their warmth of love had given place to a lifeless orthodoxy. Cf. Paul's view of faith so called without love, I Corinthians 13:2. **5. whence**—from what a height. **do the first works**—the *works* which flowed from thy *first love.* Not merely "feel thy first feelings," but do works flowing from the same principle as formerly, "faith which worketh by love." **I will come**—*Greek,* "I am coming" in special judgment on thee. **quickly**—omitted in two oldest MSS., *Vulgate* and *Coptic versions:* supported by one oldest MS.). **remove thy candlestick out of his place**—I will take away the Church from Ephesus and remove it elsewhere. "It is removal of the candlestick, not extinction of the candle, which is threatened here; judgment for some, but that very judgment the occasion of mercy for others. So it has been. The seat of the Church has been changed, but the Church itself survives. What the East has lost, the West has gained. One who lately visited Ephesus found only three Christians there, and these so ignorant as scarcely to have heard the names of St. Paul or St. John" [TRENCH].

ADAM CLARKE

it is not his particular state that is described, but the state of the people in general under his care.

THE EPISTLE TO THE CHURCH AT EPHESUS

1. *Unto the angel of the church of Ephesus.* By *angel* we are to understand the "messenger" or person sent by God to preside over this church; and to him the epistle is directed, not as pointing out his state, but the state of the church under his care. *Angel of the church* here answers exactly to that officer of the synagogue among the Jews called the messenger of the church, whose business it was to read, pray, and teach in the synagogue. The church at Ephesus is first addressed, as being the place where John chiefly resided; and the city itself was the metropolis of that part of Asia. *Holdeth the seven stars.* Who particularly preserves and guides and upholds, not only the ministers of those seven churches, but all the genuine ministers of His gospel, in all ages and places. *Walketh in the midst of the seven golden candlesticks.* Is the supreme Bishop and Head, not only of those churches, but of all the churches or congregations of His people throughout the world.

2. *I know thy works.* For the eyes of the Lord are throughout the earth, beholding the evil and the good; and, being omnipresent, all things are continually open and naked before Him. It is worthy of remark that whatsoever is praiseworthy in any of these churches is first mentioned, thereby intimating that God is more intent on finding out the good than the evil in any person or church, and that those who wish to reform such as have fallen or are not making sufficient advances in the divine life should take occasion, from the good which yet remains, to encourage them to set out afresh for the kingdom of Heaven. Exhortations and encouragements of this kind are sure to produce the most blessed effects; and under such the work of God infallibly revives.

3. *And hast borne.* The same things mentioned in the preceding verse, but in an inverted order, the particular reason of which does not appear. Perhaps it was intended to show more forcibly to this church that there was no good which they had done, nor evil which they had suffered, that was forgotten before God. *And hast not fainted.* They must therefore have had a considerable portion of this love remaining, else they could not have thus acted.

4. *Nevertheless I have somewhat against thee.* The clause should be read, according to the Greek, thus: "But I have against you that you have left your first love." They did not retain that strong and ardent affection for God and sacred things which they had when first brought to the knowledge of the truth, and justified by faith in Christ.

5. *Remember.* Consider the state of grace in which you once stood; the happiness, love, and joy which you felt when you received remission of sins; the zeal you had for God's glory and the salvation of mankind; your willing, obedient spirit, your cheerful self-denial, your fervor in private prayer, your detachment from the world, and your heavenly-mindedness. *Whence thou art fallen.* Or "Remember what a loss you have sustained." *Repent.* Be deeply humbled before God for having so carelessly guarded the divine treasure. *Do the first works.* Resume your former zeal and diligence; watch, fast, pray, reprove sin, carefully attend all the ordinances of God, walk as in His sight, and rest not till you have recovered all your lost ground, and got back the evidence of your acceptance with your Maker. *I will come unto thee quickly.* In the way of judgment. *And will remove thy candlestick.* Take away My ordinances, remove your ministers, and send you a famine of the word.

MATTHEW HENRY

(2) By an encouraging mention of what was yet good among them, *v.* 6. "Though thou hast declined in thy love to what is good, yet thou retainest thy hatred to what is evil." An indifference of spirit between truth and error, good and evil, may be called *charity* and *meekness*, but it is not pleasing to Christ.

III. We have the conclusion of this epistle.

1. A call to attention. What is said to one church concerns all the churches, in every place and age.

2. A promise of great mercy to those who overcome. We must never yield to our spiritual enemies, but fight the good fight, till we gain the victory, and the warfare and victory shall have a glorious triumph and reward. They shall *eat of the tree of life which is in the midst of the paradise of God*, not in the earthly paradise, but the heavenly.

Verses 8–11

I. The preface or inscription in both parts. 1. The superscription: *To the angel of the church in Smyrna*. 2. The subscription. Jesus Christ is the *first and the last*. It is but a little scantling of time that is allowed to us in this world, but our Redeemer is the first and the last. *He was dead and is alive*. He was dead, and died for our sins; he is alive, and he ever lives to make intercession for us.

II. The subject-matter of this epistle.

1. The improvement they had made in their spiritual state. But thou art rich. Some who are poor outwardly are inwardly rich, rich in faith and in good works. Where there is spiritual plenty, outward poverty may be better borne.

2. Their sufferings: *I know thy tribulation and thy poverty*. Jesus Christ takes particular notice of all their troubles.

3. He knows the wickedness and the falsehood of their enemies: *I know the blasphemy of those that say they are Jews, but are not;* that is, of those who

JAMIESON, FAUSSET, BROWN

6. But—How graciously, after necessary censure, He returns to praise for our consolation, and as an example to *us*, that we would show, when we reprove, we have more pleasure in praising than in fault-finding. **hatest the deeds**—We should hate men's evil *deeds*, not hate the men themselves. **Nicolaitanes**—IRENÆUS, *Hæreses* 1. 26. 3; and TERTULLIAN, *Præscriptione Hæreticorum* 46, make these followers of Nicolas, one of *the seven* (honorably mentioned, Acts 6:3, 5). They (CLEMENS ALEXANDRINUS, *Stromata* 2. 20; 3. 4 and EPIPHANIUS, *Hæreses* 25) evidently confound the latter Gnostic Nicolaitanes, or followers of one Nicolaos, with those of Revelation.

Cf. vss. 14, 15, which shows the true sense of Nicolaitanes; they are not a sect, but professing Christians who, like Balaam of old, tried to introduce into the Church a false freedom, i.e., licentiousness; this was a reaction in the opposite direction from Judaism, the first danger to the Church combated in the council of Jerusalem, and by Paul in the Epistle to Galatians. These symbolical Nicolaitanes, or followers of Balaam, abused Paul's doctrine of the grace of God into a plea for lasciviousness (II Pet. 2:15, 16, 19; Jude 4, 11 who both describe the same sort of seducers as followers of *Balaam*). **7. He that hath an ear**—This clause precedes the promise in the first three addresses, succeeds it in the last four. Thus the promises are enclosed on both sides with the precept urging the deepest attention as to the most momentous truths. Every man "hath an ear" naturally, but he alone will be able to hear spiritually to whom God has given "the hearing ear"; whose "ear God hath wakened" and "opened." Cf. "Faith, the ears of the soul" [CLEMENS ALEXANDRINUS]. **the Spirit saith**—What *Christ* saith, *the Spirit* saith; so one are the Second and Third Persons. **unto the churches**—not merely to the particular, but to the universal Church. **overcometh**—In John's Gospel (16:33) and First Epistle (2:13, 14, 5:4, 5) an object follows, viz., "the world," "the wicked one." **will I give**—as the Judge. The tree of life in Paradise, lost by the fall, is restored by the Redeemer. Allusions to it occur in Proverbs 3:18; 11:30; 13:12; 15:4, and prophetically, ch. 22:2, 14; Ezekiel 47:12; cf. John 6:51. **give . . . tree of life**—The thing promised corresponds to the kind of faithfulness manifested. They who refrain from Nicolaitane indulgences (vs. 6) and idol meats (vss. 14, 15), shall eat of meat infinitely superior, viz., the fruit of the tree of life, and the hidden manna (vs. 17). **in the midst of the paradise**—The oldest MSS. omit "the midst of." In Genesis 2:9 these words are appropriate, for there were *other* trees in the garden, but not *in the midst* of it. Here *the tree of life* is simply *in the paradise*, for no other tree is mentioned in it; in ch. 22:2 the tree of life is *"in the midst* of the street of Jerusalem"; from this the clause was inserted here. *Paradise* (a Persian, or else Semitic word), originally used of any garden of delight; then specially of Eden; then the temporary abode of separate souls in bliss; then "the Paradise *of God*," the third heaven, the immediate presence of God. **8. Smyrna**—in Ionia, a little to the north of Ephesus. POLYCARP, martyred in A.D. 168, eighty-six years after his conversion, was bishop, and probably "the angel of the Church in Smyrna" meant here. The allusions to persecutions and faithfulness unto death accord with this view. IGNATIUS (*Martyrium Ignatii*, 3), on his way to martyrdom in Rome, wrote to POLYCARP, then (A.D. 108) bishop of Smyrna; if his bishopric commenced ten or twelve years earlier, the dates will harmonize. TERTULLIAN, *Præscriptione Hæreticorum*, 32, and IRENÆUS, who had talked with POLYCARP in youth, tell us POLYCARP was consecrated bishop of Smyrna by St. John. **the first . . . the last . . . was dead . . . is alive**—The attributes of Christ most calculated to comfort the Church of Smyrna under its persecutions; resumed from ch. 1:17, 18. As death was to Him but the gate to life eternal, so it is to be to them (vs. 10, 11). **9. thy works, and**—omitted in two oldest MSS., *Vulgate*, and *Coptic*. Supported by one oldest MS. **tribulation**—owing to persecution. **poverty**—owing to "the spoiling of their goods." **but thou art rich**—in grace. Contrast Laodicea, *rich* in the world's eyes and her own, *poor* before God. "There are both poor rich-men, and rich poor-men in God's sight" [TRENCH]. **blasphemy of them**—blasphemous calumny of thee on the part of (or *arising from*) them. . . . **say they are Jews, and are not**—Jews by national descent, but not spiritually of "the true circumcision." The Jews blaspheme Christ as "the hanged one." As elsewhere, so at Smyrna they bitterly opposed Christianity; and

ADAM CLARKE

6. *The deeds of the Nicolaitanes.* These were, as is commonly supposed, a sect of the Gnostics, who taught the most impure doctrines and followed the most impure practices.

7. *He that hath an ear.* Let every intelligent person, and every Christian man, attend carefully to what the Holy Spirit, in this and the following epistles, says to the churches. See the note on Matt. xi. 15, where the same form of speech occurs.

To him that overcometh. To him who continues steadfast in the faith and uncorrupt in his life, who faithfully confesses Jesus and neither imbibes the doctrines nor is led away by the error of the wicked, *will I give to eat of the tree of life.* As he who conquered his enemies had, generally, not only great honor but also a reward, so here a great reward is promised "to the conqueror." And as in the Grecian games, to which there may be an allusion, the conqueror was crowned with the leaves of some tree, here it is promised that they should *eat of the fruit of the tree of life, which is in the midst of the paradise of God;* that is, that they should have a happy and glorious immortality. *The tree of life* is frequently spoken of by the rabbins; and by it they generally mean the immortality of the soul and a final state of blessedness.

THE EPISTLE TO THE CHURCH AT SMYRNA

8. *These things saith the first and the last.* He who is eternal; from whom all things come, and to whom all things must return. *Which was dead,* for the redemption of the world; *and is alive* to die no more forever, His glorified humanity being enthroned at the Father's right hand.

9. *I know thy works.* As He had spoken to the preceding church, so He speaks to this: I know all that you have done, and all that you have suffered. The *tribulation* here mentioned must mean persecution, either from the Jews, the heathens, or from the heretics, who, because of their flesh-pampering doctrine, might have had many partisans at Smyrna. *And poverty.* Stripped probably of all their temporal possessions because of their attachment to the gospel. *But thou art rich.* Rich in faith, and heir of the kingdom of Christ. *The blasphemy of them which say they are Jews.* There were persons there who professed Judaism, and had a synagogue in the place, and professed to worship the true God; but they had no genuine religion, and they served the devil rather than God. They

MATTHEW HENRY

pretend to be the only peculiar covenant-people of God, when indeed *they are the synagogue of Satan*. For the synagogues of Satan to give themselves out to be the church or Israel of God is no less than blasphemy.

4. He foreknows the future trials of his people. (1) He forewarns them of future trials, *v.* 10. They had been impoverished by their tribulations before; now they must be imprisoned. (2) Christ forearms them against these approaching troubles, [1] By his counsel: *Fear none of these things*. This is not only a word of command, but of efficacy. [2] By showing them how their sufferings would be alleviated and limited. They should not be universal. It would be some of them, not all. They were not to be perpetual, but for a short time: *Ten days*. It should be to try them, not to destroy them. [3] By proposing a glorious reward to their fidelity: *Be thou faithful to death, and I will give thee a crown of life*. He has said it that is able to do it; and he has undertaken that he will do it. The suitableness of it. *A crown*, to reward their poverty, their fidelity, and their conflict. *A crown of life*, to reward those who are faithful even unto death.

III. The conclusion of this message. A call to universal attention. It concerns all the inhabitants of the world to observe God's dealings with his own people. A gracious promise to the conquering Christian, *v.* 11. There is not only a first, but a second death. This second death is unspeakably worse than the first death. It is *eternal death*. From this death Christ will save all his faithful servants. The first death shall not hurt them, and the second death shall have no power over them.

Verses 12–17

I. The inscription of this message. *To the angel of the church of Pergamos*. The church of Pergamos was infested with men of corrupt minds, and Christ, being resolved to fight against them by the sword of his word, takes the title of him that *hath the sharp sword with two edges*. The word of God is a sword; it is a weapon both offensive and defensive. It is a *sharp sword*. No heart is so hard but it is able to wound it. It is a *sword with two edges*. There is the *edge* of the law against the transgressors of that dispensation, and the *edge* of the gospel against the despisers of that dispensation.

II. The contents of the epistle.

1. Christ takes notice of the trials and difficulties this church encountered, *v.* 13. Now that which added very much lustre to the good works of this church was the circumstance of the place where this church was planted, a place where *Satan's seat* was. His *circuit* is throughout the world, his *seat* is in some places that are infamous for wickedness, error, and cruelty.

2. He commends their steadfastness. "*Thou holdest fast my name;* thou art not ashamed of thy relation to me, but accountest it thine honour that my name is named on thee. That which has made thee thus faithful is the grace of faith: *thou hast not denied*, nor departed from the Christian faith." They had been steadfast *even in those days wherein Antipas his faithful martyr was slain among them*. He sealed his faith and fidelity with his blood in the place where Satan dwelt. They were not discouraged nor drawn away from their steadfastness.

JAMIESON, FAUSSET, BROWN

at POLYCARP's martyrdom they joined the heathens in clamoring for his being cast to the lions; and when there was an obstacle to this, for his being burnt alive; and with their own hands they carried logs for the pile. **synagogue of Satan**–Only once is the term "synagogue" in the New Testament used of the Christian assembly, and that by the apostle who longest maintained the union of the Church and Jewish Synagogue. The *Jews*, who might have been "the Church of God," had now, by their opposition and unbelief, become the synagogue of Satan. So "the throne of Satan" (vs. 13) represents the *heathens'* opposition to Christianity; "the depths of Satan" (vs. 24), the opposition of *heretics*. **10. Fear none . . .**–the oldest MSS. read, "Fear *not* those things. . . ." "The Captain of our salvation never keeps back what those who faithfully witness for Him may have to bear for His name's sake; never entices recruits by the promise they shall find all things easy and pleasant there" [TRENCH]. **devil**–"the accuser." He acted, through Jewish *accusers* against Christ and His people. The conflict of the latter was not with mere flesh and blood, but with the rulers of the darkness of this world. **tried**–with *temptation* by "the devil." The same event is often both a *temptation* from the devil, and a *trial* from God–God sifting and winnowing the man to separate his chaff from his wheat, the devil sifting him in the hope that nothing but chaff will be found in him [TRENCH]. **ten days**–not the ten persecutions from Nero to Diocletian. LYRA explains *ten years* on the year-day principle. The *shortness* of the duration of the persecution is evidently made the ground of consolation. **unto death**–so as even to endure death for My sake. **crown of life**–James 1:12; II Timothy 4:8, "crown of righteousness"; I Peter 5:4, "crown of glory." The *crown* is the *garland*, the mark of a *conqueror*, or of one *rejoicing*, or at a *feast;* but *diadem* is the mark of a KING. **11. shall not be hurt**–*Greek*, "shall not by any means (or possibly) be hurt." **the second death**–"the lake of fire." "The death in life of the lost, as contrasted with the life in death of the saved" [TRENCH]. The phrase "the second death" is peculiar to the Apocalypse. What matter about the first death, which sooner or later must pass over us, if we escape *the second death*? POLYCARP's noble words to his heathen judges who wished him to recant, are well known: "Fourscore and six years have I served the Lord, and He never wronged me, how then can I blaspheme my King and Saviour?" Smyrna's faithfulness is rewarded by its candlestick not having been removed out of its place (vs. 5); Christianity has never wholly left it; whence the Turks call it, "Infidel Smyrna." **12.** TRENCH prefers writing *Pergamus*, or rather, *Pergamum*, on the river Caicus. It was capital of Attalus the Second's kingdom, which was bequeathed by him to the Romans, 133 B.C. Famous for its library, founded by Eumenes (197-159), and destroyed by Caliph Omar. *Parchment*, i.e., *Pergamena charta*, was here discovered for book purposes. Also famous for the magnificent temple of Esculapius, the healing god [TACITUS, *Annals*, 3. 63]. **he which hath the sharp sword with two edges**–appropriate to His address having a twofold bearing, a searching power so as to convict and convert some (vss. 13, 17), and to convict and condemn to punishment others (vss. 14-16, especially vs. 16; cf. also *Note*, ch. 1:16). **13. I know thy works**–Two oldest MSS. omit this clause; one oldest MS. retains it. **Satan's seat**–rather as the *Greek* is translated all through Revelation, "throne." Satan, in impious mimicry of God's heavenly throne, sets up his earthly throne (ch. 4:2). Esculapius was worshipped there under the serpent form; and Satan, the old serpent, as the instigator (cf. vs. 10) of fanatical devotees of Esculapius, and, through them, of the supreme magistracy at Pergamos, persecuted one of the Lord's people (Antipas) even to death. Thus, this address is an anticipatory preface to ch. 12:1-17; *Note*, "*throne* . . . the dragon, Satan . . . war with her seed," 5:9, 17. **even in those days**–Two oldest MSS. omit "even"; two retain it. **wherein**–Two oldest MSS. omit this (then translate, "in the days of Antipas, My faithful witness," or "martyr"); two retain it. Two oldest MSS.read, "My witness, MY faithful one"; two read as *English Version*. Antipas is another form for Antipater. SIMEON METAPHRASTES has a palpably legendary story, unknown to the early Fathers, that Antipas, in Domitian's reign, was shut up in a red-hot brazen bull, and ended his life in thanksgivings and prayers. HENGSTENBERG makes the name, like other apocalyptic names, symbolical, meaning one standing out "against all" for Christ's sake. **14. few**–in comparison of the *many* tokens of thy faithfulness. **hold**

ADAM CLARKE

applied a sacred name to an unholy thing; and this is one meaning of the word *blasphemy* in this book.

10. *Ten days*. As the *days* in this book are what is commonly called "prophetic days," each answering to a year, the *ten days* of tribulation may denote "ten years of persecution"; and this was precisely the duration of the persecution under Diocletian, during which all the Asiatic churches were grievously afflicted. Others understand the expression as implying frequency and abundance, as it does in other parts of Scripture. Gen. xxxi. 7, 41: Thou hast "changed my wages ten times"; i.e., you have frequently changed my wages. Num. xiv. 22: "Those men . . . have tempted me now these ten times"; i.e., They have frequently and grievously tempted and sinned against Me. Neh. iv. 12: "The Jews which dwelt by them came . . . [and] said unto us ten times," i.e., They were frequently coming and informing us that our adversaries intended to attack us. Job xix. 3; "These ten times have ye reproached me"; i.e., you have loaded me with continual reproaches. *Be thou faithful unto death*. Be firm, hold fast the faith, confess Christ to the last and at all hazards, and you shall have *a crown of life*—you shall be crowned with life, have an eternal happy existence, though you suffer a temporal death. It is said of Polycarp that when brought before the judge, and commanded to abjure and blaspheme Christ, he firmly answered, "Eighty and six years have I served Him, and He never did me wrong. How then can I blaspheme my King, who hath saved me?" He was then adjudged to the flames, and suffered cheerfully for Christ, the Lord and Master.

11. *He that overcometh*. The "conqueror" who has stood firm in every trial and vanquished all his adveraries. *Shall not be hurt of the second death*. That is, an eternal separation from God and the glory of His power, as what we commonly mean by final perdition. This is another rabbinical mode of speech in very frequent use, and by it they understand the punishment of hell in a future life.

THE EPISTLE TO THE CHURCH AT PERGAMOS

12. *Which hath the sharp sword*. See on chap. i. 16. The "sword of the Spirit, which is the word of God," cuts every way; it convinces of sin, righteousness, and judgment; pierces between the joints and the marrow, divides between the soul and spirit, dissects the whole mind, and exhibits a regular anatomy of the soul. It not only reproves and exposes sin, but it slays the ungodly, pointing out the punishment they shall endure. Jesus has the *sword with two edges*, because He is the Saviour of sinners and the Judge of quick and dead.

13. *Where Satan's seat is*. "Where Satan has his throne"—where he reigns as king and is universally obeyed. It was a maxim among the Jews that, where the law of God was not studied, there Satan dwelt; but he was obliged to leave the place where a synagogue or academy was established. *Thou holdest fast my name*. Notwithstanding that the profession of Christianity exposed this church to the bitterest persecution, they held fast the name of Christian, which they had received from Jesus Christ, and did not deny His faith; for when brought to the trial they openly professed themselves disciples and followers of their Lord and Master. *Antipas was my faithful martyr*. Who this *Antipas* was we cannot tell. We only know that he was a Christian, and probably bore some office in the church, and became illustrious by his martyrdom in the cause of Christ.

14. *I have a few things against thee*. Their good deeds are first carefully sought out and

MATTHEW HENRY

3. He reproves them for their sinful failures (*v.* 14). The filthiness of the spirit and the filthiness of the flesh often go together. To continue in communion with persons of corrupt principles and practices draws a guilt and blemish upon the whole society.

4. He calls them to repentance, *v.* 16. It is the duty of churches and communities as well as particular persons; those who sin together should repent together. When God comes to punish the corrupt members of a church, he rebukes that church itself for allowing such to continue in its communion, and some drops of the storm fall upon the whole society. The word of God will take hold of sinners, sooner or later, either for their conviction or their confusion.

III. There is the promise of great favour to those that overcome, *v.* 17. 1. The hidden manna, the influences and comforts of the Spirit of Christ, coming down from heaven into the soul, from time to time. This is hidden from the rest of the world, and it is laid up in Christ.

2. The white stone, with a new name engraven upon it. This white stone is absolution from the guilt of sin, alluding to the ancient custom of giving a white stone to those acquitted on trial and a black stone to those condemned. The new name is the name of adoption. None can read the evidence of a man's adoption but himself.

JAMIESON, FAUSSET, BROWN

the doctrine of Balaam—"the *teaching* of Balaam," viz., that which he "taught Balak." Cf. "the counsel of Balaam," Numbers 31:16. "Balak" is dative in the *Greek,* whence BENGEL translates, "taught (the Moabites) for (i.e., to please) Balak." But though in Numbers it is not expressly said he taught *Balak,* yet there is nothing said inconsistent with his having done so; and JOSEPHUS, *Antiquities,* 4. 6. 6, says he did so. The dative is a Hebraism for the accusative. **children**—*Greek,* "*sons* of Israel." **stumbling block**—lit., that part of a trap on which the bait was laid, and which, when touched, caused the trap to close on its prey; then any entanglement to the foot [TRENCH]. **eat things sacrificed unto idols** —the act common to the Israelites of old, and the Nicolaitanes in John's day; he does not add what was peculiar to the Israelites, viz., that they *sacrificed* to idols. The temptation to eat idol meats was a peculiarly strong one to the Gentile converts. For not to do so involved almost a withdrawal from partaking of any social meal with the heathen around. For idol meats, after a part had been offered in sacrifice, were nearly sure to be on the heathen entertainer's table; so much so, that the *Greek* "to kill" (*thuein*) meant originally "to sacrifice." Hence arose the decree of the council of Jerusalem forbidding to eat such meats; subsequently some at Corinth ate unscrupulously and *knowingly* of such meats, on the ground that the idol is nothing; others needlessly fortured themselves with scruples, lest *unknowingly* they should eat of them when they got meat from the market or in a heathen friend's house. Paul handles the question in I Corinthians 8 and 10:25-33. **fornication**—often connected with idolatry. **15. thou**—emphatic: "So THOU also hast," As Balak and the Moabites of old had Balaam and his followers literally, *so hast thou also them that hold the* same Balaamite or *Nicolaitane doctrine* spiritually or symbolically. Literal eating of idol meats and fornication in Pergamos were accompanied by spiritual idolatry and fornication. **doctrine**—teaching (*Note*, vs. 6): viz., to tempt God's people to idolatry. **which thing I hate**—It is sin not to hate what God hates. The Ephesian Church (vs. 6) had this point of superiority to Pergamos. **16.** The three oldest MSS. read, "Repent, *therefore.*" Not only the Nicolaitanes, but the whole Church of Pergamos is called on to repent of not having *hated* the Nicolaitane teaching and practice. Contrast Paul, Acts 20:26. **I will come**—I am coming. **fight against them**—*Greek,* "war with them"; with the Nicolaitanes primarily; but including also *chastisement of the* whole Church at Pergamos: cf. "unto THEE." **with the sword of my mouth**—resumed from ch. 1:16, but with an allusion to the drawn *sword* with which the angel of the Lord confronted Balaam on his way to curse Israel: an earnest of *the sword* by which he and the seduced Israelites fell at last. The spritual Balaamites of John's day are to be smitten with the Lord's spiritual sword, the word or "rod of His mouth." **17. to eat**—omitted in the three oldest MSS. **the hidden manna**—the heavenly food of Israel, in contrast to the idol meats (vs. 14). A pot of manna was laid up in the holy place "before the testimony." The allusion is here to this: probably also to the Lord's discourse (John 6:31-35). Translate, "the manna which is hidden." As the manna hidden in the sanctuary was by divine power preserved from corruption, so Christ in His incorruptible body has passed into the heavens, and is hidden there until the time of His appearing. Christ Himself is the manna "hidden" from the world, but revealed to the believer, so that he has already a foretaste of His preciousness. Cf. as to Christ's own hidden food on earth, John 4:32, 34, and Job 23:12. The full manifestation shall be at His coming. **white stone . . . new name . . . no man knoweth saving he . . .**—TRENCH's explanation seems best. *White* is the color and livery of heaven. "New" implies something altogether renewed and heavenly. The white stone is a glistening diamond, the Urim borne by the high priest within the *choschen* or breastplate of judgment, with the twelve tribes' names on the twelve precious stones, next the heart. The word *Urim* means light, answering to the color *white.* None but the high priest knew the name written upon it, probably the incommunicable name of God, "Jehovah." The high priest consulted it in some divinely appointed way to get direction from God when needful. The "new name" is *Christ's* (cf. ch. 3:12, "I will write upon him *My* new name"): some new revelation of Himself which shall hereafter be imparted to His people, and which they alone are capable of receiving. The connection with the "hidden manna" will thus be clear, as none save the high priest had

ADAM CLARKE

commended; what was wrong in them is touched with a gentle but effectual hand. The followers of Balaam, the Nicolaitans, and the Gnostics were probably all the same kind of persons, but see on v. 6. What the doctrine of Balaam was, see the notes on Num. xxiv; xxv; and xxxi. It appears that there were some then in the church at Pergamos who held eating things offered to idols in honor of those idols, and fornication, indifferent things. They associated with idolaters in the heathen temples and partook with them in their religious festivals.

15. *The doctrine of the Nicolaitanes.* See on v. 6.

16. *Will fight against them with the sword of my mouth.* See on v. 12. He now speaks for their edification and salvation; but if they do not repent, He will shortly declare those judgments which shall unavoidably fall upon them.

17. *The hidden manna.* It was a constant tradition of the Jews that the ark of the covenant, the tables of stone, Aaron's rod, the holy anointing oil, and the pot of manna were hidden by King Josiah when Jerusalem was taken by the Chaldeans; and that these should all be restored in the days of the Messiah. This *manna* was *hidden,* but Christ promises to give it to him that is conqueror. Jesus is the Ark, the Oil, the Rod, the Testimony, and the Manna. He who is partaker of His grace has all those things in their spiritual meaning and perfection. *And will give him a white stone.* It is supposed that by the white stone is meant pardon or acquittance, and the evidence of it; and that there is an allusion here to the custom observed by judges in ancient times, who were accustomed to give their suffrages by *white* and black pebbles. Those who gave the former were for absolving the culprit; those who gave the latter were for his condemnation. Others suppose there is an allusion here to conquerors in the public games, who were not only conducted with great pomp into the city to which they belonged, but had a *white stone* given to them, with their name inscribed on it; which badge entitled them, during their whole life, to be maintained at the public expense. The most remarkable of these instruments were the *tesserae hospitales,* which were given as badges of friendship and alliance, and on which some device was engraved, as a testimony that a contract of friendship had been made between the parties. A small, oblong, square piece of wood, bone, stone, or ivory was taken and divided into two equal parts, on

MATTHEW HENRY

Verses 18–29

I. The inscription. *To the angel of the church of Thyatira.*

By whom it was sent: by *the Son of God,* who is here described as having *eyes like a flame of fire, and feet like as fine brass.* His eyes are like a flame of fire, signifying his piercing insight into all persons and all things. His feet are like fine brass. As he judges with perfect wisdom, so he acts with perfect strength and steadiness.

II. The contents of this epistle.

1. The honourable character and commendation Christ gives of this church. Christ makes honourable mention of their *charity*: there is no religion where there is no charity. Their *service.* Their *faith,* which was the grace that actuated all the rest. Their *patience.* Their growing fruitfulness: their last works were better than the first. It should be the ambition and earnest desire of all Christians that their last works may be their best works.

2. A faithful reproof for what was amiss. These wicked seducers are compared to Jezebel, and called by her name. The sin of these seducers was that they attempted to draw the servants of God into fornication, and to offer sacrifices to idols.

They abused the patience of God to harden themselves in their wickedness. God gave them space for repentance, but they repented not.

JAMIESON, FAUSSET, BROWN

access to the "manna hidden" in the sanctuary. Believers, as spiritual priests unto God, shall enjoy the heavenly antitypes to the hidden manna and the Urim stone. **receiveth it**—viz., "the stone"; not "the new name"; see above. The "name that no man knew but Christ Himself," He shall hereafter reveal to His people. **18. Thyatira**—in Lydia, south of Pergamos. Lydia, the purple-seller of this city, having been converted at Philippi, a Macedonian city (with which Thyatira, as being a Macedonian colony, had naturally much intercourse), was probably the instrument of first carrying the Gospel to her native town. John follows the geographical order here, for Thyatira lay a little to the left of the road from Pergamos to Sardis (STRABO, 13:4). **Son of God . . . eyes like . . . fire . . . feet . . . like fine brass**—or "glowing brass" (*Note,* ch. 1:14, 15, whence this description is resumed). Again His attributes accord with His address. The title "Son of God," is from Psalm 2:7, 9, which is referred to in vs. 27. The attribute, "eyes like a flame . . ." answers to vs. 23, "I am He which searcheth the reins and hearts." The attribute, "feet like . . . brass," answers to vs. 27, "as the vessels of a potter shall they be broken to shivers," He *treading* them *to pieces* with His strong feet. **19. The oldest MSS.** transpose the *English Version* order, and read, "faith and service." The four are subordinate to "thy works"; thus, "I know thy works, *even* the love and the faith (these two forming one pair, as 'faith works by love,' Gal. 5:6), and the service (*ministration* to the suffering members of the Church, and to all in spiritual or temporal need), and the endurance of (i.e., shown by) thee" (this pronoun belongs to all four). As *love* is inward, so *service* is its outward manifestation. Similarly, *faith* and persevering *edurance,* or "*patient continuance* (the same *Greek* as here, Rom. 2:7) in well-doing," are connected. **and thy works; and the last**—Omit the second "and," with the three oldest MSS. and the ancient versions; translate, "And (I know) thy works which are last (to be) more in number than the first"; realizing I Thessalonians 4:1; the converse of Matthew 12:45; II Peter 2:20. Instead of retrograding from "the first works" and "first love," as Ephesus, Thyatira's *last works* exceeded her *first* (vss. 4, 5). **20. a few things**—omitted in the three oldest MSS. Translate then, "I have against thee *that*. . . ." **sufferest**—The three oldest MSS. read, "lettest alone." **that woman**—Two oldest MSS. read, "THY wife"; two omit it. *Vulgate* and most ancient versions read as *English Version.* The symbolical Jezebel was to the Church of Thyatira what Jezebel, Ahab's "wife," was to him. Some self-styled prophetess (or as the feminine in *Hebrew* is often used *collectively* to express a multitude, *a set of false prophets*), as closely attached to the Church of Thyatira as a *wife* is to a husband, and as powerfully influencing for evil that Church as Jezebel did Ahab. Wholly given to Baal-worship, like Eth-baal, whose name expresses his idolatry, she, with her strong will, seduced the weak Ahab and Israel beyond the calf-worship (which was a worship of the true God under the cherub-ox form, i.e., a violation of the second commandment) to that of Baal (a violation of the first commandment also). She seems to have been herself a priestess and prophetess of Baal. Cf. II Kings 9:22, 30, "*whoredoms* of . . . Jezebel and her *witchcrafts*" (impurity was part of the worship of the Phœnician Astarte, or Venus). Her spiritual counterpart at Thyatira lured God's "servants" by pretended utterances of inspiration to the same libertinism, fornication, and eating of idol meats, as the Balaamites and Nicolaitanes (vss. 6, 14, 15). By a false spiritualism these seducers led their victims into the grossest carnality, as though things done in the flesh were outside the true man, and were, therefore, indifferent. "The deeper the Church penetrated into heathenism, the more she herself became heathenish; this prepares us for the expressions 'harlot' and 'Babylon,' applied to her afterwards" [AUBERLEN]. **to teach and to seduce**—The three oldest MSS. read, "and she teaches and seduces," or "deceives." **21. space**—*Greek,* "time." **of her fornication . . . she repented not**—The three oldest MSS. read, "and she *willeth* not *to repent of* (lit., 'out of', i.e., so as to come *out* of) *her fornication.*" Here there is a transition from *literal* to *spiritual* fornication, as appears from vs. 22. The idea arose from Jehovah's covenant relation to the Old Testament Church being regarded as a marriage, any transgression against which was, therefore, *harlotry, fornication,* or *adultery.* **22. Behold**—calling attention to her awful doom to come. **I will**—*Greek* present, "I cast her." **a bed**—The place of her sin shall be the place of her punishment. The bed of her sin shall be her bed of

ADAM CLARKE

which each of the parties wrote his own name, and then interchanged it with the other. This was carefully preserved; and by producing this when they travelled, it gave a mutual claim to the bearers of kind reception and hospitable entertainment at each other's houses. The *tessera* taken in this sense seems to have been a kind of tally, and the two parts were compared together to ascertain the truth. Now it is very probable that John may allude to this, for on this mode of interpretation every part of the verse is consistent. The word does not necessarily signify a *stone* of any kind, but a suffrage, sentence, decisive vote; and in this place seems answerable to the *tessera.* The names of the contracting persons, or some device, were written on the *tessera,* which commemorated the friendly contract; and as the parts were interchanged, none could know that name or device, or the reason of the contract, but he who received it. This, when produced, gave the bearer a right to the offices of hospitality; he was accommodated with food, lodging, as far as these were necessary; and to this the eating *of the hidden manna* may refer.

THE EPISTLE TO THE CHURCH AT THYATIRA

19. *I know thy works.* And of these he first sets forth their *charity,* their "love" to God and each other, and particularly to the poor and distressed; and hence followed their *faith,* their "fidelity," to the grace they had received; and *service,* "ministration"; properly pious and benevolent service to widows, orphans, and the poor in general. *And thy patience.* Your "perseverance" under afflictions and persecutions, and your continuance in well-doing. **I put** *faith* before *service* according to the general consent of the best MSS. and versions. *Thy works.* The continued labor of love and thorough obedience. *The last to be more than the first.* They not only retained what they had received at first, but grew in grace, and in the knowledge and love of Jesus Christ. This is a rare thing in most Christian churches; they generally lose the power of religion and rest in the forms of worship, and it requires a powerful revival to bring them to such a state that their last works shall be more than their first.

20. *That woman Jezebel.* There is an allusion here to the history of Ahab and Jezebel, as given in 2 Kings ix—x; and although we do not know who this Jezebel was, yet from the allusion we may take it for granted she was a woman of power and influence in Thyatira, who corrupted the true religion and harassed the followers of God in that city, as Jezebel did in Israel. Instead of *that woman Jezebel,* many excellent MSS., and almost all the ancient versions, read "thy wife Jezebel"; which intimates, indeed asserts, that this bad woman was the wife of the bishop of the church, and his criminality in suffering her was therefore the greater. This reading Griesbach has received into the text.

21. *I gave her space to repent.* It is worthy of remark that the Gnostics called their doctrine "the depths of God" and "the depths of Bythos," intimating that they contained the most profound secrets of divine wisdom. Christ here calls them the "depths of Satan," being masterpieces of his subtlety. Perhaps they thought them to be of God, while all the time they were deceived by the devil.

MATTHEW HENRY

3. The punishment of this seducer, *v.* 22, 23. *I will cast her into a bed*, into a bed of pain, not of pleasure. *I will kill her children with death;* that is, the second death.

4. The design of Christ in the destruction of these wicked seducers, was the instruction of others. God is known by *the judgments that he executes.*

5. The encouragement given to those who keep themselves pure and undefiled, *v.* 24. (1) What these seducers called their doctrines—*depths*, profound mysteries. (2) What Christ called them—*depths of Satan*, Satanical delusions and devices.

(3) How tender Christ is of his faithful servants, *v.* 24, 25. "I only require your attention to what you have received." If they hold fast faith and a good conscience till he come, all the difficulty and danger will be over.

III. The conclusion of this message, *v.* 26–29. 1. The promise of an ample reward to the persevering victorious believer: Very great power and dominion over the rest of the world: *Power over the nations.*

JAMIESON, FAUSSET, BROWN

sickness and anguish. Perhaps a pestilence was about to be sent. Or the bed of the grave, and of the hell beyond, where the worm dieth not. **them that commit adultery with her**—spiritually; including both the eating of *idol meats* and *fornication.* "With her," in the *Greek*, implies *participation with* her in her adulteries, viz., by *suffering her* (vs. 20), or *letting* her *alone*, and so virtually encouraging her. **except they repent**—*Greek* aorist, "repent" *at once;* shall have repented by the time limited in My purpose. **their deeds**—Two of the oldest MSS. and most ancient versions read "her." Thus, God's true servants, who by connivance, are incurring the guilt of *her deeds*, are distinguished from her. One oldest MS., ANDREAS, and CYPRIAN, support "their." **23. her children**—(Isa. 57:3; Ezek. 23:45, 47). Her proper adherents; not those who *suffer* her, but those who are begotten of her. A distinct class from the last in vs. 22 (cf. *Note* there), whose sin was less direct, being that only of connivance. **kill . . . with death**—Cf. the disaster that overtook the literal Jezebel's votaries of Baal, and Ahab's sons, I Kings 18:40; II Kings 10:6, 7, 24, 25. *Kill with death* is a Hebraism for *slay with most sure and awful death;* so "dying thou shalt die" (Gen. 2:17). Not "die the common death of men" (Num. 16:29). **all the churches shall know**—implying that these addresses are designed for the catholic Church of all ages and places. So palpably shall God's hand be seen in the judgment on Thyatira, that the whole Church shall recognize it as God's doing. **I am he**—the "I" is strongly emphatical: "that it is *I* am He who. . . ." **searcheth . . . hearts**—God's peculiar attribute is given to Christ. The "reins" are the seat of the desires; the "heart," that of the thoughts. The *Greek* for "searcheth" expresses an accurate following up of all tracks and windings. **unto every one of you**—lit., "unto you, to each." **according to your works**—to be judged not according to the mere act as it appears to man, but with reference to the motive, *faith* and *love* being the only motives which God recognizes as sound. **24. you . . . and . . . the rest**—The three oldest MSS. omit "and"; translate then, "Unto you, the rest." **as many as have not**—not only do not *hold*, but are free from contact with. **and which**—The oldest MSS. omit "and"; translate, "whosoever." **the depths**—These false prophets boasted peculiarly of their *knowledge of mysteries* and *the deep things of God;* pretensions subsequently expressed by their arrogant title, *Gnostics* ("full of knowledge"). The Spirit here declares their so-called "depths," (viz., of knowledge of divine things) to be really "depths *of Satan*"; just as in vs. 9, He says, instead of "the synagogue *of God*," "the synagogue *of Satan.*" **I will put**—Two oldest MSS. have "I put," or "cast." One oldest MS. reads as *English Version.* **none other burden**—save abstinence from, and protestation against, these abominations; no "depths" beyond your reach, such as they teach, no new doctrine, but the old faith and rule of practice once for all delivered to the saints. **25. that which ye have already**—(Jude 3, end). **hold fast**—do not let go from your grasp, however false teachers may wish to wrest it from you. **till I come**—when your conflict with evil will be at an end. The *Greek* implies *uncertainty* as to when He shall come. **26. And**—implying the close connection of the promise to the conqueror that follows, with the preceding exhortation, vs. 25. **and keepeth**—*Greek*, "and he that keepeth." Cf. the same word in the passage already alluded to by the Lord, Acts 15:28, 29, end. **my works**—in contrast to "her (*English Version*, 'their') works" (vs. 22). The works which I command and which are the fruit of My Spirit. **unto the end**—(Matt. 24:13). The image is perhaps from the race, wherein it is not enough to enter the lists, but the runner must persevere *to the end.* **give power**—*Greek*, authority." **over the nations**—at Christ's coming the saints shall possess the kingdom "under the whole heaven"; therefore over this earth; cf. Luke 19:17, "have thou *authority* [the same *word* as here] over ten cities." **27.** From Psalm 2:8, 9. **rule**—lit., "rule as a shepherd." In Psalm 2:9 it is, "Thou shalt *break* them with a rod of iron." The LXX, pointing the *Hebrew* word differently, read as Revelation here. The *English Version* of Psalm 2:9 is doubtless right, as the parallel word, "dash in pieces," proves. But the Spirit in this case sanctions the *additional* thought as true, that the Lord shall mingle mercy to some, with judgment on others; beginning by destroying His Antichristian foes, He shall reign in love over the rest.

As severity here is the primary thought, "rule as a shepherd" seems to me to be used thus: He who would have shepherded them with a pastoral

ADAM CLARKE

J. A. SEISS:

The church in Thyatira had some of the same excellencies as the church in Pergamos, but conjoined with even worse defects. It was active in services and charities, patient in reliance upon God's promises, and increasingly vigorous in its endeavors; but it was lacking in proper zeal for the maintenance of godly discipline and doctrine, and was so indulgent toward errors and errorists that falsehood and idolatry permeated, overlaid and modified the whole character of the church, obscuring the faith, deceiving the saints, and setting up in its very midst the infamous school of Satan himself. With all that is said commendatory of this church, the idea of effeminacy connects with its whole history and character. The first Christian in Thyatira was a woman. The name, Thyatira, some take as equivalent to *thygatira*, a daughter. We get the idea of feminine oppression. The false prophets who first enticed the members of this church into apostasy were women. And the great fault which Christ finds with these Christians is their toleration of the false pretences, the miserable domination, and the abominable doings, of one whom He designates as "that woman Jezebel," who, like her namesake of old, seems to have borne down what should have been the governing will, set aside the true prophets of God with falsities, and entirely taken possession of the church for her own impurities. It was a church with much activity of faith and love, but lying in the embraces of an adulteress, and, for the most part, completely in her power.—*The Apocalypse*

25. *That which ye have*—that is, the pure doctrine of the gospel; *hold fast till I come*—till I come to execute the judgments which I have threatened.

26. *Power over the nations.* Every witness of Christ has power to confute and confound all the false doctrines and maxims of the nations of the world, for Christianity shall at last rule over all; the kingdom of Christ will come, and the kingdom of this world become the kingdoms of our God and of His Christ.

MATTHEW HENRY

Knowledge and wisdom, suitable to such power and dominion: *I will give him the morning-star.* Christ is the morning-star. He brings day with him into the soul, the light of grace and of glory. 2. This epistle ends with the usual demand of attention.

CHAPTER 3

Verses 1–6

I. The preface. *To the angel of the church of Sardis,* said to have been the first city in that part of the world that was converted by the preaching of John; and, some say, the first that revolted from Christianity. By whom this message was sent—the Lord Jesus, *that hath the seven spirits of God, and the seven stars.* (1) He hath the seven spirits, that is, the Holy Spirit with his various powers. This epistle being sent to a languishing ministry and church, they are very fitly put in mind that Christ has the seven spirits, the Spirit without measure and in perfection, to whom they may apply themselves for the reviving of his work among them. (2) He hath the seven stars, the angels of the churches. The Holy Spirit usually works by the ministry, and the ministry will be of no efficacy without the Spirit; the same divine hand holds them both.

II. The body of this epistle. In this (and in the epistle to Laodicea) he begins,

1. With a reproof, and a very severe one. Hypocrisy, and a lamentable decay in religion, are the sins charged upon this church. This church had gained a great reputation; it had a name for a flourishing church. We read not of any unhappy divisions among themselves. Everything appeared well, as to what falls under the observation of men. This church was not really what it was reputed to be. There was a form of godliness, but not the power, *a name to live,* but not a principle of life. What little life was yet left among them was expiring, ready to die.

2. Our Lord proceeds to give this degenerate church the best advice, *v.* 2. (1) He advises them to be upon their watch. Whenever we are off our watch, we lose ground, and therefore must return to our watchfulness against sin, and Satan. (2) To strengthen the things that remain, and that are ready to die. Some understand this of persons. It is a difficult thing to keep up to the life and *power of godliness* ourselves, when we see a universal deadness and declension prevailing round about us. Or it may be understood of practices: *I have not found thy works perfect before God;* there is something wanting in them; there is the shell, but not the kernel. The inward thing is wanting, thy works are hollow and empty. When the spirit is wanting the form cannot long subsist. (3) To recollect themselves (*v.* 3); to remember what they had received and heard, how welcome the gospel and the grace of God were to them when they first received them. (4) To hold fast what they had received, that they might not lose all *and repent.*

3. Christ enforces his counsel with a dreadful threatening, *v.* 3. (1) When Christ leaves a people as to his gracious presence, he comes to them in judgment. (2) His judicial approach to a dead declining people will be surprising; their deadness will keep them in security.

JAMIESON, FAUSSET, BROWN

rod, shall, because of their hardened unbelief, shepherd them with a rod of iron. **shall they be broken**—So one oldest MS., *Vulgate, Syriac,* and *Coptic Versions* read. But two oldest MSS, read, "as the vessels of a potter *are* broken to shivers." *A potter's vessel dashed to pieces,* because of its failing to answer the design of the maker, is the image to depict God's sovereign power to give reprobates to destruction, not by caprice, but in the exercise of His righteous judgment. **even as I**—"as *I* also have received of (from) My Father," viz., in Psalm 2:7-9. Jesus had refused to receive the kingdom without the cross at Satan's hands; He would receive it from none but the Father, who had appointed the cross as the path to the crown. As the Father has given the authority to Me over the heathen and uttermost parts of the earth, so I impart a share of it to My victorious disciple. **28. the morning star**—i.e., I will give unto him *Myself,* who am "the morning star" (ch. 22:16); so that reflecting My perfect brightness, he shall shine like Me, the morning star, and share My *kingly glory* (of which a *star* is the symbol, Num. 21:17; Matt. 2:2).

CHAPTER 3

Vss. 1-22. The Epistles to Sardis, Philadelphia, and Laodicea. **1. Sardis**—the ancient capital of Lydia, the kingdom of wealthy Crœsus, on the river Pactolus. The address to this Church is full of rebuke. It does not seem to have been in vain; for Melito, bishop of Sardis in the second century, was eminent for piety and learning. **he that hath the seven Spirits of God**—i.e., He who hath all the fulness of the Spirit (ch. 1:4; 4:5; 5:6, with which cf. Zech. 3:9; 4:10, proving His Godhead). This attribute implies His infinite power by the Spirit to convict of sin and of a hollow profession. **and the seven stars**—(ch. 1:16, 20). His *having the seven stars,* or presiding ministers, flows, as a consequence, from His *having the seven Spirits,* or the fulness of the Holy Spirit. The human ministry is the fruit of Christ's sending down the gifts of the Spirit. *Stars* imply brilliancy and glory; the fulness of the Spirit, and the fulness of brilliant light in Him, form a designed contrast to the formality which He reproves. **name . . . livest . . . dead**—(I Tim. 5:6; II Tim. 3:5 Titus 1:16; cf. Eph. 2:1, 5; 5:14). "A name," i.e., a reputation. Sardis was famed among the churches for spiritual *vitality;* yet the Heart-searcher, who seeth not as man seeth, pronounces her *dead;* how great searchings of heart should her case create among even the best of us! Laodicea deceived herself as to her true state (vs. 17), but it is not written that she had a high *name* among the other churches, as Sardis had. **2. Be**—*Greek.* "Become," what thou art not, "watchful," or "wakeful," lit., "waking." **the things which remain**—Strengthen those thy remaining few graces, which, in thy spiritual deadly slumber, are not yet quite extinct [Alford]. **are**—The two oldest MSS. read, "were ready," lit., "were about to die," viz., at the time when you "strengthen" them. This implies that "thou art dead," vs. 1, is to be taken with limitation; for those must have some life who are told to *strengthen the things that remain.* **perfect**—lit., "filled up in full complement"; Translate, "complete." Weighed in the balance of Him who requires living faith as the motive of works, and found wanting. **before God**—*Greek,* in the sight of God." The three oldest MSS., *Vulgate, Syriac,* and *Coptic,* read, "before (in the sight of) my God"; Christ's judgment is God the Father's judgment. **3. how thou hast received**—(Col. 2:6; I Thess. 4:1; I Tim. 6:20). What Sardis is to "remember" is, not *how* joyfully she had received originally the Gospel message, but how the precious deposit was committed to her originally, so that she could not say, she had not "received and heard" it. The *Greek* is not aorist (as in ch. 2:4, as to Ephesus, "Thou *didst leave* thy first love"), but "thou hast received" (perfect), and still hast the permanent deposit of doctrine committed to thee. The word "keep" (so the *Greek* is for *English Version,* "hold fast") which follows, accords with this sense. "Keep" or observe the commandment which thou hast received and didst hear. **heard**—*Greek* aorist, "didst hear," viz., when the Gospel doctrine was committed to thee.

If therefore—seeing thou art so warned, if, nevertheless. . . . **come on thee as a thief**—in special judgment on thee as a Church, with the same stealthiness and as unexpectedly as shall be My visible second coming. As *the thief* gives no notice of his approach. Christ applies the language which

ADAM CLARKE

27. *He shall rule them with a rod of iron.* He shall restrain vice by the strictest administration of justice; and those who finally despise the word and rebel shall be *broken* and destroyed, so as never more to be able to make head against the truth.

CHAPTER 3

Epistle to the Church at Sardis

1. *The seven Spirits of God.* See the note on chap. i. 4.

Thou hast a name that thou livest. You have the reputation of Christians, and consequently of being alive to God, through the quickening influence of the divine Spirit; but *art dead*—you have not the life of God in your souls; you have not walked consistently and steadily before God, and His Spirit has been grieved with you, and He has withdrawn much of His light and power.

2. *Be watchful.* You have lost ground by carelessness and inattention. Awake, and keep awake! *Strengthen the things which remain.* The convictions and good desires, with any measure of the fear of God and of a tender conscience, which, although still subsisting, are about to perish, because the Holy Spirit, who is the Author of them, being repeatedly grieved, is about finally to depart.

Thy works perfect. "Filled up." They performed duties of all kinds, but no duty completely. They were constantly beginning, but never brought anything to a proper end. Their resolutions were languid, their strength feeble, and their light dim. They probably maintained their reputation before men, but their works were not perfect before God.

3. *Remember.* Enter into a serious consideration of your state. *How thou hast received.* With what joy, zeal, and gladness you heard the gospel of Christ when first preached to you.

Hold fast. Those good desires and heavenly influences which still remain. *And repent.* Be humbled before God.

I will come on thee as a thief. As the thief comes when he is not expected.

MATTHEW HENRY

4. Our blessed Lord does not leave this sinful people without some comfort and encouragement (*v.* 4). He makes honourable mention of the faithful remnant in Sardis, though but small. God takes notice of the smallest number of those who abide with him; and the fewer they are the more precious in his sight.

He makes a very gracious promise to them. They shall walk with Christ, and what delightful converse will there be between Christ and them when they thus walk together! Those who walk with Christ shall walk with Christ in the white robes of honour and glory in the other world.

III. The conclusion of this epistle.

1. A great reward promised to the conquering Christian (*v.* 5). The purity of grace shall be rewarded with the perfect purity of glory. Holiness, when perfected, shall be its own reward; glory is the perfection of grace.

To this is added another promise. Christ has his book of life. Christ will not blot the names of his chosen and faithful ones out of this book of life. The names of those that overcome shall never be blotted out. Christ will produce this book of life, and confess the names of the faithful who stand there, before God, and all the angels. How great will this honour and reward be!

2. The demand of universal attention finishes the message. Every word from God deserves attention from men.

Verses 7–13

I. The inscription.

1. For whom it was designed: *The angel of the church of Philadelphia.* It was its ancient name, on account of the love and kindness which the citizens had and showed to each other. This was an excellent spirit, and would render them an excellent church, as indeed they were, for here is no one fault found with this church.

2. By whom this letter was signed; even by the same Jesus. You have his personal character: *He that is holy* and *he that is true*; holy in his nature, and therefore he cannot but be true to his word.

JAMIESON, FAUSSET, BROWN

in its fullest sense describes His second coming, to describe His coming in special judgments on churches and states (as Jerusalem, Matt. 24) these special judgments being anticipatory earnests of that great last coming. **4.** The three oldest MSS. prefix "but," or "nevertheless" (notwithstanding thy spiritual deadness), and omit "even." **names**—persons *named* in the book of life (vs. 5) known by name by the Lord as His own. These had the reality corresponding to their name; not a mere *name* among men as *living,* while really *dead* (vs. 1). The gracious Lord does not overlook any exceptional cases of real saints in the midst of unreal professors. **not defiled their garments**—viz., the garments of their Christian profession, of which baptism is the initiatory seal, whence the candidates for baptism used in the ancient Church to be arrayed in white. Cf. also Ephesians 5:27, as to the spotlessness of the Church when she shall be presented to Christ; and ch. 19:8, as to the "fine linen, clean and white, the righteousness of the saints," in which it shall be granted to her to be arrayed; and "the wedding garment." Meanwhile she is not to sully her Christian profession with any defilement of flesh or spirit, but to "keep her garments." For no defilement shall enter the heavenly city. **they shall walk with me in white**—The promised reward accords with the character of those to be rewarded: keeping their *garments undefiled* and white through the blood of the Lamb now, they shall *walk with Him in while* hereafter. **are worthy**—with the worthiness (not their own, but that) which Christ has put on them (ch. 7:14). Ezekiel 16:14, "perfect through MY comeliness which I had put upon thee." Grace is glory in the bud. "The *worthiness* here denotes a congruity between the saint's *state of grace* on earth, and that of *glory,* which the Lord has appointed for them, about to be estimated by the law itself of grace" [VITRINGA]. Contrast Acts 13:46. **5. white**—not a dull white, but glittering, dazzling white [GROTIUS]. Cf. Matthew 13:43. The body transfigured into the likeness of Christ's body, and emitting beams of light reflected from Him, is probably the "white raiment" promised here. **the same**—*Greek,* "THIS man"; he and he alone. So one oldest MS. reads. But two oldest MSS., and most of the ancient versions, shall THUS be clothed...." **raiment**—*Greek,* "garments." "He that overcometh" shall receive the same reward as they who "have not defiled their garments" (vs. 4); therefore the two are identical. **I will not**—*Greek,* "I will not by any means." **blot out ... name out of ... book of life**—of the heavenly city. A register was kept in ancient cities of their citizens: the names of the dead were of course erased. So those who have a *name that they live and are dead* (vs. 1), are blotted out of God's roll of the heavenly citizens and heirs of eternal *life:* **... before**—*Greek,* **"in the presence of."** Cf. the same promise of Christ's confessing before His Father those who confessed Him, Matthew 10:32, 33; Luke 12:8, 9. He omits "in heaven" after "My Father," because there is, now that He is in heaven, no contrast between the Father *in heaven* and the Son *on earth.* He now sets His seal from heaven upon many of His words uttered on earth [TRENCH].

6. (Cf. *Note,* ch. 2:7.) **7. Philadelphia**—in Lydia, twenty-eight miles southeast of Sardis, built by Attalus Philadelphus, king of Pergamos, who died A.D. 138. It was nearly destroyed by an earthquake in the reign of Tiberius [TACITUS, *Annals,* 2. 47]. The connection of this Church with Jews there causes the address to it to have an Old Testament coloring in the images employed. It and Smyrna alone of the seven receive unmixed praise. **he that is holy**—as in the Old Testament, "*the Holy One* of Israel." Thus Jesus and the God of the Old Testament are one. None but God is absolutely holy (*Greek, hagios,* separate from evil and perfectly hating it). In contrast to "the synagogue of Satan" (vs. 9). **true**—*Greek, alethinos:* "VERY God," as distinguished from the false gods and from all those who *say that they are* what *they are not* (vs. 9): real, genuine. Furthermore, He *perfectly* realizes all that is involved in the names, GOD, *Light* (John 1:9; I John 2:8), *Bread* (John 6:32), the *Vine* (John 15:1); as distinguished from all typical, partial, and imperfect realizations of the idea. His nature answers to His name (John 17:3; I Thess. 1:9). The *Greek, alethes,* on the other hand, is "truth-speaking," "truthloving" (John 3:33; Titus 1:2). **he that hath the key of David**—the antitype of Eliakim, to whom the "key," the emblem of authority "over the house of David," was transferred from Shebna, who was removed from the office of chamberlain or treasurer, as unworthy of it. Christ, the Heir of the throne of David, shall supplant all the less wor-

ADAM CLARKE

4. *Thou hast a few names even in Sardis.* A few "persons," *names* being put for those who bore them. And as the members of the church were all enrolled, or their names entered in a book, when admitted into the church or when baptized, *names* are here put for the people themselves. *Have not defiled their garments.* Their souls. The Hebrews considered holiness as the garb of the soul, and evil actions as stains or spots on this garb.

They shall walk with me in white. They shall be raised to a state of eternal glory, and shall be forever with their Lord.

5. *I will not blot out his name.* This may be an allusion to the custom of registering the names of those who were admitted into the church in a book kept for that purpose. These are properly *book[s] of life,* as there those who were born unto God were registered. Or there may be allusions to the *white raiment* worn by the priests, and the erasing of the name of any priest out of the sacerdotal list who had either sinned or was found not to be of the seed of Aaron. "The great council of Israel sat and judged the priests. If in a priest any vice was found they stripped off his white garments and clothed him in *black,* in which he wrapped himself, went out, and departed. Him in whom no vice was found they clothed in *white,* and he went and took his part in the ministry among his brother priests." *I will confess his name.* I will acknowledge that this person is My true disciple and a member of My mystical body.

EPISTLE TO THE CHURCH AT PHILADELPHIA

7. *He that is holy.* In whom holiness essentially dwells, and from whom all holiness is derived. *He that is true.* He who is the Fountain of truth.

He that hath the key of David. See this metaphor explained, Matt. xvi. 19.

MATTHEW HENRY

The acts of his government. [1] He opens. He opens a door of opportunity to his churches; he opens a door of entrance, opens the heart; and he opens the door of admission into the church triumphant. [2] He shuts the door. When he pleases, he shuts the door of opportunity, and he shuts the door of heaven against the workers of iniquity. The way and manner in which he performs these acts is absolute sovereignty. When he works, none can hinder.

II. The subject-matter of this epistle.

1. Christ puts them in mind of what he had done for them, *v.* 8. I have set it open, and kept it open, though there be many adversaries. Wicked men envy the people of God their door of liberty, and would be glad to shut it against them. If we do not provoke Christ to shut this door against us, men cannot do it.

2. This church is commended, *v.* 8. In this there seems to be couched a gentle reproof: "*Thou hast a little strength*, a little grace." True grace, though weak, has the divine approbation; yet believers should not rest satisfied in a little, but should strive to grow in grace. True grace, though weak, will enable the Christian to keep the word of Christ, and not to deny his name.

3. The great favour God would bestow on this church, *v.* 9, 10.

(1) Christ would make this church's enemies subject to her. [1] Those enemies are described to be such as *said they were Jews*, but were really *the synagogue of Satan*. [2] Their subjection to the church is described: *They shall worship at thy feet;* shall be convinced that they have been in the wrong. How shall this great change be wrought? By the power of God upon the hearts of his enemies, and by signal discoveries of his peculiar favour to his church: *They shall know that I have loved thee.* Christ can discover this his favour to his people in such a manner that their very enemies shall see it, and be forced to acknowledge it. This will, by the grace of Christ, soften the hearts of their enemies.

(2) Another instance of favour that Christ promises (*v.* 10). The gospel of Christ is the word of his patience. It is the fruit of the patience of God to a sinful world.

After a day of patience we must expect an hour of temptation. Those who keep the gospel in a time of peace shall be kept by Christ in an hour of temptation.

4. Christ calls the church to persevere. "*Hold fast that which thou hast*; thou hast been possessed of this excellent treasure, hold it fast. *Behold, I come quickly.* I am just coming to relieve them under the trial, to reward their fidelity, and to punish those who fall away. The persevering Christian shall win the prize from backsliding professors."

III. The conclusion of this epistle, *v.* 12, 13.

1. Our Saviour promises a glorious reward to the victorious believer in two things: (1) He shall be a monumental *pillar in the temple of God*; not a pillar to support the temple, but a monument of the grace of God, a monument that shall never be defaced nor removed, as many stately pillars erected in honour to the Roman emperors and generals have been.

JAMIESON, FAUSSET, BROWN

thy stewards who have abused their trust in God's spiritual house, and "shall reign over the house of Jacob," literal and spiritual (Luke 1:32, 33), "for ever," "as a Son over His own house" (Heb. 3:2-6). It rests with Christ to open or shut the heavenly palace, deciding who is, and who is not, to be admitted: as He also opens, or shuts, the prison, *having the keys of hell (the grave) and death* (ch. 1:18). Though "the synagogue of Satan," false "Jews" (vs. 9) try to "shut" the "door" which I "set open before thee"; "no man can shut it" (vs. 8). **shutteth**—So *Vulgate* and *Syriac Versions* read. But the four oldest MSS. read, "shall shut"; so *Coptic Version* and ORIGEN. **shutteth, and no man openeth**—Two oldest MSS., B, א *Coptic Version*, and ORIGEN read, "shall open." Two oldest MSS., A, C. and *Vulgate Version* support *English Version* reading. **8. I have set**—*Greek*, "given": it is My gracious *gift* to thee. **open door** for evangelization; a door of spiritual usefulness. The *opening of a door* by Him to the Philadelphian Church accords with the previous assignation to Him of "the key of David." **and**—The three oldest MSS., A, B, C, and ORIGEN read, "*which* no man can shut." **for**—"because." **a little**—This gives the idea that Christ says, He sets before Philadelphia an open door because she has *some little* strength; whereas the sense rather is, He does so because she has "*but little* strength": being consciously weak herself, she is the fitter object for God's power to rest on [so AQUINAS], that so the Lord Christ may have all the glory. **and hast kept**—*and* so, the *littleness of thy strength* becoming the source of Almighty power to thee, as leading thee to rest wholly on My great power, *thou hast kept My word*. **9. I will make**—*Greek* present, "I make," lit., "I give" (*Note*, vs. 8). The promise to Philadelphia is larger than that to Smyrna. To Smyrna the promise was that "the synagogue of Satan" should not prevail against the faithful in her: to Philadelphia, that she should even win over some of "the synagogue of Satan" to *fall on their faces and confess God is in her of a truth*. Translate, "(some) of the synagogue." For until Christ shall come, and *all* Israel then be saved, there is but "a remnant" being gathered out of the Jews "according to the election of grace." This is an instance of how Christ set before her an "open door," some of her greatest adversaries, the Jews, being brought to the obedience of the faith. Their *worshipping before her feet* expresses the convert's willingness to take the very lowest place in the Church, doing servile honor to those whom once they persecuted, rather than dwell with the ungodly. So the Philippian jailer before Paul. **10. patience**—"endurance." "The word of My endurance" is *My Gospel word*, which teaches *patient endurance* in expectation of my coming (ch. 1:9). *My endurance* is the endurance which I require, and which I practice. Christ Himself now *endures, patiently* waiting until the usurper be cast out, and all "His enemies be made His footstool." So, too, His Church, for the joy before her of sharing His coming kingdom, *endures patiently*. Hence, in vs. 11, follows, "Behold, I come quickly." **I also**—The reward is in kind: "because thou didst keep. . . ." "I also (on My side) will keep thee. . . . **from**—*Greek*, "(so as to deliver thee) *out of*," not to exempt *from* temptation. **the hour of temptation**—the appointed *season* of affliction and temptation (so in Deut. 4:34 the plagues are called "the temptations of Egypt"), lit., "*the* temptation": the sore temptation which is coming on: the time of great tribulation before Christ's second coming. **to try them that dwell upon the earth**—those who are of earth, earthy (ch. 8:13). "Dwell" implies that their *home* is earth, not heaven. **11. Behold**—omitted by the three oldest MSS. and most ancient versions. **I come quickly**—the great incentive to persevering faithfulness, and the consolation under present trials. **that . . . which thou hast**—"The word of my patience," or "endurance" (vs. 10), which He had just commended them for keeping, and which involved with it the attaining of the kingdom; this they would lose if they yielded to the temptation of exchanging consistency and suffering for compromise and ease. **that no man take thy crown**—which otherwise thou wouldst receive: that no tempter cause thee to lose it: not that the tempter would thus secure it for himself (Col. 2:18). **12. pillar in the temple**—In one sense there shall be "no temple" in the heavenly city because there shall be no distinction of things into sacred and secular, for all things and persons shall be holy to the Lord. The city shall be all one great temple, in which the saints shall be not merely *stones*, as in the spiritual temple now on earth, but all eminent as *pillars:* immovably firm (unlike Philadelphia, the

ADAM CLARKE

Key is the emblem of authority and knowledge; *the key of David* is the regal right or authority of David. David could shut or open the kingdom of Israel to whom he pleased. The Kingdom of the gospel and the kingdom of Heaven are at the disposal of Christ. He can shut against whom He will; He can open to whom He pleases. If He shuts, no man can open; if He opens, no man can shut.

8. *I have set before thee an open door.* I have opened to you a door to proclaim and diffuse My word; and notwithstanding there are many adversaries to the spread of My gospel, yet none of them shall be able to prevent it. *Thou hast a little strength.* May refer either to the smallness of the numbers or to the littleness of their grace.

9. *I will make them,* show them to be, *of the synagogue of Satan,* who *say they are Jews,* pretending thereby to be of the synagogue of God, and consequently His true and peculiar children. *I will make them to come and worship.* I will so dispose of matters in the course of My providence that the Jews shall be obliged to seek unto the Christians for toleration, support, and protection, which they shall be obliged to sue for in the most humble and abject manner. *To know that I have loved thee.* That the love which was formerly fixed on the Jews is now removed and transferred to the Gentiles.

10. *The word of my patience.* The doctrine which has exposed you to so much trouble and persecution, and required so much patience and magnanimity to bear up under its attendant trials.

The hour of temptation. A "time" of sore and peculiar trial which might have proved too much for their strength. He who is faithful to the grace of God is often hidden from trials and difficulties which fall without mitigation on those who have been unfaithful in His covenant. Many understand by the *hour of temptation* the persecution under Trajan, which was greater and more extensive than the preceding ones under Nero and Domitian. *To try them.* That is, such persecutions will be the means of trying and proving those who profess Christianity and showing who were sound and thorough Christians and who were not.

12. *A pillar in the temple.* There is probably an allusion here to the two pillars in the Temple of Jerusalem, called Jachin and Boaz, "stability and strength." The Church is the *temple;* Christ is the Foundation on which it is built; and His ministers are the pillars by which, under Him, it is adorned and supported.

MATTHEW HENRY

(2) On this there shall be an honourable inscription, as in those cases is usual. [1] *The name of God, and the name of the city of God, the new Jerusalem, which came down from heaven.*

[2] The *new name* of Christ. By this it will appear under whose banner this conquering believer had enlisted, and under whose influence he fought the good fight, and came off victorious.

2. The epistle is closed up with the demand of attention.

Verses 14–22

We now come to the last and worst of all the seven Asian churches. Here is nothing commended.

I. The inscription. *To the angel of the church of Laodicea.* The apostle Paul was very instrumental in planting the gospel in this city, from which he wrote a letter, as he mentions in *the epistle to the Colossians.* Here our Lord Jesus styles himself *the Amen, the faithful and true witness, the beginning of the creation of God. The Amen,* one that is steady and unchangeable in all his purposes and promises.

The faithful and true witness, whose testimony of God to men ought to be received.

The beginning of the creation of God, either of the first creation, or of the second creation, the church; as it is in *ch.* i. 5.

II. The subject-matter.

1. The heavy charge drawn up against this church, *v.* 15. Lukewarmness or indifference in religion is the worst temper in the world. If religion is worth anything, it is worth everything. Here is no room for neutrality. Christ expects that men should declare themselves in earnest either for him or against him.

JAMIESON, FAUSSET, BROWN

city which was so often shaken by earthquakes, STRABO, 12 and 13), like the colossal pillars before Solomon's temple, Boaz (i.e., "In it is strength") and Jachin ("It shall be established"): only that those pillars were outside, these shall be within the temple. **my God**—(*Note,* ch. 2:7). **go no more out**—The *Greek* is stronger, *never more at all.* As the elect angels are beyond the possibility of falling, being now under (as the Schoolmen say) "the blessed necessity of goodness," so shall the saints be. **upon him the name of my God**—as belonging to God in a peculiar sense (ch. 7:3; 9:4; 14:1; and especially 23:4), therefore secure. As the name of Jehovah ("Holiness to the Lord") was on the golden plate on the high priest's forehead (Exod. 28:36-38); so the saints in their heavenly royal priesthood shall bear His name openly, as consecrated to Him.

name of the city of my God—as one of its citizens (ch. 21:2, 3, 10, which is briefly alluded to by anticipation here). The full description of the city forms the appropriate close of the book. The saint's citizenship is now hidden, but then it shall be manifested: he shall have *the right to enter in through the gates into the city* (ch. 22:14). This was the city which Abraham *looked for.* **new**—*Greek, kaine.* Not the old Jerusalem, once called "the holy city," but having forfeited the name. *Greek, nea,* would express that it had *recently come* into existence; but *Greek, kaine,* that which is *new and different,* superseding the worn-out old Jerusalem and its polity.

my new name—at present incommunicable and only known to God: to be hereafter revealed and made the believer's own in union with God in Christ. Christ's name written on him denotes he shall be *wholly Christ's. New* also relates to Christ, who shall assume a *new* character (answering to His "new name") entering with His saints on a kingdom—not that which He had with the Father before the worlds, but that earned by His humiliation as Son of man. **13.** (*Note,* ch. 2:7.) **14. Laodiceans**—The city was in the southwest of Phrygia, on the river Lycus, not far from Colosse, and lying between it and Philadelphia. It was destroyed by an earthquake, A.D. 62, and rebuilt by its wealthy citizens without the help of the state [TACITUS, *Annals* 14. 27]. This wealth (arising from the excellence of its wools) led to a self-satisfied, lukewarm state in spiritual things, as vs. 17 describes. See *Note* on Colossians 4:16, on the Epistle which is thought to have been written to the Laodicean Church by Paul. The Church in latter times was apparently flourishing; for one of the councils at which the canon of Scripture was determined was held in Laodicea in A.D. 361. Hardly a Christian is now to be found on or near its site. **the Amen**—(Isa. 65:16, *Hebrew,* "Bless Himself in the God of *Amen* . . . swear by the God of *Amen,*" II Cor. 1:20). He who not only says, but is, *the Truth.* The title happily harmonizes with the address. His unchanging faithfulness as "the Amen" contrasts with Laodicea's wavering of purpose, "neither hot nor cold" (vs. 16). The angel of Laodicea has with some probability been conjectured to be Archippus, to whom, thirty years previously, Paul had already given a monition, as needing to be stirred up to diligence in his ministry. So the *Apostolic Constitutions,* 8. 46, name him as the first bishop of Laodicea: supposed to be the son of Philemon (Philemon 2). **faithful and true witness**—As "the Amen" expresses the unchangeable truth of His promises; so "the faithful the true witness," the truth of His revelations as to the heavenly things which He has seen and testifies. "Faithful," i.e., trustworthy (II Tim. 2:11, 13). "True" is here (*Greek, alethinos*) *not truth-speaking* (*Greek, alethes*), but "perfectly realizing all that is comprehended in the name *Witness*" (I Tim. 6:13). **beginning of the creation of God**—not he whom God created first, but as in Colossians 1:15-18 (cf. *Notes* there), the *Beginner* of all creation, its originating instrument. All creation would not be represented adoring Him, if He were but one of themselves. His being the Creator is a strong guarantee for His *faithfulness* as "the Witness and Amen." **15. neither cold**—The antithesis to "hot," lit., "boiling" ("fervent," Acts 18:25; Rom. 12:11; cf. Song of Sol. 8:6; Luke 24:32), requires that "cold" should here mean more than negatively *cold;* it is rather, positively *icy cold:* having never yet been warmed. The Laodiceans were in spritual things *cold* comparatively, but not *cold* as the world outside, and as those who had never belonged to the Church. The lukewarm state, if it be the transitional stage to a warmer, is a desirable state (for

ADAM CLARKE

I will write upon him the name of my God. As the high priest had on his breastplate the names of the twelve tribes engraved, and these constituted the city or church of God, Christ here promises that in place of them the twelve apostles, representing the Christian Church, shall be written, which is called the New Jerusalem, and which God has adopted in place of the twelve Jewish tribes.

My new name. The Saviour of all, the Light that lightens the Gentiles, the Christ, the Anointed One, the only Governor of His Church, and the Redeemer of all mankind. There is here an intimation that the Christian Church is to endure forever, and the Christian ministry to last as long as time endures: *He shall go no more out* forever.

EPISTLE TO THE CHURCH OF THE LAODICEANS

14. *These things saith the Amen.* That is, He who is true or faithful; from *aman,* "he was true"; immediately interpreted, *the faithful and true witness.*

The beginning of the creation of God. That is, the Head and Governor of all creatures, the King of the creation. See on Col. i. 15. By His titles here He prepares them for the humiliating and awful truths which He was about to declare, and the authority on which the declaration was founded.

15. *Thou art neither cold nor hot.* You are neither heathens nor Christians—neither good nor evil—neither led away by false doctrine nor thoroughly addicted to that which is true. In a word, they were listless and indifferent, and seemed to care little whether heathenism or Christianity prevailed. Though they felt little zeal either for the salvation of their own souls or that of others, yet they had such a general conviction of the truth and importance of Christianity that they could not readily give it up.

MATTHEW HENRY

2. A severe punishment threatened: *I will spew thee out of my mouth.* As lukewarm water turns the stomach, and provokes to a vomit, lukewarm professors turn the heart of Christ against them. He is sick of them, and cannot long bear them. They shall be rejected.

3. We have one cause of this indifference assigned, and that is self-conceitedness or self-delusion, *v.* 17. What a difference there was between the thoughts they had of themselves and the thoughts that Christ had of them. The high thoughts they had of themselves. Perhaps they were well provided for as to their bodies, and this made them overlook the necessities of their souls. Or they thought themselves well furnished in their souls. How careful should we be not to put the cheat upon our own souls! Doubtless there are many in hell that once thought themselves to be in the way to heaven. The mean thoughts that Christ had of them. They were poor, really poor, when they said and thought they were rich. Their souls were starving in the midst of their abundance. They were *blind*; they could not see their state, nor their way; they could not see into themselves; yet they thought they saw. They could not see Christ. They could not see God. They were naked. They were without clothing, had neither the garment of justification nor that of sanctification.

4. We have good counsel given by Christ to this sinful people, *v.* 18. Our Lord Jesus Christ continues to give good counsel to those who have cast his counsels behind their backs. These people were poor; Christ counsels them to buy of him gold tried in the fire, that they might be rich. He lets them know where they might have true riches and how they might have them. Where they might have them—from himself. How must they have this true gold from him? They must buy it. "Part with self-sufficiency, and come to Christ with your poverty and emptiness, that you may be filled with his hidden treasure." These people were naked; Christ tells them where they might have clothing. This they must receive from Christ; and they must only put off their filthy rags that they might put on the white raiment which he had provided for them.

They were blind; and he *counsels them to buy of him eye-salve, that they might see*, to give up their own wisdom and reason, and resign themselves to his word and Spirit, and their eyes shall be opened.

JAMIESON, FAUSSET, BROWN

a little religion, if real, is better than none); but most fatal when, as here, an abiding condition, for it is mistaken for a safe state (vs. 17). This accounts for Christ's desiring that they were *cold* rather than *lukewarm.* For then there would not be the same "danger of mixed motive and disregarded principle" [ALFORD].

16. neither cold nor hot—So one oldest MS., B., and *Vulgate* read. But two oldest MSS., *Syriac, and Coptic* transpose thus, "hot nor cold." It is remarkable that the *Greek* adjectives are in the masculine, agreeing with the angel, not feminine, agreeing with the Church. The Lord addresses the angel as the embodiment and representative of the Church. The chief minister is answerable for his flock if he have not faithfully warned the members of it. **I will**—*Greek,* "I am about to," "I am ready to": I have it in my mind: implying graciously the possibility of the threat not being executed, if only they repent at once. His dealings towards them will depend on theirs towards Him. **spue thee out of my mouth**—reject with righteous loathing, as Canaan spued out its inhabitants for their abominations. Physicians used *lukewarm* water to cause *vomiting. Cold* and *hot* drinks were common at feasts, but never *lukewarm.* There were hot and cold springs near Laodicea. **17.** Self-sufficiency is the fatal danger of a likewarm state (*Note,* vs. 15). **thou sayest**—virtually and mentally, if not in so many words. **increased with goods**—*Greek,* "have become enriched," implying self-praise in self-acquired riches. The Lord alludes to Hosea 12:8. The riches on which they prided themselves were spiritual riches; though, doubtless, their spiritual self-sufficiency ("I have need of nothing") was much fostered by their worldly wealth; as, on the other hand, *poverty of spirit* is fostered by *poverty* in respect to worldly riches. **knowest not that thou**—in particular above all others. The "THOU" in the *Greek* is emphatic. **art wretched**—*Greek,* "art *the* wretched one." **miserable**—So one oldest MSS. reads. But two oldest MSS. prefix "the." Translate, "*the* pitiable"; "the one especially to be pitied." How different Christ's estimate of men, from their own estimate of themselves, "I have need of nothing!" **blind**—whereas Laodicea boasted of a deeper than common *insight* into divine things. They were not absolutely *blind,* else *eye-salve* would have been of no avail to them; but *short-sighted.* **18.** Gentle and loving irony. Take *My advice,* thou who fanciest thyself *in need of nothing.* Not only art thou not in need of nothing, but art in need of the commonest necessaries of existence.

"Buy" at the cost of thine own self-sufficiency (so Paul, Phil. 3:7, 8); and the giving up of all things, however dear to us, that would prevent our *receiving* Christ's salvation as a *free gift,* e.g., self and worldly desires. Cf. Isaiah 55:1, "Buy ... without money and price." **of me**—the source of "unsearchable riches" (Eph. 3:8). Laodicea was a city of extensive money transactions [CICERO]. **gold tried in ...**—lit., "*fired* (and fresh) *from* the fire," i.e., just fresh *from* the furnace which has proved its purity, and retaining its bright gloss. Sterling spiritual wealth, as contrasted with its counterfeit, in which Laodicea boasted itself. Having bought this *gold* she will be no longer *poor* (vs. 17). **mayest be rich**—*Greek,* "... enriched." **white raiment**—"garments." Laodicea's wools were famous. Christ offers infinitely whiter raiment. As "gold tried in the fire" expresses *faith* tested by fiery trials: so "white raiment," *Christ's righteousness* imputed to the believer in justification and imparted in sanctification. **appear**—*Greek,* "be manifested," viz., at the last day, when everyone without the wedding garment shall be discovered. To strip one, is in the East the image of putting to open shame. So also to clothe one with fine apparel is the image of doing him honor. Man can discover his shame, God alone can cover it, so that his nakedness shall not be manifested at last (Col. 3:10-14). Blessed is he whose sin is so *covered.* The hypocrite's shame may be manifested now; it must be so at last. **anoint ... with eye-salve**—The oldest MSS. read, "(buy of Me) eye-salve (collyrium, a roll of ointment), *to anoint* thine eyes." Christ has for Laodicea an ointment far more precious than all the costly unguents of the East. The *eye* is here the conscience or inner light of the mind. According as it is sound and "single" (*Greek, haplous,* "simple"), or otherwise, the man sees aright spiritually, or does not. The Holy Spirit's unction, like the ancient eye-salve's, first smarts with conviction of sin, then heals. He opens our eyes first to ourselves in our wretchedness, then to the Saviour in His preciousness. **19.** (Job 5:17; Prov. 3:

ADAM CLARKE

I would thou wert cold or hot. That, is, you should be decided; adopt some part or other, and be in earnest in your attachment to it. Epictetus, Ench., chap. 36: "Thou oughtest to be one kind of man, either a good man or a bad man."

16. *Because thou art lukewarm.* Irresolute and undecided. *I will spue thee out of my mouth.* He alludes here to the known effect of tepid water upon the stomach; it generally produces a nausea. I will cast you off.

17. *I am rich.* You suppose yourself to be in a safe state, perfectly sure of final salvation, because you have begun well and laid the right foundation. It was this most deceitful conviction that cut the nerves of their spiritual diligence; they rested in what they had already received, and seemed to think that once in grace must be still in grace. *Thou art wretched.* "Most wretched." Instead of being children of God, as they supposed, and infallible heirs of the Kingdom, they were, in the sight of God, in the condition of the most abject slaves. *And miserable.* Most deplorable, to be pitied by all men. *And poor.* Having no spiritual riches, no holiness of heart. *Rich* and *poor* are sometimes used by the rabbins to express the righteous and the wicked. *And blind.* The eyes of your understanding being darkened, so that you do not see your state. *And naked.* Without the image of God, not clothed with holiness and purity. A more deplorable state in spiritual things can scarcely be imagined than that of this church. And it is the true picture of many churches and of innumerable individuals.

18. *White raiment.* Holiness of heart and life.

Anoint thine eyes. Pray for, that you may receive, the enlightening influences of My Spirit, that you may be convinced of your true state, and see where your help lies.

MATTHEW HENRY

5. Great and gracious encouragement to this sinful people to take the admonition well that Christ had given them, *v.* 19, 20. "You may think I have given you hard words and severe reproofs; it is all out of love to your souls." Sinners ought to take the rebukes of God's word as tokens of his goodwill to their souls. Better are the frowns and wounds of a friend than the flattering smiles of an enemy.

If they would comply with his admonitions, he was ready to make them good to their souls, *v.* 20. Christ is graciously pleased by his word and Spirit to come to the door of the heart of sinners. He finds this door shut against him; the heart of man is by nature shut up against Christ. When he finds the heart shut, he does not immediately withdraw, but he waits to be gracious.

Those who open to him shall enjoy his presence. He will sup with them; he will accept of what is good in them; and he will bring the best part of the entertainment with him.

III. The conclusion of this epistle.

1. The promise made to the overcoming believer. It was possible that by the reproofs and counsels of Christ they might be inspired with fresh zeal and vigour, and might come off conquerors in their spiritual warfare. If they did so they should have a great reward, *v.* 21. Christ himself had met with his temptations and conflicts. He overcame them all, and was more than a conqueror. Those who are conformed to Christ in his trials and victories shall be conformed to him in his glory.

2. All is closed up with the general demand of attention (*v.* 22). Thus end the messages of Christ to the Asian churches.

JAMIESON, FAUSSET, BROWN

11, 12; Heb. 12:5, 6.) So in the case of Manasseh (II Chron 33:11-13). **As many**—All. **I love**—*Greek, philo,* the love of gratuitous *affection,* independent of any grounds for esteem in the object loved. But in the case of Philadelphia (vs. 9), "I have loved thee" (*Greek, egapesa*) with the love of *esteem,* founded on the judgment. Cf. *Note* in my *English Gnomon* of BENGEL, John 21:15-17. **I rebuke**—The "I" in the *Greek* stands first in the sentence emphatically. *I* in My dealings, so altogether unlike man's, in the case of *all whom I love, rebuke.* The *Greek, elencho,* is the same verb as in John 16:8, "(the Holy Ghost) will *convince* (rebuke unto conviction) the world of sin." **chasten**—"chastise." The *Greek, paideu,* which in classical *Greek* means to *instruct,* in the New Testament means to *instruct by chastisement* (Heb. 12:5, 6). **be zealous**—habitually. Present tense in the *Greek,* of a *lifelong course of zeal.* The opposite of "lukewarm." The *Greek* by alliteration marks this: Laodicea had not been "hot" (*Greek, zestos*), she is therefore urged to "be zealous" (*Greek, zeleue*): both are derived from the same verb, *Greek, zeo,* "to boil." **repent**—*Greek* aorist: of an act to be *once for all done,* and *done at once.* **20. stand**—waiting in wonderful condescension and long-suffering. **knock**—(Song of Sol. 5:2). This is a further manifestation of His loving desire for the sinner's salvation. He who is Himself "the Door," and who bids us "knock" that it may be "opened unto" us, is first Himself to knock at the door of our hearts. If He did not knock first, we should never come to knock at His door. **my voice**—He appeals to the sinner not only with His hand (His providences) *knocking,* but with His *voice* (His word read or heard; or rather, His Spirit inwardly applying to man's spirit the lessons to be drawn from His providence and His word). **man hear**—for man is not compelled by irresistible force: Christ *knocks,* but does not break open the door, though the violent take heaven by the force of prayer (Matt. 11:12): whosoever does hear, does so not of himself, but by the *drawings* of God's grace (John 6:44): *repentance* is Christ's gift (Acts 5:31). **I will come in to him**—as I did to Zaccheus. **sup with him, and he with me**—Delightful reciprocity! Cf. "dwelleth in me, and I in Him," John 6:56. Whereas, ordinarily, the admitted guest sups with the admitter, here the divine guest becomes Himself the host, for He is the bread of life, and the Giver of the marriage feast. **21. sit with me in my throne**—(Ch. 2:26, 27; 20:6; Matt. 19:28; 20:23; John 17:22, 24; II Tim. 2.12). The same whom Christ had just before threatened to *spue out of His mouth,* is now offered *a seat with Him on His throne!* "The highest place is within reach of the lowest; the faintest spark of grace may be fanned into the mightiest flame of love" [TRENCH]. **even as I also**—Two thrones are here mentioned: (1)His Father's, upon which He now sits, and has sat since His ascension, after His victory over death, sin, the world; upon this none can sit save God, and the God-man Christ Jesus, for it is the incommunicable prerogative of God alone; (2) the throne which shall be peculiarly *His* as the once humbled and then glorified *Son of man,* to be set up over the whole earth (heretofore usurped by Satan) at His coming again; in this the *victorious* saints shall share (I Cor. 6:2). The transfigured elect Church shall with Christ judge and reign over the nations in the flesh, and Israel the foremost of them; ministering blessings to them as angels were the Lord's mediators of blessing and administrators of His government in setting up His throne in Israel at Sinai.

ADAM CLARKE

19. *As many as I love.* So it was the love He still had to them that induced Him thus to reprehend and thus to counsel them.

Be zealous. Be in earnest to get your souls saved. They had no zeal; this was their bane. He now stirs them up to diligence in the use of the means of grace, and repentance for their past sins and remissness.

20. *Behold, I stand at the door, and knock.* There are many sayings of this kind among the ancient rabbins; thus in *Shir Hashirim Rabba,* fol. 25, 1: "God said to the Israelites, My children, open to me one door of repentance, even so wide as the eye of a needle, and I will open to you doors through which calves and horned cattle may pass." In *Sohar Levit.* fol. 8, col. 32, it is said: "If a man conceal his sin, and do not open it before the holy King. although he ask mercy, yet the door of repentance shall not be opened to him. But if he open it before the holy blessed God, God spares him, and mercy prevails over wrath; and when he laments, although all the doors were shut, yet they shall be opened to him, and his prayer shall be heard." Christ stands, waits long, at the *door* of the sinner's heart; He knocks—uses judgments, mercies, reproofs, exhortations, to induce sinners to repent and turn to Him; He lifts up His *voice*—calls loudly by His Word, ministers, and Spirit. *If any man hear.* If the sinner will seriously consider his state and attend to the voice of his Lord. *And open the door.* This must be his own act, receiving power for this purpose from his offended Lord, who will not break open the door; He will make no forcible entry. *I will come in to him.* I will manifest myself to him, heal all his backslidings, pardon all his iniquities, and love him freely. *Will sup with him.* Hold communion with him, feed him with the bread of life.

21. *To sit with me in my throne.* In every case it is *to him that overcometh,* to the "conqueror," that the final promise is made. He that conquers not is not crowned; therefore every promise is here made to him that is faithful unto death. Here is a most remarkable expression: Jesus has conquered and is set down with the Father upon the Father's throne; he who conquers through Christ sits down with Christ upon His throne; but Christ's throne and the throne of the Father are the same; and it is on this same throne that those who are faithful unto death are finally to sit!

This is the worst of the seven churches, and yet the most eminent of all the promises are made to it, showing that the worst may repent, finally conquer, and attain even to the highest state of glory.

MATTHEW HENRY — CHAPTER 4

Verses 1–8

We have here an account of a second vision with which the apostle John was favoured.

I. The preparation made for the apostle's having this vision.

1. *A door was opened in heaven.* We can know nothing of future events but what God is pleased to discover to us; they are within the veil, till God opens the door.

JAMIESON, FAUSSET, BROWN — CHAPTER 4

Vss. 1-11. VISION OF GOD'S THRONE IN HEAVEN; THE FOUR AND TWENTY ELDERS; THE FOUR LIVING CREATURES. **After this**—*Greek,* "After these things," marking the opening of the next vision in the succession. Here is the transition from "the things which are" (ch. 1:19), the existing state of the seven churches, as a type of the Church in general, in John's time, to "the things which shall be hereafter," viz., in relation to the time when John wrote. **I looked**—rather as *Greek,* "I saw" in vision; not as *English Version* means, I directed my *look* that way. **was**—Omit, as not being in the *Greek* **opened** "standing open"; not as though John saw it in the act of being opened. Cf. Ezekiel 1:1; Matthew 3: 16; Acts 7:56; 10:11. But in those visions the heavens opened, disclosing the visions to those below on

ADAM CLARKE — CHAPTER 4

1. *A door was opened in heaven.* This appears to have been a visible aperture in the sky over his head.

MATTHEW HENRY

2. To prepare John for the vision, a trumpet was sounded, and he was called up into heaven, to have a sight there of the things which were to be hereafter.

3. To prepare for this vision, *the apostle was in the Spirit.* He was in a rapture. His spirit was possessed with the spirit of prophecy, and wholly under a divine influence.

II. The vision itself. 1. He saw *a throne set in heaven,* the seat of honour, and authority, and judgment. All earthly thrones are under the jurisdiction of this throne that is set in heaven. 2. He saw a glorious one upon the throne. There was one in it who filled it, and that was God. *His countenance was like a jasper and a sardine-stone;* he is not described by any human features, so as to be represented by an image, but only by his transcendent brightness.

3. He saw *a rainbow about the throne, like unto an emerald, v.* 3. The rainbow was the seal and token of the covenant of providence that God made with Noah. This rainbow looked like *the emerald*; the most prevailing colour was a pleasant green, to show the reviving and refreshing nature of the new covenant.

4. He saw *four-and-twenty seats* round about the throne, with *four-and-twenty elders. They are clothed in white raiment,* the righteousness of the saints; they *had on their heads crowns of gold,* signifying the honour and authority given them of God, and the glory they have with him.

5. He perceived lightnings and voices proceeding out of the throne. Thus he gave forth the law on mount Sinai; and the gospel has not less glory and authority than the law.

6. He saw *seven lamps of fire burning before the throne* (*v.* 5), the various gifts, graces, and operations of the Spirit of God.

7. He saw *before the throne a sea of glass like unto crystal.* In this all those must be washed that are admitted into the gracious presence of God.

JAMIESON, FAUSSET, BROWN

earth. Whereas here, heaven, the temple of God, remains closed to those on earth, but John is transported in vision through an open door up into heaven, whence he can see things passing on earth or in heaven, according as the scenes of the several visions require. **the first voice which I heard**—the voice which I heard at first, viz., in ch. 1:10; *the former voice.* **was as it were**—Omit *was,* it not being in the *Greek.* "Behold" governs in sense both "a door . . ." and "the first voice. . . ." **Come up hither**—through the "open door." **be**—come to pass. **hereafter**—*Greek,* "after these things": after the present time (ch. 1:19). **2. And**—omitted in the two oldest MSS., *Vulgate, Syriac.* **I was . . .** —*Greek,* "I became in the Spirit" (*Note,* ch. 1:10): I was completely rapt in vision into the heavenly world. **was set**—not *was placed,* but *was situated,* lit., "lay." **one sat on the throne**—the Eternal Father: the Creator (vs. 11): also cf. vs. 8 with ch. 1:4, where also the Father is designated, "which is, and was, and is to come." **3. was**—omitted in the two oldest MSS., but supported by *Vulgate* and *Coptic.* **to look upon**—*Greek,* "in sight," or "appearance." **jasper**—From ch. 21:11, where it is called *most precious,* which the *jasper* was not, EBRARD infers it was a diamond. Ordinarily, the *jasper* is a stone of various wavy colors, somewhat transparent: in ch. 21:11 it represents watery crystalline brightness. The *sardine,* our cornelian, or else a fiery red. As the watery brightness represents God's holiness, so the fiery red His justice executing fiery wrath. The same union of white or watery brightness and fiery redness appears in ch. 1:14; 10:1; Ezekiel 1:4; 8:2; Daniel 7: 9. **rainbow round about the throne**—forming a complete circle (type of God's perfection and eternity: not a half circle as the earthly rainbow) surrounding the throne vertically. Its various colors, which combined form one pure solar ray, symbolize the varied aspects of God's providential dealings uniting in one harmonious whole. Here, however, the predominating color among the prismatic colors is green, the most refreshing of colors to look upon, and so symbolizing God's consolatory promises in Christ to His people amidst judgments on His foes. **4. seats**—rather as the *Greek* is translated in this very verse, "thrones," of course lower and smaller than the grand central *throne.* So ch. 16:10, "the seat (rather *throne*) of the beasts," in hellish parody of God's throne. **four and twenty elders**—*Greek,* "*the* four and twenty (or as one oldest MS., 'twenty-four') elders": the well-known elders [ALFORD]. But TREGELLES translates, "Upon the twenty-four thrones (*I saw:* omitted in two oldest MSS.) elders sitting": which is more probable, as *the twenty-four elders* were not mentioned before, whereas *the twenty-four thrones* were. They are not angels, for they have *white robes* and *crowns* of victory, implying a conflict and endurance, "Thou hast *redeemed us*": they represent the *Heads* of the **Old** and **New Testament** churches respectively, the Twelve Patriarchs (cf. ch. 7:5-8, not in their personal, but in their representative character), and Twelve Apostles. So in ch. 15:3, "the song of *Moses,* and of the *Lamb,*" the double constituents of the Church are implied, the Old Testament and the New Testament. **5. proceeded**—*Greek,* "proceed." **thunderings and voices** —The two oldest MSS. transpose, "voices and thunderings." Cf. at the giving of the law on Sinai, Exodus 19:16. "The *thunderings* express God's threats against the ungodly: there are voices in the thunders (ch. 10:3), i.e., not only does He threaten generally, but also predicts *special* judgments" [GROTIUS]. **seven lamps . . . seven Spirits** —The Holy Spirit in His sevenfold operation, as the light-and-life Giver (cf. ch. 5:6, *seven eyes . . . the seven Spirits of God;* 1:4; 21:23 Ps. 119:105) and fiery purifier of the godly, and consumer of the ungodly (Matt. 3:11). **6. Two oldest MSS.,** A, B, *Vulgate, Coptic,* and *Syriac* read, "*As it were* a sea of glass." **like . . . crystal**—not imperfectly transparent as the ancient common glass, but like rock crystal.

But see the analogue in the temple, the molten sea *before* the sanctuary (*Note,* vs. 4, above). There is in this sea depth and transparency, but not the fluidity and instability of the natural sea (cf. ch. 21:1). It stands solid, calm, and clear, God's *judgments* are called "a great deep" (Ps. 36:6). In ch. 15:2 it is a "sea of glass mingled with *fire.*" Thus there is symbolized here the purificatory baptism of water and the Spirit of all who are made "kings and priests unto God." In ch. 15:2 the baptism with the fire of trial is meant. Through both all the kingpriests have to pass in coming to God:

ADAM CLARKE

2. ***I was in the Spirit.*** **Rapt up in an ecstasy.**

3. ***And he that sat.*** **There is here no description of the Divine Being, so as to point out any similitude, shape, or dimensions. The description rather aims to point out the surrounding glory and effulgence than the person of the almighty King.**

4. ***Four and twenty elders.*** **Perhaps this is in reference to the smaller Sanhedrin at Jerusalem, which was composed of twenty-three elders; or to the princes of the twenty-four courses of the Jewish priests which ministered at the Tabernacle and the Temple, at first appointed by David.** ***Clothed in white raiment.*** **The garments of the priests.** ***On their heads crowns of gold.*** **An emblem of their dignity.**

5. ***Seven lamps of fire.*** **Seven angels, the attendants and ministers of the supreme King. See chap. i. 4.**

MATTHEW HENRY

8. He saw *four animals*, living creatures, between the throne and the circle of the elders (as seems most probable), standing between God and the people; these seem to signify the ministers of the gospel. The elders sit and are ministered unto; these stand and minister: they rest not night nor day.

Verses 8–11

We have considered the sights that the apostle saw in heaven: now let us observe the songs that he heard.

I. He heard the song of the four living creatures, which refers to the prophet Isaiah's vision, *ch.* vi. They adore one God, and one only, *the Lord God Almighty*. They adore three holies in this one God.

II. He heard the adorations of the *four-and-twenty elders*, *v.* 10, 11.

1. The object of their worship: *Him that sat on the throne*, the eternal everliving God. There is but one God, and he alone, as God, is worshipped by the church on earth and in heaven.

2. The acts of adoration. They *fell down before him that sat on the throne.* They *cast their crowns before the throne*; they gave God the glory of the holiness wherewith he had crowned their souls on earth and the honour and happiness with which he crowns them in heaven. It is their glory to be glorifying God.

3. The words of adoration, *v.* 11. In this they tacitly acknowledge that God is exalted far above all blessing and praise. He was worthy to receive glory, but they were not worthy to praise.

4. We have the ground of their adoration. (1) He is the Creator of all things; and none but the Creator of all things should be adored; no made thing can be the object of religious worship. (2) He is the preserver of all things. All beings but God are dependent upon the will and power of God, and no dependent being must be set up as an object of religious worship. (3) He is the final cause of all things: *For thy pleasure they are and were created.* It was his will and pleasure to create all things.

JAMIESON, FAUSSET, BROWN

His *judgments,* which overwhelm the ungodly, they stand firmly upon, as on a solid sea of glass; able like Christ to walk on the sea, as though it were solid. **round about the throne**—one in the midst of each side of the throne. **four beasts**—The *Greek* for "beasts," ch. 13:1, 11, is different, *therion,* the symbol for the carnal man by opposition to God losing his true glory, as lord, under Him, of the lower creatures, and degraded to the level of the *beast.* Here it is *zoon,* "living creatures"; not *beast.* **7. calf**—"a steer"—[ALFORD]. The LXX often uses the *Greek* term here for an *ox* (Exod. 22:1; 29:10, etc.). **as a man**—The oldest MSS. have "as of a man." **8. about him**—*Greek,* "round about him." ALFORD connects this with the following sentence: "All round and within (their wings) they are (so two oldest MSS., A, B, and *Vulgate* read) full of eyes." John's object is to show that the six wings in each did not interfere with that which he had before declared, viz., that they were "full of eyes before and behind." The eyes were *round* the outside of each wing, and up the *inside* of each when half expanded, and of the part of body in that inward recess. **rest not**—lit., "have no rest." How awfully different the reason why the worshippers of the beast "have no rest day nor night," viz., "their torment for ever and ever." **Holy, holy, holy**—The "*tris-hagion*" of the *Greek* liturgies. In Isaiah 6:3, as here, it occurs; also Psalm 99:3, 5, 9, where He is praised as "holy," (1) on account of His majesty (vs. 1) about to display itself; (2) His justice (vs. 4) already displaying itself; (3) His mercy (vss. 6-8) which displayed itself in times past. So here "Holy," as He "who was"; "Holy," as He "who is": "Holy," as He "who is to come." He showed Himself an object of holy worship in the past creation of all things: more fully He shows Himself so in governing all things: He will, in the highest degree, show Himself so in the consummation of all things. "Of (from) Him, through Him, and to Him, are all things: to whom be glory for ever. Amen." In Isaiah 6:3 there is added, "the whole EARTH is full of His glory." But in Revelation this is deferred until the glory of THE LORD fills *the earth,* His enemies having been destroyed [BENGEL]. **Almighty**—answering to "Lord of hosts" (Sabaoth), Isaiah 6:3. The cherubim here have *six* wings, like the seraphim in Isaiah 6; whereas the cherubim in Ezekiel 1:6 had *four* wings each. They are called by the same name, "living creatures." But whereas in Ezekiel each living creature has all four faces, here the four belong severally one to each.

But here the context best suits the view which regards the *four living creatures* as representing the *redeemed election-Church* in its relation of ministering king-priests to God, and ministers of blessing to the redeemed earth, and the nations on it, and the animal creation, in which *man* stands at the head of all, *the lion* at the head of wild beasts, *the ox* at the head of tame beasts, *the eagle* at the head of birds and of the creatures of the waters. **9-11.** The ground of praise here is God's *eternity,* and God's *power* and *glory* manifested in the creation of all things for His pleasure. Creation is the foundation of all God's other acts of power, wisdom, and love, and therefore forms the first theme of His creatures' thanksgivings. The four living creatures take the lead of the twenty-four elders, both in this anthem, and in that *new song* which follows on the ground of their redemption (ch. 5:8-10). **9. when**—i.e., whensoever: as often as. A simultaneous giving of glory on the part of the beasts, and on the part of the elders. **give**—"shall give" in one oldest MS. **for ever and ever**—*Greek,* "unto the ages of the ages." **10. fall**—immediately. *Greek,* "*shall* fall down": implying that this ascription of praise *shall be* repeated onward to eternity. So also, "*shall* worship . . . *shall* cast their crowns," viz., in acknowledgment that all the merit of their *crowns* (not kingly *diadems,* but the *crowns* of conquerors) is due to Him. **11. O Lord**—The two oldest MSS., A, B, *Vulgate,* and *Syriac* add, "and our God." "Our" by virtue of creation, and especially redemption. **glory . . .**—"*the* glory—*the* honor—*the* power." **thou**—emphatic in the *Greek:* "It is THOU who didst create." **all things**—*Greek,* "the all things": the universe. **for . . .**—*Greek,* "on account of"; "for the sake of Thy pleasure," or "will."

were created—by Thy definite act of creation at a definite time.

ADAM CLARKE

6. *Four beasts.* "Four living creatures." The word beast is very improperly used here and elsewhere in this description. Wycliffe first used it, and translators in general have followed him in this uncouth rendering.

7. *The first beast was like a lion.* It is supposed that there is a reference here to the four standards or ensigns of the four divisions of the tribes in the Israelitish camp, as they are described by Jewish writers. The first living creature was like a *lion;* this was, say the rabbins, the standard of Judah on the east, with the two tribes of Issachar and Zabulon. The second, like a *calf* or "ox," which was the emblem of Ephraim, who pitched on the west, with the two tribes of Manasseh and Benjamin. The third, with the *face* of a *man,* which, according to the rabbins, was the standard of Reuben, who pitched on the south, with the two tribes of Simeon and Gad. The fourth, which was like a *flying* (spread) *eagle,* was, according to the same writers, the emblem on the ensign of Dan, who pitched on the north, with the two tribes of Asher and Naphtali. This traditionary description agrees with the four faces of the cherub in Ezekiel's vision.

8. *The four beasts had each of them six wings.* I have already observed, in the preface to this book, that the phraseology is rabbinical; I might have added, and the imagery also. We have almost a counterpart of this description in *Pirkey Elieser,* chap. 4. In *Shemoth Rabba,* sec. 23, fol. 122, 4, Rabbi Abin says: "There are four which have principality in this world: among intellectual creatures, *man;* among birds, the *eagle;* among cattle, the *ox;* and among wild beasts, the *lion*: each of these has a kingdom and a certain magnificence, and they are placed under the throne of glory, Ezek. i. 10, to show that no creature is to exalt itself in this world, and that the kingdom of God is over all." These creatures may be considered the representatives of the whole creation.

10. *Cast their crowns before the throne.* Acknowledge the infinite supremacy of God, and that they have derived their being and their blessings from Him alone. This is an allusion to the custom of prostrations in the East, and to the homage of petty kings acknowledging the supremacy of the emperor.

11. *Thou art worthy, O Lord, to receive.* Thus all creation acknowledges the supremacy of God; and we learn from this song that He made all things for His pleasure; and through the same motive He preserves.

MATTHEW HENRY

CHAPTER 5

Verses 1–5

Hitherto the apostle had seen only the great God, the governor of all things. Now,

I. He is favoured with a sight of the methods of his government, as they are all written down in a book which he holds in his hand; and this we are now to consider as shut up and sealed. But there is a transcript of so much as was necessary to be known in the book of the scripture in general, in the prophetical part of scripture especially. God holds this book in his right hand, to declare the authority of the book. It is known to none but himself, till he allows it to be opened. It is *sealed with seven seals.* Each part seems to have its particular seal. These seven parts are not unsealed and opened at once, but successively, one scene of Providence introducing another, and explaining it.

II. He heard a proclamation made concerning this sealed book. The crier was *a strong angel.* This angel seems to come out as a champion, with a challenge to any or all the creatures to try the strength of their wisdom in opening the counsels of God. The cry or challenge, *v.* 2. None in heaven or earth could accept the challenge and undertake the task. *None under the earth,* none of the fallen angels. Satan himself, with all his subtlety, cannot do it; the creatures cannot open it, nor look on it; they cannot read it. God only can do it.

III. The apostle *wept much;* it was a great disappointment to him. By what he had seen in him who sat upon the throne, he was very desirous to see and know more of his mind and will. Those who have seen his glory desire to know his will.

IV. The apostle was comforted and encouraged to hope this sealed book would yet be opened. Who it was that gave John the hint: *One of the elders.* God had revealed it to his church. Who it was that would do the thing—the Lord Jesus Christ, called *the lion of the tribe of Judah,* according to his human nature, and *the root of David* according to his divine nature.

He who bears the office of Mediator between God and man, is fit and worthy to open and execute all the counsels of God towards men.

Verses 6–14

I. The apostle beholds this book taken into the hands of the Lord Jesus Christ. His place and station. He was on the same throne with the Father. Christ, as man and Mediator, is subordinate to God the Father, but is nearer to him than all the creatures.

The form in which he appeared. Before he is called *a lion;* here he appears *as a lamb slain.* He is a lion to conquer Satan, a lamb to satisfy the justice of God. He appears as a *lamb, having seven horns and*

JAMIESON, FAUSSET, BROWN

CHAPTER 5

Vss. 1-14. THE BOOK WITH SEVEN SEALS: NONE WORTHY TO OPEN IT BUT THE LAMB: HE TAKES IT AMIDST THE PRAISES OF THE REDEEMED, AND OF THE WHOLE HEAVENLY HOST. **1. in . . .**—*Greek,* "(lying) *upon* the right hand . . . ." His right hand was open and on it lay the book. On God's part there was no withholding of His future purposes as contained in the book: the only obstacle to unsealing it is stated in vs. 3 [ALFORD]. **book**—rather, as accords with the ancient form of books, and with the *writing on the backside,* "a roll." The *writing on the back* implies fulness and completeness, so that nothing more needs to be added (ch. 22:18). The roll, or book, appears from the context to be "*the title-deed of man's inheritance*" [DE BURGH] redeemed by Christ, and contains the successive steps by which He shall recover it from its usurper and obtain actual possession of the kingdom already "purchased" for Himself and His elect saints. **sealed . . . seven seals**—*Greek,* "sealed up," or "firmly sealed." The number *seven* (divided into four, the world-wide number, and three, the divine) abounds in Revelation and expresses *completeness.* Thus, the *seven seals,* representing all power given to the Lamb; the *seven trumpets,* by which the world kingdoms are shaken and overthrown, and the Lamb's kingdom ushered in; and the *seven vials,* by which the beast's kingdom is destroyed. **2. strong**—(Ps. 103:20). His voice penetrated heaven, earth, and Hades (ch. 10:1-3). **2. no man**—*Greek,* "no *one.*" Not merely *no man,* but also *no one* of any order of beings. **in earth**—*Greek,* "upon the earth." **under the earth**—viz., in Hades. **look thereon**—to look upon the contents, so as to read them. **4. and to read**—inserted in *English Version Greek* text without good authority. One oldest MS., ORIGEN, CYPRIAN, and HILARY omit the clause. "To read" would be awkward standing between "to open the book" and "to look thereon." John having been promised a revelation of "things which must be hereafter," *weeps* now at his earnest desire being apparently frustrated. He is a pattern to us to imitate, as an eager and teachable learner of the Apocalypse. **5. one of**—*Greek,* "one from among." The "elder" meant is, according to some (in LYRA), Matthew. With this accords the description here given of Christ, "the *Lion,* which is (so the *Greek*) of the tribe of Juda, the root of David"; the royal, David-descended, lion-aspect of Christ being that prominent in Matthew, whence the lion among the fourfold cherubim is commonly assigned to him. **Root of David**—(Isa. 11:1, 10). Not merely "a sucker come up from David's ancient root" (as ALFORD limits it), but also including the idea of His being Himself the root and origin of David: cf. these two truths brought together, Matthew 22:42-45. Hence He is called not merely *Son of David,* but also *David.* He is at once "the branch" of David, and "the root" of David, David's Son and David's Lord, the *Lamb* slain and therefore the *Lion* of Juda: about to reign over Israel, and thence over the whole earth. **prevailed**—*Greek,* "conquered": absolutely, as elsewhere (ch. 3:21): *gained the victory:* His past victory over all the powers of darkness entitles Him now to open the book. **to open**—i.e., *so as to open.* One oldest MS., B, reads, "He that openeth," i.e., whose office it is to open, but the weight of oldest authorities is with *English Version* reading, viz., A, *Vulgate, Coptic,* and ORIGEN. **6. I beheld, and, lo**—One oldest MS., A, omits "and, lo." Another, B, CYPRIAN, etc,. support, "and, lo," but omit, "and I beheld." **in the midst of the throne**—i.e., not *on* the throne (cf. vs. 7), but in the midst of the company (ch. 4:4) which was "round about the throne." **Lamb**—*Greek, arnion;* always found in Revelation exclusively, except in John 21:15 alone: it expresses *endearment,* viz., the endearing relation in which Christ now stands to us, as the consequence of His previous relation as the *sacrificial Lamb.* So also our relation to Him: He the *precious Lamb,* we His *dear lambs,* one with Him. BENGEL thinks there is in *Greek, arnion,* the idea of *taking the lead of the flock.* Another object of the form *Greek, arnion,* the Lamb, is to put Him in the more marked contrast to *Greek, therion,* the Beast. Elsewhere *Greek, amnos,* is found, applying to Him as the *paschal, sacrificial Lamb* (Isa. 53:7, LXX; John 1:29, 36; Acts 8:32; I Pet. 1:19). **as it had been slain**—bearing marks of His past death wounds. He was standing, though bearing the marks of one slain. In the midst of heavenly glory Christ crucified is still the prominent object. **seven horns**—i.e., *perfect might,* "seven" symbolizing *perfection;* "horns," *might,* in contrast to the

ADAM CLARKE

CHAPTER 5

1. *A book written within and on the backside.* That is, the book was full of solemn contents *within,* but it was sealed; and on the *backside* was a superscription indicating its contents. It was a labelled book, or one written on each side of the skin, which was not usual.

Sealed with seven seals. As seven is a number of perfection, it may mean that the book was so sealed that the seals could neither be counterfeited nor broken; i.e., the matter of the book was so obscure and enigmatical, and the work it enjoined and the facts it predicted so difficult and stupendous, that they could neither be known nor performed by human wisdom or power.

2. *A strong angel.* One of the chief of the angelic host. *Proclaiming.* As the "herald" of God. *To open the book, and to loose the seals.* To loose the seals that he may open the book. Who can tell what this book contains? Who can open its mysteries? The book may mean the purposes and designs of God relative to His government of the world and the Church.

3. *And no man.* No "person" or "being." *In heaven.* Among all the angels of God. *Nor in the earth.* No human being. *Neither under the earth.* No disembodied spirit, nor any demon. Neither angels, men, nor devils can fathom the decrees of God. *Neither to look thereon.* None can look into it unless it be opened, and none can open it unless the seals be unloosed.

4. *I wept much.* Because the world and the Church were likely to be deprived of the knowledge of the contents of the book.

5. *The Lion of the tribe of Juda.* Jesus Christ, who sprang from this tribe, as His genealogy proves; see on Matthew i and Luke iii. There is an allusion here to Gen. xlix. 9, "Judah is a lion's whelp"; the lion was the emblem of this tribe, and was supposed to have been embroidered on its ensigns. *The Root of David.* See Isa. xi. 1. Christ was *the Root of David* as to His divine nature; He was a "Branch" "out of the stem of Jesse" as to His human nature.

Hath prevailed. By the merit of His incarnation, passion, and death. *To open the book.* To explain and execute all the purposes and decrees of God, in relation to the government of the world and the Church.

6. *Stood a Lamb.* Christ, so called because He was a sacrificial Offering; "a little or delicate Lamb."

As it had been slain. As if now in the act of being offered. This is very remarkable; so important is the sacrificial offering of Christ in the sight of God that He is still represented as being in the very act of pouring out His blood for the offenses of man. Thus all succeeding generations find they have the continual sacrifice ready, and the newly shed Blood to offer. *Seven horns.* As horn is the emblem of power,

MATTHEW HENRY

seven eyes, perfect power to execute all the will of God and perfect wisdom to understand it all. *For he hath the seven Spirits of God*, he has received the Holy Spirit without measure. His act and deed (*v.* 7), not by violence, nor by fraud, but he prevailed to do it (as *v.* 5), he prevailed by his merit and worthiness.

II. No sooner had Christ received this book out of the Father's hand than he received the applauses and adorations of angels and men, yea, of *every creature*.

1. The church begins the doxology, as being more immediately concerned in it (*v.* 8). (1) The object of their worship—*the Lamb*, the Lord Jesus Christ. (2) Their posture: They *fell down before him*, gave him the most profound adoration. (3) The instruments used in their adoration—*harps and vials*; the harps were the instruments of praise, the vials were full of odours or incense, which signify *the prayers of the saints.*

(4) The matter of their song. *Thou art worthy to take the book, and to open the seals thereof.* They mention the grounds of this worthiness, yet they chiefly insist upon the merit of his sufferings; these more sensibly struck their souls with thankfulness and joy. They mention his suffering: *"Thou wast slain."* The fruits of his sufferings. [1] Redemption to God. [2] High exaltation, *v.* 10.

J. A. SEISS:

"And he came and took [the book] from the right hand of him that sitteth upon the throne." This is the sublimest individual act recorded in the Apocalypse. It is the act which includes all that suffering creation, and the disinherited saints of God have been sighing, and crying, and waiting for, for all these long ages. It is the act which carries with it all else that is written in the succeeding part of this glorious revelation. It is the act by virtue of which the world is subdued, Babylon judged, Antichrist destroyed, the dragon vanquished, death overthrown, the curse expunged, the earth made new, and the reign of everlasting blessedness and peace made to cover its hills and illuminate its valleys, and transform it into an unfading paradise of God. It was the lifting of the title deeds of the alienated inheritance—the legal act of repossession of all that was lost in Adam, and paid for by the blood and tears of the Son of God. Heaven looks on in solemn silence as that act is being performed. The universe is stricken with awe, and grows breathless as it views it. And the Living Ones, and Elders, and all the hosts of angels, are filled with adoring wonder and joy, as if another fiat had gone forth from God for a new creation.—*The Apocalypse*

2. The doxology is carried on by the angels, *v.* 11. They are said to be *innumerable*, and to be the attendants on the throne of God. Though they did not need a Saviour themselves, yet they rejoice in the redemption and salvation of sinners, and they agree with the church that he is *worthy to receive power*,

JAMIESON, FAUSSET, BROWN

horns of the Antichristian world powers, ch. 17:3; etc.; Daniel 7:7, 20; 8:3. **seven eyes . . . the seven Spirits . . . sent forth**—So one oldest MS., A. But B reads, "*being* sent forth." As the *seven lamps* before the throne represent the Spirit of God immanent in the Godhead, so the *seven eyes* of the Lamb represent the same sevenfold Spirit profluent from the incarnate Redeemer in His world-wide energy. The *Greek* for "sent forth," *apostellomena,* or else *apestalmenoi,* is akin to the term "apostle," reminding us of the Spirit-impelled labors of Christ's apostles and minister throughout the world: if the present tense be read, as seems best, the idea will be that of those labors *continually going on* unto the end. "Eyes" symbolize His all-watchful and wise providence for His Church, and against her foes. **7.** The book lay on the open hand of Him that sat on the throne for any to take who was found worthy [ALFORD]. The Lamb takes it from the Father in token of formal investiture into His universal and everlasting dominion as Son of man.

8. had taken—*Greek,* "took." **fell down before the Lamb**—who shares worship and the throne with the Father. **harps**—Two oldest MSS., A, B, *Syriac* and *Coptic* read, "a harp": a kind of guitar, played with the hand or a quill. **vials**—"bowls" [TREGELLES]: censers. **odours**—*Greek,* "incense." **prayers of saints**—as the angel offers their prayers (ch. 8:3) with incense (cf. Ps. 141:2). This gives not the least sanction to Rome's dogma of our praying to saints. Though *they* be employed by God in some way unknown to us to present our prayers (nothing is said of their *interceding* for us), yet *we* are told to pray only to Him (ch. 19:10; 22: 8, 9). *Their own* employment is praise (whence they all have *harps*): ours is prayer. **9. sung**—*Greek,* "sing": it is their blessed occupation continually. The theme of *redemption* is ever new, ever suggesting fresh thoughts of praise, embodied in the "new song." **us to God**—So MS. B, *Coptic, Vulgate,* and CYPRIAN. But A omits "us": and א reads instead, "to *our* God." **out of**—the present election-church gathered *out of* the world, as distinguished from the peoples gathered to Christ as the subjects, not of an election, but of a general and world-wide conversion of all nations. **kindred . . . tongue . . . people . . . nation**—The number *four* marks world-wide extension: the four quarters of the world. For "kindred," translate as *Greek,* "tribe." This term and "people" are usually restricted to *Israel:* "tongue and nation" to the *Gentiles* (ch. 7:9; 11:9; 13:7, the oldest reading; 14:6). Thus there is here marked the election-Church gathered from Jews and Gentiles. In ch. 10:11, for "tribes," we find among the four terms "kings"; in 17:15, "multitudes." **10. made us**—A, B, א, *Vulgate, Syriac,* and *Coptic* read, "them." The *Hebrew* construction of the third person for the first, has a graphic relation to *the redeemed,* and also has a more modest sound than *us, priests* [BENGEL]. **unto our God**—So B and א read. But A omits the clause. **kings**—So B reads. But A, א, *Vulgate, Coptic,* and CYPRIAN, read, "A kingdom." א reads also "a priesthood" for *priests.* They who cast their crowns before the throne, do not call themselves *kings* in the sight of the great *King* (ch. 4:10, 11); though their priestly access has such dignity that their reigning on earth cannot exceed it. So in ch. 20:6 **they are not called** "kings" [BENGEL]. **we shall reign on the earth**—This is a new feature added to ch. 1:6. א, *Vulgate,* and *Coptic* read, *"They* shall reign." A and B read, *"They reign."* ALFORD takes this reading and explains it of the Church EVEN NOW, in Christ her Head, reigning on the earth: "all things are being put under her feet, as under His; her kingly office and rank are asserted, even in the midst of persecution." But even if we read (I think the weightiest authority is against it), "They *reign,*" still it is the prophetical present for the future: the seer being transported into the future when the full number of the redeemed (represented by the *four living creatures*) shall be complete and the visible *kingdom begins.* The saints do spiritually reign now; but certainly not as they shall when the prince of this world shall be bound (*Notes,* ch. 20:2-6).

11. I beheld—the angels: who form the outer circle, while the Church, the object of redemption, forms the inner circle nearest the throne. The heavenly hosts ranged around gaze with intense love and adoration at this crowning manifestation of God's love, wisdom, and power. **ten thousand times ten thousand**—*Greek,* "myriads of myriads." **12. to receive power**—*Greek,* "*the* power." The remaining six (the whole being *seven,* the number for *perfection* and *completeness*) are

ADAM CLARKE

and *seven* the number of perfection, the *seven horns* may denote the all-prevailing and infinite might of Jesus Christ. He can support all His friends; He can destroy all His enemies; and He can save to the uttermost all that come unto God through Him. *Seven eyes.* To denote His infinite knowledge and wisdom; but as these *seven eyes* are said to be *the seven Spirits of God,* they seem to denote rather His providence, in which He often employs the ministry of angels. Therefore these are said to be *sent forth into all the earth.* See on chap. i. 4.

7. *He came and took the book.* This verse may be properly explained by John, chap. i. 18. "No man hath seen God at any time; the only begotten Son, which is in the bosom of the Father, he hath declared him." With Jesus alone are all the counsels and mysteries of God.

8. *The four beasts . . . fell down before the Lamb.* The whole Church of God, and all His children in heaven and earth, acknowledge that Jesus Christ is alone worthy and able to unfold and execute all the mysteries and counsels of God. *Having every one of them harps.* There were *harps* and *vials;* and each of the *elders* and living creatures had one. *Odours, which are the prayers of saints.* The frankincense and odors offered at the Tabernacle were emblems of the prayers and praises of the Lord. That prayers are compared to incense, see Ps. cxli. 2: "Let my prayer be set forth before thee as incense."

9. *A new song.* Composed on the matters and blessings of the gospel, which was just now opened on earth. But *new song* may signify a "most excellent song"; and by this the gospel and its blessings are probably signified. The gospel is called a *new song,* Ps. xcvi. 1. And perhaps there is an allusion in the "harps" here to Ps. cxliv. 9: "I will sing a new song unto thee, O God: upon a psaltery and an instrument of ten strings." The same form of speech is found, Isa. xlii. 10: "Sing unto the Lord a new song"; and there the prophet seems to have the gospel dispensation particularly in view. *Thou . . . hast redeemed us to God by thy blood out of every nation.* It appears, therefore, that the living creatures and the elders represent the aggregate of the followers of God; or the Christian Church in all nations, and among all kinds of people, and perhaps through the whole compass of time; and all these are said to be redeemed by Christ's *blood,* plainly showing that His life was a sacrificial offering for the sins of mankind.

10. *Kings and priests.* See Exod. xix. 6; 1 Pet. ii. 5, 9, and the notes there.

11. *The voice of many angels.* These also are represented as joining in the chorus with redeemed mortals. *Ten thousand times ten thousand.* "Myriads of myriads and chiliads of chiliads"; that is, an infinite or innumerable multitude. This is in reference to Dan. vii. 10.

12. *To receive power.* That is, Jesus Christ is worthy "to take," to have ascribed to Him, *power*—omnipotence;

MATTHEW HENRY

and riches, and wisdom, and strength, and honour, and glory, and blessing.

3. This doxology is resounded by the whole creation, *v.* 13. Heaven and earth ring with the high praises of the Redeemer. The whole creation fares the better for Christ.

That part which is made for the whole creation is a song of *blessing, and honour, and glory, and power. To him that sits on the throne,* to God the Father. *To the Lamb,* the Mediator of the new covenant. We worship and glorify one and the same God for our creation and for our redemption. Thus we have seen this sealed book passing with great solemnity from the hand of the Creator into the hand of the Redeemer.

JAMIESON, FAUSSET, BROWN

all, as well as "power," ranged under the one *Greek* article, to mark that they form *one* complete aggregate belonging to God and His coequal, the Lamb. Cf. ch. 7:12, where each of all seven has the article. **riches**—both spiritual and earthly. **blessing**—ascribed praise: the *will* on the creature's part, though unaccompanied by the *power,* to return blessing for blessing conferred [ALFORD]. **13.** The universal chorus of creation, including the outermost circles as well as the inner (of saints and angels), winds up the doxology. The *full* accomplishment of this is to be when Christ takes His great power and reigns visibly. **every creature**—"all His works in all places of His dominion" (Ps. 103:22). **under the earth**—the departed spirits in Hades. **such as are**—So B and *Vulgate.* But A omits this. **in the sea**—*Greek, "upon* the sea": the sea animals which are regarded as being on the surface [ALFORD]. **all that are in them**—So *Vulgate* reads. A omits "all (things)" here (*Greek, panta*), and reads, "I heard *all* (*Greek, pantas*) saying": implying the harmonious concert of all in the four quarters of the universe. **Blessing . . .**—*Greek, "the* blessing, *the* honor, and *the* glory, and *the might to the ages of the ages."* The *fourfold* ascription indicates *world-wide* universality. **14. said**—So A, *Vulgate,* and *Syriac* read. But B and *Coptic* read, "(I heard) *saying.*" **Amen**—So A reads. But B reads, *"the* (accustomed) Amen." As in ch. 4:11, the four and twenty elders asserted God's worthiness to receive the glory, as having *created all things,* so here the four living creatures ratify by their "Amen" the whole *creation's* ascription of the glory to Him. **four and twenty**—omitted in the oldest MSS.: *Vulgate* supports it. **him that liveth for ever and ever**—omitted in all the MSS.: inserted by commentators from ch. 4:9. But there, where the thanksgiving is *expressed,* the words are appropriate; but here less so, as their worship is that of silent prostration. "Worshipped" (viz., God and the Lamb). So in ch. 11:1, "worship" is used absolutely.

ADAM CLARKE

riches—beneficence; *wisdom*—omniscience; *strength*—power in prevalent exercise; *honour*—the highest reputation for what He has done; *glory*—the praise due to such actions; *and blessing*—the thankful acknowledgments of the whole creation. Here are seven different species of praise; and this is exactly agreeable to the rabbinical forms, which the author of this book keeps constantly in view. See *Sepher Rasiel,* fol. 39, 2: "To thee belongs glory; magnitude; might; the kingdom; the honour; the victory; and the praise."

13. *Every creature.* All parts of the creation, animate and inanimate, are represented here, by that figure of speech called "personification," as giving praise to the Lord Jesus, because by Him all things were created. We find the whole creation gives precisely the same praise, and in the same terms, to Jesus Christ, who is undoubtedly meant here by the Lamb just slain, as they give to God who sits upon the throne. Now if Jesus Christ were not properly God, this would be idolatry, as it would be giving to the creature what belongs to the Creator.

14. *The four beasts said, Amen.* Acknowledged that what was attributed to Christ was His due. *The four and twenty elders.* The word twenty-four is wanting in the most eminent MSS. and versions. *Fell down and worshipped.* Fell down on their knees, and then "prostrated themselves" before the throne. This is the Eastern method of adoration: first, the person worshipping fell down on his knees; and then, bowing down, touched the earth with his forehead. This latter act was "prostration." *Him that liveth for ever.* This clause is wanting in many MSS. and is undoubtedly spurious.

MATTHEW HENRY

CHAPTER 6

Verses 1, 2

Christ, the Lamb, opens the first seal.

We have the vision itself, *v.* 2. 1. The Lord Jesus appears riding on *a white horse.* 2. *He had a bow* in his hand. The convictions impressed by the word of God are sharp arrows, they reach at a distance. 3. *A crown was given him.* When Christ was going to war, one would think a helmet had been more proper than a crown; but a crown is given him as the earnest of victory. 4. *He went forth conquering, and to conquer.* As long as the church continues militant Christ will be conquering. He conquers his enemies in his people; their sins are their enemies and his enemies; when Christ comes with power into their soul he begins to conquer these enemies, and he goes on conquering, in the progressive work of sanctification, till he has gained us a complete victory. And he conquers his enemies in the world, wicked men. The successful progress of the gospel of Christ in the world is a glorious sight, worth beholding. Christ's work is not all done at once. We are ready to think, when the gospel goes forth, it should carry all the world before it, but it often meets with opposition, and moves slowly. Christ will do his own work effectually, in his own time and way.

Verses 3–8

The next three seals give us a sad prospect of judgments with which God punishes those who abuse the everlasting gospel.

I. Upon opening the second seal *another horse* appears, *a red horse, v.* 4. This signifies the desolating judgment of war. The sword of war is a dreadful judgment; it takes away peace from the earth. Men, who should love one another and help one another, are, in a state of war, set upon killing one another.

JAMIESON, FAUSSET, BROWN

CHAPTER 6

Vss. 1-17. THE OPENING OF THE FIRST SIX OF THE SEVEN SEALS. **1. one of the seals**—The oldest MSS., A, B, C, *Vulgate,* and *Syriac* read, "one of the *seven* seals." **noise**—The three oldest MSS. read this in the nominative or dative, not the genitive, as *English Version,* "I heard one from among the four living creatures saying, as (it were) *the voice* (or, *as with the voice*) of thunder." The first living creature was like a *lion* (ch. 4:7): his voice is in consonance. Implying the lion-like boldness with which, in the successive great revivals, the faithful have *testified for Christ,* and especially a little before His coming shall testify. Or, rather, their earnestness in praying for *Christ's coming.* **Come and see**—One oldest MS., B, has "And see." But A, C, and *Vulgate* reject it. ALFORD rightly objects to *English Version* reading: "Whither was John to come? Separated as he was by the glassy sea from the throne, was he to cross it?" Contrast the form of expression, ch. 10:8. It is much more likely to be the cry of the redeemed to the Redeemer, "Come" and deliver the groaning creature from the bondage of corruption. Thus, vs. 2 is an answer to the cry, *went* (lit., "came") forth corresponding to "Come."

2. Evidently Christ, whether in person, or by His angel, preparatory to His coming again, as appears from ch. 19:11, 12. **bow**—(Ps. 45:4, 5). **crown**—*Greek, stephanos,* the garland or wreath of a *conqueror,* which is also implied by His *white horse,* white being the emblem of victory. **and to conquer**—i.e., so as to gain a lasting victory. All four seals usher in *judgments* on the earth, as the power which opposes the reign of Himself and His Church. This, rather than the work of conversion and conviction, is primarily meant, though doubtless, secondarily, the elect will be gathered out through His word and His judgments. **3. and see**—omitted in the three oldest MSS., A, B, C, and *Vulgate.* **4. red**—the color of *blood.* The color of the horse in each case answers to the mission of the rider. Cf. Matthew 10:24-36, "Think not I am come to send *peace* on earth; I came not to send *peace,* but a *sword."* The *white* horse of Christ's bloodless victories is soon followed, through man's perversion of the Gospel, by the *red* horse of bloodshed; but this is overruled to the clearing away of the obstacles to Christ's coming kingdom. The patient *ox* is the emblem of the second *living creature* who, at the opening of this seal, saith, "Come." The saints amidst judgments on the earth in pa-

ADAM CLARKE

CHAPTER 6

1. *When the Lamb opened one of the seals.* It is worthy of remark that the opening of the seals is not merely a declaration of what God will do, but is the exhibition of a purpose then accomplished; for whenever the seal is opened, the sentence appears to be executed. It is supposed that, from chaps. vi to xi inclusive, the calamities which should fall on the enemies of Christianity, and particularly the Jews, are pointed out under various images, as well as the calamities. *One of the four beasts.* Probably that with the face of a lion. See chap. iv. 7. *Come and see.* Attend to what is about to be exhibited. It is very likely that all was exhibited before his eyes as in a scene; and he saw every act represented which was to take place, and all the persons and things which were to be the chief actors.

2. *A white horse.* Supposed to represent the gospel system, and pointing out its excellence, swiftness, and purity. *He that sat on him.* Supposed to represent Jesus Christ. *A bow.* The preaching of the gospel, darting conviction into the hearts of sinners. *A crown.* The emblem of the Kingdom which Christ was to establish on earth. *Conquering, and to conquer.* Overcoming and confounding the Jews first, and then the Gentiles, spreading more and more the doctrine and influence of the Cross over the face of the earth.

3. *The second beast.* That which had the face of an ox.

4. *Another horse that was red.* The emblem of war; perhaps also of severe persecution, and the martyrdom of the saints. *Him that sat thereon.* Some say, Christ; others, Vespasian; others, the Roman armies. *Take peace from the earth.* To deprive Judea of all tranquillity.

MATTHEW HENRY

II. Upon opening the third seal another horse appears, *a black horse*, signifying famine (*v.* 5).

One judgment seldom comes alone; the judgment of war naturally draws after it that of famine. The famine of bread is a terrible judgment; but the famine of the word is more so.

III. Upon opening the fourth seal there appears another horse, of a pale colour. 1. The name of the rider—*Death*, the king of terrors. 2. The attendants of this king of terrors—*hell*. There is a natural connection between one judgment and another: war is a wasting calamity, and draws scarcity and famine after it; and famine draws the pestilence after it. God has published threatenings against the wicked as well as promises to the righteous; and it is our duty to believe the threatenings as well as the promises.

IV. After the opening of these seals we have this general observation, *v.* 8. To the three great judgments of war, famine, and pestilence, is here added *the beasts of the earth*, another of God's sore judgments. When a nation is depopulated by the sword, famine, and pestilence, the small remnant that continue become an easy prey. Others, by *the beasts of the field*, understand brutish, cruel, savage men.

Verses 9–17

I. The fifth seal. It does not contain a new prophecy, but rather opens a spring of consolation to those who still were under great tribulation.

1. The sight this apostle saw at the opening of the fifth seal (*v.* 9). He saw the souls of the martyrs. Where he saw them—in the most holy place; he saw them in heaven, at the foot of Christ. God has provided a good place in the better world for those who are faithful to death and are not allowed a place any longer on earth. The cause in which they suffered —*the word of God and the testimony which they held*. A noble cause, the best that any man can lay down his life for.

2. The cry he heard, *v.* 10. Even *the spirits of just men made perfect* retain a proper resentment of the wrong they have sustained by their cruel enemies. They commit their cause to him to whom vengeance belongeth; they are not for avenging themselves, but leave all to God.

3. The kind return that was made to this cry (*v.* 11). What was given to them—*white robes*, the robes of victory and of honour.

JAMIESON, FAUSSET, BROWN

tience "endure to the end." **that they should kill**—The *Greek* is indicative future, "that they may, as they also shall, kill one another." **5. Come and see**—The two oldest MSS., A, C. and *Vulgate* omit "and see." B retains the words. **black**—implying *sadness* and *want*. **had**—*Greek*, "having." **a pair of balances**—the symbol of scarcity of provisions, the bread being doled out by weight. **6. a voice**—Two oldest MSS., A, C, read, "*as it were* a voice." B reads as *English Version*. The voice is heard "in the midst of the four living creatures" (as Jehovah in the Shekinah cloud manifested His presence between the cherubim); because it is only for the sake of, and in connection with, His redeemed, that God mitigates His judgments on the earth. **A measure**—"A *chœnix*." While making food scarce, do not make it so much so that a *chœnix* (about a day's provision of wheat, variously estimated at two or three pints) shall not be obtainable "for a penny" (*denarius*, about twenty cents, probably the day's wages of a laborer). *Famine* generally follows the *sword*. Ordinarily, from sixteen to twenty measures were given for a denarius. The *sword, famine, noisome beasts*, and the *pestilence*, are God's four judgments on the earth. A spiritual famine, too, may be included in the judgment. The "Come," in the case of this third seal, is said by the third of the four living creatures, whose likeness is *a man* indicative of sympathy and human compassion for the sufferers. God in it tempers judgment with mercy. Cf. Matthew 24:7, which indicates the very calamities foretold in these seals, *nation rising against nation* (the sword), *famines, pestilences* (vs. 8), and *earthquakes* (vs. 12). **three measures of barley for a penny**—the cheaper and less nutritious grain, bought by the laborer who could not buy enough wheat for his family with his day's wages, a denarius, and, therefore, buys barley. **see thou hurt not the oil, and the wine**—the luxuries of life, rather than necessaries; the oil and wine were to be spared for the refreshment of the sufferers. **7. and see**—supported by B; omitted by A, C, and *Vulgate*. The *fourth living creature*, who was "like a flying eagle," introduces this seal; implying high-soaring intelligence, and judgment descending from on high fatally on the ungodly, as the king of birds on his prey. **8. pale**—"livid" [ALFORD]. **Death**—personified. **Hell**—*Hades* personified. **unto them**—*Death* and *Hades*. So A, C read. But B and *Vulgate* read, "to him." **fourth part of the earth**—answering to the first four seals; his portion as one of the four, being a *fourth part*. **death**—pestilence; cf. Ezekiel 14:21 with the four judgments here, the *sword, famine, pestilence*, and *wild beasts;* the *famine* the consequence of the *sword; pestilence*, that of *famine;* and *beasts* multiplying by the consequent depopulation. **with the beasts**—*Greek*, "by"; more direct agency. **9.** The three last seals relate to the invisible, as the first four to the visible world; the fifth, to the martyrs who have died as believers; the sixth, to those who have died, or who shall be found at Christ's coming, unbelievers, viz., "the kings . . . great men . . . bondman . . . freeman"; the seventh, to the silence in heaven. The scene changes from earth to heaven; so that interpretations which make these three last consecutive to the first four seals, are very doubtful. **I saw**—in spirit. For souls are not naturally visible. **under the altar**—As the blood of sacrificial victims slain on the altar was poured *at the bottom of the altar*, so the souls of those sacrificed for Christ's testimony are symbolically represented as *under the altar*, in heaven; for the life or animal *soul* is in the *blood*, and blood is often represented as crying for vengeance (Gen. 4:10). **testimony which they held**—i.e., which they bore, as committed to them to bear. Cf. ch. 12:17, "*Have* (same *Greek* as here) the testimony of Jesus." **10. How long**—*Greek*, "Until when?" **Lord**—*Greek*, "Master"; implying that He has them and their foes and all His creatures as absolutely at His disposal, as a master has his *slaves;* hence, in vs. 11, "*fellow servants*," or *fellow slaves* follows. **holy**—*Greek*, "the Holy one." **avenge**—"exact vengeance for our blood." **on**—*Greek*, "*from* them." **that dwell on the earth**—the ungodly, of earth, earthly, as distinguished from the Church, whose home and heart are even now in heavenly places. **11. white robes**—The three oldest MSS., A, B, C, read, "A white robe was given." **every one of**—One oldest MS., B, omits this. A and C read, "unto them, unto each," i.e., unto them severally. Though their joint cry for the riddance of the earth from the ungodly is not yet granted, it is intimated that it will be so in due time; meanwhile, *individually* they receive the white robe, indicative of light, joy, and triumphant victory over their foes; even as the

ADAM CLARKE

They should kill one another. This was literally the case with the Jews, while besieged by the Romans. *A great sword*. Great influence and success, producing terrible carnage.

5. *The third beast*. That which had the face of a man. *A black horse*. The emblem of famine. Some think that which took place under Claudius. See Matt. xxiv. 7; the same which was predicted by Agabus, Acts xi. 28. *A pair of balances*. To show that the scarcity would be such that every person must be put under an allowance.

6. *A measure of wheat for a penny*. It contained as much as one man could consume in a day; and a *penny*, the Roman *denarius*, was the ordinary pay of a laborer. So it appears that in this scarcity each might be able to obtain a bare subsistence by his daily labor; but a man could not, in such cases, provide for a family.

Three measures of barley. This seems to have been the proportion of value between the wheat and the barley. Barley was allowed to afford a poor aliment, and was given to the Roman soldiers instead of wheat, by way of punishment. *Hurt not the oil and the wine*. Be sparing of these; use them not as delicacies, but for necessity, because neither the vines nor the olives will be productive.

7. *The fourth beast*. That which had the face of an eagle.

8. *A pale horse*. The symbol of death. Of this symbol there can be no doubt, because it is immediately said, *His name that sat on him was Death. And Hell followed with him*. The "grave," or "state of the dead," received the slain. *Over the fourth part of the earth*. One-fourth of mankind was to feel the desolating effects of this seal. *To kill with sword* (war), *and with hunger* (famine), *and with death* (pestilence), *and with the beasts of the earth* (lions, tigers, hyaenas, which would multiply in consequence of the devastations occasioned by war, famine, and pestilence).

9. *The fifth seal*. There is no animal nor any other being to introduce this seal, nor does there appear to be any new event predicted; but the whole is intended to comfort the followers of God under their persecutions, and to encourage them to bear up under their distresses. *I saw under the altar*. A symbolical vision was exhibited, in which he saw an *altar;* and under it *the souls of them that were slain for the word of God*—martyred for their attachment to Christianity—are represented as being newly slain as victims to idolatry and superstition.

10. *And they cried with a loud voice*. That is, their blood, like that of Abel, cried for vengeance; for we are not to suppose that there was anything like a vindictive spirit in those happy and holy souls who had shed their blood for the testimony of Jesus. We sometimes say, "Blood cries for blood"; that is, in the order of divine justice every murderer, and every murdering persecutor, shall be punished. *O Lord*. Sovereign Lord. *Holy*. In Thy own nature, hating threatenings. *Dost thou not judge* the persecutors, *and avenge our blood*, inflict signal punishment, *on them that dwell on the earth?* Probably meaning the persecuting Jews; they dwelt "upon that land," a form of speech by which Judea is often signified in the New Testament.

11. *White robes*. The emblems of purity, innocence, and triumph.

MATTHEW HENRY

What was said to them—that they should be easy in themselves, for it would not be long ere the number of their fellow-sufferers *should be fulfilled*. He will recompence tribulation to those who trouble them, and to those that are troubled full and uninterrupted rest.

II. We have here the sixth seal opened, *v.* 12.

1. The tremendous events that were hastening; and here are several occurrences that contribute to make that day and dispensation very dreadful (*v.* 13). It would be a judgment that should astonish all the world.

2. The dread and terror that would seize upon all sorts of men in that great and awful day, *v.* 15. The degree of their terror and astonishment; it should prevail so far as to make them call *to the mountains to fall upon them, and to the hills to cover them.* The cause of their terror—*the wrath of the Lamb.* Though God be invisible, he can make the inhabitants of this world sensible of his awful frowns.

Though Christ be a lamb, yet he can be angry, and *the wrath of the Lamb* is exceedingly dreadful. As men have their day of opportunity, and their seasons of grace, so God has his day of righteous wrath.

JAMIESON, FAUSSET, BROWN

Captain of their salvation goes forth on a *white* horse *conquering and to conquer;* also of purity and sanctity through Christ. **should**—So C reads. But A and B, "*shall* rest." **a little season**—One oldest MS., B, omits "little." A and C support it. Even if it be omitted, is it to be inferred that the "season" is short as compared with eternity? BENGEL fancifully made a *season* (*Greek, chronus,* the word here used) to be one thousand one hundred and eleven one-ninth years, and a **time** (ch. 12:12, 14, **Greek, kairos**) to be a fifth of a *season,* i.e., two hundred and twenty-two two-ninths years. The only distinction in the *Greek* is, a *season* (*Greek, chronus*) is a sort of aggregate of *times. Greek, kairos,* a specific time, and so of short duration. As to their *rest,* cf. ch. 14:13 (the same *Greek, anapauomai*); Isa. 57:2; Dan. 12:13. **until their ... brethren ... be fulfilled**—in number. Until their full number shall have been completed. The number of the elect is definitely fixed: perhaps to fill up that of the fallen angels. But this is mere conjecture. The *full* blessedness and glory of all the saints shall be simultaneous. The earlier shall not anticipate the later saints. A and C read, "shall have been accomplished"; B and ℵ read, "shall have accomplished (their course)." **12.** As vss. 4, 6-8, the sword, famine, and pestilence, answer to Matthew 24:6, 7; and vss. 9, 10, as to martyrdoms, answer to Matthew 24:9, 10; so this passage, vss. 12, 17, answers to Matthew 24:29, 30, "the sun shall be darkened, and the moon shall not give her light, and the stars shall fall from heaven; ... then shall all the tribes of the earth mourn, and they shall see the Son of man coming"; imagery describing *the portents* of the immediate coming of the day of the Lord; but *not the coming itself* until the elect are sealed, and the judgments invoked by the martyrs descend on the earth, the sea, and the trees (ch. 7). **and, lo**—So A reads. But B and C omit "lo." **earthquake**—*Greek,* "shaking" of *the heavens,* the sea, and the dry land; the shaking of these mutable things being the necessary preliminary to the setting up of those *things which cannot be shaken.* This is one of the *catchwords* [WORDSWORTH] connecting the sixth seal with the sixth trumpet (ch. 11:13) and the seventh vial (ch. 16:17-21); also the seventh seal (ch. 8:5). **sackcloth**—One kind, made of the "hair" of Cilician goats, was called "cilicium," or Cilician cloth, and was used for tents, etc. Paul, a Cilician, made such tents (Acts 18:3). **moon**—A, B, C, and oldest versions read, the whole moon"; the full moon; not merely the crescent moon. **as blood**—(Joel 2:31). **13. stars ... fell ... as a fig tree casteth her ... figs**—(Isa. 34:4, Nah. 3:12). The Church shall be then ripe for glorification, the Antichristian world for destruction, which shall be accompanied with mighty phenomena in nature. As to the stars falling to the earth, Scripture describes natural phenomena as they would appear to the spectator, not in the language of scientific accuracy; and yet, while thus adapting itself to ordinary men, it drops hints which show that it anticipates the discoveries of modern science. **14. departed**—*Greek, "was separated from"* its place; "was made to depart." Not as ALFORD, "parted *asunder*"; for, on the contrary, it was rolled *together* as a scroll which had been open is rolled up and laid aside. There is no "asunder one from another" here in the *Greek,* as in Acts 15:39, which ALFORD copies. **mountain ... moved out of ... places**—(Ps. 121:1, *Margin;* Jer. 3:23; 4:24; Nah. 1:5). This total disruption shall be the precursor of the new earth, just as the pre-Adamic convulsions prepared it for its present occupants. **15. kings ... hid themselves**—Where was now the spirit of those whom the world has so greatly feared? [BENGEL]. **great men**—statesmen and high civil officers. **rich men ... chief captains**—The three oldest MSS., A, B, C, transpose thus, "chief captains ... rich men." **mighty**—The three oldest MSS, A, B, and C read, "strong" physically (Ps. 33:16). **in**—lit., "into"; ran *into,* so as to *hide themselves* in. **dens**—"caves." **16. from the face**—(Ps. 34:16). On the whole verse, cf. Hosea 10:8; Luke 23:30. **17.** Lit., "the day, the great (day)," which can only mean the last great day. After the Lord has exhausted all His ordinary judgments, the sword, famine, pestilence, and wild beasts, and still sinners are impenitent, the great day of the Lord itself shall come.

to stand—to stand justified, and not condemned before the Judge. Thus the sixth seal brings us to the verge of the Lord's coming. The ungodly "tribes of the earth" tremble at the signs of His immediate approach. But before He actually inflicts the blow in person, "the elect" must be "gathered " out.

ADAM CLARKE

They should rest yet for a little season. This is a declaration that, when the cup of the iniquity of the Jews should be full, they should then be punished in a mass. If this book was written before the destruction of Jerusalem, as is most likely, then this destruction is that which was to fall upon the Jews and the "little time" or *season* was that which elapsed between their martyrdom, or the date of this book, and the final destruction of Jerusalem by the Romans, under Vespasian and his son Titus, about A.D. 70. What follows may refer to the destruction of the heathen Roman Empire.

12. *The sixth seal.* This seal also is opened and introduced by Jesus Christ alone. *A great earthquake.* A most stupendous change in the civil and religious constitution of the world. If it refer to Constantine the Great, the change that was made by his conversion to Christianity might be very properly represented under the emblem of an *earthquake,* and the other symbols mentioned in this and the following verses. The *sun*—the ancient pagan government of the Roman Empire—was totally darkened; and, like a black hair *sackcloth,* was degraded and humbled to the dust. The *moon*—the ecclesiastical state of the same empire—became as *blood*—was totally ruined, their sacred rites abrogated, their priests and religious institutions desecrated, their altars cast down, their temples destroyed, or turned into places for Christian worship.

13. *The stars of heaven.* The gods and goddesses, demigods, and deified heroes of their poetical and mythological heaven were prostrated indiscriminately, and lay as useless as the figs or fruit of a tree shaken down before ripe by a "tempestuous wind."

14. *And the heaven departed as a scroll.* The whole system of pagan and idolatrous worship, with all its spiritual, secular, and superstitious influence, was blasted, shrivelled up, and rendered null and void, as a parchment scroll when exposed to the action of a strong fire. *And every mountain.* All the props, supports, and dependencies of the empire, whether regal allies, tributary kings, dependent colonies, or mercenary troops, were all *moved out of their places,* so as to stand no longer in the same relation to that empire, and its worship, support, and maintenance, as they formerly did. *And island.* The heathen temples, with their precincts and enclosures, cut off from the common people, and into which none could come but the privileged, may be here represented by islands, for the same reasons.

15. *The kings of the earth.* All the secular powers who had endeavored to support the pagan worship by authority, influence, riches, political wisdom, and military skill; with *every bondman*—all "slaves," who were in life and limb addicted to their masters or owners. *And every free man.* Those who had been manumitted, commonly called "freedmen," and who were attached, through gratitude, to the families of their liberators. All *hid themselves*—were astonished at the total overthrow of the heathen empire and the revolution which had then taken place.

16. *Said to the mountains and rocks.* Expressions which denote the strongest perturbation and alarm. They preferred any kind of death to that which they apprehended from this most awful revolution. *From the face of him that sitteth on the throne.* They now saw that all these terrible judgments came from the Almighty; and that Christ, the Author of Christianity, was now judging, condemning, and destroying them for their cruel persecutions of is followers.

17. *For the great day of his wrath.* The decisive and manifest time in which He will execute judgment on the oppressors of His people. *Who shall be able to stand?* No might can prevail against the might of God. All these things may literally apply to the final destruction of Jerusalem, and to the revolution which took place in the Roman Empire under Constantine the Great. Some apply them to the "day of judgment"; but they do not seem to have that awful event in view.

MATTHEW HENRY

CHAPTER 7

Verses 1–12

I. An account of the restraint laid upon the winds. By these winds we suppose are meant those errors which would occasion a great deal of trouble and mischief to the church of God. The spirits of error are compared to *the four winds,* contrary one to another, but doing much hurt to the garden and vineyard of God. Errors are as wind, by which those who are unstable are shaken. They are restrained by the ministry of angels, *standing on the four corners of the earth;* the spirit of error cannot go forth till God permits it. Angels minister to the good of the church by restraining its enemies. Their restraint was only for a season, and that was *till the servants of God were sealed in their foreheads.*

II. An account of the sealing of the servants of God. 1. To whom this work was committed—to an angel. Another angel was employed to mark out and distinguish the faithful servants of God.

2. How they were distinguished—the seal of God was set upon their foreheads. By this mark they were set apart for mercy and safety in the worst of times.

3. The number of those that were sealed. A particular account of those that were sealed of the twelve tribes of Israel—twelve thousand out of every tribe.

J. A. SEISS:

We see that God is not yet done with the Jews. Their national restoration is not necessarily involved in this text; though such a restoration in advance of this sealing would admirably agree with the vision and with other predictions relating to the same transactions. But it is involved that the Jews shall remain a distinct people upon earth up to the day of judgment; and that, before the final consummation, God will again turn himself toward them, and begin to deal with them once more in mercy, as in the days that He brought them up out of the land of Egypt. Edom, and those who disbelieve with Edom in Jacob's birthright, may sneeringly ask: "Watchman, what of the night?" But, there is a morning coming. A stormy morning it may be; but a morning nevertheless, and not without its sunshine and its rays of blessing. They err who tell us that all God's promises to Israel as a race are dead, never again to be revived. The Giver of them does not so speak. His inspired Apostle, even after Jerusalem had fallen, wrote, with regard to this very subject, that "the gifts and calling of God are without repentance"; and that for the selfsame Israel which has fallen, and been cast down, and broken off, there is a coming fullness, recovery, and grafting in again, when the Deliverer shall come (see Rom. 11).

—*The Apocalypse*

A general account of those who were saved out of other nations (*v.* 9). Though the church of God is but a little flock, in comparison of the wicked world, yet it is no contemptible society, but really large, and to be still more enlarged.

JAMIESON, FAUSSET, BROWN

CHAPTER 7

VSS. 1-17. SEALING OF THE ELECT OF ISRAEL. THE COUNTLESS MULTITUDE OF THE GENTILE ELECT. **1. And**—so B and *Syriac.* But A, C, *Vulgate,* and *Coptic* omit "and." **after these things**—A, B, C, and *Coptic* read, "after this." The two visions in this chapter come in as an episode *after* the sixth seal, and before the seventh seal. **earth . . . sea . . . tree**—The judgments to descend on these are in answer to the martyrs' prayer under the *fifth* seal. Cf. the same judgments under the *fifth* trumpet, the sealed being exempt (ch. 9:4). **on any tree**—*Greek, "against* any tree" (*Greek, epi ti dendron:* but *on* the earth," *Greek, epi tees gees*). **2. from the east**—*Greek,* ". . . the rising of the sun." The quarter from which God's glory oftenest manifests itself. **3. Hurt not**—by letting loose the destructive winds. **till we have sealed the servants of our God**—parallel to Matthew 24:31, "His angels . . . shall gather together His elect from the four winds." God's love is such, that He *cannot do anything* in the way of judgment, till His people are secured from hurt (Gen. 19:22). Israel, at the eve of the Lord's coming, shall be found re-embodied as a nation; for its tribes are distinctly specified (Joseph, however, being substituted for Dan; whether because Antichrist is to come from Dan, or because Dan is to be Antichrist's especial tool [ARETAS, tenth century], cf. Gen. 49:17; Jer. 8:16; Amos 8:14; just as there was a Judas among the Twelve). Out of these tribes *a believing remnant* will be preserved from the judgments which shall destroy all the Antichristian confederacy (ch. 6:12-17), and *shall be transfigured with the elect Church of all nations,* viz., 144,000 (or whatever number is meant by this symbolical number), who shall faithfully resist the seductions of Antichrist, while the rest of the nation, restored to Palestine in unbelief, are his dupes, and at last his victims.

foreheads—the most conspicuous and noblest part of man's body; on which the helmet, "the hope of salvation," is worn. **4.** *Twelve* is the number of the tribes, and appropriate to *the Church:* 3 by 4:3, the *divine* number, multiplied by 4, the number for *world-wide extension.* 12 by 12 implies *fixity and completeness,* which is taken a thousandfold in 144,000. A *thousand* implies *the world perfectly pervaded by the divine;* for it is *ten,* the world number, raised to the power of *three,* the number of God. **of all the tribes**—lit., "out of every tribe"; not 144,000 of each tribe, but the aggregate of the 12,000 *from every tribe.* **children**—*Greek, "sons* of Israel." Ch. 3:12; 21:12, are no objection, as ALFORD thinks, to the literal Israel being meant; for, in consummated glory, still the Church will be that "built on the foundation of the (*Twelve*) apostles (Israelites), Jesus Christ (an Israelite) being the chief cornerstone." Gentile believers shall have *the name of Jerusalem written on them,* in that they shall share the citizenship antitypical to that of the literal Jerusalem. **5-8.** Judah (meaning *praise*) stands first, as Jesus' tribe. Benjamin, the youngest, is last; and with him is associated second last, Joseph. Reuben, as originally first-born, comes next after Judah, to whom it gave place, having by sin lost its primogeniture-right. Besides the reason given above, another akin for the omission of Dan, is, its having been the first to lapse into idolatry (Judg. 18); for which same reason the name Ephraim, also (cf. Judg. 17: Hos. 4:17), is omitted, and Joseph substituted. Also, it had been now for long almost extinct. Long before, the Hebrews say [GROTIUS], it was reduced to the one family of Hussim, which perished subsequently in the wars before Ezra's time. Hence it is omitted in I Chronicles 4-8. Dan's small numbers are joined here to Naphtali's, whose brother he was by the same mother [BENGEL]. The twelve times twelve thousand sealed ones of Israel are the nucleus of transfigured humanity [AUBERLEN], to which the elect Gentiles are joined, "a multitude which no man could number," vs. 9 (i.e., the Church of Jews and Gentiles indiscriminately, in which the Gentiles are the predominant element, Luke 21:24. The word "tribes," *Greek,* implies that *believing Israelites* are in this *countless multitude*). Both are in heaven, yet ruling over the earth, as ministers of blessing to its inhabitants: while upon earth the world of nations is added to the kingdom of Israel. The twelve apostles stand at the head of the whole. The upper and the lower congregation, though distinct, are intimately associated. **9. no man**—*Greek,* "no one." **of all nations**—*Greek,* "OUT OF *every nation.*" The human race is *one nation* by origin, but afterwards separated itself into *tribes, peoples,* and *tongues;*

ADAM CLARKE

CHAPTER 7

1. *And after these things.* Immediately after the preceding vision. *I saw four angels.* Instruments which God employs in the dispensation of His providence; we know not what. *On the four corners of the earth.* On the extreme parts of the land of Judea, called "the land," or *earth,* by way of eminence. *Holding the four winds.* Preventing evil from every quarter. *Earth . . . sea, nor on any tree;* keeping the whole of the land free from evil, till the Church of Christ should wax strong, and each of His followers have time to prepare for his flight from Jerusalem, previously to its total destruction by the Romans.

2. *The seal of the living God.* This angel is represented as the chancellor of the supreme King, and as *ascending from the east,* "from the rising of the sun." Some understand this of Christ, who is called "the east," Luke i. 78. *Four angels, to whom it was given to hurt.* Particular agents employed by divine providence in the management of the affairs of the earth, but whether spiritual or material we know not.

3. *Till we have sealed the servants of our God.* There is manifestly an allusion to Ezek. ix. 4 here. By sealing we are to understand consecrating the persons in a more especial manner to God, and showing, by this mark of God upon them, that they were under His more immediate protection, and that nothing should hurt them. It was a custom in the East, and indeed in the West too, to stamp with a hot iron the name of the owner upon the forehead or shoulder of his slave. It is worthy of remark that not one Christian perished in the siege of Jerusalem; all had left the city and escaped to Pella.

4. *I heard the number of them which were sealed.* In the number of 144,000 are included all the Jews converted to Christianity; 12,000 out of each of the 12 tribes. But this must be only a certain for an uncertain number; for it is not to be supposed that just 12,000 were converted out of each of the 12 tribes.

5-8. *Of the tribe of Juda.* First, we are to observe that the tribe of Levi is here mentioned, though that tribe had no inheritance in Israel; but they now belonged to the spiritual priesthood. Secondly, that the tribe of Dan, which had an inheritance, is here omitted, as also the tribe of Ephraim. Thirdly, that the tribe of *Joseph* is here added in the place of Ephraim. Ephraim and Dan, being the principal promoters of idolatry, are left out in this enumeration.

9. *A great multitude.* This appears to mean the Church of Christ among the Gentiles, for it was different from that collected from the twelve tribes; and it is here said to be *of all*

MATTHEW HENRY

III. We have the songs of saints and angels, *v.* 9–12. 1. The praises offered up by the saints. (1) The posture of these praising saints: they *stood before the throne, and before the Lamb*, before the Creator and the Mediator. The throne of God would be inaccessible to sinners were it not for a Mediator. (2) Their habit: they were *clothed with white robes, and had palms in their hands*, as conquerors used to appear in their triumphs.

(3) Their employment: they *cried with a loud voice, saying, Salvation to our God who sitteth upon the throne, and to the Lamb.* This may be understood either as a *hosannah*, or as a *hallelujah*. Both the Father and the Son are joined together in these praises; the Father contrived this salvation, the Son purchased it, and those who enjoy it must and will bless the Lord and the Lamb.

2. Here is the song of the angels as they fell on their faces and worshipped (*v.* 11, 12). What humility then, and what profound reverence, become us vile frail creatures, when we come into the presence of God! They consented to the praises of the saints, their *Amen* thereto; and then they added more of their own. We see what is the work of heaven, and we ought to get our hearts tuned for it, and to long for that world where our praises, as well as happiness, will be perfected.

Verses 13–17

A description of the happiness of those who have faithfully served the Lord Jesus Christ.

I. A question asked by one of the elders, not for his own information, but for John's instruction. The lowest saint in heaven knows more than the greatest apostle in the world.

II. The answer returned by the apostle, in which he tacitly acknowledges his own ignorance: *Thou knowest*.

III. The account given to the apostle concerning that noble army of martyrs. 1. The low and desolate state they had formerly been in; they had been in great tribulation. The way to heaven lies through many tribulations; but tribulation shall not *separate us from the love of God.*

2. The means by which they had been prepared for the great happiness they now enjoyed, *v.* 14. This is the only blood that makes the robes of the saints white and clean.

3. The blessedness to which they are now advanced. (1) They are happy in their station, for *they are before the throne of God night and day*; and he *dwells among them.* (2) They are happy in their employment, for they serve God continually.

JAMIESON, FAUSSET, BROWN

hence, the one singular stands first, followed by the three plurals. **kindreds**—*Greek*, "tribes." **people**—*Greek*, "peoples." The "first fruits unto the Lamb," the 144,000 (ch. 14:1-4) of Israel, are followed by a copious harvest of all nations, an election *out of* the Gentiles, as the 144,000 are an election out of Israel (*Note*, vs. 3). **white robes**—(*Note*, ch. 6:11; also ch. 3:5, 18; 4:4). **palms in . . . hands**—the antitype to Christ's entry into Jerusalem amidst the palm-bearing multitude. This shall be just when He is about to come visibly and take possession of His kingdom. The *palm branch* is the symbol of joy and triumph. It was used at the feast of tabernacles, on the fifteenth day of the seventh month, when they kept feast to God in thanksgiving for the ingathered fruits. The antitype shall be the completed gathering in of the harvest of the elect redeemed here described. **10. cried**—*Greek*, "cry," in the three oldest MSS., A, B, C, *Vulgate, Syriac,* and *Coptic*. It is their continuing, ceaseless employment. **Salvation**—lit., "THE salvation"; all the praise of our salvation be ascribed to our God. At the Lord's entry into Jerusalem, the type, similarly "salvation" is the cry of the palm-bearing multitudes. *Hosanna* means "save us now"; taken from Psalm 118:25, in which Psalm (vss. 14, 15, 21, 26) the same connection occurs between *salvation,* the *tabernacles* of the righteous, and the Jews' cry to be repeated by the whole nation at Christ's coming, "Blessed be He that cometh in the name of the Lord." **11.** The angels, as in ch. 5:11, in their turn take up the anthem of praise. There it was "*many* angels," here it is "*all* the angels." **stood**—"were standing" [ALFORD]. **12.** *Greek, "The* blessing, *the* glory, *the* wisdom, *the* thanksgiving, *the* honor, *the* power, *the* might [the doxology is *sevenfold,* implying its totality and completeness], *unto the ages of the ages.*" **13. answered**—viz., to my thoughts; spoke, asking the question which might have been expected to arise in John's mind from what has gone before. One of the twenty-four elders, representing the Old and New Testament ministry, appropriately acts as interpreter of this vision of the glorified Church. **What . . .**—*Greek* order, "These which are arrayed in white robes, WHO are they?" **14. Sir**—*Greek,* "Lord." B, C, *Vulgate, Syriac, Coptic* versions, and CYPRIAN read, "My Lord." A omits "My," as *English Version.* **thou knowest**—taken from Ezekiel 37:3. Comparatively ignorant ourselves of divine things, it is well for us to look upward for divinely communicated knowledge. **came**—rather as *Greek,* "come"; implying that they are *just come.* **great tribulation**—*Greek,* "THE great tribulation"; "the tribulation, the great one," viz., *the* tribulation to which the martyrs were exposed under the fifth seal, the same which Christ foretells as about to precede His coming (Matt. 24:21, *great tribulation*), and followed by the same signs as the sixth seal (Matt. 24:29, 30), cf. Daniel 12:1; including also retrospectively all *the tribulation* which the saints of all ages have had to pass through. Thus this seventh chapter is a recapitulation of the vision of the six seals, ch. 6, to fill up the outline there given in that part of it which affects the faithful of that day. There, however, their number was waiting to be completed, but here it is completed, and they are seen taken out of the earth before the judgments on the Antichristian apostasy; with their Lord, they, and all His faithful witnesses and disciples of past ages, wait for His coming and their coming to be glorified and reign together with Him. **washed . . . robes . . . white in the blood of . . . Lamb**—(ch. 1:5; Isa. 1:18; Heb. 9:14; I John 1:7; cf. Isa. 61:10; Zech. 3:3-5). Faith applies to the heart the purifying blood; once for all for justification, continually throughout the life for sanctification. **15. Therefore**—because they are so washed white; for without it they could never have entered God's holy heaven; ch. 22:14, "Blessed are those who *wash their robes* (the oldest MSS. reading), that they may have right to the tree of life, and may enter in through the gates into the city"; 21:27; Ephesians 5:26, 27. **before**—*Greek,* "in the presence of." Matthew 5:8; I Corinthians 13:12, "face to face." **throne . . . temple**—These are connected because we can approach the heavenly King only through priestly mediation; therefore, Christ is at once King and Priest on His throne. **day and night**—i.e., perpetually; as those approved of as priests by the Sanhedrim were clothed in white, and kept by turns a perpetual watch in the temple at Jerusalem; cf. as to the singers, I Chronicles 9:33, "day and night"; Psalm 134:1. Strictly "there is no night" in the heavenly sanctuary (ch. 22:5). **in his temple**—in what is the

ADAM CLARKE

nations, and kindreds, and people, and tongues. Clothed with white robes, as emblems of innocence and purity. With *palms in their hands,* in token of victory gained over the world, the devil, and the flesh.

10. *Salvation to our God.* That is, God alone is the Author of the salvation of man; and this salvation is procured for and given to them through the *Lamb,* as their propitiatory Sacrifice.

11. *All the angels.* As there is joy in the presence of God among these holy spirits when one sinner repents, no wonder that they take such an interest in the gathering together of such innumerable multitudes who are fully saved from their sins.

12. *Saying, Amen.* Giving their most cordial and grateful assent to the praises attributed to God and the Lamb. *Blessing, and glory.* There are here seven different species of praise attributed to God, as in chap. v. 12, where see the note.

13. *One of the elders answered.* A Hebraism for "spoke." The question is here asked, that the proposer may have the opportunity of answering it.

14. *Sir, thou knowest.* That is, I do not know, but you can inform me. *Came out of great tribulation.* Persecutions of every kind.

And have washed their robes. Have obtained their pardon and purity through the *blood of the Lamb.* Their white robes cannot mean the righteousness of Christ, for this cannot be washed and made white in His own blood. This white linen is said to be "the righteousness of saints," chap. xix. 8, and this is the righteousness in which they stand before the throne. Therefore it is not Christ's righteousness, but it is a righteousness wrought in them by the merit of His blood and the power of His Spirit.

15. *Therefore.* Because they are washed in the blood of the Lamb, *are they before the throne*—admitted to the immediate presence, of God.

And serve him day and night. Without ceasing; being filled with the spirit of prayer, faith, love, and obedience.

MATTHEW HENRY

(3) They are happy in their freedom from all the inconveniences of this present life. From all want and sense of want: *They hunger and thirst no more;* all their wants are supplied. From all sickness and pain: they shall never be scorched by *the heat of the sun any more.* (4) They are happy in the love and guidance of the Lord Jesus: *He shall feed them, he shall lead them to living fountains of waters.* (5) They are happy in being delivered from all sorrow. *God shall wipe away all tears from their eyes.* God himself, with his own gentle and gracious hand, will wipe those tears away, and they would not have been without those tears, when God comes to wipe them away. In this he deals with them as a tender father who finds his beloved child in tears, he comforts him, he wipes his eyes, and turns his sorrow into rejoicing.

CHAPTER 8

Verses 1–6

I. The opening of the last seal. This was to introduce a new set of events.

II. A profound *silence in heaven for the space of half an hour.* A silence of expectation; great things were upon the wheel of providence, and the church of God, both in heaven and earth, stood silent, to see what God was doing.

III. The trumpets were delivered to the angels who were to sound them.

JAMIESON, FAUSSET, BROWN

heavenly analogue to His temple on earth, for strictly there is "no temple therein" (ch. 21:22), "God and the Lamb are the temple" filling the whole, so that there is no distinction of sacred and secular places; the city is the temple, and the temple the city. Cf. ch. 4:8, "the four living creatures rest not *day and night,* saying, Holy . . ." shall **dwell among them**—rather (*Greek, scenosei ep' autous*), "shall be the tabernacle over them" (cf. ch. 21:3; Lev. 26:11 especially Isa. 4:5, 6; 8:14; 25:4; Ezek. 37:27). His *dwelling among them* is to be understood as a secondary truth, besides what is expressed, viz., His being their *covert.* When once He *tabernacled among us* as *the Word made flesh,* He was in great lowliness; then He shall be in great glory. **16.** (Isa. 49:10.) **hunger no more**—as they did here. **thirst any more**—(John 4:13). **the sun**—literally, scorching in the East. Also, symbolically, the sun of persecution. **neither . . . light**—*Greek,* "by no means at all . . . light" (fall). **heat**—as the sirocco. **17. in the midst of the throne**—i.e., in the middle point in front of the throne (ch. 5:6). **feed**—*Greek,* "tend as a shepherd." **living fountains of water**—A, B, *Vulgate,* and CYPRIAN read, (eternal) "*life's* fountains of waters." "Living" is not supported by the old authorities.

CHAPTER 8

VSS. 1-13. SEVENTH SEAL. PREPARATION FOR THE SEVEN TRUMPETS. THE FIRST FOUR AND THE CONSEQUENT PLAGUES. **1. was**—*Greek,* "came to pass"; "began to be." **silence in heaven about . . . half an hour**—The last seal having been broken open, the book of God's eternal plan of redemption is opened for the Lamb to read to the blessed ones in heaven. The *half hour's silence* contrasts with the previous jubilant songs of *the great multitude,* taken up by the *angels* (ch. 7:9-11). It is the solemn introduction to the employments and enjoyments of the eternal Sabbath-rest of the people of God, commencing with the Lamb's reading the book heretofore sealed up, and which we cannot know till then. In ch. 10:4, similarly at the eve of the sounding of the seventh trumpet, when the seven thunders uttered their voices, John is forbidden to write them. The seventh trumpet (ch. 11:15-19) winds up God's vast plan of providence and grace in redemption, just as the seventh seal brings it to the same consummation. So also the seventh vial, ch. 16:17. In the Jewish temple, musical instruments and singing resounded during the whole time of the offering of the sacrifices, which formed the first part of the service. But at the offering of incense, solemn silence was kept (Ps. 62:1, "My soul *waiteth* upon God." *Margin,* "is silent"; 65:1, *Margin*), the people praying secretly all the time. The *half-hour* stillness implies, too, the earnest adoring expectation with which the blessed spirits and the angels await the succeeding unfolding of God's judgments. A *short* space is implied; for even an *hour* is so used (ch. 17:12; 18:10, 19). **2. the seven angels**—Cf. the apocryphal Tobit, 12:15, "I am Raphael, one of the seven holy angels which present the prayers of the saints, and which go in and out before the glory of the Holy One." Cf. Luke 1:19, "I am Gabriel, that stand in the presence of God." **stood**—*Greek,* "stand." **seven trumpets**—These come in during the time while the martyrs *rest until their fellow servants also, that should be killed as they were, should be fulfilled;* for it is *the inhabiters of the earth* on whom the judgments fall, on whom also the martyrs prayed that they should fall (ch. 6:10). *All* the ungodly, and not merely some one portion of them, are meant, all the opponents and obstacles in the way of the kingdom of Christ and His saints, as is proved by ch. 11:15, 18, end, at the close of the seven trumpets. The Revelation becomes more special only as it advances farther (ch. 13; 16:10; 17:18). By the seven trumpets the world kingdoms are overturned to make way for Christ's universal kingdom. The first four are connected together; and the last three, which alone have *Woe, woe, woe* (vss. 7-13). **3. another angel**—not Christ, as many think; for He, in Revelation, is always designated by one of His proper titles; though, doubtless, He is the only true High Priest, the Angel of the Covenant, standing before the golden altar of incense, and there, as Mediator, offering up His people's prayers, rendered acceptable before God through

ADAM CLARKE

Shall dwell among them. He lives in is own Church, and in the heart of every true believer.

16. *They shall hunger no more.* They shall no longer be deprived of their religious ordinances and the blessings attendant on them, as they were when in a state of persecution. *Neither shall the sun light on them.* Their secular rulers, being converted to God, became nursing fathers to the Church. *Nor any heat.* Neither persecution nor affliction of any kind. These the Hebrews express by the term "heat, scorching."

17. *The Lamb.* The Lord Jesus, enthroned with His Father in ineffable glory. *Shall feed them.* Shall communicate to them everything calculated to secure, continue, and increase their happiness. *Living fountains of waters.* A "spring" in the Hebrew phraseology is termed "living water," because constantly boiling up and running on. By these perpetual fountains we are to understand endless sources of comfort and happiness, which Jesus Christ will open out of His own infinite plenitude to all glorified souls. These eternal living fountains will make an infinite variety in the enjoyments of the blessed. *God shall wipe away,* in the most affectionate and fatherly manner, *all tears from their eyes,* all causes of distress and grief. They shall have pure, unmixed happiness.

CHAPTER 8

1. *The seventh seal.* This is ushered in and opened only by the Lamb. *Silence in heaven.* This must be a mere metaphor, *silence* being put here for the deep and solemn expectation of the stupendous things about to take place, which the opening of this seal had produced. When anything prodigious or surprising is expected, all is silence, and even the breath is scarcely heard to be drawn. *Half an hour.* As *heaven* may signify the place in which all these representations were made to John, the *half an hour* may be considered as the time during which no representation was made to him, the time in which God was preparing the august exhibition which follows. There is here, and in the following verses, a strong allusion to different parts of the Temple worship; a presumption that the Temple was still standing, and the regular service of God carried on. The *silence* here refers to this fact—while the priest went in to burn incense in the holy place, all the people continued in silent mental prayer without till the priest returned. See Luke i. 10. The angel mentioned here appears to execute the office of priest, as we shall by and by see.

2. *The seven angels which stood before God.* Probably the same as those called "the seven Spirits which are before his throne," chap. i. 4. There is still an allusion here to the seven ministers of the Persian monarchs. See Tobit, chap. xii. 15.

3. *Another angel.* About to perform the office of priest.

MATTHEW HENRY

IV. To prepare for this, another angel must first offer incense, *v.* 3. This incense he was to offer up, *with the prayers of all the saints, upon the golden altar.* 1. All the saints are a praying people; none of the children of God are born dumb. 2. Times of danger should be praying times, and so should times of great expectation; both our fears and our hopes should put us upon prayer. 3. The prayers of the saints themselves stand in need of the incense and intercession of Christ to make them acceptable and effectual. No prayer, thus recommended, was ever denied audience or acceptance. These prayers that were thus accepted in heaven produced great changes upon earth.

The same angel in the same censer *took of the fire of the altar, and cast it into the earth,* and this presently caused strange commotions, *voices, and thunderings, and lightnings, and an earthquake.* And now, all things being thus prepared, the angels discharge their duty.

Verses 7-13

I. *The first angel sounded* the first trumpet, *v.* 7. It was a very terrible storm—fire, and hail, and blood: a strange mixture! The limitation of it: it fell on *the third part of the trees,* and on the third part of *the grass,* and blasted and burnt it up. The most severe calamities have their bounds and limits set them by the great God.

II. *The second angel sounded, v.* 8. Here was still a limitation to the third part, for *in the midst of judgment God remembers mercy.*

JAMIESON, FAUSSET, BROWN

the incense of His merit. Here the angel acts merely as a *ministering spirit,* just as the twenty-four elders *have vials full of odors,* or incense, *which are the prayers of saints,* and which they present before the Lamb. **there was given unto him**—The angel does not provide the incense; it is *given to him* by Christ, whose meritorious obedience and death are the incense, rendering the saints' prayers well pleasing to God. It is not the saints who give the angel the incense; nor are their prayers identified with the incense; nor do they offer their prayers to him. Christ alone is the Mediator through whom, and to whom, prayer is to be offered. **offer it with the prayers**—rather as *Greek,* "*give* it TO the prayers," so rendering them efficacious as a *sweet-smelling savor* to God. Christ's merits alone can thus *incense* our prayers, though the angelic ministry be employed to attach this incense to the prayers. The saints' praying on earth, and the angel's incensing in heaven, are simultaneous. **all saints**—The prayers both of the saints in the heavenly rest, and of those militant on earth. The martyrs' cry is the foremost, and brings down the ensuing judgments. **golden altar**—antitype to the earthly. **4. the smoke . . .** *which came* **with the prayers . . . ascended up**—rather, "the smoke of the incense FOR (or *given* TO: 'given' being understood from vs. 3) the prayers of the saints ascended up, out of the angel's hand, in the presence of God." The angel merely burns the incense given him by Christ the High Priest, so that its smoke blends with the ascending prayers of the saints. The saints themselves are priests; and the angels in this priestly ministration are but *their fellow servants* (ch. 19:10). **5. cast it into the earth**—i.e., *unto* the earth: the hot coals off the altar cast on the earth, symbolize God's fiery judgments about to descend on the Church's foes in answer to the saints' incense-perfumed prayers which have just ascended before God, and those of the martyrs. How marvellous the power of the saints' prayers! **there were**—"there took place," or "ensued." **voices . . . thunderings . . .**—B places the "voices" after "thunderings." A places it after "lightnings." **6. sound**—blow the trumpets. **7.** The common feature of the first four trumpets is, the judgments under them affect *natural objects,* the accessories of life, the earth, trees, grass, the sea, rivers, fountains, the light of the sun, moon, and stars. The last three, the *woe-trumpets* (vs. 13), affect men's life with pain, death, and hell. The language is evidently drawn from the plagues of Egypt, five or six out of the ten exactly corresponding: the *hail,* the *fire* (Exod. 9:24), the WATER *turned to blood* (Exod. 7:19), the *darkness* (Exod. 10:21), the *locusts* (Exod. 10:12), and perhaps the *death* (ch. 9:18). Judicial retribution in kind characterizes the inflictions of the first four, those elements which had been abused punishing their abusers. **mingled with**—A, B, and *Vulgate* read, *Greek,* ". . . IN blood." So in the case of the second and third vials (ch. 16:3, 4). **upon the earth**—*Greek,* "*unto* the earth." A, B, *Vulgate,* and *Syriac* add, "And the third of the earth was burnt up." So under the third trumpet, the *third* of the rivers is affected: also, under the sixth trumpet, the *third* part of men are killed. In Zechariah 13:8, 9 this tripartite division appears, but the proportions reversed, two parts killed, only a third preserved. Here, vice versa, two-thirds escape, one-third is smitten. The fire was the predominant element. **all green grass**—no longer a third, but *all* is *burnt up.* **8. as it were**—not literally a mountain: a mountain-like burning mass. There is a plain allusion to Jeremiah 51:25; Amos 7:4. **third part of the sea became blood**—In the parallel second vial, the *whole* sea (not merely *a third*) becomes *blood.* The overthrow of Jericho, the type of the Antichristian Babylon, after which Israel, under Joshua (the same name as *Jesus*), victoriously took possession of Canaan, the type of Christ's and His people's kingdom, is perhaps alluded to in the SEVEN *trumpets,* which end in the overthrow of all Christ's foes, and the setting up of His kingdom. On the *seventh* day, at the *seventh* time, when the *seven* priests blew the *seven* ram's horn trumpets, the people shouted, and the walls fell flat: and then ensued the *blood-shedding* of the foe. A mountain-like fiery mass would not naturally change water into blood; nor would the third part of *ships* be thereby destroyed. The symbolical interpreters take *the ships* here to be *churches.* For the *Greek* here for ships is not the common one, but that used in the Gospels of the apostolic vessel in which Christ taught: and the first churches were in the shape of an inverted ship: and the *Greek* for *destroyed* is also used of heretical *corruptings* (I Tim. 6:5). **10. a lamp**—*a torch.* **11.**

ADAM CLARKE

Having a golden censer. This was a preparation peculiar to the day of expiation. "On other days it was the custom of the priest to take fire from the great altar in a silver censer, but on the day of expiation the high priest took the fire from the great altar in a golden censer; and when he was come down from the great altar, he took incense from one of the priests, who brought it to him, and went with it to the golden altar; and while he offered the incense the people prayed without in silence, which is the silence in heaven for half an hour." See Sir Isaac Newton. *Much incense, that he should offer it.* Judgments of God are now about to be executed. The *saints,* the genuine Christians, pray much to God for protection. The angelic priest comes with *much incense,* standing between the living and those consigned to death, and offers his incense to God *with the prayers of all saints.*

4. *The smoke of the incense, which came with the prayers.* Though incense itself be an emblem of the prayers of the saints, Ps. cxli. 2, yet here they are said to ascend *before God,* as well as the incense. It is not said that the angel presents these prayers. He presents the incense, and the prayers ascend with it. The ascending of the incense shows that the prayers and offering were accepted.

5. *Cast it into the earth.* That is, upon the land of Judea; intimating the judgments and desolations which were now coming upon it, and which appear to be further opened in the sounding of the seven trumpets. *There were voices.* All these seem to point out the confusion, commotions, distresses, and miseries which were coming upon these people in the wars which were at hand.

6. *Prepared themselves to sound.* Each took up his trumpet, and stood prepared to blow his blast. Wars are here indicated; the trumpet was the emblem of war.

7. *Hail and fire mingled with blood.* This was something like the ninth plague of Egypt. See Exod. ix. 18-24: "The Lord sent thunder and hail . . . and fire mingled with the hail"—"and the fire ran along upon the ground. *They were cast upon the earth.* "Into that land"; viz., Judea, thus often designated. *And the third part of trees.* Before this clause the Codex Alexandrinus and some thirty-five others have, "And the third part of the land was burnt up." This reading, which is undoubtedly genuine, is found also in the Complutensian Polyglot. Griesbach has received it into the text. The land was wasted; the *trees*—the chiefs of the nation—were destroyed; and the *grass*—the common people—slain or carried into captivity. High and low, rich and poor were overwhelmed with one general destruction. This seems to be the meaning of these figures.

8. *A great mountain burning with fire. Mountain,* in prophetic language, signifies a "kingdom," Jer. li. 25, 27, 30, 58. Great disorders, especially when kingdoms are moved by hostile invasions, are represented by "mountains" being cast "into the midst of the sea," Ps. xlvi. 2. Seas mean peoples, as is shown in this book, chap. xvii. 15. Therefore great commotions in kingdoms and among their inhabitants may be here intended; but to whom, where, and when these happened, or are to happen, we know not. *The third part of the sea became blood.* Another allusion to the Egyptian plagues, Exod. vii. 20-21. *Third part* is a rabbinism expressing a considerable number. "When Rabbi Akiba prayed, wept, rent his garments, put off his shoes, and sat in the dust, the world was struck with a curse; and then the third part of the olives, the third part of the wheat, and the third part of the barley, was smitten."

9. *The third part of the ships were destroyed.* These judgments seem to be poured out upon some maritime nation, destroying much of its population, and much of its traffic.

10. *There fell a great star from heaven.* This has given rise to various conjectures. Some say the star means Attila and his Huns; others, Genseric with his Vandals falling on the city of Rome; others, Eleazer, the son of Annus,

MATTHEW HENRY

III. *The third angel sounded, v.* 10. A star from heaven fell: *Upon a third part of the rivers, and upon the fountains of waters.* It turned those springs and streams into wormwood, made them very bitter, that men were poisoned by them. The souls of men found their ruin where they sought for their refreshment.

IV. *The fourth angel sounded.* The nature of this calamity; it was darkness; it fell therefore upon the great luminaries of the heaven, that give light to the world—*the sun, and the moon, and the stars.* The limitation: it was confined to a third part of these luminaries; there was some light both of the sun by day, and of the moon and stars by night. Where the gospel comes to a people, and is but coldly received, it is usually followed with dreadful judgments. God gives warning to men of his judgments before he sends them, so that, if a people be surprised, it is their own fault. Yet God does not in this world stir up all his wrath, but sets bounds to the most terrible judgments.

V. Before the other three trumpets are sounded here is solemn warning how terrible the calamities would be that should follow them, *v.* 13. The messenger was *an angel flying in the midst of heaven,* as in haste. Here are three woes, to show how much the calamities coming should exceed those that had been already. If less judgments do not take effect, but the church and the world grow worse under them, they must expect greater.

JAMIESON, FAUSSET, BROWN

The symbolizers interpret the *star fallen from heaven* as a chief minister (ARIUS, according to BULLINGER, BENGEL, and others; or some future false teacher, if, as is more likely, the event be still future) falling from his high place in the Church, and instead of shining with heavenly light as a *star,* becoming a torch lit with earthly fire and smouldering with smoke. And "wormwood," though medicinal in some cases, if used as ordinary water would not only be disagreeable to the taste, but also fatal to life: so "heretical wormwood changes the sweet Siloas of Scripture into deadly Marahs" [WORDSWORTH]. Contrast the converse change of bitter Marah water into sweet, Exodus 15:23. **12. third part**—not a *total* obscuration as in the sixth seal (ch. 6:12, 13). This *partial* obscuration, therefore, comes between the prayers of the martyrs under the fifth seal, and the last overwhelming judgments on the ungodly under the sixth seal, at the eve of Christ's coming. **the night likewise**—withdrew a third part of the light which the bright Eastern moon and stars ordinarily afford. **13. an angel**—A, B, *Vulgate, Syriac,* and *Coptic* read for "angel," which is supported by none of the oldest MSS., "an eagle": the symbol of judgment descending fatally from on high; the king of birds pouncing on the prey. Cf. this fourth trumpet and the flying *eagle* with the fourth seal introduced by the fourth living creature, "like a flying eagle," ch. 4:7; 6:7, 8: the aspect of Jesus as presented by the fourth Evangelist. *John* is compared in the cherubim (according to the primitive interpretation) to a flying eagle: *Christ's divine majesty* in this similitude is set forth in the Gospel according to John, His *judicial visitations* in the Revelation of John. Contrast "another angel," or *messenger,* with "the everlasting Gospel," ch. 14:6. **through the midst of heaven**—*Greek,* "in the mid-heaven," i.e., in the part of the sky where the sun reaches the *meridian:* in such a position as that the eagle is an object conspicuous to all. **the inhabiters of the earth**—the ungodly, the "men of the world," whose "portion is in this life," upon whom the martyrs had prayed that their blood might be avenged (ch. 6: 10). Not that they sought personal revenge, but their zeal was for the honor of God against the foes of God and His Church. **the other**—*Greek, "the remaining* voices."

ADAM CLARKE

spurning the emperor's victims, and exciting the fury of the Zealots; others, Arius, infecting the pure Christian doctrine with his heresy. It certainly cannot mean all these, and probably none of them. Let the reader judge.

11. *The star is called Wormwood.* So called from the bitter or distressing effects produced by its influence.

12. *The third part of the sun . . . moon . . . stars . . . was darkened.* Supposed to mean Rome, with her senates, consuls, eclipsed by Odoacer, king of the Heruli, and Theodoric, king of the Ostrogoths, in the fifth century. But all this is uncertain.

13. *I . . . heard an angel flying.* Instead of *an angel flying,* almost every MS. and version of note has "an eagle flying." The eagle was the symbol of the Romans, and was always on their ensigns. The three woes which are here expressed were probably to be executed by this people, and upon the Jews and their commonwealth. Taken in this sense the symbols appear consistent and appropriate; and the reading "eagle" instead of *angel* is undoubtedly genuine, and Griesbach has received it into the text.

MATTHEW HENRY — CHAPTER 9

Verses 1–12

1. *A star falling from heaven to the earth.* 2. To this fallen star *was given the key of the bottomless pit.* It becomes the devil's turnkey, to let loose the powers of hell against the churches of Christ. 3. Upon the opening of the bottomless pit *there arose a great smoke,* which darkened the sun and the air. The devil carries on his designs by extinguishing light and knowledge. Wretched souls follow him in the dark, or they durst not follow him. 4. Out of this dark smoke there came a swarm of locusts, and these had, by the just permission of God, power to hurt those who had not the mark of God in their foreheads. 5. The hurt they were to do them was not a bodily, but a spiritual hurt. They should not in a military way destroy all by fire and sword; the trees and the grass should be untouched, and those they hurt should not be slain. 6. They had no power so much as to hurt those who had the seal of God in their foreheads.

7. The power given to these factors for hell is limited in point of time: *five months,* a certain season, and but a short season.

JAMIESON, FAUSSET, BROWN — CHAPTER 9

VSS. 1-21. THE FIFTH TRUMPET: THE FALLEN STAR OPENS THE ABYSS WHENCE ISSUE LOCUSTS. THE SIXTH TRUMPET. FOUR ANGELS AT THE EUPHRATES LOOSED. **1.** The last three trumpets of the seven are called, from ch. 8:13, *the woe-trumpets.* **fall**—rather as *Greek,* "fallen." When John saw it, it was not in the act of *falling,* but had *fallen* already. This is a connecting link of this fifth trumpet with ch. 12:8, 9, 12, "*Woe to the inhabiters of the earth,* for the *devil* is *come down.* . . ." Cf. Isaiah 14:12, "How art thou *fallen from heaven,* Lucifer, son of the morning!" **the bottomless pit**—*Greek,* "the pit of the abyss"; *the orifice of the hell* where Satan and his demons dwell. **3. upon**—*Greek,* "unto," or "into." **as the scorpions of the earth**—as contrasted with the "locusts" which come up *from hell,* and are not "of the earth." **have power**—viz., to sting.

4. not hurt the grass . . . neither . . . green thing . . . neither . . . tree—the food on which they ordinarily prey. Therefore, not natural and ordinary locusts. Their natural instinct is supernaturally restrained to mark the judgment as altogether divine. **those men which**—*Greek, "the* men whosoever." **in . . .**—*Greek, "upon* their forehead." Thus this fifth trumpet is proved to follow the *sealing* in ch. 7, under the sixth seal. None of the saints are hurt by these locusts, which is not true of the saints in Mohammed's attack, who is supposed by many to be meant by the locusts; for many true believers fell in the Mohammedan invasions of Christendom. **5. they . . . they**—The subject changes: the first "they" is *the locusts;* the second is the *unsealed.* **five months**—the ordinary time in the year during which locusts continue their ravages.

their torment—the torment of the sufferers. This fifth verse and vs. 6 cannot refer to an invading army. For an army would *kill,* and not merely *torment.*

ADAM CLARKE — CHAPTER 9

1. *A star fall from heaven.* An angel encompassed with light suddenly descended, and seemed like a *star* falling from heaven. *The key of the bottomless pit.* Power to inundate the earth with a flood of temporal calamities and moral evils.

2. *He opened the bottomless pit.* "The pit of the bottomless deep." Some think the angel means Satan, and the bottomless pit hell. Some suppose Mohammed is meant. *There arose a smoke.* False doctrine, obscuring the true light of heaven.

3. *Locusts.* Vast hordes of military troops; the description which follows certainly agrees better with the Saracens than with any other people or nation, but may also apply to the Romans. *As the scorpions of the earth have power.* Namely, to hurt men by stinging them.

4. *They should not hurt the grass.* Neither the common people, the men of middling condition, nor the nobles. However, this appears rather to refer to the prudent counsels of a military chief, not to destroy the crops and herbage, of which they might have need in their campaigns. *Which have not the seal of God.* All false, hypocritical, and heterodox Christians.

5. *To them it was given.* That is, they were *permitted. That they should be tormented five months.* Some take these months literally, and apply them to the conduct of the Zealots who, from May to September, in the year of the siege, produced dreadful contests among the people; or to the afflictions brought upon the Jews by Cestius Gallus when he came against Jerusalem, before which he lay one whole summer, or nearly five months. Others consider the *months* as being prophetical months, each day being reckoned for a year; therefore this period must amount to 150 years, counting 30 days to each month, as was the general custom of the Asiatics. *Their torment was as the torment of a scorpion.* The phraseology here is

MATTHEW HENRY

8. Though it would be short, it would be very sharp, *v.* 6. 9. These locusts were of a monstrous size and shape, *v.* 7, 8, &c. They were equipped for their work like horses prepared to battle.

They had crowns like gold on their heads; it was not a true, but a counterfeit authority.

They had the show of wisdom and sagacity, *the faces of men*, though the spirit of devils.

They had all the allurements of seeming beauty—*hair like women.* Though they appeared with the tenderness of women, they were really cruel creatures.

They had the defence and protection of earthly powers—*breastplates of iron.* They made a mighty noise in the world, and the noise of their motion was like that of an army with chariots and horses. Though at first they soothed and flattered men with a fair appearance, there was a sting in their tails.

The king and commander of this hellish squadron is here described as an angel. *The angel of the bottomless pit;* an angel still, but a fallen angel, fallen into the bottomless pit. His true name is *Abaddon, Apollyon—a destroyer*, for that is his business, to which he diligently attends.

J. A. SEISS:

Hell and hell-torments are not the mere fictions which some have pronounced them. Neither are they as remote from this present world as men often dream. There is a fiery abyss, with myriads of evil beings in it, malignant and horrible, and there is but a door between this world and that. Heaven is just as near; but heaven is above, and hell is beneath. Mortal man and his world lie between two mighty, opposite, spiritual spheres, both touching directly upon him, each operative to conform him to itself as he yields to one or the other, to be conjoined eventually to the society on high, or to companionship with devils and all evil beings beneath. To doubt this is to mistake concerning the most momentous things of our existence, and to have all our senses closed to the most startling realities of our lives. As we are heavenly in our inclinations and efforts, and open and yielding to things Divine, heaven opens to us, and spirits of heaven become our helpers, comforters, protectors, and guides; and as we are devilish in our temper, unbelieving, defiant of God, and self-sufficient, the doors of separation between us and hell gradually yield, and the smoke of the pit gathers over us, and the spirits of perdition come forth to move among us and to do us mischief. And at the last, as the saints of God are taken up out of the world on the one side, the angels of hell with their malignity and torments are let in on the other.

—The Apocalypse

Verses 13–21

I. The preface to this vision, *v.* 13, 14. When nations are ripe for punishment, those instruments of God's anger that were before restrained are let loose upon them, *v.* 14.

JAMIESON, FAUSSET, BROWN

6. shall desire—*Greek,* "eagerly desire"; set their mind on. **shall flee**—So B, *Vulgate, Syriac,* and *Coptic* read. But A and ℵ read, "fleeth," viz., continually. In ch. 6:16, which is at a later stage of God's judgments, the ungodly seek annihilation, not from the torment of their suffering, but from fear of the face of the Lamb before whom they have to stand. **7. prepared unto battle**—*Greek,* "made ready unto war." Cf. *Note,* Joel 2:4, where the resemblance of locusts to horses is traced: the plates of a horse armed for battle are an image on a larger scale of the outer shell of the locust. **crowns**—(Nah. 3:17). ELLIOTT explains this of the *turbans* of Mohammedans. But how could turbans be "like gold?" ALFORD understands it of the head of the locusts actually ending in a crown-shaped fillet which resembled gold in its material. **as the faces of men**—The "as" seems to imply the locusts here do not mean *men.* At the same time they are not natural locusts, for these do not sting *men* (vs. 5). They must be supernatural. **8. hair of women**—long and flowing. An Arabic proverb compares the antlers of locusts to the hair of girls. EWALD *in* ALFORD understands the allusion to be to the hair on the legs or bodies of the locusts: cf. "rough caterpillars," Jeremiah 51:27. **as the teeth of lions**—(Joel 1:6, as to locusts). **9. as it were breastplates of iron**—not such as forms the thorax of the natural locust. **as . . . chariots** (Joel 2:5-7). **battle**—*Greek,* "war." **10. tails like unto scorpions**—like unto *the tails of* scorpions. **and there were stings**—There is no oldest MS. for this reading. A, B, ℵ *Syriac,* and *Coptic* read, "and (they have) stings: and in their tails (is) their power (lit., 'authority': authorized power) to hurt." **11. And**—so *Syriac.* But A, B, and ℵ, omit "and." **had**—*Greek,* "have." **a king . . .** *which is* **the angel**—*English Version,* agreeing with A, ℵ, reads the (*Greek*) article before "angel," in which reading we must translate, "They have as king over them *the* angel . . ." Satan (cf. vs. 1). Omitting the article with B, we must translate, "They have as king *an* angel . . .": one of the chief demons under Satan: I prefer from vs. 1, the former. **bottomless pit**—*Greek,* "abyss." **Abaddon**—i.e., *perdition* or *destruction* (Job 26:6; Prov. 27:20). The locusts are supernatural instruments in the hands of Satan to torment, and yet not kill, the ungodly, under this fifth trumpet. Just as in the case of godly Job, Satan was allowed to torment with elephantiasis, but not to touch his *life.* In vs. 20, these two woe-trumpets are expressly called "plagues." ANDREAS OF CÆSAREA, A.D. 500, held, in his *Commentary on Revelation,* that the locusts mean *evil spirits* again permitted to come forth on earth and afflict men with various plagues. **12.** *Greek,* "*The* one woe." **hereafter**—*Greek,* "after these things." I agree with ALFORD and DE BURGH, that these *locusts from the abyss* refer to judgments about to fall on the ungodly immediately before Christ's second advent. None of the interpretations which regard them as past, are satisfactory. Joel 1:2-7; 2:1-11, is strictly parallel and expressly refers (2:11) to THE DAY OF THE LORD GREAT AND VERY TERRIBLE: vs. 10 gives the portents accompanying the day of the Lord's coming, *the earth quaking, the heavens trembling, the sun, moon, and stars, withdrawing their shining:* vs. 18. 31, 32, also point to the immediately succeeding deliverance of Jerusalem: cf. also, the previous last conflict in the valley of Jehoshaphat, and the dwelling of God thenceforth in Zion, blessing Judah. **13. a voice**—lit., "*one* voice." **from**—*Greek,* "out of." **the four horns**—A, *Vulgate* (*Amiatinus* MS.), *Coptic,* and *Syriac* omit "four." B and CYPRIAN support it. The *four* horns together gave forth their voice, not diverse, but *one.* God's revelation (e.g., the Gospel), though in its aspects fourfold (*four* expressing *world-wide* extension: whence *four* is the number of the Evangelists), still has but one and the same voice. However, from the parallelism of this sixth trumpet to the fifth seal (ch. 6:9, 10), the martyrs' cry for the avenging of their blood from the altar reaching its consummation under the sixth seal and sixth trumpet, I prefer understanding this *cry from the four corners of the altar* to refer to the saints' prayerful cry from the four quarters of the world, *incensed* by the angel, and ascending to God from the golden altar of incense, and bringing down in consequence fiery judgments. omits the whole clause, "one from the four horns." **14. in . . .**—*Greek, epi to potamo;* "on," or "at the great river." **Euphrates**—(Cf. ch. 16:12). The river whereat Babylon, the ancient foe of God's people was situated. Again, whether from the literal region of the Euphrates, or from the spiritual Babylon (*the*

ADAM CLARKE

peculiar, and probably refers to the warlike weapon called a *scorpion,* several of which, or men armed with them, Cestius Gallus brought with him in his army. Isidore describes this *scorpion* thus: "The scorpion is a poisoned arrow shot from a bow or other instrument, which, when it wounds a man, deposits the poison with which it is covered in the wound; whence it has the name of scorpion."

6. *In those days shall men seek death.* So distressing shall be their sufferings and torment that they shall long for death in any form, to be rescued from the evils of life.

7. *The locusts were like unto horses.* This description of the locusts appears to be taken from Joel ii. 4. The whole of this symbolical description of an overwhelming military force agrees very well with the troops of Mohammed. The Arabs are the most expert horsemen in the world; they live so much on horseback that the horse and his rider seem to make but one animal. The Romans also were eminent for their cavalry. *Crowns like gold.* Not only alluding to their costly turbans, but to the extent of their conquests and the multitude of powers which they subdued. *Their faces were as the faces of men.* That is, though locusts symbolically, they are really men.

8. *Hair as the hair of women.* No razor passes upon their flesh; their hair long, and their beards unshaven. *Their teeth were as the teeth of lions.* They are ferocious and cruel.

9. *They had breastplates . . . of iron.* They seemed to be invulnerable, for no force availed against them. *The sound of their wings.* Their hanging weapons and military trappings, with the clang of their shields and swords when they make their fierce onsets. This simile is borrowed from Joel ii. 5-7.

10. *They had tails like unto scorpions.* This may refer to the consequences of their victories. They infected the conquered with their pernicious doctrines. *Their power was to hurt men five months.* The locusts make their principal ravages during the five summer months. But probably these may be prophetic months, as above, in v. 5—150 years.

11. *A king over them.* A supreme head; some think Mohammed, some think Vespasian. *The angel of the bottomless pit.* The chief envoy of Satan. *Abaddon.* From *abad,* "he destroyed." *Apollyon.* From *apo,* intensive, and *ollyo,* "to destroy." The meaning is the same in both Hebrew and Greek.

12. *One woe is past.* That is, the woe or desolation by the symbolical scorpions. *There come two woes more.* In the trumpets of the sixth and seventh angels.

13. *The four horns of the golden altar.* This is another not very obscure indication that the Jewish Temple was yet standing.

14. *Loose the four angels.* These four angels *bound,* hitherto restrained, in the *Euphrates,* are by some supposed to be the Arabs, the Saracens, the Tartars, or the Turks; by others,

MATTHEW HENRY

II. The vision itself, *v.* 15, 16. 1. The time of their military operations is limited to *an hour, and a day, and a month, and a year*. Prophetic characters of time are hardly to be understood by us.

How far the execution shall prevail, even to a third part of the inhabitants of the earth. 2. The army that was to execute this great commission is mustered, and the number found to be of horsemen *two hundred thousand thousand*; but we are left to guess what the infantry must be. In general, it tells us, the armies should be vastly great.

3. Their formidable equipage and appearance, *v.* 17. As the horses were fierce, like lions, so those who sat upon them were clad in bright and costly armour. 4. The vast havoc and desolation that they made. 5. Their artillery, by which they made such slaughter, described *by fire, smoke, and brimstone*, issuing out of the mouths of their horses, and the stings that were in their tails.

6. The impenitancy of the antichristian generation under these dreadful judgments (*v.* 20). They still persisted in those sins for which God was so severely punishing them. Though God has revealed his wrath from heaven against them, they are obstinate, and impenitent. Impenitency under divine judgments is an iniquity that will be the ruin of sinners; for where God judges he will overcome.

JAMIESON, FAUSSET, BROWN

apostate Church, especially ROME), four angelic ministers of God's judgments shall go forth, assembling an army of horsemen throughout the four quarters of the earth, to slay a third of men, the brunt of the visitation shall be on Palestine. **15. were**—"which had been prepared" [TREGELLES rightly]. **for an hour . . .**—rather as *Greek,* "for (i.e., against) THE hour, and day, and month, and year," viz., appointed by God. The *Greek* article (*teen*), put once only before all the periods, implies that the hour in the day, and the day in the month, and the month in the year, and the year itself, had been definitely fixed by God. The article would have been omitted had a sum-total of periods been specified, viz., 391 years and one month (the period from A.D. 1281, when the Turks first conquered the Christians, to 1672, their last conquest of them, since which last date their empire has declined). **slay**—not merely to "hurt" (vs. 10), as in the fifth trumpet. **third part**—(*Note,* ch. 8:7-12). **of men**—viz., of earthy men, ch. 8:13, "inhabiters of the earth," as distinguished from God's sealed people (of which the sealed of Israel, ch. 7, form the nucleus). **16.** Cf. with these 200,000,000, Psalm 68:17; Daniel 7:10. The hosts here are evidently, from their numbers and their appearance (vs. 17), not merely *human* hosts, but probably *infernal,* though constrained to work out God's will (cf. vss. 1, 2). **and I heard**—A, B, ℵ, *Vulgate, Syriac, Coptic,* and CYPRIAN omit "and." **17. thus**—as follows. **of fire**—the *fiery color* of the breastplates answering to the *fire* which *issued* out of their *mouths.* **of jacinth**—lit., "of hyacinth color," the hyacinth of the ancients answering to our *dark blue iris:* thus, their *dark, dull-colored* breastplates correspond to the *smoke* out of their mouths. **brimstone**—*sulphur-colored:* answering to the *brimstone* or sulphur *out of their mouths.* **18. By these three**—A, B. C, and ℵ read (*apo for kupo*), "From"; implying the *direction* whence the slaughter came; not direct instrumentality as "by" implies. A, B, C, ℵ also add "plagues" after "three." *English Version* reading, which omits it, is not well supported. **by the fire**—*Greek,* "*owing to* the fire," lit., "out of." **19. their**—A, B, C and ℵ read, "the power *of the horses.*" **in their mouth**—whence *issued* the *fire, smoke, and brimstone* (vs. 17). Many interpreters understand the *horsemen* to refer to the myriads of Turkish cavalry arrayed in scarlet, blue, and yellow (*fire, hyacinth,* and *brimstone*), the *lion-headed horses* denoting their invincible courage, and *the fire* and *brimstone* out of their mouths, the gunpowder and artillery introduced into Europe about this time, and employed by the Turks; the tails, like serpents, having a venomous sting, the false religion of Mohammed supplanting Christianity, or, as ELLIOTT thinks, the Turkish pachas' horsetails, worn as a symbol of authority. (!) All this is very doubtful. Considering the parallelism of this sixth trumpet to the sixth seal, the likelihood is that events are intended immediately preceding the Lord's coming. "The false prophet" (as Isa. 9:15 proves), or second beast, having the horns of a lamb, but speaking as *the dragon,* who supports by lying miracles the final Antichrist, seems to me to be intended. Mohammed, doubtless, is a forerunner of him, but not the exhaustive fulfiller of the prophecy here: Satan will, probably, towards the end, bring out all the powers of hell for the last conflict (*Note,* "devils," vs. 20; cf. vss. 1, 2, 17, 18). **with them**—with the serpent heads and their venomous fangs. **20. the rest of the men**—i.e., the ungodly. **yet**—So A, *Vulgate, Syriac,* and *Coptic.* B and ℵ read, "did *not* even repent of," viz., so as to give up "the works . . . ." Like Pharaoh hardening his heart against repentance notwithstanding the plagues. **of their hands**—(Deut. 31:29). Especially the idols *made by their hands.* Cf. ch. 13:14, 15, "the image of the beast" ch. 19: 20. **that they should not**—So B reads. But A, C, and ℵ read. ". . . shall not": implying a prophecy of *certainty* that it shall be so. **devils**—*Greek,* "demons" which lurk beneath the idols which idolaters worship. **21. sorceries**—witchcrafts by means of *drugs* (so the *Greek*). One of the fruits of the unrenewed flesh: the sin of the heathen: about to be repeated by apostate Christians in the last days, ch. 22:15 "sorcerers." The heathen who shall have rejected the proffered Gospel and clung to their fleshly lusts, and apostate Christians who shall have relapsed into the same shall share the same terrible judgments. The worship of images was established in the East in A.D. 842. **fornication**—singular: whereas the other sins are in the plural. Other sins are perpetrated at intervals: those lacking purity of heart indulge in *one* perpetual fornication [BENGEL].

ADAM CLARKE

Vespasian's four generals, one in Arabia, one in Africa, one in Alexandria, and one in Palestine.

15. *For an hour, and a day, and a month, and a year.* We have in this place a year resolved into its component parts. Twenty-four hours constitute a day; seven days make a week; four weeks make a month; and twelve months make a year. Probably no more is meant than that these four angels were "at all times" prepared and permitted to inflict evil on the people against whom they had received their commission. There are some who understand these divisions of time as prophetical periods, and to these I must refer, not professing to discuss such uncertainties.

16. *Two hundred thousand thousand.* "Two myriads of myriads"; that is, 200,000,000; an army that was never yet got together from the foundation of the world, and could not find forage in any part of the earth. Perhaps it only means vast numbers, multitudes without number. Such a number might be literally true of the locusts. Those who will have their particular system supported by the images in this most obscure book tell us that the number here means all the soldiers that were employed in this war, from its commencement to its end!

17. *Breastplates of fire, and of jacinth, and brimstone.* That is, red, blue, and yellow; the first is the color of fire, the second of jacinth, and the third of sulphur. *And the heads of the horses.* Is this an allegorical description of great ordnance? Fire, smoke, and brimstone is a good allegorical representation of gunpowder. The Ottomans made great use of heavy artillery in their wars with the Greeks of the lower empire.

18. *By these three was the third part of men killed.* That is, By these was great carnage made.

19. *Their power is in their mouth.* From these the destructive balls are projected. *And in their tails,* the breech where the charge of gunpowder is lodged. *Their tails were like unto serpents, and had heads.* If cannons are intended, the description, though allegorical, is plain enough; for brass ordnance especially are frequently thus ornamented, both at their muzzles and at their breech.

20. *Yet repented not.* The commission which these horsemen had was against idolaters; and though multitudes of them were destroyed, yet the residue continued their senseless attachment to dumb idols, and therefore heavier judgments might be expected. These things are supposed to refer to the desolation brought upon the Greek church by the Ottomans, who entirely ruined that church and the Greek empire. The church which was then remaining was the Latin or Western church, which was not at all corrected by the judgments which fell upon the Eastern church, but continued its senseless adoration of angels, saints, relics, and does so to the present day. If therefore God's wrath be kindled against such, this church has much to fear.

21. *Neither repented they of their murders.* Their cruelties towards the genuine followers of God the Albigenses, and Waldenses, and others, against whom they published crusades, and hunted them down, and butchered them in the most shocking manner. The innumerable murders by the horrible Inquisition need not be mentioned. *Their sorceries.* Those who apply this also to the Romish church understand by it the various tricks, sleights of hand, or legerdemain by which they impose on the common people in causing images of Christ to bleed, and the various pretended miracles wrought at the tombs of pretended saints, holy wells, and suchlike. *Fornication.* Giving that honor to various creatures which is due only to the Creator. *Their thefts.* Their exactions and impositions on men for indulgences, pardons. These things may be intended, but it is going too far to say that this is the true interpretation. And yet to express any doubt on this subject is with some little else than heresy. If such men can see these things so clearly in such obscure prophecies, let them be thankful for their sight, and indulgent to those who still sit in darkness.

MATTHEW HENRY

CHAPTER 10

Verses 1–7
Another vision the apostle was favoured with.

I. The person communicating this discovery to John—an angel from heaven, *another mighty angel*.

II. His station and posture: *He set his right foot upon the sea and his left foot upon the earth. And he held in his hand a little book opened*, probably the same that was before sealed, but was now opened, and gradually fulfilled by him.

III. His awful voice (*v.* 3) was echoed by *seven thunders*, seven solemn and terrible ways of discovering the mind of God.

IV. The prohibition given to the apostle, *v.* 4. The apostle was for preserving and publishing everything he saw and heard in these visions, but the time had not yet come.

V. The solemn oath taken by this mighty angel. *He lifted up his hand to heaven, and swore by him that liveth for ever*, that *there shall be time no longer;* either,

1. That there shall be now no longer delay in fulfilling the predictions of this book than till the last angel should sound, *v.* 7. Or, 2. That when this mystery of God is finished time itself shall be no more.

JAMIESON, FAUSSET, BROWN

CHAPTER 10

Vss. 1-11. VISION OF THE LITTLE BOOK. **1. another mighty angel**—as distinguished from the *mighty angel* who asked as to the former and more comprehensive book (ch. 5:2), "Who is worthy to open the book?" **clothed with a cloud**—the emblem of God coming in judgment. **a**—A, B, C. and ℵ read "the"; referring to (ch. 4:3) *the rainbow* already mentioned. **rainbow upon his head**—the emblem of covenant mercy to God's people, amidst judgments on God's foes. Resumed from ch. 4:3 (see *Note* there). **face as . . . the sun**—(ch. 1:16 18:1). **feet as pillars of fire**—(ch. 1:15; Ezek. 1:7). The angel, as representative of Christ, reflects His glory and bears the insignia attributed in ch. 1:15, 16; 4:3, to Christ Himself. The *pillar of fire* by night led Israel through the wilderness, and was the symbol of God's presence. **2. he had**—*Greek,* "Having." **in his hand** in his left hand: as in vs. 5 (*Note*), *he lifts up his right hand to heaven.* **a little book**—a roll *little* in comparison with the "book" (ch. 5:1) which contained the *whole* vast scheme of God's purposes, not to be fully read till the final consummation. This other, a *less book,* contained only a portion which John was now to make his own (vss. 9, 11), and then to use in prophesying to others. **upon the sea . . . earth**—Though the beast with seven heads is about to arise out of the *sea* (ch. 13:1), and the beast with two horns like a lamb (ch. 13:11) out of the *earth,* yet it is but for a time, and that *time shall no longer be* (vss. 6, 7) when once *the seventh trumpet is about to sound;* the angel with his right foot on the sea, and his left on the earth, claims both as God's, and as about soon to be cleared of the usurper and his followers. **3. as . . . lion**—Christ, whom the angel represents, is often so symbolized (ch. 5:5, "the Lion of the tribe of Juda"). **seven thunders**—*Greek,* "*the* seven thunders." They form part of the Apocalyptic symbolism; and so are marked by the article as *well known.* Thus *thunderings* marked the opening of the seventh seal (ch. 8:1, 5); so also at the seventh vial (ch. 16:17, 18). **uttered their**—*Greek,* "*spake their own* voices"; i.e., voices peculiarly *their own,* and not now revealed to men. **4. when**—ℵ reads, "Whatsoever things." But most MSS. support *English Version.* **uttered their voices**—A, B, C, and ℵ omit "their voices." Then translate, "had spoken." **unto me**—omitted by A, B, C, ℵ, and *Syriac.* **Seal up**—the opposite command to ch. 22:20. Even though at *the time of the end* the things *sealed* in Daniel's time were to be revealed, yet not so the voices of these thunders. Though heard by John, they were not to be imparted by him to others in this book of Revelation; so terrible are they that God in mercy withholds them, since "sufficient unto the day is the evil thereof." **5. lifted up his hand**—So A and *Vulgate* read. But B, C, ℵ *Syriac,* and *Coptic,* ". . . his *right* hand." It was customary to lift up the hand towards heaven, appealing to the God of truth, in taking a solemn oath. **6. liveth for ever and ever**—*Greek,* "liveth unto the ages of the ages" (cf. Dan. 12:7). **created heaven . . . earth . . . sea . . .**—This detailed designation of God as the Creator, is appropriate to the subject of the angel's oath, viz., the consummating of the mystery of God (vs. 7), which can surely be brought to pass by the same Almighty power that created all things, and by none else. **that there should be time no longer**—*Greek,* "that time (i.e., an interval of time) no longer shall be." The martyrs shall have no longer a time to wait for the accomplishment of their prayers for the purgation of the earth by the judgments which shall remove their and God's foes from it (ch. 6:11). The appointed *season* or *time* of delay is at an end (the same *Greek* is here as in ch. 6:11, *chronus*). Not as *English Version* implies, Time shall end and eternity begin. **7. But**—connected with vs. 6. "There shall be no longer time (i.e., delay), *but* in the days of the voice of the seventh angel, when he is about to (so the *Greek*) sound his trumpet (so the *Greek*), then (lit., "also"; which conjunction often introduces the consequent member of a sentence) the mystery of God is finished," lit., "has been finished"; the prophet regarding the future as certain as if it were past. **A, C, ℵ, and *Coptic*** read the past tense (*Greek, etelesthee*). B reads, as *English Version,* the future (*Greek, telesthee*). should be finished" (cf. ch. 11:15-18). Sweet consolation to the waiting saints! The seventh trumpet shall be sounded without further delay. **the mystery of God**—the theme of the "little book," and so of the remainder of the Apocalypse. What

ADAM CLARKE

CHAPTER 10

1. *Another mighty angel,* either Christ or His representative; *clothed with a cloud,* a symbol of the divine majesty. *A rainbow was upon his head.* The token of God's merciful covenant with mankind. *His face was as it were the sun.* So intensely glorious that it could not be looked on. *His feet as pillars of fire.* To denote the rapidity and energy of his motions and the stability of his counsels.

2. *A little book open.* Meaning probably some design of God long concealed, but now about to be made manifest. But who knows what it means?

His right foot upon the sea, and his left foot on the earth. To show that he had the command of each, and that his power was universal, all things being under his feet.

3. *Seven thunders.* Seven being a number of perfection, it may here mean many, great, loud, and strong peals of thunder, accompanied with distinct voices; but what was said John was not permitted to reveal, v. 4.

5. *Lifted up his hand to heaven.* As one making an appeal to the Supreme Being.

6. *By him that liveth for ever and ever.* The eternal, self-existent Jehovah, the Maker of all things.

That there should be time no longer. That the gerat counsels relative to the events already predicted should be immediately fulfilled, and that there should be no longer "delay." This has no reference to the day of judgment.

7. *The mystery of God should be finished.* What this mystery refers to, who knows? Nor have we more knowledge concerning the

MATTHEW HENRY

Verses 8–11

I. A strict charge given to the apostle, 1. That he should *go and take the little book* out of the hands of that mighty angel.

2. To eat the book. Before he should publish what he had discovered he must more thoroughly digest the predictions.

II. An account of the taste which this little book would have; at first, while *in his mouth, sweet.* But, when this book of prophecy was more thoroughly digested by the apostle, the contents would be bitter; these were things so awful and terrible, that the foresight of them would not be pleasant.

III. The apostle's discharge of the duty he was called to (*v.* 10): he found the relish to be as was told him.

IV. This book of prophecy was not given him merely to gratify his own curiosity, but to be communicated by him to the world. He is ordered to prepare for another embassy, to convey those declarations of the mind and will of God to all the world, and such should be read and recorded in many languages.

CHAPTER 11

Verses 1, 2

This prophetical passage about measuring the temple is a plain reference to what we find in Ezekiel's vision, Ezek. xl. 3, &c. The design of this measurement seems to be the preservation of it in those times of public danger and calamity that are here foretold.

I. How much was to be measured. 1. *The temple;* the gospel church in general. 2. *The altar.* Whether the church has the true altars. 3. The worshippers too must be measured, whether they make God's glory their end and his word their rule.

JAMIESON, FAUSSET, BROWN

a grand contrast to the "mystery of iniquity—Babylon!" The mystery of God's scheme of redemption, once hidden in God's secret counsel and dimly shadowed forth in types and prophecies, but now more and more clearly revealed according as the Gospel-kingdom develops itself, up to its fullest consummation at the end. **declared to**—*Greek,* "declared the glad tidings to." "The mystery of God" is the *Gospel glad tidings.* The office of *the prophets* is to receive *the glad tidings* from God, in order to *declare* them to others. The final consummation is the great theme of the Gospel announced to, and by, the prophets (cf. Gal. 3:8). **8. spake . . . and said**—So *Syriac* and *Coptic* read. But A, B, C, "(I heard) again speaking with me, and saying" (*Greek, lalousan . . . legousan*). **little book**—So א and B read. But A and C, "the book." **9. I went**—*Greek,* "I went *away.*" John here leaves heaven, his standingpoint of observation heretofore, to be near the angel standing on the earth and sea. **Give**—A, B, C, and *Vulgate* read the infinitive, "Telling him *to give.*" **eat it up**—appropriate its contents so entirely as to be assimilated with (as food), and become part of thyself, so as to impart them the more vividly to others. **belly bitter**—parallel to Ezekiel 2:10, "There was written therein lamentations, and mourning, and woe." **as honey**—(Ps. 19:10 119:103). Honey, sweet to the mouth, sometimes turns into bile in the stomach. The thought that God would be glorified (ch. 11:3-6, 11-18) gave him the sweetest pleasure. Yet, afterwards the *belly,* or carnal natural feeling, was embittered with grief at the prophecy of the coming bitter persecutions of the Church (ch. 11:7-10); cf. John 16:1, 2. The revelation of the secrets of futurity is *sweet* to one at first, but *bitter* and distasteful to our natural man, when we learn the cross which is to be borne before the crown shall be won. John was grieved at the coming apostasy and the sufferings of the Church at the hands of Antichrist. **10. the little book**—So A and C, but B, א, and *Vulgate,* "the book." **was bitter**—*Greek,* "was embittered." **11. he said**—A, B, and *Vulgate* read, "*they say* unto me"; an indefinite expression for "it was said unto me." **Thou must**—The obligation lies upon thee, as the servant of God, to prophesy at His command. **again**—as thou didst already in the previous part of this book of Revelation. **before . . .**—rather as *Greek* (*epilaois*), "*concerning* many peoples . . .", viz., in their relation to the Church.

CHAPTER 11

Vss. 1-19. Measurement of the Temple. The Two Witnesses' Testimony: Their Death, Resurrection, and Ascension: The Earthquake: The Third Woe: The Seventh Trumpet Ushers in Christ's Kingdom. Thanksgiving of the Twenty-four Elders. This eleventh chapter is a compendious summary of, and introduction to, the more detailed prophecies of the same events to come in chs. 12, 13, 14, 15, 16, 17, 18, 19, 20.

1. and the angel stood—omitted in A, *Vulgate,* and *Coptic.* Supported by B and *Syriac.* If it be omitted, the "reed" will, in construction, agree with "saying." So Wordsworth takes it. The *reed,* the canon of Scripture, the measuring reed of the Church, our rule of faith, *speaks.* So in ch. 16:7 *the altar* is personified as *speaking* (cf. *Note* there). The Spirit speaks in the canon of Scripture (the word *canon* is derived from *Hebrew, kaneh,* "a reed," the word here used; and John it was who completed the canon). **the temple**—*Greek, naon* (as distinguished from the *Greek, hieron,* or temple in general), the Holy Place, "*the sanctuary.*" **the altar**—of incense; for it alone was in *the sanctuary* (*Greek, naos*). The measurement of the Holy place seems to me to stand parallel to the sealing of the elect of Israel under the sixth seal. God's elect are symbolized by the sanctuary at Jerusalem (I Cor. 3:16, 17, where the same *Greek* word, *naos,* occurs for "temple," as here). Literal Israel in Jerusalem, and with the temple restored (Ezek. 40: 3, 5, where also the temple is measured with the measuring reed, 41, 42, 43, 44), shall stand at the head of the elect Church. The measuring implies at once the exactness of the proportions of the temple to be restored, and the definite completeness (not one being wanting) of the numbers of the Israelite and of the Gentile elections. The literal temple at Jerusalem shall be the typical forerunner of the heavenly Jerusalem, in which there shall be all temple, and *no* portion exclusively set apart as *temple.* **2. But**—*Greek,* "And." **the court**

ADAM CLARKE

sounding of the seventh angel. On these points there is little agreement among learned men. Whether it mean the destruction of Jerusalem, or the destruction of the papal power, or something else, we know not. And yet with what confidence do men speak of the meaning of these hidden things! *Declared to his servants the prophets.* It is most likely, therefore, that this trumpet belongs to the Jewish state.

8. *Take the little book which is open.* Learn from this angel what should be published to the world.

9. *Take it, and eat it up.* Fully comprehend its meaning; study it thoroughly.

10. *It was in my mouth sweet as honey.* There was in it some pleasing, some unpleasing, intelligence. I read of the consolations and protection of the true worshippers of God, and did rejoice; I read of the persecutions of the Church, and was distressed.

11. *Thou must prophesy again.* You must write, not only for the instruction of the Jews in Palestine, but of those in the different provinces, as well as the heathens and heathen emperors and potentates in general.

CHAPTER 11

1. *And there was given me a reed.* See Ezek. xl. 3, etc.

Measure the temple of God. This must refer to the Temple of Jerusalem; and this is another presumptive evidence that it was yet standing.

MATTHEW HENRY

II. What was not to be measured (*v.* 2): *The court which is without the temple measure it not.* Herod, in the additions made to the temple, built an outer court, and called it *the court of the Gentiles.* This was no part of the temple, and therefore God would have no regard to it.

Both that and the city were trodden under foot for a certain time—*forty and two months.* Those who worship in the outer court are either such as worship in a false manner or with hypocritical hearts. Those who worship in the outer court will be rejected, and only those who worship within the veil accepted.

Verses 3–13

God has reserved to himself his faithful witnesses.

I. The number of these witnesses. 1. It is but small. One witness, when the cause is upon trial, is worth many at other times. 2. It is a sufficient number; for in the mouth of two witnesses every cause shall be established. Christ sent out his disciples two by two, to preach the gospel.

II. The time of their prophesying. *A thousand two hundred and threescore days;* that is (as many think), to the period of the reign of antichrist.

III. Their habit: they prophesy in sackcloth, as those that are deeply affected with the low and distressed state of the churches.

IV. How they were supported: they stood before the God of the whole earth. He made them to be like Zerubbabel and Joshua, the two olive-trees and candlestick in the vision of Zechariah, *ch.* iv. 2, &c.

V. Their security and defence during the time of their prophesying, *v.* 5. Some think this alludes to Elias's calling for fire from heaven, to consume the captains and their companies that came to seize him, 2 Kings i. 12, and restraining the dews of heaven, shutting heaven up, that no rain should fall for many days, as God did at the prayers of Elias, 1 Kings xvii. 1.

JAMIESON, FAUSSET, BROWN

. . . without—all outside *the Holy Place* (vs. 1). **leave out**—of thy measurement, lit.,"cast out"; reckon as unhallowed. **it**—emphatic. *It* is not to be measured; whereas the Holy Place is. **given**—by God's appointment. **unto the Gentiles**—In the wider sense, there are meant here "the times of the Gentiles," wherein Jerusalem is "*trodden* down of the Gentiles," as the parallel, Luke 21:24, proves; for the same word is used here [*Greek, patein*], tread under foot." Cf. also Psalm 79:1; Isaiah 63:18. **forty . . . two months**—(ch. 13:5). The same period as Daniel's "time, times, and half" (ch. 12:14); and vs. 3, and ch. 12:6, the woman a fugitive in the wilderness "a thousand two hundred and threescore days." In the wider sense, we may either adopt the year-day theory of 1260 years (on which, and the papal rule of 1260 years, see my *Notes,* Dan. 7:25; 8:14; 12-11), or rather, regard the 2300 days (Dan. 8:14), 1335 days (Dan. 12:11, 12). 1290 days, and 1260 days, as symbolical of the long period of the Gentile times, whether dating from the subversion of the Jewish theocracy at the Babylonian captivity (the *kingdom* having been never since restored to Israel), or from the last destruction of Jerusalem under Titus, and extending to the restoration of the theocracy at the coming of Him "whose right it is"; the different epochs marked by the 2300, 1335, 1290, and 1260 days, will not be fully cleared up till the grand consummation; but, meanwhile, our duty and privilege urge us to investigate them. The three and a half, in a word, marks the time in which the earthly rules over the heavenly kingdom. **3. I will give**—*power*—There is no "power" in the *Greek,* so that "give" must mean "give *commission,*" or some such word. **my two witnesses**—*Greek,* "*the* two witnesses of me." The article implies that the two were well known at least to John. **prophesy**—preach under the inspiration of the Spirit, denouncing judgments against the apostate. They are described by symbol as "the two olive trees" and "the two candlesticks," or *lamp-stands,* "standing before the God of the earth." The reference is to Zechariah 4:3, 12, where two *individuals* are meant, Joshua and Zerubbabel, who ministered to the Jewish Church, just as the two olive trees emptied the oil out of themselves into the bowl of the candlestick. So in the final apostasy God will raise up two inspired witnesses to minister encouragement to the afflicted, though sealed, remnant. As *two* candlesticks are mentioned in vs. 4, but only *one* in Zechariah 4, I think the twofold Church, Jewish and Gentile, may be meant by the two candlesticks represented by the two witnesses: just as in ch. 7 there are described first the sealed of Israel, then those of all nations. De Burgh thinks Elijah and Moses will again appear, as Malachi 4: 5, 6 seems to imply (cf. Matt. 17:11; Acts 3:21). Moses and Elijah appeared with Christ at the Transfiguration, which foreshadowed His coming millennial kingdom. An objection to this interpretation is that those blessed departed servants of God would have to submit to death (vss. 7, 8), and this in Moses' case a *second* time, which Hebrews 9:27 denies. **in sackcloth**—the garment of prophets, especially when calling people to mortification of their sins, and to repentance. Their very exterior aspect accorded with their teachings: so Elijah, and John who came in His spirit and power. The *sackcloth* of the witnesses is a catch word linking this episode under the sixth trumpet, with the *sun black as sackcloth* (in righteous retribution on the apostates who rejected God's witnesses) under the sixth seal (ch. 6:12). **4. standing before the God of the earth**—A, B, C, *Vulgate, Syriac, Coptic,* and Andreas read "Lord" for "God": so Zechariah 4: 14. Ministering to (Luke 1:19), and as in the sight of Him, who, though now so widely disowned on *earth,* is its rightful King, and shall at last be openly recognized as such (vs. 15). The phrase alludes to Zechariah 4:10, 14, "the two anointed ones that stand by the Lord of the whole earth." The article "the" marks this allusion. They are "the two candlesticks," not that they are the Church, the *one* candlestick, but as its representative *light-bearers* (*Greek,* Phil. 2:15, *phosteres*), and ministering for its encouragement in a time of apostasy. **5. will hurt**—*Greek,* "wishes," or "desires to hurt them." **fire . . . devoureth**—(Cf. Jer. 5:14; 23:29). **out of their mouth**—not literally, but God makes their inspired denunciations of judgment to come to pass and *devour* their enemies. **if any man will hurt them**—twice repeated, to mark the *immediate certainty* of the accomplishment. **in this manner**—so in like manner as he tries to hurt them

ADAM CLARKE

2. *But the court . . . is given unto the Gentiles.* **The measuring of the Temple probably refers to its approaching destruction, and the termination of the whole Levitical service; and this we find was to be done by the Gentiles (Romans), who were to tread it down 42 months; i.e., just 3½ years, or 1,260 days. This must be a symbolical period.**

3. *My two witnesses.* **This is extremely obscure; the conjectures of interpreters are as unsatisfactory as they are endless on this point. Those who wish to be amused or bewildered may have recourse both to ancients and moderns on this subject.**

4. *These are the two olive trees.* **Mentioned in Zech. iv. 14, which there represent Zerubbabel and Joshua, the high priest. The whole account seems taken from Zech. iv. 1-14. Whether the prophet and the apostle mean the same things by these emblems, we know not.**

5. *Fire proceedeth out of their mouth.* **That is, they are commissioned to denounce the judgments of God against all who would attempt to prevent them from proceeding in their ministry.**

MATTHEW HENRY

VI. The slaying of the witnesses. To make their testimony more strong, they must seal it with their blood. The time when they should be killed: *When they have finished their testimony*. They are immortal, till their work be done. The enemy that should overcome and slay them—*the beast that ascendeth out of the bottomless pit*.

Antichrist should make war against them with open force and violence; and God would permit his enemies to prevail against his witnesses for a time.

The barbarous usage of these slain witnesses; the malice of their enemies, pursued even their dead bodies. They would not allow them a quiet grave; their bodies were cast out in the open street.

Their death was a matter of mirth and joy to the antichristian world, *v*. 10.

VII. The resurrection of these witnesses. The time of their rising again (*v*. 11). God's witnesses may be slain, but they shall rise again. God will revive his work, when it seems to be dead in the world. *The Spirit of life from God entered into them, and they stood upon their feet.* God put not only life, but courage into them. The effect of their resurrection upon their enemies: *Great fear fell upon them.* A persecuting spirit, though cruel, is not a courageous, but a cowardly spirit.

JAMIESON, FAUSSET, BROWN

(cf. ch. 13:10). Retribution in kind. **6. These . . . power**—*Greek,* "authorized power." **it rain not**—*Greek, huetos brechee,* "rain shower not," lit., "*moisten* not" (the earth). **smite . . . with all plagues**—*Greek,* "with (lit., 'in') every plague." **7. finished their testimony**—The same verb is used of Paul's ending his ministry by a violent death. **the beast that ascended out of the bottomless pit**—*Greek,* "the wild beast . . . the abyss." This beast was not mentioned before, yet he is introduced as "*the* beast," because he had already been described by Daniel (7:3, 11), and he is fully so in the subsequent part of the Apocalypse, viz., ch. 13:1; 17:8.

make war against them—alluding to Daniel 7:21, where the same is said of *the little horn* that sprang up among the ten horns on the fourth beast. **8. dead bodies**—So *Vulgate, Syriac,* and ANDREAS. But A, B, C, the oldest MSS., and *Coptic* read the singular, "dead body." The two fallen in one cause are considered as *one.* **the great city**—*eight* times in the Revelation elsewhere used of BABYLON (ch. 14:8; 16:19; 17:18; 18:10, 16, 18, 19, 21). In ch. 21:10 (*English Version* as to *the new Jerusalem*), the oldest MSS. omit "the great" before *city,* so that it forms no exception. It must, therefore, have an anticipatory reference to the mystical Babylon. **which**—*Greek,* "the which," viz., *the* city *which.* **spiritually**—in a spiritual sense. **Sodom**—The very term applied by Isaiah 1:10 to apostate Jerusalem (cf. Ezek. 16:48). **Egypt**—the nation which the Jews' besetting sin was to lean upon. **where . . . Lord was crucified**—This identifies the city as Jerusalem, though the Lord was crucified *outside* of the city. The difficulty is, how can Jerusalem be called "the great city," i.e., Babylon? By her becoming the world's capital of idolatrous apostasy, such as Babylon originally was, and then Rome has been; just as she is here called also "Sodom and Egypt." **also our**—A, B, C, ORIGEN, ANDREAS, and others read, "also *their.*" Where *their Lord, also,* as well as they, was slain.

9. they—rather, "(*some*) of the peoples." **peoples**—*Greek,* "peoples." **kindreds**—*Greek,* "tribes"; all save the elect (whence it is not said, *The peoples . . .,* but [some] *of the peoples . . .;* or, *some of the peoples . . .* may refer to *those of the nations . . ., who at the time shall hold possession of Palestine and Jerusalem*). **shall see**—So *Vulgate, Syriac,* and *Coptic.* But A, B, C, and ANDREAS, the present, "see," or rather (*Greek, blepousin*), "look upon." The prophetic present. **dead bodies**—So *Vulgate, Syriac,* and ANDREAS. But A, B, C, and *Coptic,* singular, as in vs. 8, "dead body." Three and a half days answer to the three and a half years (*Notes,* vss. 2, 3), the half of seven, the full and perfect number. **shall not suffer**—so B, *Syriac, Coptic,* and ANDREAS. But A, C, and *Vulgate* read, "do not suffer." **in graves**—so *Vulgate* and PRIMASIUS. But B, C, *Syriac, Coptic,* and ANDREAS, *singular;* translate, "into a sepulchre," lit., "a monument." Accordingly, in righteous retribution in kind, *the flesh* of the Antichristian hosts is not buried, but given to *all the fowls in mid-heaven* to eat (ch. 19:17, 18, 21). **10. they that dwell upon . . . earth**—those who belong to the earth, as its citizens, not to heaven (ch. 3:10; 8:13; 12:12; 13:8). **shall**—so *Vulgate, Syriac,* and *Coptic.* But A, B, and C read *the present;* cf. *Note,* vs. 9, on "shall not suffer." **rejoice over them**—The Antichristianity of the last days shall probably be under the name of philosophical enlightenment and civilization, but really man's deification of himself. Fanaticism shall lead Antichrist's followers to exult in having at last seemingly silenced in death their Christian rebukers.

send gifts one to another—as was usual at a joyous festival. **tormented them**—viz., with the plagues which they had power to inflict (vss. 5, 6); also, by their testimony against the earthly. **11.** Translate as *Greek,* "After *the* three days. . . ." **the Spirit of life**—the same which breathed *life* into Israel's dry bones, Ezekiel 37:10, 11 (where see my *Notes*), "Breath *came into* them." The passage here, as there, is closely connected with *Israel's* restoration as a nation to political and religious life. Cf. also concerning the same, Hosea 6:2, where Ephraim says, "After two days will He revive us; in the *third day* He will *raise* us *up,* and we shall *live* in His sight." **into**—so B and *Vulgate.* But A reads (*Greek, en autois*), "(so as to be) IN them." **stood upon their feet**—the very words in Ezekiel 37:10, which proves the allusion to be to *Israel's* resurrection, in contrast to "the times of the Gentiles" wherein these "tread under foot the holy city." **great fear**—such as fell on the soldiers guarding Christ's tomb at His resurrection (Matt. 28:4), when also there was a great earthquake (vs. 2). **saw**

ADAM CLARKE

6. *These have power to shut heaven.* As Elijah did, 1 Kings xvii and xviii. *To turn them to blood.* As Moses did, Exodus vii. They shall have power to afflict the land with plagues, similar to those which were inflicted on the Egyptians.

7. *The beast that ascendeth out of the bottomless pit.* This may be what is called "antichrist," some power that is opposed to genuine Christianity. But what or whence, except from the bottomless pit, i.e., under the influence and appointment of the devil, we cannot tell; nor do we know by what name this power or being should be called. The conjectures concerning the "two witnesses" and the "beast" have been sufficiently multiplied. If the whole passage, as some think, refers to the persecution raised by the Jews against the Christians, then some Jewish power or person is the beast from the bottomless pit. If it refer to the early ages of Christianity, then the beast may be one of the persecuting heathen emperors. If it refer to a later age of Christianity, then the beast may be the papal power, and the Albigenses and Waldenses the two witnesses, which were nearly extinguished by the horrible persecutions raised up against them by the church of Rome. Whatever may be here intended, the earth has not yet covered their blood.

8. *The great city.* Some say Rome, which may be spiritually called *Sodom* for its abominations, *Egypt* for its tyrannous cruelty, and the place *where also our Lord was crucified* because of its persecution of the members of Christ; but Jerusalem itself may be intended. All these things I must leave to others.

9. *Shall not suffer their dead bodies to be put in graves.* They shall be treated with the greatest barbarity. Refusal of burial to the dead was allowed to be the sum of brutality and cruelty.

10. *Shall send gifts.* This was a custom in days of public rejoicing. They sent gifts to each other, and gave portions to the poor. See Esther ix. 19, 22.

11. *They stood upon their feet.* Were restored to their primitive state.

MATTHEW HENRY

VIII. The ascension of the witnesses into heaven, *v.* 12, 13. 1. Their ascension. To this honour they did not attempt to ascend, till God called them, and said, *Come up hither*. The Lord's witnesses must wait for their advancement, till God calls them.

2. The consequences of their ascension—a mighty shock and convulsion and the fall of *a tenth part of the city*.

The fear of God fell upon many. They gave glory to the God of heaven. Thus, when God's work and witnesses revive, the devil's work and witnesses fall before him.

Verses 14–19

What he before expected he now heard—the seventh angel sounding.

I. Loud and joyful acclamations of the saints and angels in heaven. They rose from their seats, *and fell upon their faces, and worshipped God*. They thankfully recognise the right of our God and Saviour to rule and reign over all the world, *v.* 15.

JAMIESON, FAUSSET, BROWN

–*Greek,* "beheld." **12. they**–so A, C, and *Vulgate*. But B, *Coptic, Syriac,* and ANDREAS read, "I heard." **a cloud**–*Greek,* "the cloud"; which may be merely the generic expression for what we are familiar with, as we say "*the* clouds." But I prefer taking the article as definitely alluding to THE cloud which received Jesus at His ascension, Acts 1:9 (where there is no article, as there is no allusion to a previous cloud, such as there is here). As they resembled Him in their three and a half years' witnessing, their three and a half days lying in death (though not for exactly the same time, nor put in a tomb as He was), so also in their ascension is the translation and transfiguration of the sealed of Israel (ch. 7), and the elect of all nations, caught up out of the reach of the Antichristian foe. In ch. 14:14, 15, 16, He is represented as sitting on a *white cloud*. **their enemies beheld them**–and were thus openly convicted by God for their unbelief and persecution of His servants; unlike Elijah's ascension formerly, in the sight of friends only.

13. "In that same (lit. 'the') hour." **great earthquake**–answering to the "great earthquake" under the sixth seal, just at the approach of the Lord (ch. 6:12).

tenth part of the city fell–i.e., of "the great city" (ch. 16:19; Zech. 14:2). Ten is the number of the *world kingdoms* (ch. 17:10-12), and the *beast's horns* (ch. 13:1), and the *dragon's* (ch. 12:3). Thus, in the Church-historical view, it is hereby implied that one of the ten apostate world kingdoms fall. But in the narrower view a tenth of Jerusalem under Antichrist falls. The nine-tenths remain and become when purified the center of Christ's earthly kingdom. **of men**–*Greek,* "names of men." The men are as accurately enumerated as if their names were given.

the remnant–consisting of the Israelite inhabitants not slain. Their conversion forms a blessed contrast to ch. 16:9; and above, ch. 9:20, 21. These repenting (Zech. 12:10-14; 13:1), become in the flesh the loyal *subjects* of Christ reigning over the earth with His transfigured saints. **gave glory to the God of heaven**–which while apostates, and worshipping the beast's image, they had not done. **God of heaven**–The apostates of the last days, in pretended scientific enlightenment, recognize no *heavenly* power, but only the natural forces in the earth which come under their observation. His receiving up into *heaven* the two witnesses who had *power* during their time on earth *to shut heaven* from raining (vs. 6), constrained His and their enemies who witnessed it, to acknowledge *the God of heaven,* to be *God of the earth* (vs. 4). As in vs. 4 He declared Himself to be *God of the earth* by His two witnesses, so now He proves Himself to be *God of heaven* also. **14. The second woe**–that under the sixth trumpet (ch. 9:12-21), including also the prophecy, ch. 11:1-13: *Woe* to the world, joy to the faithful, as *their redemption draweth nigh*. **the third woe cometh quickly**–It is not mentioned in detail for the present, until first there is given a sketch of the history of the origination, suffering, and faithfulness of the Church in a time of apostasy and persecution. **15. sounded**–with his trumpet. Evidently "the LAST trumpet." *Six* is close to *seven,* but does not reach it. The world judgments are complete in *six,* but by the fulfilment of *seven* the world kingdoms become Christ's. **kingdoms**–A, B, C, and *Vulgate* read the singular, "The *kingdom* (sovereignty) *of* (over) the world is our Lord's and His Christ's." There is no good authority for *English Version* reading. The *kingdoms* of the world give way to *the kingdom of* (over) *the world* exercised by Christ. The earth kingdoms are many: His shall be *one*. The appellation "Christ," *the Anointed,* is here, where His *kingdom* is mentioned appropriately for the first time used in Revelation. For it is equivalent to KING. Though priests and prophets also were *anointed,* yet this term is peculiarly applied to Him as King, insomuch that "the Lord's anointed" is His title as KING, in places where He is distinguished from the priests. The glorified Son of man shall rule mankind by His transfigured Church in heaven, and by His people Israel on earth: Israel shall be the priestly mediator of blessings to the whole world, realizing them first. **he**–not emphatic in the *Greek*. **shall reign for ever and ever**–*Greek,* "unto the ages of the ages." Here begins the millennial reign, the consummation of "the mystery of God" (ch. 10:7). **16. before God**–B and *Syriac* read, "before *the throne of* God." But A, C, *Vulgate,* and *Coptic* read as *English Version*. **seats**–*Greek,* "thrones." **17. thanks**–for the answer to our prayers (ch. 6:10, 11) in *destroying them which destroy the earth* (vs. 18),

ADAM CLARKE

12. *They ascended up to heaven.* Enjoyed a state of great peace and happiness.

13. *A great earthquake.* Violent commotions among the persecutors, and revolutions of states. *Slain of men seven thousand.* Many perished in these popular commotions.

The remnant were affrighted. Seeing the hand of God's judgments so remarkably stretched out. *Gave glory.* Received the pure doctrines of the gospel, and glorified God for His judgments and their conversion.

14. *The second woe is past.* That which took place under the sixth trumpet, and has been already described. *The third woe cometh.* Is about to be described under the seventh trumpet, which the angel is now prepared to sound. Of the three woes which were denounced, chap. viii. 13, the first is described in chap. ix. 1-12, the second in chap. ix. 13-21. These woes are supposed by many learned men to refer to the destruction of Jerusalem: the first woe—the seditions among the Jews themselves; the second woe—the besieging of the city by the Romans; the third woe—the taking and sacking of the city, and burning the Temple. This was the greatest of all the woes, as in it the city and Temple were destroyed, and nearly a million men lost their lives.

15. *There were great voices in heaven.* All the heavenly host—angels and redeemed human spirits—joined together to magnify God, that He had utterly discomfited His enemies and rendered His friends glorious. This will be truly the case when the kingdoms of this world become the kingdoms of God and of His Christ. But when shall this be? Some say what is meant by these words has already taken place in the destruction of the Jewish state and sending the gospel throughout the Gentile world. Others say that it refers to the millennium and to the consummation of all things.

16. *The four and twenty elders.* The representatives of the universal Church of Christ. See on chap. v. 8-10.

MATTHEW HENRY

They give him thanks because he had taken to him his great power. They rejoice that this his reign shall never end. None shall ever wrest the sceptre out of his hand.

II. Angry resentments in the world at these actings of the power of God (*v.* 18): *The nations were angry;* their hearts rose up against God. They fretted against God, and so increased their guilt and hastened their destruction.

III. The opening of the temple of God in heaven. What was seen there: the *ark of God's testament.* This was in the holy of holies; in this ark the tables of the law were kept. As before Josiah's time the law of God had been lost, but was then found, so in the reign of antichrist God's law was laid aside. Now the scriptures are opened, now they are brought to the view of all. What was heard and felt there: *Lightnings, voices, thunderings, an earthquake, and great hail.* By terrible things in righteousness God would answer those prayers that were presented in his holy temple, now opened.

JAMIESON, FAUSSET, BROWN

thereby preparing the way for setting up the kingdom of Thyself and Thy saints. **and art to come**—omitted in A, B, C, *Vulgate, Syriac,* CYPRIAN, and ANDREAS. The consummation having actually come, they do not address Him as they did when it was still future, "Thou that art to come." Cf. vs. 18, "is come." From the sounding of the seventh trumpet He is to His people JAH, the ever present Lord, WHO IS, more peculiarly than JEHOVAH "who is, was, and *is to come.*" **taken to thee thy great power**—"to Thee" is not in the *Greek.* Christ *takes* to Him the kingdom as His own of *right.* **18. the nations were angry**—alluding to Psalm 99:1, LXX, "The Lord is become King: let the peoples become *angry.*" Translate, as the *Greek* is the same. "The nations were *angered,* and Thy *anger* is come." How petty man's impotent *anger,* standing here side by side with that of the omnipotent God! **dead . . . be judged**—proving that this seventh trumpet is at the end of all things, when the judgment on Christ's foes and the reward of His saints, long prayed for by His saints, shall take place. **the prophets**—as, for instance, the two *prophesying witnesses* (vs. 3), and those who have showed them kindness for Christ's sake. Jesus shall come to effect by His presence that which we have looked for long, but vainly, in His absence, and by other means. **destroy them which destroy the earth**—Retribution in kind (cf. ch. 16:6; Luke 19:27). Daniel 7:14-18, my *Notes.* **19. temple**—the sanctuary or *Holy place* (*Greek, naos*), not the whole *temple* (*Greek, hieron*). **opened in heaven**—A and C read the article, "the temple of God *which is* in heaven, was opened." **the ark of his testament**—or ". . . His *covenant.*" As in the first verse the earthly sanctuary was *measured,* so here its heavenly antitype is laid open, and the antitype above to the *ark of the covenant* in the Holiest Place below is seen, the pledge of God's faithfulness to His covenant in saving His people and punishing their and His enemies. Thus this forms a fit close to the series of trumpet judgments and an introduction to the episode (chs. 12 and 13) as to His faithfulness to His Church. Here first His secret place, the heavenly sanctuary, is opened for the assurance of His people; and thence proceed His judgments in their behalf (ch. 14:15, 17; 15:5; 16:17), which the great company in heaven laud as "true and righteous." This then is parallel to the scene at the heavenly altar, at the close of the seals and opening of the trumpets (ch. 8:3),and at the close of the episode (chs. 12-15) and opening of the vials (ch. 15:7, 8).

ADAM CLARKE

17. *O Lord God Almighty, which art.* This gives a proper view of God in His eternity; all times are here comprehended, the present, the past, and the future. This is the infinitude of God.

Hast taken to thee. Thou hast exercised that power which Thou ever hast; and Thou hast broken the power of Thy enemies, and exalted Thy Church.

18. *The nations were angry.* Were enraged against Thy gospel and determined to destroy it. *Thy wrath is come.* The time to avenge Thy servants and to destroy all Thy enemies. *The time of the dead, that they should be judged.* The word "to judge" is often used in the sense of "to avenge." The dead, here, may mean those who were slain for the testimony of Jesus, and the judging is the avenging of their blood. *Give reward unto thy servants.* Who have been faithful unto death. *The prophets*—the faithful teachers in the Church; *the saints*—the Christians. *And them that fear thy name.* All Thy sincere followers. *Destroy them which destroy the earth.* All the authors, fomenters, and encouragers of bloody wars.

19. *The temple of God was opened in heaven.* The true worship of God was established and performed in the Christian Church; this is the true temple, that at Jerusalem being destroyed. *And there were lightnings, and voices, and thunderings, and an earthquake, and great hail.* These great commotions were intended to introduce the following vision; for the twelfth chapter is properly a continuation of the eleventh, and should be read in strict connection with it.

MATTHEW HENRY

CHAPTER 12

Verses 1–11

I. The attempts of Satan to prevent the increase of the church.

1. The church is represented, (1) As a *woman,* the spouse of Christ, and the mother of the saints. (2) As *clothed with the sun.* Having put on Christ, who is *the Sun of righteousness,* she shines in his rays. (3) As having *the moon under her feet.* Her heart and hope are not set upon sublunary things, but on the things that are in heaven, where her head is.

(4) As having on her head *a crown of twelve stars,* that is, the doctrine of the gospel preached by the twelve apostles. (5) As in travail and now in pain, to bring forth a holy progeny to Christ.

JAMIESON, FAUSSET, BROWN

CHAPTER 12

Vss. 1-17. VISION OF THE WOMAN, HER CHILD, AND THE PERSECUTING DRAGON. **1.** This episode (chs. 12, 13, 14, and 15) describes *in detail* the persecution of Israel and the elect Church by the beast, which had been *summarily* noticed, ch. 11:7-10, and the triumph of the faithful, and torment of the unfaithful. **great**—in size and significance. **wonder**—*Greek,* "sign": significant of momentous truths. **in heaven**—not merely the sky, but the *heaven* beyond just mentioned, ch. 11:19; cf. vss. 7-9. **woman clothed with the sun . . . moon under her feet**—the Church, Israel first, and then the Gentile Church; clothed with Christ, "the Sun of righteousness." "Fair as the moon, clear as the sun." Clothed with the Sun, the Church is the bearer of divine supernatural light in the world. So the seven churches (i.e., the Church universal, the woman) are represented as lightbearing *candlesticks* (ch. 1). On the other hand, the *moon,* though standing above the sea and earth, is altogether connected with them and is an earthly light: *sea, earth,* and *moon* represent the worldly element, in opposition to the kingdom of God—heaven, the sun. The moon cannot disperse the darkness and change it into day: thus she represents the world religion (heathenism) in relation to the supernatural world. The Church has the moon, therefore, under her feet; but the stars, as heavenly lights, on her head. The devil directs his efforts against the stars, the angels of the churches, about hereafter to shine for ever. The twelve stars, the crown around her head, are the twelve tribes of Israel [AUBERLEN]. **2. pained**—*Greek,* "tormented" (*basanizomene*). DE BURGH explains this of the bringing in of the first-begotten into the world AGAIN, when Israel shall at last welcome Him, and when "the man-child shall rule all nations with the rod of iron." But there is a plain contrast between the *painful travailing* of the woman here,

ADAM CLARKE

CHAPTER 12

1. *There appeared a great wonder in heaven; a woman clothed with the sun.* That the woman here represents the true Church of Christ most commentators are agreed. In other parts of the Apocalypse, the pure Church of Christ is evidently portrayed by a woman (19:7; 21:9). That the Christian Church is meant will appear also from her being *clothed with the sun,* a striking emblem of Jesus Christ, the Sun of righteousness, the light and glory of the Church. *The moon under her feet.* Bishop Newton understands this of the Jewish typical worship; and indeed the Mosaic system of rites and ceremonies could not have been better represented, for it was the shadow of good things to come. The moon is the less light, ruling over the night, and deriving all its illumination from the sun; in like manner the Jewish dispensation was the bright moonlight night of the world, and possessed a portion of the glorious light of the Gospel. At the rising of the sun the night is ended, and the lunar light no longer necessary, as the sun which enlightens her shines full upon the earth; exactly in the same way has the whole Jewish system of types and shadows been superseded by the birth, life, crucifixion, death, resurrection, ascension, and intercession of Jesus Christ. *A crown of twelve stars.* A very significant representation of the twelve apostles, who were the first founders of the Christian Church, and by whom the Gospel was preached in great part of the Roman empire with astonishing success.

2. *And she being with child cried, travailing in birth.* This, when taken in connection with the following verses, is a striking figure of the great persecution which the Church of Christ should suffer under the heathen Roman emperors, but more especially of that long and most dreadful one under Diocletian. The woman is represented as *being with child,* to show

MATTHEW HENRY

2. How the grand enemy of the church is represented. (1) A dragon for strength and terror—a red dragon for fierceness and cruelty. (2) As *having seven heads.* It is probable that pagan Rome is here meant. (3) As having *ten horns,* divided into ten provinces, as the Roman empire was by Augustus Cæsar. (4) As having *seven crowns upon his head,* which is afterwards expounded to be seven kings, *ch.* xvii. 10.

(5) As drawing with his tail a *third part of the stars in heaven* and *casting them down to the earth.*

(6) As standing *before the woman, to devour her child as soon as it should be born,* very vigilant to crush the Christian religion in its birth.

II. The unsuccessfulness of these attempts. She was safely delivered of a *man-child* (*v.* 5). Care was taken of this child. The Christian religion has been from its infancy the special care of *the great God and our Saviour Jesus Christ.*

Care was taken of the mother as well as of the child, *v.* 6. Furthermore her obscure and private state was for a limited time.

JAMIESON, FAUSSET, BROWN

and Christ's second coming to the Jewish Church, the believing remnant of Israel, *"Before she travailed* she brought forth . . . a MAN-CHILD," i.e., almost *without travail-pangs,* she receives (at His second advent), as if born to her, Messiah and a numerous seed. **3. appeared**—"was seen." **wonder**—*Greek; semeion* "sign." **red**—So A and *Vulgate* read. But B, C, and *Coptic* read, "of fire." In either case, the *color* of the dragon implies his fiery rage as a *murderer from the beginning.* His representative, *the beast,* corresponds, *having seven heads and ten horns* (the number of horns on the fourth beast of Daniel 7:7; ch. 13:1. But there, *ten* crowns are on the *ten horns* (for before the end, the fourth empire is divided into *ten* kingdoms); here, *seven* crowns (rather, "diadems," *Greek, diademata,* not *stephanoi,* "wreaths") are *upon his seven heads.* In Daniel 7 the Antichristian powers up to Christ's second coming are represented by four beasts, which have among them *seven* heads, i.e., the first, second, and fourth beasts having *one* head each, the third, *four* heads. His universal dominion as prince of this fallen world is implied by the *seven diadems* (contrast the "many diadems on Christ's head," ch. 19:12, when coming to destroy him and his), the caricature of the *seven* Spirits of God. His worldly instruments of power are marked by the *ten horns,* ten being the number of the world. It marks his self-contradictions that he and the beast bear both the number *seven* (the divine number) and *ten* (the world number). **4. drew**—*Greek,* present, "draweth," "drags down." His *dragging down the stars* with *his tail* (lashed back and forward in his fury) implies his persuading to apostatize, like himself, and to become earthy, those angels and also once eminent human teachers who had formerly been heavenly (cf. vs. 1; ch. 1:20; Isa. 14:12). **stood**—"stands" [ALFORD]: perfect, *Greek, hesteken.* **ready to be delivered**—"about to bring forth." **for to devour . . .**—"that when she brought forth, he might devour her child." So the dragon, represented by his agent Pharaoh (a name common to all the Egyptian kings, and meaning, according to some, *crocodile,* a reptile like the dragon, and made an Egyptian idol), was ready to devour Israel's *males* at the birth of the nation. Antitypically the true Israel, Jesus, when born, was sought for destruction by Herod, who slew all the *males* in and around Bethlehem. **5. man-child**—*Greek,* "a son, a male." On the deep significance of this term, cf. *Notes,* vss. 1, 2. **rule**—*Greek, poimainein,* "tend as a shepherd"; (see *Note,* ch. 2:27). **rod of iron**—A rod is for long-continued obstinacy until they submit themselves to obedience [BENGEL]: ch. 2:27; Psalm 2:9, which passages prove the Lord Jesus to be meant. Any interpretation which ignores this must be wrong. The *male son's* birth cannot be the origin of the Christian state (Christianity triumphing over heathenism under Constantine), which was not a divine child of the woman, but had many impure worldly elements. In a secondary sense, *the ascending of the witnesses up to heaven* answers to Christ's own ascension, "caught up unto God, and unto His throne": as also His ruling the nations with a rod of iron is to be shared in by believers (ch. 2:27). **6. woman fled**—Mary's flight with Jesus into Egypt is a type of this. **where she hath**—So C reads. But A and B add "there." **a place**—that portion of the heathen world which has received Christianity professedly, viz., mainly the fourth kingdom, having its seat in the modern Babylon, Rome, implying that *all* the heathen world would not be Christianized in the present order of things. **prepared of God**—lit., "*from* God." Not by human caprice or fear, but by the determined counsel and foreknowledge of God, the *woman,* the Church, *fled into the wilderness.* **they should feed her**—*Greek,* "nourish her." Indefinite for, "she should be fed." The heathen world, *the wilderness,* could not nourish the Church, but only afford her an outward shelter. Here, as in Daniel 4:26, and elsewhere, the third person plural refers to *the heavenly powers* who minister from God *nourishment* to the Church. As Israel had its time of first bridal love, on its first going out of Egypt into the wilderness, so the Christian Church's *wilderness*-time of *first love* was the apostolic age, when it was separate from the *Egypt* of this world, having no city here, but seeking one to come; having only a *place in the wilderness prepared of God* (vss. 6, 14). **thousand two hundred and threescore days**—anticipatory of vs. 14, where the persecution which caused her to flee is mentioned in its place: ch. 13 gives the details of the persecution. It is most unlikely that the transi-

ADAM CLARKE

that the time would speedily arrive when God's patient forbearance with the heathen would be terminated, and that a deliverer should arise in the Christian world who would execute the Divine vengeance upon paganism.

3. *There appeared another wonder—a great red dragon.* The dragon here is a symbol, not of the Roman empire in general, but of the heathen Roman empire. But what is a dragon? An entirely fabulous beast of antiquity, consequently, in this respect, a most proper emblem of the heathen worship, which consisted in paying adoration to numerous imaginary beings, termed gods, goddesses, etc. *Having seven heads.* As the dragon is an emblem of the heathen Roman power, its heads must denote heathen forms of government (17:10). *And ten horns.* That these ten horns signify as many kingdoms is evident from the seventh chapter of Daniel, where the angel, speaking of the fourth beast, says, that "the ten horns out of this kingdom are ten kings that shall arise"; and in this view of the passage many commentators are agreed, who also admit that the ten kingdoms are to be met with "amid the broken pieces of the Roman empire." And it is evident that nothing less than the dismemberment of the Roman empire, and its division into ten independent kingdoms, can be intended by the angel's interpretation just quoted. *And seven crowns upon his head.* In the seven Roman forms of government already enumerated, heathenism has been the crowning or dominant religion.

4. *And his tail drew the third part of the stars of heaven.* The *tail* of the dragon is the heathen Roman power in its seventh or last form of government, the imperial power; and is not to be restricted to the last heathen Roman emperors. The heathen imperial power is said to draw *the third part of the stars of heaven.* As the Christian Church has upon her head a crown of twelve stars, which signifies that she is under the guidance of the twelve apostles, so has the dragon also his stars or ministers. The stars therefore which the dragon draws with his tail must represent the whole body of pagan priests, who were the stars or lights of the heathen world. The religious world in the time of St. John was divided into three grand branches: the Christian world, the Jewish world, and the heathen world. Consequently, as a dragon is an emblem of a civil power supporting a religion founded in fable, it necessarily follows that the stars or ministers of the Jews and Christians cannot be numbered among those which he draws with his tail, as they were not the advocates of his idolatry, and consequently formed no part of the pagan world, though they were in subjection in secular matters to the pagan Roman empire.

5. *And she brought forth a man child.* The Christian Church, when her full time came, obtained a deliverer. *To rule all nations.* The heathen Roman empire. *With a rod of iron.* A strong figure to denote the very great restraint that should be put upon paganism, so that it should not be able longer to persecute the Christian Church. The *man child* mentioned in this verse is the dynasty of Christian emperors, beginning with Constantine's public acknowledgment of his belief in the divinity of the Christian religion, which happened in the latter part of A.D. 312, after the defeat of the Emperor Maxentius.

6. *And the woman fled into the wilderness.* The account of the woman's flying into the wilderness immediately follows that of her child being caught up to the throne of God, to denote the great and rapid increase of heresies in the Christian Church after the time that Christianity was made the religion of the empire. *Where she hath a place prepared of God.* See on verse 14.

MATTHEW HENRY

III. The attempts of the dragon not only proved unsuccessful against the church, but fatal to his own interests (*v.* 7). *Heaven* will espouse the quarrel of the church.

1. The seat of this war—*in heaven*, in the church, which is *the kingdom of heaven* on earth, under the care of heaven.

2. The parties: Christ, the great Angel of the covenant, and his faithful followers; and Satan and all his instruments. The strength of the church lies in having the Lord Jesus for the captain of their salvation.

3. The success of the battle: *The dragon and his angels fought and prevailed not.* The victory fell to Christ and his church, and the dragon and his angels were not only conquered, but cast out.

4. The triumphant song that was composed and used on this occasion, *v.* 10, 11. The conqueror is adored.

The salvation and strength of the church are all to be ascribed to the king and head of the church. The conquered enemy is described.

By his malice he appeared before God as an adversary to the church. Though he hates the presence of God, yet he is willing to appear there to accuse the people of God.

JAMIESON, FAUSSET, BROWN

tion should be made from the birth of Christ to the last Antichrist, without notice of the long intervening Church-historical period. Probably the 1260 days, or periods, representing this long interval, are RECAPITULATED on a shorter scale analogically during the last Antichrist's short reign. They are equivalent to three and a half years, which, as half of the divine number *seven,* symbolize the seeming victory of the world over the Church. As they include the whole *Gentile times* of *Jerusalem's being trodden of the Gentiles,* they must be much longer than 1260 years; for, above several centuries more than 1260 years have elapsed since Jerusalem fell. **7.** In Job 1 and 2, Satan appears among the sons of God, presenting himself before God in heaven, as the accuser of the saints: again in Zechariah 3:1, 2. **there was**—*Greek,* "there came to pass," or "arose." **war in heaven**—What a seeming contradiction in terms, yet true! Contrast the blessed result of Christ's triumph, Luke 19:38, "peace in heaven." Colossians 1:20, "made peace through the blood of His cross, by Him to *reconcile* all things unto Himself; whether . . . things in earth, or things *in heaven.*" **Michael and his angels . . . the dragon . . . and his angels**—It was fittingly ordered that, as the rebellion arose from unfaithful angels and their leader, so they should be encountered and overcome by faithful angels and their archangel, in heaven. On earth they are fittingly encountered, and shall be overcome, as represented by the beast and false prophet, by the Son of man and His armies of human saints (ch. 19:14-21). The conflict in heaven, though judicially decided already against Satan from the time of Christ's resurrection and ascension, receives its actual completion in the execution of judgment by the angels who cast out Satan from heaven. From Christ's ascension he has no standing-ground judicially against the believing elect. Luke 10:18, "I beheld (in the earnest of the future full fulfilment given in the subjection of the demons to the disciples) Satan as lightning fall from heaven." As Michael fought before with Satan about the body of the mediator of the old covenant (Jude 9), so now the mediator of the new covenant, by offering His sinless body in sacrifice, arms Michael with power to renew and finish the conflict by a complete victory. **against**—A, B, and C read, "with." **8. prevailed not**—A and *Coptic* read, "*He* prevailed not." But B and C read as *English Version.* **neither**—A, B, and C read, "not even" (*Greek, oude*): a climax. Not only did they not prevail, but *not even their place was found any more in heaven.* **9. that old serpent**—alluding to Genesis 3:1, 4. **Devil**—the *Greek,* for "accuser," or "slanderer." **Satan** the *Hebrew* for "adversary," especially in a court of justice. The twofold designation, Greek and Hebrew, marks the twofold objects of his accusations and temptations, the elect Gentiles and the elect Jews. **world**—*Greek,* "habitable world." **10. Now**—*Now* that Satan has been cast out of heaven. Primarily fulfilled in part at Jesus' resurrection and ascension, when He said (Matthew 28:18), "All power [*Greek, exousia,* 'authority,' as here; see below] is given unto Me in heaven and in earth"; connected with vs. 5, "Her child was *caught up unto God and to His throne.*" In the ulterior sense, it refers to the eve of Christ's second coming, when Israel is about to be restored as mother-church of Christendom, Satan, who had resisted her restoration on the ground of her unworthiness, having been cast out by the instrumentality of Michael, Israel's angelic *prince* (*Note,* vs. 7). Thus this is parallel, and the necessary preliminary to the glorious event similarly expressed, ch. 11:15, "The kingdom of this world is become (the very word here, *Greek egeneto,* 'is come,' 'hath come to pass') our Lord's and His Christ's," the result of Israel's resuming her place. **salvation . . .**—*Greek, "the salvation* (viz., fully, finally, and victoriously accomplished, Heb. 9:28; cf. Luke 3:6, yet future; hence, not till *now* do the blessed raise the fullest hallelujah for *salvation* to the Lamb, ch. 7:10; 19:1) *the power* (*Greek, dunamis*), and *the authority (Greek, exousia; legitimate power; see above)* of His Christ." **accused them before our God day and night**—Hence the need that the oppressed Church, *God's own elect* (like the widow, *continually coming,* so as even to *weary* the unjust judge), should *cry day and night unto Him.* **11. they**—emphatic in the *Greek.* "They" in particular. They and they alone. They were the persons who overcame. **overcame**—(Rom. 8:33, 34, 37; 16:20). **him**—(I John 2:14, 15). It is the same *victory* (a peculiarly Johannean phrase) over Satan and the world which the Gospel of John describes in the life of Jesus, his

ADAM CLARKE

7. *And there was war in heaven.* As *heaven* means here the throne of the Roman empire, the war in heaven consequently alludes to the breaking out of civil commotions among the governors of this empire. *Michael and his angels fought against the dragon.* Michael was the man child which the woman brought forth, as is evident from the context, and therefore signifies, as has been shown already, the dynasty of Christian Roman emperors. This dynasty is represented by Michael, because his is "the great prince which standeth for the children of God's people" (Dan. 12:1). *And the dragon fought and his angels.* Or ministers.

8. *And prevailed not.* Against the cause of Christianity. *Neither was their place found any more in heaven.* The advocates of the heathen idolatry were prevented from having any further share in the government of the empire. The wonderful success of Constantine over all his enemies, and his final triumph over Licinius, correspond exactly to the symbolical language in this verse.

9. *And the great dragon was cast out.* If by the *dragon* be meant the *devil,* then we are necessarily led to this conclusion, that the great apostate spirit is a monster, having seven heads and ten horns; and also that he has a *tail,* with which he drags after him the third part of the stars of heaven. The appelations, *old serpent, devil,* and *Satan,* must, therefore, be understood figuratively. The heathen power is called *that old serpent which deceived the whole world,* from its subtlety against the Christians, and its causing the whole Roman world, as far as it was in its power to embrace the absurdities of paganism.

10. *And I heard a loud voice, saying, Now is come salvation.* This is a song of triumph of the Christian Church over the heathen idolatry, and is very expressive of the great joy of the Christians upon this most stupendous event. The loud voice of triumph is said to be heard in heaven, to show that the Christian religion was now exalted to the heaven or throne of the Roman empire. "It is very remarkable," as Bishop Newton observes, "that Constantine himself, and the Christians of his time, describe his conquests under the image of a *dragon,* as if they had understood that this prophecy had received its accomplishment in him.

11. *And they overcame him by the blood of the Lamb.* Here is given the reason why the followers of Christ prevailed at this time against all their adversaries. It was because they fought against the dragon in the armor of God.

MATTHEW HENRY

How the victory was gained. The servants of God overcame Satan, (1) *By the blood of the Lamb.* (2) *By the word of their testimony*—by a resolute powerful preaching of the everlasting gospel.

By their courage and patience in sufferings; *they loved not their lives unto the death;* their love to their own lives was overcome by stronger affections of another nature.

Verses 12–17

I. The warning given of the distress that should fall upon the inhabitants of the world in general. Being defeated in his designs against the church, he is resolved to give all the disturbance he can to the world in general, *v.* 12.

II. His second attempt upon the church now in the wilderness, *v.* 13.

1. The care that God had taken of his church. He had conveyed her as on eagles' wings, into a place of safety provided for her.

2. The continual malice of the dragon against the church. Her obscurity could not altogether protect her. 3. The seasonable help provided in this dangerous juncture, *v.* 16.

JAMIESON, FAUSSET, BROWN

Epistle in the life of each believer, and his Apocalypse in the life of the Church. **by . . .**—*Greek* (*dia to haima;* accusative, not genitive, as *English Version* would require, cf. Heb. 9:12), "*on account of* (on the ground of) the blood of the Lamb"; "because of . . ."; on account of and by virtue of its having been shed. Had that blood not been shed, Satan's accusations would have been unanswerable; as it is, that blood meets every charge. **by the word of their testimony**—*Greek,* "on account of the word of their testimony." On the ground of their faithful testimony, even unto death, they are constituted victors. Their testimony evinced their victory over him by virtue of the blood of the Lamb. Hereby they confess themselves worshippers of the slain Lamb and overcome the beast, Satan's representative; an anticipation of ch. 15:2, "them that had gotten the victory over the beast" (cf. ch. 13:15, 16). **unto**—*Greek, achri,* "even as far as." They carried their not-love of life *as far as even unto* death. **12. Therefore**—because Satan is cast out of heaven (vs. 9). **dwell**—lit., "tabernacle." Not only angels and the souls of the just with God, but also the faithful militant on earth, who already in spirit tabernacle in heaven, having their home and citizenship there, *rejoice* that Satan is cast out of their home. **the inhabiters of**—So ANDREAS reads. But A, B, and C omit. The words probably, were inserted from ch. 8:13. **is come down**—rather as *Greek, catebee,* "is *gone* down"; John regarding the heaven as his standing-point of view whence he looks down on the earth. **unto you**—*earth and sea,* with their inhabitants; those who lean upon, and essentially belong to, the *earth* (contrast John 3:7, *Margin,* with John 3:31; 8:23; Phil. 3:19, end; I John 4:5) and its *sea*-like troubled politics. Furious at his expulsion from heaven, and knowing that his time on earth is short until he shall be cast down lower, when Christ shall come to set up *His* kingdom (ch. 20:1, 2), Satan concentrates all his power to destroy as many souls as he can. Though no longer able to accuse the elect in heaven, he can tempt and persecute on earth. **short time**—*Greek, kairon,* "season": *opportunity* for his assaults. **13.** Resuming from vs. 6 the thread of the discourse, which had been interrupted by the episode, vss. 7-12 (giving in the invisible world the ground of the corresponding conflict between light and darkness in the visible world), this verse accounts for her *flight into the wilderness* (vs. 6). **14. were given**—by God's determinate appointment, not by human chances (Acts 9:11). **two**—*Greek, "the* two wings of *the* great eagle." Alluding to Exodus 19:4: proving that the Old Testament Church, as well as the New Testament Church, is included in "the woman." All believers are included (Isa. 40:30, 31). *The great eagle* is the world power; in Ezekiel 17:3, 7, *Babylon* and *Egypt:* in early Church history, *Rome,* whose standard was the *eagle,* turned by God's providence from being hostile into a protector of the Christian Church. As "wings" express remote parts of the earth, the *two* wings may here mean the east and west divisions of the Roman empire. **wilderness**—the land of the heathen, the Gentiles: in contrast to Canaan, the *pleasant* and *glorious land.* God dwells in the glorious land; demons (the rulers of the heathen world, ch. 9:20; I Cor. 10:20), in the wilderness. Heathendom, in its essential nature, being without God, is a desolate *wilderness.* Thus, the woman's flight into the wilderness is the passing of the kingdom of God from the Jews to be among the Gentiles (typified by Mary's flight with her child from Judea into Egypt). **her place**—the chief seat of the then world empire, Rome. The Acts of the Apostles describe the passing of the Church from Jerusalem to Rome. The Roman protection was the eagle wing which often shielded Paul, the great instrument of this transmigration, and Christianity, from Jewish opponents who stirred up the heathen mobs. Israel was in the wilderness forty years, and had forty-two stages in her journey, so the Church for *forty-two* months, three and a half years or *times* [lit., *seasons,* used for *years* in Hellenistic Greek (MŒRIS, the Atticist), *Greek, kairous,* Dan. 7:25; 12:7], or 1260 days (vs. 6) between the overthrow of Jerusalem and the coming again of Christ, shall be a wilderness sojourner before she reaches her millennial rest (answering to Canaan of old). **15, 16. flood**—*Greek,* "river" (cf. Exod. 2:3; Matt. 2:20; and especially Exod. 14). The *flood,* or river, is the stream of Germanic tribes which, pouring on Rome, threatened to destroy Christianity. But *the earth helped the woman,* by *swallowing up the flood.* The earth, as contradistinguished from water, is the world

ADAM CLARKE

By the blood of the Lamb—by proclaiming salvation to sinners at the throne of grace for the conversion of the heathen world.

And by the word of their testimony. By constantly testifying against the errors and follies of mankind. *And they loved not their lives unto the death.* They regarded not their present temporal estate, but even gladly delivered up their lives to the fury of their persecutors, and thus sealed the truth of what they spake with their blood.

12. *Therefore rejoice, ye heavens, and ye that dwell in them.* Let the Christians, who are now partakers of the present temporal prosperity, and advanced to places of trust in the empire, praise and magnify the Lord who has thus so signally interfered in their behalf. But it is added, *Woe to the inhabiters of the earth, and of the sea! for the devil is come down unto you.* By *the inhabiters of the earth* are meant the people in subjection to the Roman empire; and by the *sea,* those parts of the Roman dominions appear to be intended that were reduced to a state of anarchy by the incursion of the barbarous nations. *Having great wrath, because he knoweth that he hath but a short time.* The Christian religion, the pagan party see with great regret, is rapidly gaining ground everywhere; and, if not timely checked, must soon brave all opposition.

13. *And when the dragon saw that he was cast unto the earth.* When the heathen party saw that they were no longer supported by the civil power, *he persecuted the woman which brought forth the man child.* The heathens persecuted the Christian Church in the behalf of which Divine Providence had raised up a dynasty of Christian Roman emperors.

14. *And to the woman were given two wings of a great eagle.* The great eagle here mentioned is an emblem of the Roman empire in general, and therefore differs from the dragon, which is a symbol of the heathen Roman empire in particular. The Roman power is called an eagle from its legionary standard. The two wings of the great eagle refer to the two grand independent divisions of the Roman empire, which took place January 17, A.D. 395, and were given to the woman, Christianity being the established religion of both empires. *That she might fly into the wilderness, into her place.* The meaning therefore of verses 6 and 14, when taken in connection with their respective contexts, is, that the woman began to make rapid strides towards the desert almost immediately after her elevation to the heaven or throne of the Roman empire, and in the course of her flight was furnished with the wings of the great eagle that she might fly into that place prepared of God, where she should be fed a thousand two hundred and threescore days. The one thousand two hundred and threescore days must be understood symbolically, and consequently denote as many natural years. The wilderness into which the woman flies is the Greek and Latin worlds, for she is conveyed into her place by means of the two wings of the great eagle.

15. *And the serpent cast out of his mouth water as a flood.* The water here evidently means *great multitudes of nations and peoples* (17:15). This water, then, which the dragon cast out of his mouth, must be an inundation of heathen barbarous nations upon the Roman empire; and the purpose which the dragon has in view by this inundation is, that he might cause the woman, or Christian Church, *to be carried away of the flood.* Entirely swept away from the face of the earth.

MATTHEW HENRY

4. His malice against the woman pushes him on to *make war with the remnant of her seed.* Fidelity will expose men still, to the end of the world, when *the last enemy shall be destroyed.*

CHAPTER 13

Verses 1-10

An account of the first beast. He seemed to the apostle to stand upon *the sea-shore.* Whence this beast came—*out of the sea.*

The form and shape of this beast. In some part of this description there seems to be an allusion to Daniel's vision of the four beasts, which represented the four monarchies, Dan. vii. 1-3, &c. The seven heads and the ten horns seem to design its several powers; the ten crowns, its tributary princes;

the word blasphemy on its forehead proclaims its direct enmity to the glory of God.

The source and spring of his authority—*the dragon.* He was set up by the devil, and the devil lent him all the assistance he could. A dangerous wound given him, and yet unexpectedly healed, *v.* 3.

JAMIESON, FAUSSET, BROWN

consolidated and civilized. The German masses were brought under the influence of Roman civilization and Christianity [AUBERLEN]. **17. wroth with**—*Greek,* "*at.*" **went**—*Greek,* "went *away.*" **the remnant of her seed**—distinct in some sense from the woman herself. Satan's first effort was to root out the Christian Church, so that there should be no visible profession of Christianity. Foiled in this, he *wars* (ch. 11:7; 13:7) against the invisible Church, viz., "those who keep the commandments of God, and have the testimony of Jesus" (A, B, and C omit "Christ"). These are "the remnant," or *rest of her seed,* as distinguished from her seed, "the man-child" (vs. 5), on one hand, and from mere professors on the other.

CHAPTER 13

VSS. 1-18. VISION OF THE BEAST THAT CAME OUT OF THE SEA: THE SECOND BEAST, OUT OF THE EARTH, EXERCISING THE POWER OF THE FIRST BEAST, AND CAUSING THE EARTH TO WORSHIP HIM. **1. I stood** So B, ℵ, and *Coptic* read. But A, C, *Vulgate,* and *Syriac,* "*He* stood." Standing on the sand of the *sea,* HE *gave* his power to the beast that rose out of the sea. **upon the sand of the sea**—where *the four winds* were to be seen *striving upon the great sea* (Dan. 7:2). **beast**—*Greek,* "wild beast." Man becomes "brutish" when he severs himself from God, the archetype and true ideal, in whose image he was first made, which ideal is realized by the man Christ Jesus. **out of the sea**—(Dan. 7:3; cf. my *Note,* ch. 8:8)—out of the troubled waves of *peoples, multitudes, nations, and tongues.* The *earth* (vs. 11), on the other hand, means the consolidated, ordered world of nations, with its culture and learning. **seven heads and ten horns**—A, B, and C transpose, "ten horns and seven heads." The ten horns are now put first (contrast the order, ch. 12:3) because they are crowned. They shall not be so till the last stage of the fourth kingdom (the Roman), which shall continue until the fifth kingdom, Christ's, shall supplant it and destroy it utterly; this last stage is marked by the *ten toes* of the two feet of the image in Daniel 2. The *seven* implies the world power setting up itself as God, and caricaturing the *seven* Spirits of God; yet its true character as God-opposed is detected by the number *ten* accompanying the seven. Dragon and beast both wear crowns, but the former on the heads, the latter on the horns (ch. 12:3; 13: 1). Therefore, both heads and horns refer to kingdoms; cf. ch. 17:7, 10, 12, "kings" representing the kingdoms whose heads they are.

The seven heads are the seven world monarchies, Egypt, Assyria, Babylon, Persia, Greece, Rome, the Germanic empire, under the last of which we live [AUBERLEN], and which devolved for a time on Napoleon, after Francis, emperor of Germany and king of Rome, had resigned the title in 1806. **crowns**—*Greek,* "diadems." **name of blasphemy**—So C, *Coptic,* and ANDREAS. A, B, and *Vulgate* read, "names . . ." viz., a name on each of the heads; blasphemously arrogating attributes belonging to God alone (cf. *Note,* ch. 17:3). A characteristic of the *little horn* in Daniel 7:8, 20, 21; II Thessalonians 2:4. **2. leopard . . . bear . . . lion**—This beast unites in itself the God-opposed characteristics of the three preceding kingdoms, resembling respectively the *leopard, bear,* and *lion.* It rises up out *of the sea,* as Daniel's four beasts, and has *ten horns,* as Daniel's fourth beast, *and seven heads,* as Daniel's four beasts had in all, viz., one on the first, one on the second, four on the third, and one on the fourth. Thus it represents comprehensively in one figure *the world power* (which in Daniel is represented by four) *of all times and places,* not merely of one period and one locality, viewed as opposed to God; just as the *woman* is the Church of all ages. This view is favored also by the fact, that the beast is the vicarious representative of Satan, who similarly has *seven heads* and *ten horns:* a general description of his universal power in all ages and places of the world. Satan appears as a serpent, as being the archetype of the beast nature (ch. 12:9). **3. one of**—lit., "from among." **wounded . . . healed**—twice again repeated emphatically (vs. 12, 14); cf. ch. 17:8, 11, "the beast that *was, and is not, and shall ascend* out of the bottomless pit" (cf. vs. 11 below); the Germanic empire, the seventh head (revived in *the eighth*), as yet future in John's time (ch. 17:10). Contrast the change whereby Nebuchadnezzar, being humbled from his selfdeifying pride, was converted from his *beast*-like form and character to MAN's form and

ADAM CLARKE

17. *And the dragon was wroth with the woman.* The heathen party, foiled in their subtle attempt to destroy Christianity, were greatly enraged, and endeavored to excite the hatred of the multitude against the religion of Jesus. *Went to make war with the remnant of her seed.* The dragon departed into the wilderness, whither the woman had fled; and in another form commenced a new species of persecution, directed only against *the remnant of her seed, who keep the commandments of God, and have the testimony of Jesus Christ.*

CHAPTER 13

1. *And I stood upon the sand of the sea, and saw a beast rise up out of the sea.* An earthly belligerent power is evidently designed. And the comparison is peculiarly appropriate; for as several species of wild beasts carry on perpetual warfare with the animal world, so most governments, influenced by ambition, promote discord and depopulation. This beast is said to *rise up out of the sea,* in which particular it corresponds with the four beasts of Daniel; the *sea* is therefore the symbol of a *great multitude of nations,* as has already been proven; and the meaning is, that every mighty empire is raised upon the ruins of a great number of nations, which it has successfully contended against and incorporated with its dominions. *Having seven heads and ten horns, and upon his horns ten crowns.* The beast here described is the Latin empire, which supported the Romish or Latin Church; for it has *upon his horns ten crowns,* i.e., is an empire composed of ten distinct monarchies in the interest of the Latin Church.

And upon his heads the name of blasphemy. Blasphemy, in Scripture, signifies impious speaking when applied to God, and injurious speaking when directed against our neighbor. A name of blasphemy is the prostitution of a sacred name to an unholy purpose. A name of blasphemy, or blasphemous appellation, is said to be upon all the seven heads of the beast. The heads signify the seven electorates of the German empire, and also seven forms of Latin government. The name of blasphemy will consequently be found upon the seven electorates of Germany. This, therefore, can be no other than that which was common, not only to the electorates but also to the whole empire of Germany, "The Sacred (or Holy) Roman Empire." Here is a sacred appellation blasphemed by its application to the principal power of the beast. No kingdom can properly be called holy but that of Jesus; therefore it would be blasphemy to unite this epithet with any other power.

2. *And the beast which I saw was like unto a leopard.* This similitude of the beast to a leopard appears to be an allusion to the third beast of Daniel, which is well known to represent the empire of the Greeks. The Latin empire greatly resembled the modern empire of the Greeks. Though in its general appearance it resembles a leopard, yet differs from it in having feet like those *of a bear.* The second beast of Daniel was likened to a bear, and there can be no doubt that the kingdom of the Medes and Persians was intended; and it is very properly likened to this animal, because it was one of the most inhuman governments that ever existed, and a *bear* is the well-known Scripture emblem of cruelty.

3. *And I saw one of his heads as it were wounded to death.* The head that was wounded to death can be no other than the seventh draconic head, which was the sixth head of the beast, viz., the imperial power; for "this head," as Bishop Newton observes, "was, as it were, wounded to death when the Roman empire was overturned by the northern nations, and an end was put to the very name of emperor in Momyllus Augustulus." *And his deadly wound was healed.* This was effected by Charlemagne, who with his successors as-

MATTHEW HENRY

The honour and worship paid to this infernal monster: *All the world wondered after the beast.* They paid honour and subjection to the devil and his instruments, and thought there was no power able to withstand them.

How he exercised his infernal power and policy: He had *a mouth, speaking great things, and blasphemies; and he made war with the saints, and overcame them.* And *against those that dwell in heaven.* The malice of the devil shows itself against heaven and the blessed inhabitants of heaven. These are above the reach of his power. All he can do is to blaspheme them; but the saints on earth are more exposed to his cruelty, and he sometimes is permitted to triumph over them. The limitation of the devil's power and success. He is limited in point of time (*v.* 5).

He is also limited as to the persons that he shall entirely subject to his will. It will be only those *whose names are not written in the Lamb's book of life.*

Those who have killed with the sword shall themselves fall by the sword (*v.* 10), and those who led the people of God into captivity shall themselves be made captives.

JAMIESON, FAUSSET, BROWN

true position towards God; symbolized by his *eagle wings being plucked,* and himself made to stand upon his feet as a *man* (Dan. 7:4). Here, on the contrary, the *beast's* head is not changed into a *human* head, but receives a deadly wound, i.e., the world kingdom which this head represents does not truly turn to God, but for a time its God-opposed character remains paralyzed ("as it were slain"; the very words marking the beast's outward resemblance to the Lamb, "as it were slain," *Notes,* ch. 5:6. Cf. also the second beast's resemblance to the *Lamb,* vs. 11). Though seemingly *slain* (*Greek* for "wounded"), it remains the beast still, to rise again in another form (vs. 11). The first six heads were heathenish, Egypt, Assyria, Babylon, Persia, Greece, Rome; the new seventh world power (the pagan German hordes pouring down on Christianized Rome), whereby Satan had hoped to stifle Christianity (ch. 11:15, 16), became itself Christianized (answering to the beast's, *as it were, deadly wound: it was slain,* and *it is not,* ch. 17:11). Its *ascent out of the bottomless pit answers* to the *healing of its deadly wound* (ch. 17:8). No essential change is noticed in Daniel as effected by Christianity upon the fourth kingdom; it remains essentially God-opposed to the last. The beast, *healed* of its temporary and external *wound,* now returns, not only from the *sea,* but from the *bottomless pit,* whence it draws new Antichristian strength of hell (vss. 3, 11, 12, 14; ch. 11:7; 17:8). **wondered after**—followed with wondering gaze. **4. which gave**—A, B, C, *Vulgate, Syriac,* and ANDREAS read, "*because* he gave." **power**—*Greek,* "*the authority*" which it had; *its* authority. **Who is like unto the beast?**—The very language appropriated to *God,* Exodus 15:11 (whence, in the *Hebrew,* the Maccabees took their name; the opponents of the Old Testament Antichrist, Antiochus); Psalm 35:10; 71:19; 113:5; Micah 7:18; *blasphemously* (vss. 1, 5) assigned to the beast. It is a parody of the name "Michael" (cf. ch. 12:7), meaning, "Who is like unto God?" **5. blasphemies**—So ANDREAS reads. B reads "blasphemy." A, "blasphemous things" (cf. Dan. 7:8; 11:25). **power**—"authority"; *legitimate power* (*Greek, exousia*). **to continue**—*Greek, poiesai,* "to act," or "work." B reads, "to make *war*" (cf. vs. 4). But A, C, *Vulgate, Syriac,* and ANDREAS omit "war." **forty . . . two months**—(*Notes,* ch. 11:2, 3; 12:6). **6. opened . . . mouth**—The usual formula in the case of a set speech, or series of speeches. Vss. 6, 7 expand vs. 5. **blasphemy**—So B and ANDREAS. A and C read "blasphemies." **and them**—So *Vulgate, Coptic,* ANDREAS, and PRIMASIUS read. A and C omit "and": "them that dwell (lit., 'tabernacle') in heaven," mean not only angels and the departed souls of the righteous, but believers on earth who have their citizenship in heaven, and whose true life is hidden from the Antichristian persecutor in *the secret of God's tabernacle. Note,* ch. 12:12; John 3:7. **7. power**—*Greek,* "authority." **all kindreds . . . tongues . . . nations**—*Greek,* "every tribe . . . tongue . . . nation." A, B, C, *Vulgate, Syriac,* ANDREAS, and PRIMASIUS add "and people," after "tribe" or "kindred." **8. all that dwell upon the earth**—being of earth earthy; in contrast to "them that dwell in heaven." **whose names are not written**—A, B, C, *Syriac, Coptic,* and ANDREAS read singular, "(every one) whose (*Greek, hou;* but B, *Greek, hon,* plural) *name* is not written." **Lamb slain from the foundation of the world**—The *Greek* order of words favors this translation. He was *slain* in the Father's eternal counsels: cf. I Peter 1:19, 20, virtually parallel. The other way of connecting the words is, "Written from the foundation of the world in the book of life of the Lamb slain." So in ch. 17:8. The elect. The former is in the *Greek* more obvious and simple.

9. A general exhortation. Christ's own words of monition calling solemn attention. **10. He that leadeth into captivity**—A, B, C, and *Vulgate* read, "if any one (be) for captivity." **shall go into captivity**—*Greek* present, "goeth into captivity." Cf. Jeremiah 15:2, which is alluded to here. ℵ, B, and C read simply, "he goeth away," and omit "into captivity." But A and *Vulgate* support the words. **he that killeth with the sword, must be killed with the sword**—So B and C read. But A reads, "if any (is for) being (lit., 'to be') killed. . . ." As of old, so now, those to be persecuted by the beast in various ways, have their trials severally appointed them by God's fixed counsel. *English Version* is quite a different sense, viz., a warning to the persecutors that they shall be punished with retribution in kind. **Here**—"Herein": in bearing their appointed sufferings lies the *patient endurance . . . of the saints.* This is to be the motto and

ADAM CLARKE

sumed all the marks of the ancient emperors of the west. *And all the world wondered after the beast.* As the original word signifies *earth,* and not *world* as in our translation, the Latin word, which is the *earth* of the beast, is here intended; and the meaning of the passage consequently is that the whole body of the Roman Catholics were affected with great astonishment at the mighty sway of the Latin empire, considering it as a great and holy power.

4. *And they worshiped the dragon.* Not only the dragon or revived western empire was worshiped; the beast, the whole Latin empire, is a partaker in the adoration. The manner in which it is worshiped consists in the subjects of it—*Saying, Who is like unto the beast?* Is it not the only holy power in the universe? Is it possible for any person not a subject of it to be saved?

5. *And there was given unto him a mouth speaking great things.* That is, there was given to the rulers of the Latin empire, who are the mouth of the beast, power to assume great and pompous titles, indicative of their mighty sway over many subjugated countries, and also to utter against their opponents the most terrible edicts.

6. *And he opened his mouth in blasphemy against God, to blaspheme his name.* The Latin empire is here represented as a blasphemous power. *And them that dwell in heaven.* By *heaven* is here meant the throne of God, and not the throne of the beast, because it is against God the beast blasphemes. This must therefore allude to his impious adoration of the saints and angels, whose residence is in heaven. He blasphemes against God by paying that adoration to the celestial inhabitants which belong to God alone.

8. *And all that dwell upon the earth shall worship him, whose names are not written in the book of life of the Lamb.* The *earth* here is the Latin world, as has been observed before in similar cases. The meaning therefore is, that all the corrupt part of mankind who are inhabitants of the Latin world shall submit to the religion of the empire, except, as Bishop Newton expresses it, "those faithful few whose names, as citizens of heaven, were enrolled in the registers of life." *Slain from the foundation of the world.* That is, of the Christian world; for this has been shown to be the meaning of *all kindreds, and tongues, and nations.* The years of the crucifixion is properly the commencement of Christianity, as the apostles then first began to promulgate the religion of Christ with the Holy Ghost sent down from heaven. But as Jesus Christ was in the Divine purpose appointed from the foundation of the world to redeem man by his blood, he therefore is, in a very eminent sense, the Lamb slain from the foundation of the world, i.e., from the creation.

MATTHEW HENRY

Verses 11–18

I. The form and shape of this second beast: *He had two horns like a lamb*, but a mouth that *spoke like the dragon.* All agree that this must be some great impostor, who, under a pretence of religion, shall deceive the souls of men.

II. The power which he exercises (*v.* 12) to draw men off from worshipping the true God to worship those who by nature are no gods.

III. The methods by which this second beast carried on his designs. Lying wonders, pretended miracles, by which they should be deceived. They would pretend to bring down fire from heaven. God sometimes permits his enemies to do things that seem very wonderful, and by which unwary persons may be deluded.

JAMIESON, FAUSSET, BROWN

watchword of the elect during the period of the world kingdom. As the first beast is to be met by *patience* and *faith* (vs. 10), the second beast must be opposed by true *wisdom* (vs. 18). **11. another beast**—"the false prophet." **out of the earth**—out of society civilized, consolidated, and ordered, but still, with all its culture, of earth earthy: as distinguished from "the sea," the troubled agitations of various peoples out of which the world power and its several kingdoms have emerged. As the first beast was like the Lamb in being, *as it were, wounded to death,* so the second is like the Lamb in having *two lamb-like horns* (its essential difference from the Lamb is marked by its having TWO, but the Lamb SEVEN horns, ch. 5:6). The former paganism of the world power, seeming to be wounded to death by Christianity, revives. In its second beast-form it is Christianized heathendom ministering to the former, and having earthly culture and learning to recommend it. The second beast's, or false prophet's rise, coincides in time with the healing of the beast's deadly wound and its revival (ch. 13:12-14). Its *manifold* character is marked by the Lord (Matt. 24:11, 24), "*Many* false prophets shall rise," where He is speaking of the last days. As the former beast corresponds to the first four beasts of Daniel, so the second beast, or the false prophet, to the little horn starting up among the ten horns of the fourth beast. **12. power**—*Greek,* "authority." **before him**—"in his presence"; as ministering to, and upholding him. "The non-existence of the beast embraces the whole Germanic Christian period. The healing of the wound and return of the beast is represented [in regard to its *final* Antichristian manifestation though including also, meanwhile, its healing and return under Popery, which is baptized heathenism] in that principle which, since 1789, has manifested itself in beast-like outbreaks" [AUBERLEN]. **which dwell therein**—the earthly-minded. The Church becomes the *harlot:* the world's political power, the Antichristian *beast;* the world's wisdom and civilization, *the false prophet.* But in the last days all these God-opposed powers which have succeeded each other shall *co-operate,* and raise each other to the most terrible and intense power of their nature: *the false prophet causes men to worship the beast, and the beast carries the harlot.* These three forms of apostasy are reducible to two: *the apostate Church* and *the apostate world, pseudo-Christianity* and *Antichristianity,* the harlot and the beast; for the false prophet is also a beast; and the two beasts, as different manifestations of the same beast-like principle, stand in contradistinction to the harlot, and are finally judged together, whereas separate judgment falls on the harlot [AUBERLEN]. **deadly wound**—*Greek,* "wound of death." **13. wonders**—*Greek,* "signs." **so that**—so *great* that. **maketh fire**—*Greek,* "maketh even fire." This is the very miracle which the two witnesses perform, and which Elijah long ago had performed; this the beast from the bottomless pit, or the false prophet, mimics. Not merely tricks, but miracles of a demoniacal kind, and by demon aid, like those of the Egyptian magicians, shall be wrought, most calculated to deceive; wrought "after the working (*Greek,* 'energy') of Satan." **14. deceiveth them that dwell on the earth**—the earthly-minded, but not *the elect.* Even a miracle is not enough to warrant belief in a professed revelation unless that revelation be in harmony with God's already revealed will. **by the means of those miracles**—rather as *Greek,* "*on account of* (because of; in consequence of) those miracles." **which he had power to do**—*Greek,* "which were given him to do." **in the sight of the beast**—"before him" (vs. 12). **which**—A, B, and C read, "who"; marking, perhaps, a personal Antichrist. **had**—So B and ANDREAS read. But A, C, and *Vulgate* read, "hath." **15. he had power**—*Greek,* "it was given to him." **to give life**—*Greek,* "breath," or "spirit." **image**—Nebuchadnezzar set up in Dura a golden *image* to be worshipped, probably of himself; for his dream had been interpreted, "Thou art this head of gold"; the three Hebrews who refused to worship the image were cast into a burning furnace. All this typifies the last apostasy. **speak**—"False doctrine will give a spiritual, philosophical appearance to the foolish apotheosis of the creaturely personified by Antichrist" [AUBERLEN]. JEROME, on Daniel 7, says, Antichrist shall be "one of the human race in whom the whole of Satan shall dwell bodily." Rome's *speaking* images and winking pictures of the Virgin Mary and the saints are an earnest of the future demoniacal miracles of the false prophet in making the beast's or Antichrist's image to speak. **16. to receive a mark**—lit., "that

ADAM CLARKE

11. *And I beheld another beast coming up out of the earth.* As a *beast* has already been shown to be the symbol of a kingdom or empire, the rising up of this second beast must consequently represent the rising up of another empire. This beast comes up *out of the earth;* therefore it is totally different from the preceding, which rose up out of the *sea. Earth* here means the Latin world, for this word has been shown to import this already in several instances; the rising up of the beast out of the *earth* must, consequently, represent the springing up of some power out of a state of subjection to the Latin empire: therefore the beast, here called *another beast*, is another Latin empire. This beast is the spiritual Latin empire, or, in other words, the Romish hierarchy; for with no other power can the prophetic description yet to be examined be shown to accord. *And he had two horns.* Two horns must represent two kingdoms; for if horns of a beast mean kingdoms in one part of the Apocalypse, kingdoms must be intended by this symbol whenever it is used in a similar way in any other part of this book. As the second beast is the spiritual Latin empire, the two horns of this best denote that the empire thus represented is composed of two distinct spiritual powers. These, therefore, can be no other, as Bishop Newton and Faber properly observe, than the two grand independent branches of the Romish hierarchy, viz., the Latin clergy, regular and secular. *Like a lamb.* The two horns of the beast, or the regular and secular clergy, profess to be the ministers of Christ, to be like him in meekness and humility, and to teach nothing that is contrary to godliness. The two-horned beast, or spiritual Latin empire, has in reality the name, and in the eyes of the Latin world the appearance, of a Christian power. But he is only so in appearance, and that alone among his deluded votaries.

12. *And he exerciseth all the power of the first beast before him.* Here he is represented as having obtained the direction and management of all the power of the first beast or secular Latin empire *before him.* That the Romish hierarchy has had the extensive power here spoken of, is evident from history; for the civil power was in subjection to the ecclesiastical. *The earth and them which dwell therein to worship the first beast, whose deadly wound was healed.* That is, he causes the whole Latin world to submit to the authority of the Latin empire, with the revived western empire at its head, persuading them that such submission is beneficial to their spiritual interests, and absolutely necessary for their salvation.

13. *Maketh fire come down from heaven—in the sight of men. Fire,* in Scripture, when it signifies wrath, represents that species of indignation which is attended with the destruction of whatever is the cause of it. Therefore the *fire* which the false prophet bringeth down from heaven upon the earth, is the fiery indignation which he causes to come down from heaven or throne of the Latin empire upon all those of the earth or Latin world who rebel against his authority. All this has been fulfilled in the Romish hierarchy; the Latin clergy have denominated all those that oppose their authority heretics, they have instituted tribunals to try the cause of heresy, and all those that would not submit to their idolatry they have condemned to various kinds of tortures and deaths.

MATTHEW HENRY

They have *the mark of the beast in their forehead* and *in their right hand*, and they have *the name of the beast* and *the number of his name*. They make an open profession of their subjection.

IV. We have here *the number of the beast*, given in such a manner as will sufficiently exercise all the wisdom and accuracy of men: *The number* is *the number of a man*, and it is 666. Only this we know, God has written *Mene Tekel* upon all his enemies; he has numbered their days, and they shall be finished, but his own kingdom shall endure for ever.

JAMIESON, FAUSSET, BROWN

they should give them a mark"; such a brand as masters stamp on their slaves, and monarchs on their subjects. Soldiers voluntarily punctured their arms with marks of the general under whom they served. Votaries of idols branded themselves with the idol's cipher or symbol. Thus Antiochus Epiphanes branded the Jews with the ivy leaf, the symbol of Bacchus (II Maccabees 6:7; III Maccabees 2:29). **17. And**—So A, B, and *Vulgate* read. C, IRENÆUS, 316, *Coptic*, and *Syriac* omit it. **might buy**—*Greek*, "may be able to buy." **the mark, or the name**—*Greek*, "the mark (viz.), the name of the beast." The mark may be, as in the case of the sealing of the saints in the forehead, not a visible mark, but symbolical of allegiance. So the sign of the cross in Popery. The Pope's interdict has often shut out the excommunicate from social and commercial intercourse. Under the final Antichrist this shall come to pass in its most violent form. **number of his name**—implying that the name has some numerical meaning. **18. wisdom**—the armory against the second beast, as *patience and faith* against the first. Spiritual *wisdom* is needed to solve the *mystery* of iniquity, so as not to be beguiled by it. **count . . . for**—The "for" implies the possibility of our calculating or counting the beast's number. **the number of a man**—i.e., counted as men generally count. So the phrase is used in ch. 21:17. **six hundred threescore and six**—A and *Vulgate* write the numbers in full in the *Greek*. But B writes merely the three *Greek* letters standing for numbers, *Ch, X, St*. "C reads" 616, but IRENÆUS, 328, opposes this and maintains "666." IRENÆUS, in the second century, disciple of POLYCARP, John's disciple, explained this number as contained in the *Greek* letters of *Lateinos* (L being 30; A, 1; T, 300; E, 5; I, 10; N, 50; O, 70; S, 200). The Latin is peculiarly the language of the Church of Rome in all her official acts; the forced unity of language in ritual being the counterfeit of the true unity; the premature and spurious anticipation of the real unity, only to be realized at Christ's coming, when all the earth shall speak "one language" (Zeph. 3:9).

ADAM CLARKE

16. *And he caused all, both small and great, rich and poor, free and bound, to receive a mark.* The mark imposed by the two-horned beast is called *the mark of his name.* The *name of the beast* is the Latin empire: the *mark of his name* must therefore be his Latin worship: for this very reason, that it is the two-horned beast, or false prophet, who causes all descriptions of persons to receive it.

17. *And that no man might buy or sell, save he that had the mark.* "If any," observes Bishop Newton, "dissent from the stated and authorized forms, they are condemned and excommunicated as heretics; and in consequence of that they are no longer suffered to buy or sell; they are interdicted from traffic and commerce, and all the benefits of civil society."

18. *Here is wisdom. Let him that hath understanding count the number of the beast; for it is the number of a man; and his number is six hundred threescore and six.* It is said *the number of the beast is the number of a man*; consequently the numbered beast must be a man, that is, it must be represented elsewhere in the Revelation under this emblem, for in no other sense can an empire be denominated *a man*. Therefore, it is not the ten-horned beast, for this is uniformly styled *The Beast* in every part of the Apocalypse where there has been occasion to mention this power. It can therefore be no other than the two-horned beast, or Romish hierarchy; which, on account of its preaching to the world its most antichristian system of doctrines, and calling it Christianity, is likewise named The False Prophet.

MATTHEW HENRY

CHAPTER 14

Verses 1–5

The Lord Jesus Christ at the head of his faithful. 1. How Christ appears: as a Lamb standing upon *Mount Zion.* A counterfeit lamb is mentioned as rising out of the earth in the last chapter, which was really a dragon; here Christ appears as the true paschal Lamb. 2. How his people appear. All who were sealed; not one of them lost in all the tribulations through which they had gone. They had *the name of God written in their foreheads.*

Their songs of praise (*v.* 3). They are described by their chastity and purity: *They are virgins.*

JAMIESON, FAUSSET, BROWN

CHAPTER 14

VSS. 1-20. THE LAMB SEEN ON ZION WITH THE 144,000. THEIR SONG. THE GOSPEL PROCLAIMED BEFORE THE END BY ONE ANGEL: THE FALL OF BABYLON, BY ANOTHER: THE DOOM OF THE BEAST WORSHIPPERS, BY A THIRD. THE BLESSEDNESS OF THE DEAD IN THE LORD. **1. a**—A, B, C, *Coptic*, and ORIGEN read, "*the.*" **Lamb . . . on . . . Sion**—having left His position "in the midst of the throne," and now taking His stand *on Sion*. **his Father's name**—A, B, and C read, "*His name and* His Father's name." **in**—*Greek*, "upon." God's and Christ's *name* here answers to the *seal* "upon their foreheads" in ch. 7:3. As the 144,000 of Israel are "the first fruits" (vs. 4), so "the harvest" (vs. 15) is the general assembly of Gentile saints to be translated by Christ as His first act in assuming His kingdom, prior to His judgment (ch. 16, the last seven vials) on the Antichristian world, in executing which His saints shall share. **2. from**—*Greek*, "out of." **voice of many waters**—as is the voice of Himself, such also is the voice of His people **I heard the voice of harpers**—A, B, C, and ORIGEN read, "the voice which I heard (was) as of harpers." **3. sung**—*Greek*, "sing." **as it were**—So A, C, and *Vulgate* read. It is "as it were" a *new song;* for it is, in truth, as old as God's eternal purpose. But B, *Syriac, Coptic,* ORIGEN, and ANDREAS omit these words. **new song**—(ch. 5:9, 10). The song is that of victory after conflict with the dragon, beast, and false prophet: never sung before, for such a conflict had never been fought before; therefore *new:* till now the kingdom of *Christ* on earth had been usurped; they sing the new song in anticipation of His blood-bought kingdom with His saints. **four beasts**—rather as *Greek*, "four living creatures." The harpers and singers evidently include the 144,000: so the parallel proves (ch. 15:2, 3), where the same act is attributed to *the general company of the saints,* the *harvest* (vs. 15) from all nations. Not as ALFORD, "the harpers and song are in heaven, but the 144,000 are on earth." **redeemed**—lit., "purchased." Not even the angels can learn that song, for they know not *experimentally* what it is to have "come out of the great tribulation, and washed their robes white in the blood of the Lamb" (ch. 7:14). **4. virgins**—spiritually (Matt. 25:1); in contrast to the apostate Church, Babylon (vs. 8),

ADAM CLARKE

CHAPTER 14

1. *A Lamb stood on the mount Sion.* This represents Jesus Christ in His sacrificial office; *mount Sion* was a type of the Christian Church. *And with him an hundred forty and four thousand.* Representing those who were converted to Christianity from among the *Jews.* See chap. vii. 4. *His Father's name written in their foreheads.* They were professedly, openly, and practically the children of God by faith in Christ Jesus. Different sects of idolaters have the peculiar mark of their god on their foreheads. Almost every MS. of importance, as well as most of the versions and many of the fathers, read this clause thus: "Having His name and His Father's name written upon their foreheads." This is undoubtedly the true reading, and is properly received by Griesbach into the text.

2. *The voice of many waters.* That is, of multitudes of various nations. *The voice of harpers.* Though the sounds were many and apparently confused, yet both harmony and melody were preserved.

3. *They sung . . . a new song.* See on chap. v. 9. *No man could learn that song.* As none but genuine Christians can worship God acceptably, because they approach Him through the only Mediator, so none can understand the deep things of God but such; nor can others know the cause why true believers exult so much in God through Christ, because they know not the communion which such hold with the Father and the Son through the Holy Ghost.

MATTHEW HENRY

They had not defiled themselves either with corporal or spiritual adultery. By their loyalty and steadfast adherence to Christ: *They follow the Lamb whithersoever he goes.* By their former designation to this honour, *v.* 4. *They were the first-fruits to God and to the Lamb,* and the earnest of many more who should *be followers of them, as they were of Christ.*

There was no guile found in them, and *they were without fault before the throne of God.* Their hearts were right with God, and they were freely pardoned in Christ.

Verses 6-12

Three angels or messengers sent from heaven to give notice of the fall of Babylon.

I. The first angel was sent on an errand antecedent to it, *v.* 6, 7. The gospel is an everlasting gospel. It is a work fit for an angel to preach this everlasting gospel. The everlasting gospel is of great concern to all the world. The gospel is the great means whereby men are brought to fear God, and to give glory to him. It is by the preaching of the gospel that men are *turned from idols to serve the living God, v.* 7.

II. The second angel follows the other, and proclaims the actual fall of Babylon. By Babylon is generally understood Rome. The wickedness of Babylon will make her fall just, *v.* 8.

III. A third angel follows the other two, *v.* 9, 10. If after this any should persist in their idolatry, they must expect *to drink deep of the wine of the wrath of God.* Those who refuse to come out of Babylon must receive of her plagues.

JAMIESON, FAUSSET, BROWN

spiritually "a harlot" (ch. 17:1-5; Isa. 1:21; contrast II Cor. 11:2; Eph. 5:25-27). Their not being *defiled with women* means they were not led astray from Christian faithfulness by the tempters who jointly constitute the spiritual "harlot." **follow the Lamb whithersoever he goeth**—in glory, being especially near His person; the fitting reward of their following Him so fully on earth. **redeemed**—"purchased." *being* **the**—rather, "*as a* first fruit." Not merely a "first fruit" in the sense in which *all* believers are so, but Israel's 144,000 elect are the *first fruit,* the Jewish and Gentile elect Church is the *harvest;* in a further sense, the whole of the transfigured and translated Church which reigns with Christ at His coming, is the *first fruit,* and the consequent general ingathering of Israel and the nations, ending in the last judgment, is the full and final harvest. **5. guile**—So ANDREAS in one copy. But A, B, C, ORIGEN, and ANDREAS in other copies read, "falsehood." Cf. with *English Version* reading Psalm 32:2; Isaiah 53:9; John 1:47. **for**—So B, *Syriac, Coptic,* ORIGEN, and ANDREAS read. But A and C omit. **without fault**—*Greek,* "blameless": in respect to the sincerity of their fidelity to Him. Not absolutely, and in themselves *blameless;* but regarded as such on the ground of His righteousness in whom alone they trusted, and whom they faithfully served by His Spirit in them. The allusion seems to be to Psalm 15:1, 2. Cf. vs. 1, "*stood on* Mount Sion." **before the throne of God**—A, B, C, *Syriac, Coptic,* ORIGEN, and ANDREAS omit these words. The oldest *Vulgate* MS. supports them. **6.** Here begins the portion relating to the Gentile world, as the former portion related to Israel. Before the *end* the Gospel is to be preached for a WITNESS *unto all nations:* not that all nations shall be converted, but all nations shall have had the opportunity given them of deciding whether they will be for, or against, Christ. **everlasting gospel**—the Gospel which announces the *glad tidings* of the *everlasting* kingdom of Christ, about to ensue immediately after the "judgment" on Antichrist, announced as imminent in vs. 7. As the former angel "flying through the midst of heaven" (ch. 8:13) announced "woe," so this angel "flying in the midst of heaven" announced *joy.* **7. Fear God**—the forerunner to embracing the *love* of God manifested in *the Gospel.* Repentance accompanies faith. **give glory to him**—and not to the beast (cf. ch. 13:4; Jer. 13:16). **the hour of his judgment**—"The hour" implies the *definite time.* "Judgment," not the general judgment, but that upon Babylon, the beast, and his worshippers (vss. 8-12). **worship him that made heaven**—not Antichrist (cf. Acts 14:15). **sea . . . fountains**—distinguished also in ch. 8:8, 10. **8. another**—so *Vulgate.* But A, B, *Syriac,* and ANDREAS add, "a second"; "another, a second angel." **Babylon**—here first mentioned; identical with *the harlot,* the apostate Church; distinct from *the beast,* and judged separately. **is fallen**—anticipation of ch. 18:2. A, *Vulgate, Syriac,* and ANDREAS support the second "is fallen." But B, C, and *Coptic* omit it. **that great city**—A, B, C, *Vulgate, Syriac,* and *Coptic* omit "city." Then translate, "Babylon the great." The ulterior and exhaustive fulfilment of Isaiah 21:9. **because**—so ANDREAS. But A, C, *Vulgate,* and *Syriac* read, "which." B and *Coptic* omit it. Even reading "which," we must understand it as giving the *reason* of her fall. **all nations**—A, B and C read, "all *the* nations." **the wine of the wrath of her fornication**—*the wine of the wrath* of God, the consequence *of her fornication.* As she made the nations drunk with the wine of her fornication, so she herself shall be made drunk with the wine of God's wrath. **9.** A, B, C, and ANDREAS read, "another, a third angel." Cf. with this verse ch. 13:15, 16. **10. The same**—*Greek,* "he also," as the just and inevitable retribution. **wine of . . . wrath of God**—(Ps. 75:8). **without mixture**—whereas wine was so commonly *mixed* with water that to *mix* wine is used in *Greek* for to *pour out* wine; *this* wine of God's wrath is *undiluted;* there is no drop of water to cool its heat. **indignation**—*Greek, orges,* "abiding wrath." But the *Greek* for "wrath" above (*Greek, thumou*) is *boiling indignation,* from (*Greek, thuo*) a root meaning "to boil"; this is temporary ebullition of anger; that is lasting [AMMONIUS], and accompanied with a purpose of vengeance [ORIGEN on Ps. 2:5]. **tormented . . . in the presence of . . . angels**—(Ps. 49:14; 58:10; 139:21; Isa. 66:24). God's enemies are regarded by the saints as their enemies, and when the day of probation is past, their mind shall be so entirely one with God's, that they shall rejoice in witnessing visibly the judicial vindication of God's righteousness in sinners' punishment. **11. for ever**

ADAM CLARKE

4. *These are they which were not defiled with women.* They are pure from idolatry, and are presented as unspotted virgins to their Lord and Saviour, Christ. There may be an allusion here to the Israelites committing idolatry, through the means of their criminal connection with the Midianitish women. See Num. xxv. 1-4 and xxxi. 16. *The firstfruits unto God.* The reference appears to be to those Jews who were the first converts to Christianity.

5. *In their mouth was found no guile.* When brought before kings and rulers they did not dissemble, but boldly confessed the Lord Jesus.

6. *Another angel fly in the midst of heaven, having the everlasting gospel.* Whether this angel means any more than a particular dispensation of providence and grace, by which the gospel shall be rapidly sent throughout the whole world; or whether it means any especial messenger, order of preachers, people, or society of Christians, whose professed object it is to send the gospel of the Kingdom throughout the earth, we know not. But the vision seems truly descriptive of a late institution entitled "The British and Foreign Bible Society," whose object it is to print and circulate the Scriptures of the Old and New Testaments through all the habitable world, and in all the languages spoken on the face of the earth.

7. *Fear God, and give glory to him.* This is the general language of the sacred writings. Worship the true God, the Creator and Governor of all things; and give Him glory; for to Him alone, not to idols or men, all glory and honor belong.

8. *Babylon is fallen, is fallen.* This is generally understood to be a prediction concerning Rome; and it is certain that Rome, in the rabbinical writings, is termed Babylon. *That great city.* Among the same writers this city is styled "the great city" and "the great Rome." But which Rome is meant? Pagan or papal Rome? Some parts of the description apply best to the former. *The wine of the wrath of her fornication.* There is an allusion here to a custom of impure women, who give love potions to those whom they wish to seduce and bind to their will; and these potions are generally of an intoxicating nature, greatly inflaming the blood, and disturbing the intellect. Fornication and adultery are frequently used in Scripture as emblems of idolatry and false worship. No nation of the earth spread their idolatries so far as the ancient Romans; they were as extensive as their conquests. And papal Rome has been not less active in disseminating her superstitions. She has given her rituals, but not the everlasting gospel, to most nations of the earth.

10. *The wine of the wrath of God.* As they have drunk the intoxicating wine of idolatry or spiritual fornication, they shall now drink the wine of God's wrath, which is poured out into the cup of His indignation. This is an allusion to the poisoned cup which certain criminals were obliged to drink, on which ensued speedy death. *Shall be tormented with fire and brimstone.* An allusion to the punishment of Sodom and Gomorrah for their unnatural crimes. *Presence of the holy angels, and . . . of the Lamb,* these being the instruments employed in their destruction; the *Lamb*—the Lord Jesus Christ—acting as Judge.

MATTHEW HENRY

When the treachery and rebellion of others shall be punished, then it will be said, to the honour of the faithful (*v.* 12): *Here is the patience of the saints;* you have before seen their patience exercised, now you see it rewarded.

Verses 13–20

The vision of the harvest and vintage.

I. The preface, *v.* 13. This prophecy came down from heaven, and not from men, and therefore it is of certain truth. It was to be preserved and published—by writing; it was to be matter of record, that the people of God might have recourse to it for their comfort upon all occasions. It principally intended to show the blessedness of all the faithful servants of God, both in death and after death: *Blessed are the dead that die in the Lord from henceforth,* &c. The description of those that are and shall be blessed—such as die in the Lord.

They are blessed in their rest. They are blessed in their recompence: *Their works follow them;* as their evidence of having lived and died in the Lord.

II. The vision itself.

1. A harvest (*v.* 14, 15), an emblem that sometimes signifies the cutting down of the wicked, and sometimes the gathering in of the righteous. This seems rather to represent God's judgments against the wicked.

(1) The Lord of the harvest—one so *like unto the Son of man* that he was the same, even the Lord Jesus. The chariot in which he sat—*a white cloud,* a cloud that had a bright side turned to the church, how dark soever it might be to the wicked. The ensign of his power: *On his head was a golden crown,* authority to do whatsoever he would do. The instrument of his providences: *In his hand a sharp sickle.*

(2) The harvest-work, to thrust the sickle into the corn, and reap the field.

(3) The harvest-time; when the corn is ripe, when the measure of the sin of men is filled up. Then he will spare them no longer; he will thrust in his sickle, and the earth shall be reaped.

2. A vintage, *v.* 17. To whom this vintage-work was committed—*another angel that came out from the altar.* The work of the vintage, which consists of two parts: (1) *Gathering the clusters of the vine, fully ripe, v.* 18.

(2) Casting these grapes *into the wine-press* (*v.* 19). It was *the wrath of God, without the city,* where the army lay that came against Babylon. The quantity of the wine, that is, of the blood that was drawn forth by this judgment (*v.* 20). But here we are left to doubtful conjectures.

JAMIESON, FAUSSET, BROWN

and ever—*Greek,* "unto ages of ages." **no rest day nor night**—Contrast the very different sense in which the same is said of the four living creatures in heaven, "They rest not day and night, saying, Holy, holy, holy . . ."; yet they do "rest" in another sense; they rest from sin and sorrow, weariness and weakness, trial and temptation (vs. 13); the lost have no rest from sin and Satan, terror, torment, and remorse. **12. Here . . .**—resumed from ch. 13:10, where see the *Note.* In the fiery ordeal of persecution which awaits all who will not worship the beast, the *faith* and *patience* of the followers of *God and Jesus* shall be put to the test, and proved. **patience**—*Greek, hupomene,* "patient, persevering endurance." The second "here" is omitted in A, B, C, *Vulgate, Syriac, Coptic,* and PRIMASIUS. Translate, "Here is the endurance of the saints, who keep . . . ." **the faith of Jesus**—the faith which has Jesus for its object. **13.** Encouragement to cheer those persecuted under the beast. **Write**—to put it on record for ever. **Blessed**—in *resting from their toils,* and, in the case of the saints just before alluded to as persecuted by the beast, in *resting from persecutions.* Their full *blessedness* is now "from henceforth," i.e., FROM THIS TIME, when the judgment on the beast and the harvest gatherings of the elect are imminent. The time so earnestly longed for by former martyrs is now all but come; the full number of their fellow servants is on the verge of completion; they have no longer to "*rest* (the same *Greek* as here, *anapausis*) yet for a little season," their eternal *rest,* or *cessation* from toils (II Thessalonians 1:7; *Greek, anesis,* relaxation after hardships. **the Spirit**—The words of God the Father (the "voice from heaven") are echoed back and confirmed by the Spirit (speaking in the Word, ch. 2:7; 22:17; and in the saints, II Cor. 5:5; I Pet. 4:14). All "God's promises in Christ are yea" (II Cor. 1:20). **unto me**—omitted in A, B, C, *Vulgate, Syriac,* and *Coptic.* **that they may**—The *Greek* includes also the idea, They are blessed, *in that they* SHALL *rest from their toils* (so the *Greek*). **and**—So B and ANDREAS read. But A, C, *Vulgate,* and *Syriac* read "for." They rest from their toils *because* their time for toil is past; they enter on the *blessed rest because* of their faith evinced by their works which, therefore, "follow WITH (so the *Greek*) them." Their *works* are specified because respect is had to the coming judgment, wherein every man shall be "judged according to his works." **crown**—*Greek, stephanon,* "garland" of victory; not His *diadem* as a king. The victory is described in detail, ch. 19:11-21. **one sat**—"one sitting," *Greek, cathemenon homoion,* is the reading of A, B, C, *Vulgate,* and *Coptic.* **15. Thrust in**—*Greek,* "Send." The angel does not command the "Son of man" (vs. 14), but is the mere messenger announcing to the Son the will of *God the Father,* in whose hands are kept *the times and the seasons.* **thy sickle**—alluding to Mark 4:29, where also it is "*sendeth* the sickle." The Son sends His sickle-bearing angel to reap the righteous when fully ripe. **harvest**—the harvest crop. By the *harvest*-reaping the elect righteous are gathered out; by the *vintage* the Antichristian offenders are removed out of the earth, the scene of Christ's coming kingdom. The Son of man Himself, with a golden crown, is introduced in the *harvest*-gathering of the elect, a mere angel in the *vintage* (vss. 18-20). **is ripe**—lit., "is dried." Ripe for glory. **16. thrust in**—*Greek,* "cast." **17. out of the temple . . . in heaven**—(ch. 11:19). **18. from the altar**—upon which were offered the incense-accompanied prayers of all saints, which bring down in answer God's fiery judgment on the Church's foes, the *fire* being *taken from the altar and cast upon the earth.* **fully ripe**—*Greek,* "come to their acme"; ripe for punishment. **19.** "The vine" is what is the subject of judgment because its grapes are not what God looked for considering its careful culture, but "wild grapes' (Isa. 5). The apostate world of Christendom, not the world of heathendom who have not heard of Christ, is the object of judgment. Cf. the emblem, ch. 19: 15; Isaiah 63:2, 3; Joel 3:13. **20. without the city**—Jerusalem. The scene of the blood-shedding of Christ and His people shall be also the scene of God's vengeance on the Antichristian foe. Cf. the "horsemen," ch. 9:16, 17. **blood**—answering to the red wine. The slaughter of the apostates is what is here spoken of, not their eternal punishment. **even unto the horse bridles**—of the avenging "armies of heaven." **by the space of a thousand . . . six hundred furlongs**—lit., "a thousand six hundred furlongs *off*" [W. KELLY].

ADAM CLARKE

11. *The smoke of their torment.* Still an allusion to the destruction of Sodom and Gomorrah.

12. *Here is the patience of the saints.* Here the faith of the true Christians shall be proved; they will "follow the Lamb whithersoever he goeth"; they keep the commandments of God, and are steadfast in the faith of our Lord Jesus Christ. Sometimes *patience* or "perseverance" is taken for the reward of these virtues. The text therefore may be thus understood: Here is the reward of the perseverance of the true Christians; for although they die for the testimony of Jesus, yet they shall be unutterably blessed. See the next verse.

13. *I heard a voice from heaven.* As the information now to be given was of the utmost importance, it is solemnly communicated by a voice from heaven, and the apostle is commanded to write or record what is said. *Blessed are the dead.* Happy are they. They do not see the evil that shall come upon the world, and are exempted from any further sufferings. "Happy are the dead" is a proverb frequently to be met in the Greek and Roman poets. *From henceforth.* "From this time; now; immediately." This word is joined to the following by many MSS. and some versions. It was a maxim among the Jews that as soon as the souls of the just departed from this life they ascended immediately to heaven. *Yea, saith the Spirit.* The Holy Spirit confirms the declaration from heaven and assigns the reasons of it. *That they may rest from their labours.* Have no more tribulation and distress. *And their works do follow them.* "And their works follow with them." Here is an elegant personification; their good works, sufferings, etc., are represented as so many companions escorting them on their way to the kingdom of God.

14. *A white cloud.* It is supposed that, from this verse to the end of the chapter, the destruction of Rome is represented under the symbols of harvest and vintage; images very frequent among the ancient prophets, by which they represented the destruction and excision of nations. See Joel iii. 12-14; Isa. xvii. 5; lxiii. 1; and Matt. xiii. 37 *A golden crown* In token of victory and regal power.

15. *Thrust in thy sickle.* Execute the judgments which God has decreed. *For the harvest of the earth is ripe.* The cup of the people's iniquity is full.

16. *The earth was reaped.* The judgments were executed.

18. *Power over fire.* Probably meaning the same angel which is mentioned in chap. viii. 3; ix. 13, who stood by the altar of burnt offering, having authority over its fire to offer that incense to God which represents the prayers of the saints.

19. *The great winepress of the wrath of God.* The place or kingdom where God executes His judgments on the workers of iniquity, whether pagans or persecuting Christians—Rome pagan or Rome papal.

20. *Even unto the horse bridles.* A hyperbolical expression, to denote a great effusion of blood. The Jews said, "When Hadrian besieged the city called Bitter, he slew so many that the horses waded in blood up to their mouths."

MATTHEW HENRY

CHAPTER 15

Verses 1–4

The pouring out of the seven vials, which was committed to seven angels. The work they had to do, which was to finish the destruction of antichrist.

The spectators and witnesses of this their commission: all *that had gotten the victory over the beast,* &c.

These stood on a *sea of glass singing the song of Moses.* They extol the greatness of God's works.

They call upon all nations to render unto God the fear due to such a discovery of his truth and justice: *Who shall not fear thee?* (*v.* 4).

Verses 5–8

I. How these angels appeared, *v.* 5. Here is an allusion to the holiest of all in the tabernacle and temple, where was *the mercy-seat, covering the ark of the testimony.* In the judgments God was now about to execute he was fulfilling the prohecies and promises of his word and covenant, which were there always before him.

JAMIESON, FAUSSET, BROWN

CHAPTER 15

Vss. 1-8. THE LAST SEVEN VIALS OF PLAGUES. SONG OF THE VICTORS OVER THE BEAST. **1. the seven last plagues**—*Greek,* "seven plagues which are the last." **is filled up**—lit., "was finished," or "consummated": the prophetical past for the future, the future being to God as though it were past, so sure of accomplishment is His word. This verse is the summary of the vision that follows: the angels do not actually receive the vials till vs. 7; but here, in vs. 1, by anticipation they are spoken of as *having* them. There are no more plagues after these until the Lord's coming in judgment. The destruction of Babylon (ch. 18) is the last: then in ch. 19 He appears. **2. sea of glass**—Answering to the molton sea or great brazen laver before the mercy seat of the earthly temple, for the purification of the priests; typifying the baptism of water and the Spirit of all who are made kings and priests unto God. **mingled with fire**—answering to the *baptism* on earth *with fire,* i.e., fiery trial, as well as with the Holy Ghost, which Christ's people undergo to purify them, as gold is purified of its dross in the furnace. **them that had gotten the victory over**—*Greek,* "those (coming) off from (the conflict with) the beast-conquerors." **over the number of his name** A, B, C, *Vulgate, Syriac,* and *Coptic* omit the words in *English Version,* "over his mark." *The mark,* in fact, is the *number of his name* which the faithful refused to receive, and so were victorious over it. **stand on the sea of glass**—ALFORD and DE BURGH explain "on (the shore of) the sea": *at* the sea. So the preposition, *Greek, epi,* with the accusative, is used for *at,* ch. 3:20. It has a pregnant sense: "standing" implies *rest, Greek epi* with the accusative implies motion *towards.* Thus the meaning is, Having come TO the sea, and now *standing* AT it. As the sea typifies the troubled state out of which the beast arose, and which is to be no more in the blessed world to come (ch. 21:1), so the victorious saints stand on it, having it *under their feet* (as the *woman* had the *moon,* ch. 12:1, see *Note*); but it is now no longer treacherous wherein the feet sink, but solid like glass, as it was under the feet of Christ, whose triumph and power the saints now share. Firmness of footing amidst apparent instability is thus represented.
harps of God—in the hands of these heavenly *virgins,* infinitely surpassing the timbrels of Miriam and the Israelitesses. **3. song of Moses . . . and . . . the Lamb**—The New Testament song of the Lamb (i.e., the song which the Lamb shall lead, as being "the Captain of our salvation," just as Moses was leader of the Israelites, the song in which those who conquer through Him [Rom. 8:37] shall join, ch. 12:11) is the antitype to the triumphant Old Testament song of Moses and the Israelites at the Red Sea (Exod. 15). The Churches of the Old and New Testament are essentially one in their conflicts and triumphs.
servant of God—(Exod. 14:31; Num. 12:7; Josh. 22:5). The Lamb is more: He is the SON. **Great and marvellous are thy works . . .**—part of Moses' last song. The vindication of the justice of God that so He may be glorified is the grand end of God's dealings. Hence His servants again and again dwell upon this in their praises (ch. 16:7; 19:2; Prov. 16:4; Jer. 10:10; Dan. 4:37). Especially at the judgment (Ps. 50:1-6; 145:17). **saints**—There is no MS. authority for this. A, B, *Coptic,* and CYPRIAN read, "of the NATIONS." C reads "of the ages," and so *Vulgate* and *Syriac.* The point at issue in the Lord's controversy with the earth is, whether He, or Satan's minion, the beast, is "the King of the nations"; here at the eve of the judgments descending on the kingdom of the beast, the transfigured saints hail Him as "the King of the nations" (Ezek. 21:27). **4. Who shall not**—*Greek,* "Who is there but must fear Thee?" Cf. Moses' song, Exodus 15:14-16, on the fear which God's judgments strike into the foe. **thee**—so *Syriac.* But A, B, C, *Vulgate,* and CYPRIAN reject "thee." **all nations shall come**—alluding to Psalm 22:27-31; cf. Isaiah 66:23; Jeremiah 16:19. The conversion of *all nations,* therefore, shall be when Christ shall come, and not till then; and the first moving cause will be Christ's *manifested judgments* preparing all hearts for receiving Christ's mercy.
judgment—*Greek,* "righteousness." **5.** So ch. 11:19; cf. ch. 16:17. "The tabernacle of the testimony" appropriately here comes to view, where God's faithfulness in avenging His people with judgments on their foes is about to be set forth. We need to get a glimpse within the Holy place to "understand" the secret spring

ADAM CLARKE

CHAPTER 15

1. *Seven angels having the seven last plagues.* Under the emblems of harvest and vintage God's judgments on the enemies of His Church have already been pointed out; but these are further signified by the seven vials, which are called *the seven last plagues* of God. *The seven last plagues* appear to fall under the seventh and last trumpet. As the seventh seal contained the seven trumpets, so the seventh trumpet contains the seven vials. And as seven angels sounded the seven trumpets, so seven angels are appointed to pour out the seven vials, angels being always the ministers of Providence. This chapter contains the opening vision which is preparatory to the pouring out of the vials.

2. *A sea of glass.* A spacious, lucid plain around the throne, from which fiery coruscations were continually emitted; or the reflection of the light upon this lucid plain produced the prismatic colors of the most vivid rainbow.

3. *They sing the song of Moses.* That which Moses sang, Exod. xv. 1, when he and the Israelites, by the miraculous power of God, had got safely through the Red Sea, and saw their enemies all destroyed. *And the song of the Lamb.* The same song adapted to the state of the suffering, but now delivered, Christians.

Great and marvellous are thy works. God's works are descriptive of His infinite power and wisdom. *Lord God Almighty.* Nearly the same as "Jehovah God of hosts." *Just and true are thy ways.* Every step God takes in grace or providence is according to justice, and He carefully accomplishes all His threatenings and all His promises; to this He is bound by His truth.

4. *Who shall not fear thee?* That is, "All should fear" and worship this true God, because He is just and true and *holy;* and His saints should love and obey Him, because He is their King; and they and all men should acknowledge His *judgments,* because they are *made manifest.*

5. *The temple of the tabernacle of the testimony.* The *temple* which succeeded the *tabernacle,* in which was the *testimony,* viz., the two tables, Aaron's rod, pot of manna, holy anointing oil, etc. All bearing testimony to the truth of God and His miraculous interposition in their behalf.

MATTHEW HENRY

II. How they were equipped. Their array, *v.* 6. This was the habit of the high priests when they went in to enquire of God, and came out with an answer from him. They do everything in a pure and holy manner.

Their artillery was *seven vials filled with the wrath of God;* they were armed with the wrath of God against his enemies.

III. They were all wrapt up in clouds of smoke, which filled the temple, from the glorious and powerful presence of God; so that *no man was able to enter into the temple*, till the work was finished. God himself was now preaching to the church and to all the world, by terrible things in righteousness; but when this work was done, the temple would be opened.

JAMIESON, FAUSSET, BROWN

and the end of God's righteous dealings. **are**—lit., "were": the prophetical past for the immediate future. **5. behold**—omitted by A, B, C, *Syriac*, and ANDREAS. It is supported only by *Vulgate, Coptic,* and PRIMASIUS, but no MS. **6. having**—So B reads. But A and C, read "who have": not that they had them yet (cf. vs. 7), but they are by anticipation described according to their office. **linen**—So B reads. But A, C, and *Vulgate,* "a stone." On the principle that the harder reading is the one least likely to be an interpolation, we should read, "a stone pure ('and' is omitted in A, B, C, and ANDREAS), brilliant" (so the *Greek*): probably the diamond. With *English Version,* cf. Acts 1:10; 10:30. **golden girdles**—resembling the Lord in this respect (ch. 1:13). **7. one of the four beasts**—*Greek,* "living creatures." The presentation of the vials to the angels by one of the living creatures implies the ministry of the Church as the medium for manifesting to angels the glories of redemption (Eph. 3:10). **vials**—"bowls"; a broad shallow cup or bowl. The breadth of the vials in their upper part would tend to cause their contents to pour out *all at once,* implying the overwhelming suddenness of the woes. **full of . . . wrath**—How sweetly do the *vials full of odors,* i.e., the incense-perfumed prayers of the saints, contrast with these! **8. temple . . . filled**—Isaiah 6:4; cf. Exodus 40:34; II Chronicles 5:14, as to the earthly temple, of which this is the antitype. **the glory of God and . . . power**—then fully manifested. **no man was able to enter . . . the temple**—because of God's presence in His manifested glory and power during the execution of these judgments.

ADAM CLARKE

6. *The seven angels came out of the temple.* To show that they were sent from God himself. *Clothed in pure and white linen.* Habited as priests. For these habits see Exod. xxviii. 6, 8; and see the note on chap. i. 13.

8. *The temple was filled with smoke.* So was the Tabernacle when consecrated by Moses, Exod. xl. 34-35, and the Temple when consecrated by Solomon, 1 Kings viii. 10-11; 2 Chron. v. 14. See Isa. vi. 4. This account seems at least partly copied from those above.

MATTHEW HENRY

CHAPTER 16

Verses 1-7

I. Though everything was made ready before, yet nothing was to be put in execution without an order from God; and this he gave out of the temple.

II. No sooner was the word of command given than it was immediately obeyed. God says, *Go your ways, and pour out the vials;* and immediately the work is begun. We have here a reference and allusion to several of the plagues of Egypt. Their sins were alike, and so were their punishments. These vials have a plain reference to the seven trumpets, which represented the rise of antichrist. The fall of antichrist shall be gradual; as Rome was not built in one day, so neither shall it fall in one day. The fall of the antichristian interest shall be universal. Everything that any ways belonged to them, all consigned over to ruin, all accursed for the sake of the wickedness of that people.

1. The first angel, *v.* 2. Where the vial fell—*upon the earth,* upon the common people. What it produced—*noisome and grievous sores on all who had the mark of the beast.* They had marked themselves by their sin, now God marks them out by his judgments.

2. *The second angel poured out his vial.* Where it fell—*upon the sea.* It turned the sea into blood, *as the blood of a dead man, and every living soul died in the sea.* God discovered not only the vanity and falsehood of their religion, but the pernicious and deadly nature of it.

The next angel poured out his vial. Where it fell—*upon the rivers, and upon the fountains of waters. It turned them into blood.*

The following doxology (*v.* 5, 6). The instrument that God makes use of in this work is here called *the angel of the waters,* who extols the righteousness of God in this retaliation, to which another angel answered by full consent, *v.* 7.

JAMIESON, FAUSSET, BROWN

CHAPTER 16

VSS. 1-21. THE SEVEN VIALS AND THE CONSEQUENT PLAGUES. **1. a great voice**—viz., God's. These seven vials (the detailed expansion of *the vintage,* ch. 14:18-20) being called "the last," must belong to the period just when the term of the beast's power has expired (whence reference is made in them all to the worshippers of the beast as the objects of the judgments), close to the end or coming of the Son of man. **the temple**—B and *Syriac* omit. But A, C, *Vulgate,* and ANDREAS support the words. **the vials**—so *Syriac* and *Coptic.* But A, B, C, *Vulgate,* and ANDREAS read, "the *seven* vials." **upon**—*Greek,* "into." **2. went**—*Greek,* "went away." **poured out**—So the angel cast fire into the earth previous to the series of trumpets (ch. 8:5). **upon**—*so Coptic.* But A, B, C, *Vulgate,* and *Syriac* read, "into." **noisome**—lit., "evil" (cf. Deut. 28:27, 35). The very same *Greek* word is used in the LXX as here, *Greek, helkos.* The reason why the sixth Egyptian plague is the *first* here is because it was directed against the Egyptian magicians, Jannes and Jambres, so that they could not stand before Moses; and so here the plague is sent upon those who in the beast worship had practiced sorcery. As they submitted to the mark of the beast, so they must bear the mark of the avenging God. Contrast ch. 7:3; Ezekiel 9:4, 6. **grievous**—distressing to the sufferers. **sore upon the men**—antitype to the sixth Egyptian plague. **which had the mark of the beast**—Therefore this first vial is subsequent to the period of the beast's rule. **3. angel**—So B and ANDREAS. But A, C, and *Vulgate* omit it. **upon**—*Greek,* "into." **became as . . . blood**—answering to another Egyptian plague. **of a dead man**—putrefying. **living soul**—So B and ANDREAS. But A, C, and *Syriac,* "soul of life" (cf. Gen. 1:30; 7:21, 22). **in the sea**—So B and ANDREAS. But A, C, and *Syriac* read, "(as respects) the things in the sea." **4.** Exodus 7:20. **angel**—so *Syriac, Coptic,* and ANDREAS. But A, B, C, and *Vulgate* omit it. **5. angel of the waters**—i.e., presiding over the waters. **O Lord**—omitted by A, B, C, *Vulgate, Syriac, Coptic,* and ANDREAS. **and shalt be**—A, B, C, *Vulgate,* and ANDREAS for this clause read, "(which art and wast) *holy.*" The Lord is now no longer He that *shall* come, for He *is come* in vengeance and therefore the third of the three clauses found in ch. 1:4, 8; and 4:8 is here and in ch. 11:17 omitted. **judged thus**—lit., "these things." "Thou didst inflict this judgment." **6.** (Ch. 11:18, end; Gen. 9:6; Isa. 49:26.) An anticipation of ch. 18:20, 24; cf. ch. 13:15. **For**—A, B, C, and ANDREAS omit. **7. another out of**—omitted in A, C, *Syriac,* and *Coptic.* Translate then, "I heard the altar [personified] saying." On it the prayers of saints are presented before God: beneath it are the souls of the martyrs crying for vengeance on the foes of God. **8. angel**—so *Coptic* and ANDREAS. But A, B, C, *Vulgate,* and *Syriac* omit it. **upon**—not as in

ADAM CLARKE

CHAPTER 16

1. *Go your ways, and pour out.* These ministers of the divine justice were ready to execute vengeance upon transgressors, having full power, but could do nothing in this way till they received especial commission. Nothing can be done without the permission of God, and in the manifestation of justice or mercy by divine agency there must be positive command.

2. *A noisome and grievous sore.* This is a reference to the sixth Egyptian plague, boils and blains, Exod. ix. 8, etc.

3. *As the blood of a dead man.* Either meaning blood in a state of putrescency or an effusion of blood in naval conflicts; even the sea was tinged with the blood of those who were slain in these wars. This is most probably the meaning of this vial. These engagements were so sanguinary that both the conquerors and the conquered were nearly destroyed; *every living soul died in the sea.*

4. *Upon the rivers and fountains of waters.* This is an allusion to the first Egyptian plague. Exod. vii. 20; and to those plagues in general there are allusions throughout this chapter. It is a sentiment of the rabbins that "whatever plagues God inflicted on the Egyptians in former times, he will inflict on the enemies of his people in all later times."

5. *The angel of the waters.* The rabbins attribute angels, not only to the four elements so called, but to almost everything besides. We have already seen the "angel of the bottomless pit," chap. ix. 11, and "the angel of the fire," chap. xiv. 18.

6. *Thou hast given them blood to drink.* They thirsted after blood and massacred the saints of God, and now they have got blood to drink!

MATTHEW HENRY

Verses 8–11

The fourth angel poured out his vial, and that fell upon the sun. That sun which before cherished them with warm and benign influences shall now grow hot against these idolaters, and shall scorch them, which yet will be so far from bringing them to repentance, that it will cause them to curse God. They will be hardened to their ruin.

The fifth angel, *v.* 10. Where this vial fell—*upon the seat of the beast,* upon Rome itself. The whole kingdom of the beast *was full of darkness.* Darkness is opposed to wisdom and penetration, and forebodes the confusion and folly which the idolaters should discover at that time. It is opposed to pleasure and joy.

Verses 12–16

The sixth angel poured out his vial.

I. Where it fell—*upon the great river Euphrates.* Some take it literally. Others take it for the river Tiber.

II. What did this vial produce? The drying up of the river. A way is hereby prepared *for the kings of the east.* The last effort of the great dragon; he is resolved to have another push for it.

The instruments he makes use of: *Three unclean spirits like frogs.* These would muster up the devil's forces for a decisive battle.

The means these instruments would use. They would work pretended miracles.

JAMIESON, FAUSSET, BROWN

vss. 2, 3, "into." **sun**—Whereas by the fourth trumpet the sun is darkened (ch. 8:12) in a third part, here by the fourth vial the sun's bright scorching power is intensified. **power was given unto him**—rather, "unto *it,*" the sun. **men**—*Greek,* "the men," viz., those who had the mark of the beast (vs. 2). **9. men**—*Greek, "the* men." **repented not to give him glory**—(ch. 9:20). Affliction, if it does not melt, hardens the sinner. Cf. the better result on others, ch. 11:13; 14:7; 15:4. **10. angel**—omitted by A, B, C, *Vulgate,* and *Syriac.* But *Coptic* and ANDREAS support it. **seat**—*Greek, "throne* of the beast": set up in arrogant mimicry of God's throne; the dragon gave his throne to the beast (ch. 13:2). **darkness**—parallel to the Egyptian plague of darkness, Pharaoh being the type of Antichrist (cf. ch. 15:2, 3, *Notes*; cf. the fifth trumpet, ch. 9:2). **gnawed their tongues for pain**—*Greek, "owing to the* pain" occasioned by the previous plagues, rendered more appalling by the darkness. Or, as "gnashing of teeth" is one of the accompaniments of hell, so this "gnawing of their tongues" is through rage at the baffling of their hopes and the overthrow of their kingdom. **11. sores**—This shows that each fresh plague was accompanied with the continuance of the preceding plagues: there was an accumulation, not a mere succession, of plagues. **repented not**—(Cf. vs. 9). **12. angel**—so *Coptic* and ANDREAS. A, B, C, *Vulgate,* and *Syriac* omit. **kings of the east**—*Greek,* "the kings who are from the rising of the sun." Reference to *the Euphrates* similarly occurs in the sixth trumpet. The drying up of the *Euphrates,* I think, is to be taken figuratively, as *Babylon* itself, which is situated on it, is undoubtedly so, ch. 17:5. The waters of the Euphrates (cf. Isa. 8:7, 8) are spiritual Babylon's, i.e., the apostate Church's (of which Rome is the chief, though not exclusive representative) spiritual and temporal powers. The drying up of the waters of Babylon expresses the same thing as the ten kings stripping, eating, and burning the whore. The phrase, "way may be prepared for," is that applied to *the Lord's coming* (Isa. 40:3; Matt. 3:3; Luke 1:76). He shall come *from the East* (Matt. 24:27; Ezek. 43:2, "the glory of the God of Israel came *from the way of the East*"): not alone, for His elect transfigured saints of Israel and the Gentiles shall accompany Him, who are *"kings* and priests unto God" (ch. 1:6). **13. unclean spirits like frogs**—the antitype to the plague of frogs sent on Egypt. The presence of the "unclean spirit" in the land (Palestine) is foretold, Zechariah 13:2, in connection with idolatrous *prophets.* Beginning with infidelity as to Jesus Christ's coming in the flesh, men shall end in the grossest idolatry of the beast, the incarnation of all that is self-deifying and God-opposed in the world powers of all ages; having rejected Him that came in the Father's name, they shall worship one that comes in his own, though really the devil's representative; as frogs croak by night in marshes and quagmires, so these unclean spirits in the darkness of error teach lies amidst the mire of filthy lusts. The unclean spirit out of the mouth of *the dragon* symbolizes the proud infidelity which opposes God and Christ. That out of the *beast's* mouth is the spirit of the world, which in the politics of men, whether lawless democracy or despotism, sets man above God. That out of the mouth of the *false prophet* is lying spiritualism and religious delusion, which shall take the place of the harlot when she shall have been destroyed. **the dragon**—Satan, who *gives his power and throne* (ch. 13:2) *to the beast.* **false prophet**—distinct from the harlot, the apostate Church (of which Rome is the chief, though not sole, representative), ch. 17:1-3, 16; and identical with *the second beast,* ch. 13:11-15, as appears by comparing ch. 19:20 with ch. 13:13; ultimately consigned to the lake of fire with the first beast; as is also the dragon a little later (ch. 20:10). **14. devils**—*Greek,* "demons." **working miracles**—*Greek,* "signs." **go forth unto**—or "for," i.e., to tempt them to the battle with Christ. **the kings of the earth and . . .**—A, B, *Syriac,* and ANDREAS omit "of the earth and," which clause is not in any MS. Translate, "kings of the whole habitable world," who are "of this world," in contrast to "the kings of (from) the East" (the sunrising), vs. 12, viz., the saints to whom Christ *has appointed a kingdom,* and who are "children of light." God, in permitting Satan's *miracles,* as in the case of the Egyptian magicians who were His instruments in hardening Pharaoh's heart, gives the reprobate up to judicial delusion preparatory to their destruction. **battle**—*Greek,* "war"; the final conflict for the kingship of the world described in

ADAM CLARKE

10. *The seat of the beast.* "Upon the throne of the wild beast." The regal family was smitten by the fourth vial; they did not repent; then the fifth angel pours out his vial on the throne of the wild beast, or anti-Christian idolatrous power. *Was full of darkness.* Confusion, dismay, and distress.

11. *Blasphemed the God of heaven.* Neither did they repent; therefore other judgments must follow.

12. *Upon the great river Euphrates.* Probably meaning the people in the vicinity of this river, though some think that the Tiber is intended. *The water thereof was dried up.* The people discomfited and all impediments removed. *The kings of the east.* There seems to be an allusion here to the ruin of Babylon by Cyrus, predicted by the Prophet Jeremiah, chaps. l and li.

13. *Three unclean spirits.* Perhaps false teachers, called afterwards "spirits of devils," which persuade the kings of the earth by lying miracles to come forth to the place of general slaughter, vv. 14, 16.

J. A. SEISS:

To tell exactly who and what these seducing devils are, and exactly how they manage their infernal mission, may not be in our power. This is not the only place where their agency and successes are mentioned. Paul tells us that the Spirit speaketh expressly, that in the latter times seducing spirits shall manifest themselves, even teaching demons, deceiving men with their lies (1 Tim. 4:1, 2). They are spirits; they are "unclean spirits"; they are "demon spirits"; they are sent forth into activity by the Dragon Trinity; they are the elect agents to awaken the world to the attempt to abolish God from the earth; and they are frog-like in that they come forth out of the pestiferous quagmires of the universe, do their work amid the world's evening shadows, and creep, and croak, and defile, and fill the ears of the nations with their noisy demonstrations, till they set all the kings and armies of the whole earth in enthusiastic commotion for the final crushing out of the Lamb and all His powers. As in chapter 9, the seven Spirits of God and of Christ went forth into all the earth to make up and gather together into one holy fellowship the great congregation of the sanctified; so these spirits of hell go forth upon the kings and potentates of the world, to make up and gather together the grand army of the devil's worshipers.—*The Apocalypse*

MATTHEW HENRY

The warning which God gives of this great and decisive trial, *v*. 15. When God's cause comes to be tried, and his battles to be fought, all his people shall be ready and be faithful and valiant in his service.

The field of battle—a place called *Armageddon*; that is, say some, the mount of Megiddo. The further account of it is suspended till we come to the nineteenth chapter, *v*. 19, 20.

Verses 17–21

An account of the seventh and last angel pouring forth his vial, which was the finishing stroke.

I. Where this plague fell—*on the air*, upon the prince of the power of the air, that is, the devil. Here is a vial poured out upon his kingdom, and he is not able to support his tottering cause and interest any longer.

II. What it produced. 1. A thankful voice from heaven, pronouncing that now the work was done. It is finished.

2. An earthquake, so great as never was before, and this ushered in by thunder and lightnings.

3. The fall of Babylon (*v*. 19). God now remembered this great and wicked city. Now he gives unto her *the cup of the wine of the fierceness of his wrath*, and every island and every mountain, that seemed by nature and situation the most secured, were carried away in the deluge of this ruin.

III. How the antichristian party were affected with it. Though it fell upon them as a dreadful storm, as if the stones of the city, tossed up into the air, came down upon their heads, like hailstones of a talent weight each, yet they were so far from repenting that they blasphemed that God who thus punished them.

CHAPTER 17

Verses 1–6

Here we have a new vision. 1. The invitation given to the apostle, *v*. 1. This is a name of great infamy. She had been a prostitute to the kings of the earth, whom she had intoxicated *with the wine of her fornication*.

JAMIESON, FAUSSET, BROWN

ch. 19:17-21. **15.** The gathering of the world kings with the beast against the Lamb is the signal for Christ's coming; therefore He here gives the charge to be watching for His coming and clothed in the garments of justification and sanctification, so as to be accepted. **thief**—(Matt. 24:43; II Pet. 3:10), **they**—saints and angels. **shame**—lit., "unseemliness" (*Greek, aschemosunee*): Greek, I Corinthians 13:5: a different word from the *Greek* in ch. 3:18 (*Greek, aischunee*). **16. he**—rather, "they (the three unclean spirits) gathered them together." If *English Version* be retained, "He" will refer to *God* who gives them over to the delusion of the three unclean spirits; or else *the sixth angel* (vs. 12). **Armageddon**—*Hebrew, Har*, a mountain, and *Megiddo* in Manasseh in Galilee, the scene of the overthrow of the Canaanite kings by God's miraculous interposition under Deborah and Barak; the same as the great plain of Esdraelon. Josiah, too, as the ally of Babylon, was defeated and slain at Megiddo; and the mourning of the Jews at the time just before God shall interpose for them against all the nations confederate against Jerusalem, is compared to the mourning for Josiah at Megiddo. Megiddo comes from a root, *gadad*, "cut off," and means *slaughter*. Cf. Joel 3:2, 12, 14, where "the valley of Jehoshaphat" (meaning in *Hebrew*, "judgment of God") is mentioned as the scene of God's final vengeance on the God-opposing foe. Probably some great plain, antitypical to the valleys of Megiddo and Jehoshaphat, will be the scene. **17. angel**—so ANDREAS. But A, B, *Vulgate*, and *Syriac* omit it. **into**—so ANDREAS (*Greek, eis*). But A and B, "upon" (*Greek, epi*). **great**—so B, *Vulgate, Syriac, Coptic*, and ANDREAS. But A omits. **of heaven**—so B and ANDREAS But A, *Vulgate, Syriac*, and *Coptic* omit. **It is done**—"It is come to pass." God's voice as to the final consummation, as Jesus' voice on the cross when the work of expiation was completed, "It is finished." **18. voice . . . thunders . . . lightnings**—A has the order, "lightnings . . . voices . . . thunders." This is the same close as that of the seven seals and the seven thunders; but with the difference that they do not merely form the conclusion, but introduce the consequence, of the last vial, viz., the utter destruction of Babylon and then of the Antichristian armies. **earthquake**—which is often preceded by a lurid state of air, such as would result from the vial poured upon it. **men were**—so B, *Vulgate, Syriac*, and ANDREAS. But A and *Coptic* read, "A man was." **so mighty**—*Greek*, "such." **19. the great city**—the capital and seat of the apostate Church, spiritual Babylon (of which Rome is the representative, if one literal city be meant). The city in ch. 11:8 (see *Note*), is probably distinct, viz., Jerusalem under Antichrist (*the beast*, who is distinct from *the harlot* or apostate Church). In ch. 11:13 only a *tenth* of Jerusalem falls whereas here the city (Babylon) "became (*Greek*) into three parts" by the earthquake. **cities of the nations**—other great cities in league with spiritual Babylon. **great . . . came in remembrance**—*Greek*, "Babylon the great was remembered" (ch. 18:5). It is now that the last call to escape from Babylon is given to God's people in her (ch. 18:4). **fierceness**—the *boiling over* outburst of His wrath (*Greek, thumou orgees*), cf. *Note*, ch. 14:10. **20.** Plainly parallel to ch. 6:14-17, and by anticipation descriptive of the last judgment. **the mountains**—rather as *Greek*, "there were found no mountains." **21. fell**—*Greek*, "descends." **upon men**—*Greek*, "*the* men." **men**—not those struck who died, but the rest. Unlike the result in the case of Jerusalem (ch. 11:13), where "the remnant . . . affrighted . . . gave glory to the God of heaven." **was**—*Greek*, "is."

CHAPTER 17

VSS. 1-18. THE HARLOT BABYLON'S GAUD: THE BEAST ON WHICH SHE RIDES, HAVING SEVEN HEADS AND TEN HORNS, SHALL BE THE INSTRUMENT OF JUDGMENT ON HER.

1. unto me—A, B, *Vulgate, Syriac*, and *Coptic* omit. **many**—So A. But B, "*the* many waters" (Jer. 51:13); vs. 15, below, explains the sense. The whore is the apostate Church, just as *the woman* (ch. 12) is *the Church while faithful*. **drunk with**—*Greek*, "owing to." It cannot be pagan Rome, but papal Rome, if a particular seat of error be meant, but I incline to think that the judgment (ch. 18:2) and the spiritual fornication (ch. 18:3), though finding their culmination in Rome, are not restricted to it, but comprise the whole apostate Church, Roman, Greek, and even Protestant, so far as it has been seduced from its "first love" (ch. 2:4)

ADAM CLARKE

15. *Behold, I come as a thief*. Here is a sudden but timely warning to put every man on his guard, when this sudden and generally unexpected tribulation should take place. *Keepeth his garments, lest he walk naked*. Here is a plain allusion to the office of him who was called the prefect or overseer of the mountain of the Temple. His custom was to go his rounds during the watches of the night; and if he found any of the Levites sleeping on his watch, he had authority to beat him with a stick and burn his vestments. Such a person being found on his return home *naked*, it was at once known that he had been found asleep at his post, had been beaten, and his clothes burned; thus his *shame* was seen—he was reproached for his infidelity and irreligion.

16. *Armageddon*. The original of this word has been variously formed and variously translated. It is "the mount of the assembly"; or "the destruction of their army"; or it is "Mount Megiddo," the valley of which was remarkable for two great slaughters: one of the Israelites, 2 Kings xxiii. 29, the other of the Canaanites, Judg. iv. 16; v. 19. But what is the battle of Armageddon? How ridiculous have been the conjectures of men relative to this point! Within the last twenty years this battle has been fought at various places, according to our purblind seers and self-inspired prophets! At one time it was Austerlitz, at another Moscow, at another Leipsic, and now Waterloo! And thus they have gone on, and will go on, confounding and being confounded.

17. *Poured out his vial into the air*. To signify that this plague was to be widely diffused, and perhaps to intimate that pestilences and various deaths would be the effect of this vial. *It is done*. It is said, chap. x. 7, that in the days of the seventh trumpet "the mystery of God should be finished"; so here we find it completed. "All's over!"

18. *A great earthquake*. Most terrible commotions, both civil and religious. Or a convulsion, shaking, or revolution.

19. *The great city*. Some say Jerusalem, others Rome pagan, others Rome papal.

The cup of the wine of the fierceness of his wrath. Alluding to the mode of putting certain criminals to death, by making them drink a cup of poison.

20. *Every island fled away*. Probably meaning the capture of seaport towns, and fortified places.

21. *A great hail . . . every stone about the weight of a talent*. Has this any reference to cannon balls and bombs? It is very doubtful; we are all in the dark in these matters. The words "as a talent" are used to express something "great, excessively oppressive."

CHAPTER 17

1. *Come hither; I will show unto thee the judgment of the great whore that sitteth upon many waters*. That idolatrous worship is frequently represented in Scripture under the character of a *whore* or whoredom, is evident from numerous passages which it is unnecessary to quote. The woman mentioned here is called a *great whore*, to denote her excessive depravity, and the awful nature of her idolatry. She is also represented as *sitting upon many waters*, to show the vast extent of her influence.

MATTHEW HENRY

2. The appearance she made, *v.* 4. 3. Her principal seat and residence—*upon the beast that had seven heads and ten horns;* that is to say, Rome, the city on seven hills.

4. Her name, which *was written on her forehead.* She is named from her place of residence—*Babylon the great.*

She is named from her infamous way and practice; not only a harlot, but a mother of harlots.

5. Her diet: she satiated herself with *the blood of the saints and martyrs of Jesus.* She drank their blood with such greediness that she intoxicated herself with it.

Verses 7–13

Here we have the mystery of this vision explained. But it is so explained as still to need further explanation. 1. This beast *was, and is not, and yet is;*

JAMIESON, FAUSSET, BROWN

to Christ, the heavenly Bridegroom, and given its affections to worldly pomps and idols. The *woman* (ch. 12:1) is the congregation of God in its purity under the Old and New Testament, and appears again as the Bride of the Lamb, the transfigured Church prepared for the marriage feast. The woman, the invisible Church, is latent in the apostate Church, and is the Church militant; the Bride is the Church triumphant. **3. the wilderness**—Contrast her in ch. 12:6, 14, having *a place in the wilderness*-world, but not a home; a sojourner here, looking for the city to come. Now, on the contrary, she is contented to have her portion in this moral wilderness. **upon a scarlet . . . beast**—The same as in ch. 13:1, who there is described as here, "having seven heads and ten horns (therein betraying that he is representative of the dragon, ch. 12:3), and upon his heads names (so the oldest MSS. read) of blasphemy"; cf. also vss. 12-14, below, with ch. 19:19, 20, and ch. 17:13, 14, 16. Rome, resting on the world power and ruling it by the claim of supremacy, is the chief, though not the exclusive, representative of this symbol. As the dragon is fiery-*red,* so the beast is blood-red in color; implying its *blood-guiltiness,* and also deep-dyed sin. The *scarlet* is also the symbol of kingly authority. **full**—all over; not merely "on his heads," as in ch. 13:1, for its opposition to God is now about to develop itself in all its intensity. Under the harlot's superintendence, the world power puts forth blasphemous pretensions worse than in pagan days. **4.** The color scarlet, it is remarkable, is that reserved for popes and cardinals. Whenever and wherever (not in Rome alone) the Church, instead of being "clothed (as at first, ch. 12:1) with the sun" of heaven, is arrayed in earthly meretricious gauds, compromising the truth of God through fear, or flattery, of the world's power, science, or wealth, she becomes the harlot seated on the beast, and doomed in righteous retribution to be judged by the beast (vs. 16). Soon, like Rome, and like the Jews of Christ's and the apostles' time leagued with the heathen Rome, she will then become the persecutor of the saints (vs. 6). Instead of drinking her Lord's "cup" of suffering, she has "a cup full of abominations and filthinesses." **decked**—lit., "gilded." **stones**—*Greek,* "stone." **filthiness**—A, B, and ANDREAS read, "the filthy (impure) things. **5. upon . . . forehead . . . name**—as harlots usually had. What a contrast to "HOLINESS TO THE LORD," inscribed on the miter *on* the high priest's *forehead*! **mystery**—implying a spiritual fact heretofore hidden, and incapable of discovery by mere reason, but now revealed. As the union of Christ and the Church is a "**great** mystery" (a spiritual truth of momentous interest, once hidden, now revealed, Eph. 5:31, 32), so the Church conforming to the world and thereby becoming a harlot is a counter "mystery" (or spiritual truth, symbolically now revealed). As iniquity in the harlot is a leaven working in "*mystery,*" and therefore called "the *mystery* of iniquity," so when she is destroyed, the iniquity heretofore working (comparatively) latently in her, shall be *revealed* in *the man of iniquity,* the open embodiment of all previous evil. The name Babylon, which in the image, Daniel 2, is given to the *head,* is here given to the harlot, which marks her as being connected with the fourth kingdom, Rome, the last part of the image. **of harlots**—*Greek,* "of *the* harlots and of *the* abominations." Not merely Rome, but Christendom as a whole, even as formerly Israel as a whole, has become a harlot. The invisible Church of true believers is hidden and dispersed in the visible Church. The boundary lines which separate harlot and woman are not denominational nor drawn externally, but can only be spiritually discerned. **6. martyrs**—witnesses. **I wondered with great admiration**—As the *Greek* is the same in the verb and the noun, translate the latter "wonder." John certainly did not *admire* her in the modern English sense. Elsewhere (vs. 8; ch. 13:3), all the earthly-minded ("they that dwell on the earth") *wonder* in admiration of the beast. Here only is John's *wonder* called forth; not the *beast,* but the woman sunken into the harlot, the Church become a world-loving apostate, moves his sorrowful astonishment at so awful a change. That the world should be beastly is natural, but that the faithful bride should become the whore is monstrous, and excites the same amazement in him as the same awful change in Israel excited in Isaiah and Jeremiah. **8. beast . . . was, and is not**—(Cf. vs. 11). The time when the beast "is not" is the time during which it has "the deadly wound"; the time of *the seventh*

ADAM CLARKE

3. *So he carried me away in the spirit into the wilderness.* This wilderness into which the apostle was carried is the desolate state of the Church of Christ, in one of the wings of the once mighty Roman empire. It was a truly awful sight, a terrible desert, a waste howling wilderness. *Saw a woman sit upon a scarlet-colored beast, full of names of blasphemy, having seven heads and ten horns.* No doubt can now be entertained that this woman is the Latin Church, for she sits upon the beast with seven heads and ten horns, which has been already proven to be the Latin empire, because his empire alone contains the number 666. This is a representation of the Latin Church in her highest state of antichristian prosperity, for she sits upon the scarlet-colored beast, a striking emblem of her complete domination over the secular Latin empire.

4. *And the woman was arrayed in purple and scarlet color, and decked with gold, and precious stones, and pearls, having a golden cup in her hand full of abominations and filthiness of her fornication.* This strikingly represents the most pompous and costly manner in which the Latin Church has held forth to the nations the rites and ceremonies of its idolatrous and corrupt worship.

5. *And upon her forehead was a name written, Mystery, Babylon the Great, the Mother of Harlots, and Abominations of the Earth.* This inscription being written upon her forehead is intended to show that she is not ashamed of her doctrines, but publicly professes and glories in them before the nations: she has indeed *a whore's forehead, she has refused to be ashamed.* The inscription upon her forehead is exactly the portraiture of the Latin Church.

7. *And the angel said unto me, Wherefore didst thou marvel? I will tell thee the mystery of the woman, and of the beast that carrieth her, which hath the seven heads and ten horns.* The apostle was greatly astonished, as well he might be, at the woman's being *drunk with the blood of the saints,* when the beast which carried her abounded with sacred appellations, such as holy, most holy, most Christian, sacred, most sacred. The angel undertakes to explain to St. John the vision which had excited in him so great astonishment; and the explication is of such great importance, that, had it not been given, the mystery of the dragon and the beast could never have been satisfactorily explained in all its particulars.

8. *The beast that thou sawest was, and is not; and shall ascend out of the bottomless pit, and go into perdition.* The beast is the Latin kingdom; consequently, the beast *was,* that is, was in existence previously to

MATTHEW HENRY

it *was* a seat of idolatry and persecution; *and is not*, not in the ancient form, *and yet it is* truly the seat of idolatry and tyranny. *It ascends out of the bottomless pit*, and it shall return thither and go into perdition.

2. *This beast has seven heads*, which have a double signification. *Seven mountains*—the seven hills on which Rome stands. *Seven kings*—seven sorts of government.

Five of these were extinct; one was then in being; and the other was yet to come, *v.* 10. This beast makes an eighth.

J. A. SEISS:

By these seven great powers then, filling up the whole interval of this world's history, this great Harlot is said to be carried. On these she rides, according to the vision. It is not upon one alone, nor upon any particular number of them, but upon all of them, the whole seven-headed Beast, that she sits. These seven powers, each and all, support the Woman as their joy and pride; and she accepts and uses them, and sways their administrations, and rides in glory by means of them. They are her devotees, lovers, and most humble servants; and she is their patronizing and most noble lady, with a mutuality of favors and inter-communion belonging to her designation. This is the picture as explained by the angel. But, to say that the Romish Papacy was thus carried, nurtured, and sustained by the ancient empires of Greece, Persia, Babylon, Assyria, and Egypt, would be a great lie on history. It was not so. In the nature of things it could not be so. By no means then can this Harlot be the Papacy alone. Furthermore, it is a matter of fact, that as surely as Rome in John's day, and Greece, Persia, Babylon, Assyria, and Egypt, before Rome, existed and bore sway on earth as regal mountains, so surely and conspicuously were they each and all ridden by this great Harlot. They were each and all the lovers, supporters, and defenders of organized falsehood in religion, the patrons of idolatry, the foster friends of all manner of spiritual harlotry.—*The Apocalypse*

JAMIESON, FAUSSET, BROWN

head becoming Christian externally, when its beastlike character was put into suspension temporarily. The *healing of its wound* answers to its *ascending out of the bottomless pit.* The beast, or Antichristian world power, returns worse than ever, with satanic powers from hell (ch. 11:7), not merely from *the sea* of convulsed nations (ch. 13:1). **go**—So B, *Vulgate*, and ANDREAS read the future tense. But A and IRENÆUS, "goeth." **into perdition**—The continuance of this revived seventh (i.e., the eighth) head is short: it is therefore called "the son of perdition," who is essentially doomed to it almost immediately after his appearance. **names were**—so *Vulgate* and ANDREAS. But A, B, *Syriac*, and *Coptic* read the singular, "name is." **written in**—*Greek*, *"upon."* **which**—rather, "when they behold the beast *that* it was .... So *Vulgate*. **was, and is not, and yet is**—A, B, and ANDREAS read, "... and shall come" (lit., "be present," viz., again: *Greek, kai parestai*). The *Hebrew, tetragrammaton*, or sacred four letters in *Jehovah* "who is, who was, and who is to come," the believer's object of worship, has its contrasted counterpart in the beast "who was, and is not, and shall be present," the object of the earth's worship [BENGEL].

9. Cf. ch. 13:18; Daniel 12:10, where similarly spiritual discernment is put forward as needed in order to understand the symbolical prophecy. **seven heads and seven mountains**—The connection between *mountains and kings* must be deeper than the mere outward fact to which incidental allusion is made, that Rome (the then world city) is on seven hills (whence heathen Rome had a national festival called *Septimontium*, the feast of the seven-hilled city [PLUTARCH]; and on the imperial coins, just as here, she is represented as a *woman seated on seven hills.* As nature shadows forth the great realities of the spiritual world, so seven-hilled Rome is *a* representative of the seven-headed world power of which the dragon has been, and is the prince. The seven universal God-opposed monarchies are Egypt (the first world power which came into collision with God's people,) Assyria, Babylon, Greece, Medo-Persia, Rome, the Germanic-Slavonic empire (the *clay* of the fourth kingdom mixed with its iron in Nebuchadnezzar's image, a *fifth* material, Dan. 2:33, 34, 42, 43, symbolizing this last head). *The woman sitting on the seven hills* implies the Old and New Testament Church conforming to, and resting on, the world power, i.e., on all the seven world kingdoms. **10. there are**—Translate, "they (the seven heads) are seven kings." **five ... one**—*Greek*, "the five ... the one"; the first five of the seven are *fallen* (a word applicable not to *forms of government passing away*, but to the *fall* of once powerful empires: Egypt, Ezek. 29 and 30; Assyria and Nineveh, Nah. 3:1-19; Babylon, ch. 18: 2; Jer. 50 and 51; Medo-Persia, Dan. 8:3-7, 20-22; 10:13; 11:2; Greece, Dan. 11:4). *Rome* was "the one" existing in John's days. "Kings" is the Scripture phrase for *kingdoms*, because these kingdoms are generally represented in character by some one prominent head, as Babylon by Nebuchadnezzar, Medo-Persia by Cyrus, Greece by Alexander, etc. **the other is not yet come**—not as ALFORD, inaccurately representing AUBERLEN, *the Christian empire beginning with Constantine;* but, the *Germanic-Slavonic* empire *beginning* and continuing in its beastlike, i.e., HEATHEN Antichristian character for only "a short space." The time when it is said of it, "it is not" (vs. 11), is the *time* during which it is "wounded to death," and has the "deadly wound" ch. 13:3). **11. beast that ... is not**—his beastly character being kept down by outward Christianization of the state until he starts up to life again as "the eighth" king, his "wound being healed" (ch. 13:3), Antichrist manifested in fullest and most intense opposition to God. The "he" is emphatic in the Greek. *He*, peculiarly and preeminently: answering to "the little horn" with eyes like the eyes of a man, and a mouth speaking great things, before whom *three of the ten horns were plucked up by the roots*, and to whom the whole ten "give their power and strength" (vss. 12, 13, 17). That a *personal* Antichrist will stand at the head of the Antichristian kingdom, is likely from the analogy of Antiochus Epiphanes, the Old Testament Antichrist, "the little horn" in Daniel 8:9-12; also, "the man of sin, son of perdition" (II Thess. 2:3-8), answers here to "goeth into perdition," and is applied to an individual, viz., Judas, in the only other passage where the phrase occurs (John 17:12). He is essentially a child of destruction, and hence he has but a little time ascended

ADAM CLARKE

the time of St. John; *is not* now, because the Latin nation has ceased long ago to be an independent power, and is now under the domination of the Romans; but *shall ascend out of the bottomless pit*, that is, the Latin kingdom, the antichristian power, or that which ascendeth out of the abyss or bottomless pit, is yet in futurity. *And they that dwell on the earth shall wonder, whose names were not written in the book of life from the foundation of the world, when they behold the beast.* By the *earth* is here meant the Latin world; therefore the meaning is, that all who dwell in the Latin world shall adhere to the idolatrous and blasphemous religion of the Latin Church, which is supported by the Latin empire, except those who abide by the sacred Scriptures, receiving them as the only rule of faith and practice. These believe in the true Sacrifice, and keep themselves unspotted from the corruption that is in the world.

9. *The seven heads are seven mountains, on which the woman sitteth.* This verse has been almost universally considered to allude to the seven hills upon which Rome originally stood. But it has been objected that modern Rome is not thus situated, and that, consequently, pagan Rome is intended in the prophecy. This is certainly a very formidable objection against the generally received opinion among Protestants, that papal Rome is the city meant by the woman sitting upon seven mountains. It has been already shown that *the woman* here mentioned is an emblem of the Latin Church in her highest state of antichristian prosperity; and therefore the city of Rome, seated upon seven mountains, is not at all designed in the prophecy. In order to understand this scripture aright, the word *mountains* must be taken in a figurative and not a literal sense. The mountains upon which the woman sitteth must be seven great powers; and as the mountains are *heads* of the beast, they must be the seven greatest eminences of the Latin world.

10. *And there are seven kings.* Before, it was said, they are *seven mountains*; here, they are also *seven kings*, which is a demonstration that kingdoms are not here meant by *mountains*: and this is a further argument that the seven electorates are represented by seven mountains, for though the sovereigns of these states ranked with kings, they were not kings; that is to say, they were not absolute and sole lords of the territories they possessed, independently of the emperor, for their states formed a part of the Germanic body. But the seven heads of the beast are also seven kings, that is to say, the Latin empire has had seven supreme forms of government; for king is used in the prophetical writings for any supreme governor of a state or people.

11. *And the beast, that was, and is not, even he is the eighth, and is of the seven, and goeth into perdition.* That is to say, the Latin kingdom that has already been, but is now no longer nominally in existence, shall immediately follow the dissolution of the seventh form of Latin government; and this dominion is called *an eighth*, because it succeeds to the seventh. Yet it is not an eighth head of the beast, because the beast has only seven heads; for to constitute a new head of the beast the form of government must not only differ in nature, but also in name. This head of the beast is, therefore, one of the seven. Consequently the form of government represented by this head is the restoration of one of the preceding seven. The restored head can be therefore no other than the regal state of the Latins, or in other words, the Latin kingdom.

MATTHEW HENRY

3. This beast had ten horns; which are said to be *ten kings which have as yet received no kingdoms.*

Verses 14-18

I. War begun between the beast and his followers, and the Lamb and his followers. One would think an army with a lamb at the head of them could not stand before *the great red dragon.*

II. Victory gained by the Lamb: *The Lamb shall overcome.* He will be sure to meet with many enemies, but he will also be sure to gain the victory.

III. The ground or reason of the victory. 1. From the character of the Lamb: *He is King of kings and Lord of lords.* All the powers of earth and hell are subject to his check and control. 2. From the character of his followers: *They are called, and chosen, and faithful.* Such an army, under such a commander, will at length carry all the world before them.

IV. The victory is justly aggrandized. 1. By the vast multitude who paid obedience and subjection to the beast and to the whore, *v.* 15, 18.

2. By the powerful influence which God hereby showed he had over the minds of great men. It was of God, and to fulfil his will, that these kings *agreed to give their kingdom unto the beast.* It was of God that afterwards their hearts were turned against the whore.

JAMIESON, FAUSSET, BROWN

out of the bottomless pit, when he "goes into perdition" (vss. 8, 11). "While the Church passes through death of the flesh to glory of the Spirit, the beast passes through the glory of the flesh to death" [AUBERLEN]. **is of the seven**—rather "springs *out of* the seven." The eighth is not merely one of the seven restored, but a new power or person proceeding *out of* the seven, and at the same time embodying all the God-opposed features of the previous seven concentrated and consummated; for which reason there are said to be not *eight,* but only *seven* heads, for the eighth is the embodiment of all the seven. **12. ten kings . . . received no kingdom as yet; but receive power as kings . . . with the beast**—Hence and from vss. 14, 16, it seems that these ten kings or kingdoms, are to be contemporaries with the beast in its last or eighth form, viz., Antichrist. Cf. Daniel 2:34, 44, "the stone smote the image upon *his feet,*" i.e., upon the *ten* toes, which are, in vss. 41-44, interpreted to be "*kings.*" The ten kingdoms are not, therefore, ten which arose in the overthrow of Rome (heathen), but are to rise out of the last state of the fourth kingdom under the eighth head. **one hour**—a definite *time* of *short* duration, during which "the devil is come down to the inhabitant of the earth and of the sea, having great wrath, because he knoweth that he hath but a *short time.*" Probably the three and a half years (ch. 11:2. 3; 13:5). **13. one mind**—one *sentiment.* **shall give**—so *Coptic.* But A, B, and *Syriac,* "give." **strength**—*Greek,* "authority." They become his dependent allies (vs. 14). Thus Antichrist sets up to be *King of kings,* but scarcely has he put forth his claim when the true KING OF KINGS appears and dashes him down in a moment to destruction. **14. These shall . . . war with the Lamb**—in league with the beast. This is a summary anticipation of ch. 19:19. This shall not be till *after* they have first executed judgment on the harlot (vss. 15, 16). **Lord of lords . . .**—anticipating ch. 19:16. *are*—not in the *Greek.* Therefore translate, "And they that are with Him, called chosen, and faithful (shall overcome them, viz., the beast and his allied kings)." These have been with Christ in heaven unseen, but now appear with Him. **15.** (Vs. 1; Isa. 8:7.) An impious parody of Jehovah who "sitteth upon the flood" [ALFORD]. Also, contrast the "many waters" ch. 19:6, "Alleluia." The "peoples . . ." here mark the universality of the spiritual fornication of the Church. The "tongues" remind us of the original Babel, the confusion of *tongues,* the beginning of Babylon, and the first commencement of idolatrous apostasy after the flood, as the tower was doubtless dedicated to the deified heavens. Thus, Babylon is the appropriate name of the harlot. **16. upon the beast**—But A, B, *Vulgate,* and *Syriac* read, "*and* the beast." **shall make her desolate**—having first dismounted her from her seat on the beast (vs. 3). **naked**—stripped of all her gaud (vs. 4). As Jerusalem used the world power to crucify her Saviour, and then was destroyed by that very power, Rome; so the Church, having apostatized to the world, shall have judgment executed on her first by the world power, the beast and his allies; and these afterwards shall have judgment executed on them by Christ Himself in person.

eat her flesh—*Greek* plural, "masses of flesh," i.e., "carnal possessions"; implying the fulness of carnality into which the Church is sunk. The judgment on the harlot is again and again described (ch. 18:1; 19:5); first by an "angel having great power" (ch. 18:1), then by "another voice from heaven" (ch. 18:4-20), then by "a mighty angel" (ch. 18:21-24). Cf. Ezekiel 16:37-44, orginally said of Israel, but further applicable to the New Testament Church when fallen into spiritual fornication. On the phrase, "eat . . . flesh" for prey upon one's property, and injure the character and person, cf. Psalm 14:4; 27:2; Jeremiah 10:25; Micah 3:3.

burn . . . with fire—the legal punishment of an abominable fornication. **17. hath put**—the prophetical past tense for the future. **fulfil**—*Greek,* "do," or "accomplish." The *Greek, poiesai,* is distinct from that which is translated, "fulfilled," *Greek, telesthesontai,* below. **his will**—*Greek,* "his mind," or *purpose;* while they think only of doing their own purpose. **to agree**—lit., "to do (or *accomplish*) one mind" or "purpose." A and *Vulgate* omit this clause, but B supports it. **the words of God**—foretelling the rise and downfall of the beast; *Greek, hoi logoi,* in A, B, and ANDREAS. *English Version* reading is *Greek, ta rhemata,* which is not well supported. No mere articulate utterances, but the efficient *words* of Him who is *the Word: Greek, logos.* **fulfilled**—(ch. 10:7). **18.**

ADAM CLARKE

12. *And the ten horns which thou sawest are ten kings, which have received no kingdom as yet; but receive power as kings one hour with the beast.* Though the Latin empire be now in existence, the ten horns refer to ten Latin kingdoms yet in futurity, and consequently they have received no dominion as yet; for that part of the Latin domination now in power is the sixth head, or imperial government of the heathen Caesars. But the ten states of the Latins receive dominion as monarchies at the same time with the beast, or that which ascendeth out of the bottomless pit; consequently, the Latin empire here intended is the one which was in futurity in the apostolic age.

13. *These have one mind, and shall give their power and strength unto the beast.* Therefore the ten horns must constitute the principal strength of the Latin empire; that is to say, this empire is to be composed of the dominions of ten monarchs independent of each other in every other sense except in their implicit obedience to the Latin Church.

14. *These shall make war with the Lamb, and the Lamb shall overcome them.* The ten powers of the beast must compose the secular kingdom of antichrist, for they make war *with the Lamb,* who is Christ Jesus. This is perfectly true of all popish states, for they have constantly opposed, as long as they have had any secular power, the progress of pure Christianity. They make war with the Lamb by persecuting his followers.

16. *And the ten horns which thou sawest upon the beast, these shall hate the whore, and shall make her desolate and naked, and shall eat her flesh, and burn her with fire.* It is said the *ten horns* shall *hate* the whore; by which is evidently meant, when connected with what follows, that the whole of the ten kingdoms in the interest of the Latin Church shall finally despise her doctrines, be reformed from popery, assist in depriving her of all influence and in exposing her follies, and in the end consign her to utter destruction. From this it follows that no Roman Catholic power which did not exist so late as the Reformation can be numbered among the horns of the beast; the horns must, therefore, be found among the great states of Europe at the commencement of the Reformation.

17. *For God hath put in their hearts to fulfil his will, and to agree, and give their kingdom unto the beast, until the words of God shall be fulfilled.* Let no one imagine that these ten Latin kingdoms, because they support an idolatrous worship, have been raised up merely by the power of man or the chances of war. No kingdom or state can exist without the will of God; therefore let the inhabitants of the world tremble when they see a wicked monarchy rise to power, and let them consider that it is raised up by the Lord to execute his vengeance upon the idolatries and profligacies of the times.

MATTHEW HENRY | JAMIESON, FAUSSET, BROWN | ADAM CLARKE

reigneth—lit., "*hath kingship* over the kings." The harlot cannot be a mere *city* literally, but is called so in a spiritual sense (ch. 11:8). Also the beast cannot represent a spiritual power, but a world power. In this verse the harlot is presented before us ripe for judgment. The 18th chapter details that judgment.

MATTHEW HENRY — CHAPTER 18

Verses 1–8

Here is another angel sent from heaven, *v.* 1. He had not only light in himself, to discern the truth of his own prediction, but to inform and enlighten the world about that great event. This angel publishes the fall of Babylon, as a thing already come to pass. Here seems to be an allusion to the prediction of the fall of pagan Babylon (Isa. xxi. 9), where the word is repeated as it is here: *has fallen, has fallen, v.* 2. This is also borrowed from Isa. xxi. 9, and seems to describe not so much her sin as her punishment, it being a common notion that unclean spirits, as well as ominous and hateful birds, used to haunt a city or house that lay in its ruins. The reason of this ruin is declared (*v.* 3). She had not only forsaken the true God herself, and set up idols, but had drawn all sorts of men into the spiritual adultery, and by her wealth and luxury had retained them in her interest.

All that expect mercy from God should not only *come out of her*, but be assisting in her destruction, *v.* 4, 5 God may have a people even in Babylon.

Those that are resolved to partake with wicked men in their sins must receive of their plagues. Though private revenge is forbidden, yet God will have his people act under him, when called to it, in pulling down his and their implacable enemies, *v.* 6.

God will proportion the punishment of sinners to the measure of their pride, and security, *v.* 7.

JAMIESON, FAUSSET, BROWN — CHAPTER 18

Vss. 1-24. BABYLON'S FALL: GOD'S PEOPLE CALLED OUT OF HER: THE KINGS AND MERCHANTS OF THE EARTH MOURN, WHILE THE SAINTS REJOICE AT HER FALL. **1. And**—so *Vulgate* and ANDREAS. But A, B, *Syriac,* and *Coptic* omit "And." **power**—Greek, "authority." **lightened**—"illumined." **with**—*Greek,* "owing to." **2. mightily . . . strong**—not supported by MSS. But A, B, *Vulgate, Syriac,* and *Coptic* read, "with (lit., 'in' a mighty voice." **is fallen, is fallen**—so A, *Vulgate, Syriac,* and ANDREAS. But B and *Coptic* omit the second "is fallen" (Isa. 21:9; Jer. 51:8). This phrase is here prophetical of her fall, still future, as vs. 4 proves. **devils**—*Greek,* "demons." **the hold**—a keep or prison. **3. drunk**—ch. 14:8, from which perhaps "the wine" may have been interpolated. They have *drunk of her fornication,* the consequence of which will be *wrath* to themselves. But A, B, and C read, "(owing to the wrath of her fornication all nations) have *fallen." Vulgate* and most versions read as *English Version,* which may be the right reading though not supported by the oldest MSS. Babylon, the whore, is destroyed before the beast slays the two witnesses (ch. 11), and then the beast himself is destroyed. **the wine**—so B, *Syriac,* and *Coptic.* But A, C, and *Vulgate* omit. **abundance**—lit., "power." **delicacies**—*Greek,* "luxury." See *Note,* I Timothy 5:11, where the *Greek* verb "wax wanton" is akin to the noun here. Translate, "wanton luxury." The reference is not to earthly merchandise, but to spiritual wares, indulgences, idolatries, superstitions, worldly compromises, wherewith the harlot, i.e., the apostate Church, has made *merchandise* of men.

4. Come out of her, my people—quoted from Jeremiah 50:8; 51:6, 45. Even in the Romish Church God has a people: but they are in great danger; their only safety is in coming out of her at once. So also in every apostate or world-conforming church there are some of God's invisible and true Church, who, if they would be safe, must come out. Especially at the eve of God's judgment on apostate Christendom: as Lot was warned to come out of Sodom just before its destruction, and Israel to come from about the tents of Dathan and Abiram. So the first Christians came out of Jerusalem when the apostate Jewish Church was judged. **partakers**—*Greek,* "have no *fellowship with* her sins." **that ye receive not of her plagues**—as Lot's wife, by lingering too near the polluted and doomed city. **5. her sins**—as a great heap. **reached**—*Greek,* "reached so far as to come into close contact with, and to *cleave* unto." **6.** Addressed to the executioners of God's wrath. **Reward**—*Greek,* "repay." **she rewarded**—*English Version* reading adds "you" with none of the oldest MSS. But A, B, C, *Vulgate, Syriac,* and *Coptic* omit it. She had not *rewarded* or *repaid* the world power for some injury which the world power had inflicted on her; but she had *given* the world power that which was its *due,* viz., spiritual delusions, because it did not like to retain God in its knowledge; the unfaithful Church's principle was, *Populus vult decipi, et decipiatur,* "The people like to be deceived, and let them be deceived." **double**—of sorrow. Contrast with this the *double* of joy which Jerusalem shall receive for her past suffering (Isa. 61:7; Zech. 9:12); even as she has received *double* punishment for her sins (Isa. 40:2). **unto her**—So *Syriac, Coptic,* and ANDREAS. A, B, and C omit it. **in the cup**—(vs. 3; ch. 14:8; 17:4). **filled**—lit., mixed. **fill to her double**—of the Lord's cup of wrath. **7. How much**—i.e., in proportion as. **lived deliciously**—luxuriously: *Note,* vs. 3, where the *Greek* is akin. **sorrow**—*Greek,* "mourning," as for a dead husband. **I sit**—so *Vulgate.* But A, B, and C prefix "that." **I . . . am no widow**—for the world power is my husband and my supporter. **shall see no sorrow**—*Greek,* "mourning." "I am seated (*this long time*) . . . I *am* no widow . . . I *shall* see no sorrow," marks her complete unconcerned security as to the past, present, and future [BENGEL]. I shall never have to mourn as one bereft of her husband. As Babylon was queen of the East, so Rome has been queen of the West, and is called on Imperial coins "the *eternal* city."

ADAM CLARKE — CHAPTER 18

1. *The earth was lightened with his glory.* This may refer to some extraordinary messenger of the everlasting gospel, who, by his preaching and writings, should be the means of diffusing the light of truth and true religion over the earth.

2. *Babylon the great is fallen, is fallen.* This is a quotation from Isa. xxi. 9: "And he . . . said, Babylon is fallen, is fallen; and all the graven images of her gods he hath broken unto the ground." This is applied by some to Rome pagan, by others to Rome papal, and by others to Jerusalem. *Is become . . . the hold of every foul spirit.* See the parallel passages in the margin. The figures here point out the most complete destruction. A city utterly sacked and ruined, never to be rebuilt.

3. *The wine of the wrath.* The punishment due to her transgressions, because they have partaken with her in her sins. See the note on chap. xiv. 8.

4. *Come out of her, my people.* These words appear to be taken from Isa. xlviii. 20; Jer. i. 8; li. 6, 45.

5. *Her sins have reached unto heaven.* They are become so great and enormous that the long-suffering of God must give place to His justice.

6. *Reward her even as she rewarded you.* These words are a prophetic declaration of what shall take place: God will deal with her as she dealt with others.

MATTHEW HENRY

When destruction comes on a people suddenly, the surprise is a great aggravation of their misery, *v.* 8.

Verses 9–24

I. A doleful lamentation made by Babylon's friends for her fall.

1. The mourners, those who had been bewitched by her fornication, and those who had been gainers by her wealth and trade—the kings and the merchants of the earth.

2. The manner of their mourning. They stood afar off. Even Babylon's friends will stand at a distance from her fall. Though they had been partakers with her in her sinful pleasures and profits, they were not willing to bear a share in her plagues. They made a grievous outcry, *v.* 19. Those who have most indulged themselves in pride and pleasure are the least able to bear calamities.

3. The cause of their mourning; not their sin, but their punishment. The spirit of antichrist is a worldly spirit, and their sorrow is a mere worldly sorrow. The wealth and merchandise of this city, all which was suddenly lost (*v.* 12, 13), and lost irrecoverably (*v.* 14).

The church of God may fall for a time, but she shall rise again; but the fall of Babylon will be an utter overthrow. Godly sorrow is some support under affliction, but mere worldly sorrow adds to the calamity.

JAMIESON, FAUSSET, BROWN

8. death—on herself, though she thought herself secure even from the death of her husband. **mourning**—instead of her feasting. **famine**—instead of her *luxurious delicacies* (vss. 3, 7). **fire**—(*Note,* ch. 17:16). Literal fire may burn the literal city of Rome, which is situated in the midst of volcanic agencies. But as the harlot is mystical (the whole faithless Church), the *burning* may be mainly mystical, symbolizing utter destruction and removal. **the Lord**—so B, C, *Syriac,* and ANDREAS. But A and *Vulgate* omit. "Strong" is the meaning of God's *Hebrew* name, EL. **judgeth**—But A, B, and C read the *past* tense (*Greek, krinas*), "who *hath judged* her": the prophetical past for the future: the charge in vs. 4 to God's people to *come out of her* implies that the judgment was not yet actually executed. **9. lived deliciously**—*Greek,* luxuriated. The faithless Church, instead of reproving, connived at the self-indulgent luxury of the great men of this world, and sanctioned it by her own practice. Contrast the world's *rejoicing* over the dead bodies of the two witnesses (ch. 11:10) who had tormented it by their faithfulness, with its *lamentations* over the harlot who had made the way to heaven smooth, and had been found a useful tool in keeping subjects in abject tyranny. Men's carnal mind relishes a religion like that of the apostate Church, which gives an opiate to conscience, while leaving the sinner license to indulge his lusts. **bewail her**—A, B, C, *Syriac, Coptic,* and CYPRIAN omit "her." **10.** God's judgments inspire fear even in the worldly, but it is of short duration, for the kings and great men soon attach themselves to the beast in its last and worst shape, as open Antichrist, claiming all that the harlot had claimed in blasphemous pretensions and more, and so making up to them for the loss of the harlot. **mighty**—*Rome* in *Greek* means *strength;* though that derivation is doubtful. **11. shall**—So. B. But A and C read the present, "weep and mourn." **merchandise**—*Greek,* "cargo": wares carried in *ships*: ship-lading (cf. vs. 17). Rome was not a commercial city, and is not likely from her position to be so. The *merchandise* must therefore be spiritual, even as the harlot is not literal, but spiritual. She did not witness against carnal luxury and pleasure-seeking, the source of the *merchants'* gains, but conformed to them (vs. 7). **12.** (*Note,* ch. 17:4.) **stones . . . pearls**—*Greek,* "stone . . . pearl." **fine linen**—A, B, and C read *Greek, bussinou* for *bussou,* i.e., fine linen manufacture" [ALFORD]. The manufacture for which *Egypt* (the type of the apostate Church, ch. 11:8) was famed. Contrast "the fine linen" (Ezek. 16:10) put on Israel, and on the New Testament Church (ch. 19:8), the Bride, by God (Ps. 132:9). **thyine wood**—the *citrus* of the Romans: probably the *cypressus thyoyides,* or the *thuia articulata.* "Citron wood" [ALFORD]. A sweet-smelling tree of Cyrene in Lybia, used for incense. **all manner vessels**—*Greek,* "every vessel," or "furniture." **13. cinnamon**—designed by God for better purposes: being an ingredient in the holy anointing oil, and a plant in the garden of the Beloved (Song of Sol. 4:14); but desecrated to vile uses by the adulteress (Prov. 7:17). **odours**—of incense. A, C, *Vulgate,* and *Syriac* prefix "and amomium" (a precious hair ointment made from an Asiatic shrub). *English Version* reading is supported by *Coptic* and ANDREAS, but not oldest MSS. **ointments**—*Greek,* "ointment." **frankincense**—Contrast the true "incense" which God loves (Ps. 141: 2; Mal. 1:11). **fine flour**—the *similago* of the Latins [ALFORD]. **beasts**—of burden: cattle. **slaves**—*Greek,* "bodies." **souls of men**—(Ezek. 27:13). Said of *slaves.* Appropriate to the spiritual harlot, apostate Christendom, especially Rome, which has so often *enslaved* both *bodies* and *souls* of men. **14.** Direct address to Babylon. **the fruits that thy soul lusted after**—*Greek,* "thy autumn-ripe fruits of the lust (eager desire) of the soul." **dainty**—*Greek,* "fat": "sumptuous" in food. **goodly**—"splendid," "bright," in dress and equipage. **departed**—supported by none of our MSS. But A, B, C, *Vulgate, Syriac,* and *Coptic* read, "perished." **thou shalt**—A, C, *Vulgate,* and *Syriac* read, "*They* (men) *shall* no more find them at all." **15. of these things**—of the things mentioned, vss. 12, 13. **which**—"*who.*" **made rich by**—*Greek,* "derived riches *from* her." **stand afar off for the fear**—(Cf. vs. 10). **wailing**—*Greek,* "mourning." **16. And**—so *Vulgate* and ANDREAS. But A, B, and C omit. **decked**—lit., "gilded." **stones . . . pearls**—*Greek,* "stone . . . pearl." B and ANDREAS read "pearls." But A and C, "pearl." **17. is come to naught**—*Greek,* "is desolated." **shipmaster**—*Greek,* "steersman," or "pilot." **all the company in ships**—A, C, *Vulgate,*

ADAM CLARKE

8. *Therefore shall her plagues come. Death,* by the sword of her adversaries; *mourning,* on account of the slaughter; and *famine,* the fruits of the field being destroyed by the hostile bands.

9. *The kings of the earth.* Those who copied her superstitions and adopted her idolatries.

10. *Standing afar off.* Beholding her desolations with wonder and astonishment, utterly unable to afford her any kind of assistance.

11. *The merchants of the earth.* These are represented as mourning over her, because their traffic with her was at an end.

J. A. SEISS:

The destruction of Great Babylon is an illustrious exhibition of the truth and righteousness of the divine administrations. Often it would seem as if God had forgotten his word, so great is the posterity of the wicked, the triumph of injustice, the wrongs and afflictions which those who most honor him suffer. But it is not so. He is true. His ways are just. Everything will come out fully equalized at the last. And here is a signal demonstration of the fact. The godless wisdom and pride of men are left to work themselves out to the full, but when the harvest is ripe the sweep of the sharp sickle of judgment comes against it and it suddenly falls, and all its just deservings it gets. The harlot has her day; but then comes her night with never a star of hope to rise upon her anymore. She is permitted to lure, delude, and debauch the world, because men preferred her abominations to the truth and kingdom of God; but only that her judgment may be the more conspicuous, and her destruction the more signal and complete. And the halleluia of eternity is all the louder and more intense because her judgment comes as it does. Ah, yes, God's ways are right; his judgments are true and righteous. Perplexing and trying as they may be for the time, our halleluias will be all the deeper and the sweeter by reason of what we may now deplore.

—The Apocalypse

13. *Slaves.* The "bodies of men"; probably distinguished here from *souls of men,* to express bondmen and freemen.

14. *Dainty and goodly.* "Delicacies for the table"; what is "splendid and costly in apparel."

16. *Clothed in fine linen, and purple.* The verb which we here translate *clothed* signifies often "to abound, be enriched, laden with," and is so used by the best Greek writers. These articles are not to be considered here as personal ornaments, but as articles of trade or merchandise, in which this city trafficked.

17. *Every shipmaster.* Captains of vessels; some think pilots are meant, and this is most likely to be the meaning of the original word. This description appears to be at least partly taken from Ezek. xxvii. 26-28. *And all the company in ships.* The crowd or passengers

MATTHEW HENRY

II. The joy and triumph there was both in heaven and earth at the irrecoverable fall of Babylon, *v.* 20. 1. How universal this joy would be: heaven and earth, angels and saints, would join in it. 2. How just and reasonable. (1) Because the fall of Babylon was an act of God's justice. Though they did not take pleasure in the miseries of any, yet they had reason to rejoice in the discoveries of the glorious justice of God.

(2) Because it was an irrecoverable ruin (*v.* 21). The place shall be no longer habitable by man, no work shall be done there, no comfort enjoyed, no light seen there, but utter darkness and desolation, as the reward of her great wickedness, *v.* 24. Such abominable sins deserved so great a ruin.

JAMIESON, FAUSSET, BROWN

and *Syriac* read, "Every one who saileth to a place" (B has "... to *the* place") *every voyager.* **18. when they saw**–*Greek, horontes.* But A, B, C, and ANDREAS read, *Greek, blepontes,* "looking at." *Greek, blepo,* is to *use the eyes,* to *look:* the act of seeing without thought of the object seen. *Greek, horao,* refers to the thing *seen* or presented to the eyes [TITTMANN]. **smoke**–so B, C. But A reads "place." **What city is like**–Cf. the similar beast as to *the beast,* ch. 13: 4: so closely do the harlot and beast approximate one another. **19. wailing**–"mourning." **that had ships**–A, B, and C read, "that had *their* ships": lit., "*the* ships." **costliness**–her costly treasures: abstract for concrete. **20. holy apostles**–So C reads. But A, B, *Vulgate, Syriac, Coptic,* and ANDREAS read, "Ye *saints and ye* apostles." **avenged you on her**–*Greek,* "judged your judgment on (lit., exacting it *from*) her." "There is more joy in heaven at the harlot's downfall than at that of the two beasts. For the most heinous of all sin is the sin of those who know God's word of grace, and keep it not. The worldliness of the Church is the most worldly of all worldliness. **21. a**–*Greek,* "one." **millstone**–Cf. the judgment on the Egyptian hosts at the Red Sea, Exodus 15:5, 10; Nehemiah 9:11, and the foretold doom of Babylon, the world power, Jeremiah 51:63, 64. **with violence**–*Greek,* "with impetus." This verse shows that this prophecy is regarded as still to be fulfilled. **22. pipers**–flute players. "Musicians," painters and sculptors, have desecrated their art to lend fascination to the sensuous worship of corrupt Christendom. **craftsman**–artisan. **23.** What a blessed contrast is ch. 22:5, respecting the city of God: "They need *no candle* (just as Babylon shall *no more* have *the light of a candle,* but for a widely different reason), for the Lord God giveth them light." **candle**–Translate as *Greek,* "lamp." **bridegroom ... bride ... no more ... in thee**–Contrast the heavenly city, with its *Bridegroom, Bride,* and blessed *marriage supper* (ch. 19:7, 9; 21:2, 9; Isa. 62:4, 5). **thy merchants were**–So most of the best authorities read. But A omits the *Greek* article before "merchants," and then translates, "The great men of ... were thy merchants." **sorceries**–*Greek,* "sorcery." **24.** Applied by Christ (Matt. 23:35) to apostate Jerusalem, which proves that not merely the literal city Rome, and the Church of Rome (though the *chief* representative of the apostasy), but the WHOLE of the faithless Church of both the Old and New Testament is meant by Babylon the harlot; just as the whole Church (Old and New Testament) is meant by "the woman" (ch. 12:1).

ADAM CLARKE

aboard. But the best MSS. and versions have "those who sail from place to place."

18. *What city is like unto this great city!* Viz., in magnitude, power, and luxury.

19. *They cast dust on their heads.* They showed every sign of the sincerest grief. The lamentation over this great ruined city, from vv. 9 to 19, is exceedingly strong and well-drawn. Here is no dissembled sorrow; all is real to the mourners, and affecting to the spectators.

20. *Rejoice over her, thou heaven.* This is grand and sublime; the fall of this bad city was cause of grief to bad men. But as this city was a persecutor of the godly and an enemy to the works of God, angels, apostles, and prophets are called to rejoice over her fall.

21. *Thus with violence shall that great city Babylon be thrown down.* This action is finely and forcibly expressed by the original words. The millstone will in falling have not only an accelerated force from the law of gravitation, but that force will be greatly increased by the projectile force impressed upon it by the power of the destroying angel. *Shall be found no more at all.* In her government, consequence, or influence. This is true of ancient Babylon. It is also true of Jerusalem; her government, consequence, and influence are gone. It is not true of Rome pagan; nor, as yet, of Rome papal.

22. *The voice of harpers.* This seems to indicate not only a total destruction of influence, etc., but also of being. It seems as if this city was to be swallowed up by an earthquake, or burnt up by fire from heaven.

23. *By thy sorceries.* Political arts, state tricks, counterfeit miracles, and deceptive maneuvers of every kind. This may be spoken of many great cities of the world, which still continue to flourish.

24. *In her was found the blood of prophets.* She was the persecutor and murderer of prophets and of righteous men. *And of all that were slain upon the earth.* This refers to her counsels and influence, exciting other nations and people to persecute and destroy the real followers of God.

MATTHEW HENRY — CHAPTER 19

Verses 1–4

The fall of Babylon being finished, and declared to be irrecoverable, this begins with a holy triumph over her. The form of their thanksgiving, *Alleluia, praise you the Lord*: with this they begin, with this they go on, and with this they end (*v.* 4); their prayers are now turned into praises, their hosannas end in halleluias.

They praise him for the truth of his word, and the righteousness of his providential conduct, especially in this great event—the ruin of Babylon (*v.* 2).

JAMIESON, FAUSSET, BROWN — CHAPTER 19

Vss. 1-21. THE CHURCH'S THANKSGIVING IN HEAVEN FOR THE JUDGMENT ON THE HARLOT. THE MARRIAGE OF THE LAMB: THE SUPPER: THE BRIDE'S PREPARATION: JOHN IS FORBIDDEN TO WORSHIP THE ANGEL: THE LORD AND HIS HOSTS COME FORTH FOR WAR: THE BEAST AND THE FALSE PROPHET CAST INTO THE LAKE OF FIRE: THE KINGS AND THEIR FOLLOWERS SLAIN BY THE SWORD OUT OF CHRIST'S MOUTH. **1. And**–so ANDREAS. But A, B, C, *Vulgate, Syriac,* and *Coptic* omit. **a great voice**–A, B, C, *Vulgate, Coptic,* and ANDREAS read, "*as it were* a great voice." What a contrast to the lamentations ch. 18! Cf. Jeremiah 51:48. The *great* manifestation of God's power in destroying Babylon calls forth a *great voice* of praise *in heaven.* **people**–*Greek,* "multitude." **Alleluia**–*Hebrew,* "Praise ye JAH," or JEHOVAH: here first used in Revelation, whence ELLICOTT infers the *Jews* bear a prominent part in this thanksgiving. JAH is not a contraction of JEHOVAH, as it sometimes occurs jointly with the latter. It means "He who IS": whereas Jehovah is "He who will be, is, and was." It implies God experienced as a PRESENT help; so that "Hallelujah," says KIMCHI in BENGEL, is found first in the Psalms *on the destruction of the ungodly.* "Hallelu-Jah" occurs four times in this passage. Cf. Psalm 149: 4-9, which is plainly parallel, and indeed identical in many of the phrases, as well as the general idea. Israel, especially, will join in the Hallelujah, when "her warfare is accomplished" and her foe destroyed. **Salvation ...**–*Greek,* "*The* salvation ... the glory ... the power." **and honour**–so *Coptic.* But A, B, C, and *Syriac* omit. **unto the Lord our God**–so ANDREAS. But A, B, C, and *Coptic* read, "(Is) of our God," i.e., belongs to Him. **2. which did corrupt the earth**–*Greek,* "*used* to corrupt" continually. "Instead of opposing and lessening,

ADAM CLARKE — CHAPTER 19

1. *I heard a great voice of much people in heaven.* The idolatrous city being destroyed, and the blood of the martyred saints being avenged, there is a universal joy among the redeemed of the Lord, which they commence with the word Hallelu-Yah, "Praise ye Jah or Jehovah"; which the Septuagint, and John from them, put into Greek letters thus: *Allelou-ia.*

Salvation. He is the sole Author of deliverance from sin; the *glory* of this belongs to Him, the *honour* should be ascribed to Him, and His *power* is that alone by which it is effected.

2. *For true and righteous.* His judgments displayed in supporting His followers and punish-

MATTHEW HENRY

When the angels and saints cried *Alleluia*, her fire burned more fiercely, *v.* 3. Praising God for what we have is praying in the most effectual manner for what is yet further to be done for us; the praises of the saints blow up the fire of God's wrath against the common enemy. The blessed harmony between the angels and the saints in this triumphant song, *v.* 4.

Verses 5-10

An epithalamium, or marriage-song, begins, *v.* 6. I. The concert of heavenly music. The chorus was large and loud, *as the voice of many waters and of mighty thunderings.*

II. The occasion of this song, *v.* 7.

1. A description of the bride, how she appeared; not in the gay and gaudy dress of the mother of harlots, but *in fine linen, clean and white,* which *is the righteousness of saints;* in the robes of Christ's righteousness. These her nuptial ornaments she did not purchase by any price of her own, but received them as the grant of her blessed Lord.

2. The marriage-feast which is declared to be such as would make all those happy who were called to it, a feast made up of the promises of the gospel, *the true sayings of God, v.* 9.

3. The transport of joy which the apostle felt. *He fell down at the feet of the angel to worship him.* The angel refused it, and this was with some resentment: "*See thou do it not. I am thy fellow-servant, and of thy brethren which have the testimony of Jesus.* Thou, as an apostle, having *the Spirit of prophecy,* hast the same testimony to give in; and therefore we are in this brethren and fellow-servants. *Worship God,* and him alone."

JAMIESON, FAUSSET, BROWN

she promoted the sinful life and decay of the world by her own earthliness, allowing the salt to lose its savor" [AUBERLEN]. **avenged**—*Greek,* "exacted in retribution." A particular application of the principle (Gen. 9:5). **blood of his servants**—literally shed by the Old Testament adulterous Church, and by the New Testament apostate Church; also virtually, though not literally, by all who, though called Christians, hate their brother, or love not the brethren of Christ, but shrink from the reproach of the cross, and show unkindness towards those who bear it. **3. again**—*Greek,* "a second time." **rose up**—*Greek,* "goeth up." **for ever and ever**—*Greek,* "to the ages of the ages." **4. beasts**—rather, "living creatures." **sat**—*Greek,* "sitteth." **5. out of**—*Greek,* "out from the throne" in A, B, C. **Praise our God**—Cf. the solemn act of praise performed by the Levites I Chronicles 16:36; 23:5, especially when the house of God was filled with the divine glory (II Chron. 5:13). **both**—omitted in A, B, C, *Vulgate, Coptic,* and *Syriac.* Translate as *Greek,* "*the* small and *the* great." **6. many waters**—Contrast the "many waters" on which the whore sitteth (ch. 17:1). This verse is the hearty response to the stirring call, "Alleluia! Praise our God" (vs. 4, 5). **the Lord God omnipotent**—*Greek,* "*the* Omnipotent." **reigneth**—lit., "reigned": hence *reigneth once for all.* His reign is a fact already established. Babylon, the harlot, was one great hindrance to His reign being recognized. **Her overthrow now clears** the way for His advent to reign; therefore, not merely Rome, but the whole of Christendom in so far as it is carnal and compromised Christ for the world, is comprehended in the term "harlot." The beast hardly arises when he at once "goeth into perdition": so that Christ is prophetically considered as already reigning, so soon does His advent follow the judgment on the harlot. **7. glad ... rejoice**—*Greek,* "rejoice ... exult." **give**—so B and ANDREAS. But A reads, "we *will* give." **glory**—*Greek,* "*the* glory." **the marriage of the Lamb is come**—The *full* and *final* consummation is at ch. 21:2-9, etc. Previously there must be the overthrow of the beast, etc., at the Lord's coming, the binding of Satan, the millennial reign, the loosing of Satan and his last overthrow, and the general judgment. The elect-Church, the heavenly Bride, soon after the destruction of the harlot, is transfigured at the Lord's coming, and joins with Him in His triumph over the beast.

8. granted—Though in one sense *she* "made herself ready," having by the Spirit's work in her put on "the wedding garment," yet in the fullest sense it is not she, but her Lord, who makes her ready by "*granting* to her that she be arrayed in fine linen." It is He who, by *giving Himself for* her, *presents her to Himself a glorious Church, not having spot, but holy and without blemish.* It is He also who *sanctifies* her, naturally vile and without beauty, *with the washing of water by the word,* and *puts His own comeliness on her,* which thus becomes hers. **clean and white**—so ANDREAS. But A and B transpose. Translate, "bright and pure"; at once brilliantly *splendid* and *spotless* as in the bride herself. **righteousness**—*Greek,* "righteousnesses"; distributively used. *Each* saint must have this righteousness: not merely be justified, as if the righteousness belonged to the Church *in the aggregate;* the saints together have *righteousnesses;* viz., He is *accounted as* "the Lord our righteousness" to each saint on his believing, their robes being made *white in the blood of the Lamb.* **9. He**—God by His angel *saith unto me.* **called**—effectually, not merely externally. The "unto," or into," seems to express this: not merely invited *to* (*Greek, epi*), but called INTO, so as to be *partakers of* (*Greek, eis*); cf. I Corinthians 1:9. **marriage supper**—*Greek,* "the supper of the marriage." Typified by the Lord's Supper. **true**—*Greek,* "genuine"; veritable sayings which shall surely be fulfilled, viz., all the previous revelations. **10. at**—*Greek,* "before." John's intending to worship the angel here, as in ch. 22:8, on having revealed to him the glory of the new Jerusalem, is the involuntary impulse of adoring joy at so blessed a prospect. It forms a marked contrast to the sorrowful *wonder* with which he had looked on the Church in her apostasy as the harlot (ch. 17:6). **thy brethren**—i.e., *a fellow servant* of thy brethren. **have the testimony of Jesus**—(*Note,* ch. 12:17). **the testimony of**—i.e., *respecting* Jesus. **is the spirit of prophecy**—is the result of the same spirit of prophecy in you as in myself. We angels, and you apostles, all alike have the testimony of (bear testimony concerning) Jesus by the operation of one and the same Spirit, who enables me to show you these revelations and enables you to record them: wherefore

ADAM CLARKE

ing His enemies are *true*—according to His predictions; and *righteous,* being all according to infinite justice and equity.

3. *Her smoke rose up.* There was, and shall be, a continual evidence of God's judgments executed on this great whore or idolatrous city; nor shall it ever be restored.

4. *The four and twenty elders.* The true Church of the Lord Jesus converted from among the Jews. See chap. iv. 10; v. 14.

5. *Praise our God.* Let all, whether redeemed from among Jews or Gentiles, give glory to God.

6. *The voice of a great multitude.* This is the catholic or universal Church of God gathered from among the Gentiles. *The Lord God omnipotent reigneth.* Many excellent MSS., most of the versions, add "our," and according to this the text reads emphatically thus: "Our Lord God, the Almighty, reigneth." What consolation to every genuine Christian that his Lord and God is the Almighty, and that this Almighty never trusts the reins of the government of the universe out of His hands!

7. *The marriage of the Lamb is come.* The meaning of these figurative expressions appears to be this: After this overthrow of idolatry and superstition, and the discomfiture of Antichrist, there will be a more glorious state of Christianity than ever was before.

8. *Arrayed in fine linen.* A prediction that the Church should become more pure in her doctrines, more pious in her experience, and more righteous in her conduct than she had ever been from her formation. *The fine linen* here spoken of is not the righteousness of Christ imputed to believers, for it is here called *the righteousness of the saints*—that which the grace and Spirit of Christ have wrought in them.

9. *Blessed are they which are called unto the marriage supper.* This is an evident allusion to the marriage of the king's son, Matt. xxii. 2, etc., where the incarnation of our Lord and the calling of Jews and Gentiles are particularly pointed out. *Blessed* are all they who hear the gospel, and are thus invited to lay hold on everlasting life.

10. *I fell at his feet to worship him.* Great as this angel was, John could not mistake him either for Jesus Christ or for God the Father; nor was his prostration intended as an act of religious worship. It was merely an act of that sort of reverence which any Asiatic would pay to a superior. His mistake was the considering that he was under obligation to the angel for the information which he had now received. This mistake the angel very properly corrects, showing him that it was from God alone this intelligence came, and that to Him alone the praise was due. *I am thy fellowservant.* No higher in dignity than yourself; employed by the same God, on the same errand, and with the same testimony; and therefore not entitled to your prostration. *Worship God*—prostrate yourself to Him, and to Him give thanks. *The testimony of Jesus is the spirit of prophecy.* As this is a reason given by the angel why he should not worship him, the meaning must be this: I, who have received this *spirit of prophecy,* am not superior to you, who have received the *testimony* of Christ, to preach Him among the Gentiles. Or the spirit of prophecy is a general

MATTHEW HENRY

Verses 11–21

The glorious head of the church is called out to a new expedition, which seems to be the great battle that was to be fought at Armageddon.

I. The description of the great Commander. The seat of his empire; and that is *heaven.* His equipage: he is again described as sitting *on a white horse.* He is *faithful and true,* he is righteous in all his proceedings, he has a penetrating insight into all the strength of his enemies, he has a large and extensive dominion, many crowns.

J. A. SEISS:

"In righteousness he judgeth and warreth." In the letter to the Laodiceans he was "the Faithful and True Witness," reproving and instructing his friends; here he is the Faithful and True Warrior and Judge, for the punishment of his enemies. Heaven cannot be at peace with iniquity, and justice cannot be at amity with falsehood and rebellion. When sin is once incorrigible, and incurable by remedial measures, it must be put down by force of arms. Mercy slighted and abused brings the executioner. The world banded together in arms against its true Sovereign brings against it the sword of insulted majesty. Not as human kings and nations war—out of covetousness, pride, and an ambition for selfish greatness and dominion—but in absolute justice and right, and in strictest accord with every holy principle and every holy interest he now unsheaths and wields the sword of infinite power. Dreadful is the carnage which follows, but no one can ever say that it is not precisely what was merited and demanded.
—The Apocalypse

His armour; and that is *a vesture dipped in blood.*

His name: *The Word of God,* a name that none fully knows but himself. His perfections are incomprehensible by any creature.

II. The army which he commands (*v.* 14).

III. The weapons of his warfare—*a sharp sword* proceeding from *his mouth* (*v.* 15).

IV. The ensigns of his authority, his coat of arms, *v.* 16.

JAMIESON, FAUSSET, BROWN

we are *fellow servants,* not I your lord to be worshipped by you. Cf. ch. 22:9, "I am fellow servant of thee and of thy brethren *the prophets*"; whence the "FOR the testimony . . ." here, may be explained as giving the reason for his adding "and (fellow servant) of thy brethren that have the testimony of Jesus." **11. behold a white horse; and he that sat upon him**—identical with ch. 6:2. Here as there he comes forth "conquering and to conquer." Compare the *ass*-colt on which He rode into Jerusalem. The *horse* was used for war: and here He is going forth to war with the beast. The *ass* is for peace. His riding on it into Jerusalem is an earnest of His reign in Jerusalem over the earth, as the *Prince of peace,* after all hostile powers have been overthrown. When the security of the world power, and the distress of the people of God, have reached the highest point, the Lord Jesus shall appear visibly from heaven to put an end to the whole course of the world, and establish His kingdom of glory. He comes to judge with vengeance the world power, and to bring to the Church redemption, transfiguration, and power over the world. Distinguish between this *coming* (Matt. 24:27, 29, 37, 39; *Greek, parousia*) and *the end,* or final judgment (Matt. 25:31; I Cor. 15:23). Powerful natural phenomena shall accompany His advent [AUBERLEN]. **12.** Identifying Him with the Son of man similarly described, ch. 1:14. **many crowns**—*Greek,* "diadems": not merely (*Greek, stephanoi*) garlands of victory, but royal crowns, as KING OF KINGS. Christ's diadem comprises all the diadems of the earth and of heavenly powers too. **name . . . that no man knew but . . . himself**—(Judg. 13:18; I Cor. 2:9, 11; I John 3:2). The same is said of the "new name" of believers. In this, as in all other respects, the disciple is made like his Lord. The Lord's own "new name" is to be theirs, and to be "in their foreheads"; whence we may infer that His as yet *unknown* name also is written on His forehead; as the high priest had "Holiness to the Lord" inscribed on the miter on his brow. John saw it as "written," but *knew not* its meaning. It is, therefore, a name which in all its glorious significancy can be only understood when the union of His saints with Him, and His and their joint triumph and reign, shall be perfectly manifested at the final consummation. **13. vesture dipped in blood**—Isaiah 63:2 is alluded to here, and in vs. 15, end. There the *blood* is not His own, but that of His foes. So here the blood on His "vesture," reminding us of *His own blood* shed for even the ungodly who trample on it, is a premonition of the shedding of *their blood* in righteous retribution. He sheds the blood, not of the godly, as the harlot and beast did, but of the blood-stained ungodly, including them both. **The Word of God**—who made the world, is He also who under the same character and attributes shall make it anew. His title, *Son of God,* is applicable in a lower sense, also to His people; but "the Word of God" indicates His incommunicable Godhead, joined to His manhood, which He shall then manifest in glory. **14. the armies . . . in heaven**—Cf. "the horse bridles," ch. 14:20. The glorified saints whom God "will bring with" Christ at His advent; cf. ch. 17:14, "they that are with Him, called, chosen, faithful"; as also "His mighty angels." **white and clean**—*Greek,* "pure." A, B, *Vulgate, Syriac,* and CYPRIAN omit "and," which ORIGEN and ANDREAS retain, as *English Version.* **15. out of his mouth . . . sword**—(ch. 1:16; 2:12, 16). Here in its *avenging* power, II Thessalonians 2:8, "consume with the Spirit *of His mouth*" (Isa. 11:4, to which there is allusion here); not in its convicting and converting efficacy (Eph. 6:17; Heb. 4:12, 13, where also the judicial keenness of the sword-like word is included). The Father commits the judgment to the Son. **he shall rule**—The HE is emphatic, He and none other, in contrast to the usurpers who have misruled on earth. "Rule," lit., "tend as a shepherd"; but here in a punitive sense. He, who would have *shepherded* them with pastoral rod and with the golden scepter of His love, shall dash them in pieces, as refractory rebels, with "a rod of iron." **treadeth . . . wine press**—(Isa. 63:3). **of the fierceness and wrath**—So ANDREAS reads. But A, B, *Vulgate, Coptic,* and ORIGEN read, "of the fierceness (or *boiling indignation*) of the wrath," omitting "and." **Almighty**—The fierceness of Christ's wrath against His foes will be executed with the resources of omnipotence. **16.** "His name written on His vesture and on His thigh," was written partly on the vesture, partly on the thigh itself, at the part where in an equestrian figure the robe drops from the thigh. The *thigh* symbolizes Christ's humanity as having come, after

ADAM CLARKE

testimony concerning Jesus, for He is the Scope and Design of the whole Scriptures.

11. *A white horse.* This is an exhibition of the triumph of Christ after the destruction of His enemies. The white horse is the emblem of this, and *Faithful and True* are characters of Christ. See chap. iii. 14. *In righteousness he doth judge and make war.* The wars which He wages are from no principle of ambition, lust of power, or extension of conquest and dominion; they are righteous in their principle and in their object.

12. *His eyes were as a flame of fire.* To denote the piercing and all-penetrating nature of His wisdom. *On his head were many crowns.* To denote the multitude of His conquests and the extent of His dominion. *A name written, that no man knew.* This is a reference to what the rabbins call the tetragrammaton, YHVH; or what we call "Jehovah." This name the Jews never attempt to pronounce; when they meet with it in the Bible, they read *Adonai* for it. But, to a man, they all declare that no man can pronounce it; and that the true pronunciation has been lost, at least since the Babylonish captivity; and that God alone knows its true interpretation and pronunciation. This, therefore, is the *name . . . that no man knew, but he himself.*

13. *He was clothed with a vesture dipped in blood.* To show that He was just come from recent slaughter. The description is taken from Isa. lxiii. 2-3.

The Word of God. Written in the Targum, and in other Jewish writings, "The word of Jehovah;" by which they always mean a Person, and not a word spoken.

14. *The armies which were in heaven.* Angels and saints, over whom Jesus Christ is Captain. *Clothed in fine linen.* All holy, pure, and righteous.

15. *Out of his mouth goeth a sharp sword.* See on chap. i. 16. This appears to mean the word of the gospel, by which His enemies are confounded and His friends supported and comforted.

With a rod of iron. He shall execute the severest judgment on the opposers of His truth. *He treadeth the winepress.* As the grapes are trodden to express the juice, so His enemies shall be bruised and beaten, so that their life's blood shall be poured out.

MATTHEW HENRY

V. An invitation given *to the fowls of heaven,* that they should come and share in the spoil and pillage of the field (*v.* 17, 18).

VI. The battle joined. The enemy falls on with great fury; the powers of earth and hell gathered, to make their utmost effort, *v.* 19.

VII. The victory gained by the great head of the church: *The beast and the false prophet* are taken prisoners, and *cast into the burning lake,* and their followers are given up to military execution, and made a feast for *the fowls of heaven.*

JAMIESON, FAUSSET, BROWN

the flesh, from the *loins* of David, and now appearing as the glorified "Son of man." On the other hand, His incommunicable divine name, "which no man knew," is on His head (vs. 12), [MENOCHIUS]. KING OF KINGS–Cf. ch. 17:14, in contrast with vs. 17, the beast being in attempted usurpation a *king of kings,* the ten kings delivering their kingdom to him. **17. an**–*Greek,* "one." **in the sun**–so as to be conspicuous in sight of the whole world. **to all the fowls**–(Ezek. 39:17-20). **and gather yourselves**–A, B, *Vulgate, Syriac, Coptic,* and ANDREAS read, "be gathered," omitting "and." **of the great God**–A, B, *Vulgate, Syriac, Coptic,* and ANDREAS read, "the great supper (i.e., banquet) of God." **18.** Contrast with this "supper," vs. 17, 18, *the marriage supper of the Lamb,* vs. 9. **captains**–*Greek,* "captains of thousands," i.e., *chief captains.* The "kings" are "the ten" who "give their power unto the beast." **free and bond**–specified in ch. 13:16, as "receiving the mark of the beast." The repetition of *flesh* (in the *Greek* it is plural: *masses of flesh*) five times in this verse, marks the gross *carnality* of the followers of the beast. Again, the giving of their flesh to the fowls to eat, is a righteous retribution for their not suffering *the dead bodies* of Christ's *witnesses to be put in graves.* **19. gathered together**–at Armageddon, under the sixth vial. For "*their* armies" in B and ANDREAS, there is found "*His* armies" in A. **war**–so ANDREAS. But A and B read, "*the* war," viz., that foretold, ch. 16:14; 17:4. **20. and with him . . .**–A reads, "and those with him." B reads, "and he who was with him, the false prophet." **miracles**–*Greek,* "*the* miracles" (lit., "signs") recorded already (ch. 13:14) as wrought by *the second beast before* (lit., in sight of) *the first beast.* Hence it follows the *second beast* is identical with *the false prophet.* I think it not unlikely that the false prophet will be the successor of the spiritual pretensions of the papacy; while the beast in its last form as the fully revealed Antichrist will be the secular representative and embodiment of the fourth world kingdom, Rome, in its last form of intensified opposition to God. Cf. with this prophecy, Ezekiel 38:39; Daniel 2:34, 35, 44; 11:44, 45; 12:1; Joel 3:9-17; Zechariah 12: 13; 14. **had received**–rather as *Greek,* "received," *once for all.* **them ; that worshipped**–lit., "them worshipping" not an act *once for all done,* as the "received" implies, but those *in the habit of* "worshipping." **These both were cast . . . into a lake**– *Greek,* ". . . *the* lake of fire," Gehenna. Satan is subsequently cast into it, at the close of the outbreak which succeeds the millennium (ch. 20:10). Then Death and Hell, as well those not found at the general judgment "written in the book of life"; this constitutes "the second death." **alive**–a living death; not mere annihilation. "Their worm dieth not, their fire is not quenched." **21. the remnant**–*Greek,* "the rest," i.e., "the kings and their armies" (vs. 19) classed together in one indiscriminate mass. A solemn confirmation of the warning in Psalm 2:10.

ADAM CLARKE

17. *An angel standing in the sun.* Exceedingly luminous, every part of Him emitting rays of light.

18. *That ye may eat the flesh of kings.* There shall be a universal destruction; the kings, generals, captains, and all their host shall be slain.

J. A. SEISS:

"And the Beast was taken." The great judgment strikes the head and leader first. He is not a system; or he would not fall till the myriads of his supporters fall. He is a *person,* as truly as his Captor is a person. He is distinct from his armies, as Christ is distinct from his; or he could not be taken in advance of his armies. He is the living god and confidence of all his hosts, and all this war is for his glory; therefore the assault is first made upon him. He is a supernatural being, a man resurrected from the dead by the devil's power, and seemingly incapable of corporeal death; for he is not slain. No sword smites him. He does not die. In contradistinction from all save his companion, the False Prophet, it is specifically stated that he is simply "taken"—taken "alive," and "cast alive into the lake of fire." His worshipers held him to be invincible. They asked in the utmost confidence and triumph, "Who is like unto the Beast? Who can war with him?" But, without the striking of a blow, and with all his worshipers in arms around him, he is "taken," captured as a lion seizes his prey, dragged away from the field as a helpless prisoner.—*The Apocalypse*

20. *That worshipped his image.* The *beast* has been represented as the Latin empire; the image of the beast, the popes of Rome; and the *false prophet,* the papal clergy. *Were cast alive into a lake of fire.* Were discomfited when alive, in the zenith of their power, and destroyed with an utter destruction.

21. *With the sword of him that sat upon the horse.* He who sat on the white horse is Christ; and His sword is His word—the unadulterated gospel.

MATTHEW HENRY

CHAPTER 20

Verses 1–10

I. A prophecy of *the binding of Satan.* To whom this work of binding Satan is committed—to *an angel from heaven.* Christ never wants proper powers and instruments to break the power of Satan. The execution of this work, *v.* 2, 3. Neither the strength of the dragon, nor the subtlety of the serpent, was sufficient to rescue him. He *cast him into the bottomless pit.* He is brought back to that prison, and there laid in chains. He is *shut up, and a seal set upon him.* We have the term of this confinement of Satan—*a thousand years,* after which he was to *be loosed* again for *a little season.*

JAMIESON, FAUSSET, BROWN

CHAPTER 20

Vss. 1-15. SATAN BOUND, AND THE FIRST-RISEN SAINTS REIGN WITH CHRIST, A THOUSAND YEARS; SATAN LOOSED, GATHERS THE NATIONS, GOG AND MAGOG, ROUND THE CAMP OF THE SAINTS, AND IS FINALLY CONSIGNED TO THE LAKE OF FIRE; THE GENERAL RESURRECTION AND LAST JUDGMENT. **1.** The destruction of his representatives, the beast and the false prophet, to whom he had given his *power, throne,* and *authority,* is followed by the binding of Satan himself for a thousand years. **the key of the bottomless pit**–now transferred from Satan's hands, who had heretofore been permitted by God to use it in letting loose plagues on the earth; he is now to be made to feel himself the torment which he had inflicted on men, but his full torment is not until he is cast into "the lake of fire" (vs. 10). **2. that old**–ancient serpent (ch. 12:9). **thousand years**–As *seven* mystically implies universality, so a *thousand* implies *perfection,* whether in good or evil [AQUINAS *on* ch. 11]. *Thousand* symbolizes that the world is perfectly leavened and pervaded by the divine; since *thousand* is *ten,* the number of the world, raised to the *third* power, *three* being the number of God [AUBERLEN]. It may denote *literally* also a *thousand years.* **3. shut him**–A, B, *Vulgate, Syriac,* and ANDREAS omit "him." **set a seal upon him**–*Greek,* "*over* him," i.e., sealed up the door of the abyss over his head. A surer seal to keep him from getting out than his seal over Jesus in the tomb of Joseph, which was burst on the resurrection morn. Satan's binding at this juncture

ADAM CLARKE

CHAPTER 20

1. *An angel came down from heaven.* One of the executors of the divine justice, who receives criminals, and keeps them in prison, and delivers them up only to be tried and executed. The *key* of the prison and the *chain* show who He is; and as the *chain* was *great,* it shows that the culprit was impeached of no ordinary crimes.

2. *That old serpent, which is the Devil, and Satan.* He who is called the *old serpent* is the *Devil*—the "calumniator," and *Satan*—the "opposer." *A thousand years.* In what this binding of Satan consists, who can tell? How many visions have been seen on this subject both in ancient and modern times! This and what is said in vv. 3-5 no doubt refer to a time in which the influence of Satan will be greatly restrained, and the true Church of God enjoy great prosperity, which shall endure for a long time. But it is not likely that the number, *a thousand years,* is to be taken literally here, and "year" symbolically and figuratively in all the book beside. The doctrine of the "millennium," or of the saints reigning on earth a thousand years, with Christ for their Head, has been illustrated and defended by many Christian writers, among both the ancients and the mod-

MATTHEW HENRY

J. A. SEISS:

Is this a literal transaction? Certainly it is. The battle is literal; the taking of the Beast and the False Prophet is literal; the slaying of the kings and their armies is literal; Satan is literal; and his binding must be equally literal. Some have asked with an air of triumph, "How can a chain of iron or brass bind a spirit, and that spirit an archangel?" But the record does not say that it is a chain of iron, or brass, or steel, or any other material of earthly chains. It is a chain of divine make, as the sword that proceeds from the mouth of the Son of God. It is a spirit-chain, as the horses of the celestial army are spirit-horses. It is a chain of a character that can bind spirit and fetter angels. Jude tells of such chains, actually holding now (Jude 6), and which not even the angels can break. What they are made of, and how they serve to bind the freedom of spiritual natures, it is not for us to know or show; but they are not therefore any less real as literal chains. Figures, tropes, and shadows cannot bind anybody, unless it be some commentators, who seem to be hopelessly entangled in them. The abyss is a reality, and the chain is also a reality, or it is not what inspiration says it is. It is called "a great chain"; and "great" it must be to hold and confine the great Red Dragon. But it is adequate to its purpose. Heaven makes no miscalculations. It is fastened on the limbs of the old monster. He cannot resist it, nor shake it off. Archangel as he is, he is compelled to submit, bound as a helpless prisoner, and violently cast into his dungeon, there to lie in his fetters for a decade of centuries.—*The Apocalypse*

II. An account of the reign of the saints for the same space of time in which Satan continued bound (*v.* 4–6). Who those were that received such honour —those who had suffered for Christ, and all who had faithfully adhered to him. The honour bestowed upon them.

They were raised from the dead, and restored to life. *They reigned with Christ a thousand years.* Those who suffer with Christ shall reign with Christ.

This is called *the first resurrection*, which none but those who have served Christ and suffered for him shall be favoured with.

The happiness of these servants of God. They are *blessed and holy*, *v.* 6. None can be blessed but those that are holy; and all that are holy shall be blessed. They are secured from the power of the second death. Those who have had experience of a spiritual resurrection are saved from the power of the second death.

JAMIESON, FAUSSET, BROWN

is not arbitrary, but is the necessary consequence of the events (ch. 19:20); just as Satan's being cast out of heaven, where he had previously been the accuser of the brethren, was the legitimate judgment which passed on him through the death, resurrection, and ascension of Christ (ch. 12:7-10). He had thought to destroy God's people on earth by Antichristian persecutions (just as he had thought previously to destroy Christ); but the Church is not destroyed from the earth but is raised to rule over it, and Satan himself is shut up for a thousand years in the "abyss" (*Greek* for "bottomless pit"), the preparatory prison to the "lake of fire," his final doom. As before he ceased by Christ's ascension to be an accuser in heaven, so during the millennium he ceases to be the seducer and the persecutor on earth. **that he should deceive**—so A. But B reads, "that he deceive" (*Greek, plana,* for *planeesee*). **and**—so *Coptic* and ANDREAS. But A, B. and *Vulgate* omit "and." **4, 5. they sat**—the twelve apostles, and the saints in general. **judgment was given unto them**—(*Note,* Dan. 7:22). The office of judging was given to them. Though in one sense having to stand before the judgment seat of Christ, yet in another sense they "do not come into judgment (*Greek*), but have already passed from death unto life." **souls**—This term is made a plea for denying the literality of the first resurrection, as if the resurrection were the spiritual one of the *souls* of believers in this life; the life and reign being that of the soul raised in this life from the death of sin by vivifying faith. But "souls" expresses their disembodied state (cf. ch. 6:9) as John saw them at first; "and they lived" implies their *coming to life in the body again,* so as to be visible, as the phrase, vs. 5, "this is the first resurrection," proves; for as surely as "the rest of the dead lived not (again) until . . ." refers to the *bodily* general resurrection, so must *the first resurrection* refer to the body. **beheaded**—lit., "smitten with an axe"; a *Roman* punishment, though crucifixion, casting to beasts, and burning, were the more common modes of execution. The guillotine in revolutionary France was a revival of the mode of capital punishment of pagan imperial Rome. **for**—*Greek,* "for the sake of"; on account of"; "because of." **and which**—*Greek,* "and the *which.*" And prominent among this class (the beheaded), such as did not worship the beast. The martyrs are put first, because most like Jesus in their sufferings and death, therefore nearest Him in their life and reign; for Christ indirectly affirms there are relative degrees and places of honor in His kingdom, the highest being for those who drink his cup of suffering. Next shall be those who have not bowed to the world power, but have looked to the things unseen and eternal. **neither**—"not yet." **foreheads . . . hands**—*Greek,* "forehead . . . hand." **reigned with Christ**—over the earth. **5. But**—B, *Coptic,* and ANDREAS read, "and." A and *Vulgate* omit it. **again**—A, B, *Vulgate, Coptic,* and ANDREAS omit it. "Lived" is used for *lived again,* as in ch. 2:8. John saw them not only when restored to life, but when in the act of reviving [BENGEL]. **first resurrection**—"the resurrection of the just." Earth is not yet transfigured, and cannot therefore be the meet locality for the transfigured Church; but from heaven the transfigured saints with Christ rule the earth, there being a much freer communion of the heavenly and earthly churches (a type of which state may be seen in the forty days of the risen Saviour during which He appeared to His disciples), and they know no higher joy than to lead their brethren on earth to the same salvation and glory as they share themselves. The millennial reign on earth does not rest on an isolated passage of the Apocalypse, but all Old Testament prophecy goes on the same view (cf. Isa. 4:3; 11:9; 35:8). **6. Blessed**—(Cf. ch. 14:13; 19:9). **on such the second death hath no power**—even as it has none on Christ now that He is risen. **priests of God**— The heavenly Church is elected not merely to salvation, but to rule in love, and minister blessings over the whole earth, as king-priests. The glory of the transfigured saints shall be felt by men in the flesh with the same consciousness of blessing as on the Mount of Transfiguration the three disciples experienced in witnessing the glory of Jesus, and of Moses and Elias, when Peter exclaimed, "It is good for us to be here"; in II Peter 1:16-18, the Transfiguration is regarded as the earnest of Christ's coming in glory. The privilege of "our high *calling* in Christ" is limited to the present time of Satan's reign; when he is bound, there will be no scope for suffering for, and so afterwards *reigning* with, Him (ch. 3:

ADAM CLARKE

erns. Were I to give a collection of the conceits of the primitive fathers on this subject, my readers would have little reason to applaud my pains. It has long been the idle expectation of many persons that the millennium, in their sense, was at hand; and its commencement has been expected in every century since the Christian era. It has been fixed for several different years, during the short period of my own life! I believed those predictions to be vain, and I have lived to see them such. Yet there is no doubt that the earth is in a state of progressive moral improvement; and that the light of true religion is shining more copiously everywhere, and will shine more and more to the perfect day. But when the religion of Christ will be at its meridian of light and heat, we know not. In each believer this may speedily take place; but probably no such time shall ever appear, in which evil shall be wholly banished from the earth, till after the day of judgment, when the earth having been burned up, a new heaven and a new earth shall be produced out of the ruins of the old, by the mighty power of God; righteousness alone shall dwell in them. The phraseology of the apostle here seems partly taken from the ancient prophets and partly rabbinical; and it is from the Jewish use of those terms that we are to look for their interpretation.

3. *He should deceive the nations no more.* Be unable to blind men with superstition and idolatry as he had formerly done.

4. *I saw thrones.* Christianity established in the earth, the kings and governors being all Christians. *Reigned with Christ a thousand years.* I am satisfied that this period should not be taken literally. It may signify that there shall be a long and undisturbed state of Christianity; and so universally shall the gospel spirit prevail that it will appear as if Christ reigned upon earth; which will in effect be the case, because His Spirit shall rule in the hearts of men; and in this time the martyrs are represented as living again; their testimony being revived, and the truth for which they died, and which was confirmed by their blood, being now everywhere prevalent. As to the term *thousand years,* it is a mystic number among the Jews. It appears therefore that this phraseology is purely rabbinical.

5. *The rest of the dead lived not again.* It is generally supposed from these passages that all who have been martyred for the truth of God shall be raised a thousand years before the other dead, and reign on earth with Christ during that time, after which the dead in general shall be raised; but this also is very doubtful.

6. *Blessed* ("happy") *and holy.* He was holy and therefore he suffered for the testimony of Jesus in the time when nothing but holiness was called to such a trial. *The first resurrection.* Supposed to be that of the martyrs, mentioned above. *The second death.* Punishment in the eternal world; such is the acceptation of the phrase among the ancient Jews. *Hath no power.* "Hath no authority"—no dominion over him. This is also a rabbinical mode of speech.

MATTHEW HENRY	JAMIESON, FAUSSET, BROWN	ADAM CLARKE

MATTHEW HENRY

III. An account of another mighty conflict, very sharp, but short and decisive. The restraints laid on Satan are at length taken off. While this world lasts, Satan's power in it will not be wholly destroyed. No sooner is Satan let loose than he falls to his old work, *deceiving the nations*, and so stirring them up to make a war with the saints and servants of God. His last efforts seem to be the greatest, *v.* 8. The principal commanders in this army under the dragon—*Gog and Magog*. Of *Gog and Magog* together we only read in Ezek. xxxviii. 2, a prophecy whence this in the Revelation borrows many of its images. The march and military disposition of this formidable army (*v.* 9).

The doom and punishment of the grand enemy, *the devil*: he is now cast into hell, with his two great officers, *the beast and the false prophet*, to be there *tormented night and day, for ever and ever.*

Verses 11–15

The utter destruction of the devil's kingdom leads to an account of the day of judgment. This will be a great day, *the great day, when all shall appear before the judgment-seat of Christ.* 1. We behold *the throne, great* and *white*, very glorious and perfectly just and righteous. 2. The Judge, the Lord Jesus Christ. *The earth and the heaven flee from his face, and there is no place found for them.* 3. The persons to be judged (*v.* 12). None are so mean but they have some talents to account for, and none so great as to avoid the jurisdiction of this court; not only those that are found alive at the coming of Christ, but all who have died before.

4. The rule of judgment settled: *The books were opened.* The book of God's omniscience, and the book of the sinner's conscience. *And another book* shall be *opened*—the book of the scriptures, the statute-book of heaven, the rule of life.

JAMIESON, FAUSSET, BROWN

21; cf. *Note*, I Cor. 6:2). Moreover, none can be saved in the present age and in the pale of the Christian Church who does not also reign with Christ hereafter, the necessary preliminary to which is suffering with Christ now. If we fail to lay hold of the crown, we lose all, "*the gift of grace* as well as the *reward of service*" [DE BURGH]. **7. expired**—*Greek*, "finished." **8. Gog and Magog**—(*Notes*, Ezek. 38 and 39). Magog is a general name for northern nations of Japheth's posterity, whose ideal head is Gog (Gen. 10:2). A has but one Greek article to "Gog and Magog," whereby the two, viz., the prince and the people, are marked as having the closest connection. B reads the second article before Magog wrongly. HILLER (*Onomasticon*) explains both words as signifying "lofty," "elevated." For "quarters" the *Greek* is "corners." **to battle**—*Greek*, "to *the* war," in A and B. But ANDREAS omits "the." **9. on the breadth of the earth**—so as completely to overspread it. Perhaps we ought to translate, ". . . of the [holy] *land*." **the camp of the saints . . . and the beloved city**—the camp of the saints encircling *the beloved city*, Jerusalem (Ecclesiasticus 24:11). Contrast "hateful" in Babylon (ch. 18:2; Deut. 32:15, LXX). Ezekiel's prophecy of Gog and Magog (38 and 39) refers to the attack made by Antichrist on Israel *before* the millennium: but this attack is made *after* the millennium, so that "Gog and Magog" are mystical names representing the final adversaries led by Satan in person. Ezekiel's Gog and Magog come from *the north*, but those here come "from the four corners of the earth." *Gog* is by some connected with a *Hebrew* root, "covered." **from God**—so B, *Vulgate, Syriac, Coptic*, and ANDREAS. But A omits the words. Even during the millennium there is a separation between heaven and earth, transfigured humanity and humanity in the flesh. Hence it is possible that an apostasy should take place at its close. In the judgment on this apostasy the world of nature is destroyed and renewed, as the world of history was before the millennial kingdom; it is only then that the new heaven and new earth are realized in final perfection. **10. that deceived**—*Greek*, "that deceiveth." **lake of fire**—his final doom: as the bottomless pit" (vs. 1) was his temporary prison. **where**—so *Coptic*. But A, B, *Vulgate*, and *Syriac* read, "where *also*." **the beast and the false prophet are**—(ch. 19:20). **day and night**—figurative for *without intermission* (ch. 22:5), such as now is caused by night interposing between day and day. The same phrase is used of the *external* state of the blessed (ch. 4:8). As the bliss of these is eternal, so the woe of Satan and the lost must be. As the beast and the false prophet led the former conspiracy against Christ and His people, so Satan in person heads the last conspiracy. **for ever and ever**—*Greek*, "to the ages of the ages." **11. great**—in contrast to the "thrones," vs. 4. **white**—the emblem of purity and justice. **him that sat on it**—the Father [ALFORD]. Rather, the Son, to whom "the Father hath committed all judgment." God in Christ, i.e., the Father represented by the Son, is He before whose judgment seat we must all stand.
earth and heaven fled away—The final conflagration, therefore, precedes the general judgment. This is followed by the new heaven and earth (ch. 21). **12. the dead**—"the rest of the dead" who did not share the first resurrection, and those who died during the millennium. **small and great**—B has "*the* small and *the* great." A, *Vulgate, Syriac*, and ANDREAS have "the great and the small." The wicked who had died from the time of Adam to Christ's second advent, and all the righteous and wicked who had died during and after the millennium, shall then have their eternal portion assigned to them. The godly who were transfigured and reigned with Christ during it, shall also be present, not indeed to have their portion assigned as if for the first time (for that shall have been fixed long before, John 5:24), but to have it *confirmed* for ever, and that God's righteousness may be vindicated in the case of both the saved and the lost, in the presence of an assembled universe. Cf. "*We* must ALL appear. . . ." Romans 14:10; II Corinthians 5:10. The saints having been first pronounced just themselves by Christ out of "the book of life," shall sit as assessors of the Judge.
books . . . opened—(Dan. 7:10). The books of God's remembrance, alike of the evil and the good (Ps. 56:8; 139:4; Mal. 3:16): conscience (Rom. 2:15, 16), the word of Christ (John 12:48), the law (Gal. 3:10), God's eternal counsel (Ps. 139:16).
book of life—(ch. 3:5; 13:8; 21:27; Exod. 32:32, 33; Ps. 69:28; Dan. 12:1; Phil. 4:3). Besides the general book recording the works of all, there is a special book for believers in which their names are

ADAM CLARKE

7. *Satan shall be loosed.* How can this bear any kind of literal interpretation? Satan is bound a thousand years, and the earth is in peace; righteousness flourishes, and Jesus Christ alone reigns. This state of things may continue forever if the imprisonment of Satan be continued. Satan, however, is loosed at the end of the thousand years, and goes out and deceives the nations, and peace is banished from the face of the earth, and a most dreadful war takes place. These can be only symbolical representations, utterly incapable of the sense generally put upon them.

8. *Gog and Magog.* This seems to be almost literally taken from the Jerusalem Targum, and that of *Jonathan ben Uzziel*, on Num. xi. 26. I shall give the words at length: "And there were two men left in the camp, the name of the one was Eldad, the name of the other was Medad, and on them the spirit of prophecy rested. Then they both prophesied together, and said, 'In the very end of time Gog and Magog and their army shall come up against Jerusalem, and they shall fall by the hand of the King Messiah; and for seven whole years shall the children of Israel light their fires with the wood of their warlike engines, and they shall not go to the wood nor cut down any tree.'" This account seems most evidently to have been copied by John, but how he intended it to be applied is a question too difficult to be solved by the skill of man; yet both the account in the rabbins and in John is founded on Ezekiel xxxviii—xxxix. The rabbinical writings are full of accounts concerning *Gog and Magog.* Under these names the enemies of God's truth are generally intended.

9. *The beloved city.* Primarily, Jerusalem; typically, the Christian Church.

10. *And the devil . . . was cast into the lake.* Before Satan was "bound," that is, his power was curtailed and restrained; now he is *cast into the lake of fire*, his power being totally taken away.

11. *A great white throne.* Refulgent with glorious majesty. *Him that sat on it.* The indescribable Jehovah. *From whose face the earth and the heaven fled away.* Even the brightness of His countenance dissolved the universe, and annihilated the laws by which it was governed. This is a very majestic figure, and finely expressed. *There was found no place for them.* The glorious majesty of God filling all things, and being all in all.

12. *The dead, small and great.* All ranks, degrees, and conditions of men. This description seems to refer to Dan. vii. 9-10.

And the books were opened. See Dan. xii. 1. "Rab Jehuda said: All the actions of men, whether good or bad, are written in a book, and of all they shall give account" (*Sohar* Gen., fol. 79, col. 298). "In the first day of the new year the holy blessed God sits that he may judge the world; and all men, without exception, give an account of themselves; and the books of the living and the dead are opened" (*Sohar Chadash*, fol. 19, 1).

MATTHEW HENRY

5. The cause to be tried; *the works of men*, what they have done and whether it be good or evil.

6. The issue of the trial and judgment. All those who have *made a covenant with death*, and an *agreement with hell*, shall then be condemned with their infernal confederates, cast with them into the lake of fire.

But those whose names are written in that book shall then be justified and acquitted by the Judge.

JAMIESON, FAUSSET, BROWN

written, not for their works, but for the work of Christ *for*, and *in*, them. Therefore it is called, "*the Lamb's* book of life." Electing grace has singled them out from the general mass. **according to their works**—We are justified *by* faith, but judged *according to* (not *by*) our works. For the general judgment is primarily designed for the final vindication of *God's righteousness before* the whole world, which in this checkered dispensation of good and evil, though really ruling the world, has been for the time less manifest. *Faith* is appreciable by God and the believer alone (ch. 2:17). But *works* are appreciable by all. These, then, are made the evidential test to decide men's eternal state, thus showing that God's administration of judgment is altogether righteous. **13. death and hell**—*Greek*, "Hades." The essential identity of the dying and risen body is hereby shown; for the *sea* and *grave* give up *their dead*. The body that sinned or served God shall, in righteous retribution, be the body also that shall suffer or be rewarded. The "sea" may have a symbolical [CLUVER *from* AUGUSTINE], besides the literal, meaning, as in ch. 8:8; 12:12; 13:1; 18:17, 19; so "death" and "hell" are personifications (cf. ch. 21:1). But the literal sense need hardly be departed from: all the different regions wherein the bodies and souls of men had been, gave them up. **14.** Death and Hades, as personified representatives of the enemies of Christ and His Church, are said to be cast into the lake of fire to express the truth that Christ and His people shall never more die, or be in the state of disembodied spirits. **This is the second death**—"the lake of fire" is added in A, B, and ANDREAS. *English Version*, which omits the clause, rests on inferior MSS. In hell the ancient form of death, which was one of the enemies destroyed by Christ, shall not continue, but a death of a far different kind reigns there, "*everlasting* destruction from the presence of the Lord": an abiding testimony of the victory of Christ. **15.** The blissful lot of the righteous is not here specially mentioned as their bliss had commenced *before* the final judgment. Cf., however, Matthew 25:34, 41, 46.

ADAM CLARKE

The books mentioned here were the books of the living and the dead, or the "book of life" and the "book of death"; that is, the account of the good and evil actions of men; the former leading to life, the latter to death. John evidently alludes here to Dan. vii. 10, on which the rabbinical account of the books appears to be founded. The expressions are figurative in both.

13. *The sea gave up the dead.* Those who had been drowned in it. *And death.* All who died by any kind of disease. Death is here personified, and represented as a keeper of defunct human beings; probably no more than earth or the grave is meant, as properly belonging to the empire of death. *And hell. Hades,* the place of separate spirits. The sea and death have the bodies of all human beings; *hades* has their spirits. That they may be judged, and punished or rewarded according to their works, their bodies and souls must be reunited; *hades,* therefore, gives up the spirits; and the sea and the earth give up the bodies.

14. *And death and hell were cast into the lake.* Death himself is now abolished, and the place for separate spirits is no longer needful. All dead bodies and separated souls being rejoined, and no more separation of bodies and souls by death to take place, consequently the existence of these things is no further necessary. *This is the second death.* The first death consisted in the separation of the soul from the body for a season; the second death in the separation of body and soul from God forever. The first death is that from which there may be a resurrection; the second death is that from which there can be no recovery.

MATTHEW HENRY

CHAPTER 21

Verses 1–8

I. A new world now opens to our view (*v.* 1). To make way for the commencement of this new world, the old world *passed away*.

II. In this new world the apostle *saw the holy city, the new Jerusalem, coming down from heaven.* This new Jerusalem is the church of God in its new and perfect state, *prepared as a bride adorned for her husband.*

JAMIESON, FAUSSET, BROWN

CHAPTER 21

Vss. 1-27. THE NEW HEAVEN AND EARTH: NEW JERUSALEM OUT OF HEAVEN. **1. the first**—i.e., the former. **passed away**—*Greek*, in A and B is "were departed" (*Greek, apeelthon,* not as in *English Version, pareelthe*). **was**—*Greek*, "is," which graphically sets the thing before our eyes as present. **no more sea**—The sea is the type of perpetual unrest. Hence our Lord rebukes it as an unruly hostile troubler of His people. It symbolized the political tumults out of which "the beast" arose, ch. 13:1. As the physical corresponds to the spiritual and moral world, so the absence of *sea,* after the metamorphosis of the earth by *fire,* answers to the unruffled state of solid peace which shall then prevail. **2. And I John**—"John" is omitted in A, B, *Vulgate, Syriac, Coptic,* and ANDREAS; also the "I" in the *Greek* of these authorities is not emphatic. The insertion of "I John" in the *Greek* would somewhat interfere with the close connection which subsists between "the new heaven and earth," vs. 1, and the "new Jerusalem" in this verse. **Jerusalem . . . out of heaven**—(ch. 3:12; Gal. 4:26, "Jerusalem which is above"; Heb. 11:10; 12:22; 13:14). The *descent* of the new Jerusalem *out of heaven* is plainly distinct from the *earthly* Jerusalem in which Israel in the flesh shall dwell during the millennium, and follows on the creation of the new heaven and earth. John in his Gospel always writes [*Greek*] *Hierosoluma* of the old city; in the Apocalypse always *Hierousaleem* of the heavenly city (ch. 3:12). *Hierousaleem* is a *Hebrew* name, the original and holy appellation. *Hierosoluma* is the common Greek term, used in a political sense. Paul observes the same distinction when refuting Judaism (Gal. 4:26; cf. 1:17, 18; 2:1; Heb. 12:22), though not so in the Epistles to Romans and Corinthians [BENGEL]. **bride**—made up of the blessed citizens of "the holy city." There is no longer merely a Paradise as in Eden (though there is that also, ch. 2:7), no longer a mere garden, but now *the city of* God on earth, costlier, statelier, and more glorious, but at the same time the result of labor and pains such as had not to be expended by man in dressing the primitive garden of Eden. **3. out of heaven**—so ANDREAS. But A and *Vulgate* read, "out of the throne." **the tabernacle**—alluding to the tabernacle of God in the wilderness (wherein many signs of His presence were given): of which this is the antitype, having previously been in heav-

ADAM CLARKE

CHAPTER 21

1. *A new heaven and a new earth.* See the notes on 2 Pet. iii. 13. The ancient Jews believed that God would renew the heavens and the earth at the end of seven thousand years. The general supposition they founded on Isa. lxv. 17. *There was no more sea.* The sea no more appeared than did the first heaven and earth. All was made new; and probably the new sea occupied a different position and was differently distributed from that of the old sea.

2. *And I John.* The writer of this book.

New Jerusalem. See the notes on Gal. iv. 24-27. This doubtless means the Christian Church in a state of great prosperity and purity, but some think eternal blessedness is intended.

MATTHEW HENRY

III. The blessed presence of God with his people is here proclaimed, *v.* 3. The presence of God with his church is the glory of the church.

The presence of God with his people in heaven will not be interrupted as it is on earth, but he will dwell with them continually. *They shall be his people. God himself will be their God.*

IV. This new and blessed state will be free from all trouble and sorrow. *All tears shall be wiped away.* God himself, as their tender Father, with his own kind hand, *shall wipe away the tears* of his children; and they would not have been without those tears when God shall come and wipe them away. All the causes of future sorrow shall be for ever removed: *There shall be neither death nor pain;* and therefore *no sorrow nor crying; former things have passed away.*

V. The truth and certainty of this blessed state are ratified by the word and promise of God, *v.* 5, 6. God would have it committed to writing, for perpetual memory, and continual use to his people. *These words are faithful and true;* and it follows, *It is done,* is as sure as if it were done already. We may and ought to take God's promise as present payment; if he has said that he *makes all things new, it is done.*

His titles of honour as a pledge of the full performance, *Alpha and Omega, the beginning and the end.* As his power and will were the first cause of all things, his pleasure and glory are the last end, and he will not lose his design. Men may begin designs which they can never bring to perfection; but *the counsel of God shall stand.* It would be inconsistent with the goodness of God, and his love to his people, to create in them holy desires, and then deny them their proper satisfaction; and therefore they may be assured that *he will give them of the fountain of the water of life freely.*

VI. The greatness of this future felicity is declared. The freeness of it: *He gives of the water of life freely.* The fulness of it. They *inherit all things* (*v.* 7). He is all in all. The tenure and title by which they enjoy this blessedness as *the sons of God,* a title most sure and indefeasible.

The vastly different state of the wicked, *v.* 8. The sins of those who perish. *The fearful* lead the van in this black list. Those who were so dastardly as not to dare to take up the cross of Christ, were yet so desperate as to run into all manner of abominable wickedness. Their punishment. They could not burn at a stake for Christ, but they must burn in hell for sin. They must die another death after their natural death; the agonies and terrors of the first death will consign them over to the far greater terrors and agonies of eternal death.

JAMIESON, FAUSSET, BROWN

en: ch. 11:19; 15:5, "the temple of the tabernacle of the testimony in heaven"; also 13:6. Cf. the contrast in Hebrews 9:23, 14, between "the patterns" and "the heavenly things themselves," between "the figures" and "the true." The earnest of the true and heavenly tabernacle was afforded in the Jerusalem temple described in Ezekiel 40, etc., as about to be, viz., during the millennium. **dwell with them**—lit., "*tabernacle* with them"; the same *Greek* word as is used of the divine Son "*tabernacling* among us." Then He was in the weakness of the *flesh:* but at the new creation of heaven and earth He shall tabernacle among us in the glory of His manifested Godhead (ch. 22:4). **they**—in *Greek* emphatic, "*they*" (in particular). **his people**—*Greek,* "His *peoples*": "the nations of the saved" being all peculiarly His, as Israel was designed to be. So A reads. But B, *Vulgate, Syriac,* and *Coptic* read, "His *people*": singular. **God himself . . . with them**—realizing fully His name Immanuel. **4. all tears**—*Greek,* "every tear." **no more death**—*Greek,* "death shall be no more." Therefore it is not the millennium, for in the latter there is *death* (Isa. 65:20; I Cor. 15:26, 54, "the *last* enemy . . . destroyed is *death*," ch. 20:14, *after* the millennium). **sorrow**—*Greek,* "mourning." **passed away**—*Greek,* "departed," as in vs. 1. **5. sat**—*Greek,* "sitteth." **all things new**—not -recent, but *changed from the old* (*Greek, kaina,* not *nea*). An earnest of this regeneration and transfiguration of nature is given already in the regenerate soul. **unto me**—so *Coptic* and ANDREAS. But A, B, *Vulgate,* and *Syriac* omit. **true and faithful**—so ANDREAS. But A, B, *Vulgate, Syriac,* and *Coptic* transpose, "faithful and true" (lit., "genuine"). **6. It is done** the same *Greek* as in ch. 16:17. "It is come to pass." So *Vulgate* reads with *English Version.* But A reads, "They (*these words,* vs. 5) are come to pass." All is as sure as if it actually had been fulfilled for it rests on the word of the unchanging God. When the consummation shall be, God shall rejoice over the work of His own hands, as at the completion of the first creation God *saw everything that He had made, and behold it was very good.* **Alpha . . . Omega**—*Greek* in A and B, "*the* Alpha . . . *the* Omega" (ch. 1:18). **give unto . . . athirst . . . water of life**—(ch. 22:17; Isa. 12:3; 55:1; John 4:13, 14; 7:37, 38). This is added lest any should despair of attaining to this exceeding weight of glory. In our present state we may drink of the stream, then we shall drink at the *Fountain.* **freely**—*Greek,* "gratuitously": the same *Greek* as is translated, "(They hated Me) without a cause," John 15:25. As *gratuitous* as was man's hatred of God, so *gratuitous* is God's love to man: there was every cause in Christ why man should love Him, yet man hated Him; there was every cause in man why (humanly speaking) God should have hated man, yet God loved man: the very reverse of what might be expected took place in both cases. Even in heaven our drinking at the Fountain shall be God's *gratuitous* gift. **7. He that overcometh**—another aspect of the believer's life: a conflict with sin, Satan, and the world is needed. *Thirsting* for salvation is the first beginning of, and continues for ever (in the sense of an appetite and relish for divine joys) a characteristic of the believer. In a different sense, the believer "shall never thirst." **inherit all things**—A, B, *Vulgate,* and CYPRIAN read, "*these* things," viz., the blessings described in this whole passage. With "all things," cf. I Corinthians 3:21-23. **I will be his God**—*Greek,* ". . . to him a God," i.e., all that is implied of blessing in the name "God." **he shall be my son**—"He" is emphatic: *He* in particular and in a peculiar sense, above others: *Greek,* "shall be *to me* a son," in fullest realization of the promise made in type to Solomon, son of David, and antitypically to the divine Son of David. **8. the fearful**—*Greek,* "the cowardly," who do not *quit themselves like men* so as to "overcome" in the good fight; who have the spirit of slavish "fear," not love, towards God; and who through fear of man are not bold for God, or "draw back." Cf. vs. 27; ch. 22:15. **unbelieving**—*Greek,* "faithless." **abominable**—who have drank of the harlot's "cup of abominations." **sorcerers**—one of the characteristics of Antichrist's time. **all liars**—*Greek,* "all *the* liars": or else "all *who are* liars"; cf. I Timothy 4:1, 2, where similarly *lying* and dealings with *spirits* and *demons,* are joined together as features of the latter times." **second death**—ch. 20:14: "*everlasting* destruction," II Thessalonians 1:9; Mark 9:44, 46, 48, "Where THEIR worm dieth not, and the fire is not quenched."**9.** The same angel who had shown John *Babylon the harlot,* is appropriately employed to show him in contrast *new Jerusalem, the Bride* (ch. 17:1-5). The angel so employed is

ADAM CLARKE

3. *The tabernacle of God is with men.* God, in the most especial manner, dwells among His followers, diffusing His light and life everywhere.

4. *There shall be no more death.* Because there shall be a general resurrection. And this is the inference which Paul makes from his doctrine of a general resurrection, 1 Cor. xv. 26, where he says, "The last enemy that shall be destroyed is death."

5. *Behold, I make all things new.* As the creation of the world at the beginning was the work of God alone, so this new creation. *These words are true and faithful.* Truth refers to the promise of these changes; faithfulness, to the fulfillment of these promises.

6. *It is done.* All is determined, and shall be fulfilled in due time. The great drama is finished, and what was intended is now completed, referring to the period alluded to by the angel. *I am Alpha and Omega.* See on chap. i. 8. *The fountain of the water of life.* See on John iv. 10, 14; vii. 37, etc. The rabbins consider "the fountain of the world to come" as one of the particular blessings of a future state.

7. *Inherit all things.* Here he had no inheritance; there he shall inherit the kingdom of Heaven, and be with God and Christ, and have every possible degree of blessedness.

8. *But the fearful.* Those who, for fear of losing life or their property, either refused to receive the Christian religion, though convinced of its truth and importance, or having received it, in times of persecution fell away, not being willing to risk their lives. *And unbelieving.* Those who resist against full evidence. *The abominable.* Those who are polluted with unnatural lust. *And murderers.* Those who take away the life of man for any cause but the murder of another, and those who hate a brother in their heart. *And whoremongers.* Adulterers, fornicators, whores, prostitutes, and rakes of every description. *Idolaters.* Those who offer any kind of worship or religious reverence to anything but God. *And all liars.* Everyone who speaks contrary to the truth when he knows the truth, and even he who speaks the truth with the intention to deceive; i.e., to persuade a person that a thing is different from what it really is, by telling only a part of the truth, or suppressing some circumstance which would have led the hearer to a different and to the true conclusion. All these shall have their portion, their "share," what belongs to them, their right, *in the lake which burneth with fire and brimstone: which is the second death,* from which there is no recovery.

MATTHEW HENRY

Verses 9–27

We now come to the vision itself.

I. The person that opened the vision to the apostle, *v.* 9. God has a variety of work and employment for his holy angels. They readily execute every commission they receive from God.

II. The place from which the apostle had this glorious view. He was taken into *a high mountain.* Those who would have clear views of heaven must get as near heaven as they can, into the mount of vision.

III. The subject-matter of the vision (*v.* 10); the church of God in her glorious, perfect, triumphant state.

1. The exterior part of the city—*the wall* and *the gates.*

(1) The wall for security. Heaven is a safe state. The height of it (*v.* 17), sufficient both for ornament and security. The matter of it: *It was as jasper, v.* 11. This city has a wall that is impregnable as well as precious. The form of it: In the new Jerusalem all shall be equal in purity and perfection. The measure of the wall (*v.* 15, 16). Here is room sufficient for all the people of God—*many mansions in their Father's house.* The foundation of the wall (*v.* 19). The foundations are described by their number—*twelve,* alluding to the twelve apostles (*v.* 14). The matter of these foundations, it was various and precious, set forth by twelve sorts of precious stones.

(2) The gates for entrance. Heaven is not inaccessible; there is a free admission to all those that are sanctified. Their number—*twelve gates,* answering to the twelve tribes of Israel. All the true Israel of God shall have entrance into the new Jerusalem. Their guards—*twelve angels,* to admit and receive the several tribes of the spiritual Israel. The inscription on the gates—*the names of the twelve tribes,* to show that they have a right to the tree of life, and to enter through the gates into the city.

The situation of the gates. As the city had four equal sides, answering to the four quarters of the world, so on each side there were three gates, signifying that there is as free entrance from one part of the world as from the other.

JAMIESON, FAUSSET, BROWN

the one that had the last seven plagues, to show that the ultimate blessedness of the Church is one end of the divine judgments on her foes. **unto me**—A, B, and *Vulgate* omit. **the Lamb's wife**—in contrast to her *who sat on many waters* (ch. 17:1), (i.e., intrigued with many peoples and nations of the world, instead of giving her undivided affections, as the Bride does, to the Lamb. **10.** The words correspond to ch. 17:3, to heighten the contrast of the bride and harlot. **mountain**—Cf. Ezekiel 40:2, where a similar vision is given from a *high mountain.* **that great**—omitted in A, B, *Vulgate, Syriac, Coptic,* and CYPRIAN. Translate then, "the holy city Jerusalem." **descending**—Even in the millennium the earth will not be a suitable abode for transfigured saints, who therefore shall then reign in heaven over the earth. But after the renewal of the earth at the close of the millennium and judgment, they shall *descend* from heaven to dwell on an earth assimilated to heaven itself. "From God" implies that "we (the city) are God's workmanship." **11. Having the glory of God**—not merely the Shekinah cloud, but God Himself as her glory dwelling in the midst of her. Cf. the type, the earthly Jerusalem in the millennium (Zech. 2:5; cf. vs. 23, below). **her light**—*Greek,* "light-giver": properly applied to the heavenly *luminaries* which diffuse light. Cf. *Note,* Philippians 2:15, the only other passage where it occurs. The "and" before "her light' is omitted in A, B, and *Vulgate.* **even like**—*Greek,* "as it were." **jasper**—representing *watery crystalline brightness.* **12. And**—A and B omit. Ezekiel 48:30-35, has a similar description, which implies that the millennial Jerusalem shall have its exact antitype in the heavenly Jerusalem which shall descend on the finally regenerated earth. **wall great and high**—setting forth the security of the Church. Also, the exclusion of the ungodly. **twelve angels**—guards of the twelve gates: an additional emblem of perfect security, while the gates being never shut (vs. 25) imply perfect liberty and peace. Also, angels shall be the brethren of the heavenly citizens. **names of . . . twelve tribes**—The inscription of the names on the gates implies that none but the spiritual Israel, God's elect, shall enter the heavenly city. **13. On the north . . . on the south**—A, B, *Vulgate, Syriac,* and *Coptic* read, "*And* on the north *and* on the *south.* In Ezekiel 48:32, Joseph, Benjamin, Dan (for which Manasseh is substituted in ch. 7:6), are on the east. Reuben, Judah, Levi, are on the *north.* Simeon, Issachar, Zebulun, on the *south.* Gad, Asher, Naphtali, on the *west.* In Numbers 2, Judah, Issachar, Zebulun, are on the east. Reuben, Simeon, Gad, on the south. Ephraim, Manasseh, Benjamin, on the *west.* Dan, Asher, Naphtali, on the *north.* **14. twelve foundations**—Joshua, the type of Jesus, chose twelve men out of the people, to carry twelve stones over the Jordan with them, as Jesus chose twelve apostles to be the twelve foundations of the heavenly city, of which He is Himself the Chief cornerstone. Peter is not the only apostolic rock on whose preaching Christ builds His Church. Christ Himself is the true foundation: the twelve are foundations only in regard to their apostolic testimony concerning Him. Though Paul was an apostle besides the twelve, yet the mystical number is retained, 12 representing the Church, viz. 3, the divine number, multiplied by 4, the world number. **in them the names . . .**—As architects often have their names inscribed on their great works, so the names of the apostles shall be held in everlasting remembrance. **15. had a golden reed**—so *Coptic.* But A, B, *Vulgate,* and *Syriac* read, "had (as) *a measure,* a golden reed." In ch. 11:2 the non-measuring of the outer courts of the temple implied its being given up to secular and heathen desecration. So here, on the contrary, the city being measured implies the entire consecration of every part, all things being brought up to the most exact standard of God's holy requirements, and also God's accurate guardianship henceforth of even the most minute parts of His holy city from all evil. **twelve thousand furlongs**—lit., "*to 12,000 stadii*": one thousand furlongs being the space between the several twelve gates.

17, hundred . . . forty . . . four cubits—twelve times twelve: the Church-number squared. The wall is far beneath the height of the city. **measure of a man, that is, of the angel**—The ordinary measure used by *men* is the measure here used by the *angel,* distinct from "the measure of the sanctuary." Men shall then be *equal to the angels.* **18. the building**—"the structure" [TREGELLES], *Greek, endomeesis.* **gold, like . . . clear glass**—Ideal gold, transparent as no gold here is [ALFORD]. Excellencies will be combined in the heavenly city

ADAM CLARKE

9. *The bride, the Lamb's wife.* The pure and holy Christian Church.

10. *To a great and high mountain.* That, being above this city, he might see every street and lane of it.

11. *Having the glory of God.* Instead of the sun and moon, it has the splendor of God to enlighten it. *Unto a stone most precious, even like a jasper stone, clear as crystal.* Among precious stones there are some even of the same species more valuable than others; for their value is in proportion to their being free from flaws, and of a uniform and brilliant transparency. A *crystal* is perfectly clear; the Oriental *jasper* is a beautiful sea-green.

12. *Had a wall great and high.* An almighty defense. *Twelve gates.* A gate for every tribe of Israel, in the vicinity of which gate that tribe dwelt, so that in coming in and going out they did not mix with each other. This description of the city is partly taken from Ezek. xlviii. 30-35.

13. *On the east three gates.* The city is here represented as standing to the four cardinal points of heaven, and presenting one side to each of these points.

14. *The wall of the city had twelve foundations.* Probably twelve stones, one of which served for a foundation or "threshold" to each gate; and on these were inscribed the names of the twelve apostles, to intimate that it was by the doctrine of the apostles that souls enter into the Church, and thence into the New Jerusalem.

15. *Had a golden reed.* Several excellent MSS. add "a measure"; he had "a measuring rod made of gold." This account of measuring the city seems to be copied, with variations, from Ezek. xl. 3, etc.

16. *The city lieth foursquare.* The quadrangular form intimates its perfection and stability, for the square figure was a figure of perfection among the Greeks; the "square" or "cubical man" was, with them, a man of unsullied integrity, perfect in all things.

17. *The wall . . . an hundred and forty and four cubits.* This is twelve, the number of the apostles, multiplied by itself. *The measure of a man, that is, of the angel.* The cubit, so called from *cubitus,* the "elbow," is the measure from the tip of the elbow to the tip of the middle finger, and is generally reckoned at one foot and a half, or eighteen inches. By the cubit of a man we may here understand the ordinary cubit, and that this was the angel's cubit who appeared in the form of a man.

18. *The building of the wall of it was of jasper.* The Oriental jasper is exceedingly hard and almost indestructible. Pillars made of this stone have lasted some thousands of years, and appear to have suffered scarcely anything from the tooth of time. *Pure gold, like unto clear glass.* Does not this imply that the walls were made of some beautifully bright yellow stone, very highly polished? This description has been most injudiciously applied to heaven; and in some public discourses, for the comfort and edification of the pious, we hear of heaven with its golden walls, golden pavements, gates of pearl, not considering that nothing of this description was ever intended to be literally understood, and that gold and jewels can have no place in the spiritual and eternal world.

MATTHEW HENRY

The materials of these gates—they were all of pearls: *Every gate one pearl.* Christ is the pearl of great price, and he is our way to God. There is nothing magnificent enough in this world fully to set forth the glory of heaven.

2. The interior part of the new Jerusalem, *v.* 22-27. The first thing which we observe there is the street of the city, *v.* 21. The saints in heaven tread upon gold. The saints are then at rest, but it is not a mere passive rest; but a state of delightful motion: *The nations that are saved walk in the light of it.* They walk with Christ in white. They have communion not only with God, but with one another.

(1) The temple of the new Jerusalem, which was no material temple, *for the Lord God Almighty, and the Lamb, are the temple thereof.*

(2) The light of this city, *v.* 23. There is no want of the light of the sun, *for the glory of God lightens that city, and the Lamb is the light thereof.* There is no need of the sun or moon, any more than we here need to set up candles at noon day.

(3) The inhabitants of this city. Their numbers—whole nations of saved souls. All those multitudes who were sealed on earth are saved in heaven. Their dignity—some of the kings and princes of the earth. God will have some of all ranks and degrees of men to fill the heavenly mansions, high and low. Their continual accession and entrance into this city: *The gates shall never be shut.* Those that are sanctified always find the gates open.

(4) The accommodations of this city: All the *glory and honour of the nations shall be brought into it.* Whatever is excellent and valuable in this world shall be there enjoyed in a more refined kind, and to a far greater degree.

(5) The unmixed purity of all who belong to the new Jerusalem, *v.* 27. There the saints shall have no impure thing remaining in them. Now they feel a sad mixture of corruption with their graces; but, at their entance into the holy of holies, they are washed in the laver of Christ's blood, and presented to the Father without spot. There the saints shall have no impure persons admitted among them. In the new Jerusalem there is a society perfectly pure. Free from such as are openly profane. There are none admitted into heaven who work abominations. Free from hypocrites, such as make lies. They cannot intrude into the new Jerusalem.

CHAPTER 22

Verses 1-5

The heavenly state is here described as a paradise. A paradise in a city, or a whole city in a paradise! In the first paradise there were only two persons to behold the beauty of it; but in this second paradise whole cities and nations shall find abundant delight and satisfaction.

I. The river of paradise. Its fountain-head—*the throne of God and the Lamb.* All our springs of

JAMIESON, FAUSSET, BROWN

which now seem incompatible. **19. And**—so *Syriac, Coptic,* and ANDREAS. But A, B, and *Vulgate* omit. Cf. vs. 14 with this verse; also Isaiah 54:11. **all manner of precious stones**—Contrast ch. 18:12 as to the harlot, Babylon. These precious stones constituted the "foundations." **chalcedony**—agate from Chalcedon: semi-opaque, sky-blue, with stripes of other colors [ALFORD].

20. sardonyx—a gem having the redness of the cornelian, and the whiteness of the onyx. **sardius**—(*Note,* ch. 4:3). **chrysolite**—described by PLINY as transparent and of a golden brightness, like our topaz: different from our pale green crystallized *chrysolite.* **beryl**—of a sea-green color. **topaz**—PLINY, 37. 32, makes it *green* and transparent, like our chrysolite. **chrysoprasus**—somewhat pale, and having the purple color of the amethyst [PLINY, 37, 20, 21]. **jacinth**—The flashing violet brightness in the amethyst is diluted in the jacinth [PLINY, 37. 41]. **21. every several**—*Greek,* "each one severally." **22. no temple . . . God . . . the temple**—As God now dwells in the spiritual Church, His "temple" (*Greek, naos,* shrine; I Cor. 3:17; 6:19), so the Church when perfected shall dwell in Him as her "temple" (*naos:* the same *Greek*). As the Church was "His sanctuary," so He is to be their sanctuary. Means of grace shall cease when the end of grace is come. Church ordinances shall give place to the God of ordinances. Uninterrupted, immediate, direct, communion with Him and the Lamb (cf. John 4:23), shall supersede intervening ordinances. **23. in it**—so *Vulgate.* But A, B, and ANDREAS read, "(shine) *on* it," or lit., "*for* her." **the light**—*Greek,* "the lamp" (Isa. 60:19, 20). The direct light of God and the Lamb shall make the saints independent of God's creatures, the sun and moon, for light. **24. of them which are saved . . . in**—*A, B, Vulgate, Coptic,* and ANDREAS read, (the nations shall walk) "*by means* of her light": omitting "of them which are saved." Her brightness shall supply them with light. **the kings of the earth**—who once had regard only to their glory, having been converted, now in the new Jerusalem do bring their glory into it, to lay it down at the feet of their God and Lord. **and honour**—so B, *Vulgate,* and *Syriac.* But A omits the clause. **25. not be shut . . . by day**—therefore shall never be shut: for it shall *always* be day. Gates are usually shut by night: but in it shall be no night. There shall be continual free ingress into it, so as that all which is blessed and glorious may continually be brought into it. So in the millennial type. **26.** All that was truly glorious and excellent in the earth and its converted *nations* shall be gathered into it; and while all shall form *one* Bride, there shall be various orders among the redeemed, analogous to the divisions of *nations* on earth constituting the one great human family, and to the various orders of angels. **27. anything that defileth**—*Greek, koinoun.* A and B read [*koinon*], "anything *unclean.*" **in the Lamb's book of life**—*Note,* ch. 20:12, 15). As all the filth of the old Jerusalem was carried outside the walls and burnt there, so nothing defiled shall enter the heavenly city, but be burnt *outside* (cf. ch. 22:15). It is striking that the apostle of love, who shows us the glories of the heavenly city, is he also who speaks most plainly of the terrors of hell. On vss. 26, 27, ALFORD writes a *Note,* rash in speculation, about the heathen *nations,* above what is written, and not at all required by the sacred text: cf. my *Note,* **vs. 26.**

CHAPTER 22

VSS. 1-21. THE RIVER OF LIFE: THE TREE OF LIFE: THE OTHER BLESSEDNESSES OF THE REDEEMED. JOHN FORBIDDEN TO WORSHIP THE ANGEL. NEARNESS OF CHRIST'S COMING TO FIX MAN'S ETERNAL STATE. TESTIMONY OF JESUS, HIS SPIRIT, AND THE BRIDE, ANY ADDITION TO WHICH, OR SUBTRACTION FROM WHICH, SHALL BE ETERNALLY PUNISHED. CLOSING BENEDICTION. **1. pure**—A, B, *Vulgate,* and HILARY 22, omit. **water of life**—infinitely superior to the typical waters in the first Paradise (Gen. 2: 10-14); and even superior to those figurative ones in the millennial Jerusalem (Ezek. 47:1, 12; Zech. 14:8), as the matured fruit is superior to the flower. The millennial waters represent full Gospel grace;

ADAM CLARKE

19. *The foundations of the wall.* Does not this mean the foundations or "thresholds" of the gates? The gates represented the twelve tribes, v. 12; and these foundations or thresholds, the twelve apostles, v. 14. There was no entrance into the city but through those gates, and none through the gates but over these thresholds. *The first foundation was jasper.* A stone very hard, some species of which are of a sea-green color; but it is generally a bright reddish brown. *The second, sapphire.* This is a stone of a fine blue color, next in hardness to the diamond. *The third, a chalcedony.* A genus of the semi-pellucid gems. *The fourth, an emerald.* This is of a bright green color without any mixture, and is one of the most beautiful of all the gems.

20. *The fifth, sardonyx.* The onxy is an accidental variety of the agate kind; it is of a dark horny color, in which is a plate of a bluish white, and sometimes of red. *The sixth, sardius.* The sardius is a precious stone of a blood-red color. *The seventh, chrysolite.* The gold stone. It is of a dusky green with a cast of yellow. It is a species of the topaz. *The eighth, beryl.* This is a pellucid gem of a bluish green color. *The ninth, a topaz.* A pale, dead green, with a mixture of yellow. It is considered by the mineralogists as a variety of the sapphire. *The tenth, a chrysoprasus.* A variety of the chrysolite, called by some a yellowish green and cloudy topaz. *The eleventh, a jacinth.* A precious stone of a dead red color, with a mixture of yellow. *The twelfth, an amethyst.* A gem generally of a purple or violet color, composed of a strong blue and deep red. These stones are nearly the same with those on the breastplate of the high priest, Exod. xxviii. 17 ff., and probably were intended to express the meaning of the Hebrew words there used.

21. *The twelve gates were twelve pearls.* This must be merely figurative, for it is out of all the order of nature to produce a pearl large enough to make a gate to such an immense city.

22. *I saw no temple.* There was no need of a temple where God and the Lamb were manifestly present.

23. *No need of the sun.* This is also one of the traditions of the ancient Jews, that "in the world to come the Israelites shall have no need of the sun by day, nor the moon by night" (*Yalcut Rubeni,* fol. 7, 3). God's light shines in this city, and in the Lamb that light is concentrated, and from Him everywhere diffused.

24. *The nations of them which are saved.* This is an allusion to the promise that the Gentiles should bring their riches, glory, and excellence to the Temple at Jerusalem, after it should be rebuilt.

25. *The gates of it shall not be shut at all.* The Christian Church shall ever stand open to receive sinners of all sorts, degrees, and nations. *There shall be no night there.* No more idolatry, no intellectual darkness; the Scriptures shall be everywhere read, the pure Word everywhere preached, and the Spirit of God shall shine and work in every heart.

26. *The glory and honour of the nations into it.* Still alluding to the declarations of the prophets that the Gentiles would be led to contribute to the riches and glory of the Temple by their gifts.

27. *There shall in no wise enter into it any thing that defileth.* See Isa. xxxv. 8; lii. 1. Neither an impure person—he who turns the grace of God into lasciviousness, nor a liar—he that holds and propagates false doctrines.

CHAPTER 22

1. *Pure river of water of life.* This is evidently a reference to the garden of paradise, and the river by which it was watered; and there is also a reference to the account, Ezek. xlvii. 7-12. *Water of life,* as we have seen before, generally signifies spring or running water; here it may signify incessant communications of happiness proceeding from God.

MATTHEW HENRY

grace, comfort, and glory, are in God; and all our streams from him are through the Lamb. Its quality —*pure and clear as crystal.* All the streams of earthly comfort are muddy; but these are clear, giving life, to those who drink of them.

II. The tree of life, in this paradise. Such a tree there was in the earthly paradise, Gen. ii. 9. This far excels it. The situation of it—*in the midst of the street, and on either side the river.* This tree of life is fed by the pure waters of the river that comes from the throne of God.

The fruitfulness of this tree. It brings forth many sorts of fruit—*twelve sorts.* It brings forth fruit at all times—*yields its fruit every month.* There is always fruit upon it.

The fruit is not only pleasant, but wholesome. The presence of God in heaven is the health and happiness of the saints.

III. The perfect freedom of this paradise from everything that is evil (*v.* 3). No serpent there, as there was in the earthly paradise. The devil has nothing to do there.

IV. The supreme felicity of this paradisaical state. There the saints shall see the face of God. God will own them, as having his seal and name on their foreheads.

They shall reign with him for ever. All this shall be with perfect knowledge and joy, walking in the light of the Lord; and this not for a time, *but for ever and ever.*

Verses 6–19

We have here a solemn ratification of the contents of this book. 1. This is confirmed by the name and nature of that God who gave out these discoveries: he is *the Lord God, faithful and true.*

JAMIESON, FAUSSET, BROWN

these waters of new Jerusalem represent Gospel glory perfected. Their continuous flow from God, the Fountain of life, symbolizes the uninterrupted continuance of life derived by the saints, ever fresh, from Him: life in fulness of joy, as well as perpetual vitality. Like pure crystal, it is free from every taint: cf. ch. 4:6, "before the throne a sea of glass, like crystal." **clear**—*Greek,* "bright." **2. street of it**—i.e., of the city. **on either side of the river**—ALFORD translates, "In the midst of the street of it (the city) and of the river, on one side and on the other" (for the second *Greek, enteuthen,* A, B, and *Syriac* read, *ekeithen:* the sense is the same; cf. *Greek,* John 19: 18); thus the trees were on each side in the middle of the space between the street and the river. But from Ezekiel 47:7, I prefer *English Version.* The antitype exceeds the type: in the first Paradise was only *one* tree of life; now there are "*very many* trees *at the bank of the river, on the one side and on the other.*" To make good sense, supposing there to be but *one* tree, we should either, as MEDE, suppose that the *Greek* for *street* is a *plain* washed on both sides by the river (as the first Paradise was washed on one side by the Tigris, on the other by the Euphrates), and that in the midst of the plain, which itself is in the midst of the river's branches, stood the tree: in which case we may translate, "In the midst of the street (plain) *itself,* and of the river (having two branches flowing) on this and on that side, was there the tree of life." Or else with DURHAM suppose, *the tree* was in the midst of the river, and extending its branches to both banks. But cf. Ezekiel 47:12, the millennial type of the final Paradise; which shows that there are several trees of the one kind, all termed "the tree of life." Death reigns now because of sin; even in the millennial earth sin, and therefore death, though much limited, shall not altogether cease. But in the final and heavenly city on earth, sin and death shall utterly cease. **yielded her fruit every month**—*Greek,* "according to each month"; each month had its own proper fruit, just as different seasons are now marked by their own productions; only that then, unlike now, there shall be *no season without its fruit,* and there shall be an endless variety, answering to *twelve,* the number symbolical of the worldwide Church (cf. *Notes,* ch. 12:1; 21:14). **leaves . . . for . . . healing**—(Ezek. 47:9, 12). The *leaves* shall be the *health-giving* preventive securing the redeemed against, not healing them of, sicknesses, while "the fruit shall be for meat." In the millennium described in Ezekiel 47 and ch. 20, the Church shall give the Gospel-tree to the nations outside Israel and the Church, and so shall heal their spiritual malady; but in the *final* and *perfect* new Jerusalem here described, the state of all is eternally fixed, and no saving process goes on any longer (cf. vs. 11). **3. no more curse**—of which the earnest shall be given in the millennium (Zech. 14:11). God can only dwell where the curse and its cause, the cursed thing sin (Josh. 7:12), are removed. So there follows rightly, "But the throne of God and of the Lamb (who redeemed us from the curse, Gal. 3:10, 13) shall be in it." Cf. in the millennium, Ezekiel 48:35. **serve him**—with *worship* (ch. 7:15). **4. see his face**—revealed in divine glory, *in Christ Jesus.* They shall see and know Him with intuitive knowledge of Him, *even as they are known by Him* (I Cor. 13:9-12), and face to face. Cf. I Tim. 6:16, with John 14:9. God the Father can only be seen in Christ. **in**—*Greek,* "*on* their foreheads." Not only shall they personally and in secret (ch. 3:17) know their sonship, but they shall be known as sons of God to all the citizens of the new Jerusalem, so that the free flow of mutual love among the members of Christ's family will not be checked by suspicion as here. **5. there**—so ANDREAS. But A, B, *Vulgate,* and *Syriac* read, "(there shall be no night) any longer"; *Greek, eti,* for *ekei.* **they need**—A, *Vulgate,* and *Coptic* read the future, "they *shall* not have need." B reads, "(and there shall be) no need." **candle**—*Greek,* "lamp." A, *Vulgate, Syriac,* and *Coptic* insert "light (*of a candle,* or *lamp*)." B omits it. **of the sun**—so A. But B omits it. **giveth . . . light**—"illumines." So *Vulgate* and *Syriac.* But A reads, "*shall* give light." **them**—so B and ANDREAS. But A reads, "*upon* them." **reign**—with a glory probably transcending that of their reign in heaven with Christ over the millennial nations in the flesh described in ch. 20:4, 6; that reign was but for a limited time, "a thousand years"; this final reign is "unto the ages of the ages." **6. These sayings are true**—thrice repeated (ch. 19:9; 21:5). For we are slow to believe that God is as good as He is. The news seems to us, habituated

ADAM CLARKE

2. *In the midst of the street of it.* That is, of the city which was described in the preceding chapter. *The tree of life.* An allusion to Gen. ii. 9. The account in Ezekiel is this: "And by the river upon the bank thereof, on this side and on that side, shall grow all trees for meat, whose leaf shall not fade . . . it shall bring forth new fruit according to his months . . . and the fruit thereof shall be for meat, and the leaf thereof for medicine," chap. xlvii. 12.

Twelve manner of fruits. "Twelve fruits"; that is, fruit twelve times in the year, as is immediately explained, *yielded her fruit every month.* As this was a great and spacious city, one fountain was not sufficient to provide water for it; therefore a river is mentioned, a great river, by which it was sufficiently watered. Some think that by this *tree of life* the gospel is indicated; the *twelve . . . fruits* are the twelve apostles; and the *leaves* are gospel doctrines by which nations—the Gentiles—are healed of the disease of sin. But this seems to be a fanciful interpretation.

3. *No more curse.* Instead of *curse* the best MSS., versions, etc., read "cursed person." As there shall be no more sinning against God, so there shall be no more curse of God upon the people; for they shall all be His *servants,* and *serve him.* Our first parents came under the curse by sinning against their Maker in paradise. These shall never apostatize; therefore neither they nor the earth shall be cursed.

4. *See his face.* Enjoy what is called the beatific vision; and they shall exhibit the fullest evidence that they belong entirely to Him, for *his name* shall be written *on their foreheads.*

5. *There shall be no night there.* See the twenty-third and twenty-fifth verses of the preceding chapter.

6. *These sayings are faithful and true.* See the preceding chapter, v. 5. From this verse to the end of the chapter is reckoned the epilogue of this book. (1) The angel affirms the truth

MATTHEW HENRY

2. By the messengers he chose. The holy angels showed them to holy men of God.

3. They will soon be confirmed by their accomplishment. Christ will make haste, *he will come quickly.* 4. By the integrity of that angel who had been the apostle's guide and interpreter in these visions.

5. By the order given to leave the book of the prophecy open, to be perused by all. He does not speak in secret.

6. By the effect this book will have upon men; those that are filthy and unjust will take occasion thence to be more so, but it will further sanctify those that are upright with God.

7. It will be Christ's rule of judgment at the great day; he will dispense rewards and punishments to men according as their works agree or disagree with the word of God. 8. It is the word of him who is the author, finisher, and rewarder of the faith and holiness of his people, *v.* 13, 14. He is *the first and the last.*

He will by this word give to his people *a right to the tree of life,* and an entrance into heaven.

9. It condemns and excludes from heaven all wicked persons, and particularly *those that love and make lies* (*v.* 15).

JAMIESON, FAUSSET, BROWN

as we are to the misery of this fallen world, too good to be true [NANGLE]. They are no dreams of a visionary, but the realities of God's sure word. **holy**—so ANDREAS. But A, B, *Vulgate, Syriac,* and *Coptic* read, ("the Lord God of the) *spirits* (of the prophets.)" The Lord God who with His Spirit inspired their spirits so as to be able to prophesy. There is but one Spirit, but individual prophets, according to the measure given them [I Cor. 12: 4-11], had their own spirits [BENGEL] (I Pet. 1:11; II Peter 1:21). **be done**—*Greek,* "come to pass." **7.** "And" is omitted in *Coptic* and ANDREAS with *English Version,* but is inserted by A, B, *Vulgate* and *Syriac.* **blessed**—(ch. 1:3). **8.** Both here and in ch. 19:9, 10, the apostle's falling at the feet of the angel is preceded by a glorious promise to the Church, accompanied with the assurance, that "These are the true sayings of God," and that those are "blessed" who keep them. Rapturous emotion, gratitude, and adoration, at the prospect of the Church's future glory transport him out of himself, so as all but to fall into an unjustifiable act; contrast his opposite feeling at the prospect of the Church's deep fall [AUBERLEN], ch. 17:6, where cf.the *Note,* and on ch. 19:9, 10. **9.** Lit., "See not"; the abruptness of the phrase marking the angel's abhorrence of the thought of *his* being worshipped however indirectly. Contrast the fallen angel's temptation to Jesus, "Fall down and worship me" (Matt. 4:9). **for**—A, B, *Vulgate, Syriac, Coptic,* ANDREAS, and CYPRIAN omit "for"; which accords with the abrupt earnestness of the angel's prohibition of an act derogatory to God. **and of**—"and (the fellow servant) of thy brethren." **10. Seal not**-But in Daniel 12:4, 9 (cf. 8:26), the command is, "Seal the book," for the vision shall be "for many days." The fulfilment of Daniel's prophecy was distant, that of John's prophecy is near. The New Testament is the time of the end and fulfilment. The Gentile Church, for which John wrote his Revelation, needs more to be impressed with the shortness of the period, as it is inclined, owing to its Gentile origin, to conform to the world and forget the coming of the Lord.
11. unjust—"unrighteous"; in relation to one's fellow men; opposed to "righteous," or "just" (as the *Greek* may be translated) below. More literally, "he that *doeth unjustly,* let him *do unjustly* still." **filthy**—in relation to one's own soul as unclean before God; opposed to holy," consecrated to God as pure.
The solemn lesson derivable from this verse is, Be converted now in the short time left (vs. 10, end) before "I come" (vss. 7, 12), or else you must remain unconverted for ever; sin in the eternal world will be left to its own natural consequences; holiness in germ will there develop itself into perfect holiness, which is happiness. **12. And**—in none of our MSS. But A, B, *Vulgate, Syriac, Coptic,* and CYPRIAN omit it. **behold, I come quickly**—(Cf. vs. 7). **my reward is with me**—(Isa. 40:10; 62:11). **to give**—*Greek,* "to render." **every man**—*Greek,* "to *each.*" **shall be**—so B in MAI. But B in TISCHENDORF, and *A, Syriac,* read, "is." **13. I am Alpha**—*Greek,* " . . . *the* Alpha and *the* Omega." A, B, *Vulgate, Syriac,* ORIGEN, and CYPRIAN transpose thus, "the First and the Last, the Beginning and the End." ANDREAS supports *English Version.* Cf. with these divine titles assumed here by the Lord Jesus, ch. 1:8, 17; 21:6. At the winding up of the whole scheme of revelation He announces Himself as the One *before whom and after whom there is no God.* **14. do his commandments**—*so B, Syriac, Coptic,* and CYPRIAN. But A, ℵ, and *Vulgate* read, (Blessed are they that) "*wash their robes,*" viz., *in the blood of the Lamb* (cf. ch. 7:14). This reading takes away the pretext for the notion of salvation by works. But even *English Version* reading is quite compatible with salvation by grace; for God's first and grand Gospel "commandment" is to believe on Jesus. Thus our "right" to (*Greek,* "privilege" or "lawful authority over") the tree of life is due not to our doings, but to what He has done for us. The *right,* or *privilege,* is founded, not on our merits, but on God's grace. **through**—*Greek,* "*by* the gates." **15. But**—so *Coptic.* But A, B, HIPPOLYTUS, ANDREAS, and CYPRIAN omit. **dogs**—*Greek,* "the dogs"; the impure, filthy (vs. 11; cf. Phil. 3:2). **maketh**—including also "whosoever *practiceth* a lie" [W. KELLY]. **16. mine angel**—for Jesus is Lord of the angels. **unto you**—ministers and people in the seven representative churches, and, through you, to testify to Christians of all times and places. **root . . . offspring of David**—appropriate title here where assuring His Church of "the sure mercies of David," secured to Israel first, and through Israel to the Gentiles. *Root* of David, as

ADAM CLARKE

of all that had been spoken, vv. 6-11. (2) Jesus Christ confirms what has been affirmed, and pledges himself for the fulfilment of all the prophecies contained in it, vv. 12-17. (3) John cautions his readers against adding or diminishing, and concludes with the apostolical blessing, vv. 18-21.

8. *I fell down to worship.* I prostrated myself before him as before a superior being, to express my gratitude, and give him thanks for the communications he had made. See on chap. xix. 10.

10. *Seal not the sayings.* Do not lay them up for future generations; they concern the present times; "They must shortly come to pass," *for the time is at hand.* See above, v. 6. What concerned the Jews was certainly *at hand.*

11. *He that is unjust, let him be unjust still.* The time of fulfilment will come so suddenly that there will be but little space for repentance and amendment. What is done must be done instantly; and let him that is holy persevere, and hold fast what he has received.

12. *Behold, I come quickly.* I come to establish My cause, comfort and support My followers, and punish the wicked.

13. *I am Alpha and Omega.* See on chap. i. 8, 18.

14. *Blessed are they that do his commandments.* They are happy who are obedient. *That they may have right to the tree of life.* The original is much more expressive, "That they may have authority over the tree of life"; an authority founded on right, this right founded on obedience to the commandments of God, and that obedience produced by the grace of God working in them.

15. *Without are dogs.* All those who are uncircumcised in heart. The Jews call all the uncircumcised *dogs.* "Who is a dog? Ans. He who is not circumcised" (*Pirkey Elieser,* chap. 29).

16. *I Jesus.* The Maker, the Redeemer, and Judge of all men. *Have sent mine angel.* An especial messenger from heaven. *I am the root and the offspring of David.* Christ is the *root* of David as to His divine nature, for from that all the human race sprang. And He is the *offspring* of David as to His human nature, for that He took of the stock of David.

MATTHEW HENRY

10. It is confirmed by *the testimony of Jesus, which is the Spirit of prophecy*. He is the fountain of all light, the *bright and the morning star*, and has given to his churches this morning light of prophecy, to assure them of the light of that perfect day which is approaching.

11. It is confirmed by an open invitation to all to come and partake of the streams of the water of life; these are tendered to all who feel in their souls a thirst which nothing in this world can quench. 12. It is confirmed by the joint testimony of the Spirit of God, and that gracious Spirit that is in all the true members of the church of God; *the Spirit and the bride*.

13. It is confirmed by a most solemn sanction, *v*. 18, 19. This sanction is like a flaming sword, to guard the canon of the scripture from profane hands.

Verses 20, 21

We have now come to the conclusion of the whole.

I. Christ's farewell to his church. *Behold, I come quickly*. As when he ascended into heaven, after his resurrection, he parted with a promise of his gracious presence, so here he parts with a promise of a speedy return. The vision is for an appointed time, and will not tarry. *He will come quickly*.

II. The church's hearty echo to Christ's promise. Her firm belief of it: *Amen, so it is*, so it shall be. Her earnest desire of it: *Even so, come, Lord Jesus*. We should never be satisfied till we find such a spirit breathing in us. This is the language of the church of the first-born, and we should join with them. What comes from heaven in a promise should be sent back to heaven in a prayer, "*Come, Lord Jesus*. Finish thy great design, and fulfil all that word in which thou hast caused thy people to hope."

III. The apostolical benediction, which closes the whole: *The grace of our Lord Jesus Christ be with you all, Amen*. Nothing should be more desired by us than that the grace of Christ may be with us in this world, to prepare us for the glory of Christ in the other world. To this most comprehensive prayer we should all add our hearty *Amen*, most earnestly thirsting after greater measures of the gracious influences of the blessed Jesus in our souls, and his gracious presence with us, till glory has perfected all his grace towards us.

JAMIESON, FAUSSET, BROWN

being Jehovah; the offspring of David as man. David's Lord, yet David's son (Matt. 22:42-45). **the morning star**—that ushered in the day of grace in the beginning of this dispensation and that shall usher in the everlasting day of glory at its close. **17.** Reply of the spiritual Church and John to Christ's words (vss. 7, 12, 16). **the Spirit**—in the churches and in the prophets. **the bride**—not here called "wife," as that title applies to her only when the full number constituting the Church shall have been completed. The invitation, "Come," only holds good while the Church is still but an affianced *Bride*, and not the actually wedded *wife*. However, "Come" may rather be the prayer of the Spirit in the Church and in believers in reply to Christ's "I come quickly," crying, Even so, "Come" (vss. 7, 12); vs. 20 confirms this view. The whole question of your salvation hinges on this, that you be able to hear with joy Christ's announcement, "I come," and to reply, "Come" [BENGEL]. Come to fully glorify Thy Bride. **let him that heareth**—i.e., let him that heareth the Spirit and Bride saying to the Lord Jesus, "Come," join the Bride as a true believer, become part of her, and so say with her to Jesus, "Come." On "heareth" means "obeyeth"; for until one has *obeyed* the Gospel call, he cannot pray to Jesus "Come"; so "hear" is used, ch. 1:3; John 10:16. **let him that is athirst come**—As the Bride, the Church, prays to Jesus, "Come," so she urges all whosoever *thirst* for participation in the full manifestation of redemption-glory at *His coming to us*, to COME in the meantime and drink of the living waters, which are the earnest of "the water of life pure as crystal . . . out of the throne of God of the Lamb" (vs. 1) in the regenerated heaven and earth. **And**—so *Syriac*. But A, B, *Vulgate*, and *Coptic* omit "and." **whosoever will**—i.e., is willing and desirous. There is a descending climax; Let him that *heareth* effectually and savingly Christ's voice, pray individually, as the Bride, the Church, does collectively, "Come, Lord Jesus" (vs. 20). Let him who, though not yet having actually *heard* unto salvation, and so not yet able to join in the prayer, "Lord Jesus, come, "still *thirsts* for it, *come* to Christ. Whosoever is even *willing*, though his desires do not yet amount to positive *thirsting*, let him take the water of life freely, i.e., gratuitously. **18. For**—None of our MSS. have this. A, B, *Vulgate*,, and ANDREAS read, "I" emphatic in the *Greek*. "*I testify*." **unto these things**—A, B, and ANDREAS read, "unto them." **add . . . add**—just retribution in kind. **19. book**—None of our MSS. read this. A, B, א, *Vulgate, Syriac*, and *Coptic* read, "(take away his part, i.e., portion) from the *tree* of life," i.e., shall deprive him of participation in the tree of life. **and from the things**—so *Vulgate*. But A, B, א, *Syriac, Coptic*, and ANDREAS omit "and"; then "which are written in this book" will refer to "the holy city and the tree of life." As in the beginning of this book (ch. 1:3) a blessing was promised to the devout, obedient student of it, so now at its close a curse is denounced against those who add to, or take from, it. **20. Amen. Even so, come**—The Song of Solomon (8:14) closes with the same yearning prayer for Christ's coming. A, B, and א omit "Even so," *Greek, nai:* then translate for *Amen*, "*So be it*, come, Lord Jesus"; joining the "Amen," or "So be it," not with Christ's saying (for He calls Himself the "Amen" at the beginning of sentences, rather than puts it as a confirmation at the end), but with John's reply. Christ's "I come," and John's "Come," are almost coincident in time; so truly does the believer reflect the mind of his Lord. **21. our**—so *Vulgate, Syriac*, and *Coptic*. But A, B, and א omit. **Christ**—so B, *Vulgate, Syriac, Coptic*, and ANDREAS. But A and א omit. **with you all**—so none of our MSS. B has, "with all the saints." A and *Vulgate* have, "with all." א has, "with the saints." This closing benediction, Paul's mark in his Epistles, was after Paul's death taken up by John. The Old Testament ended with a "curse" in connection with the *law;* the New Testament ends with a blessing in union with the Lord Jesus. **Amen**—so B, א, and ANDREAS. A and *Vulgate Fuldensis* omit it.

May the Blessed Lord who has caused all holy Scriptures to be written for our learning, bless this humble effort to make Scripture expound itself, and make it an instrument towards the conversion of sinners and the edification of saints, to the glory of His great name and the hastening of His kingdom! Amen.

ADAM CLARKE

The bright and morning star. I am splendor and glory to My kingdom; as the *morning star* ushers in the sun, so shall I usher in the unclouded and eternal glories of the everlasting Kingdom.

17. *The Spirit and the bride*. All the prophets and all the apostles; the Church of God under the Old Testament, and the Church of Christ under the New. *Say, Come*. Invite men to Jesus, that by Him they may be saved and prepared for this Kingdom.

Let him that heareth. Let all who are privileged with reading and hearing the Word of God join in the general invitation to sinners.

Him that is athirst. He who feels his need of salvation and is longing to drink of the living fountain.

And whosoever will. No soul is excluded: Jesus died for every man; every man may be saved; therefore let him who wills, who wishes for salvation, come and *take the water of life freely*—without money or price!

18. *If any man shall add*. Shall give any other meaning to these prophecies, or any other application of them, than God intends, he, though not originally intended, shall have the plagues threatened in this book for his portion.

19. *If any man shall take away*. If any man shall lessen this meaning, curtail the sense, explain away the spirit and design, of these prophecies, *God shall take away his part out of the book of life*, etc. Thus Jesus Christ warns all those who consider this book to beware of indulging their own conjectures concerning it. I confess that this warning has its own powerful influence upon my mind, and has prevented me from indulging my own conjectures concerning its meaning, or of adopting the conjectures of others. These visions and threatenings are too delicate and awful a subject to trifle with, or even to treat in the most solemn manner, where the meaning is obscure. I must leave these things to time and event, the surest interpreters. This is termed a revelation, but it is a revelation of symbols; an exhibition of enigmas, to which no particular solution is given, and to which God alone can give the solution.

20. *Surely I come quickly*. This may be truly said to every person in every age; Jesus, the Judge, is at the door! *Even so, come, Lord Jesus*. The wish and desire of the suffering Church, and of all the followers of God, who are longing for the coming of His kingdom.

21. *The grace of our Lord Jesus Christ*. May the favor and powerful influence of Jesus Christ *be with you all;* you of the seven churches, and the whole Church of Christ in every part of the earth, and through all the periods of time.